# Biblical Books in Alphabetical Order

| Book | Abbreviation | Page | Book | Abbreviation | Page |
|------|------|------|------|------|------|
| Acts | Acts | 1770 | 1 Kings | 1 Kgs | 535 |
| Amos | Am | 1451 | 2 Kings | | 575 |
| Baruch | Bar | 1330 | Lamentations | | |
| Ben Sira | Sir | 1091 | Leviticus | | |
| 1 Chronicles | 1 Chr | 607 | Luke | Lk | |
| 2 Chronicles | 2 Chr | 639 | 1 Maccabees | 1 Mc | 770 |
| Colossians | Col | 1944 | 2 Maccabees | 2 Mc | 806 |
| 1 Corinthians | 1 Cor | 1855 | Malachi | Mal | 1532 |
| 2 Corinthians | 2 Cor | 1884 | Mark | Mk | 1626 |
| Daniel | Dn | 1401 | Matthew | Mt | 1557 |
| Deuteronomy | Dt | 341 | Micah | Mi | 1478 |
| Ecclesiastes | Eccl | 1036 | Nahum | Na | 1490 |
| Ephesians | Eph | 1921 | Nehemiah | Neh | 692 |
| Esther | Est | 753 | Numbers | Nm | 290 |
| Exodus | Ex | 196 | Obadiah | Ob | 1466 |
| Ezekiel | Ez | 1342 | 1 Peter | 1 Pt | 2041 |
| Ezra | Ezr | 676 | 2 Peter | 2 Pt | 2051 |
| Galatians | Gal | 1907 | Philemon | Phlm | 1996 |
| Genesis | Gn | 128 | Philippians | Phil | 1932 |
| Habakkuk | Hb | 1496 | Proverbs | Prv | 990 |
| Haggai | Hg | 1510 | Psalms | Ps(s) | 881 |
| Hebrews | Heb | 2001 | Revelation | Rev | 2079 |
| Hosea | Hos | 1426 | Romans | Rom | 1828 |
| Isaiah | Is | 1164 | Ruth | Ru | 462 |
| James | Jas | 2032 | 1 Samuel | 1 Sm | 470 |
| Jeremiah | Jer | 1247 | 2 Samuel | 2 Sm | 508 |
| Job | Jb | 842 | Song of Songs | Sg | 1051 |
| Joel | Jl | 1443 | 1 Thessalonians | 1 Thes | 1955 |
| 1 John | 1 Jn | 2059 | 2 Thessalonians | 2 Thes | 1963 |
| 2 John | 2 Jn | 2067 | 1 Timothy | 1 Tm | 1970 |
| 3 John | 3 Jn | 2070 | 2 Timothy | 2 Tm | 1982 |
| John | Jn | 1716 | Titus | Ti | 1990 |
| Jonah | Jon | 1471 | Tobit | Tb | 712 |
| Joshua | Jos | 403 | Wisdom | Wis | 1062 |
| Jude | Jude | 2074 | Zechariah | Zec | 1516 |
| Judges | Jgs | 432 | Zephaniah | Zep | 1503 |
| Judith | Jdt | 732 | | | |

# Abbreviations, Terms, and Citations for Study Bible

| | |
|---|---|
| BCE | before the Common Era |
| ca. | *circa* (about) |
| CE | Common Era |
| cf. | *confer* (compare) |
| ch. | chapter |
| chs. | chapters |
| d. | date of death |
| ff. | the following verses |
| LORD* | the divine name |
| LXX | Septuagint |
| NT | New Testament |
| OT | Old Testament |
| v. | verse |
| vv. | verses |
| Yahweh* | the divine name |
| // | parallel passage |
| [] | in quotations, indicates a word or phrase that has been added or altered for sense |

*In the OT, the divine name was written as a series of four consonants: YHWH. Many scholars cite the divine name in this form, often to show respect for Jewish tradition, in which the divine name is never uttered. Traditionally, the word *Lord* was spoken in place of the divine name, and the text of the NABRE follows the practice of substituting this word where the divine name occurs in the Hebrew text: LORD. The small capitals indicate that this word represents the divine name. Other scholars cite the divine name in the form in which it probably was pronounced: Yahweh. The articles in this study Bible use the latter form, as it is the form students are most likely to encounter in other works on the Bible.

## Scripture citations

Scriptures are cited by name of book, then chapter number, then (following a colon) verse number. Thus "1 Cor 13:1" indicates First Corinthians, chapter 13, verse 1. In the case of very short works without chapter divisions, the number given indicates the verse. Thus "Phlm 3" indicates Philemon, verse 3.

# ANSELM ACADEMIC
# STUDY BIBLE

New American Bible Revised Edition

*For the text of the articles and introductions*

*Nihil Obstat:* Rev. William M. Becker, STD
            Censor Deputatus
            November 9, 2012

*Imprimatur:* †Most Rev. John Quinn
            Bishop of Winona
            November 9, 2012

The *nihil obstat* and *imprimatur* are official declarations that a book or pamphlet is free of doctrinal or moral error. No implication is contained therein that those who have granted the *nihil obstat* or *imprimatur* agree with the contents, opinions, or statements expressed, nor do they assume any legal responsibility associated with publication.

*For the text of the New American Bible, Revised Edtion*

NEW TESTAMENT

*Nihil Obstat:* Stephen J. Hartdegen, OFM, LSS
            Censor Deputatus

*Imprimatur:* †James A. Hickey, STD, JCD
            Archbishop of Washington
            August 27, 1986

OLD TESTAMENT

RESCRIPT

In accord with canon 825 §I of the Code of Canon Law, the United States Conference of Catholic Bishops hereby approves for publication The New American Bible, Revised Old Testament, a translation of the Sacred Scriptures authorized by the Confraternity of Christian Doctrine, Inc.

The translation was approved by the Administrative Committee of the United States Conference of Catholic Bishops in November 2008 and September 2010. It is permitted by the undersigned for private use and study. Given in the city of Washington, the District of Columbia, on the Feast of Saint Jerome, Priest and Doctor of the Church, the 30th day of September, in the year of our Lord 2010.

       Francis Cardinal George, OMI
       Archbishop of Chicago
       President, USCCB

Created by the publishing team of Anselm Academic.

Cover and Interior Design: Laurie Nelson; Typesetting: Blue Heron Bookcraft; Proofreading: Peachtree Editorial and Proofreading Services

Copyright © 2013 by Anselm Academic, Christian Brothers Publications, 702 Terrace Heights, Winona, MN 55987-1320, www.anselmacademic.org. All rights reserved. No part of this book may be reproduced by any means without the written permission of the publisher.

Printed in the United States of America

ISBN- 978-1-59982-124-5 [PB]
ISBN- 978-1-59982-163-4 [HB]

Library of Congress Cataloging-in-Publication Data

Bible. English. New American. 2013.

    Anselm Academic study Bible : New American Bible revised edition / general editor, Carolyn Osiek, RSCJ ; associate editor, Old Testament, Leslie J. Hoppe, OFM.

    pages cm

Includes index.

ISBN 978-1-59982-124-5 (pbk.) — ISBN 978-1-59982-163-4 (hardbound)

I. Osiek, Carolyn. II. Hoppe, Leslie J. III. Title.

BS192.3.A12013 .W56 2013

220.5'2054—dc23

                       2012043065

# ANSELM ACADEMIC
# STUDY BIBLE

## New American Bible Revised Edition

### General Editor
## Carolyn Osiek, RSCJ

### Associate Editor, Old Testament
## Leslie J. Hoppe, OFM

**ANSELM**
ACADEMIC

# Contents

## Introduction  17

## The Old Testament  113

## Wisdom Books

## Prophets

# The New Testament  1541

## Gospels and the Acts of the Apostles

## New Testament Charts

## Letters and Revelation

# Index to Articles and Introductions  2110

# Additional Study Aids  C1

# Online Supplements

Online resources for the *Anselm Academic Study Bible* are available at www.anselmacademic. com/studybible. Resources include bibliographies for further reading that correspond to the academic articles and introductions to Scripture in the *Anselm Academic Study Bible,* Web resources for related Church and other documents, as well as links to other related sites. Also available are materials from the *Saint Mary's Press College Study Bible* (now out of print).

# List of Maps, Charts, and Photographs

## Old Testament

## New Testament

## Additional Charts

# Contributors

**Patricia D. Ahearne-Kroll** Assistant Professor of Hebrew Bible and Jewish Studies at Ohio Wesleyan University in Delaware. *1 and 2 Maccabees*

**Dianne Bergant, CSA** Professor of Biblical Studies at Catholic Theological Union in Chicago and Past President of the Catholic Biblical Association of America. *Song of Songs; Wisdom; Ben Sira*

**Stephen J. Binz** Independent scholar in Baton Rouge, Louisiana, specializing in biblical pedagogy; founder and author of Ancient-Future Bible Study, Lectio Divina Bible Study, and Threshold Bible Study. *Critical Issues in Contemporary Biblical Interpretation* (with Anselm Academic); *Sacred Scripture in the Catholic Tradition; Contextual and Transformative Interpretation*

**Mary Katherine Birge, SSJ** Associate Professor of Theology at Mount St. Mary's University in Emmitsburg, Maryland. *The Catholic Letters and the Letter to the Hebrews; Hebrews; James; 1 and 2 Peter; 1, 2, and 3 John; Jude*

**Regina Boisclair** Professor of Religious Studies and Cardinal Newman Chair of Catholic Theology at Alaska Pacific University in Anchorage. *The Lectionary: A Canon within the Canon*

**François Bovon** Frothingham Research Professor at Harvard Divinity School in Cambridge, Massachusetts. *Deuterocanonical and Noncanonical Scriptures: Early Christian Apocrypha*

**Mary C. Boys, SNJM** Skinner and McAlpin Professor of Practical Theology at Union Theological Seminary in New York City. *The Christian Bible and the Jews*

**Laurie Brink, OP** Associate Professor of New Testament Studies at Catholic Theological Union in Chicago and Associate Editor for The Bible Today. *Introduction to Pauline Literature; Romans; 1 and 2 Corinthians*

**Susan Calef** Assistant Professor of New Testament Studies at Creighton University in Omaha, Nebraska. *Introduction to the Gospels*

**Warren Carter** Professor of New Testament at Brite Divinity School, Texas Christian University in Fort Worth, Texas. *Matthew*

**Raymond F. Collins** Visiting Scholar at Brown University in Providence, Rhode Island, and former Professor of New Testament at the Catholic University of Leuven in Belgium and the Catholic University of America in Washington, D.C. *Ephesians; Colossians; 1 and 2 Timothy; Titus*

**Mary Coloe** Associate Professor in New Testament at the Australian Catholic University in Melbourne. *John*

**Linda Day** Professor of Religious Studies at Hiram College in Hiram, Ohio, and General Editor of The Catholic Biblical Quarterly. *Joshua*

**Carol J. Dempsey, OP** Professor of Theology at the University of Portland in Oregon. *Introduction to the Pentateuch; Introduction to the Prophets; Isaiah; Jeremiah; Lamentations*

**John Endres, SJ** Professor of Sacred Scripture at the Jesuit School of Theology of Santa Clara University in Berkeley, California, past president of the Catholic Biblical Association, and member of the Society of Biblical Literature. *Deuterocanonical and Noncanonical Scriptures: Old Testament Apocrypha and Pseudepigrapha*

**Marielle Frigge, OSB** Former Professor of Scripture at Mount Marty College, Yankton, SD. Currently teaches for ongoing formation at Sacred Heart Monastery, other religious communities, lay ministry and adult education programs. *A Brief History and Practice of Biblical Criticism*

**Garrett Galvin, OFM** Assistant Professor of Sacred Scripture at the Franciscan School of Theology and the Graduate Theological Union in Berkley, California. *Jonah; Micah; Zephaniah; Haggai*

**Andrew T. Glicksman** Assistant Professor of Theology at the University of Dallas in Irving, Texas. *Introduction to the Wisdom Books; Ecclesiastes*

**Michael D. Guinan, OFM** Professor Emeritus of Old Testament and Semitic Languages at the Franciscan School of Theology and Graduate Theological Union in Berkeley, California. *Baruch; Joel; Amos; Habakkuk; Zechariah*

**Leslie J. Hoppe, OFM** Professor of Old Testament Studies at Catholic Theological Union in Chicago. Associate Editor, Old Testament, *Anselm Academic Study Bible*. *Geography, Archaeology, and the Scriptures; Introduction to the Historical Books; Judges; Ruth; 1 and 2 Samuel; 1 and 2 Kings; 1 and 2 Chronicles; Ezra; Nehemiah*

**James A. Kelhoffer** Professor of Old and New Testament Exegesis at Uppsala University in Sweden and Associate Editor of the series *Wissenschaftliche Untersuchungen zum Neuen Testament* (Scientific Studies of the New Testament). *Mark*

**Dale Launderville, OSB** Professor of Old Testament at the School of Theology and Seminary at Saint John's University in Collegeville, Minnesota. *Hosea; Obadiah; Nahum; Malachi*

**Amy-Jill Levine** University Professor of New Testament and Jewish Studies, E. Rhodes and Leona B. Carpenter Professor of New Testament Studies, and Professor of Jewish Studies at Vanderbilt Divinity School and Vanderbilt University in Nashville, Tennessee, and Affiliated Professor in the Centre for the Study of Jewish-Christian Relations at Woolf Institute in Cambridge, United Kingdom. *Jewish Biblical Interpretation*

**Seán Charles Martin** Associate Professor of Biblical Studies at the Aquinas Institute of Theology in St. Louis, Missouri. *The Distinctiveness of Jesus; The Many Faces of Jesus*

**Geoffrey Miller** Assistant Professor of Scripture at St. Louis University in St. Louis, Missouri. *Tobit; Judith; Esther; Job*

**Harry P. Nasuti** Professor of Biblical Studies and Old Testament at Fordham University in the Bronx, New York. *Psalms*

**James Chukwuma Okoye, CSSp** Director, Center for Spiritan Studies, Duquesne University, Pittsburgh. *The Formation of the Bible*

**Carolyn Osiek, RSCJ** Charles Fischer Catholic Professor of New Testament *emerita* at Brite Divinity School. Past president of the Catholic Biblical Association and the Society of Biblical Literature (SBL), former associate editor of *The Bible Today,* and book review editor of *Catholic Biblical Quarterly.* General editor, *Anselm Academic Study Bible*

**Clare K. Rothschild** Associate Professor of Scripture at Lewis University in Romeoville, Illinois. *Luke; Acts of the Apostles*

**Jean-Pierre Ruiz** Associate Professor of Biblical Studies at St. John's University and Senior Research Fellow of the Vincentian Center for Church and Society in Queens, New York. *Revelation*

**Eric Stewart** Assistant Professor of Religion at Augustana College in Rock Island, Illinois. *Social Context of the Bible*

**Pauline A. Viviano** Associate Professor of Theology at Loyola University in Chicago. *Leviticus; Numbers; Deuteronomy*

**Jerome Walsh** Former Professor of Old Testament at St. John's University, Queens, New York; the University of Botswana in Africa; and the University of Dallas in Irving, Texas. *Ezekiel; Daniel*

**Tatha Wiley** Former Professor of Theology at the Universities of St. Thomas and St. Catherine in St. Paul, Minnesota, and Editor of the Engaging Theology series. *Galatians; Philippians; 1 and 2 Thessalonians; Philemon*

**Christine Roy Yoder** Associate Professor of Old Testament Language, Literature, and Exegesis at Columbia Theological Seminary in Decatur, Georgia. *Proverbs*

# Collaborators on the Old Testament
## of the New American Bible 1970

**Bishops' Committee of the Confraternity of Christian Doctrine**

Most Rev. Charles P. Greco, D.D., Chairman

Most Rev. Joseph T. McGucken, S.T.D.

Most Rev. Vincent S. Waters, D.D.

Most Rev. Romeo Blanchette, D.D.

Most Rev. Christopher J. Weldon, D.D.

**Editors in Chief**

Rev. Louis F. Hartman, C.SS.R., S.S.L., LING.
OR. L., Chairman

Rev. Msgr. Patrick W. Skehan, S.T.D., LL.D.,
Vice-Chairman

Rev. Stephen J. Hartdegen, O.F.M., S.S.L.,
Secretary

**Associate Editors and Translators**

Rev. Edward P. Arbez, S.S., S.T.D.

Rev. Msgr. Edward J. Byrne, PH.D., S.T.D.

Rev. Edward A. Cerny, S.S., S.T.D.

Rev. James E. Coleran, S.J., S.T.L., S.S.L.

Rev. John J. Collins, S.J., M.A., S.S.L.

Sr. M. Emmanuel Collins, O.S.F., PH.D.

Prof. Frank M. Cross Jr., PH.D.

Rev. Patrick Cummins, O.S.B., S.T.D.

Rev. Antonine A. DeGuglielmo, O.F.M., S.T.D.,
S.S.L., S.S.LECT. Gen.

Rev. Alexander A. Di Lella, O.F.M., S.T.L.,
S.S.L., PH.D.

Most Rev. John J. Dougherty, S.T.L., S.S.D.

William A. Dowd, S.J., S.T.D., S.S.L.

Prof. David Noel Freedman, PH.D.

Rev. Michael J. Fruenthaner, S.J., S.T.D., S.S.D.

Rev. Msgr. Maurice A. Hofer, S.S.L

Rev. Justin Krellner, O.S.B., S.T.D.

Rev. Joseph L. Lilly, C.M., S.T.D., S.S.L.

Rev. Roderick F. MacKenzie, S.J., M.A., S.S.D.

Rev. Edward A. Mangan, C.SS.R., S.S.L.

Rev. Daniel W. Martin, C.M., S.T.L., S.S.L.

Rev. William H. McClellan, S.J.

Rev. James McGlinchey, C.M., S.T.D.

Rev. Frederick Moriarty, S.J., S.S.L., S.T.D.

Rev. Richard T. Murphy, O.P., S.T.D., S.S.D.

Rev. Roland E. Murphy, O. Carm., M.A., S.T.D.,
S.S.L.

Rev. Msgr. William R. Newton, M.S., S.S.D.

Rev. Everhard Olinger, O.S.B.

Rev. Charles H. Pickar, O.S.A., S.T.L., S.S.L.

Rev. Christopher Rehwinkel, O.F.M., S.T.D.,
S.S. LECT. GEN.

Rev. Msgr. John R. Rowan, S.T.D., S.S.L.,

Prof. J. A. Sanders, PH.D.

Rev. Edward F. Siegman, C.PP.S., S.T.D., S.S.L.

Rev. Msgr. Matthew P. Stapleton, S.T.D., S.S.L.

Rev. Msgr. John E. Steinmueller, S.T.D., S.S.L.

Rev. John Ujlaki, O.S.B., LITT.D.

Rev. Bruce Vawter, C.M., S.T.L., S.S.D.

Rev. John B. Weisengoff, S.T.D., S.S.L.

# Collaborators on the Revised Psalms
# of the New American Bible 1991

**Bishops' Ad Hoc Committee**

Most Rev. Enrique San Pedro, S.J.

Most Rev. Richard Sklba, D.D.

Most Rev. Donald W. Trautman, S.T.D., S.S.L.

Most Rev. Emil A. Wcela

Most Rev. John F. Whealon, S.S.L., Chairman

**Board of Editors**

Rev. Richard Clifford, S.J.

Br. Aloysius Fitzgerald, F.S.C.

Rev. Joseph Jensen, O.S.B.

Rev. Roland Murphy, O.Carm.

Sr. Irene Nowell, O.S.B.

Dr. Judith Sanderson

**Revisers**

Prof. Gary Anderson

Rev. Michael L. Barré, S.S.

Rev. Christopher T. Begg

Dr. Joseph Blenkinsopp

Rev. Anthony R. Ceresko, O.S.F.S.

Rev. Richard J. Clifford, S.J.

Rev. Aelred Cody, O.S.B.

Prof. Michael D. Coogan

Rev. Alexander A. Di Lella, O.F.M.

Dr. Robert A. Di Vito

Br. Aloysius Fitzgerald, F.S.C.

Rev. Michael D. Guinan, O.F.M.

Rev. William L. Holladay

Rev. William Irwin, C.S.B.

Rev. Joseph Jensen, O.S.B.

Rev. John S. Kselman

Rev. Leo Laberge, O.M.I.

Dr. Conrad E. L'Heureux

Dr. Paul G. Mosca

Rev. Dr. Roland E. Murphy, O.Carm.

Dr. Michael Patrick O'Connor

Rev. Brian J. Peckham, S.J.

Prof. Jimmy J. Roberts

Sr. Eileen M. Schuller, O.S.U.

Dr. Byron E. Shafer

Prof. Mark S. Smith

Prof. Matitiahu Tesvat

Dr. Eugene C. Ulrich

Prof. James C. VanderKam

Rev. Jerome T. Walsh

**English Consultants**

Dr. Catherine Dunn

Br. Daniel Burke, F.S.C.

**Business Manager**

Charles A. Buggé

# Collaborators on the Revised New Testament of the New American Bible 1986

**Bishops' Ad Hoc Committee**

Most Rev. Theodore E. McCarrick, D.D.

Most Rev. Richard J. Sklba, D.D.

Most Rev. J. Francis Stafford, D.D.

Most Rev. John F. Whealon, D.D., Chairman

**Board of Editors**

Rev. Msgr. Myles M. Bourke

Rev. Francis T. Gignac, S.J., Chairman

Rev. Stephen J. Hartdegen, O.F.M., Secretary

Rev. John H. Reumann

**Revisers**

Rev. Msgr. Myles M. Bourke

Rev. Frederick W. Danker

Rev. Alexander A. Di Lella, O.F.M.

Rev. Charles H. Giblin, S.J.

Rev. Francis T. Gignac, S.J.

Rev. Stephen J. Hartdegen, O.F.M.

Dr. Maurya P. Horgan

Rev. John R. Keating, S.J.

Rev. John Knox

Dr. Paul J. Kobelski

Dr. J. Rebecca Lyman

Br. Elliott C. Maloney, O.S.B.

Dr. Janet A. Timbie

**Consultants**

Rev. Joseph Jensen, O.S.B.

Rev. Aidan Kavanagh, O.S.B.

Dr. Marianne Sawicki

**Business Manager**

Charles A. Buggé

**Word Processor**

Suzanna Jordan

13

# Collaborators on the Old Testament of the New American Bible 2010

**Bishops' Committee on Doctrine**
**Subcommittee on the Translation of Scripture Text**

Most Rev. Arthur J. Serratelli, Chairman

Justin Cardinal Rigali

Most Rev. Blase J. Cupich

Most Rev. Richard J. Sklba

Most Rev. Anthony B. Taylor

**Board of Editors**

Dr. Deirdre A. Dempsey

Dr. Robert A. Di Vito

Rev. Francis T. Gignac, S.J.

Rev. Joseph Jensen, O.S.B., Chairman

Rev. Dale Launderville, O.S.B.

Rev. Roland E. Murphy, O.Carm. +

Dr. Kathleen S. Nash

Sr. Irene Nowell, O.S.B.

Rev. James P. M. Walsh, S.J.

**Revisers**

Dr. Gary A. Anderson

Rev. Michael L. Barré, S.S.

Rev. Christopher T. Begg

Dr. Joseph Blenkinsopp

Rev. Lawrence Boadt, C.S.P. +

Prof. Edward F. Campbell

Prof. Anthony Ceresko, OSFS +

Rev. Richard J. Clifford, S.J.

Rev. Aelred Cody, O.S.B.

Dr. John J. Collins

Prof. Michael D. Coogan

Rev. T.J. Jeremy Corley

Dr. Toni Craven

Dr. James L. Crenshaw

Rev. Alexander A. Di Lella, O.F.M.

Dr. Robert A. Di Vito

Br. Aloysius Fitzgerald, F.S.C. +

Rev. Joseph A. Fitzmyer, S.J.

Dr. Carole R. Fontaine

Rev. Daniel J. Harrington, S.J.

Dr. Richard S. Hess

Dr. Theodore Hiebert

Dr. William L. Holladay

Dr. Tod Linafelt

Dr. P. Kyle McCarter, Jr.

Dr. Carol Meyers

Dr. Eric Meyers

Dr. Patrick D. Miller, Jr.

Rev. Craig E. Morrison, O. Carm.

Dr. Paul G. Mosca

Dr. Kathleen S. Nash

Prof. Robert A. Oden, Jr.

Rev. Gregory J. Polan, O.S.B.

Dr. James J. M. Roberts

Dr. William M. Soll

Dr. Gene M. Tucker

Dr. Eugene C. Ulrich

Rev. Walter A. Vogels, W.F.

Rev. Jerome T. Walsh

Rev. Addison G. Wright, S.S.

Dr. David P. Wright

**Business Managers**

Charles Buggé

Mary Elizabeth Sperry

**Word Processors**

Ellen Coughlin

Nancy Hartnagel

14

# Collaborators on the Book of Psalms of the New American Bible 2010

**Bishops' Committee on Doctrine**
**Subcommittee on the Translation of Scripture Text**

Most Rev. Arthur J. Serratelli, Chairman

Justin Cardinal Rigali

Most Rev. Blase J. Cupich

Most Rev. Richard J. Sklba

Most Rev. Anthony B. Taylor

**Board of Editors**

Rev. Joseph Mindling, OFM Cap.

Rev. J. Edward Owens, O.SS.T.

**Revisers**

Rev. Michael L. Barré, S.S.

Dr. Corrine L. Carvalho

Dr. Robert A. Di Vito

Dr. Robert D. Miller II, SFO

Rev. Joseph Mindling, OFM Cap.

Rev. J. Edward Owens, O.SS.T.

Dr. Eugene C. Ulrich

**Business Manager**

Mary Elizabeth Sperry

# General Editor Acknowledgments

Just at the time that I was retiring from thirty-two years of graduate teaching in New Testament, this project was offered to me. It seemed a good way to put to use the years of experience and professional contacts that I had accumulated. We needed a consulting editor for intricacies of Old Testament commentary for which I did not think I was completely knowledgeable, and Leslie Hoppe, OFM, has admirably fulfilled that role. My gratitude goes to the many who contributed articles, commentary, and peer reviews, whose names appear in the book, and to the people with whom I dealt at Anselm Academic Press: Penny Koehler for communicating with authors and reviewers and keeping track of it all; Kristi Gudmundson for her expertise with layout, charts and maps; Paul Peterson, copy editor extraordinaire whom nary a stray reference escaped; and especially Jerry Ruff, editorial director, who kept the whole multi-ring circus going with balance, wisdom, and humor.

Carolyn Osiek, RSCJ

# Publisher Acknowledgments

*Thank you to the following individuals who reviewed this work in progress:*

**Coleman A. Baker**
*Brite Divinity School, Texas Christian University, Fort Worth, Texas*

**Richard J. Bautch**
*St. Edward's University, Austin, Texas*

**Ann Marie Caron**
*University of Saint Joseph, West Hartford, Connecticut*

**Corrine Carvalho**
*University of St. Thomas, Saint Paul, Minnesota*

**Kelley Coblentz-Bautch**
*St. Edward's University, Austin, Texas*

**Chris Franke**
*St. Catherine University, Saint Paul, Minnesota*

**Tod Linafelt**
*Georgetown University, Washington, DC*

**Maria Pascuzzi**
*School of Theology and Ministry, St. Thomas University, Miami Gardens, Florida*

**Robert H. von Thaden, Jr.**
*Mercyhurst University, Erie, Pennsylvania*

*The following contributors also reviewed this work in progress:*

Regina Boisclair, Mary Coloe, Leslie J. Hoppe, James A. Kelhoffer

*The publisher also thanks those other individuals who have generously and without recognition given of their scholarship, talent, and passion in the creation of the Anselm Academic Study Bible.*

# Introduction

# Introduction

"When I found your words, I devoured them; / your words were my joy, the happiness of my heart." So proclaimed the prophet Jeremiah in a moment of great distress (Jer 15:16). In return, God promised that if Jeremiah spoke the words of God's truth, he would endure and be a pillar of strength to others.

From age to age, the words of the Scriptures have been a source of inspiration for communities and persons who seek the face of God. They are sometimes not easy words, but rather "sharper than any two-edged sword . . . and able to discern reflections and thoughts of the heart" (Heb 4:12). To understand the Scriptures requires study and prayer, alone and in community.

From the beginning of Christian history, disciples of Jesus found in the Scriptures of Israel answers to their questions about the identity of Jesus. They realized that they needed to know as much as possible about the time, the place, and the people of biblical passages in order to understand the intended meaning of these Scriptures. All the while, these disciples were discovering new dimensions of interpretation that could respond to their new faith. These new dimensions became the expression of their own faith, in what we now call the New Testament. Together, the Bible of Israel, what we typically call the Old Testament, and the New Testament, are the foundation of the church's faith.

The Bible is the book of all Christians. Its proper home is in the faith community. Yet over the centuries its readers have also come to understand that the use of academic methods of history, archaeology, the social sciences, linguistics, and literary theory can enlighten and deepen their appreciation for the rich heritage of the Scriptures.

The following pages are intended to be an aid to the search for an ever deepening understanding of the words of Scripture. Here you will find what the best scholarship today has to tell us about how these remarkable writings came to be. We hope that you will find them helpful for your study and that you will, like so many before you, be amazed and attracted by the power of these Scriptures.

"This study is never finished; each age must in its own way newly seek to understand the sacred books" (*Interpretation of the Bible in the Church*, Pontifical Biblical Commission, Preface). You who now study the Bible are part of this process.

Carolyn Osiek, RSCJ
General Editor

# The Formation of the Bible

## James Chukwuma Okoye, CSSp

## Introduction

The word "Bible" comes from the Greek *ta biblia* ("the books"), for the Bible is a library of books spanning many centuries that Jews and Christians regard as inspired by God. It is Judeo-Christian belief that God's people first transmitted God's word orally. There came a time when oral traditions were put into writing, adapted, or added to, in order to reflect the Judeo-Christian community's fresh experiences of God. The term "Scripture" is used for such writings considered inspired and religiously authoritative.

The idea of inspiration is portrayed metaphorically in the account of God showing Moses the blueprint of the tabernacle (Ex 25–31) and dictating the Ten Commandments (Ex 20:1–17) and other laws for the community. It is found also in 2 Pt 1:21: "For no prophecy ever came through human will; but rather human beings moved by the holy Spirit spoke under the influence of God" (cf. 2 Tm 3:16).

In due time, lists of Scripture writings began to be formed. In different places and at different times these lists varied as to which writings to include and which to exclude until the community reached agreement on a delimited list called the canon. "Canon" (Greek, *kanōn*) means a rule or measuring cane, and it is used also to name a list of works that set the standard in literature or art. In reference to the Bible, canon is "a fixed collection of Scriptures that comprise [the] authoritative witness for a religious body."[1] A canon is not finalized until the text is standardized and henceforth adapts to fresh experiences only through interpretation, not the addition of more texts. However, a canon may allow tensions to stand. For example, the deuteropauline letters, those bearing Paul's name but written by others,

stand alongside the authentic letters of Paul and serve to integrate certain difficult Pauline teachings into the common pool of faith. A more striking example of tension is found in Ex 20:5–6 and Dt 7:10. The former says that the punishment for crimes committed by fathers will fall upon their children, while the latter asserts that God "repays with destruction *those who hate him*; he does not delay with those who hate him, but makes *them* pay for it" (NABRE; italics added)—rejecting trans-generational retribution for individual retribution.

Canons also differ among and even within traditions. For example, the Hebrew Bible contains thirty-nine books arranged in tripartite form. The name of this collection, "Tanak," is an acronym of the letters TNK, representing the three divisions of the collection: Torah (Law), Nebi'im (Prophets), and Ketubim (Writings). The ancient Greek version, called the "Septuagint" (discussed below), had about fifty books in a fourfold arrangement: Pentateuch (Law), Historical Books, Poetic Books, and Prophets. In the various Christian traditions, the books of the Old Testament follow the divisions of the Septuagint. The Protestant Old Testament has the same number of books as the Hebrew Bible (thirty-nine), while the Roman Catholic has forty-six, the Greek Orthodox forty-seven, and the Ethiopian Orthodox fifty. For Jews, Torah is the center of revelation and Judges– 2 Kings are "prophets." For Christians Judges– 2 Kings (with the addition, in many denominations, of certain books from the Septuagint) are "history," while the entire Old Testament is "prophecy" in the sense that Christians believe it foreshadows Christ. The Christian Old Testament is arranged so that it ends with the promise of the coming of Elijah (Mal 3:23), whom Mk 1:2–4 identifies as John the Baptist, herald of Christ.

The picture is much simpler with regard to the New Testament. All Christians now accept the same twenty-seven books.

---

1. Lee Martin McDonald and James A. Sanders, eds., *The Canon Debate* (Peabody: Hendrickson Publishers, 2002), 11.

## The Hebrew Bible—Christian Old Testament

Paul referred to the Scriptures of Israel as the "old covenant" (2 Cor 3:14). Jeremiah 31:31–34 promised a "new covenant." Jesus, relying on the promise of a new covenant, proclaimed "the new covenant" in his blood (Lk 22:20). The Septuagint rendered Hebrew *berit* (covenant) with *diathēkē* (testament). Irenaeus of Lyon (130–200 CE) was the first to speak of an "Old Testament" and a "New Testament." Out of sensitivity for Jewish belief and tradition, some Christian scholars prefer to speak of the "First Testament." However, by "Old Testament" Christians do not mean that the Hebrew Scriptures are outmoded or obsolete; rather, they are the foundational revelation for understanding the New Testament.

# Early Biblical Pieces

## The Pentateuch

Some of the poetic pieces of the Pentateuch appear to be as early as the twelfth century BCE: Ex 15:1–18 (the Song of Moses), Jgs 5, and Dt 33. Outside the Pentateuch, Ps 29 seems quite ancient and has a parallel in Ugaritic. Ugaritic is an ancient language related to Hebrew; it is known from a trove of writings dating from the fourteenth to twelfth centuries BCE found in the ruins of Ugarit (modern Ras Shamra in Syria).

Such early examples remind us that pre-literate communities generally preserve communal history through oral tradition. Literacy did not become widespread in Israel till the sixth century BCE. Gerhard von Rad believed that Genesis, Exodus, Leviticus, Numbers, Deuteronomy, and Joshua grew out of a "cultic credo" (Dt 26:5–9) recited in the central shrines of Gilgal and Shechem, with the following broad themes: Exodus from Egypt, entry into the promised land, patriarchal stories, wilderness wanderings, and Sinai and covenant.[2] These credos would have been expanded into written historical units by the Yahwist, a tenth-century

writer under Solomon. The Yahwist was one of four written documents underlying the Pentateuch in Julius Wellhausen's 1878 Documentary Hypothesis: The Yahwist ("J," since "Yahwist" begins with a "J" in German), Elohist ("E"), Deuteronomy ("D"), and Priestly sources ("P"). These four sources range from the tenth century BCE till about 400 BCE respectively. The hinge for this thesis was "the book of the law" (*torah*) discovered in 621 during repairs in the temple (2 Kgs 22–23). The reforms that King Josiah subsequently enacted show that this book of the Torah contained parts of Deuteronomy. The term "torah" ("law, instruction") was thus first applied to Deuteronomy and later to the Pentateuch.

More recent evaluation of the sources of the Pentateuch tends to lower both their complexity and the dates. A minority of scholars, though, think that Israel's national and religious traditions were handed on orally till they merged in two exilic written strands: Genesis to Numbers (attributable to P), and Deuteronomy to 2 Kings (the work of the D circle). The Pentateuch was finalized before 300 BCE, for the Samaritans, who split from Judea about that time, retained a Pentateuch (Samaritan Pentateuch) close in form to the Hebrew Torah, but with multiple variations.

## The Historical Books

Many scholars believe that the Deuteronomistic History (Deuteronomy–2 Kings) was composed in the seventh century BCE under King Hezekiah (716–687). Some think that around 550 BCE it was combined with Genesis–Numbers (known to scholars as the Tetrateuch). According to this theory, the resultant collection, which scholars call the Primary History (Genesis to Kings), was the Bible of the exiles. Others propose that the corpus of Deuteronomy–2 Kings was the work of an exilic editor. Deuteronomy was later detached from this corpus and attached to Genesis–Numbers to close the period of Mosaic revelation. Still others propose a double edition of the Deuteronomistic History, the first edition being compiled in the seventh century as propaganda for King Josiah, the second during the exile.

---

2. Gerhard von Rad, "The Form-Critical Problem of the Hexateuch," in *The Problem of the Hexateuch and Other Essays*, trans. E. W. Trueman Dicken (New York: McGraw-Hill, 1966), 1–78.

## The Prophets

Already in the eighth century, Isaiah recorded and sealed an apparently unfulfilled prophecy (Is 8:16). Jeremiah wrote down all his prophecies and repeated the exercise after King Jehoiakim burned the first scroll (Jer 36). The book of Isaiah is paradigmatic for the formation of the prophetic corpus. It originated in three diverse contexts: Is 1–39 (largely the eighth century), Is 40–55 (the exilic context, 586–539 BCE) and Is 56–66 (the postexilic context, around the fifth century BCE). It is possible that Is 40–55 never existed independently of Is 1–39, Deutero-Isaiah being the one who bound the two parts of the work together.[3] Isaiah 24–27 (called the Isaiah Apocalyse) was added in the third century BCE. The book of Jeremiah exists in at least two recensions: the Masoretic and the Septuagint, which is one-eighth shorter (see also next page, "The Dead Sea Scrolls"). The Masoretic Text (MT) is the Hebrew text as standardized and equipped with marginal and other notes by Tiberian Masoretes of the fifth to the tenth centuries CE. The parallel between the Masoretic Text of Jer 52 and 2 Kgs 24:18–25:30 suggests the same circle of editors for both (also the parallel between Is 36–39 and 2 Kg 18:13–20:19).

The Twelve Minor Prophets were written on one scroll. Many scholars agree that the collection started with the books of Hosea and Amos, and that retouches were made to both together. Beyond this, consensus eludes scholars. One proposal[4] is that next to be added was an early corpus of Hosea, Amos, Micah, and Zephaniah (related to the Deuteronomistic History and centered on Yahweh's judgment), followed by a Haggai-Zechariah 1–8 corpus, and finally the Joel-related corpus of Joel, Obadiah, Nahum, Habakkuk, and Malachi in the fifth/fourth century BCE. In the Hellenistic era, Zec 9–14 and Jonah were added. Daniel, which the Hebrew Bible places among the Writings, not the Prophets, bears the date of 165 BCE. Rabbinic tradition has it that prophecy ceased in Israel after the time of Ezra (b. Yoma 9b; b. Sanh 11a). Similarly, Josephus, a writer of Jewish history around 90–100 CE, claims that the succession of prophets ceased under Artaxerxes about the same time (*Against Apion* 1.43). Several texts bewail the lack of prophets (1 Mc 4:45–46; 14:41; Ps 74:9; Zec 13:2–6). Joel 3:1–2 pushes the renewed gift of prophecy to eschatological times. The text of the prophets was stabilized in the first century BCE/CE.[5]

## The Septuagint

The *Letter of Aristeas* (between 130 and 70 BCE) narrated the myth of seventy-two translators, six from each of the twelve tribes, summoned from Palestine to Alexandria by the Hellenistic king, Ptolemy II Philadelphus (285–46), to translate the Torah into Greek. That this translation came to be called the Septuagint, meaning "Seventy" (abbreviated LXX), rather than "Seventy-Two" may reflect the fact that Greek was the lingua franca and Jews counted the number of nations at seventy. That at first the Torah (Genesis–Deuteronomy) alone was translated indicates that only it had reached some fixity. By the second to early third centuries CE, "Septuagint" referred to the entire Greek Bible. It was also the first Christian Bible, preserved uniquely by Christians: "More than ninety percent of the quotations from the Old Testament in the New are from it."[6] It featured in textual debates in the early second century CE between Jews and Christians (Justin, *Dialogue with Trypho*, 71–73, citing the Septuagint of Is 7:14, "behold a virgin shall conceive" [cf. Mt 1:23] versus the Hebrew text, "behold a young woman shall conceive"). About this time, Jews commissioned more literal Greek translations (the versions of Aquila, Symmachus, and Theodotion). They equally rejected the messianism

---

3. H. G. Williamson, *The Book Called Isaiah: Deutero-Isaiah's Role in Composition and Redaction* (Oxford: Clarendon Press, 1994), 241. "In order to locate his message in relation to the earlier and continuing ways of God with Israel [Deutero-Isaiah] included a version of the earlier prophecies with his own and edited them in such a way as to bind the two parts of the work together" (24–41).

4. James Nogalski, *Literary Precursors to the Book of the Twelve* (Berlin: Walter de Gruyter, 1993), 282.

5. James Sanders, "Canon: Hebrew Bible," *ABD*, I:837–52, at 843.

6. Lee Martin McDonald, *The Biblical Canon: Its Origin, Transmission, and Authority* (Peabody: Hendrickson Publishers, 1995), xvii, 35.

and apocalypticism of those Scriptures that influenced the wars with Rome in 66–70 and 132–135 CE.

## The Dead Sea Scrolls

The Dead Sea Scrolls were discovered in the Judean wilderness around Qumran from 1947 to 1956. They gave evidence of scriptures even broader than the LXX and thus of the fluid state of the text of the Old Testament around the first century BCE/CE. Hebrew and Aramaic copies of Ben Sira (already known from the Cairo Geniza collection of 280,000 fragments of Jewish writings discovered in 1901), Tobit, Ps 151, and the Letter of Jeremiah (in Hebrew and Greek) turned up among the Dead Sea Scrolls, suggesting that the LXX circulated in Palestine and that the broader Christian canon (preserved in the LXX) came from Palestine and not from Alexandria. Fragments of a Greek version of the book of the Twelve Prophets from Muraba'at (dating ca. 50–100 CE) confirmed the early circulation of Greek Scriptures in Palestine itself. This text proved to be a revision of a Greek translation older than the LXX. The six Jeremiah fragments from Qumran divide into two recensions: a shorter one resembling the LXX, which is one-eighth shorter than the Masoretic Text (4QJer[b] and 4QJer[d]), and a longer one resembling the Masoretic Text (4QJer[a] and 4QJer[c]).[7]

Thus toward the end of the first century BCE, the text of the Hebrew Bible was still fluid, with at least the two recensions above and the Samaritan Pentateuch. It seems that the sectarians of Qumran considered 1 Enoch, Jubilees, the Temple Scroll, and some other texts as Scripture, perhaps Jubilees, the Temple Scroll, and the Reworked Pentateuch as even belonging to the books of Moses.[8] Qumran scribes apparently felt free to delete sentences from the text of Scripture and make other changes, so the text was not yet fixed. The mid-second century BCE sectarian text 4QMMT (Miqsat Maaseh Torah = Some of the Works of the

Torah) yields some evidence of an emerging canon when it speaks of blessings and curses "in the book of Moses [and] in the book[s of the Pr]ophets and in Davi[d and in the events] of ages past."[9] This suggests a canon of Torah and Prophets, possibly an emerging third section (indicated by "David," that is, the Psalms), and maybe even a fourth section that covers historical writings (just like the LXX). Texts unknown before Qumran include the Genesis Apocryphon, Melchisedek texts, and many psalms.

The New Testament cites 1 Enoch, Jubilees, and elements of the emerging Testaments of the Twelve Patriarchs, texts not in the LXX but found in Qumran, thus confirming the broader Palestinian provenance of Old Testament Scriptures (see above). It also cites the Assumption of Moses, Jannes and Jambres, and the Martyrdom and Ascension of Isaiah found neither in Qumran nor the LXX. It thus appears that the more restricted Hebrew canon was a result of a de-canonization process among Jews in response to Christian use of Jewish texts, and not of Christian additions of books to a closed Hebrew canon. We mentioned above the early second-century debates between Jews and Christians and the Jewish commissioning of Greek translations more literal than the LXX about the same time.

## The Canonization of the Old Testament

Before discovery of the Dead Sea Scrolls, the consensus among scholars was that the collection of Torah closed by about 400 BCE, Prophets by 200 BCE, and the Writings at the Council of Jamnia by about 90 CE. Ezra was called a "scribe, well-versed in the law of Moses given by the LORD" (Ezr 7:6), so many scholars opined that he brought with him the full Pentateuch. However, the Dead Sea Scrolls have shown that by 68 CE (date of the fall of Qumran) the text of the Old Testament was still in flux and that the sectarians, if perhaps not all Jews, admitted a broader collection of books of the Torah. Ben Sira 44–50 (Praise

---

7. Cf. James VanderKam and Peter Flint, The Meaning of the Dead Sea Scrolls (HarperSanFrancisco: 2002), 134.

8. Ibid., 177–79; see also Canon Debate, ed. McDonald and Sanders, 91–109, at 108.

9. VanderKam and Flint, The Meaning of the Dead Sea Scrolls, 170.

of Famous Men), early second century BCE, is the first text to refer to prophetic writings by name. It follows the order of the five books of Moses, Joshua–2 Kings, Isaiah, Jeremiah, Job, the Twelve Prophets, and Nehemiah (surprisingly he does not mention Ezra). Job may have been included as among the Prophets; in fact, any non-Torah book of Scripture was relegated to the Prophets. The foreword to the Greek translation of Ben Sira ca. 117 BCE (the original Hebrew was ca. 182 BCE) presents apparently closed sections of "Law and Prophets" and an indeterminate third section, referred to as "the rest of the books," and "the authors who followed them."

In Lk 24:44, Jesus speaks of "the law of Moses and . . . the prophets and psalms." Here, just as in 4QMMT (see above), "law" and "prophets" are definite sections, with "psalms" standing for an emerging section. Also in the late first century, Josephus (*Against Apion* 1.37–42) was the first to list the books of a supposedly closed Hebrew canon. This list numbered twenty-two books, the number of the Hebrew alphabet: five books of Moses, the prophets in thirteen books covering the history from Moses to Artaxerxes, then four books of hymns to God and precepts. In the extra-biblical *4 Ezra* 14:23–28 (ca. 100 CE), Ezra dictated ninety-four books, twenty-four for everybody (corresponds to the number of the current Hebrew canon) and seventy reserved for the wise. *B. Baba Batra* 14b, in discussions between rabbis of the end of the second century CE, lists by name the current twenty-four books of the Hebrew Bible in its three sections.

*Mishnah Yadayim* 3:5 (the Mishnah dates to 200 CE) reports a discussion in the Academy at Jamnia (Hebrew, *Yabneh*) toward the end of the first century CE about whether Qohelet (Ecclesiastes) and the Song of Songs "defile the hands," that is, are sacred Scripture. Rabbi Akiba's spiritual interpretation facilitated the acceptance of the Song of Songs. Many scholars today argue that Jamnia was no "synod" in the modern sense and, besides, the canon was not closed there. However, the Jamnia Academy represented Judaism in the eyes of the Romans. Some authority commissioned the late-first-century CE Jewish Greek translations mentioned above and by 130 CE rejected

the LXX altogether. The most likely candidate seems to be the Jamnia Academy. Already in early first century CE, the schools of Hillel and Shammai had discussed rules of interpretation of Scripture, suggesting that the text of parts of the Hebrew Bible was fixed or becoming so. Hillel came from Babylon and may have accepted only writings ostensibly dating to the times of Ezra-Nehemiah, and so may have influenced the shorter listing of Hebrew Scriptures, which rabbinic Judaism adopted in the second century CE.[10]

# The New Testament

Christ is the center of the Christian revelation. Most important to the early church were the sayings of Jesus and traditions about him from witnesses who knew him. First Corinthians 7:10, 25; 9:4–18 refer to the words of Jesus as normative. Joachim Jeremias compiled a list of 266 extrabiblical sayings of Jesus.[11] Until toward the end of the second century CE, Scripture for the early church meant the Greek Old Testament, which was reinterpreted to predict or explain the events of Jesus. The oral tradition of the sayings of Jesus found written form in the earliest strata of Q and the Gospel of Thomas.[12]

*Euangelion* ("gospel") referred primarily to the oral preaching about Jesus Christ. The move of Christians to Pella (in Jordan) in 66 CE, the destruction of the Temple in 70, and the death of the apostles necessitated written accounts of this gospel, beginning with the Gospel of Mark. Marcion, however (mid-second century), was the first to use the term *euangelion* for a book or writing. He identified apostolic preaching with Paul and accepted as Scripture only ten of Paul's letters and an edited Gospel of Luke. The Gnostics used mainly the same writings as the wider church, but interpreted them differently. In his

---

10. McDonald, *Biblical Canon*, 113, 158, 223.

11. Joachim Jeremias, *The Unknown Sayings of Jesus*, trans. R. H. Fuller (London: SPCK, 1958).

12. Q is a sayings source posited by scholars to explain the agreements of Matthew and Luke. The Gospel of Thomas is a gnostic work containing sayings of Jesus in gnostic clothing. Some scholars think it preceded the Christian Gospels, but the majority hold it to be early second century CE.

argument with the Gnostics, Irenaeus of Lyon (ca. 170–180) developed the doctrine of the *regula fidei* ("rule of faith"). The rule of faith consisted of varying lists of affirmations drawn from the Scriptures themselves but upheld as parameters for genuine faith and the authenticity of scriptural writings. Irenaeus was also one of the first to call Christian writings Scripture.[13]

An influence toward the Christian canon was the Christian preference for the codex from at least 100 CE. The codex was bound like modern books and so could contain the entire Bible within the same cover, unlike the scrolls used earlier. The letters of Paul were the first to be collected; 2 Pt 3:15–16 (ca. 130–150 CE) refers to them as Scripture. By about 200 CE, the four Gospels and thirteen letters of Paul were accepted everywhere.[14] The Gospel of John was beloved by Gnostics. The second-century gnostic Heracleon wrote the first ever Christian biblical commentary on it. As such, John came under suspicion in Rome and was not accepted until much later.

Several gospels circulated in the second century, mostly named after apostles, for example, the *Protoevangelium of James*, the *Gospel of Peter*, and the *Gospel of the Hebrews*. It was customary for each Christian community to have only one gospel. Soon the divergences between the various gospels raised questions. Tatian, a student of Justin Martyr, harmonized the four Gospels in his *Diatessaron*, which became the gospel of the Syrian church till well into the fifth century CE. Irenaeus solved the problem of divergences by speaking of *the* fourfold Gospel, that is, the one Gospel with four faces. He limited the Gospels to the current four. In the mid-second century, "the gospel according to . . ." came to be attached to the hitherto anonymous four Gospels. According to Eusebius (*Ecclesiastical History* 5.8.2–8, completed around 325 CE), Irenaeus accepted as Scripture Matthew, Mark, Luke, John, Revelation, Paul (the individual books of Paul were not listed), 1 John, 1 Peter, *Shepherd*

of Hermas, and Wisdom of Solomon. Other fathers of the church accepted *1 Clement, Didache, Barnabas,* and other writings. The book of Revelation was current in the West in the second century. It was also accepted in the East, until in the third century Bishop Dionysius proved it could not be from the same author as the Gospel of John.

When Constantine moved the capital from Rome to Byzantium (Constantinople) in 324, he asked Eusebius to produce fifty copies of the Scriptures for churches in the city. Eusebius himself rejected Revelation, but included it because Constantine liked it.[15] The Epistle to the Hebrews occurs in an Egyptian papyrus of the second century (P46) but was not accepted generally in the West until the fourth century. Of the Catholic Epistles, only 1 Peter and 1 John were current in the second/third century CE, Eusebius being the first to speak of "Catholic Epistles" as a group of seven.[16] The Muratorian Fragment, which used to be considered the earliest New Testament canon and of Roman origin of the second century CE, is now seen by many as of eastern provenance and dating from the late fourth century.[17]

The formation of the canon was no designed process, but the result of the interplay of contingent factors. However, certain criteria did play a role. The first was *apostolicity*—a writing had to be seen as deriving from the era of the apostles (or simply in agreement with what the church took to be apostolic teaching). Another was *catholicity*—a writing had to be relevant to the church at large and not esoteric. *Orthodoxy* required that a writing not contradict the "rule of faith." For example, bishop Serapion of Antioch initially allowed the *Gospel of Peter* to be read in church until he found its content to be contrary to the accepted faith, then banned it (*Ecclesiastical History* 6.12.3–6). Finally, a writing should be *traditional*, that is, in use in worship in most churches and from early times. Eusebius (*Ecclesiastical History* 3.25.1–17), ca. 320–342, set out the first identifiable list of New Testament Scriptures, dividing them into

---

13. Harry Y. Gamble, "Canon: New Testament," *ABD*, I:852–61, at 855.

14. Harry Y. Gamble, "The Formation of the New Testament Canon," in *A History of Biblical Interpretation*, ed. Alan Hauser and Duane Watson (Grand Rapids: Eerdmans, 2003), 1:409–29, at 416.

15. McDonald, *Biblical Canon*, 318–20.

16. Gamble, "Canon: New Testament," 855.

17. Ibid., 856.

three categories: *recognized* as Scripture were four Gospels, fourteen Letters of Paul, 1 John, 1 Peter, (Revelation?); *disputed* were James, Jude, 2 Peter, 2 John, and 3 John; and *spurious* were *Acts of Paul*, *Shepherd of Hermas*, *Apocalypse of Peter, Barnabas, Didache*, and possibly Revelation. Finally Athanasius's thirty-ninth Easter Letter (367 CE) was the first to give the current canon of the New Testament, a canon reaffirmed in the Council of Hippo, 393 (which distinguished Hebrews from Paul).

## Translations

Many ancients, including Augustine, considered the LXX inspired, as the Greek Orthodox Church still does. When Aramaic, the official language of Persia, became the language of Jews, the custom developed of accompanying the reading of the Hebrew text with running translations in Aramaic, called "Targums" (the verb *targem* means to explain, translate), already in Neh 8:8. It was forbidden to write down these Targums till about the second to fifth centuries CE. Today Targum studies are very important to Bible studies, especially the New Testament. Until the second and third centuries CE, Greek was the language of the eastern Roman Empire. As Latin became more popular, several Latin translations emerged until Pope Damasus (366–384) commissioned his secretary, Saint Jerome, to revise the Old Latin translations in accordance with the Hebrew and Greek. His translation of the Old Testament, called the Vulgate (*editio vulgata*, the common version), was completed around 404, but did not win universal currency in Christendom until about the ninth century.

Martin Luther was the first to deviate from the Vulgate for what he called the *Hebraica veritas* (the Hebrew truth), the Hebrew canon of the Old Testament, though retaining the fourfold order of the LXX. Protestants have followed him in this, and hence regard as noncanonical (also called apocryphal) seven books included in the Catholic canon, namely, Tobit, Judith, Wisdom of Solomon, Ben Sira (Ecclesiasticus), Baruch (with the Letter of Jeremiah), and 1 and 2 Maccabees. Luther's German translation of the New Testament printed

James, Jude, Hebrews, and Revelation at the end as deficient.

In 1546, the Council of Trent countered Luther by declaring the full New and Old Testaments (including the books declared apocryphal by Protestants) as sacred and canonical, affirming centuries of their inclusion beginning with Pope Damasus, who promulgated the Catholic canons at the Synod of Rome in 382 CE. From the Council of Trent until Vatican Council II (1962–1965) the Latin Vulgate was the official Catholic version. John Wycliffe completed the first English translation of the Vulgate in 1382. In 1408, a conference called at Oxford by Archbishop Arundel forbade, under pain of excommunication, any translation of Scripture into English or any other language.[18] In 1415, the Council of Constance excommunicated Wycliffe and had his remains exhumed and dishonored. William Tyndale produced the first printed English New Testament in 1525. Of the Old Testament, the Pentateuch appeared in 1530, the rest surviving his execution for heresy in manuscript form only.[19] There were other English versions until the second authorized Bible made an indelible mark as the *King James Version* (1611); it has had a tremendous impact on English language and literature. Revisions appeared as the *Revised Version* (1885), the *Revised Standard Version, with Apocrypha* (1956, revised for Catholic use, 1965), and the moderately inclusive *New Revised Standard Version* (1989).

On the Catholic side, English seminarians in Rheims (France) produced a translation of the Vulgate New Testament in 1582 and the Old Testament in 1610 after moving to the English College at Douay, Flanders. Hence this version is known as the *Douay-Rheims Version*. The *Confraternity Bible* (between 1941 and 1969) revised the Douay-Rheims version for American Catholics. Vatican II Dogmatic Constitution on Divine Revelation, *Dei Verbum*, 22, mandated translations from the original texts. Such translations, compared with the LXX,

---

18. Derek Wilson, *The People's Bible* (Oxford: Lion Hudson, 2010), 23.

19. Frederick W. Danker, *Multipurpose Tools for Bible Study*, rev. and expanded ed. (Minneapolis: Fortress Press, 1993), 178.

the Vulgate, the Targums, and other ancient versions, are often done in ecumenical collaboration, especially through the United Bible Societies and the World Catholic Biblical Federation established by Pope Paul VI in 1968.

The *New American Bible* was translated from the original languages and appeared in 1970. Its revised New Testament appeared in 1986, revised Psalms in 1991, and the revised Old Testament in 2010. A newer version, the *New American Bible, Revised Edition* (NABRE), incorporating the revisions, appeared in 2011. The current Anselm edition of the NABRE is a Study Bible intended primarily for college and university students. The *Jerusalem Bible* (1966)

was inspired by the French *Bible de Jérusalem,* which had been prepared by scholars of École Biblique, Jerusalem, from the original texts. A revision in 1985 was less dependent on the French version. The *New International Version* (1984) was an evangelical ecumenical translation. Useful for Christian-Jewish dialogue and for the history of interpretation is the *Jewish Publication Society Bible* (1917, revised 1985), available in *The Jewish Study Bible* (Oxford University Press, 2004).[20] ∎

---

20. For more information on these and other English versions, and advice about using these versions for interpretation and theology, the reader may consult Danker, *Multipurpose Tools,* 177–202.

# Geography, Archaeology, and the Scriptures

## Leslie J. Hoppe, OFM

## Geography of Palestine and the Levant

The territory controlled by the ancient Israelite kingdoms was relatively small—about the size of New Jersey. From Dan to Beersheba (see 1 Sm 3:20; 2 Sm 3:10; 17:11; 24:2; 1 Kgs 4:25), it is just 125 miles. From the Mediterranean Sea to the Jordan River (running through Jerusalem), it is about fifty miles. Still, because of its geographical location, this area had significance that transcended its size. It was the crossroads of the ancient Near East.

There are three geographical barriers to efficient east-west communications in the globe's eastern hemisphere: mountains, deserts, and seas. There are mountains from the Pyrenees in Western Europe to the Tsingling Shan in Western Asia. Deserts stretch from the Sahara in North Africa to the Gobi in Mongolia. In antiquity, travelers had to contend with five seas: the Mediterranean, Black, Caspian, and Red Seas, and the Persian Gulf. The Levant, the territory now controlled by the modern states of Syria, Lebanon, Jordan, and Israel, and the Palestinian Authority, provided the only land passage that was relatively free of obstructions, making possible communication and trade between Egypt, Africa, and Arabia to the south, Asia Minor to the north, and Mesopotamia to the east. Travelers, merchants, soldiers, and refugees all met on this 125-mile long, 50-mile wide corridor between the Mediterranean Sea and the Arabian Desert. Controlling this area was important to every nation with an expansionist agenda.

During the Iron Age in the Levant (twelfth to sixth century BCE), the small national states in the area (Aram, Israel, Judah, Ammon, Moab, and Edom) vied with one another for control of the region's resources and trade routes. Beginning in the eighth century, these states lived in the shadow of the Mesopotamian states. By the middle of the sixth century BCE, Israel and Judah succumbed to the imperialist policies of neo-Assyrian and neo-Babylonian kingdoms. Conflicts among the nations of the Levant and with the Mesopotamian states explain the animosity toward the nations frequently exhibited in the Hebrew Scriptures, for example, in the prophetic oracles against the nations (see Is 13–23; Jer 46–51; Ez 25–32; Jl 4:1–16; Am 1–2; Obadiah; and Nahum). In the fourth century BCE, Alexander the Great added the Levant to his empire, adding the West to what was already a volatile mix.

The Fertile Crescent is another name for the land mass where the east-west lines of communication meet in the Eastern Hemisphere. This sickle-shaped piece of land north of the Arabian Desert has water supplies sufficient to support agriculture and, in turn, enable settlement in towns and villages. The Fertile Crescent is divided into two subsections. The eastern section is known as "Mesopotamia," a Greek name meaning "[the land] between the rivers." In the northern part of this region, the two rivers—the Tigris and the Euphrates—supplied water necessary for agriculture. In addition, the amount of rainfall allowed for settlements away from the rivers as well. The south was subject to spring flooding because the melting winter snows in the mountains ran off into its low-lying areas. At times, these floods were catastrophic and probably occasioned the composition of epics similar to the biblical flood story (Gn 6–9). Here the kingdoms of Sumer, Babylon, and Assyria held sway from the fourth millennium BCE until the Greeks came in the fourth century followed by the Romans in the first century BCE.

The western part of the Fertile Crescent extends from the mountains of Lebanon in the north to the Red Sea in the south—a distance of five hundred miles. It is a geographically complex area. There are four topographical zones that run north-south in the region: the Coastal Plain along the Mediterranean Sea, the Western Highlands, the Central Rift Valley, and the Eastern Plateau. Besides these zones, there is, in Israel, an important depression that runs northwest to southeast—the Jezreel Valley that extends from the Carmel Range to the Rift Valley.

At the foot of Mount Hermon in the north, a major transverse fault causes the Rift Valley to drop suddenly as it begins its descent to the Red Sea. For most of that descent, the valley is below sea level. The Jordan River flows south from the Sea of Galilee in the center of the Rift Valley to the Dead Sea. The Coastal Plain widens, beginning just south of Mount Carmel, until it reaches Gaza along the shore of the Mediterranean Sea in the south. The Western Highlands descend in two steps (Upper and Lower Galilee) to the low-lying Jezreel Valley that connects the Jordan Valley with the Mediterranean coast at Acco. South of the Jezreel Valley are the highlands of Manasseh, Ephraim, and Judah. It is in these highlands that the Israelite tribes emerged. Exploiting this region for agriculture was difficult, requiring intense and constant labor. The hills had to be terraced both to provide a suitable place for the cultivation of grain and to control the run-off water. The Israelite tribes prospered there because most other peoples preferred to work the soil in the Coastal Plain or the foothills, which did not pose the obstacles to agriculture that were characteristic of the highlands.

Other important geographical subdivisions of the Levant include the area north of the territory of the kingdom of Israel. This region receives more than thirty inches of rain annually, making possible the grain production and lush pastures for which it was renowned. Tyre and Sidon, the principal cities of the Syro-Phoenician region along the Levant's northwestern coast, were prosperous ports and commercial centers. The southwestern coastal region did not have much agricultural potential or viable port facilities, but the Via Maris and other caravan routes crisscrossed through the area, and people lived off trade. The southern region received barely enough rain to support village agriculture. People living in these subdivisions of the Levant did not easily cooperate with one another—perhaps due to the geographical barriers separating them. People here had a strong regional consciousness and regarded outsiders with suspicion.

The Central Rift Valley, the Jezreel Valley, and several of the valleys along the Coastal Plain are covered by fertile alluvial soil, which could produce substantial crops when the supply of water was sufficient. The Plain of Sharon located in the center of the Coastal Plain, however, had a red, sandy soil that was not good for the grain, grapes, and olives that were staples in antiquity. The region was only marginally exploited for agriculture until modern times and remained a sandy marsh throughout the biblical period.

The soil in the highlands is formed from decomposing limestone, a hard sedimentary rock that turns into a rich, soft, red, and porous soil that sops up the winter rains and releases moisture during the dry summer months. Olive trees, in particular, thrive in this soil. Limestone also served as an excellent building material and was used extensively in antiquity for private dwellings and public, monumental structures. Above the limestone is a layer of chalk and above this is sometimes another limestone layer.

Soil with high chalk content is easier to plow because the soft chalk erodes more easily than limestone. The downside is that the soil is not as fertile as that made from the much harder limestone.

While the soil in the western part of the Fertile Crescent is rich enough to support agriculture, the region does not have anything like the two great rivers (the Tigris and the Euphrates) of the eastern part. Most rivers in Israel flow only during the rainy season (November to March). The Jordan River, a perennial stream, is located in the Rift Valley, which rendered it useless for irrigation in antiquity because people were not able to move the water from the low elevation of the river to the land where it was needed, since the valley in which the river is located is narrow and deep. There are springs in the highlands, but they could not support intensive agriculture. The water for the soil and its crops had to come as rain. The agriculture of Palestine, then, is known as *dry* agriculture, that is, without irrigation.

Having enough rain was a cause of great anxiety in ancient Israel. Many people relieved that anxiety through worshiping Baal, the Ca-naanite god of storms, who was believed to bring rain (see 1 Kgs 17–18). Baal was the main rival of Yahweh, the ancestral deity of ancient Israel, for the loyalty of the people through most of the monarchic period.

## Weather Patterns

One can only speculate about the general weather patterns in antiquity. The data neces-sary to make definite conclusions are simply not available. Meteorological statistics were kept in the region beginning only in the nine-teenth century. It is probably a mistake to think that the climate in the Levant has not changed appreciably since the Old Testament period. What follows is a description of the climate today; one must remember that there may have been some variations in the biblical period.

There are several features of the Levant's geographical setting that shape its weather pat-terns. First, it is close enough to the Sahara and Arabian deserts to feel intense heat in the sum-mer, and to the Russian and Siberian Plains to experience their cold in the winter. Second, the Mediterranean Sea and the Arabian Desert are separated by only one hundred miles and the proximity of these two to the Levant has a distinct bearing on the region's climate. Third, weather patterns usually run west to east while the Central Highlands run north to south. The effect of this is to stall weather systems west of the mountains. The combination of these factors leads to the following: there are two seasons in most of the Levant. One is a dry season that begins about June 15 and runs to about September 15. The beginning and end of this season are quite regular. It almost never rains during this time. Before and after this dry season, there are transition periods of between four and six weeks. The other principal season is the wet season. Its beginning unfortunately is not as predictable as that of the dry season. This is what caused farmers in antiquity so much anxiety.

The rains that do come fall unevenly throughout the land. It rains more in the north than in the south and more in the west than in the east. The far north can receive as much as thirty inches of rain annually while Beer-sheba

in the south receives about eight inches and is totally dry for five months (May–September). Jerusalem, which is in the center, receives about twenty-two inches of rain per year. Rain-fall is always greater on the western side of the Central Highlands than on the eastern side, since the former is closer to the sea.

## Livelihoods

The Levant was able to support farmers, shep-herds, and merchants quite well. The shep-herds led their flocks from one pasture to another, taking advantage of every hill and valley that had grass to feed their sheep. They could not stay in one place for long because the sheep would soon deplete the available resources. For shepherds, mobility was the key to survival. For farmers, by contrast, the keys to success included stability, rain, and fertile soil. In difficult times, farmers sometimes converted their land holdings to flocks and herds. This broke their tie to a particular plot of land and allowed them to move to more fertile areas and to avoid oppressive taxation. The merchants re-quired safe roads, enabling them to move from place to place without trouble. The farmers, shepherds, and merchants needed each other. For example, the merchants depended on ani-mals bred by the shepherds and farmers. They also needed guides in unfamiliar areas. The shepherd provided animals to help the farmer with both the plowing and the threshing. The merchant facilitated exchange of goods among the people of the Levant.

The Levant's geographical setting made the growing of crops sufficient to provide enough food a chancy affair. As a consequence, hav-ing enough food to eat was a source of great anxiety among the people of the region. They relieved this anxiety, in part, through religious practices. Because people believed that the Canaanite god Baal would provide the rain necessary to grow their crops, ancient Ca-naanite religious practices were very attractive to the ancient Israelites. It took a long time for the prophets to convince the people of ancient Israel to recognize their ancestral deity as the giver of the grain, wine, and oil (see Hos 2:10) and their responsibility to serve Yahweh alone.

# Biblical Archaeology

Archaeology is the study of the material remains of antiquity as opposed to its literary remains. Material remains include anything that is evidence of human activity, from monumental architecture to microscopic pollens from cultivated plants. Archaeology uncovers these objects, identifies them, reconstructs them when possible and necessary, and then classifies them. Once these preliminary tasks have been completed, the more difficult ones begin: the artifacts are compared with examples from other regions, arranged in a chronological sequence, and related to previously known information about antiquity.

The goal of archaeological projects is to reconstruct life in the ancient world, to profile the culture of the people who left these remains behind, and to help define the various types of human responses to different situations reflected in the archaeological record. Archaeology fills a void where literary sources are insufficient or nonexistent. The Bible is, after all, literature that comes from an elite group in ancient Israel. While all the people who composed the books of the Bible may not have been part of the social and economic upper class, they were people who had a keen sense of the values and beliefs of their ancestral religious tradition. But did they represent the way most Israelites believed and lived? Through its study of material remains, archaeology puts the Bible into a living context. To say this in a more theological key: archaeology makes one sensitive to the incarnational aspect of revelation.

Biblical archaeology is a relatively new field of study. At the beginning of the twentieth century, a growing number of scholars believed that excavation would settle the question of the historical value of Old Testament narratives—especially regarding the settlement of the Israelite tribes in Canaan. Archaeology has shown that the emergence of the Israelites in Canaan was a complex affair, which the biblical narratives simplify. The high hopes of the first scholars who excavated in what is now the modern state of Israel and the Palestinian Authority were never really realized. Biblical archaeologists were certain that their new

discipline would support the historical value of biblical narratives, but the excavation of sites like Jericho and Ai (see Jos 6–8) has shown that these places were largely unoccupied in the Late Bronze Age (ca. thirteenth century BCE) when the Israelite tribes supposedly conquered them. As the methods of excavation and interpretation became more sophisticated, however, some archaeologists have virtually abandoned the goal of proving the Bible's historicity. They hold that the Torah and Former Prophets have a theological purpose and do not provide the kind of data necessary to reconstruct the history of ancient Israel. Some attempts at reconstructing that history are often little more than paraphrases of the biblical text. A genuinely scientific account of ancient Israel's past needs to take into account the archaeological record as well as the available literary sources.

Most of the early archaeologists focused their attention almost entirely on sites related to the Old Testament. Few bothered with New Testament sites since the question of historicity was framed differently in relationship to the Christian Scriptures. No historian questions the existence of Jesus or Paul. Also, the historical period reflected in the New Testament was miniscule as compared to the Old Testament and was illumined by a wealth of contemporary secular and religious literature. Finally, many scholars located the principal contribution of the New Testament in the area of theology so it was thought that archaeology had little or nothing to contribute to illuminating the theological affirmations of the Christian Scriptures.

The rise of the sociological and anthropological approaches to New Testament interpretation effected a dramatic change in the relationship between archaeology and the Christian Scriptures. It is clear that religious texts are bound to the societies that produced them. A prerequisite of informed biblical interpretation, then, is knowledge of those societies in which the biblical tradition took shape. Archaeology supplies the raw data necessary to profile the Jewish and Greco-Roman contexts in which the books of the New Testament emerged. Archaeology helps cultural anthropologists describe the people who wrote and first read the Christian Scriptures by defining the characteristics of the "Mediterranean person" in the first century and all that this involves.

Today the goal of archaeology is to recreate the world of the Bible using the material remains left by the people of that world. This assumes that the Bible is the product of real people, who lived at a real time, had certain values, and functioned with political, economic, and social structures. It also assumes that the more we know about these people, the more we can know about the literature that they produced.

## Science and Art

Archaeology is both a science and an art. It is the one science that systematically destroys a good part of its evidence. As excavation proceeds, each successive occupation layer is destroyed to reach the one below. To compensate for this, archaeologists have developed detailed and exact methods for excavation and the recording of finds. This allows the progress of the excavation to be reviewed by archaeologists who did not actually participate in the excavation project. Mounting a successful project requires a team of specialists: a surveyor, a stratigrapher, a ceramicist, a numismatist, a bone specialist, a botanist, an architect, a historian, a photographer, an artist, and a reconstruction specialist. More complex projects, such as those requiring underwater excavation, require additional expertise.

The method used in excavating biblical sites is usually some variation of the Wheeler-Kenyon method. Mortimer Wheeler developed the technique of stratigraphic excavation for use with sites from the classical period and Kathleen Kenyon adapted it for use on biblical sites. The basic approach is to peel off occupational layer by occupational layer, recovering artifacts and other evidence of human presence at the site. While the excavation needs to be done carefully, the recording of data requires even greater care. Those who study biblical texts all have the same basic data before them. Those who study the material remains of an ancient society have only one opportunity to see these remains in their context unless the progress of the excavation has been duly and carefully recorded in such detail that it can be reconstructed from the final reports.

The excavation of a site is the easy part of any archaeological project. Interpretation of the artifacts uncovered in the process of excavation is more akin to an art, requiring imagination and creativity from its practitioners. Without insightful interpretation, excavation cannot advance knowledge. Interpretation transforms a mass of data into a form that is accessible to the scholarly community. Pottery, coins, bones, seeds, artifacts (metal, stone, and wood), and structures must all be related in a coherent fashion. The interpretation of data is crucial in the archaeology of Israel because significant literary remains are so rarely found during excavations there. The goal of the interpretive process is to relate the site that has been excavated to other sites in the region, to understand the culture at the site, to reconstruct the diet, the work, the religion, the politics, the economy, the aesthetics, and the moral values of the people who lived at the site in antiquity.

Before the development of archaeology as an academic discipline in the twentieth century, excavations were often little more than treasure-hunting expeditions that sought to uncover monumental buildings and to find interesting and valuable artifacts for private collectors or museums. Biblical archaeology developed as an ancillary discipline to biblical studies especially to provide the data for reconstructing the history of ancient Israel. Today archaeology is an independent field of study—a branch of Near Eastern archaeology with an agenda and a methodology independent of biblical studies. Its goal is to reconstruct the shape of ancient societies on the basis of the material remains left behind by the people of those societies. This involves much more than historical reconstruction. It includes every aspect of human endeavor, from the growing and preparation of food to the development of moral and religious values. There has been a debate among archaeologists who work in the Levant about the appropriateness of calling their discipline "biblical archaeology" since archaeology has become a field of study in its own right. One scholar suggested calling the discipline "Syro-Palestinian archaeology." This nomenclature has not really caught on. While people may continue to use the term "biblical archaeology," they now recognize its independence from biblical studies.

The early biblical archaeologists thought that their work would serve to establish the historical accuracy of Old Testament narratives—especially those dealing with the Exodus, the emergence of the Israelite tribes in Canaan, and the early monarchic period. This goal was not met. Archaeology has uncovered no evidence of a mass migration in the Sinai during the Late Bronze Age (1400–1250 BCE) when the escaped Hebrew slaves were thought to have made their way through this area. Excavations of Jericho and Ai (see Jos 6–8) suggest that these two sites were not occupied in the Late Bronze Age. Excavations in Jerusalem have not revealed the type of structures that one expects of the capital of the kind of national state from the time that David established his kingdom. This concern for demonstrating the historicity of biblical narratives has, in part, spawned the production of archaeological frauds. By one estimate, almost one third of the artifacts in the possession of the Israel Museum are fakes. It is not surprising, then, that some archaeologists wish to break the close connection between biblical studies and archaeology.

The positive contribution that archaeology can make is to describe the world that produced the Bible. What archaeology provides to readers and interpreters of the Bible is what journalists call "deep background," i.e., information that provides a context for a story. Being familiar with that "deep background" helps the interpreter to avoid making unwarranted conclusions about the text and helps the reader to read the Bible without reading "into" it. Still, some archaeologists suggest that archaeology break any connection with biblical studies and that the archaeological enterprise ought to be pursued as a humanistic enterprise—simply to understand the world of antiquity. Of course, important components

of that world were people's religious beliefs, practices, and values, which many people still consider normative for their lives today. It is very difficult to divorce archaeology in the Middle East from biblical studies.

Archaeology does, however, need to distance itself from contemporary political controversies. The interpretation of data from early excavations at Masada and Hazor reflects the nationalistic tendencies of the excavators more than a dispassionate interpretation of data. The destruction of the archaeological record as a result of renovations to structures on the Haram es-Sharif (the Temple Mount) in Jerusalem is inexcusable. Of course, archaeologists do not work in a vacuum. The Middle East is a cauldron of seething political and religious conflicts that can compromise the integrity of the archaeological enterprise. Archaeology should not be used to undergird any political or nationalistic agenda.

The growing sophistication of techniques employed by excavators and the genuinely scientific methods used to identify and interpret the results of excavation projects have transformed biblical archaeology. Those who study the biblical texts can no longer afford to ignore the growing body of knowledge about the world of the Bible that archaeology has produced in the last one hundred years. Archaeology helps us realize that the Bible is not a collection of timeless truths that have descended from the heavens, but is the principal artifact that discloses the beliefs of ancient Israelites, early Jews, and early Christians. To understand the affirmations, negations, emphases, and patterns in the books that make up the Bible it is necessary to understand the people—their world and their culture—whose beliefs find expression in the Bible. Archaeology helps one understand those people and their culture. It makes authentic dialogue with one's ancestors in the faith a genuine possibility. Biblical archaeology is one way that some people express their fascination with the origins of their religious tradition. ∎

# Social Context of the Bible

## Eric Stewart

There is no single cultural context of the Bible. The biblical texts were not composed in a single social context, nor do they describe events related to a single social context. Though they vary broadly, these contexts exhibit some closely related "cultural patterns."

The major historical and cultural contexts of the Bible are called by historians the Ancient Near East, the Hellenistic empires, and the Roman Empire. The Ancient Near East refers primarily to what is now called southwest Asia and northern Africa, and it included, among other civilizations, those of Assyria, Babylonia, Egypt, and Persia. The Hellenistic empires, beginning in Greece, stretched from Greece in the west to India in the east and included part of Egypt to the south. The Romans eventually conquered all of the kingdoms that ringed the Mediterranean Sea, and by 63 BCE, Judea was under Roman control. During the period in which the New Testament texts were composed, the Romans ruled virtually all of the inhabited territory from modern-day Iran in the east to the Straits of Gibraltar in the west, from northern Africa in the south to Ireland in the north.

Though the civilizations of the Ancient Near East, Hellenistic, and Roman periods differed from one another in many ways, and Israelite culture was different as well from each of these other civilizations, all also had broad similarities as agrarian, "Mediterranean" cultures. Such cultures are marked by certain key features that remain broadly similar throughout these cultures. These features include collectivism, honor, patronage, and kinship structures.

## Collectivism

Ancient Israel and the surrounding societies were collectivist cultures. Collectivism is the idea that one's identity derives largely from one's place within a social collective. Individualism, the primary way of conceiving the self in modern North America, largely developed during and after the period of the Enlightenment (seventeenth and eighteenth centuries CE). Individualism stresses that people are integrated wholes themselves, independent of others for their identity. Collectivism, on the other hand, identifies people by their key social relationships. "In collectivistic cultures people are interdependent within their in-groups (family, tribe, nation, etc.), give priority to the goals of their in-groups, shape their behavior primarily on the basis of in-group norms, and behave in a communal way."[1]

The biblical genealogies serve to indicate family, clan, and tribe membership (Gn 46:8–27; Jos 15:20–62; Mt 1:1–16; Lk 3:23–38). Children are known as sons and daughters of their parents (chiefly their fathers in ancient Mediterranean societies). Child rearing in collectivist cultures emphasizes conformity to in-group norms. Ben Sira 30:1–6 relates the expectations of a son toward his father in a collectivist context. At the death of the father, a son who is "one like himself" will make it seem as though the father is not dead. The son maintains his father's relationships, extending kindness to the friends of his father and exacting vengeance upon his father's enemies (Sir 30:4, 6). Even the God of Israel is known to the Israelites by a collective designation—the God of Abraham, Isaac, and Jacob (Ex 3:6). In this way, this God is designated as the God associated with ancestors of the Israelites, cementing Yahweh's place as the deity to be honored by the Israelites.

Societies in which mobility is limited, as was the case in most cultures of the biblical period, are often collectivist in outlook. Collectivists frequently are known by the place of their origin or residences. Ruth the Moabite, Jesus of Nazareth, Mary of Magdala, and Paul of Tarsus are a few of many biblical examples of people being associated with a particular place. Travel, though more common into the

---

1. Harry C. Triandis, "Individualism-Collectivism and Personality," *Journal of Personality* 69 (2001), 909.

Hellenistic and Roman periods, was fairly restricted for the majority of the population in ancient Mediterranean societies. Carol Meyers argues that the prohibitions against permanently ceding ancestral territory in the Hebrew Bible (Lv 25:23–28) are related to the intimate knowledge of the particular soils and growth patterns acquired by people who have farmed the same land for generations.[2]

Collectivists take their social cues from the group, and they put the needs and welfare of the group ahead of individual interests. In agricultural societies, in which the subsistence of the group is continually challenged due to droughts, storms, illness, warfare, and other potential calamities, members of extended family groups tend to focus on the preservation of the group, sometimes at the expense of the welfare of the individual. Situations in which the survival of the group is at stake generally increase the emphasis on group needs. In the absence of forced population shifts or severe hardship, families live in the same place, farming the same land, often for generations.

People in collectivist cultures tend to value highly their own in-groups, but they often "report negative attitudes toward their out-groups."[3] In the biblical texts, out-groups are frequently the focus of derision and scorn (Gn 34; 1 Kgs 18:20–29), and the numerous warnings against intermarriage with people (especially women) of other ethnic groups serve to reinforce the cohesion and solidarity of the Israelites (Ex 34:16; Ezr 9:12; Neh 10:31). Such attitudes toward out-groups can also be found in the Gospels and Paul's letters (Jn 4:9; Gal 2:15).

# Honor

Perhaps the most significant of the broad similarities among Mediterranean cultures is the notion of honor. All of the cultures of the Ancient Near East, along with Greek and

Roman cultures, were honor cultures. Such cultures share some basic features, though what is viewed as honorable in one culture might not be viewed as honorable in another culture. Honor is the claim a person makes to status within a community or society, plus the social acknowledgement of that claim. A person might claim to be the "best" or the "most" something, but without public recognition of that claim, it is merely seen as arrogance or conceit. Honor can be earned or achieved through various means.

David, for example, earns significant honor when he slays Goliath (1 Sm 17:49–50). Two interesting elements of the story only make sense within the context of honor cultures. When Goliath is killed, despite the Philistines' marked superiority in battle to that point, the Philistines turn and run and are slain from behind by the charging Israelite army (1 Sm 17:51–54). The defeat of their champion clearly indicates that the Israelite champion, and with him the Israelite army, are more honorable than the Philistine army. While such a victory was roundly celebrated by the Israelites, it was problematic for Saul, their king. Saul recognized that his reputation as the most honorable figure had been surpassed by David's growing honor rating (1 Sm 18:6–9). Since the slaying of "tens of thousands" is attributed to David, while Saul is only recognized as killing "thousands," Saul suspected that David would become king. For this reason, "Saul kept a jealous eye on David" (1 Sm 18:9). David's honor and social prestige had grown greater than Saul's in the eyes of the Israelites. Some other notable figures who acquired honor through battle in the Bible are Joshua (Jos 8:1–29) and Judith (Jdt 13:1–10).

Beside battle, there were other ways of achieving honor. Success in education, poetry, athletics, and many other endeavors could bring honor. Honor could also be given to someone by a more powerful person or figure. Abraham was granted honor by God. Three things are promised to Abraham: progeny, land, and a great name (Gn 12:1–2). The acquisition of a great name means that Abraham's reputation will be widely known. David received honor bestowed upon him by God (1 Sm 16:12) when God chose him to replace

---

2. Carol Meyers, "The Family in Early Israel," in *Families in Ancient Israel*, ed. Leo G. Perdue, Joseph Blenkinsopp, John J. Collins, and Carol Meyers, The Family, Religion, and Culture (Louisville: Westminster John Knox, 1997), 1–47, at 28.

3. Triandis, "Individualism-Collectivism and Personality," 914.

Saul as the king of the Israelites. Great wisdom could also be recognized and honored, as in the case of Solomon (1 Kgs 3:28). Solomon's honor was not achieved, but rather it was ascribed to him by God (1 Kgs 3:12).

God's honor was of paramount importance to the Israelites. Israel's praise of God granted God public recognition of God's honor status. The Psalms are full of praise from Israel to God (Pss 65:2; 66:1–4; 107). The Israelites know that their God is honorable, but God's honor is not always recognized outside of Israel. On various occasions it is challenged by the opponents of Israel, as when Pharaoh asks, "Who is the LORD, that I should obey him and let Israel go? I do not know the LORD, and I will not let Israel go." (Ex 5:2). The text of Exodus relates that God took this question as a challenge and made known the name of Yahweh to the Egyptians. "All the Egyptians will know that I am the LORD, when I stretch out my hand against Egypt and bring the Israelites out of their midst" (Ex 7:5). In fact, the Israelites came to know that Yahweh was their God through the benefactions extended to them while they were in Egypt (Ex 6:7). The demonstration of God's power served as a means for the furtherance of God's honor. When such power is revealed, it results in the public acknowledgement of honor (Ex 15:1-21). Honoring Yahweh is the reason for passages that mock idols in the Bible (Is 44:18–20; Wis 15:7–17), and it is also the logic behind the commandment that the Israelites are to "have no other gods beside me" (Ex 20:3). In heaven God is always honored. Yahweh is honored as the leader of the divine council (Ps 82:1–6). Within the heavenly throne room, God is constantly praised and honored by angelic beings (Is 6:3; Rev 4:8–11).

Honor operates somewhat differently for men and women. In ancient Near Eastern and Mediterranean societies, the public realm of political life, as well as work away from home in the fields or at war, pertained to men. The realm of domestic life, of maintaining and operating the household, pertained to women. These realms frequently overlapped because various parts of homes were open to the pub-lic, particularly in the Roman world.[4] Many studies of honor cultures have focused on the public world of men, and the notion of honor among women has received considerably less attention. Though fewer, studies that have focused on the domestic realm suggest that women have their own honor codes. Among women, "honesty, confidence, friendship, and industriousness" are honorable values.[5] The protection of the sexual exclusivity of women was an important part of the honor code in ancient Mediterranean societies. Failure to protect the sexual reputations of the females of a family made it harder to arrange marriages for the women of the family with other honorable families.

# Patronage and Other Patterns of Exchange

Ancient Mediterranean societies were agrarian. When compared to horticultural societies, agrarian societies are advanced in technology and production, advanced in military technology, control more expansive empires with much larger territories, have increased population sizes, regular warfare, (generally) monarchical governments, development of preindustrial cities, limited literacy, political religion, and marked social inequality.[6] Increased harnessing of animal power, the development of better and stronger metal instruments, especially iron plows, and the development of the wheel characterized agrarian societies. These developments made possible more sophisticated weaponry for war—which also meant that a given individual was no longer capable of producing weapons of the same quality and sophistication as another individual with greater means. These technological advancements, together with an increase in warfare and the increased size of the territory of empires, increased the social distance between those at

---

4. Carolyn Osiek and David L. Balch, *Families in the New Testament World: Households and House Churches* (Louisville: Westminster John Knox, 1997), 24–35.

5. Ibid., 40.

6. Gerhard Lenski, *Power and Privilege: A Theory of Social Stratification*. Chapel Hill, NC: University of North Carolina Press, 1994), 190–242.

the top of the social order and those further down. This social distance contributed to a marked increase in social inequality.

The social structure of agrarian societies might be best imagined as a pyramid.[7] Those at the top of the social structure, the ruler and the elites, comprised a small percentage of the population. In the Roman Empire, for example, estimates are that less than two percent of the population comprised the elite. The elites were those who were appointed by the ruler and included officers, personal advisers to the ruler, military leaders, priests, and local rulers. The elite typically held large landholdings that were granted to them by the ruler, who technically possessed all of the territory of the empire. Elites were rich, but in agrarian societies, the rich were not necessarily elite. Due to issues of honor and collectivism, some people who were able to amass fortunes lacked the social and political connections to turn their fortunes into influence. For this reason, these people were not able to secure a place among the elite. Often in the Bible, the elite are considered those who pervert justice and otherwise make life miserable for the peasants (1 Sm 8:11–18; Prv 17:5; Is 1:15–17; Am 6:3–7; Mi 3:9; 7:3; Lk 16:19–31; Rev 18:1–18).

Just below the elites on the pyramid were a group of "retainers" who served the elites. These retainers comprised about five percent of the population. The duties, rights, and responsibilities of the retainers varied greatly depending upon which of the elite they served and what position they occupied within that service. Retainers served as soldiers (sometimes as a full-time occupation, but more frequently in limited campaigns), household servants, and slaves who were responsible for seeing to all of the daily activities of the household including child-rearing (Ex 2:9–10) and advisers to the elites (Gn 39:4–6; 41:37–49; Dn 2:46–49). The services of the retainers as a class were especially important to maintaining the elites' grip on power, but the individual members of the retainer class were, for the most part, replaced easily (Mt 25:24–30; Lk 16:2).

The vast majority of people in agrarian societies were the peasants who worked the land. Among the chief developments in agrarian societies, owing largely to the increased technology of production, were the creation of a surplus of food and goods. The elites extracted this surplus from the peasants through rents and taxes. Estimates for rents and taxes in agrarian societies range from ten percent to seventy percent of the total production of peasant farms. The production of food was the lifeblood of agrarian societies, and the elites needed it to feed themselves and their retainers and to provide food for areas in which droughts and famines made it impossible to maintain local populations without importing food from elsewhere. In the absence of forced population shifts, peasants typically worked their ancestral lands, but during difficult times it was not uncommon for peasants to have to sell ancestral lands and go to work as tenant farmers. These tenant farmers worked on the estates of the elites, and they were paid a percentage of the crops or sometimes wages from which they had to purchase the crops that they themselves had grown. When peasants were unable to produce enough food or earn enough money to feed themselves, elites might offer them patronage. Though in most agrarian societies the elites showed negligible interest in the needs and desires of the peasant class, the elites also recognized that, if a large segment of the population of any part of their territory were to starve, it might be harder to produce enough in future years to maintain their control. Apart from the peasant class, there were also artisans, those who produced other things besides food. Artisans in agrarian societies were typically lower in social status than peasants because they were often displaced peasants who had lost their land. In the ancient Mediterranean societies, beneath the artisans in social status were classes of people who were unable to care for themselves and lacked the requisite safety net of family or friends to care for them. These people included beggars and ill people with no access to health care (Jn 5:5–7).

One of the characteristics of agrarian societies is urbanization or the building of cities. The elites in Mediterranean agrarian societies typically had two residences. One was located

---

7. Ibid., 210–96.

within the city walls, and the other was usually some type of countryside villa or estate. These two residences served different functions. Ancient cities, in most respects, were unlike modern cities.[8] The cities were populated almost exclusively by elites, their retainers, and those who served them in other capacities. The vast majority of the population of agrarian societies lived in villages located outside of the cities. Cities functioned as places of retreat for elites, especially during times of warfare. The cities were also the places in which public matters of the elites were attended to. The city was the province of politics. It is estimated that no more than ten percent of the population of any agrarian society ever lived within cities. During the growing season, the elites usually lived in their countryside estates, overseeing the production of crops by their slaves and clients. These countryside villas could serve as respite from the endless attempts to maintain and improve one's honor rating in the city, and they also provided a place to flee should epidemics of illness break out in the cities.

There were no institutions like Social Security or Medicaid in ancient Near Eastern, Hellenistic, or Roman cultures. When people found themselves unable to work due to disease, old age, or physical or mental disability, they were at the mercy of others to provide care for them. In such societies that have marked social inequality, systems of exchange are needed in order to ensure that those at the lower ends of the social spectrum have access to needed goods and services. The family was the first line of support for people unable to care for themselves. This familial reciprocity, or exchange, was open-ended; aid was provided even if the recipient was unable to reciprocate.

Among neighbors and friends, balanced reciprocity was most common. Balanced reciprocity involves even exchange and the immediate discharge of debts so that people would not have outstanding obligations to one another. Generalized reciprocity is characterized by unequal exchange among unequal parties.

Patronage is a form of generalized reciprocity in which those who are able provide access to first-order goods like food or land for clients who receive such benefactions and reciprocate loyalty to their patrons. Patrons and clients are bound by the ability of the patron to supply the goods and the willingness of the clients to offer praise to the patron. When patrons do not supply goods, clients may seek new sources of patronage, while patrons who are not honored are not likely to continue to provide patronage. Jesus teaches his disciples a prayer that appeals to God's patronage (Lk 11:2–4). Women offer patronage to Jesus (Lk 8:2–3), and Jesus' followers were commonly patrons to early Christian missionaries (Acts 15:4; Rom 16:3–4).[9] Where those among the lower strata of society were unable to access patrons directly, brokers who had established relationships with patrons could arrange for patronage, usually for a price.[10]

## Kinship

Kinship refers to the whole range of relationship based on ethnicity and the household. One's kin group extended beyond the household to include all of those to whom one was related by blood. Within the household, kin could include multiple generations as well as friends, guests, and slaves of the owner of the house. Most of the biblical texts describe the ideal family similarly. A powerful male figure rules and directs the family's affairs. Such father figures are responsible for raising sons (Sir 30:1–6), for blessing them (Gn 27:26–29), for protecting daughters (Sir 42:9–14) and finding them suitable marriage partners (Gn 29:15–30), and for maintaining the relationships of the family with other groups. Children obey their parents (Dt 5:16), and failure to do so is punishable by death (Dt 21:18–21). Ideal women raise children, manage the affairs of the household, and contribute to the

8. Eric C. Stewart, "The City in Mark," in *In Other Words: Essays on Social Science Methods and the New Testament in Honor of Jerome H. Neyrey*, ed. Anselm C. Hagedorn, Zeba A. Crook, and Eric Stewart (Sheffield: Sheffield Phoenix, 2007), 202–20, at 204–11.

9. Carolyn Osiek and Margaret Y. MacDonald with Janet H. Tulloch, *A Woman's Place: House Churches in Earliest Christianity* (Minneapolis: Fortress, 2006), 194–219.

10. Alicia Batten, "Brokerage: Jesus as Social Entrepreneur," in *Understanding the Social World of the New Testament*, ed. Dietmar Neufeld and Richard E. DeMaris (London: Routledge, 2010), 167–77.

good name of their husbands (Jdt 8:1–8; Prv 31:10–31).

These idealized versions of family relationships, especially those contained in the Wisdom literature, ought to be read *prescriptively* rather than *descriptively*.[11] Many families did not fit this ideal due to a variety of factors. Early deaths among marital relationships were common enough to merit attention in the story of Ruth (Ru 1:3–5). Widows were a distinct class among early groups of Jesus' followers, and contention about their status is evident in some cases (1 Tm 5:9–16). In other cases, infighting among family members might lead to the death of one or more of the members of the family (Gn 4:8) or other precarious situations (Gn 37:25–28).

Households within the periods in which the biblical texts were written varied considerably. Among the peasants who farmed the land, most households were located within village contexts. These villages were most often populated by extended kinship networks. Within these villages a small number of families, frequently from the same tribe or ethnic group, lived in close proximity to one another. Families within the village structure were sometimes composed of more than two generations. The oldest male in the household ran the household, at least from a legal perspective. Generally speaking, the ancestral lands were passed on to the eldest son (or the majority of the land was so passed on), and the other children either continued to live within the village structure, subservient in some ways to the eldest son, or else were forced to leave the ancestral land due to the size of the land relative to the consumption needs of the family.

Some of those who left the land wound up serving the elites in cities, working as artisans, becoming clients for elites, or were forced into slavery due to mounting debts.

Slaves were part of the kinship structure of families in the biblical worlds. There are relatively few restrictions on the treatment of slaves by their masters within the biblical texts, though for Hebrew slaves, some restrictions were mandated, such as freedom after a six-year period of enslavement (Ex 21:2–9; Dt 15:12–18). Slaves in ancient Near Eastern and Mediterranean contexts were teachers for children, cooks, launderers, field hands, and wet nurses. Children of slaves grew up alongside the children of their owners. Slaves had no legal rights within these societies, and they could be bought and sold at the whim of their owners. Slave marriages were not legally recognized. Many slaves in the Roman world in particular were granted freedom at some point in their lives. These slaves were freedmen and freedwomen and had legal and ethical obligations to act as clients of their former masters.[12] One of the features of slaves in these contexts was their sexual availability (Gn 16:1–6; 30:3–13). Both male and female slaves were considered sexually available to their masters.

Though the historical and social contexts of the Bible are varied, some commonalities, including a collectivist orientation, a concern for honor, marked social stratification, and kinship patterns that incorporated more than just biological, nuclear families characterized the biblical societies. Basic knowledge of these cultural features enables modern Western readers of the Bible to understand, to some extent, the cultural codes of the biblical texts. ■

11. Osiek and MacDonald, with Tulloch, *A Woman's Place: House Churches in Earliest Christianity*, 118–43.

12. Zeba A. Crook, "BTB Readers Guide: Loyalty," *Biblical Theology Bulletin* 34 (2004), 167–77, at 170–71.

# Deuterocanonical and Noncanonical Scriptures

A number of the literary works produced by ancient Jewish and Christian communities have, for various reasons, not been universally accepted as inspired Scripture. Some of these works—the Apocrypha—are accepted as "deuterocanonical" by some, but not all, Christian groups. Others—pseudepigraphical Old Testament works and apocryphal early Christian writings—have been rejected. The following articles offer a brief introduction to these works.

## Old Testament Apocrypha and Pseudepigrapha

### John C. Endres, SJ

During the Second Temple era (approximately 538 BCE until 132 CE) various Jewish groups authored an enormous amount of literature that was not included in the Hebrew Bible. The Septuagint (LXX) includes a number of writings not found in the Hebrew Bible, but which were widely accepted in the early Christian church. Saint Jerome held the Hebrew books as inspired and coined the term "Apocrypha" for the others, even though he was persuaded to translate the additional books into Latin for the Vulgate. Saint Augustine instead favored the wider canon of the LXX, and the Vulgate translation, with the Apocrypha, continued to be the biblical text in use by the Catholic Church until the time of the Reformation. Martin Luther, describing these books as apocryphal, denied that they were inspired Scripture but did allow them to be included in his Bible—in a special section between the books of Malachi and Matthew. The Catholic Church at Trent in 1546 included seven of these books from the Vulgate (1–2 Maccabees, Judith, Tobit, Baruch [with the Letter of Jeremiah], Wisdom of Solomon, and Ben Sira) plus expansions of Esther and Daniel (found in the LXX and Vulgate) as part of its canon (see also "The Formation of the Bible"). As a result, these "deuterocanonical books" appear in Catholic Bibles,

interspersed with historical, poetical, and prophetic books. Protestant Bibles, beginning with early Luther Bibles, either exclude these books completely or relegate them to a special section, between the Old Testament (Malachi) and the New Testament (Matthew); sometimes this added section also includes other apocryphal works (*Prayer of Manasseh*, *3 Ezra*, *4 Ezra*, and *3 Maccabees*). A related term for such books, "intertestamental," seemingly refers to the approximately four centuries between Malachi and Matthew, but it may be that the physical (spatial) location of these books in Protestant Bibles rendered this description popular.

In this Study Bible the deuterocanonical books and texts are discussed where they appear in the *New American Bible Revised Edition* (NABRE), adding to the collection of historical (Tobit, Judith, 1 and 2 Maccabees), poetic (Wisdom of Solomon, Ben Sira), and prophetic books (Baruch). All texts connected with Ezra (Esdras) are discussed in the essay on the book of Ezra. This essay comments only on the four other apocryphal texts: *Prayer of Manasseh*, *Psalm 151*, and *3 and 4 Maccabees*.

A much larger collection of extra-biblical Jewish texts, however, stands alongside the Hebrew Bible and the Apocrypha/Deuterocanonicals, often described as "Pseudepigrapha." Some use the term "pseudepigraphical" to refer to texts that have been falsely ascribed to an ancient author whose name would have commanded respect and lent authority to the particular text. Even when they fail to lend "canonical" status to a work, they witness to the lively religious imagination of people schooled in the Scriptures of the Old Testament. These writings often present more details about the great biblical figures in Genesis. They often answer questions that ordinary folk might have asked about such biblical figures. Some questions also emerged in the Aramaic Targums (cf. "The Formation of the Bible"), while others incited religious imaginations to compose new texts that interpreted the biblical stories for people in a new context or different historical era. Most of these texts are preserved in Greek, Latin, or Slavonic, and date from the second century BCE to first century CE. The term "Pseudepigrapha" does not refer to a fixed collection of texts, so it is not possible to give an exact list or number of them.

This essay thus focuses on the way the Jewish religious imagination questioned, reflected on, re-told, and interpreted important biblical characters in the Apocrypha and Pseudepigrapha. This approach differs from the historical approach of many scholars (where the books are considered in their presumed historical context)[1] or from the literary approach (in which these books are grouped with those of similar literary type or genre, such as testaments, narratives, histories, or apocalypses).[2] Our approach aligns more closely with the study of exegetical traditions (linked to biblical texts).[3]

We begin with two comprehensive works that refer to or "retell" a great amount of the Old Testament and mention many "biblical persons" known from those Scriptures. Then we examine texts that clearly connect with single biblical figures.[4]

*Jubilees*, written in Hebrew, is available now partially in Latin, wholly in Ethiopic; it narrates a revelation of the Angel of Presence to Moses, of the "events" and laws of the Torah, from the creation to the Exodus, including much material not found in the Bible. Its narratives

feature many biblical characters—like Adam and Eve, Enoch, Noah, Abraham, Rebekah, Jacob, Joseph, and Moses—with more positive attention to women than is found in the Bible. This book reflects a great desire to understand better all the stories and issues raised by a reading of Gn 1 to Ex 12.

Pseudo-Philo's *Biblical Antiquities* was written in Hebrew but is preserved fully only in a Latin text. It narrates the biblical history from Adam to the death of Saul, with numerous interpretive touches and a significant focus on women in the story.

Now we turn to biblical characters (Adam and Eve, Enoch, Noah, Abraham, Rebekah, Jacob, Dinah, Joseph, Moses, Baruch, Job, David, Solomon, Manasseh, and the Maccabees) clearly connected to apocryphal and pseudepigraphical works.

**Adam and Eve** feature in the *Life of Adam and Eve*, a Latin text that may be based on a Greek work known as the *Apocalypse of Moses*. It explores issues such as the sin of Eve and Adam, their death, burial, and resurrection on the last day, and also on the character Satan.

**Enoch** received little attention in the Bible. He appears in a genealogy (Gn 4:17–18) and his life is summarized in Gn 5:22–24, which states only that he "walked with God" and "God took him." Since Genesis does not mention his death, the brief notice spawned a great deal of interest and speculation, and Jewish thinkers concluded that he was located in heavenly circles, in the company of the angels. So much material attaches to his name (three "books" of Enoch) that he can be considered the most important biblical character in this era. *First Enoch* is composed of five distinct booklets; it stands out as the most unusual and important of the pseudepigraphical books. Written in Aramaic, the whole book is preserved only in Ethiopic and includes: the Book of the Watchers, chs. 1–36 (also preserved in Greek); the Parables of Enoch, chs. 37–71; the Book of the Luminaries (or the Astronomical Book), chs. 72–82; the Book of Dreams, chs. 83–90 (which includes the Animal Apocalypse), chs. 85–90; and the Epistle of Enoch, chs. 91–105. Enoch emerges as a type of prophetic-apocalyptic figure, delivering words

---

1. Cf. George W. E. Nickelsburg, *Jewish Literature between the Bible and the Mishnah*, 2nd ed. (Minneapolis: Fortress Press, 2005).

2. Cf. Michael E. Stone, ed., *Jewish Writings of the Second Temple Period: Apocrypha, Pseudepigrapha, Qumran Sectarian Writings, Philo, Josephus* (Van Gorcum: Assen; Philadelphia: Fortress, 1984); also Robert A. Kraft and George W. E. Nickelsburg, *Early Judaism and its Modern Interpreters* (Philadelphia: Fortress; Atlanta: Scholars Press, 1986).

3. Cf. James L. Kugel, *Traditions of the Bible: A Guide to the Bible As It Was at the Start of the Common Era* (Cambridge, MA; London, England: Harvard University Press, 1998).

4. There are three collections of these works widely available in English translation. R. H. Charles, *The Apocrypha and Pseudepigrapha of the Old Testament* (Oxford: Clarendon, 1903); J. H. Charlesworth, ed., *The Old Testament Pseudepigrapha*, 2 vols. (Garden City, NY: Doubleday, 1983 and 1985). H. F. D. Sparks, *The Apocryphal Old Testament* (Oxford: Clarendon, 1984).

and teachings of great significance; ultimately he appears as a kind of savior figure. Additional Enoch traditions appear in later texts: *2 Enoch* (Slavonic) and *3 Enoch* (*Hebrew Apocalypse of Enoch*, also known as the *Book of Hekhalot*). *Jubilees* also treats Enoch (Jub 4:16–26). In this text Enoch demonstrates great cultural learning, and is removed from his family and taken to the Garden of Eden.

**Noah** appears in several works that elaborate on the narratives in Genesis. The *Genesis Apocryphon*, an Aramaic text found at Qumran, narrates his birth and his blameless life. *Jubilees* also interprets his role, connecting him with the covenant, the calendar, and feast of Shavuot. Finally, several references to a lost document about Noah led some scholars to postulate a lost *Apocalypse of Noah*.

**Abraham**'s portrayal in Genesis is expanded in the *Testament of Abraham,* where God gives him an opportunity to compose a testament before his death. More surprising is a drama in which Death and Michael the archangel struggle with him, but the book ends without the writing of a testament. This work survives in two recensions: one in Greek, and the other a Slavonic *Apocalypse of Abraham,* where Abraham perceives the idols of his father's house, and then takes a heavenly journey described in seven visions, including a view of the sins of human beings on the earth. Abraham in *Jubilees* also gives three testaments, chs. 20, 21, and 22.

**Rebekah** does not have a text associated with her name, but she is a major character in *Jubilees*, where she preserves the covenant by orchestrating the lives of her sons Jacob and Esau, and especially by blessing Jacob and giving a last testament.

**Jacob** plays an important role in *Jubilees* 19–45, where he appears as the central covenant mediator for Judaism. One of the most important pseudepigraphical texts is the *Testaments of the Twelve Patriarchs*, featuring the sons of Jacob and his wives and concubines. Drawing from the scene in Gn 49 where Jacob at his deathbed gathers his sons around him and predicts future events for them and their descendants, these testaments offer a distinct literary document for each son. Each text recalls an incident in the life of a patriarch where a particular ethical virtue was highlighted; then the patriarch exhorts his offspring to emulate that ethical stance. Some examples are Reuben, concerning thoughts; Simeon, concerning envy; Levi, concerning priesthood and arrogance; Joseph, concerning self-control when tempted by the wife of Potiphar, and fraternal love for his brothers who had wronged him. These texts deal with common human failings—lust, anger, envy, deceit, hatred, love of money—and they are intended to warn people against such impulses. The present text clearly contains Christian terminology and notions, sparking a continuing debate about their Jewish or Christian origins.

**Dinah**, daughter of Jacob and Leah, was raped by Shechem, son of Hamor (in Gn 34). This vivid narrative sparked much interest for Jewish writers of the era. In *Jubilees* 30 the violent reaction of her brothers Simeon and Levi (killing the men of Shechem) was justified as an act opposing intermarriage with non-Jews. Other texts reflecting this incident include: *Testament of Levi*, chs. 2–7, *Aramaic Levi Document*, chs. 1–2; 6; *Judith* 9; *Pseudo Philo*, ch. 8, and Josephus, *Jewish Antiquities*, 1.337–41.

**Joseph**, son of Jacob, was included in the *Testaments of the Twelve Patriarchs*, and also in *Jubilees*, chs. 39–46. Joseph's story also inspired another Hellenistic work, *Joseph and Aseneth*; expanding on Gn 41:45, this romance narrates the conversion of the daughter of Potiphera (required for her to be available for marriage with Joseph). This Jewish work was preserved only by Christians, where its popularity may be due to its focus on conversion and a scene that might remind people of the Eucharist.

**Moses** figures prominently in two pseudepigraphs and one history. *Jubilees* opens at Mount Sinai, where Moses receives from the Angel of Presence revelation (the law and testimony) that he should pass on to Israel. Here many laws related to stories of the patriarchs and matriarchs actually derive from later Mosaic laws. In the *Testament of Moses*, the leader addresses his final words to Joshua with predictions about the future life of his people. Preserved in only one Latin manuscript, the text focusing Moses' prayer for divine compassion reflects a crisis situation. The *Exagogē* (leading out) section of *Ezekiel the Tragedian* offers numerous interpretive details about Moses and the Exodus.

Texts connected to prophetic figures also abound. **Isaiah** is featured in the *Martyrdom of Isaiah*, a Jewish work forming the first section of the Christian text, *Ascension of Isaiah*. The prophet is about to be put to death by agents of the evil King Manasseh; this story of martyrdom resembles similar scenes in 2 Mc 6–7.

**Baruch**, the scribe of **Jeremiah**, appears in the deuterocanonical book of Baruch; the Letter of Jeremiah forms the last chapter of this deuterocanonical book. *Second Baruch*, or the *Syriac Apocalypse of Baruch*, was probably a Hebrew text but is now extant only in Syriac. It portrays Baruch in an account of the sixth-century BCE fall of Jerusalem, where he utters laments and questions about God's justice. It holds out some hope for the future, while reflecting theologically on Rome's destruction of Jerusalem (cf. also *4 Ezra* [=*2 Esdras*]).

The *Sibylline Oracles* presents itself as a text given by the Sibyl, an aging Greek prophetess whose oracles usually interpret historical-political situations. This collection of twelve books in Greek includes both Christian and Jewish texts. In the late Middle Ages these female prophetic figures held prominence in Christian art and spirituality. The Sistine Chapel intersperses Sibyls and prophets of the Old Testament; the *Dies Irae*, a Latin sequence used in Requiem Masses, mentions the Sybil along with David. In Book 3 this Sibyl identifies herself as daughter-in-law of Noah (*Sib. Or.* 3.827).

**Job**, a wisdom figure in the Bible, stars in the *Testament of Job*, a Greek text that obviously depends on the LXX version of Job. In this testament, the narrative section (with Satan as adversary) stands out more than the ethical advice, which focuses on patient endurance. Job undergoes conversion and demonstrates great knowledge of heavenly realities; at its conclusion, his soul is taken to heaven in a chariot.

**David** appears in *Psalm 151*, found in the LXX and also at Qumran (Psalms Scroll from Cave 11). It recounts God's choice of David and his conquest of Goliath in 1 Sm 16–17.

Because it appears in the LXX it comprises part of the Apocrypha.

**Solomon** added authority to OT texts connected with wisdom, such as Proverbs and Ecclesiastes. Inspired by Ps 72, the *Psalms of Solomon*, also found in the LXX, offers eighteen poems attributed to him and oriented to the situation of Pompey's conquest of Jerusalem in 63 BCE. Psalm 17 of this collection features a Messiah figure and suggests a sensibility about suffering from oppression. The *Odes of Solomon* is a collection of forty-two odes attributed to Solomon. Preserved in Syriac, Greek, and Coptic, it has affinities with the Qumran *Hodayoth* (Thanksgiving Songs), and also with the Gospel of John; they likely were composed by a Jew in early second century CE.

**Manasseh** was considered the most wicked king of Judah by the Deuteronomistic Historian (2 Kgs 21), but the Chronicler relates that he repented and was rehabilitated (2 Chr 33). The Latin *Prayer of Manasseh*, from Christian sources, could easily be imagined as the prayer mentioned in 2 Chr 33:18–19. Its heartfelt sense of penitence and trust in God's compassion continue to attract worshipers. Found in medieval Vulgate manuscripts, it was considered part of the Apocrypha by Luther and also in the King James Version.

The **Maccabees** figured prominently in two deuterocanonical books, *1* and *2 Maccabees*, part of the Catholic canon. *Third Maccabees*, which is actually about Jews living in Egypt, offers assurance that God protects his people, especially at critical points of suffering. Memorable scenes include the saving of the Jews in a stadium from elephants intended to kill them, but who became inebriated and unable to carry out their task. A Greek historical romance, it appears in the LXX and in Luther's Apocrypha, but not in the Vulgate.

*Fourth Maccabees* argues that reason can dominate over the force of one's passions. Another text from Alexandria, it develops its point by retelling martyrdom scenes known from 2 Mc 6–7. The notion of expiatory suffering, justifying the noble deaths narrated in those chapters, is well developed. It appears in the Greek Orthodox Bible.

Although other examples could be adduced,

this collection amply demonstrates how the Apocrypha and especially the Pseudepigrapha basically derive from fascination with texts considered sacred among Jews, and which we know from the Bible. Testaments and apocalypses, re-told narratives, prophetic poems and psalms—all witness to the ongoing power of the Scriptures. Readers and hearers of these texts—individuals and communities—cannot help but wonder how these stories and persons might impact and inspire their own lives if they allow their religious imagination greater scope.

# Early Christian Apocrypha

## François Bovon

The first Christians were not a unified body of believers. We know several different communities existed. Their common denominator was that they lived with the Old Testament as Scripture and the apostolic preaching as good news. Around the year 50 CE the first letters were written; then the first Gospels, called "memories" in the second century by Justin Martyr, were born. To minimize divisiveness, the different Christian groups established bonds of faith and love, bringing to the common table their first writings. The grouping of the Gospels according to Matthew, Luke, and Mark in the first half of the second century CE gives evidence of an attempt to reach unity. A little later, in the second half of the second century CE, the Gospel of John was added.

Before going further one must make a distinction: the grouping of texts does not constitute canonization, that is, an official collection of books as Scripture. Even though the three, then four, Gospels were brought together, they were not immediately considered to be sacred. When Polycarp of Smyrna, writing around 115–125, mentions the Pauline Epistles (*To the Philippians* 3.2), he still considers them to be simply a corpus of documents, authoritative but not yet part of the canon of Holy Scripture. The passage, however, from a corpus to a canon then occurred relatively rapidly, since in the time of Irenaeus, around 180 CE, the four Gospels had received the status of canonical writings.

## Noncanonical Gospels and Epistles

Not all of the texts in circulation became part of this process from corpus to canon, however, because not all of the Christian communities joined the early orthodox church. An ancient gospel that did not make it into the canon is the *Gospel of Peter*. In this gospel, a long Greek passage tells of Jesus' passion, while smaller fragments, especially some verses of Jesus' missionary speech, relate to Jesus' ministry in Galilee. Therefore this was not only a gospel of Jesus' passion, as is commonly accepted, but a full gospel of the genre and the age of the Synoptic Gospels. In his *Ecclesiastical History* (6.12.3–6), Eusebius of Caesarea preserved the opinion of Serapion, Bishop of Antioch in Syria in the second half of the second century CE. Serapion first showed benevolence toward the *Gospel of Peter*, for he considered that, since the readers of that gospel were good, orthodox people, their holy writings should be acceptable. The same sympathy was not shown toward all noncanonical gospels: the early church disapproved of the *Gospel of Philip* (among the Nag Hammadi Codices), the *Gospel of Mary* (Mary Magdalene; in the Berlin Codex 8502), and the *Gospel of Judas* (in the Tchacos Codex), all recently discovered.

Unavoidable incidents, like the death of the apostles or of Jesus' family, and tragic events, like Nero's persecution in 64–65 CE, the fall of Jerusalem in 70 CE, or the delay of Jesus' second coming, brought new problems to the forefront. Faithful to the origins of their faith, early Christian leaders tried to find new solutions by digging into the old traditions, but most often they declared that their own works were of apostolic origin when in reality they were post-apostolic responses. Some of Paul's disciples, writing with good conscience in his name, tried to answer the needs of the present time. An exchange between Paul and the Corinthian community, named *3 Corinthians,* was written in the middle of the second century CE—as well as an *Epistle to the Laodiceans*.

These documents came too late to be integrated into the canon of the New Testament.

The same motives that led Christians to write letters in Paul's name pushed other believers to write in the name of Peter or James. Most of these epistles are of an ethical nature and recommend strict but generous ethical attitudes. For example, besides the two letters of Peter in the New Testament, there is a Coptic *Epistle of Peter to Philip* and a Greek *Epistle of Peter to James* (a preface to the *Pseudo-Clementine Homilies*). The author of an enigmatic *Epistle of Titus* argues in favor of an ascetical tendency and tries to impose sexual abstinence.

## The Term "Apocryphal"

The term "apocryphal" does not appear to have been used before the second century for Christian documents. Literally, it means "hidden." Humans "hide" either what they cherish or what makes them ashamed. Agreeing with other believers on the elementary core of the Christian faith, some spiritual groups—rapidly condemned as Gnostics because they tried to earn salvation through knowledge (*gnōsis*)—claimed with pride to possess additional teachings that they preferred to hide and to reveal only to the happy few. They called these secret writings "apocryphal" (in a positive sense) and often used the period after the Resurrection as a literary trope to develop their esoteric teachings (in this case, modern scholars call their writings "Dialogues with the Savior"). Such treatises as *The Book of Thomas the Contender* are particularly abundant among the Nag Hammadi Codices. The *Gospel of Thomas*—in its present form a second-century CE document—claims from its very beginning to offer a secret, an "apocryphal" (again, in the positive sense) path to eternal life. Such a claim can also be heard in other writings of the Nag Hammadi Codices, for example the *Apocryphon of James* and the *Apocryphon of John*.

About the same time, the first orthodox church writers opposed what they considered heretical teaching, and they rejected documents that their adversaries collected with respect. Justin Martyr, Irenaeus, and Tertullian, and later Eusebius and Jerome, describe these condemned documents as "false," "corrupt,"

"bastard," or "apocryphal" (in the negative sense).

Nevertheless, writings that paralleled the four Gospels and the Pauline Epistles continued to exist and even develop. In the second century CE different Jewish-Christian congregations in Palestine, Egypt, and Transjordan, still practicing the Mosaic law but believing in Jesus as the Messiah, had preserved their own memories of Jesus. Their gospels are lost, but we know of the existence of such documents and we even possess quotations from them. Among these were a *Gospel of the Nazarenes*, a *Gospel of the Hebrews*, and a *Gospel of the Ebionites* (a modern title).

While the faith of the first Christians in Jerusalem was oriented more toward the end of Jesus' life and the end of history, an interest in Jesus' birth and the origin of the world arose a few years later among the Christian Hellenists, particularly in Antioch in Syria. This interest appears in the two canonical infancy narratives, Mt 1–2 and Lk 1–2. It then developed into two forms that arrived too late to be integrated into the New Testament canon. This does not mean that they were rejected immediately as "apocryphal." The first form is related to *time*, to the past in the life of Jesus and his family: the most ancient witness, written in the second century CE, is the Greek *Birth of Mary*, claiming to have been written by James, the brother of the Lord. It is known by its modern title *Protevangelium of James*. This book was never declared apocryphal in the Greek Orthodox world, even if it remained outside the canon and was considered a historical document. It has been condemned in the West since the time of Jerome but survived for a time in Latin translations. It was then rewritten in an orthodox way to avoid further condemnations. This Latin rewriting, called the *Gospel of Pseudo-Matthew* (sixth to eighth centuries CE), was soon eclipsed by the *Birth of the Virgin Mary* (ninth to tenth centuries CE). The names of Anne and Joachim for Mary's parents come ultimately from the *Protevangelium of James*.

The second form is to speculate on *space* and to imagine Christ's incarnation: the descent of the preexistent Son through the seven heavens. Such a speculation is attested in three Christian documents, the *Ascension of Isaiah*, the *Epistle of the Apostles*, both from the second century CE, and the *Pistis Sophia*, probably from the third century.

Later in the fifth century CE, when theologians and bishops gathered for a council at Ephesus and meditated on Mary as the "Mother of God," Christian writers generated stories of the Virgin Mary's death and assumption. At least sixty-seven parallel versions of that story—called the *Transitus Mariae* (*Mary's Crossing*) or the *Dormitio Mariae* (*Mary's Last Sleep*)—are known.

## Noncanonical Acts of Apostles

In the first half of the second century, the Johannine community split (see 1 Jn 2:19). While one wing tried to give an orthodox understanding of Jesus Christ and favored the canonization of the Fourth Gospel, another wing developed independent traditions, some of which are preserved in the *Acts of John*. This writing was condemned by the church at an early stage because a section of it denied the reality of Jesus' incarnation and death. The *Acts of Andrew* faced a similar fate. Because of these drastic condemnations these literary pieces were destroyed and only fragments or revised sections survive.

Stories told in the oral tradition of Peter, Paul, Thecla, Thomas, Philip, and Matthew were gathered into large written tomes on the lives, miracles, and martyrdoms of these apostles. These writings—the *Acts of Peter*, the *Acts of Paul* including the story of Thecla, the *Acts of Thomas*, the *Acts of Philip*, and the *Martyrdom of Matthew*—focus on one apostle each and present his martyrdom after a ministry marked by ascetical recommendations and miraculous acts. This literary form is closer to the canonical Gospels than to the book of Acts. Because these noncanonical *Acts* were not so different from the Gospels and not antagonistic to the canonical book of Acts, they were at first accepted by certain theologians. Teachers in theological schools more than bishops in the cities liked these noncanonical works—and the monks favored them more than secular priests. While Origen knew and appreciated the *Acts of Paul*, Tertullian disliked it because it conferred a ministerial role on a woman; for

others, the excessive ascetic tendency attested in several sections of the *Acts of Andrew*, the *Acts of Thomas*, and the *Acts of Philip* was despicable.

## Noncanonical Apocalypses

The New Testament book of Revelation elaborates its visions in a cosmic framework and describes the end of the world through large symbolic frescoes. The same is true of another Apocalypse, the *Apocalypse of Peter*. Written probably a generation after the Johannine book of Revelation, in association with the second Jewish revolt of 132–135 CE, the *Apocalypse of Peter* also is oriented toward the end of the world with an apocalyptic perspective. Interestingly, although the original form of this apocalypse was amazingly preserved in Ethiopic, it is also partly known in a revised form in a long Greek fragment. In this fragment the context is no longer the end of the world but the end of human life. This *Apocalypse of Peter* was very popular in Antiquity: the Canon of Muratori (end of the second century CE—rather than fourth century, as has also been proposed) put it on the same level as the *Apocalypse of John*, even though the author knows of others who refused to read it in church. Building on 2 Cor 12:1–4, several writers created *Apocalypses of Paul*. One is present in the Nag Hammadi Library and another in the Greek apocryphal literature. This last *Apocalypse of Paul* was never condemned and it circulated widely in the Middle Ages. Dante knew one of its versions.

## The Reception of the Apocryphal Literature

We can point to the impact of apocryphal literature on many aspects of Christian life in late antiquity, the Byzantine period, and the Middle Ages—on liturgy, Christian art, literature, history, and theology. At Notre-Dame at Semur-en-Auxois (Burgundy, France), for example, the tympanum of the north doorway to the transept relates Saint Thomas's doubts at the Resurrection and his later travels to India as narrated in the *Acts of Thomas*.

How was it possible that works condemned

in the fourth–fifth centuries CE by major theologians—like Eusebius and Amphilochius in the East and Jerome and Augustine in the West—continued to be so influential? To explain this paradox one has to recognize two contradictory forces among early Christian thinkers. On the one side, there is the tendency to close the canon and to remain, thereafter, as biblical as possible. On the other, there are new liturgical, pastoral, and monastic needs requiring noncanonical texts. One solution was to revise, to purify, and finally to select noncanonical documents in addition to the biblical canon. So rewritten, these documents became part of the tradition. Gregory, bishop of Tours in the sixth century, saved for us the plot of the *Acts of Andrew*. In his preface to his *Life of Andrew* he reports finding a book, probably a Latin version of the old apocryphal *Acts of Andrew*. He liked the narrative but felt that the many speeches of the apostle were heretical in many respects (diplomatically he says that they were too long). Therefore he rewrote the book, respecting the narrative but eradicating the speeches.

Without becoming canonical these revised apocryphal texts nevertheless ceased to be despicable, heretical, and rejected. They became part of the Christian tradition. But their identity did not exactly correspond to the definition of the apostolic tradition set forth at the Council of Trent in the sixteenth century. While the council admitted that the magisterium of the Catholic Church has control over Scripture and tradition, the historians and theologians of today believe that these documents, neither canonical nor apocryphal, were composed by the spontaneous desires of local communities under the pressure of ecclesiastical needs in a nonrational and nonjuridical way. They were not written by powerful church authorities but by local Christian leaders. Later they were revised by theologians eager to reach church people and curious to discover unusual but respectable documents. In their new versions these books can be called profitable or useful for the soul. ∎

# The Christian Bible and the Jews

## Mary C. Boys, SNJM

To residents of the first-century CE Mediterranean world, the title of this essay would be puzzling. In that era, "Christians" and "Jews" did not yet designate members of separate religions. They are complicated terms even today, and what they meant in the first several centuries differs from their current meaning. "Jew" originally meant a person from the territory of Judea and expanded to refer to a way of life and culture, including distinctive religious practices. Followers of Jesus were originally called followers of "the Way" (see Acts 19:9, 23; 22:4; 24:14, 22). Acts 11:26 notes, "It was in Antioch that the disciples were first called Christians," but the term encompassed both Jesus-believing Jews and Jesus-believing non-Jews. The process by which Judaism and Christianity became distinct religious traditions took several centuries. Until well into the third century, "Christian" and "Jew" were more like dialects of a single language (e.g., Spanish as spoken in Mexico and Puerto Rico) than separate languages. There was no single turning point of separation; the dialects became separate languages at different times, under different circumstances, and in different locations.

Nor did the "Christian Bible" exist in the first-century Mediterranean world. As an anthology of texts composed by numerous authors and editors over a course of some 1500 years, the Bible was still in formation. First-century Jews—including those who believed in Jesus—regarded the Bible as a collection of texts vital to their identity. Although five texts of Torah took precedence (Genesis, Exodus, Leviticus, Numbers, Deuteronomy), there was as yet no consensus about the full list of writings constituting the Scriptures—and in fact to this day, various traditions, both Jewish and Christian, differ in what books of the First Testament/Hebrew Bible they include in their official lists of sacred books or "canon" (see also articles "The Formation of the Bible" and "Sacred Scripture in the Catholic Tradition").

Jews and Protestants include the same books in their canons, although in a different order. The Catholic and Eastern Orthodox churches have more books in their canons, though their lists are not identical. Most Bibles produced under Catholic auspices, including the *New American Bible, Revised Edition*, place these additional ("deuterocanonical") books within the Old Testament; in contrast, Protestant publishers often designate a separate section for these additional books, categorizing them as "apocryphal" (hidden books). By the beginning of the second century, most of the texts that constitute the New Testament had been written. By the middle of that century, the Gospels and the letters of Paul were regarded as authoritative. Not until the fourth century, however, do we have an official canon of the books constituting the Christian Bible. Yet even after this, various communities continued for centuries to recognize disparate lists as canonical.

Respect for the complexity of the Bible must be the foundation on which Christians build if they are to understand their relation with Jews and Judaism. Three dimensions of this complexity are essential: valuing the relation between the two primary parts of the Christian Bible, the "Old" and "New" Testaments; teasing out what the New Testament *appears* to say about Jews from what the fuller context implies; and learning from the developing traditions of interpretation that many Christian churches articulate today.

## The Relation of the "Old" and "New" Testaments

What Christians today term the Old Testament was the Bible of Jesus. It was to those Scriptures that his disciples turned as they searched for words and images to articulate their experience of the life, death, and Resurrection of Jesus. So it is that the New Testament is filled with citations from and allusions to that Bible—the older Testament.

Precisely how the older and newer Testaments were related was hotly debated in the early centuries as the followers of the Way discerned the identity of their movement. Around the mid-second century, Marcion (d. ca. 160) proposed a radical solution for what should be included in their Bible. He proposed they jettison the Old Testament altogether; he argued that the Bible should consist only of selected letters of Paul and an edited version of Luke's Gospel. In his view, the creator God revealed in the Old Testament was different from and inferior to the God revealed by Jesus. Although other early church figures rejected Marcion's elimination of the books of the older Testament, they found themselves in another dilemma: If they retained the books so central to Jewish identity, then what was distinct about their movement? And as the writings of the New Testament coalesced and became part of the canon of the biblical books, what was their status in relation to the books of the Old Testament?

Various solutions were proposed. Justin Martyr (ca. 100–165) argued that Jews were unable to interpret their own Scriptures correctly. In his *Dialogue with Trypho,* composed about 155, he alleged that "you [Jews], though you read them, do not catch the spirit that is in them" (*Dial.,* 29). Similarly, Augustine of Hippo (354–430) believed that Jews were ignorant of the true identity of Jesus because they misread their own Scriptures. Although Jews preserved faithfully the books of Scripture, Augustine said they read them "as the face of a blind man appears in a mirror—by others it is seen, but by himself it is not seen" (*The City of God,* 18.46). Augustine offered a formula for the relation of the Testaments that has had lasting influence: "In the Old Testament the New Testament is concealed. In the New Testament the Old Testament is revealed" (*Questiones in Heptateuchum,* 2.73). In the early church, such arguments were frequently accompanied by a harsh polemic against the synagogue: Jews had not heeded the prophets,

and so had failed to recognize Jesus Christ. Worse, they had crucified him, God's Son, so Jews were faithless and unbelieving. The harshness of the rhetoric echoes the traditions of the prophets of the Hebrew Bible and the polemical rhetoric of both Jews and Gentiles in the Greco-Roman world.

This polemic became part of the theological reasoning through which Christian thinkers ultimately gave expression to a distinctive identity apart from Judaism. Yet the rhetoric did not match social reality. Even in the second, third, and fourth centuries, when anti-Jewish rhetoric flourished, there is copious evidence of close social interaction between Jews and Christians. But once Christianity gained political power in the fourth century, the boundaries between the two traditions became more firmly fixed, and Jews became the principal "other" against which Christians defined themselves.

This differentiation came with a loss. Christianity largely lost sight of the way in which the Scriptures continued to sustain and nourish Jewish communities. The rabbis and sages interpreted the Tanak (a term formed from the initial letters of the three major parts of the Jewish Bible: Torah, Nevi'im [Prophets] and Kethubim [Writings]: TNK), compiling an impressive array of literature. Central to this literature are the compilations of diverse commentary in the Jerusalem Talmud (ca. 400) and in the Babylonian Talmud (ca. 500). These "Talmudim" (plural) include biblical interpretation, legal enactments, midrash or commentary on the books of the Bible, ritual, and liturgy. Because the church was largely unaware of these developments, its understanding of Judaism was constricted.

Another loss for many Christians was that the Old Testament was in effect reduced to a book of divine promises fulfilled only in the life of Jesus and in the New Testament. Often this meant that the Old Testament "types" were considered mere shadows of their fuller New Testament realities. In more recent years, many Christians have rightly come to recognize the richness of the Old Testament and the intricate interweaving of its stories, images, and prayers in the New Testament.

# The New Testament and Jews

Several guidelines are useful for understanding roles Jews play in the New Testament. The first involves recognition of what a complicated term "Jew" is. It is used differently in various texts. On occasion, it seems to mean primarily "Judean." More frequently, it describes Jesus, his family and disciples, and most of those he interacts with, with the exception of Gentiles (e.g., Roman officials such as Pontius Pilate, the governor of Judea, and the woman variously described as "Canaanite" or "Syro-Phoenecian"). In still other texts, especially in the Gospel of John, "Jews" often are depicted as enemies of Jesus. Moreover, different "schools" of belief and practice are evident, such as Pharisees, Sadducees, and scribes. Certain Jews, such as the high priests, hold prominent positions and interact with Roman officials, while others have little or no status in society. While common boundary markers distinguished Jews—such as the circumcision of Jewish males, and the observance of *kashrut* (dietary norms) and of *Shabbat* (sabbath)—they constituted a diverse community spread across the Mediterranean and Middle Eastern world. There was no single way of being Jewish, no official and normative ruling on what Jews should believe and how they should engage in religious practice.

A second guideline flows from the nature of the New Testament texts. They may appear to be historical writings. The Gospels, for example, seem to be documentaries of the life of Jesus. Closer reading, however, reveals that they differ from one another in many details, and that those differences provide entrée to each evangelist's distinctive portrait of Jesus. Moreover, because the Gospels were composed in the latter third of the first century, they layer concerns of the evangelist's community with their narrative of the ministry of Jesus. At times this layering has resulted in misinterpretations that have fostered negative views of Jews and Judaism.

## Texts Giving Rise to Negative Views of Jews and Judaism, I: The Pharisees

A vivid example of this is Mt 23:1–36, in which Jesus uses highly charged language characterizing the Pharisees as "hypocrites," "blind guides," "blind fools," "serpents, . . . brood of vipers," and "whitewashed tombs, which appear beautiful on the outside, but inside are full of dead men's bones and every kind of filth." As a result of such passages, the Pharisees became fixed in the Christian imagination as the epitome of hypocrisy, absolutists with regard to trivial laws who had lost sight of the wideness of God's mercy. When this view of the Pharisees was joined to interpretations of Paul's letters as contrasting the demands of the law with the grace of Christ, many Christians came to regard Judaism as a legalistic religion much inferior to the freedom Christ brought.

That Jesus may have differed with the Pharisees on certain matters is not surprising, as Jews debated with each other on how best to live according to Torah. But recent scholarship provides a quite different perspective on their negative depiction in Matthew. The Pharisees were neither Jesus' principal opponents nor the dominant force in first-century Judaism. For the most part, Pharisees served the governing class as subordinate officials. Their interest in law did not mean they were self-righteous hypocrites and legalists, absorbed by trivia and externals. Rather, they were committed to drawing upon Torah for wisdom about everyday life, and this translated into an interest in law. Emphasis on practices that served as boundary markers of Jewish identity did not mean that the Pharisees were preoccupied with ritualism and arcane rules.

What scholarship makes clear is that polemic rather than precision shaped Matthew's portrayal of the Pharisees. If, as most scholars believe, Matthew was written about 85, after the chaos following the Jewish War with Rome that ended with the destruction of the Temple and the devastation of Jerusalem in 70 CE, he was likely involved in a debate with the

Pharisees about who were to be the true leaders of this wounded community. In the literary style of the day, Matthew re-situated this later debate into the ministry of Jesus, even though in large measure Jesus and the Pharisees shared a common vision.

The Gospels tell stories on two levels: what Jesus said and did, as well as how later communities of his followers made meaning of his life, death, and Resurrection. In the case of Mt 23:1–36, what Jesus is saying against the Pharisees should be more accurately regarded as Matthew's argument with them, expressed in the polemical style of the day. In the formulation of the U.S. Catholic bishops in a 1988 publication, the evangelists "tended to telescope the long historical process whereby the gospels were set down some generations after Jesus' death. Thus, certain controversies that may have actually taken place between church leaders and rabbis toward the end of the first century were 'read back' into the life of Jesus" (*God's Mercy Endures Forever* §20).

It can be a shock to one's sensibilities to find polemics in sacred texts—but these texts did not drop down pure and undefiled from heaven. While Christians speak of the Bible as the "word of God," this revelatory word comes only through the medium of human language. God speaks in the images, customs, and idioms of particular people in specific cultures, not in some timeless, abstract mode. A helpful analogy is that of the Incarnation: just as Christ took on human nature, so, too, did God "take on" human language in the revelatory process. Acknowledging the interplay of divine and human in the Bible means that the authors whom God inspired were, nevertheless, finite and scarred by cultural biases and ignorance. Moreover, polemical attacks on rival groups, such as that of Mt 23, were characteristic of the Greco-Roman world. When reading passages that depict groups of Jews (or "the Jews" more generally), it is important to keep in mind that the "way the New Testament talks about Jews is just about the way all opponents talked about each other back then."[1]

_____
1. Luke Timothy Johnson, "The New Testament's Anti-Jewish Slander and the Conventions of Ancient Polemic," *Journal of Biblical Literature* 108, no. 3 (1989), 429.

Recognition of the polemical aspect of Mt 23 and similar passages allows contemporary readers to move beyond constricted readings. Rather than merely repeating the charges of hypocrisy against a particular Jewish group of the first century, interpreters today should read this passage as an invitation to examine their own religious beliefs and practices. Do they lead to a deeper awareness of God's mercy and call to live justly? Or do they result in self-righteousness and pretense?

By placing the polemical passages of the Bible in their literary and cultural contexts, the Scriptures invite readers of every generation to see their own lives mirrored.

## Texts Giving Rise to Negative Views of Jews and Judaism, II: Jews and the Death of Jesus

In many respects, the narratives of the passion, death, and Resurrection of Jesus are the most sacred stories of the Christian tradition. They also may be the most familiar of the biblical accounts because of the emphasis each of the four canonical Gospels devotes to these events, as well as their centrality to the preaching of the apostle Paul. Yet the texts themselves exist in a far larger universe. Each year in Holy Week, churches enact solemn rituals retelling the story; many participate in devotions such as the Stations of the Cross or services for the "Seven Last Words" of Jesus. Passion plays enhance the drama; pilgrims retrace Jesus' journey to Golgotha as they walk the *Via Crucis*—Way of the Cross—in Jerusalem and in places around the world. Music—from Bach's two monumental works for chorus and orchestra, *St. Matthew's Passion* and *St. John's Passion*, to the simplest of chants and spirituals—evokes deep emotions. Artists over the ages and throughout the world have depicted the death of Jesus in a range of media and with various intentions.

As sacred as these stories are, and as formative as they have been for Christian self-understanding, they have a shadow side because they attributed responsibility for the crucifixion to the Jews. In the popular imagination of later generations, Jews were "Christ killers"—a designation that led to tragic consequences.

The accusation that Jews were responsible for the death of Jesus, while rooted in New Testament texts, evolved over the centuries. It was an important component of preaching in the early church, still in the process of forming its own identity. It was a key element in its rivalry with the synagogue in the complex and extended process by which Christianity ultimately separated from Judaism. As a fundamental part of the "us/them" binary, this was the key polemic that stood at the center of the assertion that the Way of Christ, the crucified Savior, was the only faithful way to God and that the followers of Christ had now become God's people. God had rejected the Jews, the former people of God, because of their infidelity in killing Jesus.

Tragically, the polemical aspect of this charge was not recognized. Over the centuries, Christians continued to preach and teach about Jewish faithlessness and treachery. In the High Middle Ages, the "Christ-killer" charge moved out of the realm of rhetoric and sanctioned violence against Jews. In addition, Jews were further stereotyped as usurers, bribers, and secret killers. A more affective piety developed in which forms of meditation centered on entering into the suffering of Jesus. This intense focus on his sufferings stirred up emotions against those who had caused the suffering: Jews. Jews were accused of ritual crucifixion (crucifying Christian children) and of ritual cannibalism or "blood libel" (drinking the blood of Christian children). The famous Passion play in the Bavarian village of Oberammergau in Germany, enacted before huge crowds virtually every decade since 1680, heightened Jewish opposition to Jesus and further inflamed feelings against Jews. The vilification of Jews that had become a part of the Christian tradition was used to justify persecution and as fuel for pogroms. It became linked with German nationalist fervor and anti-Semitism in the nineteenth century, and paved the way for Nazi ideology. As the Catholic bishops of France said in their 1997 "Declaration of Repentance":

An anti-Jewish tradition stamped its mark in differing ways on Christian doctrine and teaching, in theology, apologetics, preaching and in the liturgy. It was on such ground that the venomous plant of hatred for the Jews was able to flourish. Hence, the heavy inheritance we still bear in our century, with all its consequences, which are so difficult to wipe out. Hence, our still open wounds.[2]

# Rethinking Christian Interpretations of the Bible

The "Declaration of Repentance" suggests that at least in some quarters of the church, a fundamental change in attitudes toward the Jewish people is happening. Two related developments help to explain the reasons for this sea change: reassessments in many sectors of Christianity, and biblical scholarship.

## A New Relation between Jews and Christians

Shortly after the end of World War II, sixty-five Jews and Christians from nineteen nations gathered in the summer of 1947 for an emergency conference on anti-Semitism in the Swiss village of Seelisberg. The participants met to express their profound grief over the Holocaust, their determination to combat anti-Semitism, and their desire to foster a better relationship between their traditions. They acknowledged anti-Semitism not only as a sin against God and humanity, but also as dangerous to modern civilization. They also placed interpretation of the death of Jesus at the center of their deliberations. At the conclusion of the conference, the Christian participants (Protestant, Catholic, and Orthodox) issued a statement to the churches that included ten recommendations, four of which dealt with how the churches should teach and preach

2. The full text of the declaration is available online at *http://www.bc.edu/dam/files/research_sites/cjl/texts/cjrelations/resources/documents/catholic/french_repentance.htm.*

differently about the alleged Jewish responsibility for the death of Jesus:

6. Avoid using the word "Jews" in the exclusive sense of the enemies of Jesus and the words "The Enemies of Jesus" to designate the whole Jewish people.

7. Avoid presenting the Passion in such a way as to bring the odium of the killing of Jesus upon all Jews or upon Jews alone. . . .

8. Avoid referring to the scriptural curses, or the cry of a raging mob: "His Blood be Upon Us and Our Children" [Mt 27:25], without remembering that this cry should not count against the infinitely more weighty words of our Lord: Father "Forgive Them, for They Know not What They Do" [Lk 23:34].

9. Avoid promoting the superstitious notion that the Jewish people are reprobate, accursed, reserved for a destiny of suffering.[3]

These points anticipated later statements from various churches, the most famous of which is the Second Vatican Council's 1965 declaration, *Nostra Aetate*. This brief document, consisting of five sections in its final form, went through a lengthy and contentious drafting process. The fourth section, the longest, expresses an understanding of the passion and death never previously articulated in official teachings of the Catholic Church. Without explanation of what had changed from previous teachings, the document asserted that "what happened in His passion cannot be charged against all the Jews, without distinction, then alive, nor against the Jews of today."

In the nearly fifty years since that promulgation, many Christian churches have issued similar statements and expressed desire for reconciliation with Jews. In the meantime, biblical scholars have opened up a broader horizon within which to understand the history surrounding the death of Jesus.

## New Insights on Ancient Texts

Complementing the work of the churches is that of scholars, particularly in the field of biblical studies. More extensive knowledge of the world in which the New Testament was composed has enabled more nuanced readings of polemical texts. This is especially the case with the passion accounts in the Gospels, which take on new dimensions when read in the context of the Roman Empire. The rule of Rome over the Jews in first-century Palestine becomes the critical "back story" for the passion and death of Jesus.

As Jesus preached, in God's reign the powerful are brought down from their thrones and the lowly lifted up (see Lk 1:52–53). But the Roman Empire had not become the West's regnant superpower by extending an olive branch. Conquest and victory were its watchwords, not peace. Rome's foreign policy was intended to dominate and humiliate the enemy—to inspire fear and awe in those it conquered.

This context of brutality and dehumanization reveals the function of crucifixion, which the Romans used commonly. What greater mechanism to inspire fear and keep order than crucifixion? Crucifixion was "highly organized, massive state terrorism, intended to intimidate the vast peasant and slave populations of the empire into passivity."[4] As a public humiliation—the naked body hanging for all to see, sometimes for days—it was torture designed as the ultimate deterrent. Rome reserved crucifixion only for peasants, foreigners, and slaves it deemed guilty of heinous crimes, such as fomenting rebellion, treason, and murder. Roman citizens were generally not subject to crucifixion.

Many scholars believe that the Roman governor of Judea, Pontius Pilate, may well have put Jesus to death as a messianic pretender. It was not that Jesus himself was dangerous, but that the crowds that he inspired by his preaching of the nearness of the kingdom threatened the sort of kingdom Rome represented. Roman officials associated such teaching with revolt in first-century Judea—and the threat of civil unrest was one of Rome's great concerns. Thus, many scholars conclude, Jesus was put

---

3. "The Ten Points of Seelisberg." See *http://www.jcrelations.net/en/?item=983*.

4. Stephen J. Patterson, *Beyond the Passion: Rethinking the Death and Life of Jesus* (Minneapolis: Fortress, 2004), 8.

to death under the authority of the Roman governor for an alleged violation of Roman law, likely similar to the charges of Lk 23:2 that Jesus was "misleading" the nation, forbidding the payment of taxes to the emperor, and claiming to be the Messiah, the king. Jesus was put to death under the Roman governor's authority in alliance with the power class, particularly the Temple priesthood.

The crucifixion of Jesus was the consequence of the politics of Roman-ruled Judea, in which thousands, if not tens of thousands, of Jews were crucified. Pontius Pilate would likely have had no scruples about doing away with a Jewish teacher from Galilee who attracted crowds and seemed to fear no human power. The Romans had far more power than any Jewish authorities; even the high priest served at the permission of the governor.

Why then do the Gospels place more emphasis on Jewish culpability for the death of Jesus than they do on Pilate? There is no assured answer for this. It is helpful to remember that when the Gospels were composed, "Christian" and "Jew" were not separate religions. It may well have been that Jesus-believing Jews were bitter toward *other* Jews, whom they believed should have followed Christ. It also may have been the case that the followers of the Way knew that in claiming Christ as "Savior" and "Lord" rather than Caesar, the Roman emperor, they were putting themselves in danger. The One they followed had, after all, been crucified by imperial power.

If the historical sources do not permit a resolution of this question, the largely tragic history of relations between Jews and Christians points to the significance of interpreting texts with respect for the contexts in which they originated and with sensitivity to their potential to contradict the gospel.

A new age of biblical interpretation has been under way for more than a half century. Its discoveries and methods provide opportunities for Christian readers of the Bible to understand their relationship with the Jewish people in ways that enhance a more peaceful world. ∎

# Jewish Biblical Interpretation

## Amy-Jill Levine

## Studying the Text

According to Ben Bag-Bag, a rabbinic contemporary of Jesus, Israel's Scripture is both ground of and guide to life: "Turn it and turn it again, for everything is in it; contemplate it and grow grey and old over it, and stir not from it, because you can have no better rule than it" (*Mishnah Avot* 5.22). This statement presents several initial details necessary for the understanding of Jewish biblical interpretation.

First, Scripture study is the responsibility of all the people of Israel. To make the text accessible, especially given high illiteracy rates in antiquity, Jews read the text aloud to the congregation (see Lk 4; Acts 15:21). In Aramaic-speaking settings (Aramaic came to replace Hebrew as the language in the land of Israel and points east in the Second Temple period), congregations offered Aramaic paraphrases (called "targumim," meaning "translations") for Jews unable to understand Hebrew. Today in most synagogues, the biblical material is chanted out loud in Hebrew while congregants have copies of the vernacular.

All Jews can and should participate in Torah study, including women (although like that of Christian women, Jewish women's formal participation in scriptural interpretation was rare before the late twentieth century). According to legend, Beruriah, the daughter of the martyred Rabbi Haninah ben Teradyon (early second century CE) and the wife of Rabbi Meir, daily studied three hundred legal matters (*Babylonian Talmud Pesahim* 62b), offered authoritative legal rulings (*Tosefta Bava Qamma* 4.9), and gave profound pastoral counseling (*Midrash Proverbs*).

Second, the text speaks to each reader; its manifold richness cannot be constrained to one interpretation. The traditional form of Jewish study is to debate texts with a fellow student. Much like United States Supreme Court records, rabbinical texts preserve debates and record minority opinions (*mahloket*). As *Mishnah Avot* 5.17 states, "Every dispute that is for the sake of heaven will endure." *Babylonian Talmud Eruvim* 13b concurs: sages may disagree, but "the statements of both are the words of the living God."

This approach is consistent with Judaism's nonhierarchical structure: Jews have no single authority such as a pope or a bishop. Just as certain interpreters have major influence in Christian thought (e.g., Augustine, Aquinas), so within Judaism certain interpreters have recognized authority (e.g., Rashi [1040–1105], Maimonides [1135–1204]), but disagreement with their teaching exists. Hasidic movements have leaders who determine interpretation, but these leaders have authority only over their specific group. Modern Jewish movements (Reform, Reconstructionist, Renewal, Conservative, Orthodox, etc.) have different approaches and cite different authorities to interpret Scripture, and individual Jews may and do disagree with their rabbi's interpretation.

Appreciation for multiple readings is connected to the self-definition of the Jewish community. Judaism is not simply a religion (i.e., a movement one enters because of a particular faith or belief), although people do convert to Judaism. Jews are also a "people" who generally claim common ancestry (from Abraham and Sarah) and a homeland (Israel). From the second century CE, Jews have recognized any child of a Jewish mother as a Jew; more liberal branches of Judaism today recognize as Jewish the child of either a Jewish mother or father, provided the child is raised as a Jew.

This sense of peoplehood more easily allows for multiple readings and internal disagreement: readers may disagree, but still be in the fold. In religions where membership is determined by "belief," multiple readings may be discouraged, since incorrect belief (i.e., heresy) removes the reader from the community.

Third, Judaism has a history of biblical interpretation, as the sources cited above portend. When informed Jews study Scripture, they engage in dialogue and debate with other interpreters over two millennia.

# The Scriptures of Synagogue and Church[1]

## Translation

The Bible of Judaism today is the "Masoretic Text," twenty-four Hebrew books standardized sometime between the ninth and eleventh centuries CE. Because written Hebrew originally consisted only of consonants (compare shorthand, or text-messaging), the Masoretes (the name is derived from a Hebrew term connoting the handing down of tradition) added vowels. Also controlling accuracy is the *Masorah*, a medieval commentary providing details on vocalization, variant readings, brief explanatory annotations, the counting of letters and words, and other details to ensure the standardization of copies. In antiquity, although the text was not fully standardized, the deep connections between the biblical materials found among the Dead Sea Scrolls and the medieval version suggest that the text remained relatively secure for two millennia.

New Testament writers did not follow the Hebrew Scriptures that became the Masoretic Text, however; they based their writings on Greek translations (e.g., the Septuagint) developed by Jewish communities outside the land of Israel. The differences in the texts inevitably created different interpretations.

Isaiah 7:14 provides the most famous example of this translation difference. The Hebrew describes a "young woman" (*'almah*) whose pregnancy (she is thus presumably not a virgin; cf. the NABRE "the young woman, pregnant and about to bear a son") serves as a sign to King Uzziah that his political problems will abate (7:16). The Septuagint translates *'almah* as *parthenos* (cf. the Parthenon, the temple of the virgin Athena). *Parthenos* need not mean "virgin," as the Septuagint of Gn 34:3 indicates

by calling Dinah a *parthenos* after her relations with Shechem. However, the First Gospel follows this connotation. Matthew 1:23 reads Is 7:14, in Greek, as referring to a "virgin" and finds this prediction fulfilled in Jesus' miraculous conception.

Understandings of Is 7:14 separated Jewish and Christian interpreters as early as the second century. The church father Justin Martyr (*Dialogue with Trypho* 67 [ca. 160]) records the Jewish view that the text refers to a "young woman" rather than a "virgin," and that "the whole prophecy refers to King Hezekiah." Justin responds, "Your teachers . . . have altogether taken away many Scriptures from the [Greek] translation." That is, Jews changed the text. The charge is illegitimate, as the Dead Sea Scrolls demonstrate.

## Punctuation

Early biblical manuscripts not only lack vowels, they also lack punctuation, and the Jewish tradition delights in finding multiple messages. Isaiah 40:3–4 offers an excellent example of how new pnctuation can change meaning. The original reads: "A voice proclaims: 'In the wilderness prepare the way of the LORD!'" Speaking to Jewish exiles in Babylon, Isaiah announces the good news that they will return home.

But removed from its original context, the text can read, "A voice proclaims in the wilderness: 'Prepare the way of the Lord.'" This reading appears in the Gospel of Mark (1:2–4) and it is one possible interpretation of the abbreviated quotation of Isaiah (the "voice" is not mentioned) in the Dead Sea Scrolls, given the Qumran community's desert location (1QS [the *Community Rule* from Cave 1] 8:14–16).

## Canonical Order

The terms by which Jews and Christians identify their Scriptures also highlight differences. The church's "Old Testament" necessarily portends a "New Testament." For Jews, the text is called *Miqra* (Hebrew, "that which is read, reading") and, more commonly, the "Tanak," an acronymn for Torah [the Pentateuch], Nebi'im [Prophets], and Ketubim [Writings]. The Jewish

---

1. Additional discussion related to history of various canons can be found in the article "The Formation of the Bible." For discussion of issues related to translation, see especially "Sacred Scripture in the Catholic Tradition" and "Critical Issues in Contemporary Biblical Interpretation." For discussion related to Christianity, Judaism, and Scripture, see "The Christian Bible and the Jews," "The Distinctiveness of Jesus," and "Introduction to the Prophets," particularly the section, "The Literature of the Prophetic Books and the New Testament."

Bible is thus a complete text, not "Part 1" of a larger revelation.

Complicating the identification of the Bibles of Synagogue and Church is the list of contents in the Christian "Old Testament." For Catholic and Orthodox readers, the "Old Testament" includes the deuterocanonical texts—Judith, the additions to Daniel and Esther, 1 and 2 Maccabees, Ben Sira (Ecclesiasticus), etc.—written by Jews before the time of Jesus and preserved in Greek. Many Protestants reject these texts as "Old Testament Apocrypha." Anglicans and some Lutherans, although they would not consider these books to be "deuterocanonical" in the same way that Catholics and Orthodox do, allow for reading of these works in liturgical context and as such deem them worthy of respect. Jewish tradition displays knowledge of these texts, but the books are not in the Jewish canon.

Canonical order creates a second distinction. Christian canons place the book of Ruth between Judges and 1 Samuel; in Jewish canons, Ruth appears in the Ketubim, the Writings. More telling of the distinction between Synagogue and Church is the placement of the prophetic books. The Old Testament ends with Malachi's prediction of Elijah's return "before the day of the LORD" (3:23–24). The Gospels associate John the Baptist with Elijah (Mk 1:2–4), and read the prophets as predicting Jesus' advent. For the Church, the Old Testament, beginning with sin in Eden and ending with eschatological prophecy, anticipates the New Testament, wherein sin is redressed and prophecy fulfilled.

Judaism tells a different story. Tucking the prophets (Nebi'im) in the middle of the canon, the Tanak ends with the Ketubim. This order is ancient: Josephus knows the "five books of Moses," "the Prophets" and "remaining . . . books" (*Against Apion*, 1.39–41; cf. Lk 24:32, 44). The Ketubim concludes in 2 Chr 36:23 with Cyrus of Persia's edict to the Jews in Babylon: "The LORD, the God of heaven, has given to me all the kingdoms of the earth. He has also charged me to build him a house in Jerusalem, which is in Judah. All among you, therefore, who belong to his people, may their God be with them; let them go up." A few medieval Hebrew manuscripts end not with Chronicles but with Ezra-Nehemiah. Nevertheless, the same message prevails, since Nehemiah's final verse, "Remember this in my favor, my God!" (13:31b) echoes "God" ('*elohim*) and "good" (*tob*) from Gn 1. Both Jewish canonical orders thus do not point forward to new teachings or a new canon; instead, they encourage readers to return home both literally and textually, to look again, to turn it and turn it.

# Hermeneutical Lenses

## Scriptural Emphases

Judaism emphasizes the Pentateuch or Torah (Hebrew, "instruction"). Some congregations read the entire Pentateuch, divided into fifty-four *parashiyyot* (Hebrew, "divisions"; singular: *parshah*), annually; others follow a trienniel cycle. Each *parshah* has an accompanying reading (*haftarah*, Hebrew, "conclusion, departing") from the Nebi'im (Prophets) or Ketubim (Writings). Thus texts interpret one another. Christian lectionaries (readings from the Old Testament, Psalms, Gospels, and Epistles) create different principal intertexts and thus different interpretive emphases. Further, Christian lectionaries draw primarily from the Prophets rather than the Pentateuch; therefore many laws that define Jewish identity are not proclaimed in Christian worship. In turn, passages associated with Jesus, such as Isaiah 61:1 (see Lk 4:18), do not appear in the Jewish liturgical readings.

Liturgy yields another difference in scriptural emphasis. Most Jewish holidays have assigned readings (as the Gospel Passion Narratives are read during Holy Week): on Purim, the book of Esther; on Shavuot (Hebrew, "weeks"; compare the Christian "Pentecost"), to celebrate both the Spring harvest and the giving of the Torah, the book of Ruth; on the ninth of the month of Av (early August), the date on which both Temples were destroyed, Lamentations (other communities also read Job). Only a few passages from these books are scattered in Christian lectionaries. Consequently, Jewish biblical familiarity differs from Christian familiarity.

Two more differences between Christian and Jewish understanding arise in the form by which Scripture is presented. In synagogues, the Torah is chanted in Hebrew from a handwriten scroll. In most churches the text is read in the vernacular, from a book.

## Theological and Anthropological Presuppositions

Jews and Christians, broadly speaking, read through different theological and anthropological positions. For example, the church traditionally finds in Gn 1:26, "God said: Let us make human beings in our image," indication of the Trinity, for "In the beginning was the Word" (Jn 1:1). Judaism proffers several understandings: God takes council with the angels to model the practice of the greater consulting with the lesser (*Genesis Rabbah* 8.3–4); God tests readers, who might fall into the heresy of polytheism (*Genesis Rabbah* 8.8); the plural signals divine majesty, and so on. Likely the original meaning reflected the ancient Near Eastern notion of the heavenly court (cf. 1 Kgs 22:19–22; Ps 29:1–2; 82; Is 6:8; etc.).

The story of Adam and Eve (who disappear from the Tanak after Gn 5) also receives distinct interpretations. For traditional Judaism, the disobedience of the first couple neither alienates humanity from God nor creates the sinful urge. Rather, Judaism views humanity as having both a good inclination (*yetzer ha-tob*) and an evil inclination (*yetzer ha-ra´*) and thus with moral choice. Following Torah stems the evil inclination (*Babylonian Talmud Kiddushin* 30b).

Attention to Adam and Eve developed in early Hellenistic Judaism (see Sir 25:24), a development found also in Rom 5:12–20 (cf. 5:19, "just as through the disobedience of one person the many were made sinners, so through the obedience of the one the many will be made righteous"), and 1 Tm 2:12–15 appeals to Eve's sin to restrict women's roles. Augustine claimed that "the deliberate sin of the first man is the cause of original sin" (*Marriage and Concupiscence*, 2.26.43), an idea alien to Jewish thought.

A third major place where Jewish and Christian understandings part concerns the identification of Isaiah's Suffering Servant. For the church, the servant is Jesus, "pierced for our sins. . . . by his wounds we were healed. . . . Like a lamb led to slaughter" (Is 53:5, 7; cf. Acts 8:30–36; also Jn 19:34, 37; Rev 1:7). Jewish tradition principally understands the Servant as the people Israel, wounded in exile, whose return to Zion demonstrates divine power and providence. The debate over the Servant's identification appears as early as Origen's *Against Celsus* 1.55 (248 CE): "In a discussion with some whom the Jews regard as learned I used these prophecies. At this the Jew said that these prophecies referred to the whole people as though of a single individual, since they were scattered in the dispersion and smitten, that as a result of the scattering of the Jews among the other nations many might become proselytes."

However, given Judaism's affirmation of multiple readings, individual interpretations of the Servant appear. *Babylonian Talmud Sotah* 14a connects Is 53:12 to Moses, and *Jerusalem Talmud Sheqalim* connects Is 53:4 to Rabbi Akiba. *Babylonian Talmud Sanhedrin* 98b queries: "The Messiah—what is his name? . . . The Rabbis say, The Leper Scholar, as it is said, *'surely he has borne our griefs and carried our sorrows:* yet we did esteem him a man with leprosy, *smitten of God and afflicted'*" (see also *Targum Jonathan* on Is 42:1; 52:13, which says something similar).

## *Halakah:* "Oral Law" or "Oral Torah"

The Torah does not come with an instruction manual for following each commandment (traditionally numbered at 613), and therefore Jewish communities always have had to determine the correct path. Such interpretation is called *halakah*, from the Hebrew "to walk." For example, Ex 31:14 forbids "work" on the sabbath (also 31:15; Dt 5:15; Neh 13:22; Is 56:6; Jer 17:22–27), but what constitutes work? *Mishnah Shabbat* 7.2 delineates thirty-nine labors forbidden on the sabbath. There are also codicils, e.g., cutting is forbidden but circumcision is not; laws can be overridden to save a life.

Such interpretation, initially transmitted orally, becomes known as the "oral Torah"; Gospel references to the "tradition of the elders" (Mt 15:2; Mk 7:3–4) are likely connected to this practice. Around 200 CE these interpretations were codified in the *Mishnah* (Hebrew, "instruction, repetition"), a compendium of Jewish law and lore. Interpretation continued in the *Tosefta* (Aramaic, "additional [material]" or "supplement"; completed ca. 250). Then commentaries on the Mishnah developed: the *Yerushalmi* (*Jerusalem Talmud*, completed ca. 400) and the *Bavli* (*Babylonian Talmud*, completed ca. 600). The *Bavli* is the principal authoritative text for contemporary Judaism. Printings of the Talmud display the text of the *Mishnah* surrounded by Talmudic commentary (known as *gemara*, Aramaic for "study"), surrounded by other commentaries; the text visually suggests that if the pages could be larger, ever-new readings would appear. Halakhic discussion continues to this day.

Rabbinic thought ascribes equal value and antiquity to both Written and Oral Torahs. *Mishnah Avot* 1.1 records, "Moses received the Torah from Sinai and transmitted it to Joshua. Joshua transmitted it to the Elders, the Elders to the Prophets, and the Prophets to the Men of the Great Assembly." Subsequent verses bring the tradition to the date of the Mishnah.

Knowledge of the Oral Torah provides important correctives to the view that Jewish teaching is restricted to the Tanak. For example, Mt 5:38–39 references "An eye for an eye and a tooth for a tooth" (Ex 21:23–24; Lv 24:19–20; Dt 19:21). Like Jesus, Jewish interpretation resists a retributive approach. The rabbis (*Mishnah Bava Qamma* 8.1; *Babylonian Talmud Bava Qamma* 84a) observe that the commandment cannot literally be fulfilled for no two eyes or limbs are equal. Therefore, they conclude, in the case of injury, the responsible party pays for damages, pain, medical expenses, loss of work due to injury, and anguish or embarrassment.

## Aggadah: Jewish Storytelling or Midrash

Complementing *halakhah* is *aggadah* (Aramaic, "tales" or "narratives"; compare the Hebrew *haggadah* ["narrative, tale"], the book read in Jewish homes at the Passover meal). Aggadic materials convey moral lessons and practical advice, but they are not legally binding. The principal form of *aggadah* is *midrash* (Hebrew, "to seek" or "to ask").

Some midrashic materials provide additional information about biblical figures such as Abraham and Moses (*Genesis Rabbah; Exodus Rabbah*), just as Christian writings recounted stories about Jesus and Mary's childhood (*Infancy Gospel of Thomas; Protevangelium of James*). Such accounts are more common in Jewish, Catholic, and Orthodox settings than in Protestant thought, given Protestant emphasis on *sola scriptura* (Latin, "Scripture alone").

Early Jewish interpreters believed that every word of the text had purpose—there were no superfluous terms, or even letters. For example, Gn 22:2 reads in the NABRE, "Then God said: Take your son Isaac, your only one, whom you love, and go to the land of Moriah. There offer him up as a burnt offering on one of the heights that I will point out to you." The Hebrew, literally, states, "Take your son, your only [son], [the son] whom you love, Isaac." Jewish commentators queried the descriptions and order—son, only son, loved son, Isaac—and found a dialogue. "Take your son," says God; "I have two sons," replies Abraham, "Ishmael and Isaac." God replies, "Your only son." Abraham parries, "I have only one son with Sarah, and only one son with Hagar." God replies, "The one whom you love." Given that Abraham had just banished Ishmael and his mother, his response is poignant: "I love them both." Only then does God specify, "Isaac" (from Rashi, following *Babylonian Talmud Sanhedrin* 89b, commenting on Gn 22:2).

*Midrash* can also convey profound moral views. Commenting on Israel's Exodus from Egyptian slavery, the Talmud (*Babylonian Talmud Megillah* 10b) states that the angels wanted to sing songs of joy, but God responded, "The creations of My hands are drowning in the sea, and you are singing songs?!" God was referring to the Egyptians.

The rabbis use the metaphor of a hammer

on a rock to describe this phenomenon of stories generating new stories. Commenting on Jer 23:29, "Is not my word like fire . . . like a hammer shattering rock?" *Babylonian Talmud Shabbat* 88b interprets, "Just as a hammer is divided into many sparks, so every word that went forth from the Holy One, blessed be He, split up into seventy languages." Scripture thus generates different sparks, different interpretations.

## Reading Strategies

Rabbinic readers resisted idiosyncratic interpretations that dismiss plain meanings, rely on special knowledge gained through revelation, or rest on the exclusive authority of an individual. This emphasis on the communal and logical versus the individual and inspired is epitomized by the famous account of the "oven of Akhni" (*Babylonian Talmud Bava Metzi'a* 59b). Although one rabbi makes his case that the oven is kosher on the basis of miracles, ranging from a river flowing backwards to a voice from heaven (a "*bat qol*," cf. the divine voice in Gospel accounts of Jesus' baptism and transfiguration), his case is defeated by the argument that the sages' opinions override mystical and individual reading, citing Dt 30:12 ("It [i.e., the Torah] is not in the heavens"). The responsibility for interpreting Scripture rests with the community.

The various strategies for interpretation include:

A. *Middot* (Hebrew for "measurements, norms") comprise sets of hermeneutical rules, from the seven ascribed to Rabbi Hillel, an older contemporary of Jesus, to the thirteen associated with the early-second-century CE Rabbi Ishmael, to the thirty-two ascribed to the late-second-century Rabbi Eliezer ben Jose the Galilean. Of the various techniques, the following two are the most well known.

   *Qal vahomer,* or "from the lesser to the greater" (an *a fortiori* or *a minori ad maius* argument), known also in classical and Christian contexts, argues that if a minor premise is accepted, then "how much more so" (the standard formulation) is something major acceptable (see, e.g., Mt 12:11–12).

   *Gematria,* a Hebrew term likely derived from the Greek *geometria* (i.e., "geometry"), assigns numerical values to Hebrew letters (Alef=1, Bet=2, and so on), and then compares the value of the word or phrase to another word or phrase with the same value. Gematria explains Rev 13:18: the Hebrew letters spelling "Nero Caesar" add to 666.

B. *Pardes* (Hebrew for "orchard"; "paradise" is a cognate term) is an acronym for four reading strategies presented in the *Zohar*, the thirteenth-century Spanish text (ascribed to the second-century CE Rabbi Simeon Bar-Yohai) that provides instruction in *Kabbalah* (Hebrew, "tradition, that which is received"; simplistically described as "Jewish mysticism"). P stands for *peshat*, the plain or "literal" meaning. R is for *remez* ("hint"); this approach seeks allegorical or symbolic interpretations. D is for *darash*, "inquire" or "seek"; it looks for the metaphorical meaning. S is for *sod*, "mystery" or "secret"; here interpretation derives from inspiration. These readings possibly both informed and were informed by Christian hermeneutics. From the patristic era, the church recognized multiple approaches: literal/historical, allegorical, moral (tropological), and anagogical (metaphysical/eschatological/symbolic/mystical/inspired).

C. *Allegory,* in which a textual reference has a corollary in the external world, is in Jewish interpretation principally associated with Philo of Alexandria (ca. 20 BCE–50 CE), whose works were preserved by the church (see Eusebius, *Ecclesiastical History* 2.17; Jerome, *On Illustrious Men* 11). For example, Philo describes circumcision as symbolizing "the excision of the pleasures which delude the mind" (*On the Special Laws* 1.9). Allegories appear in the New Testament (for example, Paul's allegory of

Sarah and Hagar in Gal 4) and remained popular in Christian exegesis. Generally, Jewish thought, maintaining that the plain meaning (*peshat*) should also be valued, resisted complete allegory.

D. **Pesher** (Hebrew, "interpretation") is associated primarily with the Dead Sea Scrolls. *Pesher* finds in biblical texts meanings accessible only to select readers. For example, 1QpHab (*Pesher Habakkuk* from Qumran Cave 1) 7.1–5 comments on Hb 2:1ff., "God commanded Habakkuk to write the things that were coming on the last generation, but the fulfillment of the epoch He did not make known to him. And as for the words, that a person may read it swiftly; their interpretation (*pesher*) concerns the Teacher of Righteousness, to whom God made known all the mysteries of the words of His servant the prophets."

This approach, which lifts the texts from their historical and narrative context and finds contemporary applications, resembles the Gospels' fulfillment citations (e.g., Matthew's reading [1:23] of Is 7:14). Although *pesher*-type readings appear in later books of the Tanak—Dn 9:2, 24 interprets Jeremiah's prophecy (Jer 25:11–12; 29:10) of a seventy-year exile as referring to the author's own circumstances—*pesher* interpretation, associated with revelatory rather than logical or intertextual argument, substantially drops out of Jewish exegetical practice.

E. **Typology** suggests that anterior texts present a type or a first draft of something found in the present or that something on earth has its real existence in heavenly spheres. In the New Testament, the approach is notable in the Epistle to the Hebrews. This type of interpretation also lacks much purchase in Jewish sources, in part because it limits textual meaning (once the prophecy is "fulfilled" or "completed," it has done its job and thus is no longer relevant) and in part because it requires specialized or inspired interpretation.

# Modern and Post-Modern Approaches

Jewish biblical interpreters, like Christian ones, come from and speak to various communities, from the ultra-Orthodox to the secular. Feminist, Queer, Liberationist, Ecological, Diasporic, and other readings that emphasize the author's subject position appear in Jewish interpretation, as they do in Christian and secular contexts. Jewish and non-Jewish interpreters familiar with earlier Jewish commentary draw on rabbinic/midrashic interpretation, with its attention to multiple meanings, plays on words, and intertextual conversations, to enhance literary-critical approaches. Today, increasing numbers of Jews are studying the New Testament and early Christian literature: this focus both recovers parts of Judaism not preserved by the rabbinic tradition and corrects interpretations that use Judaism as the negative foil for Jesus and the early church. ■

# The Distinctiveness of Jesus

## Séan Charles Martin

The periodic intervention of God into human history is a foundational conviction of the Judeo-Christian tradition. The call of Abraham (Gn 12:1–3), the commissioning of Moses (Ex 3:1–10), the raising up of prophets like Isaiah (Is 6), Jeremiah (Jer 1:4–10), Ezekiel (Ez 2:1–3:15), or Amos (Am 7:14–15) represent privileged instances in which the divine plan comes to light in the words and deeds of particular people living in specific times, places, and cultures. But Christians claim that the birth, ministry, suffering, death, and Resurrection of Jesus signify a new moment in the relationship between God and humanity, since, in Jesus, God has entered into human history (Jn 1:14; Phil 2:6–11; Heb 1:1–2). Human history, in this view, becomes the arena in which the power and presence of God can be discerned.

## The Gospels and Jesus

One can better understand Jesus by analyzing his deeds and sayings that are preserved in the Gospels according to Matthew, Mark, Luke, and John. The four Gospels do not purport to be biographies of Jesus in the contemporary sense of the term—that is, comprehensive accounts, chronologically arranged, of an individual's life and influences. The author of John's Gospel, for example, admits that "Jesus did many other signs in the presence of [his] disciples that are not written in this book" (Jn 20:30). The Gospels, instead, should be understood as narrative Christologies—reflections on the significance of Jesus' life and ministry, arranged in story form, so that those who hear or read the narrative might come to believe in Jesus as messiah and son of God "and that through this belief [they] might have life in his name" (Jn 20:31).

Even though the Gospels are not chronicles of the life of Jesus, they are nevertheless grounded in the specific history of first-century Galilee and Judea. They depict a figure who was born in Bethlehem in Judea (Mt 2:1; Lk 2:4–7); who grew up in Nazareth in Galilee (Mt 2:23; Mk 1:9; Lk 2:39); who embarked upon a public ministry when he was around thirty (Lk 3:23); who initially ministered in the towns and villages bordering the Sea of Galilee (Mt 4:13; Mk 1:14; Lk 4:31; Jn 1:43); who traveled to Jerusalem (perhaps frequently; see Jn 2:13; 5:1; 7:10; 12:12); who, while in Jerusalem, was betrayed by Judas Iscariot, one of his followers (Mt 26:47–50; Mk 14:43–45; Lk 22:47–48; Jn 13:21–30; 18:1–3); who was then abandoned by the rest of the Twelve; and who was arrested, tried, tortured, and executed by crucifixion (Mt 26:47–27:66; Mk 14:43–16:8; Lk 22:47–23:56; Jn 18:1–19:42). Furthermore, the Gospels include the discovery of his empty tomb by Mary Magdalene and, at least in the Synoptics, other women as well (Mt 28:1–10; Mk 16:1–8; Lk 24:1–11; Jn 20:1–2, 11–18).

But this skeletal description of signal events in the life of Jesus hardly does justice to his person and mission, any more than a *curriculum vitae* describes what might inspire someone to take up a lifelong vocation of service. To find out what moves someone to undertake his or her life's work, one has to listen to stories, to celebrate accomplishments, to ponder tragedies. In a similar way, to discover the distinctiveness of Jesus, one has to listen to what he has to say, to analyze his aphorisms, and to meditate upon the meaning of his life and works.

## Jesus, the Wonder-Worker

In his own day, Jesus was regarded as a wonder-worker. The Gospels report that he cast out demons (Mt 15:21–28; Mk 1:21–28; Lk 8:26–39), healed the sick, especially lepers (Mt 8:1–4; Mk 1:40–45; Lk 17:11–19), and raised the dead (Lk 7:11–17; Jn 11:1–44). His earliest followers specifically cited his capacity to work wonders in their preaching about his Resurrection (Acts 2:22).

In the Hebrew Scriptures, the capacity to

work miracles is imputed to the prophets, especially Elijah (1 Kgs 17:7–24) and Elisha (2 Kgs 4:1–37). Likewise, in the Acts of the Apostles, Peter and John are portrayed as wonder-workers (Acts 3:1–10), as is Paul of Tarsus (Acts 20:7–12; 28:7–9). The capacity to work wonders is not, then, an unambiguous sign of the divine status of the wonder-worker, but rather serves as an indicator of sanctity. That Jesus was holy is, of course, acknowledged throughout the New Testament (Mk 1:24; Jn 6:69; Acts 3:14; 4:27, 30; Heb 7:26).

What distinguishes Jesus' wonder-working from both that of his predecessors and that of his followers is its connection to the kingdom of God, the central theme of his preaching. In the Gospels of Matthew and Mark, Jesus' first public speech calls people to repentance (or "conversion," *metanoia* in Greek) because the kingdom of God is at hand (Mt 4:17; Mk 1:15). And while nowhere in the four Gospels is the kingdom defined, Jesus' wonder-working gives a glimpse into what the kingdom is like, especially since his miracles constitute a response to human suffering.

Whether he is depicted as expelling an unclean spirit (Mk 1:21–28) or curing a leper (Mt 8:1–4), restoring life to the only son of the widow of Nain (Lk 7:11–17) or feeding the hungry multitude in the desert (Mt 14:13–21; 15:32–39; Mk 6:34–44; 8:1–9; Lk 9:11–17; Jn 6:1–15), Jesus confronts the reality of human suffering at its most concrete: hunger, disease, and death. In feeding the hungry, healing the afflicted, and restoring life to the dead, Jesus manifests the power and the presence of God to the very people who would have had the greatest reason to wonder whether God had abandoned them. Jesus' miracles indicate, then, that efforts to relieve human suffering are signs of the in-breaking of the kingdom. The typically joyful reaction to these wonders—"God has visited his people," exclaim those who witness the raising of the son of the widow of Nain (Lk 7:16)—suggests that the bystanders see the connection between wonder-working and the kingdom.

But according to the Gospels not everyone who witnesses Jesus' miracles reacts so positively. Some people accuse him of being in league with the demonic (Mt 9:34; 12:24// Lk 11:15), to which Jesus logically replies that, in such a scenario, evil defeats itself (Mt 12:25b–26//Lk 11:17b–18). And then he presses the point home: "But if it is by the finger of God (or "Spirit of God," in the Matthean version of the saying) that [I] drive out demons, then the kingdom of God has come upon you" (Mt 12:28//Lk 11:20). Jesus' miracles thus herald the advent of the kingdom of God, and give people a foretaste of what they might hope for—a world in which God "will wipe every tear from their eyes, and there shall be no more death or mourning, wailing or pain, [for] the old order has passed away" (Rev 21:4).

## The Aphorisms of Jesus

An aphorism is a brief and memorable saying. In the Gospel accounts, the aphorisms of Jesus provide some striking and original insight into their author. In analyzing these aphorisms, one can see what Jesus thinks about morality ("Do to others whatever you would have them do to you," Mt 7:12//Lk 6:31), or the paradox of self-sacrifice ("Whoever finds his life will lose it, and whoever loses his life for my sake will find it," Mt 10:39; 16:25//Mk 8:35//Lk 9:24; 17:33// Jn 12:25); one can even discover what Jesus thinks about himself ("The Son of Man did not come to be served but to serve and to give his life as a ransom for many," Mt 20:28//Mk 10:45). The aphorisms of Jesus, as conveyed in the Gospels, thus give privileged access to his thinking, and more specifically, how he thinks about himself.

Although Jesus was at least bilingual, since he spoke Aramaic, the language of ordinary interchange in first-century Galilee and Judea, as well as Hebrew, the language of liturgical worship, his sayings have survived only in Koine Greek, the language in which the Gospels of Matthew, Mark, Luke, and John were written. Consequently, readers of the Gospels need to remember that they are working from at least one linguistic remove, if they are reading the Greek of the New Testament, and at least two removes, if they are reading the New Testament in translation.

# Aphorisms and Authority

Nevertheless, there are a number of features of the speech of Jesus that survive the trauma of (multiple) translation. One of the most striking aspects of the aphorisms of Jesus is the tone of authority in which they are delivered. For example, in the Gospels, Jesus expects his followers to withhold judgment: "Stop judging and you will not be judged. Stop condemning and you will not be condemned. Forgive and you will be forgiven" (Lk 6:37//Mt 7:1). The use of the so-called "divine passive" in these sayings ("you will be forgiven") indicates that the unnamed agent who refrains from condemnation, and who thus forgives, is God. The fact that Jesus speaks on behalf of God here gives an important indication of the way he thinks about himself. Israelite prophets had also spoken on behalf of God, but their speeches were typically prefaced by the formula, "Thus says the Lord" (Hebrew, *ki 'amar YHWH*; see, e.g., Am 1:3, 6, 9, 11). No such formula introduces the aphorisms of Jesus. It is as though he expects his hearers to recognize in his own voice the voice of God.

This assumption of the voice of God is particularly apparent in the Antitheses (Mt 5:21–48), found in the Sermon on the Mount in Matthew's Gospel (Mt 5:3–7:29). There Jesus recalls some important stipulation in the Torah ("You have heard that it was said to your ancestors . . . "), and then counterpoises it to some new teaching ("But I say to you . . . "). Some of the time, the new teaching of Jesus internalizes the values that are protected by the prohibition in the Torah. So, for instance, the law forbidding adultery (Ex 20:14//Dt 5:18) is internalized when Jesus prohibits looking at someone with lust (Mt 5:28). But, more frequently, the new teaching of Jesus rejects the Torah in favor of a new moral standard, as when he prohibits divorce (Mt 5:31–32), the taking of oaths (Mt 5:33–37), violent retaliation (Mt 5:38–42), and hatred for one's enemies (Mt 5:43–48). Here, too, the tone of authority bespeaks an awareness of his own capacity to revise the provisions of Torah.

# Jesus, the Son of Man

One should note that all four Gospels present Jesus as using the phrase "the Son of Man" to refer to himself (see, e.g., Mt 8:20; Mk 10:45; Lk 7:34; Jn 5:27). In the Hebrew Scriptures, the term "son of man" (Hebrew, *ben 'adam*) occurs 107 times, 94 of which appear in Ezekiel alone. Originally the term seems to have designated any human being (see Nm 23:19; Pss 8:5; 144:3), much as the expression "every mother's child" in English can refer to any human being. In this earliest Hebrew usage, however, "son of man" also connotes the frailty of the human condition, especially the brevity of human life in view of the inevitability of death (see, e.g., Ps 144:4, where men and women are said to be "but a breath, / [their] days are like a passing shadow").

In Ezekiel (ca. 623–571 BCE), however, the term takes on the added connotation of a human being who has been called to be a prophet, and to act as an intermediary between human beings and God. God addresses Ezekiel as "son of man" (Ez 2:1–8) at the time of his calling, and throughout the book, "son of man" becomes the ordinary way by which Ezekiel is summoned to deliver a prophetic oracle (see Ez 6:1; 37:1).

This prophetic usage is taken up in the book of Daniel, a work composed around 165 BCE, in which "one like a son of man" is presented before the Ancient of Days and rewarded with "dominion, splendor, and kingship" (Dn 7:13–14). The book of Daniel was written during the Maccabean revolt to encourage Jews to remain faithful despite persecution under the administration of Antiochus IV Epiphanes (ca. 215–164 BCE), the Seleucid king who ruled over Judea, and who had outlawed traditional Jewish practices like circumcision and worship on the sabbath (2 Mc 6:1–11). In Daniel, then, "one like a son of man" connotes fidelity to God in spite of persecution by outsiders, a faithfulness that is recognized and rewarded by God.

Jesus' use of the term "the Son of Man" as a term of self-designation, especially in Mark's Gospel, the earliest of the Synoptics, builds upon all of these previous usages and extends them. So, like the composer of Ps 144, he is conscious of the brevity of human life. And, like Ezekiel, he stands as an intermediary between God and human beings. Like the "one like a son of man" in Daniel, he has remained faithful despite the very real prospect of persecution. Nine of the fourteen times in which the expression is found in Mark indicate the inevitability of Jesus' suffering and death (Mk 8:31; 9:9, 12, 31; 10:33, 45; 14:21a, 21b, 41). In Mark's Gospel, it seems clear that Jesus knows that he will suffer for what he has been saying and doing; though for Jesus, in contrast to the "one like a son of man" in Daniel, the persecution comes from insiders: "A prophet is not without honor except in his native place and among his own kin and in his own house" (Mk 6:4//Mt 13:57//Lk 4:24//Jn 4:44).

The remaining five Son of Man sayings in Mark's Gospel (Mk 2:10, 28; 8:38; 13:26; 14:62) reflect Jesus' sense of his authority, both present and future. In the first two, the Son of Man exercises powers in the here-and-now ordinarily thought to belong to God: the forgiveness of sins (Mk 2:10) and regulation of sabbath practices (Mk 2:28). The remaining three speak of the Son of Man who "comes in his Father's glory with the holy angels" (Mk 8:38), or who comes "in the clouds with great power and glory" (Mk 13:26), or who will be "seated at the right hand of the Power / and coming with the clouds of heaven" (Mk 14:62). In these five Son of Man sayings, as in the Antitheses of the Sermon on the Mount (Mt 5:21–48), Jesus' language displays a consciousness of divine status.

## Jesus, the Son of God

In the Synoptic Gospels, Jesus is identified as the Son of God by other figures: by the angel Gabriel at the annunciation of his birth (Lk 1:35), by the disciples on the boat after they witness Jesus walking on the water (Mt 14:33), by Simon Peter at Caesarea Philippi (Mt 16:16), and by a Roman centurion immediately after Jesus dies (Mt 27:54//Mk 15:39). Even the devil (Mt 4:3, 6//Lk 4:3, 9) and various unclean spirits (Mt 8:29; Mk 3:11//Lk 4:41) call him the Son of God.

In John's Gospel, as in the Synoptics, the title "Son of God" is used by other people to refer to Jesus: John the Baptist (Jn 1:34), Nathaniel (Jn 1:49), and Martha (Jn 11:27). But John's Gospel also includes the title as a term of self-designation by Jesus himself (Jn 5:25; 10:36; 11:4).

The term as Jesus uses it with respect to himself clearly signifies a privileged relationship with God and, like the expression "Son of Man," has deep roots in the Hebrew Scriptures. Israel is called God's son in Exodus: "Israel is my son, my firstborn. . . . Let my son go, that he may serve me" (Ex 4:22–23). In a similar way, Hosea (ca. 780–725 BCE) uses the language of sonship in reference to God's choice of Israel: "When Israel was a child I loved him, / out of Egypt I called my son" (Hos 11:1). Jeremiah (ca. 655–586 BCE) likewise refers to the nation as the son of God: "For I am a father to Israel, / Ephraim is my firstborn" (Jer 31:9). This understanding of divine sonship is closely linked to that of divine election, so that in calling Israel God's son, the authors of Exodus, Hosea, and Jeremiah point to the uniquely privileged status the nation enjoys with God.

Divine sonship also appears in the Hebrew Scriptures to signify the special relationship between God and the house of David. Nathan's oracle to David (2 Sm 7:4–16) describes the king who will succeed David as God's son: "I will be a father to him, and he shall be a son to me" (2 Sm 7:14//1 Chr 17:13). Here, as in Exodus and Hosea, the image of divine sonship indicates divine election, though the one identified here as the son of God is an individual—indeed, a royal figure—and not the nation as a whole. This royal usage of the term is also reflected in Ps 2:7, probably originally intended for use at an enthronement ceremony when the Davidic king succeeded his predecessor, and Ps 89:27–38, another psalm celebrating the status of the house of David.

In John's Gospel, Jesus' own use of the term "Son of God" always has a singular reference, like Nathan's oracle and Pss 2 and 89. But the title denotes, in addition to the notions of election and privileged relationship found in the Hebrew Scriptures, a complete identification of Jesus' own mission with that of God: "Can you say that the one whom the Father has consecrated and sent into the world blasphemes because I said, 'I am the Son of God'? . . . The Father is in me and I am in the Father" (Jn 10:36–38). Similarly, in describing the outcome of Lazarus's illness, Jesus says, "This illness is not to end in death, but is for the glory of God, that the Son of God may be glorified through it" (Jn 11:4). This complete identification with God thus allows Jesus to exercise divine powers and prerogatives: "The hour is coming and is now here when the dead will hear the voice of the Son of God, and those who hear will live. For just as the Father has life in himself, so also he gave to his Son the possession of life in himself. And he gave him the power to exercise judgment, because he is the Son of Man" (Jn 5:25–27). Both of the two major titles by which Jesus refers to himself—Son of God and Son of Man—are united in this saying, identifying Jesus as the one who gives life to the dead (see Is 26:19; Ez 37:12) and exercises divine judgment (see Ps 7:12; Is 2:4).

## Jesus, Son of God in the Pauline Literature

The use of the title "Son of God" in the letters of Paul constitutes a unique witness to the person and mission of Jesus in the first several decades after his death and Resurrection. In the letter to the Romans, Paul makes use of an early creedal statement, probably originating among Torah-observant Christians, when he describes Jesus as "descended from David according to the flesh, but established as Son of God in power according to the spirit of holiness through resurrection from the dead" (Rom 1:3–4). The contrast between David and God, as well as that between flesh and "spirit of holiness," signifies the contrast between the human and the divine, and stresses the dual role of Jesus, who simultaneously represents the human race to God, and God to the human race. "Son of God" in the letter to the Romans expresses faith in the transformation wrought by the Resurrection, in which the human ancestry of Jesus, however distinguished it might have been thanks to his family connection to the house of David, is nevertheless eclipsed when God raises him from the dead.

The point cannot have been lost on the Torah-observant Christians who constituted, at least in part, the original audience to whom Paul addressed the letter to the Romans. These believers would have claimed that their own family connections to Abraham, ancestor of the chosen people, gave them privileged access to God, since God had made a covenant with Abraham and his descendants (Gn 17). But for Paul, no one's ancestry, no matter how distinguished or how faithful, counts for anything in the aftermath of the Jesus-event: "What occasion is there then for boasting? It is ruled out" (Rom 3:27). Depicting Jesus as Son of God thus diminishes anyone's claim on God apart from that afforded the believer by Jesus himself. To call Jesus Son of God, as Paul does here, is to make a claim that Jesus alone opens the way to God.

If Paul addresses Torah-observant Christians in the letter to the Romans, his second letter to the Corinthians addresses Christian converts from Greco-Roman polytheism. In this letter, probably an anthology of letter-fragments preserved by the Christians of Corinth after Paul's death, Paul describes Jesus as the Son of God specifically in connection with preaching in the Pauline mission: "For the Son of God, Jesus Christ, who was proclaimed to you by us, Silvanus and Timothy and me, was not 'yes' and 'no', but 'yes' has been in him" (2 Cor 1:19). The subject of preaching in the Pauline mission, whether by Paul himself or by assistants like Silvanus or Timothy, was always Jesus. The task was admittedly difficult: (1) Paul and his assistants had to persuade their Gentile audiences to abandon their polytheistic intuitions and to commit themselves to the one God, the Father of Jesus Christ; and (2) the Pauline preachers had to demonstrate that Jesus of Nazareth, crucified and raised from the dead, offered these Gentiles exclusive access to God. "Son of God," in this context, indicates Jesus' own fidelity to his mission, a faithfulness that took him through the cross to the Resurrection. Such fidelity becomes in Paul's view a model that can inspire these Corinthian Christians to become ever more faithful to their newly-adopted religious commitments.

In the letter to the Galatians, Paul describes Jesus as the Son of God in extraordinarily personal terms: "I have been crucified with Christ; yet I live, no longer I, but Christ lives in me; insofar as I now live in the flesh, I live by faith in the Son of God who has loved me and given himself up for me" (Gal 2:19–20). For Paul, the death of Jesus is not merely a historical event, the way one today might view any tragic death—an event to be mourned and chronicled for the sake of posterity. In his own radical identification with the crucified and risen Jesus ("Christ lives in me"), Paul sees the hope of his own transformation, and, by extension, the transformation of any believer who likewise identifies with the crucified and risen Jesus. Paul's characterization of Jesus as "Son of God" thus denotes a self-sacrificing love which transforms even the most unlikely person—like Paul himself.

In Paul's thought, to call Jesus the Son of God is to present him as the one who alone gives people access to God; the one who alone gives a witness of faithfulness unto death; the one who alone transforms humanity through self-sacrifice. So persuasive was Paul's presentation of the person and mission of Jesus that the title "Son of God" has become the church's norm against which every other understanding of Jesus is measured.

# Jesus, the Pre-Existent One

Two important early Christian hymns depict Jesus in terms that move beyond a narrative description of his teaching, preaching, and wonder-working in Galilee and Judea. Instead, they show that the early Christians who sang these hymns believed in the divine origin of Jesus and accounted for his activities in this way. These two hymns were probably originally composed for use in the liturgies of early Christianity, and were subsequently incorporated into Paul's letter to the Philippians and the Gospel of John.

The hymn in Paul's letter to the Philippians (Phil 2:6-11) comprises two stanzas. In the first stanza (vv. 6–8) Jesus is said to empty himself and to enter into the human condition, accepting the inevitability of death, even the

most painful, shameful death imaginable in the first century, death on a cross (v. 8b). And yet, according to the second stanza (vv. 9–11), that willing acceptance of suffering and death is precisely the reason God raised Jesus from the dead: "Because of this, God greatly exalted him / and bestowed on him the name / that is above every name" (v. 9), an exaltation that is hailed by the entirety of creation ("those in heaven and on earth and under the earth," v. 10), in both gesture ("every knee should bend," v. 10b) and acclamation ("and every tongue confess that / Jesus Christ is Lord, / to the glory of God the Father," v. 11).

The primary contrast in the Philippians hymn is between the self-emptying of Jesus described in the first stanza, and his exaltation described in the second. But even within the first stanza, the hymn depicts a contrast between the "form of God" (Phil 2:6a) and the "form of a slave" (v. 7b). The hymn's depiction of Jesus as one who is initially "in the form of God," with all the attributes associated with divinity—immortality, immutability and omniscience, to name but three—makes his willing embrace of humanity and its limitations all the more striking. The language of slavery in v. 7 probably alludes to the Septuagint translation of the Suffering Servant songs (Is 42:1–4; 49:1–7; 50:4–11; and 52:13–53:12), especially Is 49:3, 5 and 53:11 where the Servant is specifically said to be God's slave (*doulos* in Greek; the same term found in Phil 2:7b). By characterizing Jesus as a slave like the Suffering Servant, the hymn introduces the theme of divine vindication for the one who shoulders such suffering (see Is 49:6–7; 52:13; 53:12).

The Philippians hymn thus ascribes a descending and ascending pattern to the person and mission of Jesus. Originating in God, he empties himself of any privilege to which he has claim, endures suffering and death, and returns to God with "the name / that is above every name" (Phil 2:9b).

A descending pattern can be detected in the Prologue to the Gospel of John (Jn 1:1–18). This Prologue, which incorporates an early Christian hymn, depicts Jesus as the Word made flesh (v. 14) who reveals God to the human race (v. 18). Like the Philippians hymn, the Johannine Prologue makes reference to the Hebrew Scriptures, especially Genesis, Exodus, the Psalms, and the book of Proverbs. The opening words of the hymn, "In the beginning," echo the opening words of Genesis, and describe Jesus as the Word through whom the universe was made: "All things came to be through him," (Jn 1:3). To speak of the Word as present at the moment of creation is to situate that Word outside of time, in eternity, the technical term for which is pre-existence. This understanding of the identity of Jesus as the pre-existent Word of God alludes to the description of Wisdom in the book of Proverbs: "When he established the heavens, there was I, / . . . When he fixed the foundations of earth, / then was I beside him as artisan" (Prv 8:27, 29b–30).

The Word is described in the Prologue initially as light (Jn 1:4, 9), a probable allusion to Ps 119:105, which celebrates the power of God to save those who are afflicted. The descending action of the hymn appears in Jn 1:9–11: "The true light, which enlightens everyone, was coming into the world," and speaks of the obstacles encountered by the Word: "The world did not know him / . . . his own people did not accept him"—a compact set of expressions summarizing Jesus' suffering and death.

Unlike the Philippians hymn, which posits an ascending action of exaltation to counterbalance the descending action of self-emptying, the Prologue to John's Gospel depicts a Word that became flesh "and made his dwelling among us" (literally, "pitched his tent among us," Jn 1:14, a probable allusion to Ex 25:8–9). Just as the tent of meeting in Exodus was the privileged place of encounter between God and Israel, so, according to the Prologue, the person of Jesus becomes the meeting place between God and humanity. It is precisely in becoming flesh that the Word reveals God: "We saw his glory, / the glory as of the Father's only Son, / full of grace and truth," (Jn 1:14b).

To speak of Jesus as the pre-existent Word made flesh, as the Prologue to John's Gospel does, is to situate the subsequent Johannine narrative of his life and ministry in Galilee and Judea within the framework of eternity. To ponder his words and to contemplate his deeds as presented in John's Gospel is to see the divine plan, in place for all eternity, come to fruition.

## Jesus, the Risen One

Paul of Tarsus provides the earliest written witness to the Resurrection of Jesus, a witness that involves two convictions: first, that Jesus had been raised from the dead by the power of God (1 Cor 15:3–28) and, second, that Paul had personally encountered the risen Christ and had received a mandate to preach about Jesus "to the Gentiles" (Gal 1:16). For Paul, Jesus' terrible death by crucifixion was only comprehensible in light of his ultimate triumph over death. Jesus' Resurrection becomes the basis for Paul's understanding of discipleship. He argues, for example, that if Christ is not raised, our faith is "empty" (1 Cor 15:14), and that the Christian life consists in conformity to Jesus' death, symbolized in baptism, so as to have conformity to his Resurrection (Rom 6:1–11).

The Gospel narratives of the empty tomb on Easter morning (Mk 16:1–8//Lk 24:1–11) and the appearances of the risen Jesus there to the women (Mt 28:9–10; Jn 20:11–18) and later elsewhere to the larger groups of disciples (Mt 28:16–20; Lk 24:13–53; Jn 20:19–21:25), augmented by the intriguing account of many appearances that Paul received and passed on (1 Cor 15:5–7), likewise testify to the widespread conviction that in the early church the Resurrection of Jesus was the basis upon which their faith rested.

Indeed, it can be argued that Jesus' earliest followers preserved his aphorisms, parables, and accounts of wonder-working, first in the oral tradition, and subsequently in the Gospels of Mark, Matthew, Luke, and John, precisely because they were convinced that God had raised him from the dead. His status as the risen Lord gave his sayings and stories an authority beyond the instruction of any other sage or teacher, and caused his followers to spread his teaching "to the ends of the earth" (Acts 1:8).

# Conclusion

By both deed and word, Christians believe, Jesus seeks to bring those who hear him to recognize the in-breaking of the kingdom of God. In so doing, he presents insights into what that kingdom is like, while at the same time, he presents himself as the one who alone has authority on earth to inaugurate that kingdom.

His followers believe that in Jesus the power of God is fully present in the world, and that his distinctive claims to authority are vindicated by God in his Resurrection from the dead. Pondering the words and deeds of Jesus thus permits contemporary readers of the Gospels to appropriate the hope of the kingdom and deepen their understanding of the one who proclaims it with such authority. ■

# The Many Faces of Jesus

## Séan Charles Martin

Jesus has many faces by which he is recognized. In the New Testament, he appears in the likeness of Moses in the Gospel of Matthew, or as a high priest in the Letter to the Hebrews, as a suffering servant in the First Letter of Peter, or even as a lamb with horns in the book of Revelation. This diversity of images doubtless reflects the diversity of the earliest Christian communities in which the stories about Jesus, the stories by Jesus, and the sayings attributed to Jesus were originally preserved. But as ethnically and geographically diverse as these earliest Christian communities were, their members were typically conversant with the Torah, the Prophets, and the Writings—what today are called the Hebrew Scriptures or the Old Testament. Members of these earliest Christian communities would have used the Hebrew Scriptures in their public worship, in their communal study, and in their private prayer. Thus these first Christians, reflecting upon the wealth of concepts and images found in that sacred literature, came to understand the person and mission of Jesus as the new Adam, the new Son of David, the new Passover, and the New Covenant that the Hebrew Scriptures foretold.

## Jesus and Judaism

There were good reasons for looking to the Hebrew Scriptures in order to understand the ministry of Jesus. Jesus was born a Jew and brought up in a Jewish household. His earliest followers were all Jews. With few exceptions (Mt 8:5–13; Mk 7:24–30), Jesus ministered exclusively among his own people. His name—*Yeshua'* in Aramaic, or *Yehoshua'* in Hebrew—is a traditional Jewish name (more conventionally transliterated into English as Joshua), indicating that he was named after the successor of Moses (Jos 1:1–9), just as his mother Mary was named after Miriam, the sister of Moses (Ex 15:20), and her husband Joseph was named after Joseph, the eleventh of

the patriarch Jacob's twelve sons (Gn 37–50). As a Jew living in first-century Galilee, Jesus would have been circumcised eight days after his birth as a sign of the covenant between God and the descendants of Abraham and Sarah (Lk 2:21); he would have studied the Hebrew Scriptures (Lk 2:41–52); he would have taught in the synagogue (Mt 4:23; Mk 1:21; Lk 4:15); he would have observed the rhythm of the Jewish liturgical seasons by participating in periodic pilgrimages to the Temple in Jerusalem (Mt 21:1; Mk 11:1; Lk 2:41–51; Jn 2:13, 23; 5:1; 7:10; 10:22; 12:12); and he would have abided by the dietary restrictions that were required of his people and prescribed in the Torah. Apart from the faith and traditions of his people, Jesus cannot be understood.

So it is no wonder that Jesus' earliest followers turned to their own Jewish religious traditions and sacred literature in the effort to make sense of his life and ministry. One way by which they sought to understand Jesus was through typology, or the interpretation of Jesus in the light of his resemblance to some other figure from the Hebrew Scriptures. In this interpretative approach, the figure from the Hebrew Scriptures is the "type" (Greek, *typos*, "dent," "mark," or "original form"). Thus Paul of Tarsus uses typology when he calls Adam a "type of the one who was to come," i.e., Jesus (Rom 5:14). The author of the Letter to the Hebrews makes use of typological comparisons in associating Jesus with the figure of Melchizedek, who appears in Gn 14 (Heb 7:1–10), just as the author of the Gospel according to Matthew uses typology in relating Jesus to the figure of Moses (Mt 2:16–18; 5:1–7:29).

Typological readings of the Torah, the Prophets, and the Writings were intended by their Christian practitioners to illustrate the unity of salvation history. The resemblance between Jesus and persons like Adam, Melchizedek, Isaac, or Moses was thought to indicate the consistent plan of God, according to this typological interpretation. Thus typology sought to offer a way of understanding Jesus based on the theological categories that are found in the Torah, the Prophets, and the Writings.

## Jesus and Greco-Roman Culture

But as Christianity began to expand beyond its geographic homeland of Galilee and Judea, and beyond the Jewish diaspora communities of Antioch (in present-day Syria), Ephesus (in present-day Turkey), or Alexandria (in present-day Egypt), it encountered peoples whose familiarity with the Hebrew Scriptures, even in translation, was limited. Furthermore, the world of the ancient Mediterranean basin into which Christianity first began to expand was rich with philosophical and theological concepts and images that could be deployed in the effort to understand Jesus. Consequently, one is able to trace new ways of understanding Jesus as a consequence of early Christianity's engagement with the wider culture of Mediterranean antiquity.

Chief among those non-Christian thinkers whose body of work influenced the way in which Christians began to think about Jesus was the Greek philosopher Plato (ca. 428–348/347 BCE). Thirty-six dialogues are attributed to Plato, in which one can find his foundational conviction that what is perceived by the senses—that is, what is visible, tactile, or audible—is a mere copy or shadow (Greek, skia) of the real, which, by definition, is beyond the reach of sense-experience. Plato uses the term "form" (Greek, eidos or "idea") to refer to the essence of a thing—what makes a thing what it is. As such, forms exist beyond space, beyond time, and beyond change (Timaeus 52a).

Plato's privileging of the eternal over the temporal, the one over the many, and the invisible over the visible helped some early Christians in their efforts to understand the relationship between Jesus and the religious practices and institutions of first-century Judaism. So, for instance, in the New Testament, the author of the Letter to the Hebrews uses Platonic language in contrasting the priesthood of Aaron to that of Jesus: "They (i.e.,

the priests of Aaron) worship in a copy and shadow (Greek, skia) of the heavenly sanctuary" (Heb 8:5). The use of Platonic language in the Letter to the Hebrews thus allows the author to contrast the temporary service of the priests of Aaron with the eternal priesthood of Jesus (see Heb 9:11–12), the many priests of Aaron with the one Jesus (Heb 7:23), and the earthly Temple with the heavenly sanctuary in which Christ appears (Heb 9:23–26). And while this Platonic language permits the author of the Letter to the Hebrews to highlight the distinctiveness of Jesus, it does so at the expense of the religious traditions that nurtured Jesus' own identity and mission. This way of thinking about Jesus effectively disconnects him from his own cultural, historical, and religious context, even as it renders a portrait of Jesus that is accessible to people who subscribe to the Platonic worldview.

## Jesus and the Gnostics

Many ancient philosophical speculations seem, at first glance, to have little bearing on the identity and mission of Jesus. However, they were adopted and adapted by the religious movement called Gnosticism (Greek, gnostikos, "learned" or "knowledgeable"). In gnostic understanding, material creation, including humanity, still bears within itself a spark of that divinity from which it originated. But humanity has forgotten its origin, and needs a teacher who will give human beings the knowledge (gnōsis) that will enable them to return to their origin in God. Gnostic Christianity saw Jesus as that teacher.

Prior to 1945, gnostic teachings were known primarily by quotation in polemical works like Adversus haereses (Against Heresies), a five-volume work written in 180 CE by Irenaeus, bishop of Lugdunum in Gaul (present-day Lyon, France) to oppose gnostic teachers. In 1945, however, twelve codices, dating to the third or fourth century of the Common Era, were discovered in the town of Nag Hammadi in Upper Egypt. These codices contained fifty-two treatises, most of which were gnostic, though one treatise was a partial translation of

Plato's *Republic* from Greek into the Coptic language.

One of the treatises recovered at Nag Hammadi was the *Gospel of Thomas*, a work that comprises 114 sayings attributed to Jesus. Approximately half of the sayings in the *Gospel of Thomas* resemble the aphorisms of Jesus found in the Gospels of Matthew, Mark, Luke, and John. The rest of the sayings in the *Gospel of Thomas* are otherwise unattested in the New Testament, and some are strikingly poetic:

> Jesus said, "I am the light that is over all things. I am all: From me all came forth, and to me all attained. Split a piece of wood; I am there. Lift up the stone, and you will find me there." (*Gospel of Thomas*, 77)

The first part of the saying probably echoes Jn 8:12, "I am the light of the world," while the second and third parts seem to reflect the gnostic understanding of Jesus' role as the one who leads an ignorant humanity back to its origin in God. Finding Jesus within the wood or underneath the rock utilizes the paradox of light within the most solid of objects, and thus functions as a message of hope to gnostic Christians, who considered their earthly existence as a kind of exile.

The gnostic emphasis on Jesus as a teacher who brings enlightenment to humanity is not without its foundation in the New Testament: Nicodemus calls Jesus a "teacher who has come from God" (Jn 3:2), and the crowds who come to hear Jesus hail him for teaching as "one having authority and not as the scribes" (Mk 1:22; cf. Mt 7:29). Yet the *Gospel of Thomas* presents a curiously abstract image of Jesus: absent is any presentation of Jesus who heals the sick, restores sight to the blind, and feeds the hungry (Mk 6:30–44). And, if the *Gospel of Thomas* were the sole source of information about Jesus' life and ministry, one would never know about his suffering and death—or the fact that those who followed him during his ministry soon began to preach that he had risen from the dead.

## Jesus and the Stoics

Another school of Greek philosophy also exercised an influence over the way in which Christians eventually began to think about Jesus. Stoicism, so called because the adherents of this particular school of philosophy initially met on the "Painted Porch" (Greek, *stoa poikilē*), was founded in Athens by Zeno of Citium (ca. 334–262 BCE). In the effort to account for the intelligibility of the world, Stoic philosophers postulated the existence of a universal *Logos*, or rational principle that pervades the universe. Human beings, according to Stoic thought, possess the "seed of reason" (Greek, *logos spermatikos*) that enables them to recognize and identify that rational principle in the world around them.

The second-century Christian philosopher and apologist Justin (ca. 103–165 CE) made use of the notion of the *logos spermatikos* in his attempt to show the compatibility of Christian thought with Greek philosophy. The Gospel of John had already identified Jesus as the incarnate Word (*Logos*) of God (Jn 1:1–18); Justin built upon that conviction with his assertion that those who live a life in accordance with reason (*logos*) are already Christians, even if they lived centuries before Jesus:

> We are taught that Christ is the First-born of God, and we have explained above that he is the Word (Greek, *Logos*) of whom all humankind have a share, and that those who lived according to reason (Greek, *meta logou*) are Christians, even though they were classified as atheists, as among the Greeks, Socrates and Heraclitus, and men like them. (*First Apology*, 46)

To declare that Heraclitus (ca. 535–475 BCE) and Socrates (ca. 469–399 BCE) were Christians, even though they lived more than 400 years before Jesus of Nazareth, was to make a claim that was breathtaking in its audacity. For Justin, though, the claim was made not simply for the sake of its shock value: Justin was convinced that the truth that the philosophers proclaimed—and in the case of Socrates, the truth for which he died—is a participation in the truth of the gospel.

Justin's assertion that those who live "according to reason" are Christian, whether they know it or not, has also enjoyed a long tenure. More than 1800 years after Justin, the Second Vatican Council (1962–1965) taught that those also can attain to salvation who through no fault of their own do not know the Gospel of Christ or His Church, yet sincerely seek God and moved by grace strive by their deeds to do His will as it is known to them through the dictates of conscience. Nor does Divine Providence deny the helps necessary for salvation to those who, without blame on their part, have not yet arrived at an explicit knowledge of God and with His grace strive to live a good life. Whatever good or truth is found amongst them is looked upon by the Church as a preparation for the Gospel. (*Lumen Gentium*, 16)

If Justin's insight came about as the result of his encounter with ancient Mediterranean culture and his attempt to appropriate the best of its achievements, the Second Vatican Council's teaching developed as a pastoral response to the world's religious and cultural diversity. The bishops at Vatican II wished to salute in the diverse religions and cultures of the world whatever is good or true, and to see in that goodness and truth a way by which people might eventually meet Jesus.

# Jesus and Church Teaching

Vatican II was not the first time bishops from across the world came together to consider the state of the church. Over the centuries, the bishops, as leaders of Christianity, have gathered periodically to address theological controversies and to develop dogmatic definitions, which were subsequently enshrined in creeds to be recited by believers. These periodic gatherings are called ecumenical councils, and the first of them, the Council of Nicaea (held in what is now Iznik, in present-day Turkey), convened in 325 CE to respond to the challenge posed by Arius and his followers, who had denied the divinity of Christ.

Arius, a presbyter of the church of Alexandria, Egypt, had claimed that Jesus could not be called God. In Arius's view, Jesus was begotten by God and, as God's Son, was the first and greatest of all creatures, and the one through whom everything else was made (Jn 1:3). Arius pointed to passages in the Bible that seemed to support his conviction that the Son could not be divine: "The LORD begot me, the beginning of his works, / the forerunner of his deeds of long ago" (Prv 8:22); "the Father is greater than I" (Jn 14:28); "He is . . . the firstborn of all creation" (Col 1:15). Arius also composed a poem, *Thalia*, to disseminate his views in memorable form; he may even have been the author of popular slogans—"There was [a time] when he was not!"—that were designed to rally his followers.

After long discussion, the approximately 300 bishops who attended the Council of Nicaea developed a summary of Christian belief—the first Christian creed—in which the Son's relationship to the Father is described as "light from light, true God from true God." In a phrase specifically designed to counter Arian claims that Jesus was the first and greatest of all creatures, the Nicene Creed describes the Son as "begotten, not made." The technical philosophical term "homoousios" ("one in being," or "consubstantial") appears in the creed to further specify the relationship between the Father and the Son, so that for Christians the Son is as fully divine as the Father. Church fathers such as Athanasius, patriarch of Alexandria, who drew on the teaching of Justin and Irenaeus, saw in the Scriptures the basis for this understanding of Christ as well as the Trinity. These church fathers found numerous parallels between the Hebrew Scriptures and the New Testament in the titles, attributes, and actions assigned to Yahweh and to Christ, further explaining and establishing Christian belief.

The Nicene Creed was revised at the Council of Constantinople in 381. Versions of the creed continue to be recited today at the liturgies of the Roman Catholic Church, the Orthodox Churches, the Anglican Communion, the Lutheran Church, and many of the Reformed Churches.

More Christological disputes followed in the next centuries. They can bewilder the twenty-first-century observer, but the theological stakes at issue for Christians were these: as the intercessor between God and humanity, Jesus must be wholly and completely divine in order to represent God to the human race; and he must be wholly and completely human in order to represent the human race to God. From a Christian perspective, then, any theological statement about Jesus must do equal justice to his divinity and his humanity. The Scriptures serve as the foundation for this belief.

## Jesus and Women

If the analytic tools of philosophy and theology tend to abstract Jesus away from the concrete circumstances in which he lived and ministered, feminist interpretation analyzes gender bias in these traditional interpretations. Reading the Gospels from a feminist perspective reveals the importance of women to Jesus, and the importance of Jesus to women.

Women and their concerns occupy an important place in the ministry of Jesus. He heals a number of women who are ill—the "daughter of Abraham" who had been disabled for eighteen years (Lk 13:10–17), the woman with the hemorrhage who had been sick for twelve years (Mt 9:20–22; Mk 5:25–34; Lk 8:40–48), as well as the daughter of the Syro-Phoenician woman (Mt 15:21–28; Mk 7:24–30). He raises the daughter of Jairus from the dead (Mt 9:18–19, 23–26; Mk 5:22–24, 35–43; Lk 8:40–42, 49–56), and saves the woman caught in adultery from execution (Jn 8:2–11).

The preaching of Jesus also draws upon the experience of women and their work. So he likens the reign of God to the image of a woman making bread (Mt 13:33; Lk 13:20). And he compares the joy in heaven over the reconciliation of a sinner to the relief of a woman who has found the money she had misplaced (Lk 15:8–10). He commends the generosity of the poor widow (Mk 12:41–44; Lk 21:1–4), even as he condemns those who would exploit her generosity (Mk 12:38–40; Lk 20:46–47).

And if the Gospels testify to the importance of women to Jesus, the Gospels also testify to the importance of Jesus to women. The Gospel narratives preserve the names of women who accompanied Jesus during his mission, notably Mary Magdalene (Mt 27:55–56; Mk 15:40–41; Lk 8:2–3), as well as the names of those who provided hospitality to him during his travels (Lk 8:1–3; Jn 12:3), particularly the sisters, Martha and Mary (Lk 10:38–42). Furthermore, while his closest male followers fled

once Jesus was arrested (Mt 26:56; Mk 14:50), the women did not desert him (Mt 27:55; Mk 15:40; Lk 23:49; Jn 19:25), despite the very real risk of arrest. Clearly, Jesus was important to these women.

All four Gospels testify that the first witnesses to the Resurrection of Jesus were women (Mt 28:1–10; Mk 16:1–8; Lk 24:1–11; Jn 20:1–2, 11–18). In all of these accounts, Mary Magdalene is always mentioned first in the list of women who had come to the grave of Jesus, intending to finish the funeral rites that had been interrupted by his hasty burial. She and the other women are commissioned to bring the news to the disciples that Jesus has been raised from the dead (Mt 28:7; Mk 16:7; Lk 24:9; Jn 20:17). That the testimony of women was popularly considered inadmissible constitutes the four-fold tradition's strongest case for historical verifiability: such stories, so potentially damaging to the claim that Jesus had been raised from the dead, would hardly have been preserved unless they had actually happened.

## Jesus and Greco-Roman Art

The encounter between Christianity and the Greco-Roman world produced more than new ways of conceptualizing the person and mission of Jesus; it produced an entire body of artwork unimaginable in the Judaism in which Jesus was raised. First-century Judaism was aniconic: the Torah forbade the making of images in the "likeness of anything in the heavens above or on the earth below or in the waters beneath the earth" (Ex 20:4). But as Christianity moved into the wider Greco-Roman world, it encountered an artistic tradition that was already highly developed. Christian artists began to appropriate that Greco-Roman artistic tradition, and to portray images of Jesus in sculpture, in mosaic, and in fresco, many of which can still be seen in churches, museums, and ancient Christian burial grounds.

Initially, Christian art seems to have been little more than graffiti scratched into plaster or stone, as in the depiction of the profile of a fish by crossing two arcs—seemingly, a coded reference to Jesus, since *ichthys*, the Greek word for fish, could be construed as an acronym for **Iēsous Christos, Theou Yios, Sōtēr**, or "Jesus Christ, Son of God, Savior." Occasionally, the Greek capital letters were superimposed on one another, so that the resulting image resembled a wheel with eight spokes. Such images may date back as early as the late first or early second century CE. Certainly by the early third century CE, Clement of Alexandria (ca. 150–215 CE) can recommend that his readers have their signet rings engraved with the image of a fish (*Christ the Educator* 2.11). The image functions as a handy reminder of the Gospel narrative as a whole, since fish figure prominently therein. Jesus promises Simon Peter, Andrew, James, and John that he will make them "fishers of men" (Mt 4:19; Mk 1:17; Lk 5:10). Both Lk 5:1–11 and Jn 21:1–14 relate the story of a miraculous catch of fish, and all four Gospels preserve at least one account of the multiplication of loaves and fish in the wilderness (Mt 14:13–21 and 15:32–39; Mk 8:1–9 and 6:31–44; Lk 9:10–17; Jn 6:5–15). Even today, the image of the fish—now found on such artifacts as bumper stickers and key chains—serves as a kind of identity-marker, reminding their owners of their religious commitments, and signaling those commitments to the wider public.

Christian artistic representations of Jesus soon moved beyond graffiti. One of the earliest images of Jesus to be depicted was that of the Good Shepherd. Inspired by Jn 10:11–18 and Mt 18:12–14 and its parallel in Lk 15:3–7, Christian artists typically portrayed Jesus as a young shepherd, usually beardless, carrying a lamb on his shoulders. The earliest of these depictions can be found in the Roman catacombs as frescos: the fresco of the Good Shepherd in the Catacomb of Priscilla on the Via Salaria in Rome probably dates to the second half of the third century CE, as does the fresco of the Good Shepherd in the Catacomb of San Callisto on the Via Appia Antica. The Vatican Museums preserve a marble sculpture of the Good Shepherd, which was probably made in the early fourth century CE.

Whether in two dimensions or in three, the artistic conventions associated with the Good Shepherd were derived from ancient Greek depictions of the *Kriophoros* ("ram-bearer") sculptures, which honored the messenger-god Hermes, who is said to have saved a city from the plague by carrying a ram upon his shoulders while walking around the city walls (Pausanias, *Description of Greece*, 9.22.1–2). When the otherwise anonymous Christian artists adopted and adapted these extant artistic conventions in order to depict Jesus as the Good Shepherd, they communicated an understanding of Jesus in terms that recent converts to Christianity would have found congenial and comprehensible—and comforting as well, since both the *Kriophoros* and the Good Shepherd signify deliverance from danger.

Another prominent artistic image of Jesus was that of the Pantocrator (from the Greek *pan* "all" and *kratōr* "ruler," hence a depiction of Jesus as ruler of the universe). Typically such portraits of Jesus, done in fresco or mosaic, were placed high in the apses of large Christian basilicas, where they gazed down upon the worshipers below. In such images, the face of Jesus is generally solemn, and his right hand is raised in blessing over the worshiping assembly. Unlike the beardless, short-haired Good Shepherd, the Pantocrator is heavily bearded, with long hair parted in the middle and flowing over his shoulders.

While the image of Jesus as the Pantocrator has multiple points of inspiration in the New Testament, from the parable of the sheep and the goats (Mt 25:31–46) to multiple mentions in the book of Revelation (Rev 1:8; 4:8; 11:17; 15:3; 16:7, 14; 19:6, 15; 21:22), the iconography of the Pantocrator takes its inspiration as much from Greco-Roman imperial insignia as it does from the New Testament. Indeed, the churches themselves in which such images were installed were called "basilicas," literally "royal halls," and were architectural adaptations of edifices commonly found in major Greco-Roman cities in which imperial magistrates would render their legal decisions. In this view, the depiction of Jesus as the Pantocrator assures those who gather under his image that justice will be meted out to them by Jesus himself.

The depiction of Jesus as the Pantocrator has had an extraordinarily long tenure, artistically speaking. The earliest known depiction of Jesus as Pantocrator dates from the sixth century, and is found at St. Catherine's Monastery in the Sinai Desert. Visitors to the city of Monreale in Sicily can see a twelfth-century mosaic of the Pantocrator in the apse of the cathedral. The Basilica of the National Shrine of the Immaculate Conception in Washington, D.C. houses a twentieth-century Pantocrator, Jan Henryk de Rosen's *Christ in Majesty*.

The image of the crucified Jesus, commonly seen today in Catholic, Orthodox, and Anglican churches, is a relatively late arrival in Christian art. The earliest known artistic depiction of the crucifixion can be found on the wooden doors of the fifth-century basilica of Santa Sabina on the Aventine Hill in Rome. In this panel, Jesus is portrayed on dark cypress wood in bas-relief between the two thieves (Mt 27:38; Mk 15:27; Lk 23:32–33; Jn 19:18). In addition, he is considerably taller than the other two figures. Behind the three crucified figures appears to be the city of Jerusalem, represented by three classical pediments.

Like the depiction of Jesus as the Pantocrator, the portrait of the crucified Jesus has enjoyed a long artistic tradition. Sometimes, the crucified Jesus is depicted in stark solitude, as if to emphasize his isolation from the rest of humanity. Sometimes, the crucified Jesus is portrayed in conjunction with his mother and the Beloved Disciple (Jn 19:26–27). And sometimes, the crucified Jesus is surrounded by figures who lived long after the first century— people like Dominic de Guzmán, founder of the Order of Preachers (1170–1221), or Francis of Assisi, founder of the Order of Friars Minor (1181–1226)—in order to show the centrality of the death of Jesus to their own spirituality.

Today the image of the crucified Jesus is probably the best-known way in which Jesus is portrayed. The image appears almost everywhere and in virtually every artistic medium—as stone-hewn crucifixes brooding in cemeteries as paradoxical signs of grief and hope, as oil paintings exhibited in the hushed galleries of international museums, even as gold or silver jewelry that simultaneously displays both wealth and piety. The crucifix has become artistic shorthand for Christianity.

# Jesus, Islam, and the Qu'ran

Many Christians will be surprised to find that Jesus (Arabic, *'Isa*) receives prominent mention in the Qu'ran, the most sacred text of Islam. The most common way by which Jesus is identified in the Qu'ran is "son of Mary" (Arabic, *Ibn Maryam*; see 3.45), though he is also called "the Messiah" (Arabic, *al-Masih*; see 3.45; 4.151), and "the word of God" (Arabic, *kalimat Allah*; see 4.171), and "prophet" (Arabic, *nabi*; see 19.30), titles for Jesus that will be familiar to readers of the New Testament. And while the Qu'ran does not retell the story of Jesus as it is found in the four canonical Gospels, it makes a number of allusions to events in the life and ministry of Jesus.

In the Qu'ran, the circumstances of Jesus' birth and infancy bear both similarities and dissimilarities to the Infancy Narratives in Mt 1–2 and Lk 1–2. In the Qu'ran, as in Matthew and Luke, Mary (Arabic, *Maryam*) is identified as the mother of Jesus (19.16). And in the Qu'ran, as in Lk 1:26–38, the angel Gabriel (Arabic, *Jibrail*) announces the birth of Jesus to Mary (3.43–47; 19.17–21). But, unlike the accounts in Matthew and Luke, the Qu'ran makes no mention of Joseph, Mary's spouse. When the time comes for Jesus to be born, according to the Qu'ran, Mary goes to a remote place by herself (19.22), where she gives birth to Jesus beneath a date palm tree, on whose fruit she feeds (19.23–25). She then takes the newborn child back to her people, where the infant Jesus miraculously speaks (3.46; 5.113; 19.30–33).

The brief allusion to Jesus' childhood in the Qu'ran (3.49; 5.110) bears a close resemblance to the story preserved in the *Infancy Gospel of Thomas* 1.2 in which the child Jesus fashions birds from clay, and then brings them to life. But for the most part, what allusions the Qu'ran makes to the life and ministry of Jesus seem to imply knowledge of the canonical Gospels. So, for instance, according to the Qu'ran (3.49; 5.110) as in the Gospels of Matthew, Mark, Luke, and John, Jesus heals lepers, restores sight to the blind, and raises the dead. But the gospel in the Qu'ran is not so much a collection of stories about Jesus and stories by

Jesus, as it is for Christians: in the Qu'ran, the gospel (Arabic, *Injil*, undoubtedly, a reference to the Greek word *euangelion*—"good news" or "gospel") is understood to be a revelation given by God to Jesus, in which there is "guidance and light" (5.46).

As in the four canonical Gospels, Jesus in the Qu'ran is rejected by his people, who intend to kill him (4.157; 5.70). Unlike the Gospels, however, which are unambiguous about the manner of Jesus' death by crucifixion, the Qu'ranic passages that deal with the end of Jesus' life are open to differing interpretations. On the one hand, the infant Jesus refers to "the day I die, and the day I am raised to life again" (19.33). On the other hand, the Qu'ran seems to envision an ascension without a prior death:

They said (in boast), "We killed the Messiah 'Isa son of Maryam, the Messenger of Allah;" but they killed him not, nor crucified him, but so it was made to appear to them, and those who differ therein are full of doubts, with no (certain) knowledge, but only conjecture to follow, for of a surety they killed him not—nay, Allah raised him up unto Himself. (4.157–58)

Where the Qu'ran differs most from Christianity with respect to the person of Jesus is its rejection of any claims in favor of Jesus' divinity:

And they say: The Beneficent God has taken (to himself) a son. Certainly you have made an abominable assertion! The heavens may almost be rent thereat, and the earth cleave asunder, and the mountains fall down in pieces, that they ascribe a son to the Beneficent God. And it is not worthy of the Beneficent God that he should take (to himself) a son. (19.88–91)

Similarly, the Qu'ran rejects any understanding of God as a Trinity:

O followers of the Book! do not exceed the limits in your religion, and do not speak (lies) against Allah, but (speak) the truth; the Messiah, 'Isa son of Maryam is only an apostle of Allah and His Word which He communicated to Maryam and a spirit from Him; believe therefore in Allah and His messengers, and say not, "Three." Desist, it is better for you; Allah is only one God; far be it from His glory that He should have a son. (4.171)

Like Justin, who believed that Heraclitus and Socrates could be identified as Christians even though they lived centuries before Jesus, the Qu'ran identifies a number of figures from the Bible as Muslim—from Abraham to Ishmael to Jacob to Moses to Jesus—all of whom precede Mohammed (2.131–37; 3.67). This Qu'ranic claim seems to have been animated by the same conviction that moved Justin in the second century, and for that matter, the bishops at the Second Vatican Council in the twentieth century—the desire to recognize goodness and truth wherever and whenever it may be found, and the deeply-held belief that goodness and truth will lead humanity into a transforming encounter with God.

## Conclusion

The variety of ways by which Jesus has been understood over centuries and across cultures, informed first and foremost through reading the Scriptures, speaks to the fascination he continues to exercise over the minds and hearts of people. Teacher, Healer, High Priest, Good Shepherd, Pantocrator, Son of Mary—all of these images of Jesus reveal some feature of his mission, and uncover some aspect of his identity. In the end, the many faces of Jesus reflect the many faces that have gazed upon him, who have found in the stories of his life the meaning of their own. ■

# The Lectionary: A Canon within the Canon

## Regina Boisclair

## Introduction

Christian worship in general and Catholic liturgy in particular makes use of the Bible in diverse ways. The liturgical year recalls the biblical history of salvation; liturgical rituals renew, enrich, and interpret the biblical witness; words and phrases in the rites and many hymns reproduce or paraphrase biblical passages. As Gerard Sloyan notes, "From the opening sign of the cross (see Mt 28:19) to the final dismissal (see Ps 29:11b; Jdt 8:35), the participants are invited to live in the world of the Bible as one people with its people."[1] The most sustained use of the Bible, however, is the reading of biblical passages. For Catholics, Orthodox, Anglicans, and many Protestants, these readings are predetermined in tables, lists of preselected passages from the Bible appointed to specific occasions on the church calendar. The Catholic Church calls these tables an "ordo" or lectionary. Catholics also use the word "lectionary" to identify volumes that print the passages in their assigned sequence in order to facilitate public reading. This article concerns the tables, not the printed volumes.

The Second Vatican Council called for a revision of a lectionary that had been used in the Roman Rite since 1570. *The Constitution on the Liturgy (Sacrosanctum Concilium)* called for "a more ample, more varied and more suitable reading from sacred scripture" (35:1). The Council Fathers intended that "the treasure of the Bible be opened up more lavishly so that a richer fare may be provided for the faithful at the table of God's word. In this way a more representative part of the sacred scripture will be read to the people in the course of a prescribed number of years" (*Sacrosanctum Concilium*, 51). The Council considered that in the

proclamation of texts, understood as the Word of God, "Christ is present since it is He Himself who speaks when the holy Scriptures are read in the church" (*Sacrosanctum Concilium,* 7).

*The Revised Lectionary of the Roman Missal for Sundays and Solemnities* was promulgated in 1969 and modestly revised in 1981. It became mandatory for use in Roman Catholic worship worldwide on the first Sunday of Advent in 1971. This lectionary had three major innovations: (1) it replaced an annual cycle of readings with a three-year table, (2) it provided for three biblical selections together with a psalm or canticle in place of a Gospel passage that had been preceded by a brief segment from an epistle, and (3) it appointed regular readings from the Old Testament that were rarely included in the 1570 ordo. The three-year lectionary for Sundays and Solemnities was accompanied by a two-year table of selections for weekdays, with proper or common readings for Saints' days, as well as selections for sacramental, votive, and various other occasions. A complete weekday lectionary for Mass was an innovation; the 1570 lectionary assigned readings for Solemnities, Holy Week, some Saints' days and the sacraments, otherwise the Sunday readings were repeated throughout the week. Both the new Sunday and weekday lectionaries follow the same liturgical calendar, although they are independent one from the other.

The three-year Sunday lectionary is a highly popular change. This lectionary not only vastly increased the number of biblical texts proclaimed in public worship, but also inaugurated a new appreciation of sacred Scripture among Catholics. In addition, it had an unanticipated ecumenical influence; various Anglican and Protestant churches quickly adopted the three-year Catholic lectionary and adapted it for their own use. The denominational lectionaries changed some of the first and second readings but retained nearly all the Gospel

---

1. Gerard Sloyan, "Overview of the Lectionary for Mass: Introduction," in *The Bible Documents: A Parish Resource* (Chicago: Liturgical Training Publications, 2001), 72–73.

selections on the same occasions as the Catholic lectionary as an expression of Christian unity. Today, all the original denominational lectionaries have been effectively replaced by the 1992 *Revised Common Lectionary*. The three-year Sunday lectionary is considered "Catholicism's greatest gift to Protestant preaching."[2]

Amid enormous conflicts that followed the changes in Catholic liturgy after Vatican II, the lectionary never became the focus of opposition. Questions concerning the new lectionary focus primarily on ways it might be improved. What follows sketches the history of lectionaries, discusses the formulation of the present lectionaries, and identifies issues of concern. Lectionaries by their very nature establish a canon within the canon of interpretations of the Bible that distinguish liturgical readings from biblical texts.

## Lectionary History

While we cannot determine if Jesus' reading from Is 61:1–2, reported in Lk 4:17–20, was assigned by a lectionary, "a list of continuous readings of the Torah for Sabbaths, festivals, and also Mondays and Thursdays was fixed a century before Christ."[3] The Mishnah (ca. 200 CE) assumes that the public reading of Torah and the Prophets was an ancient practice (*Megillah* 3.4–6) and reports that the passages concerning events being commemorated were appointed for the observance of fasts and feasts such as Passover, Hanukkah, and Purim.[4] Apart from specific readings chosen for feasts or fasts, Torah portions are continuous—the next assigned reading picks up exactly where the last left off so that today the whole Torah is proclaimed over the course of one year. The second reading (the Haftorah portion) from the Prophets was and is selected to correspond thematically to that of the Torah.

There is no evidence that gatherings of the earliest Jesus movement read from the Scriptures while they continued to worship at the Temple or attend synagogues. There is no doubt, however, that once Jewish Christians left or were expelled from the synagogue, some began to include the practice of reading from the Scriptures in Christian worship. "The extent to which the church took over the synagogue system . . . is unclear, except for Ex 12 which was used at the Jewish Passover and the Christian Pascha."[5]

In the second century Justin reports that readings were proclaimed "as long as time allows" (*Apology* 1.67). In the third century individuals were ordained to the office of reader. The fourth century *Apostolic Constitutions* (8.5.11) identified a five-reading sequence "of the law and the prophets, of our epistles and the Acts, as well as the Gospels." By the fifth century, both Rome and Constantinople reduced the readings to three; sometime in the sixth century, Rome began to proclaim only two readings. The first reading came to be called the "Epistle" even when the selection was from the Old Testament, the Acts of the Apostles, or the book of Revelation, since most were from an epistle.[6] Rome's was not the only Latin liturgical tradition in the West. While the Celtic, Hispanic, and Ambrosian rites followed the Roman practice of two readings, the Gallican system retained three.[7]

Liturgical readings devised for the whole year emerged between the fourth and seventh centuries. The most ancient extant Christian lectionary codex is an Armenian lectionary that is dated between 405 and 417. A number of complete or partial lists of Western lectionaries survive from the sixth through the eleventh centuries. Before the Council of Trent no specific lectionary was mandated for the Western Church. The *Würzburg Comes*, the *Episto-*

2. James White, *Christian Worship in Transition* (Nashville: Abingdon, 1976), 139.

3. John Reumann, "A History of Lectionaries from the Synagogue in Nazareth to Post-Vatican II, *Interpretation* 31 (1977), 116–30, at 119.

4. Jacob Neusner, *The Mishnah* (New Haven and London: Yale University Press, 1988), 320–21.

5. Reginald Fuller, "Lectionaries," in *A Dictionary of Liturgy and Worship*, ed. J. G. Davies (New York: Macmillan, 1972), 211.

6. F. E. Warren, *The Liturgy and Ritual of the Ante-Nicene Church*, 2nd rev. ed. (London: Society for Promoting Christian Knowledge, 1912), 257–83.

7. Gerard Sloyan, "Some Suggestions for a Biblical Three-Year Lectionary," *Worship* (1963), 521–35, at 527.

lary of *Alcuin*, and the *Comes Murbacensis* are important examples of medieval practice.

The origin of the lectionary for the 1570 *Missale Romanum* is unknown. Since similar lectionaries were adopted by Lutheran and Anglican reformers, this ordo predated the Council of Trent (1545–1563) and was used throughout Europe. This lectionary assigns a one-year cycle of suitable Gospel readings to the solemnities and seasons; the many Sundays after Epiphany and Pentecost (now called the Sundays of the Year or Ordinary Time) introduced accounts from Jesus' ministry taken from the Gospel that seemed to present the most complete version of the story. Some "epistles" read before these Gospels were chosen to suit the occasion; a few seem suggested by the Gospel selection; most appear to be remnants of an earlier system of semi-continuous readings that has no discernable connection either to the Gospels or to the occasion. Use of this lectionary in the 1962 edition of the *Missale Romanum* has been recently revived for celebrations of the Extraordinary Form of the Mass; it provides for the proclamation of a very limited amount of the biblical witness.

## The Vatican II Revision

Work on implementing the changes mandated by *The Constitution on the Liturgy* began in 1964 when Pope Paul VI established the Council for the Implementation of the Constitution on the Sacred Liturgy, which came to be called The Consilium. The work was divided among fourteen study groups. Study Group One was charged with revising the calendar; Study Group Eleven was charged with devising the lectionary. It took three years to prepare resources, consult international exegetical, liturgical, catechetical and pastoral scholars, hold discussions, and devise preliminary schemas for the revised calendar.

The compilers clearly understood that the creation of a lectionary for Sundays and Solemnities was primary, and those passages that were considered the most important would be assigned to these occasions. The foundational principle of this effort describes the intent of biblical passages assigned to Sundays and Solemnities:

"The mystery of Christ and the history of salvation" must be presented in the readings such that the new system of readings must contain the whole nucleus of the apostolic preaching about Jesus as "Lord and Christ" (Acts 2:36) who fulfilled the Scriptures by his life, his preaching and above all, his paschal mystery and who gives life to the Church until his glorious return.[8]

The first major decision was to abandon the Tridentine Lectionary so that there would be internal coherence to a multi-year system. At the same time there was a concern to preserve historical lectionary selections, arrangements, and assignments, whenever possible. Charts of more than fifty lectionary systems, ancient and modern, occidental and oriental, Catholic, Orthodox, Anglican, and Protestant, were assembled to identify past traditions so that these could be honored.

The most significant decisions were to adopt a three-year cycle for Sundays, to assign each year to a Synoptic Gospel (Year A= Matthew; Year B=Mark; Year C=Luke), and to appoint passages from John every year during Lent and Easter—as was common in the past— as well as to supplement Mark's short Gospel in Year B. The Gospel selections that were assigned for Sundays and Solemnities range between sixty and sixty-five percent of each Gospel.

Another major decision was to appoint three readings with a psalm or canticle to each Sunday and Solemnity, although the general instructions in the introduction allow for bishops' conferences to choose to use only two readings "for pastoral reasons."[9]

The first readings are from the Old Testament, excepting for the Sundays of Easter when the First Readings from Acts maintain an ancient practice. Most Old Testament selections were assigned for some perceived correspondence, usually typological, to the Gospel. However, during the first five Sundays of Lent, the Old Testament lessons review highlights of Israel's salvation history (Year A 1, creation and fall; 2, the call of Abraham; 3, God pro-

8. Annibale Bugnini, *The Reform of the Liturgy 1948–1975*, trans. Matthew J. O'Connell (Collegeville, MN: Liturgical Press, 1990), 410.

9. Sloyan, "Introduction," 79.

vides water from the desert rock; 4, Samuel anoints David; 5, God's promise of restoration after exile; Year B 1, the covenant with Noah; 2, Abraham's sacrifice of Isaac; 3, God's gift of the Decalogue; 4, exile and restoration; 5, the promise of a new covenant; Year C 1, Moses recounts Israel's history from Abraham's wanderings to Israel's deliverance; 2, God's covenant with Abraham; 3, God reveals his name to Moses; 4, Israel enters the land; 5, God promises a new Exodus). A psalm or canticle was chosen to link with and respond to the first reading.

During Advent, Christmas, and Lent the three selections with a psalm or canticle foster themes of each season. Gospel selections are either a traditional reading for that season or chosen to support and supplement the seasonal theme(s). For instance, during the Easter Season not only are the first readings from Acts of the Apostles, but the second readings are semi-continuous selections from 1 Peter, Revelation, or 1 John, since these books were assigned during Easter in ancient lectionaries. On the Sundays of the Year (Ordinary Time) semi-continuous selections from the Gospel of the year were appointed with a corresponding Old Testament passage and psalm. For the second readings during Ordinary Time the compilers devised a separate cycle of semi-continuous selections from the epistles (Year A: 1 Cor 1–4, Rom, Phil, 1 Thes; Year B: 1 Cor 6–11, 2 Cor, Eph, Jas, Heb 2–10; Year C: 1 Cor 12–15, Gal, Col, Heb 11–12, Phlm, 1 Tm, 2 Tm, 2 Thes).

Advent anticipates Christ's second coming while we prepare to celebrate the memorial of his first. The first readings are passages understood as messianic prophecies. The Gospel for the first Sunday is a selection from Jesus' eschatological discourse from the Gospel of the year; the second and third Sunday feature accounts of the Baptist; on the fourth and final Sunday the Gospels recount the episodes from Matthew or Luke that occur before Jesus' birth.

During the Christmas, Lent, and Easter seasons, the selections follow the ancient practices of featuring John's Gospel. However, the Gospels assigned for the first two Sundays of Lent are the account of Jesus' temptation and transfiguration from the Gospel of the year. At first the readings assigned to Lent in Year A were intended for all three years. While the compilers subsequently added other readings for Years B and C, the readings for Year A are so tied into the Rite of Christian Initiation that parishes engaged in preparing adults for baptism at Easter use Year A every year.

The weekday lectionary provides enrichment for those who attend daily Mass. It contains many passages that are not in the Sunday readings. While the weekday table is called a two-year lectionary, all readings for the seasons of Advent, Christmas, Lent, Holy Week, and Easter and the Gospels for the Weekdays of the Year (Ordinary Time) are assigned to the identical occasion for both years. Only the first readings for Ordinary Time differ for each of the two years.

Like the Sunday readings, weekday selections emphasize the themes of the season: anticipation during Advent, celebration of the Incarnation during Christmas, penance and baptism during Lent. During Easter the daily lectionary continues the Sunday readings from Acts and after recounting the various Resurrection appearances in the Gospels during the week following Easter, weekday Gospels feature semi-continuous selections from Jesus' final discourse from Jn 13–17.

Weekdays of the Year (Ordinary Time) are semi-continuous selections from the Synoptic Gospels (weeks 1–9: Mk 1–12; weeks 10–21: Mt 5–25; weeks 22–34: Lk 4–21) ending with Jesus' eschatological discourse according to Luke. During Ordinary Time there are two years of selections for the first readings from both Testaments. In a two-year period only Obadiah, Zephaniah, and Judith are not represented in at least one weekday lection. Over the course of two years, those who attend daily Mass hear a representative selection from almost every book of the Bible.

## Concerns

The fact that the three-year Sunday lectionary includes, excludes, or limits certain passages concerns some biblical and liturgical scholars. Noting how Vatican II intended a Sunday lectionary to be "more ample, more varied and more suitable" (*Sacrosanctum Concilium*, 35), the Pontifical Biblical Commission observed "in its present state, it only partially fulfills this goal."[10] Biblical scholars note that the lectionaries tend to present a Gospel harmony more than a re-presentation of the distinctive thrust of each evangelist. Liturgical scholars tend to dislike the fact that the second readings follow a separate sequence of semi-continuous selections from the epistles during the Sundays of the Year (Ordinary Time); any affinity between the epistle and the other readings of Ordinary Time is serendipitous. Today, many have observed that because many selections are so abbreviated, they lose the essential message of the sacred author. However, the three most prominent concerns involve readings that foster a teaching of contempt toward Jews and Judaism; the omission of stories of the women and female images from the biblical world; and the nature of the selections from the Old Testament.

## Misperception of Jews

A number of passages in the New Testament express the pain and polemic of the Jesus movement as it separated from emerging Rabbinic Judaism. There is an unbroken trajectory between the animus of New Testament authors toward Jews who rejected Christian insights in the second half of the first century and the subsequent nineteen centuries of animosity on the part of Christians toward Judaism.

Matthew 27:25, "His blood be upon us and upon our children," has lent support to the idea that Jews of all generations were and are culpable for the death of Jesus. While this one line in the long Gospel proclaimed once in three years on Palm Sunday in Year A could be lost to an assembly (or taken correctly to apply to everyone), several readings from Acts appointed to the Sundays of Easter repeatedly assert that the Jews killed Jesus. The speeches of Peter assigned as the first reading for Easter Sunday every year (Acts 10:34, 37–43), twice again in Years A and B (A: Acts 2:14, 22–28; 2:14, 36–41; B: Acts 3:1–15, 17–19; 4:8–12),

and once again in Year C (Acts 5:27b–32, 40b–41), accuse Jews of killing Jesus. The accusation is underscored by the Church calendar since Christ's death as prelude to the Resurrection is part of the focus of the Easter Season.[11]

*Nostra Aetate*, issued in 1965 by Vatican II, states, "What happened in His passion cannot be charged against all the Jews, without distinction, then alive, nor against the Jews of today."[12] Liturgical readings that reiterate traditional teachings of contempt allow anti-Judaism to smolder like an underground fire with the potential to flare. Too many churchgoing Christians still believe the Jews killed Jesus when in fact he was crucified under the order of a Roman procurator by Roman soldiers.

The solution here would be to follow lectionary guidelines that allow the elimination of segments of the text that present pastoral problems.[13] It is unfortunate that this problem was not resolved by the compilers, who acknowledge they chose to omit verses on pastoral grounds.[14] Admittedly some of the discussions of this issue relate to the reality that eliminating these verses would be expurgating the Bible and suggest that this problem be explained in the homily that follows Gospel readings. The fact is, however, that the lectionaries are already selections and the homilies that follow the readings most often need to address other issues. A discussion of the problem of New Testament anti-Judaic polemics is more appropriate in Bible studies when questions can be asked and where it is possible to extend clarifications.

## Missing Women

The Catholic Sunday Lectionary tends to omit passages that introduce women, eliminate women from approved shorter readings, hide women in long lections, and emphasize and reinforce patriarchal premises. From the Old

---

10. Pontifical Biblical Commission, "The Interpretation of the Bible in the Church," in *Biblical Documents: A Parish Resource* (Collegeville, MN: Liturgical Press, 2001), 24.

11. Regina A. Boisclair, "Conflicting Messages: Sunday Lections/Official Catholic Teachings," in *Scripture and Theology: Proceedings of the College Theology Society 2001*, ed. Carol Dempsey and William Loewe (Maryknoll, NY: Orbis, 2002), 166–68.

12. 4:13.

13. Sloyan, "Introduction," 76.

14. Ibid., 77.

Testament, four readings include Eve, two mention Sarah, one identifies Hagar, two introduce the widow of Zarephath, one features the Shunammite woman, and another mentions Hannah. Eleven selections introduce only six women as participants in the story of Israel over a period of three years. Selections call attention to dozens of male heroes and holy men, but Rebekah, Rachel, Leah, Tamar, Shiphrah, Puah, Moses' mother, Zipporah, Miriam, Rahab, Deborah, Jael, Naomi, Ruth, Abigail, Bathsheba, Huldah, Judith, and Esther are never mentioned.

Worshiping assemblies do hear the female imagery associated with Lady Wisdom at least three times each year (C Trinity, Prv 8:22–31; B 20th, Prv 9:1–6; A 32nd, Wis 6:12–16; B 28th, Wis 7:7–11; ABC 2nd after Christmas, Sir 24:1–12; ABC Easter Vigil, Bar 3:9–15, 32–4:4); but other female images for God are only heard twice and both are introduced in the same year. Isaiah 49:15, "Can a mother forget her infant" (C 8th Sunday) and Is 66:13, "as a mother comforts her child" (C 14th Sunday) are overwhelmed when images of God as King, Lord of Hosts, and Father are pervasive. What is proclaimed suggests that women are derivative of men (B 27th Sunday, Gn 2:18–24), disposable by men (C 16th Sunday, Gn 18:1–10a), and dangerous to everyone (A 1 Lent, Gn 2:7–9, 3:1–7).[15]

Many women who were important in the early church were omitted from the Sunday lectionary. Mary the mother of Jesus and Chloe are named in passing, but Mary the mother of John Mark, Rhoda, Tabitha, Lydia, Prisca, the four prophet daughters of Philip, Phoebe, Mary of Rome, Junia, Tryphaena, Tryphosa, Persis, the mother of Rufus, Julia, the sister of Nereus, Euodia, Syntyche, Apphia, Nympha, Eunice, Lois, and Claudia are never mentioned.

Gospel stories that feature Jesus' male disciples in a favorable light are apt to be included from more than one Gospel. Excepting the accounts at the empty tomb, none of the accounts that feature an encounter between Jesus and one or more women are included more than once. Luke's story of Jesus healing a woman he identifies as a "daughter of Abraham" (who likely suffered from osteoporosis) in Lk 13:10–17 is the only miracle story not appointed as a Sunday Gospel. Many Gospel passages that include women are abbreviated, hidden, or eliminated. The story of Jesus' encounter with the Samaritan woman (A Lent 3, Jn 4:5–42) offers an approved shorter reading (Jn 4:5–15, 19b–26, 39a, 40–42) that eliminates the report that she evangelized her town.

In Mk 14:3–9 an anonymous woman from Bethany anoints Jesus' head—a symbolic Christological confession. This story is reproduced in Mt 26:6–13. In Lk 7:36–50 a sinful woman in Galilee washes Jesus and anoints Jesus' feet. In Jn 12:1–8, Mary of Bethany washes Jesus' feet. Affinities among the four accounts are evident and well recognized. The Sunday lectionary features Luke's story of the sinful woman, but neither John's accounts of Mary of Bethany's loving act nor Matthew's report of an anonymous woman's Christological confession are found in a Sunday Gospel. Mark's account is assigned to Palm Sunday in Year B but this story is hidden by the long Passion Narrative or eliminated from the shorter Gospel reading.

While all Christians are sinners and should model their lives on the repentant woman from Luke, the Sunday lectionary that balances good and sinful features of men eliminates or hides these stories in which the women exemplify ideals other than repentance. Marjorie Procter-Smith, commenting on the omission of these passages, is convinced that this story is emblematic of the fact that an androcentric hermeneutic unconsciously influenced both the selection and the way the collections of three readings were put together.[16] The lectionary appears to exemplify the admonition: "I do not permit a woman to teach or to have

---

15. Eileen Schuller, "Women in the Lectionary," *National Bulletin on Liturgy* 27, no. 137 (1994), 108–14, at 110–11.

16. Marjorie Proctor-Smith, *In Her Own Rite: Constructing Feminist Liturgical Tradition* (Nashville: Abingdon, 1990), 125–26.

authority over a man. She must be quiet" (1 Tm 2:12).[17]

## Misrepresenting the Old Testament

Since all but the Lenten readings from the Old Testament were chosen by some form of correspondence, usually typological, to a Gospel passage, the Old Testament selections fail to offer a true representation of these canonical texts. The compilers claim that the "entire Old Testament is presupposed in the Lord's preaching, his actions and his passion."[18] While this premise is assumed by New Testament authors and true to Christian faith, today scholars recognize that the principle of correspondence does not fully represent both Testaments and the Old Testament witness particularly suffers as a result.

If one were to follow the premise that selections are intended to introduce the most important parts of the Bible in the readings for Sundays and Solemnities, one might conclude that the most important parts of the Old Testament are those that correspond to the New. This is not just disputable, it is incorrect. Important accounts are missing. Significant accounts in the story of Israel and the Wisdom tradition that do not link to a Gospel passage are not heard. For example, Sunday selections fail to include an account of the flood and Noah's ark, to mention but one astonishing omission. Individual selections are frequently far too short to do much more than to set a stage for the Gospel. When passages only foreshadow what was fulfilled in Christ, the important story of God's benevolence to Israel is never heard.[19]

## Conclusion

The Bible re-presents ancient traditions that in their present canonical form are received as sacred Scripture by the churches. Lectionaries, which are the product of the churches, represent these sacred texts. James Sanders calls the whole effort of revising and preserving ancient traditions the "canonical process" and considers the contemporary lectionaries the most recent example of the same process.[20]

A lectionary is in effect a canon within the canon. It is a canon shaped by collections of selected readings assigned to the context of observances on the church calendar. Since selection excludes as well as includes, collection distorts as well as highlights, and context overlooks as well as memorializes, each of these features has interpretive effects that have the capacity either to underscore or alter the meaning of the biblical message. These effects are "set into" lectionaries by the selections, "provided by" lectionaries by their collections and contexts, and "heard from" lections by worshiping assemblies who come with preexisting attitudes and beliefs that will influence how and what they hear when the lections are proclaimed.[21]

However, while lectionary readings are not the same as the canonical texts, they are designed to foster what might be rightly understood as a liturgical process whereby believing Christians enter into these stories and respond with an affirmation of faith. Their influence also extends beyond the limits of public worship since many catechetical programs, parochial Bible studies, and popular guides for spiritual growth follow their selections. They are the only Bible that is heard, read, preached, and studied by a substantial number of churchgoing Christians. ■

17. Regina A. Boisclair, "Amnesia in the Catholic Sunday Lectionary: Women—Silenced from the Memories of Salvation History," in *Women and Theology: Proceedings of the College Theology Society, 1994*, ed. Mary Ann Hinsdale and Phyllis H. Kaminski (Maryknoll, NY: Orbis, 1995), 128.

18. Bugnini, *Reform of the Liturgy*, 411.

19. Eileen Schuller, "Some Criteria for the Choice of Scripture Texts in the Roman Lectionary," in *Shaping English Liturgy*, ed. by P. Finn and J. Schellman, (Washington, DC: Pastoral Press, 1990), 385–404, at 390–92.

20. James A. Sanders, *Canon and Community: A Guide to Canon Criticism* (Philadelphia: Fortress, 1984), 78.

21. Boisclair, "Amnesia in the Catholic Sunday Lectionary," xxiii.

# A Brief History and Practice of Biblical Criticism

## Marielle Frigge, OSB

## How Do Christians Interpret the Bible?

Over the centuries, the Bible has been interpreted differently by various people; the fundamental question, "What does the Bible mean?" has been approached in diverse ways. Through the centuries, some people have assumed that the Bible means exactly what it says, no more and no less; it is to be read and understood at face value. At times the Bible has been read as an allegory, in which every person and event is thought to represent a deeper meaning. Sometimes the Bible has been given a typological interpretation, that is, earlier characters and events are seen as foreshadowings or "types" of later ones. Some people have consulted and interpreted the Bible strictly as instruction for a moral life; others have interpreted it solely in the light of prayerful reading and reflection. At times, different persons have attempted to combine various approaches in order to interpret the Bible, always seeking to answer the basic question, "What does it mean?"

## Development of Biblical Criticism

In the eleventh through sixteenth centuries, several educational and cultural developments in Christian Europe brought new questions to the Bible, opening the way for new modes of interpretation. Universities were founded, riches of other cultures were brought to bear on European thought, and rediscovery of ancient philosophies as well as growth of new ones influenced both the content of long-accepted ideas and modes of reflecting upon those ideas. Since the Church always exists within human culture, it was inevitable that these new winds blowing across Europe's intellectual landscape would find their way into Christian thought as well. What is commonly called "biblical criticism" grew out of these

centuries of change. The word "criticism" here does not have a negative connotation; it refers to critical thinking that poses the kinds of questions one might ask about these ancient writings, questions such as: Was Noah actually six hundred years old at the time of the flood? How could Jonah survive for three days and nights in the belly of a huge fish? Why is the Lord's Prayer not the same in Matthew and Luke? Biblical criticism then, as it developed and is used today, is a reasoned process of exploring a biblical book or passage in its historical, cultural, literary, and religious contexts in order to discover what the original author meant to communicate to the original audience.

Most biblical scholars date the beginnings of biblical criticism to a French priest, Richard Simon, who produced a lengthy study of the Old Testament ca. 1650.[1] One element of the priest's work that drew particular attention was his view of authorship of the Pentateuch. Simon proposed that Moses was not, as Christians had assumed for centuries, the single author of these five books. Simon's ideas were considered shocking to many at the time, and his work was even placed on the Catholic Index of Forbidden Books in 1682.

Others, however, took up Simon's ideas and continued to ask questions of the Bible that had not been asked before. In the eighteenth century other European scholars applied language studies and historical investigation to the Bible. Jean Astruc, ca. 1750, suggested that two different names for God (*Elohim* and *Yahweh*) used in Genesis indicated two distinct sources for this first book of the Old Testament. The further work of Hermann Gunkel provided

---

1. One can trace elements of biblical criticism, such as the allegorical reading of some Scripture, at least as far back as the early third century and the writings of Clement of Alexandria and Origen; Jewish critical interpretation goes back even further. Augustine of Hippo had a profound influence in the fourth and fifth centuries.

a transition from the eighteenth to the nineteenth century. Later called the "father of form criticism," Gunkel identified various distinct oral forms within the biblical books, each with its own particular usage and intended meaning.

In the late 1870s, Julius Wellhausen offered a theory that is widely accepted today. From his study of the Pentateuch, he concluded that these five books represent a combination of four earlier written sources, code-named J, E, D, and P for the writing tradition from which each developed, i.e., Yahwist, Elohist, Deuteronomist, and Priestly. Wellhausen's proposal further threatened the traditional view that Moses was the sole author of the five books of the Pentateuch. Some Protestant scholars were uncomfortable with this idea, and many Catholics felt even more threatened. Other long-held teachings and practices were under attack at the time, and so Catholic scholars tended to repeat and emphasize traditional views. Nevertheless, study of the Bible through various methods of historical, linguistic, and literary analysis continued, but Protestant scholars were more active in biblical study using critical approaches than were Catholics at that time.

## Changing Catholic Response to Biblical Criticism

Near the end of the nineteenth century, Catholic resistance to critical analysis and interpretation of the Bible was reinforced at the highest level of authority. Fascination with human influence on the composition of biblical books had led some scholars to claim that divine inspiration had nothing to do with the formation of Scripture. For the pope at that time, such claims offered ample reason for suspicion of the new, modern methods of biblical study. In 1893, Pope Leo XIII published an encyclical, "On the Study of Holy Scripture" (*Providentissimus Deus*), warning that the new modes of biblical interpretation could easily undermine Catholic faith. In effect, the pope's letter discouraged Catholic biblical scholars from using the "new criticism," and so Catholic scholars

produced few critical studies of the Bible in the early twentieth century.

Just fifty years after Pope Leo's letter, however, Pope Pius XII published the encyclical "On the Most Opportune Way to Promote Biblical Studies" (*Divino afflante Spiritu*). His 1943 letter pointed out that conditions of biblical studies and the sciences that support them had changed greatly in fifty years. Using a different approach from that of Pope Leo, Pius XII encouraged study of the biblical languages, historical and cultural background, and the many forms of literature found in the Bible. At this time, however, most people were far more preoccupied with World War II than with the world of biblical scholarship. Therefore, Catholics did not make a great deal of progress in modern approaches to biblical study for another two decades.

Catholic scholars were not, however, completely idle. In 1964, the Pontifical Biblical Commission, an international committee of Bible scholars appointed by the pope, published the statement "On the Historical Truth of the Gospels." This document recognized that the canonical Gospels are not objective history containing only factual events written down exactly as they happened; rather, they represent three distinct stages of time and thought development. The first, earliest stage is that of Jesus himself, who used concepts and language of his own day and his Jewish culture. The second stage is that of the apostles, who after the Resurrection began to deepen their understanding of Jesus as divine, and so reinterpreted his earthly life in light of this belief. The third stage or level comes from the Gospel writers (evangelists) who collected and edited oral and written traditions circulating in various Christian communities. Each evangelist selected certain elements from among these earlier sources, interpreting them in order to fit his particular audience and historical situation.

When "On the Historical Truth of the Gospels" was published, Vatican Council II, an ecumenical (worldwide) council of the Catholic Church, was already in session. In 1965, Vatican II released an important statement on the Bible in Catholic life, the "Dogmatic Constitution on Divine Revelation" (*Dei Verbum*). In this document, the council's bishops emphasized sacred Scripture, along with Tradition, as the essential source of all Christian theology, the "study of God." They also strongly promoted the use of modern biblical criticism, paired with prayerful reflection, to interpret the Scriptures. Within about seventy years, the Catholic position on biblical criticism had shifted completely, from emphatic rejection of this approach to strong support for its use. Many Catholic Scripture scholars today are among the best in the field.

## Contextual Approach to Interpretation

As the name implies, a contextual approach to interpreting the Bible insists that a text must always be interpreted in its context. The context includes all the circumstances surrounding a text that can affect its meaning. Those who interpret the Bible contextually examine historical, literary, and theological aspects of context, which usually overlap and so affect one another. An overview of these major aspects of context follows, with some of the important questions any interpreter of the Bible needs to explore in order to understand the author's intended meanings for the original audience.

To understand the historical context of any biblical text, one inquires about the time and place and social/cultural circumstances in which a book was written, as well as the particular audience to whom the book was originally addressed. If there is a long history of oral and written transmission, the interpreter also examines the historical situation in which particular traditions formed. Events and circumstances of the time in which a book is composed normally influence what content is included or excluded, which ideas and themes receive major emphasis, and so on. For example, in modern times a book about the 1968 assassination of Rev. Martin Luther King written within a year of his death could not possibly have the same perspective as a book written today, when the civil rights movement is more advanced and Americans have a much greater understanding of the role that Dr. King played in that movement.

Theological context might involve theological perspectives, questions, or struggles of the time and place of writing, especially issues that affected the originally intended audience. This aspect of context also includes theological points that the author intends to present or perhaps question, or both. The Gospel of Matthew, for example, is addressed to a Christian community of converted Jews who were searching for the connections and disconnections between the Jewish religion they had previously followed and their new faith founded on Jesus. As a result, the author strongly emphasizes how Jesus fulfills the Hebrew Scriptures, reassuring his Jewish Christian audience that they are not completely disconnected from their former religious way of life.

By investigating the literary context of any part of the Bible, interpreters recognize the fact that though it is a literature of faith, the Bible is still literature and therefore uses the types and forms of writing of the times and cultures in which these books were written. Interpretation greatly benefits from knowledge of the literary genre of a biblical book or any particular part of it, and the purpose or intention of that kind of literature. For example, a reader who understands that a particular book of the Bible is poetry will not read it like a historical report. One who realizes that a particular text is fiction will search for the intended point or meaning, not verifiable historical or scientific facts. Interpreting a biblical text in its literary context also involves analysis of structure, plot, characters, translation, and the like. In some cases, a biblical text might be compared to other similar literature, in order to understand better the thought and ways of expressing meaning of the time and place in which the book was composed.

## Catholic Interpretation of Scripture Today

As discussed above, several Catholic teaching documents indicate a major shift within recent times from noncontextual to contextual approaches to the Bible. In recent decades, two significant statements were published in order to clarify and elaborate Catholic teaching on two important matters: the most suitable modes of interpreting sacred Scripture, and the central position the Bible holds in the life of the Church and each of its members. (In referring to these documents below, number/letter notations refer to paragraphs or sections.)

## "Dogmatic Constitution on Divine Revelation" (*Dei Verbum*), 1965

The first of these documents presents the consensus of all the Catholic bishops of the world who gathered for Vatican Council II in the early 1960s. On November 8, 1965, the council published its "Dogmatic Constitution on Divine Revelation" (*Dei Verbum*). Repeatedly the bishops clarified and promoted a contextual reading of Scripture. *Dei Verbum* describes inspiration as God's action in and through the biblical writers, and so it follows that these writings "must be acknowledged as teaching solidly, faithfully and without error that truth which God wanted to put into the sacred writings for the sake of our salvation" (11). However, the document continues, since God speaks through human beings "in human fashion, the interpreter of Sacred Scripture, in order to see clearly what God wanted to communicate to us, should carefully investigate what meaning the sacred writers really intended, and what God wanted to manifest by means of their words" (12).

To discover these intended meanings, interpreters are encouraged to work with the best translations from manuscripts written in the Bible's original languages. Further, readers need to consider the historical and cultural context of the Bible and the literary forms it employs: "For truth is set forth and expressed differently in texts which are variously historical, prophetic, poetic, or other forms of discourse, [and] due attention must be paid to the customary and characteristic styles of feeling, speaking and narrating which prevailed at the time of the sacred writer" (12).

In its comments on New Testament interpretation, *Dei Verbum* includes several ideas that had been published in 1964 by the Pontifical Biblical Commission. Both documents recognize three layers of material in the Gospels: that which comes from Jesus himself, interpretations of the earliest apostles, and the message that each Gospel writer wished to communicate to his particular audience. "The sacred authors wrote the four gospels, selecting some things from the many which had been handed on by word of mouth or in writing, reducing some of them to a synthesis, explaining some things in view of the situation of their churches, . . . but always in such fashion that they told us the honest truth about Jesus" (19). Finally, interpreters are reminded to seek understanding of a particular biblical text in light of the whole of Scripture and the Church's ongoing, living Tradition. Catholics understand tradition as all that helps the community to grow in faith, as it is handed on not only in Scripture but in the shared life, worship, and teaching of the Catholic Church.

Following these guidelines for interpretation, the Vatican II document addresses the role of Scripture in the life of the Church. The council repeatedly underscores the importance of God's guiding presence for accurate understanding, urging that "prayer should accompany the reading of Sacred Scripture" (25). Catholics will be aided by reflecting on the Bible in light of their own spiritual experience and the teaching authority of the Church's bishops, which "is not above the word of God but serves it" (10). All of the Church's "theology rests on the written word of God, together with sacred tradition, as its primary and perpetual foundation" (24), and the Bible ought to shape all preaching and catechetical instruction. Therefore, the bishops strongly recommend frequent prayerful reading of Scripture for "all the Christian faithful," since "ignorance of the Scriptures is ignorance of Christ" (25), and that "easy access to Sacred Scripture should be provided for all" (22).

## "The Interpretation of the Bible in the Church," 1993

Nearly three decades after Vatican Council II, many Catholic preachers and teachers noticed that much of the council's teaching that promoted a contextual reading of Scripture had not reached or affected many Catholics, who seemed to be influenced by biblical fundamentalism and other noncontextual modes of interpretation. In response, the Pontifical Biblical Commission published "The Interpretation of the Bible in the Church" in 1993, which contains one of the Catholic Church's strongest rejections of biblical fundamentalism. Repeating its critique of fundamentalist resistance to viewing the Bible as God's word in human language, the document states that this approach "injects into life a false certitude, for it unwittingly confuses the divine substance of the biblical message with what are in fact its human limitations." Such an emphatically noncontextual approach "often historicizes material which from the start never claimed to be historical" and fails to consider any "possibility of symbolic or figurative meaning" (I.F.).

"Interpretation of the Bible in the Church" further describes, analyzes, and evaluates several kinds of biblical criticism currently in use. On the one hand, the international committee of scholars again emphasizes the value of biblical criticism, often described as the historical-critical method of interpretation. On the other hand, the authors also reiterate that by itself this approach cannot reach truly theological understanding. In elaborating these points, the commission uses the ancient, traditional terminology of literal and spiritual senses of Scripture.

Since these terms have been used in different ways through Christian history, the commission first clarified the literal sense, stressing that it should "not be confused with the 'literalist' sense to which fundamentalists are attached." In other words, the literal sense is not at all the same as a literal reading that takes the words of the Bible at face value, without attention to their original context. Rather, the "literal sense of scripture is that which has been expressed directly by the inspired human authors." Note that this description again implies a kind of partnership between God and the human authors. As inspired, the literal sense is "intended by God," but in order to discover meanings that the human authors communicated, interpreters must analyze texts in their own historical and literary settings. Strongly endorsing a contextual approach, the commission states that "one must reject as inauthentic every interpretation alien to the meaning expressed by the human authors in

their written text," for such interpretation is often carried out in "a wildly subjective" manner (II.B.1).

An example of the last point can be seen in the use of numbers in the Bible. The "beast" of Rev 13:11–18, associated with the number 666, has been identified by various persons and groups as the Soviet Union, the United States, Russia, China, the pope, the Catholic Church, Protestantism, and Saddam Hussein, to name a few. But in order to understand the literal sense or "what was directly expressed by the human authors," one would investigate how numbers were used in the author's context, ca. 95 CE during a Roman persecution of Christians. First of all, at that time several numbers, especially seven and ten, commonly symbolized completion or perfection; further, all numbers were represented by letters of the alphabet. Revelation 13:18 says that 666 "stands for a person," and the one most likely indicated by this number is the Roman Caesar Nero (d. 68), whose name is a numerical equivalent of 666. A person who as 666 fell far short of perfection (777), Nero was the first Roman emperor to order the death of Christians, a "beastly" action repeated by some of his successors. With even a little knowledge of context, the literal sense, or what the biblical author expressed by the number 666, emerges, and other interpretations are seen as subjective meanings very different from that of the original writer.

Like Vatican II's *Dei Verbum*, the Pontifical Biblical Commission's "Interpretation of the Bible in the Church" insists that biblical criticism can assist readers to arrive at an accurate understanding of the Bible, but is insufficient by itself. The literal sense of Scripture must be integrated with the spiritual sense, the meaning that results from reading texts "under the influence of the Holy Spirit" and in the context of Christ's life, death, and Resurrection and "the new life that flows from it." Christian use of Psalm 2 offers an example of interpretation in the spiritual sense. In Psalm 2:7, God says to the king, "You are my son; / today I have begotten you." When the psalm was composed, Israelite kings were thought to be God's agent; as such, the king was sometimes described as an adopted "son" of God. Christians, however, also apply this passage to Christ. When used in relation to Jesus Christ, the psalm takes on a deeper level of meaning, referring to him as not only an agent of God but as divine in his own being. As another caution against purely subjective interpretation, however devotional it might be, the document adds that "the spiritual sense can never be stripped of its connection with the literal sense" (II.B.2).

As is evident from the preceding brief survey, there is no single, universal Christian approach to interpreting the Bible. It is also apparent that *how* Christians set about determining what the Bible means has tremendous influence on the outcome of that process. As the above review of various modes of biblical interpretation suggests, although all Christians regard the Bible as the foundation of their faith, different Christians derive meaning from these Scriptures in many different ways.

The contextual approach is most often used in academic study of the Judeo-Christian Bible. Strictly speaking, this mode of interpretation involves a two-part process in order to determine what the Bible means for twenty-first-century Christians. First, by placing the text in its context, the reader tries to discover as accurately as possible what a biblical passage would have expressed to its original audience in its own time and place; the technical name for this kind of analysis is "exegesis." At this stage, one seeks to understand the historical, literary, and theological contexts of the passage. Such insight can be discovered through careful use of study Bibles and biblical handbooks, dictionaries, and commentaries. In the second step of interpretation, readers reflect upon messages communicated to the original audience, so that the meaning of the word of God can shape and reshape the daily life of today's Christians in their own time and place; this part of the process is called "hermeneutics." Hermeneutical conclusions thus are formed within individual reader's faith perspectives and communities.

## A Closer Look at Biblical Criticism

For those seeking to understand the sacred Scriptures by means of exegesis, a wealth of resources can assist in determining historical, literary, and theological contexts of various books of the Bible. Among the most basic resources are these: *study Bibles*, which contain introductions to each book, footnotes to the biblical text, and other aids such as maps, charts, and photographs; *biblical dictionaries*, which clarify biblical persons, places, and concepts or symbols as they are used in both Old Testament and New Testament; and *biblical commentaries*, which provide section by section or verse by verse explanation of numerous elements of context in order to clarify the writer's original meanings.

## Major Types of Biblical Criticism

The major types or branches of biblical criticism are outlined below, with key questions each one explores in seeking to understand a biblical passage.

### 1. TEXT CRITICISM

This type of biblical criticism is normally done by specialists skilled in ancient manuscripts and languages, and so most readers must use secondary sources containing the results of their work. These scholars search for the most ancient and most trustworthy manuscripts (handwritten copies, on papyrus or animal skin) of biblical books. Then these manuscripts are compared, to determine the most accurate, complete version of a book. In some cases, text critics will discover copyists' errors or glosses (additions or changes) in a manuscript. The work of text criticism is important for translators, who need complete, correct manuscripts in order to produce a translation that is true to the original meanings of a biblical book.

**Questions text criticism might ask:** Are there existing complete manuscripts of a biblical book? How many? How old? How do they compare? Where different manuscripts disagree, which has the correct reading?

### 2. SOURCE CRITICISM

Source criticism is so named because it

inquires about the written or oral sources used by a biblical author, and the life setting and major purposes of each source. The set of Old Testament books called the Pentateuch, for example, most likely was compiled from four earlier written sources, composed by different persons or groups in various life settings during a five-hundred-year span. These four written compositions, in turn, drew from even earlier sources, both oral and written. A New Testament example can be found in the fourth Gospel. Scholars believe that Jn 1:1–18 makes use of an already-existing hymn that praised Christ as the Word of God.

**Questions source criticism might ask:** What sources, oral or written, group or individual, were used to construct a biblical book? What was the life setting of each earlier source, and how did its life setting shape material in that source?

## 3. FORM CRITICISM

Form criticism attempts to identify and analyze parts of biblical writing that began as oral forms of literature. Form criticism tries to uncover the original fixed oral form, the life setting in which it was used, and the actual purpose or intention of each form. Today as in the ancient past, certain oral forms often intend to communicate something other than their surface meaning. For example, today's question-and-answer oral form, "How are you?"/"Fine," does not actually mean to inquire about someone's health or feelings. Its real purpose, in today's American life setting, is simply to greet someone; it is a common substitute for "Hello."

**Questions form criticism might ask:** What is the structure of original oral forms used in the written biblical text? What was the original life setting of each oral form? What was the purpose of each oral form?

## 4. REDACTION CRITICISM

Redaction criticism analyzes the editorial work done by biblical authors on earlier (source) material. The evidence of editorial activity ("redaction") can provide important clues as to the life situation and specific interests, emphases, and perhaps even prejudices of the redactor, the final author or editor of a biblical book. Redaction criticism also seeks to determine what stages of editing a book might have gone through on its way to a final version. The Gospel of John, for example, shows signs of having undergone several stages of editing before it reached the form in which it now appears.

**Questions redaction criticism might ask:** What evidence of redaction is there in a particular biblical text? What were the redactor's particular interests, emphases, and purposes? How did they affect content, form, and major emphases of the book?

## 5. TRADITION CRITICISM

A "tradition" is a body of material passed on in oral or written form by a particular group or community and later used to compile a book or books of the Bible. A community that gathered and handed on a specific tradition ordinarily emphasized or downplayed certain aspects, according to its life setting. Tradition criticism, then, seeks to understand the origins of a tradition and the community that shaped and passed it on. For example, the Old Testament historical books often refer to the establishment of Israel as a nation ruled by a king. The Bible contains both positive and negative opinions about Israelite kingship, sometimes within the same book. Tradition criticism resolves much of the apparent contradiction: final compilers of the historical books selected portions of several different traditions, without trying to create a single, unified point of view. In this example, tradition criticism would further inquire about the community behind each strand of tradition concerning Israelite kingship, and the circumstances that led to each community's understanding and opinion of that tradition.

**Questions tradition criticism might ask:** What community began or passed on a particular tradition? What was this community's life setting? How did the community's life setting influence the content and viewpoint of this tradition?

## 6. LITERARY CRITICISM

The first task of literary criticism is analyzing the Bible as literature, exploring elements such as structure, style, characters, plot, setting, and so on. For example, the Gospel of Mark uses a structure called "framing," which sets off a key point with a pair of similar elements just before and after the important content; two stories in which a blind man is healed frame Jesus' threefold statement that he must go to Jerusalem to suffer and die. Awareness of such literary techniques helps readers recognize what the author considers most meaningful. Second, literary criticism also compares a biblical book or passage to other literature of the time, seeking to discover changes, additions, or omissions. Such differences suggest what the biblical author considered most important to communicate about a commonly circulating story. The biblical account of Noah and the flood, for example, has many parallels with ancient Mesopotamian flood stories. But there are a number of differences. The nonbiblical accounts tell of many gods involved in this disaster, while the Bible speaks of only one God, Yahweh. The author wished to emphasize that the Israelites, unlike all their neighbors, believed in one and only one God.

**Questions literary criticism might ask:** What genre or type of literature is the biblical book as a whole? What are the structure, style, and purpose of the book? What subgenres are used within the book, and what is the structure and intended meaning of each? How does the book or passage compare and contrast with other, nonbiblical literature of the time?

## 7. SOCIAL-SCIENTIFIC CRITICISM

This type of biblical criticism is so named because it explores the social and cultural background of the Bible by means of research in the social sciences. Such exploration, for instance, shows that a particular action or gesture can mean quite different things in various cultures and societies. Today in the United States, for example, waving the hand with palm outward means "Good-bye," but in Italy, it means "Come here." Social structures can also vary a great deal. In the United States today, the elderly are often placed in nursing homes, away from family and friends. In China, where aged persons are highly respected, this would be unthinkable. In order to discover the meaning of the Bible, then, we need to inquire about social and cultural structures, customs, and values of biblical peoples.

**Questions social-scientific criticism might ask:** What can be discovered about the social and cultural organization, customs, beliefs, and values of the people described in a biblical text? What social or cultural factors influenced the redactor and the redactor's sources? How might these factors affect this text?

Today more types of biblical criticism are developing, including rhetorical criticism, narrative criticism, reader-response criticism, and many others. Since there are multiple questions of context to be explored, the best biblical study aids combine the findings of many different kinds of biblical criticism. With the help of such resources, anyone who seeks to better understand the words of Scripture by exploring the text in its context can do so. Biblical criticism offers much help in the process of exegesis, discovering the meaning that a biblical book or passage would have had for its original intended audience. The audience of thousands of years later must do its own work of hermeneutics, applying that ancient meaning to Christian living in a specific twenty-first century time and place. ■

# The Historical-Critical Method of Scripture Analysis

Christians hold the sacred Scriptures as the word of God, written in the words of human beings. The following represent the foundational approaches used by students of the Bible for scriptural research.

| Method | Description and Analysis of the Text Used |
| --- | --- |
| **Historical Criticism** | Uncovers the historical situation *(Sitz im Leben)* of the world of the writer or editor. Examines the following:<br>• the date and location of the writing community<br>• the major social issues faced in a particular period<br>• the cultural worldview of the writers or editors<br>• the influence of the historical situation on the writing |
| **Textual Criticism** | Compares variant readings found in the ancient manuscript copies of the Scriptures in the original languages in an effort to determine what was the text as originally written. |
| **Comparison of Translations** | Compares and contrasts various translations of the Scriptures to understand more clearly the meaning of a given passage. Examines the following:<br>• a minimum of three mainline translations<br>• whether or not modern translations utilize the oldest versions of the Scriptures available<br>• key words in a passage from the perspective of the original languages, comparing them to other uses of the word |
| **Form Criticism** | Identifies the literary form and its function within the writing and the world of the writer. Asks the following:<br>• Did the writer use a particular literary form, such as a poem, a historical story, a prophecy, a letter, a gospel?<br>• Did the writer use a literary device such as a metaphor, an allegory, a midrash, a pun, a parable, or an exaggeration?<br>• What was the cultural function of a particular literary form or device in the world of the writer? |
| **Source Criticism** | Identifies other writings known in the ancient cultures outside of the Scriptures that influenced the writer of a specific passage. Asks the following:<br>• Did the writer build on an existing story, myth, or on other literature as the basis for the writer's work?<br>• Does the theology or justice ethic of the biblical version vary from that of the cultural source?<br>• How are similar biblical texts related to one another? |
| **Redaction Criticism** | Analyzes the role and style of the editor who compiled various writings to produce the final version of a biblical work. Identifies the following:<br>• unifying themes that the editor used to clarify teachings<br>• particular symbols and wording used by the editor to teach biblical theology and ethics<br>• the didactic or instructional intent of the editor |

# Critical Issues in Contemporary Biblical Interpretation

## Stephen J. Binz and Anselm Academic

### Translation as Interpretation

The first step in interpreting the Bible, for those who don't read Hebrew or Greek, is already done for us when we read a translation. For to read a translation of the Bible is to take for granted the interpretations of other people, because a translation into any other language is always based on the interpretive decisions of the translators as to the meaning of the text in the original language.

Translating is the process of "carrying over" meaning from one linguistic culture into another. Because the process of translation is always also an interpretation, translators of the Bible must be experts in both the original language and the language of the translation. There is never a perfect, word-for-word correspondence between one language and another, especially between ancient Hebrew and Greek, and modern languages like English. The translator is always trying to communicate the meaning of words from an ancient culture in words of a very different culture, yet always aware that the meaning of the original can never be fully captured.

There are two predominant ways to translate the Bible from its original texts into English, and each of the many translations of the Bible can be categorized under one of these two. The first type of translation is called the formal equivalence method, or word-for-word translation. This type of translation aims at adhering as closely as possible to the form of the original writing. The translator tries to match word for word and phrase for phrase as closely as possible. Because these translations retain many of the subtleties and nuances of the original languages, they are generally better for serious study of the Bible.

The other type of translation is called the dynamic equivalence method, or meaning-for-meaning translation. This type of translation is not so much concerned with matching words, but with matching the ideas and thoughts of the original text. The translator aims at identifying the meaning intended by the author and then expressing it as it would naturally be rendered in English. These translations are sometimes best for reflective and prayerful reading of the Bible, though they are generally less exacting.

There are two principle considerations when choosing a Bible in English. First, the Bible must be an accurate translation. It should faithfully give us the meaning of the original Hebrew and Greek texts. Second, the Bible must convey that meaning in English that is clear and readable. For both of these reasons, a modern version of the Bible, translated in the past few decades, is best. Older translations, like the King James Version and the Douay-Reims Bible from the sixteenth century, are not as accurate in translating from the original texts in Hebrew and Greek as the more recent works. Scripture scholars have made very significant advances in the past few decades in the study of ancient languages and the discovery of ancient biblical manuscripts. Contemporary translations are able to be much more accurate and faithful to what the biblical writers actually intended to communicate than was ever possible before.

The *New American Bible, Revised Edition* is a formal equivalence translation that is both faithful to the original texts and clearly written in contemporary English. Since every translation is also an interpretation, comparing one translation with another can also bring out different nuances and is always a helpful exercise in seeking fresh insights into the meaning of a text.

### Inclusive Language

The fact that judgments are required of translators has become more obvious with the question of how to translate gendered terms into English. The issue is more apparent with Hebrew texts, because Hebrew has only two grammatical genders, masculine and feminine; there is no neuter in Hebrew. Feminine gender is used when referring to an individual who is female, a group of people who are all female, or a noun that is feminine (like "wisdom" or "city"). Masculine gender has the same function (person[s] who are male and nouns that are masculine), but the masculine gender is also used when either the gender of the person is not known or is not important, or when referring to a group of people that includes both men and women. Although Greek does have a grammatical neuter gender, it also uses masculine to refer to a person whose gender is unknown or unimportant. For example, if an ancient text references a person who could be either a man or a woman, in both Hebrew and Greek it would refer to that person using the masculine pronoun.

In addition, some Hebrew and Greek words that can be translated as male in English, such as "man," can also be used for "anyone." When translating biblical texts, translators must determine whether a given masculine noun or pronoun in the ancient text should be translated as referring only to males or if in a given case the author intends both men and women. For example, Ps 1:1 starts, "Blessed is the 'ish (Hebrew for "man, person")." Should this be translated as "Blessed is the man . . ." referring only to a male individual, or should it be translated as "Blessed is the one . . ." because it pertains equally to men and women? Or should the translator retain "man," as the NABRE does, on the assumption that gender here is unimportant or that the reader is sufficiently familiar with biblical phrasing to know that "man" can mean "any individual"? Either translation is grammatically correct; either translation requires a judgment by the translator. Sometimes the context of the passage helps determine which translation is best, but that is not always the case.

Until recently, the divide between the ancient languages and modern English was not so stark. It used to be that English also used "man" to refer to all people, but the androcentric perspective of this language has caused

significant shifts in English. Most scholars and most educated public discourse no longer use "man" to refer to persons, people, or humanity in general. "Mankind" has been replaced by "humanity," or "humankind" as a way to better express that women and men comprise the whole of humanity. This change in English usage has prompted a majority of biblical scholars, responding to modern sensitivities and the potential for misunderstanding if gender-specific language is used, to use gender-inclusive language in their translations when referring to both men and women.

The Bible is not just an ancient text. It is a text read and proclaimed in churches and synagogues around the world. The translation of terms meant to address a contemporary audience has to be part of the judgment of the translation. As a result, most translators today, when faced with a situation where the gender of the pronoun is unclear, prefer to translate it in a way that is inclusive of both men and women, since the Bible as sacred text addresses congregations of men and women. Even in places where someone could argue that the original author might have had only men in mind, translators can still choose a gender-neutral term when the topic is one that today we know is pertinent for both genders. Therefore, when the psalmist might indeed be saying that "men" who pursue wisdom are happy (since only men were educated), today when a psalm addresses a modern audience, it can be argued that "anyone" is more applicable as men and women have equal access to education.

Lastly, there have been debates about the best way to translate pronouns referring to God in the Old Testament. In Hebrew, the pronouns for God are masculine, but the canon includes both male and female metaphors to describe God. Genesis 1:27 states that male and female (and here the Hebrew has the terms that mean biological males and biological females) are both created in the image and likeness of God. Did the Israelites consider their God to be only male? While there are certainly more male metaphors than female ones in the Bible, they are not exclusively male. The masculine pronoun would have been used if they understood God as encompassing both male and female attributes.

Translators vary on how they treat pronouns for God. Some use masculine pronouns only when the language of a given text clearly depicts God as male (such as Ez 16, where God is a husband). Others retain the traditional male pronouns throughout the text, although usually without explanation for why they do so. Some Christian biblical scholars maintain that Jesus' references to God as "Father" require male pronouns for God, assuming that by "Father" Jesus meant a male and not what could also be translated as "parent."

Debates about inclusive language for both humans and God continue to this day. The United States bishops, in the revision of the *New American Bible,* wanted to restore traditional language throughout the text so that the people in the pews would recognize echoes with other prayers and teachings in the Catholic tradition. This means that this revision of the Bible has less inclusive language than its predecessor. However, the translation was created specifically for liturgical use, rather than scholarly study. Therefore, translations that differ on gendered language are still helpful when studying the text both in its historical context and to understand its influence on contemporary society.

## Biblical Fundamentalism

Yet a third critical issue in biblical interpretation is correct understanding of texts in context. Biblical fundamentalism arises when readers fail to interpret texts contextually. A purely subjective and superficial reading of a biblical text can result in simplistic and distorted understandings. These historical and literary texts require careful attention to the context and cultural situations in which they were written. Authentic interpretation must seek first to understand the meaning intended by their original authors and the understanding of their original audience at the time in which they were written.

Fundamentalism is characterized by a rigid, dogmatic, uncompromising, and often uneducated adherence to simplistic perspectives in biblical interpretation. Yet fundamentalism is difficult to define because it is so highly individualistic in character and because there is no overarching authority that guides and governs fundamentalist communities and theology.

The following are some of the claims of biblical fundamentalism and the correctives offered by contextual interpretation:

- **The meaning of the Bible is self-evident.** Fundamentalist thought holds that any individual is capable of reading the Bible and receiving God's message accurately and fully. Because the Bible's plain sense is easily comprehensible, there is no need for outside assistance to explain what the Bible clearly teaches. The Bible means exactly what it says.

  In contrast, contextual interpretation insists that it is necessary to read the Bible with the guidance of good scholarship and pastoral helps. Since there is a substantial gap in time, language, and culture between the world of the biblical authors and the world of today's reader, the meaning of the Bible is not entirely self-evident. Interpreting the Bible accurately is a realistic goal, but it is not something that most readers can accomplish immediately and automatically.

- **Inspiration assures us that the Bible is written with infallible accuracy.** Fundamentalists hold that, because the Bible is inspired, it is completely and totally inerrant (free from all errors). For many, this view is reinforced by the theory of "plenary verbal inspiration," which asserts that every word of the original manuscripts of the Bible is exactly what God wanted it to be—and since God cannot err, the Bible cannot err. This understanding of inspiration is so absolute that the Bible could not possibly contain any factual, historical, scientific, or geographical inaccuracies or contradictions. The result of this uncompromising position is summarized in the popular slogan: "God said it; I believe it; that settles it." Since inspiration applies to every word, there is no possibility that it could have been said any better or any differently.

  The contextual understanding respects the human and historical elements of the biblical writings. While God may be the primary cause and ultimate source, the human authors were people of their own time and culture, conditioned by their own limited understandings and abilities. For this reason, contextual interpreters are not bothered by antiquated viewpoints and the incidental inconsistencies and inaccuracies that the Bible shares with other examples of ancient literature. (See also, "Contextual and Transformative Interpretation.")

• **The Bible is the sole source and authority for God's revelation.** Fundamentalists hold that only the Bible can communicate divine truth and the divine will for our lives. It contains all one needs to know, and there is no need to supplement it with other doctrines, creeds, or moral teachings. Fundamentalism discounts the very notion of a historical community, like the church or the synagogue, as the mediator of revelation and of authoritative teaching.

Contextual interpretation, on the other hand, acknowledges the communal context in which biblical literature was written and the necessity of tradition, human experience, and reasonable deliberation in understanding God's truth and will. Most contextualist interpreters would also acknowledge the necessity for an authoritative community and normative tradition outside the Bible to determine which books would be included in the biblical canon and to communicate divine revelation from age to age.

• **Only factual history is reliable truth.** For the fundamentalist, any challenge to the historical reliability of biblical accounts is a challenge to its truthfulness. The fundamentalist often historicizes texts that were written in a form that never claimed to be historical. To admit that any part might not be historically reliable is a challenge to the whole. So, for example, to question the historicity of the account of Adam, Eve, and the talking serpent of the garden could be a threat to the historical reign of King David. To suggest that the talking donkey in the tale of Balaam

in the book of Numbers might be legendary is as serious as questioning the historical crucifixion of Christ. To admit that any part is not historical is to question the authority of the Bible itself and thus threaten its sacred character.

The contextual understanding acknowledges that the Bible is made up of a variety of literary forms. Religious truth is expressed in this variety of forms, some of which are intended to be historical and some of which are not. The mythological language of the creation accounts, the legendary literature of biblical stories, the symbolic visions of the prophets, and the historical account of David are all ways in which divine truth is communicated in the biblical writings.

• **Biblical prophecy is meant to speak about events for our day and prepare us for the end of time.** Because fundamentalists see much of the Bible as a matter of prophecy and fulfillment, they consider it essential to determine how prophecy is fulfilled through events in the world today. Fundamentalist literature tends to divide the world into good and evil, attempting to demonstrate that the forces of evil are increasing in strength, and worsening world events demonstrate that the climactic events foretold in prophecy will soon take place. The end of the world scenario is mapped out through a literalist reading of selected verses cut from their context to form future scripts anticipated by current events.

A contextual understanding of the biblical prophets understands that this literature is primarily a call to justice and repentance, a challenge to change and to seek God's will. Although the prophets proclaim important truths for every age, their message is not intended to predict the details of a countdown to the end. The prophets of the Hebrew Scriptures as well as the apocalyptic teachings of the New Testament testify that God's will cannot be imprisoned in a predetermined script, and the time of creation's fulfillment is known only to God. The words of biblical prophets and the teachings of Jesus about the end call people to live in hopeful expectation of the coming of the Messiah and the completion of God's plan, while focused on the imperatives of conversion, justice, and forgiveness.

- **The Bible offers secure and certain answers in the midst of life's complexities.** Within the fundamentalist perspective, the Bible offers an emotional comfort to help people cope with the ambiguities and confusing choices offered by today's world. The Bible is a comprehensive answer book that contains all that is necessary for living a righteous life. Selectively chosen Bible verses offer a form of concrete certainty and ready answers to life's problems.

This overly simplistic approach to biblical study can be deceptive, offering interpretations that are pious but illusory. It injects into life a false certitude, for it unwittingly confuses the divine substance of the biblical message with what are in fact its human limitations. A contextual interpretation acknowledges that studying the Bible unfolds for the reader a long history of revelation accomplished through the communities of ancient Israel and the church of Jesus Christ and invites the reader into the grand narrative of salvation history. ■

# Sacred Scripture in the Catholic Tradition

## Stephen J. Binz

One of the great exhortations of the Second Vatican Council, enshrined today within the *Catechism of the Catholic Church*, is this: "Access to sacred Scripture ought to be open wide to the Christian faithful."[1] Catholic teaching goes on to clarify that prayerful study of the Bible should be a regular part of the life of Christ's disciples. This opening of Scripture to all does not mean just making the Bible available to everyone and encouraging them to read. In the Catholic tradition, the Bible must always be read in light of the contexts from which it came; that is, in the environment of covenant, community, and church. Likewise, the Bible must always be read in a way that considers the purposes toward which it leads; that is, word, worship, and witness. In other words, sacred Scripture must always be read within the framework of sacred Tradition.

Sacred Tradition, in the Catholic understanding, does not refer to beliefs and practices that are separate from biblical revelation. Instead, Tradition is the process of handing on God's revelation through the centuries. Scripture and Tradition are in no way separate from each other. Rather, Scripture is the heart of Tradition as the word of God is proclaimed, studied, celebrated in liturgy, and lived out within the church.

## Covenant, Community, and Church

The grand drama of revelation, in which God communicates with humanity in words and in deeds, takes place in the context of human history. In Christian understanding, the natural inclinations of all people to seek transcendence and to see the hand of God in the works of creation manifest God's self-revelation planted in the hearts of all people. The unity of Adam and Eve with God in the garden symbolically expresses this natural longing of humankind for God and God's desire to make known to all people his loving goodness. The choice of sin, though obscuring intimacy with God, did not end the human longing for God or God's relentless desire to bring salvation to the world.

According to Scripture, this divine desire to enter into a relationship with humanity results in a covenant. The story of God's covenant with Noah, remembered in the sign of the rainbow, expresses God's bond with the earth and God's promises to every living being. In covenant with Abraham, God began to choose a particular people who would be a blessing to all the nations of the earth. God revealed himself even more personally to Moses, and entered a covenant with the people of Israel by giving them the Torah. This covenant at Mount Sinai offered Israel a plan of obedience to God's commands and a system of sacrificial worship to celebrate and renew the covenant in every generation. The covenant with King David promised Israel a royal descendant of David who would rule over God's kingdom forever. Through the prophets, God formed his people in the hope of salvation with the expectation of a new and everlasting covenant written on the hearts of all people.

As the biblical narrative unfolds, God establishes a covenant with the family of Abraham, liberates Israel from slavery, and forms a kingdom under David. Through these acts, God prepared the foundations of the church, which he would call into existence through his Messiah. God revealed himself most fully to humankind through the sending of his Son, Jesus Christ. In him, God established his covenant forever, fulfilling all the ancient promises. In the church's liturgy and sacramental worship, God completes the pattern of temple and sacrifice established with Israel and continually renews this new and everlasting covenant.

Jesus inaugurated the church by preaching the good news and ushering in the reign of

---

1. *Dei Verbum*, 22; *CCC*, 131.

God. The chosen Twelve, with Peter as their head, formed the foundation stones of the church and, with the other disciples, shared in his mission and uniquely in the apostolic origins of the church. Christians believe that Christ, in his total self-giving, anticipated in the institution of the Eucharist and completed on the cross, accomplished the Father's saving plan and gave birth to the church. As he died on the cross, the wondrous sacrament of the whole church flowed from his pierced heart and open side. As the risen head of his church, Jesus Christ continues to fill her with his presence and saving grace.

Many people today desire to share in the life of Jesus Christ but choose not to associate themselves with his church. They claim that the Christian way has to do only with individual salvation and personal spirituality. This mindset is a striking break with the faith of early Christians. The New Testament demonstrates that denying the necessity of the church is a distortion of authentic Christian faith, that excluding the church is a loss of something absolutely essential to the gospel of Jesus Christ. From the very first, Christians have always believed that God reveals himself and establishes his covenant through community. Jesus formed a community of disciples who would continue his mission in the world and through whom his saving grace would be offered to all people. There are no Christians in the New Testament who are not members of this community called the church. Although biblical books and passages occasionally address individuals, the Scriptures usually address this public assembly of believers who are together working out their salvation in Christ. And since God "wills everyone to be saved and to come to the knowledge of the truth" (1 Tm 2:4), the gospel of Jesus Christ must be proclaimed to all people, so that God's revelation may reach to the ends of the earth.

Christians believe that God reveals himself in community before he is revealed in the written word. God was guiding the history of Israel and forming his people before a word of the Old Testament was written. Likewise, God was revealed through the earthly life of Jesus and the formation of his church before a word of the New Testament was written. The church was flourishing through evangelization, worship, teaching, and service before written narratives were even considered. In other words, God did not reveal himself or form his covenant through a written book but through the lived experiences of his people. The Bible was written by the people of God: the Old Testament by the people of Israel and the New Testament by Christ's church. The Bible is, then, the sacred literature of God's people, the inspired and lasting testimony to the community's experience of God's salvation.

In order to appreciate and understand the Bible most fully, the reader must be a part of that community from which it came. God's people hear, experience, and live God's word in the midst of that Spirit-guided community that God formed through divine revelation. This lived experience of God's people, handing on the good news of Jesus Christ, in preaching, teaching, and worship, is sacred Tradition. The church, ultimately, is not a "people of the book"; rather, it is a people of the Word of God, a Word that is living and incarnate, a Word who is, ultimately, Jesus Christ.

# Inspiration and Truth of Scripture

The Catholic Church teaches that all of the books of Scripture, in all of their parts, are sacred because they have been written under the inspiration of the Holy Spirit. Teaching that the books of the Bible are inspired literally means that they are "breathed in" by God. It is the breath of God, or his Holy Spirit, acting through human authors, that makes sacred Scripture the word of God. Paul's writing to Timothy declares this belief of the early church: "All Scripture is inspired by God and is useful for teaching, for refutation, for correction, and for training in righteousness" (2 Tm 3:16). Notice that the word for "inspired" is *theopneustos* ("God-breathed") and not *theograptos* ("God-written"). The Catholic Church does not teach that God sent the Bible direct from heaven, or that God dictated every word to the human writers. As God established his church at Pentecost through the divine wind and tongues of fire (Acts 2:3),

God formed the Scriptures through the divine breath and placed a flash of fire into the sacred word. Like the wind and fire of Pentecost that continues to form the church in every age, the same Spirit of God continues to breathe into the Scriptures. Inspiration is not just the experience of the human authors of Scripture thousands of years ago. God continues to breathe into the texts of Scripture so that they are always inspired and filled with the Holy Spirit, enabling God's people to experience the whole Bible as the living word of God.

The teachings of the Catholic Church express this mysterious reality whereby God is the author of Scripture who used human authors to produce the writing he desires to communicate to his church:

The divinely revealed realities, which are contained and presented in the text of Sacred Scripture, have been written down under the inspiration of the Holy Spirit. For Holy Mother Church, relying on the faith of the apostolic age, accepts as sacred and canonical the books of the Old and New Testaments, whole and entire, with all their parts, on the grounds that, written under the inspiration of the Holy Spirit (cf. John 20:31; 2 Tim 3:16; 2 Pet 1:19–21; 3:15–16), they have God as their author and have been handed on as such to the church herself.[2]

The Bible is the word of God in human words. This means that the human authors used their own talents and abilities, writing through their own understanding, in their own individual styles, and with their own personal creativity, to produce the inspired Scriptures. "Though [God] acted in them and by them, it was as true authors that they consigned to writing whatever he wanted written, and no more."[3]

In effect, the Catholic Church asserts that the process whereby the Bible took shape is incarnational; that is, it is both a divine and human development. While God is the primary author of Scripture and communicates with his people in a preeminent way through Scripture, it was written by human beings in particular times and circumstances, with all the limitations and historical conditions that are characteristic of the literature of humanity. The document on Divine Revelation from the Second Vatican Council expresses this dual nature of sacred Scripture: "The words of God, expressed in the words of men, are in every way like human speech, just as the Word of the eternal Father, when he took on himself the weak flesh of human beings, became like them."[4] Jesus is the Word made flesh; the Bible is the word of God in human words. If we undervalue either the divine inspiration or the human character of the Scriptures, we will not understand the Bible correctly as God intends it for his people.

The divine inspiration of the Bible does not guarantee the perfection of its human authors. However, because the Bible is inspired by God, the reader can have absolute confidence that the limitations of its human authors do not distort the truth that God desires to teach through his word. While this truth is communicated through the humanity of its writers, the reader can trust that the truth that God wishes to communicate through his word is "without error":

Since, therefore, all that the inspired authors, or sacred writers affirm should be regarded as affirmed by the Holy Spirit, we must acknowledge that the books of Scripture, firmly, faithfully, and without error, teach that truth which God, for the sake of our salvation, wished to see confided to the Sacred Scriptures.[5]

Some commentators interpret this important teaching to mean that Scripture is "without error" only in those parts that teach truths "for the sake of our salvation." This doctrinal text, however, affirms that the whole Bible, in all of its parts, teaches God's inerrant truth. The challenge of biblical interpretation is to discern what truth God wished to reveal in each particular passage. Clearly scientific accuracy is not part of the truth God wished to reveal in the book of Genesis. Likewise, historical precision is not the mode of truth God

2. *Dei Verbum*, 11; *CCC*, 105.

3. *Dei Verbum*, 11; *CCC*, 106.

4. *Dei Verbum*, 13; *CCC*, 101.

5. *Dei Verbum* 11; *CCC*, 107

communicates in the book of Exodus. However, each of those books is filled with saving truth that God wishes to reveal to the people he has created and redeemed. This truth is affirmed by the Holy Spirit, assuring the reader that the books of Scripture teach this truth "firmly, faithfully, and without error."

# Methods and Criteria for the Interpretation of Scripture

The Catholic Church has long encouraged a rigorous effort at interpreting Scripture objectively and faithfully. In 1943, Pope Pius XII wrote an encyclical that supported new methods of biblical scholarship. His teaching approved new scientific research, literary criticism, and historical study to shed new light on the meaning of the biblical texts. Pope Pius wrote: "Let the interpreter, with all care and without neglecting any light derived from recent research, endeavor to determine the peculiar character and circumstances of the sacred writer, the age in which he lived, the sources written and oral to which he had recourse, and the forms of expression he employed."[6]

In seeking the meaning intended by the inspired writers, the interpreter must take into account the fact that truth is expressed using various literary techniques and genres. Biblical truth is expressed, for example, in literary forms such as historical narratives, fictional parables, poetry, prophecy, prayers, visions, proverbs, and songs. Each of these different types of literature communicates God's truth in a unique way. The language of Scripture is often metaphorical or figurative, a means of expressing truth that is often deeper and richer than scientific or factual language. All of Scripture is God's inspired word, communicating God's truth expressed in the rich literary anthology that is the Bible.

The meaning intended by the biblical writers, that is, the literal sense of the text, must be the foundation of biblical interpretation. As Thomas Aquinas taught, "All other senses of Sacred Scripture are based in the literal."[7] This original or foundational meaning of the text is determined through various forms of historical-critical analysis, such as examining literary sources, stages of editing, grammar and rhetoric, and other forms of critical study.

Yet, Catholic scholarship does not identify itself with any single method of study and interpretation. A 1993 document from the Pontifical Biblical Commission examines a great variety of methods and approaches to Scripture, offering strengths and weaknesses of each.[8] While affirming the foundational importance of the historical-critical method, the document explores rhetorical and narrative analysis as well as sociological, psychological, liberationist, and feminist approaches. Each method can offer valid and fruitful understanding of biblical texts. The only approach to Scripture that receives an exclusively negative assessment in this document is the fundamentalist approach, which it describes as seriously flawed. (See also, "Critical Issues in Contemporary Biblical Interpretation.")

Catholic teaching insists that biblical interpretation be especially attentive to the content and unity of the whole of Scripture. The Bible is not just a collection of seventy-three individual books; it is also a single book with Jesus Christ at its center because of the unity of God's saving plan. Each part of sacred Scripture relates to all the other parts. No one passage contains all the truth on any given topic. Therefore, each passage of Scripture must be read in the context that surrounds it: first within the context of surrounding passages, then within the book which contains it, and finally within the complete canon, the whole Bible.

Documents within Scripture are often linked together thematically through quotations, allusions with key words, and thematic parallels. So, for example, Jesus' discourse on the Bread of Life in John's Gospel refers back to the passage in Exodus in which God gives his people bread from heaven in the wilderness. This link is expressed in the church's Eucharistic liturgy, as the first reading on the gift of manna in the

---

6. Pope Pius XII, *Divino afflante Spiritu*, 33

7. Thomas Aquinas, *STh* I, 1, 10, ad 1.

8. Pontifical Biblical Commission, *The Interpretation of the Bible in the Church.*

desert is followed by the Gospel proclaiming Jesus' gift of the true living bread. The unity of the biblical canon indicates that each passage sheds light on the other and that the fuller meaning of these texts is understood through these links within the canon.

Catholic teaching insists, finally, that Scripture be interpreted within the living Tradition of the church. This means interpreting in light of the doctrinal tradition of the church, including the Apostles' Creed, the Nicene Creed, and the dogmatic teachings of church councils. These authoritative sources of the church's Tradition play a critical role in Catholic interpretation of biblical passages. The church's magisterium, the authoritative teachings of the bishops united with the pope, has been entrusted by Christ with the task of interpreting the word of God authentically. In addition, other authoritative sources of interpretation must also be considered, especially the early church fathers, such as Ignatius of Antioch, Jerome, John Chrysostom, and Augustine. In addition, the doctors of the church, the writings of the saints, papal encyclicals, and other authoritative sources of the church's Tradition form the living context of the church's interpretation of Scripture. This rich tradition of teaching and commentary on the Bible helps Catholic interpreters to read the texts within the ecclesial contexts from which they came and enhances their understanding of both the literal and the fuller senses of biblical passages. (See also, "Contextual and Transformative Interpretation.")

# Apostolic Authority and the Formation of the Canon

The biblical canon is the list of writings defined as inspired by God and which form the norm of faith for God's people. It was not at all clear to the people of God which of the many writings of the Israelite and Christian communities were to be accepted as the word of God, or indeed, whether such a distinctive collection of books was needed.

The same Spirit-led community that was the source of these writings was also the authority that came to see which writings expressed its own faith. The inspired writings nourished the beliefs, teachings, and prayers of the community, and slowly but steadily these books were judged to be authentic reflections of their communal faith. The process of selection involved the reflection, inspiration, and authority of the church.

Although there was a developing sense of canonicity within Judaism during the first century, no definitive canon of the Hebrew Scriptures existed at that time. The Christian church began to set forth its Old Testament canon in the early councils. In the fourth century, church councils defined the wider collection of writings found in the Catholic and Orthodox versions of the Bible as it is today (see also, "The Formation of the Bible"). Yet it was not until that canon was challenged in the sixteenth century that the complete canon was solemnly verified at the Council of Trent.

The formation of the New Testament canon was likewise a gradual and steady development within the early church. By the middle of the second century, the Gospels and the writings of the apostles were being read in conjunction with the Old Testament in the Christian liturgy. By the beginning of the third century, the title "New Testament" was being used to refer to many of these Christian writings, and by that time most of the twenty-seven books of the New Testament canon were recognized as inspired Scripture.

Disputes continued over a few books, namely Hebrews, James, 2 Peter, 2 and 3 John, and Revelation. Other books that are not part of the canon were considered sacred by some segments within the church, especially *1* and *2 Clement*, the *Didache*, *Barnabas*, the *Apocalypse of Peter*, and the *Shepherd of Hermas* (see also, "Deuterocanonical and Noncanonical Scriptures"). By the end of the fourth century, there was general agreement throughout the church on the present twenty-seven books of the New Testament.

Again, the church from which these writings arose also determined which of them would be considered normative for the faith. Through the collective deliberation of the successors of the apostles, the bishops meeting in councils during the early centuries, the church determined her own sacred writings. The New Testament canon was settled using several criteria:

- **The writing originated with the apostles.** Apostolic authorship does not necessarily mean that a work was handwritten by an apostle, but certainly that it originated within the tradition of thought derived from an apostle.

- **The writing faithfully reflected the church's faith.** Works that were doctrinally questionable or contained esoteric messages were rejected, while those that expressed the Tradition handed down through the church from the apostles were understood to be inspired writings.

- **The writing expressed teachings for the whole church.** Works that contained messages only for a particular local community were seen as less important, while those that seemed significant for the catholic or universal church became widely known and were judged to be canonical.

- **The writing was used for liturgical reading.** Works that were read regularly as the church gathered for Eucharist came to be seen as sacred, enjoying the same status as the inspired writings of the Jewish Scriptures that had always been read in the synagogue and at the worship of Jewish Christians.

In this way, the church accepted that these works were inspired by God and that they proclaimed the truth that God wished to reveal to the world through Jesus Christ. The church cherished its sacred canon through the centuries as its standard for discerning God's continuing presence and revelation within the community of faith. The Bible became the anchor of the church's living Tradition.

## Word, Worship, and Witness

The church understands itself as living under the authority of the word of God. Consequently, it must be in continual dialogue with that word as it serves God's saving plan in history and looks toward its final accomplishment. The biblical texts must always be read in a way that considers the meaning of these texts within the dogmatic, liturgical, and pastoral tradition of the church. The Scriptures become only a dead letter from the past without this continual dialogue between the word of God and the people of God. The church listens to God's word and then responds to that word in worship and in witness.

The church is the living voice of God's word, bearing the living memory of God's saving acts in history. Its mission is to proclaim and spread the word of God throughout the world so that all people may come to the experience of faith. All the elements of the church's Tradition—the biblical canon, apostolic succession, the church's teachings, the creeds, the liturgy and sacraments—are oriented to this mission. These elements provide the continuity of the church's witness to the word of God throughout history.

In the encounter of the risen Christ with his disciples on the road to Emmaus, the church sees a pattern for its continuing encounter with Christ through the Holy Spirit. The Risen One first leads his disciples to Scripture, demonstrating how Moses and all the prophets are fulfilled in himself (Lk 24:27). He then leads them to the table of the Eucharist where he makes himself known to them (Lk 24:30–31). After encountering the Lord , the disciples then run to proclaim their experience of Christ to others (Lk 24:33–35). The word in the church is always a summons to worship and witness, to the encounter with Christ in the church's liturgy and to the work of evangelization and service.

The whole of God's saving work narrated in Scripture, completed in the death and glorification of Christ, is actualized in the church's Eucharistic worship. Here God's saving acts become present for the redemption and transformation of those sharing in the worship. As the old covenant was ratified and renewed in the sacrificial worship of God's people in the Temple of Jerusalem, the new covenant is celebrated and continually renewed by a new people with a new worship and a new temple, the body of the risen Christ.

## Sacred Scripture in the Catholic Tradition

In the church's understanding, the Scriptures emerged from the covenant renewal and liturgical worship of God's people in both the old and new covenants. The church's worship remains the living context for God's biblical word. The Bible leads to the Mass, and nearly every word of the Eucharistic liturgy is a quotation from or an allusion to Scripture. The Liturgy of the Word unfolds saving history through its proclamation of the Torah and Prophets, the Psalms, the apostolic writings, and the Gospels. In the liturgy, the divine word speaks to God's people in the present with life-changing power. During the course of the liturgical year, the Scriptural readings of the lectionary present the whole sweep of saving history and gradually transform believers into persons living in Christ. Then, in the Eucharistic Prayer, the word of God listened to in Scripture becomes the Word of God enfleshed in Christ. God's saving presence in word and sacrament brings worshipers into the great historical process by which the whole world moves toward its fulfillment as God's kingdom. ■

# Contextual and Transformative Interpretation

## Stephen J. Binz

Reading the Bible with understanding always requires some kind of interpretation. This necessity of interpretation is rooted in the differences in time, language, and culture between the writer and the reader that prevent immediate understanding. The greater the differences, the greater the necessity for a conscious effort at interpretation.

The issues involved with interpretation of the Bible fall under the field of biblical studies called "hermeneutics," rooted in the Greek verb "to interpret." Hermeneutics is the study of how to make the biblical text meaningful to a reader or community of readers separated from the original author and the community to whom the text was originally directed.

Biblical texts offer continually fuller and richer meaning to each person and to each generation without sacrificing their essential and foundational truth. As a living text, no passage of Scripture can be exhausted by a single explanation. Studying the Bible, in this sense, can never be complete; one can always go deeper into its riches.

The critical challenge of all who study the Bible is learning how to interpret the Bible properly. The meaning of any given biblical passage is multilayered, but the foundational layer is always its original meaning, the sense intended by the original author in the context in which it was written. For this reason, interpreting passages within their original historical and literary contexts is essential for probing their meaning.

The original meaning, however, is not the only aspect of the text to be considered in interpretation. Understanding the meaning of a text must consider the world of the author, the world formed by the text itself independent of its author, and the world of the present reader. Each of these contexts offers insights into the many-layered message of a biblical passage. Together they provide a treasure of meaning for understanding the Bible.

In Roman Catholic biblical interpretation, a primary role is reserved for the Church—its magisterium and living Tradition—in determining a normative understanding of the text. This understanding is reflected in the *New American Bible, Revised Edition* translation in the *Anselm Academic Study Bible* (see also the article "Sacred Scripture in the Catholic Tradition," for an exploration of Catholic biblical interpretation). In addition, this understanding is deepened by appreciation of the distinctive features of Jewish approaches to the Old Testament (see "Jewish Biblical Interpretation," for a fuller exploration of biblical understandings in that tradition).

## What the Text Meant and What It Means

Discovering rich layers of meaning in the biblical texts is part of what makes studying the Bible so interesting and rewarding. The sages of Rabbinical Judaism and the patristic writers of ancient Christianity considered their interpretation complete only when they had found a meaning pertinent and applicable to the situation of Jews and Christians in their own day. Interpretation means seeking to understand the text as a living word in the present, but always in continuity with the earliest meaning of the text in its original context.

The original meaning of a text is called the literal sense, the meaning directly intended by the original author and understood by the original hearers. This literal meaning must be distinguished from a "literalist" reading of a text; that is, reading it on the surface without any historical understanding. Scholars probe the literal sense of a text through the use of the historical-critical method, trying to understand its historical context and its literary history. This original meaning, intended by the author, is the text's foundational meaning. Any fuller or additional meaning discovered in a text must always rest upon the foundation of the literal sense. There can be no shortcuts to interpreting a biblical passage that bypass the historical aspects of its authorship.

In addition to the literal sense, biblical texts contain fuller meanings that could not have been understood by their original authors. This is a characteristic of any classical work of literature being read at a later period and in a different context, but it is particularly true of the Bible because these books are the foundational literature of living traditions. The religious communities continue to see richer meanings in their foundational literature as they confront new eras of history and new issues in their life as a community. When the writings were joined into the compilation called the Bible, this collection itself formed connections between the texts that no author could have foreseen, enlarging the meaning originally intended. Nonetheless, the fuller senses of Scripture can never be derived from the text in a wholly subjective way. Any meaning that is alien to the literal meaning can never be considered an authentic meaning of the text. Fuller meaning must always be built upon the original meaning and must be an organic development from the literal meaning.

The Jewish and Christian understandings of inspiration, that God is the primary source of the Bible, assures readers of faith that the biblical texts have vital meaning and contain divine truth for all times. This ongoing encounter over the centuries between the sacred texts and the community of faith uncovers meanings in biblical passages beyond what the original authors could have envisioned in their limited circumstances and adds fuller meaning to the original sense of the text.

The challenge of determining fuller meanings of a text beyond the literal sense is an issue of authentic interpretation. How can it be determined whether a later interpretation is legitimate or not? When does an interpretation

of the text cease to be *exegesis* (discovering meaning in the text itself) and become *eisegesis* (imposing a meaning upon a text that cannot be found in the text itself)? The challenge of genuine and faithful interpretation of the Bible is an ongoing quest in biblical scholarship, especially for Jews and Christians.

## Fuller Meanings within Biblical Texts

Here are a few different types of meaning within biblical texts that can be described as fuller senses:

- **The messianic meaning.** Following the destruction of Jerusalem and the Babylonian exile, the people of Israel began to look at the ancient covenant promises and the prophetic oracles concerning the house of King David in a new light. Since the monarchy had ended and many of God's assurances to Israel remained incompletely fulfilled, they began to expect a completion of God's work in the future age of the Messiah. This new meaning of ancient texts does not replace the original meaning, but enriches it with fuller implications and hopeful meaning.

  For Christian believers, the life, death, and Resurrection of Jesus established a radically new historical context for all the texts of the ancient covenant. The new covenant in Christ shed fresh light on the Old Testament writings and brought them fuller meaning. This Christological sense is the meaning expressed by the biblical texts when read in the context of the paschal mystery of Christ and guided by his Spirit. It always demonstrates a profound conformity with the literal sense of the text, while, at the same time, giving the text a fuller sense. The new meaning does not replace the meaning of the Old Testament text, but remains in continuity with it, retaining its original meaning while expressing its inspired fullness.

- **The canonical meaning.** Although each biblical book and passages within those books have their own unique meanings, these texts take on fuller meaning as they are understood within the context of the whole

Bible. Individual Hebrew texts achieved fuller meaning when read in the context of the Jewish Torah, prophets, and writings (Tanak). Older texts were often quoted in new contexts, giving those texts a new and enlarged significance. This fuller meaning of Old Testament texts was often expressed by New Testament writers. Through quotations and references, they demonstrated how the ancient texts pointed to the new covenant. For Christians, this canonical sense of the texts brings out the truth of St. Augustine's saying: "The New Testament lies hidden in the Old, and the Old becomes clear in the New."[1]

One way in which this canonical meaning is expressed is through *the typical sense*. This is the deeper meaning of persons, places, and events in the Bible when they are understood as foreshadowing future aspects of God's work of salvation. The "type" is a shadow or silhouette of the future reality. For example, the paschal lamb of Exodus is a type of the sacrifice of Christ (Jn 1:29); the passage of Israel through the sea is a type of Christian baptism (1 Cor 10:2). God's saving plan is characterized by a pattern of promise and fulfillment in which God's future realization is prepared through past revelation.

- **The communal meaning.** The Bible developed within the ancient traditions of Israel and the apostolic church, and the faith of these communities found expression in its texts. These sacred texts have shaped the development and renewal of these living communities in the synagogue and the church through the ages. The communal meaning of a biblical text is the fuller meaning of that text as it is understood in light of the ongoing experience of these active communities. After the biblical text has left the hands of its original author, the dialogue between the text and the believing community through time unfolds the text's fuller meaning. Because of this living, communal tradition, the act of interpreting is open-ended, and

no one interpretation of a complex text can claim to be the final, once-and-for-all meaning. The ultimate question of meaning is not simply, "What does the text mean?" as if the words had some abstract and isolated meaning, but "What is the meaning of the text for the believing community?" Understanding the Bible as divine revelation presumes a community that receives and responds to that divine communication.

# Considerations for Contextual Interpretation

In order to interpret the Bible in a genuine and reliable way, it is essential that we consider the context in which particular texts are situated. Failure to interpret passages in their context leads to superficial, simplistic, and fundamentalist readings.

- **Interpret in light of the historical and cultural background.** An immense historical and cultural gap divides the world of the Bible and the world of the modern-day reader. Just as it would be difficult for Ezekiel or Paul to enter the twenty-first century and understand our world, it is challenging to try to enter the world of the biblical authors. Yet learning something of the setting, situation, and customs of biblical times can help us immensely when interpreting the Scriptures. If we knew nothing about the Samaritans, for instance, we would read the parable of the Good Samaritan (Lk 10:25–37) simply as a story about a good person who helps another person in need. It would be a good lesson, but not the radical teaching Jesus intended it to be. When we understand that the Samaritans were despised as foreigners and heretics by the Jewish people, the parable becomes a sweeping support for universal justice and love of the outcast.

- **Interpret in light of the author's purpose.** Since the meaning intended by the original author is the foundational meaning of the passage, we must always try to understand the passage first from the author's point of view. Often authors will give hints as to the purpose of their writing within the book

---

1. Augustine, *Quaestiones in Heptateuchum* 2.73 (*Patrologia Latina* 34, 623).

itself. At the end of John's Gospel, for example, the evangelist states his intention in writing the Gospel: "These are written that you may [come to] believe that Jesus is the Messiah, the Son of God, and that through this belief you may have life in his name" (Jn 20:31). He wrote in order to enhance the faith of his readers in Jesus as the Messiah and Son of God, not to give us a detailed and precise biography of Jesus. By keeping John's purpose in mind, we will not be too concerned with why John's Gospel is so different from the other Gospels in respect to order and details.

- **Interpret in light of the literary type.** As an anthology of religious literature, the Bible contains epic history, poetry, laws, parables, prayers, symbolic visions, songs, and proverbs. The Bible contains all the rich diversity we would expect of a religious culture that spanned nearly two thousand years, from the life of Abraham to the apostolic church. Understanding the type of writing we are reading when we study any part of the Bible can carry us far in understanding the type of truth and the religious message of the text. For example, we cannot begin to interpret the book of Revelation unless we know that it is apocalyptic writing, a literary type that is written in situations of crisis. Knowing that this type of literature is filled with symbolic and mysterious imagery, we can come to understand that Revelation is not a factual forecast of the future, but a hopeful view of God's conquest of sin and death in the midst of trials and persecution.

- **Interpret in light of the literary context.** By reading a passage along with its surrounding verses and within the context of the entire book, we will be led to understand it better, and not force a meaning opposed to the intention of its author. For example, many throughout history have taken Paul's words, "Slaves, be obedient to your human masters with fear and trembling" (Eph 6:5), as biblical justification for slavery. But those words must be interpreted within the context of that passage, which is discussing how people in all relationships should be mutually

submissive toward one another (Eph 5:21). When read in the context of Paul's writings about the freedom the gospel provides, we understand that Paul was not promoting the institution of slavery, but was promoting new relationships within the accepted institutions of the time.

- **Interpret in light of the canon of Scripture.** The biblical texts take on fuller meaning when read in the context of the whole Bible. So, when we read a violent text of Scripture that doesn't sound as if it should be coming from the merciful God we have come to know, we realize that every Scripture passage is only a small part of the whole. When the people of Israel exact a destructive and vengeful conquest of their enemies in pursuit of what seems to be the direction of God, we can read that passage in the context of God's further revelation in the prophets, which speaks of God's merciful concern for all people.

- **Interpret in light of human reason and experience.** Rational thinking and sensible experience form a kind of lens through which we view and interpret the Bible. So philosophy and social sciences can be important auxiliary fields to biblical studies to aid understanding. For instance, if an ancient precept in the Bible seems to contradict the norms of universal ethics—for instance, the Old Testament justice imperative of "eye for an eye"—it would be important to explore the purpose of that law in its context rather than simply apply it to contemporary practice. The norms of reason and experience can help us establish a rational and consistent approach to rightly interpreting and correctly understanding the teachings of Scripture.

- **Interpret in light of the ongoing tradition of the community.** The history of Israel and of the church is the living tradition in which the books of the Bible were written, and it is the ongoing Jewish and Christian tradition in which these writings continue to be interpreted. We read in the light of the believing communities that have continued to understand new meanings within the text in every age. The Talmud of Judaism and the patristic writers of Christianity, for example, provide important matrices in which to interpret biblical texts. The traditions of the synagogue and of the church represent the ongoing life, teaching, prayer, worship, scholarship, and theological reflection of each community. (See also articles, "Jewish Biblical Interpretation" and "Sacred Scripture in the Catholic Tradition" for a fuller exploration of biblical scholarship in these traditions.)

## Transformative Interpretation

The Bible's written text resembles a musical score or the script of a play. The score is not itself the music, and the script itself is not the play. To become music and a drama, the score and the script must be performed. Similarly, the interpretation of the biblical text is the interaction between the written text and the reader. Each reader personally and uniquely engages the text, and in doing so further actualizes the potential meaning residing in the text.

When artists play a musical score or actors produce a work of theater, their interpretations are always many and various. However, not all interpretations are valid, nor are all interpretations equal in quality. The score and the script are always the norm. The objective identity of the piece has been established in the original act of composition. Likewise, there are many interpretations of a biblical text, yet they all must be in continuity with the text's original meaning. In the structuring of the literary work by the author, a text takes on a normative meaning. Though this meaning will certainly expand beyond the intentions of the author, the meaning built into the original composition forms the foundation upon which all other meaning must be established..

In an effective performance of a work of music or drama, the audience is pulled into the work. The music resounds through one's body and becomes one's own, or one gets caught up in the drama and that world replaces one's own. Similarly, when the reader gets caught up in the biblical work, so that the world of the text becomes the world of the reader, the reader more truly understands the text. When the Bible is interpreted in this way, it becomes transformative. No longer is it just a written, objective text to be analyzed; it has become a truth or a body of truths to be incorporated into one's worldview and made one's own.

Though the process of interpretation is unique to each reader, there is no such person as a totally independent reader. Our interpretation is always at least partly shaped by the social world in which we are members and the assumptions we bring to the act of reading. Our ethnic, national, political, and religious cultures predispose our judgments, influence our preferences, and shape the way we perceive reality. Our race, class, age, gender, sexual orientation, and religious denomination also influence the way we experience and understand life, and therefore, the way we read the Bible. Our pre-understanding provides insights into what is presented in the text and also limits our perception to aspects of our own life experience. The more we are explicitly aware of our predispositions, the more we can understand the ways the text either supports or challenges our beliefs and way of life.

One can read the Bible primarily for information, that is, to be intellectually enlightened, or for transformation, that is, to be personally changed. Though the two objectives are closely related, they are not the same. Transformative interpretation occurs in the interaction between a self-aware reader and the truth contained in the text itself. Here the objective is to go beyond the discovery of what the text says to the exploration of how the text is true and the personal consequences of that truth for the reader. The complete process of understanding takes place when one not only comprehends the text but also appropriates the text's meaning and incorporates it into one's world. This entry of the reader into the world of the text means different things for different people, but in terms of the Jewish and Christian tradition, it is variously called conversion of heart, entering the covenant, joining the people of God, and becoming a disciple of Jesus. This integration of the meaning of the text and the world of the reader is the ultimate goal of interpretation. The world of the text and that of the reader are fused in such a way that the reader becomes a changed person. When the reader engages the truth of the text in this way, the world of the reader is altered in such a way that he or she comes to live a transformed reality.

This transformative interpretation of the Bible can occur in any context, like personal reading or academic learning, but it is more likely to occur in a context similar to that in which the text was written and originally received—in a believing community. In the context of meditative prayer or communal worship, the biblical texts become more personal and immediate. The epic journey becomes my quest; the parable becomes my story; the characters become my ancestors; the psalm becomes my song. The discourses of Moses and the prophets, of Jesus and his apostles, are spoken to me, and to the community in which I live and worship. It is the difference between studying the score of a Beethoven sonata in a classroom and playing it in a concert hall. It is the difference between reading *Antigone* of Sophocles for a literature class, and experiencing it acted on a stage. This experiential, transformative interpretation is the highest form of biblical understanding.

# The Tradition of Lectio Divina

This quest for transformative interpretation of the biblical text is expressed in the ancient practice of lectio divina. This time-tested way of interpreting Scripture is rooted in Rabbinical Judaism and the patristic tradition of the early church. Through the movements of lectio divina, the reader of a biblical text is led to an encounter with God, who speaks through the pages of the inspired text. This meeting with the divine subject of Scripture invites the reader to a personal response and a gradual transformation of life.

Throughout history this practice of sacred reading has taken many forms through the writings of the saints and spiritual masters. Latin terms like *lectio, cogitatio, meditatio, compassio, oratio, contemplatio, consolatio,* *discretio, deliberatio,* and *operatio* have filled the spiritual literature to express dimensions of this ancient practice. The ancient art of lectio divina is not a rigid system or a set of required steps for a transformative interpretation of the Bible. It is rooted, rather, in an attitude toward the sacred text, a way of approaching the text with faith, openheartedness, reverence, and expectation. It trusts that the same divine Spirit who inspired the writers will work profoundly in the mind and heart of the contemporary reader.

This ancient practice, which was nurtured through the fathers and mothers of the desert and the church's monastic history, is today being revived throughout the world. The following are the primary movements of lectio divina along the path of transformative interpretation of Scripture:

- **Lectio—Reading the Text with a Listening Ear.** This first movement invites the reader to hear and understand the biblical text with as much care and understanding as possible. Lectio encourages the reader to use commentaries and other tools to uncover the rich history of interpretation and the multilayered meaning of the text. The reader carefully studies the words, metaphors, images, characters, and literary forms of the passage. The more one can comprehend something of the original historical, cultural, literary, and religious context of the passage, the better one is able to probe all the potential the text can offer. Yet lectio is not just an intellectual comprehension of the biblical text. Rather, it is a deep and personal listening. Saint Benedict, in the sixth century, described lectio as hearing Scripture "with the ear of our heart." Lectio encourages one to create a space within for the new wisdom and understanding God wants to give through the inspired Scripture.

- **Meditatio—Reflecting on the Meaning and Message of the Text.** This next movement seeks to bridge the gap between the world of the biblical writers and the contemporary world of the reader. By establishing a reflective dialogue between the ancient Scripture and the reader's own experiences, thoughts, challenges, and questions, meditatio can form connections between the text of yesterday and the circumstances of today. This more personal consideration of the text allows the sacred words to infuse our minds and hearts, permeate our approach to life, and lead us to embody the truth, goodness, and beauty of biblical writings.

- **Oratio—Praying in Response to Scripture.** Lectio divina is essentially a dialogue: listening to the inspired text and responding to its divine source. If God's Spirit has entered and inflamed one's heart through the sacred word, then one's natural response is prayer. Whether that response takes the form of praise of God, repentance for sin, petition for needs, or gratitude, the prayer resonates with the faith, hope, and love that fill the pages of the Bible. As spiritual writers have taught in every century, the style and vocabulary of one's personal prayer are molded and enriched by the biblical tradition. One's prayer becomes a healthy balance between the words, images, and sentiments of the biblical texts and the thoughts, needs, and desires arising within the one praying.

- **Contemplatio—Quietly Resting in God.** Another form of response to the biblical text is wordless contemplation. This is analogous to the response of awe and wonder that fills

a person after hearing a powerful poem or seeing a beautiful work of art. Unlike oratio, which is a response consisting of words, contemplatio is generally silent and wordless. When words are unnecessary or even impossible, one's quiet response is at a level beyond the intellect and reason. Spiritual writers have described contemplatio as a grace, a resting in God's Spirit that is beyond one's rational control.

- **Operatio—Faithful Witness in Daily Life.** The final type of response to the biblical text is the transformed life resulting from engagement with Scripture. The biblical writers teach that encountering the divine word must affect the way one lives. One cannot fully interpret Scripture without being personally changed. As James says, those who approach the text in this way become "doers of the word and not hearers only" (Jas 1:22). They become instruments of God's work, bringing about God's purposes in the world.

The complete process of understanding a biblical text takes place when one not only comprehends the text but also takes personal possession of the text and incorporates it into one's world. This transformative interpretation enables the reader to understand the breadth and length and height and depth of Scripture.

# Old Testament

# PREFACE TO THE NEW AMERICAN BIBLE

## OLD TESTAMENT

On September 30, 1943, His Holiness Pope Pius XII issued his now famous encyclical on scripture studies, *Divino afflante Spiritu*. He wrote: "We ought to explain the original text which was written by the inspired author himself and has more authority and greater weight than any, even the very best, translation whether ancient or modern. This can be done all the more easily and fruitfully if to the knowledge of languages be joined a real skill in literary criticism of the same text."

Early in 1944, in conformity with the spirit of the encyclical, and with the encouragement of Archbishop Cicognani, Apostolic Delegate to the United States, the Bishops' Committee of the Confraternity of Christian Doctrine requested members of The Catholic Biblical Association of America to translate the sacred scriptures from the original languages or from the oldest extant form of the text, and to present the sense of the biblical text in as correct a form as possible.

The first English Catholic version of the Bible, the Douay-Rheims (1582–1609/10), and its revision by Bishop Challoner (1750) were based on the Latin Vulgate. In view of the relative certainties more recently attained by textual and higher criticism, it has become increasingly desirable that contemporary translations of the sacred books into English be prepared in which due reverence for the text and strict observance of the rules of criticism would be combined.

*The New American Bible* has accomplished this in response to the need of the church in America today. It is the achievement of some fifty biblical scholars, the greater number of whom, though not all, are Catholics. In particular, the editors-in-chief have devoted twenty-five years to this work. The collaboration of scholars who are not Catholic fulfills the directive of the Second Vatican Council, not only that "correct translations be made into different languages especially from the original texts of the sacred books," but that, "with the approval of the church authority, these translations be produced in cooperation with separated brothers" so that "all Christians may be able to use them."

The text of the books contained in *The New American Bible* is a completely new translation throughout. From the original and the oldest available texts of the sacred books, it aims to convey as directly as possible the thought and individual style of the inspired writers. The better understanding of Hebrew and Greek, and the steady development of the science of textual criticism, the fruit of patient study since the time of St. Jerome, have allowed the translators and editors in their use of all available materials to approach more closely than ever before the sense of what the sacred authors actually wrote.

Where the translation supposes the received text—Hebrew, Aramaic, or Greek, as the case may be—ordinarily contained in the best-known editions, as the original or the oldest extant form, no additional remarks are necessary. But for those who are happily able to study the original text of the scriptures at firsthand, a supplementary series of textual notes pertaining to the Old Testament was added originally in an appendix to the typical edition. (It is now obtainable in a separate booklet from The Catholic Biblical Association of America, The Catholic University of America, Washington, DC 20064.) These notes furnish a guide in those cases in which the editorial board judges that the manuscripts in the original languages, or the evidence of the ancient versions, or some similar source, furnish the correct reading of a passage, or at least a reading more true to the original than that customarily printed in the available editions.

The Massoretic text of 1 and 2 Samuel has in numerous instances been corrected by the more ancient manuscripts Samuel a, b, and c from Cave 4 of Qumran, with the aid of important evidence from the Septuagint in both its oldest form and its Lucianic recension. Fragments of the lost Book of Tobit in Aramaic and in Hebrew, recovered from Cave 4 of Qumran, are in substantial agreement with the Sinaiticus Greek recension used for the translation of this book. The lost original Hebrew text of 1 Maccabees is replaced by its oldest extant form in Greek. Judith, 2 Maccabees, and parts of Esther are also translated from the Greek.

The basic text for the Psalms is not the Massoretic but one which the editors considered closer to the original inspired form, namely the Hebrew text underlying the new Latin Psalter of the Church, the *Liber Psalmorum* (1944[1], 1945[2]). Nevertheless they retained full liberty to establish the reading of the original text on sound critical principles.

The translation of Sirach, based on the original Hebrew as far as it is preserved and corrected from the ancient versions, is often interpreted in the light of the traditional Greek text. In the Book of Baruch the basic text is the Greek of the Septuagint, with some readings derived from an underlying Hebrew form no longer extant. In the deuterocanonical sections of Daniel (3:24–90; 13:1–14:42), the basic text is the Greek text of Theodotion, occasionally revised according to the Greek text of the Septuagint.

In some instances in the Book of Job, in Proverbs, Sirach, Isaiah, Jeremiah, Ezekiel, Hosea, Amos, Micah, Nahum, Habakkuk, and Zechariah there is good reason to believe that the original order of lines was accidentally disturbed in the transmission of the text. The verse numbers given in such cases are always those of the current Hebrew text, though the arrangement differs. In these instances the textual notes advise the reader of the difficulty. Cases of exceptional dislocation are called to the reader's attention by footnotes.

The Books of *Genesis to Ruth* were first published in 1952; the Wisdom Books, *Job to Sirach,* in 1955; the Prophetic Books, *Isaiah to Malachi,* in 1961; and the Historical Books, *Samuel to Maccabees,* in 1969. In the present edition of *Genesis to Ruth* there are certain new features: a general introduction to the Pentateuch, a retranslation of the text of Genesis with an introduction, cross-references, and revised textual notes, besides new and expanded exegetical notes which take into consideration the various sources or literary traditions.

The revision of *Job to Sirach* includes changes in strophe division in Job and Proverbs and in titles of principal parts and sections of Wisdom and Ecclesiastes. Corrections in the text of Sirach are made in 39:27–44:17 on the basis of the Masada text, and in 51:13–30 on the basis of the occurrence of this canticle in the Psalms scroll from Qumran Cave 11. In this typical edition, new corrections are reflected in the textual notes of Job, Proverbs, Wisdom, and Sirach. In the Psalms, the enumeration found in the Hebrew text is followed instead of the double enumeration, according to both the Hebrew and the Latin Vulgate texts, contained in the previous edition of this book.

In the Prophetic Books *Isaiah to Malachi,* only minor revisions have been made in the structure and wording of the texts, and in the textual notes.

The spelling of proper names in *The New American Bible* follows the customary forms found in most English Bibles since the Authorized Version.

The work of translating the Bible has been characterized as "the sacred and apostolic work of interpreting the word of God and of presenting it to the laity in translations as clear as the difficulty of the matter and the limitations of human knowledge permit" (A. G. Cicognani, Apostolic Delegate, in *The Catholic Biblical Quarterly,* 6, [1944], 389–90). In the appraisal of the present work, it is hoped that the words of the encyclical *Divino afflante Spiritu* will serve as a guide: "Let all the sons of the church bear in mind that the efforts of these resolute laborers in the vineyard of the Lord should be judged not only with equity and justice but also with the greatest charity; all moreover should abhor that intemperate zeal which imagines that whatever is new should for that very reason be opposed or suspected."

Conscious of their personal limitations for the task thus defined, those who have prepared this text cannot expect that it will be considered perfect; but they can hope that it may deepen in its readers "the right understanding of the divinely given Scriptures," and awaken in them "that piety by which it behooves us to be grateful to the God of all providence, who from the throne of his majesty has sent these books as so many personal letters to his own children" *(Divino afflante Spiritu).* ∎

# PREFACE TO THE REVISED NEW AMERICAN BIBLE

## OLD TESTAMENT

The first step in the genesis of *The New American Bible* was taken in 1936 when His Excellency, the Most Reverend Edwin V. O'Hara, D.D., chairman of the Episcopal Committee of the Confraternity of Christian Doctrine, invited a group of Catholic Scripture scholars to plan for a revised edition of the Challoner-Rheims New Testament, primarily on the basis of the Vulgate; the plans soon expanded to include the revision of the Old Testament. Archbishop O'Hara's initiative resulted in the formation of the Catholic Biblical Association, whose principal activity in its early years was this work of revision and translation. (For information on the work done on the New Testament, see the "Preface to *The New American Bible*: First Edition of the New Testament" and "Preface to the Revised Edition.") In 1943 His Holiness Pope Pius XII issued the encyclical *Divino afflante Spiritu*, which encouraged Scripture scholars to translate the Scriptures from the original languages. He wrote: "We ought to explain the original text which was written by the inspired author himself and has more authority and greater weight than any, even the very best, translation whether ancient or modern. This can be done all the more easily and fruitfully if to the knowledge of languages be joined a real skill in literary criticism of the same text." Although at this point work on almost twenty of the Old Testament books was completed or near completion, that work was abandoned and the new project of translating from the Hebrew, Greek, and Aramaic was undertaken.

The completed books of the Old Testament were initially published, as they became available, in four volumes: Genesis–Ruth (1952), Job–Sirach (1955), Isaiah–Malachi (1961), and Samuel–Maccabees (1969). Some fifty scholars collaborated on this project; these were mainly Catholics, but, in accord with the suggestion of Vatican II that "with the approval of the church authority, these translations be produced in cooperation with separated brothers" so that "all Christians may be able to use them" (*Dei Verbum*, No. 22), non-Catholics also participated in the work. To this point the translation had been known under the name of the "Confraternity of Christian Doctrine" or CCD for short, but when these parts of the Old Testament were combined with the New Testament in a single volume, it was given the name *"New American Bible,"* in part to reflect its ecumenical character. In producing the new volume certain changes were made from the original four volumes: a retranslation of the Book of Genesis, cross-references, new and expanded exegetical notes.

New translations and revision of existing translations are required from time to time for various reasons. For example, it is important to keep pace with the discovery and publication of new and better ancient manuscripts (e.g., the Dead Sea scrolls) so that the best possible textual tradition will be followed, as required by *Divino afflante Spiritu*. There are advances in linguistics of the biblical languages which make possible a better understanding and more accurate translation of the original languages. And there are changes and developments in vocabulary and the cultural background of the receptor language. An obvious example of this is the abandonment in English of the second person singular (use of "thee," "thou," "sayest," "hearest"), which had a major impact on Bible translations. Other changes are less obvious but are nevertheless present. There have been changes in vocabulary; for example, the term "holocaust" is now normally reserved for the sacrilegious attempt to destroy the Jewish people by the Third Reich. Concerns such as these are reflected in what Pope John Paul II spoke of as the "three pillars" of good biblical translation: "A good translation is based on three pillars that must contemporaneously support the entire work. First, there must be a deep knowledge of the language and the cultural world at the point of origin. Next, there must be a good familiarity with the language and cultural context at the point where the work will arrive. Lastly, to crown the work with success, there must be an adequate mastery of the contents and meaning of what one is translating"—and he praised the translation that "utilizes the vocabulary and idioms of everyday speech" ("le parole e le forme della lingua di tutti i giorni"). (From an address to the United Bible Societies, November 26, 2001.)

This new edition is a thorough revision of the already excellent *New American Bible* Old Testament of 1970. Work on most books of the Old Testament, begun in 1994 and completed in 2001, was done by forty revisers and a board of eight editors. The 1991 revision of the Psalter, the work of thirty revisers and six editors, was further revised by seven revisers and two editors between 2009 and 2010. As suggested in the comments above, the revision aimed at making use of the best manuscript traditions available (see below), translating as accurately as possible, and rendering the result in good contemporary English. In many ways it is a more literal translation than the original *NAB* and has attempted to be more consistent in rendering Hebrew (or Greek) words and idioms, especially in technical contexts, such as regulations for sacrifices. In translating the Psalter special effort was made to provide a smooth, rhythmic translation for easy singing or recitation, and to retain the concrete imagery of the Hebrew.

Where the Old Testament translation supposes the received text—Hebrew, Aramaic, or Greek, as the case may be—ordinarily contained in the best-known editions, as the original or the oldest extant form, no additional remarks are necessary. Where the translators have departed from those received texts, e.g., by following the Septuagint rather than the Masoretic text, accepting a reading of what is judged to be a better textual tradition, as from a Qumran manuscript, or by emending a reading apparently corrupted in transmission, such changes are recorded in the revised edition of the *Textual Notes on The New American Bible*. Additional information on the textual tradition for some books may be found in the introduction to the book in the same *Textual Notes*.

In particular, important manuscripts from Cave 4 of Qumran, as well as the most useful recensions of the Septuagint, have been consulted in the preparation of 1 and 2 Samuel. Fragments of the lost Book of Tobit in Aramaic and in Hebrew, recovered from Cave 4 of Qumran, are in substantial agreement with the Sinaiticus Greek recension used for the translation of this book. The lost original Hebrew text of 1 Maccabees is replaced by its oldest extant form in Greek. Judith, 2 Maccabees, and parts of Esther are also translated from the Greek. The translation of The Wisdom of Ben Sira is based on the original Hebrew as far as it is preserved, with corrections from the ancient versions; otherwise, the Greek of the Septuagint is followed. In the Book of Baruch the basic text is the Greek of the Septuagint, with some readings derived from an underlying Hebrew form no longer extant. In the deuterocanonical sections of Daniel (3:24–90; 13:1–14:42), the basic text is the Greek text of so-called Theodotion, occasionally revised according to the Greek text of the Septuagint. ∎

# Introduction to the Pentateuch

## Carol J. Dempsey, OP

"In the beginning, when God created the heavens and the earth . . ." (Gn 1:1) are the opening words of the Bible and the initial words of the Bible's first main division, known as the Pentateuch. The Pentateuch begins the dramatic and rich story of God's relationship with all of creation, and specifically with the human community. In general, the Pentateuch, also known as the Torah, is a body of literature that contains not only a wide variety of narratives and literary forms but also many laws, ordinances, and law codes. As a work of literature, the Pentateuch provides a window into primeval history and the ancient Near Eastern world and thought, beginning with a story about creation (Gn 1) and ending with Moses on Mount Nebo (Dt 34), viewing the land that has been divinely promised to the Israelite people.

Although the Pentateuch reads, at times, like a history book, the contents are not meant to be an accurate historical account of what took place, beginning with creation and extending down through the final days of Moses. Thus the writers and later editors of the Pentateuch were oftentimes more interested in describing and explaining why something happened instead of recording actual details of events. The Pentateuch proposes history, but relatively little of the Pentateuch's story can be verified historically.

The Pentateuch also proposes a religious and theological agenda that always needs to be considered in the context of ongoing critical theological reflection. The religious and theological lessons conveyed by the Pentateuchal narratives are just that: lessons. The Pentateuch ought not to be treated as a scientific document, especially with regard to the creation account, nor should the Pentateuch be viewed as a textbook or compilation of religious and theological truth statements. The Pentateuchal stories reflect the ancient people's experience of the sacred, which, like other biblical stories, are historically, culturally, socially, politically, and theologically conditioned. And yet the beauty of the Pentateuch is its ability not only to inspire but also to transform the lives of readers down through the ages.

## Title and Books of the Pentateuch

The title "Pentateuch" is Greek for *pentateuchos*, "five volumes." The title is not attested to before the second century CE. The Pentateuch consists of five separate books, each with its own integrity, but the books have been woven together by later redactors so as to present one continuous story. In the Jewish tradition, the Pentateuch is known as the Torah—the Law—and it is considered the most important division of the Hebrew Bible. Within the Jewish canon, these five books are regarded as having even greater authority than the Prophets and the Writings, the other two divisions of the Jewish canon, because the Torah was thought to have been written by Moses.

The five books of the Pentateuch are Genesis, Exodus, Leviticus, Numbers, and Deuteronomy. Genesis, the first book, can be divided into two segments: Gn 1–11, primeval history, and Gn 12–50, ancestral history. The book opens with the story of creation (chs. 1–2), which begins on a cosmic scale with the creation of the universe and the earth and all it contains (1:1–2:4a), followed by a more detailed description of the creation of plants, animals, and human beings from an anthropocentric perspective (2:4b–25). Clearly, the garden is the locus of activity, with human beings having a prominent role to play in creation (2:7–8, 15–25). The story of creation is followed by a series of narratives describing the transgressions of humankind (chs. 3–11) and God's response to such transgressions. Genesis 12–50 captures the story of four generations of a family: Abraham, Isaac, Jacob, and Jacob's descendants. Thus the narratives describe the origins of Israel as a people. These narratives fall into three cycles of stories: the Abrahamic Cycle (11:27–25:18), the Isaac and Jacob

Cycles (25:19–36:43), and the Joseph Cycle (chs. 37–50). In each of these cycles of narratives, the great patriarchs and matriarchs of Israel, namely, Abraham, Sarah, Isaac, Rebekah, Jacob, Rachel, Leah, Zilpah, and Bildad, as well as their children and other great women and men like Hagar, Laban, Dinah, Tamar, Potiphar, and many more characters come to life and provide a glimpse into the struggle of daily life lived under divine promise (see ch. 15) and, at times, divine judgment (see, e.g., 19:1–29). Genesis closes with Jacob's family reunited in Egypt, the place where Joseph eventually dies (50:22–26).

Egypt becomes the initial setting for Exodus, the second book of the Pentateuch. This book describes the oppression and suffering of the Israelites under the control of a despotic pharaoh who, unlike the benevolent pharaoh of Joseph's day (see Gn 47:1–12), feels threatened by the Israelites and thus oppresses them with forced labor (see Ex 1:8–22). Such suffering becomes the impetus for the raising up of Moses (Ex 3:1–12) who, under divine compunction, leads the people out of bondage (Ex 14–15) and through the wilderness (Ex 16–40) en route to the promised land. The climax of the Exodus story occurs when the Israelites reach Mount Sinai. There they receive not only a mutual covenant between their God and themselves (Ex 19:1–25) but also their God's law (Ex 20–24; 34). The Israelites have now become a "people" and not just a "family" as they were in Genesis.

Leviticus, the third book of the Pentateuch, continues the covenant law begun in Exodus. The contents of this book include many regulations dealing with sacrifices (e.g., Lv 1–7), the priesthood (chs. 8–9, 21), obligations of holiness (e.g., chs. 19–20), and feasts (e.g., ch. 23). Leviticus is the shortest book of the Pentateuch, and its main theme is Israel's call to holiness (20:26).

The fourth book of the Pentateuch is Numbers, which opens with the numbering of the Israelite tribes and their organization as a people on the march (Nm 1–2). This book describes the wanderings of the people in the wilderness for forty years. Such a long trek to the promised land of Canaan is on account of the people's rebellion against their God and their leader Moses (Nm 14:13–45).

During these wanderings, the Israelites have many different experiences and learn many lessons (e.g., Nm 21:1–9; 31). In the wilderness, Moses' successor, Joshua, is named (Nm 27:12–23; cf. Ex 33:11).

The last book of the Pentateuch, Deuteronomy, is often referred to as "the Second Law," which is what its name means in Greek. The text is almost entirely Moses' final instructional address to the Israelites (Dt 5–26), which includes an entire code of laws (Dt 12–26). The setting is the plains of Moab, located on the east side of the River Jordan. The book closes with the death of Moses in the land of Moab, which occurs right after Moses sees the land promised to the Israelites (Dt 34:1–8). Introduced in Exodus as Moses' assistant (Ex 33:11) and then as Moses' successor (Nm 27:12–23), Joshua now assumes his role as leader of the Israelites (Dt 34:9), which sets the stage for the group of texts that follow the Pentateuch.

# Authorship of the Pentateuch

The study of the authorship of the Pentateuch has a long and rich history. Originally and traditionally, Moses was and is thought to be author of those five books of the Bible. Only within the last few centuries has a thorough challenge to Mosaic authorship been launched. Among the first scholars who paved the way for questioning Mosaic authorship were Richard Simon and Baruch Spinoza, who noted that the five books were full of repetitions and contradictions and thus seemed to lack a single author. Though Jean Astruc supported Mosaic authorship, Astruc noted that Moses seemed to have used two different sources, A and B, in the compilation of Genesis. Johann Gottfried Eichhorn developed Astruc's approach and pointed out two strands in Genesis that he identified as the Yahwist (J) and the Elohist (E). Karl David Ilgen identified two strands of E and one of J, thus arguing for three sources.

Soon various hypotheses emerged with respect to the formation of the Pentateuch. Alexander Geddes proposed the Fragmentary Hypothesis. He argued that a series of unrelated fragmentary sources, which accumulated throughout many years, resulted in the completed Pentateuch. Heinrich Ewald suggested the Supplementary Hypothesis whereby a single core document E was supplemented by J and strands from the book of Deuteronomy. Lastly, Julius Wellhausen proposed the Documentary Hypothesis. According to this hypothesis, the Pentateuch is the product of four separate written documents, J, E, D, P, otherwise known as the Yahwist, Elohist, Deuteronomic, and Priestly writers. Formulated in the late nineteenth century, Wellahusen's hypothesis continues to be one of the leading theories of Pentateuchal composition, but many scholars today are more inclined to suggest that JEDP were originally four traditions that were passed down orally and eventually written down. Since Wellhausen, others who have made significant contributions to the question of the Pentateuch's formation include Hermann Gunkel, Albrecht Alt, Martin Noth, and Gerhard von Rad. Not until the 1970s did Wellhausen's hypothesis come under serious doubt by such scholars as John Van Seters, who questioned the existence of E, and Rolf Rendtorff who denied the existence of J and E as self-contained documents. The end of the twentieth century saw less of a concern for authorship and more interest in the theological message of the received form of the canon (canonical criticism) as well as an interest in the literary artistry of the Pentateuch. Although the Documentary Hypothesis has been seriously challenged, and the nature of the sources and their respective dates of composition remain much in doubt, scholars continue to work with the theory and its many modifications. Thus the authorship and the formation of the Pentateuch remain open questions, ripe for further study and investigation.

## Literary Fabric of the Pentateuch

The Pentateuch has a colorful literary fabric. First of all, within the body of the Pentateuch as a whole there are about twenty-five doublets, resulting in many contradictions. For example, Gn 1 and 2 contain one creation account but two different versions of it. The first version (Gn 1:1–2:4a) is typically classified as the Priestly version. The second version (Gn 2:4b–25) is traditionally labeled the Yahwist version. Other examples of doublets include the genealogy of Adam (Gn 4:17–26 and 5:1–28, 30–32); the flood story that has completely different versions woven together; the genealogy from Shem (Gn 10:21–31 and 11:10–26); and the Abraham and Sarah wife-sister scenario (Gn 12:10–20 and ch. 20), among others. Several historical places and sites are called by two different names such as Horeb/Sinai (Ex 3:1 and Ex 19:1–6, 16–25) and Hebron/Mamre (Gn 13:18 and Gn 18:1).

The Pentateuch contains a variety of literary forms. Laws take up a large portion of the Pentateuch. These laws extend from Exodus to Deuteronomy (e.g., Ex 20–22; Lv 12–15; and Dt 14–15), among other texts. Another form is genealogies (e.g., Gn 25:12–18; 36:1–43). Other forms include etiologies, narratives that provide explanations for a certain name or situation (e.g., Gn 47:13–26); rituals, which are descriptions of the way in which a community is to carry out significant ceremonies, such as the offering of first fruits (Dt 26:1–11); sacred traditions, references to the origins of holy places (e.g., Gn 28:10–22; 33:18–20); blessings such as Moses' final blessing on Israel (Dt 33); myths such as the story about the sons of the gods[1] (Gn 6:1–4); call narratives, especially with respect to Abraham (Gn 12) and Moses (Ex 3); poetic songs (Ex 15); and sagas, which are long, prosaic, traditional narratives that have episodic structures and that are developed around stereotyped themes, ideas, or objects as in the case of the family narratives about Abraham (Gn 12:1–25:10) and Moses (Ex 2–6). The Pentateuch as a whole is composed of both prose and poetry that expresses

---

1. Although the NABRE (and many other translations) render this phrase "the sons of God," a growing number of scholars are suggesting that "the sons of the gods" is more accurate. In Hebrew the word for "God" is ʾélōhîm, which is a plural noun form and thus can also be translated as "gods." What is significant in Gn 6:2 and 6:4 is the Hebrew definite article hā, "the." Hence the English translation for hā ʾélōhîm can be "the gods." In the context of Gn 6:1–4, "the gods" appears to be the more accurate translation over the typical rendering, "God," since the passage concerns the quest for immortality and refers to the Nephilim and the mythic warriors of old, i.e., Hercules, Odysseus, etc.

both narrative continuity and unity as well as diversity.

# Themes within the Pentateuch

Many themes emerge from the Pentateuch. One major theme is creation (Gn 1–2). Everything that has been created is not only good (1:4, 10, 12, 18, 21, 25) but very good (1:31). Another theme is promise. Various narratives within the Pentateuch describe promises made and promises fulfilled. Noah is the recipient of a divine promise that never again will the earth be destroyed by a flood (9:11). Abraham and his descendants are promised a land (12:1), which comes to fulfillment later on in the book of Joshua. They are also promised progeny (12:2).

Covenant, another major theme, is heard in the promise that God makes with Noah (Gn 9:1–17). Divine covenants are also made with Abraham (Gn 15, 17) and, by extension, his ancestors, Isaac and Jacob. A covenant is also made with Moses and the Israelites, which becomes known as the Sinai Covenant (Ex 19:4–6). For Israel, covenant means a sharing in blessing and righteousness, and Israel's responsibility is to act justly and rightly, to be in "right relationship" with God, with one another, and with all of creation. The Pentateuch contains covenants that are irrevocable, irreversible, and unconditional with respect to the God of Israel's love for the people. Besides divine covenants, the Israelites also make covenants with other individuals, as in the case of Abraham and Abimelech (Gn 21:22–34).

Complementing the covenant theme is the theme of law. Much of the material from Exodus to Deuteronomy concerns law. Two forms that the laws take are apodictic and casuistic. An apodictic law gives a simple command or prohibition (e.g., Ex 20:13–16), while a casuistic law indicates how to deal with a specific situation, if and when it happens to arise (e.g., Ex 21:20–21, 22–25, 26–27; Lv 5:1–6). Within the Pentateuch, many laws and ordinances are set down to preserve the "common good" among the Israelites (e.g., Ex 21:12–37). Other laws are of a social and religious nature (e.g.,

Ex 22:15–30). The Pentateuch also gives expression to an ancient Near Eastern law called *lex talionis*, otherwise known as "an eye for an eye and a tooth for a tooth" (e.g., Ex 21:23–25). This law was meant to be humane. For example, if someone violated the property of another, it was considered wrong to take the life of the offender; only if someone took the life of another could the offender's life be required.

Many of the laws found throughout the Pentateuch are grouped in law codes. Within the Pentateuch several law codes can be identified: the Covenant Code (Ex 20:22–23:19), the Holiness Code (Lv 17–26), the Priestly Code (various passages throughout the Torah), the Ritual Decalogue (Ex 34:14-26), and the Decalogue (Ex 20:2-17), otherwise known as the Ten Commandments. The Decalogue is the most famous of all law codes and is reiterated in Dt 5:6–21. The first part of the Decalogue calls the Israelites to be in right relationship with their God (Ex 20:2–7); the second part calls the people to embrace sabbath rest and to remember that this day is holy to their God (Ex 20:8–11); the third part calls the Israelites to be in right relationship with one another and with the natural world (Ex 20:12–17). The Pentateuch provides a rich understanding of the law which, for the Israelite people, is more than a set of rules and regulations. Torah—"the Law"—is a way of life that emphasizes an ethical vision of love for God, for one's self, for one another, for all creation. Within the law is a preferential option for those who are the most vulnerable within the society, namely, the poor, widows, orphans (the fatherless), and resident aliens or sojourners (Dt 14:28–29; 24:17, 19–21). Israel is called to obey the law so that the people can live on the land securely (Lv 25:18–19).

One major Pentateuchal theme is salvation, or redemption. The Pentateuch features a wide variety of stories and poems that celebrate Israel's God at work throughout history and through people, helping to save and redeem the Israelites from whatever is binding them or causing them suffering and hardship: famine (Gn 41:25–36; 47:1–6; Nm 11:1–9, 31–35); physical oppression (Ex 1; 3:1–10; Dt 26:5–9); transgression (Gn 9:1–17), etc. Israel's story of salvation begins with the bold and daring acts of two Hebrew midwives, Shiphrah and Puah (Ex 1:15–22), continues with the selfless act of a Levite woman (Moses' mother) who lets go of her baby son to protect him from slaughter by the Egyptians (Ex 1:22–2:4), and reaches its high point when an Egyptian woman—the daughter of the pharaoh—rescues the Hebrew baby boy who is sealed in a papyrus basket that has been sent down the Nile River. Pharaoh's daughter takes the baby as her own son and names him "Moses" (Ex 2:5–10). The Egyptian pharaoh has sent out an edict ordering the massacre of all boys born to Hebrew women; Pharaoh's daughter defies this edict. Through Moses, his deeds, and his leadership, the Israelites are freed from Egyptian bondage (Ex 3:1–15). Even as the Israelites approach the land that has been promised to them, the Pentateuch features Israel's God hard at work helping the people to defeat their enemies (Dt 2:26–3:22).

Other themes include forgiveness and reconciliation as exemplified through the story of Joseph and his brothers (Gn 42:1–47:26), deception and trickery as related in the stories about Isaac, Esau, and Rebekah (Gn 27), Joseph and Potiphar's wife (Gn 39), and Tamar and Judah (Gn 38), among others. Finally, within the Pentateuch, the dream motif comes to life. Several characters within the Pentateuch have dreams or are able to interpret dreams, all of which advances the plot and narrative action of various stories. Joseph's dreams will have a dramatic effect on his life and the lives of his entire family (Gn 37:1–11). Joseph's ability to interpret Pharaoh's dreams will secure him a position in Pharaoh's household (Gn 41). Jacob's dream gives direction to his life and brings him consolation (Gn 28:10–22). Thus the Pentateuch is a wonderfully crafted unit within the Bible, rich in literary form and technique with a variety of themes that bring to life an ancient people whose stories continue to inform, instruct, and inspire audiences today.

## Theologies of the Pentateuch

Many different theologies are present within the five books of the Pentateuch. From the book of Genesis, and specifically Gn 1–2, emerges a theology of creation. The first two chapters of Genesis describe how an ordered universe came forth from chaos and how each aspect of creation functions not only independently but also interdependently (e.g., Gn 2:3). Everything in creation is good; nothing is evil and nothing is to be feared (Gn 1:31). All of creation has intrinsic goodness by virtue of its existence and not because of its utilitarian purpose or worth (Gn 1:10, 18, 21, 25). The Priestly writer makes clear that all creation comes into existence by means of and through the Spirit or "breath" of God (Gn 1:1; cf. Gn 2:7) and that this God's spoken word is efficacious. In other words, according to Gn 1:1–2:4a, when God speaks, something happens. Within the creation story is also a theology of blessing extended to both the animals (Gn 1:22) and human beings (Gn 1:28). In the ancient world, blessing was a sign of affirmation that brought with it the gift of fertility and the ability to procreate (Gn 1:22, 28). Human beings are said to be created in God's image, according to God's likeness, which implies that they will have a share in the divine tasks of blessing, of participating fully in creation, and being good governors of and within creation (cf. Ps 104). With respect to creation, human beings are to exercise dominion, which means to care for all of creation—to "cultivate" and "care for" the garden (Gn 2:15). When viewed together, both the Priestly version (Gn 1:1–2:4a) and the Yahwist version (Gn 2:4b–25) offer a portrait of human beings that is complementary. Although sexual differentiation exists between the male and the female, both human beings are depicted as having intrinsic equality: "Male and female he created them" (Gn 1:27); "This one, at last, is bone of my bones and flesh of my flesh" (Gn 2:23). Finally, both the human beings and the animals share a common origin: they both come from the ground (Gn 2:7, 19).

Together, the Priestly and Yahwist versions of creation show that the relationship between human beings and the natural world, specifically the animals, is a harmonious order based on the Creator's justice and righteousness that overflows into the Creator's care for all creation. Furthermore, nowhere in Gn 1–2 is there any evidence of bloodshed or violence on the part of human beings or the animals.

Human beings do not hunt or kill animals for food; both are sustained by a vegetarian diet (Gn 1:29–30). Thus both the Priestly and the Yahwist versions of creation speak of relationships that exist among all aspects of creation in general, and among the Creator, human beings, nonhuman beings, and the natural world in particular.

A theology of liberation emerges from the book of Exodus. According to the text, Israel's God not only hears the groans of the oppressed Israelites (Ex 2:24) and observes their misery (3:7) but also acts to free them from their unjust bondage (chs. 3–15). How this liberation takes place, however, is in need of ongoing theological reflection. For example, the Israelites' initial liberation occurs through a series of divine "wondrous deeds" (3:20), otherwise known as plagues (see 7:14–10:29; 12:29–32), the worst of which is the tenth, the death of the Egyptians' firstborn children. The accounts of the plagues are both highly imaginative and fantastic, and their actual occurrence is debatable. For the Israelites the plagues are a welcome experience since they are directed against their Egyptian oppressors. For the Egyptians, however, the plagues are a heartbreak, and they symbolize liberation attained through violence. As it stands, the Exodus text seems to legitimize the use of violence to counteract injustice. History has borne out that violence begets violence and oftentimes only escalates violence without being transformative for all parties involved.

Two of the theologies that emerge from the book of Deuteronomy are a theology of retribution and a theology of love. Deuteronomy 28 outlines a series of blessings for those who follow God's commands (Dt 28:1–14) and a series of curses for those who are disobedient (Dt 28:15–68). This Deuteronomic theology of retribution becomes part of the fabric of the later books of the Bible and is countered by the Deuteronomic theology of love that reminds the Israelites that they are a chosen people, chosen out of love (Dt 7:7–11) and called to love their God (Dt 6:1–9) and to love their neighbors as themselves (Lv 19:18). For Israel, the essence of the law is love of God, love of self, and love of neighbor (Dt 10:12–22). To this end, they are to circumcise their hearts (Dt 10:12; cf. Dt 30:6; Jer 4:4) so that they can be a people of love. The book of Deuteronomy, as well as the Pentateuch as a whole, also makes clear that Israel's God is "the God of gods, the Lord of lords" (Dt 10:17). Israel's God is sovereign.

Other theological themes that can be found in the Pentateuch include a theology of remembering (e.g., Gn 8:1; 9:15–16; Ex 32:13; Lv 26:42; Nm 15:39–40; Dt 5:15; 8:18; 9:7, 27). The Israelites are called to remember their ancestry, their past experiences, and their God. Israel's God is called to remember the covenant. Worship is another theological theme. The Israelites honor their God through worship (Ex 33:10) and are warned against serving other gods (Dt 8:19; 11:16; 30:17). The Israelites are called to be holy because their God is holy (Lv 20:26), and they spend their whole lives trying to embody and live out this call. Finally, the Pentateuch presents a myriad of images of God, including images of God as creator, liberator, lawgiver, and judge.

In sum, the Pentateuch is a rich collection of five books whose authorship remains unknown but whose content continues to inspire and challenge people down through the ages. ■

# THE PENTATEUCH
## New American Bible, Introduction

The Pentateuch (Greek for "five books") designates the first five books of the Jewish and Christian Bible (Genesis, Exodus, Leviticus, Numbers, and Deuteronomy). Jewish tradition calls the five books Torah (Teaching, Law) because of the centrality of the Sinai covenant and legislation mediated through Moses.

The unity of the Pentateuch comes from the single story it tells. God creates the world and destines human beings for the blessings of progeny and land possession (Gn 1–3). As the human race expands, its evil conduct provokes God to send the flood to wipe out all but righteous Noah's family. After the flood, the world is repopulated from his three sons, Ham, Shem, and Japheth (Gn 4–9). From them are descended the seventy nations of the civilized world whose offense this time (building a city rather than taking their assigned lands, Gn 10–11) provokes God to elect one family from the rest. Abraham and his wife, Sarah, landless and childless, are promised a child and the land of Canaan. Amid trials and fresh promises, a son (Isaac) is born to them and Abraham takes title to a sliver of Canaanite land, a kind of down payment for later possession (Gn 12–25). Gn 25–36 tells how their descendant Jacob becomes the father of twelve sons (because of which he is called "Israel"), and Gn 37–50 tells how the rejected brother Joseph saves the family from famine and brings them to Egypt.

In Egypt, a pharaoh who knew not Joseph subjects "the seventy sons of Jacob" ("the Hebrews") to hard labor, keeping them from their land and destroying their male progeny (Ex 1). Moses is commissioned to lead the people out of Egypt to their own land (Ex 2–6). In ten plagues, the Lord defeats Pharaoh. Free at last, the Hebrews leave Egypt and journey to Mount Sinai (Ex 7–18), where they enter into a covenant to be the people of the Lord and be shaped by the Ten Commandments and other laws (Ex 19–24). Though the people commit apostasy when Moses goes back to the mountain for the plans of the dwelling (tabernacle), Moses' intercession prevents the abrogation of the covenant by God (Ex 32–34). A principle has been established, however: even the people's apostasy need not end their relationship with God. The book ends with the cloud and the glory taking possession of the tent of meeting (Ex 36:34–38). "The sons of Israel" in Ex 1:1 are the actual sons of Jacob/Israel the patriarch, but at the end of the book they are the nation Israel, for all the elements of nationhood in antiquity have been granted: a god (and temple), a leader, a land, and an authoritative tradition.

Israel remains at the holy mountain for almost a year. The entire block of material from Ex 19:1 to Nm 10:11 is situated at Sinai. The rituals of Leviticus and Numbers are delivered to Moses at the holy mountain, showing that Israel's worship was instituted by God and part of the very fabric of the people's life. Priestly material in the Book of Exodus (chaps. 25–31, 35–40) describes the basic institutions of Israelite worship (the tabernacle, its furniture, and priestly vestments). Leviticus, aptly called in rabbinic tradition the Priests' Manual, lays down the role of priests to teach Israel the distinction between clean and unclean and to see to their holiness. In Nm 10:11–22:1, the journey is resumed, this time from Sinai through the wilderness to Transjordan; Nm 22:2–36:13 tells of events and laws in the plains of Moab.

The final book of the Pentateuch, Deuteronomy, consists of four speeches by Moses to the people who have arrived at the plains of Moab, ready to conquer the land: 1:1–4:43; 4:44–28:68; 29:1–32:52; 33:1–34:12. Each speech is introduced by the formula "This is the law/words/blessing."

The Priestly editor used literary formulas. The formula "These are the generations (the wording can vary) of . . ." occurs five times in the primordial history (Gn 2:4a; 5:1; 6:9; 10:1; 11:10) and five times in the ancestral history (11:27; 25:12; 25:19; 36:1 [v. 9 is secondary]; 37:2). In Exodus and Numbers the formula (with slight variations) "They departed from (place name) and encamped at (place name)" occurs in two groups of six: A. Ex 12:37a; 13:20; 14:1–2; 15:22a; 16:1; 17:1a; and B. 19:2; Nm 10:12; 20:1a; 20:22; 21:10–11; 22:1.

Who wrote the Pentateuch, and when? Up to the seventeenth century, the virtually unanimous answer of Jews and Christians was "Moses." Moses wrote the Pentateuch as David wrote the Psalter and Solomon wrote the wisdom literature. Though scholars had noted inconsistencies (compare Ishmael's age in Gn 16:16 and 21:5, 14) and duplications (Gn 12, 20, and 26), they assumed Mosaic authorship because of the prevalent theory of inspiration: God inspired authors while they wrote. With the rise of historical criticism, scholars began to use the doublets and inconsistencies as clues to different authors and traditions.

By the late nineteenth century, one theory of the sources of the Pentateuch had been worked out that proved acceptable in its main lines to the majority of scholars (apart from Christian and Jewish conservatives) then and now. It can be quickly sketched. In the premonarchic period of the Judges (ca. 1220–1020 B.C.), the twelve tribes had an oral form of their story from creation to the taking of the land. With the beginnings of monarchy in the late eleventh and tenth centuries, the oral material was written down, being known as the Yahwist account (from its use of the divine name Yhwh). Its abbreviation, "J," comes from the German spelling of the divine name. In the following century, another account took shape in the Northern Kingdom (called E after its use of Elohim as a divine name); some believe the E source is simply a supplement to J. After the fall of the Northern Kingdom in 722/721 B.C., the E version was taken to Jerusalem where it was combined with the J version to produce J-E. During the exile (conventionally dated 587–539 B.C.) or thereafter, an editor recast J-E to make it relevant for the exiled population. This editor is conventionally known as P (= Priestly) because of the chronological and ritual interests apparent in the work. P can also designate archival material and chronological notices. The audience for the Priestly edition no longer lived in the land and was deeply concerned about its survival and its claim on the land.

Deuteronomy (= D) stands alone in style, genre (preaching rather than narrative), and content. How did it come to be the fifth book of the Pentateuch? The J-E narrative actually ends in Numbers, when Israel arrives at the plains of Moab. Many scholars believe that Deuteronomy was secondarily attached to Numbers by moving the account of Moses' death from its original place in the J-E version in Numbers to the end of Deuteronomy (chap. 34). Deuteronomy was attached to Genesis–Numbers to link it to another great work, the Deuteronomistic History (Joshua to Kings). Deuteronomy is now the fifth book of the Pentateuch and the first book of the Deuteronomistic History.

In the last three decades, the above consensus on the composition of the Pentateuch has come under attack. Some critics are extremely skeptical about the historical value of the so-called early traditions, and a few doubt there ever was a preexilic monarchy of any substance. For such scholars, the Pentateuch is a retrojection from the fourth or third centuries B.C. Other scholars postulate a different sequence of sources, or understand the sources differently.

How should a modern religiously minded person read the Pentateuch? First, readers have before them the most significant thing, the text of the Pentateuch. It is accurately preserved, reasonably well understood, and capable of touching audiences of every age. Take and read! Second, the controversies are about the sources of the Pentateuch, especially their antiquity and character. Many details will never be known, for the evidence is scanty. Indeed, the origin of many great literary works is obscure.

The Pentateuch witnesses to a coherent story that begins with the creation of the world and ends with Israel taking its land. The same story is in the historical Ps 44, 77, 78, 80, 105, 114, and 149, and in the confessions Dt 26:5–9, Jos 24:2–13, and 1 Sm 12:7–13. Though the narrative enthralls and entertains, as all great literature does, it is well to remember that it is a theopolitical charter as well, meant to establish how and why descendants of the patriarchs are a uniquely holy people among the world's nations.

The destruction of the Jerusalem Temple and

deportation of Israelites in the sixth century B.C. seemed to invalidate the charter, for Israel no longer possessed its land in any real sense. The last chapter of the ancient narrative—Israel dwelling securely in its land—no longer held true. The story had to be reinterpreted, and the Priestly editor is often credited with doing so. A preface (Gn 1) was added, emphasizing God's intent that human beings continue in existence through their progeny and possess their own land. Good news, surely, to a devastated people wondering whether they would survive and repossess their ancestral land. The

ending of the old story was changed to depict Israel at the threshold of the promised land (the plains of Moab) rather than in it. Henceforth, Israel would be a people oriented toward the land rather than possessing it. The revised ending could not be more suitable for Jews and Christians alike. Both peoples can imagine themselves on the threshold of the promised land, listening to the word of God in order to be able to enter it in the future. For Christians particularly, the Pentateuch portrays the pilgrim people waiting for the full realization of the kingdom of God. ■

# The Book of

# Genesis

## INTRODUCTION

The book of Genesis introduces the biblical canon in virtually every version of the Bible that exists. It describes the history of Israel from the creation of the universe until the death of the patriarch Jacob. Although it contains various genres, from mythic tale to genealogical list, as a whole it is a collection of narratives about the origins of ancient Israel's world.

## Significance of the Book of Genesis

The book of Genesis is an iconic narrative for Western culture. The power of the narrative is seen in how many of these biblical stories have become cultural icons. The most obvious example of this is the temptation of Adam and Eve (often misrepresented as involving only Eve), which is recognizable even to many people who feel no religious connection to the Bible. Although the contemporary cultural memory of the narrative often misreads the text, it still functions as a way to symbolize human failings.

Other Genesis stories have also fed the theological imagination. The story of the near-sacrifice of Isaac is a classic tale of what happens when deep human commitments, in this case to God and to family, clash. For the ancient Israelites, the name "Jacob" could be used to symbolize the whole nation of Israel. For early Christians, the figure of Abraham became a metaphor of how God saves those who have faith (Rom 4:1–3). The story of Joseph remains a powerful symbol of fate directed by the hand of a caring God.

In spite of the influence of this ancient text, many people today have little experience reading the book as a whole. Practicing Christians often rely on hearing only the portions of Genesis proclaimed in the lectionary, even though the lectionary presumes that the congregation

## Outline of Genesis

studies the Bible outside of Eucharist. When the book is read from start to finish, the artistry of the author, who weaves together a story fraught with tensions, becomes apparent. The actions of Abraham, for example, often defy what God has promised. Jacob, who is the very personification of the nation, is manipulative and stubborn. The ancient Israelites' account of their origins is not a story of heroes and heroines. These are people with all human frailties. God makes his covenant, not with a perfect people, but with real ones.

In all of these narratives, the central theme of the text is the intimate connection between the God called Yahweh and this particular people, Israel. God's promises of everlasting security, through land and offspring, are not revoked when the patriarchs act in all too human fashion.

## Genre and Themes

Scholars have long debated the genre of the book of Genesis. The preface to the NABRE alludes to this when it says that the book is neither fully myth nor fully history, although it has elements of both. Chapters 12–50 have been described as "saga," the tale of a family. But that definition does not fit well with chs. 1–11, which are closer to an account of the primeval period (i.e., the period of the formation of the world as we know it). This contemporary difficulty with reading the book as a whole is evident in a variety of contexts. For example, introductory textbooks usually discuss the creation material separately from the stories of the patriarchs and matriarchs. Even readers who think of Gn 1–11 as myth often mistakenly assume that chs. 12–50 are history.

The question of genre is crucial, as the Vatican II document *Dei Verbum* asserts. It is important to interpret the details of a text within the context of its genre. For example, poetic works, such as the Psalms, might use hyperbole and figurative language, which is improperly understood when read literally. In Genesis, Catholics have become quite used to the idea that the stories of creation in chs. 1–11 were not meant to be a literal description of the events of creation. These chapters use mythic motifs, metaphors, and story to get across the truths they intend to convey. Should one assume chs. 12–50 employ these same literary techniques? Do these chapters also use metaphor and story instead of reporting historical accounts of actual people? Are Abraham, Isaac, and Jacob mythic figures?

The biblical text offers at least one clue that the stories of the patriarchs are stories of a mythic era: the age of the patriarchs and matriarchs. In the cultures that surrounded Israel, one way of depicting a mythic age, that is, a time before the human and divine realms

were separated, was by having the people in the stories live exceedingly long lives. This was often coupled with the notion that people could converse with gods, and that people and gods could even intermarry. In Genesis, Abraham argues with God (Gn 18:22–33), Jacob wrestles with a divine figure (32:22–30), and "sons of God" sleep with human women (6:1–4), again, all signs that at least one of the sources for the book of Genesis viewed these people as belonging to a mythic age.

When the book of Genesis is read as a whole, it becomes clearer that this book preserves a number of stories that explain the origins of ancient Israelite society. The creation stories do so overtly. Genesis 1 describes the cosmos as an ordered whole, ruled over by humans created in God's image in order to exercise divine dominion over the world. Genesis 2 explains the origin of intimacy, the need of humans to have a suitable partner to share their life, their work, their vocation. The curses in Gn 3 reflect the hard economic life of the ancient Israelites, where the well-being of the family unit depended on men's ability to till the ground and women's ability to bear children. In the ancient world, both toils were heavy burdens that often ended in vain. Crops failed, women died in childbirth.

Genesis 12–50 is also concerned with the origins of aspects of ancient Israelite life. The saga of a four-generation family, these chapters narrate the adventures of a man whose name becomes "Israel" and who sires twelve sons, each a founder or "patriarch" of a tribe of Israel. These stories are not primarily about historical figures; they are personifications of kinship groups told through the narratives of each group's founder. The function of these stories as personification might be best seen in the story of the founding of Israel's nemeses, the Moabites and the Ammonites. Their father is Lot, whose daughters get him drunk and then sleep with him while he is passed out (Gn 19:30–38). This story reflects an Israelite attitude toward the moral inferiority of the Moabites and Ammonites.

A major theme in the book of Genesis is the covenant that God makes with Abraham, a covenant passed on to each successive generation. This covenant promises that the descendants of Abraham will become a great nation in the land that becomes Israel. Thus kinship, nationhood, and land possession are all linked in this foundational text. The sign of God's covenant with Abraham is circumcision, which marks the male body part through which the covenant is passed down to the next generation.

Kinship ties were the basis of Israelite society. Even in late Israelite texts, such as the book of Judith, genealogy is an important part of Judith's characterization. The covenant is transmitted through the family, but in ancient Israel that family structure was not the same as in modern society. The details in the book of Genesis presume the ancient understanding of family structure. Israelite society was patriarchal, that is, it was a social hierarchy where only men could own property, and only ownership of property gave the benefits of full citizenship. Women shared in those benefits by being either the daughter, wife, or mother of a land-owning male. Men could also have more than one wife. Wives were differentiated on the basis of kinship: daughters of landowners were usually wives, while lower-class women were concubines or slaves. Because women's economic security depended on having sons, wives are often depicted as competing among themselves for the attention of their husband. Wives also worried about infertility; an infertile woman could give her female slave to her husband to act as a surrogate for her.

In Genesis, we see all of these relational configurations. Abraham has a wife, Sarah, who has a slave, Hagar. When Abraham sleeps with Hagar, it is not at first clear if he claims her as his "concubine" or if she remains Sarah's slave. When Sarah asks him to clarify the situation, he states that he considers her Sarah's slave (Gn 16:6). This means she serves as a surrogate mother for Sarah. Later the text notes he has another wife, Keturah, with whom he has a number of children (25:1–2). Isaac marries only Rebekah, a kinswoman, but Jacob has two wives, each of whom has a maid that he sleeps with. Judah is seduced by his daughter-in-law Tamar, an act that is blessed by God because Judah had not provided a husband for her as he should have (ch. 38). Joseph marries an Egyptian woman, probably

signaling that some of Israel's tribes had Egyptian roots (41:45, 50–52).

What is important to note in these stories is that women are featured in Genesis more than in many other biblical books. In chs. 12–17, God repeats the covenant to Abraham three times, each time becoming more specific about what is being promised. In the last, clearest version, God states that Sarah (not Hagar or any other woman) must be the biological mother of the son to whom the promised land will pass. It is obvious that the identities of the matriarchs were also important to the covenant.

## Composition and Date

Internal evidence suggests that the book of Genesis is the result of a long process of compilation. Repetitions in certain sections of the book, contradictions, differences in literary style, and changes in the way the text refers to God all point to a text that preserves various oral and literary traditions. Although these inconsistencies were noticed at least as early as the Middle Ages, it was after the Enlightenment that scholars began constructing models of how the final author had woven together at least two written sources to compose this book (see the NAB introduction to the Pentateuch). In the late nineteenth century the seminal work of Julius Wellhausen fleshed out a four-source model for the composition of the whole Pentateuch, although only three of those sources could be found in Genesis. At around the same time, Hermann Gunkel demonstrated traces of oral traditions in this material as well.

Today biblical scholars identify at least one continuous source in Genesis, the Priestly writer (P), who has created a unified account through genealogies and other historical elements. Scholars disagree whether this Priestly writer (P) was the final redactor of this work, or whether the P material comes from an independent version of Genesis spliced in by a later redactor. The bulk of Genesis, however, is non-P material. Some scholars divide non-P material into a southern Yahwistic source (J) and a northern Elohistic source (E). The terms "Yahwist" and "Elohist" derive from the preferred terms for God (Yahweh and Elohim) in these two sources. This model can account for much but not all of the non-P material. Some scholars aver that the non-P material is too diverse to be neatly fit into only two sources, positing instead a rolling corpus of oral and written traditions.

The difficulty of ascribing only one model of composition for the book is that different sections seem to utilize different compositional techniques. The story of Joseph, a long narrative at the end of the book (chs. 37, 39–50), has fewer of the kinds of repetitions that led to the initial proposal of multiple sources. The flood narrative (chs. 6–9), in contrast, is a text full of repetitions and contradictions that has resulted from a final redactor splicing together two independent accounts of the flood. These differing compositional techniques have led to the conclusion that the final text in some way preserves older written sources and oral traditions within the same book.

Scholars debate the date when Genesis reached its final form, but it was certainly not before Israel became a nation-state around 1000 BCE. Even so, the stories have a timeless quality that make them capable of addressing audiences in a variety of historical circumstances. The focus on securely possessing the land promised by God could reflect an audience in exile, separated from that land. The notion that the ownership of this land is a God-given right could reflect an audience returning to that land after exile (sixth century BCE). Some scholars even suggest that the complex narrative style reflects Hellenistic storytelling, and date the final text to this late date (third to second centuries BCE).

Whenever it was written, the final author places the story in a by-gone era. The events that it describes are not datable, but the lifestyle of the patriarchs, their religion, and their economy place them in a time before urbanization. Just as modern stories of Sleeping Beauty situate her in an ambiguous time of castles and chivalry, so here the story draws on stock presentations of an era long ago.

The lifestyle of the patriarchs reflects this setting. They seem to wander from settlement to settlement. They own only one piece of property, a cave for burial (Gn 23:12–20). Their religion is that of nomadic people as well. They build altars at various holy sites and they worship God as a god of their ancestors. One of the elements of this bygone era is the way that God is portrayed in the book. In Genesis, God often takes on anthropomorphic characteristics. God walks in the garden (3:8), forms Adam out of the dirt (2:7), and enters into negotiations with Abraham over the fate of Sodom and Gomorrah (18:22–33).

## Conclusion

The book of Genesis contains masterfully told narratives of the origins of ancient Israelite society compiled by a final author who weaves together earlier oral traditions and written sources to create a text that remains iconic in Western culture. The book focuses on God's creation of the whole world, and the calling of a particular people through whom God will bless the whole world. Although the narrative provides background for the creation of a nation-state called Israel, it locates that foundation in the family, and asserts that God's blessings and promises are passed down through kinship groups, the most basic unit of Israelite society. These families carry forward that promise, not because they are heroes or saints, but simply because God chooses to act through them. ∎

# THE BOOK OF GENESIS

## New American Bible, Introduction

Genesis is the first book of the Pentateuch (Genesis, Exodus, Leviticus, Numbers, Deuteronomy), the first section of the Jewish and the Christian Scriptures. Its title in English, "Genesis," comes from the Greek of Gn 2:4, literally, "the book of the generation (*genesis*) of the heavens and earth." Its title in the Jewish Scriptures is the opening Hebrew word, *Bereshit*, "in the beginning."

The book has two major sections—the creation and expansion of the human race (2:4–11:9), and the story of Abraham and his descendants (11:10–50:26). The first section deals with God and the nations, and the second deals with God and a particular nation, Israel. The opening creation account (1:1–2:3) lifts up two themes that play major roles in each section—the divine command to the first couple (standing for the whole race) to produce offspring and to possess land (1:28). In the first section, progeny and land appear in the form of births and genealogies (chaps. 2–9) and allotment of land (chaps. 10–11), and in the second, progeny and land appear in the form of promises of descendants and land to the ancestors. Another indication of editing is the formulaic introduction, "this is the story; these are the descendants" (Hebrew *tōledôt*), which occurs five times in Section I (2:4; 5:1; 6:9; 10:1; 10:31) and five times in Section II (11:10; 25:12, 19; 36:1 [v. 9 is an addition]; 37:2).

**The Composition of the Book.** For the literary sources of Genesis, see Introduction to the Pentateuch. As far as the sources of Genesis are concerned, contemporary readers can reasonably assume that ancient traditions (J and E) were edited in the sixth or fifth century B.C. for a Jewish audience that had suffered the effects of the exile and was now largely living outside of Palestine. The editor highlighted themes of vital concern to this audience: God intends that every nation have posterity and land; the ancestors of Israel are models for their descendants who also live in hope rather than in full possession of what has been promised; the

ancient covenant with God is eternal, remaining valid even when the human party has been unfaithful. By highlighting such concerns, the editor addressed the worries of exiled Israel and indeed of contemporary Jews and Christians.

**Genesis 1–11.** The seven-day creation account in Gn 1:1–2:3 tells of a God whose mere word creates a beautiful universe in which human beings are an integral and important part. Though Gn 2:4–3:24 is often regarded as "the second creation story," the text suggests that the whole of 2:4–11:9 tells one story. The plot of Gn 2–11 (creation, the flood, renewed creation) has been borrowed from creation-flood stories attested in Mesopotamian literature of the second and early first millennia. In the Mesopotamian creation-flood stories, the gods created the human race as slaves whose task it was to manage the universe for them—giving them food, clothing, and honor in temple ceremonies. In an unforeseen development, however, the human race grew so numerous and noisy that the gods could not sleep. Deeply angered, the gods decided to destroy the race by a universal flood. One man and his family, however, secretly warned of the flood by his patron god, built a boat and survived. Soon regretting their impetuous decision, the gods created a revised version of humankind. The new race was created mortal so they would never again grow numerous and bother the gods. The authors of Genesis adapted the creation-flood story in accord with their views of God and humanity. For example, they attributed the fault to human sin rather than to divine miscalculation (6:5–7) and had God reaffirm without change the original creation (9:1–7). In the biblical version God is just, powerful, and not needy.

How should modern readers interpret the creation-flood story in Gn 2–11? The stories are neither history nor myth. "Myth" is an unsuitable term, for it has several different meanings and connotes untruth in popular English. "History" is equally misleading, for it suggests that the events actually took place. The best term is creation-flood story. Ancient Near Eastern thinkers did not have our methods of exploring serious questions. Instead, they used narratives for issues that we would call philosophical and theological. They added and subtracted narrative details and varied the plot as they sought meaning in the ancient stories. Their stories reveal a privileged time, when divine decisions were made that determined the future of the human race. The origin of something was thought to explain its present meaning, e.g., how God acts with justice and generosity, why human beings are rebellious, the nature of sexual attraction and marriage, why there are many peoples and languages. Though the stories may initially strike us as primitive and naive, they are in fact told with skill, compression, and subtlety. They provide profound answers to perennial questions about God and human beings.

**Genesis 11–50.** One Jewish tradition suggests that God, having been rebuffed in the attempt to forge a relationship with the nations, decided to concentrate on one nation in the hope that it would eventually bring in all the nations. The migration of Abraham's family (11:26–31) is part of the general movement of the human race to take possession of their lands (see 10:32–11:9). Abraham, however, must come into possession of his land in a manner different from the nations, for he will not immediately possess it nor will he have descendants in the manner of the nations, for he is old and his wife is childless (12:1–9). Abraham and Sarah have to live with their God in trust and obedience until at last Isaac is born to them and they manage to buy a sliver of the land (the burial cave at Machpelah, chap. 23). Abraham's humanity and faith offer a wonderful example to the exilic generation.

The historicity of the ancestral stories has been much discussed. Scholars have traditionally dated them sometime in the first half of the second millennium, though a few regard them as late (sixth or fifth century B.C.) and purely fictional. There is unfortunately no direct extra-biblical evidence confirming (or disproving) the stories. The ancestral stories have affinities, however, to late second-millennium stories of childless ancestors, and their proper names fit linguistic patterns attested in the second millennium. Given the lack of decisive evidence, it is reasonable to accept the Bible's own chronology that the patriarchs were the ancestors of Israel and that they lived well before the exodus that is generally dated in the thirteenth century.

Gn 25:19–35:43 are about Jacob and his twelve sons. The stories are united by a geographical frame: Jacob lives in Canaan until his theft of the right of the firstborn from his brother Esau forces him to flee to Paddan-Aram (alternately Aram-Naharaim). There his uncle Laban tricks him as he earlier tricked his brother. But Jacob is blessed with wealth and sons. He returns to Canaan to receive the final blessing, land, and on the way is reconciled with his brother Esau. As the sons have reached the number of twelve, the patriarch can be given the name Israel (32:28; 35:10). The blessings given to Abraham are reaffirmed to Isaac and to Jacob.

The last cycle of ancestor stories is about Jacob's son Joseph (37:1–50:26, though in chaps. 48–49 the focus swings back to Jacob). The Joseph stories are sophisticated in theme, deftly plotted, and show keen interest in the psychology of the characters. Jacob's favoring of Joseph, the son of his beloved wife Rachel, provokes his brothers to kill him. Joseph escapes death through the intercession of Reuben, the eldest, and of Judah, but is sold into slavery in Egypt. In the immediately following chap. 38, Judah undergoes experiences similar to Joseph's. Joseph, endowed by God with wisdom, becomes second only to Pharaoh in Egypt. From that powerful position, he encounters his unsuspecting brothers who have come to Egypt because of the famine, and tests them to see if they have repented. Joseph learns that they have given up their hatred because of their love for Israel, their father. Judah, who seems to have inherited the mantle of the failed oldest brother Reuben, expresses the brothers' new and profound appreciation of their father and Joseph (chap. 44). At the end of Genesis, the entire family of Jacob/Israel is in Egypt, which prepares for the events in the Book of Exodus.

**Genesis in Later Biblical Books.** The historical and prophetic books constantly refer to the covenant with the ancestors Abraham, Isaac, and Jacob. Hos 10 sees the traits of Jacob in the behavior of the Israel of his own day. Is 51:2 cites Abraham and Sarah as a model for his dispirited community, for though only a couple, they became a great nation. Jn 1, "In the beginning was the word," alludes to Gn 1:1 (and Prv 8:22) to show that Jesus is creating a new world. St. Paul interprets Jesus as the New Adam in Rom 5:14 and 1 Cor 15:22, 24, whose obedience brings life just as the Old Adam's disobedience brought death. In Rom 4, Paul cites Abraham as someone who was righteous in God's eyes centuries before the Law was given at Sinai.

### Outline of Genesis

Preamble. The Creation of the World (1:1–2:3)

I. The Story of the Nations (2:4–11:26)
  A. The Creation of the Man and the Woman, Their Offspring, and the Spread of Civilization (2:4–4:26)
  B. The Pre-flood Generations (5:1–6:8)
  C. The Flood and the Renewed Blessing (6:9–9:29)
  D. The Populating of the World and the Prideful City (10:1–11:9)
  E. The Genealogy from Shem to Terah (11:10–26)

II. The Story of the Ancestors of Israel (11:27–50:26)
  A. The Story of Abraham and Sarah (11:27–25:18)
  B. The Story of Isaac and Jacob (25:19–36:43)
  C. The Story of Joseph (37:1–50:26) ∎

# GENESIS

## PREAMBLE. THE CREATION OF THE WORLD

**1** **The Story of Creation.**† [1] In the beginning, when God created the heavens and the earth*—[2]† and the earth was without form or shape, with darkness over the abyss and a mighty wind sweeping over the waters—*

[3] Then God said: Let there be light, and there was light.* [4] God saw that the light was good. God then separated the light from the darkness. [5] God called the light "day," and the darkness he called "night." Evening came, and morning followed—the first day.†

[6] Then God said: Let there be a dome in the middle of the waters, to separate one body of water from the other. [7] God made the dome,† and it separated the water below the dome from the water above the dome. And so it happened.* [8] God called the dome "sky." Evening came, and morning followed—the second day.

[9] Then God said: Let the water under the sky be gathered into a single basin, so that the dry land may appear. And so it happened: the water under the sky was gathered into its basin, and the dry land appeared.* [10] God called the dry land "earth," and the basin of water he called "sea." God saw that it was good. [11]* Then God said: Let the earth bring forth vegetation: every kind of plant that bears seed and every kind of fruit tree on earth that bears fruit with its seed in it. And so it happened: [12] the earth brought forth vegetation: every kind of plant that bears seed and every kind of fruit tree that bears fruit with its seed in it. God saw that it was good. [13] Evening came, and morning followed—the third day.

[14] Then God said: Let there be lights in the dome of the sky, to separate day from night. Let them mark the seasons, the days and the years,* [15] and serve as lights in the dome of the sky, to illuminate the earth. And so it happened: [16] God made the two great lights, the greater one to govern the day, and the lesser one to govern the night, and the stars.* [17] God set them in the dome of the sky, to illuminate the earth, [18] to govern the day and the night, and to separate the light from the darkness. God saw that it was good. [19] Evening came, and morning followed—the fourth day.

[20]* Then God said: Let the water teem with an abundance of living creatures, and on the earth let birds fly beneath the dome of the sky. [21] God created the great sea monsters and all kinds of crawling living creatures with which the water teems, and all kinds of winged birds. God saw that it was good, [22] and God blessed

---

† **1:1–2:3** This section, from the Priestly source, functions as an introduction, as ancient stories of the origin of the world (cosmogonies) often did. It introduces the primordial story (2:4–11:26), the stories of the ancestors (11:27–50:26), and indeed the whole Pentateuch. The chapter highlights the goodness of creation and the divine desire that human beings share in that goodness. God brings an orderly universe out of primordial chaos merely by uttering a word. In the literary structure of six days, the creation events in the first three days are related to those in the second three.

1. light (day)/darkness (night) = 4. sun/moon
2. arrangement of water = 5. fish + birds from waters
3. a) dry land = 6. a) animals
   b) vegetation      b) human beings:
                        male/female

The seventh day, on which God rests, the climax of the account, falls outside the six-day structure.

Until modern times the first line was always translated, "In the beginning God created the heavens and the earth." Several comparable ancient cosmogonies, discovered in recent times, have a "when...then" construction, confirming the translation "when...then" here as well. "When" introduces the pre-creation state and "then" introduces the creative act affecting that state. The traditional translation, "In the beginning," does not reflect the Hebrew syntax of the clause.

**1:2** This verse is parenthetical, describing in three phases the pre-creation state symbolized by the chaos out of which God brings order: "earth," hidden beneath the encompassing cosmic waters, could not be seen, and thus had no "form"; there was only darkness; turbulent wind swept over the waters. Commenc-

ing with the last-named elements (darkness and water), vv. 3–10 describe the rearrangement of this chaos: light is made (first day) and the water is divided into water above and water below the earth so that the earth appears and is no longer "without outline." *The abyss:* the primordial ocean according to the ancient Semitic cosmogony. After God's creative activity, part of this vast body forms the salt-water seas (vv. 9–10); part of it is the fresh water under the earth (Ps 33:7; Ez 31:4), which wells forth on the earth as springs and fountains (Gn 7:11; 8:2; Prv 3:20). Part of it, "the upper water" (Ps 148:4; Dn 3:60), is held up by the dome of the sky (vv. 6–7), from which rain descends on the earth (Gn 7:11; 2 Kgs 7:2, 19; Ps 104:13). *A mighty wind:* literally, "spirit or breath [ruah] of God"; cf. Gn 8:1.

**1:5** In ancient Israel a day was considered to begin at sunset.

**1:7** *The dome:* the Hebrew word suggests a gigantic metal dome. It was inserted into the middle of the single body of water to form dry space within which the earth could emerge. The Latin Vulgate translation *firmamentum*, "means of support (for the upper waters); firmament," provided the traditional English rendering.

---

* **1:1** Gn 2:1, 4; 2 Mc 7:28; Ps 8:4; 33:6; 89:12; 90:2; Wis 11:17; Sir 16:24; Jer 10:12; Acts 14:15; Col 1:16–17; Heb 1:2–3; 3:4; 11:3; Rev 4:11. **1:2** Jer 4:23. **1:3** 2 Cor 4:6.
**1:7** Prv 8:27–28; 2 Pt 3:5. **1:9** Jb 38:8; Ps 33:7; Jer 5:22. **1:11** Ps 104:14. **1:14** Jb 26:10; Ps 19:2–3; Bar 3:33. **1:16** Dt 4:19; Ps 136:7–9; Wis 13:2–4; Jer 31:35. **1:20** Jb 12:7–10.

them, saying: Be fertile, multiply, and fill the water of the seas; and let the birds multiply on the earth.* [23] Evening came, and morning followed—the fifth day.

[24]* Then God said: Let the earth bring forth every kind of living creature: tame animals, crawling things, and every kind of wild animal. And so it happened: [25] God made every kind of wild animal, every kind of tame animal, and every kind of thing that crawls on the ground. God saw that it was good. [26]* Then God said: Let us make† human beings in our image, after our likeness. Let them have dominion over the fish of the sea, the birds of the air, the tame animals, all the wild animals, and all the creatures that crawl on the earth.

[27]  God created mankind in his image;
      in the image of God he created them;
      male and female† he created them.

[28] God blessed them and God said to them: Be fertile and multiply; fill the earth and subdue it.† Have dominion over the fish of the sea, the birds of the air, and all the living things

that crawl on the earth.* [29]†* God also said: See, I give you every seed-bearing plant on all the earth and every tree that has seed-bearing fruit on it to be your food; [30] and to all the wild animals, all the birds of the air, and all the living creatures that crawl on the earth, I give all the green plants for food. And so it happened. [31] God looked at everything he had made, and found it very good. Evening came, and morning followed—the sixth day.*

**2** [1] Thus the heavens and the earth and all their array were completed.* [2]† On the seventh day God completed the work he had been doing; he rested on the seventh day from all the work he had undertaken.* [3] God blessed the seventh day and made it holy, because on it he rested from all the work he had done in creation.*

## I. THE STORY OF THE NATIONS

**The Garden of Eden.** [4] This is the story† of the heavens and the earth at their creation. When the LORD God made the earth and the

---

**1:26** *Let us make*: in the ancient Near East, and sometimes in the Bible, God was imagined as presiding over an assembly of heavenly beings who deliberated and decided about matters on earth (1 Kgs 22:19–22; Is 6:8; Ps 29:1–2; 82; 89:6–7; Jb 1:6; 2:1; 38:7). This scene accounts for the plural form here and in Gn 11:7 ("Let us then go down…"). Israel's God was always considered "Most High" over the heavenly beings. *Human beings*: Hebrew *'ādām* is here the generic term for humankind; in the first five chapters of Genesis it is the proper name Adam only at 4:25 and 5:1–5. *In our image, after our likeness*: "image" and "likeness" (virtually synonyms) express the worth of human beings who have value in themselves (human blood may not be shed in 9:6 because of this image of God) and in their task, dominion (1:28), which promotes the rule of God over the universe.
**1:27** *Male and female*: as God provided the plants with seeds (vv. 11, 12) and commanded the animals to be fertile and multiply (v. 22), so God gives sexuality to human beings as their means to continue in existence.
**1:28** *Fill the earth and subdue it*: the object of the verb "subdue" may be not the earth as such but earth as the territory each nation must take for itself (chaps. 10–11), just as Israel will later do (see Nm 32:22, 29; Jos 18:1). The two divine commands define the basic tasks of the human race—to continue in existence through generation and to take possession of one's God-given territory. The dual command would have had special meaning when Israel was in exile and deeply anxious about whether they would continue as a nation and return to their ancient territory. *Have dominion*: the whole human race is made in the "image" and "likeness" of God and has "dominion." Comparable literature of the time used these words of kings rather than of human beings in general; human beings were invariably thought of as slaves of the gods created to provide menial service for the divine world. The royal language here does not, however, give human beings unlimited power, for kings in the Bible had limited dominion and were subject to prophetic critique.
**1:29** According to the Priestly tradition, the human race was originally intended to live on plants and fruits as were the animals (see v. 30), an arrangement that God will later change (9:3) in view of the human inclination to violence.

**2:2** The mention of the seventh day, repeated in v. 3, is outside the series of six days and is thus the climax of the account. The focus of the account is God. The text does not actually institute the practice of keeping the Sabbath, for it would have been anachronistic to establish at this point a custom that was distinctively Israelite (Ex 31:13, 16, 17), but it lays the foundation for the later practice. Similarly, ancient creation accounts often ended with the construction of a temple where the newly created human race provided service to the gods who created them, but no temple is mentioned in this account. As was the case with the Sabbath, it would have been anachronistic to institute the temple at this point, for Israel did not yet exist. In Ex 25–31 and 35–40, Israel builds the tabernacle, which is the precursor of the Temple of Solomon.
**2:4** *This is the story*: the distinctive Priestly formula introduces older traditions, belonging to the tradition called Yahwist, and gives them a new setting. In the first part of Genesis, the formula "this is the story" (or a similar phrase) occurs five times (2:4; 5:1; 6:9; 10:1; 11:10), which corresponds to the five occurrences of the formula in the second part of the book (11:27; 25:12, 19; 36:1[9]; 37:2). Some interpret the formula here as retrospective ("Such is the story"), referring back to chap. 1, but all its other occurrences introduce rather than summarize. It is introductory here; the Priestly source would hardly use the formula to introduce its own material in chap. 1.
The cosmogony that begins in v. 4 is concerned with the nature of human beings, narrating the story of the essential institutions and limits of the human race through their first ancestors. This cosmogony, like 1:1–3 (see note there), uses the "when…then" construction common in ancient cosmogonies.

**1:22** Gn 8:17.
**1:24** Sir 16:27–28.
**1:26–27** Gn 5:1, 3; 9:6; Ps 8:5–6; Wis 2:23; 10:2; Sir 17:1, 3–4; Mt 19:4; Mk 10:6; Jas 3:7; Eph 4:24; Col 3:10.
**1:28** Gn 8:17; 9:1; Ps 8:6–9; 115:16; Wis 9:2.
**1:29–30** Gn 9:3; Ps 104:14–15.
**1:31** 1 Tm 4:4.
**2:1** Is 45:12; Jn 1:3.
**2:2** Ex 20:9–11; 31:17; Heb 4:4, 10.
**2:3** Ex 20:11; Dt 5:14; Neh 9:14.

heavens— [5] there was no field shrub on earth and no grass of the field had sprouted, for the LORD God had sent no rain upon the earth and there was no man† to till the ground, [6] but a stream† was welling up out of the earth and watering all the surface of the ground— [7] then the LORD God formed the man† out of the dust of the ground and blew into his nostrils the breath of life, and the man became a living being.*

[8] The LORD God planted a garden in Eden, in the east,† and placed there the man whom he had formed.* [9]† Out of the ground the LORD God made grow every tree that was delightful to look at and good for food, with the tree of life in the middle of the garden and the tree of the knowledge of good and evil.*

[10] A river rises in Eden† to water the garden; beyond there it divides and becomes four branches. [11] The name of the first is the Pishon; it is the one that winds through the whole land of Havilah, where there is gold. [12] The gold of that land is good; bdellium and lapis lazuli are also there. [13] The name of the second river is the Gihon; it is the one that winds all through the land of Cush.* [14] The name of the third river is the Tigris; it is the one that flows east of Asshur. The fourth river is the Euphrates.

[15] The LORD God then took the man and settled him in the garden of Eden, to cultivate and care for it.* [16] The LORD God gave the man this order: You are free to eat from any of the trees of the garden* [17] except the tree of knowledge of good and evil. From that tree you shall not eat; when you eat from it you shall die.†*

[18] The LORD God said: It is not good for the man to be alone. I will make a helper suited to him.†* [19] So the LORD God formed out of the

---

† The account is generally attributed to the Yahwist, who prefers the divine name "Yhwh" (here rendered LORD) for God. God in this story is called "the LORD God" (except in 3:1–5); "LORD" is to be expected in a Yahwist account but the additional word "God" is puzzling.

**2:5** *Man*: the Hebrew word *'adam* is a generic term meaning "human being." In chaps. 2–3, however, the archetypal human being is understood to be male (Adam), so the word *'adam* is translated "man" here.

**2:6** *Stream*: the water wells up from the vast flood below the earth. The account seems to presuppose that only the garden of God was irrigated at this point. From this one source of all the fertilizing water on the earth, water will be channeled through the garden of God over the entire earth. It is the source of the four rivers mentioned in vv. 10–14. Later, with rain and cultivation, the fertility of the garden of God will appear in all parts of the world.

**2:7** God is portrayed as a potter molding the human body out of earth. There is a play on words in Hebrew between *'adam* ("human being," "man") and *'adama* ("ground"). It is not enough to make the body from earth; God must also breathe into the man's nostrils. A similar picture of divine breath imparted to human beings in order for them to live is found in Ez 37:5, 9–10; Jn 20:22. The Israelites did not think in the (Greek) categories of body and soul.

**2:8** *Eden, in the east*: the place names in vv. 8–14 are mostly derived from Mesopotamian geography (see note on vv. 10–14). Eden may be the name of a region in southern Mesopotamia (modern Iraq), the term derived from the Sumerian word *eden*, "fertile plain." A similar-sounding Hebrew word means "delight," which may lie behind the Greek translation, "The Lord God planted a paradise [= pleasure park] in Eden." It should be noted, however, that the garden was not intended as a paradise for the human race, but as a pleasure park for God; the man tended it for God. The story is not about "paradise lost."

The garden in the precincts of Solomon's Temple in Jerusalem seems to symbolize the garden of God (like gardens in other temples); it is apparently alluded to in Ps 1:3; 80:10; 92:14; Ez 47:7–12; Rev 22:1–2.

**2:9** The second tree, the tree of life, is mentioned here and at the end of the story (3:22, 24). It is identified with Wisdom in Prv 3:18; 11:30; 13:12; 15:4, where the pursuit of wisdom gives back to human beings the life that is made inaccessible to them in Gn 3:24. In the new creation described in the Book of Revelation, the tree of life is once again made available to human beings (Rev 2:7; 22:2, 14, 19). *Knowledge of good and evil*:

the meaning is disputed. According to some, it signifies moral autonomy, control over morality (symbolized by "good and evil"), which would be inappropriate for mere human beings; the phrase would thus mean refusal to accept the human condition and finite freedom that God gives them. According to others, it is more broadly the knowledge of what is helpful and harmful to humankind, suggesting that the attainment of adult experience and responsibility inevitably means the loss of a life of simple subordination to God.

**2:10–14** *A river rises in Eden*: the stream of water mentioned in v. 6, the source of all water upon earth, comes to the surface in the garden of God and from there flows out over the entire earth. In comparable religious literature, the dwelling of god is the source of fertilizing waters. The four rivers represent universality, as in the phrase "the four quarters of the earth." In Ez 47:1–12; Zec 14:8; Rev 22:1–2, the waters that irrigate the earth arise in the temple or city of God. The place names in vv. 11–14 are mainly from southern Mesopotamia (modern Iraq), where Mesopotamian literature placed the original garden of God. The Tigris and the Euphrates, the two great rivers in that part of the world, both emptied into the Persian Gulf. Gihon is the modest stream issuing from Jerusalem (2 Sm 5:8; 1 Kgs 1:9–10; 2 Chr 32:4), but is here regarded as one of the four great world rivers and linked to Mesopotamia, for Cush here seems to be the territory of the Kassites (a people of Mesopotamia) as in Gn 10:8. The word Pishon is otherwise unknown but is probably formed in imitation of Gihon. Havilah seems, according to Gn 10:7 and 1 Chr 1:9, to be in Cush in southern Mesopotamia though other locations have been suggested.

**2:17** *You shall die*: since they do not die as soon as they eat from the forbidden tree, the meaning seems to be that human beings have become mortal, destined to die by virtue of being human.

**2:18** *Helper suited to him*: lit., "a helper in accord with him." "Helper" need not imply subordination, for God is called a helper (Dt 33:7; Ps 46:2). The language suggests a profound affinity between the man and the woman and a relationship that is supportive and nurturing.

---

* **2:7** Gn 3:19; 18:27; Tb 8:6; Jb 34:15; Ps 103:14; 104:29; Eccl 3:20; 12:7; Wis 7:1; Sir 33:10; 1 Cor 15:45. **2:8** Is 51:3; Ez 31:9. **2:9** Gn 3:22; Prv 3:18; Rev 2:7; 22:2, 14. **2:13** Sir 24:25. **2:15** Sir 7:15. **2:16** Ps 104:14–15. **2:17** Gn 3:2–3; Rom 6:23. **2:18** Tb 8:6; Sir 36:24; 1 Cor 11:9; 1 Tm 2:13.

ground all the wild animals and all the birds of the air, and he brought them to the man to see what he would call them; whatever the man called each living creature was then its name. ²⁰ The man gave names to all the tame animals, all the birds of the air, and all the wild animals; but none proved to be a helper suited to the man.

²¹ So the LORD God cast a deep sleep on the man, and while he was asleep, he took out one of his ribs and closed up its place with flesh. * ²² The LORD God then built the rib that he had taken from the man into a woman. When he brought her to the man, ²³ the man said:

"This one, at last, is bone of my bones
    and flesh of my flesh;
This one shall be called 'woman,'
    for out of man this one has been
        taken." †

²⁴ * That is why a man leaves his father and mother and clings to his wife, and the two of them become one body. †

²⁵ The man and his wife were both naked, yet they felt no shame. †

**3** **Expulsion from Eden.** ¹ Now the snake was the most cunning † of all the wild animals that the LORD God had made. He asked the woman, "Did God really say, 'You shall not eat from any of the trees in the garden'?" ² The woman answered the snake: "We may eat of the fruit of the trees in the garden; ³ * it is only about the fruit of the tree in the middle of the garden that God said, 'You shall not eat it or even touch it, or else you will die.'" ⁴ But the snake said to the woman: "You certainly will not die! * ⁵ God knows well that when you eat of it your eyes will be opened and you will be

like gods, who know† good and evil." ⁶ The woman saw that the tree was good for food and pleasing to the eyes, and the tree was desirable for gaining wisdom. So she took some of its fruit and ate it; and she also gave some to her husband, who was with her, and he ate it. * ⁷ Then the eyes of both of them were opened, and they knew that they were naked; so they sewed fig leaves together and made loincloths for themselves.

⁸ When they heard the sound of the LORD God walking about in the garden at the breezy time of the day, † the man and his wife hid themselves from the LORD God among the trees of the garden. * ⁹ The LORD God then called to the man and asked him: Where are you? ¹⁰ He answered, "I heard you in the garden; but I was afraid, because I was naked, so I hid." ¹¹ Then God asked: Who told you that you were naked? Have you eaten from the tree of which I had forbidden you to eat? ¹² The man replied, "The woman whom you put here with me—she gave me fruit from the tree, so I ate it." ¹³ The LORD God then asked the woman: What is this you have done? The woman answered, "The snake tricked me, so I ate it." *

¹⁴ Then the LORD God said to the snake:

Because you have done this,
    cursed are you
        among all the animals, tame or wild;
On your belly you shall crawl,
    and dust you shall eat
        all the days of your life. † *
15  I will put enmity between you and the
        woman,
    and between your offspring and hers;
They will strike at your head,
    while you strike at their heel. † *

---

† **2:23** The man recognizes an affinity with the woman God has brought him. Unlike the animals who were made from the ground, she is made from his very self. There is a play on the similar-sounding Hebrew words *'ishsha* ("woman," "wife") and *'ish* ("man," "husband").

**2:24** *One body*: lit., "one flesh." The covenant of marriage establishes kinship bonds of the first rank between the partners.

**2:25** *They felt no shame*: marks a new stage in the drama, for the reader knows that only young children know no shame. This draws the reader into the next episode, where the couple's disobedience results in their loss of innocence.

**3:1** *Cunning*: there is a play on the words for "naked" (2:25) and "cunning/wise" (Heb. *'arum*). The couple seek to be "wise" but end up knowing that they are "naked."

**3:5** *Like gods, who know*: or "like God who knows."

**3:8** *The breezy time of the day*: lit., "the wind of the day." Probably shortly before sunset.

**3:14** Each of the three punishments (the snake, the woman,

the man) has a double aspect, one affecting the individual and the other affecting a basic relationship. The snake previously stood upright, enjoyed a reputation for being shrewder than other creatures, and could converse with human beings as in vv. 1–5. It must now move on its belly, is more cursed than any creature, and inspires revulsion in human beings (v. 15).

**3:15** *They will strike…at their heel*: the antecedent for "they" and "their" is the collective noun "offspring," i.e., all the descendants of the woman. Christian tradition has seen in this passage, however, more than unending hostility between snakes and hu-

---

**2:21** Sir 17:1; 1 Cor
    11:8–9; 1 Tm 2:13.
**2:24** Mt 19:5; Mk 10:7;
    1 Cor 7:10–11; Eph
    5:31.
**3:3** Gn 2:17; Rom 6:23.
**3:4–5** Wis 2:24; Sir 25:14; Is
    14:14; Jn 8:44;

2 Cor 11:3.
**3:6** Gn 3:22; 1 Tm 2:14.
**3:8** Jer 23:24.
**3:13** 2 Cor 11:3.
**3:14** Is 65:25; Mi 7:17; Rev
    12:9.
**3:15** Rom 16:20; 1 Jn 3:8;
    Rev 12:17.

<sup>16</sup>To the woman he said:

> I will intensify your toil in childbearing;
>     in pain† you shall bring forth
>         children.
> Yet your urge shall be for your husband,
>     and he shall rule over you.

<sup>17</sup>To the man he said: Because you listened to your wife and ate from the tree about which I commanded you, You shall not eat from it,

> Cursed is the ground† because of you!
>     In toil you shall eat its yield
>     all the days of your life. *
> <sup>18</sup>    Thorns and thistles it shall bear for you,
>         and you shall eat the grass of the field.
> <sup>19</sup>    By the sweat of your brow
>         you shall eat bread,
>     Until you return to the ground,
>         from which you were taken;
>     For you are dust,
>         and to dust you shall return. *

<sup>20</sup>The man gave his wife the name "Eve," because she was the mother of all the living.†

<sup>21</sup>The LORD God made for the man and his wife garments of skin, with which he clothed them. <sup>22</sup>Then the LORD God said: See! The man has become like one of us, knowing good and evil! Now, what if he also reaches out his hand to take fruit from the tree of life, and eats of it and lives forever? * <sup>23</sup>The LORD God therefore banished him from the garden of Eden, to till the ground from which he had been taken. <sup>24</sup>He expelled the man, stationing the cherubim and the fiery revolving sword east of the garden of Eden, to guard the way to the tree of life.

# 4 Cain and Abel.

<sup>1</sup>The man had intercourse with his wife Eve, and she conceived and gave birth to Cain, saying, "I have produced a male child with the help of the LORD." † <sup>2</sup>Next she gave birth to his brother Abel. Abel became a herder of flocks, and Cain a tiller of the ground. † <sup>3</sup>In the course of time Cain brought an offering to the LORD from the fruit of the ground, <sup>4</sup>while Abel, for his part, brought the fatty portion† of the firstlings of his flock. * The LORD looked with favor on Abel and his offering, <sup>5</sup>but on Cain and his offering he did not look with favor. So Cain was very angry and dejected. <sup>6</sup>Then the LORD said to Cain: Why are you angry? Why are you dejected? <sup>7</sup>If you act rightly, you will be accepted;† but if not, sin lies in wait at the door: its urge is for you, yet you can rule over it. *

---

man beings. The snake was identified with the devil (Wis 2:24; Jn 8:44; Rev 12:9; 20:2), whose eventual defeat seemed implied in the verse. Because "the Son of God was revealed to destroy the works of the devil" (1 Jn 3:8), the passage was understood as the first promise of a redeemer for fallen humankind, the *protoevangelium*. Irenaeus of Lyons (ca. A.D. 130–200), in his *Against Heresies* 5.21.1, followed by several other Fathers of the Church, interpreted the verse as referring to Christ, and cited Gal 3:19 and 4:4 to support the reference. Another interpretive translation is *ipsa*, "she," and is reflected in Jerome's Vulgate. "She" was thought to refer to Mary, the mother of the messiah. In Christian art Mary is sometimes depicted with her foot on the head of the serpent.

**3:16** *Toil...pain*: the punishment affects the woman directly by increasing the toil and pain of having children. *He shall rule over you*: the punishment also affects the woman's relationship with her husband. A tension is set up in which her urge (either sexual urge or, more generally, dependence for sustenance) is for her husband but he rules over her. But see Sg 7:11.

**3:17–19** *Cursed is the ground*: the punishment affects the man's relationship to the ground (*'adam* and *'adamah*). *You are dust*: the punishment also affects the man directly insofar as he is now mortal.

**3:20** The man gives his wife a more specific name than "woman" (2:23). The Hebrew name *hawwa* ("Eve") is related to the Hebrew word *hay* ("living"); "mother of all the living" points forward to the next episode involving her sons Cain and Abel.

**4:1** The Hebrew name *qayin* ("Cain") and the term *qaniti* ("I have produced") present a wordplay that refers to metalworking; such wordplays are frequent in Genesis.

**4:2** Some suggest the story reflects traditional strife between the farmer (Cain) and the nomad (Abel), with preference for the latter reflecting the alleged nomadic ideal of the Bible. But there is no disparagement of farming here, for Adam was created to till the soil. The story is about two brothers (the word "brother" occurs seven times) and God's unexplained preference for one, which provokes the first murder. The motif of the preferred younger brother will occur time and again in the Bible, e.g., Isaac, Jacob, Joseph, and David (1 Sm 16:1–13).

**4:4** *Fatty portion*: it was standard practice to offer the fat portions of animals. Others render, less satisfactorily, "the choicest of the firstlings." The point is not that Abel gave a more valuable gift than Cain, but that God, for reasons not given in the text, accepts the offering of Abel and rejects that of Cain.

**4:7** *You will be accepted*: the text is extraordinarily condensed and unclear. "You will be accepted" is a paraphrase of one Hebrew word, "lifting." God gives a friendly warning to Cain that his right conduct will bring "lifting," which could refer to acceptance (*lifting*) of his future offerings or of himself (as in the Hebrew idiom "*lifting* of the face") or *lifting* up of his head in honor (cf. note on 40:13), whereas wicked conduct will make him vulnerable to sin, which is personified as a force ready to attack. In any case, Cain has the ability to do the right thing. *Lies in wait*: sin is personified as a power that "lies in wait" (Heb. *robes*) at a place. In Mesopotamian religion, a related word (*rabisu*) refers to a malevolent god who attacks human beings in particular places like roofs or canals.

---

* 

**3:17** Gn 5:29; Rom 5:12; 8:20; Heb 6:8.
**3:19** Gn 2:7; Jb 10:9; 34:15; Ps 90:3; 103:14; Eccl 3:20; 12:7; Wis 15:8;

Sir 10:9; 17:2; Rom 5:12; 1 Cor 15:21; Heb 9:27.
**3:22** Gn 2:9; Rev 22:2, 14.
**4:4** Ex 34:19; Heb 11:4.
**4:7** Sir 7:1; Jude 11.

8 Cain said to his brother Abel, "Let us go out in the field."† When they were in the field, Cain attacked his brother Abel and killed him.* 9 Then the LORD asked Cain, Where is your brother Abel? He answered, "I do not know. Am I my brother's keeper?" 10 God then said: What have you done? Your brother's blood cries out to me from the ground! 11 Now you are banned from the ground† that opened its mouth to receive your brother's blood from your hand.* 12 If you till the ground, it shall no longer give you its produce. You shall become a constant wanderer on the earth. 13 Cain said to the LORD: "My punishment is too great to bear. 14 Look, you have now banished me from the ground. I must avoid you and be a constant wanderer on the earth. Anyone may kill me at sight." 15 Not so! the LORD said to him. If anyone kills Cain, Cain shall be avenged seven times. So the LORD put a mark† on Cain, so that no one would kill him at sight. 16 Cain then left the LORD's presence and settled in the land of Nod,† east of Eden.

**Descendants of Cain and Seth.** 17† Cain had intercourse with his wife, and she conceived and bore Enoch. Cain also became the founder of a city, which he named after his son Enoch. 18 To Enoch was born Irad, and Irad became the father of Mehujael; Mehujael became the father of Methusael, and Methusael became the father of Lamech. 19 Lamech took two wives; the name of the first was Adah, and the name of the second Zillah. 20 Adah gave birth to Jabal, who became the ancestor of those who dwell in tents and keep livestock. 21 His brother's name was Jubal, who became the ancestor of all who play the lyre and the reed pipe. 22 Zillah, on her part, gave birth to Tubalcain, the ancestor of all who forge instruments of bronze and iron. The sister of Tubalcain was Naamah. 23† Lamech said to his wives:

"Adah and Zillah, hear my voice;
    wives of Lamech, listen to my
        utterance:
I have killed a man for wounding me,
    a young man for bruising me.
24  If Cain is avenged seven times,
    then Lamech seventy-seven times."

25† Adam again had intercourse with his wife, and she gave birth to a son whom she called Seth. "God has granted me another offspring in place of Abel," she said, "because Cain killed him." 26 To Seth, in turn, a son was born, and he named him Enosh.

At that time people began to invoke the LORD by name.*

**5** **Generations: Adam to Noah.**† 1* This is the record of the descendants of Adam. When God created human beings, he made

---

† **4:8** *Let us go out in the field*: to avoid detection. The verse presumes a sizeable population which Genesis does not otherwise explain.

**4:11** *Banned from the ground*: lit., "cursed." The verse refers back to 3:17 where the ground was cursed so that it yields its produce only with great effort. Cain has polluted the soil with his brother's blood and it will no longer yield any of its produce to him.

**4:15** *A mark*: probably a tattoo to mark Cain as protected by God. The use of tattooing for tribal marks has always been common among the Bedouin of the Near Eastern deserts.

**4:16** *The land of Nod*: a symbolic name (derived from the verb *nûd*, to wander) rather than a definite geographic region.

**4:17–24** Cain is the first in a seven-member linear genealogy ending in three individuals who initiate action (Jabal, Jubal, and Tubalcain). Other Genesis genealogies also end in three individuals initiating action (5:32 and 11:26). The purpose of this genealogy is to explain the origin of culture and crafts among human beings. The names in this genealogy are the same (some with different spellings) as those in the ten-member genealogy (ending with Noah), which has a slightly different function. See note on 5:1–32.

**4:23–24** Lamech's boast shows that the violence of Cain continues with his son and has actually increased. The question is posed to the reader: how will God's creation be renewed?

**4:25–26** The third and climactic birth story in the chapter, showing that this birth, unlike the other two, will have good results. The name Seth (from the Hebrew verb *shat*, "to place, re-

place") shows that God has replaced Abel with a worthy successor. From this favored line Enosh ("human being/humankind"), a synonym of Adam, authentic religion began with the worship of Yhwh; this divine name is rendered as "the LORD" in this translation. The Yahwist source employs the name Yhwh long before the time of Moses. Another ancient source, the Elohist (from its use of the term *Elohim*, "God," instead of *Yhwh*, "LORD," for the pre-Mosaic period), makes Moses the first to use Yhwh as the proper name of Israel's God, previously known by other names as well; cf. Ex 3:13–15.

**5:1–32** The second of the five Priestly formulas in Part I ("This is the record of the descendants…"; see 2:4a; 6:9; 10:1; 11:10) introduces the second of the three linear genealogies in Gn 1–11 (4:17–24 and 11:10–26). In each, a list of individuals (six in 4:17–24, ten in 5:1–32, or nine in 11:10–26) ends in three people who initiate action. Linear genealogies (father to son) in ancient societies had a communicative function, grounding the authority or claim of the last-named individual in the first-named. Here, the genealogy has a literary function as well, advancing the story by showing the expansion of the human race after Adam, as well as the transmission to his descendant Noah of the divine image given to Adam. Correcting the impression one might get from the genealogy in 4:17–24, this genealogy traces the line through Seth rather than through Cain. Most of the names in the series are

---
| | |
|---|---|
| **4:8** Wis 10:3; Mt 23:35; Lk 11:51; 1 Jn 3:12; Jude 11. | **4:26** 1 Chr 1:1; Lk 3:38. **5:1** Gn 1:27; Wis 2:23; Sir 17:1; Jas 3:9. |
| **4:11** Dt 27:24. | |

them in the likeness of God; [2] he created them male and female. When they were created, he blessed them and named them humankind.

[3]* Adam was one hundred and thirty years old when he begot a son in his likeness, after his image; and he named him Seth.* [4] Adam lived eight hundred years after he begot Seth, and he had other sons and daughters. [5] The whole lifetime of Adam was nine hundred and thirty years; then he died.

[6] When Seth was one hundred and five years old, he begot Enosh. [7] Seth lived eight hundred and seven years after he begot Enosh, and he had other sons and daughters. [8] The whole lifetime of Seth was nine hundred and twelve years; then he died.

[9] When Enosh was ninety years old, he begot Kenan. [10] Enosh lived eight hundred and fifteen years after he begot Kenan, and he had other sons and daughters. [11] The whole lifetime of Enosh was nine hundred and five years; then he died.

[12] When Kenan was seventy years old, he begot Mahalalel. [13] Kenan lived eight hundred and forty years after he begot Mahalalel, and he had other sons and daughters. [14] The whole lifetime of Kenan was nine hundred and ten years; then he died.

[15] When Mahalalel was sixty-five years old, he begot Jared. [16] Mahalalel lived eight hundred and thirty years after he begot Jared, and he had other sons and daughters. [17] The whole lifetime of Mahalalel was eight hundred and ninety-five years; then he died.

[18] When Jared was one hundred and sixty-two years old, he begot Enoch. [19] Jared lived eight hundred years after he begot Enoch, and he had other sons and daughters. [20] The whole lifetime of Jared was nine hundred and sixty-two years; then he died.

[21] When Enoch was sixty-five years old, he begot Methuselah. [22] Enoch walked with God after he begot Methuselah for three hundred years, and he had other sons and daughters. [23] The whole lifetime of Enoch was three hundred and sixty-five years. [24] Enoch walked with God,† and he was no longer here, for God took him.*

[25] When Methuselah was one hundred and eighty-seven years old, he begot Lamech. [26] Methuselah lived seven hundred and eighty-two years after he begot Lamech, and he had other sons and daughters. [27] The whole lifetime of Methuselah was nine hundred and sixty-nine years; then he died.

[28] When Lamech was one hundred and eighty-two years old, he begot a son [29]* and named him Noah, saying, "This one shall bring us relief from our work and the toil of our hands, out of the very ground that the LORD has put under a curse."† [30] Lamech lived five hundred and ninety-five years after he begot Noah, and he had other sons and daughters. [31] The whole lifetime of Lamech was seven hundred and seventy-seven years; then he died.

[32] When Noah was five hundred years old, he begot Shem, Ham, and Japheth.†*

**6** **Origin of the Nephilim.**† [1] When human beings began to grow numerous on the earth and daughters were born to them, [2] the

---

† the same as the names in Cain's line in 4:17–19 (Enosh, Enoch, Lamech) or spelled with variant spellings (Mahalalel, Jared, Methuselah). The genealogy itself and its placement before the flood shows the influence of ancient Mesopotamian literature, which contains lists of cities and kings before and after the flood. Before the flood, the ages of the kings ranged from 18,600 to 36,000 years, but after it were reduced to between 140 and 1,200 years. The biblical numbers are much smaller. There are some differences in the numbers in the Hebrew and Greek manuscripts.

**5:24** Enoch is in the important seventh position in the ten-member genealogy. In place of the usual formula "then he died," the change to "Enoch walked with God" implies that he did not die, but like Elijah (2 Kgs 2:11–12) was taken alive to God's abode. This mysterious narrative spurred much speculation and writing (beginning as early as the third century B.C.) about Enoch the sage who knew the secrets of heaven and who could communicate them to human beings (see Sir 44:16; 49:14; Heb 11:5; Jude 14–15 and the apocryphal work 1 Enoch).

**5:29** The sound of the Hebrew word *noah*, "Noah," is echoed in the word *yenahamenu*, "he will bring us relief"; the latter refers both to the curse put on the soil because of human disobedience (3:17–19) and to Noah's success in agriculture, especially in raising grapes for wine (9:20–21).

**5:32** *Shem, Ham, and Japheth:* like the genealogies in 4:17–24 and 11:10–26, the genealogy ends in three individuals who engage in important activity. Their descendants will be detailed in chap. 10, where it will be seen that the lineage is political-geographical as well as "ethnic."

**6:1–4** These enigmatic verses are a transition between the expansion of the human race illustrated in the genealogy of chap. 5 and the flood depicted in chaps. 6–9. The text, apparently alluding to an old legend, shares a common ancient view that the heavenly world was populated by a multitude of beings, some of whom were wicked and rebellious. It is incorporated here, not only in order to account for the prehistoric giants, whom the Israelites called the Nephilim, but also to introduce the story of the flood with a moral orientation—the constantly increasing wickedness of humanity. This increasing wickedness leads God to reduce the human life span imposed on the first couple. As the ages in the preceding genealogy show, life spans had been exceptionally long in the early period, but God further reduces them to something near the ordinary life span.

---

**5:3–32** 1 Chr 1:1–4; Lk 3:36–38.
**5:3** Gn 4:25.
**5:24** Wis 4:10–11;
Sir 44:16; 49:14; Heb 11:5.
**5:29** Gn 3:17–19.
**5:32** Gn 6:10; 10:1.

sons of God† saw how beautiful the daughters of human beings were, and so they took for their wives whomever they pleased.* ³Then the LORD said: My spirit shall not remain in human beings forever, because they are only flesh. Their days shall comprise one hundred and twenty years.

⁴The Nephilim appeared on earth in those days, as well as later,† after the sons of God had intercourse with the daughters of human beings, who bore them sons. They were the heroes of old, the men of renown.*

## Warning of the Flood. ⁵† When the LORD saw how great the wickedness of human beings was on earth, and how every desire that their heart conceived was always nothing but evil,* ⁶the LORD regretted making human beings on the earth, and his heart was grieved.†

⁷So the LORD said: I will wipe out from the earth the human beings I have created, and not only the human beings, but also the animals and the crawling things and the birds of the air, for I regret that I made them.† ⁸But Noah found favor with the LORD.

⁹These are the descendants of Noah. Noah was a righteous man and blameless in his generation;* Noah walked with God. ¹⁰Noah begot three sons: Shem, Ham, and Japheth.

¹¹But the earth was corrupt† in the view of God and full of lawlessness.* ¹²When God saw how corrupt the earth had become, since all mortals had corrupted their ways on earth,* ¹³God said to Noah: I see that the end of all mortals has come, for the earth is full of lawlessness because of them. So I am going to destroy them with the earth.*

## Preparation for the Flood. ¹⁴Make yourself an ark of gopherwood,† equip the ark with various compartments, and cover it inside and out with pitch. ¹⁵This is how you shall build it: the length of the ark will be three hundred cubits, its width fifty cubits, and its height thirty cubits.† ¹⁶Make an opening for daylight† and finish the ark a cubit above it. Put the ark's entrance on its side; you will make it with bottom, second and third decks. ¹⁷I, on my part, am about to bring the flood waters on the earth, to destroy all creatures under the sky in which there is the breath of life; everything on earth shall perish.* ¹⁸I will establish my covenant with you. You shall go into the ark, you and your sons, your wife and your sons' wives with you.* ¹⁹Of all living creatures you shall bring two of every kind into the ark, one male and one female,† to keep them alive along with you.

---

† **6:2** *The sons of God*: other heavenly beings. See note on 1:26.
**6:4** *As well as later*: the belief was common that human beings of gigantic stature once lived on earth. In some cultures, such heroes could make positive contributions, but the Bible generally regards them in a negative light (cf. Nm 13:33; Ez 32:27). The point here is that even these heroes, filled with vitality from their semi-divine origin, come under God's decree in v. 3.
**6:5–8:22** The story of the great flood is commonly regarded as a composite narrative based on separate sources woven together. To the Yahwist source, with some later editorial additions, are usually assigned 6:5–8; 7:1–5, 7–10, 12, 16b, 17b, 22–23; 8:2b–3a, 6–12, 13b, 20–22. The other sections are usually attributed to the Priestly writer. There are differences between the two sources: the Priestly source has two pairs of every animal, whereas the Yahwist source has seven pairs of clean animals and two pairs of unclean; the floodwater in the Priestly source is the waters under and over the earth that burst forth, whereas in the Yahwist source the floodwater is the rain lasting forty days and nights. In spite of many obvious discrepancies in these two sources, one should read the story as a coherent narrative. The biblical story ultimately draws upon an ancient Mesopotamian tradition of a great flood, preserved in the Sumerian flood story, the eleventh tablet of the Gilgamesh Epic, and (embedded in a longer narrative) the Atrahasis Epic.
**6:6** *His heart was grieved*: the expression can be misleading in English, for "heart" in Hebrew is the seat of memory and judgment rather than emotion. The phrase is actually parallel to the first half of the sentence ("the LORD regretted…").
**6:7** Human beings are an essential part of their environment, which includes all living things. In the new beginning after the flood, God makes a covenant with human beings and every

living creature (9:9–10). The same close link between human beings and nature is found elsewhere in the Bible; e.g., in Is 35, God's healing transforms human beings along with their physical environment, and in Rom 8:19–23, all creation, not merely human beings, groans in labor pains awaiting the salvation of God.
**6:11** *Corrupt*: God does not punish arbitrarily but simply brings to its completion the corruption initiated by human beings.
**6:14** *Gopherwood*: an unidentified wood mentioned only in connection with the ark. It may be the wood of the cypress, which in Hebrew sounds like "gopher" and was widely used in antiquity for shipbuilding.
**6:15** Hebrew "cubit," lit., "forearm," is the distance from the elbow to the tip of the middle finger, about eighteen inches (a foot and a half). The dimensions of Noah's ark were approximately 440 × 73 × 44 feet. The ark of the Babylonian flood story was an exact cube, 120 cubits (180 feet) in length, width, and height.
**6:16** *Opening for daylight*: a conjectural rendering of the Hebrew word *sohar*, occurring only here. The reference is probably to an open space on all sides near the top of the ark to admit light and air. The ark also had a window or hatch, which could be opened and closed (8:6).
**6:19–21** *You shall bring two of every kind…, one male and one female*: For the Priestly source (P), there is no distinction between clean and unclean animals until Sinai (Lv 11), no altars or sacrifice until Sinai, and all diet is vegetarian (Gn 1:29–30); even after the flood P has no distinction between clean and

---

* **6:2** Mt 24:38; Lk 17:26–27.
**6:4** Wis 14:6; Bar 3:26.
**6:5** Ps 14:2–3.
**6:9** Wis 10:4; Sir 44:17.
**6:11** Jb 22:15–17.
**6:12** Ps 14:2.
**6:13** Sir 40:9–10; 44:17; Mt 24:37–39.
**6:17** Gn 7:4, 21; 2 Pt 2:5.
**6:18** Gn 9:9; Wis 14:6; Heb 11:7; 1 Pt 3:20.

<sup>20</sup>Of every kind of bird, of every kind of animal, and of every kind of thing that crawls on the ground, two of each will come to you, that you may keep them alive. <sup>21</sup>Moreover, you are to provide yourself with all the food that is to be eaten, and store it away, that it may serve as provisions for you and for them. <sup>22</sup>Noah complied; he did just as God had commanded him.†

7 <sup>1</sup>Then the LORD said to Noah: Go into the ark, you and all your household, for you alone in this generation have I found to be righteous before me.* <sup>2</sup>Of every clean animal, take with you seven pairs, a male and its mate; and of the unclean animals, one pair, a male and its mate; <sup>3</sup>likewise, of every bird of the air, seven pairs, a male and a female, to keep their progeny alive over all the earth. <sup>4</sup>For seven days from now I will bring rain down on the earth for forty days and forty nights, and so I will wipe out from the face of the earth every being that I have made.* <sup>5</sup>Noah complied, just as the LORD had commanded.

**The Great Flood.** <sup>6</sup>Noah was six hundred years old when the flood came upon the earth. <sup>7</sup>Together with his sons, his wife, and his sons' wives, Noah went into the ark because of the waters of the flood.* <sup>8</sup>Of the clean animals and the unclean, of the birds, and of everything that crawls on the ground, <sup>9</sup>two by two, male and female came to Noah into the ark, just as God had commanded him.* <sup>10</sup>When the seven days were over, the waters of the flood came upon the earth.

<sup>11</sup>In the six hundredth year of Noah's life, in the second month, on the seventeenth day of the month: on that day

> All the fountains of the great abyss†
>   burst forth,
> and the floodgates of the sky were
>   opened.

<sup>12</sup>For forty days and forty nights heavy rain poured down on the earth.

<sup>13</sup>On the very same day, Noah and his sons Shem, Ham, and Japheth, and Noah's wife, and the three wives of Noah's sons had entered the ark, <sup>14</sup>together with every kind of wild animal, every kind of tame animal, every kind of crawling thing that crawls on the earth, and every kind of bird. <sup>15</sup>Pairs of all creatures in which there was the breath of life came to Noah into the ark. <sup>16</sup>Those that entered were male and female; of all creatures they came, as God had commanded Noah. Then the LORD shut him in.

<sup>17</sup>The flood continued upon the earth for forty days. As the waters increased, they lifted the ark, so that it rose above the earth. <sup>18</sup>The waters swelled and increased greatly on the earth, but the ark floated on the surface of the waters. <sup>19</sup>Higher and higher on the earth the waters swelled, until all the highest mountains under the heavens were submerged. <sup>20</sup>The waters swelled fifteen cubits higher than the submerged mountains. <sup>21</sup>All creatures that moved on earth perished: birds, tame animals, wild animals, and all that teemed on the earth, as well as all humankind.* <sup>22</sup>Everything on dry land with the breath of life in its nostrils died. <sup>23</sup>The LORD wiped out every being on earth: human beings and animals, the crawling things and the birds of the air; all were wiped out from the earth. Only Noah and those with him in the ark were left.

<sup>24</sup>And when the waters had swelled on the earth for one hundred and fifty days,

8 <sup>1</sup>God remembered Noah and all the animals, wild and tame, that were with him in the ark. So God made a wind sweep over the earth, and the waters began to subside. <sup>2</sup>The fountains of the abyss and the floodgates of the sky were closed, and the downpour from the sky was held back. <sup>3</sup>Gradually the waters receded from the earth. At the end of one hundred and fifty days, the waters had

---

† unclean, since "any living creature that moves about" may be eaten (9:3). Thus P has Noah take the minimum to preserve all species, one pair of each, without distinction between clean and unclean, but he must also take on provisions for food (6:21). The Yahwist source (J), which assumes the clean-unclean distinction always existed but knows no other restriction on eating meat (Abel was a shepherd and offered meat as a sacrifice), requires additional clean animals ("seven pairs") for food and sacrifice (7:2–3; 8:20).

**6:22** *Just as God had commanded him*: as in the creation of the world in chap. 1 and in the building of the tabernacle in

Ex 25–31, 35–40 (all from the Priestly source), everything takes place by the command of God. In this passage and in Exodus, the commands of God are carried out to the letter by human agents, Noah and Moses. Divine speech is important. God speaks to Noah seven times in the flood story.

**7:11** *Abyss*: the subterranean ocean; see note on 1:2.

**7:1** Wis 10:4; Sir 44:17; 2 Pt 2:5.
**7:4** Gn 6:17; 2 Pt 2:5.
**7:7** Wis 14:6; 1 Pt 3:20;
2 Pt 2:5.
**7:9** Gn 6:19.
**7:21–23** Jb 22:16; Mt 24:39; Lk 17:27; 2 Pt 3:6.

so diminished [4] that, in the seventh month, on the seventeenth day of the month, the ark came to rest on the mountains of Ararat.† [5] The waters continued to diminish until the tenth month, and on the first day of the tenth month the tops of the mountains appeared.

[6] At the end of forty days Noah opened the hatch of the ark that he had made, [7] † and he released a raven. It flew back and forth until the waters dried off from the earth. [8] Then he released a dove, to see if the waters had lessened on the earth. [9] But the dove could find no place to perch, and it returned to him in the ark, for there was water over all the earth. Putting out his hand, he caught the dove and drew it back to him inside the ark. [10] He waited yet seven days more and again released the dove from the ark. [11] In the evening the dove came back to him, and there in its bill was a plucked-off olive leaf! So Noah knew that the waters had diminished on the earth. [12] He waited yet another seven days and then released the dove; but this time it did not come back.

[13] † In the six hundred and first year, in the first month, on the first day of the month, the water began to dry up on the earth. Noah then removed the covering of the ark and saw that the surface of the ground had dried. [14] In the second month, on the twenty-seventh day of the month, the earth was dry.

[15] Then God said to Noah: [16] Go out of the ark, together with your wife and your sons and your sons' wives. [17] Bring out with you every living thing that is with you—all creatures, be they birds or animals or crawling things that crawl on the earth—and let them abound on the earth, and be fertile and multiply on it.* [18] So Noah came out, together with his sons and his wife and his sons' wives; [19] and all the animals, all the birds, and all the crawling creatures that crawl on the earth went out of the ark by families.

[20] Then Noah built an altar to the LORD, and choosing from every clean animal and every clean bird, he offered burnt offerings on the altar. [21] When the LORD smelled the sweet odor, the LORD said to himself: Never again will I curse the ground because of human beings, since the desires of the human heart are evil from youth; nor will I ever again strike down every living being, as I have done. *

22　　All the days of the earth,
　　　　seedtime and harvest,
　　　　cold and heat,
　　　Summer and winter,
　　　　and day and night
　　　shall not cease. *

**9** **Covenant with Noah.** [1] † God blessed Noah and his sons and said to them: Be fertile and multiply and fill the earth.* [2] † Fear and dread of you shall come upon all the animals of the earth and all the birds of the air, upon all the creatures that move about on the ground and all the fishes of the sea; into your power they are delivered. [3] * Any living creature that moves about shall be yours to eat; I give them all to you as I did the green plants. [4] * Only meat with its lifeblood still in it you shall not eat.† [5] Indeed for your own lifeblood I will demand an accounting: from every animal I will demand it, and from a human being, each one for the blood of another, I will demand an accounting for human life. *

6† 　　Anyone who sheds the blood of a
　　　　human being,

---

† **8:4** *The mountains of Ararat*: the mountain country of ancient Arartu in northwest Iraq, which was the highest part of the world to the biblical writer. There is no Mount Ararat in the Bible.

**8:7–12** In the eleventh tablet of the Gilgamesh Epic, Utnapishtim (the equivalent of Noah) released in succession a dove, a swallow, and a raven. When the raven did not return, Utnapishtim knew it was safe to leave the ark. The first century A.D. Roman author Pliny tells of Indian sailors who release birds in order to follow them toward land.

**8:13–14** On the first day of the first month, the world was in the state it had been on the day of creation in chap. 1. Noah had to wait another month until the earth was properly dry as in 1:9.

**9:1** God reaffirms without change the original blessing and mandate of 1:28. In the Mesopotamian epic Atrahasis, on which the Genesis story is partly modeled, the gods changed their original plan by restricting human population through such means as childhood diseases, birth demons, and mandating celibacy among certain groups of women.

**9:2–3** Pre-flood creatures, including human beings, are depicted as vegetarians (1:29–30). In view of the human propensity to violence, God changes the original prohibition against eating meat.

**9:4** Because a living being dies when it loses most of its blood, the ancients regarded blood as the seat of life, and therefore as sacred. Jewish tradition considered the prohibition against eating meat with blood to be binding on all, because it was given by God to Noah, the new ancestor of all humankind; therefore the early Christian Church retained it for a time (Acts 15:20, 29).

**9:6** The image of God, given to the first man and woman and transmitted to every human being, is the reason that no violent attacks can be made upon human beings. That image is the basis

---

* 
**8:17** Gn 1:22, 28.　　　　　　　Dt 12:15.
**8:21** Sir 44:18; Is 54:9;　　　　**9:4** Lv 7:26–27; 17:4;
　　　 Rom 7:18.　　　　　　　　　 Dt 12:16, 23; 1 Sm
**8:22** Jer 33:20, 25.　　　　　　　14:33; Acts 15:20.
**9:1** Gn 1:22, 28; 8:17.　　　　**9:5** Gn 4:10–11; Ex
**9:3** Gn 1:29–30;　　　　　　　　21:12.

by a human being shall that one's
    blood be shed;
For in the image of God
    have human beings been made.*

⁷ Be fertile, then, and multiply; abound on earth and subdue it.*

⁸† God said to Noah and to his sons with him: ⁹ See, I am now establishing my covenant with you and your descendants after you* ¹⁰ and with every living creature that was with you: the birds, the tame animals, and all the wild animals that were with you—all that came out of the ark. ¹¹ I will establish my covenant with you, that never again shall all creatures be destroyed by the waters of a flood; there shall not be another flood to devastate the earth.* ¹² God said: This is the sign of the covenant that I am making between me and you and every living creature with you for all ages to come: ¹³* I set my bow in the clouds to serve as a sign of the covenant between me and the earth. ¹⁴ When I bring clouds over the earth, and the bow appears in the clouds, ¹⁵ I will remember my covenant between me and you and every living creature—every mortal being—so that the waters will never again become a flood to destroy every mortal being.* ¹⁶ When the bow appears in the clouds, I will see it and remember the everlasting covenant between God and every living creature—every mortal being that is on earth. ¹⁷ God told Noah: This is the sign of the covenant I have established between me and every mortal being that is on earth.

**Noah and His Sons.** ¹⁸† The sons of Noah who came out of the ark were Shem, Ham

and Japheth. Ham was the father of Canaan.* ¹⁹ These three were the sons of Noah, and from them the whole earth was populated.

²⁰ Noah, a man of the soil, was the first to plant a vineyard. ²¹ He drank some of the wine, became drunk, and lay naked inside his tent.* ²² Ham, the father of Canaan, saw his father's nakedness, and he told his two brothers outside. ²³ Shem and Japheth, however, took a robe, and holding it on their shoulders, they walked backward and covered their father's nakedness; since their faces were turned the other way, they did not see their father's nakedness. ²⁴ When Noah woke up from his wine and learned what his youngest son had done to him, ²⁵ he said:

> "Cursed be Caanan!
>     The lowest of slaves
>     shall he be to his brothers."*

²⁶ He also said:

> "Blessed be the Lᴏʀᴅ, the God of Shem!
>     Let Canaan be his slave.
> ²⁷    May God expand Japheth,†
>     and may he dwell among the tents of
>         Shem;
>     and let Canaan be his slave."

²⁸ Noah lived three hundred and fifty years after the flood. ²⁹ The whole lifetime of Noah was nine hundred and fifty years; then he died.

**10** **Table of the Nations.**† ¹ These are the descendants of Noah's sons, Shem, Ham and Japheth, to whom children were born after the flood.

---

† of the dignity of every individual who, in some sense, "represents" God in the world.

**9:8–17** God makes a covenant with Noah and his descendants and, remarkably, with all the animals who come out of the ark: never again shall the world be destroyed by flood. The sign of this solemn promise is the appearance of a rainbow.

**9:18–27** The character of the three sons is sketched here. The fault is not Noah's (for he could not be expected to know about the intoxicating effect of wine) but Ham's, who shames his father by looking on his nakedness, and then tells the other sons. Ham's conduct is meant to prefigure the later shameful sexual practices of the Canaanites, which are alleged in numerous biblical passages. The point of the story is revealed in Noah's curse of Ham's son Canaan and his blessing of Shem and Japheth.

**9:27** In the Hebrew text there is a play on the words *yapt* ("expand") and *yepet* ("Japheth").

**10:1–32** Verse 1 is the fourth of the Priestly formulas (2:4; 5:1; 6:9; 11:10) that structure Part I of Genesis; it introduces 10:2–11:9, the populating of the world and the building of the city. In a sense, chaps. 4–9 are concerned with the first of the

two great commands given to the human race in 1:28, "Be fertile and multiply!" whereas chaps. 10–11 are concerned with the second command, "Fill the earth and subdue it!" ("Subdue it" refers to each nation's taking the land assigned to it by God.) Gn 9:19 already noted that all nations are descended from the three sons of Noah; the same sentiment is repeated in 10:5, 18, 25, 32; 11:8. The presupposition of the chapter is that every nation has a land assigned to it by God (cf. Dt 32:8–9). The number of the nations is seventy (if one does not count Noah and his sons, and counts Sidon [vv. 15, 19] only once), which is a traditional biblical number (Jgs 8:30; Lk 10:1, 17). According to Gn 46:27 and Ex 1:5, Israel also numbered seventy persons, which shows that it in some sense represents the nations of the earth.

---

**9:6** Gn 1:26–27; Lv 24:17; Nm 35:33; Jas 3:9.
**9:7** Gn 1:28; 8:17; 9:2; Jas 3:7.
**9:9** Gn 6:18.
**9:11** Sir 44:18; Is 54:9.
**9:13** Sir 43:12.
**9:15** Is 54:9.
**9:18** Gn 5:32; 10:1.
**9:21** Lam 4:21; Hb 2:15.
**9:25** Dt 27:16; Wis 12:11.

2* The descendants of Japheth: Gomer,† Magog, Madai, Javan, Tubal, Meshech and Tiras.* ³The descendants of Gomer: Ashkenaz,† Diphath and Togarmah. ⁴The descendants of Javan: Elishah,† Tarshish, the Kittim and the Rodanim. ⁵From these branched out the maritime nations.

These are the descendants of Japheth by their lands, each with its own language, according to their clans, by their nations.

⁶The descendants of Ham: Cush,† Mizraim, Put and Canaan. ⁷The descendants of Cush: Seba, Havilah, Sabtah, Raamah and Sabteca. The descendants of Raamah: Sheba and Dedan.

⁸Cush† became the father of Nimrod, who was the first to become a mighty warrior on earth. ⁹He was a mighty hunter in the eyes of the Lord; hence the saying, "Like Nimrod, a mighty hunter in the eyes of the Lord." ¹⁰His kingdom originated in Babylon, Erech and Accad, all of them in the land of Shinar.† ¹¹From that land he went forth to Assyria, where he built Nineveh, Rehoboth-Ir† and Calah, ¹²as well as Resen, between Nineveh and Calah,† the latter being the principal city.

¹³* Mizraim became the father of the Ludim, the Anamim, the Lehabim, the Naphtuhim, ¹⁴the Pathrusim,† the Casluhim, and the Caphtorim from whom the Philistines came.

¹⁵Canaan became the father of Sidon, his firstborn, and of Heth;† ¹⁶also of the Jebusites, the Amorites, the Girgashites, ¹⁷the Hivites, the Arkites, the Sinites, ¹⁸the Arvadites, the Zemarites, and the Hamathites. Afterward, the clans of the Canaanites spread out, ¹⁹so that the Canaanite borders extended from Sidon all the way to Gerar, near Gaza, and all the way to Sodom, Gomorrah, Admah and Zeboiim, near Lasha.

²⁰These are the descendants of Ham, according to their clans, according to their languages, by their lands, by their nations.

²¹To Shem also, Japheth's oldest brother and the ancestor of all the children of Eber,† children were born. ²²* The descendants of Shem: Elam, Asshur, Arpachshad, Lud and Aram. ²³The descendants of Aram: Uz, Hul, Gether and Mash.

²⁴Arpachshad became the father of Shelah, and Shelah became the father of Eber. ²⁵To Eber two sons were born: the name of the first was Peleg, for in his time the world was divided;† and the name of his brother was Joktan.

²⁶Joktan became the father of Almodad, Sheleph, Hazarmaveth, Jerah, ²⁷Hadoram, Uzal, Diklah, ²⁸Obal, Abimael, Sheba, ²⁹Ophir, Havilah and Jobab. All these were descendants of Joktan. ³⁰Their settlements extended all the way from Mesha to Sephar, the eastern hill country.

³¹These are the descendants of Shem, according to their clans, according to their languages, by their lands, by their nations.

³²These are the clans of Noah's sons, according to their origins and by their nations. From

† This chapter classifies the various peoples known to the ancient Israelites; it is theologically important as stressing the basic family unity of all peoples on earth. It is sometimes called the Table of the Nations. The relationship between the various peoples is based on linguistic, geographic, or political grounds (v. 31). In general, the descendants of Japheth (vv. 2–5) are the peoples of the Indo-European languages to the north and west of Mesopotamia and Syria; the descendants of Ham (vv. 6–20) are the Hamitic-speaking peoples of northern Africa; and the descendants of Shem (vv. 21–31) are the Semitic-speaking peoples of Mesopotamia, Syria and Arabia. But there are many exceptions to this rule; the Semitic-speaking peoples of Canaan are considered descendants of Ham, because at one time they were subject to Hamitic Egypt (vv. 6, 15–19). This chapter is generally considered to be a composite from the Yahwist source (vv. 8–19, 21, 24–30) and the Priestly source (vv. 1–7, 20, 22–23, 31–32). Presumably that is why certain tribes of Arabia are listed under both Ham (v. 7) and Shem (vv. 26–28).

**10:2** *Gomer*: the Cimmerians; *Madai*: the Medes; *Javan*: the Greeks.

**10:3** *Ashkenaz*: an Indo-European people, which later became the medieval rabbinic name for Germany. It now designates one of the great divisions of Judaism, Eastern European Yiddish-speaking Jews.

**10:4** *Elishah*: Cyprus; *the Kittim*: certain inhabitants of Cyprus; *the Rodanim*: the inhabitants of Rhodes.

**10:6** *Cush*: biblical Ethiopia, modern Nubia. *Mizraim*: Lower (i.e., northern) Egypt; *Put*: either Punt in East Africa or Libya.

**10:8** *Cush*: here seems to be Cossea, the country of the Kassites; see note on 2:10–14. *Nimrod*: possibly Tukulti-Ninurta I (thirteenth century B.C.), the first Assyrian conqueror of Babylonia and a famous city-builder at home.

**10:10** *Shinar*: the land of ancient Babylonia, embracing Sumer and Akkad, present-day southern Iraq, mentioned also in 11:2; 14:1.

**10:11** *Rehoboth-Ir*: lit., "wide-streets city," was probably not the name of another city, but an epithet of Nineveh; cf. Jon 3:3.

**10:12** *Calah*: Assyrian Kalhu, the capital of Assyria in the ninth century B.C.

**10:14** *The Pathrusim*: the people of Upper (southern) Egypt; cf. Is 11:11; Jer 44:1; Ez 29:14; 30:13. *Caphtorim*: Crete; for Caphtor as the place of origin of the Philistines, cf. Dt 2:23; Am 9:7; Jer 47:4.

**10:15** *Heth*: the biblical Hittites; see note on 23:3.

**10:21** *Eber*: the eponymous ancestor of the Hebrews, that is, the one to whom they traced their name.

**10:25** In the Hebrew text there is a play on the name *Peleg* and the word *niplega*, "was divided."

**10:2–8** 1 Chr 1:5–10.  **10:2** Ez 38:2.  **10:13–18** 1 Chr 1:11–16.  **10:22–29** 1 Chr 1:17–23.

these the nations of the earth branched out after the flood.

# 11 Tower of Babel.† [1] The whole world had the same language and the same words. [2] When they were migrating from the east, they came to a valley in the land of Shinar† and settled there. [3] They said to one another, "Come, let us mold bricks and harden them with fire." They used bricks for stone, and bitumen for mortar. [4] Then they said, "Come, let us build ourselves a city and a tower with its top in the sky,† and so make a name for ourselves; otherwise we shall be scattered all over the earth."

[5] The LORD came down to see the city and the tower that the people had built. [6] Then the LORD said: If now, while they are one people and all have the same language, they have started to do this, nothing they presume to do will be out of their reach. [7] Come, let us go down and there confuse their language, so that no one will understand the speech of another. [8] So the LORD scattered them from there over all the earth, and they stopped building the city. [9] That is why it was called Babel,† because there the LORD confused the speech of all the world. From there the LORD scattered them over all the earth.

## Descendants from Shem to Abraham.†
[10]* These are the descendants of Shem. When Shem was one hundred years old, he begot Arpachshad, two years after the flood. [11] Shem lived five hundred years after he begot Arpachshad, and he had other sons and daughters. [12] When Arpachshad was thirty-five years old,

he begot Shelah.† [13] Arpachshad lived four hundred and three years after he begot Shelah, and he had other sons and daughters.

[14] When Shelah was thirty years old, he begot Eber. [15] Shelah lived four hundred and three years after he begot Eber, and he had other sons and daughters.

[16] When Eber† was thirty-four years old, he begot Peleg. [17] Eber lived four hundred and thirty years after he begot Peleg, and he had other sons and daughters.

[18] When Peleg was thirty years old, he begot Reu. [19] Peleg lived two hundred and nine years after he begot Reu, and he had other sons and daughters.

[20] When Reu was thirty-two years old, he begot Serug. [21] Reu lived two hundred and seven years after he begot Serug, and he had other sons and daughters.

[22] When Serug was thirty years old, he begot Nahor. [23] Serug lived two hundred years after he begot Nahor, and he had other sons and daughters.

[24] When Nahor was twenty-nine years old, he begot Terah. [25] Nahor lived one hundred and nineteen years after he begot Terah, and he had other sons and daughters.

[26] When Terah was seventy years old, he begot Abram,† Nahor and Haran.*

## II. THE STORY OF THE ANCESTORS OF ISRAEL

**Terah.** [27] These are the descendants of Terah.† Terah begot Abram, Nahor, and Haran, and Haran begot Lot. [28] Haran died before Terah

---

† **11:1–9** This story illustrates increasing human wickedness, shown here in the sinful pride that human beings take in their own achievements apart from God. Secondarily, the story explains the diversity of languages among the peoples of the earth.

**11:2** *Shinar*: see note on 10:10.

**11:4** *Tower with its top in the sky*: possibly a reference to the chief ziggurat of Babylon, *E-sag-ila*, lit., "the house that raises high its head."

**11:9** *Babel*: the Hebrew form of the name "Babylon"; the Babylonians interpreted their name for the city, *Bab-ili*, as "gate of god." The Hebrew word *balal*, "he confused," has a similar sound.

**11:10–26** The second Priestly genealogy goes from Shem to Terah and his three sons Abram, Nahor, and Haran, just as the genealogy in 5:3–32 went from Adam to Noah and his three sons Shem, Ham, and Japheth. This genealogy marks the important transition in Genesis between the story of the nations in 1:1–11:26 and the story of Israel in the person of its ancestors (11:27–50:26). As chaps. 1–11 showed the increase and spread of the nations, so chaps. 12–50 will show the increase and spread of Israel. The contrast between Israel and the nations is a persistent biblical theme. The ages given here are from the Hebrew text; the Samaritan and Greek texts have divergent sets of

numbers in most cases. In comparable accounts of the pre-flood period, enormous life spans are attributed to human beings. It may be an attempt to show that the pre-flood generations were extraordinary and more vital than post-flood human beings.

**11:12** The Greek text adds Kenan (cf. 5:9–10) between Arpachshad and Shelah. The Greek listing is followed in Lk 3:36.

**11:16** *Eber*: the eponymous ancestor of the Hebrews, "descendants of Eber" (10:21, 24–30); see note on 14:13.

**11:26** Abram is a dialectal variant of Abraham. God will change his name in view of his new task in 17:4.

**11:27** *Descendants of Terah*: elsewhere in Genesis the story of the son is introduced by the name of the father (25:12, 19; 36:1; 37:2). The Abraham-Sarah stories begin (11:27–32) and end with genealogical notices (25:1–18), which concern, respectively, the families of Terah and of Abraham. Most of the traditions in the cycle are from the Yahwist source. The so-called Elohist source (E) is somewhat shadowy, denied by some scholars but recognized by others in passages that duplicate other narratives (20:1–18 and 21:22–34). The Priestly source consists mostly of brief editorial notices, except for chaps. 17 and 23.

---

* **11:10–26** 1 Chr 1:24–27; Lk 3:34–36.     **11:26** Jos 24:2; 1 Chr 1:26–27.

his father, in his native land, in Ur of the Chaldeans.† ²⁹ Abram and Nahor took wives; the name of Abram's wife was Sarai,† and the name of Nahor's wife was Milcah, daughter of Haran, the father of Milcah and Iscah.* ³⁰ Sarai was barren; she had no child.

³¹ Terah took his son Abram, his grandson Lot, son of Haran, and his daughter-in-law Sarai, the wife of his son Abram, and brought them out of Ur of the Chaldeans, to go to the land of Canaan. But when they reached Haran, they settled there.* ³² The lifetime of Terah was two hundred and five years; then Terah died in Haran.†

# 12 Abram's Call and Migration. ¹ The LORD said to Abram: Go forth† from your land, your relatives, and from your father's house to a land that I will show you.* ²† I will make of you a great nation, and I will bless you; I will make your name great, so that you will be a blessing.* ³* I will bless those who bless you and curse those who curse you. All the families of the earth will find blessing in you.†

⁴* Abram went as the LORD directed him, and Lot went with him. Abram was seventy-five years old when he left Haran. ⁵† Abram took his wife Sarai, his brother's son Lot, all the possessions that they had accumulated, and the persons they had acquired in Haran, and they set out for the land of Canaan. When they came to the land of Canaan, ⁶† Abram passed through the land as far as the sacred place at Shechem, by the oak of Moreh. The Canaanites were then in the land.

⁷ The LORD appeared to Abram and said: To your descendants I will give this land. So Abram built an altar there to the LORD who had appeared to him.* ⁸ From there he moved on to the hill country east of Bethel, pitching his tent with Bethel to the west and Ai to the east. He built an altar there to the LORD and invoked the LORD by name. ⁹ Then Abram journeyed on by stages to the Negeb.†

**Abram and Sarai in Egypt.**† ¹⁰ There was famine in the land; so Abram went down to Egypt to sojourn there, since the famine in the land

---

† **11:28** *Ur of the Chaldeans*: Ur was an extremely ancient city of the Sumerians (later, of the Babylonians) in southern Mesopotamia. The Greek text has "the land of the Chaldeans." After a millennium of relative unimportance, Ur underwent a revival during the Neo-Babylonian/Chaldean empire (625–539 B.C.). The sixth-century author here identified the place by its contemporary name. As chap. 24 shows, Haran in northern Mesopotamia is in fact the native place of Abraham. In the Genesis perspective, the human race originated in the East (3:24; 4:16) and migrated from there to their homelands (11:2). Terah's family moved from the East (Ur) and Abraham will complete the journey to the family's true homeland in the following chapters.

**11:29** *Sarai*: like Abram, a dialectal variant of the more usual form of the name Sarah. In 17:15, God will change it to Sarah in view of her new task.

**11:32** Since Terah was seventy years old when his son Abraham was born (v. 26), and Abraham was seventy-five when he left Haran (12:4), Terah lived in Haran for sixty years after Abraham's departure. According to the tradition in the Samaritan text, Terah died when he was one hundred and forty-five years old, therefore, in the same year in which Abraham left Haran. This is the tradition followed in Stephen's speech: Abraham left Haran "after his father died" (Acts 7:4).

**12:1–3** *Go forth…find blessing in you*: the syntax of the Hebrew suggests that the blessings promised to Abraham are contingent on his going to Canaan.

**12:2** The call of Abraham begins a new history of blessing (18:18; 22:15–18), which is passed on in each instance to the chosen successor (26:2–4; 28:14). This call evokes the last story in the primeval history (11:1–9) by reversing its themes: Abraham goes forth rather than settle down; it is God rather than Abraham who will make a name for him; the families of the earth will find blessing in him.

**12:3** *Will find blessing in you*: the Hebrew conjugation of the verb here and in 18:18 and 28:14 can be either reflexive ("shall bless themselves by you" = people will invoke Abraham as an example of someone blessed by God) or passive ("by you all the families of earth will be blessed" = the religious privileges of Abraham and his descendants ultimately will be extended

to the nations). In 22:18 and 26:4, another conjugation of the same verb is used in a similar context that is undoubtedly reflexive ("bless themselves"). Many scholars suggest that the two passages in which the sense is clear should determine the interpretation of the three ambiguous passages: the privileged blessing enjoyed by Abraham and his descendants will awaken in all peoples the desire to enjoy those same blessings. Since the term is understood in a passive sense in the New Testament (Acts 3:25; Gal 3:8), it is rendered here by a neutral expression that admits of both meanings.

**12:5** The ancestors appear in Genesis as pastoral nomads living at the edge of settled society, and having occasional dealings with the inhabitants, sometimes even moving into towns for brief periods. Unlike modern nomads such as the Bedouin, however, ancient pastoralists fluctuated between following the herds and sedentary life, depending on circumstances. Pastoralists could settle down and farm and later resume a pastoral way of life. Indeed, there was a symbiotic relationship between pastoralists and villagers, each providing goods to the other. *Persons*: servants and others who formed the larger household under the leadership of Abraham; cf. 14:14.

**12:6** Abraham's journey to the center of the land, Shechem, then to Bethel, and then to the Negeb, is duplicated in Jacob's journeys (33:18; 35:1, 6, 27; 46:1) and in the general route of the conquest under Joshua (Jos 7:2; 8:9, 30). Abraham's journey is a symbolic "conquest" of the land he has been promised. In building altars here (vv. 7, 8) and elsewhere, Abraham acknowledges his God as Lord of the land.

**12:9** *The Negeb*: the semidesert land south of Judah.

**12:10–13:1** Abraham and Sarah's sojourn in Egypt and encounter with Pharaoh foreshadow their descendants' experience, suggesting a divine design in which they must learn to trust. The

---

| | |
|---|---|
| **11:29** Gn 17:15. | **12:3** Gn 18:18; 22:18; Acts |
| **11:31** Jos 24:3; Neh 9:7; Jdt | 3:25; Gal 3:8. |
| 5:6–9; Acts 7:4. | **12:4–5** Gn 11:31; Jos 24:3; |
| **12:1** Acts 7:3; Heb 11:8. | Acts 7:4. |
| **12:2** Gn 17:6; Sir 44:20– | **12:7** Ex 33:1; Dt 34:4; Acts |
| 21; Rom 4:17–22. | 7:5. |

was severe.* ¹¹When he was about to enter Egypt, he said to his wife Sarai: "I know that you are a beautiful woman. ¹²When the Egyptians see you, they will say, 'She is his wife'; then they will kill me, but let you live. ¹³Please say, therefore, that you are my sister,† so that I may fare well on your account and my life may be spared for your sake."* ¹⁴When Abram arrived in Egypt, the Egyptians saw that the woman was very beautiful. ¹⁵When Pharaoh's officials saw her they praised her to Pharaoh, and the woman was taken into Pharaoh's house. ¹⁶Abram fared well on her account, and he acquired sheep, oxen, male and female servants, male and female donkeys, and camels.†

¹⁷But the LORD struck Pharaoh and his household with severe plagues because of Sarai, Abram's wife.* ¹⁸Then Pharaoh summoned Abram and said to him: "How could you do this to me! Why did you not tell me she was your wife? ¹⁹Why did you say, 'She is my sister,' so that I took her for my wife? Now, here is your wife. Take her and leave!"

²⁰Then Pharaoh gave his men orders concerning Abram, and they sent him away, with his wife and all that belonged to him.

# 13 Abram and Lot Part. ¹From Egypt Abram went up to the Negeb with his wife and all that belonged to him, and Lot went with him.* ²† Now Abram was very rich in livestock, silver, and gold.* ³From the Negeb he traveled by stages toward Bethel, to the place between Bethel and Ai where his tent had formerly stood, ⁴the site where he had first built the altar; and there Abram invoked the LORD by name.*

⁵Lot, who went with Abram, also had flocks and herds and tents, ⁶so that the land could not support them if they stayed together; their possessions were so great that they could not live together. ⁷There were quarrels between the herders of Abram's livestock and the herders of Lot's livestock. At this time the Canaanites and the Perizzites were living in the land.

⁸So Abram said to Lot: "Let there be no strife between you and me, or between your herders and my herders, for we are kindred. ⁹Is not the whole land available? Please separate from me. If you prefer the left, I will go to the right; if you prefer the right, I will go to the left." ¹⁰Lot looked about and saw how abundantly watered the whole Jordan Plain was as far as Zoar, like the LORD's own garden, or like Egypt. This was before the LORD had destroyed Sodom and Gomorrah. ¹¹Lot, therefore, chose for himself the whole Jordan Plain and set out eastward. Thus they separated from each other. ¹²Abram settled in the land of Canaan, while Lot settled among the cities of the Plain, pitching his tents near Sodom. ¹³Now the inhabitants of Sodom were wicked, great sinners against the LORD.*

¹⁴After Lot had parted from him, the LORD said to Abram: Look about you, and from where you are, gaze to the north and south, east and west;* ¹⁵all the land that you see I will give to you and your descendants forever.* ¹⁶I will make your descendants like the dust of the earth; if anyone could count the dust of the earth, your descendants too might be counted.* ¹⁷Get up and walk through the land, across its length and breadth, for I give it to you. ¹⁸Abram moved his tents and went on to settle near the oak of Mamre, which is at Hebron. There he built an altar to the LORD.*

# 14 The Four Kings. ¹† When Amraphel king of Shinar, Arioch king of Ellasar, Chedorlaomer king of Elam, and Tidal

---

† story of Sarah, the ancestor in danger, is told again in chap. 20, and also in 26:1–11 with Rebekah instead of Sarah. Repetition of similar events is not unusual in literature that has been orally shaped.

**12:13** *You are my sister*: the text does not try to excuse Abraham's deception, though in 20:12 a similar deception is somewhat excused.

**12:16** *Camels*: domesticated camels did not come into common use in the ancient Near East until the end of the second millennium B.C. Thus the mention of camels here (24:11–64; 30:43; 31:17, 34; 32:8, 16; 37:25) is seemingly an anachronism.

**13:2–18** In this story of Abraham and Lot going their separate ways, Abraham resolves a family dispute by an act that shows both trust in God and generosity toward his nephew. The story suggests Lot rather than Abraham is the natural choice to be the ancestor of a great family; he is young and he takes the most fertile land (outside the land of Canaan). In contrast to Lot, who lifts his eyes to choose for himself (vv. 10–11), Abraham waits for

God to tell him to lift his eyes and see the land he will receive (v. 14). Chaps. 18–19 continue the story of Abraham and Lot. Abraham's visionary possession of the land foreshadows that of Moses (Dt 3:27; 34:4).

**14:1** Abraham plays a role with other world leaders. He defeats a coalition of five kings from the east (where, later, Israel's enemies lived) and is recognized by a Canaanite king as blessed by God Most High. The historicity of the events is controverted; apart from Shinar (Babylon), Tidal (Hittite Tudhaliya), and Elam,

---

12:10 Gn 26:1.
12:13 Gn 20:12–13; 26:7.
12:17 Ps 105:14.
13:1 Gn 12:9.
13:2 Ps 112:1–3; Prv 10:22.
13:4 Gn 12:8.

13:13 Gn 18:20; Ez 16:49; 2 Pt 2:6–8; Jude 7.
13:14 Gn 28:14.
13:15 Gn 12:7; Mt 5:5; Lk 1:55, 73; Acts 7:5; Rom 4:13; Gal 3:16.
13:16 Gn 22:17; Nm 23:10.
13:18 Gn 14:13.

king of Goiim ²made war on Bera king of Sodom, Birsha king of Gomorrah, Shinab king of Admah, Shemeber king of Zeboiim, and the king of Bela (that is, Zoar), ³all the latter kings joined forces in the Valley of Siddim (that is, the Salt Sea†). ⁴For twelve years they had served Chedorlaomer, but in the thirteenth year they rebelled. ⁵In the fourteenth year Chedorlaomer and the kings allied with him came and defeated the Rephaim in Ashteroth-karnaim, the Zuzim in Ham, the Emim in Shaveh-kiriathaim, ⁶and the Horites in the hill country of Seir, as far as El-paran, close by the wilderness.* ⁷They then turned back and came to En-mishpat (that is, Kadesh), and they subdued the whole country of both the Amalekites and the Amorites who lived in Hazazon-tamar. ⁸Thereupon the king of Sodom, the king of Gomorrah, the king of Admah, the king of Zeboiim, and the king of Bela (that is, Zoar) marched out, and in the Valley of Siddim they went into battle against them: ⁹against Chedorlaomer king of Elam, Tidal king of Goiim, Amraphel king of Shinar, and Arioch king of Ellasar—four kings against five. ¹⁰Now the Valley of Siddim was full of bitumen pits; and as the king of Sodom and the king of Gomorrah fled, they fell into these, while the rest fled to the mountains. ¹¹The victors seized all the possessions and food supplies of Sodom and Gomorrah and then went their way. ¹²They took with them Abram's nephew Lot, who had been living in Sodom, as well as his possessions, and departed.*

¹³A survivor came and brought the news to Abram the Hebrew,† who was camping at the oak of Mamre the Amorite, a kinsman of Eshcol and Aner; these were allies of Abram. ¹⁴When Abram heard that his kinsman had been captured, he mustered three hundred and eighteen of his retainers,† born in his house, and went in pursuit as far as Dan. ¹⁵He and his servants deployed against them at night, defeated them, and pursued them as far as Hobah, which is north of Damascus. ¹⁶He recovered all the possessions. He also recovered his kinsman Lot and his possessions, along with the women and the other people.

¹⁷When Abram returned from his defeat of Chedorlaomer and the kings who were allied with him, the king of Sodom went out to greet him in the Valley of Shaveh (that is, the King's Valley).

¹⁸Melchizedek, king of Salem,† brought out bread and wine. He was a priest of God Most High. ¹⁹He blessed Abram with these words:*

"Blessed be Abram by God Most High,
    the creator of heaven and earth;
20   And blessed be God Most High,
    who delivered your foes into your
      hand."

Then Abram gave him a tenth of everything. ²¹The king of Sodom said to Abram, "Give me the captives; the goods you may keep." ²²But Abram replied to the king of Sodom: "I have sworn to the LORD, God Most High,† the creator of heaven and earth, ²³that I would not take so much as a thread or a sandal strap from anything that is yours, so that you cannot say, 'I made Abram rich.' ²⁴Nothing for

---

† the names and places cannot be identified with certainty. The five cities were apparently at the southern end of the Dead Sea, and all but Bela (i.e., Zoar) were destined for destruction (19:20–24; Hos 11:8). The passage belongs to none of the traditional Genesis sources; it has some resemblance to reports of military campaigns in Babylonian and Assyrian royal annals.

**14:3** *The Salt Sea*: the Dead Sea.

**14:13** *Abram the Hebrew*: "Hebrew" was used by biblical writers for the pre-Israelite ancestors. Linguistically, it is an ethnic term; it may be built on the root Eber, who is the eponymous ancestor of the Israelites, that is, the one to whom they traced their name (10:21, 24–25; 11:14–17), or it may reflect the tradition that the ancestors came from beyond (*eber*) the Euphrates. It is used only by non-Israelites, or by Israelites speaking to foreigners.

**14:14** *Retainers*: the Hebrew word *hanik* is used only here in the Old Testament. Cognate words appear in Egyptian and Akkadian texts, signifying armed soldiers belonging to the household of a local leader.

**14:18** Melchizedek, king of Salem (Jerusalem, cf. Ps 76:3), appears with majestic suddenness to recognize Abraham's great victory, which the five local kings were unable to achieve. He prepares a feast in his honor and declares him blessed or made

powerful by God Most High, evidently the highest God in the Canaanite pantheon. Abraham acknowledges the blessing by giving a tenth of the recaptured spoils as a tithe to Melchizedek. The episode is one of several allusions to David, king at Jerusalem, who also exercised priestly functions (2 Sm 6:17). Heb 7 interprets Melchizedek as a prefiguration of Christ. *God Most High*: in Heb. *El Elyon*, one of several "El names" for God in Genesis, others being *El Olam* (21:33), *El* the God of Israel (33:20), *El Roi* (16:13), *El Bethel* (35:7), and *El Shaddai* (the usual P designation for God in Genesis). All the sources except the Yahwist use El as the proper name for God used by the ancestors. The god El was well-known across the ancient Near East and in comparable religious literature. The ancestors recognized this God as their own when they encountered him in their journeys and in the shrines they found in Canaan.

**14:22** In vv. 22–24, Abraham refuses to let anyone but God enrich him. Portrayed with the traits of a later Israelite judge or tribal hero, Abraham acknowledges that his victory is from God alone.

---

| | |
|---|---|
| **14:6** Dt 2:12. | **14:19** Ps 110:4; Heb 5:6, |
| **14:12** Gn 13:10–12. | 10; 7:1. |

me except what my servants have consumed and the share that is due to the men who went with me—Aner, Eshcol and Mamre; let them take their share."

# 15 The Covenant with Abram.† ¹Some time afterward, the word of the LORD came to Abram in a vision: Do not fear, Abram! I am your shield; I will make your reward very great.

²But Abram said, "Lord GOD, what can you give me, if I die childless and have only a servant of my household, Eliezer of Damascus?" ³Abram continued, "Look, you have given me no offspring, so a servant of my household will be my heir." ⁴Then the word of the LORD came to him: No, that one will not be your heir; your own offspring will be your heir.* ⁵He took him outside and said: Look up at the sky and count the stars, if you can. Just so, he added, will your descendants be.* ⁶* Abram put his faith in the LORD, who attributed it to him as an act of righteousness.†

⁷He then said to him: I am the LORD who brought you from Ur of the Chaldeans to give you this land as a possession.* ⁸"Lord GOD," he asked, "how will I know that I will possess it?" ⁹† He answered him: Bring me a three-year-old heifer, a three-year-old female goat, a three-year-old ram, a turtledove, and a young pigeon.* ¹⁰He brought him all these, split them in two, and placed each half opposite

the other; but the birds he did not cut up. ¹¹Birds of prey swooped down on the carcasses, but Abram scared them away. ¹²As the sun was about to set, a deep sleep fell upon Abram, and a great, dark dread descended upon him.

¹³† Then the LORD said to Abram: Know for certain that your descendants will reside as aliens in a land not their own, where they shall be enslaved and oppressed for four hundred years.* ¹⁴But I will bring judgment on the nation they must serve, and after this they will go out with great wealth.* ¹⁵You, however, will go to your ancestors in peace; you will be buried at a ripe old age. ¹⁶In the fourth generation† your descendants will return here, for the wickedness of the Amorites is not yet complete.*

¹⁷When the sun had set and it was dark, there appeared a smoking fire pot and a flaming torch, which passed between those pieces. ¹⁸† On that day the LORD made a covenant with Abram, saying: To your descendants I give this land, from the Wadi of Egypt to the Great River, the Euphrates,* ¹⁹* the land of the Kenites, the Kenizzites, the Kadmonites, ²⁰the Hittites, the Perizzites, the Rephaim, ²¹the Amorites, the Canaanites, the Girgashites, and the Jebusites.

# 16 Birth of Ishmael.† ¹Abram's wife Sarai had borne him no children. Now she

---

† **15:1–21** In the first section (vv. 1–6), Abraham is promised a son and heir, and in the second (vv. 7–21), he is promised a land. The structure is similar in both: each of the two promises is not immediately accepted; the first is met with a complaint (vv. 2–3) and the second with a request for a sign (v. 8). God's answer differs in each section—a sign in v. 5 and an oath in vv. 9–21. Some scholars believe that the Genesis promises of progeny and land were originally separate and only later combined, but progeny and land are persistent concerns especially of ancient peoples and it is hard to imagine one without the other.

**15:6** Abraham's act of faith in God's promises was regarded as an act of righteousness, i.e., as fully expressive of his relationship with God. St. Paul (Rom 4:1–25; Gal 3:6–9) makes Abraham's faith a model for Christians.

**15:9–17** Cutting up animals was a well-attested way of making a treaty in antiquity. Jer 34:17–20 shows the rite is a form of self-imprecation in which violators invoke the fate of the animals upon themselves. The eighth-century B.C. Sefire treaty from Syria reads, "As this calf is cut up, thus Matti'el shall be cut up." The smoking fire pot and the flaming torch (v. 17), which represent God, pass between the pieces, making God a signatory to the covenant.

**15:13–16** The verses clarify the promise of the land by providing a timetable of its possession: after four hundred years of servitude, your descendants will actually possess the land in the fourth generation (a patriarchal generation seems to be one hundred years). The iniquity of the current inhabitants (called here the Amorites) has not yet reached the point where God must intervene in punishment. Another table is given in Ex 12:40, which is not compatible with this one.

**15:16** *Generation:* the Hebrew term *dor* is commonly rendered as "generation," but it may signify a period of varying length. A "generation" is the period between the birth of children and the birth of their parents, normally about twenty to twenty-five years. The actual length of a generation can vary, however; in Jb 42:16 it is thirty-five and in Nm 32:13 it is forty. The meaning may be life spans, which in Gn 6:3 is one hundred twenty years and in Is 65:20 is one hundred years.

**15:18–21** The *Wadi,* i.e., a gully or ravine, *of Egypt* is the Wadi-el-'Arish, which is the boundary between the settled land and the Sinai desert. Some scholars suggest that the boundaries are those of a Davidic empire at its greatest extent; others that they are idealized boundaries. Most lists of the ancient inhabitants of the promised land give three, six, or seven peoples, but vv. 19–21 give a grand total of ten.

**16:1–16** In the previous chapter Abraham was given a timetable of possession of the land, but nothing was said about when the child was to be born. In this chapter, Sarah takes matters into her own hands, for she has been childless ten years since

---

**15:4** Gn 17:16.
**15:5** Gn 22:17; 28:14; Ex 32:13; Dt 1:10; Sir 44:21; Rom 4:18; Heb 11:12.
**15:6** 1 Mc 2:52; Rom 4:3, 9, 22; Gal 3:6–7; Jas 2:23.
**15:7** Gn 11:31; 12:1; Ex 32:13; Neh 9:7–8;

**15:9** Lv 1:14.
**15:13** Ex 12:40; Nm 20:15; Jdt 5:9–10; Is 52:4; Acts 13:20; Gal 3:17.
**15:14** Ex 3:8, 21–22.
**15:16** 1 Kgs 21:26.
**15:18** Ex 32:13; Neh 9:8; Ps 105:11; Sir 44:21.
**15:19–20** Dt 7:1.

Acts 7:2–3.

establish my covenant, and I will multiply you exceedingly.*

³ Abram fell face down and God said to him: ⁴ For my part, here is my covenant with you: you are to become the father of a multitude of nations.* ⁵ No longer will you be called Abram; your name will be Abraham,† for I am making you the father of a multitude of nations.* ⁶ I will make you exceedingly fertile; I will make nations of you; kings will stem from you. ⁷ I will maintain my covenant between me and you and your descendants after you throughout the ages as an everlasting covenant, to be your God and the God of your descendants after you.* ⁸ I will give to you and to your descendants after you the land in which you are now residing as aliens, the whole land of Canaan, as a permanent possession; and I will be their God.* ⁹ God said to Abraham: For your part, you and your descendants after you must keep my covenant throughout the ages. ¹⁰ This is the covenant between me and you and your descendants after you that you must keep: every male among you shall be circumcised.†* ¹¹ Circumcise the flesh of your foreskin. That will be the sign of the covenant between me and you.* ¹² Throughout the ages, every male among you, when he is eight days old, shall be circumcised, including houseborn slaves and those acquired with money from any foreigner who is not of your descendants.* ¹³ Yes, both the houseborn slaves and those acquired with money must be circumcised. Thus my covenant will be in your flesh as an everlasting covenant. ¹⁴ If a male is uncircumcised, that is, if the flesh of his foreskin has not been cut away, such a one will be cut off from his people; he has broken my covenant.

¹⁵ God further said to Abraham: As for Sarai your wife, do not call her Sarai; her name will be Sarah.† ¹⁶ I will bless her, and I will give you a son by her. Her also will I bless; she will give rise to nations, and rulers of peoples will issue from her.* ¹⁷ Abraham fell face down and laughed† as he said to himself, "Can a child be born to a man who is a hundred years old? Can Sarah give birth at ninety?"* ¹⁸ So Abraham said to God, "If only Ishmael could live in your favor!" ¹⁹ God replied: Even so, your wife Sarah is to bear you a son, and you shall call him Isaac. It is with him that I will maintain my covenant as an everlasting covenant and with his descendants after him.* ²⁰ Now as for Ishmael, I will heed you: I hereby bless him. I will make him fertile and will multiply him exceedingly. He will become the father of twelve chieftains, and I will make of him a great nation.* ²¹ But my covenant I will maintain with Isaac, whom Sarah shall bear to you by this time next year.* ²² When he had finished speaking with Abraham, God departed from him.

²³ Then Abraham took his son Ishmael and all his slaves, whether born in his house or acquired with his money—every male among the members of Abraham's household—and he circumcised the flesh of their foreskins on that same day, as God had told him to do. ²⁴ Abraham was ninety-nine years old when the flesh of his foreskin was circumcised,* ²⁵ and his son Ishmael was thirteen years old when the flesh of his foreskin was circumcised. ²⁶ Thus, on that same day Abraham and his son Ishmael were circumcised; ²⁷ and all the males of his household, including the slaves born in his house or acquired with his money from foreigners, were circumcised with him.

# 18 Abraham's Visitors. ¹† The Lord appeared to Abraham by the oak of

---

**17:5** Abram and Abraham are merely two forms of the same name, both meaning, "the father is exalted"; another variant form is Abiram (Nm 16:1; 1 Kgs 16:34). The additional -ha- in the form Abraham is explained by popular etymology as coming from *abhamon goyim*, "father of a multitude of nations."

**17:10** *Circumcised*: circumcision was widely practiced in the ancient world, usually as an initiation rite for males at puberty. By shifting the time of circumcision to the eighth day after birth, biblical religion made it no longer a "rite of passage" but the sign of the eternal covenant between God and the community descending from Abraham.

**17:15** Sarai and Sarah are variant forms of the same name, both meaning "princess."

**17:17** *Laughed: yishaq*, which is also the Hebrew form of the name "Isaac"; similar explanations of the name are given in Gn 18:12 and 21:6.

**18:1** Chapters 18 and 19 combined form a continuous narrative, concluding the story of Abraham and his nephew Lot that began in 13:2–18. The mysterious men visit Abraham in Mamre to promise him and Sarah a child the following year (18:1–15) and then visit Lot in Sodom to investigate and then to punish the corrupt city (19:1–29). Between the two visits, Abraham questions God about the justice of punishing Sodom (18:16–33). At the end of the destruction of Sodom, there is a short narrative about Lot as the ancestor of Moab and the Ammonites (19:30–38).

---

**17:2** Gn 12:2; 13:16; Ex 32:13.
**17:4** Sir 44:21; Rom 4:17.
**17:5** Neh 9:7.
**17:7** Ps 105:42; Lk 1:72–73; Gal 3:16.
**17:8** Ex 32:13; Dt 1:8; 14:2; Lk 1:55; Acts 7:5.
**17:10** Jn 7:22; Acts 7:8; Rom 4:11.
**17:11** Sir 44:20.
**17:12** Lv 12:3; Lk 1:59; 2:21.
**17:16** Gn 18:10; Gal 4:23.
**17:17** Rom 4:19; Heb 11:11–12.
**17:19** Gn 11:30; 21:2; Ex 32:13; Sir 44:22.
**17:20** Gn 16:10; 21:13, 18; 25:12–16.
**17:21** Gn 18:14; 21:2; 26:2–5; Rom 9:7.
**17:24** Gn 17:10; Rom 4:11.

Mamre, as he sat in the entrance of his tent, while the day was growing hot. ²Looking up, he saw three men standing near him. When he saw them, he ran from the entrance of the tent to greet them; and bowing to the ground, * ³he said: "Sir,† if it please you, do not go on past your servant. ⁴Let some water be brought, that you may bathe your feet, and then rest under the tree. ⁵Now that you have come to your servant, let me bring you a little food, that you may refresh yourselves; and afterward you may go on your way." "Very well," they replied, "do as you have said."

⁶Abraham hurried into the tent to Sarah and said, "Quick, three measures† of bran flour! Knead it and make bread." ⁷He ran to the herd, picked out a tender, choice calf, and gave it to a servant, who quickly prepared it. ⁸Then he got some curds† and milk, as well as the calf that had been prepared, and set these before them, waiting on them under the tree while they ate.

⁹"Where is your wife Sarah?" they asked him. "There in the tent," he replied. ¹⁰One of them† said, "I will return to you about this time next year, and Sarah will then have a son." Sarah was listening at the entrance of the tent, just behind him. * ¹¹Now Abraham and Sarah were old, advanced in years, and Sarah had stopped having her menstrual periods. * ¹²So Sarah laughed† to herself and said, "Now that I am worn out and my husband is old, am I still to have sexual pleasure?" ¹³But the LORD said to Abraham: "Why did Sarah laugh and say, 'Will I really bear a child, old as I am?' ¹⁴Is anything too marvelous for the LORD to do? At the appointed time, about this time next year, I will return to you, and Sarah will have a son." * ¹⁵Sarah lied, saying, "I did not laugh," because she was afraid. But he said, "Yes, you did."

**Abraham Intercedes for Sodom.** ¹⁶With Abraham walking with them to see them on their way, the men set out from there and looked down toward Sodom. ¹⁷The LORD considered: Shall I hide from Abraham what I am about to do, ¹⁸now that he is to become a great and mighty nation, and all the nations of the earth are to find blessing in him? * ¹⁹Indeed, I have singled him out that he may direct his children and his household in the future to keep the way of the LORD by doing what is right and just, so that the LORD may put into effect for Abraham the promises he made about him. ²⁰ * So the LORD said: The outcry against Sodom and Gomorrah is so great, and their sin so grave,† ²¹that I must go down to see whether or not their actions are as bad as the cry against them that comes to me. I mean to find out.

²²As the men turned and walked on toward Sodom, Abraham remained standing before the LORD. ²³Then Abraham drew near and said: "Will you really sweep away the righteous with the wicked? ²⁴Suppose there were fifty righteous people in the city; would you really sweep away and not spare the place for the sake of the fifty righteous people within it? ²⁵Far be it from you to do such a thing, to kill the righteous with the wicked, so that the righteous and the wicked are treated alike! Far be it from you! Should not the judge of all the world do what is just?" * ²⁶The LORD replied: If I find fifty righteous people in the city of Sodom, I will spare the whole place for their sake. ²⁷Abraham spoke up again: "See how I am presuming to speak to my Lord, though I am only dust and ashes! * ²⁸What if there are five less than fifty righteous people? Will you destroy the whole city because of those five?" I will not destroy it, he answered, if I find forty-five there. ²⁹But Abraham persisted, saying,

---

†
**18:3** Abraham addresses the leader of the group, whom he does not yet recognize as the Lord; in the next two verses he speaks to all three men. The other two are later (Gn 19:1) identified as angels. The shifting numbers and identification of the visitors are a narrative way of expressing the mysterious presence of God.

**18:6** *Three measures*: Hebrew *seah*; three seahs equal one ephah, about half a bushel.

**18:8** *Curds*: a type of soft cheese or yogurt.

**18:10** *One of them*: i.e., the Lord.

**18:12** *Sarah laughed*: a play on the verb "laugh," which prefigures the name of Isaac; see note on 17:17.

**18:20** The immorality of the cities was already hinted at in 13:13, when Lot made his choice to live there. The "outcry" comes from the victims of the injustice and violence rampant in the city, which will shortly be illustrated in the treatment of the

visitors. The outcry of the Hebrews under the harsh treatment of Pharaoh (Ex 3:7) came up to God who reacts in anger at mistreatment of the poor (cf. Ex 22:21–23; Is 5:7). Sodom and Gomorrah became types of sinful cities in biblical literature. Is 1:9–10; 3:9 sees their sin as lack of social justice, Ez 16:46–51, as disregard for the poor, and Jer 23:14, as general immorality. In the Genesis story, the sin is violation of the sacred duty of hospitality by the threatened rape of Lot's guests.

---

*
| | |
|---|---|
| **18:2** Heb 13:1–2. | Rom 4:21. |
| **18:10** Gn 17:19; 21:1; 2 Kgs | **18:18** Lk 1:55. |
| 4:16; Rom 9:9. | **18:20** Gn 19:13; Is 3:9; Lk |
| **18:11** Gn 17:17; Rom 4:19; | 17:28; Jude 7. |
| Heb 11:11–12. | **18:25** Dt 32:4; Jb 8:3, 20; |
| **18:14** Mt 19:26; Mk 10:27; | Wis 12:15. |
| Lk 1:37; 18:27; | **18:27** Sir 10:9; 17:27. |

"What if only forty are found there?" He replied: I will refrain from doing it for the sake of the forty. [30]Then he said, "Do not let my Lord be angry if I go on. What if only thirty are found there?" He replied: I will refrain from doing it if I can find thirty there. [31]Abraham went on, "Since I have thus presumed to speak to my Lord, what if there are no more than twenty?" I will not destroy it, he answered, for the sake of the twenty. [32]But he persisted: "Please, do not let my Lord be angry if I speak up this last time. What if ten are found there?" For the sake of the ten, he replied, I will not destroy it. *

[33]The Lord departed as soon as he had finished speaking with Abraham, and Abraham returned home.

**19** **Destruction of Sodom and Gomorrah.†** [1]The two angels reached Sodom in the evening, as Lot was sitting at the gate of Sodom. When Lot saw them, he got up to greet them; and bowing down with his face to the ground, [2]he said, "Please, my lords,† come aside into your servant's house for the night, and bathe your feet; you can get up early to continue your journey." But they replied, "No, we will pass the night in the town square." * [3]He urged them so strongly, however, that they turned aside to his place and entered his house. He prepared a banquet for them, baking unleavened bread, and they dined.

[4]* Before they went to bed, the townsmen of Sodom, both young and old—all the people to the last man—surrounded the house. [5]They called to Lot and said to him, "Where are the men who came to your house tonight? Bring them out to us that we may have sexual relations with them." [6]Lot went out to meet them at the entrance. When he had shut the door behind him, [7]he said, "I beg you, my brothers, do not do this wicked thing! [8]I have two daughters who have never had sexual relations

with men. Let me bring them out to you,† and you may do to them as you please. But do not do anything to these men, for they have come under the shelter of my roof." [9]They replied, "Stand back! This man," they said, "came here as a resident alien, and now he dares to give orders! We will treat you worse than them!" With that, they pressed hard against Lot, moving in closer to break down the door. * [10]But his guests put out their hands, pulled Lot inside with them, and closed the door; [11]they struck the men at the entrance of the house, small and great, with such a blinding light† that they were utterly unable to find the doorway.

[12]Then the guests said to Lot: "Who else belongs to you here? Sons-in-law, your sons, your daughters, all who belong to you in the city—take them away from this place! * [13]We are about to destroy this place, for the outcry reaching the Lord against those here is so great that the Lord has sent us to destroy it." * [14]So Lot went out and spoke to his sons-in-law, who had contracted marriage with his daughters.† "Come on, leave this place," he told them; "the Lord is about to destroy the city." But his sons-in-law thought he was joking.

[15]As dawn was breaking, the angels urged Lot on, saying, "Come on! Take your wife with you and your two daughters who are here, or you will be swept away in the punishment of the city." [16]When he hesitated, the men, because of the Lord's compassion for him, seized his hand and the hands of his wife and his two daughters and led them to safety outside the city. [17]As soon as they had brought them outside, they said: "Flee for your life! Do not look back or stop anywhere on the Plain. Flee to the hills at once, or you will be swept away." * [18]"Oh, no, my lords!" Lot replied to them. [19]"You have already shown favor to your servant, doing me the great kindness of saving my life. But I cannot flee to the hills, or

---

**19:1–29** The story takes place in one day (counting a day from the previous evening): evening (v. 1), dawn (v. 15), and sunrise (v. 23). The passage resembles Jgs 19:15–25, which suggests dependence of one story on the other.

**19:2** *My lords*: Lot does not yet know that the men are God's messengers; cf. 18:3.

**19:8** *Let me bring them out to you*: the authority of a patriarch within his house was virtually absolute. Lot's extreme response of offering his daughters to a violent mob seems to be motivated by the obligation of hospitality.

**19:11** *Blinding light*: an extraordinary flash that temporarily dazed the wicked men and revealed to Lot the true nature of his guests.

**19:14** It is uncertain whether Lot's sons-in-law were fully married to his daughters or only "engaged" to them (Israelite "engagement" was the first part of the marriage ceremony), or even whether the daughters involved were the same as, or different from, the two daughters who were still in their father's house.

---

**18:32** Jer 5:1; Ez 22:30.
**19:2** Heb 13:1–2.
**19:4–9** Jgs 19:22–25; Jude 7.
**19:9** Gn 13:12; 2 Pt 2:7–8.
**19:12** 2 Pt 2:7–9.
**19:13** Is 1:7, 9; Ez 16:49–50; Zep 2:9.
**19:17** Wis 10:6.

the disaster will overtake and kill me. ²⁰ Look, this town ahead is near enough to escape to. It is only a small place.† Let me flee there—is it not a small place?—to save my life." ²¹ "Well, then," he replied, "I grant you this favor too. I will not overthrow the town you have mentioned. ²² Hurry, escape there! I cannot do anything until you arrive there." That is why the town is called Zoar.*

²³ The sun had risen over the earth when Lot arrived in Zoar, ²⁴ and the Lᴏʀᴅ rained down sulfur upon Sodom and Gomorrah, fire from the Lᴏʀᴅ out of heaven.* ²⁵ He overthrew† those cities and the whole Plain, together with the inhabitants of the cities and the produce of the soil.* ²⁶ But Lot's wife looked back, and she was turned into a pillar of salt.*

²⁷ The next morning Abraham hurried to the place where he had stood before the Lᴏʀᴅ. ²⁸ As he looked down toward Sodom and Gomorrah and the whole region of the Plain,† he saw smoke over the land rising like the smoke from a kiln.*

²⁹ When God destroyed the cities of the Plain, he remembered Abraham and sent Lot away from the upheaval that occurred when God overthrew the cities where Lot had been living.

**Moabites and Ammonites.**† ³⁰ Since Lot was afraid to stay in Zoar, he and his two daughters went up from Zoar and settled in the hill country, where he lived with his two daughters in a cave. ³¹ The firstborn said to the younger: "Our father is getting old, and there is not a man in the land to have intercourse with us as is the custom everywhere. ³² Come, let us ply our father with wine and then lie with

him, that we may ensure posterity by our father." ³³ So that night they plied their father with wine, and the firstborn went in and lay with her father; but he was not aware of her lying down or getting up. ³⁴ The next day the firstborn said to the younger: "Last night I lay with my father. Let us ply him with wine again tonight, and then you go in and lie with him, that we may ensure posterity by our father." ³⁵ So that night, too, they plied their father with wine, and then the younger one went in and lay with him; but he was not aware of her lying down or getting up.

³⁶ Thus the two daughters of Lot became pregnant by their father. ³⁷ The firstborn gave birth to a son whom she named Moab, saying, "From my father."† He is the ancestor of the Moabites of today.* ³⁸ The younger one, too, gave birth to a son, and she named him Ammon, saying, "The son of my kin."† He is the ancestor of the Ammonites of today.*

# 20 **Abraham at Gerar.**† ¹ From there Abraham journeyed on to the region of the Negeb, where he settled between Kadesh and Shur.† While he resided in Gerar as an alien, ² Abraham said of his wife Sarah, "She is my sister." So Abimelech, king of Gerar, sent and took Sarah. ³ But God came to Abimelech in a dream one night and said to him: You are about to die because of the woman you have taken, for she has a husband. ⁴ Abimelech, who had not approached her, said: "O Lord, would you kill an innocent man? ⁵ Was he not the one who told me, 'She is my sister'? She herself also stated, 'He is my brother.' I acted with pure heart and with clean hands." ⁶† God

---

† **19:20** *A small place*: the Hebrew word *misar*, lit., "a little thing," has the same root consonants as the name of the town Zoar in v. 22.

**19:25** *Overthrew*: this term, lit., "turned upside down," is used consistently to describe the destruction of the cities of the Plain. The imagery of earthquake and subsequent fire fits the geology of this region.

**19:28–29** In a deft narrative detail, Abraham looks down from the height east of Hebron, from which he could easily see the region at the southern end of the Dead Sea, where the cities of the Plain were probably located.

**19:30–38** This Israelite tale about the origin of Israel's neighbors east of the Jordan and the Dead Sea was told partly to ridicule this ethnically related but rival nations and partly to give popular etymologies for their names. The stylized nature of the story is seen in the names of the daughters ("the firstborn" and "the younger"), the ease with which they fool their father, and the identical descriptions of the encounters.

**19:37** *From my father*: in Hebrew, *me'abi*, similar in sound to the name "Moab."

**19:38** *The son of my kin*: in Hebrew, *ben-ammi*, similar in sound to the name "Ammonites."

**20:1–18** Abraham again passes off his wife Sarah as his sister to escape trouble in a foreign land (cf. 12:10–13:1, the J source). The story appears to be from a different source (according to some, E) and deals with the ethical questions of the incident. Gn 26:6–11 is yet another retelling of the story, but with Isaac and Rebekah as characters instead of Abraham and Sarah.

**20:1** *Kadesh and Shur*: Kadesh-barnea was a major oasis on the southernmost border of Canaan, and Shur was probably the "way to Shur," the road to Egypt. Gerar was a royal city in the area, but has not been identified with certainty.

**20:6** Abimelech is exonerated of blame, but by that fact not cleared of the consequences of his act. He is still under the sentence of death for abducting another man's wife; the consequences result from the deed not the intention.

**19:22** Wis 10:6.
**19:24** Ps 9:6; 11:6; 107:34; Wis 10:7; Sir 16:8; Is 1:9; Lk 17:29; 2 Pt 2:6.
**19:25** Dt 29:22; Is 13:19;
Jer 50:40; Lam 4:6; Am 4:11.
**19:26** Wis 10:7; Lk 17:32.
**19:28** Rev 9:2; 14:10–11.
**19:37** Dt 2:9.
**19:38** Dt 2:19.

answered him in the dream: Yes, I know you did it with a pure heart. In fact, it was I who kept you from sinning against me; that is why I did not let you touch her. [7] So now, return the man's wife so that he may intercede for you, since he is a prophet,† that you may live. If you do not return her, you can be sure that you and all who are yours will die.

[8] Early the next morning Abimelech called all his servants and informed them of everything that had happened, and the men were filled with fear. [9] Then Abimelech summoned Abraham and said to him: "What have you done to us! What wrong did I do to you that you would have brought such great guilt on me and my kingdom? You have treated me in an intolerable way. [10] What did you have in mind," Abimelech asked him, "that you would do such a thing?" [11] Abraham answered, "I thought there would be no fear of God† in this place, and so they would kill me on account of my wife. [12] Besides, she really is my sister,† but only my father's daughter, not my mother's; and so she became my wife. [13] When God sent me wandering from my father's house, I asked her: 'Would you do me this favor? In whatever place we come to, say: He is my brother.'"*

[14] Then Abimelech took flocks and herds and male and female slaves and gave them to Abraham; and he restored his wife Sarah to him. [15] Then Abimelech said, "Here, my land is at your disposal; settle wherever you please." [16] To Sarah he said: "I hereby give your brother a thousand shekels of silver. This will preserve your honor before all who are with you and will exonerate you before everyone." [17] Abraham then interceded with God, and God restored health to Abimelech, to his wife,

and his maidservants, so that they bore children; [18] for the LORD had closed every womb in Abimelech's household on account of Abraham's wife Sarah.

# 21 Birth of Isaac.† [1] The LORD took note of Sarah as he had said he would; the LORD did for her as he had promised.* [2] Sarah became pregnant and bore Abraham a son in his old age, at the set time that God had stated.* [3] Abraham gave the name Isaac to this son of his whom Sarah bore him.* [4] When his son Isaac was eight days old, Abraham circumcised him, as God had commanded.* [5] Abraham was a hundred years old when his son Isaac was born to him. [6] Sarah then said, "God has given me cause to laugh,† and all who hear of it will laugh with me.* [7] Who would ever have told Abraham," she added, "that Sarah would nurse children! Yet I have borne him a son in his old age." [8] The child grew and was weaned, and Abraham held a great banquet on the day of the child's weaning.

[9] Sarah noticed the son whom Hagar the Egyptian had borne to Abraham playing with her son Isaac; [10] so she demanded of Abraham: "Drive out that slave and her son! No son of that slave is going to share the inheritance with my son Isaac!"* [11] Abraham was greatly distressed because it concerned a son of his.† [12] But God said to Abraham: Do not be distressed about the boy or about your slave woman. Obey Sarah, no matter what she asks of you; for it is through Isaac that descendants will bear your name.* [13] As for the son of the slave woman, I will make a nation of him also,† since he too is your offspring.

[14] Early the next morning Abraham got some

---

† **20:7** *Prophet:* only here is Abraham explicitly called "prophet," Hebrew *nabi* (cf. Ps 105:15).

**20:11** *Fear of God* is the traditional though unsatisfactory rendering of Hebrew *yir'at YHWH,* literally, "revering Yahweh." The phrase refers neither to the emotion of fear nor to religious reverence of a general kind. Rather it refers to adherence to a single deity (in a polytheistic culture), honoring that deity with prayers, rituals, and obedience. The phrase occurs again in 26:24; 43:23; and 50:19. It is very common in the wisdom literature of the Bible.

**20:12** *My sister:* marrying one's half sister was prohibited later in Israel's history.

**21:1–21** The long-awaited birth of Isaac parallels the birth of Ishmael in chap. 16, precipitating a rivalry and expulsion as in that chapter. Though this chapter is unified, the focus of vv. 1–7 is exclusively on Sarah and Isaac, and the focus of vv. 8–21 is exclusively on Hagar and Ishmael. The promise of a son to the barren Sarah and elderly Abraham has been central to the previous chapters and now that promise comes true with the birth of Isaac. The other great promise, that of land, will be resolved, at

least in an anticipatory way, in Abraham's purchase of the cave at Machpelah in chap. 23. The parallel births of the two boys has influenced the Lucan birth narratives of John the Baptist and Jesus (Lk 1–2).

**21:6** *Laugh:* for the third time (cf. 17:17 and 18:12) there is laughter, playing on the similarity in Hebrew between the pronunciation of the name Isaac and words associated with laughter.

**21:11** *A son of his:* Abraham is the father of both boys, but Sarah is the mother only of Isaac. Abraham is very concerned that Ishmael have a sufficient inheritance.

**21:13** *I will make a nation of him also:* Ishmael's descendants are named in 25:12–18.

---

**20:13** Gn 12:13.
**21:1** Gn 17:19; 18:10.
**21:2** Gal 4:23; Heb 11:11.
**21:3** Mt 1:2; Lk 3:34.
**21:4** Gn 17:10–14; Acts 7:8.
**21:6** Gn 17:17.
**21:10** Jgs 11:2; Gal 4:30.
**21:12** Rom 9:7; Heb 11:18.

bread and a skin of water and gave them to Hagar. Then, placing the child on her back,† he sent her away. As she roamed aimlessly in the wilderness of Beer-sheba, <sup>15</sup> the water in the skin was used up. So she put the child down under one of the bushes, <sup>16</sup> and then went and sat down opposite him, about a bowshot away; for she said to herself, "I cannot watch the child die." As she sat opposite him, she wept aloud. <sup>17</sup> God heard the boy's voice, and God's angel called to Hagar from heaven: "What is the matter, Hagar? Do not fear; God has heard the boy's voice in this plight of his.* <sup>18</sup> Get up, lift up the boy and hold him by the hand; for I will make of him a great nation." <sup>19</sup> Then God opened her eyes, and she saw a well of water. She went and filled the skin with water, and then let the boy drink.

<sup>20</sup> God was with the boy as he grew up. He lived in the wilderness and became an expert bowman. <sup>21</sup> He lived in the wilderness of Paran. His mother got a wife for him from the land of Egypt.

**The Covenant at Beer-sheba.** <sup>22</sup>† At that time Abimelech, accompanied by Phicol, the commander of his army, said to Abraham: "God is with you in everything you do. <sup>23</sup> So now, swear to me by God at this place† that you will not deal falsely with me or with my progeny and posterity, but will act as loyally toward me and the land in which you reside as I have acted toward you." <sup>24</sup> Abraham replied, "I so swear."

<sup>25</sup> Abraham, however, reproached Abimelech about a well that Abimelech's servants had seized by force. <sup>26</sup> "I have no idea who did that," Abimelech replied. "In fact, you never told me about it, nor did I ever hear of it until now."

<sup>27</sup> Then Abraham took sheep and cattle and gave them to Abimelech and the two made a covenant. <sup>28</sup> Abraham also set apart seven ewe lambs of the flock, <sup>29</sup> and Abimelech asked him, "What is the purpose of these seven ewe lambs that you have set apart?" <sup>30</sup> Abraham answered, "The seven ewe lambs you shall accept from me that you may be my witness that I dug this well." <sup>31</sup> This is why the place is called Beer-sheba; the two of them took an oath there. <sup>32</sup> When they had thus made the covenant in Beer-sheba, Abimelech, along with Phicol, the commander of his army, left to return to the land of the Philistines.†

<sup>33</sup> Abraham planted a tamarisk at Beer-sheba, and there he invoked by name the LORD, God the Eternal.† <sup>34</sup> Abraham resided in the land of the Philistines for a long time.

# 22

**The Testing of Abraham.**† <sup>1</sup> Some time afterward, God put Abraham to the test and said to him: Abraham! "Here I am!" he replied.* <sup>2</sup> Then God said: Take your son Isaac, your only one, whom you love, and go to the land of Moriah. There offer him up as a burnt offering on one of the heights that I will point out to you.* <sup>3</sup> Early the next morning Abraham saddled his donkey, took with him

---

† **21:14** *Placing the child on her back*: a reading based on an emendation of the traditional Hebrew text. In the traditional Hebrew text, Abraham put the bread and the waterskin on Hagar's back, while her son apparently walked beside her. In this way the traditional Hebrew text harmonizes the data of the Priestly source, in which Ishmael would have been at least fourteen years old when Isaac was born; compare 16:16 with 21:5; cf. 17:25. But in the present Elohist (?) story, Ishmael is obviously a little boy, not much older than Isaac; cf. vv. 15, 18.

**21:22** Of the two related promises of progeny and land, that of progeny has been fulfilled in the previous chapter. Now the claim on the land begins to be solidified by Abimelech's recognition of Abraham's claim on the well at Beer-sheba; it will be furthered by Abraham's purchase of the cave at Machpelah in chap. 23. Two levels of editing are visible in the story: (1) vv. 22–24, 27, 32, the general covenant with Abimelech; (2) vv. 25–26, 28–30, 31, Abraham's claim on the well. Both versions play on the root of the Hebrew word *sheba'*, which means "seven" and "swear," and the place name Beer-sheba.

**21:23** *This place*: Beer-sheba (v. 31). Abimelech had come from Gerar (20:2), about thirty miles west of Beer-sheba.

**21:32** *Philistines*: one of the Sea Peoples, who migrated from Mycenaean Greece around 1200 B.C. and settled on the coastland of Canaan, becoming a principal rival of Israel. Non-biblical texts do not use the term "Philistine" before ca. 1200 B.C.; it is probable that this usage and those in chap. 26 are

anachronistic, perhaps applying a later ethnic term for an earlier, less-known one.

**21:33** *God the Eternal*: in Hebrew, *'el 'olam*, perhaps the name of the deity of the pre-Israelite sanctuary at Beer-sheba, but used by Abraham as a title of God; cf. Is 40:28.

**22:1–19** The divine demand that Abraham sacrifice to God the son of promise is the greatest of his trials; after the successful completion of the test, he has only to buy a burial site for Sarah and find a wife for Isaac. The story is widely recognized as a literary masterpiece, depicting in a few lines God as the absolute Lord, inscrutable yet ultimately gracious, and Abraham, acting in moral grandeur as the great ancestor of Israel. Abraham speaks simply, with none of the wordy evasions of chaps. 13 and 21. The style is laconic; motivations and thoughts are not explained, and the reader cannot but wonder at the scene. In vv. 15–18, the angel repeats the seventh and climactic promise. *Moriah*: the mountain is not given a precise geographical location here, though 2 Chr 3:1 identifies Moriah as the mountain of Jerusalem where Solomon built the Temple; Abraham is thus the first to worship there. The word "Moriah" is a play on the verb "to see" (Heb. *ra'ah*); the wordplay is continued in v. 8, "God will provide (lit., "see")" and in v. 14, Yahweh-yireh, meaning "the Lord will see/provide."

---

two of his servants and his son Isaac, and after cutting the wood for the burnt offering, set out for the place of which God had told him.

⁴ On the third day Abraham caught sight of the place from a distance. ⁵ Abraham said to his servants: "Stay here with the donkey, while the boy and I go on over there. We will worship and then come back to you." ⁶ So Abraham took the wood for the burnt offering and laid it on his son Isaac, while he himself carried the fire and the knife. As the two walked on together, ⁷ Isaac spoke to his father Abraham. "Father!" he said. "Here I am," he replied. Isaac continued, "Here are the fire and the wood, but where is the sheep for the burnt offering?" ⁸ "My son," Abraham answered, "God will provide the sheep for the burnt offering." Then the two walked on together.

⁹ When they came to the place of which God had told him, Abraham built an altar there and arranged the wood on it. Next he bound† his son Isaac, and put him on top of the wood on the altar.* ¹⁰ Then Abraham reached out and took the knife to slaughter his son.* ¹¹ But the angel of the LORD called to him from heaven, "Abraham, Abraham!" "Here I am," he answered. ¹² "Do not lay your hand on the boy," said the angel. "Do not do the least thing to him. For now I know that you fear God, since you did not withhold from me your son, your only one."* ¹³ Abraham looked up and saw a single ram caught by its horns in the thicket. So Abraham went and took the ram and offered it up as a burnt offering in place of his son.† ¹⁴ Abraham named that place Yahweh-yireh;† hence

people today say, "On the mountain the LORD will provide."

¹⁵ † A second time the angel of the LORD called to Abraham from heaven ¹⁶ * and said: "I swear by my very self—oracle of the LORD— that because you acted as you did in not withholding from me your son, your only one, ¹⁷ I will bless you and make your descendants as countless as the stars of the sky and the sands of the seashore; your descendants will take possession of the gates of their enemies,* ¹⁸ and in your descendants all the nations of the earth will find blessing, because you obeyed my command."*

¹⁹ Abraham then returned to his servants, and they set out together for Beer-sheba, where Abraham lived.

**Nahor's Descendants.**† ²⁰ Some time afterward, the news came to Abraham: "Milcah too has borne sons to your brother Nahor: ²¹ Uz, his firstborn, his brother Buz, Kemuel the father of Aram, ²² Chesed, Hazo, Pildash, Jidlaph, and Bethuel." ²³ Bethuel became the father of Rebekah. These eight Milcah bore to Nahor, Abraham's brother. ²⁴ His concubine, whose name was Reumah, also bore children: Tebah, Gaham, Tahash, and Maacah.

# 23 Purchase of a Burial Plot.† ¹ The span of Sarah's life was one hundred and twenty-seven years. ² She died in Kiriath-arba—now Hebron—in the land of Canaan, and Abraham proceeded to mourn and weep for her. ³ Then he left the side of his deceased wife and addressed the Hittites:† ⁴ "Although I

---

† **22:9** *Bound:* the Hebrew verb is ʿaqad, from which is derived the noun Akedah, "the binding (of Isaac)," the traditional Jewish name for this incident.

**22:13** While the Bible recognizes that firstborn males belong to God (Ex 13:11–16; 34:19–20), and provides an alternate sacrifice to redeem firstborn sons, the focus here is on Abraham's being tested by God (v. 1). But the widely attested practice of child sacrifice underscores, for all its horror today, the realism of the test.

**22:14** *Yahweh-yireh:* a Hebrew expression meaning "the Lord will see/provide." See note on vv. 1–19.

**22:15–19** The seventh and climactic statement of the blessings to Abraham. Unlike the other statements, which were purely promissory, this one is presented as a reward for Abraham's extraordinary trust.

**22:20–24** The descendants to the second generation of Nahor, Abraham's brother, who married Milcah. Of Terah's three sons (11:27), the oldest, Abraham, fathered Isaac (21:1–7), and the youngest, Haran (who died in Ur), fathered Lot. Abraham is now told that Nahor had eight children by Milcah and four by his concubine Reumah. Apart from the notice about the children born to Abraham by his second wife, Keturah (25:1–6), all the information about Terah's family to the second generation is now

complete. It is noteworthy that Jacob will, like Nahor, have eight children by his wives and four by his concubines.

**23:1–20** The occasion for purchasing the land is the need for a burial site for Sarah, for it would be unthinkable to bury Sarah outside of the promised land. One of the two great promises to Abraham, that of progeny, has been fulfilled (21:1–7). And now the promise of land is to be fulfilled, through a kind of down payment on the full possession that will take place only with the conquest under Joshua and during the reign of David. This purchase has been prepared for by Abimelech's recognition of Abraham's claim to the well at Beer-sheba (21:22–34). Among the ancestral stories this narrative is one of two that are entirely from the P source (chap. 17 being the other). The Priestly writers may have intended to encourage the generation of the exile to a renewed hope of repossessing their land.

**23:3** *The Hittites:* in the Bible the term is applied to several different groups—inhabitants of the second-millennium Hittite empire in Asia Minor and northern Syria, residents of the Neo-

---

**22:9** Jas 2:21.
**22:10** Wis 10:5.
**22:12** Rom 8:32; 1 Jn 4:9.
**22:16–17** Gn 15:5; Ex 32:13; Lk 1:73; Rom 4:13;

Heb 6:13–14; 11:12.
**22:17** Gn 24:60.
**22:18** Gn 12:3; 18:18; 26:4; Sir 44:21; Acts 3:25; Gal 3:16.

am a resident alien† among you, sell me from your holdings a burial place, that I may bury my deceased wife."* ⁵The Hittites answered Abraham: "Please, ⁶sir, listen to us! You are a mighty leader among us. Bury your dead in the choicest of our burial sites. None of us would deny you his burial ground for the burial of your dead." ⁷Abraham, however, proceeded to bow low before the people of the land, the Hittites, ⁸and said to them: "If you will allow me room for burial of my dead, listen to me! Intercede for me with Ephron, son of Zohar, ⁹so that he will sell me the cave of Machpelah that he owns; it is at the edge of his field. Let him sell it to me in your presence at its full price for a burial place."

¹⁰Now Ephron was sitting with the Hittites. So Ephron the Hittite replied to Abraham in the hearing of the Hittites, all who entered the gate of his city: ¹¹"Please, sir, listen to me! I give you both the field and the cave in it; in the presence of my people I give it to you. Bury your dead!" ¹²But Abraham, after bowing low before the people of the land, ¹³addressed Ephron in the hearing of these men: "If only you would please listen to me! I will pay you the price of the field. Accept it from me, that I may bury my dead there." ¹⁴Ephron replied to Abraham, "Please, ¹⁵sir, listen to me! A piece of land worth four hundred shekels† of silver—what is that between you and me? Bury your dead!" ¹⁶*Abraham accepted Ephron's terms; he weighed out to him the silver that Ephron had stipulated in the hearing of the Hittites, four hundred shekels of silver at the current market value.†

¹⁷*Thus Ephron's field in Machpelah, facing Mamre, together with its cave and all the trees anywhere within its limits, was conveyed ¹⁸to Abraham by purchase in the presence of the Hittites, all who entered the gate of Ephron's city. ¹⁹After this, Abraham buried his wife Sarah in the cave of the field of Machpelah, facing Mamre—now Hebron—in the land of Canaan. ²⁰Thus the field with its cave was transferred from the Hittites to Abraham as a burial place.

# 24 Isaac and Rebekah.†

¹Abraham was old, having seen many days, and the LORD had blessed him in every way. ²*Abraham said to the senior servant of his household, who had charge of all his possessions: "Put your hand under my thigh,† ³and I will make you swear by the LORD, the God of heaven and the God of earth, that you will not take a wife for my son from the daughters of the Canaanites among whom I live, * ⁴but that you will go to my own land and to my relatives to get a wife for my son Isaac." ⁵The servant asked him: "What if the woman is unwilling to follow me to this land? Should I then take your son back to the land from which you came?" ⁶Abraham told him, "Never take my son back there for any reason! ⁷The LORD, the God of heaven, who took me from my father's house and the land of my relatives, and who confirmed by oath the promise he made to me, 'I will give this land to your descendants'—he will send his angel before you, and you will get a wife for my son there.* ⁸If the woman is unwilling to follow you, you will be released from this oath to me. But never take my son back there!" ⁹So the servant put his

---

† Hittite kingdoms in northern Syria in the first part of the first millennium, and (following Assyrian terminology) the inhabitants of Syria and Palestine. The third group is meant here.

**23:4** *A resident alien*: such a one would normally not have the right to own property. The importance of Abraham's purchase of the field in Machpelah, which is worded in technical legal terms, lies in the fact that it gave his descendants their first, though small, land rights in the country that God had promised the patriarch they would one day inherit as their own. Abraham therefore insists on purchasing the field and not receiving it as a gift.

**23:15** *Four hundred shekels*: probably an exorbitant sum; Jeremiah (32:9) paid only seventeen shekels for his field in Anathoth, though the Babylonian invasion no doubt helped to reduce the price.

**23:16** *The current market value*: the standard weight called a shekel varied according to time and place.

**24:1–67** The story of Abraham and Sarah is drawing to a close. The promises of progeny (21:1–7) and land (chap. 23) have been fulfilled and Sarah has died (23:1–2). Abraham's last duty is to ensure that his son Isaac shares in the promises. Isaac must take a wife from his own people (vv. 3–7), so the promises may

be fulfilled. The extraordinary length of this story and its development of a single theme contrast strikingly with the spare style of the preceding Abraham and Sarah stories. It points ahead to the Jacob and Joseph stories.

The length of the story is partly caused by its meticulous attention to the sign (vv. 12–14), its fulfillment (vv. 15–20), and the servant's retelling of sign and fulfillment to Rebekah's family to win their consent (vv. 34–49).

**24:2** *Put your hand under my thigh*: the symbolism of this act was apparently connected with the Hebrew concept of children issuing from their father's "thigh" (the literal meaning of "direct descendants" in 46:26; Ex 1:5). Perhaps the man who took such an oath was thought to bring the curse of sterility on himself if he did not fulfill his sworn promise. Jacob made Joseph swear in the same way (Gn 47:29). In both these instances, the oath was taken to carry out the last request of a man upon his death.

---

**23:4** Gn 33:19; Acts 7:16; Heb 11:9.
**23:16** Acts 7:16.
**23:17–18** Gn 49:29–30.
**24:2–3** Gn 47:29.
**24:3** Gn 24:37; 28:1–2; Jgs 14:3; Tb 4:12.
**24:7** Gn 12:7; Ex 6:8; Tb 5:17; Gal 3:16.

hand under the thigh of his master Abraham and swore to him concerning this matter.

[10] The servant then took ten of his master's camels, and bearing all kinds of gifts from his master, he made his way to the city of Nahor† in Aram Naharaim. [11] Near evening, at the time when women go out to draw water, he made the camels kneel by the well outside the city. [12] Then he said: "LORD, God of my master Abraham, let it turn out favorably for me† today and thus deal graciously with my master Abraham. [13] While I stand here at the spring and the daughters of the townspeople are coming out to draw water, [14] if I say to a young woman, 'Please lower your jug, that I may drink,' and she answers, 'Drink, and I will water your camels, too,' then she is the one whom you have decided upon for your servant Isaac. In this way I will know that you have dealt graciously with my master."

[15] * He had scarcely finished speaking when Rebekah—who was born to Bethuel, son of Milcah, the wife of Abraham's brother Nahor—came out with a jug on her shoulder. [16] The young woman was very beautiful, a virgin, untouched by man. She went down to the spring and filled her jug. As she came up, [17] the servant ran toward her and said, "Please give me a sip of water from your jug." [18] "Drink, sir," she replied, and quickly lowering the jug into her hand, she gave him a drink. [19] When she had finished giving him a drink, she said, "I will draw water for your camels, too, until they have finished drinking." [20] With that, she quickly emptied her jug into the drinking trough and ran back to the well to draw more water, until she had drawn enough for all the camels. [21] The man watched her the whole time, silently waiting to learn whether or not the LORD had made his journey successful. [22] When the camels had finished drinking, the man took out a gold nose-ring weighing half a shekel, and two gold bracelets weighing ten shekels for her wrists. [23] Then he asked her: "Whose daughter are you? Tell me, please. And

is there a place in your father's house for us to spend the night?" [24] She answered: "I am the daughter of Bethuel the son of Milcah, whom she bore to Nahor. [25] We have plenty of straw and fodder," she added, "and also a place to spend the night." [26] The man then knelt and bowed down to the LORD, [27] saying: "Blessed be the LORD, the God of my master Abraham, who has not let his kindness and fidelity toward my master fail. As for me, the LORD has led me straight to the house of my master's brother."

[28] Then the young woman ran off and told her mother's household what had happened. [29] * Now Rebekah had a brother named Laban. Laban rushed outside to the man at the spring. [30] † When he saw the nose-ring and the bracelets on his sister's arms and when he heard Rebekah repeating what the man had said to her, he went to him while he was standing by the camels at the spring. [31] He said: "Come, blessed of the LORD! Why are you standing outside when I have made the house ready, as well as a place for the camels?" [32] The man then went inside; and while the camels were being unloaded and provided with straw and fodder, water was brought to bathe his feet and the feet of the men who were with him. [33] But when food was set before him, he said, "I will not eat until I have told my story." "Go ahead," they replied.

[34] "I am Abraham's servant," he began. [35] "The LORD has blessed my master so abundantly that he has become wealthy; he has given him flocks and herds, silver and gold, male and female slaves, and camels and donkeys. [36] My master's wife Sarah bore a son to my master in her old age, and he has given him everything he owns. [37] My master put me under oath, saying: 'You shall not take a wife for my son from the daughters of the Canaanites in whose land I live; [38] instead, you must go to my father's house, to my own family, to get a wife for my son.' [39] When I asked my master, 'What if the woman will not follow me?'

---

† **24:10** *Nahor*: it is uncertain whether this is the place where Abraham's brother Nahor (11:27) had lived or whether it is the city Nahur, named in the Mari documents (nineteenth and eighteenth centuries B.C.), near the confluence of the Balikh and Middle Euphrates rivers. *Aram Naharaim*: lit., "Aram between the two rivers," is the Yahwist designation for Terah's homeland. The two rivers are the Habur and the Euphrates. The Priestly designation for the area is Paddan-aram, which is from the Assyrian *padana*, "road or garden," and Aram, which refers to the people or land of the Arameans.

**24:12** *Let it turn out favorably for me*: let me have a favorable sign; cf. end of v. 14.
**24:30** Laban becomes hospitable only when he sees the servant's rich gifts, which is in humorous contrast to his sister's spontaneous generosity toward the servant. Laban's opportunism points forward to his behavior in the Jacob stories (31:14–16).

**24:15** Gn 22:23.                **24:29** Gn 27:43.

GN

[40] he replied: 'The LORD, in whose presence I have always walked, will send his angel with you and make your journey successful, and so you will get a wife for my son from my own family and my father's house.* [41] Then you will be freed from my curse. If you go to my family and they refuse you, then, too, you will be free from my curse.'†

[42] "When I came to the spring today, I said: 'LORD, God of my master Abraham, please make successful the journey I am on. [43] While I stand here at the spring, if I say to a young woman who comes out to draw water, 'Please give me a little water from your jug,' [44] and she answers, 'Drink, and I will draw water for your camels, too—then she is the woman whom the LORD has decided upon for my master's son.'

[45] "I had scarcely finished saying this to myself when Rebekah came out with a jug on her shoulder. After she went down to the spring and drew water, I said to her, 'Please let me have a drink.' [46] She quickly lowered the jug she was carrying and said, 'Drink, and I will water your camels, too.' So I drank, and she watered the camels also. [47] When I asked her, 'Whose daughter are you?' she answered, 'The daughter of Bethuel, son of Nahor, borne to Nahor by Milcah.' So I put the ring on her nose and the bracelets on her wrists. [48] Then I knelt and bowed down to the LORD, blessing the LORD, the God of my master Abraham, who had led me on the right road to obtain the daughter of my master's kinsman for his son. [49] Now, if you will act with kindness and fidelity toward my master, let me know; but if not, let me know that too. I can then proceed accordingly."

[50]* Laban and Bethuel said in reply: "This thing comes from the LORD; we can say nothing to you either for or against it. [51] Here is Rebekah, right in front of you; take her and go, that she may become the wife of your master's son, as the LORD has said." [52] When Abraham's servant heard their answer, he bowed to the ground before the LORD. [53] Then he brought out objects of silver and gold and clothing and presented them to Rebekah; he also gave costly presents to her brother and mother. [54] After he and the men with him had eaten and drunk, they spent the night there.

When they got up the next morning, he said, "Allow me to return to my master."* [55] Her brother and mother replied, "Let the young woman stay with us a short while, say ten days; after that she may go." [56] But he said to them, "Do not detain me, now that the LORD has made my journey successful; let me go back to my master." [57] They answered, "Let us call the young woman and see what she herself has to say about it." [58] So they called Rebekah and asked her, "Will you go with this man?" She answered, "I will."† [59] At this they sent off their sister Rebekah and her nurse with Abraham's servant and his men. [60] They blessed Rebekah and said:

> "Sister, may you grow
>     into thousands of myriads;
> And may your descendants gain possession
>     of the gates of their enemies!"*

[61] Then Rebekah and her attendants started out; they mounted the camels and followed the man. So the servant took Rebekah and went on his way.

[62] Meanwhile Isaac had gone from Beer-lahai-roi and was living in the region of the Negeb.* [63] One day toward evening he went out to walk in the field, and caught sight of camels approaching. [64] Rebekah, too, caught sight of Isaac, and got down from her camel. [65] She asked the servant, "Who is the man over there, walking through the fields toward us?" "That is my master," replied the servant. Then she took her veil and covered herself. [66] The servant recounted to Isaac all the things he had done. [67] Then Isaac brought Rebekah into the tent of his mother Sarah. He took Rebekah as his wife. Isaac loved her and found solace after the death of his mother.

# 25

**Abraham's Sons by Keturah.** [1]†* Abraham took another wife, whose name was Keturah. [2] She bore him Zimran, Jokshan,

---

† **24:41** *Curse:* this would be the consequence of failing to carry out the oath referred to in v. 3.

**24:58** Marriages arranged by the woman's father did not require the woman's consent, but marriages arranged by the woman's brother did. Laban is the brother and Rebekah is therefore free to give her consent or not.

**25:1–11** As with the story of Terah in 11:27–32, this section lists all the descendants of Abraham as a means of concluding

---

**24:40** Tb 5:17; 10:13.
**24:50–51** Tb 7:11–12.
**24:54** Tb 7:14; 8:20.
**24:60** Gn 22:17.
**24:62** Gn 16:13–14; 25:11.
**25:1–4** 1 Chr 1:32–33.

Medan, Midian, Ishbak, and Shuah.† ³Jokshan became the father of Sheba and Dedan. The descendants of Dedan were the Asshurim, the Letushim, and the Leummim.* ⁴The descendants of Midian were Ephah, Epher, Hanoch, Abida, and Eldaah. All of these were descendants of Keturah.

⁵Abraham gave everything that he owned to his son Isaac.† ⁶To the sons of his concubines, however, he gave gifts while he was still living, as he sent them away eastward, to the land of Kedem,† away from his son Isaac.

**Death of Abraham.** ⁷The whole span of Abraham's life was one hundred and seventy-five years. ⁸Then he breathed his last, dying at a ripe old age, grown old after a full life; and he was gathered to his people. ⁹His sons Isaac and Ishmael buried him in the cave of Machpelah, in the field of Ephron, son of Zohar the Hittite, which faces Mamre,* ¹⁰the field that Abraham had bought from the Hittites; there he was buried next to his wife Sarah. ¹¹After the death of Abraham, God blessed his son Isaac, who lived near Beer-lahai-roi.

**Descendants of Ishmael.** ¹²† These are the descendants of Abraham's son Ishmael, whom Hagar the Egyptian, Sarah's slave, bore to Abraham. ¹³* These are the names of Ishmael's sons, listed in the order of their birth: Ishmael's firstborn Nebaioth, Kedar, Adbeel, Mibsam,* ¹⁴Mishma,

Dumah, Massa, ¹⁵Hadad, Tema, Jetur, Naphish, and Kedemah. ¹⁶These are the sons of Ishmael, their names by their villages and encampments; twelve chieftains of as many tribal groups.*

¹⁷The span of Ishmael's life was one hundred and thirty-seven years. After he had breathed his last and died, he was gathered to his people. ¹⁸The Ishmaelites ranged from Havilah, by Shur, which is on the border of Egypt, all the way to Asshur; and they pitched camp† alongside their various kindred.*

**Birth of Esau and Jacob.** ¹⁹† These are the descendants of Isaac, son of Abraham; Abraham begot Isaac. ²⁰Isaac was forty years old when he married Rebekah, the daughter of Bethuel the Aramean of Paddan-aram† and the sister of Laban the Aramean.* ²¹Isaac entreated the LORD on behalf of his wife, since she was sterile. The LORD heard his entreaty, and his wife Rebekah became pregnant. ²²But the children jostled each other in the womb so much that she exclaimed, "If it is like this,† why go on living!" She went to consult the LORD, ²³and the LORD answered her:

> Two nations are in your womb,
>     two peoples are separating while still
>         within you;
> But one will be stronger than the other,
>     and the older will serve the
>         younger.†*

---

† the story. The Jacob story ends similarly with the listing of the twelve sons (35:22–26), the death of Isaac (35:27–29), and the descendants of Esau (chap. 36). *Abraham took another wife*: though mentioned here, Abraham's marriage to a "concubine," or wife of secondary rank, is not to be understood as happening chronologically after the events narrated in the preceding chapter.

**25:2** Three of the six names can be identified: the Midianites are a trading people, mentioned in the Bible as dwelling east of the Gulf of Aqaba in northwest Arabia; Ishbak is a north Syrian tribe; Shuah is a city on the right bank of the Middle Euphrates. The other names are probably towns or peoples on the international trade routes.

**25:5** Amid so many descendants, Abraham takes steps that Isaac will be his favored heir.

**25:6** *The land of Kedem*: or "the country of the East," the region inhabited by the Kedemites or Easterners (29:1; Jgs 6:3, 33; Jb 1:3; Is 11:14). The names mentioned in vv. 2–4, as far as they can be identified, are those of tribes in the Arabian desert.

**25:12** Like the conclusion of the Jacob story (chap. 36), where the numerous descendants of the rejected Esau are listed, the descendants of the rejected Ishmael conclude the story.

**25:18** *Pitched camp*: lit., "fell"; the same Hebrew verb is used in Jgs 7:12 in regard to the hostile encampment of desert tribes. The present passage shows the fulfillment of the prediction contained in Gn 16:12.

**25:19–36:43** The Jacob cycle is introduced as the family history of Isaac (Jacob's father), just as the Abraham stories were introduced as the record of the descendants of Terah (Abraham's

father, 11:27). The cycle, made up of varied stories, is given unity by several recurring themes: birth, blessing and inheritance, which are developed through the basic contrasts of barrenness/fertility, non-blessing/blessing, and inheritance/exile/homeland. The large story has an envelope structure in which Jacob's youth is spent in Canaan striving with his older brother Esau (25:19–28:22), his early adulthood in Paddan-aram building a family and striving with his brother-in-law Laban (chaps. 29–31), and his later years back in Canaan (chaps. 32–36).

**25:20** *Paddan-aram*: the name used by the Priestly tradition for the northwest region of Mesopotamia, between the Habur and the Euphrates rivers. In Assyrian, *padana* is a road or a garden, and Aram refers to the people or the land of the Arameans. The equivalent geographical term in the Yahwist source is Aram Naharaim, "Aram between two rivers."

**25:22** *If it is like this*: in Hebrew, the phrase *lamah zeh* is capable of several meanings; it occurs again in v. 32 ("What good...?"), 32:30 ("Why do you want...?"), and 33:15 ("For what reason?"). It is one of several words and motifs that run through the story, suggesting that a divine pattern (unknown to the actors) is at work.

**25:23** *The older will serve the younger*: Rebekah now knows something that no one else knows, that God favors Jacob over Esau. The text does not say if she shared this knowledge with any-

---

* **25:3** Is 21:13.                          **25:18** Gn 16:12.
**25:9–10** Gn 23:3–20.                  **25:20** Gn 24:67.
**25:13–16** 1 Chr 1:29–31.            **25:23** Gn 27:29; Nm 24:18;
**25:13** Is 60:7.                                    Mal 1:2–5; Rom
**25:16** Gn 17:20.                                 9:10–13.

<sup>24</sup>When the time of her delivery came, there were twins in her womb.* <sup>25</sup>The first to emerge was reddish,† and his whole body was like a hairy mantle; so they named him Esau. <sup>26</sup>Next his brother came out, gripping Esau's heel;† so he was named Jacob. Isaac was sixty years old when they were born.*

<sup>27</sup>When the boys grew up, Esau became a skillful hunter, a man of the open country; whereas Jacob was a simple† man, who stayed among the tents.* <sup>28</sup>Isaac preferred Esau, because he was fond of game; but Rebekah preferred Jacob. <sup>29</sup>Once, when Jacob was cooking a stew, Esau came in from the open country, famished. <sup>30</sup>He said to Jacob, "Let me gulp down some of that red stuff;† I am famished." That is why he was called Edom. <sup>31</sup>But Jacob replied, "First sell me your right as firstborn."†* <sup>32</sup>"Look," said Esau, "I am on the point of dying. What good is the right as firstborn to me?" <sup>33</sup>But Jacob said, "Swear to me first!" So he sold Jacob his right as firstborn under oath.* <sup>34</sup>Jacob then gave him some bread and the lentil stew; and Esau ate, drank, got up, and went his way. So Esau treated his right as firstborn with disdain.

# 26

**Isaac and Abimelech.** <sup>1</sup>†* There was a famine in the land, distinct from the earlier one that had occurred in the days of Abraham, and Isaac went down to Abimelech, king of the Philistines in Gerar.* <sup>2</sup>The LORD appeared to him and said: Do not go down to Egypt, but camp in this land wherever I tell you. <sup>3</sup>Sojourn in this land, and I will be with you and bless you; for to you and your descendants I will give all these lands, in fulfillment of the oath that I swore to your father Abraham.* <sup>4</sup>I will make your descendants as numerous as the stars in the sky, and I will give them all these lands, and in your descendants all the nations of the earth will find blessing—* <sup>5</sup>this because Abraham obeyed me, keeping my mandate, my commandments, my ordinances, and my instructions.

<sup>6</sup>† So Isaac settled in Gerar. <sup>7</sup>When the men of the place asked questions about his wife, he answered, "She is my sister." He was afraid that, if he called her his wife, the men of the place would kill him on account of Rebekah, since she was beautiful. <sup>8</sup>But when they had been there for a long time, Abimelech, king of the Philistines, looked out of a window and saw Isaac fondling his wife Rebekah. <sup>9</sup>He called for Isaac and said: "She must certainly be your wife! How could you have said, 'She is my sister'?" Isaac replied, "I thought I might lose my life on her account." <sup>10</sup>"How could you have done this to us!" exclaimed Abimelech. "It would have taken very little for one of the people to lie with your wife, and so you would have brought guilt upon us!" <sup>11</sup>Abimelech then commanded all the people: "Anyone who maltreats this man or his wife shall be put to death."

<sup>12</sup>† Isaac sowed a crop in that region and

† one or kept it to herself, but, from their actions, it seems unlikely that either Isaac or Esau knew. That fact must be borne in mind in assessing Rebekah's role in chap. 27, the theft of Esau's blessing.

**25:25** *Reddish*: in Hebrew, *'admoni*, a reference to Edom, another name for Esau (v. 30; 36:1). Edom was also the name of the country south of Moab (southeast of the Dead Sea) where the descendants of Esau lived. It was called the "red" country because of its reddish sandstone. Moreover, "red" points ahead to the red stew in the next scene. *Hairy*: in Hebrew, *se'ar*, a reference to Seir, another name for Edom (36:8).

**25:26** *Heel*: in Hebrew *'aqeb*, a wordplay on the name Jacob; cf. 27:36. The first of three scenes of striving with Esau. The second is vv. 27–34, and the third, chap. 27. In all the scenes, Jacob values the blessing more than his ardent but unreflective brother Esau does.

**25:27** *Simple*: the Hebrew word denotes soundness, integrity, health, none of which fit here. Whatever its precise meaning, it must be opposite to the qualities of Esau.

**25:30** *Red stuff*: in Hebrew, *'adom*; another play on the word Edom, the "red" land.

**25:31** *Right as firstborn*: the privilege that entitled the firstborn son to a position of honor in the family and to a double share in the possessions inherited from the father. There is a persistent wordplay between *bekorah*, "right of the firstborn," and *berakah*, "the blessing." Contrary to custom, the preference here is for the younger son, as it was in the choice of Isaac over Ishmael.

**26:1** The promise of land and numerous descendants given to Abraham (12:1–3; 15; 17; 22:17–18) is renewed for his son Isaac. The divine blessing to Isaac is mentioned also in vv. 12, 24, and 29.

**26:6–11** This scene is the third version of the wife-in-danger story (cf. chaps. 12 and 20). The mention of the famine in 26:1 recalls the famine in 12:10; the name Abimelech, king of Gerar, recalls 20:2. The deception, according to all the stories, is the claim that the wife is a sister. This story (from the Yahwist source) departs from the two previous accounts in that the wife is not taken into the harem of the foreign king.

**26:12–33** The dispute is over water rights. In a sparsely watered land, wells were precious and claims on water could function as a kind of claim on the land. Scholars generally judge the account of the dispute over water rights and its settlement by a legal agreement between Isaac and Abimelech to be a Yahwist version of the similar story about Abraham in 21:22–34. Here, Abimelech realizes that Isaac has brought blessing to his people and thus desires a covenant with him. The feast in v. 30 is part of the covenant ceremony.

25:24 Hos 12:4.
25:26 Mt 1:2.
25:27 Gn 27:6–7.
25:31 Dt 21:17.
25:33 Heb 12:16.
26:1–14 Gn 12:10–20.

26:1 Gn 12:10.
26:3 Gn 12:7; 15:18; Ex 32:13; Ps 105:9; Sir 44:22; Heb 11:9.
26:4 Gn 12:3; 22:17–18; 28:14; Ex 32:13.

reaped a hundredfold the same year. Since the LORD blessed him, [13]* he became richer and richer all the time, until he was very wealthy. [14] He acquired flocks and herds, and a great work force, and so the Philistines became envious of him. [15]* The Philistines had stopped up and filled with dirt all the wells that his father's servants had dug back in the days of his father Abraham. [16] So Abimelech said to Isaac, "Go away from us; you have become far too numerous for us." [17] Isaac left there and camped in the Wadi Gerar where he stayed. [18] Isaac reopened the wells which his father's servants had dug back in the days of his father Abraham and which the Philistines had stopped up after Abraham's death; he gave them names like those that his father had given them. [19] But when Isaac's servants dug in the wadi and reached spring water in their well, [20] the shepherds of Gerar argued with Isaac's shepherds, saying, "The water belongs to us!" So he named the well Esek,† because they had quarreled there. [21] Then they dug another well, and they argued over that one too; so he named it Sitnah.† [22] So he moved on from there and dug still another well, but over this one they did not argue. He named it Rehoboth,† and said, "Because the LORD has now given us ample room, we shall flourish in the land."

[23] From there Isaac went up to Beer-sheba. [24] The same night the LORD appeared to him and said: I am the God of Abraham, your father. Do not fear, for I am with you. I will bless you and multiply your descendants for the sake of Abraham, my servant.* [25] So Isaac built an altar there and invoked the LORD by name. After he had pitched his tent there, Isaac's servants began to dig a well nearby.

[26]* Then Abimelech came to him from Gerar, with Ahuzzath, his councilor, and Phicol, the general of his army. [27] Isaac asked them, "Why have you come to me, since you hate me and have driven me away from you?" [28] They answered: "We clearly see that the LORD has been with you, so we thought: let there be a sworn agreement between our two sides—between you and us. Let us make a covenant with you: [29] you shall do no harm to us, just as we have not maltreated you, but have always acted kindly toward you and have let you depart in peace. So now, may you be blessed by the LORD!" [30] Isaac then made a feast for them, and they ate and drank. [31] Early the next morning they exchanged oaths. Then Isaac sent them on their way, and they departed from him in peace.

[32] That same day Isaac's servants came and informed him about the well they had been digging; they told him, "We have reached water!" [33] He called it Shibah;† hence the name of the city is Beer-sheba to this day. [34]† When Esau was forty years old, he married Judith, daughter of Beeri the Hittite, and Basemath, daughter of Elon the Hivite.* [35] But they became a source of bitterness to Isaac and Rebekah.

# 27 Jacob's Deception.† 
[1] When Isaac was so old that his eyesight had failed him, he called his older son Esau and said to him, "My son!" "Here I am!" he replied. [2] Isaac then said, "Now I have grown old. I do not know when I might die. [3] So now take your hunting gear—your quiver and bow—and go out into the open country to hunt some game for me. [4] Then prepare for me a dish in the way I like, and bring it to me to eat, so that I may bless you† before I die."

---

† **26:20** *Esek:* "quarrel."
**26:21** *Sitnah:* "opposition."
**26:22** *Rehoboth:* "wide spaces," i.e., ample room to live; site is probably SW of modern day Beer-sheba.
**26:33** *Shibah:* the place name Shibah is a play on two Hebrew words, *shebu'ah,* "oath," and *shwebaa',* "seven." In v. 31, they exchanged oaths.
**26:34–35** These verses from the Priestly source introduce the next section on Esau's loss of his right as firstborn by suggesting a motivation for this in Isaac's and Rebekah's dislike for Esau's Canaanite wives.
**27:1–45** The chapter, a literary masterpiece, is the third and climactic wresting away of the blessing of Esau. Rebekah manages the entire affair, using perhaps her privileged information about Jacob's status (25:23); Jacob's only qualm is that if his father discovers the ruse, he will receive a curse instead of a blessing (vv. 11–12). Isaac is passive as he was in chaps. 22 and 24. The deception is effected through clothing (Jacob wears Esau's

clothing), which points ahead to a similar deception of a patriarch by means of clothing in the Joseph story (37:21–33). Such recurrent acts and scenes let the reader know a divine purpose is moving the story forward even though the human characters are unaware of it.
**27:4** *I may bless you:* Isaac's blessing confers fertility (vv. 27–28) and dominion (v. 29). The "dew of heaven" is rain that produces grain and wine, two of the principal foodstuffs of the ancient Near East. The "fertility of the earth" may allude to oil, the third basic foodstuff. The full agricultural year may be implied here: the fall rains are followed by the grain harvests of the spring and the grape harvest of late summer, and then the olive harvest of the fall (cf. Dt 11:14; Ps 104:13–15).

* **26:13–14** Jb 1:3.   **26:15–24** Gn 21:25–31.   **26:24** Gn 46:3.   **26:26–33** Gn 21:22–31; Prv 16:7.   **26:34–35** Gn 27:46.

⁵Rebekah had been listening while Isaac was speaking to his son Esau. So when Esau went out into the open country to hunt some game for his father,* ⁶Rebekah said to her son Jacob, "Listen! I heard your father tell your brother Esau, ⁷'Bring me some game and prepare a dish for me to eat, that I may bless you with the Lord's approval before I die.' ⁸Now, my son, obey me in what I am about to order you. ⁹Go to the flock and get me two choice young goats so that with these I might prepare a dish for your father in the way he likes. ¹⁰Then bring it to your father to eat, that he may bless you before he dies." ¹¹But Jacob said to his mother Rebekah, "But my brother Esau is a hairy man and I am smooth-skinned!* ¹²Suppose my father feels me? He will think I am making fun of him, and I will bring on myself a curse instead of a blessing." ¹³His mother, however, replied: "Let any curse against you, my son, fall on me! Just obey me. Go and get me the young goats."

¹⁴So Jacob went and got them and brought them to his mother, and she prepared a dish in the way his father liked. ¹⁵Rebekah then took the best clothes of her older son Esau that she had in the house, and gave them to her younger son Jacob to wear; ¹⁶and with the goatskins she covered up his hands and the hairless part of his neck. ¹⁷Then she gave her son Jacob the dish and the bread she had prepared.

¹⁸Going to his father, Jacob said, "Father!" "Yes?" replied Isaac. "Which of my sons are you?" ¹⁹Jacob answered his father: "I am Esau, your firstborn. I did as you told me. Please sit up and eat some of my game, so that you may bless me." ²⁰But Isaac said to his son, "How did you get it so quickly, my son?" He answered, "The Lord, your God, directed me." ²¹Isaac then said to Jacob, "Come closer, my son, that I may feel you, to learn whether you really are my son Esau or not." ²²So Jacob moved up closer to his father. When Isaac felt him, he said, "Although the voice is Jacob's, the hands are Esau's." ²³(He failed to identify him because his hands were hairy, like those of his brother Esau; so he blessed him.) ²⁴Again Isaac said, "Are you really my son Esau?" And Jacob said, "I am." ²⁵Then Isaac said, "Serve me, my son, and let me eat of the game so that I may bless you." Jacob served it to him, and Isaac ate; he brought him wine, and he drank. ²⁶Finally his father Isaac said to him, "Come closer, my son, and kiss me." ²⁷As Jacob went up to kiss him, Isaac smelled the fragrance of his clothes. With that, he blessed him, saying,

"Ah, the fragrance of my son
   is like the fragrance of a field
   that the Lord has blessed!*
²⁸ May God give to you
   of the dew of the heavens
And of the fertility of the earth
   abundance of grain and wine.
²⁹* May peoples serve you,
   and nations bow down to you;
Be master of your brothers,
   and may your mother's sons bow
       down to you.
Cursed be those who curse you,
   and blessed be those who bless you."

³⁰Jacob had scarcely left his father after Isaac had finished blessing him, when his brother Esau came back from his hunt. ³¹Then he too prepared a dish, and bringing it to his father, he said, "Let my father sit up and eat some of his son's game, that you may then give me your blessing." ³²His father Isaac asked him, "Who are you?" He said, "I am your son, your firstborn son, Esau." ³³Isaac trembled greatly. "Who was it, then," he asked, "that hunted game and brought it to me? I ate it all just before you came, and I blessed him. Now he is blessed!" ³⁴As he heard his father's words, Esau burst into loud, bitter sobbing and said, "Father, bless me too!" ³⁵When Isaac said, "Your brother came here by a ruse and carried off your blessing," ³⁶Esau exclaimed, "He is well named Jacob, is he not! He has supplanted me† twice! First he took away my right as firstborn, and now he has taken away my blessing." Then he said, "Have you not saved a blessing for me?"* ³⁷Isaac replied to Esau: "I have already appointed him your master, and I have assigned to him all his kindred as his servants; besides, I have sustained him with grain and wine. What then can I do for you,

† 27:36 He has supplanted me: in Hebrew, wayyaqebeni, a wordplay on the name Jacob, ya'aqob; see Jer 9:3 and Gn 25:26. There is also a play between the Hebrew words bekorah ("right of the firstborn") and berakah ("blessing").

27:5 Gn 25:28.
27:11 Gn 25:25.
27:27 Gn 22:17–18; Heb 11:20.
27:29 Gn 25:23; 49:8; Nm 24:9.
27:36 Gn 25:26, 29–34; Hos 12:4.

my son?" [38] But Esau said to his father, "Have you only one blessing, father? Bless me too, father!" and Esau wept aloud. * [39] His father Isaac said in response:

> "See, far from the fertile earth
>     will be your dwelling;
>     far from the dew of the heavens
>         above! *
> [40]   By your sword you will live,
>     and your brother you will serve;
>     But when you become restless,
>         you will throw off his yoke from your
>             neck." *

[41] Esau bore a grudge against Jacob because of the blessing his father had given him. Esau said to himself, "Let the time of mourning for my father come, so that I may kill my brother Jacob." * [42] When Rebekah got news of what her older son Esau had in mind, she summoned her younger son Jacob and said to him: "Listen! Your brother Esau intends to get his revenge by killing you. [43] So now, my son, obey me: flee at once to my brother Laban in Haran, [44] and stay with him a while until your brother's fury subsides— [45] until your brother's anger against you subsides and he forgets what you did to him. Then I will send for you and bring you back. Why should I lose both of you in a single day?"

**Jacob Sent to Laban.** [46] Rebekah said to Isaac: "I am disgusted with life because of the Hittite women. If Jacob also should marry a Hittite woman, a native of the land, like these women, why should I live?" *

**28** [1] † Isaac therefore summoned Jacob and blessed him, charging him: "You shall not marry a Canaanite woman! * [2] Go now to Paddan-aram, to the home of your mother's father Bethuel, and there choose a wife for yourself from among the daughters of Laban, your mother's brother. * [3] May God Almighty bless you and make you fertile, multiply you that you may become an assembly of peoples. [4] May God extend to you and your descendants the blessing of Abraham, so that you may gain possession of the land where you are residing, which he assigned to Abraham." * [5] Then Isaac sent Jacob on his way; he went to Paddan-aram, to Laban, son of Bethuel the Aramean, and brother of Rebekah, the mother of Jacob and Esau. *

[6] Esau noted that Isaac had blessed Jacob when he sent him to Paddan-aram to get himself a wife there, and that, as he gave him his blessing, he charged him, "You shall not marry a Canaanite woman," [7] and that Jacob had obeyed his father and mother and gone to Paddan-aram. [8] Esau realized how displeasing the Canaanite women were to his father Isaac, [9] so Esau went to Ishmael, and in addition to the wives he had, married Mahalath, the daughter of Abraham's son Ishmael and sister of Nebaioth. *

**Jacob's Dream at Bethel.** † [10] Jacob departed from Beer-sheba and proceeded toward Haran. [11] When he came upon a certain place, † he stopped there for the night, since the sun had already set. Taking one of the stones at the place, he put it under his head and lay down in that place. [12] Then he had a dream: a stairway †

---

† **28:1–9** A glimpse of Rebekah's shrewdness is provided by 27:42–28:2. She is aware of Esau's murderous plot against Jacob (27:42–45) but realizes the episode of the stolen blessing is still painful to Isaac; she therefore uses another motive to persuade Isaac to send Jacob away—he must marry within the family (endogamy), unlike Esau. Esau, unreflective as usual, realizes too late he also should marry within the family but, significantly, marries from Abraham's rejected line. At this point in the story, Jacob (and his mother) have taken the blessing for themselves. Their actions have put Jacob in a precarious position: he must flee the land because of his brother's murderous intent and find a wife in a far country. One might ask how God's blessing can be given to such an unworthy schemer. There is a biblical pattern of preferring the younger brother or sister over the older—Isaac over Ishmael, Jacob over Esau, Rachel over Leah, Joseph over his older brothers, Ephraim over Manasseh (Gn 48:14), David over his older brothers.

**28:10–22** As Jacob is leaving the land on his way to an uncertain future in Paddan-aram, God appears to him at a sacred place that Jacob had visited only to take a night's rest. Jacob's unawareness of the holiness of the place underscores the graciousness of the gift. On his return to Canaan, he will again encounter a

divine visitor in the form of the mysterious attacker (32:23–33) and, after his return and reconciliation with Esau, he will again go to Bethel (35:1–15).

**28:11** *Place:* the Hebrew word is often used specifically of a sacred site. The ambiguous word "place" is used here, for the text emphasizes that Jacob has no idea the place he has come upon is sacred; only when he wakes up does he realize it is sacred. The place was Bethel (v. 19), a sacred site as early as the time of Abraham (12:8).

**28:12** *Stairway:* in Hebrew, *sullam,* traditionally but inaccurately translated as "ladder." The corresponding verb, *salal,* means "to heap up" something, such as dirt for a highway or a ramp. The imagery in Jacob's dream may be derived from the Babylonian ziggurat or temple tower, "with its top in the sky" (11:4), and with brick steps leading up to a small temple at the top.

---

27:38 Heb 12:17.
27:39 Heb 11:20.
27:40 2 Kgs 8:20, 22; 2 Chr 21:8.
27:41 Wis 10:10; Ob 10.
27:46 Gn 26:34–35.

28:1 Gn 24:3–4; 26:35.
28:2 Gn 22:22.
28:4 Ex 32:13.
28:5 Jdt 8:26.
28:9 Gn 36:2–3.

rested on the ground, with its top reaching to the heavens; and God's angels were going up and down on it.* [13] And there was the LORD standing beside him and saying: I am the LORD, the God of Abraham your father and the God of Isaac; the land on which you are lying I will give to you and your descendants.* [14] Your descendants will be like the dust of the earth, and through them you will spread to the west and the east, to the north and the south. In you and your descendants all the families of the earth will find blessing.* [15] I am with you and will protect you wherever you go, and bring you back to this land. I will never leave you until I have done what I promised you.*

[16] When Jacob awoke from his sleep, he said, "Truly, the LORD is in this place and I did not know it!" [17] He was afraid and said: "How awesome this place is! This is nothing else but the house of God, the gateway to heaven!" [18] Early the next morning Jacob took the stone that he had put under his head, set it up as a sacred pillar,† and poured oil on top of it.* [19] He named that place Bethel,† whereas the former name of the town had been Luz.*

[20] Jacob then made this vow:† "If God will be with me and protect me on this journey I am making and give me food to eat and clothes to wear, [21] and I come back safely to my father's house, the LORD will be my God. [22] This stone that I have set up as a sacred pillar will be the house of God. Of everything you give me, I will return a tenth part to you without fail."

# 29

**Arrival in Haran.**† [1]* After Jacob resumed his journey, he came to the land of the Kedemites. [2] Looking about, he saw a well in the open country, with three flocks of sheep huddled near it, for flocks were watered from that well. A large stone covered the mouth of the well.* [3] When all the shepherds were assembled there they would roll the stone away from the mouth of the well and water the sheep. Then they would put the stone back again in its place over the mouth of the well.

[4] Jacob said to them, "My brothers, where are you from?" "We are from Haran," they replied. [5] Then he asked them, "Do you know Laban, son of Nahor?" "We do," they answered.* [6] He inquired further, "Is he well?" "He is," they answered; "and here comes his daughter Rachel with the sheep." [7] Then he said: "There is still much daylight left; it is hardly the time to bring the animals home. Water the sheep, and then continue pasturing them." [8] They replied, "We cannot until all the shepherds are here to roll the stone away from the mouth of the well; then can we water the flocks."

[9] While he was still talking with them, Rachel arrived with her father's sheep, for she was the one who tended them. [10] As soon as Jacob saw Rachel, the daughter of his mother's brother Laban, and the sheep of Laban, he went up, rolled the stone away from the mouth of the well, and watered Laban's sheep. [11] Then Jacob kissed Rachel and wept aloud. [12] Jacob told Rachel that he was her father's relative, Rebekah's son. So she ran to tell her father. [13] When Laban heard the news about Jacob, his sister's son, he ran to meet him. After embracing and kissing him, he brought him to his house. Jacob then repeated to Laban all these things, [14] and Laban said to him, "You are indeed my bone and my flesh."†

---

† **28:18** *Sacred pillar:* in Hebrew, *masseba,* a stone which might vary in shape and size, set upright and usually intended for some religious purpose. The custom of erecting such sacred pillars in Palestine went back to its pre-Israelite period; but since their polytheistic associations were often retained, later Israelite religion forbade their erection (Lv 26:1; Dt 16:22) and ordered the destruction of those that were associated with other religions (Ex 34:13; Dt 12:3).

**28:19** *Bethel:* i.e., "house of God"; the reference is to the house of God in v. 17.

**28:20** *This vow:* knowing well that Esau's murderous wrath stands between him and the possession of the land promised him, Jacob makes his vow very precise. He vows to make the God who appeared to him his own if the God guides him safely to Paddan-aram and back to this land.

**29:1–14** Jacob's arrival in Haran. The sight of Rachel inspires Jacob to the superhuman feat of rolling back the enormous stone by himself. The scene evokes the meeting of Abraham's steward and Jacob's mother Rebekah at a well (24:11–27).

The verse begins the story of Jacob's time in Mesopotamia (29:1–31:54), which is framed on either side by Jacob's time in Canaan, 25:19–28:22 and 32:1–36:43. In these chapters, Jacob suffers Laban's duplicity as Esau had to suffer his, though eventually Jacob outwits Laban and leaves Mesopotamia a wealthy man. An elaborate chiastic (or envelope) structure shapes the diverse material: (A) Jacob's arrival in Haran in 29:1–4; (B) contract with Laban in 29:15–20; (C) Laban's deception of Jacob in 29:21–30; (D) the center, the birth of Jacob's children in 29:31–30:24; (C´) Jacob's deception of Laban in 30:25–43; (B´) dispute with Laban in 31:17–42; (A´) departure from Laban in 31:43–54. As the chiasm reverses, so do the fortunes of Laban and Jacob. *Kedemites:* see note on 25:6.

**29:14** *Bone and...flesh:* the Hebrew idiom for English "flesh and blood" (cf. 2:23; Jgs 9:2; 2 Sm 5:1 = 1 Chr 11:1).

---

**28:12** Jn 1:51.
**28:13** Dt 1:8; Mi 7:20.
**28:14** Gn 12:3; 13:14–15; 15:5–6; 18:18; 22:17–18; 26:4; Dt 19:8; Sir 44:21.
**28:15** Gn 31:3.
**28:18** Gn 31:13; 35:14–15.
**28:19** Gn 35:6; 48:3; Jos 18:13; Jgs 1:23; Hos 12:5.
**29:1** Wis 10:10.
**29:2** Gn 24:11–12.
**29:5** Tb 7:4.

**Marriage to Leah and Rachel.** After Jacob had stayed with him a full month, [15]† Laban said to him: "Should you serve me for nothing just because you are a relative of mine? Tell me what your wages should be." [16] Now Laban had two daughters; the older was called Leah, the younger Rachel. [17] Leah had dull eyes,† but Rachel was shapely and beautiful. [18] Because Jacob loved Rachel, he answered, "I will serve you seven years for your younger daughter Rachel."† [19] Laban replied, "It is better to give her to you than to another man. Stay with me." [20] So Jacob served seven years for Rachel, yet they seemed to him like a few days because of his love for her.*

[21] Then Jacob said to Laban, "Give me my wife, that I may consummate my marriage with her, for my term is now completed." [22] So Laban invited all the local inhabitants and gave a banquet. [23] At nightfall he took his daughter Leah and brought her to Jacob, and he consummated the marriage with her. [24] Laban assigned his maidservant Zilpah to his daughter Leah as her maidservant. [25] In the morning, there was Leah! So Jacob said to Laban: "How could you do this to me! Was it not for Rachel that I served you? Why did you deceive me?" [26] Laban replied, "It is not the custom in our country to give the younger daughter before the firstborn. [27] Finish the bridal week† for this one, and then the other will also be given to you in return for another seven years of service with me."*

[28] Jacob did so. He finished the bridal week for the one, and then Laban gave him his daughter Rachel as a wife. [29] Laban assigned his maidservant Bilhah to his daughter Rachel as her maidservant. [30] Jacob then consummated his marriage with Rachel also, and he loved her more than Leah. Thus he served Laban another seven years.*

**Jacob's Children.**† [31] When the LORD saw that Leah was unloved, he made her fruitful, while Rachel was barren. [32] Leah conceived and bore a son, and she named him Reuben;† for she said, "It means, 'The LORD saw my misery; surely now my husband will love me.'"* [33] She conceived again and bore a son, and said, "It means, 'The LORD heard that I was unloved,' and therefore he has given me this one also"; so she named him Simeon.† [34] Again she conceived and bore a son, and she said, "Now at last my husband will become attached to me, since I have now borne him three sons"; that is why she named him Levi.† [35] Once more she conceived and bore a son, and she said, "This time I will give thanks to the LORD"; therefore she named him Judah.† Then she stopped bearing children.*

# 30

[1] When Rachel saw that she had not borne children to Jacob, she became envious of her sister. She said to Jacob, "Give me children or I shall die!"* [2] Jacob became angry with Rachel and said, "Can I take the place of God, who has denied you the fruit of the womb?"* [3] She replied, "Here is my maidservant Bilhah. Have intercourse with her, and let her give birth on my knees,† so that

---

† **29:15–30** Laban's deception and Jacob's marriages. There are many ironies in the passage. Jacob's protest to Laban, "How could you do this to me?" echoes the question put to Abraham (20:9) and Isaac (26:10) when their deceptions about their wives were discovered. The major irony is that Jacob, the deceiver of his father and brother about the blessing (chap. 27), is deceived by his uncle (standing in for the father) about his wife.

**29:17** *Dull eyes*: in the language of beauty used here, "dull" probably means lacking in the luster that was the sign of beautiful eyes, as in 1 Sm 16:12 and Sg 4:1.

**29:18** Jacob offers to render service (Jos 15:16–17; 1 Sm 17:25; 18:17) to pay off the customary bridal price (Ex 22:15–16; Dt 22:29).

**29:27** *The bridal week*: an ancient wedding lasted for seven days; cf. Jgs 14:12, 17.

**29:31–30:24** The note of strife, first sounded between Jacob and Esau in chaps. 25–27, continues between the two wives, since Jacob loved Rachel more than Leah (29:30). Jacob's neglect of Leah moves God to make her fruitful (29:31). Leah's fertility provokes Rachel. Leah bears Jacob four sons (Reuben, Levi, Simeon, and Judah) and her maidservant Zilpah, two (Gad and Asher). Rachel's maidservant Bilhah bears two (Dan and Naphtali). After the mandrakes (30:14–17), Leah bears Issachar and Zebulun and a daughter Dinah. Rachel then bears Joseph and,

later in the land of Canaan, Benjamin (35:18).

**29:32** *Reuben*: the literal meaning of the Hebrew name is disputed. One interpretation is *re'u ben*, "look, a son!", but here in Genesis (as also with the names of all the other sons of Jacob), it is given a symbolic rather than an etymological interpretation. Name and person were regarded as closely interrelated. The symbolic interpretation of Reuben's name, according to the Yahwist source, is based on the similar-sounding *ra'a be'onyi*, "he saw my misery." In the Elohist source, the name is explained by the similar-sounding *ye'ehabani*, "he will love me."

**29:33** *Simeon*: in popular etymology, related to *shama'*, "he heard."

**29:34** *Levi*: related to *yillaweh*, "he will become attached."

**29:35** *Judah*: related to *'odeh*, "I will give thanks, praise."

**30:3** *On my knees*: in the ancient Near East, a father would take a newborn child in his lap to signify that he acknowledged it as his own; Rachel uses the ceremony in order to adopt the child and establish her legal rights to it.

---

| | |
|---|---|
| **29:20** Hos 12:13. | **29:35** Mt 1:2; Lk 3:33. |
| **29:27** Hos 12:13. | **30:1** Prv 30:16. |
| **29:30** Dt 21:15–17. | **30:2** 2 Kgs 5:7. |
| **29:32** Gn 49:3. | |

I too may have children through her."* [4] So she gave him her maidservant Bilhah as wife,† and Jacob had intercourse with her. [5] When Bilhah conceived and bore a son for Jacob, [6] Rachel said, "God has vindicated me; indeed he has heeded my plea and given me a son." Therefore she named him Dan.† [7] Rachel's maidservant Bilhah conceived again and bore a second son for Jacob, [8] and Rachel said, "I have wrestled strenuously with my sister, and I have prevailed." So she named him Naphtali.†

[9] When Leah saw that she had ceased to bear children, she took her maidservant Zilpah and gave her to Jacob as wife. [10] So Leah's maidservant Zilpah bore a son for Jacob. [11] Leah then said, "What good luck!" So she named him Gad.† [12] Then Leah's maidservant Zilpah bore a second son to Jacob; [13] and Leah said, "What good fortune, because women will call me fortunate!" So she named him Asher.†

[14] One day, during the wheat harvest, Reuben went out and came upon some mandrakes† in the field which he brought home to his mother Leah. Rachel said to Leah, "Please give me some of your son's mandrakes." [15] Leah replied, "Was it not enough for you to take away my husband, that you must now take my son's mandrakes too?" Rachel answered, "In that case Jacob may lie with you tonight in exchange for your son's mandrakes." [16] That evening, when Jacob came in from the field, Leah went out to meet him. She said, "You must have intercourse with me, because I have hired you with my son's mandrakes." So that night he lay with her, [17] and God listened to Leah; she conceived and bore a fifth son to Jacob. [18] Leah then said, "God has given me my wages for giving my maidservant to my husband"; so she named him Issachar.† [19] Leah conceived again and bore a sixth son to Jacob; [20] and Leah said, "God has brought me a precious gift. This time my husband will honor me, because I have borne him six sons"; so she named him Zebulun.† [21] Afterwards she gave birth to a daughter, and she named her Dinah.

[22] Then God remembered Rachel. God listened to her and made her fruitful. [23] She conceived and bore a son, and she said, "God has removed my disgrace."* [24] She named him Joseph,† saying, "May the LORD add another son for me!"

**Jacob Outwits Laban.**† [25] After Rachel gave birth to Joseph, Jacob said to Laban: "Allow me to go to my own region and land. [26] Give me my wives and my children for whom I served you and let me go, for you know the service that I rendered you." [27] Laban answered him: "If you will please! I have learned through divination that the LORD has blessed me because of you." [28] He continued, "State the wages I owe you, and I will pay them." [29] Jacob replied: "You know what work I did for you and how well your livestock fared under my care; [30] the little you had before I came has grown into an abundance, since the LORD has blessed you in my company. Now, when can I do something for my own household as well?" [31] Laban asked, "What should I give you?" Jacob answered: "You do not have to give me anything. If you do this thing for me, I will again pasture and tend your sheep. [32] Let me go through your whole flock today and remove from it every dark animal among the lambs and every spotted or speckled one among the goats.† These will be my wages.

---

† **30:4** *As wife*: in 35:22 Bilhah is called a "concubine" (Heb. *pilegesh*). In v. 9, Zilpah is called "wife," and in 37:2 both women are called wives. The basic difference between a wife and a concubine was that no bride price was paid for the latter. The interchange of terminology shows that there was some blurring in social status between the wife and the concubine.

**30:6** *Dan*: explained by the term *dannanni*, "he has vindicated me."

**30:8** *Naphtali*: explained by the Hebrew term *naftulim*, lit., "contest" or "struggle."

**30:11** *Gad*: explained by the Hebrew term *begad*, lit., "in luck," i.e., "what good luck!"

**30:13** *Asher*: explained by the term *be'oshri*, lit., "in my good fortune," i.e., "what good fortune," and by the term *ye'ashsheruni*, "they call me fortunate."

**30:14** *Mandrakes*: an herb whose root was thought to promote conception. The Hebrew word for mandrakes, *duda'im*, has erotic connotations, since it sounds like the words *daddayim* ("breasts") and *dodim* ("sexual pleasure").

**30:18** *Issachar*: explained by the terms, *sekari*, "my reward,"

and in v. 16, *sakor sekartika*, "I have hired you."

**30:20** *Zebulun*: explained by the terms, *zebadani...zebed tob*, "he has brought me a precious gift," and *yizbeleni*, "he will honor me."

**30:24** *Joseph*: explained by the words *yosep*, "may he add," and in v. 23, *'asap*, "he has removed."

**30:25–43** Jacob's deception of Laban. Jacob has been living in Laban's household as an indentured worker paying off the bride price. Having paid off all his obligations, he wants to settle his accounts with Laban. His many children attest to the fulfillment of the Lord's promise of numerous progeny; the birth of Joseph to his beloved Rachel signals the fulfillment in a special way. To enter into the Lord's second promise, the land, he must now return to Canaan.

**30:32** *Dark...lambs...spotted or speckled...goats*: in the Near East the normal color of sheep is light gray, whereas that of goats is dark brown or black. A minority of sheep in that part of the world have dark patches, and a minority of goats, white

33 In the future, whenever you check on my wages, my honesty will testify for me: any animal that is not speckled or spotted among the goats, or dark among the lambs, got into my possession by theft!" 34 Laban said, "Very well. Let it be as you say."

35 That same day Laban removed the streaked and spotted he-goats and all the speckled and spotted she-goats, all those with some white on them, as well as every dark lamb, and he put them in the care of his sons.† 36 Then he put a three days' journey between himself and Jacob, while Jacob was pasturing the rest of Laban's flock.

37 Jacob, however, got some fresh shoots of poplar, almond and plane† trees, and he peeled white stripes in them by laying bare the white core of the shoots. 38 The shoots that he had peeled he then set upright in the watering troughs where the animals came to drink, so that they would be in front of them. When the animals were in heat as they came to drink, 39 the goats mated by the shoots, and so they gave birth to streaked, speckled and spotted young. 40 The sheep, on the other hand, Jacob kept apart, and he made these animals face the streaked or completely dark animals of Laban. Thus he produced flocks of his own, which he did not put with Laban's flock. 41 Whenever the hardier animals were in heat, Jacob would set the shoots in the troughs in full view of these animals, so that they mated by the shoots; 42 but with the weaker animals he would not put the shoots there. So the feeble animals would go to Laban, but the hardy ones to Jacob. 43 So the man grew exceedingly prosperous, and he owned large flocks, male and female servants, camels, and donkeys.

# 31 Flight from Laban. †

1 Jacob heard that Laban's sons were saying, "Jacob has taken everything that belonged to our father,

and he has produced all this wealth from our father's property." 2 Jacob perceived, too, that Laban's attitude toward him was not what it had previously been. 3 Then the LORD said to Jacob: Return to the land of your ancestors, where you were born, and I will be with you.*

4 So Jacob sent for Rachel and Leah to meet him in the field where his flock was. 5 There he said to them: "I have noticed that your father's attitude toward me is not as it was in the past; but the God of my father has been with me. 6 You know well that with all my strength I served your father; 7 yet your father cheated me and changed my wages ten times. God, however, did not let him do me any harm.* 8 Whenever your father said, 'The speckled animals will be your wages,' the entire flock would bear speckled young; whenever he said, 'The streaked animals will be your wages,' the entire flock would bear streaked young. 9 So God took away your father's livestock and gave it to me. 10 Once, during the flock's mating season, I had a dream in which I saw he-goats mating that were streaked, speckled and mottled. 11 In the dream God's angel said to me, 'Jacob!' and I replied, 'Here I am!' 12 Then he said: 'Look up and see. All the he-goats that are mating are streaked, speckled and mottled, for I have seen all the things that Laban has been doing to you. 13 I am the God of Bethel, where you anointed a sacred pillar and made a vow to me. Get up now! Leave this land and return to the land of your birth.'"*

14 Rachel and Leah answered him: "Do we still have an heir's portion in our father's house? 15 Are we not regarded by him as outsiders?† He not only sold us; he has even used up the money that he got for us! 16 All the wealth that God took away from our father really belongs to us and our children. So do whatever God has told you."* 17 Jacob proceeded to put his children and wives on

---

† markings. Laban is quick to agree to the offer, for Jacob would have received only a few animals. But Jacob gets the better of him, using two different means: (1) he separates out the weaker animals and then provides visual impressions to the stronger animals at mating time (a folkloric belief); (2) in 31:8–12, he transmits the preferred characteristics through controlled propagation. It should be noted that Jacob has been told what to do in a dream (31:10) and that God is behind the increase in his flocks.

30:35 By giving the abnormally colored animals to his sons, Laban not only deprived Jacob of his first small wages, but he also schemed to prevent the future breeding of such animals in the flock entrusted to Jacob.

30:37 Plane: also called the Oriental Plane, a deciduous tree found in riverine forests and marshes.

31:1–54 Jacob flees with his family from Laban. The strife

that has always accompanied Jacob continues as Laban's sons complain, "he has taken everything that belonged to our father"; the brothers' complaint echoes Esau's in 27:36. Rachel and Leah overcome their mutual hostility and are able to leave together, a harbinger of the reconciliation with Esau in chap. 33.

31:15 Outsiders: lit., "foreign women"; they lacked the favored legal status of native women. Used up: lit., "eaten, consumed"; the bridal price that a man received for giving his daughter in marriage was legally reserved as her inalienable dowry. Perhaps this is the reason that Rachel took the household images belonging to Laban.

31:3 Gn 26:3; 28:15; 32:10.    31:13 Gn 28:18.
31:7 Jdt 8:26.    31:16 Wis 10:10–11.

camels, ¹⁸ and he drove off all his livestock and all the property he had acquired in Paddan-aram, to go to his father Isaac in the land of Canaan.

¹⁹ Now Laban was away shearing his sheep, and Rachel had stolen her father's household images.†* ²⁰ Jacob had hoodwinked† Laban the Aramean by not telling him that he was going to flee. ²¹ Thus he fled with all that he had. Once he was across the Euphrates, he headed for the hill country of Gilead.

²² On the third day, word came to Laban that Jacob had fled. ²³ Taking his kinsmen with him, he pursued him for seven days† until he caught up with him in the hill country of Gilead. ²⁴ But that night God appeared to Laban the Aramean in a dream and said to him: Take care not to say anything to Jacob.*

**Jacob and Laban in Gilead.** ²⁵ When Laban overtook Jacob, Jacob's tents were pitched in the hill country; Laban also pitched his tents in the hill country of Gilead. ²⁶ Laban said to Jacob, "How could you hoodwink me and carry off my daughters like prisoners of war?† ²⁷ Why did you dupe me by stealing away secretly? You did not tell me! I would have sent you off with joyful singing to the sound of tambourines and harps. ²⁸ You did not even allow me a parting kiss to my daughters and grandchildren! Now what you have done makes no sense. ²⁹ I have it in my power to harm all of you; but last night the God of your father said to me, 'Take care not to say anything to Jacob!' ³⁰ Granted that you had to leave because you were longing for your father's house, why did you steal my gods?" ³¹ Jacob replied to Laban, "I was frightened at the thought that you might take your daughters away from me by force. ³² As for your gods, the

one you find them with shall not remain alive! If, with our kinsmen looking on, you identify anything here as belonging to you, take it." Jacob had no idea that Rachel had stolen the household images.

³³ Laban then went in and searched Jacob's tent and Leah's tent, as well as the tents of the two maidservants; but he did not find them. Leaving Leah's tent, he went into Rachel's. ³⁴† Meanwhile Rachel had taken the household images, put them inside the camel's saddlebag, and seated herself upon them. When Laban had rummaged through her whole tent without finding them,* ³⁵ she said to her father, "Do not let my lord be angry that I cannot rise in your presence; I am having my period." So, despite his search, he did not find the household images.

³⁶ Jacob, now angered, confronted Laban and demanded, "What crime or offense have I committed that you should hound me? ³⁷ Now that you have rummaged through all my things, what have you found from your household belongings? Produce it here before your kinsmen and mine, and let them decide between the two of us.

³⁸ "In the twenty years that I was under you, no ewe or she-goat of yours ever miscarried, and I have never eaten rams of your flock. ³⁹* I never brought you an animal torn by wild beasts; I made good the loss myself. You held me responsible for anything stolen by day or night.† ⁴⁰ Often the scorching heat devoured me by day, and the frost by night, while sleep fled from my eyes! ⁴¹ Of the twenty years that I have now spent in your household, I served you fourteen years for your two daughters and six years for your flock, while you changed my wages ten times. ⁴² If the God of my father, the God of Abraham and the Fear of Isaac, had not

---

† **31:19** *Household images*: in Hebrew, *teraphim*, figurines used in divination (Ez 21:26; Zec 10:2). Laban calls them his "gods" (v. 30). The traditional translation "idols" is avoided because it suggests false gods, whereas Genesis seems to accept the fact that the ancestors did not always live according to later biblical religious standards and laws.

**31:20** *Hoodwinked*: lit., "stolen the heart of," i.e., lulled the mind of. *Aramean*: the earliest extra-biblical references to the Arameans date later than the time of Jacob, if Jacob is dated to the mid-second millennium; to call Laban an Aramean and to have him speak Aramaic (Jegar-sahadutha, v. 47) is an apparent anachronism. The word may have been chosen to underscore the growing estrangement between the two men and the fact that their descendants will be two different peoples.

**31:23** *For seven days*: lit., "a way of seven days," a general term to designate a long distance; it would actually have taken a camel caravan many more days to travel from Haran to Gilead,

the region east of the northern half of the Jordan. The mention of camels in this passage is apparently anachronistic since camels were not domesticated until the late second millennium.

**31:26** *Prisoners of war*: lit., "women captured by the sword"; the women of a conquered people were treated as part of the victor's spoil; cf. 1 Sm 30:2; 2 Kgs 5:2.

**31:34** As in chap. 27, a younger child (Rachel) deceives her father to gain what belongs to him.

**31:39** Jacob's actions are more generous than the customs suggested in the Code of Hammurabi: "If in a sheepfold an act of god has occurred, or a lion has made a kill, the shepherd shall clear himself before the deity, and the owner of the fold must accept the loss" (par. 266); cf. Ex 22:12.

**31:19** Gn 31:34; 1 Sm 19:13.
**31:24** Wis 10:12.
**31:34** Gn 31:19.
**31:39** Ex 22:12.

been on my side, you would now have sent me away empty-handed. But God saw my plight and the fruits of my toil, and last night he reproached you."*

[43]† Laban replied to Jacob: "The daughters are mine, their children are mine, and the flocks are mine; everything you see belongs to me. What can I do now for my own daughters and for the children they have borne? [44]† Come, now, let us make a covenant, you and I; and it will be a treaty between you and me."

[45] Then Jacob took a stone and set it up as a sacred pillar.* [46] Jacob said to his kinsmen, "Gather stones." So they got stones and made a mound; and they ate there at the mound. [47] Laban called it Jegar-sahadutha,† but Jacob called it Galeed. [48] Laban said, "This mound will be a witness from now on between you and me." That is why it was named Galeed— [49] and also Mizpah,† for he said: "May the LORD keep watch between you and me when we are out of each other's sight. [50] If you mistreat my daughters, or take other wives besides my daughters, know that even though no one else is there, God will be a witness between you and me."

[51] Laban said further to Jacob: "Here is this mound, and here is the sacred pillar that I have set up between you and me. [52] This mound will be a witness, and this sacred pillar will be a witness, that, with hostile intent, I may not pass beyond this mound into your territory, nor may you pass beyond it into mine. [53] May the God of Abraham and the God of Nahor, the God of their father, judge between us!" Jacob took the oath by the Fear of his father Isaac.† [54] He then offered a sacrifice on the mountain and invited his kinsmen to share in the meal. When they had eaten, they passed the night on the mountain.

# 32

[1]† Early the next morning, Laban kissed his grandchildren and his daughters and blessed them; then he set out on his journey back home. [2] Meanwhile Jacob continued on his own way, and God's angels encountered him. [3] When Jacob saw them he said, "This is God's encampment." So he named that place Mahanaim.†

**Envoys to Esau.** [4] Jacob sent messengers ahead to his brother Esau in the land of Seir, the country of Edom,* [5] ordering them: "Thus you shall say to my lord Esau: 'Thus says your servant Jacob: I have been residing with Laban and have been delayed until now. [6] I own oxen, donkeys and sheep, as well as male and female servants. I have sent my lord this message in the hope of gaining your favor.'" [7] When the messengers returned to Jacob, they said, "We found your brother Esau. He is now coming to meet you, and four hundred men are with him."

[8] Jacob was very much frightened. In his anxiety, he divided the people who were with him, as well as his flocks, herds and camels, into two camps. [9] "If Esau should come and attack one camp," he reasoned, "the remaining camp may still escape." [10] Then Jacob prayed: "God of my father Abraham and God of my father Isaac! You, LORD, who said to me, 'Go back to your land and your relatives, and I will be good to you.'* [11] I am unworthy of all the acts of kindness and faithfulness that you have performed for your servant: although I crossed the Jordan here with nothing but my staff, I have now grown into two camps. [12] Save me from the hand of my brother, from the hand of Esau! Otherwise I fear that he will come and strike me down and the mothers with the children. [13] You yourself said, 'I will be very good to you, and I will make your descendants like

---

† **31:43–54** In this account of the non-aggression treaty between Laban and Jacob, the different objects that serve as witness (sacred pillar in v. 45, cairn of stones in v. 46), their different names (Jegar-sahadutha in v. 47, Mizpah in v. 49), and the two references to the covenant meal (vv. 46, 54) suggest that two versions have been fused. One version is the Yahwist source, and another source has been used to supplement it.

**31:44–54** The treaty is a typical covenant between two parties: Jacob was bound to treat his wives (Laban's daughters) well, and Laban was bound not to cross Jacob's boundaries with hostile intent.

**31:47–48** *Jegar-sahadutha*: an Aramaic term meaning "mound of witness." *Galeed*: in Hebrew, "the mound of witness."

**31:49** *Mizpah*: a town in Gilead; cf. Jgs 10:17; 11:11, 34; Hos 5:1. The Hebrew name *mispa* ("lookout") is allied to *yisep yhwh*

("may the Lord keep watch"), and also echoes the word *massebā* ("sacred pillar").

**31:53** *Fear of…Isaac*: an archaic title for Jacob's God of the Father.

**32:1–22** Jacob's negotiations with Esau. Laban kisses his daughters and grandchildren good-bye but not Jacob. On leaving Mesopotamia, Jacob has an encounter with angels of God (vv. 2–3), which provokes him to exclaim, "This is God's encampment," just as he exclaimed upon leaving Canaan, "This is the house of God, the gateway to heaven" (28:11–17).

**32:3** *Mahanaim*: a town in Gilead (Jos 13:26, 30; 21:38; 2 Sm 2:8; etc.). The Hebrew name means "two camps." There are other allusions to the name in vv. 8, 11.

---

*

| 31:42 Gn 31:24, 29. | 32:4 Gn 36:6. |
| 31:45 Gn 28:18; 35:14. | 32:10 Gn 31:3. |

GN

the sands of the sea, which are too numerous to count.'"*

<sup>14</sup>After passing the night there, Jacob selected from what he had with him a present for his brother Esau: <sup>15</sup>two hundred she-goats and twenty he-goats; two hundred ewes and twenty rams; <sup>16</sup>thirty female camels and their young; forty cows and ten bulls; twenty female donkeys and ten male donkeys. <sup>17</sup>He put these animals in the care of his servants, in separate herds, and he told the servants, "Go on ahead of me, but keep some space between the herds." <sup>18</sup>He ordered the servant in the lead, "When my brother Esau meets you and asks, 'To whom do you belong? Where are you going? To whom do these animals ahead of you belong?' <sup>19</sup>tell him, 'To your servant Jacob, but they have been sent as a gift to my lord Esau. Jacob himself is right behind us.'" <sup>20</sup>He also ordered the second servant and the third and all the others who followed behind the herds: "Thus and so you shall say to Esau, when you reach him; <sup>21</sup>and also tell him, 'Your servant Jacob is right behind us.'" For Jacob reasoned, "If I first appease him with a gift that precedes me, then later, when I face him, perhaps he will forgive me." <sup>22</sup>So the gifts went on ahead of him, while he stayed that night in the camp.

**Jacob's New Name.**† <sup>23</sup>That night, however, Jacob arose, took his two wives, with the two maidservants and his eleven children, and crossed the ford of the Jabbok. <sup>24</sup>After he got them and brought them across the wadi and brought over what belonged to him, <sup>25</sup>Jacob was left there alone. Then a man† wrestled with him until the break of dawn. <sup>26</sup>When

the man saw that he could not prevail over him, he struck Jacob's hip at its socket, so that Jacob's socket was dislocated as he wrestled with him.* <sup>27</sup>The man then said, "Let me go, for it is daybreak." But Jacob said, "I will not let you go until you bless me." <sup>28</sup>"What is your name?" the man asked. He answered, "Jacob."* <sup>29</sup>Then the man said, "You shall no longer be named Jacob, but Israel,† because you have contended with divine and human beings and have prevailed." <sup>30</sup>Jacob then asked him, "Please tell me your name." He answered, "Why do you ask for my name?" With that, he blessed him. <sup>31</sup>Jacob named the place Peniel,† "because I have seen God face to face," he said, "yet my life has been spared."*

<sup>32</sup>At sunrise, as he left Penuel, Jacob limped along because of his hip. <sup>33</sup>That is why, to this day, the Israelites do not eat the sciatic muscle that is on the hip socket, because he had struck Jacob's hip socket at the sciatic muscle.

# 33

**Jacob and Esau Meet.**† <sup>1</sup>Jacob looked up and saw Esau coming, and with him four hundred men. So he divided his children among Leah, Rachel, and the two maidservants, <sup>2</sup>putting the maidservants and their children first, Leah and her children next, and Rachel and Joseph last. <sup>3</sup>He himself went on ahead of them, bowing to the ground seven times, until he reached his brother. <sup>4</sup>Esau ran to meet him, embraced him, and flinging himself on his neck, kissed him as he wept.

<sup>5</sup>Then Esau looked up and saw the women and children and asked, "Who are these with you?" Jacob answered, "They are the children with whom God has graciously favored your

32:23–33 As Jacob crosses over to the land promised him, worried about the impending meeting with Esau, he encounters a mysterious adversary in the night with whom he wrestles until morning. The cunning Jacob manages to wrest a blessing from the night stranger before he departs. There are folkloric elements in the tale—e.g., the trial of the hero before he can return home, the nocturnal demon's loss of strength at sunrise, the demon protecting its river, the power gained by knowledge of an opponent's name—but these have been worked into a coherent though elliptical narrative. The point of the tale seems to be that the ever-striving, ever-grasping Jacob must eventually strive with God to attain full possession of the blessing.

32:25 A man: as with Abraham's three visitors in chap. 18, who appear sometimes as three, two, and one (the latter being God), this figure is fluid; he loses the match but changes Jacob's name (v. 29), an act elsewhere done only by God (17:5, 15). A few deft narrative touches manage to express intimate contact with Jacob while preserving the transcendence proper to divinity.

32:29 Israel: the first part of the Hebrew name Yisrael is given a popular explanation in the word saritha, "you contended"; the second part is the first syllable of 'elohim, "divine beings." The present incident, with a similar allusion to the name Israel, is re-

ferred to in Hos 12:5, where the mysterious wrestler is explicitly called an angel.

32:31 Peniel: a variant of the word Penuel (v. 32), the name of a town on the north bank of the Jabbok in Gilead (Jgs 8:8–9, 17; 1 Kgs 12:25). The name is explained as meaning "the face of God," peni-'el. Yet my life has been spared: see note on 16:13.

33:1–20 The truly frightening confrontation seems to have already occurred in Jacob's meeting the divine stranger in the previous chapter. In contrast, this meeting brings reconciliation. Esau, impulsive but largehearted, kisses the cunning Jacob and calls him brother (v. 9). Jacob in return asks Esau to accept his blessing (berakah, translated "gift," v. 11), giving back at least symbolically what he had taken many years before and responding to Esau's erstwhile complaint ("he has taken away my blessing," 27:36). Verses 12–17 show that the reconciliation is not total and, further, that Jacob does not intend to share the ancestral land with his brother.

32:13 Gn 28:14; 48:16; Ex 32:13; Heb 11:12.
32:26 Hos 12:5.
32:28 Gn 35:10; 1 Kgs 18:31; 2 Kgs 17:34.
32:31 Jgs 13:22.

servant." [6] Then the maidservants and their children came forward and bowed low; [7] next, Leah and her children came forward and bowed low; lastly, Joseph and Rachel came forward and bowed low. [8] Then Esau asked, "What did you intend with all those herds that I encountered?" Jacob answered, "It was to gain my lord's favor." [9] Esau replied, "I have plenty; my brother, you should keep what is yours." [10] "No, I beg you!" said Jacob. "If you will do me the favor, accept this gift from me, since to see your face is for me like seeing the face of God—and you have received me so kindly. [11] Accept the gift I have brought you. For God has been generous toward me, and I have an abundance." Since he urged him strongly, Esau accepted.

[12] Then Esau said, "Let us break camp and be on our way; I will travel in front of you." [13] But Jacob replied: "As my lord knows, the children are too young. And the flocks and herds that are nursing are a concern to me; if overdriven for even a single day, the whole flock will die. [14] Let my lord, then, go before his servant, while I proceed more slowly at the pace of the livestock before me and at the pace of my children, until I join my lord in Seir." [15] Esau replied, "Let me at least put at your disposal some of the people who are with me." But Jacob said, "Why is this that I am treated so kindly, my lord?" [16] So on that day Esau went on his way back to Seir, [17] and Jacob broke camp for Succoth.† There Jacob built a home for himself and made booths for his livestock. That is why the place was named Succoth.

[18] Jacob arrived safely at the city of Shechem, which is in the land of Canaan, when he came from Paddan-aram. He encamped in sight of the city.* [19] The plot of ground on which he had pitched his tent he bought for a hundred pieces of money† from the descendants of Hamor, the father of Shechem.* [20] He set up an altar there and invoked "El, the God of Israel."*

# 34 **The Rape of Dinah.** [1] † Dinah, the daughter whom Leah had borne to Jacob, went out to visit some of the women of the land. [2] When Shechem, son of Hamor the Hivite,† the leader of the region, saw her, he seized her and lay with her by force. [3] He was strongly attracted to Dinah, daughter of Jacob, and was in love with the young woman. So he spoke affectionately to her. [4] Shechem said to his father Hamor, "Get me this young woman for a wife."

[5] Meanwhile, Jacob heard that Shechem had defiled his daughter Dinah; but since his sons were out in the field with his livestock, Jacob kept quiet until they came home. [6] Now Hamor, the father of Shechem, went out to discuss the matter with Jacob, [7] just as Jacob's sons were coming in from the field. When they heard the news, the men were indignant and extremely angry. Shechem had committed an outrage in Israel by lying with Jacob's daughter; such a thing is not done.* [8] Hamor appealed to them, saying: "My son Shechem has his heart set on your daughter. Please give her to him as a wife. [9] Intermarry with us; give your daughters to us, and take our daughters for yourselves. [10] Thus you can live among us. The land is open before you. Settle and move about freely in it and acquire holdings here."† [11] Then Shechem appealed to Dinah's father and brothers: "Do me this favor, and whatever you ask from me, I will give. [12] No matter how high you set the bridal price and gift, I will give you whatever you ask from me; only give me the young woman as a wife."

**Revenge of Jacob's Sons.** [13] Jacob's sons replied to Shechem and his father Hamor with guile, speaking as they did because he had defiled

---

† **33:17** *Succoth*: an important town near the confluence of the Jabbok and the Jordan (Jos 13:27; Jgs 8:5–16; 1 Kgs 7:46). *Booths*: in Hebrew, *sukkot*, of the same sound as the name of the town.

**33:19** *Pieces of money*: in Hebrew, *qesita*, a monetary unit of which the value is unknown. *Descendants of Hamor*: Hamorites, "the people of Hamor"; cf. Jgs 9:28. Hamor was regarded as the eponymous ancestor of the pre-Israelite inhabitants of Shechem.

**34:1–31** The story of the rape of Dinah and the revenge of Jacob's sons on the men of the city of Shechem may reflect the relations of the tribes of Simeon and Levi to their Canaanite neighbors around Shechem; the tribes are represented by their eponymous ancestors. Jacob's farewell testament (49:5–7) cites this incident as the reason for the decline of the tribes of Simeon and Levi. Ominously, vv. 30–31 leave the situation unresolved,

with Jacob concerned about the welfare of the whole family, and Simeon and Levi concerned only about the honor of their full sister. The danger to the family from narrow self-interest will continue in the Joseph story.

**34:2** *Hivite*: the Greek text has "Horite"; the terms were apparently used indiscriminately to designate the Hurrian or other non-Semitic elements in Palestine.

**34:10** Hamor seems to be making concessions to Jacob's family in the hope of avoiding warfare between the two families.

*

**33:18** Gn 12:6; Jn 4:5.  **33:20** Jgs 6:24.
**33:19** Jos 24:32; Jn 4:5; Acts  **34:7** 2 Sm 13:12.
7:16.

their sister Dinah. [14]They said to them, "We are not able to do this thing: to give our sister to an uncircumcised man. For that would be a disgrace for us. [15]Only on this condition will we agree to that: that you become like us by having every male among you circumcised. [16]Then we will give you our daughters and take your daughters in marriage; we will settle among you and become one people. [17]But if you do not listen to us and be circumcised, we will take our daughter and go."

[18]Their proposal pleased Hamor and his son Shechem. [19]The young man lost no time in acting on the proposal, since he wanted Jacob's daughter. Now he was more highly regarded than anyone else in his father's house. [20]So Hamor and his son Shechem went to the gate of their city and said to the men of their city: [21]"These men are friendly toward us. Let them settle in the land and move about in it freely; there is ample room in the land for them. We can take their daughters in marriage and give our daughters to them. [22]But only on this condition will the men agree to live with us and form one people with us: that every male among us be circumcised as they themselves are. [23]Would not their livestock, their property, and all their animals then be ours? Let us just agree with them, so that they will settle among us."

[24]All who went out of the gate of the city listened to Hamor and his son Shechem, and all the males, all those who went out of the gate of the city,† were circumcised. [25]On the third day, while they were still in pain, two of Jacob's sons, Simeon and Levi, brothers of Dinah, each took his sword, advanced against the unsuspecting city and massacred all the males.* [26]After they had killed Hamor and his son Shechem with the sword, they took Dinah from Shechem's house and left.* [27]Then the other sons of Jacob followed up the slaughter and sacked the city because their sister had been defiled. [28]They took their sheep, cattle and donkeys, whatever was in the city and in the surrounding country. [29]They carried off all their wealth, their children, and their women, and looted whatever was in the houses.*

[30]Jacob said to Simeon and Levi: "You have brought trouble upon me by making me repugnant to the inhabitants of the land, the Canaanites and the Perizzites. I have so few men that, if these people unite against me and attack me, I and my household will be wiped out." [31]But they retorted, "Should our sister be treated like a prostitute?"

# 35 Bethel Revisited.
[1]† God said to Jacob: Go up now to Bethel. Settle there and build an altar there to the God who appeared to you when you were fleeing from your brother Esau.* [2]So Jacob told his household and all who were with him: "Get rid of the foreign gods† among you; then purify yourselves and change your clothes. [3]Let us now go up to Bethel so that I might build an altar there to the God who answered me in the day of my distress and who has been with me wherever I have gone." [4]They gave Jacob all the foreign gods in their possession and also the rings they had in their ears† and Jacob buried them under the oak that is near Shechem. [5]Then, as they set out, a great terror fell upon the surrounding towns, so that no one pursued the sons of Jacob.

[6]Thus Jacob and all the people who were with him arrived in Luz (now Bethel) in the land of Canaan.* [7]There he built an altar and called the place El-Bethel,† for it was there that God had revealed himself to him when he was fleeing from his brother.*

[8]Deborah, Rebekah's nurse, died. She was buried under the oak below Bethel, and so it was named Allon-bacuth.†

---

† **34:24** *All those who went out of the gate of the city*: apparently meaning all the residents. By temporarily crippling the men through circumcision, Jacob's sons deprived the city of its defenders.

**35:1–7** Jacob returns to Bethel and founds the sanctuary, an event that forms a "bookend" to the first visit to Bethel in 28:10–22. To enter the Lord's sanctuary, one must purify oneself and get rid of all signs of allegiance to other gods (Jos 24:23; Jgs 10:16). Jacob also seems to initiate the custom of making a pilgrimage to Bethel (see Ps 122:1 and Is 2:3, 5).

**35:2** *Foreign gods*: divine images, including those of household deities (see note on 31:19), that Jacob's people brought with them from Paddan-aram.

**35:4** *Rings…their ears*: the earrings may have belonged to the

gods because earrings were often placed on statues.

**35:7** *El-Bethel*: probably to be translated "the god of Bethel." This is one of several titles of God in Genesis that begin with *El* (= God), e.g., *El Olam* (21:33), *El Elyon* (14:18), *El* the God of Israel (33:20), *El Roi* (16:13), and *El Shaddai*. Most of these (except *El Shaddai*) are tied to specific Israelite shrines.

**35:8** *Allon-bacuth*: the Hebrew name means "oak of weeping."

---

**34:25** Gn 49:6.
**34:26** Jdt 9:2.
**34:29** Jdt 9:3–4.
**35:1** Gn 28:12–13.
**35:6** Gn 28:19; Jos 18:13; Jgs 1:22–23.
**35:7** Gn 28:12–13.

⁹On Jacob's arrival from Paddan-aram, God appeared to him again and blessed him. ¹⁰God said to him:

> Your name is Jacob.
> You will no longer be named Jacob,
> but Israel will be your name.*

So he was named Israel. ¹¹Then God said to him: I am God Almighty; be fruitful and multiply. A nation, indeed an assembly of nations, will stem from you, and kings will issue from your loins. ¹²The land I gave to Abraham and Isaac I will give to you; and to your descendants after you I will give the land.* ¹³Then God departed from him. ¹⁴In the place where God had spoken with him, Jacob set up a sacred pillar, a stone pillar, and upon it he made a libation and poured out oil.* ¹⁵Jacob named the place where God spoke to him Bethel.

**Jacob's Family.** ¹⁶Then they departed from Bethel; but while they still had some distance to go to Ephrath, Rachel went into labor and suffered great distress. ¹⁷When her labor was most intense, the midwife said to her, "Do not fear, for now you have another son." ¹⁸With her last breath—for she was at the point of death—she named him Ben-oni;† but his father named him Benjamin. ¹⁹Thus Rachel died; and she was buried on the road to Ephrath (now Bethlehem).†* ²⁰Jacob set up a sacred pillar on her grave, and the same pillar marks Rachel's grave to this day.

²¹Israel moved on and pitched his tent beyond Migdal-eder. ²²While Israel was encamped in that region, Reuben went and lay with Bilhah, his father's concubine. When Israel heard of it, he was greatly offended.†*

The sons of Jacob were now twelve. ²³The sons of Leah: Reuben, Jacob's firstborn, Simeon, Levi, Judah, Issachar, and Zebulun; ²⁴† the sons of Rachel: Joseph and Benjamin; ²⁵the sons of Rachel's maidservant Bilhah: Dan and Naphtali; ²⁶the sons of Leah's maidservant Zilpah: Gad and Asher. These are the sons of Jacob who were born to him in Paddan-aram.

²⁷Jacob went home to his father Isaac at Mamre, in Kiriath-arba (now Hebron), where Abraham and Isaac had resided. ²⁸The length of Isaac's life was one hundred and eighty years; ²⁹then he breathed his last. He died as an old man and was gathered to his people. After a full life, his sons Esau and Jacob buried him.

**36 Edomite Lists.**† ¹These are the descendants of Esau (that is, Edom). ²† Esau took his wives from among the Canaanite women: Adah, daughter of Elon the Hittite; Oholibamah, the daughter of Anah the son of Zibeon the Hivite;* ³and Basemath, daughter of Ishmael and sister of Nebaioth. ⁴Adah bore Eliphaz to Esau; Basemath bore Reuel;* ⁵and Oholibamah bore Jeush, Jalam and Korah. These are the sons of Esau who were born to him in the land of Canaan.*

⁶Esau took his wives, his sons, his daughters, and all the members of his household, as well as his livestock, all his cattle, and all the property he had acquired in the land of Canaan, and went to the land of Seir, away from his brother Jacob.* ⁷Their possessions

---

† **35:18** *Ben-oni*: means either "son of my vigor" or, more likely in the context, "son of affliction." *Benjamin*: "son of the right hand," meaning a son who is his father's help and support.

**35:19** *Bethlehem*: the gloss comes from a later tradition that identified the site with Bethlehem, also called Ephrath or Ephratha (Jos 15:59; Ru 4:11; Mi 5:1). But Rachel's grave was actually near Ramah (Jer 31:15), a few miles north of Jerusalem, in the territory of Benjamin (1 Sm 10:2).

**35:22** The genealogy in vv. 23–29 is prefaced by a notice about Reuben's sleeping with Bilhah, his father's concubine. Such an act is a serious challenge to the authority of the father (cf. 2 Sm 3:7 and 16:21). In his final testament in chap. 49, Jacob cites this act of Reuben as the reason for Reuben's loss of the authority he had as firstborn son (49:4). Reuben's act is one more instance of strife in the family and of discord between father and son.

**35:24–26** Benjamin is here said to have been born in Paddan-aram, apparently because all twelve sons of Jacob are considered as a unit.

**36:1–43** The line of Esau. In the preceding chapter (35:22–26), the list of Jacob's children completes the narrative of Jacob; in this chapter, the narrative of Esau is complete when his de-

scendants are listed. The notice of Abraham's death and burial in 25:7–10 was followed by a list of the line of his elder son Ishmael (25:12–18) and here Isaac's death and burial are followed by the line of Esau. The lines of both Ishmael and Esau are introduced by the same double formula, "These are the descendants of…" (25:12; 36:9) and "These are the names of the sons of…" (25:13; 36:10). The chapter consists of diverse material: vv. 1–3, Esau's wives; vv. 9–14, Esau's descendants; vv. 15–19, the clans of Esau; vv. 20–30, the Horites of Seir; vv. 31–39, the Edomite kings; vv. 40–43, the Edomites.

**36:2–14** The names of Esau's wives and of their fathers given here differ considerably from their names cited from other old sources in 26:34 and 28:9. *Zibeon the Hivite*: in v. 20 he is called a "Horite"; see note on 34:2.

---

**35:10** 1 Kgs 18:31; 2 Kgs 17:34.
**35:12** Ex 32:13; Heb 11:9.
**35:14** Gn 28:18; 31:45.
**35:19** Gn 48:7; 1 Sm 10:2; Mi 5:1.
**35:22** Gn 49:4; 1 Chr 5:1.
**36:2** Gn 26:34.
**36:4** 1 Chr 1:35.
**36:5** 1 Chr 1:35.
**36:6** Gn 32:4.

had become too great for them to dwell together, and the land in which they were residing could not support them because of their livestock. ⁸ So Esau settled in the highlands of Seir. (Esau is Edom.)* ⁹ These are the descendants of Esau,† ancestor of the Edomites, in the highlands of Seir.

¹⁰ These are the names of the sons of Esau: Eliphaz, son of Adah, wife of Esau, and Reuel, son of Basemath, wife of Esau. ¹¹* The sons of Eliphaz were Teman, Omar, Zepho, Gatam, and Kenaz. ¹² Timna was a concubine of Eliphaz, the son of Esau, and she bore Amalek to Eliphaz. Those were the sons of Adah, the wife of Esau. ¹³ These were the sons of Reuel: Nahath, Zerah, Shammah, and Mizzah. Those were the sons of Basemath, the wife of Esau.* ¹⁴ These were the sons of Esau's wife Oholibamah—the daughter of Anah, son of Zibeon—whom she bore to Esau: Jeush, Jalam, and Korah.*

¹⁵ These are the clans of the sons of Esau. The sons of Eliphaz, Esau's firstborn: the clans of Teman, Omar, Zepho, Kenaz, ¹⁶ Korah, Gatam, and Amalek. These are the clans of Eliphaz in the land of Edom; they are the sons of Adah. ¹⁷ These are the sons of Reuel, son of Esau: the clans of Nahath, Zerah, Shammah, and Mizzah. These are the clans of Reuel in the land of Edom; they are the sons of Basemath, wife of Esau. ¹⁸ These were the sons of Oholibamah, wife of Esau: the clans of Jeush, Jalam, and Korah. These are the clans of Esau's wife Oholibamah, daughter of Anah. ¹⁹ These are the sons of Esau—that is, Edom—according to their clans.

²⁰ These are the sons of Seir the Horite,† the inhabitants of the land: Lotan, Shobal, Zibeon, Anah,* ²¹ Dishon, Ezer, and Dishan; those are the clans of the Horites, sons of Seir in the land of Edom. ²²* The sons of Lotan were Hori and Hemam, and Lotan's sister was Timna. ²³ These are the sons of Shobal: Alvan, Mahanath, Ebal, Shepho, and Onam. ²⁴ These are the sons of Zibeon: Aiah and Anah. He is

the Anah who found water in the desert while he was pasturing the donkeys of his father Zibeon. ²⁵ These are the children of Anah: Dishon and Oholibamah, daughter of Anah. ²⁶ These are the sons of Dishon: Hemdan, Eshban, Ithran, and Cheran. ²⁷ These are the sons of Ezer: Bilhan, Zaavan, and Akan. ²⁸ These are the sons of Dishan: Uz and Aran. ²⁹ These are the clans of the Horites: the clans of Lotan, Shobal, Zibeon, Anah, ³⁰ Dishon, Ezer, and Dishan; those are the clans of the Horites, clan by clan, in the land of Seir.

³¹* These are the kings who reigned in the land of Edom before any king reigned over the Israelites.† ³² Bela, son of Beor, became king in Edom; the name of his city was Dinhabah. ³³ When Bela died, Jobab, son of Zerah, from Bozrah, succeeded him as king. ³⁴ When Jobab died, Husham, from the land of the Temanites, succeeded him as king. ³⁵ When Husham died, Hadad, son of Bedad, succeeded him as king. He is the one who defeated Midian in the country of Moab; the name of his city was Avith. ³⁶ When Hadad died, Samlah, from Masrekah, succeeded him as king. ³⁷ When Samlah died, Shaul, from Rehoboth-on-the-River, succeeded him as king. ³⁸ When Shaul died, Baal-hanan, son of Achbor, succeeded him as king. ³⁹ When Baal-hanan, son of Achbor, died, Hadad succeeded him as king; the name of his city was Pau. His wife's name was Mehetabel, the daughter of Matred, son of Mezahab.

⁴⁰ These are the names of the clans of Esau identified according to their families and localities: the clans of Timna, Alvah, Jetheth, ⁴¹ Oholibamah, Elah, Pinon, ⁴² Kenaz, Teman, Mibzar, ⁴³ Magdiel, and Iram. Those are the clans of the Edomites, according to their settlements in their territorial holdings—that is, of Esau, the ancestor of the Edomites.

# 37 Joseph Sold into Egypt. ¹ Jacob settled in the land where his father had sojourned, the land of Canaan.† ² This is the

---

36:9 *These are the descendants of Esau*: the original heading of the genealogy is preserved in v. 10 ("These are the names of the sons of Esau"). This use of the Priestly formula is secondary and should not be counted in the list of ten such formulas in Genesis.

36:20 *Seir the Horite*: according to Dt 2:12, the highlands of Seir were inhabited by Horites before they were occupied by the Edomites.

36:31 *Before any king reigned over the Israelites*: obviously this statement was written after the time of Saul, Israel's first king. According to 1 Sm 14:47, Saul waged war against the Edomites;

according to 2 Sm 8:2, 13–14 and 1 Kgs 11:14–17, David made Edom a vassal state and nearly wiped out the royal line. These events reflect the words of the Lord to Rebekah at the birth of the boys, "the older shall serve the younger" (25:23).

37:1 The statement points ahead to 47:27, "Thus Israel settled in the land of Egypt, in the region of Goshen." These two statements frame the Joseph narrative; the later material

| | |
|---|---|
| 36:8 Dt 2:4–5; Jos 24:4. | 36:20–21 1 Chr 1:38. |
| 36:11–12 1 Chr 1:36. | 36:22–28 1 Chr 1:39–42. |
| 36:13 1 Chr 1:37. | 36:31–43 1 Chr 1:43–54. |
| 36:14 1 Chr 1:35. | |

story of the family of Jacob.† When Joseph was seventeen years old, he was tending the flocks with his brothers; he was an assistant to the sons of his father's wives Bilhah and Zilpah, and Joseph brought their father bad reports about them. ³Israel loved Joseph best of all his sons, for he was the child of his old age; and he had made him a long ornamented tunic.† ⁴When his brothers saw that their father loved him best of all his brothers, they hated him so much that they could not say a kind word to him.

⁵† Once Joseph had a dream, and when he told his brothers, they hated him even more.* ⁶He said to them, "Listen to this dream I had. ⁷There we were, binding sheaves in the field, when suddenly my sheaf rose to an upright position, and your sheaves formed a ring around my sheaf and bowed down to it." ⁸His brothers said to him, "Are you really going to make yourself king over us? Will you rule over us?" So they hated him all the more because of his dreams and his reports.*

⁹Then he had another dream, and told it to his brothers. "Look, I had another dream," he said; "this time, the sun and the moon and eleven stars were bowing down to me." ¹⁰When he told it to his father and his brothers, his father reproved him and asked, "What is the meaning of this dream of yours? Can it be that I and your mother and your brothers are to come and bow to the ground before you?" ¹¹So his brothers were furious at him but his father kept the matter in mind.

¹²One day, when his brothers had gone to pasture their father's flocks at Shechem, ¹³Israel said to Joseph, "Are your brothers not tending our flocks at Shechem? Come and I will send you to them." "I am ready," Joseph answered. ¹⁴"Go then," he replied; "see if all is well with your brothers and the flocks, and bring back word." So he sent him off from the valley of Hebron. When Joseph reached Shechem, ¹⁵a man came upon him as he was wandering about in the fields. "What are you looking for?" the man asked him. ¹⁶"I am looking for my brothers," he answered. "Please tell me where they are tending the flocks." ¹⁷The man told him, "They have moved on from here; in fact, I heard them say, 'Let us go on to Dothan.'" So Joseph went after his brothers and found them in Dothan. ¹⁸They saw him from a distance, and before he reached them, they plotted to kill him. ¹⁹They said to one another: "Here comes that dreamer! ²⁰Come now, let us kill him and throw him into one of the cisterns here; we could say that a wild beast devoured him. We will see then what comes of his dreams."*

²¹† But when Reuben heard this, he tried to save him from their hands, saying: "We must not take his life." ²²Then Reuben said, "Do not shed blood! Throw him into this cistern in the wilderness; but do not lay a hand on him." His purpose was to save him from their hands and restore him to his father.*

²³So when Joseph came up to his brothers, they stripped him of his tunic, the long

---

† (47:28–49:33) is about Jacob; chap. 50 brings to a conclusion themes remaining from the earlier story. One aim of the Joseph story is to explain how Israel came to Egypt after sojourning so long in Canaan.

**37:2** The Joseph story is great literature not only in its themes but in its art. The stories show an interest in the psychology of the characters; everyone acts "in character" yet there is never a doubt that a divine purpose is bringing events to their conclusion. According to a literary analysis, vv. 1–4 set the scene; vv. 5–36 introduce the dramatic tension in the form of a conflict within the family; chaps. 38–41 describe the journeys away from their family of the eponymous ancestors of the two great tribes of later times, Judah (chap. 38) and Joseph (chaps. 39–41) and their preliminary conclusions; chaps. 42–44 detail the famine and journeys for food (chaps. 42, 43) that bring the brothers and (indirectly) the father into fresh contact with a mature Joseph who now has the power of life and death over them; 45:1–47:27 is the resolution (reconciliation of Joseph to his brothers) and the salvation of the family.

**37:3** Jacob's favoring Joseph over his other sons is a cause of the brothers' attempt on his life. Throughout the story, Jacob is unaware of the impact of his favoritism on his other sons (cf. vv. 33–35; 42:36). *Long ornamented tunic:* the meaning of the Hebrew phrase is unclear. In 2 Sm 13:18–19, it is the distinctive dress of unmarried royal daughters. The "coat of many colors"

in the Septuagint became the traditional translation. Ancient depictions of Semites in formal dress show them with long, ornamented robes and that is the most likely meaning here. Possibly, the young Joseph is given a coat that symbolizes honor beyond his years. Later, Pharaoh will clothe Joseph in a robe that symbolizes honor (41:42).

**37:5–10** Joseph's dreams of ruling his brothers appear at first glance to be merely adolescent grandiosity, and they bring him only trouble. His later successes make it clear, however, that they were from God. Another confirmation of their divine source is the doubling of dreams (cf. 41:32).

**37:21–36** The chapter thus far is from the Yahwist source, as are also vv. 25–28a. But vv. 21–24 and 28b–36 are from another source (sometimes designated the Elohist source). In the latter, Reuben tries to rescue Joseph, who is taken in Reuben's absence by certain Midianites; in the Yahwist source, it is Judah who saves Joseph's life by having him sold to certain Ishmaelites. Although the two variant forms in which the story was handed down in early oral tradition differ in these minor points, they agree on the essential fact that Joseph was brought as a slave into Egypt because of the jealousy of his brothers.

**37:5** Gn 42:9.          **37:20** Gn 44:28.
**37:8** Gn 50:17–18.      **37:22** Gn 42:22.

ornamented tunic he had on; <sup>24</sup> then they took him and threw him into the cistern. The cistern was empty; there was no water in it.

<sup>25</sup> Then they sat down to eat. Looking up, they saw a caravan of Ishmaelites coming from Gilead, their camels laden with gum, balm, and resin to be taken down to Egypt. * <sup>26</sup> Judah said to his brothers: "What is to be gained by killing our brother and concealing his blood? * <sup>27</sup> Come, let us sell him to these Ishmaelites, instead of doing away with him ourselves. After all, he is our brother, our own flesh." His brothers agreed.

<sup>28</sup> Midianite traders passed by, and they pulled Joseph up out of the cistern. They sold Joseph for twenty pieces of silver† to the Ishmaelites, who took him to Egypt. * <sup>29</sup> When Reuben went back to the cistern and saw that Joseph was not in it, he tore his garments,† <sup>30</sup> and returning to his brothers, he exclaimed: "The boy is gone! And I—where can I turn?" <sup>31</sup> They took Joseph's tunic, and after slaughtering a goat, dipped the tunic in its blood. <sup>32</sup> Then they sent someone to bring the long ornamented tunic to their father, with the message: "We found this. See whether it is your son's tunic or not." <sup>33</sup> He recognized it and exclaimed: "My son's tunic! A wild beast has devoured him! Joseph has been torn to pieces!" * <sup>34</sup> Then Jacob tore his garments, put sackcloth on his loins, and mourned his son many days. <sup>35</sup> Though his sons and daughters tried to console him, he refused all consolation, saying, "No, I will go down mourning to my son in Sheol."† Thus did his father weep for him. *

<sup>36</sup> The Midianites, meanwhile, sold Joseph in Egypt to Potiphar, an official of Pharaoh and his chief steward. *

# 38 Judah and Tamar.†

<sup>1</sup> About that time Judah went down, away from his brothers, and pitched his tent near a certain Adullamite named Hirah. <sup>2</sup> There Judah saw the daughter of a Canaanite named Shua; he married her, and had intercourse with her. * <sup>3</sup> She conceived and bore a son, whom she named Er. <sup>4</sup> Again she conceived and bore a son, whom she named Onan. <sup>5</sup> Then she bore still another son, whom she named Shelah. She was in Chezib† when she bore him. *

<sup>6</sup> Judah got a wife named Tamar for his firstborn, Er. <sup>7</sup> But Er, Judah's firstborn, greatly offended the LORD; so the LORD took his life. * <sup>8</sup> * Then Judah said to Onan, "Have intercourse with your brother's wife, in fulfillment of your duty as brother-in-law, and thus preserve your brother's line."† <sup>9</sup> Onan, however, knew that the offspring would not be his; so whenever he had intercourse with his brother's wife, he wasted his seed on the ground, to avoid giving offspring to his brother. <sup>10</sup> What he did greatly offended the LORD, and the LORD took his life too. <sup>11</sup> Then Judah said to his daughter-in-law Tamar, "Remain a widow in your father's house until my son Shelah grows up"—for he feared that Shelah also might die like his brothers. So Tamar went to live in her father's house.

<sup>12</sup> Time passed, and the daughter of Shua, Judah's wife, died. After Judah completed the period of mourning, he went up to Timnah, to those who were shearing his sheep, in company with his friend Hirah the Adullamite. <sup>13</sup> Then Tamar was told, "Your father-in-law is on his way up to Timnah to shear his sheep." <sup>14</sup> So she took off her widow's garments, covered herself with a shawl, and having wrapped

---

† **37:28** *They sold Joseph…silver*: editors tried to solve the confusion, created by different sources, by supposing that it was the Midianite traders who pulled Joseph out of the pit and sold him to Ishmaelites. In all probability, one source had the brothers selling Joseph to Ishmaelites, whereas the other had them cast him into the pit whence he was taken by Midianite traders.

**37:29** *Tore his garments*: the traditional sign of mourning in the ancient Near East.

**37:35** *Sheol*: see note on Ps 6:6.

**38:1–30** This chapter has subtle connections to the main Joseph story. It tells of the eponymous founder of the other great tribe of later times, Judah. Having already been introduced as one of the two good brothers in 37:26–27, he appears here as the father-in-law of the twice-widowed Tamar; he has reneged on his promise to provide his son Shelah to her in a levirate marriage. Unjustly treated, Tamar takes matters into her own hands and tricks Judah into becoming the father of her children, Perez and Zerah. Judah ultimately acknowledges that his daughter-in-law was right ("She is in the right rather than I," v. 26). In contrast to Judah's expectations, the family line does not continue through

his son Shelah, but through the children of Tamar. Similarities relate this little story to the main narrative: the deception involving an article of clothing (the widow's garments of Tamar, Judah's seal, cord, and staff) point back to the bloody tunic that deceives Jacob in 37:31–33; a woman attempts the seduction of a man separated from his family, for righteous purposes in chap. 38, for unrighteous purposes in chap. 39.

**38:5** *Chezib*: a variant form of Achzib (Jos 15:44; Mi 1:14), a town in the Judean Shephelah.

**38:8** *Preserve your brother's line*: lit., "raise up seed for your brother": an allusion to the law of levirate, or "brother-in-law," marriage; see notes on Dt 25:5; Ru 2:20. Onan's violation of this law brought on him God's punishment (vv. 9–10).

**37:25** Gn 43:11.
**37:26** Jb 16:18.
**37:28** Ps 105:17; Wis 10:13; Acts 7:9.
**37:33** Gn 44:28.
**37:35** Gn 42:38.
**37:36** Ps 105:17.
**38:2** 1 Chr 2:3.
**38:5** 1 Chr 4:21.
**38:7** 1 Chr 2:3.
**38:8** Dt 25:5; Mt 22:24; Mk 12:19; Lk 20:28.

herself sat down at the entrance to Enaim, which is on the way to Timnah; for she was aware that, although Shelah was now grown up, she had not been given to him in marriage.* [15] When Judah saw her, he thought she was a harlot, since she had covered her face. [16] So he went over to her at the roadside and said, "Come, let me have intercourse with you," for he did not realize that she was his daughter-in-law. She replied, "What will you pay me for letting you have intercourse with me?" [17] He answered, "I will send you a young goat from the flock." "Very well," she said, "provided you leave me a pledge until you send it." [18] Judah asked, "What pledge should I leave you?" She answered, "Your seal and cord,† and the staff in your hand." So he gave them to her and had intercourse with her, and she conceived by him. [19] After she got up and went away, she took off her shawl and put on her widow's garments again.

[20] Judah sent the young goat by his friend the Adullamite to recover the pledge from the woman; but he did not find her. [21] So he asked the men of that place, "Where is the prostitute,† the one by the roadside in Enaim?" But they answered, "No prostitute has been here." [22] He went back to Judah and told him, "I did not find her; and besides, the men of the place said, 'No prostitute has been here.'" [23] "Let her keep the things," Judah replied; "otherwise we will become a laughingstock. After all, I did send her this young goat, but you did not find her."

[24] About three months later, Judah was told, "Your daughter-in-law Tamar has acted like a harlot and now she is pregnant from her harlotry." Judah said, "Bring her out; let her be burned." [25] But as she was being brought out, she sent word to her father-in-law, "It is by the man to whom these things belong that I am pregnant." Then she said, "See whose seal and cord and staff these are." [26] Judah recognized them and said, "She is in the right rather than I, since I did not give her to my

son Shelah." He had no further sexual relations with her.

[27] When the time of her delivery came, there were twins in her womb.* [28] While she was giving birth, one put out his hand; and the midwife took and tied a crimson thread on his hand, noting, "This one came out first." [29]* But as he withdrew his hand, his brother came out; and she said, "What a breach you have made for yourself!" So he was called Perez.† [30] Afterward his brother, who had the crimson thread on his hand, came out; he was called Zerah.†*

# 39 Joseph's Temptation.

[1] When Joseph was taken down to Egypt, an Egyptian, Potiphar, an official of Pharaoh and his chief steward, bought him from the Ishmaelites who had brought him there. [2]* The LORD was with Joseph and he enjoyed great success and was assigned to the household of his Egyptian master. [3] When his master saw that the LORD was with him and brought him success in whatever he did, [4] he favored Joseph and made him his personal attendant; he put him in charge of his household and entrusted to him all his possessions.* [5] From the moment that he put him in charge of his household and all his possessions, the LORD blessed the Egyptian's house for Joseph's sake; the LORD's blessing was on everything he owned, both inside the house and out. [6] Having left everything he owned in Joseph's charge, he gave no thought, with Joseph there, to anything but the food he ate.

Now Joseph was well-built and handsome. [7] After a time, his master's wife looked at him with longing and said, "Lie with me." [8] But he refused and said to his master's wife, "Look, as long as I am here, my master does not give a thought to anything in the house, but has entrusted to me all he owns. [9] He has no more authority in this house than I do. He has withheld from me nothing but you, since you are his wife. How, then, could I do this great

---

**38:18** *Seal and cord*: the cylinder seal, through which a hole was bored lengthwise so that it could be worn from the neck by a cord, was a distinctive means of identification. Apparently one's staff could also be marked with some sign of identification (cf. Nm 17:17–18).

**38:21** *Prostitute*: the Hebrew term *qedesha*, lit., "consecrated woman," designates a woman associated with a sanctuary whose activities could include prostitution; cf. Dt 23:18; Hos 4:14, where the same Hebrew word is used. In 38:15 and 24 the common word for prostitute, *zona*, is used.

**38:29** *He was called Perez*: the Hebrew word means "breach."

**38:30** *He was called Zerah*: a name connected here by popular etymology with a Hebrew word for the red light of dawn, alluding apparently to the crimson thread.

**38:14** Prv 7:10.
**38:27** 1 Chr 2:4.
**38:29** Ru 4:12; Mt 1:3; Lk 3:33.
**38:30** Nm 26:20; 1 Chr 2:4;

Mt 1:3.
**39:2** 1 Sm 3:19; 10:7; 18:14; 2 Sm 5:10; 2 Kgs 18:7; Acts 7:9.
**39:4** Dn 1:9.

wrong and sin against God?" [10]Although she spoke to him day after day, he would not agree to lie with her, or even be near her.*

[11]One such day, when Joseph came into the house to do his work, and none of the household servants were then in the house, [12]she laid hold of him by his cloak, saying, "Lie with me!" But leaving the cloak in her hand, he escaped and ran outside. [13]When she saw that he had left his cloak in her hand as he escaped outside, [14]she cried out to her household servants and told them, "Look! My husband has brought us a Hebrew man to mock us! He came in here to lie with me, but I cried out loudly. [15]When he heard me scream, he left his cloak beside me and escaped and ran outside."

[16]She kept the cloak with her until his master came home. [17]Then she told him the same story: "The Hebrew slave whom you brought us came to me to amuse himself at my expense. [18]But when I screamed, he left his cloak beside me and escaped outside." [19]When the master heard his wife's story in which she reported, "Thus and so your servant did to me," he became enraged. [20]Joseph's master seized him and put him into the jail where the king's prisoners were confined.* And there he sat, in jail.

[21]But the LORD was with Joseph, and showed him kindness by making the chief jailer well-disposed toward him.* [22]The chief jailer put Joseph in charge of all the prisoners in the jail. Everything that had to be done there, he was the one to do it. [23]The chief jailer did not have to look after anything that was in Joseph's charge, since the LORD was with him and was bringing success to whatever he was doing.

# 40 The Dreams Interpreted. [1]† Some time afterward, the royal cupbearer and baker offended their lord, the king of Egypt. [2]Pharaoh was angry with his two officials, the chief cupbearer and the chief baker, [3]and he put them in custody in the house of the chief steward, the same jail where Joseph was confined. [4]The chief steward assigned Joseph to them, and he became their attendant.

After they had been in custody for some time, [5]the cupbearer and the baker of the king of Egypt who were confined in the jail both had dreams on the same night, each his own dream and each dream with its own meaning. [6]When Joseph came to them in the morning, he saw that they looked disturbed. [7]So he asked Pharaoh's officials who were with him in custody in his master's house, "Why do you look so troubled today?" [8]They answered him, "We have had dreams, but there is no one to interpret them." Joseph said to them, "Do interpretations not come from God? Please tell me the dreams."*

[9]Then the chief cupbearer told Joseph his dream. "In my dream," he said, "I saw a vine in front of me, [10]and on the vine were three branches. It had barely budded when its blossoms came out, and its clusters ripened into grapes. [11]Pharaoh's cup was in my hand; so I took the grapes, pressed them out into his cup, and put it in Pharaoh's hand." [12]Joseph said to him: "This is its interpretation. The three branches are three days; [13]within three days Pharaoh will single you out† and restore you to your post. You will be handing Pharaoh his cup as you formerly did when you were his cupbearer. [14]Only think of me when all is well with you, and please do me the great favor of mentioning me to Pharaoh, to get me out of this place. [15]The truth is that I was kidnapped from the land of the Hebrews, and I have not done anything here that they should have put me into a dungeon."

[16]When the chief baker saw that Joseph had given a favorable interpretation, he said to him: "I too had a dream. In it I had three bread baskets on my head; [17]in the top one were all kinds of bakery products for Pharaoh, but the birds were eating them out of the basket on my head." [18]Joseph said to him in reply: "This is its interpretation. The three baskets are three days; [19]within three days Pharaoh will single you out and will impale you on a stake, and the birds will be eating your flesh."

[20]And so on the third day, which was Pharaoh's birthday, when he gave a banquet to all his servants, he singled out the chief cupbearer and chief baker in the midst of his servants. [21]He restored the chief cupbearer to his office, so that he again handed the cup to Pharaoh;

---

† **40:1** Joseph interprets the dreams of the Pharaoh's two officials. His ability to interpret the dreams shows that God is still with him and points forward to his role of dream interpreter for Pharaoh in chap. 41.

**40:13** *Single you out:* lit., "lift up your head" (see also vv. 19, 20).

**39:10** 1 Mc 2:53.      **39:21** Acts 7:9–10.
**39:20** Ps 105:18.      **40:8** Gn 41:16.

²²but the chief baker he impaled—just as Joseph had told them in his interpretation. ²³Yet the chief cupbearer did not think of Joseph; he forgot him.

# 41 Pharaoh's Dream. ¹† After a lapse of two years, Pharaoh had a dream. He was standing by the Nile, ²when up out of the Nile came seven cows, fine-looking and fat; they grazed in the reed grass. ³Behind them seven other cows, poor-looking and gaunt, came up out of the Nile; and standing on the bank of the Nile beside the others, ⁴the poor-looking, gaunt cows devoured the seven fine-looking, fat cows. Then Pharaoh woke up.

⁵He fell asleep again and had another dream. He saw seven ears of grain, fat and healthy, growing on a single stalk. ⁶Behind them sprouted seven ears of grain, thin and scorched by the east wind; ⁷and the thin ears swallowed up the seven fat, healthy ears. Then Pharaoh woke up—it was a dream!

⁸Next morning his mind was agitated. So Pharaoh had all the magicians† and sages of Egypt summoned and recounted his dream to them; but there was no one to interpret it for him. ⁹Then the chief cupbearer said to Pharaoh: "Now I remember my negligence! ¹⁰Once, when Pharaoh was angry with his servants, he put me and the chief baker in custody in the house of the chief steward. ¹¹Later, we both had dreams on the same night, and each of our dreams had its own meaning. ¹²There was a Hebrew youth with us, a slave of the chief steward; and when we told him our dreams, he interpreted them for us and explained for each of us the meaning of his dream.* ¹³Things turned out just as he had told us: I was restored to my post, but the other man was impaled."

¹⁴Pharaoh therefore had Joseph summoned, and they hurriedly brought him from the dungeon. After he shaved and changed his clothes, he came to Pharaoh.* ¹⁵Pharaoh then said to Joseph: "I had a dream but there was no one to interpret it. But I hear it said of you, 'If he hears a dream he can interpret it.'" ¹⁶"It is not

I," Joseph replied to Pharaoh, "but God who will respond for the well-being of Pharaoh."*

¹⁷Then Pharaoh said to Joseph: "In my dream, I was standing on the bank of the Nile, ¹⁸when up from the Nile came seven cows, fat and well-formed; they grazed in the reed grass. ¹⁹Behind them came seven other cows, scrawny, most ill-formed and gaunt. Never have I seen such bad specimens as these in all the land of Egypt! ²⁰The gaunt, bad cows devoured the first seven fat cows. ²¹But when they had consumed them, no one could tell that they had done so, because they looked as bad as before. Then I woke up. ²²In another dream I saw seven ears of grain, full and healthy, growing on a single stalk. ²³Behind them sprouted seven ears of grain, shriveled and thin and scorched by the east wind; ²⁴and the seven thin ears swallowed up the seven healthy ears. I have spoken to the magicians, but there is no one to explain it to me."

²⁵Joseph said to Pharaoh: "Pharaoh's dreams have the same meaning. God has made known to Pharaoh what he is about to do. ²⁶The seven healthy cows are seven years, and the seven healthy ears are seven years—the same in each dream. ²⁷The seven thin, bad cows that came up after them are seven years, as are the seven thin ears scorched by the east wind; they are seven years of famine. ²⁸Things are just as I told Pharaoh: God has revealed to Pharaoh what he is about to do. ²⁹Seven years of great abundance are now coming throughout the land of Egypt; ³⁰but seven years of famine will rise up after them, when all the abundance will be forgotten in the land of Egypt. When the famine has exhausted the land, ³¹no trace of the abundance will be found in the land because of the famine that follows it, for it will be very severe. ³²That Pharaoh had the same dream twice means that the matter has been confirmed by God and that God will soon bring it about.

³³"Therefore, let Pharaoh seek out a discerning and wise man and put him in charge of the land of Egypt. ³⁴Let Pharaoh act and appoint overseers for the land to organize it during the

---

† **41:1–57** Joseph correctly interprets Pharaoh's dream and becomes second in command over all Egypt.

**41:8** *Magicians*: one of the tasks of the "magicians" was interpreting dreams. The interpretation of dreams was a long-standing practice in Egypt. A manual of dream interpretation has been found, written in the early second millennium and re-published later in which typical dreams are given ("If a man sees himself in a dream…") followed by a judgment of "good" or "bad." Interpreters were still needed for dreams, however, and Pharaoh complains that none of his dream interpreters can interpret his unprecedented dream. The same term will be used of Pharaoh's magicians in Exodus.

*
**41:12** Dn 1:17.
**41:14** Ps 105:20.

**41:16** Gn 40:8.

seven years of abundance. [35] They should collect all the food of these coming good years, gathering the grain under Pharaoh's authority, for food in the cities, and they should guard it. [36] This food will serve as a reserve for the country against the seven years of famine that will occur in the land of Egypt, so that the land may not perish in the famine."

[37] This advice pleased Pharaoh and all his servants.* [38] "Could we find another like him," Pharaoh asked his servants, "a man so endowed with the spirit of God?" [39] So Pharaoh said to Joseph: "Since God has made all this known to you, there is no one as discerning and wise as you are. [40] You shall be in charge of my household, and all my people will obey your command. Only in respect to the throne will I outrank you."* [41] Then Pharaoh said to Joseph, "Look, I put you in charge of the whole land of Egypt." [42] With that, Pharaoh took off his signet ring† and put it on Joseph's finger. He dressed him in robes of fine linen and put a gold chain around his neck. [43] He then had him ride in his second chariot, and they shouted "Abrek!"† before him.

Thus was Joseph installed over the whole land of Egypt. [44] "I am Pharaoh," he told Joseph, "but without your approval no one shall lift hand or foot in all the land of Egypt." [45] Pharaoh also bestowed the name of Zaphenath-paneah† on Joseph, and he gave him in marriage Asenath, the daughter of Potiphera, priest of Heliopolis. And Joseph went out over the land of Egypt. [46] Joseph was thirty years old when he entered the service of Pharaoh, king of Egypt.

After Joseph left Pharaoh, he went throughout the land of Egypt. [47] During the seven years of plenty, when the land produced abundant crops, [48] he collected all the food of these years

of plenty that the land of Egypt was enjoying and stored it in the cities, placing in each city the crops of the fields around it. [49] Joseph collected grain like the sands of the sea, so much that at last he stopped measuring it, for it was beyond measure.

[50] Before the famine years set in, Joseph became the father of two sons, borne to him by Asenath, daughter of Potiphera, priest of Heliopolis.* [51] Joseph named his firstborn Manasseh,† meaning, "God has made me forget entirely my troubles and my father's house"; [52] and the second he named Ephraim,† meaning, "God has made me fruitful in the land of my affliction."

[53] When the seven years of abundance enjoyed by the land of Egypt came to an end, [54] the seven years of famine set in, just as Joseph had said. Although there was famine in all the other countries, food was available throughout the land of Egypt.* [55] When all the land of Egypt became hungry and the people cried to Pharaoh for food, Pharaoh said to all the Egyptians: "Go to Joseph and do whatever he tells you." [56] When the famine had spread throughout the land, Joseph opened all the cities that had grain and rationed it to the Egyptians, since the famine had gripped the land of Egypt. [57] Indeed, the whole world came to Egypt to Joseph to buy grain, for famine had gripped the whole world.

# 42 The Brothers' First Journey to Egypt.†
[1] When Jacob learned that grain rations were for sale in Egypt, he said to his sons: "Why do you keep looking at one another?" [2] He went on, "I hear that grain is for sale in Egypt. Go down there and buy some for us, that we may stay alive and not die."* [3] So ten

---

**41:42** *Signet ring:* a finger ring in which was set a stamp seal, different from the cylinder seal such as Judah wore; see note on 38:18. By receiving Pharaoh's signet ring, Joseph was made vizier of Egypt (v. 43); the vizier was known as "seal-bearer of the king of Lower Egypt." The gold chain was a symbol of high office in ancient Egypt.
**41:43** *Abrek:* apparently a cry of homage, though the word's derivation and actual meaning are uncertain.
**41:45** *Zaphenath-paneah:* a Hebrew transcription of an Egyptian name meaning "the god speaks and he (the newborn child) lives." *Asenath:* means "belonging to (the Egyptian goddess) Neith." *Potiphera:* means "he whom Ra (the Egyptian god) gave"; a shorter form of the same name was borne by Joseph's master (37:36). *Heliopolis:* in Hebrew, *On,* a city seven miles northeast of modern Cairo, site of the chief temple of the sun god; it is mentioned also in v. 50; 46:20; Ez 30:17.
**41:51** *Manasseh:* an allusion to this name is in the Hebrew expression, *nishshani,* "he made me forget."

**41:52** *Ephraim:* related to the Hebrew expression *hiphrani,* "(God) has made me fruitful." The name originally meant something like "fertile land."
**42:1–38** The first journey of the brothers to Egypt. Its cause is famine, which was also the reason Abraham and Sarah undertook their dangerous journey to Egypt. The brothers bow to Joseph in v. 6, which fulfills Joseph's dream in 37:5–11. Endowed with wisdom, Joseph begins a process of instruction or "discipline" for his brothers that eventually forces them to recognize the enormity of their sin against him and the family. He controls their experience of the first journey with the result that the second journey in chaps. 43–44 leads to full acknowledgment and reconciliation.

**41:37** Acts 7:10.
**41:40** 1 Mc 2:53; Ps 105:21; Wis 10:14; Acts 7:10.
**41:50** Gn 46:20; 48:5.
**41:54** Ps 105:16; Acts 7:11.
**42:2** Acts 7:12.

of Joseph's brothers went down to buy grain from Egypt. [4] But Jacob did not send Joseph's brother Benjamin with his brothers, for he thought some disaster might befall him. [5] And so the sons of Israel were among those who came to buy grain, since there was famine in the land of Canaan. *

[6] Joseph, as governor of the country, was the one who sold grain to all the people of the land. When Joseph's brothers came, they bowed down to him with their faces to the ground. * [7] He recognized them as soon as he saw them. But he concealed his own identity from them and spoke harshly to them. "Where do you come from?" he asked them. They answered, "From the land of Canaan, to buy food."

[8] When Joseph recognized his brothers, although they did not recognize him, [9] he was reminded of the dreams he had about them. He said to them: "You are spies. * You have come to see the weak points† of the land." [10] "No, my lord," they replied. "On the contrary, your servants have come to buy food. [11] All of us are sons of the same man. We are honest men; your servants have never been spies." [12] But he answered them: "Not so! It is the weak points of the land that you have come to see." [13] "We your servants," they said, "are twelve brothers, sons of a certain man in Canaan; but the youngest one is at present with our father, and the other one is no more." * [14] "It is just as I said," Joseph persisted; "you are spies. [15] This is how you shall be tested: I swear by the life of Pharaoh that you shall not leave here unless your youngest brother comes here. [16] So send one of your number to get your brother, while the rest of you stay here under arrest. Thus will your words be tested for their truth; if they are untrue, as Pharaoh lives, you are spies!" [17] With that, he locked them up in the guardhouse for three days.

[18] On the third day Joseph said to them: "Do this, and you shall live; for I am a God-fearing man. [19] If you are honest men, let one of your brothers be confined in this prison, while the rest of you go and take home grain for your starving families. [20] But you must bring me your youngest brother. Your words will thus be verified, and you will not die." To this they agreed. * [21] To one another, however, they said: "Truly we are being punished because of our brother. We saw the anguish of his heart when he pleaded with us, yet we would not listen. That is why this anguish has now come upon us." * [22] Then Reuben responded, "Did I not tell you, 'Do no wrong to the boy'? But you would not listen! Now comes the reckoning for his blood." * [23] They did not know, of course, that Joseph understood what they said, since he spoke with them through an interpreter. [24] But turning away from them, he wept. When he was able to speak to them again, he took Simeon from among them and bound him before their eyes. [25] Then Joseph gave orders to have their containers filled with grain, their money replaced in each one's sack, and provisions given them for their journey. After this had been done for them, [26] they loaded their donkeys with the grain and departed.

[27] At the night encampment, when one of them opened his bag to give his donkey some fodder, he saw his money there in the mouth of his bag. [28] He cried out to his brothers, "My money has been returned! Here it is in my bag!" At that their hearts sank. Trembling, they asked one another, "What is this that God has done to us?"

[29] When they got back to their father Jacob in the land of Canaan, they told him all that had happened to them. [30] "The man who is lord of the land," they said, "spoke to us harshly and put us in custody on the grounds that we were spying on the land. [31] But we said to him: 'We are honest men; we have never been spies. [32] We are twelve brothers, sons of the same father; but one is no more, and the youngest one is now with our father in the land of Canaan.' [33] Then the man who is lord of the land said to us: 'This is how I will know if you are honest men: leave one of your brothers with me, then take grain for your starving families and go. [34] When you bring me your youngest brother, and I know that you are not spies but honest men, I will restore your brother to you, and you may move about freely in the land.'"

[35] When they were emptying their sacks, there in each one's sack was his moneybag! At the sight of their moneybags, they and their father were afraid. [36] Their father Jacob said to

† **42:9, 12** *Weak points*: lit., "the nakedness of the land"; the military weakness of the land, like human nakedness, should not be seen by strangers.

**42:5** Jdt 5:10; Acts 7:11.   **42:6** Ps 105:21.   **42:9** Gn 37:5.   **42:13** Gn 44:20.   **42:20** Gn 43:5.   **42:21** Gn 37:18–27.   **42:22** Gn 37:22.

them: "Must you make me childless? Joseph is no more, Simeon is no more, and now you would take Benjamin away! All these things have happened to me!" [37] Then Reuben told his father: "You may kill my own two sons if I do not return him to you! Put him in my care, and I will bring him back to you." [38] But Jacob replied: "My son shall not go down with you. Now that his brother is dead, he is the only one left. If some disaster should befall him on the journey you must make, you would send my white head down to Sheol in grief."*

# 43 The Second Journey to Egypt.†

[1] Now the famine in the land grew severe. [2] So when they had used up all the grain they had brought from Egypt, their father said to them, "Go back and buy us a little more food." [3] But Judah replied: "The man strictly warned us, 'You shall not see me unless your brother is with you.'* [4] If you are willing to let our brother go with us, we will go down to buy food for you. [5] But if you are not willing, we will not go down, because the man told us, 'You shall not see me unless your brother is with you.'"* [6] Israel demanded, "Why did you bring this trouble on me by telling the man that you had another brother?" [7] They answered: "The man kept asking about us and our family: 'Is your father still living? Do you have another brother?' We answered him accordingly. How could we know that he would say, 'Bring your brother down here'?"

[8] Then Judah urged his father Israel: "Let the boy go with me, that we may be off and on our way if you and we and our children are to keep from starving to death.* [9] I myself will serve as a guarantee for him. You can hold me responsible for him. If I fail to bring him back and set him before you, I will bear the blame before you forever.* [10] Had we not delayed, we could have been there and back twice by now!"

[11] Israel their father then told them: "If it must be so, then do this: Put some of the land's best products in your baggage and take them down to the man as gifts: some balm and honey, gum and resin, and pistachios and almonds.* [12] Also take double the money along, for you must return the amount that was put back in the mouths of your bags; it may have been a mistake. [13] Take your brother, too, and be off on your way back to the man. [14] May God Almighty grant you mercy in the presence of the man, so that he may let your other brother go, as well as Benjamin. As for me, if I am to suffer bereavement, I shall suffer it."

[15] So the men took those gifts and double the money and Benjamin. They made their way down to Egypt and presented themselves before Joseph. [16] When Joseph saw them and Benjamin, he told his steward, "Take the men into the house, and have an animal slaughtered and prepared, for they are to dine with me at noon." [17] Doing as Joseph had ordered, the steward conducted the men to Joseph's house. [18] But they became apprehensive when they were led to his house. "It must be," they thought, "on account of the money put back in our bags the first time, that we are taken inside—in order to attack us and take our donkeys and seize us as slaves." [19] So they went up to Joseph's steward and talked to him at the entrance of the house. [20] "If you please, sir," they said, "we came down here once before to buy food.* [21] But when we arrived at a night's encampment and opened our bags, there was each man's money in the mouth of his bag—our money in the full amount! We have now brought it back.* [22] We have brought other money to buy food. We do not know who put our money in our bags." [23] He replied, "Calm down! Do not fear! Your God and the God of your father must have put treasure in your bags for you. As for your money, I received it." With that, he led Simeon out to them.

[24] The steward then brought the men inside Joseph's house. He gave them water to wash their feet, and gave fodder to their donkeys. [25] Then they set out their gifts to await Joseph's arrival at noon, for they had heard that they were to dine there. [26] When Joseph came home, they presented him with the gifts they had brought inside, while they bowed down before him to the ground. [27] After inquiring how they were, he asked them, "And how is your aged father, of whom you spoke? Is he still alive?"* [28] "Your servant our father is still

---

† 43:1–34 The second journey to Egypt. Joseph the sage has carefully prepared the brothers for a possible reconciliation. In this chapter and the following one Judah steps forward as the hero, in contrast to chaps. 37 and 42 where Reuben was the hero. Here Judah serves as guarantee for Benjamin.

42:38 Gn 37:35.
43:3 Gn 44:23.
43:5 Gn 42:20.
43:8 Gn 42:37.
43:9 Gn 44:32.
43:11 Gn 45:23.
43:20 Gn 42:3.
43:21 Gn 42:27–28.
43:27 Tb 7:4.

alive and doing well," they said, as they knelt and bowed down. ²⁹ Then Joseph looked up and saw Benjamin, his brother, the son of his mother. He asked, "Is this your youngest brother, of whom you told me?" Then he said to him, "May God be gracious to you, my son!"* ³⁰ With that, Joseph hurried out, for he was so overcome with affection for his brother that he was on the verge of tears. So he went into a private room and wept there.

³¹ After washing his face, he reappeared and, now having collected himself, gave the order, "Serve the meal." ³² It was served separately to him,† to the brothers, and to the Egyptians who partook of his board. Egyptians may not eat with Hebrews; that is abhorrent to them. ³³ When they were seated before him according to their age, from the oldest to the youngest, they looked at one another in amazement; ³⁴ and as portions were brought to them from Joseph's table, Benjamin's portion was five times as large as† anyone else's. So they drank freely and made merry with him.

# 44

**Final Test.**† ¹ Then Joseph commanded his steward: "Fill the men's bags with as much food as they can carry, and put each man's money in the mouth of his bag. ² In the mouth of the youngest one's bag put also my silver goblet, together with the money for his grain." The steward did as Joseph said. ³ At daybreak the men and their donkeys were sent off. ⁴ They had not gone far out of the city when Joseph said to his steward: "Go at once after the men! When you overtake them, say to them, 'Why did you repay good with evil? Why did you steal my silver goblet? ⁵ Is it not the very one from which my master drinks and which he uses for divination?† What you have done is wrong.'"

⁶ When the steward overtook them and repeated these words to them, ⁷ they said to him: "Why does my lord say such things? Far be it from your servants to do such a thing! ⁸ We even brought back to you from the land of Canaan the money that we found in the mouths of our bags. How could we steal silver or gold from your master's house? ⁹ If any of your servants is found to have the goblet, he shall die, and as for the rest of us, we shall become my lord's slaves." ¹⁰ But he replied, "Now what you propose is fair enough, but only the one who is found to have it shall become my slave, and the rest of you can go free." ¹¹ Then each of them quickly lowered his bag to the ground and opened it; ¹² and when a search was made, starting with the oldest and ending with the youngest, the goblet turned up in Benjamin's bag. ¹³ At this, they tore their garments. Then, when each man had loaded his donkey again, they returned to the city.

¹⁴ When Judah and his brothers entered Joseph's house, he was still there; so they flung themselves on the ground before him. ¹⁵ "How could you do such a thing?" Joseph asked them. "Did you not know that such a man as I could discern by divination what happened?" ¹⁶ Judah replied: "What can we say to my lord? How can we plead or how try to prove our innocence? God has uncovered your servants' guilt.† Here we are, then, the slaves of my lord—the rest of us no less than the one in whose possession the goblet was found." ¹⁷ Joseph said, "Far be it from me to act thus! Only the one in whose possession the goblet was found shall become my slave; the rest of you may go back unharmed to your father."

¹⁸ Judah then stepped up to him and said: "I beg you, my lord, let your servant appeal to my lord, and do not become angry with your servant, for you are the equal of Pharaoh. ¹⁹ My lord asked his servants,† 'Have you

---

† **43:32** *Separately to him*: that Joseph did not eat with the other Egyptians was apparently a matter of rank.

**43:34** *Five times as large as*: probably an idiomatic expression for "much larger than." Cf. 45:22.

**44:1–34** Joseph's pressure on his brothers and Judah's great speech. Judah has the longest speech in the Book of Genesis; it summarizes the recent past (vv. 18–29), shows the pain Joseph's actions have imposed on their aged father (vv. 30–32), and ends with the offer to take the place of Benjamin as servant of Joseph (vv. 33–34). The role of Judah in the entire story is exceedingly important and is easily underrated: he tries to rescue Joseph (37:26–27), his "going down away from the brothers" is parallel to Joseph's (chap. 38) and prepares him (as it prepares Joseph) for the reconciliation, his speech in chap. 44 persuades Joseph to reveal himself and be reconciled to his brothers. Here, Judah effectively replaces Reuben as a spokesman for the brothers.

Jacob in his testament (chap. 49) devotes the most attention to Judah and Joseph. In one sense, the story can be called the story of Joseph and Judah.

**44:5** *Divination*: seeking omens through liquids poured into a cup or bowl was a common practice in the ancient Near East; cf. v. 15. Even though divination was frowned on in later Israel (Lv 19:31), it is in this place an authentic touch which is ascribed to Joseph, the wisest man in Egypt.

**44:16** *Guilt*: in trying to do away with Joseph when he was young.

**44:19** *My lord asked his servants*: such frequently repeated expressions in Judah's speech show the formal court style used by a subject in speaking to a high official.

---

**43:29** Gn 42:13.

a father, or another brother?' 20 So we said to my lord, 'We have an aged father, and a younger brother, the child of his old age. This one's full brother is dead, and since he is the only one by his mother who is left, his father is devoted to him.'* 21 Then you told your servants, 'Bring him down to me that I might see him.' 22 We replied to my lord, 'The boy cannot leave his father; his father would die if he left him.' 23 But you told your servants, 'Unless your youngest brother comes down with you, you shall not see me again.'* 24 When we returned to your servant my father, we reported to him the words of my lord.

25 "Later, our father said, 'Go back and buy some food for us.' 26 So we reminded him, 'We cannot go down there; only if our youngest brother is with us can we go, for we may not see the man if our youngest brother is not with us.' 27 Then your servant my father said to us, 'As you know, my wife bore me two sons. 28 One of them, however, has gone away from me, and I said, "He must have been torn to pieces by wild beasts!" I have not seen him since.* 29 If you take this one away from me too, and a disaster befalls him, you will send my white head down to Sheol in grief.'

30 "So now, if the boy is not with us when I go back to your servant my father, whose very life is bound up with his, he will die as soon as he sees that the boy is missing; 31 and your servants will thus send the white head of your servant our father down to Sheol in grief. 32 Besides, I, your servant, have guaranteed the boy's safety for my father by saying, 'If I fail to bring him back to you, father, I will bear the blame before you forever.'* 33 So now let me, your servant, remain in place of the boy as the slave of my lord, and let the boy go back with his brothers. 34 How could I go back to my father if the boy were not with me? I could not bear to see the anguish that would overcome my father."

# 45

**The Truth Revealed.**† 1 Joseph could no longer restrain himself in the presence of all his attendants, so he cried out, "Have everyone withdraw from me!" So no one attended him when he made himself known to his brothers. 2 But his sobs were so loud that the Egyptians heard him, and so the news reached Pharaoh's house. 3* "I am Joseph," he said to his brothers. "Is my father still alive?" But his brothers could give him no answer, so dumbfounded were they at him.

4 "Come closer to me," Joseph told his brothers. When they had done so, he said: "I am your brother Joseph, whom you sold into Egypt. 5 But now do not be distressed, and do not be angry with yourselves for having sold me here. It was really for the sake of saving lives that God sent me here ahead of you.* 6 The famine has been in the land for two years now, and for five more years cultivation will yield no harvest. 7 God, therefore, sent me on ahead of you to ensure for you a remnant on earth and to save your lives in an extraordinary deliverance. 8 So it was not really you but God who had me come here; and he has made me a father to Pharaoh,† lord of all his household, and ruler over the whole land of Egypt.

9† "Hurry back, then, to my father and tell him: 'Thus says your son Joseph: God has made me lord of all Egypt; come down to me without delay.* 10 You can settle in the region of Goshen,† where you will be near me—you and your children and children's children, your flocks and herds, and everything that you own. 11 I will provide for you there in the five years of famine that lie ahead, so that you and your household and all that are yours will not suffer want.' 12 Surely, you can see for yourselves, and Benjamin can see for himself, that it is I who am speaking to you. 13 Tell my father all about my high position in Egypt and all that you have seen. But hurry and bring my father down here." 14 Then he threw his arms around his brother Benjamin and wept on his shoulder. 15 Joseph then kissed all his brothers and wept over them; and only then were his brothers able to talk with him.

16 The news reached Pharaoh's house:

---

† **45:1–28** Joseph reveals his identity and the family is reconciled.
**45:8** *Father to Pharaoh*: a term applied to a vizier in ancient Egypt.
**45:9–15** In these verses, as in 46:31–47:5a, all from the Yahwist source, Joseph in his own name invites his father and brothers to come to Egypt. Only after their arrival is Pharaoh informed of the fact. On the other hand, in 45:16–20, which scholars have traditionally attributed to the Elohist source, it is Pharaoh himself

who invites Joseph's family to migrate to his domain.
**45:10** *The region of Goshen*: the meaning of the term is unknown. It is found in no Egyptian source. It is generally thought to be in the modern Wadi Tumilat in the eastern part of the Nile Delta.

**44:20** Gn 42:13.        **45:3–4** Acts 7:13.
**44:23** Gn 43:3.          **45:5** Gn 50:20.
**44:28** Gn 37:20, 33.     **45:9** Acts 7:14.
**44:32** Gn 43:9.

"Joseph's brothers have come." Pharaoh and his officials were pleased. [17] So Pharaoh told Joseph: "Say to your brothers: 'This is what you shall do: Load up your animals and go without delay to the land of Canaan. [18] There get your father and your households, and then come to me; I will assign you the best land in Egypt, where you will live off the fat of the land.'* [19] Instruct them further: 'Do this. Take wagons from the land of Egypt for your children and your wives and bring your father back here. [20] Do not be concerned about your belongings, for the best in the whole land of Egypt shall be yours.'"

[21] The sons of Israel acted accordingly. Joseph gave them the wagons, as Pharaoh had ordered, and he supplied them with provisions for the journey. [22] He also gave to each of them a set of clothes, but to Benjamin he gave three hundred shekels of silver and five sets of clothes. [23] Moreover, what he sent to his father was ten donkeys loaded with the finest products of Egypt and another ten loaded with grain and bread and provisions for his father's journey. [24] As he sent his brothers on their way, he told them, "Do not quarrel on the way."

[25] So they went up from Egypt and came to the land of Canaan, to their father Jacob. [26] When they told him, "Joseph is still alive—in fact, it is he who is governing all the land of Egypt," he was unmoved, for he did not believe them. [27] But when they recounted to him all that Joseph had told them, and when he saw the wagons that Joseph had sent to transport him, the spirit of their father Jacob came to life. [28] "Enough," said Israel. "My son Joseph is still alive! I must go and see him before I die."

# 46 Migration to Egypt.

[1]† Israel set out with all that was his. When he arrived at Beer-sheba, he offered sacrifices to the God of his father Isaac. [2] There God, speaking to Israel in a vision by night, called: Jacob! Jacob! He answered, "Here I am." [3] Then he said: I am God,† the God of your father. Do not be afraid to go down to Egypt, for there I will make you a great nation. [4] I will go down to Egypt with you and I will also bring you back here, after Joseph has closed your eyes.

[5] So Jacob departed from Beer-sheba, and the sons of Israel put their father and their wives and children on the wagons that Pharaoh had sent to transport him. [6] They took with them their livestock and the possessions they had acquired in the land of Canaan. So Jacob and all his descendants came to Egypt.* [7] His sons and his grandsons, his daughters and his granddaughters—all his descendants—he took with him to Egypt.

[8] These are the names of the Israelites, Jacob and his children, who came to Egypt.

Reuben, Jacob's firstborn,* [9]† and the sons of Reuben: Hanoch, Pallu, Hezron, and Carmi.* [10] The sons of Simeon: Jemuel, Jamin, Ohad, Jachin, Zohar, and Shaul, son of a Canaanite woman.* [11] The sons of Levi: Gershon, Kohath, and Merari.* [12] The sons of Judah: Er, Onan, Shelah, Perez, and Zerah—but Er and Onan had died in the land of Canaan; and the sons of Perez were Hezron and Hamul.* [13] The sons of Issachar: Tola, Puah, Jashub, and Shimron.* [14] The sons of Zebulun: Sered, Elon, and Jahleel.* [15] These were the sons whom Leah bore to Jacob in Paddan-aram, along with his daughter Dinah—thirty-three persons in all, sons and daughters.

[16] The sons of Gad: Zephon, Haggi, Shuni, Ezbon, Eri, Arod, and Areli.* [17] The sons of Asher: Imnah, Ishvah, Ishvi, and Beriah, with their sister Serah; and the sons of Beriah: Heber and Malchiel.* [18] These are the children of Zilpah, whom Laban had given to his daughter Leah; these she bore to Jacob—sixteen persons in all.

[19] The sons of Jacob's wife Rachel: Joseph and Benjamin. [20] In the land of Egypt Joseph became the father of Manasseh and Ephraim, whom Asenath, daughter of Potiphera, priest of Heliopolis, bore to him.* [21] The sons of Benjamin: Bela, Becher, Ashbel, Gera, Naaman, Ahiram, Shupham, Hupham, and Ard.*

---

† **46:1–47:26** Jacob and his family settle in Egypt. Joseph's economic policies.
  **46:3** *I am God*: more precisely according to the Hebrew text, "I am El." "El" is here a divine name, not the common noun "god."
  **46:9–27** This genealogical list is based on the clan lists (Nm 26:5–50) from the Mosaic period.

* **45:18** Acts 7:14.  **46:6** Ex 1:1; Jos 24:4;

Jdt 5:10; Acts 7:15.
**46:8** Ex 1:2.
**46:9** Ex 6:14; Nm 26:5; 1 Chr 5:3.
**46:10** Ex 6:15; Nm 26:12; 1 Chr 4:24.
**46:11** Ex 6:16; Nm 3:17; 26:57; 1 Chr 6:1.
**46:12** Gn 38:3–10, 29–30; Nm 26:19; Ru 4:12; 1 Chr 2:5.
**46:13** Nm 26:23–24; 1 Chr 7:1.
**46:14** Nm 26:26.
**46:16** Nm 26:15–16.
**46:17** Nm 26:44; 1 Chr 7:30–31.
**46:20** Gn 41:50; Nm 26:28, 35.
**46:21** Nm 26:38; 1 Chr 7:6; 8:1–4.

²²These are the sons whom Rachel bore to Jacob—fourteen persons in all.

²³The sons of Dan: Hushim.* ²⁴The sons of Naphtali: Jahzeel, Guni, Jezer, and Shillem.* ²⁵These are the sons of Bilhah, whom Laban had given to his daughter Rachel; these she bore to Jacob—seven persons in all.

²⁶Jacob's people who came to Egypt—his direct descendants, not counting the wives of Jacob's sons—numbered sixty-six persons in all.* ²⁷Together with Joseph's sons who were born to him in Egypt—two persons—all the people comprising the household of Jacob who had come to Egypt amounted to seventy persons† in all.*

²⁸Israel had sent Judah ahead to Joseph, so that he might meet him in Goshen. On his arrival in the region of Goshen, ²⁹Joseph prepared his chariot and went up to meet his father Israel in Goshen. As soon as Israel made his appearance, Joseph threw his arms around him and wept a long time on his shoulder. ³⁰And Israel said to Joseph, "At last I can die, now that I have seen for myself that you are still alive."

³¹Joseph then said to his brothers and his father's household: "I will go up and inform Pharaoh, telling him: 'My brothers and my father's household, whose home is in the land of Canaan, have come to me. ³²The men are shepherds, having been owners of livestock;† and they have brought with them their flocks and herds, as well as everything else they own.' ³³So when Pharaoh summons you and asks what your occupation is, ³⁴you must answer, 'We your servants, like our ancestors, have been owners of livestock from our youth until now,' in order that you may stay in the region of Goshen, since all shepherds are abhorrent to the Egyptians."

# 47 Settlement in Goshen. ¹Joseph went and told Pharaoh, "My father and my brothers have come from the land of Canaan, with their flocks and herds and everything

else they own; and they are now in the region of Goshen." ²He then presented to Pharaoh five of his brothers whom he had selected from their full number. ³When Pharaoh asked them, "What is your occupation?" they answered, "We, your servants, like our ancestors, are shepherds. ⁴We have come," they continued, "in order to sojourn in this land, for there is no pasture for your servants' flocks, because the famine has been severe in the land of Canaan. So now please let your servants settle in the region of Goshen."* ⁵Pharaoh said to Joseph, "Now that your father and your brothers have come to you, ⁶the land of Egypt is at your disposal; settle your father and brothers in the pick of the land. Let them settle in the region of Goshen. And if you know of capable men among them, put them in charge of my livestock." ⁷Then Joseph brought his father Jacob and presented him to Pharaoh. And Jacob blessed Pharaoh. ⁸Then Pharaoh asked Jacob, "How many years have you lived?" ⁹Jacob replied: "The years I have lived as a wayfarer amount to a hundred and thirty. Few and hard have been these years of my life, and they do not compare with the years that my ancestors lived as wayfarers."† ¹⁰Then Jacob blessed Pharaoh and withdrew from his presence.

¹¹Joseph settled his father and brothers and gave them a holding in Egypt on the pick of the land, in the region of Rameses,† as Pharaoh had ordered. ¹²And Joseph provided food for his father and brothers and his father's whole household, down to the youngest.

**Joseph's Land Policy.** ¹³Since there was no food in all the land because of the extreme severity of the famine, and the lands of Egypt and Canaan were languishing from hunger, ¹⁴Joseph gathered in, as payment for the grain that they were buying, all the money that was to be found in Egypt and Canaan, and he put it in Pharaoh's house. ¹⁵When all the money in Egypt and Canaan was spent, all the Egyptians came to Joseph, pleading, "Give us food!

---

**46:27** *Seventy persons*: it is difficult to get this exact number by adding up the persons mentioned in the preceding genealogies. One might assume it refers to Jacob and sixty-nine descendants, excluding Er and Onan but including Dinah. Ex 1:5 repeats the number but excludes Jacob. Dt 10:22 refers to seventy persons descending to Egypt. The best solution is to take the number as expressing totality. Since there are seventy nations in chap. 10, it is likely that the text is drawing a parallel between the two entities and suggesting that Israel "represents" the nations before God.

**46:32** *Owners of livestock*: the phrase occurs only here and

in v. 34. The difference between this term and "shepherds" is not clear, for the brothers do not mention it to Pharaoh in 47:3.

**47:9** *Wayfarer…wayfarers*: human beings are merely sojourners on earth; cf. Ps 39:13.

**47:11** *The region of Rameses*: same as the region of Goshen; see note on 45:10.

**46:23** Nm 26:42.
**46:24** Nm 26:48–49; 1 Chr 7:13.
**46:26** Ex 1:5.
**46:27** Ex 1:5; Dt 10:22; Acts 7:14.
**47:4** Ex 23:9; Dt 23:8.

Why should we perish in front of you? For our money is gone." <sup>16</sup>"Give me your livestock if your money is gone," replied Joseph. "I will give you food in return for your livestock." <sup>17</sup>So they brought their livestock to Joseph, and he gave them food in exchange for their horses, their flocks of sheep and herds of cattle, and their donkeys. Thus he supplied them with food in exchange for all their livestock in that year. <sup>18</sup>That year ended, and they came to him in the next one and said: "We cannot hide from my lord that, with our money spent and our livestock made over to my lord, there is nothing left to put at my lord's disposal except our bodies and our land. <sup>19</sup>Why should we and our land perish before your very eyes? Take us and our land in exchange for food, and we will become Pharaoh's slaves and our land his property; only give us seed, that we may survive and not perish, and that our land may not turn into a waste."

<sup>20</sup>So Joseph acquired all the land of Egypt for Pharaoh. Each of the Egyptians sold his field, since the famine weighed heavily upon them. Thus the land passed over to Pharaoh, <sup>21</sup>and the people were reduced to slavery, from one end of Egypt's territory to the other. <sup>22</sup>Only the priests' lands Joseph did not acquire. Since the priests had a fixed allowance from Pharaoh and lived off the allowance Pharaoh had granted them, they did not have to sell their land.

<sup>23</sup>Joseph told the people: "Now that I have acquired you and your land for Pharaoh, here is your seed for sowing the land. <sup>24</sup>But when the harvest is in, you must give a fifth of it to Pharaoh, while you keep four-fifths as seed for your fields and as food for yourselves and your households and as food for your children." <sup>25</sup>"You have saved our lives!" they answered. "We have found favor with my lord; now we will be Pharaoh's slaves." <sup>26</sup>Thus Joseph made

it a statute for the land of Egypt, which is still in force, that a fifth of its produce should go to Pharaoh. Only the land of the priests did not pass over to Pharaoh.

**Israel Blesses Ephraim and Manasseh.** <sup>27</sup>Thus Israel settled in the land of Egypt, in the region of Goshen. There they acquired holdings, were fertile, and multiplied greatly.* <sup>28</sup>† Jacob lived in the land of Egypt for seventeen years; the span of his life came to a hundred and forty-seven years. <sup>29</sup>When the time approached for Israel to die, he called his son Joseph and said to him: "If it pleases you, put your hand under my thigh as a sign of your enduring fidelity to me; do not bury me in Egypt. <sup>30</sup>When I lie down with my ancestors, take me out of Egypt and bury me in their burial place."* "I will do as you say," he replied. <sup>31</sup>But his father demanded, "Swear it to me!" So Joseph swore to him. Then Israel bowed at the head of the bed.†

**48** <sup>1</sup>† Some time afterward, Joseph was informed, "Your father is failing." So he took along with him his two sons, Manasseh and Ephraim. <sup>2</sup>When Jacob was told, "Your son Joseph has come to you," Israel rallied his strength and sat up in bed.

<sup>3</sup>* Jacob then said to Joseph: "God Almighty appeared to me at Luz† in the land of Canaan, and blessing me, <sup>4</sup>he said, 'I will make you fertile and multiply you and make you into an assembly of peoples, and I will give this land to your descendants after you as a permanent possession.' <sup>5</sup>So now your two sons who were born to you in the land of Egypt before I joined you here, shall be mine; Ephraim and Manasseh shall be mine as much as Reuben and Simeon are mine. <sup>6</sup>Progeny born to you after them shall remain yours; but their heritage shall be recorded in the names of their

---

† **47:28–50:26** Supplements to the Joseph story. Most of the material in this section centers on Jacob—his blessing of Joseph's sons, his farewell testament, and his death and burial in Canaan. Only the last verses (50:15–26) redirect attention to Joseph's sons, the twelve brothers; they are assured that the reconciliation will not collapse after the death of the patriarch.

**47:31** *Israel bowed at the head of the bed*: meaning perhaps that he gave a nod of assent and appreciation as he lay on his bed. The oath and gesture are the same as Abraham's in 24:2. Israel's bowing here suggests the fulfillment of Joseph's dreams in 37:9–10, when parents and brothers bowed down to Joseph (cf. 42:6; 43:26). By using different vowels for the Hebrew word for "bed," the Greek version translated it as "staff," and understood the phrase to mean that he bowed in worship, leaning on the top of his staff; it is thus quoted in Heb 11:21.

**48:1–22** Jacob continues his preparations for death. In a scene that evokes the nearly blind Isaac blessing Jacob and Esau (chap. 27), Jacob blesses Joseph's two sons. He adopts them, elevating them to a status equal to that of Jacob's first sons Reuben and Simeon (cf. 1 Chr 5:1). The adoption is one more instance of Jacob's favoring Rachel and those born of her. The mention of Jacob's failing eyesight and his selection of the younger son over the older evokes the great deathbed scene in chap. 27. He reaffirms to Joseph the ancient divine promise of progeny and land.

**48:3** *Luz*: an older name of Bethel (28:19).

47:27 Ex 1:7.          48:3–4 Gn 28:12–15; 35:6.
47:30 Gn 50:5.

brothers. [7]* I do this because, when I was returning from Paddan, your mother Rachel died, to my sorrow, during the journey in Canaan, while we were still a short distance from Ephrath; and I buried her there on the way to Ephrath [now Bethlehem]."†

[8] When Israel saw Joseph's sons, he asked, "Who are these?" [9] "They are my sons," Joseph answered his father, "whom God has given me here." "Bring them to me," said his father, "that I may bless them." [10] Now Israel's eyes were dim from age; he could not see well. When Joseph brought his sons close to him, he kissed and embraced them. [11] Then Israel said to Joseph, "I never expected to see your face again, and now God has allowed me to see your descendants as well!"

[12] Joseph removed them from his father's knees and bowed down before him with his face to the ground. [13] Then Joseph took the two, Ephraim with his right hand, to Israel's left, and Manasseh with his left hand, to Israel's right, and brought them up to him. [14] But Israel, crossing his hands, put out his right hand and laid it on the head of Ephraim, although he was the younger, and his left hand on the head of Manasseh, although he was the firstborn. [15] Then he blessed them with these words:

> "May the God in whose presence
>     my fathers Abraham and Isaac walked,
> The God who has been my shepherd
>     from my birth to this day,*
[16] The angel who has delivered me from all
>         harm,
>     bless these boys
> That in them my name be recalled,
>     and the names of my fathers,
>         Abraham and Isaac,
> And they may become teeming
>         multitudes
>     upon the earth!"

[17] When Joseph saw that his father had laid his right hand on Ephraim's head, this seemed wrong to him; so he took hold of his father's hand, to remove it from Ephraim's head to Manasseh's, [18] saying, "That is not right, father; the other one is the firstborn; lay your right hand on his head!" [19] But his father refused. "I know it, son," he said, "I know. That one too shall become a people, and he too shall be great. Nevertheless, his younger brother shall surpass him, and his descendants shall become a multitude of nations." [20] So he blessed them that day and said, "By you shall the people of Israel pronounce blessings, saying, 'God make you like Ephraim and Manasseh.'" Thus he placed Ephraim before Manasseh.*

[21] Then Israel said to Joseph: "I am about to die. But God will be with you and will restore you to the land of your ancestors. [22]* As for me, I give to you, as to the one above his brothers, Shechem, which I captured from the Amorites with my sword and bow."†

# 49

**Jacob's Testament.**† [1] Jacob called his sons and said: "Gather around, that I may tell you what is to happen to you in days to come.

[2]    "Assemble and listen, sons of Jacob,
>     listen to Israel, your father.

[3]    "You, Reuben, my firstborn,
>     my strength and the first fruit of my
>         vigor,
>     excelling in rank and excelling in
>         power!
[4]    Turbulent as water, you shall no longer
>         excel,
>     for you climbed into your father's
>         bed
>     and defiled my couch to my sorrow.*

---

**48:7** Since her early death prevented Rachel from bearing more than two sons, Jacob feels justified in treating her two grandsons as if they were her own offspring.
**48:22** Both the meaning of the Hebrew and the historical reference in this verse are obscure. By taking the Hebrew word for Shechem as a common noun meaning shoulder or mountain slope, some translators render the verse, "I give you one portion more than your brothers, which I captured…" The reference may be to the capture of Shechem by the sons of Jacob (34:24–29). Shechem lay near the border separating the tribal territory of Manasseh from that of Ephraim (Jos 16:4–9; 17:1–2, 7).
**49:1–27** The testament, or farewell discourse, of Jacob, which has its closest parallel in Moses' farewell in Dt 33:6–25. From his privileged position as a patriarch, he sees the future of his children (the eponymous ancestors of the tribes) and is able to describe

how they will fare and so gives his blessing. The dense and archaic poetry is obscure in several places. The sayings often involve word-plays (explained in the notes). The poem begins with the six sons of Leah (vv. 2–15), then deals with the sons of the two secondary wives, and ends with Rachel's two sons, Joseph and Benjamin. Reuben, the oldest son, loses his position of leadership as a result of his intercourse with Bilhah (35:22), and the words about Simeon and Levi allude to their taking revenge for the rape of Dinah (chap. 34). The preeminence of Judah reflects his rise in the course of the narrative (mirroring the rise of Joseph). See note on 44:1–34.

**48:7** Gn 35:19.
**48:15** Heb 11:21.
**48:20** Heb 11:21.

**48:22** Jos 17:14, 17–18; Jn 4:5.
**49:4** Gn 35:22; 1 Chr 5:1–2.

5† "Simeon and Levi, brothers indeed,
     weapons of violence are their knives.†
6   Let not my person enter their council,
     or my honor be joined with their
       company;
   For in their fury they killed men,
     at their whim they maimed oxen.*
7   Cursed be their fury so fierce,
     and their rage so cruel!
   I will scatter them in Jacob,
     disperse them throughout Israel.

8   "You, Judah, shall your brothers praise
     —your hand on the neck of your
       enemies;
   the sons of your father shall bow
     down to you.
9   Judah is a lion's cub,
     you have grown up on prey, my son.
   He crouches, lies down like a lion,
     like a lioness—who would dare rouse
       him?*
10  The scepter shall never depart from
       Judah,
     or the mace from between his feet,
   Until tribute comes to him,†
     and he receives the people's
       obedience.
11  He tethers his donkey to the vine,
     his donkey's foal to the choicest stem.
   In wine he washes his garments,
     his robe in the blood of grapes.†
12  His eyes are darker than wine,
     and his teeth are whiter than milk.

13  "Zebulun shall dwell by the seashore;
     he will be a haven for ships,
     and his flank shall rest on Sidon.

14  "Issachar is a rawboned donkey,
     crouching between the saddlebags.

15  When he saw how good a settled life was,
     and how pleasant the land,
   He bent his shoulder to the burden
     and became a toiling serf.

16  "Dan shall achieve justice† for his
       people
     as one of the tribes of Israel.
17  Let Dan be a serpent by the roadside,
     a horned viper by the path,
   That bites the horse's heel,
     so that the rider tumbles backward.

18  "I long for your deliverance, O LORD!†

19  "Gad shall be raided by raiders,
     but he shall raid at their heels.†

20  "Asher's produce is rich,
     and he shall furnish delicacies for
       kings.

21  "Naphtali is a hind let loose,
     which brings forth lovely fawns.

22  "Joseph is a wild colt,
     a wild colt by a spring,
     wild colts on a hillside.
23  Harrying him and shooting,
     the archers opposed him;
24  But his bow remained taut,
     and his arms were nimble,
   By the power of the Mighty One of
       Jacob,
     because of the Shepherd, the Rock of
       Israel,
25  The God of your father, who helps you,†
     God Almighty, who blesses you,
   With the blessings of the heavens above,
     the blessings of the abyss that
       crouches below,

---

† **49:5–7** This passage probably refers to their attack on the city of Shechem (Gn 34). Because there is no indication that the warlike tribe of Levi will be commissioned as a priestly tribe (Ex 32:26–29; Dt 33:11), this passage reflects an early, independent tradition.

**49:5** *Knives:* if this is the meaning of the obscure Hebrew word here, the reference may be to the knives used in circumcising the men of Shechem (34:24; cf. Jos 5:2).

**49:10** *Until tribute comes to him:* this translation is based on a slight change in the Hebrew text, which, as it stands, would seem to mean, "until he comes to Shiloh." A somewhat different reading of the Hebrew text would be, "until he comes to whom it belongs." This last has been traditionally understood in a messianic sense. In any case, the passage aims at the supremacy of the tribe of Judah and of the Davidic dynasty.

**49:11** *In wine...the blood of grapes:* Judah's clothes are poetically pictured as soaked with grape juice from trampling in the wine press, the rich vintage of his land; cf. Is 63:2.

**49:16** In Hebrew the verb for "achieve justice" is from the same root as the name Dan.

**49:18** This short plea for divine mercy has been inserted into the middle of Jacob's testament.

**49:19** In Hebrew there is assonance between the name Gad and the words for "raided," "raiders," and "raid."

**49:25–26** A very similar description of the agricultural riches of the tribal land of Joseph is given in Dt 33:13–16.

---

**49:6** Gn 34:25.                    **49:9** 1 Chr 5:2.

GN

The blessings of breasts and womb,
26      the blessings of fresh grain and
             blossoms,
       the blessings of the everlasting
             mountains,
       the delights of the eternal hills.
May they rest on the head of Joseph,
       on the brow of the prince among his
             brothers.

27   "Benjamin is a ravenous wolf;
       mornings he devours the prey,
       and evenings he distributes the
             spoils."

**Farewell and Death.** 28 All these are the twelve tribes of Israel, and this is what their father said about them, as he blessed them. To each he gave a suitable blessing. 29 Then he gave them this charge: "Since I am about to be gathered to my people, bury me with my ancestors in the cave that lies in the field of Ephron the Hittite, 30 the cave in the field of Machpelah, facing on Mamre, in the land of Canaan, the field that Abraham bought from Ephron the Hittite for a burial ground.* 31 There Abraham and his wife Sarah are buried, and so are Isaac and his wife Rebekah, and there, too, I buried Leah— 32 the field and the cave in it that had been purchased from the Hittites."

33 When Jacob had finished giving these instructions to his sons, he drew his feet into the bed, breathed his last, and was gathered to his people.

50 **Jacob's Funeral.** 1 Joseph flung himself upon his father and wept over him as he kissed him. 2 Then Joseph ordered the physicians in his service to embalm his father. When the physicians embalmed Israel, 3 they spent forty days at it, for that is the full period of embalming; and the Egyptians mourned him for seventy days. 4 When the period of mourning was over, Joseph spoke to Pharaoh's

household. "If you please, appeal to Pharaoh, saying: 5 My father made me swear: 'I am dying. Bury me in my grave that I have prepared for myself in the land of Canaan.' So now let me go up to bury my father. Then I will come back."* 6 Pharaoh replied, "Go and bury your father, as he made you promise on oath."

7 So Joseph went up to bury his father; and with him went all of Pharaoh's officials who were senior members of his household and all the other elders of the land of Egypt, 8 as well as Joseph's whole household, his brothers, and his father's household; only their children and their flocks and herds were left in the region of Goshen. 9 Chariots, too, and horsemen went up with him; it was a very imposing retinue.

10 When they arrived at Goren-ha-atad,† which is beyond the Jordan, they held there a very great and solemn memorial service; and Joseph observed seven days of mourning for his father. 11 When the Canaanites who inhabited the land saw the mourning at Goren-ha-atad, they said, "This is a solemn funeral on the part of the Egyptians!" That is why the place was named Abel-mizraim. It is beyond the Jordan.

12 Thus Jacob's sons did for him as he had instructed them. 13 They carried him to the land of Canaan and buried him in the cave in the field of Machpelah, facing on Mamre, the field that Abraham had bought for a burial ground from Ephron the Hittite.*

14 After Joseph had buried his father he returned to Egypt, together with his brothers and all who had gone up with him for the burial of his father.

**Plea for Forgiveness.** 15 † Now that their father was dead, Joseph's brothers became fearful and thought, "Suppose Joseph has been nursing a grudge against us and now most certainly will pay us back in full for all the wrong we did him!" 16 So they sent to Joseph and said:

---

† **50:10–11** *Goren-ha-atad:* "Threshing Floor of the Brambles." *Abel-mizraim:* although the name really means "watercourse of the Egyptians," it is understood here, by a play on the first part of the term, to mean "mourning of the Egyptians." The site has not been identified through either reading of the name. But it is difficult to see why the mourning rites should have been held in the land beyond the Jordan when the burial was at Hebron. Perhaps an earlier form of the story placed the mourning rites beyond the Wadi of Egypt, the traditional boundary between Canaan and Egypt (Nm 34:5; Jos 15:4, 47).
**50:15–26** The final reconciliation of the brothers. Fearful of what may happen after the death of their father, the brothers

engage in a final deception, inventing the dying wish of Jacob. Again, Joseph weeps, and, again, his brothers fall down before him, offering to be his slaves (44:16, 33). Joseph's assurance is also a summation of the story: "Even though you meant harm to me, God meant it for good, to achieve this present end, the survival of many people" (v. 20). Joseph's adoption of the children of Manasseh's son Machir recalls Jacob's adoption of his grandchildren (48:5, 13–20); the adoptions reflect tribal history (cf. Jgs 5:14).

**49:30** Gn 23:17.     **50:13** Gn 23:16; Jos 24:32;
**50:5** Gn 47:30.                    Acts 7:16.

"Before your father died, he gave us these instructions: [17] 'Thus you shall say to Joseph: Please forgive the criminal wrongdoing of your brothers, who treated you harmfully.' So now please forgive the crime that we, the servants of the God of your father, committed." When they said this to him, Joseph broke into tears. [18] Then his brothers also proceeded to fling themselves down before him and said, "We are your slaves!" [19] But Joseph replied to them: "Do not fear. Can I take the place of God? [20] Even though you meant harm to me, God meant it for good, to achieve this present end, the survival of many people.* [21] So now, do not fear. I will provide for you and for your children." By thus speaking kindly to them, he reassured them.*

[22] Joseph remained in Egypt, together with his father's household. He lived a hundred and ten years. [23] He saw Ephraim's children to the third generation, and the children of Manasseh's son Machir were also born on Joseph's knees.*

**Death of Joseph.** [24] Joseph said to his brothers: "I am about to die. God will surely take care of you and lead you up from this land to the land that he promised on oath to Abraham, Isaac and Jacob."* [25] Then, putting the sons of Israel under oath, he continued, "When God thus takes care of you, you must bring my bones up from this place."* [26] Joseph died at the age of a hundred and ten. He was embalmed and laid to rest in a coffin in Egypt.*

---

50:20 Gn 45:5.
50:21 Gn 47:12.
50:23 Nm 32:39; Jos 17:1.
50:24 Ex 3:8; Heb 11:22.
50:25 Ex 13:19; Heb 11:22.
50:26 Sir 49:15.

# The Book of

# Exodus

## INTRODUCTION

The book of Exodus is named for the central event narrated in the book: the liberation of the Israelites, also called Hebrews in this book, from slavery in Egypt. It covers the history of Israel from their time of slavery until the building of a portable tent shrine used to worship Yahweh while they were in the wilderness. Although the book features Moses as the reluctant hero of this epic story, it highlights God's role in freeing this oppressed group and shaping them into a people who worship only Yahweh.

The book of Exodus cannot be understood apart from the books that surround it. The Priestly material (P) that begins Genesis 1 does not dissipate until the end of the book of Numbers, suggesting that Exodus is the second of a four-book epic comprised of Genesis, Exodus, Leviticus, and Numbers. Exodus itself, however, introduces a four-book arc (Exodus, Leviticus, Numbers, and Deuteronomy) that covers the life of Moses. The hero who is born in Ex 2 does not die until the end of Deuteronomy, making him the focus of more books in the Old Testament than any other biblical figure. Beyond this arc, the narrative of the deliverance of the Israelites begun in Exodus does not reach its culmination until the book of Joshua with their arrival in the promised land. In short, although it is relatively clear where the book of Exodus begins and ends, it is less clear whether it was an independent book, or whether it always circulated with the material that surrounds it.

The book itself is comprised of three interlocking epic narratives: the story of the enslavement, oppression, and deliverance of the Hebrews (chs. 1–15); the account of God's revelation of the law at Sinai (chs. 15–34); and the focus on the question of how Yahweh should be properly worshiped (chs. 35–40). Each mini-narrative has its own style and focus.

## Outline of Exodus

I. Introduction: The Oppression of the Israelites in Egypt (1:1–2:22)

II. The Call and Commission of Moses (2:23–7:7)

III. The Contest with Pharaoh (7:8–13:16)

IV. The Deliverance of the Israelites from Pharaoh and Victory at the Sea (13:17–15:21)

V. The Journey in the Wilderness to Sinai (15:22–18:27)

VI. Covenant and Legislation at Mount Sinai (19:1–31:18)

VII. Israel's Apostasy and God's Renewal of the Covenant (32:1–34:35)

VIII. The Building of the Tabernacle and the Descent of God's Glory upon It (35:1–40:38)

## Composition

The book of Exodus in its final form is the result of a compilation of written sources and oral traditions. The most easily identifiable written source is a continuous account of the Exodus written by the Priestly writer (P), who depicts the conflict between Yahweh and Pharaoh as a cosmic battle. Many of the most important scenes in the narrative, however, are non-P material, including two additional versions of how the Israelites crossed the sea, stories of rebellion, and the account of the worship of the golden calf. The book also contains non-narrative material, such as an ancient poem in Ex 15, and an old legal code in chs. 21–23.

Some scholars identify the bulk of the non-P

material as stemming from either a southern source (Yahwist) or a northern source (Elohist). There are additional traces of the Deuteronomistic source, seen most clearly in the account of the golden calf in Ex 32. Other scholars would see less continuity in the non-P material, arguing instead for a final redactor who has woven together a number of written and oral traditions. In this model of authorship, the addition of material from both D and P significantly shape the final text.

While the story that mentions the building of the cities of Pithom and Raamses (Ex 1:11) is set sometime around 1200 BCE, the date of the final redaction of the book is also debated. It certainly stems from after the period of Jeroboam I (ca. 920 BCE), whose construction of golden calves in 1 Kgs 12:28 is parodied in Ex 32:4. Most scholars, however, would date the final text much later than that, many opting for a date at the end of or even after the exile (ca. 550–400 BCE), i.e., at least 600 years after the time of Moses.

## Content

While the genealogy that starts the book (Ex 1:1–5) links the narrative to Genesis, the description of new circumstances in Ex 1:6–8 signals a clear beginning to the book of Exodus. Throughout the book the Hebrews are depicted as a people rather uninformed about who Yahweh is and how they should respond to this deity.

Moses arises as a heroic figure, miraculously saved in infancy from certain death. After such an auspicious beginning, Moses dominates the rest of the book. He has a series of direct revelations from Yahweh, instructs the people about their God, leads them as they escape their slavery, and delivers to them the law made known by this God. Moses plays many roles in this book. He is portrayed as a political leader, unsuccessfully negotiating with Pharaoh to secure the release of these Hebrew slaves. He functions as a military leader, leading the people in their confrontation with Pharaoh's army at the Reed Sea (so named in the Hebrew text). He acts like a king when he mediates the law that God has revealed at Mount Sinai (also called Mount Horeb in 3:1a,

17:6, and 33:6). Like a prophet, he intercedes with God on behalf of the people, early on securing them food and water, later saving them from God's mortal wrath.

The principal character of the book of Exodus, however, is God. The narration goes out of its way to depict Moses as God's instrument. All action in the book is precipitated by God. God saves the infant Moses, God tells Moses how to negotiate with Pharaoh, God parts the sea and drowns the Egyptians, and God gives Moses the law. The account of the plagues in the first part of the book, which casts the strife as a contest between God and Pharaoh, establishes God's central role in the book.

Exodus ends with a long description of the building of a tent shrine, called the tabernacle, used by the Israelites to worship God in the desert. Thirteen out of the forty chapters in the book are devoted to its construction, first with God's detailed command on how they should build it (Ex 25–31), then with an equally detailed description of its realization (chs. 35–40). Although the ending of the book is not as clearly marked as the book's beginning, it culminates with a clear focus on God as the deliverer of the Israelites.

## Deliverance from Slavery

Each section in the book of Exodus has its own theme and focus. The book opens with the dramatically told story of the deliverance of the Hebrews, which continues to be retold today. It is cast as a classic story of good versus evil. The text expects the audience to cheer at the destruction of the evil Pharaoh and his army. The hardening of Pharaoh's heart is just one of the many elements that highlight Yahweh's complete control over an enemy characterized by hubris. The narrative builds to two key moments: the account of the final plague and the descriptions of the crossing of the sea.

When the book of Exodus is read as a whole, the slaying of the firstborn in the Passover account is anticipated by Pharaoh's slaughter of Hebrew male babies (Ex 1–2). In light of this narrative framing, the slaying of the firstborn of the Egyptians becomes a kind of "just deserts": Pharaoh suffers the fate he had tried to impose on the Hebrews. To modern audiences, the expectation that the slaying of the firstborn of the Egyptians is a glorious event presents difficulties. For the ancient audience, however, the notion that a deity could demand the life of a person or their child goes unquestioned. For example, Achan's whole family is killed as punishment when he violates God's command (Jos 7:24–25). One way that Job's faith is tested is with the death of his children (Jb 1:18–19).

The tenth plague is not only the culmination of a series of divine acts that prove who is the real god, it also contains instructions on how to commemorate it in Ex 12. From this description, it appears that the ancient celebrations of Passover included a ritual re-enactment of the deliverance of the people from slavery. Exodus 12:11 states that Israelite families must eat with their sandals on, their staffs in their hands, ready to leave on a moment's notice.

Outside of Ex 12, however, the celebration of Passover is not as prominent. The legal codes in Nm 28 and Dt 16 only mention a temple ritual on that day, not one that takes place at home. Except for Ex 12 and Dt 16, the legal codes give greater prominence to the Feast of Unleavened Bread to which Passover is attached; in fact, Passover is not even mentioned in the description of the Feast of Unleavened Bread in Ex 23. In the historical books of the Old Testament, the fact that King Josiah must "re-instate" Passover (2 Kgs 23:21–23) implies that Passover was either not celebrated at many points in Israel's history or not celebrated properly (although 2 Chr 30:1–3 assumes Passover was kept before the reign of Hezekiah). It could be that one of the purposes of the final book of Exodus is to give much more prominence and centrality to the observance of Passover.

The ritual elements in the story of the Passover invite the reader to recognize ritual elements in other parts of the narrative. For example, in the account of the deliverance at the Red Sea, the people are miraculously saved by God's presence, as angel, cloud, fire (Ex 14:19, 24), and wind (14:21), rather than by the people engaging in battle. Outside of this text, God appears as cloud and fire at sacred places, like God's holy mountain as well as the tabernacle. In the ancient poem in Ex 15 the ultimate destination of the freed slaves is the mountain on which Yahweh's temple will be built. The Israelites are freed, not just to avoid oppression, but in order to praise God. These clues in the text suggest that the book of Exodus in part reflects traditions developed in and around ritual retellings of the Exodus events.

# The Giving of the Law

The notion that the Israelites are freed in order to *do* something is further established by their first stopping point after their deliverance: Mount Sinai. This is the same mountain on which God had revealed the divine name to Moses in Ex 3, there called Mount Horeb, through a bush that burned but was not consumed. For the final author, Sinai was a place for theophany, i.e., a place where God would appear. In this episode God initially wants to reveal the law to the whole assembly of people, but when they see the fire, storm, and earthquake that accompany the theophany, they beg that Moses receive the revelation alone.

Many Christians assume that the law that Moses receives is only the Ten Commandments, but this is a false conclusion. The Ten Commandments are only a small part of what is revealed. The bulk of the rest of the whole Pentateuch consists of laws that are presented in the narrative as directly revealed by God; Jewish tradition counts 613 laws in the Pentateuch. The Ten Commandments, which are less law than they are general categories into which some laws will fit, serve as the preamble for the actual law codes.

The legal material found in most of the rest of the books of Exodus, Leviticus, Numbers, and Deuteronomy have a number of repetitions, which lead scholars to conclude that the final form of the Pentateuch contains a number of law codes from different periods of Israel's history. The laws in Ex 21–23 are rather brief compared to those in the other Pentateuchal texts. They reflect a less urbanized period of Israelite society. As a result they are less concerned with the kind of social stratification that resulted from the rise of cities and monarchies. They cover a wide variety of topics, from the ritual calendar to laws about livestock, slavery, and rape.

The style of the legal material changes in the laws about the construction of the tabernacle (Ex 25–31 and 35–40). These laws are long, detailed, meticulous, and reflect the establishment of a professional priestly class. The cost of the tabernacle is lavish, beyond the reach of a group of slaves fleeing their oppressors. Yet the tabernacle account is also presented as part of the law given at Sinai.

The law-giving in Exodus is interrupted by the story of the idolatrous worship of the golden calf. This story highlights how detailed the law was: Moses was on Sinai so long that the people assumed he was dead. In his place they beg Aaron, Moses' brother, to make them a representation of Yahweh in the form of a calf or heifer (the Hebrew word in Ex 32:4 can mean either), thus making Aaron their leader in Moses' stead. When the noise of their celebration of the idol comes up the mountain, God vows to kill this rebellious people and make Moses a new people whom he can lead (again highlighting the importance of Moses to this story). Moses in his anger breaks the tablets on which God had inscribed the law, but he still begs God to spare those who would repent. After the non-repentant have been slain, Moses returns to the mountain to receive another set of laws.

## Proper Worship

The intertwining of the accounts of the tabernacle and the story of the golden calf highlight the fact that one theme central to the book of Exodus is the question of the proper worship of Yahweh. The books of Kings report that when the northern tribes set up their own kingdom, they built temples where Yahweh was represented with a calf or heifer. Archaeology reveals that bull icons were common in this part of the world, not as direct representatives of the god, but rather as pedestals for deities who stand on their backs. The northern Israelites probably assumed, not that Yahweh was a bovine, but that God was invisibly present above the calves.

The southern kingdom of Judah used the combination of the ark of the covenant, a gold-lined box which may have contained the law given at Sinai, along with two cherubim as the pedestal on which Yahweh rested. This combination is called God's throne and footstool in various Israelite texts (see 1 Chr 28:2; Ps 132:7; Is 6:1; Jer 17:12; Ez 43:7). This throne and footstool could never be confused with God, and so there was no danger that people would worship the ark as if it were a god. The southern critique of the northern temples probably reflects the conviction that people in the north worshiped the bovine rather than God.

The construction of the ark of the covenant, the "proper" alternative to represent God's presence in this holy space, is the centerpiece in the account of the tabernacle. This is the only place in the Bible that gives the dimensions and materials of the ark (25:10–22 and 37:1–9). God states that he will meet the people from between the two cherubim that are placed on either end of the ark. This promise is fulfilled at the end of the book: once Moses erects the tabernacle and places the ark and all of the other furnishings within it, the "glory" of Yahweh fills the tabernacle and remains there for the rest of the Israelites' journey.

## The Creation of a People

The book of Exodus from start to finish not only tells the story of the deliverance of the Israelites from slavery to a life dedicated to Yahweh, it does so by emphasizing the role of the law—including those laws directing proper worship—for their identity as a people. The story begins with their enslavement to Pharaoh, a man who claimed to be a god but who was unable to rule over the lowest people in his realm. They are delivered by a God whose name they do not even know, but who saves them by laying claim on the firstborn of the Egyptians and then by slaying, with wind and sea, the evil army that pursues them. They see the effects of this God when the Lord appears on Sinai, a reality that frightens them so much that they ask their mediator, Moses, to stand in their place. They try to invent their own form of worship, creating a calf to represent this god who has delivered them, an attempt that is sorely misguided. For this book, proper worship comes in the form of a tabernacle, whose plan is revealed by God, where Yahweh will appear to them "in all the stages of their journey" (Ex 40:38).

Proper worship is part of the whole law given to the Israelites at Sinai. The book of Exodus depicts obedience to the law, in all of its details, as securing the safety of the Israelites in their wanderings. They are freed, not for their sake alone, but in order to embark on a journey that will lead them to a land where God will reign from the divinely chosen holy temple (Ex 15:17–18). Once there, obedience to the law will signify that the descendants of this group of freed slaves are God's chosen people. ∎

# THE BOOK OF EXODUS

## New American Bible, Introduction

The second book of the Pentateuch is called Exodus, from the Greek word for "departure," because its central event was understood by the Septuagint's translators to be the departure of the Israelites from Egypt. Its Hebrew title, *Shemoth* ("Names"), is from the book's opening phrase, "These are the names...." Continuing the history of Israel from the point where the Book of Genesis leaves off, Exodus recounts the Egyptian oppression of Jacob's ever-increasing descendants and their miraculous deliverance by God through Moses, who led them across the Red Sea to Mount Sinai where they entered into a covenant with the Lord. Covenantal laws and detailed prescriptions for the tabernacle (a portable sanctuary foreshadowing the Jerusalem Temple) and its service are followed by a dramatic episode of rebellion, repentance, and divine mercy. After the broken covenant is renewed, the tabernacle is constructed, and the cloud signifying God's glorious presence descends to cover it.

These events made Israel a nation and confirmed their unique relationship with God. The "law" (Hebrew *torah*) given by God through Moses to the Israelites at Mount Sinai constitutes the moral, civil, and ritual legislation by which they were to become a holy people. Many elements of it were fundamental to the teaching of Jesus (Mt 5:21–30; 15:4) as well as to New Testament and Christian moral teaching (Rom 13:8–10; 1 Cor 10:1–5; 1 Pt 2:9).

The principal divisions of Exodus are:

I. Introduction: The Oppression of the Israelites in Egypt (1:1–2:22)
II. The Call and Commission of Moses (2:23–7:7)
III. The Contest with Pharaoh (7:8–13:16)
IV. The Deliverance of the Israelites from Pharaoh and Victory at the Sea (13:17–15:21)
V. The Journey in the Wilderness to Sinai (15:22–18:27)
VI. Covenant and Legislation at Mount Sinai (19:1–31:18)
VII. Israel's Apostasy and God's Renewal of the Covenant (32:1–34:35)
VIII. The Building of the Tabernacle and the Descent of God's Glory upon It (35:1–40:38) ■

# EXODUS

## I. INTRODUCTION: THE OPPRESSION OF THE ISRAELITES IN EGYPT

**1** **Jacob's Descendants in Egypt.** [1] These are the names of the sons of Israel† who, accompanied by their households, entered into Egypt with Jacob: [2]† Reuben, Simeon, Levi and Judah; [3] Issachar, Zebulun and Benjamin; [4] Dan and Naphtali; Gad and Asher. [5] The total number of Jacob's direct descendants† was seventy. * Joseph was already in Egypt.

[6] Now Joseph and all his brothers and that whole generation died. * [7] But the Israelites were fruitful and prolific. They multiplied and became so very numerous that the land was filled with them. †

**The Oppression.** [8] * Then a new king, who knew nothing of Joseph, † rose to power in Egypt. [9] He said to his people, "See! The Israelite people have multiplied and become more numerous than we are! [10] Come, let us deal shrewdly with them to stop their increase; † otherwise, in time of war they too may join our enemies to fight against us, and so leave the land."

[11] Accordingly, they set supervisors over the Israelites to oppress them with forced labor. * Thus they had to build for Pharaoh† the garrison cities of Pithom and Raamses. [12] Yet the more they were oppressed, the more they multiplied and spread, so that the Egyptians began to loathe the Israelites. [13] So the Egyptians reduced the Israelites to cruel slavery, [14] making life bitter for them with hard labor, at mortar† and brick and all kinds of field work—cruelly oppressed in all their labor.

**Command to the Midwives.** [15] The king of Egypt told the Hebrew midwives, one of whom was called Shiphrah and the other Puah, [16] "When you act as midwives for the Hebrew women, look on the birthstool:† if it is a boy, kill him; but if it is a girl, she may live." [17] The midwives, however, feared God; they did not do as the king of Egypt had ordered them, but let the boys live. [18] So the king of Egypt summoned the midwives and asked them, "Why have you done this, allowing the boys to live?" [19] The midwives answered Pharaoh, "The Hebrew women are not like the Egyptian women. They are robust and give birth before the midwife arrives." [20] Therefore God dealt well with the midwives; and the people multiplied and grew very numerous. [21] And because the midwives feared God, God built up families for them. [22] Pharaoh then commanded all his people, "Throw into the Nile every boy that is born, * but you may let all the girls live."

**2** **Birth and Adoption of Moses.** [1] Now a man† of the house of Levi married a Levite woman, * [2] and the woman conceived and bore a son. Seeing what a fine child he was, she hid him for three months. * [3] But when she

---

† **1:1** *Sons of Israel*: here literally the first-generation sons of Jacob/Israel. Cf. v. 5. However, beginning with v. 7 the same Hebrew phrase refers to Jacob's more remote descendants; hence, from there on, it is ordinarily rendered "the Israelites." *Households*: the family in its fullest sense, including wives, children and servants.

**1:2** Jacob's sons are listed here according to their respective mothers. Cf. Gn 29:31; 30:20; 35:16–26.

**1:5** *Direct descendants*: lit., "persons coming from Jacob's loins"; hence, wives of Jacob's sons and servants are not included. Cf. Gn 46:26. *Seventy*: Gn 46:26, along with the Septuagint for the verse, agrees on a total of sixty-six coming down to Egypt with Jacob, but in v. 27 the Hebrew text adds the two sons born to Joseph in Egypt and presupposes Jacob himself and Joseph for a total of seventy; the Septuagint adds "nine sons" born to Joseph to get a total of seventy-five. This is the figure the Septuagint and 4QExᵃ have here in Ex 1:5.

**1:7** *Fruitful...multiplied...the land was filled with them*: the language used here to indicate the fecundity of the Israelite population echoes the divine blessing bestowed upon humanity at creation (Gn 1:28) and after the flood (Gn 9:1) as well as suggesting fulfillment of the promises to the ancestors Abraham, Isaac, and Jacob (Gn 12:2; 13:16; 15:5; 28:14; passim).

**1:8** *Who knew nothing of Joseph*: the nuance intended by the Hebrew verb "know" here goes beyond precise determination. The idea may be not simply that a new king came to power who had not heard of Joseph but that this king ignored the services that Joseph had rendered to Egypt, repudiating the special relationship that existed between Joseph and his predecessor on the throne.

**1:10** *Increase*: Pharaoh's actions thereby immediately pit him against God's will for the Israelites to multiply; see note on v. 7 above.

**1:11** *Pharaoh*: not a personal name, but a title common to all the kings of Egypt.

**1:14** *Mortar*: either the wet clay with which the bricks were made, as in Na 3:14, or the cement used between the bricks in building, as in Gn 11:3.

**1:16** *Birthstool*: apparently a pair of stones on which the mother is seated for childbirth opposite the midwife. The Hebrew word elsewhere is used to refer to the stones of a potter's wheel.

**2:1** *Now a man*: the chapter begins abruptly, without names for the man or woman (in contrast to the midwives of 1:15), who in 6:20 are identified as Amram and Jochebed.

* **1:5** Gn 46:26–27; Dt 10:22; Acts 7:14.
**1:6** Gn 50:26.
**1:8–10** Acts 7:18–19.
**1:11** Dt 26:6.
**1:22** Acts 7:19.
**2:1** Ex 6:20; Nm 26:59.
**2:2** Acts 7:20; Heb 11:23.

© Daniel Blatt

"Then Pharaoh's daughter came down to bathe at the Nile, while her attendants walked along the bank of the Nile. Noticing the basket among the reeds, she sent her handmaid to fetch it" (Ex 2:5). Above, the Nile River in Egypt.

could no longer hide him, she took a papyrus basket,† daubed it with bitumen and pitch, and putting the child in it, placed it among the reeds on the bank of the Nile. ⁴His sister stationed herself at a distance to find out what would happen to him.

⁵Then Pharaoh's daughter came down to bathe at the Nile, while her attendants walked along the bank of the Nile. Noticing the basket among the reeds, she sent her handmaid to fetch it. ⁶On opening it, she looked, and there was a baby boy crying! She was moved with pity for him and said, "It is one of the Hebrews' children." ⁷Then his sister asked

Pharaoh's daughter, "Shall I go and summon a Hebrew woman to nurse the child for you?" ⁸Pharaoh's daughter answered her, "Go." So the young woman went and called the child's own mother. ⁹Pharaoh's daughter said to her, "Take this child and nurse him for me, and I will pay your wages."† So the woman took the child and nursed him. ¹⁰When the child grew,† she brought him to Pharaoh's daughter, and he became her son.* She named him Moses; for she said, "I drew him out of the water."

**Moses' Flight to Midian.** ¹¹* On one occasion, after Moses had grown up,† when he had

---

† **2:3** *Basket*: the same Hebrew word is used in Gn 6:14 and throughout the flood narrative for Noah's ark, but nowhere else in the Bible. Here, however, the "ark" or "chest" was made of papyrus stalks. Presumably the allusion to Genesis is intentional. Just as Noah and his family were preserved safe from the threatening waters of the flood in the ark he built, so now Moses is preserved from the threatening waters of the Nile in the ark prepared by his mother. *Among the reeds*: the Hebrew noun for "reed" is overwhelmingly used in the phrase "Reed Sea," traditionally translated "Red Sea."

**2:9** *And I will pay your wages*: the idea that the child's mother will be paid for nursing her child—and by Pharaoh's own daughter—heightens the narrative's irony.

**2:10** *When the child grew*: while v. 9 implies that the boy's mother cared for him as long as he needed to be nursed (presumably, between two and four years), the same verb appears in v. 11 to describe the attainment of adulthood. *And he became her son*: Pharaoh's daughter adopts Moses, thus adding to the irony of the account. The king of Egypt had ordered the killing of all the sons of the Hebrews, and one now becomes the son of his own

daughter! *Moses*: in Hebrew, *mosheh*. There is a play on words here: Hebrew *mosheh* echoes *meshithihu* ("I drew him out"). However, the name Moses actually has nothing to do with that Hebrew verb, but is probably derived from Egyptian "beloved" or "has been born," preserved in such Pharaonic names as Thutmoses (meaning approximately "Beloved of the god Thoth" or "The god Thoth is born, has given birth to [the child]"). The original meaning of Moses' name was no longer remembered (if it was Egyptian, it may have contained an Egyptian divine element as well, perhaps the name of the Nile god Hapi), and a secondary explanation was derived from this story (or gave rise to it, if the drawing from the water of the Nile was intended to foreshadow the Israelites' escape from Egypt through the Red Sea).

**2:11** *After Moses had grown up*: cf. 7:7, where Moses is said to be eighty years old at the time of his mission to Pharaoh. *Striking*: probably in the sense of "flogging"; in v. 12, however, the same verb is used in the sense of "killing."

**2:10** Acts 7:21; Heb 11:24.      **2:11–14** Acts 7:23–28.

gone out to his kinsmen and witnessed their forced labor, he saw an Egyptian striking a Hebrew, one of his own kinsmen. [12] Looking about and seeing no one, he struck down the Egyptian and hid him in the sand. [13] The next day he went out again, and now two Hebrews were fighting! So he asked the culprit, "Why are you striking your companion?" [14] But he replied, "Who has appointed you ruler and judge over us? Are you thinking of killing me as you killed the Egyptian?" Then Moses became afraid and thought, "The affair must certainly be known." [15] When Pharaoh heard of the affair, he sought to kill Moses. But Moses fled from Pharaoh and went to the land of Midian.†* There he sat down by a well.

[16] Now the priest of Midian had seven daughters, and they came to draw water and fill the troughs to water their father's flock. [17] But shepherds came and drove them away. So Moses rose up in their defense and watered their flock. [18] When they returned to their father Reuel,† he said to them, "How is it you have returned so soon today?" [19] They answered, "An Egyptian† delivered us from the shepherds. He even drew water for us and watered the flock!" [20] "Where is he?" he asked his daughters. "Why did you leave the man

there? Invite him to have something to eat." [21] Moses agreed to stay with him, and the man gave Moses his daughter Zipporah in marriage. [22] She conceived and bore a son, whom he named Gershom;† for he said, "I am a stranger residing in a foreign land."*

## II. THE CALL AND COMMISSION OF MOSES

**The Burning Bush.** [23] A long time passed, during which the king of Egypt died. The Israelites groaned under their bondage and cried out, and from their bondage their cry for help went up to God.* [24] God heard their moaning and God was mindful of his covenant* with Abraham, Isaac and Jacob. [25] God saw the Israelites, and God knew....†

**3** [1]† Meanwhile Moses was tending the flock of his father-in-law Jethro, the priest of Midian. Leading the flock beyond the wilderness, he came to the mountain of God, Horeb.† [2] There the angel of the LORD† appeared to him as fire flaming out of a bush.* When he looked, although the bush was on fire, it was not being consumed. [3] So Moses decided, "I must turn aside to look at this

---

**2:15** *Land of Midian*: the territory under the control of a confederation made up, according to Nm 31:8, of five Midianite tribes. According to Gn 25:1–2, Midian was a son of Abraham by Keturah. In view of the extreme hostility in later periods between Israel and Midian (cf. Nm 31; Jgs 6–8), the relationship is striking, as is the account here in Exodus of good relations between Moses and no less than a Midianite priest.

**2:18** *Reuel*: also called Jethro. Cf. 3:1; 4:18; 18:1.

**2:19** *An Egyptian*: Moses was probably wearing Egyptian dress, or spoke Egyptian to Reuel's daughters.

**2:22** *Gershom*: the name is explained unscientifically as if it came from the Hebrew word *ger*, "sojourner, resident alien," and the Hebrew word *sham*, "there." *Stranger residing*: Hebrew *ger*, one who seeks and finds shelter and a home away from his or her own people or land.

**2:25** *God knew*: in response to the people's cry, God, mindful of the covenant, looks on their plight and acknowledges firsthand the depth of their suffering (see 3:7). In vv. 23–25, traditionally attributed to the Priestly writer, God is mentioned five times, in contrast to the rest of chaps. 1–2, where God is rarely mentioned. These verses serve as a fitting transition to Moses' call in chap. 3.

**3:1–4:17** After the introduction to the narrative in 2:23–25, the commissioning itself falls into three sections: God's appearance under the aspect of a burning bush (3:1–6); the explicit commission (3:7–10); and an extended dialogue between Moses and God, in the course of which Moses receives the revelation of God's personal name. Although in the J source of the Pentateuch people have known and invoked God's personal name in worship since the time of Seth (Gn 4:26), for the E and P sources (see 6:2–4) God first makes this name publicly available here through Moses.

**3:1** *The mountain of God, Horeb*: traditionally, "Horeb" is taken to be an alternate name in E source material and Deu-

teronomy (e.g., Dt 1:2) for what in J and P is known as Mount Sinai, the goal of the Israelites' journey after leaving Egypt and the site of the covenant God makes with Israel. However, it is not clear that originally the two names reflect the same mountain, nor even that "Horeb" refers originally to a mountain and not simply the dry, ruined region (from Hebrew *horeb*, "dryness, devastation") around the mountain. Additionally, the position of "Horeb" at the end of the verse may indicate that the identification of the "mountain of God" with Horeb (= Sinai?) represents a later stage in the evolution of the tradition about God's meeting with Moses. The phrase "mountain of God" simply anticipates the divine apparitions which would take place there, both on this occasion and after the Israelites' departure from Egypt; alternatively, it means that the place was already sacred or a place of pilgrimage in pre-Israelite times. In any case, the narrative offers no indications of its exact location.

**3:2** *The angel of the LORD*: Hebrew *mal'ak* or "messenger" is regularly translated *angelos* by the Septuagint, from which the English word "angel" is derived, but the Hebrew term lacks connotations now popularly associated with "angel" (such as wings). Although angels frequently assume human form (cf. Gn 18–19), the term is also used to indicate the visual form under which God occasionally appeared and spoke to people, referred to indifferently in some Old Testament texts either as God's "angel," *mal'ak*, or as God. Cf. Gn 16:7, 13; Ex 14:19, 24–25; Nm 22:22–35; Jgs 6:11–18. *The bush*: Hebrew *seneh*, perhaps "thorny bush," occurring only here in vv. 2–4 and in Dt 33:16. Its use here is most likely a wordplay on Sinai (Hebrew *sinay*), implying a popular etymology for the name of the sacred mountain.

---

**2:15** Acts 7:29; Heb 11:27.    **2:24** Ex 6:5; Ps 105:8–9; 106:44–45.
**2:22** Ex 18:3.
**2:23** Ex 3:7, 9; Dt 26:7.    **3:2–10** Acts 7:30–35.

remarkable sight. Why does the bush not burn up?" ⁴When the LORD saw that he had turned aside to look, God called out to him from the bush: Moses! Moses! He answered, "Here I am." ⁵God said: Do not come near! Remove your sandals from your feet, for the place where you stand is holy ground.* ⁶I am the God of your father,† he continued, the God of Abraham, the God of Isaac, and the God of Jacob.* Moses hid his face, for he was afraid to look at God.

**The Call and Commission of Moses.** ⁷But the LORD said: I have witnessed the affliction of my people in Egypt and have heard their cry against their taskmasters, so I know well what they are suffering. ⁸Therefore I have come down† to rescue them from the power of the Egyptians and lead them up from that land into a good and spacious land, a land flowing with milk and honey, the country of the Canaanites, the Hittites, the Amorites, the Perizzites, the Girgashites, the Hivites and the Jebusites.* ⁹Now indeed the outcry of the Israelites has reached me, and I have seen how the Egyptians are oppressing them. ¹⁰Now, go! I am sending you to Pharaoh to bring my people, the Israelites, out of Egypt.

¹¹But Moses said to God, "Who am I† that I should go to Pharaoh and bring the Israelites out of Egypt?" ¹²God answered: I will be with you; and this will be your sign† that I have sent you. When you have brought the people out of Egypt, you will serve God at this mountain. ¹³"But," said Moses to God, "if I go to the Israelites and say to them, 'The God of your ancestors has sent me to you,' and they ask me, 'What is his name?' what do I tell them?" ¹⁴God replied to Moses: I am who I am.† Then he added: This is what you will tell the Israelites: I AM has sent me to you.

¹⁵God spoke further to Moses: This is what you will say to the Israelites: The LORD, the God of your ancestors, the God of Abraham,

---

† **3:6** *God of your father*: a frequently used epithet in Genesis (along with the variants "my father" and "your father") for God as worshiped by the ancestors. As is known from its usage outside of the Bible in the ancient Near East, it suggests a close, personal relationship between the individual and the particular god in question, who is both a patron and a protector, a god traditionally revered by the individual's family and whose worship is passed down from father to son. *The God of Abraham…Jacob*: this precise phrase (only here and in v. 15; 4:5) stresses the continuity between the new revelation to Moses and the earlier religious experience of Israel's ancestors, identifying the God who is now addressing Moses with the God who promised land and numerous posterity to the ancestors. Cf. Mt 22:32; Mk 12:26; Lk 20:37. *Afraid to look at God*: the traditions about Moses are not uniform in regard to his beholding or not being able to look at God (cf. 24:11; 33:11, 18–23; 34:29–35). Here Moses' reaction is the natural and spontaneous gesture of a person suddenly confronted with a direct experience of God. Aware of his human frailty and the gulf that separates him from the God who is holy, he hides his face. To encounter the divine was to come before an awesome and mysterious power unlike any other a human being might experience and, as such, potentially threatening to one's very identity or existence (see Gn 32:30).

**3:8** *I have come down*: cf. Gn 11:5, 7; 18:21. *Flowing with milk and honey*: an expression denoting agricultural prosperity, which seems to have been proverbial in its application to the land of Canaan. Cf. Ex 13:5; Nm 13:27; Jos 5:6; Jer 11:5; 32:22; Ez 20:6, 15.

**3:11** *Who am I*: this question is always addressed by an inferior to a superior (to the ruler in 1 Sm 18:18; to God in 2 Sm 7:18 and its parallel, 1 Chr 17:16; 1 Chr 29:14; 2 Chr 2:5). In response to some special opportunity or invitation, the question expresses in a style typical of the ancient Near East the speaker's humility or gratitude or need of further assistance, but never unwillingness or an outright refusal to respond. Instead the question sets the stage for further support from the superior should that be needed (as here).

**3:12** *Sign*: a visible display of the power of God. The ancient notion of a sign from God does not coincide with the modern understanding of "miracle," which suggests some disruption in the laws governing nature. While most any phenomenon can become a vehicle for displaying the purposes and providence of God, here the sign intended to confirm Moses' commission by God seems to be the burning bush itself. Since normally the giving of such a sign would follow the commission rather than precede it (see Jgs 6:11–24), some see Israel's service of God at Sinai after the exodus from Egypt as the confirmatory sign, albeit retroactively. It is more likely, however, that its mention here is intended to establish the present episode with Moses alone as a prefiguration of God's fiery theophany to all Israel on Mount Sinai. *Serve God*: Hebrew ʿ-b-d, "serve," includes among its meanings both the notion of "serving or working for another" and the notion of "worship." The implication here is that the Israelites' service/worship of God is incompatible with their service to Pharaoh.

**3:14** *I am who I am*: Moses asks in v. 13 for the name of the One speaking to him, but God responds with a wordplay which preserves the utterly mysterious character of the divine being even as it appears to suggest something of the inner meaning of God's name: ʾehyeh "I am" or "I will be(come)" for "Yhwh," the personal name of the God of Israel. While the phrase "I am who I am" resists unraveling, it nevertheless suggests an etymological linking between the name "Yhwh" and an earlier form of the Hebrew verbal root h-y-h "to be." On that basis many have interpreted the name "Yhwh" as a third-person form of the verb meaning "He causes to be, creates," itself perhaps a shortened form of a longer liturgical name such as "(God who) creates (the heavenly armies)." Note in this connection the invocation of Israel's God as "LORD (Yhwh) of Hosts" (e.g., 1 Sm 17:45). In any case, out of reverence for God's proper name, the term Adonai, "my Lord," was later used as a substitute. The word LORD (in small capital letters) indicates that the Hebrew text has the sacred name (Yhwh), the tetragrammaton. The word "Jehovah" arose from a false reading of this name as it is written in the current Hebrew text. The Septuagint has egō eimi ho ōn, "I am the One who is" (ōn being the participle of the verb "to be"). This can be taken as an assertion of God's aseity or self-existence, and has been understood as such by the Church, since the time of the Fathers, as a true expression of God's being, even though it is not precisely the meaning of the Hebrew.

---

*
**3:5** Jos 5:15.                              Mk 12:26; Lk 20:37.
**3:6** Ex 4:5; Mt 22:32;            **3:8** Gn 15:19–21.

the God of Isaac, and the God of Jacob, has sent me to you.

> This is my name forever; *
> this is my title for all generations.

¹⁶ Go and gather the elders of the Israelites, and tell them, The LORD, the God of your ancestors, the God of Abraham, Isaac, and Jacob, has appeared to me and said: I have observed you and what is being done to you in Egypt; ¹⁷ so I have decided to lead you up out of your affliction in Egypt into the land of the Canaanites, the Hittites, the Amorites, the Perizzites, the Girgashites, the Hivites and the Jebusites, a land flowing with milk and honey. ¹⁸ They will listen to you. Then you and the elders of Israel will go to the king of Egypt and say to him: * The LORD, the God of the Hebrews, has come to meet us. So now, let us go a three days' journey in the wilderness to offer sacrifice to the LORD, our God. ¹⁹ Yet I know that the king of Egypt will not allow you to go unless his hand is forced. ²⁰ So I will stretch out my hand and strike Egypt with all the wondrous deeds I will do in its midst. After that he will let you go. ²¹ * I will even make the Egyptians so well-disposed toward this people that, when you go, you will not go empty-handed. ²² Every woman will ask her neighbor and the resident alien in her house for silver and gold articles† and for clothing, and you will put them on your sons and daughters. So you will plunder the Egyptians.

**4** ¹ "But," objected Moses, "suppose they do not believe me or listen to me? For they may say, 'The LORD did not appear to you.'" ² The LORD said to him: What is in your hand? "A staff," he answered. ³ God said: Throw it on the ground. So he threw it on the ground and it became a snake, * and Moses backed away from it. ⁴ Then the LORD said to Moses: Now stretch out your hand and take hold of its tail. So he stretched out his hand and took hold of it, and it became a staff in his hand. ⁵ That is

so they will believe that the LORD, the God of their ancestors, the God of Abraham, the God of Isaac, and the God of Jacob, did appear to you.

⁶ Again the LORD said to him: Put your hand into the fold of your garment. So he put his hand into the fold of his garment, and when he drew it out, there was his hand covered with scales, like snowflakes. ⁷ Then God said: Put your hand back into the fold of your garment. So he put his hand back into the fold of his garment, and when he drew it out, there it was again like his own flesh. ⁸ If they do not believe you or pay attention to the message of the first sign, they should believe the message of the second sign. ⁹ And if they do not believe even these two signs and do not listen to you, take some water from the Nile and pour it on the dry land. The water you take from the Nile will become blood on the dry land. *

**Aaron's Office as Assistant.** ¹⁰ Moses, however, said to the LORD, "If you please, my Lord, I have never been eloquent, neither in the past nor now that you have spoken to your servant; but I am slow of speech and tongue." * ¹¹ The LORD said to him: Who gives one person speech? Who makes another mute or deaf, seeing or blind? Is it not I, the LORD? ¹² Now go, I will assist you in speaking† and teach you what you are to say. ¹³ But he said, "If you please, my Lord, send someone else!"† ¹⁴ Then the LORD became angry with Moses and said: I know there is your brother, Aaron the Levite, who is a good speaker; even now he is on his way to meet you. When he sees you, he will truly be glad. ¹⁵ You will speak to him and put the words in his mouth. I will assist both you and him in speaking and teach you both what you are to do. ¹⁶ He will speak to the people for you: he will be your spokesman,† and you will be as God to him. * ¹⁷ Take this staff† in your hand; with it you are to perform the signs.

**Moses' Return to Egypt.** ¹⁸ After this Moses returned to Jethro† his father-in-law and said to

---

3:22 *Articles:* probably jewelry.
4:12 *Assist you in speaking:* lit., "be with your mouth"; cf. v. 15, lit., "be with your mouth and with his mouth."
4:13 *Send someone else:* lit., "send by means of him whom you will send," that is, "send whom you will."
4:16 *Spokesman:* lit., "mouth"; Aaron was to serve as a mouthpiece for Moses, as a prophet does for God; hence the relation between Moses and Aaron is compared to that between God and his prophet: Moses "will be as God to," i.e., lit., "will

become God for him." Cf. 7:1.
4:17 *This staff:* probably the same as that of vv. 2–4; but some understand that a new staff is now given by God to Moses.
4:18 *Jethro:* the Hebrew text has "Jether," apparently a variant form of "Jethro" found in the same verse. *To see whether they are*

3:15 Ps 135:13.    4:9 Ex 7:17, 19–20.
3:18 Ex 5:3.    4:10 Ex 6:12.
3:21–22 Ex 11:2–3; 12:35–36.    4:16 Ex 7:1.
4:3 Ex 7:10.

him, "Let me return to my kindred in Egypt, to see whether they are still living." Jethro replied to Moses, "Go in peace." [19] Then the LORD said to Moses in Midian: Return to Egypt, for all those who sought your life are dead. [20] So Moses took his wife and his sons, mounted them on the donkey, and started back to the land of Egypt. Moses took the staff of God with him. [21] The LORD said to Moses: On your return to Egypt, see that you perform before Pharaoh all the wonders I have put in your power. But I will harden his heart† and he will not let the people go. [22]* So you will say to Pharaoh, Thus says the LORD: Israel is my son, my firstborn. [23] I said to you: Let my son go, that he may serve me. Since you refused to let him go, I will kill your son, your firstborn.*

[24]† On the journey, at a place where they spent the night, the LORD came upon Moses and sought to put him to death. [25]* But Zipporah took a piece of flint and cut off her son's foreskin and, touching his feet,† she said, "Surely you are a spouse of blood to me." [26] So God let Moses alone. At that time she said, "A spouse of blood," in regard to the circumcision.

[27] The LORD said to Aaron: Go into the wilderness to meet Moses. So he went; when meeting him at the mountain of God, he kissed him. [28] Moses told Aaron everything the LORD had sent him to say, and all the signs he had commanded him to do. [29] Then Moses and Aaron went and gathered all the elders of the Israelites. [30] Aaron told them everything the LORD had said to Moses, and he performed the signs before the people. [31] The people believed, and when they heard that the LORD had observed the Israelites and had seen their affliction,† they knelt and bowed down.

**5 Pharaoh's Hardness of Heart.** [1] Afterwards, Moses and Aaron went to Pharaoh and said, "Thus says the LORD, the God of Israel: Let my people go, that they may hold a feast† for me in the wilderness." [2] Pharaoh answered, "Who is the LORD, that I should obey him and let Israel go? I do not know the LORD,† and I will not let Israel go." [3] They replied, "The God of the Hebrews has come to meet us. Let us go a three days' journey in the wilderness, that we may offer sacrifice to the LORD, our God,* so that he does not strike us with the plague or the sword." [4] The king of Egypt answered them, "Why, Moses and Aaron, do you make the people neglect their work? Off to your labors!" [5] Pharaoh continued, "Look how they are already more numerous† than the people of the land, and yet you would give them rest from their labors!"

[6] That very day Pharaoh gave the taskmasters

---

† *still living*: Moses did not tell his father-in-law his main reason for returning to Egypt.

**4:21** *Harden his heart*: in the biblical view, the heart, whose actual function in the circulation of blood was unknown, typically performs functions associated today more with the brain than with the emotions. Therefore, while it may be used in connection with various emotional states ranging from joy to sadness, it very commonly designates the seat of intellectual and volitional activities. For God to harden Pharaoh's heart is to harden his resolve against the Israelites' desire to leave. In the ancient world, actions which are out of character are routinely attributed not to the person but to some "outside" superhuman power acting upon the person (Jgs 14:16; 1 Sm 16:10). Uncharacteristically negative actions or states are explained in the same way (1 Sm 16:14). In this instance, the opposition of Pharaoh, in the face of God's displays of power, would be unintelligible to the ancient Israelites unless he is seen as under some divine constraint. But this does not diminish Pharaoh's own responsibility. In the anthropology of the ancient Israelites there is no opposition between individual responsibility and God's sovereignty over all of creation. Cf. Rom 9:17–18.

**4:24–26** This story continues to perplex commentators and may have circulated in various forms before finding its place here in Exodus. Particularly troublesome is the unique phrase "spouse of blood." Nevertheless, v. 26, which apparently comes from the hand of a later commentator on the original story, is intended to offer some clarification. It asserts that when Zipporah used the problematic expression (addressing it either to Moses or her son), she did so with reference to the circumcision performed on her son—the only place in the Bible where this rite is performed by a woman. Whatever the precise meaning of the phrase "spouse of blood," circumcision is the key to understanding it as well as the entire incident. One may conclude, therefore, that God was angry with Moses for having failed to keep the divine command given to Abraham in Gn 17:10–12 and circumcise his son. Moses' life is spared when his wife circumcises their son.

**4:25** *Touching his feet*: a euphemism most probably for the male sexual organ (see 2 Kgs 18:27; Is 7:20); whether the genitals of the child (after Zipporah circumcised him) or of Moses (after the circumcision of his son) is not clear.

**4:31** *Observed…their affliction*: the same phrases used in God's dialogue with Moses in 3:16–17.

**5:1** *Hold a feast*: the Hebrew verb used here, *hagag* ("to celebrate a feast or a festival"; see 12:14; 23:14), refers to a community celebration marked above all by a procession to the sanctuary. It is used especially of three major feasts: Unleavened Bread, Pentecost (in 23:16, "the Feast of Harvest," but customarily "the Feast of Weeks" [*Shavuot*]), and Succoth/Sukkoth (in 34:16, "the Feast of Ingathering," but more frequently "of Booths, or Tabernacles," as in Dt 16:13, 16; 31:10; Lv 23:34; Zec 14:16; *passim*) and—along with the related noun *hag*—the Passover in 12:14. See 23:14–18; 34:18–25.

**5:2** *I do not know the LORD*: whether or not he had heard of the Lord, the God of Israel, Pharaoh here refuses to acknowledge the Lord's authority. See note on 1:8.

**5:5** *They are already more numerous*: a recollection of Pharaoh's earlier words to his subjects in 1:9.

4:22 Sir 36:11.                    4:25 Is 6:2; 7:20.
4:23 Ex 11:5; 12:29.            5:3 Ex 3:18.

of the people and their foremen† this order: ⁷"You shall no longer supply the people with straw for their brickmaking† as before. Let them go and gather their own straw! ⁸Yet you shall levy upon them the same quota of bricks as they made previously. Do not reduce it. They are lazy; that is why they are crying, 'Let us go to offer sacrifice to our God.' ⁹Increase the work for the men, so that they attend to it and not to deceitful words."

¹⁰So the taskmasters of the people and their foremen went out and told the people, "Thus says Pharaoh,† 'I will not provide you with straw. ¹¹Go and get your own straw from wherever you can find it. But there will not be the slightest reduction in your work.'" ¹²The people, then, scattered throughout the land of Egypt to gather stubble for straw, ¹³while the taskmasters kept driving them on, saying, "Finish your work, the same daily amount as when the straw was supplied to you." ¹⁴The Israelite foremen, whom the taskmasters of Pharaoh had placed over them, were beaten, and were asked, "Why have you not completed your prescribed amount of bricks yesterday and today, as before?"

**Complaint of the Foremen.** ¹⁵Then the Israelite foremen came and cried out to Pharaoh:† "Why do you treat your servants in this manner? ¹⁶No straw is supplied to your servants, and still we are told, 'Make bricks!' Look how your servants are beaten! It is you who are at fault." ¹⁷He answered, "Lazy! You are lazy! That is why you keep saying, 'Let us go and offer sacrifice to the Lord.' ¹⁸Now off to work! No straw will be supplied to you, but you must supply your quota of bricks."

¹⁹The Israelite foremen realized they were in trouble, having been told, "Do not reduce your daily amount of bricks!" ²⁰So when they left Pharaoh they assailed Moses and Aaron, who were waiting to meet them, ²¹and said to them, "The Lord look upon you and judge! You have made us offensive to Pharaoh and his servants, putting a sword into their hands to kill us."

**Renewal of God's Promise.** ²²Then Moses again had recourse to the Lord and said, "Lord, why have you treated this people badly? And why did you send me? ²³From the time I went to Pharaoh to speak in your name, he has treated this people badly, and you have done nothing to rescue your people."

**6** ¹The Lord answered Moses: Now you will see what I will do to Pharaoh. For by a strong hand, he will let them go; by a strong hand,† he will drive them from his land.

**Confirmation of the Promise to the Ancestors.** ²†Then God spoke to Moses, and said to him: I am the Lord. ³As God the Almighty† I appeared* to Abraham, Isaac, and Jacob, but by my name, Lord, I did not make myself known to them. ⁴I also established my covenant with them, to give them the land of Canaan, the land in which they were residing as aliens.* ⁵Now that I have heard the groaning of the Israelites, whom the Egyptians have reduced to slavery, I am mindful of my covenant.* ⁶Therefore, say to the Israelites: I am the Lord. I will free you from the burdens of the Egyptians and will deliver you from their slavery. I will redeem you by my outstretched arm and with mighty acts of judgment. ⁷I will take you as my own people, and I will be your God;*

**5:6** *The taskmasters of the people and their foremen*: the former were higher officials and probably Egyptians; the latter were lower officials (perhaps recordkeepers or clerks), chosen from the Israelites themselves. Cf. v. 14.
**5:7** Straw was mixed with clay to give sun-dried bricks greater cohesion and durability.
**5:10** *Thus says Pharaoh*: the standard formula for prophetic oracles, but with Pharaoh rather than the Lord as the subject. This heightens the sense of personal conflict between Pharaoh, who acts as if he were God, and the Lord, whose claims are spurned by Pharaoh.
**5:15** *Cried out to Pharaoh*: the Hebrew verb translated "cry out" and its related noun are normally used of appeals to God by Moses (8:8; 14:15; 15:25; 17:4), the people (3:7, 9; 14:10), or an oppressed individual (22:22, 26). Here, by implication, these minor Israelite officials appeal to Pharaoh as if he were their God. See v. 10.
**6:1** *By a strong hand*: by God's hand or Pharaoh's hand? The Hebrew is ambiguous; although it may be an allusion to God's hand of 3:19–20, both interpretations are possible.
**6:2–7:7** According to the standard source criticism of the Pentateuch, 6:2–7:7 represents a Priestly version of the JE call narrative in 3:1–4:17. But in context the present account does more than simply repeat the earlier passage. See note below.
**6:3** *God the Almighty*: in Hebrew, *El Shaddai*. This traditional translation does not have a firm philological basis. *But by my name…I did not make myself known to them*: although the text implies that the name Lord was unknown previously, in context the emphasis in the passage falls on the understanding of God that comes with knowledge of the name. In this way God responds to the worsening plight of the Israelites and Moses' complaint in 5:23 that God has done nothing at all to rescue them.

**6:3** Gn 17:1; 35:11.    **6:5** Ex 2:24.
**6:4** Gn 15:18; 17:4–8.    **6:7** Lv 26:12.

and you will know that I, the LORD, am your God who has freed you from the burdens of the Egyptians [8] and I will bring you into the land which I swore to give to Abraham, Isaac, and Jacob. I will give it to you as your own possession—I, the LORD! [9] But when Moses told this to the Israelites, they would not listen to him because of their dejection and hard slavery.

[10] Then the LORD spoke to Moses: [11] Go, tell Pharaoh, king of Egypt, to let the Israelites leave his land. [12] However, Moses protested to the LORD, "If the Israelites did not listen to me, how is it possible that Pharaoh will listen to me, poor speaker†* that I am!" [13] But the LORD spoke to Moses and Aaron regarding the Israelites and Pharaoh, king of Egypt, and charged them to bring the Israelites out of the land of Egypt.

**Genealogy of Moses and Aaron.** [14] These are the heads of their ancestral houses.† The sons of Reuben,* the firstborn of Israel: Hanoch, Pallu, Hezron and Carmi; these are the clans of Reuben. [15] The sons of Simeon:* Jemuel, Jamin, Ohad, Jachin, Zohar and Shaul, the son of a Canaanite woman; these are the clans of Simeon. [16] These are the names of the sons of Levi,* in their genealogical order: Gershon, Kohath and Merari. Levi lived one hundred and thirty-seven years.

[17] The sons of Gershon,* by their clans: Libni and Shimei. [18] The sons of Kohath:* Amram, Izhar, Hebron and Uzziel. Kohath lived one hundred and thirty-three years. [19] The sons of Merari:* Mahli and Mushi. These are the clans of Levi in their genealogical order.

[20] Amram married his aunt† Jochebed,* who bore him Aaron, Moses, and Miriam. Amram lived one hundred and thirty-seven years. [21] The sons of Izhar: Korah, Nepheg and Zichri.

[22] The sons of Uzziel: Mishael, Elzaphan and Sithri. [23] Aaron married Elisheba, Amminadab's* daughter, the sister of Nahshon; she bore him Nadab, Abihu, Eleazar and Ithamar. [24] The sons of Korah: Assir, Elkanah and Abiasaph. These are the clans of the Korahites. [25] Eleazar, Aaron's son, married one of Putiel's daughters, who bore him Phinehas.† These are the heads of the ancestral houses of the Levites by their clans. [26] These are the Aaron and the Moses to whom the LORD said, "Bring the Israelites out from the land of Egypt, company by company." [27] They are the ones who spoke to Pharaoh, king of Egypt, to bring the Israelites out of Egypt—the same Moses and Aaron.

[28] When the LORD spoke to Moses in the land of Egypt [29] the LORD said to Moses: I am the LORD. Say to Pharaoh, king of Egypt, all that I tell you. [30] But Moses protested to the LORD, "Since I am a poor speaker, how is it possible that Pharaoh will listen to me?"

**7** [1] The LORD answered Moses: See! I have made you a god to Pharaoh,* and Aaron your brother will be your prophet.† [2] You will speak all that I command you. In turn, your brother Aaron will tell Pharaoh to let the Israelites go out of his land. [3] Yet I will make Pharaoh so headstrong that, despite the many signs and wonders that I work in the land of Egypt, [4] Pharaoh will not listen to you. Therefore I will lay my hand on Egypt and with mighty acts of judgment I will bring my armies, my people the Israelites, out of the land of Egypt. [5] All Egyptians will know that I am the LORD, when I stretch out my hand against Egypt and bring the Israelites out of their midst.

[6] This, then, is what Moses and Aaron did. They did exactly as the LORD had commanded them. [7] Moses was eighty years old, and Aaron eighty-three, when they spoke to Pharaoh.

---

† **6:12** *Poor speaker*: lit., "uncircumcised of lips": a metaphor expressing the hindrance of good communication expressed as "slow of speech and tongue" (4:10). Also used as a metaphor for impeded "heart" (Lv 26:41; Dt 10:16).
**6:14** The purpose of the genealogy here is to give the line from which Moses and Aaron sprang, with special emphasis placed on the line of Aaron. Reuben and Simeon are mentioned first because, as older brothers of Levi, their names occur before his in the genealogy.
**6:20** *His aunt*: more exactly, "his father's sister." Later on such a marriage was forbidden. Cf. Lv 18:12. Hence, the Greek and Latin versions render here, "his cousin."
**6:25** *Phinehas*: according to Nm 25:13, Phinehas was given by God "the covenant of an everlasting priesthood" because of his zeal for God when the Israelites committed apostasy

by worshiping the Baal of Peor in the plains of Moab (see Nm 25:1–18).
**7:1** *Prophet*: Hebrew *nabi*, one who can legitimately speak for God and in God's name to another or others. Just as God spoke to Moses, so Moses will speak to Aaron, who will be a "prophet" to Pharaoh. Cf. 4:16.

---

**6:12** Ex 4:10.
**6:14** Nm 26:5–6; 1 Chr 5:3.
**6:15** Nm 26:12; 1 Chr 4:24.
**6:16** Nm 3:17; 1 Chr 6:1; 23:6.
**6:17** Nm 3:21; 1 Chr 6:2; 23:7.
**6:18** Nm 3:27; 1 Chr 6:3, 18.
**6:19** Nm 3:20; 1 Chr 6:4, 14; 23:21.
**6:20** Nm 26:59.
**6:23** Ru 4:19–20; 1 Chr 2:10.
**7:1** Ex 4:15–16.

EX

## III. THE CONTEST WITH PHARAOH

**The Staff Turned into a Serpent.** [8] The LORD spoke to Moses and Aaron: [9] When Pharaoh demands of you, "Produce a sign or wonder," you will say to Aaron: "Take your staff and throw it down before Pharaoh, and it will turn into a serpent."* [10] Then Moses and Aaron went to Pharaoh and did just as the LORD had commanded. Aaron threw his staff down before Pharaoh and his servants, and it turned into a serpent. [11] Pharaoh, in turn, summoned the wise men and the sorcerers, and they also, the magicians* of Egypt, did the same thing by their magic arts. [12] Each one threw down his staff, and they turned into serpents. But Aaron's staff swallowed their staffs. [13] Pharaoh, however, hardened his heart and would not listen to them, just as the LORD had foretold.

**First Plague: Water Turned into Blood.†** [14] Then the LORD said to Moses: Pharaoh is obstinate† in refusing to let the people go. [15] In the morning, just when he sets out for the water, go to Pharaoh and present yourself by the bank of the Nile, holding in your hand the staff that turned into a snake.† [16] Say to him: The LORD, the God of the Hebrews, sent me to you with the message: Let my people go to serve me in the wilderness. But as yet you have not listened. [17] Thus says the LORD: This is how you will know that I am the LORD. With the staff here in my hand, I will strike the water in the Nile and it will be changed into blood.* [18] The fish in the Nile will die, and the Nile itself will stink so that the Egyptians will be unable to drink water from the Nile.

[19] The LORD then spoke to Moses: Speak to Aaron: Take your staff and stretch out your hand over the waters of Egypt—its streams, its canals, its ponds, and all its supplies of water—that they may become blood. There will be blood throughout the land of Egypt, even in the wooden pails and stone jars.

[20] This, then, is what Moses and Aaron did, exactly as the LORD had commanded. Aaron raised his staff and struck the waters in the Nile in full view of Pharaoh and his servants, and all the water in the Nile was changed into blood. [21] The fish in the Nile died, and the Nile itself stank so that the Egyptians could not drink water from it. There was blood throughout the land of Egypt. [22] But the Egyptian magicians did the same† by their magic arts. So Pharaoh hardened his heart and would not listen to them, just as the LORD had said. [23] Pharaoh turned away and went into his house, with no concern even for this. [24] All the Egyptians had to dig round about the Nile for drinking water, since they could not drink any water from the Nile.

**Second Plague: The Frogs.** [25] Seven days passed after the LORD had struck the Nile. [26] Then the LORD said to Moses: Go to Pharaoh and tell him:* Thus says the LORD: Let my people go to serve me. [27] If you refuse to let them go, then I will send a plague of frogs over all your territory. [28] The Nile will teem with frogs. They will come up and enter into your palace and into your bedroom and onto your bed, into the houses of your servants, too, and among your people, even into your ovens and your kneading bowls. [29] The frogs will come up over you and your people and all your servants.

**8** [1] The LORD then spoke to Moses: Speak to Aaron: Stretch out your hand with your staff over the streams, the canals, and the ponds, and make frogs overrun the land of Egypt. [2] So Aaron stretched out his hand over the waters of Egypt, and the frogs came up and covered the land of Egypt. [3] But the magicians

---

**7:14–12:30** After a brief preface (vv. 8–13) drawn from the Priestly source, a narrative depicting the series of ten disasters that God brings upon Pharaoh because of his stubbornness ensues. Although most of these disasters, known traditionally as the "ten plagues of Egypt," could be interpreted as naturally occurring phenomena, they are clearly represented by the biblical authors as extraordinary events indicative of God's intervention on behalf of Israel and as occurring exactly according to Moses' commands. See Ps 78:43–51 and 105:27–36 for poetic versions of these plagues, which also differ significantly from the account here.

**7:14** *Pharaoh is obstinate*: lit., "Pharaoh's heart is heavy" (*kabed*); thus not precisely the same Hebrew idiom as found in vv. 13 and 22, "stubborn," lit., "Pharaoh's heart was hard(ened)" (*hazaq*) (cf. the related idiom with Pharaoh as the object, e.g., 4:21).

**7:15** *The staff that turned into a snake*: the allusion is to 4:2–4 rather than 7:9–12. The latter comes from the hand of the Priestly writer and features Aaron—with his staff—as the principal actor.

**7:22** *The Egyptian magicians did the same*: this is an exaggeration, presumably influenced by the similar statement in v. 11; whereas the magicians could turn their staffs into snakes after Aaron had done so, after Aaron's sign there should not have been any water in Egypt still unchanged to blood for the magicians "to do the same" with it (cf. v. 24).

---

| | |
|---|---|
| **7:9** Ex 4:3. | **7:17–21** Ex 4:9; Ps 78:44; |
| **7:11** 2 Tm 3:8. | 105:29; Wis 11:5–7. |
| | **7:26–29** Ps 78:45; 105:30. |

did the same by their magic arts and made frogs overrun the land of Egypt.

⁴Then Pharaoh summoned Moses and Aaron and said, "Pray to the LORD to remove the frogs from me and my people, and I will let the people go to sacrifice to the LORD." ⁵Moses answered Pharaoh, "Please designate for me the time when I am to pray for you and your servants and your people, to get rid of the frogs from you and your houses. They will be left only in the Nile." ⁶"Tomorrow," he said. Then Moses replied, "It will be as you have said, so that you may know that there is none like the LORD, our God. ⁷The frogs will leave you and your houses, your servants and your people; they will be left only in the Nile."

⁸After Moses and Aaron left Pharaoh's presence, Moses cried out to the LORD on account of the frogs that he had inflicted on Pharaoh; ⁹and the LORD did as Moses had asked. The frogs died off in the houses, the courtyards, and the fields. ¹⁰Heaps of them were piled up, and the land stank. ¹¹But when Pharaoh saw there was a respite, he became obstinate and would not listen to them, just as the LORD had said.

**Third Plague: The Gnats.** ¹²Thereupon the LORD spoke to Moses: Speak to Aaron: Stretch out your staff and strike the dust of the earth, and it will turn into gnats†* throughout the land of Egypt. ¹³They did so. Aaron stretched out his hand with his staff and struck the dust of the earth, and gnats came upon human being and beast alike. All the dust of the earth turned into gnats throughout the land of Egypt. ¹⁴Though the magicians did the same thing to produce gnats by their magic arts, they could not do so.* The gnats were on human being and beast alike, ¹⁵and the magicians said to Pharaoh, "This is the finger of God."† Yet Pharaoh hardened his heart and

would not listen to them, just as the LORD had said.

**Fourth Plague: The Flies.** ¹⁶Then the LORD spoke to Moses: Early tomorrow morning present yourself to Pharaoh when he sets out toward the water, and say to him: Thus says the LORD: Let my people go to serve me. ¹⁷For if you do not let my people go, I will send swarms of flies upon you and your servants and your people and your houses. The houses of the Egyptians and the very ground on which they stand will be filled with swarms of flies. ¹⁸But on that day I will make an exception of the land of Goshen, where my people are, and no swarms of flies will be there, so that you may know that I the LORD am in the midst of the land. ¹⁹I will make a distinction† between my people and your people. This sign will take place tomorrow. ²⁰This the LORD did. Thick swarms of flies entered the house of Pharaoh and the houses of his servants; throughout Egypt the land was devastated on account of the swarms of flies.*

²¹Then Pharaoh summoned Moses and Aaron and said, "Go sacrifice to your God within the land." ²²But Moses replied, "It is not right to do so, for what we sacrifice to the LORD, our God, is abhorrent to the Egyptians.† If we sacrifice what is abhorrent to the Egyptians before their very eyes, will they not stone us? ²³We must go a three days' journey in the wilderness and sacrifice to the LORD, our God, as he commands us." ²⁴Pharaoh said, "I will let you go to sacrifice to the LORD, your God, in the wilderness, provided that you do not go too far away. Pray for me." ²⁵Moses answered, "As soon as I leave you I will pray to the LORD that the swarms of flies may depart tomorrow from Pharaoh, his servants, and his people. Pharaoh, however, must not act deceitfully again and refuse to let the people go to

---

† **8:12, 17** *Gnats, flies:* it is uncertain what species of troublesome insects are meant here in vv. 12–14 and then in vv. 17–27, the identification as "gnat" (vv. 12–14) and as "fly" (vv. 17–27) being based on the rendering of the Septuagint. Others suggest "lice" in vv. 12–14, while rabbinic literature renders Hebrew *'arob* in vv. 17–27 as a "mixture of wild animals." In the Hebrew of the Old Testament, the word occurs only in the context of the plagues (see also Ps 78:45 and 105:31).

**8:15** *The finger of God:* previously the magicians had, for the most part, been able to replicate the signs and wonders Moses performed to manifest God's power—turning their staffs into snakes (7:11–12), turning water into blood (7:22), and producing frogs to overrun the land of Egypt (8:3). But now for the first time they are unable to compete, and confess a power greater than their own is at work. Cf. Lk 11:20.

**8:19** *A distinction:* while some uncertainty surrounds the Hebrew here rendered as "distinction," it is clear that now the Israelites begin to be set apart from the Egyptians, a separation that reaches a climax in the death of the Egyptian firstborn (11:7).

**8:22** Perhaps Moses is deceiving the Pharaoh much like the "God-fearing" midwives (1:16–20), although ancient historians writing about Egypt some time after the period in which the exodus is set do note Egyptian prohibitions on sacrificing cattle or slaughtering sacred animals. As such, the Egyptians might well have fiercely resented certain sacrificial practices of the Israelites. Certain animals were held sacred in Egypt, as the representations of various deities.

---

**8:12–13** Ps 105:31. **8:14** Wis 17:7.　**8:20** Ps 78:45; 105:31; Wis 16:9.

sacrifice to the LORD." [26] When Moses left Pharaoh, he prayed to the LORD; [27] and the LORD did as Moses had asked, removing the swarms of flies from Pharaoh, his servants, and his people. Not one remained. [28] But once more Pharaoh became obstinate and would not let the people go.

# 9 Fifth Plague: The Pestilence.

[1] Then the LORD said to Moses: Go to Pharaoh and tell him: Thus says the LORD, the God of the Hebrews: Let my people go to serve me. [2] For if you refuse to let them go and persist in holding them, [3] the hand of the LORD will strike your livestock in the field—your horses, donkeys, camels, herds and flocks—with a very severe pestilence. [4] But the LORD will distinguish between the livestock of Israel and that of Egypt, so that nothing belonging to the Israelites will die. [5] And the LORD set a definite time, saying: Tomorrow the LORD will do this in the land. [6] And on the next day the LORD did it. All the livestock of the Egyptians died,* but not one animal belonging to the Israelites died. [7] But although Pharaoh found upon inquiry that not even so much as one of the livestock of the Israelites had died, he remained obstinate and would not let the people go.

**Sixth Plague: The Boils.** [8] So the LORD said to Moses and Aaron: Each of you take handfuls of soot from a kiln, and in the presence of Pharaoh let Moses scatter it toward the sky. [9] It will turn into fine dust over the whole land of Egypt and cause festering boils† on human being and beast alike throughout the land of Egypt.

[10] So they took the soot from a kiln and appeared before Pharaoh. When Moses scattered it toward the sky, it caused festering boils on human being and beast alike. [11] Because of the boils the magicians could not stand in Moses' presence, for there were boils on the magicians as well as on the rest of the Egyptians. [12] But the LORD hardened Pharaoh's heart, and he would not listen to them, just as the LORD had said to Moses.

**Seventh Plague: The Hail.** [13] Then the LORD spoke to Moses: Early tomorrow morning present yourself to Pharaoh and say to him: Thus says the LORD, the God of the Hebrews: Let my people go to serve me, [14] for this time I will unleash all my blows upon you and your servants and your people, so that you may know that there is none like me anywhere on earth. [15] For by now I should have stretched out my hand and struck you and your people with such pestilence that you would have vanished from the earth. [16] But this is why I have let you survive: to show you† my power and to make my name resound throughout the earth!* [17] Will you continue to exalt yourself over my people and not let them go? [18] At this time tomorrow, therefore, I am going to rain down such fierce hail as there has never been in Egypt from the day it was founded up to the present. [19] Therefore, order your livestock and whatever else you have in the open fields to be brought to a place of safety. Whatever human being or animal is found in the fields and is not brought to shelter will die when the hail comes down upon them. [20] Those of Pharaoh's servants who feared the word of the LORD hurried their servants and their livestock off to shelter. [21] But those who did not pay attention to the word of the LORD left their servants and their livestock in the fields.

[22] The LORD then said to Moses: Stretch out your hand toward the sky, that hail may fall upon the entire land of Egypt, on human being and beast alike and all the vegetation of the fields in the land of Egypt. [23] So Moses stretched out his staff toward the sky, and the LORD sent forth peals of thunder and hail.* Lightning flashed toward the earth, and the LORD rained down hail upon the land of Egypt. [24] There was hail and lightning flashing here and there through the hail, and the hail was so fierce that nothing like it had been seen in Egypt since it became a nation. [25] Throughout the land of Egypt the hail struck down everything in the fields, human being and beast alike; it struck down all the vegetation of the fields and splintered every tree in the fields. [26] Only in the land of Goshen, where the Israelites were, was there no hail.

[27] Then Pharaoh sent for Moses and Aaron and said to them, "I have sinned this time! The

---

† **9:9** *Boils*: the exact nature of the disease is not clear. Semitic cognates, for example, suggest the Hebrew root means "to be hot" and thus point to some sort of inflammation. The fact that soot taken from the kiln is the agent of the disease would point in the same direction. See further Lv 13:18–23; Dt 28:35; 2 Kgs 20:7.

**9:16** *To show you*: some ancient versions such as the Septuagint read, "to show through you." Cf. Rom 9:17.

*
**9:6** Ps 78:48.　　　　**9:23–24** Ps 78:47; 105:32–33.
**9:16** Rom 9:17.

L<small>ORD</small> is the just one, and I and my people are the ones at fault. 28 Pray to the L<small>ORD</small>! Enough of the thunder† and hail! I will let you go; you need stay no longer." 29 Moses replied to him, "As soon as I leave the city I will extend my hands to the L<small>ORD</small>; the thunder will cease, and there will be no more hail so that you may know that the earth belongs to the L<small>ORD</small>. 30 But as for you and your servants, I know that you do not yet fear the L<small>ORD</small> God."

31 Now the flax and the barley were ruined, because the barley was in ear and the flax in bud. 32 But the wheat and the spelt were not ruined, for they grow later.

33 When Moses had left Pharaoh and gone out of the city, he extended his hands to the L<small>ORD</small>. The thunder and the hail ceased, and the rain no longer poured down upon the earth. 34 But Pharaoh, seeing that the rain and the hail and the thunder had ceased, sinned again and became obstinate, both he and his servants. 35 In the hardness of his heart, Pharaoh would not let the Israelites go, just as the L<small>ORD</small> had said through Moses.

# 10 Eighth Plague: The Locusts. 1 Then the L<small>ORD</small> said to Moses: Go to Pharaoh, for I have made him and his servants obstinate in order that I may perform these signs of mine among them 2 and that you may recount to your son and grandson how I made a fool of the Egyptians and what signs I did among them, so that you may know that I am the L<small>ORD</small>.*

3 So Moses and Aaron went to Pharaoh and told him, "Thus says the L<small>ORD</small>, the God of the Hebrews: How long will you refuse to submit to me? Let my people go to serve me. 4 For if you refuse to let my people go, tomorrow I will bring locusts into your territory. 5 They will cover the surface of the earth, so that the earth itself will not be visible. They will eat up the remnant you saved undamaged from the hail, as well as all the trees that are growing in your fields. 6 They will fill your houses and the houses of your servants and of all the Egyptians—something your parents and your grandparents have not seen from the day they appeared on this soil until today." With that he turned and left Pharaoh.

7 But Pharaoh's servants said to him, "How long will he be a snare for us? Let the people go to serve the L<small>ORD</small>, their God. Do you not yet realize that Egypt is being destroyed?" 8 So Moses and Aaron were brought back to Pharaoh, who said to them, "Go, serve the L<small>ORD</small>, your God. But who exactly will go?" 9 Moses answered, "With our young and old we must go; with our sons and daughters, with our flocks and herds we must go. It is a pilgrimage feast of the L<small>ORD</small> for us." 10 "The L<small>ORD</small> help you,"† Pharaoh replied, "if I let your little ones go with you! Clearly, you have some evil in mind. 11 By no means! Just you men go and serve the L<small>ORD</small>.† After all, that is what you have been asking for." With that they were driven from Pharaoh's presence.

12* The L<small>ORD</small> then said to Moses: Stretch out your hand over the land of Egypt for the locusts, that they may come upon it and eat up all the land's vegetation, whatever the hail has left. 13 So Moses stretched out his staff over the land of Egypt, and the L<small>ORD</small> drove an east wind† over the land all that day and all night. When it was morning, the east wind brought the locusts. 14 The locusts came up over the whole land of Egypt and settled down over all its territory. Never before had there been such a fierce swarm of locusts, nor will there ever be again. 15 They covered the surface of the whole land, so that it became black. They ate up all the vegetation in the land and all the fruit of the trees the hail had spared. Nothing green was left on any tree or plant in the fields throughout the land of Egypt.

16 Pharaoh hurriedly summoned Moses and Aaron and said, "I have sinned against the L<small>ORD</small>, your God, and against you. 17 But now, do forgive me my sin only this once, and pray to the L<small>ORD</small>, your God, only to take this death from me." 18 When Moses left Pharaoh, he prayed to the L<small>ORD</small>, 19 and the L<small>ORD</small> caused the wind to shift to a very strong west wind, which took up the locusts and hurled them into the Red Sea.† Not a single locust remained within

---

9:28 *Thunder*: lit., "divine voices," "voices of God," or the like.

10:10 *The L<small>ORD</small> help you…*: lit., "May the Lord be with you in the same way as I let you…"; a sarcastic blessing intended as a curse.

10:11 Pharaoh realized that if the men alone went they would have to return to their families. He suspected that the Hebrews had no intention of returning.

10:13 *East wind*: coming across the desert from Arabia, the strong east wind brings Egypt the burning sirocco and, at times, locusts. Cf. 14:21.

10:19 *The Red Sea*: the traditional translation, cf. Septuagint and other Versions; but the Hebrew literally means "sea of reeds" or "reedy sea," which could probably be applied to a number of

10:2 Dt 6:20–25.     10:12–15 Ps 78:46; 105:34–35.

the whole territory of Egypt. <sup>20</sup> Yet the LORD hardened Pharaoh's heart, and he would not let the Israelites go.

**Ninth Plague: The Darkness.** <sup>21</sup>* Then the LORD said to Moses: Stretch out your hand toward the sky, that over the land of Egypt there may be such darkness† that one can feel it. <sup>22</sup> So Moses stretched out his hand toward the sky, and there was dense darkness throughout the land of Egypt for three days. <sup>23</sup> People could not see one another, nor could they get up from where they were, for three days. But all the Israelites had light where they lived.

<sup>24</sup> Pharaoh then summoned Moses and Aaron and said, "Go, serve the LORD. Only your flocks and herds will be detained. Even your little ones may go with you." <sup>25</sup> But Moses replied, "You also must give us sacrifices and burnt offerings to make to the LORD, our God. <sup>26</sup> Our livestock also must go with us. Not an animal must be left behind, for some of them we will select for service† to the LORD, our God; but we will not know with which ones we are to serve the LORD until we arrive there." <sup>27</sup> But the LORD hardened Pharaoh's heart, and he was unwilling to let them go. <sup>28</sup> Pharaoh said to Moses, "Leave me, and see to it that you do not see my face again! For the day you do see my face you will die!" <sup>29</sup> Moses replied, "You are right! I will never see your face again."

**11** **Tenth Plague: The Death of the First-born.** <sup>1</sup> Then the LORD spoke to Moses: One more plague I will bring upon Pharaoh and upon Egypt. After that he will let you depart. In fact, when he finally lets you go, he will drive you away. <sup>2</sup>* Instruct the people that every man is to ask his neighbor, and every woman her neighbor, for silver and gold articles and for clothing. <sup>3</sup> The LORD indeed made the Egyptians well-disposed toward the people; Moses himself was very highly regarded by Pharaoh's servants and the people in the land of Egypt.

<sup>4</sup> Moses then said, "Thus says the LORD: About midnight I will go forth through Egypt.* <sup>5</sup>* Every firstborn in the land of Egypt will die, from the firstborn of Pharaoh who sits on his throne to the firstborn of the slave-girl who is at the handmill,† as well as all the firstborn of the animals. <sup>6</sup> Then there will be loud wailing throughout the land of Egypt, such as has never been, nor will ever be again. <sup>7</sup> But among all the Israelites, among human beings and animals alike, not even a dog will growl, so that you may know that the LORD distinguishes between Egypt and Israel. <sup>8</sup> All these servants of yours will then come down to me and bow down before me, saying: Leave, you and all your followers!* Then I will depart." With that he left Pharaoh's presence in hot anger.

<sup>9</sup> The LORD said to Moses: Pharaoh will not listen to you so that my wonders may be multiplied in the land of Egypt. <sup>10</sup> Thus, although Moses and Aaron performed all these wonders in Pharaoh's presence, the LORD hardened Pharaoh's heart, and he would not let the Israelites go from his land.

**12** **The Passover Ritual Prescribed.**† <sup>1</sup> The LORD said to Moses and Aaron in the land of Egypt: <sup>2</sup>† This month will stand at the head of your calendar; you will reckon it the first month of the year.* <sup>3</sup> Tell the whole community of Israel: On the tenth of this month every family must procure for itself a lamb, one apiece for each household. <sup>4</sup> If a household is too small for a lamb, it along

---

bodies of shallow water, most likely somewhat to the north of the present deep Red Sea.

**10:21** *Darkness:* commentators note that at times a storm from the south, called the *khamsin*, blackens the sky of Egypt with sand from the Sahara; the dust in the air is then so thick that the darkness can, in a sense, "be felt." But such observations should not obscure the fact that for the biblical author what transpires in each of the plagues is clearly something extraordinary, an event which witnesses to the unrivaled power of Israel's God.

**10:26** *Service:* as is obvious from v. 25, the service in question here is the offering of sacrifice. The continued use of the verb *'bd* "to serve" and related nouns for both the people's bondage in Egypt and their subsequent service to the Lord dramatizes the point of the conflict between Pharaoh and the God of Israel, who demands from the Israelites an attachment which is exclusive. See Lv 25:55.

**11:5** *Handmill:* two pieces of stone were used to grind grain.

A smaller upper stone was moved back and forth over a larger stationary stone. This menial work was done by slaves and captives.

**12:1–20** This section, which interrupts the narrative of the exodus, contains later legislation concerning the celebration of Passover.

**12:2** As if to affirm victory over Pharaoh and sovereignty over the Israelites, the Lord proclaims a new calendar for Israel. *This month:* Abib, the month of "ripe grain." Cf. 13:4; 23:15; 34:18; Dt 16:1. It occurred near the vernal equinox, March–April. Later it was known by the Babylonian name of Nisan. Cf. Neh 2:1; Est 3:7.

* **10:21–22** Ps 105:28.    **11:5–6** Ex 12:29–30.
**11:2–3** Ex 3:21–22;    **11:8** Ex 12:31–33.
    12:35–36.    **12:2–20** Lv 23:5–8; Nm 9:2–5;
**11:4** Ex 12:12.      28:16–25; Dt 16:1–8.

with its nearest neighbor will procure one, and apportion the lamb's cost† in proportion to the number of persons, according to what each household consumes. ⁵Your lamb must be a year-old male and without blemish. You may take it from either the sheep or the goats. ⁶You will keep it until the fourteenth day of this month, and then, with the whole community of Israel assembled, it will be slaughtered during the evening twilight. ⁷They will take some of its blood and apply it to the two doorposts and the lintel of the houses in which they eat it. ⁸They will consume its meat that same night, eating it roasted with unleavened bread and bitter herbs. ⁹Do not eat any of it raw or even boiled in water, but roasted, with its head and shanks and inner organs. ¹⁰You must not keep any of it beyond the morning; whatever is left over in the morning must be burned up. ¹¹This is how you are to eat it: with your loins girt, sandals on your feet and your staff in hand, you will eat it in a hurry. It is the LORD's Passover. ¹²For on this same night I will go through Egypt, striking down every firstborn in the land, human being and beast alike, and executing judgment on all the gods of Egypt—I, the LORD!* ¹³But for you the blood will mark the houses where you are. Seeing the blood, I will pass over you; thereby, when I strike the land of Egypt, no destructive blow will come upon you.*

¹⁴This day will be a day of remembrance for you, which your future generations will celebrate with pilgrimage to the LORD; you will celebrate it as a statute forever. ¹⁵For seven days you must eat unleavened bread. From the very first day you will have your houses clear of all leaven. For whoever eats leavened bread from the first day to the seventh will be cut off† from Israel. ¹⁶On the first day you will hold a sacred assembly, and likewise on the seventh. On these days no sort of work shall be done, except to prepare the food that everyone needs. ¹⁷Keep, then, the custom of the unleavened bread,* since it was on this very day that I brought your armies out of the land of Egypt. You must observe this day throughout your generations as a statute forever. ¹⁸From the evening of the fourteenth day of the first month until the evening of the twenty-first day of this month you will eat unleavened bread. ¹⁹For seven days no leaven may be found in your houses; for anyone, a resident alien or a native, who eats leavened food will be cut off from the community of Israel. ²⁰You shall eat nothing leavened; wherever you dwell you may eat only unleavened bread.

**Promulgation of the Passover.** ²¹Moses summoned all the elders of Israel and said to them, "Go and procure lambs for your families, and slaughter the Passover victims. ²²* Then take a bunch of hyssop,† and dipping it in the blood that is in the basin, apply some of this blood to the lintel and the two doorposts. And none of you shall go outdoors until morning. ²³For when the LORD goes by to strike down the Egyptians, seeing the blood on the lintel and the two doorposts, the LORD will pass over that door and not let the destroyer come into your houses to strike you down.

²⁴"You will keep this practice forever as a statute for yourselves and your descendants. ²⁵Thus, when you have entered the land which the LORD will give you as he promised, you must observe this rite. ²⁶* When your children ask you, 'What does this rite of yours mean?' ²⁷you will reply, 'It is the Passover sacrifice for the LORD, who passed over the houses of the Israelites in Egypt; when he struck down the Egyptians, he delivered our houses.'"

Then the people knelt and bowed down, ²⁸and the Israelites went and did exactly as the LORD had commanded Moses and Aaron.

**Death of the Firstborn.** ²⁹* And so at midnight the LORD struck down every firstborn in the land of Egypt, from the firstborn of Pharaoh sitting on his throne to the firstborn of the prisoner in the dungeon, as well as all the firstborn of the animals. ³⁰Pharaoh arose in the night, he and all his servants and all

---

† **12:4** *The lamb's cost:* some render the Hebrew, "reckon for the lamb the number of persons required to eat it." Cf. v. 10.

**12:15** *Cut off:* a common Priestly term, not easily reduced to a simple English equivalent, since its usage appears to involve a number of associated punishments, some or all of which may come into play in any instance of the term's use. These included the excommunication of the offender from the Israelite community, the premature death of the offender, the eventual eradication of the offender's posterity, and finally the loss by the offender of all ancestral holdings.

**12:22** *Hyssop:* a plant with many small woody branches that was convenient for a sprinkling rite.

*
| 12:12 Nm 33:4. | Dt 6:20–25. |
| 12:13 Heb 11:28. | 12:29–30 Ex 11:4–6; Nm |
| 12:17 Ex 13:3. | 33:4; Ps 78:51; |
| 12:22–23 Ex 12:7, 13. | 105:36; 136:10; Wis |
| 12:26–27 Ex 13:8, 14–15; | 18:10–16. |

the Egyptians; and there was loud wailing throughout Egypt, for there was not a house without its dead.

**Permission to Depart.** ³¹During the night Pharaoh summoned Moses and Aaron and said, "Leave my people at once, you and the Israelites! Go and serve the LORD as you said. ³²Take your flocks, too, and your herds, as you said, and go; and bless me, too!"†

³³The Egyptians, in a hurry to send them away from the land, urged the people on, for they said, "All of us will die!" ³⁴The people, therefore, took their dough before it was leavened, in their kneading bowls wrapped in their cloaks on their shoulders. ³⁵* And the Israelites did as Moses had commanded: they asked the Egyptians for articles of silver and gold and for clothing. ³⁶Indeed the LORD had made the Egyptians so well-disposed toward the people that they let them have whatever they asked for. And so they despoiled the Egyptians.

**Departure from Egypt.** ³⁷The Israelites set out from Rameses* for Succoth, about six hundred thousand men on foot, not counting the children. ³⁸A crowd of mixed ancestry† also went up with them, with livestock in great abundance, both flocks and herds. ³⁹The dough they had brought out of Egypt they baked into unleavened loaves. It was not leavened, because they had been driven out of Egypt and could not wait. They did not even prepare food for the journey.

⁴⁰The time the Israelites had stayed in Egypt† was four hundred and thirty years.* ⁴¹At the end of four hundred and thirty years, on this very date, all the armies of the LORD left the land of Egypt. ⁴²This was a night of vigil for the LORD, when he brought them out of the land of Egypt; so on this night all Israelites must keep a vigil for the LORD throughout their generations.

**Law of the Passover.** ⁴³The LORD said to Moses and Aaron: This is the Passover statute. No foreigner may eat of it. ⁴⁴However, every slave bought for money you will circumcise; then he may eat of it. ⁴⁵But no tenant or hired worker may eat of it. ⁴⁶It must be eaten in one house; you may not take any of its meat outside the house.* You shall not break any of its bones.† ⁴⁷The whole community of Israel must celebrate this feast. ⁴⁸If any alien* residing among you would celebrate the Passover for the LORD, all his males must be circumcised, and then he may join in its celebration just like the natives. But no one who is uncircumcised may eat of it. ⁴⁹There will be one law† for the native and for the alien residing among you.

⁵⁰All the Israelites did exactly as the LORD had commanded Moses and Aaron. ⁵¹On that same day the LORD brought the Israelites out of the land of Egypt company by company.

**13** **Consecration of Firstborn.** ¹The LORD spoke to Moses and said: ²Consecrate to me every firstborn; whatever opens the womb among the Israelites,* whether of human being or beast, belongs to me.

³* Moses said to the people, "Remember this day on which you came out of Egypt, out of a house of slavery. For it was with a strong hand that the LORD brought you out from there. Nothing made with leaven may be eaten. ⁴This day on which you are going out is in the month of Abib.† ⁵Therefore, when the LORD, your God, has brought you into the land of the Canaanites, the Hittites, the Amorites, the Perrizites, the Girgashites, the Hivites, and the Jebusites, which he swore to your ancestors to give you, a land flowing with milk and honey, you will perform the following service†

---

**12:32** *Bless me, too*: in a final and humiliating admission of defeat, once again Pharaoh asks Moses to intercede for him (cf. 8:24). However, Pharaoh may be speaking sarcastically.

**12:38** *Mixed ancestry*: not simply descendants of Jacob; cf. Nm 11:4; Lv 24:10–11.

**12:40** *In Egypt*: according to the Septuagint and the Samaritan Pentateuch "in Canaan and Egypt," thus reckoning from the time of Abraham. Cf. Gal 3:17.

**12:46** *You shall not break any of its bones*: the application of these words to Jesus on the cross (Jn 19:36) sees the Paschal lamb as a prophetic type of Christ, sacrificed to free men and women from the bondage of sin. Cf. also 1 Cor 5:7; 1 Pt 1:19.

**12:49** *One law*: the first appearance of the word torah, traditionally translated as "law," though it can have the broader meaning of "teaching" or "instruction." Elsewhere, too, it is said

that the "alien" is to be accorded the same treatment as the Israelite (e.g., Lv 19:34).

**13:4** *Abib*: lit., "ear (of grain)," the old Canaanite name for this month; Israel later called it "Nisan." It was the first month in their liturgical calendar (cf. Ex 12:2).

**13:5** *The following service*: the celebration of the feast of Unleavened Bread now constitutes the Israelites' service, in contrast to the "service" they performed for Pharaoh as his slaves.

---

12:35–36 Ex 3:21–22; 11:2–3; Ps 105:37–38.
12:37 Nm 33:3–5.
12:40 Gn 15:13; Acts 7:6; Gal 3:17.
12:46 Nm 9:12; Jn 19:36.
12:48 Nm 9:14.
13:2 Ex 13:12–15.
13:3–10 Ex 12:2–20.

in this month. ⁶ For seven days you will eat un-leavened bread, and the seventh day will also be a festival to the LORD. ⁷ Unleavened bread may be eaten during the seven days, but noth-ing leavened and no leaven may be found in your possession in all your territory. ⁸ And on that day you will explain to your son, 'This is because of what the LORD did for me when I came out of Egypt.' ⁹ It will be like a sign† on your hand and a reminder on your forehead,* so that the teaching of the LORD will be on your lips: with a strong hand the LORD brought you out of Egypt. ¹⁰ You will keep this statute at its appointed time from year to year.

¹¹ "When the LORD, your God, has brought you into the land of the Canaanites, just as he swore to you and your ancestors, and gives it to you, ¹²* you will dedicate to the LORD every newborn that opens the womb; and every first-born male of your animals will belong to the LORD. ¹³ Every firstborn of a donkey you will ransom with a sheep. If you do not ransom it, you will break its neck. Every human first-born of your sons you must ransom. ¹⁴ And when your son asks you later on, 'What does this mean?' you will tell him, 'With a strong hand the LORD brought us out of Egypt, out of a house of slavery. ¹⁵ When Pharaoh stub-bornly refused to let us go, the LORD killed ev-ery firstborn in the land of Egypt, the firstborn of human being and beast alike. That is why I sacrifice to the LORD every male that opens the womb, and why I ransom every firstborn of my sons.' ¹⁶ It will be like a sign on your hand and a band on your forehead that with a strong hand the LORD brought us out of Egypt."*

## IV. THE DELIVERANCE OF THE ISRAELITES FROM PHARAOH AND VICTORY AT THE SEA

**Toward the Red Sea.** ¹⁷ Now, when Pharaoh let the people go, God did not lead them by way of the Philistines' land,† though this was the nearest; for God said: If the people see that they have to fight, they might change their minds and return to Egypt. ¹⁸ Instead, God rerouted them toward the Red Sea by way of the wilderness road, and the Israelites went up out of the land of Egypt arrayed for battle. ¹⁹ Moses also took Joseph's bones* with him, for Joseph had made the Israelites take a sol-emn oath, saying, "God will surely take care of you, and you must bring my bones up with you from here."

²⁰ Setting out from Succoth, they camped at Etham* near the edge of the wilderness. ²¹* The LORD preceded them, in the day-time by means of a column of cloud to show them the way, and at night by means of a column of fire† to give them light. Thus they could travel both day and night. ²² Neither the column of cloud by day nor the column of fire by night ever left its place in front of the people.

**14** ¹ Then the LORD spoke to Moses: ² Speak to the Israelites: Let them turn about and camp before Pi-hahiroth, between Migdol and the sea.* Camp in front of Baal-zephon,† just opposite, by the sea. ³ Pharaoh will then say, "The Israelites are wandering about aimlessly in the land. The wilderness has closed in on them." ⁴ I will so harden Pharaoh's heart that he will pursue them. Thus I will receive glory through Pharaoh and all his army, and the Egyptians will know that I am the LORD.

This the Israelites did. ⁵* When it was re-ported to the king of Egypt that the people had fled, Pharaoh and his servants had a change of heart about the people. "What in the world have we done!" they said. "We have released Israel from our service!" ⁶ So Pharaoh harnessed his chariots and took his army with him. ⁷ He took six hundred select chariots and

---

**13:9** *Sign:* while here observance of the feast of Unleavened Bread is likened only metaphorically to a physical sign of one's piety that can be worn as a kind of badge in commemoration of the ex-odus, from ancient times Jews have seen in this verse also the basis for the wearing of phylacteries. These are small receptacles for cop-ies of biblical verses which Jewish men bind to the arms and fore-head as a kind of mnemonic device for the observance of the Law.

**13:17** *By way of the Philistines' land:* the most direct route from Egypt to Palestine, along the shore of the Mediterranean.

**13:21** *A column of cloud...a column of fire:* probably one and the same extraordinary phenomenon, a central nucleus of fire surrounded by smoke; only at night was its luminous nature visible; cf. 40:38.

**14:2** *Pi-hahiroth...Migdol...Baal-zephon:* these places have not been definitively identified. Even the relative position of Pi-hahiroth and Baal-zephon is not clear; perhaps the former was on the west shore of the sea, where the Israelites were, and the latter on the opposite shore.

**13:9** Ex 13:16; Dt 6:8; 11:18.
**13:12–15** Ex 13:2; 22:28–29; 34:19–20; Nm 3:12–13; 8:16–17; 18:15; Dt 15:19.
**13:16** Ex 13:9.
**13:19** Gn 50:25; Jos 24:32.
**13:20** Nm 33:6.
**13:21–22** Ex 40:38; Nm 9:15–22; Dt 1:33; Neh 9:19; Ps 78:14; 105:39; Wis 10:17.
**14:2** Nm 33:7–8.
**14:5–8** Wis 19:3; 1 Mc 4:9.

EX

all the chariots of Egypt, with officers† on all of them. 8The Lord hardened the heart of Pharaoh, king of Egypt, so that he pursued the Israelites while they were going out in triumph. 9The Egyptians pursued them—all Pharaoh's horses, his chariots, his horsemen,† and his army—and caught up with them as they lay encamped by the sea, at Pi-hahiroth, in front of Baal-zephon.

**Crossing the Red Sea.** 10Now Pharaoh was near when the Israelites looked up and saw that the Egyptians had set out after them. Greatly frightened, the Israelites cried out to the Lord. 11To Moses they said, "Were there no burial places in Egypt that you brought us to die in the wilderness? What have you done to us, bringing us out of Egypt? 12Did we not tell you this in Egypt, when we said, 'Leave us alone that we may serve the Egyptians'? Far better for us to serve the Egyptians than to die in the wilderness." 13But Moses answered the people, "Do not fear! Stand your ground and see the victory the Lord will win for you today. For these Egyptians whom you see today you will never see again. 14The Lord will fight for you; you have only to keep still."

15Then the Lord said to Moses: Why are you crying out to me? Tell the Israelites to set out. 16And you, lift up your staff and stretch out your hand over the sea, and split it in two, that the Israelites may pass through the sea on dry land. 17But I will harden the hearts of the Egyptians so that they will go in after them, and I will receive glory through Pharaoh and all his army, his chariots and his horsemen. 18The Egyptians will know that I am the Lord, when I receive glory through Pharaoh, his chariots, and his horsemen.

19The angel of God,† who had been leading Israel's army, now moved and went around behind them. And the column of cloud, moving

from in front of them, took up its place behind them, 20so that it came between the Egyptian army and that of Israel. And when it became dark, the cloud illumined the night; and so the rival camps did not come any closer together all night long.† 21*Then Moses stretched out his hand over the sea; and the Lord drove back the sea with a strong east wind all night long and turned the sea into dry ground. The waters were split, 22so that the Israelites entered into the midst of the sea on dry land, with the water as a wall to their right and to their left.

**Rout of the Egyptians.** 23The Egyptians followed in pursuit after them—all Pharaoh's horses and chariots and horsemen—into the midst of the sea. 24But during the watch just before dawn, the Lord looked down from a column of fiery cloud upon the Egyptian army and threw it into a panic; 25and he so clogged their chariot wheels that they could drive only with difficulty. With that the Egyptians said, "Let us flee from Israel, because the Lord is fighting for them against Egypt."

26Then the Lord spoke to Moses: Stretch out your hand over the sea, that the water may flow back upon the Egyptians, upon their chariots and their horsemen. 27So Moses stretched out his hand over the sea, and at daybreak the sea returned to its normal flow. The Egyptians were fleeing head on toward it when the Lord cast the Egyptians into the midst of the sea. 28*As the water flowed back, it covered the chariots and the horsemen. Of all Pharaoh's army which had followed the Israelites into the sea, not even one escaped. 29But the Israelites had walked on dry land through the midst of the sea, with the water as a wall to their right and to their left. 30Thus the Lord saved Israel on that day from the power of Egypt. When Israel saw the Egyptians lying dead on the seashore 31and saw the great

---

**14:7** *Officers:* cf. 1 Kgs 9:22; Ez 23:15. The Hebrew word *shalish*, rendered in 1 Kgs 9:22 as "adjutant," has yet to have its meaning convincingly established. Given the very possible etymological connection with the number "three," others suggest the translation "three-man crew" or, less likely, the "third man in the chariot" although Egyptian chariots carried two-man crews. The author of the text may have been describing the chariots of his experience without direct historical knowledge of Egyptian ways.
**14:9** *Horsemen:* the usage here may be anachronistic, since horsemen, or cavalry, play a part in warfare only at the end of the second millennium B.C.
**14:19** *Angel of God:* Hebrew *mal'ak ha'elohim* (Septuagint *ho angelos tou theou*) here refers not to an independent spiritual

being but to God's power at work in the world; corresponding to the column of cloud/fire, the expression more clearly preserves a sense of distance between God and God's creatures. The two halves of the verse are parallel and may come from different narrative sources.
**14:20** The reading of the Hebrew text here is uncertain. The image is of a darkly glowing storm cloud, ominously bright, keeping the two camps apart.

**14:21–22** Ex 15:19; Ps 66:6; 78:13; 136:13–14; Wis 10:18; 19:7–8; Is 63:12–13; Heb 11:29. **14:28–29** Dt 11:4; Ps 106:11.

power that the LORD had shown against Egypt, the people feared the LORD. They believed in the LORD* and in Moses his servant.

# 15

¹Then Moses and the Israelites sang* this song to the LORD:†

I will sing to the LORD, for he is
　　gloriously triumphant;
　　horse and chariot he has cast into the
　　sea.
² My strength and my refuge is the LORD,
　　and he has become my savior.*
　This is my God, I praise him;
　　the God of my father, I extol him.
³ The LORD is a warrior,
　　LORD is his name!
⁴ Pharaoh's chariots and army he hurled
　　into the sea;
　　the elite of his officers were drowned
　　in the Red Sea.†
⁵ The flood waters covered them,
　　they sank into the depths like a stone.*
⁶ Your right hand, O LORD, magnificent in
　　power,
　　your right hand, O LORD, shattered the
　　enemy.
⁷ In your great majesty you overthrew
　　your adversaries;
　　you loosed your wrath to consume
　　them like stubble.
⁸ At the blast of your nostrils the waters
　　piled up,
　　the flowing waters stood like a
　　mound,
　　the flood waters foamed in the midst
　　of the sea.

⁹ The enemy boasted, "I will pursue and
　　overtake them;
　　I will divide the spoils and have my
　　fill of them;
　　I will draw my sword; my hand will
　　despoil them!"
¹⁰ When you blew with your breath, the
　　sea covered them;
　　like lead they sank in the mighty
　　waters.
¹¹ Who is like you among the gods,
　　O LORD?
　　Who is like you, magnificent among
　　the holy ones?
　Awe-inspiring in deeds of renown,
　　worker of wonders,
¹² when you stretched out your right
　　hand, the earth swallowed them!
¹³ In your love† you led the people you
　　redeemed;
　　in your strength you guided them to
　　your holy dwelling.
¹⁴ The peoples heard and quaked;
　　anguish gripped the dwellers in
　　Philistia.
¹⁵ Then were the chieftains of Edom
　　dismayed,
　　the nobles of Moab seized by
　　trembling;
　All the inhabitants of Canaan melted
　　away;
¹⁶* terror and dread fell upon them.
　By the might of your arm they became
　　silent like stone,
　　while your people, LORD, passed over,
　　while the people whom you created
　　passed over.†

---

**15:1–21** This poem, regarded by many scholars as one of the oldest compositions in the Bible, was once an independent work. It has been inserted at this important juncture in the large narrative of Exodus to celebrate God's saving power, having miraculously delivered the people from their enemies, and ultimately leading them to the promised land.

Although the victory it describes over the Egyptians at the sea bears a superficial resemblance in v. 8 to the preceding depiction of the water standing like a wall (14:22), the poem (as opposed to the following prose verse, v. 19) suggests a different version of the victory at sea than that found in chap. 14. There is no splitting of the sea in an act reminiscent of the Lord's combat at creation with the sea monsters Rahab and Leviathan (Jb 9:13; 26:12; Ps 74:13–14; 89:11; Is 51:9–10); nor is there mention of an east wind driving the waters back so that the Israelites can cross. In this version it is by means of a storm at sea, caused by a ferocious blast from his nostrils, that the Lord achieves a decisive victory against Pharaoh and his army (vv. 1–12). The second half of the poem (vv. 13–18) describes God's guidance into the promised land.

**15:4** *Red Sea*: the traditional translation of the Hebrew *yam*

*suph*, which actually means "Sea of Reeds" or "reedy sea." The location is uncertain, though in view of the route taken by the Israelites from Egypt to Sinai, it could not have been the Red Sea, which is too far south. It was probably a smaller body of water south of the Gulf of Suez. The term occurs also in Exodus at 10:19; 13:18; and 23:31.

**15:13** *Love*: the very important Hebrew term *hesed* carries a variety of nuances depending on context: love, kindness, faithfulness. It is often rendered "steadfast love." It implies a relationship that generates an obligation and therefore is at home in a covenant context. Cf. 20:6.

**15:16** *Passed over*: an allusion to the crossing of the Jordan River (cf. Jos 3–5), written as if the entry into the promised land had already occurred. This verse suggests that at one time there was a ritual enactment of the conquest at a shrine near the Jordan River which included also a celebration of the victory at the sea.

---

**14:31** Ex 4:31; Ps 106:12;
　Wis 10:20.
**15:1** Ex 15:21.

**15:2** Ps 118:14; Is 12:2.
**15:5** Neh 9:11.
**15:16–17** Ps 78:53–55.

<sup>17</sup> You brought them in, you planted them
    on the mountain that is your own—
The place you made the base of your
    throne, L ORD,
    the sanctuary, L ORD, your hands
        established.
<sup>18</sup> May the L ORD reign forever and ever!

<sup>19</sup> When Pharaoh's horses and chariots and
horsemen entered the sea, the L ORD made the
waters of the sea flow back upon them, though
the Israelites walked on dry land through the
midst of the sea.* <sup>20</sup> Then the prophet Miriam,
Aaron's sister, took a tambourine in her hand,
while all the women went out after her with
tambourines, dancing; <sup>21</sup> and she responded†
to them:

Sing to the L ORD, for he is gloriously
    triumphant;
    horse and chariot he has cast into the
        sea.*

## V. THE JOURNEY IN THE WILDERNESS TO SINAI

**At Marah and Elim.** <sup>22</sup>* Then Moses led Israel
forward from the Red Sea,† and they marched
out to the wilderness of Shur. After traveling
for three days through the wilderness without
finding water, <sup>23</sup> they arrived at Marah, where
they could not drink its water, because it was
too bitter. Hence this place was called Marah.
<sup>24</sup> As the people grumbled against Moses, say-
ing, "What are we to drink?" <sup>25</sup> he cried out to
the L ORD, who pointed out to him a piece of
wood. When he threw it into the water, the
water became fresh.*

It was here that God, in making statutes
and ordinances for them, put them to the test.
<sup>26</sup> He said: If you listen closely to the voice of
the L ORD, your God, and do what is right in his
eyes: if you heed his commandments and keep

all his statutes, I will not afflict you with any
of the diseases with which I afflicted the Egyptians;* for I, the L ORD, am your healer.
<sup>27</sup> Then they came to Elim, where there were
twelve springs of water and seventy palm trees,
and they camped there near the water.*

# 16 **The Wilderness of Sin.** <sup>1</sup> Having set out
from Elim, the whole Israelite commu-
nity came into the wilderness of Sin, which is
between Elim and Sinai, on the fifteenth day
of the second month† after their departure
from the land of Egypt. <sup>2</sup> Here in the wilderness the whole Israelite community grumbled
against Moses and Aaron. <sup>3</sup> The Israelites said
to them, "If only we had died at the L ORD's
hand in the land of Egypt, as we sat by our kettles of meat and ate our fill of bread! But you
have led us into this wilderness to make this
whole assembly die of famine!"

**The Quail and the Manna.** <sup>4</sup> Then the L ORD
said to Moses:* I am going to rain down bread
from heaven† for you. Each day the people are
to go out and gather their daily portion; thus
will I test them, to see whether they follow my
instructions or not. <sup>5</sup> On the sixth day, however, when they prepare what they bring in,
let it be twice as much as they gather on the
other days. <sup>6</sup> So Moses and Aaron told all the
Israelites,* "At evening you will know that it
was the L ORD who brought you out of the land
of Egypt; <sup>7</sup> and in the morning you will see the
glory of the L ORD, when he hears your grumbling against him. But who are we that you
should grumble against us?" <sup>8</sup> And Moses said,
"When the L ORD gives you meat to eat in the
evening and in the morning your fill of bread,
and hears the grumbling you utter against
him, who then are we? Your grumbling is not
against us, but against the L ORD."

<sup>9</sup> Then Moses said to Aaron, "Tell the whole
Israelite community: Approach the L ORD, for

---

**15:21** *She responded*: Miriam's refrain echoes the first verse
of this song and was probably sung as an antiphon after each
verse.
**15:22** *Red Sea*: see note on Ex 15:4.
**16:1** *On the fifteenth day of the second month*: just one full
month after their departure from Egypt. Cf. 12:2, 51; Nm 33:3–4.
The Septuagint takes the date to be the beginning of the Israelites' grumbling.
**16:4** *Bread from heaven*: as a gift from God, the manna is
said to come down from the sky. Cf. Ps 78:24–25; Wis 16:20.
Perhaps it was similar to a natural substance that is still found in
small quantities on the Sinai peninsula—probably the honey-like
resin from the tamarisk tree—but here it is, at least in part, clearly

an extraordinary sign of God's providence. With reference to Jn
6:32, 49–52, the Christian tradition has regarded the manna as
a type of the Eucharist. *Test*: as the text stands, it seems to leave
open the question whether the test concerns trusting in God to
provide them with the daily gift of food or observing the sabbath
instructions.

**15:19** Ex 14:21–29.                **15:27** Nm 33:9.
**15:21** Ex 15:1.                     **16:4** Ps 78:24–25; 105:40;
**15:22–23** Nm 33:8.                     Jn 6:31–32; 1 Cor
**15:25** Sir 38:5.                        10:3.
**15:26** Dt 7:15.                     **16:6–7** Ex 16:12.

he has heard your grumbling." <sup>10</sup> But while Aaron was speaking to the whole Israelite community, they turned in the direction of the wilderness, and there the glory of the LORD appeared in the cloud! <sup>11</sup> The LORD said to Moses: <sup>12</sup> I have heard the grumbling of the Israelites. Tell them: In the evening twilight you will eat meat, and in the morning you will have your fill of bread, and then you will know that I, the LORD, am your God.

<sup>13</sup> In the evening, quail* came up and covered the camp. In the morning there was a layer of dew all about the camp, <sup>14</sup> and when the layer of dew evaporated, fine flakes were on the surface of the wilderness, fine flakes like hoarfrost on the ground. <sup>15</sup> On seeing it, the Israelites asked one another, "What is this?"† for they did not know what it was. But Moses told them, "It is the bread which the LORD has given you to eat.*

**Regulations Regarding the Manna.** <sup>16</sup> "Now, this is what the LORD has commanded. Gather as much of it as each needs to eat, an omer† for each person for as many of you as there are, each of you providing for those in your own tent." <sup>17</sup> The Israelites did so. Some gathered a large and some a small amount. <sup>18</sup>† But when they measured it out by the omer, the one who had gathered a large amount did not have too much, and the one who had gathered a small amount did not have too little. They gathered as much as each needed to eat. <sup>19</sup> Moses said to them, "Let no one leave any of it over until morning." <sup>20</sup> But they did not listen to Moses, and some kept a part of it over until morning, and it became wormy and stank. Therefore Moses was angry with them.

<sup>21</sup> Morning after morning they gathered it, as much as each needed to eat; but when the sun grew hot, it melted away. <sup>22</sup> On the sixth day they gathered twice as much food, two omers for each person. When all the leaders of the community came and reported this to Moses, <sup>23</sup> he told them, "That is what the LORD

has prescribed. Tomorrow is a day of rest, a holy sabbath of the LORD. Whatever you want to bake, bake; whatever you want to boil, boil; but whatever is left put away and keep until the morning." <sup>24</sup> When they put it away until the morning, as Moses commanded, it did not stink nor were there worms in it. <sup>25</sup> Moses then said, "Eat it today, for today is the sabbath of the LORD. Today you will not find any in the field. <sup>26</sup> Six days you will gather it, but on the seventh day, the sabbath, it will not be there." <sup>27</sup> Still, on the seventh day some of the people went out to gather it, but they did not find any. <sup>28</sup> Then the LORD said to Moses: How long will you refuse to keep my commandments and my instructions? <sup>29</sup> Take note! The LORD has given you the sabbath. That is why on the sixth day he gives you food for two days. Each of you stay where you are and let no one go out on the seventh day. <sup>30</sup> After that the people rested on the seventh day.

<sup>31</sup> The house of Israel named this food manna.* It was like coriander seed,† white, and it tasted like wafers made with honey.

<sup>32</sup> Moses said, "This is what the LORD has commanded. Keep a full omer of it for your future generations, so that they may see the food I gave you to eat in the wilderness when I brought you out of the land of Egypt." <sup>33</sup> Moses then told Aaron, "Take a jar† and put a full omer of manna in it. Then place it before the LORD to keep it for your future generations." <sup>34</sup> As the LORD had commanded Moses, Aaron placed it in front of the covenant† to keep it.

<sup>35</sup> The Israelites ate the manna for forty years, until they came to settled land;* they ate the manna until they came to the borders of Canaan. <sup>36</sup> (An omer is one tenth of an ephah.)†

# 17 **Water from the Rock.** <sup>1</sup> From the wilderness of Sin the whole Israelite community journeyed by stages, as the LORD directed, and encamped at Rephidim.*

But there was no water for the people to

---

† **16:15** *What is this*: the Hebrew *man hu* is thus rendered by the ancient versions, which understood the phrase as a popular etymology of the Hebrew word *man*, "manna"; but some render *man hu*, "This is manna."

**16:16** *Omer*: a dry measure of approximately two quarts.

**16:18** Paul cites this passage as an example of equitable sharing (2 Cor 8:15).

**16:31** *Coriander seed*: small, round, aromatic seeds of bright brown color; the comparison, therefore, refers merely to the size and shape, not to the taste or color of the manna.

**16:33** *Jar*: according to the Greek translation, which is followed in Heb 9:4, this was a golden vessel.

**16:34** *The covenant*: i.e., the ark of the covenant, in which were placed the two tablets of the Ten Commandments. Cf. 25:16, 21–22.

**16:36** *Omer...ephah*: see note on Is 5:10.

**16:13** Nm 11:31; Ps 78:27–28.
**16:15** Dt 8:3.
**16:31** Nm 11:7.
**16:35** Jos 5:12.
**17:1** Nm 33:12–14.

drink, 2* and so they quarreled with Moses and said, "Give us water to drink." Moses replied to them, "Why do you quarrel with me? Why do you put the LORD to a test?" 3 Here, then, in their thirst for water, the people grumbled against Moses, saying, "Why then did you bring us up out of Egypt? To have us die of thirst with our children and our livestock?" 4 So Moses cried out to the LORD, "What shall I do with this people? A little more and they will stone me!" 5 The LORD answered Moses: Go on ahead of the people, and take along with you some of the elders of Israel, holding in your hand, as you go, the staff with which you struck the Nile. 6 I will be standing there in front of you on the rock in Horeb. Strike the rock, and the water will flow from it for the people to drink.* Moses did this, in the sight of the elders of Israel. 7 The place was named Massah and Meribah,† because the Israelites quarreled there and tested the LORD, saying, "Is the LORD in our midst or not?"*

**Battle with Amalek.** 8 Then Amalek† came and waged war against Israel in Rephidim.* 9 So Moses said to Joshua, "Choose some men for us, and tomorrow go out and engage Amalek in battle. I will be standing on top of the hill with the staff of God in my hand." 10 Joshua did as Moses told him: he engaged Amalek in battle while Moses, Aaron, and Hur climbed to the top of the hill. 11 As long as Moses kept his hands raised up, Israel had the better of the fight, but when he let his hands rest, Amalek had the better of the fight. 12 Moses' hands, however, grew tired; so they took a rock and put it under him and he sat on it. Meanwhile Aaron and Hur supported his hands, one on one side and one on the other, so that his hands remained steady until sunset. 13 And Joshua defeated Amalek and his people with the sword.

14 Then the LORD said to Moses: Write this down in a book as something to be remembered, and recite it to Joshua:* I will completely blot out the memory of Amalek from under the heavens. 15 Moses built an altar there, which he named Yahweh-nissi;† 16 for he said, "Take up the banner of the LORD!† The LORD has a war against Amalek through the ages."

**18 Meeting with Jethro.** 1 Now Moses' father-in-law Jethro, the priest of Midian, heard of all that God had done for Moses and for his people Israel: how the LORD had brought Israel out of Egypt. 2 So his father-in-law Jethro took along Zipporah, Moses' wife—now this was after Moses had sent her back—† 3 and her two sons. One of these was named Gershom;* for he said, "I am a resident alien in a foreign land." 4 The other was named Eliezer; for he said, "The God of my father is my help; he has rescued me from Pharaoh's sword." 5 Together with Moses' wife and sons, then, his father-in-law Jethro came to him in the wilderness where he was encamped at the mountain of God,† 6 and he sent word to Moses, "I, your father-in-law Jethro, am coming to you, along with your wife and her two sons."

7 Moses went out to meet his father-in-law, bowed down, and then kissed him. Having greeted each other, they went into the tent. 8 Moses then told his father-in-law of all that the LORD had done to Pharaoh and the Egyptians for the sake of Israel, and of all the hardships that had beset them on their journey, and how the LORD had rescued them. 9 Jethro rejoiced over all the goodness that the LORD had shown Israel in rescuing them from the power of the Egyptians. 10 "Blessed be the LORD," he said, "who has rescued you from the power of the Egyptians and of Pharaoh. 11 Now I know that the LORD is greater than

---

**17:7** *Massah…Meribah*: Hebrew words meaning, respectively, "the place of the test" and "the place of strife, of quarreling."
**17:8** *Amalek*: the Amalekites appear in the Bible as early inhabitants of southern Palestine and the Sinai peninsula prior to the appearance of the Israelites in the region. Cf. Nm 24:20.
**17:15** *Yahweh-nissi*: meaning, "the Lord is my banner."
**17:16** *Take up the banner of the LORD*: lit., "a hand on the LORD's banner," apparently a war cry for the Israelite troops in the conduct of Holy War; however, the Hebrew text is difficult to interpret.
**18:2** *Moses had sent her back*: a later gloss which attempts to harmonize Zipporah's presence with Jethro here in this story and the account of Moses' return to Egypt with Zipporah in 4:20.
**18:5** The allusion to meeting Moses encamped at the moun-

tain of God, prior to the arrival of the Israelites at Sinai in chap. 19, might well suggest a different narrative context for this story from an earlier stage of the biblical tradition's development. It is noteworthy that immediately after the Sinai pericope (Ex 19:1–Nm 10:28), recounting the theophany at Sinai and the giving of the law, the narrative of Israel's march through the wilderness resumes with an apparent doublet of the visit by Moses' father-in-law (Nm 10:29–32).

---

**17:2–7** Nm 20:2–13.
**17:5–6** Dt 8:15; Ps 78:15–16; 105:41; Wis 11:4; Is 43:20; 48:21.
**17:7** Ps 95:8–9.
**17:8** Dt 25:17–19; 1 Sm 15:2.
**17:14** Nm 24:20; 1 Sm 15:3, 20.
**18:3** Ex 2:22.

all the gods; for he rescued the people from the power of the Egyptians when they treated them arrogantly." [12] Then Jethro, the father-in-law of Moses, brought a burnt offering† and sacrifices for God, and Aaron came with all the elders of Israel to share with Moses' father-in-law in the meal before God.

**Appointment of Minor Judges.** [13] The next day Moses sat in judgment for the people, while they stood around him from morning until evening. [14] When Moses' father-in-law saw all that he was doing for the people, he asked, "What is this business that you are conducting for the people? Why do you sit alone while all the people have to stand about you from morning till evening?" [15] Moses answered his father-in-law, "The people come to me to consult God. [16] Whenever they have a disagreement, they come to me to have me settle the matter between them and make known to them God's statutes and instructions."

[17] "What you are doing is not wise," Moses' father-in-law replied. [18] "You will surely wear yourself out, both you and these people with you. The task is too heavy for you;* you cannot do it alone. [19]† Now, listen to me, and I will give you some advice, and may God be with you. Act as the people's representative before God, and bring their disputes to God. [20] Enlighten them in regard to the statutes and instructions, showing them how they are to conduct themselves and what they are to do. [21] But you should also look among all the people for able and God-fearing men, trustworthy men who hate dishonest gain, and set them over the people as commanders of thousands, of hundreds, of fifties, and of tens.* [22] Let these render decisions for the people in all routine cases. Every important case they should refer to you, but every lesser case they can settle themselves. Lighten your burden by letting them bear it with you! [23] If you do this, and God so commands you,† you will be able to stand the strain, and all these people, too, will go home content."

[24] Moses listened to his father-in-law and did all that he had said. [25] He picked out able men from all Israel and put them in charge of the people as commanders of thousands, of hundreds, of fifties, and of tens. [26] They rendered decisions for the people in all routine cases. The more difficult cases they referred to Moses, but all the lesser cases they settled themselves. [27] Then Moses said farewell to his father-in-law, who went off to his own country.

## VI. COVENANT AND LEGISLATION AT MOUNT SINAI

**19 Arrival at Sinai.** [1]* In the third month after the Israelites' departure from the land of Egypt, on the first day, they came to the wilderness of Sinai. [2] After they made the journey from Rephidim and entered the wilderness of Sinai, they then pitched camp in the wilderness.†

While Israel was encamped there in front of the mountain, [3] Moses went up to the mountain of God. Then the LORD called to him from the mountain, saying: This is what you will say to the house of Jacob; tell the Israelites: [4] You have seen how I treated the Egyptians and how I bore you up on eagles' wings and brought you to myself.* [5] Now, if you obey me completely and keep my covenant,† you will be my treasured possession among all peoples,* though all the earth is mine. [6] You

† **18:12** That a non-Israelite, such as Jethro, should bless Israel's God by way of acknowledging what God had done for Israel (v. 10) is not entirely surprising; but the Midianite priest's sacrifice to the God of Israel, including his presiding over a sacrificial meal with Aaron and the elders of Israel, is unusual, suggesting that he was himself already a worshiper of Yhwh, Israel's God. Note further in this connection the role Jethro takes in the following narrative (vv. 13–27) in instituting a permanent judiciary for the Israelites. *Burnt offering*: a sacrifice wholly burnt up as an offering to God.
**18:19–20** By emphasizing Moses' mediatorial role for the people before God in regard to God's statutes and instructions, this story about the institution of Israel's judiciary prepares for Moses' role in the upcoming revelation of the law at Sinai.
**18:23** *And God so commands you*: i.e., God approves.
**19:2** Apparently from a different source (P) than v. 1, which notes the date, v. 2 from the J source includes a second notice of the arrival in the wilderness of Sinai. The Israelites now will

be camped at Sinai from this point on all the way to Nm 10:10. This is a striking indication of the centrality and importance of the Sinai narrative in the overall composition of the Pentateuch.
**19:5** *Covenant*: while covenants between individuals and between nations are ubiquitous in the ancient Near East, the adaptation of this concept to express the relationship that will henceforth characterize God's relationship to Israel represents an important innovation of biblical faith. Other gods might "choose" nations to fulfill a special destiny or role in the world; but only Israel's God is bound to a people by covenant. Thereby Israel's identity as a people is put upon a foundation that does not depend upon the vicissitudes of Israelite statehood or the normal trappings of national existence. Israel will be a covenant people.

**18:18** Nm 11:14.
**18:21, 25** Dt 1:15; 16:18.
**19:1–2** Nm 33:15.
**19:4** Dt 32:11–12.
**19:5** Dt 7:6; 14:2; 26:18–19; 32:8–9.

© Dennis Kurtz

On Mount Sinai, also called Mount Horeb (Ex 3), God gives his law to Moses and, through him, the people of Israel. Above, the Sinai mountain range, located on the Sinai Peninsula in Egypt.

will be to me a kingdom of priests,† a holy nation.* That is what you must tell the Israelites. ⁷ So Moses went and summoned the elders of the people. When he set before them all that the LORD had ordered him to tell them, ⁸ all the people answered together, "Everything the LORD has said, we will do." Then Moses brought back to the LORD the response of the people.

⁹ The LORD said to Moses: I am coming to you now in a dense cloud,* so that when the people hear me speaking with you, they will also remain faithful to you.

When Moses, then, had reported the response of the people to the LORD, ¹⁰ the LORD said to Moses: Go to the people and have them sanctify themselves today and tomorrow. Have them wash their garments ¹¹ and be ready for the third day; for on the third day the LORD will come down on Mount Sinai in the sight of all the people. ¹² Set limits for the people all around,* saying: Take care not to go up the mountain, or even to touch its edge. All who touch the mountain must be put to death. ¹³ No hand shall touch them, but they must be stoned to death or killed with arrows. Whether human being or beast, they must not be allowed to live. Only when the ram's horn sounds may they go up on the mountain.† ¹⁴ Then Moses came down from the mountain to the people and had them sanctify themselves, and they washed their garments. ¹⁵ He said to the people, "Be ready for the third day. Do not approach a woman."

**The Great Theophany.** ¹⁶ * On the morning of the third day there were peals of thunder and lightning, and a heavy cloud over the mountain, and a very loud blast of the shofar,† so that all the people in the camp trembled. ¹⁷ But Moses led the people out of the camp to meet God, and they stationed themselves at

---

† **19:6** *Kingdom of priests*: inasmuch as this phrase is parallel to "holy nation," it most likely means that the whole Israelite nation is set apart from other nations and so consecrated to God, or holy, in the way priests are among the people (cf. Is 61:6; 1 Pt 2:5, 9).

**19:13** *May they go up on the mountain*: in vv. 12–13a, a later Priestly reshaping of an earlier version of the instructions governing how the people are to prepare for the encounter with God (vv. 10–11, 13b), the people are to be restrained from ascending the mountain, which is suffused with the holiness of God and

too dangerous for their approach. In the earlier version, as v. 13b suggests, the sanctified people must come near, in order to hear God speaking with Moses (v. 9) and in this way receive confirmation of his special relationship with God.

**19:16** *Shofar*: a ram's horn used like a trumpet for signaling both for liturgical and military purposes.

**19:6** 1 Pt 2:9.
**19:9** Ex 20:21; 24:15–18.
**19:12–13** Ex 34:3; Heb 12:18–19.
**19:16–19** Dt 4:10–12.

the foot of the mountain. [18] Now Mount Sinai was completely enveloped in smoke, because the LORD had come down upon it in fire. The smoke rose from it as though from a kiln, and the whole mountain trembled violently. [19] The blast of the shofar grew louder and louder, while Moses was speaking and God was answering him with thunder.

[20] † When the LORD came down upon Mount Sinai, to the top of the mountain, the LORD summoned Moses to the top of the mountain, and Moses went up. [21] Then the LORD told Moses: Go down and warn the people not to break through to the LORD in order to see him; otherwise many of them will be struck down. [22] For their part, the priests, who approach the LORD must sanctify themselves; else the LORD will break out in anger against them. [23] But Moses said to the LORD, "The people cannot go up to Mount Sinai, for you yourself warned us, saying: Set limits around the mountain to make it sacred." [24] So the LORD said to him: Go down and come up along with Aaron. But do not let the priests and the people break through to come up to the LORD; else he will break out against them." [25] So Moses went down to the people and spoke to them.

# 20 The Ten Commandments.† [1] Then God spoke all these words:

[2] * I am the LORD your God, who brought you out of the land of Egypt, * out of the house of slavery. [3] You shall not have other gods beside me. † [4] You shall not make for yourself an idol * or a likeness of anything † in the heavens above or on the earth below or in the waters beneath the earth; [5] you shall not bow down before them or serve them. * For I, the LORD, your God, am a jealous God, inflicting punishment for their ancestors' wickedness on the children of those who hate me, down to the third and fourth generation†; [6] but showing love down to the thousandth generation of those who love me and keep my commandments.

[7] You shall not invoke the name of the LORD, your God, in vain. †* For the LORD will not leave unpunished anyone who invokes his name in vain.

[8] Remember the sabbath day—keep it holy. † [9] Six days you may labor and do all your work, [10] but the seventh day is a sabbath of the LORD your God. * You shall not do any work, either you, your son or your daughter, your male or female slave, your work animal, or the resident

---

† **19:20–25** At this point the Priestly additions of vv. 12–13a are elaborated with further Priestly instructions, which include the priests' sanctifying themselves apart from the people (v. 22) and Aaron accompanying Moses to the top of the mountain (v. 24).

**20:1–17** The precise numbering and division of these precepts into "ten commandments" is somewhat uncertain. Traditionally among Catholics and Lutherans vv. 1–6 are considered as only one commandment, and v. 17 as two. The Anglican, Greek Orthodox, and Reformed churches count vv. 1–6 as two, and v. 17 as one. Cf. Dt 5:6–21. The traditional designation as "ten" is not found here but in 34:28 (and also Dt 4:13 and 10:4), where these precepts are alluded to literally as "the ten words." That they were originally written on two tablets appears in Ex 32:15–16; 34:28–29; Dt 4:13; 10:2–4.

The present form of the commands is a product of a long development, as is clear from the fact that the individual precepts vary considerably in length and from the slightly different formulation of Dt 5:6–21 (see especially vv. 12–15 and 21). Indeed they represent a mature formulation of a traditional morality. Why this specific selection of commands should be set apart is not entirely clear. None of them is unique in the Old Testament and all of the laws which follow are also from God and equally binding on the Israelites. Even so, this collection represents a privileged expression of God's moral demands on Israel and is here set apart from the others as a direct, unmediated communication of God to the Israelites and the basis of the covenant being concluded on Sinai.

**20:3** *Beside me:* this commandment is traditionally understood as an outright denial of the existence of other gods except the God of Israel; however, in the context of the more general prohibitions in vv. 4–5, v. 3 is, more precisely, God's demand for Israel's exclusive worship and allegiance.

The Hebrew phrase underlying the translation "beside me" is, nonetheless, problematic and has been variously translated, e.g., "except me," "in addition to me," "in preference to me," "in defiance of me," and "in front of me" or "before my face."

The latter translation, with its concrete, spatial nuances, has suggested to some that the prohibition once sought to exclude from the Lord's sanctuary the cult images or idols of other gods, such as the asherah, or stylized sacred tree of life, associated with the Canaanite goddess Asherah (34:13). Over the course of time, as vv. 4–5 suggest, the original scope of v. 3 was expanded.

**20:4** *Or a likeness of anything:* compare this formulation to that found in Dt 5:8, which understands this phrase and the following phrases as specifications of the prohibited idol (Hebrew *pesel*), which usually refers to an image that is carved or hewn rather than cast.

**20:5** *Jealous:* demanding exclusive allegiance. *Inflicting punishment…the third and fourth generation:* the intended emphasis is on God's mercy by the contrast between punishment and mercy ("to the thousandth generation"—v. 6). Other Old Testament texts repudiate the idea of punishment devolving on later generations (cf. Dt 24:16; Jer 31:29–30; Ez 18:2–4). Yet it is known that later generations may suffer the punishing effects of sins of earlier generations, but not the guilt.

**20:7** *In vain:* i.e., to no good purpose, a general framing of the prohibition which includes swearing falsely, especially in the context of a legal proceeding, but also goes beyond it (cf. Lv 24:16; Prv 30:8–9).

**20:8** *Keep it holy:* i.e., to set it apart from the other days of the week, in part, as the following verse explains, by not doing work that is ordinarily done in the course of a week. The special importance of this command can be seen in the fact that, together with vv. 9–11, it represents the longest of the Decalogue's precepts.

---

**20:2–17** Dt 5:6–21.
**20:2** Lv 26:13; Ps 81:11; Hos 13:4.
**20:4** Ex 34:17; Lv 26:1; Dt 4:15–19; 27:15.
**20:5** Ex 34:7, 14; Nm 14:18; Dt 4:24; 6:15.
**20:7** Lv 19:12; 24:16.
**20:8–11** Ex 23:12; 31:13–16; 34:21; 35:2; Lv 23:3.

alien within your gates. [11] For in six days the LORD made the heavens and the earth, the sea and all that is in them; but on the seventh day he rested.* That is why the LORD has blessed the sabbath day and made it holy.†

[12]†* Honor your father and your mother, that you may have a long life in the land the LORD your God is giving you.*

[13] You shall not kill.†*

[14] You shall not commit adultery.*

[15] You shall not steal.*

[16] You shall not bear false witness against your neighbor.*

[17] You shall not covet your neighbor's house. You shall not covet your neighbor's wife, his male or female slave, his ox or donkey, or anything that belongs to your neighbor.*

**Moses Accepted as Mediator.** [18] Now as all the people witnessed the thunder and lightning, the blast of the shofar and the mountain smoking, they became afraid and trembled.* So they took up a position farther away [19] and said to Moses, "You speak to us, and we will listen; but do not let God speak to us, or we shall die." [20] Moses answered the people, "Do not be afraid, for God has come only to test you and put the fear of him upon you so you do not sin." [21] So the people remained at a distance, while Moses approached the dark cloud where God was.

**The Covenant Code.** [22]† The LORD said to Moses: This is what you will say to the Israelites: You have seen for yourselves that I have spoken to you from heaven. [23] You shall not make alongside of me gods of silver, nor shall you make for yourselves gods of gold.* [24] An altar of earth make for me, and sacrifice upon it your burnt offerings and communion sacrifices, your sheep and your oxen.* In every place where I cause my name to be invoked† I will come to you and bless you. [25] But if you make an altar of stone for me,* do not build it of cut stone, for by putting a chisel to it you profane it. [26] You shall not ascend to my altar by steps, lest your nakedness be exposed.

# 21

**Laws Regarding Slaves.** [1] These are the ordinances† you shall lay before them. [2]* When you purchase a Hebrew slave,† he is to serve you for six years, but in the seventh year he shall leave as a free person without any payment. [3] If he comes into service alone, he shall leave alone; if he comes with a wife, his wife shall leave with him. [4] But if his master gives him a wife and she bears him sons or daughters, the woman and her children belong to her master and the man shall leave alone. [5] If, however, the slave declares, 'I love my master and my wife and children; I will not leave as a free person,' [6] his master shall bring him to God† and there, at the door or

---

† **20:11** Here, in a formulation which reflects Priestly theology, the veneration of the sabbath is grounded in God's own hallowing of the sabbath in creation. Compare 31:13; Dt 5:15.

**20:12–17** The Decalogue falls into two parts: the preceding precepts refer to God, the following refer primarily to one's fellow Israelites.

**20:13** *Kill*: as frequent instances of killing in the context of war or certain crimes (see vv. 12–18) demonstrate in the Old Testament, not all killing comes within the scope of the commandment. For this reason, the Hebrew verb translated here as "kill" is often understood as "murder," although it is in fact used in the Old Testament at times for unintentional acts of killing (e.g., Dt 4:41; Jos 20:3) and for legally sanctioned killing (Nm 35:30). The term may originally have designated any killing of another Israelite, including acts of manslaughter, for which the victim's kin could exact vengeance. In the present context, it denotes the killing of one Israelite by another, motivated by hatred or the like (Nm 35:20; cf. Hos 6:9).

**20:22–23:33** This collection consists of the civil and religious laws, both apodictic (absolute) and casuistic (conditional), which were given to the people through the mediation of Moses. They will be written down by Moses in 24:4.

**20:24** *Where I cause my name to be invoked*: i.e., at the sacred site where God wishes to be worshiped. Dt 12 will demand the centralization of all sacrificial worship in one place chosen by God.

**21:1** *Ordinances*: judicial precedents to be used in settling questions of law and custom. More than half of the civil and religious laws in this collection (20:22–23:33), designated in 24:7

as "the book of the covenant," have parallels in the cuneiform laws of the ancient Near East. It is clear that Israel participated in a common legal culture with its neighbors.

**21:2** *Slave*: an Israelite could become a slave of another Israelite as a means of paying a debt, or an Israelite could be born into slavery due to a parent's status as a slave. Here a time limit is prescribed for such slavery; other stipulations (vv. 20–21, 26–27) tried to reduce the evils of slavery, but slavery itself is not condemned in the Old Testament.

**21:6** *To God*: the ritual of the piercing of the slave's ear, which signified a lifetime commitment to the master, probably took place at the door of the household, where God as protector of the household was called upon as a witness. Another possible location for the ritual would have been the door of the sanctuary, where God or judges would have witnessed the slave's promise of lifetime obedience to his master.

---

* 
**20:11** Ex 31:17; Gn 2:2–3.
**20:12–16** Mt 19:18–19; Mk 10:19; Lk 18:20; Rom 13:9.
**20:12** Lv 20:9; Mt 15:4; Mk 7:10; Eph 6:2–3.
**20:13** Mt 5:21.
**20:14** Lv 18:20; 20:10; Dt 22:22; Mt 5:27.
**20:15** Lv 19:11.

**20:16** Ex 23:1; Dt 19:16–19; Prv 19:5, 9; 24:28.
**20:17** Rom 7:7.
**20:18–21** Dt 4:11; 5:22–27; 18:16; Heb 12:18–19.
**20:23** Ex 20:3–4.
**20:24** Dt 12:5, 11; 14:23; 16:6.
**20:25** Dt 27:5; Jos 8:31.
**21:2–6** Lv 25:39–55; Dt 15:12–18; Jer 34:14.

doorpost, he shall pierce his ear with an awl, thus keeping him as his slave forever.

⁷When a man sells his daughter as a slave, she shall not go free as male slaves do. ⁸But if she displeases her master, who had designated her† for himself, he shall let her be redeemed. He has no right to sell her to a foreign people, since he has broken faith with her. ⁹If he designates her for his son, he shall treat her according to the ordinance for daughters. ¹⁰If he takes another wife, he shall not withhold her food, her clothing, or her conjugal rights. ¹¹If he does not do these three things for her, she may leave without cost, without any payment.

**Personal Injury.** ¹²†Whoever strikes someone a mortal blow must be put to death.* ¹³However, regarding the one who did not hunt another down, but God caused death to happen by his hand, I will set apart for you a place to which that one may flee. ¹⁴But when someone kills a neighbor after maliciously scheming to do so, you must take him even from my altar and put him to death. ¹⁵Whoever strikes father or mother shall be put to death.†

¹⁶A kidnapper, whether he sells the person or the person is found in his possession, shall be put to death.*

¹⁷Whoever curses† father or mother shall be put to death.*

¹⁸When men quarrel and one strikes the other with a stone or with his fist, not mortally, but enough to put him in bed, ¹⁹the one who struck the blow shall be acquitted, provided the other can get up and walk around with the help of his staff. Still, he must compensate him for his recovery time and make provision for his complete healing.

²⁰When someone strikes his male or female slave with a rod so that the slave dies under his hand, the act shall certainly be avenged. ²¹If, however, the slave survives for a day or two, he is not to be punished, since the slave is his own property.

²²†When men have a fight and hurt a pregnant woman, so that she suffers a miscarriage, but no further injury, the guilty one shall be fined as much as the woman's husband demands of him, and he shall pay in the presence of the judges. ²³*But if injury ensues, you shall give life for life, ²⁴eye for eye, tooth for tooth, hand for hand, foot for foot, ²⁵burn for burn, wound for wound, stripe for stripe.

²⁶When someone strikes his male or female slave in the eye and destroys the use of the eye, he shall let the slave go free in compensation for the eye. ²⁷If he knocks out a tooth of his male or female slave, he shall let the slave go free in compensation for the tooth.

²⁸When an ox gores a man or a woman to death, the ox must be stoned; its meat may not be eaten. The owner of the ox, however, shall be free of blame. ²⁹But if an ox was previously in the habit of goring people and its owner, though warned, would not watch it; should it then kill a man or a woman, not only must the ox be stoned, but its owner also must be put to death. ³⁰If, however, a fine is imposed on him, he must pay in ransom† for his life whatever amount is imposed on him. ³¹This ordinance applies if it is a boy or a girl that the ox gores. ³²But if it is a male or a female slave that it gores, he must pay the owner of the slave thirty shekels of silver, and the ox must be stoned.

**Property Damage.** ³³When someone uncovers or digs a cistern and does not cover it over again, should an ox or a donkey fall into it, ³⁴the owner of the cistern must make good by

---

**21:8** *Designated her*: intended her as a wife of second rank.
**21:12–14** Unintentional homicide is to be punished differently from premeditated, deliberate murder. One who kills unintentionally can seek asylum by grasping the horns of the altar at the local sanctuary. In later Israelite history, when worship was centralized in Jerusalem, cities throughout the realm were designated as places of refuge. Apparently the leaders of the local community were to determine whether or not the homicide was intentional.
**21:15** The verb used most often signifies a violent, sometimes deadly, attack. The severe penalty assigned is intended to safeguard the integrity of the family.
**21:17** *Curses*: not merely an angrily uttered expletive at one's parents, but a solemn juridical formula of justifiable retribution which was considered to be legally binding and guaranteed by God.
**21:22–25** This law of talion is applied here in the specific case of a pregnant woman who, as an innocent bystander, is injured by two fighting men. The law of talion is not held up as a general principle to be applied throughout the book of the covenant. (But see note on Lv 24:19–20.) Here this principle of rigorous accountability aimed to prevent injury to a woman about to give birth by apparently requiring the assailant to have his own wife injured as she was about to bring new life into his family. However, it is debatable whether talion was ever understood or applied literally in Israel. In his Sermon on the Mount, Jesus challenges his audience to find a deeper form of justice than the supposed equilibrium offered by talion (Mt 5:38–40).
**21:30** *Ransom*: the amount of money or material goods required to restore the relationship between the relatives of the victim and the negligent owner of the goring ox.

**21:12** Lv 24:17; Nm 35:15–29; Dt 4:41–42; 19:2–5.
**21:16** Dt 24:7.
**21:17** Lv 20:9; Prv 20:20; Mt 15:4; Mk 7:10.
**21:23–25** Lv 24:18–21; Dt 19:21; Mt 5:38.

restoring the value of the animal to its owner, but the dead animal he may keep.

35 When one man's ox hurts another's ox and it dies, they shall sell the live ox and divide this money as well as the dead animal equally between them. 36 But if it was known that the ox was previously in the habit of goring and its owner would not watch it, he must make full restitution, an ox for an ox; but the dead animal he may keep.

37 When someone steals an ox or a sheep and slaughters or sells it, he shall restore five oxen for the one ox, and four sheep for the one sheep.*

**22** 1 [If a thief is caught† in the act of housebreaking and beaten to death, there is no bloodguilt involved. 2 But if after sunrise he is thus beaten, there is bloodguilt.] He must make full restitution. If he has nothing, he shall be sold to pay for his theft. 3 If what he stole is found alive in his possession, be it an ox, a donkey or a sheep, he shall make twofold restitution.

4 When someone causes a field or a vineyard to be grazed over, by sending his cattle to graze in another's field, he must make restitution with the best produce of his own field or vineyard. 5 If a fire breaks out, catches on to thorn bushes, and consumes shocked grain, standing grain, or the field itself, the one who started the fire must make full restitution.

**Trusts and Loans.** 6 When someone gives money or articles to another for safekeeping and they are stolen from the latter's house, the thief, if caught, must make twofold restitution. 7 If the thief is not caught, the owner of the house shall be brought to God,† to swear that he himself did not lay hands on his neighbor's property. 8 In every case of dishonest appropriation, whether it be about an ox, or a donkey, or a sheep, or a garment, or anything else that has disappeared, where another claims that the thing is his, the claim of

both parties shall be brought before God; the one whom God convicts must make twofold restitution to the other.

9 When someone gives an ass, or an ox, or a sheep, or any other animal to another for safekeeping, if it dies, or is maimed or snatched away, without anyone witnessing the fact, 10 there shall be an oath before the LORD between the two of them that the guardian did not lay hands on his neighbor's property; the owner must accept the oath, and no restitution is to be made. 11 But if the guardian has actually stolen from it, then he must make restitution to the owner. 12 If it has been killed by a wild beast, let him bring it as evidence; he need not make restitution for the mangled animal.*

13 When someone borrows an animal from a neighbor, if it is maimed or dies while the owner is not present, that one must make restitution. 14 But if the owner is present, that one need not make restitution. If it was hired, this was covered by the price of its hire.

**Social Laws.** 15 * When a man seduces a virgin who is not betrothed, and lies with her, he shall make her his wife by paying the bride price. 16 If her father refuses to give her to him, he must still pay him the bride price for virgins.†

17 You shall not let a woman who practices sorcery live.*

18 Anyone who lies with an animal shall be put to death.*

19 Whoever sacrifices to any god, except to the LORD alone, shall be put under the ban.*

20 You shall not oppress or afflict a resident alien, for you were once aliens residing in the land of Egypt.* 21 You shall not wrong any widow or orphan. 22 If ever you wrong them and they cry out to me, I will surely listen to their cry. 23 My wrath will flare up, and I will kill you with the sword; then your own wives will be widows, and your children orphans.

24 * If you lend money to my people, the poor

---

† **22:1–2** *If a thief is caught*: this seems to be a fragment of what was once a longer law on housebreaking, which has been inserted here into the middle of a law on stealing animals. At night the householder would be justified in killing a burglar outright, but not so in the daytime, when the burglar could more easily be caught alive. *He must make full restitution*: this stood originally immediately after 21:37.
**22:7** *Brought to God*: either within the household or at the sanctuary, the owner of the house is required to take an oath before God.

**22:16** *The bride price for virgins*: fifty shekels according to Dt 22:29.

**21:37** 2 Sm 12:6.
**22:12** Gn 31:39.
**22:15–16** Dt 22:28–29.
**22:17** Lv 19:26, 31; 20:6, 27; Dt 18:10–11.
**22:18** Lv 18:23; Dt 27:21.
**22:19** Dt 13; 17:2–7.
**22:20–23** Ex 23:9; Lv 19:33–34; Dt 10:18–19; 24:17–18; 27:19; Zec 7:10.
**22:24** Lv 25:35–38; Dt 23:19–20; 24:10–13; Ez 18:7–8, 17–18.

among you, you must not be like a money lender; you must not demand interest from them. <sup>25</sup> If you take your neighbor's cloak as a pledge, you shall return it to him before sunset; <sup>26</sup> for this is his only covering; it is the cloak for his body. What will he sleep in? If he cries out to me, I will listen; for I am compassionate.*

<sup>27</sup> You shall not despise God,† nor curse a leader of your people.*

<sup>28</sup> You shall not delay the offering of your harvest and your press. You shall give me the firstborn of your sons. <sup>29</sup> You must do the same with your oxen and your sheep; for seven days the firstling may stay with its mother, but on the eighth day you must give it to me.*

<sup>30</sup> You shall be a people sacred to me. Flesh torn to pieces in the field you shall not eat; you must throw it to the dogs.*

# 23

<sup>1</sup> You shall not repeat a false report. Do not join your hand with the wicked to be a witness supporting violence.* <sup>2</sup> You shall not follow the crowd in doing wrong. When testifying in a lawsuit, you shall not follow the crowd in perverting justice. <sup>3</sup> You shall not favor the poor in a lawsuit.*

<sup>4</sup> When you come upon your enemy's ox or donkey going astray, you must see to it that it is returned.* <sup>5</sup> When you notice the donkey of one who hates you lying down under its burden, you should not desert him; you must help him with it.

<sup>6</sup> You shall not pervert justice for the needy among you in a lawsuit. <sup>7</sup> You shall keep away from anything dishonest. The innocent and the just you shall not put to death, for I will not acquit the guilty. <sup>8</sup> Never take a bribe, for a bribe blinds the clear-sighted and distorts the words of the just.* <sup>9</sup> You shall not oppress a resident alien; you well know how it feels to be an alien, since you were once aliens yourselves in the land of Egypt.*

**Religious Laws.** <sup>10</sup>* For six years you may sow your land and gather in its produce. <sup>11</sup> But the seventh year you shall let the land lie untilled and fallow, that the poor of your people may eat of it and their leftovers the wild animals may eat. So also shall you do in regard to your vineyard and your olive grove.

<sup>12</sup> For six days you may do your work, but on the seventh day you must rest,* that your ox and your donkey may have rest, and that the son of your maidservant and the resident alien may be refreshed. <sup>13</sup> Give heed to all that I have told you.

You shall not mention the name of any other god; it shall not be heard from your lips.

<sup>14</sup>* Three times a year you shall celebrate a pilgrim feast to me.† <sup>15</sup> You shall keep the feast of Unleavened Bread. As I have commanded you, you must eat unleavened bread for seven days at the appointed time in the month of Abib, for it was then that you came out of Egypt. No one shall appear before me† empty-handed. <sup>16</sup> You shall also keep the feast of the grain harvest with the first fruits of the crop that you sow in the field; and finally, the feast of Ingathering at the end of the year, when you collect your produce from the fields. <sup>17</sup> Three times a year shall all your men appear before the LORD God.

<sup>18</sup> You shall not offer the blood of my sacrifice with anything leavened;* nor shall the fat of my feast be kept overnight till the next day. <sup>19</sup> The choicest first fruits of your soil you shall bring to the house of the LORD, your God.

You shall not boil a young goat in its mother's milk.†

**Reward of Fidelity.** <sup>20</sup> See, I am sending an angel* before you, to guard you on the way and bring you to the place I have prepared. <sup>21</sup> Be attentive to him and obey him. Do not rebel against him, for he will not forgive your sin. My authority is within him.† <sup>22</sup> If you obey

---

† **22:27** *Despise God*: a turning away from God's authority and so failing to honor God (cf. 1 Sm 2:30).

**23:14** These three feasts—Passover/Unleavened Bread, Weeks (Pentecost), and Booths (Tabernacles or Succoth/Sukkoth)—are also listed in 34:18–26; Lv 23; Dt 16.

**23:15** *Appear before me*: the original expression was "see my face"; so also in several other places, as 23:17; 34:23–24; Dt 16:16; 31:11.

**23:19** *Boil a young goat in its mother's milk*: this command, repeated in 34:26 and Dt 14:21, is difficult to understand. It may originate from a taboo that forbade killing the young that were still nursing from the mother, or that forbade the mixing of life and death: the slaughtered young goat with the milk that previously had nourished its life. The Jewish dietary custom of keeping meat and dairy products separate is based on this command.

**23:21** *My authority is within him*: lit., "My name is within him."

| | |
|---|---|
| **22:25–26** Dt 24:10–13; Jb 22:6; Prv 20:16; 27:13; Am 2:8. | **23:8** Dt 16:19; 27:25; Sir 20:28. |
| **22:27** Acts 23:5. | **23:9** Ex 22:20. |
| **22:29** Ex 13:2; 34:19; Lv 22:27; Dt 15:19. | **23:10–11** Lv 25:3–7. |
| **22:30** Lv 7:24; 17:15; 22:8. | **23:12** Ex 20:8–10. |
| **23:1–2** Dt 19:16–21. | **23:14–17** Ex 34:18, 22–24; Lv 23; Dt 16:1–17. |
| **23:3** Lv 19:15. | **23:18–19** Ex 34:25–26. |
| **23:4** Dt 22:1–4. | **23:20** Ex 14:19; 32:34; 33:2. |

him and carry out all I tell you, I will be an enemy to your enemies and a foe to your foes. ²³My angel will go before you and bring you to the Amorites, Hittites, Perizzites, Canaanites, Hivites and Jebusites; and I will wipe them out. ²⁴Therefore, you shall not bow down to their gods and serve them, nor shall you act as they do; rather, you must demolish them and smash their sacred stones.†* ²⁵You shall serve the LORD, your God; then he will bless your food and drink, and I will remove sickness from your midst; ²⁶no woman in your land will be barren or miscarry; and I will give you a full span of life.

²⁷I will have the terror of me precede you, so that I will throw into panic every nation you reach.* I will make all your enemies turn from you in flight, ²⁸and ahead of you I will send hornets† to drive the Hivites, Canaanites and Hittites out of your way. ²⁹But I will not drive them all out before you in one year, lest the land become desolate and the wild animals multiply against you. ³⁰Little by little I will drive them out before you, until you have grown numerous enough to take possession of the land. ³¹*I will set your boundaries from the Red Sea to the sea of the Philistines,† and from the wilderness to the Euphrates; all who dwell in this land I will hand over to you and you shall drive them out before you. ³²You shall not make a covenant with them or their gods. ³³They must not live in your land. For if you serve their gods, this will become a snare to you.*

# 24 Ratification of the Covenant.

¹Moses himself was told: Come up to the LORD, you and Aaron, with Nadab, Abihu, and seventy of the elders of Israel. You shall bow down at a distance. ²Moses alone is to come close to the LORD; the others shall not come close, and the people shall not come up with them.

³When Moses came to the people and related all the words and ordinances of the LORD, they all answered with one voice, "We will do everything that the LORD has told us."* ⁴Moses then wrote down all the words of the LORD and, rising early in the morning, he built at the foot of the mountain an altar and twelve sacred stones† for the twelve tribes of Israel. ⁵*Then, having sent young men of the Israelites to offer burnt offerings and sacrifice young bulls as communion offerings to the LORD, ⁶Moses took half of the blood and put it in large bowls; the other half he splashed on the altar. ⁷Taking the book of the covenant, he read it aloud to the people, who answered, "All that the LORD has said, we will hear and do." ⁸Then he took the blood and splashed it on the people, saying, "This is the blood of the covenant which the LORD has made with you according to all these words."

⁹Moses then went up with Aaron, Nadab, Abihu, and seventy elders of Israel, ¹⁰and they beheld the God of Israel. Under his feet there appeared to be sapphire tilework, as clear as the sky itself. ¹¹Yet he did not lay a hand on these chosen Israelites. They saw God,† and they ate and drank.

**Moses on the Mountain.** ¹²The LORD said to Moses: Come up to me on the mountain and, while you are there, I will give you the stone tablets* on which I have written the commandments intended for their instruction. ¹³So Moses set out with Joshua, his assistant, and went up to the mountain of God. ¹⁴He told the elders, "Wait here for us until we return to you. Aaron and Hur are with you. Anyone with a complaint should approach them." ¹⁵Moses went up the mountain. Then the cloud covered the mountain. ¹⁶The glory of the LORD settled upon Mount Sinai. The cloud covered it for six days, and on the seventh day he called to Moses from the midst of

---

23:24 *Sacred stones:* objects that symbolized the presence of Canaanite deities. In general, standing stones served as memorials for deities, persons, or significant events such as military victories or covenant-making. See 24:4.

23:28 *Hornets:* the Hebrew *sirʿah* is a disputed term, but according to ancient interpreters it refers to hornets that were unleashed against the enemy to sting them and cause panic (cf. Dt 7:20; Jos 24:12; Wis 12:8). Others associate the word with plagues or troublesome afflictions.

23:31 *The sea of the Philistines:* the Mediterranean. Only in the time of David and Solomon did the territory of Israel come near to reaching such distant borders.

24:4 *Sacred stones:* stone shafts or slabs, erected as symbols

of the fact that each of the twelve tribes had entered into this covenant with God; see 23:24; Gn 28:18.

24:11 *They saw God:* the ancients thought that the sight of God would bring instantaneous death. Cf. 33:20; Gn 16:13; 32:31; Jgs 6:22–23; 13:22. *Ate and drank:* partook of the sacrificial meal.

23:23–24 Ex 34:10–16; Nm 33:51–52; Dt 7:24–26.
23:27–30 Dt 2:25; 7:20–22.
23:31 Gn 15:18; Dt 11:24; Jos 1:4.
23:32–33 Ex 34:12–16; Dt 7:2–6.
24:3 Ex 19:8.
24:5–8 Heb 9:18–20.
24:12 Ex 31:18; 32:15–16; Dt 5:22.

the cloud. * [17] To the Israelites the glory of the LORD was seen as a consuming fire on the top of the mountain. * [18] But Moses entered into the midst of the cloud and went up on the mountain. He was on the mountain for forty days and forty nights. *

# 25 Collection of Materials. [1] The LORD spoke to Moses: * [2] Speak to the Israelites: Let them receive contributions for me. From each you shall receive the contribution that their hearts prompt them to give me. [3] These are the contributions you shall accept from them: gold, silver, and bronze; * [4] violet, purple, and scarlet yarn; fine linen and goat hair; [5] rams' skins dyed red, and tahash † skins; acacia wood; [6] oil for the light; spices for the anointing oil and for the fragrant incense; [7] onyx stones and other gems for mounting on the ephod and the breastpiece. [8] They are to make a sanctuary for me, that I may dwell in their midst. * [9] According to all that I show you regarding the pattern of the tabernacle and the pattern of its furnishings, so you are to make it. *

## Plan of the Ark. [10] You shall make an ark of acacia wood, * two and a half cubits † long, one and a half cubits wide, and one and a half cubits high. [11] Plate it inside and outside with pure gold, and put a molding of gold around the top of it. [12] Cast four gold rings and put them on the four supports of the ark, two rings on one side and two on the opposite side. [13] Then make poles of acacia wood and plate them with gold. [14] These poles you are to put through the rings on the sides of the ark, for carrying it; [15] they must remain in the rings of the ark and never be withdrawn. [16] In the ark you are to put the covenant which I will give you.

[17] You shall then make a cover † of pure gold, two and a half cubits long, and one and a half cubits wide. [18] Make two cherubim † of beaten gold for the two ends of the cover; [19] make one cherub at one end, and the other at the other end, of one piece with the cover, at each end. [20] The cherubim shall have their wings spread out above, sheltering the cover with them; they shall face each other, with their faces looking toward the cover. [21] This cover you shall then place on top of the ark. In the ark itself you are to put the covenant which I will give you. [22] There I will meet you and there, from above the cover, between the two cherubim on the ark of the covenant, I will tell you all that I command you regarding the Israelites.

## The Table. [23] You shall also make a table of acacia * wood, two cubits long, a cubit wide, and a cubit and a half high. [24] Plate it with pure gold and make a molding of gold around it. [25] Make a frame † for it, a handbreadth high, and make a molding of gold around the frame. [26] You shall also make four rings of gold for it and fasten them at the four corners, one at each leg. [27] The rings shall be alongside the frame as holders for the poles to carry the table. [28] These poles for carrying the table you shall make of acacia wood and plate with gold. [29] You shall make its plates † and cups, as well as its pitchers and bowls for pouring libations; make them of pure gold. [30] On the table you shall always keep showbread set before me. *

## The Menorah. [31] You shall make a menorah † of pure beaten gold *—its shaft and branches—with its cups and knobs and petals springing directly from it. [32] Six branches are to extend from its sides, three branches on one side, and three on the other. [33] † On one

---

**25:5** *Tahash*: perhaps a kind of specially finished leather. The Greek and Latin versions took it for the color hyacinth.

**25:10** *Cubits*: the distance between the elbow and tip of the middle finger of an average-size person, about eighteen inches. The dimensions of the ark of the covenant were approximately 3 3/4 feet long, 2 1/4 feet wide, and 2 1/4 feet high.

**25:17** *Cover*: the Hebrew term, *kapporet*, has been connected with *kippur*, as in the feast of Yom Kippur or Day of Atonement (Lv 16; 23:26–32): hence, influenced by the Greek and Latin versions, and Luther's German, English translations have rendered it "propitiatory," "mercy seat," and the like.

**25:18–20** *Cherubim*: probably in the form of human-headed winged lions. The cherubim over the ark formed the throne for the invisible Lord. Cf. Ps 80:2. For a more detailed description of the somewhat different cherubim in the Temple of Solomon, see 1 Kgs 6:23–28; 2 Chr 3:10–13.

**25:25** *A frame*: probably placed near the bottom of the legs to keep them steady. The golden table of Herod's Temple is pictured

thus on the Arch of Titus.

**25:29–30** The plates held the showbread, that is, the holy bread which was placed upon the table every sabbath as an offering to God, and was later eaten by the priests. The cups held the incense which was strewn upon the bread. Cf. Lv 24:5–9. The libation wine was poured from the pitchers into the bowls. All these vessels were kept on the golden table.

**25:31** *Menorah*: this traditional lampstand is still used today in Jewish liturgy.

**25:33** In keeping with the arrangement of the ornaments on the shaft, the three sets of ornaments on each branch were probably so placed that one was at the top and the other two equally

---

24:16 Sir 45:5.
24:17 Ex 19:18; Heb 12:18.
24:18 Ex 34:28; Dt 9:9.
25:1–7 Ex 35:4–9, 20–29.
25:3 Ex 35:4–9.
25:8–9 Ex 26:1–30; 36:8–38.
25:9 Acts 7:44.
25:10–22 Ex 37:1–9; Heb 9:1–5.
25:23–30 Ex 37:10–16.
25:30 Lv 24:5–9.
25:31–40 Ex 37:17–24.

branch there are to be three cups, shaped like almond blossoms, each with its knob and petals; on the opposite branch there are to be three cups, shaped like almond blossoms, each with its knob and petals; and so for the six branches that extend from the menorah. <sup>34</sup> On the menorah there are to be four cups,† shaped like almond blossoms, with their knobs and petals. <sup>35</sup> The six branches that go out from the menorah are to have a knob under each pair. <sup>36</sup> Their knobs and branches shall so spring from it that the whole will form a single piece of pure beaten gold. <sup>37</sup>† You shall then make seven lamps* for it and so set up the lamps that they give their light on the space in front of the menorah. <sup>38</sup> These, as well as the trimming shears and trays,† must be of pure gold. <sup>39</sup> Use a talent† of pure gold for the menorah and all these utensils. <sup>40</sup> See that you make them according to the pattern shown you on the mountain.*

## 26 The Tent Cloth.

<sup>1</sup> The tabernacle itself you shall make out of ten sheets† woven of fine linen twined and of violet, purple, and scarlet yarn, with cherubim embroidered on them.* <sup>2</sup> The length of each shall be twenty-eight cubits, and the width four cubits; all the sheets shall be of the same size. <sup>3</sup> Five of the sheets are to be joined one to another; and the same for the other five. <sup>4</sup> Make loops of violet yarn along the edge of the end sheet in one set, and the same along the edge of the end sheet in the other set. <sup>5</sup> Make fifty loops along the edge of the end sheet in the first set, and fifty loops along the edge of the corresponding sheet in the second set, and so placed that the loops are directly opposite each other. <sup>6</sup> Then make fifty clasps of gold and join the two sets of sheets, so that the tabernacle forms one whole.

<sup>7</sup> Also make sheets woven of goat hair for a tent† over the tabernacle. Make eleven such sheets; <sup>8</sup> the length of each shall be thirty cubits, and the width four cubits: all eleven sheets shall be of the same size. <sup>9</sup> Join five of the sheets into one set, and the other six sheets into another set. Use the sixth sheet double at the front of the tent.† <sup>10</sup> Make fifty loops along the edge of the end sheet in one set, and fifty loops along the edge of the end sheet in the second set. <sup>11</sup> Also make fifty bronze clasps and put them into the loops, to join the tent into one whole. <sup>12</sup> There will be an extra half sheet of tent covering, which shall be allowed to hang down over the rear of the tabernacle. <sup>13</sup> Likewise, the sheets of the tent will have an extra cubit's length to be left hanging down on either side of the tabernacle to cover it. <sup>14</sup> Over the tent itself make a covering of rams' skins dyed red, and above that, a covering of tahash skins.

**The Framework.** <sup>15</sup>* You shall make frames for the tabernacle, acacia-wood uprights. <sup>16</sup> The length of each frame is to be ten cubits, and its width one and a half cubits. <sup>17</sup> Each frame shall have two arms† joined one to another; so you are to make all the frames of the tabernacle. <sup>18</sup> Make the frames of the tabernacle as follows: twenty frames on the south side, <sup>19</sup> with forty silver pedestals under the twenty frames, two pedestals under each frame for its two arms; <sup>20</sup> twenty frames on the other side of the tabernacle, the north side, <sup>21</sup> with their forty silver pedestals, two pedestals under each frame. <sup>22</sup> At the rear of the tabernacle, to the west, six frames, <sup>23</sup> and two frames for the corners of the tabernacle, at its rear. <sup>24</sup> These two shall be double at the bottom, and likewise double at the top, to the first ring. That is how both corner frames are to be made. <sup>25</sup> Thus, there shall be eight frames, with their sixteen silver pedestals, two pedestals under each frame. <sup>26</sup> Also

---

make bars of acacia wood: five for the frames on one side of the tabernacle, 27 five for those on the other side, and five for those at the rear, to the west. 28 The center bar, at the middle of the frames, shall reach across from end to end. 29 Plate the frames with gold, and make gold rings on them as holders for the bars, which are also to be plated with gold. 30 You shall set up the tabernacle according to its plan, which you were shown on the mountain.

**The Veils.** 31 You shall make a veil woven of violet, purple, and scarlet yarn,* and of fine linen twined, with cherubim embroidered on it.* 32 It is to be hung on four gold-plated columns of acacia wood, which shall have gold hooks† and shall rest on four silver pedestals. 33 Hang the veil from clasps. The ark of the covenant you shall bring inside, behind this veil which divides the holy place from the holy of holies. 34 Set the cover on the ark of the covenant in the holy of holies.

35 Outside the veil you shall place the table and the menorah, the latter on the south side of the tabernacle, opposite the table, which is to be put on the north side. 36 For the entrance of the tent make a variegated† curtain of violet, purple, and scarlet yarn and of fine linen twined. 37 Make five columns of acacia wood for this curtain; plate them with gold, with their hooks of gold; and cast five bronze pedestals for them.

# 27

**The Altar for Burnt Offerings.** 1 You shall make an altar* of acacia wood, on a square, five cubits long and five cubits wide; it shall be three cubits high. 2 At the four corners make horns† that are of one piece with the altar. You shall then plate it with bronze. 3 Make pots for removing the ashes, as well as shovels, basins, forks, and fire pans; all these utensils you shall make of bronze. 4 Make for it a grating,† a bronze network; make four bronze rings for it, one at each of its four corners. 5 Put it down around the altar, on the ground. This network is to be half as high as the altar. 6 You shall also make poles of acacia wood for the altar, and plate them with bronze. 7 These poles are to be put through the rings, so that they are on either side of the altar when it is carried. 8 Make the altar itself in the form of a hollow† box. Just as it was shown you on the mountain, so it is to be made.

**Court of the Tabernacle.** 9* You shall also make a court for the tabernacle. On the south side the court shall have hangings, of fine linen twined, a hundred cubits long, 10 with twenty columns and twenty pedestals of bronze; the hooks and bands on the columns shall be of silver. 11 On the north side there shall be similar hangings, a hundred cubits long, with twenty columns and twenty pedestals of bronze; the hooks and bands on the columns shall be of silver. 12 On the west side, across the width of the court, there shall be hangings, fifty cubits long, with ten columns and ten pedestals. 13 The width of the court on the east side shall be fifty cubits. 14 On one side there shall be hangings to the extent of fifteen cubits, with three columns and three pedestals; 15 on the other side there shall be hangings to the extent of fifteen cubits, with three columns and three pedestals.

16 At the gate of the court there shall be a variegated curtain, twenty cubits long, woven of violet, purple, and scarlet yarn and of fine linen twined. It shall have four columns and four pedestals.

17 All the columns around the court shall have bands and hooks of silver, and pedestals of bronze. 18 The court is to be one hundred cubits long, fifty cubits wide, and five cubits high. Fine linen twined must be used, and the pedestals must be of bronze. 19 All the fittings of the tabernacle, whatever be their use, as well as all its tent pegs and all the tent pegs of the court, must be of bronze.

**Oil for the Lamps.** 20 You shall command the Israelites to bring you clear oil of crushed olives, to be used for the light, so that you may keep lamps burning always.* 21 From evening

---

† **26:32** *Hooks*: probably placed near the tops of the columns, to hold the rope from which the veils and curtains hung.
**26:36** *Variegated*: without definite designs such as the cherubim on the inner veil.
**27:2** *Horns*: the horn of a ram, goat or ox is a common Old Testament figure for strength and dignity; they represent the divine character of the altar itself or the deity worshiped there.
**27:4** *Grating*: it is not clear whether this was flush with the altar or at some small distance from it; in the latter case the space

between the altar and the grating would be filled with stones and serve as a platform around the altar, which would otherwise be too high for the priest to reach conveniently.
**27:8** *Hollow*: probably filled with earth or stones when in use. Cf. 20:24–25.

*
**26:31** 2 Chr 3:14.          **27:9–19** Ex 38:9–20.
**26:31** Ex 36:35–38.         **27:20–21** Lv 24:1–4.
**27:1–8** Ex 38:1–7.

to morning Aaron and his sons shall maintain them before the Lord in the tent of meeting, outside the veil which hangs in front of the covenant. This shall be a perpetual statute for the Israelites throughout their generations.

# 28 The Priestly Vestments.

¹* Have your brother Aaron, and with him his sons, brought to you, from among the Israelites, that they may be my priests: Nadab and Abihu, Eleazar and Ithamar, Aaron's sons. ²For the glorious adornment of your brother Aaron you shall have sacred vestments made. ³Therefore, tell the various artisans whom I have endowed with skill† to make vestments for Aaron to consecrate him as my priest. ⁴These are the vestments they shall make: a breastpiece, an ephod, a robe, a brocade tunic, a turban, and a sash. In making these sacred vestments which your brother Aaron and his sons are to wear in serving as my priests, ⁵they shall use gold, violet, purple, and scarlet yarn and fine linen.

## The Ephod and Breastpiece.

⁶The ephod† they shall make of gold thread and of violet, purple, and scarlet yarn, embroidered on cloth of fine linen twined.* ⁷It shall have a pair of shoulder straps joined to its two upper ends. ⁸The embroidered belt of the ephod shall extend out from it and, like it, be made of gold thread, of violet, purple, and scarlet yarn, and of fine linen twined.

⁹Get two onyx stones and engrave on them the names of the sons of Israel: ¹⁰six of their names on one stone, and the names of the remaining six on the other stone, in the order of their birth. ¹¹As a gem-cutter engraves a seal, so shall you have the two stones engraved with the names of the sons of Israel and then mounted in gold filigree work. ¹²Set these two stones on the shoulder straps of the ephod as memorial stones of the sons of Israel. Thus Aaron shall bear their names on his shoulders as a reminder before the Lord. ¹³Make filigree

rosettes of gold,* ¹⁴as well as two chains of pure gold, twisted like cords, and fasten the cordlike chains to the filigree rosettes.

¹⁵* The breastpiece† of decision you shall also have made, embroidered like the ephod with gold thread and violet, purple, and scarlet yarn on cloth of fine linen twined. ¹⁶It is to be square when folded double, a span high and a span wide. ¹⁷† On it you shall mount four rows of precious stones: in the first row, a carnelian, a topaz, and an emerald; ¹⁸in the second row, a garnet, a sapphire, and a beryl; ¹⁹in the third row, a jacinth, an agate, and an amethyst; ²⁰in the fourth row, a chrysolite, an onyx, and a jasper. These stones are to be mounted in gold filigree work, ²¹twelve of them to match the names of the sons of Israel, each stone engraved like a seal with the name of one of the twelve tribes.

²²When the chains of pure gold, twisted like cords, have been made for the breastpiece, ²³you shall then make two rings of gold for it and fasten them to the two upper ends of the breastpiece. ²⁴The gold cords are then to be fastened to the two rings at the upper ends of the breastpiece, ²⁵the other two ends of the cords being fastened in front to the two filigree rosettes which are attached to the shoulder straps of the ephod. ²⁶Make two other rings of gold and put them on the two lower ends of the breastpiece, on its edge that faces the ephod. ²⁷Then make two more rings of gold and fasten them to the bottom of the shoulder straps next to where they join the ephod in front, just above its embroidered belt. ²⁸Violet ribbons shall bind the rings of the breastpiece to the rings of the ephod, so that the breastpiece will stay right above the embroidered belt of the ephod and not swing loose from it.

²⁹Whenever Aaron enters the sanctuary, he will thus bear the names of the sons of Israel on the breastpiece of decision over his heart as a constant reminder before the Lord. ³⁰In this breastpiece of decision* you shall put the

---

**28:3** *Artisans…endowed with skill:* lit., "wise of heart," and "filled with a spirit of wisdom." In Hebrew wisdom includes practical skills. Cf. 35:35; 36:1–2.

**28:6** *Ephod:* this Hebrew word is retained in the translation because it is the technical term for a peculiar piece of the priestly vestments, the exact nature of which is uncertain. It seems to have been a sort of apron that hung from the shoulders of the priest by shoulder straps (v. 7) and was tied around his waist by the loose ends of the attached belt (v. 8).

**28:15–30** *Breastpiece:* an approximately nine-inch square, pocketlike receptacle for holding the Urim and Thummim (v. 30). It formed an integral part of the ephod, to which it was attached

by an elaborate system of rings and chains. Both the ephod and its breastpiece were made of brocaded linen. *Span:* Heb. *zeret,* the distance between the top of the little finger and the thumb; one half a cubit, approximately nine inches.

**28:17–20** The translation of the Hebrew names of some of these gems is quite conjectural.

**28:1–5** Ex 39:1; Sir 45:7.
**28:6–12** Ex 39:2–7; Sir 45:8–14.
**28:13–14** Ex 28:22, 25; 39:15, 18.
**28:15–21** Ex 39:15–21.
**28:30** Lv 8:8; Sir 45:11.

Urim and Thummim,† that they may be over Aaron's heart whenever he enters the presence of the LORD. Thus he shall always bear the decisions for the Israelites over his heart in the presence of the LORD.

**Other Vestments.** ³¹The robe of the ephod* you shall make entirely of violet material. ³²It shall have an opening for the head in the center, and around this opening there shall be a selvage, woven as at the opening of a shirt, to keep it from being torn. ³³At the hem at the bottom you shall make pomegranates, woven of violet, purple, and scarlet yarn and fine linen twined, with gold bells between them; ³⁴a gold bell, a pomegranate, a gold bell, a pomegranate, all around the hem of the robe. ³⁵Aaron shall wear it when ministering, that its sound may be heard as he enters and leaves the LORD's presence in the sanctuary; else he will die.

³⁶You shall also make a plate of pure gold and engrave on it, as on a seal engraving, "Sacred to the LORD." ³⁷This plate is to be tied over the turban with a violet ribbon in such a way that it rests on the front of the turban,* ³⁸over Aaron's forehead. Since Aaron bears whatever guilt the Israelites may incur in consecrating any of their sacred gifts, this plate must always be over his forehead, so that they may find favor with the LORD.

³⁹* The tunic of fine linen shall be brocaded. The turban shall be made of fine linen. The sash shall be of variegated work.

⁴⁰Likewise, for the glorious adornment of Aaron's sons you shall have tunics and sashes and skullcaps made, for glorious splendor. ⁴¹With these you shall clothe your brother Aaron and his sons. Anoint and install them,† consecrating them as my priests. ⁴²You must also make linen pants for them, to cover their naked flesh from their loins to their thighs.* ⁴³Aaron and his sons shall wear them whenever they go into the tent of meeting or approach the altar to minister in the sanctuary, lest they incur guilt and die. This shall be a

perpetual ordinance for him and for his descendants.

**29** **Consecration of the Priests.** ¹This is the rite you shall perform in consecrating them as my priests.* Procure a young bull and two unblemished rams. ²With bran flour make unleavened cakes mixed with oil, and unleavened wafers spread with oil, ³and put them in a basket. Take the basket of them along with the bull and the two rams. ⁴Aaron and his sons you shall also bring to the entrance of the tent of meeting, and there wash them with water. ⁵Take the vestments and clothe Aaron with the tunic, the robe of the ephod, the ephod itself, and the breastpiece, fastening the embroidered belt of the ephod around him. ⁶Put the turban on his head, the sacred diadem on the turban. ⁷Then take the anointing oil and pour it on his head, and anoint him. ⁸Bring forward his sons also and clothe them with the tunics, ⁹gird them with the sashes, and tie the skullcaps on them.* Thus shall the priesthood be theirs by a perpetual statute, and thus shall you install Aaron and his sons.

**Installation Sacrifices.** ¹⁰* Now bring forward the bull in front of the tent of meeting. There Aaron and his sons shall lay their hands on its head. ¹¹Then slaughter the bull before the LORD, at the entrance of the tent of meeting. ¹²Take some of its blood and with your finger put it on the horns of the altar. All the rest of the blood you shall pour out at the base of the altar. ¹³All the fat that covers its inner organs, as well as the lobe of its liver and its two kidneys, together with the fat that is on them, you shall take and burn on the altar. ¹⁴But the meat and hide and dung of the bull you must burn up outside the camp, since this is a purification offering.* ¹⁵Then take one of the rams, and after Aaron and his sons have laid their hands on its head, ¹⁶slaughter it. The blood you shall take and splash on all the sides of the altar. ¹⁷Cut the

---

† **28:30** *Urim and Thummim*: both the meaning of these Hebrew words and the exact nature of the objects so designated are uncertain. They were apparently lots of some kind which were drawn or cast by the priest to ascertain God's decision on particular questions. Hence, the pocket in which they were kept was called "the breastpiece of decision."
**28:41** *Install them*: lit., "fill their hands," a technical expression used for the installation of priests.

**28:31–35** Ex 39:20–25; Lv 8:9;
        Sir 45:10.
    **28:37** Ex 39:31; Lv 8:9.
**28:39–43** Ex 39:27–31.
    **28:42** Ez 44:18.

**29:1–8** Lv 8:1–9.
    **29:9** Lv 8:13.
**29:10–26** Lv 8:14–30.
    **29:14** Heb 13:11.

E
X

ram into pieces; you shall wash its inner organs and shanks and put them with the pieces and with the head. [18] Then you shall burn the entire ram on the altar, since it is a burnt offering, a sweet-smelling oblation to the LORD.

[19] After this take the other ram, and when Aaron and his sons have laid their hands on its head, [20] slaughter it. Some of its blood you shall take and put on the tip of Aaron's right ear and on the tips of his sons' right ears and on the thumbs of their right hands and the great toes of their right feet. Splash the rest of the blood on all the sides of the altar. [21] Then take some of the blood that is on the altar, together with some of the anointing oil, and sprinkle this on Aaron and his vestments, as well as on his sons and their vestments, that he and his sons and their vestments may be sacred.

[22] Now, from this ram you shall take its fat: its fatty tail,[†] the fat that covers its inner organs, the lobe of its liver, its two kidneys with the fat that is on them, and its right thigh, since this is the ram for installation; [23] then, out of the basket of unleavened food that you have set before the LORD, you shall take one of the loaves of bread, one of the cakes made with oil, and one of the wafers. [24] All these things you shall put into the hands of Aaron and his sons, so that they may raise them as an elevated offering[†] before the LORD. [25] After you receive them back from their hands, you shall burn them on top of the burnt offering on the altar as a sweet-smelling oblation to the LORD. [26] Finally, take the brisket of Aaron's installation ram and raise it as an elevated offering before the LORD; this is to be your own portion.

[27][†] Thus shall you set aside the brisket of whatever elevated offering is raised,[*] as well as the thigh of whatever contribution is raised up, whether this be the installation ram or anything else belonging to Aaron or to his sons. [28] Such things are due to Aaron and his sons from the Israelites by a perpetual statute as a contribution. From their communion offerings, too, the Israelites shall make a contribution, their contribution to the LORD.

[29] The sacred vestments[*] of Aaron shall be passed down to his sons after him, that in them they may be anointed and installed. [30] The son who succeeds him as priest and who is to enter the tent of meeting to minister in the sanctuary shall be clothed with them for seven days.

[31][*] You shall take the installation ram and boil its meat in a holy place. [32] At the entrance of the tent of meeting Aaron and his sons shall eat the meat of the ram and the bread that is in the basket. [33] They themselves are to eat of these things by which atonement was made at their installation and consecration; but no unauthorized person may eat of them, since they are sacred. [34] If some of the meat of the installation sacrifice or some of the bread remains over on the next day, this remnant you must burn up; it is not to be eaten, since it is sacred.

[35] Carry out all these commands in regard to Aaron and his sons just as I have given them to you.[*] Seven days you shall spend installing them, [36][*] sacrificing a bull each day as a purification offering, to make atonement. Thus you shall purify the altar[†] by purging it, and you shall anoint it in order to consecrate it. [37] Seven days you shall spend in purging the altar and in consecrating it. Then the altar will be most sacred, and whatever touches it will become sacred.

[38][†] Now, this is what you shall regularly offer on the altar: two yearling lambs[*] as the sacrifice established for each day; [39] one lamb in the morning and the other lamb at the evening twilight. [40] With the first lamb there shall be a tenth of an ephah of bran flour mixed with a fourth of a hin[†] of oil of crushed olives and, as its libation, a fourth of a hin of wine. [41] The other lamb you shall offer at the

[†] **29:22** *Fatty tail*: the thick layer of fat surrounding the tails of sheep and rams bred in the Middle East. It is regarded as a choice food. Cf. Lv 3:9.

**29:24–26** *Elevated offering*: the portions of a communion offering, brisket and right thigh, which the officiating priest raised in the presence of the Lord. They were reserved for Aaron and his sons.

**29:27–30** These verses are a parenthetical interruption of the installation ritual; v. 31 belongs logically immediately after v. 26.

**29:36–37** *Purify the altar*: the purpose of the purification offering here is to cleanse, or purify, the newly constructed altar of any defilement resulting from presumably minor and inadvertent sins, but the text is not explicit about what the offenses were or who committed them. So various theories have been proposed to explain the cause of the altar's contamination. Note, however, that the offering appears to be demanded of Aaron and his sons; they are the ones who lay hands upon it (v. 10).

**29:38–42** A parenthesis inserted into the rubrics for consecrating the altar; v. 43 belongs directly after v. 37.

**29:40** *Hin*: see note on Ez 45:24.

29:27–28 Lv 7:31–34; 10:14– 15; Nm 18:18–19; Dt 18:3.
29:29 Nm 20:26, 28.
29:31–34 Lv 8:31–32.
29:35 Lv 8:36.
29:36–37 Lv 8:33–35.
29:38–42 Nm 28:3–8.

evening twilight, with the same grain offering and libation as in the morning. You shall offer this as a sweet-smelling oblation to the Lord. [42] Throughout your generations this regular burnt offering shall be made before the Lord at the entrance of the tent of meeting, where I will meet you and speak to you.

[43] There, at the altar, I will meet the Israelites; hence, it will be made sacred by my glory.* [44] Thus I will consecrate the tent of meeting and the altar, just as I also consecrate Aaron and his sons to be my priests. [45] I will dwell in the midst of the Israelites and will be their God. [46] They shall know that I, the Lord, am their God who brought them out of the land of Egypt, so that I, the Lord, their God, might dwell among them.

# 30 Altar of Incense.
[1] For burning incense you shall make an altar of acacia wood,* [2] with a square surface, a cubit long, a cubit wide, and two cubits high, with horns that are of one piece with it. [3] Its grate on top, its walls on all four sides, and its horns you shall plate with pure gold. Put a gold molding around it. [4] Underneath the molding you shall put gold rings, two on one side and two on the opposite side, as holders for the poles used in carrying it. [5] Make the poles, too, of acacia wood and plate them with gold. [6] This altar you are to place in front of the veil that hangs before the ark of the covenant where I will meet you.*

[7] On it Aaron shall burn fragrant incense. Morning after morning, when he prepares the lamps, [8] and again in the evening twilight, when he lights the lamps, he shall burn incense. Throughout your generations this shall be the regular incense offering before the Lord. [9] On this altar you shall not offer up any profane incense, or any burnt offering or grain offering; nor shall you pour out a libation upon it. [10] Once a year Aaron shall purge its horns.* Throughout your generations he is to purge it once a year with the blood of the atoning purification offering. This altar is most sacred to the Lord.

**Census Tax.** [11] The Lord also told Moses: [12] When you take a census* of the Israelites who are to be enrolled, each one, as he is

enrolled, shall give the Lord a ransom for his life, so that no plague may come upon them for being enrolled. [13] This is what everyone who is enrolled must pay: a half-shekel, according to the standard of the sanctuary shekel—twenty gerahs to the shekel—a half-shekel contribution to the Lord.* [14] Everyone who is enrolled, of twenty years or more, must give the contribution to the Lord. [15] The rich need not give more, nor shall the poor give less, than a half-shekel in this contribution to the Lord to pay the ransom for their lives. [16]* When you receive this ransom money from the Israelites, you shall donate it to the service of the tent of meeting, that there it may be a reminder of the Israelites before the Lord of the ransom paid for their lives.

**The Basin.** [17] The Lord told Moses: [18] For ablutions you shall make a bronze basin with a bronze stand. Place it between the tent of meeting and the altar, and put water in it.* [19] Aaron and his sons shall use it in washing their hands and feet.* [20] When they are about to enter the tent of meeting, they must wash with water, lest they die. Likewise when they approach the altar to minister, to offer an oblation to the Lord, [21] they must wash their hands and feet, lest they die. This shall be a perpetual statute for him and his descendants throughout their generations.

**The Anointing Oil.** [22] The Lord told Moses: [23] Take the finest spices: five hundred shekels of free-flowing myrrh; half that amount, that is, two hundred and fifty shekels, of fragrant cinnamon; two hundred and fifty shekels of fragrant cane; [24] five hundred shekels of cassia—all according to the standard of the sanctuary shekel; together with a hin of olive oil; [25] and blend them into sacred anointing oil,* perfumed ointment expertly prepared.* With this sacred anointing oil [26] you shall anoint the tent of meeting and the ark of the covenant, [27] the table and all its utensils, the menorah and its utensils, the altar of incense [28] and the altar for burnt offerings with all its utensils, and the basin with its stand. [29] When you have consecrated them, they shall be most sacred; whatever touches them shall be sacred. [30] Aaron and his sons you shall also anoint

29:43 Ex 25:22.
30:1–5 Ex 37:25–28.
30:6 Ex 40:26.
30:10 Lv 16:18.
30:12 Nm 1:2–3; 26:2.
30:13 Mt 17:24–27.
30:16 Ex 38:25.
30:18 Ex 38:8; 40:7, 30.
30:19–21 Ex 40:31–32.
30:25 Ex 37:29.
30:25–29 Ex 40:9–11; Lv 8:10; Nm 7:1.

and consecrate as my priests.* ³¹ Tell the Israelites: As sacred anointing oil this shall belong to me throughout your generations. ³² It may not be used in any ordinary anointing of the body, nor may you make any other oil of a like mixture. It is sacred, and shall be treated as sacred by you. ³³ Whoever prepares a perfume like this, or whoever puts any of this on an unauthorized person, shall be cut off from his people.

**The Incense.** ³⁴* The LORD told Moses: Take these aromatic substances: storax and onycha and galbanum, these and pure frankincense in equal parts; ³⁵ and blend them into incense. This fragrant powder, expertly prepared, is to be salted and so kept pure and sacred. ³⁶ Grind some of it into fine dust and put this before the covenant in the tent of meeting where I will meet you. This incense shall be treated as most sacred by you. ³⁷ You may not make incense of a like mixture for yourselves; you must treat it as sacred to the LORD. ³⁸ Whoever makes an incense like this for his own enjoyment of its fragrance, shall be cut off from his people.

# 31

**Choice of Artisans.** ¹* The LORD said to Moses: ² See, I have singled out† Bezalel, son of Uri, son of Hur, of the tribe of Judah, ³ and I have filled him with a divine spirit of skill and understanding and knowledge in every craft: ⁴ in the production of embroidery, in making things of gold, silver, or bronze, ⁵ in cutting and mounting precious stones, in carving wood, and in every other craft. ⁶ As his assistant I myself have appointed Oholiab, son of Ahisamach, of the tribe of Dan. I have also endowed all the experts with the necessary skill to make all the things I have commanded you: ⁷* the tent of meeting, the ark of the covenant with its cover, all the furnishings of the tent, ⁸ the table with its utensils, the pure gold menorah with all its utensils, the altar of incense, ⁹ the altar for burnt offerings with all its utensils, the basin with its stand, ¹⁰ the service cloths,† the sacred vestments for Aaron

the priest, the vestments for his sons in their ministry, ¹¹ the anointing oil, and the fragrant incense for the sanctuary. According to all I have commanded you, so shall they do.

**Sabbath Laws.** ¹²* The LORD said to Moses: ¹³ You must also tell the Israelites: Keep my sabbaths, for that is to be the sign between you and me throughout the generations, to show that it is I, the LORD, who make you holy. ¹⁴† Therefore, you must keep the sabbath for it is holiness for you. Whoever desecrates it shall be put to death. If anyone does work on that day, that person must be cut off from the people. ¹⁵ Six days there are for doing work, but the seventh day is the sabbath of complete rest, holy to the LORD. Anyone who does work on the sabbath day shall be put to death. ¹⁶ So shall the Israelites observe the sabbath, keeping it throughout their generations as an everlasting covenant. ¹⁷ Between me and the Israelites it is to be an everlasting sign; for in six days the LORD made the heavens and the earth, but on the seventh day he rested at his ease.

¹⁸ When the LORD had finished speaking to Moses on Mount Sinai, he gave him the two tablets of the covenant, the stone tablets inscribed by God's own finger.*

# VII. ISRAEL'S APOSTASY AND GOD'S RENEWAL OF THE COVENANT

# 32

**The Golden Calf.** ¹ When the people saw that Moses was delayed in coming down from the mountain, they gathered around Aaron and said to him, "Come, make us a god who will go before us; as for that man Moses who brought us out of the land of Egypt, we do not know what has happened to him."* ² Aaron replied, "Take off the golden earrings that your wives, your sons, and your daughters are wearing, and bring them to me." ³ So all the people took off their earrings and brought them to Aaron. ⁴ He received their offering, and fashioning it with a tool, made a molten calf. Then they cried out, "These are your gods, Israel, who brought you† up from

---

**31:2** *Singled out:* lit., "called by name"; cf. 35:30.

**31:10** *The service cloths:* so the Greek. They were perhaps the colored cloths mentioned in Nm 4:4–15.

**31:14–15** For the distinction between work proscribed on certain festivals and weekly Sabbaths, see note on Lv 23:3.

**32:4–5** *Who brought you...a feast of the LORD:* it seems that the golden calf was intended as an image, not of another god, but of the Lord, whose strength was symbolized by the strength

of a young bull. The Israelites, however, had been forbidden to represent the Lord under any visible form. Cf. 20:4. In the tenth century Jeroboam made golden calves for the shrines at Bethel

**30:30** Ex 29:7; Lv 8:12.　　**31:12–17** Ex 20:8–11; 35:1–3.
**30:34–38** Ex 25:6; 37:29.　　**31:18** Ex 24:12; 32:15–16;
**31:1–6** Ex 35:30–35.　　　　　　Dt 5:22.
**31:7–11** Ex 35:10–19.　　**32:1** Ex 32:23; Acts 7:40.

the land of Egypt."* 5 On seeing this, Aaron built an altar in front of the calf and proclaimed, "Tomorrow is a feast of the LORD." 6 Early the next day the people sacrificed burnt offerings and brought communion sacrifices. Then they sat down to eat and drink, and rose up to revel.*

7* Then the LORD said to Moses: Go down at once because your people, whom you brought out of the land of Egypt, have acted corruptly. 8 They have quickly turned aside from the way I commanded them, making for themselves a molten calf and bowing down to it, sacrificing to it and crying out, "These are your gods, Israel, who brought you up from the land of Egypt!" 9* I have seen this people, how stiffnecked they are, continued the LORD to Moses. 10 Let me alone, then, that my anger may burn against them to consume them. Then I will make of you a great nation.

11† But Moses implored the LORD, his God, saying,* "Why, O LORD, should your anger burn against your people, whom you brought out of the land of Egypt with great power and with a strong hand? 12 Why should the Egyptians say, 'With evil intent he brought them out, that he might kill them in the mountains and wipe them off the face of the earth'? Turn from your burning wrath; change your mind about punishing your people. 13 Remember your servants Abraham, Isaac, and Israel, and how you swore to them by your own self, saying,* 'I will make your descendants as numerous as the stars in the sky; and all this land that I promised, I will give your descendants as their perpetual heritage.'" 14 So the LORD changed his mind about the punishment he had threatened to inflict on his people.

15 Moses then turned and came down the mountain with the two tablets of the covenant in his hands,* tablets that were written on both sides, front and back. 16 The tablets were made by God; the writing was the writing of God, engraved on the tablets.* 17 Now, when

Joshua heard the noise of the people shouting, he said to Moses, "That sounds like a battle in the camp." 18 But Moses answered,

> "It is not the noise of victory,
>   it is not the noise of defeat;
>   the sound I hear is singing."

19 As he drew near the camp, he saw the calf and the dancing. Then Moses' anger burned, and he threw the tablets down and broke them on the base of the mountain.* 20 Taking the calf they had made, he burned it in the fire and then ground it down to powder, which he scattered on the water† and made the Israelites drink.*

21† Moses asked Aaron, "What did this people do to you that you should lead them into a grave sin?" 22 Aaron replied, "Do not let my lord be angry. You know how the people are prone to evil. 23 They said to me, 'Make us a god to go before us; as for this man Moses who brought us out of the land of Egypt, we do not know what has happened to him.' 24 So I told them, 'Whoever is wearing gold, take it off.' They gave it to me, and I threw it into the fire, and this calf came out."

25 Moses saw that the people were running wild because Aaron had lost control—to the secret delight of their foes. 26 Moses stood at the gate of the camp and shouted, "Whoever is for the LORD, come to me!" All the Levites* then rallied to him, 27 and he told them, "Thus says the LORD, the God of Israel: Each of you put your sword on your hip! Go back and forth through the camp, from gate to gate, and kill your brothers, your friends, your neighbors!" 28 The Levites did as Moses had commanded, and that day about three thousand of the people fell. 29 Then Moses said, "Today you are installed as priests† for the LORD, for you went against your own sons and brothers, to bring a blessing upon yourselves this day."

---

† and Dan, presumably to function as thrones for the Lord as the ark did in Jerusalem (see 1 Kgs 12:27–30).

**32:11–13** Moses uses three arguments to persuade the Lord to remain faithful to the Sinai covenant even though the people have broken it: (1) they are God's own people, redeemed with God's great power; (2) God's reputation will suffer if they are destroyed; (3) the covenant with Abraham still stands. The Lord's change of mind is a testimony to Israel's belief in the power of intercessory prayer.

**32:20** *The water:* according to Dt 9:21, this was the stream that flowed down Mount Sinai.

**32:21–24** Aaron attempts to persuade Moses not to act in an-

ger, just as Moses persuaded the Lord. He also shifts the blame from himself to the people.

**32:29** *Installed as priests:* lit., "fill your hands," a term for the ordination of priests (see 28:41; 29:9, 29, 33, 35; Nm 3:3). Because of their zeal for the true worship of the Lord, the Levites were chosen to be special ministers of the ritual service.

---

**32:4** Ex 32:8; 1 Kgs 12:28.  
**32:6** 1 Cor 10:7.  
**32:7–8** Dt 9:12, 16.  
**32:9–10** Dt 9:13.  
**32:11–12** Nm 14:13–19; Dt 9:28–29; Ps 106:23.  
**32:13** Gn 22:16–17.  
**32:15** Dt 9:15.  
**32:16** Ex 31:18.  
**32:19** Dt 9:16–17.  
**32:20** Dt 9:21.  
**32:26–29** Dt 33:8–9.

**The Atonement.** [30] On the next day Moses said to the people,* "You have committed a grave sin. Now I will go up to the LORD; perhaps I may be able to make atonement for your sin." [31] So Moses returned to the LORD and said, "Ah, this people has committed a grave sin in making a god of gold for themselves! [32] Now if you would only forgive their sin! But if you will not, then blot me out of the book that you have written."† [33] The LORD answered Moses: Only the one who has sinned against me will I blot out of my book. [34] Now, go and lead the people where I have told you. See, my angel will go before you. When it is time for me to punish, I will punish them for their sin.

[35] Thus the LORD struck the people for making the calf, the one that Aaron made.

# 33

[1] The LORD spoke to Moses: Go! You and the people whom you have brought up from the land of Egypt are to go up from here to the land about which I swore to Abraham, Isaac, and Jacob: I will give it to your descendants.* [2] Driving out the Canaanites, Amorites, Hittites, Perizzites, Hivites and Jebusites, I will send an angel before you* [3] to a land flowing with milk and honey. But I myself will not go up in your company, because you are a stiff-necked people; otherwise I might consume you on the way. [4] When the people heard this painful news, they mourned, and no one wore any ornaments.

[5] The LORD spoke to Moses: Speak to the Israelites: You are a stiff-necked people. Were I to go up in your company even for a moment, I would destroy you. Now off with your ornaments! Let me think what to do with you. [6] So, from Mount Horeb onward, the Israelites stripped off their ornaments.

**Moses' Intimacy with God.** [7] Moses used to pitch a tent* outside the camp at some distance. It was called the tent of meeting. Anyone who wished to consult the LORD would go to the tent of meeting outside the camp.

[8] Whenever Moses went out to the tent, the people would all rise and stand at the entrance of their own tents, watching Moses until he entered the tent. [9] As Moses entered the tent, the column of cloud would come down and stand at its entrance while the LORD spoke with Moses. [10] On seeing the column of cloud stand at the entrance of the tent, all the people would rise and bow down at the entrance of their own tents. [11] The LORD used to speak to Moses face to face,* as a person speaks to a friend. Moses would then return to the camp, but his young assistant, Joshua, son of Nun, never left the tent. [12] Moses said to the LORD, "See, you are telling me: Lead this people.* But you have not let me know whom you will send with me. Yet you have said: You are my intimate friend;† You have found favor with me. [13] Now, if I have found favor with you, please let me know your ways so that, in knowing you, I may continue to find favor with you. See, this nation is indeed your own people. [14] The LORD answered: I myself† will go along, to give you rest. [15] Moses replied, "If you are not going yourself, do not make us go up from here. [16] For how can it be known that I and your people have found favor with you, except by your going with us? Then we, your people and I, will be singled out from every other people on the surface of the earth." [17] The LORD said to Moses: This request, too, which you have made, I will carry out, because you have found favor with me and you are my intimate friend.

[18] Then Moses said, "Please let me see your glory!" [19] The LORD answered: I will make all my goodness pass before you, and I will proclaim my name, "LORD," before you; I who show favor to whom I will, I who grant mercy to whom I will.* [20] But you cannot see my face,* for no one can see me and live.† [21] Here, continued the LORD, is a place near me where you shall station yourself on the rock. [22] When my glory passes I will set you in the cleft of the rock and will cover you with my hand until I have passed by. [23] Then I will remove my hand,

---

† **32:32** *The book that you have written*: a symbolic reference to the list of God's faithful people.

**33:12** *Intimate friend*: lit., "know by name." The root word meaning "know" or "make known" appears four times in vv. 12–13.

**33:14** *I myself*: lit., "my face," that is, "my presence." The making of the calf (32:1–4) is an attempt to control the Lord's presence. In response the Lord refuses to accompany the people (33:3) until Moses persuades him.

**33:20** *No one can see me and live*: reflecting the tradition

that to see God meant instant death. This is contradicted by the statements that Hagar (Gn 16:13), Jacob (Gn 32:31), and Manoah and his wife (Jgs 13:22) all "see God" and yet live (see also Ex 24:10–11).

**32:30–34** Dt 9:18–19.  **33:11** Nm 12:8; Dt 34:10;
  **33:1** Gn 12:7.              Sir 45:4–5.
  **33:2** Ex 23:23.        **33:12** Ex 32:34.
  **33:7** Ex 29:42–43.     **33:19** Rom 9:15.
                             **33:20** Jn 1:18; 1 Tm 6:16.

so that you may see my back; but my face may not be seen.

# 34 Renewal of the Tablets.

[1]The LORD said to Moses: "Cut two stone tablets like the former,* that I may write on them the words† which were on the former tablets that you broke. [2]Get ready for tomorrow morning, when you are to go up Mount Sinai and there present yourself to me on the top of the mountain. [3]No one shall come up with you, and let no one even be seen on any part of the mountain;* even the sheep and the cattle are not to graze in front of this mountain." [4]Moses then cut two stone tablets like the former, and early the next morning he went up Mount Sinai as the LORD had commanded him, taking in his hand the two stone tablets.

[5]The LORD came down in a cloud and stood with him there and proclaimed the name, "LORD." [6]So the LORD passed before him and proclaimed: The LORD, the LORD, a God gracious and merciful, slow to anger and abounding in love and fidelity,† [7]continuing his love for a thousand generations, and forgiving wickedness, rebellion, and sin; yet not declaring the guilty guiltless, but bringing punishment for their parents' wickedness on children and children's children to the third and fourth generation!* [8]Moses at once knelt and bowed down to the ground. [9]Then he said, "If I find favor with you, Lord, please, Lord, come along in our company. This is indeed a stiff-necked people; yet pardon our wickedness and sins, and claim us as your own."

**Religious Laws.** [10]The LORD said: Here is the covenant I will make. Before all your people I will perform marvels never before done† in any nation anywhere on earth, so that all the people among whom you live may see the work of the LORD. Awe-inspiring are the deeds I will perform with you! [11]As for you, observe what I am commanding you today.*

See, I am about to drive out before you the Amorites, Canaanites, Hittites, Perizzites, Hivites and Jebusites. [12]*Take care not to make a covenant with the inhabitants of the land that you are to enter; lest they become a snare among you. [13]Tear down their altars; smash their sacred stones, and cut down their asherahs.† [14]You shall not bow down to any other god, for the LORD—"Jealous"† his name—is a jealous God. [15]Do not make a covenant with the inhabitants of the land; else, when they prostitute themselves with their gods and sacrifice to them, one of them may invite you and you may partake of the sacrifice. [16]And when you take their daughters as wives for your sons, and their daughters prostitute themselves with their gods, they will make your sons do the same.

[17]You shall not make for yourselves molten gods.*

[18]You shall keep the festival of Unleavened Bread.* For seven days at the appointed time in the month of Abib you are to eat unleavened bread, as I commanded you; for in the month of Abib you came out of Egypt.

[19]To me belongs every male that opens the womb among all your livestock, whether in the herd or in the flock.* [20]The firstling of a donkey you shall redeem with a lamb; if you do not redeem it, you must break its neck. The firstborn among your sons you shall redeem.

No one shall appear before me empty-handed.

[21]Six days you may labor,* but on the seventh day you shall rest; even during the seasons of plowing and harvesting you must rest.

[22]*You shall keep the feast of Weeks with the first fruits of the wheat harvest, likewise, the feast of the Ingathering at the close of the year.† [23]Three times a year all your men shall appear before the Lord, the LORD God of Israel.

---

† **34:1** *Words:* a common term for commandments, especially the Decalogue (see v. 28). In v. 27 "words" connotes the commands given in vv. 11–26.

**34:6** *Gracious…fidelity:* this succinct poetic description of God is an often-repeated statement of belief (see Nm 14:18; Ps 103:8; 145:8; Jl 2:13; Jon 4:2). All the terms describe God's relationship to the covenant people.

**34:10** *Never before done:* lit., "created." The verb used here (Heb. *baraʾ*) is predicated only of God (see Gn 1:1, 21, 27; Ps 51:12). These wonders are a new creation and can be performed only by God.

**34:13** Asherah was the name of a Canaanite goddess. In her honor wooden poles (*asherot*) were erected, just as stone pillars (*massebot*) were erected in honor of the god Baal. Both were placed near the altar in a Canaanite shrine.

**34:14** *Jealous:* see note on 20:5. Some, by a slight emendation, render, "The Lord is jealous for his name." Cf. Ez 39:25.

**34:22** *Feast of Weeks:* the festival of thanksgiving for the harvest, celebrated seven weeks or fifty days after the beginning of the harvest. It was also called Pentecost (fiftieth) and coincided with the giving of the law on Mount Sinai, fifty days after the offering of the first fruits; cf. Lv 23:10–11; Dt 16:9. *Feast of the Ingathering:* feast of Booths.

**34:1** Dt 10:1–2.
**34:3** Ex 19:12–13, 21.
**34:6–7** Ex 20:5–6; Nm 14:18; Dt 5:9–10; Jer 32:18.
**34:11** Ex 13:5; 33:2.
**34:12–16** Ex 23:32–33; Dt 7:1–5; 12:2–3.
**34:17** Lv 19:4; Dt 5:8–9.
**34:18** Ex 12:15–20; 13:3–4.
**34:19–20** Ex 13:2, 12–13; 23:15.
**34:21** Ex 20:9–10.
**34:22–23** Ex 23:16–17; Dt 16:10, 13, 16.

E X

24 Since I will drive out the nations before you and enlarge your territory, no one will covet your land when you go up three times a year to appear before the LORD, your God.

25 You shall not offer me the blood of sacrifice with anything leavened, nor shall the sacrifice of the Passover feast be kept overnight for the next day.

26 The choicest first fruits of your soil you shall bring to the house of the LORD, your God.

You shall not boil a young goat in its mother's milk. *

**Radiance of Moses' Face.** 27 Then the LORD said to Moses: Write down these words, for in accordance with these words I have made a covenant with you and with Israel. 28 So Moses was there with the LORD for forty days and forty nights, * without eating any food or drinking any water, and he wrote on the tablets the words of the covenant, the ten words.

29 As Moses came down from Mount Sinai with the two tablets of the covenant in his hands, he did not know that the skin of his face had become radiant† while he spoke with the LORD. 30 When Aaron, then, and the other Israelites saw Moses and noticed how radiant the skin of his face had become, they were afraid to come near him. 31 Only after Moses called to them did Aaron and all the leaders of the community come back to him. Moses then spoke to them. 32 Later, all the Israelites came up to him, and he enjoined on them all that the LORD had told him on Mount Sinai. 33 When Moses finished speaking with them, he put a veil over his face. 34 Whenever Moses entered the presence of the LORD to speak with him, he removed the veil until he came out again. * On coming out, he would tell the Israelites all that he had been commanded. 35 Then the Israelites would see that the skin of Moses' face was radiant; so he would again put the veil over his face until he went in to speak with the LORD.

## VIII. THE BUILDING OF THE TABERNACLE AND THE DESCENT OF GOD'S GLORY UPON IT

# 35

**Sabbath Regulations.** 1 Moses assembled the whole Israelite community

and said to them, * "These are the words the LORD has commanded to be observed. 2 On six days work may be done, but the seventh day shall be holy to you as the sabbath of complete rest to the LORD. Anyone who does work on that day shall be put to death. 3 You shall not even light a fire in any of your dwellings on the sabbath day."

**Collection of Materials.** 4 Moses said to the whole Israelite community, "This is what the LORD has commanded: 5 * Receive from among you contributions for the LORD. Everyone, as his heart prompts him, shall bring, as a contribution to the LORD, gold, silver, and bronze; 6 violet, purple, and scarlet yarn; fine linen and goat hair; 7 rams' skins dyed red, and tahash skins; acacia wood; 8 oil for the light; spices for the anointing oil and for the fragrant incense; 9 onyx stones and other gems for mounting on the ephod and on the breastpiece.

**Call for Artisans.** 10 * "Let every artisan among you come and make all that the LORD has commanded: 11 the tabernacle, with its tent, its covering, its clasps, its frames, its bars, its columns, and its pedestals; 12 the ark, with its poles, the cover, and the curtain veil; 13 the table, with its poles and all its utensils, and the showbread; 14 the menorah, with its utensils, the lamps, and the oil for the light; 15 the altar of incense, with its poles; the anointing oil, and the fragrant incense; the entrance curtain for the entrance of the tabernacle; 16 the altar for burnt offerings, with its bronze grating, its poles, and all its utensils; the basin, with its stand; 17 the hangings of the court, with their columns and pedestals; the curtain for the gate of the court; 18 the tent pegs for the tabernacle and for the court, with their ropes; 19 the service cloths for use in the sanctuary; the sacred vestments for Aaron, the priest, and the vestments for his sons in their ministry."

**The Contribution.** 20 When the whole Israelite community left Moses' presence, 21 all, as their hearts moved them and their spirit prompted, brought a contribution to the LORD for the work of the tent of meeting, for all its services, and for the sacred vestments. 22 Both the men

---

† **34:29** *Radiant:* the Hebrew word translated "radiant" is spelled like the term for "horns." Thus the artistic tradition of portraying Moses with horns.

**34:25–26** Ex 23:18–19.
**34:28** Ex 24:18; Dt 9:9, 18; 10:2, 4.
**34:33–34** 2 Cor 3:13, 16.

**35:1–3** Ex 31:13–17.
**35:5–9** Ex 25:2–7.
**35:10–19** Ex 31:6–11.

and the women, all as their heart prompted them, brought brooches, earrings, rings, necklaces, and various other gold articles.* Everyone who could presented an offering of gold to the LORD. 23 Everyone who happened to have violet, purple, or scarlet yarn, fine linen or goat hair, rams' skins dyed red or tahash skins, brought them. 24 Whoever could make a contribution of silver or bronze offered it to the LORD; and everyone who happened to have acacia wood for any part of the work, brought it. 25 All the women who were expert spinners brought hand-spun violet, purple, and scarlet yarn and fine linen thread. 26 All the women, as their hearts and skills moved them, spun goat hair. 27 The tribal leaders brought onyx stones and other gems for mounting on the ephod and on the breastpiece; 28 as well as spices, and oil for the light, anointing oil, and fragrant incense. 29 Every Israelite man and woman brought to the LORD such voluntary offerings as they thought best, for the various kinds of work which the LORD, through Moses, had commanded to be done.

**The Artisans.** 30 Moses said to the Israelites:* "See, the LORD has singled out Bezalel, son of Uri, son of Hur, of the tribe of Judah, 31 and has filled him with a divine spirit of skill and understanding and knowledge in every craft: 32 in the production of embroidery, in making things of gold, silver, or bronze, 33 in cutting and mounting precious stones, in carving wood, and in every other craft. 34 He has also given both him and Oholiab, son of Ahisamach, of the tribe of Dan, the ability to teach others. 35 He has endowed them with skill to execute all types of work: engraving, embroidering, the making of variegated cloth of violet, purple, and scarlet yarn and fine linen thread, weaving, and all other arts and crafts.

**36** 1 "Bezalel, therefore, will set to work with Oholiab and with all the artisans whom the LORD has endowed with skill and understanding in knowing how to do all the work for the service of the sanctuary, just as the LORD has commanded."* 2 Moses then called Bezalel and Oholiab and all the other artisans whom the LORD had endowed with skill, men whose hearts moved them to come and do the work. 3 They received from Moses all the contributions which the Israelites had brought for the work to be done for the sanctuary service. Still, morning after morning the people continued to bring their voluntary offerings to Moses. 4 Thereupon all the artisans who were doing the work for the sanctuary came from the work each was doing, 5 and told Moses, "The people are bringing much more than is needed to carry out the work which the LORD has commanded us to do." 6 Moses, therefore, ordered a proclamation to be made throughout the camp: "Let neither man nor woman make any more contributions for the sanctuary." So the people stopped bringing their offerings; 7 there was already enough at hand, and more than enough, to complete the work to be done.

**The Tent Cloth and Coverings.** 8* The various artisans who were doing the work made the tabernacle with its ten sheets woven of fine linen twined, having cherubim embroidered on them with violet, purple, and scarlet yarn. 9 The length of each sheet was twenty-eight cubits, and the width four cubits; all the sheets were the same size. 10 Five of the sheets were joined together, edge to edge; and the other five sheets likewise, edge to edge. 11 Loops of violet yarn were made along the edge of the end sheet in the first set, and the same along the edge of the end sheet in the second set. 12 Fifty loops were thus put on one inner sheet, and fifty loops on the inner sheet in the other set, with the loops directly opposite each other. 13 Then fifty clasps of gold were made, with which the sheets were joined so that the tabernacle formed one whole.

14 Sheets of goat hair were also woven as a tent over the tabernacle. Eleven such sheets were made. 15 The length of each sheet was thirty cubits and the width four cubits; all eleven sheets were the same size. 16 Five of these sheets were joined into one set, and the other six sheets into another set. 17 Fifty loops were made along the edge of the end sheet in one set, and fifty loops along the edge of the corresponding sheet in the other set. 18 Fifty bronze clasps were made with which the tent was joined so that it formed one whole. 19 A covering for the tent was made of rams' skins dyed red and, above that, a covering of tahash skins.

**The Framework.** 20 * Frames were made for the tabernacle, acacia-wood uprights. 21 The length of each frame was ten cubits, and the width one and a half cubits. 22 Each frame had two arms, fastening them one to another. In this way all the frames of the tabernacle were made. 23 The frames for the tabernacle were made as follows: twenty frames on the south side, 24 with forty silver pedestals under the twenty frames, two pedestals under each frame for its two arms; 25 twenty frames on the other side of the tabernacle, the north side, 26 with their forty silver pedestals, two pedestals under each frame. 27 At the rear of the tabernacle, to the west, six frames were made, 28 and two frames were made for the corners of the tabernacle, at its rear. 29 These were double at the bottom, and likewise double at the top, to the first ring. That is how both corner frames were made. 30 Thus, there were eight frames, with their sixteen silver pedestals, two pedestals under each frame. 31 Bars of acacia wood were also made, five for the frames on one side of the tabernacle, 32 five for those on the other side, and five for those at the rear, to the west. 33 The center bar, at the middle of the frames, was made to reach across from end to end. 34 The frames were plated with gold, and gold rings were made on them as holders for the bars, which were also plated with gold.

**The Veil.** 35 * The veil was made of violet, purple, and scarlet yarn, and of fine linen twined, with cherubim embroidered on it. 36 Four gold-plated columns of acacia wood, with gold hooks, were made for it, and four silver pedestals were cast for them.

37 The curtain for the entrance of the tent was made of violet, purple, and scarlet yarn, and of fine linen twined, woven in a variegated manner. 38 Its five columns, with their hooks as well as their capitals and bands, were plated with gold; their five pedestals were of bronze.

# 37 **The Ark.** 1 Bezalel made the ark of acacia wood, two and a half cubits long, one and a half cubits wide, and one and a half cubits high. 2 The inside and outside were plated with gold, and a molding of gold was put around it. 3 Four gold rings were cast for its four supports, two rings on one side and two

on the opposite side. 4 Poles of acacia wood were made and plated with gold; 5 these poles were put through the rings on the sides of the ark, for carrying it.

6 The cover was made of pure gold, two and a half cubits long and one and a half cubits wide. 7 Two cherubim of beaten gold were made for the two ends of the cover; 8 one cherub was at one end, the other at the other end, made of one piece with the cover, at each end. 9 The cherubim had their wings spread out above, sheltering the cover. They faced each other, with their faces looking toward the cover.*

**The Table.** 10 * The table was made of acacia wood, two cubits long, a cubit wide, and a cubit and a half high. 11 It was plated with pure gold, and a molding of gold was put around it. 12 A frame a handbreadth high was also put around it, with a molding of gold around the frame. 13 Four rings of gold were cast for it and fastened at the four corners, one at each leg. 14 The rings were alongside the frame as holders for the poles to carry the table. 15 These poles for carrying the table were made of acacia wood and plated with gold. 16 The vessels that were set on the table, its plates and cups, as well as its pitchers and bowls for pouring libations, were made of pure gold.

**The Menorah.** 17 * The menorah was made of pure beaten gold—its shaft and branches—with its cups and knobs and petals springing directly from it. 18 Six branches extended from its sides, three branches on one side and three on the other. 19 On one branch there were three cups, shaped like almond blossoms, each with its knob and petals; on the opposite branch there were three cups, shaped like almond blossoms, each with its knob and petals; and so for the six branches that extended from the menorah. 20 On the menorah there were four cups, shaped like almond blossoms, with their knobs and petals. 21 The six branches that went out from the menorah had a knob under each pair. 22 The knobs and branches so sprang from it that the whole formed but a single piece of pure beaten gold. 23 Its seven lamps, as well as its trimming shears and trays, were made of pure gold. 24 A talent of pure gold was used for the menorah and its various utensils.

**The Altar of Incense.** 25* The altar of incense was made of acacia wood, on a square, a cubit long, a cubit wide, and two cubits high, having horns that sprang directly from it. 26 Its grate on top, its walls on all four sides, and its horns were plated with pure gold; and a gold molding was put around it. 27 Underneath the molding gold rings were placed, two on one side and two on the opposite side, as holders for the poles used in carrying it. 28 The poles, too, were made of acacia wood and plated with gold.

29 The sacred anointing oil and the fragrant incense were prepared in their pure form by a perfumer.*

**38** **The Altar for Burnt Offerings.** 1 The altar for burnt offerings* was made of acacia wood, on a square, five cubits long and five cubits wide; its height was three cubits. 2 At the four corners horns were made that sprang directly from the altar. It was then plated with bronze. 3 All the utensils of the altar, the pots, shovels, basins, forks and fire pans, were likewise made of bronze. 4 A grating, a bronze network, was made for the altar and placed around it, on the ground, half as high as the altar itself. 5 Four rings were cast for the four corners of the bronze grating, as holders for the poles, 6 which were made of acacia wood and plated with bronze. 7 The poles were put through the rings on the sides of the altar for carrying it. The altar was made in the form of a hollow box.

8 The bronze basin,* with its bronze stand, was made from the mirrors of the women who served† at the entrance of the tent of meeting.

**The Court of the Tabernacle.** 9* The court was made as follows. On the south side the hangings of the court were of fine linen twined, a hundred cubits long, 10 with twenty columns and twenty pedestals of bronze, the hooks and bands of the columns being of silver. 11 On the north side there were similar hangings, a hundred cubits long, with twenty columns and twenty pedestals of bronze; the hooks and bands of the columns were of silver. 12 On the west side there were hangings, fifty cubits long, with ten columns and ten pedestals; the hooks

and bands of the columns were of silver. 13 On the east side the court was fifty cubits. 14 On one side there were hangings to the extent of fifteen cubits, with three columns and three pedestals; 15 on the other side, beyond the gate of the court, there were likewise hangings to the extent of fifteen cubits, with three columns and three pedestals. 16 The hangings on all sides of the court were woven of fine linen twined. 17 The pedestals of the columns were of bronze, while the hooks and bands of the columns were of silver; the capitals were silver-plated, and all the columns of the court were banded with silver.

18 At the gate of the court there was a variegated curtain, woven of violet, purple, and scarlet yarn and of fine linen twined, twenty cubits long and five cubits wide, in keeping with the hangings of the court. 19 There were four columns and four pedestals of bronze for it, while their hooks were of silver, and their capitals and their bands silver-plated. 20 All the tent pegs for the tabernacle and for the court around it were of bronze.

**Amount of Metal Used.** 21 The following is an account of the various amounts used on the tabernacle, the tabernacle of the covenant, drawn up at the command of Moses by the Levites under the direction of Ithamar, son of Aaron the priest. 22 However, it was Bezalel, son of Uri,* son of Hur, of the tribe of Judah, who made all that the LORD commanded Moses, 23 and he was assisted by Oholiab, son of Ahisamach, of the tribe of Dan, who was an engraver, an embroiderer, and a weaver of variegated cloth of violet, purple, and scarlet yarn and of fine linen.

24 All the gold used in the entire construction of the sanctuary, having previously been given as an offering, amounted to twenty-nine talents and seven hundred and thirty shekels, according to the standard of the sanctuary shekel. 25 The silver of those of the community who were enrolled was one hundred talents and one thousand seven hundred and seventy-five shekels, according to the standard of the sanctuary shekel; 26 one bekah apiece, that is, a half-shekel, according to the standard of the sanctuary shekel, was received from everyone

---

† **38:8** The reflecting surface of ancient mirrors was usually of polished bronze. *The women who served*: cf. 1 Sm 2:22.

37:25–28 Ex 30:1–5.
37:29 Ex 30:23–25, 34–36.
38:1–7 Ex 27:1–8; 2 Chr 1:5.
38:8 Ex 30:18–21.
38:9–20 Ex 27:9–19.
38:22–23 Ex 31:2, 6; 35:30, 34; 36:1.
38:26 Nm 1:46.

who was enrolled, of twenty years or more, namely, six hundred and three thousand five hundred and fifty men.* 27 One hundred talents of silver were used for casting the pedestals of the sanctuary and the pedestals of the veil, one talent for each pedestal, or one hundred talents for the one hundred pedestals. 28 The remaining one thousand seven hundred and seventy-five shekels were used for making the hooks on the columns, for plating the capitals, and for banding them with silver. 29 The bronze, given as an offering, amounted to seventy talents and two thousand four hundred shekels. 30 With this were made the pedestals at the entrance of the tent of meeting, the bronze altar with its bronze gratings, and all the utensils of the altar, 31 the pedestals around the court, the pedestals at the gate of the court, and all the tent pegs for the tabernacle and for the court around it.

# 39 The Priestly Vestments. 1 With violet, purple, and scarlet yarn were woven the service cloths for use in the sanctuary, as well as the sacred vestments* for Aaron, as the LORD had commanded Moses.

2* The ephod was woven of gold thread and of violet, purple, and scarlet yarn and of fine linen twined. 3 Gold was first hammered into gold leaf and then cut up into threads, which were woven with the violet, purple, and scarlet yarn into an embroidered pattern on the fine linen. 4 Shoulder straps were made for it and joined to its two upper ends. 5 The embroidered belt on the ephod extended out from it, and like it, was made of gold thread, of violet, purple, and scarlet yarn, and of fine linen twined, as the LORD had commanded Moses. 6 The onyx stones were prepared and mounted in gold filigree work; they were engraved like seal engravings with the names of the sons of Israel. 7 These stones were set on the shoulder straps of the ephod as memorial stones of the sons of Israel, just as the LORD had commanded Moses.

8* The breastpiece was embroidered like the ephod, with gold thread and violet, purple, and scarlet yarn on cloth of fine linen twined. 9 It was square and folded double, a span high and a span wide in its folded form. 10 Four rows of precious stones were mounted on it: in the first row a carnelian, a topaz, and an emerald; 11 in the second row, a garnet, a sapphire, and a beryl; 12 in the third row a jacinth, an agate, and an amethyst; 13 in the fourth row a chrysolite, an onyx, and a jasper. They were mounted in gold filigree work. 14 These stones were twelve, to match the names of the sons of Israel, and each stone was engraved like a seal with the name of one of the twelve tribes.

15* Chains of pure gold, twisted like cords, were made for the breastpiece, 16 together with two gold filigree rosettes and two gold rings. The two rings were fastened to the two upper ends of the breastpiece. 17 The two gold chains were then fastened to the two rings at the ends of the breastpiece. 18 The other two ends of the two chains were fastened in front to the two filigree rosettes, which were attached to the shoulder straps of the ephod. 19 Two other gold rings were made and put on the two lower ends of the breastpiece, on the edge facing the ephod. 20 Two more gold rings were made and fastened to the bottom of the two shoulder straps next to where they joined the ephod in front, just above its embroidered belt. 21 Violet ribbons bound the rings of the breastpiece to the rings of the ephod, so that the breastpiece stayed right above the embroidered belt of the ephod and did not swing loose from it. All this was just as the LORD had commanded Moses.

**Other Vestments.** 22 The robe of the ephod was woven entirely of violet yarn, 23 with an opening in its center like the opening of a shirt, with selvage around the opening to keep it from being torn. 24 At the hem of the robe pomegranates were made of violet, purple, and scarlet yarn and of fine linen twined; 25 bells of pure gold were also made and put between the pomegranates all around the hem of the robe: 26 a bell, a pomegranate, a bell, a pomegranate, all around the hem of the robe which was to be worn in performing the ministry—all this, just as the LORD had commanded Moses.

27 For Aaron and his sons there were also woven tunics of fine linen;* 28 the turban of fine linen; the ornate skullcaps of fine linen; linen pants of fine linen twined; 29 and sashes of variegated work made of fine linen twined and of violet, purple, and scarlet yarn, as the LORD had commanded Moses. 30* The plate of

39:1 Ex 31:10.          39:8–14 Ex 28:15–21.          39:27–29 Ex 28:39–42.          39:30–31 Ex 28:36–37.
39:2–10 Ex 28:6–12.     39:15–21 Ex 28:31–35.

the sacred diadem was made of pure gold and inscribed, as on a seal engraving: "Sacred to the LORD." [31] It was tied over the turban with a violet ribbon, as the LORD had commanded Moses.

### Presentation of the Work to Moses.
[32] Thus the entire work of the tabernacle of the tent of meeting was completed. The Israelites did the work just as the LORD had commanded Moses; so it was done. [33] They then brought to Moses the tabernacle, the tent with all its furnishings, the clasps, the frames, the bars, the columns, the pedestals, [34] the covering of rams' skins dyed red, the covering of tahash skins, the curtain veil; [35] the ark of the covenant with its poles, the cover, [36] the table with all its utensils and the showbread, [37] the pure gold menorah with its lamps set up on it and with all its utensils, the oil for the light, [38] the golden altar, the anointing oil, the fragrant incense; the curtain for the entrance of the tent, [39] the altar of bronze with its bronze grating, its poles and all its utensils, the basin with its stand, [40] the hangings of the court with their columns and pedestals, the curtain for the gate of the court with its ropes and tent pegs, all the equipment for the service of the tabernacle of the tent of meeting; [41] the service cloths for use in the sanctuary, the sacred vestments for Aaron the priest, and the vestments to be worn by his sons in their ministry. [42] Just as the LORD had commanded Moses, so the Israelites had carried out all the work. [43] So when Moses saw that all the work was done just as the LORD had commanded, he blessed them.

## 40 Setting Up the Tabernacle.
[1] Then the LORD said to Moses: [2] * On the first day of the first month† you shall set up the tabernacle of the tent of meeting. * [3] Put the ark of the covenant in it, and screen off the ark with the veil. * [4] Bring in the table and set it. Then bring in the menorah and set up the lamps on it. [5] Put the golden altar of incense in front of the ark of the covenant, and hang the curtain at the entrance of the tabernacle. [6] Put the altar for burnt offerings in front of the entrance of the tabernacle of the tent of meeting. [7] Place

the basin between the tent of meeting and the altar, and put water in it. [8] Set up the court round about, and put the curtain at the gate of the court.

[9] * Take the anointing oil and anoint the tabernacle and everything in it, consecrating it and all its furnishings, so that it will be sacred. [10] Anoint the altar for burnt offerings and all its utensils, consecrating it, so that it will be most sacred. [11] Likewise, anoint the basin with its stand, and thus consecrate it.

[12] * Then bring Aaron and his sons to the entrance of the tent of meeting, and there wash them with water. [13] Clothe Aaron with the sacred vestments and anoint him, thus consecrating him as my priest. [14] Bring forward his sons also, and clothe them with the tunics. [15] As you have anointed their father, anoint them also as my priests. Thus, by being anointed, shall they receive a perpetual priesthood throughout all future generations.

[16] Moses did just as the LORD had commanded him. [17] On the first day of the first month of the second year the tabernacle was set up. [18] It was Moses who set up the tabernacle. He placed its pedestals, set up its frames, put in its bars, and set up its columns. [19] He spread the tent over the tabernacle and put the covering on top of the tent, as the LORD had commanded him. [20] * He took the covenant and put it in the ark; he placed poles alongside the ark and set the cover upon it. [21] He brought the ark into the tabernacle and hung the curtain veil, thus screening off the ark of the covenant, as the LORD had commanded him. [22] He put the table in the tent of meeting, on the north side of the tabernacle, outside the veil, [23] and arranged the bread on it before the LORD, as the LORD had commanded him. * [24] He placed the menorah in the tent of meeting, opposite the table, on the south side of the tabernacle, [25] and he set up the lamps before the LORD, as the LORD had commanded him. [26] He placed the golden altar in the tent of meeting, in front of the veil, [27] and on it he burned fragrant incense, as the LORD had commanded him. [28] He hung the curtain at the entrance of the tabernacle. [29] He put the altar

---

† 40:2 *On the first day of the first month*: almost a year after the departure of the Israelites from Egypt. Cf. v. 17.

* 40:2–8 Ex 40:16–33.
40:2 Ex 26:30.
40:3–8 Ex 26:33–37.
40:9–11 Ex 30:26–29.
40:12–15 Ex 28:41; 29:4–9; Lv 8:1–13.
40:20–29 Ex 25:16, 21; 26:33–37.
40:23 Ex 25:30.

for burnt offerings in front of the entrance of the tabernacle of the tent of meeting, and sacrificed burnt offerings and grain offerings on it, as the LORD had commanded him. 30*He placed the basin between the tent of meeting and the altar, and put water in it for washing. 31Moses and Aaron and his sons used to wash their hands and feet there, 32for they washed themselves whenever they went into the tent of meeting or approached the altar, as the LORD had commanded Moses. 33Finally, he set up the court around the tabernacle and the altar and hung the curtain at the gate of the court.

Thus Moses finished all the work.

**God's Presence in the Tabernacle.** 34*Then the cloud covered the tent of meeting, and the glory of the LORD filled the tabernacle. 35Moses could not enter the tent of meeting, because the cloud settled down upon it and the glory of the LORD filled the tabernacle. 36Whenever the cloud rose from the tabernacle, the Israelites would set out on their journey. 37But if the cloud did not lift, they would not go forward; only when it lifted did they go forward. 38The cloud of the LORD was over the tabernacle by day, and fire in the cloud at night, in the sight of the whole house of Israel in all the stages of their journey.

---

40:30–32 Ex 30:18–21.          40:34–38 Nm 9:15–22.

# The Book of
# Leviticus

## INTRODUCTION

### Pauline A. Viviano

The book of Leviticus ushers the contemporary reader into the realm of the sacred as it confronts the realm of the common and mundane. It is concerned with a holy God who requires Israel to be holy in every aspect of its life. The rules and regulations of the book of Leviticus are often seen as unnecessary and obsolete for they reflect a religious worldview not shared by many today, but Israel's concern with how to live in the presence of a holy God is a concern that is ever present in communities of faith.

## Context, Origin, and Date of Leviticus

As part of the Pentateuch the book of Leviticus is drawn into the larger narrative of Israel's Exodus from Egypt and the establishment of a covenant relationship with Yahweh on Mount Sinai. Its immediate literary context is the series of laws on priestly matters from Ex 25:1 to Nm 10:10. It is difficult to determine precisely the prehistory of the book of Leviticus. It is clear that the book grew over time from material that was composed and preserved within Priestly circles. It is generally accepted that Lv 1–16 is a collection with its own stages of development and that the Holiness Code (Lv 17–26) and Lv 27 were independent works edited into the book of Leviticus. The dating of Priestly material is notoriously difficult, for ritual laws and practices are very slow to change. The book of Leviticus probably did not receive its final form until the postexilic period, but much of the material in the book surely comes from an earlier time. The book of Leviticus represents cultic observances as practiced in the Second Temple, but many of these observances have been drawn into the Second Temple period from the preexilic period.

## Outline of Leviticus

I.   **Ritual of Sacrifices (1:1–7:38)**

   A. **Instructions for the Israelites (1:1–5:26)**

   B. **Instructions for the Priests (6:1–7:38)**

II.  **Ceremony of Ordination (8:1–10:20)**

III. **Laws Regarding Ritual Purity (11:1–16:34)**

IV.  **Holiness Laws (17:1–26:46)**

V.   **Redemption of Offerings (27:1–34)**

## Holiness and the Clean and Unclean

The concept of ritually clean and ritually unclean grounds many of the regulations in Leviticus. Clean and unclean do not have to do with hygienic practices, but with whether one is able to participate in cultic rituals or is barred from doing so. Ritually unclean is not the same as dirty or immoral, although immorality could render one unclean. Rather the concern with ritually clean and unclean focuses on what makes it acceptable or unacceptable for a person to come into the presence of the holy. Even today when one comes into the presence of a holy or powerful person, one prepares for that encounter by bathing and putting on clean and appropriate dress. So too, in ancient Israel one prepared to come before God by ensuring that one was fit to do so by being in a state of ritual purity, that is, by being "clean."

Israel's concern with clean/unclean is bound up with Israel's understanding of holiness. The root meaning of the Hebrew word for holiness (qdsh) is "to be separate or set apart." God is utterly holy, for God is completely set apart from the created order; God is "Other." Holiness is not an attribute of God among other attributes, but it defines who God is and thus grounds all attributes. The holiness of God is manifest in God's power over all of creation. The experience of the holiness of God is awe-inspiring and leads one to acknowledge the absolute supremacy of God and to bow before this God in worship. The phrase "fear of God" captures the feeling of reverence and humility that is generated by the experience of the awesome power of the deity. To come into the presence of the holy is fraught with danger. To move from the common, mundane realm of daily life into the sacred realm where one has access to God requires preparation.

Israel is called to be a holy nation (Lv 19:2), a people set apart from all other nations. This call to holiness will affect every aspect of Israel's life. The people of Israel are called to abide by moral and ritual codes that allow them to live as Yahweh's holy people. Israel is to set apart certain objects, times, places, and even people as sacred. The book of Leviticus instructs Israel and its priests about the proper ordering of its life as a holy nation dedicated to a holy God. Though much of Leviticus focuses on cultic matters and the ordering of the community in terms of holiness, it is also concerned with issues of justice in the daily affairs of the community. A holy people do not engage in deceitful business practices (19:35–36), slander (19:16), or mistreatment of the weak and handicapped (19:14). Judgment is to be rendered fairly and impartially (19:15). Israel is to care for the poor and the alien in the land (19:9–10); Israelites are to show love not only to their neighbor (19:18) but also to the immigrant (19:33–34).

## Sacrifices

The opening chapters of Leviticus set out the various kinds of sacrifice: burnt offerings (Lv 1:1–17), grain offerings (2:1–16), communion sacrifices (3:1–17), purification offerings (4:1–5:13), and reparation offerings (5:14–26). These offerings are distinguished by what is to

be offered (animals and grains), how it is to be offered (burnt or slaughtered), and on what occasion (festival or atonement) it is to be offered. It is easy to get lost in the details surrounding the kinds of sacrifice and the rules regulating the offering of sacrifice, but for today's reader, why sacrifices were offered is probably a more important issue. Building upon the few hints given in the biblical text and drawing upon the research of anthropologists, biblical scholars have advanced three major reasons for offering sacrifice in ancient Israel: as a gift, to achieve union with God, and to atone for sin.

### As a Gift

In Israel sacrifice was offered as a gift to recognize Yahweh as sovereign Lord much as one would offer tribute to a king. The earth and all that is in it belongs to Yahweh as the creator God; Israel's use of the gifts of creation depends upon its recognition that all rightfully belongs to Yahweh. Sacrifice as gift could represent one's devotion and homage to the deity, but it could also express contrition and supplication. It could be an offering accompanied by joyful praise and gratitude for Yahweh's many blessings.

### To Achieve Union with God

In Israel sacrifice was offered to achieve union with Yahweh. Many sacrifices, though not all, were eaten symbolically by God and literally by the priest and the offerer with his family. Israel did not think that Yahweh literally ate food; Yahweh's part was burned to symbolize its transference to the heavenly realm in the "going up" of the smoke. The priest received part of the sacrifice as payment for his services, but the bulk of the offering was returned to the offerer and was eaten as a sacred meal by the offerer with his family and friends. It was thought that in sharing a meal with the deity a bond was created between Yahweh and Israel analogous to the familial bond created among those who share a meal together.

### To Atone for Sin

In Israel some sacrifices were offered to

atone for sin. In these sacrifices the removal of sin or impurity is indicated by the word *kippur,* which is often translated "atone," but this word includes other meanings such as "ransom," "cleanse," "purge," or "cover up." Sin is removed by the use of blood in these sacrifices, but exactly how this is to be understood is not clear. Blood was thought to contain the life-force of an animal or person. The blood/life of the animal may substitute for the blood/life of the sinner, thus serving as ransom for the life of the sinner. Repentance and restitution played a role in purification and reparation sacrifices.

## Festivals

In all religions certain times of the year are set apart as sacred. In the book of Leviticus these days are the sabbath (Lv 23:3) and the annual feasts (Passover and Unleavened Bread, 23:4–14; Weeks, also called Pentecost, 23:15–22; New Year's Day, 23:23–25; Day of Atonement, 16:1–34; 23:26–32; Booths, 23:33–43). These festivals gave the Israelites an opportunity to rest from their labors and focus on Yahweh's gracious deliverance from oppression, guidance in difficult times, gift of the law, blessing of an abundant harvest, and forgiveness of their sins. Two additional periods of time were set apart: the sabbatical year (25:1–7), and the jubilee year (25:8–22). During the sabbatical year the land was to lie fallow and during the jubilee year, not only was the land to lie fallow, but property bought in the last fifty years was to be returned to its owner. Though 1 Mc 6:48–54 attests to the observance of a sabbatical year, scholars debate whether the sabbatical year and the jubilee year as envisaged by Leviticus represent an ideal or actual practice.

## Priests

The main function of the priest in the book of Leviticus is to serve at the altar. This involves participating in and overseeing all aspects of sacrifice: the slaughtering of the animals, the sprinkling of blood when necessary, and the burning of animals as required. All of these actions are filled with symbolism and meaning and given religious significance. As those closest to the altar, priests must embody a greater degree of holiness than the average person and thus regulations surrounding the ritual purity of priests are more rigorous (Lv 21:1–22:16). Priests are given detailed instructions regarding the rubrics of sacrifice (6:1–7:27); even how they are to be paid is included in the book of Leviticus (7:28–38).

The book of Leviticus presents the ritual of anointing and consecration of Aaron and his sons in which they are symbolically moved from the common, everyday realm into the realm of the sacred in a ceremony that includes purification, offerings, washings, anointing, and ordination (Lv 8:1–9:24). The seriousness of approaching the altar without strict adherence to ritual regulations is indicated by the deaths of Nadab and Abihu when they make an unauthorized offering of fire (10:1–5). Only the Aaronide priesthood is authorized to preside at the altar. The Levites are mentioned only once in the book of Leviticus and that is only in reference to property claims (25:32–34). The lack of interest in the Levites may reflect the subordination of the levitical priesthood to the Aaronide priesthood that occurred in the late post-exilic period.

## Daily Life, Ritual Purity, and the Holiness Code

By the sanctification of daily life Israel lives out its call to be a holy nation. In the Exodus Israel experienced the holiness of Yahweh by being led from slavery to freedom, but the book of Leviticus shifts focus from Yahweh's act of liberation to what it means to live every day as a holy people. In the wilderness Yahweh sanctifies Israel by his presence in the tabernacle (Lv 26:11–12), but Israel is to sanctify itself by worshiping Yahweh and keeping the law (11:44; 20:7; 22:31–32). Holiness is to permeate every aspect of Israel's relationship with Yahweh and with one another. Thus there are regulations regarding what to eat (11:1–47) and the consecration of property and objects to Yahweh (27:1–33). There are laws covering skin diseases (13:1–46; 14:1–32), and mold and fungus on clothes and in homes (13:47–59; 14:33–57), as well as uncleanness associated with childbirth (12:1–8) and with bodily discharges (15:1–33). There are laws that cover sexual behavior (18:1–30) and a variety of other actions (19:1–37).

The concern behind all of these laws is with the holiness of Israel, which becomes explicit in the Holiness Code (Lv 17–26): "Be holy, for I, the LORD your God, am holy" (19:2). Many theories have been advanced as to why these laws developed, but no theory accounts for all

of the laws. These laws reflect the social and religious attitudes of the society that produced them. They give order to life, enabling those who live these laws to find that order. Behind these laws is a concept of holiness that sees the holy as whole, complete, and perfect. Anything that is imperfect and incomplete, contaminated in some way, renders one unclean. In many cases uncleanness is easily remedied by various rituals, but not in all cases. Few today find meaning in these laws, but the call to holiness remains as urgent as ever. ∎

# THE BOOK OF LEVITICUS

## New American Bible, Introduction

The name "Leviticus" was given to the third book of the Pentateuch by the ancient Greek translators because a good part of this book deals with concerns of the priests, who are of the tribe of Levi.

The book mainly treats cultic matters (i.e., sacrifices and offerings, purity and holiness, the priesthood, the operation of the sanctuary, and feast days) but is also interested in various behavioral, ethical, and economic issues (e.g., sexual practices, idolatrous worship, treatment of others, the sale of land, slavery). The goal of the laws is not merely legislative. For the most part they cohere as a system and attempt to inculcate a way of life in the book's hearers and readers. In addition to these concerns, Leviticus, comprising as it does the center of the Pentateuch, carries forward the narrative of Exodus (cf. chaps. 1, 8–9, 10, 16, 24).

The book is part of the Priestly tradition (P) of the Pentateuch, to which belong various narratives and legal passages (e.g., Gn 1:1–2:4; 9:1–17; 17:1–27; Ex 12:1–20, 40–50; 25:1–31:18; 35:1–40:38; Nm 1:1–10:28; 15:1–14; 17:1–19:22; 25:6–31:54). Within the Priestly material itself there are signs of variant traditions and development.

The main divisions of Leviticus are:

I. Ritual of Sacrifices (1:1–7:38)
   A. Instructions for the Israelites (1:1–5:26)
   B. Instructions for the Priests (6:1–7:38)
II. Ceremony of Ordination (8:1–10:20)
III. Laws Regarding Ritual Purity (11:1–16:34)
IV. Holiness Laws (17:1–26:46)
V. Redemption of Offerings (27:1–34) ∎

# LEVITICUS

## I. RITUAL OF SACRIFICES

### A. Instructions for the Israelites

**1** **Burnt Offerings.** [1]The LORD called Moses, and spoke to him from the tent of meeting:* [2]Speak to the Israelites and tell them: When any one of you† brings an offering of livestock to the LORD, you shall bring your offering from the herd or from the flock.*

[3]†* If a person's offering is a burnt offering† from the herd, the offering must be a male without blemish.* The individual shall bring it to the entrance of the tent of meeting to find favor with the LORD, [4]and shall lay a hand† on the head* of the burnt offering, so that it may be acceptable* to make atonement* for the one who offers it. [5]The bull shall then be slaughtered† before the LORD, and Aaron's sons, the priests, shall offer its blood by splashing it on all the sides of the altar which is at the entrance of the tent of meeting.* [6]Then the burnt offering shall be flayed and cut into pieces. [7]After Aaron's sons, the priests, have put burning embers on the altar and laid wood on them, [8]they shall lay the pieces of meat, together with the head and the suet, on top of the wood and the embers on the altar; [9]but the inner organs and the shanks shall

be washed with water. The priest shall then burn all of it on the altar as a burnt offering, a sweet-smelling oblation to the LORD.*

[10]If a person's burnt offering is from the flock, that is, a sheep or a goat, the offering must be a male without blemish. [11]It shall be slaughtered on the north side of the altar before the LORD, and Aaron's sons, the priests, shall splash its blood on all the sides of the altar. [12]When it has been cut into pieces, the priest shall lay these, together with the head and suet, on top of the wood and the embers on the altar; [13]but the inner organs and the shanks shall be washed with water. The priest shall then offer all of it, burning it on the altar. It is a burnt offering, a sweet-smelling oblation to the LORD.

[14]If a person offers a bird as a burnt offering to the LORD, the offering brought must be a turtledove or a pigeon.* [15]Having brought it to the altar, the priest shall wring its head off and burn it on the altar. The blood shall be drained out against the side of the altar.* [16]He shall remove its crissum† by means of its feathers and throw it on the ash heap at the east side of the altar. [17]Then, having torn the bird open by its wings without separating the halves, the priest shall burn it on the altar, on the wood and the embers. It is a burnt offering, a sweet-smelling oblation to the LORD.

**2** **Grain Offerings.** [1]†* When anyone brings a grain offering to the LORD, the offering must consist of bran flour. The offerer shall

---

† 

**1:2** *Any one of you*: women as well as men bring sacrifices (see 12:6–8; 15:28–30) and are explicitly obligated in other ritual matters (e.g., 13:29, 38; Nm 5:6; 6:2; Lk 2:24). Thus, though the Hebrew formulates sacrificial and other law with male reference, the translation reflects the inclusion of women in ritual requirements. *From the herd or from the flock*: the only animals which could be used as sacrificial victims were domestic animals either of the bovine class (bulls, cows and calves) or the ovine class (sheep and lambs, goats and kids). Excluded, therefore, were not only all wild animals, but also such "unclean" domestic animals as the camel and the donkey (cf. 11:1–47; 27:26–27).

**1:3–5** *Entrance of the tent of meeting…before the LORD*: probably the forecourt from the entrance of the court to the entrance of the tent (cf. Ex 27). Thus the altar in front of the tent was entirely accessible to the laity.

**1:3** The burnt offering is used for regular daily (6:1–6) offerings, public festivals (Nm 28–29), purification rituals (Lv 12:6–8; 14:19–20; 15:15, 30), and individuals' vows and voluntary offerings (22:18–20).

**1:4** *Lay a hand*: the imposition of a single hand for the sacrifices in chaps. 1–5 may be a means of designating the animal as belonging to the offerer. See note on 16:21. *Atonement*: see note on 16:6.

**1:5** *Shall then be slaughtered*: lit., "he shall slaughter the bull." Slaughtering is not something the offerer must do (as opposed to, for example, hand placement [v. 4] or the presentation

of sacrificial portions as an elevated offering [7:29–34]). Thus the verb is construed impersonally here.

**1:16** *Crissum*: the area around the anus of the bird, lying beneath the bird's tail.

**2:1** Grain offerings are used as independent offerings (those in this chapter and cf. 6:12–16; 8:26–27; 23:10–11), as substitutes for other offerings in a case of poverty (5:11–13), and as accompaniments to animal offerings (cf. Nm 15:1–12; 28:1–29:39; Lv 14:20; 23:12, 18, 37). Chapter 2 describes two basic types of grain offering: uncooked (vv. 1–3) and cooked (vv. 4–10). The flour (*sōlet*) used was made of wheat (Ex 29:2) and Jewish

---

**1:1** Ex 40.
**1:2** Lv 1:3, 10; 3:1, 6, 12.
**1:3** Lv 6:1–6; 22:18–19.
**1:3** Lv 22:17–25; Ex 12:5.
**1:4** Lv 3:2, 8, 13; 4:4, 15, 24, 29, 33; 8:14, 18, 22; Nm 8:12; 2 Chr 29:23; cf. Lv 16:21; 24:14; Nm 27:18, 23; Dt 34:9.
**1:4** Lv 19:5; 22:19–29; Gn 4:3–5; Mal 1:8–14.
**1:4** Lv 9:7; 14:20; Jb 1:5; 42:8; cf. Gn 32:21; Ex 29:36–37; 30:15;

Lv 16:16–20; 17:11; Ez 43:20, 26.
**1:5** Lv 1:11, 15; 3:2, 8, 13; cf. Lv 4:5–7, 25.
**1:9** Lv 2:2; 3:5; 4:31; 26:31; Gn 8:20–21; Nm 28:2; cf. Lv 3:11; 21:6, 21; 22:25.
**1:14** Lv 5:7; 12:8; 15:14–15; Lk 2:24.
**1:15** Lv 5:8–9.
**2:1** Lv 5:11–13; 6:7–16; 7:9–14; 24:5–9; Nm 15:1–21; cf. Gn 4:3–5.

pour oil on it and put frankincense* over it, [2] and bring it to Aaron's sons, the priests. A priest shall take a handful of the bran flour and oil, together with all the frankincense, and shall burn it on the altar as a token of the offering,† a sweet-smelling oblation to the LORD.* [3] The rest of the grain offering belongs to Aaron and his sons,* a most holy* portion from the oblations to the LORD.

[4] When you offer a grain offering baked in an oven, it must be in the form of unleavened cakes made of bran flour mixed with oil, or of unleavened wafers spread with oil.* [5] If your offering is a grain offering that is fried on a griddle,* it must be of bran flour mixed with oil and unleavened. [6] Break it into pieces, and pour oil over it. It is a grain offering. [7] If your offering is a grain offering that is prepared in a pan, it must be made of bran flour, fried in oil. [8] A grain offering that is made in any of these ways you shall bring to the LORD. It shall be presented to the priest, who shall take it to the altar. [9] The priest shall then remove from the grain offering a token and burn it on the altar as a sweet-smelling oblation to the LORD. [10] The rest of the grain offering belongs to Aaron and his sons, a most holy portion from the oblations to the LORD.

[11] † Every grain offering that you present to the LORD shall be unleavened, for you shall not burn any leaven or honey as an oblation to the LORD.* [12] Such you may present to the LORD in the offering of the first produce that is processed,* but they are not to be placed on the altar for a pleasing odor. [13] You shall season all your grain offerings with salt. Do not let the salt of the covenant with your God† be lacking from your grain offering. On every offering you shall offer salt.* [14] If you offer a grain offering of first ripe

fruits to the LORD, you shall offer it in the form of fresh early grain, roasted by fire and crushed as a grain offering of your first ripe fruits. [15] You shall put oil on it and set frankincense on it. It is a grain offering. [16] The priest shall then burn some of the groats and oil, together with all the frankincense, as a token of the offering, an oblation to the LORD.

# 3 Communion Sacrifices. [1] †* If a person's offering is a communion sacrifice, if it is brought from the herd, be it a male or a female animal, it must be presented without blemish* before the LORD. [2] The one offering it shall lay a hand on the head* of the offering. It shall then be slaughtered at the entrance of the tent of meeting. Aaron's sons, the priests, shall splash its blood on all the sides of the altar. [3] * From the communion sacrifice the individual shall offer as an oblation to the LORD the fat† that covers the inner organs, and all the fat that adheres to them, [4] as well as the two kidneys, with the fat on them near the loins, and the lobe of the liver, which is removed with the kidneys. [5] Aaron's sons shall burn this on the altar with the burnt offering that is on the wood and the embers, as a sweet-smelling oblation to the LORD. *

[6] If the communion sacrifice one offers to the LORD is from the flock, be it a male or a female animal, it must be presented without blemish. [7] If one presents a lamb as an offering, that person shall bring it before the LORD, [8] and after laying a hand on the head of the offering, it shall then be slaughtered before the tent of meeting. Aaron's sons shall splash its blood on all the sides of the altar. [9] From the communion sacrifice the individual shall present as an oblation to the LORD its fat: the whole fatty tail, which is removed close to

---

tradition and Semitic cognates indicate that it is a coarse rather than a fine flour.

**2:2** *Token of the offering:* lit., "reminder." Instead of burning the whole grain offering, only this part is burned on the altar.

**2:11–12** No grain offering that is leavened can be offered on the altar. Those in 7:13 and 23:17 are leavened but not offered on the altar. The Hebrew word for "honey" may refer to fruit syrup as well as to bee honey.

**2:13** *The salt of the covenant with your God:* partaking of salt in common was an ancient symbol of friendship and alliance. Cf. Mark 9:49–50 and Col 4:6.

**3:1** The exact meaning of Hebrew *shelamim,* "communion sacrifice," is not clear. It has also been rendered "gift," "(re)-payment," "peace," "well-being," or "covenant" offering. This offering may be brought for a vow or voluntary offering (cf. 22:21). A distinct version of the communion sacrifice is the thanksgiving offering (7:11–15 vis-à-vis vv. 16–18).

**3:3–5** *Fat:* only part of the offering is devoted to God, as opposed to the burnt offering (chap. 1), which is wholly burnt (except for the skin). The meat is distributed among the offerer (and the offerer's party) and the priests (cf. 7:11–36).

| | |
|---|---|
| **2:1** Cf. Ex 30:1–10; Lv 16:11–13; Prv 27:9. | **2:13** Nm 18:19; Ezr 6:9; 7:22; Ez 43:24. |
| **2:2** Lv 1:9. | **3:1** Lv 7:11–36. |
| **2:3** Lv 6:9; 7:9–10. | **3:1** Lv 22:21. |
| **2:3** Lv 6:10, 18, 22; 10:12, 17; 24:9. | **3:2** Lv 1:4. |
| **2:4** 1 Chr 23:29. | **3:3–5** Lv 3:9–10, 14–16; 4:8–9, 31, 35; 6:5; |
| **2:5** Lv 6:14. | 7:3–4, 30–31; 8:16, |
| **2:11** Mt 16:12; Mk 8:15; Lk 12:1; 1 Cor 5:7; Gal 5:9. | 25; 16:25; 17:6; Ex 29:13, 22; cf. Ez 44:15. |
| **2:12** Nm 18:12–13, 27; 15:20–21. | **3:5** Lv 1:9. |

the spine, the fat that covers the inner organs, and all the fat that adheres to them, ¹⁰ as well as the two kidneys, with the fat on them near the loins, and the lobe of the liver, which is removed with the kidneys. ¹¹ The priest shall burn this on the altar as food,* an oblation to the Lord.

¹² If a person's offering is a goat, the individual shall bring it before the Lord, ¹³ and after laying a hand on its head, it shall then be slaughtered before the tent of meeting. Aaron's sons shall splash its blood on all the sides of the altar. ¹⁴ From this the one sacrificing shall present an offering as an oblation to the Lord: the fat that covers the inner organs, and all the fat that adheres to them, ¹⁵ as well as the two kidneys, with the fat on them near the loins, and the lobe of the liver, which is removed with the kidneys. ¹⁶ The priest shall burn these on the altar as food, a sweet-smelling oblation.

All the fat belongs to the Lord. ¹⁷ This shall be a perpetual ordinance for your descendants wherever they may dwell. You shall not eat any fat or any blood.†*

**Purification Offerings.** ¹ The Lord said to Moses: ²* Tell the Israelites: When a person inadvertently† does wrong by violating any one of the Lord's prohibitions—

**For the Anointed Priest.** ³ If it is the anointed priest† who thus does wrong and thereby makes the people guilty, he shall offer to the Lord an unblemished bull of the herd as a purification offering for the wrong he committed. ⁴ Bringing the bull to the entrance of the tent of meeting, before the Lord, he shall lay his hand on its head* and slaughter it before the Lord. ⁵† The anointed priest shall then take some of the bull's blood and bring

it into the tent of meeting, ⁶ where, dipping his finger in the blood, he shall sprinkle some of it seven times before the Lord, toward the veil of the sanctuary.* ⁷ The priest shall also put some of the blood on the horns of the altar of fragrant incense which stands before the Lord in the tent of meeting. The rest of the bull's blood he shall pour out at the base of the altar for burnt offerings which is at the entrance of the tent of meeting. ⁸ He shall remove all the fat of the bull of the purification offering: the fat that covers the inner organs, and all the fat that adheres to them, ⁹ as well as the two kidneys, with the fat on them near the loins, and the lobe of the liver, which is removed with the kidneys, ¹⁰ just as the fat pieces are removed from the ox of the communion sacrifice.* The priest shall burn these on the altar for burnt offerings. ¹¹† But the hide of the bull and its meat, with its head, shanks, inner organs and dung, ¹² that is, the whole bull, shall be brought outside the camp to a clean place† where the ashes are deposited and there be burned in a wood fire. At the place of the ash heap, there it must be burned.*

**For the Community.** ¹³ If the whole community of Israel errs† inadvertently and without even being aware of it violates any of the Lord's prohibitions, and thus are guilty, ¹⁴ when the wrong that was committed becomes known, the community shall offer a bull of the herd as a purification offering. They shall bring it before the tent of meeting. ¹⁵ The elders of the community shall lay their hands on the bull's head before the Lord. When the bull has been slaughtered before the Lord, ¹⁶ the anointed priest shall bring some of its blood into the tent of meeting, ¹⁷ and dipping his finger in the blood, he shall sprinkle it seven times

---

**3:17** *Any fat or any blood*: this prohibition is mentioned here because portions of this offering could be eaten by lay Israelites, who may not be entirely familiar with the prohibition (cf. 7:22–27; 19:26). The fat prohibited is only the visceral fat mentioned in 3:9–10, 14–15, not muscular fat.

**4:2** *Inadvertently*: the concern in this chapter, and much of chap. 5, is wrongs done unintentionally. Intentional ("high-handed") sins are punished with being "cut off" from the people (Nm 15:30–31). See note on Lv 7:20. *Lord's prohibitions*: not included in the faults figured here is failure to perform positive commandments. Failing to perform positive commands, however, still renders the individual liable to other punishment (e.g., failing to observe the Passover, Nm 9:13). Cf. Nm 15:22–31.

**4:3** *The anointed priest*: the chapter presents four cases of inadvertent wrong, arranged in descending order according to the status of the wrongdoer: high priest (vv. 3–12), entire community (vv. 13–21), tribal leader (vv. 22–26), and general populace (vv. 27–35). The higher one's position, the more deeply the sin affects

the sanctuary (vv. 5–7, 17–18 versus vv. 25, 29, 34). See note on 16:6. *Purification offering*: the Hebrew verb *ḥiṭṭēʾ* means "remove sin, purify" (Lv 8:15; Ez 43:20–23; 45:18–19; cf. Ex 29:36). The offering cleansed the various places to which the blood was applied or the rooms in which it was sprinkled.

**4:5–7** On the structure of the sanctuary, see Ex 26–27.

**4:11–12** See note on 6:17–23.

**4:12** *Clean place*: i.e., ritually "clean" or pure. It has nothing to do with the presence of dirt or waste. See 6:4.

**4:13** *Whole community...errs*: this case probably complements that of vv. 3–12. There the high priest sins so that the people become guilty. Those verses deal with his requirements for atonement; vv. 13–21 deal with the people's requirements.

**3:11** Lv 9:19.
**3:17** Lv 17:10.
**4:2** Lv 6:17–23; Nm 15:22–31.
**4:4** Lv 1:4.
**4:6–7** Lv 4:17–18; 16:16; cf. 4:25.
**4:10** Lv 3:3.
**4:12** Lv 6:23.

before the Lord, toward the veil. [18] He shall also put some of the blood on the horns of the altar which is before the Lord in the tent of meeting. The rest of the blood he shall pour out at the base of the altar for burnt offerings which is at the entrance of the tent of meeting. [19] He shall remove all of its fat and burn it on the altar, [20] doing with this bull just as he did with the other bull of the purification offering; he will do the same thing. Thus the priest shall make atonement* on their behalf, that they may be forgiven. [21] This bull shall also be brought outside the camp and burned,* just as the first bull. It is a purification offering for the assembly.

**For the Tribal Leader.** [22] Should a tribal leader* do wrong inadvertently by violating any one of the prohibitions of the Lord his God, and thus be guilty, [23] when he learns of the wrong he committed, he shall bring as his offering an unblemished male goat. [24] He shall lay his hand on its head and it shall be slaughtered in the place where the burnt offering is slaughtered, before the Lord. It is a purification offering. [25] The priest shall then take some of the blood of the purification offering on his finger and put it on the horns* of the altar for burnt offerings. The rest of the blood he shall pour out at the base of the altar. [26] All of its fat he shall burn on the altar like the fat of the communion sacrifice. Thus the priest shall make atonement on the tribal leader's behalf for his wrong, that he may be forgiven.

**For the General Populace.** [27] If anyone of the general populace does wrong inadvertently by violating one of the Lord's prohibitions, and thus is guilty, [28] upon learning of the wrong committed, that person shall bring an unblemished she-goat as the offering for the wrong committed. [29] The wrongdoer shall lay a hand on the head of the purification offering, and the purification offering shall be slaughtered at the place of the burnt offerings. [30] The priest shall then take some of its blood on his finger and put it on the horns of the altar for burnt offerings. The rest of the blood he shall pour out at the base of the altar. [31] He shall remove all the fat, just as the fat is removed from the communion sacrifice. The priest shall burn it on the altar for a sweet odor to the Lord. Thus the priest shall make atonement, so that the individual may be forgiven.

[32] If, however, a person brings a lamb as a purification offering, that person shall bring an unblemished female, and [33] lay a hand on its head. It shall be slaughtered as a purification offering in the place where the burnt offering is slaughtered. [34] The priest shall then take some of the blood of the purification offering on his finger and put it on the horns of the altar for burnt offerings. The rest of the blood he shall pour out at the base of the altar. [35] He shall remove all its fat just as the fat is removed from the lamb of the communion sacrifice. The priest shall burn these on the altar with the other oblations for the Lord. Thus the priest shall make atonement on the person's behalf for the wrong committed, that the individual may be forgiven.

**5 Special Cases for Purification Offerings.**† [1] If a person, either having seen or come to know something, does wrong by refusing as a witness under oath to give information,* that individual shall bear the penalty; [2] or if someone, without being aware of it, touches any unclean thing, such as the carcass of an unclean wild animal, or an unclean domestic animal, or an unclean swarming creature,† and thus is unclean and guilty;* [3] or if someone, without being aware of it, touches some human uncleanness,* whatever kind of uncleanness this may be, and then subsequently becomes aware of guilt; [4] or if someone, without being aware of it, rashly utters an oath with bad or good intent,* whatever kind of oath this may be, and then subsequently becomes aware of guilt in regard to any of these matters— [5] when

---

† **5:1–13** This differs from the prescriptions for purification offerings in chap. 4 by listing four specific wrongs for which a purification offering is brought and allowing the substitution of birds and grain offerings in the case of poverty.
**5:2** *Swarming creature*: a rather imprecise categorization that includes various small creatures in the seas, such as fish that go about in large groups or swarms (Gn 1:20; Lv 11:10); or, similarly, various winged insects that mass in the skies (Lv 11:20; Dt 14:19); and, finally, various small creatures that move in swarms on land, whether crawlers, quadrupeds, or of the multilegged variety (Lv 11:41–42). According to 11:29–30,

even various rodents and lizards can be included in this category.

*
| | |
|---|---|
| **4:20** Lv 1:4. | **17**:15–16. |
| **4:21** Lv 6:23. | **5:3** Lv 12:4; 13:35–36; |
| **4:22** Nm 10:4; 25:14. | 15:2–12, 19–27; Nm |
| **4:25** Lv 4:30, 34; 8:15; 9:9; | 19:14–22. |
| 16:18; Ex 29:12; Ez | **5:4** Nm 30:3; Jgs 11:30– |
| 43:20; cf. Lv 4:7. | 36; 1 Sm 14:24–30; |
| **5:1** Jgs 17:2–3; Prv 29:24. | Mk 6:23–26; Acts |
| **5:2** Lv 11:1–45; 15:31; | 23:12. |

someone is guilty in regard to any of these matters, that person shall confess the wrong committed, [6] and make reparation to the LORD for the wrong committed: a female animal from the flock, a ewe lamb or a she-goat, as a purification offering. Thus the priest shall make atonement on the individual's behalf for the wrong.

[7] If, however, the person cannot afford an animal of the flock,* that person shall bring to the LORD as reparation for the wrong committed two turtledoves or two pigeons, one for a purification offering and the other for a burnt offering. [8] The guilty party shall bring them to the priest, who shall offer the one for the purification offering first.* Wringing its head at the neck, yet without breaking it off, [9] he shall sprinkle some of the blood of the purification offering against the side of the altar. The rest of the blood shall be drained out against the base of the altar. It is a purification offering. [10] The other bird he shall offer as a burnt offering according to procedure. Thus the priest shall make atonement on the person's behalf for the wrong committed, so that the individual may be forgiven.

[11] If the person is unable to afford even two turtledoves or two pigeons, that person shall bring as an offering for the wrong committed one tenth of an ephah† of bran flour for a purification offering. The guilty party shall not put oil or place frankincense on it, because it is a purification offering.* [12] The individual shall bring it to the priest, who shall take a handful as a token of the offering and burn it on the altar with the other oblations for the LORD. It is a purification offering. [13] Thus the priest shall make atonement on the person's behalf for the wrong committed in any of the above cases, so that the individual may be forgiven. The rest of the offering, like the grain offering, shall belong to the priest.

**Reparation Offerings.**† [14] The LORD said to Moses: [15]* When a person commits sacrilege by inadvertently misusing any of the LORD's sacred objects,* the wrongdoer shall bring to the LORD as reparation an unblemished ram from the flock, at the established value† in silver shekels according to the sanctuary shekel, as a reparation offering. [16] The wrongdoer shall also restore what has been misused of the sacred objects, adding a fifth of its value,* and give this to the priest. Thus the priest shall make atonement for the person with the ram of the reparation offering, so that the individual may be forgiven.

[17] If someone does wrong and violates one of the LORD's prohibitions without realizing it, that person is guilty* and shall bear the penalty. [18] The individual shall bring to the priest an unblemished ram of the flock, at the established value, for a reparation offering. The priest shall then make atonement on the offerer's behalf for the error inadvertently and unknowingly committed so that the individual may be forgiven. [19] It is a reparation offering. The individual must make reparation to the LORD.

[20] The LORD said to Moses: [21] When someone does wrong and commits sacrilege against the LORD by deceiving* a neighbor about a deposit or a pledge or a stolen article, or by otherwise retaining a neighbor's goods unjustly;* [22] or if, having found a lost article, the person lies about it, swearing falsely about any of the things that a person may do wrong— [23] when someone has thus done wrong and is guilty, that person shall restore the thing that was stolen, the item unjustly retained, the item left as deposit, or the lost article that was found [24] or whatever else the individual swore falsely about. That person shall make full restitution of the thing itself, and add one fifth of its value to it, giving it to its owner at the time of reparation. [25] Then that person shall bring to the priest as reparation to the LORD an unblemished ram of the flock, at the established value, as a reparation offering. [26] The priest shall make atonement on the person's behalf

---

† **5:11** *Ephah:* see note on Is 5:10.

**5:14–26** This last half of the chapter deals with a distinct sacrifice, the reparation offering (Heb. *'asham*). The Hebrew root for this term has a basic meaning of "be guilty." The noun can have a consequential sense of "that which is due from guilt," i.e., "compensation, indemnification, reparation"; hence the translation "reparation offering," rather than the alternatives "guilt offering" or "trespass offering." This offering is brought most often in cases of sacrilege.

**5:15** *At the established value:* the Hebrew term *'erkĕkā,*

which in context means "(established) value," may indicate that a person could bring the monetary equivalent of a ram instead of an actual animal. See vv. 18, 25.

* **5:7** Cf. Lv 5:11; 12:8; 14:21.
**5:8** Lv 1:14–17.
**5:11** Lv 2:1–3; Nm 5:15.
**5:15** Lv 7:1–6; Nm 5:5–8.
**5:15** Lv 22:14.
**5:16** Lv 22:14; 27:13, 15, 19, 27.
**5:17** Ps 19:13; Jb 1:5.
**5:21** Ps 59:13; Hos 4:2.
**5:21** Ex 22:6–12.

before the Lord, so that the individual may be forgiven for whatever was done to incur guilt.

## B. Instructions for the Priests

**6** **The Daily Burnt Offering.** [1] The Lord said to Moses: [2]†* Give Aaron and his sons the following command: This is the ritual† for the burnt offering—the burnt offering that is to remain on the hearth of the altar all night until the next morning, while the fire is kept burning on the altar. [3] The priest, clothed in his linen robe and wearing linen pants underneath, shall take away the ashes to which the fire has reduced the burnt offering on the altar, and lay them at the side of the altar. [4] Then, having taken off these garments and put on other garments, he shall carry the ashes to a clean place outside the camp. [5] The fire on the altar is to be kept burning; it must not go out. Every morning the priest shall put firewood on it. On this he shall lay out the burnt offering* and burn the fat of the communion offering. [6] The fire is to be kept burning continuously on the altar; it must not go out.

**The Grain Offering.** † [7] This is the ritual of the grain offering. Aaron's sons shall offer it before the Lord, in front of the altar. [8] A priest shall then take from the grain offering a handful of bran flour and oil, together with all the frankincense that is on it,* and this he shall burn on the altar as a token of the offering, a sweet aroma to the Lord. [9] The rest of it Aaron and his sons may eat; but it must be eaten unleavened in a sacred place:* in the court of the tent of meeting they shall eat it. [10] It shall not be baked with leaven. I have given it to them as their portion from the oblations for the Lord; it is most holy,* like the purification offering and the reparation offering. [11] Every male of

Aaron's descendants may eat of it perpetually throughout your generations as their rightful due from the oblations for the Lord. Whatever touches the oblations becomes holy.

**High Priest's Daily Grain Offering.** † [12] The Lord said to Moses: [13] This is the offering that Aaron and his sons shall present to the Lord on the day he is anointed: one tenth of an ephah of bran flour for the regular grain offering, half of it in the morning and half of it in the evening. [14] You shall bring it well kneaded and fried in oil on a griddle.* Having broken the offering into pieces, you shall present it as a sweet aroma to the Lord. [15] The anointed priest descended from Aaron who succeeds him shall do likewise. This is the Lord's due forever. The offering shall be wholly burned.* [16] Every grain offering of a priest shall be a whole offering; it may not be eaten.

**Purification Offerings.** † [17] The Lord said to Moses: [18]* Tell Aaron and his sons: This is the ritual for the purification offering. At the place where the burnt offering is slaughtered, there also, before the Lord, shall the purification offering be slaughtered. It is most holy.* [19] The priest who offers the purification offering shall eat of it; it shall be eaten in a sacred place,* in the court of the tent of meeting. [20] Whatever touches its flesh becomes holy. If any of its blood spatters on a garment, the stained part must be washed in a sacred place. [21] A clay vessel in which it has been boiled shall be broken; if it is boiled in a copper vessel, this shall be scoured afterward and rinsed with water.* [22] Every male of the priestly line may eat it. It is most holy. [23] But no purification offering of which some blood has been brought into the tent of meeting* to make atonement in the sanctuary shall be eaten; it must be burned with fire.*

---

**6:2–6** This passage may have reference to the burnt offering that is offered in the morning and late afternoon each day (cf. Ex 29:38–42; Nm 28:3–8).

**6:2** *Ritual:* Hebrew *torah,* which also has the broader meaning of "instruction." The treatment of sacrifices in chaps. 6–7 recapitulates the offerings treated in 1–5 but now with more emphasis on priestly duties and prerogatives.

**6:7–11** The passage is apparently concerned with the raw grain offering of 2:1–3.

**6:12–16** This seems to refer to a grain offering offered twice daily by the high priest, perhaps identical to the regular grain offering in Nm 4:16 (cf. Neh 10:34). This offering is distinct from the grain offering that accompanies the daily burnt offering.

**6:17–23** There are two types of purification offering: one whose blood is used inside the tent sanctuary (4:1–12, 13–21) and another whose blood was only used at the outer sacrificial

altar (4:22–26, 27–31, 32–35). The carcasses of the former, as well as of purification offerings brought by the priests themselves (cf. 8:14–17; 9:8–11), are not eaten by priests but disposed of at the ash heap outside the camp, which itself is set up around the sanctuary (Ex 29:14; Lv 4:11–12, 21; 6:23; 8:17; 9:11; 16:27). The Letter to the Hebrews compares Jesus' suffering "outside the gate" to the disposal of purification offering carcasses outside the camp (Heb 13:11–13).

---

* 6:2 Lv 1.
6:5 Lv 9:17.
6:8 Lv 2:1–3.
6:9 Lv 6:19; 7:6; 10:13, 17; 24:9.
6:10 Lv 2:3.
6:14 Lv 2:5.
6:15 Lv 2:9.

6:18 Lv 4:1–5:13.
6:18 Lv 2:3.
6:19 Lv 6:9.
6:21 Lv 11:32–33; 15:12.
6:23 Lv 4:5; Heb 13:11.
6:23 Lv 4:11–12, 21; 8:17; 9:11; 16:27.

# 7

**Reparation Offerings.** ¹†* This is the ritual for the reparation offering. It is most holy. ²At the place where the burnt offering is slaughtered, the reparation offering shall also be slaughtered.* Its blood shall be splashed on all the sides of the altar. ³* All of its fat shall be offered: the fatty tail, the fat that covers the inner organs, and all the fat that adheres to them, ⁴as well as the two kidneys with the fat on them near the loins, and the lobe of the liver, which is removed with the kidneys. ⁵The priest shall burn these on the altar as an oblation to the LORD. It is a reparation offering. ⁶Every male of the priestly line may eat of it; but it must be eaten in a sacred place.* It is most holy.*

⁷Because the purification offering and the reparation offering are alike, both have the same ritual. The reparation offering belongs to the priest who makes atonement with it. ⁸As for the priest who offers someone's burnt offering, to him belongs the hide of the burnt offering that is offered. ⁹†* Also, every grain offering that is baked in an oven or made in a pan or on a griddle shall belong to the priest who offers it, ¹⁰whereas all grain offerings* that are mixed with oil or are dry shall belong to all of Aaron's sons without distinction.

**Communion Sacrifices.**† ¹¹* This is the ritual for the communion sacrifice that is offered to the LORD. ¹²† If someone offers it for thanksgiving, that person shall offer it with unleavened cakes mixed with oil, unleavened wafers spread with oil, and cakes made of bran flour mixed with oil and well kneaded. ¹³One shall present this offering together with loaves of leavened bread along with the thanksgiving communion sacrifice. ¹⁴From this the individual shall offer one bread of each type of offering as a contribution† to the LORD; this shall belong to the priest who splashes the blood of the communion offering.

¹⁵†* The meat of the thanksgiving communion sacrifice shall be eaten on the day it is offered; none of it may be kept till the next morning.* ¹⁶However, if the sacrifice offered is a votive or a voluntary offering,† it shall be eaten on the day the sacrifice is offered, and on the next day what is left over may be eaten.* ¹⁷But what is left over of the meat of the sacrifice on the third day must be burned in the fire. ¹⁸If indeed any of the flesh of the communion sacrifice is eaten on the third day, it shall not be accepted; it will not be reckoned to the credit of the one offering it. Rather it becomes a desecrated meat. Anyone who eats of it shall bear the penalty.†

¹⁹† Should the meat touch anything unclean, it may not be eaten, but shall be burned in the fire.* As for other meat, all who are clean may eat of it. ²⁰If, however, someone in a state of uncleanness eats the meat of a communion sacrifice belonging to the LORD, that person shall be cut off†* from the people. ²¹Likewise, if someone touches anything

---

**7:1–6** These prescriptions may appear here rather than in 5:14–26 where this offering is first treated because the monetary equivalent of the offering might have been brought instead of an actual animal. See note on 5:15.

**7:9–10** For the distinction between uncooked and cooked grain offerings, see 2:1–10 and note on 2:1. The contradiction between v. 9 and 2:10 may reflect a development in custom, with the distribution in v. 9 coming from earlier times, when sanctuary personnel was more limited.

**7:11–36** This section discusses three types of communion sacrifice: the thanksgiving offering (vv. 12–15), a votive offering, and a voluntary offering (vv. 16–18). The latter two are similar and are thus mentioned together. Verses 19–36 apply to all types of communion sacrifice.

**7:12–13** Four types of breads accompany the thanksgiving offering. Three types are cooked grain offerings comparable to those in 2:4–10. Also required are loaves of leavened bread (see 2:11).

**7:14** *Contribution*: Hebrew *terumah*. This does not indicate a particular ritual action. The word simply means "gift, something set apart."

**7:15–18** Sacrifices must be properly consumed for them to be effective (cf. also 19:5–8; 22:30). Similar rules obtain for the Passover offering (Ex 12:10; Nm 9:12; cf. Ex 23:18; 34:25; Dt 16:4) and the ordination offering (Ex 29:34; Lv 8:32).

**7:16** *Votive or a voluntary offering*: these are not specific types of offerings but rather motivations for bringing the communion sacrifice (cf. 22:18). A votive offering is brought as the consequence of a promise (vow) made to God. A voluntary offering is a spontaneous gift to God independent of a prior promise. See note on 27:2–13.

**7:18** *Bear the penalty*: this refers in many cases to punishment by God (cf. 17:16; 19:8; 20:17, 19; Nm 18:1, 23; 30:16).

**7:19–21** For ritual impurity, see note on 11:1–15:33.

**7:20** *Cut off*: a common term in the Priestly source that cannot always be reduced to a simple English equivalent, since its usage appears to involve a number of associated punishments, some or all of which may come into play in any one instance (see Ex 12:15 and note). All the same, as a punishment from God, to be "cut off" (from one's people) frequently appears to refer to termination of the offender's family line (and perhaps in some cases an early death); see Lv 20:2–3, 20–21; Ru 4:10; Ps 109:13; Mal 2:12.

**7:1** Lv 5:14–26.
**7:2** Lv 6:18.
**7:3** Lv 3:4.
**7:6** Lv 6:9.
**7:6** Lv 2:3.
**7:9** Lv 2:3–10; Nm 18:9; Ez 44:29.
**7:10** Lv 2:14–15.
**7:11** Lv 3.

**7:15** Lv 19:6–7.
**7:15** Lv 22:29–30.
**7:16** Lv 19:5–8.
**7:19** Lv 12:4.
**7:20** Lv 17:4, 9–10, 14; 18:29; 20:3, 5–6, 17–18; Gn 17:14; Ex 30:33; Nm 15:31; Ps 37:9, 28, 34; 109:13.

unclean, whether it be human uncleanness or an unclean animal or an unclean loathsome creature, and then eats the meat of the communion sacrifice belonging to the LORD, that person, too, shall be cut off from the people.

**Prohibition Against Blood and Fat.** 22 The LORD said to Moses: 23 Tell the Israelites: You shall not eat the fat of any ox or sheep or goat.* 24 Although the fat of an animal that has died a natural death or has been killed by wild beasts may be put to any other use, you may not eat it.* 25 If anyone eats the fat of an animal from which an oblation is made to the LORD, that person shall be cut off from the people. 26* Wherever you dwell, you shall not eat any blood, whether of bird or of animal. 27 Every person who eats any blood shall be cut off from the people.

**Portions from the Communion Sacrifice for Priests.** 28 The LORD said to Moses: 29 Tell the Israelites: The person who offers a communion sacrifice to the LORD shall be the one to bring from it the offering to the LORD. 30 The offerer's own hands shall carry the oblations for the LORD: the person shall bring the fat together with the brisket, which is to be raised as an elevated* offering† before the LORD. 31 The priest shall burn the fat on the altar,* but the brisket belongs to Aaron and his sons. 32 Moreover, from your communion sacrifices you shall give to the priest the right leg as a contribution. 33 The one among Aaron's sons who offers the blood and the fat of the communion offering shall have the right leg as his portion, 34 for from the communion sacrifices of the Israelites I have taken the brisket that is elevated and the leg that is a contribution, and I have given them to Aaron, the priest, and to his sons as their due from the Israelites forever.*

35 This is the priestly share from the oblations for the LORD, allotted to Aaron and his sons on the day they were brought forth to be the priests of the LORD, 36 which the LORD ordered to be given them from the Israelites on the day they were anointed, as their due throughout their generations forever.

**Summary.** 37 This is the ritual for the burnt offering, the grain offering, the purification offering, the reparation offering, the ordination offering,* and the communion sacrifice, 38 which the LORD enjoined on Moses at Mount Sinai at the time when he commanded the Israelites in the wilderness of Sinai to bring their offerings to the LORD.*

## II. CEREMONY OF ORDINATION

**8** **Ordination of Aaron and His Sons.**† 1* The LORD said to Moses: 2 Take Aaron along with his sons, the vestments, the anointing oil, the bull for a purification offering, the two rams, and the basket of unleavened bread, 3 then assemble the whole community† at the entrance of the tent of meeting. 4 Moses did as the LORD had commanded. When the community* had assembled at the entrance of the tent of meeting, 5 Moses told them: "This is what the LORD has ordered to be done." 6 Bringing forward Aaron and his sons, Moses first washed them with water. 7† Then he put the tunic on Aaron,* girded him with the sash, clothed him with the robe, placed the ephod on him, and girded him with the ephod's embroidered belt, fastening the ephod on him with it. 8 He then set the breastpiece on him, putting the Urim and Thummim† in it. 9 He put the turban on his head, attaching the gold medallion, the sacred headband,† on the front

---

† **7:30** *Raised as an elevated offering:* these portions of the sacrifices were specially dedicated by lifting them in presentation before God's abode. The sanctifying effect of this action is clearly seen in 23:17–20; Nm 6:19–20.

**8:1–2** This chapter presents the fulfillment of the commands in Ex 28–29; 30:26–30; and 40:9–15.

**8:3–4** *Community:* this word (Heb. *'edah*) may refer to tribal leaders, all adult males, or the entire nation. The last is probably intended here.

**8:7–9, 13** On the priestly clothing, see Ex 28–29. *Ephod:* according to Ex 28:6–14, the term for one of Aaron's special vestments made of gold thread, with multicolored woolen thread woven into it as well as fine linen. In appearance it resembled a kind of apron, hung on the priest by shoulder straps and secured by an embroidered belt. A somewhat simpler "apron" was presumably worn by other priests (1 Sm 22:18).

**8:8** *The Urim and Thummim:* see Ex 28:30 and note there.

Although these terms and the object(s) they refer to are still unexplained, they appear to be small objects that functioned like dice or lots to render a decision for those making an inquiry of God, perhaps originally in legal cases where the guilt of the accused could not otherwise be determined (cf. Ex 28:30; Nm 27:21; Dt 33:8; 1 Sm 28:6; Ezr 2:63; Neh 7:65).

**8:9** *Headband:* see Ex 39:30–31. The gold medallion, together with its cords, comprises the sacred headband.

---

| | |
|---|---|
| **7:23** Lv 3:17. | **7:34** Ex 29:27–28. |
| **7:24** Lv 22:8. | **7:37** Lv 8:22. |
| **7:26** Lv 17:10. | **7:38** Lv 26:46; 27:34. |
| **7:30** Lv 8:27, 29; 9:21; | **8:1** Cf. Ex 28–29; 39; |
| 10:15; 14:12, 21, 24; | 40:12–15. |
| 23:17, 20; Nm 6:20; | **8:4** Nm 27:19. |
| 8:13; 18:18. | **8:7–9** Sir 45:8–13; Heb |
| **7:31** Lv 3:11, 16. | 5:1–4; 7:1–28. |

of the turban, as the LORD had commanded Moses to do.

10† Taking the anointing oil, Moses anointed and consecrated the tabernacle and all that was in it.* 11 Then he sprinkled some of the oil seven times on the altar, and anointed the altar, with all its utensils, and the laver, with its base, to consecrate them. 12 He also poured some of the anointing oil on Aaron's head and anointed him, to consecrate him.* 13 Moses likewise brought forward Aaron's sons, clothed them with tunics, girded them with sashes, and put skullcaps on them, as the LORD had commanded him to do.

**Ordination Sacrifices.** 14 He brought forward the bull for a purification offering, and Aaron and his sons laid their hands on its head. 15 When it was slaughtered, Moses took the blood† and with his finger he put it on the horns around the altar, thus purifying the altar.* He poured out the rest of the blood at the base of the altar. Thus he consecrated it so that atonement could be made on it. 16 Taking all the fat that was over the inner organs, as well as the lobe of the liver and the two kidneys with their fat,* Moses burned them on the altar. 17 The bull, however, with its hide and flesh and dung he burned in the fire outside the camp, as the LORD had commanded Moses to do.*

18 He next brought forward the ram of the burnt offering,* and Aaron and his sons laid their hands on its head. 19 When it was slaughtered, Moses splashed the blood on all sides of the altar. 20 After the ram was cut up into pieces, Moses burned the head, the cut-up pieces and the suet. 21 After the inner organs and the shanks were washed with water, Moses burned these remaining parts of the ram on the altar. It was a burnt offering for a sweet aroma, an oblation to the LORD, as the LORD had commanded Moses.

22† Then he brought forward the second ram, the ordination ram,* and Aaron and his sons laid their hands on its head. 23 When it was slaughtered, Moses took some of its blood and put it on the lobe of Aaron's right ear, on the thumb of his right hand, and on the big toe† of his right foot.* 24 Moses had the sons of Aaron also come forward, and he put some of the blood on the lobes of their right ears, on the thumbs of their right hands, and on the big toes of their right feet. The rest of the blood he splashed on all the sides of the altar. 25 He then took the fat: the fatty tail and all the fat over the inner organs, the lobe of the liver and the two kidneys with their fat, and likewise the right thigh; 26 from the basket of unleavened bread that was set before the LORD he took one unleavened cake, one loaf of bread made with oil, and one wafer; these he placed on top of the portions of fat and the right thigh. 27 He then put all these things upon the palms of Aaron and his sons, whom he had raise them as an elevated offering before the LORD.* 28 When Moses had removed them from their palms, he burned them on the altar with the burnt offering. They were an ordination offering for a sweet aroma, an oblation to the LORD. 29 He then took the brisket and raised it as an elevated offering before the LORD; this was Moses' own portion of the ordination ram, as the LORD had commanded Moses. 30 Taking some of the anointing oil and some of the blood that was on the altar, Moses sprinkled it upon Aaron and his vestments, as well as his sons and their vestments, thus consecrating both Aaron and his vestments and his sons and their vestments.*

31 Moses said to Aaron and his sons, "Boil the meat at the entrance of the tent of meeting, and there eat it with the bread that is in the basket of the ordination offering, in keeping with the command I have received: 'Aaron and his sons shall eat of it.' 32 What is left over of the meat and the bread you shall burn in the fire. 33 Moreover, you are not to depart†

---

8:10–12 Anointing with the specially prepared oil (cf. Ex 30:22–33) is one of the means of making objects and persons holy by setting them apart for a special function or purpose.

8:15 *Moses took the blood*: Moses is acting as a priest in this chapter.

8:22–32 The priestly ordination offering is a unique type of sacrifice but similar in many respects to the communion sacrifice (chap. 3; 7:11–34).

8:23–24 *Lobe...thumb...toe*: these parts of the body are meant to represent the body as a whole. The application of the blood symbolizes the priests' passing from a profane to a holy state. Cf. 14:14–17.

8:33–35 *You are not to depart*: the tenor and context of this requirement in vv. 33 and 35 seem to indicate that the priests are not to leave the sanctuary precincts for any reason. *Your ordination is to last for seven days...what has been done today...be done*: the consecration rites in Exodus are to be performed every day for seven days (cf. Ex 29:30, 35–37).

| | |
|---|---|
| 8:10 Ex 30:26. | 8:18 Lv 1:10–13. |
| 8:12 Sir 45:15. | 8:22 Lv 7:37. |
| 8:15 Heb 9:22. | 8:23 Lv 14:14, 17. |
| 8:16–17 Lv 3:4–5; 4:8–11. | 8:27 Lv 7:30. |
| 8:17 Lv 6:23. | 8:30 Ex 40:15. |

from the entrance of the tent of meeting for seven days, until the days of your ordination are completed; for your ordination is to last for seven days. [34] What has been done today the LORD has commanded be done, to make atonement for you. [35] You must remain at the entrance of the tent of meeting day and night for seven days, carrying out the prescriptions of the LORD, so that you do not die, for this is the command I have received."* [36] So Aaron and his sons did all that the LORD had commanded through Moses.

**9 Octave of the Ordination.** [1] On the eighth day†* Moses summoned Aaron and his sons, together with the elders of Israel, [2] and said to Aaron, "Take a calf of the herd for a purification offering and a ram for a burnt offering, both without blemish, and offer them before the LORD. [3]† Tell the Israelites, too: Take a he-goat for a purification offering, a calf and a lamb, both unblemished yearlings, for a burnt offering, [4] and an ox and a ram for a communion sacrifice, to sacrifice before the LORD, along with a grain offering mixed with oil; for today the LORD will appear to you." [5] So they brought what Moses had ordered before the tent of meeting. When the whole community had come forward and stood before the LORD, [6]† Moses said, "This is what the LORD orders you to do, that the glory of the LORD may appear to you. [7] Approach the altar," Moses then told Aaron, "and make your purification offering and your burnt offering in atonement for yourself and for your household;† then make the offering of the people in atonement for them, as the LORD has commanded."*

[8] Approaching the altar, Aaron first slaughtered the calf of the purification offering that was his own offering. [9] When his sons presented the blood to him, he dipped his finger in the blood and put it on the horns of the altar.* The rest of the blood he poured out at the base of the altar. [10] He then burned on the altar the fat, the kidneys and the lobe of the liver from the purification offering, as the LORD had commanded Moses; [11] but the flesh and the hide he burned in the fire outside the camp.* [12] Then Aaron slaughtered the burnt offering. When his sons brought him the blood, he splashed it on all sides of the altar. [13] They then brought him the pieces and the head of the burnt offering, and he burned them on the altar. [14] Having washed the inner organs and the shanks, he burned these also with the burnt offering on the altar.*

[15] Then he had the people's offering brought. Taking the goat that was for the people's purification offering, he slaughtered it and offered it as a purification offering as before. [16] Then he brought forward the burnt offering and offered it according to procedure. [17] He then presented the grain offering; taking a handful of it, he burned it on the altar, in addition to the morning burnt offering.* [18] Finally he slaughtered the ox and the ram, the communion sacrifice of the people. When his sons brought him the blood, Aaron splashed it on all sides of the altar.* [19] The portions of fat from the ox and from the ram, the fatty tail, the covering fat, the kidneys, and the lobe of the liver [20] they placed on top of the briskets. Aaron burned the fat pieces on the altar, [21] but the briskets and the right thigh he raised as an elevated offering* before the LORD, as the LORD had commanded Moses.

**Revelation of the Lord's Glory.** [22]† Aaron then raised his hands over the people and blessed* them. When he came down from offering the purification offering, the burnt offering, and the communion offering, [23] Moses and Aaron went into the tent of meeting. On coming out they blessed the people. Then the glory of the LORD appeared to all the people. [24]† Fire came forth from the LORD's presence and consumed

---

9:1 *Eighth day*: this is the conclusion of the priestly initiation ceremony.

9:3–4 The seven-day consecration of the priests in chap. 8 did not require sacrifices from the community. Now communal sacrifices as well as priestly sacrifices are required.

9:6–21 Aaron and his sons now perform the offerings, instead of Moses (see note on 8:15).

9:7 *For your household*: unlike the Septuagint, the Hebrew reads *be'ad ha'am*, "for the people."

9:22–23 The people are blessed twice. For the possible content of the blessing, compare the priestly blessing in Nm 6:22–27. Solomon offers a double blessing at the dedication of the Temple (1 Kgs 8:14–21, 55–61).

9:24 The theophany consists of a fire that apparently comes from the tent of meeting. God's fiery glory is also manifested in the pillar of cloud and fire that led the Israelites and rested over the tent of meeting (Ex 13:21; 40:38; Nm 9:15–23; 10:11). On God's fiery glory, see also Ex 24:17; Ez 1:27–28.

8:35 Lv 10:7.
9:1 Lv 8:33.
9:7 Lv 16:3–5.
9:9 Lv 4:25, 30, 34.
9:11 Lv 6:23.
9:14 Lv 1:5–9.
9:17 Nm 28:23; 2 Kgs 16:15; Ez 46:13–15.
9:18 Lv 3:2.
9:21 Lv 7:30–34.
9:22 Nm 6:22–27.

the burnt offering and the fat on the altar.* Seeing this, all the people shouted with joy and fell prostrate.

**10** **Nadab and Abihu.** ¹† Aaron's sons Nadab and Abihu took their censers and, putting incense on the fire they had set in them,* they offered before the LORD unauthorized fire, such as he had not commanded. ² Fire therefore came forth from the LORD's presence and consumed them,* so that they died in the LORD's presence. ³ Moses then said to Aaron, "This is as the LORD said:

Through those near to me I will be
    sanctified;
in the sight of all the people I will
    obtain glory."†*

But Aaron said nothing. ⁴† Then Moses summoned Mishael and Elzaphan, the sons of Aaron's uncle Uzziel, with the order, "Come, carry your kinsmen from before the sanctuary to a place outside the camp." ⁵ So they drew near and carried them by means of their tunics outside the camp, as Moses had commanded.

**Conduct of the Priests.** ⁶ Moses said to Aaron and his sons Eleazar and Ithamar, "Do not dishevel your hair* or tear your garments,* lest you die and bring God's wrath also on the whole community. While your kindred, the rest of the house of Israel, may mourn for those whom the LORD's fire has burned up, ⁷ you shall not go beyond the entrance of the tent of meeting,* else you shall die; for the anointing oil of the LORD is upon you." So they did as Moses told them.

⁸ The LORD said to Aaron: ⁹ When you are to go to the tent of meeting, you and your sons are forbidden, by a perpetual statute throughout your generations, to drink any wine or strong drink, lest you die.* ¹⁰ You must be able to distinguish between what is sacred and what is profane, and between what is clean and what is unclean;†* ¹¹ and you must be able to teach the Israelites all the statutes that the LORD has given them through Moses.

**The Eating of the Priestly Portions.** ¹² Moses said to Aaron and his surviving sons, Eleazar and Ithamar, "Take the grain offering† left over from the oblations to the LORD, and eat it beside the altar in the form of unleavened cakes, since it is most holy. ¹³ You must eat it in a sacred place because it is your and your sons' due from the oblations to the LORD; such is the command I have received. ¹⁴* The brisket of the elevated offering and the leg† of the contribution, however, you and your sons and daughters may eat, in a clean place; for these have been assigned to you and your children as your due from the communion sacrifices of the Israelites. ¹⁵ The leg of the contribution and the brisket of the elevated offering shall be brought in with the oblations of fat to be raised as an elevated offering before the LORD. They shall belong to you and your children as your due forever, as the LORD has commanded."

¹⁶ Moses inquired closely about the goat of the purification offering† and discovered that it had all been burned. So he was angry

---

† **10:1–2** Nadab and Abihu are the older sons of Aaron (Ex 6:23–24). Their sin apparently involves using embers from an unapproved source instead of the altar (cf. 16:12). The fire that destroys them is the same type found in 9:24.
**10:3** The explanation for the divine reaction indicates that improper cultic actions desecrate God and compromise God's glory. Desecration evokes divine punishment (cf. Ex 28:43; Nm 4:15, 19–20). *Those near to me:* i.e., cultic officials.
**10:4–5** Moses has lay people remove the bodies so that the priests can continue their cultic activities free of contamination by a corpse (cf. Nm 19).
**10:10** *Sacred and...profane...clean and...unclean:* something or someone may be either sacred or profane (i.e., ordinary, not set apart), and at the same time clean or unclean. Priests would be particularly concerned about keeping what is unclean away from the sacred.
**10:12–13** *Grain offering:* this is the grain offering of the people of 9:4, 17. Only the token offering had been offered; the rest was for the priests' consumption.
**10:14** *Brisket...leg:* these are from the Israelites' communion sacrifices in 9:4, 18–21.

**10:16–20** *Goat of the purification offering:* this is the people's purification offering of 9:3, 15. Since its blood is not brought into the sanctuary, then, according to 6:17–23, this is the type of purification offering which is to be eaten by the priests in a holy place. *Eleazar and Ithamar:* they burned the entire goat of the people's purification offering (9:15) instead of eating it in a sacred place (6:19) to remove ritually the sin of the community by the ingestion of the meat of the offering. Aaron's defense of this action of his sons is somewhat vague: he merely alludes to the loss suffered in the death of Nadab and Abihu, without giving an explicit reason for Eleazar and Ithamar's not eating the people's purification offering, as required.

| | |
|---|---|
| **9:24** 1 Kgs 18:38; 2 Chr 7:1; 2 Mc 2:10; cf. Ex 24:16–17. | Nm 20:12. |
| **10:1** Lv 16:1; Nm 3:4; 26:61; 1 Chr 24:2. | **10:6** Lv 13:45. |
| | **10:6** Lv 21:5–6, 10–12. |
| | **10:7** Lv 8:33–35; 21:12. |
| **10:2** Nm 16:35; cf. Lv 9:24. | **10:9** Ez 44:21. |
| | **10:10** Lv 11:47; 20:25; Ez 22:26; 44:23. |
| **10:3** Lv 21:17, 21; | **10:14** Lv 7:34. |

with the surviving sons of Aaron, Eleazar and Ithamar, and said, 17*"Why did you not eat the purification offering in the sacred place, since it is most holy? It has been given to you that you might remove the guilt of the community and make atonement for them before the LORD. 18 Since its blood was not brought inside the sanctuary, you should certainly have eaten the offering in the sanctuary, as I was commanded." 19 Aaron answered Moses, "Even though they presented their purification offering and burnt offering before the LORD today, still this misfortune has befallen me. Had I then eaten of the purification offering today, would it have been pleasing to the LORD?" 20 On hearing this, Moses was satisfied.

## III. LAWS REGARDING RITUAL PURITY†

**11** **Clean and Unclean Meats.**† 1* The LORD said to Moses and Aaron: 2 Speak to the Israelites and tell them: Of all land animals these are the ones you may eat: 3 Any animal that has hoofs you may eat, provided it is cloven-footed and chews the cud. 4 But you shall not eat* any of the following from among those that only chew the cud or only have hoofs: the camel, which indeed chews the cud, but does not have hoofs and is therefore unclean for you; 5 the rock hyrax,† which indeed chews the cud, but does not have hoofs and is therefore unclean for you; 6 the hare, which indeed chews the cud, but does not have hoofs and is therefore unclean for you; 7 and the pig,* which does indeed have hoofs and is cloven-footed, but does not chew the cud and is therefore unclean for you. 8 You shall not eat their meat, and you shall not touch their carcasses; they are unclean for you.

9 Of the various creatures that live in the water, you may eat the following: whatever in the seas or in river waters that has both fins and scales you may eat.* 10 But of the creatures that swarm in the water or of animals that otherwise live in the water, whether in the sea or in the rivers, all those that lack either fins or scales are loathsome for you, 11 and shall always be loathsome to you. Their meat you shall not eat, and their carcasses you shall loathe. 12 Every water creature that lacks fins or scales is loathsome for you.

13 Of the birds,† these you shall loathe; they shall not be eaten, they are loathsome: the griffon vulture, the bearded vulture, the black vulture, 14 the kite, the various species of falcons, 15 the various species of crows, 16 the eagle owl, the kestrel, the long-eared owl, the various species of hawks, 17 the little owl, the cormorant, the screech owl, 18 the barn owl, the horned owl, the osprey, 19 the stork, the various species of herons, the hoopoe, and the bat.

20 The various winged insects that walk on all fours are loathsome for you. 21 But of the various winged insects that walk on all fours you may eat those that have legs jointed above their feet for leaping on the ground; 22 hence of these you may eat the following: the various kinds of locusts, the various kinds of bald locusts, the various kinds of crickets, and the various kinds of grasshoppers.* 23 All other winged insects that have four legs are loathsome for you.

24 You become unclean by the following— anyone who touches their carcasses shall be unclean until evening,* 25 and anyone who carries any part of their carcasses shall wash his garments and be unclean until evening— 26 by all hoofed animals that are not cloven-footed or do not chew the cud; they are

---

† **11:1–15:33** Priestly legislation manifests two types of impurity or uncleanness: tolerated and prohibited. Prohibited impurity arises from various sins (e.g., 4:1–5; 5:2–3; 18:6–23; 20:2–5; Nm 5:13–14; 6:6–7). Tolerated impurity has three main sources: certain dead bodies (animal and human; cf. Lv 11 and Nm 19), various regular and abnormal genital discharges (Lv 12; 15), and diseases (specifically "scaly infection," chaps. 13–14). An additional tolerated impurity is that generated by the cult in order to rectify the effect of these impurities or sins (cf. chap. 4; 16:26, 28).

**11:1–47** Apart from the introduction and conclusion (vv. 1–2a, 46–47), this chapter has three sections: (1) prohibitions against eating certain land, water, and air animals (vv. 2b–23); (2) consequences of contact with various animals (vv. 24–41); (3) a prohibition against eating small land animals, which is motivated by the requirement that Israel be holy as God is holy (vv. 41–45). These animals are impure only when dead. Cf. Dt 14:3–21.

**11:5–6** According to modern zoology, the rock hyrax (*Hyrax syriacus*) is classified as an ungulate, and the hare as a rodent; neither is a ruminant. They appear to chew their food as the true ruminants do, and it is upon this appearance that the classification in the text is based.

**11:13–23, 30** Birds: the term is broader, including all animals that fly (including bats, v. 19, and flying insects, vv. 20–23). The identification of the various Hebrew names for these birds and reptiles is in many cases uncertain.

---

10:17 Lv 6:18–19.
11:1 Lv 27:11, 27; Gn 7:2–3, 8–9; Dt 14:3–21.
11:4 Jgs 13:4, 7; Is 66:17; Ez 4:12–14.
11:7 Prv 11:22; Is 65:4; 66:17; Mt 7:6; 8:30–32; Mk 5:11–16; Lk 8:32–33; 15:15–16.
11:9 Jn 21:9–13.
11:22 Mt 3:4; Mk 1:6.
11:24 Lv 5:2; 7:21.

unclean for you; anyone who touches them becomes unclean. 27 Also by the various quadrupeds that walk on paws; they are unclean for you; anyone who touches their carcasses shall be unclean until evening, 28 and anyone who carries their carcasses shall wash his garments and be unclean until evening. They are unclean for you.

29 Of the creatures that swarm on the ground, the following are unclean for you: the rat, the mouse, the various kinds of lizards, 30 the gecko, the spotted lizard, the agama, the skink, and the chameleon. 31 Among the various swarming creatures, these are unclean for you. Everyone who touches them when they are dead shall be unclean until evening. 32 Everything on which one of them falls when dead becomes unclean, including any article of wood, cloth, leather or goat hair—any article of which use can be made. It must be immersed in water and remain unclean until evening, when it again becomes clean. 33 Should any of these creatures fall into a clay vessel, everything in it becomes unclean, and the vessel itself you must break. 34 Any food that can be eaten which makes contact with water, and any liquid that may be drunk, in any such vessel become unclean. 35 Any object on which any part of their carcasses falls becomes unclean; if it is an oven or stove, this must be broken to pieces; they are unclean and shall always be unclean to you. 36 However, a spring or a cistern for collecting water remains clean; but whoever touches such an animal's carcass becomes unclean. 37 If any part of their carcasses falls on any sort of grain that is to be sown, it remains clean; 38 but if the grain has become moistened, it becomes unclean to you when any part of their carcasses falls on it.

39 †* When one of the animals that you could otherwise eat dies of itself, anyone who touches its carcass shall be unclean until evening; 40 and anyone who eats any part of its carcass shall wash his garments and be unclean until evening;* so also, anyone who carries its carcass shall wash his garments and be unclean until evening.

41 All the creatures that swarm on the ground are loathsome and shall not be eaten. 42 Whether it crawls on its belly, goes on all fours, or has many legs—any creature that swarms on the earth—you shall not eat them; they are loathsome. 43 Do not make yourselves loathsome by any swarming creature nor defile yourselves with them and so become unclean by them.* 44 For I, the LORD, am your God. You shall make and keep yourselves holy,† because I am holy.* You shall not make yourselves unclean, then, by any swarming creature that crawls on the ground. 45 Since I, the LORD, am the one who brought you up from the land of Egypt that I might be your God, you shall be holy, because I am holy.

46 This is the instruction for land animals, birds, and all the creatures that move about in the water, as well as any animal that swarms on the ground, 47 that you may distinguish between the clean and the unclean, and between creatures that may be eaten and those that may not be eaten.*

## 12 Uncleanness of Childbirth. 1 The LORD said to Moses: 2 Tell the Israelites: When a woman has a child, giving birth to a boy, she shall be unclean† for seven days, with the same uncleanness as during her menstrual period.* 3 On the eighth day, the flesh of the boy's foreskin shall be circumcised,†* 4 and then she shall spend thirty-three days more in a state of blood purity; she shall not touch anything sacred nor enter the sanctuary till the days of her purification are fulfilled. 5 If she gives birth to a girl, for fourteen days she shall be as unclean as during her menstrual period, after which she

---

† 11:39–40 These animals create uncleanness, but are not prohibited as food (cf. 17:15–16). Priests who have a higher degree of holiness than other Israelites may not eat these animals (22:8; cf. Ez 44:31). Cf. Ex 22:30; Dt 14:21.

11:44–45 *Keep yourselves holy…you shall be holy:* a similar idea is expressed in 20:25–26. There, distinguishing between the animals is compared to God's distinguishing between the peoples and choosing Israel.

12:2–5 The mother has two stages of uncleanness or impurity: the first where her uncleanness is as severe as during her menstrual period and is contagious to profane persons and objects (cf. 15:19–24), and the second where she does not contaminate persons and objects but is still impure to what is holy, such as

the sanctuary (12:4) or sacrifices. The implication is that in the second stage she may resume sexual relations with her husband (which would be prohibited in the first stage according to 18:19).

12:3 Circumcision is the sign of the covenant between God and Israel (Gn 17:1–27) and allows full participation in the religious community (Ex 12:43–49; Jos 5:2–10). This command was fulfilled after Jesus' birth (Lk 2:21).

| | |
|---|---|
| **11:39** Lv 17:15–16; 22:8; Ex 22:30; Ez 4:12–14; 44:31. | **11:44** Lv 19:2; 20:7, 26; Mt 5:48; 1 Pt 1:16. |
| **11:40** Lv 17:15; 22:8. | **11:47** Lv 10:10. |
| **11:43–44** Lv 20:25–26. | **12:2** Lv 15:19. |
| | **12:3** Gn 17:12; Jn 7:22. |

shall spend sixty-six days† in a state of blood purity.

⁶† When the days of her purification for a son or for a daughter are fulfilled,* she shall bring to the priest at the entrance of the tent of meeting a yearling lamb for a burnt offering and a pigeon or a turtledove for a purification offering. ⁷ The priest shall offer them before the LORD to make atonement for her, and thus she will be clean again after her flow of blood. Such is the ritual for the woman who gives birth to a child, male or female. ⁸ If, however, she cannot afford a lamb,* she may take two turtledoves or two pigeons,* the one for a burnt offering and the other for a purification offering. The priest shall make atonement for her, and thus she will again be clean.

# 13 Scaly Infection.† ¹ The LORD said to Moses and Aaron: ²* When someone has on the skin a mark, lesion, or blotch which appears to develop into a scaly infection, the person shall be brought to Aaron, the priest, or to one of the priests among his sons. ³ If the priest, upon examination of the skin's infection, finds that the hair on the infection has turned white and the infection itself appears to be deeper than the skin, † it is indeed a scaly infection; the priest, on seeing this, shall declare the person unclean. ⁴† If, however, the blotch on the skin is white, but does not seem to be deeper than the skin, nor has the hair turned white, the priest shall quarantine the afflicted person for seven days.† ⁵ Should the priest,

upon examination on the seventh day, find that the infection has remained unchanged in color and has not spread on the skin, the priest shall quarantine the person for another seven days. ⁶ Should the priest, upon examination again on the seventh day, find that the infection is now faded and has not spread on the skin, the priest shall declare the person clean; it was merely a scab. The person shall wash his garments† and so become clean. ⁷ But if, after the person was examined by the priest and declared clean, the scab spreads at all on the skin, the person shall once more be examined by the priest. ⁸ Should the priest, upon examination, find that the scab has indeed spread on the skin, he shall declare the person unclean; it is a scaly infection.

⁹ When someone is afflicted with a scaly infection, that person shall be brought to the priest. ¹⁰ Should the priest, upon examination, find that there is a white mark on the skin which has turned the hair white and that there is raw flesh in it, ¹¹ it is a chronic scaly infection on the skin. The priest shall declare the person unclean without quarantine, since the individual is certainly unclean. ¹²† If the scaly infection breaks out on the skin and, as far as the priest can see, covers all the skin of the afflicted person from head to foot, ¹³ should the priest then, upon examination, find that the scaly infection does cover the whole body, he shall declare the afflicted person clean; since the person has turned completely white; that individual is clean. ¹⁴ But as soon as raw

---

† **12:5** *If she gives birth to a girl…sixty-six days:* while the longer period of uncleanness following the birth of a girl, compared to that following the birth of a boy, might reflect the relative disparity in social status between men and women in ancient Israel (and attested in other cultures), this is by no means certain. There is no simple correlation in the Bible between the worth of something and the degree of impurity it can occasion.

**12:6–8** Certain tolerated impurities (see note on 11:1–15:33) are strong enough to pollute the sanctuary and require purification offerings, including the parturient (see also 14:10–32; 15:13–15, 28–30). Cf. note on 4:3. Mary fulfilled the command of bringing sacrifices after the birth of Jesus (Lk 2:22–24).

**13:1–14:57** These chapters deal with scaly or fungal infections (Hebrew *ṣāraʿat*). The older translation "leprosy" is misleading because *ṣāraʿat* refers to not just one but several chronic and enduring skin diseases in human beings. The disease known as "leprosy" (Hansen's disease) is probably not included among the conditions described in the chapter. Also the term *ṣāraʿat* refers to fungal growths in fabrics and on the walls of houses. The reason why these conditions, and not other diseases, were considered unclean was that they were quite visible, associated with death (cf. Nm 12:9–12), and traditionally connected with punishment by the deity (Lv 14:34; Dt 28:27, 35; 2 Sm 3:29; 2 Kgs 5:26–27; 2 Chr 26:16–21).

**13:3** The symptoms of white hair and depth (perhaps a subcutaneous lesion) do not clearly correlate with known skin diseases

or lesions. It may be that the symptoms are a hybrid ideal that do not reflect reality and are the result of priestly systematization. The same judgment applies to the conditions in vv. 10–11, 20, 25; cf. note on vv. 12–17.

**13:4–8** The symptoms here involve a flaky patch of skin that spreads after one week or stays the same after two. This correlates with many skin diseases, such as psoriasis, seborrhoeic dermatitis, certain mycotic infections, patchy eczema, and pityriasis rosea.

**13:4** *Quarantine…seven days:* unless lesions have unmistakable symptoms of scaly infection, time is needed to distinguish disease from a condition which is following the natural course of healing and remission. Cf. vv. 5, 21, 26, 27, 31, 33, 50, 54; 14:38.

**13:6** *Wash his garments:* even suspected scaly infections create some impurity, not just diagnosed infections (vv. 45–46).

**13:12–17** This is not a paradox, namely where a limited lesion is impure but one that covers the whole body is pure. Rather, a white lesion that lacks ulcerated skin ("raw flesh") is pure, even if it covers the whole body. This formulation reflects priestly interest in systematization.

---

**12:6** Lk 2:22–24.
**12:8** Lv 14:21–22.
**12:8** Lv 1:14; Lk 2:24.
**13:2** Lv 22:4; Ex 4:6;

Nm 5:2–3; Dt 24:8;
2 Sm 3:29; 2 Kgs
5:1, 3–7, 11, 27; Mk
1:40–45.

flesh appears, the individual is unclean; [15] on observing the raw flesh, the priest shall declare the person unclean, because raw flesh is unclean; it is a scaly infection. [16] If, however, the raw flesh again turns white, the person shall return to the priest; [17] should the latter, upon examination, find that the infection has indeed turned white, he shall declare the afflicted person clean; the individual is clean.

[18] If a boil appeared on a person's skin which later healed, [19] should now in the place of the boil a white mark or a reddish white blotch develop, the person shall be examined by the priest. [20] If the latter, upon examination, finds that it is deeper than the skin and that the hair has turned white, he shall declare the person unclean; it is a scaly infection that has broken out in the boil. [21] But if the priest, upon examination, finds that there is no white hair in it and that it is not deeper than the skin and is faded, the priest shall quarantine the person for seven days. [22] If it has then spread on the skin, the priest shall declare the person unclean; it is an infection. [23] But if the blotch remains the same without spreading, it is merely the scar of the boil; the priest shall therefore declare the person clean.

[24] If there was a burn on a person's skin, and the burned area now becomes a reddish white or a white blotch, [25] when the priest, upon examination, finds that the hair has turned white in the blotch and this seems to be deeper than the skin, it is a scaly infection that has broken out in the burn; the priest shall therefore declare the person unclean; it is a scaly infection. [26] But if the priest, upon examination, finds that there is no white hair in the blotch and that this is not deeper than the skin and is faded, the priest shall quarantine the person for seven days. [27] Should the priest, upon examination on the seventh day, find that it has spread at all on the skin, he shall declare the person unclean; it is a scaly infection. [28] But if the blotch remains the same without spreading on the skin and is faded, it is merely the spot of the burn; the priest shall therefore declare the person clean, since it is only the scar of the burn.

[29]† When a man or a woman has an infection on the head or in the beard, [30] should the priest, upon examination, find that the infection appears to be deeper than the skin and that there is fine yellow hair in it, the priest shall declare the person unclean; it is a scall. It is a scaly infection of the head or beard. [31] But if the priest, upon examining the scall infection, finds that it does not appear to be deeper than the skin, though the hair in it may not be black, the priest shall quarantine the scall-stricken person for seven days. [32] Should the priest, upon examining the infection on the seventh day find that the scall has not spread and has no yellow hair in it and does not seem to be deeper than the skin, [33] the person shall shave, but not the scall spot. Then the priest shall quarantine the scall-diseased person for another seven days. [34] If the priest, upon examining the scall on the seventh day, finds that it has not spread on the skin and that it does not appear to be deeper than the skin, he shall declare the person clean; the latter shall wash his garments, and will thus be clean. [35] But if the scall spreads at all on the skin after the person has been declared clean— [36] should the priest, upon examination, find that the scall has indeed spread on the skin, he need not look for yellow hair; the individual is unclean. [37] If, however, the scall has remained unchanged in color and black hair has grown in it, the disease has been healed; the person is clean, and the priest shall declare the individual clean.

[38]† When the skin of a man or a woman is spotted with several white blotches, [39] if the priest, upon examination, finds that the blotches on the skin are pale white, it is only tetter that has broken out on the skin, and the person therefore is clean.

[40] When a man loses the hair of his head, he is simply bald on the crown and not unclean.* [41] So too, if he loses the hair on the front of his head, he is simply bald on the forehead and not unclean. [42] But when there is a reddish white infection on his bald crown or bald forehead, it is a scaly infection that is breaking out there. [43] If the priest, upon examination, finds that the infection spot on the bald area on the crown or forehead has the same reddish white appearance as that of a scaly infection of the

---

† **13:29–37** The symptoms in this unit may include either favus (a mycotic infection) or a protein deficiency syndrome (Kwashiorkor) where the hair may be fine and copper-red to yellow.

**13:38–39** This may refer to vitiligo, where patches of the skin and hair lose pigmentation.

**13:40** 2 Kgs 2:23.

skin, ⁴⁴ the man has a scaly infection and is unclean. The priest shall declare him unclean; his infection is on his head.

⁴⁵† The garments of one afflicted with a scaly infection shall be rent and the hair disheveled,* and the mustache covered.* The individual shall cry out, "Unclean, unclean!" ⁴⁶ As long as the infection is present, the person shall be unclean. Being unclean, that individual shall dwell apart, taking up residence outside the camp.*

### Fungal Infection of Fabrics and Leather.

⁴⁷ When a fungal infection is on a garment of wool or of linen, ⁴⁸ or on the warp and woof† of linen or wool, or on a hide or anything made of leather, ⁴⁹ if the infection on the garment or hide, or on the warp or woof, or on any leather article is greenish or reddish, the thing is indeed a fungal infection and must be examined by the priest. ⁵⁰ Having examined the infection, the priest shall quarantine the infected article for seven days. ⁵¹ If the priest, upon inspecting the infection on the seventh day, finds that it has spread on the garment, or on the warp or woof, or on the leather, whatever be its use, the infection is a harmful fungus; the article is unclean. ⁵² He shall therefore burn up the garment, or the warp or woof, be it of wool or linen, or any leather article which is infected; since it is a harmful fungus, it must be destroyed by fire. ⁵³ But if the priest, upon examination, finds that it has not spread on the garment, or on the warp or woof, or on the leather article, ⁵⁴ he shall give orders to have the infected article washed and then quarantined for another seven days. ⁵⁵ If the priest, upon examination after the infection was washed, finds that it has not changed its color, even though it may not have spread, the article is unclean. You shall burn it with fire. It is a fray, be it on its inner or outer side. ⁵⁶ But if the priest, upon examination, finds that the infection has faded after the washing, he shall cut it out of the garment, or the leather, or the warp or woof. ⁵⁷ If, however, the infection again appears on the garment, or on the warp or woof, or on the leather article, it is still virulent and you shall burn the thing infected with fire. ⁵⁸ But if, after the washing, the infection has disappeared from the garment, or the warp or woof, or the leather article, the thing shall be washed a second time, and thus it will be clean. ⁵⁹ This is the instruction for a fungal* infection on a garment of wool or linen, or on a warp or woof, or on any leather article, to determine whether it is clean or unclean.

## 14 Purification After Scaly Infection.

¹† The LORD said to Moses: ²* This is the ritual for someone that had a scaly infection at the time of that person's purification.* The individual shall be brought to the priest, ³ who is to go outside the camp.* If the priest, upon inspection, finds that the scaly infection has healed in the afflicted person, ⁴ he shall order that two live, clean birds,† as well as some cedar wood, scarlet yarn, and hyssop be obtained for the one who is to be purified.* ⁵† The priest shall then order that one of the birds be slaughtered over an earthen vessel with fresh water in it. ⁶ Taking the living bird with the cedar wood, the scarlet yarn and the hyssop, the priest shall dip them, including the live bird, in the blood of the bird that was slaughtered over the fresh water, ⁷ and then sprinkle seven times on the person to be purified from the scaly infection. When he has thus purified that person, he shall let the living bird fly away over the countryside.* ⁸ The

---

† **13:45–46** The symbolic association with death is found in the mourning activities in which those diagnosed with these afflictions engage: rending clothes, disheveling the hair, and covering the mouth. They are also excluded from the camp. Cf. examples of exclusion in Nm 5:1–4; 12:14–15; 2 Kgs 7:3–10; 15:5; 2 Chr 26:21. Persons with scaly infections must have been able to pollute others in the priestly system, though this is not stated. Hence, they must cry out "Unclean, unclean!" to warn others of their presence.

**13:48** *Warp and woof*: it is possible that the nature of the weave allowed fungus to grow separately along warp or woof. Otherwise, this may refer to the yarns before they are woven together.

**14:1–32** The rites here are for purification from human scaly infections after recovery, not for healing (but cf. 2 Kgs 5:10–14).

**14:4–7** The bird rite is also found for purifying a house from a fungus (vv. 49–53). The rite apparently removes impurity from

the individual and, by means of the live bird, sends it away to unpopulated areas (v. 7). This is similar to the dispatch of a goat laden with sins on the Day of Atonement (16:21–22).

**14:5–7** The blood from the bird serves as a ritual detergent, much like the blood from the purification offering (see notes on 4:3). It is not a sacrifice, however, since it is not performed at the sanctuary. *Fresh water*: lit., "living water," taken from some source of running water, not from a cistern.

* **13:45** Lv 10:6.
**13:45** Mi 3:7.
**13:46** Lv 14:3; Nm 5:2; 12:14–15; 2 Kgs 7:3–10; 15:5; 2 Chr 26:21; Mt 26:6; Mk 14:3; Lk 17:11–19.
**13:59** Lv 14:54–57.
**14:2** 2 Kgs 5:10, 14; Mt 8:4; 10:8; Mk 1:44; Lk 4:27; 5:14.
**14:2** Lv 14:48–53.
**14:3** Lv 13:46.
**14:4** Nm 19:6.
**14:7** Lv 16:21–22.

person being purified shall then wash his garments, shave off all hair, and bathe in water,† and so become clean. After this the person may come inside the camp, but shall still remain outside his or her tent for seven days.* ⁹On the seventh day this individual shall again shave off all hair, of the head, beard, and eyebrows—all hair must be shaved—and also wash his garments and bathe the body in water, and so become clean.

¹⁰On the eighth day the individual shall take two unblemished male lambs, one unblemished yearling ewe lamb, three tenths of an ephah of bran flour mixed with oil for a grain offering, and one log† of oil. ¹¹The priest who performs the purification ceremony shall place the person who is being purified, as well as all these offerings, before the LORD at the entrance of the tent of meeting. ¹²Taking one of the male lambs, the priest shall present it as a reparation offering,* along with the log of oil, raising them as an elevated* offering before the LORD. ¹³This lamb shall be slaughtered in the sacred place where the purification offering and the burnt offering are slaughtered, because the reparation offering is like the purification offering; it belongs to the priest and is most holy. ¹⁴†* Then the priest shall take some of the blood of the reparation offering and put it on the lobe of the right ear, the thumb of the right hand, and the big toe of the right foot of the person being purified. ¹⁵The priest shall also take the log of oil and pour some of it into the palm of his own left hand; ¹⁶then, dipping his right finger in the oil on his left palm, he shall sprinkle some of it with his finger seven times before the LORD. ¹⁷Of the oil left in his hand the priest shall put some on the lobe of the right ear, the thumb of the right hand, and the big toe of the right foot of the person being purified, over the blood of the reparation offering. ¹⁸The rest of the oil in his hand the priest shall put on the head* of the one being purified. Thus shall the priest make atonement for the individual before the LORD. ¹⁹The priest shall next offer the purification offering,* thus making atonement on behalf of the one being purified from the uncleanness. After this the burnt offering shall be slaughtered. ²⁰The priest shall offer the burnt offering* and the grain offering on the altar before the LORD. Thus shall the priest make atonement for the person, and the individual will become clean.

**Poor Person's Sacrifices.** ²¹If a person is poor and cannot afford so much,* that person shall take one male lamb for a reparation offering, to be used as an elevated offering in atonement, one tenth of an ephah of bran flour mixed with oil for a grain offering, a log of oil, ²²and two turtledoves or pigeons, which the individual can more easily afford, the one as a purification offering and the other as a burnt offering. ²³On the eighth day of purification the person shall bring them to the priest, at the entrance of the tent of meeting before the LORD. ²⁴Taking the lamb of the reparation offering, along with the log of oil, the priest shall raise them as an elevated offering before the LORD. ²⁵When the lamb of the reparation offering has been slaughtered, the priest shall take some of its blood, and put it on the lobe of the right ear, on the thumb of the right hand, and on the big toe of the right foot of the person being purified. ²⁶The priest shall then pour some of the oil into the palm of his own left hand ²⁷and with his right finger sprinkle some of the oil in his left palm seven times before the LORD. ²⁸Some of the oil in his hand the priest shall also put on the lobe of the right ear, the thumb of the right hand, and the big toe of the right foot of the person being purified, where he had sprinkled the blood of the reparation offering. ²⁹The rest of the oil in his hand the priest shall put on the head of the one being purified. Thus shall he make atonement for the individual before the LORD. ³⁰Then, of the turtledoves or pigeons, such as the person can afford, ³¹the priest shall offer one as a purification offering and the other as a burnt offering,* along with the grain

---

† **14:8** *Bathe in water*: This phrase occurs frequently in Lv 14–16 and is imprecise. It can refer to both ordinary and cultic washing. The context will determine the meaning. At this early period in Israel's history it is probably not a reference to cultic immersion in a Mikveh—a Second Temple period ritual.

**14:10** *Log*: a liquid measure of capacity attested in the Bible only here. It is apparently equal in capacity to one-half liter.

**14:14–17** The application of blood and oil here facilitates the movement of the person from the severely impure to the pure profane sphere; it reintegrates him or her into the community. Cf. 8:23–24.

* 
| | |
|---|---|
| **14:8** Lv 15:13, 28. | **14:19** Lv 4. |
| **14:12** Lv 7:1–10. | **14:20** Lv 1. |
| **14:12** Lv 7:30. | **14:21** Lv 5:7, 11; 12:8. |
| **14:14** Lv 8:23–24. | **14:31** Lv 1:14–17; 5:7–10. |
| **14:18** Lv 8:12, 30. | |

offering. Thus shall the priest make atonement before the LORD for the person who is being purified. ³²This is the ritual for one afflicted with a scaly infection who has insufficient means for purification.

**Fungal Infection of Houses.** ³³†The LORD said to Moses and Aaron: ³⁴When you come into the land of Canaan, which I am giving you to possess, if I put* a fungal infection in any house of the land you occupy, ³⁵the owner of the house shall come and report to the priest, "Something like an infection has appeared in my house." ³⁶The priest shall then order the house to be cleared out before he goes in to examine the infection, lest everything in the house become unclean. Only after this is he to go in to examine the house. ³⁷If the priest, upon inspection, finds that the infection on the walls of the house consists of greenish or reddish spots* which seem to go deeper than the surface of the wall, ³⁸he shall go out of the house to the doorway and quarantine the house for seven days. ³⁹On the seventh day the priest shall return. If, upon inspection, he finds that the infection has spread on the walls, ⁴⁰he shall order the infected stones to be pulled out and cast in an unclean place outside the city. ⁴¹The whole inside of the house shall then be scraped, and the mortar that has been scraped off shall be dumped in an unclean place outside the city. ⁴²Then other stones shall be brought and put in the place of the old stones, and new mortar obtained and plastered on the house. ⁴³If the infection breaks out once more in the house after the stones have been pulled out and the house has been scraped and replastered, ⁴⁴the priest shall come; and if, upon inspection, he finds that the infection has spread in the house, it is a corrosive fungus in the house, and it is unclean. ⁴⁵It shall be pulled down, and all its stones, beams and mortar shall be hauled away to an unclean place outside the city. ⁴⁶*Whoever enters a house while it is quarantined shall be unclean until evening.

⁴⁷Whoever sleeps or eats in such a house shall also wash his garments.

⁴⁸*If the priest finds, when he comes to the house, that the infection has in fact not spread in the house after the plastering, he shall declare the house clean, since the infection has been healed. ⁴⁹To purify the house, he shall take two birds, as well as cedar wood, scarlet yarn, and hyssop. ⁵⁰One of the birds he shall slaughter over an earthen vessel with fresh water in it. ⁵¹Then, taking the cedar wood, the hyssop and the scarlet yarn, together with the living bird, he shall dip them all in the blood of the slaughtered bird and the fresh water, and sprinkle the house seven times. ⁵²Thus he shall purify the house with the bird's blood and the fresh water, along with the living bird, the cedar wood, the hyssop, and the scarlet yarn. ⁵³He shall then let the living bird fly away over the countryside outside the city. Thus he shall make atonement for the house, and it will be clean.

⁵⁴This is the ritual for every kind of human scaly infection and scall, ⁵⁵and for fungus diseases in garments and houses— ⁵⁶for marks, lesions and blotches— ⁵⁷to give direction when there is a state of uncleanness and when a state of cleanness. This is the ritual for scaly infection.

**15** **Sexual Uncleanness.**† ¹The LORD said to Moses and Aaron: ²†Speak to the Israelites and tell them: When any man has a genital discharge, he is thereby unclean.* ³Such is his uncleanness from this discharge, whether his body† drains freely with the discharge or is blocked up from the discharge. His uncleanness is on him all the days that his body discharges or is blocked up from his discharge; this is his uncleanness. ⁴Any bed on which the man with the discharge lies is unclean, and any article on which he sits is unclean. ⁵Anyone who touches his bed shall wash his garments, bathe in water, and be unclean until evening. ⁶Whoever sits on an article on which the man with the discharge

---

† **14:33–53** Discussion of fungi in houses is probably delayed until here because it deals with a case pertaining to living in the land (v. 34) as opposed to the foregoing cases which apply even in the wilderness. The rules on fabrics (13:47–58) apply to the tent dwellings in the wilderness.

**15:1–33** Sexual discharges may be unclean partly because they involve the loss of life fluids or are otherwise involved with phenomena at the margins of life and death.

**15:2–3** The uncleanness here is perhaps a discharge of

pus because of urethritis (often but not solely associated with gonorrhea).

**15:3** *Body:* here a euphemism in the Hebrew for "penis."

---

**14:34** Nm 12:9–15; 2 Kgs 15:4–5; 2 Chr 26:16–21.
**14:37** Lv 13:49.
**14:46–47** cf. Lv 15:10.
**14:48** Lv 14:2–9.
**15:2** Nm 5:2.

was sitting shall wash his garments, bathe in water, and be unclean until evening. [7] Whoever touches the body of the man with the discharge shall wash his garments, bathe in water, and be unclean until evening. [8] If the man with the discharge spits on a clean person, the latter shall wash his garments, bathe in water, and be unclean until evening. [9] Any saddle on which the man with the discharge rides is unclean. [10] Whoever touches anything that was under him shall be unclean until evening; whoever carries any such thing shall wash his garments, bathe in water, and be unclean until evening.* [11] Anyone whom the man with the discharge touches with his unrinsed hands shall wash his garments, bathe in water, and be unclean until evening. [12] Earthenware touched by the man with the discharge shall be broken; and every wooden article shall be rinsed with water.

[13] When a man with a discharge becomes clean† of his discharge, he shall count seven days* for his purification. Then he shall wash his garments and bathe his body in fresh water, and so he will be clean. [14] On the eighth day he shall take two turtledoves or two pigeons,* and going before the Lord, to the entrance of the tent of meeting, he shall give them to the priest, [15] who shall offer them up, the one as a purification offering and the other as a burnt offering. Thus shall the priest make atonement before the Lord for the man because of his discharge.

[16] † When a man has an emission of semen, he shall bathe his whole body in water and be unclean until evening.* [17] Any piece of cloth or leather with semen on it shall be washed with water and be unclean until evening.

[18] If a man has sexual relations with a woman, they shall both bathe in water and be unclean until evening.

[19] † When a woman has a flow of blood from her body, she shall be in a state of menstrual uncleanness for seven days. Anyone who touches her shall be unclean until evening.* [20] Anything on which she lies or sits during her menstrual period shall be unclean. [21] Anyone who touches her bed shall wash his garments, bathe in water, and be unclean until evening. [22] Whoever touches any article on which she was sitting shall wash his garments, bathe in water, and be unclean until evening. [23] Whether an object† is on the bed or on something she sat upon, when the person touches it, that person shall be unclean until evening. [24] If a man lies with her, he contracts her menstrual uncleanness and shall be unclean for seven days;* every bed on which he then lies also becomes unclean.

[25] † When a woman has a flow of blood for several days outside her menstrual period, or when her flow continues beyond the ordinary period, as long as she suffers this unclean flow she shall be unclean, just as during her menstrual period.* [26] Any bed on which she lies during such a flow becomes unclean, as it would during her menstrual period, and any article on which she sits becomes unclean just as during her menstrual period. [27] Anyone who touches them becomes unclean; that person shall wash his garments, bathe in water, and be unclean until evening.

[28] * When she becomes clean from her flow, she shall count seven days; after this she becomes clean. [29] On the eighth day she shall take two turtledoves or two pigeons and bring them to the priest at the entrance of the tent of meeting. [30] The priest shall offer one of them as a purification offering and the other as a burnt offering. Thus shall the priest make atonement before the Lord for her because of her unclean flow.

---

† **15:13** *Becomes clean*: i.e., when his discharge ceases. The rite that follows is for purification, not a cure; see note on 14:1–32.

**15:16–18** Menstrual blood, semen, and other impurities in Lv 11–15 are considered "impure" either because they are force of life whose "loss" represents death or because, as uniquely human conditions, they are symbolically incompatible with the deity and the divine abode, the sanctuary. Lv 15:16 refers to a spontaneous nocturnal emission, and either because this marks life and death boundaries or because of its uniquely human (versus divine) character, any contact with it renders the object or person ritually unclean. Thus, in 15:18 it is not the marital act itself that is polluting, but only semen.

**15:19–24** This is normal menstruation.

**15:23** *An object*: the Hebrew is unclear. This translation means that even an object on the woman's unclean bed or chair

can mediate uncleanness to another, but only if all the object touched is still on the bed or article sat upon, thus forming a chain of simultaneous contact.

**15:25–30** This is menstruation outside the normal cycle or for periods longer than normal. A woman with a chronic blood flow was healed by touching the tassel of Jesus' cloak (Mt 9:20–22; Mk 5:25–34; Lk 8:43–48).

---

**15:10** Lv 11:24–25, 27–28, 39–40; 14:46–47.
**15:13** Lv 14:8.
**15:14** Lv 12:8; 14:22.
**15:16** Ex 19:15; Dt 23:11–12; 1 Sm 21:6.
**15:19** Lv 12:2, 5; 2 Sm 11:4; Ez 36:17.
**15:24** Lv 18:19; 20:18; Ez 18:6.
**15:25** Mt 9:20–22; Mk 5:25–34; Lk 8:43–48.
**15:28** Lv 15:13–15.

³¹ You shall warn the Israelites of their uncleanness, lest they die through their uncleanness by defiling my tabernacle,* which is in their midst.

³² This is the ritual for the man with a discharge, or who has an emission of semen, and thereby becomes unclean; ³³ as well as for the woman who has her menstrual period; or one who has a discharge, male or female; and also for the man who lies with an unclean woman.

# 16 The Day of Atonement.

¹† After the death of Aaron's two sons,* who died when they encroached on the LORD's presence, the LORD spoke to Moses ² and said to him: Tell your brother Aaron that he is not to come whenever he pleases† into the inner sanctuary, inside the veil,* in front of the cover on the ark, lest he die, for I reveal myself in a cloud above the ark's cover. ³ Only in this way may Aaron enter the inner sanctuary. He shall bring a bull of the herd for a purification offering and a ram for a burnt offering. ⁴ He shall wear the sacred linen tunic, with the linen pants underneath, gird himself with the linen sash and put on the linen turban.* But since these vestments are sacred, he shall not put them on until he has first bathed his body in water.* ⁵ From the Israelite community he shall receive two male goats for a purification offering and one ram for a burnt offering.

⁶ Aaron shall offer the bull, his purification offering, to make atonement† for himself and for his household. ⁷ Taking the two male goats and setting them before the LORD at the entrance of the tent of meeting, ⁸ he shall cast lots* to determine which one is for the LORD and which for Azazel.†* ⁹ The goat that is determined by lot for the LORD, Aaron shall present and offer up as a purification offering. ¹⁰ But the goat determined by lot for Azazel he shall place before the LORD alive, so that with it he may make atonement by sending it off to Azazel in the desert.

¹¹ Thus shall Aaron offer his bull for the purification offering, to make atonement for himself and for his family. When he has slaughtered it, ¹² he shall take a censer full of glowing embers from the altar before the LORD, as well as a double handful of finely ground fragrant incense, and bringing them inside the veil, ¹³ there before the LORD he shall put incense on the fire, so that a cloud of incense may shield the cover that is over the covenant, else he will die. ¹⁴ Taking some of the bull's blood, he shall sprinkle it with his finger on the front of the ark's cover and likewise sprinkle some of the blood with his finger seven times in front of the cover.

¹⁵ Then he shall slaughter the goat of the people's purification offering, and bringing its blood inside the veil, he shall do with it as he did with the bull's blood, sprinkling it on the ark's cover and in front of it. ¹⁶ Thus he shall purge the inner sanctuary† of all the Israelites' impurities and trespasses, including all their sins. He shall do the same for the tent of meeting,* which is set up among them in the midst of their uncleanness. ¹⁷ No one else may be in the tent of meeting from the time he enters the inner sanctuary to make atonement until he departs. When he has made atonement for himself and his household, as well as for the whole Israelite assembly, ¹⁸† he shall come

---

† **16:1–34** This is the narrative sequel of the story in chap. 10. The ritual in chapter 16 originally may have been an emergency rite in response to unexpected pollution of the sanctuary.

**16:2** *Not to come whenever he pleases:* access to the various parts of the sanctuary is strictly controlled. Only the high priest can enter the most holy place, and only once a year. *The veil:* the Letter to the Hebrews makes use of the imagery of the Day of Atonement (in Hebrew *Yom Kippur*) to explain Jesus' sacrifice (Heb 9:1–14, 23–28). *Ark's cover:* the meaning of *kappōret* is not certain. It may be connected with the verb *kipper* "to atone, purge" (see note on v. 6) and thus refer to this part of the ark as a focus of atonement or purification.

**16:6** *Make atonement:* the Hebrew verb *kipper* refers specifically to the removal of sin and impurity (cf. Ex 30:10; Lv 6:23; 8:15; 16:16, 18, 20, 27, 33; Ez 43:20, 26; 45:20), thus "to purge" in vv. 16, 18, 20, and 33, and more generally to the consequence of the sacrificial procedure, which is atonement (cf. Lv 17:11). "Atonement" is preeminently a function of the purification sacrifice, but other sacrifices, except apparently the communion sacrifice, achieve this as well.

**16:8** *Azazel:* a name for a demon (meaning something like "angry/fierce god"). See note on 17:7.

**16:16** *Inner sanctuary:* this refers to the most holy room (vv. 2, 11–15). *Trespasses, including all their sins:* the term for "trespasses" (Heb. *pesha'im*), which has overtones of rebellion, and the phrase "all their sins" indicate that even sins committed intentionally are included (such as when the sinner "acts defiantly," as in Nm 15:30–31). This complements the scheme found in Lv 4 (see note on 4:3): intentional sins pollute the sanctuary more and penetrate even further than inadvertent sins, namely to the most holy place. *The same for the tent of meeting:* this rite may be that found in 4:5–7, 16–18 where blood is sprinkled in the anterior room and blood is placed on the horns of the incense altar there. Cf. Ex 30:10.

**16:18–19** Thus a third locale in the sanctuary complex, the open-air altar, is purified. See the summaries in 16:20, 33.

---

*

| | |
|---|---|
| **15:31** Lv 5:2–3; 22:9; Nm 19:13, 20. | **16:4** Lv 8:6. |
| **16:1** Lv 10:1–5. | **16:8** Jos 7:14–20; Acts 1:26. |
| **16:2** Lv 23:26–32; Nm 29:7–11; Heb 9:6–28. | **16:8** Lv 17:7. |
| **16:4** Lv 8:7; Ex 28:1–40. | **16:16** Lv 4:5–7, 16–18. |

out to the altar before the Lord and purge it also. Taking some of the bull's and the goat's blood, he shall put it on the horns around the altar, [19] and with his finger sprinkle some of the blood on it seven times.* Thus he shall purify it and sanctify it from the impurities of the Israelites.

**The Scapegoat.** [20] When he has finished purging the inner sanctuary, the tent of meeting and the altar, Aaron shall bring forward the live goat. [21] Laying both hands† on its head, he shall confess over it all the iniquities of the Israelites and their trespasses, including all their sins, and so put them on the goat's head.* He shall then have it led into the wilderness by an attendant. [22] The goat will carry off all their iniquities to an isolated region.*

When the goat is dispatched into the wilderness, [23] Aaron shall go into the tent of meeting, strip off the linen vestments he had put on when he entered the inner sanctuary, and leave them in the tent of meeting. [24] After bathing his body with water in a sacred place, he shall put on his regular vestments, and then come out and offer his own and the people's burnt offering, in atonement for himself and for the people, [25] and also burn the fat of the purification offering on the altar.

[26] The man who led away the goat for Azazel shall wash his garments and bathe his body in water; only then may he enter the camp. [27] The bull and the goat of the purification offering whose blood was brought to make atonement in the inner sanctuary, shall be taken outside the camp,* where their hides and flesh and dung shall be burned in the fire. [28] The one who burns them shall wash his garments and bathe his body in water; only then may he enter the camp.

**The Fast.** [29]* This shall be an everlasting statute for you: on the tenth day of the seventh month every one of you, whether a native or a resident alien, shall humble yourselves† and shall do no work. [30] For on this day atonement is made for you to make you clean; of all your sins you will be cleansed before the Lord. [31] It shall be a sabbath of complete rest for you, on which you must humble yourselves—an everlasting statute.

[32] This atonement is to be made by the priest who has been anointed and ordained to the priesthood in succession to his father. He shall wear the linen garments, the sacred vestments, [33] and purge the most sacred part of the sanctuary, as well as the tent of meeting, and the altar. He shall also make atonement for the priests and all the people of the assembly. [34] This, then, shall be an everlasting statute for you: once a year atonement shall be made on behalf of the Israelites for all their sins. And Moses did as the Lord had commanded him.

## IV. HOLINESS LAWS

**17** **Sacredness of Blood.** [1] The Lord said to Moses: [2] Speak to Aaron and his sons, as well as to all the Israelites, and tell them: This is what the Lord has commanded: [3]† Any Israelite who slaughters an ox or a sheep or a goat, whether in the camp or outside of it, [4] without first bringing it to the entrance of the tent of meeting to present it as an offering to the Lord in front of the Lord's tabernacle, shall be judged guilty of bloodshed†*—that individual has shed blood, and shall be cut off* from the people. [5] This is so that such sacrifices as they used to offer in the open field the Israelites shall henceforth bring to the Lord at the entrance of the tent of meeting, to the priest, and sacrifice them there as communion sacrifices to the Lord.* [6] The priest will splash the blood on the altar of the Lord at the entrance of the tent of meeting and burn the fat for an odor pleasing to the Lord. [7] No

---

† **16:21** *Both hands:* this gesture is for transferring sins to the head of the goat and is apparently different in meaning from the one-handed gesture that precedes the slaughtering of sacrificial animals (1:4; 3:2; 4:4; see note on 1:4).

**16:29** *Humble yourselves:* also v. 31. The idiom used here (Heb. *'innâ nephesh*) involves mainly fasting (Ps 35:13), but probably prohibits other activities such as anointing (Dn 10:3) and sexual intercourse (2 Sm 12:15–24). Such acts of self-denial display the need for divine favor. Fasting is often undertaken in times of emergency and mourning (cf. 1 Sm 14:24; 2 Sm 1:12; 3:35; cf. Mk 2:18–22).

**17:3–4** Any animal slaughtered must be brought to the tent of meeting as an offering. This differs from Dt 12:15–28, which allows those living too far from the temple to slaughter an animal for food at home without offering it as a sacrifice.

**17:4** *Guilty of bloodshed:* human beings and animals can incur blood guilt for killing human beings (cf. Gn 9:5–6); human beings can incur blood guilt for killing animals (see note on Lv 24:17–22).

**16:19** Lv 4:25, 30, 34.
**16:21** Is 53:6; 2 Cor 5:21.
**16:22** Lv 14:7, 53; Is 53:11–12; Jn 1:29; 1 Pt 2:24.
**16:27** Lv 4:11–12; 6:23;
Heb 13:11–13.
**16:29** Lv 23:27, 32; Nm 29:7.
**17:4** Lv 24:18.
**17:4** Lv 7:20.
**17:5** Lv 3:1–2, 7–8, 13.

longer shall they offer their sacrifices to the demons† with whom they prostituted themselves.* This shall be an everlasting statute for them and their descendants.

⁸Tell them, therefore: Anyone, whether of the house of Israel or of the aliens residing among them, who offers a burnt offering or sacrifice ⁹without bringing it to the entrance of the tent of meeting to offer it to the LORD, shall be cut off from the people. ¹⁰* As for anyone, whether of the house of Israel or of the aliens residing among them, who consumes any blood, I will set myself against that individual and will cut that person off from among the people, ¹¹since the life of the flesh is in the blood,* and I have given it to you to make atonement† on the altar for yourselves, because it is the blood as life that makes atonement. ¹²That is why I have told the Israelites: No one among you, not even a resident alien, may consume blood.

¹³Anyone hunting,† whether of the Israelites or of the aliens residing among them, who catches an animal or a bird that may be eaten, shall pour out its blood and cover it with earth,* ¹⁴since the life of all flesh is its blood. I have told the Israelites: You shall not consume the blood of any flesh. Since the life of all flesh is its blood, anyone who consumes it shall be cut off.

¹⁵Everyone, whether a native or an alien, who eats of an animal that died of itself or was killed by a wild beast, shall wash his garments, bathe in water, and be unclean until evening, and then become clean.* ¹⁶If one does not wash his garments and bathe, that person shall bear the penalty.

# 18 Laws Concerning Sexual Behavior.

¹The LORD said to Moses: ²Speak to the Israelites and tell them: I, the LORD, am your God.† ³You shall not do as they do in the land of Egypt, where you once lived, nor shall you do as they do in the land of Canaan, where I am bringing you; do not conform to their customs.* ⁴My decrees you shall carry out, and my statutes you shall take care to follow. I, the LORD, am your God. ⁵Keep, then, my statutes and decrees, for the person who carries them out will find life† through them. I am the LORD.*

⁶† None of you shall approach a close relative† to have sexual intercourse. I am the LORD. ⁷† You shall not disgrace your father by having intercourse with your mother.* She is your own mother; you shall not have intercourse with her. ⁸You shall not have intercourse with your father's wife, for that would be a disgrace to your father. ⁹You shall not have intercourse with your sister,†* your father's daughter or your mother's daughter, whether she was born in your own household or born elsewhere. ¹⁰You shall not have intercourse with your son's daughter or with your daughter's daughter,† for that would be a disgrace to you. ¹¹You shall not have intercourse with the daughter whom your father's wife bore to him in his household,* since she, too, is your sister. ¹²You shall not have intercourse with your father's sister,* since she is your father's relative. ¹³You shall not have intercourse with your mother's sister, since she is your mother's relative. ¹⁴You shall not disgrace your father's brother by having sexual relations with his wife,* since she, too, is your aunt. ¹⁵You shall

---

**17:7** *Demons*: for Hebrew *śĕ'îrîm*, lit., "goats." Like the demon Azazel (cf. 16:8, 10, 21–22), they dwell in the open country (17:5). Cf. Is 13:21; 34:14.

**17:11** *To make atonement*: this is probably to be understood in the context of liability for shedding animal blood (cf. v. 4). Placing the blood on the altar exonerates the slaughterer from guilt for the killing. See note on 16:6.

**17:13** *Hunting*: game animals are not permitted as offerings. One nonetheless has to treat the blood of these animals carefully by covering it with earth. Cf. Dt 12:16, 24.

**17:2** *I, the LORD, am your God*: this declaration appears frequently elsewhere throughout chaps. 17–26, sometimes with a statement of God's holiness or his sanctifying activity. It emphasizes the importance of the laws and the relationship of the divine lawgiver to the people.

**18:5** *Find life*: in Dt 30:15–20 Moses sets before the people life and death. The alternatives are set out in detail in Lv 26 and Dt 28. Cf. Lv 20:11, 13, 21.

**18:6–23** These laws deal with illicit sexual behavior. Lv 20:10–21 reiterates most of these cases, with penalties. Cf. also Dt 27:15–26; Ez 22:7–12. The ordering of the cases in Lv 18 seems to be: blood relatives (vv. 6–13), those related by marriage

(vv. 14–18), then other cases (vv. 19–23).

**18:6** *Close relative*: this refers to a blood relative and includes those not specifically mentioned in the list, such as one's own daughter and a full sister. *Have sexual intercourse*: lit., "to uncover nakedness."

**18:7–8** Cf. the story of Reuben lying with Bilhah, his father's concubine and Rachel's maid (Gn 35:22; 49:4).

**18:9, 11** Cf. actual or possible marriage to a half sister in Gn 20:12 and 2 Sm 13:13.

**18:10** Daughter incest is found in the story of Lot (Gn 19:30–38).

---

**17:7** Ex 34:15; Dt 32:17; 2 Chr 11:15; 1 Cor 10:20.
**17:10–14** Lv 3:17; 7:26–27; Gn 9:4; Dt 12:16, 23–24.
**17:11** Gn 9:4.
**17:13** Dt 12:15–16.
**17:15** Lv 11:39–40; 22:8.
**18:3** Lv 20:22–23.
**18:5** Ez 20:11, 13, 21; Gal 3:12.
**18:7** Lv 20:11; Dt 23:1; 27:20; 1 Cor 5:1.
**18:9** Lv 20:17; Dt 27:22.
**18:11** Lv 20:17.
**18:12** Lv 20:19.
**18:14** Lv 20:20.

L V

not have intercourse with your daughter-in-law;†* she is your son's wife; you shall not have intercourse with her. 16 You shall not have intercourse with your brother's wife;†* that would be a disgrace to your brother. 17 You shall not have intercourse with a woman and also with her daughter, nor shall you marry and have intercourse with her son's daughter or her daughter's daughter;* they are related to her. This would be shameful. 18 While your wife is still living you shall not marry her sister as her rival and have intercourse with her.*

19 You shall not approach a woman to have intercourse with her while she is in her menstrual uncleanness.* 20 You shall not have sexual relations with your neighbor's wife,†* defiling yourself with her. 21* You shall not offer any of your offspring for immolation to Molech,† thus profaning the name of your God. I am the LORD. 22 You shall not lie with a male as with a woman;* such a thing is an abomination. 23 You shall not have sexual relations with an animal, defiling yourself with it; nor shall a woman set herself in front of an animal to mate with it; that is perverse.*

24 Do not defile yourselves by any of these things, because by them the nations whom I am driving out of your way have defiled themselves. 25 And so the land has become defiled, and I have punished it for its wickedness, and the land has vomited out its inhabitants.* 26 You, however, must keep my statutes and decrees, avoiding all these abominations, both the natives and the aliens resident among you— 27 because the previous inhabitants did all these abominations and the land became

defiled; 28 otherwise the land will vomit you out also for having defiled it, just as it vomited out the nations before you. 29 For whoever does any of these abominations shall be cut off from the people. 30 Heed my charge, then, not to observe the abominable customs that have been observed before your time, and thus become impure by them.* I, the LORD, am your God.

# 19 Various Rules of Conduct. 1 The LORD said to Moses: 2 Speak to the whole Israelite community and tell them: Be holy, for I, the LORD your God, am holy.†* 3† Each of you revere your mother and father,* and keep my sabbaths.* I, the LORD, am your God.

4 Do not turn aside to idols, nor make molten gods for yourselves.* I, the LORD, am your God.

5 When you sacrifice your communion sacrifice to the LORD, you shall sacrifice it so that it is acceptable on your behalf. 6 It must be eaten on the day of your sacrifice or on the following day. Whatever is left over until the third day shall be burned in fire. 7 If any of it is eaten on the third day, it will be a desecrated offering and not be accepted;* 8 whoever eats of it then shall bear the penalty for having profaned what is sacred to the LORD. Such a one shall be cut off* from the people.

9† When you reap the harvest of your land, you shall not be so thorough that you reap the field to its very edge, nor shall you gather the gleanings of your harvest.* 10 Likewise, you shall not pick your vineyard bare, nor gather up the grapes that have fallen. These things

---

† 18:15 Judah had intercourse with his daughter-in-law Tamar (Gn 38), but did not know her true identity until her pregnancy was discovered.

18:16 This refers to cohabiting with one's sister-in-law not only while the brother is alive, but also after he is dead. Dt 25:5–10 allows for the marriage to the wife of a brother when that brother died without a male heir. Cf. Gn 38:6–14. It was the violation of this law of Leviticus which aroused the wrath of John the Baptist against Herod Antipas (Mt 14:4; Mk 6:18).

18:20 Adultery in the Hebrew Bible and the ancient Near East is intercourse between a married or betrothed woman and any male. In the Bible it is generally punishable by the death of both individuals (20:10; cf. Dt 22:22–27). Intercourse with an unmarried or unbetrothed woman is not prohibited but carries responsibilities and fines (cf. Ex 22:15–16; Dt 22:28–29). Cf. Lv 19:20–22.

18:21 Immolation to Molech: the reference is to the custom of sacrificing children to the god Molech. Cf. Ez 16:20–21; 20:26, 31; 23:37. See note on Lv 20:1–5.

19:2 Be holy, for I...am holy: in the writings commonly attributed to the Priestly collection, Israel is called to be holy through obeying God's precepts (11:44–45; 20:7–8, 24–26; Nm 15:40–41). Cf. Dt 14:2, 21; 26:19; and Ex 19:6.

19:3–4 Cf. the Decalogue laws on revering parents (Ex 20:12; Dt 5:16), keeping sabbaths (Ex 20:8–11; Dt 5:12–15), and not making or worshiping idols (Ex 20:2–6; Dt 5:7–10).

19:9–10 The Israelites maintain the poor in part by letting them gather unharvested portions of fields and vineyards. Cf. 23:22; Ru 2:1–10.

* 18:15 Lv 20:12.
18:16 Lv 20:21; Dt 25:5–10; Mt 14:3–4; Mk 6:18.
18:17 Lv 20:14; Dt 27:23.
18:18 Gn 29:27–28.
18:19 Lv 15:24, 33; 20:18; Ez 18:6; 22:10.
18:20 Lv 20:10; Ex 20:14; Dt 5:18; 22:22; Mt 5:27–30; Jn 8:4–5.
18:21 Lv 20:2–5; Dt 18:10; 1 Kgs 11:7; 2 Kgs 16:3.
18:22 Lv 20:13; Gn 19:4–11; Jgs 19:22–30;
Rom 1:27; 1 Cor 6:9.
18:23 Lv 20:15–16; Ex 22:18; Dt 27:21.
18:25 Lv 20:22.
18:30 Lv 20:23; Dt 18:9.
19:2 Lv 11:44.
19:3 Lv 20:9; Ex 20:12.
19:3 Lv 23:3.
19:4 Lv 26:1; Ex 20:3–5; 34:17; Dt 5:8; 27:15.
19:7 Lv 7:15–18.
19:8 Lv 7:20.
19:9 Lv 23:22; Dt 24:19–22.

you shall leave for the poor and the alien. I, the LORD, am your God.

¹¹† You shall not steal. You shall not deceive or speak falsely to one another.* ¹²You shall not swear falsely by my name, thus profaning the name of your God.* I am the LORD.

¹³You shall not exploit your neighbor. You shall not commit robbery. You shall not withhold overnight the wages of your laborer.* ¹⁴† You shall not insult the deaf, or put a stumbling block in front of the blind, but you shall fear your God. I am the LORD.

¹⁵You shall not act dishonestly in rendering judgment. Show neither partiality to the weak nor deference to the mighty, but judge your neighbor justly.* ¹⁶You shall not go about spreading slander among your people; nor shall you stand by idly when your neighbor's life is at stake. I am the LORD.

¹⁷† You shall not hate any of your kindred in your heart. Reprove your neighbor openly so that you do not incur sin because of that person.* ¹⁸Take no revenge and cherish no grudge against your own people. You shall love your neighbor as yourself. I am the LORD.*

¹⁹† Keep my statutes: do not breed any of your domestic animals with others of a different species; do not sow a field of yours with two different kinds of seed; and do not put on a garment woven with two different kinds of thread.*

²⁰†* If a man has sexual relations with a female slave who has been acquired by another man but has not yet been redeemed or given her freedom, an investigation shall be made. They shall not be put to death, because she has not been freed. ²¹The man shall bring to the entrance of the tent of meeting as his reparation to the LORD a ram as a reparation offering.* ²²With the ram of the reparation offering the priest shall make atonement before the LORD for the wrong the man has committed, so that he will be forgiven for the wrong he has committed.

²³When you come into the land and plant any fruit tree there,* first look upon its fruit as if it were uncircumcised. For three years, it shall be uncircumcised for you; it may not be eaten. ²⁴In the fourth year, however, all of its fruit shall be dedicated to the LORD in joyous celebration. ²⁵Not until the fifth year may you eat its fruit, to increase the yield for you. I, the LORD, am your God.

²⁶Do not eat anything with the blood still in it.* Do not recite charms or practice soothsaying.†* ²⁷Do not clip your hair at the temples, nor spoil the edges of your beard. ²⁸Do not lacerate your bodies for the dead, and do not tattoo yourselves.†* I am the LORD.

²⁹You shall not degrade your daughter by making a prostitute of her;* otherwise the land will prostitute itself and become full of lewdness. ³⁰Keep my sabbaths, and reverence my sanctuary.* I am the LORD.

³¹Do not turn to ghosts or consult spirits, by which you will be defiled.* I, the LORD, am your God.

³²Stand up in the presence of the aged, show respect for the old, and fear your God. I am the LORD.

³³When an alien resides with you in your land, do not mistreat such a one.* ³⁴You shall

---

**19:11–13** Cf. the Decalogue commandments against stealing (Ex 20:15; Dt 5:19), wrongly using God's name (Ex 20:7; Dt 5:11), and swearing falsely against another (Ex 20:16; Dt 5:20).

**19:14** In Dt 27:18 a curse falls on the head of the one who misleads the blind.

**19:17–18** These verses form a unit and describe different attitudes and actions towards one's fellow Israelites. A separate passage is necessary to advise a similar attitude toward aliens (vv. 33–34). Cf. 25:39–46. The admonition at the end of v. 18 came to be viewed in Judaism and Christianity as one of the central commandments. (See Mt 22:34–40; Mk 12:28–34; Lk 10:25–28; cf. Mt 19:19; Rom 13:8–10; Gal 5:14). The New Testament urges love for enemies as well as neighbors (Mt 5:43–48; Lk 6:27–36; cf. Prv 25:21–22).

**19:19** One reason why mixtures are prohibited seems to be that they are holy (see Dt 22:9, 10–11). Israelites are allowed mixtures in the wearing of fringes on the edges or corners of their clothing (Nm 15:37–41; Dt 22:12). Some mixtures are considered abominations (cf. Lv 18:23; Dt 22:5).

**19:20–22** On adultery, see note on 18:20. Here it is not adultery in the technical sense since the woman is not free. A reparation offering is required as a penalty (see 5:14–26).

**19:26** *Recite charms...soothsaying:* methods of divination (cf. Gn 44:5, 15; Is 2:6; Ez 21:26–28). Legitimate means of learning the future or God's will were through the Urim and Thummim stones (see Lv 8:8), lots (see Lv 16:8) and prophets (cf. Dt 18:9–22; 1 Sm 28:6–7).

**19:28** *Do not tattoo yourselves:* see note on Gn 4:15. This prohibition probably refers only to the common ancient Near Eastern practice of branding a slave with its owner's name as well as branding the devotees of a god with its name.

| | |
|---|---|
| **19:11** Ex 20:15–16. | **19:21** Lv 5:14–26. |
| **19:12** Ex 20:7; Mt 5:33–37. | **19:23** Dt 20:19–20. |
| **19:13** Dt 24:14–15. | **19:26** Lv 17:10. |
| **19:15** Ex 23:2–3; Dt 1:17; 16:19; Ps 82:2; Prv 24:23. | **19:26** Dt 18:10; 2 Kgs 17:17; 21:6; 2 Chr 33:6. |
| **19:17** Mt 18:15; Lk 17:3; Gal 6:1. | **19:28** Lv 21:5. |
| **19:18** Mt 5:43; 19:19; 22:39; Mk 12:31; Rom 13:9; Gal 5:14; Jas 2:8; 1 Jn 3:14. | **19:29** Lv 21:7, 14. |
| | **19:30** Lv 19:3. |
| | **19:31** Lv 20:6, 27; Dt 18:11; Is 8:19. |
| **19:19** Dt 22:9–12. | **19:33** Ex 22:20; 23:9; Jer 22:3; Mal 3:5. |
| **19:20** Dt 22:22–29. | |

treat the alien who resides with you no differently than the natives born among you; you shall love the alien as yourself; for you too were once aliens in the land of Egypt.* I, the LORD, am your God.

³⁵ Do not act dishonestly in using measures of length or weight or capacity. ³⁶ You shall have a true scale and true weights, an honest ephah and an honest hin.†* I, the LORD, am your God, who brought you out of the land of Egypt. ³⁷ Be careful, then, to observe all my statutes and decrees. I am the LORD.

## 20 Penalties for Various Sins. ¹† The LORD said to Moses: ²Tell the Israelites: Anyone, whether an Israelite or an alien residing in Israel, who gives offspring to Molech shall be put to death.* The people of the land shall stone that person. ³* I myself will turn against and cut off* that individual from among the people; for in the giving of offspring to Molech, my sanctuary was defiled* and my holy name was profaned. ⁴ If the people of the land condone the giving of offspring to Molech, by failing to put the wrongdoer to death, ⁵ I myself will turn against that individual and his or her family, and I will cut off from their people both the wrongdoer and all who follow this person by prostituting themselves with Molech.

⁶ Should anyone turn to ghosts and spirits and prostitute oneself with them,* I will turn against that person and cut such a one off from among the people. ⁷ Sanctify yourselves, then, and be holy; for I, the LORD, your God,* am holy. ⁸ Be careful, therefore, to observe my statutes. I, the LORD, make you holy.

⁹ Anyone who curses father or mother shall be put to death;†* and having cursed father or mother, such a one will bear the bloodguilt.† ¹⁰† If a man commits adultery with his neighbor's wife,* both the adulterer and the adulteress shall be put to death. ¹¹ If a man disgraces his father by lying with his father's wife,* the two of them shall be put to death; their bloodguilt is upon them. ¹² If a man lies with his daughter-in-law,* both of them shall be put to death; they have done what is perverse; their bloodguilt is upon them. ¹³ If a man lies with a male as with a woman,* they have committed an abomination; the two of them shall be put to death; their bloodguilt is upon them. ¹⁴ If a man marries a woman and her mother also,* that is shameful conduct; the man and the two women as well shall be burned to death, so that shamefulness may not be found among you. ¹⁵ If a man has sexual relations with an animal,* the man shall be put to death, and you shall kill the animal. ¹⁶ If a woman goes up to any animal to mate with it,* you shall kill the woman and the animal; they shall both be put to death; their bloodguilt is upon them. ¹⁷ If a man marries his sister,* his father's daughter or his mother's daughter, and they have intercourse with each other, that is disgraceful; they shall be publicly cut off† from the people; the man shall bear the penalty of having had intercourse with his own sister. ¹⁸ If a man lies with a woman during her menstrual period and has intercourse with her, he has laid bare the source of her flow and she has uncovered it.* The two of them shall be cut off from the people. ¹⁹ You shall not have intercourse with your mother's sister or your father's sister,* because that dishonors one's own flesh; they shall bear their penalty. ²⁰ If a man lies with his uncle's wife, he disgraces his uncle;* they shall bear the

† **19:36** *Ephah*: see note on Is 5:10; *hin*: see note on Ez 45:24.
**20:1–5** The term Molech may refer to a deity, perhaps with an underworld association, and the activity forbidden here may be connected with divination. Cf. Dt 18:10; 2 Kgs 17:17; 21:6. In the kingdom of Judah the cult appears to have been practiced in the Valley of Hinnom, just outside Jerusalem on the west and south (2 Kgs 23:10; Jer 32:35).
**20:9** *Curses father or mother…put to death*: this is more than a simple expletive uttered in anger against one's parents. See note on Ex 21:17.
**20:9–21** *Bloodguilt*: these penalties, beginning with cursing one's parents, reflect the concerns of a patriarchal society that the breakdown of one's relations with one's parents can lead to the breakdown of all other familial relationships, resulting in the breakdown of society.
**20:10–21** See 18:6–23 and notes there. It appears that the inclusion of various penalties in 20:10–21 accounts for the different order of the cases here compared to the order found in

18:6–23. The reason why the offenses in 20:10–21 carry different penalties, however, is not clear. Perhaps the cases in vv. 17–21 were considered slightly less serious, being condemned but not criminally prosecuted.
**20:17** *Cut off*: see note on 7:20.

* **19:34** Dt 10:19.
**19:36** Dt 25:13–16; Prv 16:11; Am 8:5; Mi 6:10–11.
**20:2** Lv 18:21; Dt 12:31; 18:10; 2 Kgs 16:3; 17:17; 21:6; 23:10; Jer 32:35.
**20:3** Ez 23:39.
**20:3** Lv 7:20.
**20:3** Lv 15:31.
**20:6** Lv 19:31.
**20:7** Lv 11:44.
**20:9** Lv 19:3; Ex 21:17; Dt 21:18–21; Prv 20:20; Mt 15:4; Mk 7:10.
**20:10** Lv 18:20.
**20:11** Lv 18:8.
**20:12** Lv 18:15.
**20:13** Lv 18:22.
**20:14** Lv 18:17.
**20:15** Lv 18:23.
**20:16** Lv 18:23.
**20:17** Lv 18:9.
**20:18** Lv 18:19.
**20:19** Lv 18:12–13.
**20:20** Lv 18:14.

penalty; they shall die childless. ²¹If a man takes his brother's wife, it is severe defilement and he has disgraced his brother;* they shall be childless.

²²Be careful to observe all my statutes and all my decrees; otherwise the land where I am bringing you to dwell will vomit you out.* ²³Do not conform, therefore, to the customs of the nations* whom I am driving out of your way, because all these things that they have done have filled me with disgust for them. ²⁴But to you I have said:* You shall take possession of their land. I am giving it to you to possess, a land flowing with milk and honey. I, the LORD, am your God, who have set you apart from other peoples. ²⁵* You, too, must set apart, then, the clean animals from the unclean, and the clean birds from the unclean, so that you do not make yourselves detestable through any beast or bird or any creature which creeps on the ground that I have set apart for you as unclean. ²⁶To me, therefore, you shall be holy; for I, the LORD, am holy,* and I have set you apart from other peoples to be my own.

²⁷A man or a woman who acts as a medium or clairvoyant* shall be put to death. They shall be stoned to death; their bloodguilt is upon them.

# 21 Sanctity of the Priesthood.

¹† The LORD said to Moses: Speak to the priests, Aaron's sons, and tell them: None of you shall make himself unclean for any dead person among his kindred,* ²except for his nearest relatives, his mother or father, his son or daughter, his brother* ³or his unmarried sister, who is of his own family while she remains single; for these he may make himself unclean. ⁴But as a husband among his kindred† he shall not make himself unclean and thus profane himself.

⁵The priests shall not make bald the crown of their head, nor shave the edges of their beard, nor lacerate their body.* ⁶They shall be holy to their God, and shall not profane their God's name, since they offer the oblations of the LORD, the food of their God; so they must be holy.

⁷† A priest shall not marry a woman debased by prostitution, nor a woman who has been divorced by her husband; for the priest is holy to his God.* ⁸Honor him as holy for he offers the food* of your God; he shall be holy to you, because I, the LORD, am holy who make you holy.

⁹If a priest's daughter debases herself by prostitution, she thereby debases her father; she shall be burned with fire.*

¹⁰The most exalted of the priests, upon whose head the anointing oil has been poured and who has been ordained to wear the special vestments, shall not dishevel his hair or rend his garments, ¹¹nor shall he go near any dead person.* Not even for his father or mother may he thus become unclean; ¹²nor shall he leave the sanctuary and profane the sanctuary of his God, for the consecration of the anointing oil of his God is upon him.* I am the LORD.

¹³He shall marry only a woman who is a virgin. ¹⁴He shall not marry a widow or a woman who has been divorced or one who has been debased by prostitution, but only a virgin, taken from his kindred, he shall marry,* ¹⁵so that he not profane his offspring among his kindred. I, the LORD, make him holy.

## Priestly Blemishes.

† ¹⁶The LORD said to Moses: ¹⁷Say to Aaron: None of your descendants, throughout their generations, who has any blemish shall come forward to offer the food of his God. ¹⁸Anyone who has any of the

---

**21:1–12** While off duty the regular priests are not to become corpse-contaminated except for the close relatives listed in vv. 2–3. While on duty they presumably could not become impure at all. The high priest is restricted from all corpse contamination, on or off duty (vv. 11–12). Lay Israelites are not restricted from corpse contamination, except when in contact with what is holy (cf. Dt 26:14). See note on Lv 11:39–40. Israelites who undertake a nazirite vow enter into a sanctified state and cannot contact corpses (Nm 6:6–12). Cf. Ez 44:25–27.

**21:4** *Husband among his kindred*: this probably refers to relatives by marriage and may even include his wife.

**21:7** The ideal seems to be that a priest marry a virgin. This is explicitly stated for the high priest (cf. vv. 13–14; so also Ez 44:22, except there priests may marry widows of priests). The high priest has the added limitation that his wife must come from his kindred, i.e., the priestly family (cf. Ez 44:22).

**21:16–23** Though priests with certain bodily imperfections cannot serve at the altar (vv. 18–20), they are not impure, since they may still eat of the offerings, which are holy, and do so within the sanctuary precincts since it is there the most holy offerings are to be eaten (v. 22).

20:21 Lv 18:16.
20:22 Lv 18:25, 28.
20:23 Lv 18:30.
20:24 Ex 3:8, 17.
20:25 Lv 11:2–47; Dt 14:4–20.
20:26 Lv 11:44.
20:27 Lv 19:31; Ex 22:17; Dt 18:11.
21:1 Ez 44:25–27.
21:2 Lv 10:6–7.
21:5 Lv 19:27–28; Ez 44:20.
21:7 Lv 19:29; Ez 44:22.
21:8 Lv 1:9.
21:9 Gn 38:24.
21:11 Lv 10:4–7.
21:12 Lv 10:7.
21:14 Ez 44:22.

following blemishes may not come forward:* he who is blind, or lame, or who has a split lip, or a limb too long, ¹⁹ or a broken leg or arm, ²⁰ or who is a hunchback or dwarf or has a growth in the eye, or who is afflicted with sores, scabs, or crushed testicles. ²¹ No descendant of Aaron the priest who has any such blemish may draw near to offer the oblations of the LORD; on account of his blemish he may not draw near to offer the food of his God. ²² He may, however, eat the food of his God: of the most sacred as well as sacred offerings.* ²³ Only, he may not enter through the veil nor draw near to the altar on account of his blemish; he shall not profane my sacred precincts, for it is I, the LORD, who make them holy.

²⁴ Moses, therefore, told this to Aaron and his sons and to all the Israelites.

# 22 Priestly Purity.† ¹ The LORD said to Moses: ² Tell Aaron and his sons to treat with respect the sacred offerings which the Israelites consecrate to me; otherwise they will profane my holy name. I am the LORD.

³ † Tell them: If any one of you, or of your descendants in any future generation, dares, while he is in a state of uncleanness, to draw near the sacred offerings which the Israelites consecrate to the LORD, such a one shall be cut off from my presence.* I am the LORD.

⁴ No descendant of Aaron who is stricken with a scaly infection,* or who suffers from a genital discharge,* may eat of the sacred offerings, until he again becomes clean. Moreover, if anyone touches a person who has become unclean by contact with a corpse,* or if anyone has had an emission of semen,* ⁵ or if anyone touches any swarming creature* whose uncleanness is contagious or any person whose uncleanness, of whatever kind it may be, is contagious—*⁶ the one who touches such as these shall be unclean until evening and may not eat of the sacred portions until he has first

bathed his body in water.* ⁷ Then, when the sun sets, he shall be clean.* Only then may he eat of the sacred offerings, for they are his food. ⁸ † He shall not make himself unclean by eating of any animal that has died of itself or has been killed by wild beasts.* I am the LORD.

⁹ They shall keep my charge so that they will not bear the punishment in this matter and die* for their profanation. I am the LORD who makes them holy.

¹⁰ Neither an unauthorized person nor a priest's tenant or laborer may eat of any sacred offering.* ¹¹ But a slave† whom a priest acquires by purchase or who is born in his house may eat of his food. ¹² † A priest's daughter who is married to an unauthorized person may not eat of the sacred contributions. ¹³ But if a priest's daughter is widowed or divorced and, having no children, returns to her father's house, she may then eat of her father's food as in her youth. No unauthorized person, however, may eat of it. ¹⁴ * If such a one eats of a sacred offering through inadvertence, that person shall make restitution to the priest for the sacred offering, with an increment of one fifth of the amount. ¹⁵ The priests shall not allow the sacred offerings which the Israelites contribute to the LORD to be profaned* ¹⁶ nor make them incur a penalty when they eat their sacred offerings. For I, the LORD, make them holy.

## Unacceptable Victims. ¹⁷ † The LORD said to Moses: ¹⁸ Speak to Aaron and his sons and to all the Israelites, and tell them: When anyone of the house of Israel, or any alien residing in Israel, who presents an offering, brings a burnt offering* as a votive offering or as a voluntary offering to the LORD, ¹⁹ if it is to be acceptable for you, it must be an unblemished male of the herd, of the sheep or of the goats.* ²⁰ You shall not offer one that has any blemish, for such a one would not be acceptable on your

---

† **22:1–16** While priests with bodily imperfections may eat the holy sacrifices (21:16–23), those impure and those not of the priestly household may not.

**22:3–8** On uncleanness, see chaps. 11–15 and notes there.

**22:8** See note on 11:39–40.

**22:11** *Slave:* in contrast to the tenant or hired worker of v. 10, the slave, who is by definition a foreigner, is part of the priest's household and therefore may eat of sacrifices.

**22:12–13** A priest's daughter, when a dependent of her father, may eat of the lesser holy offerings.

**22:17–25** This passage complements the section on the bodily imperfections of priests in 21:16–23. The laws taken

together indicate that whoever and whatever approaches and contacts the altar needs to be physically unimpaired.

**21:18** Lv 22:19–25; Dt 23:2–9.
**21:22** Lv 2:3, 10; 6:29; 7:6, 34.
**22:3** Lv 7:20–21.
**22:4** Lv 13–14.
**22:4** Lv 15:2–18.
**22:4** Nm 19:14–22.
**22:4** Lv 15:16.
**22:5** Lv 11:29–31.
**22:5** Lv 15:2–12, 18–27.
**22:6** Lv 17:15; Nm 19:7–8, 19; Heb 10:22.
**22:7** Dt 23:12.
**22:8** Lv 11:39–40; Ez 44:31.
**22:9** Lv 15:31.
**22:10** Mt 12:4.
**22:14** Lv 5:15–16.
**22:15** Lv 19:8; Nm 18:32.
**22:18** Lv 1:3.
**22:19** Lv 21:16–23.

behalf.* ²¹When anyone presents a communion sacrifice* to the LORD from the herd or the flock in fulfillment of a vow, or as a voluntary offering, if it is to find acceptance, it must be unblemished; it shall not have any blemish. ²²One that is blind or lame or maimed, or one that has running lesions or sores or scabs, you shall not offer to the LORD; do not put such an animal on the altar as an oblation to the LORD. ²³† An ox or a sheep that has a leg that is too long or is stunted you may indeed present as a voluntary offering, but it will not be acceptable as a votive offering. ²⁴One that has its testicles bruised or crushed or torn out or cut off you shall not offer to the LORD. You shall neither do this in your own land ²⁵nor receive from a foreigner any such animals to offer up as the food of your God; since they are deformed or blemished, they will not be acceptable on your behalf.

²⁶† The LORD said to Moses: ²⁷When an ox or a lamb or a goat is born, it shall remain with its mother for seven days; only from the eighth day onward will it be acceptable, to be offered as an oblation to the LORD.* ²⁸You shall not slaughter an ox or a sheep on one and the same day with its young. ²⁹Whenever you offer a thanksgiving sacrifice to the LORD, so offer it that it may be acceptable on your behalf; ³⁰it must be eaten on the same day; none of it shall be left over until morning.* I am the LORD.

³¹Be careful to observe my commandments. I am the LORD. ³²Do not profane my holy name, that in the midst of the Israelites I may be hallowed. I, the LORD, make you holy, ³³who led you out of the land of Egypt to be your God. I am the LORD.

# 23 Holy Days.†
¹The LORD said to Moses: ²Speak to the Israelites and tell them: The following are the festivals* of the LORD, which you shall declare holy days. These are my festivals:

³For six days work may be done; but the seventh day is a sabbath of complete rest,† a declared holy day; you shall do no work. It is the LORD's sabbath wherever you dwell.*

**Passover.** ⁴These are the festivals of the LORD, holy days which you shall declare at their proper time.* ⁵The Passover of the LORD† falls on the fourteenth day of the first month, at the evening twilight.* ⁶The fifteenth day of this month is the LORD's feast of Unleavened Bread. For seven days you shall eat unleavened bread.* ⁷On the first of these days you will have a declared holy day; you shall do no heavy work. ⁸On each of the seven days you shall offer an oblation to the LORD. Then on the seventh day you will have a declared holy day; you shall do no heavy work.

⁹† The LORD said to Moses: ¹⁰Speak to the Israelites and tell them: When you come into the land which I am giving you, and reap its harvest, you shall bring the first sheaf of your harvest to the priest, ¹¹who shall elevate* the sheaf before the LORD that it may be acceptable on your behalf.* On the day after the sabbath† the priest shall do this. ¹²On this day, when your sheaf is elevated, you shall offer to the LORD for a burnt offering an unblemished yearling lamb. ¹³Its grain offering shall be two tenths of an ephah of bran flour mixed with oil, as a sweet-smelling oblation to the LORD; and its libation shall be a fourth of a hin of

wine. [14] You shall not eat any bread or roasted grain or fresh kernels until this day, when you bring the offering for your God. This shall be a perpetual statute throughout your generations wherever you dwell.

**Pentecost.** [15] Beginning with the day after the sabbath, the day on which you bring the sheaf for elevation, you shall count seven full weeks; * [16] you shall count to the day after the seventh week, fifty days.†* Then you shall present a new grain offering to the LORD. [17] For the elevated offering of your first-ripened fruits to the LORD, you shall bring with you from wherever you live two loaves of bread made of two tenths of an ephah of bran flour and baked with leaven. [18] Besides the bread, you shall offer to the LORD a burnt offering of seven unblemished yearling lambs, one bull of the herd, and two rams, along with their grain offering and libations, as a sweet-smelling oblation to the LORD. [19] One male goat shall be sacrificed as a purification offering, and two yearling lambs as a communion sacrifice. [20] The priest shall elevate them—that is, the two lambs—with the bread of the first-ripened fruits as an elevated offering before the LORD; these shall be sacred to the LORD and belong to the priest. [21] On this same day you shall make a proclamation: there shall be a declared holy day for you; no heavy work may be done. This shall be a perpetual statute through all your generations wherever you dwell.

[22] * When you reap the harvest of your land, you shall not be so thorough that you reap the field to its very edge, nor shall you gather the gleanings of your harvest. These things you shall leave for the poor and the alien. I, the LORD, am your God.

**New Year's Day.** [23] The LORD said to Moses: [24] Tell the Israelites: On the first day of the seventh month †* you will have a sabbath rest, with trumpet blasts as a reminder, a declared holy day; [25] you shall do no heavy work, and you shall offer an oblation to the LORD.

**The Day of Atonement.** [26] The LORD said to Moses: [27] Now the tenth day of this seventh month is the Day of Atonement. †* You will have a declared holy day. You shall humble yourselves and offer an oblation to the LORD. [28] On this day you shall not do any work, because it is the Day of Atonement, when atonement is made for you before the LORD, your God. [29] Those who do not humble themselves on this day shall be cut off from the people. [30] If anyone does any work on this day, I will remove that person from the midst of the people. [31] You shall do no work; this is a perpetual statute throughout your generations wherever you dwell; [32] it is a sabbath of complete rest for you. You shall humble yourselves. Beginning on the evening of the ninth of the month, you shall keep your sabbath from evening to evening.

**The Feast of Booths.** [33] The LORD said to Moses: [34] Tell the Israelites: The fifteenth day of this seventh month is the LORD's feast of Booths, †* which shall continue for seven days. [35] On the first day, a declared holy day, you shall do no heavy work. [36] For seven days you shall offer an oblation to the LORD, and on the eighth day you will have a declared holy day. You shall offer an oblation to the LORD. It is the festival closing. You shall do no heavy work.

[37] † These, therefore, are the festivals of the LORD which you shall declare holy days, in order to offer as an oblation to the LORD burnt offerings and grain offerings, sacrifices and libations, as prescribed for each day, [38] in addition to the LORD's sabbaths, your donations, your various votive offerings, and the

---

† **23:16–21** *Fifty days:* Pentecost. This festival occurs on a single day, fifty days after the feast of Unleavened Bread, elsewhere called the "feast of the Harvest" (Ex 23:16), "Day of First Fruits" (Nm 28:26), and "feast of Weeks" (Ex 34:22; Dt 16:10, 16). The name Pentecost comes from the later Greek term for the holy day (cf. Acts 2:1; 20:16; 1 Cor 16:8), referring to the fiftieth day. This is the occasion for bringing the first fruits of the wheat harvest.

**23:24** *First day of the seventh month:* the seventh new moon is counted from a new year beginning in the spring (cf. v. 5). Like the seventh day in the week, it is preeminent among the new moon days (cf. Nm 28:11–15; 29:1–6).

**23:27** *Day of Atonement:* see chap. 16 and notes there.

**23:34** *Feast of Booths:* this is the final harvest festival of the

year celebrating the remaining harvest. It is called the "feast of Ingathering" (Ex 23:16; 34:22), the "feast of Booths" (Lv 23:34; Dt 16:13), or simply the "feast" (1 Kgs 8:65). It is a seven-day festival with an eighth closing day. The first and eighth days are rest days (see note on v. 3).

**23:37–38** This appears to be the original conclusion of the chapter.

---

* 
| | |
|---|---|
| **23:15** Ex 23:16; 34:22; Nm 28:26–31; Dt 16:9–12. | **23:27** Lv 16:1–34; 25:9; Nm 29:7–11. |
| **23:16** Acts 2:1. | **23:34** Ex 23:16; 34:22; Dt 16:13–15; 31:10; |
| **23:22** Lv 19:9–10. | 2 Mc 1:9, 18; Jn 7:2. |
| **23:24** Nm 29:1–6. | |

voluntary offerings that you present to the LORD.

³⁹ On the fifteenth day, then, of the seventh month, when you have gathered in the produce of the land, you shall celebrate the feast of the LORD† for a whole week. The first and the eighth day shall be days of rest. ⁴⁰ On the first day you shall gather fruit of majestic trees, branches of palms, and boughs† of leafy trees and valley willows. Then for a week you shall make merry before the LORD, your God. ⁴¹ You shall keep this feast of the LORD for one whole week in the year. By perpetual statute throughout your generations in the seventh month of the year, you shall keep it. ⁴² You shall dwell in booths for seven days; every native-born Israelite shall dwell in booths, ⁴³ that your descendants may realize that, when I led the Israelites out of the land of Egypt, I made them dwell in booths. I, the LORD, am your God.

⁴⁴ Thus did Moses announce to the Israelites the festivals of the LORD.

# 24

**The Sanctuary Light.†** ¹ The LORD said to Moses: ² Order the Israelites to bring you clear oil of crushed olives for the light, so that you may keep the lamp burning regularly.* ³ In the tent of meeting, outside the veil that hangs in front of the covenant, Aaron shall set up the lamp to burn before the LORD regularly, from evening till morning, by a perpetual statute throughout your generations. ⁴ He shall set up the lamps on the pure gold menorah to burn regularly before the LORD.

**The Showbread.†** ⁵ You shall take bran flour and bake it into twelve cakes,* using two tenths of an ephah of flour for each cake.

⁶ These you shall place in two piles, six in each pile, on the pure gold table before the LORD. ⁷ With each pile put some pure frankincense, which shall serve as an oblation to the LORD, a token of the bread offering. ⁸ Regularly on each sabbath day the bread* shall be set out before the LORD on behalf of the Israelites by an everlasting covenant. ⁹ It shall belong to Aaron and his sons, who must eat it in a sacred place, since it is most sacred,* his as a perpetual due from the oblations to the LORD.

**Punishment of Blasphemy.†** ¹⁰ A man born of an Israelite mother and an Egyptian father went out among the Israelites, and in the camp a fight broke out between the son of the Israelite woman and an Israelite man. ¹¹ The son of the Israelite woman uttered the LORD's name in a curse and blasphemed. So he was brought to Moses—now his mother's name was Shelomith, daughter of Dibri, of the tribe of Dan— ¹² and he was kept in custody till a decision from the LORD should settle the case for them.* ¹³ The LORD then said to Moses: ¹⁴ Take the blasphemer outside the camp, and when all who heard him have laid their hands† on his head,* let the whole community stone him. ¹⁵ Tell the Israelites: Anyone who blasphemes God shall bear the penalty; ¹⁶ whoever utters the name of the LORD in a curse shall be put to death.* The whole community shall stone that person; alien and native-born alike must be put to death for uttering the LORD's name in a curse.

¹⁷ † Whoever takes the life of any human being shall be put to death;* ¹⁸ whoever takes the life of an animal shall make restitution of another animal, life for a life.* ¹⁹ † Anyone who

---

**23:39–43** *The feast of the LORD*: the feast of Booths, the pre-eminent festival. This section supplements vv. 33–36 by prescribing the popular activities for the festival.

**23:40–43** *Fruit…branches…boughs*: the fruit and/or foliage from these trees is to be gathered, but it is not said how they are used. The command to make merry suggests they may have been used in a procession or even circumambulation of the altar (cf. Ps 26:6). Later tradition understood these prescriptions as referring to making the booths out of the foliage (Neh 8:15).

**24:1–4** On the lamp, see Ex 25:31–40; 26:35; 27:20–21; 37:17–24; 40:24–25; Nm 8:1–4. It occupies the south side of the anterior room of the sanctuary tent and provides light for that room.

**24:5–9** On the bread table, see Ex 25:23–29; 26:35; 37:10–16; 40:22–23. It occupies the north side of the anterior room of the sanctuary tent. The bread is a type of grain offering (see note on 2:1).

**24:10–22** This is a narrative where an offense leads to clarifying revelation similar to the cases in Lv 10:1–7 and 16:1–34; Nm 9:6–14 and 15:32–36.

**24:14** *Laid their hands*: see notes on 1:4 and 16:21. It may be

that blasphemy generated a type of pollution which the hearers return to the culprit by this gesture.

**24:17–22** A digression dealing with bodily injury follows the blasphemy rules. It may have been appended since the first case is another example of the death penalty. But the section develops according to its own logic. All legal traditions require death for homicide: Gn 9:5–6; Ex 21:12–14; Nm 35:9–34; Dt 19:1–13; cf. Ex 20:13 and Dt 5:17.

**24:19–20** The phrase "life for a life" in v. 18 leads to introducing the law of talion in vv. 19–20. Some have interpreted the law here and the similar expressions in Ex 21:23–25 and Dt 19:21 to mean that monetary compensation equal to the injury is to

---

| **24:2** Ex 25:31–40; | **24:16** Ex 22:27; 1 Kgs |
| 27:20–21. | 21:10, 13; Mt |
| **24:5** Ex 25:23–30; 1 Kgs | 26:65–66; Jn 10:33. |
| 7:48; 2 Chr 13:11; | **24:17** Gn 9:5–6; Ex 21:12– |
| Heb 9:2. | 14; Nm 35:9–34; Dt |
| **24:8** 1 Chr 9:32. | 19:11–13. |
| **24:9** 1 Sm 21:5. | **24:18** Ex 21:33–34; cf. Lv |
| **24:12** Nm 15:34. | 17:4. |
| **24:14** Lv 16:21. | |

inflicts a permanent injury on his or her neighbor shall receive the same in return: [20] fracture for fracture, eye for eye, tooth for tooth. The same injury that one gives another shall be inflicted in return.* [21] Whoever takes the life of an animal shall make restitution, but whoever takes a human life shall be put to death. [22] You shall have but one rule, for alien and native-born alike.* I, the LORD, am your God.

[23] When Moses told this to the Israelites, they took the blasphemer outside the camp and stoned him;* they did just as the LORD commanded Moses.

# 25

**The Sabbatical Year.** [1] The LORD said to Moses on Mount Sinai: [2]† Speak to the Israelites and tell them: When you enter the land that I am giving you, let the land, too, keep a sabbath for the LORD. [3] For six years you may sow your field, and for six years prune your vineyard, gathering in their produce.* [4] But during the seventh year the land shall have a sabbath of complete rest, a sabbath for the LORD,* when you may neither sow your field nor prune your vineyard. [5] The aftergrowth of your harvest you shall not reap, nor shall you pick the grapes of your untrimmed vines. It shall be a year of rest for the land. [6] While the land has its sabbath, all its produce will be food to eat for you yourself and for your male and female slave, for your laborer and the tenant who live with you, [7] and likewise for your livestock and for the wild animals on your land.

**The Jubilee Year.** [8]† You shall count seven weeks of years—seven times seven years—such that the seven weeks of years amount to forty-nine years. [9] Then, on the tenth day of the seventh month† let the ram's horn resound; on this, the Day of Atonement,* the ram's horn blast shall resound throughout your land. [10] You shall treat this fiftieth year as sacred. You shall proclaim liberty in the land for all its inhabitants.* It shall be a jubilee for you, when each of you shall return to your own property, each of you to your own family. [11] This fiftieth year is your year of jubilee; you shall not sow, nor shall you reap the aftergrowth or pick the untrimmed vines, [12] since this is the jubilee. It shall be sacred for you. You may only eat what the field yields of itself.

[13] In this year of jubilee, then, each of you shall return to your own property. [14] Therefore, when you sell any land to your neighbor or buy any from your neighbor, do not deal unfairly with one another. [15] On the basis of the number of years since the last jubilee you shall purchase the land from your neighbor;* and so also, on the basis of the number of years of harvest, that person shall sell it to you. [16] When the years are many, the price shall be so much the more; when the years are few, the price shall be so much the less. For it is really the number of harvests that the person sells you. [17] Do not deal unfairly with one another, then; but stand in fear of your God. I, the LORD, am your God.

[18] Observe my statutes and be careful to keep my ordinances, so that you will dwell securely in the land. [19] The land will yield its fruit and you will eat your fill, and live there securely.* [20] And if you say, "What shall we eat in the seventh year, if we do not sow or reap our crop?"* [21] I will command such a blessing for you in the sixth year that there will be crop enough for three years, [22] and when you sow in the eighth year, you will still be eating from the old crop; even into the ninth year, until the crop comes in, you will still be eating from the old crop.*

---

†
be paid, though the wording of the law here and the context of Dt 19:21 indicate an injury is to be inflicted upon the injurer.

**25:2–7** As every seventh day is to be a day of rest (cf. 23:3), so every seventh year is a year of rest (cf. 26:34–35, 43). The rest consists in not doing agricultural work. The people are to live off what grows naturally in the fields (vv. 6–7). Verses 19–22 add insurance by saying that God will make the sixth-year crop abundant such that its excess will stretch over the seventh sabbatical year as well as the eighth year when new crops are not yet harvested (cf. 26:10). Cf. Ex 23:10–11.

**25:8–17** The fiftieth year is the jubilee, determined by counting off "seven weeks of years." It is sacred, like the sabbath day. Specifically, in it indentured Israelites return to their own households and land that has been sold returns to its original owner. Different laws are found in Ex 21:1–6; Dt 15:1–3, 12–18 (cf. Jer 34:8–22).

**25:9** Seventh month: the priestly laws reflect the use of two calendars, one starting in the spring (cf. chap. 23) and one in the fall. The jubilee is calculated on the basis of the latter. Ram's horn: Hebrew shophar. The name for the year, jubilee (Heb. yobel), also means "ram's horn" and comes from the horn blown to announce the occasion.

**24:20** Ex 21:23–25; Dt 19:21; Mt 5:38.
**24:22** Lv 19:34; Ex 12:49; Nm 15:16.
**24:23** Acts 7:57–58.
**25:3** Ex 23:10–11.
**25:4** Lv 26:34; 1 Mc 6:49, 53.
**25:9** Lv 16:29.
**25:10** Nm 36:4; Is 61:2; Jer 34:8–22; Ez 46:17; Lk 4:19.
**25:15** Lv 27:18, 23.
**25:19** Lv 26:5–6.
**25:20** Mt 6:25, 31–34; Lk 12:22, 29.
**25:22** Lv 26:10.

**Redemption of Property.**† ²³ The land shall not be sold irrevocably; for the land is mine, and you are but resident aliens and under my authority. ²⁴ Therefore, in every part of the country that you occupy, you must permit the land to be redeemed. ²⁵ When one of your kindred is reduced to poverty and has to sell some property, that person's closest relative,† who has the duty to redeem it, shall come and redeem what the relative has sold.* ²⁶ If, however, the person has no relative to redeem it, but later on acquires sufficient means to redeem it, ²⁷ the person shall calculate the years since the sale, return the balance to the one to whom it was sold, and thus regain the property.* ²⁸ But if the person does not acquire sufficient means to buy back the land, what was sold shall remain in the possession of the purchaser until the year of the jubilee, when it must be released and returned to the original owner.*

²⁹† When someone sells a dwelling in a walled town, it can be redeemed up to a full year after its sale—the redemption period is one year. ³⁰ But if such a house in a walled town has not been redeemed at the end of a full year, it shall belong irrevocably to the purchaser throughout the generations; it shall not be released in the jubilee. ³¹ However, houses in villages that are not encircled by walls shall be reckoned as part of the surrounding farm land; they may be redeemed, and in the jubilee they must be released.

³²† In levitical cities* the Levites shall always have the right to redeem the houses in the cities that are in their possession. ³³ As for levitical property that goes unredeemed—houses sold in cities of their possession shall be released in the jubilee; for the houses in levitical cities are their possession in the midst of the Israelites. ³⁴ Moreover, the pasture land* belonging to their cities shall not be sold at all; it must always remain their possession.

³⁵ When one of your kindred is reduced to poverty and becomes indebted to you, you shall support that person like a resident alien; let your kindred live with you. ³⁶ Do not exact interest in advance or accrued interest,† but out of fear of God let your kindred live with you. ³⁷* Do not give your money at interest or your food at a profit. ³⁸ I, the LORD, am your God, who brought you out of the land of Egypt to give you the land of Canaan and to be your God.

³⁹† When your kindred with you, having been so reduced to poverty, sell themselves to you, do not make them work as slaves.* ⁴⁰ Rather, let them be like laborers or like your tenants, working with you until the jubilee year, ⁴¹ when, together with any children, they shall be released from your service and return to their family and to their ancestral property. ⁴² Since they are my servants, whom I brought out of the land of Egypt, they shall not sell themselves as slaves are sold. ⁴³ Do not lord it over them harshly, but stand in fear of your God.

⁴⁴† The male and female slaves that you possess—these you shall acquire from the nations round about you.* ⁴⁵ You may also acquire them from among the resident aliens who reside with you, and from their families who are with you, those whom they bore in your land. These you may possess, ⁴⁶ and bequeath to your children as their hereditary possession forever. You may treat them as slaves. But none of you shall lord it harshly over any of your fellow Israelites.*

† **25:23–55** This is a series of laws dealing mainly with situations of poverty in which one has to sell land, obtain a loan, or become indentured. Many of the laws are connected with the release of debts in the jubilee year.
**25:25** A close family member is responsible for redemption. Some of these are specified in v. 49.
**25:29–31** Not being able to redeem a house in a walled city after one year is probably due to the demographic and economic situation of large towns as opposed to small villages and open agricultural areas. The agricultural lands associated with the latter were the foundation for the economic viability of the Israelite family, and as such, God—who is the ultimate owner of the land (25:23)—has assigned them to the Israelites as permanent holdings.
**25:32–34** An exception to the rule in vv. 29–31 is made for levitical cities (Nm 35:1–8), since the Levites have no broad land holdings. Their houses can be redeemed and are to be released in the jubilee year.
**25:36** *Interest in advance or accrued interest:* two types of

interest are mentioned here. The former may refer to interest subtracted from the loaned amount in advance, and the latter, to interest or a payment in addition to the loaned amount.
**25:39–43** Here the individual Israelite has no assets and must become indentured to another Israelite for economic survival. No provision is given for redemption before the jubilee year, though such is probably allowed.
**25:44–46** While Israelites may not be held as permanent slaves (vv. 39–43, 47–55), foreigners may be. They are not released in the jubilee, but may be bequeathed to one's children. They may be treated as "slaves," i.e., harshly (cf. Ex 21:20–21).

* **25:25** Ru 2:20; 4:4, 6; Jer 32:7–8.
**25:27** Lv 27:18, 23.
**25:28** Lv 27:24.
**25:32** Nm 35:1–8.
**25:34** Nm 35:3.
**25:37** Ex 22:24; Dt 23:20.
**25:39** Ex 21:2–11; Dt 15:12–18; 1 Kgs 9:22; Jer 34:8–22.
**25:44** Dt 21:10–14.
**25:46** Is 14:1–2.

47 When your kindred, having been so reduced to poverty, sell themselves to a resident alien who has become wealthy or to descendants of a resident alien's family, 48 even after having sold themselves, they still may be redeemed by one of their kindred, 49 by an uncle or cousin, or by some other relative from their family; or, having acquired the means, they may pay the redemption price themselves. 50 With the purchaser they shall compute the years from the sale to the jubilee, distributing the sale price over these years as though they had been hired as laborers. 51 The more years there are, the more of the sale price they shall pay back as the redemption price; 52 the fewer years there are before the jubilee year, the more they have as credit; in proportion to the years of service they shall pay the redemption price. 53 The tenant alien shall treat those who sold themselves as laborers hired on an annual basis, and the alien shall not lord it over them harshly before your very eyes. 54 And if they are not redeemed by these means, they shall nevertheless be released, together with any children, in the jubilee year. 55 For the Israelites belong to me as servants; they are my servants, whom I brought out of the land of Egypt, I, the LORD, your God.

## 26 The Reward of Obedience. 1† Do not make idols for yourselves. You shall not erect a carved image or a sacred stone for yourselves, nor shall you set up a carved stone for worship in your land;* for I, the LORD, am your God. 2 Keep my sabbaths,* and reverence my sanctuary. I am the LORD.

3†* If you live in accordance with my statutes and are careful to observe my commandments, 4 I will give you your rains in due season, so that the land will yield its crops, and the trees their fruit;* 5 your threshing will last till vintage time, and your vintage till the time for sowing, and you will eat your fill of food, and live securely in your land.* 6 I will establish peace in the land, and you will lie down to rest with no one to cause you anxiety. I will rid the country of ravenous beasts, and no sword shall sweep across your land. 7 You will rout your enemies, and they shall fall before your sword. 8 Five of you will put a hundred of your foes to flight, and a hundred of you will put to flight ten thousand, till your enemies fall before your sword.* 9 I will look with favor upon you, and make you fruitful and numerous,* as I carry out my covenant with you. 10 You shall eat the oldest stored harvest, and have to discard it to make room for the new.* 11* I will set my tabernacle in your midst, and will not loathe you. 12 Ever present in your midst, I will be your God, and you will be my people; 13 I, the LORD, am your God, who brought you out of the land of Egypt to be their slaves no more, breaking the bars of your yoke and making you walk erect.*

**The Punishment of Disobedience.†** 14* But if you do not heed me and do not keep all these commandments, 15 if you reject my statutes and loathe my decrees, refusing to obey all my commandments and breaking my covenant, 16 then I, in turn, will do this to you: I will bring terror upon you—with consumption and fever to dim the eyes and sap the life. You will sow your seed in vain, for your enemies will consume the crop. 17 I will turn against you, and you will be beaten down before your enemies* and your foes will lord it over you. You will flee though no one pursues you.

18 If even after this you do not obey me, I will increase the chastisement for your sins sevenfold,* 19 to break your proud strength. I will make the sky above you as hard as iron, and your soil as hard as bronze, 20 so that your strength will be spent in vain; your land will bear no crops, and its trees no fruit.

21 If then you continue hostile, unwilling to

---

† **26:1–46** This chapter concludes the revelation of laws at Mount Sinai (cf. v. 46). Blessings and curses are also found at the end of Deuteronomy's law collection (Dt 28). Similar lists of blessings and curses appear in the conclusions of ancient Near Eastern treaties.

**26:3–13** The blessings are concerned with the well-being of the nation and its land and involve agricultural bounty, national security, military success and population growth.

**26:14–46** To encourage obedience, the list of punishments is longer than the blessings (cf. a similar proportion in Dt 28). The punishments are presented in waves (vv. 14–17, 18–20, 21–22, 23–26, 27–39), one group following another if the people do not return to obedience. Punishments involve sickness, pestilence, agricultural failure and famine, attack of wild animals, death of the people's children, destruction of illicit and even licit cults, military defeat, panic, and exile.

| | |
|---|---|
| **26:1** Lv 19:4; Nm 33:52. | **26:9** Gn 1:28; Ex 1:7. |
| **26:2** Lv 23:3. | **26:10** Lv 25:22. |
| **26:3** Dt 28:1–69. | **26:11–12** Ex 29:45; Ez |
| **26:4** Dt 11:14; Ps 85:13; Ez | 37:26–28; 2 Cor 6:16. |
| 34:26–27. | **26:13** Ez 34:27; Na 1:13. |
| **26:5** Lv 25:18–19; Dt | **26:14** Dt 28:15–69. |
| 12:10. | **26:17** 2 Kgs 8:33–34. |
| **26:8** Dt 32:30; Jos 23:10. | **26:18** Ps 79:12; Prv 6:31. |

obey me, I will multiply my blows sevenfold, as your sins deserve. <sup>22</sup> I will unleash wild beasts against you, to rob you of your children and wipe out your livestock, till your population dwindles away and your roads become deserted.

<sup>23</sup> If, with all this, you still do not accept my discipline and continue hostile to me, <sup>24</sup>* I, too, will continue to be hostile to you and I, for my part, will smite you for your sins sevenfold. <sup>25</sup> I will bring against you the sword, the avenger of my covenant. Though you then huddle together in your cities, I will send pestilence among you, till you are delivered to the enemy. <sup>26</sup> When I break your staff of bread, ten women will need but one oven for baking your bread, and they shall dole it out to you by weight;* and though you eat, you shall not be satisfied.

<sup>27</sup> If, despite all this, you disobey and continue hostile to me, <sup>28</sup> I will continue in my hostile rage toward you, and I myself will discipline you for your sins sevenfold, <sup>29</sup> till you begin to eat the flesh of your own sons and daughters.* <sup>30</sup> I will demolish your high places, overthrow your incense stands, and cast your corpses upon the corpses of your idols.* In my loathing of you, <sup>31</sup> I will lay waste your cities and desolate your sanctuaries, refusing your sweet-smelling offerings. <sup>32</sup> So devastated will I leave the land that your enemies who come to live there will stand aghast at the sight of it.* <sup>33</sup> And you I will scatter among the nations* at the point of my drawn sword, leaving your countryside desolate and your cities deserted. <sup>34</sup> Then shall the land, during the time it lies waste, make up its lost sabbaths, while you are in the land of your enemies; then shall the land have rest and make up for its sabbaths* <sup>35</sup> during all the time that it lies desolate, enjoying the rest that you would not let it have on your sabbaths when you lived there.

<sup>36</sup> Those of you who survive in the lands of their enemies, I will make so fainthearted that the sound of a driven leaf will pursue them,

and they shall run as if from the sword, and fall though no one pursues them; <sup>37</sup> stumbling over one another as if to escape a sword, while no one is after them—so helpless will you be to take a stand against your foes! <sup>38</sup> You shall perish among the nations, swallowed up in your enemies' country. <sup>39</sup> Those of you who survive will waste away in the lands of their enemies, for their own and their ancestors' guilt.*

<sup>40</sup>† They will confess* their iniquity and the iniquity of their ancestors in their treachery against me and in their continued hostility toward me, <sup>41</sup> so that I, too, had to be hostile to them and bring them into their enemies' land. Then, when their uncircumcised hearts are humbled and they make amends for their iniquity, <sup>42</sup> I will remember my covenant with Jacob, and also my covenant with Isaac; and also my covenant with Abraham I will remember.* The land, too, I will remember. <sup>43</sup> The land will be forsaken by them, that in its desolation without them, it may make up its sabbaths, and that they, too, may make good the debt of their guilt for having spurned my decrees and loathed my statutes. <sup>44</sup> Yet even so, even while they are in their enemies' land, I will not reject or loathe them to the point of wiping them out, thus making void my covenant with them; for I, the LORD, am their God. <sup>45</sup> I will remember for them the covenant I made with their forebears, whom I brought out of the land of Egypt before the eyes of the nations,* that I might be their God. I am the LORD.

<sup>46</sup> These are the statutes, decrees and laws which the LORD established between himself and the Israelites through Moses on Mount Sinai.*

## V. REDEMPTION OF OFFERINGS

**27** **Votive Offerings and Dedications.** <sup>1</sup> The LORD said to Moses: <sup>2</sup>† Speak to the Israelites and tell them: When anyone makes a vow to the LORD* with respect to the value of

---

† **26:40–45** Even though the people may be severely punished, God will remember the covenant when the people repent.

**27:2–13** Vows are conditional promissory oaths. One covenants to do something for the benefit of God, usually to make a dedication, if God fulfills the individual's accompanying request (cf. Gn 28:20–21; Jgs 11:30–31; 1 Sm 1:11; 2 Sm 15:7–8; Ps 56:13–14). Vows must be fulfilled (Nm 30:3; Dt 23:22; cf. Ps 66:13–15). Verses 2–8 deal with votive offerings involving human beings. Actual dedication of human beings (cf. Jgs 11:30–31, 34–40; 1 Sm 1:11, 24–28) is obviated by payment

**26:24–25** Jer 2:30; Ez 5:17; 14:17.
**26:26** Is 9:19; Ez 4:16; 5:16; 14:13; Mi 6:14.
**26:29** Lam 2:20.
**26:30** 2 Chr 14:5; 34:3–4, 7; Ez 6:3–6.
**26:32** 1 Kgs 9:8; Jer 9:11; 18:16; 19:8; 25:18.
**26:33** Ps 44:12; Jer 15:7; Ez 6:8.

**26:34** Lv 25:2; 2 Chr 36:21.
**26:39** Ez 4:17; 24:23; 33:10.
**26:40** Nm 16:21; Nm 5:7; Neh 1:6.
**26:42** Ex 6:5; 2 Kgs 13:23; Ps 106:45; Ez 16:60.
**26:45** Ex 12:51.
**26:46** Lv 7:38; Nm 36:13.
**27:2** Dt 23:22–24; Jgs 11:30–31; Eccl 5:3–4.

a human being, [3] the value for males between the ages of twenty and sixty shall be fifty silver shekels, by the sanctuary shekel; [4] and for a female, the value shall be thirty shekels. [5] For persons between the ages of five and twenty, the value for a male shall be twenty shekels, and for a female, ten shekels. [6] For persons between the ages of one month and five years, the value for a male shall be five silver shekels, and for a female, three shekels. [7] For persons of sixty or more, for a male the value shall be fifteen shekels, and ten shekels for a female. [8] However, if the one who made the vow is too poor to meet the sum,* the person must be set before the priest, who shall determine a value; the priest will do this in keeping with the means of the one who made the vow.

[9] If the offering vowed to the LORD is an animal that may be sacrificed, every such animal given to the LORD becomes sacred.* [10] The offerer shall not substitute or exchange another for it, either a worse or a better one. If the offerer exchanges one animal in place of another, both the original and its substitute shall become sacred. [11] If any unclean animal which is unfit for sacrifice* to the LORD is vowed, it must be set before the priest, [12] who shall determine its value† in keeping with its good or bad qualities, and the value set by the priest shall stand. [13] If the offerer wishes to redeem the animal, the person shall pay one fifth more than this valuation.*

[14]† When someone dedicates a house as sacred to the LORD,† the priest shall determine its value in keeping with its good or bad qualities, and the value set by the priest shall stand. [15] A person dedicating a house who then wishes to redeem it shall pay one fifth more than the price thus established, and then it will again belong to that individual.*

[16] If someone dedicates to the LORD a portion of hereditary land, its valuation shall be made according to the amount of seed required to sow it, the acreage sown with a homer† of barley seed being valued at fifty silver shekels. [17] If the dedication of a field is made at the beginning of a jubilee period, the full valuation shall hold; [18] but if it is some time after this, the priest shall estimate its money value according to the number of years left until the next jubilee year, with a corresponding reduction on the valuation.* [19] A person dedicating a field who then wishes to redeem†* it shall pay one fifth more than the price thus established, and so reclaim it. [20] If, instead of redeeming such a field, one sells it† to another, it may no longer be redeemed; [21] but at the jubilee it shall be released* as sacred† to the LORD; like a field that is put under the ban, it shall become priestly property.

[22] If someone dedicates to the LORD a field that was purchased and was not part of hereditary property, [23] the priest shall compute its value in proportion to the number of years until the next jubilee, and on the same day the person shall pay the price thus established, a sacred donation to the LORD; [24] at the jubilee the field shall revert to the hereditary owner of this land from whom it had been purchased.†

[25] Every valuation shall be made according to the standard of the sanctuary shekel. There are twenty gerahs to the shekel.

---

† of the person's value (mentioned in the temple income in 2 Kgs 12:5). The values reflect the different economic and administrative roles of people in different age and gender groups within ancient Israelite society. Verses 9–13 concern the bringing of animals for a vow.

**27:12** *Determine its value*: in contrast to human beings (vv. 3–7) there are no set values for unclean animals, and the condition of the animal is taken into consideration (cf. vv. 14, 27).

**27:14–24** These verses deal with dedications. They take effect when uttered and, unlike vows, they are not conditional. They are related to the jubilee year laws in 25:23–31.

**27:14** *House as sacred to the LORD*: the house becomes sanctuary property and presumably may be sold to another if the owner does not redeem it (cf. notes on vv. 20 and 21). While 25:31 requires that unredeemed houses in unwalled towns be returned to the original owners at the jubilee, in the laws here such houses apparently become the property of the sanctuary (cf. v. 21). It is likely that dedicated houses in a walled city needed to be redeemed within one year, following 25:29–30.

**27:16** *Homer*: see note on Is 5:10.

**27:19** *Redeem*: the person apparently can redeem the land up to the jubilee year, following 25:23–28. See note on v. 21.

**27:20** *If…one sells it*: the verse is difficult since the person should not be able to sell the land after it is dedicated. The verb "sells" may be construed impersonally here: "If…it is sold," i.e., by the sanctuary.

**27:21** *Released as sacred*: the dedication changes the ownership of the land. It now belongs to the sanctuary. It returns to the sanctuary's possession after leasing it out (v. 20). Presumably if the land remained in the sanctuary's possession until the jubilee, and it was not redeemed, the land would belong permanently to the sanctuary and priests.

**27:24** In contrast to the cases in vv. 14–15 and 16–21, this land returns to the original owner since that individual did not personally make the dedication. The principle is that one cannot permanently dedicate what one does not own. Cf. 2 Sm 24:22–25.

---

27:8 Lv 5:7, 11.
27:9 Lv 27:11, 27.
27:11 Lv 11:2–8; Ex 13:13; 34:20.
27:13 Lv 5:16, 24.

27:15 Lv 22:14.
27:18 Lv 25:15–16, 26–27, 50–52.
27:19 Lv 25:25.
27:21 Lv 25:28, 31.

**Irredeemable Offerings.** [26]† Note that a first-born animal,* which as such already belongs to the LORD, may not be dedicated. Whether an ox or a sheep, it is the LORD's. [27] But if it is an unclean animal,† it may be redeemed by paying one fifth more than its value. If it is not redeemed, it shall be sold at its value.

[28] Note, also, that any possession which someone puts under the ban† for the LORD, whether it is a human being, an animal, or a hereditary field, shall be neither sold nor redeemed; everything that is put under the ban becomes most holy to the LORD.* [29] All human beings that are put under the ban cannot be redeemed; they must be put to death.*

[30]† All tithes of the land, whether in grain from the fields or in fruit from the trees, belong to the LORD; they are sacred to the LORD.* [31] If someone wishes to redeem any of the tithes, the person shall pay one fifth more than their value. [32] The tithes of the herd and the flock, every tenth animal that passes under the herdsman's rod, shall be sacred to the LORD. [33] It shall not matter whether good ones or bad ones are thus chosen, and no exchange may be made. If any exchange is made, both the original animal and its substitute become sacred and cannot be redeemed.

[34] These are the commandments which the LORD gave Moses on Mount Sinai for the Is-raelites.*

---

**27:26** Firstborn animals and human beings already belong to God (cf. Ex 13:1–2, 12; 34:19); they cannot be vowed or dedicated. Cf. Nm 18:15–18; Dt 15:19–23.

**27:27** *An unclean animal*: such as the firstborn of a donkey, which was unfit for sacrifice. According to Ex 13:13; 34:20, a firstborn donkey was to be redeemed by offering a sheep in its stead, or was to have its neck broken.

**27:28** *Puts under the ban*: this is a higher form of dedication to God than that found in vv. 14–24. Anything so dedicated is beyond redemption and cannot be sold by the sanctuary and priests (contrast vv. 15, 19, 20). This type of dedication is found mostly

in contexts of war (e.g., Jos 6:17–21; 8:26; 10:1, 28). Lv 27:28 shows that the ban can apply to one's own property.

**27:30–33** On the regulation concerning the tithes see Dt 14:22–29.

---

**27:26** Ex 13:2.
**27:28** Nm 18:14; Dt 7:26; Jos 7:1; 1 Sm 15:21; Ez 44:29.
**27:29** 1 Kgs 20:42.
**27:30** Nm 18:25–32; Dt 14:22–24; Mal 3:8, 10.
**27:34** Lv 7:38.

# The Book of

# Numbers

## INTRODUCTION

Pauline A. Viviano

The book of Numbers is the fourth book of the Pentateuch and as such is part of a larger story that began in Genesis with creation and will end in 2 Kings with the destruction of Jerusalem and its Temple, the exile of many of the leading citizens from the land of Judah, followed by a brief notice of the release of the exiled king, Jehoiachin, from prison in 561 BCE. Coming after the Exodus and the establishment of the covenant relationship with Yahweh on Mount Sinai, the book of Numbers continues the story with Israel on its way through the wilderness. The book ends with Israel poised to enter the land of Canaan, the promised land. On this journey Israel will have many opportunities to learn what it means to live as Yahweh's covenanted people. They will learn from Yahweh's guidance and laws, but they will also learn from their failure to trust and obey their covenant Lord and their leaders in the wilderness. Of the promises to Abraham (Gn 12:1–3), it is the promise of the land that looms on the horizon in the book of Numbers.

## Origin, Date, and Structure of Numbers

It is generally recognized that the author of the book of Numbers drew upon preexilic sources in the composition of this book; indeed, he mentions the "Book of the Wars of the LORD" (Nm 21:14) as a source. Many scholars find evidence of the Pentateuchal sources, J, E, and especially P, throughout the book, but the very existence of these sources continues to be debated. The rough transitions in the book between stories and laws and the occasional inconsistencies bear witness to its long history of editing and reediting. The final shaping of this material was done during the period of the exile or in the early postexilic period.

## Outline of Numbers

I. Census and Preparation for the Departure from Sinai (1:1–10:10)

II. Departure, Rebellion, and Wandering in the Wilderness for Forty Years (10:11–25:18)

III. Second Census of a New Generation and Preparation to Enter the Promised Land (25:19–36:13)

The book of Numbers appears to be a rather eclectic collection of material pulled together to fill in the time between the Sinai experience and entrance into the land of Canaan. Lists, laws, narratives, prose, and poetry are repeatedly intermixed according to a logic that eludes contemporary readers. Various attempts have been made to organize the material chronologically or geographically, but no organizational principle accounts for the entire book. The journey motif provides a backdrop against which to read the diverse material contained in the book of Numbers. The events along the journey become opportunities for Israel to prepare for its entry into the land of Canaan. At stopping points along that journey, laws are given to inform Israel how they are to live as the people of Yahweh in the land. The lists provide structuring for the people in the wilderness and for Israel's future life as a nation in the promised land.

## The Lists

There are census lists (Nm 1–4, 26) and other kinds of lists (e.g., 7:1–88; 33:1–49) throughout the book of Numbers. These lists probably derive from documents of a later period, but they were drawn into the book of Numbers as part of the preparation for the conquest of the land of Canaan. This is most evident in the census lists, the stated purpose of which is to enroll those able to serve in the military (1:3; 26:2), but even the other lists, along with many of the laws, are concerned to ready the people to enter into the land of Canaan and take possession of it. The arrangement of Israel in the camp (2:1–34) and on the move (10:11–28) suggests an army in military formation preparing for battle (33:50–56). Concern about what to do with the spoils of war (31:25–54), the future boundaries of the land (34:1–15), and how that land is to be allotted to the tribes of Israel (26:52–56; 34:16–29) underscore the military concerns associated with this journey through the wilderness.

Throughout the book of Numbers much attention is given to priests and Levites by including their number, status, arrangement, duties, and payment. It may be that the priests and Levites had a dominant role in the shaping of the book of Numbers, but the inclusion of these matters reflects the importance of the priesthood in offering sacrifice and in the rule of the community in the postexilic period. Priests and Levites mediate Yahweh's will to the people and they bring Israel before Yahweh by means of prayer and sacrifice.

## Legal Material in the Book of Numbers

Laws are inserted at various points in Israel's journey to the promised land. These laws concern how Israel is to live as the people of Yahweh, but they cover a wide range of disparate matters and often overlap with or vary from the laws of Exodus and Leviticus. It is not clear why these laws are inserted between the narratives of the book of Numbers, but they will define for Israel how to live as Yahweh's people. Many of the laws concern the offering of sacrifice (Nm 7:1–88; 15:1–31; 28:1–30:1), but there are also regulations regarding cultic objects (8:1–4), tassels (15:37–41), and even the use of trumpets (10:1–10). Some laws cover murder and manslaughter (35:16–34),

restitution for theft (5:5–10), vows of Nazirites (6:1–21), as well as other kinds of vows (30:2–17). Problems arise in the community regarding what is to be done with one who violates the sabbath (15:32–36), how the guilt of a wife accused of adultery is to be determined (5:11–31), and whether daughters can inherit (27:1–11; 36:1–12). These laws became part of Israel's legal traditions as it sought to define its life as the covenanted people of Yahweh.

## The Wilderness Experience

The wilderness experience runs deep in Israel's traditions and is remembered both positively and negatively. The prophets Hosea (Hos 2:16–17) and later Jeremiah (Jer 2:2–3) saw the wilderness period as a time of "courtship" between Yahweh and his people, a time when Yahweh graciously cared for Israel and Israel remained faithful to Yahweh. In the book of Numbers, however, the journey through the wilderness is remembered as a time of complaint and rebellion on Israel's part, of impatience and anger on Yahweh's part. With each act of defiance and its subsequent punishment Israel learns what it means to live in trust and dependence upon Yahweh.

The people complain about the lack of food and water (Nm 20:2–6a; 21:4–5) or they are dissatisfied with the food they have been given (11:1–15; 21:5). Yahweh's angry response is often allayed by Moses' intercession, but at times it erupts and the people are punished (11:31–35; 21:6–9). Complaints regarding leadership surface now and again on Israel's journey. Moses himself complains about the burden of leadership and is provided with seventy elders to share his burden (11:1–30), but other complaints about leadership lead to punishment. Aaron and Miriam question Moses' leadership and Miriam is stricken with leprosy (12:1–15). Korah, along with Dathan and Abiram, rebel against the leadership of both Moses and Aaron and each dies as a result (16:1–35). The people even complain about Yahweh's leadership (14:1–38) and turn to the worship of other gods (25:1–5); those who led them astray are executed. Each act of rebellion is punished

## Battles

Israel is prepared for the conquest of Canaan through the experiences of victory and defeat in battle. Victories are briefly recounted (over Arad, Nm 21:1–3; over Sihon, 21:21–32; and over Og, 21:33–22:1) and the land beyond the Jordan comes under the control of Israel for the tribes of Gad, Reuben, and Manasseh (32:1–42); but it is the unsuccessful attempt to take the land of Canaan (14:39–45) that provides Israel's greatest lesson about what success entails. After hearing from its scouts that the Canaanites are "giants" (nephilim), the people of Israel are convinced that they will be unsuccessful in battle against them. This lack of trust in Yahweh, especially in light of the Exodus and Yahweh's promise of the land, provokes Yahweh's anger. Moses is able to intercede on behalf of the people and Yahweh does not strike them with pestilence, but none of those who doubted Yahweh will enter the land. They will die in the wilderness; their children will enter the land after wandering for forty years. Motivated by remorse and guilt the people take it upon themselves to invade Canaan, but as this invasion is not backed by Yahweh, it is doomed to fail. War had to be authorized by Yahweh, as in the war against the Midianites (31:1–12; cf. 25:16–18), and the directives for fighting battles had to be followed exactly if Israel was to succeed.

Biblical scholars often use the phrase "holy war" to speak of the practice of war as described in the Old Testament, especially in the books of Numbers through 2 Samuel, but war in the Bible is not to be confused with the "holy war" (jihad) of Islam. The involvement of Yahweh in the wars of the Old Testament may be disconcerting for contemporary readers, but for Israel Yahweh was involved in all aspects of its life as a nation, including war. Yahweh was identified as a "warrior" (Ex 15:3) and in Israel war was thought to be a sacral act, authorized, directed, and even fought (e.g., Jos 10:14) by Yahweh. Those who participated in Yahweh's battles were to maintain themselves in a state of ritual purity (e.g., Jos 3:5), and all that was

won as a result of war was to be sacrificed to Yahweh (e.g., Jos 6:17), a practice known as herem. In an earlier age herem may have been associated with the need for purification following a battle, but as found in the Old Testament it may represent a theological construct that shows Israel's utter dependence upon Yahweh and that Israel is to radically separate itself from the religions and customs of other nations. There is no archaeological evidence that the Canaanites were destroyed wholesale as Yahweh commanded (Dt 7:2; 20:17). Even the biblical text indicates that the command was not fully carried out, for the Canaanites are still a force to be reckoned with in the book of Judges (e.g., Jgs 1:1; 4:2), as are Midianites and Amalekites, two other groups subjected to herem. Knowing the historical and theological context of these stories of war helps to put into perspective the role of the deity in war for ancient Israel, but one needs to proceed with caution when drawing upon these texts in contemporary discussions of war.

## Balaam's Story (Nm 22–24)

The story of Balaam is delightfully comic. Its main characters, Balaam and Balak, act with utter seriousness, but their buffoonish behavior cannot help but elicit laughter. Balak, the king of Moab, has an exaggerated fear of the Israelites, whom he sees as so numerous that he declares, "They have covered up the earth" (Nm 22:5). Balak's repeated attempts to get Balaam to curse Israel are outlandish as he drags him up and down one mountain after another. Balaam is forbidden by God to go to curse Israel, but after Balak's second request Balaam is at first allowed to go, only to be stopped en route by the angel of Yahweh. Balaam's donkey is more attuned to the presence of the divine than Balaam, for he sees the angel of Yahweh blocking his way with a drawn sword. Balaam sees neither the angel nor the sword, but he wishes he had a sword to kill the donkey who has come to a halt and refuses to go on. Balaam's brutal beating of his donkey deserves a rebuke, and the rebuke comes from the donkey himself. Yahweh opens the mouth of the donkey; similarly it is Yahweh who will control what Balaam says when he arrives at his destination. Balaam is allowed to continue his journey, but each attempt by Balaam to curse Israel becomes instead an occasion to bless Israel. Yahweh will not allow his people to be cursed. Balaam's first three oracles speak of Israel as a nation chosen by Yahweh and under his protection; Yahweh secures blessing for Israel (23:1–10, 18–24; 24:3–9). The fourth oracle (24:15–19) announces the destruction of Moab and Edom, and the rise of Israel as a mighty nation.

## Conclusion

The diverse material in the book of Numbers— the lists and laws, the complaints and rebellion in the wilderness, the battles fought and blessings given—contributes each in its own way to Israel's preparation for entry into the land of Canaan. The organization of Israel on its march through the wilderness and the experiences of battle prepare Israel to shoulder the burden of conquest when it comes into the land. The laws guide Israel in living as Yahweh's people, but it is the experience of the wilderness and Israel's response to that experience that teach Israel how to live in relationship to its God. Israel learns the necessity of trust in Yahweh when its faith is challenged by the lack of food and water in the wilderness. It learns the necessity of obedience when it rebels against Yahweh and its leaders in the wilderness.

The book of Numbers reflects a period of transition for Israel, a transition from slavery to freedom. That in-between time in the wilderness enables Israel to remove the shackles of slavery and begin to learn what it means to be a free people, but it is not an easy transition. Nostalgia for the past and fear of what the future might bring results in rebellion and disobedience. Nevertheless Yahweh continues to guide and direct his people, and also to punish them when necessary, hoping to strengthen Israel's faith and to encourage Israel to live in trust and obedience that the blessings spoken by Balaam might become a reality. ■

N
M

# THE BOOK OF NUMBERS

## New American Bible, Introduction

The Book of Numbers derives its name from the account of the two censuses taken of the Hebrew people, one near the beginning and the other toward the end of the journey in the wilderness (chaps. 1 and 26). It continues the story of that journey begun in Exodus, and describes briefly the experiences of the Israelites for a period of thirty-eight years, from the end of their encampment at Sinai to their arrival at the border of the promised land. Numerous legal ordinances are interspersed in the account, making the book a combination of law and history.

The book divides neatly into two parts. Each part begins with a census of the people (chaps. 1 and 26) and inaugurates a period of preparation prior to entering the promised land. In the first case these preparations come to a tragic end when scouts are sent forth to survey the promised land (chaps. 13–14). Upon their return, the people are so disheartened by the description of the native inhabitants and the seemingly impossible task that lies in front of them that they refuse to enter the land. This results in a decision to doom that entire generation to death and to allow another generation the chance to enter. After the death of the first generation, then, a second census is taken (chap. 26) and again preparations are made to enter the land. In this case, however, the birth of a new generation suggests these preparations will not be in vain. The book ends with the Israelites across the Jordan outside the land of Canaan, underscoring a chief theme of the Pentateuch as a whole: the people anticipating the fulfillment of God's promise of the land.

In the New Testament numerous allusions to incidents in the Book of Numbers appear: the bronze serpent (Jn 3:14–15), the sedition of Korah and its consequences (1 Cor 10:10), the prophecies of Balaam (2 Pt 2:15–16), and the water gushing from the rock (1 Cor 10:4).

The chief divisions of the Book of Numbers are as follows:

I. Census and Preparation for the Departure from Sinai (1:1–10:10)

II. Departure, Rebellion, and Wandering in the Wilderness for Forty Years (10:11–25:18)

III. Second Census of a New Generation and Preparation to Enter the Promised Land (25:19–36:13) ■

# NUMBERS

## I. CENSUS AND PREPARATION FOR THE DEPARTURE FROM SINAI

**The Census.** ¹ In the second year after the Israelites' departure from the land of Egypt, on the first day of the second month, the LORD said to Moses at the tent of meeting in the wilderness of Sinai: ² † Take a census of the whole community of the Israelites, * by clans and ancestral houses, registering by name each male individually. ³ You and Aaron shall enroll in companies all the men in Israel of twenty years or more who are fit for military service.

**Moses' Assistants.** ⁴ With you there shall be a man from each tribe, each the head of his ancestral house. ⁵ * These are the names of those who are to assist you:

from Reuben: Elizur, son of Shedeur;
⁶ from Simeon: Shelumiel, son of Zurishaddai;
⁷ from Judah: * Nahshon, son of Amminadab;
⁸ from Issachar: Nethanel, son of Zuar;
⁹ from Zebulun: Eliab, son of Helon;
¹⁰ for the descendants of Joseph: from Ephraim: Elishama, son of Ammihud; and from Manasseh: Gamaliel, son of Pedahzur;
¹¹ from Benjamin: Abidan, son of Gideoni;
¹² from Dan: Ahiezer, son of Ammishaddai;
¹³ from Asher: Pagiel, son of Ochran;
¹⁴ from Gad: Eliasaph, son of Reuel;
¹⁵ from Naphtali: Ahira, son of Enan.

¹⁶ * These were the elect of the community, leaders of their ancestral tribes, heads of the clans of Israel. ¹⁷ So Moses and Aaron took these men who had been designated by name, ¹⁸ and assembled the whole community on the first day of the second month. Every man of twenty years or more then registered individually his name and lineage according to clan and ancestral house, ¹⁹ as the LORD had commanded Moses. So he enrolled them in the wilderness of Sinai.

**Count of the Twelve Tribes.** ²⁰ Of the descendants of Reuben, the firstborn of Israel, registered individually by name and lineage according to their clans and ancestral houses, every male of twenty years or more, everyone fit for military service: ²¹ those enrolled from the tribe of Reuben were forty-six thousand five hundred.

²² Of the descendants of Simeon, registered individually by name and lineage according to their clans and ancestral houses, every male of twenty years or more, everyone fit for military service: ²³ those enrolled from the tribe of Simeon were fifty-nine thousand three hundred.

²⁴ Of the descendants of Gad, registered by name and lineage according to their clans and ancestral houses, every male of twenty years or more, everyone fit for military service: ²⁵ those enrolled from the tribe of Gad were forty-five thousand six hundred and fifty.

²⁶ Of the descendants of Judah, registered by name and lineage according to their clans and ancestral houses, every male of twenty years or more, everyone fit for military service: ²⁷ those enrolled from the tribe of Judah were seventy-four thousand six hundred.

²⁸ Of the descendants of Issachar, registered by name and lineage according to their clans and ancestral houses, every male of twenty years or more, everyone fit for military service: ²⁹ those enrolled from the tribe of Issachar were fifty-four thousand four hundred.

³⁰ Of the descendants of Zebulun, registered by name and lineage according to their clans and ancestral houses, every male of twenty years or more, everyone fit for military service: ³¹ those enrolled from the tribe of Zebulun were fifty-seven thousand four hundred.

³² Of the descendants of Joseph:

Of the descendants of Ephraim, registered by name and lineage according to their clans and ancestral houses, every male of twenty years or more, everyone fit for military service: ³³ those enrolled from the tribe of Ephraim were forty thousand five hundred.

³⁴ Of the descendants of Manasseh, registered by name and lineage according to their clans and ancestral houses, every male of

---

**1:2** All Israel was divided into tribes, each tribe into clans, and each clan into ancestral houses.

**1:2–3** Nm 14:29; 26:2–51.
**1:5–15** Nm 10:14–28.
**1:7** Mt 1:4; Lk 3:32–33.
**1:16** Ex 18:21, 25.

twenty years or more, everyone fit for military service: ³⁵ those enrolled from the tribe of Manasseh were thirty-two thousand two hundred.

³⁶ Of the descendants of Benjamin, registered by name and lineage according to their clans and ancestral houses, every male of twenty years or more, everyone fit for military service: ³⁷ those enrolled from the tribe of Benjamin were thirty-five thousand four hundred.

³⁸ Of the descendants of Dan, registered by name and lineage according to their clans and ancestral houses, every male of twenty years or more, everyone fit for military service: ³⁹ those enrolled from the tribe of Dan were sixty-two thousand seven hundred.

⁴⁰ Of the descendants of Asher, registered by name and lineage according to their clans and ancestral houses, every male of twenty years or more, everyone fit for military service: ⁴¹ those enrolled from the tribe of Asher were forty-one thousand five hundred.

⁴² Of the descendants of Naphtali, registered by name and lineage according to their clans and ancestral houses, every male of twenty years or more, everyone fit for military service: ⁴³ those enrolled from the tribe of Naphtali were fifty-three thousand four hundred.

⁴⁴ It was these who were enrolled, each according to his ancestral house, by Moses and Aaron and the twelve leaders of Israel. ⁴⁵ The total enrollment of the Israelites of twenty years or more, according to their ancestral houses, everyone fit for military service in Israel— ⁴⁶ the total enrollment was six hundred and three thousand, five hundred and fifty.

**Levites Omitted in the Census.** ⁴⁷ Now the Levites were not enrolled* by their ancestral tribe with the others.† ⁴⁸ For the LORD had told Moses, ⁴⁹ The tribe of Levi alone you shall not enroll nor include in the census along with the other Israelites. ⁵⁰ You are to give the Levites charge of the tabernacle of the covenant with all its equipment and all that belongs to it. It is they who shall carry the tabernacle with all its equipment and who shall be its ministers;* and they shall camp all around

the tabernacle. ⁵¹ When the tabernacle is to move on, the Levites shall take it down; when the tabernacle is to be pitched, it is the Levites who shall set it up. Any unauthorized person who comes near† it shall be put to death.* ⁵² The other Israelites shall camp according to their companies, each in their own divisional camps,* ⁵³ but the Levites shall camp around the tabernacle of the covenant to ensure that God's wrath will not fall upon the Israelite community. The Levites shall keep guard over the tabernacle of the covenant.* ⁵⁴ The Israelites complied; they did just as the LORD had commanded Moses.

**2 Arrangement of the Tribes.** ¹ The LORD said to Moses and Aaron: ² The Israelites shall camp, each in their own divisions, under the ensigns of their ancestral houses.* They shall camp at some distance all around the tent of meeting.

³† Encamped on the east side, toward the sunrise, shall be the divisional camp of Judah, arranged in companies. The leader of the Judahites is Nahshon, son of Amminadab, ⁴ and the enrollment of his company is seventy-four thousand six hundred. ⁵ Encamped beside it is the tribe of Issachar. The leader of the Issacharites is Nethanel, son of Zuar, ⁶ and the enrollment of his company is fifty-four thousand four hundred. ⁷ Also the tribe of Zebulun. The leader of the Zebulunites is Eliab, son of Helon, ⁸ and the enrollment of his company is fifty-seven thousand four hundred. ⁹ The total enrollment of the camp of Judah by companies is one hundred and eighty-six thousand four hundred. They shall be first on the march.

¹⁰ The divisional camp of Reuben shall be on the south side, by companies. The leader of the Reubenites is Elizur, son of Shedeur, ¹¹ and the enrollment of his company is forty-six thousand five hundred. ¹² Encamped beside it is the tribe of Simeon. The leader of the Simeonites is Shelumiel, son of Zurishaddai, ¹³ and the enrollment of his company is fifty-nine thousand three hundred. ¹⁴ Next is the tribe of Gad. The leader of the Gadites is Eliasaph, son

---

**1:47** The Levites were not enrolled in this census, which was principally for military purposes, but a separate census was made of them. Cf. 3:15–16, 39.

**1:51** *Comes near*: here and in 3:10, 38; 17:5; 18:4, 7 the Hebrew word rendered "comes near" is very nearly a technical term for someone who intrudes upon or violates a space set apart as holy and for which they have not been qualified by priesthood.

**2:3–31** A similar arrangement of the tribes around the central sanctuary in the ideal Israel is given in Ez 48.

**1:47** Nm 2:33; 3:14–39; 26:57–62.
**1:50** Nm 3:7–8; 4:2–49; 1 Chr 6:33.
**1:51** Nm 3:10, 38; 18:7; 2 Sm 6:6–7;
1 Chr 13:10.
**1:52** Nm 2:2, 34.
**1:53** Nm 3:7–8, 38; 8:19; 18:4–5.
**2:2** Nm 1:52.

of Reuel, 15 and the enrollment of his company is forty-five thousand six hundred and fifty. 16 The total enrollment of the camp of Reuben by companies is one hundred and fifty-one thousand four hundred and fifty. They shall be second on the march.

17 Then the tent of meeting and the camp of the Levites shall set out in the midst of the divisions. As they camp, so also they will march, each in place, by their divisions.

18 The divisional camp of Ephraim shall be on the west side, by companies. The leader of the Ephraimites is Elishama, son of Ammihud, 19 and the enrollment of his company is forty thousand five hundred. 20 Beside it shall be the tribe of Manasseh. The leader of the Manassites is Gamaliel, son of Pedahzur, 21 and the enrollment of his company is thirty-two thousand two hundred. 22 Also the tribe of Benjamin. The leader of the Benjaminites is Abidan, son of Gideoni, 23 and the enrollment of his company is thirty-five thousand four hundred. 24 The total enrollment of the camp of Ephraim by companies is one hundred and eight thousand one hundred. They shall be third on the march.

25 The divisional camp of Dan shall be on the north side, by companies. The leader of the Danites is Ahiezer, son of Ammishaddai, 26 and the enrollment of his company is sixty-two thousand seven hundred. 27 Encamped beside it shall be the tribe of Asher. The leader of the Asherites is Pagiel, son of Ochran, 28 and the enrollment of his company is forty-one thousand five hundred. 29 Also the tribe of Naphtali. The leader of the Naphtalites is Ahira, son of Enan, 30 and the enrollment of his company is fifty-three thousand four hundred. 31 The total enrollment of the camp of Dan is one hundred and fifty-seven thousand six hundred. They shall be the last on the march, by divisions.

32 * These are the enrollments of the Israelites according to their ancestral houses. The total enrollment of the camps by companies is six hundred and three thousand five hundred and fifty. 33 The Levites, however, were not enrolled with the other Israelites, just as the LORD had commanded Moses. 34 The Israelites did just as the LORD had commanded Moses; both

in camp and on the march they were in their own divisions, everyone by clan and according to ancestral house.

# 3 The Sons of Aaron.
1 These are the offspring of Aaron and Moses at the time the LORD spoke to Moses on Mount Sinai. 2 These are the names of Aaron's sons: Nadab, the firstborn, Abihu, Eleazar, and Ithamar.* 3 These are the names of Aaron's sons, the anointed priests whom he ordained to serve as priests. 4 But Nadab and Abihu died* in the presence of the LORD when they offered unauthorized fire before the LORD in the wilderness of Sinai; and they left no sons. So only Eleazar and Ithamar served as priests during the lifetime of their father Aaron.

**Levites in Place of the Firstborn.** 5 Now the LORD said to Moses: 6 Summon the tribe of Levi and station them before Aaron the priest to serve him.* 7 They shall discharge his obligations and those of the whole community before the tent of meeting* by maintaining the tabernacle. 8 They shall have responsibility for all the furnishings of the tent of meeting and discharge the obligations of the Israelites by maintaining the tabernacle. 9 You shall assign the Levites to Aaron and his sons;* they have been assigned unconditionally to him from among the Israelites. 10 But you will appoint only Aaron and his descendants to exercise the priesthood.* Any unauthorized person who comes near shall be put to death.

11 The LORD said to Moses: 12 I hereby take the Levites from the Israelites in place of every firstborn that opens the womb among the Israelites.* The Levites, therefore, are mine, 13 because every firstborn is mine. When I struck down all the firstborn in the land of Egypt, I consecrated to me every firstborn in Israel, human being and beast alike. They belong to me; I am the LORD.

**Census of the Levites.** 14 The LORD said to Moses in the wilderness of Sinai: 15 Enroll the Levites by their ancestral houses and clans, enrolling every male of a month or more.* 16 Moses, therefore, enrolled them at the direction of the LORD, just as the LORD had charged.

---

2:32–33 Nm 1:44–49.
3:2 Ex 6:23; 1 Chr 24:1.
3:4 Nm 26:61; Lv 10:1–2;

1 Chr 24:2.
3:6 Nm 18:2.
3:7 Nm 8:24.

3:9 Nm 8:19.
3:10 Nm 1:51; 18:7.

3:12–13 Nm 3:41; 8:16–18; Ex 13:2, 12, 15.
3:15 Nm 3:39; 26:62.

17* These were the sons of Levi by name: Gershon, Kohath and Merari. 18 These were the names of the sons of Gershon, by their clans: Libni and Shimei. 19 The sons of Kohath, by their clans, were Amram, Izhar, Hebron and Uzziel. 20 The sons of Merari, by their clans, were Mahli and Mushi. These were the clans of the Levites by their ancestral houses.

**Duties of the Levitical Clans.** 21 To Gershon belonged the clan of the Libnites and the clan of the Shimeites; these were the clans of the Gershonites. 22 Their enrollment, registering every male of a month or more, was seven thousand five hundred. 23 The clans of the Gershonites camped behind the tabernacle, to the west. 24 The leader of the ancestral house of the Gershonites was Eliasaph, son of Lael. 25* At the tent of meeting their responsibility was the tabernacle:† the tent and its covering, the curtain at the entrance of the tent of meeting, 26 the hangings of the court, the curtain at the entrance of the court enclosing both the tabernacle and the altar, and the ropes—whatever pertained to their maintenance.

27 To Kohath belonged the clans of the Amramites, the Izharites, the Hebronites, and the Uzzielites; these were the clans of the Kohathites. 28 Their enrollment, registering every male of a month or more, was eight thousand three hundred. They were the ones who performed the duties of the sanctuary. 29 The clans of the Kohathites camped on the south side of the tabernacle. 30 And the leader of their ancestral house of the clan of the Kohathites was Elizaphan, son of Uzziel. 31 Their responsibility was the ark, the table, the menorah, the altars, the utensils of the sanctuary with which the priests minister, the veil, and everything pertaining to their maintenance.† 32 The chief of the leaders of the Levites, however, was Eleazar, son of Aaron the priest; he was in charge of those who performed the duties of the sanctuary.

33 To Merari belonged the clans of the Mahlites and the Mushites; these were the clans of Merari. 34 Their enrollment, registering every male of a month or more, was six thousand two hundred. 35 The leader of the ancestral house of the clans of Merari was Zuriel, son of Abihail. They camped at the north side of the tabernacle. 36† The Merarites were assigned responsibility for the boards of the tabernacle, its bars, columns, pedestals, and all its fittings—and everything pertaining to their maintenance, 37 as well as the columns of the surrounding court with their pedestals, pegs and ropes.

38 East of the tabernacle, that is, in front of the tent of meeting, toward the sunrise, were camped Moses and Aaron and the latter's sons, performing the duties of the sanctuary incumbent upon the Israelites. Any unauthorized person who came near was to be put to death. 39 The total enrollment of the Levites whom Moses and Aaron enrolled at the direction of the Lord, by clans, every male a month old or more, was twenty-two thousand.

**Census and Ransom of Firstborn.** 40 The Lord then said to Moses: Enroll every firstborn male of the Israelites a month old or more, and count the number of their names. 41 Then take the Levites for me—I am the Lord—in place of all the firstborn of the Israelites, as well as the Levites' cattle, in place of all the firstborn among the cattle of the Israelites. 42 So Moses enrolled all the firstborn of the Israelites, as the Lord had commanded him. 43 All the firstborn males, registered by name, of a month or more, numbered twenty-two thousand two hundred and seventy-three.

44 The Lord said to Moses: 45 Take the Levites in place of all the firstborn of the Israelites, and the Levites' cattle in place of their cattle, that the Levites may belong to me. I am the Lord. 46 As a redemption-price for the two hundred and seventy-three firstborn of the Israelites over and above the number of the Levites, 47 you shall take five shekels for each individual, according to the sanctuary shekel, twenty gerahs to the shekel.* 48 Give this

---

† **3:25–26** The Gershonites had two wagons for transporting these things; cf. 7:7. For a description of the tabernacle, see Ex 26:1–6; the tent, Ex 26:7–13; its covering, Ex 26:14; the curtain at the entrance, Ex 26:36; the hangings of the court, Ex 27:9–15; the curtain at the entrance of the court, Ex 27:16; the ropes of the tabernacle, Ex 35:18.
**3:31** The Kohathites had to carry these sacred objects on their shoulders; cf. 7:9. For a description of the ark, see Ex 25:10–22; the table, Ex 25:23–30; the menorah, Ex 25:31–40; the altars, Ex 27:1–8; 30:1–10.

**3:36–37** The Merarites had four wagons for transporting this heavy material; cf. 7:8. For a description of the boards, bars, etc., of the tabernacle, see Ex 26:15–30; the columns, pedestals, etc., of the court, Ex 27:9–19.

* 
**3:17–20** Nm 26:57; Gn 46:11; Ex 6:16–19; 1 Chr 6:1–2, 16–19.
**3:25–26** Ex 26:7, 14, 36; 36:14.
**3:47** Nm 18:16; Ex 30:13; Lv 27:25; Ez 45:12.

money to Aaron and his sons as a redemption-price for the extra number. ⁴⁹ So Moses took the redemption money for those over and above the ones redeemed by the Levites. ⁵⁰ From the firstborn of the Israelites he took the money, one thousand three hundred and sixty-five shekels according to the sanctuary shekel. ⁵¹ He then gave this redemption money to Aaron and his sons, at the direction of the LORD, just as the LORD had commanded Moses.

**Duties Further Defined.** ¹ The LORD said to Moses and Aaron: ² Take a census among the Levites of the Kohathites, by clans and ancestral houses, ³ all between thirty† and fifty years of age, who will join the personnel for doing tasks in the tent of meeting.*

⁴ This is the task of the Kohathites in the tent of meeting: the most sacred objects. ⁵ In breaking camp, Aaron and his sons shall go in and take down the screening curtain† and cover the ark of the covenant with it. ⁶ Over these they shall put a cover of yellow-orange skin, and on top of this spread an all-violet cloth and put the poles in place. ⁷ On the table of the Presence they shall spread a violet cloth and put on it the plates and cups, as well as the bowls and pitchers for libations; the established bread offering shall remain on the table. ⁸ Over these they shall spread a scarlet cloth and cover it with a covering of yellow-orange skin, and put the poles in place. ⁹ They shall use a violet cloth to cover the menorah of the light with its lamps, tongs, and trays, as well as the various containers of oil from which it is supplied. ¹⁰ The menorah with all its utensils they shall then put in a covering of yellow-orange skin, and place on a litter. ¹¹ Over the golden altar† they shall spread a violet cloth, and cover this also with a covering of yellow-orange skin, and put the poles in place. ¹² Taking the utensils of the sanctuary service, they shall put them all in violet cloth and cover them with a covering of yellow-orange skin. They shall then place them on a litter. ¹³ After cleansing the altar† of its ashes, they shall spread a purple cloth over it. ¹⁴ On this they shall put all the utensils with which it is served: the fire pans, forks,† shovels, basins, and all the utensils of the altar. They shall then spread a covering of yellow-orange skin over this, and put the poles in place.

¹⁵ Only after Aaron and his sons have finished covering the sacred objects and all the utensils on breaking camp, can the Kohathites enter to carry them. But they shall not touch the sacred objects; if they do they will die.* These, then, are the objects in the tent of meeting that the Kohathites shall carry.

¹⁶ Eleazar, son of Aaron the priest, shall be in charge of the oil for the light, the fragrant incense, the established grain offering, and the anointing oil. He shall be in charge of the whole tabernacle with all the sacred objects and utensils that are in it.

¹⁷ The LORD said to Moses and Aaron: ¹⁸ Do not let the group of Kohathite clans perish from among the Levites. ¹⁹ That they may live and not die when they approach the most sacred objects, this is what you shall do for them: Aaron and his sons shall go in and assign to each of them his task and what he must carry; ²⁰ but the Kohathites shall not go in to look upon the sacred objects even for an instant, or they will die.*

²¹ The LORD said to Moses: ²² Take a census of the Gershonites also, by ancestral houses and clans, ²³ enrolling all between thirty and fifty years of age who will join the personnel to do the work in the tent of meeting. ²⁴ This is the task of the clans of the Gershonites, what they must do and what they must carry: ²⁵ they shall carry the curtains of the tabernacle, the tent of meeting with its covering and the outer wrapping of yellow-orange skin, the curtain at the entrance of the tent of meeting, ²⁶ the hangings of the court, the curtain at the entrance to the gate of the court that encloses both the tabernacle and the altar, together with their ropes and all other objects necessary for their use. Whatever is to be done to maintain these things, they shall do. ²⁷ The service of the Gershonites shall be entirely under the direction of Aaron and his sons, with regard to

---

**4:3** *Thirty:* according to other passages the Levites began to serve when they were twenty-five (8:24) or even only twenty years old (1 Chr 23:24, 27; 2 Chr 31:17; Ezr 3:8; but cf. 1 Chr 23:3).

**4:5** *The screening curtain:* the veil between the inner and the outer rooms of the sanctuary. Cf. Ex 26:31–33.

**4:11** *The golden altar:* the altar of incense. Cf. Ex 30:1–6.

**4:13** *The altar:* the bronze altar for animal sacrifices. Cf. Ex 27:1–8.

**4:14** *Forks:* used in turning over the sacrificed animal on the fire of the altar. *Basins:* to receive the sacrificial blood; cf. Zec 9:15.

---

**4:3** Nm 8:24; 1 Chr 23:24–27.
**4:15** 2 Sm 6:6–7; 1 Chr 13:9–10.
**4:20** 1 Sm 6:19–20.

what they must carry and what they must do; you shall list for them by name what they are to carry. <sup>28</sup>This, then, is the task of the clans of the Gershonites in the tent of meeting; and they shall be under the supervision of Ithamar, son of Aaron the priest.

<sup>29</sup>The Merarites, too, you shall enroll by clans and ancestral houses, <sup>30</sup>enrolling all between thirty and fifty years of age who will join the personnel to maintain the tent of meeting. <sup>31</sup>* This is what they shall be responsible for carrying, with respect to all their service in the tent of meeting: the boards of the tabernacle with its bars, columns and pedestals, <sup>32</sup>and the columns of the surrounding court with their pedestals, pegs and ropes, including all their accessories and everything for their maintenance. You shall list by name the objects they shall be responsible for carrying. <sup>33</sup>This, then, is the task of the clans of the Merarites with respect to all their service in the tent of meeting under the supervision of Ithamar, son of Aaron the priest.

**Number of Adult Levites.** <sup>34</sup>So Moses and Aaron and the leaders of the community enrolled the Kohathites, by clans and ancestral houses, <sup>35</sup>all between thirty and fifty years of age who will join the personnel to work in the tent of meeting; <sup>36</sup>their enrollment by clans was two thousand seven hundred and fifty. <sup>37</sup>Such was the enrollment of the clans of the Kohathites, everyone who was to serve in the tent of meeting, whom Moses enrolled, together with Aaron, as the Lord directed through Moses.

<sup>38</sup>As for the enrollment of the Gershonites, by clans and ancestral houses, <sup>39</sup>all between thirty and fifty years of age who will join the personnel to work in the tent of meeting— <sup>40</sup>their enrollment by clans and ancestral houses was two thousand six hundred and thirty. <sup>41</sup>Such was the enrollment of the clans of the Gershonites, everyone who was to serve in the tent of meeting, whom Moses enrolled, together with Aaron, as the Lord directed.

<sup>42</sup>As for the enrollment of the clans of the Merarites, by clans and ancestral houses, <sup>43</sup>all from thirty up to fifty years of age who will join the personnel to work in the tent of meeting— <sup>44</sup>their enrollment by clans was three thousand two hundred. <sup>45</sup>Such was the enrollment of the clans of the Merarites, whom Moses enrolled, together with Aaron, as the Lord directed through Moses.

<sup>46</sup>As for the total enrollment of the Levites, which Moses and Aaron and the Israelite leaders had made, by clans and ancestral houses, <sup>47</sup>all between thirty and fifty years of age who were to undertake tasks of service or transport for the tent of meeting— <sup>48</sup>their total enrollment was eight thousand five hundred and eighty. <sup>49</sup>As the Lord directed through Moses, they gave each of them their assignments for service and for transport; just as the Lord had commanded Moses.

**5** **The Unclean Expelled.** <sup>1</sup>The Lord said to Moses: <sup>2</sup>Order the Israelites to expel from camp everyone with a scaly infection, and everyone suffering from a discharge, and everyone who has become unclean by contact with a corpse.†* <sup>3</sup>Male and female alike, you shall expel them. You shall expel them from the camp so that they do not defile their camp, where I dwell in their midst.* <sup>4</sup>This the Israelites did, expelling them from the camp; just as the Lord had commanded Moses, so the Israelites did.

**Unjust Possession.**† <sup>5</sup>The Lord said to Moses: <sup>6</sup>* Tell the Israelites: If a man or a woman commits any offense against another person, thus breaking faith with the Lord, and thereby becomes guilty, <sup>7</sup>that person shall confess the wrong that has been done, make restitution in full, and in addition give one fifth of its value to the one that has been wronged. <sup>8</sup>However, if there is no next of kin,† one to whom restitution can be made, the restitution shall be made to the Lord and shall fall to the priest; this is apart from the ram of atonement with which the priest makes atonement for the guilty individual. <sup>9</sup>Likewise, every

---

† **5:2** For the laws regarding victims of skin disease, see Lv 13–14; those suffering from a discharge, Lv 15; those unclean by contact with a corpse, Nm 19:11–22; Lv 21:1–4.
**5:5–10** The basic law on unjust possession is given in Lv 5:14–26. The new item here concerns the case where the injured party has died and left no heirs, in which case the restitution must be made to the priest.
**5:8** *Next of kin:* Hebrew *go'el* ("redeemer"), a technical term denoting the nearest relative, upon whom devolved the obligation of "redeeming" the family property, in order to keep it within the family. Cf. Lv 25:25; Ru 4:1–6.

* **4:31** Nm 3:36–37.
**5:2** Nm 19:11, 13; Lv 13:46; 21:1; 22:4.
**5:3** Nm 35:34.
**5:6–10** Lv 5:21–25.

contribution among the sacred offerings that the Israelites present to the priest will belong to him.* 10 Each shall possess his own sacred offerings; what is given to a priest shall be his.*

**Ordeal for Suspected Adultery.** 11 The LORD said to Moses: 12 Speak to the Israelites and tell them: If a man's wife goes astray and becomes unfaithful to him 13 by virtue of a man having intercourse with her* in secret from her husband and she is able to conceal the fact that she has defiled herself for lack of a witness who might have caught her in the act; 14 or if a man is overcome by a feeling of jealousy that makes him suspect his wife, and she has defiled herself; or if a man is overcome by a feeling of jealousy that makes him suspect his wife and she has not defiled herself— 15 then the man shall bring his wife to the priest as well as an offering on her behalf, a tenth of an ephah† of barley meal. However, he shall not pour oil on it nor put frankincense over it, since it is a grain offering of jealousy, a grain offering of remembrance which recalls wrongdoing.

16 The priest shall first have the woman come forward and stand before the LORD. 17 In an earthen vessel he shall take holy water,† as well as some dust from the floor of the tabernacle and put it in the water.* 18 Making the woman stand before the LORD, the priest shall uncover her head and place in her hands the grain offering of remembrance, that is, the grain offering of jealousy, while he himself shall hold the water of bitterness that brings a curse. 19 Then the priest shall adjure the woman, saying to her, "If no other man has had intercourse with you, and you have not gone astray by defiling yourself while under the authority of your husband, be immune to this water of bitterness that brings a curse. 20 But if you have gone astray while under the authority of your husband, and if you have defiled yourself and a man other than your husband has had intercourse with you"— 21 so shall the priest adjure the woman with this imprecation—"may the LORD make you a curse and malediction† among your people by causing your uterus to fall and your belly to swell! 22 May this water, then, that brings a curse, enter your bowels to make your belly swell and your uterus fall!"* And the woman shall say, "Amen, amen!"† 23 The priest shall put these curses in writing and shall then wash them off into the water of bitterness, 24 and he will have the woman drink the water of bitterness that brings a curse, so that the water that brings a curse may enter into her to her bitter hurt. 25 But first the priest shall take the grain offering of jealousy from the woman's hand, and having elevated the grain offering before the LORD, shall bring it to the altar, 26 where he shall take a handful of the grain offering as a token offering and burn it on the altar.* Only then shall he have the woman drink the water. 27 Once he has had her drink the water, if she has defiled herself and been unfaithful to her husband, the water that brings a curse will enter into her to her bitter hurt, and her belly will swell and her uterus will fall, so that she will become a curse among her people. 28 If, however, the woman has not defiled herself, but is still pure, she will be immune and will still be fertile.

29 This, then, is the ritual for jealousy when a woman goes astray while under the authority of her husband and defiles herself, 30 or when such a feeling of jealousy comes over a man that he becomes suspicious of his wife; he shall have her stand before the LORD, and the priest shall perform this entire ritual for her. 31 The man shall be free from punishment,† but the woman shall bear her punishment.

**6** **Laws Concerning Nazirites.** 1 The LORD said to Moses: 2 Speak to the Israelites and tell them: When men or women solemnly take the nazirite† vow to dedicate themselves to him. For her part, the woman (if guilty) must bear her punishment.

5:15 *Ephah:* see note on Is 5:10.
5:17 *Holy water:* water from the basin that stood in the court of the tabernacle.
5:21 *Curse and malediction:* the woman's name would be used in curses and oaths to invoke a similar misfortune on another person or on oneself. Cf. Is 65:15; Jer 29:22.
5:22 *Amen:* a Hebrew word meaning "certainly, truly," used to give assent to a statement, a curse, a blessing, a prayer, or the like, in the sense of "so be it."
5:31 *Free from punishment:* the point is that a husband will not suffer a harmful consequence if his accusation is not borne out by the ordeal; if he's right, his wife's punishment vindicates

6:2–21 *Nazirite:* from the Hebrew word *nazir,* meaning "set apart as sacred, dedicated, vowed." The nazirite vow could be either for a limited period or for life. Those bound by this vow had to abstain from all the products of the grapevine, from cutting or shaving their hair, and from contact with a corpse. They were regarded as men and women of God like the prophets; cf. Am 2:11–12. Examples of lifelong nazirites

5:9 Dt 18:3–4; Ez 44:29–30.
5:10 Lv 10:12–15.
5:13 Lv 18:20; Jn 8:4.
5:17 Nm 19:17.
5:22 Ps 109:18.
5:26 Lv 5:12.

the LORD, [3] they shall abstain from wine and strong drink;* they may neither drink wine vinegar, other vinegar, or any kind of grape juice, nor eat either fresh or dried grapes. [4] As long as they are nazirites they shall not eat anything of the produce of the grapevine; not even the seeds or the skins. [5] While they are under the nazirite vow, no razor shall touch their hair.* Until the period of their dedication to the LORD is over, they shall be holy, letting the hair of their heads grow freely. [6] As long as they are dedicated to the LORD, they shall not come near a dead person.* [7] Not even for their father or mother, sister or brother, should they defile themselves, when these die, since their heads bear their dedication to God. [8] As long as they are nazirites they are holy to the LORD.

[9] If someone dies very suddenly in their presence, defiling their dedicated heads, they shall shave their heads on the day of their purification, that is, on the seventh day. [10] On the eighth day they shall bring two turtledoves or two pigeons to the priest at the entrance of the tent of meeting. [11] The priest shall offer up the one as a purification offering and the other as a burnt offering, thus making atonement for them for the sin they committed with respect to the corpse. On the same day they shall reconsecrate their heads [12] and rededicate themselves to the LORD for the period of their dedication, bringing a yearling lamb as a reparation offering. The previous period is not valid, because they defiled their dedicated heads.

[13] This is the ritual for the nazirites:* When the period of their dedication is complete they shall go to the entrance of the tent of meeting, [14] bringing their offerings to the LORD, one unblemished yearling lamb for a burnt offering, one unblemished yearling ewe lamb for a purification offering, one unblemished ram as a communion offering, [15] and a basket of unleavened cakes of bran flour mixed with oil and of unleavened wafers spread with oil, along with their grain offerings and libations. [16] The priest shall present them before the LORD, and shall offer up the purification offering and the burnt offering for them. [17] He shall then offer up the ram as a communion sacrifice to the LORD, along with the basket of unleavened cakes, and the priest will offer the grain offering and libation. [18] Then at the entrance of the tent of meeting the nazirite shall shave his or her dedicated head, take the hair of the dedicated head, and put it in the fire under the communion sacrifice. [19] After the nazirite has shaved off the dedicated hair, the priest shall take a boiled shoulder of the ram, as well as one unleavened cake from the basket and one unleavened wafer, and shall put them in the hands of the nazirite. [20] The priest shall then elevate them as an elevated offering before the LORD. They are an offering belonging to the priest, along with the brisket of the elevated offering and the leg of the contribution. Only after this may the nazirite drink wine.

[21] This, then, is the law for the nazirites, that is, what they vow as their offering to the LORD in accord with their dedication, apart from anything else which their means may allow. In keeping with the vow they take so shall they do, according to the law of their dedication.

**The Priestly Blessing.** [22] The LORD said to Moses: [23] Speak to Aaron and his sons and tell them: This is how you shall bless the Israelites. Say to them:

[24]    The LORD bless you and keep you!
[25]    The LORD let his face shine upon you,
      and be gracious to you!
[26]    The LORD look upon you kindly and give
      you peace!†

[27] So shall they invoke my name upon the Israelites, and I will bless them.

**7** **Offerings of the Tribal Leaders.** [1] Now, when Moses had completed the erection of the tabernacle, he anointed and consecrated it with all its equipment,* as well as the altar with all its equipment. After he anointed and consecrated them, [2] an offering was made by

---

were Samson (Jgs 13:4–5, 7; 16:17), Samuel (1 Sm 1:11), and John the Baptist (Lk 1:15). At the time of Jesus the practice of taking the nazirite vow for a limited period seems to have been quite common, even among the early Christians; cf. Acts 18:18; 21:23–24, 26.

  **6:26** *Peace*: the Hebrew word *Shalom* includes the idea of happiness, good health, prosperity, friendship, and general well-being. To use this term as a greeting was to pray for all these things upon the one greeted.

  **6:5** Jgs 13:5; 16:17; 1 Sm 1:11.
  **6:6** Nm 19:11, 16; Lv 21:11.
  **6:13** Acts 21:24, 26.
  **7:1** Ex 40:17.

the tribal leaders of Israel, who were heads of ancestral houses, the same leaders of the tribes who supervised those enrolled. ³The offering they brought before the LORD consisted of six wagons for baggage and twelve oxen, that is, a wagon for every two tribal leaders, and an ox for each. These they presented before the tabernacle.

⁴The LORD then said to Moses: ⁵Accept their offering, that these things may be put to use to maintain the tent of meeting. Assign them to the Levites, to each according to his duties. ⁶So Moses accepted the wagons and oxen, and assigned them to the Levites. ⁷He gave two wagons and four oxen to the Gershonites* according to their duties, ⁸and four wagons and eight oxen to the Merarites according to their duties, under the supervision of Ithamar, son of Aaron the priest. ⁹He gave none to the Kohathites, because they were responsible for maintenance of the sacred objects that had to be carried on their shoulders.*

¹⁰For the dedication of the altar also, the tribal leaders brought offerings when it was anointed;* the leaders presented their offering before the altar. ¹¹But the LORD said to Moses: Let one leader each day present his offering for the dedication of the altar.

¹²† The one who presented his offering on the first day was Nahshon, son of Amminadab, of the tribe of Judah. ¹³His offering consisted of one silver plate weighing a hundred and thirty shekels and one silver basin weighing seventy shekels according to the sanctuary shekel, both filled with bran flour mixed with oil for a grain offering; ¹⁴one gold cup of ten shekels' weight filled with incense; ¹⁵one bull from the herd, one ram, and one yearling lamb for a burnt offering; ¹⁶one goat for a purification offering; ¹⁷and two bulls, five rams, five he-goats, and five yearling lambs for a communion sacrifice. This was the offering of Nahshon, son of Amminadab.

¹⁸On the second day Nethanel, son of Zuar, tribal leader of Issachar, made his offering. ¹⁹He presented as his offering one silver plate weighing a hundred and thirty shekels and one silver basin weighing seventy shekels according to the sanctuary shekel, both filled with bran flour mixed for a grain

offering; ²⁰one gold cup of ten shekels' weight filled with incense; ²¹one bull from the herd, one ram, and one yearling lamb for a burnt offering; ²²one goat for a purification offering; ²³and two bulls, five rams, five he-goats, and five yearling lambs for a communion sacrifice. This was the offering of Nethanel, son of Zuar.

²⁴On the third day it was the turn of the tribal leader of the Zebulunites, Eliab, son of Helon. ²⁵His offering consisted of one silver plate weighing a hundred and thirty shekels and one silver basin weighing seventy shekels according to the sanctuary shekel, both filled with bran flour mixed with oil for a grain offering; ²⁶one gold cup of ten shekels' weight filled with incense; ²⁷one bull from the herd, one ram, and one yearling lamb for a burnt offering; ²⁸one goat for a purification offering; ²⁹and two bulls, five rams, five he-goats, and five yearling lambs for a communion sacrifice. This was the offering of Eliab, son of Helon.

³⁰On the fourth day it was the turn of the tribal leader of the Reubenites, Elizur, son of Shedeur. ³¹His offering consisted of one silver plate weighing a hundred and thirty shekels and one silver basin weighing seventy shekels according to the sanctuary shekel, both filled with bran flour mixed with oil for a grain offering; ³²one gold cup of ten shekels' weight filled with incense; ³³one bull from the herd, one ram, and one yearling lamb for a burnt offering; ³⁴one goat for a purification offering; ³⁵and two bulls, five rams, five he-goats, and five yearling lambs for a communion sacrifice. This was the offering of Elizur, son of Shedeur.

³⁶On the fifth day it was the turn of the tribal leader of the Simeonites, Shelumiel, son of Zurishaddai. ³⁷His offering consisted of one silver plate weighing a hundred and thirty shekels and one silver basin weighing seventy shekels according to the sanctuary shekel, both filled with bran flour mixed with oil for a grain offering; ³⁸one gold cup of ten shekels' weight filled with incense; ³⁹one bull from the herd, one ram, and one yearling lamb for a burnt offering; ⁴⁰one goat for a purification offering; ⁴¹and two bulls, five rams, five he-goats, and five yearling lambs for a communion sacrifice. This was the offering of Shelumiel, son of Zurishaddai.

---

† **7:12–88** The repetitive account of the same offerings brought by each of the twelve tribal leaders and the summary of them are characteristic of an official registration.

**7:7–8** Nm 4:24–33.      **7:10** Nm 7:84.
    **7:9** Nm 3:31; 4:4–15.

⁴² On the sixth day it was the turn of the tribal leader of the Gadites, Eliasaph, son of Reuel. ⁴³ His offering consisted of one silver plate weighing a hundred and thirty shekels and one silver basin weighing seventy shekels according to the sanctuary shekel, both filled with bran flour mixed with oil for a grain offering; ⁴⁴ one gold cup of ten shekels' weight filled with incense; ⁴⁵ one bull from the herd, one ram, and one yearling lamb for a burnt offering; ⁴⁶ one goat for a purification offering; ⁴⁷ and two bulls, five rams, five he-goats, and five yearling lambs for a communion sacrifice. This was the offering of Eliasaph, son of Reuel.

⁴⁸ On the seventh day it was the turn of the tribal leader of the Ephraimites, Elishama, son of Ammihud. ⁴⁹ His offering consisted of one silver plate weighing a hundred and thirty shekels and one silver basin weighing seventy shekels according to the sanctuary shekel, both filled with bran flour mixed with oil for a grain offering; ⁵⁰ one gold cup of ten shekels' weight filled with incense; ⁵¹ one bull from the herd, one ram, and one yearling lamb for a burnt offering; ⁵² one goat for a purification offering; ⁵³ and two bulls, five rams, five he-goats, and five yearling lambs for a communion sacrifice. This was the offering of Elishama, son of Ammihud.

⁵⁴ On the eighth day it was the turn of the tribal leader of the Manassites, Gamaliel, son of Pedahzur. ⁵⁵ His offering consisted of one silver plate weighing a hundred and thirty shekels and one silver basin weighing seventy shekels according to the sanctuary shekel, both filled with bran flour mixed with oil for a grain offering; ⁵⁶ one gold cup of ten shekels' weight filled with incense; ⁵⁷ one bull from the herd, one ram, and one yearling lamb for a burnt offering; ⁵⁸ one goat for a purification offering; ⁵⁹ and two bulls, five rams, five he-goats, and five yearling lambs for a communion sacrifice. This was the offering of Gamaliel, son of Pedahzur.

⁶⁰ On the ninth day it was the turn of the tribal leader of the Benjaminites, Abidan, son of Gideoni. ⁶¹ His offering consisted of one silver plate weighing a hundred and thirty shekels and one silver basin weighing seventy shekels according to the sanctuary shekel, both filled with bran flour mixed with oil for a grain offering; ⁶² one gold cup of ten shekels' weight filled with incense; ⁶³ one bull from the herd, one ram, and one yearling lamb for a burnt offering; ⁶⁴ one goat for a purification offering; ⁶⁵ and two bulls, five rams, five he-goats, and five yearling lambs for a communion sacrifice. This was the offering of Abidan, son of Gideoni.

⁶⁶ On the tenth day it was the turn of the tribal leader of the Danites, Ahiezer, son of Ammishaddai. ⁶⁷ His offering consisted of one silver plate weighing a hundred and thirty shekels and one silver basin weighing seventy shekels according to the sanctuary shekel, both filled with bran flour mixed with oil for a grain offering; ⁶⁸ one gold cup of ten shekels' weight filled with incense; ⁶⁹ one bull from the herd, one ram, and one yearling lamb for a burnt offering; ⁷⁰ one goat for a purification offering; ⁷¹ and two bulls, five rams, five he-goats, and five yearling lambs for a communion sacrifice. This was the offering of Ahiezer, son of Ammishaddai.

⁷² On the eleventh day it was the turn of the tribal leader of the Asherites, Pagiel, son of Ochran. ⁷³ His offering consisted of one silver plate weighing one hundred and thirty shekels and one silver basin weighing seventy shekels according to the sanctuary shekel, both filled with bran flour mixed with oil for a grain offering; ⁷⁴ one gold cup of ten shekels' weight filled with incense; ⁷⁵ one bull from the herd, one ram, and one yearling lamb for a burnt offering; ⁷⁶ one goat for a purification offering; ⁷⁷ and two bulls, five rams, five he-goats, and five yearling lambs for a communion sacrifice. This was the offering of Pagiel, son of Ochran.

⁷⁸ On the twelfth day it was the turn of the tribal leader of the Naphtalites, Ahira, son of Enan. ⁷⁹ His offering consisted of one silver plate weighing a hundred and thirty shekels and one silver basin weighing seventy shekels according to the sanctuary shekel, both filled with bran flour mixed with oil for a grain offering; ⁸⁰ one gold cup of ten shekels' weight filled with incense; ⁸¹ one bull from the herd, one ram, and one yearling lamb for a burnt offering; ⁸² one goat for a purification offering; ⁸³ and two bulls, five rams, five he-goats, and five yearling lambs for a communion sacrifice. This was the offering of Ahira, son of Enan.

⁸⁴ These were the offerings for the dedication of the altar, given by the tribal leaders of Israel on the occasion of its anointing: twelve silver plates, twelve silver basins, and twelve

gold cups. ⁸⁵Each silver plate weighed a hundred and thirty shekels, and each silver basin seventy, so that all the silver of these vessels amounted to two thousand four hundred shekels, according to the sanctuary shekel. ⁸⁶The twelve gold cups that were filled with incense weighed ten shekels apiece, according to the sanctuary shekel, so that all the gold of the cups amounted to one hundred and twenty shekels. ⁸⁷The animals for the burnt offerings were, in all, twelve bulls, twelve rams, and twelve yearling lambs, with their grain offerings; those for the purification offerings were twelve goats. ⁸⁸The animals for the communion sacrifices were, in all, twenty-four bulls, sixty rams, sixty he-goats, and sixty yearling lambs. These, then, were the offerings for the dedication of the altar after it was anointed.

**The Voice.** ⁸⁹When Moses entered the tent of meeting to speak with God, he heard the voice addressing him from above the cover* on the ark of the covenant, from between the two cherubim; and so it spoke to him.

**8** **The Menorah.** ¹The LORD said to Moses: ²Speak to Aaron and say: "When you set up the menorah-lamps,* have the seven lamps throw their light in front of the menorah."† ³Aaron did so, setting up the menorah-lamps to face the area in front of the menorah, just as the LORD had commanded Moses. ⁴This is the construction of the menorah: hammered gold,* from its base to its bowls† it was hammered; according to the pattern which the LORD had shown Moses, so he made the menorah.

**Purification of the Levites.** ⁵The LORD said to Moses: ⁶Take the Levites from among the Israelites and cleanse them.† ⁷This is what you shall do to them to cleanse them. Sprinkle them with the water of purification, have them shave their whole bodies and wash their garments, and so cleanse themselves. ⁸Then they shall take a bull from the herd, along with its grain offering of bran flour mixed with

oil; and you shall take another bull from the herd for a purification offering. ⁹Bringing the Levites before the tent of meeting, you shall assemble also the whole community of the Israelites. ¹⁰When you have brought the Levites before the LORD, the Israelites shall lay their hands upon them. ¹¹Aaron shall then present the Levites before the LORD as an elevated offering from the Israelites, that they may perform the service of the LORD. ¹²The Levites in turn shall lay their hands on the heads of the bulls, offering one as a purification offering and the other as a burnt offering to the LORD, to make atonement for the Levites. ¹³Then you shall have the Levites stand before Aaron and his sons, and you shall present them as an elevated offering to the LORD; ¹⁴thus you shall separate the Levites from the rest of the Israelites, and the Levites shall belong to me.*

¹⁵Only then shall the Levites enter upon their service in the tent of meeting, when you have cleansed them and presented them as an elevated offering. ¹⁶For they, among the Israelites, are totally dedicated to me; I have taken them for myself in place of everyone that opens the womb, the firstborn of all the Israelites.* ¹⁷Indeed, all the firstborn among the Israelites, human being and beast alike, belong to me; I consecrated them to myself on the day I killed all the firstborn in the land of Egypt.* ¹⁸But I have taken the Levites in place of all the firstborn Israelites; ¹⁹and from among the Israelites I have given to Aaron and his sons these Levites, who are to be dedicated,* to perform the service of the Israelites in the tent of meeting and to make atonement for them, so that no plague may strike among the Israelites should they come too near the sanctuary.

²⁰This, then, is what Moses and Aaron and the whole community of the Israelites did with respect to the Levites; the Israelites did exactly as the LORD had commanded Moses concerning them. ²¹When the Levites had purified themselves† and washed their garments, Aaron presented them as an elevated offering before the LORD, and made atonement for them to cleanse them. ²²Only then did they

---

† **8:2** *Menorah:* a seven-branched lampstand; see Ex 25:31–40; 37:17–24.
  **8:4** *Bowls:* lit., "blossom," a designation for the blossom-shaped cups holding the lamps of the menorah.
  **8:6** *Cleanse them:* in the language of the Pentateuch only the priests were "consecrated," that is, made sacred or set aside for the Lord, in an elaborate ceremony described in Ex 29 and in this chapter. The Levites were "cleansed," that is, made ritually clean

for their special work.
  **8:21** *Purified themselves:* by having the "water of purification" sprinkled on them as prescribed in v. 7.

| | |
|---|---|
| **7:89** Ex 25:22. | **8:16** Nm 3:12, 45. |
| **8:2** Ex 25:37. | **8:17** Nm 3:13; Lk 2:23. |
| **8:4** Ex 25:31, 40. | **8:19** Nm 3:9–10. |
| **8:14** Nm 3:45. | |

enter upon their service in the tent of meeting under the supervision of Aaron and his sons. Exactly as the LORD had commanded Moses concerning the Levites, so it was done with regard to them.

**Age Limits for Levitical Service.** 23 The LORD said to Moses: 24 This is the rule for the Levites. Everyone twenty-five years old or more shall join the personnel in the service of the tent of meeting.* 25 But everyone fifty on up shall retire from the work force and serve no more. 26 They shall assist their fellow Levites in the tent of meeting in performing their duties, but they shall not do the work. This, then, is how you are to regulate the duties of the Levites.

**9** **Second Passover.** 1 The LORD said to Moses in the wilderness of Sinai, in the first month of the second year following their departure from the land of Egypt: 2 Tell the Israelites to celebrate the Passover at the prescribed time. 3 In the evening twilight of the fourteenth day of this month* you shall celebrate it at its prescribed time, in accord with all its statutes and regulations. 4 So Moses told the Israelites to celebrate the Passover, 5 and they did celebrate the Passover on the fourteenth day of the first month during the evening twilight in the wilderness of Sinai. Just as the LORD had commanded Moses, so the Israelites did.

6 There were some, however, who were unclean because of a human corpse and so could not celebrate the Passover that day. These men came up to Moses and Aaron that same day 7 and they said to them, "Although we are unclean because of a human corpse, why should we be deprived of presenting the LORD's offering at its prescribed time along with other Israelites?" 8 Moses answered them, "Wait so that I can learn what the LORD will command in your regard."

9 The LORD then said to Moses: 10 Speak to the Israelites: "If any one of you or of your descendants is unclean because of a human corpse, or is absent on a journey, you may still celebrate the LORD's Passover. 11 But you shall celebrate it in the second month,* on the fourteenth day of that month during the evening

twilight, eating it with unleavened bread and bitter herbs, 12 and not leaving any of it over till morning, nor breaking any of its bones,* but observing all the statutes of the Passover. 13 However, anyone who is clean and not away on a journey, who yet fails to celebrate the Passover, shall be cut off from the people, for not presenting the LORD's offering at the prescribed time. That person shall bear the consequences of this sin.

14 "If an alien† who lives among you would celebrate the LORD's Passover, it shall be celebrated according to the statutes and regulations for the Passover. You shall have the same law for the resident alien as for the native of the land."*

**The Fiery Cloud.** 15 On the day when the tabernacle was erected, the cloud† covered the tabernacle, the tent of the covenant; but from evening until morning it took on the appearance of fire over the tabernacle.* 16 It was always so: during the day the cloud covered the tabernacle and at night had the appearance of fire. 17 Whenever the cloud rose from the tent, the Israelites would break camp; wherever the cloud settled, the Israelites would pitch camp.* 18 At the direction of the LORD the Israelites broke camp, and at the LORD's direction they pitched camp.* As long as the cloud stayed over the tabernacle, they remained in camp.

19 Even when the cloud lingered many days over the tabernacle, the Israelites kept the charge of the LORD and would not move on. 20 Yet if it happened the cloud was over the tabernacle only for a few days, at the direction of the LORD they stayed in camp; and at the LORD's direction they broke camp. 21 If it happened the cloud remained there only from evening until morning, when the cloud rose in the morning, they would break camp. Whether the cloud lifted during the day or the night they would then break camp. 22 Whether the cloud lingered over the tabernacle for two days or for a month or longer, the Israelites remained in camp and did not break camp; but when it lifted, they broke camp. 23 At the direction of the LORD they pitched camp, and

---

† **9:14** *An alien:* compare this passage with the Passover legislation in Ex 12:48, where circumcision is required of the alien who would celebrate the feast.

**9:15** *The cloud:* already mentioned at the departure from Egypt; cf. Ex 13:21–22.

**8:24** Nm 4:3, 23.          **9:14** Ex 12:48–49.
**9:3** Ex 12:6; Lv 23:5.          **9:15** Ex 13:21.
**9:11** 2 Chr 30:2–15.          **9:17** Wis 18:3.
**9:12** Ex 12:46; Jn 19:36.          **9:18** 1 Cor 10:1.

at the LORD's direction they broke camp; they kept the charge of the LORD, as the LORD directed them through Moses.

# 10 The Silver Trumpets.

¹The LORD said to Moses: ²Make two trumpets of silver, making them of hammered silver, for you to use in summoning the community and in breaking camp. ³When both are blown, the whole community shall gather round you at the entrance of the tent of meeting; ⁴but when one of them is blown, only the tribal leaders, the heads of the clans of Israel, shall gather round you. ⁵When you sound the signal, those encamped on the east side shall break camp; ⁶when you sound a second signal, those encamped on the south side shall break camp; when you sound a third signal, those encamped on the west side shall break camp; when you sound a fourth signal, those encamped on the north side shall break camp. Thus shall the signal be sounded for them to break camp. ⁷But in calling forth an assembly you are to blow a blast, without sounding the signal.

⁸The sons of Aaron, the priests, shall blow the trumpets; this is prescribed forever for you and your descendants. ⁹*When in your own land you go to war against an enemy that is attacking you, you shall sound the alarm on the trumpets, and you shall be remembered before the LORD, your God, and be saved from your foes. ¹⁰And when you rejoice† on your festivals, and your new-moon feasts, you shall blow the trumpets over your burnt offerings and your communion sacrifices,* so that this serves as a reminder of you before your God. I, the LORD, am your God.

## II. DEPARTURE, REBELLION, AND WANDERING IN THE WILDERNESS FOR FORTY YEARS

## Departure from Sinai.

¹¹In the second year, on the twentieth day of the second month, the cloud rose from the tabernacle of the covenant, ¹²and the Israelites moved on from the

wilderness of Sinai by stages, until the cloud came to rest in the wilderness of Paran.

¹³The first time that they broke camp at the direction of the LORD through Moses, ¹⁴* the divisional camp of the Judahites, arranged in companies, was the first to set out. Over its whole company was Nahshon, son of Amminadab, ¹⁵with Nethanel, son of Zuar, over the company of the tribe of Issacharites, ¹⁶and Eliab, son of Helon, over the company of the tribe of Zebulunites. ¹⁷Then, after the tabernacle was dismantled, the Gershonites and Merarites who carried the tabernacle set out. ¹⁸The divisional camp of the Reubenites, arranged in companies, was the next to set out. Over its whole company was Elizur, son of Shedeur, ¹⁹with Shelumiel, son of Zurishaddai, over the company of the tribe of Simeonites, ²⁰and Eliasaph, son of Reuel, over the company of the tribe of Gadites. ²¹The Kohathites, who carried the sacred objects, then set out. Before their arrival the tabernacle would be erected. ²²The divisional camp of the Ephraimites set out next, arranged in companies. Over its whole company was Elishama, son of Ammihud, ²³with Gamaliel, son of Pedahzur, over the company of the tribe of Manassites, ²⁴and Abidan, son of Gideoni, over the company of the tribe of Benjaminites. ²⁵Finally, as rear guard for all the camps, the divisional camp of the Danites set out, arranged in companies. Over its whole company was Ahiezer, son of Ammishaddai, ²⁶with Pagiel, son of Ochran, over the company of the tribe of Asherites, ²⁷and Ahira, son of Enan, over the company of the tribe of Naphtalites. ²⁸This was the order of march for the Israelites, company by company, when they set out.

## Hobab as Guide.

²⁹Moses said to Hobab,† son of Reuel the Midianite, Moses' father-in-law, "We are setting out for the place concerning which the LORD has said, 'I will give it to you.' Come with us, and we will be generous toward you, for the LORD has promised prosperity to Israel." ³⁰But he answered, "No, I will not come. I am going instead to the land of my

---

10:10 *When you rejoice:* cf. Dt 16:14. *Festivals:* the great annual feasts of the Passover, Pentecost and Booths described in Lv 23; Nm 28–29.

10:29–32 *Hobab:* one of three names for the father-in-law of Moses (see Ex 2:18; 4:18; 18:6; Jgs 4:11). Here perhaps Hobab's initial refusal indicates he wished to be coaxed before granting the favor. From Jgs 1:16 it seems probable that he did accede to Moses' request. However, Ex 18:27 suggests Moses'

father-in-law returned to his own land. Indeed, to the extent Nm 10:29–32 appears to repeat Ex 18:27, it may indicate a resumption of the narrative of Israel's march through the wilderness after the "digression" formed by the Israelite sojourn at Sinai, Ex 19:1–Nm 10:28.

10:9 2 Chr 13:14.                    2 Chr 29:26–28.
10:10 Nm 29:1;                       10:14–16 Nm 2:3, 5, 7.

birth." [31] Moses said, "Please, do not leave us; you know where we can camp in the wilderness, and you can serve as our guide. [32] If you come with us, we will share with you the prosperity the LORD will bestow on us."

### Into the Wilderness.
[33] * From the mountain of the LORD† they made a journey of three days, and the ark of the covenant of the LORD went before them for the three-day journey to seek out a resting place for them. [34] And the cloud of the LORD was over them by day when they set out from camp.

[35] Whenever the ark set out, Moses would say,

> "Arise, O LORD, may your enemies be
> scattered,
> and may those who hate you flee
> before you."

[36] And when it came to rest, he would say,

> "Bring back, O LORD, the myriads of
> Israel's troops!"

# 11

### Discontent of the People.
[1] Now the people complained bitterly in the hearing of the LORD;* and when he heard it his wrath flared up, so that the LORD's fire burned among them and consumed the outskirts of the camp. [2] But when the people cried out to Moses, he prayed to the LORD and the fire died out. [3] Hence that place was called Taberah,† because there the fire of the LORD burned among them.

[4] The riffraff among them were so greedy for meat that even the Israelites lamented again,* "If only we had meat for food! [5] We remember the fish we used to eat without cost in Egypt, and the cucumbers, the melons, the leeks, the onions, and the garlic. [6] But now we are famished; we have nothing to look forward to but this manna."*

[7] * Manna was like coriander seed† and had the appearance of bdellium. [8] When they had gone about and gathered it up, the people would grind it between millstones or pound it in a mortar, then cook it in a pot and make it into loaves, with a rich creamy taste. [9] At night, when the dew fell upon the camp, the manna also fell.*

[10] When Moses heard the people, family after family, crying at the entrance of their tents, so that the LORD became very angry, he was grieved. [11] "Why do you treat your servant so badly?" Moses asked the LORD. "Why are you so displeased with me that you burden me with all this people? [12] Was it I who conceived all this people? or was it I who gave them birth, that you tell me to carry them at my breast, like a nurse carrying an infant, to the land you have promised under oath to their fathers? [13] Where can I get meat to give to all this people? For they are crying to me, 'Give us meat for our food.' [14] I cannot carry all this people by myself, for they are too heavy for me. [15] If this is the way you will deal with me, then please do me the favor of killing me at once, so that I need no longer face my distress."

### The Seventy Elders.
[16] Then the LORD said to Moses: Assemble for me seventy of the elders of Israel, whom you know to be elders and authorities among the people, and bring them to the tent of meeting. When they are in place beside you, [17] I will come down and speak with you there. I will also take some of the spirit that is on you and will confer it on them, that they may share the burden of the people with you. You will then not have to bear it by yourself.

[18] To the people, however, you shall say: "Sanctify yourselves for tomorrow, when you shall have meat to eat. For in the hearing of the LORD you have cried, 'If only we had meat for food! Oh, how well off we were in Egypt!' Therefore the LORD will give you meat to eat, [19] and you will eat it, not for one day, or two days, or five, or ten, or twenty days, [20] but for a whole month—until it comes out of your very nostrils and becomes loathsome to you. For you have rejected the LORD who is in your midst, and in his presence you have cried, 'Why did we ever leave Egypt?'"

---

† 10:33 *The mountain of the LORD*: Sinai (Horeb), elsewhere always called "the mountain of God."
11:3 *Taberah*: means "the burning."
11:7 *Coriander seed*: see note on Ex 16:31. *Bdellium*: a transparent, amber-colored gum resin, which is also mentioned in Gn 2:12.

* 10:33 Dt 1:33.
11:1 Dt 9:22.
11:4 Ps 78:18.
11:5–6 Nm 21:5; Ex 16:3; Acts 7:39.
11:7–8 Ex 16:14–15, 31; Ps 78:24; Wis 16:20; Jn 6:31.
11:9 Ex 16:14–15.

21 But Moses said, "The people around me include six hundred thousand soldiers; yet you say, 'I will give them meat to eat for a whole month.' 22 Can enough sheep and cattle be slaughtered for them? If all the fish of the sea were caught for them, would they have enough?" 23 The LORD answered Moses: Is this beyond the LORD's reach? You shall see now whether or not what I have said to you takes place.

**The Spirit on the Elders.** 24 So Moses went out and told the people what the LORD had said. Gathering seventy elders of the people, he had them stand around the tent. 25 The LORD then came down in the cloud and spoke to him. Taking some of the spirit that was on Moses, he bestowed it on the seventy elders; and as the spirit came to rest on them, they prophesied† but did not continue.

26 Now two men, one named Eldad and the other Medad, had remained in the camp, yet the spirit came to rest on them also. They too had been on the list, but had not gone out to the tent; and so they prophesied in the camp. 27 So, when a young man ran and reported to Moses, "Eldad and Medad are prophesying in the camp," 28 Joshua, son of Nun, who from his youth had been Moses' aide, said, "My lord, Moses, stop them." 29 But Moses answered him, "Are you jealous for my sake? If only all the people of the LORD were prophets! If only the LORD would bestow his spirit on them!" 30 Then Moses retired to the camp, along with the elders of Israel.

**The Quail.** 31 There arose a wind* from the LORD that drove in quail from the sea and left them all around the camp site, to a distance of a day's journey and at a depth of two cubits upon the ground.† 32* So all that day, all night, and all the next day the people set about to gather in the quail. Even the one who got the least gathered ten homers† of them. Then they spread them out all around the camp. 33 But while the meat was still between their teeth, before it could be chewed, the LORD's wrath flared up against the people, and the LORD struck them with a very great plague. 34 So that place was named Kibroth-hattaavah,† because it was there that the greedy people were buried.

35 From Kibroth-hattaavah the people set out for Hazeroth, where they stayed.

**12** **Jealousy of Aaron and Miriam.** 1 Miriam and Aaron spoke against Moses on the pretext of the Cushite woman he had married; for he had in fact married a Cushite woman.† 2 They complained,† "Is it through Moses alone that the LORD has spoken? Has he not spoken through us also?" And the LORD heard this. 3* Now the man Moses was very humble, more than anyone else on earth. 4 So at once the LORD said to Moses and Aaron and Miriam: Come out, you three, to the tent of meeting. And the three of them went. 5 Then the LORD came down in a column of cloud, and standing at the entrance of the tent, called, "Aaron and Miriam." When both came forward, 6 the LORD said: Now listen to my words:

If there are prophets among you,
in visions I reveal myself to them,
in dreams I speak to them;
7 Not so with my servant Moses!
Throughout my house he is worthy of trust:†*
8 face to face I speak to him,*
plainly and not in riddles.
The likeness of the LORD he beholds.

Why, then, do you not fear to speak against my servant Moses? 9 And so the LORD's wrath flared against them, and he departed.

---

11:25 *They prophesied*: in the sense, not of foretelling the future, but of speaking in enraptured enthusiasm. Such manifestations are mentioned in the early days of Hebrew prophecy (1 Sm 10:10–12; 19:20–21; Jl 3:1) and in the first years of the Church (Acts 2:6–11, 17; 19:6; 1 Cor 12–14).
11:31 The heaps of quail lying upon the ground all around the Israelites' camp suggest the ambiguity of God's response to the people's lament for meat in v. 4 and foreshadow the plague which God will now bring upon Israel (v. 33). Their request had been nothing less than a rejection of what God has done for them (v. 20).
11:32 *Homers*: see note on Is 5:10. *They spread them out*: to cure by drying.
11:34 *Kibroth-hattaavah*: means "graves of greed."

12:1 *Cushite woman*: apparently Zipporah, the Midianite, is meant; cf. Ex 2:21.
12:2 The apparent reason for Miriam's and Aaron's quarrel with their brother Moses was jealousy of his authority; his Cushite wife served only as an occasion for the dispute.
12:7 *Worthy of trust*: the text is open to a variety of interpretations. Thus, the word of Moses may be relied upon by Israel because God speaks to him directly; or, Moses alone is worthy of God's trust in God's household (heavenly or earthly). An alternative translation, however, is: "with all my house he is entrusted."

11:31 Ps 78:26–28.
11:32–33 Ps 78:26–31.
12:3 Sir 45:1–2.
12:7 Heb 3:2, 5.
12:8 Ex 33:1; Dt 34:10; Sir 45:3.

**Miriam's Punishment.** [10] Now the cloud withdrew from the tent, and there was Miriam,* stricken with a scaly infection, white as snow! † When Aaron turned toward Miriam and saw her stricken with snow-white scales, [11] he said to Moses, "Ah, my lord! Please do not charge us with the sin that we have foolishly committed! [12] Do not let her be like the stillborn baby that comes forth from its mother's womb with its flesh half consumed." [13] Then Moses cried to the LORD, "Please, not this! Please, heal her!" [14] But the LORD answered Moses: Suppose her father had spit in her face, would she not bear her shame for seven days? Let her be confined outside the camp for seven days; afterwards she may be brought back. [15] So Miriam was confined outside the camp for seven days, and the people did not start out again until she was brought back.

[16] After that the people set out from Hazeroth and encamped in the wilderness of Paran.

# 13

**The Twelve Scouts.** [1] The LORD said to Moses: [2] Send men to reconnoiter the land of Canaan, which I am giving the Israelites. You shall send one man from each ancestral tribe, every one a leader among them. [3]* So Moses sent them from the wilderness of Paran, at the direction of the LORD. All of them were leaders among the Israelites. [4] These were their names:

from the tribe of Reuben, Shammua, son of Zaccur;
[5] from the tribe of Simeon, Shaphat, son of Hori;
[6] from the tribe of Judah, Caleb, son of Jephunneh;
[7] from the tribe of Issachar, Igal;
[8] for the Josephites, from the tribe of Ephraim, Hoshea, son of Nun;
[9] from the tribe of Benjamin, Palti, son of Raphu;

[10] from the tribe of Zebulun, Gaddiel, son of Sodi;
[11] for the Josephites, from the tribe of Manasseh, Gaddi, son of Susi;
[12] from the tribe of Dan, Ammiel, son of Gemalli;
[13] from the tribe of Asher, Sethur, son of Michael;
[14] from the tribe of Naphtali, Nahbi, son of Vophsi;
[15] from the tribe of Gad, Geuel, son of Machi.

[16] These are the names of the men whom Moses sent to reconnoiter the land. But Hoshea, son of Nun, Moses called Joshua.†

[17] In sending them to reconnoiter the land of Canaan, Moses said to them, "Go up there in the Negeb, up into the highlands, [18] and see what kind of land it is and whether the people living there are strong or weak, few or many. [19] Is the country in which they live good or bad? Are the towns in which they dwell open or fortified? [20] Is the soil fertile or barren, wooded or clear? And do your best to get some of the fruit of the land." It was then the season for early grapes.

[21] So they went up and reconnoitered the land from the wilderness of Zin† as far as where Rehob adjoins Lebo-hamath. [22]* Going up by way of the Negeb, they reached Hebron, where Ahiman, Sheshai and Talmai, descendants of the Anakim,† were. (Now Hebron had been built seven years before Zoan in Egypt.) [23] They also reached the Wadi Eshcol,† where they cut down a branch with a single cluster of grapes on it, which two of them carried on a pole, as well as some pomegranates and figs. [24] It was because of the cluster the Israelites cut there that they called the place Wadi Eshcol.*

**Their Report.** [25] They returned from reconnoitering the land forty days later. [26]* Proceeding

---

† **12:10** *Stricken with a scaly infection, white as snow*: see note on Lv 13:1–14:47. The point of the simile lies either in the flakiness or the whiteness of snow.
**13:16** *Joshua*: in Hebrew, "Jehoshua," which was later modified to "Jeshua," the Hebrew name for "Jesus." Hoshea and Joshua are variants of one original name meaning "the LORD saves." Cf. Lk 1:21.
**13:21** *The wilderness of Zin*: north of Paran and southwest of the Dead Sea. It is quite distinct from "the wilderness of Sin" near the border of Egypt (Ex 16:1; 17:1; Nm 33:11). *Lebo-hamath*: a town near Riblah (Jer 39:5–6) at the southern border of Hamath, an independent kingdom in southern Syria. David's conquests extended as far as Hamath (2 Sm 8:9–11), and Lebo-hamath

thus formed the northern border of the ideal extent of Israel's possessions (Nm 34:7–9; Ez 47:15; 48:1). This may suggest that this verse was inserted precisely to extend the scope of the reconnaissance; cf. Dt 1:24.
**13:22, 28** *Anakim*: an aboriginal race in southern Palestine, largely absorbed by the Canaanites. Either because of their tall stature or because of the massive stone structures left by them, the Israelites regarded them as giants.
**13:23** *Eshcol*: means "cluster."

---

*
**12:10** Dt 24:9.                    **13:24** Nm 32:9; Dt 1:24–25.
**13:3–33** Dt 1:22–28.              **13:26–27** Ex 3:8, 17.
**13:22** Jos 11:21–22.

directly to Moses and Aaron and the whole community of the Israelites in the wilderness of Paran at Kadesh, they made a report to them and to the whole community, showing them the fruit of the land. 27 They told Moses: "We came to the land to which you sent us. It does indeed flow with milk and honey, and here is its fruit. 28 However, the people who are living in the land are powerful, and the towns are fortified and very large.* Besides, we saw descendants of the Anakim there. 29 Amalekites live in the region of the Negeb; Hittites, Jebusites and Amorites dwell in the highlands, and Canaanites along the sea and the banks of the Jordan."

30 Caleb, however, quieted the people before Moses and said, "We ought to go up and seize the land, for we can certainly prevail over it." 31 But the men who had gone up with him said, "We cannot attack these people; they are too strong for us." 32 They spread discouraging reports* among the Israelites about the land they had reconnoitered, saying, "The land that we went through and reconnoitered is a land that consumes its inhabitants. And all the people we saw there are huge. 33 * There we saw the Nephilim† (the Anakim are from the Nephilim); in our own eyes we seemed like mere grasshoppers, and so we must have seemed to them."

**14** **Threats of Revolt.** 1 At this, the whole community broke out with loud cries, and the people wept into the night. 2 * All the Israelites grumbled against Moses and Aaron, the whole community saying to them, "If only we had died in the land of Egypt," or "If only we would die here in the wilderness! 3 Why is the LORD bringing us into this land only to have us fall by the sword? Our wives and little ones will be taken as spoil. Would it not be better for us to return to Egypt?" 4 So they said to one another, "Let us appoint a leader and go back to Egypt."

5 But Moses and Aaron fell prostrate before the whole assembled community of the Israelites; 6 while Joshua, son of Nun, and Caleb, son of Jephunneh, who had been among those that reconnoitered the land, tore their garments 7 and said to the whole community of the Israelites,* "The land which we went through and reconnoitered is an exceedingly good land. 8 If the LORD is pleased with us, he will bring us in to this land and give it to us, a land which flows with milk and honey. 9 * Only do not rebel against the LORD! You need not be afraid of the people of the land, for they are but food for us!† Their protection has left them, but the LORD is with us. Do not fear them."

**The Lord's Sentence.** 10 The whole community threatened to stone them. But the glory of the LORD appeared at the tent of meeting to all the Israelites. 11 And the LORD said to Moses: How long will this people spurn me? How long will they not trust me, despite all the signs I have performed among them?* 12 I will strike them with pestilence and disown them. Then I will make of you a nation greater and mightier than they.*

13 * But Moses said to the LORD: "The Egyptians will hear of this, for by your power you brought out this people from among them. 14 They will tell the inhabitants of this land, who have heard that you, LORD, are in the midst of this people; you, LORD, who directly revealed yourself! Your cloud stands over them, and you go before them by day in a column of cloud and by night in a column of fire.* 15 If now you slay this people all at once, the nations who have heard such reports of you will say, 16 'The LORD was not able to bring this people into the land he swore to give them; that is why he slaughtered them in the wilderness.'* 17 Now then, may my Lord's forbearance be great, even as you have said, 18 * 'The LORD is slow to anger and abounding in kindness, forgiving iniquity and rebellion; yet certainly not declaring the guilty guiltless, but punishing children to the third and fourth generation for their parents' iniquity.' 19 Pardon, then, the iniquity of this people in keeping with your great kindness, even as you have forgiven them from Egypt until now."*

---

13:33 Nephilim: i.e., "fallen ones" (in the Septuagint, "giants"), a reference to fallen heroes of old. Cf. Gn 6:4.
14:9 They are but food for us: lit., "for they are our bread." "Bread" (Heb. lechem) is here used in the sense of "prey, spoils" to be consumed by an invader. This is the answer to the pessimistic report that this land "consumes its inhabitants" (13:32).

13:28–29 Dt 9:1–2.
13:32 Nm 32:9; Jos 14:8.
13:33 Dt 2:10.
14:2 Ex 16:3; Ps 106:25.
14:7–8 Dt 1:25.
14:9 Dt 7:18.
14:11 Ps 78:22, 32.
14:12 Ex 32:10.
14:13–16 Ex 32:12; Dt 9:26–29; Ps 106:23.
14:14 Ex 13:21; Jos 2:9–10.
14:16 Ex 32:12; Dt 9:28.
14:18 Ex 20:5; 34:6–7; Ps 103:8; 145:8.
14:19 Ps 78:38.

20 The LORD answered: I pardon them as you have asked. 21 Yet, by my life and the LORD's glory that fills the whole earth, 22 of all the people who have seen my glory and the signs I did in Egypt and in the wilderness,* and who nevertheless have put me to the test ten times already and have not obeyed me, 23 not one shall see the land which I promised on oath to their ancestors. None of those who have spurned me shall see it. 24 But as for my servant Caleb, because he has a different spirit and follows me unreservedly,* I will bring him into the land which he entered, and his descendants shall possess it. 25 But now, since the Amalekites and Canaanites are living in the valleys,† turn away tomorrow and set out into the wilderness by way of the Red Sea road.

26 The LORD also said to Moses and Aaron: 27 How long will this wicked community grumble against me?* I have heard the grumblings of the Israelites against me. 28 Tell them:† "By my life"—oracle of the LORD—"I will do to you just what I have heard you say. 29 Here in the wilderness* your dead bodies shall fall. Of all your men of twenty years or more, enrolled in your registration, who grumbled against me, 30 not one of you shall enter the land where I solemnly swore to settle you, except Caleb, son of Jephunneh, and Joshua, son of Nun. 31 Your little ones, however, who you said would be taken as spoil, I will bring in, and they shall know the land you rejected.* 32 But as for you, your bodies shall fall here in the wilderness, 33 while your children will wander for forty years, suffering for your infidelity, till the last of you lies dead in the wilderness.* 34 Corresponding to the number of days you spent reconnoitering the land—forty days—you shall bear your punishment one year for each day: forty years. Thus you will realize what it means to oppose me. 35 I, the LORD, have spoken; and I will surely do this to this entire wicked community that conspired against me: here in the wilderness they shall come to their end and there they will die."

36 And the men whom Moses had sent to reconnoiter the land* and who on returning had set the whole community grumbling against him by spreading discouraging reports about the land— 37 these men who had spread discouraging reports about the land were struck down by the LORD and died. 38 Only Joshua, son of Nun, and Caleb, son of Jephunneh, survived of all the men who had gone to reconnoiter the land.*

**Unsuccessful Invasion.** 39 When Moses repeated these words to all the Israelites, the people mourned greatly. 40 Early the next morning they started up high into the hill country, saying, "Here we are, ready to go up to the place that the LORD spoke of:* for we did wrong." 41 But Moses said, "Why are you now transgressing the LORD's order? This cannot succeed. 42 Do not go up, because the LORD is not in your midst; do not allow yourself to be struck down by your enemies.* 43 For there the Amalekites and Canaanites will face you, and you will fall by the sword. You have turned back from following the LORD; therefore the LORD will not be with you."

44 Yet they dared to go up high into the hill country,* even though neither the ark of the covenant of the LORD nor Moses left the camp. 45 And the Amalekites and Canaanites who dwelt in that hill country came down and defeated them, beating them back as far as Hormah.†

**15** **Secondary Offerings.** 1 The LORD spoke to Moses: 2† Speak to the Israelites and say to them: When you enter the land that I am giving you for your settlements, 3 if you make to the LORD an oblation from the herd or from the flock—either a burnt offering or a sacrifice, to fulfill a vow, or as a voluntary offering, or for one of your festivals—to produce

---

† **14:25** *The valleys:* the low-lying plains in the Negeb and along the seacoast and in the Jordan depression, as well as the higher valleys in the mountains farther north: cf. v. 45.

**14:28–29** God punished the grumblers by giving them their wish; cf. v. 2. Their lack of trust in God is cited in 1 Cor 10:10 and Heb 3:12–18 as a warning for Christians.

**14:45** *Hormah:* one of the Canaanite royal cities in southern Judah, according to the tradition attested in Jos 12:14, although Nm 21:1–3 gives it as the new name for the city of Arad when it was destroyed by Israel. According to the list of conquered cities preserved in Jgs 1, the earlier name for the city of Hormah was Zephath. The precise location is unknown.

**15:2–16** These laws on sacrifice are complementary to those of Lv 1–3. Since the food of the Israelites consisted not only of meat but also of bread, oil and wine, they offered flour, wine and oil in sacrifice to the Lord besides the animal oblations.

---

* 
14:22–23 Dt 1:35.
14:24 Jos 14:8–9.
14:27 Ex 16:7, 12.
14:29 Dt 1:35; Heb 3:17.
14:31 Dt 1:39.
14:33–34 Nm 13:26; 32:13; Ps 95:10; Ez 4:6.
14:36–37 Nm 13:17, 32–33; 1 Cor 10:10.
14:38 Nm 26:65.
14:40 Nm 13:18; Dt 1:41.
14:42 Dt 1:42.
14:44 Dt 1:43.

a pleasing aroma for the LORD, [4] the one presenting the offering shall also present to the LORD a grain offering, a tenth of a measure[†] of bran flour mixed with a fourth of a hin of oil, [5] as well as wine for a libation, a fourth of a hin. You will do this with the burnt offering or the sacrifice, for each lamb. [6] Alternatively for a ram you shall make a grain offering of two tenths of a measure of bran flour mixed with a third of a hin of oil, [7] and for a libation, a third of a hin of wine, thereby presenting a pleasing aroma to the LORD. [8] If you make an offering from the herd—either a burnt offering, or a sacrifice, to fulfill a vow, or as a communion offering to the LORD, [9] with it a grain offering of three tenths of a measure of bran flour mixed with half a hin of oil will be presented; [10] and you will present for a libation, half a hin of wine—a sweet-smelling oblation to the LORD. [11] The same is to be done for each ox, ram, lamb or goat. [12] Whatever the number you offer, do the same for each of them.

[13] All the native-born shall make these offerings in this way, whenever they present a sweet-smelling oblation to the LORD. [14] Likewise, in any future generation, any alien residing with you or anyone else in your midst, who presents an oblation of pleasing aroma to the LORD, must do as you do. [15] There is but one statute for you and for the resident alien, a perpetual statute throughout your generations. You and the resident alien will be alike before the LORD; [16] you and the alien residing with you will have the same rule and the same application of it.

[17] The LORD spoke to Moses: [18] Speak to the Israelites and say to them: When you enter the land into which I am bringing you [19] and eat of the bread of the land, you shall offer the LORD a contribution. [20] A round loaf from your first batch of dough[†] you shall offer as a contribution. Just like a contribution from the threshing floor you shall offer it.[*] [21] Throughout your generations you shall give a contribution to the LORD from your first batch of dough.

**Purification Offerings.**[†] [22] If through inadvertence you fail to do any of these commandments which the LORD has given to Moses—[*] [23] anything the LORD commanded you through Moses from the time the LORD first gave the command down through your generations— [24] if it was done inadvertently without the community's knowledge, the whole community shall sacrifice one bull from the herd as a burnt offering of pleasing aroma to the LORD, along with its prescribed grain offering and libation, as well as one he-goat as a purification offering. [25] [*] Then the priest shall make atonement for the whole Israelite community; and they will be forgiven, since it was inadvertence, and for their inadvertence they have brought their offering: an oblation to the LORD as well as their purification offering before the LORD. [26] Not only the whole Israelite community but also the aliens residing among you shall be forgiven, since the inadvertent fault affects all the people.

[27] If it is an individual who sins inadvertently,[*] this person shall bring a yearling she-goat as a purification offering. [28] And the priest shall make atonement before the LORD for the one who erred, since the sin was inadvertent, making atonement for the person to secure forgiveness. [29] You shall have but one rule for the person who sins inadvertently, whether a native-born Israelite or an alien residing among you.

[30] But anyone who acts defiantly,[*] whether a native or an alien, reviles the LORD, and shall be cut off from among the people. [31] [*] For having despised the word of the LORD and broken his commandment, he must be cut off entirely and bear the punishment.

**The Sabbath-breaker.** [32] While the Israelites were in the wilderness, a man was discovered gathering wood on the sabbath day. [33] Those who caught him at it brought him to Moses and Aaron and the whole community. [34] But they put him in custody, for there was no clear decision[†] as to what should be done with

---

† **15:4** *Measure*: the word, supplied from the context, does not appear in the Hebrew (as also in vv. 6, 9; 28:9, 12, 20, 28; 29:3, 9, 14). Probably the ephah (which is named in 5:15; 28:5) is intended. *Hin*: see note on Ez 45:24.

**15:20** *Dough*: the meaning of the Hebrew term is uncertain; some render, "baking utensils." This word is used elsewhere only in Ez 44:30 and Neh 10:33; a related Hebrew word is used in Lv 2:14.

**15:22–31** See note on Lv 4:2. Although Lv 4–5 and Nm 15:22–31 both concern inadvertent sins, the emphasis here, as

opposed to Lv 4–5, is on the failure of the community to perform "positive commands" rather than on doing what is prohibited.

**15:34** *No clear decision*: either it was not clear that gathering wood constituted "work" and as such a willful violation of the sabbath and a capital offense; or they did not yet know how the death penalty was to be inflicted.

**15:19–20** Ez 44:30.          **15:27–28** Lv 4:27–28.
**15:22–23** Lv 4:13–14.        **15:30** Dt 17:12.
**15:25** Lv 4:20.              **15:31** Prv 13:13.

him.* <sup>35</sup> Then the LORD said to Moses: This man shall be put to death; let the whole community stone him outside the camp. <sup>36</sup> So the whole community led him outside the camp and stoned him to death, as the LORD had commanded Moses.

**Tassels on the Cloak.** <sup>37</sup> The LORD said to Moses: <sup>38</sup> Speak to the Israelites and tell them that throughout their generations they are to make tassels† for the corners of their garments, fastening a violet cord to each corner.* <sup>39</sup> When you use these tassels, the sight of the cord will remind you of all the commandments of the LORD and you will do them, without prostituting yourself going after the desires of your hearts and your eyes. <sup>40</sup> Thus you will remember to do all my commandments and you will be holy to your God. <sup>41</sup> I, the LORD, am your God who brought you out of the land of Egypt to be your God: I, the LORD your God.*

**16** **Rebellion of Korah.** <sup>1</sup>† Korah, son of Izhar, son of Kohath, son of Levi, and the Reubenites Dathan and Abiram, sons of Eliab, and On, son of Peleth,† son of Reuben took <sup>2</sup> two hundred and fifty Israelites who were leaders in the community, members of the council and men of note, and confronted Moses. <sup>3</sup> Holding an assembly against Moses and Aaron, they said,* "You go too far! The whole community, all of them, are holy; the LORD is in their midst. Why then should you set yourselves over the LORD's assembly?"

<sup>4</sup> When Moses heard this, he fell prostrate. <sup>5</sup> Then he said to Korah and to all his faction, "May the LORD make known tomorrow morning who belongs to him and who is the holy one and whom he will have draw near to him! The one whom he chooses, he will have draw near to him. <sup>6</sup> Do this: take your censers, Korah

and all his faction, <sup>7</sup> and put fire in them and place incense in them before the LORD tomorrow. He whom the LORD then chooses is the holy one. You Levites go too far!"

<sup>8</sup> Moses also said to Korah, "Hear, now, you Levites! <sup>9</sup>* Are you not satisfied that the God of Israel has singled you out from the community of Israel, to have you draw near him to maintain the LORD's tabernacle, and to attend upon the community and to serve them? <sup>10</sup> He has allowed you and your Levite kinsmen with you to approach him, and yet you seek the priesthood too. <sup>11</sup> It is therefore against the LORD that you and all your faction are conspiring. As for Aaron, what has he done that you should grumble against him?"

**Rebellion of Dathan and Abiram.** <sup>12</sup> Moses summoned Dathan and Abiram, sons of Eliab, but they answered, "We will not go.† <sup>13</sup> Are you not satisfied that you have brought us here from a land flowing with milk and honey to have us perish in the wilderness, that now you must also lord it over us? <sup>14</sup> Far from bringing us to a land flowing with milk and honey, or giving us fields and vineyards for our inheritance, will you gouge out our eyes?† No, we will not go."

<sup>15</sup> Then Moses became very angry and said to the LORD, "Pay no attention to their offering. I have never taken a single donkey from them, nor have I wronged any one of them."*

**Korah.** <sup>16</sup> Moses said to Korah, "You and all your faction shall appear before the LORD tomorrow—you and they and Aaron too. <sup>17</sup> Then each of you take his own censer, put incense in it, and present it before the LORD, two hundred and fifty censers; and you and Aaron, each with his own censer, do the same." <sup>18</sup> So each of them took their censers, and laying

---

<sup>†</sup> **15:38** *Tassels:* at the time of Jesus these tassels were worn by all pious Jews, including Jesus (Mt 9:20–21; Mk 6:56); some Pharisees wore very large ones in a display of their zeal for the law (Mt 23:5).

**16:1–3** The evidence seems to show that accounts of two, if not more, distinct rebellions have been combined in this chapter. The most obvious are the rebellions of Korah and his faction (Nm 27:3) and of Dathan and Abiram (Dt 11:6); cf. Ps 106. The present account combines both events into one narrative; but even here it is rather easy to separate the two. The rebellion of the Reubenites, Dathan and Abiram, was more political in character, against Moses alone as the civil leader (cf. v. 13); these rebels were punished by being swallowed alive in an earthquake. The rebellion of Korah was more religious in character, directed primarily against the religious leadership of Aaron (though in vv. 19–22 it is Korah and the whole community against both Moses

and Aaron). About two hundred and fifty malcontents joined Korah's faction, and they are punished by fire. The parts of the present section which refer to the rebellion of Dathan and Abiram are vv. 12–15 and vv. 25–34 of chap. 16; the rest of chap. 16 and all of chap. 17 chiefly concern the rebellion of Korah.

**16:1** *The Reubenites…son of Peleth:* some suggest on the basis of 26:5, 8 and Gn 46:9 reading instead of the traditional Hebrew text: "son of Levi, and Dathan and Abiram, sons of Eliab, son of Pallu, son of Reuben."

**16:12** *We will not go:* to appear before Moses' "tribunal."

**16:14** *Gouge out our eyes:* blind us to the real state of affairs.

---

15:34 Lv 24:12.
15:38 Dt 22:12.
15:41 Lv 22:32–33.

16:3 Ps 106:16–18; Sir 45:19.
16:9 Dt 10:8.
16:15 1 Sm 12:3.

incense on the fire they had put in them, they took their stand by the entrance of the tent of meeting along with Moses and Aaron. ¹⁹ Then, when Korah had assembled all the community against them at the entrance of the tent of meeting, the glory of the LORD appeared to the entire community, ²⁰ and the LORD said to Moses and Aaron: ²¹ Stand apart from this community, that I may consume them at once. ²² But they fell prostrate and exclaimed, "O God, God of the spirits of all living creatures, if one man sins will you be angry with the whole community?" ²³ The LORD answered Moses: ²⁴ Speak to the community and tell them: Withdraw from the area around the tent† of Korah, Dathan and Abiram.

**Punishment of Dathan and Abiram.** ²⁵ Moses, followed by the elders of Israel, arose and went to Dathan and Abiram.† ²⁶ Then he spoke to the community, "Move away from the tents of these wicked men and do not touch anything that is theirs; otherwise you too will be swept away because of all their sins." ²⁷ So they withdrew from the area around the tents of Korah, Dathan and Abiram. When Dathan and Abiram had come out and were standing at the entrance of their tents with their wives, their children, and their little ones, ²⁸ Moses said, "This is how you shall know that the LORD sent me to do all I have done, and that it was not of my own devising: ²⁹ if these die an ordinary death, merely suffering the fate common to all humanity, the LORD has not sent me. ³⁰ But if the LORD makes a chasm, and the ground opens its mouth and swallows them with all belonging to them, and they go down alive to Sheol,† then you will know that these men have spurned the LORD." ³¹* No sooner had he finished saying all this than the ground beneath them split open, ³² and the earth opened its mouth and swallowed them and their families and all of Korah's people† with all their possessions. ³³ They went down alive to Sheol with all belonging to them; the earth

closed over them, and they disappeared from the assembly. ³⁴ But all the Israelites near them fled at their shrieks, saying, "The earth might swallow us too!"

**Punishment of Korah.** ³⁵ And fire from the LORD came forth which consumed the two hundred and fifty men who were offering the incense.

**17** ¹ The LORD said to Moses: ² Tell Eleazar, son of Aaron the priest, to remove the censers from the embers; and scatter the fire some distance away, for they have become holy— ³† the censers of those who sinned at the cost of their lives. Have them hammered into plates to cover the altar, because in being presented before the LORD they have become holy. In this way they shall serve as a sign to the Israelites. ⁴ So taking the bronze censers which had been presented by those who were burned, Eleazar the priest had them hammered into a covering for the altar, ⁵ just as the LORD had directed him through Moses. This was to be a reminder to the Israelites that no unauthorized person, no one who was not a descendant of Aaron, should draw near to offer incense before the LORD, lest he meet the fate of Korah and his faction.

⁶ The next day the whole Israelite community grumbled against Moses and Aaron, saying, "You have killed the people of the LORD." ⁷ But while the community was assembling against them, Moses and Aaron turned toward the tent of meeting, and the cloud now covered it and the glory of the LORD appeared. ⁸ Then Moses and Aaron came to the front of the tent of meeting, ⁹ and the LORD said to Moses: ¹⁰ Remove yourselves from this community, that I may consume them at once. But they fell prostrate.

¹¹ Then Moses said to Aaron, "Take your censer, put fire from the altar in it, lay incense on it, and bring it quickly to the community to make atonement for them; for wrath has

---

**16:24** *Withdraw from the area around the tent:* the word for "tent," *mishkan,* here and in v. 27, is otherwise used in the singular only for the tent of meeting, suggesting possibly the erection of a rival sanctuary by the rebels. Note further, as an indication of the fact that various accounts of rebellion have been fused here, that in v. 19 the entire community had been assembled by Korah at the tent of meeting.

**16:25** Since Dathan and Abiram had refused to go to Moses (vv. 12–14), he, with the elders as witnesses, was obliged to go to their tents.

**16:30** *Sheol:* see note on Ps 6:6.

**16:32** *And all of Korah's people:* the implication of this secondary addition to the text is, on the one hand, that Korah met his death elsewhere, presumably with the two hundred and fifty offering incense (vv. 16–17, 35); or, on the other hand, he died along with Dathan and Abiram in the splitting of the earth.

**17:3** Whatever was brought into intimate contact with something holy shared in its holiness. See note on 19:20.

**16:31–34** Nm 26:10; Lv 10:2;        Ps 106:17–18.
Dt 11:6;

come forth from the LORD and the plague has begun."* ¹²Aaron took his censer just as Moses directed and ran in among the assembly, where the plague had already begun among the people. Then he offered the incense and made atonement for the people, ¹³while standing there between the living and the dead. And so the scourge was checked. ¹⁴There were fourteen thousand seven hundred dead from the scourge, in addition to those who died because of Korah. ¹⁵When the scourge had been checked, Aaron returned to Moses at the entrance of the tent of meeting.

**Aaron's Staff.** ¹⁶The LORD now said to Moses: ¹⁷Speak to the Israelites and get from them a staff† for each ancestral house, twelve staffs in all, from all the leaders of their ancestral houses. Write each man's name on his staff; ¹⁸and write Aaron's name on Levi's staff.† For each head of an ancestral house shall have a staff. ¹⁹Then deposit them in the tent of meeting, in front of the covenant, where I meet you. ²⁰The staff of the man whom I choose shall sprout. Thus I will rid myself of the Israelites' grumbling against you.

²¹So Moses spoke to the Israelites, and all their leaders gave him staffs, twelve in all, one from each leader of their ancestral houses; and Aaron's staff was among them. ²²Then Moses deposited the staffs before the LORD in the tent of the covenant. ²³The next day, when Moses entered the tent of the covenant, Aaron's staff, representing the house of Levi, had sprouted. It had put forth sprouts, produced blossoms, and borne ripe almonds! ²⁴So Moses brought out all the staffs from the LORD's presence to all the Israelites, and each one identified his own staff and took it. ²⁵Then the LORD said to Moses: Put back Aaron's staff in front of the covenant, for safe keeping as a sign to the rebellious, so

that their grumbling against me may cease and they might not die. ²⁶Moses did this. Just as the LORD had commanded him, so he did.

**Charge of the Sacred Things.** ²⁷† Then the Israelites exclaimed to Moses, "We will perish; we are lost, we are all lost! ²⁸Anyone who approaches the tabernacle of the LORD will die! Will there be no end to our perishing?"

**18** ¹The LORD said to Aaron:† You and your sons as well as your ancestral house with you† shall be responsible for any sin with respect to the sanctuary; but only you and your sons with you shall be responsible for any sin with respect to your priesthood. ²You shall also present with you your kinsmen of the tribe of Levi, your ancestral tribe, that they may be joined to you† and assist you, while you and your sons with you are in front of the tent of the covenant. ³They shall discharge your obligations and those with respect to the whole tent; however, they shall not come near the utensils of the sanctuary or the altar, or else both they and you will die. ⁴They will be joined to you to perform the duties associated with the tent of meeting, all the labor pertaining to the tent. But no unauthorized person† shall come near you. ⁵You shall perform the duties of the sanctuary and of the altar, that wrath may not fall again upon the Israelites.

⁶I hereby take your kinsmen, the Levites, from among the Israelites; they are a gift to you,* dedicated to the LORD for the labor they perform for the tent of meeting. ⁷* But you and your sons with you must take care to exercise your priesthood in whatever concerns the altar and the area within the veil.† I give you your priesthood as a gift. Any unauthorized person who comes near shall be put to death.

---

† **17:17** The staff was not merely an article of practical use, but also a symbol of authority; cf. Gn 49:10; Nm 24:17; Jer 48:17. Therefore, the staff of a leader of a tribe was considered the emblem of the tribe; in fact, certain Hebrew words such as *matteh*, the word for "staff" here, also mean "tribe." Perhaps for this reason, to avoid confusion, the author here uses the term *bet'ab*, "ancestral house," for "tribe" instead of one of the ordinary words for "tribe."

**17:18** *Levi's staff*: it is not clear whether this is considered as one of the twelve mentioned in the preceding verse, or as a thirteenth staff. Sometimes Levi is reckoned as one of the twelve tribes (e.g., Dt 27:12–13), but more often the number twelve is arrived at by counting the two sub-tribes of Joseph, i.e., Ephraim and Manasseh, as distinct tribes. In this passage also it seems probable that the tribe of Levi is considered apart from the other twelve tribes.

**17:27–28** The people's distress here echoes their panic in 16:34, and may be heightened further by the death of the two hundred and fifty leaders offering incense in 16:35.

**18:1–3** This law, which kept unqualified persons from contact with holy things, is in response to the Israelites' cry in 17:28. It is followed by other laws concerning priests and Levites.

**18:1** *With you*: not only in the present but also those of his house in the future.

**18:2** *Be joined to you*: in Hebrew a pun on the popular etymology of the name "Levi." Cf. Gn 29:34.

**18:4** *Unauthorized person*: here, "one who is not a Levite"; in v. 7, "one who is not a priest."

**18:7** *Veil*: the outer veil, or "curtain," is probably meant.

---

**17:11** Wis 18:20–21.          **18:7** Nm 3:10.
**18:6** Nm 3:9; 8:19.

**The Priests' Share of the Sacrifices.** ⁸ The Lord said to Aaron:† I hereby give to you charge of the contributions made to me, including the various holy offerings of the Israelites;* I assign them to you and to your sons as a perquisite, a perpetual due. ⁹ This is what you shall have from the oblations that are most holy: every offering of theirs—namely, all their grain offerings, purification offerings, and reparation offerings which they must return to me—shall be most holy for you and for your sons. ¹⁰ You shall eat them in a most holy place;† every male may partake of them. As holy, they belong to you.

¹¹ This also you shall have: the contributions that are their gifts, including the elevated offering† of the Israelites; I assign them to you and to your sons and daughters with you as a perpetual due.* All in your household who are clean may eat them. ¹² I also assign to you all the best* of the new oil and of the new wine and grain that they give to the Lord as their first produce that has been processed. ¹³ The first-ripened fruits of whatever is in their land, which they bring to the Lord, shall be yours; all of your household who are clean may eat them. ¹⁴ Whatever is under the ban† in Israel shall be yours. ¹⁵ Every living thing that opens the womb, human being and beast alike, such as are to be offered to the Lord, shall be yours;* but you must redeem the firstborn of human beings, as well as redeem the firstborn of unclean animals. ¹⁶ For the redemption price of a son, when he is a month old, you shall pay the equivalent of five silver shekels according to the sanctuary shekel, that is, twenty gerahs. ¹⁷ But the firstborn of cattle, or the firstborn of sheep or the firstborn of goats you shall not redeem; they are holy. Their blood you must splash on the altar and their fat you must burn as an oblation of pleasing aroma to the Lord. ¹⁸* Their meat, however, shall be yours, just as the brisket of the elevated offering and the right thigh belong to you. ¹⁹ As a perpetual due I assign to you and to your sons and daughters with you all the contributions of holy things which the Israelites set aside for the Lord; this is a covenant of salt† to last forever before the Lord, for you and for your descendants with you. ²⁰* Then the Lord said to Aaron:† You shall not have any heritage in their land nor hold any portion among them; I will be your portion and your heritage among the Israelites.

**Tithes Due the Levites.** ²¹ To the Levites, however, I hereby assign all tithes in Israel as their heritage in recompense for the labor they perform, the labor pertaining to the tent of meeting.* ²² The Israelites may no longer approach the tent of meeting, thereby incurring the penalty of death. ²³ Only the Levites are to perform the labor pertaining to the tent of meeting, and they shall incur the penalty for the Israelites' sin;† this is a permanent statute for all your generations. But they shall not have any heritage among the Israelites, ²⁴ for I have assigned to the Levites as their heritage the tithes which the Israelites put aside as a contribution to the Lord. That is why I have said, they will not have any heritage among the Israelites.

**Tithes Paid by the Levites.** ²⁵ The Lord said to Moses: ²⁶ Speak to the Levites and say to them: When you take from the Israelites the tithes I have assigned you from them as your heritage, you are to make a contribution from them to the Lord, a tithe of the tithe; ²⁷ and your contribution will be credited to you as if

---

† **18:8–10** Two classes of offerings are here distinguished: the most holy offering, of which only the male members of the priestly families could eat (vv. 8–10), and the other offerings, which the women of the priestly families could eat (vv. 11–19).
**18:10** *In a most holy place:* in the court of the tabernacle, according to Lv 6:9, 19.
**18:11** *Elevated offering:* this included the brisket and right thigh (v. 18), the shoulder of the peace offering (Lv 7:30–34), and portions of the nazirite sacrifice (Nm 6:19–20). *With you:* see note on v. 1. Aaron had no daughters; see also v. 19.
**18:14** *Under the ban:* in Hebrew, *herem*, which means here "set aside from profane use and made sacred to the Lord." Cf. Lv 27:21, 28.
**18:19** *A covenant of salt:* cf. 2 Chr 13:5. The reference may perhaps be to the preservative power of salt (cf. Mt 5:13); but more likely the phrase refers to the custom of eating salt together to render a contract unbreakable. See note on Lv 2:13.

**18:20** The priests and Levites were forbidden to own hereditary land such as the other Israelites possessed; therefore in the allotment of the land (chap. 34) they did not receive any portion of it. Certain cities, however, were assigned to them for their residence; cf. 35:1–8.
**18:23** *Incur the penalty for the Israelites' sin:* the Levites are responsible for protecting the sanctuary from illegitimate encroachment and in this sense pay the penalty for the Israelites' iniquity. This responds further to the fears of the people expressed in 17:27–28.

---

**18:8** Nm 5:9.
**18:11** Ex 29:27–28; Lv 7:34; 10:14.
**18:12–13** Dt 18:4; 26:2.
**18:15** Ex 13:2.
**18:18** Lv 7:31–34.
**18:20** Dt 10:9; 18:1–2; Jos 13:33; Ez 44:28.
**18:21** Heb 7:5.

it were grain from the threshing floor or new wine from the vat. ²⁸ Thus you too shall make a contribution to the Lord from all the tithes you take from the Israelites, handing over to Aaron the priest the contribution to the Lord. ²⁹ From all the gifts to you, you shall make every contribution due to the Lord—from their best parts, that is the part to be consecrated from them.

³⁰ Say to them also: Once you have made your contribution from the best part, the rest of the tithe will be credited to the Levites as if it were produce of the threshing floor or the produce of the vat. ³¹ You and your households may eat it anywhere, since it is your recompense in exchange for labor in the tent of meeting. ³² You will incur no punishment when you contribute the best part of it. But do not profane the holy offerings of the Israelites or else you shall die.

# 19 Ashes of the Red Heifer. ¹ The Lord spoke to Moses and Aaron: ² This is the statute for the ritual which the Lord has commanded. Tell the Israelites to procure for you a red heifer without defect and free from every blemish and on which no yoke has ever been laid. ³ You will give it to Eleazar the priest, and it will be led outside the camp† and slaughtered in his presence. ⁴ Eleazar the priest will take some of its blood on his finger and sprinkle it seven times toward the front of the tent of meeting.† ⁵ Then the heifer will be burned in his sight; it will be burned with its hide and flesh, its blood and dung; ⁶ and the priest will take cedar wood, hyssop and scarlet yarn and throw them into the fire in which the heifer is being burned. ⁷ The priest shall then wash his garments and bathe his body in water, afterward he may enter the camp. The priest remains unclean until the evening. ⁸ Likewise, the one who burned the heifer shall wash his garments in water, bathe his body in water, and be unclean until evening. ⁹ Then somebody who is clean shall gather up the ashes of the heifer and deposit them in a clean place outside the camp. There they are to be kept

to prepare purification water for the Israelite community. This is a purification offering. ¹⁰ The one who has gathered up the ashes of the heifer shall also wash his garments and be unclean until evening. This is a permanent statute, both for the Israelites and for the alien residing among them.

**Use of the Ashes.** ¹¹ Those who touch the corpse of any human being will be unclean for seven days; ¹² they shall purify themselves with the water on the third and on the seventh day, and then be clean. But if they fail to purify themselves on the third and on the seventh day, they will not become clean. ¹³* Those who touch the corpse of a human being who dies and who fail to purify themselves defile the tabernacle of the Lord and these persons shall be cut off from Israel. Since the purification water has not been splashed over them, they remain unclean: their uncleanness is still on them.

¹⁴ This is the ritual: When someone dies in a tent, everyone who enters the tent, as well as everyone already in it, will be unclean for seven days; ¹⁵ and every open vessel with its lid unfastened will be unclean. ¹⁶ Moreover, everyone who in the open country touches a person who has been slain by the sword or who has died naturally, or who touches a human bone or a grave, will be unclean for seven days. ¹⁷ For anyone who is thus unclean, ashes shall be taken from the burnt purification offering, and spring water will be poured on them from a vessel.* ¹⁸ Then someone who is clean will take hyssop, dip it in this water, and sprinkle it on the tent and on all the vessels and persons that were in it, or on the one who touched the bone, the slain person or the other corpse, or the grave. ¹⁹ The clean will sprinkle the unclean on the third and on the seventh day, and thus purify them on the seventh day. Then they will wash their garments and bathe in water, and in the evening be clean. ²⁰† Those who become unclean and fail to purify themselves—those people will be cut off from the assembly, because they defile the sanctuary of the Lord.

---

† **19:3** *Outside the camp:* several early Christian writers saw in this a prefiguring of the sacrificial death of Jesus outside the walls of Jerusalem; cf. Jn 19:20; Heb 13:12; in the purifying water, into which the ashes of the red heifer were put, they saw a type of the water of Baptism.
**19:4** *Toward the front of the tent of meeting:* since the tabernacle faced the east (Ex 26:15–30), the killing of the heifer would

take place east of the camp; in later times it was done on the Mount of Olives, east of the Temple.
**19:20** Ritual uncleanness is, as it were, contagious; so also sacredness; see note on 17:3.

**19:13** Lv 15:31.        **19:17–19** Heb 9:13–14.

"The Israelites, the whole community, arrived in the wilderness of Zin in the first month, and the people stayed at Kadesh. It was here that Miriam died, and here that she was buried" (Nm 20:1). Above, the desert of Zin, a barren area southwest of the Dead Sea.

The purification water has not been splashed over them; they remain unclean. ²¹ This will be a permanent statute for you.

Those who sprinkle the purification water will wash their garments, and those who come in contact with the purification water will be unclean until evening. ²² Moreover, anything that the unclean person touches becomes unclean itself, and the one who touches such a person becomes unclean until evening.

# 20 †Death of Miriam. ¹ The Israelites, the whole community, arrived in the wilderness of Zin† in the first month, and the people stayed at Kadesh. It was here that Miriam died, and here that she was buried.

**Need for Water at Kadesh.** ² Since the community had no water, they held an assembly against Moses and Aaron. ³ The people quarreled with Moses, exclaiming, "Would that we had perished when our kindred perished before the LORD! ⁴ Why have you brought the

LORD's assembly into this wilderness for us and our livestock to die here? ⁵ Why have you brought us up out of Egypt, only to bring us to this wretched place? It is not a place for grain nor figs nor vines nor pomegranates! And there is no water to drink!" ⁶ But Moses and Aaron went away from the assembly to the entrance of the tent of meeting, where they fell prostrate.

**Sin of Moses and Aaron.** Then the glory of the LORD appeared to them, ⁷ and the LORD said to Moses: ⁸ Take the staff and assemble the community, you and Aaron your brother, and in their presence command the rock to yield its waters. Thereby you will bring forth water from the rock for them, and supply the community and their livestock with water. ⁹ So Moses took the staff from its place before the LORD, as he was ordered. ¹⁰ Then Moses and Aaron gathered the assembly in front of the rock, where he said to them,* "Just listen, you rebels! Are we to produce water for you out of

---

† **20:1–29** In this chapter the deaths of the three wilderness leaders are either intimated or explicitly reported: Miriam, v. 1; Moses, v. 12; Aaron, vv. 12, 22–29.

**20:1** *The wilderness of Zin*: a barren region with a few good oases, southwest of the Dead Sea. See note on 13:21. *The first month*: we would expect the mention also of the day and of the year (after the exodus) when this took place; cf. similar dates in 1:1; 10:11; 33:38; Dt 1:3. Here the full date is left unspecified.

According to one chronology, the Israelites arrived in Kadesh in the third year after the exodus (cf. Dt 1:46). But the itinerary in chap. 33 would suggest the fortieth year, the year in which Aaron died (33:38).

**20:10** Ex 17:5–6.

this rock?" 11* Then, raising his hand, Moses struck the rock twice† with his staff, and water came out in abundance, and the community and their livestock drank. 12† But the LORD said to Moses and Aaron: Because you did not have confidence in me, to acknowledge my holiness before the Israelites, therefore you shall not lead this assembly into the land I have given them.

13 These are the waters of Meribah,* where the Israelites quarreled with the LORD, and through which he displayed his holiness.

**Edom's Refusal.** 14 From Kadesh Moses sent messengers to the king of Edom: "Thus says your brother Israel:† You know of all the hardships that have befallen us, 15 how our ancestors went down to Egypt, and we stayed in Egypt a long time, and the Egyptians treated us and our ancestors harshly. 16 When we cried to the LORD,* he heard our cry and sent an angel who led us out of Egypt. Now here we are at Kadesh, a town at the edge of your territory. 17 Please let us pass through your land. We will not cross any fields or vineyards, nor drink any well water, but we will go straight along the King's Highway† without turning to the right or to the left, until we have passed through your territory."

18 But Edom answered him, "You shall not pass through here; if you do, I will advance against you with the sword." 19 The Israelites said to him, "We will go up along the highway. If we or our livestock drink any of your water, we will pay for it. It is nothing—just let us pass through on foot." 20 But Edom replied, "You shall not pass through,"* and advanced against them with a large and heavily armed force. 21 Therefore, since Edom refused to let Israel pass through their territory, Israel turned away from them.

**Death of Aaron.** 22* Setting out from Kadesh, the Israelites, the whole community, came to Mount Hor.† 23 There at Mount Hor, on the border of the land of Edom, the LORD said to Moses and Aaron: 24 Let Aaron be gathered to his people, for he shall not enter the land I have given to the Israelites, because you both rebelled against my directions at the waters of Meribah. 25 Take Aaron and Eleazar his son and bring them up on Mount Hor.* 26 Then strip Aaron of his garments and put them on Eleazar, his son; but there Aaron shall be gathered up in death.

27 Moses did as the LORD commanded. When they had climbed Mount Hor in view of the whole community, 28 Moses stripped Aaron of his garments and put them on Eleazar his son. Then Aaron died there on top of the mountain.* When Moses and Eleazar came down from the mountain, 29 all the community understood that Aaron had breathed his last; and for thirty days the whole house of Israel mourned Aaron.

**21 Victory over Arad.** 1 When the Canaanite, the king of Arad,† who ruled over the Negeb,* heard that the Israelites were coming along the way of Atharim, he engaged Israel in battle and took some of them captive. 2 Israel then made this vow to the LORD: "If you deliver this people into my hand, I will put their cities under the ban."* 3 The LORD paid attention to Israel and delivered up the Canaanites,* and they put them and their cities under the ban. Hence that place was named Hormah.†

**The Bronze Serpent.** 4 From Mount Hor they set out by way of the Red Sea, to bypass the land of Edom, but the people's patience was worn out by the journey; 5 so the people

---

**20:11** *Twice:* perhaps because he did not have sufficient faith to work the wonder with the first blow. Cf. v. 12.

**20:12–13** What lay behind Moses and Aaron's lack of confidence is not made explicit in the text. *Holiness:* an allusion to the name of the place, Kadesh, which means "holy, sanctified, sacred." Meribah means "contention." Cf. Ex 17:7.

**20:14** *Your brother Israel:* according to biblical tradition, the Edomites were descended from Esau, the brother of Jacob. Their country, to the southeast of the Dead Sea, was also known as Seir; cf. Gn 25:24–26; 36:1, 8–9.

**20:17** *The King's Highway:* an important highway, running north and south along the plateau east of the Dead Sea. In ancient times it was much used by caravans and armies; later it was improved by the Romans, and large stretches of it are still clearly recognizable.

**20:22** *Mount Hor:* not definitively identified, but probably to

be sought in the vicinity of Kadesh. According to Dt 10:6, Aaron died at Moserah (cf. "Moseroth" in Nm 33:30–31), which is apparently the name of the region in which Mount Hor is situated.

**21:1–3** The account of this episode seems to be a later insertion here, since logically v. 4 belongs immediately after 20:29. Perhaps this is the same event as that mentioned in Jgs 1:16–17.

**21:3** *Hormah:* related to the Hebrew word *herem*, meaning "put under the ban." See notes on 14:45; 18:14.

**20:11** Ps 78:15–16; Wis 11:4; 1 Cor 10:4.
**20:13** Nm 27:14; Ex 17:7.
**20:16** Ex 2:23.
**20:20** Jgs 11:17.
**20:21–22** Nm 33:37.
**20:25–26** Dt 32:50.
**20:28** Nm 33:38.
**21:1** Nm 33:40.
**21:2** Jos 6:17; Jgs 1:17.
**21:3** Nm 14:45.

complained* against God and Moses, "Why have you brought us up from Egypt to die in the wilderness, where there is no food or water? We are disgusted with this wretched food!"†

⁶ So the LORD sent among the people seraph† serpents, which bit* the people so that many of the Israelites died. ⁷ Then the people came to Moses and said, "We have sinned in complaining against the LORD and you. Pray to the LORD to take the serpents from us." So Moses prayed for the people, ⁸ and the LORD said to Moses: Make a seraph and mount it on a pole, and everyone who has been bitten will look at it and recover.† ⁹ Accordingly Moses made a bronze serpent† and mounted it on a pole, and whenever the serpent bit someone, the person looked at the bronze serpent and recovered.*

**Journey Around Moab.** ¹⁰ The Israelites moved on and encamped in Oboth.* ¹¹ Then they moved on from Oboth and encamped in Iye-abarim† in the wilderness facing Moab on the east. ¹² Moving on from there, they encamped in the Wadi Zered. ¹³ Moving on from there, they encamped on the other side of the Arnon, in the wilderness that extends from the territory of the Amorites; for the Arnon forms Moab's boundary, between Moab and the Amorites. ¹⁴ Hence it is said in the "Book of the Wars of the LORD":†

"Waheb in Suphah and the wadies,
15      Arnon and the wadi gorges
    That reach back toward the site of Ar†
        and lean against the border of Moab."

¹⁶ From there they went to Beer,† which is the well of which the LORD said to Moses, Gather the people together so that I may give them water. ¹⁷ Then Israel sang this song:

Spring up, O well!—so sing to it—
18  The well that the princes sank,
        that the nobles of the people dug,
    With their scepters and their staffs—
        from the wilderness, a gift.

¹⁹ From Beer to Nahaliel, from Nahaliel to Bamoth, ²⁰ from Bamoth to the valley in the country of Moab at the headland of Pisgah that overlooks Jeshimon.†

**Victory over Sihon.** ²¹ Now Israel sent messengers to Sihon, king of the Amorites, with the message, ²² "Let us pass through your land. We will not turn aside into any field or vineyard, nor will we drink any well water, but we will go straight along the King's Highway until we have passed through your territory." ²³ Sihon,* however, would not permit Israel to pass through his territory, but mustered all his forces and advanced against Israel into the wilderness. When he reached Jahaz, he engaged Israel in battle. ²⁴ But Israel put him to the sword, and took possession of his land from the Arnon to the Jabbok and as far as Jazer of the Ammonites, for Jazer is the boundary of the Ammonites. ²⁵* Israel seized all the towns here, and Israel settled in all the towns of the Amorites, in Heshbon and all its dependencies. ²⁶ For Heshbon was the city of Sihon, king of the Amorites, who had fought against the former king of Moab and had taken all his land from him as far as the Arnon. ²⁷ That is why the poets say:

"Come to Heshbon, let it be rebuilt,
    let Sihon's city be firmly constructed.
28  For fire went forth from Heshbon
    and a blaze from the city of Sihon;
    It consumed Ar of Moab
    and swallowed up the high places of
        the Arnon.

---

† **21:5** *This wretched food*: apparently the manna is meant.
**21:6** *Seraph*: the Hebrew name for a certain species of venomous snake; etymologically the word might signify "the fiery one." Compare the winged throne guardians in Is 6:2, 6; see also Is 14:29; 30:6.
**21:8** *Everyone who has been bitten will look at it and recover*: in the Gospel of John this scene is regarded as a type for the crucifixion of Jesus (Jn 3:14–15).
**21:9** King Hezekiah, in his efforts to reform Israelite worship, "smashed the bronze serpent Moses had made" (2 Kgs 18:4).
**21:11** *Iye-abarim*: probably means "the ruins in the Abarim (Mountains)." See note on 27:12.
**21:14** The "Book of the Wars of the LORD": an ancient collection of Israelite songs, now lost. *Waheb in Suphah*: since neither place is mentioned elsewhere, it is uncertain whether these Hebrew words are to be considered as place names; some Hebrew words, now lost, must have preceded this phrase.
**21:15** *Ar*: a city or district in Moab, located on the Arnon; see v. 28; Dt 2:18.
**21:16** *Beer*: "a well," here used as a place name.
**21:20** *Jeshimon*: "the wasteland"; in 1 Sm 23:19, 24 and 26:1, 3, this is the wilderness of Judah on the western side of the Dead Sea, but here and in Nm 23:28, it seems to refer to the southern end of the Jordan valley where Beth-jeshimoth was situated.

* **21:5** Nm 11:6; Ex 16:3.      Jn 3:14–15.
**21:6** Dt 8:15; Wis 16:5;      **21:10** Nm 33:43–44.
    1 Cor 10:9.      **21:23** Dt 2:32; Jgs 11:20.
**21:9** Wis 16:6–7, 10;      **21:25–26** Jos 21:39; Jgs 11:26.

<sup>29</sup>    Woe to you, Moab!
        You are no more, people of
            Chemosh!†
        He let his sons become fugitives
            and his daughters be taken captive by
                the Amorite king Sihon.
<sup>30</sup>    From Heshbon to Dibon their
            dominion is no more;
        Ar is laid waste; fires blaze as far as
            Medeba."

<sup>31</sup> So Israel settled in the land of the Amorites. <sup>32</sup> Moses sent spies to Jazer; and the Israelites captured it with its dependencies and dispossessed the Amorites who were there.

**Victory over Og.** <sup>33</sup>* Then they turned and went up along the road to Bashan. But Og, king of Bashan, advanced against them with all his forces to give battle at Edrei. <sup>34</sup> The LORD, however, said to Moses: Do not fear him; for into your hand I deliver him with all his forces and his land. You will do to him as you did to Sihon, king of the Amorites, who reigned in Heshbon.* <sup>35</sup> So they struck him down with his sons and all his forces, until not a survivor was left to him, and they took possession of his land.

**22** <sup>1</sup> Then the Israelites moved on and encamped in the plains of Moab† on the other side of the Jordan opposite Jericho.

**Balaam Summoned.** <sup>2</sup> Now Balak, son of Zippor, saw all that Israel did to the Amorites, <sup>3</sup> and Moab feared the Israelites greatly because they were numerous. Moab was in dread of the Israelites. <sup>4</sup> So Moab said to the elders of Midian, "Now this horde will devour everything around us as an ox devours the grass of the field." At that time Balak, son of Zippor, was king of Moab; <sup>5</sup> and he sent messengers to Balaam, son of Beor, at Pethor on the river, in the land of the Ammonites,† to summon him

with these words, "A people has come out of Egypt! They have covered up the earth and are settling down opposite me! <sup>6</sup> Now come, curse this people for me,† since they are stronger than I am. Perhaps I may be able to defeat them and drive them out of the land. For I know that whoever you bless is blessed and whoever you curse is cursed." <sup>7</sup> So the elders of Moab and the elders of Midian, themselves experts in divination,† left and went to Balaam, to whom they gave Balak's message. <sup>8</sup> He said to them, "Stay here overnight, and I will give you whatever answer the LORD gives me." So the princes of Moab lodged with Balaam.

<sup>9</sup> Then God came to Balaam and said: Who are these men with you? <sup>10</sup> Balaam answered God, "Balak, son of Zippor, king of Moab, sent me the message: <sup>11</sup> 'This people that has come out of Egypt has covered up the earth. Now come, lay a curse on them for me; perhaps I may be able to fight them and drive them out.'" <sup>12</sup> But God said to Balaam: Do not go with them and do not curse this people, for they are blessed. <sup>13</sup> The next morning Balaam arose and told the princes of Balak, "Go back to your own country, for the LORD has refused to let me go with you." <sup>14</sup> So the princes of Moab went back to Balak with the report, "Balaam refused to come with us."

**Second Appeal to Balaam.** <sup>15</sup> Balak yet again sent princes, who were more numerous and more distinguished than the others. <sup>16</sup> On coming to Balaam they told him, "Thus says Balak, son of Zippor: Please do not refuse to come to me. <sup>17</sup> I will reward you very handsomely and will do anything you ask of me. Come, lay a curse on this people for me." <sup>18</sup>* But Balaam replied to Balak's servants, "Even if Balak gave me his house full of silver and gold, I could not do anything, small or great, contrary to the command of the LORD, my God. <sup>19</sup> But, you too stay here overnight, so that I may learn what else the LORD may

---

**21:29** *Chemosh*: the chief god of the Moabites, mentioned in the famous inscription of Mesha, king of Moab, who ruled at the same time as the Omrides in Israel. Cf. 1 Kgs 11:7, 33; 2 Kgs 23:13; Jer 48:7, 13.

**22:1** *The plains of Moab*: the lowlands to the northeast of the Dead Sea, between the Jordan and the foothills below Mount Nebo. Here the Israelites remained until they crossed the Jordan, according to Jos 1–4. Jericho lay to the west of the Jordan.

**22:5** *In the land of the Ammonites*: the translation rests on a slight emendation of the traditional Hebrew text in accordance with the tradition represented by the Vulgate. While Pethor remains unidentified, this verse supports an identification of

Balaam's homeland in the Transjordan (cf. the Deir 'Alla Inscriptions), over against other traditions in the text which connect Balaam with Syria (23:7; Dt 23:5).

**22:6** *Curse this people for me*: Balak believed that Balaam, known in the tradition as a diviner (cf. Jos 13:22), could utter a curse upon Israel which would come to pass.

**22:7** *Experts in divination*: lit., "divination was in their hand," i.e., "in their possession"; cf. Ezr 7:25.

**21:33** Dt 3:1–7.          **22:18** Nm 24:13.
**21:34** Ps 136:17–22.

say to me." [20] That night God came to Balaam and said to him: If these men have come to summon you, go back with them; yet only on the condition that you do exactly as I tell you. [21] So the next morning when Balaam arose, he saddled his donkey,† and went off with the princes of Moab.

**The Talking Donkey.** [22] But now God's anger flared up† at him for going, and the angel of the LORD took up a position on the road as his adversary. As Balaam was riding along on his donkey, accompanied by two of his servants, [23] the donkey saw the angel of the LORD standing in the road with sword drawn. The donkey turned off the road and went into the field, and Balaam beat the donkey to bring her back on the road. [24] Then the angel of the LORD stood in a narrow lane between vineyards with a stone wall on each side. [25] When the donkey saw the angel of the LORD there, she pressed against the wall; and since she squeezed Balaam's leg against the wall, he beat her again. [26] Then the angel of the LORD again went ahead, and stood next in a passage so narrow that there was no room to move either to the right or to the left. [27] When the donkey saw the angel of the LORD there, she lay down under Balaam. Balaam's anger flared up and he beat the donkey with his stick.

[28]* Then the LORD opened the mouth of the donkey, and she asked Balaam, "What have I done to you that you beat me these three times?" [29] "You have acted so willfully against me," said Balaam to the donkey, "that if I only had a sword at hand, I would kill you here and now." [30] But the donkey said to Balaam, "Am I not your donkey, on which you have always ridden until now? Have I been in the habit of treating you this way before?" "No," he replied. [31] Then the LORD opened Balaam's eyes, so that he saw the angel of the LORD standing on the road with sword drawn; and he knelt and bowed down to the ground. [32] But the angel of the LORD said to him: "Why have you beaten your donkey these three times? I have come as an adversary because this rash journey of yours is against my will. [33] When the donkey saw me,

she turned away from me these three times. If she had not turned away from me, you are the one I would have killed, though I would have spared her." [34] Then Balaam said to the angel of the LORD, "I have sinned. Yet I did not know that you took up a position to oppose my journey. Since it has displeased you, I will go back home." [35] But the angel of the LORD said to Balaam: "Go with the men; but you may say only what I tell you." So Balaam went on with the princes of Balak.

[36] When Balak heard that Balaam was coming, he went out to meet him at Ar-Moab on the border formed by the Arnon, at its most distant point. [37] And Balak said to Balaam, "Did I not send an urgent summons to you? Why did you not come to me? Did you think I could not reward you?" [38] Balaam answered Balak, "Well, I have come to you after all. But what power have I to say anything? I can speak only what God puts in my mouth." [39] Then Balaam went with Balak, and they came to Kiriath-huzoth. [40] Here Balak sacrificed oxen and sheep, and sent portions to Balaam and to the princes who were with him.

**The First Oracle.** [41] The next morning Balak took Balaam up on Bamoth-baal, and from there he could see some of the people.

# 23

[1] Then Balaam said to Balak, "Build me seven altars here, and here prepare seven bulls and seven rams for me." [2] So Balak did as Balaam had ordered, and Balak and Balaam offered a bull and a ram on each altar. [3] Balaam said to Balak, "Stand here by your burnt offering while I go over there. Perhaps the LORD will meet me, and then I will tell you whatever he lets me see." And so he went out on the barren height. [4] Then God met Balaam, and Balak said to him: "I have erected the seven altars, and have offered a bull and a ram on each altar." [5] The LORD put an utterance in Balaam's mouth, and said: Go back to Balak, and speak accordingly. [6] So he went back to Balak, who was still standing by his burnt offering together with all the princes of Moab. [7] Then Balaam recited his poem:

---

† **22:21** *Donkey:* technically a she-donkey; Heb. *aton.*
**22:22** *God's anger flared up:* God's apparent change of mind became a source of much speculation in the tradition. So, for example, God was angry, not merely because Balaam was going to Balak, for he had God's permission for the journey (v. 20), but perhaps because he was tempted by greed to curse Israel against

God's command (cf. 2 Pt 2:15; Jude 11; compare Nm 22:32). *Adversary:* Heb. *satan;* see also v. 32; cf. 1 Sm 29:4; 2 Sm 19:22; 1 Kgs 11; Jb 1–2; Ps 109:6; Zec 3:1–2; 1 Chr 21:1.

---

* **22:28** 2 Pt 2:15–16.

From Aram† Balak has led me here,
  Moab's king, from the mountains of
    Qedem:*
  "Come, curse for me Jacob,
    come, denounce Israel."
8 How can I lay a curse on the one whom
    God has not cursed?
  How denounce the one whom the
    LORD has not denounced?
9 For from the top of the crags I see him,
    from the heights I behold him.
  Here is a people that lives apart†
    and does not reckon itself among the
     nations.
10 Who has ever counted the dust of
    Jacob,
  who numbered Israel's dust-cloud?†
  May I die the death of the just,
    may my end be like theirs!

11 "What have you done to me?" cried Balak to Balaam. "It was to lay a curse on my foes that I brought you here; but instead, you have blessed them!" 12 Balaam replied, "Is it not what the LORD puts in my mouth that I take care to repeat?"

**The Second Oracle.** 13 Then Balak said to him, "Please come with me to another place† from which you can see them; but you will see only some, not all of them, and from there lay a curse on them for me." 14 So he brought him to a lookout post on the top of Pisgah, where he built seven altars and offered a bull and a ram on each of them. 15 Balaam then said to Balak, "Stand here by your burnt offering, while I seek a meeting over there." 16 Then the LORD met Balaam, and, having put an utterance in his mouth, said to him: Return to Balak, and speak accordingly. 17 So he went to Balak, who was still standing by his burnt offering together with the princes of Moab. When Balak asked him, "What did the LORD say?" 18 Balaam recited his poem:

  Rise, Balak, and listen;
    give ear to my testimony, son of
     Zippor!
19 God is not a human being who speaks
    falsely,
  nor a mortal, who feels regret.
  Is God one to speak and not act,
    to decree and not bring it to pass?
20 I was summoned to bless;
    I will bless; I cannot revoke it!
21 Misfortune I do not see in Jacob,
    nor do I see misery† in Israel.
  The LORD, their God, is with them;
    among them is the war-cry of their
     King.
22 They have the like of a wild ox's horns:†
    God who brought them out of Egypt.*
23 No, there is no augury against Jacob,
    nor divination against Israel.
  Now it is said of Jacob,
    of Israel, "Look what God has done!"
24 Here is a people that rises up like a
    lioness,
  and gets up like a lion;
  It does not rest till it has devoured its
    prey
  and has drunk the blood of the
    slain.*

25 "Neither lay a curse on them nor bless them," said Balak to Balaam. 26 But Balaam answered Balak, "Did I not tell you, 'Everything the LORD tells me I must do'?"

**The Third Oracle.** 27 Then Balak said to Balaam, "Come, let me bring you to another place; perhaps God will approve of your laying a curse on them for me from there." 28 So he took Balaam to the top of Peor, that overlooks Jeshimon. 29 Balaam then said to Balak, "Build me seven altars here; and here prepare for me seven bulls and seven rams." 30 And Balak did as Balaam had ordered, offering a bull and a ram on each altar.

---

**23:7** *Aram*: the ancient name of the region later known as Syria. *The mountains of Qedem*: Qedem is the name for a region in northern Syria. Qedem also means "eastern." Perhaps this designates the low ranges in the Syrian desert. The "mountains of old" is also a possible translation.
**23:9** *A people that lives apart*: that is, "securely"; cf. Dt 33:28.
**23:10** *The dust of Jacob…Israel's dust-cloud*: the Israelites will be as numerous as the dust kicked up by Israel in its march through the wilderness.
**23:13** *To another place*: Balak thought that if Balaam would

view Israel from a different site, he could deliver a different kind of omen.
**23:21** *Misfortune…misery*: Balaam states that he is unable to see any evils for Israel.
**23:22** *A wild ox's horns*: Israel possesses the strength of a wild ox because of God's presence among them. Compare the claim by the psalmist, the Lord is "my rock…my saving horn" (Ps 18:3).

**23:7** Nm 22:6.
**23:22** Nm 24:8.
**23:24** Nm 24:9; Gn 49:9.

# 24

¹ Balaam, however, perceiving that the LORD was pleased to bless Israel, did not go aside as before to seek omens, but turned his gaze toward the wilderness. ² When Balaam looked up and saw Israel encamped, tribe by tribe, the spirit of God came upon him, ³ and he recited his poem:

The oracle of Balaam, son of Beor,
the oracle of the man whose eye is true,
⁴ The oracle of one who hears what God says,
and knows what the Most High knows,
Of one who sees what the Almighty sees,
in rapture† and with eyes unveiled:
⁵ How pleasant are your tents, Jacob;
your encampments, Israel!
⁶ Like palm trees spread out,
like gardens beside a river,
Like aloes the LORD planted,
like cedars beside water;
⁷ Water will drip from their buckets,
their seed will have plentiful water;
Their king will rise higher than Agag†
and their dominion will be exalted.
⁸ They have the like of a wild ox's horns:
God who brought them out of Egypt.
They will devour hostile nations,
break their bones, and crush their loins.*
⁹ Crouching, they lie like a lion,
or like a lioness; who will arouse them?
Blessed are those who bless you,
and cursed are those who curse you!*

¹⁰ In a blaze of anger at Balaam, Balak clapped his hands† and said to him, "It was to lay a curse on my foes that I summoned you here; yet three times now you have actually blessed them!* ¹¹ Now flee to your home. I promised to reward you richly, but the LORD has withheld the reward from you!" ¹² Balaam replied to Balak, "Did I not even tell the messengers whom you sent to me, ¹³ 'Even if Balak gave me his house full of silver and gold, I could not of my own accord do anything, good or evil, contrary to the command of the LORD'? Whatever the LORD says I must say.*

**The Fourth Oracle.** ¹⁴ "But now that I am about to go to my own people, let me warn you what this people will do to your people in the days to come." ¹⁵ Then he recited his poem:

The oracle of Balaam, son of Beor,
the oracle of the man whose eye is true,
¹⁶ The oracle of one who hears what God says,
and knows what the Most High knows,
Of one who sees what the Almighty sees,
in rapture and with eyes unveiled.
¹⁷ I see him, though not now;
I observe him, though not near:
A star shall advance from Jacob,
and a scepter† shall rise from Israel,
That will crush the brows of Moab,*
and the skull of all the Sethites,
¹⁸ Edom will be dispossessed,
and no survivor is left in Seir.
Israel will act boldly,
¹⁹ and Jacob will rule his foes.

---

† **24:4** *In rapture:* lit., "falling," therefore possibly "in a trance." However, this interpretation is uncertain.

**24:7** *Agag:* during Saul's reign, king of Amalek (1 Sm 15:8), fierce enemy of Israel during the wilderness period; see v. 20 (Ex 17:8–16).

**24:10** *Balak clapped his hands:* a gesture suggesting contempt or derision, apparently made in anger (cf. Jb 27:23; Lam 2:15).

**24:17** *A star...a scepter:* some early Christian writers, as well as rabbinic interpreters, understood this prophecy in messianic terms. So, for example, Rabbi Akiba designates Bar Kosiba the messiah in the early second century A.D. by calling him Bar Kokhba, i.e., son of the star, alluding to this passage. Although this text is not referred to anywhere in the New Testament, in a Christian messianic interpretation the star would refer to Jesus, as also the scepter from Israel; cf. Is 11:1. But it is doubtful whether this passage is to be connected with the "star of the Magi" in Mt 2:1–12. *The brows of Moab, and the skull of all the Sethites:* under the figure of a human being, Moab is specified as the object of conquest by a future leader of Israel. The

personification of peoples or toponyms is common enough in the Old Testament; see, e.g., Hos 11:1; Ps 98:8. In Jer 48:45, which paraphrases the latter part of our verse, Moab is depicted as someone whose boasting warrants its ruin. In view of the use of Heb. *pe'ah* (here "brows") in Nm 34:3 to indicate a boundary, some see in the "brows" of Moab and the "skull" of the Sethites a representation of features of Moab's topography, i.e., the borderlands and the interior plateau. *The Sethites:* cf. Gn 4:25; here probably a general designation for nomadic/tribal groups on the borders of Palestine, unless they are to be identified with the Shutu mentioned in Execration texts of the early second millennium B.C. and the fourteenth century Amarna tablets from Egypt; however, the Shutu are not attested in Moab. On the basis of Gn 4:25 and Gn 25, one might also think of a reference to humanity in general.

---

**24:8** Nm 23:22.           **24:10** Nm 23:11.
**24:9** Nm 23:24; Gn 12:3;  **24:13** Nm 22:18.
   27:29; 49:9.              **24:17** 2 Sm 8:2.

20 Upon seeing Amalek, Balaam recited his poem:

> First† of the nations is Amalek,
>   but their end is to perish forever.*

21 Upon seeing the Kenites,† he recited his poem:

> Though your dwelling is safe,
>   and your nest is set on a cliff;
> 22   Yet Kain will be destroyed
>   when Asshur† takes you captive.

23 Upon seeing† [the Ishmaelites?] he recited his poem:

> Alas, who shall survive of Ishmael,
> 24   to deliver them from the hands of the Kittim?
> When they have conquered Asshur and
>   conquered Eber,
> They too shall perish forever.

25 Then Balaam set out on his journey home; and Balak also went his way.

# 25

**Worship of Baal of Peor.** 1 While Israel was living at Shittim,† the people profaned themselves by prostituting themselves with the Moabite women.* 2 These then invited the people to the sacrifices of their god, and the people ate of the sacrifices* and bowed down to their god. 3 Israel thereby attached itself to the Baal of Peor,* and the LORD's anger flared up against Israel. 4* The LORD said to Moses: Gather all the leaders of the people, and publicly execute them† before the LORD, that the blazing wrath of the LORD may turn away from Israel. 5 So Moses told the Israelite judges, "Each of you kill those of his men who have attached themselves to the Baal of Peor."†

**Zeal of Phinehas.** 6 At this a certain Israelite came and brought in a Midianite woman† to his kindred in the view of Moses and of the whole Israelite community, while they were weeping at the entrance of the tent of meeting. 7* When Phinehas, son of Eleazar, son of Aaron the priest, saw this, he rose up from the assembly, and taking a spear in his hand, 8 followed the Israelite into the tent where he pierced the two of them, the Israelite and the woman. Thus the plague upon the Israelites was checked; 9 but the dead from the plague were twenty-four thousand.

10 Then the LORD said to Moses: 11 Phinehas, son of Eleazar, son of Aaron the priest, has turned my anger from the Israelites by his being as jealous among them as I am; that is why I did not put an end to the Israelites in my jealousy.† 12* Announce, therefore, that I hereby give him my covenant of peace,† 13 which shall be for him and for his descendants after him the covenant of an everlasting priesthood, because he was jealous on behalf of his God and thus made expiation for the Israelites.

14† The name of the slain Israelite, the one

---

**24:20** *First*: lit., "the beginning." In the Bible, Amalek is a people indigenous to Palestine and therefore considered as of great antiquity. There is a deliberate contrast here between the words "first" and "end."

**24:21** *The Kenites* lived in high strongholds in the mountains of southern Palestine and the Sinai Peninsula, and were skilled in working the various metals found in their territory. Their name is connected, at least by popular etymology, with the Hebrew word for "smith"; of similar sound to *qayin*, i.e., "Kain" or "smith," is the Hebrew word for "nest," *qen*—hence the play on words in the present passage.

**24:22** *Asshur*: the mention of Asshur, i.e., Assyria, is not likely before the ninth or eighth centuries B.C.

**24:23–24** *Upon seeing*: this phrase, lacking the Hebrew text, is found in the Septuagint, but without "the Ishmaelites" designated as the subject of the oracle. The Hebrew text of the oracle itself shows considerable disarray; the translation therefore relies on reconstruction of the putative original and is quite uncertain.

**25:1** *Shittim*: the full name was Abel-shittim, a locality at the foot of the mountains in the northeastern corner of the plains of Moab (33:49). *Prostituting themselves*: the application to men of such traditional language for apostasy clearly suggests apostasy was taken to be an inevitable consequence of intermarriage with the Midianite women.

**25:4** *Publicly execute them*: the same phrase occurs in 2 Sm 21:6–14, where the context shows that at least a part of the penalty consisted in being denied honorable burial. In both passages, dismemberment or impalement (perhaps subsequent to the actual execution) as a punishment for the breaking of covenant pledges, is a possible interpretation of the Hebrew phrase.

**25:5** Thereby Moses apparently alters the Lord's command to execute all the leaders.

**25:6** *Midianite woman*: according to 22:4, 7, the Midianites were allied with the Moabites in opposing Israel, while 31:16 claims that Balaam had induced the Midianite women to lure the Israelites away from the Lord. *They were weeping*: on account of the plague that had struck them; cf. v. 8.

**25:11** *My jealousy*: God's desire to maintain an exclusive hold on the allegiance of the Israelites.

**25:12** *Covenant of peace*: by means of this covenant between God and Phinehas, Phinehas can expect God's protection, especially from any threat of reprisal for his action; cf. Is 54:10; Ez 34:25; 37:26.

**25:14–15** The noble lineage of the slain couple is mentioned in order to stress the courage of Phinehas in punishing them. The zeal of Phinehas became proverbial; cf. Ps 106:30; Sir 45:23; 1 Mc 2:26, 54.

---

**24:20** Ex 17:14; 1 Sm 15:3.
**25:1** Nm 31:16.
**25:2** Ex 34:15–16.
**25:3** Ps 106:28; Hos 9:10.
**25:4** Dt 4:3.
**25:7** Ps 106:30.
**25:12–13** 1 Mc 2:26, 54; Ps 106:31; Sir 45:23–24.

slain with the Midianite woman, was Zimri, son of Salu, prince of a Simeonite ancestral house. <sup>15</sup>The name of the slain Midianite woman was Cozbi, daughter of Zur, who was head of a clan, an ancestral house, in Midian.

**Vengeance on the Midianites.** <sup>16</sup>† The LORD then said to Moses: <sup>17</sup>* Treat the Midianites as enemies and strike them, <sup>18</sup>for they have been your enemies by the deceitful dealings they had with you regarding Peor and their kinswoman Cozbi, the daughter of a Midianite prince, who was slain at the time of the plague because of Peor.

## III. SECOND CENSUS OF A NEW GENERATION AND PREPARATION TO ENTER THE PROMISED LAND

**26** **The Second Census.** <sup>19</sup>After the plague <sup>1</sup>the LORD said to Moses and Eleazar, son of Aaron the priest: <sup>2</sup>Take a census, by ancestral houses, throughout the community of the Israelites of all those of twenty years or more who are eligible for military service in Israel.* <sup>3</sup>So on the plains of Moab along the Jordan at Jericho, Moses and Eleazar the priest enrolled them, <sup>4</sup>those of twenty years or more, as the LORD had commanded Moses.

The Israelites who came out of the land of Egypt were as follows:†

<sup>5</sup>* Reuben, the firstborn of Israel. The descendants of Reuben by their clans were: through Hanoch, the clan of the Hanochites; through Pallu, the clan of the Palluites; <sup>6</sup>through Hezron, the clan of the Hezronites; through Carmi, the clan of the Carmites. <sup>7</sup>These were the clans of the Reubenites, and those enrolled numbered forty-three thousand seven hundred and thirty.

<sup>8</sup>From Pallu descended Eliab. <sup>9</sup>The sons of Eliab were Nemuel, Dathan, and Abiram* — the same Dathan and Abiram, ones designated by the community, who contended with Moses and Aaron as part of Korah's faction when they contended with the LORD. <sup>10</sup>The earth opened its mouth and swallowed them, along with Korah, as a warning. The faction was destroyed when the fire consumed two hundred and fifty men. <sup>11</sup>The descendants of Korah, however, did not die out.

<sup>12</sup>The descendants of Simeon by clans were: through Nemuel,† the clan of the Nemuelites; through Jamin, the clan of the Jaminites; through Jachin, the clan of the Jachinites; <sup>13</sup>through Zerah, the clan of the Zerahites; through Shaul, the clan of the Shaulites. <sup>14</sup>These were the clans of the Simeonites, twenty-two thousand two hundred.

<sup>15</sup>The descendants of Gad by clans were: through Zephon, the clan of the Zephonites; through Haggi, the clan of the Haggites; through Shuni, the clan of the Shunites; <sup>16</sup>through Ozni, the clan of the Oznites; through Eri, the clan of the Erites; <sup>17</sup>through Arod, the clan of the Arodites; through Areli, the clan of the Arelites. <sup>18</sup>These were the clans of the descendants of Gad, of whom there were enrolled forty thousand five hundred.

<sup>19</sup>The sons of Judah were Er and Onan. Er and Onan died in the land of Canaan.* <sup>20</sup>The descendants of Judah by their clans were: through Shelah, the clan of the Shelahites; through Perez, the clan of the Perezites; through Zerah, the clan of the Zerahites. <sup>21</sup>The descendants of Perez were: through Hezron, the clan of the Hezronites; through Hamul, the clan of the Hamulites. <sup>22</sup>These were the clans of Judah, of whom there were enrolled seventy-six thousand five hundred.

<sup>23</sup>The descendants of Issachar by their clans were: through Tola, the clan of the Tolaites; through Puvah, the clan of the Puvahites; <sup>24</sup>through Jashub, the clan of the Jashubites; through Shimron, the clan of the Shimronites. <sup>25</sup>These were the clans of Issachar, of whom there were enrolled sixty-four thousand three hundred.

<sup>26</sup>The descendants of Zebulun by their clans were: through Sered, the clan of the Seredites; through Elon, the clan of the Elonites; through Jahleel, the clan of the Jahleelites. <sup>27</sup>These were the clans of the Zebulunites, of whom there were enrolled sixty thousand five hundred.

---

**25:16–18** The account of the execution of this command is given in 31:1–18.

**26:4** This introduction to the census seems to contradict vv. 64–65 by including those who came out of Egypt.

**26:12** *Nemuel:* so also in 1 Chr 4:24. In Gn 46:10 and Ex 6:15, a son of Simeon with the same position in the genealogy bears the name "Jemuel"; it is uncertain which form is correct.

See above, v. 9, where the name "Nemuel" occurs for a person descended from Pallu. Some speculate this name was inserted from v. 12 to provide a continuing line for Pallu.

**25:17–18** Nm 31:2–12.  **26:9–10** Nm 16:1, 32.
**26:2** Nm 1:2–3.  **26:19** Gn 38:7, 10; 46:12;
**26:5–6** 1 Chr 5:3.        1 Chr 2:3.

28 The sons of Joseph were Manasseh and Ephraim. 29 The descendants of Manasseh by clans were: through Machir, the clan of the Machirites. Now Machir begot Gilead: through Gilead, the clan of the Gileadites. 30 The descendants of Gilead were: through Iezer, the clan of the Iezrites; through Helek, the clan of the Helekites; 31 through Asriel, the clan of the Asrielites; through Shechem, the clan of the Shechemites; 32 through Shemida, the clan of the Shemidaites; through Hepher, the clan of the Hepherites. 33 * As for Zelophehad, son of Hepher—he had no sons, but only daughters. The names of the daughters of Zelophehad were Mahlah, Noah, Hoglah, Milcah and Tirzah. 34 These were the clans of Manasseh, and those enrolled numbered fifty-two thousand seven hundred.

35 These were the descendants of Ephraim by their clans: through Shuthelah, the clan of the Shuthelahites; through Becher, the clan of the Becherites; through Tahan, the clan of the Tahanites. 36 These were the descendants of Shuthelah: through Eran, the clan of the Eranites. 37 These were the clans of the Ephraimites, of whom there were enrolled thirty-two thousand five hundred.

These were the descendants of Joseph by their clans.

38 The descendants of Benjamin by their clans were: through Bela, the clan of the Belaites; through Ashbel, the clan of the Ashbelites; through Ahiram, the clan of the Ahiramites; 39 through Shupham, the clan of the Shuphamites; through Hupham, the clan of the Huphamites. 40 The sons of Bela were Ard and Naaman: through Ard, the clan of the Ardites; through Naaman, the clan of the Naamites. 41 These were the descendants of Benjamin by their clans, of whom there were enrolled forty-five thousand six hundred.

42 These were the descendants of Dan by their clans: through Shuham the clan of the Shuhamites. These were the clans of Dan, 43 of whom there were enrolled sixty-four thousand four hundred.

44 The descendants of Asher by their clans were: through Imnah, the clan of the Imnites; through Ishvi, the clan of the Ishvites; through Beriah, the clan of the Beriites; 45 through Heber, the clan of the Heberites; through Malchiel, the clan of the Malchielites. 46 The name of Asher's daughter was Serah. 47 These were the clans of the descendants of Asher, of whom there were enrolled fifty-three thousand four hundred.

48 The descendants of Naphtali by their clans were: through Jahzeel, the clan of the Jahzeelites; through Guni, the clan of the Gunites; 49 through Jezer, the clan of the Jezerites; through Shillem, the clan of the Shillemites. 50 These were the clans of Naphtali, of whom there were enrolled forty-five thousand four hundred.

51 These were the Israelites who were enrolled: six hundred and one thousand seven hundred and thirty.

**Allotment of the Land.** † 52 The LORD said to Moses: 53 * Among these the land shall be divided as their heritage in keeping with the number of people named. 54 * To a large tribe you shall assign a large heritage, to a small tribe a small heritage, each receiving its heritage in proportion to the number enrolled in it. 55 But the land shall be divided by lot, all inheriting according to the lists of their ancestral tribes. 56 As the lot falls the heritage of each tribe, large or small, will be assigned.

**Census of the Levites.** 57 These were the Levites enrolled by clans: through Gershon, the clan of the Gershonites; through Kohath, the clan of the Kohathites; through Merari, the clan of the Merarites. 58 These were clans of Levi: the clan of the Libnites, the clan of the Hebronites, the clan of the Mahlites, the clan of the Mushites, the clan of the Korahites. †

Now Kohath begot Amram, 59 whose wife was named Jochebed. She was the daughter of Levi, born to Levi in Egypt. To Amram she bore Aaron and Moses and Miriam their sister. 60 To Aaron were born Nadab and Abihu, Eleazar and Ithamar. 61 But Nadab and Abihu died

---

**26:52–56** The division of Canaan among the various tribes and clans and families was determined not only by the size of each group but also by lot. Perhaps the lots determined the respective locality of each tribal land and the section reserved for each clan, while the relative size of the allotted locality and section depended on the numerical strength of each group. The Israelites considered the outcome of the drawing of lots as an expression of God's will; cf. Lv 16:8–10; Jos 14:2; 15:1; etc.; Acts 1:23–26.

**26:58** Compare 3:18–20 for a different listing.

**26:33** Nm 27:1; 36:11; Jos 17:3.

**26:53** Jos 11:23.
**26:54** Nm 33:54; 35:8.

when they offered unauthorized fire before the Lord. [62] The Levites enrolled were twenty-three thousand, every male one month or more of age.* They were not enrolled with the other Israelites, however, for no heritage was given them among the Israelites.

[63] These, then, were those enrolled by Moses and Eleazar the priest, when they enrolled the Israelites on the plains of Moab along the Jordan at Jericho. [64] Among them there was not one of those who had been enrolled by Moses and Aaron the priest, when they enrolled the Israelites in the wilderness of Sinai. [65]* For the Lord had told them that they would surely die in the wilderness, and not one of them was left except Caleb, son of Jephunneh, and Joshua, son of Nun.

# 27

**Zelophehad's Daughters.** [1] The daughters of Zelophehad, son of Hepher, son of Gilead, son of Machir, son of Manasseh, came forward. (Zelophehad belonged to the clans of Manasseh, son of Joseph.) The names of his daughters were Mahlah, Noah, Hoglah, Milcah and Tirzah.* [2] Standing before Moses, Eleazar the priest, the princes, and the whole community at the entrance of the tent of meeting, they said: [3] "Our father died in the wilderness. Although he did not join the faction of those who conspired against the Lord,† Korah's faction, he died for his own sin without leaving any sons. [4] But why should our father's name be cut off from his clan merely because he had no son? Give us land among our father's kindred."

**Laws Concerning Heiresses.**† [5] So Moses laid their case before the Lord, [6] and the Lord said to him: [7] The plea of Zelophehad's daughters is just; you shall give them hereditary land among their father's kindred and transfer their father's heritage to them. [8] Tell the Israelites:

If a man dies without leaving a son, you shall transfer his heritage to his daughter; [9] if he has no daughter, you shall give his heritage to his brothers; [10] if he has no brothers, you shall give his heritage to his father's brothers; [11] if his father had no brothers, you shall give his heritage to his nearest relative in his clan, who shall then take possession of it.

This will be the statutory procedure for the Israelites, as the Lord commanded Moses.*

**Joshua to Succeed Moses.** [12] The Lord said to Moses: Go up into this mountain of the Abarim range† and view the land that I have given to the Israelites.* [13] When you have viewed it, you will be gathered to your people, as was Aaron your brother.* [14] For in the rebellion of the community in the wilderness of Zin you both rebelled against my order to acknowledge my holiness before them by means of the water.* (These were the waters of Meribah of Kadesh in the wilderness of Zin.)

[15] Then Moses said to the Lord, [16] "May the Lord, the God of the spirits of all humanity,† set over the community someone [17] who will be their leader in battle and who will lead them out and bring them in, that the Lord's community may not be like sheep without a shepherd." [18] And the Lord replied to Moses: Take Joshua, son of Nun,* a man of spirit,† and lay your hand upon him. [19] Have him stand before Eleazar the priest and the whole community, and commission him in their sight. [20] Invest him with some of your own power, that the whole Israelite community may obey him. [21] He shall present himself to Eleazar the priest, who will seek for him the decision of the Urim† in the Lord's presence; and as it directs, Joshua, all the Israelites with him, and the whole community will go out for battle; and as it directs, they will come in.

[22] Moses did as the Lord had commanded

---

† 27:3 *He did not join…against the Lord:* had he done so, he and his heirs could have been deprived of a portion in the promised land.

27:5–11 The purpose of this law, as also that of the related laws in 36:2–10 (marriage within the same tribe), Dt 25:5–10 (levirate marriage), and Lv 25:10 (return of property in the jubilee year), was to keep the landed property within the proper domain of each tribe.

27:12 *The Abarim range:* the mountains on the eastern side of the Dead Sea. The peak of this chain is Mount Nebo where Moses views the promised land before he dies (Dt 32:49).

27:16 *The God of the spirits of all humanity:* the sense is that God knows the character and abilities of all people and therefore knows best whom to appoint (cf. Jgs 6:34; 11:29; 1 Sm 16:13); see the same phrase in Nm 16:22, where "spirit" evidently

means the life principle.

27:18 *A man of spirit:* lit., "a man in whom there is spirit," that is, probably one who is endowed with a courageous spirit (Jos 2:11); compare Gn 41:38; Dt 34:9.

27:21 *The Urim:* certain sacred objects which Israelite priests employed to discern the divine will, probably by obtaining a positive or negative answer to a given question. The full expression was "the Urim and Thummim"; cf. Ex 28:30; Lv 8:8; Dt 33:8; Ezr 2:63; Neh 7:65. Joshua ordinarily did not receive direct revelations from God as Moses had received them.

---

26:62 Nm 3:39.
26:65 Nm 14:22–24, 29.
27:1 Nm 26:33; Jos 17:3.
27:11 Jer 32:6–9.
27:12 Dt 3:27; 32:49; 34:1.
27:13–14 Nm 20:12, 24.
27:14 Dt 32:51.
27:18 Dt 34:9.

him. Taking Joshua and having him stand before Eleazar the priest and the whole community, ²³he laid his hands on him and commissioned him, as the LORD had directed through Moses.

# 28 General Sacrifices.
¹The LORD said to Moses: ²Give the Israelites this commandment: At their prescribed times, you will be careful to present to me the food offerings that are due me, oblations of pleasing aroma to me.

**Each Morning and Evening.** ³* You will tell them therefore: This is the oblation which you will offer to the LORD: two unblemished yearling lambs each day as the regular burnt offering,† ⁴offering one lamb in the morning and the other during the evening twilight, ⁵each with a grain offering of one tenth of an ephah of bran flour mixed with a fourth of a hin of oil of crushed olives.† ⁶This is the regular burnt offering that was made at Mount Sinai for a pleasing aroma, an oblation to the LORD. ⁷And as the libation for the first lamb, you will make a libation to the LORD in the sanctuary† of a fourth of a hin of strong drink. ⁸The other lamb you will offer during the evening twilight, making the same grain offering and the same libation as in the morning, as an oblation of pleasing aroma to the LORD.

**On the Sabbath.** ⁹On the sabbath day: two unblemished yearling lambs, with a grain offering of two tenths of an ephah of bran flour mixed with oil, and its libation. ¹⁰This is the sabbath burnt offering each sabbath, in addition to the regular burnt offering and its libation.

**At the New Moon Feast.** ¹¹On your new moons† you will offer as a burnt offering to the LORD two bulls of the herd, one ram, and seven unblemished yearling lambs, ¹²with

three tenths of an ephah of bran flour mixed with oil as the grain offering for each bull, two tenths of an ephah of bran flour mixed with oil as the grain offering for the ram, ¹³and one tenth of an ephah of bran flour mixed with oil as the grain offering for each lamb, a burnt offering with a pleasing aroma, an oblation to the LORD. ¹⁴Their libations will consist of a half a hin of wine for each bull, a third of a hin for the ram, and a fourth of a hin for each lamb. This is the burnt offering for the new moon, for every new moon through the months of the year. ¹⁵Moreover, there will be one goat for a purification offering to the LORD; it will be offered in addition to the regular burnt offering and its libation.

**At the Passover.** ¹⁶The fourteenth day† of the first month is the Passover of the LORD, * ¹⁷and the fifteenth day of this month is the pilgrimage feast. For seven days unleavened bread is to be eaten. ¹⁸On the first day you will declare a holy day, and you shall do no heavy work.† * ¹⁹You will offer an oblation, a burnt offering to the LORD: two bulls of the herd, one ram, and seven yearling lambs that you are sure are unblemished. ²⁰Their grain offerings will be of bran flour mixed with oil; you will offer three tenths of an ephah for each bull and two tenths for the ram. ²¹You will offer one tenth for each of the seven lambs; ²²and one goat as a purification offering to make atonement for yourselves. ²³These offerings you will make in addition to the morning burnt offering which is part of the regular burnt offering. ²⁴You will make exactly the same offerings each day for seven days as food offerings, oblations of pleasing aroma to the LORD; they will be offered in addition to the regular burnt offering with its libation. ²⁵On the seventh day you will declare a holy day: you shall do no heavy work. *

**At Pentecost.** ²⁶On the day of first fruits,† on your feast of Weeks, * when you present to the

---

**28:3** *The regular burnt offering:* "the *tamid* burnt offering," the technical term for the daily sacrifice. The lambs—as well as the goats for the purification offering (vv. 15, 22, 30)—are all specified as males.
**28:5** *Oil of crushed olives:* this oil, probably made in a mortar, was purer and more expensive than oil extracted in the olive press.
**28:7** *In the sanctuary:* i.e., the tent of meeting. But according to Sir 50:15, the libation was poured at the base of the outer altar.
**28:11** *On your new moons:* beginning on the evening when the crescent of the new moon first appeared. The beginning of the month is reckoned according to the new moon.

**28:16** *The fourteenth day:* toward evening at the end of this day; cf. Ex 12:6, 18.
**28:18** *Heavy work:* apparently, some sorts of activity are permitted on a day such as this, whereas "any work" is prohibited by 29:7 on the Day of Atonement. See note on Lv 23:3.
**28:26** *The day of first fruits:* a unique term for this feast, which is usually called "the feast of Weeks"; it was celebrated as a thanksgiving for the wheat harvest seven weeks after the barley

**28:3–8** Ex 29:38–42.
**28:16** Ex 12:18; Lv 23:5; Dt 16:1.
**28:18** Ex 12:16; Lv 23:7.
**28:25** Ex 12:16; 13:6; Lv 23:8.
**28:26** Ex 34:22.

LORD an offering of new grain, you will declare a holy day: you shall do no heavy work. ²⁷You will offer burnt offering for a pleasing aroma to the LORD: two bulls of the herd, one ram, and seven yearling lambs that you are sure are unblemished. ²⁸Their grain offerings will be of bran flour mixed with oil: three tenths of an ephah for each bull, two tenths for the ram, ²⁹and one tenth for each of the seven lambs. ³⁰One goat will be for a purification offering to make atonement for yourselves. ³¹You will make these offerings, together with their libations, in addition to the regular burnt offering with its grain offering.

# 29 On New Year's Day. ¹In the seventh month on the first day† you will declare a holy day, and do no heavy work; it shall be a day on which you sound the trumpet.* ²You will offer a burnt offering for a pleasing aroma to the LORD: one bull of the herd, one ram, and seven unblemished yearling lambs. ³Their grain offerings will be of bran flour mixed with oil: three tenths of an ephah for the bull, two tenths for the ram, ⁴and one tenth for each of the seven lambs. ⁵One goat will be a purification offering to make atonement for yourselves. ⁶These are in addition to the burnt offering for the new moon with its grain offering, and in addition to the regular burnt offering with its grain offering, together with the libations prescribed for them, for a pleasing aroma, an oblation to the LORD.

## On the Day of Atonement. ⁷On the tenth day of this seventh month† you will declare a holy day, humble yourselves, and do no sort of work.* ⁸You will offer a burnt offering to the LORD, a pleasing aroma: one bull of the herd, one ram, and seven yearling lambs that you are sure are unblemished. ⁹Their grain offerings of bran flour mixed with oil: three tenths of an ephah for the bull, two tenths for the one ram, ¹⁰and one tenth for each of the seven lambs. ¹¹One goat will be a purification

offering. These are in addition to the purification offering for purging,† the regular burnt offering with its grain offering, and their libations.

## On the Feast of Booths. ¹²† On the fifteenth day of the seventh month you will declare a holy day:* you shall do no heavy work. For the following seven days you will celebrate a pilgrimage feast to the LORD. ¹³You will offer a burnt offering, an oblation of pleasing aroma to the LORD: thirteen bulls† of the herd, two rams, and fourteen yearling lambs that are unblemished. ¹⁴Their grain offerings will be of bran flour mixed with oil: three tenths of an ephah for each of the thirteen bulls, two tenths for each of the two rams, ¹⁵and one tenth for each of the fourteen lambs. ¹⁶One goat will be a purification offering. These are in addition to the regular burnt offering with its grain offering and libation.

¹⁷On the second day: twelve bulls of the herd, two rams, and fourteen unblemished yearling lambs, ¹⁸with the grain offerings and libations for the bulls, rams and lambs in their prescribed number, ¹⁹as well as one goat as a purification offering, besides the regular burnt offering with its grain offering and libation.

²⁰On the third day: eleven bulls, two rams, and fourteen unblemished yearling lambs, ²¹with the grain offerings and libations for the bulls, rams and lambs in their prescribed number, ²²as well as one goat for a purification offering, besides the regular burnt offering with its grain offering and libation.

²³On the fourth day: ten bulls, two rams, and fourteen unblemished yearling lambs, ²⁴the grain offerings and libations for the bulls, rams and lambs in their prescribed number, ²⁵as well as one goat as a purification offering, besides the regular burnt offering, its grain offering and libation.

²⁶On the fifth day: nine bulls, two rams, and fourteen unblemished yearling lambs, ²⁷* with the grain offerings and libations for the bulls,

---

† harvest (Passover). In the time of Jesus it was commonly known by the Greek word "Pentecost," that is, "fiftieth" (day after the Passover); see note on Lv 23:16–21.

**29:1** *In the seventh month on the first day*: (about September–October) now the Jewish New Year's Day. In the older calendar the year began with the first of Nisan (March–April), which is still known as the first month; cf. Ex 12:2.

**29:7** *The tenth day of this seventh month*: the Day of Atonement. *Humble yourselves*: that is, with fasting.

**29:11** *The purification offering for purging*: the bull prescribed in Lv 16:11–12 for the purging of the tent sanctuary.

**29:12** This feast of Booths (Tabernacles or Sukkot) celebrating the vintage harvest was the most popular of all and therefore had the most elaborate ritual. See note on Lv 23:34.

**29:13** *Thirteen bulls*: the number of bulls sacrificed before the octave day was seventy, arranged on a descending scale so that the number on the seventh day was the sacred number seven.

**29:1** Nm 10:10; Lv 23:24.          **29:12** Lv 23:34–35.
**29:7** Lv 16:29; 23:27–28,          **29:27** Nm 29:30, 37.
32.

rams and lambs in their prescribed number, [28] as well as one goat as a purification offering, besides the regular burnt offering with its grain offering and libation.

[29] On the sixth day: eight bulls, two rams, and fourteen unblemished yearling lambs, [30] with the grain offerings and libations for the bulls, rams and lambs in their prescribed number, [31] as well as one goat as a purification offering, besides the regular burnt offering, its grain offering and libation.

[32] On the seventh day: seven bulls, two rams, and fourteen unblemished yearling lambs, [33] with the grain offerings and libations for the bulls, rams and lambs in their prescribed number, [34] as well as one goat as a purification offering, besides the regular burnt offering, its grain offering and libation.

[35] On the eighth day* you will hold a public assembly:† you shall do no heavy work. [36] You will offer a burnt offering, an oblation of pleasing aroma to the LORD: one bull, one ram, and seven unblemished yearling lambs, [37] with the grain offerings and libations for the bulls, rams and lambs in their prescribed number, [38] as well as one goat as a purification offering, besides the regular burnt offering with its grain offering and libation.

[39] These are the offerings you will make to the LORD on your festivals, besides your votive or voluntary offerings of burnt offerings, grain offerings, libations, and communion offerings.

# 30

[1] So Moses instructed the Israelites exactly as the LORD had commanded him.

**Validity and Annulment of Vows.** [2] Moses said to the heads of the Israelite tribes, "This is what the LORD has commanded: [3] When a man makes a vow to the LORD or binds himself under oath to a pledge,† he shall not violate his word, but must fulfill exactly the promise he has uttered.*

[4] "When a woman makes a vow to the LORD, or binds herself to a pledge, while still in her father's house in her youth, [5] and her father learns of her vow or the pledge to which she bound herself and says nothing to her about it, then any vow or any pledge to which she bound herself remains valid. [6] But if on the day he learns of it her father opposes her, then any vow or any pledge to which she bound herself becomes invalid; and the LORD will release her from it, since her father opposed her.

[7] "If she marries while under a vow or under a rash pledge to which she bound herself, [8] and her husband learns of it, yet says nothing to her on the day he learns it, then the vows or the pledges to which she bound herself remain valid. [9] But if on the day her husband learns of it he opposes her, he thereby annuls the vow she had made or the rash pledge to which she had bound herself, and the LORD will release her from it. [10] (The vow of a widow or of a divorced woman, however, any pledge to which such a woman binds herself, is valid.)

[11] "If it is in her husband's house† that she makes a vow or binds herself under oath to a pledge, [12] and her husband learns of it yet says nothing to her to oppose her, then all her vows remain valid or any pledge to which she has bound herself. [13] But if on the day he learns of them her husband annuls them, then whatever she has expressly promised in her vows or in her pledge becomes invalid; since her husband has annulled them, the LORD will release her from them.

[14] "Any vow or any pledge that she makes under oath to humble herself, her husband may either confirm or annul. [15] But if her husband, day after day, says nothing at all to her, he thereby confirms all her vows or all the pledges incumbent upon her; he has confirmed them, because on the day he learned of them he said nothing to her. [16] If, however, he annuls them† some time after he first learned of them, he will be responsible for her guilt."

[17] These are the statutes which the LORD commanded Moses concerning a husband and his wife, as well as a father and his daughter

---

**29:35** *A public assembly:* the Hebrew word is the technical term for the closing celebration of the three major feasts of the Passover, Pentecost and Booths, or of other special feasts that lasted for a week. Cf. Lv 23:36; Dt 16:8; 2 Chr 7:9; Neh 8:18.

**30:3** *A vow…a pledge:* here the former signifies the promise to dedicate either a person, an animal, or a thing or their equivalent to the sanctuary upon the fulfillment of some specified conditions (Lv 27:1–13); the latter signifies the assumption of either a positive or a negative obligation—that is, the promise either to

do something or to abstain from something; cf. v. 14.

**30:11** *In her husband's house:* after her marriage. This contrasts with the case given in vv. 7–9.

**30:16** *He annuls them:* he prevents their fulfillment. Since he has first allowed the vows to remain valid, he can no longer annul them.

**29:35** Lv 23:36; Jn 7:37.          **30:3** Dt 23:22; Eccl 5:3–4.

while she is still in her youth in her father's house.

# 31 Campaign Against the Midianites.

[1] The LORD said to Moses:† [2] Avenge the Israelites on the Midianites, and then you will be gathered to your people. [3] So Moses told the people, "Arm some men among you for the campaign, to attack Midian and to execute the LORD's vengeance on Midian. [4] From each of the tribes of Israel you will send a thousand men to the campaign." [5] From the contingents of Israel, therefore, a thousand men of each tribe were levied, so that there were twelve thousand men armed for war. [6] Moses sent them out on the campaign, a thousand from each tribe, with Phinehas, son of Eleazar, the priest for the campaign, who had with him the sacred vessels and the trumpets for sounding the alarm. [7] They waged war against the Midianites, as the LORD had commanded Moses, and killed every male. [8] Besides those slain in battle, they killed the kings of Midian: Evi, Rekem, Zur, Hur and Reba, the five kings of Midian;† and they also killed Balaam, son of Beor, with the sword. [9] But the Israelites took captive the women of the Midianites with their children, and all their herds and flocks and wealth as loot, [10] while they set on fire all the towns where they had settled and all their encampments. [11] Then they took all the plunder, with the people and animals they had captured, and brought the captives, together with the spoils and plunder, [12] to Moses and Eleazar the priest and to the Israelite community at their camp on the plains of Moab by the Jordan opposite Jericho.

## Treatment of the Captives. 

[13] When Moses and Eleazar the priest, with all the leaders of the community, went outside the camp to meet them, [14] Moses became angry with the officers of the army, the commanders of thousands and the commanders of hundreds, who were returning from the military campaign. [15] "So you have spared all the women!" he exclaimed. [16] "These are the very ones who on Balaam's advice were behind the Israelites' unfaithfulness to the LORD in the affair at Peor,* so that plague struck the LORD's community. [17]† Now kill, therefore, every male among the children and kill every woman who has had sexual relations with a man. [18] But you may spare for yourselves all the girls who have not had sexual relations.

## Purification After Combat. 

[19] "Moreover, remain outside the camp for seven days; every one of you who has killed anyone or touched someone killed will purify yourselves on the third and on the seventh day—both you and your captives. [20] You will also purify every garment, every article of leather, everything made of goats' hair, and every article of wood."

[21] Eleazar the priest told the soldiers who had taken part in the battle: "This is the prescribed ritual which the LORD has commanded Moses: [22] gold, silver, bronze, iron, tin and lead— [23] whatever can stand fire—you shall put into the fire, that it may become clean; however, it must also be purified with water of purification.† But whatever cannot stand fire you must put into the water. [24] On the seventh day you will wash your garments, and then you will again be clean. After that you may enter the camp."

## Division of the Spoils. 

[25] The LORD said to Moses: [26] With the help of Eleazar the priest and of the heads of the ancestral houses of the community, inventory all the spoils captured, human being and beast alike; [27] then divide the spoils† between the warriors who went on the campaign and the whole community. [28] You will levy a tax for the LORD on the soldiers who went on the campaign: one out of every five hundred persons, oxen, donkeys, and sheep. [29] From their half you will take it and give it to Eleazar the priest as a contribution to the LORD. [30] From the Israelites' half you will take one captive from every fifty human beings, oxen, donkeys, and sheep—all

---

† **31:1–3** The narrative of Israel's campaign against Midian, which was interrupted after 25:18, is now resumed.

**31:8** *The five kings of Midian*: they are called Midianite princes, Sihon's vassals, in Jos 13:21.

**31:17** There are later references to Midian in Jgs 6–8; 1 Kgs 11:18; Is 60:6. The present raid was only against those Midianites who were dwelling at this time near the encampment of the Israelites.

**31:23** *Water of purification*: water mixed with the ashes of the

red heifer as prescribed in 19:9.

**31:27** *Divide the spoils*: for a similar division of the plunder into two equal parts, between those who engaged in the battle and those who stayed with the baggage, cf. 1 Sm 30:24. But note that here the tax on the plunder of the noncombatants is ten times as much as that on the soldiers' plunder.

* **31:16** 2 Pt 2:15; Rev 2:14.

the animals—and give them to the Levites, who perform the duties of the LORD's tabernacle. [31] So Moses and Eleazar the priest did this, as the LORD had commanded Moses.

**Amount of the Plunder.** [32] This plunder, what was left of the loot which the troops had taken, amounted to six hundred and seventy-five thousand sheep, [33] seventy-two thousand oxen, [34] sixty-one thousand donkeys, [35] and thirty-two thousand women who had not had sexual relations.

[36] The half-share that fell to those who had gone out on the campaign was in number: three hundred and thirty-seven thousand five hundred sheep, [37] of which six hundred and seventy-five fell as tax to the LORD; [38] thirty-six thousand oxen, of which seventy-two fell as tax to the LORD; [39] thirty thousand five hundred donkeys, of which sixty-one fell as tax to the LORD; [40] and sixteen thousand persons, of whom thirty-two persons fell as tax to the LORD. [41] Moses gave the taxes contributed to the LORD to Eleazar the priest, exactly as the LORD had commanded Moses.

[42] As for the Israelites' half, which Moses had taken from the men who had fought— [43] the community's half was three hundred and thirty-seven thousand five hundred sheep, [44] thirty-six thousand oxen, [45] thirty thousand five hundred donkeys, [46] and sixteen thousand persons. [47] From the Israelites' half, Moses took one captive from every fifty, from human being and beast alike, and gave them to the Levites, who performed the duties of the LORD's tabernacle, exactly as the LORD had commanded Moses.

**Gifts of the Officers.** [48] Then those who were officers over the contingents of the army, commanders of thousands and commanders of hundreds, came up to Moses [49] and said to him, "Your servants have counted the soldiers under our command, and not one of us is missing. [50]† So, we have brought as an offering to the LORD articles of gold that each

of us has picked up—anklets, bracelets, rings, earrings, or pendants—to make atonement for ourselves before the LORD." [51] Moses and Eleazar the priest accepted the gold from them, all fashioned pieces. [52] The gold that was given as a contribution to the LORD—from the commanders of thousands and the commanders of hundreds—amounted in all to sixteen thousand seven hundred and fifty shekels. [53] What the common soldiers had looted each one kept for himself.† [54] So Moses and Eleazar the priest accepted the gold from the commanders of thousands and of hundreds, and put it in the tent of meeting as a reminder on behalf of the Israelites before the LORD.

# 32

**Request of Gad and Reuben.** [1] Now the Reubenites and Gadites had a very large number of livestock. Noticing that the land of Jazer and of Gilead† was a place suited to livestock, [2] the Gadites and Reubenites came to Moses and Eleazar the priest and to the leaders of the community and said, [3]† "The region of Ataroth, Dibon, Jazer, Nimrah, Heshbon, Elealeh, Sebam, Nebo and Baal-meon— [4] the land which the LORD has laid low before the community of Israel, is a land for livestock, and your servants have livestock." [5] They continued, "If we find favor with you, let this land be given to your servants as their possession. Do not make us cross the Jordan."

**Moses' Rebuke.** [6] But Moses answered the Gadites and Reubenites: "Are your kindred, then, to go to war, while you remain here? [7] Why do you wish to discourage the Israelites from crossing to the land the LORD has given them? [8] That is just what your ancestors did when I sent them from Kadesh-barnea to reconnoiter the land.* [9] They went up to the Wadi Eshcol and reconnoitered the land, then so discouraged the Israelites that they would not enter the land the LORD had given them. [10]* At that time the anger of the LORD flared up, and he swore: [11] None of the men twenty years old or more who have come up from

---

† **31:50** The precise nature and use of some of these articles of gold is not certain.

**31:53** Apparently because of the commanders' generosity the common troops were under no sort of obligation to make their own offerings and could keep their loot.

**32:1** *Gilead:* the name of the western part of the plateau east of the Jordan, sometimes signifying the whole region from the Yarmuk to the Jordan, sometimes only the northern part of this region, and sometimes, as here, only its southern part. Jazer lay

to the east of southern Gilead.

**32:3** The places named in this verse, as well as the additional ones given in vv. 34–38, were all in the former kingdom of Sihon, that is, in the region between the Jabbok and the Arnon. Cf. 21:23–24; Jos 13:19–21, 24–27.

---

**32:8–9** Nm 13:31–33; Dt 1:22.　　**32:10–11** Dt 1:34–35.

Egypt will see the land I promised under oath to Abraham and Isaac and Jacob, because they have not followed me unreservedly— 12* except the Kenizzite† Caleb, son of Jephunneh, the Kenizzite, and Joshua, son of Nun, since they have followed the LORD unreservedly. 13 So the anger of the LORD flared up against the Israelites and he made them wander in the wilderness forty years, until the whole generation that had done evil in the sight of the LORD had disappeared. 14 And now here you are, offspring of sinful stock, rising up in your ancestors' place to add still more to the LORD's blazing anger against the Israelites. 15 If you turn away from following him, he will again abandon them in the wilderness, and you will bring about the ruin of this entire people."

**Counter Proposal.** 16 But they approached him and said: "We will only build sheepfolds here for our flocks and towns for our families; 17 but we ourselves will march as troops in the vanguard before the Israelites,* until we have led them to their destination. Meanwhile our families will remain in the fortified towns because of the land's inhabitants. 18 We will not return to our homes until all the Israelites have taken possession of their heritage. 19* But we will not claim any heritage with them across the Jordan and beyond, because we have received a heritage for ourselves on the eastern side of the Jordan."

**Agreement Reached.** 20† Moses said to them in reply: "If you do this—if you march as troops before the LORD into battle 21 and cross the Jordan in full force before the LORD until he has driven his enemies out of his way 22 and the land is subdued before the LORD, then you may return here, free from every obligation to the LORD and to Israel, and this land will be your possession before the LORD.* 23 But if you do not do this, you will have sinned against the LORD, and you can be sure that the consequences of your sin will overtake you. 24 Build the towns, then, for your families, and the folds for your flocks, but fulfill what you have promised."

25 The Gadites and Reubenites answered Moses, "Your servants will do as my lord commands. 26* While our wives and children, our livestock and other animals remain there in the towns of Gilead, 27 all your servants will go across as armed troops before the LORD to battle, just as my lord says."

28 So Moses gave this command in their regard to Eleazar the priest, to Joshua, son of Nun, and to the heads of the ancestral houses of the Israelite tribes: 29 He said to them, "If all the Gadites and Reubenites cross the Jordan with you in full force before the LORD into battle, the land will be subdued before you, and you will give them Gilead as a possession. 30 But if they will not go across in force with you before the LORD, you will bring their wives and children and livestock across before you into Canaan, and they will possess a holding among you in the land of Canaan."

31 To this the Gadites and Reubenites replied, "We will do what the LORD has ordered your servants. 32 We ourselves will go across in force before the LORD into the land of Canaan, but we will retain our hereditary property on this side of the Jordan."† 33 So Moses gave them—†the Gadites and Reubenites, as well as half the tribe of Manasseh, son of Joseph—the kingdom of Sihon, king of the Amorites, and the kingdom of Og, king of Bashan, the land with its towns, and the districts of the surrounding towns.*

34 The Gadites rebuilt the cities of Dibon, Ataroth, Aroer, 35 Atroth-shophan, Jazer, Jogbehah, 36 Beth-nimrah and Beth-haran—fortified cities—and sheepfolds. 37 The Reubenites rebuilt Heshbon, Elealeh, Kiriathaim, 38 Nebo, Baal-meon (names to be changed!),† and

---

† **32:12** *Kenizzite*: a member of the clan of Kenaz, which, according to Gn 36:11, 15, 42, was Edomite; but, according to Nm 13:6; 34:19, Caleb belonged to the tribe of Judah; cf. also Jos 14:6, 14.

**32:20–22** Since the ark of the Lord was carried into battle with the Israelite army, the vanguard was said to march before the Lord (see Jos 6:6–9).

**32:32** *This side of the Jordan*: lit., "beyond the Jordan"; the perspective in Hebrew is from the west bank looking toward the east bank where the Reubenites and Gadites finally settled.

**32:33** The preceding is concerned solely with the two tribes of Gad and Reuben and with the land of the former kingdom of Sihon; it seems probable that the sudden reference here to the half-tribe of Manasseh and to their territory in Bashan, the former kingdom of Og, is a later addition to the text.

**32:38** The phrase in parentheses is probably a gloss, warning the reader perhaps to substitute some other word for Nebo and Baal, the names of foreign deities mentioned in the last two city names. *They called by their old names*: lit., "they called by their names"; however, some understand the current Hebrew text to mean, "they called by new names," or "their own names."

---

**32:12** Nm 14:24; Dt 1:36.
**32:17** Jos 4:12–13.
**32:19** Jos 13:8.
**32:22** Jos 1:15.
**32:26** Jos 1:14.
**32:33** Dt 3:12; 29:7; Jos 12:6; 13:8.

Sibmah. These towns, which they rebuilt, they called by their old names.

**Other Conquests.** 39 The descendants of Machir, son of Manasseh, went to Gilead and captured it, dispossessing the Amorites who were there. 40 (Moses gave Gilead to Machir,* son of Manasseh, and he settled there.) 41 Jair,* a descendant of Manasseh, went and captured their tent villages, and called them Havvoth-jair.† 42 Nobah went and captured Kenath with its dependencies and called it Nobah after his own name.

# 33 Stages of the Journey. 1 The following are the stages by which the Israelites went out by companies from the land of Egypt under the guidance of Moses and Aaron.† 2 Moses recorded the starting points of the various stages at the direction of the LORD. These are the stages according to their starting points: 3 They set out from Rameses in the first month, on the fifteenth day of the first month. On the day after the Passover the Israelites went forth in triumph, in view of all Egypt, 4 while the Egyptians buried those whom the LORD had struck down, every firstborn; on their gods, too, the LORD executed judgments.*

**From Egypt to Sinai.** 5 Setting out from Rameses, the Israelites camped at Succoth. 6 Setting out from Succoth, they camped at Etham near the edge of the wilderness. 7 Setting out from Etham, they turned back to Pi-hahiroth, which is opposite Baal-zephon, and they camped opposite Migdol.* 8 Setting out from Pi-hahiroth, they crossed over through the sea into the wilderness,* and after they traveled a three days' journey in the wilderness of Etham, they camped at Marah. 9 Setting out from Marah, they came to Elim; at Elim there were twelve springs of water and seventy palm trees, and they camped there.* 10 Setting out from Elim, they camped beside the Red Sea. 11 Setting out from the Red Sea, they camped in the wilderness of Sin. 12 Setting out from the wilderness of Sin, they camped at Dophkah. 13 Setting out from Dophkah, they camped at Alush. 14 Setting out from Alush, they camped at Rephidim, where there was no water for the people to drink.* 15 Setting out from Rephidim, they camped in the wilderness of Sinai.*

**From Sinai to Kadesh.** 16 Setting out from the wilderness of Sinai, they camped at Kibroth-hattaavah. 17 Setting out from Kibroth-hattaavah, they camped at Hazeroth.* 18 Setting out from Hazeroth, they camped at Rithmah. 19 Setting out from Rithmah, they camped at Rimmon-perez. 20 Setting out from Rimmon-perez, they camped at Libnah. 21 Setting out from Libnah, they camped at Rissah. 22 Setting out from Rissah, they camped at Kehelathah. 23 Setting out from Kehelathah, they camped at Mount Shepher. 24 Setting out from Mount Shepher, they camped at Haradah. 25 Setting out from Haradah, they camped at Makheloth. 26 Setting out from Makheloth, they camped at Tahath. 27 Setting out from Tahath, they camped at Terah. 28 Setting out from Terah, they camped at Mithkah. 29 Setting out from Mithkah, they camped at Hashmonah. 30† Setting out from Hashmonah, they camped at Moseroth. 31 Setting out from Moseroth, they camped at Bene-jaakan. 32 Setting out from Bene-jaakan, they camped at Mount Gidgad. 33 Setting out from Mount Gidgad, they camped at Jotbathah. 34 Setting out from Jotbathah, they camped at Abronah. 35 Setting out from Abronah, they camped at Ezion-geber.† 36 Setting out from Ezion-geber, they camped in the wilderness of Zin, that is, Kadesh.*

---

† **32:41** *Havvoth-jair:* that is, "villages of Jair."

**33:1–3** According to v. 2, this list of camping sites was drawn up by Moses as an itinerary recording Israel's trek through the wilderness. Comparison with the more detailed accounts of the journey as given elsewhere suggests that the list is not necessarily comprehensive. It records just forty camping sites, not counting the starting place, Rameses, and the terminus, the plains of Moab. This number, which corresponds exactly to the forty years of wandering in the wilderness, is probably a schematic device. Moreover, it seems that in its present form the order of some of the names here has been disturbed. Several names listed here are not recorded elsewhere.

**33:30–36** Moseroth is mentioned in Dt 10:6 (in the form of "Moserah") as the place where Aaron died, apparently a variant

of the tradition here in v. 38 regarding the place of Aaron's death; so also Nm 20:22–24 and Dt 32:50. Perhaps Moseroth was close to Mount Hor.

**33:35** *Ezion-geber:* Solomon conducted sea trade with Ophir from this port (1 Kgs 9:26), today probably identified on the northern coast of the Gulf of Elath between the Jordanian city of Aqabah and the Israeli city of Elath.

---

*
| | |
|---|---|
| **32:40** Dt 3:15. | **33:9** Ex 15:27. |
| **32:41** Dt 3:14. | **33:14** Ex 17:1. |
| **33:4–5** Ex 12:12, 29, 37. | **33:15** Ex 19:2. |
| **33:7** Ex 14:2. | **33:17–18** Nm 11:34–35. |
| **33:8** Ex 15:22. | **33:36–37** Nm 20:1, 22. |

**From Kadesh to the Plains of Moab.** [37] Setting out from Kadesh, they camped at Mount Hor on the border of the land of Edom.

[38] Aaron the priest ascended Mount Hor* at the Lord's direction, and there he died in the fortieth year after the departure of the Israelites from the land of Egypt, on the first day of the fifth month. [39] Aaron was a hundred and twenty-three years old when he died on Mount Hor.

[40]† When the Canaanite, the king of Arad, who ruled over the Negeb in the land of Canaan, heard that the Israelites were coming....

[41]† Setting out from Mount Hor, they camped at Zalmonah. [42] Setting out from Zalmonah, they camped at Punon. [43] Setting out from Punon, they camped at Oboth. [44] Setting out from Oboth, they camped at Iye-abarim on the border of Moab. [45] Setting out from Iye-abarim, they camped at Dibon-gad. [46] Setting out from Dibon-gad, they camped at Almon-diblathaim. [47] Setting out from Almon-diblathaim, they camped in the Abarim range opposite Nebo. [48] Setting out from the Abarim range, they camped on the plains of Moab by the Jordan opposite Jericho. [49] They camped by the Jordan on the plains of Moab extended from Beth-jeshimoth to Abel-shittim.

**Conquest and Division of Canaan.** [50] The Lord spoke to Moses on the plains of Moab by the Jordan opposite Jericho: [51] Speak to the Israelites and say to them: When you go across the Jordan into the land of Canaan, [52] dispossess all the inhabitants of the land before you; destroy all their stone figures, destroy all their molten images, and demolish all their high places.* [53] You will take possession of the land and settle in it, for I have given you the land to possess. [54] You will apportion the land among yourselves by lot, clan by clan, assigning a large heritage to a large clan and a small heritage to a small clan.* Wherever anyone's lot falls, there will his possession be; you will

apportion these shares within your ancestral tribe.

[55] But if you do not dispossess the inhabitants of the land before you, those whom you allow to remain will become barbs in your eyes and thorns in your sides, and they will harass you in the land where you live,* [56] and I will treat you as I had intended to treat them.

# 34 **The Boundaries.** [1] The Lord spoke to Moses: [2] Give the Israelites this order: When you enter the land of Canaan, this is the territory that shall fall to you as your heritage—the land of Canaan with its boundaries:

[3] Your southern boundary will be at the wilderness of Zin along the border of Edom;* on the east your southern boundary will begin at the end of the Salt Sea. [4] Then your boundary will turn south of the Akrabbim Pass and cross Zin. Terminating south of Kadesh-barnea, it extends to Hazar-addar and crosses to Azmon.* [5] Then the boundary will turn from Azmon to the Wadi of Egypt and terminate at the Sea.*

[6] For your western boundary you will have the Great Sea† with its coast; this will be your western boundary.

[7] This will be your boundary on the north: from the Great Sea you will draw a line to Mount Hor,† [8] and draw it from Mount Hor to Lebo-hamath, with the boundary terminating at Zedad. [9] Then the boundary extends to Ziphron and terminates at Hazar-enan. This will be your northern boundary.

[10] For your eastern boundary you will draw a line from Hazar-enan to Shepham. [11] From Shepham the boundary will go down to Riblah, east of Ain, and descending further, the boundary will strike the ridge on the east side of the Sea of Chinnereth;† [12] then the boundary will descend along the Jordan and terminate with the Salt Sea.

This will be your land, with the boundaries that surround it.

[13] Moses also gave this order to the Israelites:

---

†
**33:40** The verse repeats almost verbatim the same introduction to the account of the victory over Arad as is given in 21:1–3, where it also follows the account of Aaron's death. Perhaps the isolated verse here is intended by the editor(s) of Numbers to point the reader to the fuller account given there.
**33:41b–49** It seems that this section stood originally immediately after v. 36a.
**34:6** *The Great Sea*: the Mediterranean.
**34:7–8** *Mount Hor*: different from the one where Aaron died;

cf. 20:22; 33:37–38.
**34:11** *Sea of Chinnereth*: in the New Testament known as the Sea of Galilee; today called Lake Kinneret.

---
*
| | |
|---|---|
| **33:38** Nm 20:25; Dt 32:50. | **33:55** Jos 23:13; Jgs 2:3. |
| **33:52** Ex 23:31; 34:13; Dt | **34:3** Jos 15:1–2. |
| 7:5; 12:3. | **34:4** Jos 15:3. |
| **33:54** Nm 26:53–56. | **34:5** Jos 15:4. |

"This is the land, to be apportioned among you by lot, which the LORD has commanded to be given to the nine and a half tribes. [14] For the tribe of the Reubenites according to their ancestral houses, and the tribe of the Gadites according to their ancestral houses, as well as half of the tribe of Manasseh, have already received their heritage; [15] these two and a half tribes have received their heritage across the Jordan opposite Jericho, in the east, toward the sunrise."

**Supervisors of the Allotment.** [16] The LORD spoke to Moses: [17] These are the names of the men who shall apportion the land among you: Eleazar the priest, and Joshua, son of Nun; [18]* and you will designate one leader from each of the tribes to apportion the land. [19] These are the names of the men:

from the tribe of Judah: Caleb, son of Jephunneh,
[20] from the tribe of the Simeonites: Samuel, son of Ammihud;
[21] from the tribe of Benjamin: Elidad, son of Chislon;
[22] from the tribe of the Danites: a leader, Bukki, son of Jogli;
[23] for the descendants of Joseph: from the tribe of the Manassites: a leader, Hanniel, son of Ephod; and
[24] from the tribe of the Ephraimites: a leader, Kemuel, son of Shiphtan;
[25] from the tribe of the Zebulunites: a leader, Elizaphan, son of Parnach;
[26] from the tribe of the Issacharites: a leader, Paltiel, son of Azzan;
[27] from the tribe of the Asherites: a leader, Ahihud, son of Shelomi;
[28] from the tribe of the Naphtalites: a leader, Pedahel, son of Ammihud.

[29] These are the ones whom the LORD commanded to apportion to the Israelites their heritage in the land of Canaan.

# 35 **Cities for the Levites.** [1] The LORD spoke to Moses on the plains of Moab by the Jordan opposite Jericho: [2]* Command the Israelites out of the heritage they possess to give the Levites cities to dwell in; you will also give the Levites the pasture lands around the cities. [3] The cities will be for them to dwell in, and the pasture lands will be for their cattle, their flocks, and all their other animals. [4] The pasture lands of the cities to be assigned the Levites shall extend a thousand cubits out from the city walls in every direction. [5] You will measure out two thousand cubits outside the city along the east side, two thousand cubits along the south side, two thousand cubits along the west side, and two thousand cubits along the north side, with the city lying in the center. These will be the pasture lands of their cities. [6]* Now these are the cities you will give to the Levites: the six cities of asylum which you must establish for the homicide to run to, and in addition forty-two other cities— [7] a total of forty-eight cities with their pasture lands which you will assign to the Levites. [8]† In assigning the cities from what the Israelites possess, take more from a larger group and fewer from a smaller one, so that each will cede cities to the Levites in proportion to the heritage which it receives.

**Cities of Asylum.** [9]* The LORD spoke to Moses: [10] Speak to the Israelites and say to them: When you go across the Jordan into the land of Canaan, [11] select for yourselves cities to serve as cities of asylum, where a homicide who has killed someone inadvertently may flee. [12] These cities will serve you as places of asylum from the avenger of blood,† so that a homicide will not be put to death until tried before the community. [13] As for the cities you assign, you will have six cities of asylum: [14] you will designate three cities beyond the Jordan, and you will designate three cities in the land of Canaan. These will be cities of asylum. [15] These six cities will serve as places of asylum for the Israelites, and for the resident or transient aliens among them, so that anyone who has killed a person inadvertently may flee there.

**Murder and Manslaughter.** [16]† If someone strikes another with an iron instrument and

---

† **35:8** This provision was hardly observed in the actual assignment of the levitical cities as narrated in Jos 21.
**35:12** *The avenger of blood*: Hebrew, *go'el*, often translated as "redeemer," one who, as next of kin to the slain (2 Sm 14:7), and here, as executor of public justice, had the right and duty to take the life of the murderer; cf. Dt 19:6, 12; Jos 20:3, 5, 9.

**35:16–25** Here, as also in Dt 19:1–13, there is a casuistic development of the original law as stated in Ex 21:12–14.

* 

34:18 Nm 1:4.
35:2 Jos 14:3–4; 21:2.

35:6 Dt 4:41–42; Jos 20:2.
35:9–15 Dt 19:2; Jos 20:2–6.

causes death, that person is a murderer, and the murderer must be put to death.* ¹⁷ If someone strikes another with a death-dealing stone in the hand and death results, that person is a murderer, and the murderer must be put to death. ¹⁸ Or if someone strikes another with a death-dealing club in the hand and death results, that person is a murderer, and the murderer must be put to death. ¹⁹ The avenger of blood is the one who will kill the murderer, putting the individual to death on sight.

²⁰ If someone pushes another out of hatred, or throws something from an ambush, and death results,* ²¹ or strikes another with the hand out of enmity and death results, the assailant must be put to death as a murderer. The avenger of blood will kill the murderer on sight.

²²* However, if someone pushes another without malice aforethought, or without lying in ambush throws some object at another, ²³ or without seeing drops upon another some death-dealing stone and death results, although there was neither enmity nor malice— ²⁴ then the community will judge between the assailant and the avenger of blood in accordance with these norms. ²⁵ The community will deliver the homicide from the avenger of blood and the community will return the homicide to the city of asylum where the latter had fled;* and the individual will stay there until the death of the high priest who has been anointed with sacred oil. ²⁶ If the homicide leaves at all the bounds of the city of asylum to which flight had been made, ²⁷ and is found by the avenger of blood beyond the bounds of the city of asylum, and the avenger of blood kills the homicide, the avenger incurs no bloodguilt; ²⁸ for the homicide was required to stay in the city of asylum until the death of the high priest. Only after the death of the high priest may the homicide return to the land of the homicide's possession.

²⁹ This is the statute for you throughout all your generations, wherever you live, for rendering judgment.

**Judgment.** ³⁰ Whenever someone kills another, the evidence of witnesses is required to kill the murderer.* A single witness does not suffice for putting a person to death.

**No Indemnity.** ³¹ You will not accept compensation in place of the life of a murderer who deserves to die, but that person must be put to death. ³² Nor will you accept compensation to allow one who has fled to a city of asylum to return to live in the land before the death of the high priest. ³³ You will not pollute the land where you live. For bloodshed pollutes the land, and the land can have no expiation for the blood shed on it except through the blood of the one who shed it. ³⁴ Do not defile the land in which you live and in the midst of which I dwell;* for I the LORD dwell in the midst of the Israelites.

**36** **Inheritance of Daughters.** ¹ The heads of the ancestral houses in a clan of the descendants of Gilead, son of Machir, son of Manasseh—one of the Josephite clans—came up and spoke before Moses and Eleazar the priest and before the leaders who were the heads of the ancestral houses of the Israelites. ² They said: "The LORD commanded my lord to apportion the land by lot for a heritage among the Israelites;* and my lord was commanded by the LORD to give the heritage of Zelophehad our kinsman to his daughters. ³ But if they marry into one of the other Israelite tribes, their heritage will be withdrawn from our ancestral heritage and will be added to that of the tribe into which they marry; thus the heritage that fell to us by lot will be diminished. ⁴ When the Israelites celebrate the jubilee year,† the heritage of these women will be added to that of the tribe into which they marry and their heritage will be withdrawn from that of our ancestral tribe."

⁵† So Moses commanded the Israelites at the direction of the LORD: "The tribe of the Josephites are right in what they say. ⁶ This is what the LORD commands with regard to the daughters of Zelophehad: They may marry anyone they please, provided they marry into a clan of their ancestral tribe, ⁷ so that no heritage of the Israelites will pass from one tribe to another, but all the Israelites will retain

---

† **36:4** Before the jubilee year various circumstances, such as divorce, could make such property revert to its original tribal owners; but in the jubilee year it became irrevocably attached to its new owners.
**36:5–9** This is a supplement to the law given in 27:5–11.

35:16 Ex 21:12; Lv 24:17.
35:20 Ex 21:14; Dt 19:11.
35:22 Jos 20:3.
35:25 Jos 20:6.
35:30 Dt 17:6; 19:15;
Jn 8:17; 2 Cor 13:1;
1 Tm 5:19.
35:34 Ex 29:45.
36:2 Nm 26:55; 27:6; Jos 17:3–4.

their own ancestral heritage. [8]Every daughter who inherits property in any of the Israelite tribes will marry someone belonging to a clan of her own ancestral tribe, in order that all the Israelites may remain in possession of their own ancestral heritage. [9]Thus, no heritage will pass from one tribe to another, but all the Israelite tribes will retain their own ancestral heritage."

[10]The daughters of Zelophehad did exactly as the LORD commanded Moses. [11]Mahlah, Tirzah, Hoglah, Milcah and Noah, Zelophehad's daughters, married sons of their uncles on their father's side. [12]They married within the clans of the descendants of Manasseh, son of Joseph; hence their heritage remained in the tribe of their father's clan.

**Conclusion.** [13]These are the commandments and decisions which the LORD commanded the Israelites through Moses, on the plains of Moab beside the Jordan opposite Jericho.

# The Book of
# Deuteronomy

## INTRODUCTION

### Pauline A. Viviano

The book of Deuteronomy brings the Pentateuch to a close with the death of Moses, but at the same time it introduces the next phase of Israel's life as Yahweh's people in the promised land. In Deuteronomy Israel is in an "in-between" time. The journey through the wilderness has come to an end, and now on the banks of the Jordan the people of Israel pause to listen as Moses addresses them before they enter into the land of Canaan. These last words of Moses bring his leadership to an end and provide a theological lens for viewing the events recounted in the books of Joshua, Judges, 1–2 Samuel, and 1–2 Kings.

## The Discovery of a Law Code (621 BCE)

Second Kings 22:3–23:3 recounts the discovery of a "book of the law" in the Temple during the reign of King Josiah of Judah. After Huldah, a prophet, authenticates this law code as the word of Yahweh, the king gathers the people, reads the book to them, and binds himself by covenant in obedience to the law of that book. In the subsequent reform described in 2 Kgs 23:4–24 the king purges the Temple of images and other objects associated with the worship of other gods. He removes priests who have been engaged in idolatrous practices, defiles altars and sites where other gods were worshiped, suppresses various divination practices, and commands the people to observe the Passover. King Josiah receives high praise for his actions: "Before him there had been no king who turned to the LORD as he did, with his whole heart, his whole being, and his whole strength, in accord with the entire law of Moses" (2 Kgs 23:25).

Many scholars identify the "book of the law" discovered at that time as the Deuteronomic

---

## Outline of Deuteronomy

I.  **First Address (1:1–4:43)**

II. **Second Address (4:44–28:69)**

   A. **The Lord's Covenant with Israel (4:44–11:32)**

   B. **The Deuteronomic Code (12:1–28:69)**

III. **Third Address (29:1–33:29)**

IV. **The Death of Moses (34:1–12)**

---

law code (or, more likely, an earlier version of it) because of the similarities between the reform initiated by King Josiah and the content of that law code. Some scholars dismiss the story of the discovery of a law code as propaganda created to justify the reform of King Josiah, but whether grounded in historical event or created as propaganda, Deuteronomic theology (as described below) begins to dominate in the late seventh century BCE and will result in the production of the book of Deuteronomy and the collection of books that scholars call the Deuteronomistic History. This collection consists of Joshua, Judges, 1–2 Samuel, and 1–2 Kings, with the book of Deuteronomy as its introduction.

## The Development of Deuteronomy

There is broad agreement that the book of Deuteronomy was shaped over centuries, but the exact stages and details of its development continue to be debated. At the core of Deuteronomy is a collection of laws with an exhortation to obedience and an affirmation that Israel is Yahweh's special possession. Other

D
T

law collections would be added over time, and it would be edited and reedited until it came to its present shape as the Deuteronomic law code (Dt 12–26). In this process about 50 percent of the ancient law collection known as the book of the covenant (Ex 20:23–23:33) was incorporated into the Deuteronomic Code. The book of the covenant was not simply absorbed into the Deuteronomic Code. Rather it was taken up, revised, and updated. Some parts of Dt 5–11 may have been added at this early stage of development, connecting the law collection with covenant-making and the giving of the Ten Commandments (Dt 5:1–21).

The material surrounding this inner core came together through a series of revisions by editors most likely from the Deuteronomic School that had emerged in the late preexilic period and continued into the exilic and postexilic periods. The added material expanded the historical introduction to the law collection and brought to the fore the parenetic overtones for which the book of Deuteronomy is known. There were at least two stages of development from the Deuteronomic School. At the first stage of editing, Dt 1–3 and parts of chs. 31 and 34 were added, and at a second stage, Dt 4:1–40. At the latest stage of development the death of Moses (34:4–8), which is attributed to the Priestly author, was added, as were the Song of Moses (ch. 31), the Blessing of Moses (ch. 32), and parts of ch. 31. The process of the development of the book of Deuteronomy began in the early seventh century BCE, but the book likely did not reach its present form until the postexilic period (after 538 BCE).

# The Form and Language of Deuteronomy

The book of Deuteronomy is in the form of a "farewell speech," indeed a series of farewell speeches of Moses. In literature, as in life, the final words of a person have special importance. A "farewell speech" from a leading character in a narrative provides an opportunity to summarize key lessons from the past and give guidance to future generations, and this is precisely what is done in the book of Deuteronomy. In the early chapters Moses

recounts Israel's journey through the wilderness and the covenant issued on Mount Horeb, which is used in Deuteronomy as an alternate name for Mount Sinai. The Deuteronomic law provides guidance to the people of Israel on how to live in the land. Toward the end of Deuteronomy, Moses prepares the people for the conquest and commissions Joshua as his successor. Interwoven throughout Moses' speeches is a sustained exhortation to fidelity in the worship of Yahweh and Yahweh alone and to obedience to the laws set out in Deuteronomy.

The book of Deuteronomy bears the imprint of the suzerainty treaty form. In the ancient Near East this treaty form was used to define relationships between conquering and conquered nations, between empires and their vassal states. Elements of the Hittite suzerainty treaty form and the treaty forms used by the Assyrians and Babylonians in the ninth to seventh centuries make their way into the book of Deuteronomy, probably from the hands of the Deuteronomic editors. Treaties between a suzerain (or overlord) and a vassal generally consisted of six elements: introduction of the speaker, historical prologue, stipulations, attention to the treaty document, witnesses, and sanctions. In the book of Deuteronomy the speaker is identified as Moses (Dt 4:45), but Yahweh also speaks (5:6ff.). Israel's history is recounted by Moses (chs. 1–3) and the stipulations are found in the Deuteronomic law code of chs. 12–26, although some stipulations are already worked into 4:44–6:25. Attention to the treaty document is found in 27:8; 31:9–13, 24–29, followed by sanctions in the form of curses (27:14–26; 28:15–68) and blessings (28:1–14). There are no witnesses in the book of Deuteronomy, for witnesses to treaties were often the gods and goddesses of the ancient Near East and in the book of Deuteronomy Yahweh and Yahweh alone is Israel's God.

The suzerainty treaty form influenced not only the formal content of the book of Deuteronomy but also its terminology. Words such as "love," "know," and "fear" are typically found in treaties to describe the relationship between suzerain and vassal. To "walk after," "obey the voice of," and "serve" define the behavior of the vassal. "Peace" and "prosperity" are rewards for obedience to the overlord. The Deuteronomists use these terms so frequently they have become identified as characteristically Deuteronomic terminology.

# The Theology of Deuteronomy

In the book of Deuteronomy the people of Israel are the elect people of Yahweh, their God. As Yahweh's elect they are called to live in a covenant relationship with Yahweh and to obey the laws of that covenant in the land that Yahweh has given them. The theory of retribution, that is, the notion that obedience leads to success and disobedience leads to failure, is the underlying theological principle that grounds the exhortation to fidelity in obedience to the law. Legalism is avoided in the book of Deuteronomy by placing obedience to the law in the context of the relationship of love between Yahweh and Israel. The pervasive theological perspective of the book of Deuteronomy is seen especially in its treatment of the following areas: God and Israel, election and covenant, law, and land.

## God and Israel

Clearly stated in the book of Deuteronomy is that Yahweh and Yahweh alone is Israel's God (Dt 4:34; 6:4) and Israel's response to its God is to "love the LORD, your God, with your whole heart, and with your whole being, and with your whole strength" (6:5). God and people are in relationship, a relationship based in Yahweh's initiative and realized in Israel's response. Though Yahweh speaks from the heavenly realm (4:36), it is the nearness of Yahweh (4:7) that receives emphasis in Deuteronomy. Yahweh is present with Israel (23:15) and active in Israel's history, a history recounted in the opening chapters of Deuteronomy. Yahweh is present when Israel comes to worship (12:7; 16:11, 16). Yahweh is a jealous God (4:24; 5:9; 6:15), that is, he is passionately devoted to Israel. Yahweh is a great and awesome God (7:21), but Israel is not to be terrified by Yahweh for Yahweh is also a faithful (7:9) and merciful God (4:31).

Israel is a people defined by its relationship to Yahweh. Their loyalty to Yahweh is not to be compromised and thus any source of temptation to worship other gods is to be removed (Dt 7:1–6; 13:1–19) and becoming involved with idols is strongly denounced (4:15–24; 12:29–13:19). Israel is a community that is held together by the common worship of Yahweh. Israel is not a state in Deuteronomy, but a people bound to one God and to the law issued by that God. Behind Israel's identity stands Yahweh's election of Israel and the covenant between God and the people. "All Israel" is the focus of the book of Deuteronomy for it sees the people as one people united in worship at one shrine where Yahweh, who made them his people, is worshiped. The book of Deuteronomy addresses Israel on the banks of the Jordan; thus the people are outside the land and situated in the time before they became corrupted in the land. The "you" addressed in Deuteronomy, however, is the Israel of the age of the compilers of the book. The Deuteronomists' generation thus is brought to an earlier age before the time of sin and rebellion and asked to consider the importance of their relationship to Yahweh and the demands attached to that relationship as they contemplate their future.

## Election and Covenant

The notion that the people of Israel as a whole are chosen by Yahweh (Dt 4:37; 7:6; 10:15; 14:2), and are thus his elect people, is a distinctive part of Deuteronomic faith. It is the people as a whole who are set apart to be in special relationship with Yahweh. Being "chosen" in the past was applied to kings, but with Deuteronomy there is a democratization of the notion of election: all are the elect. In Deuteronomy Yahweh's choice of Israel is based on his love and fulfills the promise made to Israel's ancestors (7:7–8). As the elect, Israel is to be a holy people and Yahweh's own possession (7:6; 26:18). Yahweh's actions on behalf of his people, specifically bringing Israel out of Egypt and giving them the promised land, reflect his love for them. In the Deuteronomic law code the election of Israel will extend to the election of one sanctuary where Israel is to worship Yahweh. It is the place that Yahweh chooses and the place where Yahweh will cause his name to dwell (12:5, 11, 14, 18, 21, 26; 14:23, 25; 15:20; 16:2, 6, 11, 15; 17:8, 10; 18:6; 26:2). The location of the one sanctuary is never identified in Deuteronomy, but as Israel's history unfolds, the one sanctuary will be identified as the Temple in Jerusalem.

The Deuteronomic School adopts "covenant" as the primary way to speak of the relationship between Yahweh and Israel. The notion of covenant pervades the entire Deuteronomistic History, but is especially dominant in the book of Deuteronomy. In Deuteronomy it is acknowledged that the covenant has already been made with Israel's ancestors (Dt 4:31; 29:24) or promised to them (29:13), but Deuteronomy also says the covenant at Mount Horeb is made with "us" (5:2–3), that is, the Israelites presently on the banks of the Jordan, and it is being made with them "today" (29:11). The confusion may result from later editing of the book, but the effect is to make the covenant a present reality for Moses' audience, an audience that includes even the reader. The covenant is sworn by oath (29:11, 13) and Yahweh will not forget it (4:31; 7:9), but the preservation of the covenant depends upon the people's obedience to its ordinances (7:12).

Israel is exhorted not to forget the covenant (Dt 4:23), but it is clear that they will break and forsake the covenant (31:16, 20) and be destroyed as a result (29:21–27). Israel is to heed Yahweh's ordinances (7:12), but loyalty to the covenant is grounded foremost in the First Commandment (5:7–9). In obedience to that commandment Israel is not to make idols (4:23), or go after other gods (6:14), or worship, serve, and sacrifice to other gods (31:20). At worship Israel is to express its love, gratitude, and loyalty to Yahweh and Yahweh alone.

## Law

Law figures prominently in the book of Deuteronomy, but not simply in its listing of specific laws. Rather, throughout the book there is a sustained exhortation to obey the law. The tone is one of persuasion and encouragement, often accompanying the law with motivations for obedience (e.g., Dt 4:1). The law is

to be learned and passed on to subsequent generations (4:9). Knowledge of Israel's laws is important, but the book of Deuteronomy is concerned to impress upon Israel the religious convictions that provide a basis for obedience to the law. Prominent among these convictions is the recognition that the covenant relationship between Yahweh and Israel is the context of the law. The law is grounded in a relationship and gives expression to that relationship. Obedience to the law is Israel's response to the love initiated by the deity; disobedience disrupts the relationship of love between God and people.

The Ten Commandments occupy a position of prominence in the book of Deuteronomy (Dt 5:6–21) and as the law code of chs. 12–26 unfolds, specific laws are based on principles drawn from the Ten Commandments. The laws of Deuteronomy direct Israel to be the holy people of Yahweh in the context of the daily life of the community in its religious, social, and political dimensions. No distinction is made between religious and secular law, because all areas of life are under the purview of Yahweh. Laws regulating such matters as sacrifices and festivals are included along with laws that attend to the concern for the poor and the conduct of war. Among its many laws the Deuteronomic law code covers what to eat, how to mourn, proper sexual behavior, and what is expected of judges, priests, prophets, and kings. That so many and such diverse aspects of Israel's life are covered in these laws suggests that living the covenant relationship involves a commitment of one's whole life to Yahweh, a commitment that finds expression in worship and in how Israel conducts its life as a just and holy people.

## Land

In the setting of the book of Deuteronomy Israel is encamped on the banks of the Jordan, poised to enter the land of Canaan and take it over. It is an appropriate time to reflect upon the land and its meaning and indeed references to the land are interspersed in Moses' farewell speeches and in the Deuteronomic law code. The promises to Abraham included a promise of land (Dt 1:8; cf. Gn 12:7; 13:15, 17) and the fulfillment of that promise is about to be realized in the book of Joshua with the conquest of the land (Dt 1:8). The land is part of the promise to the ancestors; it is gift and inheritance, but it is also a reward for obedience (4:40; 5:32). The land is the place where covenant is to be lived and the law is to be obeyed (e.g., 4:5, 14; 6:1–2), but possession of the land can be lost by disobedience. In the history of Israel as found in the books of Joshua to 2 Kings it is the worship of other gods that is the primary cause of Israel's loss of the land. As in the suzerainty treaties of the ancient Near East, destruction and exile are punishments for betrayal of the overlord, but in the book of Deuteronomy the loss of the land is never presented as final. The future is open-ended. If Israel returns to the worship of Yahweh, and if it lives in obedience to the law as it is spelled out, especially in the book of Deuteronomy, then Israel will be allowed to return to the land and dwell in it in prosperity and peace.

# The Song of Moses and Blessing of Moses

Before Deuteronomy closes with the death of Moses (Dt 34:1–12), there are two poems inserted at the end of Moses' final speech: the Song of Moses (32:1–43) and the Blessing of Moses (33:1–29). The Song of Moses is not a song of praise, but rather a poem that draws upon prophetic and wisdom traditions to highlight Israel's future. It is a future in which the people of Israel fail to live in fidelity to Yahweh in spite of Yahweh's care for them. They will experience punishment, but Yahweh in his compassion will vindicate them. The Blessing of Moses is a blessing of the tribes of Israel that echoes the blessing of Jacob upon his sons (Gn 49). It points to the future destinies of the tribes and ends by acknowledging that Israel's blessedness rests upon Yahweh and what he has done on its behalf. ■

D
T

# THE BOOK OF DEUTERONOMY

## New American Bible, Introduction

The title of Deuteronomy in Hebrew is *Debarim*, "words," from its opening phrase. The English title comes from the Septuagint of 17:18, *deuteronomion*, "copy of the law"; this title is appropriate because the book replicates much of the legal content of the previous books, serving as a "second law." It brings to a close the five books of the Torah or Pentateuch with a retrospective account of Israel's past—the exodus, the Sinai covenant, and the wilderness wanderings—and a look into Israel's future as they stand poised to enter the land of Canaan and begin their life as a people there.

The book consists of three long addresses by Moses. Each of these contains narrative, law, and exhortation, in varying proportions. In an expansion of the first commandment of the decalogue (Ex 20:5–6; Dt 5:9–10), Moses tells the Israelites how to make a success of their life as a people once they are settled in the land. The choice presented to Israel is to love the Lord and keep his commandments, or to serve "other gods." That choice will determine what kind of life they will make for themselves in the land. Whichever choice they make as a people carries consequences, which Deuteronomy terms "blessing" and "curse." Thus the book can be seen as a kind of survival manual for Israel in their life as a people: how to live and what to avoid. This gives the book its hortatory style and tone of life-or-death urgency.

One defining concern of the book is centralization of worship. As Israel's God is one (6:4–5), so its worship must be focused in one place, which the Lord "will choose from among your tribes"; there the Lord will "make his name dwell" (see note on 12:5). Thus the privileged status of the Jerusalem Temple is asserted; all other places and all other modes of worship of the God of Israel (the local shrines, the "high places," "under every green tree") are proscribed.

The book was probably composed over the course of three centuries, from the eighth century to the exile and beyond. It bears some relation to "the Book of the Law" discovered in the Jerusalem Temple around 622 B.C. during the reign of King Josiah (2 Kgs 22:8–13). It gives evidence of later editing: cf. the references to exile in 4:1–40; 28:63–68; 29;21–28; 30:1–10.

Over the book looms the disaster of 722/721, the fall of the Northern Kingdom, Israel. The detailed description of siege (28:49–57) especially echoes the fate the North suffered at the hands of the Assyrian invader. The book draws the minds of its intended readers back to a time before disastrous mistakes were made and their disastrous effects felt, and serves to explain the political and theological dynamics that led to the destruction of the North as well as to warn the surviving Southern Kingdom, Judah, to reform by keeping faith with Israel's covenant Lord.

The characteristic and highly recognizable language and theology of Deuteronomy are seen in editorial comments structuring the works that follow it in the Hebrew canon, the Books of Joshua, Judges, Samuel, and Kings. Together with Deuteronomy, these present a history of Israel from Moses to the time of the Babylonian exile. Conventionally this great multivolume work is termed the Deuteronomistic History. The Book of Deuteronomy itself was also incorporated into the Torah as its fifth volume.

The book presents three discourses by Moses, as follows:

# DEUTERONOMY

## I. FIRST ADDRESS

**1** **Introduction.** ¹† These are the words that Moses spoke to all Israel beyond the Jordan in the wilderness, in the Arabah, opposite Suph, between Paran and Tophel, Laban, Hazeroth, and Dizahab. ² It is a journey of eleven days from Horeb† to Kadesh-barnea by way of the highlands of Seir.

³ In the fortieth year,† on the first day of the eleventh month, Moses spoke to the Israelites according to all that the LORD had commanded him to speak to them, ⁴ after he had defeated Sihon, king of the Amorites, who reigned in Heshbon,* and Og, king of Bashan, who reigned in Ashtaroth and in Edrei. ⁵ Beyond the Jordan, in the land of Moab, Moses undertook to explain this law:

**Departure from Horeb.** ⁶†* The LORD, our God, said to us at Horeb:† You have stayed long enough at this mountain. ⁷ Leave here and go to the hill country of the Amorites† and to all the surrounding regions, the Arabah, the mountains, the Shephelah, the Negeb and the seacoast—the land of the Canaanites and the Lebanon as far as the Great River, the Euphrates. ⁸ See, I have given that land over to you.* Go now and possess the land that the LORD swore to your ancestors, Abraham, Isaac, and Jacob, to give to them and to their descendants after them.

**Appointment of Elders.** ⁹* At that time I said to you, "I am unable to carry you by myself.*

¹⁰ The LORD, your God, has made you numerous, and now you are as numerous as the stars of the heavens.* ¹¹ May the LORD, the God of your ancestors, increase you a thousand times over, and bless you as he promised! ¹² But how can I, by myself, bear the weight, the contentiousness of you? ¹³ Provide wise, discerning, and reputable persons for each of your tribes, that I may appoint them as your leaders." ¹⁴ You answered me, "What you have proposed is good." ¹⁵ So I took the leaders of your tribes, wise and reputable, and set them as leaders over you, commanders over thousands, over hundreds, over fifties and over tens, and other tribal officers. ¹⁶* I charged your judges at that time, "Listen to complaints among your relatives, and administer true justice to both parties even if one of them is a resident alien. ¹⁷ In rendering judgment, do not consider who a person is; give ear to the lowly and to the great alike, fearing no one, for the judgment is God's. Any case that is too difficult for you bring to me and I will hear it." ¹⁸ Thus I charged you, at that time, with all the things you were to do.

**The Twelve Scouts.** ¹⁹* Then we set out from Horeb and journeyed through that whole vast and fearful wilderness that you have seen, in the direction of the hill country of the Amorites, as the LORD, our God, had commanded; and we came to Kadesh-barnea.* ²⁰ I said to you, "You have come to the hill country of the Amorites, which the LORD, our God, is giving us. ²¹ See, the LORD, your God, has given this land over to you. Go up and take possession of it, as the LORD, the God of your ancestors, has promised you. Do not fear or be dismayed." ²² Then all of you approached me and said, "Let us send men ahead to spy out the land

**1:1** The entire book of Deuteronomy is set "beyond the Jordan," in the land of Moab (cf. v. 5; Nm 36:13), on the eve of the Israelites' crossing of the Jordan (Jos 3). *The Arabah*: the valley of the Jordan and the depression south of the Dead Sea.
**1:2** *Horeb*: an alternative name for Mount Sinai, the wilderness mountain where the Israelites received revelation from God (cf. Ex 3; 19). *Kadesh-barnea*: the southern gateway to the land of Canaan, from which Moses sent spies to reconnoiter the land (cf. Nm 13:26; 32:8). *Seir*: Edom, the land just south of Moab.
**1:3** *Fortieth year*: counting from the exodus from Egypt (cf. Ex 12:2; 13:20–22).
**1:6–3:29** Throughout this section Moses is reviewing the events following the departure from Horeb, as a basis for the exhortation beginning in 4:1. Most of these events are narrated with some variation in the Book of Numbers.
**1:6** *Horeb*: the name given to the mountain of revelation in the Elohist and Deuteronomic traditions; this mountain is called Sinai in the Yahwist and Priestly traditions.

**1:7** *The hill country of the Amorites*: the central mountain range of Palestine. *The Negeb*: the arid land in southern Palestine. *The Lebanon*: the mountain range of Phoenicia, north of Palestine. This is an idealized presentation of the land the Israelites were to occupy; Israel never held power as far as the "Great River" (the Euphrates). The Amorites and the Canaanites were only two of several different peoples occupying the land (cf. 7:1).

**1:4** Dt 2:24–3:11; Nm 21:21–35.   **1:9** Dt 1:31.
**1:6–8** Ex 32:34–33:3.   **1:10** Dt 10:22; Gn 15:5; 22:17; 26:3–4; Ex 32:13.
**1:8** Dt 6:10, 23; 9:5, 27; 29:13; 30:20; 34:4; Gn 12:7; 13:14–15; 15:18–21; 17:8; 26:3–5; 28:13–14.
**1:9–18** Ex 18:13–26;   **1:9** Nm 11:16–30.
**1:16–17** Dt 10:17–18; 16:18–20.
**1:19–25** Nm 13:1–27.
**1:19** Nm 11:11–36.

for us and report to us on the road we should follow and the cities we will come upon." ²³Agreeing with the proposal, I took twelve men from your number, one from each tribe. ²⁴They set out into the hill country as far as the Wadi Eshcol, and explored it. ²⁵Then, taking along some of the fruit of the land, they brought it down to us and reported, "The land the LORD, our God, is giving us is good."

**Threats of Revolt.** ²⁶* But you refused to go up;* you defied the command of the LORD, your God. ²⁷You set to murmuring in your tents, "Out of hatred for us the LORD has brought us out of the land of Egypt,* to deliver us into the power of the Amorites and destroy us. ²⁸What shall we meet with up there? Our men have made our hearts melt by saying, 'The people are bigger and taller than we, and their cities are large and fortified to the sky; besides, we saw the Anakim† there.'"*

²⁹But I said to you, "Have no dread or fear of them. ³⁰* The LORD, your God, who goes before you, is the one who will fight for you, just as he acted with you before your very eyes in Egypt, ³¹as well as in the wilderness, where you saw how the LORD, your God, carried you, as one carries his own child, all along your journey until you arrived at this place." ³²Despite this, you would not trust the LORD, your God, ³³who journeys before you to find you a place to camp—by night in the fire, and by day in the cloud, to show you the way to go.* ³⁴When the LORD heard your words, he was angry, and took an oath: ³⁵Not a single one of this evil generation shall look upon the good land I swore to give to your ancestors, ³⁶except Caleb,† son of Jephunneh. He shall see it, for to him and to his descendants I will give the land he trod upon,* because he has fully followed the LORD.

³⁷The LORD was angered against me also on your account, and said, You shall not enter there either,* ³⁸but Joshua,* son of Nun, your attendant, shall enter. Encourage him, for he is the one who is to give Israel its possession.

³⁹Your little ones, who you said would become plunder, and your children, who as yet do not know good from evil—they shall enter there; to them I will give it, and they shall take possession of it. ⁴⁰But as for yourselves: turn back and proceed into the wilderness on the Red Sea road.

**Unsuccessful Invasion.** ⁴¹* In reply you said to me, "We have sinned against the LORD. We will go up ourselves and fight, just as the LORD, our God, commanded us." And each of you girded on his weapons, making light of going up into the hill country. ⁴²But the LORD said to me, Warn them: Do not go up and fight—for I will not be in your midst—lest you be beaten down before your enemies. ⁴³I gave you this warning but you would not listen. You defied the LORD's command and arrogantly went off into the hill country. ⁴⁴Then the Amorites living in that hill country came out against you and put you to flight the way bees do, cutting you down in Seir as far as Hormah. ⁴⁵On your return you wept before the LORD, but the LORD did not listen to your voice or give ear to you. ⁴⁶That is why you had to stay as long as you did at Kadesh.

**2** **Northward Along Edom.** ¹* Then we turned and proceeded into the wilderness on the Red Sea road,* as the LORD had told me, and circled around the highlands of Seir for a long time. ²Finally the LORD said to me, ³You have wandered round these highlands long enough; turn and go north. ⁴Command the people: You are now about to pass through the territory of your relatives, the descendants of Esau, who live in Seir. Though they are afraid of you, be very careful ⁵not to come in conflict with them, for I will not give you so much as a foot of their land, since I have already given Esau possession of the highlands of Seir.* ⁶You shall purchase from them with money the food you eat; even the water you drink you shall buy from them with money. ⁷Surely, the LORD, your God, has blessed you in all your

---

† 
**1:28** *Anakim:* a people proverbially notable for height, mentioned in pre-Israelite Egyptian texts, and in the biblical tradition associated with the region of Hebron and the hill country of Judah (Nm 13:22, 28, 33; Jos 11:21; 14:12, 15).
**1:36** *Except Caleb:* and Joshua (v. 38).

*
**1:26–40** Nm 13:28–14:38.
**1:26** Dt 9:23.

21; 9:2; Nm 13:22, 28, 33; Jos 11:21–22; 14:12, 15; 15:13–14; 21:11; Jgs 1:20.
**1:27** Dt 9:28.
**1:28** Dt 1:28; 2:10–11,
**1:30–31** Dt 3:22; 8:15; 32:10; Ex 14:13–14.
**1:33** Ex 13:21; 40:38; Nm 9:15–16; 10:33–34; 14:14.
**1:36** Jos 14:6–14.

**1:37** Dt 4:21; 34:4; Nm 20:12.
**1:38** Dt 31:3, 7–8; Nm 27:18–23; 34:17; Jos 1:1–9.
**1:41–46** Nm 14:39–45.
**2:1–8** Nm 20:14–21; Jgs 11:15–17.
**2:1** Dt 1:40; Nm 14:25.
**2:5** Gn 36:6–8.

undertakings; he has been concerned† about your journey through this vast wilderness. It is now forty years that the LORD, your God, has been with you, and you have lacked nothing.* ⁸ So we passed by our relatives, the descendants of Esau who live in Seir, leaving behind us the Arabah route, Elath, and Ezion-geber.

**Along Moab.** Then we turned and passed on toward the wilderness of Moab. ⁹* And the LORD said to me, Do not show hostility to the Moabites or engage them in battle, for I will not give you possession of any of their land, since I have given Ar to the descendants of Lot as their possession.* ¹⁰ (Formerly the Emim lived there, a people great and numerous and as tall as the Anakim;* ¹¹ like the Anakim they are considered Rephaim, though the Moabites call them Emim.* ¹² In Seir, however, the former inhabitants were the Horites;* the descendants of Esau dispossessed them, clearing them out of the way and dwelling in their place, just as Israel has done in the land of its possession which the LORD gave it.) ¹³ Now get ready to cross the Wadi Zered.

So we crossed the Wadi Zered. ¹⁴* Now thirty-eight years had elapsed between our departure from Kadesh-barnea and the crossing of the Wadi Zered; in the meantime the whole generation of soldiers had perished from the camp, as the LORD had sworn they should. ¹⁵ Indeed the LORD's own hand was against them, to rout them from the camp completely.

**Along Ammon.** ¹⁶* When at length death had put an end to all the soldiers among the people, ¹⁷ the LORD said to me, ¹⁸ You are now about to leave Ar and the territory of Moab behind. ¹⁹ As you come opposite the Ammonites,* do not show hostility or come in conflict with them, for I will not give you possession of any land of the Ammonites, since I have given it to the descendants of Lot as their possession. ²⁰ (This also is considered a country of the Rephaim; formerly the Rephaim dwelt there.

The Ammonites call them Zamzummim,* ²¹ a people great and numerous and as tall as the Anakim. But these, too, the LORD cleared out of the way for the Ammonites, so that they dispossessed them and dwelt in their place.* ²² He did the same for the descendants of Esau, who live in Seir, by clearing the Horites out of their way, so that they dispossessed them and dwelt in their place down to the present.* ²³ As for the Avvim, who once lived in villages in the vicinity of Gaza,† the Caphtorim, migrating from Caphtor, cleared them away and dwelt in their place.)*

**Defeat of Sihon.** ²⁴* Advance now across the Wadi Arnon. I now deliver into your power Sihon, the Amorite king of Heshbon, and his land. Begin to take possession; engage him in battle.* ²⁵ This day I will begin to put a fear and dread of you into the peoples everywhere under heaven, so that at the mention of your name they will quake and tremble before you.

²⁶ So I sent messengers from the wilderness of Kedemoth to Sihon, king of Heshbon, with this offer of peace: ²⁷ "Let me pass through your country. I will travel only on the road. I will not turn aside either to the right or to the left. ²⁸ The food I eat you will sell me for money, and the water I drink, you will give me for money. Only let me march through, ²⁹ as the descendants of Esau who dwell in Seir and the Moabites who dwell in Ar have done, until I cross the Jordan into the land the LORD, our God, is about to give us."* ³⁰ But Sihon, king of Heshbon, refused to let us pass through his land, because the LORD, your God, made him stubborn in mind and obstinate in heart that he might deliver him into your power, as indeed he has now done.

³¹ Then the LORD said to me, Now that I have already begun to give over to you Sihon and his land, begin to take possession. ³² So Sihon and all his people advanced against us to join battle at Jahaz; ³³ but since the LORD, our God, had given him over to us, we defeated him and

---

† 2:7 *Concerned:* lit., "known"; cf. Ex 2:25.
2:23 *Gaza:* later a stronghold of the Philistines (cf. Jos 13:3). *Caphtor:* the island of Crete.

2:7 Dt 8:2–5.
2:9–13 Nm 21:12–15; Jgs 11:17–18.
2:9 Gn 19:36–38.
2:10 Dt 1:28.
2:11 Dt 2:20; 3:11, 13; Gn 14:5; 15:20; Jos 12:4; 13:12; 17:15.
2:12 Gn 14:6; 36:20–30.
2:14–15 Nm 14:28–35.
2:16–19 Nm 21:24.
2:19 Gn 19:36–38.
2:20 Dt 2:11; 3:11, 13; Gn 14:5; 15:20; Jos 12:4; 13:12; 17:15.
2:21 Dt 1:28.
2:22 Gn 14:6; 36:6–8, 20–30.
2:23 Gn 10:14; Jos 13:3; 18:23; 1 Chr 1:12; Jer 47:4; Am 9:7.
2:24–3:11 Dt 1:4; 29:7; 31:4; Jos 2:10; 9:10; 12:1–6; Neh 9:22; Ps 135:10–12; 136:17–22.
2:24–37 Nm 21:21–32; Jgs 11:19–22.
2:29 Dt 2:4–9.

his sons and all his people. [34]* At that time we captured all his cities and put every city under the ban,† men, women and children; we left no survivor. [35] Our only plunder was the livestock and the spoils of the captured cities. [36] From Aroer on the edge of the Wadi Arnon and from the town in the wadi itself, as far as Gilead,* no city was too well fortified for us. All of them the LORD, our God, gave over to us. [37] However, just as the LORD, our God, commanded us, you did not encroach upon any of the Ammonite land, neither the region bordering on the Wadi Jabbok, nor the cities of the highlands.*

**3 Defeat of Og.** [1] Then we turned and proceeded up the road to Bashan. But Og, king of Bashan,* came out against us with all his people to give battle at Edrei. [2] The LORD said to me, Do not be afraid of him, for I have delivered him into your power with all his people and his land. Do to him as you did to Sihon, king of the Amorites, who reigned in Heshbon. [3] And thus the LORD, our God, delivered into our power also Og, king of Bashan, with all his people. We defeated him so completely that we left him no survivor. [4] At that time we captured all his cities; there was no town we did not take: sixty cities in all, the whole region of Argob, the kingdom of Og in Bashan— [5] all these cities were fortified with high walls and gates and bars—besides a great number of unwalled towns. [6]* As we had done to Sihon, king of Heshbon, so also here we put all the towns under the ban, men, women and children; [7] but all the livestock and the spoils of each city we took as plunder for ourselves.

[8] And so at that time we took from the two kings of the Amorites beyond the Jordan the territory from the Wadi Arnon to Mount Hermon [9] (the Sidonians call Hermon Sirion and the Amorites call it Senir), [10] all the towns of the plateau, all of Gilead, and all of Bashan as far as Salecah and Edrei, towns of the kingdom of Og in Bashan. [11] (Og, king of Bashan, was the last remaining survivor of the Rephaim. He had a bed of iron,† nine regular cubits long and four wide, which is still preserved in Rabbah of the Ammonites.)*

**Allotment of the Conquered Lands.** [12]* As for the land we took possession of at that time, I gave Reuben and Gad the territory from Aroer, on the edge of the Wadi Arnon, halfway up into the highlands of Gilead, with its cities. [13] The rest of Gilead and all of Bashan, the kingdom of Og, I gave to the half-tribe of Manasseh. (The whole Argob region, all that part of Bashan, was once called a land of the Rephaim.* [14] Jair, a Manassite,* took all the region of Argob as far as the border of the Geshurites and Maacathites, and named them—Bashan, that is—after himself, Havvoth-jair, the name it bears today.) [15] To Machir† I gave Gilead, [16] and to Reuben and Gad the territory from Gilead to the Wadi Arnon—the middle of the wadi being its boundary—and to the Wadi Jabbok, which is the border of the Ammonites, [17] as well as the Arabah with the Jordan and its banks from Chinnereth† to the Salt Sea of the Arabah, under the slopes of Pisgah on the east.

[18]* At that time I charged you: The LORD, your God, has given you this land as your possession. But all your troops equipped for battle must cross over in the vanguard of your fellow Israelites. [19] But your wives and children, as well as your livestock, of which I know you have a large number, shall remain behind in the towns I have given you, [20] until the LORD has settled your relatives as well, and they too possess the land which the LORD, your God, will give them on the other side of the Jordan. Then you may all return to the possessions I have given you.

[21] And I charged Joshua as well, "Your own eyes have seen all that the LORD, your God,

---

† **2:34** *Under the ban:* in Hebrew, *herem*, which means to devote to the Lord (cf. 7:1–5; 20:10–18). The biblical text often presents *herem* as the total extermination of a population as a manifestation of the will of the Lord. It is historically doubtful that Israel ever literally carried out this theological program.

**3:11** *Bed of iron:* some translate, "a sarcophagus of basalt"; its dimensions would be approximately thirteen and a half feet by six feet.

**3:15** *Machir:* a clan of the tribe of Manasseh (cf. Gn 50:23).

**3:17** *Chinnereth:* later known as the Lake of Gennesaret and the Sea of Galilee. *The Salt Sea:* the Dead Sea. *Pisgah:* a mountain range to the northeast of the Salt Sea; Mount Nebo, from which Moses viewed the promised land, is in this range (cf. v. 27; 34:1).

**2:34–35** Dt 3:6; 7:2, 26; 13:16, 18; 20:16–18; Jos 10:40; 11:11–12.
**2:36** Dt 3:12–13; Jos 13:8–13, 15–23.
**2:37** Nm 21:24; Jos 12:2.
**3:1–11** Nm 21:33–35.
**3:6–7** Dt 2:34–35; 7:2, 26; 13:16, 18; 20:16–18; Jos 10:40; 11:11–12.
**3:11** Dt 2:11, 20; 3:13; Gn

14:5; 15:20; Jos 12:4; 13:12; 17:15.
**3:12–22** Nm 32:1–42; Jos 13:8–33.
**3:13** Dt 2:11, 20; 3:11; Gn 14:5; 15:20; Jos 12:4; 13:12; 17:15.
**3:14** Nm 32:41; Jgs 10:4; 1 Chr 2:23.
**3:18–20** Jos 1:12–15; 4:12; 22:1–4.

has done to both these kings; so, too, will the LORD do to all the kingdoms into which you will cross over. [22] Do not fear them, for it is the LORD, your God, who will fight for you."*

## Moses Excluded from the Promised Land.
[23]* It was then that I entreated the LORD, [24] "Lord GOD, you have begun to show to your servant your greatness and your mighty hand. What god in heaven or on earth can perform deeds and powerful acts like yours? [25] Ah, let me cross over and see the good land beyond the Jordan, that fine hill country, and the Lebanon!" [26] But the LORD was angry with me on your account† and would not hear me.* The LORD said to me, Enough! Speak to me no more of this. [27] Go up to the top of Pisgah and look out to the west, and to the north, and to the south, and to the east. Look well, for you shall not cross this Jordan.* [28] Commission Joshua,* and encourage and strengthen him, for it is he who will cross at the head of this people and he who will give them possession of the land you are to see.

[29] So we remained in the valley opposite Beth-peor.

**4 Advantages of Fidelity.** [1] Now therefore, Israel, hear the statutes and ordinances I am teaching you to observe, that you may live, and may enter in and take possession of the land which the LORD, the God of your ancestors, is giving you.* [2] In your observance of the commandments of the LORD, your God,* which I am commanding you, you shall not add to what I command you nor subtract from it. [3] You have seen with your own eyes what the LORD did at Baal-peor:* the LORD, your God, destroyed from your midst everyone who followed the Baal of Peor; [4] but you, who held fast to the LORD, your God, are all alive today. [5] See, I am teaching you the statutes and ordinances as the LORD, my God, has commanded me, that you may observe them in the land

you are entering to possess. [6] Observe them carefully, for this is your wisdom and discernment in the sight of the peoples, who will hear of all these statutes and say, "This great nation is truly a wise and discerning people."* [7]* For what great nation is there that has gods so close to it as the LORD, our God, is to us whenever we call upon him? [8] Or what great nation has statutes and ordinances that are as just as this whole law which I am setting before you today?*

## Revelation at Horeb.
[9] However, be on your guard and be very careful not to forget the things your own eyes have seen, nor let them slip from your heart as long as you live, but make them known to your children* and to your children's children, [10] that day you stood before the LORD, your God, at Horeb, when the LORD said to me: Assemble the people for me, that I may let them hear my words, that they may learn to fear† me as long as they live in the land and may so teach their children. [11]* You came near and stood at the foot of the mountain, while the mountain blazed to the heart of the heavens with fire and was enveloped in a dense black cloud. [12] Then the LORD spoke to you from the midst of the fire.* You heard the sound of the words, but saw no form; there was only a voice. [13] He proclaimed to you his covenant, which he commanded you to keep: the ten words,† which he wrote on two stone tablets.* [14] At that time the LORD charged me to teach you the statutes and ordinances for you to observe in the land you are about to cross into and possess.

## Danger of Idolatry.
[15] Because you saw no form at all on the day the LORD spoke to you at Horeb from the midst of the fire, be strictly on your guard [16] not to act corruptly by fashioning an idol for yourselves to represent any figure, whether it be the form of a man or of a woman,* [17] the form of any animal on the

---

† 
**3:26** *On your account*: that Moses saw but never entered the promised land is attested by every Pentateuchal tradition, but different reasons are given in different places. Nm 20:12 and Dt 32:51 present Moses as being at fault. Here, as in 1:37 and 4:21, the fault lies in the people but affects Moses.
**4:10** *Fear*: not in the sense of "be terrified," but rather "manifest reverence or awe."
**4:13** *Ten words*: the ten commandments, or decalogue (cf. 5:22; Ex 34:28).

**3:22** Dt 1:30; Ex 14:13–14.
**3:23–29** Nm 27:12–23.
**3:26** Dt 4:21.
**3:27** Dt 3:17; 32:48–52;
  34:1–4.
**3:28** Dt 1:38; 31:7–8.
**4:1** Dt 4:45; 5:1, 31; 6:1,
  17, 20; 11:32; 12:1;
  26:16.
**4:2** Dt 13:1.
**4:3** Nm 25:1–13; Ps
  106:28; Hos 9:10.
**4:6** Dt 26:5; Gn 12:2;
  18:18; 46:3; Ex 32:10.
**4:7–8** 2 Sm 7:23.
**4:8** Dt 4:44.
**4:9** Dt 6:7, 20–25;
  11:19–21; 29:29;
  31:12–13; Ps 78:3–6.
**4:11–13** Ex 19:7–20:21.
**4:12** Dt 4:33, 36; 5:4.
**4:13** Dt 5:6–21; 10:4;
  Ex 20:1–17; 24:12;
  31:18; 34:27–28.
**4:16** Dt 5:8; Ex 20:4.

earth, the form of any bird that flies in the sky, [18] the form of anything that crawls on the ground, or the form of any fish in the waters under the earth. [19] And when you look up to the heavens and behold the sun or the moon or the stars, the whole heavenly host, do not be led astray into bowing down to them and serving them. * These the LORD, your God, has apportioned to all the other nations under the heavens; [20] but you the LORD has taken and led out of that iron foundry, Egypt, that you might be his people, his heritage, as you are today. * [21] But the LORD was angry with me on your account* and swore that I should not cross the Jordan nor enter the good land which the LORD, your God, is giving you as a heritage. [22] I myself shall die in this country; I shall not cross the Jordan; but you are going to cross over and take possession of that good land. * [23] Be careful, therefore, lest you forget the covenant which the LORD, your God, has made with you, and fashion for yourselves against his command an idol in any form whatsoever. * [24] For the LORD, your God, is a consuming fire, a jealous God.†*

**God's Fidelity and Love.** [25] * When you have children and children's children, and have grown old in the land, should you then act corruptly by fashioning an idol in the form of anything, and by this evil done in his sight provoke the LORD, your God, [26] I call heaven and earth this day to witness against you, that you shall all quickly perish from the land which you are crossing the Jordan to possess. You shall not live in it for any length of time but shall be utterly wiped out. * [27] The LORD will scatter you among the peoples, and there shall remain but a handful of you among the nations to which the LORD will drive you. [28] There you shall serve gods that are works of human hands, of wood and stone, gods which can neither see nor hear, neither eat nor smell. * [29] Yet when you seek the LORD, your God, from there, you shall indeed find him if you search after him with all your heart and soul. * [30] In your distress, when all these things shall have come upon you, you shall finally return to the LORD, your God, and listen to his voice. [31] Since the LORD, your God, is a merciful God, he will not abandon or destroy you, nor forget the covenant with your ancestors that he swore to them. *

[32] Ask now of the days of old, before your time, ever since God created humankind upon the earth; ask from one end of the sky to the other: Did anything so great ever happen before? Was it ever heard of? [33] Did a people ever hear the voice of God speaking from the midst of fire, as you did, and live? * [34] Or did any god venture to go and take a nation for himself from the midst of another nation, by testings, by signs and wonders, * by war, with strong hand and outstretched arm, and by great terrors, all of which the LORD, your God, did for you in Egypt before your very eyes? [35] All this you were allowed to see that you might know that the LORD is God; there is no other. * [36] Out of the heavens he let you hear his voice to discipline you; on earth he let you see his great fire, and you heard him speaking out of the fire. [37] For love of your ancestors he chose their descendants after them and by his presence and great power led you out of Egypt, [38] dispossessing before you nations greater and mightier than you, so as to bring you in and to give their land to you as a heritage, as it is today. [39] This is why you must now acknowledge, and fix in your heart, that the LORD is God in the heavens above and on earth below, and that there is no other. * [40] And you must keep his statutes and commandments which I command you today, that you and your children after you may prosper, and that you may have

---

† **4:24** *A jealous God:* Hebrew *'el qanna.* The root of the adjective *qanna* expresses the idea of intense feeling focused on solicitude for someone or something; see, e.g., Ps 69:10; Sg 8:6; Is 9:6; 37:32; Ez 39:25. The Septuagint translated the adjective as *zelotes,* and the Vulgate followed suit; hence the traditional English rendering "jealous" (and sometimes "zealous") found in the Douai-Rheims and King James versions. In modern usage, however, "jealous" denotes unreasonable, petty possessiveness, a meaning, even as nuance, wanting in the Hebrew. In the first commandment (5:6–10; Ex 20:2–6) and passages derived from it (like 4:24; 6:15; Ex 34:14; Jos 24:19; Na 1:2), Israel's God is represented as totally committed to his purpose, and Israel is put on notice to take him and his directives for their life as a people with equal seriousness.

**4:19** Dt 17:3; Jb 31:26–28.
**4:20** 1 Kgs 8:51; Is 48:10; Jer 11:4.
**4:21** Dt 1:37; 3:26.
**4:22** Dt 3:27; 34:1–12; Jos 1–12.
**4:23** Dt 4:16; 9:12–14; Ex 32:1–10.
**4:24** Dt 5:9; 6:15; 9:3; Ex 24:17; 34:14.
**4:25–27** Dt 28:64–67.
**4:26** Dt 30:19; 31:28; 32:1; Is 1:2.
**4:28** Dt 28:64; 29:17; Lv 26:30–39; Ps 115:4–8; 135:15–18;
Is 44:9–20.
**4:29** Dt 6:5; Jer 29:13–14.
**4:31** Dt 31:8; Gn 9:9–17; 15:18–21; 17:1–21; Ex 34:6–7.
**4:33** Dt 4:36; 5:24, 26; Ex 20:19.
**4:34** Dt 7:19; 26:8; 29:2; Ex 7:3; 15:3–10; Jer 32:21.
**4:35** Dt 4:39; 32:39; 1 Kgs 8:60; Is 43:10–13; Jl 2:27.
**4:39** Dt 4:35; 32:39; 1 Kgs 8:60; Is 43:10–13; Jl 2:27.

long life on the land which the LORD, your God, is giving you forever.*

**Cities of Refuge.** 41* Then Moses set apart three cities in the region east of the Jordan, 42 to which a homicide might flee who killed a neighbor unintentionally, where there had been no hatred previously, so that the killer might flee to one of these cities and live: 43 Bezer in the wilderness, in the region of the plateau, for the Reubenites; Ramoth in Gilead for the Gadites; and Golan in Bashan for the Manassites.

## II. SECOND ADDRESS

### A. The Lord's Covenant with Israel

**Introduction.** 44 This is the law† which Moses set before the Israelites.* 45 These are the decrees, and the statutes and ordinances† which Moses proclaimed to the Israelites after they came out of Egypt,* 46* beyond the Jordan in the valley opposite Beth-peor, in the land of Sihon, king of the Amorites, who reigned in Heshbon, whom Moses and the Israelites defeated after they came out of Egypt.* 47 They took possession of his land and the land of Og, king of Bashan, as well—the land of these two kings of the Amorites in the region beyond the Jordan to the east: 48 from Aroer on the edge of the Wadi Arnon to Mount Sion† (that is, Hermon) 49 and all the Arabah beyond the Jordan to the east, as far as the Arabah Sea† under the slopes of Pisgah.

**5** **The Covenant at Horeb.** 1 Moses summoned all Israel and said to them, Hear, O Israel, the statutes and ordinances which

I proclaim in your hearing this day, that you may learn them and take care to observe them.* 2 The LORD, our God, made a covenant with us at Horeb; 3 not with our ancestors† did the LORD make this covenant, but with us, all of us who are alive here this day. 4* Face to face, the LORD spoke with you on the mountain from the midst of the fire,* 5 while I was standing between the LORD and you at that time, to announce to you these words of the LORD, since you were afraid of the fire and would not go up the mountain:

**The Decalogue.** 6* I am the LORD your God, who brought you out of the land of Egypt,* out of the house of slavery. 7* You shall not have other gods beside me. 8 You shall not make for yourself an idol or a likeness of anything in the heavens above or on the earth below or in the waters beneath the earth; 9† you shall not bow down before them or serve them. For I, the LORD, your God, am a jealous† God, bringing punishment for their parents' wickedness on the children of those who hate me, down to the third and fourth generation, 10 but showing love down to the thousandth generation of those who love me and keep my commandments.

11 You shall not invoke the name of the LORD, your God, in vain.* For the LORD will not leave unpunished anyone who invokes his name in vain.

12* Observe the sabbath day—keep it holy, as the LORD, your God, commanded you. 13 Six days you may labor and do all your work, 14 but the seventh day is a sabbath of the LORD your God. You shall not do any work, either

---

† 4:44 *Law:* Hebrew *torah*, meaning "instruction," "law," "teaching"; the standard translation "law" comes from the influence of the Septuagint's *nomos*, "law," and the extensive legislation in Ex 20–Nm 10.
  4:45 *Statutes and ordinances:* terms referring to the legal corpus in 12:1–26:19.
  4:48 *Sion:* another name for Mount Hermon, besides those mentioned in 3:9 (to be distinguished from the Mount Zion of Jerusalem).
  4:49 *The Arabah Sea:* the Dead Sea, cf. 3:17.
  5:3 *Not with our ancestors:* in fact, the covenant was made with the ancestors, but these had died out during the "forty" years. The covenant is considered to be ongoing—for Israel in Moab and beyond.
  5:9–10 Israel is confronted with a choice, to "love" or to "hate" the Lord, and with the consequences of each choice. "Wickedness" works destruction not only on those who do it but also down the generations, in a sort of ripple effect. Yet, if Israel keeps the commandments, they will experience the Lord's *hesed* ("love") down to the thousandth generation. Thus the Lord's merciful love is disproportionate to the evil results of iniquity ("down to the third and fourth generation"). *To the thousandth*

*generation:* lit., "to thousands"; cf. 7:9.
  5:9 *Jealous:* see note on 4:24.

---

| | |
|---|---|
| **4:40** Dt 6:3; 12:28. | 24:16; 27:15; Ex |
| **4:41–43** Dt 19:1–13; Nm | 20:3–6; 34:6–7, 14; |
| 35:10–28; Jos 20:1–9. | Lv 26:1; Nm 14:18; Ps |
| **4:44** Dt 4:8; 17:18–19; | 81:10; 97:7; Jer 7:9; |
| 30:10; 31:11–12. | 31:29–30; 32:18–19; |
| **4:45** Dt 4:1; 5:1, 31; 6:1, | Ez 18:1–24. |
| 17, 20; 11:32; 12:1; | **5:11** Dt 6:13; 10:20; 18:20; |
| 26:16; Ps 25:10. | 23:21–23; Ex 20:7; |
| **4:46–49** Dt 2:24–3:29. | Lv 19:12; 24:10–23; |
| **4:46** Dt 3:29; 34:6. | Ps 24:4; Jer 29:23; Mt |
| **5:1** Dt 4:1, 45; 5:31; 6:1, | 5:33–37. |
| 17, 20; 11:32; 12:1; | **5:12–15** Dt 14:22–16:17; |
| 26:16. | 24:18, 22; Ex 20:8– |
| **5:4–5** Ex 19:3–25; | 11; 23:12; 31:12–17; |
| 20:18–19; 24:2. | 34:21; Is 58:13–14; |
| **5:4** Dt 34:10; Nm 12:8. | Jer 17:21–27; |
| **5:6–21** Ex 20:2–17. | Mt 12:1–14; Mk |
| **5:6** Dt 20:2; Ps 81:11. | 2:23–3:6; Lk 6:1–11; |
| **5:7–10** Dt 4:23–24, 31; | 13:10–17; 14:1–6; Jn |
| 6:4–5; 7:9–10; 12:2– | 5:2–18; 7:22–23. |
| 13:18; 17:3; 18:20; | |

you, your son or your daughter, your male or female slave, your ox or donkey or any work animal, or the resident alien within your gates, so that your male and female slave may rest as you do. ¹⁵ Remember that you too were once slaves in the land of Egypt, and the LORD, your God, brought you out from there with a strong hand and outstretched arm. That is why the LORD, your God, has commanded you to observe the sabbath day.

¹⁶* Honor your father and your mother, as the LORD, your God, has commanded you, that you may have a long life and that you may prosper in the land the LORD your God is giving you.

¹⁷* You shall not kill.†

¹⁸* You shall not commit adultery.

¹⁹* You shall not steal.

²⁰* You shall not bear dishonest witness against your neighbor.

²¹* You shall not covet your neighbor's wife.

You shall not desire your neighbor's house or field, his male or female slave, his ox or donkey, or anything that belongs to your neighbor.

**Moses as Mediator.** ²² These words the LORD spoke with a loud voice to your entire assembly on the mountain from the midst of the fire and the dense black cloud, and added no more. He inscribed them on two stone tablets and gave them to me.* ²³ But when you heard the voice from the midst of the darkness, while the mountain was ablaze with fire, you came near to me, all your tribal heads and elders, ²⁴ and said, "The LORD, our God, has indeed let us see his glory and his greatness, and we have heard his voice from the midst of the fire.* Today we have found out that God may speak to a mortal and that person may still live. ²⁵ Now, why should we die? For this great

fire will consume us. If we hear the voice of the LORD, our God, any more, we shall die.* ²⁶ For what mortal has heard the voice of the living God speaking from the midst of fire, as we have, and lived? ²⁷ You go closer and listen to all that the LORD, our God, will say, and then tell us what the LORD, our God, tells you; we will listen and obey."*

²⁸ The LORD heard your words as you were speaking to me and said to me, I have heard the words these people have spoken to you, which are all well said.* ²⁹ Would that they might always be of such a mind, to fear me and to keep all my commandments! Then they and their descendants would prosper forever. ³⁰ Go, tell them: Return to your tents. ³¹ Then you stand here near me and I will give you all the commandments, the statutes and the ordinances; you must teach them, that they may observe them in the land I am giving them to possess.*

³² Be careful, therefore, to do as the LORD, your God, has commanded you, not turning aside to the right or to the left, ³³ but following exactly the way that the LORD, your God, commanded you that you may live and prosper, and may have long life in the land which you are to possess.*

**6** ¹ This then is the commandment, the statutes and the ordinances,* which the LORD, your God, has commanded that you be taught to observe in the land you are about to cross into to possess, ² so that you, that is, you, your child, and your grandchild, may fear the LORD, your God, by keeping, as long as you live, all his statutes and commandments* which I enjoin on you, and thus have long life. ³ Hear then, Israel, and be careful to observe them, that it may go well with you and that you may increase greatly; for the LORD, the God of your

---

† **5:17** Kill: see note on Ex 20:13.

**5:16** Dt 21:18–21; 27:16; Ex 20:12; 21:15, 17; Sir 3:1–16; Mt 10:34–39; 12:46–50; 15:4; 19:19; Mk 3:31–35; 7:10; 10:19; Lk 8:19–21; 14:26; 18:20, 28–30; Eph 6:1–4.
**5:17** Dt 4:41–43; 19:1–13; 20:1–21:9; 21:18–23; Gn 4:8–16; Ex 20:13; 21:12–14; Nm 35:16–34; Jer 7:9; Hos 4:2; Mt 5:21–26;

19:18; Mk 10:19; Lk 18:20; Jas 2:11.
**5:18** Dt 22:13–23:1; Gn 20:1–18; 39:7–20; Ex 20:14; Lv 18:20; 20:10; 2 Sm 11:1–12:25; Jer 7:9; Hos 4:2; Mt 5:27–30; 19:18; Mk 10:19; Lk 18:20; Jas 2:11.
**5:19** Dt 23:24; 24:7; Gn 40:15; Ex 20:15; 21:16, 37; 22:1–3, 12; Lv 19:11, 13; 1 Kgs 21:1–19; Jer 7:9;

Hos 4:2; Mt 19:18; Mk 10:19; Lk 18:20.
**5:20** Dt 19:15–19; Ex 20:16; 23:1–3; Lv 19:11, 15–16; 1 Kgs 21:1–19; Ps 5:6–10; 10:7–9; 27:12; Prv 25:18; 30:8–10; Jer 7:9; Hos 4:2; Mt 19:18; 26:59–60; Mk 10:19; Lk 18:20.
**5:21** Dt 7:25; Ex 20:17; Jos 7:21; 2 Sm 11:1–12:25; 1 Kgs 21:1–19; Is 5:8; Mi 2:2; Mt 5:27–30; Lk 12:13–21; Eph 5:5; Col 3:5.

Hos 4:2; Mt 19:18; Mk 10:19; Lk 18:20.
**5:22** Dt 4:13; 9:9–11, 17; 10:1–5; Ex 24:12; 31:18; 32:15–20; 34:1–5.
**5:24** Dt 4:33, 36; Ex 20:19.
**5:25** Dt 18:16.
**5:27** Ex 20:19.
**5:28** Dt 18:17.
**5:31** Dt 4:1, 45; 5:1; 6:1, 17, 20; 11:32; 12:1; 26:16.
**5:33** Dt 4:40.
**6:1** Dt 4:1, 45; 5:1, 31; 6:17, 20; 11:32; 12:1; 26:16.
**6:2** Dt 4:10, 40; 5:29; 6:24; 10:12–13.

ancestors, promised you a land flowing with milk and honey.*

**The Great Commandment.**† ⁴* Hear, O Israel!† The LORD is our God, the LORD alone! ⁵Therefore, you shall love the LORD, your God, with your whole heart, and with your whole being, and with your whole strength.* ⁶* Take to heart these words which I command you today.* ⁷Keep repeating them to your children. Recite them when you are at home and when you are away, when you lie down and when you get up.* ⁸Bind them on your arm as a sign† and let them be as a pendant on your forehead.* ⁹Write them on the doorposts of your houses and on your gates.*

**Fidelity in Prosperity.** ¹⁰* When the LORD, your God, brings you into the land which he swore to your ancestors, to Abraham, Isaac, and Jacob, that he would give you, a land with fine, large cities that you did not build,* ¹¹with houses full of goods of all sorts that you did not garner, with cisterns that you did not dig, with vineyards and olive groves that you did not plant; and when, therefore, you eat and are satisfied,* ¹²* be careful not to forget the LORD, who brought you out of the land of Egypt, that house of slavery. ¹³* The LORD, your God, shall you fear; him shall you serve,† and by his name shall you swear. ¹⁴* You shall not go after other gods, any of the gods of the surrounding peoples— ¹⁵for the LORD, your God who is in your midst, is a passionate God—lest the anger of the LORD, your God, flare up against you and he destroy you from upon the land.

¹⁶You shall not put the LORD, your God, to the test, as you did at Massah.* ¹⁷But keep the commandments of the LORD, your God, and the decrees and the statutes he has commanded you. ¹⁸Do what is right and good in the sight of the LORD, that it may go well with you, and you may enter in and possess the good land which the LORD promised on oath to your ancestors, ¹⁹driving all your enemies out of your way, as the LORD has promised.*

**Instruction to Children.** ²⁰* Later on, when your son asks you, "What do these decrees and statutes and ordinances mean?"* which the LORD, our God, has enjoined on you, ²¹* you shall say to your son, "We were once slaves of Pharaoh in Egypt, but the LORD brought us out of Egypt with a strong hand* ²²and wrought before our eyes signs and wonders, great and dire, against Egypt and against Pharaoh and his whole house. ²³He brought us from there to bring us in and give us the land he had promised on oath to our ancestors.* ²⁴* The LORD commanded us to observe all these statutes in fear of the LORD, our God, that we may always have as good a life as we have today. ²⁵This is our justice before the LORD, our God: to observe carefully this whole commandment he has enjoined on us."

**7** **Destruction of the Nations in the Land.** ¹* When the LORD, your God, brings you into the land which you are about to enter to possess, and removes many nations before you—the Hittites, Girgashites, Amorites,

---

† **6:4–5** This passage, an expansion of the first commandment (5:6–10), contains the basic principle of the whole Mosaic law, the keynote of the Book of Deuteronomy: since the Lord alone is God, Israel must love him with an undivided heart. Jesus cited these words as "the greatest and the first commandment," embracing in itself the whole law of God (Mt 22:37–38; Mk 12:29–30; Lk 10:27).

**6:4** *Hear, O Israel!*: in Hebrew, *shema yisra'el*; hence this passage (vv. 4–9), containing the Great Commandment, is called the Shema. In later Jewish tradition, 11:13–21 and Nm 15:37–41 were added to form a prayer recited every evening and morning. *The LORD is our God, the LORD alone*: other possible translations are "the Lord our God is one Lord"; "the Lord our God, the Lord is one"; "the Lord is our God, the Lord is one."

**6:8** *Bind them . . . as a sign*: these injunctions were probably meant merely in a figurative sense; cf. Ex 13:9, 16. In the late postexilic period, they were taken quite literally, and devout Jews tied on their arms and foreheads "phylacteries," boxes containing strips of parchment on which these words were inscribed; cf. Mt 23:5.

**6:13** *Him shall you serve*: the verb could be translated as either "serve" or "worship" (cf. 5:9).

**6:3** Ex 3:8.
**6:4–5** Dt 4:35, 39; 5:6–10; 6:13–14; 10:17; 1 Kgs 8:60; 18:39; 2 Kgs 5:15; 19:15, 19; Is 44:6; 45:5–6; Mt 22:37–38; Mk 12:29–30; Lk 10:27.
**6:5** Dt 4:29; 10:12; 11:13; 13:4; 26:16; 30:2, 10; 1 Sm 7:3; 2 Kgs 23:3, 25.
**6:6–9** Dt 11:18–21.
**6:6** Dt 11:18; 30:14; 32:46; Ps 37:31; Prv 3:3; Is 51:7; Jer 31:33.
**6:7** Dt 4:9–10; 6:20–25; 11:1–7, 19; 31:13; 32:46; Prv 6:22.
**6:8** Dt 11:18; Ex 13:9, 16; Prv 3:3; 6:21.
**6:9** Dt 11:20.
**6:10–19** Dt 5:6–10.
**6:10** Dt 1:8.
**6:10–11** Dt 8:7–14; 32:11–14; Jos 24:13; Neh 9:25.
**6:12** Dt 5:6.
**6:13** Dt 10:20; Is 48:1; Jer 4:2; 12:16; Mt 4:10; Lk 4:8.
**6:14–15** Dt 4:23–26; 8:19–20; 11:16–17, 28; 29:18–20; 30:17–18; 2 Kgs 17:7–18.
**6:16** Ex 17:1–7; Ps 95:8–9; Mt 4:7; Lk 4:12.
**6:19** Ex 23:27; 34:11; Jos 1–12.
**6:20–25** Dt 6:6–9.
**6:20** Ex 12:26; 13:14; Jos 4:6, 21.
**6:21–23** Dt 26:5–10.
**6:21** Dt 5:3, 6.
**6:23** Dt 1:8.
**6:24–25** Dt 4:1–4; 30:15–20.
**7:1–11** Dt 4:23–33; 34:11–16; Nm 33:51–56.

Canaanites, Perizzites, Hivites, and Jebusites,* seven nations more numerous and powerful than you— ²and when the LORD, your God, gives them over to you and you defeat them, you shall put them under the ban. Make no covenant with them* and do not be gracious to them. ³* You shall not intermarry with them, neither giving your daughters to their sons nor taking their daughters for your sons. ⁴For they would turn your sons from following me to serving other gods, and then the anger of the LORD would flare up against you and he would quickly destroy you.

⁵But this is how you must deal with them:* Tear down their altars, smash their sacred pillars, chop down their asherahs,† and destroy their idols by fire. ⁶For you are a people holy to the LORD, your God; the LORD, your God, has chosen you from all the peoples on the face of the earth to be a people specially his own.* ⁷It was not because you are more numerous than all the peoples that the LORD set his heart on you and chose you; for you are really the smallest of all peoples.* ⁸It was because the LORD loved you and because of his fidelity to the oath he had sworn to your ancestors, that the LORD brought you out with a strong hand and redeemed you from the house of slavery, from the hand of Pharaoh, king of Egypt.* ⁹* Know, then, that the LORD, your God, is God: the faithful God who keeps covenant mercy to the thousandth generation toward those who love him and keep his commandments,* ¹⁰but who repays with destruction those who hate him; he does not delay with those who hate him, but makes them pay for it. ¹¹Therefore carefully observe the commandment, the statutes and the ordinances which I command you today.

**Blessings of Obedience.** ¹²* As your reward for heeding these ordinances and keeping them carefully, the LORD, your God, will keep with you the covenant mercy he promised on oath to your ancestors. ¹³He will love and bless and multiply you; he will bless the fruit of your womb and the produce of your soil, your grain and wine and oil, the young of your herds and the offspring of your flocks, in the land which he swore to your ancestors he would give you. ¹⁴You will be blessed above all peoples; no man or woman among you shall be childless nor shall your livestock be barren. ¹⁵The LORD will remove all sickness from you; he will not afflict you with any of the malignant diseases that you know from Egypt, but will leave them with all those who hate you.

¹⁶You shall consume all the peoples which the LORD, your God, is giving over to you. You are not to look on them with pity, nor serve their gods, for that would be a snare to you.* ¹⁷* If you say to yourselves, "These nations are more numerous than we. How can we dispossess them?" ¹⁸do not be afraid of them. Rather, remember clearly what the LORD, your God, did to Pharaoh and to all Egypt: ¹⁹the great testings which your own eyes have seen, the signs and wonders, the strong hand and outstretched arm with which the LORD, your God, brought you out. The same also will he do to all the peoples of whom you are now afraid. ²⁰Moreover, the LORD, your God, will send hornets among them, until those who are left and those who are hiding from you are destroyed.* ²¹Therefore, do not be terrified by them, for the LORD, your God, who is in your midst, is a great and awesome God. ²²He will remove these nations before you little by little. You cannot finish with them quickly, lest the wild beasts become too numerous for you.* ²³The LORD, your God, will give them over to you and throw them into utter panic until they are destroyed.* ²⁴He will deliver their kings into

---

† **7:5** *Sacred pillars . . . asherahs:* cut or uncut stones and wooden poles or trees (cf. 16:21) that had some cultic function. Fairly common religious artifacts, their association with the non-Israelite cults of Canaan and perhaps with Canaanite gods and goddesses, specifically the goddess Asherah, led to their condemnation in the Deuteronomic reform and possibly earlier.

*

**7:1** Dt 1:7; Gn 10:16–17; 13:7; 15:19–21; 23:3–20; 34:2, 30; 49:29–30; Ex 3:8; 23:23; 33:2; Nm 13:29; Jos 1:4; 3:10; 9:1–7; 15:63; 17:15; 24:11; Jgs 1:4–5; 3:3, 5; 2 Sm 5:6–10; 1 Kgs 9:20; Ez 16:3, 45.

**7:2** Dt 2:34–35; 3:6; 7:26; 13:16, 18; 20:16–18; Ex 23:32–33; 34:12, 15; Jos 9:3–27; 10:40; 11:11–12; Jgs 2:2.

**7:3–4** Gn 34:9–10; Ex 34:16; Jos 23:12–13; Jgs 3:5–6;

1 Kgs 11:1–6.
**7:5** Dt 12:2–3, 29–31; 16:21–22; Ex 34:13; 2 Kgs 18:4; 23:4–24.
**7:6** Dt 14:2, 21; 26:18–19; 32:8–14; Ex 19:5–6; Ps 135:4; Mal 3:17.
**7:7** Dt 10:15.
**7:8** Dt 5:6; 9:26; 13:5; 15:15; 21:8; 24:18; Ps 78:42.
**7:9–10** Dt 4:31; 5:9–10; 24:16; Ex 20:5–6; 34:6–7; Nm 14:18; Jer 31:29–30; 32:18–19; Ez 18:1–24; Jn 9:1–3.
**7:9** Dt 5:9–10; 7:12; 32:4;

1 Kgs 8:23–24; Neh 1:5; 9:32; Ps 89:1–2, 24, 28, 33–34; 98:3; Is 49:7; 54:10; 55:3; Dn 9:4; Jon 4:2; Mi 7:20.
**7:12–15** Dt 15:6; 28:1–14; 30:1–10; Ex 23:22–33; Lv 26:3–13.
**7:16** Dt 5:7–10.
**7:17–19** Dt 1:28–31; 3:22; 4:34, 37–38; 9:1–3; 20:1; 29:2–3; Jos 23:3, 9–10.
**7:20** Ex 23:28.
**7:22** Ex 23:29–30; Jgs 3:1–6.
**7:23** Dt 7:2.

your power, that you may make their names perish from under the heavens. No one will be able to stand up against you,* till you have destroyed them. 25* The images of their gods you shall destroy by fire. Do not covet the silver or gold on them, nor take it for yourselves, lest you be ensnared by it; for it is an abomination to the LORD, your God.* 26 You shall not bring any abominable thing into your house, so as to be, like it, under the ban; loathe and abhor it utterly for it is under the ban.†

## 8 God's Care.
8 ¹ Be careful to observe this whole commandment* that I enjoin on you today, that you may live and increase, and may enter in and possess the land which the LORD promised on oath to your ancestors. ² Remember how for these forty years the LORD, your God, has directed all your journeying in the wilderness,* so as to test you by affliction, to know what was in your heart: to keep his commandments, or not. ³ He therefore let you be afflicted with hunger, and then fed you with manna,* a food unknown to you and your ancestors, so you might know that it is not by bread alone† that people live, but by all that comes forth from the mouth of the LORD. ⁴ The clothing did not fall from you in tatters, nor did your feet swell these forty years.* ⁵ So you must know in your heart that, even as a man disciplines his son, so the LORD, your God, disciplines you.* ⁶ Therefore, keep the commandments of the LORD, your God, by walking in his ways and fearing him.

## Cautions About Prosperity.
⁷* For the LORD, your God, is bringing you into a good country, a land with streams of water, with springs and fountains welling up in the hills and valleys, ⁸ a land of wheat and barley, of vines and fig trees and pomegranates, of olive trees and of honey, ⁹ a land where you will always have bread and where you will lack nothing, a land whose stones contain iron and in whose hills you can mine copper. ¹⁰ But when you have eaten and are satisfied, you must bless the LORD, your God, for the good land he has given you. ¹¹* Be careful not to forget the LORD, your God, by failing to keep his commandments and ordinances and statutes which I enjoin on you today: ¹² lest, when you have eaten and are satisfied, and have built fine houses and lived in them, ¹³ and your herds and flocks have increased, your silver and gold has increased, and all your property has increased, ¹⁴ you then become haughty of heart and forget the LORD, your God, who brought you out of the land of Egypt, that house of slavery; ¹⁵ he guided you through the vast and terrible wilderness with its saraph† serpents and scorpions, its parched and waterless ground; he brought forth water for you from the flinty rock* ¹⁶ and fed you in the wilderness with manna, a food unknown to your ancestors, that he might afflict you and test you, but also make you prosperous in the end. ¹⁷ Otherwise, you might say in your heart,* "It is my own power and the strength of my own hand that has got me this wealth." ¹⁸ Remember then the LORD, your God, for he is the one who gives you the power to get wealth, by fulfilling, as he has now done, the covenant he swore to your ancestors. ¹⁹ But if you do forget the LORD, your God, and go after other gods, serving and bowing down to them,* I bear witness to you this day that you will perish utterly. ²⁰ Like the nations which the LORD destroys before you, so shall you too perish for not listening to the voice of the LORD, your God.

## 9 Unmerited Success.
9 ¹ Hear, O Israel! You are now about to cross the Jordan to enter in and dispossess nations greater and stronger than yourselves, having large cities fortified to the heavens,* ² the Anakim, a people great and tall.* You yourselves know of them and

---

**7:26** *Under the ban*: and therefore doomed to destruction; see note on 2:34.

**8:3** *Not by bread alone*: Deuteronomic theology puts the good things promised faithful Israel into the context of the Lord's gratuitous love. As in 6:10–12, the goods of life must be seen as gift. Israel is to seek what really matters; all else will be added (cf. Mt 6:33).

**8:15** *Saraph*: see note on Nm 21:6.

---

**7:24** Dt 11:25; Jos 12:7–24.
**7:25–26** Dt 5:8–9; 9:21; Jos 6:18–19; 7:1, 20–21;

Jgs 8:24–27; 17:2–4; 1 Kgs 15:13; 2 Kgs 23:4.
**7:25** Dt 12:31; 17:1;

18:12; 22:5; 23:18; 24:4; 25:16; Prv 6:16; 15:8–9, 26.
**8:1** Dt 4:1; 6:1.
**8:2** Dt 1:3; 2:7; 29:4; Ps 95:10; Am 2:10.
**8:3** Ex 16:11–36; Nm 11:5–9; Jos 5:12; Mt 4:4; Lk 4:4.
**8:4** Dt 29:4; Neh 9:21.
**8:5** Dt 4:36; 11:2; 21:18–21; Ps 94:12; Prv 3:11–12.
**8:7–9** Dt 1:25; 11:10–12;

32:13–14; 33:28.
**8:11–14** Dt 6:10–12.
**8:15** Dt 32:13; Ex 17:6; Nm 20:8–11; 21:6–9; Ps 114:8; Wis 11:4.
**8:17** Dt 9:4–5.
**8:19** Dt 4:25–26; 30:18; 2 Kgs 17:7–18.
**9:1** Dt 1:28; 4:38.
**9:2** Dt 1:28; 2:10–11, 21; Nm 13:22, 28, 33; Jos 11:21–22; 14:12, 15; 15:13–14; 21:11; Jgs 1:20.

have heard it said of them, "Who can stand up against the Anakim?" [3] Know, then, today that it is the LORD, your God, who will cross over before you as a consuming fire; he it is who will destroy them and subdue them before you, so that you can dispossess and remove them quickly, as the LORD promised you.* [4] After the LORD, your God, has driven them out of your way, do not say in your heart, "It is because of my justice the LORD has brought me in to possess this land,* and because of the wickedness of these nations the LORD is dispossessing them before me."† [5] No, it is not because of your justice or the integrity of your heart that you are going in to take possession of their land; but it is because of their wickedness that the LORD, your God, is dispossessing these nations before you and in order to fulfill the promise he made on oath to your ancestors, Abraham, Isaac, and Jacob.* [6] Know this, therefore: it is not because of your justice that the LORD, your God, is giving you this good land to possess, for you are a stiff-necked people.*

**The Golden Calf.** [7] Remember and do not forget how you angered the LORD, your God, in the wilderness. From the day you left the land of Egypt until you came to this place, you have been rebellious toward the LORD.* [8]* At Horeb you so provoked the LORD that he was angry enough to destroy you,* [9] when I had gone up the mountain to receive the stone tablets of the covenant which the LORD made with you.* Meanwhile I stayed on the mountain forty days and forty nights; I ate no food and drank no water. [10] The LORD gave me the two stone tablets inscribed, by God's own finger,* with a copy of all the words that the LORD spoke to you on the mountain from the midst of the fire on the day of the assembly. [11] Then, at the end of the forty days and forty nights, when the LORD had given me the two stone tablets, the tablets of the covenant, [12]* the LORD said to me, Go down from here now, quickly, for your people whom you have brought out of

Egypt are acting corruptly; they have already turned aside from the way I commanded them and have made for themselves a molten idol. [13] I have seen now how stiff-necked this people is, the LORD said to me. [14] Let me be, that I may destroy them and blot out their name from under the heavens. I will then make of you a nation mightier and greater than they.

[15] When I had come down again from the blazing, fiery mountain, with the two tablets of the covenant in both my hands,* [16] I saw how you had sinned against the LORD, your God, by making for yourselves a molten calf. You had already turned aside from the way which the LORD had commanded you.* [17] I took hold of the two tablets and with both hands cast them from me and broke them before your eyes.* [18] Then, as before, I lay prostrate before the LORD for forty days and forty nights; I ate no food, I drank no water, because of all the sin you had committed in the sight of the LORD, doing wrong and provoking him.* [19] For I dreaded the fierce anger of the LORD against you: his wrath would destroy you.* Yet once again the LORD listened to me. [20] With Aaron, too, the LORD was deeply angry, and would have destroyed him; but I prayed for Aaron also at that time.* [21] Then, taking the calf, the sinful object you had made, I burnt it and ground it down to powder as fine as dust, which I threw into the wadi that went down the mountainside.*

[22] At Taberah, at Massah, and at Kibroth-hattaavah likewise, you enraged the LORD.* [23] And when the LORD sent you up from Kadesh-barnea saying, Go up and take possession of the land I have given you, you rebelled against this command of the LORD, your God, and would not believe him or listen to his voice.* [24] You have been rebels against the LORD from the day I first knew you.

[25]* Those forty days, then, and forty nights, I lay prostrate before the LORD, because he had threatened to destroy you. [26] And I prayed to the Lord and said: O Lord GOD, do not destroy your people, the heritage you redeemed

---

† **9:4** *Before me:* Hebrew reads "before you."

**9:3** Dt 4:24; 31:3.
**9:4** Dt 8:17.
**9:5** Dt 1:8.
**9:6** Dt 9:13; 10:16; 31:27; Ex 32:9; 33:3; 34:9; Is 48:4; Jer 17:23; 19:15.
**9:7** Dt 31:27; Ex 14:10–14; 2 Kgs 21:15; Jer 7:25–26.
**9:8–21** Ex 32:1–34:29.
**9:8** Ex 32:10.
**9:9** Dt 4:13–14; 5:22; 9:11, 18, 25; 10:10;

Ex 24:12–18; 34:28.
**9:10** Dt 5:22; 10:4; Ex 31:18.
**9:12–14** Dt 5:6–10; Ex 32:7–10.
**9:15** Ex 32:15.
**9:16** Dt 5:6–10; Ex 32:1–6; Ps 106:19–22.
**9:17** Ex 32:19.
**9:18** Dt 10:10; Ex 32:31; 34:28.
**9:19** Dt 10:10; Ex 32:11–14.
**9:20** Ex 32:1–6, 21–25, 35.
**9:21** Ex 32:20.
**9:22** Dt 6:16; Ex 17:1–7; Nm 11:1–34.
**9:23** Dt 1:19–33.
**9:25–29** Ex 32:11–14.

in your greatness and have brought out of Egypt with your strong hand. * 27 Remember your servants, Abraham, Isaac, and Jacob. Do not look upon the stubbornness of this people nor upon their wickedness and sin, * 28 lest the land from which you have brought us say, "The LORD was not able to bring them into the land he promised them, and out of hatred for them, he brought them out to let them die in the wilderness." * 29 They are your people and your heritage, whom you have brought out by your great power and with your outstretched arm. *

10 1 * At that time the LORD said to me, Cut two stone tablets like the first ones * and come up the mountain to me. Also make an ark out of wood. 2 I will write upon the tablets the words that were on the tablets that you broke, and you shall place them in the ark. 3 So I made an ark of acacia wood, and cut two stone tablets like the first ones, and went up the mountain with the two tablets in my hand. * 4 The LORD then wrote on the tablets, as he had written before, the ten words† that the LORD had spoken to you on the mountain from the midst of the fire on the day of the assembly; and the LORD gave them to me. 5 Then I turned and came down from the mountain, and placed the tablets in the ark I had made. * There they have remained, as the LORD commanded me.

6 * The Israelites set out from Beeroth Benejaakan for Moserah; Aaron died there and was buried. His son Eleazar succeeded him as priest. * 7 From there they set out for Gudgodah, and from Gudgodah for Jotbathah, a region where there is water in the wadies. 8 At that time the LORD set apart the tribe of Levi to carry the ark of the covenant of the LORD, * to stand before the LORD to minister to him, and to bless in his name, as they have done to this day. 9 For this reason, Levi has no hereditary portion with his relatives; * the LORD himself is his portion, as the LORD, your God, promised him.

10 Meanwhile I stayed on the mountain as I did before, forty days and forty nights, and once again the LORD listened to me. The LORD was unwilling to destroy you. 11 The LORD said to me, Go now and set out at the head of the people, * that they may enter in and possess the land that I swore to their ancestors I would give them.

**The Lord's Majesty and Compassion.** 12 * Now, therefore, Israel, what does the LORD, your God, ask of you but to fear the LORD, your God, to follow in all his ways, to love and serve the LORD, your God, with your whole heart and with your whole being, * 13 to keep the commandments and statutes of the LORD that I am commanding you today for your own well-being? * 14 Look, the heavens, even the highest heavens, belong to the LORD, your God, as well as the earth and everything on it. * 15 Yet only on your ancestors did the LORD set his heart to love them. He chose you, their descendants, from all the peoples, as it is today. * 16 Circumcise therefore the foreskins of your hearts,† and be stiff-necked no longer. 17 For the LORD, your God, is the God of gods, the Lord of lords, the great God, mighty and awesome, who has no favorites, accepts no bribes, * 18 who executes justice for the orphan and the widow, and loves the resident alien, giving them food and clothing. * 19 So you too should love the resident alien, for that is what you were in the land of Egypt. * 20 The LORD, your God, shall you fear, and him shall you serve; to him hold fast and by his name shall you swear. * 21 He is your praise; he is your God, who has done for you those great and awesome things that your own eyes have

---

† **10:4** *Ten words:* the ten commandments (cf. 4:13).

**10:16** *Circumcise therefore the foreskins of your hearts:* cf. 30:6; Jer 4:4; Rom 2:29. The "uncircumcised heart" (Lv 26:41; Jer 9:25; Ez 44:7, 9) is closed and unreceptive to God, just as "uncircumcised ears" (Jer 6:10) are closed to the word of the Lord, and "uncircumcised lips" (Ex 6:12, 30) are a hindrance to speaking on behalf of the Lord.

---

**9:26** Dt 4:20; 7:8.
**9:27** Dt 7:8.
**9:28** Dt 32:26–27; Nm 14:13–16.
**9:29** Dt 4:20; Ex 6:6–7.
**10:1–11** Ex 34:1–28.

**10:1** Ex 34:1.
**10:3** Ex 34:4.
**10:4** Dt 4:13; 5:22; Ex 20:1–17; 34:1–4, 27–29.
**10:5** Ex 40:20; 1 Kgs 8:9.

**10:6–7** Nm 33:31–33.
**10:6** Nm 3:1–4, 32; 20:22–29.
**10:8** Dt 21:5; 33:8–11; Ex 32:25–29; Nm 3:6–10; 6:22–27; 8:23–26.
**10:9** Dt 18:1–8; Nm 18:20.
**10:11** Dt 1:6; Ex 32:34; 33:1.
**10:12–13** Ps 15; 24:3–5; Mi 6:6–8.
**10:12** Dt 6:5, 13; 8:6; 11:13.
**10:13** Dt 4:1; 5:10, 29–33; 6:2; 7:9; 11:1, 13, 22.
**10:14** 1 Kgs 8:27; Neh 9:6;

Ps 148:4.
**10:15** Dt 7:6–8; Ex 19:5–6.
**10:17** Dt 1:17; 16:19; Ex 15:11; 2 Chr 19:7; Jb 34:19; Ps 47:2; 136:2–3; Dn 2:47; Acts 10:34; Rom 2:11; Gal 2:6; 1 Tm 6:15; Rev 17:14; 19:16.
**10:18** Ps 68:5–6; 99:4; 146:7–9.
**10:19** Dt 24:17–22; Ex 22:21–24; 23:9; Lv 19:33–34.
**10:20** Dt 6:13; Mt 4:10; Lk 4:8.

seen.* ²²Seventy strong your ancestors went down to Egypt,* and now the Lord, your God, has made you as numerous as the stars of heaven.

# 11 Recalling the Wonders of the Lord.
¹Love the Lord, your God, therefore, and keep his charge, statutes, ordinances, and commandments always.* ²Recall today that it was not your children, who have neither known nor seen the discipline of the Lord, your God—his greatness, his strong hand and outstretched arm;* ³the signs and deeds he wrought in the midst of Egypt, on Pharaoh, king of Egypt, and on all his land;* ⁴what he did to the Egyptian army and to their horses and chariots, engulfing them in the waters of the Red Sea† as they pursued you,* so that the Lord destroyed them even to this day; ⁵what he did for you in the wilderness until you came to this place; ⁶and what he did to the Reubenites Dathan and Abiram, sons of Eliab, when the earth opened its mouth and swallowed them up out of the midst of Israel, with their families and tents and every living thing that belonged to them—* ⁷but it was you who saw with your own eyes all these great deeds that the Lord has done.

**The Gift of Rain.** ⁸* So keep all the commandments I give you today, that you may be strong enough to enter in and take possession of the land that you are crossing over to possess, ⁹and that you may have long life on the land which the Lord swore to your ancestors he would give to them and their descendants, a land flowing with milk and honey. ¹⁰The land you are to enter and possess is not like the land of Egypt from which you have come, where you would sow your seed and then water it by hand,† as in a vegetable garden. ¹¹* No, the land into which you are crossing to take possession is a land of mountains and valleys that drinks in rain from the heavens, ¹²a land which the Lord, your God, looks after; the eyes of the Lord, your God, are upon it continually through the year, from beginning to end.

¹³† * If, then, you truly listen to my commandments which I give you today, loving and serving the Lord, your God, with your whole heart and your whole being, ¹⁴I will give the seasonal rain to your land, the early rain† and the late rain, that you may have your grain, wine and oil to gather in; ¹⁵and I will bring forth grass in your fields for your animals. Thus you may eat and be satisfied. ¹⁶* But be careful lest your heart be so lured away that you serve other gods and bow down to them.* ¹⁷For then the anger of the Lord will flare up against you and he will close up the heavens, so that no rain will fall, and the soil will not yield its crops, and you will soon perish from the good land the Lord is giving you.

**Need for Fidelity.** ¹⁸* Therefore, take these words of mine into your heart and soul. Bind them on your arm as a sign, and let them be as a pendant on your forehead. ¹⁹Teach them to your children, speaking of them when you are at home and when you are away, when you lie down and when you get up, ²⁰and write them on the doorposts of your houses and on your gates, ²¹so that, as long as the heavens are above the earth, you and your children may live on in the land which the Lord swore to your ancestors he would give them.

²²* For if you are careful to observe this entire commandment I am giving you, loving the Lord, your God, following his ways exactly, and holding fast to him, ²³the Lord will dispossess all these nations before you, and you will dispossess nations greater and mightier than yourselves. ²⁴* Every place where you set foot shall be yours: from the wilderness and the Lebanon, from the Euphrates River to the Western Sea,† shall be your territory. ²⁵None shall

**11:4** *The Red Sea*: Hebrew *yam suph*, that is, "sea of reeds" or "reedy sea."
**11:10** *By hand*: lit., "by foot," probably referring to a kind of mechanism for irrigation from the Nile.
**11:13–15** Here as elsewhere Moses shifts between speaking of the Lord in the third person and speaking for the Lord in the first person.
**11:14** *The early rain*: the rains which begin in October or November and continue intermittently throughout the winter. *The late rain*: the heavy showers of March and April. In Palestine crops are sown in autumn and harvested in spring and summer.
**11:24** *The Western Sea*: the Mediterranean.

**10:21** Ps 109:1; Jer 17:14.
**10:22** Dt 1:10; Gn 46:8–27; Ex 1:5; Acts 7:14.
**11:1** Gn 26:5; 1 Kgs 2:3.
**11:2** Dt 4:9; 6:20–25.
**11:3** Dt 6:22; 7:18–19; 26:8; 29:1–2; 34:11; Ps 78:42–51.
**11:4** Ex 14:26–31; 15:1–10; Jos 24:6–7; Ps 78:53; 106:9–11.
**11:6** Nm 16:1–35; Ps 106:16–17.
**11:8–9** Dt 5:33; 6:1–3.
**11:11–12** Dt 8:7–10.
**11:13–15** Dt 7:12–14; 10:12–13; 28:1–14; Lv 26:3–5; Ps 104:14; Jer 5:24.
**11:16–17** Dt 4:25–27; 6:14–15; 28:15–68.
**11:16** Dt 5:6–10; 7:1–6; 13:2–19; 1 Kgs 8:35–36.
**11:18–21** Dt 6:6–9.
**11:22–23** Dt 7:1; 9:1–3; 10:12–13.
**11:24** Dt 1:7; Ex 23:31; Jos 1:3.

stand up against you; the LORD, your God, will spread the fear and dread of you through any land where you set foot, as he promised you.*

**Blessing and Curse.** 26* See, I set before you this day a blessing and a curse: 27 a blessing for obeying the commandments of the LORD, your God, which I give you today; 28 a curse if you do not obey the commandments of the LORD, your God, but turn aside from the way I command you today, to go after other gods, whom you do not know.* 29 When the LORD, your God, brings you into the land which you are to enter and possess, then on Mount Gerizim you shall pronounce the blessing,* on Mount Ebal, the curse.† 30 (These are beyond the Jordan, on the other side of the western road in the land of the Canaanites who live in the Arabah, opposite Gilgal beside the oak of Moreh.)* 31 Now you are about to cross the Jordan to enter and possess the land which the LORD, your God, is giving you. When, therefore, you take possession of it and settle there, 32 be careful to observe all the statutes and ordinances that I set before you today.

## B. The Deuteronomic Code

**12** **One Center of Worship.** 1 These are the statutes and ordinances which you must be careful to observe in the land which the LORD, the God of your ancestors, has given you to possess, throughout the time you live on its soil.* 2* Destroy entirely all the places where the nations you are to dispossess serve their gods, on the high mountains, on the hills, and under every green tree.* 3 Tear down their altars, smash their sacred pillars, burn up their asherahs, and chop down the idols of their gods, that you may destroy the very name of them from that place.

4 That is not how you are to act toward the LORD, your God. 5 Instead,* you shall seek out the place which the LORD, your God, chooses out of all your tribes and designates as his dwelling to put his name there.†* There you shall go, 6 bringing your burnt offerings and sacrifices, your tithes and personal contributions, your votive and voluntary offerings, and the firstlings of your herds and flocks.* 7 There, too, in the presence of the LORD, your God, you and your families shall eat and rejoice in all your undertakings, in which the LORD, your God, has blessed you.*

8 You shall not do as we are doing here today, everyone doing what is right in their own sight,* 9 since you have not yet reached your resting place, the heritage which the LORD, your God, is giving you. 10 But after you have crossed the Jordan and dwell in the land which the LORD, your God, is giving you as a heritage, when he has given you rest from all your enemies round about and you live there in security,* 11†* then to the place which the LORD, your God, chooses as the dwelling place for his name you shall bring all that I command you: your burnt offerings and sacrifices, your tithes and personal contributions, and every special offering you have vowed to the LORD. 12 You shall rejoice in the presence of the LORD, your God, with your sons and daughters, your male and female slaves, as well as with the Levite within your gates, who has no hereditary portion with you.

13* Be careful not to sacrifice your burnt offerings in any place you like, 14 but offer them

---

**11:29** For the full ceremony of blessing and curse, see chaps. 27–28. Gerizim and Ebal are mountains in Samaria, separated by a deep ravine.

**12:5** *The place . . . to put his name there*: Moses thus designates Jerusalem (Mt. Zion), in accordance with the Deuteronomic doctrine that the Lord "chooses" Zion, as the place where eventually the Temple will be built, as he chooses the house of David to reign over Israel; see 2 Sm 7; 1 Kgs 8; Ps 132. But the Lord's presence in Jerusalem consists in putting his "name" there (12:11, 21; 14:23–24; 16:2, 6, 11; 26:2; 1 Kgs 8:44, 49; 9:3; 11:36; 14:21; 2 Kgs 17:34; 21:4, 7; 23:27). The Lord himself "cannot be contained" in an earthly dwelling (1 Kgs 8:27), but because he says of the Jerusalem Temple that "my name will be there" (1 Kgs 8:16, 29), he is present. This theology allows God in a way to dwell with Israel and at the same time preserves divine transcendence. See note on 1 Kgs 8:12–13.

**12:11** Sacrifice is to be confined to the single place that the Lord has chosen; eventually this was Jerusalem.

**11:25** Dt 2:25; 7:23–24; Ex 23:27.
**11:26–28** Dt 28:1–68; 30:1, 15–20; Lv 26:3–45.
**11:28** Dt 32:16–18.
**11:29** Dt 27:12–13; Jos 8:30–35.
**11:30** Gn 12:6; 35:4.
**12:1** Dt 4:44–45.
**12:2–28** Dt 5:7–10; Ex 20:24–26; 2 Kgs 18:3–6, 22; 23:4–9.
**12:2–3** Dt 7:5, 24–25; Ex 23:23–24; 34:11–14; Nm 33:51–52; Jgs 17:3–5; 1 Kgs 12:28–30; 14:22–24; 2 Kgs 16:4; 17:7–12; Jer 2:20; 3:6–10; Hos 4:12–13.
**12:5–7** Dt 12:11–12; 14:22–26; 15:19–20; 16:2, 6, 10–11, 14–15; 26:2.

**12:5** 2 Sm 7:13; 1 Kgs 8:16–21, 27–30.
**12:6** Dt 14:22–27; 15:19–23; 23:21–23; 26:12–15; Lv 1:3–17; 3:1–17; 6:2–6; 7:29–36; 27:1–8; Nm 15:18–21; 28:2–8; 30:2–15; Am 4:4–5; 5:22.
**12:7** Dt 12:12, 18–19; 14:26–27; 15:20; 16:11, 14; 26:11.
**12:8** Dt 6:18; 12:28; Jgs 17:6; 21:25.
**12:10** Dt 3:18–20; 11:22–25; Jos 23:1; 2 Sm 7:1; 1 Kgs 5:17–18; 8:56.
**12:11–12** Dt 12:5–7; 14:22–26; 15:19–20; 16:2, 6, 10–11, 14–15; 26:2.
**12:13–14** Jos 22:10–34.

in the place which the LORD chooses in one of your tribal territories; there you shall do what I command you.

**Profane and Sacred Slaughter.** [15]† However, in any of your communities you may slaughter and eat meat freely, according to the blessing that the LORD, your God, has given you; the unclean as well as the clean may eat it, as they do the gazelle or the deer.* [16]† Only, you shall not eat of the blood, but must pour it out on the ground like water.* [17] Moreover, you may not, in your own communities, partake of your tithe of grain or wine or oil, of the first-born of your herd or flock, of any offering you have vowed, of your voluntary offerings, or of your personal contributions. [18] These you must eat in the presence of the LORD, your God, in the place that the LORD, your God, chooses, along with your son and daughter, your male and female slave, and the Levite within your gates; and there, in the presence of the LORD, you shall rejoice in all your undertakings. [19] Be careful, also, that you do not neglect the Levite as long as you live in your land.*

[20]* After the LORD, your God, has enlarged your territory, as he promised you,* and you think, "I will eat meat," as it is your desire to eat meat, you may eat it freely; [21] and if the place where the LORD, your God, chooses to put his name is too far, you may slaughter in the manner I have commanded you any of your herd or flock that the LORD has given you, and eat it freely in your own community. [22] You may eat it as you would the gazelle or the deer: the unclean and the clean eating it together. [23]* But make sure that you do not eat of the blood; for blood is life; you shall not eat that life with the flesh. [24] Do not eat of the blood, therefore, but pour it out on the ground like water. [25] Do not eat of it, that you and your children after you may prosper for doing what is right in the sight of the LORD. [26] However, any sacred gifts or votive offerings

that you may have, you shall bring with you to the place which the LORD chooses, [27] and there you must sacrifice your burnt offerings, both the flesh and the blood, on the altar of the LORD, your God; of your other sacrifices the blood indeed must be poured out against the altar of the LORD, your God,* but their flesh you may eat.

[28] Be careful to heed all these words I command you today, that you and your descendants after you may forever prosper for doing what is good and right in the sight of the LORD, your God.*

**Warning Against Abominable Practices.** [29]* When the LORD, your God, cuts down from before you the nations you are going in to dispossess, and you have dispossessed them and are settled in their land, [30] be careful that you not be trapped into following them after they have been destroyed before you. Do not inquire regarding their gods, "How did these nations serve their gods, so I might do the same." [31] You shall not worship the LORD, your God, that way, because they offered to their gods every abomination that the LORD detests, even burning their sons and daughters to their gods.*

# 13 Penalties for Enticing to Idolatry. [1] Every word that I command you, you shall be careful to observe, neither adding to it nor subtracting from it.

[2]* If there arises in your midst a prophet or a dreamer† who promises you a sign or wonder, [3] saying, "Let us go after other gods," whom you have not known, "and let us serve them," and the sign or wonder foretold to you comes to pass, [4] do not listen to the words of that prophet or that dreamer; for the LORD, your God, is testing you to know whether you really love the LORD, your God, with all your heart and soul.* [5] The LORD, your God, shall you follow, and him shall you fear; his

---

† **12:15** At this point a distinction is being made between cultic sacrifice and slaughter of animals for food. *In any of your communities:* lit., "within your gates."

**12:16** The blood was understood to be the source or vehicle of life and so was not to be consumed. Cf. Gn 9:4.

**13:2, 4, 6** *Dreamer:* a false prophet who pretended to have received revelations from God in a dream; cf. Jer 23:25–32; 27:9; Zec 10:2. But dreams could also be a means of true prophecy (Nm 12:6; Jl 3:1) and of genuine revelations (Gn 20:3, 6; 31:11, 24; 37:5, 9; Mt 1:20; 2:12, 13, 19; etc.).

* **12:15** Dt 12:20–22; 15:22;
    Lv 7:19–21.
**12:16** Dt 12:23–27; 15:23;
    Gn 9:4; Lv 3:17;
    17:10–14; 19:26;
    1 Sm 14:31–35.
**12:19** Dt 14:27.
**12:20–27** Lv 17:3–9.
**12:20** Dt 19:8; Gn 28:14; Ex
    34:24.
**12:23–25** Dt 12:16; 15:23;
    Gn 9:4; Lv 3:17;
    17:10–14; 19:26;
    1 Sm 14:31–35.

**12:27** Lv 17:11.
**12:28** Dt 4:40; 5:29; 6:2–3,
    17–18; 12:25.
**12:29–31** Dt 7:1–5, 25; Ex
    23:33; 34:12; Jgs
    2:2–3.
**12:31** Dt 18:10; Lv 18:21;
    20:2–5; 2 Kgs 3:27;
    16:3; 21:6; 23:10; Jer
    7:31; 19:5.
**13:2–19** Dt 6:4, 14–15;
    17:2–7.
**13:4** Dt 8:2, 16.

commandments shall you observe, and to his voice shall you listen; him you shall serve, and to him you shall hold fast.* ⁶ But that prophet or that dreamer shall be put to death, because, in order to lead you astray from the way which the LORD, your God, has commanded you to take, the prophet or dreamer has spoken apostasy against the LORD, your God, who brought you out of the land of Egypt and redeemed you from the house of slavery. Thus shall you purge the evil from your midst.*

⁷ If your brother, your father's child or your mother's child, your son or daughter, your beloved spouse, or your intimate friend entices you secretly, saying, "Come, let us serve other gods," whom you and your ancestors have not known, ⁸ any of the gods of the surrounding peoples, near to you or far away, from one end of the earth to the other: ⁹ do not yield or listen to any such person; show no pity or compassion and do not shield such a one,* ¹⁰* but kill that person. Your hand shall be the first raised to put such a one to death; the hand of all the people shall follow. ¹¹ You shall stone that person to death, for seeking to lead you astray from the LORD, your God, who brought you out of the land of Egypt, out of the house of slavery. ¹² And all Israel shall hear of it and fear, and never again do such evil as this in your midst.*

¹³ If you hear it said concerning one of the cities which the LORD, your God, gives you to dwell in, ¹⁴ that certain scoundrels have sprung up in your midst and have led astray the inhabitants of their city, saying, "Come, let us serve other gods," whom you have not known, ¹⁵ you must inquire carefully into the matter and investigate it thoroughly. If you find that it is true and an established fact that this abomination has been committed in your midst,* ¹⁶* you shall put the inhabitants of that city to the sword, placing the city and all that is in it, even its livestock, under the ban. ¹⁷ Having heaped up all its spoils in the middle of its square, you shall burn the city with all its spoils as a whole burnt offering to the LORD, your God. Let it be a heap of ruins forever, never to be rebuilt. ¹⁸ You shall not hold on to anything that is under the ban; then the LORD will turn from his burning anger and show you mercy, and in showing you mercy multiply you as he swore to your ancestors, ¹⁹ because you have listened to the voice of the LORD, your God, keeping all his commandments, which I give you today, doing what is right in the sight of the LORD, your God.

# 14 Improper Mourning Rites. ¹ You are children of the LORD, your God. You shall not gash yourselves nor shave the hair above your foreheads for the dead.* ² For you are a people holy to the LORD, your God; the LORD, your God, has chosen you from all the peoples on the face of the earth to be a people specially his own.*

**Clean and Unclean Animals.** ³ You shall not eat any abominable thing.* ⁴* These are the animals you may eat: the ox, the sheep, the goat, ⁵ the deer, the gazelle, the roebuck, the wild goat, the ibex, the antelope, and the mountain sheep. ⁶ Any among the animals that has divided hooves, with the foot cloven in two, and that chews the cud you may eat. ⁷ But you shall not eat any of the following that chew the cud or have cloven hooves: the camel, the hare, and the rock badger, which indeed chew the cud, but do not have divided hooves; they are unclean for you. ⁸ And the pig, which indeed has divided hooves, with cloven foot, but does not chew the cud, is unclean for you. Their flesh you shall not eat, and their dead bodies you shall not touch.

⁹ These you may eat, of all that live in the water: whatever has both fins and scales you may eat, ¹⁰ but all those that lack either fins or scales you shall not eat; they are unclean for you.

¹¹ You may eat all clean birds. ¹²† But you shall not eat any of the following: the griffon vulture, the bearded vulture, the black vulture, ¹³ the various kites and falcons, ¹⁴ all kinds of crows, ¹⁵ the eagle owl, the kestrel, the long-eared owl, all species of hawks, ¹⁶ the little owl,

---

† **14:12–18** The identification of several of the birds in these verses is uncertain.

*
**13:5** Dt 6:4–5; 10:20; 11:22.
**13:6** Dt 17:7, 12; 19:19; 21:21; 22:21–22, 24; 24:7;
Jer 28:16; 29:32.
**13:9** Dt 7:16; 19:13, 21; 25:12.
**13:10–11** Dt 17:5–7; 21:21; 22:20–24; Jos 7:25–
26; 1 Kgs 21:13–14.
**13:12** Dt 17:13; 21:21.
**13:15** Dt 17:4; 19:18.
**13:16–17** Dt 20:16–18; Jos 6:17, 24; 7:25–26; 8:28.
**14:1** Dt 32:5–6, 18–20; Lv 19:27–28; 21:5;
Ps 103:13; Is 1:2, 4; 30:1; Jer 3:14, 19, 22; 16:6; 31:9, 20; 41:4–5; Hos 2:1; 11:1–4.
**14:2** Dt 7:6; Ex 19:5–6.
**14:3** Acts 10:14.
**14:4–20** Lv 11:2–23.

the screech owl, the barn owl, [17] the horned owl, the osprey, the cormorant, [18] the stork, any kind of heron, the hoopoe, and the bat. [19]† All winged insects are also unclean for you and shall not be eaten. [20] Any clean winged creatures you may eat.

[21] You shall not eat the carcass of any animal that has died of itself; but you may give it to a resident alien within your gates to eat, or you may sell it to a foreigner. For you are a people holy to the Lord, your God.*

You shall not boil a young goat in its mother's milk.†

**Tithes.** [22] Each year you shall tithe all the produce of your seed that grows in the field;* [23] then in the place which the Lord, your God, chooses as the dwelling place of his name* you shall eat in his presence the tithe of your grain, wine and oil, as well as the firstlings of your herd and flock, that you may learn always to fear the Lord, your God. [24]* But if, when the Lord, your God, blesses you, the journey is too much for you and you are not able to bring your tithe, because the place which the Lord, your God, chooses to put his name is too far for you, [25] you may exchange the tithe for money, and with the money securely in hand, go to the place which the Lord, your God, chooses. [26] You may then exchange the money for whatever you desire, oxen or sheep, wine or beer, or anything else you want, and there in the presence of the Lord, your God, you shall consume it and rejoice, you and your household together.* [27] But do not neglect the Levite within your gates, for he has no hereditary portion with you.*

[28]* At the end of every third year you shall bring out all the tithes of your produce for that year and deposit them within your own communities, [29] that the Levite who has no hereditary portion with you, and also the resident alien, the orphan and the widow within your gates, may come and eat and be satisfied; so that the Lord, your God, may bless you in all that you undertake.

# 15

**Debts and the Poor.** [1] At the end of every seven-year period† you shall have a remission of debts,* [2] and this is the manner of the remission. Creditors shall remit all claims on loans made to a neighbor, not pressing the neighbor, one who is kin, because the Lord's remission has been proclaimed. [3] You may press a foreigner, but you shall remit the claim on what your kin owes to you.* [4]* However, since the Lord, your God, will bless you abundantly in the land the Lord, your God, will give you to possess as a heritage, there shall be no one of you in need [5] if you but listen to the voice of the Lord, your God, and carefully observe this entire commandment which I enjoin on you today. [6] Since the Lord, your God, will bless you as he promised, you will lend to many nations, and borrow from none;* you will rule over many nations, and none will rule over you.

[7]* If one of your kindred is in need in any community in the land which the Lord, your God, is giving you, you shall not harden your heart nor close your hand against your kin who is in need. [8] Instead, you shall freely open your hand and generously lend what suffices to meet that need.* [9] Be careful not to entertain the mean thought, "The seventh year, the year of remission, is near," so that you would begrudge your kin who is in need and give nothing, and your kin would cry to the Lord against you and you would be held guilty.* [10] When you give, give generously and not with a stingy heart; for that, the Lord, your God, will bless you in all your works and undertakings. [11] The land will never lack for needy persons; that is why I command you: "Open your

---

† **14:19–20** Lv 11:20–23 suggests that the unclean winged insects are those that walk on the ground; the clean winged creatures are those that leap on the ground, such as certain species of locusts.
**14:21** *Boil a young goat in its mother's milk:* the meaning of this regulation is obscure but it may have a humane concern similar to the prohibitions against slaughtering an animal and its young on the same day (Lv 22:27–28) and capturing a mother bird along with her fledgling or eggs (Dt 22:6–7). See note on Ex 23:19.
**15:1** *At the end of every seven-year period:* in every seventh, or sabbatical, year. Cf. 15:9; 31:10; and compare Dt 15:12. *A remission of debts:* it is debated whether a full cancellation of debts is meant, or merely a suspension of payment on them or on their interest, but the former is more likely. Cf. Ex

23:11 where the same Hebrew root is used of a field that is "let lie fallow" in the sabbatical year.

| | |
|---|---|
| **14:21** Ex 22:30; 23:19; 34:26; Lv 17:15; 22:8; Ez 44:31. | **14:28–29** Dt 26:12–15. |
| **14:22** Gn 14:20; 28:22; Lv 27:30–33; Nm 18:21–32; 1 Sm 8:15, 17; 2 Chr 31:2–19; Neh 12:44; Am 4:4. | **15:1** Dt 31:10; Lv 25:1–55; Neh 10:31. |
| | **15:3** Dt 23:20. |
| | **15:4–6** Dt 7:12–14; 28:1–14. |
| | **15:6** Dt 28:12. |
| **14:23** Dt 12:5–7, 11–12, 17–18; 15:19–20. | **15:7–11** Ex 22:25. |
| | **15:8** Dt 24:19; Lv 25:35; Ps 37:21–22; Prv 19:17; Sir 29:1–2; Mt 5:42. |
| **14:24–26** Mk 11:15; Jn 2:13–14. | |
| **14:26** Dt 12:7. | **15:9** Dt 24:15; Ex 22:23–24, 27. |
| **14:27** Dt 12:12, 19. | |

hand freely to your poor and to your needy kin in your land."*

**Hebrew Slaves.** 12* If your kin, a Hebrew man or woman, sells himself or herself to you, he or she is to serve you for six years, but in the seventh year you shall release him or her as a free person. 13* When you release a male from your service, as a free person, you shall not send him away empty-handed, 14 but shall weigh him down with gifts from your flock and threshing floor and wine press; as the LORD, your God, has blessed you, so you shall give to him. 15 For remember that you too were slaves in the land of Egypt, and the LORD, your God, redeemed you. That is why I am giving you this command today.* 16* But if he says to you, "I do not wish to leave you," because he loves you and your household, since he is well off with you, 17 you shall take an awl and put it through his ear† into the door, and he shall be your slave forever. Your female slave, also, you shall treat in the same way. 18 Do not be reluctant when you let them go free, since the service they have given you for six years was worth twice a hired laborer's salary; and the LORD, your God, will bless you in everything you do.

**Firstlings.** 19* You shall consecrate to the LORD, your God, every male firstling born in your herd and in your flock. You shall not work the firstlings of your cattle, nor shear the firstlings of your flock. 20 In the presence of the LORD, your God, you shall eat them year after year, you and your household, in the place that the LORD will choose.* 21* But if a firstling has any defect, lameness or blindness, any such serious defect, you shall not sacrifice it to the LORD, your God, 22 but in your own communities you may eat it, the unclean and the clean eating it together, as you would a gazelle or a deer. 23 Only, you must not eat of its blood; you shall pour it out on the ground like water.

**16 Feast of the Passover.** 1 Observe the month of Abib† by keeping the Passover of the LORD, your God,* since it was in the month of Abib that the LORD, your God, brought you out of Egypt by night. 2 You shall offer the Passover sacrifice from your flock and your herd to the LORD, your God, in the place the LORD will choose as the dwelling place of his name.* 3* You shall not eat leavened bread with it. For seven days you shall eat with it only unleavened bread, the bread of affliction, so that you may remember as long as you live the day you left the land of Egypt; for in hurried flight you left the land of Egypt. 4 No leaven is to be found with you in all your territory for seven days, and none of the meat which you sacrificed on the evening of the first day shall be kept overnight for the next day.

5 You may not sacrifice the Passover in any of the communities which the LORD, your God, gives you; 6 only at the place which the LORD, your God, will choose as the dwelling place of his name, and in the evening at sunset, at the very time when you left Egypt, shall you sacrifice the Passover.* 7 You shall cook and eat it at the place the LORD, your God, will choose; then in the morning you may return to your tents. 8 For six days you shall eat unleavened bread, and on the seventh day there shall be a solemn assembly for the LORD, your God; on that day you shall do no work.*

**Feast of Weeks.** 9* You shall count off seven weeks; begin to count the seven weeks from the day when the sickle is first put to the standing grain. 10 You shall then keep the feast of Weeks† for the LORD, your God, and the measure of your own voluntary offering which you will give shall be in proportion to the blessing the LORD, your God, has given you. 11 You shall rejoice in the presence of the LORD, your God, together with your son and daughter, your male and female slave, and the Levite within your gates, as well as the resident alien,

**15:17** *His ear:* cf. Ex 21:6 and note there.
**16:1** *Abib:* "ear of grain, ripe grain," the name of the month in which the barley harvest fell, corresponding to our March and April; at a later period this month received the Babylonian name of "Nisan."
**16:10** *Feast of Weeks:* a celebration of the grain harvest, later known as "Pentecost"; cf. Acts 2:1.

**15:11** Dt 15:8; Mt 26:11.
**15:12–18** Ex 21:2–11; Jer 34:8–22.
**15:13–15** Ex 3:21–22; 12:35–36.
**15:15** Dt 5:15; 10:19; 16:12;
24:18, 22.
**15:16–17** Ex 21:5–6.
**15:19** Ex 13:2, 11–16; 22:29–30; 34:19–20; Lv 22:27; 27:26; Nm 18:15–18.
**15:20** Dt 12:6–7, 17–18; 14:23.
**15:21–23** Dt 12:15–16, 22–24; 17:1; Lv 22:17–25; Mal 1:8.
**16:1–8** Ex 12:2–13:10; 23:15; 34:18; Lv 23:5–8; Nm 28:16–25; Jos
5:10–12; 2 Kgs 23:21–23; 2 Chr 30:1–27; 35:1–19; Ez 45:21–24.
**16:2** Dt 12:5, 11; 16:6.
**16:3–4** Ex 12:34, 39; 13:6–7; 34:18.
**16:6** Dt 12:5, 11; 16:2.
**16:8** Ex 13:6; Lv 23:36; Nm 29:35; Is 1:13; Am 5:21.
**16:9–12** Ex 23:16; 34:22; Lv 23:15–21; Nm 28:26–31.

the orphan, and the widow among you, in the place which the LORD, your God, will choose as the dwelling place of his name.* 12 Remember that you too were slaves in Egypt, so carry out these statutes carefully.

**Feast of Booths.** 13* You shall celebrate the feast of Booths† for seven days, when you have gathered in the produce from your threshing floor and wine press. 14 You shall rejoice at your feast,* together with your son and daughter, your male and female slave, and also the Levite, the resident alien, the orphan and the widow within your gates. 15 For seven days you shall celebrate this feast for the LORD, your God, in the place which the LORD will choose; since the LORD, your God, has blessed you in all your crops and in all your undertakings, you will be full of joy.

16 Three times a year,* then, all your males shall appear before the LORD, your God, in the place which he will choose: at the feast of Unleavened Bread, at the feast of Weeks, and at the feast of Booths. They shall not appear before the LORD empty-handed, 17 but each with his own gift, in proportion to the blessing which the LORD, your God, has given to you.

**Justice.** 18* In all the communities which the LORD, your God, is giving you, you shall appoint judges and officials throughout your tribes to administer true justice for the people. 19 You must not distort justice: you shall not show partiality;* you shall not take a bribe, for a bribe blinds the eyes even of the wise and twists the words even of the just. 20 Justice, justice alone shall you pursue, so that you may live and possess the land the LORD, your God, is giving you.

**Illicit Worship.** 21* You shall not plant an asherah† of any kind of wood next to the altar of the LORD, your God, which you will build;* 22 nor shall you erect a sacred pillar, such as the LORD, your God, hates.

**17** 1 You shall not sacrifice to the LORD, your God, an ox or a sheep with any serious defect;* that would be an abomination to the LORD, your God.

2* If there is found in your midst, in any one of the communities which the LORD, your God, gives you, a man or a woman who does evil in the sight of the LORD, your God, and transgresses his covenant,* 3 by going to serve other gods, by bowing down to them, to the sun or the moon or any of the host of heaven, contrary to my command;* 4 and if you are told or hear of it, you must investigate it thoroughly. If the truth of the matter is established that this abomination has been committed in Israel, 5 you shall bring the man or the woman who has done this evil deed out to your gates† and stone the man or the woman to death. 6 Only on the testimony of two or three witnesses shall a person be put to death;* no one shall be put to death on the testimony of only one witness. 7 The hands of the witnesses shall be the first raised to put the person to death, and afterward the hands of all the people.* Thus shall you purge the evil from your midst.

**Judges.** 8* If there is a case for judgment proves too baffling for you to decide, in a matter of bloodshed or of law or of injury, matters of dispute within your gates, you shall then go up to the place which the LORD, your God, will choose, 9 to the levitical priests or to the judge who is in office at that time. They shall investigate the case and then announce to you the decision.* 10 You shall act according to the decision they announce to you in the place which the LORD will choose, carefully observing everything as they instruct you. 11 You shall

---

† **16:13** *Feast of Booths:* also called Tabernacles; a harvest festival at the end of the agricultural year. In later times, during the seven days of the feast the Israelites camped in booths made of branches erected on the roofs of their houses or in the streets in commemoration of their wanderings in the wilderness, where they dwelt in such temporary shelters.
**16:21–22** *Asherah . . . sacred pillar:* see note on 7:5; Ex 34:13.
**17:5** *Out to your gates:* outside the gates, so as not to defile the city; cf. Lv 24:14; Nm 15:36; Acts 7:58; Heb 13:12.

* **16:11** Dt 12:5–7, 11–12, 18.
**16:13–15** Dt 31:10–13; Ex 23:16; 34:22; Lv 23:34–43;
Nm 29:12–38; 1 Kgs 8:2, 62–66; Ezr 3:4; Neh 8:14; Ez 45:25.
**16:14** Dt 16:11.

**16:16** Dt 12:7; 16:11, 14; Ex 23:14–15, 17; 34:23–24; 2 Chr 8:13.
**16:18–20** Dt 1:13–17; 17:8–13; 19:17; 21:5; Ex 18:13–26; 2 Chr 19:5–11.
**16:19** Dt 1:16–17; 10:17–18; Ex 23:2–3, 6–8; Lv 19:15; Prv 17:23; 18:5; 24:23; Is 1:23; Mi 7:3; Jn 7:24; Jas 2:9.
**16:21–17:7** Dt 5:7–10; 6:4–5; 12:29–14:2.
**16:21–22** Dt 7:5; Ex 34:13; 1 Kgs 14:15;
2 Kgs 23:6, 15; 2 Chr 33:3.
**17:1** Lv 22:20.
**17:2–7** Dt 13:2–19.
**17:2** Jos 7:11, 15; 23:16; Jgs 2:20; 2 Kgs 18:12; Jer 34:18; Hos 6:7; 8:1.
**17:3** Dt 4:19; 2 Kgs 17:16; 21:3; 23:5; Jer 8:2; Ez 8:16.
**17:6** Dt 19:15; Nm 35:30; Jn 8:17; 2 Cor 13:1.
**17:7** Dt 13:6, 10.
**17:8–9** Ex 18:13–26.
**17:9** Dt 21:5; 2 Chr 19:8; Ezr 7:25.

carry out the instruction they give you and the judgment they pronounce, without turning aside either to the right or left from the decision they announce to you. [12] Anyone who acts presumptuously and does not obey the priest† who officiates there in the ministry of the LORD, your God, or the judge, shall die. Thus shall you purge the evil from Israel. [13] And all the people, on hearing of it, shall fear, and will never again act presumptuously.*

**The King.** [14]* When you have come into the land which the LORD, your God, is giving you, and have taken possession of it and settled in it, should you then decide, "I will set a king over me, like all the surrounding nations,"* [15] you may indeed set over you a king whom the LORD, your God, will choose.* Someone from among your own kindred you may set over you as king; you may not set over you a foreigner, who is no kin of yours. [16]† But he shall not have a great number of horses; nor shall he make his people go back again to Egypt to acquire many horses, for the LORD said to you, Do not go back that way again.* [17] Neither shall he have a great number of wives, lest his heart turn away,* nor shall he accumulate a vast amount of silver and gold. [18] When he is sitting upon his royal throne, he shall write a copy of this law† upon a scroll from the one that is in the custody of the levitical priests.* [19]†* It shall remain with him and he shall read it as long as he lives, so that he may learn to fear the LORD, his God, and to observe carefully all the words of this law and these statutes, [20] so that he does not exalt himself over his kindred or turn aside from

this commandment to the right or to the left, and so that he and his descendants may reign long in Israel.

**18 Priests.** [1] The levitical priests, the whole tribe of Levi, shall have no hereditary portion with Israel; they shall eat the fire offerings of the LORD and the portions due to him.* [2] They shall have no heritage among their kindred; the LORD himself is their heritage, as he has told them.* [3] This shall be the due of the priests from the people: those who are offering a sacrifice, whether an ox or a sheep, shall give the priest the shoulder, the jowls and the stomach. [4] The first fruits of your grain, your wine, and your oil,* as well as the first shearing of your flock, you shall also give him. [5] For the LORD, your God, has chosen him out of all your tribes to be in attendance to minister in the name of the LORD, him and his descendants for all time.*

[6] When a Levite goes from one of your communities anywhere in Israel in which he has been residing, to visit, as his heart may desire, the place which the LORD will choose, [7] and ministers there in the name of the LORD, his God, like all his fellow Levites who stand before the LORD there, [8] he shall receive the same portions to eat, along with his stipends and patrimony.†

**Prophets.** [9] When you come into the land which the LORD, your God, is giving you, you shall not learn to imitate the abominations of the nations there.* [10]* Let there not be found among you anyone who causes their son or daughter to pass through the fire,† or

---

† **17:12** *The priest*: the high priest; *the judge*: a layman. The court system here, involving lay and priestly officials, resembles the one whose establishment is attributed to King Jehoshaphat in 2 Chr 19:8–11 (cf. Ex 18:17–23 and Dt 1:17).

**17:16–17** This restriction on royal acquisitions may have in mind the excesses of Solomon's reign mentioned in 1 Kgs 10:1–11:6. *Horses*: chariotry for war. Egypt engaged in horse trading, and the danger envisioned here is that some king might make Israel a vassal of Egypt for military aid.

**17:18** *A copy of this law*: the source of the name Deuteronomy, which in Hebrew is literally "double" or "copy"; in the Septuagint translated as *deuteronomion*, literally "a second law." In Jerome's Latin Vulgate as *deuteronium*.

**17:19** The only positive requirement imposed upon the king is strict adherence to the Mosaic or Deuteronomic law. In that respect, the king's primary task was to be a model Israelite.

**18:8** *His stipends and patrimony*: meaning of the Hebrew is uncertain.

**18:10–11** *Causes their son or daughter to pass through the fire*: to Molech. See note on Lv 18:21. Such human sacrifices are classed here with various occult and magical practices because they were believed to possess powers for averting a calamity;

cf. 2 Kgs 3:27. Three other categories of magic are listed here: divination of the future (by a soothsayer or augur); black magic (by a sorcerer or one who casts spells); and necromancy (by one who consults ghosts and spirits, or seeks oracles from the dead to divine the future).

---

| | |
|---|---|
| * | |
| **17:13** Dt 13:12. | 1 Kgs 2:4; Ps |
| **17:14–20** 1 Sm 10–25. | 132:11–18. |
| **17:14** Dt 26:1; 1 Sm 8:5, | **18:1** Nm 18:8–9, 20–24; |
| 19–20. | Jos 13:14; 18:7; 2 Chr |
| **17:15** 1 Sm 9:16; 10:24; | 31:2–19; 1 Cor 9:13. |
| 16:1–13; 1 Kgs | **18:2** Nm 18:20; Jos 13:33. |
| 19:15–16; 2 Kgs | **18:4** Dt 26:1–11; Nm |
| 9:1–13. | 18:12; 2 Chr 31:5; |
| **17:16** Dt 28:68; 1 Sm | Neh 13:10–13. |
| 8:10–12; 1 Kgs 4:26; | **18:5** Dt 10:8; Jer 33:18. |
| 10:26–29; Is 2:7. | **18:9** Dt 12:29–31; Lv |
| **17:17** 1 Kgs 10:10–25; | 18:24–30. |
| 11:1–8; Neh 13:26; Is | **18:10–11** Dt 12:31; Ex 22:18; |
| 2:7. | Lv 18:21; 19:31; 20:6, |
| **17:18** Dt 31:9, 24–26; Jos | 27; 1 Sm 28:7–19; |
| 8:32. | 2 Kgs 17:17; 21:6; |
| **17:19–20** Dt 5:32–6:3; 2 Sm | 23:10, 24; Is 8:19–20; |
| 7:12–16; | Ez 21:21. |

practices divination, or is a soothsayer, augur, or sorcerer, [11] or who casts spells, consults ghosts and spirits, or seeks oracles from the dead. [12] Anyone who does such things is an abomination to the LORD, and because of such abominations the LORD, your God, is dispossessing them before you.* [13] You must be altogether sincere with the LORD, your God. [14] Although these nations whom you are about to dispossess listen to their soothsayers and diviners, the LORD, your God, will not permit you to do so.

[15] A prophet like me† will the LORD, your God, raise up for you from among your own kindred; that is the one to whom you shall listen.* [16] This is exactly what you requested of the LORD, your God, at Horeb on the day of the assembly, when you said, "Let me not again hear the voice of the LORD, my God, nor see this great fire any more, or I will die."* [17] And the LORD said to me, What they have said is good. [18] I will raise up for them a prophet like you from among their kindred, and will put my words into the mouth of the prophet; the prophet shall tell them all that I command.* [19] Anyone who will not listen to my words which the prophet speaks in my name, I myself will hold accountable for it.* [20] But if a prophet presumes to speak a word in my name* that I have not commanded, or speaks in the name of other gods, that prophet shall die.

[21] Should you say to yourselves, "How can we recognize that a word is one the LORD has not spoken?", [22] if a prophet speaks in the name of the LORD but the word does not come true, it is a word the LORD did not speak. The prophet has spoken it presumptuously; do not fear him.

# 19 Cities of Refuge. [1]* When the LORD, your God, cuts down the nations whose land the LORD, your God, is giving you, and you have dispossessed them and settled in their cities and houses,* [2] you shall set apart three cities† in the land the LORD, your God, is giving you to possess. [3] You shall measure the distances and divide into three regions the land of which the LORD, your God, is giving you possession, so that every homicide will be able to find a refuge.

[4] This is the case of a homicide who may take refuge there and live: when someone strikes down a neighbor unintentionally and not out of previous hatred. [5] For example, if someone goes with a neighbor to a forest to cut wood, wielding an ax to cut down a tree, and its head flies off the handle and hits the neighbor a mortal blow, such a person may take refuge in one of these cities and live. [6] Should the distance be too great, the avenger of blood† might in hot anger pursue, overtake, and strike the killer dead, even though that one does not deserve the death penalty since there had been no previous hatred; [7] for this reason I command you: Set apart three cities.

[8]* But if the LORD, your God, enlarges your territory, as he swore to your ancestors, and gives you all the land he promised your ancestors he would give, [9] because you carefully observe this whole commandment which I give you today, loving the LORD, your God, and ever walking in his ways, then add three more cities to these three. [10] Thus, in the land which the LORD, your God, is giving you as a heritage, innocent blood will not be shed and you will not become guilty of bloodshed.*

[11] However, if someone, hating a neighbor, lies in wait, attacks, and strikes the neighbor dead, and then flees to one of these cities, [12] the elders of the killer's own city shall send and have the killer taken from there, to be handed over to the avenger of blood and slain. [13] Do not show pity, but purge from Israel the innocent blood, so that it may go well with you.*

---

† **18:15** *A prophet like me*: from the context (opposition to the practices described in vv. 10–11) it seems that Moses is referring in general to all the true prophets who were to succeed him. This passage came to be understood in a quasi-Messianic sense in the New Testament (Mt 17:5; Jn 6:14; 7:40; Acts 3:22; 7:37).

**19:2** *Set apart three cities*: the Israelites were to have at least six cities of refuge, three in the land east of the Jordan and three in the land of Canaan west of the Jordan; but since the three cities east of the Jordan had now been appointed (Dt 4:41–43), reference is made here only to the three west of the Jordan. The execution of this command is narrated in Jos 20.

**19:6** *The avenger of blood*: see note on Nm 35:12.

---

| | |
|---|---|
| **18:12** Dt 9:4. | 14:13–16; 23:9–40; |
| **18:15** Mt 17:5; Mk 9:7; Lk | 28:1–17; Ez 13:1–23. |
| 9:35; Jn 1:45; 6:14; | **19:1–13** Dt 4:41–43; Ex |
| 7:40; Acts 3:22; 7:37. | 21:12–14; Nm |
| **18:16** Ex 20:19. | 35:9–34; Jos 20:1–9. |
| **18:18** Ex 4:10–16; Jer 1:9; | **19:1** Dt 6:10–11; 12:29. |
| 15:19; Ez 3:1–4. | **19:8** Dt 11:22–25; 12:20; |
| **18:19** Jer 11:21–23; Am | Gn 15:18–21; 28:14; |
| 7:10–17; Acts 3:23. | Ex 23:31. |
| **18:20, 22** Dt 13:2–6; 1 Kgs | **19:10** Dt 21:8–9. |
| 22:1–40; Jer | **19:13** Dt 13:6, 9. |

**Removal of Landmarks.** 14 You shall not move your neighbor's boundary markers† erected by your forebears in the heritage that will be allotted to you in the land the LORD, your God, is giving you to possess.*

**False Witnesses.** 15* One witness alone shall not stand against someone in regard to any crime or any offense that may have been committed; a charge shall stand only on the testimony of two or three witnesses.*

16 If a hostile witness rises against someone to accuse that person of wrongdoing, 17 the two parties in the dispute shall appear in the presence of the LORD, in the presence of the priests and judges in office at that time,* 18* and the judges must investigate it thoroughly. If the witness is a false witness and has falsely accused the other,* 19 you shall do to the false witness just as that false witness planned to do to the other. Thus shall you purge the evil from your midst. 20 The rest shall hear and be afraid, and never again do such an evil thing as this in your midst.* 21 Do not show pity. Life for life,† eye for eye, tooth for tooth, hand for hand, and foot for foot!*

**20** **Courage in War.** 1 When you go out to war against your enemies and you see horses and chariots and an army greater than your own, you shall not be afraid of them, for the LORD, your God, who brought you up from the land of Egypt, will be with you.

2 When you are drawing near to battle, the priest shall come forward and speak to the army, 3 and say to them, "Hear, O Israel! Today you are drawing near for battle against your enemies. Do not be weakhearted or afraid, alarmed or frightened by them. 4 For it is the LORD, your God, who goes with you to fight for you against your enemies and give you victory."*

5 Then the officials shall speak to the army:* "Is there anyone who has built a new house

and not yet dedicated it? Let him return home, lest he die in battle and another dedicate it. 6 Is there anyone who has planted a vineyard and not yet plucked its fruit? Let him return home, lest he die in battle and another pluck its fruit. 7 Is there anyone who has betrothed a woman and not yet married her? Let him return home, lest he die in battle and another marry her."* 8 The officials shall continue to speak to the army: "Is there anyone who is afraid and weakhearted?* Let him return home, or else he might make the hearts of his fellows melt as his does."

9 When the officials have finished speaking to the army, military commanders shall be appointed over them.

**Cities of the Enemy.** 10* When you draw near a city to attack it, offer it terms of peace. 11 If it agrees to your terms of peace and lets you in, all the people to be found in it shall serve you in forced labor. 12* But if it refuses to make peace with you and instead joins battle with you, lay siege to it, 13 and when the LORD, your God, delivers it into your power, put every male in it to the sword; 14 but the women and children and livestock and anything else in the city—all its spoil—you may take as plunder for yourselves, and you may enjoy this spoil of your enemies, which the LORD, your God, has given you.

15† That is how you shall deal with any city at a considerable distance from you, which does not belong to these nations here. 16* But in the cities of these peoples that the LORD, your God, is giving you as a heritage, you shall not leave a single soul alive. 17 You must put them all under the ban—the Hittites, Amorites, Canaanites, Perizzites, Hivites, and Jebusites—just as the LORD, your God, has commanded you, 18 so that they do not teach you to do all the abominations that they do for their gods, and you thus sin against the LORD, your God.

---

† **19:14** *Move your neighbor's boundary markers*: a prohibition against furtively extending one's property by moving a neighbor's boundary stone.

**19:21** *Life for life . . .*: this phrasing of the *lex talionis* may seem exaggerated, but the law itself is meant to ensure equity and proportional punishment; cf. note on Ex 21:22–25.

**20:15** Deuteronomy makes a distinction between treatment of nations far away and those close at hand whose abhorrent religious practices might, or did, influence Israel's worship. This harsh policy was to make sure the nations nearby did not pass their practices on to Israel (cf. chap. 7).

* **19:14** Dt 27:17; Jb 24:2; Prv 22:28; 23:10; Hos 5:10.
**19:15–21** Dt 5:20; Ex 20:16; 23:1.
**19:15** Dt 17:6; Nm 35:30; Mt 18:16; Jn 8:17; 2 Cor 13:1.
**19:17** Dt 1:17; 17:8–12.
**19:18–19** Dn 13:61–62.
**19:18** Dt 13:15; 17:4.
**19:20** Dt 13:11.
**19:21** Ex 21:23–25;

Lv 24:19–20; Mt 5:38.
**20:4** Dt 1:30; 3:22; Ex 14:14; 15:3; Jos 23:10; Jgs 4:14.
**20:5–8** 1 Mc 3:56.
**20:7** Dt 24:5.
**20:8** Jgs 7:3.
**20:10–11** Jos 9:23–27; 11:19; 2 Sm 10:19.
**20:12–14** Nm 31:7, 9, 11; Jos 22:8.
**20:16–18** Dt 7:1–2; 12:29–31; Jos 10:40; 11:11, 14.

**Trees of a Besieged City.** [19]* When you are at war with a city and have to lay siege to it for a long time before you capture it, you shall not destroy its trees by putting an ax to them. You may eat of them, but you must not cut them down. Are the trees of the field human beings, that they should be included in your siege? [20] However, those trees which you know are not fruit trees you may destroy. You may cut them down to build siegeworks against the city that is waging war with you, until it falls.

# 21

**Absolution of Untraced Murder.**† [1] If the corpse of someone who has been slain is found lying in the open, in the land the LORD, your God, is giving you to possess, and it is not known who killed the person, [2] your elders and judges shall go out and measure the distances to the cities that are in the neighborhood of the corpse. [3]* When it is established which city is nearest the corpse, the elders of that city shall take a heifer that has never been put to work or worn a yoke; [4] the elders of that city shall bring the heifer down to a wadi with an everflowing stream at a place that has not been plowed or sown, and shall break the heifer's neck there in the wadi. [5] The priests, the descendants of Levi, shall come forward, for the LORD, your God, has chosen them to minister to him and to bless in the name of the LORD, and every case of dispute or assault shall be for them to decide. [6] Then all the elders of that city nearest the corpse shall wash their hands† over the heifer whose neck was broken in the wadi, [7] and shall declare, "Our hands did not shed this blood,† and our eyes did not see the deed. [8] Absolve, O LORD, your people Israel, whom you have redeemed, and do not let the guilt of shedding innocent blood remain in the midst of your people Israel." Thus they shall be absolved from the guilt of bloodshed, [9] and you shall purge the innocent blood from your midst, and do what is right in the eyes of the LORD.*

**Marriage with a Female Captive.** [10]* When you go out to war against your enemies and the LORD, your God, delivers them into your power, so that you take captives, [11] if you see a beautiful woman among the captives and become so enamored of her that you wish to have her as a wife, [12] and so you take her home to your house, she must shave her head,† cut her nails, [13] lay aside her captive's garb, and stay in your house, mourning her father and mother for a full month. After that, you may come to her, and you shall be her husband and she shall be your wife. [14] If later on you lose your liking for her, you shall give her her freedom, if she wishes it; you must not sell her for money. Do not enslave her, since you have violated her.*

**Rights of the Firstborn.** [15]* If a man has two wives, one loved and the other unloved, and if both the loved and the unloved bear him sons, but the firstborn is the son of the unloved wife: [16] when he comes to bequeath his property to his sons he may not consider as his firstborn the son of the wife he loves, in preference to the son of the wife he does not love, the firstborn. [17] On the contrary, he shall recognize as his firstborn the son of the unloved wife, giving him a double share of whatever he happens to own, since he is the first fruits of his manhood, and to him belong the rights of the firstborn.*

**The Stubborn and Rebellious Son.** [18]* If someone has a stubborn and rebellious son who will not listen to his father or mother, and will not listen to them even though they discipline him,* [19] his father and mother shall take hold of him and bring him out to the elders at the gate† of his home city, [20] where they shall say to the elders of the city, "This son of ours is a stubborn and rebellious fellow who will not listen to us; he is a glutton and a drunkard."* [21] Then all his fellow citizens shall stone him

---

† **21:1–9** This law has to do with absolving the community of bloodguilt that accrues to it and to the land when a homicide occurs and the murderer cannot be identified and punished.

**21:6** *Wash their hands:* a symbolic gesture in protestation of one's own innocence when human blood is unjustly shed; cf. Mt 27:24.

**21:7** *This blood:* the blood of the slain, or the bloodguilt effected by the killing.

**21:12–13** *Shave her head . . . :* these symbolic actions probably signified the transition or change of status of the woman or perhaps the end of her period of mourning for her previous husband or family.

**21:19** *The gate:* in the city walls. This open space served as the forum for the administration of justice. Cf. 22:15; 25:7; Ru 4:1, 2, 11; Is 29:21; Am 5:10, 12, 15.

---

| | |
|---|---|
| **20:19–20** 2 Kgs 3:18, 25. | 1 Kgs 1:5–21. |
| **21:3–4** Nm 19:2–3. | **21:17** Gn 49:3–4. |
| **21:9** Dt 19:13. | **21:18–21** Dt 5:16; 27:16; Ex |
| **21:10–14** Dt 20:14. | 20:12; 21:15, 17; Lv |
| **21:14** Dt 15:12–18; | 20:9. |
| 22:13–19, 20–29; | **21:18** Ps 78:8; Jer 5:23. |
| 24:1–3; Jer 34:15–16. | **21:20** Prv 23:20–21; 28:7; |
| **21:15–17** Gn 21:9–13; | Mt 11:19; Lk 7:34. |

to death. Thus shall you purge the evil from your midst, and all Israel will hear and be afraid.*

**Corpse of a Criminal.** 22 * If a man guilty of a capital offense is put to death and you hang him on a tree,† 23 his corpse shall not remain on the tree overnight.* You must bury it the same day; anyone who is hanged is a curse of God.† You shall not defile the land which the LORD, your God, is giving you as a heritage.

22 **Concern for the Neighbor.** 1 * You shall not see your neighbor's ox or sheep going astray and ignore it; you must bring it back. 2 If this neighbor does not live near you, or you do not know who the owner may be, take it to your own house and keep it with you until your neighbor claims it; then return it. 3 You shall do the same with a donkey; you shall do the same with a garment; and you shall do the same with anything else which your neighbor loses and you happen to find. You may not ignore them.

4 You shall not see your neighbor's donkey or ox fallen on the road and ignore it; you must help in lifting it up.

**Various Precepts.** 5 A woman shall not wear a man's garment, nor shall a man put on a woman's clothing; for anyone who does such things is an abomination to the LORD, your God.*

6 * If, while walking along, you come across a bird's nest with young birds or eggs in it, in any tree or on the ground, and the mother bird is sitting on them, you shall not take away the mother bird along with her brood. 7 You must let the mother go, taking only her brood, in order that you shall prosper and have a long life.

8 When you build a new house, put a parapet around the roof, so that you do not bring bloodguilt upon your house if someone falls off.*

9 †* You shall not sow your vineyard with two different kinds of seed, or else its produce shall become forfeit, both the crop you have sown and the yield of the vineyard. 10 You shall not plow with an ox and a donkey harnessed together. 11 You shall not wear cloth made from wool and linen woven together.

12 You shall put tassels on the four corners of the cloak that you wrap around yourself.*

**Marriage Legislation.** 13 If a man, after marrying a woman and having relations with her, comes to dislike her,* 14 and accuses her of misconduct and slanders her by saying, "I married this woman, but when I approached her I did not find evidence of her virginity," 15 the father and mother of the young woman shall take the evidence of her virginity† and bring it to the elders at the city gate. 16 There the father of the young woman shall say to the elders, "I gave my daughter to this man in marriage, but he has come to dislike her, 17 and now accuses her of misconduct, saying: 'I did not find evidence of your daughter's virginity.' But here is the evidence of my daughter's virginity!" And they shall spread out the cloth before the elders of the city. 18 Then these city elders shall take the man and discipline him,† 19 and fine him one hundred silver shekels, which they shall give to the young woman's father, because the man slandered a virgin in Israel. She shall remain his wife, and he may not divorce her as long as he lives. 20 But if this charge is true, and evidence of the young woman's virginity is not found, 21 they shall bring the young woman to the entrance of her father's house and there the men of her town shall stone her to death, because she committed a shameful crime in Israel by prostituting herself in her father's house. Thus shall you purge the evil from your midst.*

22 If a man is discovered lying with a woman who is married to another, they both shall die, the man who was lying with the woman as

---

† **21:22** *You hang him on a tree*: some understand, "impaled on a stake." In any case the hanging or impaling was not the means used to execute the criminal; he was first put to death by the ordinary means, stoning, and his corpse was then exposed on high as a warning for others. Cf. Jos 8:29; 10:26; 1 Sm 31:10; 2 Sm 21:9.
**21:23** Gal 3:13 applies these words to the crucifixion of Jesus, who "redeemed us from the curse of the law, becoming a curse for us."
**22:9–11** Some understand these laws as serving to preserve distinctions set by God in the creation. *Become forfeit*: to the sanctuary; lit., "be holy"; cf. Lv 19:19; Jos 6:19.

**22:15** *The evidence of her virginity*: the bridal garment or sheet stained with blood from the first nuptial relations.
**22:18** *Discipline him*: whip him, as prescribed in 25:1–3.

**21:21** Dt 13:6, 11–12; 22:21, 24; Lv 20:2; 24:14–16.
**21:22–23** Jos 8:29; 10:26–27; 1 Sm 31:8–13; 2 Sm 4:12.
**21:23** Gal 3:13.
**22:1** Ex 23:4–5.
**22:5** Dt 7:25–26.
**22:6–7** Lv 22:28.
**22:8** Dt 19:10.
**22:9–11** Lv 19:19.
**22:12** Nm 15:38–41; Mt 23:5.
**22:13** Dt 24:1.
**22:21** Dt 13:6; Gn 34:7; 2 Sm 13:12.

well as the woman.* Thus shall you purge the evil from Israel.

²³ If there is a young woman, a virgin who is betrothed,† and a man comes upon her in the city and lies with her, ²⁴ you shall bring them both out to the gate of the city and there stone them to death: the young woman because she did not cry out though she was in the city, and the man because he violated his neighbor's wife. Thus shall you purge the evil from your midst. ²⁵ But if it is in the open fields that a man comes upon the betrothed young woman, seizes her and lies with her, only the man who lay with her shall die. ²⁶ You shall do nothing to the young woman, since the young woman is not guilty of a capital offense. As when a man rises up against his neighbor and murders him, so in this case:†* ²⁷ it was in the open fields that he came upon her, and though the betrothed young woman may have cried out, there was no one to save her.

²⁸* If a man comes upon a young woman, a virgin who is not betrothed, seizes her and lies with her, and they are discovered, ²⁹ the man who lay with her shall give the young woman's father fifty silver shekels and she will be his wife, because he has violated her. He may not divorce her as long as he lives.

# 23

¹ A man shall not marry his father's wife,† nor shall he dishonor his father's bed.*

**Membership in the Assembly.** ²† No one whose testicles have been crushed or whose penis has been cut off may come into the assembly of the Lord.* ³ No one born of an illicit union may come into the assembly of the Lord, nor any descendant of such even to the tenth generation may come into the assembly of the Lord.* ⁴* No Ammonite or Moabite may ever come into the assembly of the Lord,

nor may any of their descendants even to the tenth generation come into the assembly of the Lord, ⁵ because they would not come to meet you with food and water on your journey after you left Egypt, and because they hired Balaam, son of Beor, from Pethor in Aram Naharaim, to curse you. ⁶ The Lord, your God, would not listen to Balaam but turned his curse into a blessing for you, because the Lord, your God, loves you. ⁷ Never seek their welfare or prosperity as long as you live.* ⁸* Do not abhor the Edomite: he is your brother. Do not abhor the Egyptian: you were a resident alien in his country. ⁹ Children born to them may come into the assembly of the Lord in the third generation.

**Cleanliness in Camp.** ¹⁰ When in camp during an expedition against your enemies, you shall keep yourselves from anything bad. ¹¹* If one of you becomes unclean because of a nocturnal emission, he shall go outside the camp; he shall not come back into the camp. ¹² Toward evening, he shall bathe in water; then, when the sun has set, he may come back into the camp. ¹³ Outside the camp you shall have a place set aside where you shall go. ¹⁴ You shall keep a trowel in your equipment and, when you go outside to relieve yourself, you shall dig a hole with it and then cover up your excrement. ¹⁵ Since the Lord, your God, journeys along in the midst of your camp to deliver you and to give your enemies over to you, your camp must be holy, so that he does not see anything indecent in your midst and turn away from you.*

**Various Precepts.** ¹⁶* You shall not hand over to their master any slaves who have taken refuge with you from their master. ¹⁷ Let them live among you in any place they choose, in any one of your communities† that seems good to them. Do not oppress them.

---

**22:23** *A young woman, a virgin who is betrothed*: a girl who is married but not yet brought to her husband's home and whose marriage is therefore still unconsummated.

**22:26** *So in this case*: in the absence of witnesses ("in the open field"), the presumption must be that the woman is the victim, and so guiltless.

**23:1** *Father's wife*: stepmother.

**23:2** Exclusion of an emasculated male may have had to do with association of emasculation with the practices of other peoples, or it may have been rejection of someone with a significant blemish who was thus not suitable for participation in the sacral assembly.

**23:17** *In any one of your communities*: from this it would seem that the slave in question is a fugitive from a foreign country.

**22:22** Dt 5:18; Ex 20:14; Lv 20:10; Ez 16:38–40; Jn 8:3–5.
**22:26** Dt 19:4–6.
**22:28–29** Dt 22:19; Ex 22:16–17.
**23:1** Dt 27:20; Gn 9:20–27; 49:4; Lv 18:6–19; 20:11; Ez 22:10.
**23:2** Lv 21:16–24.
**23:3** Gn 19:30–38; Lv 18:6–18.
**23:4–6** Nm 22:1–24:25; Ru 4:9–17; Ezr 10:10–44; Neh 13:1–3, 23–27.
**23:7** Ezr 9:12.
**23:8** Dt 2:2–8; 26:5; Gn 12:10–20; 25:19–26; 36:6–9; 46:5–7; 47:27.
**23:11–12** Lv 15:16–17.
**23:15** Dt 1:30; 20:4; 31:6, 8; 2 Sm 7:6.
**23:16–17** 1 Kgs 2:39–40.

<sup>18</sup>There shall be no temple prostitute† among the Israelite women, nor a temple prostitute among the Israelite men.* <sup>19</sup>You shall not offer a prostitute's fee or a dog's pay† as any kind of votive offering in the house of the LORD, your God; both these things are an abomination to the LORD, your God.*

<sup>20</sup>* You shall not demand interest from your kindred on a loan of money or of food or of anything else which is loaned. <sup>21</sup>From a foreigner you may demand interest, but you may not demand interest from your kindred, so that the LORD, your God, may bless you in all your undertakings on the land you are to enter and possess.

<sup>22</sup>* When you make a vow to the LORD, your God, you shall not delay in fulfilling it; for the LORD, your God, will surely require it of you and you will be held guilty. <sup>23</sup>Should you refrain from making a vow, you will not be held guilty. <sup>24</sup>But whatever your tongue utters you must be careful to do, just as you freely vowed to the LORD, your God, with your own mouth.

<sup>25</sup>When you go through your neighbor's vineyard, you may eat as many grapes as you wish, until you are satisfied, but do not put them in your basket. <sup>26</sup>When you go through your neighbor's grainfield, you may pluck some of the ears with your hand, but do not put a sickle to your neighbor's grain.

# 24

**Marriage Legislation.**† <sup>1</sup>* When a man, after marrying a woman, is later displeased with her because he finds in her something indecent, and he writes out a bill of divorce and hands it to her, thus dismissing her from his house, <sup>2</sup>if on leaving his house she goes and becomes the wife of another man, <sup>3</sup>and the second husband, too, comes to dislike her and he writes out a bill of divorce and hands it to her, thus dismissing her from his house, or if this second man who has married her dies, <sup>4</sup>then her former husband, who dismissed her, may not again take her as his wife after she has become defiled. That would be an abomination before the LORD, and you shall not bring such guilt upon the land the LORD, your God, is giving you as a heritage.*

<sup>5</sup>* When a man is newly wed, he shall not go out on a military expedition, nor shall any duty be imposed on him. He shall be exempt for one year for the sake of his family, to bring joy to the wife he has married.

**Pledges and Kidnappings.** <sup>6</sup>† No one shall take a hand mill or even its upper stone as a pledge for debt, for that would be taking as a pledge the debtor's life.

<sup>7</sup>If anyone is caught kidnapping a fellow Israelite, enslaving or selling the victim, that kidnapper shall be put to death.* Thus shall you purge the evil from your midst.

**Skin Diseases.** <sup>8</sup>* In an attack of scaly infection† you shall be careful to observe exactly and to carry out all the instructions the levitical priests give you, as I have commanded them: observe them carefully. <sup>9</sup>* Remember what the LORD, your God, did to Miriam on the journey after you left Egypt.

**Loans and Wages.** <sup>10</sup>When you make a loan of any kind to your neighbor, you shall not enter the neighbor's house to receive the pledge, <sup>11</sup>but shall wait outside until the person to whom you are making the loan brings the pledge outside to you. <sup>12</sup>If the person is poor, you shall not sleep in the pledged garment,

---

† **23:18–19** *Temple prostitute:* Heb. *qedesha*, lit., "holy one," a title of the goddess of fertility. The role or function of the *qedesha* is debated; some see this as simply a term for a prostitute (Heb. *zona*). Others see it as designating a cultic role but not necessarily one involving sexual activity. The evidence is insufficient to give a final answer.

**23:19** *Dog's pay:* "dog" is a derogatory term for a male temple prostitute.

**24:1–4** This law is directly concerned only with forbidding a divorced man from remarrying his former wife, and indirectly with checking hasty divorces, by demanding sufficient cause and certain legal formalities. Divorce itself is taken for granted and tolerated as an existing custom whose potential evils this law seeks to lessen. Cf. 22:19, 29; Mal 2:14–16. *Something indecent:* a rather indefinite phrase, meaning perhaps "immodest conduct," but possibly including any kind of objectionable conduct. By New Testament times Jewish opinion differed concerning what was sufficient ground for divorce; cf. Mt 19:3.

**24:6** Since the Israelites ground their grain into flour only in

sufficient quantity for their current need, to deprive a debtor of his hand mill was equivalent to condemning him to starvation.

**24:8** *Scaly infection:* the Hebrew word seems to have to do with one or more skin diseases that produce scales, such as psoriasis. Its precise meaning is uncertain. See note on Lv 13:1–14:57.

---

**23:18** Gn 38:21–22; 1 Kgs
14:24; 15:12; 22:46;
2 Kgs 23:7; Hos 4:14.
**23:19** Dt 7:25–26; Is
23:17–18.
**23:20–21** Dt 15:1–11;
24:10–13; Ex 22:25;
Lv 25:35–38; Ez 18:8,
13, 17; 22:12; Lk
6:34–35.
**23:22–24** Gn 28:20–22; Nm
21:2–3; 30:1–15;

Jgs 11:30–40; 1 Sm
1:11; Ps 56:12–13;
66:13–15; 132:1–5;
Eccl 5:3–5.
**24:1–4** Dt 22:13–19, 28–29;
Sir 7:26; Jer 3:1; Mt
5:31–32; 19:3–9.
**24:4** Dt 7:25–26.
**24:5** Dt 20:7.
**24:7** Dt 13:6; Ex 21:16.
**24:8** Lv 13:1–14:57.
**24:9** Nm 12:10–15.

13 but shall definitely return it at sunset, so that your neighbor may sleep in the garment* and bless you. That will be your justice before the LORD, your God.

14 * You shall not exploit a poor and needy hired servant, whether one of your own kindred or one of the resident aliens who live in your land, within your gates.* 15 On each day you shall pay the servant's wages before the sun goes down, since the servant is poor and is counting on them. Otherwise the servant will cry to the LORD against you, and you will be held guilty.*

**Individual Responsibility.** 16 Parents shall not be put to death for their children, nor shall children be put to death for their parents; only for one's own crime shall a person be put to death.*

**Rights of the Unprotected.** 17 * You shall not deprive the resident alien or the orphan of justice, nor take the clothing of a widow as pledge. 18 For, remember, you were slaves in Egypt, and the LORD, your God, redeemed you from there; that is why I command you to do this.

19 * When you reap the harvest in your field and overlook a sheaf in the field, you shall not go back to get it; let it be for the resident alien, the orphan, and the widow, so that the LORD, your God, may bless you in all your undertakings. 20 When you knock down the fruit of your olive trees, you shall not go over the branches a second time; let what remains be for the resident alien, the orphan, and the widow. 21 When you pick your grapes, you shall not go over the vineyard a second time; let what remains be for the resident alien, the orphan, and the widow. 22 For remember that you were slaves in the land of Egypt; that is why I command you to do this.

**25** **Limits on Punishments.** 1 When there is a dispute and the parties draw near for judgment, and a decision is given, declaring one party in the right and the other in the wrong, 2 if the one in the wrong deserves whipping, the judge shall have him lie down and in the presence of the judge receive the number of lashes the crime warrants. 3 Forty lashes† may be given, but no more;* or else, if more lashes are added to these many blows, your brother will be degraded in your sight.

**Treatment of Oxen.** † 4 You shall not muzzle an ox when it treads out grain.*

**Levirate Marriage.** 5 * When brothers live together† and one of them dies without a son, the widow of the deceased shall not marry anyone outside the family; but her husband's brother shall come to her, marrying her and performing the duty of a brother-in-law.* 6 The firstborn son she bears shall continue the name of the deceased brother, that his name may not be blotted out from Israel. 7 But if a man does not want to marry his brother's wife, she shall go up to the elders at the gate and say, "My brother-in-law refuses to perpetuate his brother's name in Israel and does not intend to perform his duty toward me." 8 Thereupon the elders of his city shall summon him and speak to him. If he persists in saying, "I do not want to marry her," 9 † his sister-in-law, in the presence of the elders, shall go up to him and strip his sandal from his foot and spit in his face, declaring, "This is how one should be treated who will not build up his brother's family!" 10 And his name shall be called in Israel, "the house of the man stripped of his sandal."

**Various Precepts.** 11 When two men are fighting and the wife of one intervenes to save her

---

25:3 *Forty lashes:* while the punishment is severe, the law seeks to limit it from being overly harsh and inhumane. Later Jewish practice limited the number to thirty-nine; cf. 2 Cor 11:24.

25:4 This is comparable in spirit to 22:6–7; Israelites are not to be grasping and calculating. St. Paul argues from this verse that laborers have the right to live on the fruits of their labor; cf. 1 Cor 9:9; 1 Tm 5:18.

25:5 *When brothers live together:* when relatives of the same clan, though married, hold their property in common. It was only in this case that the present law was to be observed, since one of its purposes was to keep the property of the deceased within the same clan. Such a marriage of a widow with her brother-in-law is known as a "levirate" marriage from the Latin word *levir,* meaning "a husband's brother."

25:9–10 The penalty decreed for a man who refuses to comply with this law of family loyalty is public disgrace; the widow is to spit in his face. Some commentators connect this symbolic act with the ceremony mentioned in Ru 4:7, 8.

| | |
|---|---|
| **24:13** Dt 6:25; Ex 22:25–26; Am 2:8. | Ex 22:21–24; 23:9. |
| **24:14–15** Lv 19:13; Sir 34:26–27; Jer 22:13. | **24:19–22** Ex 23:10–11; Lv 19:9–10; 23:22; Ru 2:1–23. |
| **24:14** Dt 1:16. | **25:3** 2 Cor 11:24. |
| **24:15** Dt 15:9; Mt 20:1–16. | **25:4** Prv 12:10; 1 Cor 9:9; 1 Tm 5:18. |
| **24:16** Dt 7:10; 2 Kgs 14:6; 2 Chr 25:4; Jer 31:29–30; Ez 18:20. | **25:5–10** Gn 38:1–30; Ru 4:5–10; Lk 20:27–33. |
| **24:17–18** Dt 10:17–19; 15:15; 24:22; 27:19; | **25:5** Mt 22:24; Mk 12:19; Lk 20:28. |

husband from the blows of his opponent, if she stretches out her hand and seizes the latter by his genitals, 12 you shall chop off her hand; show no pity.

13 * You shall not keep two differing weights in your bag, one heavy and the other light; 14 nor shall you keep two different ephahs† in your house, one large and the other small. 15 But use a full and just weight, a full and just ephah, so that you may have a long life on the land the LORD, your God, is giving you. 16 For everyone who does these things, everyone who does what is dishonest, is an abomination to the LORD, your God. *

17 †* Bear in mind what Amalek did to you on the journey after you left Egypt, 18 how he surprised you along the way, weak and weary as you were, and struck down at the rear all those who lagged behind; he did not fear God. 19 Therefore, when the LORD, your God, gives you rest from all your enemies round about in the land which the LORD, your God, is giving you to possess as a heritage, you shall blot out the memory of Amalek from under the heavens. Do not forget!

# 26 Thanksgiving for the Harvest. 1 * When you have come into the land which the LORD, your God, is giving you as a heritage, and have taken possession and settled in it, 2 you shall take some first fruits* of the various products of the soil which you harvest from the land the LORD, your God, is giving you; put them in a basket and go to the place which the LORD, your God, will choose as the dwelling place for his name. 3 There you shall go to the priest in office at that time and say to him, "Today I acknowledge to the LORD, my God, that I have indeed come into the land which the LORD swore to our ancestors to give us."* 4 The priest shall then take the basket from your hands and set it in front of the altar of the LORD, your God. 5 Then you shall declare

in the presence of the LORD, your God, "My father was a refugee Aramean† who went down to Egypt with a small household and lived there as a resident alien.* But there he became a nation great, strong and numerous. 6 * When the Egyptians maltreated and oppressed us, imposing harsh servitude upon us, 7 we cried to the LORD, the God of our ancestors, and the LORD heard our cry and saw our affliction, our toil and our oppression. 8 Then the LORD brought us out of Egypt with a strong hand and outstretched arm, with terrifying power, with signs and wonders,* 9 and brought us to this place, and gave us this land, a land flowing with milk and honey.* 10 Now, therefore, I have brought the first fruits of the products of the soil which you, LORD, have given me." You shall set them before the LORD, your God, and you shall bow down before the LORD, your God. 11 Then you and your household, together with the Levite and the resident aliens who live among you, shall celebrate with all these good things which the LORD, your God, has given you.*

**Declaration Concerning Tithes.** 12 When you have finished setting aside all the tithes of your produce in the third year,* the year of the tithes, and have given them to the Levite, the resident alien, the orphan and the widow, that they may eat and be satisfied in your own communities, 13 you shall declare before the LORD, your God, "I have purged my house of the sacred portion and I have given it to the Levite, the resident alien, the orphan and the widow, just as you have commanded me. I have not transgressed any of your commandments, nor forgotten any. 14 † I have not eaten any of the tithe while in mourning; I have not brought any of it while unclean; I have not offered any of it to the dead. I have thus obeyed the voice of the LORD, my God, and done just as you have commanded me.* 15 Look down,

25:14 Ephahs: see note on Is 5:10.
25:17–19 This attack on Israel by Amalek is not mentioned elsewhere in the Old Testament, although it probably was connected with the battle mentioned in Ex 17:8. A campaign against Amalek was carried out by Saul; cf. 1 Sm 15.
26:5 Aramean: probably in reference to the origin of the patriarchs from Aram Naharaim (cf. Gn 24:10; 25:20; 28:5; 31:20, 24).
26:14 These are allusions to foreign religious practices. To the dead: to feed the spirits of the dead, or perhaps to worship Baal.

25:13–16 Lv 19:35–36; Prv 16:11; 20:23; Ez 45:10; Hos 12:7; Mi 6:11.
25:16 Dt 7:25–26.
25:17–19 Ex 17:8–16; 1 Sm 15:2–33.
26:1–11 Dt 14:22–29; 16:1–17; Ex 22:29; Lv 23:9–21; Nm 28:26–31.
26:2 Dt 12:5, 11; 18:4; Ex 23:19; 34:26; Tb 1:6–7.
26:3 Dt 1:8, 20–21.
26:5 Gn 46:5–7, 26–27; Ex 1:7, 9; Acts 7:14–15.
26:6–7 Ex 1:8–22; 2:23–25; 3:7–10; 6:9; Nm 20:15–16; 1 Kgs 12:4.
26:8 Dt 4:34; 6:21–22; Ex 12:51.
26:9 Ex 3:8.
26:11 Dt 12:7, 12.
26:12 Dt 14:28–29.
26:14 Dt 14:1; Lv 11:24–25; 22:3; Jer 16:7.

then, from heaven, your holy abode, and bless your people Israel and the fields you have given us, as you promised on oath to our ancestors, a land flowing with milk and honey."*

**The Covenant.** 16* This day the LORD, your God, is commanding you to observe these statutes and ordinances. Be careful, then, to observe them with your whole heart and with your whole being. 17 Today you have accepted the LORD's agreement: he will be your God, and you will walk in his ways, observe his statutes, commandments, and ordinances, and obey his voice. 18 And today the LORD has accepted your agreement: you will be a people specially his own, as he promised you, you will keep all his commandments, 19 and he will set you high in praise and renown and glory above all nations he has made, and you will be a people holy to the LORD, your God, as he promised.

## 27 The Altar on Mount Ebal. 1 Then Moses, with the elders of Israel, commanded the people, saying: Keep this whole commandment which I give you today. 2 On the day you cross the Jordan into the land which the LORD, your God, is giving you, set up some large stones and coat them with plaster. 3 Write on them,* at the time you cross, all the words of this law, so that you may enter the land which the LORD, your God, is giving you, a land flowing with milk and honey, just as the LORD, the God of your ancestors, promised you. 4 When you cross the Jordan, on Mount Ebal you shall set up these stones concerning which I command you today, and coat them with plaster, 5* and you shall build there an altar to the LORD, your God, an altar made of stones that no iron tool has touched. 6 You shall build this altar of the LORD, your God, with unhewn stones, and shall offer on it burnt offerings to the LORD, your God. 7 You

shall also offer communion sacrifices† and eat them there, rejoicing in the presence of the LORD, your God. 8 On the stones you shall inscribe all the words of this law very clearly.

9 Moses, with the levitical priests, then said to all Israel: Be silent, Israel, and listen! This day you have become the people of the LORD, your God.* 10 You shall obey the voice of the LORD, your God, and keep his commandments and statutes which I am giving you today.

**Preparation for Blessings and Curses.** 11 That same day Moses commanded the people, saying: 12* When you cross the Jordan, these shall stand on Mount Gerizim to bless the people: Simeon, Levi, Judah, Issachar, Joseph and Benjamin. 13 And these shall stand on Mount Ebal for the curse: Reuben, Gad, Asher, Zebulun, Dan and Naphtali.

**The Twelve Curses.** 14 The Levites shall proclaim in a loud voice to all the Israelites: 15† "Cursed be anyone who makes a carved or molten idol,* an abomination to the LORD, the work of a craftsman's hands, and sets it up in secret!" And all the people shall answer, "Amen!"

16 "Cursed be anyone who dishonors father or mother!"* And all the people shall answer, "Amen!"

17 "Cursed be anyone who moves a neighbor's boundary markers!"* And all the people shall answer, "Amen!"

18 "Cursed be anyone who misleads the blind on their way!"* And all the people shall answer, "Amen!"

19 "Cursed be anyone who deprives the resident alien, the orphan or the widow of justice!"* And all the people shall answer, "Amen!"

20 "Cursed be anyone who has relations with his father's wife, for he dishonors his father's bed!"* And all the people shall answer, "Amen!"

---

27:7 *Communion sacrifices:* The principal feature of this ritual (see Lv 3:1–17) is the sharing of the sacrifice with God, the priest and the person offering the sacrifice, who eat it as a holy thing (cf. Ex 24:5).

27:15–26 The ceremony described here reflects the structure of covenant. The people assent to the directives their covenant Lord sets forth; their "Amen" ratifies the proscription of idolatry, injustice, incest, murder, and infidelity in general. Thus the "love" of the Lord which is at the heart of Israel's existence as his covenant people (6:4–5) is spelled out in terms of particular actions. The "Amen" is an acceptance of the curses or sanctions entailed by breaking faith with the Lord. Cf. 30:15–20, a concise statement of covenant theology.

**26:15** 1 Kgs 8:39, 43, 49; Ps 102:19.
**26:16–19** Dt 7:6; 8:6; 10:12–13; 11:22; 14:2; 27:9; 28:1, 9; 29:12–13; Ex 6:7; 19:5–6; 24:7; Lv 26:12; 2 Sm 7:24; Jer 7:23; 31:33; Ez 11:20; Hos 2:23.
**27:3** Jos 8:32.
**27:5–7** Ex 20:24–25; Jos 8:30–31.
**27:9** Dt 26:17–19.
**27:12–13** Dt 11:26–29;

Jos 8:33–35.
**27:15** Dt 4:15–20; 5:8–9; Ex 20:4, 23; 34:17; Lv 19:4; 26:1; Ps 115:4–8; Wis 14:8.
**27:16** Dt 5:16; 21:18–21; Ex 20:12; 21:17; Lv 20:9.
**27:17** Dt 19:14.
**27:18** Lv 19:14.
**27:19** Dt 24:17–18; Ex 22:21–24; 23:9; Lv 19:33–34.
**27:20** Dt 23:1; Lv 18:7–8; 20:11.

21 "Cursed be anyone who has relations with any animal!"* And all the people shall answer, "Amen!"

22 "Cursed be anyone who has relations with his sister, whether his father's daughter or his mother's daughter!"* And all the people shall answer, "Amen!"

23 "Cursed be anyone who has relations with his mother-in-law!"* And all the people shall answer, "Amen!"

24 "Cursed be anyone who strikes down a neighbor in secret!"* And all the people shall answer, "Amen!"

25 "Cursed be anyone who accepts payment to kill an innocent person!"* And all the people shall answer, "Amen!"

26 "Cursed be anyone whose actions do not uphold the words of this law!"* And all the people shall answer, "Amen!"

# 28

**Blessings for Obedience.** 1 Now,* * if you diligently obey the voice of the LORD, your God, carefully observing all his commandments which I give you today, the LORD, your God, will set you high above all the nations of the earth.* 2 All these blessings will come upon you and overwhelm you when you obey the voice of the LORD, your God:

3*    May you be blessed in the city,
        and blessed in the country!

4    Blessed be the fruit of your womb,
        the produce of your soil and the
          offspring of your livestock,
        the issue of your herds and the young
          of your flocks!*

5    Blessed be your grain basket and your
        kneading bowl!

6    May you be blessed in your coming in,
        and blessed in your going out!†*

**Victory and Prosperity.** 7 The LORD will beat down before you the enemies that rise up against you; they will come out against you from one direction, and flee before you in seven.†* 8 The LORD will affirm the blessing upon you, on your barns and on all your undertakings; he will bless you in the land that the LORD, your God, is giving you. 9 The LORD will establish you as a holy people, as he swore to you,* if you keep the commandments of the LORD, your God, and walk in his ways. 10 All the peoples of the earth will see that the name of the LORD is proclaimed over you,† and they will be afraid of you.* 11 The LORD will generously increase the fruit of your womb, the offspring of your livestock, and the produce of your soil, upon the land which the LORD swore to your ancestors he would give you.* 12 The LORD will open up for you his rich storehouse, the heavens, to give your land rain in due season and to bless all the works of your hands. You will lend to many nations but borrow from none.* 13 The LORD will make you the head not the tail, the top not the bottom, if you obey the commandments of the LORD, your God, which I am giving you today, observing them carefully, 14 not turning aside, either to the right or to the left, from any of the words which I am giving you today, following other gods and serving them.*

**Curses for Disobedience.** 15 But if you do not obey the voice of the LORD, your God,* carefully observing all his commandments and statutes which I give you today, all these curses shall come upon you and overwhelm you:

16 * May you be cursed in the city, and cursed in the country! 17 Cursed be your grain basket and your kneading bowl! 18 Cursed be the fruit of your womb, the produce of your soil and the offspring of your livestock, the issue of your herds and the young of your flocks! 19 May you be cursed in your coming in, and cursed in your going out!

**Sickness and Defeat.** 20 The LORD will send on you a curse, panic, and frustration in

---

28:6 *In your coming in . . . in your going out:* at the beginning and end of every action, or in all actions in general. The rhetorical figure is called merismus. See also 6:7.

28:7 *From one direction . . . in seven:* in one disciplined body, contrasted with many scattered groups.

28:10 *The name of the LORD is proclaimed over you:* an expression signifying ownership and protection. Cf. 2 Sm 12:28; 1 Kgs 8:43; Is 4:1; 63:19; Jer 7:10–11; 14:9; 15:16; 25:29; Am 9:12.

---

27:21 Ex 22:18; Lv 18:23; 20:15–16.
27:22 Lv 18:9; 20:17.
27:23 Lv 18:17; 20:14.
27:24 Dt 5:17; 21:1; Ex 20:13; 21:12; Nm 35:20–21.
27:25 Dt 16:19; Ex 23:7–8.
27:26 Jer 11:3; Gal 3:10.
28:1–68 Lv 26:3–45.
28:1–14 Dt 7:12–16; 11:13–15.
28:1 Dt 26:19; Ps 89:27; Is 55:3–5.
28:3–6 Dt 28:16–19.
28:4 Dt 7:13–14; 30:9; Ex 23:26; Lv 26:9.
28:6 Ps 121:8.
28:7 Dt 9:1–3; Ex 23:27–28; Dt 26:6–8.
28:9 Dt 26:18–19; Ex 19:5–6.
28:10 Dt 2:25; 11:25; Is 61:9.
28:11 Dt 28:4.
28:12 Dt 15:6.
28:14 Dt 5:32.
28:15 Bar 1:20; Dn 9:11; Mal 2:2.
28:16–19 Dt 28:3–6.

everything you set your hand to, until you are speedily destroyed and perish for the evil you have done in forsaking me. ²¹* The LORD will make disease cling to you until he has made an end of you from the land you are entering to possess. ²²The LORD will strike you with consumption, fever, and inflammation, with fiery heat and drought, with blight and mildew, that will pursue you until you perish. ²³The heavens over your heads will be like bronze and the earth under your feet like iron.* ²⁴For rain the LORD will give your land powdery dust, which will come down upon you from the heavens until you are destroyed. ²⁵The LORD will let you be beaten down before your enemies; though you advance against them from one direction, you will flee before them in seven,† so that you will become an object of horror to all the kingdoms of the earth.* ²⁶Your corpses will become food for all the birds of the air and for the beasts of the field, with no one to frighten them off.* ²⁷The LORD will strike you with Egyptian boils* and with tumors, skin diseases and the itch, from none of which you can be cured. ²⁸* And the LORD will strike you with madness, blindness and panic, ²⁹so that even at midday you will grope in the dark as though blind, unable to find your way.

**Despoilment.** You will be oppressed and robbed continually, with no one to come to your aid. ³⁰Though you betroth a wife, another will have her. Though you build a house, you will not live in it. Though you plant a vineyard, you will not pluck its fruits.* ³¹* Your ox will be slaughtered before your eyes, but you will not eat its flesh. Your donkey will be stolen in your presence, but you will never get it back. Your flocks will be given to your enemies, with no one to come to your aid. ³²Your sons and daughters will be given to another people while you strain your eyes looking for them every day, having no power to do anything. ³³A people you do not know will consume the fruit of your soil and of all your labor, and you will be thoroughly oppressed and continually crushed, ³⁴until you are driven mad by what your eyes must look upon. ³⁵The LORD will strike you with malignant boils of which you cannot be cured, on your knees and legs, and from the soles of your feet to the crown of your head.

**Exile.** ³⁶* The LORD will bring you, and your king whom you have set over you, to a nation which you and your ancestors have not known, and there you will serve other gods, of wood and stone, ³⁷and you will be a horror, a byword, a taunt among all the peoples to which the LORD will drive you.

**Fruitless Labors.** ³⁸* Though you take out seed to your field, you will harvest but little, for the locusts will devour it. ³⁹Though you plant and cultivate vineyards, you will not drink or store up the wine, for the worms will eat them. ⁴⁰Though you have olive trees throughout your country, you will have no oil for ointment, for your olives will drop off. ⁴¹Though you beget sons and daughters, they will not remain with you, for they will go into captivity. ⁴²Buzzing insects will take possession of all your trees and the crops of your soil. ⁴³* The resident aliens among you will rise above you higher and higher, while you sink lower and lower. ⁴⁴They will lend to you, not you to them. They will become the head, you the tail.

⁴⁵All these curses will come upon you, pursuing you and overwhelming you, until you are destroyed, because you would not obey the voice of the LORD, your God, by keeping his commandments and statutes which he gave you.* ⁴⁶They will be a sign and a wonder† for you and your descendants for all time. ⁴⁷Since you would not serve the LORD, your God, with heartfelt joy for abundance of every kind, ⁴⁸in hunger and thirst, in nakedness and utter want, you will serve the enemies whom the LORD will send against you. He will put an iron yoke on your neck, until he destroys you.*

---

† **28:25** *From one direction . . . in seven:* see note on v. 7.
**28:46** *A sign and a wonder:* an ominous example, attracting attention; cf. 29:21–28.

**28:21–22** Lv 26:16, 25; Jer 14:12; Am 4:9–10; Hg 2:17.
**28:23** Lv 26:19.
**28:25** Dt 1:44; 28:7; Lv 26:17, 37.
**28:26** Ps 79:2; Jer 7:33; 34:20.
**28:27** Dt 7:15; 28:60; Ex 9:8–12.
**28:28–29** Is 59:10.
**28:30** Dt 20:5–7; Am 5:11.
**28:31–34** Jer 5:17; Lam 5:1–18; Am 7:17.
**28:36–37** Dt 4:27–28; 1 Kgs 9:6–9; 2 Kgs 25:6–7, 11; 2 Chr 7:19–22;
33:11; 36:6, 20; Jer 16:13; 24:8–9; 25:8–11; Ez 17:12.
**28:38–42** Dt 28:18; Lv 26:20; Lam 1:5; Mi 6:15; Zep 1:13; Hg 1:6.
**28:43–44** Dt 15:6; 28:12–13.
**28:45** Dt 28:15.
**28:48** Jer 28:14.

**Invasion and Siege.** [49]* The LORD will raise up against you a nation from afar, from the end of the earth, that swoops down like an eagle, a nation whose language you do not understand, [50] a nation of fierce appearance, that shows neither respect for the aged nor mercy for the young. [51] They will consume the offspring of your livestock and the produce of your soil, until you are destroyed; they will leave you no grain or wine or oil, no issue of herd, no young of flock, until they have brought about your ruin. [52] They will besiege you in each of your communities, until the great, fortified walls, in which you trust, come tumbling down all over your land. They will besiege you in every community throughout the land which the LORD, your God, has given you, [53]* and because of the siege and the distress to which your enemy subjects you, you will eat the fruit of your womb, the flesh of your own sons and daughters whom the LORD, your God, has given you. [54] The most refined and fastidious man among you will begrudge his brother and his beloved wife and his surviving children, [55] any share in the flesh of his children that he himself is using for food because nothing else is left him—such the siege and distress to which your enemy will subject you in all your communities. [56] The most fastidious woman among you, who would not venture to set the sole of her foot on the ground, so refined and fastidious is she, will begrudge her beloved husband and her son and daughter [57] the afterbirth that issues from her womb and the infants she brings forth because she secretly eats them for want of anything else—such the siege and distress to which your enemy will subject you in your communities.

**Plagues.** [58] If you are not careful to observe all the words of this law which is written in this book, and to fear this glorious and awesome name, the LORD, your God,* [59]* the LORD will bring upon you and your descendants wondrous calamities, severe and constant calamities, and malignant and constant sicknesses.

[60] He will bring back upon you all the diseases of Egypt† which you dread, and they will cling to you. [61] Even any sickness or calamity not written in this book of the law, that too the LORD will bring upon you until you are destroyed. [62] You who were numerous as the stars of the heavens* will be left few in number, because you would not obey the voice of the LORD, your God.

**Exile.** [63]* Just as the LORD once took delight in making you prosper and grow, so will the LORD now take delight in ruining and destroying you, and you will be plucked out of the land you are now entering to possess. [64] The LORD will scatter you among all the peoples from one end of the earth to the other, and there you will serve other gods, of wood and stone, which you and your ancestors have not known. [65] Among these nations you will find no rest, not even a resting place for the sole of your foot, for there the LORD will give you an anguished heart and wearied eyes† and a trembling spirit. [66] Your life will hang in suspense and you will stand in dread both day and night, never sure of your life. [67] In the morning you will say, "Would that it were evening!" and in the evening you will say, "Would that it were morning!" because of the dread that your heart must feel and the sight that your eyes must see. [68] The LORD will send you back in ships to Egypt, by a route which I told you that you would never see again;* and there you will offer yourselves for sale to your enemies as male and female slaves, but there will be no buyer.

[69] These are the words of the covenant which the LORD commanded Moses to make with the Israelites in the land of Moab, in addition to the covenant he made with them at Horeb.

## III. THIRD ADDRESS

# 29

**Past Favors Recalled.** [1] Moses summoned all Israel and said to them, You have seen with your own eyes all that the LORD did in the land of Egypt to Pharaoh and all his

---

**28:60** *He will bring back upon you all the diseases of Egypt*: such as the Lord had promised to remove from the people (7:15); cf. v. 27.

**28:65** *Wearied eyes*: cf. v. 32.

**28:49–52** Jer 5:15–17; 6:22–26; Bar 4:15–16.
**28:53–57** Lv 26:29; 2 Kgs 6:28–29; Jer 19:9; Lam 2:20; 4:10; Bar 2:3.
**28:58** Dt 6:13; Jos 24:14.
**28:59–61** Dt 7:15; 28:21–22, 27.
**28:62** Dt 1:10; 10:22; 26:5; Jer 42:2.
**28:63–67** Dt 4:26–28; 30:9; Lv 26:33–39.
**28:68** Jer 42–44; Hos 8:13; 9:3, 6; 11:5.

servants and to all his land, [2] the great testings your own eyes have seen, and those great signs and wonders.* [3] But the LORD has not given you a heart to understand, or eyes to see, or ears to hear until this day.* [4]* I led you for forty years in the wilderness. Your clothes did not fall from you in tatters nor your sandals from your feet; [5] it was not bread that you ate, nor wine or beer that you drank—so that you might know that I, the LORD, am your God. [6]* When you came to this place, Sihon, king of Heshbon, and Og, king of Bashan, came out to engage us in battle, but we defeated them [7] and took their land, and gave it as a heritage to the Reubenites, Gadites, and the half-tribe of Manasseh.* [8] Observe carefully the words of this covenant, therefore, in order that you may succeed in whatever you do.*

**All Israel Bound by Covenant.** [9] You are standing today, all of you, in the presence of the LORD, your God—your tribal heads, elders, and officials, all of the men of Israel, [10] your children, your wives, and the resident alien who lives in your camp, from those who cut wood to those who draw water for you— [11] to enter into the covenant of the LORD, your God, which the LORD, your God, is making with you today, with its curse, [12] so that he may establish you today as his people and he may be your God, as he promised you and as he swore to your ancestors, to Abraham, Isaac and Jacob. [13]* But it is not with you alone that I am making this covenant, with its curse, [14] but with those who are standing here with us today in the presence of the LORD, our God, and with those who are not here with us† today.

**Warning Against Idolatry.** [15] You know that we lived in the land of Egypt and that we passed through the nations, that you too passed through [16] and saw the loathsome things and idols of wood and stone, of gold and silver, that they possess. [17] There may be among you

a man or woman, or a clan or tribe, whose heart is now turning away from the LORD, our God, to go and serve the gods of these nations; there may be among you a root bearing poison and wormwood; [18] if any such persons, after hearing the words of this curse, should congratulate themselves, saying in their hearts, "I am safe, even though I walk in stubbornness of heart," thereby sweeping away moist and dry alike,†* [19] the LORD will never consent to pardon them. Instead, the LORD's burning wrath will flare up against them; every curse written in this book will pounce on them, and the LORD will blot out their names from under the heavens.* [20] The LORD will single them out from all the tribes of Israel for doom, in keeping with all the curses of the covenant written in this book of the law.

**Punishment for Idolatry.** [21]* Future generations, your descendants who will rise up after you, as well as the foreigners who will come here from distant lands, when they see the calamities of this land and the ills the LORD has inflicted upon it— [22] all its soil burned out by sulphur and salt, unsown and unfruitful, without a blade of grass, like the catastrophe of Sodom and Gomorrah,* Admah and Zeboiim,† which the LORD overthrew in his furious wrath— [23]* they and all the nations will ask, "Why has the LORD dealt thus with this land? Why this great outburst of wrath?" [24] And they will say, "Because they abandoned the covenant of the LORD, the God of their ancestors, which he had made with them when he brought them out of the land of Egypt, [25] and they went and served other gods and bowed down to them, gods whom they did not know and whom he had not apportioned to them.* [26]* So the anger of the LORD flared up against this land and brought on it every curse written in this book. [27] The LORD uprooted them from their soil in anger, fury, and great wrath, and cast them out into another

---

† **29:14** *Not here with us:* this includes future generations. This attitude appears also in 5:3.
**29:18** *Sweeping away moist and dry alike:* possibly a proverbial expression: because of Israel's infidelity the Lord will punish the just with the wicked (cf. Gn 18:25), rooting out good plants in irrigated soil, together with worthless plants growing in dry ground.
**29:22** *Admah and Zeboiim:* neighboring cities of Sodom and Gomorrah in the Jordan Plain and identified in the tradition as destroyed with them. Cf. Hos 11:8; Jer 50:40.

* **29:1–2** Dt 4:34, 37–38; 6:21–23; 7:19; 26:5–9.
**29:3** Is 6:9–10; Jer 5:21; Ez 12:2; Mt 13:14–15; Mk 4:12; Lk 8:10; Jn 12:40; Acts 28:26–27.
**29:4–5** Dt 8:2–4.
**29:6** Dt 1:4; 2:31–33; 3:1–3; Nm 21:23–24, 33–35.
**29:7** Dt 3:16–17; Nm 32:33.
**29:8** Jos 1:7–8; 1 Kgs 2:3.
**29:13–14** Dt 5:3.
**29:18** Jer 7:10.
**29:19** Dt 9:14; 25:19.
**29:21–27** Dt 4:25–28.
**29:22** Gn 19:24–25; Hos 11:8.
**29:23–24** 1 Kgs 9:8–9; Jer 5:19; 9:12–16; 16:10–13; 22:8–9.
**29:25** Dt 4:19; 32:8–9.
**29:26–27** Dt 29:20–21; Dn 9:11–14.

land, as they are today." [28] The hidden things† belong to the LORD our God, but the revealed things are for us and for our children forever, to observe all the words of this law.

# 30 Compassion for the Repentant.

[1]†* When all these things, the blessing and the curse which I have set before you, come upon you,* and you take them to heart in any of the nations where the LORD, your God, has dispersed you, [2]* and return to the LORD, your God, obeying his voice, according to all that I am commanding you today, you and your children, with your whole heart and your whole being, [3] the LORD, your God, will restore your fortunes and will have compassion on you; he will again gather you from all the peoples where the LORD, your God, has scattered you. [4] Though you may have been dispersed to the farthest corner of the heavens, even from there will the LORD, your God, gather you; even from there will he bring you back.* [5] The LORD, your God, will then bring you into the land your ancestors once possessed, that you may possess it; and he will make you more prosperous and numerous than your ancestors.* [6] The LORD, your God, will circumcise your hearts† and the hearts of your descendants,* so that you will love the LORD, your God, with your whole heart and your whole being, in order that you may live. [7] The LORD, your God, will put all those curses on your enemies and the foes who pursued you.* [8] You, however, shall again obey the voice of the LORD and observe all his commandments which I am giving you today. [9] Then the LORD, your God, will generously increase your undertakings, the fruit of your womb, the offspring of your livestock, and the produce of your soil;* for the LORD, your God, will again take delight in your prosperity, just as he took delight in your ancestors', [10] because you will obey the voice of the LORD, your God, keeping the commandments and statutes that

are written in this book of the law, when you return to the LORD, your God, with your whole heart and your whole being.

[11]* For this command which I am giving you today is not too wondrous or remote for you. [12] It is not in the heavens, that you should say, "Who will go up to the heavens to get it for us and tell us of it, that we may do it?" [13] Nor is it across the sea, that you should say, "Who will cross the sea to get it for us and tell us of it, that we may do it?" [14] No, it is something very near to you, in your mouth† and in your heart, to do it.

**The Choice Before Israel.** [15] See, I have today set before you life and good, death and evil.* [16] If you obey the commandments of the LORD, your God, which I am giving you today, loving the LORD, your God, and walking in his ways, and keeping his commandments, statutes and ordinances, you will live and grow numerous, and the LORD, your God, will bless you in the land you are entering to possess.* [17]* If, however, your heart turns away and you do not obey, but are led astray and bow down to other gods and serve them, [18] I tell you today that you will certainly perish; you will not have a long life on the land which you are crossing the Jordan to enter and possess. [19] I call heaven and earth today to witness against you:* I have set before you life and death, the blessing and the curse. Choose life, then, that you and your descendants may live, [20] by loving the LORD, your God, obeying his voice, and holding fast to him. For that will mean life for you, a long life for you to live on the land which the LORD swore to your ancestors, to Abraham, Isaac, and Jacob, to give to them.*

# 31 The Lord's Leadership.

[1] When Moses had finished speaking these words to all Israel, [2] he said to them, I am now one hundred and twenty years old* and am no longer

**29:28** *The hidden things*: probably the events of the future. *The revealed things*: the covenant and its provisions, including the sanctions of blessing and curse. This aphorism may mean: leave "hidden things" to God; what matters is to keep the law.
**30:1–5** Text such as this suggests a postexilic perspective; cf. also chaps. 31–32.
**30:6** *Circumcise your hearts*: see note on 10:16.
**30:14** *In your mouth*: that is, memorized and recited; cf. 6:7; 11:19. *And in your heart*: internalized and appropriated; cf. 6:6; 11:18.

**30:1–10** Dt 4:29–31; Lv 26:40–45.
**30:1** Dt 11:26–28; 27:11–28:69.
**30:2–3** Dt 4:29–30; 6:5; 30:10; 1 Kgs 8:47–48; Jer 24:7; 29:14; 33:26; Ez 39:25; Am 9:14; Zep 3:20.
**30:4** Neh 1:9; Is 43:5–7; Jer 31:10; 32:37; Ez 36:24; 37:21.
**30:5** Jer 23:3.
**30:6** Dt 6:5; 10:16; Ez 11:19–20; 36:26–28.
**30:7** Dt 7:15.
**30:9** Dt 28:4, 11; 30:2.
**30:11–14** Dt 6:6; 11:18; Jer 1:9; Bar 3:29–31; Rom 10:6–8.
**30:15** Dt 11:26–28; Jer 21:8.
**30:16** Dt 4:1; 8:1; 11:22.
**30:17–18** Dt 5:7; 6:4; 8:19–20.
**30:19** Dt 4:26; 11:26–28; 28:2, 15; 31:28.
**30:20** Dt 1:8; 4:1, 40.
**31:2** Dt 1:37; 3:23–28; 4:21–24; 34:7; Gn 6:3; Ex 7:7; Nm 20:12; Acts 7:23, 30.

able to go out and come in; besides, the Lord has said to me, Do not cross this Jordan. ³ It is the Lord, your God, who will cross before you; he will destroy these nations before you, that you may dispossess them.* (It is Joshua who will cross before you, as the Lord promised.) ⁴* The Lord will deal with them just as he dealt with Sihon and Og, the kings of the Amorites, and with their country, when he destroyed them. ⁵ When, therefore, the Lord delivers them up to you, you shall deal with them according to the whole commandment which I have given you.* ⁶ Be strong and steadfast; have no fear or dread of them, for it is the Lord, your God, who marches with you; he will never fail you or forsake you.*

**Call of Joshua.** ⁷ Then Moses summoned Joshua and in the presence of all Israel said to him,* "Be strong and steadfast, for you shall bring this people into the land which the Lord swore to their ancestors he would give them; it is you who will give them possession of it. ⁸ It is the Lord who goes before you; he will be with you and will never fail you or forsake you. So do not fear or be dismayed."*

**The Reading of the Law.** ⁹* When Moses had written down this law, he gave it to the levitical priests who carry the ark of the covenant of the Lord, and to all the elders of Israel.* ¹⁰ Moses commanded them, saying, On the feast of Booths,* at the prescribed time in the year for remission† which comes at the end of every seven-year period, ¹¹ when all Israel goes to appear before the Lord, your God, in the place which he will choose, you shall read this law aloud in the presence of all Israel. ¹² Assemble the people—men, women and children, as well as the resident aliens who live in your communities—that they may hear and so learn to fear the Lord, your God, and to observe carefully all the words of this law. ¹³ Their children also, who do not know it yet, shall hear and learn to fear the Lord, your God, as long as you live on the land which you are about to cross the Jordan to possess.

**Commission to Joshua.** ¹⁴* The Lord said to Moses, The time is now approaching for you to die. Summon Joshua, and present yourselves at the tent of meeting that I may commission him. So Moses and Joshua went and presented themselves at the tent of meeting. ¹⁵ And the Lord appeared at the tent in a column of cloud; the column of cloud stood at the entrance of the tent.

**A Command to Moses.** ¹⁶ The Lord said to Moses, Soon you will be at rest with your ancestors, and then this people will prostitute themselves† by following the foreign gods among whom they will live in the land they are about to enter.* They will forsake me and break the covenant which I have made with them. ¹⁷* At that time my anger will flare up against them; I will forsake them and hide my face from them; they will become a prey to be devoured, and much evil and distress will befall them. At that time they will indeed say, "Is it not because our God is not in our midst that these evils have befallen us?" ¹⁸ Yet I will surely hide my face at that time because of all the evil they have done in turning to other gods. ¹⁹ Now, write out this song* for yourselves. Teach it to the Israelites and have them recite it, so that this song may be a witness for me against the Israelites. ²⁰ For when I have brought them into the land flowing with milk and honey which I promised on oath to their ancestors, and they have eaten and are satisfied and have grown fat, if they turn to other gods and serve them, despising me and breaking my covenant, ²¹ then, when great evil and distress befall them, this song will speak to them as a witness, for it will not be forgotten if their descendants recite it. For I know what they are inclined to do even at the present time, before I have brought them into the land which I promised on oath. ²² So Moses wrote this song that same day, and he taught it to the Israelites.

**Commission of Joshua.** ²³ Then he commissioned Joshua, son of Nun, and said to him,

---

† **31:10** *The year for remission*: cf. 15:1–3 and note there.
   **31:16** *Prostitute themselves*: lit., "whore after," a play on the phrase "go after," viz. after other gods.

*
   **31:3** Dt 1:30–33; 3:22, 28;
       9:3.
   **31:4** Dt 2:26–3:7; 3:21–22;
       Nm 21:21–35.
   **31:5** Dt 7:1–5; 20:16–18.
   **31:6** Dt 1:29; 20:3–4.
   **31:7–8** Dt 1:21; 31:23; Jos
       1:6–9; 10:25.

   **31:8** Ex 3:12; Jos 1:5, 17;
       3:7; 2 Sm 7:9.
   **31:9–13** Dt 31:24–27.
   **31:9** Dt 10:1–5, 8.
   **31:10–12** Dt 12:5; 15:1–11;
       16:13–15; 2 Kgs 23:2;
       Neh 8:1–8.
   **31:14–15** Dt 33:7–11; Nm 12:5.
   **31:16** Dt 32:16–17;

   Ex 34:15–16; Jgs
       2:11–23; 8:27, 33;
   1 Kgs 11:1–10; 2 Kgs
       17:7–41; Jer 11:9–10;
       Hos 4:12; 9:1.
   **31:17–18** Dt 1:42; 32:19–25;
       Nm 14:42.
   **31:19** Dt 6:6–9; 31:21;
       32:1–43.

Be strong and steadfast, for it is you who will bring the Israelites into the land which I promised them on oath.* I myself will be with you.

**The Law Placed in the Ark.** 24 When Moses had finished writing out on a scroll the words of this law in their entirety, 25 Moses gave the Levites* who carry the ark of the covenant of the LORD this order: 26 Take this book of the law and put it beside the ark of the covenant of the LORD, your God, that there it may be a witness against you.* 27 For I already know how rebellious and stiff-necked you will be. Why, even now, while I am alive among you, you have been rebels against the LORD! How much more, then, after I am dead!* 28 * Assemble all your tribal elders and your officials before me, that I may speak these words for them to hear and so may call heaven and earth to witness against them. 29 * For I know that after my death you are sure to act corruptly and to turn aside from the way along which I commanded you, so that evil will befall you in time to come because you have done what is evil in the LORD's sight, and provoked him by your deeds.

**The Song of Moses.** 30 Then Moses recited the words of this song in their entirety, for the whole assembly of Israel to hear:

# 32

1 † Give ear, O heavens, and let me speak;
    let the earth hear the words of my mouth!*
2 May my teaching soak in like the rain,
    and my utterance drench like the dew,
  Like a downpour upon the grass,
    like a shower upon the crops.
3 For I will proclaim the name of the LORD,
    praise the greatness of our God!

4 The Rock—how faultless are his deeds,
    how right all his ways!
  A faithful God, without deceit,
    just and upright is he!*
5 Yet his degenerate children have treated him basely,
    a twisted and crooked generation!*
6 Is this how you repay the LORD,
    so foolish and unwise a people?
  Is he not your father who begot you,
    the one who made and established you?*
7 Remember the days of old,
    consider the years of generations past.
  Ask your father, he will inform you,
    your elders, they will tell you:*
8 When the Most High allotted each nation its heritage,
    when he separated out human beings,*
  He set up the boundaries of the peoples
    after the number of the divine beings;†
9 But the LORD's portion was his people;
    his allotted share was Jacob.*
10 He found them in a wilderness,
    a wasteland of howling desert.
  He shielded them, cared for them,
    guarded them as the apple of his eye.*
11 As an eagle incites its nestlings,
    hovering over its young,
  So he spread his wings, took them,
    bore them upon his pinions.*
12 The LORD alone guided them,
    no foreign god was with them.*
13 * He had them mount the summits of the land,†
    fed them the produce of its fields;

---

† **32:1–43** The whole song is a poetic sermon, having for its theme the Lord's benefits to Israel (vv. 1–14) and Israel's ingratitude and idolatry in turning to the gods of the nations; these sins will be punished by the nations themselves (vv. 15–29); in turn, the foolish pride of the nations will be punished, and the Lord's honor will be vindicated (vv. 30–43).
**32:8** *Divine beings:* lit., "sons of God" (see also v. 43); members of the divine assembly; cf. 1 Kgs 22:19; Jb 1:6; 2:1; 38:7; Ps 82; 89:6–7. The nations are portrayed as having their respective tutelary deities.
**32:13** *The land:* Canaan.

---

**31:23** Dt 31:7–8; Nm 27:15–23; Jos 1:1–9.
**31:24–25** Dt 31:9.
**31:26** Dt 10:1–5; Ex 40:20; 1 Kgs 8:9.
**31:27** Dt 9:6–7, 22–24.
**31:28** Dt 31:12–13, 19–22; 30:19; 32:1–43.
**31:29** Jgs 2:11–23.
**32:1** Dt 4:26; 30:19; 31:28.
**32:4** Dt 7:9; 32:15, 18, 30–31; 2 Sm 22:3; Ps 18:2, 31, 46; 92:15; Is 17:10; Hb 1:12; Rev 15:3.
**32:5** Dt 9:12; 14:1; 31:29; Ps 78:8; Is 1:2–4; Lk 9:41.
**32:6** Ex 4:22–23; Is 63:16; 64:8; Jer 31:9; Hos 11:1–4.
**32:7** Dt 4:32–34.
**32:8** Gn 14:18–22; Nm 24:16; Jb 1:6; 2:1; Ps 29:1; 47:2; 82:6; 83:18; 89:5–7; Is 14:14; Acts 17:26.
**32:9** Dt 7:6; Ex 19:5–6; Ps 33:12; Sir 17:17; Jer 10:16; Zec 2:16.
**32:10** Dt 1:31; 2:7; 8:15; Ps 17:8; Prv 7:2; Jer 2:2–3, 6; Hos 2:15; 13:5–6; Zec 2:12.
**32:11** Ex 19:4.
**32:12** Ex 15:13; Is 43:12; Hos 13:4.
**32:13–14** Dt 8:7–10; Ps 81:16.

He suckled them with honey from the
    crags
  and olive oil from the flinty rock;
14 Butter from cows and milk from sheep,
    with the best of lambs;
Bashan† bulls and goats,
    with the cream of finest wheat;
  and the foaming blood of grapes you
    drank.

15 So Jacob ate and was satisfied,
  Jeshurun† grew fat and kicked;
    you became fat and gross and gorged.
They forsook the God who made them
  and scorned the Rock of their
    salvation.*
16 With strange gods they incited him,
  with abominations provoked him to
    anger.*
17 They sacrificed to demons, to "no-gods,"
  to gods they had never known,
Newcomers from afar,
  before whom your ancestors had
    never trembled.
18 You were unmindful of the Rock that
    begot you,
  you forgot the God who gave you
    birth.*

19 The Lord saw and was filled with
    loathing,
  provoked by his sons and daughters.*
20 He said, I will hide my face from them,
  and see what becomes of them.
For they are a fickle generation,
  children with no loyalty in them!*
21 Since they have incited me with a "no-
    god,"
  and provoked me with their empty
    idols,
I will incite them with a "no-people";†
  with a foolish nation I will provoke
    them.*

22 For by my wrath a fire is kindled
  that has raged to the depths of Sheol,
It has consumed the earth with its yield,
  and set on fire the foundations of the
    mountains.*
23 I will heap evils upon them
  and exhaust all my arrows against
    them:*
24 Emaciating hunger and consuming fever
  and bitter pestilence,
And the teeth of wild beasts I will send
    among them,
  with the venom of reptiles gliding in
    the dust.*
25 Out in the street the sword shall bereave,
  and at home the terror
For the young man and the young
    woman alike,
  the nursing babe as well as the gray
    beard.*
26 I said: I will make an end of them
  and blot out their name from human
    memory,
27 Had I not feared the provocation by the
    enemy,
  that their foes might misunderstand,
And say, "Our own hand won the
    victory;
  the Lord had nothing to do with any
    of it."*
28 For they are a nation devoid of reason,†
  having no understanding.
29 If they had insight they would realize
    this,
  they would understand their end:
30 "How could one rout a thousand,
  or two put ten thousand to flight,
Unless it was because their Rock sold
    them,
  the Lord delivered them up?"

31 Indeed, their "rock" is not like our Rock;
  our enemies are fools.

---

**32:14** *Bashan:* a fertile grazing land east of the Jordan, famous for its sleek, strong cattle. Cf. Ps 22:13; Ez 39:18; Am 4:1.
    **32:15** *Jeshurun:* a term for Israel from *yashar,* meaning "upright"; its use here is possibly ironic.
    **32:21** *"No-god" . . . "no-people":* worship of the gods of the nations brings destruction at the hands of a foreign invader. A false god cannot sustain or protect (cf. Jer 14:22); and though the nations seem "foolish" (see their characterization in such passages as Ps 114:1; Is 28:11; 33:19), they will prove to be anything but nonentities when the Lord stirs them up against Israel (Is 9:10–12). For the "no-" or "not-" construction, see Hos 1:6, 9; 2:1, 25.
    **32:28–35** The reference is to the nations, not to Israel.

---

**32:15** Dt 8:12–18; 31:20;
    33:5, 26; Neh 9:25; Is
    44:2.
**32:16–17** Dt 31:16; Ps 78:58;
    81:9; 106:34–39.
**32:18** Is 49:15; Jer 2:32.
**32:19** Dt 4:24.
**32:20** Dt 31:17–18; Nm
    6:25–26.
**32:21** Dt 28:49–50; Jgs
    2:14–15; Is 9:11–12;

Rom 10:19.
**32:22** Dt 4:24; Ps 18:7–8;
    50:3; Lam 4:11.
**32:23** Dt 32:42; Ps 7:12–13;
    18:14; Ez 5:16.
**32:24** Dt 28:21–22.
**32:25** Lv 26:25; Jer 6:11;
    Lam 1:20; 2:21; Ez
    7:15.
**32:27** Dt 9:26–29; Ex
    32:11–14; Ps 74:18.

D
T

32 For their vine is from the vine of
       Sodom,
     from the vineyards of Gomorrah.
   Their grapes are grapes of poison,
     and their clusters are bitter.*

33 Their wine is the venom of serpents,
     the cruel poison of vipers.

34 Is not this stored up with me,
     sealed up in my storehouses?

35 Vengeance is mine and recompense,
     for the time they lose their footing;
   Because the day of their disaster is at
       hand
     and their doom is rushing upon
       them!*

36 Surely, the LORD will do justice for his
       people;
     on his servants he will have pity.
   When he sees their strength is gone,
     and neither bond nor free† is left,*

37 He will say, Where are their gods,*
     the rock in whom they took refuge,

38 Who ate the fat of their sacrifices
     and drank the wine of their
       libations?
   Let them rise up now and help you!
   Let them be your protection!

39 See now that I, I alone, am he,
     and there is no god besides me.
   It is I who bring both death and life,
     I who inflict wounds and heal them,
     and from my hand no one can
       deliver.*

40 For I raise my hand to the heavens
     and will say: As surely as I live
       forever,

41 When I sharpen my flashing sword,
     and my hand lays hold of judgment,
   With vengeance I will repay my foes
     and requite those who hate me.*

42 I will make my arrows drunk with
       blood,
     and my sword shall devour
       flesh—

   With the blood of the slain and the
       captured,
     from the long-haired heads of the
       enemy.

43 Exult with him, you heavens,
     bow to him, all you divine beings!
   For he will avenge the blood of his
       servants,
     take vengeance on his foes;
   He will requite those who hate him,
     and purge his people's land.*

44 So Moses, together with Hoshea,† son of Nun, went and spoke all the words of this song in the hearing of the people.*

**Final Appeal.** 45 When Moses had finished speaking all these words to all Israel, 46 he said to them,* Take to heart all the words that I am giving in witness against you today, words you should command your children, that they may observe carefully every word of this law. 47 For this is no trivial matter for you, but rather your very life; by this word you will enjoy a long life on the land you are crossing the Jordan to possess.*

**Moses Looks upon Canaan.** 48 On that very day the LORD said to Moses, 49 Ascend this mountain of the Abarim,† Mount Nebo in the land of Moab facing Jericho, and view the land of Canaan, which I am giving to the Israelites as a possession.* 50 Then you shall die on the mountain you are about to ascend, and shall be gathered to your people, just as your brother Aaron died on Mount Hor† and there was gathered to his people,* 51 because both of you broke faith with me among the Israelites at the waters of Meribath-kadesh in the wilderness of Zin: you did not manifest my holiness among the Israelites.†* 52 You may indeed see the land from a distance, but you shall not enter that land which I am giving to the Israelites.*

---

† **32:36** *Neither bond nor free*: an all-inclusive expression; cf. 1 Kgs 14:10; 2 Kgs 9:8.
**32:44** *Hoshea*: a variant of "Joshua." Cf. note on Nm 13:16.
**32:49** *Abarim*: probably the mountain range to the east of the Dead Sea.
**32:50** *Mount Hor*: on the western border of Seir or Edom; cf. Nm 20:23–28; 33:37–38. Dt 10:6 locates elsewhere the place of Aaron's death.
**32:51** Cf. note on 3:26.

**32:32** Dt 29:23.
**32:35** Ps 94:1; Is 59:18; 61:2; Hos 9:7.
**32:36** 2 Mc 7:6; Ps 9:8; 135:14.
**32:37–38** Jgs 10:14; 1 Kgs 18:27; Jer 2:28.
**32:39** Dt 4:35; 6:4; 1 Sm 2:6–8; Tb 13:2; Jb 5:18; Wis 16:13; Is 30:26; 43:10–13; 44:6; Hos 6:1–2.
**32:41** Is 1:24; Na 1:2.
**32:43** Dt 32:1, 8; Is 49:13.
**32:44** Dt 31:14–15, 23.
**32:46** Dt 4:9.
**32:47** Dt 4:40; 6:1–2.
**32:49** Dt 34:1; Nm 27:12.
**32:50** Dt 10:6; Nm 20:23–29; 27:13; 33:38–39.
**32:51** Ex 17:1–7; Nm 20:1–13; 27:14; Ps 106:32–33.
**32:52** Dt 3:27; 34:4.

# 33

**Blessing upon the Tribes.**† ¹This is the blessing with which Moses, the man of God, blessed the Israelites before he died.* ²* He said:

> The LORD came from Sinai
>     and dawned on his people from Seir;
>     he shone forth from Mount Paran.
> With him were myriads of holy ones;
>     at his right hand advanced the gods.†

³   Indeed, lover of the peoples,
>     all the holy ones are at your side;
> They follow at your heels,
>     carry out your decisions.

⁴   Moses charged us with the law,
>     as a possession for the assembly of
>         Jacob.*

⁵   A king arose† in Jeshurun
>     when the chiefs of the people
>         assembled,
>     and the tribes of Israel united.*

⁶   May Reuben live and not die out,*
>     but let his numbers be few.

⁷Of Judah he said this:

> Hear, LORD, the voice of Judah,
>     and bring him to his people.†
> His own hands defend his cause;
>     be a help against his foes.*

⁸Of Levi he said:*

> Give to Levi your Thummim,
>     your Urim† to your faithful one;
> Him you tested at Massah,
>     contended against him at the waters
>         of Meribah.*

⁹†  He said of his father and mother,
>     "I have no regard for them";
> His brothers he would not acknowledge,
>     and his own children he did not
>         recognize.
> For they kept your words,
>     and your covenant they upheld.*

¹⁰*  They teach your ordinances to Jacob,
>     your law to Israel.
> They bring incense to your nostrils,
>     and burnt offerings to your altar.

¹¹   Bless, LORD, his strength,
>     be pleased with the work of his hands.
> Crush the loins of his adversaries
>     and of his foes, that they may not
>         rise.

¹²Of Benjamin he said:

> The beloved of the LORD,
>     he abides in safety beside him;
> He shelters him all day long;
>     the beloved abides at his breast.†*

¹³Of Joseph he said:*

> Blessed by the LORD is his land
>     with the best of heaven above
>     and of the abyss crouching beneath;
¹⁴   With the best of the produce of the sun,
>     and the choicest yield of the months;
¹⁵   With the finest gifts of the ancient
>         mountains
>     and the best from the everlasting
>         hills;
¹⁶   With the best of the earth and its
>         fullness,
>     and the favor of the one who dwells
>         on Sinai.

---

**33:1–29** This poem, called the Blessing of Moses, consists of a series of poetic characterizations of each of the tribes of Israel (vv. 6–25), introduced (vv. 2–3) and concluded (vv. 26–27) by a theophany; vv. 4–5 lead into the blessing proper; and the poem ends with a blessing on Israel as a whole (vv. 28–29). This catalog of the tribal units of the people Israel resembles the Blessing of Jacob (Gn 49) and the Song of Deborah (Jgs 5, especially vv. 14–18); all three poems seem to date from the early premonarchic period.

**33:2** *Gods:* the divine beings who constitute the armies of the Lord, the heavenly hosts (Sabaoth); see note on 32:8. These "holy ones" (v. 3) are the retinue of the Lord, the warrior God, in his march from the southern mountains (Sinai, Seir, Paran).

**33:5** *A king arose:* it is unclear whether this refers to divine kingship or the beginning of the monarchy in Israel. *Jeshurun:* see note on 32:15.

**33:7** *Bring him to his people:* this probably refers to the isolated position of the tribe of Judah (cf. Jgs 1:17–19); according to some commentators the reference is to the divided kingdom.

**33:8** *Thummim . . . Urim:* devices priests used for divination (cf. note on Ex 28:30).

**33:9** The reference is probably to the Levites' slaughter of other Israelites after the incident of the golden calf; cf. Ex 32:27–29.

**33:12** *Abides at his breast:* an image of security under divine protection.

---

**33:1** Jos 14:6; Ps 90:1.
**33:2–3** Ex 15:14–17;
19:18–20; Nm 10:36;
Jgs 5:4–5; Ps 68:7–8,
17; 89:7; Hb 3:3–6.
**33:4** Dt 4:44; Jn 1:17; 7:19.
**33:5** Dt 32:15.
**33:6** Gn 49:3–4.
**33:7** Gn 49:8–12.
**33:8–11** Gn 49:5–7.
**33:8** Dt 6:16; 9:22; 32:51;

Ex 17:1–7; 28:30; Lv
8:8; Nm 20:1–13;
1 Sm 14:41–42.
**33:9** Lk 14:26.
**33:10–11** Dt 10:8; 17:9–11;
18:1–8; Ex 30:7–8;
Lv 10:11; 2 Kgs
17:27–28; Mal 2:4–9.
**33:12** Gn 49:27.
**33:13–17** Gn 49:22–26.
**33:16** Ex 3:1–6; Jgs 5:6.

Let these come upon the head of Joseph
   and upon the brow of the prince
      among his brothers.*
17 His firstborn bull, majesty is his!
   His horns are the horns of a wild ox;
   With them he gores the peoples,
      attacks the ends of the earth.
   These are the myriads of Ephraim,
   and these the thousands of
      Manasseh.

18 Of Zebulun he said:*

Rejoice, Zebulun, in your expeditions,
   exult, Issachar, in your tents!
19 They invite peoples to the mountain
   where they offer right sacrifices,
   Because they suck up the abundance of
      the seas†
   and the hidden treasures of the
      sand.

20 Of Gad he said:*

Blessed be the one who has made Gad
      so vast!
   He lies there like a lion;
   he tears the arm, the head as well.
21 He saw that the best should be his,
   for there the commander's portion
      was assigned;
   he came at the head of the people.
   He carried out the justice of the LORD
   and his ordinances for Israel.*

22 Of Dan he said:

Dan is a lion's cub,*
   that springs away from a viper!

23 Of Naphtali he said:

Naphtali, abounding with favor,
   filled with the blessing of the LORD,
take possession of the west and
   south.*
24 Of Asher he said:*

Most blessed† of sons be Asher!
   May he be the favorite among his
      brothers,
   and may he dip his foot in oil!
25 May the bolts of your gates be iron and
      bronze;
   may your strength endure through all
      your days!
26 There is none like the God of
      Jeshurun,
   who rides the heavens in his power,
   who rides the clouds in his
      majesty;*
27 The God of old is a refuge;
   a support are the arms of the
      Everlasting.
   He drove the enemy out of your way
   and he said, "Destroy!"*
28 Israel abides securely,
   Jacob dwells apart,
   In a land of grain and wine,
   where the heavens drip with dew.*
29 Happy are you, Israel! Who is like you,
   a people delivered by the LORD,
   Your help and shield,
   and the sword of your glory.
   Your enemies cringe before you;
   you stride upon their backs.*

## IV. THE DEATH OF MOSES

34 ¹Then Moses went up from the plains of Moab to Mount Nebo,* the peak of Pisgah which faces Jericho, and the LORD showed him all the land—Gilead, and as far as Dan, ²all Naphtali, the land of Ephraim and Manasseh, all the land of Judah as far as the Western Sea,* ³the Negeb, the plain (the

---

† **33:19** *The abundance of the seas*: perhaps the wealth that comes from sea trade or from fishing. *The hidden treasures of the sand*: possibly an allusion to the valuable purple dye extracted from certain marine shells found on the coast of northern Palestine.
**33:24** *Most blessed*: Hebrew *baruk*; but the name Asher may suggest a play on the Hebrew *'ashre*, "happy"; cf., e.g., v. 29; Ps 1:1. *Oil*: the land of the tribe of Asher was covered with olive groves.

**33:18–19** Gn 49:13–15.
**33:20–21** Gn 49:19.
  **33:21** Nm 32:1–32; Jos 1:12–15; 1 Chr 5:18–22; 12:8–15.
  **33:22** Gn 49:16–17.
  **33:23** Gn 49:21; Jos 19:32–39.
**33:24–25** Gn 49:20.
  **33:26** Dt 32:15; Ps 18:10;
68:4, 33; 104:3;
Is 19:1.
**33:27** Dt 7:1, 17–24.
**33:28** Dt 7:12–16; Gn 27:28; Nm 23:9.
**33:29** Dt 4:7–8; Gn 15:1; 2 Sm 22:3; Ps 28:7; 119:114.
  **34:1** Dt 3:27; 32:49.
  **34:2** Dt 11:24.

valley of Jericho, the City of Palms), and as far as Zoar. <sup>4</sup> The LORD then said to him, This is the land* about which I promised on oath to Abraham, Isaac, and Jacob, "I will give it to your descendants." I have let you see it with your own eyes, but you shall not cross over. <sup>5</sup> So there, in the land of Moab, Moses, the servant of the LORD, died* as the LORD had said; <sup>6</sup> and he was buried in a valley in the land of Moab, opposite Beth-peor; to this day no one knows the place of his burial.* <sup>7</sup> Moses was one hundred and twenty years old* when he died, yet his eyes were undimmed and his vigor unabated. <sup>8</sup> The Israelites wept for Moses in the plains of Moab for thirty days, till they had completed the period of grief and mourning for Moses.

<sup>9</sup> Now Joshua, son of Nun,* was filled with the spirit of wisdom, since Moses had laid his hands upon him; and so the Israelites gave him their obedience, just as the LORD had commanded Moses.

<sup>10</sup>* Since then no prophet has arisen in Israel like Moses, whom the LORD knew face to face, <sup>11</sup>* in all the signs and wonders the LORD sent him to perform in the land of Egypt against Pharaoh and all his servants and against all his land, <sup>12</sup> and all the great might and the awesome power that Moses displayed in the sight of all Israel.

---

34:4 Dt 1:8; 3:27; 32:52;
  Gn 12:7; 15:18–21.
34:5 Dt 32:50; Ex 14:31;
  Nm 12:7–8;

Jos 1:1–2, 7, 13, 15;
  1 Kgs 8:53, 56;
  Mal 3:22.
34:6 Dt 3:29.

34:7 Dt 31:2.
34:9 Nm 27:18–23; Jos 1:17.
34:10 Dt 5:4; 18:15; Ex
  33:11; Nm 12:8;

Sir 45:5.
34:11–12 Dt 4:34; Ex 4:21; 7:1,
  8–12.

# Deities of the Ancient Near East

Ancient Israel's belief in the existence of only one God developed over centuries against the backdrop of the polytheism of the ancient Near East (ANE). In the ANE, each nation had its patron deity. The people of early Israel worshiped Yahweh while assuming the existence of these other gods. The prophets insisted that Israel worship Yahweh alone and criticized popular religion and the national cult of polytheism. By the late sixth century BCE, monotheism, championed by prophets such as Second Isaiah, became the norm.

| Name | Significance | Reference |
|---|---|---|
| strange (foreign) gods; other gods; gods of the nations | Biblical expressions for gods other than Yahweh, ancient Israel's patron deity. | Ex 20:3; Dt 31:16; 2 Kgs 18:33 |
| El | The common Semitic word for "god," originally the chief god of the Canaanite pantheon; occurs 230 times in Bible, often referring to Yahweh. | Num 23:22; Ez 28:2 |
| Baal | A title meaning "lord" used of several Canaanite deities, especially Hadad, the Canaanite deity of storms and fertility; chief rival for the loyalty Israel owed to Yahweh. | Jgs 2:11; 1 Kgs 16:31–33; 1 Kgs 18 |
| Anath | The goddess of war in Ugartic texts; sister of Baal; never mentioned in the Hebrew Scriptures except as a component proper name; some identify her as the "Queen of Heaven." | Jos 19:38; Jgs 1:33; Jer 7:18 |
| Molech | A Canaanite deity associated with the ritualistic killing of human beings, especially children. | Lv 18:21; 20:2–5; Jer 32:35 |
| Asherah | Ugartic texts (14th century BCE) portray this goddess as the spouse of El and the mother of 70 children, including Baal; in the Bible, Asherah most often refers to wooden poles used in the cult of the goddess. | Ex 34:13; Deut 7:5; Jgs 3:7 |
| Ashtart; Astarte; Ashtaroth; Ashtoreth | "Ashtart" and "Astarte" in the Bible (NABRE), a Canaanite goddess, identified with the evening star; Ashtaroth is the plural form; Ashtoreth is a Hebrew parody of the goddess's name. | Jgs 10:6; 1 Sm 31:10; 1 Kgs 11:5, 33; 2 Kgs 23:13 |
| Ishtar (Akkadian); Inanna (Sumerian) | The principal goddess of the Mesopotamian pantheon; never mentioned in the Hebrew Scriptures; some identify her as the "Queen of Heaven." | Jer 7:18; 44:17–19, 25 |
| Tammuz (Akkadian); Dumuzi (Sumerian) | A Mesopotamian deity; husband of Ishtar; dies prematurely; Ezekiel condemns the practice of women weeping for Tammuz, which he found even in the Temple of Jerusalem. | Ez 8:14 |
| Dagon | A Semitic deity who became the national god of the Philistines; Dagon's popular cult continued after the Philistines ceased to exist as a nation. | Jgs 16:23; 1 Sm 5:1–5, 7; 1 Chr 10:10; 1 Mc 10:83–84 |
| Host of Heaven | Can refer to Yahweh's military retinue and to the divine council; under Canaanite influence, an object of worship equated with the worship of "other gods"; celestial bodies and the signs of the zodiac. | 1 Kgs 22:19; 2 Kgs 17:16; 23:5; Sir 17:32 |
| Marduk; Merodach | The principal deity of the Babylonian pantheon in the first millennium BCE; sometimes appears in the Hebrew Scriptures under the title "bel," i.e., Lord. | 2 Kgs 25:27; Isa 46:1; Jer 50:2; 51:44 |
| Apis | An Egyptian bull-deity, worshiped in the region of Memphis. | Jer 46:15 |
| Amon; Amun | Self-created Egyptian god; as Amun-Ra, he became the principal deity of Upper Egypt. | Jer 46:25 |

# Spiritual Ancestors of the Monotheistic Faiths

The stories of the mothers and fathers of the Abrahamic faiths provided the founding narrative that the postexilic redactor used to teach that God's covenant promise to Abraham and his descendants continued. Abraham, Sarah, Isaac, Hagar, and Ishmael are the spiritual ancestors of all who practice the Jewish, Christian, and Muslim faiths.

| Name | Significance and Reference |
|---|---|
| **Abraham** | Abraham responded to the call of God and journeyed into the unknown land of Canaan, where he received God's covenant promises. He is regarded as the ancestor of the monotheistic faiths: Judaism, Christianity, and Islam (Gn 12:1–5; 15:1–18; 17:1–8). |
| **Sarah** | With her husband, Abraham, Sarah journeyed to the land of Canaan. She became the mother of Isaac and the mother of the Hebrew people (Gn 12–25). |
| **Lot** | Lot's family escaped the destruction of Sodom and Gomorrah. His wife looked back and was turned into a pillar of salt (Gn 19). |
| **Melchizedek** | Priest of "God Most High" and king of peace, Melchizedek offered a sacrifice of bread and wine for Abraham and blessed him (Gn 14:18–20). |
| **Hagar** | Sarah's Egyptian slave who was given to Abraham as a concubine, Hagar received an angelic annunciation regarding the destiny of her son Ishmael; thereupon she proclaimed that she had seen God. She became the mother of the Arab people (Gn 16:1–16). |
| **Keturah** | Keturah was Abraham's wife (Gn 25:1–4) or concubine (1 Chr 1:32–33) after the death of Sarah. |
| **Ishmael** | Abraham's son with Hagar, Ishmael was ancestor of the Arab people (Gn 16; 25:12–18). |
| **Isaac** | Isaac was the son promised to the elderly Abraham and Sarah. Isaac's life symbolized God's continual love for Israel (Gn 21:1–8). |
| **Rebekah** | Beautiful daughter of Abraham's nephew Bethuel, Rebekah married Isaac. She mothered twin sons: Jacob and Esau (Gn 24; 25:19–26). |
| **Esau** | Esau was Jacob's twin, firstborn son of Isaac and Rebekah. Esau and Jacob began their conflict in the womb (Gn 25:22–26). |
| **Jacob, or Israel** | Second son of Isaac and Rebekah, Jacob was Esau's twin and ancestor of the twelve tribes, who came to symbolize Israel's struggle with God across history (Gn 25:26; 35:9–12). Israel would also become the name of the northern kingdom (1 Kgs 12:1–20). |
| **Rachel** | Rachel was the younger daughter of Rebekah's brother Laban. Jacob served Laban for seven years in order to marry Rachel but was tricked into marrying Leah. After satisfying "the bridal week" with Leah, Jacob also was given Rachel (his beloved) to marry; he then worked seven more years to satisfy Laban. Rachel bore Joseph and Benjamin and died in labor (Gn 29:13–30:24; 35:16–19). |
| **Leah** | Older daughter of Laban, Leah gave birth to Jacob's sons Reuben, Simeon, Levi, Judah, Issachar, and Zebulun, and one daughter, Dinah (Gn 29:31–30:21). |
| **Bilhah** | Slave woman of Rachel, Bilhah gave birth to Jacob's sons Dan and Naphtali (Gn 30:1–8). |

*(continued on next page)*

| Name | Significance and Reference |
|------|---------------------------|
| Zilpah | Slave woman of Leah, Zilpah gave birth to Jacob's sons Gad and Asher (Gn 30:9–13). |
| Reuben | Reuben, the firstborn of Jacob and Leah, was kind to Joseph when his other brothers plotted his murder. Reuben seduced Bilhah (Gn 37:21; 1 Chr 5:1). |
| Simeon | Simeon was Leah and Jacob's raging son who, with his brother Levi, exacted blood revenge for Dinah and Shechem's union. The brothers' act resulted in tense relations between the family of Jacob and their Canaanite neighbors (Gn 34:25–31). |
| Levi | Son of Leah and Jacob, Levi was the ancestor of the Levites, the priests who would be caretakers of the tabernacle and Temple (Gn 29:34; Nm 3:5–13). |
| Issachar | Issachar was the son of Leah and Jacob. Jacob's blessing affirmed this tribe's agrarian lifestyle (Gn 30:18; 49:14–15; Nm 1:28–29; Jos 19:17–23). |
| Zebulun | Zebulun was the sixth son of Jacob and Leah (Gn 30:20; Jos 19:10–16). |
| Judah | Leah's fourth son with Jacob, Judah was the ancestor of the most powerful tribe of Israel, in whose territory Jerusalem would be located (Gn 29:35; Jos 15:1–12). |
| Tamar | The widow of Er and Onan, Tamar used trickery to gain her right to a child from Judah. She was an ancestor of the house of David (Gn 38:6–26; Mt 1:3). |
| Gad | Son of Jacob and Zilpah, Gad was the ancestor of a tribe sharing the borders of the Jabbok and Aroer rivers with Reuben (Gn 30:10–11; Jos 13:24–28). |
| Asher | Asher was the son of Zilpah and Jacob. His tribe consisted of merchants, ranchers, and exporters (Gn 30:12–13; Dt 33:24–25; Jos 19:24–31; 1 Chr 6:59). |
| Dan | Dan was the son of Jacob and Bilhah. Warriors, deliverers, seafarers, merchants, craftsmen, and teachers would be among the members of this clan that settled in the far north (Gn 30:5–6; Ex 31:1–11; Jos 19:40–48; Jgs 5:17). |
| Naphtali | Son of Bilhah and Jacob, his blessing affirmed the virility of the tribe (Gn 30:7–8; 49:21). |
| Benjamin | Benjamin was the son of Jacob and Rachel, who died at his birth. The tribe of Benjamin consisted of hunters, warriors, and betrayers (Gn 35:16–19; 49:27; Jgs 19:14–21:25). Saul, first king of Israel, was of the tribe of Benjamin (1 Sm 9:1–2; 10:17–24). In the New Testament, Saul, also called Paul the apostle, was of the tribe of Benjamin (Rom 11:1). |
| Joseph | Favored son of Rachel and Jacob, his legendary multicolored coat revealed his future status in Egypt. His brothers sold him into slavery but he thrived in Egypt, as would his descendants until the time of Moses (Gn 30:22–24; 37; 49:22–26). |

# Prophets and Kings (Eleventh to Sixth Centuries BCE)

By the ninth century BCE, there were two Israelite national states: Judah in the south and Israel in the north. The Bible asserts that before this time three kings, Saul, David, and Solomon, ruled a unified nation, though it is more likely that they were local chieftains rather than rulers of a national state. Until its fall in the sixth century, the kingdom of Judah was ruled by members of the Davidic dynasty, while no single dynasty was

| Prophets Date and Reference | Kings of the "United Monarchy" – Date and Reference | |
| --- | --- | --- |
| **Samuel:** Seer, judge, and prophet, associated with the rise of the monarchy (1 Sm 3:20; 7:15–16; 8:1–22; 9:19; 10:1–27). | **Saul** (end of eleventh century BCE): A Benjaminite who became the first king of Israel. First Samuel reflects different viewpoints on Saul and the institution of the monarchy (1 Sm 9:1–10:27; 11:1–15). | |
| **Gad:** David's seer (1 Sm 22:5; 2 Sm 24:11–19). | **David** (early tenth century BCE): Succeeded Saul because of his success in conflicts with the Philistines and his marriages to women of important families. His descendants ruled Judah for 400 years (1 Sm 18:8, 20–29; 25:40–43; 2 Sm 11:26–27). | |
| **Nathan:** announced God's choice of Davidic dynasty (2 Sm 7) and supported Solomon's succession (1 Kgs 1:38). | **Solomon** (961–922 BCE): Son of David and Bathsheba, known for his wisdom, wealth, and construction of the Temple in Jerusalem. First Kings suggests that the deterioration of Solomon's reign was due to the influence of his non-Israelite wives (1 Kgs 3:4–14; 6:1–2; 10:14–29; 11:1–10). | |
| | **Kings of Judah** | **Kings of Israel** |
| **Ahijah** (end of tenth century BCE): announced the division of Solomon's kingdom (1 Kgs 11:29–39). | **Rehoboam** (931–913 BCE): chose not to compromise with the elders of Israel, who then refused to acknowledge his succession (1 Kgs 12:1–25). | **Jeroboam** (931–910 BCE): founder of the kingdom of Israel; established temples at Dan and Bethel (1 Kgs 12:16–20, 26–31). |
| **Shemaiah:** advised Rehoboam against engaging in a civil war over the division of the kingdom (1 Kgs 12:21–24). | **Abijam** (Abijah) (913–911 BCE): fought a border conflict with Jeroboam; the book of Kings presents his reign negatively (1 Kgs 15:3–5), while Chronicles views him as pious (2 Chr 13). | **Nadab** (910–909 BCE): son and successor of Jeroboam; assassinated after a two-year reign (1 Kgs 15:25–30).  **Baasha** (909–886 BCE): killed all Jeroboam's descendants, made Tirzah his capital, and fought with Asa (1 Kgs 15:33–34). |
| **Jehu** (ninth century BCE): Condemned Baasha and predicted the fall of his dynasty (1 Kgs 16:1–4); criticized Jehoshaphat for his alliance with Ahab (2 Chr 19:2–3). | **Asa** (911–870 BCE): purged the Temple cult of foreign accretions and fought a border war with Israel; ruled for 41 years (1 Kgs 15). | **Elah** (886–885 BCE): son of Baasha, assassinated by Zimri, one of his generals, who then assumed the throne (1 Kgs 16:8–14).  **Zimri** (885 BCE): killed all members of the royal family, ruled for only one week; Omri, another Israelite general, revolted. Rather than surrender, Zimri committed suicide (1 Kgs 16:18). |
| **Eliezer** (ninth century BCE): criticized Jehoshaphat for his alliance with Ahaziah (2 Chr 20:37). | **Jehoshaphat** (870–848 BCE): supported the exclusive worship of Yahweh, made peace with Israel, and initiated gold trade with Ophir (1 Kgs 22:41–51). | **Omri** (885–874 BCE): assumed throne after defeating Tibni in a civil war (1 Kgs 16:21); most capable king of Israel, made Samaria his capital and turned Israel into a commercial, political, and military power (1 Kgs 16:23–28). |
| **Elijah** (middle of ninth century BCE): a staunch Yahwist; opposed royal policy that promoted worship of Baal (1 Kgs 17–19; 21; 2 Kgs 1:1–2:18). | **Jehoram** (Joram) (848–841 BCE): married Athaliah, Ahab's daughter; considered an apostate (2 Kgs 8:18); Edomites revolted against rule by Judah (2 Kgs 8:21); killed his brothers (2 Chr 21:11–13). | **Ahab** (874–854 BCE): The Bible ignores Ahab's achievement as a builder and political and military leader, portraying him as a weak, evil, and unjust king who promoted the worship of foreign gods (1 Kgs 16:29–33; 20:1–22:40). |
| **Micaiah,** son of Imlah (ninth century BCE): announced that the forces of Israel and Judah would be defeated by the Arameans (1 Kgs 22). | **Ahaziah** (841 BCE): ruled for one year; killed during Jehu's revolt against Joram (2 Kgs 9:27–28). | **Ahaziah** (853–852 BCE): son and successor of Ahab, promoted worship of Baal and joined Jehoshaphat of Judah in commercial dealings; seriously injured in a fall, he consulted the god of Ekron about his recovery; Elijah announced that his injury was fatal (1 Kgs 22:52–54; 2 Kgs 1; 2 Chr 20:35–37). |

*(continued on next page)*

able to establish itself in the kingdom of Israel. The Bible presents the prophets as the defenders of traditional Israelite religion and morality against the kings, most of whom introduced cultic practices at odds with the exclusive worship of Israel's God and oversaw an oppressive social and economic system. The dates given in the chart below are approximate.

*(Prophets and Kings — continued from previous page)*

| Prophets Date and Reference | Kings of Judah Date and Reference | Kings of Israel Date and Reference |
|---|---|---|
| **Zedekiah** (ninth century BCE): along with 400 other prophets, erroneously predicted victory because God gave them a "lying spirit" to induce Ahab to fight a battle he could not win. Zedekiah slapped Micaiah for contradicting him (1 Kgs 22:24). | **Athaliah** (841–835 BCE): Jehoram's widow; killed all male members of the royal family upon Ahaziah's death and ruled as queen; only woman and non-Davidide to rule Judah; promoted the worship of Baal; assassinated after a rule of six years (2 Kgs 11:13–20). | **Jehoram** (Joram) (852–841 BCE): brother of Ahab and successor of Ahaziah; did not support Baal worship but supported the Yahwistic shrines at Dan and Bethel; Moab successfully revolted against Israelite rule; Jehoram resisted Arameans, assassinated by Jehu (2 Kgs 9:1–25). |
| **Elisha** (ninth century BCE): presented as a disciple and successor of Elijah; subject of a cycle of miracle stories and legends related to a war between Israel and Aram. He and Elijah supported Jehu's coup (2 Kgs 2:1–8:15; 9–10; 13:14–25). | **Joash** (Jehoash) (835–796 BCE): survived Athaliah's massacre of the royal family and succeeded her; Kings puts a positive spin on his 40-year reign while Chronicles gives the credit to the priest Jehoiada; paid tribute to the Arameans; assassinated by his own officials (2 Kgs 11—12; 2 Chr 22:10—24:27). | **Jehu** (841–814 BCE): led a successful revolt against the Omride dynasty after the failure of a campaign against the Arameans; ended the cult of Baal in Israel; submitted to Assyria (2 Kgs 9–10). |
| **Amos** (eighth century BCE): a Judean agricultural worker who preached in Israel; not a professional prophet; proclaimed that Israel's religious institutions were corrupt. | | **Jehoahaz** (814–798 BCE): son and successor of Jehu; Israel dominated by Arameans; supported shrines at Dan and Bethel (2 Kgs 13:1–9). |
| | | **Jehoash** (Joash) (798–782 BCE): supported shrines at Dan and Bethel; defeated Amaziah of Judah (2 Kgs 13:10–25; 14:8–16). |
| **Jonah** (eighth century BCE): prophesied Jeroboam's military success (2 Kgs 14:25–26). | **Amaziah** (796–767 BCE): executed his father's assassins; defeated Edom but was defeated by Israel; assassinated after a 29-year reign (2 Kgs 14:1–20). | **Jeroboam II** (782–753 BCE): was responsible for military success and economic prosperity, though the poor did not benefit (2 Kgs 14:23–29). |
| **Hosea** (eighth century BCE): preached during the years of the decline of the kingdom of Israel and condemned its citizens for their infidelity; his experience of an unhappy marriage became an image of God's relationship with Israel. | **Azariah** (Uzziah) (767–740 BCE): failed to end worship on high places, developed leprosy; a capable military leader (2 Kgs 15:1–7; 2 Chr 26). | **Zechariah** (753–752 BCE): last king of the Jehu dynasty, ruled for six months; assassinated by Shallum (2 Kgs 15:8–12). |
| | | **Shallum** (752 BCE): his one-month reign was the beginning of the end for the kingdom of Israel; assassinated by Menahem, who took the throne (2 Kgs 15:13–16). |
| | **Jotham** (740–732 BCE): regent because of Azariah's leprosy; rule began in prosperity but his last years saw the beginning of Assyria's move into the region (2 Kgs 15:32–38). | **Menahem** (752–742 BCE): paid a heavy tribute to Assyria to stay on the throne; levied taxes to pay tribute (2 Kgs 15:17–22). |
| | | **Pekahiah** (742–740 BCE): continued pro-Assyrian policies of Menahem; assassinated by Pekah (2 Kgs 15:22–26). |
| **Isaiah of Jerusalem** (eighth century BCE): condemned Judeans for religious rituals that were not accompanied by social justice. He believed that rebellious Judah could change, so his view of Judah's future was hopeful. The prophet encouraged Ahaz to refrain from any alliance with Assyria. | **Ahaz** (732–716 BCE): responded to the Assyrian crisis by becoming a vassal of Assyria; introduced Assyrian religious symbols into the Temple; refused to join an anti-Assyrian coalition (2 Kgs 16:1–20). | **Pekah** (740–732 BCE): reversed the pro-Assyrian policies of his predecessors; attempted to persuade Ahaz to bring Judah into his anti-Assyrian coalition; assassinated by Hoshea with encouragement from the Assyrians (2 Kgs 15:25–31). |
| | | **Hoshea** (732–721 BCE): pro-Assyrian at first; later rebelled. Assyrians conquered Israel and incorporated its territory into its provincial system (2 Kgs 17:1–6). |

*(continued on next page)*

(Prophets and Kings – continued from previous page)

## Prophet of Assyrian Destruction

**Micah** (eighth century BCE): a contemporary of Isaiah, Hosea, and Amos; the prophet's oracles expect the fall of both Israelite kingdoms, speaking of both divine judgment and salvation.

| Prophets of Judah | Kings of Judah: Post-Destruction of Israel |
|---|---|
| **Nahum** (seventh century BCE): A Judean prophet who gave a nationalistic message, envisioning the fall of the Assyrian Empire. | **Hezekiah** (716–687 BCE): a reformer of Judean religious practices, a patron of the sages (2 Kgs 18:1–20:21; Prv 25:1), and a builder who prepared for the defense of Jerusalem in view of the Assyrian threat; though Jerusalem did not fall, Judah became an Assyrian vassal. |
| **Zephaniah** (sixth century BCE): supported the religious reforms of Josiah (Zep 1; 3:14–20). | **Manasseh** (687–642 BCE): regarded as the most wicked king of Judah; completely subservient to Assyria; Chronicles suggests that he repented late in life while Kings holds him responsible for Judah's fall; longest reign of any king (2 Kgs 21:1–18; 2 Chr 33). |
| **Jeremiah** (seventh to sixth century BCE): a priest from Anathoth, was active from the time of Josiah to the fall of Jerusalem. The prophet called for Judah to submit to Babylon, which was God's instrument of judgment on its infidelity. Jeremiah believed, however, that Judah had a future beyond judgment. | **Amon** (642–640 BCE): continued subservience to Assyria; assassinated by people whose motives are unclear (2 Kgs 21:19–26).

**Josiah** (640–608 BCE): placed on the throne by landed gentry who executed his father's assassins; remembered for his religious reforms; despite his fidelity, he died a tragic death in battle (2 Kgs 21:26—23:30). |
| **Uriah** (seventh century BCE): Jeremiah asserts that this prophet was killed by Jehoiakim for prophesying against Judah and Jerusalem (Jer 26:20–23). | **Jehoahaz** (608 BCE): deposed by the Egyptians after a three-month reign; taken to Egypt in exile (2 Kgs 23:30–33).

**Jehoiakim** (609–597 BCE): a brother of Jehoahaz, placed on the throne by the Egyptians. When Egypt was defeated by Babylon, Judah became a vassal of the latter. Jehoiakim was an unwilling vassal and revolted. He died during the siege of Jerusalem (2 Kgs 23:33–37). |
| **Hananiah** (sixth century BCE): a prophet who opposed Jeremiah's call for Judah to submit to Babylon (Jer 28). | **Jehoiachin (Jeconiah)** (597 BCE): succeeded his father Jehoiakim; surrendered to the Babylonians and was taken as an exile to Babylon, where he died sometime after 560 (2 Kgs 24:6–16; 25:27–30). |
| **Ezekiel** (sixth century BCE): a priest who prophesied in Babylon during the exile; saw a future for Judah in which there would be a place for a Davidic "prince" (Ez 33–37). | **Zedekiah (Mattaniah)** (597–586 BCE): Jehoiachin's uncle, placed on the throne by the Babylonians. After an 11-year reign, he withheld tribute from the Babylonians, who besieged Jerusalem, destroyed the Temple, and executed the royal family except for Zedekiah, who was taken to Babylon in exile. Jeremiah regarded him as weak and unfit (1 Kgs 24:17–25:11; Jer 52:1–11). |

# Wonders, Miracles, and Signs in the Old Testament

In the Bible, miraculous events function as signs of God's commitment to the eternal covenant. The powers of nature submit to the will and purpose of the Lord God of Israel. Biblical stories and liturgical celebrations honor the memory of these mysterious events as manifestations of God's will.

| Wonders | Mysterious Event and Reference |
|---|---|
| Power over the creation | God calls forth life from the void (Gn 1–2). |
| | The sun and the moon stand still (Jos 10:12–14). |
| | The shadow of the sun reverses its direction (2 Kgs 20:9–11; Is 38:8). |
| Miraculous fires | Moses and God commune at the burning bush (Ex 3:2–6). |
| | The Israelites are led by fire at night and a cloud by day (Ex 13:21). |
| | The Lord to give Moses the Ten Commandments (Ex 19:18). |
| | Elijah calls fire from the sky (1 Kgs 18:38; 2 Kgs 1:10–12). |
| Wondrous births and annunciations | The sterile wives, Sarah, Rebekah, and Rachel, give birth to sons and fulfill the covenant (Gn 17:17; 18:12–14; 21:2; 25:21; 30:22–23). |
| | An angel announces Samson's birth (Jgs 13:3). |
| The plagues of Egypt | Moses' staff changes into a serpent (Ex 4:2–5; 7:8–12). |
| | God sends ten plagues on Egypt to convince Pharaoh to free the Israelites (Ex 7:14–12:30). |
| Power over the waters | The Israelites cross the waters of the sea on dry land (Ex 14:22). |
| | The Jordan's waters are halted for Joshua (Jos 3:14–17; 4:16–18). |
| | Elijah's prayers bring rain (1 Kgs 18:41–45). |
| Healings and afflictions | Aaron's atonement cures a plague (Nm 17:9–13). |
| | The bronze serpent of Moses heals (Nm 21:6–9). |
| | Elisha can cure or inflict leprosy (2 Kgs 5:1–14, 26–27). |
| Extraordinary interventions and rescues | Israelites win a battle when Moses lifts his staff (Ex 17:9–13). |
| | The walls of Jericho fall (Jos 6:6–20). |
| | An angel of the Lord kills 185,000 Assyrians (2 Kgs 19:35; Is 37:36). |
| | Daniel's three friends survive the fiery furnace (Dn 3:19–24, 91–94). |
| | Jonah lives in the belly of the great fish (Jon 2:1–11). |
| Extraordinary powers | Gideon discerns God's will with his fleece (Jgs 6:37–40). |
| | Samson has wondrous strength (Jgs 14:6; 16:3, 29–30). |
| | Elisha reads minds and can heal or inflict blindness (2 Kgs 6:8–20). |
| Multiplication of food and oil | The Israelites receive manna in the desert (Ex 16:21–35). |
| | Elijah and Elisha can increase meal and oil (1 Kgs 17:9–16; 2 Kgs 4:1–7). |
| | Elisha feeds many (2 Kgs 4:42–44). |
| Power over death—restoration to life | Elijah raises the widow's son to life (1 Kgs 17:17–24). |
| | Elisha raises the Shunammite child (2 Kgs 4:18–37). |
| | A dead man is raised to life in contact with the bones of Elisha (2 Kgs 13:21). |

# Introduction to the Historical Books

## Leslie J. Hoppe, OFM

## The Arrangement of the Books of the Bible

The books of the Bible originally were copied and transmitted on parchment strips sewn together to form scrolls. The Romans developed the book format and by the seventh century CE, it replaced the scroll. The rabbis, however, held that the book format was not acceptable for public reading so Jews continued to use scrolls in worship. But as the book format became more popular, the order in which the individual books of the Scriptures were to be arranged became an issue.

The rabbis divided the books of the Hebrew Bible into three general categories: the Torah (the five books ascribed to Moses), the Prophets, and the Writings (see Lk 24:44). The Prophets were subdivided into two subcategories: the Former Prophets (Joshua, Judges, Samuel, and Kings) and the Latter Prophets (Isaiah, Jeremiah, Ezekiel, and the Twelve, i.e., the "minor" prophets). The third division, the Writings, included all the books that did not fit into the previous two categories. When the books of the Hebrew Scriptures were transmitted in book format, the order of the books reflected this arrangement.

Beginning in the third century BCE, the Jews living in Egypt began translating the Hebrew Scriptures into Greek because their facility with Hebrew had diminished. They produced several versions of their sacred books in Greek. The first Christians adopted the Greek translation that has become known as the Septuagint as their preferred Bible. When the Septuagint was published in book format, two significant differences between it and the rabbinic Bible became obvious. First, there were several books in the Septuagint that did not appear in the rabbinic Bible and, second, the books in the Septuagint were arranged differently from those in the rabbinic Bible.

The books found in the Septuagint but not in the Hebrew Bible are called the *Apocrypha*, i.e., "hidden" books. The Catholic Church accepts several books of the Apocrypha as canonical, referring to them as *deuterocanonical* books. This term implies that it was necessary to resolve questions about the appropriateness of including these books in the canon of Scripture. These questions were resolved for the Catholic Church by the Council of Trent (1545–1563), which accepted the following books of the Apocrypha as canonical: Tobit, Judith, 1–2 Maccabees, Wisdom, Ben Sira (Ecclesiasticus), Baruch, and additions to the books of Esther and Daniel. Protestant churches, however, have rejected the canonicity of these books since the time of the Reformation. (See the article "The Formation of the Bible.")

Like the rabbinic Bible, the Septuagint begins with Genesis, Exodus, Leviticus, Numbers, and Deuteronomy, in that order. The Septuagint arranges the rest of the books by two criteria: chronology and literary type. Jerome and other early Christian theologians accepted the Septuagint ordering of books, which was standardized by the Council of Trent. Following the five books of the Torah, which is also known by the Greek name *Pentateuch* ("five volumes"), are books that have been termed "historical books." These include Joshua, Judges, Ruth, 1–2 Samuel, 1–2 Kings, Ezra, Nehemiah, Tobit, Judith, Esther, and 1–2 Maccabees. Following the historical books are poetic and wisdom texts such as Psalms, Proverbs, and Job. The final division of the Septuagint contains the "prophetic books." Included in this group are books of the so-called "writing prophets" plus the books of Daniel, Baruch, and Lamentations. Following Luther, Protestant churches accept only the books found in the Hebrew Bible as canonical, though the arrangement of books of the Old Testament in Bibles used by Protestants follows that of the Septuagint rather than that of the rabbinic Bible.

# The Historical Books

This introduction deals with the second division of the collection of canonical books accepted by the Catholic Church, i.e., the "historical books." The Church's first theologians used the term "historical books" to refer to the books from Genesis to Esther, but over time this term became restricted to the books from Joshua to 2 Maccabees for Catholics and Joshua to Esther for Protestants. It is important to realize that these books are not histories in the contemporary sense of the word; rather, they are narratives or stories—some are about individuals, e.g., Esther and Tobit, while others are about the people of Israel and Judah. At least three are most probably works of fiction (Tobit, Judith, Esther) while others, such as the books of Kings, do contain information that historians have used to reconstruct the history of Israel. Still it is essential that readers today recognize that these books are intended to communicate religious ideas rather than to provide historical information. The stories found in these books are vehicles used to express religious beliefs. They contain theology in story form similar to the parables of Jesus found in the New Testament.

## Joshua–2 Kings

Among the "historical books" are two multi-volume collections: the Deuteronomistic History of Israel and the Chronicler's History. The former includes the books of Joshua, Judges, 1–2 Samuel, and 1–2 Kings. Jewish tradition held that these books were written under prophetic inspiration by Joshua, Samuel, and Jeremiah. Of course, like most books of the Bible, Joshua–2 Kings are anonymous works. The Deuteronomistic History tells the story of the people of Israel in their land from the time they entered it under the leadership of Joshua until the time of the exile of Judah under the Babylonians. Biblical scholars use the term "Deuteronomistic" to describe these books because the principles for interpreting ancient Israel's life in its land were derived primarily from the book of Deuteronomy, which at one time probably served to introduce the story of Israel found in Joshua to 2 Kings. Foremost among these principles is that obedience to the Torah brings God's blessings upon Israel while disobedience brings divine judgment.

The Deuteronomistic History of Israel is best understood as "the past turned into a sermon." Israel's story is told not to provide information but motivation. Its purpose is to convince its readers that the people of Israel can have a future only if they choose the way of obedience. The story of Israel in its land illustrates the consequences of choosing the path of disobedience and infidelity, in order to persuade readers to be absolutely faithful to God alone and to live by the commandments in the Torah.

While there is general agreement about the basic religious thought of the Deuteronomistic History, there is no agreement about its date, authorship, and composition. It is clear that sources were used in the composition of this work, e.g., the stories of the individual judges in the book of Judges, the stories about the rise of David to kingship (1 Sm 16–2 Sm 5) and the succession to his throne (2 Sm 9–20, 1 Kgs 1–2), and the stories about Elijah and Elisha (1 Kgs 17–2 Kgs 8). But was the Deuteronomistic History finally the work of a single author or did multiple authors contribute, with an editor putting the books together as we now have them? Dates for its composition range from the seventh to the fourth centuries. It is most likely that the books received their final form sometime after the fall of Jerusalem, and that they were intended to explain the reasons for the fall of the two Israelite kingdoms and the end of the Davidic dynasty, the destruction of Jerusalem's Temple and the scattering of its priesthood, and the exile of the leadership classes of Judah to Babylon.

The Deuteronomistic History is a literary and theological masterpiece. Its engrossing stories about ancient Israel's heroes and villains, its kings and prophets, and some ordinary folk are vehicles for persuading readers that obedience to the written, authoritative law found in the book of Deuteronomy is the way to restore their nation's relationship with God and secure a future in the land promised to their ancestors. The central importance that the book of Deuteronomy came to have in Judaism is a testament to the achievement of the unnamed author of the Deuteronomistic History.

## Ruth

The Septuagint ordering of books places the book of Ruth immediately after the book of Judges since the setting for Ruth's story is the time of the judges (Ru 1:1). The book has its own value and charm, but its placement in Christian Bibles interrupts the flow of the Deuteronomistic History. The rabbis placed Ruth in their third division of the canon: the Writings.

## 1-2 Chronicles

Following the books that comprise the Deuteronomistic History comes another multi-volume "history": the Chronicler's History. At one time, scholars held that this history included 1–2 Chronicles, Ezra, and Nehemiah, but that view is no longer widely held. The Chronicler's History begins with nine chapters that are almost exclusively taken up with genealogies, beginning with Adam (1 Chr 1:1) and concluding with the family of Saul (1 Chr 9:35–44). The Chronicler's story of Israel ends with the decree of Cyrus the Persian, urging the exiles from Judah to return to Jerusalem and rebuild the Temple (2 Chr 36:22–23). One function of the genealogies is to assure the returnees that they stand in continuity with the ancestors of all Israel. From the Chronicler's perspective, it is this continuity that gives legitimacy to the restoration.

The Chronicler's narratives begin with the death of Saul and the consequent accession of David (1 Chr 10:1–11:3), who is the central figure in 1 Chronicles. While the Deuteronomistic Historian's portrait of David gives a prominent place to the description of David's flaws, the Chronicler totally ignores these and describes David as almost exclusively concerned with preparing for the building of the Temple, arranging the duties of the priests and Levites who will serve there, and instructing the Temple's musicians and other personnel.

The Chronicler's portrait of David reveals the author's belief in the centrality of worship in Jerusalem's Temple for the life of all Israel. While the Deuteronomist underscores the importance of obedience to the Torah, the Chronicler points to David as an example of one devoted entirely to the worship of Israel's ancestral Deity. The Chronicler's portrait of Solomon likewise omits details that may detract from his picture of a monarch almost totally consumed with the proper worship of God in the Temple of Jerusalem. For example, Solomon's descent into idolatry (1 Kgs 11) goes unmentioned in the Chronicler's description of his reign.

The Chronicler's story of the two Israelite kingdoms is colored by the significance he attaches to the Temple of Jerusalem. For example, in 2 Chr 13, the speech of Abijah makes it clear that the principal offense of the kingdom of Israel is its failure to recognize Jerusalem as the only legitimate setting for Israel's worship of its God. The Chronicler is clearly calling the Samaritans, who live in the territory of the former kingdom of Israel, to recognize the exclusive claims on the Temple of Jerusalem. For the Chronicler, the future of all Israel depends on its commitment to the worship of its God in the only place where legitimate worship may be offered: the Temple of Jerusalem. The rabbinic arrangement of the books of the Hebrew Scriptures underscores this. The Hebrew Bible ends with 2 Chr 36:22–23, which calls the exiles to return to Jerusalem and rebuild the Temple.

## Ezra-Nehemiah

Another form of the decree of Cyrus, which concludes 2 Chronicles, appears at the beginning of the book of Ezra (Ezr 1:1–4), pointing to continuity between the stories in the books of Chronicles and those found in the next two books: Ezra and Nehemiah. It is likely that Ezra and Nehemiah were composed as sequels to Chronicles as they describe the progress of the restoration following the return of the exiles, who were encouraged by Cyrus to return to Jerusalem. According to the books of Ezra and Nehemiah, the restoration resulted from implementing the policies of Persian kings Cyrus and Artaxerxes.

Ezra 1–6 describes the rebuilding of the

Jerusalem Temple in accordance with Cyrus's decree. In Ezr 7 the focus shifts to the restoration of Jewish life through obedience to the Torah. The Persians allowed subject peoples to have a measure of autonomy by upholding local, traditional laws as long as these did not undermine Persian rule. The narratives from Ezr 7 to the end of Nehemiah describe how the imposition of Mosaic law affected the Jewish community in Jerusalem, which was to be rebuilt and repopulated in accord with the wishes of the Persian king Artaxerxes.

A special feature of both Ezra and Nehemiah is their insistence on separation from non-Jews. The book of Ezra ends with the requirement that Jewish men abandon their foreign wives and any children from their marriage with these women (Ezr 10:6–44). Nehemiah builds a wall around Jerusalem—a visible sign of the separation of Jews from all Gentiles (Neh 6:1–19; 12:27–43; 13:1–3). Despite the efforts of Ezra and Nehemiah, the restoration is far from satisfactory since Judah is still a subject people, a subprovince of the Persian Empire. The books of Ezra and Nehemiah do not hint at how or when the restoration will be complete. These books describe the beginning of the restoration: the rebuilding of the Temple, the re-establishment and repopulation of Jerusalem, and the people's commitment to the Torah.

## Tobit

From narratives about the people of Israel as a whole, the focus of the next three books shifts to three individuals, each of whom faces formidable personal struggles. The first is the story of Tobit, a Galilean who finds himself living as an exile in Nineveh. He tries to lead a good life, but he meets misfortune when he is accidentally blinded. His story is woven with that of a certain Sarah who lives in Media. She married seven times, with each of her husbands dying during their wedding night. Tobit's son Tobiah is the bridge connecting the two stories. In the course of finding a cure for his father, he meets and marries Sarah. With the help of the angel Raphael, he is able to survive his wedding night with Sarah and effect the cure of his father's blindness. As a coda to the story, Tobiah lives long enough to hear of Nineveh's fall, for which he thanks God.

The book of Tobit is among the most skillfully crafted stories in the Bible. It is set in Assyria, where Tobit and his family were taken as exiles following the fall of the kingdom of Israel in the eighth century, though the book was likely composed in the third or early second century BCE. Its message is directed to all Jews living outside their ancestral homeland, encouraging them to remain faithful to the values and practices of their ancestral faith even among peoples that do not share these values. Doing so may be difficult, but they can count on God's support in their struggles to remain faithful. The underlying theological idea is derived from the book of Deuteronomy: in the end God will bless those who are faithful. While Tobit is numbered among the "historical" books of the Old Testament, its purpose is not to provide historical data but to affirm traditional Israelite morality—especially the values connected with family life and charity toward those in need. Luther considered Tobit a fictional tale—a position that most interpreters hold today. Indeed, Tobit has several motifs similar to ancient Near Eastern folktales.

Despite the book's promotion of traditional Jewish values of family, good deeds, prayer, and the importance of Jerusalem and the Temple, Tobit is not among the books of the Hebrew Scriptures. Some Jews of antiquity valued it—several copies of Tobit were found among the Dead Sea Scrolls. The Catholic Church has included Tobit in the canon of the Old Testament since the earliest canon lists. The book's reception in the East has been mixed, but the Orthodox Church now accepts it as canonical. Catholics regard Tobit as a deuterocanonical book, while Protestants consider it apocryphal.

## Judith

Although Tobit and his family are exiles in Assyria, the book does display a welcoming attitude toward Gentiles (Tb 13:11; 14:6–7). In contrast, the book of Judith, which follows Tobit in the Catholic canon, views Gentiles as threats to Judah's existence. In the book, this threat comes in the person of Nebuchadnezzar, who sent his army under Holofernes to punish those nations that did not support his war against Arphaxad, the king of the Medes. Holofernes enjoys success in his campaigns until he comes to the village of Bethulia in Judah. There he is assassinated and his army routed through the actions of Judith.

On the surface, the story of Judith reads like a historical account, but there are so many historical and geographical errors in the text that those who first heard or read the book of Judith no doubt recognized the story for what it really was: an entertaining and engrossing tale of a great Israelite victory against extraordinarily long odds—a victory that was possible because of the initiative taken by a woman. The story is not about some actual battle. It is rather a thinly veiled critique of the community's male leadership, whose failures are magnified by the intervention of a woman who accomplishes what they could not. This is the supreme irony of a book filled with ironies.

The book purports to relate events that took place shortly after the return from exile (Jdt 4:3). It is more likely that it comes from some time after the Maccabees defeated the forces of the Seleucid Empire (165 BCE). Indeed, the book presents Judith as a female Maccabee, defeating the enemies of Judah when that seemed all but impossible. One of the goals of Holofernes's expedition was to "destroy all the gods of the land" so that people would then worship Nebuchadnezzar alone (3:8). The worship of the king as a god places this story squarely in the Greek period. Antiochus IV (who ruled 175–164 BCE) thought of himself as Zeus manifest.

Despite its Deuteronomic flavoring, there is no evidence that the Jews of Palestine ever considered Judith as canonical. No fragments of the Aramaic or Hebrew versions of Judith were found at Qumran. Christians were divided on the question of canonicity. Jerome was skeptical while Augustine, typically, accepted the book as inspired. Protestant Christians consider Judith apocryphal while Catholics number it among the deutercanonical books of the Old Testament.

## Esther

The books of Judith and Esther are tales

featuring beautiful Jewish women whose courageous exploits save their people from impending disaster. The book of Judith mentions God frequently. It portrays Judith as living a life of fasting and prayer. It alludes to characteristic Jewish beliefs and practices. The Hebrew version of Esther, however, never mentions God or any Jewish religious practices or institutions, except for Purim. And yet the book of Esther found its way into the rabbinic Bible while the book of Judith did not.

Like Judith, Esther sees Gentiles as potential threats to the existence of the Jewish people. It is set in the court of Persia. The king of Persia chooses Esther as his queen after his first wife displeases him. Esther's uncle Mordecai, a high official in the Persian court, discovers a plot against the king and saves the king from assassination. The king is understandably grateful. This arouses the jealousy of Haman, another court official, who decides to eliminate his rival Mordecai and all Jews residing in Persia. Mordecai learns of Haman's plot and enlists Esther in a plan to turn the king against Haman. Mordecai's plan is successful and the Jews of Persia are safe. Mordecai orders the Jews to celebrate their deliverance during the two-day festival of Purim (9:23).

When the Hebrew Esther was translated into Greek, 107 verses were added to give the book a more religious flavor. The Hebrew text is a secular tale about the persecution of the Jews, illustrating how Jews can take control of the situation to ensure their survival. The additions found in the Greek version make the deliverance of the Jews the result of prayer to God, who controls the fate of Israel. Perhaps the secular character of the Hebrew Esther was the reason the rabbis were slow to embrace the book. As late as the fourth century CE, there were rabbis who did not include the book of Esther among the books they considered sacred. Christians too had questions about the book's canonical character. Luther regarded Esther as apocryphal with its Greek additions while the Council of Trent included the additions among the deuterocanonical texts.

## 1-2 Maccabees

The last two of the historical books refocus

attention on the Jewish community in Palestine. First Maccabees covers a seventy-year period (175–104 BCE) that witnesses the improbable rise of an obscure priestly family to political and religious leadership of the Jewish community. The story of the Maccabees begins with a notice of Alexander the Great's death (323 BCE) and the events in Palestine following the accession of Antiochus IV as ruler of the Seleucid Kingdom (175 BCE). Antiochus's anti-Jewish policies prompted a priest named Mattathias and his sons to take up armed resistance. Their success led to their receiving the sobriquet of *Maccabee*, i.e., "Hammer." Following the death of Mattathias, each of his sons in succession assumed the leadership of the Jewish community. At first their leadership was primarily military in nature but eventually came to include the religious and political spheres as well (1 Mc 14:25–49). One purpose of 1 Maccabees is to support the sons of Mattathias in the role they came to play in the Jewish community of Palestine.

Second Maccabees does not continue the story of the family of Mattathias. Rather it offers another version of that story—one that focuses on the purification of the Temple that was necessary because of its desecration by Antiochus IV. The book claims to be an abridgement of a five-volume work of a certain Jason of Cyrene (2 Mc 2:23) and covers events from 180 to 161 BCE. Second Maccabees is less interested in crediting the leadership of the Maccabees, but ascribes the victories that led to the rededication of the Temple to God's powerful intervention (e.g., 2 Mc 11:1–13).

Neither 1 nor 2 Maccabees is part of the Hebrew Scriptures. They came into the Christian canon of the Old Testament through their inclusion in the Septuagint. The church's early theologians considered these two books as authoritative, but Luther, followed by Protestant churches, included them among those considered apocryphal. The Septuagint also contains *3* and *4 Maccabees*, which are considered canonical by the Greek Orthodox Church.

# The Value of the Historical Books

At one time, modern histories of ancient Israel were little more than paraphrases of the biblical narratives. Today that is no longer the case, primarily because of archaeological excavations in the Holy Land. Excavation of places such as Jericho, Ai, and Jerusalem has shown that the stories of the Israelite tribes' settlement and the reigns of David and Solomon do not reflect the realities of the historical periods in which these stories are set. Also, most of the historical books place a heavy emphasis on the divine causation of events. For example, the fall of the kingdom of Israel is blamed on Israel's sins and the failure to heed the message of the prophets (2 Kgs 17). The expansionist policies of the aggressively militaristic neo-Assyrian Empire are largely ignored. The biblical histories are quite selective in what is reported. For example, Omri was among the greatest kings of Israel, yet the Deuteronomist basically dismisses him, summing up his reign in a mere six verses (1 Kgs 16:23–28). In the Deuteronomist's view, Omri's achievements are not worth mentioning since he was guilty of the sin of Jeroboam. The Chronicler virtually ignores Omri, mentioning him only in passing (2 Chr 22:2).

At the same time, one cannot dismiss the historical books as without merit as resources for the modern historian of Israel, but readers need to recognize that the goal of each of these histories was to make it clear that Israel had a future—despite its infidelity to its God. They affirm that judgment was not God's last word to Israel, despite Israel's failures. These affirmations transcend the judgments that historians usually make, but they represent the fundamental beliefs of those unnamed writers who gave us the historical books. ■

# THE HISTORICAL BOOKS

## New American Bible, Introduction

Where the Hebrew Bible comprises three sections—Torah or Pentateuch; Prophetic Books, both the Former and the Latter Prophets; and the Writings, including everything else in the Hebrew Canon—the Christian Old Testament has traditionally been arranged along different lines. After the Pentateuch comes a series of books that continue, in roughly chronological order, the history of Israel. The Book of Joshua depicts Israel taking possession of the land of Canaan. Judges collects stories about the leaders of early Israel in the two hundred years before the emergence of the monarchy. After the tale of Ruth, a sort of interlude in the narrative sweep of these books, 1 and 2 Samuel tell of the rise and fall of Saul, Israel's first king, and the succession and successes of David. The Books of Kings take us from the death of David and the enthronement of Solomon, through the division of the people into the two kingdoms of Israel and Judah, to the destruction of the Northern Kingdom, Israel, at the hands of the Assyrian invader (722/721 B.C.), and the fall of Judah, the Southern Kingdom, to the Babylonians (587 B.C.) and its ensuing exile, the Babylonian captivity.

Except for Ruth, these writings bear the marks of a specific theological outlook, that of the Book of Deuteronomy, and together with that book as its introductory volume constitute what is called the Deuteronomistic History. In this theology, what has characterized Israel's history, in the six hundred years from Moses to the Babylonian exile, has been a dynamic of fidelity or infidelity to Israel's covenant Lord, and the consequent destiny Israel forges for itself of covenant blessing or covenant curse.

This dynamic of choice and consequences serves to explain the disasters Israel incurs throughout its history, from the so-called conquest and the days of the Judges to the fall of the North. In its preexilic edition, the Deuteronomistic History would have stood also as warning and wake-up call to the surviving Southern Kingdom.

The Books of Chronicles recycle much of the material found in the previous works, but the author ("the Chronicler") treats it selectively, with a characteristic theological point of view; its focus is the Jerusalem Temple and its cultic arrangements, which by way of legitimation are attributed to David, the ideal king. The Chronicler's interests carry through the Books of Ezra and Nehemiah, which recount the restoration of Jewish worship and life in the period of Persian rule following release from exile in Babylon.

The Books of Maccabees give us two overlapping but somewhat differing accounts of Jewish resistance to Seleucid persecution in the early second century B.C., and the assumption of power by the leaders of the resistance, the Maccabees or Hasmoneans.

The traditional designation of these books as "historical" describes their scope and contents, and is not meant to assert factual verifiability; while they contain much valuable historical information, in the narrow sense, their purpose is theological rather than historiographic.

The Books of Tobit, Judith, and Esther are sometimes reckoned among the historical books, but they differ from the writings sketched above, and call for special treatment; see the introduction to those books. ■

# Joshua

## INTRODUCTION

### Linda Day

In the ongoing story of Israel, after the giving of the Torah and the people's experiences traveling through the wilderness, the book of Joshua answers the question, how did Israel come to acquire the land that had been promised to them? It includes familiar tales (e.g., the battle of Jericho, Rahab and the spies) along with lesser-known stories and other materials, many of which are no less dramatic. Joshua plays a pivotal role in the development of theology in the biblical tradition, while also exhibiting ethical tensions. Through its representation of an emerging people establishing their place and practices, the book challenges its readers also to be faithful, obedient, and courageous, and gives them hope of divine presence and protection.

## Structure and Content

Of its total twenty-four chapters, the book divides straightforwardly into two halves. Chapters 1–12 depict the various military conquests to obtain territory, and chs. 13–24 relate the allotment of this territory and settlement in the land. Each half concludes with a summary that ties up its respective narrative movement (12:1–24; 24:29–33). Within each primary section are two subdivisions. Chapters 1–5 describe the various necessary preparations for the invasion and chs. 6–12, the actual campaigns. Chapters 13–21 give details of the land apportionment, and chs. 22–24 describe two national assemblies.

The narrative opens with the people of Israel camped east of the Jordan River. Yahweh appoints Joshua as the new leader of Israel, to replace Moses, and promises Israel a vast land (ch. 1). Joshua sends two spies to scope out Jericho, where Rahab assists them in their mission (ch. 2). The people cross the Jordan in

## Outline of Joshua

I.  **Conquest of Canaan (1:1–12:24)**

II. **Division of the Land (13:1–21:45)**

III. **Return of the Transjordan Tribes and Joshua's Farewell (22:1–24:33)**

formal array (led by the ark of the covenant) with miraculous aid (the waters part on either side), after which they erect a twelve-stone memorial (chs. 3–4). In the final preparations for battle, all the men are circumcised and the Israelites celebrate their first Passover west of the Jordan (ch. 5). Ritual marching around Jericho in various increments of "sevens" defeats the city (ch. 6). The unfaithfulness of Achan initially leads to defeat at the hands of Ai, but victory follows his punishment (chs. 7–8). Hearing of Israel's military success, the people of Gibeon engage in a ruse to ensure their survival (ch. 9). The Israelites defeat local kings in southern (ch. 10) and northern (ch. 11) campaigns, and the conquered kings are listed (ch. 12).

As the narrative turns to divisions of territory, first mentioned are the allotments east of the Jordan River, earlier granted by Moses to the tribes of Reuben, Gad, and half-Manasseh (Jos 13). In the land of Canaan, Joshua grants inheritance to Caleb, one of the original spies sent by Moses (ch. 14); to the tribes of Judah and Joseph (chs. 15–17); and by lot to the tribes of Benjamin, Simeon, Zebulun, Issachar, Asher, Naphtali, and Dan (chs. 18–19). Cities of refuge are established as asylums for persons committing unintentional murder (ch. 20), and other cities provide grazing rights for the Levites (ch. 21). Joshua sends the eastern tribes home across the Jordan, but the purpose

JOS

of an altar they build is initially misunderstood and causes disagreement (ch. 22). An elderly Joshua charges Israel's leaders to be faithful and gathers all the people for a covenant renewal ceremony (chs. 23–24). The book concludes with his death.

## Canonical Context

The book of Joshua looks both backward and forward. It follows the book of Deuteronomy in the canon and continues many of Deuteronomy's themes and unique characteristics. Deuteronomy is, in essence, a series of speeches by Moses as the people of Israel stand poised to set foot in the promised land. The book of Joshua enters immediately into this context, reporting Moses' death and beginning another lengthy speech, one of many throughout the narrative. It continues an explicit connection with Deuteronomy through references to the fulfillment of Moses' instructions, the use of distinctive vocabulary, and even the repetition of specific texts. The larger narrative structure echoes Deuteronomy's expectations for the acquisition and division of the land, including its warnings of potential difficulties and divisions. Moreover, Joshua strongly emphasizes the theological message of Yahweh's choice of this people and gift of this land, requiring a response of the people's faithfulness and obedience to the commandments.

At the same time, Joshua also points forward. It stands as the first book in the Former Prophets (Joshua through Kings), and in many ways it serves as the prologue to this collection, initiating Israel's life as a unified people dwelling in Canaan and anticipating their persistent struggles and ongoing challenges to do so effectively and faithfully. Scholars use the term Deuteronomistic History to refer to these books along with Deuteronomy. As part of this larger collection, the book of Joshua reflects its character as what might be considered "theological history," that is, an interest not in verifiable historical facts about Israel's past but instead in outlining national origins and stressing national identity and behavior. The book contains a variety of material: folktales and traditional stories, battle reports, etiologies, sermons, city lists, border descriptions, and summary accounts. The references to the tent of meeting and the prominence of the priests Phineas and Eleazar also give portions of the book a Priestly flavor. These materials appear to have been gathered together in a complex process that occurred over some time and in various stages of development. The date of Joshua's final editing is uncertain but can best be considered as no earlier than the sixth century BCE with the rest of the Deuteronomistic History.

## Themes

**Obedience**. The command to obey Yahweh opens the book (see Yahweh's initial directives to Joshua, 1:7–8) and also closes it (in the form of Joshua's final directives to the people, 24:16–28). In between it represents a series of tests that provide opportunities to see whether the people of Israel will choose to be obedient. Israel is commanded not only to fight but also to obey, and they will be allowed to keep the land only to the degree that they are faithful to the instruction of their God. Devotion to Yahweh is illuminated through various religious rituals: the Passover sacrifice, circumcision, the erection of stone memorials, and respect for the ark of the covenant. Disobedience is similarly highlighted, particularly through the negative example of Achan (ch. 7). The incident with the altar built by the eastern tribes demonstrates that what may at first glance appear disobedient is not necessarily so if one's motives are honorable (22:10–34).

The Torah—Yahweh's instruction for the people of Israel, given through the teaching of Moses—is central to the book. Torah is the vital principle for Israel's life in Canaan, and obedience and disobedience to it determines their ultimate success or failure in the land. Joshua makes the entirety of the Torah accessible to the people, and no one is exempted from its obligations (Jos 8:30–35). One of the tenets of the Torah is the concept of *herem*, or the "ban." *Herem* requires that, in any victory, all the spoils be dedicated to Yahweh: all opponents are to be killed and no booty is to be taken. The people are not to benefit materially from war, and God is honored as the proper victor.

JOS

**Leadership**. In the work that bears his name, Joshua is the primary character—a stage he shares with the divine character, Yahweh. Joshua exemplifies a model of centralized leadership for the organization of the nation, a leader who is invested by Yahweh and supported by Yahweh throughout. At first the servant of Moses (1:1), by the end of his life Joshua has fully become the "servant of the LORD" (24:29). In many ways, the book presents Joshua as a royal figure, looking forward to the role played by the king in later Israelite history. Such leadership is difficult, however, and requires personal fortitude, as the repeated injunction to "be strong and steadfast" makes explicit. Joshua is the protégé of and now successor to Moses, the ideal leader whom the narrative will not let readers forget. Repeatedly Joshua's actions echo those of Moses, through the overarching agenda of conquering and allotting land as well as sending out spies, miraculously leading the people across a body of water, and stretching out an arm to initiate action. Joshua's role is as mediator between Yahweh and Israel, conveying the divine word to the people. At the same time, he is also the model Israelite, exemplifying for the people how to serve Yahweh (24:14–15).

**National Unity**. Countless times the narrative stresses that "all Israel" and "all the congregation" act together. The unity of the people of Israel is of great importance. The people act with one accord in their military endeavors and their obedience to Yahweh and Joshua. Thus national unity serves as a marker of Israel's identity and an affirmation of its uniqueness, in contrast to the "otherness" of non-Israelites. Israel's unified national identity stands in opposition to the fractured identity of the Canaanites, with their plurality of many ethnic designations, many kings, many worship sites, and many gods. Joshua's final warning is for separation from the other peoples out of fear that intermingling will lead to unfaithfulness and ultimate abandonment of Yahweh (Jos 23:1–13).

Punctuating the book, however, are stories of individuals that present a different impression. Lived situations do not always hew to the national ideal of complete segregation. Upon crossing the Jordan, the people of Israel meet sympathetic and virtuous persons among the indigenous population. Indeed, the first person in the promised land to acknowledge Yahweh is a Canaanite prostitute. The report that Rahab's family and the Gibeonites live in the land alongside Israel for generations (Jos 6:25; 9:21, 27) stands in contrast to the idea that the nation should be, or ever was, ethnically homogenous. When individuals who typically would not be allowed to have land—the Canaanite Caleb, the female Achsah, and the daughters of Zelophehad—ask for a claim to territory, it is granted. And Israel itself shows moments of interior dividedness, as the western tribes threaten war against the eastern tribes (22:12) and the tribe of Joseph complains about its allotment (17:14–18). Such accounts serve to counter the official rhetoric of Israel's exclusivity and complete separation.

**Geography**. The book as a whole brings to fulfillment Yahweh's promise to Israel's ancestors for a land of their own. Fittingly, detailed geographic description punctuates the narrative depicting the winning of this land. Physical space and physical boundaries are of great concern. The first boundary is the Jordan River, its central importance illuminated by the elaborate and ceremonial activity of its crossing. Geographical location guides the two main movements of the book, first as the conquest engages in campaigns in the central territories and then moves on to the south and the north, and second as the boundaries of the territories allotted to the twelve tribes are fixed. The detail devoted to these descriptions, although they are idealized, provides a sense of satisfaction in Israel's settlement life. Moreover, the delineation of large swaths of yet-unconquered Canaanite territory (Jos 1:4–5; 13:2–6) holds out a hopeful expectation of further geographic expansion for Israel's future life in the promised land.

**Violence**. The amount and level of violence in this book can unsettle readers. The narrative includes shocking activity that highlights death and destruction, the wholesale slaughter of populations. Israel's gift of its long-anticipated national home comes at great loss of life. And as the repeated creedal declaration "the LORD fought for Israel" affirms, the people are called to obey and worship a warlike God, a militant divine warrior. For modern readers, Israel's appropriation of property belonging to others can seem similar to more recent occasions of colonization, and its practice of *herem* to instances of genocide.

The book's portrayal of how Israel came to be is dramatic but unrealistic. Archaeological and historical evidence does not support its version of a quick military conquest by a people arriving from outside Canaan. Cities prominent in the book of Joshua either were not occupied during this period or show no evidence of destruction and resettlement. It appears more likely that Israelite culture and identity developed indigenously and peacefully, predominantly from within Canaan itself. Therefore the book provides an idealized portrait of Israel's origin, and its violent battle reports are legendary rather than factual. This literature was collected, produced, and read much later, by a people who were militarily weak, vulnerable in the face of more powerful nations, and frequently in danger of losing their land. The book of Joshua, in its depiction of forceful military conquest, can resonate with any nation that likewise has memories of a violent origin. It remains problematic in all times when cultures wrestle with instances of ethnic violence and the rhetoric of divine sanction. ■

# THE BOOK OF JOSHUA

## New American Bible, Introduction

The Book of Joshua presents a narrative of the way Israel took possession of the land of Canaan, making it the land of Israel. This process is swift and inexorable, and is followed by an orderly division and disposition of the land among the twelve tribes, with a concluding ceremony of covenant renewal.

The theological message of the book is unmistakable. God has been faithful to the promise of the land. If Israel relies totally on the Lord for victory; if Israel is united as a people; if the law of *herem* is kept and no one grows rich from victory in war—then and only then will Israel possess the land.

The Israelites are led by Joshua, the successor of Moses, and the book is at pains to show not only how Joshua carries on the work of Moses but how the "conquest" of Canaan is continuous with the exodus from Egypt. This is seen in the repeated insistence that, as the Lord was with Moses, so he is with Joshua; and, especially, in the crossing of the Jordan River, which is patterned after the crossing of the Red Sea.

The book preserves older traditions of Israel's settlement in the land, especially in the division of the land among the tribes. As with Deuteronomy and the whole Deuteronomistic History (see introduction to Deuteronomy), the fall of the Northern Kingdom in 722/721 B.C. shows its influence throughout. As addressed to the needs of a late preexilic audience, then, the book should be read not so much as imparting information about how Israel took over the land of Canaan, many centuries before the composition of the book, as teaching a lesson about how Israel is to avoid losing the land.

Modern readers may be put off by the description of battles and their aftermath, the destruction of everyone and everything in the cities taken under the "ban" (*herem*). The ban was practiced in the ancient Near East, in Israel and elsewhere, but in Joshua the wholesale destruction of the Canaanites is an idealization of the deuteronomic idea that pagans are to be wiped out so they will not be an occasion for apostasy from the Lord (cf. Dt 7:1–6); note in particular the artificial, formalized description of destruction of towns in Jos 10:28–39. It should be remembered that by the time the book was written, the Canaanites were long gone. Progressive revelation throughout Israel's history produced far more lofty ideals, as when the prophets see all the nations embracing faith in Yahweh, being joined to Israel, and living in peace with one another (Is 2:2–4; 19:23–25; 45:22–25; Zec 8:22–23), and the New Testament teaches us to love even our enemies (Mt 5:43–45).

A comparison of Joshua with the account of Israel's early history found in the first chapter of the Book of Judges shows that Israel's emergence as the dominant presence in the land was a slow and piecemeal affair, not achieved at one stroke and with great ease: the Book of Joshua, with its highly idealized depiction of the "conquest," is a theologically programmatic cautionary tale about what the people are to do and not do in order to avoid the fate of the Northern Kingdom in losing the land.

The Book of Joshua may be divided as follows:

I. Conquest of Canaan (1:1–12:24)
II. Division of the Land (13:1–21:45)
III. Return of the Transjordan Tribes and Joshua's Farewell (22:1–24:33) ■

# JOSHUA

## I. CONQUEST OF CANAAN

**1** **Divine Promise of Assistance.** [1]After Moses, the servant of the LORD, had died, the LORD said to Moses' aide Joshua, son of Nun: [2]† Moses my servant is dead. So now, you and the whole people with you, prepare to cross the Jordan to the land that I will give the Israelites. [3]* Every place where you set foot I have given you, as I promised Moses. [4]† All the land of the Hittites, from the wilderness and the Lebanon east to the great river Euphrates and west to the Great Sea, will be your territory.* [5]No one can withstand you as long as you live. As I was with Moses, I will be with you:* I will not leave you nor forsake you. [6]Be strong and steadfast, so that you may give this people possession of the land I swore to their ancestors that I would give them. [7]* Only be strong and steadfast, being careful to observe the entire law which Moses my servant enjoined on you. Do not swerve from it either to the right or to the left, that you may succeed wherever you go. [8]Do not let this book of the law depart from your lips. Recite it by day and by night,* that you may carefully observe all that is written in it; then you will attain your goal; then you will succeed. [9]I command you: be strong and steadfast! Do not fear nor be dismayed, for the LORD, your God, is with you wherever you go.

[10]* So Joshua commanded the officers of the people: [11]"Go through the camp and command the people, 'Prepare your provisions, for three days from now you shall cross the Jordan here, to march in and possess the land the LORD, your God, is giving as your possession.'"

**The Transjordan Tribes.** [12]* Joshua addressed the Reubenites, the Gadites, and the half-tribe of Manasseh: [13]"Remember what Moses, the servant of the LORD, commanded you when he said, 'The LORD, your God, is about to give you rest; he will give you this land.' [14]Your wives, your children, and your livestock may remain in the land Moses gave you here beyond the Jordan. But all the warriors among you must cross over armed, ahead of your kindred, and you must help them [15]until the LORD has settled your kindred, and they like you possess the land the LORD, your God, is giving them. Afterward you may return and possess your own land, which Moses, the servant of the LORD, has given you east of the Jordan."* [16]They answered Joshua, "We will do all you have commanded us, and we will go wherever you send us. [17]As completely as we obeyed Moses, we will obey you. Only, may the LORD, your God, be with you as God was with Moses. [18]Anyone who rebels against your orders and does not obey all your commands shall be put to death. Only be strong and steadfast."

**2** **Spies Saved by Rahab.** [1]Then Joshua, son of Nun, secretly sent out two spies from Shittim, saying, "Go, reconnoiter the land and Jericho." When the two reached Jericho, they went into the house of a prostitute named Rahab,* where they lodged. [2]But a report was brought to the king of Jericho: "Some men came here last night, Israelites, to spy out the land." [3]So the king of Jericho sent Rahab the order, "Bring out the men who have come to you and entered your house, for they have come to spy out the entire land." [4]The woman* had taken the two men and hidden them, so she said, "True, the men you speak of came to me, but I did not know where they came from. [5]At dark, when it was time to close the gate, they left, and I do not know where they went. You will have to pursue them

---

† **1:2–9** The beginning of the Book of Joshua strongly emphasizes the credentials of Joshua as Moses' worthy successor (vv. 2, 3, 4, 7; cf. v. 17; 3:7; 4:14; 5:15). The movement Joshua leads, whereby the Israelites take possession of the land of Canaan, is thus made continuous with the exodus from Egypt, even though (except for Joshua and Caleb) the generation that left Egypt under Moses' leadership has died out (5:4, 6), and the people who will make the land of Canaan the land of Israel are a new generation. Thus the book is at pains to establish the continuity between exodus and conquest.

**1:4** The frontiers are as follows: in the south the wilderness of Sinai, in the north the Lebanon range, in the east the Euphrates,

and in the west the Great Sea, the Mediterranean. These boundaries are ideal rather than actual.

**1:3–4** Jos 14:9; Gn 15:18; Dt 11:24–25; 34:4.
**1:4** Gn 10:19; Nm 13:17, 21–22; 34:3–12.
**1:5** Dt 3:21–22; 31:8, 23; Heb 13:5.
**1:7–8** Dt 2:27; 5:29; 17:11, 20; 28:14; Ps 1:1–3.
**1:8** Ps 1:2.
**1:10–11** Dt 20:5–9.
**1:12–18** Nm 32; Dt 3:12–20.
**1:15** Jos 22:4; Dt 3:20.
**2:1** Dt 1:22; Mt 1:5; Jas 2:25.
**2:4** Jos 6:17; Heb 11:31.

quickly to overtake them." ⁶Now, she had led them to the roof, and hidden them among her stalks of flax spread out† there. ⁷But the pursuers set out along the way to the fords of the Jordan. As soon as they had left to pursue them, the gate was shut.

⁸Before the spies lay down, Rahab went up to them on the roof ⁹and said:† "I know that the LORD has given you the land, that a dread of you has come upon us, and that all the inhabitants of the land tremble with fear because of you.* ¹⁰For we have heard how the LORD dried up the waters of the Red Sea before you when you came out of Egypt,* and what you did to Sihon and Og, the two kings of the Amorites beyond the Jordan, whom you destroyed under the ban. ¹¹We heard, and our hearts melted within us; everyone is utterly dispirited because of you, since the LORD, your God, is God in heaven above and on earth below.* ¹²*Now then, swear to me by the LORD that, since I am showing kindness to you, you in turn will show kindness to my family.* Give me a reliable sign ¹³that you will allow my father and mother, brothers and sisters, and my whole family to live, and that you will deliver us from death." ¹⁴"We pledge our lives for yours," they answered her. "If you do not betray our mission, we will be faithful in showing kindness to you when the LORD gives us the land."

¹⁵Then she let them down through the window with a rope; for she lived in a house built into the city wall.† ¹⁶"Go up into the hill country," she said, "that your pursuers may not come upon you. Hide there for three days, until they return; then you may go on your way." ¹⁷They answered her, "We are free of this oath that you made us take, unless, ¹⁸when we come into the land, you tie this scarlet cord in the window through which you are letting us down. Gather your father and mother, your brothers, and all your family into your house. ¹⁹Should any of them pass outside the doors

of your house, their blood will be on their own heads, and we will be guiltless. But if anyone in your house is harmed, their blood will be on our heads. ²⁰If, however, you betray our mission, we will be free of the oath you have made us take." ²¹"Let it be as you say," she replied, and sent them away. When they were gone, she tied the scarlet cord in the window.

²²They went up into the hill country, where they stayed three days until their pursuers, who had sought them all along the road without finding them, returned. ²³Then the two came back down from the hills, crossed the Jordan to Joshua, son of Nun, and told him all that had happened to them. ²⁴They assured Joshua, "The LORD has given all this land into our power; indeed, all the inhabitants of the land tremble with fear because of us."

## 3 Preparations for Crossing the Jordan.

¹Early the next morning, Joshua and all the Israelites moved from Shittim and came to the Jordan, where they stayed before crossing over. ²*Three days later the officers went through the camp ³*and issued these commands to the people: "When you see the ark of the covenant of the LORD, your God, which the levitical priests will carry, you must break camp and follow it, ⁴that you may know the way to take, for you have not gone over this road before. But let there be a space of two thousand cubits between you and the ark: do not come nearer to it." ⁵Joshua also said to the people, "Sanctify yourselves, for tomorrow the LORD will perform wonders among you." ⁶And he told the priests, "Take up the ark of the covenant and cross ahead of the people"; so they took up the ark of the covenant and went before the people.

⁷*Then the LORD said to Joshua: Today I will begin to exalt you in the sight of all Israel, that they may know that, as I was with Moses, so I will be with you.* ⁸Now command the priests carrying the ark of the covenant, "When

---

† **2:6** *Stalks of flax spread out*: to dry in the sun, after they had been soaked in water, according to the ancient process of preparing flax for linen-making. In the Near East the flax harvest occurs near the time of the feast of the Passover (4:19; 5:10); cf. Ex 9:31.

**2:9–11** Rahab's speech is Deuteronomic in content and style. Through her, the author expresses a theological conviction: the Lord, the God of Israel, is God above all gods; the formation of the people Israel and its success is the Lord's doing; and all the rulers of the neighboring nations do well to panic at what the Lord is doing (cf. 5:1). Rahab the prostitute is pointedly mentioned in the Matthean genealogy of Jesus (Mt 1:5) and in Jas 2:25.

**2:15** *A house built into the city wall*: the city wall formed the back wall of the house; remains of such houses have been found at ancient sites. The upper story of Rahab's house was evidently higher than the city wall. It was through the window of such a house that St. Paul escaped from Damascus; cf. Acts 9:25; 2 Cor 11:33.

* **2:9** Ex 15:15–16; 23:27.
**2:10** Jos 4:23; Ex 14:21; Nm 21:23–26, 33–35.
**2:11** Jos 5:1; Dt 4:39; Rom 10:9.
**2:12–13** Jgs 1:22–26.
**2:12** Jos 2:18; 6:23, 25.
**3:2** Jos 2:1.
**3:3** Nm 10:33.
**3:7** Jos 1:5; Dt 31:23.
**3:7** Jos 1:5; 4:14.

you come to the edge of the waters of the Jordan, there take your stand."

⁹ So Joshua said to the Israelites, "Come here and listen to the words of the LORD, your God." ¹⁰ He continued: "By this you will know that there is a living God in your midst: he will certainly dispossess before you the Canaanites, Hittites, Hivites, Perizzites, Girgashites, Amorites, and Jebusites.* ¹¹ The ark of the covenant of the Lord of the whole earth will cross the Jordan before you. ¹² Now choose twelve men,* one from each of the tribes of Israel. ¹³ When the soles of the feet of the priests carrying the ark of the LORD, the Lord of the whole earth, touch the waters of the Jordan, it will cease to flow; the water flowing down from upstream will halt in a single heap."†

**The Crossing Begun.** ¹⁴ The people set out from their tents to cross the Jordan, with the priests carrying the ark of the covenant ahead of them. ¹⁵ When those bearing the ark came to the Jordan and the feet of the priests bearing the ark were immersed in the waters of the Jordan—which overflows all its banks during the entire season of the harvest—† ¹⁶ the waters flowing from upstream halted, standing up in a single heap* for a very great distance indeed, from Adam, a city in the direction of Zarethan; those flowing downstream toward the Salt Sea of the Arabah disappeared entirely.† Thus the people crossed over opposite Jericho. ¹⁷ The priests carrying the ark of the covenant of the LORD stood on dry ground in the Jordan riverbed* while all Israel crossed on dry ground, until the whole nation had completed the crossing of the Jordan.

**4 Memorial Stones.** ¹ After the entire nation had completed the crossing of the Jordan, ² the LORD said to Joshua: Choose twelve men* from the people, one from each tribe, ³ and command them, "Take up twelve stones

from this spot in the Jordan riverbed where the priests have been standing.* Carry them over with you, and place them where you are to stay tonight."

⁴ Summoning the twelve men he had selected from among the Israelites, one from each tribe, ⁵ Joshua said to them: "Go to the Jordan riverbed in front of the ark of the LORD, your God; lift to your shoulders one stone apiece, so that they will equal in number the tribes of the Israelites. ⁶ In the future, these are to be a sign among you. When your children ask you, † 'What do these stones mean to you?'* ⁷ you shall answer them, 'The waters of the Jordan ceased to flow before the ark of the covenant of the LORD when it crossed the Jordan.'* Thus these stones are to serve as a perpetual memorial to the Israelites." ⁸ The twelve Israelites did as Joshua had commanded: they took up twelve stones from the Jordan riverbed as the LORD had said to Joshua, one for each of the tribes of the Israelites. They carried them along to the camp site, and there they placed them. ⁹ Joshua set up the twelve stones that had been in the Jordan riverbed on the spot where the priests stood who were carrying the ark of the covenant. They are there to this day.

¹⁰ † The priests carrying the ark stood in the Jordan riverbed until everything had been done that the LORD had commanded Joshua to tell the people, just as Moses had commanded Joshua. The people crossed over quickly, ¹¹ and when all the people had completed the crossing, the ark of the LORD also crossed; and the priests were now in front of them. ¹² The Reubenites, Gadites, and half-tribe of Manasseh, armed, marched in the vanguard of the Israelites, as Moses had ordered. ¹³ About forty thousand troops, equipped for battle, crossed over before the LORD to the plains of Jericho for war.

¹⁴ That day the LORD exalted Joshua in the

---

**3:13** *Heap:* Heb. *nēd,* the same word found in Ex 15:8; the narrative echoes the ancient Song of Miriam (Ex 15:1–18), which celebrates the crossing of the Red Sea. Thus the language provides another parallel between Joshua and Moses, conquest and exodus.

**3:15** *Season of the harvest:* toward the end of March and the beginning of April, when the barley and other crops that grew during the rainy season of winter were reaped. The crossing took place "on the tenth day of the first month" of the Hebrew year, which began with the first new moon after the spring equinox; cf. 4:19. At this time of the year the Jordan would be swollen as a result of the winter rains and the melting snow of Mount Hermon.

**3:16** Some scholars have suggested that this account may

reflect an annual ritual reenactment of the event near the sanctuary of Gilgal.

**4:6** *When your children ask you:* reminiscent of the question and response at the Passover meal, Ex 12:26–27.

**4:10–18** After the digression about the memorial stones, the author resumes the narrative by briefly repeating the story of the crossing, which had already been told in 3:14–17.

---

| | |
|---|---|
| **3:10** Ex 33:2; Dt 7:1. | **4:3** Jos 3:13; 4:8–9; Dt |
| **3:12** Jos 4:2, 4. | 27:2. |
| **3:16** Ps 114:3. | **4:6** Ex 12:26–27; Dt 6:7, |
| **3:17** Jos 4:7, 22. | 20–25. |
| **4:2** Jos 3:12. | **4:7** Jos 3:13, 16. |

sight of all Israel, * and so during his whole life they feared him as they had feared Moses.

[15] Then the LORD said to Joshua: [16] Command the priests carrying the ark of the covenant to come up from the Jordan. [17] Joshua commanded the priests, "Come up from the Jordan," [18] and when the priests carrying the ark of the covenant of the LORD had come up from the Jordan riverbed, as the soles of their feet regained the dry ground, the waters of the Jordan resumed their course and as before overflowed all its banks.

[19] The people came up from the Jordan on the tenth day of the first month, and camped in Gilgal on the eastern limits of Jericho. * [20] At Gilgal Joshua set up the twelve stones that had been taken from the Jordan, [21] saying to the Israelites, "In the future, when your children ask their parents, 'What do these stones mean?' [22] you shall inform them, 'Israel crossed the Jordan here on dry ground.' [23] For the LORD, your God, dried up the waters of the Jordan in front of you until you crossed over, just as the LORD, your God, had done at the Red Sea, drying it up in front of us until we crossed over, * [24] in order that all the peoples of the earth may know that the hand of the LORD is mighty, and that you may fear the LORD, your God, forever." *

**5** **Rites at Gilgal.** [1] When all the kings of the Amorites to the west of the Jordan and all the kings of the Canaanites by the sea heard that the LORD had dried up the waters of the Jordan before the Israelites until they crossed over, their hearts melted and they were utterly dispirited because of the Israelites.

[2] * On this occasion the LORD said to Joshua: Make flint knives and circumcise Israel for the second time. [3] So Joshua made flint knives and circumcised the Israelites at Gibeath-haaraloth. † [4] This was the reason for the

circumcision: Of all the people who had come out of Egypt, every male of military age had died in the wilderness * during the journey after they came out of Egypt. [5] Though all the men who came out were circumcised, none of those born in the wilderness during the journey after the departure from Egypt were circumcised. [6] Now the Israelites wandered forty years in the wilderness, until all the warriors among the people that came forth from Egypt died off because they had not listened to the voice of the LORD. For the LORD swore * that he would not let them see the land he had sworn to their ancestors to give us, a land flowing with milk and honey. [7] * It was the children God raised up in their stead whom Joshua circumcised, for these were yet with foreskins, not having been circumcised on the journey. [8] When the circumcision of the entire nation was complete, they remained in camp where they were, until they recovered. [9] Then the LORD said to Joshua: Today I have removed the reproach of Egypt from you. * Therefore the place is called Gilgal † to the present day.

[10] * While the Israelites were encamped at Gilgal on the plains of Jericho, they celebrated the Passover on the evening of the fourteenth day of the month. † [11] On the day after the Passover they ate of the produce of the land in the form of unleavened cakes and parched grain. On that same day [12] after they ate of the produce of the land, the manna ceased. No longer was there manna for the Israelites, who that year ate of the yield of the land of Canaan. *

**Siege at Jericho.** [13] † While Joshua was near Jericho, he raised his eyes and saw one who stood facing him, drawn sword in hand. * Joshua went up to him and asked, "Are you one of us or one of our enemies?" [14] He replied, "Neither. I am the commander † of the

---

† **5:3** *Gibeath-haaraloth:* "Hill of the Foreskins."

**5:9** *The place is called Gilgal:* by popular etymology, because of the similarity of sound with the Hebrew word *gallothi,* "I have removed." Gilgal probably means "circle," i.e., the place of the circle of standing stones. Cf. 4:4–8.

**5:10** *The month:* the first month of the year, later called Nisan; see note on 3:15. The crossing of the Jordan occurred, therefore, about the same time of the year as did the crossing of the Red Sea; cf. Ex 12–14.

**5:13–6:26** The account of the siege of Jericho embraces: (1) the command of the Lord to Joshua (5:13–6:5); (2) Joshua's instructions to the Israelites, with a brief summary of how these orders were carried out (6:6–11); (3) a description of the action on each of the first six days (6:12–14); (4) the events on the seventh day (6:15–26).

**5:14** *Commander:* the leader of the heavenly army of the Lord of hosts is either the Lord or an angelic warrior; if the latter, he is a messenger who speaks in the person of the one who sent him. *I have come:* the solemn language of theophany; cf., e.g., Ps 50:3; 96:13.

---

| | |
|---|---|
| **4:14** Jos 3:7. | **5:6** Nm 14:33–34; Heb |
| **4:19** Ex 12:2–3. | 3:11, 17. |
| **4:23** Ex 14:21. | **5:7** Gn 17:8–14. |
| **4:24** Ex 9:3; 14:31; 16:3. | **5:9** Jos 4:19; Eph |
| **5:2** Gn 17; 34; Ex | 2:11–22. |
| 4:24–26. | **5:10** Ex 12:6; Nm 9:3–5. |
| **5:4** Nm 14:29; 26:64–65; | **5:12** Ex 16:35. |
| 1 Cor 10:5. | **5:13** Ex 23:20. |

army of the LORD: now I have come." Then Joshua fell down to the ground in worship, and said to him, "What has my lord to say to his servant?" 15 The commander of the army of the LORD replied to Joshua, "Remove your sandals from your feet, for the place on which you are standing is holy."* And Joshua did so.

6 1 Now Jericho was in a state of siege because of the presence of the Israelites. No one left or entered. 2 And to Joshua the LORD said: I have delivered Jericho, its king, and its warriors into your power. 3* Have all the soldiers circle the city, marching once around it. Do this for six days, 4 with seven priests carrying ram's horns ahead of the ark. On the seventh day march around the city seven times, and have the priests blow the horns. 5 When they give a long blast on the ram's horns and you hear the sound of the horn, all the people shall shout aloud. The wall of the city will collapse, and the people shall attack straight ahead.

6 Summoning the priests, Joshua, son of Nun, said to them, "Take up the ark of the covenant with seven of the priests carrying ram's horns in front of the ark of the LORD." 7 And he ordered the people, "Proceed and surround the city, with the picked troops marching ahead of the ark of the LORD." 8 When Joshua spoke to the people, the seven priests who carried the ram's horns before the LORD marched and blew their horns, and the ark of the covenant of the LORD followed them. 9 In front of the priests with the horns marched the picked troops; the rear guard followed the ark, and the blowing of horns was kept up continually as they marched. 10 But Joshua had commanded the people, "Do not shout or make any noise or outcry until I tell you, 'Shout!' Then you must shout." 11 So he had the ark of the LORD circle the city, going once around it, after which they returned to camp for the night.

12 Early the next morning, Joshua had the priests take up the ark of the LORD. 13 The seven priests bearing the ram's horns marched in front of the ark of the LORD, blowing their horns. Ahead of these marched the picked troops, while the rear guard followed the ark of the LORD, and the blowing of horns was kept up continually. 14 On this second day they again marched around the city once before returning to camp; and for six days in all they did the same.

15 On the seventh day, beginning at daybreak, they marched around the city seven times in the same manner; on that day only did they march around the city seven times. 16 The seventh time around, the priests blew the horns and Joshua said to the people, "Now shout, for the LORD has given you the city. 17* The city and everything in it is under the ban. Only Rahab the prostitute and all who are in the house with her are to live, because she hid the messengers we sent. 18* But be careful not to covet or take anything that is under the ban;† otherwise you will bring upon the camp of Israel this ban and the misery of it. 19 All silver and gold, and the articles of bronze or iron, are holy to the LORD. They shall be put in the treasury of the LORD."

**The Fall of Jericho.** 20 As the horns blew, the people began to shout. When they heard the sound of the horn, they raised a tremendous shout. The wall collapsed,† and the people attacked the city straight ahead and took it.* 21 They observed the ban by putting to the sword all living creatures* in the city: men and women, young and old, as well as oxen, sheep and donkeys.

22* To the two men who had spied out the land, Joshua said, "Go into the prostitute's house and bring out the woman with all her family, as you swore to her you would do." 23 The spies entered and brought out Rahab, with her father, mother, brothers, and all her family; her entire family they led forth and placed outside the camp of Israel. 24 The city itself they burned with all that was in it;* but the silver, gold, and articles of bronze and iron they placed in the treasury of the house

† **6:18** *Under the ban*: doomed to destruction; see notes on Lv 27:28; Nm 18:14; 21:3.
**6:20** The blowing of the horns and the shouting, features of the ritual procession with the ark of the covenant (cf. 1 Chr 15:28; 2 Chr 5:11–14), are the people's counterpart of the Lord's theophany; cf. note on Jgs 5:4–5; and Jgs 7:15–22; 2 Chr 13:15. The Lord gives the victory; this is the theological point of the story.

**5:15** Ex 3:5; Acts 7:33. / **6:3–5** Nm 10:2–9; 2 Sm 6:15–16. / **6:17** Jos 2:4; Dt 20:17; Heb 11:31. / **6:18** Jos 7:12, 25; Dt 13:18. / **6:20** 2 Mc 12:15; Heb 11:30. / **6:21** Gn 15:16; Dt 7:2. / **6:22–23** Jos 2:13–14. / **6:24** Jos 8:2.

of the LORD. 25† Because Rahab the prostitute had hidden the messengers whom Joshua had sent to reconnoiter Jericho, Joshua let her live, along with her father's house and all her family, who dwell in the midst of Israel to this day.

26* On that occasion Joshua imposed the oath: Cursed before the LORD be the man who attempts to rebuild this city, Jericho. At the cost of his firstborn will he lay its foundation, and at the cost of his youngest son will he set up its gates.†

27 Thus the LORD was with Joshua so that his fame spread throughout the land.*

**7 Defeat at Ai.** 1 But the Israelites acted treacherously with regard to the ban; Achan, son of Carmi, son of Zabdi, son of Zerah of the tribe of Judah, took goods that were under the ban,* and the anger of the LORD flared up against the Israelites.

2* Joshua next sent men from Jericho to Ai, which is near Beth-aven and east of Bethel, with the order, "Go up and reconnoiter the land." When they had explored Ai, 3 they returned to Joshua and advised, "Do not send all the people up; if only about two or three thousand go up, they can attack and overcome Ai. You need not tire all the people: the enemy there are few." 4 About three thousand of the people made the attack, but they fled before the army at Ai, 5 who killed some thirty-six of them. They pursued them from the city gate to the Shebarim, and defeated them on the descent, so that the confidence of the people melted away like water.

6 Joshua, together with the elders of Israel, tore their garments and fell face down before the ark of the LORD until evening; and they threw dust on their heads. 7 "Alas, Lord GOD," Joshua prayed, "why did you ever allow this people to cross over the Jordan, delivering us into the power of the Amorites, that they might destroy us? Would that we had been content to dwell on the other side of the Jordan. 8 Please, Lord, what can I say, now that Israel has turned its back to its enemies? 9 When the Canaanites and the other inhabitants of the land hear of it, they will close in around us and efface our name from the earth. What will you do for your great name?"*

10 The LORD replied to Joshua: Stand up. Why are you lying there? 11* Israel has sinned: they have transgressed the covenant† which I enjoined on them. They have taken goods subject to the ban. They have stolen and lied, placing the goods in their baggage. 12 If the Israelites cannot stand up to their enemies, but must turn their back to them, it is because they are under the ban. I will not continue to be with you unless you remove that which is banned from among you. 13 Get up, sanctify the people.* Tell them, "Sanctify yourselves before tomorrow, for thus says the LORD, the God of Israel: That which is banned is in your midst, Israel. You cannot stand up to your enemies until you remove it from among you. 14 In the morning you must come forward by tribes. The tribe which the LORD designates shall come forward by clans; the clan which the LORD designates shall come forward by families; the family which the LORD designates shall come forward one by one. 15 Whoever is designated as having incurred the ban shall be destroyed by fire, with all that is his, because he has trangressed the covenant of the LORD and has committed a shameful crime in Israel."*

**Achan's Guilt and Punishment.** 16 Early the next morning Joshua had Israel come forward by tribes, and the tribe of Judah was designated.† 17 Then he had the clans of Judah come forward, and the clan of Zerah was designated. He had the clan of Zerah* come forward by families, and Zabdi was designated. 18 Finally he had that family come forward one by one, and Achan, son of Carmi, son of Zabdi, son of Zerah of the tribe of Judah,

---

**6:25** The genealogy of Jesus in Matthew (1:2–16) presents Rahab the prostitute as the wife of Salmon (1:5) and so the ancestor of David (Ru 4:18–22) and of Jesus.

**6:26** *At the cost of his firstborn…its gates:* this curse was fulfilled when Hiel rebuilt Jericho as a fortified city during the reign of Ahab, king of Israel; cf. 1 Kgs 16:34.

**7:11** *Transgressed the covenant:* the Hebrew word translated "transgressed" appears frequently in the first five chapters where it is used to describe how Israel "crossed" the Jordan River. There is a wordplay here to emphasize Israel's responsibility to follow God to the promised land and so to obey and not transgress the

divine command.

**7:16–18** *Was designated:* probably by means of the Urim and Thummim; cf. 1 Sm 14:38–42. See note on Ex 28:30.

---

**6:26** Jos 9:23; 1 Kgs 16:34.
**6:27** Jos 1:5.
**7:1** Jos 6:18; 22:20; 1 Chr 2:7.
**7:2** Nm 13:17–20.
**7:9** Nm 14:13–19.
**7:11–12** Jos 6:17–19.
**7:13** Jos 3:5; Lv 20:7; 1 Sm 16:5.
**7:15** Dt 13:15–16.
**7:17** Nm 26:20.

was designated. ¹⁹Joshua said to Achan, "My son, give glory to the LORD, the God of Israel, and praise him by telling me what you have done; do not hide it from me." ²⁰Achan answered Joshua, "I have indeed sinned against the LORD, the God of Israel. This is what I have done: ²¹Among the spoils, I saw a beautiful Babylonian mantle, two hundred shekels of silver, and a bar of gold fifty shekels in weight; I coveted them and I took them. They are now hidden in the ground inside my tent, with the silver underneath." ²²Joshua sent messengers and they ran to the tent and there they were, hidden in the tent, with the silver underneath. ²³They took them from the tent, brought them to Joshua and all the Israelites, and spread them out before the LORD.

²⁴Then Joshua and all Israel took Achan, son of Zerah, with the silver, the mantle, and the bar of gold, and with his sons and daughters, his ox, his donkey and his sheep, his tent, and all his possessions, and led them off to the Valley of Achor. ²⁵Joshua said, "What misery have you caused us? May the LORD bring misery upon you today!"* And all Israel stoned him to death. They burnt them with fire and they stoned them. ²⁶Over Achan they piled a great heap of stones, which remains to the present day.* Then the LORD turned from his anger. That is why the place is called the Valley of Achor† to this day.

**8** **Capture of Ai.** ¹*The LORD then said to Joshua: Do not be afraid or dismayed. Take all the army with you and prepare to attack Ai.* I have delivered the king of Ai into your power, with his people, city, and land. ²Do to Ai and its king what you did to Jericho and its king—except that you may take its spoil and livestock as plunder.* Set an ambush behind the city. ³So Joshua and all the soldiers prepared to attack Ai. Picking out thirty thousand warriors,† Joshua sent them off by night ⁴with these orders: "See that you ambush the city from the rear. Do not be very far from the city. All of you must be ready. ⁵The rest of the people and I will come up to the city, and

when they make a sortie against us as they did the last time, we will flee from them. ⁶They will keep coming out after us until we have drawn them away from the city, for they will think, 'They are fleeing from us as they did the last time.' When we flee, ⁷then you rise from ambush and take possession of the city, which the LORD, your God, will deliver into your power. ⁸When you have taken the city, set it on fire in obedience to the LORD's command. These are my orders to you."* ⁹Then Joshua sent them away. They went to the place of ambush, taking up their position to the west of Ai, toward Bethel. Joshua, however, spent that night with the army.

¹⁰Early the next morning Joshua mustered the army and went up to Ai at its head, with the elders of Israel. ¹¹When all the troops he led were drawn up in position before the city, they pitched camp north of Ai, on the other side of the ravine. ¹²He took about five thousand warriors and set them in ambush between Bethel and Ai, west of the city. ¹³Thus the people took up their stations, with the main body north of the city and the ambush west of it, and Joshua waited overnight in the valley. ¹⁴The king of Ai saw this, and he and all his army came out very early in the morning to engage Israel in battle at the place in front of the Arabah, not knowing that there was an ambush behind the city. ¹⁵Joshua and the main body of the Israelites fled toward the wilderness, pretending defeat, ¹⁶until the last of the soldiers in the city had been called out to pursue them. Since they were drawn away from the city, with everyone pursuing Joshua, ¹⁷not a soldier remained in Ai or Bethel. They abandoned the city, leaving it open, as they pursued Israel.

¹⁸Then the LORD directed Joshua: Stretch out the javelin in your hand toward Ai, for I will deliver it into your power. Joshua stretched out the javelin in his hand toward the city, ¹⁹and as soon as he did so, the men in ambush rose from their post, rushed in, captured the city, and immediately set it on fire. ²⁰By the time the army of Ai looked back, the smoke from

---

† **7:26** *Achor*: "misery," or "disaster." The reference is to the saying of Joshua in v. 25, with an allusion also to the similar-sounding name of Achan.

**8:3** *Thirty thousand warriors*: this figure of the Hebrew text, which seems extremely high, may be due to a copyist's error; some manuscripts of the Septuagint have "three thousand," which is the number of the whole army in the first, unsuccessful attack (7:4); the variant reading in v. 12 mentions "five thou-

sand." More likely, the word for "thousand" here and in other military contexts may designate a squad or fighting unit, itself composed of significantly fewer warriors.

**7:25** Jos 6:18; 22:20; Dt 13:15–16; 1 Chr 2:7.
**7:26** Jos 8:29; Dt 13:18.
**8:1–26** Jgs 20:20–38.
**8:1** Jos 2:24; Dt 1:21.
**8:2** Jos 6:21, 24; Dt 20:14.
**8:8** Jos 6:24.

JOS

the city was going up to the heavens. Escape in any direction was impossible, because the Israelites retreating toward the wilderness now turned on their pursuers; 21 for when Joshua and the main body of Israelites saw that the city had been taken by ambush and was going up in smoke, they struck back at the forces of Ai. 22 Since those in the city came out to intercept them, Ai's army was hemmed in by Israelites on both sides, who cut them down without any fugitives or survivors* 23 except the king, whom they took alive and brought to Joshua.

24 When Israel finished killing all the inhabitants of Ai in the open, who had pursued them into the wilderness, and all of them to the last man fell by the sword, then all Israel returned and put to the sword those inside the city. 25 There fell that day a total of twelve thousand men and women, the entire population of Ai. 26* Joshua kept the javelin in his hand stretched out until he had carried out the ban on all the inhabitants of Ai. 27 However, the Israelites took for themselves as plunder the livestock and the spoil of that city, according to the command of the LORD issued to Joshua. 28 Then Joshua destroyed Ai by fire, reducing it to an everlasting mound of ruins, as it remains today.* 29 He had the king of Ai hanged on a tree until evening;* then at sunset Joshua ordered the body removed from the tree and cast at the entrance of the city gate, where a great heap of stones was piled up over it, which remains to the present day.

**Altar on Mount Ebal.** 30†* Later, on Mount Ebal, Joshua built to the LORD, the God of Israel, an altar 31 of unhewn stones on which no iron tool had been used,* just as Moses, the servant of the LORD, had commanded the Israelites, as recorded in the book of the law. On this altar they sacrificed burnt offerings to the LORD and made communion sacrifices. 32 There, in the presence of the Israelites, Joshua inscribed upon the stones a copy of the law written by Moses. 33 And all Israel, resident

alien and native alike, with their elders, officers, and judges, stood on either side of the ark facing the levitical priests who were carrying the ark of the covenant of the LORD.* Half of them were facing Mount Gerizim and half Mount Ebal, just as Moses, the servant of the LORD, had first commanded for the blessing of the people of Israel. 34* Then were read aloud all the words of the law, the blessings and the curses, exactly as written in the book of the law. 35* Every single word that Moses had commanded, Joshua read aloud to the entire assembly, including the women and children, and the resident aliens among them.

# 9 Confederacy Against Israel. 1 When the news reached all the kings west of the Jordan, in the mountain regions and in the Shephelah, and all along the coast of the Great Sea as far as the Lebanon: Hittites, Amorites, Canaanites, Perizzites, Hivites, and Jebusites,* 2 they gathered together to launch a common attack against Joshua and Israel.

**The Gibeonite Deception.** 3 On hearing what Joshua had done to Jericho and Ai, the inhabitants of Gibeon* 4 formed their own scheme. They chose provisions for a journey, making use of old sacks for their donkeys, and old wineskins, torn and mended. 5 They wore old, patched sandals and shabby garments; and all the bread they took was dry and crumbly. 6 Thus they journeyed to Joshua in the camp at Gilgal, where they said to him and to the Israelites, "We have come from a far-off land; now, make a covenant with us."* 7 But the Israelites replied to the Hivites,† "You may be living in land that is ours. How, then, can we make a covenant with you?" 8 But they answered Joshua, "We are your servants." Then Joshua asked them, "Who are you? Where do you come from?" 9 They answered him, "Your servants have come from a far-off land, because of the fame of the LORD, your God. For we have heard reports of all that he did in Egypt* 10 and all that he did to the two kings of the Amorites

---

**8:30–35** These ceremonies were prescribed in Dt 11:29 and 27:2–26.

**9:7** *The Hivites:* apparently the Gibeonites belonged to this larger ethnic group (cf. also 11:19), although in 2 Sm 21:2 they are classed as Amorites; both groups are listed among the seven nations of Canaan whom, according to Dt 7:1–2, the Israelites were to dispossess.

**8:22** Dt 7:2.
**8:26** Ex 17:11–13.
**8:28** Dt 13:16.
**8:29** Jos 10:26–27; Dt 21:22–23; Jn 19:31.
**8:30–35** Dt 27:1–8, 12–13.
**8:31** Ex 20:24–25.
**8:33** Jos 3:3; Dt 11:27; 31:9, 12.
**8:34** Dt 28:2–68; 30:19; 31:11; Neh 8:2–3.
**8:35** Dt 31:12.
**9:1** Jos 3:10; 5:1; Ex 3:8, 17; 23:23; Dt 1:7.
**9:3** Jos 6:21, 24.
**9:6** Ex 23:32; Dt 7:2.
**9:9–10** Jos 2:10–11.

beyond the Jordan,* Sihon, king of Heshbon, and Og, king of Bashan, who lived in Ashtaroth. [11] So our elders and all the inhabitants of our land said to us, 'Take along provisions for the journey and go to meet them. Say to them: "We are your servants; now make a covenant with us."' [12] This bread of ours was still warm when we brought it from home as provisions the day we left to come to you, but now it is dry and crumbly. [13] Here are our wineskins, which were new when we filled them, but now they are torn. Look at our garments and sandals; they are worn out from the very long journey." [14] Then the Israelite leaders partook of their provisions, without inquiring of the LORD.* [15] So Joshua made peace with them and made a covenant to let them live,* which the leaders of the community sealed with an oath.

**Gibeonites Made Vassals.** [16] Three days after the covenant was made, the Israelites heard that these people were from nearby, and would be living in Israel. [17] The third day on the road, the Israelites came to their cities of Gibeon, Chephirah, Beeroth, and Kiriathjearim, [18] but did not attack them, because the leaders of the community had sworn to them by the LORD, the God of Israel. When the entire community grumbled against the leaders, [19] these all remonstrated with the community, "We have sworn to them by the LORD, the God of Israel, and so we cannot harm them. [20] Let us therefore let them live, and so deal with them that no wrath fall upon us because of the oath we have sworn to them."* [21] Thus the leaders said to them, "Let them live, and become hewers of wood and drawers of water† for the entire community." So the community did as the leaders advised them.*

[22] Joshua summoned the Gibeonites and said to them, "Why did you deceive us and say, 'We live far off from you'?—You live among us! [23] Now are you accursed: every one of you shall always be a slave, hewers of wood and drawers of water, for the house of my God." [24] They answered Joshua, "Your servants were fully informed of how the LORD, your God,

commanded Moses his servant that you be given the entire land and that all its inhabitants be destroyed before you. Since, therefore, at your advance, we were in great fear for our lives, we acted as we did.* [25] And now that we are in your power, do with us what is good and right in your eyes." [26] † Joshua did what he had decided: while he saved them from being killed by the Israelites, [27] on that day he made them, as they still are, hewers of wood and drawers of water for the community and for the altar of the LORD, in the place the LORD would choose.

# 10

**The Siege of Gibeon.** [1] Now when Adonizedek, king of Jerusalem, heard that Joshua had captured Ai and put it under the ban, and had done to that city and its king as he had done to Jericho and its king,* and that the inhabitants of Gibeon had made their peace with Israel, remaining among them, [2] there was great fear abroad, because Gibeon was a great city, like one of the royal cities, greater even than Ai, and all its men were warriors. [3] So Adonizedek, king of Jerusalem, sent to Hoham, king of Hebron, Piram, king of Jarmuth, Japhia, king of Lachish, and Debir, king of Eglon, with this message: [4] "Come and help me attack Gibeon, for it has made peace with Joshua and the Israelites."* [5] The five Amorite kings, of Jerusalem, Hebron, Jarmuth, Lachish, and Eglon, † gathered with all their forces, and marched against Gibeon to make war on it. [6] Thereupon, the Gibeonites sent an appeal to Joshua in his camp at Gilgal: "Do not abandon your servants. Come up here quickly and save us. Help us, because all the Amorite kings of the mountain country have joined together against us."*

**Joshua's Victory.** [7] So Joshua marched up from Gilgal with all his army and all his warriors. [8] The LORD said to Joshua: Do not fear them, for I have delivered them into your power. Not one of them will be able to withstand you. [9] After an all-night march from Gilgal, Joshua made a surprise attack upon them, [10] and the LORD threw them into disorder before Israel.

---

**9:21** *Hewers of wood and drawers of water:* proverbial terms for those who do menial work; cf. Dt 29:10–11.
**9:26–27** Later on, Saul violated the immunity of the Gibeonites, but David vindicated it; cf. 2 Sm 21:1–9.
**10:5** *Hebron…Eglon:* these four cities were to the south and southwest of Jerusalem.

**9:10** Nm 21:25, 33–35; Dt 1:4.
**9:14** Nm 27:21.
**9:15** Jos 11:19; 2 Sm 21:2.
**9:20** Jos 22:20.
**9:21** Dt 29:11.
**9:24** Ex 23:27–28; Dt 7:1–2.
**10:1** Jgs 6:21, 24; 8:26–29.
**10:4** Jos 9:15.
**10:6** Jos 9:6.

The Israelites inflicted a great slaughter on them at Gibeon and pursued them down the Beth-horon slope, attacking them as far as Azekah and Makkedah.

¹¹While they fled before Israel along the descent of Beth-horon, the LORD hurled great stones from the heavens† above them all the way to Azekah, killing many. * More died from these hailstones than the Israelites killed with the sword. ¹²It was then, when the LORD delivered up the Amorites to the Israelites, that Joshua prayed to the LORD, and said in the presence of Israel:

Sun, stand still at Gibeon,
 Moon, in the valley of Aijalon!
¹³ The sun stood still,
 the moon stayed,
 while the nation took vengeance on
  its foes. *

This is recorded† in the Book of Jashar. The sun halted halfway across the heavens; not for an entire day did it press on. ¹⁴Never before or since was there a day like this, when the LORD obeyed the voice of a man; for the LORD fought for Israel. ¹⁵Then Joshua and all Israel returned to the camp at Gilgal.

**Execution of Amorite Kings.** ¹⁶The five kings who had fled hid in the cave at Makkedah. ¹⁷When Joshua was told, "The five kings have been found, hiding in the cave at Makkedah," ¹⁸he said, "Roll large stones to the mouth of the cave and post guards over it. ¹⁹But do not remain there yourselves. Pursue your enemies, and harry them in the rear. Do not allow them to reach their cities, for the LORD, your God, has delivered them into your power."

²⁰Once Joshua and the Israelites had finally inflicted the last blows in this very great slaughter, and the survivors had escaped from them into the fortified cities, ²¹all the army returned to Joshua and the camp at Makkedah in victory; no one uttered a sound against the Israelites. ²²Then Joshua said, "Open the mouth of the cave and bring me those five kings from the cave." ²³They did so; they brought out to him from the cave the five kings, of Jerusalem, Hebron, Jarmuth, Lachish, and Eglon. ²⁴When they brought the five kings out to Joshua, he summoned all the army of Israel and said to the commanders of the soldiers who had marched with him, "Come forward and put your feet on the necks of these kings." They came forward and put their feet upon their necks. ²⁵ * Then Joshua said to them, "Do not be afraid or dismayed, be firm and steadfast. This is what the LORD will do to all the enemies against whom you fight." ²⁶ * Thereupon Joshua struck and killed the kings, and hanged them on five trees, where they remained hanging until evening. ²⁷At sunset Joshua commanded that they be taken down from the trees and be thrown into the cave where they had hidden; over the mouth of the cave large stones were placed, which remain until this very day.

**Conquest of Southern Canaan.** ²⁸ * Makkedah, too, Joshua captured and put to the sword at that time. He put the city, its king, and every person in it under the ban, leaving no survivors. Thus he did to the king of Makkedah what he had done to the king of Jericho. ²⁹Joshua then passed on with all Israel from Makkedah to Libnah, and attacked it, ³⁰and the LORD delivered it, with its king, into the power of Israel. He put it to the sword with every person there, leaving no survivors. Thus he did to its king what he had done to the king of Jericho. ³¹Joshua next passed on with all Israel from Libnah to Lachish, where they set up a camp during the attack. ³²The LORD delivered Lachish into the power of Israel, so that on the second day Joshua captured it and put it to the sword with every person in it, just as he had done to Libnah. ³³At that time Horam, king of Gezer, came up to help Lachish, but Joshua defeated him and his people, leaving him no survivors. ³⁴From Lachish, Joshua passed on with all Israel to Eglon; encamping

† **10:11** *Great stones from the heavens*: the hailstones mentioned in the next sentence.
**10:13** *This is recorded*: the reference is to the preceding poetic passage. Evidently the *Book of Jashar*, like the *Book of the Wars of the Lord* (Nm 21:14), recounted in epic style the exploits of Israel's early heroes. *The sun halted*: lit., "the sun stood"; this obscure passage may suppose a longer than natural day caused when the sun stopped moving across the sky, or it may refer to

the sun stopping its light-giving function, perhaps through an eclipse. In any case it was seen as a sign that God fought Israel's battle (v. 42; cf. Ex 14:14).

* **10:11** Jb 38:22–23. **10:26–27** Jos 8:29; Dt
**10:13** Sir 46:4; Is 28:21. 21:22–23.
**10:25** Jos 1:9. **10:28** Jos 6:21.

near it, they attacked it [35] and captured it the same day, putting it to the sword. On that day he put under the ban every person in it, just as he had done at Lachish. [36] From Eglon, Joshua went up with all Israel to Hebron, which they attacked [37] and captured. They put it to the sword with its king, all its cities, and every person there, leaving no survivors, just as Joshua had done to Eglon. He put it under the ban and every person in it. [38] Then Joshua and all Israel turned back to Debir and attacked it, [39] capturing it with its king and all its cities. They put them to the sword and put under the ban every person in it, leaving no survivors. Thus he did to Debir and its king what he had done to Hebron, as well as to Libnah and its king.

[40]* Joshua conquered the entire land; the mountain regions, the Negeb, the Shephelah, and the mountain slopes, with all their kings. He left no survivors, but put under the ban every living being, just as the LORD, the God of Israel, had commanded. [41] Joshua conquered them from Kadesh-barnea to Gaza, and all the land of Goshen† to Gibeon. [42] All these kings and their lands Joshua captured all at once, for the LORD, the God of Israel, fought for Israel. [43] Thereupon Joshua with all Israel returned to the camp at Gilgal.

## 11 Northern Confederacy.

[1] When Jabin, king of Hazor,† learned of this, he sent a message to Jobab, king of Madon, to the king of Shimron, to the king of Achshaph, [2] and to the northern kings in the mountain regions and in the Arabah near Chinneroth, in the Shephelah, and in Naphath-dor to the west.* [3] These were Canaanites to the east and west, Amorites, Hittites, Perizzites, and Jebusites in the mountain regions, and Hivites at the foot of Hermon in the land of Mizpah.* [4] They came out with all their troops, an army numerous as the sands on the seashore, and with a multitude of horses and chariots.* [5] All these kings made a pact and together they marched to the waters of Merom,† where they encamped to fight against Israel.

[6] The LORD said to Joshua, "Do not fear them, for by this time tomorrow I will present them slain to Israel. You must hamstring their horses and burn their chariots." [7] Joshua with his whole army came upon them suddenly at the waters of Merom and fell upon them. [8] The LORD delivered them into the power of the Israelites, who defeated them and pursued them to Greater Sidon, to Misrephoth-maim,* and eastward to the valley of Mizpeh. They struck them all down, leaving no survivors. [9] Joshua did to them as the LORD had commanded: he hamstrung their horses and burned their chariots.

### Conquest of Northern Canaan.

[10] At that time Joshua, turning back, captured Hazor and struck down its king with the sword; for Hazor formerly was the chief of all those kingdoms. [11] He also struck down with the sword every person there, carrying out the ban, till none was left alive. Hazor itself he burned. [12] All the cities of those kings, and the kings themselves, Joshua captured and put to the sword, carrying out the ban on them, as Moses, the servant of the LORD, had commanded.* [13] However, Israel did not destroy by fire any of the cities built on their mounds, except Hazor, which Joshua burned. [14] All the spoil and livestock of these cities the Israelites took as plunder; but the people they put to the sword, until they had destroyed the last of them, leaving none alive. [15] As the LORD had commanded his servant Moses, so Moses commanded Joshua, and Joshua acted accordingly.* He left nothing undone that the LORD had commanded Moses should be done.

### Survey of the Conquest.

[16] So Joshua took all this land: the mountain regions, the entire Negeb, all the land of Goshen, the Shephelah, the Arabah, as well as the mountain regions and Shephelah of Israel,* [17] from Mount Halak that rises toward Seir* as far as Baal-gad in the Lebanon valley at the foot of Mount Hermon. All their kings he captured and put to death. [18] Joshua waged war against all these

---

† **10:41** *Goshen:* a town and its surrounding district at the southern end of the Judean mountains (cf. 11:16; 15:51); not to be confused with the land of Goshen in northeastern Egypt (Gn 45:10).

**11:1–3** *Hazor, Madon, Shimron,* and *Chinneroth:* cities and their surrounding districts in eastern Galilee. *Achshaph* and *Naphath-dor:* southwest of Galilee. *The mountain regions:* in central and northern Galilee.

**11:5** *The waters of Merom:* of uncertain identification, per-

haps Tel Qarnei Hittin, about seven and a half kilometers west of modern Tiberias.

---

*
| | |
|---|---|
| **10:40** Dt 20:16–17. | **11:12** Dt 7:2; 20:16–17. |
| **11:2** Jos 12:3. | **11:15** Dt 7:2; 31:7–8. |
| **11:3** Jos 3:10. | **11:16** Jos 10:41; 12:8. |
| **11:4** Ex 15:1, 21. | **11:17** Jos 12:7; Dt 7:24. |
| **11:8** Jos 13:6. | |

kings for a long time. ¹⁹ With the exception of the Hivites who lived in Gibeon, no city made peace with the Israelites; all were taken in battle.* ²⁰ For it was the LORD's doing to make their hearts obstinate to meet Israel in battle, that they might be put under the ban without mercy, and be destroyed as the LORD had commanded Moses.*

²¹ † At that time Joshua penetrated the mountain regions and exterminated the Anakim in Hebron,* Debir, Anab, the entire mountain region of Judah, and the entire mountain region of Israel. Joshua put them and their cities under the ban, ²² so that no Anakim were left in the land of the Israelites. However, some survived in Gaza, in Gath, and in Ashdod. ²³ * Thus Joshua took the whole land, just as the LORD had said to Moses. Joshua gave it to Israel as their heritage, apportioning it among the tribes. And the land had rest from war. †

# 12 † Lists of Conquered Kings.

¹ These are the kings of the land whom the Israelites conquered and whose lands they occupied, east of the Jordan, from the River Arnon to Mount Hermon, including all the eastern section of the Arabah: ² * First, Sihon, king of the Amorites, who lived in Heshbon. His domain extended from Aroer, which is on the bank of the Wadi Arnon, to include the wadi itself, and the land northward through half of Gilead to the Wadi Jabbok at the border with the Ammonites, ³ as well as the Arabah from the eastern side of the Sea of Chinnereth, as far south as the eastern side of the Salt Sea of the Arabah in the direction of Beth-jeshimoth,* southward under the slopes of Pisgah. ⁴ Secondly, the border of Og, king of Bashan, a survivor of the Rephaim, who lived at Ashtaroth and Edrei.* ⁵ He ruled over Mount Hermon, Salecah, and all Bashan as far as the boundary of the Geshurites and Maacathites, and over half of Gilead as far as the territory of Sihon,

king of Heshbon. ⁶ It was Moses, the servant of the LORD, and the Israelites who conquered them; Moses, the servant of the LORD, gave possession of their land to the Reubenites, the Gadites, and the half-tribe of Manasseh.*

⁷ This is a list of the kings of the land whom Joshua and the Israelites conquered west of the Jordan, from Baal-gad in the Lebanon valley to Mount Halak which rises toward Seir; Joshua apportioned their land and gave possession of it to the tribes of Israel; ⁸ it included the mountain regions and Shephelah, the Arabah, the slopes, the wilderness, and the Negeb, belonging to the Hittites, Amorites, Canaanites, Perizzites, Hivites, and Jebusites: ⁹ The king of Jericho, one;* the king of Ai, which is near Bethel, one; ¹⁰ the king of Jerusalem, one; the king of Hebron, one; ¹¹ the king of Jarmuth, one; the king of Lachish, one;* ¹² the king of Eglon, one; the king of Gezer, one;* ¹³ the king of Debir, one; the king of Geder, one;* ¹⁴ the king of Hormah, one; the king of Arad, one; ¹⁵ the king of Libnah, one; the king of Adullam, one;* ¹⁶ the king of Makkedah, one; the king of Bethel, one;* ¹⁷ the king of Tappuah, one; the king of Hepher, one;* ¹⁸ the king of Aphek, one; the king of Lasharon, one;* ¹⁹ the king of Madon, one; the king of Hazor, one;* ²⁰ the king of Shimron, one; the king of Achshaph, one;* ²¹ the king of Taanach, one; the king of Megiddo, one;* ²² the king of Kedesh, one; the king of Jokneam, at Carmel, one;* ²³ the king of Dor, in Naphath-dor, one; the king of Goyim at Gilgal, one;* ²⁴ and the king of Tirzah, one—thirty-one kings in all.

## II. DIVISION OF THE LAND

# 13 Division of Land Commanded.

¹ When Joshua was old and advanced in years, the LORD said to him:* Though now you are old and advanced in years, a very large part of the land still remains to be possessed. ² This

† **11:21–23** Most of the land assigned to the tribe of Judah was not conquered by it until the early period of the Judges. See note on Jgs 1:1–36.
**11:23** *The land had rest from war*: later passages (15:13–17; 17:12–13) show individual tribes still fighting against the remaining Canaanites. This verse forms the conclusion to the first part of the book.
**12:1–24** This chapter, inserted between the two principal parts of the book (chaps. 1–11 and 13–21), resembles the lists of conquered cities which are inscribed on monuments of Egyptian and Assyrian rulers. Perhaps this list was copied here from some such public Israelite record.

**11:19** Jos 9:3, 7, 15.
**11:20** Dt 2:30; 20:16–17.
**11:21** Jos 15:13–14; Nm 13:22; Dt 1:28; 9:1–3.
**11:23** Jos 14:1–19:51; Nm 34:2–12; Heb 4:8–10.
**12:2–5** Nm 21:21–35; Dt 1:4; 2:24–37.
**12:3** Jos 13:20.
**12:4** Nm 34:11–12.
**12:6** Nm 32:33; Dt 3:12–13.
**12:9** Jos 6:2; 8:23.
**12:10–11** Jos 10:23.
**12:12** Jos 10:23, 33.
**12:13** Jos 10:38–39; 15:36.
**12:15** Jos 10:29–30; 15:35.
**12:16** Jos 8:17; 10:28.
**12:17** Jos 15:34.
**12:18** Jos 15:53.
**12:19** Jos 11:1, 10.
**12:20** Jos 11:1.
**12:21** Jos 17:11.
**12:22** Jos 19:37.
**12:23** Jos 11:2.
**13:1** Jos 23:1.

is the remaining land: all Geshur† and all the districts of the Philistines ³(from the stream adjoining Egypt to the boundary of Ekron in the north is reckoned Canaanite territory, though held by the five lords of the Philistines in Gaza, Ashdod, Ashkelon, Gath, and Ekron); ⁴also where the Avvim are in the south;* all the land of the Canaanites from Mearah of the Sidonians to Aphek, and the boundaries of the Amorites;* ⁵and the Gebalite territory; and all the Lebanon on the east, from Baal-gad at the foot of Mount Hermon to Lebo-hamath. ⁶All the inhabitants of the mountain regions between Lebanon and Misrephoth-maim, all Sidonians, I will drive out before the Israelites;* at least include these areas in the division of the Israelite heritage, just as I have commanded you. ⁷Now, therefore, apportion among the nine tribes and the half-tribe of Manasseh the land which is to be their heritage.

**The Eastern Tribes.** ⁸* Now the other half of the tribe of Manasseh, as well as the Reubenites and Gadites, had taken as their heritage what Moses, the servant of the LORD, had given them east of the Jordan: ⁹from Aroer on the bank of the Wadi Arnon and the city in the wadi itself, through the tableland of Medeba and Dibon, ¹⁰with the rest of the cities of Sihon, king of the Amorites, who reigned in Heshbon, to the boundary of the Ammonites; ¹¹also Gilead and the territory of the Geshurites and Maacathites, all Mount Hermon, and all Bashan as far as Salecah, ¹²the entire kingdom in Bashan of Og, who was king at Ashtaroth and Edrei (he was a holdover from the remnant of the Rephaim). These Moses defeated and dispossessed. ¹³But the Israelites did not dispossess the Geshurites and Maacathites, so that Geshur and Maacath dwell in the midst of Israel to this day. ¹⁴* However, Moses assigned no heritage to the tribe of Levi; the LORD, the God of Israel, is their heritage, as the LORD had promised them.

**Reuben.** ¹⁵* This is what Moses gave to the tribe of the Reubenites by their clans:* ¹⁶Their territory reached from Aroer, on the bank

of the Wadi Arnon, and the city in the wadi itself, through the tableland about Medeba, ¹⁷to include Heshbon and all its towns on the tableland, Dibon, Bamoth-baal, Beth-baal-meon, ¹⁸Jahaz, Kedemoth, Mephaath, ¹⁹Kiriathaim, Sibmah, Zereth-shahar on the knoll within the valley, ²⁰Beth-peor, the slopes of Pisgah, Beth-jeshimoth, ²¹and the other cities of the tableland and of the whole kingdom of Sihon. This Amorite king, who reigned in Heshbon, Moses had defeated, with the princes of Midian, vassals of Sihon who were settled in the land: Evi, Rekem, Zur, Hur, and Reba;* ²²Balaam, son of Beor, the diviner, the Israelites killed with the sword, together with those they struck down.* ²³The boundary of the Reubenites was the Jordan. These cities and their villages were the heritage of the Reubenites by their clans.

**Gad.** ²⁴* This is what Moses gave to the tribe of the Gadites by their clans: ²⁵Their territory included Jazer, all the cities of Gilead, and half the land of the Ammonites as far as Aroer, toward Rabbah ²⁶(that is, from Heshbon to Ramath-mizpeh and Betonim, and from Mahanaim to the boundary of Lo-debar); ²⁷and in the Jordan valley: Beth-haram, Beth-nimrah, Succoth, Zaphon, the other part of the kingdom of Sihon, king of Heshbon, with the bank of the Jordan to the southeastern tip of the Sea of Chinnereth. ²⁸These cities and their villages were the heritage of the clans of the Gadites.

**Manasseh.** ²⁹* This is what Moses gave to the half-tribe of Manasseh; the half-tribe of the Manassites, by their clans, had ³⁰territory including Mahanaim, all of Bashan, the entire kingdom of Og, king of Bashan, and all the villages of Jair, which are sixty cities in Bashan. ³¹Half of Gilead, with Ashtaroth and Edrei, royal cities of Og in Bashan, fell to the descendants of Machir, son of Manasseh, to half the Machirites, by their clans.

³²These are the heritages which Moses gave when he was in the plains of Moab, beyond the Jordan east of Jericho. ³³But Moses gave no heritage to the tribe of Levi: the LORD, the God

---

**13:2** *Geshur*: not to be confused with the large Aramean district of the same name in Bashan (vv. 11–13; Dt 3:14); here it is a region to the south of the Philistine country, since vv. 2–5 list the unconquered lands along the coast from south to north; cf. also 1 Sm 27:8.

**13:4** Jgs 3:3.
**13:4** Jos 1:4.
**13:6** Jos 11:8.
**13:8** Jos 12:6; Nm 32:33.
**13:14** Jos 14:3–4; Nm 18:20–24.
**13:15–31** Dt 3:12–17.
**13:15–23** Nm 21:25–31; 32:37–38.
**13:21** Nm 21:24; 31:8; Dt 3:10.
**13:22** Nm 31:8.
**13:24–28** Nm 32:34–36.
**13:29–31** Nm 32:39–42.

of Israel, is their heritage, as he had promised them.*

**14** **The Western Tribes.** [1] These are the portions which the Israelites received as heritage in the land of Canaan.* Eleazar the priest, Joshua, son of Nun, and the heads of families in the tribes of the Israelites determined [2] their heritage by lot, as the LORD had commanded through Moses concerning the remaining nine and a half tribes.* [3] To two and a half tribes Moses had already given a heritage beyond the Jordan; to the Levites he had given no heritage among them:* [4] the descendants of Joseph formed two tribes, Manasseh and Ephraim. But the Levites were given no share of the land except cities to live in, with their pasture lands for the herds and flocks.*

[5] As the LORD had commanded Moses, so the Israelites did: they apportioned the land.

**Caleb's Portion.** [6]* When the Judahites approached Joshua in Gilgal, the Kenizzite Caleb, son of Jephunneh, said to him: "You know the word the LORD spoke to Moses, the man of God, concerning you and concerning me in Kadesh-barnea. [7]* I was forty years old when Moses, the servant of the LORD, sent me from Kadesh-barnea to reconnoiter the land; and I brought back to him a frank report. [8]* My fellow scouts who went up with me made the people's confidence melt away, but I was completely loyal to the LORD, my God. [9] On that occasion Moses swore this oath, 'The land where you have set foot shall become your heritage and that of your descendants forever, because you have been completely loyal to the LORD, my God.' [10] Now, as he promised, the LORD has preserved me these forty-five years since the LORD spoke thus to Moses while Israel journeyed in the wilderness; and now I am eighty-five years old,* [11] but I am still as strong today as I was the day Moses sent me forth, with no

less vigor whether it be for war or for any other tasks.†* [12] Now give me this mountain region which the LORD promised me that day, as you yourself heard. True, the Anakim are there, with large fortified cities, but if the LORD is with me I shall be able to dispossess them, as the LORD promised."* [13] Joshua blessed Caleb, son of Jephunneh, and gave him Hebron as his heritage.* [14] Therefore Hebron remains the heritage of the Kenizzite Caleb, son of Jephunneh, to the present day, because he was completely loyal to the LORD, the God of Israel. [15] Hebron was formerly called Kiriath-arba, for Arba, the greatest among the Anakim.* And the land had rest from war.

**15** **Boundaries of Judah.** [1] The lot for the tribe of Judah by their clans fell toward the boundary of Edom, the wilderness of Zin in the Negeb, in the extreme south.* [2]* Their southern boundary ran from the end of the Salt Sea,† from the tongue of land that faces the Negeb, [3] and went southward below the pass of Akrabbim, across through Zin, up to a point south of Kadesh-barnea, across to Hezron, and up to Addar; from there, looping around Karka, [4] it crossed to Azmon and then joined the Wadi of Egypt† before coming out at the sea. (This is your southern boundary.) [5] The eastern boundary was the Salt Sea as far as the mouth of the Jordan.

The northern boundary climbed northward from the tongue of the sea, toward the mouth of the Jordan, [6]* up to Beth-hoglah, and ran north of Beth-arabah, up to Eben-Bohan-ben-Reuben. [7] Thence the boundary climbed to Debir, north of the Valley of Achor,* in the direction of the Gilgal that faces the pass of Adummim, on the south side of the wadi; from there it crossed to the waters of En-shemesh and emerged at En-rogel. [8] Climbing again to the Valley of Ben-hinnom† on the southern flank of the Jebusites (that is,

---

† **14:11** War...other tasks: lit., "to go forth and to come in," i.e., to conduct military expeditions and to return after victory; cf. 1 Sm 18:16; 2 Sm 5:2.

**15:2** Salt Sea: the Dead Sea. The "tongue," a prominent feature of the landscape, is a spit of land thrusting into the Dead Sea from its eastern shore; it is now called by its Arabic name, 'el lisân, "tongue."

**15:4** Wadi of Egypt: the natural boundary between Gaza and the Sinai Peninsula.

**15:8** The Valley of Ben-hinnom: the southern limit of Jerusalem. Ben-hinnom means "son of Hinnom." The place was also called Valley of Hinnom, in Hebrew ge-hinnom, whence the word "Gehenna" is derived.

**13:33** Jos 18:7; Nm 18:20.
**14:1** Jos 17:4; 21:1; Nm 27:19–22; 34:17–18.
**14:2** Nm 26:55; 33:54; 34:13.
**14:3** Jos 13:8, 14, 33.
**14:4** Jos 21:3–40; Gn 48:5.
**14:6** Nm 14:24, 30; 32:12; Dt 1:36, 38.
**14:7** Nm 14:6–9.
**14:8** Nm 13:31–33; 14:24;
32:12; Dt 1:36.
**14:10** Nm 14:30.
**14:11** Sir 46:1–10.
**14:12** Jos 11:21–22.
**14:13** Jos 10:36–37; 15:13–19; 21:11–12.
**14:15** Jgs 1:10.
**15:1** Nm 34:3.
**15:2–4** Nm 34:3–12.
**15:6** Jos 18:18–19, 22.
**15:7** Jos 7:26; 18:16–18.

Jerusalem), the boundary rose to the top of the mountain at the northern end of the Valley of Rephaim,* which bounds the Valley of Hinnom on the west. ⁹From the top of the mountain it ran to the fountain of waters of Nephtoah,* extended to the cities of Mount Ephron, and continued to Baalah, or Kiriath-jearim. ¹⁰From Baalah the boundary curved westward to Mount Seir and passed north of the ridge of Mount Jearim (that is, Chesalon); it descended to Beth-shemesh, and ran across to Timnah. ¹¹It then extended along the northern flank of Ekron, continued through Shikkeron, and across to Mount Baalah, from there to include Jabneel, before it came out at the sea. ¹²The western boundary was the Great Sea† and its coast. This was the complete boundary of the Judahites by their clans.

**Conquest by Caleb.** ¹³*As the LORD had commanded, Joshua gave Caleb, son of Jephunneh,* a portion among the Judahites, namely, Kiriath-arba (Arba was the father of Anak), that is, Hebron. ¹⁴*And Caleb dispossessed from there the three Anakim, the descendants of Anak: Sheshai, Ahiman, and Talmai. ¹⁵From there he marched up against the inhabitants of Debir,* which was formerly called Kiriath-sepher. ¹⁶Caleb said, "To the man who attacks Kiriath-sepher and captures it, I will give my daughter Achsah in marriage." ¹⁷†Othniel captured it, the son of Caleb's brother Kenaz; so Caleb gave him his daughter Achsah in marriage. ¹⁸When she came to him, she induced him to ask her father for some land. Then, as she alighted from the donkey, Caleb asked her, "What do you want?" ¹⁹She answered, "Give me a present! Since you have assigned to me land in the Negeb, give me also pools of water." So he gave her the upper and the lower pools.

**Cities of Judah.**† ²⁰This is the heritage of the tribe of Judahites by their clans: ²¹The cities of the tribe of the Judahites in the extreme southern district toward Edom were: Kabzeel, Eder, Jagur, ²²Kinah, Dimonah, Adadah,

²³Kedesh, Hazor, and Ithnan; ²⁴Ziph, Telem, Bealoth, ²⁵Hazor-hadattah, and Kerioth-hezron (that is, Hazor); ²⁶Amam, Shema, Moladah, ²⁷Hazar-gaddah, Heshmon, Beth-pelet, ²⁸Hazar-shual, Beer-sheba, and Biziothiah; ²⁹Baalah, Iim, Ezem, ³⁰Eltolad, Chesil, Hormah, ³¹Ziklag, Madmannah, Sansannah, ³²Lebaoth, Shilhim, and Ain and Rimmon; a total of twenty-nine cities with their villages.

³³In the Shephelah: Eshtaol, Zorah, Ashnah, ³⁴Zanoah, Engannim, Tappuah, Enam, ³⁵Jarmuth, Adullam, Socoh, Azekah, ³⁶Shaaraim, Adithaim, Gederah, and Gederothaim; fourteen cities and their villages. ³⁷Zenan, Hadashah, Migdal-gad, ³⁸Dilean, Mizpeh, Joktheel, ³⁹Lachish, Bozkath, Eglon, ⁴⁰Cabbon, Lahmas, Chitlish, ⁴¹Gederoth, Beth-dagon, Naamah, and Makkedah; sixteen cities and their villages. ⁴²Libnah, Ether, Ashan, ⁴³Iphtah, Ashnah, Nezib, ⁴⁴Keilah, Achzib, and Mareshah; nine cities and their villages. ⁴⁵Ekron and its towns and villages; ⁴⁶from Ekron to the sea, all the towns that lie alongside Ashdod, and their villages; ⁴⁷Ashdod and its towns and villages; Gaza and its towns and villages, as far as the Wadi of Egypt and the coast of the Great Sea.

⁴⁸In the mountain regions: Shamir, Jattir, Socoh, ⁴⁹Dannah, Kiriath-sannah (that is, Debir), ⁵⁰Anab, Eshtemoh, Anim, ⁵¹Goshen, Holon, and Giloh; eleven cities and their villages. ⁵²Arab, Dumah, Eshan, ⁵³Janim, Beth-tappuah, Aphekah, ⁵⁴Humtah, Kiriath-arba (that is, Hebron), and Zior; nine cities and their villages. ⁵⁵Maon, Carmel, Ziph, Juttah, ⁵⁶Jezreel, Jokdeam, Zanoah, ⁵⁷Kain, Gibbeah, and Timnah; ten cities and their villages. ⁵⁸Halhul, Beth-zur, Gedor, ⁵⁹Maarath, Beth-anoth, and Eltekon; six cities and their villages. Tekoa, Ephrathah (that is, Bethlehem), Peor, Etam, Kulom, Tatam, Zores, Karim, Gallim, Bether, and Manoko; eleven cities and their villages. ⁶⁰Kiriath-baal (that is, Kiriath-jearim) and Rabbah; two cities and their villages.*

⁶¹In the wilderness:† Beth-arabah, Middin, Secacah, ⁶²Nibshan, Ir-hamelah, and En-gedi; six cities and their villages. ⁶³But the Jebusites

---

**15:12** *Great Sea*: the Mediterranean.
**15:17–19** The story of Othniel is told again in Jgs 1:13–15; cf. also Jgs 3:9–11.
**15:20–62** This elaborate list of the cities of Judah was probably taken from a document made originally for administrative purposes; the cities are divided into four provincial districts, some of which have further subdivisions. For similar lists of the cities of Judah, cf. 19:2–7; 1 Chr 4:28–32; Neh 11:25–30. This

list has suffered in transmission, so that the totals given in vv. 32 and 36 are not exact; many of the cities cannot be identified.
**15:61** *In the wilderness*: in the Jordan rift near the Dead Sea.

**15:8** Jos 18:16.
**15:9** Jos 18:15.
**15:13–19** Jgs 1:10–15.
**15:13** Jos 14:13–15.
**15:14** Nm 13:22; Jgs 1:20.
**15:15** Jos 10:38.
**15:60** Jos 18:14.

JOS

who lived in Jerusalem the Judahites could not dispossess; so the Jebusites dwell in Jerusalem beside the Judahites to the present day. *

**16** **The Joseph Tribes.**† [1]The lot that fell to the Josephites extended from the Jordan at Jericho to the waters of Jericho east of the wilderness; then the boundary went up from Jericho to the heights at Bethel. † [2]Leaving Bethel for Luz, it crossed the ridge to the border of the Archites at Ataroth, [3]and descended westward to the border of the Japhletites, to that of the Lower Beth-horon, and to Gezer, and from there to the sea. *

**Ephraim.** [4]Within the heritage of Manasseh and Ephraim, sons of Joseph, [5]the dividing line † for the heritage of the Ephraimites by their clans ran from east of Ataroth-addar to Upper Beth-horon * [6]and thence to the sea. From Michmethath * on the north, their boundary curved eastward around Taanath-shiloh, and continued east of it to Janoah; [7]from there it descended to Ataroth and Na-arah, and reaching Jericho, it ended at the Jordan. [8]From Tappuah the boundary ran westward to the Wadi Kanah and ended at the sea. This was the heritage of the Ephraimites by their clans, [9]including the villages that belonged to each city set aside for the Ephraimites within the heritage of the Manassites. [10]But they did not dispossess the Canaanites living in Gezer; * they live within Ephraim to the present day, though they have been put to forced labor.

**17** **Manasseh.** [1]* Now as for the lot that fell to the tribe of Manasseh * as the firstborn of Joseph: since Manasseh's eldest son, Machir, the father of Gilead, was a warrior, who had already obtained Gilead and Bashan, [2]the allotment was now made to the rest of the Manassites by their clans: the descendants of Abiezer, Helek, Asriel, Shechem,

Hepher, and Shemida; these are the other male children of Manasseh, son of Joseph, by their clans.

[3]* Furthermore, Zelophehad, son of Hepher, son of Gilead, son of Machir, son of Manasseh, had no sons, but only daughters, whose names were Mahlah, Noah, Hoglah, Milcah, and Tirzah. [4]These presented themselves to Eleazar the priest, to Joshua, son of Nun, and to the leaders, saying, "The LORD commanded Moses to give us a heritage among our relatives." So in accordance with the command of the LORD a heritage was given them among their father's relatives. [5]Thus ten shares fell to Manasseh apart from the land of Gilead and Bashan beyond the Jordan, * [6]since these female descendants of Manasseh received each a portion among his sons. The land of Gilead fell to the rest of the Manassites.

[7]Manasseh bordered on Asher. † From Michmethath, near Shechem, another boundary ran southward to include the inhabitants of En-Tappuah, [8]because the district of Tappuah belonged to Manasseh, although Tappuah itself was an Ephraimite city on the border of Manasseh. [9]This same boundary continued down to the Wadi Kanah. * The cities that belonged to Ephraim from among the cities in Manasseh were those to the south of that wadi; thus the territory of Manasseh ran north of the wadi and ended at the sea. [10]The land on the south belonged to Ephraim and that on the north to Manasseh; with the sea as their common boundary, they reached Asher on the north and Issachar on the east.

[11]* Moreover, in Issachar and in Asher Manasseh was awarded Beth-shean and its towns, Ibleam and its towns, the inhabitants of Dor and its towns, the inhabitants of Endor and its towns, the inhabitants of Taanach and its towns, the inhabitants of Megiddo and its towns (the third is Naphath-dor). [12]Since the Manassites were not able to dispossess these cities, the Canaanites continued to inhabit this

---

† **16:1–17:18** After the boundaries and cities of Judah, the most important tribe, are given, the land of the next most important group, the two Joseph tribes of Ephraim and Manasseh, is described, though it was separated from Judah by the territories of Benjamin (18:11–20) and Dan (19:40–48).
**16:1–3** This line formed the southern boundary of Ephraim and the northern boundaries of Benjamin and of Dan.
**16:5** *The dividing line*: separating Ephraim from Manasseh. Ephraim's northern border (v. 5) is given in an east-to-west direction; its eastern border (vv. 6–7) in a north-to-south direction.
**17:7** *Manasseh bordered on Asher*: only at the extreme northwestern section of Manasseh's territory. The boundary given in

the following sentences (vv. 7–10) is a more detailed description of the one already mentioned in 16:5–7, as separating Manasseh from Ephraim.

**15:63** Jgs 1:21; 2 Sm 5:6.        **17:1** Gn 41:51; 46:20;
**16:3** Jos 10:10, 33.                  48:18; 50:23; Dt 3:13,
**16:5** Jos 18:13.                        15.
**16:6–9** Jos 17:7–9.               **17:3–6** Nm 27:1–7; 36:2.
**16:10** Jgs 1:29.                      **17:5** Nm 13:30–31.
**17:1–3** Nm 26:29–33.            **17:9** Jos 16:8–9.
                                                **17:11** 1 Chr 7:29.

region. ¹³When the Israelites grew stronger they put the Canaanites to forced labor, but they did not dispossess them.

**Protest of Joseph Tribes.** ¹⁴The descendants of Joseph said to Joshua, "Why have you given us only one lot and one share as our heritage?* Our people are too many, because of the extent to which the LORD has blessed us." ¹⁵Joshua answered them, "If you are too many, go up to the forest and clear out a place for yourselves there in the land of the Perizzites and Rephaim, since the mountain regions of Ephraim are so narrow." ¹⁶For the Josephites said, "Our mountain regions are not enough for us; on the other hand, the Canaanites living in the valley region all have iron chariots, in particular those in Beth-shean and its towns, and those in the valley of Jezreel." ¹⁷Joshua therefore said to Ephraim and Manasseh, the house of Joseph, "You are a numerous people and very strong. You shall not have merely one share, ¹⁸for the mountain region which is now forest shall be yours when you clear it. Its adjacent land shall also be yours if, despite their strength and iron chariots, you dispossess the Canaanites."

**18** ¹The whole community of the Israelites assembled at Shiloh, where they set up the tent of meeting; and the land was subdued before them.*

**The Seven Remaining Portions.** ²There remained seven tribes among the Israelites that had not yet received their heritage. ³Joshua therefore said to the Israelites, "How much longer will you put off taking steps to possess the land which the LORD, the God of your ancestors, has given you? ⁴Choose three representatives from each of your tribes; I will send them to go throughout the land and describe it for purposes of acquiring their heritage. When they return to me ⁵you shall divide it into seven parts. Judah is to retain its territory in the south,* and the house of Joseph its territory in the north. ⁶You shall bring to me here the description of the land in seven sections. I will then cast lots for you here before

the LORD, our God. ⁷For the Levites have no share among you,* because the priesthood of the LORD is their heritage; while Gad, Reuben, and the half-tribe of Manasseh have already received the heritage east of the Jordan which Moses, the servant of the LORD, gave them."

⁸When those who were to describe the land were ready for their journey, Joshua commanded them, "Go throughout the land and describe it; return to me and I will cast lots for you here before the LORD in Shiloh." ⁹So they went through the land, described its cities in writing in seven sections, and returned to Joshua in the camp at Shiloh. ¹⁰Joshua then cast lots for them before the LORD in Shiloh, and divided up the land for the Israelites into their separate shares.

**Benjamin.** ¹¹One lot fell to the tribe of Benjaminites by their clans. The territory allotted them lay between the descendants of Judah and those of Joseph. ¹²* Their northern boundary† began at the Jordan and went over the northern flank of Jericho, up westward into the mountains, until it reached the wilderness of Beth-aven. ¹³From there it crossed over to the southern flank of Luz (that is, Bethel). Then it ran down to Ataroth-addar, on the mountaintop south of Lower Beth-horon.* ¹⁴For the western border, the boundary line swung south from the mountaintop opposite Beth-horon until it reached Kiriath-baal (that is, Kiriath-jearim; this city belonged to the Judahites). This was the western boundary. ¹⁵The southern boundary began at the limits of Kiriath-jearim and projected to the spring at Nephtoah. ¹⁶* It went down to the edge of the mountain on the north of the Valley of Rephaim, where it faces the Valley of Ben-hinnom; and continuing down the Valley of Hinnom along the southern flank of the Jebusites, reached En-rogel. ¹⁷Inclining to the north, it extended to En-shemesh, and thence to Geliloth, opposite the pass of Adummim. Then it dropped to Eben-Bohan-ben-Reuben, ¹⁸across the northern flank of the Arabah overlook, down into the Arabah. ¹⁹From there the boundary continued across the northern flank of Beth-hoglah and extended northward to the

---

† **18:12–20** Benjamin's northern boundary (vv. 12–13) corresponded to part of the southern boundary of Ephraim (16:1–2). Their western border (v. 14) was the eastern border of Dan (cf. 19:40–47). Their southern boundary (vv. 15–19) corresponded to part of the northern boundary of Judah (15:5–9).

**17:14** Jos 16:4; Gn 48:19–22.
**18:1** Jos 11:23; 14:15; 19:51.
**18:5** Jos 15:1–17:18.
**18:7** Jos 13:8, 33.
**18:12–13** Jos 16:1–5.
**18:13** Gn 28:19.
**18:16–18** Jos 15:6–8.

tongue of the Salt Sea, toward the southern end of the Jordan. This was the southern boundary. ²⁰The Jordan bounded it on the east. This was how the heritage of the Benjaminites by their clans was bounded on all sides.

²¹Now the cities belonging to the tribe of the Benjaminites by their clans were: Jericho, Beth-hoglah, Emek-keziz, ²²Beth-arabah, Zemaraim, Bethel, ²³Avvim, Parah, Ophra, ²⁴Chephar-ammoni, Ophni, and Geba; twelve cities and their villages. ²⁵Also Gibeon, Ramah, Beeroth, ²⁶Mizpeh, Chephirah, Mozah, ²⁷Rekem, Irpeel, Taralah, ²⁸Zela, Haeleph, the Jebusite city (that is, Jerusalem), Gibeah, and Kiriath; fourteen cities and their villages. This was the heritage of the clans of Benjaminites.

# 19 Simeon.
¹The second lot fell to Simeon. The heritage of the tribe of Simeonites by their clans lay within that of the Judahites. ²*For their heritage they received Beer-sheba, Shema, Moladah, ³Hazar-shual, Balah, Ezem, ⁴Eltolad, Bethul, Hormah, ⁵Ziklag, Bethmarcaboth, Hazar-susah, ⁶Beth-lebaoth, and Sharuhen; thirteen cities and their villages. ⁷Also Ain, Rimmon, Ether, and Ashan; four cities and their villages, ⁸besides all the villages around these cities as far as Baalath-beer (that is, Ramoth-negeb). This was the heritage of the tribe of the Simeonites by their clans. ⁹This heritage of the Simeonites was within the confines of the Judahites; for since the portion of the latter was too large for them, the Simeonites obtained their heritage within it.

**Zebulun.** ¹⁰†The third lot fell to the Zebulunites by their clans. The boundary of their heritage was at Sarid. ¹¹Their boundary went up west and through Mareal, reaching Dabbesheth and the wadi that is near Jokneam. ¹²From Sarid eastward it ran to the district of Chisloth-tabor, on to Daberath, and up to Japhia. ¹³From there it continued eastward to Gath-hepher and to Eth-kazin, extended to Rimmon, and turned to Neah. ¹⁴Skirting north of Hannathon, the boundary ended at the valley of Iphtahel. ¹⁵Thus, with Kattath, Nahalal, Shimron, Idalah, and Bethlehem, there were twelve cities and their villages. ¹⁶This was the heritage of the Zebulunites by their clans, these cities and their villages.

**Issachar.** ¹⁷†The fourth lot fell to Issachar. The territory of the Issacharites by their clans ¹⁸included Jezreel, Chesulloth, Shunem, ¹⁹Hapharaim, Shion, Anaharath, ²⁰Rabbith, Kishion, Ebez, ²¹Remeth, En-gannim, En-haddah, and Beth-pazzez. ²²The boundary reached Tabor, Shahazumah, and Beth-shemesh, ending at the Jordan: sixteen cities and their villages. ²³This was the heritage of the Issacharites by their clans, these cities and their villages.

**Asher.** ²⁴†The fifth lot fell to the Asherites by their clans. ²⁵Their territory included Helkath, Hali, Beten, Achshaph, ²⁶Allammelech, Amad, and Mishal, and reached Carmel on the west, and Shihor-libnath. ²⁷In the other direction, it ran eastward of Beth-dagon, reached Zebulun and the valley of Iphtahel; then north of Beth-emek and Neiel, it extended northward to Cabul, ²⁸Ebron, Rehob,* Hammon, and Kanah, near Greater Sidon. ²⁹Then the boundary turned back to Ramah and to the fortress city of Tyre; thence it cut back to Hosah and ended at the sea. Thus, with Mahalab, Achzib, ³⁰Ummah, Acco, Aphek, and Rehob, there were twenty-two cities and their villages. ³¹This was the heritage of the tribe of the Asherites by their clans, these cities and their villages.

**Naphtali.** ³²†The sixth lot fell to the Naphtalites. ³³Their boundary extended from Heleph, from the oak at Zaanannim, including Adaminekeb and Jabneel, to Lakkum, and ended at the Jordan. ³⁴In the opposite direction,

---

† **19:10–16** Zebulun's territory was in the central section of the Jezreel Valley and of southern Galilee; it was bounded on the south by Manasseh, on the southeast by Issachar, on the northeast and north by Naphtali, and on the west by Asher. The site of the later city of Nazareth was within its borders. Bethlehem of Zebulun was, of course, distinct from the city of the same name in Judah. *Twelve cities*: apparently seven of the names are missing from v. 15, unless some of the places mentioned in vv. 12–14 are to be included in the number.

**19:17–23** Issachar's land was on the eastern watershed of the Jezreel Valley, but also included the southeastern end of the Galilean mountains. It was surrounded by Manasseh on the south and east, by Naphtali on the north, and by Zebulun on the west.

Jezreel (v. 18) dominated the valley to which it gave its name, the later form of which was Esdraelon.

**19:24–31** Asher inherited the western slope of the Galilean hills as far as the Mediterranean, with Manasseh to the south, Zebulun and Naphtali to the east, and Phoenicia to the north.

**19:32–39** Naphtali received eastern Galilee; Asher was to the west and Zebulun and Issachar were to the south, while the upper Jordan and Mount Hermon formed the eastern border. Part of the tribe of Dan later on occupied the northern extremity of Naphtali's lands, at the sources of the Jordan (v. 47).

---

**19:2–8** 1 Chr 4:28–33.   **19:28–30** Jgs 1:31.

westerly, it ran through Aznoth-tabor and from there extended to Hukkok; it reached Zebulun on the south, Asher on the west, and the Jordan on the east. [35] The fortified cities were Ziddim, Zer, Hammath, Rakkath, Chinnereth, [36] Adamah, Ramah, Hazor, [37] Kedesh, Edrei, En-hazor, [38] Yiron, Migdal-el, Horem, Beth-anath, and Beth-shemesh;* nineteen cities and their villages. [39] This was the heritage of the tribe of the Naphtalites by their clans, these cities and their villages.

**Dan.** [40]† The seventh lot fell to the tribe of Danites by their clans. [41] Their heritage was the territory of Zorah, Eshtaol, Ir-shemesh, [42] Shaalabbin, Aijalon, Ithlah,* [43] Elon, Timnah, Ekron, [44] Eltekoh, Gibbethon, Baalath, [45] Jehud, Beneberak, Gath-rimmon, [46] Me-jarkon, and Rakkon, with the coast at Joppa. [47]* But the territory of the Danites was too small for them; so the Danites marched up and attacked Leshem,† which they captured and put to the sword. Once they had taken possession of Leshem, they dwelt there and named it after their ancestor Dan. [48] This was the heritage of the tribe of the Danites by their clans, these cities and their villages.

**Joshua's City.** [49] When the last of them had received the portions of the land they were to inherit, the Israelites assigned a heritage in their midst to Joshua, son of Nun. [50] According to the command of the LORD, they gave him the city he requested, Timnah-serah* in the mountain region of Ephraim. He rebuilt the city and made it his home.

[51] These are the heritages which Eleazar the priest, Joshua, son of Nun, and the heads of families in the tribes of the Israelites apportioned by lot in the presence of the LORD, at the door of the tent of meeting in Shiloh. Thus they finished dividing the land.

# 20 Cities of Refuge. [1]* The LORD said to Joshua:† [2] Tell the Israelites: Designate

for yourselves the cities of refuge of which I spoke to you through Moses, [3] to which anyone guilty of inadvertent and unintentional homicide may flee for asylum from the avenger of blood. [4] To one of these cities the killer shall flee, and standing at the entrance of the city gate, shall plead his case in the hearing of the elders of the city, who must receive him and assign him a place in which to live among them. [5] Though the avenger of blood pursues him, they shall not deliver up to him the one who killed a neighbor unintentionally, when there had been no hatred previously. [6] Once he has stood judgment before the community, he shall live on in that city until the death of the high priest who is in office at the time. Then the killer may return home to the city from where he originally fled.

**List of Cities.** [7] So they set apart Kedesh in Galilee in the mountain region of Naphtali, Shechem in the mountain region of Ephraim, and Kiriath-arba (that is, Hebron) in the mountain region of Judah.* [8] And beyond the Jordan east of Jericho they designated Bezer in the wilderness on the tableland in the tribe of Reuben, Ramoth in Gilead in the tribe of Gad, and Golan in Bashan in the tribe of Manasseh.* [9] These are the designated cities to which any Israelite or alien residing among them who had killed a person unintentionally might flee to escape death at the hand of the avenger of blood, until the killer could appear before the community.

# 21 Levitical Cities. [1] The heads of the Levite families† approached Eleazar the priest, Joshua, son of Nun, and the heads of families of the other tribes of the Israelites* [2] at Shiloh in the land of Canaan, and said to them, "The LORD commanded, through Moses, that cities be given us to dwell in, with pasture lands for our livestock."* [3] Out of their own heritage, according to the command of the

---

† **19:40–46** The original territory of Dan was a small enclave between Judah, Benjamin, Ephraim, and the Philistines.
**19:47** *Leshem*: called Laish in Jgs 18, where the story of the migration of the Danites is told at greater length.
**20:1–9** The laws concerning the cities of refuge are given in Nm 35:9–28; Dt 19:1–13; see notes on Nm 35:16–25; Dt 19:2.
**21:1** The order to establish special cities for the Levites is given in Nm 35:1–8. The forty-eight cities listed here were hardly the exclusive possession of the Levites; at least the more important of them, such as Hebron, Shechem, and Ramoth in Gilead, were certainly peopled for the most part by the tribe in whose

territory they were situated. But in all these cities the Levites had special property rights which they did not possess in other cities; cf. Lv 25:32–34.

* **19:38** Jgs 1:33.
**19:42** Jgs 1:35.
**19:47** Jgs 18:27–29.
**19:50** Jos 24:30; Jgs 2:9.
**20:1–9** Ex 21:12–14; Nm 35:9–15; Dt 4:41–43; 19:1–10.
**20:7** Jos 15:13; 19:37; 21:21.
**20:8** Jos 21:27, 36.
**21:1** Ex 6:16–19; Nm 3:17–20.
**21:2–3, 8** Nm 35:1–8.

LORD, the Israelites gave the Levites the following cities with their pasture lands.

⁴ When the first lot among the Levites fell to the clans of the Kohathites, the descendants of Aaron the priest obtained by lot from the tribes of Judah, Simeon, and Benjamin, thirteen cities. ⁵ From the clans of the tribe of Ephraim, from the tribe of Dan, and from the half-tribe of Manasseh, the rest of the Kohathites obtained by lot ten cities.* ⁶ From the clans of the tribe of Issachar, from the tribe of Asher, from the tribe of Naphtali, and from the half-tribe of Manasseh, the Gershonites obtained by lot thirteen cities. ⁷ From the tribes of Reuben, Gad, and Zebulun, the clans of the Merarites obtained twelve cities. ⁸ These cities with their pasture lands the Israelites gave by lot to the Levites, as the LORD had commanded through Moses.

**Cities of the Priests.** ⁹* From the tribes of the Judahites and Simeonites they gave the following cities ¹⁰ and assigned them to the descendants of Aaron in the Kohathite clan of the Levites, since the first lot fell to them: ¹¹ first, Kiriath-arba (Arba was the father of Anak), that is, Hebron, in the mountain region of Judah, with the adjacent pasture lands, ¹² although the open country and villages belonging to the city had been given to Caleb, son of Jephunneh, as his holding.* ¹³ Thus to the descendants of Aaron the priest were given the city of refuge for homicides at Hebron, with its pasture lands; also, Libnah with its pasture lands, ¹⁴ Jattir with its pasture lands, Eshtemoa with its pasture lands, ¹⁵ Holon with its pasture lands, Debir with its pasture lands, ¹⁶ Ain with its pasture lands, Juttah with its pasture lands, and Beth-shemesh with its pasture lands: nine cities from these two tribes. ¹⁷ From the tribe of Benjamin they obtained Gibeon with its pasture lands, Geba with its pasture lands, ¹⁸ Anathoth* with its pasture lands, and Almon with its pasture lands: four cities. ¹⁹ These cities which with their pasture lands belonged to the priestly descendants of Aaron, were thirteen in all.

**Cities of the Other Kohathites.** ²⁰* The rest of the Kohathite clans among the Levites obtained by lot, from the tribe of Ephraim, four cities. ²¹ They were assigned, with its pasture lands, the city of refuge for homicides at Shechem in the mountain region of Ephraim; also Gezer with its pasture lands, ²² Kibzaim with its pasture lands, and Beth-horon with its pasture lands. ²³ From the tribe of Dan they obtained Elteke with its pasture lands, Gibbethon with its pasture lands, ²⁴ Aijalon with its pasture lands, and Gath-rimmon with its pasture lands: four cities. ²⁵ From the half-tribe of Manasseh, Taanach with its pasture lands, and Gath-rimmon with its pasture lands: two cities. ²⁶ These cities which with their pasture lands belonged to the rest of the Kohathite clans were ten in all.

**Cities of the Gershonites.** ²⁷* The Gershonite clan of the Levites received from the half-tribe of Manasseh the city of refuge for homicides at Golan in Bashan, with its pasture lands; and also Beth-Astharoth with its pasture lands: two cities. ²⁸ From the tribe of Issachar they obtained Kishion with its pasture lands, Daberath with its pasture lands, ²⁹ Jarmuth with its pasture lands, and En-gannim with its pasture lands: four cities. ³⁰ From the tribe of Asher, Mishal with its pasture lands, Abdon with its pasture lands, ³¹ Helkath with its pasture lands, and Rehob with its pasture lands: four cities. ³² From the tribe of Naphtali, the city of refuge for homicides at Kedesh in Galilee, with its pasture lands; also Hammath with its pasture lands, and Kartan with its pasture lands: three cities. ³³ The cities which belonged to the Gershonite clans, with their pasture lands, were thirteen in all.

**Cities of the Merarites.** ³⁴* The Merarite clans, the last of the Levites, received, from the tribe of Zebulun, Jokneam with its pasture lands, Kartah with its pasture lands, ³⁵ Dimnah with its pasture lands, and Nahalal with its pasture lands: four cities. ³⁶ Also, across the Jordan, from the tribe of Reuben, the city of refuge for homicides at Bezer with its pasture lands, Jahaz with its pasture lands, ³⁷ Kedemoth with its pasture lands, and Mephaath with its pasture lands: four cities. ³⁸ From the tribe of Gad, the city of refuge for homicides at Ramoth in Gilead with its pasture lands, Mahanaim with its pasture lands, ³⁹ Heshbon with its pasture

J
O
S

lands, and Jazer with its pasture lands: four cities in all. <sup>40</sup>The cities allotted to the Merarite clans, the last of the Levites, were therefore twelve in all.

<sup>41</sup>Thus the total number of cities* within the territory of the Israelites which, with their pasture lands, belonged to the Levites, was forty-eight. <sup>42</sup>With each and every one of these cities went the pasture lands round about it.

<sup>43</sup>And so the LORD gave Israel the entire land he had sworn to their ancestors he would give them.* Once they had taken possession of it, and dwelt in it, <sup>44</sup>the LORD gave them peace on every side, just as he had promised their ancestors. Not one of their enemies could withstand them; the LORD gave all their enemies into their power. <sup>45</sup>Not a single word of the blessing* that the LORD had promised to the house of Israel failed; it all came true.

## III. RETURN OF THE TRANSJORDAN TRIBES AND JOSHUA'S FAREWELL

**22** **The Eastern Tribes Dismissed.** <sup>1</sup>At that time Joshua summoned the Reubenites, the Gadites, and the half-tribe of Manasseh <sup>2</sup>and said to them:* "You have observed all that Moses, the servant of the LORD, commanded you, and have listened to my voice in everything I commanded you. <sup>3</sup>For many years now, even until today, you have not abandoned your allies, but have taken care to observe the commands of the LORD, your God. <sup>4</sup>Now that the LORD, your God, has settled your allies as he promised them, you may return to your tents, to your own land, which Moses, the servant of the LORD, gave you, across the Jordan.* <sup>5</sup>But be very careful to observe the commandment and the law which Moses, the servant of the LORD, commanded you: love the LORD, your God,* follow him in all his ways, keep his commandments, hold fast to him, and serve him with your whole heart and your whole self." <sup>6</sup>Joshua then

blessed them and sent them away, and they went to their tents.

<sup>7</sup>(For, to half of the tribe of Manasseh Moses had assigned land in Bashan;* and to the other half Joshua had given a portion along with their allies west of the Jordan.) When Joshua sent them away to their tents and blessed them, <sup>8</sup>he said, "Now that you are returning to your own tents with great wealth, with abundant livestock, with silver, gold, bronze and iron, and with a very large supply of clothing, divide these spoils of your enemies with your allies there."* <sup>9</sup>So the Reubenites, the Gadites, and the half-tribe of Manasseh left the other Israelites at Shiloh in the land of Canaan and returned to the land of Gilead, their own land, which they had received according to the LORD's command through Moses.*

**The Altar Beside the Jordan.** <sup>10</sup>When the Reubenites, the Gadites, and the half-tribe of Manasseh came to the region of the Jordan in the land of Canaan, they built an altar there at the Jordan, an impressively large altar. <sup>11</sup>The other Israelites heard the report:* "The Reubenites, the Gadites, and the half-tribe of Manasseh have built an altar" in the region of the Jordan facing the land of Canaan,† across from the Israelites. <sup>12</sup>When the Israelites heard this, they assembled at Shiloh, as the entire Israelite community to take military action against them.†

**Accusation of the Western Tribes.** <sup>13</sup>The Israelites sent Phinehas, son of Eleazar the priest, to the Reubenites, the Gadites, and the half-tribe of Manasseh in the land of Gilead,* <sup>14</sup>and with him ten leaders, one from each tribe of Israel, each one the head of an ancestral house among the clans of Israel. <sup>15</sup>When these came to the Reubenites, the Gadites, and the half-tribe of Manasseh in the land of Gilead, they said to them: <sup>16</sup>"Thus says the whole community of the LORD: What act of treachery is this

---

† **22:11** In the region of the Jordan facing the land of Canaan: on the eastern side of the Jordan valley. The river itself formed the boundary between these eastern tribes and the rest of the tribes who lived in what was formerly Canaan—though the term "Canaan" could also be used of both sides of the Jordan valley (cf. v. 10). The Transjordan tribes naturally built their altar in their own territory.

**22:12** To take military action against them: the western Israelites considered this altar, which seemed to violate the customary unity of the sanctuary (cf. Lv 17:1–9; Dt 12:4–14), as constituting rebellion against the Lord and compromising national unity.

**21:41** Nm 35:7.
**21:43** Gn 12:7; 13:15; 15:18; 26:3; 28:4, 13.
**21:45** Jos 23:14–15.
**22:2–6** Jos 1:12–17; Nm 32:20–32; Dt 3:18–20.
**22:4** Jos 13:8.
**22:5** Dt 6:5–6, 17; 10:12; 11:1, 13, 22.
**22:7** Jos 17:5.
**22:8** Nm 31:27.
**22:9** Jos 18:1; Nm 32:1, 26, 29.
**22:11** Dt 12:5, 11–14; 13:13–17.
**22:13** Ex 6:25; Sir 45:23–24.

you have committed against the God of Israel? This day you have turned from following the LORD; by building an altar of your own you have rebelled against the LORD this day. [17] Is the iniquity of Peor not enough, by which we made ourselves impure, even to this day, and a plague came upon the community of the LORD?* [18] If today you turn away from following the LORD, and rebel against the LORD, tomorrow he will be angry with the whole community of Israel! [19] If you consider the land you now possess unclean,† cross over to the land the LORD possesses, where the tabernacle of the LORD stands, and share that with us. But do not rebel against the LORD, nor involve us in rebellion, by building an altar of your own in addition to the altar of the LORD, our God. [20] When Achan, son of Zerah,* acted treacherously by violating the ban, was it not upon the entire community of Israel that wrath fell? Though he was but a single man, he did not perish alone† for his guilt!"

**Reply of the Eastern Tribes.** [21] The Reubenites, the Gadites, and the half-tribe of Manasseh replied to the heads of the Israelite clans: [22] "The LORD is the God of gods. The LORD, the God of gods,† knows and Israel shall know. If now we have acted out of rebellion or treachery against the LORD, our God, do not try to save us this day, [23] and if we have built an altar of our own to turn from following the LORD, or to sacrifice burnt offerings, grain offerings, or communion sacrifices upon it, the LORD himself will exact the penalty. [24] We did it rather out of our anxious concern lest in the future your children should say to our children: 'What have you to do with the LORD, the God of Israel? [25] For the LORD has placed the Jordan as a boundary between you and us, you Reubenites and Gadites. You have no share in the LORD.' Thus your children would prevent ours from revering the LORD. [26] So we thought, 'Let us act for ourselves by building this altar of our own'—not for burnt offerings or sacrifice,

[27]* but as witness between us and you and our descendants, that we have the right to provide for the service of the LORD in his presence with our burnt offerings, sacrifices, and communion sacrifices. Now in the future your children cannot say to our children, 'You have no share in the LORD.' [28] Our thought was that, if in the future they should speak thus to us or to our descendants, we could answer: 'Look at the copy of the altar of the LORD which our ancestors made, not for burnt offerings or for sacrifices, but to witness† between you and us.' [29] Far be it from us to rebel against the LORD or to turn now from following the LORD by building an altar for burnt offering, grain offering, or sacrifice in addition to the altar of the LORD, our God, which stands before his tabernacle."

[30] When Phinehas the priest and the leaders of the community, the heads of the Israelite clans, heard what the Reubenites, the Gadites, and the Manassites had to say, they were satisfied. [31] Phinehas, son of Eleazar the priest, said to the Reubenites, the Gadites, and the Manassites, "Today we know that the LORD is in our midst. Since you have not rebelled against the LORD by this act of treachery, you have delivered the Israelites from the hand of the LORD."

[32] Phinehas, son of Eleazar the priest, and the leaders returned from the Reubenites and the Gadites in the land of Gilead to the Israelites in the land of Canaan, and reported the matter to them. [33] The report satisfied the Israelites, who blessed God and decided not to take military action against the Reubenites and Gadites nor to ravage the land where they lived.

[34] The Reubenites and the Gadites gave the altar its name† as a witness among them that the LORD is God.

# 23 Joshua's Final Plea. [1] Many years later, after the LORD had given the Israelites rest from all their enemies round about them, and when Joshua was old and advanced in years,* [2] he summoned all Israel, including

---

† 
**22:19** *Unclean:* not sanctified by the tabernacle.
**22:20** *Achan...did not perish alone:* his guilt caused the failure of the first attack on Ai (7:4–23); this fact is adduced as an argument for the solidarity and mutual responsibility of all the Israelites.
**22:22** *The LORD, the God of gods:* the Hebrew, which cannot be adequately rendered in English here, adds to the divine name Yhwh ("the LORD") two synonymous words for "God," *'el* and *'elohim.* The repetition of these three sacred words adds force to the protestations of fidelity and innocence.

**22:28** *To witness:* far from being destined to form a rival sanctuary, the copy of the altar is intended by the eastern tribes solely as a means of teaching their children to be faithful to the one true sanctuary beyond the Jordan.
**22:34** The name of this altar was the Hebrew word for "witness," *'ed.*

**22:17** Nm 25:3–4; Dt 4:3.        **22:27** Ex 27:1–8; Dt 12:5–6,
**22:20** Jos 7:1, 5.                          11–14.
                                                        **23:1** Jos 13:1.

their elders, leaders, judges, and officers, and said to them: "I am old and advanced in years.* ³ You have seen all that the LORD, your God, has done for you against all these nations; for it has been the LORD, your God, who fought for you. ⁴* See, I have apportioned among your tribes as their heritage the nations that survive, as well as those I destroyed, between the Jordan and the Great Sea in the west. ⁵ The LORD, your God, will drive them out and dispossess them at your approach, so that you will take possession of their land as the LORD, your God, promised you. ⁶ Therefore be strong and be careful to observe all that is written in the book of the law of Moses, never turning from it right or left,* ⁷ or mingling with these nations that survive among you. You must not invoke their gods by name, or swear by them, or serve them, or bow down to them,* ⁸ but you must hold fast to the LORD, your God, as you have done up to this day. ⁹ At your approach the LORD has dispossessed great and strong nations; not one has withstood you up to this day. ¹⁰ One of you puts to flight a thousand, because it is the LORD, your God, himself who fights for you,* as he promised you. ¹¹ As for you, take great care to love the LORD, your God. ¹² For if you ever turn away from him and join with the remnant of these nations that survive among you, by intermarrying and intermingling with them,* ¹³ know for certain that the LORD, your God, will no longer dispossess these nations at your approach. Instead they will be a snare and a trap for you, a scourge for your sides and thorns for your eyes, until you perish from this good land which the LORD, your God, has given you.*

¹⁴ "Today, as you see, I am going the way of all the earth.† So now acknowledge with your whole heart and soul that not one of all the promises the LORD, your God, made concerning you has failed. Every one has come true for you; not one has failed. ¹⁵* But just as every promise the LORD, your God, made to you has come true for you, so will he bring upon you every threat,† even so far as to exterminate

you from this good land which the LORD, your God, has given you. ¹⁶ If you transgress the covenant of the LORD, your God, which he enjoined on you, to go and serve other gods and bow down to them, the anger of the LORD will flare up against you and you will quickly perish from the good land he has given you."

# 24 **Covenant Ceremony.** ¹* Joshua gathered together all the tribes of Israel at Shechem, summoning the elders, leaders, judges, and officers of Israel. When they stood in ranks before God, ² Joshua addressed all the people: "Thus says the LORD, the God of Israel: In times past your ancestors, down to Terah,* father of Abraham and Nahor, lived beyond the River† and served other gods. ³ But I brought your father Abraham from the region beyond the River and led him through the entire land of Canaan.* I made his descendants numerous, and gave him Isaac. ⁴ To Isaac I gave Jacob and Esau.* To Esau I assigned the mountain region of Seir to possess, while Jacob and his children went down to Egypt.

⁵ "Then I sent Moses and Aaron, and struck Egypt with the plagues and wonders that I wrought in her midst.* Afterward I led you out. ⁶ And when I led your ancestors out of Egypt, you came to the sea, and the Egyptians pursued your ancestors to the Red Sea with chariots and charioteers.* ⁷ When they cried out to the LORD,* he put darkness between you and the Egyptians, upon whom he brought the sea so that it covered them. Your eyes saw what I did to Egypt. After you dwelt a long time in the wilderness, ⁸* I brought you into the land of the Amorites who lived east of the Jordan. They fought against you, but I delivered them into your power. You took possession of their land, and I destroyed them at your approach. ⁹* Then Balak, son of Zippor, king of Moab, prepared to war against Israel. He summoned Balaam, son of Beor, to curse you, ¹⁰* but I would not listen to Balaam. Instead, he had to bless you, and I delivered you from his power. ¹¹ Once you crossed the Jordan* and came to

---

† **23:14** *Going the way of all the earth*: drawing near to death, the inevitable end of all; cf. 1 Kgs 2:1–2.
    **23:15** *Every threat*: mentioned especially in the list of curses in Dt 28:15–68.
    **24:2** *Beyond the River*: east of the Euphrates; cf. Gn 11:28–31.

*

**23:2** Dt 29:10.                          18:10; Ps 78:55.
**23:4** Jos 13:2–7; 14:2;          **23:6** Jos 1:7.

**23:7** Ex 20:3–6; Dt 5:7–10;          **24:3** Gn 12:1; Acts 7:2–4.
    7:2–11.                                        **24:4** Gn 36:8; 46:1, 6; Acts
**23:10** Ex 14:14; Lv 26:8; Dt          7:15.
    3:22.                                        **24:5** Ex 3:10; 7:14; 12:30.
**23:12** Ex 34:16; Dt 7:3.          **24:6** Ex 12:37, 51; 14:9.
**23:13** Nm 33:55.                          **24:7** Ex 14:10, 20, 27–28.
**23:15** Lv 26:14–39; Dt          **24:8** Nm 21:21–35.
    28:15–68.                                  **24:9** Nm 22:2–5.
**24:1** Ex 19:17.                          **24:10** Nm 23:1–24:25.
**24:2** Gn 11:26, 31; 31:53.          **24:11** Jos 3:14; 6:1.

Jericho, the citizens of Jericho fought against you, but I delivered them also into your power. [12] And I sent the hornets† ahead of you which drove them—the Amorites, Perizzites, Canaanites, Hittites, Girgashites, Hivites, and Jebusites—out of your way; it was not your sword or your bow.* [13] I gave you a land you did not till and cities you did not build, to dwell in; you ate of vineyards and olive groves you did not plant.*

[14]* "Now, therefore, fear the LORD and serve him completely and sincerely. Cast out the gods your ancestors served beyond the River and in Egypt, and serve the LORD. [15]* If it is displeasing to you to serve the LORD, choose today whom you will serve, the gods your ancestors served beyond the River or the gods of the Amorites in whose country you are dwelling. As for me and my household, we will serve the LORD."

[16] But the people answered, "Far be it from us to forsake the LORD to serve other gods. [17] For it was the LORD, our God, who brought us and our ancestors up out of the land of Egypt, out of the house of slavery. He performed those great signs before our very eyes and protected us along our entire journey and among all the peoples through whom we passed. [18] At our approach the LORD drove out all the peoples, including the Amorites who dwelt in the land. Therefore we also will serve the LORD, for he is our God."

[19] Joshua in turn said to the people, "You may not be able to serve the LORD, for he is a holy God; he is a passionate God* who will not forgive your transgressions or your sins. [20] If you forsake the LORD and serve strange gods, he will then do evil to you and destroy you, after having done you good."

[21] But the people answered Joshua, "No! We will serve the LORD." [22] Joshua therefore said to the people, "You are witnesses against yourselves that you have chosen to serve the LORD." They replied, "We are witnesses!" [23] "Now, therefore, put away the foreign gods that are among you and turn your hearts to the LORD, the God of Israel." [24] Then the people promised Joshua, "We will serve the LORD, our God, and will listen to his voice."

[25] So Joshua made a covenant with the people that day and made statutes and ordinances for them at Shechem. [26] Joshua wrote these words in the book of the law of God. Then he took a large stone and set it up there under the terebinth that was in the sanctuary of the LORD.* [27] And Joshua said to all the people, "This stone shall be our witness,* for it has heard all the words which the LORD spoke to us. It shall be a witness against you, should you wish to deny your God." [28] Then Joshua dismissed the people, each to their own heritage.*

**Death of Joshua.** [29]* After these events, Joshua, son of Nun, servant of the LORD, died at the age of a hundred and ten, [30] and they buried him within the borders of his heritage at Timnath-serah* in the mountain region of Ephraim north of Mount Gaash.† [31] Israel served the LORD during the entire lifetime of Joshua, and of those elders who outlived Joshua and who knew all the work the LORD had done for Israel. [32]* The bones of Joseph,† which the Israelites had brought up from Egypt, were buried in Shechem in the plot of ground Jacob had bought from the sons of Hamor, father of Shechem, for a hundred pieces of money. This was a heritage of the descendants of Joseph. [33] When Eleazar, son of Aaron, also died, he was buried on the hill which had been given to his son Phinehas* in the mountain region of Ephraim.

---

**24:12** The hornets: see note on Ex 23:28.

**24:30** Following this verse the Greek translation of the Bible (the Septuagint) adds: "They laid with him there, in the tomb where they buried him, the flint knives with which he had circumcised the Israelites at Gilgal, when he brought them out of Egypt, as Yhwh commanded them. There they are to this very day."

**24:32** Joseph's bones (Gn 50:24–26) and Jacob's purchase of the burial ground (Gn 33:18–20) relate Joshua with Genesis. *A hundred pieces of money*: see note on Gn 33:19.

**24:12** Jos 3:10; 11:20; Ex 23:28; Dt 7:20; Ps 44:3.
**24:13** Dt 6:10–11.
**24:14** Dt 10:12; 1 Sm 7:3; 12:24; Tb 14:9.
**24:15** Dt 30:15–19; Jgs 2:11–13.
**24:19** Ex 20:5; 23:21; 34:14; Lv 19:2; Dt 5:9.
**24:26** Gn 28:18; 31:45; Jgs 9:6.
**24:27** Jos 4:1–9; Gn 31:48, 52; Dt 31:19, 21, 26.
**24:28** Jgs 2:6.
**24:29–31** Jgs 2:7–9.
**24:30** Jos 19:50.
**24:32** Gn 33:19; 50:24; Ex 13:19.
**24:33** Jos 22:13.

# The Book of

# Judges

## INTRODUCTION

### Leslie J. Hoppe, OFM

The book of Judges is a series of stories, some edifying and others horrifying, that cover the period from the death of Joshua to just before the establishment of the Israelite monarchy. The book focuses on the issue of legitimate and effective leadership after the deaths of Moses and Joshua. Religious rather than historiographic in orientation, the book's basic assumption is that Israel's continued presence in the land is dependent on its fidelity to God and the ability of the leaders of the various Israelite tribes to maintain that fidelity. The book calls these leaders "judges" (Jgs 2:18), hence its name. Originally these stories of the judges were likely local traditions that memorialized leaders of tribal militias in localized conflicts over the land and its agricultural produce. These local traditions are given an "all-Israel" significance in the book of Judges, though these heroes who made it possible for the Israelite tribes to maintain their presence in Canaan receive almost no mention in the rest of the Hebrew Bible.

This book is a part of a more extensive literary work that Jewish tradition calls the "Former Prophets" and scholarly usage terms the "Deuteronomistic History" of Israel. The hand of the Deuteronomist in Judges, however, is slight, evident primarily in the introduction to the book (Jgs 1:1–3:6) and in the final verdict on the period of ancient Israel's life in the land: "In those days there was no king in Israel; everyone did what was right in their own sight" (21:25). This text appears to suggest that the monarchy could put an end to the self-destructive behavior of the tribes described in the book's final chapters. It also provides a link with 1 Samuel, which describes the rise of the Israelite monarchy. In the rest of the book, the Deuteronomistic author remains in the background, allowing the stories of the judges to speak for themselves.

The Israelite tribes settled in the central highlands of Canaan toward the end of the Late Bronze Age (1550–1150 BCE) during a period of still unexplained political turmoil and economic collapse in the eastern Mediterranean region. The highlands were settled by people who wanted no part of the conflicts among the Canaanite city-states that were the by-products of the breakdown of political order in the region. Such people established villages throughout the highlands. This area was less attractive to farmers than Canaan's coastal plain, foothills, and valleys, and therefore had been only lightly populated. In addition, the invention of the cistern, which allowed for the storage of rainwater for use in the dry season, made increased agricultural activity in the highlands possible. Still, without a strong central authority and the order that such authority imposed, there were inevitable conflicts over environmental resources and agricultural produce. Such conflicts are reflected in the stories of the judges, who were successful in maintaining the hold of the Israelite tribes on the land.

The book is divided into three sections. The first part (Jgs 1:1–3:6) recapitulates in summary form the settlement of the Israelite tribes in

## Outline of Judges

I. **The Situation in Canaan Following the Israelite Conquest (1:1–3:6)**

II. **Stories of the Judges (3:7–16:31)**

III. **Further Stories of the Tribes of Dan and Benjamin (17:1–21:25)**

JGS

the land of Canaan and provides a theological framework for understanding the events leading up to the establishment of the monarchy. The beginning of the book of Judges stands in tension with the book of Joshua, which immediately precedes it. Joshua describes Israel's acquisition of the land as the achievement of the Israelite tribes coming into Canaan from the east. United under the leadership of Joshua, the tribes made quick thrusts into Canaan—first in the central area and then in the south and finally in the north—with great success. Almost half of Joshua is devoted to dividing up the land among the victorious Israelite tribes (Jos 13–21). The book of Judges, on the other hand, begins with a question about who will lead the tribes in battle against the Canaanites (Jgs 1:1).

The rest of the Deuteronomistic introduction to the book (Jgs 2:1–3:6) offers a theological explanation for the failure of several of the tribes to secure the land assigned to them. The book asserts that the Israelite tribes were disobedient and disloyal to the God who brought their ancestors out of Egypt (2:2b). They were to avoid assimilating with the Canaanite population—especially in religious matters. But Judges states that following the passing of Joshua and his generation, the Israelites took up the worship of Baal, a Canaanite deity (2:10–12). Baal was the god of the storms that brought the rain that was absolutely essential for the type of agriculture practiced in Canaan. Unlike Egypt and Mesopotamia, Canaan was not blessed with a river system capable of providing irrigation for crops. Almost all the water necessary for farming had to come as rain. The patron deity of the Israelites came from southern arid regions (see Hb 3:3). While the Israelites celebrated the fact that their God had liberated their ancestors from slavery in Egypt, they assumed that their new life in Canaan required a god who could bring rain—so they thought it necessary to turn to Baal for help. Who would be better suited to bring needed rain than Baal, who was known as "the Rider of the Clouds"?

The second part of Judges (Jgs 3:7–15:20) presents the Israelite acquisition of the land as a long, drawn-out struggle against powerful and well-organized enemies, who contested the claims of the Israelite tribes on the land. When these enemies were successful, the Israelites cried out for help and God responded by raising up judges who led the tribal militias against the forces threatening them. Some of the judges receive little more than a passing reference (Shamgar, 3:31; Tola, 10:1–2; Jair, 10:3–5; Ibzan, 12:8–10; Elon, 12:11–12; and Abdon, 12:13–15) while others are the subject of engrossing narratives and, in one case, an epic-like poem (ch. 5). One interesting feature of these stories is that each judge appears to be an unlikely candidate for military leadership: Deborah was a woman (4:4), Gideon was an obscure farmer with no military experience (6:15), Jephthah was a social outcast because he was the son of a prostitute (11:1), Samson was totally self-absorbed and deluded (chs. 13–16). Even Ehud's left-handedness (3:21) put him outside what was considered socially acceptable. This served to underscore the belief that the deliverance of the tribes was not a human achievement but was the result of God's power.

After describing a tribal leader's military success, the book states that the leader "judged" Israel during his lifetime, maintaining the people's loyalty to their God. The leadership provided by the judges is best described as "charismatic," i.e., leadership that depended upon the individual's gifts and the people's recognition of those gifts. There was one failed attempt to institutionalize this pattern of leadership by establishing a monarchy (see Jgs 9). Consequently the leadership provided by the judges was temporary and local in nature.

Though the arrangement of the narrative of the book of Judges implies a chronological succession of judges from Othniel (Jgs 3:7) to Samson (13:24–25), the stories likely celebrated regional heroes. When the Israelite tribes developed a national consciousness, it was natural that these originally independent local traditions received an "all-Israel" significance though none of the judges was ever able to marshal all of the tribes in response to any threat. Only the tribes immediately affected usually responded to the judges' call to arms. The Song of Deborah criticizes several of the tribes for their failure to join the forces

J
G
S

that Deborah and Barak were assembling (4:15b–17).

The final section of the book (Jgs 17:1–21:25) contains various stories from the end of the tribal period. Chapters 17–18 describe cultic matters and the migration of the tribe of Dan to the north of Canaan after the Danites were unable to secure the territory originally allotted to them. The final three chapters of the book describe a horrendous act of gang rape, murder, and the internecine war among the tribes that these outrages provoked. These stories were meant to show how terribly disordered the life of the Israelite tribes had become. The book's final verse gives the verdict on these developments: "In those days there was no king in Israel; everyone did what was right in their own sight" (21:25). The books that follow (1–2 Samuel, 1–2 Kings) tell the story of the Israelite monarchy, which in the end proved incapable of providing the kind of leadership needed to maintain just inter-societal relationships in Israel and the commitment to serve the Lord alone.

The book of Judges preserves the memory that the presence of the Israelite tribes in Canaan was contested by other peoples and that Israel's possession of the land was secured in part by violence. The transition between the Late Bronze Age and Early Iron Age was marked by economic and political disruptions that led people to seek means of avoiding the violent consequences of these disruptions. While the cause of all this remains a mystery, it is clear that the Israelite tribes emerged in Canaan during these unsettled times, which the book of Judges reflects. This book, however, offers a theological explanation for the difficulties the Israelite tribes experienced: their failure to remain loyal to the God who brought their ancestors out of Egypt. Can the book of Judges be used to reconstruct the

history of ancient Israel in the period before the establishment of the monarchy? No judge is mentioned in any ancient Near Eastern text outside of the Bible. The book of Judges offers a glimpse into the early history of Israel, but only in a general way. Its purpose is not historiographic but homiletic. The book of Judges describes the consequences of Israel's infidelities as an encouragement to its readers to remain faithful to their ancestral religious traditions.

God's response to Israel's infidelities is forbearance. Despite the tribes' repeated failures God raises up one judge after another. The judges first furnish the military leadership to blunt the threat to the tribes from other groups contending for the land and its produce. Once the military threat is removed, the judge then provides the religious leadership that keeps Israel faithful during the judge's lifetime. Unfortunately, Israel invariably fails to maintain its loyalty to God and a military crisis follows, leading the tribes to call upon God for help. God then raises up still another judge. The question that the attentive reader asks is, how long can this go on?

The Deuteronomistic verdict on the period of the judges (Jgs 21:25) implies that the monarchy could put an end to Israel's dalliance with Baal, its conflicts with its neighbors, and its own self-destructive behavior. Unfortunately, that was not to be the case. The story of the Israelite monarchy and the two Israelite national states that follows in the books of Samuel and Kings is a story of an unrelenting downward spiral. In the end, the territory of the Israelite states was incorporated into the provincial system of the Mesopotamian empires while the Israelites themselves were sent into exile. The narrative in the book of Judges is a harbinger of what is to come in the story of ancient Israel in the land promised to the descendants of Abraham. ∎

# THE BOOK OF JUDGES

## New American Bible, Introduction

The Hebrew word translated "Judges" in the English title of the book refers not to specialized judicial officers or magistrates but to leaders in general. According to the biblical narrative these judges led Israel from the end of the conquest of Canaan until the beginning of the monarchy. The period of the Judges, therefore, extended from the death of Joshua (Jos 24:29–31; cf. Jgs 1:1) until the installation of Saul as Israel's first king by the prophet Samuel, who was also the last judge (see 1 Sm 7:15–17).

The Book of Judges begins with two introductory passages. The first (chap. 1) gives a description of the situation in Canaan after the Israelite conquest. It emphasizes the continued existence of the indigenous inhabitants of Canaan in many parts of the land because of Israel's inability to drive them out completely. The second passage (2:1–3:6) is a thematic introduction to the period of the Judges, describing a cyclical pattern of infidelity, oppression, "crying out," and deliverance (see note on 2:10–19).

The main part of the book (3:7–16:31) consists of a series of stories about thirteen leaders whose careers are described in greater or lesser detail. The exploits of six of these—Othniel, Ehud, Deborah, Gideon, Jephthah, and Samson—are related at length, and all are shown to have delivered Israel from oppression or danger. They are customarily called "major judges," whereas the other six—Shamgar, Tola, Jair, Ibzan, Elon, and Abdon—who appear only in brief notices, are designated "minor judges." The thirteenth, Abimelech, is included in neither group, since his story is essentially a continuation of that of Gideon and his career is presented as deplorable, a cautionary tale of royal ambition.

The final section of the book consists of two episodes, one about the migration of the tribe of Dan (chaps. 17–18) and the other about an intertribal war directed against the tribe of Benjamin (chaps. 19–21). These stories illustrate the religious and political disorder that prevailed at the time when, as yet, "there was no king in Israel" (see note on 17:6).

The principal contribution of the Deuteronomistic historian to the Book of Judges is the thematic introduction to—and theological evaluation of—the period of the Judges in 2:1–3:6, as well as editorial comments structuring the narrative throughout, e.g., 3:7; 4:1; etc. The historian drew the stories of the judges themselves from older sources, which could have existed in written form but derive ultimately from oral tradition.

Thus the principal divisions of the book in outline are as follows:

I. The Situation in Canaan Following the Israelite Conquest (1:1–3:6)
II. Stories of the Judges (3:7–16:31)
III. Further Stories of the Tribes of Dan and Benjamin (17:1–21:25) ■

# JUDGES

## I. THE SITUATION IN CANAAN FOLLOWING THE ISRAELITE CONQUEST

**1** **Canaanites in Palestine.** ¹† After the death of Joshua the Israelites consulted the LORD, asking, "Who shall be first among us to attack the Canaanites and to do battle with them?" ²The LORD answered: Judah shall attack: I have delivered the land into his power.* ³Judah then said to his brother Simeon, "Come up with me into the territory allotted to me, and let us do battle with the Canaanites. I will likewise go with you into the territory allotted to you." So Simeon went with him.*

⁴When Judah attacked, the LORD delivered the Canaanites and Perizzites into their power, and they struck down ten thousand of them in Bezek. ⁵* They came upon Adonibezek in Bezek and fought against him. When they struck down the Canaanites and Perizzites, ⁶Adonibezek fled. They pursued him, and when they caught him, they cut off his thumbs and big toes. ⁷"Seventy kings," said Adonibezek, "used to pick up scraps under my table with their thumbs and big toes cut off. As I have done, so has God repaid me." He was brought to Jerusalem, and he died there. ⁸† The Judahites fought against Jerusalem, captured it, and put it to the sword, setting the city itself on fire.*

⁹Afterward the Judahites went down to fight against the Canaanites who lived in the mountain region, in the Negeb, and in the foothills.* ¹⁰Judah also marched against the Canaanites who lived in Hebron, which was formerly called Kiriath-arba, and defeated Sheshai, Ahiman, and Talmai.* ¹¹They marched from there against the inhabitants of Debir, which was formerly called Kiriath-sepher. ¹²Caleb said, "To the man who attacks Kiriath-sepher and captures it, I will give my daughter Achsah in marriage." ¹³* Othniel captured it, the son of Caleb's younger brother Kenaz; so Caleb gave him his daughter Achsah in marriage. ¹⁴When she came to him, she induced him to ask her father for some land. Then, as she alighted from the donkey, Caleb asked her, "What do you want?" ¹⁵She answered, "Give me a present. Since you have put me in the land of the Negeb, give me pools of water." So Caleb gave her what she wanted, both the upper and the lower pool.

¹⁶* The descendants of Hobab the Kenite, Moses' father-in-law,† came up with the Judahites from the City of Palms to the wilderness of Arad, which is in the Negeb, and they settled among the Amalekites. ¹⁷* Then Judah went with his brother Simeon, and they defeated the Canaanites who lived in Zephath. They put the city under the ban and renamed it Hormah.†* ¹⁸Judah captured Gaza with its territory, Ashkelon with its territory, Ekron with its territory, and Ashdod† with its territory.* ¹⁹The LORD was with Judah, so they gained possession of the mountain region. But they could not dispossess those who lived on the plain, because they had iron chariots. ²⁰* As Moses had commanded, they gave Hebron to Caleb, who then drove the three sons of Anak away from there.

²¹† As for the Jebusites dwelling in Jerusalem,

---

† **1:1–36** The chapter depicts the Israelite settlement of Canaan as a gradual and incomplete process (cf. Ex 23:29–30; Dt 7:22). This picture contrasts sharply with that found in Joshua, where the conquest is rapid and total. Accordingly, some scholars believe that Jgs 1 derives from an early account, which is less idealized and more realistic than that on which Joshua is based. Others, noting that Judah is presented as the only tribe that was completely successful in driving foreigners from its territory, think that the account was written at a late date and reflects suspicion in Judah about foreign elements in the Israelite populations of outlying areas (cf. 2 Kgs 17:24–33).

**1:8** See note on 1:21 below.

**1:16** *Hobab the Kenite, Moses' father-in-law*: as in 4:11. However, in Nm 10:29 Hobab is identified as Moses' brother-in-law, while Reuel is identified as Moses' father-in-law (see also Ex 2:18). The more common name of Moses' father-in-law is Jethro, also a Midianite (e.g., Ex 3:1). It is impossible to sort out the relationships among these three men in the ancient traditions. *City of Palms*: Jericho (cf. Dt 34:3) or a town in the Negeb.

**1:17** *The ban…Hormah*: the narrator relates the city-name "Hormah" to "the ban" (Hebrew *herem*), which commanded the Israelites to devote to the Lord—and thus to destroy—whatever

was captured within the land (cf. Dt 20:10–18).

**1:18** *Gaza…Ashkelon…Ekron…Ashdod*: four of the five major cities of the Philistines (see note on 3:3). Since these cities were on the coastal plain, the statement that Judah captured them is contrary to v. 19, which notes Judah's failure to drive out the inhabitants of the lowlands. In the Septuagint the problem is removed by changing the beginning of this verse to read "Judah did not dispossess…."

**1:21** According to Jos 18:16, Jerusalem was assigned to the tribe of Benjamin. According to the notice in 1:8 above, the city was burned by the Judahites, but elsewhere (2 Sm 5:6–9) we learn that it was not actually taken from the Jebusites until David captured it and made it his capital.

* —
**1:2** Jgs 20:18.    Nm 13:22; Jos 14:15.
**1:3** Jgs 1:17.    **1:13** Jgs 3:9.
**1:5** Jos 10:1.    **1:16** Jgs 4:11; Nm
**1:8** Jos 10:1–27; 2 Sm    10:29–32.
   5:6–9.    **1:17** Jos 1:3.
**1:9** Jos 10:40; 11:16;    **1:17** Nm 21:3; Jos 12:14.
   12:8.    **1:18** Jos 11:22.
**1:10** Jos 15:13–19;    **1:20** Jos 14:6–15.

the Benjaminites did not dispossess them, so that the Jebusites live with the Benjaminites in Jerusalem to the present day.*

²²The house of Joseph, too, went up against Bethel, and the LORD was with them. ²³The house of Joseph reconnoitered Bethel, which formerly was called Luz.* ²⁴The scouts saw a man coming out of the city and said to him, "Tell us the way into the city, and we will show you mercy." ²⁵He showed them the way into the city, and they put the city to the sword; but they let the man and his whole clan go free. ²⁶The man then went to the land of the Hittites, where he built a city and called it Luz, which is its name to this day.

²⁷*Manasseh did not take possession of Beth-shean with its towns or of Taanach with its towns. Nor did they dispossess the inhabitants of Dor and its towns, those of Ibleam and its towns, or those of Megiddo and its towns. The Canaanites continued to live in this district. ²⁸When Israel grew stronger, they conscripted the Canaanites as laborers, but did not actually drive them out. ²⁹*Ephraim did not drive out the Canaanites living in Gezer, and so the Canaanites lived among them in Gezer.

³⁰*Nor did Zebulun dispossess the inhabitants of Kitron or those of Nahalol; the Canaanites lived among them and became forced laborers.

³¹*Nor did Asher dispossess the inhabitants of Acco or those of Sidon, or take possession of Mahaleb, Achzib, Helbah, Aphik, or Rehob. ³²So the Asherites settled among the Canaanite inhabitants of the land, for they had not dispossessed them.

³³*Nor did Naphtali drive out the inhabitants of Beth-shemesh or those of Beth-anath. They settled among the Canaanite inhabitants of the land and the inhabitants of Beth-shemesh and Beth-anath became forced laborers for them.

³⁴The Amorites hemmed in the Danites in the mountain region, not permitting them to come down onto the plain. ³⁵So the Amorites continued to live in Harheres, Aijalon, and Shaalbim, but as the power of the house of Joseph grew, they were conscripted as laborers.

³⁶The territory of the Amorites extended from the Akrabbim pass, from Sela and upward.

**2 Infidelities of the Israelites.** ¹A messenger of the LORD went up from Gilgal to Bochim and said, I brought you up from Egypt and led you into the land which I promised on oath to your ancestors. I said, I will never break my covenant with you, ²but you must not make a covenant with the inhabitants of this land; you must pull down their altars.* But you did not listen to me. Look what you have done! ³For I also said,† I will not clear them out of your way; they will become traps for you, and their gods a snare for you.*

⁴When the messenger of the LORD had spoken these things to all the Israelites, the people wept aloud. ⁵They named that place Bochim,† and they offered sacrifice there to the LORD.

⁶*Then Joshua dismissed the people, and the Israelites went, each to their own heritage, to take possession of the land. ⁷The people served the LORD during the entire lifetime of Joshua, and of those elders who outlived Joshua and who had seen all the great work the LORD had done for Israel. ⁸Joshua, son of Nun, the servant of the LORD, died at the age of a hundred and ten, ⁹and they buried him within the borders of his heritage at Timnath-heres in the mountain region of Ephraim north of Mount Gaash.*

¹⁰†When the rest of that generation were also gathered to their ancestors, and a later generation arose that did not know the LORD or the work he had done for Israel, ¹¹*the Israelites did what was evil in the sight of the LORD. They served the Baals,† ¹²and abandoned the

† 2:3 *I also said*: the Lord explicitly warned the Israelites of the consequences of disobedience; see Nm 33:55 and especially Jos 23:13.

2:5 *Bochim*: Hebrew for "weepers."

2:10–19 This long thematic passage establishes the cyclical pattern for the stories found in the rest of the book. When the Israelites are secure, they forsake the Lord and worship other gods. In punishment the Lord places them in the power of a foreign oppressor. But when they cry out in distress, the Lord takes pity on them and raises up a judge, who delivers them from the oppressor. The Israelites remain faithful to the Lord during the lifetime of the judge, but when the judge dies they again abandon the Lord, and the cycle begins anew.

2:11 *The Baals*: the title "Baal," meaning "lord" or "master," belonged to a large number of Canaanite, Phoenician, and Syrian deities, including especially the great storm god Hadad Baal, widely revered as lord of the earth. The plural form, which occurs here, was used by the biblical writers to refer to foreign gods in general.

1:21 Jos 15:63; 18:16; 2 Sm 5:6–9.
1:23 Gn 28:19; Jos 18:13.
1:27–28 Jos 17:11–13.
1:29 Jos 16:10.
1:30 Jos 19:10–16.
1:31–32 Jos 19:24–31.
1:33 Jos 19:32–39.
2:2 Ex 23:32; 34:12–13; Dt 7:2, 5; 12:2–3.
2:3 Ex 23:33; Dt 7:16; Jos 23:13.
2:6–9 Jos 24:28–31.
2:9 Jos 19:49–50.
2:11–14 Jgs 3:7–8, 12; 4:1–2; 6:1; 10:6–8; 13:1.

LORD, the God of their ancestors, the one who had brought them out of the land of Egypt. They followed other gods, the gods of the peoples around them, and bowed down to them, and provoked the LORD.

[13] Because they had abandoned the LORD and served Baal and the Astartes,† [14] the anger of the LORD flared up against Israel, and he delivered them into the power of plunderers who despoiled them. He sold them into the power of the enemies around them, and they were no longer able to withstand their enemies. [15] Whenever they marched out, the hand of the LORD turned against them, as the LORD had said, and as the LORD had sworn to them;* and they were in great distress. [16] But the LORD raised up judges to save them from the power of their plunderers; [17] but they did not listen to their judges either, for they prostituted themselves by following other gods, bowing down to them. They were quick to stray from the way their ancestors had taken, who obeyed the commandments of the LORD; but these did not. [18] When the LORD raised up judges for them, he would be with the judge and save them from the power of their enemies as long as the judge lived. The LORD would change his mind when they groaned in their affliction under their oppressors. [19] But when the judge died, they would again do worse than their ancestors, following other gods, serving and bowing down to them, relinquishing none of their evil practices or stubborn ways.*

[20]* The anger of the LORD flared up against Israel, and he said: Because this nation has transgressed my covenant, which I enjoined on their ancestors, and has not listened to me, [21] I for my part will not clear away for them any more of the nations Joshua left when he died. [22]* They will be made to test Israel, to see whether or not they will keep to the way of the LORD and continue in it as their ancestors did. [23] Therefore the LORD allowed these nations to remain instead of expelling them immediately. He had not delivered them into the power of Joshua.

**3** [1] These are the nations the LORD allowed to remain, so that through them he might test Israel, all those who had not experienced any of the Canaanite wars— [2] to teach warfare to those generations of Israelites who had never experienced it: [3]* the five lords of the Philistines,† and all the Canaanites, the Sidonians, and the Hivites who lived in the mountain region of the Lebanon between Baal-hermon and Lebo-hamath. [4] These served as a test for Israel, to know whether they would obey the commandments the LORD had enjoined on their ancestors through Moses. [5] So the Israelites settled among the Canaanites, Hittites, Amorites, Perizzites, Hivites, and Jebusites.* [6] They took their daughters in marriage, and gave their own daughters to their sons in marriage,* and served their gods.

## II. STORIES OF THE JUDGES

**Othniel.** [7]* Then the Israelites did what was evil in the sight of the LORD; they forgot the LORD, their God, and served the Baals and the Asherahs,† [8] and the anger of the LORD flared up against them. He sold them into the power of Cushan-rishathaim,† king of Aram Naharaim; and the Israelites served Cushan-rishathaim for eight years. [9] But when the Israelites cried out to the LORD,* he raised up a savior for them, to save them. It was Othniel, son of Caleb's younger brother Kenaz.* [10] The spirit of the LORD came upon him,* and he judged Israel. When he marched out to war, the LORD delivered Cushan-rishathaim, king of Aram, into his power, and his hold on Cushan-rishathaim was firm. [11] So the land was at rest for forty years,* until Othniel, son of Kenaz, died.

---

**2:13** *The Astartes*: Ashtoreth, or Astarte, was an important Canaanite and Phoenician goddess. The plural form used here probably refers to foreign goddesses in general.

**3:3** *The Philistines*: a people of Aegean origin who settled on the coastal plain of southern Canaan in the twelfth century B.C.; from their name derives the geographic designation Palestine. Israel competed for control of the country against a group of their cities: Gaza, Ashkelon, Ashdod, Gath, and Ekron.

**3:7** *The Asherahs*: Asherah was an important goddess, whose presence in the cult was represented by a wooden pole, also called an "asherah"; see notes on Ex 34:13 and Dt 7:5. Here the plural is used to refer to goddesses in general.

**3:8** *Cushan-rishathaim*: this king is not known from other biblical or extrabiblical sources. His title, "king of Aram Naharaim," indicates that he was a Mesopotamian ruler.

---

**2:15** Lv 26:14–39; Dt 28:15–68.
**2:19** Jgs 3:12; 4:1; 8:33–34.
**2:20–21** Jos 23:13; Jgs 2:2–3.
**2:22** Jgs 3:1, 4.
**3:3** Jos 13:2–5.
**3:5** Ex 3:8, 17; 23:23; 33:2; 34:11; Dt 7:1; 20:17; Jos 3:10; 24:11.
**3:6** Ex 34:16; Dt 7:3; Jos 23:12.
**3:7–8** Jgs 2:11–14.
**3:9** Jgs 3:15; 4:3; 6:6, 7; 10:10; 1 Sm 12:8, 10.
**3:9** Jgs 1:13.
**3:10** Jgs 6:34; 11:29; 13:25; 14:6, 19; 15:14; 1 Sm 11:6.
**3:11** Jgs 3:30; 5:31; 8:28.

**Ehud.** <sup>12</sup> Again the Israelites did what was evil in the sight of the Lord, so he strengthened Eglon, king of Moab, against Israel because they did what was evil in the sight of the Lord. <sup>13</sup> Taking the Ammonites and Amalek as allies, he went and defeated Israel, taking possession of the City of Palms. <sup>14</sup> So the Israelites served Eglon, king of Moab, for eighteen years.

<sup>15</sup> But when the Israelites cried out to the Lord, he raised up for them a savior, Ehud, son of Gera, a Benjaminite who was left-handed.† The Israelites would send their tribute to Eglon, king of Moab, by him. <sup>16</sup> Ehud made himself a two-edged dagger a foot long, and strapped it under his clothes on his right thigh. <sup>17</sup> He presented the tribute to Eglon, king of Moab; now Eglon was a very fat man. <sup>18</sup> When he had finished presenting the tribute, he dismissed the troops who had carried the tribute. <sup>19</sup> But he himself turned back at the sculptured stones near Gilgal, and said, "I have a secret message for you, O king." And the king said, "Silence!" Then when all his attendants had left his presence, <sup>20</sup> Ehud went in to him where he sat alone in his cool upper room. Ehud said, "I have a word from God for you." So the king rose from his throne. <sup>21</sup> Then Ehud with his left hand drew the dagger from his right thigh, and thrust it into Eglon's belly. <sup>22</sup> The hilt also went in after the blade, and the fat closed over the blade because he did not withdraw the dagger from the body.

<sup>23</sup> Then Ehud went out onto the porch, shutting the doors of the upper room on Eglon and locking them. <sup>24</sup> When Ehud had left and the servants had come, they saw that the doors of the upper room were locked, and thought, "He must be easing himself in the cool chamber." <sup>25</sup> They waited until they were at a loss when he did not open the doors of the upper room. So they took the key and opened them, and there was their lord lying on the floor, dead.

<sup>26</sup> During their delay Ehud escaped and, passing the sculptured stones, took refuge in Seirah. <sup>27</sup> On his arrival he sounded the horn in the mountain region of Ephraim, and the Israelites went down from the mountains with him as their leader. <sup>28</sup> "Follow me," he said to them, "for the Lord has delivered your enemies the Moabites into your power."* So they followed him down and seized the fords of the Jordan against the Moabites, permitting no one to cross. <sup>29</sup> On that occasion they slew about ten thousand Moabites, all of them strong warriors. Not one escaped. <sup>30</sup> So Moab was brought under the power of Israel* at that time; and the land had rest for eighty years.*

**Shamgar.** <sup>31</sup> After him there was Shamgar,† son of Anath,* who slew six hundred Philistines with an oxgoad.* He, too, was a savior for Israel.

**4 Deborah and Barak.** <sup>1</sup>* The Israelites again did what was evil in the sight of the Lord; Ehud was dead. <sup>2</sup> So the Lord sold them into the power of the Canaanite king, Jabin, who reigned in Hazor. The general of his army was Sisera, who lived in Harosheth-ha-goiim.* <sup>3</sup>* But the Israelites cried out to the Lord; for with his nine hundred iron chariots Jabin harshly oppressed the Israelites for twenty years.

<sup>4</sup> At that time the prophet Deborah, wife of Lappidoth, was judging Israel. <sup>5</sup> She used to sit under Deborah's palm tree, between Ramah and Bethel in the mountain region of Ephraim, where the Israelites came up to her for judgment. <sup>6</sup> She had Barak, son of Abinoam,* summoned from Kedesh of Naphtali. She said to him, "This is what the Lord, the God of Israel, commands: Go, march against Mount Tabor, and take with you ten thousand men from Naphtali and Zebulun. <sup>7</sup> I will draw Sisera, the general of Jabin's army, out to you at the Wadi Kishon,* together with his chariots and troops, and I will deliver them into your power." <sup>8</sup> But Barak answered her, "If you come with me, I will go; if you do not come with me, I will not go." <sup>9</sup> "I will certainly go with you," she replied, "but you will not gain glory for the expedition on which you are setting out, for it is into a woman's power that

---

† **3:15** *Left-handed*: this detail is important because it shows why Ehud is able to conceal a weapon on his right thigh (3:16). There is also a wordplay involved, since "Benjaminite" in Hebrew could also mean "right-handed man."

**3:31** Shamgar is the first of the so-called minor judges; cf. Introduction.

**3:28** Nm 21:34; Dt 2:24; Jos 2:24; Jgs 4:7, 14; 7:7, 9, 15.
**3:30** Jgs 8:28; 11:23; 1 Sm 7:13.
**3:30** Jgs 3:11; 5:31; 8:28.
**3:31** Jgs 5:6.
**3:31** Jgs 15:15; 2 Sm 23:8, 18.
**4:1** Jgs 2:19; 3:12; 8:33–34.
**4:2** Jos 11:1–15; Ps 83:10; 1 Sm 12:9.
**4:3** Jgs 3:9, 15; 6:6, 7; 10:10; 1 Sm 12:8, 10.
**4:6** Heb 11:32.
**4:7** Jgs 5:21; Ps 83:10.

the LORD is going to sell Sisera." So Deborah arose and went with Barak and journeyed with him to Kedesh.

[10] Barak summoned Zebulun and Naphtali to Kedesh, and ten thousand men followed him.* Deborah also went up with him. [11]† Now Heber the Kenite had detached himself from Cain, the descendants of Hobab, Moses' father-in-law,* and had pitched his tent by the terebinth of Zaanannim, which was near Kedesh.

[12] It was reported to Sisera that Barak, son of Abinoam, had gone up to Mount Tabor. [13] So Sisera called out all nine hundred of his iron chariots and all his forces from Harosheth-ha-goiim to the Wadi Kishon. [14] Deborah then said to Barak, "Up! This is the day on which the LORD has delivered Sisera into your power. The LORD marches before you." So Barak went down Mount Tabor, followed by his ten thousand men. [15] And the LORD threw Sisera and all his chariots and forces into a panic before Barak.* Sisera himself dismounted from his chariot and fled on foot, [16] but Barak pursued the chariots and the army as far as Harosheth-ha-goiim. The entire army of Sisera fell beneath the sword, not even one man surviving.

[17] Sisera fled on foot to the tent of Jael, wife of Heber the Kenite, for there was peace between Jabin, king of Hazor, and the family of Heber the Kenite. [18] Jael went out to meet Sisera and said to him, "Turn aside, my lord, turn aside with me; do not be afraid." So he went into her tent, and she covered him with a rug. [19] He said to her, "Please give me a little water to drink. I am thirsty." So she opened a skin of milk, gave him a drink, and then covered him.* [20] "Stand at the entrance of the tent," he said to her. "If anyone comes and asks, 'Is there someone here?' say, 'No!'" [21] Jael, wife of Heber, got a tent peg and took a mallet in her hand. When Sisera was in a deep sleep from exhaustion, she approached him stealthily and drove the peg through his temple and down

into the ground, and he died.* [22] Then when Barak came in pursuit of Sisera, Jael went out to meet him and said to him, "Come, I will show you the man you are looking for." So he went in with her, and there lay Sisera dead, with the tent peg through his temple.

[23] Thus on that day God humbled the Canaanite king, Jabin, before the Israelites; [24] their power weighed ever more heavily on him, until at length they finished off the Canaanite king, Jabin.

# 5 Song of Deborah. [1]* On that day Deborah sang this song—and Barak, son of Abinoam:

[2]†   When uprising broke out in Israel,
     when the people rallied for duty—
       bless the LORD!

[3]   Hear, O kings! Give ear, O princes!
     I will sing, I will sing to the LORD,
     I will make music to the LORD, the
       God of Israel.

[4]†*   LORD, when you went out from Seir,
     when you marched from the plains of
       Edom,
   The earth shook, the heavens poured,
     the clouds poured rain,

[5]   The mountains streamed,
     before the LORD, the One of Sinai,
     before the LORD, the God of Israel.

[6]   In the days of Shamgar, son of Anath,*
     in the days of Jael, caravans ceased:
   Those who traveled the roads
     now traveled by roundabout paths.*

[7]   Gone was freedom beyond the walls,
     gone indeed from Israel.
   When I, Deborah, arose,
     when I arose, a mother in Israel.†

[8]   New gods were their choice;
     then war was at the gates.
   No shield was to be found, no spear,
     among forty thousand in Israel!

[9]   My heart is with the leaders of Israel,

---

† **4:11** It was characteristic of the Kenites that they encamped alongside or among other nomadic groups, such as the Amalekites (cf. 1:16; 1 Sm 15:6). They are most often mentioned in connection with tribes living in the southern part of Judah, but Heber's group seems to have moved north and pitched its tents in the lower Galilee. *Cain*: in this case a collective term for the Kenites. For Hobab, see 1:16.

**5:2–31** This canticle is an excellent example of early Hebrew poetry, even though some of its verses are now obscure.

**5:4–5** The Lord himself marches to war in support of Israel. Storm and earthquake are part of the traditional imagery

of theophany; cf. Ex 19:16, 18–20; Dt 33:2–3; Ps 18:7–15; 77:17–20; 144:5–7.

**5:7** *A mother in Israel*: the precise meaning of the term "mother" is unclear, except that it seems to indicate Deborah's position of leadership, and so may be a title (cf. 2 Sm 20:19).

* **4:10** Jgs 5:18.
**4:11** Nm 10:29; Jgs 1:16.
**4:15** Ex 14:24; Jos 10:10; 1 Sm 7:10.
**4:19** Jgs 5:25.
**4:21** Jgs 5:26.
**5:1** Ex 15:1.
**5:4–5** Dt 33:2; Ps 68:8–9; Hb 3:3–15.
**5:6** Jgs 3:31.
**5:6** Is 33:8.

with the dedicated ones of the
    people—bless the Lord;

10 Those who ride on white donkeys,
    seated on saddle rugs,
    and those who travel the road,
Sing of them

11     to the sounds of musicians at the
    wells.
There they recount the just deeds of the
    Lord,
    his just deeds bringing freedom to
    Israel.

12 Awake, awake, Deborah!
    Awake, awake, strike up a song!
Arise, Barak!
    Take captive your captors, son of
    Abinoam!

13 Then down went Israel against the
    mighty,
    the army of the Lord went down for
    him against the warriors.

14† From Ephraim, their base in the valley;
    behind you, Benjamin, among your
    troops.
From Machir came down commanders,
    from Zebulun wielders of the
    marshal's staff.

15 The princes of Issachar were with
    Deborah,
Issachar, faithful to Barak;
    in the valley they followed at his
    heels.
Among the clans of Reuben
    great were the searchings of heart!

16 Why did you stay beside your hearths
    listening to the lowing of the herds?
Among the clans of Reuben
    great were the searchings of heart!

17 Gilead stayed beyond the Jordan;
    Why did Dan spend his time in ships?
Asher remained along the shore,
    he stayed in his havens.

18 Zebulun was a people who defied death,
    Naphtali, too, on the open heights! *

19 The kings came and fought;
    then they fought, those kings of
    Canaan,
At Taanach by the waters of Megiddo;
    no spoil of silver did they take.

20 From the heavens the stars† fought;
    from their courses they fought against
    Sisera. *

21 The Wadi Kishon swept them away;
    the wadi overwhelmed them, the
    Wadi Kishon. *
    Trample down the strong!†

22 Then the hoofs of the horses hammered,
    the galloping, galloping of steeds.

23 "Curse Meroz,"† says the messenger of
    the Lord,
    "curse, curse its inhabitants!
For they did not come when the Lord
    helped,
    the help of the Lord against the
    warriors."

24 Most blessed of women is Jael, *
    the wife of Heber the Kenite,
    blessed among tent-dwelling women!

25 He asked for water, she gave him milk,
    in a princely bowl she brought him
    curds. *

26* With her hand she reached for the peg,
    with her right hand, the workman's
    hammer.
She hammered Sisera, crushed his head;
    she smashed, pierced his temple.

27 At her feet he sank down, fell, lay still;
    down at her feet he sank and fell;
    where he sank down, there he fell,
    slain.

28† From the window she looked down,
    the mother of Sisera peered through
    the lattice:
"Why is his chariot so long in coming?
    why are the hoofbeats of his chariots
    delayed?"

29 The wisest of her princesses answers her;

---

† **5:14–22** The poet praises the tribes that participated in the war against Sisera: Ephraim, Benjamin, Machir (later regarded as a clan of Manasseh), Zebulun, Issachar, and Naphtali, the tribe of Barak (cf. 4:6). By contrast, the tribes of Reuben, Gilead (elsewhere a region occupied by Reubenites and Gadites), Dan, and Asher are chided for their lack of participation. The more distant tribes of Judah and Simeon are not mentioned, and some historians believe they were not part of Israel at this time.
**5:20–21** *Stars:* the heavenly host, or angelic army. The roles played by the stars and the flash floods underscore the divine involvement in the battle (cf. 5:4–5).
**5:21** *Trample down the strong!:* the meaning of these words

is obscure. If this interpretation is correct, Deborah is the one addressed.
**5:23** *Meroz:* an unknown locality in which Israelites probably resided, since its inhabitants are cursed for their failure to participate in the battle.
**5:28–30** The scene shifts to the household of the slain Canaanite general, where the anxious foreboding of Sisera's mother is countered by the assurances of the noblewomen.

| | |
|---|---|
| **5:18** Jgs 4:10. | **5:24** Jgs 4:17; Jdt 13:18; Lk |
| **5:20** Jgs 4:15. | 1:42. |
| **5:21** Jgs 4:7, 13; Ps 83:10. | **5:25** Jgs 4:19. |
| | **5:26–27** Jgs 4:21. |

she even replies to herself,

30 "They must be dividing the spoil they
took:
a slave woman or two for each man,
Spoil of dyed cloth for Sisera,
spoil of ornate dyed cloth,
a pair of ornate dyed cloths for my
neck in the spoil."

31 So perish all your enemies, O LORD!*
But may those who love you be like
the sun rising in its might!

And the land was at rest for forty years.*

# 6 The Call of Gideon.
¹The Israelites did what was evil in the sight of the LORD, who therefore delivered them into the power of Midian for seven years, ²so that Midian held Israel subject. From fear of Midian the Israelites made dens in the mountains, the caves, and the strongholds.* ³For it used to be that whenever the Israelites had completed sowing their crops, Midian, Amalek, and the Kedemites† would come up, ⁴encamp against them, and lay waste the produce of the land as far as the outskirts of Gaza, leaving no sustenance in Israel, and no sheep, ox, or donkey. ⁵For they would come up with their livestock, and their tents would appear as thick as locusts. They would be too many to count when they came into the land to lay it waste. ⁶*Israel was reduced to utter poverty by Midian, and so the Israelites cried out to the LORD.

⁷When Israel cried out to the LORD because of Midian, ⁸*the LORD sent a prophet to the Israelites who said to them: Thus says the LORD, the God of Israel: I am the one who brought you up from Egypt; I brought you out of the house of slavery. ⁹I rescued you from the power of Egypt and all your oppressors. I drove them out before you and gave you their land. ¹⁰And I said to you: I, the LORD, am your God; you shall not fear the gods of the Amorites in whose land you are dwelling. But you did not listen to me.

¹¹Then the messenger of the LORD came and sat under the terebinth in Ophrah that belonged to Joash the Abiezrite. Joash's son Gideon* was beating out wheat in the wine press to save it from the Midianites, ¹²and the messenger of the LORD appeared to him and said: The LORD is with you, you mighty warrior! ¹³"My lord," Gideon said to him, "if the LORD is with us, why has all this happened to us? Where are his wondrous deeds about which our ancestors told us when they said, 'Did not the LORD bring us up from Egypt?' For now the LORD has abandoned us and has delivered us into the power of Midian." ¹⁴*The LORD turned to him and said: Go with the strength you have, and save Israel from the power of Midian. Is it not I who send you? ¹⁵But he answered him, "Please, my Lord, how can I save Israel? My family is the poorest in Manasseh, and I am the most insignificant in my father's house."* ¹⁶The LORD said to him: I will be with you,† and you will cut down Midian to the last man. ¹⁷He answered him, "If you look on me with favor, give me a sign that you are the one speaking with me. ¹⁸Please do not depart from here until I come to you and bring out my offering and set it before you." He answered: I will await your return.

¹⁹So Gideon went off and prepared a young goat and an ephah† of flour in the form of unleavened cakes. Putting the meat in a basket and the broth in a pot, he brought them out to him under the terebinth and presented them. ²⁰*The messenger of God said to him: Take the meat and unleavened cakes and lay them on this rock; then pour out the broth. When he had done so, ²¹the messenger of the LORD stretched out the tip of the staff he held. When he touched the meat and unleavened cakes, a fire came up from the rock and consumed the meat and unleavened cakes. Then the messenger of the LORD disappeared from sight. ²²†Gideon, now aware that it had been the

---

**6:3** *Midian, Amalek, and the Kedemites:* three groups of camel nomads, whose raids were a constant threat to settled peoples like the Israelites during the period of the Judges.

**6:16** *I will be with you:* narratives telling how the Lord commissions someone for a task depict the person's reactions of reluctance, confusion, or sense of inadequacy, and the Lord's reassurance ("I will be with you"), sometimes accompanied by a sign (cf. Ex 3:12; Jer 1:8). Lk 1:28–37 is modeled on this pattern.

**6:19** *Ephah:* see note on Is 5:10.

**6:22** Ancient Israel thought that seeing God face to face

meant mortal danger, as Ex 33:20 indicates and as Gideon's reaction here shows. Compare the reaction of Samson's parents (13:22–23) when they realize they have been conversing with the Lord.

---

5:31 Ps 83.
5:31 Jgs 3:11, 30; 8:28.
6:2 1 Sm 13:6.
6:6–7 Jgs 3:9, 15; 4:3;
10:10; 1 Sm 12:8, 10.

6:8–10 Jgs 2:1–3; 10:11–14.
6:11 Heb 11:32.
6:14 Ex 3:10–12.
6:15 1 Sm 9:21.
6:20–22 Jgs 13:19–22.

messenger of the LORD, said, "Alas, Lord GOD, that I have seen the messenger of the LORD face to face!"* ²³The LORD answered him: You are safe. Do not fear. You shall not die. ²⁴So Gideon built there an altar to the LORD and called it Yahweh-shalom.†* To this day it is still in Ophrah of the Abiezrites.

²⁵That same night the LORD said to him: Take your father's bull, the bull fattened for seven years, and pull down your father's altar to Baal. As for the asherah† beside it, cut it down ²⁶and build an altar to the LORD, your God, on top of this stronghold with the pile of wood. Then take the fattened bull and offer it as a whole-burnt sacrifice on the wood from the asherah you have cut down. ²⁷So Gideon took ten of his servants and did as the LORD had commanded him. But he was too afraid of his family and of the townspeople to do it by day; he did it at night. ²⁸Early the next morning the townspeople found that the altar of Baal had been dismantled, the asherah beside it cut down, and the fattened bull offered on the altar that was built. ²⁹They asked one another, "Who did this?" They inquired and searched until they were told, "Gideon, son of Joash, did it." ³⁰So the townspeople said to Joash, "Bring out your son that he may die, for he has dismantled the altar of Baal and cut down the asherah that was beside it." ³¹But Joash replied to all who were standing around him, "Is it for you to take action for Baal, or be his savior? Anyone who takes action for him shall be put to death by morning. If he is a god, let him act for himself,* since his altar has been dismantled!" ³²So on that day Gideon was called Jerubbaal,†* because of the words, "Let Baal take action against him, since he dismantled his altar."

³³Then all Midian and Amalek and the Kedemites mustered and crossed over into the valley of Jezreel, where they encamped.

³⁴And Gideon was clothed with the spirit of the LORD,†* and he blew the horn summoning Abiezer to follow him. ³⁵He sent messengers throughout Manasseh, and they, too, were summoned to follow him; he also sent messengers throughout Asher, Zebulun, and Naphtali, and they advanced to meet the others. ³⁶Gideon said to God, "If indeed you are going to save Israel through me, as you have said, ³⁷I am putting this woolen fleece on the threshing floor, and if dew is on the fleece alone, while all the ground is dry, I shall know that you will save Israel through me, as you have said." ³⁸That is what happened. Early the next morning when he wrung out the fleece, he squeezed enough dew from it to fill a bowl. ³⁹Gideon then said to God, "Do not be angry with me if I speak once more. Let me make just one more test with the fleece. Let the fleece alone be dry, but let there be dew on all the ground." ⁴⁰That is what God did that night: the fleece alone was dry, but there was dew on all the ground.

**7** **Defeat of Midian.** ¹Early the next morning Jerubbaal* (that is, Gideon) encamped by the spring of Harod with all his soldiers. The camp of Midian was north of him, beside the hill of Moreh in the valley. ²The LORD said to Gideon: You have too many soldiers with you for me to deliver Midian into their power, lest Israel vaunt itself against me and say, "My own power saved me."†* ³So announce in the hearing of the soldiers, "If anyone is afraid or fearful, let him leave!* Let him depart from Mount Gilead!"† Twenty-two thousand of the soldiers left, but ten thousand remained. ⁴The LORD said to Gideon: There are still too many soldiers. Lead them down to the water and I will test them for you there. If I tell you that a certain man is to go with you, he must go with you. But no one is to go if I tell you he must

6:24 *Yahweh-shalom*: a reference to the Lord's words, "You are safe" (v. 23), lit., "Peace be to you!"
6:25 *The asherah*: see note on Ex 34:13.
6:32 *Jerubbaal*: similar in sound to the Hebrew words meaning, "Let Baal take action."
6:34 *Clothed with the spirit of the LORD*: narratives about the selection of leaders in early Israel typically attribute their prowess to "the spirit of the Lord," not to their own qualities (cf. v. 15). The Lord's spirit "comes upon" them (3:10; 11:29; 13:25) or "rushes upon" them (14:6, 19; 15:14; 1 Sm 11:6), and they are transformed into effective leaders. Here, Gideon is "clothed" with the Lord's spirit; cf. the clothing or vesture imagery in Is 59:17; 61:10; Ez 16:10–14; Jb 29:14.
7:2 *My own power saved me*: Deuteronomic theology constantly warns Israel against attributing success to their own ef-

forts; cf. Dt 6:10–12; 8:17.
7:3 *Mount Gilead*: since the well-known highlands of Gilead were east of the Jordan River, some other hill of Gilead must be intended here. Perhaps its name is preserved in Ain Jalud (or Galud), the modern Arabic name of the spring of Harod, where Gideon's army is encamped (v. 1). The narrator plays on the Hebrew word "fearful" (*hared*) and the name of the spring, *harod*.

6:22 Gn 32:31; Dt 5:24–26; Jgs 13:22.
6:24 Gn 33:20; 35:7; Ex 7:15.
6:31 1 Kgs 18:27.
6:32 1 Sm 12:11.
6:34 Jgs 3:10; 11:29; 13:25; 14:6, 19; 15:14; 1 Sm 11:6.
7:1 Jgs 6:32.
7:2 Dt 8:17; 9:4.
7:3 Dt 20:8.

not. [5]† When Gideon led the soldiers down to the water, the Lord said to him: Everyone who laps up the water as a dog does with its tongue you shall set aside by himself; and everyone who kneels down to drink raising his hand to his mouth you shall set aside by himself. [6]Those who lapped up the water with their tongues numbered three hundred, but all the rest of the soldiers knelt down to drink the water. [7]The Lord said to Gideon: By means of the three hundred who lapped up the water I will save you and deliver Midian into your power. So let all the other soldiers go home. [8]They took up such supplies as the soldiers had with them, as well as their horns, and Gideon sent the rest of the Israelites to their tents, but kept the three hundred men. Now the camp of Midian was below him in the valley.

[9]That night the Lord said to Gideon: Go, descend on the camp, for I have delivered it into your power. [10]If you are afraid to attack, go down to the camp with your aide Purah [11]and listen to what they are saying. After that you will have the courage to descend on the camp. So he went down with his aide Purah to the outposts of the armed men in the camp. [12]* The Midianites, Amalekites, and all the Kedemites were lying in the valley, thick as locusts. Their camels could not be counted, for they were as many as the sands on the seashore. [13]† When Gideon arrived, one man was telling another about a dream. "I had a dream," he said, "that a round loaf of barley bread was rolling into the camp of Midian. It came to a certain tent and struck it and turned it upside down, and the tent collapsed." [14] "This can only be the sword of the Israelite Gideon, son of Joash," the other replied. "God has delivered Midian and all the camp into his power." [15]When Gideon heard the account of the dream and its explanation, he bowed down. Then returning to the camp of Israel, he said, "Arise, for the Lord has delivered the camp of Midian into your power."

[16]He divided the three hundred men into three companies, and provided them all with horns and with empty jars and torches inside

the jars. [17] "Watch me and follow my lead," he told them. "I shall go to the edge of the camp, and as I do, you must do also. [18]When I and those with me blow horns, you too must blow horns all around the camp and cry out, 'For the Lord and for Gideon!'" [19]So Gideon and the hundred men who were with him came to the edge of the camp at the beginning of the middle watch,† just after the posting of the guards. They blew the horns and broke the jars they were holding. [20]When the three companies had blown their horns and broken their jars, they took the torches in their left hands, and in their right the horns they had been blowing, and cried out, "A sword for the Lord and for Gideon!" [21]They all remained standing in place around the camp, while the whole camp began to run and shout and flee. [22]When they blew the three hundred horns, the Lord set the sword of one against another throughout the camp, and they fled as far as Beth-shittah in the direction of Zeredah, near the border of Abel-meholah at Tabbath.

[23]* The Israelites were called to arms from Naphtali, from Asher, and from all Manasseh, and they pursued Midian. [24]Gideon also sent messengers throughout the mountain region of Ephraim to say, "Go down to intercept Midian, and seize the water courses against them as far as Beth-barah, as well as the Jordan." So all the Ephraimites were called to arms, and they seized the water courses as far as Beth-barah, and the Jordan as well. [25]* They captured the two princes of Midian, Oreb and Zeeb, killing Oreb at the rock of Oreb and Zeeb at the wine press of Zeeb. Then they pursued Midian, but they had the heads of Oreb and Zeeb brought to Gideon beyond the Jordan.

**8** [1]* But the Ephraimites said to him, "What have you done to us, not summoning us when you went to fight against Midian?" And they quarreled bitterly with him. [2]But he answered them, "What have I done in comparison with you? Is not the gleaning of Ephraim better than the vintage of Abiezer?* [3]It was into your power God

---

**7:5** The point of this selection process is clear: the battle against the nomadic raiders is going to be won not because of the numerical superiority of the Israelite troops but because of the power of the Lord.

**7:13** The dream seems to foretell the victory of the agricultural Israelites (the barley loaf) over the nomadic Midianites (the tent).

**7:19** *At the beginning of the middle watch*: at the start of the

second of the three watches into which the night was divided. The sentinels were changed at the beginning of a watch, thus making the camp momentarily vulnerable.

*

**7:12** Jgs 6:3.
**7:23** Jgs 6:35.
**7:25** Ps 83:12; Is 10:26.

**8:1** Jgs 12:1.
**8:2** Jgs 6:34.

delivered the princes of Midian, Oreb and Zeeb.* What have I been able to do in comparison with you?" When he said this, their anger against him subsided.

⁴ When Gideon reached the Jordan and crossed it, he and his three hundred men were exhausted and famished. ⁵ So he said to the people of Succoth, "Will you give my followers some loaves of bread? They are exhausted, and I am pursuing Zebah and Zalmunna, kings of Midian." ⁶ But the princes of Succoth replied, "Are the hands of Zebah and Zalmunna already in your possession, that we should give food to your army?"† ⁷ Gideon said, "Very well; when the LORD has delivered Zebah and Zalmunna into my power, I will thrash your bodies with desert thorns and briers." ⁸ He went up from there to Penuel and made the same request of them, but the people of Penuel answered him as had the people of Succoth. ⁹ So to the people of Penuel, too, he said, "When I return in peace, I will demolish this tower."

¹⁰ Now Zebah and Zalmunna were in Karkor with their force of about fifteen thousand men; these were all who were left of the whole Kedemite army, a hundred and twenty thousand swordsmen having fallen. ¹¹ Gideon went up by the route of the tent-dwellers east of Nobah and Jogbehah, and attacked the force when it felt secure. ¹² Zebah and Zalmunna fled and Gideon pursued them. He captured the two kings of Midian, Zebah and Zalmunna, terrifying the entire force.

¹³ Then Gideon, son of Joash, returned from battle by the pass of Heres. ¹⁴ He captured a young man of Succoth and questioned him, and he wrote down for him the seventy-seven princes and elders of Succoth. ¹⁵ So he went to the princes of Succoth and said, "Here are Zebah and Zalmunna, with whom you taunted me, 'Are the hands of Zebah and Zalmunna already in your possession, that we should give food to your weary men?'" ¹⁶ He seized the elders of the city, and with desert thorns and briers he thrashed the people of Succoth. ¹⁷ He also demolished the tower of Penuel and killed the people of the city.

¹⁸ Then he said to Zebah and Zalmunna, "What about the men you killed at Tabor?" "They were all like you," they replied. "They appeared to be princes." ¹⁹ "They were my brothers, my mother's sons," he said. "As the LORD lives, if you had spared their lives, I would not kill you." ²⁰ Then he said to his firstborn, Jether, "Go, kill them." But the boy did not draw his sword, for he was afraid, for he was still a boy. ²¹* Zebah and Zalmunna said, "Come, kill us yourself, for as a man is, so is his strength." So Gideon stepped forward and killed Zebah and Zalmunna. He also took the crescents that were on the necks of their camels.

²²* The Israelites then said to Gideon, "Rule over us—you, your son, and your son's son—for you saved us from the power of Midian." ²³ But Gideon answered them, "I will not rule over you, nor shall my son rule over you. The LORD must rule over you."*

²⁴ Gideon went on to say, "Let me make a request of you. Give me, each of you, a ring from his spoils." (Since they were Ishmaelites,† the enemy had gold rings.) ²⁵ "We will certainly give them," they replied, and they spread out a cloak into which everyone threw a ring from his spoils. ²⁶ The gold rings he had requested weighed seventeen hundred gold shekels, apart from the crescents and pendants, the purple garments worn by the kings of Midian, and apart from the trappings that were on the necks of their camels. ²⁷* Gideon made an ephod out of the gold and placed it in his city, Ophrah. All Israel prostituted themselves there, and it became a snare to Gideon and his household.

²⁸ Midian was brought into subjection by the Israelites; they no longer held their heads high, and the land had rest for forty years,* during the lifetime of Gideon.

**Gideon's Son Abimelech.** ²⁹ Then Jerubbaal, son of Joash, went to live in his house. ³⁰* Now Gideon had seventy sons, his own

---

† **8:6** *Are the hands…already in your possession…?*: i.e., can you already boast of victory? The hands of slain enemies were sometimes cut off and counted as trophies.

**8:24** *Ishmaelites*: evidently used here as a general term for nomads, whose wealth was in the form of gold and flocks. The genealogies in Genesis place the Midianites as descendants of Abraham and his wife Keturah (Gn 25:1–2), and the Ishmaelites as the descendants of Ishmael, son of Abraham and Hagar, Sarah's Egyptian slave (Gn 25:12–16).

| | |
|---|---|
| **8:3** Jgs 7:25. | **8:27** Jgs 17:5; 18:14. |
| **8:21** Ps 83:12. | **8:28** Jgs 3:11, 30; 5:31. |
| **8:22** 1 Sm 8:5; Hos 13:10. | **8:30** Jgs 9:2, 5; 10:4; 12:9, |
| **8:23** 1 Sm 8:7; 10:19; | 14. |
| 12:12. | |

offspring, for he had many wives. ³¹ His concubine† who lived in Shechem also bore him a son, whom he named Abimelech. ³² At a good old age Gideon, son of Joash, died and was buried in the tomb of Joash his father in Ophrah of the Abiezrites. ³³* But after Gideon was dead, the Israelites again prostituted themselves by following the Baals, making Baal-berith† their god. ³⁴ The Israelites did not remember the LORD, their God, who had delivered them from the power of their enemies all around them. ³⁵ Nor were they loyal to the house of Jerubbaal (Gideon) for all the good he had done for Israel.

**9** ¹ Abimelech, son of Jerubbaal, went to his mother's kin in Shechem,* and said to them and to the whole clan to which his mother's family belonged, ² "Put this question to all the lords of Shechem: 'Which is better for you: that seventy men, all Jerubbaal's sons, rule over you, or that one man rule over you?' You must remember that I am your own flesh and bone."* ³ When his mother's kin repeated these words on his behalf to all the lords of Shechem, they set their hearts on Abimelech, thinking, "He is our kin." ⁴ They also gave him seventy pieces of silver from the temple of Baal-berith, with which Abimelech hired worthless men and outlaws as his followers. ⁵ He then went to his father's house in Ophrah, and killed his brothers, the seventy sons of Jerubbaal, on one stone. Only the youngest son of Jerubbaal, Jotham, escaped, for he was hidden. ⁶ Then all the lords of Shechem and all Beth-millo came together and made Abimelech king by the terebinth at the memorial pillar in Shechem.

⁷ When this was reported to Jotham, he went and stood at the top of Mount Gerizim and cried out in a loud voice:

"Hear me, lords of Shechem,
    and may God hear you!
⁸ One day the trees went out
    to anoint a king over themselves.
So they said to the olive tree,

'Reign over us.'
⁹ But the olive tree answered them,
    'Must I give up my rich oil,
    whereby gods and human beings are
        honored,†
    and go off to hold sway over the
        trees?'
¹⁰ Then the trees said to the fig tree,
    'Come; you reign over us!'
¹¹ But the fig tree answered them,
    'Must I give up my sweetness
    and my sweet fruit,
    and go off to hold sway over the
        trees?'
¹² Then the trees said to the vine,
    'Come you, reign over us.'
¹³ But the vine answered them,
    'Must I give up my wine
    that cheers gods† and human beings,
    and go off to hold sway over the
        trees?'
¹⁴ Then all the trees said to the buckthorn,
    'Come; you reign over us!'
¹⁵ The buckthorn answered the trees,
    'If you are anointing me in good faith,
    to make me king over you,
    come, and take refuge in my shadow.
    But if not, let fire come from the
        buckthorn
    and devour the cedars of Lebanon.'*

¹⁶ "Now then, if you have acted in good faith and integrity in appointing Abimelech your king, if you have acted with good will toward Jerubbaal and his house, and if you have treated him as he deserved— ¹⁷ for my father fought for you at the risk of his life when he delivered you from the power of Midian, ¹⁸ but you have risen against my father's house today and killed his seventy sons upon one stone and made Abimelech, the son of his maidservant,* king over the lords of Shechem, because he is your kin— ¹⁹ if, then, you have acted in good faith and integrity toward Jerubbaal and his house today, then rejoice in Abimelech and may he in turn rejoice in you! ²⁰ But if not, let fire come forth from Abimelech and devour

---

† **8:31** *Concubine:* a wife of secondary rank.
**8:33** *Baal-berith:* a divine epithet meaning "lord of the covenant." The same deity is called El-berith, "god of the covenant," in 9:46.
**9:9** *Whereby gods and human beings are honored:* olive oil had a variety of cultic uses (e.g., Lv 2:1, 6, 15; 24:2), and it was also used in the consecration of priests and kings for office (e.g., Ex 30:25, 30; 1 Sm 10:1; 16:13).

**9:13** *Cheers gods:* wine was part of a number of types of offerings in the Israelite cult (cf. Ex 29:40; Lv 23:13; Nm 15:7, 10), and it was also used widely in the worship of foreign gods (cf. Dt 32:37–38; Is 65:11).

**8:33–34** Jgs 2:19; 3:12; 4:1.    **9:15** 2 Kgs 14:9.
**9:1** Jgs 8:31.    **9:18** Jgs 8:31.
**9:2** 2 Sm 5:1; 19:12, 13.

the lords of Shechem and Beth-millo, and let fire come forth from the lords of Shechem and Beth-millo and devour Abimelech." ²¹ Then Jotham fled and escaped to Beer, where he remained for fear of his brother Abimelech.

²² When Abimelech had ruled Israel for three years, ²³ God put an evil spirit* between Abimelech and the lords of Shechem, and the lords of Shechem broke faith with the house of Abimelech. ²⁴ This was to repay the violence done to the seventy sons of Jerubbaal and to avenge their blood upon their brother Abimelech, who killed them, and upon the lords of Shechem, who encouraged him to kill his brothers. ²⁵ The lords of Shechem then set men in ambush for him on the mountaintops, and they robbed all who passed them on the road. It was reported to Abimelech.

²⁶ Now Gaal, son of Ebed, and his kin came, and when they passed through Shechem, the lords of Shechem put their trust in him. ²⁷ They went out into the fields, harvested the grapes from their vineyards, trod them out, and held a festival. Then they went to the temple of their god, where they ate and drank and cursed Abimelech. ²⁸* Gaal, son of Ebed, said, "Who is Abimelech? And who is Shechem that we should serve him? Did not the son of Jerubbaal and his lieutenant Zebul serve the men of Hamor, father of Shechem?* So why should we serve him? ²⁹ Would that these troops were entrusted to my command! I would depose Abimelech. I would say to Abimelech, 'Get a larger army and come out!'"

³⁰ When Zebul, the ruler of the city, heard what Gaal, son of Ebed, had said, he was angry ³¹ and sent messengers to Abimelech in Arumah to say, "Gaal, son of Ebed, and his kin have come to Shechem and are stirring up the city against you. ³² So take action tonight, you and the troops who are with you, and set an ambush in the fields. ³³ Promptly at sunrise tomorrow morning, make a raid on the city. When he and the troops who are with him come out against you, deal with him as best you can."

³⁴ During the night Abimelech went into action with all his soldiers and set up an ambush outside of Shechem in four companies. ³⁵ Gaal, son of Ebed, went out and stood at the entrance of the city gate. When Abimelech and his soldiers rose from their place of ambush, ³⁶ Gaal saw the soldiers and said to Zebul, "There are soldiers coming down from the mountaintops!" But Zebul answered him, "It is the shadow of the hills that you see as men." ³⁷ But Gaal went on to say, "Soldiers are coming down from the region of Tabbur-haarez, and one company is coming by way of Elon-meonenim." ³⁸ Zebul said to him, "Where now is your boast, when you said, 'Who is Abimelech that we should serve him?' Are these not the troops for whom you expressed contempt? Go out now and fight with them." ³⁹ So Gaal went out at the head of the lords of Shechem to fight against Abimelech; ⁴⁰ but when Abimelech went after him, he fled from him. Many fell slain right up to the entrance of the gate. ⁴¹ Abimelech returned to Arumah, and Zebul drove Gaal and his kin away so that they could no longer remain at Shechem.

⁴² The next day, the army marched out into the field, and it was reported to Abimelech. ⁴³ He divided the troops he had into three companies, and set up an ambush in the fields. He watched until he saw the army leave the city and then went on the attack against them. ⁴⁴ Abimelech and the company with him rushed in and stood by the entrance of the city gate, while the other two companies rushed upon all who were in the field and attacked them. ⁴⁵ That entire day Abimelech fought against the city. He captured it, killed the people who were in it, and demolished the city itself, sowing it with salt.†*

⁴⁶ When they heard of this, all the lords of the Migdal-shechem went into the crypt of the temple of El-berith. ⁴⁷ It was reported to Abimelech that all the lords of the Migdal-shechem were gathered together. ⁴⁸ So he went up Mount Zalmon with all his soldiers, took his ax in his hand, and cut down some brushwood. This he lifted to his shoulder, then said to the troops with him, "Hurry! Do just as you have seen me do." ⁴⁹ So all the soldiers likewise cut down brushwood and, following Abimelech, placed it against the crypt. Then they set the crypt on fire over them, so that every one of the people of the Migdal-shechem, about a thousand men and women, perished.

† 9:45 *Sowing it with salt*: a severe measure, since it rendered the soil barren and useless.

9:23 1 Sm 16:14; 18:10; 19:9; 1 Kgs 22:19–23.
9:28 1 Sm 25:10.
9:28 Gn 33:19; 34:2.
9:45 Dt 29:23; Jer 17:6; Ps 107:34.

⁵⁰Abimelech proceeded to Thebez, encamped, and captured it. ⁵¹Now there was a strong tower in the middle of the city, and all the men and women and all the lords of the city fled there, shutting themselves in and going up to the roof of the tower. ⁵²Abimelech came up to the tower and fought against it. When he came close to the entrance of the tower to set it on fire, ⁵³a certain woman cast the upper part of a millstone† down on Abimelech's head, and it fractured his skull.* ⁵⁴He immediately called his armor-bearer and said to him, "Draw your sword and put me to death so they will not say about me, 'A woman killed him.'"* So his attendant ran him through and he died. ⁵⁵When the Israelites saw that Abimelech was dead, they all left for their homes.

⁵⁶Thus did God repay the evil that Abimelech had done to his father in killing his seventy brothers. ⁵⁷God also brought all the wickedness of the people of Shechem back on their heads, for the curse of Jotham, son of Jerubbaal, overtook them.

# 10

**Tola.** ¹After Abimelech, Tola,† son of Puah, son of Dodo, a man of Issachar, rose up to save Israel; he lived in Shamir in the mountain region of Ephraim. ²When he had judged Israel twenty-three years, he died and was buried in Shamir.

**Jair.** ³Jair the Gileadite came after him and judged Israel twenty-two years. ⁴*He had thirty sons who rode on thirty donkeys† and possessed thirty cities in the land of Gilead (these are called Havvoth-jair to the present day).* ⁵Jair died and was buried in Kamon.

**Oppression by the Ammonites.** ⁶*The Israelites again did what was evil in the sight of the LORD, serving the Baals and Ashtarts, the gods of Aram, the gods of Sidon, the gods of Moab, the gods of the Ammonites, and the gods of the Philistines. Since they had abandoned the LORD and would not serve him, ⁷the LORD became angry with Israel and he sold them into the power of the Philistines and the Ammonites. ⁸For eighteen years they afflicted and oppressed the Israelites in Bashan, and all the Israelites in the Amorite land beyond the Jordan in Gilead. ⁹The Ammonites also crossed the Jordan to fight against Judah, Benjamin and the house of Ephraim, so that Israel was in great distress.

¹⁰*Then the Israelites cried out to the LORD, "We have sinned against you, for we have abandoned our God and served the Baals." ¹¹*The LORD answered the Israelites: Did not the Egyptians, the Amorites,* the Ammonites, the Philistines, ¹²the Sidonians, the Amalekites, and the Midianites* oppress you? Yet when you cried out to me, and I saved you from their power, ¹³you still abandoned me and served other gods. Therefore I will save you no more.* ¹⁴Go and cry out to the gods you have chosen; let them save you in your time of distress. ¹⁵But the Israelites said to the LORD, "We have sinned. Do to us whatever is good in your sight. Only deliver us this day!" ¹⁶And they cast out the foreign gods from their midst and served the LORD, so that he grieved over the misery of Israel.

¹⁷The Ammonites were called out for war and encamped in Gilead, while the Israelites assembled and encamped at Mizpah. ¹⁸The captains of the army of Gilead said to one another, "The one who begins the war against the Ammonites shall be leader of all the inhabitants of Gilead."*

# 11

**Jephthah.** ¹Jephthah* the Gileadite was a warrior. He was the son of a prostitute, fathered by Gilead. ²Gilead's wife had also borne him sons. When they grew up the sons of the wife had driven Jephthah away, saying to him, "You shall inherit nothing in our father's house, for you are the son of another woman." ³So Jephthah had fled from his brothers and taken up residence in the land of Tob.* Worthless men had joined company with him, and went out with him on raids.*

---

**9:53** *The upper part of a millstone:* a common hand mill consisted of a large flat stone base and a smaller upper stone (cf. Dt 24:6) shaped so that it could be held in the hands and rolled or ground against the lower stone. It is an upper stone that the woman hurls over the wall to kill Abimelech.

**10:1–5** *Tola...Jair:* two more of the so-called "minor judges"; see Introduction.

**10:4** *Donkeys:* mounts signifying rank and wealth; cf. 5:10; 12:14.

**9:53** 2 Sm 11:21.
**9:54** 1 Sm 31:4; 2 Sm 1:9; 1 Chr 10:4.
**10:4** Jgs 8:30; 9:2, 5; 12:9, 14.
**10:4** Dt 3:14.
**10:6–8** Jgs 2:11–14; 3:7–8, 12; 4:1–2; 6:1; 13:1.
**10:10** Jgs 3:9, 15; 4:3; 6:6,
7; 1 Sm 12:8, 10.
**10:11–14** Jgs 2:1–3; 6:8–10.
**10:11** Nm 21:21–32.
**10:12** Jgs 6:1–6.
**10:13** Jgs 2:21.
**10:18** Jgs 11:5–11.
**11:1** Heb 11:32.
**11:3** 2 Sm 10:6, 8.
**11:3** Jgs 9:4; 1 Sm 22:2.

⁴Some time later, the Ammonites went to war with Israel. ⁵As soon as the Ammonites were at war with Israel, the elders of Gilead went to bring Jephthah from the land of Tob. ⁶"Come," they said to Jephthah, "be our commander so that we can fight the Ammonites." ⁷"Are you not the ones who hated me and drove me from my father's house?" Jephthah replied to the elders of Gilead, "Why do you come to me now, when you are in distress?" ⁸* The elders of Gilead said to Jephthah, "This is the reason we have come back to you now: if you go with us to fight against the Ammonites, you shall be the leader of all of the inhabitants of Gilead." ⁹Jephthah answered the elders of Gilead, "If you bring me back to fight against the Ammonites and the LORD delivers them up to me, I will be your leader." ¹⁰The elders of Gilead said to Jephthah, "The LORD is witness between us that we will do as you say." ¹¹So Jephthah went with the elders of Gilead, and the army made him their leader and commander. Jephthah gave all his orders in the presence of the LORD in Mizpah.

¹²Then he sent messengers to the king of the Ammonites to say, "What do you have against me that you come to fight with me in my land?" ¹³The king of the Ammonites answered the messengers of Jephthah, "Israel took away my land from the Arnon to the Jabbok and the Jordan when they came up from Egypt.* Now restore it peaceably."

¹⁴Again Jephthah sent messengers to the king of the Ammonites, ¹⁵saying to him, "This is what Jephthah says: 'Israel did not take the land of Moab or the land of the Ammonites.* ¹⁶For when they came up from Egypt, Israel went through the wilderness to the Red Sea and came to Kadesh. ¹⁷Israel then sent messengers to the king of Edom saying, "Let me pass through your land." But the king of Edom did not give consent.* They also sent to the king of Moab, but he too was unwilling. So Israel remained in Kadesh.* ¹⁸Then they went through the wilderness, and bypassing the land of Edom and the land of Moab, they arrived east of the land of Moab and encamped across the Arnon.* Thus they did not enter the territory of Moab, for the Arnon is the boundary of Moab.* ¹⁹* Then Israel sent messengers to the Amorite king Sihon, who was king of Heshbon. Israel said to him, "Let me pass through your land to my own place." ²⁰But Sihon refused to let Israel pass through his territory. He gathered all his soldiers, and they encamped at Jahaz and fought Israel. ²¹But the LORD, the God of Israel, delivered Sihon and his entire army into the power of Israel, who defeated them and occupied all the land of the Amorites who lived in that region. ²²They occupied all of the Amorite territory from the Arnon to the Jabbok and the wilderness to the Jordan.* ²³Now, then, it was the LORD, the God of Israel, who dispossessed the Amorites for his people, Israel. And you are going to dispossess them? ²⁴Should you not take possession of that which your god Chemosh† gave you to possess, and should we not take possession of all that the LORD, our God, has dispossessed for us? ²⁵Now, then, are you any better than Balak, son of Zippor, king of Moab? Did he ever quarrel with Israel or make war against them?* ²⁶Israel has dwelt in Heshbon and its villages, Aroer and its villages, and all the cities on the banks of the Arnon for three hundred years.* Why did you not recover them during that time? ²⁷As for me, I have not sinned against you, but you wrong me by making war against me. Let the LORD, who is judge, decide this day between the Israelites and the Ammonites!'" ²⁸But the king of the Ammonites paid no heed to the message Jephthah sent him.

**Jephthah's Vow.** ²⁹The spirit of the LORD came upon Jephthah.* He passed through Gilead and Manasseh, and through Mizpah of Gilead as well, and from Mizpah of Gilead he crossed over against the Ammonites. ³⁰† Jephthah

---

† **11:24** *Chemosh:* the god of the Moabites (1 Kgs 11:7; 2 Kgs 23:13) not the Ammonites, whose god was Milcom (1 Kgs 11:5; 2 Kgs 23:13). Much of the disputed land, which lay between the Jabbok and Arnon Rivers, was actually in Moab, and many of the details of this passage (vv. 12–28) seem more applicable to a quarrel with the king of the Moabites than with the king of the Ammonites.
**11:30–40** Jephthah's rash vow and its tragic consequences reflect a widespread folklore motif, most familiar in the Greek story of Iphigenia and her father, Agamemnon. The sacrifice of children was strictly forbidden by Mosaic law (Lv 18:21; 20:2–5), and when the biblical writers report its occurrence, they usually condemn it in strong terms (2 Kgs 16:3; 21:6; Jer 7:31; 19:5). In this case, however, the narrator simply records the old story, offering no comment on the acceptability of Jephthah's extreme

* 
**11:8–11** Jgs 10:18.
**11:13** Nm 21:24.
**11:15** Dt 2:9, 19.
**11:17** Nm 21:14–21.
**11:17** Dt 1:46.
**11:18** Nm 20:21; 21:4, 10–12; Dt 2:8.
**11:18** Nm 21:13; 22:36.
**11:19–21** Nm 21:21–26; Dt 2:26–36.
**11:22** Jgs 11:13.
**11:25** Nm 22–24; Jos 24:9–10; Mi 6:5.
**11:26** Nm 21:25; Dt 2:36.
**11:29** Jgs 3:10; 6:34; 13:25; 14:6, 19; 15:14; 1 Sm 11:6.

made a vow to the Lord.* "If you deliver the Ammonites into my power," he said, [31] "whoever comes out of the doors of my house to meet me when I return from the Ammonites in peace shall belong to the Lord. I shall offer him up as a burnt offering."

[32] Jephthah then crossed over against the Ammonites to fight against them, and the Lord delivered them into his power. [33] He inflicted a very severe defeat on them from Aroer to the approach of Minnith—twenty cities in all—and as far as Abel-keramin. So the Ammonites were brought into subjection by the Israelites. [34] When Jephthah returned to his house in Mizpah, it was his daughter who came out to meet him, with tambourine-playing and dancing. She was his only child: he had neither son nor daughter besides her. [35] When he saw her, he tore his garments and said, "Ah, my daughter! You have struck me down and brought calamity upon me. For I have made a vow† to the Lord and I cannot take it back."* [36] "Father," she replied, "you have made a vow to the Lord. Do with me as you have vowed, because the Lord has taken vengeance for you against your enemies the Ammonites." [37] Then she said to her father, "Let me have this favor. Do nothing for two months, that I and my companions may go wander in the mountains to weep for my virginity." [38] "Go," he replied, and sent her away for two months. So she departed with her companions and wept for her virginity in the mountains. [39] At the end of the two months she returned to her father, and he did to her as he had vowed. She had not had relations with any man.

It became a custom in Israel [40] for Israelite women to go yearly to mourn the daughter of Jephthah the Gileadite for four days of the year.

# 12 The Shibboleth Incident. [1] The men of Ephraim were called out, and they crossed over to Zaphon. They said to Jephthah, "Why did you go to fight with the Ammonites

without calling us to go with you?* We will burn your house on top of you." [2] Jephthah answered them, "My soldiers and I were engaged in a contest with the Ammonites. They were pressing us hard, and I cried out to you, but you did not come to save me from their power. [3] When I saw that you were not coming to save me, I took my life in my own hand and crossed over against the Ammonites, and the Lord delivered them into my power. Why, then, should you come up against me this day to fight with me?"

[4] Then Jephthah gathered together all the men of Gilead and fought against Ephraim. The men of Gilead defeated Ephraim, [5] and Gilead seized the fords of the Jordan against Ephraim. When any of the fleeing Ephraimites said, "Let me pass," the men of Gilead would say to him, "Are you an Ephraimite?" If he answered, "No!" [6] they would ask him to say "Shibboleth."† If he said "Sibboleth," not pronouncing it exactly right, they would seize him and kill him at the fords of the Jordan. Forty-two thousand Ephraimites fell at that time.

[7] Jephthah judged Israel for six years, and Jephthah the Gileadite died and was buried in his city in Gilead.*

**Ibzan.** [8] After him Ibzan† of Bethlehem judged Israel. [9] * He had thirty sons and thirty daughters whom he gave in marriage outside the family, while bringing in thirty wives for his sons from outside the family. He judged Israel for seven years. [10] Ibzan died and was buried in Bethlehem.

**Elon.** [11] After him Elon the Zebulunite judged Israel; he judged Israel for ten years. [12] Elon the Zebulunite died and was buried at Aijalon in the land of Zebulun.

**Abdon.** [13] After him Abdon, son of Hillel, the Pirathonite, judged Israel. [14] * He had forty sons and thirty grandsons, who rode on seventy donkeys. He judged Israel for eight years. [15] Abdon, son of Hillel, the Pirathonite, died

---

† gesture. The story may have been preserved because it provided an explanation of the custom described in vv. 39–40 according to which Israelite women mourned Jephthah's daughter annually in a four-day ceremony.

**11:35** *Made a vow:* lit., "opened my mouth"; so in v. 36.

**12:6** *Shibboleth:* Hebrew meaning "ear of grain" or "torrent of water." Though the Ephraimites probably spoke the same dialect of Hebrew as their Gileadite neighbors, there was enough regional variation in their pronunciation of the initial sound of

this word to betray them to their enemies.

**12:8–15** *Ibzan…Elon…Abdon:* three more of the so-called "minor judges"; see Introduction.

---

| | |
|---|---|
| **11:30** Gn 28:20–22; 1 Sm 1:11; 2 Sm 15:7–8. | **12:7** Jgs 10:2, 5; 12:10, 12, 15; 15:20. |
| **11:35** Nm 30:3; Dt 23:22; Eccl 5:4. | **12:9** Jgs 8:30; 9:2, 5; 10:4; 12:14. |
| **12:1** Jgs 8:1. | **12:14** Jgs 9:2; 10:4; 12:9. |

and was buried in Pirathon in the land of Ephraim in the mountain region of the Amalekites.

# 13 The Birth of Samson.
¹* The Israelites again did what was evil in the sight of the Lord, who therefore delivered them into the power of the Philistines for forty years.

²There was a certain man from Zorah, of the clan of the Danites,† whose name was Manoah. His wife was barren and had borne no children.* ³* An angel of the Lord appeared to the woman and said to her: Though you are barren and have had no children, you will conceive and bear a son. ⁴* Now, then, be careful to drink no wine or beer and to eat nothing unclean, ⁵for you will conceive and bear a son. No razor shall touch his head, for the boy is to be a nazirite for God† from the womb. It is he who will begin to save Israel from the power of the Philistines.

⁶The woman went and told her husband, "A man of God came to me; he had the appearance of an angel of God, fearsome indeed. I did not ask him where he came from, nor did he tell me his name. ⁷But he said to me, 'You will conceive and bear a son. So drink no wine or beer, and eat nothing unclean. For the boy shall be a nazirite for God from the womb, until the day of his death.'" ⁸Manoah then prayed to the Lord. "Please, my Lord," he said, "may the man of God whom you sent return to us to teach us what to do for the boy who is to be born."

⁹God heard the prayer of Manoah, and the angel of God came again to the woman as she was sitting in the field; but her husband Manoah was not with her. ¹⁰The woman ran quickly and told her husband. "The man who came to me the other day has appeared to me," she said to him; ¹¹so Manoah got up and followed his wife. When he reached the man, he said to him, "Are you the one who spoke to my wife?" I am, he answered. ¹²Then Manoah asked, "Now, when what you say comes true, what rules must the boy follow? What must he do?" ¹³The angel of the Lord answered Manoah: Your wife must be careful about all the things of which I spoke to her. ¹⁴She must not eat anything that comes from the vine, she must not drink wine or beer, and she must not eat anything unclean. Let her observe all that I have commanded her. ¹⁵Then Manoah said to the angel of the Lord, "Permit us to detain you, so that we may prepare a young goat for you." ¹⁶But the angel of the Lord answered Manoah: Though you detained me, I would not eat your food. But if you want to prepare a burnt offering, then offer it up to the Lord. For Manoah did not know that he was the angel of the Lord. ¹⁷† Then Manoah said to the angel of the Lord, "What is your name, that we may honor you when your words come true?" ¹⁸* The angel of the Lord answered him: Why do you ask my name? It is wondrous. ¹⁹* Then Manoah took a young goat with a grain offering and offered it on the rock to the Lord, who works wonders. While Manoah and his wife were looking on, ²⁰as the flame rose to the heavens from the altar, the angel of the Lord ascended in the flame of the altar. When Manoah and his wife saw this, they fell on their faces to the ground; ²¹but the angel of the Lord was seen no more by Manoah and his wife.* Then Manoah, realizing that it was the angel of the Lord, ²²said to his wife, "We will certainly die,† for we have seen God." ²³But his wife said to him, "If the Lord had meant to kill us, he would not have accepted a burnt offering and grain offering from our hands! Nor would he have let us see all this, or hear what we have heard."

²⁴The woman bore a son and named him Samson, and when the boy grew up the Lord blessed him. ²⁵The spirit of the Lord came upon him for the first time* in Mahaneh-dan, between Zorah and Eshtaol.

---

† **13:2** *The clan of the Danites:* before the migration described in chap. 18 the tribe of Dan occupied a small territory west of Benjamin, adjacent to the Philistine plain; see note on 3:3.

**13:5** *A nazirite for God:* according to the rules for nazirites set forth in Nm 6:2–8, Samson's vows would have obliged him to abstain from wine and other products of the vine and to keep his hair uncut. As the story that follows shows, the last requirement proved especially fateful in Samson's life.

**13:17–19** Manoah asks for a name so that he will know how to acknowledge the help of the visitor, but the angel will say only that his name is "wondrous," i.e., beyond human comprehension. Manoah's response is to dedicate his offering to "the Lord, who works wonders."

**13:22** *We will certainly die:* seeing God face to face was believed to be fatal, as explained in note on 6:22, where Gideon's reaction is similar to that of Manoah here.

**13:1** Jgs 2:11–14; 3:7–8, 12; 4:1–2; 6:1; 10:6–8.
**13:2** 1 Sm 1:2; Lk 1:7.
**13:3** 1 Sm 1:20; Lk 1:13, 31.
**13:4–5** Nm 6:1–5; 1 Sm 1:11;
Lk 1:15.
**13:18** Gn 32:30.
**13:19–20** Jgs 6:19–21.
**13:21–23** Jgs 6:22–23.
**13:25** Jgs 3:10; 6:34; 11:29; 14:6, 19; 15:14; 1 Sm 11:6.

JGS

# 14

**Marriage of Samson.** [1] Samson went down to Timnah where he saw one of the Philistine women. [2] On his return he told his father and mother, "I saw in Timnah a woman, a Philistine. Get her for me as a wife." [3]* His father and mother said to him, "Is there no woman among your kinsfolk or among all your people, that you must go and take a woman from the uncircumcised Philistines?" But Samson answered his father, "Get her for me, for she is the one I want." [4]* Now his father and mother did not know that this had been brought about by the LORD, who was seeking an opportunity against the Philistines;† for at that time they ruled over Israel.*

[5] So Samson went down to Timnah with his father and mother. When he turned aside to the vineyards of Timnah, a young lion came roaring out toward him. [6]* But the spirit of the LORD rushed upon Samson, and he tore the lion apart barehanded,* as one tears a young goat. Without telling his father or mother what he had done, [7] he went down and spoke to the woman. He liked her. [8] Later, when he came back to marry her, he turned aside to look at the remains of the lion, and there was a swarm of bees in the lion's carcass, and honey. [9] So he scooped the honey out into his hands and ate it as he went along. When he came to his father and mother, he gave them some to eat, but he did not tell them that he had scooped the honey from the lion's carcass.

[10] His father also went down to the woman, and Samson gave a feast there, since it was customary for the young men to do this. [11] Out of their fear of him, they brought thirty men to be his companions. [12] Samson said to them, "Let me propose a riddle to you. If within the seven days of the feast you solve it for me, I will give you thirty linen tunics and thirty sets of garments. [13] But if you cannot answer it for me, you must give me thirty tunics and thirty sets of garments." "Propose your riddle," they

responded, "and we will listen to it." [14] So he said to them,

> "Out of the eater came food,
>     out of the strong came sweetness."

For three days they were unable to answer the riddle, [15] and on the fourth day they said to Samson's wife,* "Trick your husband into solving the riddle for us, or we will burn you and your family.* Did you invite us here to reduce us to poverty?" [16]†* So Samson's wife wept at his side and said, "You just hate me! You do not love me! You proposed a riddle to my people, but did not tell me the answer." He said to her, "If I did not tell even my father or my mother, must I tell you?" [17] But she wept beside him during the seven days the feast lasted, and on the seventh day, he told her the answer, because she pressed him, and she explained the riddle to her people.*

[18] On the seventh day, before the sun set, the men of the city said to him,

> "What is sweeter than honey,
>     what is stronger than a lion?"

He replied to them,

> "If you had not plowed with my heifer,
>     you would not have solved my
>         riddle."

[19]* The spirit of the LORD rushed upon him, and he went down to Ashkelon, where he killed thirty of their men and stripped them; he gave their garments to those who had answered the riddle. Then he went off to his own family in anger, [20] and Samson's wife was married to the companion who had been his best man.*

# 15

**Samson Defeats the Philistines.** [1] After some time, in the season of the wheat

---

† **14:4** *An opportunity against the Philistines:* although the story of Samson's first love might be taken as an illustration of the danger of foreign marriages, the narrator explains it differently. Samson's infatuation with the Timnite woman was the Lord's way of creating an opportunity to punish the Philistines for their oppression of Israel.

**14:16** The story of Samson and the Timnite woman is very similar in its narrative structure to the better-known story of Samson and Delilah (16:1–22). In both, Samson's success in his conflict with the Philistines depends on keeping a secret. In both stories Samson is betrayed by the Philistine woman he loves

when she importunes him to reveal the secret to her and then, when he gives in, divulges it to her people.

**14:3** Gn 24:3–4; 26:34–35; 28:1–2, 6–9.
**14:4** 1 Sm 10:14–16; Lk 2:41–51.
**14:4** 2 Kgs 5:7.
**14:6** Jgs 3:10; 6:34; 11:29; 13:25; 14:19; 15:14; 1 Sm 11:6.
**14:6** 1 Sm 17:34–36;
2 Sm 23:20.
**14:15** Jgs 16:5.
**14:15** Jgs 15:6.
**14:16** Jgs 16:15.
**14:17** Jgs 16:16–18.
**14:19** Jgs 3:10; 6:34; 11:29; 13:25; 14:6; 15:14; 1 Sm 11:6.
**14:20** Jgs 15:2, 6.

harvest, Samson visited his wife, bringing a young goat. But when he said, "Let me go into my wife's room," her father would not let him go in. 2 He said, "I thought you hated her, so I gave her to your best man. Her younger sister is better; you may have her instead." 3 Samson said to him, "This time I am guiltless if I harm the Philistines." 4 So Samson went and caught three hundred jackals, and turning them tail to tail, he took some torches and tied one between each pair of tails. 5 He then kindled the torches and set the jackals loose in the standing grain of the Philistines, thus burning both the shocks and standing grain, the vineyards and olive groves.

6* When the Philistines asked, "Who has done this?" they were told, "Samson, the son-in-law of the Timnite, because his wife was taken and given to his best man." So the Philistines went up and destroyed her and her family by fire.* 7 Samson said to them, "If this is how you act, I will not stop until I have taken revenge on you." 8 And he struck them hip and thigh—a great slaughter. Then he went down and stayed in a cleft of the crag of Etam.

9 The Philistines went up and encamped in Judah, deploying themselves against Lehi.* 10 When the men of Judah asked, "Why have you come up against us?" they answered, "To take Samson prisoner; to do to him as he has done to us." 11 Three thousand men of Judah went down to the cleft of the crag of Etam and said to Samson, "Do you not know that the Philistines are our rulers? Why, then, have you done this to us?" He answered them, "As they have done to me, so have I done to them." 12 They said to him, "We have come down to bind you and deliver you to the Philistines." Samson said to them, "Swear to me that you will not attack me yourselves." 13 "No," they replied, "we will only bind you and hand you over to them. We will certainly not kill you." So they bound him with two new ropes and brought him up from the crag. 14 When he reached Lehi, and the Philistines came shouting to meet him,* the spirit of the LORD rushed upon him: the ropes around his arms became like flax that is consumed by fire, and his

bonds melted away from his hands. 15 Coming upon the fresh jawbone of an ass, he reached out, grasped it, and with it killed a thousand men.* 16 Then Samson said,

"With the jawbone of an ass
  I have piled them in a heap;
With the jawbone of an ass
  I have slain a thousand men."

17 As he finished speaking he threw the jawbone from him; and so that place was named Ramath-lehi.† 18 Being very thirsty, he cried to the LORD and said, "You have put this great victory into the hand of your servant. Must I now die of thirst and fall into the hands of the uncircumcised?" 19 Then God split the cavity in Lehi, and water issued from it, and Samson drank till his spirit returned and he revived. Hence it is called En-hakkore† in Lehi to this day.

20 Samson judged Israel for twenty years in the days of the Philistines.*

## 16

1 Once Samson went to Gaza, where he saw a prostitute and visited her. 2 The people of Gaza were told, "Samson has come here," and they surrounded him with an ambush at the city gate all night long. And all the night they waited, saying, "At morning light we will kill him." 3 Samson lay there until midnight. Then he rose at midnight, seized the doors of the city gate and the two gateposts, and tore them loose, bar and all. He hoisted them on his shoulders and carried them to the top of the ridge opposite Hebron.

**Samson and Delilah.** 4 After that he fell in love with a woman in the Wadi Sorek whose name was Delilah. 5* The lords of the Philistines came up to her and said, "Trick him and find out where he gets his great strength, and how we may overcome and bind him so as to make him helpless. Then for our part, we will each give you eleven hundred pieces of silver."

6 So Delilah said to Samson, "Tell me where you get your great strength and how you may be bound so as to be made helpless." 7 "If they

---

† **15:17** Ramath-lehi: "Jawbone Height"; in Hebrew *lehi* means "jawbone."

**15:19** En-hakkore: understood as "the spring of the crier," an allusion to Samson's cry in v. 18. The story is used to explain the name of a well-known spring in Lehi. The Hebrew also means "Partridge Spring."

**15:6** Jgs 14:20.
**15:6** Jgs 14:15.
**15:9** 2 Sm 23:11–12.
**15:14** Jgs 3:10; 6:34; 11:29; 13:25; 14:6, 19;

1 Sm 11:6.
**15:15** Jgs 3:31; 2 Sm 23:12.
**15:20** Jgs 10:2, 5; 12:7, 10, 12, 15; 16:31.
**16:5** Jgs 14:15.

bind me with seven fresh bowstrings that have not dried," Samson answered her, "I shall grow weaker and be like anyone else." ⁸ So the lords of the Philistines brought her seven fresh bowstrings that had not dried, and she bound him with them. ⁹ She had men lying in wait in the room, and she said to him, "The Philistines are upon you, Samson!" But he snapped the bowstrings as a thread of tow is snapped by a whiff of flame; and his strength remained unexplained.

¹⁰ Delilah said to Samson, "You have mocked me and told me lies. Now tell me how you may be bound." ¹¹ "If they bind me tight with new ropes, with which no work has been done," he answered her, "I shall grow weaker and be like anyone else." ¹² So Delilah took new ropes and bound him with them. Then she said to him, "The Philistines are upon you, Samson!" For there were men lying in wait in the room. But he snapped the ropes off his arms like thread.

¹³ Delilah said to Samson again, "Up to now you have mocked me and told me lies. Tell me how you may be bound." He said to her, "If you weave the seven locks of my hair into the web and fasten them with the pin, I shall grow weaker and be like anyone else." ¹⁴ So when he went to bed, Delilah took the seven locks of his hair and wove them into the web, and fastened them with the pin. Then she said, "The Philistines are upon you, Samson!" Awakening from his sleep, he pulled out both the loom and the web.

¹⁵* Then she said to him, "How can you say 'I love you' when your heart is not mine? Three times already you have mocked me, and not told me where you get your great strength!" ¹⁶* She pressed him continually and pestered him till he was deathly weary of it. ¹⁷ So he told her all that was in his heart and said, "No razor has touched my head, for I have been a nazirite for God from my mother's womb.* If I am shaved, my strength will leave me, and I shall grow weaker and be like anyone else." ¹⁸ When Delilah realized that he had told her all that was in his heart, she summoned the lords of the Philistines, saying, "Come up this time, for he has told me all that is in his

heart." So the lords of the Philistines came to her and brought the money with them.* ¹⁹ She put him to sleep on her lap, and called for a man who shaved off the seven locks of his hair. He immediately became helpless, for his strength had left him.† ²⁰ When she said "The Philistines are upon you, Samson!" he woke from his sleep and thought, "I will go out as I have done time and again and shake myself free." He did not realize that the LORD had left him. ²¹ But the Philistines seized him and gouged out his eyes. Then they brought him down to Gaza and bound him with bronze fetters, and he was put to grinding grain in the prison. ²² But the hair of his head began to grow as soon as it was shaved.

**The Death of Samson.** ²³* The lords of the Philistines assembled to offer a great sacrifice to their god Dagon† and to celebrate. They said, "Our god has delivered Samson our enemy into our power." ²⁴ When the people saw him, they praised their god. For they said,

"Our god has delivered into our power
  our enemy, the ravager of our land,
  the one who has multiplied our
    slain."

²⁵ When their spirits were high, they said, "Call Samson that he may amuse us." So they called Samson from the prison, and he provided amusement for them. They made him stand between the columns, ²⁶ and Samson said to the attendant who was holding his hand, "Put me where I may touch the columns that support the temple, so that I may lean against them." ²⁷ The temple was full of men and women: all the lords of the Philistines were there, and from the roof about three thousand men and women looked on as Samson provided amusement. ²⁸ Samson cried out to the LORD and said, "Lord GOD, remember me! Strengthen me only this once that I may avenge myself on the Philistines at one blow for my two eyes." ²⁹ Samson grasped the two middle columns on which the temple rested and braced himself against them, one at his right, the other at his left. ³⁰ Then saying, "Let

**16:19** See note on 13:5.
**16:23** *Dagon*: an ancient Syrian grain deity (cf. Hebrew *dagan*, "grain") whom the Philistines adopted as their national god after their arrival on the coast of Canaan.

**16:15** Jgs 14:16.
**16:16–18** Jgs 14:17.
**16:17** Jgs 13:5.
**16:18** Jgs 16:5.
**16:23** 1 Sm 5:2–5.

me die with the Philistines!" Samson pushed hard, and the temple fell upon the lords and all the people who were in it. Those he killed by his dying were more than those he had killed during his lifetime.

[31] His kinsmen and all his father's house went down and bore him up for burial in the grave of Manoah his father between Zorah and Eshtaol. He had judged Israel for twenty years.*

## III. FURTHER STORIES OF THE TRIBES OF DAN AND BENJAMIN

**17** **Micah and the Levite.** [1] There was a man from the mountain region of Ephraim whose name was Micah. [2]† He said to his mother, "The eleven hundred pieces of silver that were taken from you, about which you pronounced a curse and even said it in my hearing—I have that silver. I took it. So now I will restore it to you." Then his mother said, "May my son be blessed by the LORD!" [3] When he restored the eleven hundred pieces of silver to his mother, she said, "I consecrate the silver to the LORD from my own hand on behalf of my son to make an idol overlaid with silver."†* [4] So when he restored the silver to his mother, she took two hundred pieces and gave them to the silversmith, who made of them an idol overlaid with silver. So it remained in the house of Micah. [5] The man Micah had a shrine, and he made an ephod and teraphim,†* and installed one of his sons, who became his priest.* [6]† In those days there was no king in Israel; everyone did what was right in their own eyes.*

[7] There was a young man from Bethlehem of Judah, from the clan of Judah; he was a Levite residing there.* [8] The man set out from the city, Bethlehem of Judah, to take up residence wherever he could find a place. On his journey he came into the mountain region of Ephraim as far as the house of Micah. [9] "Where do you come from?" Micah asked him. He answered him, "I am a Levite, from Bethlehem in Judah, and I am on my way to take up residence wherever I can find a place." [10] "Stay with me," Micah said to him. "Be father and priest to me,* and I will give you ten silver pieces a year, a set of garments, and your living." He pressed the Levite, [11] and he agreed to stay with the man. The young man became like one of his own sons. [12]† Micah installed the Levite, and the young man became his priest, remaining in the house of Micah. [13] Then Micah said, "Now I know that the LORD will prosper me, since I have the Levite as my priest."

**18** **Migration of the Danites.** [1] In those days there was no king in Israel.* In those days the tribe of the Danites were in search of a heritage to dwell in, for up to that time no heritage had been allotted† to them among the tribes of Israel.*

[2] So the Danites sent from their clans five powerful men of Zorah and Eshtaol, to reconnoiter the land and scout it. "Go, scout the land," they were told. They went into the mountain region of Ephraim, and they spent the night there. [3] While they were near the house of Micah,* they recognized the voice† of the young Levite,* so they turned aside. They asked him, "Who brought you here?

---

† **17:2** The narrator picks up the story after a number of events, including a theft and a mother's curse, have already taken place.

**17:3** *An idol overlaid with silver*: two nouns in Hebrew, one indicating a wooden image and the other denoting an image cast from metal. The probable interpretation is that the woman intends for her silver to be recast as a covering for an image of a god, possibly the Lord. This was forbidden in Mosaic law (cf. Ex 20:4 and Dt 5:8).

**17:5** *An ephod and teraphim*: cultic paraphernalia. An ephod was a priestly garment, especially that worn by the high priest (cf. Ex 28 and 39), which contained a pocket for objects used for divination. Teraphim were household idols (Gn 31:19, 34–35; 1 Sm 19:13), which may also have had a divinatory function.

**17:6** This refrain, which will be repeated fully or in part three more times (18:1; 19:1; 21:25), calls attention to the disorder and lawlessness that prevailed before the establishment of kingship in Israel. In this case the problem is cultic impropriety, seen not only in the making of an idol but in the establishment of a local temple, complete with an ephod and teraphim.

**17:12–13** Previously one of Micah's sons served as priest (v. 5). But Micah's family were probably Ephraimites (cf. v. 1) rather than Levites, and the story reflects a sense that only Levites were to be

consecrated as priests; cf. Nm 18:7, where descent from Aaron is further specified as a requirement to be a priest. Thus Micah believes it will be to his advantage to retain the itinerant Levite.

**18:1** *No heritage…allotted*: according to Jos 19:40–48, the Danites received an allotment in the central part of the country (cf. note on 13:2 above). The point here may be that since they were unable to take full possession of that original allotment, as indicated by the notice in Jgs 1:34, they are now seeking territory elsewhere.

**18:3** *Recognized the voice*: this might indicate that the Danite scouts were personally acquainted with the young Levite, but it is more likely to mean that, being originally from Judah, his dialect or accent was noticeably different from others in Micah's household.

---

| | |
|---|---|
| **16:31** Jgs 10:2, 5; 12:7, 10, 12, 15; 15:20. | **17:7** Jgs 19:1. |
| | **17:10** Jgs 18:19. |
| **17:3** Ex 20:4; Lv 19:4; Dt 5:8. | **18:1** Jgs 17:6; 19:1; 21:25. |
| | **18:1** Jgs 1:34; Jos 19:40–48. |
| **17:5** Jgs 18:14, 18. | |
| **17:5** 1 Sm 7:1. | **18:3** Jgs 17:1. |
| **17:6** Jgs 18:1; 19:1; 21:25. | **18:3** Jgs 17:7–12. |

What are you doing here? What is your interest here?" 4 "This is what Micah has done for me," he replied to them. "He has hired me and I have become his priest."* 5 They said to him, "Consult God, that we may know whether the journey we are making will lead to success."* 6 The priest said to them, "Go in peace! The journey you are making is under the eye of the LORD."

7 So the five men went on and came to Laish. They saw the people there living securely after the manner of the Sidonians, quiet and trusting, with no lack of any natural resource. They were distant from the Sidonians and had no dealings with the Arameans.† 8 When the five returned to their kin in Zorah and Eshtaol, they were asked, "What do you have to report?" 9 They replied, "Come, let us attack them, for we have seen the land and it is very good. Are you going to hesitate? Do not be slow to go in and take possession of the land! 10 When you go you will come to a trusting people. The land stretches out in both directions, and God has indeed given it into your power—a place where no natural resource is lacking."*

11 So six hundred of the clan of the Danites, men armed with weapons of war, set out from Zorah and Eshtaol. 12 They marched up into Judah and encamped near Kiriath-jearim; for this reason the place is called Mahaneh-dan† to this day (it lies west of Kiriath-jearim).*

13 From there they passed on into the mountain region of Ephraim and came to the house of Micah. 14 Then the five men who had gone to reconnoiter the land spoke up and said to their kindred, "Do you know that in these houses there are an ephod, teraphim, and an idol overlaid with silver?* Now decide what you must do!" 15 So turning in that direction, they went to the house of the young Levite at the home of Micah and greeted him. 16 The six hundred Danites stationed themselves at the entrance of the gate armed with weapons of war. 17 The five men who had gone to reconnoiter the land went up 18 and entered the house of Micah with the priest standing there. They took the idol, the ephod, the teraphim and the metal image. When the priest said to them, "What are you doing?" 19 they said to him, "Be still! Put your hand over your mouth! Come with us and be our father and priest.* Is it better for you to be priest for the family of one man or to be priest for a tribe and a clan in Israel?" 20 The priest, agreeing, took the ephod, the teraphim, and the idol, and went along with the troops. 21 As they turned to depart, they placed their little ones, their livestock, and their goods at the head of the column.

22* When the Danites had gone some distance from the house of Micah, Micah and the men in the houses nearby mustered and overtook them. 23 They called to the Danites, who turned and said to Micah, "What do you want that you have called this muster?" 24 "You have taken my god, which I made for myself, and you have gone off with my priest as well," he answered. "What is left for me? How, then, can you ask me, 'What do you want?'" 25 The Danites said to him, "Do not let your voice be heard near us, or aggravated men will attack you, and you will have forfeited your life and the lives of your family!" 26 Then the Danites went on their way, and Micah, seeing that they were too strong for him, turned back and went home.

27* Having taken what Micah had made and his priest, they marched against Laish, a quiet and trusting people; they put them to the sword and destroyed the city by fire. 28 No one came to their aid, since the city was far from Sidon and they had no dealings with the Arameans; the city was in the valley that belongs to Beth-rehob. The Danites then rebuilt the city and occupied it. 29 They named it Dan after their ancestor Dan, who was born to Israel.* But Laish was the name of the city formerly. 30† The Danites set up the idol for themselves,

---

**18:7** *The Sidonians...the Arameans*: the people of Laish were not in regular contact with their neighbors, including the Sidonians or Phoenicians in the coastal district to the west and the Arameans in the regions to the north and east. This isolation is mentioned to underscore the vulnerability of the peaceful and unfortified city.

**18:12** *Mahaneh-dan*: Hebrew, "camp of Dan."

**18:30** Micah's shrine is now reinstalled at Laish-Dan. In the time of the kings of Israel and Judah, Dan was the site of one of the two national sanctuaries of the Northern Kingdom, both of which are strongly condemned by the editors of the Books of Kings, who regarded Jerusalem as the only acceptable place for

a temple (1 Kgs 12:26–30). This verse draws a direct connection between Micah's temple and the later royal sanctuary at Dan. Seen in this light the account of the establishment of Micah's shrine, with its idol cast from stolen silver, becomes a highly polemical foundation story for the temple at Dan. *Jonathan, son*

**18:4** Jgs 17:10.
**18:5** Jgs 1:1; 1 Sm 14:18–19, 36–44; 23:2, 4, 9–12; 30:7–8.
**18:10** 1 Chr 5:40.
**18:12** Jgs 13:25.
**18:14** Jgs 17:4–5.
**18:19** Jgs 17:10.
**18:22–26** Gn 31:22–32:1.
**18:27–29** Jos 19:47.
**18:29** Gn 30:5–6.

and Jonathan, son of Gershom, son of Moses,* and his descendants were priests for the tribe of the Danites until the time the land went into captivity. <sup>31</sup>They maintained the idol Micah had made as long as the house of God was in Shiloh.†

# 19 The Levite from Ephraim.
<sup>1</sup>In those days, when there was no king in Israel,†* there was a Levite residing in remote parts of the mountain region of Ephraim* who had taken for himself a concubine from Bethlehem of Judah. <sup>2</sup>But his concubine spurned him and left him for her father's house in Bethlehem of Judah, where she stayed for some four months. <sup>3</sup>Her husband then set out with his servant and a pair of donkeys, and went after her to soothe her and bring her back. He arrived at her father's house, and when the young woman's father saw him, he came out joyfully to meet him. <sup>4</sup>His father-in-law, the young woman's father, urged him to stay, and so he spent three days eating and drinking and passing the night there. <sup>5</sup>On the fourth day they rose early in the morning and he prepared to go. But the young woman's father said to his son-in-law, "Fortify yourself with a little food; you can go later on." <sup>6</sup>So they stayed and the two men ate and drank together. Then the young woman's father said to the husband, "Why not decide to spend the night here and enjoy yourself?" <sup>7</sup>The man made a move to go, but when his father-in-law pressed him he went back and spent the night there.

<sup>8</sup>On the fifth morning he rose early to depart, but the young woman's father said, "Fortify yourself!" He coaxed him, and he tarried until the afternoon, and the two of them ate. <sup>9</sup>Then when the husband was ready to go with his concubine and servant, the young woman's father said to him, "See, the day is wearing on toward evening. Stay for the night. See, the day is coming to an end. Spend the night here and enjoy yourself. Early tomorrow you can start your journey home." <sup>10</sup>The man, however, refused to stay another night; he and his concubine set out with a pair of saddled donkeys, and traveled until they came opposite Jebus, which is Jerusalem. <sup>11</sup>Since they were near Jebus with the day far gone, the servant said to his master, "Come, let us turn off to this city of the Jebusites and spend the night in it." <sup>12</sup>But his master said to him, "We will not turn off to a foreigner's city,* where there are no Israelites. We will go on to Gibeah. <sup>13</sup>Come," he said to his servant, "let us make for some other place and spend the night in either Gibeah or Ramah."* <sup>14</sup>So they continued on their way until the sun set on them when they were opposite Gibeah of Benjamin.

<sup>15</sup>† There they turned off to enter Gibeah for the night.* The man went in and sat down in the town square, but no one took them inside to spend the night. <sup>16</sup>In the evening, however, an old man came from his work in the field; he was from the mountain region of Ephraim, though he was living in Gibeah where the local people were Benjaminites. <sup>17</sup>* When he noticed the traveler in the town square, the old man asked, "Where are you going, and where have you come from?" <sup>18</sup>He said to him, "We are traveling from Bethlehem of Judah far up into the mountain region of Ephraim, where I am from. I have been to Bethlehem of Judah, and now I am going home; but no one has taken me into his house. <sup>19</sup>We have straw and fodder for our donkeys, and bread and wine for myself and for your maidservant and the young man who is with your servant; there is nothing else we need." <sup>20</sup>"Rest assured," the old man said to him, "I will provide for all your needs, but do not spend the night in the public square." <sup>21</sup>So he led them to his house and mixed fodder for the donkeys. Then they washed their feet, and ate and drank.*

† *of Gershom, son of Moses*: Micah's Levite is now identified as the son or descendant of Gershom, Moses' eldest son (Ex 2:22; 18:3). In the traditional Hebrew text an additional letter has been suspended over the name "Moses" to alter it to "Manasseh," thus protecting Moses from association with idol worship. *Captivity*: although Samaria fell in 722/721 B.C., much of the northern part of the country, probably including Dan, had been subjugated about a decade earlier by the Assyrian emperor Tilgath-pileser III.

**18:31** *Shiloh*: a major sanctuary which has a role in the final episode of Judges (21:12, 21).

**19:1** *No king in Israel*: see note on 17:6. The violent story that follows is offered as another example of the disorder that prevailed before the inauguration of the monarchy.

**19:15–21** The narrative casts a very unfavorable light on Gibeah of Benjamin, the town from which Israel's first king would come (cf. 1 Sm 9:1–2). No Benjaminite offers hospitality to the Levite and his travel party, who are obliged to wait at night in the town square until an Ephraimite residing in Gibeah welcomes them into his home.

| | |
|---|---|
| **18:30** Ex 2:22; 18:3. | **19:15** Jgs 20:4. |
| **19:1** Jgs 17:6; 18:1; 21:25. | **19:17–21** Gn 19:1–3. |
| **19:1** Jgs 17:7. | **19:21** Gn 18:4; 24:32; |
| **19:12** Jgs 1:21; 2 Sm 5:6. | 43:24. |
| **19:13** Jos 18:25. | |

JGS

**The Outrage at Gibeah.** 22†* While they were enjoying themselves, the men of the city, a bunch of scoundrels, surrounded the house and beat on the door. They said to the old man who was the owner of the house, "Bring out the man who has come into your house, so that we may get intimate with him." 23 The man who was the owner of the house went out to them and said, "No, my brothers; do not be so wicked. This man has come into my house; do not commit this terrible crime. 24 Instead, let me bring out my virgin daughter and this man's concubine. Humiliate them, or do whatever you want; but against him do not commit such a terrible crime." 25 But the men would not listen to him. So the man seized his concubine and thrust her outside to them. They raped her and abused her all night until morning, and let her go as the sun was coming up. 26 At the approach of morning the woman came and collapsed at the entrance of the house in which her husband was, and lay there until morning. 27 When her husband rose in the morning and opened the door of the house to start out again on his journey, there was the woman, his concubine, collapsed at the entrance of the house with her hands on the threshold. 28 "Come, let us go," he said to her, but there was no answer. So the man placed her on a donkey and started out again for home.

29† On reaching home, he got a knife and took hold of the body of his concubine. He cut her up limb by limb into twelve pieces and sent them throughout the territory of Israel.* 30 He instructed the men whom he sent, "Thus you shall say to all the men of Israel: 'Has such a thing ever happened from the day the Israelites came up from the land of Egypt to this day?†* Take note of it; form a plan and give orders.'"

# 20 Assembly of Israelites. 1 So all the Israelites came out as one, from Dan to Beer-sheba†* including the land of Gilead,

and the assembly gathered to the LORD at Mizpah. 2 The leaders of all the people, all the staff-bearers of Israel,† presented themselves in the assembly of the people of God—four hundred thousand foot soldiers who carried swords. 3 Meanwhile, the Benjaminites heard that the Israelites had gone up to Mizpah. The Israelites asked, "How did this evil thing happen?" 4 and the Levite, the husband of the murdered woman, testified: "It was at Gibeah of Benjamin, which my concubine and I had entered for the night.* 5* The lords of Gibeah rose up against me and surrounded me in the house at night. I was the one they intended to kill, but they abused my concubine and she died. 6* So I took my concubine and cut her up and sent her through every part of the territory of Israel, because of the terrible thing they had done in Israel. 7 So now, all you Israelites, give your judgment and counsel in this matter."* 8 All the people rose as one to say, "None of us will leave for our tents or return to our homes. 9 Now as for Gibeah, this is what we will do: We will go up against it by lot, 10 taking from all the tribes of Israel ten men for every hundred, a hundred for every thousand, a thousand for every ten thousand, and procuring supplies for the soldiers who will go to exact from Gibeah of Benjamin the full measure of the terrible thing it committed in Israel."

11 So all the men of Israel gathered against the city, united as one. 12 The tribes of Israel sent men throughout the tribe of Benjamin to say, "What is this evil that has occurred among you? 13 Now give up the men, the scoundrels who are in Gibeah, that we may put them to death and thus purge the evil from Israel." But the Benjaminites refused to listen to their kindred, the Israelites. 14 Instead, the Benjaminites assembled from their cities at Gibeah, to march out to battle with the Israelites. 15 On that day the Benjaminites mustered from their cities twenty-six thousand swordsmen, in addition to the inhabitants of Gibeah, who mustered seven hundred picked men 16† who were

---

† **19:22–25** This part of the grim story closely parallels that of the assault on Lot's angelic visitors in Gn 19:4–8.

**19:29** The Levite's gruesome way of summoning the tribes is a drastic version of that used by Saul in 1 Sm 11:7, where he dismembers a yoke of oxen.

**19:30** *Has such a thing ever happened…?*: the outrage became a byword in Israel, so that in the eighth century the prophet Hosea could invoke "the days of Gibeah" (Hos 9:9; cf. 10:9) to signify corruption and wrongdoing.

**20:1** *From Dan to Beer-sheba*: the entire country, from north

to south. *The land of Gilead*: Israelite territory east of the Jordan.

**20:2** *The staff-bearers of Israel*: the tribal leaders.

**20:16** The strange notice that the Gibeahite warriors were left-handed was probably added here under the influence of the Ehud story; cf. 3:15 and the note there.

---

**19:22–25** Gn 19:4–9.                    1 Kgs 5:5.
  **19:29** 1 Sm 11:7.          **20:4** Jgs 19:15.
  **19:30** Hos 9:9; 10:9.     **20:5** Jgs 19:22–28.
  **20:1** 1 Sm 3:20; 2 Sm 3:10;     **20:6** Jgs 19:29.
    17:11; 24:2, 15;          **20:7** Jgs 19:30.

J
G
S

left-handed, every one of them able to sling a stone at a hair without missing. ¹⁷The men of Israel, without Benjamin, mustered four hundred thousand swordsmen, all of them warriors. ¹⁸They went up to Bethel and consulted God. When the Israelites asked, "Who shall go up first for us to do battle with the Benjaminites?" the LORD said: Judah first.†* ¹⁹† The Israelites rose in the morning and encamped against Gibeah.

**War with Benjamin.** ²⁰The men of Israel marched out to do battle with Benjamin and drew up in battle array against them at Gibeah. ²¹The Benjaminites marched out of Gibeah that day and felled twenty-two thousand men of Israel. ²²† But the army of the men of Israel took courage and again drew up for battle in the place where they had drawn up on the previous day. ²³Then the Israelites went up and wept before the LORD until evening. "Shall I again engage my brother Benjamin in battle?" they asked the LORD; and the LORD answered: Attack! ²⁴When the Israelites drew near to the Benjaminites on the second day, ²⁵Benjamin marched out of Gibeah against them again and felled eighteen thousand Israelites, all of them swordsmen. ²⁶So the entire Israelite army went up and entered Bethel, where they sat weeping before the LORD. They fasted that day until evening and presented burnt offerings and communion offerings before the LORD. ²⁷The Israelites consulted the LORD (for the ark of the covenant of the LORD was there in those days, ²⁸and Phinehas, son of Eleazar, son of Aaron,† was standing in his presence in those days), and asked, "Shall I again go out to battle with my brother Benjamin, or shall I stop?" The LORD said: Attack! For tomorrow I will deliver him into your power. ²⁹†* So Israel set men in ambush around Gibeah.

³⁰When the Israelites went up against the Benjaminites on the third day, they drew up against Gibeah as on other occasions. ³¹When the Benjaminites marched out to meet the army, they began, as on other occasions, to strike down some of the troops along the highways, one of which goes up to Bethel and one to Gibeah in the open country; about thirty Israelites were slain. ³²The Benjaminites thought, "They are routed before us as previously." The Israelites, however, were thinking, "We will flee and draw them out from the city onto the highways." ³³And then all the men of Israel rose from their places, forming up at Baal-tamar, and the Israelites in ambush rushed from their place west of Gibeah ³⁴and advanced against Gibeah with ten thousand picked men from all Israel. The fighting was severe, but no one knew that a disaster was closing in. ³⁵The LORD defeated Benjamin before Israel; and on that day the Israelites killed twenty-five thousand one hundred men of Benjamin, all of them swordsmen.

³⁶Then the Benjaminites saw that they were defeated. The men of Israel gave ground to Benjamin, trusting in the ambush they had set at Gibeah. ³⁷Then the men in ambush, having made a sudden dash against Gibeah, marched in and put the whole city to the sword. ³⁸The arrangement the men of Israel had with the men in ambush was that they would send up a smoke signal from the city, ³⁹and the men of Israel would then wheel about in the battle. Benjamin, having begun by killing off some thirty of the men of Israel, thought, "Surely they are completely routed before us, as in the earlier fighting." ⁴⁰But when the signal, the column of smoke, began to rise up from the city, Benjamin looked back and there was the whole city going up in smoke toward heaven. ⁴¹Then when the men of Israel wheeled about, the men of Benjamin were thrown into confusion, for they realized that disaster was closing in on them. ⁴²They retreated before the men of Israel in the direction of the wilderness, but

J G S

20:18 *Judah first*: as in 1:2, where the enemy is the Canaanites. This time the attack is against fellow Israelites, an indication of how far things have deteriorated in these days when as yet "there was no king in Israel"; see note on 17:6.
20:19–25 The Israelites are defeated twice by the Benjaminites.
20:22–23 These two verses seem to be transposed. The day of supplication described in v. 23 must have preceded the assembly for battle reported in v. 22.
20:28 *Phinehas, son of Eleazar, son of Aaron*: the main line of the priesthood was traced through a grandson of Aaron by this name; see Ex 6:25 and Nm 25:10–13. Whether the priest identified here is the same man or his lineal descendant, the mention of his name adds authority to the sanctuary at Bethel. The reference to the ark of the covenant in the preceding verse has the same effect.
20:29–46 The Israelites are successful in their third attempt to defeat Benjamin. Leaving an ambush behind, they decoy the enemy troops out of the city by pretending to be routed as on the two previous occasions. The stratagem is strongly reminiscent of that employed in the conquest of Ai (Jos 8). Two accounts of the present battle against Gibeah are preserved, one in 20:29–36a and another in 20:36b–46.

20:18 Jgs 1:1–2.     20:29–46 Jos 8:3–24.

the fighting kept pace with them, and those who had been in the city were spreading destruction in between. ⁴³They surrounded the men of Benjamin, pursued them from Nohah and drove them along to a point east of Gibeah. ⁴⁴Eighteen thousand from Benjamin fell, all of them warriors. ⁴⁵They turned and fled into the wilderness to the crag of Rimmon. The Israelites picked off five thousand men on the highways and kept pace with them as far as Gidom, where they struck down another two thousand of them. ⁴⁶The total of those from Benjamin who fell that day was twenty-five thousand swordsmen, all of them warriors. ⁴⁷Six hundred men turned and fled into the wilderness to the crag of Rimmon, where they remained for four months.*

⁴⁸Then the men of Israel turned back against the Benjaminites, putting them to the sword—the inhabitants of the cities, the livestock, and all they came upon.* Moreover they destroyed by fire all the cities they came upon.

# 21

**Ensuring a Future for Benjamin.** ¹† The men of Israel took an oath at Mizpah: "None of us will give his daughter in marriage to anyone from Benjamin." ²So the people went to Bethel and remained there before God until evening, raising their voices in bitter weeping.* ³They said, "LORD, God of Israel, why has this happened in Israel that today one tribe of Israel should be lacking?" ⁴Early the next day the people built an altar there and offered burnt offerings and communion offerings. ⁵Then the Israelites asked, "Are there any among all the tribes of Israel who did not come up to the LORD for the assembly?" For there was a solemn oath that anyone who did not go up to the LORD at Mizpah should be put to death.*

⁶The Israelites were disconsolate over their brother Benjamin and said, "Today one tribe has been cut off from Israel. ⁷What can we do

about wives for the survivors, since we have sworn by the LORD not to give them any of our daughters in marriage?" ⁸And when they asked, "Is there one among the tribes of Israel who did not come up to the LORD in Mizpah?" they found that none of the men of Jabesh-gilead had come to the encampment for the assembly. ⁹A roll call of the people was taken, and none of the inhabitants of Jabesh-gilead* was present. ¹⁰So the assembly sent twelve thousand warriors there with orders, "Go put the inhabitants of Jabesh-gilead to the sword. ¹¹This is what you are to do: Every male and every woman who has had relations with a male you shall put under the ban."†* ¹²Finding among the inhabitants of Jabesh-gilead four hundred young virgin women, who had not had relations with a man, they brought them to the camp at Shiloh, in the land of Canaan.* ¹³Then the whole assembly sent word to the Benjaminites at the crag of Rimmon,* offering them peace. ¹⁴† So Benjamin returned at that time, and they were given as wives the women of Jabesh-gilead who had been spared; but these proved to be not enough for them.

¹⁵The people had regrets about Benjamin because the LORD had made a breach among the tribes of Israel.* ¹⁶The elders of the assembly said, "What shall we do for wives for the survivors? For the women of Benjamin have been annihilated."* ¹⁷They said, "There must be heirs for the survivors of Benjamin, so that a tribe will not be wiped out from Israel. ¹⁸Yet we cannot give them any of our daughters in marriage." For the Israelites had taken an oath, "Cursed be he who gives a wife to Benjamin!" ¹⁹Then they thought of the yearly feast of the LORD at Shiloh,* north of Bethel, east of the highway that goes up from Bethel to Shechem, and south of Lebonah. ²⁰And they instructed the Benjaminites, "Go and set an ambush in the vineyards. ²¹When you see the women of Shiloh come out to join in the dances, come

---

† **21:1–7** The victorious Israelites now become concerned about the survival of the tribe they have defeated. Despite the large number of Benjaminites killed in the final battle (20:46) and the general carnage that followed (20:48), there does not seem to be a shortage of wives for the surviving men. The problem is rather a shortage of wives for the surviving men, the result of a previously unmentioned vow the Israelites took not to permit their daughters to marry Benjaminites.

**21:11** *Under the ban*: see note on 1:17. In this case the sanction is imposed not because of the rules for the conquest of the promised land (cf. Dt 20:10–18) but because of the failure of the men of Jabesh-gilead to honor their oath and report for the assembly.

**21:14** Very strong political ties existed between the people of Jabesh-gilead and the Benjaminites, especially those involving Saul, the Benjaminite king of Israel. See 1 Sm 11, where Saul rescues Jabesh from an Ammonite siege, and 1 Sm 31:11–13, where the people of Jabesh exert themselves to ensure that the bodies of Saul and his sons should receive honorable burial.

**20:47** Jgs 21:13.
**20:48** Dt 13:15–17.
**21:2** Jgs 20:26.
**21:5** Jgs 20:8–10.
**21:9** 1 Sm 11:1–11; 31:11–13; 2 Sm 2:4–7; 21:11–14.
**21:11** Nm 31:17.
**21:12** Jos 21:2; 22:9.
**21:13** Jgs 20:47.
**21:15** 2 Sm 6:8.
**21:16** Jgs 20:48.
**21:19** 1 Sm 1:3, 21.

out of the vineyards and catch a wife for each of you from the women of Shiloh; then go on to the land of Benjamin. 22 When their fathers or their brothers come to complain to us, we shall say to them, 'Release them to us as a kindness, since we did not take a woman for every man in battle. Nor did you yourselves give your daughters to them, thus incurring guilt.'†

23 The Benjaminites did this; they carried off wives for each of them from the dancers they had seized, and they went back each to his own heritage, where they rebuilt the cities and settled them. 24 At that time the Israelites dispersed from there for their own tribes and clans; they set out from there each to his own heritage.

25† In those days there was no king in Israel; everyone did what was right in their own sight.*

---

**21:22** *Release them…guilt*: this verse is difficult. Evidently the elders intend to make two arguments in support of their request that the men of Shiloh release their claims on the abducted women. The first argument seems to be that an insufficient number of women were taken "in battle"—i.e., the raid on Jabesh-gilead—to provide "a woman for every man"—i.e., a wife for every Benjaminite. The second argument is that since the women have been kidnapped, the men of Shiloh will not be guilty of having violated the oath mentioned above in 21:1, 7, and 18.

**21:25** See note on 17:6. This final editorial comment calls attention to the chaos that followed the Benjaminite civil war and the near anarchy that characterized the various efforts to meet the need for wives for the Benjaminites.

---

**21:25** Jgs 17:6; 18:1; 19:1.

# The Book of

# Ruth

## INTRODUCTION

### Leslie J. Hoppe, OFM

The book of Ruth is a charming and engaging story of love and commitment that developed in most unexpected circumstances. An Israelite family from Bethlehem left their home for Moab in order to escape the effects of one of the periodic famines that afflicted the land of Israel. Those who first heard or read this story recognized this as an act of desperation. The Israelites and the Moabites were political and religious enemies. The Bible contains frequent denunciations of the Moabites (Is 15–16; Jer 48:1–47; Am 2:1–3; Zep 2:8–11). A tenth-century Moabite text speaks of the Israelites as oppressors and celebrates a victory over them.

Sometime after settling in Moab, Elimelech, the father of the Israelite family, died. Surviving him were his widow Naomi and their two sons, both of whom married women from Moab. Ten years later, both of Naomi's sons died. Naomi decided to return to her home in Bethlehem since she heard that the famine had ended. Her daughters-in-law decided to accompany her. She advised them to stay in Moab and remarry in order to secure their future. While one of Naomi's daughters-in-law reluctantly took her advice, the second, named Ruth, refused to leave Naomi to fend for herself. When Naomi realized that Ruth could not be dissuaded, she said no more. Both women made their way back to Bethlehem.

Fortunately, Naomi and Ruth arrived at the beginning of the barley harvest, which takes place in early April. Since they were without means of support, Ruth was able to follow the harvesters through the fields and pick the ears of grain that they missed so that she and Naomi would have something to eat. Ruth gleaned in a field owned by Boaz, a wealthy relative of Naomi's deceased husband. Eventually, Ruth and Boaz married with encouragement from Naomi. Boaz was impressed with what Ruth had done for her mother-in-law by leaving her own parents, her native country, and accompanying Naomi to a land populated by people who were not expected to welcome her (Ru 2:11–12). But when the two married, the people of Bethlehem wished them both all the best (4:11–12).

The union of Boaz and Ruth produces a child, who is destined to be the grandfather of David (Ru 4:17). Ruth generously shares her child with Naomi. The text even asserts that Naomi becomes the child's nurse. The story has a happy ending for all—especially for Naomi, whose grandson helps fill the void in her life caused by the deaths of her husband and sons.

The early rabbis saw this story as a paradigm of conversion to Judaism. Because Naomi told Ruth to return to her family and homeland three times (Ru 1:8, 12, 15), rabbis suggested that any potential converts to Judaism should be turned away three times as well. If would-be converts are determined to become Jews despite these rejections, they can be accepted. This process was necessary not only to determine the sincerity of any convert but also to impress upon the convert that fidelity to Judaism is not easy. The rabbis also had the book of Ruth read during the synagogue service on the Feast of Shavuot, also known as the Feast of Weeks or Pentecost. This feast takes place during the spring harvest of grain. Finally, they included it among the third division of the Hebrew Bible, i.e., the Writings. The Bibles used by Christians, however, follow the ordering of books in the Septuagint, which places this book following the book of Judges since it is set in the "time of the judges" (1:1).

Modern interpreters of the book of Ruth have discerned several levels of meaning in the book. Some see the book weighing in on the question of admitting Gentiles to the Jewish community. Indeed, the book explains how even the enemies of Israel could become part of the people of Israel. Deuteronomy 23:2–6 asserts that no Moabite can become part of the community of those who worship Yahweh—even to the "tenth generation." According to the Bible, the Moabites and Israelites were related through Abraham. Lot, Abraham's nephew, was the ancestor of the Moabites (Gn 19:37). But the Bible also describes the interaction between these two peoples as generally hostile (Nm 21–24; Jgs 3:12–30; 11:25–26; 1 Sm 14:47; 2 Sm 8:2; 2 Kgs 3). Solomon's fall from God's favor is blamed in part on the Moabite women who were in his harem. The king built a shrine to the Moabite god Chemosh for them (1 Kgs 11:1, 7, 33). Moab was a frequent object of prophetic criticism. The book of Ruth, then, stands in dramatic contrast to the hostility toward Moabites evident in the biblical tradition.

The Moabites were not the only neighbors of ancient Israel toward whom the Hebrew Bible shows hostility. The people of the two Israelite kingdoms experienced their neighbors as potential threats to their political, economic, and religious well-being. A regular feature of prophetic books is the oracle against the nations, e.g., Is 13–23; Jer 46–51; Ez 25–32. Indeed the prophecies of Obadiah and Nahum are extended oracles of judgment against two of ancient Israel's neighbors. At the same time, a significant motif in the biblical tradition is Israel's calling to be a "blessing" (Gn 12:3) and a "light" (Is 42:6) to the nations. Some interpreters see the book of Ruth as moving its readers to see beyond their unfortunate experiences with other peoples to Israel's calling to be a blessing and a light to the nations.

Other interpreters have looked to the book of Ruth to illuminate an ancient Near Eastern custom that was enshrined in Israelite law: the levirate marriage. (The word *levir* is Latin for "brother-in-law.") In antiquity, people considered the death of a man with no male heir to be a great tragedy since there would be no one to remember the deceased. Also, the death of a man without male heirs made the question of inheritance complicated. Levirate marriage also helped provide for the widow

of the deceased. It became a custom for the nearest kinsman to marry the widow of a man who died without sons. Deuteronomy 25:5–10 obliges a surviving brother to marry the widow of his brother who died without a male heir if the brothers had not already divided the inheritance they had from their father.

The people of Bethlehem bless Boaz for marrying Ruth and "rais[ing] up a family for her late husband" (Ru 4:10). Evidently, the action of a deceased man's nearest relative in marrying his widow and providing him with an heir was recognized as something to be commended. While the marriage of Boaz and Ruth is not actually a fulfillment of the Deuteronomic law, since Boaz was not the brother of Ruth's late husband, the story sheds light on a custom that served to deal with potentially serious problems that arose when a married man died without leaving a male heir.

A related issue is the question of ownership of arable land. Ancient Israel had an agricultural economy. To survive in such an economy people needed to have access to the means of production, i.e., to land. According to Ru 4, Naomi was putting up for sale land owned by her husband Elimelech. The male heir of Elimelech's field, Naomi's son, died without a male heir. A relative of Elimelech was able to "redeem" that land and keep it in the possession of Elimelech's extended family. He declined to do so because he would be required to marry Ruth as well. This clears the way for Boaz to marry Ruth and claim Elimelech's land.

The custom of having relatives claim the land of a man without male heirs ensured that the land would remain under control of the extended family. Presumably the elders of that family would distribute the land fairly among the members of the extended family. This was necessary to keep people from falling into poverty simply because they did not have enough land to feed themselves and their families. This custom served to prevent the development of large landed estates controlled by a wealthy few and worked by agricultural day laborers or debt-slaves. The prophets criticize those who take advantage of the predicaments in which people sometimes find themselves to amass large estates from the small family holdings (see Is 5:8–9).

R
U

The story of Boaz's action toward Ruth and Naomi also illustrates how people of means should act toward those who have few economic resources to sustain their lives. The poor had the right to follow reapers who harvested the ripe grain from the fields. In fact, Deuteronomy counsels a type of studied incompetence in the harvesting process so that "the resident alien, the orphan, and the widow" could find some sustenance from what remained after the harvest was complete (Dt 24:19–22). Boaz makes certain that Ruth's efforts in his fields will be successful. In fact, he allows her to join the professional harvesters. She need not wait until they are finished. He even instructs the harvesters to let some grain fall to the earth so Ruth can gather it easily (Ru 2:15–16). Boaz does all this to ensure the well-being of a Moabite. The clear conclusion to be drawn is that Israelite farmers are to be at least this generous toward their brothers and sisters in need.

Finally, the book of Ruth ends with a genealogy of David (Ru 4:17–22). Who would have imagined that an act of kindness and love that an obscure Moabite widow offered to her Israelite mother-in-law would lead to connect these people with the great national hero of the people of Israel: David? This is the power of faith and love. The New Testament follows the example of the author of the book of Ruth. The Gospel of Matthew mentions Ruth as an ancestor of Jesus, the son of David (Mt 1:5).

The book of Ruth shows that human relationships are not a matter of duty and obligation but of love and concern for the vulnerable. Such relationships have consequences beyond the people directly involved, as the story of Ruth illustrates. The ethnic and religious boundaries that serve to keep people from extending love and concern for each other are meant to be crossed as Ruth does. The happy ending of Ruth's story has its heroine find her trust and happiness as she forgets her own comfort and security. The book of Ruth presents this young Moabite woman to its readers and suggests that they follow her example if they wish to find their own happiness and security. ■

# THE BOOK OF RUTH

## New American Bible, Introduction

The Book of Ruth is named for the Moabite woman who commits herself to the Israelite people by an oath to her mother-in-law Naomi and becomes the great-grandmother of David by marriage to Boaz of Bethlehem. Thus she is an ancestor in the messianic line that leads to Jesus (Mt 1:5).

The book portrays the love and loyalty of human beings in working their way through tragic circumstances to participation in the community of the faithful people of God. The key is responsible and loving decision-making: Ruth's loyalty (2:11), her generosity (1:15–17; 2:2, 7) and her willingness to take risks for the sake of righteousness set in motion a chain of beneficial events, while behind the scenes God blesses each step in the developing drama. Ruth is so frequently designated "the Moabite" in the book that the audience of the story is constantly reminded of the universality of the embrace of salvation.

In the Greek and Latin canons, Ruth follows Judges, to which it is related by its opening time reference ("Once back in the time of the judges..."), and precedes Samuel, serving as transition from Israel as tribal union to monarchy. In the present sequence of the Hebrew canon it is placed among the "Writings" immediately after the Book of Proverbs, which ends with a powerful portrayal of "the woman of worth" (Prv 31:10–31; cf. Ru 3:11). Ruth is the primary liturgical text in Judaism for the celebration of the feast of Weeks (Shabuot).

The beauty of the story's construction, its use of dialogue (nearly two thirds of the text), and the sheer drama of its content mark it as one of the classic short stories of world literature. Based on the recollection of an historical figure, a story is developed which grips its audience with profound insight into divine and human relationships. The story is presented from a point some time after the course of events, as is indicated by the explanation of an obscure custom in 4:7. Wherever and whenever it was told, its claim of God's universal concern for humankind and the attractiveness of caring human responsibility shines forth.

The date of composition is disputed. Many authors date it early in the monarchy, and valid arguments can be presented for that position. Others argue for a postexilic date; they see the favorable presentation of a Moabite woman who became David's grandmother as a counter to the stringent measures of Ezra and Nehemiah against marriage with Moabites and other non-Jews (Ezr 9–10; Neh 13:23–29). ■

R
U

# RUTH

**1 Naomi in Moab.** [1] Once back in the time of the judges† there was a famine in the land; so a man from Bethlehem of Judah left home with his wife and two sons to reside on the plateau of Moab. [2] The man was named Elimelech, his wife Naomi, and his sons Mahlon and Chilion; they were Ephrathites from Bethlehem of Judah. Some time after their arrival on the plateau of Moab, [3] Elimelech, the husband of Naomi, died, and she was left with her two sons. [4] They married Moabite women, one named Orpah, the other Ruth. When they had lived there about ten years, [5] both Mahlon and Chilion died also, and the woman was left with neither her two boys† nor her husband.

[6] She and her daughters-in-law then prepared to go back from the plateau of Moab because word had reached her there that the LORD had seen to his people's needs† and given them food. [7] She and her two daughters-in-law left the place where they had been living. On the road back to the land of Judah, [8] Naomi said to her daughters-in-law, "Go back, each of you to your mother's house.† May the LORD show you the same kindness as you have shown to the deceased and to me. [9]* May the LORD guide each of you to find a husband and a home in which you will be at rest." She kissed them good-bye, but they wept aloud, [10] crying, "No! We will go back with you, to your people." [11] Naomi replied, "Go back, my daughters. Why come with me?

Have I other sons in my womb who could become your husbands?† [12] Go, my daughters, for I am too old to marry again. Even if I had any such hope, or if tonight I had a husband and were to bear sons, [13] would you wait for them and deprive yourselves of husbands until those sons grew up? No, my daughters, my lot is too bitter for you, because the LORD has extended his hand against me." [14] Again they wept aloud; then Orpah kissed her mother-in-law good-bye, but Ruth clung to her.

[15] "See now," she said, "your sister-in-law has gone back to her people and her god. Go back after your sister-in-law!" [16]† But Ruth said, "Do not press me to go back and abandon you!

> Wherever you go I will go,
>     wherever you lodge I will lodge.
> Your people shall be my people
>     and your God, my God.
> [17] Where you die I will die,
>     and there be buried.

May the LORD do thus to me, and more, if even death separates me from you!" [18] Naomi then ceased to urge her, for she saw she was determined to go with her.

**The Return to Bethlehem.** [19] So they went on together until they reached Bethlehem. On their arrival there, the whole town was excited about them, and the women asked: "Can this be Naomi?" [20]* But she said to them, "Do not call me Naomi ['Sweet']. Call me Mara ['Bitter'], for the Almighty has made my life very bitter. [21]†* I went away full, but the LORD has

---

† **1:1–2** *Back in the time of the judges:* the story looks back three generations before King David (4:17) into the time of the tribal confederation described in the Book of Judges. David's Moabite connections are implied in 1 Sm 22:3–4. *Bethlehem of Judah:* Bethlehem, a town in which part of the Judean clan-division called Ephrathah lived; cf. 1 Chr 2:50–51; 4:4; Mi 5:1. Jos 19:15 mentions a different Bethlehem in the north. *The plateau of Moab:* on the east side of the Jordan valley rift, where the hills facing west get more rain, and where agricultural conditions differ from those in Judah. *Ephrathites:* a reminder of David's origins; cf. Mi 5:1.

**1:5** *Boys:* the way the storyteller chooses certain words as guides is shown here; "boy" will not appear again until 4:16.

**1:6** *Had seen to his people's needs:* lit., "had visited his people."

**1:8** *Mother's house:* the women's part of the home, but also perhaps the proper location for arranging marriage; Sg 3:4; 8:2; Gn 24:28. *Kindness:* Hebrew *hesed.* The powerful relationship term used here will recur in 2:20 and 3:10; kindness operates on both the divine-human and human-human level in Ruth.

**1:11** *Other sons…husbands:* a reference to a customary practice known from Dt 25:5–10, levirate marriage, which assigns

responsibility to the brother-in-law to produce heirs in order to perpetuate the name and hold the patrimonial land of a man who died childless. How far the responsibility extended beyond blood brothers is unclear; cf. Gn 38:8 and the upcoming scene in Ru 4:5–6. Naomi imagines the impossible: were she to have more sons they could take Ruth and Orpah as their wives.

**1:16–17** Ruth's adherence to her mother-in-law in 1:14 is now expressed in a profound oath of loyalty, culminating in a formulary found frequently in Samuel and Kings; cf. especially 1 Sm 20:13. *Even death:* burial in Naomi's family tomb means that not even death will separate them.

**1:21** Naomi's despair is made clear by her play on the meaning of her name in v. 20 and now by her accusation, like that in many psalms and in Job, that God has acted harshly toward her. The language belongs to the realm of judicial proceedings. By crying out in this way, the faithful Israelite opens the door to change, since the cry assumes that God hears and will do something about such seemingly unjust circumstances.

---

brought me back empty. Why should you call me 'Sweet,' since the LORD has brought me to trial, and the Almighty has pronounced evil sentence on me." [22]Thus it was that Naomi came back with her Moabite daughter-in-law Ruth, who accompanied her back from the plateau of Moab. They arrived in Bethlehem at the beginning of the barley harvest.†

**2** **The Meeting.** [1]† Naomi had a powerful relative named Boaz,* through the clan of her husband Elimelech. [2]† Ruth the Moabite said to Naomi, "I would like to go and glean grain in the field of anyone who will allow me." Naomi said to her, "Go ahead, my daughter." [3]So she went. The field she entered to glean after the harvesters happened to be the section belonging to Boaz, of the clan of Elimelech. [4]† Soon, along came Boaz from Bethlehem and said to the harvesters, "The LORD be with you," and they replied, "The LORD bless you." [5]Boaz asked the young man overseeing his harvesters, "Whose young woman is this?" [6]The young man overseeing the harvesters answered, "She is the young Moabite who came back with Naomi from the plateau of Moab.* [7]† She said, 'I would like to gather the gleanings into sheaves after the harvesters.' Ever since she came this morning she has remained here until now, with scarcely a moment's rest."

[8]Boaz then spoke to Ruth, "Listen, my daughter. Do not go to glean in anyone else's field; you are not to leave here. Stay here with my young women. [9]Watch to see which field is to be harvested, and follow them. Have I not commanded the young men to do you no harm? When you are thirsty, go and drink from the vessels the young people have filled." [10]Casting herself prostrate upon the ground,

she said to him, "Why should I, a foreigner, be favored with your attention?" [11]* Boaz answered her: "I have had a complete account of what you have done for your mother-in-law after your husband's death; you have left your father and your mother and the land of your birth, and have come to a people whom previously you did not know. [12]* May the LORD reward what you have done! May you receive a full reward from the LORD, the God of Israel, under whose wings you have come for refuge." [13]She said, "May I prove worthy of your favor, my lord. You have comforted me. You have spoken to the heart of your servant†—and I am not even one of your servants!" [14]At mealtime Boaz said to her, "Come here and have something to eat; dip your bread in the sauce." Then as she sat near the harvesters, he handed her some roasted grain and she ate her fill and had some left over. [15]As she rose to glean, Boaz instructed his young people: "Let her glean among the sheaves themselves without scolding her, [16]and even drop some handfuls and leave them for her to glean; do not rebuke her."

[17]She gleaned in the field until evening, and when she beat out what she had gleaned it came to about an ephah† of barley, [18]which she took into the town and showed to her mother-in-law. Next she brought out what she had left over from the meal and gave it to her. [19]So her mother-in-law said to her, "Where did you glean today? Where did you go to work? May the one who took notice of you be blessed!" Then she told her mother-in-law with whom she had worked. "The man at whose place I worked today is named Boaz," she said. [20]* "May he be blessed by the LORD, who never fails to show kindness to the living and to the dead," Naomi exclaimed to her

R
U

---

† **1:22** Barley and wheat harvests come in succession, from as early as April–May into June–July; Dt 16:9–12 suggests that the grain harvest lasts about seven weeks. The time reference leads effectively to the next episode.

**2:1** Kinship ties and responsibilities now become very important. Boaz is introduced as one of a group surrounding Naomi through her husband's kin who are expected to extend care. The particular term used here (*moda'*, "relative") is picked up in 3:2; otherwise, most of the terminology about this responsibility to care will use the vocabulary of redeeming (*go'el*, "redeemer").

**2:2** Israelite custom made provision for the poor, the widow, the stranger and the orphan to gather what was left behind by the harvesters, and warned farmers not to cut to the edges of their fields, for the sake of these marginalized; Lv 19:9–10; 23:22; Dt 24:19–22.

**2:4** The story brings Boaz upon the scene quickly, but he moves among his workers with the grace of a man of promi-

nence, greeting them and being received with courtesy. The Hebrew blessing formulas used are frequent in Jewish and Christian liturgies.

**2:7** The verse is somewhat garbled, but the points are clear that Ruth has been appropriately deferential in seeking permission to glean, and has worked steadily since arriving. Or perhaps she has waited patiently until Boaz arrives to gain permission.

**2:13** *Servant*: only here is the language of servanthood used. Ruth has spoken with very deferential words to Boaz, but then seems to think that she has assumed too much.

**2:17** *Ephah*: see note on Is 5:10.

**2:1** Ru 3:2, 12; Mt 1:5.   **2:12** Ru 3:9; Dt 32:37; Ps
**2:6** Ru 1:22.                        91:4.
**2:11** Ru 1:14–17.             **2:20** Gn 24:27; Lv 25:25;
                                              27:9–33.

daughter-in-law. She continued, "This man is a near relative of ours, one of our redeemers."† [21] "He even told me," added Ruth the Moabite, "Stay with my young people until they complete my entire harvest." [22] "You would do well, my daughter," Naomi rejoined, "to work with his young women; in someone else's field you might be insulted." [23] So she stayed gleaning with Boaz's young women until the end of the barley and wheat harvests.

## 3 Ruth Again Presents Herself.

When Ruth was back with her mother-in-law, [1] Naomi said to her, "My daughter, should I not be seeking a pleasing home for you?* [2]† Now! Is not Boaz,* whose young women you were working with, a relative of ours? This very night he will be winnowing barley at the threshing floor. [3] Now, go bathe and anoint yourself; then put on your best attire and go down to the threshing floor. Do not make yourself known to the man before he has finished eating and drinking. [4] But when he lies down, take note of the place where he lies; then go uncover a place at his feet† and you lie down. He will then tell you what to do." [5] "I will do whatever you say," Ruth replied. [6] She went down to the threshing floor and did just as her mother-in-law had instructed her.

[7] Boaz ate and drank to his heart's content, and went to lie down at the edge of the pile of grain. She crept up, uncovered a place at his feet, and lay down. [8] Midway through the night, the man gave a start and groped about, only to find a woman lying at his feet. [9] "Who are you?" he asked. She replied, "I am your servant Ruth. Spread the wing of your cloak† over your servant, for you are a redeemer."

[10] He said, "May the Lord bless you, my daughter! You have been even more loyal now than before in not going after the young men, whether poor or rich. [11] Now rest assured, my daughter, I will do for you whatever you say; all my townspeople know you to be a worthy woman.† [12]* Now, I am in fact a redeemer, but there is another redeemer closer than I.† [13] Stay where you are for tonight, and tomorrow, if he will act as redeemer for you, good. But if he will not, as the Lord lives, I will do it myself. Lie there until morning."* [14] So she lay at his feet until morning, but rose before anyone could recognize another, for Boaz had said, "Let it not be known that this woman came to the threshing floor." [15] Then he said to her, "Take off the shawl you are wearing; hold it firmly." When she did so, he poured out six measures of barley and helped her lift the bundle; then he himself left for the town.

[16] She, meanwhile, went home to her mother-in-law, who asked, "How did things go, my daughter?" So she told her all the man had done for her, [17] and concluded, "He gave me these six measures of barley and said, 'Do not go back to your mother-in-law empty.'"* [18] Naomi then said, "Wait here, my daughter, until you learn what happens, for the man will not rest, but will settle the matter today."

## 4 Boaz Marries Ruth.

[1] Boaz went to the gate† and took a seat there. Along came the other redeemer* of whom he had spoken. Boaz called to him by name, "Come, sit here." And he did so. [2] Then Boaz picked out ten of the elders† of the town and asked them to sit nearby. When they had done this, [3] he said to the other redeemer: "Naomi, who has come

---

† **2:20** For the first time, the story uses the Hebrew word *go'el*, "redeemer," for the responsibilities of the circle of kinship surrounding Naomi and Ruth and their deceased relatives. Involved are the recovery or retention of family land (Lv 25:25; 27:9–33; Jer 32:6–25), release of a relative from voluntary servitude to pay debts (Lv 25:47–55), and "redeeming blood" or vengeance, attested in passages which regulate such vengeance. No explicit connection is made elsewhere in the Bible between marriage responsibilities and redeeming.

**3:2** Ruth's determined action to bring relief to Naomi's and her own circumstances now impels Naomi to move, using means available in Israelite custom which no one in the story has up to this point brought into play.

**3:4** *Uncover a place at his feet*: Naomi advocates a course of action that will lead Boaz to act. Israelite custom and moral expectations strongly suggest that there is no loss of virtue involved in the scene.

**3:9** *Spread the wing of your cloak*: Ez 16:8 makes it clear that this is a request for marriage. Ruth connects it to "redeemer" responsibility. A wordplay on "wing" links what Boaz is asked to

do to what he has asked God to do for Ruth in 2:12.

**3:11** *Worthy woman*: the language corresponds to the description of Boaz in 2:1 (lit., "strong and worthy"); the two worthy people are linked in character to one another, as they have already proven to be in their generous behavior toward the ones in need of their care. The townspeople, lit., "all the gate of my people," will ratify this at the gate in the sequel.

**3:12** *Another redeemer closer than I*: Boaz knows of a closer relative who would have a prior right to buy the field and marry Ruth.

**4:1** The gate of an Israelite town was the place where commercial and other legal matters were dealt with in publicly witnessed fashion.

**4:2** *Ten of the elders*: to serve as judges in legal matters as well as witnesses of the settlement of business affairs; cf. Dt 25:7–9.

---

**3:1** Ru 1:9.       **3:13** Ru 1:16; 4:5.
**3:2** Ru 2:1.       **3:17** Ru 1:21.
**3:12** Ru 4:1.       **4:1** Ru 3:12.

back from the plateau of Moab, is putting up for sale the piece of land that belonged to our kinsman Elimelech. ⁴† So I thought I would inform you. Before those here present, including the elders of my people, purchase the field; act as redeemer.* But if you do not want to do it, tell me so, that I may know, for no one has a right of redemption prior to yours, and mine is next." He answered, "I will act as redeemer."

⁵† Boaz continued, "When you acquire the field from Naomi, you also acquire responsibility for Ruth the Moabite,* the widow of the late heir, to raise up a family for the deceased on his estate." ⁶The redeemer replied, "I cannot exercise my right of redemption for that would endanger my own estate. You do it in my place, for I cannot." ⁷* Now it used to be the custom in Israel that, to make binding a contract of redemption or exchange, one party would take off a sandal† and give it to the other. This was the form of attestation in Israel. ⁸So the other redeemer, in saying to Boaz, "Acquire it for yourself," drew off his sandal. ⁹Boaz then said to the elders and to all the people, "You are witnesses today that I have acquired from Naomi all the holdings of Elimelech, Chilion and Mahlon. ¹⁰I also acquire Ruth the Moabite, the widow of Mahlon, as my wife, in order to raise up a family for her late husband on his estate, so that the name of the deceased may not perish from his people and his place. Do you witness this today?"

¹¹* All those at the gate, including the elders, said, "We do. May the LORD make this woman come into your house like Rachel and Leah, who between them built up the house of Israel. Prosper in Ephrathah! Bestow a name in Bethlehem! ¹²With the offspring the LORD will give you from this young woman, may your house become like the house of Perez, whom Tamar bore to Judah."†

¹³Boaz took Ruth. When they came together as husband and wife, the LORD enabled her to conceive and she bore a son. ¹⁴Then the women said to Naomi, "Blessed is the LORD who has not failed to provide you today with a redeemer. May he become famous in Israel! ¹⁵He will restore your life and be the support of your old age, for his mother is the daughter-in-law who loves you. She is worth more to you than seven sons!" ¹⁶Naomi took the boy, cradled him† against her breast, and cared for him. ¹⁷The neighbor women joined the celebration: "A son has been born to Naomi!"* They named him Obed. He was the father of Jesse, the father of David.

¹⁸* These are the descendants of Perez: Perez was the father of Hezron,* ¹⁹Hezron was the father of Ram, Ram was the father of Amminadab, ²⁰* Amminadab was the father of Nahshon, Nahshon was the father of Salma, ²¹Salma was the father of Boaz, Boaz was the father of Obed, ²²* Obed was the father of Jesse, and Jesse became the father of David.

---

† **4:4** Although the laws governing inheritance by Israelite widows are not specified in the Bible, Naomi seems to have the right of disposal of a piece of Elimelech's land. The redemption custom in Lv 25:25 would then guide the procedure.

**4:5–6** Although redemption and levirate practices are not otherwise linked in the Bible, they belong in the same area of need. Boaz claims that buying Elimelech's field obligates the other redeemer to produce an heir for Mahlon, who would then inherit the land. That would jeopardize this redeemer's overall holdings, since he would lose the land he had paid for. He can afford the first step but not the second, and cedes his responsibility to Boaz, who is willing to do both.

**4:7** Take off a sandal: the legislation in Dt 25:8–10 provides that if a "redeemer" refuses to carry out the obligation of marrying his brother's wife, the woman shall strip off his sandal as a gesture of insult. In later years, when the obligation of carrying out this function of the "redeemer" was no longer keenly felt, the removal of the sandal may have become a formalized way of renouncing the rights/obligations of the "redeemer," as in this text.

**4:12** Gn 38 contains a story about Tamar similar to Ruth's in levirate marriage. Judah, under less laudable circumstances, fulfills the same role as Boaz will, and Perez, son of Judah and Tamar, perpetuates the line. Thus two non-Israelite women, Tamar and Ruth, are important links in David's genealogy.

**4:16** Cradled him: the child belongs to Naomi in the sense that he now becomes the redeemer in the family, as stated in 4:14. This tender act by Naomi is not necessarily adoptive and differs from the relationship in Gn 30:3; cf. Nm 11:12. Naomi now has a "boy" to replace her two lost "boys" in 1:5.

*
**4:4** Lv 25:25.
**4:5** Ru 3:13.
**4:7** Dt 25:9.
**4:11** Gn 29:31–30:24; 35:16–19.
**4:17** Lk 1:58.
**4:18–22** 1 Chr 2:4–15; Mt 1:3–6.
**4:18** Gn 46:12; Nm 26:21; 1 Chr 4:1.
**4:20** Ex 6:23; Nm 1:7; 2:3; 7:12–17; 10:14.
**4:22** 1 Sm 16:2–13.

# The Books of
# Samuel

## INTRODUCTION

### Leslie J. Hoppe, OFM

The story of Israel in its land continues with the books of 1 and 2 Samuel, which tell of the beginnings of the Israelite monarchy and Israel's first two kings: Saul and David. Originally these stories took up a single scroll. When the Hebrew Bible was translated into Greek in the third and second centuries BCE, the translators divided the book into two, calling the resulting works 1 and 2 Kingdoms. Eventually Jewish Bibles accepted this division, but called the two books 1 and 2 Samuel. The name is appropriate since the figure of Samuel plays a prominent role in 1 Samuel, and 1 Chr 29:29 credits Samuel, together with Nathan and Gad, with writing "the deeds of King David."

The narratives in the books of Samuel fall into three overlapping cycles. Stories with Samuel as the main character come first (1 Sm 1–25), but in the course of those stories a second major character emerges—Saul (1 Sm 9–2 Sm 1). These books reach their climax with the story of David (1 Sm 16–2 Sm 24). The books chronicle the move toward centralized, official leadership for the Israelite tribes. The regional and charismatic leadership characteristic of the judges' period did not offer a permanent solution to the religious, military, and political challenges that the Israelite tribes continued to face as they tried to maintain their hold on the land of Canaan. The threat posed by the Philistines, first described in the book of Judges, had become acute. Though Shamgar (Jgs 3:31) and Samson (Jgs 13–16) had some success against the Philistines, the tribe of Dan, likely because of relentless Philistine incursions into its territory along Canaan's central coast, chose to move to the far north of Canaan (Jgs 18). Until the Philistines could be neutralized, Israel's continued presence in the land remained in doubt.

The origins of the Philistines remain

## Outline of 1–2 Samuel

I. **The Last Judges, Eli and Samuel (1 Sm 1:1–7:17)**

II. **Establishment of the Monarchy (1 Sm 8:1–12:25)**

III. **Saul and David (1 Sm 13:1–2 Sm 2:7)**

IV. **The Reign of David (2 Sm 2:8–20:26)**

V. **Appendixes (2 Sm 21:1–24:25)**

unknown, though they were probably refugees from the tidal wave of destruction that resulted from the collapse of the political and economic systems in the eastern Mediterranean region. These refugees became a potent military threat to the peace of the region at the end of the Late Bronze Age (ca. 1206–1150 BCE) as they were searching for territory to call their own. The prize they sought was Egypt. Rameses III, however, prevented a Philistine takeover in 1190 BCE and settled the Philistines along the southern coast of Canaan, which Egypt controlled. After Rameses's death, the Philistines overthrew their Egyptian overlords and began consolidating their hold on the southwest of Canaan in preparation for expanding their holdings to the north and east. They eventually reached as far north as the fertile Jezreel Valley and the city of Beth Shean. As the Philistines continued to expand their holdings, they brought large swaths of Israelite territory under their control. Something had to be done to end the Philistine threat to Israel's continued presence in the land. The books of Samuel chronicle how that threat was removed.

Though Samuel enjoyed initial success against the Philistines (1 Sm 7:7–17), the elders of the Israelite tribes recognized that the Philistines posed the kind of challenge that could not be adequately met by the temporary and regional leadership of the judges, of whom Samuel was the last. The elders wanted the permanent, centralized leadership provided by a king. Saul was the first king of Israel and his reign was marked from beginning (1 Sm 13) to end (1 Sm 31) by wars with the Philistines. Though Saul managed to keep the Philistines from attaining complete hegemony over Israel, he lost his life during one of his campaigns against them (1 Sm 31:1–7). It was David, Saul's successor, who eventually ended the Philistine threat, enabling the Israelite tribes to live in peace and security.

The stories of Saul's reign present him as an incompetent, plagued by paranoia and depression. It is not a flattering portrait of Israel's first king. Though the text presents David as having been chosen by God to succeed the hapless Saul (1 Sm 16), it also makes it clear that David took great care to position himself to take Saul's throne. He became a member of Saul's court and family. He befriended Jonathan, Saul's son and presumed heir, who became David's most vocal supporter. He married Michal, Saul's daughter. But at Saul's death, only Judah, David's own tribe, acclaimed him king (2 Sm 2:1–4a) while Ishbaal, one of Saul's sons, was made king over the other tribes (2 Sm 2:8–11). There was a war of succession (2 Sm 3:1), at the end of which all the male members of Saul's family were dead except for Meribbaal, Jonathan's disabled son. With the assassination of Ishbaal, David's path to Saul's throne was unobstructed (2 Sm 4:1–5:5).

Though the books of Samuel describe David's victories over the Philistines, beginning with his defeat of Goliath (1 Sm 17) to his rout of the Philistines in the Valley of Rephaim (2 Sm 5:17–25), there is nonetheless a strong undercurrent of suspicion and even opposition to David and his attempts to consolidate his power. There were those who objected to the centralizing tendencies of David's actions. They feared that this would compromise the freedom of action enjoyed by the Israelite tribes and their elders. The request for a king is followed by a description of the transformation of Israelite society that will come with the monarchy (1 Sm 8). That transformation will effectively turn all Israelites into the king's servants, who will be obliged to do his bidding. David's plans to build a temple (2 Sm 7:1–3) were countered by God's rejection of those plans (2 Sm 7:4–7). Temple-building was a royal prerogative in the ancient Near East and represented David's attempt at centralization. Finally, David authorized a census to facilitate taxation and conscription (2 Sm 24:2–9). A plague that followed the census-taking was characterized as divine punishment for the census (2 Sm 24:10–17).

Perhaps the most negative assessment of the monarchy is found in the story of the succession to David, which takes up 2 Sm 9–20 and concludes in 1 Kgs 1–2. Second Samuel 9 depicts David as securing his own succession to Israel's throne by having Meribbaal, the last male survivor of Saul's household, move to Jerusalem. It is a thinly disguised attempt to keep a close watch on a person around whom those who opposed David's kingship could rally. The scene moves to a war David waged on the Ammonites (2 Sm 10–11). It was not a war to protect the Israelite tribes from oppression. It was a war to extend the borders of David's kingdom. Peasant farmers had to fight and die for David's glory. During a second campaign against the Ammonites, David did not even bother to join his troops, but stayed in Jerusalem where he had an affair with Bathsheba, the wife of an officer in his army. When she became pregnant, David had the officer brought home in order that he might sleep with his wife so that David's child would appear to have been fathered by Bathsheba's husband. When the officer refused to go along with this scheme, David ordered his return to the front so that he would be killed in battle (2 Sm 11). David then married Bathsheba, but their child died a week after birth (2 Sm 12:18). The prophet Nathan reprimanded David for his abuse of power. David's acknowledgment of responsibility spared him further punishment (2 Sam 12:1–12).

Following this sordid episode, David's family life deteriorated. Amnon, David's eldest son, raped Tamar, Amnon's half sister (2 Sm 13:1–22). When David did not punish Amnon (his favored firstborn son), Absalom, Tamar's

**1 S M**

full brother, avenged this outrage by having Amnon killed (2 Sm 13:23–28). Absalom fled to Geshur, the homeland of his mother, and remained there until David forgave him and allowed him to return (2 Sm 14:28–33). Absalom, however, never really forgave his father for overlooking Amnon's crime. He sought to depose his father and take the throne for himself. After some initial success, Absalom's revolution ended in failure and Absalom was killed by one of David's generals (2 Sm 18:9–17). By recounting this tragic and sad story of David's family, the Deuteronomist appears to be saying to the reader: "If you want a monarchy, this is what you get." Subsequently, David had to face another revolt—this one led by Sheba, who belonged to the tribe of Benjamin, which was Saul's tribe (2 Sm 20). Though this revolt failed, it is clear that David did not enjoy the support of all Israel.

At one time, the narratives about David's reign were considered examples of early attempts at history writing, with some of the narratives being composed by eyewitnesses. Few interpreters hold that position today. Archaeology has undercut confidence in the historical value of these books. According to 2 Samuel, David ruled an empire that extended from the Mediterranean Sea in the west and the northern Sinai in the south. It included most of the Transjordan in the east and approached the River Euphrates in the north. Excavation has found no evidence that eleventh-century BCE Jerusalem was the kind of administrative center that such an empire would have needed. It is likely that both David and Saul were local chieftains and that the establishment of the Israelite national states had yet to take place. While the books of Samuel may help reconstruct the history of ancient Israel, extreme care must be taken in assessing the historical value of individual texts.

There is, however, one artifact from antiquity that does mention David: a stele erected in the ninth century BCE by a king of Aram in celebration of his victory over "the king of Israel" and a king of "the house of David." The Aramaic inscription is the only ancient Near Eastern text other than the Bible that mentions David. There is general agreement that the David named in the inscription is the David of the Bible. It is clear then that by the ninth century even non-Israelites thought of David as the founder of the dynasty that ruled the kingdom of Judah.

It is essential to remember that 1–2 Samuel are part of a larger work that also includes Joshua, Judges, and 1–2 Kings. Although biblical scholars call this extended work the Deuteronomistic *History*, it is not a historical work in the modern sense of the term. Its purpose is religious and homiletical. The belief that Israel's future depended on its fidelity to God and obedience to God's written, authoritative law guided the author in telling the story of Israel in its land. The goal of the storyteller was to persuade the people of Israel to live lives of fidelity and obedience. The stories of Saul and David as told in 1–2 Samuel illustrate the story of the people of Israel in microcosm. What began so well ended so badly. The books of Samuel affirm that both Saul and David were chosen by God to be king over the Israelite tribes (1 Sm 9:14–21; 16:1–13), yet both failed to fulfill the expectations of those who acclaimed them king. The people of Israel were chosen by God to be a people "specially his own" (Dt 7:6; 14:2; 26:18). They too failed to remain committed to the God who chose them.

While later biblical and early Jewish tradition rehabilitated David's reputation, the books of Samuel are equivocal in their portrait of David. The same can be said of their portrait of Saul and indeed the monarchic system. The monarchy introduced social, political, and economic systems that ran contrary to those of early Israel. The centripetal forces generated by the monarchy consolidated power at the center and helped create a social and economic dynamic that was excoriated by prophets such as Isaiah, Jeremiah, Micah, and Amos. The book of Deuteronomy offered a needed but hopelessly unrealistic remedy: "When [the king] is sitting upon his royal throne, he shall write a copy of this law upon a scroll from the one that is in the custody of the levitical priests. It shall remain with him and he shall read it as long as he lives, so that he may learn to fear the LORD . . . so that he does not exalt himself over his kindred" (Dt 17:18–20). ▪

# THE BOOKS OF SAMUEL

## New American Bible, Introduction

These books describe the rise and development of kingship in Israel. Samuel is a pivotal figure. He bridges the gap between the period of the Judges and the monarchy, and guides Israel's transition to kingship. A Deuteronomistic editor presents both positive and negative traditions about the monarchy, portraying it both as evidence of Israel's rejection of the Lord as their sovereign (1 Sm 8:6–22; 12:1–25) and as part of God's plan to deliver the people (1 Sm 9:16; 10:17–27; 2 Sm 7:8–17). Samuel's misgivings about abuse of royal power foreshadow the failures and misdeeds of Saul and David and the failures of subsequent Israelite kings.

Although the events described in 1 and 2 Samuel move from the last of the judges to the decline of David's reign and the beginning of a legendary "Golden Age" under Solomon's rule, this material does not present either a continuous history or a systematic account of this period. The author/editor developed a narrative timeline around freely composed speeches, delivered by prophets like Samuel (e.g., 1 Sm 15:10–31; 28:15–19) and Nathan (2 Sm 12:1–12), who endorse Deuteronomistic perspectives regarding the establishment of the monarchy, the relationship between worship and obedience, and the divine covenant established with the house of David.

These books include independent blocks (e.g., the Ark Narrative [1 Sm 4:1–7:1], Saul's rise to power [1 Sm 9:1–11:15], David's ascendancy over Saul [1 Sm 16–31], the Succession Narrative [2 Sm 9–20; 1 Kgs 1–2]), which the editor shaped into three narrative cycles, the last two marked by transitional passages in 1 Sm 13:1 and 2 Sm 1:1. Each section focuses on a major figure in the development of the monarchy: Samuel, the reluctant king maker (1 Sm 1–12); Saul, the king whom the Lord rejects (1 Sm 13–31); David, the king after the Lord's own heart (2 Sm 1–24). A common theme unites these narratives: Israel's God acts justly, prospering those who remain faithful and destroying those who reject his ways (1 Sm 2:9). Along with the rest of the Deuteronomistic History, the Books of Samuel become an object lesson for biblical Israel as it tries to re-establish its religious identity after the destruction of Jerusalem and the loss of its homeland (587/586 B.C.).

The contents of the Books of Samuel may be divided as follows:

I. The Last Judges, Eli and Samuel (1 Sm 1:1–7:17)
II. Establishment of the Monarchy (1 Sm 8:1–12:25)
III. Saul and David (1 Sm 13:1–2 Sm 2:7)
IV. The Reign of David (2 Sm 2:8–20:26)
V. Appendixes (2 Sm 21:1–24:25) ■

# FIRST SAMUEL

## I. THE LAST JUDGES, ELI AND SAMUEL

**1 Elkanah and His Family at Shiloh.** [1]There was a certain man from Ramathaim, a Zuphite from the hill country of Ephraim. His name was Elkanah, the son of Jeroham, son of Elihu, son of Tohu, son of Zuph, an Ephraimite. * [2]He had two wives, one named Hannah, the other Peninnah; Peninnah had children, but Hannah had no children. [3]Each year this man went up from his city to worship and offer sacrifice to the LORD of hosts at Shiloh, where the two sons of Eli, Hophni and Phinehas, were ministering as priests of the LORD. * [4]When the day came for Elkanah to offer sacrifice, he used to give portions to his wife Peninnah and to all her sons and daughters, [5]but he would give a double portion to Hannah because he loved her, though the LORD had closed her womb. * [6]Her rival, † to upset her, would torment her constantly, since the LORD had closed her womb. * [7]Year after year, when she went up to the house of the LORD, Peninnah would provoke her, and Hannah would weep and refuse to eat. † [8]Elkanah, her husband, would say to her: "Hannah, why are you weeping? Why are you not eating? Why are you so miserable? Am I not better for you than ten sons?" *

**Hannah's Prayer.** [9]Hannah rose after one such meal at Shiloh, and presented herself before the LORD; at the time Eli the priest was sitting on a chair near the doorpost of the LORD's temple. [10]In her bitterness she prayed to the LORD, weeping freely, [11]and made this vow: "O LORD of hosts, if you look with pity on the hardship of your servant, if you remember me and do not forget me, if you give your handmaid a male child, I will give him to the LORD all the days of his life. No razor shall ever touch his head." † * [12]As she continued praying before the LORD, Eli watched her mouth, [13]for Hannah was praying silently; though her lips were moving, her voice could not be heard. Eli, thinking she was drunk, [14]said to her, "How long will you make a drunken spectacle of yourself? Sober up from your wine!" [15]"No, my lord!" Hannah answered. "I am an unhappy woman. I have had neither wine nor liquor; I was only pouring out my heart to the LORD. [16]Do not think your servant a worthless woman; my prayer has been prompted by my deep sorrow and misery." [17]Eli said, "Go in peace, and may the God of Israel grant you what you have requested." [18]She replied, "Let your servant find favor in your eyes," and left. She went to her quarters, ate and drank with her husband, and no longer appeared downhearted. [19]Early the next morning they worshiped before the LORD, and then returned to their home in Ramah. When they returned Elkanah had intercourse with his wife Hannah, and the LORD remembered her.

**Hannah Bears a Son.** [20]She conceived and, at the end of her pregnancy, bore a son whom she named Samuel. † "Because I asked the LORD for him." [21]The next time her husband Elkanah was going up with the rest of his household to offer the customary sacrifice to the LORD and to fulfill his vows, [22]Hannah did not go, explaining to her husband, "Once the child is weaned, I will take him to appear before the LORD and leave him there forever." † [23]Her husband Elkanah answered her: "Do what you think best; wait until you have weaned him. Only may the LORD fulfill his word!" And so she remained at home and nursed her son until she had weaned him. *

---

† **1:6** *Her rival*: Hebrew *sara*, "rival wife, co-wife"; in the Talmud, a technical term for a second or co-wife.

**1:7** In biblical narrative, the social status gained by producing children, especially males, often set woman against woman; cf. e.g., Gn 16, 21, 30. Peninnah's provocations may be the arrogant boasting mentioned in 2:3.

**1:11** *No razor…*: the Septuagint adds "he shall drink neither wine nor liquor." This addition is a further suggestion that Samuel is dedicated to God under a nazirite vow (Nm 6:4–5); see note on v. 22.

**1:20** *Samuel*: Hannah's explanation associates her son's name with the narrative's wordplay on the Hebrew verbs *s'l* ("ask," vv. 17, 27), *his'il* ("hand over, dedicate," v. 28), *sa'ul* ("dedicated," v. 28), and the noun *se'elah* ("request," vv. 17, 27). The name, however, is related to the Hebrew root *s'l* only through assonance. It means "his name is El/God," not "the one requested of or dedicated (*sa'ul*) to God" (v. 28), which is the meaning of the name Saul. The author may have lifted the *s'l* wordplay from a narrative about Saul to portray Samuel as God's gracious answer to Hannah's request.

**1:22** *Leave him there forever*: a Qumran manuscript adds "I will give him as a nazirite forever"; it interprets v. 11 to mean that Hannah dedicates Samuel under a nazirite vow (cf. Nm 6:4–5).

* **1:1** 1 Chr 6:19–20.
**1:3** Ex 23:14–17; 34:23; Dt 16:16; Jgs 21:19.
**1:5** Dt 21:15–17.
**1:6** Gn 16:4–5; 29:31; Jgs 13:2; Lk 1:7.
**1:8** Ru 4:15.
**1:11** Nm 6:1–5; Jgs 13:2–5; 16:17; Lk 1:15.
**1:23** Dt 9:5; 2 Sm 7:25; 1 Kgs 2:4.

**Hannah Presents Samuel to the Lord.** 24 Once he was weaned, she brought him up with her, along with a three-year-old bull, an ephah† of flour, and a skin of wine, and presented him at the house of the LORD in Shiloh. 25 After they had slaughtered the bull, they brought the child to Eli. 26 Then Hannah spoke up: "Excuse me, my lord! As you live, my lord, I am the woman who stood here near you, praying to the LORD. 27 I prayed for this child, and the LORD granted my request. 28 Now I, in turn, give him to the LORD; as long as he lives, he shall be dedicated to the LORD." Then they worshiped there before the LORD.

2 ¹ And Hannah prayed:†

"My heart exults in the LORD,
my horn is exalted by my God.
I have swallowed up my enemies;
I rejoice in your victory. *
² There is no Holy One like the LORD;
there is no Rock like our God. *
³ Speak boastfully no longer,
Do not let arrogance issue from your
mouths.†
For an all-knowing God is the LORD,
a God who weighs actions. *
⁴ "The bows of the mighty are broken,
while the tottering gird on strength. *
⁵ The well-fed hire themselves out for
bread,
while the hungry no longer have to
toil.
The barren wife bears seven sons,
while the mother of many
languishes. *
⁶ "The LORD puts to death and gives life,
casts down to Sheol and brings up
again. *
⁷ The LORD makes poor and makes rich,
humbles, and also exalts.
⁸ He raises the needy from the dust;

from the ash heap lifts up the poor,
To seat them with nobles
and make a glorious throne their
heritage.

"For the pillars of the earth are the
LORD's,
and he has set the world upon them. *
⁹ He guards the footsteps of his faithful
ones,
but the wicked shall perish in the
darkness;
for not by strength does one prevail.
¹⁰ The LORD's foes shall be shattered;
the Most High in heaven thunders;
the LORD judges the ends of the earth.
May he give strength to his king,
and exalt the horn of his anointed!" *

¹¹ When Elkanah returned home to Ramah, the child remained in the service of the LORD under the priest Eli.

**Wickedness of Eli's Sons.** 12 Now the sons of Eli were wicked; they had respect neither for the LORD 13 nor for the priests' duties toward the people. When someone offered a sacrifice, the priest's servant would come with a three-pronged fork, while the meat was still boiling, * 14 and would thrust it into the basin, kettle, caldron, or pot. Whatever the fork brought up, the priest would take for himself. They treated all the Israelites who came to the sanctuary at Shiloh in this way. 15 In fact, even before the fat was burned, the priest's servant would come and say to the one offering the sacrifice, "Give me some meat to roast for the priest. He will not accept boiled meat from you, only raw meat." 16 And if this one protested, "Let the fat be burned first, then take whatever you wish," he would reply, "No, give it to me now, or else I will take it by force." * 17 Thus the young men sinned grievously in the presence of the LORD, treating the offerings to the LORD with disdain.

---

† 1:24 *Ephah:* see note on Is 5:10.
**2:1–10** Hannah appeals to a God who maintains order by keeping human affairs in balance, reversing the fortunes of the arrogant, who, like Peninnah, boast of their good fortune (vv. 1, 3, 9) at the expense of those like Hannah who receive less from the Lord. Hannah's admission places her among the faithful who trust that God will execute justice on their behalf. The reference "his king…his anointed" (v. 10) recalls the final sentence of the Book of Judges and introduces the kingship theme that dominates the Books of Samuel.

**2:3** *Speak…mouths:* addressed to the enemies mentioned in v. 1.

---

| | |
|---|---|
| **2:1** Dt 33:17; 2 Sm 22:3; Ps 18:2; 89:18; Is 61:10; Lk 1:47, 69. | Jb 5:11; Ps 30:4; Wis 16:13; Lk 1:52. |
| **2:2** 2 Sm 22:3; Ps 18:2. | **2:8** Jb 9:6; 38:6; Ps 75:4; 104:5; 113:8; 121:3. |
| **2:3** Ps 75:5–6. | **2:10** Ps 98:9. |
| **2:4** Is 40:29. | **2:13–15** Ex 29:27–28; Lv |
| **2:5** Ru 4:15; Jer 15:9. | 7:29–36; Dt 18:3. |
| **2:6** Dt 32:39; Tb 4:19; | **2:16** Lv 3:3–5; Nm 18:17. |

**The Lord Rewards Hannah.** [18]Meanwhile the boy Samuel, wearing a linen ephod,† was serving in the presence of the LORD. [19]His mother used to make a little garment for him, which she would bring him each time she went up with her husband to offer the customary sacrifice. [20]And Eli would bless Elkanah and his wife, as they were leaving for home. He would say, "May the LORD repay you with children from this woman for the gift she has made to the LORD!" [21]The LORD favored Hannah so that she conceived and gave birth to three more sons and two daughters, while young Samuel grew up in the service of the LORD.*

**Eli's Futile Rebuke.** [22]When Eli was very old, he kept hearing how his sons were treating all Israel, and that they were behaving promiscuously† with the women serving at the entry of the meeting tent. [23]So he said to them: "Why are you doing such things? I hear from everyone that your behavior is depraved. [24]Stop this, my sons! The report that I hear the LORD's people spreading is not good. [25]If someone sins against another, anyone can intercede for the sinner with the LORD; but if anyone sins against the LORD, who can intercede† for the sinner?" But they disregarded their father's warning, since the LORD wanted them dead. [26]Meanwhile, young Samuel was growing in stature and in worth in the estimation of the LORD and the people.*

**The Fate of Eli's House.**† [27]A man of God came to Eli and said to him: "Thus says the LORD: I went so far as to reveal myself to your father's house when they were in Egypt as slaves to the house of Pharaoh. [28]I chose them out of all the tribes of Israel to be my priests, to go up to my altar, to burn incense, and to wear

the ephod† in my presence; and I assigned all the fire offerings of the Israelites to your father's house.* [29]Why do you stare greedily at my sacrifices and at the offerings that I have prescribed? Why do you honor your sons more than you honor me, fattening yourselves with the choicest part of every offering of my people Israel? [30]*This, therefore, is the oracle of the LORD, the God of Israel: I said in the past that your family and your father's house should minister in my presence forever. But now—oracle of the LORD: Far be it from me! I will honor those who honor me, but those who despise me shall be cursed. [31]Yes, the days are coming when I will break your strength and the strength of your father's house, so that no one in your family lives to old age. [32]You shall witness, like a disappointed rival, all the benefits enjoyed by Israel, but no member of your household shall ever grow old. [33]I will leave you one man at my altar to wear out his eyes and waste his strength, but the rest of your family shall die by the sword. [34]This is a sign for you—what happens to your two sons, Hophni and Phinehas. Both of them will die on the same day.* [35]I will choose a faithful priest who shall do what I have in heart and mind. I will establish a lasting house for him and he shall serve in the presence of my anointed forever. [36]Then whoever is left of your family will grovel before him for a piece of silver or a loaf of bread, saying: Please assign me a priestly function, that I may have a crust of bread to eat."*

**3** **Revelation to Samuel.** [1]During the time young Samuel was minister to the LORD under Eli, the word of the LORD was scarce and vision infrequent. [2]† One day Eli was asleep in his usual place. His eyes had lately grown

---

† **2:18** *Linen ephod:* not the same as the high priest's ephod (Ex 28:6–14) or the ephod used in divination (v. 28). Samuel wore the same kind of a ceremonial garment as the priests did (1 Sm 22:18). David also wore an ephod when he danced before the ark (2 Sm 6:14).

**2:22** *Behaving promiscuously:* this part of the verse, which recalls Ex 38:8, is a gloss; it is lacking in the oldest Greek translation, and in 4QSamᵃ.

**2:25** *Who can intercede:* Eli's sons fail to understand that their crime is directly against God and that God will punish them for it. Their behavior is set in sharp contrast to Samuel's, which meets with God's approval.

**2:27–36** These verses describe the punishment of Eli from a point of view contemporary with the reform of Josiah (2 Kgs 23:9; cf. v. 36); they hint at the events recorded in 1 Sm 22:18–23 and 1 Kgs 2:27. The older story of this divine warning occurs in 1 Sm 3:11–14. *A man of God:* often an anonymous figure

whose speech foreshadows events in the near future. Cf. 1 Sm 9:6; 1 Kgs 13:1; 2 Kgs 23:16–17.

**2:28** *Ephod:* a portable container, presumably of cloth, for the lots used in ritual consultation of God during the days of the Judges (Jgs 17:5; 18:14–15) and into the time of David (1 Sm 14:3; 23:6–9; 30:7–8). Attached to the ephod of the high priest described in Ex 28:6–8 is a "breastpiece of decision" which symbolized, but did not facilitate, such consultation. The Exodus text codifies a later form of the tradition.

**3:2–18** The call of Samuel: This section may be divided as follows: 1. the triple summons (vv. 2–9); 2. God's revelation (vv. 10–14); 3. Samuel informs Eli (vv. 15–18).

---

*
| | |
|---|---|
| **2:21** 1 Sm 3:19. | **2:30–31** 2 Sm 22:26; 1 Kgs |
| **2:26** Lk 2:52. | 2:27; Ps 18:25. |
| **2:28** 1 Sm 23:9; 30:7–8; Jgs | **2:34** 1 Sm 4:11. |
| 17:5. | **2:36** 2 Kgs 23:9. |

so weak that he could not see. ³The lamp of God was not yet extinguished,† and Samuel was sleeping in the temple of the LORD where the ark of God was.* ⁴The LORD called to Samuel, who answered, "Here I am." ⁵He ran to Eli and said, "Here I am. You called me." "I did not call you," Eli answered. "Go back to sleep." So he went back to sleep. ⁶Again the LORD called Samuel, who rose and went to Eli. "Here I am," he said. "You called me." But he answered, "I did not call you, my son. Go back to sleep."

⁷Samuel did not yet recognize the LORD, since the word of the LORD had not yet been revealed to him. ⁸The LORD called Samuel again, for the third time. Getting up and going to Eli, he said, "Here I am. You called me." Then Eli understood that the LORD was calling the youth. ⁹So he said to Samuel, "Go to sleep, and if you are called, reply, 'Speak, LORD, for your servant is listening.'" When Samuel went to sleep in his place, ¹⁰the LORD came and stood there, calling out as before: Samuel, Samuel! Samuel answered, "Speak, for your servant is listening." ¹¹The LORD said to Samuel: I am about to do something in Israel that will make the ears of everyone who hears it ring.* ¹²On that day I will carry out against Eli everything I have said about his house, beginning to end. ¹³I announce to him that I am condemning his house once and for all, because of this crime: though he knew his sons were blaspheming God, he did not reprove them.* ¹⁴Therefore, I swear to Eli's house: No sacrifice or offering will ever expiate its crime.† ¹⁵Samuel then slept until morning, when he got up early and opened the doors of the temple of the LORD. He was afraid to tell Eli the vision, ¹⁶but Eli called to him, "Samuel, my son!" He replied, "Here I am." ¹⁷Then Eli asked, "What did he say to you? Hide nothing from me! May God do thus to you, and more,† if you hide from me a single thing he

told you." ¹⁸So Samuel told him everything, and held nothing back. Eli answered, "It is the LORD. What is pleasing in the LORD's sight, the LORD will do."

**Samuel Acknowledged as Prophet.** ¹⁹Samuel grew up, and the LORD was with him, not permitting any word of his to go unfulfilled.* ²⁰*Thus all Israel from Dan to Beer-sheba came to know that Samuel was a trustworthy prophet of the LORD. ²¹The LORD continued to appear at Shiloh, manifesting himself to Samuel at Shiloh through his word. Samuel's word spread throughout Israel.

**4** **Defeat of the Israelites.**† ¹At that time, the Philistines gathered for an attack on Israel. Israel went out to engage them in battle and camped at Ebenezer, while the Philistines camped at Aphek. ²The Philistines then drew up in battle formation against Israel. After a fierce struggle Israel was defeated by the Philistines, who killed about four thousand men on the battlefield. ³When the troops retired to the camp, the elders of Israel said, "Why has the LORD permitted us to be defeated today by the Philistines? Let us fetch the ark of the LORD from Shiloh that it may go into battle among us and save us from the grasp of our enemies."*

**Loss of the Ark.** ⁴So the people sent to Shiloh and brought from there the ark of the LORD of hosts, who is enthroned upon the cherubim.† The two sons of Eli, Hophni and Phinehas, accompanied the ark of God.* ⁵When the ark of the LORD arrived in the camp, all Israel shouted so loudly that the earth shook. ⁶The Philistines, hearing the uproar, asked, "What does this loud shouting in the camp of the Hebrews mean?" On learning that the ark of the LORD had come into the camp, ⁷the Philistines were frightened, crying out, "Gods have come

---

3:3 *Not yet extinguished*: referring to the nighttime setting of this narrative (cf. Ex 27:20–21) and foreshadowing a permanently extinguished lamp when the ark is captured and Shiloh destroyed.
3:14 Lv 4:3–12 presents another view: the offering of a bull can expiate priestly sin.
3:17 *May God do thus to you, and more*: an oath formula which strengthens Eli's demand by threatening divine punishment if Samuel does not obey. Cf. 14:44; 20:13; 25:22; 2 Sm 3:9, 35; 19:14.
4:1–7:1 The Ark Narrative: A striking indication that this is an independent narrative is the absence of any mention of Samuel. *The Philistines*: one of the Sea Peoples, of Aegean origin, who oc-

cupied the coastal plain of Palestine and threatened the Israelites who settled the inland hills.
4:4 *Enthroned upon the cherubim*: this divine title first occurs in the Old Testament at the sanctuary at Shiloh (cf. 2 Sm 6:2); God is represented seated upon a throne borne through the heavens by cherubim, creatures partly human being, partly beast (cf. Ez 1 and 10).

---

3:3 Ex 27:20–22.     3:20 Jgs 20:1; 2 Sm 3:10;
3:11 2 Kgs 21:12.          17:11; 24:2.
3:13 1 Sm 2:27–36.   4:3 Nm 10:35; 14:42–44.
3:19 1 Sm 2:21.      4:4 Ez 25:21–22.

to their camp. Woe to us! This has never happened before. [8]Woe to us! Who can deliver us from the power of these mighty gods?† These are the gods who struck the Egyptians with various plagues in the desert. [9]Take courage and act like soldiers, Philistines; otherwise you will become slaves to the Hebrews, as they were your slaves. Fight like soldiers!" [10]The Philistines fought and Israel was defeated; everyone fled to their own tents.† It was a disastrous defeat; Israel lost thirty thousand foot soldiers. [11]The ark of God was captured, and Eli's two sons, Hophni and Phinehas, were dead.*

**Death of Eli.** [12]A Benjaminite fled from the battlefield and reached Shiloh that same day, with his clothes torn and his head covered with dirt.* [13]When he arrived, Eli was sitting in his chair beside the gate, watching the road, for he was troubled at heart about the ark of God. The man, however, went into the city to announce his news; then the whole city cried out. [14]When Eli heard the uproar, he wondered why there was such commotion. Just then the man rushed up to inform him. [15]Eli was ninety-eight years old, and his eyes would not focus. So he could not see. [16]The man said to Eli: "I have come from the battlefield; today I fled from there." He asked, "What happened, my son?" [17]And the messenger answered: "Israel fled from the Philistines; in fact, the troops suffered heavy losses. Your two sons, Hophni and Phinehas, are dead, and the ark of God has been captured." [18]At this mention of the ark of God, Eli fell backward from his chair into the gateway; he died of a broken neck since he was an old man and heavy. He had judged Israel for forty years.

[19]His daughter-in-law, the wife of Phinehas, was pregnant and about to give birth. When she heard the news about the capture of the ark of God and the deaths of her father-in-law and her husband, she crouched down in labor, and gave birth. [20]She was about to die when the women standing around her said to her, "Do not be afraid, you have given birth to a son." Yet she neither answered nor paid any attention.* [21]She named the child Ichabod, saying, "Gone is the glory from Israel," referring to the capture of the ark of God and to her father-in-law and her husband. [22]She said, "Gone is the glory from Israel," because the ark of God had been captured.*

**5** **The Ark in the Temple of Dagon.** [1]†* The Philistines, having captured the ark of God, transferred it from Ebenezer to Ashdod.* [2]They then took the ark of God and brought it into the temple of Dagon, placing it beside Dagon. [3]When the people of Ashdod rose early the next morning, Dagon was lying face down on the ground before the ark of the LORD. So they picked Dagon up and put him back in his place. [4]But early the next morning, when they arose, Dagon lay face down on the ground before the ark of the LORD, his head and hands broken off and lying on the threshold, his trunk alone intact. [5]For this reason, neither the priests of Dagon nor any others who enter the temple of Dagon tread on the threshold of Dagon in Ashdod to this very day.

**The Ark Is Carried About.** [6]Now the hand of the LORD weighed heavily on the people of Ashdod, ravaging them and afflicting the city and its vicinity with tumors.†* [7]On seeing how matters stood, the people of Ashdod decided, "The ark of the God of Israel must not remain with us, for his hand weighs heavily on us and Dagon our god." [8]So they summoned all the Philistine leaders and inquired of them, "What shall we do with the ark of the God of Israel?" The people of Gath replied, "Let them move the ark of the God of Israel to us." So they moved the ark of the God of Israel to Gath. [9]But after it had been brought there, the hand of the LORD was against the city, resulting

---

4:8 *These mighty gods*: the Philistines, who were polytheists, presume that the Israelites also honored several gods.

4:10 *To their own tents*: the defeat is so catastrophic that the soldiers abandon the army for home; cf. 2 Sm 18:17.

5:1–12 The Philistines take the ark to Dagon's temple in Ashdod to confirm their victory. Their action, however, underscores Dagon's impotence and the Lord's power. The narrator relates the transfer of the ark from Ashdod to Gath and then Ekron as the progress of a conquering warrior king through the Philistine cities along the central plain. The Philistines' humiliation recalls the climax of the Samson story (Jgs 16:13–21).

5:6 *Tumors*: the Septuagint adds that mice, suggestive of bubonic plague, infested their fields, thus anticipating the golden mice in 6:4–5. One symptom of bubonic plague is swollen lymph nodes ("tumors").

4:11 1 Sm 2:34.
4:12 Jos 7:6; 2 Sm 1:2; Jer 7:12.
4:20 1 Sm 14:3; Gn 35:16–20.
4:22 Ps 78:61.
5:1–5 Jgs 16:23–30; Is 45:5–6, 20–21.
5:1 Jos 13:3.
5:6 Ps 32:4.

in utter turmoil: the LORD afflicted its inhabitants, young and old, and tumors broke out on them. [10]The ark of God was next sent to Ekron; but as it entered that city, the people there cried out, "Why have they brought the ark of the God of Israel here to kill us and our kindred?" [11]Then they, too, sent a summons to all the Philistine leaders and pleaded: "Send away the ark of the God of Israel. Send it back to its place so it does not kill us and our kindred." A deadly panic had seized the whole city, since the hand of God lay heavy upon it. [12]Those who escaped death were afflicted with tumors. Thus the outcry from the city went up to the heavens.

**6** **The Ark Is Returned.** [1]The ark of the LORD had been in the land of the Philistines seven months [2]when they summoned priests and diviners to ask, "What shall we do with the ark of the LORD? Tell us what we should send back with it." [3]They replied: "If you intend to send back the ark of the God of Israel, you must not send it alone, but must, by all means, make amends to God through a reparation offering.† Then you will be healed, and will learn why God continues to afflict you." [4]When asked further, "What reparation offering should be our amends to God?" they replied: "Five golden tumors and five golden mice to correspond to the number of Philistine leaders, since the same plague has struck all of you and your leaders. [5]Therefore, make images of the tumors and of the mice that are devastating your land and so give glory to the God of Israel. Perhaps then God will lift his hand from you, your gods, and your land. [6]Why should you become stubborn, the way the Egyptians and Pharaoh were stubborn? Was it not after he had dealt ruthlessly with them that the Israelites were released and departed?* [7]So now set to work and make a new cart. Then take two milk cows that have not borne the yoke; hitch them to the cart, but drive their calves indoors away from them.†* [8]You shall next take the ark of the LORD and

place it on the cart, putting the golden articles that you are offering as reparation for your guilt in a box beside it. Start it on its way, and let it go. [9]Then watch! If it goes up to Beth-shemesh† along the route to the LORD's territory, then it was the LORD who brought this great calamity upon us; if not, we will know that it was not the LORD's hand, but a bad turn, that struck us."

**The Ark in Beth-shemesh.** [10]They acted upon this advice. Taking two milk cows, they hitched them to the cart but shut up their calves indoors. [11]Then they placed the ark of the LORD on the cart, along with the box containing the golden mice and the images of the tumors. [12]The cows went straight for the route to Beth-shemesh and continued along this road, mooing as they went, turning neither right nor left. The Philistine leaders followed them as far as the border of Beth-shemesh. [13]The people of Beth-shemesh were harvesting the wheat in the valley. They looked up and rejoiced when they saw the ark. [14]The cart came to the field of Joshua the Beth-shemite and stopped there. At a large stone in the field, the wood of the cart was split up and the cows were offered as a burnt offering to the LORD.* [15]The Levites, meanwhile, had taken down the ark of God and the box beside it, with the golden articles, and had placed them on the great stone. The people of Beth-shemesh also offered other burnt offerings and sacrifices to the LORD that day.* [16]After witnessing this, the five Philistine leaders returned to Ekron the same day.

[17]The golden tumors the Philistines sent back as a reparation offering to the LORD were as follows: one for Ashdod, one for Gaza, one for Ashkelon, one for Gath, and one for Ekron. [18]The golden mice, however, corresponded to the number of all the cities of the Philistines belonging to the five leaders, including fortified cities and open villages.† The large stone on which the ark of the LORD was placed is still in the field of Joshua the Beth-shemite at the present time.*

---

† **6:3** *A reparation offering*: an offering to make amends for unwitting transgressions against holy things or property rights; cf. Lv 6:1–3.

**6:7** *But drive their calves indoors away from them*: a test to confirm the source of the Philistines' trouble. Left to their instincts, milk cows would remain near their calves rather than head for the road to Beth-shemesh.

**6:9** *Beth-shemesh*: a border city (about twenty-four miles west of Jerusalem) between Philistine and Israelite territory.

**6:18** *Open villages*: the plague devastated both fortified cities and villages, an indication of the Lord's power over the Philistines.

**6:6** Ex 7:14; 8:15; 9:34.  **6:15** Dt 31:25; 1 Chr 15:2.
**6:7** Nm 19:2; Dt 21:3;  **6:18** 1 Sm 7:12; Gn 31:52;
2 Sm 6:3.  Jos 24:27.
**6:14** 2 Sm 24:21–25.

## Penalty for Irreverence.

**Penalty for Irreverence.** [19]The descendants of Jeconiah did not join in the celebration with the inhabitants of Beth-shemesh when they saw the ark of the LORD, and seventy of them were struck down. The people mourned over this great calamity which the LORD had inflicted upon them. [20]The men of Beth-shemesh asked, "Who can stand in the presence of the LORD, this Holy God? To whom can the ark go so that we are rid of it?" [21]They then sent messengers to the inhabitants of Kiriath-jearim, saying, "The Philistines have returned the ark of the LORD; come down and get it."

**7** [1]So the inhabitants of Kiriath-jearim came for the ark of the LORD and brought it into the house of Abinadab on the hill, appointing his son Eleazar as guardian of the ark of the LORD.

**Samuel the Judge.** [2]From the day the ark came to rest in Kiriath-jearim, a long time, twenty years, elapsed, and the whole house of Israel turned to the LORD. [3]Then Samuel addressed the whole house of Israel: "If you would return to the LORD with your whole heart, remove your foreign gods and your Astartes, fix your hearts on the LORD, and serve him alone, then the LORD will deliver you from the hand of the Philistines." * [4]So the Israelites removed their Baals and Astartes, † and served the LORD alone. [5]Samuel then gave orders, "Gather all Israel to Mizpah, that I may pray to the LORD for you." * [6]When they had gathered at Mizpah, they drew water and poured it out† on the ground before the LORD, and they fasted that day, saying, "We have sinned against the LORD." It was at Mizpah that Samuel began to judge the Israelites. *

**Rout of the Philistines.** [7]When the Philistines heard that the Israelites had gathered at Mizpah, their leaders went up against Israel.

Hearing this, the Israelites became afraid of the Philistines [8]and appealed to Samuel, "Do not stop crying out to the LORD our God for us, to save us from the hand of the Philistines." * [9]Samuel therefore took an unweaned lamb and offered it whole as a burnt offering to the LORD. * He cried out to the LORD for Israel, and the LORD answered him. [10]While Samuel was sacrificing the burnt offering, the Philistines drew near for battle with Israel. That day, however, the LORD thundered loudly against the Philistines, and threw them into such confusion that they were defeated by Israel. * [11]Thereupon the Israelites rushed out from Mizpah and pursued the Philistines, striking them down even beyond Beth-car. [12]Samuel then took a stone and placed it between Mizpah and Jeshanah; he named it Ebenezer, † explaining, "As far as this place the LORD has been our help." [13]Thus were the Philistines subdued, never again to enter the territory of Israel, for the hand of the LORD was against them as long as Samuel lived. * [14]The cities from Ekron to Gath which the Philistines had taken from Israel were restored to them. Israel also freed the territory of these cities from Philistine domination. There was also peace between Israel and the Amorites. †

[15]Samuel judged Israel as long as he lived. [16]He made a yearly circuit, passing through Bethel, Gilgal and Mizpah† and judging Israel at each of these places. [17]Then he used to return to Ramah, for that was his home. There, too, he judged Israel and built an altar to the LORD. *

## II. ESTABLISHMENT OF THE MONARCHY

**8** **Request for a King.** [1]† In his old age Samuel appointed his sons judges over Israel. * [2]His firstborn was named Joel, his second son, Abijah; they judged at Beer-sheba. [3]His sons did not follow his example, but looked to

---

† **7:4** *Baals and Astartes*: a Deuteronomistic phrase; cf. Jgs 2:13; 10:6; 1 Sm 12:10. Baal and Astarte were Canaanite divinities.
**7:6** *Drew water and poured it out*: this ritual act does not appear elsewhere in the Old Testament. Linked with fasting and admission of sin, it seems to function as a purification ritual that washes away the guilt incurred by worshiping the Canaanite Baal and his consort Astarte. Its effectiveness is immediately evident when the Lord thunders a response to Samuel's offering.
**7:12** *Ebenezer*: "stone of the helper," i.e., the Lord.
**7:14** *The Amorites*: enemies in Transjordan. Israel is now secure, safe from external and internal threat.
**7:16** *Bethel, Gilgal and Mizpah*: Bethel and Mizpah are located about five and eight miles north of Jerusalem respectively,

in the district around Ramah, Samuel's home. Perhaps Gilgal, which has not been definitively located, was also in this area.
**8:1–22** From this chapter on, the editors of 1 Samuel provide two and sometimes three perspectives on the same event: e.g., the selection of Saul as king is recounted in chap. 8; 10:17–24; chap. 12.

**7:3** 1 Sm 12:10, 20, 24; Jos 24:23; Jgs 6:6–10; 10:10–16.
**7:5** 1 Sm 10:17; Jgs 20:1.
**7:6** Jgs 20:26; Ps 22:14; Lam 2:19.
**7:8** Jos 24:7; Jgs 3:9, 15;
6:6; 10:15.
**7:9–10** 2 Sm 22:14–15; Sir 46:16–18.
**7:10** Ex 9:23; 2 Sm 22:14.
**7:13** Jgs 3:20; 8:28; 11:33.
**7:17** 1 Sm 9:12; 14:35.
**8:1** 1 Chr 6:13.

their own gain, accepting bribes and perverting justice. * [4] Therefore all the elders of Israel assembled and went to Samuel at Ramah [5] and said to him, "Now that you are old, and your sons do not follow your example, appoint a king over us, like all the nations, to rule us." *

[6] Samuel was displeased when they said, "Give us a king to rule us." But he prayed to the LORD. [7] The LORD said: Listen to whatever the people say. You are not the one they are rejecting. They are rejecting me as their king. * [8] They are acting toward you just as they have acted from the day I brought them up from Egypt to this very day, deserting me to serve other gods. [9] Now listen to them; but at the same time, give them a solemn warning and inform them of the rights of the king who will rule them.

**The Governance of the King.** [10] Samuel delivered the message of the LORD in full to those who were asking him for a king. [11] He told them: "The governance of the king who will rule you will be as follows: He will take your sons and assign them to his chariots and horses, and they will run before his chariot. * [12] He will appoint from among them his commanders of thousands and of hundreds. He will make them do his plowing and harvesting and produce his weapons of war and chariotry. * [13] He will use your daughters as perfumers, cooks, and bakers. [14] He will take your best fields, vineyards, and olive groves, and give them to his servants. * [15] He will tithe your crops and grape harvests to give to his officials † and his servants. * [16] He will take your male and female slaves, as well as your best oxen and donkeys, and use them to do his work. [17] He will also tithe your flocks. As for you, you will become his slaves. * [18] On that day you will cry out because of the king whom you have chosen, but the LORD will not answer you on that day."

**Persistent Demand.** [19] The people, however, refused to listen to Samuel's warning and said,

"No! There must be a king over us. * [20] We too must be like all the nations, with a king to rule us, lead us in warfare, and fight our battles." [21] Samuel listened to all the concerns of the people and then repeated them to the LORD. [22] The LORD said: Listen to them! Appoint a king to rule over them. Then Samuel said to the people of Israel, "Return, each one of you, to your own city." †

**9** **Saul.** [1] There was a powerful man from Benjamin named Kish, who was the son of Abiel, son of Zeror, son of Becorath, son of Aphiah, a Benjaminite. * [2] He had a son named Saul, who was a handsome young man. There was no other Israelite more handsome than Saul; he stood head and shoulders above the people. *

**The Lost Donkeys.** [3] Now the donkeys of Saul's father, Kish, had wandered off. Kish said to his son Saul, "Take one of the servants with you and go out and hunt for the donkeys." [4] So they went through the hill country of Ephraim, and through the land of Shalishah. Not finding them there, they continued through the land of Shaalim without success. They also went through the land of Benjamin, but they failed to find the animals. [5] When they came to the land of Zuph, Saul said to the servant who was with him, "Come, let us turn back, lest my father forget about the donkeys and become anxious about us." [6] The servant replied, "Listen! There is a man of God in this city, a man held in high esteem; everything he says comes true. Let us go there now! Perhaps he can advise us about the journey we have undertaken." [7] * But Saul said to his servant, "If we go, what can we offer the man? The food in our bags has run out; we have no present to give the man of God. What else do we have?" [8] Again the servant answered Saul, "I have a quarter shekel of silver. † If I give that to the man of God, he will advise us about the journey." [9] * (In former times in Israel, anyone who went to consult God used to say, "Come,

---

† **8:15** *Officials*: lit., eunuchs. These high-ranking administrators were not necessarily emasculated.
**8:22** *To your own city*: Samuel will later reassemble the people at Mizpah (10:17) to acclaim Saul as their king.
**9:8** *A quarter shekel of silver*: about a tenth of an ounce of silver.

**8:3** 1 Sm 2:12–17; Ex 23:8; Dt 16:19;
Prv 17:23.
**8:5–6** Dt 17:14–15; Hos
13:10; Acts 13:21.
**8:7–8** 1 Sm 12:1, 12–13; Jgs 8:22–23; 10:13; 1 Kgs 9:9.
**8:11** 1 Sm 10:25; Dt 17:14–20; 1 Kgs 12.
**8:12** 2 Sm 15:1; 1 Kgs 1:5.
**8:14** Dt 14:22–23.
**8:15** 1 Sm 22:7; 1 Kgs 21:1–24; Ez 46:18.
**8:17** 1 Kgs 12:4.
**8:19** 1 Sm 10:19.
**9:1** 1 Sm 14:51; 1 Chr 8:33.
**9:2** 1 Sm 10:23; 16:12.
**9:7–8** Nm 22:7; 1 Kgs 14:3; 2 Kgs 4:42; 5:15; 8:8–9.
**9:9** Sir 46:15.

let us go to the seer." For the one who is now called prophet was formerly called seer.) [10] Saul then said to his servant, "You are right! Come on, let us go!" So they headed toward the city where the man of God lived.

**Meeting the Young Women.** [11]* As they were going up the path to the city, they met some young women coming out to draw water and they asked them, "Is the seer in town?" [12]* The young women answered, "Yes, there—straight ahead. Hurry now; just today he came to the city, because the people have a sacrifice today on the high place.† [13] When you enter the city, you may reach him before he goes up to the high place to eat. The people will not eat until he arrives; only after he blesses the sacrifice will the invited guests eat. Go up immediately, for you should find him right now."

**Saul Meets Samuel.** [14] So they went up to the city. As they entered it—there was Samuel coming toward them on his way to the high place. [15] The day before Saul's arrival, the LORD had revealed to Samuel:* [16] At this time tomorrow I will send you a man from the land of Benjamin whom you are to anoint as ruler of my people Israel. He shall save my people from the hand of the Philistines. I have looked upon my people; their cry has come to me.* [17] When Samuel caught sight of Saul, the LORD assured him: This is the man I told you about; he shall govern my people. [18] Saul met Samuel in the gateway and said, "Please tell me where the seer lives." [19] Samuel answered Saul: "I am the seer. Go up ahead of me to the high place and eat with me today. In the morning, before letting you go, I will tell you everything on your mind. [20] As for your donkeys that were lost three days ago, do not worry about them, for they have been found. Whom should Israel want if not you and your father's family?" [21] Saul replied: "Am I not a Benjaminite, from the smallest of the tribes of Israel,† and is not my clan the least among the clans of the tribe of Benjamin? Why say such things to me?"*

**The Meal.**† [22] Samuel then took Saul and his servant and brought them into the room. He seated them at the head of the guests, of whom there were about thirty. [23] He said to the cook, "Bring the portion I gave you and told you to put aside." [24] So the cook took up the leg and what went with it, and placed it before Saul. Samuel said: "This is a reserved portion that is set before you. Eat, for it was kept for you until this time; I explained that I was inviting some guests." Thus Saul dined with Samuel that day. [25] When they came down from the high place into the city, a mattress was spread for Saul on the roof, [26] and he slept there.

**Saul's Anointing.** At daybreak Samuel called to Saul on the roof, "Get up, and I will send you on your way." Saul got up, and he and Samuel went outside the city together. [27] As they were approaching the edge of the town, Samuel said to Saul, "Tell the servant to go on ahead of us, but you stay here for a moment, that I may give you a word from God."

**10** [1] Then, from a flask he had with him, Samuel poured oil on Saul's head and kissed him, saying: "The LORD anoints you ruler over his people Israel. You are the one who will govern the LORD's people and save them from the power of their enemies all around them.*

**The Signs Foretold.** "This will be the sign† for you that the LORD has anointed you ruler over his heritage: [2] When you leave me today, you will meet two men near Rachel's tomb† at Zelzah in the territory of Benjamin. They will say to you, 'The donkeys you went to look for have been found. Now your father is no longer worried about the donkeys, but is anxious about you and says: What shall I

---

† 
**9:12** *On the high place:* the local sanctuary on the top of a hill, where the sacrifice was offered and the sacrificial meal eaten.
**9:21** *Smallest of the tribes of Israel:* Saul's objection is a common element in call narrative, e.g., Ex 3:11; 4:10; Jgs 6:15.
**9:22–24** At this ritual meal, Samuel treats the youthful Saul as if he were already king. Saul receives the part of the sacrificed animal reserved for the priest and his family, perhaps the sheep's fat tail. Legal texts (Ex 29:22; Lv 3:9; 7:3–4) require the priest to burn this portion of the sheep on the altar.
**10:1** *The sign:* the role of the new ruler is confirmed by specific signs; cf. Ex 7:9.

**10:2** Here, as in Jer 31:15, Rachel's tomb is placed at Ramah, north of Jerusalem. Later tradition understood Ephrath (Gn 35:19–20) as Bethlehem and placed the tomb farther south (Mt 2:16–18).

**9:11** Gn 24:11–14; Ex 2:16.
**9:12** 1 Sm 7:17; 16:2, 5; 20:6, 29; Dt 12:13; 1 Kgs 3:2, 4.
**9:15** Acts 13:21.
**9:16** 1 Sm 10:1; Jgs 6:14.
**9:21** 1 Sm 15:17.
**10:1** 1 Sm 9:16–17; 16:13; 24:7; Jos 9:9; 1 Kgs 1:39; Acts 13:21.

do about my son?'* ³ Farther on, when you arrive at the oak of Tabor,† three men will meet you as they go up to God at Bethel; one will be bringing three young goats, another three loaves of bread, and the third a skin of wine. ⁴ They will greet you and offer you two elevated offerings of bread, which you should accept from them. ⁵ * After that you will come to Gibeath-elohim, where the Philistine garrison† is located. As you enter that city, you will meet a band of prophets coming down from the high place. They will be preceded by lyres, tambourines, flutes, and harps, and will be in prophetic ecstasy. ⁶ The spirit of the LORD will rush upon you, and you will join them in their prophetic ecstasy and will become a changed man.* ⁷ When these signs have come to pass, do whatever lies to hand, because God is with you. ⁸ * Now go down ahead of me to Gilgal, for I shall come down to you, to offer burnt offerings and to sacrifice communion offerings. Wait seven days until I come to you; I shall then tell you what you must do."†

**The Signs Come to Pass.** ⁹ As Saul turned to leave Samuel, God changed his heart. That very day all these signs came to pass.… ¹⁰† From there they arrived at Gibeah, where a band of prophets met Saul, and the spirit of God rushed upon him, so that he joined them in their prophetic ecstasy.* ¹¹ When all who had known him previously saw him in a prophetic state among the prophets, they said to one another, "What has happened to the son of Kish? Is Saul also among the prophets?"* ¹² And someone from that district responded, "And who is their father?" Thus the saying arose, "Is Saul also among the prophets?" ¹³ When he came out of the prophetic ecstasy, he went home.

**Silence About the Kingship.** ¹⁴ Saul's uncle asked him and his servant, "Where have you been?" Saul replied, "Looking for the donkeys. When we could not find them, we went to Samuel." ¹⁵ Saul's uncle said, "Tell me, then, what Samuel said to you." ¹⁶ Saul said to his uncle, "He assured us that the donkeys had been found." But Saul told him nothing about what Samuel had said about the kingship.

**Saul Chosen King.** ¹⁷ Samuel called the people together to the LORD at Mizpah* ¹⁸ and addressed the Israelites: "Thus says the LORD, the God of Israel: It was I who brought Israel up from Egypt and delivered you from the power of the Egyptians and from the power of all the kingdoms that oppressed you.* ¹⁹ But today you have rejected your God, who saves you from all your evils and calamities, by saying, 'No! You must appoint a king over us.' Now, therefore, take your stand before the LORD according to your tribes and families."* ²⁰ So Samuel had all the tribes of Israel come forward, and the tribe of Benjamin was chosen.† ²¹ Next he had the tribe of Benjamin come forward by clans, and the clan of Matri was chosen, and finally Saul, son of Kish, was chosen. But when they went to look for him, he was nowhere to be found. ²² * Again they consulted the LORD, "Is there still someone else to come forward?" The LORD answered: He is hiding among the baggage. ²³ They ran to bring him from there; when he took his place among the people, he stood head and shoulders above all the people.* ²⁴ Then Samuel addressed all the people, "Do you see the man whom the LORD has chosen? There is no one like him among all the people!" Then all the people shouted out, "Long live the king!"*

²⁵ Samuel next explained to the people the rules of the monarchy,† wrote them in a book,

---

† **10:3** *Oak of Tabor*: or terebinth. Such a tree often indicates a shrine.
  **10:5** *The Philistine garrison*: the Hebrew word for "garrison" has been explained alternatively to mean a stele established to mark the Philistine occupation, or an inspector or officer for the collection of taxes. *Prophetic ecstasy*: a condition of religious enthusiasm often induced by communal rituals of music and dancing.
  **10:8** By inserting this verse, with its seven days, an editor has named in the very context of Saul's anointing the condition which in a later narrative will be the grounds for the rejection of the dynastic character of Saul's kingship (13:8–15).
  **10:10** An editor has abridged a longer version of this story by omitting mention of the first two signs Samuel has given (vv. 2–4).

**10:20** *Was chosen*: probably by casting lots; cf. 14:40–42; Jos 7:14, 17.
**10:25** *Rules of the monarchy*: a charter describing the relationship between the king and the people.

---

| | |
|---|---|
| **10:2** Jer 31:15; Mk 14:13. | **10:17** 1 Sm 7:5. |
| **10:5–6** 1 Sm 13:3; 16:13; | **10:18** Ex 20:2; Lv 11:45; |
| 19:20–21. | 25:38; Nm 15:41; Dt |
| **10:6** 1 Sm 11:6; 16:13; Jgs | 5:6; Jgs 6:8–9. |
| 14:6, 19; 15:14; 2 Kgs | **10:19** 1 Sm 8:19. |
| 3:15. | **10:22** 1 Sm 30:24. |
| **10:8** 1 Sm 13:8; Lv 3:1. | **10:23** 1 Sm 9:2; 16:7. |
| **10:10** 1 Sm 19:20–24; Nm | **10:24** 2 Sm 16:16; 1 Kgs |
| 11:25. | 1:25; 2 Kgs 11:12. |
| **10:11** 1 Sm 19:24. | |

and placed them before the presence of the LORD. Samuel then sent the people back to their own homes.* ²⁶ Saul also went home to Gibeah, accompanied by warriors whose hearts the LORD had touched. ²⁷ But some worthless people said, "How can this fellow save us?" They despised him and brought him no tribute.†*

11 **Defeat of the Ammonites.** ¹† About a month later, Nahash the Ammonite went up and besieged Jabesh-gilead. All the people of Jabesh begged Nahash, "Make a treaty with us, and we will serve you."* ² But Nahash the Ammonite replied, "This is my condition for making a treaty with you: I will gouge out the right eye of every man,† and thus bring shame on all Israel." ³ The elders of Jabesh said to him: "Give us seven days to send messengers throughout the territory of Israel. If there is no one to save us, we will surrender to you." ⁴ When the messengers arrived at Gibeah of Saul and reported the news in the people's hearing, they all wept aloud. ⁵ Just then Saul came in from the field, behind his oxen. "Why are the people weeping?" he asked. They repeated the message of the inhabitants of Jabesh for him. ⁶ As he listened to this report, the spirit of God rushed upon him and he became very angry.* ⁷ Taking a yoke of oxen, he cut them into pieces and sent them throughout the territory of Israel† by messengers saying, "If anyone does not come out to follow Saul and Samuel, the same thing will be done to his oxen!" The dread of the LORD came upon the people and they went forth as one.* ⁸ When Saul reviewed them in Bezek,† there were three hundred thousand Israelites and seventy thousand Judahites.

⁹ To the messengers who had come he said, "Tell the inhabitants of Jabesh-gilead that tomorrow, when the sun grows hot, they will be saved." The messengers went and reported this to the inhabitants of Jabesh, and they rejoiced. ¹⁰ The men of Jabesh said to Nahash, "Tomorrow we will surrender to you, and you may do with us whatever you want." ¹¹ The next day, Saul arranged his troops in three companies and invaded the camp during the dawn watch. They slaughtered Ammonites until the day had gotten hot; by then the survivors were so scattered that no two of them were left together.

**Saul Accepted as King.** ¹²† The people then said to Samuel: "Who questioned whether Saul should rule over us? Hand them over and we will put them to death."* ¹³ But Saul objected, "No one will be put to death this day, for today the LORD has rescued Israel."* ¹⁴ Samuel said to the people, "Come, let us go to Gilgal to renew the kingship there." ¹⁵ So all the people went to Gilgal, and there they made Saul king in the LORD's presence. They also sacrificed communion offerings there before the LORD, and Saul and all the Israelites rejoiced greatly.

12 †**Samuel's Integrity.** ¹† Samuel addressed all Israel: "I have granted your request in every respect," he said. "I have set a king over you* ² and now the king will lead you. As for me, I am old and gray, and my sons are among you. I was your leader from my youth to the present day. ³ Here I stand! Answer me in the presence of the LORD and the LORD's anointed. Whose ox have I taken? Whose donkey have I taken? Whom have I cheated? Whom have I wronged? From whom have I

---

**10:27** *Tribute*: a gift to honor a new ruler as a pledge of one's loyalty; see Gn 32:14; Jgs 3:15; 2 Sm 8:2.

**11:1** A text from Qumran (1QSamᵃ) introduces this chapter with the report that Nahash, king of the Ammonites, had attacked the Gadites and the Reubenites, gouging out their right eyes. Seven thousand of them had fled to Jabesh-gilead. This additional information would explain why Nahash besieged Jabesh-gilead. There is no consensus among scholars whether the Qumran text represents an original reading or a secondary expansion.

**11:2** *Right eye of every man*: thus rendering them incapable of military action.

**11:7** *Throughout the territory of Israel*: Saul's gesture summons the Israelite confederacy to a coordinated response against Nahash; cf. Jgs 19:29 for a similar action. *Dread of the LORD*: often a panic that immobilizes Israel's enemies; here, however, it has the opposite effect and incites the Israelites to battle.

**11:8** *Bezek*: probably modern Khirbet Ibziq, northeast of Shechem, on the west slope of the Jordan valley, opposite Jabesh-gilead.

**11:12–14** With the defeat of the Ammonites, Saul demon-

strates his ability to command Israel's army and defend the land. At Gilgal, Saul's kingship is ratified; ironically, he loses his kingship at the same place (13:7).

**12:1–25** This chapter narrates the transition from the leadership of the judges to the rule of the king. The Deuteronomistic redactor has Samuel contrast the wickedness of Israel's ancestors with the Lord's gracious deliverance (vv. 6–12). The people realize that their demand for a king has compounded that wickedness. Now that the Lord has given them a king, Samuel urges the people and their king to serve the Lord wholeheartedly (vv. 13–25).

**12:1–5** Samuel's upright leadership is set in sharp contrast to the despotic powers of the king described in chap. 8. By their testimony, the people witness to Samuel's righteousness.

---

| | |
|---|---|
| **10:25** 1 Sm 8:11; Dt | Jgs 14:6, 19; 15:14. |
| 17:14–20. | **11:7** 1 Kgs 11:30; 2 Kgs |
| **10:27** 1 Sm 11:12. | 13:18. |
| **11:1** 1 Sm 12:12; 31:11; | **11:12** 1 Sm 10:27. |
| 2 Sm 10:2. | **11:13** 2 Sm 19:23. |
| **11:6** 1 Sm 16:13; | **12:1** 1 Sm 8:7, 9, 22. |

accepted a bribe and shut my eyes because of it? I will make restitution to you."* [4]They replied, "You have neither cheated us, nor oppressed us, nor accepted anything from anyone." [5]So he said to them, "The LORD is witness against you this day, and the LORD's anointed is witness, that you have found nothing in my possession." "The LORD is witness," they said.

**Samuel Admonishes the People.** [6]Samuel continued: "The LORD is witness, who appointed Moses and Aaron and brought your ancestors up from the land of Egypt.* [7]Now take your stand, that I may judge you in the presence of the LORD according to all the gracious acts that the LORD has done for you and your ancestors. [8]When Jacob and his sons went to Egypt and the Egyptians oppressed them, your ancestors cried out to the LORD. The LORD then sent Moses and Aaron to bring them out of Egypt and settled them in this place.* [9]But they forgot the LORD their God; and so the LORD sold them into the power of Sisera, the captain of the army of Hazor, the power of the Philistines, and the power of the king of Moab, who made war against them.* [10]They cried out to the LORD and said, 'We have sinned because we abandoned the LORD and served the Baals and Astartes. Now deliver us from the power of our enemies, and we will serve you.'* [11]The LORD sent Jerubbaal, Barak, Jephthah, and Samuel; he delivered you from the power of your enemies on every side, so that you could live in security.* [12]Yet, when you saw Nahash, king of the Ammonites, advancing against you, you said to me, 'No! A king must rule us,' even though the LORD your God is your king.*

**Warnings for People and King.** [13]"Now here is the king you chose. See! The LORD has given you a king.* [14]If you fear and serve the LORD, if you listen to the voice of the LORD and do not rebel against the LORD's command, if both

you and the king, who rules over you, follow the LORD your God—well and good. [15]But if you do not listen to the voice of the LORD and if you rebel against the LORD's command, the hand of the LORD will be against you and your king. [16]Now then, stand ready to witness the great marvel the LORD is about to accomplish before your eyes. [17]Are we not in the harvest time for wheat?† Yet I will call upon the LORD, and he will send thunder and rain. Thus you will see and understand how great an evil it is in the eyes of the LORD that you have asked for a king."* [18]Samuel called upon the LORD, and the LORD sent thunder and rain that day.

**Assistance Promised.** Then all the people feared the LORD and Samuel. [19]They said to Samuel, "Pray to the LORD your God for us, your servants, that we may not die for having added to all our other sins the evil of asking for a king." [20]"Do not fear," Samuel answered them. "You have indeed committed all this evil! Yet do not turn from the LORD, but serve him with your whole heart. [21]Do not turn aside to gods who are nothing,† who cannot act and deliver. They are nothing.* [22]For the sake of his own great name† the LORD will not abandon his people, since the LORD has decided to make you his people.* [23]As for me, far be it from me to sin against the LORD by ceasing to pray for you and to teach you the good and right way.* [24]But you must fear the LORD and serve him faithfully with all your heart, for you have seen the great things the LORD has done among you. [25]If instead you continue to do evil, both you and your king shall be swept away."

## III. SAUL AND DAVID

**13** [1][Saul was…years old when he became king and he reigned…-two years over Israel.]†

---

**12:17** *Harvest time for wheat*: in May–June. Since this is a period of little or no rainfall in Israel, the people will not mistake the sign for a natural phenomenon.

**12:21** *Gods who are nothing*: Hebrew *tohu*, lit., "emptiness," cf. Gn 1:2 (*…webohu*); here, idols without power or substance, as in Is 41:29.

**12:22** *His own great name*: were the Lord to abandon his people, even if they abandon him, he would diminish his stature or reputation in the divine council or among the nations (e.g., Ez 20:9). Throughout the Old Testament the Lord is encouraged to deliver Israel, despite its evil, "for the sake of his name."

**13:1** A formula like that of 2 Sm 5:4 was introduced here at some time; but the age of Saul when he became king remains a

blank, and the two years assigned for his reign in the Masoretic text cannot be correct. Acts 13:21 offers the round number of forty years.

**12:3** Ex 20:17; 23:8; Nm 16:15; Dt 16:19; Sir 46:19.
**12:6** Mi 6:4.
**12:8** Gn 46:5; Ex 1:11; 2:23–25.
**12:9** Jgs 3:12–15; 4:2–3; 10:7; 13:1.
**12:10** 1 Sm 7:3–4; Jgs 10:10.
**12:11** Jgs 6:14, 32; 11:1.

**12:12** 1 Sm 8:6–7, 19; 11:1–2; Jgs 8:23.
**12:13** 1 Sm 8:7.
**12:17** Ex 9:23, 28–30; 1 Kgs 18:1.
**12:21** Dt 32:37–39; Is 41:29; 44:9–10.
**12:22** Ex 18:10; Dt 4:34; Jos 7:9; Is 48:9; Jer 14:21; Dn 3:34.
**12:23** Ex 32:11.

**Saul Offers Sacrifice.** [2] Saul chose three thousand of Israel, of whom two thousand remained with him in Michmash and in the hill country of Bethel, and one thousand were with Jonathan in Gibeah of Benjamin. He sent the rest of the army back to their tents. [3] Now Jonathan struck the Philistine garrison† in Gibeah, and the Philistines got word of it. Then Saul sounded the horn throughout the land, saying, "Let the Hebrews hear!" * [4] Then all Israel heard the report, "Saul has struck the garrison of the Philistines! Israel has become odious to the Philistines!" Then the army was called up to Saul in Gilgal. [5] The Philistines also assembled for battle against Israel, with thirty thousand chariots,† six thousand horsemen, and foot soldiers as numerous as the sand on the seashore. * They came up and encamped in Michmash, east of Beth-aven. * [6] When the soldiers saw they were in danger because the army was hardpressed, they hid themselves in caves, thickets, rocks, caverns, and cisterns. [7] Other Hebrews crossed the Jordan into the land of Gad and Gilead. Saul, however, held out in Gilgal, all his army trembling in fear behind him.† [8] He waited seven days, until the appointed time Samuel had set, but Samuel did not come, and the army deserted Saul. * [9] He then said, "Bring me the burnt offering and communion offerings!" Then he sacrificed the burnt offering.

**King Saul Reproved.** [10] As he finished sacrificing the burnt offering, there came Samuel! So Saul went out toward him in order to greet him. [11] Samuel asked him, "What have you done?" Saul explained: "When I saw that the army was deserting me and you did not come on the appointed day, and that the Philistines were assembling at Michmash, [12] I said to myself, 'Now the Philistines will come down against me at Gilgal, and I have not yet sought the LORD's blessing.' So I thought I should sacrifice the burnt offering." [13] Samuel replied to Saul: "You have acted foolishly! Had you kept the command the LORD your God gave you, the LORD would now establish your kingship in Israel forever; [14] but now your kingship shall not endure. The LORD has sought out a man after his own heart† to appoint as ruler over his people because you did not observe what the LORD commanded you." *

**Philistine Invasion.** [15] Then Samuel set out from Gilgal and went his own way; but what was left of the army went up after Saul to meet the soldiers, going from Gilgal to Gibeah of Benjamin. Saul then counted the soldiers he had with him, about six hundred. * [16] Saul, his son Jonathan, and the soldiers they had with them were now occupying Geba of Benjamin, and the Philistines were encamped at Michmash. [17] Meanwhile, raiders left the camp of the Philistines in three bands. * One band took the Ophrah road toward the district of Shual; [18] another turned in the direction of Beth-horon; and the third took the road for Geba that overlooks the Valley of the Hyenas toward the desert.

**Disarmament of Israel.**† [19] Not a single smith was to be found anywhere in Israel, for the Philistines had said, "Otherwise the Hebrews will make swords or spears." * [20] All Israel, therefore, had to go down to the Philistines to sharpen their plowshares, mattocks, axes, and sickles. [21] The price for the plowshares and mattocks was two thirds of a shekel, and a third of a shekel for sharpening the axes and for setting the ox-goads. [22] And so on the day of battle neither sword nor spear could be found in the hand of any of the soldiers with Saul or Jonathan. Only Saul and his son Jonathan had them.

**Jonathan's Exploit.** [23] An outpost of the Philistines had pushed forward to the pass of Michmash. *

---

† **13:3–4** *The Philistine garrison:* see note on 10:5. *Let the Hebrews hear:* a different reading of these verses, based on the Greek, would yield: "And the Philistines heard that the Hebrews (or: the slaves) had revolted. Saul in the meantime sounded the trumpet throughout all the land (v. 4), and all Israel heard that Saul...."

**13:5** *Thirty thousand chariots:* some Greek manuscripts read "three thousand chariots."

**13:7–15** These verses, like 10:8, anticipate the rejection of Saul; a different occasion and motivation for this are given in chap. 15 and 28:17–18.

**13:14** *After his own heart:* i.e., of his choosing, for his purpose. While the verse undoubtedly refers to David, it concerns the Lord's decision to continue the kingship, even though he has rejected Saul, by selecting the heir to Saul's throne.

**13:19–22** These details emphasize the Philistines' military power and superior technology, a reminder that an Israelite victory depends on God.

* ——————————

| | |
|---|---|
| **13:3** 1 Sm 14:1–15; Jgs 3:27; 6:34; 2 Sm 20:1–2. | **13:14** 1 Sm 15:28; 25:30; 2 Sm 7:15–16; Ps 78:70; Acts 13:22. |
| **13:5** Gn 22:17; 41:49; Jgs 7:12. | **13:15** 1 Sm 14:2. |
| **13:5** 1 Sm 14:22. | **13:17** 1 Sm 14:15. |
| **13:8** 1 Sm 10:8. | **13:19** Jgs 5:8. |
| | **13:23** 1 Sm 14:15. |

# 14

[1] One day Jonathan, son of Saul, said to his armor-bearer, "Come, let us go over to the Philistine outpost on the other side." But he did not inform his father— * [2] Saul was sitting under the pomegranate tree in Migron on the outskirts of Gibeah; with him were about six hundred men. [3] Ahijah, son of Ahitub, brother of Ichabod, the son of Phinehas, son of Eli, the priest of the LORD at Shiloh, was wearing the ephod—nor did the soldiers know that Jonathan had gone. * [4] Flanking the ravine through which Jonathan intended to cross to the Philistine outpost were rocky crags on each side, one named Bozez and the other Seneh. [5] One crag was to the north, toward Michmash; the other to the south, toward Geba. [6] Jonathan said to his armor-bearer: "Come, let us go over to that outpost of the uncircumcised. Perhaps the LORD will help us, because it is no more difficult for the LORD to grant victory by means of a few than it is by means of many." * [7] His armor-bearer replied, "Do whatever you think best; I am with you in whatever you decide." [8] Jonathan continued: "When we cross over to those men, we will be visible to them. [9] If they say to us, 'Stay there until we can come to you,' we will stop where we are; we will not go up to them. [10] But if they say, 'Come up to us,' we will go up, because the LORD has delivered them into our hand. That will be our sign." † * [11] When the two of them came into the view of the Philistine outpost, the Philistines remarked, "Look, some Hebrews † are coming out of the holes where they have been hiding." [12] The men of the outpost called to Jonathan and his armor-bearer. "Come up here," they said, "and we will teach you a lesson." So Jonathan said to his armor-bearer, "Climb up after me, for the LORD has delivered them into the hand of Israel." [13] Jonathan clambered up with his armor-bearer behind him. As the Philistines fell before Jonathan, his armor-bearer, who followed him, would finish them off. [14] In this first attack Jonathan and his armor-bearer killed about twenty men within half a furlong. [15] Then terror spread through the camp and the countryside; all the soldiers in the outpost and in the raiding parties shuddered in terror. The earth shook with an awesome shuddering. † *

**Rout of the Philistines.** [16] Saul's sentinels in Gibeah of Benjamin saw that the enemy camp had scattered and were running in all directions. [17] Saul said to those around him, "Count the troops and find out if any of us are missing." When they had taken the count, they found Jonathan and his armor-bearer missing. [18] Saul then said to Ahijah, "Bring the ephod here." (Ahijah was wearing the ephod before the Israelites at that time.) [19] While Saul was speaking to the priest, the uproar in the Philistine camp kept increasing. So he said to the priest, "Withdraw your hand." [20] And Saul and all his men rallied and rushed into the fight, where the Philistines, wholly confused, were thrusting swords at one another. * [21] The Hebrews who had previously sided with the Philistines and had gone up with them to their camp turned to join the Israelites under Saul and Jonathan. * [22] Likewise, all the Israelites who were hiding in the hill country of Ephraim, hearing that the Philistines were fleeing, kept after them in the battle. * [23] † Thus the LORD saved Israel that day.

**Saul's Oath.** The battle continued past Beth-aven. [24] Even though the Israelites were exhausted that day, Saul laid an oath on them, saying, "Cursed be the one who takes food before evening, before I am able to avenge myself on my enemies." So none of the people tasted food. [25] Now there was a honeycomb lying on the ground, [26] and when the soldiers came to the comb the honey was flowing; yet no one raised a hand from it to his mouth, because the people feared the oath.

**Violation of the Oath.** [27] Jonathan, who had not heard that his father had put the people under oath, thrust out the end of the staff he was holding and dipped it into the

---

† **14:10** *That will be our sign:* Jonathan acknowledges that the battle is in God's hands.

**14:11** *Hebrews:* while this term is often used by foreigners of Israelites, in this verse it seems to be a derogatory epithet for soldiers who deserted Saul's army while he was waiting for Samuel to arrive in Gilgal.

**14:15** *Awesome shuddering:* lit., "shuddering caused by God"; the panic in the Philistine camp is the work of Israel's warrior God.

**14:23** The victory apparently cleared the Philistines off the main ridge of mountains in the territories of Benjamin and Ephraim.

---

**14:1** 1 Sm 13:3.
**14:3** 1 Sm 2:28; 4:21; 14:18; 23:9; 30:7.
**14:6** 1 Sm 17:26, 36, 47; Jgs 14:3; Sir 39:18; 1 Mc 3:19.
**14:10** Jos 8:1; 10:8; Jgs 12:3.
**14:15** 2 Sm 22:8; Jl 2:10–11.
**14:20** Jgs 7:22.
**14:21** 1 Sm 29:4.
**14:22** 1 Sm 13:6.

honeycomb. Then he raised it to his mouth and his eyes brightened. 28 At this, one of the soldiers spoke up: "Your father put the people under a strict oath, saying, 'Cursed be the one who takes food today!' As a result the people are weakened." 29* Jonathan replied: "My father brings trouble to the land. Look how bright my eyes are because I had this little taste of honey. 30 What is more, if the army had eaten freely of the enemy's plunder when they came across it today, surely the slaughter of the Philistines would have been the greater by now!"

**Consuming the Blood.** 31 After the Philistines were routed that day from Michmash to Aijalon, the people were completely exhausted. 32 So the army pounced upon the plunder and took sheep, oxen, and calves, slaughtering them on the ground and eating the meat with the blood in it.* 33 Informed that the army was sinning against the LORD by eating the meat with blood in it, Saul said: "You have broken faith. Roll a large stone here for me." 34 He continued: "Mingle with the people and tell each of them, 'Bring an ox or sheep to me. Slaughter them here and then eat. But you must not sin against the LORD by eating meat with blood in it.'" So that night they all brought whatever oxen they had seized, and they slaughtered them there; 35 and Saul built an altar to the LORD—this was the first time he built an altar to the LORD.*

**Jonathan in Danger of Death.** 36 Then Saul said, "Let us go down in pursuit of the Philistines by night, to plunder them until daybreak and leave no one alive." They replied, "Do what you think best." But the priest said, "Let us consult God." 37 So Saul inquired of God: "Shall I go down in pursuit of the Philistines? Will you deliver them into the hand of Israel?" But he received no answer on this occasion.* 38 "All officers of the army," Saul announced, "come forward. Find out how this sin was committed today. 39 As the LORD lives

who has given victory to Israel, even if my son Jonathan has committed it, he shall surely die!" But none of the people answered him. 40 So he said to all Israel, "Stand on one side, and my son Jonathan and I will stand on the other." The people responded, "Do what you think best."* 41 And Saul said to the LORD, the God of Israel: "Why did you not answer your servant this time? If the blame for this resides in me or my son Jonathan, LORD, God of Israel, respond with Urim; but if this guilt is in your people Israel, respond with Thummim."† Jonathan and Saul were designated, and the people went free.* 42 Saul then said, "Cast lots between me and my son Jonathan." And Jonathan was designated. 43 Saul said to Jonathan, "Tell me what you have done." Jonathan replied, "I only tasted a little honey from the end of the staff I was holding. Am I to die for this?" 44 Saul declared, "May God do thus to me, and more, if you do not indeed die, Jonathan!"*

**Rescue of Jonathan.** 45 But the soldiers protested to Saul: "Is Jonathan to die, the man who won this great victory for Israel? This must not be! As the LORD lives, not a single hair of his head shall fall to the ground, for God was with him in what he did today!" Thus the soldiers rescued† Jonathan and he did not die.* 46 After that Saul gave up the pursuit of the Philistines, who returned to their own territory.

**Saul's Victories.** 47 After taking possession of the kingship over Israel, Saul waged war on its enemies all around—Moab, the Ammonites, Edom, the kings of Zobah, and the Philistines. Wherever he turned, he was successful* 48 and fought bravely. He defeated Amalek and delivered Israel from the hand of those who were plundering them.*

**Saul's Family.** 49 The sons of Saul were Jonathan, Ishvi, and Malchishua; the name of his firstborn daughter was Merob; the name of the younger was Michal.* 50 The name of Saul's

---

† **14:41** *Urim…Thummim:* objects, one representing a positive response and the other a negative response, kept in the front pocket of the priest's ephod, a garment worn as a breastplate, and used to ascertain God's will in certain instances, e.g., whether Saul should help rout the Philistines. Saul consults the priest but is too impatient to finish the consultation and hurries impulsively into battle.
**14:45** *Rescued:* the Hebrew word used is that for the "redemption" of the firstborn (Ex 13:13–15).

**14:29** Jos 7:25; 1 Kgs 18:17–18.
**14:32** 1 Sm 15:19, 21; Gn 4:9; Lv 3:17; 7:26–27; 17:10–14; Acts 15:20, 29.
**14:35** 1 Sm 7:17; Jgs 6:24.
**14:37** 1 Sm 28:6, 15.
**14:40** Jos 7:13–15.
**14:41** 1 Sm 10:20; 28:6; Ex 28:30; Dt 33:8.
**14:44** 1 Sm 3:17; Ru 1:17.
**14:45** 2 Sm 14:11; 1 Kgs 1:52.
**14:47** 2 Sm 1:22; 8:2–5.
**14:48** 1 Sm 15:7.
**14:49** 1 Sm 18:20, 25; 31:2; 1 Chr 8:33; 9:39; 10:2.

wife was Ahinoam, daughter of Ahimaaz. The name of his general was Abner, son of Ner, Saul's uncle; [51] Kish, Saul's father, and Ner, Abner's father, were sons of Abiel.*

[52] There was heavy fighting with the Philistines during Saul's lifetime. Whenever Saul saw any strong or brave man, he took him into his service.

# 15 †Disobedience of Saul.

[1] Samuel said to Saul: "It was I the LORD sent to anoint you king over his people Israel. Now, therefore, listen to the message of the LORD.* [2] Thus says the LORD of hosts: I will punish what Amalek did to the Israelites when he barred their way as they came up from Egypt.* [3] Go, now, attack Amalek, and put under the ban† everything he has. Do not spare him; kill men and women, children and infants, oxen and sheep, camels and donkeys."*

[4] Saul alerted the army, and at Telaim reviewed two hundred thousand foot soldiers and ten thousand men of Judah.† [5] Saul went to the city of Amalek and set up an ambush in the wadi. [6]* He warned the Kenites: "Leave Amalek, turn aside and come down so I will not have to destroy you with them, for you were loyal to the Israelites when they came up from Egypt."† After the Kenites left, [7] Saul routed Amalek from Havilah to the approaches of Shur, on the frontier of Egypt.* [8] He took Agag, king of Amalek, alive, but the rest of the people he destroyed by the sword, putting them under the ban. [9] He and his troops spared Agag and the best of the fat sheep and oxen, and the lambs. They refused to put under the ban anything that was worthwhile, destroying only what was worthless and of no account.

**Samuel Rebukes Saul.** [10] Then the word of the LORD came to Samuel: [11] I regret having made Saul king, for he has turned from me and has not kept my command. At this Samuel grew angry and cried out to the LORD all night.* [12] Early in the morning he went to meet Saul, but was informed that Saul had gone to Carmel, where he set up a monument in his own honor, and that on his return he had gone down to Gilgal. [13] When Samuel came to him, Saul greeted him: "The LORD bless you! I have kept the command of the LORD." [14] But Samuel asked, "What, then, is this bleating of sheep that comes to my ears, the lowing of oxen that I hear?" [15] Saul replied: "They were brought from Amalek. The people spared the best sheep and oxen to sacrifice to the LORD, your God; but the rest we destroyed, putting them under the ban." [16] Samuel said to Saul: "Stop! Let me tell you what the LORD said to me last night." "Speak!" he replied. [17] Samuel then said: "Though little in your own eyes, are you not chief of the tribes of Israel? The LORD anointed you king of Israel* [18] and sent you on a mission, saying: Go and put the sinful Amalekites under a ban of destruction. Fight against them until you have exterminated them.* [19] Why then have you disobeyed the LORD? You have pounced on the spoil, thus doing what was evil in the LORD's sight."* [20] Saul explained to Samuel: "I did indeed obey the LORD and fulfill the mission on which the LORD sent me. I have brought back Agag, the king of Amalek, and, carrying out the ban, I have destroyed the Amalekites. [21] But from the spoil the army took sheep and oxen, the best of what had been banned, to sacrifice to the LORD your God in Gilgal."* [22] But Samuel said:

"Does the LORD delight in burnt
    offerings and sacrifices
  as much as in obedience to the LORD's
    command?
Obedience is better than sacrifice,
  to listen, better than the fat of rams.†
[23]  For a sin of divination is rebellion,
  and arrogance, the crime of idolatry.

1 SM

---

† 
**15:1–35** The rejection of Saul sets the stage for the remainder of 1 Samuel. The audience knows that, in the ensuing struggle between David and Saul, David will triumph as king.
**15:3** *Put under the ban*: this terminology mandates that all traces of the Amalekites (people, cities, animals, etc.) be exterminated. No plunder could be seized for personal use. In the light of Dt 20:16–18, this injunction would eliminate any tendency toward syncretism. The focus of this chapter is that Saul fails to execute this order.
**15:4** The numbers here are not realistic; compare 14:2.
**15:6** The Kenites honored the terms of an alliance with Israel.
**15:22** Samuel's reprimand echoes that of the prophets. Cultic

practice is meaningless, even hypocritical, unless accompanied by an attentiveness to God's will.

---

**14:51** 1 Sm 9:1.
**15:1** Jos 3:9; 2 Kgs 20:16; Is 28:14.
**15:2** Ex 17:8–10, 16; Dt 25:17–19.
**15:3** 1 Sm 27:8; 30:17; Ex 17:16; Nm 24:20; Jos 6:17.
**15:6** Nm 24:21.
**15:7** 1 Sm 27:8.
**15:11** 1 Sm 15:35; Gn 6:6–7.
**15:17** 1 Sm 9:21.
**15:18** 1 Sm 28:18.
**15:19** 1 Sm 14:32.
**15:21** Lv 27:28.
**15:22** Prv 21:3; Hos 6:6; Am 5:21–25; Zec 10:2; Mt 9:13; 12:7; Heb 10:9.

Because you have rejected the word of
the LORD,
the LORD in turn has rejected you as
king."*

**Rejection of Saul.** [24] Saul admitted to Samuel: "I have sinned, for I have transgressed the command of the LORD and your instructions. I feared the people and obeyed them.* [25] Now forgive my sin, and return with me, that I may worship the LORD." [26] But Samuel said to Saul, "I will not return with you, because you rejected the word of the LORD and the LORD has rejected you as king of Israel."* [27] As Samuel turned to go, Saul seized a loose end of his garment, and it tore off.* [28] So Samuel said to him: "The LORD has torn the kingdom of Israel from you this day, and has given it to a neighbor of yours, who is better than you.* [29] The Glory of Israel neither deceives nor repents,† for he is not a mortal who repents."* [30] But Saul answered: "I have sinned, yet honor me now before the elders of my people and before Israel. Return with me that I may worship the LORD your God." [31] And so Samuel returned with him, and Saul worshiped the LORD.

**Samuel Executes Agag.** [32] Afterward Samuel commanded, "Bring Agag, king of Amalek, to me." Agag came to him struggling and saying, "So it is bitter death!" [33] And Samuel said,

"As your sword has made women
childless,
so shall your mother be childless
among women."

Then he cut Agag to pieces before the LORD in Gilgal.* [34] Samuel departed for Ramah, while Saul went up to his home in Gibeah of Saul. [35] Never again, as long as he lived, did Samuel see Saul. Yet he grieved over Saul, because the LORD repented that he had made him king of Israel.*

**16** **Samuel Is Sent to Bethlehem.** [1]* The LORD said to Samuel: How long will you grieve for Saul, whom I have rejected as king of Israel? Fill your horn with oil, and be on your way. I am sending you to Jesse of Bethlehem, for from among his sons I have decided on a king.† [2] But Samuel replied: "How can I go? Saul will hear of it and kill me." To this the LORD answered: Take a heifer along and say, "I have come to sacrifice to the LORD." [3] Invite Jesse to the sacrifice, and I myself will tell you what to do; you are to anoint for me the one I point out to you.*

**Samuel Anoints David.** [4] Samuel did as the LORD had commanded him. When he entered Bethlehem, the elders of the city came trembling to meet him and asked, "Is your visit peaceful, O seer?" [5] He replied: "Yes! I have come to sacrifice to the LORD. So purify yourselves and celebrate with me today." He also had Jesse and his sons purify themselves and invited them to the sacrifice.* [6] As they came, he looked at Eliab and thought, "Surely the anointed is here before the LORD." [7] But the LORD said to Samuel: Do not judge from his appearance or from his lofty stature, because I have rejected him. God does not see as a mortal, who sees the appearance. The LORD looks into the heart.* [8]* Then Jesse called Abinadab and presented him before Samuel, who said, "The LORD has not chosen him." [9] Next Jesse presented Shammah, but Samuel said, "The LORD has not chosen this one either." [10] In the same way Jesse presented seven sons before Samuel, but Samuel said to Jesse, "The LORD has not chosen any one of these." [11] Then Samuel asked Jesse, "Are these all the sons you have?" Jesse replied, "There is still the youngest, but he is tending the sheep." Samuel said to Jesse, "Send for him; we will not sit down to eat until he arrives here."* [12] Jesse had the young man brought to them. He was ruddy, a youth with beautiful eyes, and good looking.

---

† **15:29** *Nor repents:* the apparent contradiction between this verse and vv. 11, 35 leads some scholars to consider it a gloss (cf. Nm 23:19). However, this phrase can be understood to underscore the definitive character of Samuel's declaration that Saul has lost the kingship.

**16:1** David is anointed two more times after Saul's death (2 Sm 2:4; 5:3). In 17:28, his brother Eliab is not aware of David's selection. These repetitions and inconsistencies reflect the final editor's use of multiple sources.

**15:23** Dt 18:10.
**15:24** 1 Sm 26:21.
**15:26** 1 Kgs 11:11, 30–31.
**15:27** 1 Sm 24:6; 1 Kgs 11:29–31.
**15:28** 1 Sm 28:17; 2 Sm 7:15–16.
**15:29** Nm 23:19.
**15:33** Ex 21:23; Jgs 8:21.
**15:35** 1 Sm 28:15.
**16:1** Ru 4:17–22; 1 Kgs 1:39; 1 Chr 11:3; Is 11:1; Mt 2:6; Lk 2:4.
**16:3** 1 Sm 9:13, 22, 24.
**16:5** 1 Sm 9:12–13; 20:26; Ex 19:10; Jb 1:5.
**16:7** 1 Sm 10:23–24; 1 Kgs 11:4; 1 Chr 28:9; Prv 15:11; Jer 17:10; 20:12; Lk 16:15; Acts 1:24.
**16:8–11** 1 Sm 17:12–13; 1 Chr 2:13–15.
**16:11** 1 Sm 17:15, 28, 34; 2 Sm 7:8; Ps 78:70–71.

1
S
M

The LORD said: There—anoint him, for this is the one!* 13 Then Samuel, with the horn of oil in hand, anointed him in the midst of his brothers, and from that day on, the spirit of the LORD rushed upon David. Then Samuel set out for Ramah.*

**David Wins Saul's Approval.** 14†* The spirit of the LORD had departed from Saul, and he was tormented by an evil spirit from the LORD. 15 So the servants of Saul said to him: "Look! An evil spirit from God is tormenting you. 16 If your lordship will order it, we, your servants here attending to you, will look for a man skilled in playing the harp. When the evil spirit from God comes upon you, he will play and you will feel better." 17 Saul then told his servants, "Find me a good harpist and bring him to me." 18* One of the servants spoke up: "I have observed that a son of Jesse of Bethlehem is a skillful harpist. He is also a brave warrior, an able speaker, and a handsome young man. The LORD is certainly with him."

**David Made Armor-Bearer.** 19 Accordingly, Saul dispatched messengers to ask Jesse to send him his son David, who was with the flock. 20 Then Jesse took five loaves of bread, a skin of wine, and a young goat, and sent them to Saul with his son David.* 21 Thus David came to Saul and entered his service. Saul became very fond of him and made him his armor-bearer.* 22 Saul sent Jesse the message, "Let David stay in my service, for he meets with my approval." 23 Whenever the spirit from God came upon Saul, David would take the harp and play, and Saul would be relieved and feel better, for the evil spirit would leave him.

# 17 **The Challenge of Goliath.** 1 The Philistines rallied their forces for battle at Socoh in Judah and camped between Socoh

and Azekah at Ephes-dammim. 2 Saul and the Israelites rallied and camped in the valley of the Elah, drawing up their battle line to meet the Philistines. 3 The Philistines were stationed on one hill and the Israelites on an opposite hill, with a valley between them.

4 A champion named Goliath of Gath came out from the Philistine camp; he was six cubits and a span† tall. 5 He had a bronze helmet on his head and wore a bronze breastplate of scale armor weighing five thousand shekels, 6 bronze greaves, and had a bronze scimitar slung from his shoulders. 7 The shaft of his javelin was like a weaver's beam, and its iron head weighed six hundred shekels.† His shield-bearer went ahead of him.* 8 He stood and shouted to the ranks of Israel: "Why come out in battle formation? I am a Philistine, and you are Saul's servants. Choose one of your men, and have him come down to me. 9 If he beats me in combat and kills me, we will be your vassals; but if I beat him and kill him, you shall be our vassals and serve us." 10 The Philistine continued: "I defy the ranks of Israel today. Give me a man and let us fight together." 11 When Saul and all Israel heard this challenge of the Philistine, they were stunned and terrified.

**David Comes to the Camp.** † 12 David was the son of an Ephrathite named Jesse from Bethlehem in Judah who had eight sons. In the days of Saul Jesse was old and well on in years.* 13 The three oldest sons of Jesse had followed Saul to war; the names of these three sons who had gone off to war were Eliab the firstborn; Abinadab the second; and Shammah the third. 14 David was the youngest. While the three oldest had joined Saul, 15 David would come and go from Saul's presence to tend his father's sheep at Bethlehem.* 16 Meanwhile the Philistine came forward

---

**16:14–23** These verses explain Saul's loss of divine favor and David's rise to power. By approving the young man, Saul identifies David as his legitimate successor. Of the two traditions in the Hebrew text about David's entry into Saul's service, the Greek translation retains only the one found in vv. 14–23; 17:1–11, 32–54. *An evil spirit from the LORD:* Saul's erratic behavior is attributed to a change in the Lord's relationship with him. Cf. Jgs 9:23, where the Lord puts an evil spirit between Abimelech and the citizens of Shechem.

**17:4** *Six cubits and a span:* about nine feet nine inches (a cubit equals about eighteen inches; a span equals about eight inches). The Greek text and 4QSam² read: "four cubits and a span" (six feet nine inches). The description of the Philistine's might and his powerful weapons contrasts with the picture of the

youthful David who trusts in God.
**17:7** *Six hundred shekels:* over fifteen pounds.
**17:12–31** Here the final editor begins an alternative account of David's encounter with the Philistine hero, which continues in vv. 50–51 and concludes in 17:55–18:5.

**16:12** 1 Sm 9:2.
**16:13** 1 Sm 10:6; 11:6; Jgs 3:10; 9:9; Sir 46:13.
**16:14** 1 Sm 18:10–11.
**16:18** 1 Sm 18:12, 14, 28; 2 Sm 5:10; 17:8; Jn 3:2.
**16:20** 1 Sm 9:7–8; 10:3–4; 16:1; 17:17–19.
**16:21** 1 Sm 18:2.
**17:7** 2 Sm 21:19; 1 Chr 11:23; 20:5.
**17:12** 1 Sm 16:1, 10; Ru 1:2.
**17:15** 1 Sm 16:11; 18:2; 2 Sm 7:8; Ps 78:70–71.

and took his stand morning and evening for forty days.

[17] Now Jesse said to his son David: "Take this ephah of roasted grain and these ten loaves for your brothers, and bring them quickly to your brothers in the camp. [18] Also take these ten cheeses for the field officer. Greet your brothers and bring home some token from them. [19] Saul and your brothers, together with all Israel, are at war with the Philistines in the valley of the Elah." [20] Early the next morning, having left the flock with a shepherd, David packed up and set out, as Jesse had commanded him. He reached the barricade of the camp just as the army, on their way to the battleground, were shouting their battle cry.* [21] The Israelites and the Philistines drew up opposite each other in battle array. [22] David entrusted what he had brought to the keeper of the baggage and hastened to the battle line, where he greeted his brothers.* [23] While he was talking with them, the Philistine champion, by name Goliath of Gath, came up from the ranks of the Philistines and spoke as before, and David listened. [24] When the Israelites saw the man, they all retreated before him, terrified. [25] The Israelites had been saying: "Do you see this man coming up? He comes up to insult Israel. The king will make whoever kills him a very wealthy man. He will give his daughter to him and declare his father's family exempt from taxes in Israel."* [26] David now said to the men standing near him: "How will the man who kills this Philistine and frees Israel from disgrace be rewarded? Who is this uncircumcised Philistine that he should insult the armies of the living God?"* [27] They repeated the same words to him and said, "That is how the man who kills him will be rewarded." [28] When Eliab, his oldest brother, heard him speaking with the men, he grew angry with David and said: "Why did you come down? With whom have you left those sheep in the wilderness? I know your arrogance and dishonest heart. You came down to enjoy the battle!"* [29] David protested, "What have I done now? I was only talking." [30] He turned from him to another and asked the same question; and everyone gave him the same answer as before. [31] The words

that David had spoken were overheard and reported to Saul, who sent for him.

**David Challenges Goliath.** [32] Then David spoke to Saul: "My lord should not lose heart. Let your servant go and fight this Philistine." [33] But Saul answered David, "You cannot go up against this Philistine and fight with him, for you are only a youth, while he has been a warrior from his youth." [34] * Then David told Saul: "Your servant used to tend his father's sheep, and whenever a lion or bear came to carry off a sheep from the flock, [35] I would chase after it, attack it, and snatch the prey from its mouth. If it attacked me, I would seize it by the throat, strike it, and kill it. [36] Your servant has killed both a lion and a bear. This uncircumcised Philistine will be as one of them, because he has insulted the armies of the living God."

[37] David continued: "The same LORD who delivered me from the claws of the lion and the bear will deliver me from the hand of this Philistine." Saul answered David, "Go! the LORD will be with you."*

**Preparation for the Encounter.** [38] Then Saul dressed David in his own tunic, putting a bronze helmet on his head and arming him with a coat of mail. [39] David also fastened Saul's sword over the tunic. He walked with difficulty, however, since he had never worn armor before. He said to Saul, "I cannot go in these, because I am not used to them." So he took them off. [40] Then, staff in hand, David selected five smooth stones from the wadi and put them in the pocket of his shepherd's bag. With his sling in hand, he approached the Philistine.

**David's Victory.** [41]† With his shield-bearer marching before him, the Philistine advanced closer and closer to David. [42] When he sized David up and saw that he was youthful, ruddy, and handsome in appearance, he began to deride him. [43] He said to David, "Am I a dog that you come against me with a staff?" Then the Philistine cursed David by his gods [44] and said to him, "Come here to me, and I will feed your flesh to the birds of the air and the beasts of the field."* [45] David answered him: "You

---

† **17:41–47** The two combatants trade theological taunts. God uses the most unlikely opponent to destroy Goliath.

* **17:20** 1 Sm 26:5.          **17:22** 1 Sm 25:13.

**17:25** 1 Sm 18:17; Jos 15:16.
**17:26** 1 Sm 18:25; Dt 5:26; Jgs 15:18; 2 Kgs 19:4; Is 37:4; Jer 10:10.
**17:28** 1 Sm 16:6.
**17:34–35** Jgs 14:6; Sir 47:3.
**17:37** Prv 28:1.
**17:44** Dt 28:26; Ps 79:2–3; Is 18:6; Jer 7:33; 15:3.

come against me with sword and spear and scimitar, but I come against you in the name of the LORD of hosts, the God of the armies of Israel whom you have insulted. ⁴⁶Today the LORD shall deliver you into my hand; I will strike you down and cut off your head. This very day I will feed your dead body and the dead bodies of the Philistine army to the birds of the air and the beasts of the field; thus the whole land shall learn that Israel has a God. ⁴⁷All this multitude, too, shall learn that it is not by sword or spear that the LORD saves. For the battle belongs to the LORD, who shall deliver you into our hands."*

⁴⁸The Philistine then moved to meet David at close quarters, while David ran quickly toward the battle line to meet the Philistine. ⁴⁹David put his hand into the bag and took out a stone, hurled it with the sling, and struck the Philistine on the forehead. The stone embedded itself in his brow, and he fell on his face to the ground. ⁵⁰Thus David triumphed over the Philistine with sling and stone; he struck the Philistine dead, and did it without a sword in his hand.* ⁵¹Then David ran and stood over him; with the Philistine's own sword which he drew from its sheath he killed him, and cut off his head.*

**Flight of the Philistines.** When the Philistines saw that their hero was dead, they fled. ⁵²Then the men of Israel and Judah sprang up with a battle cry and pursued them to the approaches of Gath and to the gates of Ekron, and Philistines fell wounded along the road from Shaaraim as far as Gath and Ekron. ⁵³When they returned from their pursuit of the Philistines, the Israelites looted their camp. ⁵⁴*David took the head of the Philistine and brought it to Jerusalem; but he kept Goliath's armor in his own tent.†

**David Presented to Saul.** ⁵⁵As Saul watched David go out to meet the Philistine, he asked his general Abner, "Abner, whose son is that

young man?" Abner replied, "On your life, O king, I have no idea."* ⁵⁶And the king said, "Find out whose son the lad is." ⁵⁷So when David returned from slaying the Philistine, Abner escorted him into Saul's presence. David was still holding the Philistine's head. ⁵⁸Saul then asked him, "Whose son are you, young man?" David replied, "I am the son of your servant Jesse of Bethlehem."

**18 David and Jonathan.** ¹By the time David finished speaking with Saul, Jonathan's life became bound up with David's life; he loved him as his very self.* ²Saul retained David on that day and did not allow him to return to his father's house.* ³Jonathan and David made a covenant, because Jonathan loved him as his very self. ⁴Jonathan took off† the cloak he was wearing and handed it over to David, along with his military dress, even his sword, bow, and belt.* ⁵David then carried out successfully every mission on which Saul sent him. So Saul put him in charge of his soldiers; this met with the approval of the whole army, even Saul's officers.

**Saul's Jealousy.** ⁶At the approach of Saul and David, on David's return after striking down the Philistine, women came out from all the cities of Israel to meet Saul the king, singing and dancing, with tambourines, joyful songs, and stringed instruments.†* ⁷The women played and sang:

"Saul has slain his thousands,
    David his tens of thousands."*

⁸Saul was very angry and resentful of the song, for he thought: "They give David tens of thousands, but only thousands to me. All that remains for him is the kingship." ⁹From that day on, Saul kept a jealous eye on David.

¹⁰*The next day an evil spirit from God rushed upon Saul, and he raged in his house. David was in attendance, playing the harp as at

**17:54** Jerusalem was a Jebusite city; it came under Israelite control only at the beginning of David's rule. As a young shepherd, David would not have had a military tent. In 21:10, Goliath's sword is in the Nob temple.
**18:4** *Jonathan took off*: with the details in this verse, the narrator identifies David as Jonathan's replacement and Saul's heir to the throne. Cf. 23:17 and Gn 41:39–43.
**18:6** *Stringed instruments*: perhaps a lute-like instrument with three strings; the Hebrew word, *shalshim*, perhaps related to the root *shlsh* ("three"), occurs only here in the Old Testament.

**17:47** 1 Sm 14:6, 10; Ps 33:16.
**17:50** 1 Mc 4:30; Sir 47:4.
**17:51** 1 Sm 21:10.
**17:54** 1 Sm 31:9.
**17:55** 1 Sm 14:50.
**18:1** 1 Sm 19:1–7; 20:17; 23:16; 2 Sm 1:26; 9:1.
**18:2** 1 Sm 16:21; 17:15.
**18:4** 2 Sm 1:22.
**18:6** Ex 15:20–21; Jgs 11:34; Jdt 15:12.
**18:7** 1 Sm 21:12; 29:5; Ps 91:7; Sir 47:6–7.
**18:10–11** 1 Sm 16:14; 19:9–10; 20:33; 22:6; 26:8.

1SM

other times, while Saul was holding his spear. [11] Saul poised the spear, thinking, "I will nail David to the wall!" But twice David escaped him. [12] Saul then began to fear David because the LORD was with him but had turned away from Saul. [13] Saul sent him out of his presence and appointed him a field officer. So David led the people on their military expeditions [14] and prospered in all his ways, for the LORD was with him. [15] Seeing how he prospered, Saul feared David. [16] But all Israel and Judah loved David, since he led them on their expeditions.†*

**Saul Plots Against David.** [17] Saul said to David, "Look, I will give you my older daughter, Merob, in marriage if you become my warrior and fight the battles of the LORD." Saul thought, "I will not lay a hand on him. Let the hand of the Philistines strike him."* [18] But David answered Saul: "Who am I? And who are my kindred or my father's clan in Israel that I should become the king's son-in-law?" [19] But when the time came for Saul's daughter Merob to be given to David, she was given as wife to Adriel the Meholathite instead.*

[20] Now Saul's daughter Michal loved David. When this was reported to Saul, he was pleased.* [21] He thought, "I will offer her to him as a trap, so that the hand of the Philistines may strike him." So for the second time Saul said to David, "You shall become my son-in-law today." [22] Saul then ordered his servants, "Speak to David privately and say: The king favors you, and all his officers love you. You should become son-in-law to the king." [23] But when Saul's servants mentioned this to David, he said: "Is becoming the king's son-in-law a trivial matter in your eyes? I am poor and insignificant." [24] When his servants reported David's answer to him, [25] Saul commanded them, "Say this to David: The king desires no other price for the bride than the foreskins of one hundred Philistines, that he may thus take vengeance on his enemies." Saul intended to have David fall into the hands of the Philistines.* [26] When the servants reported this offer to David, he was pleased with the prospect of becoming the king's son-in-law.

Before the year was up, [27] David arose and went with his men and slew two hundred Philistines. He brought back their foreskins and counted them out before the king that he might become the king's son-in-law. So Saul gave him his daughter Michal as wife. [28] Then Saul realized that the LORD was with David and that his own daughter Michal loved David. [29] So Saul feared David all the more and was his enemy ever after.

[30] The Philistine chiefs continued to make forays, but each time they took the field, David was more successful against them than any of Saul's other officers, and his name was held in great esteem.

**19** **Persecution of David.** [1] Saul discussed his intention to kill David with his son Jonathan and with all his servants. But Saul's son Jonathan, who was very fond of David,* [2] told him: "My father Saul is trying to kill you. Therefore, please be on your guard tomorrow morning; stay out of sight and remain in hiding. [3] I, however, will go out and stand beside my father in the countryside where you are, and will speak to him about you. If I learn anything, I will let you know."

[4] Jonathan then spoke well of David to his father Saul, telling him: "The king should not harm his servant David. He has not harmed you, but has helped you very much by his deeds.† [5] When he took his life in his hands and killed the Philistine, and the LORD won a great victory for all Israel, you were glad to see it. Why, then, should you become guilty of shedding innocent blood by killing David without cause?"* [6] Saul heeded Jonathan's plea and swore, "As the LORD lives, he shall not be killed." [7] So Jonathan summoned David and repeated the whole conversation to him. He then brought David to Saul, and David served him as before.

**David Escapes from Saul.** [8] When war broke out again, David went out to fight against the Philistines and inflicted such a great defeat upon them that they fled from him. [9]* Then an evil spirit from the LORD came upon Saul as he was sitting in his house with spear in hand

---

† **18:16** *Led them on their expeditions:* lit., "go out and come in," i.e., through the city gates; an idiom for military victory.

**19:4** Jonathan reminds Saul that David has served him loyally and done nothing to earn a traitor's death. Cf. 24:18–20.

**18:16** 2 Sm 5:2.
**18:17** 1 Sm 14:49; 17:25.
**18:19** 1 Sm 21:8; 24:16.
**18:20** 1 Sm 14:49; 25:44; 26:23; 2 Sm 3:13.
**18:25** 1 Sm 17:26;
Gn 34:12.
**19:1** 1 Sm 18:1; 20:1–3.
**19:5** 1 Sm 17:55–56; Dt 19:10; Ps 119:109.
**19:9–10** 1 Sm 16:14; 18:10–11.

while David was playing the harp nearby. [10] Saul tried to pin David to the wall with the spear, but David eluded Saul, and the spear struck only the wall, while David got away safely.

[11] The same night, Saul sent messengers to David's house to guard it, planning to kill him in the morning. David's wife Michal informed him, "Unless you run for your life tonight, tomorrow you will be killed."† [12] Then Michal let David down through a window, and he made his escape in safety.* [13] Michal took the teraphim† and laid it in the bed, putting a tangle of goat's hair at its head and covering it with a blanket.* [14] When Saul sent officers to arrest David, she said, "He is sick." [15] Saul, however, sent the officers back to see David and commanded them, "Bring him up to me in his bed, that I may kill him." [16] But when the messengers entered, they found the teraphim in the bed, with the tangle of goat's hair at its head. [17] Saul asked Michal: "Why did you lie to me like this? You have helped my enemy to get away!" Michal explained to Saul: "He threatened me, saying 'Let me go or I will kill you.'"

**David and Saul in Ramah.** [18] When David got safely away, he went to Samuel in Ramah, informing him of all that Saul had done to him. Then he and Samuel went to stay in Naioth.† [19] When Saul was told that David was at Naioth in Ramah, [20] he sent officers to arrest David. But when they saw the band of prophets presided over by Samuel in a prophetic state, the spirit of God came upon them and they too fell into the prophetic ecstasy.* [21] Informed of this, Saul sent other messengers, who also fell into the prophetic ecstasy. For the third time Saul sent messengers, but they too fell into a prophetic ecstasy.

**Saul Among the Prophets.** [22] Finally Saul went to Ramah himself. Arriving at the large cistern in Secu, he asked, "Where are Samuel and David?" Someone answered, "At Naioth in Ramah." [23] As he walked from there to Naioth in Ramah, the spirit of God came upon him also, and he continued on, acting like a prophet until he reached Naioth in Ramah. [24] Then he, too, stripped himself of his garments and remained in a prophetic state in the presence of Samuel;† all that day and night he lay naked. That is why they say, "Is Saul also among the prophets?"*

**20** **David Consults with Jonathan.** [1] David fled from Naioth in Ramah, and went to Jonathan. "What have I done?" he asked him. "What crime or what offense does your father hold against me that he seeks my life?"* [2] Jonathan answered him: "Heaven forbid that you should die! My father does nothing, great or small, without telling me. Why, then, should my father conceal this from me? It cannot be true!" [3] But David replied: "Your father is well aware that I am favored with your friendship, so he has decided, 'Jonathan must not know about this or he will be grieved.' Nevertheless, as the Lord lives and as you live, there is only a step between me and death." [4] Jonathan then said to David, "I will do whatever you say." [5] David answered: "Tomorrow is the new moon, when I should in fact dine with the king. Let me go and hide in the open country until evening.* [6] If it turns out that your father misses me, say, 'David urged me to let him go on short notice to his city Bethlehem, because his whole clan is holding its seasonal sacrifice there.'* [7] If he says, 'Very well,' your servant is safe. But if he becomes quite angry, you can be sure he has planned some harm. [8]* Do this kindness for your servant because of the Lord's covenant into which you brought us: if I am guilty, kill me yourself! Why should you give me up to your father?" [9] But Jonathan answered: "Not I! If ever I find out that my father is determined to harm you,

† **19:11** This story may have originally followed 18:29, placing the episode of David's escape on the night of his marriage with Michal.

**19:13** *Teraphim:* a life-sized image of a household god in human form; cf. also note on Gn 31:19. Elsewhere in the Deuteronomistic History, use of teraphim is condemned (15:23; 2 Kgs 23:24).

**19:18** *Naioth:* meaning "the pastures." This place appears only in chaps. 19–20 and is associated with Ramah.

**19:24** *In the presence of Samuel:* this verse, which disagrees with 15:35, is further evidence of the diverse origins of these accounts. *"Is Saul also among the prophets?":* although similar to the story of Saul's prophetic ecstasy in 10:10–13, this account offers a more disparaging portrait of Saul.

| | |
|---|---|
| **19:12** Jos 2:15; Acts 9:25; | 2 Sm 6:20. |
| 2 Cor 11:33. | **20:1** 1 Sm 19:1–7, 11–17; |
| **19:13** Gn 31:19; Jgs 17:5; | 21:11; 27:4; Gn |
| 18:14, 18, 20; Ez | 31:36. |
| 21:26. | **20:5** Nm 10:10; 28:11–15; |
| **19:20** 1 Sm 10:5–6, 10; Nm | Ezr 3:5; Neh 10:34. |
| 11:25. | **20:6** 1 Sm 17:12. |
| **19:24** 1 Sm 10:10–12; | **20:8–9** 1 Sm 18:3; 23:17–18. |

I will certainly let you know." [10] David then asked Jonathan, "Who will tell me if your father gives you a harsh answer?"

**Mutual Agreement.** [11] Jonathan replied to David, "Come, let us go out into the field." When they were out in the open country together, [12] Jonathan said to David: "As the Lord, the God of Israel, lives, I will sound out my father about this time tomorrow. Whether he is well disposed toward David or not, I will inform you. [13]* Should it please my father to bring any harm upon you, may the Lord do thus to Jonathan and more,† if I do not inform you of it and send you on your way in peace. May the Lord be with you even as he was with my father. [14] Only this: if I am still alive, may you show me the kindness of the Lord. But if I die, [15] never cut off your kindness from my house. And when the Lord cuts off all the enemies of David from the face of the land, [16] the name of Jonathan must never be cut off from the family of David, or the Lord will make you answer for it." [17] And in his love for David, Jonathan renewed his oath to him, because he loved him as he loved himself.

[18] Jonathan then said to him: "Tomorrow is the new moon; you will be missed, since your place will be vacant. [19] On the third day you will be missed all the more. Go to the spot where you hid on the other occasion and wait near the mound there.* [20] On the third day of the month I will shoot arrows to the side of it, as though aiming at a target. [21] I will then send my attendant to recover the arrows. If in fact I say to him, 'Look, the arrow is this side of you; pick it up,' come, for you are safe. As the Lord lives, there will be nothing to fear. [22] But if I say to the boy, 'Look, the arrow is beyond you,' go, for the Lord sends you away. [23] However, in the matter which you and I have discussed, the Lord shall be between you and me forever." [24] So David hid in the open country.

**David's Absence.** On the day of the new moon, when the king sat down at the feast to dine, [25] he took his usual place against the wall. Jonathan sat facing him, while Abner sat at the king's side. David's place was vacant. [26]* Saul, however, said nothing that day, for he thought, "He must have become unclean by accident."† [27] On the next day, the second day of the month, David's place was still vacant. So Saul asked his son Jonathan, "Why has the son of Jesse not come to table yesterday or today?" [28] Jonathan explained to Saul: "David pleaded with me to let him go to Bethlehem. [29] 'Please let me go,' he begged, 'for we are having a clan sacrifice in our city, and my brothers insist on my presence. Now then, if you think well of me, give me leave to visit my brothers.' That is why he has not come to the king's table." [30] But Saul grew angry with Jonathan and said to him: "Son of a rebellious woman, do I not know that, to your own disgrace and to the disgrace of your mother's nakedness, you are the companion of Jesse's son? [31] For as long as the son of Jesse lives upon the earth, you cannot make good your claim to the kingship!† Now send for him, and bring him to me, for he must die."* [32] But Jonathan argued with his father Saul: "Why should he die? What has he done?" [33] At this Saul brandished his spear to strike him, and thus Jonathan learned that his father was determined to kill David.* [34] Jonathan sprang up from the table in a rage and ate nothing that second day of the month, because he was grieved on David's account, and because his father had humiliated him.

**Jonathan's Farewell.** [35] The next morning Jonathan, accompanied by a young boy, went out into the field for his appointment with David. [36] There he said to the boy, "Run and find the arrows." And as the boy ran, he shot an arrow past him. [37] When the boy made for the spot where Jonathan had shot the arrow, Jonathan called after him, "The arrow is farther on!" [38] Again he called to the boy, "Hurry, be quick, don't delay!" Jonathan's boy picked up the arrow and brought it to his master. [39] The boy suspected nothing; only Jonathan and David knew what was meant. [40] Then Jonathan gave his weapons to his boy and said to him,

† **20:13** See note on 3:17.
**20:26** The meal on the first day of the month would have had religious overtones, and a ritual impurity (Lv 15:16; Dt 23:10–12) would have barred David from sharing in it.
**20:31** *Your claim to the kingship:* Saul admits his intention that Jonathan should succeed him and that David is a threat to his lineage (cf. 23:17). However Jonathan has already acknowl-

edged David's kingship (18:3–4) and his own subservient role (20:13–16).

* 
| **20:13–16** 1 Sm 10:7; 17:37; | **20:26** 1 Sm 16:5; Lv |
| 18:12, 14; 24:22–23; | 7:20–21; 15:1–3. |
| 2 Sm 9:1–13; 21:7. | **20:31** 2 Sm 12:5. |
| **20:19** 1 Sm 19:1–7. | **20:33** 1 Sm 18:11. |

"Go, take them to the city." [41] When the boy had gone, David rose from beside the mound and fell on his face to the ground three times in homage. They kissed each other and wept aloud together. [42]* At length Jonathan said to David, "Go in peace, in keeping with what the two of us have sworn by the name of the LORD: 'The LORD shall be between you and me, and between your offspring and mine forever.'"

# 21

[1] Then David departed on his way, while Jonathan went back into the city.

**The Holy Bread.** [2] David went to Ahimelech, the priest of Nob, who came trembling to meet him. He asked, "Why are you alone? Is there no one with you?"†* [3] David answered the priest: "The king gave me a commission and told me, 'Do not let anyone know anything about the business on which I have sent you or the commission I have given you.' For that reason I have arranged a particular meeting place with my men. [4]* Now what do you have on hand? Give me five loaves, or whatever you can find." [5]† But the priest replied to David, "I have no ordinary bread on hand, only holy bread; if the men have abstained from women, you may eat some of that." [6] David answered the priest: "We have indeed stayed away from women. In the past whenever I went out on a campaign, all the young men were consecrated—even for an ordinary campaign. All the more so are they consecrated with their weapons today!" [7] So the priest gave him holy bread, for no other bread was on hand except the showbread which had been removed from before the LORD and replaced by fresh bread when it was taken away.* [8] One of Saul's servants was there that day, detained before the LORD;† his name was Doeg the Edomite, the chief of Saul's shepherds.*

**The Sword of Goliath.** [9] David then asked Ahimelech: "Do you have a spear or a sword on hand? I brought along neither my sword nor my weapons, because the king's business was urgent." [10] The priest replied: "The sword of Goliath the Philistine, whom you killed in the Valley of Elah, is here wrapped in a garment behind an ephod.† If you wish to take it, do so; there is no sword here except that one." "There is none like it," David cried, "give it to me!"*

**David a Fugitive.** [11] That same day David fled from Saul, going to Achish, king of Gath.* [12] But the servants of Achish said to him, "Is this not David, the king of the land? Is it not for him that during their dances they sing out,

'Saul has slain his thousands,
    David his tens of thousands'?"*

[13] David took note of these remarks and became very much afraid of Achish, king of Gath.† [14] So, he feigned insanity in front of them and acted like a madman in their custody, drumming on the doors of the gate and drooling onto his beard. [15] Finally Achish said to his servants: "You see the man is mad. Why did you bring him to me? [16] Do I not have enough madmen, that you bring this one to rant in my presence? Should this fellow come into my house?"

# 22

[1] David left Gath and escaped to the cave of Adullam. When his brothers and the rest of his family heard about it, they came down to him there.* [2] He was joined by all those in difficulties or in debt, or embittered,† and became their leader. About four hundred men were with him.

[3] From there David went to Mizpeh of Moab

---

† **21:2** Ahimelech realizes that he risks incurring Saul's anger if David has come to Nob as a fugitive.

**21:5–6** According to Lv 24:5–9, the showbread consisted of twelve loaves that were replaced each sabbath. Since the old bread was to be consumed by the priests, Ahimelech questions David regarding the ritual purity of his men (see 2 Sm 11:11). David's answer supposes the discipline of a military campaign under the conditions of "holy war" (Dt 23:10–15).

**21:8** *Detained before the* LORD: perhaps to fulfill a ritual obligation. David's arrival at Nob seems to coincide with a festival day, since the showbread has recently been replaced with fresh bread. *Shepherds*: i.e., Saul's palace guard. Cf. 22:9–10, where Doeg has easy access to Saul.

**21:10** *Ephod*: here an object or image large enough to conceal Goliath's sword. Cf. Gideon's ephod in Jgs 8:27.

**21:13** *Gath*: a Philistine city (see note on 5:1–12), the home of Goliath.

**22:2** *Embittered*: Hebrew *mar-nephesh*, "bitter of spirit," used of Hannah, deprived of a child, in 1:10, and of David's soldiers, whose women and children the Amalekites had seized (30:6). Cf. also 2 Sm 17:8. David becomes a hero for those who have endured loss or deprivation.

---

| | |
|---|---|
| **20:42** 2 Sm 9:1; 21:7. | **21:8** 1 Sm 22:9. |
| **21:2** 1 Sm 16:4; Is 10:32; | **21:10** 1 Sm 17:51, 54. |
| Mk 2:26. | **21:11** 1 Sm 27:2; 29:5. |
| **21:4** Lv 24:5, 9. | **21:12** 1 Sm 18:7; 29:5. |
| **21:7** Lv 24:5–9; Mt 12:3–4; | **22:1** 2 Sm 23:13; Ps 63; Mi |
| Mk 2:26; Lk 6:3–5. | 1:15. |

and said to the king of Moab, "Let my father and mother stay with you, until I learn what God will do for me." [4] He left them with the king of Moab; they stayed with him as long as David remained in the stronghold.†

[5] But Gad the prophet said to David: "Do not remain in the stronghold! Leave! Go to the land of Judah." And so David left and went to the forest of Hereth.*

**Doeg Betrays Ahimelech.** [6] Now Saul heard that David and his men had been located. At the time he was sitting in Gibeah under a tamarisk tree on the high place, holding his spear, while all his servants stood by him.* [7] So he said to them: "Listen, men of Benjamin! Will the son of Jesse give all of you fields and vineyards? Will he appoint any of you an officer over a thousand or a hundred men?* [8] Is that why you have all conspired against me? Why no one told me that my son had made a pact with the son of Jesse? None of you has shown compassion for me by revealing to me that my son has incited my servant to ambush me, as is the case today."* [9]* Then Doeg the Edomite, who was standing with Saul's officers, spoke up: "I saw the son of Jesse come to Ahimelech, son of Ahitub, in Nob. [10] He consulted the LORD for him, furnished him with provisions, and gave him the sword of Goliath the Philistine."

**Slaughter of the Priests.** [11] So the king summoned Ahimelech the priest, son of Ahitub, and all his family, the priests in Nob. They all came to the king. [12] "Listen, son of Ahitub!" Saul declared. "Yes, my lord," he replied. [13] Saul questioned him, "Why have you conspired against me with the son of Jesse by giving him food and a sword and by consulting God for him, that he might rise up against me in ambush, as is the case today?" [14] Ahimelech answered the king: "Who among all your servants is as loyal as David, the king's son-in-law, captain of your bodyguard, and honored in your own house? [15] Is this the first time I have

consulted God for him? No indeed! Let not the king accuse his servant or anyone in my family of such a thing. Your servant knows nothing at all, great or small, about the whole matter." [16] But the king said, "You shall certainly die, Ahimelech, with all your family." [17] The king then commanded his guards standing by him: "Turn and kill the priests of the LORD, for they gave David a hand. They knew he was a fugitive and yet failed to inform me." But the king's servants refused to raise a hand to strike the priests of the LORD.*

[18] The king therefore commanded Doeg, "You, turn and kill the priests!" So Doeg the Edomite himself turned and killed the priests that day—eighty-five who wore the linen ephod. [19] Saul also put the priestly city of Nob to the sword, including men and women, children and infants, and oxen, donkeys and sheep.

**Abiathar Escapes.** [20] One son of Ahimelech, son of Ahitub, named Abiathar,† escaped and fled to David.* [21] When Abiathar told David that Saul had slain the priests of the LORD, [22] David said to him: "I knew that day, when Doeg the Edomite was there, that he would certainly tell Saul. I am responsible for the slaughter of all your family. [23] Stay with me. Do not be afraid; whoever seeks your life must seek my life also. You are under my protection."†

# 23

**Keilah Liberated.** [1] David was informed that the Philistines were attacking Keilah and plundering the threshing floors.* [2] So he consulted the LORD, asking, "Shall I go and attack these Philistines?" The LORD answered, Go, attack them, and free Keilah.* [3] But David's men said to him: "Even in Judah we have reason to fear. How much more so if we go to Keilah against the forces of the Philistines!" [4] Again David consulted the LORD, who answered: Go down to Keilah, for I will deliver the Philistines into your power.* [5] So David went with his men to Keilah and fought

---

† **22:4–5** *Stronghold*: seemingly connected with the cave complex in v. 1.

**22:20** *Abiathar*: the sole survivor of Eli's household (2:27–36). David now has in his service the only priest of the Lord left in the land and exclusive access to the ephod for consulting the Lord (cf. 23:9–13). David later appoints Abiathar co-high priest with Zadok in Jerusalem (2 Sm 20:25), but Solomon exiles Abiathar to Anathoth when the priest does not support his bid for the throne. Cf. 1 Kgs 2:26–27.

**22:23** *You are under my protection*: once again a sharp contrast is drawn between Saul, who kills the Lord's priests, and David, who protects the lone survivor.

**22:5** 2 Sm 24:11–13.
**22:6** 1 Sm 14:2; Jgs 4:5.
**22:7** 1 Sm 8:14.
**22:8** 1 Sm 18:3; 20:8; 23:18.
**22:9–10** 1 Sm 21:2–10; Ps 52.
**22:17** 1 Sm 2:31, 33; 21:7.
**22:20** 1 Sm 23:6; 30:7; 2 Sm 20:25; 1 Kgs 2:26–27.
**23:1** Jos 15:44.
**23:2** 1 Sm 28:6.
**23:4** 1 Sm 17:47.

against the Philistines. He drove off their cattle and inflicted a severe defeat on them, and freed the inhabitants of Keilah.

⁶Abiathar, son of Ahimelech, who had fled to David, went down with David to Keilah, taking the ephod with him.*

**Flight from Keilah.** ⁷When Saul was told that David had entered Keilah, he thought: "God has put him in my hand, for he has boxed himself in by entering a city with gates and bars." ⁸Saul then called all the army to war, in order to go down to Keilah and besiege David and his men. ⁹When David found out that Saul was planning to harm him, he said to the priest Abiathar, "Bring the ephod here."* ¹⁰"LORD God of Israel," David prayed, "your servant has heard that Saul plans to come to Keilah, to destroy the city on my account. ¹¹Will they hand me over? Will Saul come down as your servant has heard? LORD God of Israel, tell your servant." The LORD answered: He will come down. ¹²David then asked, "Will the citizens of Keilah deliver me and my men into the hand of Saul?" The LORD answered: They will deliver you. ¹³So David and his men, about six hundred in number, left Keilah and wandered from place to place. When Saul was informed that David had fled from Keilah, he did not go forth.

**David and Jonathan in Horesh.** ¹⁴David now lived in the strongholds in the wilderness, or in the barren hill country near Ziph. Though Saul sought him continually, the LORD did not deliver David into his hand. ¹⁵While David was in the wilderness of Ziph at Horesh he was afraid that Saul had come out to seek his life. ¹⁶Then Saul's son, Jonathan, came down to David at Horesh and encouraged him in the LORD.* ¹⁷He said to him: "Have no fear, my father Saul shall not lay a hand to you. You shall be king of Israel† and I shall be second to you. Even my father Saul knows this."* ¹⁸The two of them made a covenant before the LORD in Horesh, where David remained, while Jonathan returned to his home.*

**Treachery of the Ziphites.** ¹⁹Some of the Ziphites went up to Saul in Gibeah and said, "David is hiding among us in the strongholds at Horesh on the hill of Hachilah, south of Jeshimon.* ²⁰Therefore, whenever the king wishes to come down, let him do so. It will be our task to deliver him into the king's hand." ²¹Saul replied: "The LORD bless you for your compassion toward me.* ²²Go now and make sure once more! Take note of the place where he sets foot for I am told that he is very cunning. ²³Look around and learn in which of all the various hiding places he is holding out. Then come back to me with reliable information, and I will go with you. If he is in the region, I will track him down out of all the families of Judah." ²⁴So they went off to Ziph ahead of Saul. At this time David and his men were in the wilderness below Maon, in the Arabah south of the wasteland.*

**Escape from Saul.** ²⁵When Saul and his men came looking for him, David got word of it and went down to the gorge in the wilderness below Maon. Saul heard of this and pursued David into the wilderness below Maon. ²⁶As Saul moved along one side of the gorge, David and his men took to the other. David was anxious to escape Saul, while Saul and his men were trying to outflank David and his men in order to capture them. ²⁷Then a messenger came to Saul, saying, "Come quickly, because the Philistines have invaded the land." ²⁸Saul interrupted his pursuit of David and went to meet the Philistines. This is how that place came to be called the Rock of Divisions.

# 24 **David Spares Saul.**† ¹David then went up from there and stayed in the strongholds of Engedi. ²When Saul returned from the pursuit of the Philistines, he was told that David was in the desert near Engedi. ³So Saul took three thousand of the best men from all Israel and went in search of David and his men in the direction of the wild goat crags. ⁴When he came to the sheepfolds along the way, he found a cave, which he entered to

---

† **23:17** *King of Israel*: to emphasize the inevitability of the Lord's plan, the narrator frames Jonathan's statement with two accounts of David's mercy toward Saul.

**24:1** The first of two accounts (see chap. 26) in which David spares Saul's life. The two accounts, which do not make reference to each other, are probably alternative versions of the same story.

---

**23:6** 1 Sm 22:20; 30:7.
**23:9** 1 Sm 2:28.
**23:16** 1 Sm 18:1.
**23:17** 1 Sm 20:14–16.
**23:18** 1 Sm 18:3; 20:8.
**23:19** 1 Sm 26:1–3; Ps 54.
**23:21** 2 Sm 2:5.
**23:24** 1 Sm 25:2.

relieve himself. David and his men were occupying the inmost recesses of the cave.*

⁵ David's servants said to him, "This is the day about which the LORD said to you: I will deliver your enemy into your hand; do with him as you see fit." So David moved up and stealthily cut off an end of Saul's robe. ⁶ Afterward, however, David regretted that he had cut off an end of Saul's robe.* ⁷ He said to his men, "The LORD forbid that I should do such a thing to my master, the LORD's anointed, to lay a hand on him, for he is the LORD's anointed."* ⁸ With these words David restrained his men and would not permit them to attack Saul. Saul then left the cave and went on his way. ⁹ David also stepped out of the cave, calling to Saul, "My lord the king!" When Saul looked back, David bowed, his face to the ground in homage, ¹⁰ and asked Saul: "Why do you listen to those who say, 'David is trying to harm you'? ¹¹ You see for yourself today that the LORD just now delivered you into my hand in the cave. I was told to kill you, but I took pity on you instead. I decided, 'I will not raise a hand against my master, for he is the LORD's anointed.' ¹² Look here, my father. See the end of your robe which I hold. I cut off an end of your robe and did not kill you. Now see and be convinced that I plan no harm and no rebellion. I have done you no wrong, though you are hunting me down to take my life.* ¹³ May the LORD judge between me and you. May the LORD exact justice from you in my case. I shall not lay a hand on you. ¹⁴ As the old proverb says, 'From the wicked comes wickedness.' Thus I will not lay a hand on you. ¹⁵ What is the king of Israel attacking? What are you pursuing? A dead dog! A single flea!* ¹⁶ The LORD will be the judge to decide between us. May the LORD see this, defend my cause, and give me justice against you!"*

**Saul's Remorse.** ¹⁷ When David finished saying these things to Saul, Saul answered, "Is that your voice, my son David?" And he wept freely. ¹⁸ Saul then admitted to David: "You are more in the right than I am. You have treated me graciously, while I have treated you badly. ¹⁹ You have declared this day how you treated me graciously: the LORD delivered me into

Pictured above, a cave such as that in which David hid in the desert near En-gedi. When Saul entered the cave to relieve himself, David did not harm him but instead used the occasion to demonstrate his loyalty to Saul, whom he called "the LORD's anointed" (1 Sm 24:7).

your hand and you did not kill me. ²⁰ For if someone comes upon an enemy, do they send them graciously on their way? So may the LORD reward you graciously for what you have done this day. ²¹ And now, since I know that you will certainly become king and that the kingship over Israel shall come into your possession,* ²² swear to me by the LORD that you will not cut off my descendants and that you will not blot out my name from my father's house."* ²³ David gave Saul his oath and Saul returned home, while David and his men went up to the stronghold.

# 25 Death of Samuel. ¹ Samuel died, and all Israel gathered to mourn him; they buried him at his home in Ramah.* Then David went down to the wilderness of Paran.

**Nabal and Abigail.** ² There was a man of Maon who had property in Carmel; he was very wealthy, owning three thousand sheep and a thousand goats. At the time, he was present for the shearing of his flock in Carmel.* ³ The

---

24:4 Ps 57.
24:6 1 Sm 15:27.
24:7 1 Sm 10:1; 26:9; 31:4;
    2 Sm 1:14.
24:12 Rom 12:19.
24:15 2 Sm 9:8; 16:9.
24:16 1 Sm 18:19, 31;
    26:19;
Ps 35:1–3; 43:1.
24:21 1 Sm 26:25.
24:22 2 Sm 9:1–3.
25:1 1 Sm 28:3;
Sir 46:13–20.
25:2 1 Sm 23:24; Jos
    15:55.

man's name was Nabal and his wife was Abigail. The woman was intelligent and attractive, but Nabal, a Calebite, was harsh and bad-mannered.* ⁴While in the wilderness, David heard that Nabal was shearing his flock, ⁵so he sent ten young men, instructing them: "Go up to Carmel. Pay Nabal a visit and greet him in my name. ⁶Say to him, 'Peace be with you, my brother, and with your family, and with all who belong to you. ⁷I have just heard that shearers are with you. Now, when your shepherds were with us, we did them no injury, neither did they miss anything while they were in Carmel. ⁸Ask your servants and they will tell you. Look kindly on these young men, since we come at a festival time. Please give your servants and your son David† whatever you can.'"

⁹When David's young men arrived, they delivered the entire message to Nabal in David's name, and then waited. ¹⁰But Nabal answered the servants of David: "Who is David? Who is the son of Jesse? Nowadays there are many servants who run away from their masters. ¹¹Must I take my bread, my wine, my meat that I have slaughtered for my own shearers, and give them to men who come from who knows where?" ¹²So David's young men retraced their steps and on their return reported to him all that had been said. ¹³Thereupon David said to his men, "Let everyone strap on his sword." And everyone did so, and David put on his own sword. About four hundred men went up after David, while two hundred remained with the baggage.

¹⁴Abigail, Nabal's wife, was informed of this by one of the servants, who said: "From the wilderness David sent messengers to greet our master, but he screamed at them. ¹⁵Yet these men were very good to us. We were not harmed, neither did we miss anything all the while we were living among them during our stay in the open country. ¹⁶Day and night they were a wall of protection for us, the whole time we were pasturing the sheep near them. ¹⁷Now, see what you can do, for you must realize that otherwise disaster is in store for our master and for his whole house. He is such a scoundrel

that no one can talk to him." ¹⁸Abigail quickly got together two hundred loaves, two skins of wine, five dressed sheep, five seahs of roasted grain, a hundred cakes of pressed raisins, and two hundred cakes of pressed figs, and loaded them on donkeys. ¹⁹She then said to her servants, "Go on ahead; I will follow you." But to her husband Nabal she said nothing.

²⁰Hidden by the mountain, she came down riding on a donkey, as David and his men were coming down from the opposite direction. When she met them, ²¹David had just been saying: "Indeed, it was in vain that I guarded all this man's possessions in the wilderness, so that nothing of his was missing. He has repaid good with evil. ²²May God do thus to David, and more, if by morning I leave a single male alive among all those who belong to him."* ²³As soon as Abigail saw David, she dismounted quickly from the donkey and, falling down, bowed low to the ground before David in homage.

²⁴As she fell at his feet she said: "My lord, let the blame be mine. Please let your maidservant speak to you; listen to the words of your maidservant.* ²⁵My lord, do not pay any attention to that scoundrel Nabal, for he is just like his name. His name means fool,† and he acts the fool. I, your maidservant, did not see the young men whom my lord sent. ²⁶Now, therefore, my lord, as the LORD lives, and as you live, the LORD has kept you from shedding blood and from avenging yourself by your own hand. May your enemies and those who seek to harm my lord become as Nabal!†* ²⁷Accept this gift, then, which your maidservant has brought for my lord, and let it be given to the young men who follow my lord. ²⁸Please forgive the offense of your maidservant, for the LORD shall certainly establish a lasting house for my lord, because my lord fights the battles of the LORD. Let no evil be found in you your whole life long.* ²⁹If any adversary pursues you to seek your life, may the life of my lord be bound in the bundle of the living† in the care of the LORD your God; may God hurl out the lives of your enemies as

---

† 
**25:8** *Your son David*: this kinship language may reflect a political or social relationship between Nabal and David. Nabal, however, does not acknowledge it.

**25:25** Hebrew *nabal* means "fool" (cf. Is 32:5–7). Abigail, on the other hand, acts wisely to save herself and her household by offering prudent counsel to the future king of Israel.

**25:26** Abigail, encouraging David to trust in God's promise, anticipates that some misfortune will shortly overtake Nabal, as

in fact it does (vv. 37–38).

**25:29** *The bundle of the living*: the figure is perhaps taken from the practice of tying up valuables in a kerchief or bag for safekeeping. Abigail desires that David enjoy permanent peace and

*
| **25:3** 1 Sm 27:3; Dt | 2 Kgs 9:8. |
| 1:35–36; Jos 14:6–15; | **25:24** 2 Sm 14:9. |
| 1 Chr 2:42, 45. | **25:26** Dt 20:4; Jgs 7:2. |
| **25:22** 1 Kgs 16:11; 21:21; | **25:28** 1 Kgs 11:38. |

from the hollow of a sling.* [30] And when the LORD fulfills for my lord the promise of success he has made concerning you, and appoints you as ruler over Israel,* [31] you shall not have any regrets or burdens on your conscience, my lord, for having shed innocent blood or for having rescued yourself. When the LORD bestows good on my lord, remember your maidservant." [32] David said to Abigail: "Blessed is the LORD, the God of Israel, who sent you to meet me today. [33] Blessed is your good judgment and blessed are you yourself. Today you have prevented me from shedding blood and rescuing myself with my own hand. [34] Otherwise, as the LORD, the God of Israel, lives, who has kept me from harming you, if you had not come so promptly to meet me, by dawn Nabal would not have had so much as one male left alive." [35] David then took from her what she had brought him and said to her: "Go to your home in peace! See, I have listened to your appeal and have granted your request."

**Nabal's Death.** [36] When Abigail came to Nabal, he was hosting a banquet in his house like that of a king, and Nabal was in a festive mood and very drunk. So she said not a word to him until daybreak the next morning. [37] But then, when Nabal was sober, his wife told him what had happened. At this his heart died within him, and he became like a stone. [38] About ten days later the LORD struck Nabal and he died. [39] Hearing that Nabal was dead, David said: "Blessed be the LORD, who has defended my cause against the insult from Nabal, and who restrained his servant from doing evil, but has repaid Nabal for his evil deeds."

**David Marries Abigail and Ahinoam.** David then sent a proposal of marriage to Abigail.* [40] When David's servants came to Abigail in Carmel, they said to her, "David has sent us to make his proposal of marriage to you." [41] Rising and bowing to the ground, she answered, "Let your maidservant be the slave who washes the feet of my lord's servants." [42] She got up immediately, mounted a donkey, and followed David's messengers, with her five maids attending her. She became his wife. [43]* David also married Ahinoam of Jezreel. Thus both of them were his wives. [44] But Saul gave David's wife Michal, Saul's own daughter, to Palti, son of Laish, who was from Gallim.*

# 26 David Spares Saul Again.† [1]* Men from Ziph came to Saul in Gibeah, reporting that David was hiding on the hill of Hachilah at the edge of Jeshimon. [2] So Saul went down to the wilderness of Ziph with three thousand of the best warriors of Israel, to search for David in the wilderness of Ziph. [3] Saul camped beside the road on the hill of Hachilah, at the edge of Jeshimon. David, who was living in the wilderness, saw that Saul had come into the wilderness after him [4] and sent out scouts, who confirmed Saul's arrival. [5] David then went to the place where Saul was encamped and saw the spot where Saul and his general, Abner, son of Ner, had their sleeping quarters. Saul was lying within the camp, and all his soldiers were bivouacked around him.* [6] David asked Ahimelech the Hittite, and Abishai, son of Zeruiah and brother of Joab, "Who will go down into the camp with me to Saul?" Abishai replied, "I will."* [7] So David and Abishai reached Saul's soldiers by night, and there was Saul lying asleep within the camp, his spear thrust into the ground at his head and Abner and his troops sleeping around him.

[8] Abishai whispered to David: "God has delivered your enemy into your hand today. Let me nail him to the ground with one thrust of the spear; I will not need to strike him twice!"* [9] But David said to Abishai, "Do not harm him, for who can lay a hand on the LORD's anointed and remain innocent? [10] As the LORD lives," David declared, "only the LORD can strike him: either when the time comes for him to die, or when he goes out and perishes in battle.†* [11] But the LORD forbid that I lay a

---

† security, but that his enemies be subject to constant agitation and humiliation like a stone whirled about, cast out of the sling, and thereafter disregarded.

**26:1** The second account of David sparing Saul's life; cf. note on 24:1.

**26:10** *Perishes in battle*: David's words foreshadow how Saul will die (31:3–4). They also emphasize that David, unlike Saul, knows his proper place before God. David comes to the kingship innocent of Saul's blood, although the king pursues him like an enemy and David has had two opportunities to kill him.

25:29 Ps 69:28.
25:30 1 Sm 13:14; 2 Sm 3:10.
25:39 1 Kgs 2:44.
25:43 1 Sm 27:3.
25:44 1 Sm 18:20; 27:3; 30:5; 2 Sm 2:2, 13–16; 1 Chr 3:1.
26:1–2 1 Sm 23:19–20; Ps 54.
26:5 1 Sm 17:20.
26:6 2 Sm 3:30; 1 Chr 2:16.
26:8 1 Sm 18:11; 19:10; 20:33.
26:10 Ps 37:13.

hand on the LORD's anointed! Now take the spear at his head and the water jug, and let us be on our way." [12] So David took the spear and the water jug from their place at Saul's head, and they withdrew without anyone seeing or knowing or awakening. All remained asleep, because a deep slumber† from the LORD had fallen upon them.*

**David Taunts Abner.** [13] Crossing over to an opposite slope, David stood on a distant hilltop. With a great distance between them [14] David called to the army and to Abner, son of Ner, "Will you not answer, Abner?" Then Abner shouted back, "Who is it that calls me?" [15] David said to Abner: "Are you not a man? Who in Israel is your equal? Why were you not guarding your lord the king when one of his subjects came to assassinate the king, your lord? [16] What you have done is not right. As the LORD lives, you people deserve death because you have not guarded your lord, the anointed of the LORD. Go, look: where are the king's spear and the water jug that was at his head?"

**Saul Admits His Guilt.** [17] Saul recognized David's voice and asked, "Is that your voice, David my son?"† David answered, "Yes, my lord the king." [18] He continued: "Why does my lord pursue his servant? What have I done? What evil am I planning? [19] Please, now, let my lord the king listen to the words of his servant. If the LORD has incited you against me, may an offering please the LORD. But if it is the people who have done so, may they be cursed before the LORD. They have driven me away so that today I have no share in the LORD's heritage,† but am told: 'Go serve other gods!'* [20] Do not let my blood spill on the ground far from the presence of the LORD. For the king of Israel has come out to seek a single flea as if he were hunting partridge† in the mountains." [21] Then Saul said: "I have done wrong. Come back, David, my son! I will not harm you again,

because you considered my life precious today even though I have been a fool and have made a serious mistake." [22] But David answered: "Here is the king's spear. Let an attendant come over to get it. [23] The LORD repays everyone's righteousness and faithfulness. Although the LORD delivered you into my hands today, I could not lay a hand on the LORD's anointed.* [24] Just as I regarded your life as precious today, so may the LORD regard my life as precious and deliver me from all dangers." [25] Then Saul said to David: "Blessed are you, my son David! You shall certainly succeed in whatever you undertake." David went his way, and Saul returned to his place.*

# 27 **David Flees to the Philistines.** [1] David said to himself: "I shall perish some day at the hand of Saul. I have no choice but to escape to the land of the Philistines; then Saul will give up his continual search for me throughout the land of Israel, and I will be out of his reach." [2] Accordingly, David departed with his six hundred soldiers and went over to Achish, son of Maoch, king of Gath.* [3] David and his men lived in Gath with Achish; each one had his family, and David had his two wives, Ahinoam from Jezreel and Abigail, the widow of Nabal from Carmel.* [4] When Saul learned that David had fled to Gath, he no longer searched for him.

[5] David said to Achish: "If I meet with your approval, let me have a place to live in one of the country towns. Why should your servant live with you in the royal city?" [6] That same day Achish gave him Ziklag, which has, therefore, belonged to the kings of Judah† up to the present time.* [7] In all, David lived a year and four months in Philistine territory.*

**David Raids Israel's Foes.** [8] David and his men went out on raids against the Geshurites, Girzites, and Amalekites—peoples living in the land between Telam, on the approach to Shur,

---

**26:12** *Deep slumber*: as in Gn 2:21; 15:12; Is 29:10. The Lord aids David's foray into Saul's camp and allows David to come and go undetected.

**26:17** *David my son*: Saul's reference to David as his son, which appears three times in this chapter (vv. 17, 21, 25), alludes to David's role as his successor.

**26:19** *The LORD's heritage*: the land and people of Israel (Dt 32:8–9; Ps 33:12). If driven from the land, David could not take part in worship of Israel's God; nonetheless, God has blessed David (cf. v. 25).

**26:20** *Partridge*: lit., "the caller." The metaphor is built on

clever wordplay: in v. 14, David calls out to the army and Abner asks the caller's identity. David calls out the answer: "the caller" is the object of the king's pursuit.

**27:6** Ziklag was a royal city and not part of Israel's tribal land holdings. Jerusalem later enjoyed a similar status (2 Sm 5:7–9).

---

**26:12** Gn 2:21; 15:12.
**26:19** 1 Sm 24:16.
**26:23** 1 Sm 18:20.
**26:25** 1 Sm 18:14; 24:21.
**27:2** 1 Sm 21:11–16.

**27:3** 1 Sm 25:3, 44;
    30:3–5; 2 Sm 2:3.
**27:6** 1 Sm 30:1.
**27:7** 1 Sm 29:3.

and the land of Egypt.* ⁹ In attacking the land David would not leave a man or woman alive, but would carry off sheep, oxen, donkeys, camels, and clothes. Then he would return to Achish, ¹⁰ who would ask, "Against whom did you raid this time?" David would reply, "Against the Negeb of Judah,"† or "Against the Negeb of Jerahmeel," or "Against the Negeb of the Kenites."* ¹¹ David never left a man or woman alive to be brought to Gath. He thought, "They will betray us and say, 'This is what David did.'" This was his custom as long as he lived in Philistine territory. ¹² Achish trusted David, thinking, "His people Israel must certainly detest him. I shall have him as my vassal forever."

**28** ¹ In those days the Philistines mustered their military forces to fight against Israel. So Achish said to David, "You realize, of course, that you and your warriors† must march out for battle with me." ² David answered Achish, "Good! Now you shall learn what your servant can do." Then Achish said to David, "I shall appoint you as my permanent bodyguard."

³ Now, Samuel was dead. All Israel had mourned him and buried him in his city, Ramah. Meanwhile Saul had driven mediums and diviners out of the land.*

**Saul in Despair.** ⁴ The Philistines rallied and, coming to Shunem, they encamped. Saul, too, mustered all Israel; they camped on Gilboa. ⁵ When Saul saw the Philistine camp, he grew afraid and lost heart completely. ⁶ He consulted the LORD; but the LORD gave no answer, neither in dreams nor by Urim nor through prophets.* ⁷ Then Saul said to his servants, "Find me a medium† through whom I can seek counsel." His servants answered him, "There is a woman in Endor who is a medium."*

**The Medium at Endor.** ⁸ So he disguised himself, putting on other clothes, and set out with two companions. They came to the woman at night, and Saul said to her, "Divine for me; conjure up the spirit I tell you."* ⁹ But the woman answered him, "You know what Saul has done, how he expelled the mediums and diviners from the land. Then why are you trying to entrap me and get me killed?" ¹⁰ But Saul swore to her by the LORD, "As the LORD lives, you shall incur no blame for this." ¹¹ "Whom do you want me to conjure up?" the woman asked him. "Conjure up Samuel for me," he replied.

**Samuel Appears.** ¹² When the woman saw Samuel, she shrieked at the top of her voice and said to Saul, "Why have you deceived me? You are Saul!" ¹³ But the king said to her, "Do not be afraid. What do you see?" "I see a god rising from the earth," she replied. ¹⁴ "What does he look like?" asked Saul. "An old man is coming up wrapped in a robe," she replied. Saul knew that it was Samuel, and so he bowed his face to the ground in homage.

**Saul's Doom.** ¹⁵† Samuel then said to Saul, "Why do you disturb me by conjuring me up?" Saul replied: "I am in great distress, for the Philistines are waging war against me and God has turned away from me. Since God no longer answers me through prophets or in dreams, I have called upon you to tell me what I should do."* ¹⁶ To this Samuel said: "But why do you ask me, if the LORD has abandoned you for your neighbor?* ¹⁷ The LORD has done to you what he declared through me: he has torn the kingdom from your hand and has given it to your neighbor David.

¹⁸ "Because you disobeyed the LORD's directive and would not carry out his fierce anger against Amalek, the LORD has done this to you today.* ¹⁹ Moreover, the LORD will deliver Israel, and you as well, into the hands of the Philistines. By tomorrow you and your sons will be with me, and the LORD will have

---

**27:10** *The Negeb of Judah*: David deceives Achish by assuring him that he has attacked Israelite territory.

**28:1** *You and your warriors*: David is faced with a potentially dangerous dilemma: either to reveal his continuing loyalty to his own people or to obey Achish and fight against his own people.

**28:7** *A medium*: Saul's own prohibition of necromancy and divination (v. 3) was in keeping with the consistent teaching of the Old Testament (cf. Lv 19:31; 20:6, 27; Dt 18:10).

**28:15–19** The consultation with the medium serves to remind the reader that the Lord's plan for David marches onward; no sorcery can thwart it.

**27:8** 1 Sm 15:3, 7; Jos 13:2–3.
**27:10** 1 Sm 30:14, 29; 1 Chr 2:9, 25, 42.
**28:3** 1 Sm 25:1; Sir 46:20.
**28:6** 1 Sm 14:37, 41; Ex 28:30; Lv 8:8.
**28:7** Lv 19:31; 20:27;
Dt 18:10–12; 2 Kgs 21:6; 1 Chr 10:13–14; Acts 16:16.
**28:8** 1 Sm 15:23; 1 Kgs 14:2.
**28:15** 1 Sm 14:37; Sir 46:20.
**28:16** 1 Sm 15:27–28.
**28:18** 1 Sm 15:18–19, 26.

delivered the army of Israel into the hands of the Philistines."*

²⁰ Immediately Saul fell full length on the ground, in great fear because of Samuel's message. He had no strength left, since he had eaten nothing all that day and night. ²¹ Then the woman came to Saul and, seeing that he was quite terror-stricken, said to him: "Remember, your maidservant obeyed you: I took my life in my hands and carried out the request you made of me. ²² Now you, in turn, please listen to your maidservant. Let me set out a bit of food for you to eat, so that you are strong enough to go on your way." ²³ But he refused, saying, "I will not eat." However, when his servants joined the woman in urging him, he listened to their entreaties, got up from the ground, and sat on a couch. ²⁴ The woman had a stall-fed calf in the house, which she now quickly slaughtered. Then taking flour, she kneaded it and baked unleavened bread. ²⁵ She set the meal before Saul and his servants, and they ate. Then they got up and left the same night.

# 29 David's Aid Rejected.
¹ Now the Philistines had mustered all their forces in Aphek, and the Israelites were encamped at the spring in Jezreel.* ² As the Philistine lords were marching their units of a hundred and a thousand, David and his warriors were marching in the rear guard with Achish. ³ The Philistine commanders asked, "What are those Hebrews doing here?" Achish answered them: "Why, that is David, the officer of Saul, king of Israel. He has been with me for a year or two, and from the day he came over to me until now I have never found fault in him."* ⁴ But the Philistine commanders were angered at this and said to him: "Send that man back! Let him return to the place you picked out for him. He must not go down into battle with us; during the battle he might become our enemy. For how else can he win back his master's favor, if not at the expense of our soldiers?* ⁵ Is this not the David for whom they sing during their dances,

'Saul has slain his thousands,
   David his tens of thousands'?"*

⁶ So Achish summoned David and said to him: "As the LORD lives, you are honest, and I would want you with me in all my battles. To this day I have found nothing wrong with you since you came to me. But in the view of the chiefs you are not welcome. ⁷ Leave peacefully, now, and do nothing that might displease the Philistine chiefs." ⁸ But David said to Achish: "What have I done? What fault have you found in your servant from the day I entered your service until today, that I cannot go to fight against the enemies of my lord the king?" ⁹ "I recognize," Achish answered David, "that you are trustworthy, like an angel of God. But the Philistine commanders are saying, 'He must not go with us into battle.' ¹⁰ So the first thing tomorrow, you and your lord's servants who came with you, go to the place I picked out for you. Do not take to heart their worthless remarks; for you have been valuable in my service. But make an early morning start, as soon as it grows light, and be on your way." ¹¹ So David and his warriors left early in the morning to return to the land of the Philistines, and the Philistines went on up to Jezreel.

# 30 Ziklag in Ruins.
¹ Before David and his men reached Ziklag on the third day, the Amalekites had raided the Negeb and Ziklag. They stormed Ziklag, and set it on fire.* ² They took captive the women and all who were in the city, young and old, killing no one, and they herded them off when they left. ³ David and his men arrived at the city to find it burned to the ground and their wives, sons, and daughters taken captive. ⁴ Then David and those who were with him wept aloud until they could weep no more. ⁵ David's two wives, Ahinoam of Jezreel and Abigail, the widow of Nabal from Carmel, had also been carried off.* ⁶ Now David found himself in great danger, for the soldiers spoke of stoning him, so bitter were they over the fate of their sons and daughters. David took courage in the LORD his God ⁷* and said to Abiathar, the priest, son of Ahimelech, "Bring me the ephod!" When Abiathar brought him the ephod, ⁸ David inquired of the LORD, "Shall I pursue these raiders? Can I overtake them?" The LORD answered him: Go in pursuit, for you will certainly overtake them and bring about a rescue.

**28:19** 1 Sm 31:2–6; Sir 46:20.
**29:1** 1 Sm 4:1.
**29:3** 1 Sm 27:7.
**29:4** 1 Chr 12:19–20.
**29:5** 1 Sm 18:6–7; 21:12.
**30:1** 1 Sm 15:2; 27:6, 10; 1 Chr 12:21.
**30:5** 1 Sm 25:42; 27:3;
**30:5.**
**30:7–8** 1 Sm 2:28; 23:6; Ex 28:30.

1 S M

**Raid on the Amalekites.** ⁹ So David went off with his six hundred as far as the Wadi Besor, where those who were to remain behind halted. ¹⁰ David continued the pursuit with four hundred, but two hundred were too exhausted to cross the Wadi Besor and remained behind. ¹¹ An Egyptian was found in the open country and brought to David. They gave him food to eat and water to drink; ¹² they also offered a cake of pressed figs and two cakes of pressed raisins. When he had eaten, he revived, for he had not taken food nor drunk water for three days and three nights. ¹³ Then David asked him, "To whom do you belong? Where did you come from?" "I am an Egyptian, the slave of an Amalekite," he replied. "My master abandoned me three days ago because I fell sick. ¹⁴ We raided the Negeb of the Cherethites, the territory of Judah, and the Negeb of Caleb; and we set Ziklag on fire."* ¹⁵ David then asked him, "Will you lead me down to these raiders?" He answered, "Swear to me by God that you will not kill me or hand me over to my master, and I will lead you down to the raiders." ¹⁶ So he led them down, and there were the Amalekites lounging all over the ground, eating, drinking, and celebrating because of all the rich plunder they had taken from the land of the Philistines and from the land of Judah.

**The Plunder Recovered.** ¹⁷ From dawn to sundown the next day David attacked them, allowing no one to escape except four hundred young men, who mounted their camels and fled.* ¹⁸ David recovered everything the Amalekites had taken, and he rescued his two wives. ¹⁹ Nothing was missing, small or great, plunder or sons or daughters, of all that the Amalekites had taken. David brought back everything. ²⁰ Moreover, David took all the sheep and oxen, and as they drove these before him, they shouted, "This is David's plunder!"

**Division of the Plunder.** ²¹ When David came to the two hundred men who had been too exhausted to follow him, whom he had left behind at the Wadi Besor, they came out to meet David and the men with him. As David approached, he greeted them. ²² But all the greedy and worthless among those who had accompanied David said, "Since they did not accompany us, we will not give them anything from the plunder, except for each man's wife and children." ²³ But David said: "You must not do this, my brothers, after what the LORD has given us. The LORD has protected us and delivered into our hands the raiders that came against us.* ²⁴ Who could agree with this proposal of yours? Rather, the share of the one who goes down to battle shall be the same as that of the one who remains with the baggage—they share alike."* ²⁵ And from that day forward he made this a law and a custom in Israel, as it still is today.*

**David's Gifts to Judah.** ²⁶ When David came to Ziklag, he sent part of the plunder to his friends, the elders of Judah,† saying, "This is a gift to you from the plunder of the enemies of the LORD," namely, ²⁷ to those in Bethel, Ramoth-negeb, Jattir, ²⁸ Aroer, Siphmoth, Eshtemoa, ²⁹ Racal, Jerahmeelite cities and Kenite cities,* ³⁰ Hormah, Borashan, Athach, ³¹ Hebron, and to all the places that David and his men had frequented.*

**31** **Death of Saul and His Sons.** ¹* Now the Philistines went to war against Israel, and the Israelites fled before them, and fell, slain on Mount Gilboa. ² The Philistines pressed hard after Saul and his sons. When the Philistines had struck down Jonathan, Abinadab, and Malchishua, sons of Saul,* ³ the fury of the battle converged on Saul. Then the archers hit him, and he was severely wounded. ⁴ Saul said to his armor-bearer, "Draw your sword and run me through; otherwise these uncircumcised will come and abuse me." But the armor-bearer, badly frightened, refused, so Saul took his own sword and fell upon it.* ⁵* When the armor-bearer saw that Saul was dead, he too fell upon his sword and died with him. ⁶ Thus Saul, his three sons, and his armor-bearer died together on that same day. ⁷ When the Israelites on the slope of the valley

---

† **30:26** *Elders of Judah:* David consolidates his power in southern Judah in preparation for his anointing at Hebron (2 Sm 5:3).

* **30:14** 1 Sm 27:10; Ez 25:16.
**30:17** 1 Sm 15:3; Jos 6:17; Jgs 7:12.
**30:23** Dt 20:4, 14.
**30:24** 1 Sm 17:22; 25:13.
**30:25** Nm 31:27.
**30:29** 1 Sm 27:10.
**30:31** 2 Sm 2:1–4.
**31:1–13** 2 Sm 1:1–16; 4:4; 1 Chr 10:1–12.
**31:2** 1 Sm 14:49; 28:19;
1 Chr 10:2–3.
**31:4** 1 Sm 24:6; Jgs 9:54; 1 Chr 10:4.
**31:5** 1 Sm 10:1; 26:9; 2 Mc 14:42.

and those along the Jordan saw that the men of Israel had fled and that Saul and his sons were dead, they abandoned their cities and fled. Then the Philistines came and lived in those cities.

⁸On the following day, when the Philistines came to strip the slain, they found Saul and his three sons fallen on Mount Gilboa. ⁹They cut off Saul's head and stripped him of his armor; these they sent throughout the land of the Philistines to bring the good news to the temple of their idols and to the people.* ¹⁰They put

his armor in the temple of Astarte but impaled his body on the wall of Beth-shan.

**Burial of Saul.** ¹¹* When the inhabitants of Jabesh-gilead heard what the Philistines had done to Saul, ¹²all their warriors set out and traveled through the night; they removed the bodies of Saul and his sons from the wall of Beth-shan, and, returning to Jabesh, burned them.† ¹³Then they took their bones and buried them under the tamarisk tree in Jabesh, and fasted for seven days.

---

† **31:12** *Burned them:* cremation was not an Israelite custom. The people of Jabesh-gilead repay Saul's victory over the Ammonites on their behalf (chap. 11) by providing burial and funeral rites for him and his sons. Probably the damaged state of the corpus necessitated cremation.

**31:9** 1 Sm 17:54; 2 Sm 1:20; 2 Mc 15:35.

**31:11–13** 1 Sm 11:1–11; 2 Sm 2:4–7; 21:12–14.

# SECOND SAMUEL

**1** **Report of Saul's Death.** [1] After the death of Saul, David returned from his victory over the Amalekites and stayed in Ziklag two days.* [2] On the third day a man came from the field of battle, one of Saul's people, with his garments torn and his head covered with dirt. Going to David, he fell to the ground in homage. [3] David asked him, "Where have you come from?" He replied, "From the Israelite camp; I have escaped." [4] "What happened?" David said. "Tell me." He answered that the soldiers had fled the battle and many of them had fallen and were dead; and that Saul and his son Jonathan were dead. [5] Then David said to the youth who was reporting to him, "How do you know that Saul and his son Jonathan are dead?" [6]* The youth reporting to him replied: "I happened to find myself on Mount Gilboa and saw Saul leaning on his spear, with chariots and horsemen closing in on him. [7] He turned around and saw me, and called me to him. When I said, 'Here I am,' [8] he asked me, 'Who are you?' and I replied, 'An Amalekite.' [9] Then he said to me, 'Stand over me, please, and put me to death, for I am in great suffering, but still alive.' [10] So I stood over him and put him to death, for I knew that he could not survive his wound. I removed the crown from his head and the armlet from his arm and brought them here to my lord."

[11] David seized his garments and tore them, and so did all the men who were with him.* [12] They mourned and wept and fasted until evening for Saul and his son Jonathan, and for the people of the Lord and the house of Israel, because they had fallen by the sword.* [13] David said to the youth who had reported to him, "Where are you from?" He replied, "I am the son of a resident alien, an Amalekite." [14] David said to him, "How is it that you were not afraid to put forth your hand to desecrate the Lord's anointed?"* [15] David then called one of the attendants and said to him, "Come, strike him down"; so he struck him and he died. [16] David said to him, "Your blood is on your head, for you testified against yourself when you said, 'I put the Lord's anointed to death.'"

**Lament for Saul and Jonathan.** [17] Then David chanted this lament for Saul and his son Jonathan [18] (he commanded that it be taught to the Judahites; it is recorded in the Book of Jashar):*

19     Alas! the glory of Israel,
        slain upon your heights!
    How can the warriors have fallen!
20     Do not report it in Gath,
        as good news in Ashkelon's streets,
    Lest Philistine women rejoice,
        lest the women of the uncircumcised
          exult!*
21     O mountains of Gilboa,
        upon you be neither dew nor rain,
        nor surging from the deeps!†
    Defiled there the warriors' shields,
        the shield of Saul—no longer
          anointed with oil!*
22     From the blood of the slain,
        from the bodies of the warriors,
    The bow of Jonathan did not turn back,
        nor the sword of Saul return
          unstained.†*
23     Saul and Jonathan, beloved and dear,
        separated neither in life nor death,
        swifter than eagles, stronger than
          lions!
24     Women of Israel, weep over Saul,
        who clothed you in scarlet and in
          finery,
    covered your clothing with ornaments
          of gold.
25     How can the warriors have fallen
        in the thick of battle!
    Jonathan—slain upon your heights!
26     I grieve for you, Jonathan my brother!
        Most dear have you been to me;
    More wondrous your love to me
        than the love of women.*

---

† **1:21** *Surging from the deeps*: this conjectural reading of the Hebrew yields a parallelism with dew and rain: the mountains where the warriors have fallen in battle are to be desiccated, deprived of water from above (rain, dew) and below (the primordial deeps).
**1:22** *Unstained*: lit., "empty." The sword was conceived as a devouring mouth; see, e.g., 2:26.

**1:1** 1 Sm 30:17–20; 31:1–13.
**1:6–10** 2 Sm 4:10; 1 Sm 31:1–4; 1 Chr 10:1–4.
**1:11** 2 Sm 13:31.
**1:12** 1 Sm 31:13.
**1:14** 1 Sm 10:1; 24:7;
     Ps 105:15.
**1:18** Jos 10:13.
**1:20** Jgs 16:23; 1 Sm 31:9;
     Mi 1:10.
**1:21** Gn 27:28.
**1:22** 1 Sm 14:47.
**1:26** 1 Sm 18:1–4.

2 SM

27     How can the warriors have fallen,
       the weapons of war have perished!

**2 David Is Anointed King.** ¹ After this, David inquired of the LORD, "Shall I go up into one of the cities of Judah?" The LORD replied to him: Go up. Then David asked, "Where shall I go?" He replied: To Hebron. ² So David went up there, with his two wives, Ahinoam of Jezreel and Abigail, the wife of Nabal of Carmel.* ³ David also brought up his men with their families, and they dwelt in the towns of Hebron. ⁴ Then the men of Judah came there and anointed David king over the house of Judah.

A report reached David that the people of Jabesh-gilead had buried Saul.* ⁵ So David sent messengers to the people of Jabesh-gilead and said to them: "May you be blessed by the LORD for having done this kindness to your lord Saul in burying him. ⁶ And now may the LORD show you kindness and fidelity. For my part, I will show generosity to you for having done this. ⁷ So take courage and prove yourselves valiant, for though your lord Saul is dead, the house of Judah has anointed me king over them."

## IV. THE REIGN OF DAVID

**Ishbaal King of Israel.** ⁸ Abner, son of Ner, captain of Saul's army, took Ishbaal,† son of Saul, and brought him over to Mahanaim,* ⁹ where he made him king over Gilead, the Asherites, Jezreel, Ephraim, Benjamin, and the rest of Israel. ¹⁰ Ishbaal, son of Saul, was forty years old when he became king over Israel, and he reigned two years; but the house of Judah followed David. ¹¹ In all, David was king in Hebron over the house of Judah seven years and six months.*

**Combat near Gibeon.** ¹² Now Abner, son of Ner, and the servants of Ishbaal, Saul's son, set out from Mahanaim for Gibeon. ¹³ Joab, son of Zeruiah, and the servants of David also set out and encountered them at the pool of Gibeon. And they sat down, one group on one side of the pool and the other on the opposite side. ¹⁴ Then Abner said to Joab, "Let the young men rise and perform for us."† Joab replied, "All right." ¹⁵ So they rose and were counted off: twelve of the Benjaminites of Ishbaal, son of Saul, and twelve of David's servants. ¹⁶ Then each one grasped his opponent's head and thrust his sword into his opponent's side, and they all fell down together.† And so that place was named the Field of the Sides; it is in Gibeon.

**Death of Asahel.** ¹⁷ The battle that day was very fierce, and Abner and the men of Israel were defeated by David's servants. ¹⁸ The three sons of Zeruiah were there—Joab, Abishai, and Asahel.* Asahel, who was as fleet of foot as a gazelle in the open field, ¹⁹ set out after Abner, turning neither right nor left in his pursuit. ²⁰ Abner turned around and said, "Is that you, Asahel?" He replied, "Yes." ²¹ Abner said to him, "Turn right or left; seize one of the young men and take what you can strip from him." But Asahel would not stop pursuing him. ²² Once more Abner said to Asahel: "Stop pursuing me! Why must I strike you to the ground? How could I show my face to your brother Joab?"* ²³ Still he refused to stop. So Abner struck him in the abdomen with the heel of his spear, and the weapon protruded from his back. He fell there and died on the spot. All who came to the place where Asahel had fallen and died, halted. ²⁴ But Joab and Abishai continued the pursuit of Abner. The sun had gone down when they came to the hill of Ammah which lies east of the valley toward the wilderness near Geba.

**Truce Between Joab and Abner.** ²⁵ Here the Benjaminites rallied around Abner, forming a single group, and made a stand on a hilltop. ²⁶ Then Abner called to Joab and said: "Must the sword devour forever? Do you not know that afterward there will be bitterness? How long before you tell the people to stop pursuing their brothers?" ²⁷ Joab replied, "As

---

† **2:8** *Ishbaal:* here and elsewhere in the Hebrew text, his name appears as "Ishbosheth"; the second part of Ishbaal, *-baal*, refers to the Canaanite god Baal, and is therefore suppressed, replaced by *bosheth*, "shame."
**2:14** *Perform:* lit., "play."
**2:16** The nature of this gruesome game is not clear, and the place name is variously given in the older texts.

**2:2** 1 Sm 25:42–43.
**2:4** 1 Sm 31:11–13.
**2:8** 1 Sm 14:50.
**2:11** 2 Sm 5:5; 1 Kgs 2:11.
**2:18** 2 Sm 23:24; 1 Chr 2:16; 27:7.
**2:22** 2 Sm 3:27–28, 30.

2
S
M

God lives, if you had not spoken, it would be morning before the people would be stopped from pursuing their brothers." ²⁸ Joab then sounded the horn, and all the people came to a halt, pursuing Israel no farther and fighting no more. ²⁹ Abner and his men marched all night long through the Arabah, crossed the Jordan, marched all through the morning, and came to Mahanaim. ³⁰ Joab, coming from the pursuit of Abner, assembled all the men. Nineteen other servants of David were missing, besides Asahel. ³¹ But David's servants had struck down and killed three hundred and sixty men of Benjamin, followers of Abner. ³² They took up Asahel and buried him in his father's tomb in Bethlehem. Joab and his men made an all-night march, and dawn found them in Hebron.

**3** ¹ There followed a long war between the house of Saul and the house of David, in which David grew ever stronger, but the house of Saul ever weaker.

**Sons Born in Hebron.** ²* Sons were born to David in Hebron: his firstborn, Amnon, of Ahinoam from Jezreel; ³ the second, Chileab, of Abigail the wife of Nabal of Carmel; the third, Absalom, son of Maacah, who was the daughter of Talmai, king of Geshur;* ⁴ the fourth, Adonijah, son of Haggith; the fifth, Shephatiah, son of Abital;* ⁵ and the sixth, Ithream, by David's wife Eglah. These were born to David in Hebron.

**Ishbaal and Abner Quarrel.** ⁶ During the war between the house of Saul and the house of David, Abner was gaining power in the house of Saul. ⁷ Now Saul had had a concubine, Rizpah, the daughter of Aiah. And Ishbaal, son of Saul, said to Abner, "Why have you slept with my father's concubine?"†* ⁸ Enraged at the words of Ishbaal, Abner said, "Am I a dog's head from Judah? As of today, I have been loyal to the house of Saul your father, to his brothers and his friends, and I have kept you out of David's clutches; and today you charge me with a crime involving a woman! ⁹ May God do thus to Abner, and more, if I do not

carry out for David what the LORD swore to him—* ¹⁰ that is, take away the kingdom from the house of Saul and establish the throne of David over Israel as well as Judah, from Dan to Beer-sheba."* ¹¹ Ishbaal was no longer able to say a word to Abner, he feared him so.

**Abner and David Reconciled.** ¹² Then Abner sent messengers to David in Telam, where he was at the moment, to say, "Make a covenant with me, and you have me on your side, to bring all Israel over to you." ¹³ He replied, "Good, I will make a covenant with you. But one thing I require of you. You must not appear before me unless you bring back Michal, Saul's daughter, when you come to present yourself to me."* ¹⁴ At the same time David sent messengers to Ishbaal, son of Saul, to say, "Give me my wife Michal, whom I betrothed by paying a hundred Philistine foreskins." ¹⁵ Ishbaal sent for her and took her away from her husband Paltiel, son of Laish,* ¹⁶ who followed her weeping as far as Bahurim. But Abner said to him, "Go back!" So he turned back. ¹⁷ Abner then had a word with the elders of Israel: "For some time you have been wanting David as your king. ¹⁸ Now take action, for the LORD has said of David: By David my servant I will save my people Israel from the power of the Philistines and from the power of all their enemies." ¹⁹ Abner also spoke with Benjamin, and then went to speak with David in Hebron concerning all that would be agreeable to Israel and to the whole house of Benjamin. ²⁰ When Abner, accompanied by twenty men, came to David in Hebron, David prepared a feast for Abner and for the men who were with him. ²¹ Then Abner said to David, "I will now go to assemble all Israel for my lord the king, that they may make a covenant with you; you will then be king over all whom you wish to rule." So David let Abner go on his way in peace.

**Death of Abner.** ²² Just then David's servants and Joab were coming in from an expedition, bringing much plunder with them. Abner, having been dismissed by David, was no longer with him in Hebron but had gone on his way in peace. ²³ When Joab and the whole force

† **3:7** Asserting a right to the late king's harem was tantamount to claiming his kingship; cf. 16:21–22; 1 Kgs 2:21–22.

**3:2–5** 1 Chr 3:1–4.
**3:3** 2 Sm 13:37; 15:8.
**3:4** 1 Kgs 1:5.
**3:7** 2 Sm 16:21–22; 21:8–10;
1 Kgs 2:21–22.
**3:9** Ru 1:17.
**3:10** 2 Sm 5:2; 1 Sm 25:30.
**3:13** 1 Sm 18:20–27.
**3:15** 1 Sm 25:44.

he had with him arrived, he was informed, "Abner, son of Ner, came to David, and he let him go on his way in peace." 24 So Joab went to the king and said: "What have you done? Abner came to you! Why did you let him get away? 25 Don't you know Abner? He came to trick you, to learn your comings and goings, to learn everything you do." 26 Joab then left David and sent messengers after Abner to bring him back from the cistern of Sirah; but David did not know. 27 When Abner returned to Hebron, Joab took him aside within the city gate to speak with him privately. There he stabbed him in the abdomen, and he died for the blood of Asahel, Joab's brother.* 28 Later David heard of it and said: "Before the LORD, I and my kingdom are forever innocent.* 29 May the blood of Abner, son of Ner, be on the head of Joab and all his family. May Joab's family never be without one suffering from a discharge, or one with a skin disease, or a man who holds the distaff, or one falling by the sword, or one in need of food!"† 30 Joab and Abishai his brother had been lying in wait for Abner because he killed Asahel their brother in battle at Gibeon.

**David Mourns Abner.** 31 Then David said to Joab and to all the people who were with him, "Tear your garments, put on sackcloth, and mourn over Abner." King David himself followed the bier.* 32 When they had buried Abner in Hebron, the king wept aloud at the grave of Abner, and all the people wept. 33 And the king sang this lament over Abner:

Should Abner have died like a fool?
34    Your hands were not bound with chains,
        nor your feet placed in fetters;
As one falls before the wicked, you fell.

And all the people continued to weep for him. 35 Then they went to console David with food while it was still day. But David swore, "May God do thus to me, and more, if before the sun goes down I eat bread or anything else."* 36 All the people noted this with approval, just as everything the king did met with their approval. 37 So on that day all the people and all Israel came to know that it was not the king's doing that Abner, son of Ner, was put to death. 38 The king then said to his servants: "Do you not know that a prince, a great man, has fallen today in Israel. 39 Although I am the anointed king, I am weak this day, and these men, the sons of Zeruiah, are too ruthless for me. May the LORD repay the evildoer in accordance with his evil deed."*

**4 Death of Ishbaal.** 1 When Ishbaal, son of Saul, heard that Abner was dead in Hebron, he lost his resolve and all Israel was alarmed. 2 Ishbaal, son of Saul, had two company leaders named Baanah and Rechab, sons of Rimmon the Beerothite, of the tribe of Benjamin—Beeroth, too, was ascribed to Benjamin:* 3 the Beerothites fled to Gittaim, where they have been resident aliens to this day.* 4 (Jonathan, son of Saul, had a son with crippled feet. He was five years old when the news about Saul and Jonathan came from Jezreel; his nurse took him and fled, but in their hasty flight, he fell and became lame. His name was Meribbaal.)†* 5 The sons of Rimmon the Beerothite, Rechab and Baanah, came into the house of Ishbaal during the heat of the day, while he was lying on his bed in the afternoon. 6 The gatekeeper of the house had dozed off while sifting wheat, and was asleep. So Rechab and his brother Baanah slipped past her 7 and entered the house while Ishbaal was lying asleep in his bedroom. They struck and killed him, and cut off his head. Then, taking the head, they traveled on the Arabah road all night long.

**The Murder Avenged.** 8 They brought the head of Ishbaal to David in Hebron and said to the king: "This is the head of Ishbaal, son of your enemy Saul, who sought your life. Thus has the LORD this day avenged my lord the king on Saul and his posterity." 9 But David replied to Rechab and his brother Baanah, sons of Rimmon the Beerothite: "As the LORD lives, who

---

† **3:29** An assortment of imprecations, consisting of physical ailments, weakness, violent death, and poverty.
**4:4** *Meribbaal*: Hebrew has *mephiboseth*; see note on 2:8. His name, in fact, is Meribbaal; cf. 1 Chr 8:34; 9:40. He is the subject of chap. 9 below. The text of this verse may owe its present place to the fact that ancient copies of the Books of Samuel tended to confuse his name with that of his uncle

Ishbaal, Saul's son and successor, a principal figure in chaps. 2–4.

**3:27** 2 Sm 2:17–23; 1 Kgs 2:5, 31–33.
**3:28, 30** 2 Sm 2:22–23.
**3:31** 2 Sm 21:10.
**3:35** Ru 1:17.
**3:39** Ps 28:4; Is 3:11.
**4:2** 2 Sm 9:3; Jos 9:17–18.
**4:3** Jos 18:25.
**4:4** 2 Sm 9:3; 19:25.

rescued me from every distress: [10] the man who reported to me, 'Saul is dead,' and thought he was bringing good news, that man I seized and killed in Ziglag: that was the reward I gave him.* [11] How much more now, when wicked men have slain an innocent man in bed at home, must I require his blood from you and purge you from the land!" [12] So at David's command, the young men killed them and cut off their hands and feet, hanging them up near the pool in Hebron. But he took the head of Ishbaal and buried it in Abner's grave in Hebron.*

## 5 David King of Israel.

[1]* All the tribes of Israel came to David in Hebron, and they said: "Look! We are your bone and your flesh. [2] In days past, when Saul was still our king, you were the one who led Israel out in all its battles and brought it back. And the LORD said to you: You shall shepherd my people Israel; you shall be ruler over Israel."* [3] Then all the elders of Israel came to the king in Hebron, and at Hebron King David made a covenant with them in the presence of the LORD; and they anointed David king over Israel. [4] David was thirty years old when he became king, and he reigned forty years: [5] in Hebron he was king over Judah seven years and six months, and in Jerusalem he was king thirty-three years over all Israel and Judah.*

### Capture of Zion.†

[6]* Then the king and his men went to Jerusalem against the Jebusites who inhabited the land. They told David, "You shall not enter here: the blind and the lame will drive you away!" which was their way of saying, "David shall not enter here."* [7] David nevertheless captured the fortress of Zion, which is the City of David. [8] On that day David said: "All who wish to strike at the Jebusites must attack through the water shaft. The lame and the blind shall be the personal enemies of David." That is why it is said, "The blind and the lame shall not enter the palace."* [9] David took up residence in the fortress which he called the City of David. David built up the city on all sides, from the Millo toward the center.* [10] David became ever more powerful, for the LORD of hosts was with him.* [11]* Hiram, king of Tyre, sent envoys to David along with cedar wood, and carpenters and masons, who built a house for David.* [12] David now knew† that the LORD had truly established him as king over Israel and had exalted his kingdom for the sake of his people Israel.

### David's Family in Jerusalem.

[13]* David took more concubines and wives in Jerusalem after he had come from Hebron, and more sons and daughters were born to him. [14] These are the names of those who were born to him in Jerusalem: Shammua, Shobab, Nathan, Solomon, [15] Ibhar, Elishua, Nepheg, Japhia, [16] Elishama, Beeliada, and Eliphelet.

### Rout of the Philistines.

[17] When the Philistines had heard that David was anointed king over Israel, they marched out in force to come after him. When David heard this, he went down to the refuge.† [18] Meanwhile the Philistines had come and deployed themselves in the valley of Rephaim.† [19] David inquired of the LORD, "Shall I attack the Philistines, and will you deliver them into my power?" The LORD answered David: Attack, for I will surely deliver the Philistines into your power. [20] So David went to Baal-perazim,† and he defeated

---

5:6–12 David's most important military exploit, the taking of Jerusalem, is here presented before his battles with the Philistines, vv. 17–25, which took place earlier. The sense of vv. 6 and 8 is in doubt. Perhaps the Jebusites boasted that Jerusalem was impregnable, using a metaphorical or proverbial expression that claimed the city was defensible even by people not suited for military action. The saying then received a different sense (v. 8), to the effect that "the blind and the lame" were David's enemies. Mt 21:14 and Lk 14:13 seem to play off, and transform, this saying.

5:12 David now knew: Hiram's carpenters and masons built David a house of cedar, the very model of a Canaanite king's palace. This house then represented the consolidation of David's royal power, in the Canaanite mode, with Jerusalem as David's personal fiefdom and capital city.

5:17 Refuge: probably near Adullam (1 Sm 22:1–5).

5:18–25 The successive defeats of the Philistines in the valley of Rephaim southwest of Jerusalem had the effect of blocking their access to the mountain ridge near Gibeon, and confining them to their holdings on the coast and in the foothills beyond Gezer to the west and south.

5:20 Baal-perazim: here the title ba'al, "master, lord," refers to the Lord; perazim is the plural of perez, which means "breaking" or "bursting," as in 6:8.

---

4:10 2 Sm 1:6–10, 14, 16.
4:12 Dt 21:22–23; 1 Sm 31:10.
5:1–5 1 Chr 11:1–3.
5:2 2 Sm 3:10; Dt 17:15; 1 Sm 18:16.
5:5 2 Sm 2:11; 1 Kgs 2:11; 1 Chr 3:4.
5:6–10 1 Chr 11:4–9.
5:6 Jos 15:63; Jgs 1:19, 21; Is 29:3.

5:8 Lv 21:18; Mt 21:14–15.
5:9 1 Kgs 3:1; 9:15; 11:27.
5:10 Ps 78:70–72; 89; 132:13.
5:11–25 1 Chr 14:1–16.
5:11–12 1 Kgs 5:15; 1 Chr 14:1–2.
5:13–16 1 Chr 3:5–8; 14:3–7.

them there. He said, "The LORD has broken through my enemies before me just as water breaks through a dam." Therefore that place was called Baal-perazim. 21 The Philistines abandoned their gods there, and David and his men carried them away. 22 Once again the Philistines came up and deployed themselves in the valley of Rephaim, 23 and again David inquired of the LORD, who replied: Do not attack the front—circle behind them and come against them near the balsam trees. 24 When you hear the sound of marching† in the tops of the balsam trees, act decisively, for then the LORD has already gone before you to strike the army of the Philistines. 25 David did as the LORD commanded him, and routed the Philistines from Gibeon as far as Gezer.

**6** **The Ark Brought to Jerusalem.** 1* David again assembled all the picked men of Israel, thirty thousand in number. 2 Then David and all the people who were with him set out for Baala of Judah to bring up from there the ark of God, which bears the name "the LORD of hosts enthroned above the cherubim."* 3 They transported the ark of God on a new cart and took it away from the house of Abinadab on the hill. Uzzah and Ahio, sons of Abinadab, were guiding the cart,* 4 with Ahio walking before it, 5 while David and all the house of Israel danced before the LORD with all their might, with singing, and with lyres, harps, tambourines, sistrums, and cymbals.* 6 As they reached the threshing floor of Nodan, Uzzah stretched out his hand to the ark of God and steadied it, for the oxen were tipping it. 7 Then the LORD became angry with Uzzah; God struck him on that spot, and he died there in God's presence. 8 David was angry because the LORD's wrath had broken out against Uzzah. Therefore that place has been called Perez-uzzah† even to this day. 9 David became frightened of the LORD that day, and he said, "How can the ark of the LORD come

to me?" 10 So David was unwilling to take the ark of the LORD with him into the City of David. David deposited it instead at the house of Obed-edom the Gittite.

11 The ark of the LORD remained in the house of Obed-edom the Gittite for three months, and the LORD blessed Obed-edom and all his household.* 12* When it was reported to King David that the LORD had blessed the household of Obed-edom and all that he possessed because of the ark of God, David went to bring up the ark of God from the house of Obed-edom into the City of David with joy.* 13 As soon as the bearers of the ark of the LORD had advanced six steps, he sacrificed an ox and a fatling. 14 Then David came dancing before the LORD with abandon, girt with a linen ephod.†* 15 David and all the house of Israel were bringing up the ark of the LORD with shouts of joy and sound of horn. 16 As the ark of the LORD was entering the City of David, Michal, daughter of Saul, looked down from her window, and when she saw King David jumping and dancing before the LORD, she despised him in her heart. 17* They brought in the ark of the LORD and set it in its place within the tent which David had pitched for it. Then David sacrificed burnt offerings and communion offerings before the LORD. 18 When David had finished sacrificing burnt offerings and communion offerings, he blessed the people in the name of the LORD of hosts, 19 and distributed among all the people, the entire multitude of Israel, to every man and every woman, one loaf of bread, one piece of meat, and one raisin cake. Then all the people returned to their homes.

20† When David went home to bless his own house,* Michal, the daughter of Saul, came out to meet him and said, "How well the king of Israel has honored himself today, exposing himself to the view of the slave girls of his followers, as a commoner might expose himself!" 21 But David replied to Michal: "I

---

5:24 *Sound of marching*: the wind in the treetops suggestive of the footsteps of the Lord and the heavenly host.
6:8 *Perez-uzzah*: this Hebrew phrase means "the breaking out against Uzzah"; see note on 5:20.
6:14 *Girt with a linen ephod*: the ephod was some sort of priestly vestment (probably like an apron); cf. Ex 28:4; Jgs 17:5; 1 Sm 2:18, 28; 14:3; 22:18; 23:6. The cultic procession that accompanies the ark to the holy mountain, Zion, is led by King David, dancing ecstatically and wearing a priestly vestment.
6:20–23 Michal's reaction to David's dancing comes from her conception of how a king should comport himself. David

rejects this understanding, saying he needs no instruction from the house of the failed king, Saul.

6:1–11 1 Chr 13:1–14.
6:2 Ex 25:10; Jos 15:9; 1 Chr 13:6; Ps 132:8–10.
6:3 1 Sm 4:3–4; 6:7–8; 7:1; Dn 3:55.
6:5 Ps 68:24–25; 150:3–5.
6:11 1 Chr 26:4.
6:12–23 1 Chr 15:1–29; Ps 24:7–10.
6:12 1 Kgs 8:1.
6:14 1 Sm 2:18.
6:17–19 Lv 1:1–17; 3:1–17; 1 Chr 16:1–3.
6:20 1 Chr 16:43.

was dancing before the LORD. As the LORD lives, who chose me over your father and all his house when he appointed me ruler over the LORD's people, Israel, not only will I make merry before the LORD,* ²²but I will demean myself even more. I will be lowly in your eyes, but in the eyes of the slave girls you spoke of I will be somebody." ²³Saul's daughter Michal was childless to the day she died.

**7** **The Oracle of Nathan.** ¹*After the king had taken up residence in his house, and the LORD had given him rest from his enemies on every side,* ²the king said to Nathan the prophet, "Here I am living in a house of cedar, but the ark of God dwells in a tent!"* ³Nathan answered the king, "Whatever is in your heart, go and do, for the LORD is with you."* ⁴But that same night the word of the LORD came to Nathan: ⁵Go and tell David my servant, Thus says the LORD: Is it you who would build me a house to dwell in?* ⁶I have never dwelt in a house from the day I brought Israel up from Egypt to this day, but I have been going about in a tent or a tabernacle. ⁷As long as I have wandered about among the Israelites, did I ever say a word to any of the judges whom I commanded to shepherd my people Israel: Why have you not built me a house of cedar?

⁸Now then, speak thus to my servant David, Thus says the LORD of hosts:† I took you from the pasture, from following the flock, to become ruler over my people Israel.* ⁹I was with you wherever you went, and I cut down all your enemies before you. And I will make your name like that of the greatest on earth.* ¹⁰I will assign a place for my people Israel and I will plant them in it to dwell there; they will never again be disturbed, nor shall the wicked

ever again oppress them, as they did at the beginning, ¹¹and from the day when I appointed judges over my people Israel. I will give you rest from all your enemies. Moreover, the LORD also declares to you that the LORD will make a house for you:* ¹²*when your days have been completed and you rest with your ancestors, I will raise up your offspring after you, sprung from your loins, and I will establish his kingdom. ¹³He it is† who shall build a house for my name, and I will establish his royal throne forever. ¹⁴I will be a father to him, and he shall be a son to me. If he does wrong, I will reprove him with a human rod and with human punishments;* ¹⁵but I will not withdraw my favor from him as I withdrew it from Saul who was before you.* ¹⁶Your house and your kingdom are firm forever before me; your throne shall be firmly established forever.†* ¹⁷In accordance with all these words and this whole vision Nathan spoke to David.

**David's Thanksgiving.** ¹⁸Then King David went in and sat in the LORD's presence and said, "Who am I, Lord GOD, and what is my house, that you should have brought me so far?* ¹⁹And yet even this is too little in your sight, Lord GOD! For you have made a promise regarding your servant's house reaching into the future, and giving guidance to the people, Lord GOD! ²⁰What more can David say to you? You know† your servant, Lord GOD! ²¹For your servant's sake and as you have had at heart, you have brought about this whole magnificent disclosure to your servant. ²²Therefore, great are you, Lord GOD! There is no one like you, no God but you, as we have always heard.* ²³What other nation on earth is there like your people Israel? What god has ever led a

---

**7:8–16** The message Nathan delivers to David, called the Dynastic Oracle, is prompted by David's intention to build a house (i.e., a temple) for the Lord, like David's own house (i.e., palace) of cedar. David is told, in effect, not to bother building a house for the Lord; rather, the Lord will make a house for him—a dynasty, the House of David. Not only will he have descendants (v. 12) who will sit upon the throne of Israel (v. 13), their rule will last forever (vv. 13, 16); and even if they transgress the Lord's commands, the line of David will never be removed from kingship as Saul was (cf. 1 Sm 13; 15). The oracle establishes the Davidic king as standing in relationship to the Lord as a son to a father (v. 14; cf. Ps 2:7; 89:27). The Dynastic Oracle, with cognate texts in the Scriptures, is the basis for Jewish expectations of an anointed king (1 Sm 12:3, 5), son of David (Mt 21:9); cf. Acts 2:30; Heb 1:5.

**7:13** *He it is*: Solomon, in the event.

**7:16** The unconditional promise made here, and reflected in Ps 89:34–35, stands in contrast to the tradition in Ps 132:12, where the continuation of the line of David depends on their

fidelity to the Lord; cf. also 1 Kgs 2:4; 6:12; 8:25.

**7:20** *Know*: give recognition, choose, single out: cf. Gn 18:19; Ex 33:12; Am 3:2.

| | |
|---|---|
| **6:21** 1 Sm 13:14; 15:28. | 1 Chr 22:10; 2 Chr |
| **7:1–29** 1 Chr 17:1–27. | 7:18; Ps 89:4, 26–29, |
| **7:1** Dt 12:10; 25:19; | 36–37; Lk 1:32; Heb |
| 1 Kgs 5:4. | 1:5. |
| **7:2** Ex 39:32. | **7:14** Ps 2:7; 89:26; Prv |
| **7:3** Ps 132:1–5. | 3:12. |
| **7:5** 1 Kgs 5:3; 8:16, 27; | **7:15** 2 Sm 23:5; 1 Sm |
| 1 Chr 22:8; 28:3; Is | 13:14; 15:26, |
| 66:1; Acts 7:48–49. | 28; 2 Kgs 19:34; |
| **7:8** 1 Sm 16:13; 17:15– | 1 Chr 17:11–14; Ps |
| 20; Ps 78:70–71; Am | 89:33–34. |
| 7:14–15. | **7:16** 2 Sm 23:5; Dn 2:44; |
| **7:9** Ps 89:27. | 1 Mc 2:57; Mk 11:10; |
| **7:11** 2 Sm 23:5; 1 Kgs | Lk 1:32–33; Heb 1:8. |
| 2:4–24. | **7:18** 1 Chr 17:16. |
| **7:12–15** 1 Kgs 5:19; 8:19; | **7:22** Ex 15:11; Is 45:5. |

nation, redeeming it as his people and making a name by great and awesome deeds, as you drove out the nations and their gods before your people, whom you redeemed for yourself from Egypt?* 24* You have established for yourself your people Israel as your people forever, and you, Lord, have become their God. 25 Now, Lord God, confirm the promise that you have spoken concerning your servant and his house forever. Bring about what you have promised 26 so that your name may be forever great. People will say: 'The Lord of hosts is God over Israel,' when the house of your servant David is established in your presence. 27 Because you, Lord of hosts, God of Israel, have revealed to your servant, 'I will build you a house,' your servant now finds the courage to make this prayer before you. 28 Since you, Lord God, are truly God and your words are truth and you have made this generous promise to your servant,* 29 do, then, bless the house of your servant, that it may be in your presence forever—since you, Lord God, have promised, and by your blessing the house of your servant shall be blessed forever."

**8** **Summary of David's Wars.** 1* After this, David defeated the Philistines and subdued them; and David took...† from the Philistines. 2 He also defeated Moab and measured them with a line. Making them lie down on the ground, he measured two lengths of line for death, and a full length for life.† Thus the Moabites became subject to David, paying tribute. 3* David then defeated Hadadezer, son of Rehob, king of Zobah, when he went to reestablish his dominion at the River.* 4 David captured from him one thousand seven hundred horsemen and twenty thousand foot soldiers. David hamstrung all the chariot horses, but left one hundred for his chariots.* 5 The

Arameans of Damascus came to help Hadadezer, king of Zobah, but David also defeated twenty-two thousand of them in Aram. 6 David then placed garrisons in the Damascus region of Aram, and the Arameans became David's subjects, paying tribute. The Lord brought David victory in all his undertakings. 7 David took the golden shields that were carried by Hadadezer's attendants and brought them to Jerusalem. (These Shishak, king of Egypt, took away when he came to Jerusalem in the days of Rehoboam, son of Solomon.) 8 From Tebah and Berothai, cities of Hadadezer, King David removed a very large quantity of bronze. 9 When Toi, king of Hamath, heard that David had defeated the entire army of Hadadezer, 10 Toi sent his son Hadoram to wish King David well and to congratulate him on having waged a victorious war against Hadadezer; for Hadadezer had been at war with Toi. Hadoram also brought with him articles of silver, gold, and bronze. 11 These also King David consecrated to the Lord along with the silver and gold that he had taken for this purpose from all the nations he had subdued: 12 from Edom, Moab, the Ammonites, the Philistines, and Amalek, and from the spoils of Hadadezer, son of Rehob, king of Zobah.

13 On his return,† David made a name for himself by defeating eighteen thousand Edomites in the Valley of Salt.* 14 He set up garrisons in Edom, and all the Edomites became David's subjects. Thus the Lord brought David victory in all his undertakings.

**David's Officials.** 15* David was king over all Israel; he dispensed justice and right to all his people. 16 Joab, son of Zeruiah, was in command of the army. Jehoshaphat, son of Ahilud, was chancellor. 17 Zadok, son of Ahitub, and Ahimelech, son of Abiathar, were priests.†

---

**8:1** *David took...:* the original Hebrew seems irretrievable. The transmitted text gives "the bridle of the cubit"; 1 Chr 18:1 understood "Gath and its towns"; others implausibly read "dominion of the capital city."

**8:2** *Two lengths...a full length for life:* usually taken to mean that two-thirds of them were executed; but it could mean that two-thirds were spared, if the line was used full length in their case but doubled on itself to make "two lines" for those to be put to death. Note the contrasting good relations in 1 Sm 22:3–4.

**8:13** *On his return:* possibly to Jerusalem, after the revolt of Absalom (chaps. 15–18), which this catalogue of victories would avoid mentioning. 1 Chr 18:12 attributes the defeat of the Edomites to Abishai, while the superscription of Ps 60 attributes it to Joab.

**8:17** *Zadok...Ahimelech, son of Abiathar, were priests:* the names of Abiathar and Ahimelech are frequently associated

with David (1 Sm 22:20; 23:6; 30:7; 2 Sm 15:24, 29, 35; 17:15; 19:12; 20:25), but they show Abiathar acting as priest, not Ahimelech: Abiathar shared the priestly office with Zadok in David's reign and even during Solomon's early years (1 Kgs 2:26; 4:4). Ahimelech was the name of Abiathar's father. This verse and 1 Chr 18:16 may indicate that Abiathar had a son named Ahimelech who also acted as a priest, like his father and his namesake grandfather, in the last years of David.

---

| | |
|---|---|
| **7:23** Dt 4:7, 34. | **8:3** 2 Sm 10:6; 1 Kgs |
| **7:24–25** Ex 6:7; Dt 7:6; 26:17; | 11:23. |
| 29:13. | **8:4** Jos 11:6, 9. |
| **7:28** Nm 23:19; Jn 17:17. | **8:13** 2 Kgs 14:7. |
| **8:1–18** 1 Chr 18:1–17. | **8:15–18** 2 Sm 20:23–26; |
| **8:3–8** 2 Sm 10:15–19. | 1 Kgs 4:1–6; 1 Chr |
| | 18:14–17. |

Shavsha was scribe. [18]Benaiah, son of Jehoi-ada, was in command of the Cherethites and the Pelethites; and David's sons were priests.*

## 9 David and Meribbaal.

[1]David asked, "Is there any survivor of Saul's house to whom I may show kindness for the sake of Jonathan?"* [2]Now there was an official of the house of Saul named Ziba. He was summoned to David, and the king asked him, "Are you Ziba?" He replied, "Your servant."* [3]Then the king asked, "Is there any survivor of Saul's house to whom I may show God's kindness?" Ziba answered the king, "There is still Jonathan's son, the one whose feet are crippled."* [4]The king asked him, "Where is he?" and Ziba answered the king, "He is in the house of Machir, son of Ammiel, in Lodebar."* [5]So King David sent for him and had him brought from the house of Machir, son of Ammiel, from Lodebar. [6]When Meribbaal, son of Jonathan, son of Saul, came to David, he fell face down in homage. David said, "Meribbaal," and he answered, "Your servant." [7]"Do not be afraid," David said to him, "I will surely be kind to you for the sake of Jonathan your father. I will restore to you all the lands of Saul your grandfather, and you shall eat at my table always." [8]Bowing low, he answered, "What am I, your servant, that you should pay attention to a dead dog like me?"* [9]The king then called Ziba, Saul's attendant, and said to him: "All that belonged to Saul and to his entire house, I am giving to your lord's son. [10]You and your sons and servants must till the land for him. You shall bring in the produce, which shall be food for your lord's household to eat. But Meribbaal, your lord's son, shall always eat at my table." Now Ziba had fifteen sons and twenty servants. [11]Ziba answered the king, "Whatever my lord the king commands his servant, so shall your servant do." And so Meribbaal ate at David's table like one of the king's sons.* [12]Meribbaal had a young son whose name was Mica; and all the tenants of Ziba's household worked for Meribbaal.* [13]But Meribbaal lived in Jerusalem, because he always ate at the king's table. He was lame in both feet.*

## 10 Campaigns Against Ammon.

[1]* After this,† the king of the Ammonites died, and Hanun his son succeeded him as king. [2]David said, "I will show kindness to Hanun, the son of Nahash, as his father showed kindness to me." Therefore David sent his servants to Hanun to console him concerning his father. But when David's servants had entered the land of the Ammonites, [3]the Ammonite princes said to their lord Hanun, "Do you think David is doing this—sending you these consolers—to honor your father? Is it not rather to explore the city, to spy on it, and to overthrow it, that David has sent his servants to you?" [4]So Hanun seized David's servants, shaved off half their beards, cut away the lower halves of their garments at the buttocks, and sent them away.* [5]David was told of it and he sent word for them to be intercepted, for the men had been greatly disgraced. "Remain at Jericho," the king told them, "until your beards have grown again; then come back here."

[6]† When the Ammonites realized that they were in bad odor with David, they sent for and hired twenty thousand Aramean foot soldiers from Beth-rehob and Zobah, as well as the king of Maacah with one thousand men, and twelve thousand men from Tob.*

[7]When David heard of this, he sent Joab and his whole army of warriors against them.* [8]The Ammonites marched out and lined up for battle at the entrance of their city gate, while the Arameans of Zobah and Rehob and the men of Tob and Maacah remained apart in the open field. [9]When Joab saw that there was a battle line both in front of and behind him, he chose some of the best fighters of Israel and lined them up against the Arameans; [10]the rest of the army he placed under the command of his brother Abishai and lined up to oppose the Ammonites. [11]And he said, "If the Arameans prove too strong for me, you must come

**10:1** *After this:* early in the reign of David, since Hanun's father Nahash (1 Chr 19:1) had been ruling in Ammon at the beginning of Saul's reign (1 Sm 11) and Solomon was not yet born (2 Sm 11:1; 12:24).

**10:6–9** A Hebrew text from Qumran (4QSamª) comes closer in these verses to what is given in 1 Chr 19:6–9. The scene of the conflict is more likely the Ammonite capital, Rabbath-Ammon (v. 8; cf. Josephus *Ant.*, vii, 123), than Medeba (1 Chr 19:7).

| | |
|---|---|
| **8:18** 2 Sm 15:18; 20:7, 23; 23:20. | **9:8** 1 Sm 24:15. |
| **9:1** 2 Sm 21:7; 1 Sm 18:1–4; 20:8–10, 15–17, 42. | **9:11** 2 Sm 19:29. |
| | **9:12** 1 Chr 8:34. |
| | **9:13** 2 Sm 21:7. |
| **9:2** 2 Sm 16:1–4; 19:27. | **10:1–19** 1 Chr 19:1–19. |
| **9:3** 2 Sm 4:4. | **10:4** Is 20:4. |
| **9:4** 2 Sm 17:27. | **10:6** 2 Sm 8:3; 1 Sm 14:47. |
| | **10:7** 2 Sm 11:1. |

and save me; and if the Ammonites prove too strong for you, I will come to save you. ¹²Hold firm and let us show ourselves courageous for the sake of our people and the cities of our God; and may the LORD do what is good in his sight." ¹³Joab therefore advanced with his men for battle with the Arameans, but they fled before him. ¹⁴And when the Ammonites saw that the Arameans had fled, they too fled before Abishai, and reentered their city. Joab then ceased his attack on the Ammonites and came to Jerusalem. ¹⁵*Seeing themselves vanquished by Israel, the Arameans held a full muster of troops. ¹⁶Hadadezer sent for and brought Arameans from beyond the River. They came to Helam, with Shobach, the captain of Hadadezer's army, at their head. ¹⁷When this was reported to David, he gathered all Israel together, crossed the Jordan, and went to Helam. The Arameans drew up in formation against David and gave battle. ¹⁸But the Arameans fled before Israel, and David killed seven hundred of their chariot fighters and forty thousand of their foot soldiers. He struck down Shobach, commander of the army, and he died on the field. ¹⁹When Hadadezer's vassal kings saw themselves vanquished by Israel, they made peace with the Israelites and became their subjects. After this, the Arameans were afraid to give further aid to the Ammonites.

# 11 David's Sin.
¹At the turn of the year,† the time when kings go to war, David sent out Joab along with his officers and all Israel, and they laid waste the Ammonites and besieged Rabbah. David himself remained in Jerusalem.* ²One evening David rose from his bed and strolled about on the roof of the king's house. From the roof he saw a woman bathing; she was very beautiful. ³David sent people to inquire about the woman and was told, "She is Bathsheba, daughter of Eliam, and wife of Uriah the Hittite, Joab's armorbearer."* ⁴Then David sent messengers and took her. When she came to him, he took her to bed, at a time when she was just purified after her period; and she returned to her house. * ⁵But the woman had become pregnant; she sent a message to inform David, "I am pregnant."

⁶So David sent a message to Joab, "Send me Uriah the Hittite." Joab sent Uriah to David. ⁷And when he came, David asked him how Joab was, how the army was, and how the war was going, and Uriah answered that all was well. ⁸David then said to Uriah, "Go down to your house and bathe your feet." Uriah left the king's house, and a portion from the king's table was sent after him. ⁹But Uriah slept at the entrance of the king's house with the other officers of his lord, and did not go down to his own house. ¹⁰David was told, "Uriah has not gone down to his house." So he said to Uriah, "Have you not come from a journey? Why, then, did you not go down to your house?" ¹¹Uriah answered David, "The ark and Israel and Judah are staying in tents, and my lord Joab and my lord's servants are encamped in the open field. Can I go home to eat and to drink and to sleep with my wife? As the LORD lives and as you live, I will do no such thing." * ¹²Then David said to Uriah, "Stay here today also, and tomorrow I will send you back." So Uriah stayed in Jerusalem that day. On the following day, ¹³David summoned him, and he ate and drank with David, who got him drunk. But in the evening he went out to sleep on his bed among his lord's servants, and did not go down to his house. ¹⁴The next morning David wrote a letter to Joab which he sent by Uriah. ¹⁵This is what he wrote in the letter: "Place Uriah up front, where the fighting is fierce. Then pull back and leave him to be struck down dead." ¹⁶So while Joab was besieging the city, he assigned Uriah to a place where he knew the defenders were strong. ¹⁷When the men of the city made a sortie against Joab, some officers of David's army fell, and Uriah the Hittite also died.

¹⁸Then Joab sent David a report of all the details of the battle, ¹⁹instructing the messenger, "When you have finished giving the king all the details of the battle, ²⁰the king may become angry and say to you: 'Why did you go near the city to fight? Did you not know that they would shoot from the wall above? ²¹Who killed Abimelech, son of Jerubbaal? Was it not a woman who threw a millstone down on him from the wall above, so that he died in Thebez? Why did you go near the wall?' Then

---

† **11:1** *At the turn of the year*: in the spring.

**10:15–19** 2 Sm 8:3–8; 1 Chr 9:16–19.
**11:1** 2 Sm 10:7; 1 Chr 20:1.
**11:3** 2 Sm 23:39.
**11:4** Lv 15:19.
**11:11** 1 Sm 4:3–4.

you in turn are to say, 'Your servant Uriah the Hittite is also dead.'"* ²²The messenger set out, and on his arrival he reported to David everything Joab had sent him to tell.† ²³He told David: "The men had the advantage over us and came out into the open against us, but we pushed them back to the entrance of the city gate. ²⁴Then the archers shot at your servants from the wall above, and some of the king's servants died; and your servant Uriah the Hittite is also dead." ²⁵David said to the messenger: "This is what you shall say to Joab: 'Do not let this be a great evil in your sight, for the sword devours now here and now there. Strengthen your attack on the city and destroy it.' Encourage him."

²⁶When the wife of Uriah heard that her husband had died, she mourned her lord. ²⁷But once the mourning was over, David sent for her and brought her into his house. She became his wife and bore him a son. But in the sight of the LORD what David had done was evil.

**12** **Nathan's Parable.**† ¹The LORD sent Nathan to David, and when he came to him, he said: "Tell me how you judge this case: In a certain town there were two men, one rich, the other poor.* ²The rich man had flocks and herds in great numbers. ³But the poor man had nothing at all except one little ewe lamb that he had bought. He nourished her, and she grew up with him and his children. Of what little he had she ate; from his own cup she drank; in his bosom she slept; she was like a daughter to him. ⁴Now, a visitor came to the rich man, but he spared his own flocks and herds to prepare a meal for the traveler who had come to him: he took the poor man's ewe lamb and prepared it for the one who had come to him." ⁵David grew very angry with that man and said to Nathan:

"As the LORD lives, the man who has done this deserves death! ⁶He shall make fourfold restitution† for the lamb because he has done this and was unsparing."* ⁷Then Nathan said to David: "You are the man!

**Nathan's Indictment.** "Thus says the LORD God of Israel: I anointed you king over Israel. I delivered you from the hand of Saul.* ⁸I gave you your lord's house and your lord's wives for your own. I gave you the house of Israel and of Judah. And if this were not enough, I could count up for you still more. ⁹Why have you despised the LORD and done what is evil in his sight? You have cut down Uriah the Hittite with the sword; his wife you took as your own, and him you killed with the sword of the Ammonites. ¹⁰Now, therefore, the sword shall never depart from your house, because you have despised me and have taken the wife of Uriah the Hittite to be your wife.* ¹¹Thus says the LORD: I will bring evil upon you out of your own house. I will take your wives before your very eyes, and will give them to your neighbor: he shall lie with your wives in broad daylight.†* ¹²You have acted in secret, but I will do this in the presence of all Israel, in the presence of the sun itself."

**David's Repentance.** ¹³Then David said to Nathan, "I have sinned against the LORD." Nathan answered David: "For his part, the LORD has removed your sin. You shall not die,* ¹⁴but since you have utterly spurned the LORD by this deed, the child born to you will surely die." ¹⁵Then Nathan returned to his house.

The LORD struck the child that the wife of Uriah had borne to David, and it became desperately ill. ¹⁶David pleaded with God on behalf of the child. He kept a total fast, and spent the night lying on the ground clothed in sackcloth. ¹⁷The elders of his house stood beside

---

† **11:22–24** In these verses the Greek text has David, angry with Joab, repeat exactly the questions Joab had foreseen in vv. 20–21. In v. 24 of our oldest Greek text, the messenger specifies that about eighteen men were killed. The Greek is considerably longer than the transmitted Hebrew text, suggesting that the Hebrew may have lost some sentences.

**12:1–7** David has committed adultery with Bathsheba and arranged the death of her husband. Instead of directly indicting the king for this criminal abuse of his royal authority, the prophet Nathan tells David a story. In the story, a parable of David's own actions, a powerful man takes cruel advantage of his vulnerable neighbor. Hearing the story, David is outraged and denounces the rich man—thus unwittingly pronouncing judgment on himself ("You are the man," v. 7).

**12:6** *Fourfold restitution:* David's judgment foreshadows the deaths of four of his own sons: the child born of his adulterous union with Bathsheba (v. 18); Amnon (13:28–29); Absalom (18:15; 19:1); and Adonijah (1 Kgs 2:24–25).

**12:11** *In broad daylight:* lit., "before the eyes of the sun"; the phrase echoes "before your very eyes" and anticipates "in the presence of the sun itself" (v. 12). The reference is to Absalom's action in appropriating his father's harem (16:22).

*
**11:21** Jgs 9:50–54.       18:14.
**12:1** Sir 47:1.       **12:11** 2 Sm 16:21–22.
**12:6** Ex 21:37; Lk 19:8.     **12:13** 1 Kgs 21:29; Ps 32:5;
**12:7** 1 Sm 16:13.       51:4; Sir 47:11.
**12:10** 2 Sm 13:28–29;

him to get him to rise from the ground; but he would not, nor would he take food with them. 18 On the seventh day, the child died. David's servants were afraid to tell him that the child was dead, for they said: "When the child was alive, we spoke to him, but he would not listen to what we said. How can we tell him the child is dead? He may do some harm!" 19 But David noticed his servants whispering among themselves and realized that the child was dead. He asked his servants, "Is the child dead?" They said, "Yes." 20 Rising from the ground, David washed and anointed himself, and changed his clothes. Then he went to the house of the LORD and worshiped. He returned to his own house and asked for food; they set it before him, and he ate. 21 His servants said to him: "What is this you are doing? While the child was living, you fasted and wept and kept vigil; now that the child is dead, you rise and take food." 22 He replied: "While the child was living, I fasted and wept, thinking, 'Who knows? The LORD may grant me the child's life.' 23 But now he is dead. Why should I fast? Can I bring him back again? I shall go to him, but he will not return to me."* 24 Then David consoled Bathsheba his wife. He went and slept with her; and she conceived and bore him a son, who was named Solomon. The LORD loved him 25 and sent the prophet Nathan to name him Jedidiah,† on behalf of the LORD.

**End of the Ammonite War.** 26* Joab fought against Rabbah of the Ammonites and captured that royal city. 27 He sent messengers to David to say: "I have fought against Rabbah and have taken the water-city. 28 Therefore, assemble the rest of the soldiers, join the siege against the city, and capture it, lest I be the one to capture the city and mine be the name people mention, not yours." 29 So David assembled the rest of the soldiers, went to Rabbah, fought against it, and captured it. 30 He took the crown of Milcom from the idol's head, a talent† of gold in weight, with precious stones; this crown David wore on his own head. He also brought out a great amount of spoil from the city. 31 He deported the people of the city

and set them to work with saws, iron picks, and iron axes, or put them to work at the brickmold. He dealt thus with all the cities of the Ammonites. Then David and his whole army returned to Jerusalem.

**13** **Amnon's Rape of Tamar.** 1 After this, the following occurred. David's son Absalom had a beautiful sister named Tamar, and David's son Amnon loved her.* 2 He was in such anguish over his sister Tamar that he became sick; she was a virgin, and Amnon thought it impossible to do anything to her. 3 Now Amnon had a friend named Jonadab, son of David's brother Shimeah, who was very clever.†* 4 He asked him, "Prince, why are you so dejected morning after morning? Why not tell me?" So Amnon said to him, "I am in love with Tamar, my brother Absalom's sister." 5 Then Jonadab replied, "Lie down on your bed and pretend to be sick. When your father comes to visit you, say to him, 'Please let my sister Tamar come and encourage me to take food. If she prepares something in my presence, for me to see, I will eat it from her hand.'" 6 So Amnon lay down and pretended to be sick. When the king came to visit him, Amnon said to the king, "Please let my sister Tamar come and prepare some fried cakes before my eyes, that I may take food from her hand."

7 David then sent home a message to Tamar, "Please go to the house of your brother Amnon and prepare some food for him." 8 Tamar went to the house of her brother Amnon, who was in bed. Taking dough and kneading it, she twisted it into cakes before his eyes and fried the cakes. 9 Then she took the pan and set out the cakes before him. But Amnon would not eat; he said, "Have everyone leave me." When they had all left him, 10 Amnon said to Tamar, "Bring the food into the bedroom, that I may have it from your hand." So Tamar picked up the cakes she had prepared and brought them to her brother Amnon in the bedroom. 11 But when she brought them close to him so he could eat, he seized her and said to her, "Come! Lie with me, my sister!" 12 But she answered him, "No, my brother! Do not

---

† **12:25** *Jedidiah*: the name means "beloved of Yhwh."
**12:30** *A talent*: since this would normally be more than seventy-five pounds, the report may have been embellished.
**13:3** *Clever*: lit., "wise." Jonadab's "wisdom" extends only to sly cleverness in getting things done; he devises the plan that will enable Amnon to pursue his infatuation. In the

categories of the Old Testament wisdom tradition, Jonadab is a fool.

* **12:23** Jb 7:9–10.     **13:1** 2 Sm 3:2–3; 1 Chr 3:9.
**12:26–31** 1 Chr 20:1–3.     **13:3** 2 Sm 21:21.

force me! This is not done in Israel. Do not commit this terrible crime.* ¹³Where would I take my shame? And you would be labeled a fool in Israel.† So please, speak to the king; he will not keep me from you."* ¹⁴But he would not listen to her; he was too strong for her: he forced her down and raped her. ¹⁵Then Amnon felt intense hatred for her; the hatred he felt for her far surpassed the love he had had for her. Amnon said to her, "Get up, leave." ¹⁶She replied, "No, brother, because sending me away would be far worse than this evil thing you have done to me." He would not listen to her, ¹⁷but called the youth who was his attendant and said, "Send this girl outside, away from me, and bar the door after her." ¹⁸Now she had on a long tunic, for that is how virgin princesses dressed in olden days. When his attendant put her out and barred the door after her, ¹⁹Tamar put ashes on her head and tore the long tunic in which she was clothed. Then, putting her hands to her head, she went away crying loudly. ²⁰Her brother Absalom said to her: "Has your brother Amnon been with you? Keep still now, my sister; he is your brother. Do not take this so to heart." So Tamar remained, devastated, in the house of her brother Absalom. ²¹King David, when he heard of the whole affair, became very angry. He would not, however, antagonize Amnon, his high-spirited son; he loved him, because he was his firstborn. ²²And Absalom said nothing, good or bad, to Amnon; but Absalom hated Amnon for having humiliated his sister Tamar.

**Absalom's Plot.** ²³Two years went by. It was sheep-shearing time for Absalom in Baal-hazor near Ephraim, and Absalom invited all the king's sons. ²⁴Absalom went to the king and said: "Your servant has hired the shearers. Please, may the king come with all his servants to your servant." ²⁵But the king said to Absalom, "No, my son, all of us should not go lest we be a burden to you." And though Absalom urged him, he would not go but began to bid him good-bye. ²⁶Absalom then said, "If not you, then please let my brother Amnon come with us." The king asked him, "Why should he go with you?" ²⁷But at Absalom's urging, the

king sent Amnon and with him all his other sons. Absalom prepared a banquet fit for a king. ²⁸*But Absalom had instructed his attendants: "Now watch! When Amnon is merry with wine and I say to you, 'Kill Amnon,' put him to death. Do not be afraid, for it is I who order you to do it. Be strong and act like warriors."

**Death of Amnon.** ²⁹When the attendants did to Amnon as Absalom had commanded, all the king's other sons rose up, mounted their mules, and fled. ³⁰While they were still on the road, a report reached David: "Absalom has killed all the king's sons and not one of them is left." ³¹The king stood up, tore his garments, and lay on the ground. All his servants standing by him also tore their garments.* ³²But Jonadab, son of David's brother Shimeah, spoke up: "Let not my lord think that all the young men, the king's sons, have been killed! Amnon alone is dead, for Absalom was set on this ever since Amnon humiliated his sister Tamar. ³³Now let my lord the king not take so to heart that report, 'All the king's sons are dead.' Amnon alone is dead." ³⁴Meanwhile, Absalom had taken flight. Then the servant on watch looked out and saw a large group coming down the slope from the direction of Bahurim. He came in and reported this to the king: "I saw some men coming down the mountainside from the direction of Bahurim." ³⁵So Jonadab said to the king: "There! The king's sons have come. It is as your servant said." ³⁶No sooner had he finished speaking than the king's sons came in, weeping aloud. The king, too, and all his servants wept very bitterly. ³⁷But Absalom, who had taken flight, went to Talmai, son of Ammihud, king of Geshur,* ³⁸and stayed in Geshur for three years. ³⁹All that time the king continued to mourn his son; but his intention of going out against Absalom abated as he was consoled over the death of Amnon.

# 14 The Wise Woman of Tekoa. ¹Now Joab, son of Zeruiah, knew how the king felt toward Absalom. ²Joab sent to Tekoa and brought from there a wise woman, to whom he said: "Pretend to be in mourning. Put on

**13:13** *A fool in Israel*: a play on *nebala* (v. 12), "terrible crime," lit., "folly."

**13:12** Lv 18:9; 20:17; Dt 22:21; 27:22.
**13:13** Gn 34:7–8.
**13:28–29** 2 Sm 12:10.
**13:31** 2 Sm 1:11.
**13:37** 2 Sm 3:3; 15:8.

mourning apparel and do not anoint yourself with oil, that you may appear to be a woman who has long been mourning someone dead. ³Then go to the king and speak to him in this manner." And Joab told her what to say.

⁴So the woman of Tekoa went to the king and fell to the ground in homage, saying, "Help, O king!" ⁵*The king said to her, "What do you want?" She replied: "Alas, I am a widow; my husband is dead. ⁶Your servant had two sons, who quarreled in the field, with no one to part them, and one of them struck his brother and killed him. ⁷Then the whole clan confronted your servant and demanded: 'Give up the one who struck down his brother. We must put him to death for the life of his brother whom he has killed; we must do away with the heir also.' Thus they will quench my remaining hope† and leave my husband neither name nor posterity upon the earth."* ⁸The king then said to the woman: "Go home. I will issue a command on your behalf." ⁹The woman of Tekoa answered him, "Upon me and my family be the blame, my lord king; the king and his throne are innocent." ¹⁰Then the king said, "If anyone says a word to you, have him brought to me, and he shall not touch you again." ¹¹But she said, "Please, let the king remember the Lord your God, that the avenger of blood may not go too far in destruction and that my son may not be done away with." He replied, "As the Lord lives, not a hair of your son shall fall to the ground."

¹²But the woman continued, "Please let your servant say still another word to my lord the king." He replied, "Speak." ¹³So the woman said: "Why, then, do you think the way you do against the people of God? In pronouncing as he has, the king shows himself guilty, in not bringing back his own banished son. ¹⁴We must indeed die; we are then like water that is poured out on the ground and cannot be gathered up. Yet, though God does not bring back to life, he does devise means so as not to banish† anyone from him.* ¹⁵And now, if I have presumed to speak to the king of this matter, it is because the people have given me cause to fear. And so your servant thought: 'Let me speak to the king. Perhaps he will grant the petition of his servant. ¹⁶For the king must surely listen and rescue his servant from the grasp of one who would destroy both me and my son from the heritage of God.' ¹⁷And your servant says, 'Let the word of my lord the king lead to rest;† indeed, my lord the king is like an angel of God, discerning good and evil. The Lord your God be with you.'"*

¹⁸The king answered the woman, "Now do not conceal from me anything I may ask you!" The woman said, "Let my lord the king speak." ¹⁹So the king asked, "Is the hand of Joab with you in all this?" And the woman answered: "As you live, my lord the king, it is just as my lord has said, and not otherwise. It was your servant Joab who instructed me and told your servant all these things she was to say. ²⁰Your servant Joab did this in order to approach the matter in a roundabout way. But my lord is wise with the wisdom of an angel of God, knowing all things on earth."

**Absalom's Return.** ²¹Then the king said to Joab: "I am granting this request. Go and bring back young Absalom." ²²Falling to the ground in homage and blessing the king, Joab said, "This day your servant knows that I am in good favor with you, my lord king, since the king has granted the request of your servant." ²³Joab then went off to Geshur and brought Absalom to Jerusalem. ²⁴But the king said, "Let him go off to his own house; he shall not appear before† me." So Absalom went off to his house and did not appear before the king.

²⁵In all Israel there was no man more praised for his beauty than Absalom, flawless from the sole of his foot to the crown of his head. ²⁶When he shaved his head—as he used to do at the end of every year, because his hair became too heavy for him—the hair weighed two hundred shekels according to the royal standard. ²⁷Absalom had three sons born to him, besides a daughter named Tamar, who was a beautiful woman.*

† 14:7 *Hope*: lit., "glowing coal." The image is similar to that of a lighted lamp, e.g., Ps 132:17, or small hearth fire, to keep alive the ancestral name.

14:14 *Not to banish*: a possible allusion to the religious institution of cities of refuge for involuntary murderers; see Nm 35:9–15.

14:17 *Rest*: cf. Ru 1:9; Ps 95:11; Mi 2:10. The reference here is to a return home for Absalom.

14:24 *Appear before*: lit., "see the face of," a term from court etiquette; so also in vv. 28, 32.

14:5–7 2 Kgs 6:26–28.
14:7 Nm 35:19.
14:14 Jb 7:9; 14:7–12;
Ps 88:4, 10–12.
14:17, 20 1 Sm 29:9.
14:27 2 Sm 18:18.

**Absalom Is Pardoned.** [28] Absalom lived in Jerusalem for two years without appearing before the king. [29] Then he sent a message asking Joab to send him to the king, but Joab would not come to him. Although he asked him a second time, Joab would not come. [30] He therefore instructed his servants: "You see Joab's field that borders mine, where he has barley. Go, set it on fire." And so Absalom's servants set the field on fire.* Joab's farmhands came to him with torn garments and told him, "Absalom's servants set your field on fire." [31] Joab went to Absalom in his house and asked him, "Why have your servants set my field on fire?" [32] Absalom answered Joab: "I sent you a message: Come here, that I may send you to the king to say: 'Why did I come back from Geshur? I would be better off if I were still there!' Now, let me appear before the king. If I am guilty, let him put me to death." [33] Joab went to the king and reported this. The king then called Absalom; he came to him and in homage fell on his face to the ground before the king. Then the king kissed Absalom.

# 15

**Absalom's Ambition.** [1] After this, Absalom provided himself with chariots, horses, and a retinue of fifty.* [2] Moreover, Absalom used to rise early and stand alongside the road leading to the gate. If someone had a lawsuit to be decided by the king, Absalom would call to him and say, "From what city are you?" And when he replied, "Your servant is of such and such a tribe of Israel," [3] Absalom would say to him, "Your case is good and just, but there is no one to hear you in the king's name." [4] And he would continue: "If only I could be appointed judge in the land! Then everyone who has a lawsuit to be decided might come to me and I would render him justice." [5] Whenever a man approached him to show homage, he would extend his hand, hold him, and kiss him. [6] By behaving in this way toward all the Israelites who came to the king for judgment, Absalom was stealing the heart of Israel.

**Conspiracy in Hebron.** [7] After a period of four years, Absalom said to the king: "Please let me go to Hebron and fulfill a vow I made to the LORD. [8] For while living in Geshur in Aram, your servant made this vow: 'If the LORD ever brings me back to Jerusalem, I will worship him in Hebron.'"* [9] The king said to him, "Go in peace," and he went off to Hebron. [10] Then Absalom sent agents throughout the tribes of Israel to say, "When you hear the sound of the horn, say, 'Absalom is king in Hebron!'" [11] Two hundred men had accompanied Absalom from Jerusalem. They had been invited and went in all innocence, knowing nothing. [12] Absalom also sent to Ahithophel the Gilonite, David's counselor, an invitation to come from his town, Giloh, for the sacrifices he was about to offer. So the conspiracy gained strength, and the people with Absalom increased in numbers.*

**David Flees Jerusalem.** [13] An informant came to David with the report, "The Israelites have given their hearts to Absalom,* and they are following him." [14] At this, David said to all his servants who were with him in Jerusalem: "Get up, let us flee, or none of us will escape from Absalom. Leave at once, or he will quickly overtake us, and then bring disaster upon us, and put the city to the sword." [15] The king's servants answered him, "Whatever our lord the king chooses to do, we are your servants." [16] Then the king set out, accompanied by his entire household, except for ten concubines whom he left behind to care for the palace.* [17] As the king left the city, with all his officers accompanying him, they halted opposite the ascent of the Mount of Olives, at a distance, [18] while the whole army marched past him.

**David and Ittai.** As all the Cherethites and Pelethites, and the six hundred Gittites who had entered his service from that city, were passing in review before the king,* [19] the king said to Ittai the Gittite: "Why should you also go with us? Go back and stay with the king, for you are a foreigner and you, too, are an exile from your own country. [20] You came only yesterday, and today shall I have you wander off with us wherever I have to go? Return and take your brothers with you, and may the LORD show you kindness and fidelity." [21] But Ittai answered the king, "As the LORD lives, and as my lord the king lives, your servant shall be wherever my lord the king is, whether for death or for life."* [22] So the king said to Ittai,

"Go, then, march on." And Ittai the Gittite, with all his men and all the dependents that were with him, marched on. 23 The whole land wept aloud as the last of the soldiers went by, and the king crossed the Wadi Kidron with all the soldiers moving on ahead of him by way of the ascent of the Mount of Olives, toward the wilderness.

**David and the Priests.** 24 Zadok, too, and all the Levites bearing the ark of the covenant of God set down the ark of God until the whole army had finished marching out of the city; and Abiathar came up. 25 Then the king said to Zadok: "Take the ark of God back to the city. If I find favor with the LORD, he will bring me back and permit me to see it and its lodging place. 26 But if he should say, 'I am not pleased with you,' I am ready; let him do to me as he sees fit."* 27 The king also said to Zadok the priest: "Look, you and Abiathar return to the city in peace, and both your sons with you, your own son Ahimaaz, and Abiathar's son Jonathan. 28 Remember, I shall be waiting at the fords near the wilderness until a report from you comes to me." 29 So Zadok and Abiathar took the ark of God back to Jerusalem and remained there.

30 As David went up the ascent of the Mount of Olives, he wept without ceasing. His head was covered, and he was walking barefoot. All those who were with him also had their heads covered and were weeping as they went.* 31 When David was told, "Ahithophel is among the conspirators with Absalom," he said, "O LORD, turn the counsel of Ahithophel to folly!"*

**David and Hushai.** 32 When David reached the top, where God was worshiped, Hushai the Archite was there to meet him, with garments torn and dirt upon his head.* 33 David said to him: "If you come with me, you will be a burden to me; 34 but if you return to the city and say to Absalom, 'Let me be your servant, O king; I was formerly your father's servant, but now I will be yours,' you will thwart for me the counsel of Ahithophel.* 35 You will have the priests Zadok and Abiathar there with you. If you hear anything from the king's house, you shall report it to the priests Zadok and Abiathar, 36 who have there with them their two sons, Zadok's son Ahimaaz and Abiathar's son Jonathan. Through them you shall send on to me whatever you hear." 37 So David's friend Hushai went into the city, Jerusalem, as Absalom was about to enter it.

**16 David and Ziba.** 1 David went a little beyond the top and Ziba, the servant of Meribbaal, was there to meet him with saddled donkeys laden with two hundred loaves of bread, an ephah of cakes of pressed raisins, an ephah of summer fruits, and a skin of wine.* 2 The king said to Ziba, "What are you doing with all this?" Ziba replied: "The donkeys are for the king's household to ride on. The bread and summer fruits are for your servants to eat, and the wine to drink when they grow weary in the wilderness." 3 Then the king said, "And where is your lord's son?" Ziba answered the king, "He is staying in Jerusalem, for he said, 'Today the house of Israel will restore to me my father's kingdom.'"* 4 The king therefore said to Ziba, "So! Everything Meribbaal had is yours." Then Ziba said: "I pay you homage, my lord the king. May I find favor with you!"*

**David and Shimei.** 5 As King David was approaching Bahurim, there was a man coming out; he was of the same clan as the house of Saul, and his name was Shimei, son of Gera. He kept cursing as he came out,* 6 and throwing stones at David and at all King David's officers, even though all the soldiers, including the royal guard, were on David's right and on his left. 7 Shimei was saying as he cursed: "Get out! Get out! You man of blood, you scoundrel! 8 The LORD has paid you back for all the blood shed from the family of Saul,† whom you replaced as king, and the LORD has handed over the kingdom to your son Absalom. And now look at you: you suffer ruin because you are a man of blood." 9 Abishai, son of Zeruiah, said to the king: "Why should this dead dog curse my lord the king? Let me go over and take off his head."* 10 But the

---

† **16:8** *Blood shed...Saul*: probably refers to the episode recounted in 21:1–14.

* **15:26** 2 Sm 16:10.
**15:30** 2 Sm 19:5; Mi 1:8.
**15:31** 2 Sm 16:23; 17:14, 23.
**15:32** 2 Sm 16:16.
**15:34** 2 Sm 16:19.
**16:1** 2 Sm 4:4; 9:1–13; 19:18, 25.
**16:3** 2 Sm 19:26–27.
**16:4** 2 Sm 19:30.
**16:5** 2 Sm 3:16; 19:17, 22–23; 1 Kgs 2:8.
**16:9** 2 Sm 19:22; 1 Sm 24:15; 26:6.

king replied: "What business is it of mine or of yours, sons of Zeruiah, that he curses? Suppose the LORD has told him to curse David; who then will dare to say, 'Why are you doing this?'"* [11] Then David said to Abishai and to all his servants: "If my own son, who came forth from my loins, is seeking my life, how much more might this Benjaminite do so! Let him alone and let him curse, for the LORD has told him to.* [12] Perhaps the LORD will look upon my affliction and repay me with good for the curses he is uttering this day." [13] David and his men continued on the road, while Shimei kept up with them on the hillside, all the while cursing and throwing stones and dirt as he went.* [14] The king and all the soldiers with him arrived at the Jordan tired out, and stopped there to rest.

**Absalom's Counselors.** [15] In the meantime Absalom, with all the Israelites, entered Jerusalem, and Ahithophel was with him. [16] When David's friend Hushai the Archite came to Absalom, he said to him: "Long live the king! Long live the king!"* [17] But Absalom asked Hushai: "Is this your devotion to your friend? Why did you not go with your friend?" [18] Hushai replied to Absalom: "On the contrary, I am his whom the LORD and all this people and all Israel have chosen, and with him I will stay. [19] Furthermore, as I was in attendance upon your father, so will I be before you. Whom should I serve, if not his son?"*

[20] Then Absalom said to Ahithophel, "Offer your counsel on what we should do." [21] Ahithophel replied to Absalom: "Go to your father's concubines, whom he left behind to take care of the palace. When all Israel hears how odious you have made yourself to your father, all those on your side will take courage."* [22] So a tent was pitched on the roof for Absalom, and Absalom went to his father's concubines in view of all Israel.*

**Counsel of Ahithophel.** [23] Now the counsel given by Ahithophel at that time was as though one sought the word of God. Such was all the counsel of Ahithophel both to David and to Absalom.*

**17** [1] Ahithophel went on to say to Absalom: "Let me choose twelve thousand men and be off in pursuit of David tonight. [2] If I come upon him when he is weary and discouraged, I shall cause him panic, and all the people with him will flee, and I shall strike down the king alone. [3] Then I can bring back the rest of the people to you, as a bride returns to her husband. It is the death of only one man you are seeking; then all the people will be at peace." [4] This plan sounded good to Absalom and to all the elders of Israel.

**Counsel of Hushai.** [5] Then Absalom said, "Now call Hushai the Archite also; let us hear what he too has to say." [6] When Hushai came to Absalom, Absalom said to him: "This is Ahithophel's plan. Shall we follow his plan? If not, give your own." [7] Hushai replied to Absalom, "This time Ahithophel has not given good counsel." [8] And he went on to say: "You know that your father and his men are warriors, and that they are as fierce as a bear in the wild robbed of her cubs. Moreover, since your father is a skilled fighter, he will not spend the night with the army.* [9] Even now he lies hidden in one of the caves or in one of his other places. And if some of our soldiers should fall at the first attack, whoever hears of it will say, 'Absalom's followers have been slaughtered.' [10] Then even the brave man with the heart of a lion—his heart will melt. For all Israel knows that your father is a fighter and those who are with him are brave. [11] This is what I counsel: Let all Israel be assembled, from Dan to Beer-sheba, as numerous as the sands by the sea, and you yourself go with them. [12] We can then attack him wherever we find him, settling down upon him as dew alights on the ground. None shall survive—neither he nor any of his followers. [13] And if he retires into a city, all Israel shall bring ropes to that city and we can drag it into the gorge, so that not even a pebble of it can be found." [14] Then Absalom and all the Israelites said, "The counsel of Hushai the Archite is better than the counsel of Ahithophel." For the LORD had commanded that Ahithophel's good counsel should be thwarted, so that he might bring Absalom to ruin.*

**16:10** 2 Sm 15:25–26; 19:23.
**16:11** 2 Sm 12:11.
**16:13** 2 Sm 19:19–24.
**16:16** 2 Sm 15:32–37.
**16:19** 2 Sm 15:34.
**16:21** 2 Sm 15:16; 20:3.
**16:22** 2 Sm 12:11–12.
**16:23** 2 Sm 15:12, 31;
17:23.
**17:8** Hos 13:8.
**17:14** 2 Sm 15:31, 34.

2 S M

**David Told of the Plan.** [15] Then Hushai said to the priests Zadok and Abiathar: "This is the counsel Ahithophel gave Absalom and the elders of Israel, and this is what I counseled. [16] So send a warning to David immediately: 'Do not spend the night at the fords near the wilderness, but cross over without fail. Otherwise the king and all the people with him will be destroyed.'" [17] Now Jonathan and Ahimaaz were staying at En-rogel. A maidservant was to come with information for them, and they in turn were to go and report to King David. They could not risk being seen entering the city, [18] but an attendant did see them and informed Absalom. They hurried on their way and reached the house of a man in Bahurim who had a cistern in his courtyard. They let themselves down into it, [19] and the woman took the cover and spread it over the mouth of the cistern, strewing crushed grain on the cover so that nothing could be noticed. [20] When Absalom's servants came to the woman at the house, they asked, "Where are Ahimaaz and Jonathan?" The woman replied, "They went by a short while ago toward the water." They searched, but found no one, and so returned to Jerusalem. [21] As soon as they left, Ahimaaz and Jonathan came up out of the cistern and went on to report to King David. They said to him: "Leave! Cross the water at once, for Ahithophel has given such and such counsel in regard to you." [22] So David and all his people moved on and crossed the Jordan. By daybreak, there was no one left who had not crossed.

[23] When Ahithophel saw that his counsel was not acted upon, he saddled his donkey and departed, going to his home in his own city. Then, having left orders concerning his household, he hanged himself. And so he died and was buried in his father's tomb. *

[24] Now David had arrived at Mahanaim while Absalom crossed the Jordan accompanied by all the Israelites. [25] Absalom had put Amasa in command of the army in Joab's place. Amasa was the son of an Ishmaelite named Ithra, who had married Abigail, daughter of Jesse and sister of Joab's mother Zeruiah. * [26] Israel and Absalom encamped in the land of Gilead.

[27] When David came to Mahanaim, Shobi, son of Nahash from Rabbah of the Ammonites, Machir, son of Ammiel from Lodebar, and Barzillai, the Gileadite from Rogelim, * [28] brought beds and covers, basins and pottery, as well as wheat, barley, flour, roasted grain, beans, lentils, [29] honey, and butter and cheese from the flocks and herds, for David and those who were with him to eat; for they said, "The people will be hungry and tired and thirsty in the wilderness."

# 18

**Preparation for Battle.** [1] After mustering the troops he had with him, David placed officers in command of units of a thousand and units of a hundred. [2] David then divided the troops three ways, a third under Joab, a third under Abishai, son of Zeruiah and brother of Joab, and a third under Ittai the Gittite. The king said to the troops, "I intend to go out with you myself." [3] But they replied: "You must not come out with us. For if we flee, no one will care; even if half of us die, no one will care. But you are worth ten thousand of us. Therefore it is better that we have you to help us from the city." [4] The king said to them, "I will do what you think best." So the king stood by the gate as all the soldiers marched out in units of a hundred and a thousand. [5] But the king gave this command to Joab, Abishai, and Ittai: "Be gentle with young Absalom for my sake." All the soldiers heard as the king gave commands to the various leaders with regard to Absalom.

**Defeat of Absalom's Forces.** [6] David's army then took the field against Israel, and a battle was fought in the forest near Mahanaim. [7] The forces of Israel were defeated by David's servants, and the casualties there that day were heavy—twenty thousand men. [8] The battle spread out over that entire region, and the forest consumed more combatants that day than did the sword.

**Death of Absalom.** [9] Absalom unexpectedly came up against David's servants. He was mounted on a mule, and, as the mule passed under the branches of a large oak tree, his hair caught fast in the tree. He hung between heaven and earth while the mule under him kept going. [10] Someone saw this and reported

2 SM

**17:23** 2 Sm 15:31; 16:23.    **17:25** 2 Sm 19:14; 20:4–13.    **17:27** 2 Sm 9:4; 19:32; 1 Kgs 2:7; Ezr 2:61.

to Joab, "I saw Absalom hanging from an oak tree." [11] Joab said to the man who told him this: "If you saw him, why did you not strike him to the ground on the spot? Then it would have been my duty to give you fifty pieces of silver and a belt." [12] But the man replied to Joab: "Even if I already held a thousand pieces of silver in my two hands, I would not lay a hand on the king's son, for in our hearing the king gave you and Abishai and Ittai a command: 'Protect the youth Absalom for my sake.' [13] Had I been disloyal and killed him, it would all have come out before the king, and you would stand aloof." [14] Joab replied, "I will not waste time with you in this way." And taking three pikes in hand, he thrust for the heart of Absalom. He was still alive in the tree.* [15] When ten of Joab's young armor-bearers closed in on Absalom, and killed him with further blows, [16] Joab then sounded the horn, and the soldiers turned back from the pursuit of the Israelites, because Joab called them to halt. [17] They took Absalom and cast him into a deep pit in the forest, and built up a very large mound of stones over him. And all the Israelites fled to their own tents.*

[18] During his lifetime Absalom had taken a pillar and set it up for himself in the King's Valley, for he said, "I have no son to perpetuate my name." The pillar which he named for himself is called Absalom's Monument to the present day.*

**David Told of Absalom's Death.** [19] Then Ahimaaz, son of Zadok, said, "Let me run to take the good news to the king that the LORD has set him free from the power of his enemies." [20] But Joab said to him: "You are not the man to bring the news today. On some other day you may take the good news, but today you would not be bringing good news, for in fact the king's son is dead." [21] Then Joab said to a Cushite, "Go, tell the king what you have seen." The Cushite bowed to Joab and ran off. [22] But Ahimaaz, son of Zadok, said to Joab again, "Come what may, permit me also to run after the Cushite." Joab replied: "Why do you want to run, my son? You will receive no reward." [23] But he insisted, "Come what may, I want to run." Joab said to him, "Run." Ahimaaz took the way of the Jordan plain and outran the Cushite.

[24] Now David was sitting between the two gates, and a lookout mounted to the roof of the gate above the city wall, where he looked out and saw a man running all alone. [25] The lookout shouted to inform the king, who said, "If he is alone, he has good news to report." As he kept coming nearer, [26] the lookout spied another runner. From his place atop the gate he cried out, "There is another man running by himself." And the king responded, "He, too, is bringing good news." [27] Then the lookout said, "I notice that the first one runs like Ahimaaz, son of Zadok." The king replied, "He is a good man; he comes with good news."* [28] Then Ahimaaz called out and greeted the king. With face to the ground he paid homage to the king and said, "Blessed be the LORD your God, who has delivered up the men who rebelled against my lord the king." [29] But the king asked, "Is young Absalom safe?" And Ahimaaz replied, "I saw a great disturbance when the king's servant Joab sent your servant on, but I do not know what it was." [30] The king said, "Step aside and remain in attendance here." So he stepped aside and remained there. [31] When the Cushite came in, he said, "Let my lord the king receive the good news that this day the LORD has freed you from the power of all who rose up against you." [32] But the king asked the Cushite, "Is young Absalom all right?" The Cushite replied, "May the enemies of my lord the king and all who rebel against you with evil intent be as that young man!"

**19** [1] The king was shaken, and went up to the room over the city gate and wept. He said as he wept, "My son Absalom! My son, my son Absalom! If only I had died instead of you, Absalom, my son, my son!"

**Joab Reproves David.** [2] Joab was told, "The king is weeping and mourning for Absalom," [3] and that day's victory was turned into mourning for the whole army when they heard, "The king is grieving for his son." [4] The soldiers stole into the city that day like men shamed by flight in battle. [5] Meanwhile the king covered his face and cried out in a loud voice, "My son Absalom! Absalom! My son, my son!"* [6] So Joab went to the king's residence and said: "Though they saved your life and your sons'

**18:14** 2 Sm 12:10; 13:28–29.   **18:17** Jos 7:26; 8:29; 10:27.   **18:18** 2 Sm 14:27.   **18:27** 2 Kgs 9:20.   **19:5** 2 Sm 15:30.

and daughters' lives, and the lives of your wives and your concubines, you have put all your servants to shame today [7] by loving those who hate you and hating those who love you. For you have announced today that officers and servants are nothing to you. Indeed I am now certain that if Absalom were alive today and all of us dead, that would be fine with you. [8] Now then, get up! Go out and speak kindly to your servants. I swear by the LORD that if you do not go out, not a single man will remain with you overnight, and this will be a far greater disaster for you than any that has come upon you from your youth until now." [9] So the king got up and sat at the gate. When all the people were told, "The king is sitting at the gate," they came into his presence.

**The Reconciliation.** Now the Israelites had fled to their separate tents, [10] but throughout the tribes of Israel all the people were arguing among themselves, saying to one another: "The king delivered us from the grasp of our enemies, and it was he who rescued us from the grasp of the Philistines. Now, he has fled the country before Absalom, [11] but Absalom, whom we anointed over us, has died in battle. Why, then, should you remain silent about restoring the king to his palace?" When the talk of all Israel reached the king, [12] David sent word to the priests Zadok and Abiathar: "Say to the elders of Judah: 'Why should you be last to restore the king to his palace? [13] You are my brothers, you are my bone and flesh. Why should you be last to restore the king?' [14] Also say to Amasa: 'Are you not my bone and flesh? May God do thus to me, and more, if you do not become commander of my army permanently in place of Joab.'"* [15] He won the hearts of the Judahites all together, and so they sent a message to the king: "Return, with all your servants."

**David and Shimei.** [16] So the king returned, and when he reached the Jordan, Judah had come to Gilgal to meet him and to bring him across the Jordan. [17] Shimei, son of Gera, the Benjaminite from Bahurim, hurried down with the Judahites to meet King David,* [18] accompanied by a thousand men from Benjamin. Ziba, too, the servant of the house of Saul,

accompanied by his fifteen sons and twenty servants, hastened to the Jordan before the king.* [19]* They crossed over the ford to bring the king's household over and to do whatever he wished. When Shimei, son of Gera, crossed the Jordan, he fell down before the king [20] and said to him: "May my lord not hold me guilty; do not remember or take to heart the wrong that your servant did the day my lord the king left Jerusalem. [21] For your servant knows that I have done wrong. But I now am the first of the whole house of Joseph to come down today to meet my lord the king." [22] But Abishai, son of Zeruiah, countered: "Shimei must be put to death for this. He cursed the anointed of the LORD." [23] David replied: "What has come between you and me, sons of Zeruiah, that you would become my adversaries this day? Should anyone die today in Israel? Am I not aware that today I am king over Israel?"* [24] Then the king said to Shimei, "You shall not die." And the king gave him his oath.

**David and Meribbaal.** [25] Meribbaal, son of Saul, also went down to meet the king. He had not cared for his feet nor trimmed his mustache nor washed his clothes from the day the king left until he returned safely. [26] When he came from Jerusalem to meet the king, the king asked him, "Why did you not go with me, Meribbaal?"* [27] He replied: "My lord king, my servant deceived me. For your servant said to him, 'Saddle the donkey for me, that I may ride on it and go with the king'; your servant is lame.* [28] But he slandered your servant before my lord the king. But my lord the king is like an angel of God. Do whatever seems good to you. [29] For though my father's entire house deserved only death from my lord the king, yet you placed your servant among those who eat at your table. What right do I still have to make further appeal to the king?"* [30] But the king said to him: "Why do you go on talking? I say, 'You and Ziba shall divide the property.'"* [31] Meribbaal answered the king, "Indeed let him take it all, now that my lord the king has returned safely to his house."

**David and Barzillai.** [32] Barzillai the Gileadite also came down from Rogelim and escorted

19:14 2 Sm 17:25; 20:4.
19:17 2 Sm 16:5–13.
19:18 2 Sm 16:1–4;
  19:25–31.

19:19–24 2 Sm 16:13; Ex 22:27;
  1 Kgs 2:8–9.
19:23 2 Sm 16:9–10; 1 Sm
  11:13;

1 Kgs 2:8–9, 36–46.
19:26 2 Sm 16:3.
19:27 2 Sm 9:2–13.

19:29 2 Sm 9:9–11.
19:30 2 Sm 16:4.

the king to the Jordan for his crossing, taking leave of him at the Jordan. * [33] It was Barzillai, a very old man of eighty, who had provided for the king during his stay in Mahanaim; he was a very great man. [34] The king said to Barzillai, "Cross over with me, and I will provide for your old age as my guest in Jerusalem." [35] But Barzillai answered the king: "How much longer have I to live, that I should go up to Jerusalem with the king? [36] I am now eighty years old. Can I distinguish between good and evil? Can your servant taste what he eats and drinks, or still hear the voices of men and women singers? Why should your servant be any further burden to my lord the king? [37] In escorting the king across the Jordan, your servant is doing little enough! Why should the king give me this reward? [38] Please let your servant go back to die in my own city by the tomb of my father and mother. Here is your servant Chimham. Let him cross over with my lord the king. Do for him whatever seems good to you." [39] Then the king said to him, "Chimham shall cross over with me, and for him I will do whatever seems good to you. And anything else you would like me to do for you, I will do." [40] Then all the people crossed over the Jordan but the king remained; he kissed Barzillai and bade him farewell as he returned to his own place. [41] Finally the king crossed over to Gilgal, accompanied by Chimham.

**Israel and Judah Quarrel.** All of the people of Judah and half of the people of Israel had escorted the king across. [42] But then all these Israelites began coming to the king and saying, "Why did our brothers the Judahites steal you away and bring the king and his household across the Jordan, along with all David's men?" [43] All the Judahites replied to the men of Israel: "Because the king is our relative. Why are you angry over this? Have we had anything to eat at the king's expense? Or have portions from his table been given to us?" [44] The Israelites answered the Judahites: "We have ten shares in the king. Also, we are the firstborn† rather than you. Why do you slight us? Were we not first to speak of restoring our king?" Then the Judahites

in turn spoke even more fiercely than the Israelites. *

# 20

**Sheba's Rebellion.** [1] Now a scoundrel named Sheba, the son of Bichri, a Benjaminite, happened to be there. He sounded the horn and cried out,

"We have no share in David,
    nor any heritage in the son of Jesse.
Everyone to your tents, O Israel!" *

[2] So all the Israelites left David to follow Sheba, son of Bichri. But the Judahites, from the Jordan to Jerusalem, remained loyal to their king. [3] David came to his house in Jerusalem, and the king took the ten concubines whom he had left behind to care for the palace and placed them under guard. He provided for them, but never again saw them. And so they remained shut away to the day of their death, lifelong widows. *

**Amasa's Death.** [4] Then the king said to Amasa: "Summon the Judahites for me within three days. Then present yourself here." * [5] Accordingly Amasa set out to summon Judah, but delayed beyond the time set for him. [6] Then David said to Abishai: "Sheba, son of Bichri, may now do us more harm than Absalom did. Take your lord's servants and pursue him, lest he find fortified cities and take shelter while we look on." [7] So Joab and the Cherethites and Pelethites and all the warriors marched out behind Abishai from Jerusalem to campaign in pursuit of Sheba, son of Bichri. * [8] † They were at the great stone in Gibeon when Amasa met them. Now Joab had a belt over his tunic, from which was slung a sword in its sheath at his thigh; the sword would slide out downwards. * [9] Joab asked Amasa, "Is everything all right, my brother?" and with his right hand held Amasa's beard as if to kiss him. [10] And since Amasa was not on his guard against the sword in Joab's other hand, Joab stabbed him in the abdomen with it, so that his entrails burst forth to the ground, and he died; there was no second thrust. Then Joab and Abishai his brother pursued Sheba, son of Bichri. *

---

† **19:44** The firstborn had special rights over the other siblings.
**20:8** The text of this verse is quite uncertain.

* **19:32** 2 Sm 17:27–29; 1 Kgs 2:7; Ezr 2:61.
**19:44** 1 Kgs 11:31.
**20:1** 1 Kgs 12:16.
**20:3** 2 Sm 15:16;
**16:20–22.**
**20:4** 2 Sm 17:25; 19:14.
**20:7** 2 Sm 8:18.
**20:8** 2 Sm 2:13.
**20:10** 1 Kgs 2:5.

[11] One of Joab's attendants stood by Amasa and said, "Let him who favors Joab and is for David follow Joab." [12] Amasa lay covered with blood in the middle of the highroad, and the man noticed that all the soldiers were stopping. So he rolled Amasa away from the road to the field and spread a garment over him, because he saw how all who came upon him were stopping. [13] When he had been removed from the road, everyone went on after Joab in pursuit of Sheba, son of Bichri.

**Joab Pursues Sheba.** [14] Sheba had passed through all the tribes of Israel to Abel Beth-maacah. Then all the Bichrites assembled and they too entered the city after him. [15] So all Joab's troops came and besieged him in Abel Beth-maacah. They built up a mound against the city, so that it stood against the rampart, and were battering the wall to knock it down. [16] Then a wise woman from the city called out, "Listen, listen! Tell Joab, 'Come here, so I can speak with you.'" [17] When Joab had come near her, the woman said, "Are you Joab?" And he replied, "Yes." She said to him, "Listen to what your servant has to say." He replied, "I am listening." [18] Then she went on to say: "There is a saying from long ago,† 'Let them ask if they will in Abel or in Dan whether loyalty is finished [19] or ended in Israel.' You are seeking to batter down a city that is a mother in Israel. Why do you wish to swallow up the heritage of the LORD?"* [20] Joab answered, "Not at all, not at all! I do not wish to swallow or batter anything. [21] That is not the case at all. A man from the hill country of Ephraim, whose name is Sheba, son of Bichri, has rebelled against King David. Give him up, just him, and I will withdraw from the city." Then the woman said to Joab, "His head shall be thrown to you across the wall." [22] In her wisdom, the woman went to all the people, and they cut off the head of Sheba, son of Bichri, and threw it out to Joab. He then sounded the horn, and they scattered from the city to their own tents, while Joab returned to Jerusalem to the king.

**David's Officials.** [23] Joab was in command of the whole army of Israel. Benaiah, son of Jehoiada, was in command of the Cherethites and Pelethites.* [24] Adoram was in charge of the forced labor. Jehoshaphat, son of Ahilud, was the chancellor. [25] Shawsha was the scribe. Zadok and Abiathar were priests.* [26] Ira the Jairite was also David's priest.

## V. APPENDIXES

**21** **Gibeonite Vengeance.** [1] In David's time there was a famine for three years, year after year. David sought the presence of the LORD, who said: There is bloodguilt on Saul and his family because he put the Gibeonites to death.* [2] So the king called the Gibeonites and spoke to them. (Now the Gibeonites were not Israelites, but survivors of the Amorites; and although the Israelites had given them their oath, Saul had sought to kill them off in his zeal for the Israelites and for Judah.)* [3] David said to the Gibeonites, "What must I do for you and how must I make atonement, that you may bless the heritage of the LORD?" [4] The Gibeonites answered him, "We have no claim against Saul and his house for silver or gold, nor is it our place to put anyone to death in Israel." Then he said, "I will do for you whatever you propose." [5] They said to the king, "As for the man who was exterminating us and who intended to destroy us that we might have no place in all the territory of Israel, [6] let seven men from among his descendants be given to us, that we may execute them before the LORD in Gibeon, on the LORD's mountain." The king replied, "I will give them up." [7] The king, however, spared Meribbaal, son of Jonathan, son of Saul, because of the LORD's oath that formed a bond between David and Saul's son Jonathan.* [8] But the king took Armoni and Meribbaal, the two sons that Aiah's daughter Rizpah had borne to Saul, and the five sons of Saul's daughter Merob that she had borne to Adriel, son of Barzillai the Meholathite,* [9] and delivered them into the power of the Gibeonites, who then executed them on the mountain before the LORD. The seven fell at the one time; they were put to death during the first days of the harvest—that is, at the beginning of the barley harvest.

---

† **20:18–19** This proverbial expression is obscure but seems to reflect a tradition that this Danite town was associated with oracles or other sorts of revelation. Cf. Mt 16:13–17; and the intertestamental *Testament of Levi* 2:3.

**20:19** Gn 49:16.
**20:23** 2 Sm 8:16–18; 23:20.
**20:25** 2 Sm 8:17–18.
**21:1** 2 Sm 24:13.
**21:2** Jos 9:3–27.
**21:7** 2 Sm 9:13; 1 Sm 18:3;
20:8–10, 15–16, 42.
**21:8** 2 Sm 3:7.

[10] Then Rizpah, Aiah's daughter, took sackcloth and spread it out for herself on the rock from the beginning of the harvest until rain came down on them from the heavens, fending off the birds of the heavens from settling on them by day, and the wild animals by night.* [11] When David was informed of what Rizpah, Aiah's daughter, the concubine of Saul, had done, [12] he went and obtained the bones of Saul and of his son Jonathan from the citizens of Jabesh-gilead, who had stolen them away secretly from the public square of Beth-shan, where the Philistines had hanged them at the time they defeated Saul on Gilboa.* [13] When he had brought up from there the bones of Saul and of his son Jonathan, the bones of those who had been executed were also gathered up. [14] Then the bones of Saul and of his son Jonathan were buried in the land of Benjamin, at Zela, in the tomb of his father Kish. After all that the king commanded had been carried out, God granted relief to the land.*

**Exploits in Philistine Wars.** [15] There was another battle between the Philistines and Israel. David went down with his servants and fought the Philistines, but David grew tired. [16] Dadu, a descendant of the Rephaim, whose bronze spear weighed three hundred shekels, was about to take him captive. Dadu was girt with a new sword and thought he would kill David, [17] but Abishai, son of Zeruiah, came to help him, and struck and killed the Philistine. Then David's men swore to him, "You must not go out to battle with us again, lest you quench the lamp of Israel."*

[18] * After this, there was another battle with the Philistines, in Gob. On that occasion Sibbecai the Hushathite struck down Saph, a descendant of the Rephaim.* [19] * There was another battle with the Philistines, in Gob,

and Elhanan, son of Jair from Bethlehem, killed Goliath of Gath, whose spear shaft was like a weaver's beam. [20] There was another battle, at Gath, and there was a giant, who had six fingers on each hand and six toes on each foot—twenty-four in all. He too was descended from the Rephaim. [21] And when he insulted Israel, Jonathan, son of David's brother Shimei, struck him down.* [22] These four were descended from the Rephaim in Gath, and they fell at the hands of David and his servants.

# 22

**Song of Thanksgiving.**† [1] David proclaimed the words of this song to the LORD when the LORD had rescued him from the grasp of all his enemies and from the grasp of Saul.* [2] He said:*

> O LORD, my rock, my fortress, my
>           deliverer,
> [3]      my God, my rock of refuge!
> My shield, my saving horn,†
>      my stronghold, my refuge,
>      my savior, from violence you keep me
>           safe.*
> [4]  Praised be the LORD, I exclaim!
>      I have been delivered from my enemies.
>
> [5]      The breakers of death surged round
>                about me,
>      the menacing floods† terrified me;
> [6]      The cords of Sheol tightened;
>      the snares of death lay in wait for me.
> [7]      In my distress I called out: LORD!
>      I cried out to my God;
> From his temple† he heard my voice,
>      my cry reached his ears.
>
> [8]      The earth rocked and shook;†
>      the foundations of the heavens
>                trembled;

---

† **22:1–51** This psalm of thanksgiving also appears in the Psalter, with a few small variants, as Ps 18. In both places it is attributed to David. Two main sections can be distinguished. In the first part, after an introductory stanza of praise to God (vv. 2–4), the writer describes the peril he was in (vv. 5–7), and then poetically depicts, under the form of a theophany, God's intervention in his behalf (vv. 8–20), concluding with an acknowledgment of God's justice (vv. 21–31). In the second part, God is praised for having prepared the psalmist for war (vv. 32–35), given him victory over his enemies (vv. 36–39), whom he put to flight (vv. 40–43), and bestowed on him dominion over many peoples (vv. 44–46). The entire song ends with an expression of grateful praise (vv. 47–51).

**22:3** *My saving horn:* my strong savior. The horn, such as that

of an enraged bull, was a symbol of strength; cf. Lk 1:69.

**22:5–6** *Breakers…floods:* traditional Old Testament imagery for lethal danger, from which the Lord is uniquely able to rescue; cf. Ps 69:2, 15–16; 89:10–11; Jon 2:3–6.

**22:7** *His temple:* his heavenly abode.

**22:8–10** The Lord's coming is depicted by means of a storm theophany, including earthquake (vv. 8, 16) and thunderstorm (vv. 9–15); cf. Jgs 5:4–5; Ps 29; 97:2–6; Hb 3.

**21:10** 2 Sm 3:31; 12:16.
**21:12** 1 Sm 31:10–13.
**21:14** 2 Sm 24:25.
**21:17** 1 Kgs 11:36; 15:4;
     2 Kgs 8:19.
**21:18–22** 1 Chr 20:4–8.

**21:18** 2 Sm 23:27.
**21:19–20** 1 Sm 17:4, 7.
**21:21** 2 Sm 13:3.
**22:1** Ps 18:1.
**22:2–51** Ps 18:3–51.
**22:3** 1 Sm 2:1–2.

they shook as his wrath flared up.

9   Smoke rose in his nostrils,
      a devouring fire from his mouth;
      it kindled coals into flame.

10  He parted the heavens and came down,
      a dark cloud under his feet. *

11  Mounted on a cherub † he flew,
      borne along on the wings of the
        wind. *

12  He made darkness the cover about him,
      a mass of water, heavy thunderheads.

13  From the brightness of his presence
      coals were kindled to flame.

14  The LORD thundered from heaven;
      the Most High made his voice
        resound.

15  He let fly arrows and scattered them;
      lightning, and dispersed them. *

16  Then the bed of the sea appeared;
      the world's foundations lay bare,
    At the roar of the LORD,
      at the storming breath of his nostrils. *

17  He reached down from on high and
        seized me,
      drew me out of the deep waters. *

18  He rescued me from my mighty enemy,
      from foes too powerful for me.

19  They attacked me on a day of distress,
      but the LORD came to my support.

20  He set me free in the open;
      he rescued me because he loves me.

21  The LORD acknowledged my
        righteousness;
      rewarded my clean hands.

22  For I kept the ways of the LORD;
      I was not disloyal to my God.

23  His laws were all before me,
      his decrees I did not cast aside.

24  I was honest toward him;
      I was on guard against sin.

25  So the LORD rewarded my righteousness,
      the cleanness of my hands in his
        sight.

26 * Toward the faithful you are faithful; †
      to the honest you are honest;

27  Toward the sincere you are sincere;

but to the perverse you are devious.

28  Humble people you save,
      though on the haughty your eyes look
        down.

29  You are my lamp, O LORD!
      My God brightens the darkness about
        me.

30  With you I can rush an armed band,
      with my God to help I can leap a wall.

31  God's way is unerring;
      the LORD's promise is tried and true;
      he is a shield for all who trust in
        him. *

32  Truly, who is God except the LORD?
      Who but our God is the rock?

33  This God who girded me with might,
      kept my way unerring,

34  Who made my feet swift as a deer's,
      set me safe on the heights, *

35  Who trained my hands for war,
      my arms to bend even a bow of
        bronze.

36  You have given me your protecting
        shield,
      and your help has made me great.

37  You gave me room to stride;
      my feet never stumbled.

38  I pursued my enemies and overtook
        them;
      I did not turn back till I destroyed
        them.

39  I struck them down, and they did not
        rise;
      they fell dead at my feet.

40  You girded me with strength for war;
      subdued adversaries at my feet.

41  My foes you put to flight before me;
      those who hated me I destroyed.

42  They cried for help, but no one saved
        them,
      cried to the LORD but got no answer.

43  I ground them fine as the dust of the
        earth;
      like mud in the streets I trod them
        down.

---

† **22:11** *Mounted on a cherub*: in the traditional storm theophany, as here, the Lord appears with thunder, lightning, earthquake, rain, darkness, cloud, and wind. Sometimes these are represented as his retinue; sometimes he is said to ride upon the clouds or "the wings of the wind" (Ps 104:3). The parallelism in v. 11 suggests that the winged creatures called cherubim are imagined as bearing the Lord aloft. In the iconography of the ark of the covenant, the Lord was "enthroned upon the cherubim";

cf. Ex 37:7–9; 1 Sm 4:4; 2 Sm 6:2; 2 Kgs 19:15; Ps 80:2; 99:1.
**22:26–27** People are treated by God in the same way they treat him and other people.

---

| | |
|---|---|
| **22:10** Ps 144:5. | **22:17** Ps 144:7. |
| **22:11** Ex 25:18–22. | **22:26–27** 1 Sm 2:30. |
| **22:15** Ps 144:6. | **22:31** Prv 30:5. |
| **22:16** Ex 15:8. | **22:34** Ps 62:3; Hb 3:19. |

44 You rescued me from the strife of my
people;
    you made me head over nations.
  A people I had not known became my
slaves;
45 Foreigners cringed before me;
    as soon as they heard of me they
obeyed.
46 Their courage failed;
    they came trembling from their
fortresses.
47 The LORD lives! Blessed be my rock!
    Exalted be God, the rock of my
salvation.
48 O God who granted me vindication,
    subdued peoples under me,
49 and helped me escape from my
enemies,
  Truly you have exalted me above my
adversaries,
    from the violent you have rescued me.
50 Thus I will proclaim you, LORD, among
the nations;
    I will sing the praises of your name.*
51 You have given great victories to your
king,
    and shown kindness to your anointed,
  to David and his posterity forever.

# 23 The Last Words of David.† ¹These are
the last words of David:

  The oracle of David, son of Jesse;
    the oracle of the man God raised up,
  Anointed of the God of Jacob,
    favorite of the Mighty One of Israel.*
2 The spirit of the LORD spoke through
me;
    his word was on my tongue.*
3 The God of Israel spoke;
    of me the Rock of Israel said,
  "One who rules over humankind with
justice,
    who rules in the fear of God,*
4 Is like the light at sunrise

on a cloudless morning,
    making the land's vegetation glisten
after rain."*
5 Is not my house firm before God?
    He has made an eternal covenant with
me,
    set forth in detail and secured.*
  Will he not bring to fruition
    all my salvation and my every desire?
6 But the wicked are all like thorns to be
cast away;
    they cannot be taken up by hand.*
7 One wishing to touch them
    must be armed with iron or the shaft
of a spear.
  They must be utterly consumed by
fire.

**David's Warriors.** ⁸These are the names of
David's warriors.† Ishbaal, the son of Hachamoni, chief of the Three. He brandished his
spear over eight hundred whom he had slain
in a single encounter.* ⁹Next to him was Eleazar, the son of Dodo the Ahohite, one of the
Three warriors with David at Ephes-dammim,
when they insulted the Philistines who had
massed there for battle. The Israelites had retreated,* ¹⁰but he stood there and struck down
the Philistines until his hand grew tired from
clutching the sword. The LORD brought about
a great victory on that day; the army turned
back to rejoin Eleazar, but only to strip the
slain. ¹¹Next to him was Shammah, son of
Agee the Hararite. The Philistines had assembled at Lehi, where there was a plot of land
full of lentils. The people were fleeing before
the Philistines,* ¹²but he took his stand in the
middle of the plot, kept it safe, and cut down
the Philistines. Thus the LORD brought about
a great victory. Such deeds as these the Three
warriors performed.

¹³Three of the Thirty chiefs went down to
David in the cave of Adullam during the harvest, while a Philistine clan was encamped in
the Valley of Rephaim.* ¹⁴David was then in

---

**23:1–7** *The last words of David*: the text of this short composition is difficult in places; it views David's career in retrospect.
**23:8–39** There are thirty-seven warriors in all named in this
list. First there are the Three warriors most noted for single-
handed exploits (vv. 8–12). Then comes the story of a daring
adventure by three unnamed members of the larger group of
the Thirty (vv. 13–17). Next come the commanders of the king's
bodyguard, Abishai (vv. 18–19) and Benaiah (vv. 20–23), with
whom must be counted Asahel (v. 24) and Joab (vv. 18, 24, 37),
and finally the group of the Thirty (vv. 24–39).

---

**22:50** Ps 22:23; Rom 15:9.
**23:1** 1 Kgs 2:1–9; Sir 47:8.
**23:2** Is 59:21; Jer 1:9.
**23:3** Ps 72:1–4.
**23:4** Jgs 5:31; Ps 72:6.
**23:5** 2 Sm 7:11, 15–16; Ps
89:30; Is 55:3.
**23:6** Dt 13:14.
**23:8–39** 1 Chr 11:11–41;
27:1–15.
**23:9** 1 Sm 17:1.
**23:11** Jgs 15:9.
**23:13** 1 Sm 22:1; Mi 1:15.

the stronghold, and there was a garrison of Philistines in Bethlehem. ¹⁵ Now David had a craving and said, "If only someone would give me a drink of water from the cistern by the gate of Bethlehem!" ¹⁶ Thereupon the three warriors broke through the encampment of the Philistines, drew water from the cistern by the gate of Bethlehem, and carried it back to David. But he refused to drink it, and instead poured it out† to the LORD, ¹⁷ saying: "The LORD forbid that I do such a thing! Could I drink the blood of these men who went at the risk of their lives?" So he refused to drink it.

¹⁸ Abishai, the brother of Joab, son of Zeruiah, was the chief of the Thirty; he brandished his spear over three hundred whom he had slain. He made a name among the Thirty, ¹⁹ but was more famous than any of the Thirty, becoming their leader. However, he did not attain to the Three.

²⁰ Benaiah, son of Jehoiada, a valiant man of mighty deeds, from Kabzeel, killed the two sons of Ariel of Moab. Also, he went down and killed the lion in the cistern on a snowy day.* ²¹ He likewise slew an Egyptian, a huge man. The Egyptian carried a spear, but Benaiah came against him with a staff; he wrested the spear from the Egyptian's hand, and killed him with that spear. ²² Such deeds as these Benaiah, the son of Jehoiada, performed; and he made a name among the Thirty warriors ²³ but was more famous than any of the Thirty. However, he did not attain to the Three. David put him in charge of his bodyguard.* ²⁴ Asahel,* brother of Joab, was among the Thirty; Elhanan, son of Dodo, from Bethlehem; ²⁵ Shammah, from En-harod; Elika, from En-harod; ²⁶ Helez, from Beth-pelet; Ira, son of Ikkesh, from Tekoa; ²⁷ Abiezer, from Anathoth; Sibbecai, from Husha;* ²⁸ Zalmon, from Ahoh; Maharai, from Netophah; ²⁹ Heled, son of Baanah, from Netophah; Ittai, son of Ribai, from Gibeah of Benjamin; ³⁰ Benaiah, from Pirathon; Hiddai, from the valley of Gaash; ³¹ Abibaal, from Beth-arabah; Azmaveth, from Bahurim; ³² Eliahba, from Shaalbon; Jashen the Gunite; Jonathan, ³³ son of Shammah

the Hararite; Ahiam, son of Sharar the Hararite; ³⁴ Eliphelet, son of Ahasbai, from Beth-maacah; Eliam, son of Ahithophel, from Gilo; ³⁵ Hezrai, from Carmel; Paarai the Arbite; ³⁶ Igal, son of Nathan, from Zobah; Bani the Gadite; ³⁷ Zelek the Ammonite; Naharai, from Beeroth, the armor-bearer of Joab, son of Zeruiah; ³⁸ Ira, from Jattir; Gareb, from Jattir; ³⁹ Uriah the Hittite—thirty-seven in all.*

# 24

**David's Census; the Plague.** ¹ The LORD's anger against Israel flared again,* and he incited David against them: "Go, take a census of Israel and Judah." ² The king therefore said to Joab and the leaders of the army who were with him, "Tour all the tribes of Israel from Dan to Beer-sheba and register the people, that I may know their number." ³ But Joab replied to the king: "May the LORD your God increase the number of people a hundredfold for my lord the king to see it with his own eyes. But why does it please my lord to do a thing of this kind?" ⁴ However, the king's command prevailed over Joab and the leaders of the army, so they left the king's presence in order to register the people of Israel. ⁵ Crossing the Jordan, they began near Aroer, south of the city in the wadi, and turned in the direction of Gad toward Jazer. ⁶ They continued on to Gilead and to the district below Mount Hermon. Then they proceeded to Dan; from there they turned toward Sidon, ⁷ going to the fortress of Tyre and to all the cities of the Hivites and Canaanites, and ending up in the Negeb of Judah, at Beer-sheba. ⁸ Thus they toured the whole land, reaching Jerusalem again after nine months and twenty days. ⁹ Joab then reported the census figures to the king: of men capable of wielding a sword, there were in Israel eight hundred thousand, and in Judah five hundred thousand.

¹⁰ Afterward, however, David regretted having numbered the people. David said to the LORD: "I have sinned grievously in what I have done.* Take away, LORD, your servant's guilt, for I have acted very foolishly."† ¹¹ When David rose in the morning, the word of the LORD

2 SM

---

† **23:16** *Poured it out*: as a libation.
**24:10** The narrative supposes that since the people belonged to the Lord rather than to the king, only the Lord should know their exact number. Further, since such an exact numbering of the people would make it possible for the king to exercise centralized power, imposing taxation, conscription, and expropriation upon Israel, the story shares the view of monarchy found in 1 Sm 8:4–18. See also Nm 3:44–51, where census taking requires an apotropaic offering.

*

| | |
|---|---|
| **23:20** 2 Sm 8:18; 20:23; Jgs 14:6; 1 Kgs 2:29–30. | **23:39** 2 Sm 11:3. |
| **23:23** 1 Sm 22:14. | **24:1–25** 1 Chr 21:1–27. |
| **23:24** 2 Sm 2:18–23. | **24:10** 1 Sm 24:6; 1 Chr 21:7–8. |
| **23:27** 2 Sm 21:18. | |

came to the prophet Gad, David's seer, saying: [12] Go, tell David: Thus says the LORD: I am offering you three options; choose one of them, and I will give you that. [13] Gad then went to David to inform him. He asked: "Should three years of famine come upon your land; or three months of fleeing from your enemy while he pursues you; or is it to be three days of plague in your land? Now consider well: what answer am I to give to him who sent me?" * [14] David answered Gad: "I am greatly distressed. But let us fall into the hand of God, whose mercy is great, rather than into human hands." [15] Thus David chose the plague. At the time of the wheat harvest it broke out among the people. The LORD sent plague over Israel from morning until the time appointed, and from Dan to Beer-sheba seventy thousand of the people died. [16] But when the angel stretched forth his hand toward Jerusalem to destroy it, the LORD changed his mind about the calamity, and said to the angel causing the destruction among the people: Enough now! Stay your hand. * The angel of the LORD was then standing at the threshing floor of Araunah the Jebusite. * [17] When David saw the angel who was striking the people, he said to the LORD: "It is I who have sinned; it is I, the shepherd, who have done wrong. But these sheep, what have they done? Strike me and my father's family!"

**David Offers Sacrifices.** [18] On the same day Gad went to David and said to him, "Go and set up an altar to the LORD on the threshing floor of Araunah the Jebusite." [19] According to Gad's word, David went up as the LORD had commanded. [20] Now Araunah looked down and saw the king and his servants coming toward him while he was threshing wheat. So he went out and bowed down before the king, his face to the ground. [21] Then Araunah asked, "Why does my lord the king come to his servant?" David replied, "To buy the threshing floor from you, to build an altar to the LORD, that the plague may be withdrawn from the people." [22] * But Araunah said to David: "Let my lord the king take it and offer up what is good in his sight. See, here are the oxen for burnt offerings, and the threshing sledges and the yokes of oxen for wood. [23] All this does Araunah give to the king." Araunah then said to the king, "May the LORD your God accept your offering." [24] The king, however, replied to Araunah, "No, I will buy it from you at the proper price, for I cannot sacrifice to the LORD my God burnt offerings that cost me nothing." So David bought the threshing floor and the oxen for fifty silver shekels. [25] Then David built an altar to the LORD there, and sacrificed burnt offerings and communion offerings. The LORD granted relief to the land, and the plague was withdrawn from Israel.

---

**24:13** 2 Sm 21:1.

**24:16** Gn 6:6; Ex 32:14; 1 Chr 21:15; Jon 3:10.

**24:16** Ex 12:23; 2 Kgs 19:35.

**24:22–23** 1 Sm 6:14; 1 Kgs 19:21.

# The Books of
# Kings

## INTRODUCTION

### Leslie J. Hoppe, OFM

The books of Kings are the last components of the Hebrew Bible's Former Prophets, which tell the story of Israel in its land from the time of Joshua to the exile. Like the books of Samuel, 1–2 Kings originally took up a single scroll. The books were divided when the Hebrew Bible was first translated into Greek sometime in the third or second century BCE, though the division does not appear in manuscripts of the Bible in Hebrew until the Middle Ages (ca. fifteenth century). The division into two books is artificial and somewhat awkward. The succession of Ahaziah to the throne of the kingdom of Israel is noted in 1 Kgs 22:52–54 while the account of his reign is taken up immediately following in 2 Kgs 1:1–18.

First Kings begins with the accession of Solomon and 2 Kings ends with the parole of King Jehoiachin, a Judahite king who was taken into exile in 597 BCE. These books tell the sad and tragic story of how the people of Israel lost the land promised to Abraham and his descendants (Gn 12:7), and how the Davidic dynasty came to an end despite God's promise that the dynasty and kingdom would be "firmly established forever" (2 Sm 7:16). The author gives no explicit statement about the future of the people of Judah beyond the exile, offering no hint of the restoration that began with the decree of Cyrus, encouraging the exiles of Judah to return to Jerusalem and rebuild its Temple (2 Chr 36:22–23; Ezr 1:1–4). The Former Prophets then is the story of Israel's infidelity and its consequences, leaving the reader to wonder if there is any future for Israel.

First Kings 1–2 concludes the account of the succession to David begun in 2 Sm 9–20. Solomon's accession is secured by court intrigues, assassinations, and political marriage (1 Kgs 1:5–3:1). The story of Solomon's dream at the shrine in Gibeon (1 Kgs 3:4–15) provides

## Outline of 1–2 Kings

I. The Reign of Solomon (1 Kgs 1:1–11:43)

II. The Reign of Jeroboam (1 Kgs 12:1–14:20)

III. Kings of Judah and Israel (1 Kgs 14:21–16:34)

IV. The Story of Elijah (1 Kgs 17:1–19:21)

V. The Story of Ahab (1 Kgs 20:1–2 Kgs 1:18)

VI. Elisha Succeeds Elijah (2 Kgs 2:1–25)

VII. Stories of Elisha and Joram (2 Kgs 3:1–9:13)

VIII. The End of the Omrid Dynasty (2 Kgs 9:14–11:20)

IX. Kings of Judah and Israel (2 Kgs 12:1–17:5)

X. The End of Israel (2 Kgs 17:6–41)

XI. The End of Judah (2 Kgs 18:1–25:30)

divine approval for his accession. Solomon's fitness for the throne is further supported by his legendary wisdom (1 Kgs 3:16–28) and by his building of the Temple of Jerusalem (1 Kgs 6–8). But Solomon compromises the absolute loyalty he owes to God, with the result that the end of his reign is marked by internal and external threats (1 Kgs 11).

Kings suggests that the deterioration of the Solomonic kingdom led the elders of Israel to reassert themselves by requiring Rehoboam, Solomon's son and presumed heir, to provide some relief from the high taxes of the Solomonic period. When Rehoboam refused,

1
K
G
S

the elders of Israel turned to Jeroboam, whom they acclaimed as king. Only the tribe of Judah recognized Rehoboam as Solomon's successor (1 Kgs 12). According to 1 Kings, then, the two Israelite kingdoms were the result of a revolt that ended the "united monarchy" ruled by Israel's first three kings. The issue of the formation of the two Israelite states is among the most controverted issues facing the historians of ancient Israel. The biblical narratives offer a reconstruction of the early period of the Israelite monarchy that is simply not supported by the evidence brought to light by archaeological excavation. As a result, some historians assert that the Israelite national states (Israel and Judah) were founded in the ninth century BCE and that a "united monarchy" was a creation of the Deuteronomistic Historian, who offered a theological explanation for the political, economic, and social developments that led to the rise and fall of Israel and Judah.

The Deuteronomist asserts that Jeroboam's successful rebellion was the fulfillment of prophecy (1 Kgs 11:26–39). But Jeroboam and his successors, without exception, are condemned for places of worship established and maintained at Dan and Bethel, which the Deuteronomist regarded as illegitimate (1 Kgs 12:26–33). For the Deuteronomist, Jerusalem was the place that God chose to receive the worship of the people of Israel. The book of Deuteronomy asserts that there is only one setting for Israel's sacrificial worship (Dt 12). Though the Deuteronomic text does not explicitly name the place, the author of Kings makes it clear that the place is Jerusalem. In a similar fashion, the Deuteronomist excoriates most of the kings of Judah for their failure to end the cultic activities on "the high places" of Judah. From the Deuteronomist's perspective, this failure to recognize Jerusalem as the only setting for the authentic worship of Israel's God was the principal cause of the fall of the Israelite kingdoms.

From a historical point of view, Israel and Judah along with the other small national states of the Levant were able to maintain their independence because of the vacuum of imperial power in the region. While these kingdoms fought with each other in order to assert their dominance, none was in a position to exert control of the region. The political and military situation changed with the rise of the neo-Assyrian Empire under Tiglath–Pileser III (745–727 BCE), whom 2 Kgs 15:19 knows as Pul. He and two of his successors led annual military campaigns into the Levant and incorporated much of the region, including the kingdom of Israel, into the Assyrian provincial system. Judah was able to maintain nominal independence by maintaining complete subservience to the Assyrian authorities. The situation changed with the fall of Assyria to the neo-Babylonian Empire, another expansionist Mesopotamian empire. The Babylonians wished to take control of Egypt, so the kings of Judah believed they had a natural ally in Egypt and thus made an ill-advised revolt against the Babylonian Empire. The result was the end of the Judahite national state along with the Davidic dynasty, the destruction of the Temple, and the exile of the state's leading citizens to Babylon. While the Deuteronomist mentions the military activities of both the Assyrians and Babylonians, 2 Kings makes it clear that the fall of the two Israelite kingdoms was the result of the failure of its kings and people to serve God alone and to worship God only in the place of God's choice, i.e., Jerusalem (2 Kgs 17:7–23; 21:11–15; 23:26–27).

Beginning with the story of Rehoboam of Judah and Jeroboam of Israel and continuing until the fall of the kingdom of Israel, the stories of the rulers of the two Israelite kingdoms are intertwined. Sometimes the two kingdoms were at war with each other, (e.g., 1 Kgs 15:16), and at other times the two kingdoms collaborated against a common enemy (e.g., 2 Kgs 8:25–29). Certainly, the senior partner was the kingdom of Israel, which could boast of a stronger economy. The king most responsible for Israel's economic and political position was Omri (878–845 BCE), whom some historians regard as a true founder of the kingdom of Israel. Omri built his capital at Samaria and established peaceful relationships with both Sidon and Judah through treaties sealed through political marriages. He founded a dynasty that included four kings despite the penchant of the kingdom of Israel for frequent changes in ruling families. Omri sought to bring internal peace to his kingdom by treating both his Israelite and Canaanite subjects equally—to the point of supplying state support for the worship of Baal, the god worshiped by the Canaanites. It was this policy that alienated the staunch Yahwists among Omri's subjects. The Deuteronomist ignores all of Omri's achievements and gives him scant notice in the story of the kingdom of Israel (1 Kgs 16:23–28). Ahab, Omri's son and successor, receives much more attention because it was during his reign that the conflict between the Yahwists, represented by the prophets Elijah (1 Kgs 17–19; 21; 2 Kgs 1–2) and Elisha (1 Kgs 19; 2 Kgs 2–13), and the worshipers of Baal came to a head because of the aggressive promotion of the cult of Baal by Jezebel, Ahab's Sidonian wife.

The Elijah and Elisha cycle of stories illustrates the struggles and victories of the "Yahweh alone" protagonists against those in the royal establishment who promoted the worship of Baal in the kingdom of Israel. The conflict was not only over which god to worship but how society was to be structured. This is clearly illustrated by the story of Naboth's vineyard (1 Kgs 21). Ahab's Yahwistic background led him to recognize the rights of Naboth to refuse to sell him his land, while Jezebel did not understand why the king's will could be thwarted by an ordinary citizen. Baalism supported a hierarchical social and economic system in which the rights of the king were paramount. The social conflict that was the by-product of the religious conflict between Baalism and Yahwism led to an armed revolution led by Jehu and supported by Elisha against Joram, Omri's grandson and the last king of the Omride dynasty (2 Kgs 9–10). Like many armed revolutions, it became difficult to control and a century later the prophet Hosea announced God's judgment on Israel because of the blood shed in God's name (Hos 1:4).

After describing the Jehu revolution that shook the kingdom of Israel, the Deuteronomist describes how the kingdom of Judah was touched by Jehu's revolt. Ahaziah, king of Judah, happened to be visiting Israel when the revolution broke out and was one of its victims (2 Kgs 9:27). His mother Athaliah, who was a member of the Omride royal family (2 Kgs 8:26), had the members of the Judahite royal family killed. She then ruled Judah as queen for seven years until she was assassinated. Joash, one member of the royal family who escaped the bloodbath, was proclaimed king.

The two Israelite kingdoms continued to suffer because of the inept rule of their kings, though Israel appears to have enjoyed peace and prosperity during the forty-one year reign of Jeroboam II (786–746 BCE). The prophets Amos and Hosea identified the wealthy as those who benefited most from Jeroboam's policy and warned that the loyalty that God expected from Israel was compromised by the hold that Baalism had on some of the population. Soon after Jeroboam's death, the expansionist policies of the Assyrian Empire in the Levant led to the end of the kingdom of Israel. Political chaos marked the last years of that kingdom, which ceased to exist as a political entity in 721 BCE with many of its leading citizens exiled to Assyria. The Deuteronomist offers one explanation for this disaster: "The Israelites sinned against the LORD" (2 Kgs 17:7).

The kingdom of Judah also felt Assyrian domination though it was able to maintain the semblance of national independence. Hezekiah (715–687 BCE) tried to get out from under Assyrian rule, but most of Judah felt the harsh Assyrian response. Jerusalem, however, escaped destruction (2 Kgs 18–19). Manasseh ruled for an unprecedented fifty-five years (677–642 BCE; 2 Kgs 21:1). He was able to preserve the Judahite national state by being totally compliant to the wishes of the Assyrian masters of Judah and Jerusalem. Eventually, however, Assyrian power waned because of weak kings. Josiah (640–609 BCE) was able to chart an independent course until his untimely death at Megiddo in a battle he should never have fought (2 Kgs 23:29). Because he rid Jerusalem of elements of non-Yahwistic worship probably introduced during the reign of Manasseh, the Deuteronomist holds Josiah in high regard and suggests that his religious reforms were occasioned by the discovery of "the book of the law" in the temple (2 Kgs 22:8–23:20).

The end of the kingdom of Judah took place not long after Josiah's death. The last kings of Judah were unable to prevent the collapse of their kingdom occasioned by the rise of the neo-Babylonian Empire under Nebuchadnezzar, who defeated the Judahite forces in

Jerusalem in 597 BCE. He took King Jehoiachin and the many members of Jerusalem's upper class to Babylon as exiles. Zedekiah, the last king of Judah, foolishly listened to those advising a revolt against Nebuchadnezzar. In 587 the Babylonians besieged and took Jerusalem, destroyed the Temple, killed all the members of the royal family they could find, and led Zedekiah into exile along with many of Jerusalem's leading citizens. The Babylonians appointed a Judahite named Gedaliah to rule Judah in place of the Davidic king, but he was assassinated by Judahite nationalists (2 Kgs 25:22–26). Second Kings and the Former Prophets end on an ambiguous note. The Deuteronomist mentions the parole of the exiled King Jehoiachin with the implication that he died while still in Babylon (2 Kgs 25:29). What the exiled king's parole portends for the future of Judah is unclear.

The Former Prophets (the Deuteronomistic History) tells a tragic story: what began with so much promise and hope under Joshua ends with the territory of the Israelite kingdoms as subprovinces of the Babylonian Empire. In addition, foreigners were introduced into the territory of the kingdom of Israel to repopulate the region after the exile to Assyria (2 Kgs 17:24–41). The Davidic dynasty and the Judahite national state were no more. The Temple of Jerusalem lay in ruins and its priesthood was scattered. Many people found themselves in exile. For the Deuteronomist all this was a consequence of Israel's failure to serve God alone. ∎

# THE BOOKS OF KINGS
## New American Bible, Introduction

The two Books of Kings are regarded by many as the last part of a work commonly known as the Deuteronomistic History. The latter tells the story of Israel from its settlement in the land (Joshua and Judges) through the transition from judgeship to monarchy under Samuel, Saul, and David (1 and 2 Samuel) to the reign of Solomon, the disintegration of the united kingdom into the kingdoms of Israel and Judah and the eventual downfall of both kingdoms (1 and 2 Kings). The Deuteronomistic History along with the Pentateuch forms a single historical narrative stretching from creation to exile.

The Books of Kings can be approached in several ways. They contain history and are an important source of information about the Israelite kingdoms. They are also narrative that calls for careful reading; historical accuracy is sometimes sacrificed to the demands of compelling characterization and dramatic tension. Most importantly, both historical presentation and narrative creativity are shaped by a particular religious worldview.

The multifaceted character of the work means that it has a variety of focal points. The historical events themselves, of course, are important, but the patterns according to which the author organizes those events give a unity to the author's historical reconstruction. The northern kings are condemned without exception, and the royal line degenerates from the divine election of Jeroboam I through a succession of short-lived dynasties to the bloodbath of Jehu's coup d'état, and finally dies out in a series of assassinations. (It must be admitted that the author at times skews the story to preserve the pattern: the relatively prosperous forty-one-year reign of Jeroboam II is dismissed in seven verses!) Judah's kings, on the other hand, follow a cyclic pattern of infidelity followed by reform, with each reformer king (Asa, Joash, Hezekiah, Josiah) greater than the last. Unfortunately the apostate kings also progress in wickedness, until the evil of Manasseh is so great that even Josiah's fidelity cannot turn away the Lord's wrath (2 Kgs 23:26).

As a literary work, the Books of Kings are admirable. Some of the brilliance is accessible only in Hebrew: wordplays, the sounds and rhythms of poetic passages, verbal allusions to other passages of the Hebrew Bible. Scenes are drawn with a vibrancy and immediacy that English cannot reproduce without sounding overdone. But other literary techniques survive translation: symmetrical structures for narrative units (and the disruptions of symmetry at significant points), rich ambiguities (see 1 Kgs 3:26), foreshadowings (such as the way the prophet of Bethel and the man of God of Judah in 1 Kgs 13 portend the destinies of their respective kingdoms). Characterization is rich and complex (Solomon, Jeroboam, Elijah, Ahab, Elisha, Jehu, etc.), revealing deep insight into human nature.

In offering a theological interpretation of history, 1–2 Kings upholds a double principle: the justification of the political disintegration of the Davidic empire, and the necessity of the religious unity of the Lord's people. This double principle is, practically speaking, unrealistic; see Jeroboam I's reasonable assessment in 1 Kgs 12:26–27. But for the Deuteronomistic historian, that is irrelevant. Just as the separation of the kingdoms is the Lord's will (1 Kgs 12:22–24), so too is the centralization of worship at the Temple in Jerusalem (1 Kgs 9:3; see Dt 12). 1–2 Kings reflects that double principle in its organization. The story of each king is told integrally, whether the king is of Israel or Judah: both lines of kings are legitimate. But the stories of the two lines are recounted in the order in which each king came to the throne, irrespective of which kingdom he ruled: there is only one people of God, though they are under two different royal jurisdictions. Moreover, each king is evaluated on theological grounds, with no allowance made for political or economic successes or failures. All Israelite kings are condemned because they did not reverse Jeroboam I's sin of setting up sanctuaries outside Jerusalem. Judahite kings are condemned for apostasy or praised for reform, as the case may be; but a continuing source of irritation to the Deuteronomistic historian is the failure of even the praiseworthy kings to do anything about local shrines outside Jerusalem (the "high places").

Into the stories of the kings, almost as a counterpoint, are woven numerous stories of prophets, named and great (Elijah, Elisha, Isaiah), and less known or anonymous (1 Kgs 13; 22). Many of the stories are anecdotal, reflecting the everyday life of prophets and prophetic guilds (1 Kgs 17; 2 Kgs 4). But the volatile dynamics of prophetic involvement in the political realm are prominent: prophets in opposition to kings (1 Kgs 14; 21; 2 Kgs 9), prophets in support of kings (1 Kgs 20:1–34; 2 Kgs 19–20; 22:14–20). This too is part of the theological worldview of the Deuteronomistic historian. The destiny of Israel is in God's hand. Through prophets, the divine will is made known on earth to kings and people and the future consequences of their response to God's will are spelled out. It is perhaps indicative of the importance prophets have in 1 and 2 Kings that the structural center of the two books is the story of Elisha's succession to Elijah's prophetic ministry (2 Kgs 2), and that this is one of the few passages in Kings that occurs outside the account of any king's reign. Behind the temporal realm of kings and reigns lies the continuing realm of the divine word and its servants, the prophets.

1–2 Kings draws on older sources (perhaps on archival records, certainly on works called "The Book of the Chronicles of the Kings"; see, for example, 1 Kgs 14:19, 29), which it uses for its own theological purpose. The so-called Deuteronomistic History itself underwent a complex process of editorial revision whose stages are disputed by scholars. There may have been an edition sometime late in the reign of Josiah (640–609 B.C.), but in the form we have it the work comes from the time of the exile (see 2 Kgs 25:27–30). In its turn the Deuteronomistic History was one of the sources used by the Chronicler in postexilic times to compile the history presented in 1 and 2 Chronicles. Though Chronicles has little interest in the Northern Kingdom, much of the material in Kings about the kingdom of Judah reappears, sometimes in altered form, in Chronicles.

The Books of Kings may be divided as follows:

I. The Reign of Solomon (1 Kgs 1:1–11:43)
II. The Reign of Jeroboam (1 Kgs 12:1–14:20)
III. Kings of Judah and Israel (1 Kgs 14:21–16:34)
IV. The Story of Elijah (1 Kgs 17:1–19:21)
V. The Story of Ahab (1 Kgs 20:1–2 Kgs 1:18)
VI. Elisha Succeeds Elijah (2 Kgs 2:1–25)
VII. Stories of Elisha and Joram (2 Kgs 3:1–9:13)
VIII. The End of the Omrid Dynasty (2 Kgs 9:14–11:20)
IX. Kings of Judah and Israel (2 Kgs 12:1–17:5)
X. The End of Israel (2 Kgs 17:6–41)
XI. The End of Judah (2 Kgs 18:1–25:30) ∎

# FIRST KINGS

## I. THE REIGN OF SOLOMON†

**1** **David's Old Age.** ¹† When King David was old and advanced in years, though they covered him with blankets he could not get warm. ² His servants therefore said to him, "Let a young virgin be sought to attend my lord the king,† and to nurse him. If she sleeps with you, my lord the king will be warm." ³ So they sought for a beautiful girl throughout the territory of Israel, and found Abishag the Shunamite. So they brought her to the king. ⁴ The girl was very beautiful indeed, and she nursed the king and took care of him. But the king did not have relations with her.

**Adonijah's Ambition.** ⁵ Adonijah, son of Haggith, boasted, "I shall be king!" and he provided himself with chariots, horses, and a retinue of fifty to go before him.* ⁶ Yet his father would never antagonize him by asking, "Why are you doing this?" Adonijah was also very handsome, and next in age to Absalom by the same mother. ⁷ He consulted with Joab, son of Zeruiah, and with Abiathar the priest, and they became Adonijah's supporters. ⁸ However, Zadok the priest, Benaiah, son of Jehoiada, Nathan the prophet, Shimei and Rei, and David's warriors did not support Adonijah.

⁹ Adonijah slaughtered sheep, oxen, and fatlings at the stone Zoheleth near En-rogel† and invited all his brothers, the king's sons, and all the royal officials of Judah; ¹⁰ but he did not invite Nathan the prophet, or Benaiah, or the warriors, or Solomon his brother.

**Solomon Proclaimed King.** ¹¹ Then Nathan said to Bathsheba, Solomon's mother: "Have you not heard that Adonijah, son of Haggith, has become king, and our lord David does not know? ¹² Come now, let me advise you so that you may save your life and the life of your son Solomon. ¹³ Go, visit King David, and say to him, 'Did you not, my lord king, swear to your handmaid: Your son Solomon shall be king after me; it is he who shall sit upon my throne? Why, then, has Adonijah become king?' ¹⁴ And while you are still there speaking to the king, I will come in after you and confirm your words."

¹⁵ So Bathsheba visited the king in his room. The king was very old, and Abishag the Shunamite was caring for the king.† ¹⁶ Bathsheba bowed in homage to the king. The king said to her, "What do you wish?"† ¹⁷ She answered him: "My lord, you swore to your servant by the LORD, your God, 'Solomon your son will be king after me; it is he who shall sit upon my throne.' ¹⁸ But now Adonijah has become king, and you, my lord king, do not know it.† ¹⁹ He has sacrificed bulls, fatlings, and sheep in great numbers; he has invited all the king's sons, Abiathar the priest, and Joab, the commander of the army, but not your servant Solomon. ²⁰† Now, my lord king, all Israel is looking to you to declare to them who is to sit upon the

---

† **1:1–11:43** The story of the reign of Solomon comprises twelve major units, organized concentrically. That is, the first unit (1:1–2:12a) balances the last (11:26–43), the second (2:12b–46) balances the second last (11:14–25), and so forth. (See the structural notes at the beginning of each major unit.) The center of the whole story is a diptych that narrates the construction of the Temple (6:1–7:51) and its dedication (8:1–9:10).

**1:1–2:12a** The first major unit of the Solomon story concludes the so-called Succession Narrative (2 Sm 9–20; 1 Kgs 1–2). This unit tells how Solomon, a younger son, came to succeed David on the throne of Israel through the intervention of the prophet Nathan. Compare the last unit of the Solomon story, 11:26–43, where the prophet Ahijah begins the process whereby Jeroboam becomes king of the northern tribes after Solomon's death. The story of Solomon's accession is itself concentrically arranged: David's decline, Adonijah's rise, Solomon's supporters, David's decision, Solomon's inauguration, Adonijah's fall, David's death. Chronicles has no developed parallel to this story (see 1 Chr 23:1).

**1:2** The fulsome use of royal titles and the elaborate etiquette in the Succession Narrative suggest the raw ambition of the contending parties and the oppressive atmosphere of the court.

**1:9** *En-rogel*: the modern Job's Well just southeast of Jeru-

salem. It marked the ancient boundary between the tribes of Benjamin and Judah (Jos 15:7; 18:16).

**1:15** Entering the king's chambers, Bathsheba confronts two realities: he is very old; and she herself, the woman for whom David once committed adultery and murder, has been replaced at the king's side and in his bed.

**1:16** Throughout 1 Kgs 1 the key question is "Who shall be king (*malak*)?" David's feeble, two-syllable question to Bathsheba is an ironic echo of that key word: "What do you wish?" renders the Heb. *mahlak*?

**1:18** Bathsheba uses a clever wordplay to conceal the rivalry between Solomon and Adonijah and imply that the real rivalry is between David and Adonijah. She repeatedly addresses David as "my lord king" (*'adoni hammelek*), but claims that "Adonijah has become king" (*adoniya malak*). *Know*: the term means both "be aware of" and "recognize, acknowledge, ratify."

**1:20** There was no precedent for determining succession to the throne of Israel. Adonijah and his supporters assumed that primogeniture would assure the succession as it did in the monarchies of the surrounding nations. But Bathsheba persuades David that he is free to name anyone he chooses.

* 
**1:5** 2 Sm 15:1.

throne of my lord the king after him. ²¹ If this is not done, when my lord the king rests with his ancestors, I and my son Solomon will be considered criminals."

²² While she was still speaking to the king, Nathan the prophet came in. ²³ They told the king, "Nathan the prophet is here." He entered the king's presence and did him homage, bowing to the floor. ²⁴ Then Nathan said: "My lord king, did you say, 'Adonijah shall be king after me and shall sit upon my throne'? ²⁵ For today he went down and sacrificed bulls, fatlings, and sheep in great numbers; he invited all the king's sons, the commanders of the army, and Abiathar the priest, and even now they are eating and drinking in his company and saying, 'Long live King Adonijah!' ²⁶ But me, your servant, he did not invite; nor Zadok the priest, nor Benaiah, son of Jehoiada, nor your servant Solomon. ²⁷ If this was done by order of my lord the king, you did not tell me, your servant, who is to sit upon the throne of my lord the king after him."

²⁸ King David answered, "Call Bathsheba here." When she entered the king's presence and stood before him, ²⁹ the king swore, "As the LORD lives, who has redeemed my life from all distress, ³⁰ this very day I will fulfill the oath I swore to you by the LORD, the God of Israel, 'Your son Solomon shall be king after me and shall sit upon my throne in my place.'" ³¹ Bowing to the floor in homage to the king, Bathsheba said, "May my lord, King David, live forever!"

³² Then King David said, "Call Zadok the priest, Nathan the prophet, and Benaiah, son of Jehoiada." When they had entered the king's presence, ³³ he said to them: "Take with you the royal officials. Mount my son Solomon upon my own mule and escort him down to Gihon. ³⁴ There Zadok the priest and Nathan the prophet shall anoint him king over Israel, and you shall blow the ram's horn and cry, 'Long live King Solomon!' ³⁵ When you come back up with him, he is to go in and sit upon my throne. It is he that shall be king in my place: him I designate ruler of Israel and of Judah." ³⁶ Benaiah, son of Jehoiada, answered

the king: "So be it! May the LORD, the God of my lord the king, so decree! ³⁷ As the LORD has been with my lord the king, so may he be with Solomon, and make his throne even greater than that of my lord, King David!"

³⁸ So Zadok the priest, Nathan the prophet, Benaiah, son of Jehoiada, and the Cherethites and Pelethites† went down, and mounting Solomon on King David's mule, escorted him to Gihon. ³⁹ Then Zadok the priest took the horn of oil from the tent and anointed Solomon. They blew the ram's horn and all the people shouted, "Long live King Solomon!" ⁴⁰ Then all the people went up after him, playing flutes and rejoicing so much the earth split with their shouting.

**Adonijah Submits to Solomon.** ⁴¹ Adonijah and all the guests who were with him heard it, just as they ended their banquet. When Joab heard the sound of the ram's horn, he asked, "Why this uproar in the city?" ⁴² As he was speaking, Jonathan, son of Abiathar the priest, arrived. Adonijah said, "Come, you are a man of worth and must bring good news." ⁴³ Jonathan answered Adonijah, "Hardly!† Our lord, King David, has made Solomon king. ⁴⁴ The king sent with him Zadok the priest, Nathan the prophet, Benaiah, son of Jehoiada, and the Cherethites and Pelethites, and they mounted him upon the king's own mule. ⁴⁵ Zadok the priest and Nathan the prophet anointed him king at Gihon, and they went up from there rejoicing, so that the city is in an uproar. That is the noise you hear. ⁴⁶ Moreover, Solomon has taken his seat on the royal throne, ⁴⁷ and moreover the king's servants have come to pay their respects to our lord, King David, saying, 'May your God make Solomon's name more famous than your name, his throne greater than your throne!' And the king in his bed did homage. ⁴⁸ This is what the king said: 'Blessed be the LORD, the God of Israel, who has this day provided one to sit upon my throne, so that I see it with my own eyes.'" ⁴⁹ All the guests of Adonijah got up trembling, and went each their way, ⁵⁰ but Adonijah, in fear of Solomon, got up and went to grasp the horns of the altar.†

---

**1:38** *Cherethites and Pelethites*: mercenaries in David's bodyguard. They became part of his retinue after he defeated the Philistines and established himself in Jerusalem; cf. 2 Sm 8:18; 15:18; 20:23.
**1:43** *Hardly*: Jonathan's first word, *'abal*, whose meaning (such as "indeed," "on the contrary") must be discerned from the context, may be ironic. This irony is deepened by an un-

translatable wordplay in Hebrew: a very similar word means "to mourn," which is an appropriate comment about the death of Adonijah's hopes for the throne.
**1:50** *Horns of the altar*: the protuberances on each of the four corners of the altar (Ex 27:2; 29:12). By grasping the horns of the altar Adonijah is claiming asylum (Ex 21:13–14; 1 Kgs 2:28).

[51] It was reported to Solomon: "Adonijah, in fear of King Solomon, is clinging to the horns of the altar and saying, 'Let King Solomon first swear that he will not kill me, his servant, with the sword.'" [52] Solomon answered, "If he proves worthy, not a hair of his shall fall to the ground. But if evil is found in him, he shall die." [53] King Solomon sent to have him brought down from the altar, and he came and paid homage to King Solomon. Solomon then said to him, "Go to your house."

# 2 David's Last Instructions and Death.

[1] When the time of David's death drew near, he gave these instructions to Solomon his son: [2] "I am going the way of all the earth. Be strong and be a man! [3]* Keep the mandate of the LORD, your God, walking in his ways and keeping his statutes, commands, ordinances, and decrees as they are written in the law of Moses, that you may succeed in whatever you do, and wherever you turn, [4]* and that the LORD may fulfill the word he spoke concerning me: If your sons so conduct themselves that they walk before me in faithfulness with their whole heart and soul, there shall never be wanting someone of your line on the throne of Israel.

[5]†* "You yourself know what Joab, son of Zeruiah, did to me—what he did to the two commanders of Israel's armies, Abner, son of Ner, and Amasa, son of Jether: he killed them and brought the blood of war into a time of peace, and put the blood of war on the belt about his waist and the sandal on his foot. [6] Act with all the wisdom you possess; do not let his gray head go down to Sheol in peace. [7]* But be true to the sons of Barzillai the Gileadite, and have them among those who eat at your table. For they were loyal to me when I was fleeing from your brother Absalom. [8]* You also have with you Shimei, son of Gera, the Benjaminite of Bahurim, who cursed me bitterly the day I was going to Mahanaim. When he came down to meet me at the Jordan, I swore to him by the LORD: 'I will not kill you by the sword.' [9] But you must not let him go unpunished. You are wise; you will know what to do to send his gray head down to Sheol in blood."

[10]* David rested with his ancestors and was buried in the City of David. [11]* David was king over Israel for forty years: he was king seven years in Hebron and thirty-three years in Jerusalem.

## The Kingdom Made Secure.† [12] Then Solomon sat on the throne of David his father, and his kingship was established.

[13] Adonijah, son of Haggith, came to Bathsheba, the mother of Solomon. "Do you come in peace?" she asked. "In peace," he answered, [14] and he added, "I have something to say to you." She replied, "Speak." [15] So he said: "You know that the kingship was mine, and all Israel expected me to be king. But the kingship passed me by and went to my brother; by the LORD's will it went to him. [16] But now there is one favor I would ask of you. Do not refuse me." And she said, "Speak on." [17]† He said, "Please ask King Solomon, who will not refuse you, to give me Abishag the Shunamite to be my wife." [18] Bathsheba replied, "Very well, I will speak to the king for you."

[19] Then Bathsheba went to King Solomon to speak to him for Adonijah, and the king stood up to meet her and paid her homage. Then he sat down upon his throne, and a throne was provided for the king's mother, who sat at his right. [20] She said, "There is one small favor I would ask of you. Do not refuse me." The king said to her, "Ask it, my mother, for I will not refuse you." [21] So she said, "Let Abishag the Shunamite be given to your brother Adonijah

---

† **2:5–9** David urges Solomon to purge Joab and Shimei and supplies him with justification for doing so. Joab had killed Abner (2 Sm 3:22–30) and Amasa (2 Sm 20:4–12), thereby bringing blood guilt upon himself and perhaps upon his master David. Shimei had cursed David (2 Sm 16:5–8), though David pledged that Shimei would not be killed for it (2 Sm 19:16–24). David's motives, however, may have been more personal. Joab also killed David's son Absalom and chided David for his untimely public display of grief (2 Sm 18:9–19:8), and David may have felt himself free of the promise he made to Shimei because that promise was coerced by the presence of Shimei's thousand partisans backing him at the time.

**2:12–46** The second major unit of the Solomon story shows how Solomon eliminated people he considered threats to the security of his throne. It is marked by a device called "inclu-sion," where the text repeats a word, phrase, or idea at the beginning and end of a literary unit (see vv. 12b, 46b). Compare 11:14–25, where Solomon is unable to eliminate other threats to his security.

**2:17–25** Abishag had belonged to David's harem (1:3–4), which Solomon inherited. Adonijah's request could imply a challenge to Solomon's accession and so exposes Adonijah to the suspicion of insurrection that will cost him his life; cf. 2 Sm 3:6–11; 16:21–22.

* ————

**2:3** Dt 17:18–19.
**2:4** 2 Sm 7:11–16; Ps 132:11–12.
**2:5** 2 Sm 3:22–30; 20:8–10.
**2:7** 2 Sm 17:27–29; 19:32–41.
**2:8** 2 Sm 16:5–13; 19:17–24.
**2:10** Acts 2:29.
**2:11** 2 Sm 2:1–4; 5:1–5.

to be his wife." ²² King Solomon answered his mother, "And why do you ask that Abishag the Shunamite be given to Adonijah? Ask the kingship for him as well, for he is my older brother! Ask for him, for Abiathar the priest, for Joab, son of Zeruiah!" ²³ And King Solomon swore by the LORD: "May God do thus to me and more, if Adonijah has not spoken this word at the cost of his life. ²⁴* And now, as the LORD lives, who has established me and set me on the throne of David my father and made for me a house as he promised, this day shall Adonijah be put to death." ²⁵ Then King Solomon sent Benaiah, son of Jehoiada, who struck him dead.

²⁶* The king said to Abiathar the priest: "Go to your estate in Anathoth. Though you deserve to die, I will not put you to death at this time, because you carried the ark of the Lord GOD before David my father and shared in all the hardships my father endured."† ²⁷* So Solomon dismissed Abiathar from the office of priest of the LORD, thus fulfilling the word the LORD had spoken in Shiloh against the house of Eli.

²⁸ When the news came to Joab, since he had sided with Adonijah, though not with Absalom, he fled to the tent of the LORD and clung to the horns of the altar. ²⁹ King Solomon was told, "Joab has fled to the tent of the LORD and is by the altar." He sent Benaiah, son of Jehoiada, with the order, "Go, strike him down." ³⁰ Benaiah went to the tent of the LORD and said to him, "The king says, 'Come out.'" But he answered, "No! I will die here." Benaiah reported to the king, "This is what Joab said to me in reply." ³¹ The king answered him: "Do as he has said. Strike him down and bury him, and remove from me and from my father's house the blood which Joab shed without provocation. ³²* The LORD will bring blood upon his own head, because he struck down two men better and more just than himself, and slew them with the sword without my father David's knowledge: Abner, son of Ner, commander of Israel's army, and Amasa, son

of Jether, commander of Judah's army. ³³ Their blood will be upon the head of Joab and his descendants. But upon David and his descendants, upon his house and his throne, there shall be peace forever from the LORD." ³⁴ Benaiah, son of Jehoiada, went back, struck him down and killed him; he was buried in his house in the wilderness. ³⁵ The king appointed Benaiah, son of Jehoiada, over the army in his place; Zadok the priest the king put in place of Abiathar.

³⁶ Then the king summoned Shimei and said to him: "Build yourself a house in Jerusalem and stay there. Do not go anywhere else. ³⁷ For the day you leave, and cross the Wadi Kidron, be certain you shall surely die. Your blood shall be upon your own head." ³⁸ Shimei answered the king: "I accept. Your servant will do just as my lord the king has said." So Shimei stayed in Jerusalem for a long time. ³⁹ But three years later, two of Shimei's servants ran away to Achish, son of Maacah, king of Gath, and Shimei was told, "Your servants are in Gath." ⁴⁰ So Shimei rose, saddled his donkey, and went to Achish in Gath in search of his servants; and Shimei returned from Gath with his servants. ⁴¹ When Solomon was told that Shimei had gone from Jerusalem to Gath, and had returned, ⁴² the king summoned Shimei and said to him: "Did I not have you swear by the LORD and warn you clearly, 'The day you leave and go anywhere else, be certain you shall surely die'? And you answered, 'I accept and obey.'† ⁴³ Why, then, have you not kept the oath of the LORD and the command that I gave you?" ⁴⁴* And the king said to Shimei: "In your heart you know very well the evil that you did to David my father. Now the LORD is bringing your own evil upon your head. ⁴⁵ But King Solomon shall be blessed, and David's throne shall be established before the LORD forever." ⁴⁶ The king then gave the order to Benaiah, son of Jehoiada, who went out and struck him dead.

And the royal power was established in Solomon's hand.

---

**2:26** The narrator indulges in a subtle wordplay: Abiathar's exile to Anathoth (*anatot*) continues the series of hardships he has endured (*hitʾannita*).

**2:42–44** In his charge against Shimei, Solomon misrepresents the truth in two ways. He did not make Shimei take an oath. And he imposed capital punishment only on crossing the Wadi Kidron, to the east of Jerusalem. This was presumably to prevent Shimei from returning to his home, Bahurim, which lay in that

direction; Gath, however, is southwest of Jerusalem. Solomon's next words to Shimei reveal that he is really being punished for cursing David, not for violating Solomon's command.

**2:24** 2 Sm 7:11–16.
**2:26** 1 Sm 22:20–23.
**2:27** 1 Sm 2:27–33.
**2:32** 2 Sm 3:22–30; 20:8–10.
**2:44** 2 Sm 16:5–13; 19:17–24.

# 3 Early Promise of Solomon's Reign.†

[1]* Solomon allied himself by marriage with Pharaoh, king of Egypt. He married the daughter of Pharaoh and brought her to the City of David, until he should finish building his own house, and the house of the LORD, and the wall around Jerusalem. [2] The people were sacrificing on the high places, however, for up to that time no house had been built for the name of the LORD. [3] Although Solomon loved the LORD, walking in the statutes of David his father, he offered sacrifice and burned incense on the high places.

[4] The king went to Gibeon to sacrifice there, because that was the great high place. Upon its altar Solomon sacrificed a thousand burnt offerings. [5] In Gibeon the LORD appeared to Solomon in a dream at night. God said: Whatever you ask I shall give you. [6] Solomon answered: "You have shown great kindness to your servant, David my father, because he walked before you with fidelity, justice, and an upright heart; and you have continued this great kindness toward him today, giving him a son to sit upon his throne. [7] Now, LORD, my God, you have made me, your servant, king to succeed David my father; but I am a mere youth, not knowing at all how to act— [8] I, your servant, among the people you have chosen, a people so vast that it cannot be numbered or counted. [9] Give your servant, therefore, a listening heart to judge your people and to distinguish between good and evil. For who is able to give judgment for this vast people of yours?"

[10] The Lord was pleased by Solomon's request. [11] So God said to him: Because you asked for this—you did not ask for a long life for yourself, nor for riches, nor for the life of your enemies—but you asked for discernment to know what is right— [12] I now do as you request. I give you a heart so wise and discerning that there has never been anyone like you until now, nor after you will there be anyone to equal you. [13]* In addition, I give you what you have not asked for: I give you such riches and glory that among kings there will be no one like you all your days. [14] And if you walk in my ways, keeping my statutes and commandments, as David your father did, I will give you a long life. [15] Solomon awoke; it was a dream! He went to Jerusalem, stood before the ark of the covenant of the Lord, sacrificed burnt offerings and communion offerings, and gave a feast for all his servants.

## Solomon's Listening Heart.†

[16] Later, two prostitutes came to the king and stood before him. [17] One woman said: "By your leave, my lord, this woman and I live in the same house, and I gave birth in the house while she was present. [18] On the third day after I gave birth, this woman also gave birth. We were alone; no one else was in the house with us; only the two of us were in the house. [19] This woman's son died during the night when she lay on top of him. [20] So in the middle of the night she got up and took my son from my side, as your servant was sleeping. Then she laid him in her bosom and laid her dead son in my bosom. [21] I rose in the morning to nurse my son, and he was dead! But when I examined him in the morning light, I saw it was not the son I had borne." [22] The other woman answered, "No! The living one is my son, the dead one is yours." But the first kept saying, "No! the dead one is your son, the living one is mine!" Thus they argued before the king. [23] Then the king said: "One woman claims, 'This, the living one, is my son, the dead one is yours.' The other answers, 'No! The dead one is your son, the living one is mine.'" [24] The king continued, "Get me a sword." When they brought the sword before the king, [25] he said, "Cut the living child in two, and give half to one woman and half to the other." [26]† The woman whose son was alive, because she was stirred with compassion for her son, said to the king, "Please, my lord, give her the living baby—do not kill it!"

---

† **3:1–15** The third major unit of the Solomon story depicts the bright beginning of his reign. It includes the narrator's remarks about Solomon's marriage and his building projects, and a divine appearance to Solomon. Compare 11:1–13, where the same themes recur, but in negative fashion. The story of the divine appearance is told also in 2 Chr 1:1–13.

**3:16–5:14** The fourth major unit of the Solomon story shows how Solomon used the three gifts that the Lord gave him in 3:12–13: a listening heart (3:16–28), riches (4:1–5:8), universal renown (5:9–14). In each case his gifts benefited the populace, from the lowest classes (3:16–28) to his whole people (4:20;

5:5) to the whole world (5:9–14). Compare 9:26–10:29, where the same three gifts all redound to the benefit of Solomon himself.

**3:26–27** The true mother reveals herself by an uncommon and tender word for the child, "baby." With this, and the woman's willingness to give up her child, Solomon realizes that she is the true mother, and quotes her words exactly in rendering his judgment.

**3:1** 1 Kgs 7:8; 9:24.       **3:13** Eccl 1:12–13; Wis 7:7–11; Mt 6:29.

But the other said, "It shall be neither mine nor yours. Cut it in two!" [27] The king then answered, "Give her the living baby! Do not kill it! She is the mother." [28] When all Israel heard the judgment the king had given, they were in awe of him, because they saw that the king had in him the wisdom of God for giving right judgment.

# 4 Solomon's Riches: Domestic Affairs.†

[1] Solomon was king over all Israel, [2] and these were the officials he had in his service:

Azariah, son of Zadok, the priest;
[3] Elihoreph and Ahijah, sons of Shisha, scribes;
Jehoshaphat, son of Ahilud, the chancellor;
[4] Benaiah, son of Jehoiada, in charge of the army;
Zadok and Abiathar, priests;
[5] Azariah, son of Nathan, in charge of the governors;
Zabud, son of Nathan, priest and companion to the king;
[6] Ahishar, master of the palace; and Adoniram, son of Abda, in charge of the forced labor.

[7]† Solomon had twelve governors over all Israel who supplied food for the king and his household, each having to provide for one month in the year. [8] Their names were:†

the son of Hur in the hill country of Ephraim;
[9] the son of Deker in Makaz, Shaalbim, Beth-shemesh, and Elon Beth-hanan;
[10] the son of Hesed in Arubboth, as well as in Socoh and the whole region of Hepher;

[11] the son of Abinadab, in all Naphath-dor; he was married to Taphath, Solomon's daughter;
[12] Baana, son of Ahilud, in Taanach and Megiddo and all Beth-shean near Zarethan below Jezreel, from Beth-shean to Abel-meholah to beyond Jokmeam;
[13] the son of Geber in Ramoth-gilead, having charge of the villages of Jair, son of Manasseh, in Gilead; and of the district of Argob in Bashan—sixty large walled cities with gates barred with bronze;
[14] Ahinadab, son of Iddo, in Mahanaim;
[15] Ahimaaz, in Naphtali; he was married to Basemath, another daughter of Solomon;
[16] Baana, son of Hushai, in Asher and Aloth;
[17] Jehoshaphat, son of Paruah, in Issachar;
[18] Shimei, son of Ela, in Benjamin;
[19] Geber, son of Uri, in the land of Gilead, the land of Sihon, king of the Amorites, and of Og, king of Bashan.

There was one governor besides, in the land of Judah.† [20]* Judah and Israel were as numerous as the sands by the sea; they ate and drank and rejoiced.

# 5 Solomon's Riches: International Affairs.

[1]† Solomon ruled over all the kingdoms from the River† to the land of the Philistines, down to the border of Egypt; they paid Solomon tribute and served him as long as he lived. [2]† Solomon's provisions for each day were thirty kors of fine flour, sixty kors of meal, [3] ten fatted oxen, twenty pasture-fed oxen, and a hundred sheep, not counting harts, gazelles,

---

**4:1–5:8** The sub-unit on Solomon's riches is organized around domestic affairs (4:1–20) and international affairs (5:1–5), with a short appendix on Solomon's horses and chariots (5:6–8). Compare 9:26–10:29, where comparable elements reappear.

**4:7–19** The administration of the kingdom thus initiated by Solomon continued in its main features for the duration of the monarchy in Israel and Judah. Note the use of "all Israel" to mean only the northern tribes (see also 5:27). Solomon's exactions did not fall evenly on the whole people, but favored his own southern tribe of Judah. Eventually this inequity would lead to the dissolution of the union of Israel and Judah (12:1–19).

**4:8–19** Several of the governors are identified only by their fathers' names.

**4:19** *One governor...land of Judah:* the royal territory of Judah had its own peculiar administration different from that of the twelve northern districts, each of which had to supply the

king and his household with a month's provisions of food each year (v. 7).

**5:1–32** This translation follows the numeration of the Hebrew Bible, rather than the Vulgate; in many English translations, 5:1–34, and 5:15 is 5:1.

**5:1** *The River:* that is, the Euphrates. This claim may be exaggerated, but "from the Euphrates to the border of Egypt" was the traditional description of the extent of the Davidic holdings.

**5:2** The list of Solomon's supplies may have originally belonged with the list of governors in 4:7–19, but the author has placed it here to imply that Solomon's vassal kingdoms, not his own citizenry, supplied his vast daily needs. The daily provisions listed could have supported several thousand people. *Kors:* see note on Ez 45:14.

**4:20** Gn 22:17; 32:13;      Hos 1:10; Heb 11:12. Dn 3:36;

roebucks, and fatted fowl. [4] He had dominion over all the land west of the River, from Tiphsah to Gaza, and all its kings, and he had peace on all his borders round about. [5]* Thus Judah and Israel lived in security, everyone under their own vine and fig tree from Dan to Beersheba, as long as Solomon lived.

### Solomon's Riches: Chariots and Horses.

[6]* Solomon had forty thousand stalls for horses for chariots and twelve thousand horsemen. [7]† The governors, one for each month, provided food for King Solomon and for all the guests at King Solomon's table. They left nothing unprovided. [8] For the chariot horses and draft animals also, each brought his quota of barley and straw to the required place.

### Solomon's Renown.

[9]* Moreover, God gave Solomon wisdom, exceptional understanding, and knowledge, as vast as the sand on the seashore. [10] Solomon's wisdom surpassed that of all the peoples of the East and all the wisdom of Egypt. [11] He was wiser than anyone else—wiser than Ethan the Ezrahite, or Heman, Chalcol, and Darda, the musicians—and his fame spread throughout the neighboring peoples. [12] Solomon also uttered three thousand proverbs, and his songs numbered a thousand and five. [13] He spoke of plants, from the cedar on Lebanon to the hyssop growing out of the wall, and he spoke about beasts, birds, reptiles, and fishes. [14]* People from all nations came to hear Solomon's wisdom, sent by all the kings of the earth who had heard of his wisdom.

### Preparations for the Temple.

† [15] When Hiram, king of Tyre, heard that Solomon had been anointed king in place of his father, he sent an embassy to him; for Hiram had always been David's friend.† [16] Solomon sent back this message to Hiram: [17]* "You know that David my father, because of the wars that beset him, could not build a house for the name of the LORD his God until such time as the LORD should put his enemies under the soles of his feet. [18] But now the LORD, my God, has given me rest on all sides, without adversary or misfortune. [19]* So I intend to build a house for the name of the LORD, my God, as the LORD said to David my father: Your son whom I will put upon your throne in your place shall build the house for my name. [20] Give orders, then, to have cedars from the Lebanon cut down for me. My servants shall accompany yours, and I will pay you whatever you say for your servants' wages. For you know that there is no one among us who is skilled in cutting timber like the Sidonians." [21] When Hiram had heard the words of Solomon, he was overjoyed, and said, "Blessed be the LORD this day, who has given David a wise son over this numerous people." [22]† Hiram then sent word to Solomon, "I have heard the proposal you sent me, and I will provide all the cedars and fir trees you desire. [23] My servants shall bring them down from the Lebanon to the sea, and I will arrange them into rafts in the sea and bring them wherever you say. There I will break up the rafts, and you shall take the lumber. You, for your part, shall furnish the provisions I desire for my household." [24] So Hiram continued to provide Solomon with all the cedars and fir trees he desired, [25] while Solomon gave Hiram twenty thousand kors of wheat to provide for his household, and twenty kors† of handpressed oil. Solomon gave Hiram all this every year. [26] The LORD gave Solomon wisdom as he promised him. So there was peace between

---

5:7 This verse suggests that the governors also saw to the provender for Solomon's animals (v. 8).

5:15–32 The fifth major unit of the Solomon story explains the preparations Solomon made for the construction of the Temple. He negotiates with Hiram of Tyre for materiel (5:15–26), and conscripts a labor force for personnel (5:27–32). Compare 9:11–23, which returns to the same two themes after the Temple has been built and dedicated. 2 Chr 2:1–17 presents another version of the same material.

5:15 David's friend: the term "to be a friend," lit., "to love," is political, and means that David and Hiram had been allies. The purpose of Hiram's embassy is to determine whether Solomon is willing to continue the alliance. This unspoken agenda lies behind the negotiations about materials for the Temple, as the concluding v. 26 makes clear.

5:22–23 Although his reply is couched in polite, diplomatic language, Hiram renegotiates Solomon's terms in his own favor.

No Israelites are to enter Tyrian territory, and Solomon is not to pay the salary of Hiram's laborers but rather to furnish "provisions" for his household—the same language used of the tribute Solomon received from his own vassals in v. 4.

5:25 Twenty kors: this means about two thousand gallons of the finest olive oil available, hand-pressed rather than produced in large olive presses, so that no debris (such as crushed olive pits, powder from the grinding stones) would contaminate the oil. Also see note on 2 Chr 2:9.

5:5 Sir 47:13.
5:6 1 Kgs 10:26; Dt 17:16; 2 Chr 1:14; 9:25.
5:9–14 Sir 47:15–17.

5:14 1 Kgs 10:1.
5:17 2 Sm 7:5–7; 1 Chr 22:7–8.
5:19 2 Sm 7:12–13.

Hiram and Solomon, and the two of them made† a covenant.

²⁷King Solomon raised thirty thousand forced laborers from all Israel.† ²⁸He sent them to the Lebanon for a month in relays of ten thousand, so that they spent one month in the Lebanon and two months at home. Adoniram was in charge of the forced labor. ²⁹Solomon had seventy thousand carriers and eighty thousand stonecutters in the mountain, ³⁰in addition to three thousand three hundred overseers answerable to Solomon, who were in charge of the work and directed the people engaged in the work. ³¹By order of the king, fine, large blocks of stone were quarried to give the house a foundation of hewn stone. ³²Solomon's and Hiram's builders, along with others from Gebal,† shaped them, and prepared the wood and stones for building the house.

# 6 Building of the Temple.†

¹In the four hundred and eightieth year after the Israelites went forth from the land of Egypt, in the fourth year of Solomon's reign over Israel, in the month of Ziv (the second month), he began to build the house of the LORD.†

²The house which King Solomon built for the LORD was sixty cubits long, twenty wide, and thirty high. ³The porch in front of the nave of the house was twenty cubits from side to side along the width of the house, and ten cubits deep in front of the house. ⁴Windows with closed lattices were made for the house, ⁵and adjoining the wall of the house he built a substructure around its walls that enclosed the nave and the inner sanctuary, and he made side chambers all around. ⁶The lowest story was five cubits wide, the middle one six cubits wide, the third seven cubits wide, because he put recesses along the outside of the house to avoid fastening anything into the walls of the house. ⁷The house was built of stone dressed at the quarry, so that no hammer or ax, no iron tool, was to be heard in the house during its construction. ⁸The entrance to the middle story was on the south side of the house; stairs led up to the middle story and from the middle story to the third. ⁹When he had finished building the house, it was roofed in with rafters and boards of cedar. ¹⁰He built the substructure five cubits high all along the outside of the house, to which it was joined by cedar beams.

¹¹The word of the LORD came to Solomon: ¹²*As to this house you are building—if you walk in my statutes, carry out my ordinances, and observe all my commands, walking in them, I will fulfill toward you my word which I spoke to David your father. ¹³I will dwell in the midst of the Israelites and will not forsake my people Israel.

¹⁴When Solomon finished building the house, ¹⁵its inside walls were lined with cedar paneling: he covered the interior with wood from floor to ceiling, and he covered its floor with fir planking. ¹⁶At the rear of the house a space of twenty cubits was set off by cedar panels from the floor to the ceiling, enclosing the inner sanctuary, the holy of holies. ¹⁷The house was forty cubits long, that is, the nave,

---

**5:26** *Made:* lit., "cut." The story of Solomon's arrangements with Hiram is framed by references to political alliance between Israel and Tyre (vv. 15, 26). Since, in Hebrew idiom, Hiram and Solomon "cut" a covenant, this suggests that the agreement they reach for "cutting" wood (which clearly favors Hiram) reflects the terms of the larger treaty.

**5:27** *All Israel:* see note on 4:7–19.

**5:32** *Gebal:* Byblos.

**6:1–7:51** The central units of the Solomon story describe the building of the Temple (6:1–7:51) and its dedication ceremony (8:1–9:10). The account of the construction of the Temple ("the house") is organized to give the reader a guided tour. Approaching from a distance, we see ground plans (6:2–3) and structural work in stone (6:4–8) and wood (6:9–10). After a brief interruption that recounts a divine word to Solomon (6:11–13), we enter the Temple to view the paneling and ornamentation of the nave (6:14–18), the gilded walls and golden entrance of the inner sanctuary or holy of holies (6:19–22), with its priceless interior decoration and furnishings (6:23–28). As we leave, we admire the interior carvings and gilded floor of the inner sanctuary (6:29–30), return to the nave through carved and gilded doors (6:31–32), and exit from the nave through another set of carved and gilded doors (6:33–35) to the courtyard (6:36). Our guide briefly points out the nearby palace complex (7:1–12); then we

walk around the courtyard to marvel at Hiram's heroic works in bronze: the two columns (7:15–22), the "sea" (7:23–26), and the ten stands and basins set along either side of the Temple buildings (7:27–39). The account ends with the smaller bronze vessels Hiram made for the Temple services (7:40–47) and the gold vessels that Solomon made (7:48–50). Unfortunately, several factors make it impossible to use the account to produce a satisfactory model of Solomon's Temple. Throughout the account there are numerous technical architectural terms whose meaning is lost to us; and it is moreover likely that the author is describing the Temple as it stood in his own time, centuries after Solomon's day. The Chronicler also describes the construction of the Temple in 2 Chr 3:1–4:22 and its dedication in 2 Chr 5:1–7:22.

**6:1** Construction of the Temple is here dated in relation to the traditional date of the exodus from Egypt, rounded off to a conventional twelve generations of forty years each. This chronology means that the Temple was built approximately midway between Israel's two foundational deliverances, the exodus and the return from the Babylonian exile. The schematization of history implied in these figures recommends caution in using them for historical reconstruction.

**6:12** 2 Sm 7:13–16.

the part in front. [18] The cedar in the interior of the house was carved in the form of gourds and open flowers; all was of cedar, and no stone was to be seen.

[19] In the innermost part of the house† he set up the inner sanctuary to house the ark of the LORD's covenant. [20] In front of the inner sanctuary (it was twenty cubits long, twenty wide, and twenty high, and he covered it with pure gold), he made an altar of cedar. [21] Solomon covered the interior of the house with pure gold, and he drew golden chains across in front of the inner sanctuary, and covered it with gold. [22] He covered the whole house with gold, until the whole house was done, and the whole altar that belonged to the inner sanctuary he covered with gold. [23] In the inner sanctuary he made two cherubim, each ten cubits high, made of pine. [24] Each wing of a cherub was five cubits so that the span from wing tip to wing tip was ten cubits. [25] The second cherub was also ten cubits: the two cherubim were identical in size and shape; [26] the first cherub was ten cubits high, and so was the second. [27] He placed the cherubim in the inmost part of the house; the wings of the cherubim were spread wide, so that one wing of the first touched the side wall and the wing of the second touched the other wall; the wings pointing to the middle of the room touched each other. [28] He overlaid the cherubim with gold.

[29] The walls of the house on all sides of both the inner and the outer rooms had carved figures of cherubim, palm trees, and open flowers. [30] The floor of the house of both the inner and the outer rooms was overlaid with gold. [31] At the entrance of the inner sanctuary, doors of pine were made; the doorframes had five-sided posts. [32] The two doors were of pine, with carved figures of cherubim, palm trees, and open flowers. The doors were overlaid with gold, and the cherubim and the palm trees were also covered with beaten gold. [33] He did the same at the entrance to the nave, where the doorposts were of pine and were four-sided. [34] The two doors were of fir wood, each door consisting of two panels hinged together; [35] and he carved cherubim, palm trees, and open flowers, and plated them with gold. [36] He walled off the inner court with three courses of hewn stones and one course of cedar beams.

[37] The foundations of the LORD's house were laid in the month of Ziv in the fourth year, [38] and it was finished, in all particulars, exactly according to plan, in the month of Bul, the eighth month, in the eleventh year. Thus Solomon built it in seven years.

**7** [1]†* To finish the building of his own house Solomon took thirteen years. [2] He built the House of the Forest of Lebanon one hundred cubits long, fifty wide, and thirty high; it was supported by four rows of cedar columns, with cedar beams upon the columns. [3] Moreover, it had a ceiling of cedar above the rafters resting on the columns; these rafters numbered forty-five, fifteen to a row. [4] There were lattices in three rows, each row facing the next, [5] and all the openings and doorposts were squared with lintels, each facing across from the next. [6] He also made the Porch of Columns, fifty cubits long and thirty wide. The porch extended across the front, and there were columns with a canopy in front of them. [7] He also made the Porch of the Throne where he gave judgment—that is, the Porch of Judgment; it was paneled with cedar from floor to ceiling beams. [8]* The house in which he lived was in another court, set in deeper than the Porch and of the same construction. (Solomon made a house like this Porch for Pharaoh's daughter, whom he had married.)† [9] All these buildings were of fine stones, hewn to size and trimmed front and back with a saw, from the foundation to the bonding course and outside as far as the great court. [10] The foundation was made of fine, large blocks, some ten cubits and some eight cubits. [11] Above were fine stones hewn to size, and cedar wood. [12] The great court had

---

† **6:19** *The innermost part of the house*: the inner sanctuary or holy of holies reserved exclusively for the Lord, enthroned upon the cherubim over the ark of the covenant (2 Chr 3:10–13). See note on Ex 25:18–20.

**7:1–12** The account of Solomon's building of the Temple (the Lord's "house") is interrupted by an account of his building of the palace (Solomon's "house"), which contained also the main buildings of public administration. The passage is anachronistic, since 6:38–7:1 and 9:10 imply that the palace was not begun until the Temple was completed. By placing the account here, the narrator highlights the fact that Solomon spent almost twice as long on his own "house" as on the Lord's.

**7:8** Solomon did not build the house for Pharaoh's daughter until Temple and palace were finished (3:1). By mentioning this marriage, the narrator keeps before the reader a developing theme in the Solomon story: the king's building activities for his foreign wives, which eventually implicate him in idolatry (3:1; 7:8; 9:24; 11:1–8).

---

**7:1** 1 Kgs 9:10.        **7:8** 1 Kgs 3:1; 9:24.

three courses of hewn stones all around and a course of cedar beams. So also were the inner court of the house of the LORD and its porch.

[13] King Solomon brought Hiram † from Tyre. [14] He was a bronze worker, the son of a widow from the tribe of Naphtali; his father had been from Tyre. He was endowed with wisdom, understanding, and knowledge for doing any work in bronze. He came to King Solomon and did all his metal work.

[15] †* He fashioned two bronze columns, each eighteen cubits high and twelve cubits in circumference. [16] He also made two capitals cast in bronze, to be placed on top of the columns, each of them five cubits high. [17] There were meshes made like netting and braid made like chains for the capitals on top of the columns, seven for each capital. [18] † He also cast pomegranates, two rows around each netting to cover the capital on top of the columns. [19] The capitals on top of the columns (in the porch) were made like lilies, four cubits high. [20] And the capitals on the two columns, both above and adjoining the bulge where it crossed out of the netting, had two hundred pomegranates in rows around each capital. [21] He set up the columns at the temple porch; one he set up to the south, and called it Jachin, and the other to the north, and called it Boaz. † [22] The top of the columns was made like a lily. Thus the work on the columns was completed.

[23] Then he made the molten sea; † it was made with a circular rim, and measured ten cubits across, five in height, and thirty in circumference. [24] Under the brim, gourds encircled it for ten cubits around the compass of the sea; the gourds were in two rows and were cast in one mold with the sea. [25] This rested on twelve oxen, three facing north, three facing west, three facing south, and three facing east, with their haunches all toward the center; upon them was set the sea. [26] It was a handbreadth thick, and its brim resembled that of a cup, being lily-shaped. Its capacity was two thousand baths. †

[27] He also made ten stands of bronze, each four cubits long, four wide, and three high. [28] When these stands were constructed, panels were set within the framework. [29] On the panels within the frames there were lions, oxen, and cherubim; and on the frames likewise, above and below the lions and oxen, there were wreaths in hammered relief. [30] Each stand had four bronze wheels and bronze axles. The four legs of each stand had cast braces, which were under the basin; they had wreaths on each side. [31] The mouth of the basin was inside, and a cubit above, the crown, whose opening was round, made like a receptacle, a cubit and a half in depth. There was carved work at the opening, on panels that were square, not circular. [32] The four wheels were below the paneling, and the axletrees of the wheels and the stand were of one piece. Each wheel was a cubit and a half high. [33] The wheels were constructed like chariot wheels; their axletrees, rims, spokes, and hubs were all cast. [34] The four braces reached the four corners of each stand, and formed part of the stand. [35] At the top of the stand there was a raised collar half a cubit high, and the handles and panels on top of the stand formed part of it. [36] On the flat ends of the handles and on the panels, wherever there was a bare space, cherubim, lions, and palm trees were carved, as well as wreaths all around. [37] This was how he made the ten stands, all of the same casting, the same size, the same shape. [38] He made ten bronze basins, each four cubits in diameter with a capacity of forty baths, one basin atop each of the ten stands.

[39] He placed the stands, five on the south side of the house and five on the north. The sea he placed off to the southeast from the south side of the house.

[40] When Hiram had made the pots, shovels, and bowls, he finished all his work for King Solomon in the house of the LORD: [41] two columns; two nodes for the capitals on top of

---

† **7:13** *Hiram:* a craftsman, not the king of Tyre (5:15–26).

**7:15** The two bronze columns were called Jachin and Boaz (v. 21; also 2 Chr 3:17); the significance of the names is unclear. The columns stood to the right and left of the Temple porch, and may have been intended to mark the entrance to the building as the entrance to God's private dwelling. Their extraordinary size and elaborate decoration would have made them the most impressive parts of the Temple visible to the ordinary viewer, who was not permitted into the nave, let alone into the innermost sanctuary. According to Jer 52:21, the columns were hollow, the bronze exterior being "four fingers thick."

**7:18–20** The Hebrew text is corrupt in many places here, and alternative readings attested in the ancient versions are secondary attempts to make sense of the text. A clearer description of the columns and their decoration is found in vv. 41–42.

**7:21** *Jachin…Boaz:* see note on 7:15.

**7:23–26** *The molten sea:* this was a large circular tank containing about twelve thousand gallons of water.

**7:26** *Baths:* see note on Is 5:10.

the columns; two pieces of netting covering the two nodes for the capitals on top of the columns; ⁴²four hundred pomegranates in double rows on both pieces of netting that covered the two nodes of the capitals on top of the columns; ⁴³ten stands; ten basins on the stands; ⁴⁴one sea; twelve oxen supporting the sea; ⁴⁵pots, shovels, and bowls. All these articles which Hiram made for King Solomon in the house of the LORD were of burnished bronze. ⁴⁶The king had them cast in the neighborhood of the Jordan, between Succoth and Zarethan, in thick clay molds. ⁴⁷Solomon did not weigh all the articles because they were so numerous; the weight of the bronze, therefore, was not determined.

⁴⁸Solomon made all the articles that were for the house of the LORD: the golden altar; the table on which the showbread lay; ⁴⁹the lampstands of pure gold, five to the right and five to the left before the inner sanctuary; their flowers, lamps, and tongs of gold; ⁵⁰basins, snuffers, bowls, cups, and firepans of pure gold; hinges of gold for the doors of the innermost part of the house, or holy of holies, and for the doors of the outer room, the nave. ⁵¹*When all the work undertaken by King Solomon in the house of the LORD was completed,† he brought in the votive offerings of his father David, and put the silver, gold, and other articles in the treasuries of the house of the LORD.

**8** **Dedication of the Temple.**† ¹Then Solomon assembled the elders of Israel and all the heads of the tribes, the princes in the ancestral houses of the Israelites. They came to King Solomon in Jerusalem, to bring up the ark of the LORD's covenant from the city of David (which is Zion). ²All the people of Israel assembled before King Solomon during the festival in the month of Ethanim (the seventh month). † ³When all the elders of Israel had arrived, the priests took up the ark; ⁴and they brought up the ark of the LORD and the tent of meeting with all the sacred vessels that were in the tent. The priests and Levites brought them up. ⁵King Solomon and the entire community of Israel, gathered for the occasion before the ark, sacrificed sheep and oxen too many to number or count. ⁶†The priests brought the ark of the covenant of the LORD to its place, the inner sanctuary of the house, the holy of holies, beneath the wings of the cherubim. ⁷The cherubim had their wings spread out over the place of the ark, sheltering the ark and its poles from above. ⁸*The poles were so long that their ends could be seen from the holy place in front of the inner sanctuary. They cannot be seen from outside, but they remain there to this day. ⁹*There was nothing in the ark but the two stone tablets which Moses had put there at Horeb, when the LORD made a covenant with the Israelites after they went forth from the land of Egypt. ¹⁰*When the priests left the holy place, the cloud filled the house of the LORD ¹¹so that the priests could no longer minister because of the cloud, since the glory of the LORD had filled the house of the LORD. ¹²†*Then Solomon said,

---

† **7:51** The account of the Temple's construction has been punctuated by references to "building" (*banah*) or "finishing" (*killah*) it (6:1b, 9a, 14, 38; 7:40). Here, at the end of the account, the narrator uses a different verb for its "completion," *shillem*, which allows him to play on the name of Solomon (*shelomo*).
**8:1–66** The account of the Temple's dedication ceremony is organized concentrically: Solomon gathers the assembly (vv. 1–13), blesses it (vv. 14–21), utters a long dedicatory prayer (vv. 22–53), blesses the assembly again (vv. 54–61), and dismisses it (vv. 62–66). To this account is appended an appearance of the Lord to Solomon (9:2–9) that balances the divine word to Solomon in the account of the Temple's construction (6:11–13).
**8:2** "The seventh month" ("Ethanim" in the Canaanite calendar) corresponded to late September/early October. The great festival at that time of year is the feast of Booths, or Succoth/ Sukkoth (see Lv 23:33–43; Dt 16:13–15). The feast was important enough to warrant holding the dedication ceremony either a month before or eleven months after the Temple was completed in the eighth month (6:38).
**8:6–9** The transfer of the ark of the covenant into the newly constructed Temple building, God's act of possession (8:10–13), and Solomon's dedicatory prayer and sacrifices constituted the Temple's solemn dedication and made of it the place of God's

presence in the midst of Israel for which David had hoped (2 Sm 6:12–15; 7:1–3). Later God expresses approval of the Temple with an oracle (1 Kgs 9:3–9).
**8:12–13** This brief poem is rich in layered meanings. The "dark cloud" in which the Lord intends to dwell refers not only to the cloud that filled the Temple (v. 10) but to the darkness of the windowless holy of holies and to the mystery of the God enthroned invisibly upon the cherubim as well. Solomon calls the Temple he offers God a firm base, using terminology similar to that used for God's firm establishment of Solomon's own kingdom (2:12, 46). Finally, Solomon intends this as a place for God to *yashab*, but the Hebrew word *yashab* can mean "to dwell" or "to sit." In other words, the Temple can be understood both as a place where God resides and as the earthly foundation of God's heavenly throne. The double meaning allows an understanding of the divine presence as both transcendent and graciously immanent. See Solomon's sentiments in 8:27, and the frequent reference in 8:30–52 to God's hearing in heaven prayers that were offered in or toward the Temple.

---

**7:51** 2 Sm 8:9–12.
**8:8** Ex 25:13–15.
**8:9** Ex 25:16; 34:27–28; Dt 10:5; Heb 9:4.
**8:10** Ex 13:21; 40:34–38.
**8:12** Ex 20:21; Dt 4:11; 5:22; Ps 97:2.

"The LORD intends to dwell in the dark
    cloud;
13    I have indeed built you a princely
      house,
    the base for your enthronement
      forever."

14 The king turned and blessed the whole assembly of Israel, while the whole assembly of Israel stood. 15 He said: "Blessed be the LORD, the God of Israel, who with his own mouth spoke a promise to David my father and by his hand fulfilled it, saying: 16* Since the day I brought my people Israel out of Egypt, I have not chosen a city out of any tribe of Israel for the building of a house, that my name might be there; but I have chosen David to rule my people Israel. 17 When David my father wished to build a house for the name of the LORD, the God of Israel, 18 the LORD said to him: In wishing to build a house for my name, you did well. 19 But it is not you who will build the house, but your son, who comes from your loins; he shall build the house for my name. 20 Now the LORD has fulfilled the word he spoke: I have succeeded David my father, and I sit on the throne of Israel, as the LORD has spoken, and I have built this house for the name of the LORD, the God of Israel. 21 I have provided there a place for the ark in which is the covenant of the LORD that he made with our ancestors when he brought them out of the land of Egypt."

**Solomon's Prayer.** 22 Solomon stood before the altar of the LORD in the presence of the whole assembly of Israel, and stretching forth his hands toward heaven, 23 he said, "LORD, God of Israel, there is no God like you in heaven above or on earth below; you keep covenant and love toward your servants who walk before you with their whole heart, 24 the covenant that you kept toward your servant, David my father, what you promised him; your mouth has spoken and your hand has fulfilled this very day. 25* And now, LORD, God of Israel, keep toward your servant, David my father, what you promised: There shall never be wanting someone from your line to sit before me on the throne of Israel, provided that your descendants keep to their way, walking

before me as you have. 26 Now, God of Israel, may the words you spoke to your servant, David my father, be confirmed.

27 "Is God indeed to dwell on earth? If the heavens and the highest heavens cannot contain you, how much less this house which I have built! 28 Regard kindly the prayer and petition of your servant, LORD, my God, and listen to the cry of supplication which I, your servant, utter before you this day. 29 May your eyes be open night and day toward this house, the place of which you said, My name shall be there; listen to the prayer your servant makes toward this place. 30 Listen to the petition of your servant and of your people Israel which they offer toward this place. Listen, from the place of your enthronement, heaven, listen and forgive.

31* "If someone sins in some way against a neighbor and is required to take an oath sanctioned by a curse, and comes and takes the oath before your altar in this house, 32 listen in heaven; act and judge your servants. Condemn the wicked, requiting their ways; acquit the just, rewarding their justice.

33 "When your people Israel are defeated by an enemy because they sinned against you, and then they return to you, praise your name, pray to you, and entreat you in this house, 34 listen in heaven and forgive the sin of your people Israel, and bring them back to the land you gave their ancestors.

35 "When the heavens are closed, so that there is no rain, because they have sinned against you, but they pray toward this place and praise your name, and turn from their sin because you have afflicted them, 36 listen in heaven and forgive the sin of your servants, your people Israel (for you teach them the good way in which they should walk). Give rain to this land of yours which you have given to your people as their heritage.

37 "If there is famine in the land or pestilence; or if blight comes, or mildew, or locusts, or caterpillars; if an enemy of your people presses upon them in the land and at their gates; whatever plague or sickness there may be; 38 whatever prayer or petition any may make, any of your people Israel, who know heartfelt remorse and stretch out their hands toward this house, 39 listen in heaven, the place

8:16–19 2 Sm 7:5–8, 12–13.          8:25 1 Kgs 2:4; 9:5; 2 Sm 7:14–16; Jer 33:17.          8:31 Ex 22:6–10.

of your enthronement; forgive and take action. Render to each and all according to their ways, you who know every heart; for it is you alone who know the heart of every human being. [40] So may they revere you as long as they live on the land you gave our ancestors.

[41] "To the foreigners, likewise, who are not of your people Israel, but who come from a distant land for the sake of your name [42] (since people will hear of your great name and your mighty hand and your outstretched arm), when they come and pray toward this house, [43] listen in heaven, the place of your enthronement. Do all that the foreigner asks of you, that all the peoples of the earth may know your name, may revere you as do your people Israel, and may know that your name has been invoked upon this house that I have built.

[44] "When your people go out to war against their enemies, by whatever way you send them, and they pray to the LORD toward the city you have chosen and the house I have built for your name, [45] listen in heaven to their prayer and petition, and uphold their cause.

[46]* "When they sin against you (for there is no one who does not sin), and in your anger against them you deliver them to an enemy, so that their captors carry them off to the land of the enemy, far or near, [47] and they have a change of heart in the land of their captivity and they turn and entreat you in the land of their captors and say, 'We have sinned and done wrong; we have been wicked'; [48] if with their whole heart and soul they turn back to you in the land of their enemies who took them captive, and pray to you toward the land you gave their ancestors, the city you have chosen, and the house I have built for your name, [49] listen in heaven, your dwelling place, to their prayer and petition, and uphold their cause. [50] Forgive your people who have sinned against you and all the offenses they have committed against you, and grant them mercy in the sight of their captors, so that these will be merciful to them. [51] For they are your people and your heritage, whom you brought out of Egypt, from the midst of the iron furnace.

[52] "Thus may your eyes be open to the petition of your servant and to the petition of your people Israel; thus may you listen to them whenever they call upon you. [53] For you have set them apart from all the peoples of the earth to be your heritage, as you declared through Moses your servant when you brought our ancestors out of Egypt, Lord my GOD."

[54] After Solomon finished offering this entire prayer and petition to the LORD, he rose from before the altar of the LORD, where he had been kneeling, hands outstretched toward heaven. [55] He stood and blessed the whole assembly of Israel, saying in a loud voice: [56] "Blessed be the LORD who has given rest to his people Israel, just as he promised. Not a single word has gone unfulfilled of the entire gracious promise he made through Moses his servant. [57] May the LORD, our God, be with us as he was with our ancestors and may he not forsake us nor cast us off. [58] May he draw our hearts to himself, that we may walk in his ways and keep the commands, statutes, and ordinances that he enjoined on our ancestors. [59] May these words of mine, the petition I have offered before the LORD, our God, be present to the LORD our God day and night, that he may uphold the cause of his servant and the cause of his people Israel as each day requires, [60] so that all the peoples of the earth may know that the LORD is God and there is no other. [61]† Your heart must be wholly devoted to the LORD, our God, observing his statutes and keeping his commandments, as on this day."

[62] The king and all Israel with him offered sacrifices before the LORD. [63]† Solomon offered as communion offerings to the LORD twenty-two thousand oxen and one hundred twenty thousand sheep. Thus the king and all the Israelites dedicated the house of the LORD. [64] On that day the king consecrated the middle of the court facing the house of the LORD; he offered there the burnt offerings, the grain offerings, and the fat of the communion offerings, because the bronze altar before the LORD was too small to hold the burnt offering, the grain offering, and the fat of the communion offering. [65] On this occasion Solomon and all Israel with him, a great assembly from Lebo-hamath to the Wadi of Egypt, celebrated the festival before the LORD, our God, for seven days. [66] On the eighth day he dismissed the people, who blessed the king and went to their

† **8:61** In urging the people to be "wholly devoted" (*shalem*), Solomon plays on his own name (*shelomo*), as if to imply that he himself exemplifies perfect fidelity to God.

**8:63** "Communion offerings" (*shelamim*) is another wordplay on the name of Solomon.

**8:46** Eccl 7:20; 1 Jn 1:8.

tents, rejoicing and glad of heart because of all the blessings the LORD had given to David his servant and to his people Israel.

## 9 Promise and Warning to Solomon.

[1] After Solomon finished building the house of the LORD, the house of the king, and everything else that he wanted to do, [2]* the LORD appeared to Solomon a second time, as he had appeared to him in Gibeon. [3] The LORD said to him: I have heard the prayer of petition which you offered in my presence. I have consecrated this house which you have built and I set my name there forever; my eyes and my heart shall be there always. [4] As for you, if you walk before me as David your father did, wholeheartedly and uprightly, doing all that I have commanded you, keeping my statutes and ordinances, [5]* I will establish your royal throne over Israel forever, as I promised David your father: There shall never be wanting someone from your line on the throne of Israel. [6] But if ever you and your descendants turn from following me, fail to keep my commandments and statutes which I set before you, and proceed to serve other gods and bow down to them, [7] I will cut off Israel from the land I gave them and repudiate the house I have consecrated for my name. Israel shall become a proverb and a byword among all nations, [8]* and this house shall become a heap of ruins. Every passerby shall gasp in horror and ask, "Why has the LORD done such things to this land and to this house?" [9] And the answer will come: "Because they abandoned the LORD, their God, who brought their ancestors out of the land of Egypt, and they embraced other gods, bowing down to them and serving them. That is why the LORD has brought upon them all this evil."

**After Building the Temple.**† [10]* After the twenty years during which Solomon built the two houses, the house of the LORD and the house of the king—[11] Hiram, king of Tyre, supplying Solomon with all the cedar wood, fir wood, and gold he wished, and King Solomon giving Hiram in return twenty cities in the land of Galilee— [12] Hiram left Tyre to see the cities Solomon had given him, but he was not satisfied with them. [13] So he said, "What are these cities you have given me, my brother?"† And he called them the land of Cabul, as they are called to this day. [14] Hiram, however, had sent King Solomon one hundred and twenty talents of gold.†

[15] This is an account of the conscript labor force King Solomon raised in order to build the house of the LORD, his own house, Millo,† the wall of Jerusalem, Hazor, Megiddo, Gezer [16] (Pharaoh, king of Egypt, had come up and taken Gezer and, after destroying it by fire and slaying all the Canaanites living in the city, had given it as a farewell gift to his daughter, Solomon's wife; [17] Solomon then rebuilt Gezer), Lower Beth-horon, [18] Baalath, Tamar in the desert of Judah, [19] all his cities for supplies, cities for chariots and cities for cavalry, and whatever Solomon desired to build in Jerusalem, in Lebanon, and in the entire land under his dominion. [20] All the people who were left of the Amorites, Hittites, Perizzites, Hivites, and Jebusites, who were not Israelites— [21] those of their descendants who were left in the land and whom the Israelites had not been able to destroy under the ban—these Solomon conscripted as forced laborers, as they are to this day. [22] But Solomon made none of the Israelites forced laborers, for they were his fighting force, his ministers, commanders, adjutants, chariot officers, and cavalry. [23] There were five hundred fifty overseers answerable to Solomon's governors for the work, directing the people engaged in the work.

[24]* As soon as Pharaoh's daughter went up from the City of David to her house, which he had built for her, Solomon built Millo. [25] Three times a year Solomon used to offer

---

† **9:10–25** This unit of the Solomon story corresponds to 5:15–32. It comprises the same two themes, negotiations with Hiram of Tyre (vv. 10–14) and use of conscripted labor (vv. 15–23); the last two verses mark the end of the account of Solomon's building projects (vv. 24–25). Chronicles has an incomplete parallel in 2 Chr 8:1–13.

**9:13** *Brother:* a term for a treaty partner; cf. 20:32–33. *Cabul:* the meaning is uncertain; perhaps "of no value."

**9:14** The talent was a measure of weight that varied in the course of ancient Israel's history from forty-five to one hundred thirty pounds. This would mean that, at the least, Hiram sent five

thousand pounds of gold to Solomon, and the figure may be as much as three times that amount.

**9:15** *Millo:* probably means ground fill, and may refer to an artificial earthwork or platform of stamped ground south of the Temple area. It was begun by David (2 Sm 5:9); cf. 1 Kgs 9:24; 11:27.

---

*
**9:2** 1 Kgs 3:4–15; 6:11–13; 11:9–13.
**9:5** 2 Sm 7:16.
**9:8** Dt 29:23; Jer 22:8.
**9:10** 1 Kgs 6:38–7:1.
**9:24** 1 Kgs 3:1; 7:8.

burnt offerings and communion offerings on the altar which he had built to the LORD, and to burn incense before the LORD.

Thus he completed the temple.†

**Solomon's Gifts.**† [26] King Solomon also built a fleet at Ezion-geber, which is near Elath on the shore of the Red Sea in the land of Edom.† [27] To this fleet Hiram sent his own servants, expert sailors, with the servants of Solomon. [28] They went to Ophir, and obtained four hundred and twenty talents of gold and brought it to King Solomon.

# 10

**Solomon's Listening Heart: The Queen of Sheba.**† [1]* The queen of Sheba,† having heard a report of Solomon's fame, came to test him with subtle questions. [2] She arrived in Jerusalem with a very numerous retinue, and with camels bearing spices, a large amount of gold, and precious stones. She came to Solomon and spoke to him about everything that she had on her mind. [3] King Solomon explained everything she asked about, and there was nothing so obscure that the king could not explain it to her. [4] When the queen of Sheba witnessed Solomon's great wisdom, the house he had built, [5] the food at his table, the seating of his ministers, the attendance and dress of his waiters, his servers, and the burnt offerings he offered in the house of the LORD, it took her breath away. [6] "The report I heard in my country about your deeds and your wisdom is true," she told the king. [7] "I did not believe the report until I came and saw with my own eyes that not even the half

had been told me. Your wisdom and prosperity surpass the report I heard. [8] Happy are your servants, happy these ministers of yours, who stand before you always and listen to your wisdom. [9] Blessed be the LORD, your God, who has been pleased to place you on the throne of Israel. In his enduring love for Israel, the LORD has made you king to carry out judgment and justice." [10] Then she gave the king one hundred and twenty gold talents, a very large quantity of spices, and precious stones. Never again did anyone bring such an abundance of spices as the queen of Sheba gave to King Solomon.

[11] Hiram's fleet, which used to bring gold from Ophir, also brought from there a very large quantity of almug† wood and precious stones. [12] With this wood the king made supports for the house of the LORD and for the house of the king, and harps and lyres for the singers. Never again was any such almug wood brought or seen to the present day.

[13] King Solomon gave the queen of Sheba everything she desired and asked for, besides what King Solomon gave her from Solomon's royal bounty. Then she returned with her servants to her own country.

**Solomon's Riches: Domestic Affairs.**† [14]* The gold that came to Solomon in one year weighed six hundred and sixty-six gold talents, [15] in addition to what came from the tolls on travelers, from the traffic of merchants, and from all the kings of Arabia and the governors of the country. [16]* King Solomon made two hundred shields of beaten gold (six hundred shekels of gold went into each shield) [17] and

---

† **9:25** With these words the account of the construction and dedication of the Temple, which began in 6:1, comes to a close. The verb "complete" (*shillem*) is a play on Solomon's name (*shelomo*); see also the note on 7:51.
**9:26–10:29** The next major unit of the Solomon story returns to the theme of the three gifts the Lord gave Solomon in 3:12–13: a listening heart (10:1–13), riches (9:26–27; 10:14–22, 26–29), universal renown (10:23–25). In 3:16–5:14, where the same three themes structure the passage, the emphasis was on the benefits these gifts brought to the whole nation; here it is on the luxury they afford to Solomon's own court. The material in 9:26–28; 10:11–12, 22 dealing with Solomon's commercial fleet corresponds to the material on Solomon's international affairs in 5:1–5. Chronicles has a partial parallel to this material in 2 Chr 9:17–28; see also 2 Chr 1:14–17.
**9:26** *Ezion-geber…Edom*: the first mention of maritime commerce in the Israelite kingdom; Edom was subject after David conquered it; cf. 2 Sm 8:13–14.
**10:1–13** The sub-unit on Solomon's wisdom contrasts with 3:16–28. There Solomon's gifts led him to listen to the humblest of his subjects; he accomplished justice and was revered by all his people. Here the emphasis is on his clever speech to a foreign monarch. She is duly impressed by the glory of his court, but it

is she, not Solomon, who recalls the monarch's duty of establishing justice (v. 9). The unit is interrupted briefly by a remark about Solomon's maritime commerce (10:11–12).
**10:1** *Queen of Sheba*: women rulers among the Arabs are recorded in eighth-century B.C. Assyrian inscriptions. Sheba was for centuries the leading principality in what is now Yemen.
**10:11–12** *Almug*: the identification of this wood is unknown.
**10:14–29** The material on Solomon's riches, like that in 4:1–5:8, is organized around domestic affairs, international affairs, and chariots and horses (see note on 4:1–5:8), but contrasts with that earlier passage. There, Solomon's domestic administration produced prosperity for all Judah and Israel (4:20); here the focus is on the wealth and luxury of Solomon's own palace (10:14–21). There his international hegemony assured peace for all Judah and Israel (5:5); here his maritime ventures simply bring him more and more wealth (9:26–28; 10:11–12, 22). There even his livestock benefited from his prudent administration; here chariotry and horses are just another commodity to be traded (10:26–29).

---

**10:1** Mt 12:42; Lk 11:31.    **10:16** 1 Kgs 14:26–28; 2 Sm 8:7.
**10:14** Dt 17:17; Sir 47:18.

three hundred bucklers of beaten gold (three minas of gold went into each buckler); and the king put them in the house of the Forest of Lebanon. ¹⁸ The king made a large ivory throne, and overlaid it with refined gold. ¹⁹ The throne had six steps, a back with a round top, and an arm on each side of the seat, with two lions standing next to the arms, ²⁰ and twelve other lions standing there on the steps, two to a step, one on either side of each step. Nothing like this was made in any other kingdom. ²¹ All King Solomon's drinking vessels were gold, and all the utensils in the house of the Forest of Lebanon were pure gold. There was no silver, for in Solomon's time silver was reckoned as nothing. ²² For the king had a fleet of Tarshish ships† at sea with Hiram's fleet. Once every three years the fleet of Tarshish ships would come with a cargo of gold, silver, ivory, apes, and peacocks.

**Solomon's Renown.** ²³ Thus King Solomon surpassed all the kings of the earth in riches and wisdom. ²⁴ And the whole world sought audience with Solomon, to hear the wisdom God had put into his heart. ²⁵ They all brought their yearly tribute: vessels of silver and gold, garments, weapons, spices, horses and mules— what was due each year.

**Solomon's Riches: Chariots and Horses.** ²⁶* Solomon amassed chariots and horses; he had one thousand four hundred chariots and twelve thousand horses; these he allocated among the chariot cities and to the king's service in Jerusalem. ²⁷* The king made silver as common in Jerusalem as stones, and cedars as numerous as the sycamores of the Shephelah. ²⁸ Solomon's horses were imported from Egypt and from Cilicia, where the king's merchants purchased them. ²⁹ A chariot imported from Egypt cost six hundred shekels of silver, a

horse one hundred and fifty shekels; they were exported at these rates to all the Hittite and Aramean kings.

# 11 The End of Solomon's Reign. † ¹* King Solomon loved many foreign women besides the daughter of Pharaoh—Moabites, Ammonites, Edomites, Sidonians, Hittites—²* from nations of which the LORD had said to the Israelites: You shall not join with them and they shall not join with you, lest they turn your hearts to their gods. But Solomon held them† close in love. ³ He had as wives seven hundred princesses and three hundred concubines, and they turned his heart.

⁴ When Solomon was old his wives had turned his heart to follow other gods, and his heart was not entirely with the LORD, his God, as the heart of David his father had been. ⁵ Solomon followed Astarte, the goddess of the Sidonians, and Milcom, the abomination of the Ammonites. ⁶ Solomon did what was evil in the sight of the LORD, and he did not follow the LORD unreservedly as David his father had done. ⁷ Solomon then built a high place to Chemosh, the abomination of Moab, and to Molech, the abomination of the Ammonites, on the mountain opposite Jerusalem. ⁸ He did the same for all his foreign wives who burned incense and sacrificed to their gods.

⁹* The LORD became angry with Solomon, because his heart turned away from the LORD, the God of Israel, who had appeared to him twice ¹⁰ and commanded him not to do this very thing, not to follow other gods. But he did not observe what the LORD commanded. ¹¹ So the LORD said to Solomon: Since this is what you want, and you have not kept my covenant and the statutes which I enjoined on you, I will surely tear the kingdom away from you and give it to your servant. ¹²* But I will

---

**10:22** *Tarshish ships*: large, strong vessels for long voyages. Tarshish was probably the ancient Tartessus, a Phoenician colony in southern Spain. *Ivory, apes, and peacocks*: the Hebrew words are obscure and the translations conjectural; however, the reference is certainly to exotic luxury items.
**11:1–13** The next major unit of the Solomon story corresponds to 3:1–15. Like the earlier passage it includes the narrator's remarks about Solomon's foreign wives and his building projects, and a divine word commenting on Solomon's conduct. However, where 3:1–15 is generally positive toward Solomon, the present passage is unrelievedly negative. Chronicles has no parallel to this material.
**11:2** *Them*: both the nations and their gods.
**11:14–25** This unit of the Solomon story corresponds to

2:12b–46, where Solomon secured his kingdom by eliminating three men he perceived as threats. In this passage, we learn of two foreigners the Lord raised up as "adversaries" to Solomon as early as the beginning of his reign (despite Solomon's complacent claim to Hiram in 5:18 that he had no adversary). In the next section we will learn of a third opponent, Israelite rather than foreign, who turns out to be the "servant of Solomon" announced by the Lord in 11:11. Chronicles has no parallel to this material.

| *                        |                          |
|--------------------------|--------------------------|
| **10:26** 1 Kgs 5:6; Dt 17:16; | **11:2** Ex 34:16. |
| 2 Chr 1:14; 9:25. | **11:9** 1 Kgs 3:4–15; |
| **10:27** Dt 17:17; Sir 47:18. | 6:11–13; 9:2–9. |
| **11:1–3** Dt 17:17; Sir | **11:12–13** 1 Kgs 11:34–36. |
| 47:19–20. | |

not do this during your lifetime, for the sake of David your father; I will tear it away from your son's hand. [13] Nor will I tear away the whole kingdom. I will give your son one tribe for the sake of David my servant and for the sake of Jerusalem, which I have chosen.

### Threats to Solomon's Kingdom.†

[14] The LORD then raised up an adversary† against Solomon: Hadad the Edomite, who was of the royal line in Edom. [15]* Earlier, when David had conquered Edom, Joab, the commander of the army, while going to bury the slain, killed every male in Edom. [16] Joab and all Israel remained there six months until they had killed off every male in Edom. [17] But Hadad, with some Edomite servants of his father, fled toward Egypt. Hadad was then a young boy. [18] They left Midian and came to Paran; they gathered men from Paran and came to Egypt, to Pharaoh, king of Egypt; he gave Hadad a house, appointed him rations, and assigned him land. [19] Hadad won great favor with Pharaoh, so that he gave him in marriage his sister-in-law, the sister of Queen Tahpenes, his own wife. [20] Tahpenes' sister bore Hadad a son, Genubath. Tahpenes weaned him in Pharaoh's palace. And Genubath lived in Pharaoh's house, with Pharaoh's own sons. [21] When Hadad in Egypt heard that David rested with his ancestors and that Joab, the commander of the army, was dead, he said to Pharaoh, "Give me leave to return to my own land." [22] Pharaoh said to him, "What do you lack with me, that you are seeking to return to your own land?" He answered, "Nothing, but please let me go!"

[23] God raised up against Solomon another adversary, Rezon, the son of Eliada, who had fled from his lord, Hadadezer, king of Zobah, [24]* when David was slaughtering them. Rezon gathered men about him and became leader of a marauding band. They went to Damascus, settled there, and made him king in Damascus. [25] Rezon was an adversary of Israel as long as Solomon lived, in addition to the harm done by Hadad, and he felt contempt for Israel. He became king over Aram.

### Ahijah Announces Jeroboam's Kingship.†

[26] Solomon had a servant, Jeroboam, son of Nebat, an Ephraimite from Zeredah with a widowed mother named Zeruah. He rebelled against the king. [27] This is how he came to rebel. King Solomon was building Millo, closing up the breach of the City of David, his father. [28] Jeroboam was a very able man, and when Solomon saw that the young man was also a good worker, he put him in charge of all the carriers conscripted from the house of Joseph.

[29] At that time Jeroboam left Jerusalem, and the prophet Ahijah the Shilonite met him on the road. The prophet was wearing a new cloak,† and when the two were alone in the open country, [30]* Ahijah took off his new cloak, tore it into twelve pieces, [31]* and said to Jeroboam: "Take ten pieces for yourself. Thus says the LORD, the God of Israel: I am about to tear the kingdom out of Solomon's hand and will give you ten of the tribes. [32] He shall have one tribe for the sake of my servant David, and for the sake of Jerusalem, the city I have chosen out of all the tribes of Israel. [33] For they have forsaken me and have bowed down to Astarte, goddess of the Sidonians, Chemosh, god of Moab, and Milcom, god of the Ammonites. They have not walked in my ways or done what is right in my eyes, according to my statutes and my ordinances, as David his father did. [34] Yet I will not take any of the kingdom from Solomon himself, but will keep him a prince as long as he lives, for the sake of David my servant, whom I have chosen, who kept my commandments and statutes.

[35] But I will take the kingdom from his son's hand and give it to you—that is, the ten tribes. [36] I will give his son one tribe, that David my servant may always have a holding before me in Jerusalem, the city I have chosen, to set my

---

**11:14** *Adversary:* Hebrew *śatan*, one who stands in opposition; in this context a political opponent.

**11:26–43** The last major unit of the Solomon story tells how the prophet Ahijah announces the divine intention to take the larger part of Solomon's kingdom from his control and give it to Jeroboam, Solomon's servant. This counterbalances the first unit of the story, 1:1–2:12a, where another prophet, Nathan, managed to influence the royal succession and obtain the throne for Solomon. The unit is also the first part of the story of Jeroboam (11:26–14:20). It thus acts as a literary hinge connecting the two stories. Chronicles contains a death notice for Solomon in 2 Chr 9:29–31.

**11:29** The narrator uses a powerful wordplay here. In the Hebrew consonantal text, Ahijah's cloak (*slmh*) is indistinguishable from Solomon's name (*slmh*). Since a prophetic gesture such as Ahijah's was understood as effecting the event it announced, Ahijah's tearing of his cloak embodies the divine action that will tear Solomon's kingdom apart (cf. vv. 11–13).

**11:15** 2 Sm 8:13–14.    **11:30** 1 Sm 15:27–28.
**11:24** 2 Sm 8:3–6.     **11:31–32** 1 Kgs 12:20.

name there. [37] You I will take and you shall reign over all that you desire and shall become king of Israel. [38] If, then, you heed all that I command you, walking in my ways, and do what is right in my eyes by keeping my statutes and my commandments like David my servant, I will be with you. I will build a lasting house for you, just as I did for David; I will give Israel to you. [39] I will humble David's line for this, but not forever."

[40] When Solomon tried to have Jeroboam killed, Jeroboam fled to Shishak, king of Egypt. He remained in Egypt until Solomon's death.

[41] The rest of the acts of Solomon, with all that he did and his wisdom, are recorded in the book of the acts of Solomon. [42] Solomon was king in Jerusalem over all Israel for forty years. [43] Solomon rested with his ancestors and was buried in the City of David, his father, and Rehoboam his son succeeded him as king.

## II. THE REIGN OF JEROBOAM†

# 12
**Political Disunity.**† [1] Rehoboam went to Shechem,† where all Israel had come to make him king. [2] When Jeroboam, son of Nebat, heard about it, he was still in Egypt. He had fled from King Solomon and remained in Egypt, [3] and they sent for him. Then Jeroboam and the whole assembly of Israel came and they said to Rehoboam, [4] "Your father put a heavy yoke on us. If you now lighten the harsh servitude and the heavy yoke your father imposed on us, we will be your servants." [5] He answered them, "Come back to me in three days," and the people went away.

[6] King Rehoboam asked advice of the elders who had been in his father Solomon's service

while he was alive, and asked, "How do you advise me to answer this people?" [7] They replied, "If today you become the servant of this people and serve them, and give them a favorable answer, they will be your servants forever." [8] But he ignored the advice the elders had given him, and asked advice of the young men who had grown up with him and were in his service. [9] He said to them, "What answer do you advise that we should give this people, who have told me, 'Lighten the yoke your father imposed on us'?" [10] The young men who had grown up with him replied, "This is what you must say to this people who have told you, 'Your father made our yoke heavy; you lighten it for us.' You must say, 'My little finger is thicker than my father's loins. [11] My father put a heavy yoke on you, but I will make it heavier. My father beat you with whips, but I will beat you with scorpions.'" [12] Jeroboam and the whole people came back to King Rehoboam on the third day, as the king had instructed them: "Come back to me in three days." [13] Ignoring the advice the elders had given him, the king gave the people a harsh answer. [14] He spoke to them as the young men had advised: "My father made your yoke heavy, but I will make it heavier. My father beat you with whips, but I will beat you with scorpions." [15] * The king did not listen to the people, for this turn of events was from the LORD: he fulfilled the word the LORD had spoken through Ahijah the Shilonite to Jeroboam, son of Nebat. [16] * When all Israel saw that the king did not listen to them, the people answered the king:

"What share have we in David?†
We have no heritage in the son of
Jesse.

---

† **12:1–14:20** Like the story of the reign of Solomon, the story of the reign of Jeroboam is concentrically organized. Ahijah's oracle of promise to Jeroboam (11:26–43) belongs to both stories, ending that of Solomon (see note on 1:1–11:43) and beginning that of Jeroboam; it corresponds to Ahijah's oracle of condemnation in 14:1–20. Within those literary boundaries are accounts of political (12:1–20) and religious (13:11–34) disunity between Israel and Judah. The center of the story is the account of Jeroboam's heterodox cultic innovations (12:26–31).

**12:1–20** The first major unit of the Jeroboam story was Ahijah's oracle (11:26–40), followed by the notice of Solomon's death (11:41–43). This is the second major unit. It tells how Jeroboam came to the throne of Israel after the intransigence of Solomon's son Rehoboam provoked the northern tribes to secede from Jerusalem. The political disunity of the two kingdoms fulfills the word spoken by Ahijah. Compare 13:11–32, where Jeroboam's improper cultic innovations produce religious disunity

as well. The scene is concentrically arranged: narrative introduction, first interview, first consultation, second consultation, second interview, narrative conclusion. Chronicles has a parallel version of this story in 2 Chr 10:1–19.

**12:1** *Shechem:* chief city of the northern tribes, where a covenant had previously been made between the Lord and his people and a stone of witness had been erected in memory of the event (Jos 24:25–27). *All Israel:* see note on 4:7–19.

**12:16** *What share have we in David?:* even in David's time the northern tribes seemed ready to withdraw from the union with Judah (2 Sm 20:1). The unreasonable attitude of Rehoboam toward them intensified the discontent caused by the oppression of Solomon (v. 4) and thus precipitated the political separation of the two kingdoms. In the view of the Deuteronomistic historian (1 Kgs 11:35–36; 12:24), this was by the Lord's decree.

**12:15** 1 Kgs 11:26–39.　　　　**12:16** 2 Sm 20:1.

THE ISRAELITE KINGDOMS

© 2013 ANSELM ACADEMIC

A    B    C    D    E    F

ASSYRIA

PHOENICIA

• Damascus

SYRIA

The Great Sea
(Mediterranean Sea)

*Lake of
Galilee*

KINGDOM
OF ISRAEL

*Jordan River*

Samaria •

AMMON

Jerusalem •

PHILISTIA

*Salt Sea
(Dead Sea)*

KINGDOM
OF
JUDAH

MOAB

EDOM

EGYPT

*Gulf of Suez*

Ezion Geber •

*Gulf of
Aqaba*

0    50    100 miles

0    50    100 kilometers

> To your tents, Israel!
> Now look to your own house, David."

So Israel went off to their tents. [17] But Rehoboam continued to reign over the Israelites who lived in the cities of Judah.

[18] King Rehoboam then sent out Adoram,† who was in charge of the forced labor, but all Israel stoned him to death. King Rehoboam then managed to mount his chariot and flee to Jerusalem. [19] And so Israel has been in rebellion against the house of David to this day. [20] When all Israel heard that Jeroboam had returned, they summoned him to an assembly and made him king over all Israel. None remained loyal to the house of David except the tribe of Judah alone.

**Divine Approval.**† [21] On his arrival in Jerusalem, Rehoboam assembled all the house of Judah and the tribe of Benjamin—one hundred and eighty thousand elite warriors—to wage war against the house of Israel, to restore the kingdom to Rehoboam, son of Solomon. [22] However, the word of God came to Shemaiah, a man of God: [23] Say to Rehoboam, son of Solomon, king of Judah, and to all the house of Judah and to Benjamin, and to the rest of the people: [24] Thus says the LORD: You must not go out to war against your fellow Israelites. Return home, each of you, for it is I who have brought this about. They obeyed the word of the LORD and turned back, according to the word of the LORD.

[25] Jeroboam built up Shechem in the hill country of Ephraim and lived there. Then he left it and built up Penuel.

**Jeroboam's Cultic Innovations.**† [26] Jeroboam thought to himself: "Now the kingdom will return to the house of David. [27] If this people go up to offer sacrifices in the house of the LORD in Jerusalem, the hearts of this people will return to their master, Rehoboam, king of Judah, and they will kill me and return to Rehoboam, king of Judah." [28]* The king took counsel, made two calves of gold, and said to the people: "You have been going up to Jerusalem long enough. Here are your gods, O Israel, who brought you up from the land of Egypt." [29]* And he put one in Bethel, the other in Dan.† [30] This led to sin, because the people frequented these calves in Bethel and in Dan. [31] He also built temples on the high places and made priests from among the common people who were not Levites.

**Divine Disapproval.**† [32] Jeroboam established a feast in the eighth month on the fifteenth day of the month like the pilgrimage feast in Judah, and he went up to the altar. He did this in Bethel, sacrificing to the calves he had made. He stationed in Bethel the priests of the high places he had built. [33] Jeroboam went up to the altar he built in Bethel on the fifteenth day of the eighth month, the month he arbitrarily chose. He established a feast for the Israelites, and he went up to the altar to burn incense.

**13** [1] A man of God came from Judah to Bethel by the word of the LORD, while Jeroboam was standing at the altar to burn incense. [2]* He cried out against the altar by the word of the LORD: "Altar, altar, thus says the

---

† **12:18** *Adoram:* the name is a shortened form of "Adoniram" (see 4:6; 5:28). If this is the same Adoram who held the position in David's day (2 Sm 20:24), he would have been a very old man.

**12:21–25** The center of this unit is a divine oracle delivered by a man of God of the Southern Kingdom in which the Lord affirms his approval of the secession of the northern tribes. Compare 13:1–10, where another man of God from Judah proclaims the Lord's condemnation of Jeroboam's religious separatism. Chronicles has a very similar version of Shemaiah's oracle in 2 Chr 11:1–4.

**12:26–31** At the center of the story of Jeroboam the narrator describes how the king went beyond the political separation of Israel from Judah to create a separatist religious system as well. Jeroboam feared that continued worship in the single Temple in Jerusalem would threaten the political independence of his kingdom. To prevent this he established sanctuaries with non-levitical clergy in his own territory. At two of the sanctuaries he set up golden calves, which the narrator depicts as idols. Thus begins what will later be called "the sin of Jeroboam" (13:34), a theme that will be echoed throughout 1–2 Kings in the condemnations of almost every king of the Northern Kingdom. Historically,

Jeroboam's innovations were not as heterodox as our narrative portrays them. Bethel was an ancient and traditional site for worship of the Lord; and the calves were probably intended to be a dais for the deity invisibly enthroned upon them, rather like the cherubim atop the ark of the covenant.

**12:29** *Bethel...Dan:* at the southern and northern boundaries of the separate kingdom of Israel, where sanctuaries had existed in the past (Gn 12:8; 13:3–4; 28:10–22; 35:1–15; Jgs 18:1–31).

**12:32–13:10** This unit of the Jeroboam story corresponds to 12:21–25. Before Jeroboam's cultic innovations, a man of God from Judah proclaimed the Lord's approval of the political separation of the kingdoms. After Jeroboam's cultic innovations, a man of God from Judah proclaims the Lord's disapproval of Israel's religious separatism. The unit begins with a long, detailed introduction about the dedication festival Jeroboam holds at Bethel (12:32–33); then follows the scene of the ceremony disrupted by the oracle of the man of God (13:1–10).

**12:28** Ex 32:1–10.      **13:2** 2 Kgs 23:16.
**12:29** Tb 1:5.

LORD: A child shall be born to the house of David, Josiah by name, who shall slaughter upon you the priests of the high places who burn incense upon you, and they shall burn human bones upon you." [3] * He also gave a sign that same day and said: "This is the sign that the LORD has spoken: The altar shall be torn apart and the ashes on it shall be scattered." [4] When the king heard the word of the man of God which he was crying out against the altar in Bethel, Jeroboam stretched forth his hand from the altar and said, "Seize him!" But the hand he stretched forth against him withered, so that he could not draw it back. [5] (The altar was torn apart and the ashes from the altar were scattered, in accordance with the sign the man of God gave by the word of the LORD.)

[6] Then the king said to the man of God, "Entreat the LORD, your God, and intercede for me that my hand may be restored." So the man of God entreated the LORD, and the king's hand was restored as it was before. [7] The king told the man of God, "Come with me to the house for some refreshment so that I may give you a present." [8] The man of God said to the king, "If you gave me half your palace, I would not go with you, nor eat bread or drink water in this place. [9] For I was instructed by the word of the LORD: Do not eat bread or drink water, and do not return by the way you came." [10] So he departed by another road and did not go back the way he had come to Bethel.

**Prophetic Disunity.**† [11] There was an old prophet living in Bethel, whose son came and told him all that the man of God had done that day in Bethel. When his sons repeated to their father the words the man of God had spoken to the king, [12] the father asked them, "Which way did he go?" So his sons pointed out to him the road taken by the man of God who had come from Judah. [13] Then he said to his sons, "Saddle the donkey for me." When they had saddled it, he mounted [14] and followed the man of God, whom he found seated under a terebinth. When he asked him, "Are you the man of God who came from Judah?" he answered, "Yes." [15] Then he said, "Come

home with me and have some bread." [16] "I cannot return with you or go with you, and I cannot eat bread or drink water with you in this place," he answered, [17] "for I was told by the word of the LORD: You shall not eat bread or drink water there, and do not go back the way you came." [18] But he said to him, "I, too, am a prophet like you, and an angel told me by the word of the LORD: Bring him back with you to your house to eat bread and drink water." But he was lying to him. [19] So he went back with him, and ate bread and drank water in his house. [20] But while they were sitting at table, the word of the LORD came to the prophet who had brought him back, [21] and he cried out to the man of God who had come from Judah: "Thus says the LORD: Because you rebelled against the charge of the LORD and did not keep the command which the LORD, your God, gave you, [22] but returned and ate bread and drank water in the place where he told you, Do not eat bread or drink water, your corpse shall not be brought to the grave of your ancestors." [23] After he had eaten bread and drunk, they saddled for him the donkey that belonged to the prophet who had brought him back, [24] and he set out. But a lion met him on the road, and killed him. His body lay sprawled on the road, and the donkey remained standing by it, and so did the lion.

[25] Some passersby saw the body lying in the road, with the lion standing beside it, and carried the news to the city where the old prophet lived. [26] On hearing it, the prophet who had brought him back from his journey said: "It is the man of God who rebelled against the charge of the LORD. The LORD has delivered him to a lion, which mangled and killed him, according to the word which the LORD had spoken to him." [27] Then he said to his sons, "Saddle the donkey for me," and they saddled it. [28] He went off and found the body sprawled on the road with the donkey and the lion standing beside it. The lion had not eaten the body nor had it harmed the donkey. [29] The prophet lifted up the body of the man of God and put it on the donkey, and brought him back to the city to mourn and to bury him.

---

† **13:11–34** The next major unit illustrates how Jeroboam's cultic innovations begin to alienate prophetic figures of the two kingdoms. Nevertheless, the Lord's word is stronger than any human attempt to thwart it. The two prophets also foreshadow the destinies of their respective kingdoms. Israel's experiment with idolatry can tempt Judah to abandon its faithfulness to the Lord.

If Judah succumbs, and no longer speaks the word that can call Israel back to the true God, then the only hope for reuniting the two kingdoms will be when they have both died the death of exile.

* **13:3** 2 Kgs 23:15.

<sup>30</sup> He laid the man's body in his own grave, and they mourned over it: "Alas, my brother!" <sup>31</sup>* After he had buried him, he said to his sons, "When I die, bury me in the grave where the man of God is buried. Lay my bones beside his. <sup>32</sup>* For the word which he proclaimed by the word of the LORD against the altar in Bethel and against all the temples on the high places in the cities of Samaria shall certainly come to pass."

<sup>33</sup> Even after this, Jeroboam did not turn from his evil way, but again made priests for the high places from among the common people. Whoever desired it was installed as a priest of the high places. <sup>34</sup> This is the account of the sin of the house of Jeroboam for which it was to be cut off and destroyed from the face of the earth.

# 14 Ahijah Announces Jeroboam's Downfall.†

<sup>1</sup> At that time Abijah, son of Jeroboam, took sick. <sup>2</sup>* So Jeroboam said to his wife, "Go and disguise yourself so that no one will recognize you as Jeroboam's wife. Then go to Shiloh, where you will find Ahijah the prophet. It was he who spoke the word that made me king over this people. <sup>3</sup> Take along ten loaves, some cakes, and a jar of honey, and go to him. He will tell you what will happen to the child." <sup>4</sup> The wife of Jeroboam did so. She left and went to Shiloh and came to the house of Ahijah.

Now Ahijah could not see because age had dimmed his sight. <sup>5</sup> But the LORD said to Ahijah: Jeroboam's wife is coming to consult you about her son, for he is sick. Thus and so you must tell her. When she comes, she will be in disguise. <sup>6</sup> So Ahijah, hearing the sound of her footsteps as she entered the door, said, "Come in, wife of Jeroboam. Why are you in disguise? For my part, I have been commissioned to give you bitter news. <sup>7</sup> Go, tell Jeroboam, 'Thus says the LORD, the God of Israel: I exalted you from among the people and made you ruler of my people Israel. <sup>8</sup> I tore the kingdom away from the house of David and gave it to you. Yet you have not been like my servant David, who kept my commandments and followed me with his whole heart, doing only what is right in my sight. <sup>9</sup> You have done more evil than all who were before you: you have gone and made for yourself other gods and molten images to provoke me; but me you have cast behind your back. <sup>10</sup>* Therefore, I am bringing evil upon the house of Jeroboam:

I will cut off from Jeroboam's line every male
—bond or free—in Israel;
I will burn up what is left of the house of Jeroboam
as dung is burned, completely.
<sup>11</sup>*  Anyone of Jeroboam's line who dies in the city,
dogs will devour;
anyone who dies in the field,
the birds of the sky will devour.

For the LORD has spoken!' <sup>12</sup> As for you, leave, and go home! As you step inside the city, the child will die, <sup>13</sup> and all Israel will mourn him and bury him, for he alone of Jeroboam's line will be laid in the grave, since in him alone of Jeroboam's house has something pleasing to the LORD, the God of Israel, been found. <sup>14</sup> The LORD will raise up for himself a king over Israel who will cut off the house of Jeroboam—today, at this very moment! <sup>15</sup> The LORD will strike Israel like a reed tossed about in the water and will pluck out Israel from this good land which he gave their ancestors, and will scatter them beyond the River,† because they made asherahs for themselves, provoking the LORD. <sup>16</sup> He will give up Israel because of the sins Jeroboam has committed and caused Israel to commit." <sup>17</sup> So Jeroboam's wife left and went back; when she came to Tirzah and crossed the threshold of her house, the child died. <sup>18</sup> He was buried and all Israel mourned him, according to the word of the LORD spoken through his servant Ahijah the prophet.

<sup>19</sup> The rest of the acts of Jeroboam, how he fought and how he reigned, these are recorded in the book of the chronicles of the kings of Israel. <sup>20</sup> The length of Jeroboam's reign was

---

† **14:1–20** The last major unit of the Jeroboam story recounts the story of Ahijah of Shiloh's oracle condemning the entire house of Jeroboam; this is followed by a formulaic notice of Jeroboam's death and the succession of his son. Compare the first unit of the Jeroboam story, 11:26–43, which recounted Ahijah's oracle proclaiming Jeroboam's kingship, followed by the formulaic notice of the death of Solomon.

**14:15** *The River:* the Euphrates; see note on 5:1.

---

**13:31** 2 Kgs 23:17–18.
**13:32** 2 Kgs 23:19–20.
**14:2** 1 Kgs 11:29–39.
**14:10** 1 Kgs 15:29–30.
**14:11** 1 Kgs 16:4; 21:22.

© Daniel Blatt

A typical Israelite four-room house had open space in the middle where most daily activities took place. Wood pillars supported the second floor, where the owners of the house lived; animals were penned on the ground floor. Remains of houses of the four-room plan are common at archaeological sites of the biblical period.

twenty-two years. He rested with his ancestors, and Nadab his son succeeded him as king.

### III. KINGS OF JUDAH AND ISRAEL†

**Reign of Rehoboam.** ²¹† Rehoboam, son of Solomon, became king in Judah. Rehoboam was forty-one years old when he became king, and he reigned seventeen years in Jerusalem, the city in which, out of all the tribes of Israel, the LORD chose to set his name. His mother's name was Naamah the Ammonite.

²² Judah did evil in the LORD's sight and they angered him even more than their ancestors had done. ²³ They, too, built for themselves high places, sacred pillars, and asherahs,† upon every high hill and under every green tree. ²⁴ There were also pagan priests in the land. Judah imitated all the abominable practices of the nations whom the LORD had driven out of the Israelites' way. ²⁵† In the fifth year of King Rehoboam, Shishak, king of Egypt, attacked Jerusalem. ²⁶* He took everything, including the treasures of the house of the LORD and the treasures of the house of the king, even the gold shields Solomon had made. ²⁷ To replace them, King Rehoboam made bronze shields, which he entrusted to the officers of the guard on duty at the entrance of the royal house. ²⁸ Whenever the king visited the house of the LORD, those on duty would carry the shields, and then return them to the guardroom.

²⁹ The rest of the acts of Rehoboam, with all that he did, are recorded in the book of the chronicles of the kings of Judah. ³⁰ There was war between Rehoboam and Jeroboam all their days. ³¹ Rehoboam rested with his

---

† **14:21–16:34** The treatment of the events of Jeroboam's reign shows that the author believes that the political division of the kingdoms embodies the Lord's will, but that their religious separation is undesirable. The Israelites are, in effect, one people of God under two royal administrations. This complex arrangement is reflected in the way 1–2 Kings organizes the history of the divided kingdoms. Each reign is treated as a unity: the kings, whether of Israel or Judah, are legitimate rulers. But the accounts of northern and southern kings are interwoven in the order in which each came to the throne, without regard to which kingdom they ruled: the people of God is one.
**14:21** The account of each king's reign follows the same basic pattern: a formulaic introduction, a theological evaluation based

on religious fidelity, a brief account of an event from the king's reign, and a formulaic conclusion.
**14:23** *Asherahs:* see note on Ex 34:13.
**14:25–28, 30** The narrator recounts Shishak's campaign here to imply that it was punishment for Judah's evil, and perhaps to cast him as supporting Jeroboam in his constant warfare with Rehoboam. (Shishak was named as Jeroboam's protector and patron in 11:40.) Egyptian records of the campaign list one hundred fifty cities conquered in Israel as well as Judah, but Jerusalem is not one of them. Chronicles has a parallel version of this account in 2 Chr 12:9–11.

---

**14:26** 1 Kgs 10:16–17.

ancestors; he was buried with his ancestors in the City of David. His mother's name was Naamah the Ammonite. His son Abijam succeeded him as king.

# 15 Reign of Abijam.

Reign of Abijam. [1] In the eighteenth year of King Jeroboam, son of Nebat, Abijam became king of Judah; [2] he reigned three years in Jerusalem. His mother's name was Maacah, daughter of Abishalom.

[3] He followed all the sins his father had committed before him, and his heart was not entirely with the LORD, his God, as was the heart of David his father. [4] Yet for David's sake the LORD, his God, gave him a holding in Jerusalem, raising up his son after him and permitting Jerusalem to endure, [5]* because David had done what was right in the sight of the LORD and did not disobey any of his commands as long as he lived, except in the case of Uriah the Hittite.

[6] There was war between Rehoboam and Jeroboam all their days. [7] The rest of the acts of Abijam, with all that he did, are recorded in the book of the chronicles of the kings of Judah. There was war between Abijam and Jeroboam. [8] Abijam rested with his ancestors; they buried him in the City of David, and his son Asa succeeded him as king.

**Reign of Asa.** [9] In the twentieth year of Jeroboam, king of Israel, Asa, king of Judah, became king; [10] he reigned forty-one years in Jerusalem. His mother's† name was Maacah, daughter of Abishalom. [11] Asa did what was right in the sight of the LORD like David his father, [12] banishing the pagan priests from the land and removing all the idols his ancestors had made. [13] He also deposed his grandmother Maacah from her position as queen mother, because she had made an outrageous object for Asherah. Asa cut down this object and burned it in the Wadi Kidron. [14] The high places did not disappear; yet Asa's heart was entirely with the LORD as long as he lived. [15] He brought into the house of the LORD his father's and his own votive offerings of silver and gold and various vessels. [16] There was war between Asa and Baasha, king of Israel, all their days. [17] Baasha, king of Israel, attacked Judah and fortified Ramah to blockade Asa, king of Judah. [18] Asa then took all the silver and gold remaining in the treasuries of the house of the LORD and the house of the king. Entrusting them to his ministers, King Asa sent them to Ben-hadad, son of Tabrimmon, son of Hezion, king of Aram,† who ruled in Damascus. He said: [19] "There is a treaty between you and me, as there was between your father and my father. I am sending you a present of silver and gold. Go, break your treaty with Baasha, king of Israel, that he may withdraw from me." [20] Ben-hadad agreed with King Asa and sent the leaders of his troops against the cities of Israel. They attacked Ijon, Dan, Abel-beth-maacah, and all Chinnereth, besides all the land of Naphtali. [21] When Baasha heard of it, he left off fortifying Ramah, and stayed in Tirzah. [22] Then King Asa summoned all Judah without exception, and they carried away the stones and beams with which Baasha was fortifying Ramah. With them King Asa built Geba of Benjamin and Mizpah. [23] All the rest of the acts of Asa, with all his valor and all that he did, and the cities he built, are recorded in the book of the chronicles of the kings of Judah. But in his old age, Asa had an infirmity in his feet. [24] Asa rested with his ancestors; he was buried with his ancestors in the City of David his father, and his son Jehoshaphat succeeded him as king.

**Reign of Nadab.** [25] Nadab, son of Jeroboam, became king of Israel in the second year of Asa, king of Judah. For two years he reigned over Israel.

[26] He did what was evil in the LORD's sight, walking in the way of his father and the sin he had caused Israel to commit. [27] Baasha, son of Ahijah, of the house of Issachar, plotted against him and struck him down at Gibbethon of the Philistines, which Nadab and all Israel were besieging. [28] Baasha killed him in the third year of Asa, king of Judah, and

---

† **15:10** Maacah was in fact Asa's grandmother (see v. 2), but "king's mother" was perhaps a title for the *gebira*, the "Great Lady" or "queen mother" (see, for instance, 2:19). This influential position was usually held by the king's biological mother, but Maacah may have retained it after the early death of her son Abijam.

**15:18** *Ben-hadad…king of Aram*: Ben-hadad I, third successor of Rezon, who had thrown off the yoke of the Israelites during the reign of Solomon and become king of Aram (11:23–24). Chronicles has a parallel version of this account in 2 Chr 16:1–6. *Who ruled:* lit., "sitting," i.e., enthroned, possibly also meaning "resident" or "residing."

* ——————

**15:5** 2 Sm 11:1–27.

succeeded him as king. ²⁹ * Once he was king, he killed the entire house of Jeroboam, not leaving a single soul but destroying Jeroboam utterly, according to the word of the LORD spoken through his servant, Ahijah the Shilonite, ³⁰ because of the sins Jeroboam committed and caused Israel to commit, by which he provoked the LORD, the God of Israel, to anger.

³¹ The rest of the acts of Nadab, with all that he did, are recorded in the book of the chronicles of the kings of Israel. ³² There was war between Asa and Baasha, king of Israel, all their days.

**Reign of Baasha.** ³³ In the third year of Asa, king of Judah, Baasha, son of Ahijah, became king of all Israel in Tirzah for twenty-four years.

³⁴ He did what was evil in the LORD's sight, walking in the way of Jeroboam and the sin he had caused Israel to commit.

**16** ¹ The word of the LORD came to Jehu, son of Hanani, against Baasha: ² Inasmuch as I exalted you from the dust and made you ruler of my people Israel, but you have walked in the way of Jeroboam and have caused my people Israel to sin, provoking me to anger by their sins, ³ * I will burn up what is left of Baasha and his house; I will make your house like that of Jeroboam, son of Nebat:

⁴ *　One of Baasha's line who dies in the
　　　city,
　　　dogs will devour;
　　One who dies in the field,
　　　the birds of the sky will devour.

⁵ The rest of the acts of Baasha, what he did and his valor, are recorded in the book of the chronicles of the kings of Israel. ⁶ Baasha rested with his ancestors; he was buried in Tirzah, and his son Elah succeeded him as king. ⁷ (Through the prophet Jehu, son of Hanani, the word of the LORD came against Baasha and his house, because of all the evil Baasha did in the sight of the LORD, provoking him to anger by his deeds so that he became like the house of Jeroboam, and because of what he destroyed.)

**Reign of Elah.** ⁸ In the twenty-sixth year of Asa, king of Judah, Elah, son of Baasha, became king of Israel in Tirzah for two years.

⁹ His servant Zimri, commander of half his chariots, plotted against him. As he was in Tirzah, drinking to excess in the house of Arza, master of his palace in Tirzah, ¹⁰ * Zimri entered; he struck and killed him in the twenty-seventh year of Asa, king of Judah, and succeeded him as king. ¹¹ Once he was king, seated on the throne, he killed the whole house of Baasha, not sparing a single male relative or friend of his. ¹² * Zimri destroyed the entire house of Baasha, according to the word the LORD spoke against Baasha through Jehu the prophet, ¹³ because of all the sins which Baasha and his son Elah committed and caused Israel to commit, provoking the LORD, the God of Israel, to anger by their idols.

¹⁴ The rest of the acts of Elah, with all that he did, are recorded in the book of the chronicles of the kings of Israel.

**Reign of Zimri.** ¹⁵ In the twenty-seventh year of Asa, king of Judah, Zimri became king for seven days in Tirzah.

The army was encamped at Gibbethon of the Philistines ¹⁶ when they heard, "Zimri has formed a conspiracy and has killed the king." So that day in the camp all Israel made Omri, commander of the army, king of Israel. ¹⁷ Omri and all Israel with him marched up from Gibbethon and besieged Tirzah. ¹⁸ When Zimri saw that the city was captured, he entered the citadel of the king's house and burned it down over him. He died ¹⁹ because of the sins he had committed, doing what was evil in the LORD's sight by walking in the way of Jeroboam and the sin he had caused Israel to commit.

²⁰ The rest of the acts of Zimri, with the conspiracy he carried out, are recorded in the book of the chronicles of the kings of Israel.

**Civil War.** ²¹ At that time the people of Israel were divided in two, half following Tibni, son of Ginath, to make him king, and half for Omri. ²² The partisans of Omri prevailed over those of Tibni, son of Ginath. Tibni died and Omri became king.

**15:29** 1 Kgs 14:10–11.
**16:3** 1 Kgs 16:11; 21:22.
**16:4** 1 Kgs 14:11.
**16:10** 2 Kgs 9:31.
**16:12** 1 Kgs 16:2–4.

**Reign of Omri.** ²³ In the thirty-first year of Asa, king of Judah, Omri became king of Israel for twelve years; the first six of them he reigned in Tirzah.

²⁴ He then bought the mountain of Samaria from Shemer for two silver talents and built upon the mountain the city he named Samaria, after Shemer, the former owner. ²⁵ But Omri did what was evil in the LORD's sight, more than any of his predecessors. ²⁶ In every way he imitated the sinful conduct of Jeroboam, son of Nebat, and the sin he had caused Israel to commit, thus provoking the LORD, the God of Israel, to anger by their idols.

²⁷ The rest of the acts of Omri, what he did and his valor, are recorded in the book of the chronicles of the kings of Israel. ²⁸ Omri rested with his ancestors; he was buried in Samaria, and Ahab his son succeeded him as king.

**Reign of Ahab.** ²⁹ Ahab, son of Omri, became king of Israel in the thirty-eighth year of Asa, king of Judah. Ahab, son of Omri, reigned over Israel in Samaria for twenty-two years.

³⁰ Ahab, son of Omri, did what was evil in the LORD's sight more than any of his predecessors. ³¹ It was not enough for him to follow the sins of Jeroboam, son of Nebat. He even married Jezebel, daughter of Ethbaal, king of the Sidonians, and began to serve Baal, and worship him. ³² Ahab set up an altar to Baal in the house of Baal which he built in Samaria, ³³ and also made an asherah. Ahab did more to provoke the LORD, the God of Israel, to anger than any of the kings of Israel before him. ³⁴* During his reign, Hiel from Bethel rebuilt Jericho. At the cost of Abiram, his firstborn son, he laid the foundation, and at the cost of

Segub, his youngest son, he set up the gates, according to the word of the LORD spoken through Joshua, son of Nun.†

## IV. THE STORY OF ELIJAH†

**17 Elijah Proclaims a Drought.†** ¹ Elijah the Tishbite,†* from Tishbe in Gilead, said to Ahab: "As the LORD, the God of Israel, lives, whom I serve, during these years there shall be no dew or rain except at my word." ² The word of the LORD came to Elijah: ³ Leave here, go east and hide in the Wadi Cherith, east of the Jordan. ⁴ You shall drink of the wadi, and I have commanded ravens to feed you there. ⁵ So he left and did as the LORD had commanded. He left and remained by the Wadi Cherith, east of the Jordan. ⁶* Ravens brought him bread and meat in the morning, and bread and meat in the evening, and he drank from the wadi.

⁷ After some time, however, the wadi ran dry, because no rain had fallen in the land. ⁸* So the word of the LORD came to him: ⁹ Arise, go to Zarephath of Sidon and stay there. I have commanded a widow there to feed you. ¹⁰ He arose and went to Zarephath. When he arrived at the entrance of the city, a widow was there gathering sticks; he called out to her, "Please bring me a small cupful of water to drink." ¹¹ She left to get it, and he called out after her, "Please bring along a crust of bread." ¹² She said, "As the LORD, your God, lives, I have nothing baked; there is only a handful of flour in my jar and a little oil in my jug. Just now I was collecting a few sticks, to go in and prepare something for myself and my son; when we have eaten it, we shall die." ¹³ Elijah said to

---

**16:34** See note on Jos 6:26.

**17:1–19:21** The central section of 1–2 Kings tells the story of the dynasty of Omri. That dynasty begins and ends in civil war (1 Kgs 16:21–22; 2 Kgs 9–11). Most of the story is set during the reigns of Ahab of Israel (1 Kgs 16:29–22:40) and his son Joram (2 Kgs 3:1–9:26) and focuses particularly on the interaction of the king with various prophets, especially Ahab with Elijah and Joram with Elisha. The story of Ahab itself contains two large complexes, a series of narratives about Elijah (1 Kgs 17:1–19:21) and a series about hostility between Ahab and the prophets (1 Kgs 20:1–22:38).

**17:1–24** The story of Elijah is in three parts. The first (chap. 17) describes how Elijah proclaimed a drought on God's authority and how he survived during the drought. The second (chap. 18) describes how he ends the drought by bringing the populace back to exclusive worship of the Lord. The third (chap. 19) describes Elijah's despair at the failure of his prophetic mission and his consequent attempt to resign from the prophetic office.

**17:1** This verse introduces the enigmatic figure of Elijah the Tishbite. (The name "Elijah" means "the Lord is my God." The meaning of "Tishbite" is unknown; it may refer to a place or to a

social class.) His appearance before Ahab is abrupt and involves several matters that will unify the whole Elijah story. His claim to "serve the Lord" (lit., to "stand before the Lord") points forward to 19:13, where he refuses to do so; the center of narrative tension on this level is the question of the prophet's autonomy in God's service. His proclamation of a drought points forward to 18:41–45 where he announces the drought's end; the center of narrative tension on this level is the struggle between the Lord and the Canaanite fertility god Baal for the loyalties of Israel. His claim that the drought is due to his own word of power ("except at my word") points forward to 17:24 where the widow acknowledges the divine source of the word Elijah speaks; the center of narrative tension on this level is the gradual characterization of the prophet as one who receives a divine word (vv. 2, 8), obeys it (v. 5), conveys an effective divine word of threat (v. 1) or promise (vv. 14, 16), and even speaks an effective human word of entreaty to God (vv. 20, 22).

---

**16:34** Jos 6:26.
**17:1** Sir 48:1–12; Jas 5:17–18.
**17:6** Ex 16:8, 12.
**17:8–16** 2 Kgs 4:1–7; Lk 4:25–26.

her, "Do not be afraid. Go and do as you have said. But first make me a little cake and bring it to me. Afterwards you can prepare something for yourself and your son. ¹⁴ For the LORD, the God of Israel, says: The jar of flour shall not go empty, nor the jug of oil run dry, until the day when the LORD sends rain upon the earth." ¹⁵ She left and did as Elijah had said. She had enough to eat for a long time—he and she and her household. ¹⁶ The jar of flour did not go empty, nor the jug of oil run dry, according to the word of the LORD spoken through Elijah.

¹⁷* Some time later the son of the woman, the owner of the house, fell sick, and his sickness grew more severe until he stopped breathing. ¹⁸ So she said to Elijah, "Why have you done this to me, man of God? Have you come to me to call attention to my guilt and to kill my son?" ¹⁹ Elijah said to her, "Give me your son." Taking him from her lap, he carried him to the upper room where he was staying, and laid him on his own bed. ²⁰ He called out to the LORD: "LORD, my God, will you afflict even the widow with whom I am staying by killing her son?" ²¹ Then he stretched himself out upon the child three times and he called out to the LORD: "LORD, my God, let the life breath return to the body of this child." ²² The LORD heard the prayer of Elijah; the life breath returned to the child's body and he lived. ²³ Taking the child, Elijah carried him down into the house from the upper room and gave him to his mother. Elijah said, "See! Your son is alive." ²⁴ The woman said to Elijah, "Now indeed I know that you are a man of God, and it is truly the word of the LORD that you speak."

**18** **Elijah Ends the Drought.**† ¹ Long afterward, in the third year, the word of the LORD came to Elijah: Go, present yourself to Ahab, that I may send rain upon the earth. ² So Elijah went to present himself to Ahab.

Now the famine in Samaria was severe, ³ and Ahab had summoned Obadiah, master of his palace, who greatly revered the LORD. ⁴ When Jezebel was slaughtering the prophets of the LORD, Obadiah took a hundred prophets, hid them away by fifties in caves, and supplied them with food and water. ⁵ Ahab said to Obadiah, "Go through the land to all sources of water and to all the wadies. We may find grass and keep the horses and mules alive, so that we shall not have to slaughter any of the beasts." ⁶ Dividing the land to explore between them, Ahab went one way by himself, Obadiah another way by himself. ⁷ As Obadiah was on his way, Elijah met him. Recognizing him, Obadiah fell prostrate and asked, "Is it you, my lord Elijah?" ⁸ He said to him, "Yes. Go tell your lord, 'Elijah is here!'"† ⁹ But Obadiah said, "What sin has your servant committed, that you are handing me over to Ahab to be killed? ¹⁰ As the LORD, your God, lives, there is no nation or kingdom where my lord has not sent in search of you. When they replied, 'He is not here,' he made each kingdom and nation swear they could not find you. ¹¹ And now you say, 'Go tell your lord: Elijah is here!' ¹² After I leave you, the spirit of the LORD will carry you to some place I do not know, and when I go to inform Ahab and he does not find you, he will kill me—though your servant has revered the LORD from his youth! ¹³ Have you not been told, my lord, what I did when Jezebel was murdering the prophets of the LORD—that I hid a hundred of the prophets of the LORD, fifty each in caves, and supplied them with food and water? ¹⁴ And now you say, 'Go tell your lord: Elijah is here!' He will kill me!" ¹⁵ Elijah answered, "As the LORD of hosts lives, whom I serve, I will present myself to him today."

¹⁶ So Obadiah went to meet Ahab and informed him, and Ahab came to meet Elijah. ¹⁷ When Ahab saw Elijah, he said to him, "Is it you, you disturber of Israel?" ¹⁸ He answered, "It is not I who disturb Israel, but you and your father's house, by forsaking the commands of the LORD and you by following the Baals. ¹⁹ Now summon all Israel to me on Mount Carmel, as well as the four hundred and fifty

---

† **18:1–45** The story of the conflict with the prophets of Baal (vv. 21–40) is embedded in the story of the drought and its ending (vv. 1–20, 41–45). The connection between the two stories is found in Canaanite theology, in whose pantheon Baal, "the Cloud Rider," the god of rain and storm, was recognized as the one who brings fertility. Worship of many gods was virtually universal in the ancient world; the Israelite requirement of exclusive worship of the Lord (Ex 20:3) was unique. The people of Israel had apparently become comfortable worshiping both Baal and the Lord, perhaps assigning mutually exclusive spheres of influence to each. By claiming authority over the rain (17:1; 18:1),

the Lord was challenging Baal's power in Baal's own domain. The entire drought story in chaps. 17–18 implies what becomes explicit in 18:21–40: this is a struggle between the Lord and Baal for the loyalties of the people of Israel.

† **18:8** *Elijah is here*: the Hebrew *hinneh 'eliyahu* involves a pun. The sentence means both "Elijah is here," informing Ahab that the prophet has been found, and "Behold, Yhwh is my God" (the meaning of the name "Elijah").

---

**17:17–24** 2 Kgs 4:18–37; Lk 7:11–16.

prophets of Baal and the four hundred prophets of Asherah who eat at Jezebel's table." 20 So Ahab summoned all the Israelites and had the prophets gather on Mount Carmel.

21 Elijah approached all the people and said, "How long will you straddle the issue? If the LORD is God, follow him; if Baal, follow him." But the people did not answer him. 22 So Elijah said to the people, "I am the only remaining prophet of the LORD, and there are four hundred and fifty prophets of Baal. 23 Give us two young bulls. Let them choose one, cut it into pieces, and place it on the wood, but start no fire. I shall prepare the other and place it on the wood, but shall start no fire. 24 You shall call upon the name of your gods, and I will call upon the name of the LORD. The God who answers with fire is God." All the people answered, "We agree!"

25 Elijah then said to the prophets of Baal, "Choose one young bull and prepare it first, for there are more of you. Call upon your gods, but do not start the fire." 26 Taking the young bull that was turned over to them, they prepared it and called upon Baal from morning to noon, saying, "Baal, answer us!" But there was no sound, and no one answering. And they hopped around the altar they had prepared. 27 When it was noon, Elijah taunted them: "Call louder, for he is a god; he may be busy doing his business, or may be on a journey. Perhaps he is asleep and must be awakened." 28 They called out louder and slashed themselves with swords and spears according to their ritual until blood gushed over them. 29 Noon passed and they remained in a prophetic state until the time for offering sacrifice. But there was no sound, no one answering, no one listening.

30 Then Elijah said to all the people, "Come here to me." When they drew near to him, he repaired the altar of the LORD which had been destroyed. 31 He took twelve stones, for the number of tribes of the sons of Jacob, to whom the LORD had said: Israel shall be your name. 32 He built the stones into an altar to the name of the LORD, and made a trench around the altar large enough for two measures of grain. 33 When he had arranged the wood, he cut up the young bull and laid it on the wood. 34 He said, "Fill four jars with water and pour it over the burnt offering and over the wood." "Do it again," he said, and they did it again. "Do it a third time," he said, and they did it a third time. 35 The water flowed around the altar; even the trench was filled with the water. 36 At the time for offering sacrifice, Elijah the prophet came forward and said, "LORD, God of Abraham, Isaac, and Israel, let it be known this day that you are God in Israel and that I am your servant and have done all these things at your command. 37 * Answer me, LORD! Answer me, that this people may know that you, LORD, are God and that you have turned their hearts back to you." 38 The LORD's fire came down and devoured the burnt offering, wood, stones, and dust, and lapped up the water in the trench. 39 Seeing this, all the people fell prostrate and said, "The LORD is God! The LORD is God!" 40 * Then Elijah said to them, "Seize the prophets of Baal. Let none of them escape!" They seized them, and Elijah brought them down to the Wadi Kishon and there he slaughtered them. 41 Elijah then said to Ahab, "Go up, eat and drink, for there is the sound of a heavy rain." 42 So Ahab went up to eat and drink, while Elijah went up to the top of Carmel, crouched down to the earth, and put his head between his knees. 43 He said to his servant, "Go up and look out to sea." He went up and looked, but reported, "There is nothing." Seven times he said, "Go look again!" 44 And the seventh time the youth reported, "There is a cloud as small as a man's hand rising from the sea." Elijah said, "Go and say to Ahab, 'Harness up and go down the mountain before the rain stops you.'" 45 All at once the sky grew dark with clouds and wind, and a heavy rain fell. Ahab mounted his chariot and headed for Jezreel. 46 But the hand of the LORD was on Elijah. He girded up his clothing and ran before Ahab as far as the approaches to Jezreel.

# 19

**Flight to Horeb.**† 1 Ahab told Jezebel all that Elijah had done—that he had murdered all the prophets by the sword. 2 Jezebel then sent a messenger to Elijah and said, "May the gods do thus to me and more, if by this time tomorrow I have not done with your life what was done to each of them." 3 Elijah was

---

† 19:1–21 The story of Elijah's journey to Mount Horeb begins as a flight from danger, but takes a surprising turn. The prophet makes his solitary way to the mountain where the Lord had appeared to Moses and the Israelites ("Horeb" is an alternate name for "Sinai"). Like Moses on the holy mountain, Elijah experiences a theophany and receives a commission.

18:37 Ex 32:13.    18:40 Ex 32:26–28.

afraid and fled for his life, going to Beer-sheba of Judah. He left his servant there [4]* and went a day's journey into the wilderness, until he came to a solitary broom tree and sat beneath it. He prayed for death: "Enough, LORD! Take my life, for I am no better than my ancestors." [5] He lay down and fell asleep under the solitary broom tree, but suddenly a messenger† touched him and said, "Get up and eat!" [6] He looked and there at his head was a hearth cake and a jug of water. After he ate and drank, he lay down again, [7] but the angel of the LORD came back a second time, touched him, and said, "Get up and eat or the journey will be too much for you!" [8]* He got up, ate, and drank; then strengthened by that food, he walked forty days and forty nights to the mountain of God, Horeb.

[9] There he came to a cave, where he took shelter. But the word of the LORD came to him: Why are you here, Elijah? [10] He answered: "I have been most zealous for the LORD, the God of hosts, but the Israelites have forsaken your covenant. They have destroyed your altars and murdered your prophets by the sword. I alone remain, and they seek to take my life." [11]* Then the LORD said: Go out and stand on the mountain before the LORD;† the LORD will pass by. There was a strong and violent wind rending the mountains and crushing rocks before the LORD—but the LORD was not in the wind; after the wind, an earthquake—but the LORD was not in the earthquake; [12] after the earthquake, fire—but the LORD† was not in the fire; after the fire, a light silent sound.†

[13] When he heard this, Elijah hid his face in his cloak and went out and stood at the entrance of the cave. A voice said to him, Why are you here, Elijah? [14]* He replied, "I have been most zealous for the LORD, the God of hosts, but the Israelites have forsaken your covenant. They have destroyed your altars and murdered your prophets by the sword. I alone remain, and they seek to take my life."

[15]†* The LORD said to him: Go back! Take the desert road to Damascus. When you arrive, you shall anoint Hazael as king of Aram. [16]* You shall also anoint Jehu, son of Nimshi, as king of Israel, and Elisha, son of Shaphat of Abelmeholah, as prophet to succeed you. [17] Anyone who escapes the sword of Hazael, Jehu will kill. Anyone who escapes the sword of Jehu, Elisha will kill. [18]* But I will spare seven thousand in Israel—every knee that has not bent to Baal, every mouth that has not kissed him.

[19]† Elijah set out, and came upon Elisha, son of Shaphat, as he was plowing with twelve yoke of oxen; he was following the twelfth. Elijah went over to him and threw his cloak on him. [20]* Elisha left the oxen, ran after Elijah, and said, "Please, let me kiss my father and mother good-bye, and I will follow you." Elijah answered, "Go back! What have I done to you?" [21] Elisha left him and, taking the yoke of oxen, slaughtered them; he used the plowing equipment for fuel to boil their flesh, and gave it to the people to eat. Then he left and followed Elijah to serve him.

## V. THE STORY OF AHAB†

# 20

**Ahab's Victories over Aram.**† [1] Benhadad, king of Aram, gathered all his

---

† **19:5–7** Sound asleep, Elijah is startled awake by an unspecified "messenger." Only in v. 7 is the figure identified as a messenger (or "angel") of the Lord.

**19:11–13** To "stand before the Lord" is a literal translation of a Hebrew idiom meaning "to serve the Lord"; Elijah has used this idiom twice before to describe himself as the Lord's servant (17:1; 18:15). The Lord's command, then, means that Elijah is to take up once again the prophetic service to which he has been appointed. The Lord's question, "Why are you here?" (v. 9, repeated in v. 13), could imply an accusation that he is abandoning his prophetic office. In v. 15, the Lord tells him to go back.

**19:12** Compare these divine manifestations to Elijah with those to Moses on the same mountain (Ex 19:16–19; 33:18–23; 34:5–6; Dt 4:10–15). Though various phenomena, such as wind, storms, earthquakes, fire, accompany the divine presence, they do not constitute the presence itself which, like the "silent sound," is mysterious and ultimately ungraspable. Moses and Elijah, the two figures who experienced God's theophany on this mountain, reappear with Jesus on another mountain at his transfiguration (Mt 17:1–9; Mk 9:2–9; Lk 9:28–36).

**19:15–17** Elijah himself carried out only the last of the three commissions entrusted to him (vv. 19–21); Elisha performed the first himself (2 Kgs 8:7–19), and the second, the anointing of

Jehu, through one of his followers (2 Kgs 9:1–10).

**19:19–21** Elijah's act of throwing his mantle over the shoulders of Elisha associates him with Elijah as a servant (v. 21). Elisha will later succeed to Elijah's position and prophetic power (2 Kgs 2:1–15). Elisha's prompt response, destroying his plow and oxen, signifies a radical change from his former manner of living.

**20:1–22:54** Although coverage of Ahab's reign began in 16:29, he was only a secondary character in the chapters about Elijah. Now attention focuses on Ahab. Each of these chapters tells a story of the king (20:1–34; 21:1–16; 22:1–4, 29–38), to which is attached a scene of prophetic condemnation (20:30–42; 21:17–29; 22:5–28). As relations between Ahab and the prophets of the Lord deteriorate, the scenes of prophetic condemnation get longer and the condemnations themselves become more pointed. Some historians doubt that the stories of hostility between Israel and Aram (chaps. 20 and 22) originally pertained to the reign of Ahab. If this is correct, their original setting may have been decades later.

**20:1–34** This story recounts two battles through which Ahab

---

| | |
|---|---|
| **19:4** Jon 4:6–9. | **19:15** 2 Kgs 8:7–15. |
| **19:8** Ex 34:28. | **19:16** 2 Kgs 2:1–15; 9:1–10. |
| **19:11–13** Ex 33:18–23; 34:5–6. | **19:18** Rom 11:4. |
| **19:14** Rom 11:3. | **19:20** Lk 9:61–62. |

forces and, accompanied by thirty-two kings with horses and chariotry, set out to besiege and attack Samaria. ²He sent messengers to Ahab, king of Israel, within the city, ³and said to him, "This is Ben-hadad's message: 'Your silver and gold are mine, and your wives and your fine children are mine.'" ⁴The king of Israel answered, "Just as you say, my lord king, I and all I have are yours." ⁵But the messengers came again and said, "This is Ben-hadad's message: 'I sent you word: Give me your silver and gold, your wives and your children. ⁶But now I say: At this time tomorrow I will send my servants to you, and they shall ransack your house and the houses of your servants. They shall seize and take away whatever you consider valuable.'" ⁷The king of Israel then summoned all the elders of the land and said: "Understand clearly that this man is intent on evil. When he sent to me for my wives and children, my silver and my gold, I did not refuse him." ⁸All the elders and all the people said to him, "Do not listen. Do not give in." ⁹Accordingly he directed the messengers of Ben-hadad, "Say this: 'To my lord the king: I will do all that you demanded of your servant the first time. But this I cannot do.'" The messengers left and reported this. ¹⁰Ben-hadad then responded, "May the gods do thus to me and more, if there will remain enough dust in Samaria to make handfuls for all my followers." ¹¹The king of Israel replied, "Tell him, 'Let not one who puts on armor boast like one who takes it off.'" ¹²Ben-hadad was drinking in the pavilions with the kings when he heard this reply. He commanded his servants, "Get ready!"; and they got ready to storm the city.

¹³Then a prophet came up to Ahab, king of Israel, and said: "The LORD says, Do you see all this vast army? Today I am giving it into your power, that you may know that I am the LORD." ¹⁴But Ahab asked, "Through whom will it be given over?" He answered, "The LORD says, Through the aides of the provincial governors." Then Ahab asked, "Who is to attack?" He replied, "You are." ¹⁵So Ahab mustered the aides of the provincial governors, two hundred

thirty-two of them. Behind them he mustered all the Israelite soldiery, who numbered seven thousand in all. ¹⁶†They marched out at noon, while Ben-hadad was drinking heavily in the pavilions with the thirty-two kings who were his allies. ¹⁷When the aides of the provincial governors marched out first, Ben-hadad received word, "Some men have marched out of Samaria." ¹⁸He answered, "Whether they have come out for peace or for war, take them alive." ¹⁹But when these had come out of the city—the aides of the provincial governors with the army following them— ²⁰each of them struck down his man. The Arameans fled with Israel pursuing them, while Ben-hadad, king of Aram, escaped on a chariot horse. ²¹Then the king of Israel went out and destroyed the horses and chariots. Thus he inflicted a severe defeat on Aram.

²²Then the prophet approached the king of Israel and said to him: "Go, regroup your forces. Understand clearly what you must do, for at the turning of the year† the king of Aram will attack you." ²³Meanwhile the servants of the king of Aram said to him: "Their gods are mountain gods. That is why they defeated us. But if we fight them on level ground, we shall be sure to defeat them. ²⁴This is what you must do: Take the kings from their posts and put prefects in their places. ²⁵Raise an army as large as the army you have lost, horse for horse, chariot for chariot. Let us fight them on level ground, and we shall surely defeat them." He took their advice and did this. ²⁶At the turning of the year, Ben-hadad mustered Aram and went up to Aphek to fight against Israel. ²⁷The Israelites, too, were mustered and supplied with provisions; then they went out to meet the enemy. The Israelites, encamped opposite, looked like little flocks of goats, while Aram covered the land. ²⁸A man of God approached and said to the king of Israel: "The LORD says, Because Aram has said the LORD is a god of mountains, not a god of plains, I will give all this vast army into your power that you may know I am the LORD." ²⁹They were encamped opposite each other for seven days.

---

† won freedom for Israel from vassalage to Ben-hadad of Syria. The story is chiastically arranged: negotiations (vv. 1–12), battle (vv. 13–21), battle (vv. 22–30), negotiations (vv. 31–34). The ensuing prophetic condemnation is surprising, since the portrait of Ahab in vv. 1–34 is apparently quite positive.
**20:16–19** The narrator uses a sort of verbal split-screen technique to show us two separate and simultaneous scenes. At the gates of Samaria, the Israelite forces are coming out to battle (v.

16a): first the aides (lit., "young men"; v. 17a), then the whole army (v. 19). Meanwhile in the Aramean camp Ben-hadad is getting drunk (v. 16b), receiving reports (v. 17b) and issuing commands (v. 18).
**20:22** *At the turning of the year*: the idiom may mean "next year about this time" or "at the beginning of the year," i.e., the spring (cf. 2 Sm 11:1).

On the seventh day battle was joined, and the Israelites struck down one hundred thousand foot soldiers of Aram in one day. [30] The survivors fled into the city of Aphek, where the wall collapsed on twenty-seven thousand of them. Ben-hadad, too, fled, and took refuge within the city, in an inner room.

[31] His servants said to him: "We have heard that the kings of the house of Israel are merciful kings. Allow us, therefore, to garb ourselves in sackcloth, with cords around our heads, and go out to the king of Israel. Perhaps he will spare your life." [32] Dressed in sackcloth girded at the waist and wearing cords around their heads, they went to the king of Israel and said, "Your servant Ben-hadad says, 'Spare my life!'" He asked, "Is he still alive? He is my brother."† [33] Hearing this as a good omen, the men quickly took him at his word and said, "Ben-hadad is your brother." He answered, "Go and get him." When Ben-hadad came out to him, the king had him mount his chariot. [34] Ben-hadad said to him, "The cities my father took from your father I will restore, and you may set up bazaars for yourself in Damascus, as my father did in Samaria." Ahab replied, "For my part, I will set you free on those terms." So he made a covenant with him and then set him free.

**Prophetic Condemnation.** [35] Acting on the word of the LORD, one of the guild prophets said to his companion, "Strike me." But he refused to strike him. [36] Then he said to him, "Since you did not obey the voice of the LORD, a lion will attack you when you leave me." When he left him, a lion came upon him and attacked him.* [37] Then the prophet met another man and said, "Strike me." The man struck him a blow and wounded him. [38] The prophet went on and waited for the king on the road, disguising himself with a bandage

over his eyes. [39] As the king was passing, he called out to the king and said: "Your servant went into the thick of the battle, and suddenly someone turned and brought me a man and said, 'Guard this man. If he is missing, you shall have to pay for his life with your life or pay out a talent of silver.'† [40] But while your servant was occupied here and there, the man disappeared." The king of Israel said to him, "That is your sentence. You have decided it yourself." [41] He quickly removed the bandage from his eyes, and the king of Israel recognized him as one of the prophets. [42]* He said to him: "The LORD says, Because you have set free the man I put under the ban,† your life shall pay for his life, your people for his people." [43]* Disturbed and angry, the king of Israel set off for home and entered Samaria.

**21 Seizure of Naboth's Vineyard.**† [1] Naboth the Jezreelite had a vineyard in Jezreel next to the palace of Ahab, king of Samaria. Some time later, [2] Ahab said to Naboth, "Give me your vineyard to be my vegetable garden, since it is close by, next to my house. I will give you a better vineyard in exchange, or, if you prefer, I will give you its value in money." [3] Naboth said to Ahab, "The LORD forbid that I should give you my ancestral heritage."† [4] Ahab went home disturbed and angry at the answer Naboth the Jezreelite had given him: "I will not give you my ancestral heritage." Lying down on his bed, he turned away and would not eat. [5] His wife Jezebel came to him and said to him, "Why are you so sullen that you will not eat?" [6] He answered her, "Because I spoke to Naboth the Jezreelite and said to him, 'Sell me your vineyard, or, if you prefer, I will give you a vineyard in exchange.' But he said, 'I will not give you my vineyard.'" [7] Jezebel his wife said to him, "What a king of Israel you are! Get up! Eat and be cheerful. I

† 20:32 *He is my brother:* cf. note on 9:13.
20:39 The "man" is ostensibly a prisoner of war, to be kept or sold as a slave. In the event he escapes, the one charged with guarding him would be obliged either to pay a fine or to take his place as a slave. The fine, however, is exorbitant: a talent of silver is roughly one hundred times the price of an ordinary slave (see Ex 21:32). This is the only clue Ahab will get that he is being set up and that the story is really about himself in his dealings with Ben-hadad. In 2 Sm 14:1–20, the wise woman of Tekoa uses the same technique with King David: she tells a story that elicits a reaction from the king; David is tricked into pronouncing judgment on himself, as the story parallels his own situation. The prophet Nathan (2 Sm 12:1–7) likewise uses a story that leads David to see his sin for what it is.

20:42 *Under the ban:* cf. note on Dt 2:34.
21:1–16 The story tells how Jezebel manipulates important structures of Israelite social order, law, and religious observance to eliminate a faithful Israelite landowner who frustrates Ahab's will.
21:3 *Heritage:* Hebrew *naḥalah.* Naboth is unwilling to sell or exchange his vineyard. According to the Israelite system of land tenure and distribution, land was held in common within a social unit. The ancestral *naḥalah* was not private property, to be alienated at will.

20:36 1 Kgs 13:24.　20:43 1 Kgs 21:4.
20:42 1 Kgs 22:35.

will give you the vineyard of Naboth the Jezreelite."

⁸So she wrote letters in Ahab's name and, having sealed them with his seal, sent them to the elders and to the nobles who lived in the same city with Naboth. ⁹This is what she wrote in the letters: "Proclaim a fast and set Naboth at the head of the people. ¹⁰Next, set two scoundrels opposite him to accuse him: 'You have cursed God and king.' Then take him out and stone him to death."

¹¹His fellow citizens—the elders and the nobles who dwelt in his city—did as Jezebel had ordered in the letters she sent them. ¹²They proclaimed a fast and set Naboth at the head of the people. ¹³Two scoundrels came in and sat opposite Naboth, and the scoundrels accused him in the presence of the people, "Naboth has cursed God and king." And they led him out of the city and stoned him to death. ¹⁴Then they sent word to Jezebel: "Naboth has been stoned to death."

¹⁵When Jezebel learned that Naboth had been stoned to death, she said to Ahab, "Go, take possession of the vineyard of Naboth the Jezreelite which he refused to sell you, because Naboth is not alive, but dead." ¹⁶When Ahab heard that Naboth was dead, he started on his way down to the vineyard of Naboth the Jezreelite, to take possession of it.

**Prophetic Condemnation.** ¹⁷Then the word of the LORD came to Elijah the Tishbite: ¹⁸Go down to meet Ahab, king of Israel, who is in Samaria. He will be in the vineyard of Naboth, where he has gone to take possession. ¹⁹* Tell him: "Thus says the LORD: After murdering, do you also take possession?" And tell him, "Thus says the LORD: In the place where the dogs licked up the blood of Naboth, the dogs shall lick up your blood, too."

²⁰† Ahab said to Elijah, "Have you found me out, my enemy?" He said, "I have found you. Because you have given yourself up to doing evil in the LORD's sight, ²¹* I am bringing evil upon you: I will consume you and will cut off every male belonging to Ahab, whether bond or free, in Israel. ²²I will make your house like that of Jeroboam, son of Nebat, and like the house of Baasha, son of Ahijah, because you have provoked me by leading Israel into sin."

²³Against Jezebel, too, the LORD declared: The dogs shall devour Jezebel in the confines of Jezreel.

²⁴ Anyone of Ahab's line who dies in the
city,
dogs will devour;
Anyone who dies in the field,
the birds of the sky will devour.

²⁵Indeed, no one gave himself up to the doing of evil in the sight of the LORD as did Ahab, urged on by his wife Jezebel. ²⁶He became completely abominable by going after idols, just as the Amorites had done, whom the LORD drove out of the Israelites' way.

²⁷When Ahab heard these words, he tore his garments and put on sackcloth over his bare flesh. He fasted, slept in the sackcloth, and went about subdued. ²⁸Then the word of the LORD came to Elijah the Tishbite, ²⁹* Have you seen how Ahab has humbled himself before me? Since he has humbled himself before me, I will not bring the evil in his time. I will bring the evil upon his house in his son's time.

# 22

**Ahab's Defeat by Aram.**† ¹Three years passed without war between Aram and Israel. ²In the third year, however, King Jehoshaphat of Judah came down to the king of Israel. ³The king of Israel said to his servants, "Do you not know that Ramoth-gilead is ours and we are doing nothing to take it from the king of Aram?" ⁴He asked Jehoshaphat, "Will you come with me to fight against Ramoth-gilead?" Jehoshaphat answered the king of Israel, "You and I are as one, and your people and my people, your horses and my horses as well."

**21:20–26** In these verses the narrator uses against the third Israelite dynasty the same condemnation formula that was uttered against the first two dynasties, those of Jeroboam (14:9–11) and Baasha (16:2–4). Part of the formula is put in Elijah's mouth, in an oracle against Ahab and his descendants (vv. 21–22), and part of it in an aside to the reader that extends the condemnation to Ahab's wife, Jezebel, and his whole household (vv. 23–24). The oracle against Jezebel will be fulfilled in 2 Kgs 9:36; the obliteration of the dynasty will be recounted in the bloody stories of 2 Kgs 9–11.
**22:1–40** This chapter presents a contrasting parallel to chap. 20, where Ahab enjoyed victories over Aram's aggression. Here

Ahab is the aggressor, but falls in battle against Aram. Like the preceding chapters, it contains a story of Ahab plus an episode of prophetic condemnation. The story ends with the formulaic conclusion to Ahab's reign (vv. 39–40). Chronicles has a parallel version of this account in 2 Chr 18:1–34. After the story of Ahab's death come accounts of the reign of Jehoshaphat (paralleled in 2 Chr 20:31–37) and of the beginning of the reign of Ahaziah.

**21:19** 1 Kgs 22:38; 2 Kgs 9:26.    15:29; 16:3–4, 11; 2 Kgs 9:8–10, 36.
**21:21–23** 1 Kgs 14:10–11;    **21:29** 2 Kgs 9:25–26.

**Prophetic Condemnation.** [5] Jehoshaphat also said to the king of Israel, "Seek the word of the Lord at once." [6] The king of Israel assembled the prophets, about four hundred of them, and asked, "Shall I go to fight against Ramoth-gilead or shall I refrain?" They said, "Attack. The Lord will give it into the power of the king."† [7] But Jehoshaphat said, "Is there no other prophet of the Lord here we might consult?" [8] The king of Israel answered, "There is one other man through whom we might consult the Lord; but I hate him because he prophesies not good but evil about me. He is Micaiah, son of Imlah." Jehoshaphat said, "Let not the king say that." [9] So the king of Israel called an official and said to him, "Get Micaiah, son of Imlah, at once."

[10] The king of Israel and Jehoshaphat, king of Judah, were seated, each on his throne, clothed in their robes of state in the square at the entrance of the gate of Samaria, and all the prophets were prophesying before them. [11]* Zedekiah, son of Chenaanah, made himself two horns of iron† and said, "The Lord says, With these you shall gore Aram until you have destroyed them." [12] The other prophets prophesied in a similar vein, saying: "Attack Ramoth-gilead and conquer! The Lord will give it into the power of the king."

[13] Meanwhile, the messenger who had gone to call Micaiah said to him, "Look now, the prophets are unanimously predicting good for the king. Let your word be the same as any of theirs; speak a good word." [14] Micaiah said, "As the Lord lives, I shall speak whatever the Lord tells me." [15] When he came to the king, the king said to him, "Micaiah, shall we go to fight at Ramoth-gilead, or shall we refrain?" He said, "Attack and conquer! The Lord will give it into the power of the king." [16] But the king answered him, "How many times must I adjure you to tell me nothing but the truth in the name of the Lord?" [17]† So Micaiah said:

"I see all Israel
    scattered on the mountains,
    like sheep without a shepherd,
And the Lord saying,
    These have no master!
    Let each of them go back home in
      peace."

[18] The king of Israel said to Jehoshaphat, "Did I not tell you, he does not prophesy good about me, but only evil?" [19]† Micaiah continued: "Therefore hear the word of the Lord: I saw the Lord seated on his throne, with the whole host of heaven standing to his right and to his left. [20] The Lord asked: Who will deceive Ahab, so that he will go up and fall on Ramoth-gilead?† And one said this, another that, [21] until this spirit came forth and stood before the Lord, saying, 'I will deceive him.' The Lord asked: How? [22] He answered, 'I will go forth and become a lying spirit in the mouths of all his prophets.' The Lord replied: You shall succeed in deceiving him. Go forth and do this. [23] So now, the Lord has put a lying spirit in the mouths of all these prophets of yours; the Lord himself has decreed evil against you."

[24] Thereupon Zedekiah, son of Chenaanah, came up and struck Micaiah on the cheek, saying, "Has the spirit of the Lord, then, left me to speak with you?" [25] Micaiah said, "You shall find out on the day you go into an inner room to hide." [26] The king of Israel then said, "Seize Micaiah and take him back to Amon, prefect of the city, and to Joash, the king's son, [27] and say, 'This is the king's order: Put this man in prison and feed him scanty rations of bread and water until I come back in safety.'" [28]* But Micaiah said, "If you return in safety, the Lord has not spoken through me." (He also said, "Hear, O peoples, all of you.")†

**Ahab at Ramoth-gilead.** [29] The king of Israel and Jehoshaphat, king of Judah, went up to

---

† **22:6** Though Ahab is clearly intended to understand the oracle as prophesying his success, the prophets' words are ambiguous. "The lord" (not "the Lord," i.e., the proper name of Israel's God) who will give victory is unidentified, as is the king to whom it will be given.
    **22:11** The "two" horns probably symbolize the coalition of two kings, Ahab and Jehoshaphat.
    **22:17** Micaiah's oracle uses the common ancient metaphor of "shepherd" for the king. It means that the Israelite forces will be left leaderless because the king (or perhaps both kings: the word "master" could be singular or plural in Hebrew) will die in battle.
    **22:19–23** Since Ahab's intention to attack Ramoth-gilead is unshaken, Micaiah reveals God's plan to trick Ahab to his death,

and thus virtually dares Ahab to walk into the trap with his eyes open. The work of the "lying spirit" explains the ambiguities of the prophets' original oracle in v. 6. Prophets "stand in the council of the Lord" and are privy to its deliberations; cf. Jer 23:22.
    **22:20** *Fall on Ramoth-gilead*: lit., "heights of Gilead"; even the Lord's words are double-meaning. God wants Ahab to "fall on" (that is, attack) Ramoth-gilead so that he will "fall on" (that is, die on) Ramoth-gilead.
    **22:28** The last words of the verse are a scribal gloss attributing to Micaiah, son of Imlah, the opening words of the book of a different Micaiah (Micah), the prophet of Moresheth, the sixth of the twelve minor prophets of the Old Testament canon.

**22:11** Dt 33:17.        **22:28** Mi 1:2.

Ramoth-gilead, <sup>30</sup> and the king of Israel said to Jehoshaphat, "I will disguise myself and go into battle, but you put on your own robes." So the king of Israel disguised himself and entered the battle. <sup>31</sup> In the meantime the king of Aram had given his thirty-two chariot commanders the order, "Do not fight with anyone, great or small, except the king of Israel alone."

<sup>32</sup> When the chariot commanders saw Jehoshaphat, they cried out, "There is the king of Israel!" and wheeled to fight him. But Jehoshaphat cried out, <sup>33</sup> and the chariot commanders, seeing that he was not the king of Israel, turned away from him. <sup>34</sup> But someone drew his bow at random, and hit the king of Israel between the joints of his breastplate. He ordered his charioteer, "Rein about and take me out of the ranks, for I am wounded."

<sup>35</sup>* The battle grew fierce during the day, and the king, who was propped up in his chariot facing the Arameans, died in the evening. The blood from his wound flowed to the bottom of the chariot. <sup>36</sup> At sunset a cry went through the army, "Every man to his city, every man to his land!"

<sup>37</sup> And so the king died, and came back to Samaria, and they buried him there. <sup>38</sup>* When they washed out the chariot at the pool of Samaria, the dogs licked up his blood and prostitutes bathed there, as the LORD had prophesied.

<sup>39</sup> The rest of the acts of Ahab, with all that he did, including the ivory house he built and all the cities he built, are recorded in the book of the chronicles of the kings of Israel. <sup>40</sup> Ahab rested with his ancestors, and his son Ahaziah succeeded him as king.

**Reign of Jehoshaphat.** <sup>41</sup> Jehoshaphat, son of Asa, became king of Judah in the fourth year

of Ahab, king of Israel. <sup>42</sup> Jehoshaphat was thirty-five years old when he became king, and he reigned twenty-five years in Jerusalem. His mother's name was Azubah, daughter of Shilhi.

<sup>43</sup> He walked in the way of Asa his father unceasingly, doing what was right in the LORD's sight. <sup>44</sup> Nevertheless, the high places did not disappear, and the people still sacrificed on the high places and burned incense there. <sup>45</sup> Jehoshaphat also made peace with the king of Israel.

<sup>46</sup> The rest of the acts of Jehoshaphat, with his valor, what he did and how he fought, are recorded in the book of the chronicles of the kings of Judah. <sup>47</sup> He removed from the land the rest of the pagan priests who had remained in the reign of Asa his father. <sup>48</sup> There was no king in Edom, but an appointed regent. <sup>49</sup> Jehoshaphat made Tarshish ships to go to Ophir for gold; but in fact the ships did not go, because they were wrecked at Ezion-geber. <sup>50</sup> That was the time when Ahaziah, son of Ahab, had said to Jehoshaphat, "Let my servants accompany your servants in the ships." But Jehoshaphat would not agree. <sup>51</sup> Jehoshaphat rested with his ancestors; he was buried with his ancestors in the City of David his father, and his son Jehoram succeeded him as king.

**Reign of Ahaziah.**† <sup>52</sup> Ahaziah, son of Ahab, became king over Israel in Samaria in the seventeenth year† of Jehoshaphat, king of Judah; he reigned two years over Israel.

<sup>53</sup> He did what was evil in the sight of the LORD, walking in the way of his father, his mother, and Jeroboam, son of Nebat, who caused Israel to sin. <sup>54</sup> He served Baal and worshiped him, thus provoking the LORD, the God of Israel, just as his father had done.

---

† **22:52–54** The account of Ahaziah's reign continues in 2 Kings.

**22:52** *Seventeenth year:* so the present Hebrew text. This is consistent with the figures in 2 Kgs 3:1, but together those figures conflict with information in 1 Kgs 22:42 and 2 Kgs 1:17. The problem of the chronology of the kings of Israel and Judah

has never been convincingly resolved; it is complicated by the fact that the ancient Greek translation sometimes has different lengths of reign and different accession dates. See further note on 2 Kgs 3:1.

* **22:35** 1 Kgs 20:42.       **22:38** 1 Kgs 21:19.

# SECOND KINGS

## 1

**Reign of Ahaziah, Continued.** [1] After Ahab's death, Moab rebelled against Israel.* [2] Ahaziah fell through the lattice of his roof terrace at Samaria and was injured. So he sent out messengers with the instructions: "Go and inquire of Baalzebub,† the god of Ekron, whether I shall recover from this injury."

[3] Meanwhile, the messenger of the LORD said to Elijah the Tishbite: Go and meet the messengers of Samaria's king, and tell them: "Is it because there is no God in Israel that you are going to inquire of Baalzebub, the god of Ekron?" [4] For this, the LORD says: You shall not leave the bed upon which you lie; instead, you shall die. And Elijah departed. [5] The messengers then returned to Ahaziah, who asked them, "Why have you returned?" [6] They answered, "A man met us and said to us, 'Go back to the king who sent you and tell him: The LORD says: Is it because there is no God in Israel that you are sending to inquire of Baalzebub, that god of Ekron? For this you shall not leave the bed upon which you lie; instead, you shall die.'" [7] The king asked them, "What was the man like who met you and said these things to you?" [8] They replied, "He wore a hairy garment† with a leather belt around his waist." "It is Elijah the Tishbite!" he exclaimed.

[9] Then the king sent a captain with his company of fifty men after Elijah. The prophet was seated on a hilltop when he found him. He said, "Man of God, the king commands you, 'Come down.'" [10] Elijah answered the captain, "Well, if I am a man of God, may fire come down from heaven and consume you and your fifty men." And fire came down

from heaven and consumed him and his fifty men.* [11] The king sent another captain with his company of fifty men after Elijah. He shouted up and said, "Man of God, the king says, 'Come down immediately!'" [12] Elijah answered them, "If I am a man of God, may fire come down from heaven and consume you and your fifty men." And divine fire† came down from heaven and consumed him and his fifty men. [13] The king sent a third captain with his company of fifty men. When the third captain had climbed the hill, he fell to his knees before Elijah, pleading with him. He said, "Man of God, let my life and the lives of these fifty men, your servants, count for something in your sight! [14] Already fire has come down from heaven, consuming the first two captains with their companies of fifty men. But now, let my life count for something in your sight!" [15] Then the messenger of the LORD said to Elijah: Go down with him; you need not be afraid of him. So Elijah left and went down with him to the king. [16] He declared to the king: "Thus says the LORD: Because you sent messengers to inquire of Baalzebub, the god of Ekron—do you think there is no God in Israel to inquire of?—you shall not leave the bed upon which you lie; instead you shall die."*

[17] Ahaziah died according to the word of the LORD spoken by Elijah. Since he had no son, Joram† succeeded him as king, in the second year of Joram, son of Jehoshaphat, king of Judah.

[18] The rest of the acts of Ahaziah, which he did, are recorded in the book of chronicles of the kings of Israel.

## VI. ELISHA SUCCEEDS ELIJAH†

## 2

**Elijah's Journey.** [1] When the LORD was about to take Elijah up to heaven in a

---

**1:2** *Baalzebub*: in this form, "Baal of flies." The name in the Hebrew text is a derisive alteration of Baalzebul, "Prince Baal." The best New Testament evidence supports the latter form in Mt 10:25; Lk 11:15.

**1:8** *Hairy garment*: a sign of prophetic calling; see Zec 13:4. John the Baptizer wore a similarly distinctive mantle; see Mt 3:4; Mk 1:6.

**1:12** *Divine fire*: lit., "fire of God," which in Hebrew sounds quite like "man of God." The play on words is the basis for Elijah's retort. This story was told among the people to enhance the dignity of the prophet and to reflect the power of God whom he served. A similar phrase, "the LORD's fire," described the miraculous divine fire that fell from a cloudless sky to consume Elijah's offering in 1 Kgs 18:38.

**1:17** *Joram*: in 2 Kings the name "Joram" (*yoram*) and its variant "Jehoram" (*yehoram*) are used interchangeably. To avoid the impression that they are different names and designate different people, both forms are rendered "Joram" in this translation. Confusion arises, however, because the king of Israel whose reign is recounted beginning in 3:1 and the contemporary king of Judah whose reign is recounted beginning in 8:16 share this name. On the relationship of Joram of Israel to Joram of Judah, see note on 3:1.

**2:1–25** The story of Elisha's succession to Elijah's prophetic office is oddly set between the death of Ahaziah (1:17) and the

---

**1:1** 2 Kgs 3:4–27.                                    Lk 9:51–55.
**1:10** Lv 10:1–2; Sir 48:3;      **1:16** Sir 48:6.

whirlwind, he and Elisha were on their way from Gilgal.†

[2] Elijah said to Elisha, "Stay here, please. The LORD has sent me on to Bethel." Elisha replied, "As the LORD lives, and as you yourself live, I will not leave you." So they went down to Bethel. [3] The guild prophets who were in Bethel went out to Elisha and asked him, "Do you know that today the LORD will take your master from you?" He replied, "Yes, I know that. Be still."

[4] Elijah said to him, "Elisha, stay here, please. The LORD has sent me on to Jericho." Elisha replied, "As the LORD lives, and as you yourself live, I will not leave you." So they came to Jericho. [5] The guild prophets who were in Jericho approached Elisha and asked him, "Do you know that today the LORD will take your master from you?" He replied, "Yes, I know that. Be still."

[6] Elijah said to him, "Stay here, please. The LORD has sent me on to the Jordan." Elisha replied, "As the LORD lives, and as you yourself live, I will not leave you." So the two went on together. [7] Fifty of the guild prophets followed and stood facing them at a distance, while the two of them stood next to the Jordan.

**Elisha Succeeds Elijah.** [8] Elijah took his mantle, rolled it up and struck the water: it divided, and the two of them crossed over on dry ground.*

[9]* When they had crossed over, Elijah said to Elisha, "Request whatever I might do for you, before I am taken from you." Elisha answered, "May I receive a double portion of your spirit."† [10] He replied, "You have asked something that is not easy. Still, if you see me taken up from you, your wish will be granted;

otherwise not." [11] As they walked on still conversing, a fiery chariot and fiery horses came between the two of them, and Elijah went up to heaven in a whirlwind,* [12] and Elisha saw it happen. He cried out, "My father! my father!† Israel's chariot and steeds!" Then he saw him no longer.

He gripped his own garment, tore it into two pieces, [13] and picked up the mantle which had fallen from Elijah. Then he went back and stood at the bank of the Jordan. [14] Wielding the mantle which had fallen from Elijah, he struck the water and said, "The LORD, the God of Elijah—where is he now?"† He struck the water: it divided, and he crossed over.

**Elisha's Journey.** [15] The guild prophets in Jericho, who were on the other side, saw him and said, "The spirit of Elijah rests on Elisha." They went to meet him, bowing to the ground before him.* [16] They said, "Among your servants are fifty brave men. Let them go in search of your master. Perhaps the spirit of the LORD has lifted him up and left him on some mountain or in some valley." He answered, "Do not send them."* [17] But they kept urging him, until he was embarrassed and said, "Send them." So they sent the fifty men, who searched for three days without finding him.* [18] When they returned to Elisha in Jericho, where he was staying, he said to them, "Did I not tell you not to go?"

[19]* The inhabitants of the city complained to Elisha, "The site of the city is fine indeed, as my lord can see, but the water is bad and the land sterile." [20] Elisha said, "Bring me a new bowl and put salt into it." When they had brought it to him, [21] he went out to the spring and threw salt into it, saying, "Thus says the

---

† accession of his successor (3:1). The effect is to place this scene, which is the central scene in the whole of 1–2 Kings, outside of time. It thereby becomes almost mythic in its import and reminds us that, behind the transitory flow of kings and kingdoms, stand the eternal word of God and the prophets who give it voice. Just as 1–2 Kings pivots on this chapter, so this scene too is concentrically constructed. Together Elijah and Elisha journey to Bethel, thence to Jericho, and thence across the Jordan. There Elijah is taken up in the whirlwind and Elijah's mantle of power comes to Elisha. Now alone, Elisha crosses the Jordan again, returns to Jericho and thence back to Bethel.

**2:1** *Gilgal*: there are several places in the Hebrew Bible named Gilgal; the word probably means "circle," viz. of stones. Here the route of the prophets' journey rules out the most famous Gilgal (Jos 4–5), the one near Jericho. This Gilgal may have been located in the area of modern Jiljulieh, approximately seven miles north of Bethel, which seems to preserve the ancient name.

**2:9** *Double portion of your spirit*: as the firstborn son inher-

ited a double portion of his father's property (Dt 21:17), so Elisha asks to inherit from Elijah his spirit of prophecy in the degree befitting his principal disciple. In Nm 11:17–25, God bestows some of the spirit of Moses on others.

**2:12** *My father*: a religious title accorded prophetic leaders; cf. 6:21; 8:9; and 13:14, where King Joash of Israel reacts to Elisha's own impending death with the same words Elisha uses here.

**2:14** *The LORD, the God of Elijah—where is he now?*: the words in Hebrew have an incantatory quality, as if Elisha is invoking both the divine name and the name of his departed master in an attempt to duplicate Elijah's miracle.

*
**2:8** Ex 14:15–22; Jos 3:14–17.
**2:9–15** Nm 11:16–17, 24–29.
**2:11** Gn 5:24; 1 Mc 2:58; Sir 48:9–12; Acts 1:9.
**2:15** 1 Kgs 19:19; Sir 48:12.
**2:16** 1 Kgs 18:12.
**2:17** 1 Kgs 17:2; 18:10.
**2:19–22** 2 Kgs 4:38–41.

LORD: I have purified this water. Never again shall death or sterility come from it." <sup>22</sup> And the water has stayed pure even to this day, according to the word Elisha had spoken.

<sup>23</sup>† From there Elisha went up to Bethel. While he was on the way, some little boys came out of the city and jeered at him: "Go away, baldy; go away, baldy!" <sup>24</sup> The prophet turned and saw them, and he cursed them in the name of the LORD. Then two she-bears came out of the woods and tore forty-two of the children to pieces.

<sup>25</sup> From there he went to Mount Carmel, and returned to Samaria from there.

## VII. STORIES OF ELISHA AND JORAM†

3 **Reign of Joram of Israel.** <sup>1</sup> Joram, son of Ahab, became king over Israel in Samaria in the eighteenth year of Jehoshaphat, king of Judah, and he reigned twelve years.†

<sup>2</sup>* He did what was evil in the LORD's sight, though not like his father and mother. He did away with the pillar of Baal that his father had made, <sup>3</sup> but he still held fast unceasingly to the sins which Jeroboam, son of Nebat, caused Israel to commit.

**War Against Moab: Drought.** <sup>4</sup>† Now Mesha, king of Moab, who raised sheep, used to pay the king of Israel as tribute a hundred thousand lambs and the wool of a hundred thousand rams. <sup>5</sup> But when Ahab died, the king of Moab rebelled against the king of Israel. <sup>6</sup> King Joram set out from Samaria and mustered all Israel. <sup>7</sup>* Then he sent Jehoshaphat, the king of Judah, the message: "The king of Moab has rebelled against me. Will you come with me to Moab to fight?" He replied, "I will. You and I are as one, your people and my people, and your horses and my horses as well." <sup>8</sup> He said, "By what route shall we attack?" and the other said, "By way of the wilderness of Edom."

<sup>9</sup> So the king of Israel set out, accompanied by the king of Judah and the king of Edom. After a roundabout journey of seven days the water gave out for the army and for the animals with them. <sup>10</sup> The king of Israel exclaimed, "Alas! The LORD has called three kings together only to deliver us into the power of Moab." <sup>11</sup> But Jehoshaphat asked, "Is there no prophet of the LORD here through whom we may inquire of the LORD?" One of the servants of the king of Israel replied, "Elisha, son of Shaphat, who poured water on the hands of Elijah,† is here." <sup>12</sup> Jehoshaphat agreed, "He has the word of the LORD." So the king of Israel, along with Jehoshaphat and the king of Edom, went down to Elisha. <sup>13</sup> Elisha asked the king of Israel, "What do you want with me? Go to the prophets of your father and to the prophets of your mother." The king of Israel replied, "No, the LORD has called these three kings together only to deliver us into the power of Moab." <sup>14</sup> Then Elisha said, "As the LORD of hosts lives, whom I serve, were it not that I respect Jehoshaphat, the king of Judah, I should neither look at you nor notice you at all. <sup>15</sup> Now get me a

---

<sup>†</sup> **2:23–24** This story probably was told to warn children of the importance of respect for prophets.

**3:1–9:13** After the formulaic introduction to the reign of Joram of Israel, this section falls into two parts. The first contains several stories about the prophet Elisha, both in private and in public life. There are four longer stories, arranged in an ABBA pattern: drought during war with Moab (vv. 4–27), restoration of the Shunammite's son (4:8–37), healing of Naaman (5:1–27), famine during war with Aram (6:24–7:20). The last three of these stories are each preceded and followed by short anecdotal tales about Elisha. The second part of this section turns to the political realm. Elisha carries out the Lord's commissions to Elijah (1 Kgs 19:15–17) to anoint Hazael king of Aram (2 Kgs 8:7–15) and Jehu king of Israel (9:1–13). To prepare for the story of Jehu's insurrection (9:14–11:20), the narrator places between those two narratives notices about the royal succession in Judah (8:16–24, 25–29). The formulaic conclusions to the reigns of Joram of Israel and Ahaziah of Judah (8:25–29) are missing, since the deaths of both will be recounted in the story of Jehu's insurrection.

**3:1** The contradiction between 1:17 and v. 1 regarding the year when Joram succeeded Ahaziah of Israel makes any reconstruction of the chronology of Israel's and Judah's kings uncertain. Some scholars think that one or the other notice is simply incorrect. Others propose to explain the discrepancy by a co-regency: Jehoshaphat of Judah would have shared the throne with his son Joram from Jehoshaphat's seventeenth year until he died in the twenty-fifth year of his reign (1 Kgs 22:42; see also 2 Kgs 8:16). The issue is further complicated by the speculation of some historians that "Joram of Israel" ("son" of Ahab of Israel: v. 1) and "Joram of Judah" ("son-in-law" of Ahab of Israel: 8:18) were in fact the same person, in whom the royal houses and separate realms of Israel and Judah were briefly reunited.

**3:4** In the period of oral tradition, it seems that stories of kings were often told without identifying the kings by name. (Vestiges of this anonymity are still visible in 1 Kgs 3:16–28; 20:4–43; 22:1–38; 2 Kgs 6:8–7:20.) Names (such as "Ahab" in 1 Kgs 20:13–14; 22:20) were added later. As a consequence, the historical attachment of such stories to the kings about whom they are told is open to question. (See note on 1 Kgs 20:1–22:54.) The present story about a campaign against Moab by Joram and Jehoshaphat has several striking similarities to the campaign against Ramoth-gilead by Ahab and Jehoshaphat in 1 Kgs 22:1–38. There exists a Moabite inscription that contains Mesha's self-aggrandizing account of his successful rebellion against Israel, but the times and places it mentions are different from those implied in vv. 4–27.

**3:11** *Poured water on the hands of Elijah*: possibly a metaphor for "was Elijah's servant." But the phrase occurs nowhere else in the Old Testament and its meaning is not certain.

---

**3:2** 1 Kgs 16:32.          **3:7–11** 1 Kgs 22:3–8.

minstrel." When the minstrel played, the hand of the LORD came upon Elisha, ¹⁶and he announced: "Thus says the LORD: Provide many catch basins in this wadi. ¹⁷For the LORD says: Though you will see neither wind nor rain, yet this wadi will be filled with water for you to drink, and for your livestock and pack animals. ¹⁸And since the LORD does not consider this enough, he will also deliver Moab into your power. ¹⁹You shall destroy every fortified city and every choice city, fell every fruit tree, stop up all the springs, and ruin every fertile field with stones."*

²⁰In the morning, at the time of the sacrifice, water came from the direction of Edom and filled the land.

²¹Meanwhile, all Moab had heard that the kings had come to war against them; troops from the youngest on up were mobilized and stationed at the border. ²²When they rose early that morning, the sun was shining across the water. The Moabites saw the water as red as blood, ²³and said, "This is blood! The kings have fought among themselves and killed one another. Quick! To the spoils, Moab!" ²⁴But when they reached the camp of Israel, the Israelites rose up and attacked the Moabites, who fled from them. They ranged through the countryside destroying Moab— ²⁵leveling the cities, each one casting the stones onto every fertile field and filling it, stopping up every spring, felling every fruit tree, until only the stones of Kir-hareseth† remained. Then the slingers surrounded and attacked it. ²⁶When he saw that the battle was going against him, the king of Moab took seven hundred swordsmen to break through to the king of Edom, but he failed. ²⁷So he took his firstborn, who was to succeed him as king, and offered him as a burnt offering upon the wall. The wrath against Israel† was so great that they gave up the siege and returned to their own land.*

**4** **The Widow's Oil.** ¹* A certain woman, the widow of one of the guild prophets, cried out to Elisha: "My husband, your servant, is dead. You know that he revered the LORD, yet now his creditor has come to take my two

© Dennis Kurtz

"For the LORD says: Though you will see neither wind nor rain, yet this wadi will be filled with water for you to drink, and for your livestock and pack animals" (2 Kgs 3:17). A wadi is a gorge or streambed, dry most of the year. Above, the Wadi Kelt, a deep gorge in the Judean wilderness.

children into servitude."† ²Elisha answered her, "What am I to do for you? Tell me what you have in the house." She replied, "This servant of yours has nothing in the house but a jug of oil." ³He said, "Go out, borrow vessels from all your neighbors—as many empty vessels as you can. ⁴Then come back and close the door on yourself and your children; pour the oil into all the vessels, and as each is filled, set it aside." ⁵So she went out. She closed the door on herself and her children and, as they handed her the vessels, she would pour in oil. ⁶When all the vessels were filled, she said to her son, "Bring me another vessel." He answered, "There is none left." And then the oil stopped. ⁷She went and told the man of God, who said, "Go sell the oil to pay off your creditor; with what remains, you and your children can live."

---

**3:25** *Kir-hareseth:* a major city of Moab, identified with modern Kerak, east of the Dead Sea; cf. Is 16:7, 11; Jer 48:31, 36.

**3:27** *The wrath against Israel:* probably the wrath of Chemosh, the Moabite god to whom the child was offered. The Israelites, intimidated by this wrath, retreat.

**4:1** *His creditor...into servitude:* Israelite law permitted the selling of wife and children into slavery for debt; cf. Ex 21:7; Am 2:6; 8:6; Is 50:1.

**3:19** Dt 20:19.     **4:1–7** 1 Kgs 17:8–16.
**3:27** Jgs 11:30–31.

**Elisha Raises the Shunammite's Son.** [8] One day Elisha came to Shunem, where there was a woman of influence, who pressed him to dine with her. Afterward, whenever he passed by, he would stop there to dine. [9] So she said to her husband, "I know that he is a holy man of God. Since he visits us often, [10] let us arrange a little room on the roof and furnish it for him with a bed, table, chair, and lamp, so that when he comes to us he can stay there."*

[11] One day Elisha arrived and stayed in the room overnight. [12] Then he said to his servant Gehazi, "Call this Shunammite woman." He did so, and when she stood before Elisha, [13] he told Gehazi, "Say to her, 'You have troubled yourself greatly for us; what can we do for you? Can we say a good word for you to the king or to the commander of the army?'" She replied, "I am living among my own people."† [14] Later Elisha asked, "What can we do for her?" Gehazi answered, "She has no son, and her husband is old." [15] Elisha said, "Call her." He did so, and when she stood at the door, [16] Elisha promised, "This time next year you will be cradling a baby son." She said, "My lord, you are a man of God; do not deceive your servant."*

[17] Yet the woman conceived, and by the same time the following year she had given birth to a son, as Elisha had promised; [18] and the child grew up healthy.*

One day the boy went out to his father among the reapers. [19] He said to his father, "My head! My head!" And his father said to the servant, "Carry him to his mother." [20] The servant picked him up and carried him to his mother; he sat in her lap until noon, and then died. [21] She went upstairs and laid him on the bed of the man of God. Closing the door on him, she went out [22] and called to her husband, "Let me have one of the servants and a donkey. I must go quickly to the man of God, and I will be back." [23] He asked, "Why are you going to him today? It is neither the new moon nor the sabbath." But she said, "It is all right." [24] When the donkey was saddled, she said to her servant, "Lead on! Do not stop my donkey unless I tell you." [25] She kept going till she reached the man of God on Mount Carmel. When he saw her at a distance, the man of God said to his servant Gehazi: "There is the Shunammite! [26] Hurry to meet her, and ask if everything is all right with her, with her husband, and with the boy." "Everything is all right," she replied. [27] But when she reached the man of God on the mountain, she clasped his feet. Gehazi came near to push her away, but the man of God said: "Let her alone, she is in bitter anguish; the Lord hid it from me and did not let me know." [28] She said, "Did I ask my lord for a son? Did I not say, 'Do not mislead me'?" [29] He said to Gehazi, "Get ready for a journey. Take my staff with you and be off; if you meet anyone, give no greeting,† and if anyone greets you, do not answer. Lay my staff upon the boy." [30] But the boy's mother cried out: "As the Lord lives and as you yourself live, I will not release you." So he started back with her.

[31] Meanwhile, Gehazi had gone on ahead and had laid the staff upon the boy, but there was no sound, no response. He returned to meet Elisha and told him, "The boy has not awakened." [32] When Elisha reached the house, he found the boy dead, lying on the bed. [33] He went in, closed the door on them both, and prayed to the Lord. [34] Then he lay upon the child on the bed, placing his mouth upon the child's mouth, his eyes upon the eyes, and his hands upon the hands. As Elisha stretched himself over the child, the boy's flesh became warm.* [35] He arose, paced up and down the room, and then once more stretched himself over him, and the boy sneezed seven times and opened his eyes.* [36] Elisha summoned Gehazi and said, "Call the Shunammite." He called her, and she came to him, and Elisha said to her, "Take your son." [37] She came in and fell at his feet in homage; then she took her son and left.

**The Poisoned Stew.** [38]* When Elisha returned to Gilgal, there was a famine in the land. Once, when the guild prophets were seated before him, he said to his servant, "Put the large pot on, and make some vegetable stew for the

---

† **4:13** *I am living among my own people*: the Shunammite woman declines Elisha's offer. Surrounded by the support of her family and her clan, she is secure. Ironically, at some point in the future Elisha's advice will send her to live among foreigners (see 8:1–2).

**4:29** *Give no greeting*: a profuse exchange of greetings and compliments would normally surround the chance encounter of

acquaintances on the road. This would, however, take time, and Gehazi's mission was urgent. Compare Lk 10:4.

*
| | |
|---|---|
| **4:10** 1 Kgs 17:9. | Acts 20:10–12. |
| **4:16** Gn 18:9–15. | **4:34–37** Sir 48:13. |
| **4:18–37** 1 Kgs 17:17–24; Lk | **4:35** Heb 11:35. |
| 7:11–16; | **4:38–41** 2 Kgs 2:19–22. |

guild prophets." ³⁹ Someone went out into the field to gather herbs and found a wild vine, from which he picked a sackful of poisonous wild gourds. On his return he cut them up into the pot of vegetable stew without anybody's knowing it. ⁴⁰ The stew was served, but when they began to eat it, they cried, "Man of God, there is death in the pot!" And they could not eat it. ⁴¹ He said, "Bring some meal." He threw it into the pot and said, "Serve it to the people to eat." And there was no longer anything harmful in the pot.

**The Barley Loaves.** ⁴² * A man came from Baal-shalishah bringing the man of God twenty barley loaves made from the first fruits, and fresh grain in the ear. Elisha said, "Give it to the people to eat." ⁴³ But his servant objected, "How can I set this before a hundred?" Elisha again said, "Give it to the people to eat, for thus says the LORD: You will eat and have some left over." ⁴⁴ He set it before them, and when they had eaten, they had some left over, according to the word of the LORD.

**5** **Elisha Cures Naaman's Leprosy.** ¹ Naaman, the army commander of the king of Aram, was highly esteemed and respected by his master, for through him the LORD had brought victory to Aram. But valiant as he was, the man was a leper.† ² Now the Arameans had captured from the land of Israel in a raid a little girl, who became the servant of Naaman's wife. ³ She said to her mistress, "If only my master would present himself to the prophet in Samaria! He would cure him of his leprosy."

⁴ Naaman went and told his master, "This is what the girl from the land of Israel said." ⁵ The king of Aram said, "Go. I will send along a letter to the king of Israel." So Naaman set out, taking along ten silver talents, six thousand gold pieces, and ten festal garments. ⁶ He brought the king of Israel the letter, which read: "With this letter I am sending my servant Naaman to you, that you may cure

him of his leprosy." ⁷ When he read the letter, the king of Israel tore his garments and exclaimed: "Am I a god with power over life and death, that this man should send someone for me to cure him of leprosy? Take note! You can see he is only looking for a quarrel with me!"* ⁸ When Elisha, the man of God, heard that the king of Israel had torn his garments, he sent word to the king: "Why have you torn your garments? Let him come to me and find out that there is a prophet in Israel."

⁹ Naaman came with his horses and chariot and stopped at the door of Elisha's house. ¹⁰ Elisha sent him the message: "Go and wash seven times in the Jordan, and your flesh will heal, and you will be clean."* ¹¹ But Naaman went away angry, saying, "I thought that he would surely come out to me and stand there to call on the name of the LORD his God, and would move his hand over the place, and thus cure the leprous spot. ¹² Are not the rivers of Damascus, the Abana and the Pharpar, better than all the waters of Israel? Could I not wash in them and be cleansed?"† With this, he turned about in anger and left.

¹³ But his servants came up and reasoned with him: "My father, if the prophet told you to do something extraordinary, would you not do it? All the more since he told you, 'Wash, and be clean'?" ¹⁴ So Naaman went down and plunged into the Jordan seven times, according to the word of the man of God. His flesh became again like the flesh of a little child, and he was clean.*

¹⁵ He returned with his whole retinue to the man of God. On his arrival he stood before him and said, "Now I know that there is no God in all the earth, except in Israel. Please accept a gift from your servant."* ¹⁶ Elisha replied, "As the LORD lives whom I serve, I will not take it." And despite Naaman's urging, he still refused. ¹⁷ Naaman said: "If you will not accept, please let me, your servant, have two mule-loads of earth,† for your servant will no longer make burnt offerings or sacrifices to any other god except the LORD. ¹⁸ But may the

---

**5:1** *Leper*: the terms traditionally translated "leper" and "leprosy" covered a wide variety of skin disorders like psoriasis, eczema, and seborrhea, but probably not Hansen's disease (modern "leprosy"); there is no clear evidence of its existence in biblical times.

**5:12** *Wash in them and be cleansed*: typical of the ambiguity in ritual healing or cleanliness. The muddy waters of the Jordan are no match hygienically for the mountain spring waters of Damascus; ritually, it is the other way around.

**5:17** *Two mule-loads of earth*: worship of the Lord is associated with the soil of the Holy Land, where he is present.

**4:42–44** Mt 14:13–21; 15:32– 38; Mk 6:34–44; 8:1–9; Lk 9:10–17; Jn 6:1–13.

**5:7** 1 Sm 2:6; Jn 5:21.
**5:10** Jn 9:7.
**5:14** Lk 4:27.
**5:15** Lk 17:17–19.

LORD forgive your servant this: when my master enters the temple of Rimmon to bow down there, as he leans upon my arm, I too must bow down in the temple of Rimmon. When I bow down in the temple of Rimmon, may the LORD please forgive your servant this." [19] Elisha said to him, "Go in peace."†

Naaman had gone some distance [20] when Gehazi, the servant of Elisha, the man of God, thought to himself: "My master was too easy on this Aramean Naaman, not accepting what he brought. As the LORD lives, I will run after him and get something out of him." [21] So Gehazi hurried after Naaman. Seeing that someone was running after him, Naaman alighted from his chariot to wait for him. He asked, "Is everything all right?" [22] Gehazi replied, "Yes, but my master sent me to say, 'Two young men have just come to me, guild prophets from the hill country of Ephraim. Please give them a talent of silver and two festal garments.'" [23] Naaman said, "I insist! Take two talents," and he pressed him. He tied up two silver talents in bags and gave them, with two festal garments, to two of his servants, who carried them before Gehazi. [24] When he reached the hill, Gehazi received these things, appropriated them for his house, and sent the men on their way.

[25] He went in and stood by Elisha his master, who asked him, "Where have you been, Gehazi?" He answered, "Your servant has not gone anywhere." [26] But Elisha said to him: "Was I not present in spirit when someone got down from his chariot to wait for you? Is this a time to take money or to take garments, olive orchards or vineyards, sheep or cattle, male or female servants? [27] The leprosy of Naaman shall cling to you and your descendants forever." And Gehazi went out, a leper with skin like snow.†

**6** **The Lost Ax.** [1] The guild prophets once said to Elisha: "This place where we live with you is too cramped for us. [2] Let us go to the Jordan, where by getting one beam apiece we can build ourselves a place to live." Elisha said, "Go." [3] One of them requested, "Please

agree to accompany your servants." He replied, "Yes, I will come."

[4] So he went with them, and when they arrived at the Jordan they began to cut down trees. [5] While one of them was felling a tree trunk, the iron ax blade slipped into the water. He cried out, "Oh, no, master! It was borrowed!" [6] "Where did it fall?" asked the man of God. When he pointed out the spot, Elisha cut off a stick, threw it into the water, and brought the iron to the surface. [7] He said, "Pick it up." And the man stretched out his hand and grasped it.

**The Aramean Ambush.** [8] When the king of Aram was waging war on Israel, he would make plans with his servants: "I will bivouac at such and such a place." [9] But the man of God would send word to the king of Israel, "Be careful! Do not pass by this place, for Aram will attack there." [10] So the king of Israel would send word to the place which the man of God had indicated, and alert it; then they would be on guard. This happened several times.

[11] Greatly disturbed over this, the king of Aram called together his officers and asked them, "Will you not tell me who among us is for the king of Israel?" [12] "No one, my lord king," answered one of the officers. "The Israelite prophet Elisha can tell the king of Israel the very words you speak in your bedroom." [13] He said, "Go, find out where he is, so that I may take him captive."

Informed that Elisha was in Dothan, [14] he sent there a strong force with horses and chariots. They arrived by night and encircled the city. [15] Early the next morning, when the servant of the man of God arose and went out, he saw the force with its horses and chariots surrounding the city. "Alas!" he said to Elisha. "What shall we do, my lord?" [16] Elisha answered, "Do not be afraid. Our side outnumbers theirs." [17] Then he prayed, "O LORD, open his eyes, that he may see." And the LORD opened the eyes of the servant, and he saw that the mountainside was filled with fiery chariots and horses around Elisha.*

[18] When the Arameans came down to get

---

**5:19** *Go in peace:* Elisha understands and approves the situation of Naaman who, though now a worshiper of the God of Israel, is required by his courtly office to assist his master, the king ("leans upon my arm," v. 18), worshiping in the temple of the Canaanite god Baal-Rimmon.
**5:27** *With skin like snow:* "snow" is often used to describe the

skin conditions covered by the term "leprosy" (Ex 4:6; Nm 12:10; see note on 5:1). It is unclear whether the comparison is with the white color, dry flakes, or moist shine, any of which can occur in the relevant skin diseases.

**6:17** 2 Kgs 2:11; 7:6; Ps 68:18.

him, Elisha prayed to the Lord, "Strike this people blind, I pray you." And the Lord struck them blind, according to Elisha's word. ¹⁹ Then Elisha said to them: "This is the wrong road, and this is the wrong city. Follow me! I will take you to the man you want." And he led them to Samaria. ²⁰ When they entered Samaria, Elisha prayed, "O Lord, open their eyes that they may see." The Lord opened their eyes, and they saw that they were inside Samaria. ²¹ When the king of Israel saw them, he asked, "Shall I kill them, my father? Shall I kill them?" ²² Elisha replied, "You must not kill them. Do you slay those whom you have taken captive with your sword or bow?† Serve them a meal. Let them eat and drink, and then go back to their master." ²³ The king spread a great feast for them. When they had eaten and drunk he sent them away, and they went back to their master. No more Aramean raiders came into the land of Israel.

**War Against Aram: Famine.** ²⁴ After this, Benhadad, king of Aram, mustered his whole army and laid siege to Samaria. ²⁵ Because of the siege the famine in Samaria was so severe that a donkey's head sold for eighty pieces of silver, and a fourth of a kab of "dove droppings"† for five pieces of silver.

²⁶* One day, as the king of Israel was walking on the city wall, a woman cried out to him, "Save us, my lord king!" ²⁷ He replied, "If the Lord does not save you, where could I find means to save you? On the threshing floor? In the wine press?" ²⁸ Then the king asked her, "What is your trouble?" She replied: "This woman said to me, 'Give up your son that we may eat him today; then tomorrow we will eat my son.' ²⁹ So we boiled my son and ate him. The next day I said to her, 'Now give up your son that we may eat him.' But she hid her son." ³⁰ When the king heard the woman's words, he tore his garments. And as he was walking on the wall, the people saw that he was wearing sackcloth underneath, next to his skin.

³¹ The king exclaimed, "May God do thus to me, and more, if the head of Elisha, son of Shaphat, stays on him today!" ³² Meanwhile, Elisha was sitting in his house in conference with the elders. The king had sent one of his courtiers; but before the messenger reached him, Elisha said to the elders: "Do you know that this murderer is sending someone to cut off my head? When the messenger comes, see that you close the door and hold it fast against him. His master's footsteps are echoing behind him." ³³ While Elisha was still speaking, the messenger came down to him and said, "This evil is from the Lord. Why should I trust in the Lord any longer?"†

**7** ¹ Elisha replied: "Hear the word of the Lord! Thus says the Lord: At this time tomorrow a seah of fine flour will sell for a shekel, and two seahs of barley for a shekel, in the market† of Samaria." ² But the adjutant, upon whose arm the king leaned, answered the man of God, "Even if the Lord were to make windows in heaven, how could this happen?" Elisha said, "You shall see it with your own eyes, but you shall not eat of it."

³ At the city gate four lepers were asking one another, "Why should we sit here until we die?* ⁴ If we decide to go into the city, we shall die there, for there is famine in the city. If we remain here, we shall die too. So come, let us desert to the camp of the Arameans. If they let us live, we live; if they kill us, we die." ⁵ At twilight they left for the Arameans; but when they reached the edge of the camp, no one was there. ⁶* The Lord had caused the army of the Arameans to hear the sound of chariots and horses, the sound of a large army, and they had reasoned among themselves, "The king of Israel has hired the kings of the Hittites and the kings of Egypt to fight us." ⁷ Then in the twilight they had fled, abandoning their tents, their horses, and their donkeys, the whole camp just as it was, and fleeing for their lives. ⁸ After the lepers reached the edge of the

---

**6:22** *With your sword or bow*: since the king would not slay prisoners who had surrendered to his power, much less should he slay prisoners captured by God's power. This wartime practice stands in contrast to that of holy war, where prisoners were placed under the ban and so devoted to destruction (see 1 Kgs 20:35–43).

**6:25** *"Dove droppings"*: it is unclear whether this phrase is to be read literally (e.g., dung used as fuel) or as the nickname of a type of edible plant, as attested in Arabic. A kab was probably around a quart.

**6:33** The messenger speaks in the king's name. Similarly, Elisha's response in the next verse can be spoken of as delivered to the king (7:18).

**7:1** *Market*: lit., "gate," the principal place of trading in ancient walled cities in time of peace.

**6:26–29** Dt 28:53–57.
**7:3** Lv 13:46.
**7:6–7** 2 Kgs 6:17; 2 Sm 5:24.

camp, they went first into one tent, ate and drank, and took silver, gold, and clothing from it, and went out and hid them. Back they came into another tent, took things from it, and again went out and hid them. ⁹Then they said to one another: "We are not doing right. This is a day of good news, and we are keeping silent. If we wait until morning breaks, we will be blamed. So come, let us go and inform the palace." ¹⁰They came and summoned the city gatekeepers. They said, "We went to the camp of the Arameans, but no one was there—not a human voice, only the horses and donkeys tethered, and the tents just as they were left." ¹¹The gatekeepers announced this and it was reported within the palace.

¹²Though it was night, the king got up; he said to his servants, "Let me tell you what the Arameans have done to us. Knowing that we are starving, they have left their camp to hide in the field. They are thinking, 'The Israelites will leave the city and we will take them alive and enter it.'" ¹³† One of his servants, however, suggested: "Let some of us take five of the horses remaining in the city—they are just like the whole throng of Israel that has reached its limit—and let us send scouts to investigate." ¹⁴They took two chariots, and horses, and the king sent them to reconnoiter the Aramean army with the order, "Go and find out." ¹⁵They followed the Arameans as far as the Jordan, and the whole route was strewn with garments and other objects that the Arameans had thrown away in their haste. The messengers returned and told the king. ¹⁶The people went out and plundered the camp of the Arameans.

Then a seah of fine flour sold for a shekel and two seahs of barley for a shekel, according to the word of the LORD. ¹⁷The king had put in charge of the gate the officer upon whose arm he leaned; but the people trampled him to death at the gate, just as the man of God had predicted when the messenger came down to him. ¹⁸This was in accordance with the word the man of God spoke to the king: "Two seahs of barley will sell for a shekel, and a seah of fine flour for a shekel at this time tomorrow

in the market of Samaria." ¹⁹The adjutant had answered the man of God, "Even if the LORD were to make windows in heaven, how could this happen?" And Elisha had replied, "You shall see it with your own eyes, but you shall not eat of it." ²⁰And that is what happened to him, for the people trampled him to death at the gate.

**8** **The Shunammite's Return.** ¹Elisha once said to the woman whose son he had restored to life: "Get ready! Leave with your household and live wherever you can, because the LORD has decreed a seven-year famine which is coming upon the land."* ²The woman got ready and did as the man of God said, setting out with her household, and living in the land of the Philistines for seven years.

³At the end of the seven years, the woman returned from the land of the Philistines and went out to the king to appeal for her house and her field. ⁴The king was talking with Gehazi, the servant of the man of God: "Tell me all the great things that Elisha has done." ⁵Just as he was telling the king how his master had restored a dead person to life, the very woman whose son Elisha had restored to life came to the king appealing for her house and field. Gehazi said, "My lord king, this is the woman, and this is that son of hers whom Elisha restored to life." ⁶The king questioned the woman, and she told him her story. With that the king placed an official† at her disposal, saying, "Restore all her property to her, with all that the field produced from the day she left the land until now."

**Elisha and Hazael of Aram.†** ⁷*Elisha came to Damascus at a time when Ben-hadad, king of Aram, lay sick. When he was told, "The man of God has come here," ⁸the king said to Hazael, "Take a gift with you and go call on the man of God. Consult the LORD through him, 'Will I recover from this sickness?'"* ⁹Hazael went to visit him, carrying a present, and with forty camel loads of the best goods of Damascus. On his arrival, he stood before

---

† **7:13** The Hebrew of this verse is difficult and its meaning is uncertain.

**8:6** An official: lit., "eunuch," and perhaps actually so in this instance.

**8:7–15** Elisha carries out the commission the Lord gave Elijah in 1 Kgs 19:15. See note on 2 Kgs 3:1–9:13.

* **8:1** 2 Kgs 4:18–37.    **8:8** 1 Kgs 14:1–3.
**8:7–15** 1 Kgs 19:15.

Elisha and said, "Your son Ben-hadad, king of Aram, has sent me to you to ask, 'Will I recover from my sickness?'" ¹⁰Elisha answered, "Go and tell him, 'You will surely recover.' But the LORD has showed me that he will surely die." ¹¹Then he stared him down until he became ill at ease. The man of God wept, ¹²and Hazael asked, "Why are you weeping, my lord?" Elisha replied, "Because I know the evil that you will inflict upon the Israelites. You will burn their fortresses, you will slay their youth with the sword, you will dash their little children to pieces, you will rip open their pregnant women."* ¹³Hazael exclaimed, "How can your servant, a dog† like me, do anything so important?" Elisha replied, "The LORD has showed you to me as king over Aram."

¹⁴Hazael left Elisha and returned to his master, who asked, "What did Elisha tell you?" Hazael replied, "He said, 'You will surely recover.'" ¹⁵The next day, however, Hazael took a cloth, dipped it in water, and spread it over the king's face, so that he died. And Hazael succeeded him as king.

**Reign of Joram of Judah.** ¹⁶† In the fifth year of Joram, son of Ahab, king of Israel, Joram, son of Jehoshaphat, king of Judah, became king. ¹⁷He was thirty-two years old when he became king, and he reigned eight years in Jerusalem. ¹⁸He walked in the way of the kings of Israel as the house of Ahab had done, since the daughter of Ahab was his wife; and he did what was evil in the LORD's sight. ¹⁹Even so, the LORD was unwilling to destroy Judah, for the sake of his servant David. For he had promised David that he would leave him a holding in the LORD's presence for all time.* ²⁰During Joram's reign, Edom revolted against the rule of Judah and installed a king of its own. ²¹Thereupon Joram with all his chariots crossed over to Zair. He arose by night and broke through the Edomites when they had surrounded him and the commanders of his chariots. Then his army fled homeward. ²²To this day Edom has

been in revolt against the rule of Judah. Libnah also revolted at that time.*

²³The rest of the acts of Joram, with all that he did, are recorded in the book of the chronicles of the kings of Judah. ²⁴Joram rested with his ancestors; he was buried with his ancestors in the City of David, and his son Ahaziah succeeded him as king.

**Reign of Ahaziah of Judah.**† ²⁵In the twelfth year of Joram, son of Ahab, king of Israel, Ahaziah, son of Joram, king of Judah, became king. ²⁶Ahaziah was twenty-two years old when he became king, and he reigned one year in Jerusalem. His mother's name was Athaliah, daughter of Omri, king of Israel.†

²⁷He walked in the way of the house of Ahab and did what was evil in the LORD's sight like the house of Ahab, since he was related to them by marriage. ²⁸He joined Joram, son of Ahab, in battle against Hazael, king of Aram, at Ramoth-gilead, where the Arameans wounded Joram.* ²⁹King Joram returned to Jezreel to be healed of the wounds which the Arameans had inflicted on him at Ramah in his battle against Hazael, king of Aram. Then Ahaziah, son of Joram, king of Judah, went down to Jezreel to visit Joram, son of Ahab, for he was sick.

**9** **Elisha and Jehu of Israel.**† ¹*Elisha the prophet called one of the guild prophets and said to him: "Get ready for a journey. Take this flask of oil with you, and go to Ramoth-gilead. ²When you get there, look for Jehu, son of Jehoshaphat, son of Nimshi. Enter and take him away from his companions and bring him into an inner chamber. ³From the flask you have, pour oil on his head, and say, 'Thus says the LORD: I anoint you king over Israel.' Then open the door and flee without delay."

⁴The aide (the prophet's aide) went to Ramoth-gilead. ⁵When he arrived, the commanders of the army were in session. He said, "I have a message for you, commander."

---

† **8:13** To call oneself a "dog" is to admit one's insignificance (1 Sm 24:15; 2 Sm 9:8); it is not necessarily a term of contempt, as in English. Hazael focuses on the question of his power, making no comment on the atrocities Elisha predicts he will commit.
**8:16** On the apparent contradictions among 1:17, 3:1, and this verse, see note on 3:1.
**8:25–29** The narrative of Ahaziah's reign, like that of Joram of Israel, lacks the standard formulaic conclusion. The deaths of both kings, and indeed the obliteration of the whole house of Omri, will be recounted in the story of Jehu's insurrection.

**8:26** It is unclear whether Athaliah was Omri's daughter (v. 26) or his granddaughter (v. 18). Perhaps "daughter" here is being used loosely for "female descendant."
**9:1–13** Elisha carries out the commission the Lord gave Elijah in 1 Kgs 19:16. See note on 2 Kgs 3:1–9:13.

---

* **8:12** 2 Kgs 13:3–7.  **8:22** Gn 27:40.
  **8:19** 2 Sm 7:12–16; 1 Kgs  **8:28–29** 2 Kgs 9:14–15.
  11:36; 15:4.  **9:1–13** 1 Kgs 19:16.

Jehu asked, "For which one of us?" "For you, commander," he answered. ⁶Jehu got up and went into the house. Then the prophet's aide poured the oil on his head and said, "Thus says the LORD, the God of Israel: I anoint you king over the people of the LORD, over Israel. ⁷†You shall destroy the house of Ahab your master; thus will I avenge the blood of my servants the prophets, and the blood of all the other servants of the LORD shed by Jezebel. ⁸*The whole house of Ahab shall perish:

I will cut off from Ahab's line every male,
    whether bond or free in Israel.

⁹I will make the house of Ahab like that of Jeroboam, son of Nebat, and like that of Baasha, son of Ahijah. ¹⁰In the confines of Jezreel, the dogs shall devour Jezebel so that no one can bury her." Then he opened the door and fled.

¹¹When Jehu rejoined his master's servants, they asked him, "Is all well? Why did that madman come to you?" He replied, "You know that kind of man and his talk." ¹²But they said, "Tell us another lie!" So he told them, "This is what the prophet's aide said to me, 'Thus says the LORD: I anoint you king over Israel.'" ¹³At once each took his garment, spread it under Jehu on the bare steps, blew the horn, and cried out, "Jehu is king!"

## VIII. THE END OF THE OMRID DYNASTY†

**Death of Joram of Israel.** ¹⁴*Jehu, son of Jehoshaphat, son of Nimshi, formed a conspiracy against Joram. (Joram, with all Israel, had been besieging Ramoth-gilead against Hazael, king of Aram, ¹⁵but had returned to Jezreel to be healed of the wounds the Arameans had inflicted on him in the battle against Hazael, king of Aram.)

Jehu said to them, "If this is what you really want, see that no one escapes from the city to report in Jezreel."

¹⁶Then Jehu mounted his chariot and drove to Jezreel, where Joram lay ill and Ahaziah, king of Judah, had come to visit him. ¹⁷The watchman standing on the tower in Jezreel saw the troop of Jehu coming and reported, "I see chariots." Joram said, "Get a driver and send him to meet them and to ask whether all is well." ¹⁸So a horseman went out to meet him and said, "The king asks, 'Is everything all right?'" Jehu said, "What does it matter to you how things are? Get behind me." The watchman reported to the king, "The messenger has reached them, but is not returning." ¹⁹Joram sent a second horseman, who went to them and said, "The king asks, 'Is everything all right?'" "What does it matter to you how things are?" Jehu replied. "Get behind me." ²⁰The watchman reported, "He has reached them, but is not returning. The driving is like that of Jehu, son of Nimshi; he drives like a madman." ²¹*"Hitch up my chariot," said Joram, and they hitched up his chariot. Then Joram, king of Israel, and Ahaziah, king of Judah, set out, each in his own chariot, to meet Jehu. They reached him near the plot of ground of Naboth the Jezreelite.

²²When Joram recognized Jehu, he asked, "Is everything all right, Jehu?" Jehu replied, "How could everything be all right as long as all the harlotry and sorcery† of your mother Jezebel continues?" ²³Joram reined about and fled, crying to Ahaziah, "Treason, Ahaziah!" ²⁴But Jehu had drawn his bow and he shot Joram between the shoulders, so that the arrow went through his heart and he collapsed in his chariot. ²⁵Then Jehu said to his adjutant Bidkar, "Take him and throw him into the plot of ground in the field of Naboth the Jezreelite. For remember when you and I were driving teams behind Ahab his father, the LORD delivered this oracle against him: ²⁶As surely as I saw yesterday the blood of Naboth and the blood of his sons—oracle of the LORD— I will repay you for it in that very plot of

---

**9:7–10** The author has Elisha's emissary expand considerably the speech Elisha told him to deliver by adding the same type of prophetic indictments and sanctions as were invoked on previous occasions against the dynasties of Jeroboam (1 Kgs 14:10–11), of Baasha (1 Kgs 16:3–4), and of Ahab himself (1 Kgs 21:21–24).

**9:14–11:20** Death pervades this section. The dynasty founded by Omri (1 Kgs 16:23) drowns in a bloodbath, taking numberless others along with it. The scenes are in three parallel sets of three: death comes (1) to Joram of Israel, Ahab's son; to Ahaziah of Judah, his son-in-law; and to Jezebel, the Baalist

queen mother of Israel; (2) then to seventy descendants of Ahab; to forty-two relatives of Ahaziah of Judah; and to numerous Baal worshipers; (3) finally to Jehu of Israel; to the blood royal of Judah; and to Athaliah, the Baalist queen mother of Judah and last of the Omrids.

**9:22** *Harlotry and sorcery*: both terms are metaphors referring to Jezebel's worship of the foreign god Baal.

---

**9:8–10** 1 Kgs 14:10–11;          **9:14–15** 2 Kgs 8:28–29.
        16:3–4; 21:21–24.          **9:21–26** 1 Kgs 21:1–24.

ground—oracle of the LORD. So now take him and throw him into this plot of ground, in keeping with the word of the LORD."

**Death of Ahaziah of Judah.** 27* Seeing what was happening, Ahaziah, king of Judah, fled toward Beth-haggan. Jehu pursued him, shouting, "Him too!" They struck him as he rode through the pass of Gur near Ibleam, but he continued his flight as far as Megiddo and died there. 28 His servants brought him in a chariot to Jerusalem and they buried him in his grave with his ancestors in the City of David. 29 In the eleventh year of Joram, son of Ahab, Ahaziah became king over Judah.

**Death of Jezebel.** 30 Jehu came to Jezreel, and when Jezebel heard of it, she shadowed her eyes, adorned her hair, and looked down from her window. 31 As Jehu came through the gate, she cried out, "Is all well, you Zimri, murderer of your master?"* 32 Jehu looked up to the window and shouted, "Who is on my side? Who?" At this, two or three eunuchs looked down toward him. 33 "Throw her down," he ordered. They threw her down, and some of her blood spurted against the wall and against the horses. Jehu trod over her body 34 and, after eating and drinking, he said: "Attend to that accursed woman and bury her; for she was the daughter of a king." 35 But when they went to bury her, they found nothing of her but the skull, the feet, and the hands. 36 They returned to Jehu, and when they told him, he said, "This is the word the LORD spoke through his servant Elijah the Tishbite: In the confines of Jezreel the dogs shall devour the flesh of Jezebel.* 37 The corpse of Jezebel shall be like dung in the field in the confines of Jezreel, so that no one can say: This was Jezebel."

**10** **Death of the Sons of Ahab of Israel.** 1* Ahab had seventy sons in Samaria. Jehu wrote letters and sent them to Samaria, to the elders who were rulers of Jezreel and to Ahab's guardians. Jehu wrote: 2 "Since

your master's sons are with you, as well as his chariots, horses, fortified city, and weaponry, when this letter reaches you 3 decide which is the best and the fittest of your master's sons, place him on his father's throne, and fight for your master's house." 4 They were overcome with fright and said, "If the two kings could not withstand him, how can we?" 5 So the master of the palace and the chief of the city, along with the elders and the guardians, sent this message to Jehu: "We are your servants, and we will do everything you tell us. We will proclaim no one king; do whatever you think best." 6 So Jehu wrote them a second letter: "If you are on my side and will obey me, bring along the heads of your master's sons† and come to me in Jezreel at this time tomorrow." (The seventy princes were in the care of prominent men of the city, who were rearing them.)

7 When the letter arrived, they took the princes and slew all seventy of them, put their heads in baskets, and sent them to Jehu in Jezreel. 8 A messenger came in and told him, "They have brought the heads of the princes." He said, "Pile them in two heaps at the gate of the city until morning." 9 In the morning he came outside, stood there, and said to all the people: "You are guiltless, for it was I who conspired against my lord and slew him. But who killed all these? 10 Know that not a single word which the LORD has spoken against the house of Ahab shall fail. The LORD has accomplished what he decreed through his servant Elijah."* 11 (And so Jehu slew all who were left of the house of Ahab in Jezreel, as well as all his powerful supporters, intimates, and priests, leaving him no survivor.)* 12 Then he went back inside.

**Death of the Relatives of Ahaziah of Judah.** He set out for Samaria and, at Beth-eked-haroim on the way, 13 Jehu came across relatives of Ahaziah, king of Judah. "Who are you?" he asked, and they said, "We are relatives of Ahaziah. We are going down to visit the princes and the family of the queen mother."† 14 "Take

---

**10:6** *Heads of your master's sons*: Jehu's command is cleverly ambiguous. He allows the Samarian leaders to understand "heads" either literally or metaphorically as "most important individuals." Then, when the leaders decapitate Ahab's potential successors, Jehu can claim to be innocent of their blood (v. 9).

**10:13** Since Athaliah, the queen mother in Judah, was of the Israelite royal house (8:18, 26), both the "princes" (lit., the "king's sons") and the queen mother's "family" (lit., her "sons") would belong to the royal houses of both kingdoms. They may thus be numbered

among the seventy "sons of Ahab" killed in vv. 1–7. Because "sons" can refer to more remote offspring, the queen mother's "sons" may include Ahaziah's brothers, sons, nephews, as well as the "relatives" (lit., the "brothers") of Ahaziah who are speaking in this scene.

---

**9:27–28** 2 Chr 22:7–9.
**9:31** 1 Kgs 16:8–13.
**9:36** 1 Kgs 21:23.
**10:1–11** Jgs 9:5; 1 Kgs 15:29;
16:11–12; 21:8.
**10:10** 1 Kgs 21:17–29.
**10:11** Hos 1:4.

them alive," Jehu ordered. They were taken alive, forty-two in number, then slain at the pit of Beth-eked. Not one of them survived.

[15] When he set out from there, Jehu met Jehonadab, son of Rechab, on the road. He greeted him and asked, "Are you with me wholeheartedly, as I am with you?" "Yes," he replied. "If you are, give me your hand." He gave him his hand, and he had him mount his chariot,* [16] and said, "Come with me and see my zeal for the LORD." And they took him along in his chariot.

**Slaughter of the Worshipers of Baal.** [17] When he arrived in Samaria, Jehu slew all who were left of Ahab's line in Samaria, doing away with them completely, according to the word the LORD spoke to Elijah.

[18] Jehu gathered all the people together and said to them: "Ahab served Baal to some extent, but Jehu will serve him yet more.* [19] Now summon for me all Baal's prophets, all his servants, and all his priests. See that no one is absent, for I have a great sacrifice for Baal. Whoever is absent shall not live." This Jehu did as a ruse, so that he might destroy the servants of Baal.*

[20] Jehu said further, "Proclaim a solemn assembly in honor of Baal." They did so, [21] and Jehu sent word of it throughout all Israel. All the servants of Baal came; there was no one who did not come; they came to the temple of Baal, and it was filled from wall to wall. [22] Then Jehu said to the custodian of the wardrobe, "Bring out garments for all the servants of Baal." When he had brought out the garments for them, [23] Jehu, with Jehonadab, son of Rechab, entered the temple of Baal and said to the servants of Baal, "Search and be sure that there is no one who serves the LORD here with you, but only servants of Baal." [24] Then they proceeded to offer sacrifices and burnt offerings. Now Jehu had stationed eighty troops outside with this warning, "Any of you who lets someone escape of those whom I shall deliver into your hands shall pay life for life."

[25] As soon as he finished offering the burnt offering, Jehu said to the guards and aides, "Go in and slay them. Let no one escape." So the guards and aides put them to the sword

and cast them out. Afterward they went into the inner shrine of the temple of Baal, [26] and took out the pillars of the temple of Baal. They burned the shrine, [27] tore down the pillar of Baal, tore down the temple of Baal, and turned it into a latrine, as it remains today. [28] Thus Jehu destroyed Baal in Israel.

**Death of Jehu of Israel.** [29] However, Jehu did not desist from the sins which Jeroboam, son of Nebat, had caused Israel to commit, the golden calves at Bethel and at Dan.*

[30] The LORD said to Jehu: Because you have done well what is right in my eyes, and have done to the house of Ahab all that was in my heart, your sons to the fourth generation shall sit upon the throne of Israel.* [31] But Jehu was not careful to walk in the law of the LORD, the God of Israel, with all his heart, since he did not desist from the sins which Jeroboam had caused Israel to commit. [32]* At that time the LORD began to dismember Israel. Hazael defeated the Israelites throughout their territory [33] east of the Jordan (all the land of Gilead, of the Gadites, Reubenites, and Manassites), from Aroer on the wadi Arnon up through Gilead and Bashan.

[34] The rest of the acts of Jehu, with all that he did and all his valor, are recorded in the book of the chronicles of the kings of Israel. [35] Jehu rested with his ancestors and was buried in Samaria, and his son Jehoahaz succeeded him as king. [36] The length of Jehu's reign over Israel was twenty-eight years in Samaria.

# 11

**Death of the Heirs of Ahaziah of Judah.** [1]* When Athaliah, the mother of Ahaziah, saw that her son was dead, she began to kill off the whole royal family. [2] But Jehosheba,† daughter of King Joram and sister of Ahaziah, took Joash, Ahaziah's son, and spirited him away, along with his nurse, from the bedroom where the princes were about to be slain. He was concealed from Athaliah, and so he did not die. [3] For six years he remained hidden with her in the house of the LORD, while Athaliah ruled as queen over the land.

**Death of Athaliah.** [4] But in the seventh year, Jehoiada summoned the captains of the

---

**11:2** According to 2 Chr 22:11, Jehosheba was the wife of Jehoiada, the high priest. If this is historical, it would explain her access to the Temple's residential precincts.

**10:15** 1 Kgs 20:33; 1 Chr 2:55; Jer 35:1–19.
**10:18** 1 Kgs 16:30–33.
**10:19** 1 Kgs 18:19, 40.
**10:29** 1 Kgs 12:28–30.
**10:30** 2 Kgs 15:12.
**10:32** 2 Kgs 8:12; Am 1:3.
**11:1–2** Jgs 9:5.

Carians† and of the guards. He had them come to him in the house of the LORD, made a covenant with them, exacted an oath from them in the house of the LORD, and then showed them the king's son. ⁵He gave them these orders: "This is what you must do: one third of you who come on duty on the sabbath shall guard the king's house; ⁶another third shall be at the gate Sur; and the last third shall be at the gate behind the guards. You shall guard the palace on all sides, ⁷while the two of your divisions who are going off duty that week shall keep guard over the house of the LORD for the king. ⁸You shall surround the king, each with drawn weapons, and anyone who tries to approach the guard detail is to be killed; stay with the king, wherever he goes."

⁹The captains did just as Jehoiada the priest commanded. Each took his troops, both those going on duty for the week and those going off duty that week, and came to Jehoiada the priest. ¹⁰* He gave the captains King David's spear and quivers, which were in the house of the LORD. ¹¹And the guards, with drawn weapons, lined up from the southern to the northern limit of the enclosure, surrounding the altar and the temple on the king's behalf. ¹²Then Jehoiada brought out the king's son and put the crown and the testimony† upon him. They proclaimed him king and anointed him, clapping their hands and shouting, "Long live the king!"

¹³When Athaliah heard the noise made by the people, she came before them in the house of the LORD. ¹⁴When she saw the king standing by the column,† as was the custom, and the captains and trumpeters near the king, and all the people of the land rejoicing and blowing trumpets, Athaliah tore her garments and cried out, "Treason, treason!" ¹⁵Then Jehoiada the priest instructed the captains in command of the force: "Escort her with a guard detail. If anyone follows her, let him die by the sword." For the priest had said, "She must not die in the house of the LORD." ¹⁶So they seized her, and when she reached the Horse Gate of the king's house, she was put to death.

¹⁷* Then Jehoiada made a covenant between the LORD and the king and the people,† by which they would be the LORD's people; and another between the king and the people. ¹⁸Thereupon all the people of the land went to the temple of Baal and demolished it. They shattered its altars and images completely, and slew Mattan, the priest of Baal, before the altars. Jehoiada the priest appointed a detachment for the house of the LORD, ¹⁹and took the captains, the Carians, the guards, and all the people of the land, and they led the king down from the house of the LORD; they came through the guards' gate to the king's house, and Joash took his seat on the royal throne. ²⁰All the people of the land rejoiced and the city was quiet, now that Athaliah had been slain with the sword at the king's house.

## IX. KINGS OF JUDAH AND ISRAEL†

# 12 Reign of Joash of Judah. ¹Joash was seven years old when he became king. ²In the seventh year of Jehu, Joash became king, and he reigned forty years in Jerusalem. His mother's name was Zibiah, from Beersheba.

³Joash did what was right in the LORD's sight as long as he lived, because Jehoiada the priest guided him, ⁴though the high places did not disappear; the people continued to sacrifice and to burn incense on the high places.

⁵Joash said to the priests: "All the funds for sacred purposes that are brought to the house of the LORD—the census tax, personal redemption money—and all funds that are freely brought to the house of the LORD, ⁶the priests

---

**11:4** *Carians*: foreign mercenaries serving as the royal bodyguard. Compare "Cherethites and Pelethites" in 1 Kgs 1:38.

**11:12** *Testimony*: that is, the two tablets of the law preserved in the ark in the Temple. Presumably they were placed upon the king during his installation ceremony as a reminder of the law he was to uphold.

**11:14** *By the column*: the king's special place in the Temple court; cf. 23:3; 2 Chr 23:13. *People of the land*: in this period, the phrase referred to the important citizenry, whose influence sometimes extended to the selection of royal successors (cf. 2 Kgs 11:14–20; 15:5; 16:15; 21:24; 23:6, 30–35; 24:14; 25:3, 19). In postexilic times, by contrast, the phrase was used of the poor.

**11:17** There are two covenants. One is between the Lord as one party and the people, headed by the king, as the other. The second covenant, between king and people, is comparable to that made between David and the elders of Israel at Hebron (2 Sm 5:3).

**12:1–17:5** This section recounts briefly the reigns of the last several kings of Israel and the kings of Judah contemporary with them. As always, the accounts of the kings are given in the order in which each came to the throne, without regard to which kingdom they ruled. See note on the similar section that begins in 1 Kgs 14:21.

---

**11:10** 2 Sm 8:7.                    **11:17** 2 Kgs 23:3.

may take for themselves, each from his own vendor. However, they must make whatever repairs on the temple may prove necessary." [7] Nevertheless, as late as the twenty-third year of the reign of King Joash, the priests had not made needed repairs on the temple. [8] Accordingly, King Joash summoned the priest Jehoiada and the other priests. He asked, "Why do you not repair the temple? You must no longer take funds from your vendors, but you shall turn them over for the repairs." [9] So the priests agreed that they would neither take funds from the people nor make the repairs on the temple.

[10] Jehoiada the priest then took a chest, bored a hole in its lid, and set it beside the altar, on the right as one entered the house of the LORD. The priests who kept the doors would put into it all the silver that was brought to the house of the LORD. [11]* When they noticed that there was a large amount of silver in the chest, the royal scribe would come up with the high priest, and they would gather up and weigh all the silver that was in the house of the LORD. [12] The amount thus realized they turned over to the workers assigned to the house of the LORD. They in turn would pay it to the carpenters and builders working in the house of the LORD, [13] and to the masons and stone cutters, and for the purchase of the wood and hewn stone used in repairing the breaches, and for any other expenses that were necessary to repair the house of the LORD. [14] None of the valuables brought to the house of the LORD were used there to make silver basins, snuffers, bowls, trumpets, or any gold or silver article. [15] Instead, they were given to the workers, and with them they repaired the house of the LORD. [16] Moreover, no reckoning was asked of those who were provided with the funds to give to the workers, because they held positions of trust. [17] The funds from reparation offerings and from purification offerings, however, were not brought to the house of the LORD; they belonged to the priests.

[18] Then Hazael, king of Aram, came up and attacked Gath. When he had taken it, Hazael resolved to go on to attack Jerusalem. [19] Joash,† king of Judah, took all the sacred offerings presented by his forebears, Jehoshaphat, Jehoram, and Ahaziah, kings of Judah, as well as his own, and all the gold there was in the treasuries of the house of the LORD and the king's house, and sent them to King Hazael of Aram, who then turned away from Jerusalem.

[20] The rest of the acts of Joash, with all that he did, are recorded in the book of the chronicles of the kings of Judah. [21] Certain of his officials† entered into a conspiracy and struck Joash down at Beth-millo. [22] Jozacar, son of Shimeath, and Jehozabad, son of Shomer, were the officials who struck and killed him. He was buried with his ancestors in the City of David, and his son Amaziah succeeded him as king.

# 13

**Reign of Jehoahaz of Israel.** [1] In the twenty-third year of Joash, son of Ahaziah, king of Judah, Jehoahaz, son of Jehu, became king over Israel in Samaria for seventeen years.

[2] He did what was evil in the LORD's sight: he did not depart from following the sins that Jeroboam, son of Nebat, had caused Israel to commit. [3] The LORD was angry with Israel and for a long time gave them into the power of Hazael, king of Aram, and of Ben-hadad, son of Hazael. [4] Then Jehoahaz entreated the LORD, who heard him, since he saw the oppression to which the king of Aram had subjected Israel. * [5] So the LORD gave Israel a savior,† and the Israelites, freed from the power of Aram, dwelt in their own tents as formerly. [6] Nevertheless, they did not desist from the sins the house of Jeroboam had caused Israel to commit, but persisted in them. The Asherah† remained even in Samaria. * [7] No army was left to Jehoahaz, except fifty horses with ten chariots and ten thousand foot soldiers, since the king of Aram had destroyed them and trampled them like dust.

[8] The rest of the acts of Jehoahaz, with all

---

† **12:19** *Joash*: in 2 Kings the name "Joash" and its variant "Jehoash" are interchangeable (see note on "Joram" and "Jehoram" at 1:17), whether in reference to the king of Judah (vv. 1–22) or his slightly later contemporary, Joash of Israel (13:10–25). Both forms are rendered "Joash" in this translation.

**12:21** *Officials*: lit., "servants." The Hebrew *ebed* ("servant") has a wide range of meanings, always including service to another.

**13:5** *A savior*: i.e., a military leader (cf. Jgs 3:9, 15). Here the identity of the savior is unclear, but the reappearance of a militant Elisha in this chapter after an absence of several chapters and nearly thirty years suggests the narrator may have had him in mind. Two generations later Joash's grandson, Jeroboam II, will also "save" Israel (14:27).

**13:6** *Asherah*: see note on Ex 34:13.

**12:11–16** 2 Kgs 22:3–7.
**13:4** 2 Kgs 14:26–27.
**13:6** Ex 34:13; 1 Kgs 16:33.

that he did and his valor, are recorded in the book of the chronicles of the kings of Israel. ⁹Jehoahaz rested with his ancestors; he was buried in Samaria and his son Joash succeeded him as king.

**Reign of Joash of Israel.** ¹⁰In the thirty-seventh year of Joash, king of Judah, Joash, son of Jehoahaz, became king over Israel in Samaria sixteen years. ¹¹He did what was evil in the LORD's sight; he did not desist from any of the sins Jeroboam, son of Nebat, had caused Israel to commit, but persisted in them.

¹²† The rest of the acts of Joash, with all that he did and his valor, and how he fought with Amaziah, king of Judah, are recorded in the book of the chronicles of the kings of Israel. ¹³Joash rested with his ancestors. Then Jeroboam sat on his throne. Joash was buried in Samaria with the kings of Israel.

**Elisha's Deathbed Prophecy.** ¹⁴When Elisha was suffering from the sickness of which he was to die, Joash, king of Israel, went down to weep over him. "My father, my father!"† he exclaimed, "Israel's chariot and steeds!"* ¹⁵Elisha said to him, "Take bow and arrows," and he took bow and arrows. ¹⁶† Elisha said to the king of Israel, "Rest your hand on the bow," and he rested his hand on it. Elisha placed his hands over the king's hands ¹⁷and said, "Open the window toward the east." He opened it. Elisha said, "Shoot," and he shot. He said,

> "An arrow of victory for the LORD!
> An arrow of victory over Aram!
> You will beat Aram at Aphek and finish
>  him!"

¹⁸Then he said to the king of Israel, "Take the arrows," which he did. Elisha said to the king of Israel, "Beat the ground!" He beat the ground three times and stopped. ¹⁹The man of God became angry with him and said, "You should have beat five or six times. You would have beaten Aram and finished him. Now you will beat Aram only three times."

²⁰And so Elisha died and was buried.

At that time of year, bands of Moabites used to raid the land. ²¹Once some people were burying a man, when suddenly they saw such a raiding band. So they cast the man into the grave of Elisha, and everyone went off. But when the man came in contact with the bones of Elisha, he came back to life and got to his feet.*

²²King Hazael of Aram oppressed Israel all the days of Jehoahaz. ²³But the LORD was gracious with Israel and looked on them with compassion because of his covenant with Abraham, Isaac, and Jacob. He was unwilling to destroy them or to cast them out from his presence even up to now. ²⁴So when King Hazael of Aram died and his son Ben-hadad succeeded him as king, ²⁵Joash, son of Jehoahaz, took back from Ben-hadad, son of Hazael, the cities Hazael had taken in battle from Jehoahaz, his father. Three times Joash beat him, and thus recovered the cities of Israel.

**14 Reign of Amaziah of Judah.** ¹In the second year† of Joash, son of Jehoahaz, king of Israel, Amaziah, son of Joash, king of Judah, became king. ²He was twenty-five years old when he became king, and he reigned twenty-nine years in Jerusalem. His mother's name was Jehoaddin, from Jerusalem. ³He did what was right in the LORD's eyes, though not like David his father. He did just as his father Joash had done, ⁴though the high places did not disappear, and the people continued to sacrifice and to burn incense on the high places.

---

† **13:12–13** The conclusion to the reign of Joash is given again in 14:15–16. In both places it disrupts the standard pattern followed in the Books of Kings. The account of Joash's reign ends in vv. 12–13; this leaves the story of Elisha's last illness (in which Joash figures prominently) suspended between regnal accounts, much as the story of Elisha's succession to Elijah's prophetic office (chap. 2) was suspended between the accounts of Ahaziah and Joram. In 14:15–16 the concluding formula for Joash's reign interrupts the account of the reign of Amaziah of Judah (14:1–22), much as Joash himself invaded Amaziah's kingdom (14:11–14).

**13:14** *My father, my father*: the way the king addresses the dying Elisha echoes Elisha's address to Elijah in 2:12.

**13:16–19** Symbolic acts, like prophetic oracles, were understood to unleash the power they expressed. Similar symbolic acts are seen in Ex 17:8–13; Jos 8:18–20; Ez 4:1–3.

**14:1–2** *In the second year…twenty-nine years in Jerusalem*: as they stand, the chronological data in the introductions to the reigns of the kings of Judah and Israel are incompatible with one another. The kings of Judah between Athaliah and Ahaz are assigned too many years in all to correspond to the reigns in Israel from Jehu to the fall of Samaria. Various theories have been proposed in an attempt to explain the discrepancy, such as co-regencies, or textual corruption in the process of transmission.

---

*  **13:14** 2 Kgs 2:12.  **13:21** Sir 48:14.

⁵ When Amaziah had the kingdom firmly in hand, he struck down the officials who had struck down the king, his father. ⁶ But their children he did not put to death, according to what is written in the book of the law of Moses, which the LORD commanded: "Parents shall not be put to death for their children, nor shall children be put to death for their parents; only for one's own crimes shall a person be put to death."*

⁷ Amaziah struck down ten thousand Edomites in the Salt Valley. He took Sela in battle and renamed it Joktheel, the name it has to this day.*

⁸ Then Amaziah sent messengers to Joash, son of Jehoahaz, son of Jehu, king of Israel, with this message: "Come, let us meet face to face." ⁹ Joash, king of Israel, sent this reply to Amaziah, king of Judah: "A thistle of Lebanon sent word to a cedar of Lebanon, 'Give your daughter to my son in marriage,' but an animal of Lebanon passed by and trampled the thistle underfoot.* ¹⁰ You have indeed struck down Edom, and your heart is lifted up; enjoy your glory, but stay home! Why bring misfortune and failure on yourself and on Judah with you?" ¹¹ But Amaziah did not listen. So Joash, king of Israel, advanced, and he and Amaziah, king of Judah, met face to face at Beth-shemesh of Judah, ¹² and Judah was defeated by Israel, and all fled to their tents. ¹³ But Amaziah, king of Judah, son of Joash, son of Ahaziah, was captured by Joash, king of Israel, at Beth-shemesh. When they came to Jerusalem Joash tore down the wall of Jerusalem, from the Gate of Ephraim to the Corner Gate, four hundred cubits. ¹⁴ He took all the gold and silver and all the vessels found in the house of the LORD and in the treasuries of the king's house, and hostages as well. Then he returned to Samaria.

¹⁵† The rest of the acts of Joash, what he did and his valor, and how he made war against Amaziah, king of Judah, are recorded in the book of the chronicles of the kings of Israel. ¹⁶ Joash rested with his ancestors; he was buried in Samaria with the kings of Israel, and his son Jeroboam succeeded him as king.

¹⁷† Amaziah, son of Joash, king of Judah, survived Joash, son of Jehoahaz, king of Israel, by fifteen years. ¹⁸ The rest of the acts of Amaziah are recorded in the book of the chronicles of the kings of Judah. ¹⁹ When a conspiracy was formed against him in Jerusalem, he fled to Lachish. But he was pursued to Lachish and killed there. ²⁰ He was brought back on horses and was buried in Jerusalem with his ancestors in the City of David. ²¹ Thereupon all the people of Judah† took Azariah, who was only sixteen years old, and made him king to succeed Amaziah, his father. ²² It was he who rebuilt Elath and restored it to Judah, after the king rested with his ancestors.

**Reign of Jeroboam II of Israel.** ²³ In the fifteenth year of Amaziah, son of Joash, king of Judah, Jeroboam, son of Joash, king of Israel, became king in Samaria for forty-one years. ²⁴ He did evil in the LORD's sight; he did not desist from any of the sins that Jeroboam, son of Nebat, had caused Israel to commit. ²⁵ He restored the boundaries of Israel from Lebo-hamath to the sea of the Arabah,† as the LORD, the God of Israel, had foretold through his servant, the prophet Jonah, son of Amittai, from Gath-hepher. ²⁶ For the LORD saw the very bitter affliction of Israel, where there was neither bond nor free, no one at all to help Israel. ²⁷ Since the LORD had not resolved to wipe out the name of Israel from under the heavens, he saved them through Jeroboam, son of Joash.

²⁸ The rest of the acts of Jeroboam, with all that he did and his valor, how he fought, and how he regained Damascus and Hamath for Israel, are recorded in the book of the chronicles of the kings of Israel. ²⁹ Jeroboam rested with his ancestors, the kings of Israel, and his son Zechariah succeeded him as king.

# 15 **Reign of Azariah of Judah.** ¹ In the twenty-seventh year† of Jeroboam, king of Israel, Azariah, son of Amaziah, king of Judah, became king. ² He was sixteen years old when he became king, and he reigned

---

† **14:15–16** See note on 13:12–13.
**14:17** See note on vv. 1–2.
**14:21** *All the people of Judah*: this phrase may refer to the army (compare, for example, "all Israel" in 1 Kgs 16:16–17). If this is its meaning here, then Amaziah's assassination and Azariah's succession are owing to a military coup. *Azariah*: also called Uzziah in many texts.

**14:25** *Sea of the Arabah*: the Dead Sea. *Jonah, son of Amittai*: see note on Jon 1:1.
**15:1** *Twenty-seventh year*: see note on 14:1–2.

**14:6** Dt 24:16; Ez 18:20.        **14:9** Jgs 9:8–15.
**14:7** 2 Sm 8:13–14.

fifty-two years in Jerusalem. His mother's name was Jecholiah, from Jerusalem. ³ He did what was right in the LORD's sight, just as his father Amaziah had done, ⁴ though the high places did not disappear, and the people continued to sacrifice and to burn incense on the high places. ⁵ The LORD afflicted the king, and he was a leper until the day he died. He lived in a house apart, while Jotham, the king's son, was master of the palace and ruled the people of the land. †

⁶ The rest of the acts of Azariah, and all that he did, are recorded in the book of the chronicles of the kings of Judah. ⁷ Azariah rested with his ancestors, and was buried with them in the City of David, and his son Jotham succeeded him as king.

**Reign of Zechariah of Israel.** ⁸ In the thirty-eighth year of Azariah, king of Judah, Zechariah, son of Jeroboam, became king over Israel in Samaria for six months.

⁹ He did what was evil in the LORD's sight, as his ancestors had done, and did not desist from the sins that Jeroboam, son of Nebat, had caused Israel to commit. ¹⁰ Shallum, son of Jabesh, plotted against him and struck him down at Ibleam. He killed him and reigned in his place.

¹¹ As for the rest of the acts of Zechariah, these are recorded in the book of the chronicles of the kings of Israel. ¹² This was the word the LORD had spoken to Jehu: Sons of your line to the fourth generation shall sit upon the throne of Israel; and so it was. *

**Reign of Shallum of Israel.** ¹³ Shallum, son of Jabesh, became king in the thirty-ninth year of Uzziah, king of Judah; he reigned one month in Samaria.

¹⁴ Menahem, son of Gadi, came up from Tirzah to Samaria, and struck down Shallum, son of Jabesh, in Samaria. He killed him and reigned in his place.

¹⁵ As for the rest of the acts of Shallum, with the conspiracy he carried out, these are recorded in the book of the chronicles of the kings of Israel. ¹⁶ At that time, Menahem attacked Tappuah, all its inhabitants, and its whole district as far as Tirzah, because they did not let him in. He attacked them; he even ripped open all their pregnant women.

**Reign of Menahem of Israel.** ¹⁷ In the thirty-ninth year of Azariah, king of Judah, Menahem, son of Gadi, became king over Israel for ten years in Samaria. ¹⁸ He did what was evil in the LORD's sight as long as he lived, not desisting from the sins that Jeroboam, son of Nebat, had caused Israel to commit. ¹⁹ Pul, † king of Assyria, came against the land. But Menahem gave Pul a thousand talents of silver to have his help in holding onto his kingdom. ²⁰ Menahem paid out silver on behalf of Israel, that is, for all the people of substance, by giving the king of Assyria fifty shekels of silver for each one. So the king of Assyria went home and did not stay in the land.

²¹ The rest of the acts of Menahem, with all that he did, are recorded in the book of the chronicles of the kings of Israel. ²² Menahem rested with his ancestors, and his son Pekahiah succeeded him as king.

**Reign of Pekahiah of Israel.** ²³ In the fiftieth year of Azariah, king of Judah, Pekahiah, son of Menahem, became king over Israel in Samaria for two years.

²⁴ He did what was evil in the LORD's sight, not desisting from the sins that Jeroboam, son of Nebat, had caused Israel to commit. ²⁵ His adjutant Pekah, son of Remaliah, conspired against him, and struck him down at Samaria within the palace stronghold; he had with him fifty men from Gilead. He killed him and reigned in his place. ²⁶ As for the rest of the acts of Pekahiah, with all that he did, these are recorded in the book of the chronicles of the kings of Israel.

**Reign of Pekah of Israel.** ²⁷ † In the fifty-second year of Azariah, king of Judah, Pekah, son of Remaliah, became king over Israel in Samaria for twenty years.

²⁸ He did what was evil in the LORD's sight, not desisting from the sins that Jeroboam,

---

**15:5** *People of the land*: see note on 11:14.
**15:19** *Pul*: the Babylonian throne name of the Assyrian Tiglath-pileser III; cf. v. 29.
**15:27** The twenty years here ascribed to Pekah are difficult to reconcile with other chronological notices about the kings. One theory would see Pekah and Menahem as rival kings over parts

of a divided Israelite territory; this could explain Menahem's concern for Assyrian support (vv. 19–20) and Assyria's attack on Pekah (v. 29). See 16:1 and note on 14:1–2.

**15:12** 2 Kgs 10:30.

son of Nebat, had caused Israel to commit. **29** In the days of Pekah, king of Israel, Tiglath-pileser, king of Assyria, came and took Ijon, Abel-beth-maacah, Janoah, Kedesh, Hazor, Gilead, and Galilee—all the land of Naphtali—deporting the inhabitants to Assyria. **30**† Hoshea, son of Elah, carried out a conspiracy against Pekah, son of Remaliah; he struck and killed him, and succeeded him as king in the twentieth year of Jotham, son of Uzziah.

**31** As for the rest of the acts of Pekah, with all that he did, these are recorded in the book of the chronicles of the kings of Israel.

**Reign of Jotham of Judah.** **32** In the second year of Pekah, son of Remaliah, king of Israel, Jotham, son of Uzziah, king of Judah, became king. **33** He was twenty-five years old when he became king, and he reigned sixteen years in Jerusalem. His mother's name was Jerusha, daughter of Zadok.

**34** He did what was right in the LORD's sight, just as his father Uzziah had done, **35** though the high places did not disappear, and the people continued to sacrifice and to burn incense on the high places. It was he who built the Upper Gate† of the LORD's house.

**36** The rest of the acts of Jotham, with what he did, are recorded in the book of the chronicles of the kings of Judah. **37** It was at that time that the LORD began to unleash Rezin, king of Aram, and Pekah, son of Remaliah, against Judah.* **38** Jotham rested with his ancestors; he was buried with his ancestors in the City of David his father, and his son Ahaz succeeded him as king.

**16** **Reign of Ahaz of Judah.**† **1** In the seventeenth year of Pekah, son of Remaliah, Ahaz, son of Jotham, king of Judah, became king. **2** Ahaz was twenty years old when he became king, and he reigned sixteen years in Jerusalem.

He did not do what was right in the sight of the LORD his God, as David his father had done. **3** He walked in the way of the kings of Israel; he even immolated his child by fire, in accordance with the abominable practices of the nations whom the LORD had dispossessed before the Israelites.* **4** Further, he sacrificed and burned incense on the high places, on hills, and under every green tree.*

**5** Then Rezin, king of Aram, and Pekah, son of Remaliah, king of Israel, came up to Jerusalem to attack it. Although they besieged Ahaz, they were unable to do battle. **6** (In those days Rezin, king of Aram, recovered Elath for Aram, and drove the Judahites out of it. The Edomites then entered Elath, which they have occupied until the present.)

**7** Meanwhile, Ahaz sent messengers to Tiglath-pileser, king of Assyria, with the plea: "I am your servant and your son. Come up and rescue me from the power of the king of Aram and the king of Israel, who are attacking me." **8** Ahaz took the silver and gold that were in the house of the LORD and in the treasuries of the king's house and sent them as a present to the king of Assyria. **9** The king of Assyria listened to him and moved against Damascus, captured it, deported its inhabitants to Kir, and put Rezin to death.

**10** King Ahaz went to Damascus to meet Tiglath-pileser, king of Assyria. When he saw the altar in Damascus, King Ahaz sent to Uriah the priest a model of the altar and a detailed design of its construction. **11** Uriah the priest built an altar according to the plans which King Ahaz sent him from Damascus, and had it completed by the time King Ahaz returned from Damascus. **12** On his arrival from Damascus, the king inspected the altar; the king approached the altar, went up **13** and sacrificed his burnt offering and grain offering, pouring out his libation, and sprinkling the blood of his communion offerings on the altar. **14** The bronze altar that stood before the LORD he brought from the front of the temple—that is,

† **15:30** The twenty years here reckoned to Jotham of Judah may include his co-regency with Azariah (v. 5); otherwise they are impossible to reconcile with v. 33, which ascribes him only sixteen years. The verse also appears to contradict 16:1, which has Jotham's son and successor, Ahaz, coming to the throne while Pekah still reigns in Israel, and 17:1, which dates Hoshea's accession to the throne to the twelfth year of Ahaz.
**15:35** *The Upper Gate*: also called the Gate of Benjamin; cf. Jer 20:2; Ez 9:2.
**16:1–20** Firmly dated events bearing on chaps. 16–20 are: the fall of Damascus (16:9) in 732 B.C., the fall of Samaria

(18:9–11) in 722/721 B.C., and Sennacherib's invasion of Judah (18:13) in 701 B.C., which both in Kings and in Is 36:1 occurs in the fourteenth year of Hezekiah. These data make it possible to connect the chronology of Israel and Judah to the larger chronology of ancient Near Eastern history, but they also complicate further the already vexed problem of inconsistencies in the biblical data about accession years and lengths of reign.

**15:37** Is 7:1–16.　　**16:4** Dt 12:2.
**16:3** Lv 18:21; Dt 18:10.

from the space between the new altar and the house of the LORD—and set it on the north side of his altar. ¹⁵ * King Ahaz commanded Uriah the priest, "Upon the large altar sacrifice the morning burnt offering and the evening grain offering, the king's burnt offering and grain offering, and the burnt offering and grain offering of the people of the land. † Their libations you must sprinkle on it along with all the blood of burnt offerings and sacrifices. But the old bronze altar shall be mine for consultation." ¹⁶ Uriah the priest did just as King Ahaz had commanded. ¹⁷ King Ahaz detached the panels from the stands and removed the basins from them; he also took down the bronze sea from the bronze oxen that supported it, and set it on a stone pavement. ¹⁸ In deference to the king of Assyria he removed the sabbath canopy that had been set up in the house of the LORD and the king's outside entrance† to the temple.

¹⁹ The rest of the acts of Ahaz, with what he did, are recorded in the book of the chronicles of the kings of Judah. ²⁰ Ahaz rested with his ancestors; he was buried with his ancestors in the City of David, and his son Hezekiah succeeded him as king.

# 17 Reign of Hoshea of Israel.

¹ In the twelfth year of Ahaz, king of Judah, Hoshea, son of Elah, became king in Samaria over Israel for nine years. ² He did what was evil in the LORD's sight, yet not to the extent of the kings of Israel before him. ³ Shalmaneser, † king of Assyria, advanced against him, and Hoshea became his vassal and paid him tribute. * ⁴ But the king of Assyria found Hoshea guilty of conspiracy for sending messengers to the king of Egypt at Sais, and for failure to pay the annual tribute to the king of Assyria. So the king of Assyria

arrested and imprisoned him. ⁵ Then the king of Assyria† occupied the whole land and attacked Samaria, which he besieged for three years.

## X. THE END OF ISRAEL†

**Israelites Deported.** ⁶ In Hoshea's ninth year, the king of Assyria took Samaria, deported the Israelites to Assyria, and settled them in Halah, and at the Habor, a river of Gozan, and in the cities of the Medes. * ⁷ This came about because the Israelites sinned against the LORD, their God, who had brought them up from the land of Egypt, from under the hand of Pharaoh, king of Egypt. They venerated other gods, ⁸ * they followed the rites of the nations whom the LORD had dispossessed before the Israelites and those that the kings of Israel had practiced. ⁹ They adopted unlawful practices toward the LORD, their God. They built high places in all their cities, from guard post to garrisoned town. ¹⁰ They set up pillars and asherahs† for themselves on every high hill and under every green tree. ¹¹ They burned incense there, on all the high places, like the nations whom the LORD had sent into exile at their coming. They did evil things that provoked the LORD, ¹² and served idols, although the LORD had told them: You must not do this.

¹³ * The LORD warned Israel and Judah by every prophet and seer: Give up your evil ways and keep my commandments and statutes, in accordance with the entire law which I enjoined on your ancestors and which I sent you by my servants the prophets. ¹⁴ But they did not listen. They grew as stiff-necked as their ancestors, who had not believed in the LORD, their God. * ¹⁵ They rejected his statutes, the covenant he had made with their ancestors, and the warnings he had given them. They

---

**16:15** *People of the land:* see note on 11:14. *For consultation:* perhaps the introduction into Judah of the Babylonian practice of reading omens from animal sacrifices; cf. Ez 21:26.

**16:18** *Sabbath canopy...outside entrance:* the Hebrew is obscure, but as a vassal Ahaz must have had to divest himself of signs of sovereignty.

**17:3** *Shalmaneser:* son and successor of the Assyrian king Tiglath-pileser III. *Vassal:* lit., "servant"; cf. 16:7; so also in 24:1.

**17:5** *The king of Assyria:* Shalmaneser was succeeded by Sargon II, who usurped the Assyrian throne in 722/721 B.C. In his inscriptions, Sargon claims to have captured Samaria during the first year of his reign.

**17:6–41** This brief section is the Deuteronomistic historian's theological reflection on the causes and aftermath of Assyria's conquest of the Northern Kingdom. The text contrasts the Israelites, who were deported (v. 6) because they abandoned the

worship of the Lord (vv. 7–23), with the foreigners who were brought into the land (v. 24) and undertook, however imperfectly, to worship the Lord alongside their own traditional deities (vv. 25–34a). The last verses recapitulate the apostasy of the Israelites (vv. 34b–40) and the syncretism of the foreigners (v. 41). This is a deliberately disparaging, and not wholly accurate, account of the origin of the Samaritans; it reflects the hostility the Judahites continued to hold toward the inhabitants of the northern territories.

**17:10** *Asherahs:* see note on Ex 34:13.

---

**16:15** Ex 29:38–41; Nm 28:3–8.  
**17:3** 2 Kgs 18:9.  
**17:6** 2 Kgs 18:10–11; Tb 1:2.  
**17:8–12** Ex 23:24; 34:13; Dt 12:2.  
**17:13** Jer 25:5.  
**17:14** Dt 9:13.

followed emptiness and became empty; they followed the surrounding nations whom the LORD had commanded them not to imitate. * ¹⁶They abandoned all the commandments of the LORD, their God: they made for themselves two molten calves; they made an asherah; they bowed down to all the host of heaven; they served Baal. * ¹⁷ * They immolated their sons and daughters by fire. They practiced augury and divination. They surrendered themselves to doing what was evil in the LORD's sight, and provoked him.

¹⁸ * The LORD became enraged, and removed them from his presence. Only the tribe of Judah was left. ¹⁹Even the people of Judah did not keep the commandments of the LORD, their God, but followed the rites practiced by Israel. ²⁰So the LORD rejected the entire people of Israel: he afflicted them and delivered them over to plunderers, finally casting them from his presence. * ²¹When he tore Israel away from the house of David, they made Jeroboam, son of Nebat, king; but Jeroboam lured the Israelites away from the LORD, causing them to commit a great sin. * ²²The Israelites imitated Jeroboam in all the sins he committed; they would not depart from them.

²³Finally, the LORD removed Israel from his presence, just as he had declared through all his servants, the prophets. Thus Israel went into exile from their native soil to Assyria until this very day.

**Foreigners Deported to Israel.** ²⁴The king of Assyria brought people from Babylon, Cuthah, Avva, Hamath, and Sepharvaim, and settled them in the cities of Samaria in place of the Israelites. They took possession of Samaria and dwelt in its cities. ²⁵When they first settled there, they did not venerate the LORD, so he sent lions among them that killed some of them. ²⁶A report reached the king of Assyria: "The nations you deported and settled in the cities of Samaria do not know the proper worship of the god of the land, so he has sent lions among them that are killing them, since they do not know the law of the god of the land." ²⁷The king of Assyria gave the order,

"Send back some of the priests you deported, to go there and settle, to teach them the proper worship of the god of the land." ²⁸So one of the priests who had been deported from Samaria returned and settled in Bethel, and began to teach them how to venerate the LORD.

²⁹Thus each of these nations continued to make its own gods, setting them up in the shrines of the high places the Samarians had made: each nation in the cities in which they dwelt. ³⁰The Babylonians made Sukkot-Benot;† the people of Cuth made Nergal; those from Hamath made Ashima; ³¹those from Avva made Nibhaz and Tartak; and those from Sepharvaim immolated their children by fire to their city gods, King Hadad and King Anu. ³²At the same time, they were venerating the LORD, appointing from their own number priests for the high places to officiate for them in the shrines on the high places. ³³They were both venerating the LORD and serving their own gods. They followed the custom of the nations from among whom they had been deported.

³⁴To this very day they continue to act according to their former customs, not venerating the LORD nor observing the statutes and regulations, the law and commandment, that the LORD enjoined on the descendants of Jacob, whom he had named Israel. * ³⁵When the LORD made a covenant with them, he commanded them: You must not venerate other gods, nor bow down to them, nor serve them, nor offer sacrifice to them, * ³⁶but only to the LORD, who brought you up from the land of Egypt with great power and outstretched arm. Him shall you venerate, to him shall you bow down, and to him shall you offer sacrifice. ³⁷You must be careful always to observe the statutes and ordinances, the law and commandment, which he wrote for you; you must not venerate other gods. ³⁸The covenant I made with you, you must not forget; you must not venerate other gods. ³⁹You must venerate only the LORD, your God; it is he who will deliver you from the power of all your enemies. ⁴⁰But they did not listen; they continued to act according to their former customs.

† **17:30** *Sukkot-Benot*: several of the divine names in vv. 30–31 are problematic or conjectural. Sukkot-Benot is unknown, but the name may have been corrupted from that of Sarpanitu, the consort of the Babylonian god Marduk.

**17:15** Jer 2:5.
**17:16** Ex 34:13; Dt 4:19; 17:2–3; 1 Kgs 12:28; 16:33.
**17:17** Lv 18:21; Dt 18:10.
**17:18** Sir 48:15.
**17:20** Jer 25:9.
**17:21** 1 Kgs 12:20, 26–33; 13:34.
**17:34** Gn 32:29; 35:10.
**17:35–38** Ex 20:3–6.

**41** But these nations were both venerating the LORD and serving their own idols. Their children and children's children are still acting like their ancestors, to this very day.

## XI. THE END OF JUDAH†

**18** **Reign of Hezekiah.** ¹ In the third year of Hoshea, son of Elah, king of Israel, Hezekiah, son of Ahaz, king of Judah, became king. ² He was twenty-five years old when he became king, and he reigned twenty-nine years in Jerusalem. His mother's name was Abi, daughter of Zechariah.

³ He did what was right in the LORD's sight, just as David his father had done. ⁴ It was he who removed the high places, shattered the pillars, cut down the asherah,† and smashed the bronze serpent Moses had made, because up to that time the Israelites were burning incense to it. (It was called Nehushtan.)* ⁵ He put his trust in the LORD, the God of Israel; and neither before nor after him was there anyone like him among all the kings of Judah. ⁶ Hezekiah held fast to the LORD and never turned away from following him, but observed the commandments the LORD had given Moses. ⁷ The LORD was with him, and he succeeded in all he set out to do. He rebelled against the king of Assyria and did not serve him. ⁸ It was he who struck the Philistines as far as Gaza, and all its territory from guard post to garrisoned town.

⁹† In the fourth year of King Hezekiah, which was the seventh year of Hoshea, son of Elah, king of Israel, Shalmaneser, king of Assyria, attacked Samaria and laid siege to it, ¹⁰* and after three years they captured it. In the sixth year of Hezekiah, the ninth year of Hoshea, king of Israel, Samaria was taken. ¹¹ The king of Assyria then deported the Israelites to Assyria and led them off to Halah, and the Habor, a river of Gozan, and the cities of the Medes. ¹² This happened because they did not obey the LORD, their God, but violated his covenant; they did not obey nor do all that Moses, the servant of the LORD, commanded.*

**Sennacherib and Hezekiah.** ¹³† In the fourteenth year of King Hezekiah, Sennacherib, king of Assyria,† attacked all the fortified cities of Judah and captured them.* ¹⁴ Hezekiah, king of Judah, sent this message to the king of Assyria at Lachish: "I have done wrong. Leave me, and whatever you impose on me I will bear." The king of Assyria exacted three hundred talents of silver and thirty talents of gold from Hezekiah, king of Judah. ¹⁵ Hezekiah gave him all the funds there were in the house of the LORD and in the treasuries of the king's house. ¹⁶ At the same time, Hezekiah removed the nave doors and the uprights of the house of the LORD, which the king of Judah had ordered to be overlaid with gold, and gave them to the king of Assyria.*

¹⁷ The king of Assyria sent the general, the lord chamberlain, and the commander† from Lachish with a great army to King Hezekiah at Jerusalem. They went up and came to Jerusalem, to the conduit of the upper pool on the highway of the fuller's field, where they took their stand. ¹⁸ They called for the king, but Eliakim, son of Hilkiah, the master of the palace, came out, along with Shebnah the scribe and the chancellor Joah, son of Asaph.* ¹⁹ The commander said to them, "Tell

---

**18:1–25:30** The Books of Kings end, as they began, with the people of the Lord in a single kingdom, Judah, centered on the capital, Jerusalem, and the Solomonic Temple. The reigns of two reformer kings, both praised, are recounted at length: Hezekiah (chaps. 18–20) and Josiah (22:1–23:30). Each is followed by shorter accounts of two kings who are condemned: Manasseh and Amon (chap. 21) and Jehoahaz and Jehoiakim (23:31–24:7). The book ends with the last days of Judah under Jehoiachin and Zedekiah and the beginning of the Babylonian exile.

**18:4** *Asherah:* see note on Ex 34:13. *Nehushtan:* the name *nehushtan* contains several wordplays in Hebrew. It recalls the word "serpent" (*nahash*), the word "bronze" (*nehoshet*), and the word "to read omens" (*nihesh*). The sentence is also unclear about who named the bronze serpent "Nehushtan"—whether Moses when he made it, or the people when they venerated it, or Hezekiah when he destroyed it.

**18:9** The correlations between the reigns of Hezekiah and Hoshea in vv. 9–10 conflict with other biblical data and with the date for the fall of Samaria, 722/721 B.C. (see note on 16:1–20). Since Sennacherib's invasion in the fourteenth year of

Hezekiah (v. 13) took place in 701, Hezekiah cannot have been on the throne twenty years earlier. Various solutions have been proposed: scribal errors in writing the numbers; a Hezekian co-regency with his father Ahaz beginning in 729; etc. None of the solutions has won a consensus among historians.

**18:13–20:19** This material is found also in Is 36–39, with one long addition (Is 38:9–20) and only a few other changes.

**18:13** Sennacherib succeeded Sargon II as king of Assyria. His Judean campaign was waged in 701 B.C. See notes on 16:1–20 and 18:9.

**18:17** *General, the lord chamberlain…commander:* the text lists three major functionaries by their Assyrian titles, of which only the first, more nearly "lord lieutenant," is military in origin; the commander was technically the king's chief butler.

---

**18:4** Ex 23:24; 34:13; Nm 21:4–9; Dt 12:2; Wis 16:5–7; Jn 3:14.
**18:10–11** 2 Kgs 17:5–6; Tb 1:2.
**18:12** 2 Kgs 17:6–23; Ex 24:7.
**18:13–19:36** Sir 48:18–21.
**18:16** 1 Kgs 6:31–35.
**18:18** Is 22:15–25.

Hezekiah, 'Thus says the great king, the king of Assyria: On what do you base this trust of yours? <sup>20</sup> Do you think mere words substitute for strategy and might in war? In whom, then, do you place your trust, that you rebel against me? <sup>21</sup> Do you trust in Egypt, that broken reed of a staff, which pierces the hand of anyone who leans on it? That is what Pharaoh, king of Egypt, is to all who trust in him.* <sup>22</sup> Or do you people say to me, "It is in the LORD our God we trust!"? Is it not he whose high places and altars Hezekiah has removed, commanding Judah and Jerusalem, "Worship before this altar in Jerusalem"?'

<sup>23</sup> "Now, make a wager with my lord, the king of Assyria: I will give you two thousand horses if you are able to put riders on them. <sup>24</sup> How then can you turn back even a captain, one of the least servants of my lord, trusting, as you do, in Egypt for chariots and horses? <sup>25</sup> Did I come up to destroy this place without the LORD? The LORD himself said to me: Go up and destroy that land!"

<sup>26</sup> Then Eliakim, son of Hilkiah, and Shebnah and Joah said to the commander: "Please speak to your servants in Aramaic; we understand it. Do not speak to us in the language of Judah within earshot of the people who are on the wall." <sup>27</sup> But the commander replied: "Was it to your lord and to you that my lord sent me to speak these words? Was it not rather to those sitting on the wall, who, with you, will have to eat their own excrement and drink their urine?"†

<sup>28</sup> Then the commander stepped forward and cried out in a loud voice in the language of Judah, "Listen to the words of the great king, the king of Assyria. <sup>29</sup> Thus says the king: Do not let Hezekiah deceive you, for he cannot rescue you from my hand. <sup>30</sup> And do not let Hezekiah induce you to trust in the LORD, saying, 'The LORD will surely rescue us, and this city will not be handed over to the king of Assyria.' <sup>31</sup> Do not listen to Hezekiah, for thus says the king of Assyria: Make peace with me, and surrender to me! Eat, each of you, from your vine, each from your own fig tree. Drink

water, each from your own well, <sup>32</sup> until I arrive and take you to a land like your own, a land of grain and wine, a land of bread and vineyards, a land of rich olives and honey. Live, and do not die! And do not listen to Hezekiah when he would incite you by saying, 'The LORD will rescue us.' <sup>33</sup> Has any of the gods of the nations ever rescued his land from the power of the king of Assyria? <sup>34</sup> Where are the gods of Hamath and Arpad? Where are the gods of Sepharvaim, Hena, and Ivvah? Did they indeed rescue Samaria from my power?† <sup>35</sup> Which of the gods for all these lands ever rescued his land from my power? Will the LORD then rescue Jerusalem from my power?" <sup>36</sup> But the people remained silent and did not answer at all, for the king's command was, "Do not answer him."

<sup>37</sup> Then the master of the palace, Eliakim, son of Hilkiah, Shebnah the scribe, and the chancellor Joah, son of Asaph, came to Hezekiah with their garments torn, and reported to him the words of the commander.

# 19 Hezekiah and Isaiah. <sup>1</sup> When King Hezekiah heard this, he tore his garments, covered himself with sackcloth, and went into the house of the LORD. <sup>2</sup> He sent Eliakim, the master of the palace, Shebnah the scribe, and the elders of the priests, covered with sackcloth, to tell the prophet Isaiah, son of Amoz, <sup>3</sup> "Thus says Hezekiah:

A day of distress and rebuke,
a day of disgrace is this day!
Children are due to come forth,
but the strength to give birth is
lacking.†

<sup>4</sup> Perhaps the LORD, your God, will hear all the words of the commander, whom his lord, the king of Assyria, sent to taunt the living God, and will rebuke him for the words which the LORD, your God, has heard. So lift up a prayer for the remnant that is here." <sup>5</sup> When the servants of King Hezekiah had come to Isaiah, <sup>6</sup> he said to them, "Tell this to your lord: Thus

---

<sup>†</sup> **18:27** *Excrement…urine*: the reference is to the famine that results from a prolonged siege (compare 6:24–25; Dt 28:53–57). For public reading, ancient tradition (e.g., the Qere reading of the Masoretic text) softened the terms to "eat their own waste and drink their own bodies' water."
**18:34** *Did they indeed…power?*: some time after the fall of Samaria in 722/721 B.C., Hamath, Arpad, and other small states in the region formed an anti-Assyrian coalition. If the coalition

had succeeded, it could have broken Assyrian control over the whole region, including Samaria, and allowed the kingdom of Israel to free itself. When Assyria crushed the coalition, it also crushed Israel's hopes for liberation.
**19:3** See note on Is 37:3.

---

* **18:21** Is 30:1–7; 31:1–3; Ez 29:6–7.

**NEO-BABYLONIAN EMPIRE, ca. SIXTH CENTURY BCE**

☐ Extent of the Babylonian Empire, ca. 587 BCE
▦ Kingdom of Israel, fell in 721 BCE
▨ Kingdom of Judah, fell in 587 BCE

© 2013 ANSELM ACADEMIC

says the LORD: Do not be frightened by the words you have heard, by which the deputies of the king of Assyria have blasphemed me.* [7] I am putting in him such a spirit that when he hears a report he will return to his land. I will make him fall by the sword in his land."

[8] When the commander, on his return, heard that the king of Assyria had withdrawn from Lachish, he found him besieging Libnah.

**Sennacherib, Hezekiah, and Isaiah.** [9] The king of Assyria heard a report: "Tirhakah, king of Ethiopia, has come out to fight against you." Again he sent messengers to Hezekiah to say: [10] "Thus shall you say to Hezekiah, king of Judah: Do not let your God in whom you trust deceive you by saying, 'Jerusalem will not be handed over to the king of Assyria.' [11] You, certainly, have heard what the kings of Assyria have done to all the lands: they put them under the ban! And are you to be rescued? [12]* Did the gods of the nations whom my fathers destroyed deliver them—Gozan, Haran, Rezeph, or the Edenites in Telassar? [13] Where are the king of Hamath, the king of Arpad, or the kings of the cities Sepharvaim, Hena and Ivvah?"

[14] Hezekiah took the letter from the hand of the messengers and read it; then he went up to the house of the LORD, and spreading it out before the LORD, [15] Hezekiah prayed in the LORD's presence: "LORD, God of Israel, enthroned on the cherubim! You alone are God over all the kingdoms of the earth. It is you who made the heavens and the earth.* [16] Incline your ear, LORD, and listen! Open your eyes, LORD, and see! Hear the words Sennacherib has sent to taunt the living God. [17] Truly, O LORD, the kings of Assyria have laid waste the nations and their lands. [18] They gave their gods to the fire—they were not gods at all, but the work of human hands—wood and stone, they destroyed them. [19] Therefore, LORD, our God, save us from this man's power, that all the kingdoms of the earth may know that you alone, LORD, are God."*

[20] Then Isaiah, son of Amoz, sent this message to Hezekiah: "Thus says the LORD, the God of Israel, to whom you have prayed concerning Sennacherib, king of Assyria: I have listened! [21]† This is the word the LORD has spoken concerning him:

> She despises you, laughs you to scorn,
>   the virgin daughter Zion!
> Behind you she wags her head,
>   daughter Jerusalem.
> [22] Whom have you insulted and
>     blasphemed,
>   at whom have you raised your voice
> And lifted up your eyes on high?
>   At the Holy One of Israel!
> [23] Through the mouths of your messengers
>   you insulted the Lord when you said,
> 'With my many chariots I went up
>   to the tops of the peaks,
>   to the recesses of Lebanon,
> To cut down its lofty cedars,
>   its choice cypresses;
> I reached to the farthest shelter,
>   the forest ranges.
> [24] I myself dug wells
>   and drank foreign waters,
> Drying up all the rivers of Egypt
>   beneath the soles of my feet.'
> [25] "Have you not heard?
>   A long time ago I prepared it,
>   from days of old I planned it.
> Now I have brought it about:
> You are here to reduce
>   fortified cities to heaps of ruins,
> [26] Their people powerless,
>   dismayed and distraught.
> They are plants of the field,
>   green growth,
>   thatch on the rooftops,
> Grain scorched by the east wind.
> [27] I know when you stand or sit,
>   when you come or go*
>   and how you rage against me.
> [28] Because you rage against me,
>   and your smugness has reached my
>     ears,
> I will put my hook in your nose
>   and my bit in your mouth,
> And make you leave by the way you came.
> [29] "This shall be a sign for you:
> This year you shall eat the aftergrowth,
>   next year, what grows of itself;
> But in the third year, sow and reap,
>   plant vineyards and eat their fruit!

† **19:21–31** Verses 21–28 are addressed to Sennacherib, vv. 29–31 to Judah.

* **19:6** Is 10:5–14.    **19:12–13** 2 Kgs 17:6, 24; 18:34.    **19:15** Ex 25:17–22;    **19:19** 1 Kgs 18:36.    1 Kgs 6:23–28; 8:6–7.    **19:27** Ps 139:2–3.

30 The remaining survivors of the house of
    Judah
      shall again strike root below
      and bear fruit above.
31 For out of Jerusalem shall come a
    remnant,
      and from Mount Zion, survivors.
    The zeal of the LORD of hosts shall do
      this.

32 "Therefore, thus says the LORD about the king:

    He shall not come as far as this city,
      nor shoot there an arrow,
      nor confront it with a shield,
    Nor cast up a siege-work against it.
33 By the way he came he shall leave,
      never coming as far as this city,
      oracle of the LORD.
34 I will shield and save this city
      for my own sake and the sake of
        David my servant."*

35 That night the angel of the LORD went forth and struck down one hundred and eighty-five thousand men in the Assyrian camp. Early the next morning, there they were, dead, all those corpses!* 36 So Sennacherib, the king of Assyria, broke camp, departed, returned home, and stayed in Nineveh.

37 When he was worshiping in the temple of his god Nisroch, his sons Adrammelech and Sharezer struck him down with the sword and fled into the land of Ararat. His son Esarhaddon reigned in his place.

# 20 End of Hezekiah's Reign.

1* In those days, when Hezekiah was mortally ill, the prophet Isaiah, son of Amoz, came and said to him: "Thus says the LORD: Put your house in order, for you are about to die; you shall not recover." 2 He turned his face to the wall and prayed to the LORD: 3 "Ah, LORD, remember how faithfully and wholeheartedly I conducted myself in your presence, doing what was good in your sight!" And Hezekiah wept bitterly. 4 Before Isaiah had left the central courtyard, the word of the LORD came to

him: 5 Go back and tell Hezekiah, the leader of my people: "Thus says the LORD, the God of David your father:

    I have heard your prayer;
      I have seen your tears.
      Now I am healing you.
    On the third day you shall go up
      to the house of the LORD.
6 I will add to your life fifteen years.
    I will rescue you and this city
      from the hand of the king of Assyria;
    I will be a shield to this city
      for my own sake and the sake of
        David my servant."

7 Then Isaiah said, "Bring a poultice of figs and apply it to the boil for his recovery." 8 Hezekiah asked Isaiah, "What is the sign that the LORD will heal me and that I shall go up to the house of the LORD on the third day?" 9 Isaiah replied, "This will be the sign for you from the LORD that he will carry out the word he has spoken: Shall the shadow go forward or back ten steps?" 10 "It is easy for the shadow to advance ten steps," Hezekiah answered. "Rather, let it go back ten steps." 11 So Isaiah the prophet invoked the LORD. He made the shadow go back the ten steps it had descended on the staircase to the terrace of Ahaz.

12 At that time, Berodach-baladan,† son of Baladan, king of Babylon, sent letters and gifts to Hezekiah when he heard that he had been ill. 13 Hezekiah listened to the envoys and then showed off his whole treasury: his silver, gold, spices and perfumed oil, his armory, and everything in his storerooms; there was nothing in his house or in all his realm that Hezekiah did not show them. 14 Then Isaiah the prophet came to King Hezekiah and asked him: "What did these men say to you? Where did they come from?" Hezekiah replied, "They came from a distant land, from Babylon." 15 He asked, "What did they see in your house?" Hezekiah answered, "They saw everything in my house. There is nothing in my storerooms that I did not show them." 16 Then Isaiah said to Hezekiah: "Hear the word of the LORD: 17 The time is coming when all that is in your house, everything that

† **20:12** *Berodach-baladan*: this famous king's name is more correctly recorded in Is 39:1 as "Merodach-baladan." The Babylonian form, Marduk-apal-idinna, means "Marduk has granted a son." Historically, any embassy from him to Hezekiah must have been

aimed at establishing an anti-Assyrian strategy of cooperation.

\*                                
**19:34** 2 Sm 7:12.            2 Mc 8:19.
**19:35** 1 Mc 7:41;          **20:1–11** Sir 48:23.

your ancestors have stored up until this day, shall be carried off to Babylon; nothing shall be left, says the LORD. [18] Some of your own descendants, your offspring, your progeny, shall be taken and made attendants in the palace of the king of Babylon." [19] Hezekiah replied to Isaiah, "The word of the LORD which you have spoken is good." For he thought, "There will be peace and stability in my lifetime."

[20] The rest of the acts of Hezekiah, with all his valor, and how he constructed the pool and conduit† and brought water into the city, are recorded in the book of the chronicles of the kings of Judah.* [21] Hezekiah rested with his ancestors, and his son Manasseh succeeded him as king.

## 21 Reign of Manasseh.

[1] Manasseh was twelve years old when he became king, and he reigned fifty-five years in Jerusalem. His mother's name was Hephzibah.

[2] He did what was evil in the LORD's sight, following the abominable practices of the nations whom the LORD had dispossessed before the Israelites. [3] He rebuilt the high places which Hezekiah his father had destroyed. He set up altars to Baal and also made an asherah, as Ahab, king of Israel, had done. He bowed down to the whole host of heaven and served them.* [4] He built altars in the house of the LORD, of which the LORD had said: In Jerusalem I will set my name. [5] And he built altars for the whole host of heaven in the two courts of the house of the LORD. [6] He immolated his child by fire. He practiced soothsaying and divination, and reintroduced the consulting of ghosts and spirits.

He did much evil in the LORD's sight and provoked him to anger.* [7] The Asherah idol he had made, he placed in the LORD's house, of which the LORD had said to David and to his son Solomon: In this house and in Jerusalem, which I have chosen out of all the tribes of Israel, I shall set my name forever.* [8] I will no longer make Israel step out of the land I gave their ancestors, provided that they are careful to observe all I have commanded them and the entire law which Moses my servant enjoined upon them. [9] But they did not listen.

Manasseh misled them into doing even greater evil than the nations the LORD had destroyed at the coming of the Israelites. [10] Then the LORD spoke through his servants the prophets: [11] "Because Manasseh, king of Judah, has practiced these abominations, and has done greater evil than all that was done by the Amorites before him, and has led Judah into sin by his idols,* [12] therefore, thus says the LORD, the God of Israel: I am about to bring such evil on Jerusalem and Judah that, when any hear of it, their ears shall ring: [13] I will measure Jerusalem with the same cord as I did Samaria, and with the plummet I used for the house of Ahab. I will wipe Jerusalem clean as one wipes a dish, wiping it inside and out.* [14] I will cast off the survivors of my inheritance. I will deliver them into enemy hands, to become prey and booty for all their enemies, [15] because they have done what is evil in my sight and provoked me from the day their ancestors came forth from Egypt until this very day." [16] Manasseh shed so much innocent blood that it filled the length and breadth of Jerusalem, in addition to the sin he caused Judah to commit by doing what was evil in the LORD's sight.

[17] The rest of the acts of Manasseh, with all that he did and the sin he committed, are recorded in the book of the chronicles of the kings of Judah. [18] Manasseh rested with his ancestors; he was buried in his palace garden, the garden of Uzza, and his son Amon succeeded him as king.

**Reign of Amon.** [19] Amon was twenty-two years old when he became king, and he reigned two years in Jerusalem. His mother's name was Meshullemeth, daughter of Haruz, from Jotbah.

[20] He did what was evil in the LORD's sight, as his father Manasseh had done. [21] He walked in all the ways of his father; he served the idols his father had served, and bowed down to them. [22] He abandoned the LORD, the God of his ancestors, and did not walk in the way of the LORD.

[23] Officials of Amon plotted against him and killed the king in his palace, [24] but the people of the land† then slew all who had plotted

---

† **20:20** *Pool and conduit:* Hezekiah's tunnel is described in more detail in 2 Chr 32:30.
**21:24** *People of the land:* see note on 11:14.

* **20:20** Sir 48:17.
**21:3** 2 Kgs 17:16; 1 Kgs 16:31–33.
**21:6** Lv 18:21; 19:26; Dt 18:10–14; 1 Sm 28:3.
**21:7** 2 Sm 7:13; 1 Kgs 8:16; 9:3.
**21:11** Jer 15:4.
**21:13** Is 34:11; Lam 2:8; Am 7:7–9.

against King Amon, and the people of the land made his son Josiah king in his stead. ²⁵ The rest of the acts of Amon, which he did, are recorded in the book of the chronicles of the kings of Judah. ²⁶ He was buried in his own grave in the garden of Uzza, and his son Josiah succeeded him as king.

# 22
**Reign of Josiah.** ¹ Josiah was eight years old when he became king, and he reigned thirty-one years in Jerusalem. His mother's name was Jedidah, daughter of Adaiah, from Bozkath.

² He did what was right in the LORD's sight, walking in the way of David his father, not turning right or left.

**The Book of the Law.** ³ * In his eighteenth year, King Josiah sent the scribe Shaphan,† son of Azaliah, son of Meshullam, to the house of the LORD with these orders: ⁴ "Go to the high priest Hilkiah and have him calculate the valuables that have been brought to the house of the LORD, which the doorkeepers have collected from the people. ⁵ Then have him turn them over to the master workers in the house of the LORD, and have them give them to the ordinary workers who are in the house of the LORD to repair its breaches: ⁶ to the carpenters, the builders, and the masons, and to purchase wood and hewn stone. ⁷ No reckoning shall be asked of them regarding the funds provided to them, because they hold positions of trust."

⁸ The high priest Hilkiah informed the scribe Shaphan, "I have found the book of the law† in the temple of the LORD." Hilkiah gave the book to Shaphan, who read it. ⁹ Then the scribe Shaphan went to the king and reported, "Your servants have smelted down the silver deposited in the temple and have turned it over to the master workers in the house of the LORD." ¹⁰ The scribe Shaphan also informed the king, "Hilkiah the priest has given me a book," and then Shaphan read it in the presence of the king. ¹¹ When the king heard the words of the book of the law, he tore his garments.

¹² The king then issued this command to Hilkiah the priest, Ahikam, son of Shaphan, Achbor, son of Micaiah, Shaphan the scribe, and Asaiah the king's servant: ¹³ "Go, consult the LORD for me, for the people, and for all Judah, about the words of this book that has been found, for the rage of the LORD has been set furiously ablaze against us, because our ancestors did not obey the words of this book, nor do what is written for us." ¹⁴ So Hilkiah the priest, Ahikam, Achbor, Shaphan, and Asaiah went to Huldah the prophet, wife of Shallum, son of Tikvah, son of Harhas, keeper of the wardrobe; she lived in Jerusalem, in the Second Quarter. When they had spoken to her, ¹⁵ she said to them, "Thus says the LORD, the God of Israel: Say to the man who sent you to me, ¹⁶ Thus says the LORD: I am about to bring evil upon this place and upon its inhabitants—all the words of the book which the king of Judah has read. ¹⁷ Because they have abandoned me and have burned incense to other gods, provoking me by all the works of their hands, my rage is ablaze against this place and it cannot be extinguished.

¹⁸ "But to the king of Judah who sent you to consult the LORD, give this response: Thus says the LORD, the God of Israel: As for the words you have heard, ¹⁹ because you were heartsick and have humbled yourself before the LORD when you heard what I have spoken concerning this place and its inhabitants, that they would become a desolation and a curse; and because you tore your garments and wept before me, I in turn have heard, oracle of the LORD. ²⁰ I will therefore gather you to your ancestors; you shall go to your grave in peace, and your eyes shall not see all the evil I am about to bring upon this place." This they reported to the king.

# 23
¹ The king then had all the elders of Judah and of Jerusalem summoned before him. ² The king went up to the house of the LORD with all the people of Judah and all the inhabitants of Jerusalem: priests, prophets, and all the people, great and small. He read aloud to them all the words of the book of the covenant that had been found in the house of the LORD. * ³ The king stood by the column and made a covenant in the presence of the

---

† **22:3** *Shaphan:* head of a prominent family in the reign of Josiah, secretary to the king, bearer and reader of the newly found book of the law (vv. 3–13; 25:22). He and his sons favored the reform of King Josiah and supported the prophet Jeremiah; cf. Jer 26:24; 29:1–3; 36:10–12; 39:14.

**22:8** *Book of the law:* probably an early edition of material now found in the Book of Deuteronomy.

● ————————

**22:3–7** 2 Kgs 12:11–16.      **23:2** Dt 17:18–19.

LORD to follow the LORD and to observe his commandments, statutes, and decrees with his whole heart and soul, and to re-establish the words of the covenant written in this book. And all the people stood by the covenant.

**Josiah's Religious Reform.** 4 Then the king commanded the high priest Hilkiah, his assistant priests, and the doorkeepers to remove from the temple of the LORD all the objects that had been made for Baal, Asherah, and the whole host of heaven. These he burned outside Jerusalem on the slopes of the Kidron; their ashes were carried to Bethel. * 5 He also put an end to the idolatrous priests whom the kings of Judah had appointed to burn incense on the high places in the cities of Judah and in the vicinity of Jerusalem, as well as those who burned incense to Baal, to the sun, moon, and signs of the zodiac, and to the whole host of heaven. * 6 From the house of the LORD he also removed the Asherah to the Wadi Kidron, outside Jerusalem; he burned it and beat it to dust, in the Wadi Kidron, and scattered its dust over the graveyard of the people of the land. † * 7 He tore down the apartments of the cult prostitutes in the house of the LORD, where the women wove garments for the Asherah. * 8 He brought in all the priests from the cities of Judah, and then defiled, from Geba to Beersheba, the high places where they had offered incense. He also tore down the high places of the gates, which were at the entrance of the Gate of Joshua, governor of the city, north of the city gate. 9 (The priests of the high places could not function at the altar of the LORD in Jerusalem; but they, along with their relatives, ate the unleavened bread.)

10 The king also defiled Topheth in the Valley of Ben-hinnom, so that there would no longer be any immolation of sons or daughters by fire † in honor of Molech. * 11 He did away with the horses which the kings of Judah had dedicated to the sun; these were at the entrance of the house of the LORD, near the chamber of Nathan-melech the official, which was in the large building. The chariots of the sun he destroyed by fire. 12 He also demolished the altars made by the kings of Judah on the roof (the roof terrace of Ahaz), and the altars made by Manasseh in the two courts of the LORD's house. He pulverized them and threw the dust into the Wadi Kidron. * 13 The king defiled the high places east of Jerusalem, south of the Mount of the Destroyer, † which Solomon, king of Israel, had built in honor of Astarte, the Sidonian horror, of Chemosh, the Moabite horror, and of Milcom, the Ammonites' abomination. * 14 He broke to pieces the pillars, cut down the asherahs, and filled the places where they had been with human bones. *

15 Likewise the altar which was at Bethel, the high place built by Jeroboam, son of Nebat, who caused Israel to sin—this same altar and high place he tore down and burned, grinding the high place to powder and burning the asherah. * 16 When Josiah turned and saw the graves there on the mountainside, he ordered the bones taken from the graves and burned on the altar, and thus defiled it, according to the LORD's word proclaimed by the man of God as Jeroboam stood by the altar on the feast day. When the king looked up and saw the grave of the man of God who had proclaimed these words, 17 he asked, "What is that marker I see?" The people of the city replied, "The grave of the man of God who came from Judah and proclaimed the very things you have done to the altar in Bethel." 18 "Let him be," he said, "let no one move his bones." So they left his bones undisturbed together with the bones of the prophet who had come from Samaria. † 19 Josiah also removed all the temples on the high places in the cities of Samaria

---

† **23:6** *People of the land:* see note on 11:14.

**23:10** *Topheth…by fire:* Topheth was a cultic site probably in the Hinnom Valley just west of Jerusalem where, apparently, children were immolated to the deity Molech (Hebrew *melek,* "king," deformed in the biblical tradition to "Molech"). The practice was condemned by Deuteronomic law and denounced by Jeremiah (Dt 12:31; Jer 7:29–31). In Jer 19 the deity is identified as the Canaanite god Baal.

**23:13** *Mount of the Destroyer:* the name of the mountain in Hebrew is a wordplay. "The Mount of the *mashchit*" means "the Mount of the Destroyer" or perhaps "the Mount of Destruction." The word plays on *mishchah,* "anointment," and on *mashiach,* "anointed one," both of which are references to the ceremony that consecrated the king. The mountain in question was the Mount of Olives, whose trees produced oil for the royal anoint-

ing. In the present context, both sides of the wordplay allude to Solomon, the anointed king (*mashiach*), whose building of non-Yahwistic shrines on this very mountain resulted in the destruction (*mashchit*) of the Davidic realm (see 1 Kgs 11:4–13). *Horror…abomination:* all three idols are described with pejorative terms.

**23:18** *From Samaria:* an anachronistic use of the name of the later capital city for the whole region. The prophet was from Bethel; cf. 1 Kgs 13:11.

| | |
|---|---|
| **23:4** Sir 49:3. | **23:12** 2 Kgs 20:11; 21:5. |
| **23:5** Dt 4:19; 17:2–7. | **23:13** 1 Kgs 11:4–8. |
| **23:6** Dt 16:21. | **23:14** Dt 16:21; 1 Kgs |
| **23:7** Dt 23:18–19. |      14:23. |
| **23:10** Lv 18:21; Dt | **23:15–20** 1 Kgs 12:26–13:34. |
|      18:10–12. | |

which the kings of Israel had built, provoking the LORD; he did the very same to them as he had done in Bethel. [20] He slaughtered upon the altars all the priests of the high places that were there, and burned human bones upon them. Then he returned to Jerusalem.

[21] The king issued a command to all the people: "Observe the Passover of the LORD, your God, as it is written in this book of the covenant."* [22] No Passover such as this had been observed during the period when the judges ruled Israel, or during the entire period of the kings of Israel and the kings of Judah, [23] until the eighteenth year of King Josiah, when this Passover of the LORD was kept in Jerusalem.

[24] Further, Josiah purged the consultation of ghosts and spirits, with the household gods, idols,† and all the other horrors to be seen in the land of Judah and in Jerusalem, so that he might carry out the words of the law that were written in the book that Hilkiah the priest had found in the house of the LORD.*

[25] Before him there had been no king who turned to the LORD as he did, with his whole heart, his whole being, and his whole strength, in accord with the entire law of Moses; nor did any king like him arise after him.* [26] Yet the LORD did not turn from his fiercely burning anger against Judah, because of all the provocations that Manasseh had given. [27] The LORD said: Even Judah will I put out of my sight as I did Israel. I will reject this city, Jerusalem, which I chose, and the house of which I said: There shall my name be.

[28] The rest of the acts of Josiah, with all that he did, are recorded in the book of the chronicles of the kings of Judah. [29] In his time Pharaoh Neco, king of Egypt, went up toward the Euphrates River against the king of Assyria.† King Josiah set out to meet him, but was slain at Megiddo at the first encounter. [30] His servants brought his body on a chariot from Megiddo to Jerusalem, where they buried him in his own grave. Then the people of the land took Jehoahaz, son of Josiah, anointed him, and proclaimed him king to succeed his father.

**Reign of Jehoahaz.** [31] Jehoahaz was twenty-three years old when he became king, and he reigned three months in Jerusalem. His mother's name was Hamutal, daughter of Jeremiah, from Libnah.*

[32] He did what was evil in the LORD's sight, just as his ancestors had done. [33] Pharaoh Neco took him prisoner at Riblah in the land of Hamath, thus ending his reign in Jerusalem. He imposed a fine upon the land of a hundred talents of silver and a talent of gold.† [34] Pharaoh Neco then made Eliakim, son of Josiah, king in place of Josiah his father; he changed his name to Jehoiakim. Jehoahaz he took away with him to Egypt, where he died. [35] Jehoiakim gave the silver and gold to Pharaoh, but taxed the land to raise the amount Pharaoh demanded. He exacted the silver and gold from the people of the land, from each proportionately, to pay Pharaoh Neco.

**Reign of Jehoiakim.** [36] Jehoiakim was twenty-five years old when he became king, and he reigned eleven years in Jerusalem. His mother's name was Zebidah, daughter of Pedaiah, from Rumah.

[37] He did what was evil in the LORD's sight, just as his ancestors had done.

# 24

[1] During Jehoiakim's reign Nebuchadnezzar, king of Babylon, attacked, and Jehoiakim became his vassal for three years. Then Jehoiakim turned and rebelled against him. [2] The LORD loosed against him bands of Chaldeans, Arameans, Moabites, and Ammonites; he unleashed them against Judah to destroy him, according to the LORD's word spoken through his servants the prophets. [3] This befell Judah because the LORD had stated that he would put them out of his sight for the sins Manasseh had committed in all that he did, [4] and especially because of the innocent blood he shed; he filled Jerusalem with innocent blood, and the LORD would not forgive.*

[5] The rest of the acts of Jehoiakim, with all that he did, are recorded in the book of the

---

23:24 *Household gods, idols*: teraphim. See note on Gn 31:19.

23:29 *Against the king of Assyria*: the narrator depicts Neco's advance as an attack on Assyrian forces. The Babylonian record of the event, however, implies that Neco intended to support the remnant of Assyrian forces against a Babylonian onslaught in order to prop up a buffer state between Egypt and Babylon and assure Egyptian control of the Syro-Palestinian region.

23:33 *A talent of gold*: unless the fine imposed was a mere token, this figure seems too low; cf. 18:14. A number may have dropped from the Hebrew text; various ancient translations read "ten" or "one hundred" here.

23:21 Dt 16:1–8.
23:24 2 Kgs 21:6; Gn 31:19; Dt 18:10–14; Jgs 18:14.
23:25 Dt 6:5; Sir 49:1–3.
23:31 2 Kgs 24:18.
24:4 2 Kgs 21:16.

chronicles of the kings of Judah. [6] Jehoiakim rested with his ancestors, and his son Jehoiachin succeeded him as king. [7] The king of Egypt did not again leave his own land, for the king of Babylon had taken all that belonged to the king of Egypt from the wadi of Egypt to the Euphrates River.

**Reign of Jehoiachin.** [8] Jehoiachin was eighteen years old when he became king, and he reigned three months in Jerusalem. His mother's name was Nehushta, daughter of Elnathan, from Jerusalem.

[9] He did what was evil in the Lord's sight, just as his father had done.

[10]* At that time officers of Nebuchadnezzar, king of Babylon, attacked Jerusalem, and the city came under siege. [11] Nebuchadnezzar, king of Babylon, himself arrived at the city while his officers were besieging it. [12] Then Jehoiachin, king of Judah, together with his mother, his ministers, officers, and functionaries, surrendered to the king of Babylon, who, in the eighth year of his reign,[†] took him captive. [13] He carried off all the treasures of the house of the Lord and the treasures of the king's house, and broke up all the gold utensils that Solomon, king of Israel, had provided in the house of the Lord, as the Lord had decreed.* [14] He deported all Jerusalem: all the officers and warriors of the army, ten thousand in number, and all the artisans and smiths. Only the lowliest of the people of the land[†] were left. [15] He deported Jehoiachin to Babylon, and the king's mother, his wives, his functionaries, and the chiefs of the land he led captive from Jerusalem to Babylon.* [16] All seven thousand soldiers of the army, and a thousand artisans and smiths, all of them trained warriors, these too the king of Babylon brought captive to Babylon. [17] In place of Jehoiachin the king of Babylon made Mattaniah, Jehoiachin's uncle, king; he changed his name to Zedekiah.*

**Reign of Zedekiah.** [18]† Zedekiah was twenty-one years old when he became king, and he reigned eleven years in Jerusalem. His mother's name was Hamutal, daughter of Jeremiah, from Libnah.*

[19] He did what was evil in the sight of the Lord, just as Jehoiakim had done. [20] This befell Jerusalem and Judah because the Lord was so angry that he cast them out of his sight.

Zedekiah rebelled against the king of Babylon.

# 25

[1] In the tenth month of the ninth year of Zedekiah's reign, on the tenth day of the month, Nebuchadnezzar, king of Babylon, and his whole army advanced against Jerusalem, encamped around it, and built siege walls on every side. [2] The siege of the city continued until the eleventh year of Zedekiah. [3] On the ninth day of the month,[†] when famine had gripped the city, and the people of the land had no more food, [4] the city walls were breached. That night, all the soldiers came to the gate between the two walls near the king's garden (the Chaldeans had the city surrounded), while the king went toward the Arabah.[†] [5] But the Chaldean army pursued the king and overtook him in the desert near Jericho, abandoned by his whole army. [6] The king was therefore arrested and brought to Riblah to the king of Babylon, who pronounced sentence on him. [7] They slew Zedekiah's sons before his eyes; then they put out his eyes, bound him with fetters, and brought him to Babylon.

[8] On the seventh day of the fifth month (this was in the nineteenth year of Nebuchadnezzar, king of Babylon), Nebuzaradan, captain of the bodyguard, came to Jerusalem as the agent of the king of Babylon. [9] He burned the house of the Lord, the house of the king, and all the houses of Jerusalem (every noble house); he destroyed them by fire.* [10] The Chaldean troops who were with the captain of the guard tore down the walls that surrounded Jerusalem, [11] and Nebuzaradan, captain of the guard, led into exile the last of the army remaining in the city, and those

---

[†] **24:12** *The eighth year of his reign:* that is, of Nebuchadnezzar's reign, not Jehoiachin's. The year was 597 B.C.

**24:14** *People of the land:* see note on 11:14.

**24:18–25:30** Much of this material closely parallels Jer 52; some of the events are also recounted in Jer 39.

**25:3** *Ninth day of the month:* the text does not say which month; but Jer 39:2 and 52:6 set the breaching of the city walls in the fourth month; in later times that was the date of a fast commemorating the event (cf. Zec 8:19). *People of the land:*

the influential citizens (see note on 11:14); even they, whose resources went beyond those of the ordinary people, were starving.

**25:4** The Hebrew text of this verse is missing some words. The present translation is based on a likely reconstruction.

---

**24:10–17** Dn 1:1–2.　　　**24:17** Jer 37:1.
**24:13** 2 Kgs 20:17.　　**24:18** 2 Kgs 23:31.
**24:15** Est A:3; 2:6.　　**25:9** Ps 74:2–7.

who had deserted† to the king of Babylon, and the last of the commoners. ¹²But some of the country's poor the captain of the guard left behind as vinedressers and farmers.

¹³The bronze columns that belonged to the house of the LORD, and the stands and the bronze sea in the house of the LORD, the Chaldeans broke into pieces; they carried away the bronze to Babylon.* ¹⁴They took also the pots, the shovels, the snuffers, the cups and all the bronze articles used for service.* ¹⁵The fire pans and the bowls that were of solid gold or silver the captain of the guard also carried off.* ¹⁶The two columns, the one bronze sea, and the stands, which Solomon had made for the house of the LORD—the weight in bronze of all these articles was never calculated.* ¹⁷Each of the columns was eighteen cubits high; a bronze capital three cubits high surmounted each column, and a netting with pomegranates encircled the capital, all of bronze; and they were duplicated on the other column, on the netting.*

¹⁸The captain of the guard also took Seraiah, the chief priest, Zephaniah, an assistant priest, and the three doorkeepers. ¹⁹And from the city he took one officer who was a commander of soldiers, five courtiers in the personal service of the king who were still in the city, the scribe in charge of the army who mustered the people of the land,† and sixty of the people of the land still remaining in the city. ²⁰The captain of the guard, Nebuzaradan, arrested these and brought them to the king of Babylon at Riblah, and ²¹the king of Babylon struck them down and put them to death in Riblah, in the land of Hamath. And thus Judah went into exile from their native soil.

**Governorship of Gedaliah.** ²²*As for the people whom he had allowed to remain in the land of Judah, Nebuchadnezzar, king of Babylon, appointed Gedaliah, son of Ahikam, son of Shaphan, over them. ²³Hearing that the king of Babylon had appointed Gedaliah over them, all the army commanders and the troops came to him at Mizpah: Ishmael, son of Nethaniah, Johanan, son of Kareah, Seraiah, son of Tanhumeth the Netophathite, and Jaazaniah, son of the Maakite, each with his troops. ²⁴Gedaliah gave the commanders and their troops his oath. He said to them, "Do not be afraid of the Chaldean officials. Remain in the country and serve the king of Babylon, so that all will be well with you."

²⁵But in the seventh month Ishmael, son of Nethaniah, son of Elishama, of royal descent, came with ten others, attacked Gedaliah and killed him, along with the Judahites and Chaldeans who were in Mizpah with him. ²⁶Then all the people, great and small, left with the army commanders and went to Egypt for fear of the Chaldeans.

**Release of Jehoiachin.** ²⁷In the thirty-seventh year of the exile of Jehoiachin, king of Judah, on the twenty-seventh day of the twelfth month, Evil-merodach, king of Babylon, in the inaugural year of his own reign, raised up Jehoiachin, king of Judah, from prison. ²⁸He spoke kindly to him and gave him a throne higher than that of the other kings who were with him in Babylon. ²⁹Jehoiachin took off his prison garb; he ate regularly in the king's presence as long as he lived; ³⁰and for his allowance the king granted him a regular allowance, in fixed daily amounts, for as long as he lived.

---

**25:11** *Those who had deserted*: perhaps on the advice of Jeremiah; cf. Jer 38:2–3.

**25:19** *People of the land*: see note on 11:14.

| | |
|---|---|
| **25:13** 2 Kgs 16:17; 1 Kgs 7:15–39; Jer 27:19–23. | **25:16** 1 Kgs 7:47. |
| **25:14** 1 Kgs 7:40–45. | **25:17** 1 Kgs 7:15–20; Jer 52:21–23. |
| **25:15** 1 Kgs 7:50. | **25:22–26** Jer 40:7–41:18. |

# The First Book of

# Chronicles

## INTRODUCTION

### Leslie J. Hoppe, OFM

The two books of Chronicles were originally a single literary work. The Septuagint (an ancient Greek translation of the Jewish Scriptures) was responsible for the division into two books. Chronicles has also been known under several names. The rabbis called this work "The Book of the Events of the Days." The Septuagint called these books "Paraleipomenon," meaning "that which was left out"—presumably from the books of Samuel and Kings. Jerome gave Chronicles an imposing title: "The Chronicle of the Entire Divine History." The English title of this work reflects that given by Luther in his German translation.

Though the bulk of Chronicles tells the story of ancient Israel from the time of David to the end of the exile, it is not a history in the contemporary sense of the word nor is it a dry chronicle of events. It is a theological work in narrative form that begins with Adam and ends with the decree of Cyrus, calling upon the Babylonian exiles to return to Jerusalem and rebuild the Temple.

The position of Chronicles in English Bibles after 2 Kings reflects the Septuagint's ordering of books. In the Hebrew Bible, 1–2 Chronicles end the collection of books. The final verse of 2 Chronicles, with its call to return to Jerusalem, helped maintain the attachment of Jews to the Holy City through the millennia of their dispersion.

Chronicles is likely the product of an individual author living in the fourth century BCE though there were additions to his work so the final form of the book comes from a later period—perhaps as late at the second century BCE. By the time Chronicles was written most of the books of the Hebrew Bible existed in the form we now have them. Certainly the author was influenced by the theological perspectives of these books while formulating

## Outline of 1 Chronicles

his own unique understanding of the meaning of ancient Israel's experience. The way the Chronicler handles earlier tradition shows how he adapted and reformulated that tradition in order to speak to new circumstances.

The first nine chapters of 1 Chronicles consist mostly of genealogies. These genealogies begin with Adam and conclude with the descendants of Saul. While 1 Chr 1–9 has some genealogical material unique to it, these chapters show connections with Genesis, Exodus, Numbers, Joshua, Samuel, and Ruth, reflecting similar traditions and perhaps actual reliance on these traditions. The story of Saul in 1 Chr 10 is much shorter than that found in 1 Samuel and serves merely to introduce the story of David, who is the focus of the rest of 1 Chronicles.

The unique portrait of David found in Chronicles points to the book's central concern: the Temple, its rituals, and its personnel. Chronicles reflects the belief that the Temple was the institution that should occupy the center of Judah's life. To communicate this message Chronicles has the Temple as the object of all David's activity. David brings the ark to Jerusalem, prepares for the building of the Temple, organizes the Temple's personnel, instructs Solomon to build the Temple, and provides for precious metals and stones to be used in adorning the structure.

At the time Chronicles was written, faith in Judah's future was at a low point. Judah was a minor subprovince of the Persian Empire. The national state and native dynasty were no more and it was highly unlikely that the Davidic dynasty would again rule in Judah. While the people of Judah were able to live according to their ancestral traditions, their economy was hurt by heavy taxation. The Temple was a modest structure and its priests and Levites did not attract much popular support. The people of Judah wondered about prospects for the future. Chronicles affirms that a revived, rejuvenated Temple cultus was the only way that Judah could secure its future. David is presented as a model for the people of Judah to emulate. If they would only do in their day what David did in his, they would enjoy God's blessing.

Though the books of Samuel and Kings are sources for Chronicles, there are some discrepancies between them. This is most obvious in the portrait of David found in 2 Samuel and 1 Chronicles. While 2 Samuel does not hesitate to describe David's moral failures as well as his virtues, 1 Chronicles does not include any material that may detract from the positive portrait of the king that is crucial to the book's intention to present David as someone for the people of Judah to emulate—especially in his devotion to the worship of Yahweh.

The riveting focus that Chronicles has on the proper worship of Yahweh in the Temple of Jerusalem, presided over by proper priests and Levites, leads the book to ignore traditions that

are very important in other biblical literature. For example, Chronicles makes no mention of or even allusion to the Exodus, to the theophany at Sinai, or to the settlement of the Israelites in the land of Canaan. For Chronicles, Judah's relationship with its ancestral deity has its foundation in the Temple cultus. To locate Judah's self-identification elsewhere is a serious miscalculation. To focus on the issue of the historical value of the narrative in Chronicles, then, is to miss the point that Chronicles attempts to make.

For Chronicles, the issue is not historical reconstruction of Judah's past. Chronicles is essentially oriented toward the future. It assures its readers that they have a future despite the dismal political and economic prospects Judah appears to have. The Temple is Judah's key to securing its future. If the Jews who live in the Diaspora would only return to Jerusalem and join those Jews who live in Judah in worshiping the God of their ancestors in the Temple led by the priests and Levites that God had chosen and David arranged in their ranks, there would be no question about Judah's future. While the voice of Chronicles was not the only one to be heard in fourth-century Judah, it provided important direction to a discouraged and conquered people. It helped Jews and Judaism to survive when other ancient peoples and their religious traditions disappeared into the pages of history. ■

# THE FIRST BOOK OF CHRONICLES

## New American Bible, Introduction

The Greek title, *paraleipomena*, means "things omitted," or "passed over" (i.e., in the accounts found in Samuel and Kings). The Books of Chronicles, however, are much more than a supplement to Samuel and Kings; a comparison of the two histories discloses striking differences of scope and purpose. The Books of Chronicles record in some detail the lengthy span (some five hundred fifty years) from the death of King Saul to the return from the exile. Unlike today's history writing, wherein factual accuracy and impartiality of judgment are the norm, biblical history, with rare exceptions, was less concerned with reporting in precise detail all the facts of a situation than with drawing out the meaning of those facts. Biblical history was thus primarily interpretative, and its purpose was to disclose the action of the living God in human affairs. For this reason we speak of it as "sacred history."

These characteristics are apparent when we examine the primary objective of the Chronicler (the conventional designation for the anonymous author) in compiling his work. Given the situation which confronted the Jewish people at this time (the end of the fifth century B.C.), the Chronicler realized that Israel's political greatness was a thing of the past. Yet, for the Chronicler, Israel's past held the key to the people's future. In particular, the Chronicler aimed to establish and defend the legitimate claims of the Davidic monarchy in Israel's history, and to underscore the status of Jerusalem and its divinely established Temple worship as the center of religious life for the Jewish

people. If Judaism was to survive and prosper, it would have to heed the lessons of the past and devoutly serve its God in the place where he had chosen to dwell, the Temple in Jerusalem. From the Chronicler's point of view, the reigns of David and Solomon were the ideal to which all subsequent rule in Judah must aspire. The Chronicler was much more interested in David's religious and cultic influence than in his political power, however. He saw David's (and Solomon's) primary importance as deriving rather from their roles in the establishment of Jerusalem and its Temple as the center of the true worship of the Lord. Furthermore, he presents David as the one who prescribed the Temple's elaborate ritual (which, in point of fact, only gradually evolved in the Second Temple period) and who appointed the Levites to supervise the liturgical services there.

The Chronicler used a variety of sources in writing his history. Besides the canonical Books of Genesis, Exodus, Numbers, Joshua, and Ruth, and especially the Books of Samuel and Kings (specifically 1 Sm 31–2 Kings 25), he cites the titles of many other works which have not come down to us, e.g., "The Books of the Kings of Israel," or "The Books of the Kings of Israel and Judah," and "The History of Gad the Seer." In addition, the Chronicler's work contains early preexilic material not found in the Books of Kings.

The principal divisions of 1 Chronicles are as follows:

   I. Genealogical Tables (1:1–9:34)
   II. The History of David (9:35–29:30) ∎

# FIRST CHRONICLES

## I. GENEALOGICAL TABLES†

**1** **From Adam to Abraham.** ¹Adam, Seth, Enosh,* ²Kenan, Mahalalel, Jared,* ³Enoch, Methuselah, Lamech,* ⁴Noah, Shem, Ham, and Japheth.* ⁵The sons of Japheth were Gomer, Magog, Madai, Javan, Tubal, Meshech, and Tiras.* ⁶The sons of Gomer were Ashkenaz, Riphath, and Togarmah. ⁷The sons of Javan were Elishah, Tarshish, the Kittim, and the Rodanim.

⁸The sons of Ham were Cush, Mizraim, Put, and Canaan. ⁹The sons of Cush were Seba, Havilah, Sabta, Raama, and Sabteca. The sons of Raama were Sheba and Dedan. ¹⁰Cush became the father of Nimrod, who was the first to be a warrior on the earth.* ¹¹*Mizraim became the father of the Ludim, Anamim, Lehabim, Naphtuhim, ¹²Pathrusim, Casluhim, and Caphtorim, from whom the Philistines sprang. ¹³Canaan became the father of Sidon, his firstborn, and Heth, ¹⁴and the Jebusites, the Amorites, the Girgashites, ¹⁵the Hivites, the Arkites, the Sinites, ¹⁶the Arvadites, the Zemarites, and the Hamathites.

¹⁷*The sons of Shem were Elam, Asshur, Arpachshad, Lud, and Aram. The sons of Aram were Uz, Hul, Gether, and Mash. ¹⁸Arpachshad became the father of Shelah, and Shelah became the father of Eber. ¹⁹Two sons were born to Eber; the first was named Peleg (for in his time the world was divided),† and his brother was named Joktan. ²⁰Joktan became the father of Almodad, Sheleph, Hazarmaveth, Jerah, ²¹Hadoram, Uzal, Diklah, ²²Ebal, Abimael, Sheba, ²³Ophir, Havilah, and Jobab; all these were the sons of Joktan.

²⁴*Shem, Arpachshad, Shelah, ²⁵Eber, Peleg, Reu, ²⁶Serug, Nahor, Terah, ²⁷Abram, that is, Abraham.*

**From Abraham to Jacob.** ²⁸The sons of Abraham were Isaac and Ishmael.* ²⁹These were their generations:

Nebaioth, the firstborn of Ishmael, then Kedar, Adbeel, Mibsam, ³⁰Mishma, Dumah, Massa, Hadad, Tema, ³¹Jetur, Naphish, and Kedemah. These were the sons of Ishmael.*

³²The sons of Keturah, Abraham's concubine: she bore Zimran, Jokshan, Medan, Midian, Ishbak, and Shuah. The sons of Jokshan were Sheba and Dedan. ³³The sons of Midian were Ephah, Epher, Hanoch, Abida, and Eldaah. All these were the sons of Keturah.*

³⁴Abraham begot Isaac. The sons of Isaac were Esau and Israel.*

³⁵The descendants of Esau were Eliphaz, Reuel, Jeush, Jalam, and Korah. ³⁶The descendants of Eliphaz were Teman, Omar, Zephi, Gatam, Kenaz, Timna, and Amalek. ³⁷The descendants of Reuel were Nahath, Zerah, Shammah, and Mizzah.*

³⁸The sons of Seir† were Lotan, Shobal, Zibeon, Anah, Dishon, Ezer, and Dishan. ³⁹The sons of Lotan were Hori and Homam; Timna was the sister of Lotan. ⁴⁰The sons of Shobal were Alian, Manahath, Ebal, Shephi, and Onam. The sons of Zibeon were Aiah and Anah. ⁴¹The sons of Anah: Dishon. The sons of Dishon were Hemdan, Eshban, Ithran, and Cheran. ⁴²The sons of Ezer were Bilhan, Zaavan, and Jaakan. The sons of Dishan were Uz and Aran.*

⁴³*The kings who reigned in the land of Edom before the Israelites had kings were the following: Bela, son of Beor, the name of whose city was Dinhabah. ⁴⁴When Bela died, Jobab, son of Zerah, from Bozrah, succeeded him as king.* ⁴⁵When Jobab died, Husham, from the land of the Temanites, succeeded him as king.* ⁴⁶Husham died and Hadad, son of

---

† **1:1–9:34** The Chronicler's intention seems to have been to retell, from his particular viewpoint, the story of God's people from creation down to his own day. Since his primary interest was the history of David and the Davidic dynasty of Judah, he hurries through everything that preceded the death of Saul, David's predecessor as king, by the use of genealogical lists. The sources for these genealogies are mostly the books, already largely in their present form in the Chronicler's time, that eventually formed the Hebrew canon. For any given portion of these chapters, see the cross-references to their scriptural sources.

**1:19** *Divided*: see note on Gn 10:25.

**1:38** *Seir*: another name for Esau (v. 35) or Edom (v. 43).

**1:1** Gn 5:3, 6, 9.
**1:2–4** Gn 5:9–32; 10:2–32.
**1:3** Gn 4:24.
**1:4** Gn 5:32; 6:10; 9:18.
**1:5–7** Gn 10:2–4.
**1:10** Gn 10:8.
**1:11–16** Gn 10:13–18.
**1:17–23** Gn 10:22–29; 11:10–18.
**1:24–27** Gn 11:10–26; Lk 3:34–36.
**1:27** Gn 17:5; Neh 9:7.
**1:28** Gn 16:11, 15; 21:2–3; Gal 4:22–23;

Heb 11:11.
**1:29–31** Gn 25:13–16.
**1:32–33** Gn 25:1–4.
**1:34** Gn 21:2–3; 25:19, 25–26; 32:28–29; Mt 1:2; Lk 3:34.
**1:35–37** Gn 36:4–5, 10–13, 15–19.
**1:38–42** Gn 36:20–28.
**1:43–54** Gn 36:31–43.
**1:44** Is 34:6; 63:1; Jer 49:13, 22.
**1:45** Gn 36:11; Jb 2:11; Jer 49:7, 20.

Bedad, succeeded him as king. He overthrew the Midianites on the Moabite plateau, and the name of his city was Avith. ⁴⁷Hadad died and Samlah of Masrekah succeeded him as king. ⁴⁸Samlah died and Shaul from Rehoboth on the Euphrates succeeded him as king. ⁴⁹When Shaul died, Baalhanan, son of Achbor, succeeded him as king. ⁵⁰Baalhanan died and Hadad succeeded him as king. The name of his city was Pai, and his wife's name was Mehetabel. She was the daughter of Matred, who was the daughter of Mezahab. ⁵¹* After Hadad died, there were chiefs in Edom: the chiefs of Timna, Aliah, Jetheth, ⁵²Oholibamah, Elah, Pinon, ⁵³Kenaz, Teman, Mibzar, ⁵⁴Magdiel, and Iram were the chiefs of Edom.

**2** ¹These were the sons of Israel: Reuben, Simeon, Levi, Judah, Issachar, Zebulun,* ²Dan, Joseph, Benjamin, Naphtali, Gad, and Asher.*

**Judah.** ³The sons of Judah† were: Er, Onan, and Shelah; these three Bathshua, a Canaanite woman, bore to him. But Judah's firstborn, Er, was wicked in the sight of the LORD, so he took his life.* ⁴Judah's daughter-in-law Tamar bore him Perez and Zerah, so that he had five sons in all.*

⁵The sons of Perez were Hezron and Hamul.* ⁶The sons of Zerah were Zimri, Ethan, Heman, Calcol, and Darda—five in all.* ⁷The sons of Zimri: Carmi. The sons of Carmi: Achar, who brought trouble upon Israel by violating the ban.* ⁸The sons of Ethan: Azariah. ⁹The sons born to Hezron were Jerahmeel, Ram, and Chelubai.†*

¹⁰† Ram became the father of Amminadab, and Amminadab became the father of Nahshon, a prince of the Judahites.* ¹¹* Nahshon became the father of Salmah. Salmah became

the father of Boaz. ¹²Boaz became the father of Obed. Obed became the father of Jesse. ¹³* Jesse became the father of Eliab, his firstborn, of Abinadab, the second son, Shimea, the third,* ¹⁴Nethanel, the fourth, Raddai, the fifth, ¹⁵Ozem, the sixth, and David, the seventh. ¹⁶Their sisters were Zeruiah and Abigail. Zeruiah had three sons: Abishai, Joab, and Asahel.* ¹⁷Abigail bore Amasa, whose father was Jether the Ishmaelite.*

¹⁸† By his wife Azubah, Caleb, son of Hezron, became the father of a daughter, Jerioth. Her sons were Jesher, Shobab, and Ardon.* ¹⁹When Azubah died, Caleb married Ephrath, who bore him Hur.* ²⁰Hur became the father of Uri, and Uri became the father of Bezalel.* ²¹Then Hezron had relations with the daughter of Machir, the father of Gilead, whom he married when he was sixty years old. She bore him Segub.* ²²Segub became the father of Jair, who possessed twenty-three cities in the land of Gilead.* ²³Geshur and Aram took from them the villages of Jair, that is, Kenath and its towns, sixty cities in all, which had belonged to the sons of Machir, the father of Gilead.* ²⁴After the death of Hezron, Caleb had relations with Ephrathah, the widow of his father Hezron, and she bore him Ashhur, the father of Tekoa.*

²⁵The sons of Jerahmeel,† the firstborn of Hezron, were Ram, the firstborn, then Bunah, Oren, and Ozem, his brothers.* ²⁶Jerahmeel also had another wife, named Atarah, who was the mother of Onam. ²⁷The sons of Ram, the firstborn of Jerahmeel, were Maaz, Jamin, and Eker. ²⁸The sons of Onam were Shammai and Jada. The sons of Shammai were Nadab and Abishur. ²⁹Abishur's wife, who was named Abihail, bore him Ahban and Molid. ³⁰The sons of Nadab were Seled and Appaim. Seled died childless. ³¹The sons

2:3–4:23 The Chronicler had two reasons for placing his genealogy of the tribe of Judah before those of the other tribes, and for making it longer than all the others: his interest in David, who was of the tribe of Judah; and the prominence of descendants of that tribe among the Jews of the Chronicler's time.

2:9 Chelubai: a variant form of the name Caleb (vv. 18, 42), a different person from the Chelub mentioned in 4:11.

2:10–17 These verses list the immediate ancestors of David. A similar list appears in Ru 4:18–22.

2:18–24 These verses record the descendants of Caleb. In 4:15 as well as frequently in the Pentateuch (see Nm 13:6; 14:6, 30; 26:65; etc.), Caleb is called the son of Jephunneh. Here his father is called Hezron, perhaps because the Calebites were reckoned as part of the clan of the Hezronites.

2:25–41 The Jerahmeelites were a clan living in the Negeb of Judah.

1:51–54 Gn 36:40–43.
2:1 Gn 29:32–35; 30:18, 20; 35:23.
2:2 Gn 30:6, 8, 11, 13, 24; 35:18, 24–26.
2:3 1 Chr 4:21; Gn 38:1–5; 46:12.
2:4 Gn 38:7, 13–30; 46:12; Mt 1:3.
2:5 Gn 46:12.
2:6 1 Kgs 5:11.
2:7 Jos 7:1, 18–21, 24–25; 22:20.
2:9 Mt 1:3.
2:10 Mt 1:4.
2:11–12 Nm 1:7; Mt 1:4–5.
2:13–15 1 Sm 16:6–13; 17:13–14.
2:13 2 Chr 11:18.
2:16 2 Sm 2:18.
2:17 2 Sm 17:25; 19:14; 20:4–13.
2:18 1 Chr 2:24.
2:19 1 Chr 2:24.
2:20 Ex 24:14; 31:2; 35:30; 2 Chr 1:5.
2:21 Nm 26:29; 27:1; 32:39; Jos 13:31; Jgs 5:14.
2:22 Nm 32:41; 1 Kgs 4:13.
2:23 Dt 3:14; Jos 13:30.
2:24 1 Chr 2:19; 2 Sm 14:2; 2 Chr 11:6.
2:25 1 Sm 27:10; 30:29; Jb 32:2.

of Appaim: Ishi. The sons of Ishi: Sheshan. The sons of Sheshan: Ahlai.* ³²The sons of Jada, the brother of Shammai, were Jether and Jonathan. Jether died childless. ³³The sons of Jonathan were Peleth and Zaza. These were the sons of Jerahmeel. ³⁴Sheshan had no sons, only daughters; he had an Egyptian slave named Jarha. ³⁵Sheshan gave his daughter in marriage to his slave Jarha, and she bore him Attai. ³⁶Attai became the father of Nathan. Nathan became the father of Zabad. ³⁷Zabad became the father of Ephlal. Ephlal became the father of Obed. ³⁸Obed became the father of Jehu. Jehu became the father of Azariah. ³⁹Azariah became the father of Helez. Helez became the father of Eleasah. ⁴⁰Eleasah became the father of Sismai. Sismai became the father of Shallum. ⁴¹Shallum became the father of Jekamiah. Jekamiah became the father of Elishama.

⁴²The sons of Caleb,† the brother of Jerahmeel: Mesha his firstborn, who was the father of Ziph. Then the sons of Mareshah, who was the father of Hebron. ⁴³The sons of Hebron were Korah, Tappuah, Rekem, and Shema. ⁴⁴Shema became the father of Raham, who was the father of Jorkeam. Rekem became the father of Shammai. ⁴⁵The son of Shammai: Maon, who was the father of Beth-zur. ⁴⁶Ephah, Caleb's concubine, bore Haran, Moza, and Gazez. Haran became the father of Gazez. ⁴⁷The sons of Jahdai were Regem, Jotham, Geshan, Pelet, Ephah, and Shaaph. ⁴⁸Maacah, Caleb's concubine, bore Sheber and Tirhanah. ⁴⁹She also bore Shaaph, the father of Madmannah, Sheva, the father of Machbenah, and the father of Gibea. Achsah was Caleb's daughter.*

⁵⁰These were sons of Caleb, sons of Hur,† the firstborn of Ephrathah: Shobal, the father of Kiriath-jearim, ⁵¹Salma, the father of Bethlehem, and Hareph, the father of Bethgader. ⁵²The sons of Shobal, the father of Kiriath-jearim, were Reaiah, half of the Manahathites, ⁵³and the clans of Kiriath-jearim: the Ithrites, the Puthites, the Shumathites, and the Mishraites. From these the Zorahites and the Eshtaolites derived.* ⁵⁴The sons of Salma were Bethlehem, the Netophathites, Atroth-beth-Joab, half of the Manahathites, and the Zorites. ⁵⁵The clans of the Sopherim dwelling in Jabez were the Tirathites, the Shimeathites, and the Sucathites. They were the Kenites, who descended from Hammath, the ancestor of the Rechabites.*

**3** ¹†* These were the sons of David born to him in Hebron: the firstborn, Amnon, by Ahinoam of Jezreel; the second, Daniel,† by Abigail of Carmel; ²the third, Absalom, son of Maacah, who was the daughter of Talmai, king of Geshur; the fourth, Adonijah, son of Haggith; ³the fifth, Shephatiah, by Abital; the sixth, Ithream, by his wife Eglah. ⁴Six in all were born to him in Hebron, where he reigned seven years and six months. Then he reigned thirty-three years in Jerusalem.* ⁵* In Jerusalem the following were born to him: Shimea,† Shobab, Nathan, Solomon—four by Bathsheba, the daughter of Ammiel;* ⁶Ibhar, Elishua, Eliphelet, ⁷Nogah, Nepheg, Japhia, ⁸Elishama, Eliada, and Eliphelet—nine. ⁹All these were sons of David, in addition to other sons by concubines; and Tamar was their sister.*

¹⁰†* The son of Solomon was Rehoboam, whose son was Abijah, whose son was Asa, whose son was Jehoshaphat,* ¹¹whose son was Joram, whose son was Ahaziah, whose son was Joash,* ¹²whose son was Amaziah, whose son was Azariah, whose son was Jotham,* ¹³whose son was Ahaz, whose son was Hezekiah, whose son was Manasseh,* ¹⁴whose son was Amon, whose son was Josiah.* ¹⁵The sons of Josiah were: the firstborn Johanan; the second, Jehoiakim; the third, Zedekiah; the fourth, Shallum.†* ¹⁶The sons of Jehoiakim were: Jeconiah, his son; Zedekiah, his son.*

† **2:42–49** Another list (see vv. 18–24) of the Calebites, a clan inhabiting the south of Judah.
**2:50–55** The Hurites were a clan dwelling to the south and west of Jerusalem and related to the Calebites.
**3:1–9** A list of David's sons.
**3:1** *Daniel:* he is called Chileab in 2 Sm 3:3.
**3:5** *Shimea:* he bears the name Shammua in 2 Sm 5:14. *Ammiel:* Bathsheba's father is called Eliam in 2 Sm 11:3.
**3:10–16** The kings of Judah from Solomon down to the destruction of Jerusalem by the Babylonians.
**3:15** *Shallum:* another name for Jehoahaz, Josiah's immediate successor; cf. Jer 22:11.

* **2:31** 1 Chr 4:20.
**2:49** Jos 15:16; Jgs 1:12.
**2:53** Jgs 18:2.
**2:55** Nm 24:21; Jgs 1:16; 4:11; 1 Sm 15:6; Jer 35.
**3:1–4** 2 Sm 3:2–5.
**3:4** 2 Sm 2:11; 5:5.
**3:5–8** 2 Sm 5:14–16.
**3:5** 2 Sm 11:3.
**3:9** 2 Sm 13:1–2.
**3:10–17** Mt 1:7–12.
**3:10** 1 Kgs 11:43; 14:31; 15:1, 8, 24; 2 Chr 9:31; 12:16;
13:23; 17:1.
**3:11** 1 Kgs 22:51; 2 Chr 21:1; 22:1; 24:1, 27.
**3:12** 2 Kgs 12:21; 14:21; 15:7; 2 Chr 25:1; 26:1, 23; 27:1.
**3:13** 2 Kgs 15:38; 16:20; 20:21; 2 Chr 28:1, 27; 32:33.
**3:14** 2 Kgs 21:18, 26; 2 Chr 33:20, 25.
**3:15** 2 Kgs 23:34; 24:17; 2 Chr 36:4, 10.
**3:16** 2 Kgs 24:6, 17; 2 Chr 36:8, 10.

17 The sons of Jeconiah† the captive were: Shealtiel,* 18 Malchiram, Pedaiah, Shenazzar,† Jekamiah, Hoshama, and Nedabiah. 19 The sons of Pedaiah were Zerubbabel† and Shimei. The sons of Zerubbabel were Meshullam and Hananiah; Shelomith was their sister. 20 The sons of Meshullam were Hashubah, Ohel, Berechiah, Hasadiah, Jushabhesed—five. 21 The sons of Hananiah were Pelatiah, Jeshaiah, Rephaiah, Arnan, Obadiah, and Shecaniah. 22 The sons of Shecaniah were Shemaiah, Hattush, Igal, Bariah, Neariah, Shaphat—six.* 23 The sons of Neariah were Elioenai, Hizkiah, and Azrikam—three. 24 The sons of Elioenai were Hodaviah, Eliashib, Pelaiah, Akkub, Johanan, Delaiah, and Anani—seven.

4 1 † The sons of Judah were: Perez, Hezron, Carmi, Hur, and Shobal.* 2 Reaiah, the son of Shobal, became the father of Jahath, and Jahath became the father of Ahumai and Lahad. These were the clans of the Zorathites.

3 These were the sons of Hareph, the father of Etam: Jezreel, Ishma, and Idbash; their sister was named Hazzelelponi. 4 Penuel was the father of Gedor, and Ezer the father of Hushah. These were the sons of Hur, the firstborn of Ephrathah, the father of Bethlehem.

5 Ashhur, the father of Tekoa, had two wives, Helah and Naarah.* 6 Naarah bore him Ahuzzam, Hepher, the Temenites, and the Ahashtarites. These were the sons of Naarah. 7 The sons of Helah were Zereth, Izhar, Ethnan, and Koz. 8 Koz became the father of Anub and Zobebah, as well as of the clans of Aharhel, son of Harum. 9 Jabez was the most distinguished of his brothers. His mother had named him Jabez, saying, "I bore him with pain." 10 Jabez prayed to the God of Israel: "Oh, that you may truly bless me and extend my boundaries! May your hand be with me and make me free of misfortune, without pain!" And God granted his prayer.

11 Chelub, the brother of Shuhah, became the father of Mehir, who was the father of Eshton. 12 Eshton became the father of Bethrapha, Paseah, and Tehinnah, the father of the city of Nahash. These were the men of Recah.

13 The sons of Kenaz were Othniel and Seraiah. The sons of Othniel were Hathath and Meonothai;* 14 Meonothai became the father of Ophrah. Seraiah became the father of Joab, the father of Geharashim, so called because they were artisans. 15 The sons of Caleb, son of Jephunneh, were Ir, Elah, and Naam. The sons of Elah: Kenaz.* 16 The sons of Jehallelel were Ziph, Ziphah, Tiria, and Asarel. 17 The sons of Ezrah were Jether, Mered, Epher, and Jalon. Jether became the father of Miriam, Shammai, and Ishbah, the father of Eshtemoa.* 18 Mered's Egyptian wife bore Jered, the father of Gedor, Heber, the father of Soco, and Jekuthiel, the father of Zanoah. These were the sons of Bithiah, the daughter of Pharaoh, whom Mered married. 19 The sons of his Jewish wife, the sister of Naham, the father of Keilah, were Shimon the Garmite and Ishi the Maacathite. 20 The sons of Shimon were Amnon, Rinnah, Benhanan, and Tilon. The son of Ishi was Zoheth and the son of Zoheth. . . .

21 The sons of Shelah, son of Judah, were: Er, the father of Lecah; Laadah, the father of Mareshah; the clans of the linen weavers' guild in Bethashbea;* 22 Jokim; the people of Cozeba; and Joash and Saraph, who held property in Moab, but returned to Bethlehem. (These are events of old.) 23 They were potters and inhabitants of Netaim and Gederah, where they lived in the king's service.

**Simeon.** 24 The sons of Simeon were Nemuel, Jamin, Jachin, Zerah, and Shaul,* 25 whose son was Shallum, whose son was Mibsam, whose son was Mishma. 26 The sons of Mishma were his son Hammuel, whose son was Zaccur,

---

† **3:17–24** The descendants of King Jeconiah down to the time of the Chronicler. If twenty-five years are allowed for each generation, the ten generations between Jeconiah and Anani (the last name on the list) would put the birth of the latter at about 405 B.C.—an important item in establishing the approximate date of the Chronicler's work in its final form.

**3:18** Shenazzar: presumably he is the same as Sheshbazzar (Ezr 1:8, 11; 5:14–16), the prince of Judah who was the first Jewish governor of Judah after the exile. Both forms of the name probably go back to the Babylonian name Sin-ab-ussar, meaning "O [god] Sin, protect [our] father!"

**3:19** Zerubbabel: here called the son of Pedaiah, though elsewhere (Hg 1:12, 14; 2:2, 23; Ezr 3:2, 8; 5:2; Neh 12:1) his father's name is given as Shealtiel. The latter indication may

merely point to the fact that Zerubbabel succeeded Shealtiel as head of the house of David.

**4:1–43** Genealogies of the southern tribes, Judah and Simeon.

---

**3:17, 19** Ezr 2:2; 3:2, 8; 5:2; Sir 49:11; Hg 1:1, 12, 14; Mt 1:12–13; Lk 3:27.
**3:22** Neh 3:29.
**4:1** 1 Chr 2:4–5, 7, 9, 50; Gn 38:29; 46:12; Mt 1:3.
**4:5** 1 Chr 2:24.
**4:13** Jos 15:17; Jgs 1:13; 3:9, 11.
**4:15** Nm 13:6; 14:6; 32:12; Jos 14:6, 14.
**4:17** 1 Sm 30:28.
**4:21** 1 Chr 2:3; Gn 38:5; 46:12; Nm 26:20.
**4:24** Gn 46:10; Ex 6:15; Nm 26:12–13.

whose son was Shimei. ²⁷Shimei had sixteen sons and six daughters. His brothers, however, did not have many sons, and as a result all their clans did not equal the number of the Judahites.

²⁸They dwelt in Beer-sheba, Moladah, Hazar-shual, ²⁹Bilhah, Ezem, Tolad, ³⁰Bethuel, Hormah, Ziklag, ³¹Beth-marcaboth, Hazarsusim, Bethbiri, and Shaaraim. Until the reign of David, these were their cities ³²and their villages. Etam, also, and Ain, Rimmon, Tochen, and Ashan—five cities,* ³³together with all their outlying villages as far as Baal. Here is where they dwelt, and so it was inscribed of them in their family records.

³⁴Meshobab, Jamlech, Joshah, son of Amaziah, ³⁵Joel, Jehu, son of Joshibiah, son of Seraiah, son of Asiel, ³⁶Elioenai, Jaakobah, Jeshohaiah, Asaiah, Adiel, Jesimiel, Benaiah, ³⁷Ziza, son of Shiphi, son of Allon, son of Jedaiah, son of Shimri, son of Shemaiah— ³⁸these just named were princes in their clans, and their ancestral houses spread out to such an extent* ³⁹that they went to the approaches of Gedor,† east of the valley, seeking pasture for their flocks. ⁴⁰They found abundant and good pastures, and the land was spacious, quiet, and peaceful—for the Hamites dwelt there formerly. ⁴¹They who have just been listed by name set out during the reign of Hezekiah, king of Judah, and attacked their tents and also the Meunites who were there. They put them under the ban that is still in force to this day and dwelt in their place because they found pasture there for their flocks.*

⁴²Five hundred of them (the Simeonites) went to Mount Seir, with Pelatiah, Neariah, Rephaiah, and Uzziel, sons of Ishi, at their head. ⁴³They attacked the surviving Amalekites who had escaped, and have lived there to the present day.*

**5** **Reuben.** ¹†The sons of Reuben, the firstborn of Israel. (He was indeed the firstborn, but because he defiled the couch of his father his birthright was given to the sons of Joseph, son of Israel, so that he is not listed in the family records according to his birthright.*

²Judah, in fact, became powerful among his brothers, so that the ruler came from him, though the birthright had been Joseph's.)* ³The sons of Reuben, the firstborn of Israel, were Hanoch, Pallu, Hezron, and Carmi.* ⁴His son was Joel, whose son was Shemaiah, whose son was Gog, whose son was Shimei, ⁵whose son was Micah, whose son was Reaiah, whose son was Baal, ⁶whose son was Beerah, whom Tilgath-pileser, the king of Assyria, took into exile; he was a prince of the Reubenites.* ⁷His brothers who belonged to his clans, when they were listed in the family records according to their descendants, were: Jeiel, the chief, and Zechariah, ⁸and Bela, son of Azaz, son of Shema, son of Joel. The Reubenites lived in Aroer and as far as Nebo and Baal-meon;* ⁹toward the east they dwelt as far as the wilderness which extends from the Euphrates River, for they had much livestock in the land of Gilead.* ¹⁰In Saul's time they waged war with the Hagrites, and when they had defeated them they dwelt in their tents throughout the region east of Gilead.*

**Gad.** ¹¹The Gadites lived alongside them in the land of Bashan as far as Salecah.* ¹²Joel was chief, Shapham was second in command, and Janai was judge in Bashan.* ¹³Their brothers, according to their ancestral houses, were: Michael, Meshullam, Sheba, Jorai, Jacan, Zia, and Eber—seven. ¹⁴These were the sons of Abihail, son of Huri, son of Jaroah, son of Gilead, son of Michael, son of Jeshishai, son of Jahdo, son of Buz. ¹⁵Ahi, son of Abdiel, son of Guni, was the head of their ancestral houses. ¹⁶They dwelt in Gilead, in Bashan and its towns, and in all the pasture lands of Sirion to the borders. ¹⁷All were listed in the family records in the time of Jotham, king of Judah, and of Jeroboam, king of Israel.

¹⁸The Reubenites, Gadites, and the half-tribe of Manasseh were warriors, men who bore shield and sword and who drew the bow, trained in warfare—forty-four thousand seven hundred and sixty men fit for military service. ¹⁹When they waged war against the Hagrites and against Jetur, Naphish, and

---

**4:39** *Gedor*: the Greek reads Gerar, probably correctly.
**5:1–26** Genealogies of the Transjordanian tribes, Reuben, Gad, and the half-tribe of Manasseh.

**4:28–32** Jos 19:2–8.
   **4:38** Nm 1:2.
   **4:41** 2 Kgs 18:1–2;

2 Chr 29:1.
   **4:43** Ex 17:8, 14; Dt 25:17–19;

1 Sm 14:48; 15:3, 7–8; 2 Sm 8:12.
   **5:1** Gn 35:22; 48:5, 15–22; 49:3–4; Dt 33:6.
   **5:2** 1 Chr 28:4; Gn 49:8–12.
   **5:3** Gn 46:9; Ex 6:14;

Nm 26:5–6.
   **5:6** 2 Kgs 15:29.
   **5:8** Jos 13:9, 16–17; Nm 32:3, 38.
   **5:9** Jos 22:9.
   **5:10** Ps 83:6–7.
   **5:11** Jos 13:11, 24–28.
   **5:12** Gn 46:16.

Nodab, * ²⁰ they received help so that the Hagrites and all who were with them were delivered into their power. For during the battle they cried out to God, and he heard them because they had put their trust in him. * ²¹ Along with one hundred thousand persons they also captured their livestock: fifty thousand camels, two hundred fifty thousand sheep, and two thousand donkeys. ²² Many were slain and fell; for "From God the victory." They dwelt in their place until the time of the exile. *

**The Half-tribe of Manasseh.** ²³ The half-tribe of Manasseh lived in the land of Bashan as far as Baal-hermon, Senir, and Mount Hermon; they were numerous. ²⁴ The following were the heads of their ancestral houses: Epher, Ishi, Eliel, Azriel, Jeremiah, Hodaviah, and Jahdiel—men who were warriors, famous men, and heads over their ancestral houses.

²⁵ However, they acted treacherously toward the God of their ancestors by prostituting themselves to follow the gods of the peoples of the land, whom God had destroyed before them. * ²⁶ Therefore the God of Israel stirred up against them the anger of Pul, † king of Assyria, and the anger of Tilgath-pilneser [sic], king of Assyria, who deported the Reubenites, the Gadites, and the half-tribe of Manasseh and brought them to Halah, Habor, and Hara, and to the river Gozan, where they have remained to this day. *

**Levi.**† ²⁷ The sons of Levi were Gershon, Kohath, and Merari. * ²⁸ The sons of Kohath were Amram, Izhar, Hebron, and Uzziel. * ²⁹ The children of Amram were Aaron, Moses, and Miriam. The sons of Aaron were Nadab, Abihu, Eleazar, and Ithamar. * ³⁰ † Eleazar became the father of Phinehas. Phinehas became the father of Abishua. ³¹ Abishua became the father of Bukki. Bukki became the father of Uzzi. ³² Uzzi became the father of Zerahiah.

Zerahiah became the father of Meraioth. ³³ Meraioth became the father of Amariah. Amariah became the father of Ahitub. ³⁴ Ahitub became the father of Zadok. Zadok became the father of Ahimaaz. ³⁵ Ahimaaz became the father of Azariah. Azariah became the father of Johanan. ³⁶ Johanan became the father of Azariah, who served as priest in the temple Solomon built in Jerusalem. ³⁷ Azariah became the father of Amariah. Amariah became the father of Ahitub. ³⁸ Ahitub became the father of Zadok. Zadok became the father of Shallum. ³⁹ Shallum became the father of Hilkiah. Hilkiah became the father of Azariah. ⁴⁰ Azariah became the father of Seraiah. Seraiah became the father of Jehozadak. ⁴¹ Jehozadak was one of those who went into the exile which the LORD inflicted on Judah and Jerusalem through Nebuchadnezzar.

**6** ¹ The sons of Levi were Gershon, Kohath, and Merari. * ² The sons of Gershon were named Libni and Shimei. * ³ The sons of Kohath were Amram, Izhar, Hebron, and Uzziel. * ⁴ The sons of Merari were Mahli and Mushi. *

These were the clans of Levi, according to their ancestors. ⁵ Of Gershon: his son Libni, whose son was Jahath, whose son was Zimmah, ⁶ whose son was Joah, whose son was Iddo, whose son was Zerah, whose son was Jetherai.

⁷ The sons of Kohath: his son Amminadab, whose son was Korah, whose son was Assir, ⁸ whose son was Elkanah, whose son was Ebiasaph, whose son was Assir, ⁹ whose son was Tahath, whose son was Uriel, whose son was Uzziah, whose son was Shaul. ¹⁰ The sons of Elkanah were Amasai and Ahimoth, ¹¹ whose son was Elkanah, whose son was Zophai, whose son was Nahath, ¹² whose son was Eliab, whose son was Jeroham, whose son was Elkanah, whose son was Samuel. ¹³ The sons of Samuel were Joel, the firstborn, and Abijah, the second.

**5:26** *Pul:* the Chronicler seems to speak of two different kings here, but Pul was the name which the Assyrian king Tilgath-pileser III (745–727 B.C.) adopted as king of Babylon.
**5:27–6:66** The tribe of Levi. The Chronicler's list gives special prominence to Levi's son Kohath, from whom were descended both the Aaronite priests (vv. 28–41) and the leading group of Temple singers (6:18–23).
**5:30–41** The line of preexilic high priests. The list seems to become confused in vv. 36–38, which repeat the same names, mostly in inverse order, that occur in vv. 34–36. A similar but shorter list occurs, with variations, in Ezr 7:1–5.

**5:19** 1 Chr 1:31; 5:10; Gn 25:15; Ps 83:6–7.
**5:20** Dt 33:20–21.
**5:22** Nm 32:39; Dt 3:8–10; Jgs 3:3.
**5:25** Ex 34:14–16; 2 Kgs 17:7.
**5:26** 2 Kgs 15:9, 29; 17:6.
**5:27** 1 Chr 6:1; 23:6; Gn 46:11; Ex 6:16; Nm 26:57.
**5:28** 1 Chr 6:3; Ex 6:18.
**5:29** Ex 6:20; Nm 26:59–60.
**6:1** 1 Chr 5:27; 23:6; Gn 46:11; Ex 6:16; Nm 26:57.
**6:2** Ex 6:17.
**6:3** Ex 6:18; Nm 3:19; 26:59.
**6:4** 1 Chr 6:14; Ex 6:19; Nm 3:20; 26:58.

[14] The sons of Merari: Mahli, whose son was Libni, whose son was Shimei, whose son was Uzzah,* [15] whose son was Shimea, whose son was Haggiah, whose son was Asaiah.

[16] The following were established by David for the service of song† in the LORD's house at the time when the ark had a resting place. [17] They served as singers before the tabernacle of the tent of meeting until Solomon built the house of the LORD in Jerusalem, and they performed their services according to the order prescribed for them. [18] Those who so performed are the following, together with their sons.

Among the Kohathites: Heman, the chanter, son of Joel, son of Samuel, [19] son of Elkanah, son of Jeroham, son of Eliel, son of Toah, [20] son of Zuph, son of Elkanah, son of Mahath, son of Amasi, [21] son of Elkanah, son of Joel, son of Azariah, son of Zephaniah, [22] son of Tahath, son of Assir, son of Ebiasaph, son of Korah,* [23] son of Izhar, son of Kohath, son of Levi, son of Israel.

[24] His brother Asaph stood at his right hand. Asaph was the son of Berechiah, son of Shimea, [25] son of Michael, son of Baaseiah, son of Malchijah, [26] son of Ethni, son of Zerah, son of Adaiah, [27] son of Ethan, son of Zimmah,* son of Shimei, [28] son of Jahath, son of Gershon, son of Levi.

[29] Their brothers, the Merarites, stood at the left: Ethan, son of Kishi, son of Abdi, son of Malluch, [30] son of Hashabiah, son of Amaziah, son of Hilkiah, [31] son of Amzi, son of Bani, son of Shemer, [32] son of Mahli, son of Mushi, son of Merari, son of Levi.*

[33] Their brother Levites were appointed to all the other services of the tabernacle of the house of God.* [34] However, it was Aaron and his sons who made the sacrifice on the altar for burnt offerings and on the altar of incense; they alone had charge of the holy of holies and of making atonement for Israel, as Moses, the servant of God, had commanded.*

[35] These were the sons of Aaron: his son Eleazar, whose son was Phinehas, whose son was Abishua, [36] whose son was Bukki, whose son was Uzzi, whose son was Zerahiah, [37] whose son was Meraioth, whose son was Amariah, whose son was Ahitub, [38] whose son was Zadok, whose son was Ahimaaz.

[39]† The following were their dwelling places, by encampments in their territories. To the sons of Aaron who belonged to the clan of the Kohathites, since the lot fell to them, [40] was assigned Hebron in the land of Judah, with its adjacent pasture lands. [41] However, the open country and the villages belonging to the city had been given to Caleb, the son of Jephunneh. [42] There were assigned to the sons of Aaron: Hebron a city of refuge, Libnah with its pasture lands, Jattir with its pasture lands, Eshtemoa with its pasture lands, [43] Holon with its pasture lands, Debir with its pasture lands, [44] Ashan with its pasture lands, Jetta with its pasture lands, and Beth-shemesh with its pasture lands. [45] Also from the tribe of Benjamin: Gibeon with its pasture lands, Geba with its pasture lands, Almon with its pasture lands, Anathoth with its pasture lands. In all, they had thirteen cities with their pasture lands. [49] The Israelites assigned these cities with their pasture lands to the Levites, [50] designating them by name and assigning them by lot from the tribes of the Judahites, Simeonites, and Benjaminites.

[46] The other Kohathites obtained ten cities by lot for their clans from the tribe of Ephraim, from the tribe of Dan, and from the half-tribe of Manasseh. [47] The clans of the Gershonites obtained thirteen cities from the tribes of Issachar, Asher, and Naphtali, and from the half-tribe of Manasseh in Bashan. [48] The clans of the Merarites obtained twelve cities by lot from the tribes of Reuben, Gad, and Zebulun.

[51] The clans of the Kohathites obtained cities by lot from the tribe of Ephraim. [52] They were assigned cities of refuge: Shechem in the mountain region of Ephraim, with its pasture lands, Gezer with its pasture lands, [53] Kibzaim with its pasture lands, and Beth-horon with its pasture lands. [54] From the tribe of Dan: Elteke with its pasture lands, Gibbethon with its pasture lands, Aijalon with its pasture lands, and Gath-rimmon with its pasture lands. [55] From

---

† 

**6:16–32** The cultic functions performed by the levitical families in the postexilic Temple at the time of the Chronicler are here traced back to David, in a way analogous to that in which all the laws in the Pentateuch are attributed to Moses.

**6:39–66** For the rights of the Levites in the cities assigned to them, see note on Jos 21:1.

* 

**6:14** 1 Chr 6:4; Ex 6:19; Nm 3:20; 26:58.
**6:22** Ex 6:24.
**6:27** 1 Chr 6:2, 5.
**6:32** Ex 6:19; Nm 26:58.
**6:33** 1 Chr 15:17, 19; 16:41–42; 2 Chr 5:12.
**6:34** 1 Chr 16:39–40.

the half-tribe of Manasseh: Taanach with its pasture lands and Ibleam with its pasture lands. These belonged to the rest of the Kohathite clan.

<sup>56</sup> The clans of the Gershonites received from the half-tribe of Manasseh: Golan in Bashan with its pasture lands and Ashtaroth with its pasture lands. <sup>57</sup> From the tribe of Issachar: Kedesh with its pasture lands, Daberath with its pasture lands, <sup>58</sup> Ramoth with its pasture lands, and Engannim with its pasture lands. <sup>59</sup> From the tribe of Asher: Mashal with its pasture lands, Abdon with its pasture lands, <sup>60</sup> Hilkath with its pasture lands, and Rehob with its pasture lands. <sup>61</sup> From the tribe of Naphtali: Kedesh in Galilee with its pasture lands, Hammon with its pasture lands, and Kiriathaim with its pasture lands.

<sup>62</sup> The rest of the Merarites received from the tribe of Zebulun: Jokneam with its pasture lands, Kartah with its pasture lands, Rimmon with its pasture lands, and Tabor with its pasture lands. <sup>63</sup> Across the Jordan at Jericho (that is, east of the Jordan) they received from the tribe of Reuben: Bezer in the desert with its pasture lands, Jahzah with its pasture lands, <sup>64</sup> Kedemoth with its pasture lands, and Mephaath with its pasture lands. <sup>65</sup> From the tribe of Gad: Ramoth in Gilead with its pasture lands, Mahanaim with its pasture lands, <sup>66</sup> Heshbon with its pasture lands, and Jazer with its pasture lands.

# 7

**Issachar.** <sup>1</sup>† The sons of Issachar were Tola, Puah, Jashub, and Shimron: four.* <sup>2</sup> The sons of Tola were Uzzi, Rephaiah, Jeriel, Jahmai, Ibsam, and Shemuel, heads of the ancestral houses of Tola, mighty warriors in their generations. In the time of David they numbered twenty-two thousand six hundred.* <sup>3</sup> The sons of Uzzi: Izarahiah. The sons of Izarahiah were Michael, Obadiah, Joel, and Isshiah. All five of these were chiefs. <sup>4</sup> Along with them, in their generations, according to ancestral houses, were thirty-six thousand men in organized military troops, since they had more wives and children <sup>5</sup> than their fellow tribesmen. In all the clans of Issachar there was a total of eighty-seven thousand warriors listed in their family records.

**Benjamin.** <sup>6</sup> The sons of Benjamin were Bela, Becher, and Jediael—three.* <sup>7</sup> The sons of Bela were Ezbon, Uzzi, Uzziel, Jerimoth, and Iri— five. They were heads of their ancestral houses and warriors. Their family records listed twenty-two thousand and thirty-four. <sup>8</sup> The sons of Becher were Zemirah, Joash, Eliezer, Elioenai, Omri, Jeremoth, Abijah, Anathoth, and Alemeth—all these were sons of Becher.* <sup>9</sup> Their family records listed twenty thousand two hundred of their kindred who were heads of their ancestral houses and warriors. <sup>10</sup> The sons of Jediael: Bilhan. The sons of Bilhan were Jeush, Benjamin, Ehud, Chenaanah, Zethan, Tarshish, and Ahishahar. <sup>11</sup> All these were sons of Jediael, heads of ancestral houses and warriors. They numbered seventeen thousand two hundred men fit for military service…† <sup>12</sup> Shupham and Hupham.*

**Dan, Naphtali and Manasseh.** The sons of Dan: Hushim. <sup>13</sup> The sons of Naphtali were Jahziel, Guni, Jezer, and Shallum. These were sons of Bilhah.* <sup>14</sup> The sons of Manasseh, whom his Aramean concubine bore:* she bore Machir, the father of Gilead.* <sup>15</sup> Machir took a wife whose name was Maacah; his sister's name was Molecheth. Manasseh's second son was named Zelophehad, who had only daughters.* <sup>16</sup> Maacah, Machir's wife, bore a son whom she named Peresh. He had a brother named Sheresh, whose sons were Ulam and Rakem. <sup>17</sup> The sons of Ulam: Bedan. These were the sons of Gilead, the son of Machir, the son of Manasseh. <sup>18</sup> His sister Molecheth bore Ishhod, Abiezer, and Mahlah. <sup>19</sup> The sons of Shemida were Ahian, Shechem, Likhi, and Aniam.

**Ephraim.** <sup>20</sup>* The sons of Ephraim: Shuthelah, whose son was Bered, whose son was Tahath, whose son was Eleadah, whose son was Tahath, <sup>21</sup> whose son was Zabad. Ephraim's son Shuthelah, and Ezer and Elead, who were born in the land, were killed by the inhabitants of Gath because they had gone down to take away their livestock. <sup>22</sup> Their father Ephraim mourned a long time, but after his relatives had come and comforted him, <sup>23</sup> he had

---

† 
  **7:1–40** The seven northern tribes.
  **7:11** The Hebrew text appears to be defective.

*
  **7:1** Gn 46:13.                    **7:2** Nm 26:23–24;

  Jgs 10:1.                            Nm 26:48–49.
  **7:6** Gn 46:21; Nm 26:38.          **7:14–19** Nm 26:29–32.
  **7:8** Gn 46:21.                    **7:14** Nm 26:29; Jos 17:1.
  **7:12** Nm 26:39.                   **7:15** Nm 26:33; Jos 17:3.
  **7:12–13** Gn 46:24;                **7:20** Nm 26:35.

relations with his wife, who conceived and bore a son whom he named Beriah, since evil† had befallen his house. * 24 He had a daughter, Sheerah, who built Lower and Upper Beth-horon and Uzzen-sheerah. 25 Zabad's son was Rephah, whose son was Resheph, whose son was Telah, whose son was Tahan, 26 whose son was Ladan, whose son was Ammihud, whose son was Elishama, * 27 whose son was Nun, whose son was Joshua.

28 Their property and their dwellings were in Bethel and its towns, Naaran to the east, Gezer and its towns to the west, and also Shechem and its towns as far as Ayyah and its towns. * 29 Manasseh, however, had possession of Beth-shean and its towns, Taanach and its towns, Megiddo and its towns, and Dor and its towns. In these dwelt the sons of Joseph, the son of Israel. *

**Asher.** 30 The sons of Asher were Imnah, Ish-vah, Ishvi, and Beriah; their sister was Serah. * 31 Beriah's sons were Heber and Malchiel, who was the father of Birzaith. 32 Heber became the father of Japhlet, Shomer, Hotham, and their sister Shua. 33 The sons of Japhlet were Pasach, Bimhal, and Ashvath; these were the sons of Japhlet. 34 The sons of Shomer were Ahi, Roh-gah, Jehubbah, and Aram. 35 The sons of his brother Hotham were Zophah, Imna, Shelesh, and Amal. 36 The sons of Zophah were Suah, Harnepher, Shual, Beri, Imrah, 37 Bezer, Hod, Shamma, Shilshah, Ithran, and Beera. 38 The sons of Jether were Jephunneh, Pispa, and Ara. 39 The sons of Ulla were Arah, Hanniel, and Rizia. 40 All these were sons of Asher, heads of ancestral houses, distinguished men, warriors, and chiefs among the princes. Their family records numbered twenty-six thousand men fit for military service.

**8 Benjamin.** 1 † Benjamin became the father of Bela, his firstborn, Ashbel, the second son, Aharah, the third, * 2 Nohah, the fourth, and Rapha, the fifth. 3 The sons of Bela were Addar and Gera, the father of Ehud. 4 The sons of Ehud were Abishua, Naaman, Ahoah, * 5 Gera, Shephuphan, and Huram. 6 These were

the sons of Ehud, family heads over those who dwelt in Geba and were deported to Manahath. 7 Also Naaman, Ahijah, and Gera. The last, who led them into exile, became the father of Uzza and Ahihud. 8 Shaharaim became a father on the Moabite plateau after he had put away his wives Hushim and Baara. 9 By his wife Hodesh he begot Jobab, Zibia, Mesha, Malcam, 10 Jeuz, Sachia, and Mirmah. These were his sons, family heads. 11 By Hu-shim he begot Abitub and Elpaal. 12 The sons of Elpaal were Eber, Misham, Shemed (who built Ono and Lod with its nearby towns), * 13 and Beriah, and Shema. They were family heads of those who dwelt in Aijalon, and they put the inhabitants of Gath to flight. 14 Their relatives were Elpaal, Shashak, and Jeremoth. 15 Zebadiah, Arad, Eder, 16 Michael, Ishpah, and Joha were the sons of Beriah. 17 Zebadiah, Meshullam, Hizki, Heber, 18 Ishmerai, Izliah, and Jobab were the sons of Elpaal. 19 Jakim, Zichri, Zabdi, 20 Elienai, Zillethai, Eliel, 21 Ada-iah, Beraiah, and Shimrath were the sons of Shimei. 22 Ishpan, Eber, Eliel, 23 Abdon, Zichri, Hanan, 24 Hananiah, Elam, Anthothi-jah, 25 Iphdeiah, and Penuel were the sons of Shashak. 26 Shamsherai, Shehariah, Athaliah, 27 Jaareshiah, Elijah, and Zichri were the sons of Jeroham. 28 These were family heads in their generations, chiefs who dwelt in Jerusalem.

29 * In Gibeon dwelt Jeiel, the founder of Gibeon, whose wife's name was Maacah; 30 also his firstborn son, Abdon, and Zur, Kish, Baal, Ner, Nadab, 31 Gedor, Ahio, Zecher, and Mikloth. 32 Mikloth became the father of Shimeah. These, too, dwelt with their relatives in Jerusalem, opposite their fellow tribesmen. 33 * Ner became the father of Kish, and Kish became the father of Saul. Saul became the father of Jonathan, Malchishua, Abinadab, and Eshbaal. * 34 The son of Jonathan was Meribbaal, and Meribbaal became the father of Micah. * 35 The sons of Micah were Pithon, Melech, Tarea, and Ahaz. 36 Ahaz became the father of Jehoaddah, and Jehoaddah became the father of Alemeth, Azmaveth, and Zimri. Zimri became the father of Moza. * 37 Moza became the father of Binea, whose son was

---

† **7:23** *Beriah…evil:* the name sounds like the Hebrew word for "evil," with the preposition *be.*
**8:1–40** A second, variant list (cf. 7:6–11) of the Benjaminites, highlighting the family of Saul (vv. 33–40).

* **7:23** 1 Chr 8:13.

**7:26** Nm 1:10; 2:18; 7:48; 10:22.

**7:28** Gn 12:8; 1 Kgs 9:16.
**7:29** Jos 17:11.
**7:30** Gn 46:17; Nm 26:44–46.
**8:1** 1 Chr 7:6; Gn 46:21; Nm 26:38–44.
**8:4** Jgs 3:15.
**8:12** Neh 11:35.
**8:29–32** 1 Chr 9:35–38.
**8:33–38** 1 Chr 9:39–44.
**8:33** 1 Chr 10:2; 1 Sm 9:1; 14:49, 51; 31:2.
**8:34** 2 Sm 4:4; 9:6; 10:12.
**8:36** 1 Chr 9:42.

Raphah, whose son was Eleasah, whose son was Azel. <sup>38</sup>Azel had six sons, whose names were Azrikam, his firstborn, Ishmael, Sheariah, Azariah, Obadiah, and Hanan; all these were the sons of Azel.* <sup>39</sup>The sons of Eshek, his brother, were Ulam, his firstborn, Jeush, the second son, and Eliphelet, the third. <sup>40</sup>The sons of Ulam were warriors, skilled with the bow, and they had many sons and grandsons: one hundred and fifty. All these were the sons of Benjamin.

**9** <sup>1</sup>Thus all Israel was listed in family lists, and these are recorded in the book of the kings of Israel.*

Now Judah had been exiled to Babylon because of its treachery. <sup>2</sup>†* The first to settle again in their cities and dwell there were certain Israelites, the priests, the Levites, and the temple servants.*

**Jerusalemites.** <sup>3</sup>In Jerusalem lived Judahites and Benjaminites; also Ephraimites and Manassites. <sup>4</sup>Among the Judahites was Uthai, son of Ammihud, son of Omri, son of Imri, son of Bani, one of the sons of Perez, son of Judah. <sup>5</sup>Among the Shelanites were Asaiah, the firstborn, and his sons. <sup>6</sup>Among the Zerahites were Jeuel and six hundred and ninety of their relatives. <sup>7</sup>Among the Benjaminites were Sallu, son of Meshullam, son of Hodaviah, son of Hassenuah, <sup>8</sup>as well as Ibneiah, son of Jeroham; Elah, son of Uzzi, son of Michri; Meshullam, son of Shephatiah, son of Reuel, son of Ibnijah. <sup>9</sup>Their kindred of various families were nine hundred and fifty-six. All those named were heads of their ancestral houses.

<sup>10</sup>Among the priests were Jedaiah; Jehoiarib; Jachin; <sup>11</sup>Azariah, son of Hilkiah, son of Meshullam, son of Zadok, son of Meraioth, son of Ahitub, the ruler of the house of God; <sup>12</sup>Adaiah, son of Jeroham, son of Pashhur, son of Malchijah; Maasai, son of Adiel, son of Jahzerah, son of Meshullam, son of Meshillemith, son of Immer. <sup>13</sup>Their brothers, heads of their ancestral houses, were one thousand seven hundred and sixty, valiant in the work of the service of the house of God.

<sup>14</sup>Among the Levites were Shemaiah, son of Hasshub, son of Azrikam, son of Hashabiah, one of the sons of Merari; <sup>15</sup>Bakbakkar; Heresh; Galal; Mattaniah, son of Mica, son of Zichri, a descendant of Asaph; <sup>16</sup>Obadiah, son of Shemaiah, son of Galal, a descendant of Jeduthun; and Berechiah, son of Asa, son of Elkanah, whose family lived in the villages of the Netophathites.

<sup>17</sup>The gatekeepers were Shallum, Akkub, Talmon, Ahiman, and their brothers; Shallum was the chief. <sup>18</sup>Previously they had stood guard at the king's gate on the east side; now they became gatekeepers for the encampments of the Levites. <sup>19</sup>Shallum, son of Kore, son of Ebiasaph, a descendant of Korah, and his brothers of the same ancestral house of the Korahites had as their assigned task the guarding of the threshold of the tent, just as their fathers had guarded the entrance to the encampment of the Lord. <sup>20</sup>Phinehas, son of Eleazar, had been their chief in times past; the Lord was with him.* <sup>21</sup>Zechariah, son of Meshelemiah, guarded the gate of the tent of meeting.* <sup>22</sup>In all, those who were chosen for gatekeepers at the threshold were two hundred and twelve. They were inscribed in the family records of their villages. David and Samuel the seer had established them in their position of trust. <sup>23</sup>Thus they and their sons kept guard over the gates of the house of the Lord, the house which was then a tent. <sup>24</sup>The gatekeepers were stationed at the four sides, to the east, the west, the north, and the south.* <sup>25</sup>Their brothers who lived in their own villages took turns in assisting them for seven-day periods,* <sup>26</sup>while the four chief gatekeepers were on permanent duty. These were the Levites who also had charge of the chambers and treasures of the house of God. <sup>27</sup>They would spend the night near the house of God, for it was in their charge and they had the duty of opening it each morning.

<sup>28</sup>Some of them had charge of the vessels used there, tallying them as they were brought in and taken out. <sup>29</sup>Others were appointed to take care of the utensils and all the sacred vessels, as well as the fine flour, the wine, the oil, the frankincense, and the spices. <sup>30</sup>It was the sons of priests, however, who mixed the

† **9:2–34** The inhabitants of Jerusalem after the exile. A similar list, though with many variants in the names, occurs in Neh 11:3–24.

**8:38** 1 Chr 9:43.    **9:1** 2 Chr 16:11; 20:34; 25:26; 27:7; 33:18; 36:8.    **9:2–34** Neh 11:3–24.    **9:2** Ezr 2:70; 7:7; Neh 11:3.    **9:20** Ex 6:25; Nm 25:7, 11; Jgs 20:28.    **9:21** 1 Chr 26:2, 14.    **9:24** 1 Chr 26:13.    **9:25** 2 Chr 23:4–5.

spiced ointments.* [31]* Mattithiah, one of the Levites, the firstborn of Shallum the Korahite, was entrusted with preparing the cakes. [32] Benaiah the Kohathite, one of their brothers, was in charge of setting out the showbread each sabbath.*

[33] These were the singers and the gatekeepers, family heads over the Levites. They stayed in the chambers when free of duty, for day and night they had to be ready for service. [34] These were the levitical family heads by their generations, chiefs who dwelt in Jerusalem.

## II. THE HISTORY OF DAVID

**Genealogy of Saul.** [35]* Jeiel, the founder of Gibeon, dwelt in Gibeon; his wife's name was Maacah. [36] His firstborn son was Abdon; then came Zur, Kish, Baal, Ner, Nadab, [37] Gedor, Ahio, Zechariah, and Mikloth. [38] Mikloth became the father of Shimeam. These, too, with their relatives, dwelt opposite their relatives in Jerusalem. [39] Ner became the father of Kish, and Kish became the father of Saul. Saul became the father of Jonathan, Malchishua, Abinadab, and Eshbaal. [40] The son of Jonathan was Meribbaal, and Meribbaal became the father of Micah. [41] The sons of Micah were Pithon, Melech, Tahrea, and Ahaz. [42] Ahaz became the father of Jehoaddah, and Jehoaddah became the father of Alemeth, Azmaveth, and Zimri. Zimri became the father of Moza. [43] Moza became the father of Binea, whose son was Rephaiah, whose son was Eleasah, whose son was Azel. [44] Azel had six sons, whose names were Azrikam, his firstborn, Ishmael, Sheariah, Azariah, Obadiah, and Hanan; these were the sons of Azel.

**10** **Death of Saul and His Sons.** [1]* Now the Philistines went to war against Israel, and Israel fled before them, and they fell, slain on Mount Gilboa. [2] The Philistines pressed hard after Saul and his sons. When the Philistines had struck down Jonathan, Abinadab, and Malchishua, sons of Saul, [3] the fury of the battle converged on Saul. Then the archers hit him, and he was severely wounded.

[4] Saul said to his armor-bearer, "Draw your sword and run me through; otherwise these uncircumcised will come and abuse me." But the armor-bearer, badly frightened, refused, so Saul took his own sword and fell upon it. [5] When the armor-bearer saw that Saul was dead, he too fell upon his sword and died. [6] Thus Saul, and his three sons, his whole house, died together. [7] When all the Israelites in the valley saw that Saul and his sons had fled and that they had died, they abandoned their cities and fled. Then the Philistines came and lived in those cities.

[8] On the following day, when the Philistines came to strip the slain, they found Saul and his sons fallen on Mount Gilboa. [9] They stripped him, and took his head and his armor; these they sent throughout the land of the Philistines to bring the good news to their idols and to the people. [10] They put his armor in the temple of their gods, but his skull they impaled at the temple of Dagon.

**Burial of Saul.** [11] When all the inhabitants of Jabesh-gilead heard all that the Philistines had done to Saul, [12] all their warriors set out, recovered the corpses of Saul and his sons, and brought them to Jabesh. They buried their bones under the oak of Jabesh, and fasted for seven days.*

[13]† Thus Saul died because of his treason against the LORD in disobeying his word, and also because he had sought counsel from a ghost,* [14] rather than from the LORD. Therefore the LORD took his life, and turned his kingdom over to David, the son of Jesse.*

**11** **David Is Made King.** [1]* Then all Israel gathered around David in Hebron, and they said: "Look! We are your bone and your flesh. [2] In days past, when Saul was still the king, it was you who led Israel in all its battles. And now the LORD, your God, has said to you: You shall shepherd my people Israel; you shall be ruler over my people Israel."* [3] Then all the elders of Israel came to the king at Hebron, and at Hebron David made a covenant with

---

**10:13–14** The Chronicler explains why Saul met his tragic end: he had disobeyed the Lord's command given through the prophet Samuel (1 Sm 15:3–9), and had consulted a necromancer (1 Sm 28:6–19), contrary to the Mosaic law (Dt 18:10–11).

9:30 Ex 30:20–33.
9:31–32 1 Chr 23:29; Lv 2:1–15; 6:13–16; 7:11.
9:32 Ex 25:30; Lv 24:5–8.
9:35–44 1 Chr 8:29–38.
10:1–12 1 Sm 31:1–13.
10:12 2 Sm 2:5.
10:13 Dt 18:10–14; 1 Sm 13:13–14; 15:3, 11, 26.
10:14 1 Sm 15:28; 2 Sm 3:9–10.
11:1–9 2 Sm 5:1–10.
11:2 1 Sm 18:5, 13–16, 30; 19:8.

them in the presence of the LORD; and they anointed David king over Israel, in accordance with the word of the LORD given through Samuel.*

**Jerusalem Captured.** 4 Then David and all Israel went to Jerusalem, that is, Jebus, where the inhabitants of the land were called Jebusites.* 5 The inhabitants of Jebus said to David, "You shall not enter here." David nevertheless captured the fortress of Zion, which is the City of David. 6 David said, "Whoever strikes the Jebusites first shall be made chief and captain." Joab, the son of Zeruiah, was the first to attack; and so he became chief.* 7 David took up residence in the fortress, which therefore was called the City of David. 8 He built up the city on all sides, from the Millo all the way around, while Joab restored the rest of the city.* 9 David became ever more powerful, for the LORD of hosts was with him.

**David's Warriors.** 10* These were David's chief warriors who, together with all Israel, supported him in his reign in order to make him king, according to the LORD's word concerning Israel.

11 Here is the list of David's warriors:

Ishbaal, the son of Hachamoni, chief of the Three.† He brandished his spear over three hundred, whom he had slain in a single encounter.

12 Next to him was Eleazar, the son of Dodo the Ahohite, one of the Three warriors.* 13 He was with David at Pas-dammim, where the Philistines had massed for battle. There was a plot of land full of barley. The people were fleeing before the Philistines,* 14 but he took his stand in the middle of the plot, kept it safe, and cut down the Philistines. Thus the LORD brought about a great victory.

15 Three of the Thirty chiefs went down to the rock, to David, who was in the cave of Adullam while the Philistines were encamped in the valley of Rephaim.* 16 David was then in the stronghold, and a Philistine garrison was at Bethlehem. 17 David had a strong craving, and said, "If only someone would give me a drink of water from the cistern by the gate of Bethlehem!" 18 Thereupon the Three broke through the encampment of the Philistines, drew water from the cistern by the gate of Bethlehem, and carried it back to David. But David refused to drink it. Instead, he poured it out† to the LORD, 19 saying, "God forbid that I should do such a thing! Could I drink the blood of these men who risked their lives? For at the risk of their lives they brought it." So he refused to drink it. Such deeds as these the Three warriors performed.

20* Abishai, the brother of Joab, was the chief of the Thirty;† he brandished his spear over three hundred, whom he had slain. He made a name beside the Three,* 21 but was twice as famous as any of the Thirty, becoming their leader. However, he did not attain to the Three.

22 Benaiah, son of Jehoiada, a valiant man of mighty deeds, from Kabzeel, killed the two sons of Ariel of Moab. Also, he went down and killed the lion in the cistern on a snowy day. 23 He likewise slew the Egyptian, a huge man five cubits tall. The Egyptian carried a spear that was like a weaver's beam, but Benaiah came against him with a staff; he wrested the spear from the Egyptian's hand, and killed him with that spear. 24 Such deeds as these Benaiah, the son of Jehoiada, performed, and he made a name beside the Three warriors, 25 but was more famous than any of the Thirty. However, he did not attain to the Three. David put him in charge of his bodyguard.*

26 Also these warriors: Asahel, the brother of Joab; Elhanan, son of Dodo, from Bethlehem;* 27 Shammoth, from En-harod; Helez, from Beth-pelet; 28 Ira, son of Ikkesh, from Tekoa; Abiezer, from Anathoth; 29 Sibbecai, from Husha; Ilai, from Ahoh;* 30 Maharai, from Netophah; Heled, son of Baanah, from Netophah;* 31 Ithai, son of Ribai, from Gibeah of Benjamin; Benaiah, from Pirathon;* 32 Hurai, from Nahale-gaash; Abiel, from Beth-arabah;

---

11:11 *The Three*: the Chronicler actually names only two of these figures, Ishbaal and Eleazar. According to 2 Sm 23:11, the third member of the Three was Shammah.

11:18 *Poured it out*: as a libation.

11:20 *The Thirty*: they are listed by name in vv. 26–47. The parallel list in 2 Sm 23:8–39 often differs in names and spellings; for the numbers, see note on 2 Sm 23:8–39.

11:3 1 Sm 16:1, 13; 2 Sm 2:4.
11:4 Jos 15:8; Jgs 1:21; 19:10–11.
11:6 2 Sm 8:16.
11:8 1 Kgs 9:15, 24; 11:27; 2 Chr 32:5.
11:10–41 2 Sm 23:8–39.
11:12 1 Chr 27:4.
11:13 1 Sm 17:1.
11:15 1 Chr 14:9;

2 Sm 5:18, 22.
11:20–21 2 Sm 23:18–19.
11:20 1 Chr 18:12; 1 Sm 26:6–10; 2 Sm 16:9; 18:2; 21:17.
11:25 2 Sm 8:18; 20:23.
11:26 1 Chr 2:16; 27:7.
11:29 1 Chr 27:11.
11:30 1 Chr 27:13.
11:31 1 Chr 27:14.

33 Azmaveth, from Bahurim; Eliahba, from Shaalbon; 34 Jashen the Gunite; Jonathan, son of Shagee the Hararite; 35 Ahiam, son of Sachar the Hararite; Eliphelet, son of 36 Ahasbai, from Beth-maacah; Ahijah, from Gilo; 37 Hezro, from Carmel; Naarai, the son of Ezbai; 38 Joel, brother of Nathan, from Rehob, the Gadite; 39 Zelek the Ammonite; Naharai, from Beeroth, the armor-bearer of Joab, son of Zeruiah; 40 Ira, from Jattir; Gareb, from Jattir; 41 Uriah the Hittite; Zabad, son of Ahlai, 42 and, in addition to the Thirty, Adina, son of Shiza, the Reubenite, chief of the tribe of Reuben; 43 Hanan, son of Maacah; Joshaphat the Mithnite; 44 Uzzia, the Ashterathite; Shama and Jeiel, sons of Hotham, from Aroer; 45 Jediael, son of Shimri, and Joha, his brother, the Tizite; 46 Eliel the Mahavite; Jeribai and Joshaviah, sons of Elnaam; Ithmah, from Moab; 47 Eliel, Obed, and Jaasiel the Mezobian.

## 12 David's Early Followers.

1 The following men came to David in Ziklag while he was still under banishment from Saul, son of Kish; they, too, were among the warriors who helped him in his battles.* 2 They were archers who could use either the right or the left hand, both in slinging stones and in shooting arrows with the bow. They were some of Saul's kinsmen, from Benjamin. 3 Ahiezer was their chief, along with Joash, both sons of Shemaah of Gibeah; also Jeziel and Pelet, sons of Azmaveth; Beracah; Jehu, from Anathoth;* 4 Ishmaiah the Gibeonite, a warrior among the Thirty, and over the Thirty; 5 Jeremiah; Jahaziel; Johanan; Jozabad from Gederah; 6 Eluzai; Jerimoth; Bealiah; Shemariah; Shephatiah the Haruphite; 7 Elkanah, Isshiah, Azarel, Joezer, and Jashobeam, who were Korahites; 8 Joelah and Zebadiah, sons of Jeroham, from Gedor.

9 Some of the Gadites also went over to David when he was at the stronghold in the wilderness. They were valiant warriors, experienced soldiers equipped with shield and spear, fearsome as lions, swift as gazelles on the mountains.* 10 Ezer was their chief, Obadiah was second, Eliab third, 11 Mishmannah fourth, Jeremiah fifth, 12 Attai sixth, Eliel seventh, 13 Johanan eighth, Elzabad ninth, 14 Jeremiah tenth, and Machbannai eleventh.

15 These Gadites were army commanders, the lesser over hundreds and the greater over thousands. 16 It was they who crossed over the Jordan in the first month, when it was overflowing both its banks, and chased away all who were in the valleys to the east and to the west.

17 Some Benjaminites and Judahites also came to David at the stronghold. 18 David went out to meet them and addressed them in these words: "If you come peacefully, to help me, I am of a mind to have you join me. But if you have come to betray me to my enemies though my hands have done no wrong, may the God of our ancestors see and punish you."

19 Then a spirit clothed Amasai, the chief of the Thirty, and he answered David:

"We are yours, O David,
    we are with you, son of Jesse.
Peace, peace to you,
    and peace to him who helps you;
    may your God be your helper!"

So David received them and placed them among the leaders of his troops.

20 Men from Manasseh also deserted to David when he came with the Philistines to battle against Saul. However, he did not help the Philistines, for their lords took counsel and sent him home, saying, "At the cost of our heads he will desert to his master Saul." 21 As he was returning to Ziklag, therefore, these deserted to him from Manasseh: Adnah, Jozabad, Jediael, Michael, Jozabad, Elihu, and Zillethai, chiefs of thousands of Manasseh.† 22 They helped David by taking charge of his troops, for they were all warriors and became commanders of his army. 23 And from day to day men kept coming to David's help until there was a vast encampment, like God's own encampment.

## The Assembly at Hebron.

24 This is the muster of the detachments of armed troops that came to David at Hebron to bring Saul's kingdom over to him, as the LORD had ordained. 25 † Judahites bearing shields and spears: six thousand eight hundred armed troops. 26 Of the Simeonites, warriors fit for battle: seven thousand one hundred. 27 Of the Levites: four

---

† **12:21** See note on 27:1–15.
**12:25–38** The Chronicler here takes the brief account of David's installation as king in 2 Sm 5:1–3 (= 1 Chr 11:1–3) and expands it in line with his exaltation of David and his dynasty.

* **12:1** 1 Sm 27:1–7.          **12:9** Dt 33:20.
**12:3** 1 Chr 27:12.

thousand six hundred, <sup>28</sup> along with Jehoiada, leader of the line of Aaron, with another three thousand seven hundred, <sup>29</sup> and Zadok, a young warrior, with twenty-two princes of his father's house. <sup>30</sup> Of the Benjaminites, the kinsmen of Saul: three thousand—until this time, most of them had kept their allegiance to the house of Saul. <sup>31</sup> Of the Ephraimites: twenty thousand eight hundred warriors, men renowned in their ancestral houses. <sup>32</sup> Of the half-tribe of Manasseh: eighteen thousand, designated by name to come and make David king. <sup>33</sup> Of the Issacharites, their chiefs who were endowed with an understanding of the times and who knew what Israel had to do: two hundred chiefs, together with all their kinsmen under their command. <sup>34</sup> From Zebulun, men fit for military service, set in battle array with every kind of weapon for war: fifty thousand men rallying with a single purpose. <sup>35</sup> From Naphtali: one thousand captains, and with them, armed with shield and lance, thirty-seven thousand men. <sup>36</sup> Of the Danites, set in battle array: twenty-eight thousand six hundred. <sup>37</sup> From Asher, fit for military service and set in battle array: forty thousand. <sup>38</sup> From the other side of the Jordan, of the Reubenites, Gadites, and the half-tribe of Manasseh, men equipped with every kind of weapon of war: one hundred and twenty thousand.

<sup>39</sup> All these soldiers, drawn up in battle order, came to Hebron with the resolute intention of making David king over all Israel. The rest of Israel was likewise of one mind to make David king. <sup>40</sup> They remained with David for three days, eating and drinking, for their relatives had prepared for them. <sup>41</sup> Moreover, their neighbors from as far as Issachar, Zebulun, and Naphtali came bringing food on donkeys, camels, mules, and oxen—provisions in great quantity of meal, pressed figs, raisins, wine, oil, oxen, and sheep. For there was rejoicing in Israel.

# 13 Transfer of the Ark. <sup>1</sup>* After David had taken counsel with his commanders of thousands and of hundreds, that is, with

every leader, <sup>2</sup> he said to the whole assembly of Israel: "If it seems good to you, and is so decreed by the LORD our God, let us send to the rest of our kindred from all the districts of Israel, and also the priests and the Levites from their cities with pasture lands, that they may join us; * <sup>3</sup> and let us bring the ark of our God here among us, for in the days of Saul we did not consult it." <sup>4</sup> And the whole assembly agreed to do it, for it seemed right in the eyes of all the people.

<sup>5</sup> Then David assembled all Israel, from Shihor of Egypt† to Lebo-hamath, to bring the ark of God from Kiriath-jearim. * <sup>6</sup> David and all Israel went up to Baalah, that is, to Kiriath-jearim, of Judah, to bring up from there the ark of God, which was known by the name "LORD enthroned upon the cherubim." * <sup>7</sup> They transported the ark of God on a new cart from the house of Abinadab; Uzzah and Ahio were guiding the cart, <sup>8</sup> while David and all Israel danced before God with all their might, with singing, and with lyres, harps, tambourines, cymbals, and trumpets.

<sup>9</sup> As they reached the threshing floor of Chidon,† Uzzah stretched out his hand to steady the ark, for the oxen were tipping it. <sup>10</sup> Then the LORD became angry with Uzzah and struck him, because he had laid his hand on the ark; he died there in God's presence. <sup>11</sup> David was angry because the LORD's anger had broken out against Uzzah. Therefore that place has been called Perez-uzzah† even to this day.

<sup>12</sup> David was afraid of God that day, and he said, "How can I bring in the ark of God to me?" <sup>13</sup> Therefore he did not take the ark with him into the City of David, but deposited it instead at the house of Obed-edom the Gittite. <sup>14</sup> The ark of God remained in the house of Obed-edom with his family for three months, and the LORD blessed Obed-edom's household and all that he possessed. *

# 14 David in Jerusalem. <sup>1</sup>* Hiram, king of Tyre, sent envoys to David along with cedar wood, and masons and carpenters to build him a house.†* <sup>2</sup> David now knew†

---

**13:5** *Shihor of Egypt*: the eastern branch of the Nile delta. *Lebo-hamath*: in southern Syria.

**13:9** *Chidon*: in 2 Sm 6:6 the name is Nodan (variant: Nacon).

**13:11** *Perez-uzzah*: this Hebrew phrase means "the breaking out against Uzza."

**14:1** The Chronicler's account of David's establishment as king and his victories over the Philistines follows 2 Sm 5:11–25,

but makes David's rule even more prominent.

**14:2** *David now knew*: see note on 2 Sm 5:12.

**13:1–14** 2 Sm 6:1–11.
　**13:2** Nm 35:1–8; Jos 14:4; 21:2–42.
　**13:5** 1 Chr 15:3; Jos 13:3, 5; 1 Sm 6:21; 7:1–2; 2 Sm 6:1–11.
**13:6** Jos 15:9; 18:14; 1 Sm 4:4; 7:1.
**13:14** 1 Chr 26:4–5.
**14:1–16** 2 Sm 5:11–25.
**14:1** 2 Sm 5:11; 2 Chr 2:4.

that the LORD had truly established him as king over Israel, for his kingdom was greatly exalted for the sake of his people Israel. ³ David took other wives in Jerusalem and became the father of more sons and daughters. ⁴ These are the names of those who were born to him in Jerusalem: Shammua, Shobab, Nathan, Solomon, ⁵ Ibhar, Elishua, Elpelet, ⁶ Nogah, Nepheg, Japhia, ⁷ Elishama, Beeliada, and Eliphelet.*

**The Philistine Wars.** ⁸ When the Philistines had heard that David was anointed king over all Israel, they marched out in force looking for him. But when David heard of this, he went out against them. ⁹ Meanwhile the Philistines had come and raided the valley of Rephaim.* ¹⁰ David inquired of God, "Shall I attack the Philistines, and will you deliver them into my power?" The LORD answered him, "Attack, for I have delivered them into your power." ¹¹ So they attacked, at Baal-perazim, and David defeated them there. Then David said, "By my hand God has broken through my enemies just as water breaks through a dam." Therefore that place was called Baal-perazim.† ¹² The Philistines abandoned their gods there, and David ordered them to be burnt.*

¹³ Once again the Philistines raided the valley, ¹⁴ and again David inquired of God. But God answered him: Do not try to pursue them, but go around them and come against them near the balsam trees. ¹⁵ When you hear the sound of marching in the tops of the balsam trees, then go forth to battle, for God has already gone before you to strike the army of the Philistines. ¹⁶ David did as God commanded him, and they routed the Philistine army from Gibeon to Gezer.

¹⁷ Thus David's fame was spread abroad through every land, and the LORD put the fear of him on all the nations.

## 15 Preparations for Moving the Ark.
¹ David built houses for himself in the City of David and prepared a place for the ark of God, pitching a tent for it there. ² At that time he said, "No one may carry the ark of God

except the Levites, for the LORD chose them to carry the ark of the LORD and to minister to him forever."* ³ Then David assembled all Israel to Jerusalem to bring up the ark of the LORD to its place, which he had prepared for it.* ⁴ David also convened the sons of Aaron and the Levites: ⁵ of the sons of Kohath, Uriel, their chief, and one hundred and twenty of his brothers; ⁶ of the sons of Merari, Asaiah, their chief, and two hundred and twenty of his brothers; ⁷ of the sons of Gershon, Joel, their chief, and one hundred and thirty of his brothers; ⁸ of the sons of Elizaphan, Shemaiah, their chief, and two hundred of his brothers; ⁹ of the sons of Hebron, Eliel, their chief, and eighty of his brothers; ¹⁰ of the sons of Uzziel, Amminadab, their chief, and one hundred and twelve of his brothers.

¹¹ David summoned the priests Zadok and Abiathar, and the Levites Uriel, Asaiah, Joel, Shemaiah, Eliel, and Amminadab,* ¹² and said to them: "You heads of the levitical houses, sanctify yourselves along with your brothers to bring up the ark of the LORD, the God of Israel, to the place which I have prepared for it.* ¹³ Because you were not with us the first time, the LORD our God broke out against us, for we did not seek him aright."* ¹⁴ Accordingly, the priests and the Levites sanctified themselves to bring up the ark of the LORD, the God of Israel. ¹⁵ The Levites carried the ark of God on their shoulders with poles, as Moses had commanded according to the word of the LORD.*

¹⁶ David commanded the commanders of the Levites to appoint their brothers as singers and to play on musical instruments, harps, lyres, and cymbals, to make a loud sound of rejoicing.* ¹⁷ Therefore the Levites appointed Heman, son of Joel, and, among his brothers, Asaph, son of Berechiah; and among the sons of Merari, their brothers, Ethan, son of Kushaiah;* ¹⁸ and, together with these, their brothers of the second rank: the gatekeepers Zechariah, Uzziel, Shemiramoth, Jehiel, Unni, Eliab, Benaiah, Maaseiah, Mattithiah, Eliphelehu, Mikneiah, Obed-edom, and Jeiel. ¹⁹ The singers, Heman, Asaph, and Ethan, sounded brass cymbals. ²⁰ Zechariah, Uzziel, Shemiramoth,

---

*
**14:3–7** 1 Chr 3:5–8; 2 Sm 5:13–16.
**14:9** 1 Chr 11:15.
**14:12** Dt 7:5, 25.
**15:2** Nm 1:50; 7:9; Dt 10:8; 31:25; 1 Sm 6:15; Jos 3:8.
**15:3** 1 Chr 13:5; 2 Sm 6:15, 17.
**15:11** 1 Chr 16:39; 2 Sm 8:17; 15:29, 35.
**15:12** 2 Chr 29:5, 15, 34; 30:3, 15, 24.
**15:13** 1 Chr 13:3.
**15:15** Ex 25:10–22; Nm 1:50; 7:9; 2 Chr 35:3.
**15:16** 1 Chr 13:8; 16:5; 2 Chr 5:12; 29:25; Neh 12:27.
**15:17** 1 Chr 6:31–47; 25:1–8.

Jehiel, Unni, Eliab, Maaseiah, and Benaiah played on harps set to "Alamoth."† 21 But Mattithiah, Eliphelehu, Mikneiah, Obed-edom, and Jeiel led the song on lyres set to "sheminith." 22 Chenaniah was the chief of the Levites in the singing; he directed the singing, for he was skillful. * 23 Berechiah and Elkanah were gatekeepers before the ark. 24 The priests, Shebaniah, Joshaphat, Nethanel, Amasai, Zechariah, Benaiah, and Eliezer, sounded the trumpets before the ark of God. * Obed-edom and Jeiel were also gatekeepers before the ark.

**The Ark Comes to Jerusalem.** 25 * Thus David, the elders of Israel, and the commanders of thousands went to bring up the ark of the covenant of the LORD with joy from the house of Obed-edom. 26 While God helped the Levites to carry the ark of the covenant of the LORD, they sacrificed seven bulls and seven rams. * 27 David was vested in a robe of fine linen, as were all the Levites who carried the ark, the singers, and Chenaniah, the leader of song; David was also wearing a linen ephod. * 28 Thus all Israel brought up the ark of the covenant of the LORD with joyful shouting, to the sound of horns, trumpets, and cymbals, and the music of harps and lyres. 29 But as the ark of the covenant of the LORD was entering the City of David, Michal, daughter of Saul, looked down from her window, and when she saw King David leaping and dancing, she despised him in her heart. *

**16** 1 * They brought in the ark of God and set it within the tent which David had pitched for it. * Then they sacrificed burnt offerings and communion offerings to God. 2 When David had finished sacrificing the burnt offerings and communion offerings, he blessed the people in the name of the LORD, 3 and distributed to every Israelite, to every man and every woman, a loaf of bread, a piece of meat, and a raisin cake.

**David's Directives for the Levites.** 4 He then appointed certain Levites to minister before the ark of the LORD, to celebrate, thank, and praise the LORD, the God of Israel. * 5 Asaph was their chief, and second to him were Zechariah, Uzziel, Shemiramoth, Jehiel, Mattithiah, Eliab, Benaiah, Obed-edom, and Jeiel. These were to play on harps and lyres, while Asaph was to sound the cymbals, 6 and the priests Benaiah and Jahaziel were to be the regular trumpeters before the ark of the covenant of God.

7 On that same day, David appointed Asaph and his brothers to sing for the first time these praises of the LORD:

8 † Give thanks to the LORD, invoke his name; *
make known among the peoples his deeds.
9 Sing praise, play music;
proclaim all his wondrous deeds.
10 Glory in his holy name;
rejoice, O hearts that seek the LORD!
11 Rely on the mighty LORD;
constantly seek his face.
12 Recall the wondrous deeds he has done,
his signs, and his words of judgment,
13 You sons of Israel, his servants,
offspring of Jacob, the chosen ones!
14 The LORD is our God;
who rules the whole earth.
15 He remembers forever his covenant
the pact imposed for a thousand generations—
16 Which was made with Abraham,
confirmed by oath to Isaac,
17 And ratified as binding for Jacob,
an everlasting covenant for Israel:
18 "To you will I give the land of Canaan,
your own allotted heritage."
19 When they were few in number,
a handful, and strangers there,
20 Wandering from nation to nation,
from one kingdom to another,
21 He let no one oppress them;
for their sake he rebuked kings:
22 "Do not touch my anointed,
to my prophets do no harm."
23 * Sing to the LORD, all the earth,

---

15:20–21 *Alamoth…sheminith:* musical terms of uncertain meaning. *Alamoth,* lit., "young women," occurs in the superscription to Ps 46. The term *sheminith,* in v. 21, might mean "bass" or "octave"; cf. Ps 6:1; 12:1.

16:8–36 A hymn composed of parts of several psalms: vv. 8–22 = Ps 105:1–15; vv. 23–33 = Ps 96:1–13; vv. 34–36 = Ps 106:1, 47–48. There are minor textual variants between this hymn and the psalms it is drawn from.

15:22 1 Chr 26:29.
15:24 Nm 10:8; Jos 6:4–8.
15:25–29 2 Sm 6:12–16.
15:26 2 Sm 6:17; 2 Chr 29:21.
15:27 1 Sm 2:18; 2 Sm 6:14.
15:29 2 Sm 6:20–23.
16:1–3 2 Sm 6:17–19.
16:1 1 Chr 15:1.
16:4 Sir 47:9.
16:8–22 Ps 105:1–15.
16:23–33 Ps 96:1–13.

announce his salvation, day after day.

24 Tell his glory among the nations;
　　among all peoples, his wondrous
　　　deeds.

25 For great is the LORD and highly to be
　　praised;
　　to be feared above all gods.

26 For the gods of the nations all do
　　nothing,
　　but the LORD made the heavens.

27 Splendor and majesty go before him;
　　power and rejoicing are in his holy
　　　place.

28 Give to the LORD, you families of
　　nations,
　　give to the LORD glory and might;

29 Give to the LORD the glory due his
　　name!
　Bring gifts, and come before him;
　　bow down to the LORD, splendid in
　　　holiness.

30 Tremble before him, all the earth;
　　the world will surely stand fast, never
　　　to be moved.

31 Let the heavens be glad and the earth
　　rejoice;
　　let them say among the nations: The
　　　LORD is king.

32 Let the sea and what fills it resound;
　　let the plains be joyful and all that is
　　　in them!

33 Then let all the trees of the forest exult
　　before the LORD, who comes,
　　who comes to rule the earth.

34* Give thanks to the LORD, who is good,
　　whose love endures forever;

35 And say, "Save us, O God, our savior,
　　gather us and deliver us from among
　　　the nations,
　That we may give thanks to your holy
　　name
　　and glory in praising you."

36 Blessed be the LORD, the God of Israel,
　　from everlasting to everlasting!
　Let all the people say, Amen! Hallelujah.

37 Then David left Asaph and his brothers there before the ark of the covenant of the LORD to minister before the ark regularly according to the daily ritual; 38 he also left there Obed-edom and sixty-eight of his brothers, including Obed-edom, son of Jeduthun, and Hosah, to be gatekeepers.* 39 But the priest Zadok and his priestly brothers he left before the tabernacle of the LORD on the high place at Gibeon,* 40 to make burnt offerings to the LORD on the altar for burnt offerings regularly, morning and evening, and to do all that is written in the law of the LORD which he commanded Israel.* 41 With them were Heman and Jeduthun and the others who were chosen and designated by name to give thanks to the LORD, "whose love endures forever,"* 42 with trumpets and cymbals for accompaniment, and instruments for sacred song. The sons of Jeduthun kept the gate.* 43 Then all the people departed, each to their own homes, and David returned to bless his household.*

17 **The Oracle of Nathan.** 1* After David had taken up residence in his house, he said to Nathan the prophet, "See, I am living in a house of cedar, but the ark of the covenant of the LORD is under tentcloth."* 2 Nathan replied to David, "Whatever is in your heart, go and do, for God is with you." 3 But that same night the word of God came to Nathan: 4 Go and tell David my servant, Thus says the LORD: It is not you who are to build the house for me to dwell in.* 5 For I have never dwelt in a house, from the day I brought Israel up, even to this day, but I have been lodging in tent or tabernacle. 6 As long as I have wandered about with all Israel, did I ever say a word to any of the judges of Israel whom I commanded to shepherd my people, Why have you not built me a house of cedar? 7 Now then, speak thus to my servant David, Thus says the LORD of hosts: I took you from the pasture, from following the flock, to become ruler over my people Israel.* 8 I was with you wherever you went, and I cut down all your enemies before you. I will make your name like that of the greatest on the earth. 9 I will assign a place for my people Israel and I will plant them in it to dwell there; they will never again be disturbed, nor shall the wicked ever again oppress them, as they did at the

---

**16:34–36** Ps 106:1, 47–48.
**16:38** 1 Chr 15:24.
**16:39** 1 Kgs 3:4.
**16:40** Ex 29:38–42; Lv 6:9;
　　Nm 28:3, 6; 2 Chr
　　13:11.
**16:41** 2 Chr 5:12; 7:3, 6;
　　20:21; Ezr 3:11.

**16:42** 2 Chr 29:27.
**16:43** 2 Sm 6:19–20.
**17:1–27** 2 Sm 7:1–29.
**17:1** 1 Chr 15:1;
　　2 Sm 5:11.
**17:4** 1 Chr 28:3; 1 Kgs
　　8:19.
**17:7** 1 Sm 16:11.

beginning, [10] and during all the time when I appointed judges over my people Israel. And I will subdue all your enemies. Moreover, I declare to you that the LORD will build you a house: [11] when your days have been completed and you must join your ancestors, I will raise up your offspring after you who will be one of your own sons, and I will establish his kingdom.* [12] He it is who shall build me a house, and I will establish his throne forever.* [13] I will be a father to him, and he shall be a son to me, and I will not withdraw my favor from him as I withdrew it from the one who was before you;* [14] but I will maintain him in my house and in my kingdom forever, and his throne shall be firmly established forever.

[15] In accordance with all these words and this whole vision Nathan spoke to David.

**David's Thanksgiving.** [16] Then King David came in and sat in the LORD's presence, and said: "Who am I, LORD God, and what is my house, that you should have brought me so far? [17] And yet, even this is too little in your sight, O God! For you have made a promise regarding your servant's house reaching into the future, and you have looked on me as henceforth the most notable of men, LORD God.* [18] What more can David say to you? You have known† your servant. [19] LORD, for your servant's sake and in keeping with your purpose, you have done this great thing. [20] LORD, there is no one like you, no God but you, just as we have always heard.*

[21] "Is there, like your people Israel, whom you redeemed from Egypt, another nation on earth whom a god went to redeem as his people? You won for yourself a name for great and awesome deeds by driving out the nations before your people.* [22] You made your people Israel your own forever, and you, LORD, became their God. [23] Now, LORD, may the promise that you have spoken concerning your servant and his house remain firm forever. Bring about what you have promised, [24] that your name, LORD of hosts, God of Israel, may be great and abide forever, while the house of your servant is established in your presence.

[25] "Because you, my God, have revealed to your servant that you will build him a house, your servant dares to pray before you.* [26] Since you, LORD, are truly God and have made this generous promise to your servant, [27] do, then, bless the house of your servant, that it may be in your presence forever—since it is you, LORD, who blessed it, it is blessed forever."*

**18** **David's Victories.** [1]* After this, David defeated the Philistines and subdued them; and he took Gath and its towns away from the Philistines. [2] He also defeated Moab, and the Moabites became David's subjects, paying tribute.

[3] David then defeated Hadadezer, king of Zobah, toward Hamath, who was on his way to set up his victory stele at the river Euphrates. [4] David captured from him one thousand chariots, seven thousand horsemen, and twenty thousand foot soldiers. David hamstrung all the chariot horses, but left one hundred for his chariots.* [5] The Arameans of Damascus came to help Hadadezer, king of Zobah, but David also defeated twenty-two thousand of their men in Aram. [6] Then David set up garrisons in the Damascus region of Aram, and the Arameans became David's subjects, paying tribute. Thus the LORD made David victorious in all his campaigns.

[7] David took the golden shields that were carried by Hadadezer's attendants and brought them to Jerusalem. [8] David likewise took away from Tibhath and Cun, cities of Hadadezer, large quantities of bronze; Solomon later used it to make the bronze sea and the pillars and the vessels of bronze.*

[9] When Tou, king of Hamath, heard that David had defeated the entire army of Hadadezer, king of Zobah, [10] he sent his son Hadoram to wish King David well and to congratulate him on having waged a victorious war against Hadadezer; for Hadadezer had been at war with Tou. He also brought gold, silver and bronze articles of every sort.* [11] These also King David consecrated to the LORD along with all the silver and gold that he had taken from the nations: from Edom, Moab, the Ammonites, the Philistines, and Amalek.

[12] Abishai, the son of Zeruiah, also defeated

**17:18** *Known*: given David recognition, chosen him, singled him out; cf. Gn 18:19; Ex 33:12; Am 3:2.

**17:11** 2 Sm 7:12–13.       **17:12** 1 Chr 22:10; 28:6, 10.

**17:13** 2 Sm 7:14.          **18:1–13** 2 Sm 8:1–14.
**17:17** 2 Sm 7:19.          **18:4** 2 Sm 8:14; Jos 11:6, 9.
**17:20** Sir 36:4.
**17:21** Dt 4:7; 2 Sm 7:23.  **18:8** 2 Sm 8:8; 1 Kgs 7:15, 23, 27.
**17:25** 2 Sm 7:27.
**17:27** Nm 22:6.            **18:10** 2 Sm 8:10.

eighteen thousand Edomites in the Valley of Salt.* [13] He set up garrisons in Edom, and all the Edomites became David's subjects. Thus the LORD brought David victory in all his undertakings.

**David's Officials.** [14]* David was king over all Israel; he dispensed justice and right to all his people. [15] Joab, son of Zeruiah, was in command of the army; Jehoshaphat, son of Ahilud, was chancellor;* [16] Zadok, son of Ahitub, and Ahimelech, son of Abiathar, were priests; † Shavsha was scribe;* [17] Benaiah, son of Jehoiada, was in command of the Cherethites and the Pelethites; and David's sons were the chief assistants to the king. † *

# 19

**Campaigns Against Ammon.** [1]* Afterward Nahash, king of the Ammonites, died and his son succeeded him as king. [2] David said, "I will show kindness to Hanun, the son of Nahash, for his father showed kindness to me." Therefore he sent envoys to console him over his father. But when David's servants had entered the land of the Ammonites to console Hanun, [3] the Ammonite princes said to Hanun, "Do you think David is doing this—sending you these consolers—to honor your father? Have not his servants rather come to you to explore the land, spying it out for its overthrow?" [4] So Hanun seized David's servants and had them shaved and their garments cut off halfway at the hips. Then he sent them away. [5] David was told about the men, and he sent word for them to be intercepted, for the men had been greatly disgraced. "Remain at Jericho," the king told them, "until your beards have grown again; then come back here."

[6] When the Ammonites realized that they had put themselves in bad odor with David, Hanun and the Ammonites sent a thousand talents of silver to hire chariots and horsemen from Aram Naharaim, from Aram-maacah, and from Zobah. [7] They hired thirty-two thousand chariots along with the king of Maacah

and his army, who came and encamped before Medeba. The Ammonites also assembled from their cities and came out for war. [8] When David heard of this, he sent Joab and his whole army of warriors against them. [9] The Ammonites marched out and lined up for battle at the entrance of the city, while the kings who had come to their help remained apart in the open field. [10] When Joab saw that there was a battle line both in front of and behind him, he chose some of the best fighters among the Israelites and lined them up against the Arameans; [11] the rest of the army, which he placed under the command of his brother Abishai, then lined up to oppose the Ammonites. [12] And he said: "If the Arameans prove too strong for me, you must come and save me; and if the Ammonites prove too strong for you, I will save you. [13] Hold firm and let us show ourselves courageous for the sake of our people and the cities of our God; and may the LORD do what is good in his sight." [14] Joab therefore advanced with his men to engage the Arameans in battle; but they fled before him. [15] And when the Ammonites saw that the Arameans had fled, they too fled before his brother Abishai, and entered their city. Joab then came to Jerusalem.

[16] Seeing themselves vanquished by Israel, the Arameans sent messengers to bring out the Arameans from beyond the Euphrates, with Shophach, the commander of Hadadezer's army, at their head. [17] When this was reported to David, he gathered all Israel together, crossed the Jordan, and met them. With the army of David drawn up to fight the Arameans, they gave battle. [18] But the Arameans fled before Israel, and David killed seven thousand of their chariot fighters and forty thousand of their foot soldiers; he also put to death Shophach, the commander of the army. [19] When the vassals of Hadadezer saw themselves vanquished by Israel, they made peace with David and became his subjects. After this, the Arameans refused to come to the aid of the Ammonites.

---

† **18:16** *Zadok...and Ahimelech, son of Abiathar, were priests*: emendation—the Masoretic text here reads "Abimelech," not "Ahimelech"; but 2 Sm 8:17, the Chronicler's source, has "Ahimelech." See note there.

**18:17** *Chief assistants to the king*: according to 2 Sm 8:18, the Chronicler's source here, David's sons were priests. The Chronicler's modification reflects his conviction that only Aaron's descendants could be priests.

* **18:12** 2 Sm 8:13; 2 Kgs 14:7.
**18:14–17** 2 Sm 8:15–18.
**18:15** 1 Chr 16:6; 2 Sm 8:16; 1 Kgs 4:3.
**18:16** 1 Chr 24:3, 6, 31; 2 Sm 8:17.
**18:17** 1 Chr 11:22; 2 Sm 8:18; 1 Kgs 1:38, 44.
**19:1–19** 2 Sm 10:1–19.

**20** ¹At the turn of the year,† the time when kings go to war, Joab led the army out in force, laid waste the land of the Ammonites, and went on to besiege Rabbah; David himself remained in Jerusalem. When Joab had attacked Rabbah and destroyed it, ² David took the crown of Milcom from the idol's head. It was found to weigh a talent of gold, with precious stones on it; this crown David wore on his own head. He also brought out a great amount of spoil from the city. ³ He deported the people of the city and set them to work with saws, iron picks, and axes. David dealt thus with all the cities of the Ammonites. Then David and his whole army returned to Jerusalem.*

**Victories over the Philistines.** ⁴* Afterward there was another battle with the Philistines, at Gezer. At that time, Sibbecai the Hushathite struck down Sippai, one of the descendants of the Rephaim, and the Philistines were subdued.*

⁵ There was another battle with the Philistines, and Elhanan, the son of Jair, slew Lahmi, the brother of Goliath† of Gath, whose spear shaft was like a weaver's beam.*

⁶ There was another battle, at Gath, and there was a giant, who had six fingers to each hand and six toes to each foot; twenty-four in all. He too was descended from the Rephaim. ⁷ He defied Israel, and Jonathan, the son of Shimea, David's brother, slew him. ⁸ These were the descendants of the Rephaim of Gath who died at the hands of David and his servants.

**21** **David's Census; the Plague.** ¹* A satan† rose up against Israel, and he incited David to take a census of Israel.* ² David therefore said to Joab and to the other generals of the army, "Go, number the Israelites from Beer-sheba to Dan, and report back to me that

I may know their number." ³ But Joab replied: "May the LORD increase his people a hundredfold! My lord king, are not all of them my lord's subjects? Why does my lord seek to do this thing? Why should he bring guilt upon Israel?" ⁴ However, the king's command prevailed over Joab, who departed and traversed all of Israel, and then returned to Jerusalem. ⁵ Joab reported the census figures to David: of men capable of wielding a sword, there were in all Israel one million one hundred thousand, and in Judah four hundred and seventy thousand. ⁶ Levi and Benjamin, however, he did not include in the census, for the king's command was repugnant to Joab.* ⁷ This command was evil in the sight of God, and he struck Israel. ⁸ Then David said to God, "I have sinned greatly in doing this thing. Take away your servant's guilt, for I have acted very foolishly."

⁹ Then the LORD spoke to Gad, David's seer, in these words:* ¹⁰ Go, tell David: Thus says the LORD: I am laying out three options; choose one of them, and I will inflict it on you. ¹¹ Accordingly, Gad went to David and said to him: "Thus says the LORD: Decide now— ¹² will it be three years of famine; or three months of fleeing your enemies, with the sword of your foes ever at your back; or three days of the LORD's own sword, a plague in the land, with the LORD's destroying angel in every part of Israel? Now consider: What answer am I to give him who sent me?" ¹³ Then David said to Gad: "I am in serious trouble. But let me fall into the hand of the LORD, whose mercy is very great, rather than into hands of men."

¹⁴ Therefore the LORD sent a plague upon Israel, and seventy thousand Israelites died. ¹⁵ God also sent an angel to Jerusalem to destroy it; but as the angel was on the point of destroying it, the LORD saw and changed his mind about the calamity, and said to the destroying angel, "Enough now! Stay your hand!"*

---

**20:1** *At the turn of the year:* thus in 2 Sm 11 begins the story of David's adultery with Bathsheba and his murder of her husband Uriah, but the Chronicler omits it.

**20:5** *Elhanan...slew Lahmi, the brother of Goliath:* with this notice the Chronicler solves the difficulty of the apparent contradiction between 1 Sm 17:49, 51 (David killed Goliath) and 2 Sm 21:19 (Elhanan killed Goliath).

**21:1** *A satan:* in the parallel passage (2 Sm 24:1) David is led astray because of the Lord's anger. The Chronicler's modification reflects the changed theological outlook of postexilic Israel, when evil was no longer attributed directly to God. At an earlier period the Hebrew word *satan* ("adversary," or, especially in a court of law, "accuser") designated both human beings (1 Kgs

11:14) and a "son of God" who accused people before God (Jb 1:6–12; 2:1–7; Zec 3:1–2). In later Judaism (cf. Wis 2:24) and in the New Testament, *satan*, or the "devil" (from *diablos*, the Greek translation of the Hebrew word), designates an evil spirit who tempts people to do wrong.

**20:2–3** 2 Sm 12:30–31.
**20:4–8** 2 Sm 21:18–22.
**20:4** 1 Chr 11:29; 27:11.
**20:5** 1 Chr 11:26; 1 Sm 17:4, 23.
**21:1–27** 2 Sm 24:1–25.
**21:1** Zec 3:1–2.
**21:6** 1 Chr 27:24; Nm 1:49.
**21:9** 1 Chr 29:29; 1 Sm 9:9; 2 Chr 29:25.
**21:15** Gn 6:6; Ex 32:14; 2 Sm 24:16; Jon 3:10.

**Ornan's Threshing Floor.** The angel of the LORD was then standing by the threshing floor of Ornan the Jebusite. [16]When David raised his eyes, he saw the angel of the LORD standing between earth and heaven, drawn sword in hand stretched out against Jerusalem.* David and the elders, clothed in sackcloth, fell face down, [17]and David prayed to God: "Was it not I who ordered the census of the people? I am the one who sinned, I did this wicked thing. But these sheep, what have they done? O LORD, my God, strike me and my father's family, but do not afflict your people with this plague!"

[18]Then the angel of the LORD commanded Gad to tell David to go up and set up an altar to the LORD on the threshing floor of Ornan the Jebusite.* [19]David went up at the word of Gad, which he spoke in the name of the LORD. [20]Ornan turned around and saw the king; his four sons who were with him hid themselves, but Ornan kept on threshing wheat. [21]But as David came toward Ornan, he looked up and saw that it was David, and left the threshing floor and bowed down before David, his face to the ground. [22]David said to Ornan: "Sell me the site of this threshing floor, that I may build on it an altar to the LORD. Sell it to me at its full price, that the plague may be withdrawn from the people." [23]But Ornan said to David: "Take it as your own, and let my lord the king do what is good in his sight. See, I also give you the oxen for the burnt offerings, the threshing sledges for the wood, and the wheat for the grain offering. I give it all to you." [24]But King David replied to Ornan: "No! I will buy it from you properly, at its full price. I will not take what is yours for the LORD, nor bring burnt offerings that cost me nothing." [25]So David paid Ornan six hundred shekels of gold† for the place.

**Altar for Burnt Offerings.** [26]David then built an altar there to the LORD, and sacrificed burnt offerings and communion offerings. He called upon the LORD, who answered him by sending down fire from heaven upon the altar for burnt offerings.* [27]Then the LORD gave orders to the angel to return his sword to its sheath.

[28]Once David saw that the LORD had answered him at the threshing floor of Ornan the Jebusite, he continued to offer sacrifices there. [29]The tabernacle of the LORD, which Moses had made in the wilderness, and the altar for burnt offerings were at that time on the high place at Gibeon.* [30]But David could not go into his presence to inquire of God, for he was fearful of the sword of the angel of the LORD.

**22** [1]Thus David said, "This is the house of the LORD God, and this is the altar for burnt offerings for Israel."* [2]† David then ordered that the resident aliens in the land of Israel should be brought together, and he appointed them stonecutters to hew out stone blocks for building the house of God.* [3]David also laid up large stores of iron to make nails for the doors of the gates, and clamps, together with so much bronze that it could not be weighed,* [4]and cedar trees without number. The Sidonians and Tyrians brought great stores of cedar logs to David.* [5]David said: "My son Solomon is young and inexperienced; but the house that is to be built for the LORD must be made so magnificent that it will be renowned and glorious in all lands. Therefore I will make preparations for it." Thus before his death David laid up materials in abundance.*

**Charge to Solomon.** [6]Then he summoned his son Solomon and commanded him to build a house for the LORD, the God of Israel. [7]* David said to Solomon: "My son, it was my purpose to build a house myself for the name of the LORD, my God. [8]But this word of the LORD came to me: You have shed much blood, and you have waged great wars. You may not build a house for my name, because you have shed too much blood upon the earth in my sight. [9]However, a son will be born to you. He will be a peaceful man, and I will give him rest from all his enemies on every side. For Solomon shall be his name, and in his time I will

---

† **21:25** *Six hundred shekels of gold*: according to 2 Sm 24:24, David paid only fifty shekels of silver for Ornan's threshing floor; the Chronicler's higher figure reflects the value the site of the future Temple had in his eyes.

**22:2–4** According to 1 Kgs 5:15–32, Solomon himself made the material preparations for building the Temple, even though David had wished to do so (1 Kgs 5:17–19). The Chronicler, however, seeks to enhance David's role in the building of the Temple.

**21:16** Jos 5:13.
**21:18** 2 Chr 3:1.
**21:26** Lv 9:24; Jgs 6:21;
1 Kgs 18:38; 2 Chr
7:1; 2 Mc 2:10–12.
**21:29** 1 Chr 16:39; 1 Kgs
8:4; 2 Chr 1:3.
**22:1** 1 Chr 21:18, 26, 28;
2 Chr 3:1.
**22:2** 1 Kgs 5:31–32;
9:20–21; 2 Chr
2:16–17.
**22:3** 1 Chr 18:8; 1 Kgs
7:47.
**22:4** Ezr 3:7; 2 Chr 2:9.
**22:5** 1 Chr 29:1.
**22:7–10** 1 Chr 17:1–14; 28:2–
7; 2 Sm 7:1–16; 1 Kgs
5:17–19; 8:17–21.

bestow peace† and tranquility on Israel.* ¹⁰It is he who shall build a house for my name; he shall be a son to me, and I will be a father to him,* and I will establish the throne of his kingship over Israel forever.

¹¹ "Now, my son, the LORD be with you, and may you succeed in building the house of the LORD your God, as he has said you shall. ¹²But may the LORD give you prudence and discernment when he gives you command over Israel, so that you keep the law of the LORD, your God. ¹³Only then shall you succeed, if you are careful to observe the statutes and ordinances which the LORD commanded Moses for Israel. Be strong and steadfast; do not fear or be dismayed.* ¹⁴See, with great effort I have laid up for the house of the LORD a hundred thousand talents of gold,† a million talents of silver, and bronze and iron in such great quantities that they cannot be weighed. I have also laid up wood and stones, to which you must add.* ¹⁵Moreover, you have available workers, stonecutters, masons, carpenters, and experts in every craft, ¹⁶without number, skilled with gold, silver, bronze, and iron. Set to work, therefore, and the LORD be with you!"

**Charge to the Officials.** ¹⁷David also commanded all of the officials of Israel to help his son Solomon: ¹⁸"Is not the LORD your God with you? Has he not given you rest on every side? Indeed, he has delivered the inhabitants of the land into my power, and the land is subdued before the LORD and his people.* ¹⁹Therefore, devote your hearts and souls to seeking the LORD your God. Proceed to build the sanctuary of the LORD God, that the ark of the covenant of the LORD and God's sacred vessels may be brought into the house built for the name of the LORD."*

# 23

**The Levitical Divisions.** ¹When David had grown old and was near the end of his days, he made his son Solomon king over Israel.* ²He then gathered together all the officials of Israel, along with the priests and the Levites.

³The Levites thirty years old and above were counted, and their total number was found to be thirty-eight thousand.* ⁴Of these, twenty-four thousand were to direct the service of the house of the LORD, six thousand were to be officials and judges, ⁵four thousand were to be gatekeepers,* and four thousand were to praise the LORD with the instruments which [David] had devised for praise. ⁶David apportioned them into divisions according to the sons of Levi: Gershon, Kohath, and Merari.*

⁷To the Gershonites belonged Ladan and Shimei. ⁸The sons of Ladan: Jehiel the chief, then Zetham and Joel; three in all.* ⁹The sons of Shimei were Shelomoth, Haziel, and Haran; three. These were the heads of the families of Ladan. ¹⁰The sons of Shimei were Jahath, Zizah, Jeush, and Beriah; these were the sons of Shimei, four in all. ¹¹Jahath was the chief and Zizah was second to him; but Jeush and Beriah had few sons, and therefore they were classed as a single family, exercising a single office.

¹²The sons of Kohath: Amram, Izhar, Hebron, and Uzziel; four in all.* ¹³The sons of Amram were Aaron and Moses. Aaron was set apart to be consecrated as most holy, he and his sons forever, to offer sacrifice before the LORD, to minister to him, and to bless in his name forever.* ¹⁴As for Moses, however, the man of God, his sons were counted as part of the tribe of Levi. ¹⁵The sons of Moses were Gershom and Eliezer.* ¹⁶The sons of Gershom: Shubael the chief.* ¹⁷The sons of Eliezer were Rehabiah the chief—Eliezer had no other sons, but the sons of Rehabiah were very numerous. ¹⁸The sons of Izhar: Shelomith the chief. ¹⁹The sons of Hebron: Jeriah, the chief, Amariah, the second, Jahaziel, the third, and

---

† **22:9** The Hebrew word for peace, *shalom*, is reflected in the name Solomon, in Hebrew, *Shelomo*. The Chronicler draws a contrast here between Solomon, the "peaceful man," and David, who "waged great wars" (v. 8). David was prevented from building the Temple, not only because his time was taken up in waging war (1 Kgs 5:17), but also because he shed much blood (1 Chr 22:8), thereby making himself, in the Chronicler's view, ritually unfit for the task.

**22:14** *A hundred thousand talents of gold*: about 3,775 tons of gold. *A million talents of silver*: about 37,750 tons of silver. These highly exaggerated figures are intended to stress the inestimable value of the Temple as the center of Israelite worship. More modest figures are given in 1 Kgs 9:14, 28; 10:10, 14.

**22:9** 2 Sm 12:24.
**22:10** Heb 1:5.
**22:13** 1 Chr 28:7, 20; Dt 31:6, 23; Jos 1:6–7, 9; 1 Kgs 2:2–3.
**22:14** 1 Chr 29:2–5.
**22:18** 1 Chr 23:25; Jos 21:44; 23:1; 2 Sm 7:1.
**22:19** 1 Kgs 8:6, 21; 2 Chr 5:7; 6:11.
**23:1** 1 Chr 28:5; 1 Kgs 1:30.
**23:3** Nm 4:3, 23, 30, 35,
39, 43, 47; 8:23–26; 2 Chr 31:17.
**23:5** 1 Chr 9:22.
**23:6** 1 Chr 6:1, 16–30; 26:1–19; Ex 6:16; Nm 3:17; 26:57.
**23:8** 1 Chr 26:21–22; 29:8.
**23:12** 1 Chr 26:23; Ex 6:18; Nm 3:19; 26:58–61.
**23:13** 1 Chr 6:49; Ex 6:20; 28:1; Nm 6:23.
**23:15** Ex 2:22; 18:3–4.
**23:16** 1 Chr 26:24.

Jekameam, the fourth.* 20The sons of Uzziel: Micah, the chief, and Isshiah, the second.*

21The sons of Merari: Mahli and Mushi. The sons of Mahli: Eleazar and Kish.* 22Eleazar died leaving no sons, only daughters; the sons of Kish, their kinsmen, married them.* 23The sons of Mushi: Mahli, Eder, and Jeremoth; three in all.*

24These were the sons of Levi according to their ancestral houses, the family heads as they were enrolled one by one according to their names. They performed the work of the service of the house of the LORD beginning at twenty years of age.* 25David said: "The LORD, the God of Israel, has given rest to his people, and has taken up his dwelling in Jerusalem forever.* 26Henceforth the Levites need not carry the tabernacle or any of the equipment for its service."* 27For by David's last words the Levites were enlisted from the time they were twenty years old. 28Their duty is to assist the sons of Aaron in the service of the house of the LORD, having charge of the courts, the chambers, and the preservation of everything holy: they take part in the service of the house of God. 29They also have charge of the showbread, of the fine flour for the grain offering, of the wafers of unleavened bread, and of the baking and mixing, and of all measures of quantity and size.* 30They are to be present every morning to offer thanks and to praise the LORD, and likewise in the evening;* 31and at every sacrifice of burnt offerings to the LORD on sabbaths, new moons, and feast days, in such numbers as are prescribed, they must always be present before the LORD* 32and observe what is prescribed for them concerning the tent of meeting, the sanctuary, and the sons of Aaron, their kinsmen, in the service of the house of the LORD.

# 24 The Priestly Divisions. 1There were also divisions for the sons of Aaron. The sons of Aaron were Nadab, Abihu, Eleazar, and Ithamar.* 2Nadab and Abihu died before their father, leaving no sons; therefore only Eleazar and Ithamar served as priests.*

3David, with Zadok, a descendant of Eleazar, and Ahimelech, a descendant of Ithamar, apportioned them their offices in the priestly service.* 4But since the sons of Eleazar were found to be more numerous by male heads than those of Ithamar, the former were divided into sixteen groups, and the latter into eight groups, each under its family heads. 5Their functions were assigned impartially by lot, for there were officers of the holy place, and officers of God, descended both from Eleazar and from Ithamar. 6The scribe Shemaiah, son of Nethanel, a Levite, recorded them in the presence of the king, and of the officials, of Zadok the priest, and of Ahimelech, son of Abiathar, † and of the heads of the ancestral houses of the priests and of the Levites, listing two successive family groups from Eleazar before each one from Ithamar.*

7* The first lot fell to Jehoiarib, the second to Jedaiah, 8the third to Harim, the fourth to Seorim, 9the fifth to Malchijah, the sixth to Mijamin, 10the seventh to Hakkoz, the eighth to Abijah.* 11the ninth to Jeshua, the tenth to Shecaniah, 12the eleventh to Eliashib, the twelfth to Jakim, 13the thirteenth to Huppah, the fourteenth to Ishbaal, 14the fifteenth to Bilgah, the sixteenth to Immer, 15the seventeenth to Hezir, the eighteenth to Happizzez, 16the nineteenth to Pethahiah, the twentieth to Jehezkel, 17the twenty-first to Jachin, the twenty-second to Gamul, 18the twenty-third to Delaiah, the twenty-fourth to Maaziah. 19This was the appointed order of their service when they functioned in the house of the LORD according to the precepts given them by Aaron, their father, as the LORD, the God of Israel, had commanded him.*

Other Levites. 20* Of the remaining Levites, there were Shubael, of the sons of Amram, and Jehdeiah, of the sons of Shubael; 21Isshiah, the chief, of the sons of Rehabiah; 22Shelomith of the Izharites, and Jahath of the sons of Shelomith. 23The sons of Hebron were Jeriah, the chief, Amariah, the second, Jahaziel, the third, Jekameam, the fourth. 24The sons of Uzziel

† 24:6 Ahimelech, son of Abiathar: see note on 18:16.

23:19 1 Chr 24:23.
23:20 1 Chr 24:24–25.
23:21 1 Chr 6:29; 24:26, 28–29; Ex 6:19; Nm 3:20, 33.
23:22 1 Chr 24:28–29.
23:23 1 Chr 6:47; 24:30.

23:24 2 Chr 31:17; Ezr 3:8.
23:25 1 Chr 22:18; Ps 132:13.
23:26 1 Chr 15:15; 2 Chr 35:3.
23:29 1 Chr 9:29, 31–32; Lv 2:1, 4–5; 24:5–8.

23:30 Nm 28:3–8.
23:31 Nm 28:2–29:39.
23:32 Nm 3:6–9; 18:2–5.
24:1 Ex 6:23; Nm 3:2–4; 26:60.
24:2 Lv 10:1–7, 12; Nm 3:2, 4.
24:3 1 Chr 18:16; 2 Sm 8:17; 2 Chr 8:14.

24:6 1 Chr 18:16; 2 Sm 8:17.
24:7–10 1 Chr 9:10–13; Ezr 2:36–38; Neh 7:39–42; 11:10–14.
24:10 Lk 1:5.
24:19 2 Chr 23:8.
24:20–31 1 Chr 23:7–23.

were Micah; Shamir, of the sons of Micah; [25] Ishiah, the brother of Micah; and Zechariah, a descendant of Isshiah. [26] The sons of Merari were Mahli, Mushi, and the sons of his son Uzziah. [27] The sons of Merari through his son Uzziah: Shoham, Zaccur, and Ibri. [28] The sons of Mahli were Eleazar, who had no sons, [29] and Jerahmeel, of the sons of Kish. [30] The sons of Mushi were Mahli, Eder, and Jerimoth.

These were the sons of the Levites according to their ancestral houses. [31] They too, in the same manner as their kinsmen, the sons of Aaron, cast lots in the presence of King David, Zadok, Ahimelech, and the heads of the priestly and levitical families; the more important family did so in the same way as the less important one.*

# 25 The Singers.
[1] David and the leaders of the liturgy set apart for the service the sons of Asaph, Heman, and Jeduthun, who prophesied† to the accompaniment of lyres and harps and cymbals.*

This is the list of those who performed this service: [2] Of the sons of Asaph: Zaccur, Joseph, Nethaniah, and Asharelah, sons of Asaph, under the direction of Asaph, who prophesied under the guidance of the king. [3] Of Jeduthun, these sons of Jeduthun: Gedaliah, Zeri, Jeshaiah, Shimei, Hashabiah, and Mattithiah; six, under the direction of their father Jeduthun, who prophesied to the accompaniment of a lyre, to give thanks and praise to the LORD. [4] Of Heman, these sons of Heman: Bukkiah, Mattaniah, Uzziel, Shubael, and Jerimoth; Hananiah, Hanani, Eliathah, Giddalti, Romamti-ezer, Joshbekashah, Mallothi, Hothir, and Mahazioth. [5] All these were the sons of Heman, the king's seer for divine matters; to exalt him God gave Heman fourteen sons and three daughters.* [6] All these, whether of Asaph, Jeduthun, or Heman, were under their fathers' direction in the singing in the house of the LORD to the accompaniment of cymbals, harps and lyres, serving in the house of God, under the guidance of the king.* [7] Their number, together with that of their kinsmen who were trained in

singing to the LORD, all of them skilled men, was two hundred and eighty-eight. [8] They cast lots for their functions equally, young and old, master and pupil alike.*

[9] The first lot fell to Asaph, to the family of Joseph; he and his sons and his kinsmen were twelve. Gedaliah was the second; he and his kinsmen and his sons were twelve. [10] The third was Zaccur, his sons, and his kinsmen: twelve. [11] The fourth fell to Izri, his sons, and his kinsmen: twelve. [12] The fifth was Nethaniah, his sons, and his kinsmen: twelve. [13] The sixth was Bukkiah, his sons, and his kinsmen: twelve. [14] The seventh was Jesarelah, his sons, and his kinsmen: twelve. [15] The eighth was Jeshaiah, his sons, and his kinsmen: twelve. [16] The ninth was Mattaniah, his sons, and his kinsmen: twelve. [17] The tenth was Shimei, his sons, and his kinsmen: twelve. [18] The eleventh was Uzziel, his sons, and his kinsmen: twelve. [19] The twelfth fell to Hashabiah, his sons, and his kinsmen: twelve. [20] The thirteenth was Shubael, his sons, and his kinsmen: twelve. [21] The fourteenth was Mattithiah, his sons, and his kinsmen: twelve. [22] The fifteenth fell to Jeremoth, his sons, and his kinsmen: twelve. [23] The sixteenth fell to Hananiah, his sons, and his kinsmen: twelve. [24] The seventeenth fell to Joshbekashah, his sons, and his kinsmen: twelve. [25] The eighteenth fell to Hanani, his sons, and his kinsmen: twelve. [26] The nineteenth fell to Mallothi, his sons, and his kinsmen: twelve. [27] The twentieth fell to Eliathah, his sons, and his kinsmen: twelve. [28] The twenty-first fell to Hothir, his sons, and his kinsmen: twelve. [29] The twenty-second fell to Giddalti, his sons, and his kinsmen: twelve. [30] The twenty-third fell to Mahazioth, his sons, and his kinsmen: twelve. [31] The twenty-fourth fell to Romamti-ezer, his sons, and his kinsmen: twelve.

# 26 Divisions of Gatekeepers.
[1] * As for the divisions of gatekeepers: Of the Korahites was Meshelemiah, the son of Kore, one of the sons of Abiasaph. [2] Meshelemiah's sons: Zechariah, the firstborn, Jediael, the

† 25:1 This list of twenty-four classes of Temple singers balances the list of the twenty-four classes of priests (24:4–19). The last nine names in v. 4, which seem to form a special group, were perhaps originally fragments or incipits (the opening words) of hymns. With some slight changes in the vocalization, these names would mean: "Have mercy on me, O LORD," "Have mercy on me," "You are my God," "I magnify," "I extol the help of…," "Sitting in adversity," "I have fulfilled," "He made abundant," and "Visions."

24:31 1 Chr 25:8; 26:13.
25:1 1 Chr 6:16–32;
15:16–17, 19; 16:37;
2 Chr 5:12; 35:15;
Neh 12:27, 45.
25:5 2 Chr 35:15.
25:6 1 Chr 15:16.
25:8 1 Chr 24:31.
26:1 1 Chr 9:19; 2 Chr 8:14; 23:19; 35:15;
Neh 12:45.

second son, Zebadiah, the third, Jathniel, the fourth, [3] Elam, the fifth, Jehohanan, the sixth, Eliehoenai, the seventh. [4] Obed-edom's sons: Shemaiah, the firstborn, Jehozabad, a second son, Joah, the third, Sachar, the fourth, Nethanel, the fifth, [5] Ammiel, the sixth, Issachar, the seventh, Peullethai, the eighth, for God blessed him. [6] To his son Shemaiah were born sons who ruled over their family, for they were warriors. [7] The sons of Shemaiah were Othni, Rephael, Obed, and Elzabad; also his kinsmen who were men of substance, Elihu and Semachiah. [8] All these were the sons of Obed-edom, who, together with their sons and their kinsmen, were men of substance, fit for the service. Of Obed-edom, sixty-two. [9] Of Meshelemiah, eighteen sons and kinsmen, men of substance.

[10] Hosah, a descendant of Merari, had these sons: Shimri, the chief (for though he was not the firstborn, his father made him chief),* [11] Hilkiah, the second son, Tebaliah, the third, Zechariah, the fourth. All the sons and kinsmen of Hosah were thirteen.

[12] To these divisions of the gatekeepers, by their chief men, were assigned watches for them to minister in the house of the LORD, for each group in the same way. [13] They cast lots for each gate, small and large families alike. [14] When the lot was cast for the east side, it fell to Meshelemiah. Then they cast lots for his son Zechariah, a prudent counselor, and the north side fell to his lot.* [15] To Obed-edom fell the south side, and to his sons the storehouse. [16] To Hosah fell the west side with the Shallecheth gate at the ascending highway. For each family, watches were established. [17] On the east, six watched each day, on the north, four each day, on the south, four each day, and at the storehouse they were two and two; [18] as for the large building† on the west, there were four at the highway and two at the large building. [19] These were the classes of the gatekeepers, sons of Korah and Merari.

**Treasurers.** [20] Their brother Levites had oversight of the treasuries of the house of God and the treasuries of votive offerings.* [21] Among the sons of Ladan the Gershonite, the family heads were sons of Jehiel:* [22]* the sons of Jehiel, Zetham and his brother Joel, who oversaw the treasures of the house of the LORD. [23] Of the Amramites, Izharites, Hebronites, and Uzzielites, [24] Shubael, son of Gershom, son of Moses, was principal overseer of the treasures. [25]* His associate was of the line of Eliezer, whose son was Rehabiah, whose son was Jeshaiah, whose son was Joram, whose son was Zichri, whose son was Shelomith. [26] This Shelomith and his kinsmen oversaw all the treasures of the votive offerings dedicated by King David, the heads of the families, the commanders of thousands and of hundreds, and the commanders of the army;* [27] what came from wars and from spoils, they dedicated for the support of the house of the LORD. [28] Also, whatever Samuel the seer, Saul, son of Kish, Abner, son of Ner, Joab, son of Zeruiah, and all others had consecrated, was under the charge of Shelomith and his kinsmen.

**Magistrates.** [29] Among the Izharites, Chenaniah and his sons were in charge of Israel's civil affairs† as officials and judges.* [30] Among the Hebronites, Hashabiah* and his kinsmen, one thousand seven hundred men of substance, had the administration of Israel on the western side of the Jordan for all the work of the LORD and the service of the king. [31] Among the Hebronites, Jerijah was their chief according to their family records. In the fortieth year of David's reign search was made, and there were found among them warriors at Jazer of Gilead.* [32] His kinsmen were also men of substance, two thousand seven hundred heads of families. King David appointed them to the administration of the Reubenites, the Gadites, and the half-tribe of Manasseh for everything pertaining to God and to the king.

# 27 **Army Commanders.**† [1] This is the list of the Israelite family heads, commanders of thousands and of hundreds, and

---

26:18 *The large building*: parbar, mentioned also in 2 Kgs 23:11; the meaning of the word is unclear.

26:29 *Civil affairs*: lit., "external work," i.e., conduct of affairs external to the Temple.

27:1–15 This list of army commanders is similar to, but distinct from, the list of David's warriors given in 11:10–47. The schematic enumeration of the soldiers presented here appears artificial and exaggerated (12 x 24,000 = 288,000 men!). However, the Hebrew word ('eleph) translated "thousand" might also

designate a military unit of much smaller size.

| | |
|---|---|
| **26:10** 1 Chr 16:38. | 24:21. |
| **26:14** 1 Chr 9:21. | **26:26** 2 Sm 8:11. |
| **26:20** 1 Chr 28:12; 1 Kgs 7:51. | **26:29** 1 Chr 23:4. |
| **26:21** 1 Chr 23:7–8; 29:8. | **26:30** 1 Chr 27:17; Neh 11:15–16. |
| **26:22–24** 1 Chr 23:8, 12, 16. | **26:31** 1 Chr 23:19; 29:27; |
| **26:25** 1 Chr 23:17–18; | Jos 13:25. |

other officers who served the king in all that pertained to the divisions, of twenty-four thousand men each, that came and went month by month throughout the year.

² Over the first division for the first month was Ishbaal, son of Zabdiel, and in his division were twenty-four thousand men; ³ a descendant of Perez, he was chief over all the commanders of the army for the first month. ⁴ Over the division of the second month was Eleazar, son of Dodo, from Ahoh, and in his division were twenty-four thousand men.* ⁵* The third army commander, for the third month, was Benaiah, son of Jehoiada the chief priest, and in his division were twenty-four thousand men. ⁶ This Benaiah was a warrior among the Thirty and over the Thirty. His son Ammizabad was over his division. ⁷ Fourth, for the fourth month, was Asahel, brother of Joab, and after him his son Zebadiah, and in his division were twenty-four thousand men.* ⁸ Fifth, for the fifth month, was the commander Shamhuth, a descendant of Zerah, and in his division were twenty-four thousand men. ⁹ Sixth, for the sixth month, was Ira, son of Ikkesh, from Tekoa, and in his division were twenty-four thousand men. ¹⁰ Seventh, for the seventh month, was Hellez, from Beth-pelet, of the Ephraimites, and in his division were twenty-four thousand men. ¹¹ Eighth, for the eighth month, was Sibbecai the Hushathite, a descendant of Zerah, and in his division were twenty-four thousand men.* ¹² Ninth, for the ninth month, was Abiezer from Anathoth, of Benjamin, and in his division were twenty-four thousand men. ¹³ Tenth, for the tenth month, was Maharai from Netophah, a descendant of Zerah, and in his division were twenty-four thousand men. ¹⁴ Eleventh, for the eleventh month, was Benaiah the Pirathonite, of the Ephraimites, and in his division were twenty-four thousand men. ¹⁵ Twelfth, for the twelfth month, was Heldai the Netophathite, of the family of Othniel, and in his division were twenty-four thousand men.

**Tribal Leaders.** ¹⁶ Over the tribes of Israel, for the Reubenites the leader was Eliezer, son of Zichri; for the Simeonites, Shephatiah, son of Maacah; ¹⁷ for Levi, Hashabiah, son of Kemuel; for Aaron, Zadok; ¹⁸ for Judah, Eliab,* one of David's brothers; for Issachar, Omri, son of Michael; ¹⁹ for Zebulun, Ishmaiah, son of Obadiah; for Naphtali, Jeremoth, son of Azriel; ²⁰ for the Ephraimites, Hoshea, son of Azaziah; for the half-tribe of Manasseh, Joel, son of Pedaiah; ²¹ for the half-tribe of Manasseh in Gilead, Iddo, son of Zechariah; for Benjamin, Jaasiel, son of Abner; ²² for Dan, Azarel, son of Jeroham. These were the commanders of the tribes of Israel.

²³ David did not count those who were twenty years of age or younger, for the LORD had promised to multiply Israel like the stars of the heavens.* ²⁴ Joab, son of Zeruiah, began to take the census, but he did not complete it, for because of it wrath fell upon Israel. Therefore the number was not recorded in the book of chronicles of King David.*

**Overseers.** ²⁵ Over the treasuries of the king was Azmaveth,* the son of Adiel. Over the treasuries in the country, the cities, the villages, and the towers was Jonathan, son of Uzziah. ²⁶ Over the farm workers who tilled the soil was Ezri, son of Chelub. ²⁷ Over the vineyards was Shimei from Ramah, and over their produce for the wine cellars was Zabdi the Shiphmite. ²⁸ Over the olive trees and sycamores of the Shephelah was Baalhanan the Gederite, and over the stores of oil was Joash. ²⁹ Over the cattle that grazed in Sharon was Shitrai the Sharonite, and over the cattle in the valleys was Shaphat, the son of Adlai; ³⁰ over the camels was Obil the Ishmaelite; over the donkeys was Jehdeiah the Meronothite; ³¹ and over the flocks was Jaziz the Hagrite. All these were the overseers of King David's possessions.

**David's Court.** ³² Jonathan, David's uncle and a man of intelligence, was counselor and scribe; he and Jehiel, the son of Hachmoni, attended the king's sons. ³³ Ahithophel was also the king's counselor, and Hushai the Archite was the king's friend.* ³⁴ After Ahithophel† came Jehoiada, the son of Benaiah, and Abiathar. The commander of the king's army was Joab.

† **27:34** *After Ahithophel:* after Ahithophel's suicide (2 Sm 17:23), Jehoiada succeeded him as the king's counselor. *Abiathar:* David's priest, along with Zadok. See note on 18:16.

**27:4** 1 Chr 11:12; 2 Sm 23:9. **27:5–6** 1 Chr 11:22–25; 18:17; 2 Sm 23:20–23. **27:7** 2 Sm 2:18; 23:24. **27:11** 1 Chr 11:29; 20:4; 2 Sm 21:18. **27:18** 1 Chr 2:13. **27:23** Gn 22:17. **27:24** 2 Sm 24:10. **27:25** 2 Sm 23:31. **27:33** 2 Sm 15:12, 32–37; 16:16–19, 23; 17:5–16, 23.

# 28

**The Assembly at Jerusalem.** [1] David assembled at Jerusalem all the commanders of Israel, the tribal commanders, the commanders of the divisions who were in the service of the king, the commanders of thousands and of hundreds, those in command of all the king's estates and possessions, and his sons, together with the courtiers, the warriors, and every person of substance.* [2] * King David rose to his feet and said: "Hear me, my kinsmen and my people. It was my purpose to build a house of repose myself for the ark of the covenant of the LORD, the footstool for the feet of our God;† and I was preparing to build it. [3] But God said to me, You may not build a house for my name, for you are a man who waged wars and shed blood. [4] However, the LORD, the God of Israel, chose me from all my father's family to be king over Israel forever. For he chose Judah as leader, then one family of Judah, that of my father; and finally, among all the sons of my father, it pleased him to make me king over all Israel.* [5] And of all my sons—for the LORD has given me many sons—he has chosen my son Solomon to sit on the throne of the LORD's kingship over Israel.* [6] For he said to me: It is your son Solomon who shall build my house and my courts, for I have chosen him for my son, and I will be a father to him.* [7] I will establish his kingdom forever, if he perseveres in carrying out my commandments and ordinances as he does now. [8] Therefore, in the sight of all Israel, the assembly of the LORD, and in the hearing of our God: keep and carry out all the commandments of the LORD, your God, that you may continue to possess this good land and afterward leave it as an inheritance to your children forever.*

[9] "As for you, Solomon, my son, know the God of your father and serve him with a whole heart and a willing soul, for the LORD searches all hearts and understands all the mind's thoughts. If you search for him, he will be found; but if you abandon him, he will cast you off forever.* [10] See, then! The LORD has

chosen you to build a house as his sanctuary. Be strong and set to work."

**Temple Plans Given to Solomon.** [11] Then David gave to his son Solomon the design of the portico and of the house itself, with its storerooms, its upper rooms and inner chambers, and the shrine containing the cover of the ark.* [12] He provided also the design for all else that he had in mind by way of courts for the house of the LORD, with the surrounding compartments for the treasuries of the house of God and the treasuries for the votive offerings, [13] as well as for the divisions of the priests and Levites, for all the work of the service of the house of the LORD, and for all the liturgical vessels of the house of the LORD. [14] He specified the weight of gold to be used in the golden vessels for the various services and the weight of silver to be used in the silver vessels for the various services; [15] likewise for the golden menorahs and their lamps he specified the weight of gold for each menorah and its lamps, and for the silver menorahs he specified the weight of silver for each menorah and its lamps, depending on the use to which each menorah was to be put.* [16] He specified the weight of gold for each table that was to hold the showbread, and the silver for the silver tables; [17] the pure gold for the forks, basins, and pitchers; the weight of gold for each golden bowl and the weight of silver for each silver bowl; [18] the refined gold, and its weight, to be used for the altar of incense; and, finally, gold to fashion the chariot:† the cherubim spreading their wings and covering the ark of the covenant of the LORD.* [19] All this he wrote down, by the hand of the LORD, to make him understand it—the working out of the whole design.

[20] Then David said to his son Solomon: "Be strong and steadfast, and go to work; do not fear or be dismayed, for the LORD God, my God, is with you. He will not fail you or abandon you before you have completed all the work for the service of the house of the LORD.*

---

**28:2** *The ark...the footstool...of our God*: the Lord, who was invisibly enthroned upon the cherubim associated with the ark of the covenant at Shiloh and later in the Jerusalem Temple, had the ark as his footstool; cf. Ps 99:5; 132:7. There was no ark in the postexilic Temple. Cf. note on 2 Chr 5:9.
**28:18** *Chariot*: this reference is probably inspired by the vision account in Ez 1:4–24; 10:1–22.

**28:1** 1 Chr 27:2–22, 25–31; 11:10–47.
**28:2–3** 1 Chr 17:4; 22:7–10; 2 Sm 7:5; 1 Kgs 5:3; Ps 132:3–7.
**28:4** 1 Chr 17:23; Gn 49:8–12; 1 Sm 16:6–13.
**28:5** 1 Chr 3:1–9; 14:3–7; 22:9; 23:1; Wis 9:7.
**28:6** 1 Chr 17:11–14; 22:9–10; 2 Sm 7:12–13.
**28:8** Dt 4:5.
**28:9** 1 Chr 29:17; 2 Chr 15:2; 1 Kgs 8:61.
**28:11** Ex 25:9, 40; 26:30.
**28:15** Ex 25:31–37.
**28:18** Ex 25:18–22; 30:1–10; 1 Kgs 6:23–28.
**28:20** 1 Chr 22:13; Jos 1:5.

21 The divisions of the priests and Levites are ready for all the service of the house of God; they will be with you in all the work with all those who are eager to show their skill in every kind of craftsmanship. Also the commanders and all the people will do everything that you command."*

# 29

**Offerings for the Temple.** 1 King David then said to the whole assembly: "My son Solomon, whom alone God has chosen, is still young and inexperienced; the work, however, is great, for this palace is not meant for human beings, but for the LORD God.* 2 For this reason I have stored up for the house of my God, as far as I was able, gold for what will be made of gold, silver for what will be made of silver, bronze for what will be made of bronze, iron for what will be made of iron, wood for what will be made of wood, onyx stones and settings for them, carnelian and mosaic stones, every other kind of precious stone, and great quantities of marble.* 3 But now, because of the delight I take in the house of my God, in addition to all that I stored up for the holy house, I give to the house of my God my personal fortune in gold and silver: 4 three thousand talents of Ophir gold, and seven thousand talents of refined silver, for overlaying the walls of the rooms,* 5 for the various utensils to be made of gold and silver, and for every work that is to be done by artisans. Now, who else will contribute generously and consecrate themselves this day to the LORD?"*

6 Then the heads of the families, the tribal commanders of Israel, the commanders of thousands and of hundreds, and those who had command of the king's affairs came forward willingly* 7 and contributed for the service of the house of God five thousand talents and ten thousand darics of gold, ten thousand talents of silver, eighteen thousand talents of bronze, and one hundred thousand talents of iron.* 8 Those who had precious stones gave them into the keeping of Jehiel the Gershonite for the treasury of the house of the LORD.* 9 The people rejoiced over these free-will offerings, for they had been contributed to the LORD wholeheartedly. King David also rejoiced greatly.*

**David's Prayer.** 10 Then David blessed the LORD in the sight of the whole assembly. David said:

"Blessed are you, LORD,
      God of Israel our father,
      from eternity to eternity.
11    Yours, LORD, are greatness and might,
      majesty, victory, and splendor.
  For all in heaven and on earth is yours;
      yours, LORD, is kingship;
      you are exalted as head over all.
12    Riches and glory are from you,
      and you have dominion over all.
  In your hand are power and might;
      it is yours to give greatness and
      strength to all.*
13    Therefore, our God, we give you thanks
      and we praise the majesty of your
      name.

14 "But who am I, and who are my people, that we should have the means to contribute so freely? For everything is from you, and what we give is what we have from you. 15 For before you we are strangers and travelers, like all our ancestors. Our days on earth are like a shadow, without a future.* 16 LORD our God, all this wealth that we have brought together to build you a house for your holy name comes from you and is entirely yours. 17 I know, my God, that you put hearts to the test and that you take pleasure in integrity. With a whole heart I have willingly given all these things, and now with joy I have seen your people here present also giving to you generously. 18 LORD, God of our ancestors Abraham, Isaac, and Israel,* keep such thoughts in the hearts and minds of your people forever, and direct their hearts toward you. 19 Give to my son Solomon a wholehearted desire to keep your commandments, precepts, and statutes, that he may carry out all these plans and build the palace for which I have made preparation."

20 Then David told the whole assembly, "Now bless the LORD your God!" And the whole assembly blessed the LORD, the God

---

28:21 Ex 36:1–5.
  29:1 1 Chr 22:5; 28:5.
  29:2 1 Chr 22:14.
  29:4 2 Chr 9:10; 1 Kgs 9:28; 10:11.

29:5 Ex 25:2; 35:5–6.
  29:6 1 Chr 27:1, 25–31; 28:1.
  29:7 Ezr 2:69; 8:27; Neh 7:70–71.

29:8 1 Chr 23:8; 26:21.
  29:9 2 Kgs 12:4.
  29:12 2 Chr 20:6; Wis 6:3.

29:15 Lv 25:23; Wis 2:5; 5:9.
  29:18 Ex 3:6, 15; 4:5; 1 Kgs 18:36.

of their ancestors, bowing down in homage before the L ORD and before the king. ²¹ On the following day they brought sacrifices and burnt offerings to the L ORD, a thousand bulls, a thousand rams, and a thousand lambs, together with their libations and many other sacrifices for all Israel; ²² and on that day they ate and drank in the L ORD's presence with great rejoicing.

**Solomon Anointed.** Then for a second time† they proclaimed David's son Solomon king, and they anointed him for the L ORD as ruler, and Zadok as priest. ²³ Thereafter Solomon sat on the throne of the L ORD as king succeeding his father David; he prospered, and all Israel obeyed him.* ²⁴ All the commanders and warriors, and also all the other sons of King David, swore allegiance to King Solomon. ²⁵ And the

L ORD exalted Solomon greatly in the eyes of all Israel, giving him a glorious reign such as had not been enjoyed by any king over Israel before him.*

**David's Death.** ²⁶ Thus David, the son of Jesse, had reigned over all Israel. ²⁷ He was king over Israel for forty years: he was king seven years in Hebron and thirty-three years in Jerusalem.* ²⁸ He died at a ripe old age, rich in years and wealth and glory, and his son Solomon succeeded him as king.* ²⁹ Now the deeds of King David, first and last, are recorded in the history of Samuel the seer, the history of Nathan the prophet, and the history of Gad the seer,* ³⁰ together with the particulars of his reign and valor, and of the events that affected him and all Israel and all the kingdoms of the earth.

---

**29:22** *For a second time*: the first time is in 23:1 where David appoints Solomon his successor. Now there is a solemn public ratification of that appointment.

**29:23** 1 Chr 28:5; 2 Chr 9:8;
1 Kgs 2:12.
**29:25** 2 Chr 1:12; 1 Kgs
3:13.

**29:27** 2 Sm 5:5; 1 Kgs 2:11.
**29:28** 1 Chr 23:1.
**29:29** 1 Chr 21:9; 1 Sm
22:5.

# The Second Book of
# Chronicles

## INTRODUCTION

### Leslie J. Hoppe, OFM

Second Chronicles begins its narrative with Solomon. Its portrait of this king is similar to the portrait of David in 1 Chronicles. Chronicles focuses almost entirely on Solomon's activities associated with the building of the Temple. It does not repeat the details of the much darker portrait found in 1 Kgs 9–11. While it would have been impossible for Chronicles to ignore the existence of the kingdom of Israel, the book largely skips over material from 1–2 Kings related to the story of that kingdom. Chronicles focuses almost exclusively on the kingdom of Judah and its rulers. Chronicles mentions individual kings of Israel only when a king of Judah had some contact with them. The book describes the relatively good behavior of some kings and the blessings that this brings to them, along with the infidelity of other kings that results in divine judgment. While 2 Kings lays the blame for the fall of Jerusalem on Manasseh (21:11–13), Chronicles notes that he prayed for forgiveness (2 Chr 33:12–19). The reason Jerusalem fell and the people of Judah were taken to exile was because of the people's failures—they did not listen to the prophets (2 Chr 36:15–17). This democratization of responsibility for Judah's fall served to remind the people of Judah that they held their future in their own hands. That future would not be determined by kings, foreign or domestic—it would be determined by the people of Judah themselves.

Second Chronicles displays the book's keen sense of divine retribution as exemplified in the lives of Judah's kings. The notion that God rewards good deeds and punishes evil ones is, of course, not unique to Chronicles. It undergirds the moral systems of most religions and is a special emphasis in the book of Deuteronomy and in the literature that reflects its religious perspectives—especially the

## Outline of 2 Chronicles

I. The Reign of Solomon (1:1–9:31)

II. The Post-Solomonic Monarchy of Judah (10:1–36:23)

books of Joshua, Judges, Samuel, and Kings. Chronicles rejects the belief that a person can be rewarded or punished because of the deeds of another individual. The conclusion that readers were to draw from the Chronicles' rehearsal of the reason for Judah's downfall was that if they were to change their ways, they could look forward to divine blessing. The basis for this belief was God's compassion for the people of Judah (2 Chr 36:15). Solomon's prayer at the dedication of the Temple assumes that God is ready to forgive whenever God is asked for forgiveness (6:25, 27, 30, 39).

While Chronicles largely ignores the story of the kingdom of Israel, because the author believed that kingdom to be illegitimate, the book does not reject the people of the former northern kingdom. In 2 Chr 30, Hezekiah invites the people of the north to worship in the Temple of Jerusalem and assures that anyone from the north who comes to Jerusalem will be welcomed. The king affirms to the northerners that God is gracious and merciful and will turn toward those who join the people of Judah in their worship (30:6–9). Hezekiah celebrated a Passover in Jerusalem that included people from the former northern kingdom (30:25). Chronicles notes that nothing like that happened since the days of Solomon (30:26). The book states that during Josiah's reign, people from the former northern kingdom contributed funds for the repair of Jerusalem's Temple (34:9).

The author of Chronicles sought to promote the sole legitimacy of the worship of Yahweh as conducted in the Temple of Jerusalem. This is clear from the two royal speeches that frame the story of the two Israelite kingdoms. In 2 Chr 13:4–12 and in 30:6–9, first Abijah and then Hezekiah call for the people of the north to repent and join the people of Judah for worship in Jerusalem's Temple, but this was not to be. The rift between the two peoples who worshiped the same God became permanent in 128 BCE when the Jewish high priest John Hyrcanus had the Samaritan Temple on Mount Gerizim destroyed. The New Testament witnesses to the animosity that developed between the Jews and the Samaritans, the descendants of the people of the kingdom of Israel (Jn 4:9, 20).

Second Chronicles appears to be dependent upon the narratives of 1–2 Kings, though there are many differences between these two texts. Exploring the reasons for these differences will bring the purpose and achievement of Chronicles into sharper focus. Chronicles assumes that the lasting achievement of David and his dynasty was its establishment of the Temple cultus, the building and restoration of the Temple itself, and the provisions made for the personnel who served there. For Chronicles the Davidic dynasty may be gone, but the Temple and its cultus must continue. The people of Judah are the legitimate successors of the Davidic dynasty in its role as patron of the Jerusalem Temple. Chronicles is convinced that Judah's future depends upon the people's commitment to the Temple that David planned, Solomon built, and most of their successors tried to maintain.

Chronicles has not enjoyed the popularity that other biblical works have had over the centuries. Some dismiss this work as an obvious falsification of ancient Israel's history to make an ideological point. Others marginalize it as homiletical storytelling. It appears only three times in the Roman Catholic Lectionary. Even in antiquity some Jews did not consider this work very important. For example, Cave 4 at Qumran produced more than 500 fragments and complete manuscripts of a variety of biblical and other Jewish religious texts. Among these was found only one fragment from Chronicles with only four verses (2 Chr 28:27–29:3). While the under-representation of Chronicles among the Dead Sea Scrolls may be purely accidental, more likely it was intentional, since the people at Qumran withdrew from participation in worship at the Jerusalem Temple. The New Testament never quotes a text from Chronicles.

The insistence of Chronicles that Judah take responsibility for creating its future reflects faith in God's compassion and in the people's potential. Chronicles was convinced that a better future awaited the people of Judah if they only continued serving their ancestral deity in the Temple. Though Judaism has learned to live in a world without a temple, the achievement of Chronicles is still remarkable. Certainly this work was, in part, responsible for the survival of the Jewish community at a very difficult time in its history. ◾

# THE SECOND BOOK OF CHRONICLES

## New American Bible, Introduction

The Second Book of Chronicles takes up the history of the monarchy where the First Book leaves off. It begins with the account of the reign of Solomon (chaps. 1–9) from the special viewpoint of the Chronicler. The portrait of Solomon is an idealized one; he appears as second only to David. Solomon's building of the Temple and the magnificence of his court are described in detail while the serious defects of his reign as cited in 1 Kings are simply not mentioned. This procedure is in keeping with the Chronicler's purpose of stressing the supreme importance of the Temple and its worship. He wishes to impress on his readers the splendor of God's dwelling and the magnificence of the liturgy of sacrifice, prayer, and praise offered there. Judah's kings are judged by their attitude toward the Temple and its cult. To this ideal of one people, united in the worship of the one true God at the Temple of Jerusalem founded by David and Solomon, the restored community is to conform.

In treating the period of divided monarchy (chaps. 10–36), the Chronicler gives practically all his attention to the kingdom of Judah. His virtual omission of the northern Israelite kings is significant. In his view, the northern tribes of Israel were guilty of religious schism as long as they worshiped the Lord in a place other than the Temple of Jerusalem. The Chronicler makes no mention of the important sanctuaries of Yhwh at Dan and Bethel—as though they had never existed. Nevertheless, he retains the ancient ideal of "all Israel" (a phrase occurring forty-one times in Chronicles) as the people of God. This unity, however, can exist only if the worship of "the whole congregation of Israel" takes place exclusively in the Jerusalem Temple. This requirement explains the Chronicler's praise of Kings Hezekiah and Josiah for striving, after the fall of Samaria, to unite the remnants of the northern tribes of Israel with the kingdom of Judah. Nevertheless, after Josiah's death, Judah quickly careens toward its demise at the hands of the Babylonians. That catastrophe is reversed by the edict of Cyrus allowing a return to Jerusalem and rebuilding of the Temple. Thus 2 Chronicles ends.

The Second Book of Chronicles can be divided into two major segments as follows:

I. The Reign of Solomon (1:1–9:31)

II. The Post-Solomonic Monarchy of Judah (10:1–36:23) ■

# SECOND CHRONICLES

## I. THE REIGN OF SOLOMON

**1** **Solomon at Gibeon.** [1] Solomon, son of David, strengthened his hold on the kingdom, for the LORD, his God, was with him, making him ever greater. [2] Solomon summoned all Israel, the commanders of thousands and of hundreds, the judges, the princes of all Israel, and the family heads; [3]* and, accompanied by the whole assembly, Solomon went to the high place at Gibeon, because the tent of meeting of God, made in the wilderness by Moses, the LORD's servant, was there. [4] David had, however, brought up the ark of God from Kiriath-jearim to Jerusalem, where he had provided a place and pitched a tent for it; [5] the bronze altar made by Bezalel, son of Uri, son of Hur, he put in front of the tabernacle of the LORD.† There Solomon and the assembly sought out the LORD,* [6] and Solomon offered sacrifice in the LORD's presence on the bronze altar at the tent of meeting; he sacrificed a thousand burnt offerings upon it.

[7] That night God appeared to Solomon and said to him: Whatever you ask, I will give you. [8] Solomon answered God: "You have shown great favor to David my father, and you have made me king to succeed him. [9] Now, LORD God, may your word to David my father be confirmed, for you have made me king over a people as numerous as the dust of the earth.* [10] Give me, therefore, wisdom and knowledge to govern this people, for otherwise who could rule this vast people of yours?" [11] God then replied to Solomon: Because this has been your wish—you did not ask for riches, treasures, and glory, or the life of those who hate you, or even for a long life for yourself, but you have asked for wisdom and knowledge in order to rule my people over whom I have made you king— [12] wisdom and knowledge are given you. I will also give you riches, treasures, and glory, such as kings before you never had, nor will those who come after you.

**Solomon's Wealth.** [13] Solomon returned to Jerusalem from the high place at Gibeon, from before the tent of meeting, and became king over Israel. [14] Solomon amassed chariots and horses: he had one thousand four hundred chariots and twelve thousand horses; these he allocated among the chariot cities and to the king's service in Jerusalem.* [15] The king made silver and gold as common in Jerusalem as stones, and cedars as numerous as the sycamores of the Shephelah.* [16] Solomon's horses were imported from Egypt and Cilicia,† where the king's agents purchased them at the prevailing price.* [17] A chariot imported from Egypt cost six hundred shekels of silver, a horse one hundred and fifty shekels; so they were exported to all the Hittite and Aramean kings.*

**Preparations for the Temple.** [18] Solomon gave orders for the building of a house for the name of the LORD and also a king's house for himself.

**2** [1] Solomon conscripted seventy thousand men to carry stones and eighty thousand to cut the stones in the mountains, and over these he placed three thousand six hundred overseers.* [2]* Moreover, Solomon sent this message to Huram, king of Tyre: "As you dealt with David my father, and sent him cedars to build a house for his dwelling— [3] now I am going to build a house for the name of the LORD, my God, and to consecrate it to him, for the burning of fragrant incense in his presence, for the perpetual display of the showbread, for burnt offerings morning and evening, and for the sabbaths, new moons, and festivals of

---

† **1:5** *The bronze altar…the tabernacle of the LORD*: by this notice, the Chronicler justifies Solomon's worship at the high place of Gibeon. He pictures the tabernacle, i.e., the Mosaic meeting tent, and the bronze altar made at Moses' command (Ex 31:1–9) as remaining at Gibeon after David had installed the ark of the covenant in another tent in Jerusalem (1 Chr 15:1, 25; 16:1). Bezalel's altar was made of acacia wood plated with bronze (Ex 27:1–2). Later, Solomon made an all-bronze altar for the Temple in Jerusalem (2 Chr 4:1).
**1:16–17** *Egypt and Cilicia*: it seems likely that the horses came from Cilicia and the chariots from Egypt. Some scholars find a reference to Musur, a mountain district north of Cilicia, rather than to Egypt (Misrayim) in 1 Kgs 10:28–29, the Chronicler's source for this notice. The Chronicler himself probably understood the source to be speaking of Egypt; cf. 2 Chr 9:28.

* **1:3–12** 1 Kgs 3:4–15; 1 Chr 21:29.
**1:5** Ex 27:1–2; 31:2; 1 Chr 2:20.
**1:9** Gn 13:16; 28:14.
**1:14** 2 Chr 9:25; 1 Kgs 10:26–29.
**1:15** 1 Kgs 10:27.
**1:16** 1 Kgs 10:28.
**1:17** 1 Kgs 10:29.
**2:1** 2 Chr 2:17; 5:29–30.
**2:2–9** 1 Kgs 5:15–20; 1 Chr 14:1.

the LORD, our God: such is Israel's perpetual obligation.* ⁴And the house I am going to build must be great, for our God is greater than all other gods. ⁵Yet who is really able to build him a house, since the heavens and even the highest heavens cannot contain him? And who am I that I should build him a house,* unless it be to offer incense in his presence? ⁶Now, send me men skilled at work in gold, silver, bronze, and iron, in purple, crimson, and violet fabrics, and who know how to do engraved work, to join the skilled craftsmen who are with me in Judah and Jerusalem, whom David my father appointed. ⁷Also send me boards of cedar, cypress and cabinet wood from Lebanon, for I realize that your servants know how to cut the wood of Lebanon. My servants will work with yours ⁸in order to prepare for me a great quantity of wood, since the house I intend to build must be great and wonderful. ⁹I will furnish as food for your servants, the woodcutters, twenty thousand kors of wheat, twenty thousand kors of barley, twenty thousand baths of wine, and twenty thousand baths of oil."†*

¹⁰Huram, king of Tyre, wrote an answer which he sent to Solomon: "Because the LORD loves his people, he has placed you over them as king." ¹¹He added: "Blessed be the LORD, the God of Israel, who made heaven and earth, for having given King David a wise son of intelligence and understanding, who will build a house for the LORD and also his own royal house.* ¹²*I am now sending you a craftsman of great skill, Huram-abi, ¹³son of a Danite woman† and of a father from Tyre; he knows how to work with gold, silver, bronze, and iron, with stone and wood, with purple, violet, fine linen, and crimson, and also how to do all kinds of engraved work and to devise every type of design that may be given him and your craftsmen and the craftsmen of my lord

David your father. ¹⁴*And now, let my lord send to his servants the wheat, barley, oil, and wine which he has promised. ¹⁵For our part, we will cut trees on Lebanon, as many as you need, and send them down to you in rafts to the port of Joppa, whence you may take them up to Jerusalem."*

¹⁶*Thereupon Solomon took a census of all the alien men resident in the land of Israel (following the census David his father had taken of them); they were found to number one hundred fifty-three thousand six hundred. ¹⁷Of these he made seventy thousand carriers and eighty thousand cutters in the mountains, and three thousand six hundred overseers to keep the people working.*

**3** **Building of the Temple.** ¹*Then Solomon began to build the house of the LORD in Jerusalem on Mount Moriah,† which had been shown to David his father, in the place David had prepared, the threshing floor of Ornan the Jebusite. ²He began to build in the second month of the fourth year of his reign. ³These were the specifications laid down by Solomon for building the house of God: the length was sixty cubits according to the old measure, and the width was twenty cubits;* ⁴the front porch along the width of the house was also twenty cubits, and it was twenty cubits high.† He covered its interior with pure gold.* ⁵The nave he overlaid with cypress wood and overlaid that with fine gold, embossing on it palms and chains.* ⁶He also covered the house with precious stones for splendor; the gold was from Parvaim. ⁷The house, its beams and thresholds, as well as its walls and its doors, he overlaid with gold, and he engraved cherubim upon the walls. ⁸He also made the room of the holy of holies. Its length corresponded to the width of the house, twenty cubits, and its width was also twenty cubits. He overlaid it

---

† **2:9** There is probably some exaggeration here. The parallel passage in 1 Kgs 5:25 does not list the barley or the wine, and mentions only twenty kors of olive oil. *Kors:* see note on Ez 45:14; *baths:* see note on Is 5:10. The amount given in Chronicles would be one hundred times as much (20,000 baths equals 2,000 kors).

**2:13** *A Danite woman:* in 1 Kgs 7:14 she is called a widow of the tribe of Naphtali. The Danites had settled in the northern section of Naphtali's territory (Jgs 18:27–29). Bezalel, the head artisan in the time of Moses, had as his assistant a member of the tribe of Dan (Ex 31:6).

**3:1** *Mount Moriah:* Gn 22:2 speaks of a "height in the land of Moriah." This is the only place in the Bible where the Temple mount is identified with the site where Abraham was to have sacrificed Isaac.

**3:4** *The front porch...twenty cubits high:* this figure, not given in 1 Kgs 7, is based on a variant Greek text that may be due to a later revision. The Hebrew text itself has "one hundred and twenty cubits high." The Chronicler nearly doubles the height of the two free-standing columns adjacent to the porch in 2 Chr 3:15 as compared with the source, 1 Kgs 7:15–16.

**2:3** Lv 24:5–8; Nm 28–29.
**2:5** 2 Chr 6:18.
**2:9** 1 Kgs 5:25; Ezr 3:7.
**2:11** 1 Kgs 5:21.
**2:12–13** Ex 31:1–5; 1 Kgs 7:13–14.
**2:14–15** 1 Kgs 5:22–26.
**2:15** Ezr 3:7.
**2:16–17** 1 Chr 22:2.
**2:17** 2 Chr 2:1.
**3:1–2** Gn 22:2; 1 Kgs 6:1; 1 Chr 21:22–26; 22:1.
**3:3** 1 Kgs 6:2.
**3:4** 1 Kgs 6:3.
**3:5** 1 Kgs 6:15; Ez 41:1.

with fine gold to the amount of six hundred talents.* ⁹The weight of the nails was fifty gold shekels. The upper chambers he likewise overlaid with gold.

¹⁰* For the room of the holy of holies he made two cherubim of carved workmanship, which were then covered with gold. ¹¹The wings of the cherubim spanned twenty cubits: one wing of each cherub, five cubits in length, extended to a wall of the house, while the other wing, also five cubits in length, touched the corresponding wing of the other cherub. ¹²The wing of the cherub, five cubits, touched the wall of the house, and the other wing, five cubits, was joined to the wing of the other cherub. ¹³The combined wingspread of the two cherubim was thus twenty cubits. They stood upon their own feet, facing toward the nave. ¹⁴He made the veil† of violet, purple, crimson, and fine linen, and had cherubim embroidered upon it.*

¹⁵* In front of the house he set two columns thirty-five cubits high; the capital of each was five cubits. ¹⁶He devised chains in the form of a collar with which he encircled the capitals of the columns, and he made a hundred pomegranates which he set on the chains. ¹⁷He set up the columns to correspond with the nave, one for the right side and the other for the left, and he called the one to the right Jachin and the one to the left Boaz.

**4** ¹Then he made a bronze altar twenty cubits long, twenty cubits wide and ten cubits high.* ²* He also made the molten sea. It was made with a circular rim, and measured ten cubits across, five in height, and thirty in circumference. ³Under the brim a ring of figures of oxen† encircled it for ten cubits, all the way around the compass of the sea; there were two rows of oxen cast in one mold with the sea. ⁴This rested on twelve oxen, three facing north, three facing west, three facing south, and three facing east, with their haunches

all toward the center; upon them was set the sea. ⁵It was a handbreadth thick, and its brim resembled that of a cup, being lily-shaped. It had a capacity of three thousand baths.†

⁶Then he made ten basins for washing, placing five of them to the right and five to the left. In these the victims for the burnt offerings were washed; but the sea was for the priests to wash in.*

⁷He made the menorahs of gold, ten of them as was prescribed, and placed them in the nave, five to the right and five to the left.* ⁸He made ten tables and had them set in the nave, five to the right and five to the left; and he made a hundred golden bowls.* ⁹He made the court of the priests and the great courtyard* and the gates of the courtyard; the gates he covered with bronze. ¹⁰The sea he placed off to the southeast from the south side of the house.*

¹¹* When Huram had made the pots, shovels, and bowls, he finished all his work for King Solomon in the house of God: ¹²two columns; two nodes for the capitals on top of the columns; and two pieces of netting covering the two nodes for the capitals on top of the columns; ¹³four hundred pomegranates in double rows on both pieces of netting that covered the two nodes of the capitals on top of the columns. ¹⁴He made the stands, and the basins on the stands; ¹⁵one sea, and the twelve oxen under it; ¹⁶pots, shovels, forks, and all the articles Huram-abi made for King Solomon for the house of the LORD; they were of burnished bronze. ¹⁷The king had them cast in the neighborhood of the Jordan, between Succoth and Zeredah, in thick clay molds. ¹⁸Solomon made all these vessels, so many in number that the weight of the bronze could not be determined.

¹⁹Solomon made all the articles that were for the house of God: the golden altar, the tables on which the showbread lay, ²⁰the menorahs and their lamps of pure gold which were

---

† **3:14** *The veil*: this was suspended at the entrance of the holy of holies, in imitation of the veil of the Mosaic meeting tent (Ex 26:31–32). Solomon's Temple had doors at this point, according to 1 Kgs 6:31. Apparently the Temple of the Chronicler's time did have a veil, just as did Herod's Temple (Mt 27:51; Mk 15:38; Lk 23:45).
**4:3** *Oxen*: in 1 Kgs 7:24 this double row of ornaments is described as consisting of gourds. The text of Kings available to the Chronicler may have been corrupt at this point since the two words sound similar in Hebrew. In 4:16 the Chronicler speaks of forks while 1 Kgs 7:40 refers to bowls.

† **4:5** *Three thousand baths*: two thousand baths according to 1 Kgs 7:26; see note on 1 Kgs 7:23–26.

**3:8** 1 Kgs 6:16–17, 20.
**3:10–13** 1 Kgs 6:23–27.
**3:14** Mt 27:51.
**3:15–17** 1 Kgs 7:15–20; Ez 40:49.
**4:1** Ez 43:13–17.
**4:2–5** 1 Kgs 7:23–26.
**4:6** 1 Kgs 7:38–39; Ez 40:38.
**4:7** 1 Kgs 7:49.
**4:8** 1 Kgs 7:50; 1 Chr 28:16.
**4:9** 1 Kgs 7:12.
**4:10** 1 Kgs 7:39.
**4:11–22** 1 Kgs 7:40–51.

to burn as prescribed before the inner sanctuary, [21] flowers, lamps, and gold tongs (this was of purest gold), [22] snuffers, bowls, cups, and firepans of pure gold. As for the entrance to the house, its inner doors to the holy of holies, as well as the doors to the nave of the temple, were of gold.

**5** **Dedication of the Temple.** [1]* When all the work undertaken by Solomon for the house of the LORD was completed, he brought in the votive offerings of David his father, putting the silver, the gold, and other articles in the treasuries of the house of God. [2] Then Solomon assembled the elders of Israel and all the heads of the tribes, the princes in the ancestral houses of the Israelites, to Jerusalem to bring up the ark of the LORD's covenant from the City of David, which is Zion. [3] All the people of Israel assembled before the king during the festival of the seventh month.† [4]* When all the elders of Israel had arrived, the Levites† took up the ark; [5] and they brought up the ark and the tent of meeting with all the sacred vessels that were in the tent. The levitical priests brought them up.

[6] King Solomon and the entire community of Israel, gathered for the occasion before the ark, sacrificed sheep and oxen too many to number or count. [7] The priests brought the ark of the covenant of the LORD to its place: the inner sanctuary of the house, the holy of holies, beneath the wings of the cherubim. [8] The cherubim had their wings spread out over the place of the ark, covering the ark and its poles from above. [9] The poles were so long that their ends could be seen from the holy place in front of the inner sanctuary. (They cannot be seen from outside, but they remain there to this day.)† [10] There was nothing in the ark but the two tablets which Moses had put there at Horeb when the LORD made a covenant with the Israelites after they went forth from Egypt.

[11] When the priests left the holy place (all the priests who were present had purified themselves regardless of the rotation of their various divisions), [12] the Levites who were singers, all who belonged to Asaph, Heman, Jeduthun, and their sons and brothers, clothed in fine linen, with cymbals, harps, and lyres, stood east of the altar, and with them a hundred and twenty priests blowing trumpets.

[13] When the trumpeters and singers were heard as a single voice praising and giving thanks to the LORD, and when they raised the sound of the trumpets, cymbals, and other musical instruments to "Praise the LORD, who is so good, whose love endures forever," the cloud filled the house of the LORD.* [14] The priests could no longer minister because of the cloud, since the glory of the LORD had filled the house of God.*

**6** [1]* Then Solomon said:

> "The LORD intends to dwell in the dark
>      cloud;
> [2] I have built you a princely house,
>      the base for your enthronement
>      forever."

[3]* The king turned and blessed the whole assembly of Israel, while the whole assembly of Israel stood. [4] He said: "Blessed be the LORD, the God of Israel, who with his own mouth spoke a promise to David my father and by his hand fulfilled it, saying: [5] Since the day I brought my people out of the land of Egypt, I have not chosen a city out of any tribe of Israel for the building of a house, that my name might be there; nor have I chosen any man to be ruler of my people Israel; [6] but now I have chosen Jerusalem, that my name may be there, and I have chosen David† to rule my people Israel. [7] When David my father wished to build a house for the name of the LORD, the God of Israel, [8] the LORD said to him: In wishing to build a house for my name, you did well. [9] But it is not you who will build the house, but your son, who comes from your loins: he shall build the house for my name.

[10] "Now the LORD has fulfilled the word he

---

**5:3** *Festival of the seventh month*: feast of Booths (Tabernacles); cf. notes on 7:9–10; 1 Kgs 8:2.
**5:4** *The Levites*: the parallel passage in 1 Kgs 8:3 reads "the priests"; but in 2 Chr 5:5 the Deuteronomic expression "levitical priests" is used, as it is in 23:18; 30:27.
**5:9** *They remain there to this day*: the Chronicler must have copied this notice from his source (1 Kgs 8:8), losing sight of the fact that there was no ark in the Temple of his own day. (According to 2 Mc 2:4–8, the ark of Solomon's Temple was

concealed by Jeremiah at the time of the Babylonian destruction of Jerusalem.)
**6:6** *Jerusalem…David*: Ps 132:11, 13 puts in parallel the Lord's choice of David and Zion, the royal house of David and the mountain in Jerusalem as the site for the Lord's house.

**5:1–14** 1 Kgs 7:51–8:13.　　　**5:14** 2 Chr 7:2; 1 Kgs
**5:4–5** 2 Chr 35:3.　　　　　　　8:10–11.
　　**5:13** Ps 136; Jer 33:11.　　**6:1–2** 1 Kgs 8:12–13.
　　　　　　　　　　　　　　**6:3–11** 1 Kgs 8:14–21.

spoke. I have succeeded David my father, and I sit on the throne of Israel, as the LORD has said, and I have built this house for the name of the LORD, the God of Israel. [11] I have placed there the ark, in which is the covenant of the LORD that he made with the Israelites."

**Solomon's Prayer.** [12]* Then he stood before the altar of the LORD in the presence of the whole assembly of Israel and stretched forth his hands. [13]† Solomon had made a bronze platform five cubits long, five cubits wide, and three cubits high, which he had placed in the middle of the courtyard. Having ascended it, Solomon knelt in the presence of the whole assembly of Israel and stretched forth his hands toward heaven. [14] He said: "LORD, God of Israel, there is no God like you in heaven or on earth; you keep the covenant and love toward your servants who walk before you with their whole heart, [15] the covenant that you kept toward your servant, David my father. That which you promised him, your mouth has spoken and your hand has fulfilled this very day. [16] And now, LORD, God of Israel, keep toward your servant, David my father, what you promised: There shall never be wanting someone from your line to sit before me on the throne of Israel, provided that your descendants keep to their way, walking by my law, as you have. [17] Now, LORD, God of Israel, may the words which you spoke to David your servant be confirmed.

[18] "Is God indeed to dwell with human beings on earth? If the heavens and the highest heavens cannot contain you, how much less this house which I have built! [19] Regard kindly the prayer and petition of your servant, LORD, my God, and listen to the cry of supplication which I, your servant, utter before you. [20] May your eyes be open day and night toward this house, the place where you have decreed your name shall be; listen to the prayer your servant makes toward this place. [21] Listen to the petition of your servant and of your people Israel which they offer toward this place. Listen, from the place of your enthronement, heaven, and listen and forgive.

[22] "If someone sins against a neighbor and is required to take an oath sanctioned by a curse, and comes and takes the oath before your altar in this house, [23] listen in heaven: act and judge your servants. Condemn the wicked, requiting their ways; acquit the just, rewarding their justice. [24] When your people Israel are defeated by an enemy because they have sinned against you, and then they turn, praise your name, pray to you, and entreat you in this house, [25] listen from heaven and forgive the sin of your people Israel, and bring them back to the land you gave them and their ancestors. [26] When the heavens are closed so that there is no rain, because they have sinned against you, but they pray toward this place and praise your name, and turn from their sin because you have afflicted them, [27] listen in heaven and forgive the sin of your servants, your people Israel. (For you teach them the good way in which they should walk.) Give rain upon this land of yours which you have given to your people as their heritage.

[28] "If there is famine in the land or pestilence; or if blight comes, or mildew, or locusts swarm, or caterpillars; when their enemies besiege them at any of their gates; whatever plague or sickness there may be; [29] whatever prayer of petition any may make, any of your people Israel, who know affliction and pain and stretch out their hands toward this house, [30] listen from heaven, the place of your enthronement, and forgive. Render to each and all according to their ways, you who know every heart; for it is you alone who know the heart of every human being. [31] So may they revere you and walk in your ways as long as they live on the land you gave our ancestors.

[32] "To the foreigners, likewise, who are not of your people Israel, but who come from a distant land for the sake of your great name, your mighty hand and outstretched arm, and come in prayer to this house, [33] listen from heaven, the place of your enthronement. Do all that the foreigner asks of you, that all the peoples of the earth may know your name, may revere you as do your people Israel, and may know that your name has been invoked upon this house that I have built.

[34] "When your people go out to war against

---

**6:13** This verse has no equivalent in 1 Kgs 8:22–23, the Chronicler's source. Solomon is depicted as praying on "a bronze platform…in the middle of the courtyard" because in the time of the Chronicler only priests were permitted to pray before the altar.

**6:12–40** 1 Kgs 8:22–53.

their enemies, by whatever way you send them, and they pray to you toward the city you have chosen and the house I have built for your name, <sup>35</sup> listen from heaven to their prayer and petition, and uphold their cause. <sup>36</sup> When they sin against you (for there is no one who does not sin), and in your anger against them you deliver them to an enemy, so that their captors carry them off to another land, far or near, <sup>37</sup> and they have a change of heart in the land of their captivity and they turn and entreat you in the land of their captors and say, 'We have sinned and done wrong; we have been wicked,' <sup>38</sup> if with all their heart and soul they turn back to you in the land of those who took them captive, and pray toward their land which you gave their ancestors, the city you have chosen, and the house which I have built for your name, <sup>39</sup> listen from heaven, the place of your enthronement, to their prayer and petitions, and uphold their cause. Forgive your people who have sinned against you. <sup>40</sup> Now, my God, may your eyes be open and your ears be attentive to the prayer of this place. <sup>41</sup> And now:

"Arise, Lord God, come to your resting place,
    you and your majestic ark.
Your priests, Lord God, will be clothed with salvation,
    your faithful ones rejoice in good things.
<sup>42</sup>    Lord God, do not reject the plea of your anointed,
    remember the devotion of David, your servant."*

**7** <sup>1</sup>* When Solomon had ended his prayer, fire came down from heaven and consumed the burnt offerings and the sacrifices, and the glory of the Lord filled the house. <sup>2</sup> But the priests could not enter the house of the Lord, for the glory of the Lord filled the house of the Lord.* <sup>3</sup> All the Israelites looked on while the fire came down and the glory of

the Lord was upon the house, and they fell down upon the pavement with their faces to the earth and worshiped, praising the Lord, "who is so good, whose love endures forever." <sup>4</sup> The king and all the people offered sacrifices before the Lord.* <sup>5</sup> King Solomon offered as sacrifice twenty-two thousand oxen, and one hundred twenty thousand sheep.*

**End of the Dedication.** Thus the king and all the people dedicated the house of God. <sup>6</sup> The priests were standing at their stations, as were the Levites, with the musical instruments of the Lord which King David had made to give thanks to the Lord, "whose love endures forever," when David offered praise through them. The priests opposite them blew the trumpets and all Israel stood.* <sup>7</sup> Then Solomon consecrated the middle of the court facing the house of the Lord; he offered there the burnt offerings and the fat of the communion offerings, since the bronze altar which Solomon had made could not hold the burnt offering, the grain offering, and the fat.* <sup>8</sup> On this occasion Solomon and with him all Israel, a great assembly from Lebo-hamath to the Wadi of Egypt, celebrated the festival for seven days.* <sup>9</sup>* On the eighth day they held a solemn assembly, for they had celebrated the dedication of the altar for seven days and the feast† for seven days. <sup>10</sup> On the twenty-third day of the seventh month he dismissed the people to their tents, rejoicing and glad of heart because of all the blessings the Lord had given to David, to Solomon, and to his people Israel. <sup>11</sup>* Solomon finished building the house of the Lord, the house of the king, and everything else he wanted to do in regard to the house of the Lord and his own house.

**God's Promise to Solomon.** <sup>12</sup> The Lord appeared to Solomon during the night and said to him: I have heard your prayer, and I have chosen this place for my house of sacrifice. <sup>13</sup> If I close heaven so that there is no rain, if

---

<sup>†</sup> 7:9–10 *The feast*: Booths, celebrated on the fifteenth day of the seventh month and followed by a solemn octave lasting through the twenty-second day (Lv 23:33–36; Nm 29:12–35); the people are therefore sent home on the twenty-third day of the month (v. 10). The festival (v. 8) marking the dedication of the altar and of the Temple was held during the seven days prior to the feast of Booths, i.e., from the seventh to the fourteenth day of the seventh month. According to 1 Kgs 8:3, 65–66 the dedication of the Temple was celebrated concomitantly with the seven days

of the feast of Booths, after which the people were dismissed on the eighth day.

* — — — — — —
**6:41–42** Ps 132:8–10.        8:62; Ps 136:1.
**7:1–10** Jgs 6:21; 1 Kgs     **7:5** 1 Kgs 8:63.
       8:54–66; 1 Chr 21:26;   **7:6** Nm 10:8, 10; Ps 136:1.
       2 Mc 2:10.              **7:7** 1 Kgs 8:64.
**7:2** 2 Chr 5:14; Ex 24:16;  **7:8** 1 Kgs 8:65.
       1 Kgs 8:10–11.          **7:9–10** 1 Kgs 8:66.
**7:4** 2 Chr 5:13; 1 Kgs      **7:11–22** 1 Kgs 9:1–9.

I command the locust to devour the land, if I send pestilence among my people, ¹⁴ if then my people, upon whom my name has been pronounced, humble themselves and pray, and seek my face and turn from their evil ways, I will hear them from heaven and pardon their sins and heal their land. ¹⁵ Now, therefore, my eyes shall be open and my ears attentive to the prayer of this place; ¹⁶ now I have chosen and consecrated this house that my name may be there forever; my eyes and my heart shall be there always.

¹⁷ As for you, if you walk before me as David your father did, doing all that I have commanded you and keeping my statutes and ordinances, ¹⁸ I will establish the throne of your kingship as I covenanted with David your father when I said, There shall never be wanting someone from your line as ruler in Israel. ¹⁹ But if ever you turn away and forsake my commandments and statutes which I set before you, and proceed to serve other gods, and bow down to them, ²⁰ I will uproot the people from the land I gave and repudiate the house I have consecrated for my name. I will make it a proverb and a byword among all nations. ²¹ And this house which is so exalted—every passerby shall be horrified and ask: "Why has the LORD done such things to this land and to this house?" ²² And the answer will come: "Because they abandoned the LORD, the God of their ancestors, who brought them out of the land of Egypt, and they embraced other gods, bowing down to them and serving them. That is why he has brought upon them all this evil."

**8** **Public Works.** ¹* After the twenty years during which Solomon built the house of the LORD and his own house, ² he built up the cities which Huram had given him,† and settled Israelites there. ³ Then Solomon went to Hamath of Zoba and conquered it. ⁴ He built Tadmor† in the wilderness and all the supply cities, which he built in Hamath. ⁵* He built Upper Beth-horon and Lower Beth-horon, fortified cities with walls, gates, and bars; ⁶ also Baalath, all the supply cities belonging to Solomon, and all the cities for the chariots, the cities for horses, and whatever else Solomon desired to build in Jerusalem, in Lebanon, and in the entire land under his dominion. ⁷ All the people who were left of the Hittites, Amorites, Perizzites, Hivites, and Jebusites who were not Israelites— ⁸ those of their descendants who were left in the land and whom the Israelites had not destroyed—Solomon conscripted as forced laborers, as they are to this day. ⁹ But Solomon made none of the Israelites forced laborers for his works, for they were his fighting force, commanders, adjutants, chariot officers, and cavalry. ¹⁰ They were also King Solomon's two hundred and fifty overseers who directed the people.

**Solomon's Piety.** ¹¹ Solomon brought the daughter of Pharaoh up from the City of David to the house which he had built for her, for he said, "No wife of mine shall dwell in the house of David, king of Israel, for the places where the ark of the LORD has come are holy."

¹² In those times Solomon sacrificed burnt offerings to the LORD upon the altar of the LORD which he had built in front of the porch, ¹³ as was required to be done day by day according to the command of Moses, especially on the sabbaths, at the new moons, and on the fixed festivals three times a year: on the feast of the Unleavened Bread, the feast of Weeks, and the feast of Booths.*

¹⁴ And according to the ordinance of David his father he appointed the various divisions of the priests for their service, and the Levites according to their functions of praise and attendance upon the priests, as the daily duty required. The gatekeepers by their divisions stood guard at each gate, since such was the command of David, the man of God.* ¹⁵ There was no deviation from the king's command in whatever related to the priests and Levites or the treasuries. ¹⁶ All of Solomon's work was carried out successfully from the day the foundation of the house of the LORD was laid until its completion. The house of the LORD was finished.

---

† **8:2** *The cities which Huram had given him:* according to 1 Kgs 9:10–14, it was Solomon who ceded the cities to the king of Tyre as payment for the timber and gold received from him. Since, however, 1 Kgs 9:12 states that Hiram was not satisfied with the cities, the Chronicler may have inferred that he gave them back to Solomon.

**8:4** *Tadmor:* later known as Palmyra, an important caravan city in the Syrian desert. The parallel passage in 1 Kgs 9:18 has "Tamar," in southern Judah; cf. Ez 47:19; 48:28. But Solomon may well have fortified Tadmor against the Arameans.

**8:1–2** 1 Kgs 9:10–11.
**8:5–12** 1 Kgs 9:17–25.
**8:13** Ex 23:14; Nm 28–29;
1 Kgs 9:25.
**8:14** 1 Chr 23–26; Neh 12:46.

**Glories of the Court.** [17] In those times Solomon went to Ezion-geber and to Elath on the seashore of the land of Edom.* [18] Huram had his servants send him ships and his own servants, expert seamen; they went with Solomon's servants to Ophir, and obtained there four hundred and fifty talents of gold and brought it to King Solomon.*

**9** **The Queen of Sheba.** [1]* The queen of Sheba, having heard a report of Solomon's fame, came to Jerusalem to test him with subtle questions, accompanied by a very numerous retinue and by camels bearing spices, a large amount of gold, and precious stones. She came to Solomon and spoke to him about everything that she had on her mind. [2] Solomon explained to her everything she asked about, and there was nothing so obscure that Solomon could not explain it to her.*

[3]* When the queen of Sheba witnessed Solomon's great wisdom, the house he had built, [4] the food at his table, the seating of his ministers, the attendance and dress of his waiters, his cupbearers and their dress, and the burnt offerings he sacrificed in the house of the LORD, it took her breath away. [5] "The report I heard in my country about your deeds and your wisdom is true," she told the king. [6] "I did not believe the report until I came and saw with my own eyes that not even the half of your great wisdom had been told me. You have surpassed the report I heard. [7] Happy your servants, happy these ministers of yours, who stand before you always and listen to your wisdom. [8] Blessed be the LORD, your God, who was pleased to set you on his throne as king for the LORD, your God. In the love your God has for Israel, to establish them forever, he has made you king over them to carry out judgment and justice." [9] Then she gave the king one hundred and twenty gold talents, a very large quantity of spices, and precious stones. Never again did anyone bring such an abundance of spices as the queen of Sheba gave to King Solomon.

[10] The servants of Huram and of Solomon who brought gold from Ophir also brought cabinet wood and precious stones. [11] With the cabinet wood the king made stairs for the house of the LORD and the house of the king, and harps and lyres for the chanters. The like of these had not been seen before in the land of Judah.*

[12] King Solomon gave the queen of Sheba everything she desired and asked for, more than she had brought to the king. Then she returned with her servants to her own country.*

[13]* The gold that came to Solomon in one year weighed six hundred and sixty-six gold talents, [14] in addition to what came from the tolls on travelers and what the merchants brought. All the kings of Arabia also, and the governors of the country, brought gold and silver to Solomon.

[15] King Solomon made two hundred large shields of beaten gold (six hundred shekels of gold went into each shield) [16] and three hundred bucklers of beaten gold (three hundred shekels of gold went into each buckler); and the king put them in the house of the Forest of Lebanon.

[17] The king made a large ivory throne, and overlaid it with fine gold. [18] The throne had six steps; a footstool of gold was fastened to the throne, and there was an arm on each side of the seat, with two lions standing next to the arms, [19] and twelve other lions standing there on the steps, two to a step. Nothing like this was made in any other kingdom. [20] All King Solomon's drinking vessels were gold, and all the utensils in the house of the Forest of Lebanon were pure gold. There was no silver, for in Solomon's time silver was reckoned as nothing. [21] For the king had ships that went to Tarshish with the servants of Huram. Once every three years the fleet of Tarshish ships would come with a cargo of gold, silver, ivory, apes, and monkeys.

**Solomon's Renown.** [22] Thus King Solomon surpassed all the kings of the earth in riches and wisdom.

[23] All the kings of the earth sought audience with Solomon, to hear the wisdom God had put into his heart. [24] They all brought their tribute: vessels of silver and gold, garments, weapons, spices, horses, and mules—what was due each year. [25] Solomon had four thousand stalls for horses, chariots, and twelve thousand

8:17 1 Kgs 9:26.          9:1 1 Kgs 10:1–2.          9:3–9 1 Kgs 10:4–9.          9:12 1 Kgs 10:13.
8:18 1 Kgs 9:27–28.       9:2 1 Kgs 10:3.             9:10–11 1 Kgs 10:11–12.    9:13–28 1 Kgs 10:14–28.

2 CHR

horses; these he allocated among the chariot cities and to the king's service in Jerusalem. ²⁶ He was ruler over all the kings from the River to the land of the Philistines and down to the border of Egypt. ²⁷ The king made silver as common in Jerusalem as stones, and cedars as numerous as the sycamores of the Shephelah. ²⁸ † Solomon's horses were imported from Egypt and from all the lands.

**The Death of Solomon.** ²⁹ * The remainder of the acts of Solomon, first and last, are recorded in the acts of Nathan the prophet, in the prophecy of Ahijah the Shilonite, and in the visions of Iddo the seer concerning Jeroboam, son of Nebat. ³⁰ Solomon was king in Jerusalem over all Israel for forty years. ³¹ Solomon rested with his ancestors and was buried in the City of David, his father, and Rehoboam his son succeeded him as king.

## II. THE POST-SOLOMONIC MONARCHY OF JUDAH

**10** **Division of the Kingdom.** ¹ * Rehoboam went to Shechem, where all Israel † had come to make him king. ² When Jeroboam, son of Nebat, heard about it, he was in Egypt where he had fled from King Solomon; and he returned from Egypt. ³ They sent for him; Jeroboam and all Israel came and said to Rehoboam: ⁴ "Your father put on us a heavy yoke. If you now lighten the harsh servitude and the heavy yoke your father imposed on us, we will be your servants." ⁵ He answered them, "Come back to me in three days," and the people went away.

⁶ King Rehoboam asked advice of the elders who had been in his father Solomon's service while he was still alive, and asked, "How do you advise me to answer this people?" ⁷ They replied, "If you will deal kindly with this people and please them, giving them a favorable reply, they will be your servants forever." ⁸ But he ignored the advice the elders had given him and asked advice of the young men who had grown up with him and were in his service. ⁹ He said to them, "What answer do you advise us to give this people, who have told me,

'Lighten the yoke your father imposed on us'?" ¹⁰ The young men who had grown up with him replied: "This is what you must say to this people who have told you, 'Your father laid a heavy yoke on us; lighten it for us.' You must say, 'My little finger is thicker than my father's loins. ¹¹ My father put a heavy yoke on you; I will make it heavier. My father beat you with whips; I will use scorpions!'"

¹² On the third day, Jeroboam and the whole people came back to King Rehoboam as the king had instructed them: "Come back to me in three days." ¹³ Ignoring the advice the elders had given him, King Rehoboam gave the people a harsh answer. ¹⁴ He spoke to them as the young men had advised: "My father laid a heavy yoke on you; I will make it heavier. My father beat you with whips; I will use scorpions." ¹⁵ The king did not listen to the people, for this turn of events was from God: the LORD fulfilled the word he had spoken through Ahijah the Shilonite to Jeroboam, the son of Nebat. *

¹⁶ * When all Israel saw that the king did not listen to them, the people answered the king:

"What share have we in David?
We have no heritage in the son of Jesse.
Everyone to your tents, Israel!
Now look to your own house, David!"

So all Israel went off to their tents, ¹⁷ but the Israelites who lived in the cities of Judah had Rehoboam as their king. ¹⁸ King Rehoboam then sent out Hadoram, who was in charge of the forced labor, but the Israelites stoned him to death. King Rehoboam, however, managed to mount his chariot and flee to Jerusalem. ¹⁹ And so Israel has been in rebellion against the house of David to this day.

**11** ¹ * On his arrival in Jerusalem, Rehoboam assembled the house of Judah and Benjamin—one hundred and eighty thousand elite warriors—to wage war against Israel and restore the kingdom to Rehoboam. ² However, the word of the LORD came to Shemaiah, a man of God: ³ Say to Rehoboam, son

---

† **9:28** See note on 1:16–17.
**10:1** *All Israel*: as in the source (1 Kgs 12:1), this term designates the northern tribes, as distinct from Judah and Benjamin. Elsewhere the Chronicler, writing on his own, speaks comprehensively of "those Israelites who lived in the cities of Judah"

(10:17), and "all the Israelites [lit., all Israel] in Judah and Benjamin" (11:3).
*

**9:29–31** 1 Kgs 11:41–43.        12:15.
**10:1–14** 1 Kgs 12:1–14.    **10:16–19** 1 Kgs 12:16–19.
    **10:15** 1 Kgs 11:29–39;    **11:1–4** 1 Kgs 12:21–24.

of Solomon, king of Judah, and to all the Israelites in Judah and Benjamin: [4] "Thus says the LORD: You must not go out to war against your kinsmen. Return home, each of you, for it is I who have brought this about." They obeyed the word of the LORD and turned back from going against Jeroboam.

### Rehoboam's Works. † [5] Rehoboam took up residence in Jerusalem and built fortified cities in Judah. [6] He built up Bethlehem, Etam, Tekoa, [7] Beth-zur, Soco, Adullam, [8] Gath, Mareshah, Ziph, [9] Adoraim, Lachish, Azekah, [10] Zorah, Aijalon, and Hebron; these were fortified cities in Judah and Benjamin. [11] Then he strengthened the fortifications and put commanders in them, along with supplies of food, oil, and wine. [12] In every city were shields and spears, and he made them very strong. Thus Judah and Benjamin remained his.

### Refugees from the North. [13] Now the priests and Levites throughout Israel presented themselves to him from all parts of their land, [14] for the Levites left their assigned pasture lands and their holdings and came to Judah and Jerusalem, because Jeroboam and his sons rejected them as priests of the LORD.* [15] In their place, he himself appointed priests for the high places as well as for the satyrs and calves he had made.* [16] After them, all those, of every tribe of Israel, who set their hearts to seek the LORD, the God of Israel, came to Jerusalem to sacrifice to the LORD, the God of their ancestors. [17] Thus they strengthened the kingdom of Judah and made Rehoboam, son of Solomon, prevail for three years; for they walked in the way of David and Solomon three years.

### Rehoboam's Family. [18] Rehoboam married Mahalath, daughter of Jerimoth, son of David and of Abihail, daughter of Eliab, son of Jesse. [19] She bore him sons: Jehush, Shemariah, and Zaham. [20] After her, he married Maacah, daughter of Absalom, who bore him Abijah,* Attai, Ziza, and Shelomith. [21] Rehoboam loved Maacah, daughter of Absalom, more than all his other wives and concubines; he had taken eighteen wives and sixty concubines, and he fathered twenty-eight sons and sixty daughters.

[22] Rehoboam put Abijah, son of Maacah, first among his brothers, as leader, for he intended to make him king. [23] He acted prudently, distributing his various sons throughout all the districts of Judah and Benjamin, in all the fortified cities; and he gave them generous provisions and sought an abundance of wives for them.

# 12

### Rehoboam's Apostasy. [1] Once Rehoboam had established himself as king and was firmly in charge, he abandoned the law of the LORD, and so did all Israel with him.* [2] So in the fifth year of King Rehoboam, Shishak, king of Egypt, attacked Jerusalem, for they had acted treacherously toward the LORD.* [3] He had twelve hundred chariots and sixty thousand horsemen, and there was no counting the army that came with him from Egypt—Libyans, Sukkites, † and Ethiopians. [4] They captured the fortified cities of Judah and came as far as Jerusalem. [5] Then Shemaiah* the prophet came to Rehoboam and the commanders of Judah who had gathered at Jerusalem because of Shishak, and said to them: "Thus says the LORD: You have abandoned me, and so I have abandoned you to the power of Shishak."

[6] Then the commanders of Israel and the king humbled themselves saying, "The LORD is in the right." [7] When the LORD saw that they had humbled themselves, the word of the LORD came to Shemaiah: Because they have humbled themselves, I will not destroy them; I will give them some deliverance, and my wrath shall not be poured out upon Jerusalem through Shishak. [8] But they shall be his servants. Then they will know what it is to serve me and what it is to serve the kingdoms of the earth. [9]* Thereupon Shishak, king of Egypt, attacked Jerusalem and took away the treasures of the house of the LORD and the treasures of the house of the king. He took everything, including the gold shields that Solomon had made. [10] To replace them, King Rehoboam made bronze shields, which he entrusted to the officers of the attendants on duty at the entrance of the king's house. [11] Whenever the king visited the house of the LORD, the attendants would carry them, and then return them

---

† **11:5–12** These verses have no parallel in 1 Kings; they are apparently based on a separate source.
 **12:3** *Sukkites:* foreign mercenaries in the Egyptian army.

* **11:14** 1 Kgs 12:32.
**11:15** Lv 17:7; 1 Kgs 12:32.
**11:20** 1 Kgs 15:2.
**12:1** 1 Kgs 11:4; 14:22.
**12:2** 1 Kgs 14:25.
**12:5** 2 Chr 11:2.
**12:9–11** 1 Kgs 14:25–28.

to the guardroom. ¹²Because he had humbled himself, the anger of the LORD turned from him so as not to destroy him completely; in Judah, moreover, there was some good.

¹³King Rehoboam was firmly in power in Jerusalem and continued to rule. Rehoboam was forty-one years old when he became king, and he reigned seventeen years in Jerusalem, the city in which, out of all the tribes of Israel, the LORD chose to set his name. His mother's name was Naamah, the Ammonite.* ¹⁴He did evil, for he had not set his heart to seek the LORD. ¹⁵*The acts of Rehoboam, first and last, are recorded in the history of Shemaiah the prophet and of Iddo the seer (his family record). There were wars between Rehoboam and Jeroboam all their days. ¹⁶Rehoboam rested with his ancestors; he was buried in the City of David. His son Abijah† succeeded him as king.

# 13 War Between Abijah and Jeroboam.
¹*In the eighteenth year of King Jeroboam, Abijah became king of Judah; ²he reigned three years in Jerusalem. His mother was named Micaiah, daughter of Uriel of Gibeah. There was war between Abijah and Jeroboam.

³†Abijah joined battle with a force of four hundred thousand picked warriors, while Jeroboam lined up against him in battle with eight hundred thousand picked and valiant warriors. ⁴Abijah stood on Mount Zemaraim, which is in the highlands of Ephraim, and said: "Listen to me, Jeroboam and all Israel! ⁵Do you not know that the LORD, the God of Israel, has given David kingship over Israel forever, to him and to his sons, by a covenant of salt?† ⁶Yet Jeroboam, son of Nebat, the servant of Solomon, son of David, arose and rebelled against his lord!* ⁷Worthless men, scoundrels, joined him and overcame Rehoboam, son of Solomon, when Rehoboam was young and inexperienced, and no match for them. ⁸But now, do you think you are a match for the kingdom of the LORD led by the descendants of David, simply because you are a huge multitude and have with you the golden calves which Jeroboam made you for gods? ⁹Have

you not expelled the priests of the LORD, the sons of Aaron, and the Levites, and made for yourselves priests like the peoples of other lands? Everyone who comes to consecrate himself with a young bull and seven rams becomes a priest of no-gods. ¹⁰But as for us, the LORD is our God, and we have not abandoned him. The priests ministering to the LORD are sons of Aaron, and the Levites also have their offices. ¹¹They sacrifice burnt offerings to the LORD and fragrant incense morning after morning and evening after evening; they set out the showbread on the pure table, and the lamps of the golden menorah burn evening after evening; for we observe our duties to the LORD, our God, but you have abandoned him. ¹²See, God is with us, at our head, and his priests are here with trumpets to sound the attack against you. Israelites, do not fight against the LORD, the God of your ancestors, for you will not succeed!"

¹³But Jeroboam had an ambush go around them to come at them from the rear; so that while his army faced Judah, his ambush lay behind them. ¹⁴When Judah turned and saw that they had to battle on both fronts, they cried out to the LORD and the priests sounded the trumpets. ¹⁵Then the Judahites shouted; and when they shouted, God struck down Jeroboam and all Israel before Abijah and Judah. ¹⁶The Israelites fled before Judah, and God delivered them into their power. ¹⁷Abijah and his people inflicted a severe defeat upon them; five hundred thousand picked men of Israel fell slain. ¹⁸The Israelites were humbled on that occasion, while the Judahites were victorious because they relied on the LORD, the God of their ancestors. ¹⁹Abijah pursued Jeroboam and seized cities from him: Bethel and its dependencies, Jeshanah and its dependencies, and Ephron and its dependencies. ²⁰Jeroboam did not regain power during Abijah's time; the LORD struck him down and he died, ²¹while Abijah continued to grow stronger. He married fourteen wives and fathered twenty-two sons and sixteen daughters.

## Death of Abijah.
²²*The rest of the acts of Abijah, his deeds and his words, are recorded

---

† 12:16 *Abijah:* in 1 Kgs 14:31–15:8 this king is called Abijam.
13:3–21 This passage is a free composition of the Chronicler based on the reference in 1 Kgs 15:6 to the war between Abijam (so in Kings, "Abijah" in Chronicles) and Jeroboam.
13:5 *Covenant of salt:* see note on Nm 18:19.

* 12:13 1 Kgs 14:21.
12:15–16 1 Kgs 14:29–31.
13:1–2 1 Kgs 15:1–2.
13:6 1 Kgs 11:26.
13:22–23 2 Chr 12:15–16; 1 Kgs 15:7–8.

in the midrash of the prophet Iddo. ²³ Abijah rested with his ancestors; they buried him in the City of David and his son Asa succeeded him as king. During his time, the land had ten years of peace.

## 14 Asa's Initial Reforms.
¹* Asa did what was good and right in the sight of the LORD, his God. ² He removed the illicit altars and the high places, smashed the sacred pillars, and cut down the asherahs. ³ He told Judah to seek the LORD, the God of their ancestors, and to observe the law and the commandment. ⁴ He removed the high places and incense stands from all the cities of Judah, and under him the kingdom had peace. ⁵ He built fortified cities in Judah, for the land had peace and no war was waged against him during these years, because the LORD had given him rest. ⁶ He said to Judah: "Let us build these cities and surround them with walls, towers, gates and bars. The land is still ours, for we have sought the LORD, our God; we sought him, and he has given us rest on every side." So they built and prospered.

## The Ethiopian Invasion.†
⁷ Asa had an army of three hundred thousand shield- and lance-bearers from Judah, and from Benjamin two hundred and eighty thousand who carried bucklers and were archers, all of them valiant warriors. ⁸ Zerah the Ethiopian advanced against them with a force of one million men and three hundred chariots, and he came as far as Mareshah.* ⁹ Asa went out to meet him and they drew up for battle in the valley of Zephathah, near Mareshah. ¹⁰ Asa called upon the LORD, his God: "LORD, there is none like you to help the powerless against the strong. Help us, LORD, our God, for we rely on you, and in your name we have come against this multitude. You are the LORD, our God; do not let men prevail against you."* ¹¹ And so the LORD defeated the Ethiopians before Asa and Judah, and the Ethiopians fled. ¹² Asa and those with

him pursued them as far as Gerar, and the Ethiopians fell until there were no survivors, for they were crushed before the LORD and his army, which carried away enormous spoils. ¹³ Then the Judahites conquered all the cities around Gerar, for the fear of the LORD was upon them; they plundered all the cities, for there was much plunder in them. ¹⁴ They also attacked the tents of the cattle-herders and carried off a great number of sheep and camels. Then they returned to Jerusalem.

## 15 Further Reforms.
¹ The spirit of God came upon Azariah, son of Oded. ² He went forth to meet Asa and said to him: "Hear me, Asa and all Judah and Benjamin! The LORD is with you when you are with him, and if you seek him he will be found; but if you abandon him, he will abandon you.* ³ For a long time Israel was without a true God, without a priest-teacher, without instruction, ⁴ but when in their distress they turned to the LORD, the God of Israel, and sought him, he was found by them.* ⁵ At that time there was no peace for anyone to go or come; rather, there were many terrors upon the inhabitants of the lands. ⁶ Nation crushed nation and city crushed city,* for God overwhelmed them with every kind of distress. ⁷ But as for you, be strong and do not slack off, for there shall be a reward for what you do."*

⁸ When Asa heard these words and the prophecy (Oded the prophet), he was encouraged to remove the detestable idols from the whole land of Judah and Benjamin and from the cities he had taken in the highlands of Ephraim, and to restore the altar of the LORD which was before the vestibule of the LORD. ⁹ Then he gathered all Judah and Benjamin, together with those of Ephraim, Manasseh, and Simeon who were resident with them; for many had defected to him from Israel when they saw that the LORD, his God, was with him. ¹⁰ They gathered at Jerusalem in the third month† of the fifteenth year of Asa's reign,

---

**14:7–14** This Ethiopian invasion of Judah is not mentioned in 1 Kings. The account is likely a legend intended to show the pious King Asa being rewarded with divine assistance. It could, however, reflect an incursion by nomads from the Negeb in Asa's time.

**15:10–12** With this description of a covenant ceremony in "the third month" of a year beginning in the spring, the Chronicler provides a basis for the later understanding of the ancient Jewish spring feast of Weeks as a commemoration of the covenant on Mount Sinai; see Ex 19:1–3; Lv 23:16 and note on

Lv 23:16–21. In the Greek period the feast came to be called Pentecost, from the Greek word for "fifty," i.e., fifty days or seven weeks after Passover. The Chronicler's presentation here has also influenced the celebration of Christian Pentecost as the "birthday of the Church"; cf. Acts 2.

**14:1–2** 2 Chr 33:15; Ex 23:24; 34:13; 1 Kgs 15:11–12.
**14:8** 2 Chr 16:8.
**14:10** 2 Chr 32:8.
**15:2** Jer 29:13–14; Hos 3:4–5.
**15:4** Dt 4:29–30.
**15:6** Is 19:2.
**15:7** Is 7:4; Jer 31:16.

<sup>11</sup> and sacrificed to the LORD on that day seven hundred oxen and seven thousand sheep from the spoils they had brought. <sup>12</sup> * They entered into a covenant to seek the LORD, the God of their ancestors, with all their heart and soul; <sup>13</sup> and everyone who would not seek the LORD, the God of Israel, was to be put to death, from least to greatest, man or woman. <sup>14</sup> They swore an oath to the LORD with a loud voice, with shouting and with trumpets and horns. <sup>15</sup> All Judah rejoiced over the oath, for they had sworn it with their whole heart and sought him with complete desire. The LORD was found by them, * and gave them rest on every side.

<sup>16</sup> * He also deposed Maacah, the mother† of King Asa, from her position as queen mother because she had made an obscene object for Asherah; Asa cut down this object, smashed it, and burnt it in the Wadi Kidron. <sup>17</sup> The high places did not disappear from Israel, yet Asa's heart was undivided as long as he lived. <sup>18</sup> He brought into the house of God his father's and his own votive offerings: silver, gold, and vessels. <sup>19</sup> There was no war until the thirty-fifth year of Asa's reign.

# 16 Asa's Infidelity.
<sup>1</sup> * In the thirty-sixth year of Asa's reign, Baasha, king of Israel, attacked Judah and fortified Ramah to block all movement for Asa, king of Judah. <sup>2</sup> Asa then brought out silver and gold from the treasuries of the house of the LORD and the house of the king and sent them to Ben-hadad, king of Aram, who ruled in Damascus. He said: <sup>3</sup> "There is a treaty between you and me, as there was between your father and my father. I am sending you silver and gold. Go, break your treaty with Baasha, king of Israel, that he may withdraw from me." <sup>4</sup> Ben-hadad agreed with King Asa and sent the leaders of his troops against the cities of Israel. They attacked Ijon, Dan, Abel-maim, besides all the store cities of Naphtali. <sup>5</sup> When Baasha heard of it, he left off fortifying Ramah, putting an end to his work. <sup>6</sup> Then King Asa commandeered all Judah and they carried away the stones and beams with which Baasha was fortifying Ramah. With them he fortified Geba and Mizpah.

<sup>7</sup> At that time Hanani the seer came to Asa, king of Judah, and said to him: "Because you relied on the king of Aram and did not rely on the LORD, your God, the army of the king of Aram has escaped† your power. <sup>8</sup> * Were not the Ethiopians and Libyans a vast army, with great numbers of chariots and horses? And yet, because you relied on the LORD, he delivered them into your power. <sup>9</sup> The eyes of the LORD roam over the whole earth, * to encourage those who are devoted to him wholeheartedly. You have acted foolishly in this matter, for from now on you will have wars." <sup>10</sup> But Asa became angry with the seer and imprisoned him in the stocks, so greatly was he enraged at him over this. Asa also oppressed some of his people at this time.

<sup>11</sup> * Now the acts of Asa, first and last, are recorded in the book of the kings of Judah and Israel. <sup>12</sup> In the thirty-ninth year of his reign, Asa contracted disease in his feet; it became worse, but even with this disease he did not seek the LORD, only physicians. <sup>13</sup> Asa rested with his ancestors; he died in the forty-first year of his reign. <sup>14</sup> They buried him in the tomb he had hewn for himself in the City of David, after laying him on a couch that was filled with spices and various kinds of aromatics compounded into an ointment; and they kindled a huge fire for him.

# 17 Jehoshaphat's Zeal for the Law.
<sup>1</sup> His son Jehoshaphat succeeded him as king and strengthened his position against Israel. * <sup>2</sup> He placed armed forces in all the fortified cities of Judah, and set garrisons in the land of Judah and in the cities of Ephraim which Asa his father had taken. <sup>3</sup> The LORD was with Jehoshaphat,† for he walked in the earlier ways of David his father, and did not seek the Baals. <sup>4</sup> Rather, he sought the God of his father and walked in his commands, and not the practices of Israel. <sup>5</sup> Through him, the LORD made the kingdom secure, and all Judah gave Jehoshaphat gifts, so that great wealth and glory was his. <sup>6</sup> Thus he was

---

† 
15:16 *Mother:* see note on 1 Kgs 15:10.
16:7 *The king of Aram has escaped:* the Lucianic recension of the Septuagint reads, "the king of Israel escaped." This may well be the original reading, since according to the story Asa hired the king of Aram as an ally against Israel.
17:3 *The LORD was with Jehoshaphat:* along with his succes-

sors Hezekiah and Josiah, Jehoshaphat is one of the Chronicler's exemplary kings.

*
| | |
|---|---|
| **15:12–13** Neh 10:29–30. | **16:8** 2 Chr 14:8–14. |
| **15:15** Dt 4:29. | **16:9** Ps 33:13–15. |
| **15:16–18** 1 Kgs 15:13–15. | **16:11–14** 1 Kgs 15:23–24. |
| **16:1–6** 1 Kgs 15:16–21. | **17:1** 1 Kgs 15:24. |

encouraged† to follow the LORD's ways, and once again he removed the high places and the asherahs from Judah.*

⁷In the third year of his reign he sent his officials, Ben-hail, Obadiah, Zechariah, Nethanel, and Micaiah, to teach in the cities of Judah. ⁸With them he sent the Levites Shemaiah, Nethaniah, Zebadiah, Asahel, Shemiramoth, Jehonathan, Adonijah, and Tobijah, together with Elishama and Jehoram the priests.* ⁹They taught in Judah, having with them the book of the law of the LORD; they traveled through all the cities of Judah and taught among the people.*

**His Power.** ¹⁰Now the fear of the LORD was upon all the kingdoms of the countries surrounding Judah, so that they did not war against Jehoshaphat. ¹¹Some of the Philistines brought Jehoshaphat gifts and a tribute of silver; the Arabians also brought him a flock of seven thousand seven hundred rams and seven thousand seven hundred he-goats.

¹²Jehoshaphat grew ever greater. He built strongholds and store cities in Judah. ¹³He carried out many works in the cities of Judah, and he had soldiers, valiant warriors, in Jerusalem. ¹⁴This was their mustering according to their ancestral houses. From Judah, the commanders of thousands: Adnah the commander, and with him three hundred thousand valiant warriors. ¹⁵Next to him, Jehohanan the commander, and with him two hundred eighty thousand. ¹⁶Next to him, Amasiah, son of Zichri, who offered himself to the LORD, and with him two hundred thousand valiant warriors. ¹⁷From Benjamin: Eliada, a valiant warrior, and with him two hundred thousand armed with bow and buckler. ¹⁸Next to him, Jehozabad, and with him one hundred and eighty thousand equipped for war. ¹⁹These attended the king; in addition to those whom the king had stationed in the fortified cities throughout all Judah.

# 18 **Alliance with Israel.** ¹*Jehoshaphat therefore had wealth and glory in abundance; but he became related to Ahab by marriage. ²After some years he went down

to Ahab at Samaria; Ahab slaughtered numerous sheep and oxen for him and for the people with him, and incited him to go up against Ramoth-gilead. ³Ahab, king of Israel, asked Jehoshaphat, king of Judah, "Will you come with me to Ramoth-gilead?" He answered, "You and I are as one, and your people and my people as well. We will be with you in the battle." ⁴Jehoshaphat also said to the king of Israel, "Seek the word of the LORD at once."

**Prophets in Conflict.** ⁵The king of Israel assembled the prophets, four hundred of them, and asked, "Shall we go to fight against Ramoth-gilead, or shall I refrain?" They said, "Attack. God will give it into the power of the king." ⁶But Jehoshaphat said, "Is there no other prophet of the LORD here we might consult?" ⁷The king of Israel answered, "There is one other man through whom we may consult the LORD; but I hate him, because he prophesies not good but always evil about me. He is Micaiah, son of Imlah." Jeshoshaphat said, "Let not the king say that." ⁸So the king of Israel called an official, and said to him, "Get Micaiah, son of Imlah, at once." ⁹The king of Israel and Jehoshaphat, king of Judah, were seated, each on his throne, clothed in their robes of state in the square at the entrance of the gate of Samaria, and all the prophets were prophesying before them.

¹⁰Zedekiah, son of Chenaanah, made himself two horns of iron and said: "The LORD says: With these you shall gore Aram until you have destroyed them." ¹¹The other prophets prophesied in the same vein, saying: "Attack Ramoth-gilead, and conquer! The LORD will give it into the power of the king." ¹²†Meanwhile the messenger who had gone to call Micaiah said to him: "Look now, the words of the prophets are as one in speaking good for the king. Let your word be at one with theirs; speak a good word." ¹³Micaiah said, "As the LORD lives, I shall speak whatever my God says."

¹⁴When he came to the king, the king said to him, "Micah, shall we go to fight at Ramoth-gilead, or shall I refrain?" He said, "Attack

---

† **17:6** *Thus he was encouraged*: lit., "his heart was high," a phrase that ordinarily describes arrogance and rebelliousness; in this case, however, it introduces a notice of Jehoshaphat's fidelity to the Lord.

**18:12–22** See note on 1 Kgs 22:19–23.

* **17:6** 2 Chr 20:33; Ex
   34:13.
**17:8** 2 Chr 19:8.

**17:9** Ezr 7:25.
**18:1–34** 1 Kgs 22:1–35.

and conquer! They will be delivered into your power." ¹⁵ But the king answered him, "How many times must I adjure you to tell me nothing but the truth in the name of the Lord?" ¹⁶ So Micaiah said:

"I see all Israel
    scattered on the mountains,
    like sheep without a shepherd,
And the Lord saying,
    These have no masters!
    Let each of them go back home in
      peace."

¹⁷ The king of Israel said to Jehoshaphat, "Did I not tell you, he does not prophesy good about me, but only evil?" ¹⁸ Micaiah continued: "Therefore hear the word of the Lord. I saw the Lord seated on his throne, with the whole host of heaven standing to his right and to his left. ¹⁹ The Lord asked: Who will deceive Ahab, king of Israel, so that he will go up and fall on Ramoth-gilead? And one said this, another that, ²⁰ until this spirit came forth and stood before the Lord, saying, 'I will deceive him.' The Lord asked: How? ²¹ He answered, 'I will go forth and become a lying spirit in the mouths of all his prophets.' The Lord replied: You shall succeed in deceiving him. Go forth and do this. ²² So now the Lord has put a lying spirit in the mouths of these prophets of yours; but the Lord himself has decreed evil against you."

²³ Thereupon Zedekiah, son of Chenaanah, came up and struck Micaiah on the cheek, saying, "Has the spirit of the Lord, then, passed from me to speak with you?" ²⁴ Micaiah said, "You shall find out on the day you go into an innermost room to hide." ²⁵ The king of Israel then said: "Seize Micaiah and take him back to Amon, prefect of the city, and to Joash the king's son, ²⁶ and say, 'This is the king's order: Put this man in prison and feed him scanty rations of bread and water until I come back in safety!'" ²⁷ But Micaiah said, "If ever you return in safety, the Lord has not spoken through me." (He also said, "Hear, O peoples, all of you!")†

**Ahab's Death.** ²⁸ The king of Israel and Jehoshaphat, king of Judah, went up to Ramoth-gilead, ²⁹ and the king of Israel said to Jehoshaphat, "I will disguise myself and go into battle. But you, put on your own robes." So the king of Israel disguised himself and they entered the battle. ³⁰ In the meantime, the king of Aram had given his chariot commanders the order, "Fight with no one, great or small, except the king of Israel alone." ³¹ When the chariot commanders saw Jehoshaphat, they thought, "There is the king of Israel!" and wheeled to fight him. But Jehoshaphat cried out and the Lord helped him; God induced them to leave him alone. ³² The chariot commanders, seeing that he was not the king of Israel, turned away from him. ³³ But someone drew his bow at random and hit the king of Israel between the joints of his breastplate. He ordered his charioteer, "Rein about and take me out of the ranks, for I am wounded."* ³⁴ The battle grew fierce during the day, and the king of Israel braced himself up in his chariot facing the Arameans until evening. He died as the sun was setting.

**19** **Jehoshaphat Rebuked.** ¹ Jehoshaphat king of Judah returned in safety to his house in Jerusalem. ² Jehu the seer, son of Hanani,† went out to meet King Jehoshaphat and said to him: "Should you help the wicked and love those who hate the Lord? For this reason, wrath is upon you from the Lord. ³ Yet some good has been found† in you, since you have removed the asherahs from the land and have set your heart to seek God."

**Judges Appointed.** ⁴ Jehoshaphat dwelt in Jerusalem; but he went out again among the people from Beer-sheba to the highlands of Ephraim and brought them back to the Lord, the God of their ancestors. ⁵ He appointed judges in the land, in all the fortified cities of Judah, city by city, ⁶ and he said to them: "Take care what you do, for the judgment you give is not human but divine; for when it comes to judgment God will be with you.* ⁷ And now, let the fear of the Lord be upon you. Act

---

† **18:27** *"Hear, O peoples, all of you!"*: this quotation, which also appears in 1 Kgs 22:28, ascribes to the prophet Micaiah ben Imlah the opening words of the book of the prophet Micah of Moresheth (Mi 1:2), who was active a century later.

**19:2** *Jehu the seer, son of Hanani*: probably not the Jehu, son of Hanani, who prophesied against Baasha of Israel almost fifty

years earlier (1 Kgs 16:1).
**19:3** *Has been found*: theological passive, i.e., God is the implied agent.

**18:33** 2 Chr 35:23; 1 Kgs 22:34.      **19:6** Dt 1:16–18; 16:19–20.

carefully, for with the LORD, our God, there is no injustice, no partiality, no bribe-taking."* [8] In Jerusalem also, Jehoshaphat appointed some Levites and priests and some of the family heads of Israel for the LORD's judgment and the disputes of those who dwell in Jerusalem.* [9] He gave them this command: "Thus you shall act: in the fear of the LORD, with fidelity and with an undivided heart. [10] And in every dispute that comes to you from your kin living in their cities, whether it concerns bloodguilt or questions of law, command, statutes, or ordinances, warn them lest they incur guilt before the LORD and his wrath come upon you and your kin. Do that and you shall not incur guilt.* [11] See now, Amariah is chief priest over you for everything that pertains to the LORD, and Zebadiah, son of Ishmael, is leader of the house of Judah in all that pertains to the king; and the Levites will be your officials. Take firm action, and the LORD will be with the good."

**20** **Invasion from Edom.** [1]† After this the Moabites, the Ammonites, and with them some Meunites came to fight against Jehoshaphat. [2] Jehoshaphat was told: "A great multitude is coming against you from across the sea, from Edom; they are already in Hazazon-tamar" (which is En-gedi). [3] Frightened, Jehoshaphat resolved to consult the LORD. He proclaimed a fast throughout all Judah. [4] Then Judah gathered to seek the LORD's help; from every one of the cities of Judah they came to seek the LORD.*

**Jehoshaphat's Prayer.** [5] Jehoshaphat stood up in the assembly of Judah and Jerusalem in the house of the LORD before the new court, [6] and he said: "LORD, God of our ancestors, are you not God in heaven, and do you not rule over all the kingdoms of the nations? In your hand is power and might, and no one can withstand you.* [7] Was it not you, our God, who dispossessed the inhabitants of this land before your people Israel and gave it forever to the descendants of Abraham, your friend? [8] They have dwelt in it and they built in it a sanctuary for your name. They have said: [9] 'If evil comes

upon us, the sword of judgment, or pestilence, or famine, we will stand before this house and before you, for your name is in this house, and we will cry out to you in our affliction, and you will hear and save!'* [10] And now, see the Ammonites, Moabites, and those of Mount Seir whom you did not allow Israel to invade when they came from the land of Egypt, but instead they passed them by and did not destroy them:* [11] See how they are now repaying us by coming to drive us out of the possession you have given us. [12] O our God, will you not bring judgment on them? We are powerless before this vast multitude that is coming against us. We ourselves do not know what to do, so our eyes are turned toward you."

**Victory Prophesied.** [13] All Judah was standing before the LORD, with their little ones, their wives, and their children. [14] And the spirit of the LORD came upon Jahaziel, son of Zechariah, son of Benaiah, son of Jeiel, son of Mattaniah, a Levite of the clan of Asaph, in the midst of the assembly, [15] and he said: "Pay attention, all of Judah, inhabitants of Jerusalem, and King Jehoshaphat! The LORD says to you: Do not fear or be dismayed at the sight of this vast multitude, for the battle is not yours but God's. [16] Go down against them tomorrow. You will see them coming up by the ascent of Ziz, and you will come upon them at the end of the wadi which opens on the wilderness of Jeruel. [17] You will not have to fight in this encounter. Take your places, stand firm, and see the salvation of the LORD; he will be with you, Judah and Jerusalem. Do not fear or be dismayed. Tomorrow go out to meet them, and the LORD will be with you."* [18] Then Jehoshaphat knelt down with his face to the ground, and all Judah and the inhabitants of Jerusalem fell down before the LORD in worship. [19] Levites from among the Kohathites and Korahites stood up to sing the praises of the LORD, the God of Israel, their voices ever louder.

**The Invaders Destroyed.** [20] Early in the morning they went out to the wilderness of Tekoa.

2
CHR

---

**20:1–30** This account seems to be a free composition of the Chronicler. However, there could well have been a raid of nomads against Judah in the reign of Jehoshaphat, similar to the one that occurred under Asa (14:8–14). The story may also be connected in some way with the campaign of Israel and Judah against Moab launched through the territory of Edom (2 Kgs 3:4–27).

**19:7** Dt 10:17.
**19:8** 2 Chr 17:8–9; Dt 17:8–13; Ps 122:3–5.
**19:10** Dt 17:8–13.
**20:4** Jer 36:6.
**20:6** 2 Chr 32:7; Dt 4:39.
**20:9** 2 Chr 6:28–31; 7:13–14; 1 Kgs 8:37–40.
**20:10** Dt 2:4–5, 9–10, 18–19.
**20:17** Ex 14:13–14; Is 8:10.

As they were going out, Jehoshaphat halted and said: "Listen to me, Judah and inhabitants of Jerusalem! Let your faith in the LORD, your God, be firm, and you will be firm.* Have faith in his prophets and you will succeed." ²¹† After taking counsel with the people, he appointed some to sing to the LORD and some to praise the holy Splendor as it went forth at the head of the army. They sang: "Give thanks to the LORD, whose love endures forever."* ²² At the moment they began their jubilant praise, the LORD laid an ambush against the Ammonites, Moabites, and those of Mount Seir who were coming against Judah, so that they were defeated. ²³ For the Ammonites and Moabites set upon the inhabitants of Mount Seir and exterminated them according to the ban.* And when they had finished with the inhabitants of Seir, each helped to destroy the other.

²⁴ When Judah came to the watchtower of the wilderness and looked toward the throng, there were only corpses fallen on the ground, with no survivors. ²⁵ Jehoshaphat and his people came to gather the spoils, and they found an abundance of cattle and personal property, garments and precious vessels. They took so much that they were unable to carry it all; it took them three days to gather the spoils, there was so much of it. ²⁶ On the fourth day they held an assembly in the Valley of Berakah†—for there they blessed the LORD; that is why the place is called the Valley of Berakah to this day. ²⁷ Then all the men of Judah and Jerusalem, with Jehoshaphat at their head, returned to Jerusalem with joy; for the LORD had given them joy over their enemies. ²⁸ They came to Jerusalem, with harps, lyres, and trumpets, to the house of the LORD. ²⁹ And the fear of God came upon all the kingdoms of the surrounding lands when they heard how the LORD had fought against the enemies of Israel. ³⁰ Thereafter Jehoshaphat's kingdom had peace, for his God gave him rest on every side.

**Jehoshaphat's Other Deeds.** ³¹* Thus Jehoshaphat reigned over Judah. He was thirty-five years old when he became king, and he reigned twenty-five years in Jerusalem. His mother's name was Azubah, daughter of Shilhi. ³² He walked in the way of Asa his father unceasingly, doing what was right in the LORD's sight. ³³ Nevertheless, the high places did not disappear and the people had not yet set their hearts on the God of their ancestors.

³⁴ The rest of the acts of Jehoshaphat, first and last, are recorded in the chronicle of Jehu, son of Hanani, which was incorporated into the book of the kings of Israel. ³⁵ After this, Jehoshaphat king of Judah joined with Ahaziah king of Israel—he acted wickedly. ³⁶* He joined with him in building ships to go to Tarshish; the fleet was built at Ezion-geber. ³⁷ But Eliezer, son of Dodavahu from Mareshah, prophesied against Jehoshaphat. He said: "Because you have joined with Ahaziah, the LORD will shatter your work." And the ships were wrecked and were unable to sail to Tarshish.

# 21

¹ Jehoshaphat rested with his ancestors; he was buried with them in the City of David. Jehoram, his son, succeeded him as king.* ² He had brothers, Jehoshaphat's sons: Azariah, Jehiel, Zechariah, Azariah, Michael, and Shephatiah; all these were sons of King Jehoshaphat of Judah. ³ Their father gave them many gifts of silver, gold, and precious objects, together with fortified cities in Judah, but the kingship he gave to Jehoram because he was the firstborn.

**Jehoram's Evil Deeds.** ⁴ When Jehoram had acceded to his father's kingdom and was firmly in power, he killed all his brothers with the sword, and also some of the princes of Israel. ⁵* Jehoram was thirty-two years old when he became king, and he reigned eight years in Jerusalem. ⁶ He walked in the way of the kings of Israel as the house of Ahab had done, since the daughter of Ahab† was his wife; and he

---

† **20:21** In accordance with Israelite conceptions of Holy War (cf. Ex 14:13–14), this highly stylized narrative presents the Lord as active in battle, while the people have only to sing hymns of praise; the enemy, in panic, fight among themselves to their mutual destruction (v. 23). *Splendor*: the Lord "goes before," i.e., leads, the army of Israel (cf. 2 Sm 5:24) with the heavenly hosts. Israel's God is depicted as present "enthroned upon the cherubim" atop the ark of the covenant. By postexilic times, the ark had disappeared, but the Lord was still present to his people. Here that presence is described as "holy Splendor," a phrase found in Ps 29:2; 96:9. Cf. the cognate image of cloud and fire

that led Israel in the wilderness (Ex 13:21–22), or the cloud of the Lord's glory that fills the sanctuary (Ex 40:34; 1 Kgs 8:10–11).

**20:26** *Berakah*: the Hebrew word for "blessing."

**21:6** *The daughter of Ahab*: her name was Athaliah. In 22:2 (and its source, 2 Kgs 8:26) she is called the daughter of Ahab's father Omri, but this should probably be understood in the sense of granddaughter.

---

| | |
|---|---|
| **20:20** Is 7:9. | **20:36–37** 1 Kgs 22:48–49. |
| **20:21** Ps 136:1. | **21:1** 1 Kgs 22:51. |
| **20:23** Jos 6:17. | **21:5–7** 1 Kgs 8:17–19. |
| **20:31–34** 1 Kgs 22:41–45. | |

did what was evil in the Lord's sight. ⁷ Even so, the Lord was unwilling to destroy the house of David because of the covenant he had made with David and because of his promise to leave him and his sons a holding for all time.*

⁸* During his time Edom revolted against the rule of Judah and installed its own king. ⁹ Thereupon Jehoram with his officers and all his chariots crossed over. He arose by night and broke through the Edomites when they had surrounded him and the commanders of his chariots. ¹⁰ To this day Edom has been in revolt against the rule of Judah. Libnah also revolted at that time against his rule because he had abandoned the Lord, the God of his ancestors. ¹¹ He also set up high places in the mountains of Judah, prostituting the inhabitants of Jerusalem, leading Judah astray.

**Jehoram Punished.** ¹² A letter came to him from Elijah† the prophet with this message: "Thus says the Lord, the God of David your father: Because you have not walked in the way of your father Jehoshaphat, nor of Asa, king of Judah, ¹³ but instead have walked in the way of the kings of Israel, leading Judah and the inhabitants of Jerusalem into prostitution, like the harlotries of the house of Ahab, and because you have killed your brothers of your father's house, who were better than you, ¹⁴ the Lord will strike your people, your children, your wives, and all that is yours with a great plague. ¹⁵ You shall have severe pains from a disease in your bowels, which will fall out because of the disease, day after day."

¹⁶ Then the Lord stirred up against Jehoram the animosity of the Philistines and of the Arabians who were neighbors of the Ethiopians. ¹⁷ They came up against Judah, breached it, and carried away all the wealth found in the king's house, along with his sons and his wives. He was left with only one son, Jehoahaz, his youngest. ¹⁸ After these events, the Lord afflicted him with a disease of the bowels for which there was no cure. ¹⁹ Some time later, after a period of two years had elapsed, his bowels fell out because of the disease and he died in great pain. His people did not make

a fire for him as they had for his ancestors.* ²⁰ He was thirty-two years old when he became king, and he reigned eight years in Jerusalem. He departed unloved; and they buried him in the City of David, though not in the tombs of the kings.*

**22** **Ahaziah.** ¹* Then the inhabitants of Jerusalem made Ahaziah, his youngest son, king to succeed him, since all the older sons had been killed by the band that had come into the camp with the Arabians. Thus Ahaziah, son of Jehoram, reigned as the king of Judah. ² Ahaziah was twenty-two years old when he became king, and he reigned one year in Jerusalem. His mother's name was Athaliah, daughter of Omri. ³ He, too, walked in the ways of the house of Ahab, because his mother was his counselor in doing evil. ⁴ To his own destruction, he did what was evil in the sight of the Lord, like the house of Ahab, since they were his counselors after the death of his father.

⁵ He was also following their counsel when he joined Jehoram, son of Ahab, king of Israel, in battle against Hazael, king of Aram, at Ramoth-gilead, where the Arameans wounded Jehoram. ⁶ He returned to Jezreel to be healed of the wounds that had been inflicted on him at Ramah in his battle against Hazael, king of Aram. Then Ahaziah, son of Jehoram, king of Judah, went down to Jezreel to visit Jehoram, son of Ahab, for he was sick. ⁷ Now from God came Ahaziah's downfall, that he should join Jehoram; for after his arrival he rode out with Jehoram to Jehu, son of Nimshi, whom the Lord had anointed to cut down the house of Ahab.* ⁸ While Jehu was executing judgment on the house of Ahab, he also came upon the princes of Judah and the nephews of Ahaziah who were his attendants, and he killed them.* ⁹ Then he looked for Ahaziah himself. They caught him hiding in Samaria and brought him to Jehu, who put him to death. They buried him, for they said, "He was the grandson of Jehoshaphat, who sought the Lord with his whole heart."* Now the house of Ahaziah did not retain the power of kingship.†

---

† **21:12** *Elijah:* this is the Chronicler's only mention of this prophet of the Northern Kingdom. It is doubtful that Elijah was still living in the reign of Jehoram of Judah; in any case, the attribution of the letter to him has a folkloristic quality.
**22:9** This account of the death of Ahaziah of Judah does not agree with that given in 2 Kgs 9:27–28.

**21:7** 1 Kgs 11:36; 2 Kgs 8:19.
**21:8–10** Gn 27:40; 2 Kgs 8:20–22.
**21:19** 2 Chr 16:14.
**21:20** 2 Kgs 8:24.
**22:1–6** 2 Kgs 8:24–29.
**22:7** 2 Kgs 9:21.
**22:8** 2 Kgs 10:12–14.
**22:9** 2 Kgs 9:27–28.

**Usurpation of Athaliah.** ¹⁰* When Athaliah, the mother of Ahaziah, saw that her son was dead, she began to kill off the whole royal family of the house of Judah. ¹¹ But Jehosheba, a daughter of the king, took Joash, Ahaziah's son, and spirited him away from among the king's sons who were about to be slain, and put him and his nurse in a bedroom. In this way Jehosheba, the daughter of King Jehoram, a sister of Ahaziah and wife of Jehoiada the priest, concealed the child from Athaliah, so that she did not put him to death. ¹² For six years he remained hidden with them in the house of God, while Athaliah ruled as queen over the land.

## 23 **Athaliah Overthrown.** ¹* In the seventh year, Jehoiada took courage and brought into covenant with himself the captains: Azariah, son of Jehoram; Ishmael, son of Jehohanan; Azariah, son of Obed; Maaseiah, son of Adaiah; and Elishaphat, son of Zichri. ² They journeyed about Judah, gathering the Levites from all the cities of Judah and also the heads of the Israelite families, and they came to Jerusalem. ³ The whole assembly made a covenant with the king in the house of God. Jehoiada said to them: "Here is the king's son who must reign, as the LORD promised concerning the sons of David. ⁴ This is what you must do: a third of your number, both priests and Levites, who come on duty on the sabbath must guard the thresholds, ⁵ another third must be at the king's house, and the final third at the Foundation Gate, when all the people will be in the courts of the LORD's house. ⁶ Let no one enter the LORD's house except the priests and those Levites who are ministering. They may enter because they are holy; but all the other people must observe the prescriptions of the LORD. ⁷ The Levites shall surround the king on all sides, each with drawn weapon. Whoever tries to enter the house is to be killed. Stay with the king wherever he goes."

⁸ The Levites and all Judah did just as Jehoiada the priest commanded. Each took his troops, both those going on duty for the week and those going off duty that week, since Jehoiada the priest had not dismissed any of the divisions.* ⁹ Jehoiada the priest gave to the captains the spears, shields, and bucklers of King David which were in the house of God. ¹⁰ He stationed all the people, each with spear in hand, from the southern to the northern limit of the enclosure, surrounding the altar and the temple on the king's behalf. ¹¹ Then they brought out the king's son and put the crown and the testimony upon him, and proclaimed him king. Jehoiada and his sons anointed him, and they cried, "Long live the king!"

¹² When Athaliah heard the noise of the people running and acclaiming the king, she came before them in the house of the LORD. ¹³ When she saw the king standing by his column† at the entrance, the captains and the trumpeters near the king, and all the people of the land rejoicing and blowing trumpets, while the singers with their musical instruments were leading the acclaim, Athaliah tore her garments, saying, "Treason! treason!" ¹⁴ Then Jehoiada the priest brought out the captains in command of the force: "Escort her with a guard detail. If anyone follows her, let him die by the sword." For the priest had said, "You must not put her to death in the house of the LORD." ¹⁵ So they seized her, and when she reached the Horse Gate of the royal palace, they put her to death.

¹⁶ Then Jehoiada made a covenant between himself and all the people and the king, that they should be the LORD's people. ¹⁷ Thereupon all the people went to the temple of Baal and demolished it. They shattered its altars and images completely, and killed Mattan, the priest of Baal, before the altars. ¹⁸ Then Jehoiada gave the charge of the LORD's house into the hands of the levitical priests, to whom David had assigned turns in the LORD's house for sacrificing the burnt offerings of the LORD, as is written in the law of Moses, with rejoicing and song, as David had provided.* ¹⁹ Moreover, he stationed guards at the gates of the LORD's house so that no one unclean in any respect might enter. ²⁰ Then he took the captains, the nobles, the rulers among the people, and all

---

† **23:13** *By his column:* there was a special place reserved for the king in the eastern gateway of the Temple court where the altar for burnt offerings stood. The king occupied this place on feasts and sabbaths at the time of the prescribed offerings, or when he came to make voluntary offerings of his own; cf. 2 Kgs 11:14 and Ez 46:1–8.

**22:10–12** 2 Kgs 11:1–3.
**23:1–17, 19–21** 2 Kgs 11:4–20.

**23:8** 2 Kgs 11:9; 1 Chr 24:19.
**23:18** 1 Chr 23:13.

the people of the land, and led the king out of the LORD's house; they came within the upper gate of the king's house, and seated the king upon the royal throne. [21] All the people of the land rejoiced and the city was quiet, now that Athaliah had been slain with the sword.

# 24

**The Temple Restored.** [1]* Joash was seven years old when he became king, and he reigned forty years in Jerusalem. His mother's name was Zibiah, from Beer-sheba. [2] Joash did what was right in the LORD's sight as long as Jehoiada the priest lived. [3] Jehoiada provided him with two wives, and he became the father of sons and daughters.

[4] After some time, Joash decided to restore the house of the LORD. [5] He gathered together the priests and Levites and said to them: "Go out to all the cities of Judah and gather money† from all Israel that you may repair the house of your God over the years. You must hurry this project." But the Levites did not. [6] Then the king summoned Jehoiada, who was in charge, and said to him: "Why have you not required the Levites to bring in from Judah and Jerusalem the tax levied by Moses, the servant of the LORD, and by the assembly of Israel, for the tent of the testimony?"* [7] For the wicked Athaliah and her sons had damaged the house of God and had even turned over to the Baals the holy things of the LORD's house.

[8] At the king's command, therefore, they made a chest, which they put outside the gate of the LORD's house.* [9] They had it proclaimed throughout Judah and Jerusalem that the tax which Moses, the servant of God, had imposed on Israel in the wilderness should be brought to the LORD.* [10] All the princes and the people rejoiced; they brought what was asked and cast it into the chest until it was filled. [11] Whenever the chest was brought to the royal officials by the Levites and they noticed that there was a large amount of money, the royal scribe and an overseer for the chief priest would come up, empty the chest, and then take it back and return it to its place. This they did day after day until they had collected a large sum of money. [12] Then the king and Jehoiada gave it to the workers in charge of the labor on the LORD's house, who hired masons and carpenters to restore the LORD's house, and also iron- and bronze-smiths to repair it. [13] The workers labored, and the task of restoration progressed under their hands. They restored the house of God according to its original form, and reinforced it. [14] After they had finished, they brought the rest of the money to the king and to Jehoiada, who had it made into utensils for the house of the LORD, utensils for the service and the burnt offerings, and basins and other gold and silver utensils.† They sacrificed burnt offerings in the LORD's house continually all the days of Jehoiada. [15] Jehoiada grew old, full of years, and died; he was a hundred and thirty years old. [16] They buried him in the City of David with the kings, because of the good he had done in Israel, especially for God and his house.

**Joash's Apostasy.** [17] After the death of Jehoiada, the princes of Judah came and paid homage to the king; then the king listened to them. [18] They abandoned the house of the LORD, the God of their ancestors, and began to serve the asherahs and the idols;* and because of this crime of theirs, wrath came upon Judah and Jerusalem. [19] Although prophets were sent to them to turn them back to the LORD and to warn them, the people would not listen. [20]* Then the spirit of God clothed Zechariah, son of Jehoiada the priest. He took his stand above the people and said to them: "Thus says God, Why are you transgressing the LORD's commands, so that you cannot prosper? Because you have abandoned the LORD, he has abandoned you." [21] But they conspired against him, and at the king's command they stoned him in the court of the house of the LORD. [22] Thus King Joash was unmindful of the devotion shown him by Jehoiada, Zechariah's father, and killed the son. As he was dying, he said, "May the LORD see and avenge."

**Joash Punished.** [23] At the turn of the year a force of Arameans came up against Joash. They invaded Judah and Jerusalem, killed all the

---

† **24:5** *Gather money*: according to 2 Kgs 12:5 the people themselves brought the money, consisting at least in part of voluntary contributions, to the Temple. By the time of the Chronicler, a fixed head tax for the upkeep of the Temple had been introduced; see 2 Chr 34:9; Neh 10:32; Ex 30:12–16. This was still in force in New Testament times (Mt 17:24–25).

**24:14** See the parallel in 2 Kgs 12:14–15; the passages are difficult to reconcile.

| | |
|---|---|
| **24:1–14** 2 Kgs 12:1–13. | **24:9** Ex 30:13. |
| **24:6** Ex 25:1–9; Neh 10:33. | **24:18** Ex 34:13. |
| **24:8** 2 Chr 34:9. | **24:20** Jgs 6:34. |

princes of the people, and sent all their spoil to the king of Damascus.* ²⁴Though the Aramean force was small, the LORD handed over a very large force into their power,* because Judah had abandoned the LORD, the God of their ancestors. So judgment was meted out to Joash. ²⁵* After the Arameans had departed from him, abandoning him to his many injuries, his servants conspired against him because of the murder of the son of Jehoiada the priest. They killed him on his sickbed. He was buried in the City of David, but not in the tombs of the kings.

²⁶Those who conspired against him were Zabad, son of Shimeath from Ammon, and Jehozabad, son of Shimrith from Moab. ²⁷An account of his sons, the great tribute imposed on him, and his rebuilding of the house of God is written in the midrash of the book of the kings. His son Amaziah succeeded him as king.*

# 25

**Amaziah's Good Start.** ¹* Amaziah was twenty-five years old when he became king, and he reigned twenty-nine years in Jerusalem. His mother's name was Jehoaddan, from Jerusalem. ²He did what was right in the LORD's sight, though not wholeheartedly. ³When he had the kingdom firmly in hand, he struck down the officials who had struck down the king, his father. ⁴But their children he did not put to death, for he acted according to what is written in the law, in the Book of Moses, which the LORD commanded: "Parents shall not be put to death for their children, nor shall children be put to death for their parents; they shall each die for their own sin."*

⁵Amaziah gathered Judah and placed them, out of all Judah and Benjamin according to their ancestral houses, under leaders of thousands and of hundreds. When he made a count of those twenty years old and over, he found that there were three hundred thousand picked men fit for war, capable of handling lance and shield. ⁶He also hired a hundred thousand valiant warriors from Israel for a hundred talents of silver. ⁷But a man of God came to him and said: "O king, let not the army of Israel go with you, for the LORD is not with Israel—with any Ephraimite. ⁸Instead, go on your own, strongly prepared for the battle; why should the LORD hinder you in the face of the enemy: for with God is power to help or to hinder." ⁹Amaziah answered the man of God, "But what is to be done about the hundred talents that I paid for the troops of Israel?" The man of God replied, "The LORD can give you much more than that." ¹⁰Amaziah then disbanded the troops that had come to him from Ephraim, and sent them home. But they became furiously angry with Judah, and returned home blazing with anger.

¹¹Amaziah now assumed command of his army. They proceeded to the Valley of Salt, where they killed ten thousand men of Seir.* ¹²The Judahites also brought back another ten thousand alive, led them to the summit of Sela, and then threw them down from that rock† so that their bodies split open. ¹³Meanwhile, the troops Amaziah had dismissed from going into battle with him raided the cities of Judah from Samaria to Beth-horon. They struck down three thousand of the inhabitants and carried off much plunder.

**Amaziah's Apostasy.** ¹⁴When Amaziah returned from his conquest of the Edomites he brought back with him the gods of the people of Seir. He set these up as his own gods; he bowed down before them and offered sacrifice to them. ¹⁵Then the anger of the LORD blazed out against Amaziah, and he sent a prophet to him who said: "Why have you sought this people's gods that could not deliver their own people from your power?" ¹⁶While he was still speaking, however, the king said to him: "Have you been appointed the king's counselor? Stop! Why should you have to be killed?" Therefore the prophet stopped. But he said, "I know that God's counsel is your destruction, for by doing this you have refused to listen to my counsel."

**Amaziah Punished.** ¹⁷* Having taken counsel, Amaziah, king of Judah, sent word to Joash, son of Jehoahaz, son of Jehu, the king of Israel, saying, "Come, let us meet face to face."

---

† **25:12** *Sela...rock:* a pun—the name of the city, Sela, in Hebrew means "rock."

24:23 2 Kgs 12:17–18.
24:24 Dt 32:30.
24:25–26 2 Kgs 12:21–22.
24:27 2 Kgs 12:19, 22.
25:1–4 2 Kgs 14:1–6.

25:4 Dt 24:16; 2 Kgs 14:5–6; Ez 18:20.
25:11 2 Kgs 14:7.
25:17–24 2 Kgs 14:8–14.

¹⁸Joash, king of Israel, sent this reply to Amaziah, king of Judah: "A thistle of Lebanon sent word to a cedar of Lebanon, 'Give your daughter to my son in marriage,' but an animal of Lebanon passed by and trampled the thistle underfoot.* ¹⁹You are thinking,

'See, I have struck down Edom!'
    Your heart is lifted up,
And glories in it. Stay home!
Why bring misfortune and failure
    on yourself and on Judah with you?"

²⁰But Amaziah did not listen; for it was God's doing that they be handed over because they sought the gods of Edom.

²¹So Joash, king of Israel, advanced, and he and Amaziah, king of Judah, met face to face at Beth-shemesh of Judah, ²²and Judah was defeated by Israel, and all fled to their tents. ²³But Amaziah, king of Judah, son of Joash, son of Jehoahaz, was captured by Joash, king of Israel, at Beth-shemesh. Joash brought him to Jerusalem and tore down the wall of Jerusalem from the Gate of Ephraim to the Corner Gate, four hundred cubits. ²⁴He took all the gold and silver and all the vessels found in the house of God with Obed-edom,† and in the treasuries of the king's house, and hostages as well. Then he returned to Samaria.

²⁵*Amaziah, son of Joash, king of Judah, survived Joash, son of Jehoahaz, king of Israel, by fifteen years. ²⁶The rest of the acts of Amaziah, first and last, are recorded in the book of the kings of Judah and Israel. ²⁷Now from the time that Amaziah turned away from the LORD, a conspiracy was formed against him in Jerusalem, and he fled to Lachish. But he was pursued to Lachish and killed there. ²⁸He was brought back on horses and was buried with his ancestors in the City of Judah.†

**26** **Uzziah's Projects.** ¹*All the people of Judah took Uzziah, who was only sixteen years old, and made him king to succeed Amaziah his father. ²It was he who rebuilt Elath and restored it to Judah, after the king rested with his ancestors. ³Uzziah was sixteen years old when he became king, and he reigned fifty-two years in Jerusalem. His mother's name was Jecoliah, from Jerusalem. ⁴He did what was right in the LORD's sight, just as his father Amaziah had done.

⁵He was prepared to seek God as long as Zechariah† lived,* who taught him to fear God; and as long as he sought the LORD, God made him prosper. ⁶He went out and fought the Philistines and razed the walls of Gath, Jabneh, and Ashdod, and built cities in the district of Ashdod and in Philistia.* ⁷God helped him against the Philistines, against the Arabians who dwelt in Gurbaal, and against the Meunites. ⁸The Ammonites paid tribute to Uzziah and his fame spread as far as Egypt, for he grew stronger and stronger. ⁹Moreover, Uzziah built towers in Jerusalem at the Corner Gate, at the Valley Gate, and at the Angle, and he fortified them. ¹⁰He built towers in the wilderness and dug numerous cisterns, for he had many cattle. He had plowmen in the Shephelah and the plains, farmers and vinedressers in the highlands and the garden land. He was a lover of the soil.

¹¹Uzziah also had a standing army of fit soldiers divided into bands according to the number in which they were mustered by Jeiel the scribe and Maaseiah the recorder, under the command of Hananiah, one of the king's officials. ¹²The entire number of family heads over these valiant warriors was two thousand six hundred, ¹³and at their disposal was a mighty army of three hundred seven thousand five hundred fighting men of great valor to help the king against his enemies. ¹⁴Uzziah provided for them—for the entire army—bucklers, lances, helmets, breastplates, bows, and slingstones. ¹⁵He also built machines in Jerusalem, devices designed to stand on the towers and at the angles of the walls to shoot arrows and cast large stones. His name spread far and wide; the help he received was wondrous, so strong did he become.

**Pride and Fall.** ¹⁶But after he had become strong, he became arrogant to his own destruction and acted treacherously with the LORD,

---

---

† **25:24** *With Obed-edom*: perhaps an Edomite priest (cf. v. 14), or possibly a member of a levitical family of gatekeepers; cf. 1 Chr 15:18; 26:12–15.

  **25:28** *The City of Judah*: i.e., Jerusalem, the capital of Judah; the parallel passage (2 Kgs 14:20) reads "the City of David."

  **26:5** *Zechariah*: not otherwise identified, but cf. 29:1.

* **25:18** Jgs 9:7–15; 2 Kgs 14:9.
  **25:25–28** 2 Kgs 14:17–20.

  **26:1–4** 2 Kgs 14:21–22; 15:1–3.
  **26:5** 2 Chr 24:2.
  **26:6** Am 1:8.

his God. He entered the temple of the Lord to make an offering on the altar of incense. ¹⁷But Azariah the priest, and with him eighty other priests of the Lord, courageous men, followed him. ¹⁸They stood up to King Uzziah, saying to him: "It is not for you, Uzziah, to burn incense to the Lord, but for the priests, the sons of Aaron, who have been consecrated for this purpose.* Leave the sanctuary, for you have acted treacherously and no longer have a part in the glory that comes from the Lord God." ¹⁹Uzziah, who was holding a censer for burning the incense, became angry. But at the very moment he showed his anger to the priests, while they were looking at him in the house of the Lord beside the altar of incense, leprosy broke out on his forehead.* ²⁰Azariah the chief priest and all the other priests examined him, and when they saw that his forehead was leprous, they rushed him out. He let himself be expelled, for the Lord had afflicted him. ²¹*King Uzziah remained a leper till the day he died. As a leper he lived in a house apart, for he was excluded from the house of the Lord. Therefore his son Jotham was master of the palace and ruled the people of the land.

²²The rest of the acts of Uzziah, first and last, were written by Isaiah the prophet, son of Amoz. ²³Uzziah rested with his ancestors and was buried with them in the field adjoining the royal cemetery, for they said, "He was a leper." His son Jotham succeeded him as king.

# 27 Jotham.
¹*Jotham was twenty-five years old when he became king, and he reigned sixteen years in Jerusalem. His mother's name was Jerusha, daughter of Zadok. ²He did what was right in the Lord's sight, just as his father Uzziah had done, though he did not enter the temple of the Lord. The people, however, continued to act corruptly.

³It was he who built the Upper Gate of the Lord's house and did much construction on the wall of Ophel. ⁴Moreover, he built cities in the hill country of Judah, and in the

wooded areas he set up fortresses and towers. ⁵He fought with the king of the Ammonites and conquered them. That year the Ammonites paid him one hundred talents of silver, together with ten thousand kors of wheat and ten thousand of barley. They brought the same to him also in the second and in the third year. ⁶Thus Jotham continued to grow strong because he made sure to walk before the Lord, his God. ⁷*The rest of the acts of Jotham, his wars and his activities, are recorded in the book of the kings of Israel and Judah. ⁸He was twenty-five years old when he became king, and he reigned sixteen years in Jerusalem. ⁹Jotham rested with his ancestors and was buried in the City of David, and his son Ahaz succeeded him as king.

# 28 Ahaz's Misdeeds.
¹*Ahaz was twenty years old when he became king, and he reigned sixteen years in Jerusalem. He did not do what was right in the sight of the Lord as David his father had done. ²He walked in the ways of the kings of Israel and even made molten idols for the Baals. ³Moreover, he offered sacrifice in the Valley of Ben-hinnom, and immolated his children by fire in accordance with the abominable practices of the nations whom the Lord had dispossessed before the Israelites.* ⁴He sacrificed and burned incense on the high places, on hills, and under every green tree.

**Ahaz Punished.** ⁵†Therefore the Lord, his God, delivered him into the power of the king of Aram. The Arameans defeated him and carried away captive a large number of his people, whom they brought to Damascus. He was also delivered into the power of the king of Israel, who defeated him with great slaughter.* ⁶For Pekah, son of Remaliah, killed one hundred and twenty thousand of Judah in a single day, all of them valiant men, because they had abandoned the Lord, the God of their ancestors. ⁷Zichri, an Ephraimite warrior, killed Maaseiah, the king's son, and Azrikam, the

---

† **28:5–8, 16–23** The account of Ahaz's reign in 2 Kings refers to hostilities of Syria (Aram) and Israel against Judah, the revolt of the Edomites, submission to Tiglath-pileser, king of Assyria, the stripping of Temple treasures to pay him tribute, and, in deference to him, shaping the cult of the Jerusalem Temple according to patterns seen in Damascus (2 Kgs 16:5–18; cf. Is 7:1–2). The account in Kings relates all this to an attack of Syria and Israel on Judah (735 B.C.), as they attempted to force Judah into an anti-Assyrian coalition; but the Chronicler, who does not mention

the attack, depicts these troubles as the result of, or examples of, Ahaz's infidelity.

* **26:18** Ex 30:7.
**26:19** Nm 12:10.
**26:21–23** 2 Kgs 15:5–7; Lv 13:46; Nm 19:20.
**27:1–3** 2 Kgs 15:32–35.
**27:7–9** 2 Kgs 15:36–38.
**28:1–4** 2 Kgs 16:1–4.
**28:3** Lv 18:21; 2 Kgs 16:3.
**28:5** 2 Kgs 16:5; Is 7:1–9.

master of the palace, and also Elkanah, who was second to the king. ⁸The Israelites took away as captives two hundred thousand of their kinfolk's wives, sons, and daughters; they also took from them much plunder, which they brought to Samaria.

**Oded's Prophecy.** ⁹In Samaria there was a prophet of the LORD by the name of Oded. He went out to meet the army returning to Samaria and said to them: "It was because the LORD, the God of your ancestors, was angry with Judah that he delivered them into your power. You, however, have killed them with a fury that has reached up to heaven. ¹⁰And now you are planning to subjugate the people of Judah and Jerusalem as your slaves and bondwomen. Are not you yourselves, therefore, guilty of a crime against the LORD, your God? ¹¹Now listen to me: send back the captives you have carried off from among your kin, for the burning anger of the LORD is upon you."

¹²At this, some of the Ephraimite leaders, Azariah, son of Johanan, Berechiah, son of Meshillemoth, Jehizkiah, son of Shallum, and Amasa, son of Hadlai, themselves stood up in opposition to those who had returned from the war. ¹³They said to them: "Do not bring the captives here, for what you are planning will make us guilty before the LORD and increase our sins and our guilt. Great is our guilt, and there is burning anger upon Israel." ¹⁴Therefore the soldiers left their captives and the plunder before the princes and the whole assembly. ¹⁵Then the men just named proceeded to help the captives. All of them who were naked they clothed from the spoils; they clothed them, put sandals on their feet, gave them food and drink, anointed them, and all who were weak they set on donkeys. They brought them to Jericho, the City of Palms, to their kinfolk. Then they returned to Samaria.*

**Further Sins of Ahaz.** ¹⁶At that time King Ahaz sent an appeal for help to the kings of Assyria.* ¹⁷The Edomites had returned, attacked Judah, and carried off captives.* ¹⁸The Philistines too had raided the cities of the Shephelah and the

Negeb of Judah; they captured Beth-shemesh, Aijalon, Gederoth, Soco and its dependencies, Timnah and its dependencies, and Gimzo and its dependencies, and settled there. ¹⁹For the LORD had brought Judah low because of Ahaz, king of Israel,† who let Judah go its own way and committed treachery against the LORD. ²⁰Tiglath-pileser, king of Assyria, did indeed come to him, but to oppress him rather than to lend strength.* ²¹Though Ahaz plundered the LORD's house and the houses of the king and the princes to pay off the king of Assyria, it was no help to him.*

²²While he was already in distress, the same King Ahaz increased his treachery to the LORD. ²³He sacrificed to the gods of Damascus who had defeated him, saying, "Since it was the gods of the kings of Aram who helped them, I will sacrifice to them that they may help me also." However, they only furthered his downfall and that of all Israel.* ²⁴Ahaz gathered up the utensils of God's house and broke them in pieces. He closed the doors of the LORD's house and made altars for himself in every corner of Jerusalem.* ²⁵In every city throughout Judah he set up high places to offer sacrifice to other gods. Thus he provoked the LORD, the God of his ancestors, to anger.

²⁶*The rest of his words and his deeds, first and last, are recorded in the book of the kings of Judah and Israel. ²⁷Ahaz rested with his ancestors and was buried in Jerusalem—in the city, for they did not bring him to the tombs of the kings of Israel. His son Hezekiah succeeded him as king.

**29** **Hezekiah's Reforms.** ¹*Hezekiah was twenty-five years old when he became king, and he reigned twenty-nine years in Jerusalem. His mother's name was Abijah, daughter of Zechariah. ²He did what was right in the LORD's sight, just as David his father had done. ³In the first month of the first year of his reign, he opened the doors of the LORD's house and repaired them.* ⁴He summoned the priests and Levites, gathering them in the open space to the east, ⁵and said to them: "Listen to me, you Levites! Sanctify yourselves now and

† **28:19** *Ahaz, king of Israel*: in his account of the period of the divided monarchy, the Chronicler regularly uses the term "Israel" as here to designate, not the Northern Kingdom, but the entire people. See note on 10:1.

**28:15** Lk 10:25–37.
**28:16** 2 Kgs 16:7.
**28:17** 2 Kgs 16:6.
**28:20** 2 Kgs 16:10; Is 7:17–20; 8:5–8.
**28:21** 2 Kgs 16:8.
**28:23** 2 Kgs 16:12–13; Is 10:20.
**28:24** 2 Chr 29:3; 30:14; 2 Kgs 16:17.
**28:26–27** 2 Kgs 16:19–20.
**29:1–2** 2 Kgs 18:2–3.
**29:3** 2 Chr 28:24.

sanctify the house of the Lord, the God of your ancestors, and clean out the filth from the sanctuary. [6] Our ancestors acted treacherously and did what was evil in the eyes of the Lord, our God. They abandoned him, turned away their faces from the Lord's dwelling, and turned their backs on him. [7] They also closed the doors of the vestibule, extinguished the lamps, and failed to burn incense and sacrifice burnt offerings in the sanctuary to the God of Israel. * [8] * Therefore the anger of the Lord has come upon Judah and Jerusalem; he has made them an object of terror, horror, and hissing, as you see with your own eyes. [9] For our ancestors fell by the sword, and our sons, our daughters, and our wives have been taken captive because of this. [10] Now, I intend to make a covenant with the Lord, the God of Israel, that his burning anger may turn away from us. [11] My sons, do not be negligent any longer, for it is you whom the Lord has chosen to stand before him, to minister to him, to be his ministers and to offer incense."

[12] Then the Levites arose: Mahath, son of Amasai, and Joel, son of Azariah, of the Kohathites; of the descendants of Merari: Kish, son of Abdi, and Azariah, son of Jehallel; of the Gershonites: Joah, son of Zimmah, and Eden, son of Joah; [13] of the sons of Elizaphan: Shimri and Jeuel; of the sons of Asaph: Zechariah and Mattaniah; [14] of the sons of Heman: Jehuel and Shimei; of the sons of Jeduthun: Shemiah and Uzziel. [15] They gathered their kinfolk together and sanctified themselves; then they came as the king had ordered, in keeping with the words of the Lord, to cleanse the Lord's house.

[16] The priests entered the interior of the Lord's house to cleanse it. Whatever they found in the Lord's temple that was unclean they brought out to the court of the Lord's house, where the Levites took it from them and carried it out to the Wadi Kidron. [17] They began the work of consecration on the first day of the first month, and on the eighth day of the month they reached the vestibule of the Lord; they consecrated the Lord's house over an eight-day period, and on the sixteenth day of the first month, they had finished. [18] Then they went inside to King Hezekiah and said: "We have cleansed the entire house

of the Lord, the altar for burnt offerings with all its utensils, and the table for the showbread with all its utensils. [19] We have restored and consecrated all the articles which King Ahaz had thrown away during his reign because of his treachery; they are now before the Lord's altar."

**The Rite of Expiation.** [20] Then King Hezekiah hastened to convoke the princes of the city and went up to the Lord's house. [21] Seven bulls, seven rams, seven lambs, and seven he-goats were presented as a purification offering for the kingdom, for the sanctuary, and for Judah. Hezekiah ordered the sons of Aaron, the priests, to offer them on the altar of the Lord. [22] They slaughtered the bulls, and the priests collected the blood and splashed it on the altar. Then they slaughtered the rams and splashed the blood on the altar; then they slaughtered the lambs and splashed the blood on the altar. [23] Then the he-goats for the purification offering were led before the king and the assembly, who laid their hands upon them. [24] The priests then slaughtered them and offered their blood on the altar to atone for the sin of all Israel. For the king had said, "The burnt offering and the purification offering are for all Israel."

[25] He stationed the Levites in the Lord's house with cymbals, harps, and lyres, according to the command of David, of Gad the king's seer, and of Nathan the prophet; for this command was from the Lord through his prophets. [26] The Levites were stationed with the instruments of David, and the priests with the trumpets. [27] Then Hezekiah ordered the burnt offering to be sacrificed on the altar. At the very moment the burnt offering began, they also began the song of the Lord, to the accompaniment of the trumpets and the instruments of David, king of Israel. [28] The entire assembly bowed down, and the song was sung and the trumpets sounded until the burnt offering had been completed. [29] Once the burnt offering was completed, the king and all who were with him knelt and worshiped. [30] King Hezekiah and the princes then told the Levites to sing the praises of the Lord in the words of David and of Asaph the seer. They sang praises till their joy was full, then fell down and worshiped.

---

**29:7** 2 Kgs 16:15.      **29:8–9** Lv 26:32–33; Dt 28:25; Jer 25:18.

[31] Hezekiah then said: "You have dedicated yourselves to the LORD. Approach, and bring forward the sacrifices and thank offerings for the house of the LORD." Then the assembly brought forward the sacrifices and thank offerings and all their voluntary burnt offerings. [32] The number of burnt offerings that the assembly brought forward was seventy oxen, one hundred rams, and two hundred lambs: all of these as a burnt offering to the LORD. [33] As consecrated gifts there were six hundred oxen and three thousand sheep. [34] Since there were too few priests to skin all the victims for the burnt offerings, their fellow Levites assisted them until the task was completed and the priests had sanctified themselves. The Levites, in fact, were more careful than the priests to sanctify themselves.* [35] The burnt offerings were indeed many, along with the fat of the communion offerings and the libations for the burnt offerings. Thus the service of the house of the LORD was re-established. [36] Hezekiah and all the people rejoiced over what God had re-established for the people, and at how suddenly this had been done.

# 30

**Invitation to Passover.** [1] Hezekiah sent word to all Israel and Judah, and even wrote letters to Ephraim and Manasseh, saying that they should come to the house of the LORD in Jerusalem to celebrate the Passover to the LORD, the God of Israel.* [2]* The king, his princes, and the entire assembly in Jerusalem had agreed to celebrate the Passover during the second month. [3] They could not celebrate it at the regular time because the priests had not sanctified themselves in sufficient numbers, and the people were not gathered at Jerusalem. [4] This seemed right to the king and the entire assembly, [5] and they issued a decree to be proclaimed throughout all Israel from Beersheba to Dan, that everyone should come to celebrate the Passover to the LORD, the God of Israel, in Jerusalem; for not many had kept it in the prescribed manner. [6] By the king's command, the couriers, with the letters written by the king and his princes, went through all Israel and Judah. They said: "Israelites, return to the LORD, the God of Abraham, Isaac, and Israel, that he may return to you, the remnant left from the hands of the Assyrian kings. [7] Do

not be like your ancestors and your kin who acted treacherously toward the LORD, the God of their ancestors, so that he handed them over to desolation, as you yourselves now see. * [8] Do not be stiff-necked, as your ancestors were; stretch out your hands to the LORD and come to his sanctuary that he has consecrated forever, and serve the LORD, your God, that he may turn his burning anger from you. [9] If you return to the LORD, your kinfolk and your children will find mercy with their captors and return to this land. The LORD, your God, is gracious and merciful and he will not turn away his face from you if you return to him." *

[10] So the couriers passed from city to city in the land of Ephraim and Manasseh and as far as Zebulun, but they were derided and scoffed at. [11] Nevertheless, some from Asher, Manasseh, and Zebulun humbled themselves and came to Jerusalem. [12] In Judah, however, the hand of God brought it about that the people were of one heart to carry out the command of the king and the princes by the word of the LORD. [13] Thus many people gathered in Jerusalem to celebrate the feast of Unleavened Bread in the second month; it was a very great assembly.

**Passover Celebrated.** [14] They proceeded to remove the altars that were in Jerusalem as well as all the altars of incense, and cast them into the Wadi Kidron. * [15] They slaughtered the Passover on the fourteenth day of the second month. The priests and Levites were shamed into sanctifying themselves and brought burnt offerings into the house of the LORD. [16] They stood in the places prescribed for them according to the law of Moses, the man of God. The priests splashed the blood given them by the Levites; [17] for many in the assembly had not sanctified themselves, and the Levites were in charge of slaughtering the Passover victims for all who were unclean so as to consecrate them to the LORD. * [18] The greater part of the people, in fact, chiefly from Ephraim, Manasseh, Issachar, and Zebulun, had not cleansed themselves. Nevertheless they ate the Passover, contrary to the prescription; because Hezekiah prayed for them, saying, "May the good LORD grant pardon to [19] all who have set their heart to seek God, the LORD, the God of their ancestors, even though they are not clean as holiness requires." [20] The LORD heard Hezekiah and healed the people.

[21] Thus the Israelites who were in Jerusalem celebrated the feast of Unleavened Bread with great rejoicing for seven days, and the Levites and the priests sang the praises of the LORD day after day with all their strength. [22] Hezekiah spoke encouragingly to all the Levites who had shown themselves well skilled in the service of the LORD. And when they had completed the seven days of festival, sacrificing communion offerings and singing praises to the LORD, the God of their ancestors, [23] the whole assembly agreed to celebrate another seven days. So with joy they celebrated seven days more. [24] King Hezekiah of Judah had contributed a thousand bulls and seven thousand sheep to the assembly, and the princes a thousand bulls and ten thousand sheep. The priests sanctified themselves in great numbers, [25] and the whole assembly of Judah rejoiced, together with the priests and Levites and the rest of the assembly that had come from Israel, as well as the resident aliens from the land of Israel and those that lived in Judah. [26] There was great rejoicing in Jerusalem, for since the days of Solomon, son of David, king of Israel, there had been nothing like it in the city. [27] Then the levitical priests rose and blessed the people; their voice was heard and their prayer reached heaven, God's holy dwelling.

# 31

**Liturgical Reforms.** [1] After all this was over, those Israelites who had been present went forth to the cities of Judah and smashed the sacred pillars, cut down the asherahs, and tore down the high places and altars throughout Judah, Benjamin, Ephraim, and Manasseh, until they were all destroyed.* Then the Israelites returned to their cities, each to his own possession.

[2] Hezekiah re-established the divisions of the priests and the Levites according to their former divisions, assigning to each priest and Levite his proper service, whether in regard to burnt offerings or communion offerings, thanksgiving or praise, or ministering in the gates of the encampment of the LORD. [3] From his own wealth the king allotted a portion for burnt offerings, those of morning and evening and those on sabbaths, new moons, and festivals, as is written in the law of the LORD.* [4] He also commanded the people living in Jerusalem to provide for the support of the priests and Levites, that they might firmly adhere to the law of the LORD.

[5] As soon as the order was promulgated, the Israelites brought, in great quantities, the best of their grain, wine, oil, and honey, and all the produce of the fields; they gave a generous tithe of everything.* [6] Israelites and Judahites living in other cities of Judah also brought in tithes of oxen, sheep, and votive offerings consecrated to the LORD, their God; these they brought in and heaped up in piles.* [7] It was in the third month that they began to establish these heaps, and they completed them in the seventh month.† [8] When Hezekiah and the princes had come and seen the piles, they blessed the LORD and his people Israel. [9] Then Hezekiah questioned the priests and the Levites concerning the piles, [10] and the priest Azariah, head of the house of Zadok, answered him, "Since they began to bring the offerings to the house of the LORD, we have eaten, been satisfied, and had much left over, for the LORD has blessed his people. This great supply is what was left over."*

[11] Hezekiah then gave orders that chambers be constructed in the house of the LORD. When this had been done, [12] they deposited the offerings, tithes, and votive offerings there for safekeeping. The overseer of these things was Conaniah the Levite, and his brother Shimei was second in command. [13] Jehiel, Azaziah, Nahath, Asahel, Jerimoth, Jozabad, Eliel, Ismachiah, Mahath, and Benaiah were supervisors subject to Conaniah the Levite and his brother Shimei by appointment of King Hezekiah and of Azariah, the prefect of the house of God. [14] Kore, the son of Imnah, a Levite and the keeper of the eastern gate, was in charge of the voluntary offerings made to God; he distributed the offerings made to the LORD and the most holy of the votive offerings. [15] Under him in the priestly cities were Eden, Miniamin, Jeshua, Shemaiah, Amariah, and Shecaniah,

† **31:7** *Third month...seventh month*: between the late spring feast of Weeks or Pentecost and the fall feast of Booths or Tabernacles, there is seldom any rain in Palestine; at the end of this dry period the problem of storage (v. 11) would become acute.

**31:1** 2 Chr 34:3–4; 2 Kgs 18:4.
**31:3** Nm 28–29; 1 Chr 29:3; Ez 45:17.
**31:5** Nm 18:18–24; Dt 14:22–23.
**31:6** Neh 12:44–47; 13:10–13.
**31:10** Lv 25:19–22.

who faithfully made the distribution to their brothers, great and small alike, according to their divisions.

[16] There was also a register by ancestral houses of males three years of age† and over, for all priests who were eligible to enter the house of the LORD according to the daily schedule to fulfill their service in the order of their divisions.* [17] The priests were inscribed in their family records according to their ancestral houses, as were the Levites twenty years of age and over according to their various offices and divisions.* [18] A distribution was also made to all who were inscribed in the family records, for their little ones, wives, sons and daughters—thus for the entire assembly, since they were to sanctify themselves by sharing faithfully in the votive offerings. [19] The sons of Aaron, the priests who lived on the lands attached to their cities, had in every city men designated by name to distribute portions to every male of the priests and to every Levite listed in the family records.

[20] Hezekiah did this in all Judah. He did what was good, upright, and faithful before the LORD, his God. [21] Everything that he undertook, for the service of the house of God or for the law and the commandment, was to seek his God. He did this with all his heart, and he prospered.*

**32** **Sennacherib's Invasion.** [1] But after all this and all Hezekiah's fidelity, there came Sennacherib, king of Assyria. He invaded Judah and besieged the fortified cities, intending to breach and take them.* [2] When Hezekiah saw that Sennacherib was coming with the intention of attacking Jerusalem, [3] he took the advice of his princes and warriors to stop the waters of the springs outside the city; they promised their help. [4]* A large force was gathered and stopped all the springs and also the stream running nearby. For they said, "Why should the kings of Assyria come and find an abundance of water?" [5] He then looked to his defenses: he rebuilt the wall where it was broken down, raised towers upon it, and built another wall outside.* He strengthened the Millo of the City of David and made a great number

of spears and shields. [6] Then he appointed army commanders over the people. He gathered them together in his presence in the open space at the gate of the city and encouraged them with these words: [7] "Be strong and steadfast; do not be afraid or dismayed because of the king of Assyria and all the horde coming with him, for there is more with us than with him.* [8] He has only an arm of flesh, but we have the LORD, our God, to help us and to fight our battles."* And the people took confidence from the words of Hezekiah, king of Judah.

**Threat of Sennacherib.** [9]* After this, while Sennacherib, king of Assyria, himself remained at Lachish with all his forces, he sent his officials to Jerusalem with this message for Hezekiah, king of Judah, and all the Judahites who were in Jerusalem: [10] "Thus says Sennacherib, king of Assyria: In what are you trusting, now that you are under siege in Jerusalem? [11] Is not Hezekiah deceiving you, delivering you over to a death of famine and thirst, by his claim that 'the LORD, our God, will rescue us from the grasp of the king of Assyria'? [12] Has not this same Hezekiah removed the Lord's own high places and altars and commanded Judah and Jerusalem, 'You shall bow down before one altar only, and on it alone you shall offer incense'? [13] Do you not know what my fathers and I have done to all the peoples of other lands? Were the gods of the nations in those lands able to rescue their lands from my hand? [14] Who among all the gods of those nations which my fathers put under the ban was able to rescue their people from my hand? Will your god, then, be able to rescue you from my hand? [15] Let not Hezekiah mislead you further and deceive you in any such way. Do not believe him! Since no other god of any other nation or kingdom has been able to rescue his people from my hand or the hands of my fathers, how much the less shall your god rescue you from my hand!"

[16] His officials said still more against the LORD God and against his servant Hezekiah, [17] for he had written letters to deride the LORD, the God of Israel, speaking of him in these terms: "As the gods of the nations in other

---

**31:16** *Three years of age*: this may be a textual error for "thirty years." According to Nm 4:3, 23, 30, men of the priestly clans served from the ages of thirty to fifty.

**31:16** 1 Chr 23:3–4.
**31:17** 1 Chr 23:6–24.
**31:21** Ps 119:2.
　**32:1** 2 Kgs 18:13.
　**32:4** Is 22:9, 11.

**32:5** Neh 2:17–18.
**32:7** 2 Chr 14:10; 20:6–12.
**32:8** Is 31:3.
**32:9–20** 2 Kgs 18:17–37; Is 36:1–22.

lands have not rescued their people from my hand, neither shall Hezekiah's god rescue his people from my hand."* ¹⁸ In a loud voice they shouted in the language of Judah to the people of Jerusalem who were on the wall, to frighten and terrify them so that they might capture their city. ¹⁹ They spoke of the God of Israel as though he were one of the gods of the other peoples of the earth, a work of human hands. ²⁰ But because of this, King Hezekiah and Isaiah the prophet, son of Amoz, prayed and cried out to heaven.*

**Sennacherib's Defeat.** ²¹ Then the Lord sent an angel, who destroyed every warrior, leader, and commander in the camp of the Assyrian king, so that he had to return shamefaced to his own country. And when he entered the temple of his god, some of his own offspring struck him down there with the sword.* ²² Thus the Lord saved Hezekiah and the inhabitants of Jerusalem from the hand of Sennacherib, king of Assyria, as from every other power; he gave them rest on every side. ²³ Many brought gifts for the Lord to Jerusalem and costly objects for Hezekiah, king of Judah, who thereafter was exalted in the eyes of all the nations.*

**Hezekiah's Later Reign.** ²⁴ In those days Hezekiah became mortally ill. He prayed to the Lord, who answered him by giving him a sign.* ²⁵ Hezekiah, however, did not respond with like generosity, for he had become arrogant. Therefore wrath descended upon him and upon Judah and Jerusalem. ²⁶* But then Hezekiah humbled himself for his pride— both he and the inhabitants of Jerusalem; and therefore the wrath of the Lord did not come upon them during the time of Hezekiah.

²⁷* Hezekiah possessed very great wealth and glory. He made treasuries for his silver, gold, precious stones, spices, jewels, and other precious things of all kinds; ²⁸ also storehouses for the harvest of grain, for wine and oil, and barns for the various kinds of cattle and flocks. ²⁹ He built cities for himself, and he acquired sheep and oxen in great numbers, for God gave him very great riches. ³⁰ This same Hezekiah

stopped the upper outlet for water from Gihon and redirected it underground westward to the City of David. Hezekiah prospered in all his works.* ³¹ Nevertheless, in respect to the ambassadors of the Babylonian officials who were sent to him to investigate the sign that had occurred in the land, God abandoned him as a test, to know all that was in his heart.

³² The rest of Hezekiah's acts, including his good deeds, are recorded in the vision of Isaiah the prophet, son of Amoz, and in the book of the kings of Judah and Israel. ³³ Hezekiah rested with his ancestors; he was buried at the approach to the tombs† of the descendants of David. All Judah and the inhabitants of Jerusalem paid him honor at his death. His son Manasseh succeeded him as king.

# 33

**Manasseh's Impiety.** ¹* Manasseh was twelve years old when he became king, and he reigned fifty-five years in Jerusalem. ² He did what was evil in the Lord's sight, following the abominable practices of the nations whom the Lord dispossessed before the Israelites. ³ He rebuilt the high places which Hezekiah his father had torn down. He set up altars to the Baals, and also made asherahs. He bowed down to the whole host of heaven and served them. ⁴ He built altars in the house of the Lord, of which the Lord had said: In Jerusalem shall my name be forever; ⁵ and he built altars to the whole host of heaven in the two courts of the house of the Lord. ⁶ It was he, too, who immolated his children by fire in the Valley of Ben-hinnom. He practiced soothsaying and divination, and reintroduced the consulting of ghosts and spirits.

He did much evil in the Lord's sight and provoked him to anger. ⁷ An idol he had made he placed in the house of God, of which God had said to David and to his son Solomon: In this house and in Jerusalem, which I have chosen out of all the tribes of Israel, I shall set my name forever. ⁸ I will no longer make Israel step out of the land I assigned to your ancestors, provided that they are careful to observe all I commanded them, the entire law, the statutes, and the ordinances given by Moses.

---

† **32:33** *The approach to the tombs:* lit., "the ascent of the tombs," perhaps "the upper section of the tombs," i.e., their most prominent and honored place.

**32:17** 2 Kgs 19:9–13; Is 37:9–13.

**32:20** 2 Kgs 19:14–19; Is 37:14–20.

**32:21** 2 Kgs 19:35–37; Is 37:36–38.
**32:23** 2 Chr 17:10–11.
**32:24** 2 Kgs 20:1–11; Is 38:1–8.

**32:26, 31** 2 Kgs 20:12–19; Is 39:1–8.
**32:27–28** 2 Kgs 20:13; Is 39:2.
**32:30** 2 Kgs 20:20–21.
**33:1–10** 2 Kgs 21:1–9.

⁹Manasseh misled Judah and the inhabitants of Jerusalem into doing even greater evil than the nations the LORD had destroyed at the coming of the Israelites. ¹⁰The LORD spoke to Manasseh and his people, but they paid no attention.

**Manasseh's Conversion.** ¹¹* Therefore the LORD brought against them the army commanders of the Assyrian king; they captured Manasseh with hooks, shackled him with chains, and transported him to Babylon.† ¹²In his distress, he began to appease the LORD, his God. He humbled himself abjectly before the God of his ancestors, ¹³and prayed to him.† The LORD let himself be won over: he heard his prayer and restored him to his kingdom in Jerusalem. Then Manasseh knew that the LORD is indeed God.

¹⁴Afterward he built an outer wall for the City of David to the west of Gihon in the valley, extending to the Fish Gate and encircling Ophel; he built it very high. He stationed army officers in all the fortified cities of Judah. ¹⁵He removed the foreign gods and the idol from the LORD's house and all the altars he had built on the mount of the LORD's house and in Jerusalem, and cast them outside the city.* ¹⁶He restored the altar of the LORD, and sacrificed on it communion offerings and thank offerings, and commanded Judah to serve the LORD, the God of Israel. ¹⁷Though the people continued to sacrifice on the high places, they now did so to the LORD, their God.

¹⁸* The rest of the acts of Manasseh, his prayer to his God, and the words of the seers who spoke to him in the name of the LORD, the God of Israel, are written in the chronicles of the kings of Israel. ¹⁹His prayer and how his supplication was heard, all his sins and his treachery, the sites where he built high places and set up asherahs and carved images before he humbled himself, all this is recorded in the chronicles of his seers. ²⁰Manasseh rested with his ancestors and was buried in his own palace. His son Amon succeeded him as king.

**Reign of Amon.** ²¹* Amon was twenty-two years old when he became king, and he reigned two years in Jerusalem. ²²He did what was evil in the LORD's sight, as his father Manasseh had done. Amon offered sacrifice to all the idols his father Manasseh had made, and served them. ²³Moreover, he did not humble himself before the LORD as his father Manasseh had humbled himself; on the contrary, Amon only increased his guilt. ²⁴His officials plotted against him and put him to death in his palace, ²⁵but the people of the land then slew all who had plotted against King Amon, and the people of the land made his son Josiah king in his stead.

**34** **Josiah's Reforms.** ¹* Josiah was eight years old when he became king, and he reigned thirty-one years in Jerusalem. ²He did what was right in the LORD's sight, walking in the way of David his father, not turning right or left. ³* In the eighth year of his reign, while he was still a youth, he began to seek after the God of David his father. Then in his twelfth year† he began to purify Judah and Jerusalem of the high places, the asherahs, and the carved and molten images. ⁴In his presence, the altars of the Baals were torn down; the incense stands erected above them he broke down; the asherahs and the carved and molten images he smashed and beat into dust, which he scattered over the tombs of those who had sacrificed to them; ⁵and the bones of the priests he burned upon their altars. Thus he purified Judah and Jerusalem. ⁶He did likewise in the cities of Manasseh, Ephraim, Simeon, and in the ruined villages of the surrounding country as far as Naphtali; ⁷he tore down the altars and asherahs, and the carved

---

† **33:11** There is no evidence elsewhere for such an imprisonment of King Manasseh in Babylon. According to the Assyrian inscriptions, however, Manasseh did pay tribute to the Assyrian kings Esarhaddon (680–669 B.C.) and Asshurbanipal (668–627 B.C.). He may well then have been obliged to go to Nineveh, Assyria's capital (rather than to Babylon as the Chronicler has it), to take his oath of allegiance as vassal to the king of Assyria.
**33:13** *And prayed to him*: these words inspired an unknown writer to compose the apocryphal "Prayer of Manasseh," which since the Council of Trent appears as an appendix to many editions of the Vulgate Bible and is used in the Church's liturgy.
**34:3** *In his twelfth year*: ca. 628 B.C., i.e., around the time of the Assyrian emperor Asshurbanipal's death, which enabled Judah to free itself from Assyrian domination. On the basis of 2 Kgs 22:1–23:25 alone, one might suppose that Josiah's reform began only after and as a result of the discovery of the book of the law in the Temple, in the eighteenth year of his reign (622 B.C.). But the Chronicler is no doubt right in placing the beginning of the reform at an earlier period. The repair of the Temple itself, which led to the finding of the book of the law, was likely part of a cultic reform initiated by Josiah.

---

**33:11** Jb 36:8; Ez 19:9.
**33:15** 2 Chr 14:2.
**33:18, 20** 2 Kgs 21:17–18.
**33:21–25** 2 Kgs 21:19–26.

**34:1–2** 2 Kgs 22:1–2.
**34:3–7** 2 Chr 14:1–4; 31:1; 2 Kgs 23:4–20.

images he beat into dust, and broke down the incense stands throughout the land of Israel. Then he returned to Jerusalem.

**The Temple Restored.** 8 * In the eighteenth year of his reign, in order to purify the land and the temple, he sent Shaphan, son of Azaliah, Maaseiah, the ruler of the city, and Joah, son of Joahaz, the chancellor, to restore the house of the LORD, his God. 9They came to Hilkiah the high priest and turned over the money brought to the house of God which the Levites, the guardians of the threshold, had collected from Manasseh, Ephraim, and all the remnant of Israel, as well as from all of Judah, Benjamin, and the inhabitants of Jerusalem. * 10They turned it over to the master workers in the house of the LORD, and these in turn used it to pay the workers in the LORD's house who were restoring and repairing it. 11They also gave it to the carpenters and the masons to buy hewn stone and timber for the tie beams and rafters of the buildings which the kings of Judah had allowed to fall into ruin. 12The men worked faithfully at their task; their overseers were Jahath and Obadiah, Levites of the line of Merari, and Zechariah and Meshullam, of the Kohathites, who directed them. All those Levites who were skillful with musical instruments 13were in charge of the men who carried the burdens, and they directed all the workers in every kind of labor. Some of the other Levites were scribes, officials, and gatekeepers.

**The Finding of the Law.** 14 * When they brought out the money that had been deposited in the house of the LORD, Hilkiah the priest found the book of the law of the LORD given through Moses. 15He reported this to Shaphan the scribe, saying, "I have found the book of the law in the house of the LORD." Hilkiah gave the book to Shaphan, 16who brought it to the king at the same time that he made his report to him. He said, "Your servants are doing everything that has been entrusted to them; 17they have smelted down the silver deposited in the LORD's house and have turned it over to the overseers and the workers." 18Then Shaphan the scribe also informed the king, "Hilkiah the priest has given me a book," and then Shaphan read it in the presence of the king.

19When the king heard the words of the law, he tore his garments. 20The king then issued this command to Hilkiah, to Ahikam, son of Shaphan, to Abdon, son of Michah, to Shaphan the scribe, and to Asaiah, the king's servant: 21 "Go, consult the LORD for me and for those who are left in Israel and Judah, about the words of the book that has been found, for the anger of the LORD burns furiously against us, because our ancestors did not keep the word of the LORD and have not done all that is written in this book." 22Then Hilkiah and others from the king went to Huldah the prophet, wife of Shallum, son of Tokhath, son of Hasrah, keeper of the wardrobe; she lived in Jerusalem, in the Second Quarter. They spoke to her as they had been instructed, 23and she said to them: "Thus says the LORD, the God of Israel: Say to the man who sent you to me, 24Thus says the LORD: I am about to bring evil upon this place and upon its inhabitants, all the curses written in the book that was read before the king of Judah. 25Because they have abandoned me and have burned incense to other gods, provoking me by all the works of their hands, my anger burns against this place and it cannot be extinguished.

26 "But to the king of Judah who sent you to consult the LORD, give this response: Thus says the LORD, the God of Israel: As for the words you have heard, 27because you were heartsick and have humbled yourself before God when you heard his words concerning this place and its inhabitants; because you humbled yourself before me, tore your garments, and wept before me, I in turn have heard—oracle of the LORD. 28I will gather you to your ancestors and you shall go to your grave in peace, and your eyes shall not see all the evil I am about to bring upon this place and upon its inhabitants."

This they reported to the king.

**Covenant Renewal.** 29 * The king then had all the elders of Judah and of Jerusalem summoned before him. 30The king went up to the house of the LORD with all the people of Judah and the inhabitants of Jerusalem: priests, Levites, and all the people, great and small. He read aloud to them all the words of the book of the covenant that had been found in the house of the LORD. [31]The king stood by the column† and made a covenant in the presence of the LORD to follow the LORD and to observe his commandments, statutes, and decrees with his whole heart and soul, carrying out the words of the covenant written in this book. [32]He thereby committed all who were in Jerusalem and Benjamin, and the inhabitants of Jerusalem acted according to the covenant of God, the God of their ancestors. [33]Josiah removed every abomination from all the territories belonging to the Israelites, and he obliged all who were in Israel to serve the LORD, their God. During his lifetime they did not turn away from following the LORD, the God of their ancestors. *

**35** **The Passover.** [1]*Josiah celebrated in Jerusalem a Passover to honor the LORD; the Passover sacrifice was slaughtered on the fourteenth day of the first month. * [2]He reappointed the priests to their duties and confirmed them in the service of the LORD's house. [3]He said to the Levites who were to instruct all Israel, and who were consecrated to the LORD: "Put the holy ark in the house built by Solomon, son of David, king of Israel. It shall no longer be a burden on your shoulders. Serve now the LORD, your God, and his people Israel. * [4]Prepare yourselves by your ancestral houses and your divisions according to the prescriptions of David, king of Israel, and the prescriptions of his son Solomon. [5]Stand in the sanctuary according to the branches of the ancestral houses of your kin, the common people, so that the distribution of the Levites and the families may be the same. * [6]Slaughter the Passover sacrifice, sanctify yourselves, and be at the disposition of your kin, that all may be done according to the word of the LORD given through Moses." *

[7]Josiah contributed to the common people a flock of lambs and young goats, * thirty thousand in number, each to serve as a Passover victim for all who were present, and also three thousand oxen; these were from the king's property. [8]His princes also gave a voluntary offering to the people, the priests, and the Levites. Hilkiah, Zechariah, and Jehiel, prefects

of the house of God, gave to the priests two thousand six hundred Passover victims along with three hundred oxen. * [9]Conaniah and his brothers Shemaiah, Nethanel, Hashabiah, Jehiel, and Jozabad, the rulers of the Levites, contributed to the Levites five thousand Passover victims, together with five hundred oxen.

[10]When the service had been arranged, the priests took their places, as did the Levites in their divisions according to the king's command. [11]The Passover sacrifice was slaughtered, whereupon the priests splashed some of the blood and the Levites proceeded with the skinning. [12]They separated out what was destined for the burnt offering and gave it to various groups of the ancestral houses of the common people to offer to the LORD, as is written in the book of Moses. They did the same with the oxen. [13]They cooked the Passover on the fire as prescribed, and also cooked the sacred portions in pots, caldrons, and pans, then brought them quickly to all the common people. * [14]Afterward they prepared the Passover for themselves and for the priests. Indeed the priests, the sons of Aaron, were busy sacrificing burnt offerings and the fatty portions until night; therefore the Levites prepared for themselves and for the priests, the sons of Aaron. [15]The singers, the sons of Asaph, were at their posts as commanded by David and by Asaph, Heman, and Jeduthun, the king's seer. The gatekeepers were at every gate; there was no need for them to leave their stations, for their fellow Levites prepared for them. [16]Thus the entire service of the LORD was arranged that day so that the Passover could be celebrated and the burnt offerings sacrificed on the altar of the LORD, as King Josiah had commanded. [17]The Israelites who were present on that occasion kept the Passover and the feast of the Unleavened Bread for seven days. [18]*No such Passover had been observed in Israel since the time of Samuel the prophet; no king of Israel had observed a Passover like that celebrated by Josiah, the priests, and Levites, all of Judah and Israel that were present, and the inhabitants of Jerusalem. [19]It was in the eighteenth year of Josiah's reign that this Passover was observed.

**34:31** *The column:* see note on 23:13.

**34:33** 2 Kgs 23:4–20.
**35:1–19** 2 Kgs 23:21–23.
**35:1** Ex 12:1–28; 2 Kgs 23:21.
**35:3** 2 Chr 5:4; 1 Chr 15:12, 15.
**35:5** 1 Chr 24–26.
**35:6** 2 Chr 30:17.
**35:7** Ex 12:5.
**35:8** Nm 7:1–83.
**35:13** Ex 12:8–9.
**35:18–19** 2 Kgs 23:22–23.

**Josiah's End.** [20] After Josiah had done all this to restore the temple, Neco, king of Egypt, came up to fight at Carchemish on the Euphrates, and Josiah went out to meet him. [21] Neco sent messengers to him, saying: "What quarrel is between us, king of Judah? I have not come against you this day, for my war is with another kingdom, and God has told me to hasten. Do not interfere with God who is with me; let him not destroy you." [22] But Josiah would not withdraw from him, for he was seeking a pretext to fight with him. Therefore he would not listen to the words of Neco that came from the mouth of God, but went out to fight in the plain of Megiddo. [23] Then the archers shot King Josiah, who said to his servants, "Take me away, I am seriously wounded."* [24] His servants took him from his own chariot, placed him in the one he had in reserve, and brought him to Jerusalem, where he died. He was buried in the tombs of his ancestors, and all Judah and Jerusalem mourned him. [25] Jeremiah also composed a lamentation for Josiah, which is recited to this day by all the male and female singers in their lamentations for Josiah. These have been made an ordinance for Israel, and can be found written in the Lamentations.†

[26]* The rest of the acts of Josiah, his good deeds in accord with what is written in the law of the LORD, [27] and his words, first and last, are recorded in the book of the kings of Israel and Judah.

# 36

**Jehoahaz.** [1]* The people of the land took Jehoahaz, son of Josiah, and made him king in Jerusalem to succeed his father. [2] Jehoahaz was twenty-three years old when he became king, and he reigned three months in Jerusalem. [3] The king of Egypt deposed him in Jerusalem and fined the land one hundred talents of silver and a talent of gold. [4] Then the king of Egypt made Eliakim, the brother of Jehoahaz, king over Judah and Jerusalem, changing his name to Jehoiakim. Neco took Jehoahaz his brother away and brought him to Egypt.

**Jehoiakim.** [5] Jehoiakim was twenty-five years old when he became king, and he reigned eleven years in Jerusalem. He did what was evil in the sight of the LORD, his God.* [6]* Nebuchadnezzar, king of Babylon, attacked and bound him in chains to take him to Babylon.† [7] Nebuchadnezzar also carried away to Babylon some of the vessels of the house of the LORD and put them in his palace in Babylon. [8] The rest of the acts of Jehoiakim, the abominable things that he did, and what therefore happened to him, are recorded in the book of the kings of Israel and Judah. His son Jehoiachin succeeded him as king.*

**Jehoiachin.** [9] Jehoiachin was eighteen years old when he became king, and he reigned three months and ten days in Jerusalem. He did what was evil in the LORD's sight.* [10] At the turn of the year, King Nebuchadnezzar sent for him and had him brought to Babylon, along with precious vessels from the house of the LORD. He made his brother Zedekiah† king over Judah and Jerusalem.*

**Zedekiah.** [11] Zedekiah was twenty-one years old when he became king, and he reigned eleven years in Jerusalem.* [12] He did what was evil in the sight of the LORD, his God, and he did not humble himself before Jeremiah the prophet, who spoke for the LORD.* [13] He also rebelled against King Nebuchadnezzar, who had made him swear by God. He became stiff-necked and hardened his heart rather than return to the LORD, the God of Israel.* [14] Likewise all the princes of Judah, the priests, and the people added treachery to treachery, practicing all the abominations of the nations and defiling the LORD's house which he had consecrated in Jerusalem.

---

**35:25** There is no mention of such a lamentation for Josiah composed by Jeremiah in either 2 Kings or Jeremiah; but see note on Zec 12:11. *Lamentations:* probably a reference to the Book of Lamentations.

**36:6** *Nebuchadnezzar…bound him in chains to take him to Babylon:* the Chronicler does not state that Jehoiakim was actually taken to Babylon. According to 2 Kgs 24:1–6, Jehoiakim revolted after being Nebuchadnezzar's vassal for three years; he died in Jerusalem before the city surrendered to the Babylonians. Dn 1:1–2, apparently based on 2 Chr 36:6–7, does speak of Jehoiakim's deportation to Babylon.

**36:10** *His brother Zedekiah:* Zedekiah was actually the

brother of Jehoiakim and the uncle of Jehoiachin (2 Kgs 24:17; Jer 37:1), though scarcely older than his nephew (2 Kgs 24:8, 18; 2 Chr 36:9, 11).

---

| | |
|---|---|
| **35:23** 2 Chr 18:33–34. | **36:9** 2 Kgs 24:8–9. |
| **35:26** 2 Kgs 23:28. | **36:10** 2 Kgs 24:10–17. |
| **36:1–4** 2 Kgs 23:30–34; 1 Chr 3:15–16. | **36:11** 2 Kgs 24:18–19; Jer 52:1. |
| **36:5** 2 Kgs 23:36–37; Jer 22:18–19. | **36:12** Jer 37:1–2. |
| **36:6** 2 Kgs 24:1–2. | **36:13** 2 Kgs 24:20; Jer 52:4; Ez 17:13–16. |
| **36:8** 2 Kgs 24:5. | |

**The Fall of Judah.** [15] Early and often the Lord, the God of their ancestors, sent his messengers to them, for he had compassion on his people and his dwelling place.* [16] But they mocked God's messengers, despised his words, and scoffed at his prophets, until the Lord's anger against his people blazed up beyond remedy.* [17] Then he brought up against them the king of the Chaldeans, who killed their young men with the sword in their own sanctuary, with compassion for neither young men nor young women, neither the old nor the infirm; all of them he delivered into his power.* [18] All the utensils of the house of God, large and small, the treasures of the Lord's house, and the treasures of the king and his princes, all these he brought to Babylon.* [19] They burnt the house of God, tore down the walls of Jerusalem, burnt down all its palaces, and destroyed all its precious objects.* [20] Those who escaped the sword he carried captive to Babylon, where they became servants to him and his sons until the Persian kingdom came to power. [21] All this was to fulfill the word of the Lord spoken by Jeremiah: Until the land has retrieved its lost sabbaths, during all the time it lies waste it shall have rest while seventy years are fulfilled.

**Decree of Cyrus.** [22]† In the first year of Cyrus, king of Persia, in order to realize the word of the Lord spoken by Jeremiah, the Lord roused the spirit of Cyrus, King of Persia, to spread this proclamation throughout his kingdom, both by word of mouth and in writing:* [23] "Thus says Cyrus, king of Persia: The Lord, the God of heaven, has given to me all the kingdoms of the earth. He has also charged me to build him a house in Jerusalem, which is in Judah. All among you, therefore, who belong to his people, may their God be with them; let them go up."

---

† 36:22–23 These verses are identical with those of Ezr 1:1–3a and were to prevent the work from ending on a note of doom.

* 36:15 Jer 7:25; Heb 1:1.
36:16 Mt 23:34–37.
36:17 Lam 1:15; 5:11–14.
36:18 2 Kgs 25:14–15.
36:19 2 Kgs 25:9–10; Lam 2:8.
36:22 Ezr 1:1–4.

# The Book of

# Ezra

## INTRODUCTION

Leslie J. Hoppe, OFM

The book of Ezra tells the story of the early postexilic period, focusing on the restoration of the worship of Yahweh in Jerusalem and the reorganization of the personnel responsible for the Temple and its activities. A principal emphasis in the book is the continuity of postexilic religious practice with that of Judah's preexilic past. The program of restoration described in the book is said to be in conformity with the Torah of Moses (Ezr 3:2; 6:18), and Ezra is presented as an expert in the Torah. This emphasis on continuity provides legitimacy for the program of religious restoration that the book supports.

The book of Nehemiah also tells the story of the Judean restoration but devotes more attention to the repopulation and rebuilding of Jerusalem. Early rabbinic tradition considered the books of Ezra and Nehemiah to be a single unified work composed by Ezra, and the earliest Hebrew manuscripts of the Bible present the two as a single work. By the fifteenth century CE, however, Jewish Bibles began dividing the single work into what we now have as the books of Ezra and Nehemiah. English Bibles have followed suit.

The book of Ezra continues the story of the people of Judah that is the subject of Chronicles. The latter ends with the decree of Cyrus the Great, encouraging the Judean exiles in Babylon to return to Jerusalem and rebuild the Temple. Ezra begins with a longer version of the same decree. This has led some interpreters to suggest that Ezra as well as Nehemiah were products of the same hand that produced Chronicles. There is some support for this hypothesis, since the Septuagint's 1 Esdras combines portions of all the three books, the conclusion of Chronicles meshes with the beginning of Ezra, and the three books do share some theological assumptions.

But there are also significant theological differences between Ezra-Nehemiah and the book of Chronicles. For example, Ezra and Nehemiah's notion of who belongs to the people of Israel differs from that of Chronicles. The latter was open to the people of the former northern kingdom while Ezra and Nehemiah regard these people as foreigners. Similarly, Chronicles does not show as much opposition to marriage outside the Judean community as do Ezra and Nehemiah. Finally, in Chronicles David is the figure of the past whose conduct is to be emulated by the people of Judah. In Ezra and Nehemiah, it is the Torah of Moses that sets the pattern for Judah's restoration. Consequently it seems unlikely that the three books form some sort of a unity.

Moreover there is a growing consensus that the books of Ezra and Nehemiah are separate works as well, written by different individuals who drew on various sources. Ezra is much more focused on the Temple and the implementation of the Mosaic Torah while Nehemiah is concerned with reconstituting Judah's economy and rebuilding Jerusalem's defenses—especially the city's wall. There are also linguistic differences between the two books, and their genealogies differ slightly. All this points to the probability that Ezra and Nehemiah were originally separate works.

The Judean restoration, which is the subject of Ezra, was possible because of the policy of the Persians toward the various peoples of their empire. In general, the Persians found few conflicts between their religious system, which was centered on Ahura Mazda, "the greatest of gods," and the religious practices that took place in the Persian provinces. Royal policy actually encouraged the cultus of local deities. Second, temples in the ancient world were important economic as well as religious institutions. Temples facilitated the efficient redistribution of foodstuffs offered as sacrificial offering to the gods, since that which was not sacrificed would be sold by priests to the general population. Rebuilding the Jerusalem Temple would be an important component of regenerating Judah's economy, which had been devastated by the conflict with the Babylonians. Finally, the Persians allowed the various peoples of their empire a type of limited autonomy. Ethnic groups in the Persian Empire were able to govern themselves according to their traditional laws as long as they accepted Persian hegemony. In the case of Judah, the Mosaic Torah became imperial law for the subprovince of Judah known by its Aramaic name: Yehud.

Following the 538 BCE decree of Cyrus the Great, some of the Judean exiles returned to Jerusalem under Sheshbazzar, whom the Persians appointed as the leader of the returnees (Ezr 1:8), and the rebuilding of the Temple began. Progress was slow until the reign of Darius I (522–486 BCE) when the prophets Haggai and Zechariah called for renewed commitment to the project (Ezr 5:1). The second Temple was finally completed in 516 BCE. Pinpointing the actual date for the missions of Ezra and Nehemiah is a perplexing historical problem. Ezra 7:7–8 states that Ezra's work began in the seventh year of Artaxerxes while Nehemiah 2:1 gives the twentieth year of Artaxerxes as the time that Nehemiah's mission began. But there were three Persian monarchs who bore the name Artaxerxes. The biblical text leaves the impression that Ezra's mission preceded that of Nehemiah. The priority given to Ezra is due less to historical memory and more to the view that Ezra was primarily responsible for the restoration of the Jewish community in Yehud. Though there is no consensus among historians on this issue, it is probable that Nehemiah's mission preceded that of Ezra. The latter's work seems to presuppose the reconstruction and repopulation of Jerusalem, which were accomplished in part by Nehemiah. This suggests that Nehemiah arrived in Jerusalem in 445 BCE during the reign of Artaxerxes I while Ezra arrived in Jerusalem in 398 BCE during the reign of Artaxerxes II.

The book of Ezra is fond of citing official Persian court documents. Since Aramaic was the official language of the Persian administration, Ezra 4:7–6:18 and 7:12–26, which quote several such documents, are in Aramaic rather than Hebrew. This, of course, is not obvious to those who read Ezra in translation. This detail, however, is significant since it shows that the intended audience of the book of Ezra was bilingual. Aramaic was also the language of commerce in the ancient Near East, suggesting that the people of Judah were able to function in an international economy. This was necessary so that the people of Judah could achieve an acceptable level of prosperity. After the area was conquered by Alexander the Great (d. 323 BCE), Greek replaced Aramaic as the international language of commerce. However, Aramaic continued to be the most commonly used Semitic language until the seventh century CE, when it was replaced by Arabic.

Chapters 1–3 of Ezra deal with the return from exile and the start of the project whose goal was the rebuilding of the Jerusalem Temple. Chapter 4 focuses on the problems that the Jerusalem community faced in restoring the Temple. The book implies that those who opposed the restoration project were people who lived in the territory of the former northern kingdom. According to the book, this opposition party attempted to characterize the reconstruction of the Jerusalem Temple as a rejection of Persian hegemony over Yehud. The Persians, however, are not swayed by the opposition and the project is resumed and successfully completed (chs. 5–6).

The story of Ezra's mission is told in chs. 7–10. The commission Ezra receives from the Persian emperor contains an order to reconstitute Judean society on the basis of the Mosaic Torah (7:13–15, 25). By accepting or rejecting this Torah, the people of Yehud either include or exclude themselves from the Jewish community. The Torah becomes the imperial law for Yehud and the means of self-designation for those

EZR

who wished to be a part of the Jewish community. Ezra was not only a scribe but a priest as well. It is not surprising then that an important component of his activities involved having the vessels of the Temple returned so that worship there could be completely restored.

The book ends with Ezra's pronouncement that marriage outside the Jewish community is unacceptable. While the Torah does not forbid mixed marriages in general, it does forbid marriages with people from certain nations (Ex 34:11–16). Ezra represents the view that any marriage outside the community threatens the community's integrity and religious commitments.

The book of Ezra makes it clear that Ezra's great achievement was his effort to secure Jewish identity through acceptance of the Mosaic Torah. A beleaguered Jewish community found new life because of a man who led them to find their future through the observance of Torah, forever shaping Judaism as a religion of ethics and morality.

The canonical book of Ezra is just one of several early Jewish religious texts ascribed to Ezra. There is a noncanonical work in the Septuagint called *1 Esdras* which contains portions of 2 Chronicles, Ezra, and Nehemiah and an original piece not found elsewhere. The Vulgate calls this text *3 Esdras* while English Bibles that contain the Apocrypha use the Septuagint title. *Fourth Ezra* is a Jewish apocalypse from the first century CE. Jerome included it as an appendix to the Vulgate and called it *4 Esdras*. It is found in English Bibles that include the Apocrypha under the title *2 Esdras*. In addition to *4 Ezra*, *2 Esdras* also contains two Christian supplements sometimes called *5 Ezra* (*2 Esdras 1–2*) and *6 Ezra* (*2 Esdras 15–16*). These various books preserve alternate versions of the narratives about Ezra and Nehemiah. Although their nomenclature is confusing, these works provide a portrait of the Judean restoration as it continued to unfold and are crucial for understanding the development of early Judaism. ■

# A Chart of the Literature Associated with Ezra

| The Hebrew Bible | Septuagint | Vulgate | English Bibles |
|---|---|---|---|
| Ezra[1] | Esdras B[2] | 1 Esdras | Ezra |
| | | 2 Esdras | Nehemiah |
| | Esdras A | 3 Esdras | 1 Esdras |
| | | 4 Esdras | 2 Esdras[3] |

1. After the fifteenth century, Hebrew Bibles divide the book of Ezra into the book of Ezra and the book of Nehemiah.
2. Contains portions of 2 Chronicles, Ezra, Nehemiah, and an original piece.
3. *2 Esdras* is made up of an apocalypes the scholars call *4 Ezra* (*2 Esdras 3–14*) and two Christian supplements: *5 Ezra* (*2 Esdras 1–2*) and *6 Ezra* (*2 Esdras 15–16*).

# THE BOOK OF EZRA

## New American Bible, Introduction

The last four books of the Hebrew canon are Ezra, Nehemiah, and 1 and 2 Chronicles, in that order. At one time, however, Ezra and Nehemiah followed 1 and 2 Chronicles and were generally considered to be the work of one and the same author known as "the Chronicler." In recent years, however, the question of the authorship of Ezra and Nehemiah is seen to be more complex. While some scholars still maintain unity of authorship, others prefer to speak of the influence of a "Chronistic school" on the formation of Ezra-Nehemiah as a single book. The treatment of Ezra-Nehemiah as a single book by the earliest editors was undoubtedly due to the fact that in ancient times the two books were put under the one name, Ezra. The combined work Ezra-Nehemiah is our most important literary source for the formation of the Jewish religious community in the province of Judah after the Babylonian exile. This is known as the period of the Restoration, and the two men most responsible for the reorganization of Jewish life at this time were Ezra and Nehemiah.

In the present state of the Ezra-Nehemiah text, there are several dislocations of large sections so that the chronological or logical sequence is disrupted. The major instance is Ezra's public reading of the law in Neh 8; others will be pointed out in the footnotes. Since arguments in favor of the chronological priority of Nehemiah to Ezra are indecisive, we accept the order in the text according to which Ezra's activity preceded that of Nehemiah.

What is known of Ezra and his work is derived almost exclusively from Ezr 7–10 (the "Ezra Memoirs") and Neh 8–9. Strictly speaking, the term "Ezra Memoirs" should be used only of that section in which Ezra speaks in the first person, i.e., Ezr 7:27–9:15. Compare the "Nehemiah Memoirs" in Neh 1:1–7:72a; 11:1, 2; 12:27–43; 13:4–31. The author combined this material with other sources at his disposal. The personality of Ezra is not so well-known

as that of Nehemiah. Ben Sira, in his praise of the fathers (Sir 44–49), omits mention of Ezra, perhaps for polemical reasons. The genealogy of Ezra (7:1–5) traces his priesthood back to Aaron, brother of Moses. This was the accepted way of establishing the legality of one's priestly office. He is also called a scribe, well-versed in the law of Moses (7:6), indicating Ezra's dedication to the study of the Torah, which he sought to make the basic rule of life in the restored community. It was in religious and cultic reform rather than in political affairs that Ezra made his mark as a postexilic leader. Jewish tradition holds him in great esteem. The apocryphal 2 Esdras, sometimes included as an appendix to the Vulgate, where it is known as 4 Esdras, transforms him into a prophet and visionary. The Talmud regards him as a second Moses, claiming that the Torah would have been given to Israel through Ezra had not Moses preceded him.

Ezra is sometimes accused of having been a legalist who gave excessive attention to the letter of the law. His work, however, should be seen and judged within a specific historical context. He gave to his people a cohesion and spiritual unity which helped to prevent the disintegration of the small Jewish community settled in the province of Judah. Had it not been for the intransigence of Ezra and of those who adopted his ideal, it is doubtful that Judaism would have so effectively resisted Hellenism in later centuries. Ezra set the tone of the postexilic community, and it was characterized by fidelity to the Torah, Judaism's authentic way of life. It is in this light that we can judge most fairly the work of Ezra during the Restoration.

The Book of Ezra is divided as follows:

I. The Return from Exile (1:1–6:22)

II. The Work of Ezra (7:1–10:44)

The following list of the kings of Persia, with the dates of their reigns, will be useful for dating the events mentioned in Ezra-Nehemiah:

| | |
|---|---|
| Cyrus | 539–530 B.C. |
| Cambyses | 530–522 B.C. |
| Darius I | 522–486 B.C. |
| Xerxes I | 486–465 B.C. |
| Artaxerxes I | 465–424 B.C. |
| Darius II | 423–404 B.C. |
| Artaxerxes II | 404–358 B.C. |
| Artaxerxes III | 358–337 B.C. |
| End of the Persian Empire (Defeat of Darius III) | 331 B.C. ∎ |

# EZRA

## I. THE RETURN FROM EXILE

**1** **The Decree of Cyrus.** ¹*In the first year of Cyrus,† king of Persia, in order to fulfill the word of the Lord spoken by Jeremiah, the Lord stirred up the spirit of Cyrus king of Persia to issue a proclamation throughout his entire kingdom, both by word of mouth and in writing: ²"Thus says Cyrus, king of Persia: 'All the kingdoms of the earth the Lord, the God of heaven,† has given to me, and he has charged me to build him a house in Jerusalem, which is in Judah. ³Those among you who belong to any part of his people, may their God be with them! Let them go up to Jerusalem in Judah to build the house of the Lord the God of Israel, that is, the God who is in Jerusalem. ⁴Let all those who have survived, in whatever place they may have lived, be assisted by the people of that place with silver, gold, goods, and livestock, together with voluntary offerings for the house of God in Jerusalem.'"

⁵Then the heads of ancestral houses† of Judah and Benjamin and the priests and Levites—everyone, that is, whose spirit had been stirred up by God—prepared to go up to build the house of the Lord in Jerusalem. ⁶*All their neighbors gave them help in every way, with silver, gold, goods, livestock, and many precious gifts, besides all their voluntary offerings. ⁷*King Cyrus, too, had the vessels of the house of the Lord brought forth that Nebuchadnezzar had taken from Jerusalem and placed in the house of his god. ⁸Cyrus, king of Persia, had them brought forth by the treasurer Mithredath, who counted them out to Sheshbazzar, prince of Judah.† ⁹This was the inventory: baskets of goldware, thirty; baskets of silverware, one thousand and twenty-nine; ¹⁰golden bowls, thirty; silver bowls, four hundred and ten; other vessels, one thousand. ¹¹Total of the gold and silver vessels: five thousand four hundred.† All these Sheshbazzar took with him when the exiles were brought up from Babylon to Jerusalem.

**2** **A Census of the Returned Exiles.** ¹†*These are the inhabitants of the province who returned from the captivity of the exiles, whom Nebuchadnezzar, king of Babylon, had carried away to Babylon, and who came back to Jerusalem and Judah, to their various cities ²(those who returned with Zerubbabel, Jeshua, Nehemiah, Seraiah, Reelaiah, Mordecai, Bilshan, Mispar, Bigvai, Rehum, and Baanah):

The census of the people of Israel: ³descendants of Parosh, two thousand one hundred and seventy-two; ⁴descendants of Shephatiah, three hundred and seventy-two; ⁵descendants of Arah, seven hundred and seventy-five; ⁶descendants of Pahath-moab, who were descendants of Jeshua and Joab, two thousand eight hundred and twelve; ⁷descendants of Elam, one thousand two hundred and fifty-four; ⁸descendants of Zattu, nine hundred and forty-five; ⁹descendants of Zaccai, seven hundred and sixty; ¹⁰descendants of Bani, six hundred and forty-two; ¹¹descendants of Bebai, six hundred and twenty-three; ¹²descendants of Azgad, one thousand two hundred and twenty-two; ¹³descendants of Adonikam, six hundred and sixty-six; ¹⁴descendants of Bigvai, two thousand and fifty-six; ¹⁵descendants of Adin, four hundred and fifty-four; ¹⁶descendants of Ater, who were descendants of Hezekiah, ninety-eight; ¹⁷descendants of Bezai, three hundred and twenty-three; ¹⁸descendants of Jorah, one hundred and twelve; ¹⁹descendants of Hashum, two hundred and twenty-three;

---

† **1:1** *In the first year of Cyrus*: the first regnal year of Cyrus was 539 B.C., but his first year as ruler of Babylon, after the conquest of that city, was 538 B.C., the year in which he issued an edict, replicated on the famous Cyrus cylinder, permitting the repatriation of peoples deported by the Babylonians.

**1:2** *The God of heaven*: this title, used as in 7:12, 21, 23, corresponds to a title of the Zoroastrian supreme deity Ahura Mazda, though it is not certain that Cyrus was a Zoroastrian.

**1:5** *Heads of ancestral houses*: the ancestral house was the basic organizational unit of the postexilic community, consisting of an extended kinship group claiming descent from a common ancestor. The patriarchs of these units played an important role in civic government.

**1:8** *Sheshbazzar, prince of Judah*: often identified with Shenassar, fourth son of Jehoiachin, king of Judah, exiled in 598 B.C.

(see 1 Chr 3:17–18), and therefore the uncle of Zerubbabel (Ezr 3:2–4). This identification is uncertain.

**1:11** *Five thousand four hundred*: either this figure or the figures given for one or more of the items listed have been corrupted in the transmission of the text.

**2:1–67** As it now stands, this list, which also appears at Neh 7:6–72, is an expanded form of lists of Babylonian repatriates from the sixth century B.C. It served to establish membership in the reconstituted Temple community; civic status and perhaps also title to property depended on this membership.

---

* **1:1** Ezr 6:3–5; 2 Chr 36:22–23; Jer 25:11–12; 29:10; Zec 1:12.   **1:6** Ex 3:21–22; 11:2; 12:35.   **1:7** 2 Kgs 25:14–15.   **2:1** Neh 7:6–72.

<sup>20</sup> descendants of Gibeon, ninety-five; <sup>21</sup> descendants of Bethlehem, one hundred and twenty-three; <sup>22</sup> people of Netophah, fifty-six; <sup>23</sup> people of Anathoth, one hundred and twenty-eight; <sup>24</sup> people of Beth-azmaveth, forty-two; <sup>25</sup> people of Kiriath-jearim, Chephirah, and Beeroth, seven hundred and forty-three; <sup>26</sup> people of Ramah and Geba, six hundred and twenty-one; <sup>27</sup> people of Michmas, one hundred and twenty-two; <sup>28</sup> people of Bethel and Ai, two hundred and twenty-three; <sup>29</sup> descendants of Nebo, fifty-two; <sup>30</sup> descendants of Magbish, one hundred and fifty-six; <sup>31</sup> descendants of the other Elam, one thousand two hundred and fifty-four; <sup>32</sup> descendants of Harim, three hundred and twenty; <sup>33</sup> descendants of Lod, Hadid, and Ono, seven hundred and twenty-five; <sup>34</sup> descendants of Jericho, three hundred and forty-five; <sup>35</sup> descendants of Senaah, three thousand six hundred and thirty.

<sup>36</sup> The priests: descendants of Jedaiah, of the house of Jeshua, nine hundred and seventy-three; <sup>37</sup> descendants of Immer, one thousand and fifty-two; <sup>38</sup> descendants of Pashhur, one thousand two hundred and forty-seven; <sup>39</sup> descendants of Harim, one thousand and seventeen.

<sup>40</sup>* The Levites: descendants of Jeshua and Kadmiel, of the descendants of Hodaviah, seventy-four.

<sup>41</sup> The singers:† descendants of Asaph, one hundred and twenty-eight.

<sup>42</sup> The gatekeepers:† descendants of Shallum, descendants of Ater, descendants of Talmon, descendants of Akkub, descendants of Hatita, descendants of Shobai, one hundred and thirty-nine in all.

<sup>43</sup> The temple servants: descendants of Ziha, descendants of Hasupha, descendants of Tabbaoth, <sup>44</sup> descendants of Keros, descendants of Siaha, descendants of Padon, <sup>45</sup> descendants of Lebanah, descendants of Hagabah, descendants of Akkub, <sup>46</sup> descendants of Hagab, descendants of Shamlai, descendants of Hanan, <sup>47</sup> descendants of Giddel, descendants

of Gahar, descendants of Reaiah, <sup>48</sup> descendants of Rezin, descendants of Nekoda, descendants of Gazzam, <sup>49</sup> descendants of Uzza, descendants of Paseah, descendants of Besai, <sup>50</sup> descendants of Asnah, descendants of the Meunites, descendants of the Nephusites, <sup>51</sup> descendants of Bakbuk, descendants of Hakupha, descendants of Harhur, <sup>52</sup> descendants of Bazluth, descendants of Mehida, descendants of Harsha, <sup>53</sup> descendants of Barkos, descendants of Sisera, descendants of Temah, <sup>54</sup> descendants of Neziah, descendants of Hatipha.

<sup>55</sup> Descendants of Solomon's servants: descendants of Sotai, descendants of Hassophereth, descendants of Peruda, <sup>56</sup> descendants of Jaalah, descendants of Darkon, descendants of Giddel, <sup>57</sup> descendants of Shephatiah, descendants of Hattil, descendants of Pochereth-hazzebaim, descendants of Ami. <sup>58</sup> The total of the temple servants together with the descendants of Solomon's servants was three hundred and ninety-two.

<sup>59</sup> The following who returned from Telmelah, Tel-harsha, Cherub, Addan, and Immer were unable to prove that their ancestral houses and their descent were Israelite: <sup>60</sup> descendants of Delaiah, descendants of Tobiah, descendants of Nekoda, six hundred and fifty-two. <sup>61</sup>* Also, of the priests: descendants of Habaiah, descendants of Hakkoz, descendants of Barzillai (he had married one of the daughters of Barzillai the Gileadite and was named after him). <sup>62</sup> These searched their family records, but their names could not be found there, and they were excluded from the priesthood. <sup>63</sup>* The governor† ordered them not to partake of the most holy foods until there should be a priest to consult the Urim and Thummim.

<sup>64</sup> The entire assembly taken together came to forty-two thousand three hundred and sixty, <sup>65</sup> not counting their male and female servants, who numbered seven thousand three hundred and thirty-seven. They also had two hundred

---

† **2:41** *The singers*: the term covers the composition as well as the rendition of liturgical music. Since they are listed as distinct from Levites (2:40), they had not yet attained levitical status, as in Chronicles (e.g., 1 Chr 9:33–34; 23:3–6).
**2:42** *The gatekeepers*: their principal task was to protect the ritual purity of the temple area (e.g., 2 Chr 23:19). The author assumes that they were established by David as a distinct levitical category (1 Chr 15:18; 26:1–19).
**2:63** *The governor*: the honorific title was also held by Nehemiah (Neh 8:9; 10:2). The identity of the governor is unknown;

both Sheshbazzar (Ezr 5:14) and Zerubbabel (Hg 1:1, 14; 2:2, 21) are identified as governors of Judah in the early Persian period. Mal 1:8 refers to an unnamed governor, and the names of other occupants of the office (Yehoezer, Ahzai, Elnathan) occur on seal impressions, though their date is uncertain. *Urim and Thummim*: cf. Ex 28:30.

* **2:40** Neh 12:23.                    **2:63** Nm 27:21; Dt 33:8;
**2:61** 2 Sm 17:27;                         1 Sm 14:41–42; 28:6.
19:32–33; 1 Kgs 2:7.

EZR

male and female singers. ⁶⁶Their horses numbered seven hundred and thirty-six, their mules two hundred and forty-five, ⁶⁷their camels four hundred and thirty-five, their donkeys six thousand seven hundred and twenty.

⁶⁸When they arrived at the house of the LORD in Jerusalem, some of the heads of ancestral houses made voluntary offerings for the house of God, to rebuild it in its place. ⁶⁹According to their means they contributed to the treasury for the temple service: sixty-one thousand drachmas of gold, five thousand minas of silver, and one hundred priestly robes. ⁷⁰The priests, the Levites, and some of the people took up residence in Jerusalem; the singers, the gatekeepers, and the temple servants settled in their cities. Thus all the Israelites settled in their cities.

# 3

**Restoration of Worship.** ¹\* Now when the seventh month† came, after the Israelites had settled in their cities, the people gathered as one in Jerusalem. ²Then Jeshua, son of Jozadak, together with his kinsmen the priests, and Zerubbabel, son of Shealtiel, together with his kinsmen, began building the altar of the God of Israel in order to offer on it the burnt offerings prescribed in the law of Moses, the man of God. ³\* They set the altar on its foundations, for they lived in fear of the peoples of the lands,† and offered burnt offerings to the LORD on it, both morning and evening. ⁴\* They also kept the feast of Booths in the manner prescribed, and they offered the daily burnt offerings in the proper number required for each day. ⁵Thereafter they offered regular burnt offerings, the sacrifices prescribed for the new moons and all the festivals sacred to the LORD, and those which anyone might bring as a voluntary offering to the LORD.

**Laying the Foundations of the Temple.** ⁶From the first day of the seventh month they reinstituted the burnt offering to the LORD, though

the foundation of the LORD's temple had not yet been laid. ⁷\* Then they hired stonecutters and carpenters, and sent food and drink and oil to the Sidonians and Tyrians that they might ship cedar trees from the Lebanon to the port of Joppa, as Cyrus, king of Persia, had authorized. ⁸In the year after their coming to the house of God in Jerusalem, in the second month, Zerubbabel, son of Shealtiel, and Jeshua, son of Jozadak, together with the rest of their kinsmen, the priests and Levites and all who had come from the captivity to Jerusalem, began by appointing the Levites twenty years of age and over to supervise the work on the house of the LORD. ⁹Jeshua and his sons and kinsmen, with Kadmiel and Binnui, son of Hodaviah, and their sons and their kindred, the Levites, together undertook to supervise those who were engaged in the work on the house of God. ¹⁰\* While the builders were laying the foundation of the LORD's temple, the priests in their vestments were stationed with trumpets and the Levites, sons of Asaph, with cymbals to praise the LORD in the manner laid down by David, king of Israel. ¹¹\* They alternated in songs of praise and thanksgiving to the LORD, "for he is good, for his love for Israel endures forever";† and all the people raised a great shout of joy, praising the LORD because the foundation of the LORD's house had been laid. ¹²\* Many of the priests, Levites, and heads of ancestral houses, who were old enough to have seen the former house, cried out in sorrow as they watched the foundation of the present house being laid. Many others, however, lifted up their voices in shouts of joy. ¹³No one could distinguish the sound of the joyful shouting from the sound of those who were weeping; for the people raised a mighty clamor which was heard far away.

# 4

**Outside Interference.** ¹When the enemies of Judah and Benjamin heard that the exiles were building a temple for the LORD, the

---

**3:1–2** *The seventh month*: Tishri (September–October), apparently of the first year of the return (538 B.C.), followed by events in the second year (v. 8). In that case it was Sheshbazzar who laid the foundations of the Temple (5:16), and it was in the second year of Darius I (520 B.C.) that Jeshua and Zerubbabel resumed work on the Temple that had been temporarily interrupted (Ezr 4:24–5:1; Hg 1:1; 2:1). The author, or a later editor, has set the construction and dedication of the Temple under Darius I back into the earliest period of the return. Shealtiel was the oldest son of King Jehoiachin (1 Chr 3:17–19); Zerubbabel was therefore Jehoiachin's grandson; see note on Ezr 1:8.

**3:3** *Peoples of the lands*: referring either to those who had never left Judah or to neighboring peoples—Edomites, Arabs, inhabitants of Samaria—who opposed those who returned.

**3:11** *"For he is good … forever"*: a refrain occurring frequently in liturgies of ancient Israel (cf. Ps 136).

---

**3:1** Neh 7:7–78.
**3:3** Dt 9:25; 1 Kgs 8:64.
**3:4** Ex 23:16; Nm 28:3–8;
  Dt 16:13–15.
**3:7** 1 Chr 22:4; 2 Chr 2:9.

**3:10** Ezr 2:41.
**3:11** 1 Chr 16:34; 2 Chr
  5:13; 7:3; Ps 106:1;
  136:1; Jer 33:11.
**3:12** Hg 2:3.

God of Israel, [2]* they approached Zerubbabel and the heads of ancestral houses and said to them, "Let us build with you, for we seek your God just as you do, and we have sacrificed to him since the days of Esarhaddon, king of Assyria,† who brought us here." [3] But Zerubbabel, Jeshua, and the rest of the heads of ancestral houses of Israel answered them, "It is not your responsibility to build with us a house for our God, but we alone must build it for the LORD, the God of Israel, as Cyrus king of Persia has commanded us." [4] Thereupon the local inhabitants† discouraged the people of Judah and frightened them off from building. [5] They also bribed counselors to work against them and to frustrate their plans during all the years of Cyrus, king of Persia, and even into the reign of Darius,† king of Persia.

**Later Hostility.** [6] In the reign of Ahasuerus,† at the beginning of his reign, they prepared a written accusation against the inhabitants of Judah and Jerusalem.

[7]† Again, in the time of Artaxerxes, Tabeel and the rest of his fellow officials, in concert with Mithredath, wrote to Artaxerxes, king of Persia. The document was written in Aramaic and was accompanied by a translation.

[8]† Then Rehum, the governor, and Shimshai, the scribe, wrote the following letter against Jerusalem to King Artaxerxes: [9] "Rehum, the governor, Shimshai, the scribe, and their fellow officials, judges, legates, and agents from among the Persians, Urukians, Babylonians, Susians (that is, Elamites), [10] and the other peoples whom the great and illustrious Osnappar† transported and settled in the city of Samaria and elsewhere in the province West-of-Euphrates, as follows… ." [11] This is a copy of the letter that they sent to him:

"To King Artaxerxes, your servants, the men of West-of-Euphrates, as follows: [12] Let it be known to the king that the Jews who came up from you to us have arrived at Jerusalem and are now rebuilding this rebellious and evil city. They are completing its walls, and the foundations have already been laid. [13] Now let it be known to the king that if this city is rebuilt and its walls completed, they will no longer pay taxes, tributes, or tolls; eventually the throne will be harmed. [14] Now, since we eat the salt of the palace† and it is not fitting for us to look on while the king is being dishonored, we have sent this message to inform the king, [15] so that inquiry may be made in the historical records of your fathers. In the historical records you will discover and verify that this is a rebellious city, harmful to kings and provinces; its people have been acting seditiously there since ancient times. That is why this city was destroyed. [16] We therefore inform the king, that if this city is rebuilt and its walls completed again, you will thereupon not have a portion in the province West-of-Euphrates."

[17] The king sent this answer: "To Rehum, the governor, Shimshai, the scribe, and their fellow officials living in Samaria and elsewhere in the province West-of-Euphrates, greetings: [18] The communication which you sent us has been read in translation in my presence. [19] When at my command inquiry was made, it was verified that from ancient times this city has risen up against kings and that rebellion and sedition have been fostered there. [20] Powerful kings once ruled in Jerusalem who controlled all West-of-Euphrates, and taxes, tributes, and tolls were paid to them. [21] Give orders, therefore, to stop these men. This city may not be rebuilt until a further decree has been issued by me. [22] Take care that you do not neglect this matter. Why should evil increase to harm the throne?"

[23]* As soon as a copy of King Artaxerxes' letter had been read before Rehum, the governor,

---

† **4:2** *Esarhaddon, king of Assyria*: the enemies represent themselves as descendants of foreigners forcibly resettled in the Samaria region after the incorporation of the Northern Kingdom into the Assyrian empire (722 B.C.; cf. 2 Kgs 17:24). We have no record of a settlement under Esarhaddon (681–669 B.C.); the Aramaic source (Ezr 4:10) refers to a different resettlement under Osnappar/Ashurbanipal (668–627 B.C.).

**4:4** *Local inhabitants*: lit., "the people of the land."

**4:5** *Darius*: Darius I (522–486 B.C.). The Temple-building narrative continues in v. 24. In between (vv. 6–23) is a series of notices about opposition to the returned exiles voiced at the Persian court in the early fifth century B.C., after the Temple had been built.

**4:6** *Ahasuerus*: Xerxes (486–465 B.C.); the early years of his reign were occupied with revolts in several parts of the empire.

**4:7** There is a note placed in the original text to indicate a change from Hebrew to Aramaic. The Aramaic section beginning here ends with 6:18; in 7:12–26 a royal letter is cited in Aramaic.

**4:8–23** The letter to Artaxerxes I (465–424 B.C.) deals with the building of the fortification walls of Jerusalem, not the building of the Temple. The interruption of the work on the city wall some time before 445 B.C. was the occasion for the arrival of Nehemiah in the province (Neh 1:1–4; 2:1–5).

**4:10** *Osnappar*: probably Ashurbanipal; see note on 4:2.

**4:14** *Eat the salt of the palace*: the idiom signifies sharing in the benefits of the palace.

---

**4:2** Ezr 4:10.     **4:23** Neh 1:3.

Shimshai, the scribe, and their fellow officials, they immediately went to the Jews in Jerusalem and stopped their work by force of arms. 24 As a result, work on the house of God in Jerusalem ceased. This interruption lasted until the second year of the reign of Darius,† king of Persia.

# 5 The Work Resumed Under Darius; Further Problems.

1* Then the prophets Haggai and Zechariah,† son of Iddo, began to prophesy to the Jews in Judah and Jerusalem in the name of the God of Israel. 2 Thereupon Zerubbabel, son of Shealtiel, and Jeshua, son of Jozadak, began again to build the house of God in Jerusalem, with the prophets of God giving them support. 3 At that time Tattenai, governor of West-of-Euphrates, came to them, along with Shethar-bozenai, and their fellow officials, and asked of them: "Who issued the decree for you to build this house and complete this edifice? 4 What are the names of the men who are building this structure?" 5 But the eye of their God was upon the elders of the Jews, and they were not delayed during the time a report went to Darius and a written order came back concerning this matter.

6 A copy of the letter which Tattenai, governor of West-of-Euphrates, along with Shethar-bozenai and their fellow officials from West-of-Euphrates, sent to King Darius; 7 they sent him a report in which was written the following:

"To King Darius, all good wishes! 8 Let it be known to the king that we have visited the province of Judah and the house of the great God: it is being rebuilt of cut stone and the walls are being reinforced with timber; the work is being carried out diligently, prospering under their hands. 9 We then questioned the elders, addressing to them the following words: 'Who issued the decree for you to build this house and complete this edifice?' 10 We also asked them their names, in order to give you a list of the men who are their leaders. 11 This was their answer to us: 'We are the servants of the God of heaven and earth, and we are rebuilding the house built here many years ago, which a great king of Israel built and completed. 12 But because our ancestors provoked the wrath of the God of heaven, he delivered them into the power of the Chaldean, Nebuchadnezzar, king of Babylon, who destroyed this house and exiled the people to Babylon. 13* However, in the first year of Cyrus, king of Babylon, King Cyrus issued a decree for the rebuilding of this house of God. 14 Moreover, the gold and silver vessels of the house of God, which Nebuchadnezzar had taken from the temple in Jerusalem and carried off to the temple in Babylon, King Cyrus ordered to be removed from the temple in Babylon, and they were given to a certain Sheshbazzar, whom he named governor. 15 He commanded him: Take these vessels and deposit them in the temple of Jerusalem, and let the house of God be rebuilt on its former site. 16 Then this same Sheshbazzar came and laid the foundations of the house of God in Jerusalem. Since that time to the present the building has been going on, and is not yet completed.' 17 Now, if it please the king, let a search be made in the royal archives of Babylon to discover whether a decree really was issued by King Cyrus for the rebuilding of this house of God in Jerusalem. And may the king's decision in this matter be communicated to us."

# 6 The Decree of Darius.

1† Thereupon King Darius issued an order to search the archives in which the treasures were stored in Babylon. 2* However, a scroll was found in Ecbatana, the stronghold in the province of Media, containing the following text: "Memorandum. 3 In the first year of his reign, King Cyrus issued a decree: With regard to the house of God in Jerusalem: the house is to be rebuilt as a place for offering sacrifices and bringing burnt offerings. Its height is to be sixty cubits and its width sixty cubits. 4 It shall have three courses of cut stone for each one of timber. The costs are to be borne by the royal house. 5 Also, let the gold and silver vessels of the house of God which Nebuchadnezzar took

---

† 4:24 *The second year ... of Darius:* that is, 520 B.C.; it marks the beginning of the successful restoration of the Temple, completed within the five years following (5:1–6:18).

5:1 *The prophets Haggai and Zechariah:* Haggai and Zechariah were active during the early years of Darius I. They document the rebuilding of the Temple and the messianic expectations associated with the Davidic descendant Zerubbabel.

6:1–2 Babylon was the capital city of the satrapy to which Judah belonged; it was therefore the natural place to look. The decree was discovered eventually, however, in Ecbatana (Hamadan), the former capital of the Medes and summer residence of the Persian kings. Cf. the Hebrew version of the decree (1:2–4).

* 5:1 Hg 1:14–2:9; Zec 4:9.      6:2 Ezr 1:4–11.
  5:13 Ezr 1:1–5.

from the temple of Jerusalem and brought to Babylon be sent back; let them be returned to their place in the temple of Jerusalem and deposited in the house of God."

⁶"Now, therefore, Tattenai, governor of West-of-Euphrates, and Shethar-bozenai, and you, their fellow officials in West-of-Euphrates, stay away from there. ⁷Let the governor and the elders of the Jews continue the work on that house of God; they are to rebuild it on its former site. ⁸I also issue this decree concerning your dealing with these elders of the Jews in the rebuilding of that house of God: Let these men be repaid for their expenses, in full and without delay from the royal revenue, deriving from the taxes of West-of-Euphrates, so that the work not be interrupted. ⁹Whatever else is required—young bulls, rams, and lambs for burnt offerings to the God of heaven, wheat, salt, wine, and oil, according to the requirements of the priests who are in Jerusalem—let that be delivered to them day by day without fail, ¹⁰that they may continue to offer sacrifices of pleasing odor to the God of heaven and pray for the life of the king and his sons. ¹¹I also issue this decree: if any man alters this edict, a beam is to be taken from his house, and he is to be lifted up and impaled on it; and his house is to be reduced to rubble for this offense. ¹²And may the God who causes his name to dwell there overthrow every king or people who may undertake to alter this decree or to destroy this house of God in Jerusalem. I, Darius, have issued this decree; let it be diligently executed."

**The Task Finally Completed.** ¹³Then Tattenai, the governor of West-of-Euphrates, and Shethar-bozenai, and their fellow officials carried out with all diligence the instructions King Darius had sent them. ¹⁴The elders of the Jews continued to make progress in the building, supported by the message of the prophets, Haggai and Zechariah, son of Iddo. They finished the building according to the command of the God of Israel and the decrees

of Cyrus and Darius, and of Artaxerxes, king of Persia. ¹⁵They completed this house on the third day of the month Adar, in the sixth year of the reign of King Darius. ¹⁶The Israelites—priests, Levites, and the other returned exiles—celebrated the dedication of this house of God with joy. ¹⁷For the dedication of this house of God, they offered one hundred bulls, two hundred rams, and four hundred lambs, together with twelve he-goats as a sin offering for all Israel, in keeping with the number of the tribes of Israel. ¹⁸Finally, they set up the priests in their classes and the Levites in their divisions for the service of God in Jerusalem, as is prescribed in the book of Moses.

**The Passover.** ¹⁹* The returned exiles kept the Passover on the fourteenth day of the first month. ²⁰The Levites, every one of whom had purified himself for the occasion, sacrificed the Passover for all the exiles, for their colleagues the priests, and for themselves. ²¹The Israelites who had returned from the exile and all those who had separated themselves from the uncleanness of the Gentiles in the land shared in it, seeking the LORD, the God of Israel. ²²* They joyfully kept the feast of Unleavened Bread for seven days, for the LORD had filled them with joy by making the king of Assyria† favorable to them, so that he gave them help in their work on the house of God, the God of Israel.

## II. THE WORK OF EZRA

**7** **Ezra, Priest and Scribe.** ¹†* After these events, during the reign of Artaxerxes, king of Persia, Ezra, son of Seraiah, son of Azariah, son of Hilkiah, ²son of Shallum, son of Zadok, son of Ahitub, ³son of Amariah, son of Azariah, son of Meraioth, ⁴son of Zerahiah, son of Uzzi, son of Bukki, ⁵son of Abishua, son of Phinehas, son of Eleazar, son of Aaron, the high priest— ⁶* this Ezra came up from Babylon. He was a scribe, well-versed in the law of Moses given by the LORD, the God of Israel. The king granted him all that he requested,

---

† **6:22** *The king of Assyria*: "Assyria" is perhaps used in a broad sense for the Persian empire; or the editor may have in mind the account of Hezekiah's Passover which refers to those who had escaped the hand of the king of Assyria (2 Chr 30:6).

**7:1–10** The editor's introduction to Ezra's autobiographical narrative. The context suggests the seventh year of Artaxerxes I, therefore, 458 B.C., as the date of Ezra's arrival in Jerusalem. The arguments often advanced for 398 B.C., the seventh year of Artaxerxes II, or less often for the thirty-seventh year of Artaxerxes I,

that is, 428 B.C., are inconclusive. For Ezra's descent from Aaron, the editor has drawn selectively on 1 Chr 5:27–41. Seraiah, the chief priest executed by the Babylonians after the fall of Jerusalem (2 Kgs 25:18–21), cannot be Ezra's father in a literal sense, and Ezra was not himself high priest.

---

**6:19** Ex 12:1–20; 2 Chr 30:14–27; 35:1–19.  
**6:22** 2 Chr 30:6.  

**7:1** 1 Chr 5:27–41.  
**7:6** Ezr 7:28; 8:18; Neh 2:8, 18.

because the hand of the Lord, his God, was over him.

[7] Some of the Israelites and some priests, Levites, singers, gatekeepers, and temple servants also came up to Jerusalem in the seventh year of King Artaxerxes. [8] Ezra came to Jerusalem in the fifth month of that seventh year of the king. [9] On the first day of the first month he began the journey up from Babylon, and on the first day of the fifth month he arrived at Jerusalem, for the favoring hand of his God was over him. [10]* Ezra had set his heart on the study and practice of the law of the Lord and on teaching statutes and ordinances in Israel.

**The Decree of Artaxerxes.** [11] This is a copy of the rescript which King Artaxerxes gave to Ezra the priest-scribe, the scribe versed in matters concerning the Lord's commandments and statutes for Israel:

[12]* "Artaxerxes, king of kings, to Ezra the priest, scribe of the law of the God of heaven, greetings! And now, [13] I have issued this decree, that anyone in my kingdom belonging to the people of Israel, its priests or Levites, who is willing to go up to Jerusalem with you, may go, [14] for you are the one sent by the king and his seven counselors to supervise Judah and Jerusalem with regard to the law of your God which is in your possession, [15] and to bring the silver and gold which the king and his counselors have freely contributed to the God of Israel, whose dwelling is in Jerusalem, [16] as well as all the silver and gold which you may receive throughout the province of Babylon, together with the voluntary offerings the people and priests freely contribute for the house of their God in Jerusalem. [17] Therefore, you must use this money with all diligence to buy bulls, rams, lambs, and the grain offerings and libations proper to these, and offer them on the altar of the house of your God in Jerusalem. [18] You and your kinsmen may do whatever seems best to you with the remainder of the silver and gold, as your God wills. [19] The vessels given to you for the service of the house of your God you are to deposit before the God of Jerusalem. [20] Whatever else you may be

required to supply for the needs of the house of your God, you may draw from the royal treasury. [21] I, Artaxerxes the king, issue this decree to all the treasurers of West-of-Euphrates: Whatever Ezra the priest, scribe of the law of the God of heaven, requests of you, let it be done with all diligence, [22] within these limits: silver, one hundred talents; wheat, one hundred kors;† wine, one hundred baths; oil, one hundred baths; salt, without limit. [23] Let everything that is decreed by the God of heaven be carried out exactly for the house of the God of heaven, that wrath may not come upon the realm of the king and his sons. [24] We also inform you that it is not permitted to impose taxes, tributes, or tolls on any priest, Levite, singer, gatekeeper, temple servant, or any other servant of that house of God.

[25]* "As for you, Ezra, in accordance with the wisdom of your God† which is in your possession, appoint magistrates and judges to administer justice to all the people in West-of-Euphrates, to all, that is, who know the laws of your God. Instruct those who do not know these laws. [26] All who will not obey the law of your God and the law of the king, let judgment be executed upon them with all diligence, whether death, or corporal punishment, or confiscation of goods, or imprisonment."

**Ezra Prepares for the Journey.** [27] Blessed be the Lord, the God of our ancestors, who put it into the heart of the king thus to glorify the house of the Lord in Jerusalem, [28]* and who let me find favor with the king, with his counselors, and with all the most influential royal officials. I therefore took courage and, with the hand of the Lord, my God, over me, I gathered together Israelite leaders to make the return journey with me.

**8 Ezra's Caravan.** [1] These are the heads of the ancestral houses and the genealogies of those who returned with me from Babylon during the reign of King Artaxerxes: [2] Of the descendants of Phinehas, Gershon; of the descendants of Ithamar, Daniel; of the

---

† **7:22** *Kors:* see note on Ez 45:14; *baths:* see note on Is 5:10.
**7:25** *The wisdom of your God:* with reference to the law (cf. Dt 4:6). The law in question was certainly not new, since it was assumed to be known by Jews in Judah and elsewhere. It corresponded to Pentateuchal law, though perhaps this had not yet been given its final form.

**7:10** Ps 119:45.
**7:12** Ezr 1:2–4.
**7:25** Dt 4:6; 2 Chr 17:7–9; Ps 37:30–31; 119:98.
**7:28** Ezr 7:6.

descendants of David, Hattush, [3] son of Shecaniah; of the descendants of Parosh, Zechariah, and with him one hundred and fifty males were enrolled; [4] of the descendants of Pahath-moab, Eliehoenai, son of Zerahiah, and with him two hundred males; [5] of the descendants of Zattu, Shecaniah, son of Jahaziel, and with him three hundred males; [6] of the descendants of Adin, Ebed, son of Jonathan, and with him fifty males; [7] of the descendants of Elam, Jeshaiah, son of Athaliah, and with him seventy males; [8] of the descendants of Shephatiah, Zebadiah, son of Michael, and with him eighty males; [9] of the descendants of Joab, Obadiah, son of Jehiel, and with him two hundred and eighteen males; [10] of the descendants of Bani, Shelomoth, son of Josiphiah, and with him one hundred and sixty males; [11] of the descendants of Bebai, Zechariah, son of Bebai, and with him twenty-eight males; [12] of the descendants of Azgad, Johanan, son of Hakkatan, and with him one hundred and ten males; [13] of the descendants of Adonikam, younger sons, whose names were Eliphelet, Jeiel, and Shemaiah, and with them sixty males; [14] of the descendants of Bigvai, Uthai, son of Zakkur, and with him seventy males.

**Final Preparations for the Journey.** [15] I assembled them by the river that flows toward Ahava,† where we camped for three days. There I perceived that both laymen and priests were present, but I could not discover a single Levite. [16] So I sent for discerning leaders, Eliezer, Ariel, Shemaiah, Jarib, Elnathan, Nathan, Zechariah, and Meshullam, [17] with a command for Iddo, the leader in the place Casiphia, instructing them what to say to Iddo and his kinsmen, and to the temple servants in Casiphia, in order to procure for us ministers for the house of our God. [18]* Since the favoring hand of our God was over us, they sent to us a well-instructed man, one of the descendants of Mahli, son of Levi, son of Israel, namely Sherebiah, with his sons and kinsmen, eighteen men. [19] They also sent us Hashabiah, and with him Jeshaiah, descendants of Merari, and their kinsmen and their sons, twenty men. [20]* Of the temple servants, those whom David

and the princes appointed to serve the Levites, there were two hundred and twenty. All these were enrolled by name.

[21] Then I proclaimed a fast, there by the river of Ahava, that we might humble ourselves before our God to seek from him a safe journey for ourselves, our children, and all our possessions. [22]* For I was ashamed to ask the king for troops and horsemen to protect us against enemies along the way, since we had said to the king, "The favoring hand of our God is over all who seek him, but his fierce anger is against all who forsake him." [23] So we fasted, seeking this from our God, and it was granted. [24] Next I selected twelve of the priestly leaders along with Sherebiah, Hashabiah, and ten of their kinsmen, [25] and I weighed out before them the silver and the gold and the vessels offered for the house of our God by the king, his counselors, his officials, and all the Israelites of that region. [26] I weighed out into their hands these amounts: silver, six hundred and fifty talents; silver vessels, one hundred; gold, one hundred talents; [27] twenty golden bowls valued at a thousand darics; two vases of excellent polished bronze, as precious as gold. [28] I addressed them in these words: "You are consecrated to the Lord, and the vessels are also consecrated; the silver and the gold are a voluntary offering to the Lord, the God of your ancestors. [29] Watch over them carefully until you weigh them out in Jerusalem in the presence of the chief priests and Levites and the leaders of ancestral houses of Israel, in the chambers of the house of the Lord." [30] The priests and the Levites then took over the silver, the gold, and the vessels that had been weighed out, to bring them to Jerusalem, to the house of our God.

**Arrival in Jerusalem.** [31] We set out from the river of Ahava on the twelfth day of the first month to go to Jerusalem. The hand of our God remained over us, and he protected us from enemies and robbers along the way. [32] We arrived in Jerusalem, where we rested for three days. [33] On the fourth day, the silver, the gold, and the vessels were weighed out in the house of our God and given to the priest

---

† **8:15** *Ahava*: an unidentified location near Babylon; also the name of the river or canal on which it stood (vv. 21, 31). A location near water was dictated by ritual as well as practical reasons (cf. Ps 137:1; Ez 1:1, 3; 3:15).

**8:18** Ezr 7:6.          **8:22** Neh 2:9.
**8:20** Ezr 2:43.

Meremoth, son of Uriah, with whom was Eleazar, son of Phinehas; they were assisted by the Levites Jozabad, son of Jeshua, and Noadiah, son of Binnui. [34] Everything was in order as to number and weight, and the total weight was registered. At that same time, [35] those who had returned from the captivity, the exiles, offered as burnt offerings to the God of Israel twelve bulls for all Israel, ninety-six rams, seventy-seven lambs, and twelve goats as sin offerings: all these as a burnt offering to the LORD. [36]† Finally, the orders of the king were presented to the king's satraps and to the governors in West-of-Euphrates, who gave their support to the people and to the house of God.

# 9 The Crisis of Mixed Marriages.

[1]* When these matters had been concluded, the leaders approached me with this report: "Neither the Israelite laymen nor the priests nor the Levites have kept themselves separate from the peoples of the lands and their abominations—Canaanites, Hittites, Perizzites, Jebusites, Ammonites, Moabites, Egyptians, and Amorites— [2] for they have taken some of their daughters as wives for themselves and their sons, thus intermingling the holy seed with the peoples of the lands. Furthermore, the leaders and rulers have taken a prominent part in this apostasy!"

**Ezra's Reaction.** [3]* When I had heard this, I tore my cloak and my mantle, plucked hair from my head and beard, and sat there devastated. [4]* Around me gathered all who were in dread of the sentence of the God of Israel† on the apostasy of the exiles, while I remained devastated until the evening sacrifice. [5] Then, at the time of the evening sacrifice, I rose in my wretchedness, and with cloak and mantle torn I fell on my knees, stretching out my hands to the LORD, my God.

**A Penitential Prayer.** [6]†* I said: "My God, I am too ashamed and humiliated to raise my face to you, my God, for our wicked deeds are heaped up above our heads and our guilt reaches up to heaven. [7] From the time of our ancestors even to this day our guilt has been great, and for our wicked deeds we have been delivered, we and our kings and our priests, into the hands of the kings of foreign lands, to the sword, to captivity, to pillage, and to disgrace, as is the case today.

[8]* "And now, only a short time ago, mercy came to us from the LORD, our God, who left us a remnant and gave us a stake in his holy place; thus our God has brightened our eyes and given us relief in our slavery. [9]* For slaves we are, but in our slavery our God has not abandoned us; rather, he has turned the good will of the kings of Persia toward us. Thus he has given us new life to raise again the house of our God and restore its ruins, and has granted us a protective wall in Judah and Jerusalem. [10] But now, our God, what can we say after all this? For we have abandoned your commandments, [11]* which you gave through your servants the prophets: The land which you are entering to take as your possession is a land unclean with the filth of the peoples of the lands, with the abominations with which they have filled it from one end to the other by their uncleanness. [12]* Do not, then, give your daughters to their sons in marriage, and do not take their daughters for your sons. Never promote their welfare and prosperity; thus you will grow strong, enjoy the produce of the land, and leave it as an inheritance to your children forever.

[13] "After all that has come upon us for our evil deeds and our great guilt—though you, our God, have made less of our sinfulness than it deserved and have allowed us to survive as we do— [14] shall we again violate your commandments by intermarrying with these abominable peoples? Would you not become so angered with us as to destroy us without remnant or survivor? [15] LORD, God of Israel, you are just; yet we have been spared, the remnant we are today. Here we are before you in our sins. Because of all this, we can no longer stand in your presence."

---

† **8:36** The story of Ezra's mission is apparently continued from this point by Neh 7:72b–8:18, which may be read before Ezr 9:1.

**9:4** *All who were in dread … God of Israel:* lit., "all who trembled"; these people are also mentioned at 10:3, and a similar designation occurs at Is 66:2, 5, a text more or less contemporary with this passage. The allusion may be to a distinct social group of rigorist tendencies who supported Ezra's marriage reform.

**9:6–15** The prayer attributed to Ezra is a communal confession of sin, of a kind characteristic of the Second Temple period (cf. Neh 9:6–37; Dn 9:4–19; 1QS 1:4–2:1), but adapted to the present situation.

* **9:1** Dt 7:1; Neh 9:2.  **9:8** Is 4:3.
**9:3** Ps 119:136.  **9:9** Ps 106:46.
**9:4** Ezr 10:3; Is 66:2, 5.  **9:11** Lv 18:24–25; Ez
**9:6** Neh 9:6–37; Ps 38:4;  36:17.
Dn 9:4–19.  **9:12** Dt 7:3.

# 10

**Response to the Crisis.** [1]While Ezra prayed and acknowledged their guilt, weeping and prostrate before the house of God, a very large assembly of Israelites gathered about him, men, women, and children; and the people wept profusely. [2]Then Shecaniah, the son of Jehiel, one of the descendants of Elam, made this appeal to Ezra: "We have indeed betrayed our God by taking as wives foreign women of the peoples of the land. Yet in spite of this there still remains a hope for Israel. [3]Let us therefore enter into a covenant before our God to dismiss all our foreign wives and the children born of them, in keeping with what you, my lord, advise, and those who are in dread of the commandments of our God. Let it be done according to the law! [4]Rise, then, for this is your duty! We are with you, so have courage and act!"

[5]Ezra stood and demanded an oath from the leaders of the priests, from the Levites and from all Israel that they would do as had been proposed; and they swore it. [6]Then Ezra left his place before the house of God and entered the chamber of Johanan, son of Eliashib,† where he spent the night neither eating food nor drinking water, for he was in mourning over the apostasy of the exiles. [7]A proclamation was made throughout Judah and Jerusalem that all the exiles should gather together in Jerusalem, [8]and that whoever failed to appear within three days would, according to the judgment of the leaders and elders, suffer the confiscation of all his possessions, and would be excluded from the assembly of the exiles.

[9]All the men of Judah and Benjamin gathered together in Jerusalem within the three-day period: it was in the ninth month,† on the twentieth day of the month. All the people, sitting in the open place before the house of God, were trembling both over the matter at hand and because it was raining. [10]*Then Ezra, the priest, stood up and said to them: "Your apostasy in taking foreign women as wives has added to Israel's guilt. [11]But now, give praise to the LORD, the God of your ancestors, and do his will: separate yourselves from the peoples of the land and from the foreign women." [12]In answer, the whole assembly cried out with a loud voice: "Yes, it is our duty to do as you say! [13]But the people are numerous and it is the rainy season, so that we cannot remain outside; besides, this is not a task that can be performed in a single day or even two, for those of us who have sinned in this regard are many. [14]Let our leaders represent the whole assembly; then let all those in our cities who have taken foreign women for wives appear at appointed times, accompanied by the elders and magistrates of each city in question, till we have turned away from us our God's burning anger over this affair." [15]Only Jonathan, son of Asahel, and Jahzeiah, son of Tikvah, were against this proposal, with Meshullam and Shabbethai the Levite supporting them.

[16]† The exiles did as agreed. Ezra the priest appointed as his assistants men who were heads of ancestral houses, one for each ancestral house, all of them designated by name. They held sessions to examine the matter, beginning with the first day of the tenth month. [17]By the first day of the first month they had finished dealing with all the men who had taken foreign women for wives.

**The List of Transgressors.** [18]Among the priests, the following were found to have taken foreign women for wives: Of the descendants of Jeshua, son of Jozadak, and his kinsmen: Maaseiah, Eliezer, Jarib, and Gedaliah. [19]They pledged themselves to dismiss their wives, and as a guilt offering for their guilt they gave a ram from the flock. [20]Of the descendants of Immer: Hanani and Zebadiah; [21]of the descendants of Harim: Maaseiah, Elijah, Shemaiah, Jehiel, and Uzziah; [22]of the descendants of Pashhur: Elioenai, Maaseiah, Ishmael, Nethanel, Jozabad, and Elasah.

[23]* Of the Levites: Jozabad, Shimei, Kelaiah (also called Kelita), Pethahiah, Judah, and Eliezer.

---

† **10:6** *Johanan, son of Eliashib:* if this Eliashib is identical with the high priest of that name during Nehemiah's mission (Neh 3:1), it would be difficult to avoid the conclusion that Ezra followed Nehemiah. But Eliashib is a common name, and, on the hypothesis of Nehemiah's chronological priority, it would be unlikely that Ezra would consort with a family which had "defiled the priesthood" (Neh 13:28–29).
**10:9** *The ninth month:* Kislev (November–December), during the first of two rainy seasons in Palestine.
**10:16–17** The work of the committee lasted three months, from the first day of the tenth month, Tebeth (December–January), to the first day of the first month, Nisan (March–April), of the following year.

**10:10** Neh 9:2.    **10:23** Neh 8:7; 10:11.

24 Of the singers: Eliashib; of the gatekeepers: Shallum, Telem, and Uri.

25 Of the people of Israel: Of the descendants of Parosh: Ramiah, Izziah, Malchijah, Mijamin, Eleazar, Malchijah, and Benaiah; 26 of the descendants of Elam: Mattaniah, Zechariah, Jehiel, Abdi, Jeremoth, and Elijah; 27 of the descendants of Zattu: Elioenai, Eliashib, Mattaniah, Jeremoth, Zabad, and Aziza; 28 of the descendants of Bebai: Jehohanan, Hananiah, Zabbai, and Athlai; 29 of the descendants of Bani: Meshullam, Malluch, Adaiah, Jashub, Sheal, and Jeremoth; 30 of the descendants of Pahath-moab: Adna, Chelal, Benaiah, Maaseiah, Mattaniah, Bezalel, Binnui, and Manasseh; 31 of the descendants of Harim: Eliezer, Isshijah, Malchijah, Shemaiah, Shimeon, 32 Benjamin, Malluch, Shemariah; 33 of the descendants of Hashum: Mattenai, Mattattah, Zabad, Eliphelet, Jeremai, Manasseh, Shimei; 34 of the descendants of Begui: Maadai, Amram, Uel, 35 Benaiah, Bedeiah, Cheluhi, 36 Vaniah, Meremoth, Eliashib, 37 Mattaniah, Mattenai, and Jaasu; 38 of the descendants of Binnui: Shimei, 39 Shelemiah, Nathan, and Adaiah; 40 of the descendants of Zachai: Shashai, Sharai, 41 Azarel, Shelemiah, Shemariah, 42 Shallum, Amariah, Joseph; 43 of the descendants of Nebo: Jeiel, Mattithiah, Zabad, Zebina, Jaddai, Joel, Benaiah.

44 † All these had taken foreign wives; but they sent them away, both the women and their children.

---

† **10:44** Some scholars find the continuation of the account of the marriage reform in Neh 9:1–5, though the date given at Neh 9:1 would fit better after Ezr 10:15; cf. Hg 2:10–14. The abrupt conclusion to Ezr 9–10 suggests that the policy of forced separation from foreign wives, not mandated by any law known to us, did not succeed. Assuming the chronological priority of Ezra, marriage outside the community was still prevalent during Nehemiah's administration, and the remarkable demographic expansion of Judaism in the following centuries would be difficult to explain if Ezra's measures had been put into effect.

# The Book of

# Nehemiah

## INTRODUCTION

### Leslie J. Hoppe, OFM

The book of Nehemiah focuses its attention primarily on the political and administrative side of the Judean restoration. As such, it complements the book of Ezra, which focuses on the restoration's religious aspects. One notable difference between the two books is that the opening verse of this book leaves the reader with the impression that it is the product of Nehemiah himself. Indeed, a significant portion of the book is written in the first person: Neh 1:1–7:5; 12:31–43; 13:4–31. Interpreters have called these passages the "memoirs" of Nehemiah. The book of Ezra also contains a passage in the first person: Ezr 8:15–9:15. The book of Nehemiah presents Nehemiah in the most positive light possible in order to support a particular approach to the restoration. While the book cannot be used to reconstruct the history of Judah in the Persian period (539–333 BCE) without special care, it does shed some light on the challenges faced by the people of Judah in reconstituting their social, economic, political, and religious life following the end of the exile.

The book of Nehemiah presents both Ezra and Nehemiah as responding to some of the difficulties faced by the people of Judah during the Persian period. The political institutions that gave the people of Judah an identity were long gone. In the view of some, marriage outside the Jewish community undermined the community's integrity. Finally, Jerusalem's citizens were subject to marauders because the city's protective wall was in ruins. The morale of the people of Judah was at its nadir when Nehemiah began his mission.

Both Ezra and Nehemiah present the Persians in a positive light. They do not claim Davidic ancestry for either Sheshbazzar or Zerubbabel, nor do they propose a restoration of the native Judahite dynasty or state. Both

## Outline of Nehemiah

I. **The Deeds of Nehemiah (1:1–7:72)**

II. **Promulgation of the Law (8:1–10:40)**

III. **Dedication of the Wall; Other Reforms (11:1–13:31)**

books carefully circumscribe the restoration to the religious and social dimension of Judah's life. They appear to be content with maintaining the political status quo and certainly do not encourage the people of Judah to engage in any activity that could signal their desire to end Persian hegemony. Though Nehemiah's goal was the restoration of Judean society, his plans did not involve a rejection of Persian rule. On the contrary, he began his mission with the permission and support of Artaxerxes I, in whose court he served (Neh 1:11b).

The precise date of Nehemiah's mission is still debated (see the initial introduction to the book of Ezra). What follows assumes that Nehemiah's mission preceded that of Ezra and began in 445 BCE during the reign of Artaxerxes I (Neh 2:1). Nehemiah heard of the deplorable conditions in Jerusalem and approached the king for authority to do something to ameliorate the situation. There was opposition to Nehemiah's mission from the political leaders of territories surrounding Judah (4:1–3). They had an interest in keeping Judah politically and especially economically weak. Nehemiah was not deterred by this opposition and managed to complete the rebuilding of Jerusalem's walls (6:15). In addition, he ensured that people who needed financial help received it without having to pay exorbitant interest rates (5:1–13).

He did not demand that the people supply him and his associates with a food allowance. On the contrary, he fed the poor out of his own resources (5:14–19). After increasing the safety of the city's citizens by rebuilding the city wall and after dealing with some of their economic problems, Nehemiah began efforts to increase the city's population. He looked to those returning from the exile since he regarded them as the true Israel (7:5–72).

The book of Nehemiah tells the story of a most significant event in the life of Judah: Ezra's reading of the Torah at the Water Gate (Neh 8:1). What led up to this event reflected the Persian practice of allowing the various peoples of their vast empire to govern themselves according to their own legal traditions and practices as long as these did not threaten Persian rule. The Torah that Ezra read to the people became imperial law for Judah. While this certainly helped the people of Judah accept Persian rule, deterring them from the kind of rebellious activity that ultimately led to the end of the Judahite national state and the Davidic dynasty, it also had a profound effect on the transformation of the religion of ancient Israel into the religion of early Judaism. While this transformation had only begun, Ezra's promulgation of the Torah, facilitated by Nehemiah, was a most significant moment in that transformation.

The religion of ancient Israel was a communal, national religion whose goal was securing peace and prosperity for the people and dynasty through the sacrificial worship of Yahweh, the nation's patron deity. The religion of early Judaism became a religion of those Judeans who chose to live by the precepts of the Torah. Obedience to the Torah brought with it the blessings promised to the obedient (Dt 28). This focus on the Torah became the hallmark of early Judaism. This emphasis on the role of the Torah in providing an identity for the people of Judah enabled them to absorb the loss of their national states and native dynasty. Following the unsuccessful revolt against Rome in 70 CE, devotion to the Torah would enable Judaism to survive after the loss of the Temple and its priesthood. Obedience to the written, authoritative Torah became

the identity marker of those who defined themselves as Jews.

The people responded to Ezra's reading of the Torah with a mixture of joy and fear. Ezra assured them that "rejoicing in the LORD" would protect them from experiencing the judgment that comes upon the disobedient (Neh 8:10). The people expressed their commitment to the Torah through study and worship. They pledged to study the Torah as carefully as did Ezra (8:13) and they celebrated the Feast of Sukkot (Booths) in a way that it had not been celebrated since the Israelite tribes first emerged in the land of Canaan (8:17). The combination of study and worship also became another mark of Jewish identity. Torah study became an essential complement to liturgical activity. This commitment to study eventually led to the development of rabbinical academies. Their great achievement was the production of the Talmud centuries later, which remains the focus of Jewish religious study.

The confession of sins (Neh 9) is among the most theologically significant scenes in the book. The people gather for a national day of mourning, the purpose of which was to call upon God's commitment to the covenant that has been manifest throughout Israel's history despite the many instances of infidelity on the part of Judah's ancestors. The confession affirms God's loyalty to Israel and implores God to consider the many difficulties faced by the people of Judah, not the least of which was political and economic oppression. The confession is the one place in the books of Ezra and Nehemiah where the true feelings of the people regarding Persian rule of Judah are given voice with a petition for relief (9:32, 36). The confession is followed by the people's decision to set things aright (ch. 10), with special attention to liturgical matters and mixed marriages.

The books of Ezra and Nehemiah both reflect the belief that marriage within the community is the only way to preserve its integrity (Ezr 10:11; Neh 13:1–3). Mixed marriages are not forbidden unequivocally in the Torah. Indeed, Moses himself was married to women who were not Israelites (Ex 2:15b–22; Nm 12:1). Ezra and Nehemiah were convinced that marriage within the community was necessary to ensure the community's integrity. Ezra and Nehemiah were not the first voices to speak against mixed marriages, however. Deuteronomy forbids intermarriage with the indigenous population of Canaan (Dt 7:3) but permits Israelite soldiers to marry foreign women taken as prisoners of war (Dt 21:10–14). Judges blames the difficulties experienced by the Israelite tribes on mixed marriages (Jgs 3:5–6), while Solomon's fall from grace was caused by his foreign wives (1 Kgs 11:4).

Since Nehemiah's mission was authorized by the Persian authorities and a good portion of the book is written in the first person, one can have the impression that the book is a report that a civil servant writes for his superior. But clearly the superior to whom Nehemiah is reporting is not Artaxerxes but his God, the ancestral deity of the Jews. Nehemiah's "memoirs" reveal a man who is determined that his people and their religion will experience a renascence after a very difficult period in which their continued existence was in doubt. Nehemiah was a man of action who responded to the crisis in Judah as soon as he heard how serious it was. He stood up to those who opposed his work because he was convinced that his mission came from God and would therefore be successful (Neh 2:8). ■

# THE BOOK OF NEHEMIAH

## New American Bible, Introduction

Problems common to the combined books Ezra-Nehemiah have been pointed out in the Introduction to the Book of Ezra. The achievements of the two men were complementary; each helped to make it possible for Judaism to maintain its identity during the difficult days of the Restoration. Ezra was the great religious reformer who succeeded in establishing the Torah as the constitution of the returned community. Nehemiah, governor of the province of Judah, was the man of action who rebuilt the walls of Jerusalem and introduced necessary administrative reforms.

The biblical sources for Nehemiah's life and work are the autobiographical portions scattered through the book. They are called the "Memoirs of Nehemiah," and have been used more effectively by the editor than the "Memoirs of Ezra." The substantial authenticity of Nehemiah's memoirs is widely accepted. From these and other sources, the picture emerges of a man dedicated to the single purpose of the welfare of his people. While serving as cupbearer to the king at the Persian court in Susa, Nehemiah received permission from Artaxerxes I to fortify Jerusalem, and served as governor of Judah for two terms, the first lasting twelve years (445–432 B.C.), the second of unknown length (Neh 5:14; 13:6). Despite temperamental shortcomings, Nehemiah was a man of good practical sense combined with deep faith in God. He used his influence as governor of Judah to serve God and the fledgling Jewish community in Jerusalem.

The Book of Nehemiah is divided as follows:

 I. The Deeds of Nehemiah (1:1–7:72)

 II. Promulgation of the Law (8:1–10:40)

 III. Dedication of the Wall; Other Reforms (11:1–13:31) ■

# NEHEMIAH

## I. THE DEEDS OF NEHEMIAH

**1** **Nehemiah Hears Bad News.** ¹† The words of Nehemiah, son of Hacaliah.

In the month Kislev of the twentieth year, I was in the citadel of Susa ²when Hanani, one of my brothers, came with other men from Judah. I asked them about the Jews, the remnant preserved after the captivity, and about Jerusalem. ³They answered me: "The survivors of the captivity there in the province are in great distress and under reproach. The wall of Jerusalem has been breached, its gates gutted by fire." ⁴When I heard this report, I began to weep and continued mourning for several days, fasting and praying before the God of heaven.

⁵†* I prayed: "LORD, God of heaven, great and awesome God, you preserve your covenant of mercy with those who love you and keep your commandments. ⁶* May your ears be attentive, and your eyes open, to hear the prayer that I, your servant, now offer in your presence day and night for your servants the Israelites, confessing the sins we have committed against you, I and my ancestral house included. ⁷* We have greatly offended you, not keeping the commandments, the statutes, and the ordinances you entrusted to your servant Moses. ⁸* But remember the admonition which you addressed to Moses, your servant, when you said: If you prove faithless, I will scatter you among the peoples; ⁹but if you return to me and carefully keep my commandments, even though your outcasts have been driven to the farthest corner of the world, I will gather them from there, and bring them back to the place I have chosen as the dwelling place for my name. ¹⁰* They are your servants,

your people, whom you freed by your great might and strong hand. ¹¹* LORD, may your ears be attentive to the prayer of your servant and that of all your servants who willingly revere your name. Grant success to your servant this day, and let him find favor with this man"—for I was cupbearer to the king.†

**2** **Appointment by the King.** ¹In the month Nisan of the twentieth year of King Artaxerxes, when the wine was in my charge, I took some and offered it to the king. Because I had never before been sad in his presence, ²the king asked me, "Why do you look sad? If you are not sick, you must be sad at heart." Though I was seized with great fear, ³I answered the king: "May the king live forever! How could I not look sad when the city where my ancestors are buried lies in ruins, and its gates consumed by fire?" ⁴The king asked me, "What is it, then, that you wish?" I prayed to the God of heaven ⁵and then answered the king: "If it please the king, and if your servant is deserving of your favor, send me to Judah, to the city where my ancestors are buried, that I may rebuild it." ⁶Then the king, with the queen seated beside him, asked me, "How long will your journey take and when will you return?" My answer was acceptable to the king and he agreed to let me go; I set a date for my return.

⁷I asked the king further: "If it please the king, let letters be given to me for the governors of West-of-Euphrates, that they may give me safe-conduct till I arrive in Judah; ⁸* also a letter for Asaph, the keeper of the royal woods, that he may give me timber to make beams for the gates of the temple citadel, for the city wall and the house that I will occupy." Since I enjoyed the good favor of my God, the king granted my requests. ⁹* Thus I proceeded to the governors of West-of-Euphrates and presented the king's letters to them. The king also sent with me army officers and cavalry.

¹⁰When Sanballat the Horonite† and Tobiah

---

† **1:1** The first mission of Nehemiah, from the twentieth year of Artaxerxes I, lasted from the spring (2:1) of 445 B.C. until 433 B.C. (5:14). It is recounted in 1:1–6:15; 12:27–43; 6:16–7:5; 11:1–21; in terms of chronology, these texts may usefully be read in that order. *Kislev*: the ninth month (November–December). *Susa*: the winter residence of the Persian kings, in southwest Iran.

**1:5** Nehemiah's prayer is a communal confession of sin, characteristic of Second Temple piety; cf. Ezr 9:6–15; Neh 9:6–37; Dn 9:4–19.

**1:11** *Cupbearer to the king*: an important official in the royal household.

**2:10** *Sanballat the Horonite*: the governor of the province of Samaria (3:33–34), apparently a native of one of the Beth-horons. A letter from the Jews living at Elephantine in southern Egypt, dated 408–407 B.C., mentions "Delayah and Shelemyah, the sons of Sanballat, the governor of Samaria," and papyri discovered in the Wadi ed-Dâliyeh in the Jordan Valley refer to a

*

**1:5** Dt 7:9, 12; Dn 9:4.
**1:6** 2 Chr 6:40.
**1:7** Dn 3:29–30.
**1:8** Dt 30:1–5.
**1:10** Dt 9:29.
**1:11** Ps 118:25.
**2:8** Ezr 7:6.
**2:9** Ezr 8:22.

the Ammonite official had heard of this, they were very much displeased that someone had come to improve the lot of the Israelites.

**Circuit of the City.** [11]* When I arrived in Jerusalem, and had been there three days, [12] I set out by night with only a few other men and with no other animals but my own mount (for I had not told anyone what my God had inspired me to do for Jerusalem). [13]† I rode out at night by the Valley Gate, passed by the Dragon Spring, and came to the Dung Gate, observing how the walls of Jerusalem were breached and its gates consumed by fire. [14] Then I passed over to the Fountain Gate and to the King's Pool. Since there was no room here for my mount to pass with me astride, [15] I continued on foot up the wadi by night, inspecting the wall all the while, until I once more reached the Valley Gate, by which I went back in. [16] The magistrates knew nothing of where I had gone or what I was doing, for as yet I had disclosed nothing to the Jews, neither to the priests, nor to the nobles, nor to the magistrates, nor to the others who were to do the work.

**Decision to Rebuild the City Wall.** [17] Afterward I said to them: "You see the trouble we are in: how Jerusalem lies in ruins and its gates have been gutted by fire. Come, let us rebuild the wall of Jerusalem, so that we may no longer be a reproach!" [18]* Then I explained to them how God had shown his gracious favor to me, and what the king had said to me. They replied, "Let us begin building!" And they undertook the work with vigor.

[19] When they heard about this, Sanballat the Horonite, Tobiah the Ammonite official, and Geshem the Arab† mocked and ridiculed us. "What are you doing?" they asked. "Are you rebelling against the king?" [20] My answer to them was this: "It is the God of heaven who will grant us success. We, his servants, shall set about the rebuilding; but you have neither share nor claim nor memorial† in Jerusalem."

**3** **List of Workers.** [1]†* Eliashib the high priest and his priestly kinsmen took up the task of rebuilding the Sheep Gate. They consecrated it and set up its doors, its bolts, and its bars, then continued the rebuilding to the Tower of the Hundred, the Tower of Hananel. [2] At their side the men of Jericho were rebuilding, and next to them was Zaccur, son of Imri. [3]* The Fish Gate was rebuilt by the people of Hassenaah; they timbered it and set up its doors, its bolts, and its bars. [4] At their side Meremoth, son of Uriah, son of Hakkoz, carried out the work of repair; next to him was Meshullam, son of Berechiah, son of Meshezabel; and next to him was Zadok, son of Baana. [5] Next to him the Tekoites carried out the work of repair; however, some of their most powerful men would not submit to the labor asked by their masters. [6] The Mishneh Gate† was repaired by Joiada, son of Paseah; and Meshullam, son of Besodeiah; they timbered it and set up its doors, its bolts, and its bars. [7] At their side Melatiah the Gibeonite did the repairing, together with Jadon the Meronothite, and the men of Gibeon and of Mizpah, who were under the jurisdiction of the governor of

---

† Sanballat, governor of Samaria, during the last years of Persian rule. Although his own name was Babylonian—Sin-uballit, i.e., "Sin (the moon god) has given life"—his two sons had names based on the divine name Yhwh. *Tobiah the Ammonite official*: the governor of the province of Ammon in Transjordan. His title, "official," lit., "servant" (in Hebrew, *ebed*), could also be understood as "slave," and Nehemiah perhaps meant it in this derogatory sense. The Tobiads remained a powerful family even in Maccabean times, and something of their history is known from 2 Maccabees (3:11; 12:17), Josephus (*Ant.* 12:160–236), the Zeno papyri of the third century B.C., and excavation at 'Araq el-'Emir in Jordan. Sanballat and Tobiah, together with Geshem the Arab (Neh 2:19; 6:1–2), who was probably in charge of Edom and the regions to the south and southeast of Judah, opposed the rebuilding of Jerusalem's walls on political grounds; the city was the capital of a rival province.

**2:13–15** Nehemiah left Jerusalem by the Valley Gate near the northwestern end of the old City of David and went south down the Tyropoean Valley toward the Dragon Spring (or the En-rogel [Jos 15:7; 18:16; 2 Sm 17:17; 1 Kgs 1:9], now known as Job's Well) at the juncture of the Valley of Hinnom and the Kidron Valley. He then turned north at the Dung Gate (or the Potsherd Gate of Jer 19:2) at the southern end of the city and

proceeded up the wadi, that is, the Kidron Valley, passing the Fountain Gate (at the Spring of Gihon) and the King's Pool (unidentified); finally he turned west and then south to his starting point.

**2:19** *Geshem the Arab*: see also 6:1–2; in 6:6 the name occurs as Gashmu. He is known from a contemporary inscription as ruler of the Kedarite Arabs, who were threatening Judah from the south and east.

**2:20** *Neither share nor claim nor memorial*: although Sanballat and Tobiah worshiped Yhwh, Nehemiah would not let them participate in any of the activities of the religious community in Jerusalem.

**3:1–32** The construction work on the gates and walls of the city is described in counterclockwise direction, beginning and ending at the Sheep Gate (to the north of the Temple). The exact locations of many of the topographical points mentioned are uncertain.

**3:6** *The Mishneh Gate*: the gate leading into the second, expanded quarter of the city; cf. 2 Kgs 22:14; Zep 1:10.

---

**2:11** Ezr 8:32.        **3:1** Jer 31:38.
**2:18** Ezr 7:6.        **3:3** Ezr 2:35; Zep 1:10.

West-of-Euphrates. ⁸ Next to them the work of repair was carried out by Uzziel, son of Harhaiah, a member of the goldsmiths' guild, and at his side was Hananiah, one of the perfumers' guild. They restored Jerusalem as far as the Broad Wall.† ⁹ Next to them the work of repair was carried out by Rephaiah, son of Hur, administrator of half the district of Jerusalem, ¹⁰ and at his side was Jedaiah, son of Harumaph, who repaired opposite his own house. Next to him Hattush, son of Hashabneiah, carried out the work of repair. ¹¹ The adjoining sector, as far as the Oven Tower, was repaired by Malchijah, son of Harim, and Hasshub, son of Pahath-moab. ¹² At their side the work of repair was carried out by Shallum, son of Hallohesh, administrator of half the district of Jerusalem, together with his daughters. ¹³ The Valley Gate was repaired by Hanun and the inhabitants of Zanoah; they rebuilt it and set up its doors, its bolts, and its bars. They also repaired a thousand cubits of the wall up to the Dung Gate. ¹⁴ The Dung Gate was repaired by Malchijah, son of Rechab, administrator of the district of Beth-haccherem; he rebuilt it and set up its doors, its bolts, and its bars. ¹⁵ The Fountain Gate was repaired by Shallum, son of Colhozeh, administrator of the district of Mizpah; he rebuilt it, roofed it, and set up its doors, its bolts, and its bars. He also repaired the wall of the Aqueduct Pool near the King's Garden as far as the steps that lead down from the City of David. ¹⁶ After him, the work of repair was carried out by Nehemiah, son of Azbuk, administrator of half the district of Beth-zur, to a place opposite the tombs of David, as far as the Artificial Pool and the barracks.

¹⁷ After him, these Levites carried out the work of repair: Rehum, son of Bani, and next to him, for his own district, was Hashabiah, administrator of half the district of Keilah. ¹⁸ After him, their kinsmen carried out the work of repair: Binnui, son of Henadad, administrator of half the district of Keilah; ¹⁹ next to him Ezer, son of Jeshua, administrator of Mizpah, who repaired the adjoining sector, the Corner, opposite the ascent to the arsenal. ²⁰ After him, Baruch, son of Zabbai, repaired the adjoining sector from the Corner to the entrance of the house of Eliashib, the high priest. ²¹ After him, Meremoth, son of Uriah, son of Hakkoz, repaired the adjoining sector from the entrance of Eliashib's house to its end.

²² After him, the work of repair was carried out by the priests, men of the surrounding country. ²³ After them, Benjamin and Hasshub carried out the repair in front of their houses; after them, Azariah, son of Maaseiah, son of Ananiah, made the repairs alongside his house. ²⁴ After him, Binnui, son of Henadad, repaired the adjoining sector from the house of Azariah to the Corner (that is, to the Angle). ²⁵ After him, Palal, son of Uzai, carried out the work of repair opposite the Corner and the tower projecting from the Upper Palace at the quarters of the guard. After him, Pedaiah, son of Parosh, carried out the work of repair ²⁶ to a point opposite the Water Gate on the east, and the projecting tower. ²⁷ After him, the Tekoites repaired the adjoining sector opposite the great projecting tower, to the wall of Ophel.

²⁸ Above the Horse Gate the priests carried out the work of repair, each opposite his own house. ²⁹* After them Zadok, son of Immer, carried out the repair opposite his house, and after him the repair was carried out by Shemaiah, son of Shecaniah, keeper of the East Gate. ³⁰ After him, Hananiah, son of Shelemiah, and Hanun, the sixth son of Zalaph, repaired the adjoining sector; after them, Meshullam, son of Berechiah, repaired the place opposite his own lodging. ³¹ After him, Malchijah, a member of the goldsmiths' guild, carried out the work of repair as far as the quarters of the temple servants and the merchants, in front of the Gate of Inspection and as far as the upper chamber of the Angle. ³² Between the upper chamber of the Angle and the Sheep Gate, the goldsmiths and the merchants carried out the work of repair.

### Opposition from Judah's Enemies.
³³ When Sanballat heard that we were rebuilding the wall, he became angry and very much incensed. He ridiculed the Jews, ³⁴ saying in the presence of his associates and the troops of Samaria: "What are these miserable Jews trying to do? Will they complete their restoration in a single day? Will they recover these stones, burnt as they are, from the heaps of dust?" ³⁵ Tobiah the Ammonite was beside him, and he said: "Whatever they are building—if a fox

---

† **3:8** *The Broad Wall*: perhaps identical with the wall, seven meters thick, discovered in the Jewish quarter of the Old City.

* **3:29** Ez 40:6.

attacks it, it will breach their wall of stones!" [36] Hear, our God, how we were mocked! Turn back their reproach upon their own heads and deliver them up as plunder in a land of captivity! [37]* Do not hide their crime and do not let their sin be blotted out in your sight, for they insulted the builders to their faces! [38] We, however, continued to build the wall, and soon it was completed up to half its height. The people worked enthusiastically.

**4** [1] When Sanballat, Tobiah, the Arabs, the Ammonites, and the Ashdodites heard that the restoration of the walls of Jerusalem was progressing—for the gaps were beginning to be closed up—they became extremely angry. [2] They all plotted together to come and fight against Jerusalem and to throw us into confusion. [3] We prayed to our God and posted a watch against them day and night for fear of what they might do. [4] Meanwhile the Judahites were saying:

"Slackened is the bearers' strength,
        there is no end to the rubbish;
Never will we be able
        to rebuild the wall."

[5] Our enemies thought, "Before they are aware of it or see us, we will come into their midst, kill them, and put an end to the work." [6] When the Jews who lived near them had come to us from one place after another, and had told us ten times over that they were about to attack us, [7] I stationed guards down below, behind the wall, near the exposed points, assigning them by family groups with their swords, spears, and bows. [8] I made an inspection, then addressed these words to the nobles, the magistrates, and the rest of the people: "Do not fear them! Keep in mind the LORD, who is great and to be feared, and fight for your kindred, your sons and daughters, your wives and your homes." [9] When our enemies realized that we had been warned and that God had upset their plan, we all went back, each to our own task at the wall.

[10]* From that time on, however, only half my work force took a hand in the work, while the other half, armed with spears, bucklers, bows, and breastplates, stood guard behind the whole house of Judah [11] as they rebuilt the wall. The load carriers, too, were armed; each worked with one hand and held a weapon with the other. [12] Every builder, while working, had a sword tied at his side. A trumpeter stood beside me, [13] for I had said to the nobles, the magistrates, and the rest of the people: "Our work is scattered and extensive, and we are widely separated from one another along the wall; [14] wherever you hear the trumpet sound, join us there; our God will fight with us." [15] Thus we went on with the work, half with spears in hand, from daybreak till the stars came out.

[16] At the same time I told the people to spend the nights inside Jerusalem, each with an attendant, so that they might serve as a guard by night and a working force by day. [17] Neither I, nor my kindred, nor any of my attendants, nor any of the bodyguard that accompanied me took off our clothes; everyone kept a weapon at hand.

**5** **Social and Economic Problems.** [1]* Then there rose a great outcry of the people and their wives against certain of their Jewish kindred.† [2] Some said: "We are forced to pawn our sons and daughters in order to get grain to eat that we may live." [3] Others said: "We are forced to pawn our fields, our vineyards, and our houses, that we may have grain during the famine." [4] Still others said: "To pay the king's tax we have borrowed money on our fields and vineyards. [5]* And though these are our own kindred, and our children are as good as theirs, we have had to reduce our sons and daughters to slavery, and violence has been done to some of our daughters! Yet we can do nothing about it, for our fields and vineyards belong to others."

[6] I was extremely angry when I heard the reasons for their complaint. [7]* After some deliberation, I called the nobles and magistrates to account, saying to them, "You are exacting interest from your own kindred!"† I then rebuked them severely, [8]* saying to them: "As far as we were able, we bought back our Jewish

5:1 *Certain of their Jewish kindred*: probably Jews who had returned from Babylonia who formed the social and economic elite in the province.

5:7 *You are exacting interest from your own kindred!*: contrary to the Mosaic law (Dt 23:20).

3:37 Neh 6:14; 13:29; Jer 18:23.
4:10 Ps 149:6.
5:1 Jer 34:8–22.
5:5 Ex 21:7; Lv 25:39.
5:7 Dt 23:20.
5:8 Lv 25:48.

kindred who had been sold to Gentiles; you, however, are selling your own kindred, to have them bought back by us." They remained silent, for they could find no answer. ⁹I continued: "What you are doing is not good. Should you not conduct yourselves out of fear of our God rather than fear of the reproach of our Gentile enemies? ¹⁰I myself, my kindred, and my attendants have lent the people money and grain without charge. Let us put an end to this usury! ¹¹Return to them this very day their fields, vineyards, olive groves, and houses, together with the interest on the money, the grain, the wine, and the oil that you have lent them." ¹²They answered: "We will return everything and exact nothing further from them. We will do just what you ask." Then I called for the priests to administer an oath to them that they would do as they had promised. ¹³I shook out the folds of my garment, saying, "Thus may God shake from home and fortune every man who fails to keep this promise, and may he thus be shaken out and emptied!" And the whole assembly answered, "Amen," and praised the LORD. Then the people did as they had promised.

**Nehemiah's Record.** ¹⁴Moreover, from the time that King Artaxerxes appointed me governor in the land of Judah, from his twentieth to his thirty-second year—during these twelve years neither I nor my kindred lived off the governor's food allowance. ¹⁵The earlier governors,† my predecessors, had laid a heavy burden on the people, taking from them each day forty silver shekels for their food; then, too, their attendants oppressed the people. But I, because I feared God, did not do this. ¹⁶In addition, though I had acquired no land of my own, I did my part in this work on the wall, and all my attendants were gathered there for the work. ¹⁷Though I set my table for a hundred and fifty persons, Jews and magistrates, as well as the neighboring Gentiles who came to us, ¹⁸and though the daily preparations were made at my expense—one ox, six choice sheep, poultry—besides all kinds of wine in abundance every ten days, despite this I did not claim the governor's allowance, for the labor lay heavy upon this people. ¹⁹Keep in

mind, my God, to my credit all that I did for this people.

**6 Plots Against Nehemiah.** ¹When it had been reported to Sanballat, Tobiah, Geshem the Arab, and our other enemies that I had rebuilt the wall and that there was no breach left in it (though up to that time I had not yet set up the doors in the gates), ²Sanballat and Geshem sent me this message: "Come, let us hold council together at Chephirim in the plain of Ono." They were planning to do me harm. ³I sent messengers to them with this reply: "I am engaged in a great enterprise and am unable to come down. Why should the work stop, while I leave it to come down to you?" ⁴Four times they sent me this same proposal, and each time I gave the same reply. ⁵Then, the fifth time, Sanballat sent me the same message by one of his servants, who bore an unsealed letter ⁶containing this text: "Among the nations it has been reported—Gashmu† is witness to this—that you and the Jews are planning a rebellion; that for this reason you are rebuilding the wall; and that you are to be their king. ⁷Also, that you have set up prophets in Jerusalem to proclaim you king of Judah. Now, since matters like these will reach the ear of the king, come, let us hold council together." ⁸I sent him this answer: "Nothing of what you report is happening; rather, it is the invention of your own mind." ⁹They were all trying to intimidate us, thinking, "They will be discouraged from continuing with the work, and it will never be completed." But instead, I then redoubled my efforts.

¹⁰I went to the house of Shemaiah, son of Delaiah, son of Mehetabel, who was confined to his house, and he said: "Let us meet in the house of God, inside the temple building; let us lock the doors of the temple. For they are coming to kill you—by night they are coming to kill you." ¹¹My answer was: "A man like me take flight? Should a man like me enter the temple to save his life? I will not go!" ¹²For on consideration, it was plain to me that God had not sent him; rather, because Tobiah and Sanballat had bribed him, he voiced this prophecy concerning me, ¹³that I might act on it out of fear and commit this sin. Then they

---

† **5:15** *The earlier governors*: both Sheshbazzar (Ezr 5:14) and Zerubbabel (Hg 1:1, 14; 2:2, 21) are said to be governors, and Mal 1:8 mentions a governor but does not name him. Other names are known from seal impressions of uncertain date.
**6:6** *Gashmu*: elsewhere (vv. 1–2; 2:19) the name is given as Geshem.

would have had a shameful story with which to discredit me. ¹⁴* Keep in mind Tobiah and Sanballat, my God, because of these things they did; keep in mind as well Noadiah the woman prophet and the other prophets who were trying to intimidate me.

**Completion of the Work.** ¹⁵ The wall was finished on the twenty-fifth day of Elul;† the work had taken fifty-two days. ¹⁶* When all our enemies had heard of this, and all the neighboring Gentiles round about had taken note of it, they were very discouraged, for they knew that it was with our God's help that this work had been completed. ¹⁷ At that same time, however, many letters were going to Tobiah from the nobles of Judah, and Tobiah's letters were reaching them, ¹⁸ for many in Judah were in league with him, since he was the son-in-law of Shecaniah, son of Arah, and his son Jehohanan had married the daughter of Meshullam, son of Berechiah. ¹⁹ They would praise his good deeds in my presence and relate to him whatever I said; and Tobiah sent letters trying to intimidate me.

**7** ¹ Now that the wall had been rebuilt, I had the doors set up, and the gatekeepers, the singers, and the Levites were put in charge of them. ² Over Jerusalem I placed Hanani, my brother, and Hananiah, the commander of the citadel, who was more trustworthy and God-fearing than most. ³ I said to them: "The gates of Jerusalem are not to be opened until the sun is hot, and while the sun is still shining they shall shut and bar the doors. Appoint as sentinels the inhabitants of Jerusalem, some at their watch posts, and others in front of their own houses."

**Census of the Province.** ⁴ Now, the city was quite wide and spacious, but its population was small, and none of the houses had been rebuilt. ⁵ When my God had inspired me to gather together the nobles, the magistrates, and the people, and to examine their family records, I came upon the family list of those who had returned in the earliest period. There I found the following written:

⁶†* These are the inhabitants of the province who returned from the captivity of the exiles whom Nebuchadnezzar, king of Babylon, had carried away, and who came back to Jerusalem and Judah, to their own cities: ⁷ They returned with Zerubbabel, Jeshua, Nehemiah, Azariah, Raamiah, Nahamani, Mordecai, Bilshan, Mispereth, Bigvai, Nehum, and Baanah.

The census of the people of Israel: ⁸ descendants of Parosh, two thousand one hundred and seventy-two; ⁹ descendants of Shephatiah, three hundred and seventy-two; ¹⁰ descendants of Arah, six hundred and fifty-two; ¹¹ descendants of Pahath-moab who were descendants of Jeshua and Joab, two thousand eight hundred and eighteen; ¹² descendants of Elam, one thousand two hundred and fifty-four; ¹³ descendants of Zattu, eight hundred and forty-five; ¹⁴ descendants of Zaccai, seven hundred and sixty; ¹⁵ descendants of Binnui, six hundred and forty-eight; ¹⁶ descendants of Bebai, six hundred and twenty-eight; ¹⁷ descendants of Azgad, two thousand three hundred and twenty-two; ¹⁸ descendants of Adonikam, six hundred and sixty-seven; ¹⁹ descendants of Bigvai, two thousand and sixty-seven; ²⁰ descendants of Adin, six hundred and fifty-five; ²¹ descendants of Ater who were descendants of Hezekiah, ninety-eight; ²² descendants of Hashum, three hundred and twenty-eight; ²³ descendants of Bezai, three hundred and twenty-four; ²⁴ descendants of Hariph, one hundred and twelve; ²⁵ descendants of Gibeon, ninety-five; ²⁶ people of Bethlehem and Netophah, one hundred and eighty-eight; ²⁷ people of Anathoth, one hundred and twenty-eight; ²⁸ people of Beth-azmaveth, forty-two; ²⁹ people of Kiriath-jearim, Chephirah, and Beeroth, seven hundred and forty-three; ³⁰ people of Ramah and Geba, six hundred and twenty-one; ³¹ people of Michmas, one hundred and twenty-two; ³² people of Bethel and Ai, one hundred and twenty-three; ³³ people of Nebo, fifty-two; ³⁴ descendants of the other Elam, one thousand two hundred and fifty-four; ³⁵ descendants of Harim, three hundred and twenty; ³⁶ descendants of Jericho, three hundred and forty-five; ³⁷ descendants of Lod, Hadid, and Ono, seven hundred and twenty-one;

N
E
H

---

† **6:15** *Elul*: the sixth month (August–September). *Fifty-two days*: according to Josephus (*Ant.* 11:174–183), the rebuilding of the walls of Jerusalem by Nehemiah took two years and four months.

**7:6–72** See note on Ezr 2:1–67.

* **6:14** Jer 23:9–40; Zec 13:3.          **7:6** Ezr 2:1–70.
  **6:16** Ps 118:22–23; 127:1.

[38] descendants of Senaah, three thousand nine hundred and thirty.

[39] The priests: descendants of Jedaiah of the house of Jeshua, nine hundred and seventy-three; [40] descendants of Immer, one thousand and fifty-two; [41] descendants of Pashhur, one thousand two hundred and forty-seven; [42] descendants of Harim, one thousand and seventeen.

[43] The Levites: descendants of Jeshua, Kadmiel of the descendants of Hodeviah, seventy-four.

[44] The singers: descendants of Asaph, one hundred and forty-eight.

[45] The gatekeepers: descendants of Shallum, descendants of Ater, descendants of Talmon, descendants of Akkub, descendants of Hatita, descendants of Shobai, one hundred and thirty-eight.

[46] The temple servants: descendants of Ziha, descendants of Hasupha, descendants of Tabbaoth, [47] descendants of Keros, descendants of Sia, descendants of Padon, [48] descendants of Lebana, descendants of Hagaba, descendants of Shalmai, [49] descendants of Hanan, descendants of Giddel, descendants of Gahar, [50] descendants of Reaiah, descendants of Rezin, descendants of Nekoda, [51] descendants of Gazzam, descendants of Uzza, descendants of Paseah, [52] descendants of Besai, descendants of the Meunites, descendants of the Nephusites, [53] descendants of Bakbuk, descendants of Hakupha, descendants of Harhur, [54] descendants of Bazlith, descendants of Mehida, descendants of Harsha, [55] descendants of Barkos, descendants of Sisera, descendants of Temah, [56] descendants of Neziah, descendants of Hatipha.

[57] Descendants of Solomon's servants: descendants of Sotai, descendants of Sophereth, descendants of Perida, [58] descendants of Jaala, descendants of Darkon, descendants of Giddel, [59] descendants of Shephatiah, descendants of Hattil, descendants of Pochereth-hazzebaim, descendants of Amon. [60] The total of the temple servants and the descendants of Solomon's servants was three hundred and ninety-two.

[61] The following who returned from Tel-melah, Tel-harsha, Cherub, Addon, and Immer were unable to prove that their ancestral houses and their descent were Israelite: [62] descendants of Delaiah, descendants of Tobiah, descendants of Nekoda, six hundred and forty-two. [63] Also, of the priests: descendants of Hobaiah, descendants of Hakkoz, descendants of Barzillai (he had married one of the daughters of Barzillai the Gileadite and was named after him). [64] These men searched their family records, but their names could not be found written there; hence they were disqualified from the priesthood, [65] and the governor† ordered them not to partake of the most holy foods until there should be a priest to consult the Urim and Thummim.

[66] The entire assembly taken together came to forty-two thousand three hundred and sixty, [67] not counting their male and female servants, who were seven thousand three hundred and thirty-seven. They also had two hundred male and female singers. Their horses were seven hundred and thirty-six, their mules two hundred and forty-five, [68] their camels four hundred and thirty-five, their donkeys six thousand seven hundred and twenty.

[69] Certain of the heads of ancestral houses contributed to the temple service. The governor put into the treasury one thousand drachmas of gold, fifty basins, thirty vestments for priests, and five hundred minas of silver. [70] Some of the heads of ancestral houses contributed to the treasury for the temple service: twenty thousand drachmas of gold and two thousand two hundred minas of silver. [71] The contributions of the rest of the people amounted to twenty thousand drachmas of gold, two thousand minas of silver, and sixty-seven vestments for priests.

[72] The priests, the Levites, the gatekeepers, the singers, the temple servants, and all Israel took up residence in their cities.

## II. PROMULGATION OF THE LAW

**8 Ezra Reads the Law.** [1]†* Now when the seventh month came, the whole people gathered as one in the square in front of the Water Gate, and they called upon Ezra

---

† **7:65, 69** *The governor*: see note on Ezr 2:63.

**8:1–18** Chronologically this belongs after Ezr 8:36. The gloss mentioning Nehemiah in Neh 8:9 was inserted in this Ezra section after the dislocation of several parts of Ezra-Nehemiah had occurred. There is no clear evidence of a simultaneous presence of Nehemiah and Ezra in Jerusalem; Neh 12:26, 36 are also scribal glosses.

* **8:1** Ezr 3:1.

the scribe to bring forth the book of the law of Moses which the LORD had commanded for Israel. [2]* On the first day of the seventh month, therefore, Ezra the priest brought the law before the assembly, which consisted of men, women, and those children old enough to understand. [3] In the square in front of the Water Gate, Ezra read out of the book from daybreak till midday, in the presence of the men, the women, and those children old enough to understand; and all the people listened attentively to the book of the law. [4] Ezra the scribe stood on a wooden platform that had been made for the occasion; at his right side stood Mattithiah, Shema, Anaiah, Uriah, Hilkiah, and Maaseiah, and on his left Pedaiah, Mishael, Malchijah, Hashum, Hashbaddanah, Zechariah, Meshullam. [5] Ezra opened the scroll so that all the people might see it, for he was standing higher than any of the people. When he opened it, all the people stood. [6] Ezra blessed the LORD, the great God, and all the people, their hands raised high, answered, "Amen, amen!" Then they knelt down and bowed before the LORD, their faces to the ground. [7]* The Levites Jeshua, Bani, Sherebiah, Jamin, Akkub, Shabbethai, Hodiah, Maaseiah, Kelita, Azariah, Jozabad, Hanan, and Pelaiah explained the law to the people, who remained in their places. [8]* Ezra read clearly from the book of the law of God, interpreting it so that all could understand what was read. [9] Then Nehemiah, that is, the governor, and Ezra the priest-scribe, and the Levites who were instructing the people said to all the people: "Today is holy to the LORD your God. Do not lament, do not weep!"—for all the people were weeping as they heard the words of the law. [10]* He continued: "Go, eat rich foods and drink sweet drinks, and allot portions to those who had nothing prepared; for today is holy to our LORD. Do not be saddened this day, for rejoicing in the LORD is your strength!" [11] And the Levites quieted all the people, saying, "Silence! Today is holy, do not be saddened." [12] Then all the people began to eat and drink, to distribute portions, and to celebrate with great joy, for they understood the words that had been explained to them.

**The Feast of Booths.** [13] On the second day, the heads of ancestral houses of the whole people, and also the priests and the Levites, gathered around Ezra the scribe to study the words of the law. [14]* They found it written in the law commanded by the LORD through Moses that the Israelites should dwell in booths during the feast of the seventh month; [15]* and that they should have this proclamation made throughout their cities and in Jerusalem: "Go out into the hill country and bring in branches of olive, oleaster, myrtle, palm, and other trees in leaf, to make booths, as it is written." [16] The people went out and brought in branches with which they made booths for themselves, on the roof of their houses, in their courtyards, in the courts of the house of God, and in the squares of the Water Gate and the Gate of Ephraim. [17]* So the entire assembly of the returned exiles made booths and dwelt in them. Now the Israelites had done nothing of this sort from the days of Jeshua, son of Nun, until this occasion; therefore there was very great joy. [18] Ezra read from the book of the law of God day after day, from the first day to the last. They kept the feast for seven days, and the solemn assembly on the eighth day, as was required.

**9** **Public Confession of Sin.** [1]†* On the twenty-fourth day of this month, the Israelites gathered together while fasting and wearing sackcloth, their heads covered with dust. [2]* Those of Israelite descent separated themselves from all who were of foreign extraction, then stood forward and confessed their sins and the guilty deeds of their ancestors. [3] When they had taken their places, they read from the book of the law of the LORD their God, for a fourth of the day, and during another fourth they made their confession and bowed down before the LORD their God. [4] Standing on the platform of the Levites were Jeshua, Binnui, Kadmiel, Shebaniah, Bunni, Sherebiah, Bani, and Chenani, who cried

† **9:1–5** The feast of Booths is followed by a penitential liturgy. Since it includes separation from foreigners, some read it as a sequel to Ezr 9–10.

**8:2** Lv 23:23–25; Nm 29:1–6.
**8:7** Neh 10:10–13.
**8:8** Ezr 7:6.
**8:10** Est 9:19.
**8:14** Ex 23:14–16;
Lv 23:33–36; Nm 29:1–38; Ez 45:25.
**8:15** Ps 118:27.
**8:17** 2 Chr 30:26; 35:18.
**9:1** Dn 9:3.
**9:2** Ezr 9:1–2; 10:11.

out to the Lord their God, with a loud voice.
5* The Levites Jeshua, Kadmiel, Bani, Hashabneiah, Sherebiah, Hodiah, Shebaniah, and Pethahiah said,

"Arise, bless the Lord, your God,
     from eternity to eternity!"
"And may they bless your glorious
          name,
     which is exalted above all blessing
          and praise."
6† "You are the Lord, you alone;
You made the heavens,
     the highest heavens and all their host,
The earth and all that is upon it,
     the seas and all that is in them.
To all of them you give life,
     the heavenly hosts bow down before
          you.
7* You are the Lord God
     who chose Abram,
Who brought him from Ur of the
          Chaldees,
     who named him Abraham.
8* You found his heart faithful in your
          sight,
     you made the covenant with him
To give the land of the Canaanites,
     Hittites, Amorites,
Perizzites, Jebusites, and Girgashites
     to him and his descendants.
You fulfilled your promises,
     for you are just.
9* You saw the affliction of our ancestors in
          Egypt,
     you heard their cry by the Red Sea;
10* You worked signs and wonders against
          Pharaoh,
     against all his servants and the people
          of his land,
Because you knew of their insolence
          toward them;
     thus you made for yourself a name
          even to this day.
11* The sea you divided before them,
     on dry ground they passed through
          the midst of the sea;
     Their pursuers you hurled into the
          depths,

like a stone into the mighty waters.
12* With a column of cloud you led them
          by day,
     and by night with a column of fire,
To light the way of their journey,
     the way in which they must travel.
13* On Mount Sinai you came down,
     you spoke with them from heaven;
You gave them just ordinances, true laws,
     good statutes and commandments;
14* Your holy sabbath you made known to
          them,
     commandments, statutes, and law you
          prescribed for them,
     by the hand of Moses your servant.
15* Food from heaven you gave them in
          their hunger,
     water from a rock you sent them in
          their thirst.
You told them to enter and occupy the
          land
     which you had sworn to give them.
16 But they, our ancestors, proved to be
          insolent;
     they were obdurate† and did not obey
          your commandments.
17* They refused to obey and no longer
          remembered
     the wonders you had worked for
          them.
They were obdurate and appointed a
          leader
     in order to return to their slavery in
          Egypt.
But you are a forgiving God, gracious
          and merciful,
     slow to anger and rich in mercy;
     you did not forsake them.
18* Though they made for themselves a
          molten calf,
     and proclaimed, 'Here is your God
          who brought you up from Egypt,'
     and were guilty of great insults,
19 Yet in your great mercy
     you did not forsake them in the
          desert.
By day the column of cloud did not
          cease to lead them on their
          journey,

9:6–37 The Septuagint attributes the prayer to Ezra; cf. Ezr 9:6–15.
9:16 They were obdurate: lit., "they stiffened their necks."
9:5 Ps 41:14; 106:48; Dn 2:20; 3:52.
9:7 Gn 12:1; 17:5.
9:8 Gn 15:18–19.
9:9 Ex 2:23–24.
9:10 Ex 7–11; 14.
9:11 Ex 15:5, 10.
9:12 Ex 13:21–22.
9:13 Ex 19–24.
9:14 Ex 20:8.
9:15 Ex 16:4; 17:1–2.
9:17 Ex 34:6; Nm 14:1–4; Dt 9:9.
9:18 Ex 32:4, 8.

by night the column of fire did not
cease to light the way they were
to travel.

20* Your good spirit you bestowed on them,
to give them understanding;
Your manna you did not withhold from
their mouths,
and you gave them water in their
thirst.

21* Forty years in the desert you sustained
them:
they did not want;
Their garments did not become worn,
and their feet did not swell.

22* You gave them kingdoms and peoples,
which you divided among them as
border lands.
They possessed the land of Sihon, king
of Heshbon,
and the land of Og, king of Bashan.

23* You made their children as numerous as
the stars of the heavens,
and you brought them into the land
which you had commanded their
ancestors to enter and possess.

24 The children went in to possess the land;
you humbled before them the
Canaanite inhabitants
and gave them into their power,
Their kings and the peoples of the land,
to do with them as they wished.

25* They captured fortified cities and fertile
land;
they took possession of houses filled
with all good things,
Cisterns already dug, vineyards, olive
groves,
and fruit trees in abundance.
They ate and had their fill,
fattened and feasted on your great
goodness.

26* But they were contemptuous and
rebelled against you:
they cast your law behind their backs.
They murdered your prophets
who bore witness against them to
bring them back to you:
they were guilty of great insults.

27* Therefore you gave them into the power
of their enemies,
who oppressed them.

But in the time of their oppression they
would cry out to you,
and you would hear them from
heaven,
And according to your great mercy give
them saviors
to deliver them from the power of
their enemies.

28 As soon as they had relief,
they would go back to doing evil in
your sight.
Again you abandoned them to the
power of their enemies,
who crushed them.
Once again they cried out to you, and
you heard them from heaven
and delivered them according to your
mercy, many times over.

29* You bore witness against them,
to bring them back to your law.
But they were insolent
and would not obey your
commandments;
They sinned against your ordinances,
which give life to those who keep
them.
They turned stubborn backs, stiffened
their necks,
and would not obey.

30 You were patient with them for many
years,
bearing witness against them through
your spirit, by means of your
prophets;
Still they would not listen.
Therefore you delivered them into the
power of the peoples of the lands.

31 Yet in your great mercy you did not
completely destroy them
and did not forsake them, for you are
a gracious and merciful God.

32* Now, our God, great, mighty, and
awesome God,
who preserves the covenant of mercy,
do not discount all the hardship that
has befallen us,
Our kings, our princes, our priests,
our prophets, our ancestors, and your
entire people,
from the time of the kings of Assyria
until this day!

NEH

---

9:20 Dt 2:7.
9:21 Dt 8:4.
9:22 Nm 21:21–35; Dt 1:4;
2:26–3:11.
9:23 Dt 1:10.
9:25 Dt 3:5; 6:10–11;
11:11; 32:15.
9:26 Wis 2:10–20.
9:27 Dn 9:19.
9:29 Lv 18:5; Dt 30:16;
32:47.
9:32 Lam 5.

33* In all that has come upon us you have
　　been just,
　　for you kept faith while we have done
　　　evil.
34 Yes, our kings, our princes, our priests,
　　and our ancestors
　　have not kept your law;
　　They paid no attention to your
　　　commandments
　　and the warnings which you gave them.
35 While they were still in their kingdom,
　　in the midst of the many good things
　　　that you had given them
　　And in the wide, fertile land
　　　that you had spread out before them,
　　They did not serve you
　　　nor turn away from their evil deeds.
36 Today we are slaves!
　　As for the land which you gave our
　　　ancestors
　　That they might eat its fruits and good
　　　things—
　　see, we have become slaves upon it!
37 Its rich produce goes to the kings
　　you set over us because of our sins,
　　Who rule over our bodies and our cattle
　　　as they please.
　　We are in great distress!"

# 10 Signatories to the Pact. ¹† In view of
all this, we are entering into a firm
pact, which we are putting into writing. On
the sealed document appear the names of our
princes, our Levites, and our priests.

² On the sealed document: the governor Nehemiah, son of Hacaliah, and Zedekiah.

³* Seraiah, Azariah, Jeremiah, ⁴ Pashhur,
Amariah, Malchijah, ⁵ Hattush, Shebaniah,
Malluch, ⁶ Harim, Meremoth, Obadiah, ⁷ Dan-
iel, Ginnethon, Baruch, ⁸ Meshullam, Abijah,
Mijamin, ⁹ Maaziah, Bilgai, Shemaiah: these
are the priests.

¹⁰ The Levites: Jeshua, son of Azaniah; Binnui, of the descendants of Henadad; Kadmiel;
¹¹* and their kinsmen Shebaniah, Hodiah,
Kelita, Pelaiah, Hanan, ¹² Mica, Rehob, Hashabiah, ¹³ Zaccur, Sherebiah, Shebaniah, ¹⁴ Hodiah, Bani, Beninu.

¹⁵ The leaders of the people: Parosh, Pahath-moab, Elam, Zattu, Bani, ¹⁶ Bunni, Azgad, Bebai, ¹⁷ Adonijah, Bigvai, Adin, ¹⁸ Ater,
Hezekiah, Azzur, ¹⁹ Hodiah, Hashum, Bezai,
²⁰ Hariph, Anathoth, Nebai, ²¹ Magpiash, Meshullam, Hezir, ²² Meshezabel, Zadok, Jaddua,
²³ Pelatiah, Hanan, Anaiah, ²⁴ Hoshea, Hananiah, Hasshub, ²⁵ Hallhohesh, Pilha, Shobek,
²⁶ Rehum, Hashabnah, Maaseiah, ²⁷ Ahiah, Hanan, Anan, ²⁸ Malluch, Harim, Baanah.

**Provisions of the Pact.** ²⁹ The rest of the people,
priests, Levites, gatekeepers, singers, temple
servants, and all others who have separated
themselves from the local inhabitants in favor
of the law of God, with their wives, their sons,
their daughters, all who are of the age of discretion, ³⁰* join their influential kindred, and
with the sanction of a curse take this oath to
follow the law of God given through Moses,
the servant of God, and to observe carefully all
the commandments of the LORD, our Lord, his
ordinances and his statutes.

³¹* We will not marry our daughters to the
local inhabitants, and we will not accept their
daughters for our sons.

³²* When the local inhabitants bring in merchandise or any kind of grain for sale on the
sabbath day, we will not buy from them on the
sabbath or on any other holy day. In the
seventh year we will forgo the produce, and
forgive every kind of debt.

³³* We impose these commandments on
ourselves: to give a third of a shekel each year
for the service of the house of our God, ³⁴ for
the showbread, the daily grain offering, the
daily burnt offering, for the sabbaths, new
moons, and festivals, for the holy offerings
and sin offerings to make atonement for Israel, for every service of the house of our God.
³⁵* We, priests, Levites, and people, have determined by lot concerning the procurement of
wood: it is to be brought to the house of our
God by each of our ancestral houses at stated
times each year, to be burnt on the altar of the
LORD, our God, as the law prescribes. ³⁶* We
have agreed to bring each year to the house
of the LORD the first fruits of our fields and of

---

† **10:1–39** This section belongs to the Nehemiah narrative
rather than to that of Ezra. It is best read after Neh 13:31, since
the stipulations of the pact seem to presuppose Nehemiah's
measures recorded in Neh 13. *In view of all this*: considering the
situation described in Neh 13:4–31.

**9:33** Dn 3:27; 9:14.
**10:3** Neh 12:1–7, 12–26.
**10:11** Ezr 10:23.
**10:30** Neh 13:23–27.
**10:31** Dt 7:2–4; Ezr 9:2, 12;
　　Neh 13:15–22.
**10:32** Neh 5:1–13;
**13:15–22**; Ex 20:8; Lv
　　25:2–7.
**10:33** Lv 24:5–9; 2 Chr
　　24:6, 9–10.
**10:35** Neh 13:31.
**10:36** Ex 13:1, 11–16; Dt
　　26:1.

our fruit trees, of every kind; [37] also, as is prescribed in the law, to bring to the house of our God, to the priests who serve in the house of our God, the firstborn of our children and our animals, including the firstborn of our flocks and herds. [38]* The first batch of our dough, and our offerings of the fruit of every tree, of wine and oil, we will bring to the priests, to the chambers of the house of our God. The tithe of our fields we will bring to the Levites; they, the Levites, shall take the tithe in all the cities of our service. [39] An Aaronite priest shall be with the Levites when they take the tithe, and the Levites shall bring the tithe of the tithes to the house of our God, to the chambers of the treasury. [40] For to these chambers the Israelites and Levites bring the offerings of grain, wine, and oil; there also are housed the vessels of the sanctuary, and the ministering priests, the gatekeepers, and the singers. We will not neglect the house of our God.

## III. DEDICATION OF THE WALL; OTHER REFORMS

**11** **Resettlement of Jerusalem.** [1]†* The administrators took up residence in Jerusalem, and the rest of the people cast lots to bring one man in ten to reside in Jerusalem, the holy city, while the other nine would remain in the other cities. [2] The people blessed all those who willingly agreed to take up residence in Jerusalem.

[3]* These are the heads of the province who took up residence in Jerusalem. In the cities of Judah dwelt Israelites, priests, Levites, temple servants, and the descendants of Solomon's servants, each on the property they owned in their own cities.

[4] In Jerusalem dwelt both Judahites and Benjaminites. Of the Judahites: Athaiah, son of Uzziah, son of Zechariah, son of Amariah, son of Shephatiah, son of Mehallalel, of the sons of Perez; [5] Maaseiah, son of Baruch, son of Colhozeh, son of Hazaiah, son of Adaiah, son of Joiarib, son of Zechariah, a son of the Shelanites. [6] The total of the descendants of Perez who dwelt in Jerusalem was four hundred and sixty-eight people of substance.

[7] These were the Benjaminites: Sallu, son of Meshullam, son of Joed, son of Pedaiah, son of Kolaiah, son of Maaseiah, son of Ithiel, son of Jeshaiah, [8] and his kinsmen, warriors, nine hundred and twenty-eight in number. [9] Joel, son of Zichri, was their commander, and Judah, son of Hassenuah, was second in command of the city.

[10] Among the priests were: Jedaiah; Joiarib; Jachin; [11] Seraiah, son of Hilkiah, son of Meshullam, son of Zadok, son of Meraioth, son of Ahitub, the ruler of the house of God, [12] and their kinsmen who carried out the temple service, eight hundred and twenty-two; Adaiah, son of Jeroham, son of Pelaliah, son of Amzi, son of Zechariah, son of Pashhur, son of Malchijah, [13] and his kinsmen, heads of ancestral houses, two hundred and forty-two; and Amasai, son of Azarel, son of Ahzai, son of Meshillemoth, son of Immer, [14] and his kinsmen, warriors, one hundred and twenty-eight. Their commander was Zabdiel, son of Haggadol.

[15] Among the Levites were Shemaiah, son of Hasshub, son of Azrikam, son of Hashabiah, son of Bunni; [16] Shabbethai and Jozabad, levitical chiefs who were placed over the external affairs of the house of God; [17] Mattaniah, son of Micah, son of Zabdi, son of Asaph, director of the psalms, who led the thanksgiving at prayer; Bakbukiah, second in rank among his kinsmen; and Abda, son of Shammua, son of Galal, son of Jeduthun. [18] The total of the Levites in the holy city was two hundred and eighty-four.

[19] The gatekeepers were Akkub, Talmon, and their kinsmen, who kept watch over the gates; one hundred and seventy-two in number.

[20] The rest of Israel, including priests and Levites, were in all the other cities of Judah in their own inheritances.

[21] The temple servants lived on Ophel. Ziha and Gishpa were in charge of the temple servants.

[22]* The prefect of the Levites in Jerusalem was Uzzi, son of Bani, son of Hashabiah, son of Mattaniah, son of Micah; he was one of the descendants of Asaph, the singers appointed to the service of the house of God—[23] for they had been appointed by royal decree, and there was a fixed schedule for the singers assigning them their daily duties.

---

† **11:1–19** This list of the family heads who lived in Jerusalem at the time of Nehemiah is best read after Neh 7:72. It parallels at many points the list of early settlers in 1 Chr 9:2–17.

* **10:38** Neh 13:10–14; Nm 18:21–32. **11:1** Neh 7:4. **11:3** 1 Chr 9:2–34. **11:22** 2 Chr 20:14.

24 Pethahiah, son of Meshezabel, a descendant of Zerah, son of Judah, was royal deputy in all affairs that concerned the people.

**Other Settlements.** 25 As concerns their villages with their fields: Judahites lived in Kiriath-arba and its dependencies, in Dibon and its dependencies, in Jekabzeel and its villages, 26 in Jeshua, Moladah, Beth-pelet, 27 in Hazarshual, in Beer-sheba and its dependencies, 28 in Ziklag, in Meconah and its dependencies, 29 in En-rimmon, Zorah, Jarmuth, 30 Zanoah, Adullam, and their villages, Lachish and its fields, Azekah and its dependencies. They were settled from Beer-sheba to Ge-hinnom.

31 Benjaminites were in Geba, Michmash, Aija, Bethel and its dependencies, 32 Anathoth, Nob, Ananiah, 33 Hazor, Ramah, Gittaim, 34 Hadid, Zeboim, Neballat, 35 Lod, Ono, and the Valley of the Artisans.

36 Some divisions of the Levites from Judah were attached to Benjamin.

# 12

**Priests and Levites at the Time of Zerubbabel.** 1* The following are the priests and Levites who returned with Zerubbabel, son of Shealtiel, and Jeshua: Seraiah, Jeremiah, Ezra, 2 Amariah, Malluch, Hattush, 3 Shecaniah, Rehum, Meremoth, 4 Iddo, Ginnethon, Abijah, 5 Mijamin, Maadiah, Bilgah, 6 Shemaiah, and Joiarib, Jedaiah, 7 Sallu, Amok, Hilkiah, Jedaiah. These were the priestly heads and their kinsmen in the days of Jeshua.

8 The Levites were Jeshua, Binnui, Kadmiel, Sherebiah, Judah, Mattaniah, who, together with his kinsmen, was in charge of the thanksgiving hymns, 9 while Bakbukiah and Unno and their kinsmen ministered opposite them by turns.

**High Priests.** 10† Jeshua became the father of Joiakim, Joiakim the father of Eliashib, and Eliashib the father of Joiada; 11 Joiada the father of Johanan, and Johanan the father of Jaddua.

**Priests and Levites Under Joiakim.** 12* In the days of Joiakim these were the priestly family heads: for Seraiah, Meraiah; for Jeremiah, Hananiah; 13 for Ezra, Meshullam; for Amariah, Jehohanan; 14 for Malluchi, Jonathan; for Shebaniah, Joseph; 15 for Harim, Adna; for Meremoth, Helkai; 16 for Iddo, Zechariah; for Ginnethon, Meshullam; 17 for Abijah, Zichri; for Miamin,…; for Moadiah, Piltai; 18 for Bilgah, Shammua; for Shemaiah, Jehonathan; 19 and for Joiarib, Mattenai; for Jedaiah, Uzzi; 20 for Sallu, Kallai; for Amok, Eber; 21 for Hilkiah, Hashabiah; for Jedaiah, Nethanel.

22 In the time of Eliashib, Joiada, Johanan, and Jaddua, the heads of ancestral houses of the priests were written down in the Book of Chronicles, up until the reign of Darius the Persian. 23 The sons of Levi: the family heads were written down in the Book of Chronicles, up until the time of Johanan, the son of Eliashib.

24* The heads of the Levites were Hashabiah, Sherebiah, Jeshua, Binnui, Kadmiel. Their kinsmen who stood opposite them to sing praises and thanksgiving in fulfillment of the command of David, the man of God, one section opposite the other, 25* were Mattaniah, Bakbukiah, Obadiah.

Meshullam, Talmon, and Akkub were gatekeepers. They guarded the storerooms at the gates.

26 All these lived in the time of Joiakim, son of Jeshua, son of Jozadak (and in the time of Nehemiah the governor and of Ezra the priest-scribe).

**Dedication of the Wall.** 27† At the dedication of the wall of Jerusalem, the Levites were sought out wherever they lived and were brought to Jerusalem to celebrate a joyful dedication with thanksgiving hymns and the music of cymbals, harps, and lyres. 28 The levitical singers gathered together from the region about Jerusalem, from the villages of the

---

† **12:10–11** Jeshua was the high priest when Zerubbabel was governor, in the last decades of the sixth century B.C. (Hg 1:1, 12, 14; 2:2, 4). He was the grandfather of Eliashib, the high priest early in Nehemiah's governorship (445–433 B.C.; Neh 3:1, 20, 21) and perhaps later. Eliashib, the grandfather of Johanan, was a grown man, if not yet a high priest, at the time of Ezra, ca. 400 B.C. (Ezr 10:6; and note). According to Josephus (*Ant.* 11:120–183), whose testimony here is doubtful, Jaddua, son of Johanan, died as an old man about the time that Alexander the Great died, 323 B.C. If, as seems probable, this list of the postexilic high priests, at least as far as Johanan, comes from the author

himself (cf. Neh 12:23) and not from a later scribe, it is of prime importance for dating the author's work in the first decades of the fourth century B.C.

**12:27–43** The dedication of the wall of Jerusalem took place, no doubt, soon after the restoration of the wall and its gates had been completed. This section, therefore, is best read after Neh 6:15.

---

**12:1** Neh 12:12–22.  
**12:12** Neh 10:3–9; 12:1–6.  
**12:24** Ezr 2:40.  
**12:25** Neh 11:17.

Netophathites, [29] from Beth-gilgal, and from the plains of Geba and Azmaveth (for the singers had built themselves settlements about Jerusalem). [30] The priests and Levites first purified themselves, then they purified the people, the gates, and the wall.

[31] I had the administrators of Judah go up on the wall, and I arranged two great choirs. The first of these proceeded to the right, along the top of the wall, in the direction of the Dung Gate, [32] followed by Hoshaiah and half the administrators of Judah, [33] along with Azariah, Ezra, Meshullam, [34] Judah, Benjamin, Shemaiah, and Jeremiah, [35] priests with the trumpets, and also Zechariah, son of Jonathan, son of Shemaiah, son of Mattaniah, son of Micaiah, son of Zaccur, son of Asaph, [36] and his kinsmen Shemaiah, Azarel, Milalai, Gilalai, Maai, Nethanel, Judah, and Hanani, with the musical instruments of David, the man of God. Ezra the scribe was at their head. [37] At the Fountain Gate they went straight up by the steps of the City of David and continued along the top of the wall above the house of David until they came to the Water Gate on the east.

[38] The second choir proceeded to the left, followed by myself and the other half of the administrators, along the top of the wall past the Oven Tower as far as the Broad Wall, [39] then past the Ephraim Gate to the Mishneh Gate, the Fish Gate, the Tower of Hananel, and the Hundred Tower, as far as the Sheep Gate. They came to a halt at the Prison Gate.

[40] Both choirs took up a position in the house of God; I, too, and half the magistrates with me, [41] together with the priests Eliakim, Maaseiah, Minjamin, Micaiah, Elioenai, Zechariah, Hananiah, with the trumpets, [42] and Maaseiah, Shemaiah, Eleazar, Uzzi, Jehohanan, Malchijah, Elam, and Ezer. The singers were heard under the leadership of Jezrahiah. [43] Great sacrifices were offered on that day, and they rejoiced, for God had given them cause for great rejoicing. The women and the children joined in, and the rejoicing at Jerusalem could be heard from far off.

[44] † * At that time men were appointed over the chambers set aside for stores, offerings, first fruits, and tithes; in them they were to collect from the fields of the various cities the portions legally assigned to the priests and Levites. For Judah rejoiced in its appointed priests and Levites [45] who carried out the ministry of their God and the ministry of purification (as did the singers and the gatekeepers) in accordance with the prescriptions of David and Solomon, his son. [46]* For in the days of David and Asaph, long ago, there were leaders of singers for songs of praise and thanksgiving to God. [47]* All Israel, in the days of Zerubbabel and in the days of Nehemiah, gave the singers and the gatekeepers their portions, according to their daily needs. They made their consecrated offering to the Levites, and the Levites made theirs to the descendants of Aaron.

# 13

[1] † * At that time, when the book of Moses was being read in the hearing of the people, it was found written there: "No Ammonite or Moabite may ever be admitted into the assembly of God; [2]* for they did not meet the Israelites with food and water, but they hired Balaam to curse them, though our God turned the curse into a blessing." [3]* When they had heard the law, they separated all those of mixed descent from Israel.

**Reform in the Temple.** [4]† Before this, the priest Eliashib, who had been placed in charge of the chambers of the house of our God and who was an associate of Tobiah, [5]* had set aside for the latter's use a large chamber in which had previously been stored the grain offerings, incense and vessels, the tithes in grain, wine, and oil allotted to the Levites, singers, and gatekeepers, and the offerings due the priests. [6] During all this time I had not been in Jerusalem, for in the thirty-second year of Artaxerxes,† king of Babylon, I had gone back to the king. After a suitable period of time, however, I asked leave of the king [7] and returned to Jerusalem, where I discovered the evil thing that

---

† **12:44–47** This account of the provisions made for the Temple services is a composition either of the author or of a later scribe. The gloss mentioning Nehemiah is not in the Septuagint.
**13:1–3** These verses serve as an introduction to the reforms Nehemiah instituted during his second mission in Jerusalem (vv. 4–31). The part of the Book of Moses read to the people is freely quoted from Dt 23:3–6.
**13:4–31** This is part of the "Memoirs of Nehemiah"; it is continued in 10:1–40.

**13:6** In the thirty-second year of Artaxerxes: Artaxerxes I, therefore 433 B.C. After…time: it is not known when Nehemiah returned to Jerusalem or how long his second period of activity there lasted.

**12:44** 1 Chr 23–26; 2 Chr 8:14.
**12:46** 2 Chr 29:30; 35:15.
**12:47** Neh 10:39; 13:10–11; Nm 18:26.
**13:1** Dt 23:3–6.
**13:2** Nm 22–24.
**13:3** Neh 13:23–28.
**13:5** Neh 12:44.

Eliashib had done for Tobiah, in setting aside for him a chamber in the courts of the house of God. 8 This displeased me very much, so I had all of Tobiah's household goods thrown outside the chamber. 9 Then I gave orders to purify the chambers, and I brought back the vessels of the house of God, the grain offerings, and the incense.

10 I learned, too, that the portions due the Levites were no longer being given, so that the Levites and the singers who should have been carrying out the services had deserted to their own fields. 11 I reprimanded the magistrates, demanding, "Why is the house of God neglected?" Then I brought the Levites together and had them resume their stations. 12* All Judah once more brought in the tithes of grain, wine, and oil to the storerooms. 13 In charge of the storerooms I appointed Shelemiah the priest, Zadok the scribe, and Pedaiah, one of the Levites, together with Hanan, son of Zaccur, son of Mattaniah, as their assistant; for they were considered trustworthy. It was their duty to make the distribution to their kinsmen. 14 Remember this to my credit, my God! Do not forget the good deeds I have done for the house of my God and its services!

**Sabbath Observance.** 15* In those days I perceived that people in Judah were treading the wine presses on the sabbath; that they were bringing in sheaves of grain, loading them on their donkeys, together with wine, grapes, figs, and every other kind of load, and bringing them to Jerusalem on the sabbath day. I warned them to sell none of these provisions. 16 In Jerusalem itself the Tyrians residing there were importing fish and every other kind of merchandise and selling it to the Judahites on the sabbath. 17 I reprimanded the nobles of Judah, demanding: "What is this evil thing you are doing, profaning the sabbath day? 18 Did not your ancestors act in this same way, with the result that our God has brought all this evil upon us and upon this city? Would you add to the wrath against Israel by once more profaning the sabbath?"

19 When the shadows were falling on the gates of Jerusalem before the sabbath, I ordered the doors to be closed and prohibited their reopening until after the sabbath. I posted some of my own people at the gates so that no load might enter on the sabbath day. 20 The merchants and sellers of various kinds of merchandise spent the night once or twice outside Jerusalem, 21 but then I warned them: "Why do you spend the night alongside the wall? If you keep this up, I will beat you!" From that time on, they did not return on the sabbath. 22 Then I ordered the Levites to purify themselves and to watch the gates, so that the sabbath day might be kept holy. This, too, remember in my favor, my God, and have mercy on me in accordance with your great mercy!

**Mixed Marriages.** 23* Also in those days I saw Jews who had married women of Ashdod, Ammon, or Moab. 24 Of their children, half spoke the language of Ashdod,† or of one of the other peoples, and none of them knew how to speak the language of Judah. 25 So I reprimanded and cursed them; I beat some of their men and pulled out their hair; and I adjured them by God: "You shall not marry your daughters to their sons nor accept any of their daughters for your sons or for yourselves! 26* Did not Solomon, the king of Israel, sin because of them? Though among the many nations there was no king like him, and though he was beloved of his God and God had made him king over all Israel, yet even he was led into sin by foreign women. 27 Must it also be heard of you that you have done this same terrible evil, betraying our God by marrying foreign women?"

28* One of the sons of Joiada, son of Eliashib the high priest, was the son-in-law of Sanballat the Horonite! I drove him from my presence. 29 Remember against them, my God, how they defiled the priesthood and the covenant of the priesthood and the Levites!

30 So I cleansed them of all foreign contamination. I established the various functions for the priests and Levites, so that each had an appointed task. 31* I also provided for the procurement of wood at stated times and for the first fruits. Remember this in my favor, my God!

---

† **13:24** *Language of Ashdod*: more likely an Aramaic rather than a Philistine dialect. *The language of Judah*: probably Hebrew.

**13:12** Neh 10:38–39; 12:44–45, 47; 2 Chr 31:6.
**13:15** Neh 10:32; Ex 20:8.
**13:23** Neh 10:31; 13:1–3;

Dt 23:3; Ezr 9–10.
**13:26** 1 Kgs 11:1–13.
**13:28** Neh 2:10; 13:4–5, 7–9.
**13:31** Neh 10:35–36.

# BIBLICAL NOVELLAS

## New American Bible, Introduction

The Bible conveys the Word of God in many literary forms: historical narrative, poetry, prophetic exhortation, wisdom sayings, and novellas (edifying stories). In the Constitution on Divine Revelation from Vatican II (*Dei Verbum*), the council fathers give instruction on how to approach this variety: "Attention must be paid to literary forms, for the fact is that truth is differently presented and expressed in the various types of historical writing, in prophetical and poetical texts, and in other forms of literary expression. Hence the interpreter must look for that meaning which the sacred writer intended to express and did in fact express through the medium of a contemporary literary form" (DV 12).

The Books of Tobit, Judith, and Esther are often grouped together. They are stories told to instruct the people concerning the ways of God, to encourage them in critical times, and to entertain. They are aids to the imagination. While they may contain kernels of historical fact, these stories are told primarily to illustrate truths that transcend history.

The author of the Book of Tobit, writing in the second century B.C., tells a story about the life of a devout family in seventh-century Assyria. He gives the people of his own time an example to follow as they struggle with the tensions of living a faithful Jewish life in the midst of a non-Jewish civilization. Tobit, suffering from the affliction of blindness, perseveres in good works and prayer, as do the other characters in the story. God sends an angel who, while hidden from them, leads them to health and happiness. The conclusion demonstrates that God does answer prayer and that perseverance in good works does not go unrewarded.

The author of the Book of Judith gives many clues that this story is beyond history.

All the worst enemies of the people—the Assyrians of the eighth and seventh centuries, the sixth-century Babylonian king Nebuchadnezzar—are rolled into one terror. The hero, Judith, is modeled on the heroes of the Book of Judges, yet her story is also reminiscent of a second-century hero, Judas Maccabeus (1–2 Maccabees). Even the conflation of time indications—the eighteenth year of Nebuchadnezzar (2:1; the year 587 B.C., when he destroyed Jerusalem and took the Jews into exile) with the return from exile and rededication of the Temple (4:3; the events of 538 and 515 respectively)—suggests God's deliverance from the most terrible circumstances. The story may be set in a time long past, but it is meant to encourage the people of the late second century to trust in God when their way of life is threatened. God can use even the most unlikely means, such as a widow, a biblical figure of powerlessness and vulnerability, to deliver them from their enemies.

The Book of Esther includes several historical elements. The Persian king Xerxes (486–465 B.C.), the city of Susa, a court official named Marduka, are all known from other sources. But further investigation shows this is not meant to be a historical account. There is no record of Xerxes having any other queen than Amestris and no mention of such a massacre during his reign. The book has a different purpose: to suggest a historical basis to the festival of Purim, perhaps originally a Persian feast. Through the story of Esther, Purim becomes a celebration of God's rescue of the people from persecution and certain death.

The message conveyed in these stories is not confined to one geographic place or historical period. It remains a valid expression of God's care for faithful people in every time and place. ∎

# The Book of

# Tobit

## INTRODUCTION

### Geoffrey Miller

The book of Tobit exhibits all the hallmarks of a classic tale: a valiant hero conquers a powerful foe, the persecuted faithful are vindicated, and a young man finds the woman destined to be his wife. The story begins in Nineveh, the capital city of the Assyrian Empire, where Tobit's family has been exiled after the fall of the northern kingdom of Israel in 722 BCE. Many other Israelites have also been deported to Assyria, but Tobit's family alone remains faithful to God by observing the regulations of the Torah. Despite this fidelity, Tobit suffers great misfortune; he is stripped of his position in the royal court, his property is confiscated, he is driven from his home, and he eventually loses his eyesight. Meanwhile, in the land of Media, Tobit's relative Sarah leads a virtuous life but also experiences tragedy. She has been married seven times, but the demon Asmodeus kills each of her husbands on the wedding night. Without a spouse or a child, Sarah is unable to find a meaningful life in a patriarchal society, and her grief is exacerbated when a servant accuses her of killing her husbands.

Both Tobit and Sarah cry out to God in their despair, and God responds to their prayers by sending the angel Raphael to remedy their problems: to cure Tobit's blindness and to provide Sarah with a husband who will defeat the demon. Over the course of the narrative, both goals are achieved. The angel disguises himself as Tobit's kinsman "Azariah" and accompanies Tobit's son Tobiah on a journey to Media to retrieve some money his father left there. Along the way, the angel encourages Tobiah to marry Sarah, daughter of Raguel, and he instructs Tobiah how to use three fish organs to ward off the demon and to cure his father's blindness. In the ensuing chapters, Tobiah does as he is instructed, repelling the demon, marrying Sarah, and returning home to Nineveh with his new

## Outline of Tobit

wife and his father's cure. The happy resolution to Tobit's and Sarah's predicaments is cause for celebration, and the story concludes with Tobit praising God and expressing his hope for a restored Jerusalem.

Although the story is set in Assyria and Media in the eighth and seventh centuries BCE, it was composed much later. The book of Tobit was written between 225 and 175 BCE for Israelites living in the Diaspora, i.e., Israelites dispersed throughout the ancient Near East after the Assyrian and Babylonian exiles. The situation of the characters in the story is akin to that of the book's intended audience. While living in a predominantly Gentile world, many Israelites have abandoned their religious and cultural heritage. The ones who remain devout are isolated from the rest of the community, and their piety does not bring them the blessings they expect. In fact, it frequently leads to hardship. When Tobit finds the bodies of other

Israelites lying in the street, he gives them a proper burial, yet he loses his job, property, and eyesight as a result. Likewise Sarah lives a chaste life and follows the Law of Moses by marrying Israelite men, yet her reputation is besmirched by allegations of murder. Ancient and modern readers alike will quickly empathize with these characters, for too often in life, righteous deeds seem to go unrewarded.

These same readers, however, must be careful to read the book of Tobit for the lessons it conveys and not as a historical account. This is especially important for readers today since the book does not readily fit into modern categories of literature. It is often classified as a historical book, but this designation is a misnomer; although it contains some historical personages (e.g., the Assyrian kings Shalmaneser and Sennacherib), it also includes several anachronistic details. For example, Tb 1:15 says that the Assyrian king Shalmaneser was succeeded by his son Sennacherib, but historical records indicate that the two were not related to each other and that Sargon II—not Sennacherib—immediately followed Shalmaneser on the throne. Other details in the story are also erroneous, such as geographical information about Assyria and Media. Strictly speaking, the book of Tobit does not recount pure history, nor was it intended to be read this way.

The book of Tobit instead belongs to the genre of didactic novel. As a novel, the book presents an entertaining story where historical and fictitious elements are combined in a delightful tale of good triumphing over evil. Two independent subplots are carefully interwoven as the stories of Tobit and Sarah collide, and ironic moments (e.g., Tobit's blindness resulting from righteous deeds) are skillfully interspersed alongside comical ones (e.g., debilitating bird droppings and inept physicians). As a didactic piece of literature, the book serves a pedagogical function, seeking to communicate important theological truths to its audience. Some of these truths are about the nature of God, such as the fact that God is a providential deity who cares for his people in exile (Tb 3:16–17; 13:1–6), or that those who remain faithful to God's commands will ultimately be rewarded (8:1–3; 10:12–18). Other lessons are exhortatory, such as the importance of marrying a person of the same tribe (4:12–13) or choosing a spouse for altruistic reasons rather than lust (8:7). Like other didactic novels of antiquity, Tobit seeks to reshape the way its readers view the world and their role in it, bidding them to emulate the exemplary characters of the book so that they may experience a meaningful, rewarding life.

Through the medium of a creative story, the book of Tobit reiterates traditional themes but does so in innovative ways. Not surprisingly, the book devotes much attention to God, but God's role in the story is paradoxical. God is mentioned more than eighty times over the course of the narrative, yet is the subject of an action only once, commissioning the angel Raphael to ameliorate the plights of both Tobit and Sarah (Tb 3:17). As with most texts from this time period, the God of the book of Tobit is a *Deus absconditus*, a "hidden God" who seems distant from creation. God's apparent absence is especially problematic in light of the suffering of righteous men and women and the widespread apostasy described in the book, prompting readers to question God's goodness. The author therefore takes up the issue of theodicy, the defense of God's justice and benevolence despite the presence of evil. The audience discovers in chapter 3 what the characters do not learn until the end of the story, namely that God is intimately involved in the lives of human beings. God does not intervene directly in human affairs but instead operates behind the scenes, using the angel Raphael to accomplish certain objectives.

By means of this heavenly emissary, God empowers the human characters to alleviate their suffering and attain happiness. The ultimate happiness that the characters receive sends an important message to the audience: good things come to those who wait. Yet the fact that two seemingly blameless people, Tobit and Sarah, undergo such terrible misfortune illustrates another key theme in the book: probationary suffering. God sometimes tests people to ensure they are sincerely virtuous and wholeheartedly devoted to God. The reward for their loyalty will eventually come, just as it does for all of the book's principal characters, as long as they remain faithful to the end.

T
B

Other motifs also permeate the book, such as almsgiving and burial of the dead, but paramount is devotion to one's family, as evidenced by the parent-child relationship and the interaction between spouses. Both Tobiah and Sarah are dutiful children who obey their parents' wishes and care very much about their well-being. Similarly, the two sets of elder parents in the story—Tobit and Anna, and Raguel and Edna—care deeply for their children and frequently give them advice in order to guide them on the proper path. The three married couples in the story also demonstrate the many facets of the marital relationship. Cooperation and communication are vital to a healthy marriage (Edna and Raguel), and prayer is likewise essential (Tobiah and Sarah). Sometimes circumstances force a reversal of roles, as when Anna is compelled to support her disabled husband financially after he becomes blind. To be sure, marriage also entails discord at times (Tobit and Anna), but such disagreements never destroy a couple's love. All three couples in the story overcome great adversity, remaining loyal to their partners and expressing their love for each other in words and deeds.

The perseverance of these beleaguered characters is a source of inspiration for readers of every generation, and the happy outcome of their travails will surely warm the heart. Readers will also enjoy many other touching features, such as the romantic notion of a "match made in heaven" and the handful of references to the family dog. The astute reader will also appreciate the clever symbolism in the names of the characters. For example, Tobit mentions a relative named Shemaiah, whose name in Hebrew means "Yahweh listens." Likewise, the names of the story's principal characters symbolize something true about God's kindness toward human beings. In response to their calamities, God helps people (Azariah) and heals them (Raphael) of their maladies. God is good (Tobit, Tobiah) and he is a dear friend (Raguel) whose gracious favor (Anna) will bring them happiness (Edna). ∎

# THE BOOK OF TOBIT

## New American Bible, Introduction

The Book of Tobit, named after its principal character, combines Jewish piety and morality with folklore in a fascinating story that has enjoyed wide popularity in both Jewish and Christian circles. Prayers, psalms, and words of wisdom, as well as the skillfully constructed story itself, provide valuable insights into the faith and the religious milieu of its unknown author. The book was probably written early in the second century B.C.; it is not known where.

Tobit, a devout and wealthy Israelite living among the captives deported to Nineveh from the Northern Kingdom of Israel in 722/721 B.C., suffers severe reverses and is finally blinded. Because of his misfortunes he begs the Lord to let him die. But recalling the large sum he had formerly deposited in far-off Media, he sends his son Tobiah there to bring back the money. In Media, at this same time, a young woman, Sarah, also prays for death, because she has lost seven husbands, each killed in turn on his wedding night by the demon Asmodeus. God hears the prayers of Tobit and Sarah and sends the angel Raphael in human form to aid them both.

Raphael makes the trip to Media with Tobiah. When Tobiah is attacked by a large fish as he bathes in the Tigris River, Raphael orders him to seize it and to remove its gall, heart, and liver because they are useful for medicine. Later, at Raphael's urging, Tobiah marries Sarah, and uses the fish's heart and liver to drive Asmodeus from the bridal chamber. Returning to Nineveh with his wife and his father's money, Tobiah rubs the fish's gall into his father's eyes and cures him. Finally, Raphael reveals his true identity and returns to heaven. Tobit then utters his beautiful hymn of praise. Before dying, Tobit tells his son to leave Nineveh because God will destroy that wicked city. After Tobiah buries his father and mother, he and his family depart for Media, where he later learns that the destruction of Nineveh has taken place.

The inspired author of the book used the literary form of religious novel (as in Esther and Judith) for the purpose of instruction and edification. The seemingly historical data, names of kings, cities, etc., are used as vivid details not only to create interest and charm, but also to illustrate the negative side of the theory of retribution: the wicked are indeed punished.

Although the Book of Tobit is usually listed with the historical books, it more correctly stands midway between them and the wisdom literature. It contains numerous maxims like those found in the wisdom books (cf. 4:3–19, 21; 12:6–10; 14:7, 9) as well as standard wisdom themes: fidelity to the law, intercessory function of angels, piety toward parents, purity of marriage, reverence for the dead, and the value of almsgiving, prayer, and fasting. The book makes Tobit a relative of Ahiqar, a noted hero of ancient Near Eastern wisdom literature and folklore.

Written most likely in Aramaic, the original of the book was lost for centuries. Fragments of four Aramaic texts and of one Hebrew text were discovered in Qumran Cave 4 in 1952 and have only recently been published. These Semitic forms of the book are in substantial agreement with the long Greek recension of Tobit found in Codex Sinaiticus, which had been recovered from St. Catherine's Monastery (Mount Sinai) only in 1844, and in mss. 319 and 910. Two other Greek forms of Tobit have long been known: the short recension, found mainly in the mss. Alexandrinus, Vaticanus, Venetus, and numerous cursive mss.; and an intermediate Greek recension, found in mss. 44, 106, 107. The Book of Tobit has also been known from two Latin versions: the long recension in the Vetus Latina, which is closely related to the long Greek recension and sometimes is even closer to the Aramaic and Hebrew texts than the Greek is; and the short recension in the Vulgate, related to the short Greek recension. The present English translation has been based mainly on Sinaiticus, which is the most complete form of the long Greek recension, despite two lacunae

(4:7–19b and 13:6i–10b) and some missing phrases, which make succeeding verses difficult to understand and make it necessary to supplement Sinaiticus from the Vetus Latina or from the short Greek recension. Occasionally, phrases or words have been introduced from the Aramaic or Hebrew texts, when they are significantly different. Forms of the Book of Tobit are also extant in ancient Arabic, Armenian, Coptic (Sahidic), Ethiopic, and Syriac, but these are almost all secondarily derived from the short Greek recension.

The divisions of the Book of Tobit are:

# TOBIT

**1** **Tobit.** ¹This book tells the story of Tobit,†
son of Tobiel, son of Hananiel, son of
Aduel, son of Gabael, son of Raphael, son of
Raguel, of the family of Asiel and the tribe
of Naphtali. ²During the days of Shalmaneser,† king of the Assyrians, he was taken captive from Thisbe, which is south of Kedesh
Naphtali in upper Galilee, above and to the
west of Asher, north of Phogor.*

## I. TOBIT'S ORDEALS

**His Virtue.** ³I, Tobit, have walked all the days
of my life on paths of fidelity and righteousness. I performed many charitable deeds for
my kindred and my people who had been
taken captive with me to Nineveh, in the land
of the Assyrians. ⁴When I lived as a young
man in my own country, in the land of Israel,
the entire tribe of my ancestor Naphtali broke
away from the house of David, my ancestor,
and from Jerusalem, the city that had been
singled out of all Israel's tribes that all Israel
might offer sacrifice there. It was the place
where the temple, God's dwelling, had been
built and consecrated for all generations to
come. ⁵*All my kindred, as well as the house
of Naphtali, my ancestor, used to offer sacrifice on every hilltop in Galilee to the calf that
Jeroboam, king of Israel, had made in Dan.†

⁶*But I alone used to go often to Jerusalem
for the festivals, as was prescribed for all Israel
by longstanding decree.† Bringing with me the
first fruits of crops, the firstlings of the flock,

the tithes of livestock, and the first shearings
of sheep,* I used to hasten to Jerusalem ⁷*and
present them to the priests, Aaron's sons, at
the altar. To the Levites ministering in Jerusalem I used to give the tithe of grain, wine,
olive oil, pomegranates, figs, and other fruits.
Six years in a row, I used to give a second tithe
in money, which each year I would go to pay
in Jerusalem. ⁸The third-year tithe I gave to orphans, widows, and converts who had joined
the Israelites. Every third year I would bring
them this offering, and we ate it in keeping
with the decree laid down in the Mosaic law
concerning it, and according to the commands
of Deborah, the mother of my father Tobiel;
for my father had died and left me an orphan.

⁹When I reached manhood, I married Anna,
a woman of our ancestral family. By her I had
a son whom I named Tobiah. ¹⁰Now, after I
had been deported to the Assyrians and came
as a captive to Nineveh, all my kindred and my
people used to eat the food of the Gentiles,*
¹¹but I refrained from eating that Gentile food.
¹²Because I was mindful of God with all my
heart, ¹³the Most High granted me favor and
status with Shalmaneser, so that I became
purchasing agent for all his needs.* ¹⁴Until
he died, I would go to Media to buy goods for
him there. I also deposited pouches of silver
worth ten talents† in trust with my kinsman
Gabael, son of Gabri, who lived at Rages, in
the land of Media. ¹⁵When Shalmaneser died
and his son Sennacherib† came to rule in his
stead, the roads to Media became unsafe, so I
could no longer go to Media.

**Courage in Burying the Dead.** ¹⁶In the days of
Shalmaneser I had performed many charitable
deeds for my kindred, members of my people.

**1:1** *Tobit:* in the Aramaic text the name is given as Tobi, an abbreviated form of Tobiyah (Ezr 2:60) or of Tobiyahu (2 Chr 17:8), a name that means "Yhwh is my welfare." *Tobiel:* "El [God] is my welfare." *Hananiel:* "El [God] has shown mercy." The book abounds in theophoric names.
**1:2** *Shalmaneser* (V) (727–722 B.C.): began the siege of Sa-maria; the inhabitants of the Northern Kingdom were taken into captivity by his successor, Sargon II (722–705); cf. 2 Kgs 17:1–6. *Thisbe* and *Phogor:* unidentified towns of Galilee. *Kedesh Naphtali:* cf. Jos 20:7; 2 Kgs 15:29. *Asher:* probably Hazor (Jos 11:1).
**1:5** Jeroboam established sanctuaries in Dan and Bethel so that the people would no longer have to go to Jerusalem for the festivals. The gold statues of calves that he placed in the sanctu-aries were considered the throne of Yhwh; but the people may have tended to worship the images themselves. Jeroboam also encouraged high places or hilltop shrines (1 Kgs 12:26–33).
**1:6–8** *Longstanding decree:* Dt 12:11, 13–14. Refusing to worship at Jeroboam's shrines, the faithful Tobit continued to

bring his offerings to Jerusalem; see 2 Chr 11:16. For the var-ious tithes, cf. Lv 27:30–33; Nm 18:20–32; 2 Chr 31:4–6; Dt 14:22–29; 26:12–13.
**1:14** *Silver worth ten talents:* a great sum of money; about ten thousand dollars, at least. *Rages:* modern Rai, about five miles southeast of Tehran. *Media:* the northwestern part of modern Iran.
**1:15** *Sennacherib* (705–681 B.C.): the son of Sargon II; neither was descended from Shalmaneser. On such historical inconsistencies, see Introduction; also notes on 5:6; 6:2; 9:2; 14:15.

**1:2** 2 Kgs 17:3; 18:9–12.   **1:7–8** Nm 18:12–13, 24; Dt
**1:5** 1 Kgs 12:26–32.            14:22–29; 18:4–5.
**1:6** Ex 23:14–15, 17;          **1:10** Lv 11; Dt 14:3–21;
        34:23.                            Acts 15:29; 1 Cor
**1:6** Dt 16:16.                        8:7–13.
                                      **1:13** Dn 2:48–49.

¹⁷* I would give my bread to the hungry and clothing to the naked. If I saw one of my people who had died and been thrown behind the wall of Nineveh, I used to bury him.† ¹⁸Sennacherib returned from Judea, having fled during the days of the judgment enacted against him by the King of Heaven because of the blasphemies he had uttered; whomever he killed I buried. For in his rage he killed many Israelites, but I used to take their bodies away by stealth and bury them. So when Sennacherib looked for them, he could not find them. ¹⁹But a certain Ninevite went and informed the king about me, that I was burying them, and I went into hiding. When I realized that the king knew about me and that I was being hunted to be put to death, I became afraid and took flight. ²⁰All my property was confiscated; I was left with nothing. All that I had was taken to the king's palace, except for my wife Anna and my son Tobiah.†

²¹But forty days did not pass before two of the king's sons assassinated him and fled to the mountains of Ararat. A son of his, Esarhaddon,† succeeded him as king. He put Ahiqar, my kinsman Anael's son, in charge of all the credit accounts of his kingdom, and he took control over the entire administration.* ²²Then Ahiqar interceded on my behalf, and I returned to Nineveh. Ahiqar had been chief cupbearer, keeper of the signet ring, treasury accountant, and credit accountant under Sennacherib, king of the Assyrians; and Esarhaddon appointed him as Second to himself. He was, in fact, my nephew, of my father's house, and of my own family.

**2** ¹Thus under King Esarhaddon I returned to my home, and my wife Anna and my son Tobiah were restored to me. Then on our festival of Pentecost, the holy feast of Weeks,† a fine dinner was prepared for me, and I reclined to eat.* ²The table was set for me, and the dishes placed before me were many. So I said to my son Tobiah: "Son, go out and bring in whatever poor person you find among our kindred exiled here in Nineveh who may be a sincere worshiper of God to share this meal with me. Indeed, son, I shall wait for you to come back."†

³Tobiah went out to look for some poor person among our kindred, but he came back and cried, "Father!" I said to him, "Here I am, son." He answered, "Father, one of our people has been murdered! He has been thrown out into the market place, and there he lies strangled." ⁴I sprang to my feet, leaving the dinner untouched, carried the dead man from the square, and put him in one of the rooms until sundown, so that I might bury him. ⁵I returned and washed† and in sorrow ate my food.* ⁶I remembered the oracle pronounced by the prophet Amos against Bethel:*

"I will turn your feasts into mourning,
    and all your songs into dirges."

⁷Then I wept. At sunset I went out, dug a grave, and buried him.

⁸My neighbors mocked me, saying: "Does he have no fear? Once before he was hunted, to be executed for this sort of deed, and he ran away; yet here he is again burying the dead!"

**Tobit's Blindness.** ⁹That same night I washed and went into my courtyard, where I lay down to sleep beside the wall. Because of the heat I left my face uncovered. ¹⁰I did not know that sparrows were perched on the wall above me; their warm droppings settled in my eyes, causing white scales† on them. I went to doctors for a cure, but the more they applied ointments, the more my vision was obscured by the white

---

**1:17–18** Tobit risked his own life to bury the dead. Deprivation of burial was viewed with horror by the Jews. Cf. 4:3–4; 6:15; 14:12–13.
**1:20** *Tobiah:* the son bears the fuller form of his father's name; see note on 1:1.
**1:21** *Esarhaddon:* 681–669 B.C. *Ahiqar:* a hero of ancient folklore, known for his outstanding wisdom. *The Story (or Wisdom) of Ahiqar* was very popular in antiquity and is extant in many different forms: Aramaic, Syriac, Armenian, Arabic (*Arabian Nights*), Greek (*Aesop's Fables*), Slavonic, Ethiopic, and Romanian. The sacred author makes Tobit the uncle of the famous Ahiqar in order to enhance Tobit's own prestige. See note on 14:10.
**2:1** *Feast of Weeks:* also called by its Greek name, Pentecost, was celebrated fifty days after the Passover. Cf. Lv 23:15–21; Dt 16:9–12.

**2:2** Almsgiving and charity to the poor are important virtues taught by the book (4:7–11, 16–17; 12:8–9; 14:10–11). *A sincere worshiper of God:* lit., "who is mindful of God with the whole heart."
**2:5** *Washed:* because of ritual defilement from touching a corpse (Nm 19:11–13).
**2:10** *White scales:* or white films. A primitive way of describing an eye ailment that results in blindness. *Elam:* or in Greek, *Elymais,* an ancient district northeast of the head of the Persian Gulf.

**1:17** Jb 31:16–20. **1:21** 2 Kgs 19:37; 2 Chr 32:21; 2 Mc 8:19; Sir 48:21; Is 37:38. **2:1** Lv 23:15–21; Nm 28:26–31; Dt 16:9–12. **2:5** Nm 19:11–22. **2:6** 1 Mc 1:39; Am 8:10.

scales, until I was totally blind. For four years I was unable to see, and all my kindred were distressed at my condition. Ahiqar, however, took care of me for two years, until he left for Elam.

¹¹ At that time my wife Anna worked for hire at weaving cloth, doing the kind of work women do. ¹² When she delivered the material to her employers, they would pay her a wage. On the seventh day of the month of Dystrus,† she finished the woven cloth and delivered it to her employers. They paid her the full salary and also gave her a young goat for a meal. ¹³ On entering my house, the goat began to bleat. So I called to my wife and said: "Where did this goat come from? It was not stolen, was it? Give it back to its owners; we have no right to eat anything stolen!" ¹⁴ * But she said to me, "It was given to me as a bonus over and above my wages." Yet I would not believe her and told her to give it back to its owners. I flushed with anger at her over this. So she retorted: "Where are your charitable deeds now? Where are your righteous acts? Look! All that has happened to you is well known!"†

**3** ¹ Then sad at heart, I groaned and wept aloud. With sobs I began to pray:†

### Tobit's Prayer for Death

² "You are righteous, Lord,
  and all your deeds are just;
All your ways are mercy and fidelity;
  you are judge of the world. *

³ And now, Lord, be mindful of me
  and look with favor upon me.
Do not punish me for my sins,
  or for my inadvertent offenses,
  or for those of my ancestors. *

"They sinned against you,

⁴   and disobeyed your commandments.

So you handed us over to plunder,
  captivity, and death,
  to become an object lesson, a byword,
  and a reproach
in all the nations among whom you
  scattered us. *

⁵ "Yes, your many judgments are right
  in dealing with me as my sins,
  and those of my ancestors, deserve.
For we have neither kept your
  commandments,
  nor walked in fidelity before you.

⁶ "So now, deal with me as you please;
  command my life breath to be taken
  from me,
  that I may depart from the face of the
  earth and become dust.
It is better for me to die than to live,†
  because I have listened to undeserved
  reproaches,
  and great is the grief within me. *

"Lord, command that I be released from
  such anguish;
  let me go to my everlasting abode;
  Do not turn your face away from me,
  Lord.
For it is better for me to die
  than to endure so much misery in life,
  and to listen to such reproaches!"

## II. SARAH'S PLIGHT

**Sarah Falsely Accused.** ⁷† On that very day, at Ecbatana in Media, it so happened that Raguel's daughter Sarah also had to listen to reproaches from one of her father's maids. ⁸ For she had been given in marriage to seven husbands, but the wicked demon Asmodeus†

---

**2:12** *Seventh day of the month of Dystrus:* late in winter. The Macedonian month Dystros corresponds to the Jewish month of Shebat (January–February). *A meal:* lit., "for the hearth"; the gift had probably been made in view of some springtime festival like the Jewish Purim.
**2:14** Anna's sharp rebuke calls to mind the words of Job's wife (Jb 2:9).
**3:1** *Pray:* prayer is a significant theme, occurring at six major turning points in the story (3:2–6, 11–15; 8:5–8, 15–17; 11:14–15; 13:1–18).
**3:6** *It is better for me to die than to live:* in his distress Tobit uses the words of the petulant Jonah (Jon 4:3, 8), who wished to die because God did not destroy the hated Ninevites. In similar circumstances, Moses (Nm 11:15), Elijah (1 Kgs 19:4), and Job (Jb 7:15) also prayed for death. *Everlasting abode:* a reference to Sheol, the dismal abode of the dead from which no one returns

(Jb 7:9–10; 14:12; Is 26:14). See note on Tb 4:6.
**3:7** From here on, the story is told in the third person. Verse 7 relates one of the several marvelous coincidences that the storyteller uses to suggest divine providence; see also vv. 16–17; 4:1; 5:4. *Ecbatana:* Hamadan in modern Iran; this was the capital of ancient Media. *Raguel:* the Greek form of the Hebrew name *Re'u'el,* "friend of God."
**3:8** *Asmodeus:* in Persian *aeshma daeva,* "demon of wrath," adopted into Aramaic with the sense of "the Destroyer." It will be subdued (8:3) by Raphael (v. 17), whose name means "God has healed."

**2:14** Jb 2:9.
**3:2** Ps 25:10; 119:137; Dn 3:27.
**3:3** Ex 34:7.
**3:4** Dt 28:15; Bar
1:16–22; 2:4–5; 3:8; Dn 9:5–6.
**3:6** Nm 11:15; 1 Kgs 19:4; Jb 7:15; Jon 4:3, 8.

kept killing them off before they could have intercourse with her, as is prescribed for wives. The maid said to her: "You are the one who kills your husbands! Look! You have already been given in marriage to seven husbands, but you do not bear the name of a single one of them. ⁹Why do you beat us? Because your husbands are dead? Go, join them! May we never see son or daughter of yours!"

¹⁰That day Sarah was sad at heart. She went in tears to an upstairs room in her father's house and wanted to hang herself. But she reconsidered, saying to herself: "No! May people never reproach my father and say to him, 'You had only one beloved daughter, but she hanged herself because of her misfortune.' And thus would I bring my father laden with sorrow in his old age to Hades. It is far better for me not to hang myself, but to beg the Lord that I might die, and no longer have to listen to such reproaches in my lifetime."*

¹¹At that same time, with hands outstretched toward the window,† she implored favor:

### Sarah's Prayer for Death

"Blessed are you, merciful God!
Blessed be your holy and honorable
name forever!
May all your works forever bless you.*

12  Now to you, Lord, I have turned my
face
and have lifted up my eyes.

13  Bid me to depart from the earth,
never again to listen to such
reproaches.

14  "You know, Master, that I am clean
of any defilement with a man.

15  I have never sullied my own name
or my father's name in the land of my
captivity.

"I am my father's only daughter,
and he has no other child to be his
heir,

Nor does he have a kinsman or close
relative
whose wife I should wait to become.
Seven husbands of mine have already
died.
Why then should I live any longer?
But if it does not please you, Lord, to
take my life,
look favorably upon me and have pity
on me,
that I may never again listen to such
reproaches!"

**An Answer to Prayer.** ¹⁶At that very time, the prayer of both of them was heard in the glorious presence of God. ¹⁷* So Raphael was sent to heal them both: to remove the white scales from Tobit's eyes, so that he might again see with his own eyes God's light; and to give Sarah, the daughter of Raguel, as a wife to Tobiah, the son of Tobit, and to rid her of the wicked demon Asmodeus. For it fell to Tobiah's lot† to claim her before any others who might wish to marry her.

At that very moment Tobit turned from the courtyard to his house, and Raguel's daughter Sarah came down from the upstairs room.

### III. PREPARATION FOR THE JOURNEY

**4** **A Father's Instruction.** ¹That same day Tobit remembered the money he had deposited in trust with Gabael at Rages in Media. ²He thought to himself, "Now that I have asked for death, why should I not call my son Tobiah and let him know about this money before I die?" ³So he called his son Tobiah; and when he came, he said to him:† "Son, when I die, give me a decent burial. Honor your mother, and do not abandon her as long as she lives. Do whatever pleases her, and do not grieve her spirit in any way.* ⁴Remember, son, how she went through many dangers for you while you were in her womb. When she dies, bury her in the same grave with me.

**3:11** *Toward the window*: that is, looking in prayer toward Jerusalem; cf. Dn 6:11. "Blessed are you" and "Blessed be God" are traditional openings of Jewish prayers (Tb 8:5, 15; 11:14; 13:1).

**3:17** *It fell to Tobiah's lot*: according to the patriarchal custom of marriage within the family group. Tobiah was Sarah's closest eligible relative (6:12). Cf. 4:12–13; Gn 24:3; 28:2; Ru 3:9–12; 4:1–12.

**4:3–19** A collection of maxims that parallel those in the wisdom literature, especially Proverbs and Sirach (see Introduction):

duties toward parents (vv. 3–4; cf. also 14:13); perseverance in virtue and avoidance of evil (vv. 5–6, 14b); necessity and value of almsgiving and charity (vv. 7–11, 16–17); marriage within the clan (vv. 12–13a); industry (v. 13b); prompt payment of wages (v. 14a); the golden rule (v. 15a); temperance (v. 15b); docility (v. 18); prayer (v. 19).

**3:10** Tb 6:15; Gn 37:35; 42:38; 44:29, 31.
**3:11** 1 Kgs 8:44, 48; Ps 28:2; 134:2; Dn 6:11.
**3:17** Tb 4:12–13; 6:12–13; Gn 24:3–4.
**4:3** Ex 20:12; Prv 23:22; Sir 7:27.

⁵ "Through all your days, son, keep the Lord in mind, and do not seek to sin or to transgress the commandments. Perform righteous deeds all the days of your life, and do not tread the paths of wickedness. ⁶* For those who act with fidelity, all who practice righteousness, will prosper in their affairs.†

⁷ "Give alms from your possessions. Do not turn your face away from any of the poor, so that God's face will not be turned away from you.* ⁸ Give in proportion to what you own. If you have great wealth, give alms out of your abundance; if you have but little, do not be afraid to give alms even of that little. ⁹ You will be storing up a goodly treasure for yourself against the day of adversity.* ¹⁰ For almsgiving delivers from death and keeps one from entering into Darkness. ¹¹ Almsgiving is a worthy offering in the sight of the Most High for all who practice it.*

¹² "Be on your guard, son, against every kind of fornication, and above all, marry a woman of your own ancestral family. Do not marry a foreign woman, one who is not of your father's tribe, because we are descendants of the prophets, who were the first to speak the truth. Noah prophesied first, then Abraham, Isaac, and Jacob, our ancestors from the beginning of time. Son, remember that all of them took wives from among their own kindred and were blessed in their children, and that their posterity would inherit the land.* ¹³ Therefore, son, love your kindred. Do not act arrogantly toward any of them, the sons and daughters of your people, by refusing to take a wife for yourself from among them. For in arrogance there is ruin and great instability. In idleness there is loss and dire poverty, for idleness is the mother of famine.

¹⁴ "Do not keep with you overnight the wages of those who have worked for you, but pay them at once. If you serve God thus, you will receive your reward. Be on your guard,

son, in everything you do; be wise in all that you say and discipline yourself in all your conduct.* ¹⁵ Do to no one what you yourself hate. Do not drink wine till you become drunk or let drunkenness accompany you on your way.*

¹⁶* "Give to the hungry some of your food, and to the naked some of your clothing. Whatever you have left over, give away as alms; and do not let your eye begrudge the alms that you give. ¹⁷* Pour out your wine and your bread on the grave of the righteous, but do not share them with sinners.†

¹⁸ "Seek counsel from every wise person, and do not think lightly of any useful advice. ¹⁹* At all times bless the Lord, your God, and ask him that all your paths may be straight and all your endeavors and plans may prosper. For no other nation possesses good counsel, but it is the Lord who gives all good things. Whomever the Lord chooses to raise is raised; and whomever the Lord chooses to cast down is cast down to the recesses of Hades. So now, son, keep in mind these my commandments, and never let them be erased from your heart.

²⁰ "Now, I must tell you, son, that I have deposited in trust ten talents of silver with Gabael, the son of Gabri, at Rages in Media. ²¹ Do not fear, son, that we have lived in poverty. You will have great wealth, if you fear God, avoid all sin, and do what is good before the Lord your God."*

**5** **The Angel Raphael.** ¹ Then Tobiah replied to his father Tobit: "Everything that you have commanded me, father, I shall do. ² But how will I be able to get that money from him, since he does not know me, and I do not know him? What sign can I give him so that he will recognize and trust me, and give me the money? I do not even know the roads to Media, in order to go there." ³ Tobit answered his son Tobiah: "He gave me his bond,† and I gave him mine; I divided his into two parts,

---

† **4:6** It was commonly thought in the Old Testament that virtue guaranteed earthly prosperity, and sin earthly disaster (Prv 10:2; cf. Dt 28).

**4:17** Tobit counsels his son to give alms in honor of the dead or, more probably, to give the "bread of consolation" to the family of the deceased. Cf. Jer 16:7; Ez 24:17.

**5:3** *Bond*: a document called in Greek *cheirographon*. In the Middle Ages, notably in England, a deed and its duplicate were written on one piece of parchment, with the Latin word *chirographum* inscribed across the top of the sheet or between the two copies of the text. The document was then cut in two in either a straight or a wavy line, the parts being given to the persons concerned. Perhaps this procedure was derived from the present

verse of Tobit. Duplicate documents, usually one part open and the other sealed, are well known from the ancient Near East.

---

*

| 4:6 Tb 13:6; Jn 3:21; Eph | 28:1–4; 29:15–30; |
| 4:15. | Ex 34:16; Dt 7:3; Jgs |
| 4:7–8 Tb 12:8–10; Dt | 14:3. |
| 15:7–8, 11; Prv 19:17; | 4:14 Lv 19:3; Dt 24:15. |
| Sir 4:1–6; 14:13; Lk | 4:15 Mt 7:12; Lk 6:31. |
| 14:13; 1 Jn 3:17. | 4:16 Dt 15:10; Is 58:7; Mt |
| 4:9 Mt 6:20–21. | 25:35–36; 2 Cor 9:7. |
| 4:11 Sir 3:30; 29:12. | 4:17 Jer 16:7; Lk 14:13. |
| 4:12 Tb 3:15, 17; 6:12; | 4:19 Dt 4:6; Ps 119:10. |
| Gn 11:29, 31; 25:20; | 4:21 1 Tm 6:6–10. |

and each of us took one part; I put one part with the money. It is twenty years since I deposited that money! So, son, find yourself a trustworthy person who will make the journey with you, and we will give him wages when you return; but bring back that money from Gabael while I am still alive."

[4] Tobiah went out to look for someone who would travel with him to Media, someone who knew the way. He went out and found the angel Raphael standing before him (though he did not know† that this was an angel of God).* [5] Tobiah said to him, "Where do you come from, young man?" He replied, "I am an Israelite, one of your kindred. I have come here to work." Tobiah said to him, "Do you know the way to Media?" [6] "Yes," he replied, "I have been there many times. I know the place well and am acquainted with all the routes. I have often traveled to Media; I used to stay with our kinsman Gabael, who lives at Rages in Media. It is a good two days' journey from Ecbatana to Rages,† for Rages is situated in the mountains, but Ecbatana is in the middle of the plain." [7] Tobiah said to him, "Wait for me, young man, till I go in and tell my father; for I need you to make the journey with me. I will pay you your wages."* [8] He replied, "Very well, I will wait; but do not be long."

[9] Tobiah went in and informed his father Tobit: "I have found someone of our own Israelite kindred who will go with me!" Tobit said, "Call the man in, so that I may find out from what family and tribe he comes, and whether he is trustworthy enough to travel with you, son."

[10] Tobiah went out to summon him, saying, "Young man, my father is calling for you." When Raphael entered the house, Tobit greeted him first. He replied, "Joyful greetings to you!" Tobit answered, "What joy is left for me? Here I am, a blind man who cannot see the light of heaven, but must remain in darkness, like the dead who no longer see the light! Though alive, I am among the dead. I can hear people's voices, but I do not see them." The young man said, "Take courage! God's healing

is near; so take courage!" Tobit then said: "My son Tobiah wants to go to Media. Can you go with him to show him the way? I will pay you your wages, brother." He answered: "Yes, I will go with him, and I know all the routes. I have often traveled to Media and crossed all its plains so I know well the mountains and all its roads." [11] Tobit asked him, "Brother, tell me, please, from what family and tribe are you?" [12] He replied, "Why? What need do you have for a tribe? Aren't you looking for a hired man?" Tobit replied, "I only want to know, brother, whose son you truly are and what your name is."*

[13] He answered, "I am Azariah,† son of the great Hananiah, one of your own kindred." [14] Tobit exclaimed: "Welcome! God save you, brother! Do not be provoked with me, brother, for wanting to learn the truth about your family. It turns out that you are a kinsman, from a noble and good line! I knew Hananiah and Nathan, the two sons of the great Shemeliah. They used to go to Jerusalem with me, where we would worship together. They were not led astray; your kindred are good people. You are certainly of good lineage. So welcome!"

[15] Then he added: "For each day I will give you a drachma as wages,† as well as expenses for you and for my son. So go with my son, and [16] I will even add a bonus to your wages!" The young man replied, "I will go with him. Do not fear. In good health we will leave you, and in good health we will return to you, for the way is safe." [17] Tobit said, "Blessing be upon you, brother." Then he called his son and said to him: "Son, prepare whatever you need for the journey, and set out with your kinsman. May God in heaven protect you on the way and bring you back to me safe and sound; may his angel accompany you for your safety, son."

Tobiah left to set out on his journey, and he kissed his father and mother. Tobit said to him, "Have a safe journey." [18] But his mother began to weep and she said to Tobit: "Why have you sent my child away? Is he not the staff of our hands, as he goes in and out before

---

**5:4** *He did not know*: the theme of an angel in disguise occurs frequently in folklore as well as in the Old Testament (Gn 18; cf. Heb 13:2).

**5:6** *It is a good two days' journey from Ecbatana to Rages*: Alexander's army took eleven days in forced marches to cover this distance, about 180 miles. (See notes on 1:15; 3:7 and Introduction.)

**5:13–14** Azariah, "Yhwh has helped"; Hananiah, "Yhwh has

shown mercy"; Nathan is a shortened form of Nathaniah, "Yhwh has given"; Shemeliah may be a Greek corruption of the Hebrew name, Shemaiah, "Yhwh has heard."

**5:15** *A drachma as wages*: the normal wages, about seventeen cents, a day's wage for a laborer.

---

**5:4** Heb 13:2.                    **5:12** Jgs 13:17–18.
**5:7** Tb 12:2.

us? [19] Do not heap money upon money! Rather relinquish it in exchange for our child! [20] What the Lord has given us to live on is certainly enough for us." [21] Tobit reassured her: "Do not worry! Our son will leave in good health and come back to us in good health. Your own eyes will see the day when he returns to you safe and sound. So, do not worry; do not fear for them, my sister.† [22] For a good angel† will go with him, his journey will be successful, and he will return in good health." [1] Then she stopped weeping.

## IV. TOBIAH'S JOURNEY TO MEDIA

**6** **On the Way to Rages.** [2] When the young man left home, accompanied by the angel, the dog followed Tobiah out and went along with them. Both journeyed along, and when the first night came, they camped beside the Tigris River.† [3] When the young man went down to wash his feet in the Tigris River, a large fish leaped out of the water and tried to swallow his foot. He shouted in alarm. [4] But the angel said to the young man, "Grab the fish and hold on to it!" He seized the fish and hauled it up on dry land. [5] The angel then told him: "Slit the fish open and take out its gall, heart, and liver, and keep them with you; but throw away the other entrails. Its gall, heart, and liver are useful for medicine."† [6] After Tobiah had slit the fish open, he put aside the gall, heart, and liver. Then he roasted and ate part of the fish; the rest he salted and kept for the journey.

**Raphael's Instructions.** Afterward the two of them traveled on together till they drew near to Media. [7] Then the young man asked the angel this question: "Brother Azariah, what medicine is in the fish's heart, liver, and gall?" [8] He answered: "As for the fish's heart and liver, if you burn them to make smoke in the presence of a man or a woman who is afflicted by a demon or evil spirit, any affliction will flee and never return. [9] As for the gall, if you apply it to

the eyes of one who has white scales, blowing right into them, sight will be restored."

[10] When they had entered Media and were getting close to Ecbatana, [11] Raphael said to the young man, "Brother Tobiah!" He answered, "Here I am!" Raphael continued, "Tonight we must stay in the house of Raguel, who is a relative of yours. He has a beautiful daughter named Sarah, [12] but no other son or daughter apart from Sarah. Since you are Sarah's closest relative, you more than any other have the right to marry her. Moreover, her father's estate is rightfully yours to inherit. The girl is wise, courageous, and very beautiful; and her father is a good man who loves her dearly."* [13] He continued: "You have the right to marry her. So listen to me, brother. Tonight I will speak to her father about the girl so that we may take her as your bride. When we return from Rages, we will have the wedding feast for her. I know that Raguel cannot keep her from you or promise her to another man; he would incur the death penalty as decreed in the Book of Moses.† For he knows that you, more than anyone else, have the right to marry his daughter. Now listen to me, brother; we will speak about this girl tonight, so that we may arrange her engagement to you. Then when we return from Rages, we will take her and bring her back with us to your house."

[14] But Tobiah said to Raphael in reply, "Brother Azariah, I have heard that she has already been given in marriage to seven husbands, and that they have died in the bridal chamber. On the very night they approached her, they would die. I have also heard it said that it was a demon that killed them. [15] So now I too am afraid of this demon, because it is in love with her and does not harm her; but it kills any man who wishes to come close to her. I am my father's only child. If I should die, I would bring the life of my father and mother down to their grave in sorrow over me; they have no other son to bury them!"* [16] Raphael said to him: "Do you not remember your father's commands? He ordered you

---

† **5:21** *My sister:* "sister" was a term of endearment used in antiquity even for one's wife; similarly "brother" for one's husband. Cf. 7:11, 15; 8:4, 21; 10:6, 13; Sg 4:9–10, 12; 5:1–2.
**5:22** *A good angel:* a reference to a guardian angel, though Tobit does not know, of course, that Raphael himself, disguised as Azariah, is the good angel in this case.
**6:2** *Tigris River:* this river is actually west of Nineveh, so they would not have come to it on their way to Media. See note on 1:15 and the Introduction.

**6:5** *Its gall…medicine:* belief in the healing power of these organs was common among the physicians of antiquity.
**6:13** *Raguel…Book of Moses:* Nm 36:6–8 prescribed marriage within the ancestral tribe for daughters who had no brothers who might inherit the ancestral property, but no death penalty is mentioned.

to marry a woman from your own ancestral family. Now listen to me, brother; do not worry about that demon. Take Sarah. I know that tonight she will be given to you as your wife! [17] When you go into the bridal chamber, take some of the fish's liver and the heart, and place them on the embers intended for incense, and an odor will be given off. [18] As soon as the demon smells the odor, it will flee and never again show itself near her. Then when you are about to have intercourse with her, both of you must first get up to pray.† Beg the Lord of heaven that mercy and protection be granted you. Do not be afraid, for she was set apart for you before the world existed. You will save her, and she will go with you. And I assume that you will have children by her, and they will be like brothers for you. So do not worry."

When Tobiah heard Raphael's words that she was his kinswoman, and of the lineage of his ancestral house, he loved her deeply, and his heart was truly set on her.

## V. MARRIAGE AND HEALING OF SARAH

**7 At the House of Raguel.** [1] When they entered Ecbatana, Tobiah said, "Brother Azariah, bring me straight to the house of our kinsman Raguel." So he did, and they came to the house of Raguel, whom they found seated by his courtyard gate. They greeted him first, and he answered, "Many greetings to you, brothers! Welcome! You have come in peace! Now enter in peace!" And he brought them into his house. [2] He said to his wife Edna, "How this young man resembles Tobit, the son of my uncle!" [3] So Edna asked them, saying, "Where are you from, brothers?" They answered, "We are descendants of Naphtali, now captives in Nineveh." [4] She said to them, "Do you know our kinsman Tobit?" They answered her, "Indeed, we do know him!" She asked, "Is he well?" [5] They answered, "Yes, he is alive and well." Then Tobiah said, "He is my father!" [6] Raguel jumped up, kissed him, and broke into tears. [7] Then, finding words, he said, "A blessing upon you, son! You are the son of a good and noble father. What a terrible

misfortune that a man so righteous and charitable has been afflicted with blindness!" He embraced his kinsman Tobiah and continued to weep. [8] His wife Edna also wept for Tobit; and their daughter Sarah also began to weep.

**Marriage of Tobiah and Sarah.** [9] Afterward, Raguel slaughtered a ram from the flock and gave them a warm reception. When they had washed, bathed, and reclined to eat and drink, Tobiah said to Raphael, "Brother Azariah, ask Raguel to give me my kinswoman Sarah." [10] Raguel overheard the words; so he said to the young man: "Eat and drink and be merry tonight, for no man has a greater right to marry my daughter Sarah than you, brother. Besides, not even I have the right to give her to anyone but you, because you are my closest relative. However, son, I must frankly tell you the truth. [11] I have given her in marriage to seven husbands who were kinsmen of ours, and all died on the very night they approached her. But now, son, eat and drink. The Lord will look after you both." Tobiah answered, "I will neither eat nor drink anything here until you settle what concerns me."

Raguel said to him: "I will do it. She is yours as decreed by the Book of Moses. It has been decided in heaven that she be given to you! Take your kinswoman; from now on you are her brother, and she is your sister.† She is given to you today and here ever after. May the Lord of heaven prosper you both tonight, son, and grant you mercy and peace." [12] Then Raguel called his daughter Sarah, and she came to him. He took her by the hand and gave her to Tobiah with these words: "Take her according to the law. According to the decree written in the Book of Moses I give her to be your wife. Take her and bring her safely to your father. And may the God of heaven grant both of you a safe journey in peace!"* [13] He then called her mother and told her to bring writing materials. He wrote out a copy of a marriage contract stating that he gave Sarah to Tobiah as his wife as decreed by the law of Moses. Her mother brought the material, and he drew up the contract, to which he affixed his seal.*

[14] Afterward they began to eat and drink.

---

† **6:18** *Get up to pray*: prayer, combined with ritual action, drives out the demon.

**7:11** *You are her brother, and she is your sister*: the marriage formula is similar to a marriage contract from the fifth century

B.C. found at Elephantine in Egypt: "She is my wife and I am her husband from this day forever."

* ———

**7:12** Gn 24:50–51.      **7:13** Tb 6:12.

15 Later Raguel called his wife Edna and said, "My sister, prepare the other bedroom and bring Sarah there." 16 She went, made the bed in the room, as he had told her, and brought Sarah there. After she had cried over her, she wiped away her tears and said, 17 "Take courage, my daughter! May the Lord of heaven grant you joy in place of your grief! Courage, my daughter!" Then she left.

# 8 Expulsion of the Demon.
1 When they had finished eating and drinking, they wanted to retire. So they brought the young man out and led him to the bedroom. 2 Tobiah, mindful of Raphael's instructions, took the fish's liver and heart from the bag where he had them, and put them on the embers intended for incense.† 3 The odor of the fish repulsed the demon, and it fled to the upper regions of Egypt;† Raphael went in pursuit of it and there bound it hand and foot. Then Raphael returned immediately.

4 When Sarah's parents left the bedroom and closed the door behind them, Tobiah rose from bed and said to his wife, "My sister, come, let us pray and beg our Lord to grant us mercy and protection." 5 She got up, and they started to pray and beg that they might be protected. He began with these words:

"Blessed are you, O God of our
        ancestors;
    blessed be your name forever and
        ever!
    Let the heavens and all your creation
        bless you forever. *
6   You made Adam, and you made his wife
        Eve
    to be his helper and support;
    and from these two the human race
        has come.
    You said, 'It is not good for the man to
        be alone;
    let us make him a helper like
        himself.' *
7   Now, not with lust,
    but with fidelity I take this
        kinswoman as my wife.

    Send down your mercy on me and on
        her,
    and grant that we may grow old
        together.
    Bless us with children."

8 They said together, "Amen, amen!" 9 Then they went to bed for the night.

But Raguel got up and summoned his servants. They went out with him and dug a grave, 10 for he said, "Perhaps Tobiah will die; then we would be a laughingstock and an object of mockery." 11 When they had finished digging the grave, Raguel went back into the house and called his wife, 12 saying, "Send one of the maids in to see whether he is alive. If he has died, let us bury him without anyone knowing about it." 13 They sent the maid, lit a lamp, and opened the bedroom door; she went in and found them sleeping together. 14 The maid came out and told them that Tobiah was alive, and that nothing was wrong. 15 Then they praised the God of heaven in these words:

"Blessed are you, God, with every pure
        blessing!
    Let all your chosen ones bless you
        forever!
16   Blessed are you, for you have made me
        happy;
    what I feared did not happen.
    Rather you have dealt with us
        according to your abundant mercy.
17   Blessed are you, for you have shown
        mercy
    toward two only children.
    Grant them, Master, mercy and
        protection,
    and bring their lives to fulfillment
        with happiness and mercy."

18 Then Raguel told his servants to fill in the grave before dawn.

# Wedding Feast.
19 He asked his wife to bake many loaves of bread; he himself went out to the herd and brought two steers and four

---

† **8:2–3** The manner of coping with demonic influences among the ancients seems strange to us. However, the fish here is a folktale element, suggesting the hero's fight with a dragon, and not a recipe for exorcism. It is clear that the author places primary emphasis on the value of prayer to God (6:18; 8:4–8), on the role of the angel as God's agent, and on the pious disposition of Tobiah.
**8:3** The desert was considered the dwelling place of demons. Cf. Is 13:21; 34:14; Mt 4:1; 12:43.

* **8:5** Dn 3:26.     **8:6** Gn 2:18–23.

rams, which he ordered to be slaughtered. So they began to prepare the feast. [20] He summoned Tobiah and said to him, "For fourteen days† you shall not stir from here, but shall remain here eating and drinking with me; you shall bring joy to my daughter's afflicted spirit. [21] Now take half of what I own here; go back in good health to your father. The other half will be yours when I and my wife die. Take courage, son! I am your father, and Edna is your mother; we belong to you and to your sister both now and forever. So take courage, son!"

# 9 The Money Recovered.

[1] Then Tobiah called Raphael and said to him: [2] "Brother Azariah, take along with you from here four servants and two camels and travel to Rages.† Go to Gabael's house and give him this bond. Get the money and then bring him along with you to the wedding celebration. [3] For you know that my father will be counting the days. If I should delay even by a single day, I would cause him intense grief. [4] You have witnessed the oath that Raguel has sworn; I cannot violate his oath." [5] So Raphael, together with the four servants and two camels, traveled to Rages in Media, where they stayed at Gabael's house. Raphael gave Gabael his bond and told him about Tobit's son Tobiah, that he had married and was inviting him to the wedding celebration. Gabael got up and counted out for him the moneybags with their seals, and they packed them on the camels.

[6] The following morning they both got an early start and traveled to the wedding celebration. When they entered Raguel's house, they found Tobiah reclining at table. He jumped up and greeted Gabael, who wept and blessed him, exclaiming: "Good and noble child, son of a good and noble, righteous and charitable man, may the Lord bestow a heavenly blessing on you and on your wife, and on your wife's father and mother. Blessed be God, because I have seen the very image of my cousin Tobit!"

## VI. TOBIAH'S RETURN JOURNEY TO NINEVEH AND THE HEALING OF TOBIT

# 10 Anxiety of the Parents.

[1] Meanwhile, day by day, Tobit was keeping track of the time Tobiah would need to go and to return. When the number of days was reached and his son did not appear, [2] he said, "Could it be that he has been detained there? Or perhaps Gabael has died, and there is no one to give him the money?" [3] And he began to grieve. [4] His wife Anna said, "My son has perished and is no longer among the living!" And she began to weep aloud and to wail over her son: [5] "Alas, child, light of my eyes, that I have let you make this journey!" [6] But Tobit kept telling her: "Be still, do not worry, my sister; he is safe! Probably they have to take care of some unexpected business there. The man who is traveling with him is trustworthy and one of our kindred. So do not grieve over him, my sister. He will be here soon." [7] But she retorted, "You be still, and do not try to deceive me! My son has perished!" She would rush out and keep watch every day at the road her son had taken. She ate nothing. After the sun had set, she would go back home to wail and cry the whole night through, getting no sleep at all.*

**Departure from Ecbatana.** Now when the fourteen days of the wedding celebration, which Raguel had sworn to hold for his daughter, had come to an end, Tobiah went to him and said: "Send me off, now, since I know that my father and mother do not believe they will ever see me again. So I beg you, father, let me depart and go back to my own father. I have already told you how I left him." [8] Raguel said to Tobiah: "Stay, son, stay with me. I am sending messengers to your father Tobit, and they will give him news of you." [9] But Tobiah insisted, "No, I beg you to send me back to my father."

[10] Raguel then promptly handed over to Tobiah his wife Sarah, together with half of all his property: male and female slaves, oxen and sheep, donkeys and camels, clothing, money, and household goods. [11] He saw them safely off. Embracing Tobiah, he said to him: "Farewell, son. Have a safe journey. May the Lord of heaven grant prosperity to you and to your wife Sarah. And may I see children of yours before I die!" [12] Then he said to his daughter Sarah, "My daughter, honor your father-in-law

---

† **8:20** *For fourteen days*: because of the happy, and unexpected, turn of events, Raguel doubles the time of the wedding feast. When Tobiah returns home, the usual seven-day feast is held (11:18). Cf. Jgs 14:12.

**9:2** *To Rages*: see note on 5:6.

**10:7** Gn 45:26.

and your mother-in-law, because from now on they are as much your parents as the ones who brought you into the world. Go in peace, daughter; let me hear a good report about you as long as I live." Finally he said good-bye to them and let them go.

Edna also said to Tobiah: "My child and beloved kinsman, may the Lord bring you back safely, and may I live long enough to see children of you and of my daughter Sarah before I die. Before the Lord, I entrust my daughter to your care. Never cause her grief all the days of your life. Go in peace, son. From now on I am your mother, and Sarah is your sister. Together may we all prosper throughout the days of our lives." She kissed them both and saw them safely off.

[13] Tobiah left Raguel, full of happiness and joy, and he blessed the Lord of heaven and earth, the King of all, for making his journey so successful. Finally he blessed Raguel and his wife Edna, and added, "I have been commanded by the Lord to honor you all the days of your life!"

# 11 Homeward Journey.
[1] As they drew near to Kaserin, which is opposite Nineveh, [2] Raphael said: "You know how we left your father. [3] Let us hurry on ahead of your wife to prepare the house while they are still on the way." [4] So both went on ahead together, and Raphael said to him, "Take the gall in your hand!" And the dog ran along behind them.

[5] Meanwhile, Anna sat watching the road by which her son was to come. [6] When she saw him coming, she called to his father, "Look, your son is coming, and the man who traveled with him!"

[7] Raphael said to Tobiah before he came near to his father: "I know that his eyes will be opened. [8] Apply the fish gall to his eyes, and the medicine will make the white scales shrink and peel off from his eyes; then your father will have sight again and will see the light of day."

**Sight Restored.** [9] Then Anna ran up to her son, embraced him, and said to him, "Now that I have seen you again, son, I am ready

to die!" And she sobbed aloud.* [10] Tobit got up and stumbled out through the courtyard gate to meet his son. Tobiah went up to him [11] with the fish gall in his hand and blew into his eyes. Holding him firmly, he said, "Courage, father." Then he applied the medicine to his eyes, and it made them sting. [12, 13] Tobiah used both hands to peel the white scales from the corners of his eyes. Tobit saw his son and threw his arms around him. [14] Weeping, he exclaimed, "I can see you, son, the light of my eyes!" Then he prayed,

"Blessed be God,
　blessed be his great name,
　　and blessed be all his holy angels.
May his great name be with us,
　and blessed be all the angels
　　throughout all the ages.
[15]　God it was who afflicted me,
　　and God who has had mercy on me.
　　Now I see my son Tobiah!"

Then Tobit went back in, rejoicing and praising God with full voice. Tobiah related to his father how his journey had been a success; that he had brought back the money; and that he had married Raguel's daughter Sarah, who was about to arrive, for she was near the gate of Nineveh.*

[16] Rejoicing and blessing God, Tobit went out to the gate of Nineveh to meet his daughter-in-law. When the people of Nineveh saw him coming, walking along briskly, with no one leading him by the hand, they were amazed. [17] Before them all Tobit proclaimed how God had shown mercy to him and opened his eyes. When Tobit came up to Sarah, the wife of his son Tobiah, he blessed her and said: "Welcome, my daughter! Blessed be your God for bringing you to us, daughter! Blessed are your father and your mother. Blessed be my son Tobiah, and blessed be you, daughter! Welcome to your home with blessing and joy. Come in, daughter!" That day there was joy for all the Jews who lived in Nineveh. [18] Ahiqar and his nephew Nadin† were also on hand to rejoice with Tobit. Tobiah's wedding feast was celebrated with joy for seven days, and many gifts were given to him.

† 11:18 *Nadin:* see note on 14:10.

* 11:9 Gn 33:4; 45:14; 46:29–30; Lk 15:20. 11:15 Tb 13:2; Dt 32:39; 1 Sm 2:6.

## VII. RAPHAEL REVEALS HIS IDENTITY

**12** **Raphael's Wages.**† [1]When the wedding celebration came to an end, Tobit called his son Tobiah and said to him, "Son, see to it that you pay his wages to the man who made the journey with you and give him a bonus too." [2]Tobiah said: "Father, how much shall I pay him? It would not hurt to give him half the wealth he brought back with me.* [3]He led me back safe and sound, healed my wife, brought the money back with me, and healed you. How much should I pay him?" [4]Tobit answered, "It is only fair, son, that he should receive half of all that he brought back." [5]So Tobiah called Raphael and said, "Take as your wages half of all that you have brought back, and farewell!"

**Exhortation.**† [6]Raphael called the two of them aside privately and said to them: "Bless God and give him thanks before all the living for the good things he has done for you, by blessing and extolling his name in song. Proclaim before all with due honor the deeds of God, and do not be slack in thanking him.† [7]A king's secret should be kept secret, but one must declare the works of God and give thanks with due honor. Do good, and evil will not overtake you. [8]Prayer with fasting is good. Almsgiving with righteousness is better than wealth with wickedness. It is better to give alms than to store up gold,* [9]for almsgiving saves from death, and purges all sin. Those who give alms will enjoy a full life,* [10]but those who commit sin and do evil are their own worst enemies.

**Raphael's Identity.** [11]"I shall now tell you the whole truth and conceal nothing at all from you. I have already said to you, 'A king's secret should be kept secret, but one must declare

the works of God with due honor.' [12]*Now when you, Tobit, and Sarah prayed, it was I who presented the record of your prayer before the Glory of the Lord; and likewise whenever you used to bury the dead.† [13]When you did not hesitate to get up and leave your dinner in order to go and bury that dead man, [14]I was sent to put you to the test. At the same time, however, God sent me to heal you and your daughter-in-law Sarah. [15]I am Raphael, one of the seven angels who stand and serve before the Glory of the Lord."*

[16]Greatly shaken, the two of them fell prostrate in fear. [17]But Raphael said to them: "Do not fear; peace be with you! Bless God now and forever. [18]As for me, when I was with you, I was not acting out of any favor on my part, but by God's will. So bless God every day; give praise with song. [19]Even though you saw me eat and drink, I did not eat or drink anything; what you were seeing was a vision. [20]So now bless the Lord on earth and give thanks to God. Look, I am ascending to the one who sent me. Write down all that has happened to you."* And he ascended. [21]They stood up but were no longer able to see him. [22]They kept blessing God and singing his praises, and they continued to give thanks for these marvelous works that God had done, because an angel of God appeared to them.

## VIII. TOBIT'S SONG OF PRAISE

**13** [1]† Then Tobit spoke and composed a song of joyful praise; he said:

Blessed be God who lives forever,
　　because his kingship lasts for all
　　　　ages. *
[2]　For he afflicts and shows mercy,
　　casts down to the depths of Hades,
　　brings up from the great abyss.

---

† **12:1–5** Tobit and his son generously agree to give Raphael far more than the wages agreed upon in 5:15–16.

**12:6–10** In the fashion of a wisdom teacher, Raphael gives the two men a short exhortation similar to the one Tobit gave his son in 4:3–19.

**12:6–7** The faithful considered the praise of God their most esteemed privilege. Without it, life was meaningless; cf. Is 38:16–20.

**12:12** Raphael is one of the seven Angels of the Presence, specially designated intercessors who present prayers to God. Angelology was developing in this period. The names of two other of these seven angels are given in the Bible: Gabriel (Dn 8:16; 9:21; Lk 1:19, 26) and Michael (Dn 10:13, 21; 12:1; Jude 9; Rev 12:7). See 1 Enoch for the names of the rest.

**13:1–18** Tobit's hymn of praise is divided into two parts. The first part (vv. 1–8) is a song of praise that echoes themes from the psalms; the second (vv. 9–18) is addressed to Jerusalem in the style of those prophets who spoke of a new and ideal Jerusalem (Is 60; cf. Rev 21). *Joyful praise*: words for joy and gladness occur throughout this prayer (vv. 1, 7, 10, 11, 13, 14, 16, 18).

---

| | |
|---|---|
| **12:2** Tb 5:3, 7, 15–16. | Acts 10:4; Rev 8:3–4. |
| **12:8** Tb 4:7–11; Sir | **12:15** Lk 1:19; Rev 8:2. |
| 29:8–13. | **12:20** Jgs 13:20. |
| **12:9** Dn 4:24. | **13:1** Tb 3:11; 8:5, 15; |
| **12:12** Jb 33:23–24; | 1 Chr 29:10; Dn 3:26. |

What is there that can snatch from his
hand?*

3 Give thanks to him, you Israelites, in the
presence of the nations,
for though he has scattered you
among them,
4 even there recount his greatness.
Exalt him before every living being,
because he is your Lord, and he is
your God,
our Father and God forever and ever!
5 He will afflict you for your iniquities,
but will have mercy on all of you.
He will gather you from all the nations
among whom you have been
scattered.*

6 When you turn back to him with all
your heart,
and with all your soul do what is right
before him,
Then he will turn to you,
and will hide his face from you no
longer.*

Now consider what he has done for
you,
and give thanks with full voice.
Bless the Lord of righteousness,
and exalt the King of the ages.

In the land of my captivity I give thanks,
and declare his power and majesty to
a sinful nation.
According to your heart do what is right
before him:
perhaps there will be pardon for you.

7 As for me, I exalt my God,
my soul exalts the King of heaven,
and rejoices all the days of my life.
Let all sing praise to his greatness,
8 let all speak and give thanks in
Jerusalem.

9 Jerusalem, holy city,
he will afflict you for the works of
your hands,†

but will again pity the children of the
righteous.*
10 Give thanks to the Lord with
righteousness,
and bless the King of the ages,
so that your tabernacle may be rebuilt
in you with joy.
May he gladden within you all who are
captives;
may he cherish within you all who are
distressed
for all generations to come.*

11 A bright light will shine to the limits of
the earth.
Many nations will come to you from
afar,
And inhabitants of all the ends of the
earth
to your holy name,
Bearing in their hands gifts for the King
of heaven.
Generation after generation will offer
joyful worship in you;
your name will be great forever and
ever.*

12 Cursed be all who despise you and
revile you;
cursed be all who hate you and speak
a harsh word against you;
cursed be all who destroy you
and pull down your walls,
And all who overthrow your towers
and set fire to your homes.
But blessed forever be all those who
respect you.*

13 Go, then, rejoice and exult over the
children of the righteous,
for they will all be gathered together
and will bless the Lord of the ages.
14 Happy are those who love you,
and happy are those who rejoice in
your peace.
Happy too are all who grieve
over all your afflictions,
For they will rejoice over you
and behold all your joy forever.*

---

† 13:9 *Works of your hands*: idols.

---

13:2 Tb 11:15; 13:9;
  Dt 32:39; 1 Sm 2:6;
13:5 Dt 30:3; Neh 1:9.

Wis 16:13.

13:6 Dt 30:2.
13:9 Tb 11:15; Mi 7:19;
  Rev 21.
13:10 Is 44:26, 28; Am 9:11;
  Zec 1:16.

13:11 Is 2:3–4; 9:1; 49:6;
  60:1; Mi 4:2; Zec
  8:22.
13:12 Bar 4:31–32.
13:14 Ps 122:6; Is 66:10.

<sup>15</sup> My soul, bless the Lord, the great King;
<sup>16</sup>    for Jerusalem will be rebuilt as his
      house forever.
Happy too will I be if a remnant of my
      offspring survives
   to see your glory and to give thanks to
      the King of heaven!

The gates of Jerusalem will be built with
      sapphire and emerald,
   and all your walls with precious
      stones.
The towers of Jerusalem will be built
      with gold,
   and their battlements with purest
      gold.*
<sup>17</sup> The streets of Jerusalem will be paved
      with rubies and stones of Ophir;
<sup>18</sup> The gates of Jerusalem will sing hymns
      of gladness,
   and all its houses will cry out,
      Hallelujah!
Blessed be the God of Israel for all ages!
For in you the blessed will bless the holy
      name forever and ever.

## IX. EPILOGUE

**14** **Parting Advice.** <sup>1</sup> So the words of Tobit's hymn of praise came to an end. Tobit died in peace at the age of a hundred and twelve and was buried with honor in Nineveh. <sup>2</sup> He was fifty-eight years old when he lost his eyesight, and after he recovered it he lived in prosperity, giving alms; he continued to fear God and give thanks to the divine Majesty.

<sup>3</sup> As he was dying, he summoned his son Tobiah and Tobiah's seven sons, and commanded him, "Son, take your children* <sup>4</sup> and flee into Media, for I believe God's word that Nahum† spoke against Nineveh. It will all happen and will overtake Assyria and Nineveh; indeed all that was said by Israel's prophets whom God sent will come to pass. Not one of all their words will remain unfulfilled,

but everything will take place in the time appointed for it, So it will be safer in Media than in Assyria or Babylon. For I know and believe that whatever God has said will be accomplished. It will happen, and not a single word of the prophecies will fail.

As for our kindred who dwell in the land of Israel, they will all be scattered and taken into captivity from the good land. All the land of Israel will become a wilderness; even Samaria and Jerusalem will be a wilderness! For a time, the house of God will be desolate and will be burned.* <sup>5</sup> But God will again have mercy on them and bring them back to the land of Israel. They will build the house again, but it will not be like the first until the era when the appointed times will be completed.† Afterward all of them will return from their captivity, and they will rebuild Jerusalem with due honor. In it the house of God will also be rebuilt, just as the prophets of Israel said of it. * <sup>6</sup>* All the nations of the world will turn and reverence God in truth; all will cast away their idols, which have deceitfully led them into error. † <sup>7</sup> They will bless the God of the ages in righteousness. All the Israelites truly mindful of God, who are to be saved in those days, will be gathered together and will come to Jerusalem; in security will they dwell forever in the land of Abraham, which will be given to them. Those who love God sincerely will rejoice, but those who commit sin and wickedness will disappear completely from the land. *

<sup>8, 9</sup> "Now, my children, I give you this command: serve God sincerely and do what is pleasing in his sight; you must instruct your children to do what is right and to give alms, to be mindful of God and at all times to bless his name sincerely and with all their strength. Now, as for you, son, leave Nineveh; do not stay here. <sup>10</sup> The day you bury your mother next to me, do not even stay overnight within the confines of the city. For I see that there is much wickedness in it, and much treachery is practiced in it, and people are not ashamed. See,

---

† **14:4–5** *Nahum*: one of the minor prophets, whose book contains oracles of doom against Nineveh. Here, in keeping with the period in which the story is set, the author makes Tobit speak as if the punishment of Nineveh, the destruction of Jerusalem (587 B.C.), the exile from Judah and the return, would all take place in the future. The technique of using the facts of past history as seemingly future predictions is a frequent device of apocalyptic writers. *The good land*: a favorite name for the promised land. Cf. Dt 1:35; 3:25; 4:21–22.
   **14:5** *Until the era…completed*: a reference to the coming of

the day of the Lord, when a new, more perfect temple was to be expected. Cf. Heb 9:1–14.
   **14:6** Conversion of the nations is also to come with the day of the Lord.

---

**13:16** Tb 14:5; Is 54:11–13; 62:2; Rev 21:10–21.
**14:3** Gn 47:29–30.
**14:4** Na 2:2–3:19.
**14:5** Neh 12:27; Jer 31:38.
**14:6** Is 60:1–4.
**14:7** Is 60:21; Jer 32:37; Ez 34:28; 37:25; 39:26.

my son, all that Nadin† did to Ahiqar, the very one who reared him. Was not Ahiqar brought down alive into the earth? Yet God made Nadin's disgraceful crime rebound against him. Ahiqar came out again into the light, but Nadin went into the everlasting darkness, for he had tried to kill Ahiqar. Because Ahiqar had given alms he escaped from the deadly trap Nadin had set for him. But Nadin fell into the deadly trap himself, and it destroyed him. * [11] So, my children, see what almsgiving does, and also what wickedness does—it kills! But now my spirit is about to leave me."

**Death of Tobit and Tobiah.** They laid him on his bed, and he died; and he was buried with honor. [12] When Tobiah's mother died,

he buried her next to his father. He then departed with his wife and children for Media, where he settled in Ecbatana with his father-in-law Raguel. * [13] He took respectful care of his aging father-in-law and mother-in-law; and he buried them at Ecbatana in Media. Then he inherited Raguel's estate as well as that of his father Tobit. [14] He died highly respected at the age of one hundred seventeen. [15] But before he died, he saw and heard of the destruction of Nineveh. He saw the inhabitants of the city being led captive into Media by Cyaxares, † the king of Media. Tobiah blessed God for all that he had done against the Ninevites and Assyrians. Before dying he rejoiced over Nineveh, and he blessed the Lord God forever and ever.

---

† **14:10** *Nadin*: in the *Story of Ahiqar*, the hero Ahiqar, chancellor under the Assyrian kings Sennacherib and Esarhaddon, adopts his nephew Nadin and prepares him to become his successor. But Nadin treacherously plots to have his uncle put to death. Ahiqar hides in a friend's house and is finally vindicated when Nadin's scheme is discovered. Thereupon Nadin is thrown into a dungeon where he dies. It was Ahiqar's almsgiving that delivered him from death; see note on 2:2. The Greek and Latin versions of the Book of Tobit read the name as Nadab, but the

Aramaic form has the ancient name Nadin, which is also found in the fifth-century B.C. Aramaic *Story of Ahiqar*.

**14:15** *Cyaxares*: Nabopolassar, king of Babylon, and Cyaxares conquered and destroyed Nineveh in 612 B.C.; see note on 1:15.

---

**14:10** Tb 1:21–22.                          **14:12** Tb 4:4.

# The Book of

# Judith

## INTRODUCTION

### Geoffrey Miller

The book of Judith tells a remarkable tale of a woman who singlehandedly repels an invading army and rescues her people from destruction. The first half of the book vividly describes how the Assyrian army conquers nation after nation and lays siege to the Jewish town of Bethulia. The second half recounts the daring intervention of Judith, a pious widow who seduces and beheads the Assyrian commander. After a midnight escape from the enemy camp, Judith returns home to a hero's welcome, showered with accolades by her townspeople and renowned throughout the land for the remainder of her days.

Composed originally in Palestine in the late second century BCE, this fictional story was highly popular in the Middle Ages and Renaissance, inspiring numerous playwrights, composers, and painters. That popularity has waned in recent centuries, however, and the book remains unknown among many Christians today. As one of seven deuterocanonical books, Judith is absent from the Jewish Tanak and Protestant Old Testament, and despite its canonical status among Catholics, it rarely appears in the liturgy. The reason for this neglect is not readily apparent. Perhaps some contemporary readers are perturbed by the gory scene where Judith decapitates the Assyrian general Holofernes, or unnerved by what might be interpreted as the heroine's morally questionable behavior. Nonetheless, the book's central theme about the saving power of God as well as the duty of God's people to remain faithful to him is consonant with other biblical texts and relates an important message to readers of every generation.

Modern readers must be careful, however, not to approach the book as a historical record. A plethora of anachronisms and inaccuracies permeate the story, especially in the opening

## Outline of Judith

I. **Assyrian Threat (1:1–3:10)**

II. **Siege of Bethulia (4:1–7:32)**

III. **Judith, Instrument of the Lord (8:1–10:10)**

IV. **Judith Goes Out to War (10:11–13:20)**

V. **Victory and Thanksgiving (14:1–16:25)**

chapters. Nebuchadnezzar is presented as king of the Assyrians, even though he was actually king of the Babylonians. Several of the places mentioned, such as Bethulia and Bectileth, are not attested elsewhere in ancient literature and may never have existed, and the rapid movement of the Assyrian army from Nineveh to upper Cilicia is impossible. Other biblical books also contain similar errors, such as Daniel and Tobit, but the mistakes found in Judith are too egregious to be the result of careless editing or insufficient historical knowledge. On the contrary, the author has intentionally mingled references to a variety of historical periods in order to create a more universalized setting for the book. By incorporating details from the Assyrian, Babylonian, Persian, and Greek epochs, the story encompasses all of Israel's oppressors from the eighth century onward. Nebuchadnezzar thus becomes a supra-historical nemesis, a symbol of any tyrant who would oppose Yahweh and his chosen people. Bethulia, a name that appears nowhere else in or outside the Bible, is likewise symbolic; it could be a variant name for the city of Bethel, or it could be a clever way to refer to Jerusalem, the place where the "house of God" (a likely meaning of the word Bethulia) was located. If the latter, the impending Assyrian onslaught jeopardizes the epicenter of Jewish life, and by defending this beleaguered village, Judith is in effect defending the heart and soul of the Israelite nation.

The combination of garbled historical references and fictive details in a religious text might alarm modern readers, but this technique is commonplace in ancient novels, both biblical (e.g., Tobit) and non-biblical (e.g., Hellenistic romances). Such works today are normally regarded as historical fiction, but the designation of "didactic novel" is more apt. As a didactic work, the book of Judith strives to teach its audience certain theological truths and to promote a virtuous way of life; as a novel, it conveys these messages through the form of an entertaining story. Readers of Judith will marvel at how a seemingly defenseless woman captivates and slays a heinous villain. They will be moved by the heroine's stirring critique of the Bethulian leaders. And they will be impelled to embrace a robust faith that does not wilt in the face of hardship.

Ancient readers will also recognize multiple allusions to earlier biblical traditions. In fashioning his tale, the author has stitched together a variety of biblical figures to produce the consummate heroine. Like Esther, Judith uses her beauty to gain access to a powerful Gentile and thwart the enemy's efforts to destroy her people. Like Jael and Deborah, she proves that a woman can serve as God's instrument in rescuing his people from a military threat. Like a young David, she confronts a formidable foe and decapitates him to the surprise of all. These and other stories have infused this tale of valor, contributing to its timeless feel. Just as Nebuchadnezzar is the ultimate villain, so Judith is the ultimate savior, replicating the valiant deeds of earlier heroes while at the same time transcending them. In one fell swoop, she vanquishes the most devastating enemy Israel has ever seen.

In addition to the inner-biblical allusions strewn throughout the narrative, the book of Judith also exhibits literary art in its structure. The two main parts of the book (Jdt 1–7 and 8–16) are dominated by two primary characters: Holofernes (Nebuchadnezzar's representative)

and Judith (Yahweh's representative). Each part conforms to a chiastic pattern where earlier parts of the story are later repeated in reverse order. For example, in 8:9–14:5, Judith plans to save Israel (A), leaves Bethulia (B), kills Holofernes (C), returns to Bethulia (B'), and plans to destroy Israel's enemies (A'). The two main parts of the story can be subdivided further and illustrate one of the book's chief themes. In the first three chapters, Nebuchadnezzar seeks to assert his sovereignty over the entire earth. In chs. 4–7, the besieged inhabitants of Bethulia are panic-stricken as they wait to see who will truly prevail as sovereign over all, Nebuchadnezzar or Yahweh. In the final nine chapters, the audience sees that Yahweh, by the hand of Judith, triumphs over Nebuchadnezzar and emerges as the true sovereign over the world.

The Bethulians struggle to grasp this truth about divine providence, for the God of the book of Judith is a hidden deity. God does not converse directly with human beings or intervene directly in human affairs, nor does God use prophets or angels to communicate his will to the people. Readers of the book instead learn about God through the statements of its various characters, especially in the form of prayer or praise. God is not tangibly present, as in the books of Genesis or Exodus, but is nevertheless intimately involved in the world, directing the course of human events (Jdt 9:5–6). God is an omnipotent being who transcends human comprehension (8:14; 16:13), yet God is also Lord of the humble, the lowly, and the downtrodden (9:11). God listens to his people's supplications (4:13; 8:17) but does not respond to ultimatums (8:11, 16). God periodically tests people (8:25–27) but refuses to be put to the test by those same people (8:12). God eradicates warfare (16:2) but is willing to use violence to defend Israel (9:2–4, 8–10, 14; 16:17). God punishes those who disobey or oppose him, whether Jew (8:21–23) or Gentile (9:2–4; 16:17), but is also compassionate toward those who fear him (16:15).

Readers also learn about God through his instrument of salvation: Judith. The providential protection of God is manifest in an intrepid woman who delivers Israel from a menacing overlord, just as Yahweh had done in times past. Yet Judith's astonishing, even

J
D
T

paradoxical behavior shows her to be a complex woman who resists all labels. She plays the damsel in distress to Assyrian soldiers but then assassinates their leader. She is one of the most affluent citizens of Bethulia, but she pursues an ascetic lifestyle characterized by extreme fasting and the wearing of sackcloth. She acts as a reclusive widow, mourning her husband's death on her private estate, but then enters the public forum to upbraid her town's leaders and take matters into her own hands. She also contravenes societal norms for women. In a culture that regards childlessness as a curse, she opts not to remarry or have children, despite the many suitors who ask for her hand in marriage. In a culture that regards widows as vulnerable and helpless, she demonstrates unparalleled courage and resourcefulness. In a culture dominated by men, she ventures into traditionally masculine realms with great success. She lectures the town leaders on orthodoxy, proper conduct, and military strategy, and she engages the enemy while the men stay at home trembling in fear. By all accounts, Judith is an indomitable woman who refuses to be constrained by convention or custom.

Judith's moral integrity is also hard to measure. On the one hand, she is a deeply devout woman who fasts, remains chaste, prays regularly to the Lord, and observes the Jewish dietary laws. She also displays her theological wisdom when she addresses the leaders of Bethulia before departing for the Assyrian camp. On the other hand, she is a liar, a seductress, and a murderer, and an increasing number of modern readers condemn her behavior as reprehensible. One might argue that her deception and assassination of Holofernes are done for a noble purpose, namely to save the lives of her people. One could also point out that Judith's behavior is little different from other biblical heroes and tricksters who use stealth and otherwise unsavory means to achieve their objectives. One could more plausibly contend that her dire circumstances allow for violence. Bethulia is under attack, and if killing can be justified in the context of war, then deception and assassination might also be permissible.

Regardless of how one evaluates Judith's conduct, one cannot deny that she is a representative figure. Her name in Hebrew means "Jewess," and she illustrates what the ideal Jew should be like. For all her complexities and potential flaws, Judith does not lapse in her faith when times are hard but remains faithful to the Lord and courageously does what she thinks is right. For reasons such as these, she is seen as a model for all of God's people. ■

# THE BOOK OF JUDITH

## New American Bible, Introduction

The Book of Judith relates the story of God's deliverance of the Jewish people. This was accomplished "by the hand of a female"—a constant motif (cf. 8:33; 9:9, 10; 12:4; 13:4, 14, 15; 15:10; 16:5) meant to recall the "hand" of God in the Exodus narrative (cf. Ex 15:6). The work may have been written around 100 B.C., but its historical range is extraordinary. Within the reign of Nebuchadnezzar (1:1; 2:1), it telescopes five centuries of historical and geographical information with imaginary details. There are references to Nineveh, the Assyrian capital destroyed in 612 B.C., to Nebuchadnezzar, the ruler not of Assyria but of Babylon (605/604–562), and to the second Temple, built around 515. The postexilic period is presumed (e.g., governance by the High Priest). The Persian period is represented by two characters, Holofernes and Bagoas, who appear together in the military campaigns of Artaxerxes III Ochus (358–338); there seem to be allusions to the second-century Seleucid ruler Antiochus IV Epiphanes. Several mysteries remain: Judith herself, Arphaxad, and others are otherwise unknown. The geographical details, such as the narrow defile into Bethulia (an unidentified town which gives access to the heart of the land), are fanciful. The simple conclusion from these and other details is that the work is historical fiction, written to exalt God as Israel's deliverer from foreign might, not by an army, but by means of a simple widow.

There are four Greek recensions of Judith (Septuagint codices Vaticanus, Sinaiticus, Alexandrinus, and Basiliano-Vaticanus), four ancient translations (Old Latin, Syriac, Sahidic, and Ethiopic), and some late Hebrew versions, apparently translated from the Vulgate. Despite Jerome's claim to have translated an Aramaic text, no ancient Aramaic or Hebrew manuscripts have been found. The oldest extant text of Judith is the preservation of 15:1–7 inscribed on a third-century A.D. potsherd. Whatever the reasons, the rabbis did not count Judith among their scriptures, and the Reformation adopted that position. The early Church, however, held this book in high honor. The first-century Pope, St. Clement of Rome, proposes Judith as an example of courageous love (1 Corinthians 55). St. Jerome holds her up as an example of a holy widow and a type of the Church (To Salvina: Letter 79, par. 10; see also To Furia: Letter 54, par. 16) and, in another place, describes Mary as a new Judith (To Eustochium: Letter 22, par. 21). The Council of Trent (1546) included Judith in the canon; thus it is one of the seven deuterocanonical books.

Inner-biblical references are noteworthy: as God acted through Moses' hand (Ex 10:21–22; 14:27–30), so God delivers "by the hand of a female," Judith. Like Jael, who drove a tent peg through the head of Sisera (Jgs 4), Judith kills an enemy general. Like Deborah (Jgs 4–5), Judith "judges" Israel in the time of military crisis. Like Sarah, the mother of Israel's future (Gn 17:6), Judith's beauty deceives foreigners, with the result that blessings redound to Israel (Gn 12:11–20). Her Hebrew name means "Jewish woman." Her exploits captured the imagination of liturgists, artists, and writers through the centuries. The book is filled with double entendres and ironic situations, e.g., Judith's conversation with Holofernes in 11:5–8, 19, where "my lord" is ambiguous, and her declaration to Holofernes that she will lead him through Judea to Jerusalem (his head goes on such a journey).

The book can be divided into five parts:

I. Assyrian Threat (1:1–3:10)
II. Siege of Bethulia (4:1–7:32)
III. Judith, Instrument of the Lord (8:1–10:10)
IV. Judith Goes Out to War (10:11–13:20)
V. Victory and Thanksgiving (14:1–16:25) ∎

# JUDITH

## I. ASSYRIAN THREAT†

**1** **Nebuchadnezzar Against Arphaxad.**† ¹ It was the twelfth year† of the reign of Nebuchadnezzar, who ruled over the Assyrians in the great city of Nineveh. At that time Arphaxad was ruling over the Medes in Ecbatana.* ² † Around Ecbatana he built a wall of hewn stones, three cubits thick and six cubits long. He made the walls seventy cubits high and fifty cubits wide. ³ At its gates he raised towers one hundred cubits high with foundations sixty cubits wide. ⁴ He made its gates seventy cubits high and forty cubits wide to allow passage of his mighty forces, with his infantry in formation. ⁵ At that time King Nebuchadnezzar waged war against King Arphaxad in the vast plain that borders Ragau.† ⁶ Rallying to him were all who lived in the hill country, all who lived along the Euphrates, the Tigris, and the Hydaspes, as well as Arioch, king of the Elamites, in the plains. Thus many nations joined the ranks of the Chelodites.†*

⁷ Then Nebuchadnezzar, king of the Assyrians, contacted all the inhabitants of Persia† and all who lived in the west, the inhabitants of Cilicia and Damascus, Lebanon and Antilebanon, and all who lived along the seacoast,

⁸ the peoples of Carmel, Gilead, Upper Galilee, and the vast plain of Esdraelon, ⁹ and all in Samaria and its cities, and west of the Jordan as far as Jerusalem, Bethany, Chelous, Kadesh,* and the river of Egypt; Tahpanhes,* Raamses, all the land of Goshen, ¹⁰ Tanis, Memphis* and beyond, and all the inhabitants of Egypt as far as the borders of Ethiopia.

¹¹ But all the inhabitants of the whole land† made light of the summons of Nebuchadnezzar, king of the Assyrians, and would not join him in the war. They were not afraid of him, since he was only a single opponent. So they sent back his envoys empty-handed and disgraced.* ¹² Then Nebuchadnezzar fell into a violent rage against all the land, and swore by his throne and his kingdom that he would take revenge on all the territories of Cilicia, Damascus, and Syria, and would destroy with his sword all the inhabitants of Moab, Ammon, the whole of Judea, and all those living in Egypt as far as the coasts of the two seas.†

**Defeat of Arphaxad.** ¹³ In the seventeenth year† he mustered his forces against King Arphaxad and was victorious in his campaign. He routed the whole force of Arphaxad, his entire cavalry, and all his chariots, ¹⁴ and took possession of his cities. He pressed on to Ecbatana, took its towers, sacked its marketplaces, and turned its glory into shame. ¹⁵ He captured Arphaxad in the mountains of Ragau, ran him through with spears, and utterly

---

† **1:1–3:10** This section consists of an introduction to Nebuchadnezzar (1:1–16), his commissioning of Holofernes (2:1–13), and a description of the campaigns Holofernes leads against the disobedient vassal nations of the west (2:14–3:10).

**1:1–16** Introduction to Nebuchadnezzar and his campaign against Arphaxad. Nebuchadnezzar (605/4–562 B.C.), the most famous Neo-Babylonian king, destroyed Jerusalem in 587 B.C., the eighteenth year of his reign (see Jer 32:1). His depiction here as an Assyrian is an invention of the author, as is the description of Arphaxad, an otherwise unknown king of the Medes, in Ecbatana.

**1:1** *Twelfth year*: in the twelfth year of Nebuchadnezzar (593 B.C.) Zedekiah, king of Judah, refused to join a revolt against him (see Jer 27:3; 28:1). *Nineveh*: capital of Assyria, destroyed in 612 B.C.

**1:2–4** Since a cubit was the distance from the elbow to the fingertip (approximately eighteen inches), these dimensions are prodigious. The massive wall around Ecbatana is described as 105 feet high and 75 feet thick, with each stone measuring four and a half feet thick and nine feet long. The tower gates are 150 feet high and 60 feet wide. Such unlikely massive structures have never been found at Ecbatana, which lies beneath the modern city of Hamadan, located in the Zagros mountains of northwest Iran. Ecbatana is mentioned in vv. 1, 2, 14 as Arphaxad's headquarters. Tradition claims Esther and Mordecai are buried there.

**1:5** Ragau, the place where Arphaxad is slain (v. 15), one of

the oldest settlements in Iran, is located on a plain one hundred miles northeast of Ecbatana. In the Book of Tobit it is the home of Gabael (Tb 1:14; 4:1, 20; 5:6; 6:13; 9:2, 5).

**1:6** *Chelodites*: Greek *Cheleoud*, probably a corruption of "Chaldeans," i.e., the Neo-Babylonians.

**1:7** Mention of Persia suggests a postexilic setting for the book, since this area would have been designated Media before the middle of the fifth century B.C.

**1:11** References to "the whole land," "all the land" are used ten times in the first two chapters (vv. 11, 12; 2:1, 2, 5, 6, 7, 9, 10, 19). This signifies all the nations west of Persia as far as Egypt that were subject to Nebuchadnezzar, i.e., the whole earth or world (esp. 2:9). These and similar formulations throughout the book build the case that the "God of heaven" (5:8; 6:19; 11:17) is the true "Master of heaven and earth" (9:12).

**1:12** *The two seas*: probably the Mediterranean to the Persian Gulf, though possibly the Red Sea and Mediterranean.

**1:13** *Seventeenth year*: 588 B.C. Without help from the vassal nations, Nebuchadnezzar defeats Arphaxad.

---

**1:1** Gn 10:22; Ezr 6:2; Tb 3:7; 5:6; 6:10; 7:1; 14:12–13; 2 Mc 9:3; Jon 1:2; 3:2–3.
**1:6** Gn 14:1, 9.
**1:9** Nm 34:4; Dt 32:51; Jos 15:23.
**1:9** Jer 2:16; 43:7–9; 44:1; 46:14.
**1:10** Is 19:13; Jer 2:16; 44:1; 46:14, 19; Ez 30:13, 15; Hos 9:6.
**1:11** 2 Sm 17:3; Ez 33:24.

destroyed him once and for all. [16]Then he returned to Nineveh with all his consolidated forces, a very great multitude of warriors; and there he and his forces relaxed and feasted for one hundred and twenty days. *

## 2 Revenge Planned Against the Western Nations.† [1]In the eighteenth year,† on the twenty-second day of the first month, there was a discussion in the palace of Nebuchadnezzar, king of the Assyrians, about taking revenge on all the land, as he had threatened. * [2]He summoned all his attendants and officers, laid before them his secret plan, and with his own lips recounted in full detail the wickedness of all the land. [3]They decided to destroy all who had refused to obey the order he had issued.

[4]When he had fully recounted his plan, Nebuchadnezzar, king of the Assyrians, summoned Holofernes, the ranking general† of his forces, second only to himself in command, and said to him: [5]"Thus says the great king, the lord of all the earth: Go forth from my presence, take with you men of proven valor, one hundred and twenty thousand infantry and twelve thousand cavalry, * [6]and proceed against all the land of the west, because they disobeyed the order I issued. [7]Tell them to have earth and water† ready, for I will come against them in my wrath; I will cover all the land with the feet of my soldiers, to whom I will deliver them as spoils. [8]Their wounded will fill their ravines and wadies, the swelling river will be choked with their dead; [9]and I will deport them as exiles to the very ends of the earth.

[10]"Go before me and take possession of all their territories for me. If they surrender to you, guard them for me until the day of their sentencing. [11]As for those who disobey, show them no mercy, but deliver them up to slaughter and plunder in all the land you occupy. * [12]For as I live,† and by the strength of my kingdom, what I have spoken I will accomplish by my own hand. * [13]Do not disobey a single one of the orders of your lord; fulfill them exactly as I have commanded you, and do it without delay."

**Campaigns of Holofernes.**† [14]So Holofernes left the presence of his lord, and summoned all the commanders, generals, and officers of the Assyrian forces. [15]He mustered one hundred and twenty thousand picked troops, as his lord had commanded, and twelve thousand mounted archers, [16]and drew them up as a vast force organized for battle. [17]He took along a very large number of camels, donkeys, and mules for carrying their supplies; innumerable sheep, cattle, and goats for their food; * [18]abundant provisions for each man, and much gold and silver from the royal palace.

[19]Then he and all his forces set out on their expedition in advance of King Nebuchadnezzar, to overrun all the lands of the western region with their chariots, cavalry, and picked infantry. [20]A huge, irregular force, too many to count, like locusts, like the dust of the earth, went along with them. *

[21]After a three-day march† from Nineveh, they reached the plain of Bectileth, and camped opposite Bectileth near the mountains to the north of Upper Cilicia. [22]From there Holofernes took all his forces, the infantry, cavalry, and chariots, and marched into the hill country. [23]He devastated Put and Lud,† and plundered all the Rassisites and the

---

† **2:1–13** Nebuchadnezzar commissions Holofernes to take vengeance on the vassal nations that refused him auxiliary military support (see 1:7–12).
**2:1** *Eighteenth year*: 587 B.C. Most of the story is set in the catastrophic year when the historical Nebuchadnezzar, king of Babylon, destroyed Jerusalem.
**2:4** *The ranking general*: Holofernes is so identified six times in Judith. See also 4:1; 5:1; 6:1; 10:13; 13:15. Holofernes and Bagoas (12:11) are Persian names; two officers of Artaxerxes III Ochos (358–338 B.C.) were so named.
**2:7** *Earth and water*: in the Persian period, offering these to a conqueror was a symbolic gesture signifying humble submission of one asking for a treaty.
**2:12** *As I live*: an oath proper to God; see the promissory oath of God the divine warrior in Dt 32:39–42; cf. Is 49:18; Jer 22:24; Ez 5:11. *By my own hand*: in his pride, Nebuchadnezzar claims to do this by his own hand (cf. Is 10:13). In contrast, Judith claims that God will deliver Israel "by my hand" (8:33; 12:4).

**2:14–3:10** As Holofernes attacks the western nations, terror sweeps across the empire at large (2:28), then Judea (4:1–2), and finally Bethulia (7:1). In these verses, the line of advance is from Nineveh to Damascus and all who submit are nonetheless devastated and forced to worship Nebuchadnezzar.
**2:21** *A three-day march*: no ancient army could have traveled three hundred miles from Nineveh to Cilicia in three days.
**2:23** *Put and Lud*: mentioned together in Jer 46:9; Ez 27:10; 30:5. Put is thought to be in Libya in Africa; Lud is usually identified with Lydia in Asia Minor. Rather than indicating definite localities here, Put and Lud add assonance and prophetic overtones to the narrative.

---

**1:16** Est 1:3–4.                    Is 13:18.
**2:1** Jer 32:1; 52:29.              **2:12** Dt 32:39–41.
**2:5** 2 Kgs 18:19, 28; 1 Mc        **2:17** Gn 41:49.
       15:13; Is 36:4, 13;            **2:20** Ex 10:4, 13, 14; Jgs
       Hos 5:13; 10:6.                       6:5; 7:12; Ps 105:34;
**2:11** Dt 7:2; Jos 11:20;                  Jl 1:4.

Ishmaelites on the border of the wilderness toward the south of the Chelleans.*

24 Then, following the Euphrates, he went through Mesopotamia, and battered down every fortified city along the Wadi Abron, until he reached the sea. 25 He seized the territory of Cilicia, and cut down everyone who resisted him. Then he proceeded to the southern borders of Japheth, toward Arabia. 26 He surrounded all the Midianites, burned their tents, and sacked their encampments.* 27 Descending to the plain of Damascus at the time of the wheat harvest, he set fire to all their fields, destroyed their flocks and herds, looted their cities, devastated their plains, and put all their young men to the sword.*

28* Fear and dread of him fell upon all the inhabitants of the coastland, upon those in Sidon and Tyre,* and those who dwelt in Sur and Ocina, and the inhabitants of Jamnia. Those in Azotus and Ascalon also feared him greatly.†

**3** **Submission of the Vassal Nations.** 1 So they sent messengers to him to sue for peace in these words: 2 "We, the servants of Nebuchadnezzar the great king, lie prostrate before you; do with us as you will. 3 See, our dwellings and all our land and every wheat field, our flocks and herds, and all our encampments are at your disposal; make use of them as you please. 4 Our cities and their inhabitants are also at your service; come and deal with them as you see fit."

5 After the spokesmen had reached

Holofernes and given him this message, 6 he went down with his forces to the seacoast, stationed garrisons in the fortified cities, and took selected men from them as auxiliaries. 7 The people of these cities and all the inhabitants of the countryside received him with garlands and dancing to the sound of timbrels. 8 But he devastated their whole territory and cut down their sacred groves, for he was allowed to destroy all the gods of the land, so that every nation might worship only Nebuchadnezzar, and all their tongues and tribes should invoke him as a god.†* 9 At length Holofernes reached Esdraelon in the neighborhood of Dothan,† the approach to the main ridge of the Judean mountains; 10 he set up his camp between Geba† and Scythopolis, and stayed there a whole month to replenish all the supplies of his forces.

## II. SIEGE OF BETHULIA†

**4** **Israel Prepares for War.**† 1 When the Israelites who lived in Judea heard of all that Holofernes, the ranking general of Nebuchadnezzar king of the Assyrians, had done to the nations, and how he had looted all their shrines† and utterly destroyed them, 2 they were in very great fear of him, and greatly alarmed for Jerusalem and the temple of the Lord, their God. 3 Now, they had only recently returned from exile, and all the people of Judea were just now reunited, and the vessels, the altar, and the temple had been purified from profanation.†* 4 So they sent word to

---

**2:28** Symbolic of the completeness of the terror that descended on the area, seven towns are listed: Tyre, Sidon, Sur, Ocina, Jamnia, Ashdod, and Ashkelon.

**3:8** *Invoke him as a god*: Holofernes violates Nebuchadnezzar's instructions (see 2:5–13). No Assyrian, Neo-Babylonian, or Persian king is known to have claimed divinity. During Hellenistic times, Ptolemy V (203–181 B.C.) and the Seleucid Antiochus IV made claims to divinity. In Dn 3 and 6, divinity is ascribed to Nebuchadnezzar and Darius, respectively.

**3:9** *Dothan*: a town in Ephraimite territory fourteen miles north of Shechem, mentioned elsewhere only twice (Gn 37:17 and 2 Kgs 6:13), but five times in Judith (3:9; 4:6; 7:3, 18; 8:3). Destroyed in 810 B.C. by Aramean invasions, Dothan was deserted until the Hellenistic period when a small settlement was constructed. Because it is mentioned so often, Dothan is sometimes thought to be the author's home.

**3:10** *Geba*: location uncertain. Scythopolis, the Greek name for ancient Beth-shean (Jos 17:11), the only city in Judith given its Greek name, strategically guarded the eastern end of the Valley of Jezreel.

**4:1–7:32** In this section the focus narrows to Judea and specifically the little town of Bethulia. The scenes alternate between the Assyrian camp (5:1–6:13; 7:1–3, 6–18) and Judea/Bethulia

(4:1–15; 6:14–21; 7:4–5, 19–32).

**4:1–15** Here the scene shifts to Judea where Israel hears of and is greatly terrified about Holofernes' destruction of the neighboring places of worship. At Joakim's instruction they take defensive measures and then pray fervently that God will not allow their sanctuary to be destroyed.

**4:1** *Shrines*: the Greek word *hiera* is used only here and may mean holy places or things. By contrast, the sanctuary in Jerusalem is *naos*, "temple" (v. 2); *oikos*, "house" (v. 3); and *hagia*, lit., "holy things" (v. 12).

**4:3** *Returned from exile…purified from profanation*: conflated historical references associated with events in 538 B.C. (return from exile) and 515 B.C. (dedication of the Second Temple) or perhaps even 164 B.C. (the rededication of the Second Temple in the Maccabean period).

| | |
|---|---|
| **2:23** Gn 2:2; 10:6, 22; Is 66:19; Ez 30:5. | **2:28** Ez 26:7–14; 29:17–20. |
| **2:26** Gn 37:36; Ex 2:15; Jgs 6–8. | **3:8** Ex 34:13; 2 Kgs 18:4; 23:14–15; 2 Chr 14:2; 17:6; 31:1; 34:4. |
| **2:27** Gn 34:26; Jos 6:21; 1 Sm 15:8. | **4:3** 1 Mc 4:36–61; 2 Mc 10:3–5. |
| **2:28** Ex 15:16; Ps 55:6. | |

the whole region of Samaria, to Kona, Beth-horon, Belmain, and Jericho, to Choba and Aesora, and to the valley of Salem.† ⁵The people there secured all the high hilltops, fortified the villages on them, and since their fields had recently been harvested, stored up provisions in preparation for war.

⁶Joakim, who was high priest† in Jerusalem in those days, wrote to the inhabitants of Bethulia and Betomesthaim, which is opposite Esdraelon, facing the plain near Dothan,* ⁷and instructed them to keep firm hold of the mountain passes, since these offered access to Judea. It would be easy to stop those advancing, as the approach was only wide enough for two at a time.† ⁸The Israelites carried out the orders given them by Joakim, the high priest, and the senate of the whole people of Israel, in session in Jerusalem.*

**Israel at Prayer.** ⁹All the men of Israel cried to God with great fervor and humbled themselves. ¹⁰They, along with their wives, and children, and domestic animals, every resident alien, hired worker, and purchased slave, girded themselves with sackcloth.†* ¹¹And all the Israelite men, women, and children who lived in Jerusalem fell prostrate in front of the temple†* and sprinkled ashes on their heads, spreading out their sackcloth before the Lord.* ¹²The altar, too, they draped in sackcloth;† and with one accord they cried out fervently to the God of Israel not to allow their children to be seized, their wives to be taken captive, the cities of their inheritance to be ruined, or the sanctuary to be profaned and mocked for the nations to gloat over.

¹³The Lord heard their cry† and saw their distress. The people continued fasting for many days throughout Judea and before the sanctuary of the Lord Almighty in Jerusalem.* ¹⁴Also girded with sackcloth, Joakim, the high priest, and all the priests in attendance before the Lord, and those who ministered to the Lord offered the daily burnt offering, the votive offerings, and the voluntary offerings of the people.* ¹⁵With ashes upon their turbans, they cried to the Lord with all their strength to look with favor on the whole house of Israel.*

# 5 Achior in the Assyrian War Council.† ¹It was reported to Holofernes, the ranking general of the Assyrian forces, that the Israelites were ready for battle, had blocked the mountain passes, fortified the high hilltops, and placed roadblocks in the plains. ²In great anger he summoned all the rulers of Moab, the governors of Ammon, and all the satraps of the coastland* ³and said to them: "Now tell me, you Canaanites, what sort of people is this that lives in the hill country? Which cities do they inhabit? How large is their force? In what does their power and strength consist? Who has set himself up as their king and the leader of their army? ⁴Why have they alone of all the inhabitants of the west refused to come out to meet me?"

⁵†Then Achior, the leader of all the Ammonites, said to him: "My lord, please listen to a report from your servant. I will tell you the truth about this people that lives in the hill country near here. No lie shall escape your servant's lips.

⁶"These people are descendants of the Chaldeans. ⁷They formerly lived in Mesopotamia, for they did not wish to follow the gods of

---

**4:4** Of the eight cities listed, only the locations of Beth-horon, Jericho, and Samaria are known. Salem, mentioned in Gn 17:17, is thought to be an ancient name of Jerusalem.

**4:6** *Joakim, who was high priest:* see also vv. 8, 14; 15:8. Joakim exercises religious and military authority comparable to that of Jonathan in Maccabean times (cf. 1 Mc 10:18–21). *Bethulia and Betomesthaim:* unknown locations mentioned only in Judith. Bethulia may mean "House of God" (*byt 'l/yh*) or "House of Ascent" (*byt 'lyh*), perhaps a reference to either Bethel or Shechem.

**4:7** *Only wide enough for two at a time:* such a narrow pass near Esdraelon cannot be identified.

**4:10** *Sackcloth:* traditional sign of penitence and supplication is here taken to the extreme. Cf. Jon 3:8.

**4:11** *Fell prostrate in front of the temple:* for a parallel to this ceremony of entreaty see Jl 1:13, 14; 2:15–17.

**4:12** *The altar…draped in sackcloth:* attested nowhere else in the Bible.

**4:13** *The Lord heard their cry:* this anticipates the role of Judith, the instrument of deliverance (chap. 16), though the people believe God has abandoned them (7:25).

**5:1–6:13** The scene shifts to the Assyrian camp below Bethulia where Holofernes talks with Achior and then expels him to the foot of the hill below the little town.

**5:5–21** Achior (Heb. "brother of light") traces the covenant of Israel from Abraham to the exile and defends the inviolability of the people because their powerful God will defend them if they do not sin. He later identifies the head Judith displays as that of Holofernes (14:6–10). He may be modeled on the famous sage, Ahiqar (see note on Tb 1:21). Achior is wise, but the wisdom granted Judith by God is more effective than his.

**4:6** Dn 13:1, 4, 28, 29, 63.
**4:8** 2 Mc 11:27.
**4:10** Neh 9:1; Est 4:1–4; Jl 1:13, 14; Jon 3:5, 6, 8.
**4:11** 1 Chr 29:20; 2 Mc 3:15.
**4:11** 2 Sm 21:10.
**4:13** Est 4:16; Jl 2:15.
**4:14** Ex 29:38–46; Nm 28:1–8; Ezr 3:4.
**4:15** Lv 16:4; Ez 24:23; 44:18; Zec 3:5.
**5:2** Dt 2:21; 2 Kgs 24:2.

their ancestors who were in the land of the Chaldeans.* <sup>8</sup>Since they abandoned the way of their ancestors, and worshiped the God of heaven,† the God whom they had come to know, their ancestors expelled them from the presence of their gods. So they fled to Mesopotamia and lived there a long time. <sup>9</sup>Their God told them to leave the place where they were living and go to the land of Canaan. Here they settled, and grew very rich in gold, silver, and a great abundance of livestock.* <sup>10</sup>Later, when famine had gripped the land of Canaan, they went down into Egypt. They stayed there as long as they found sustenance and there they grew into such a great multitude that the number of their people could not be counted.* <sup>11</sup>* The king of Egypt, however, rose up against them, and shrewdly forced them to labor at brickmaking; they were oppressed and made into slaves. <sup>12</sup>But they cried to their God, and he struck the whole land of Egypt with plagues for which there was no remedy. So the Egyptians drove them out. <sup>13</sup>Then God dried up the Red Sea before them* <sup>14</sup>and led them along the route to Sinai and Kadesh-barnea. They drove out all the inhabitants of the wilderness <sup>15</sup>and settled in the land of the Amorites. By their strength they destroyed all the Heshbonites,* crossed the Jordan, and took possession of all the hill country.* <sup>16</sup>They drove out before them the Canaanites, the Perizzites, the Jebusites, the Shechemites,† and all the Gergesites,* and they lived there a long time.

<sup>17</sup>* "As long as the Israelites did not sin in the sight of their God, they prospered, for their God, who hates wickedness, was with them. <sup>18</sup>† But when they abandoned the way he had prescribed for them, they were utterly destroyed by frequent wars, and finally taken as captives into foreign lands. The temple of their God was razed to the ground, and their cities were occupied by their enemies.* <sup>19</sup>But now they have returned to their God, and they have come back from the Diaspora where they were scattered. They have reclaimed Jerusalem, where their sanctuary is, and have settled again in the hill country, because it was unoccupied.

<sup>20</sup>* "So now, my master† and lord, if these people are inadvertently at fault, or if they are sinning against their God, and if we verify this offense of theirs, then we will be able to go up and conquer them. <sup>21</sup>But if they are not a guilty nation, then let my lord keep his distance; otherwise their Lord and God will shield them, and we will be mocked in the eyes of all the earth."

<sup>22</sup>Now when Achior had finished saying these things, all the people standing round about the tent murmured; and the officers of Holofernes and all the inhabitants of the seacoast and of Moab alike said he should be cut to pieces. <sup>23</sup>* "We are not afraid of the Israelites," they said, "for they are a powerless people, incapable of a strong defense. <sup>24</sup>Therefore let us attack, master Holofernes. They will become fodder for your great army."

<sup>1</sup>When the noise of the crowd surrounding the council had subsided, Holofernes, the ranking general of the Assyrian forces, said to Achior, in the presence of the whole throng of foreigners, of the Moabites, and of the Ammonite mercenaries: <sup>2</sup>"Who are you,† Achior and the mercenaries of Ephraim, to prophesy among us as you have done today, and to tell us not to fight against the people of Israel because their God shields them? Who is God beside Nebuchadnezzar? He will send his force and destroy them from the face of the earth. Their God will not save them;* <sup>3</sup>but we, the servants of Nebuchadnezzar, will strike them down with one blow, for they will be unable to withstand the force of our cavalry. <sup>4</sup>We will overwhelm them with it, and their mountains shall be drunk with their blood, and their

---

**5:8** *God of heaven*: a common expression in Persian times; see also 6:19; 11:17 (cf. 7:28; 9:12; 13:18).

**5:16** *Shechemites*: perhaps anticipates the allusion in Judith's prayer (9:2) to Simeon's revenge on these people.

**5:18–19** Knowledge of the Babylonian exile is presupposed; cf. also 4:3.

**5:20** *Master*: the Greek word *despota*, usually applied to God in the Septuagint, is applied to Holofernes five times in the Book of Judith (vv. 20, 24; 7:9, 11; 11:10), and only once to God (9:12).

**6:2** *Who are you*: repeated by Judith in 8:12 to the officials of Bethulia and modified in 12:14 in her response to Bagoas' invitation on Holofernes' behalf. The question, "Who is God?" motivates the entire narrative. Holofernes defends Nebuchadnezzar; Judith defends the Lord.

**5:7** Gn 11:31.
**5:9** Gn 11:31–12:5; 13:2.
**5:10** Gn 42:1–5; 46:1–7; Ex 1:7.
**5:11–12** Ex 1:10–14; 5:1–21; 7:1–11:10.
**5:13** Ex 14:21; Jos 2:10; 4:23; Ps 106:9; Wis 19:7; Heb 11:29.
**5:15** Nm 21:25–28, 30, 34; Dt 1:4; 2:24, 26, 30; 3:2, 6; 4:46.
**5:15** Jos 3.
**5:16** Gn 10:16; 15:20; Dt 7:1; Jos 3:10; 24:12; 1 Chr 1:14.
**5:17–18** Dt 28–30; Jgs 2:11–15; Ps 106:40–46.
**5:18** 2 Kgs 25.
**5:20–21** Jdt 8:18–23; 11:10; Tb 3:3.
**5:23–24** Jdt 6:2; 9:7–8; 16:2.
**6:2** Jdt 3:8; 9:7–8; 1 Kgs 22:15–17; 2 Kgs 18:32–35; Is 36:18–20; Dn 3:14–18.

J D T

plains filled with their corpses. Not a trace of them shall survive our attack; they will utterly perish. So says King Nebuchadnezzar, lord of all the earth. For he has spoken, and his words will not be in vain. ⁵As for you, Achior, you Ammonite mercenary, for saying these things in a moment of perversity, you will not see my face after today, until I have taken revenge on this people that came out of Egypt. ⁶Then at my return, the sword of my army or the spear of my attendants will pierce your sides, and you will fall among their wounded. ⁷My servants will now conduct you to the hill country, and leave you at one of the cities beside the passes. ⁸You will not die until you are destroyed together with them. ⁹If you still harbor the hope that they will not be taken, then there is no need for you to be downcast.* I have spoken, and not one of my words will fail to be fulfilled."

¹⁰Then Holofernes ordered the servants who were standing by in his tent to seize Achior, conduct him to Bethulia, and hand him over to the Israelites. ¹¹So the servants seized him and took him out of the camp into the plain. From the plain they led him up into the hill country until they reached the springs below Bethulia.

¹²When the men of the city saw them, they seized their weapons and ran out of the city to the top of the hill, and all the slingers kept them from coming up by hurling stones at them. ¹³So, taking cover below the hill, they bound Achior and left him lying at the foot of the hill; then they returned to their lord.

**Achior in Bethulia.†** ¹⁴The Israelites came down from their city and found him, untied him, and brought him into Bethulia. They placed him before the rulers of the city, ¹⁵who in those days were Uzziah,† son of Micah of the tribe of Simeon, and Chabris, son of Gothoniel, and Charmis, son of Melchiel.* ¹⁶They then convened all the elders of the city, and all their young men, as well as the women, gathered in haste at the place of assembly.

They placed Achior in the center of the people, and Uzziah questioned him about what had happened. ¹⁷He replied by giving them an account of what was said in the council of Holofernes, and of all his own words among the Assyrian rulers, and of all the boasting threats of Holofernes against the house of Israel.

¹⁸At this the people fell prostrate and worshiped God,† and they cried out: ¹⁹"Lord, God of heaven, look at their arrogance! Have mercy on our people in their abject state, and look with favor this day on the faces of those who are consecrated to you." ²⁰Then they reassured Achior and praised him highly. ²¹Uzziah brought him from the place of assembly to his home, where he gave a banquet for the elders. That whole night they called upon the God of Israel for help.

**7 The Campaign Against Israel.†** ¹The following day Holofernes ordered his whole army, and all the troops who had come to join him, to break camp and move against Bethulia, seize the passes into the hills, and make war on the Israelites. ²That same day all their fighting men went into action. Their forces numbered a hundred and seventy thousand infantry and twelve thousand cavalry, not counting the baggage train or the men who accompanied it on foot, a very great army. ³They encamped at the spring in the valley near Bethulia, and spread crosswise toward Dothan as far as Balbaim, and lengthwise from Bethulia to Cyamon, which faces Esdraelon.

⁴When the Israelites saw how many there were, they were greatly distressed and said to one another, "Soon they will strip the whole land bare. Neither the high mountains nor the valleys nor the hills will bear their weight." ⁵Yet they all seized their weapons, lighted fires on their towers, and kept watch throughout the night.*

**The Siege of Bethulia.†** ⁶On the second day Holofernes led out all his cavalry in the sight

---

6:14–21 The scene shifts back to Bethulia where Achior tells the town leaders and citizens all that Holofernes has planned against them. The people cry out to God for help.
6:15 *Uzziah: Ozeias* is the Greek equivalent of the Hebrew *'uzziyyah,* "Yah-is-my-strength." His compromise in 7:30 highlights the irony of his name. *Chabris…Charmis:* unknown outside Judith.
6:18 *The people fell prostrate and worshiped God:* here in response to Achior's report, the people properly turn to God in their distress. See 4:12.
7:1–5 The scene returns to the Assyrian camp (vv. 1–3) and

then shifts back to Bethulia (vv. 4–5). Holofernes orders war preparations; Israel sees and is greatly terrified.
7:6–32 The scene is set first in the Assyrian camp where Holofernes moves against Bethulia (vv. 6–18), and then in Bethulia where the people cry out to God and, when their courage fails, determine it is time to surrender (vv. 19–32).

6:9 Gn 4:5; 40:7.
6:15 Gn 29:33; 34:25, 30; 35:23.
7:5 1 Mc 12:28–29; 2 Mc 10:36.

of the Israelites who were in Bethulia. [7] He reconnoitered the ascents to their city and located their springs of water; these he seized, stationing armed detachments around them, while he himself returned to his troops.

[8] All the rulers of the Edomites, all the leaders of the Moabites, together with the generals of the coastal region, came to Holofernes and said:* [9] "Master, please listen to what we have to say, that there may be no losses among your forces. [10] These Israelite troops do not rely on their spears, but on the height of the mountains where they dwell, for it is not easy to reach the summit of their mountains.* [11] Therefore, master, do not attack them in regular formation, and not a single one of your troops will fall. [12] Stay in your camp, and spare every man of your force. Have some of your servants keep control of the spring of water that flows out at the base of the mountain, [13] for that is where the inhabitants of Bethulia get their water. Then thirst will destroy them, and they will surrender their city. Meanwhile, we and our troops will go up to the nearby hilltops and encamp there to guard against anyone's leaving the city. [14] They and their wives and children will languish with hunger, and even before the sword strikes them they will be laid low in the streets where they live. [15] Thus you will render them dire punishment for their rebellion and their refusal to meet you peacefully."

[16] Their words pleased Holofernes and all his attendants, and he ordered their proposal to be carried out. [17] So the Ammonites moved camp, together with five thousand Assyrians. They encamped in the valley and held the water supply and the springs of the Israelites. [18] The Edomites and the Ammonites went up and encamped in the hill country opposite Dothan; and they sent some of their men to the southeast opposite Egrebel, near Chusi, which is on Wadi Mochmur. The rest of the Assyrian army was encamped in the plain, covering all the land. Their tents and equipment were spread out in profusion everywhere, and they formed a vast multitude.

**The Distress of the Israelites.** [19] The Israelites cried to the Lord, their God, for they were disheartened, since all their enemies had them surrounded, and there was no way of escaping from them.† [20] The whole Assyrian army, infantry, chariots, and cavalry, kept them thus surrounded for thirty-four days.† All the reservoirs of water failed the inhabitants of Bethulia, [21] and the cisterns ran dry, so that on no day did they have enough water to drink, for their drinking water was rationed. [22] Their children were listless, and the women and youths were fainting from thirst and were collapsing in the streets and gateways of the city, with no strength left in them.

[23] So all the people, including youths, women, and children, went in a crowd to Uzziah and the rulers of the city. They cried out loudly and said before all the elders: [24] "May God judge between you and us! You have done us grave injustice in not making peace with the Assyrians.* [25] There is no one to help us now! God has sold us into their hands by laying us prostrate before them in thirst and utter exhaustion.* [26] So now, summon them and deliver the whole city as plunder to the troops of Holofernes and to all his forces; [27] we would be better off to become their prey. Although we would be made slaves, at least we would live, and not have to see our little ones dying before our eyes, and our wives and children breathing their last.* [28] We adjure you by heaven and earth and by our God, the Lord of our ancestors, who is punishing us for our sins and the sins of our ancestors,† that this very day you do as we have proposed."*

[29] All in the assembly with one accord broke into shrill wailing and cried loudly to the Lord their God. [30] But Uzziah said to them, "Courage, my brothers and sisters! Let us endure patiently five days more for the Lord our God to show mercy toward us; for God will not

---

† **7:19** The prayers of the Israelites shift focus from concern for the Temple and Jerusalem (4:12), to concern that God see the arrogance of the enemy and show pity on the covenant people (6:18), to expression of fear and loss of courage regarding their own safety (7:19).

**7:20** *Thirty-four days:* the Bethulians lose heart after being without water; Judith will spend four days in the enemy camp (12:10) and the Israelites will plunder the enemy camp for thirty days (15:11).

**7:28** In keeping with the deuteronomic theme of retribution,

the Bethulians interpret their persecution as punishment for their sins and the sins of their ancestors (see Ex 20:5; 34:7; Ez 18). In 8:18–27, Judith argues that they are being tested.

* 
**7:8** Gn 36:1; 1 Mc 5:3.
**7:10** 1 Kgs 20:23, 28; 2 Kgs 19:23; Ps 95:4; Is 37:24.
**7:24** Ex 5:21.
**7:25** Est 7:4.
**7:27** Ex 14:12; 16:3; 1 Mc 1:62–63.
**7:28** Ps 106:6; Lam 5:7.

utterly forsake us. <sup>31</sup> But if these days pass and help does not come to us, I will do as you say." <sup>32</sup> Then he dismissed the people. The men returned to their posts on the walls and towers of the city, the women and children went back to their homes. Throughout the city they were in great misery.

## III. JUDITH, INSTRUMENT OF THE LORD†

**8** **Description of Judith.** <sup>1</sup>†* Now in those days Judith, daughter of Merari,* son of Ox, son of Joseph, son of Oziel, son of Elkiah, son of Ananias, son of Gideon, son of Raphain, son of Ahitub, son of Elijah, son of Hilkiah, son of Eliab, son of Nathanael, son of Salamiel, son of Sarasadai, son of Simeon, son of Israel, heard of this. <sup>2</sup> Her husband, Manasseh,† of her own tribe and clan, had died at the time of the barley harvest. <sup>3</sup> While he was supervising those who bound the sheaves in the field, he was overcome by the heat; and he collapsed on his bed and died in Bethulia, his native city. He was buried with his ancestors in the field between Dothan and Balamon. <sup>4</sup>* Judith was living as a widow† in her home for three years and four months. <sup>5</sup> She set up a tent for herself on the roof of her house, put sackcloth about her waist, and wore widow's clothing. * <sup>6</sup> She fasted all the days of her widowhood, except sabbath eves and sabbaths, new moon eves and new moons, feastdays and holidays of the house of Israel. * <sup>7</sup> She was beautiful in appearance and very lovely to behold. * Her husband, Manasseh, had left her gold and silver, male and female servants, livestock and fields, which she was maintaining.

<sup>8</sup> No one had a bad word to say about her, for she feared God greatly.

**Judith and the Elders.**† <sup>9</sup> So when Judith heard of the harsh words that the people, discouraged by their lack of water, had spoken against their ruler, and of all that Uzziah had said to them in reply, swearing that he would hand over the city to the Assyrians at the end of five days, <sup>10</sup> she sent her maid who was in charge of all her things † to summon Uzziah, Chabris, and Charmis, the elders of her city. <sup>11</sup> When they came, she said to them: "Listen to me, you rulers of the people of Bethulia. What you said to the people today is not right. You pronounced this oath, made between God and yourselves, and promised to hand over the city to our enemies unless within a certain time the Lord comes to our aid. <sup>12</sup> Who are you to put God to the test today, setting yourselves in the place of God in human affairs?†* <sup>13</sup> And now it is the Lord Almighty you are putting to the test, but you will never understand anything! <sup>14</sup> You cannot plumb the depths of the human heart or grasp the workings of the human mind; how then can you fathom God, who has made all these things, or discern his mind, or understand his plan? *

"No, my brothers, do not anger the Lord our God. <sup>15</sup>† For if he does not plan to come to our aid within the five days, he has it equally within his power to protect us at such time as he pleases, or to destroy us in the sight of our enemies. <sup>16</sup> Do not impose conditions on the plans of the Lord our God. God is not like a human being to be moved by threats, nor like a mortal to be cajoled.

---

† **8:1–10:10** In this section the hero is introduced (8:1–8) and prepares to deliver Israel (8:9–10:10).

**8:1** Judith has the longest genealogy accorded any biblical woman, with family ties back to Israel/Jacob.

**8:2** *Manasseh*: Judith's marriage was endogamous, within her own tribe. The tribe and clan are identified as hers, though usually it is the husband's tribe and clan that are noted.

**8:4** *Widow*: in a reversal of traditional property law, Judith holds title to her husband's estate (see v. 7). However, she will give a part of her inheritance to her late husband's family before her death (16:24); she chooses not to remarry (16:22).

**8:9–10:10** This section opens with a repetition of the information that Judith heard about the discouragement of the people and about Uzziah's vow (cf. v. 1). Judith's plan to save Israel then takes shape. In her own home, she meets with the elders of Bethulia (vv. 9–36), prays (9:1–14), prepares herself and the food she will need in the Assyrian camp (10:1–5), goes out to meet the elders again at the gate of Bethulia (10:6–8), and sets out with her maid for the Assyrian camp (10:9–10).

**8:10** *Her maid who was in charge of all her things*: cf. Gn 15:2; 24:2; 39:4. Judith's first act in the story is to send this unnamed maid (*habra*, lit., "graceful one" or "favorite slave," v. 33;

10:2, 5, 17; 13:9; 16:23) to summon the town officials (see also other terms for female servants, *paidiske* in 10:10 and *doule* in 12:15; 13:3). Her last act in the story will be to give this woman her freedom (16:23).

**8:12** Judith reprimands the leaders for putting God to the test (cf. Dt 6:16). She will argue that the right to test belongs to God (vv. 25–27).

**8:15–16** God's plans are in opposition to Nebuchadnezzar's plans (2:2, 4). *To protect…or to destroy*: Judith defends God's freedom (cf. Jb 1:21; 2:10).

**8:1** Gn 26:34; Jer 36:14, 21, 23.
**8:1** Gn 46:11; Ex 6:16; Nm 3:17.
**8:4** 1 Sm 25:39–42; 2 Sm 11:27; Is 54:4; Lam 1:1; 5:3.
**8:5** Jos 2:6, 8; Jgs 3:20–25; 1 Sm 9:25–26; 2 Sm 11:2; 16:22;
2 Kgs 4:10; 23:12; Ps 102:8; Acts 10:9.
**8:6** Lk 2:37.
**8:7** Gn 12:11; 29:17; Est 2:7.
**8:12** Dt 6:16; Jb 38:2; 40:2, 7–8; Ps 106:14; Mal 3:15.
**8:14** Ps 139:17–18; Wis 9:13; Is 40:13; Rom 11:33–34; 1 Cor 2:11.

¹⁷ "So while we wait for the salvation that comes from him, let us call upon him to help us, and he will hear our cry if it pleases him. ¹⁸ For there has not risen among us in recent generations, nor does there exist today, any tribe, or clan, or district, or city of ours that worships gods made by hands, as happened in former days.* ¹⁹ It was for such conduct that our ancestors were handed over to the sword and to pillage, and fell with great destruction before our enemies.* ²⁰ But since we acknowledge no other god but the Lord, we hope that he will not disdain us or any of our people. ²¹ If we are taken, then all Judea will fall, our sanctuary will be plundered, and God will demand an account from us for their profanation. ²² For the slaughter of our kindred, for the taking of exiles from the land, and for the devastation of our inheritance, he will hold us responsible among the nations. Wherever we are enslaved, we will be a scandal and a reproach in the eyes of our masters. ²³ Our servitude will not work to our advantage, but the Lord our God will turn it to disgrace.

²⁴ "Therefore, my brothers, let us set an example† for our kindred. Their lives depend on us, and the defense of the sanctuary, the temple, and the altar rests with us. ²⁵* Besides all this, let us give thanks to the Lord our God for putting us to the test as he did our ancestors.* ²⁶ Recall how he dealt with Abraham, and how he tested Isaac, and all that happened to Jacob in Syrian Mesopotamia while he was tending the flocks of Laban, his mother's brother. ²⁷ He has not tested us with fire, as he did them, to try their hearts, nor is he taking vengeance on us. But the Lord chastises those who are close to him in order to admonish them."

²⁸ Then Uzziah said to her: "All that you have said you have spoken truthfully, and no one can deny your words. ²⁹ For today is not the first time your wisdom has been evident, but from your earliest days all the people have recognized your understanding, for your heart's disposition is right. ³⁰ The people, however, were so thirsty that they forced us to do for them as we have promised, and to bind ourselves by an oath that we cannot break.†* ³¹ But now, since you are a devout woman, pray for us that the Lord may send rain to fill up our cisterns. Then we will no longer be fainting from thirst."

³² Then Judith said to them: "Listen to me! I will perform a deed that will go down from generation to generation among our descendants. ³³ Stand at the city gate tonight to let me pass through with my maid; and within the days you have specified before you will surrender the city to our enemies, the Lord will deliver Israel by my hand. ³⁴ You must not inquire into the affair, for I will not tell you what I am doing until it has been accomplished." ³⁵ Uzziah and the rulers said to her, "Go in peace, and may the Lord God go before you to take vengeance upon our enemies!" ³⁶ Then they withdrew from the tent and returned to their posts.

# 9 The Prayer of Judith.† ¹ Judith fell prostrate, put ashes upon her head, and uncovered the sackcloth she was wearing. Just as the evening incense was being offered in the temple of God in Jerusalem, Judith cried loudly to the Lord:* ² "Lord, God of my father Simeon, into whose hand you put a sword to take revenge upon the foreigners† who had defiled a virgin by violating her, shaming her by uncovering her thighs, and dishonoring her by polluting her womb. You said, 'This shall not be done!' Yet they did it. ³ Therefore you handed over their rulers to slaughter; and you handed over to bloodshed the bed in which

---

†

**8:24** *Let us set an example*: when Judith says "us," she includes herself. She proposes that she together with Uzziah, Chabris, and Charmis model a faithful response to God's test for the wavering people. "Let us give thanks to the Lord our God for putting us to the test" (v. 25) repeats her intention. "Us" for Uzziah does not include her (see vv. 30, 31).

**8:30–31** *An oath that we cannot break*: Uzziah's request that Judith pray for rain underscores his lack of imagination concerning how God's deliverance might come.

**9:1–14** Judith prepares to confront the enemy by turning to God, the source of her strength. Her prayer, an individual lament, moves from a remembrance of God's saving deeds of the past to an appeal to God to exercise the same power in the present. Judith contrasts the empty pride of the Assyrians with God's surpassing might, powerful enough to be exercised in unlikely ways,

even through the hand of a woman.

**9:2** *The foreigners*: Shechem, the Hivite, violated Dinah, Jacob and Leah's daughter (Gn 34:2). *Defiled a virgin by violating her*: meaning of the Greek is unclear; lit., "who loosened the virgin's womb (*metran*) to defilement." Some read "headdress" or "girdle" (*mitran*) instead of "womb" (*metran*).

---

* 
**8:18** Jdt 5:20–21; 11:10.
**8:19** Ps 78:56–57; 106:13–14; Jer 7:16–20.
**8:25** Dt 8:5; Tb 12:14; Ps 94:12; Prv 3:11–12; Wis 3:4–6; Sir 2:1–6; Heb 12:5–6.
**8:25** Gn 22:1–19; 32:22–32; Ex 20:20; Dt 8:16.
**8:30** Ex 32:22; 1 Sm 15:20–24.
**9:1** Ex 30:7–8; 1 Chr 28:18; Ezr 9:5; Ps 141:2; Dn 9:21.

they lay deceived, the same bed that had felt the shame of their own deceiving. You struck down the slaves together with their masters, and the masters upon their thrones.† ⁴Their wives you handed over to plunder, and their daughters to captivity, and all the spoils you divided among your favored children, who burned with zeal for you and in their abhorrence of the defilement of their blood called on you for help. O God, my God, hear me also, a widow.

⁵"It is you who were the author of those events and of what preceded and followed them. The present and the future you have also planned.* Whatever you devise comes into being. ⁶The things you decide come forward and say, 'Here we are!' All your ways are in readiness, and your judgment is made with foreknowledge.*

⁷"Here are the Assyrians, a vast force, priding themselves on horse and chariot, boasting of the power of their infantry, trusting in shield and spear, bow and sling.* They do not know that you are the Lord who crushes wars;† ⁸Lord is your name. Shatter their strength in your might, and crush their force in your wrath.* For they have resolved to profane your sanctuary, to defile the tent where your glorious name resides, and to break off the horns of your altar with the sword. ⁹† See their pride, and send forth your fury upon their heads.* Give me, a widow, a strong hand to execute my plan.* ¹⁰By the deceit of my lips, strike down slave together with ruler, and ruler together with attendant. Crush their arrogance by the hand of a female.*

¹¹†* "Your strength is not in numbers, nor does your might depend upon the powerful.* You are God of the lowly, helper of those of little account, supporter of the weak, protector of those in despair, savior of those without hope.

¹²"Please, please, God of my father, God of the heritage of Israel, Master of heaven and earth, Creator of the waters, King of all you have created, hear my prayer! ¹³Let my deceitful words†* wound and bruise those who have planned dire things against your covenant, your holy temple, Mount Zion, and the house your children possess.* ¹⁴Make every nation and every tribe know clearly that you are God, the God of all power and might, and that there is no other who shields the people of Israel but you alone."

**10 Judith Prepares to Depart.** ¹As soon as Judith had ceased her prayer to the God of Israel and finished all these words, ²she rose from the ground. She called her maid and they went down into the house, which she used only on sabbaths and feast days. ³She took off the sackcloth she had on, laid aside the garments of her widowhood, washed her body with water, and anointed herself with rich ointment. She arranged her hair, put on a diadem, and dressed in the festive attire she had worn while her husband, Manasseh, was living.* ⁴She chose sandals for her feet, and put on her anklets, bracelets, rings, earrings, and all her other jewelry.* Thus she made herself very beautiful, to entice the eyes of all the men who should see her.†

⁵She gave her maid a skin of wine and a jug

---

**9:3** Because Shechem had deceived and violated Dinah, her brothers, Simeon and Levi, tricked Shechem and the men of his city into being circumcised, and then killed them while they were recovering from the circumcision (Gn 34:13–29).

**9:7–8** *You are the Lord who crushes wars; Lord is your name*: cf. Ex 15:3, "The Lord is a warrior; Lord is his name" and Jdt 16:2, "The Lord is a God who crushes wars."

**9:9–10** In a five-fold petition, Judith asks that God see their pride, send fury on their heads, give her a strong hand, strike down the enemy through her deceit, and crush their pride by the hand of a female (*theleia*, see also 13:15 and 16:5, rather than the more usual *gyne*, woman). In an androcentric society, there was no greater dishonor for a male than that he die at the hand of a female (see Jgs 9:53–54). Nine verses emphasize that by her hand God's deliverance is accomplished: 8:33; 9:9, 10; 12:4; 13:4, 14, 15; 15:10; and 16:5.

**9:11–12** Ten titles for God are arranged in two groups of five on either side of the repeated Greek particle, *nai nai* ("verily" or "please"). The title "Master of heaven and earth" (v. 12; see notes on 1:11 and 5:20) is unique to Judith in the Septuagint, as are also "God of the heritage of Israel" and "Creator of the waters."

**9:13** *Deceitful words*: twice Judith asks God to make her a successful liar in order to preserve her people (vv. 10, 13).

**10:4** Judith's beauty overcomes all who meet her (8:7; 10:7, 14, 19, 23; 11:21, 23; 12:13).

**9:5** Is 41:22–23; 42:9; 43:9; 44:7; 46:10.
**9:6** Jb 38:35; Is 46:9–13; Bar 3:35.
**9:7** Ex 15:1, 21.
**9:8** Ex 15:3; Ps 46:9–10; 76:4–5.
**9:9** Ex 15:7.
**9:9** Ex 3:19–20; 4:2, 4, 6, 7, 17, 20; 5:21; 6:1; 7:4, 5, 15, 17, 19; 8:1, 2, 12, 13; 9:3, 22; 10:12, 21, 22; 12:11; 13:3, 9, 14, 16; 14:16, 21, 26, 27; 15:6, 9, 12, 20;

Jgs 5:26.
**9:10** Jgs 4:9.
**9:11** Ps 33:16–17.
**9:11** Ex 15:2; Jgs 7:2; 1 Sm 17:45–47; 2 Chr 16:8–9.
**9:13** Jdt 10:4; 11:20, 23; 16:6, 9; Est C:24.
**9:13** Dn 11:28.
**10:3** Gn 43:24; Lv 8:6; 22:6; Tb 6:3; Ez 16:4, 9.
**10:4** Gn 24:47, 53; 35:4; Ex 3:22; 12:35; 32:3; 35:22; Nm 31:50; Is 3:18, 21; Hos 2:15.

of oil. She filled a bag with roasted grain, dried fig cakes, and pure bread.†* She wrapped all her dishes and gave them to the maid to carry.*

⁶ Then they went out to the gate of the city of Bethulia and found Uzziah and the elders of the city, Chabris and Charmis, standing there. ⁷ When they saw Judith transformed in looks and differently dressed, they were very much astounded at her beauty and said to her, ⁸ "May the God of our ancestors grant you favor and make your design successful, for the glory of the Israelites and the exaltation of Jerusalem." ⁹ Judith bowed down to God.

**Judith and Her Maid Leave Bethulia.** Then she said to them, "Order the gate of the city opened for me, that I may go to accomplish the matters we discussed." So they ordered the young men to open the gate for her, as she had requested, ¹⁰ and they did so. Then Judith and her maidservant went out. The men of the city kept her in view as she went down the mountain and crossed the valley; then they lost sight of her.

### IV. JUDITH GOES OUT TO WAR†

¹¹ As Judith and her maid walked directly across the valley, they encountered the Assyrian patrol. ¹² The men took her in custody and asked her, "To what people do you belong? Where do you come from, and where are you going?"* She replied: "I am a daughter of the Hebrews, and I am fleeing from them, because they are about to be delivered up to you as prey. ¹³ I have come to see Holofernes, the ranking general of your forces, to give him a trustworthy report; in his presence I will show him the way by which he can ascend and take possession of the whole hill country without a single one of his men suffering injury or loss of life."*

¹⁴ When the men heard her words and gazed upon her face, which appeared marvelously beautiful to them, they said to her, ¹⁵ "By hastening down to see our master, you have saved your life. Now go to his tent; some of us will accompany you to hand you over to him. ¹⁶ When you stand before him, have no fear in your heart; give him the report you have given us, and he will treat you well." ¹⁷ So they selected a hundred of their men as an escort for her and her maid, and these conducted them to the tent of Holofernes.

¹⁸ As the news of her arrival spread among the tents, a crowd gathered in the camp. They came and stood around her as she waited outside the tent of Holofernes, while he was being informed about her. ¹⁹ They marveled at her beauty, regarding the Israelites with wonder because of her, and they said to one another, "Who can despise this people who have such women among them? It is not good to leave one of their men alive, for if any were to be spared they could beguile the whole earth."

**Judith Meets Holofernes.** ²⁰ Then the guards of Holofernes and all his attendants came out and ushered her into the tent. ²¹ Holofernes was reclining on his bed under a canopy† woven of purple, gold, emeralds, and other precious stones. ²² When they announced her to him, he came out to the front part of the tent, preceded by silver lamps. ²³ When Judith came before Holofernes and his attendants, they all marveled at the beauty of her face. She fell prostrate and paid homage to him, but his servants raised her up.*

**11** ¹ Then Holofernes said to her: "Take courage, woman! Have no fear in your heart! I have never harmed anyone who chose to serve Nebuchadnezzar, king of all the earth. ² As for your people who live in the hill country, I would never have raised my spear against them, had they not insulted me. They have brought this upon themselves. ³ But now tell me why you have fled from them and come to us? In any case, you have come to safety. Take courage! Your life is spared tonight and for the future.* ⁴ No one at all will harm you. Rather, you will be well treated, as are the servants of my lord, King Nebuchadnezzar."

---

† **10:5** Concern for Israel's dietary laws, reflected in her selection of wine, roasted grain, and bread, emphasizes Judith's religious fidelity (cf. 1 Sm 25:18 and Dn 1:8–16).

**10:11–13:20** In this section Judith and her maid arrive in the Assyrian camp (10:11–19), where Judith meets (10:20–12:9) and triumphs over Holofernes (12:10–13:10a). Then she and her maid return to Bethulia and announce the victory (13:10b–20).

† **10:21** *Canopy:* netting for protection against insects. A prized possession in this story (cf. 13:15; 16:19).

---

**10:5** 1 Sm 25:18.  **10:23** Ru 2:10; 1 Sm 25:41;
**10:5** Jdt 12:2; Est C:28.                2 Sm 14:4.
**10:12** Gn 16:8.  **11:3** 2 Mc 11:19.
**10:13** Jdt 11:5–6.

⁵Judith answered him: "Listen to the words of your servant, and let your maidservant speak in your presence! I will say nothing false to my lord† this night. ⁶If you follow the words of your maidservant, God will successfully perform a deed through you, and my lord will not fail to achieve his designs.† ⁷I swear by the life of Nebuchadnezzar, king of all the earth, and by the power of him who has sent you to guide all living things, that not only do human beings serve him through you; but even the wild animals, and the cattle, and the birds of the air, because of your strength, will live for Nebuchadnezzar and his whole house.* ⁸Indeed, we have heard of your wisdom and cleverness.* The whole earth is aware that you above all others in the kingdom are able, rich in experience, and distinguished in military strategy.

⁹* "As for Achior's speech in your council, we have heard it. When the men of Bethulia rescued him, he told them all he had said to you. ¹⁰So then, my lord and master, do not disregard his word, but bear it in mind, for it is true. Indeed our people are not punished, nor does the sword prevail against them, except when they sin against their God.* ¹¹But now their sin† has caught up with them, by which they will bring the wrath of their God upon them when they do wrong; so that my lord will not be repulsed and fail, but death will overtake them. ¹²Because their food has given out and all their water is running low, they have decided to kill their animals, and are determined to consume all the things which God in his laws has forbidden them to eat. ¹³They have decided that they would use the first fruits of grain and the tithes of wine and oil, which they had consecrated and reserved for the priests who minister in the presence of our God in Jerusalem—things which the people should not so much as touch with their hands.* ¹⁴They have sent messengers to Jerusalem to bring back permission from the senate, for even there people have done these things.* ¹⁵On the very day when the response reaches them and they act upon it, they will be handed over to you for destruction.

¹⁶"As soon as I, your servant, learned all this, I fled from them. God has sent me to perform with you such deeds as will astonish people throughout the whole earth who hear of them. ¹⁷Your servant is, indeed, a God-fearing woman, serving the God of heaven night and day. Now I will remain with you, my lord; but each night your servant will go out into the valley and pray to God. He will tell me when they have committed their offenses. ¹⁸Then I will come and let you know, so that you may march out with all your forces, and not one of them will be able to withstand you. ¹⁹I will lead you through the heart of Judea until you come to Jerusalem, and there in its center I will set up your throne. You will drive them like sheep that have no shepherd, and not even a dog will growl at you.* This was told to me in advance and announced to me, and I have been sent to tell you."

²⁰Her words pleased Holofernes and all his attendants. They marveled at her wisdom and exclaimed, ²¹"No other woman from one end of the earth to the other looks so beautiful and speaks so wisely!" ²²Then Holofernes said to her: "God has done well in sending you ahead of your people, to bring victory to our hands, and destruction to those who have despised my lord. ²³You are not only beautiful in appearance, but you are also eloquent. If you do as you have said, your God will be my God;† you will live in the palace of King Nebuchadnezzar and be renowned throughout the whole earth."

**12** ¹Then he ordered them to lead her into the room where his silver dinnerware was kept, and ordered them to set a table for her with his own delicacies to eat and his own wine to drink. ²But Judith said, "I cannot eat any† of them, because it would be a

---

† **11:5–6** Here the word "lord" has a double meaning, indicating both Holofernes and God. Much irony is evident in Judith's conversation with Holofernes (e.g., 12:4).

**11:6** *Designs*: cf. 10:8; 11:6; 13:5 where this word is used as a synonym for Judith's "affair" (8:34), which she kept secret as she carried out the plan of her God (8:15, 16), unlike her counterpart Nebuchadnezzar, who told all the details of his plan (2:2, 4).

**11:11** *Sin*: but in 8:18–20 Judith asserts that the people have not committed idolatry in recent generations.

**11:23** *Your God will be my God*: in 3:8, Holofernes insisted that Nebuchadnezzar alone is god.

**12:2** *Cannot eat any*: the food of Gentiles was avoided by pious Jews (see Dn 1:8, 13, 15; Tb 1:10–11) because it might have been prohibited as unclean (see Lv 11:13–44), sacrificed to idols (see Ex 34:15; Dt 32:37–38), or contaminated with blood (see Lv 7:26–27). In addition, eating together symbolized the sharing of life.

---

**11:7** Jgs 8:19; 1 Sm 14:45; 25:26; 28:10; 2 Sm 11:11; Ez 17:16; Dn 2:38.
**11:8** Sir 1:6; 42:18.
**11:9–10** Jdt 5:5.
**11:10** Jdt 5:21; 8:18.
**11:13** Nm 18:8–9.
**11:14** 1 Mc 2:31–41.
**11:19** Ex 11:7.

scandal.* Besides, I will have enough with the things I brought with me." ³ Holofernes asked her, "But if your provisions give out, where can we get more of the same to provide for you? None of your people are with us." ⁴ Judith answered him, "As surely as you live, my lord, your servant will not use up her supplies before the Lord accomplishes by my hand what he has determined."

⁵ Then the attendants of Holofernes led her to her tent, where she slept until the middle of the night. Toward the early morning watch, she rose* ⁶ and sent this message to Holofernes, "Give orders, my lord, to let your servant go out for prayer." ⁷ So Holofernes ordered his guards not to hinder her. Thus she stayed in the camp three days. Each night she went out to the valley of Bethulia, where she bathed herself† at the spring of the camp.* ⁸ After bathing, she prayed to the Lord, the God of Israel, to direct her way for the triumph of her people. ⁹ Then she returned purified to the tent and remained there until her food was brought to her toward evening.*

**Judith at the Banquet of Holofernes.** ¹⁰ On the fourth day Holofernes gave a banquet for his servants alone, to which he did not invite any of the officers. ¹¹ And he said to Bagoas, the eunuch in charge of his personal affairs, "Go and persuade the Hebrew woman in your care to come and to eat and drink with us. ¹² It would bring shame on us to be with such a woman without enjoying her. If we do not seduce her, she will laugh at us."*

¹³ So Bagoas left the presence of Holofernes, and came to Judith and said, "So lovely a maidservant should not be reluctant to come to my lord to be honored by him, to enjoy drinking wine with us, and to act today like one of the Assyrian women who serve in the palace of Nebuchadnezzar." ¹⁴ Judith replied, "Who am I to refuse my lord? Whatever is pleasing to him I will promptly do. This will be a joy† for me until the day of my death."

¹⁵ So she proceeded to put on her festive garments and all her finery. Meanwhile her servant went ahead and spread out on the ground opposite Holofernes the fleece Bagoas had furnished for her daily use in reclining while eating.* ¹⁶ Then Judith came in and reclined. The heart of Holofernes was in rapture over her and his passion was aroused. He was burning with the desire to possess her, for he had been biding his time to seduce her from the day he saw her.* ¹⁷ Holofernes said to her, "Drink and be happy with us!" ¹⁸ Judith replied, "I will gladly drink, my lord, for today is the greatest day of my whole life." ¹⁹ She then took the things her servant had prepared and ate and drank in his presence. ²⁰ Holofernes, charmed by her, drank a great quantity of wine, more than he had ever drunk on any day since he was born.

# 13

**Judith Beheads Holofernes.** ¹ When it grew late, his servants quickly withdrew. Bagoas closed the tent from the outside and dismissed the attendants from their master's presence. They went off to their beds, for they were all tired because the banquet had lasted so long. ² Judith was left alone in the tent with Holofernes, who lay sprawled on his bed, for he was drunk with wine. ³ Judith had ordered her maidservant to stand outside the bedchamber and to wait, as on the other days, for her to come out; she had said she would be going out for her prayer. She had also said this same thing to Bagoas.

⁴ When all had departed, and no one, small or great, was left in the bedchamber, Judith stood by Holofernes' bed and prayed silently, "O Lord, God of all might, in this hour look graciously on the work of my hands for the exaltation of Jerusalem. ⁵ Now is the time for aiding your heritage and for carrying out my design to shatter the enemies who have risen against us."* ⁶ She went to the bedpost near the head of Holofernes, and taking his sword from it, ⁷ she drew close to the bed, grasped the hair of his head, and said, "Strengthen me this day, Lord, God of Israel!" ⁸ Then with all her might she struck his neck twice and cut off his head.* ⁹ She rolled his body off the bed and took the canopy from its posts. Soon afterward, she came out and handed over the head of Holofernes to her maid, ¹⁰ who put it into

---

**12:7** *Bathed herself*: she bathes to purify herself after contact with the Gentiles. Her nightly departure from the camp provides for her escape (cf. 13:10).
**12:14** *Joy*: the irony of this response is obvious; see also the joy of 14:9 and Judith's "new song" in chap. 16.

**12:2** Tb 1:10–11; Est C:28; 1 Mc 1:62–63; 2 Mc 5:27; 6:18–7:2; Dn 1:8.
**12:5** Ex 14:24; 1 Sm 11:11.
**12:7** Tb 7:9.
**12:9** 2 Sm 3:35.
**12:12** Dn 13:37, 54, 57–58.
**12:15** Tb 9:6; Ez 23:41.
**12:16** Dn 13:20, 39.
**13:5** Gn 24:45; 1 Sm 1:13.
**13:8** Jgs 4:21; 1 Sm 17:51; 31:9.

her food bag. Then the two went out together for prayer as they were accustomed to do.

**Judith and Her Maid Return to Bethulia.** They passed through the camp, and skirting that valley, went up the mountain to Bethulia, and approached its gates. [11] From a distance, Judith shouted to the guards at the gates: "Open! Open the gate! God, our God, is with us. Once more he has shown his strength in Israel and his power against the enemy, as he has today!"

**Judith Displays the Head of Holofernes.** [12]† When the citizens heard her voice, they hurried down to their city gate and summoned the elders of the city. [13] All the people, from the least to the greatest, hurriedly assembled, for her return seemed unbelievable. They opened the gate and welcomed the two women. They made a fire for light and gathered around the two. [14] Judith urged them with a loud voice: "Praise God, give praise! Praise God, who has not withdrawn his mercy from the house of Israel, but has shattered our enemies by my hand this very night!" [15] Then she took the head out of the bag, showed it to them, and said: "Here is the head of Holofernes, the ranking general of the Assyrian forces, and here is the canopy under which he lay in his drunkenness. The Lord struck him down by the hand of a female!† [16] Yet I swear by the Lord, who has protected me in the way I have walked, that it was my face that seduced Holofernes to his ruin, and that he did not defile me with sin or shame."

[17] All the people were greatly astonished. They bowed down and worshiped God, saying with one accord, "Blessed are you, our God, who today have humiliated the enemies of your people." [18] Then Uzziah said to her, "Blessed are you, daughter, by the Most High God, above all the women on earth; and blessed be the Lord God, the creator of heaven and earth, who guided your blow at the head of the leader of our enemies.* [19] Your deed of hope will never be forgotten by those who recall the might of God.* [20] May God make this redound to your everlasting honor, rewarding you with blessings, because you risked your life when our people were being oppressed, and you averted our disaster, walking in the straight path before our God." And all the people answered, "Amen! Amen!"*

## V. VICTORY AND THANKSGIVING†

**14** **Judith's Plan of Attack.** [1] Then Judith said to them: "Listen to me,† my brothers and sisters. Take this head and hang it on the parapet of your wall.* [2] At daybreak, when the sun rises on the earth, each of you seize your weapons, and let all the able-bodied men rush out of the city under command of a captain, as if about to go down into the valley against the Assyrian patrol, but without going down. [3] The Assyrians will seize their weapons and hurry to their camp to awaken the generals of the army. When they run to the tent of Holofernes and do not find him, panic will seize them, and they will flee before you.* [4] Then you and all the other inhabitants of the whole territory of Israel will pursue them and strike them down in their tracks. [5] But before doing this, summon for me Achior the Ammonite, that he may see and recognize the one who despised the house of Israel and sent him here to meet his death."

**Achior's Conversion.**† [6] So they called Achior from the house of Uzziah. When he came

---

† **13:12–20** Elements from chaps. 8–9 are echoed here. The assembly of the people at Judith's return parallels the meeting of the town officials summoned by Judith in 8:10. Uzziah blesses Judith in 8:5 and again in 13:18–20.

**13:15** *By the hand of a female:* cf. 16:5 and note on 9:9–10.

**14:1–16:25** This section describes Judith's plan to attack the Assyrian camp (14:1–5) and its execution (14:11–15:7). Between the plan and its execution, Achior identifies the head of Holofernes and is converted to Judaism. The book concludes with the victory celebration (15:8–14), hymn of thanksgiving (16:1–20), and a description of Judith's final days (16:21–25). Elements from chaps. 8–9 recur here: Judith, widow of Manasseh (8:2; 16:22), lived alone in Bethulia on her estate (8:4; 16:22), with servants and property (8:7; 16:21). Judith's instructions begin with the words "listen to me" (8:11; 14:1). Her prayer for success (9:1–14) is balanced by a prayer and display of success in 14:14–16.

**14:1–5** *Listen to me:* an imperative (used also in 8:11, 32)

opens Judith's instruction that the people display the head of Holofernes on the parapet and themselves in ranks before the enemy at daybreak. The strategy is to throw the Assyrians into panic and strike them down in their confusion; cf. 15:1–3.

**14:6–10** Recognizing the head of Holofernes, Achior faints. Then he throws himself down before Judith, acclaiming her blessed in Judah and every nation. After listening to all she had done, Achior is circumcised and joins the house of Israel. Since this violates the prohibition of Dt 23:4 that no Ammonite or Moabite shall enter the assembly, even to the tenth generation, some suggest that the book was not included in the Hebrew scriptures for this reason. However, see Is 56:3–6.

*
**13:18** Jgs 5:24; Lk 1:42.  
**13:19** Sir 35:9.  
**13:20** Dt 27:15–26; Ps 41:14; 72:19; 89:53.  
**14:1** 1 Sm 17:54; 31:9–10; 2 Sm 20:21; 2 Kgs 10:7–8; 1 Mc 7:47; 2 Mc 15:30; Mt 14:8.  
**14:3** 1 Mc 7:44.

J
D
T

and saw the head of Holofernes in the hand of one of the men in the assembly of the people, he collapsed in a faint. ⁷Then, after they lifted him up, he threw himself at the feet of Judith in homage, saying: "Blessed are you in every tent of Judah! In every nation, all who hear your name will be struck with terror.* ⁸But now, tell me all that you did during these days." So Judith told him, in the midst of the people, all that she had done, from the day she left until the time she began speaking to them. ⁹When she had finished her account, the people cheered loudly, so that the city resounded with shouts of joy. ¹⁰Now Achior, seeing all that the God of Israel had done, believed firmly in God. He circumcised the flesh of his foreskin and he has been united with the house of Israel to the present day.*

**Panic in the Assyrian Camp.** ¹¹At daybreak they hung the head of Holofernes on the wall. Then all the Israelite men took up their weapons and went out by groups to the mountain passes.* ¹²When the Assyrians saw them, they notified their commanders, who, in turn, went to their generals, their division leaders, and all their other leaders. ¹³They came to the tent of Holofernes and said to the one in charge of all his things, "Awaken our lord, for the slaves have dared come down against us in battle, to their utter destruction." ¹⁴So Bagoas went in and knocked at the entry of the tent, presuming that Holofernes was sleeping with Judith. ¹⁵When no one answered, he parted the curtains, entered the bedchamber, and found him thrown on the floor dead, with his head gone! ¹⁶He cried out loudly, weeping, groaning, and howling, and tore his garments. ¹⁷Then he entered the tent where Judith had her quarters; and, not finding her, he rushed out to the troops and cried: ¹⁸"The slaves have duped us! One Hebrew woman has brought shame on the house of King Nebuchadnezzar. Look! Holofernes on the ground—without a head!"*

¹⁹When the leaders of the Assyrian forces heard these words, they tore their tunics and were overcome with great distress. Their loud cries and shouts were heard throughout the camp.

**15** ¹On hearing what had happened, those still in their tents were horrified. ²Overcome with fear and dread, no one kept ranks any longer. They scattered in all directions, and fled along every path, both through the valley and in the hill country.* ³Those who were stationed in the hill country around Bethulia also took to flight. Then the Israelites, every warrior among them, came charging down upon them.

⁴Uzziah sent messengers to Betomasthaim, to Choba and Kona, and to the whole territory of Israel to report what had happened and to urge them all to attack the enemy and destroy them. ⁵On hearing this, all the Israelites, with one accord, attacked them and cut them down as far as Choba. Even those from Jerusalem and the rest of the hill country took part in this, for they too had been notified of the happenings in the camp of their enemy. The Gileadites and the Galileans struck the enemy's flanks with great slaughter, even beyond Damascus and its borders. ⁶The remaining people of Bethulia swept down on the camp of the Assyrians, plundered it, and acquired great riches. ⁷The Israelites, when they returned from the slaughter, took possession of what was left. Even the towns and villages in the hill country and on the plain got an enormous quantity of spoils, for there was a tremendous amount of it.

**Israel Celebrates Judith's Victory.** ⁸Then the high priest Joakim and the senate of the Israelites who lived in Jerusalem came to see for themselves the good things that the Lord had done for Israel, and to meet and congratulate Judith. ⁹When they came to her, all with one accord blessed her, saying:

> "You are the glory of Jerusalem!†
>     You are the great pride of Israel!
>     You are the great boast of our nation!
> ¹⁰    By your own hand you have done all this.
>     You have done good things for Israel,
>     and God is pleased with them.
>     May the Almighty Lord bless you
>         forever!"

And all the people said, "Amen!"

---

† **15:9** In the Lectionary of the Catholic Church, this passage is one of several choices for feasts of Mary (e.g., the Presentation of Mary). These words of praise are also echoed in antiphons for the Liturgy of the Hours on Marian feasts.

| | |
|---|---|
| **14:7** Jgs 5:24. | **14:18** Jgs 9:54. |
| **14:10** Dt 23:4. | **15:2** Gn 9:2; Dt 11:25; |
| **14:11** 2 Mc 8:23; 12:20. | 1 Mc 7:18; Sir 4:17. |

¹¹ For thirty days† all the people plundered the camp, giving Judith the tent of Holofernes, with all his silver, his beds, his dishes, and all his furniture. She took them and loaded her mule, hitched her carts, and loaded these things on them.

¹² All the women of Israel gathered to see her, and they blessed her and performed a dance in her honor.* She took branches in her hands and distributed them to the women around her, ¹³ and she and the other women crowned themselves with olive leaves. Then, at the head of all the people, she led the women in the dance, while the men of Israel followed, bearing their weapons, wearing garlands and singing songs of praise. ¹⁴† Judith led all Israel in this song of thanksgiving, and the people loudly sang this hymn of praise:

### Judith's Hymn of Deliverance

# 16

¹ And Judith sang:

"Strike up a song to my God with
    tambourines,*
  sing to the Lord with cymbals;
Improvise for him a new song,
    exalt and acclaim his name.
² For the Lord is a God who crushes
    wars;*
  he sets his encampment among his
    people;
  he delivered me from the hands of my
    pursuers.

³ "The Assyrian came from the mountains
    of the north,
  with myriads of his forces he came;
  Their numbers blocked the wadies,
    their cavalry covered the hills.
⁴ He threatened to burn my territory,
    put my youths to the sword,
  Dash my infants to the ground,
    seize my children as plunder.
    And carry off my virgins as spoil.

⁵ "But the Lord Almighty thwarted them,
    by the hand of a female!
⁶ Not by youths was their champion
    struck down,*
  nor did Titans bring him low,
  nor did tall giants attack him;*
  But Judith, the daughter of Merari,
    by the beauty of her face brought him
    down.
⁷ She took off her widow's garb
    to raise up the afflicted in Israel.
  She anointed her face with fragrant oil;
⁸ fixed her hair with a diadem,
  and put on a linen robe to beguile
    him.
⁹ Her sandals ravished his eyes,*
  her beauty captivated his mind,
  the sword cut through his neck!*
¹⁰ "The Persians trembled at her boldness,
  the Medes were daunted at her daring.
¹¹ When my lowly ones shouted,
  and my weak ones cried out,
  The enemy was terrified,
  screamed and took to flight.
¹² Sons of maidservants pierced them
    through;
  wounded them like deserters'
    children.
  They perished before the ranks of my
    Lord.

¹³ "I will sing a new song to my God.*
  O Lord, great are you and glorious,
  marvelous in power and
    unsurpassable.
¹⁴ Let your every creature serve you;
  for you spoke, and they were made.
  You sent forth your spirit, and it created
    them;*
  no one can resist your voice.*
¹⁵ For the mountains to their bases
  are tossed with the waters;
  the rocks, like wax, melt before your
    glance.*

---

† **15:11** *Thirty days:* the central actions in each half of the book are accomplished in a total of thirty-four days. Bethulia was without water for thirty-four days (7:20). Judith spent four days in the enemy camp and the Israelites plunder the Assyrian camp for thirty days.

**15:14–16:17** Judith's hymn of deliverance is patterned on the Song of Miriam (Ex 15:20–21).

* **15:12** Ex 15:20; Jgs 11:34;    1 Sm 18:6; Jer 31:4.

**16:1** Gn 31:27; Ex 15:20; 1 Sm 18:6; 2 Sm 6:5; 1 Chr 13:8; Ps 68:26; 81:3; 149:3; Jer 31:4.
**16:2** Ex 15:3; Ps 46:10.
**16:6** 1 Sm 17:4, 51.
**16:6** Gn 6:1–4; Dt 2:10, 21; 2 Sm 21:16–22; 1 Chr 20:4–8.
**16:9** Sg 7:2; Ez 16:10.

**16:9** Jgs 5:26.
**16:13** Ps 33:3; 40:4; 96:1; 98:1; 144:9; 149:1; Is 42:10.
**16:14** Gn 1; Ps 104:30; 148:5.
**16:14** Est C:3–4; Ps 33:9; Is 55:11.
**16:15** Ps 97:5; Mi 1:4; Na 1:5.

JDT

"But to those who fear you,
    you will show mercy.
16 Though the sweet fragrance of every
        sacrifice is a trifle,
    and the fat of all burnt offerings but
        little in your sight,
    one who fears the Lord is forever
        great.

17 "Woe to the nations that rise against my
        people!
    the Lord Almighty will requite them;
    in the day of judgment he will punish
        them:
    He will send fire and worms into their
        flesh,*
    and they will weep and suffer forever."

18 When they arrived at Jerusalem, they worshiped God. As soon as the people were
purified, they offered their burnt offerings,
voluntary offerings, and donations.* 19 Judith
dedicated to God all the things of Holofernes
that the people had given her, putting under
the ban the canopy that she herself had taken
from his bedchamber.* 20 For three months

the people continued their celebration in Jerusalem before the sanctuary, and Judith remained with them.

**The Renown and Death of Judith.** 21 When
those days were over, all of them returned to
their inheritance. Judith went back to Bethulia and remained on her estate. For the rest
of her life she was renowned throughout the
land. 22 Many wished to marry her, but she
gave herself to no man all the days of her
life from the time her husband, Manasseh,
died and was gathered to his people. 23 Her
fame continued to increase, and she lived
in the house of her husband, reaching the
advanced age of one hundred and five.†* 
She set her maid free. And when she died in
Bethulia, they buried her in the cave of her
husband, Manasseh;* 24 and the house of
Israel mourned her for seven days.†* Before
she died, she distributed her property to the
relatives of her husband, Manasseh, and to
her own relatives.*

25* During the lifetime of Judith and for a
long time after her death, no one ever again
spread terror† among the Israelites.

---

**16:23** *One hundred and five*: long life was a sign of blessing
(see Jb 42:16; Prv 16:31; 20:29). The fact that the Maccabean
period was one hundred and five years long (168–63 B.C.) may
account for assigning this age to Judith.
   **16:24** *Seven days*: the customary period for mourning the
dead (1 Sm 31:13).
   **16:25** *Spread terror*: Judith is compared to the heroes of the
Book of Judges (cf. Jgs 3:11, 30).

**16:17** Sir 7:17; Is 66:24; Mk
          9:48.
**16:18** Nm 19:11–22; 31:19.
**16:19** Lv 7:16.
**16:23** Jb 42:16; Prv 16:31;
          20:29; Sir 18:9; Lk
          2:36.

**16:23** Gn 23:19; 25:9;
          49:29–32; 50:13.
**16:24** Gn 50:3; 1 Sm 31:13;
          1 Chr 10:12; Sir
          22:12.
**16:24** Nm 27:6–11.
**16:25** Jgs 3:11, 30; 5:31;
          8:28.

J
D
T

# The Book of

# Esther

## INTRODUCTION

### Geoffrey Miller

The book of Esther tells a gripping tale of palace intrigue, clandestine schemes, and the reversal of fortunes. The Jewish community in Persia faces great peril when a powerful official in the Persian court hatches a plot to exterminate them, yet his evil designs are foiled by Queen Esther—the Jewish wife of the Persian emperor—and her kinsman Mordecai. The story makes excellent use of stock characters, such as the irascible villain and the gullible king, as well as the element of surprise. The narrative begins with men asserting their dominance in the political and domestic spheres, yet it ends with a woman saving the day. Mordecai's bold behavior incites Haman to plot his death, yet Mordecai ultimately brings about the death of Haman and takes his place in the Persian court. Most astonishing is the fact that the book's title character rescues the Jewish people from Persian hands, yet she is remembered not by her Jewish name (Hadassah) but by her Persian name (Esther).

Persia constitutes both the setting for the book as well as its likely place of origin, although the time of composition is more difficult to ascertain. The original story was written some time between the fifth and second centuries BCE, but a later scribe inserted additional chapters into the book in the second or first centuries BCE. (These additional chapters are indicated by the letters A through F rather than numbers.) The longer version was preserved in Greek, and its supplementary material provides a more religious tone to an otherwise secular tale. In contrast to other Jewish writings of this time, the book of Esther contains no references to the Temple, the Mosaic Law, or the promised land of Israel. Prominent themes such as covenant, the afterlife, and observance of the dietary laws are also lacking. The original Hebrew version has two other noteworthy

## Outline of Esther

I. Prologue (A:1–17)

II. Esther Becomes Queen (1:1–2:23)

III. Haman's Plot Against the Jews (3:1–13; B:1–7; 3:14–15)

IV. Esther and Mordecai Plead for Help (4:1–17; C:1–D:16; 5:1–5)

V. Haman's Downfall (5:6–8:2)

VI. The Jewish Victory and the Feast of Purim (8:3–12; E:1–24; 8:13–9:23)

VII. Epilogue: The Rise of Mordecai (9:24–10:3; F:1–11)

omissions: there are no qualms about Esther's illicit marriage to a Gentile, and there is no mention of God whatsoever. The longer Greek text rectifies these last two problems in the prayers of Esther and Mordecai, yet the dearth of more overt religious elements is one of the reasons that the book of Esther was nearly excluded from the biblical canon.

At the same time, however, the book is not completely devoid of religious concerns. It purports to recount the origin of the Jewish festival of Purim, and, even in the Hebrew version, the book implies the activity of God. Mordecai presumes that deliverance will come to the Jews "from another source" (Est 4:14), and Zeresh intimates the same to her husband Haman when she warns that he cannot prevail against Mordecai since the man is a Jew (6:13). Moreover, Esther's call for a communal fast (4:16) makes little sense unless such an endeavor can move God to intercede on his people's behalf.

The scant references to God, both implicit and explicit, create a divine portrait that is consistent with other contemporaneous texts. As in the books of Tobit and Judith, the God of Esther remains in the background of the story, operating behind the scenes. He knows all (Est C:5) and sees all (D:2; E:4), but he refrains from direct intervention or public displays of might. Esther and Mordecai cry out to him in prayer, but he speaks to the latter only in dreams (A:1–10). His people are threatened but never witness his intercession in a tangible way, even though it is the Lord who reverses the imperial decree commanding their extermination (E:21). God also turns the heart of the Persian king from anger to gentleness so that he will be more receptive to what Esther has to tell him (D:8). Although the characters in the story never receive a divine oracle or a vision of God's glory, they nevertheless benefit from God's benevolence. This depiction of God provides comforting assurance for the book's Diaspora audience—that is, Israelites dispersed throughout the ancient Near East after the Assyrian and Babylonian exiles. They, too, might have felt as if God had abandoned them since his presence was not readily apparent, but they could be certain that God was truly watching over them and would protect them from harm.

The historical setting of the book is also instrumental in communicating an important message to the audience. The book of Esther is widely regarded today as historical fiction, although this point has sometimes been overstated. There are no historical inaccuracies, as in other biblical books such as Judith and Daniel, but there are numerous improbabilities. It is hard to believe that a government official, holding a position that requires tact, prudence, and diplomacy, would become so enraged by one man that he decides to annihilate an entire people. It is even more incredible that an imperial ruler would be oblivious to many things affecting the administration of his empire and allow others to use his signet ring to pursue their agendas in his name. Furthermore, the Persians were some of the most benign imperial powers of antiquity, and the notion that they would encourage the genocide of one of their subjugated peoples is ludicrous.

However, several aspects of the tale are historically accurate, or at least plausible. The Jews were ruled by the Persians for many years, and one of these rulers was Ahasuerus (also known as Xerxes). Archaeological evidence from Susa may even support the historicity of Mordecai, although this is far from certain. More importantly, to debate the historical veracity of the story is to miss the point. The book of Esther is neither pure fact nor pure fiction but something in between. It is a novella set in a historical period and imbued with a fictional plot intended to entertain and exhort. The story offers a model of authentic Jewish life in the Diaspora, seeking to promote solidarity among Jews who might be lured by the temptation to amalgamate with other cultures. The book does not envision a return to Palestine or anticipate the overthrow of Gentile overlords. Rather, Diaspora Jews must accept the fact that they are a minority in a Gentile land, and the survival of Jewish culture will be guaranteed not by traditional institutions, such as the Davidic monarchy or priestly aristocracy, but by resourceful people such as Esther and Mordecai who find innovative ways to preserve their Jewish heritage.

The story also uses comedy and irony to downplay the threat posed by Gentile rule. Apostasy is a real danger for Diaspora Jewry, but the Persians are not. Their king is an emotionally unstable ruler prone to mood swings. When his first queen refuses to appear before him at his behest, he overreacts by marshaling all the bureaucratic power of his administration to depose her and to ensure that such defiance will never happen again. He is a man of rash judgments and impetuous decisions, promising his new queen, Esther, up to half his kingdom before even hearing the specific details of her request. In fact, the Persians are far more interested in partying than conquering; the story opens with a lavish feast that lasts 180 days and no expense is spared. Liberal consumption of alcohol typifies the Persian court, and the ten banquets of the book help contribute to this carnivalesque atmosphere. Haman is likewise a farcical caricature. He promises the king 10,000 talents of silver (an exorbitant sum he could never muster), intends to hang Mordecai on impossibly high gallows (fifty cubits, which would approximate to seventy-five feet), and witnesses his own ploy backfire when he is hung on the gallows he has built. The original audience of the book would likely find these details amusing, but they would also be emboldened by this satirical portrayal of a Gentile superpower. They have nothing to fear from the Persians—or any foreign nation ruling over Israel—since these rulers are too inept and sated with wine to jeopardize the well-being of the Jewish people. To the contrary, the Persians are so afraid of the Jews that they are willing to pretend to be Jews themselves (Est 8:17)!

The crowning irony of the book is that the mighty Persians are no match for Esther, the most unlikely of saviors. As an orphan, a woman, and an exile living in a foreign land, she would have been counted among the most vulnerable members of society, and yet she rises to one of the most powerful positions in the Persian Empire. With the assistance of her kinsman Mordecai, she determines the fate of her people and of their nemesis, Haman. Whether she is a historical personage or not, Esther is an inspiring figure who gives hope to all who read her tale. Through virtuous conduct, clever persuasion, and timely valor, she overcomes formidable odds to save her people, risking her own life in the process, yet gaining much in return. ∎

# THE BOOK OF ESTHER

## New American Bible, Introduction

The Book of Esther tells a story of the deliverance of the Jewish people. We are shown a Persian emperor, Ahasuerus (loosely based on Xerxes, 485–464 B.C.), who makes momentous decisions for trivial reasons, and his wicked minister, Haman, who takes advantage of the king's compliance to pursue a personal vendetta against the Jews by having a royal decree issued ordering their destruction. The threat is averted by two Jews, Esther and Mordecai. Their influence and intervention allow the Jews to turn the tables on their enemies and rout their attackers. This deliverance is commemorated by the inauguration of the Jewish festival of Purim on the fourteenth and fifteenth of Adar (mid-February through mid-March). The book confronts the modern reader with important themes, the evils of genocide and racism.

Esther's character matures over the course of the narrative. As a girl she is recruited for the king's harem because of her physical beauty. But at a key moment in the book (chap. 4), she rises to the challenge to risk her life for the salvation of her people. At that point, she transforms her status as queen from a position of personal privilege to one of power and public responsibility.

Esther's uncle, Mordecai, appears first as an adoptive father, whose solicitude for Esther leads him to the king's gate, where he foils a plot to assassinate the king. When he learns of the edict against the Jews, he encourages Esther to confront the king. The book ends with Mordecai as the king's chief minister.

The book is a free composition, not a historical document. Its fictional character can be illustrated by many examples of literary motifs: the use of extensive conversation to move the plot along; the motif of concealment (Esther is a Jew, related to Mordecai, but Haman does not know it, even as he comes to her banquet in chap. 7). A whole series of banquets structure the work: two by the king, one by Vashti, three by Esther, and the joyful banqueting that ends the book. Further artificialities are clear in the way characters are paired (e.g., Mordecai

and Esther) and in the delays and the speed of the action (Esther delays the banquet in 5:3–8, but the tempo of chaps. 5–6 is particularly fast); Mordecai passes from the threat of death (5:9–14) to royal honors (6:10–11) within twenty-four hours. There are many exaggerations, and even sarcastic implausibilities (cf. the effect of Vashti's disobedience in 1:17–18), and huge ironies (e.g., Haman in 6:6, 10). The work is a composite of reversals (cf. 9:1) in the lives of individuals and communities.

The book was probably written in the third or second century B.C. It has come down to us in two versions: an older Hebrew version, and a Greek version based on a text similar to the Hebrew, but with additions and alterations as described below.

One striking feature of the Hebrew version of the Book of Esther is that no divine names or titles are employed here; God is not mentioned at all. This would not be unusual in a book whose subject matter or outlook was more secular, but Esther is a book in which the religious element is prominent: the Jews fast in order to be delivered from imminent peril, experience deliverance at the eleventh hour, and commemorate their deliverance with an annual festival. Moreover, there are indirect references to divine activity (for example, in 4:14).

The Greek additions to Esther have many explicit references to God, as well as explicit descriptions of the beliefs and emotional states of Esther and Mordecai. They also elaborate on the content of the edicts from Ahasuerus as illustrations of Gentile attitudes toward Jews. While there are only a few contradictions between these Greek additions and the older Hebrew text, reading the book with these additions is a very different experience from reading the book without them. The additions to Esther are an excellent example of a process that occurs throughout the Bible: further reflections on the story become part of the story itself. Although the Book of Esther was questioned by some early Christians, even St. Jerome, the whole book, including the Greek additions, was included in the canon of Scripture by the Council of Trent.

The Greek version of the book dates from ca. 116 to 48 B.C. (see note on F:11). In the present translation, the Greek additions are indicated by the letters A through F. The regular chapter numbers apply to the Hebrew text.

The book may be divided as follows:

I. Prologue (A:1–17)
II. Esther Becomes Queen (1:1–2:23)
III. Haman's Plot Against the Jews (3:1–13; B:1–7; 3:14–15)
IV. Esther and Mordecai Plead for Help (4:1–17; C:1–D:16; 5:1–5)

V. Haman's Downfall (5:6–8:2)
VI. The Jewish Victory and the Feast of Purim (8:3–12; E:1–24; 8:13–9:23)
VII. Epilogue: The Rise of Mordecai (9:24–10:3; F:1–11)

The order of the Vulgate text in relation to the order of the Greek text is as follows:

| | | |
|---|---|---|
| Vulg. 11:2–12:6 | = | A:1–17 at the beginning of the book. |
| 13:1–7 | = | B:1–7 after 3:13. |
| 13:8–15:3–19 | = | C:1–D:16 after 4:17. |
| 15:1–2 | = | B:8, 9 after 4:8. |
| 16:1–24 | = | E:1–24 after 8:12. |
| 10:4–13 | = | F:1–10 after 10:3. ■ |

# ESTHER

## I. PROLOGUE

**A Dream of Mordecai.** ¹ In the second year of the reign of Ahasuerus the great, on the first day of Nisan, Mordecai, son of Jair, son of Shimei, son of Kish, of the tribe of Benjamin, had a dream. †* ² † He was a Jew residing in the city of Susa, a prominent man who served at the king's court, ³ and one of the captives whom Nebuchadnezzar, king of Babylon, had taken from Jerusalem with Jeconiah, king of Judah. *

⁴ * This was his dream. † There was noise and tumult, thunder and earthquake—confusion upon the earth. ⁵ Two great dragons advanced, both poised for combat. They uttered a mighty cry, ⁶ and at their cry every nation prepared for war, to fight against the nation of the just. ⁷ It was a dark and gloomy day. Tribulation and distress, evil and great confusion, lay upon the earth. ⁸ The whole nation of the just was shaken with fear at the evils to come upon them, and they expected to perish. ⁹ * Then they cried out to God, and from their crying there arose, as though from a tiny spring, a mighty river, a flood of water. ¹⁰ The light of the sun broke forth; the lowly were exalted and they devoured the boastful.

¹¹ Having seen this dream and what God intended to do, Mordecai awoke. He kept it in mind, and tried in every way, until night, to understand its meaning.

**Mordecai Thwarts an Assassination.** † ¹² * Mordecai lodged in the courtyard with Bigthan and Teresh, two eunuchs of the king who guarded the courtyard. ¹³ He overheard them plotting, investigated their plans, and discovered that they were preparing to assassinate King Ahasuerus. So he informed the king about them. ¹⁴ The king had the two eunuchs questioned and, upon their confession, put to death. ¹⁵ Then the king had these things recorded; Mordecai, too, put them into writing. ¹⁶ The king also appointed Mordecai to serve at the court, and rewarded him for his actions. *

¹⁷ Haman, however, son of Hammedatha, a Bougean, † who was held in high honor by the king, sought to harm Mordecai and his people because of the two eunuchs of the king. *

## II. ESTHER BECOMES QUEEN

**1** **The Banquet of Ahasuerus.** ¹ † During the reign of Ahasuerus—the same Ahasuerus who ruled over a hundred and twenty-seven provinces from India to Ethiopia— ² while he was occupying the royal throne in the royal precinct of Susa, † ³ in the third year of his reign, he gave a feast for all his officials and ministers: the Persian and Median army officers, the nobles, and the governors of the provinces. * ⁴ For as many as a hundred and eighty days, he displayed the glorious riches of his kingdom and the resplendent wealth of his royal estate.

⁵ At the end of this time the king gave a feast of seven days in the garden court of the royal palace for all the people, great and small, who were in the royal precinct of Susa. ⁶ There were white cotton draperies and violet hangings, held by cords of fine crimson linen from silver rings on marble pillars. Gold and silver couches were on a mosaic pavement, which

---

†

**A:1** The genealogy of Mordecai is designed to reflect opposition to Israel's enemy Haman, an Agagite (v. 17). In 1 Sm 15:1–9, Saul (whose father's name was Kish, of the tribe of Benjamin) conquered Agag the Amalekite.

**A:2–3** Repeats information from 2:5–6, on which see note, but states that Mordecai is already a court official. In the Hebrew text, Mordecai is not given this rank until 7:10–8:2.

**A:4** An interpretation of the dream that relates its features to the plot of the book is given in F:1–6.

**A:12–17** Retells the story in 2:21–23, but with several differences. Addition A has Mordecai inform the king directly, whereas in 2:22 Mordecai informs the king through Esther after she has become queen. A:16 has Mordecai rewarded immediately after his service, whereas the Hebrew text defers the reward of Mordecai to 6:3–13. In A:17, the failure of the eunuchs' plot becomes Haman's reason for seeking the destruction of Mordecai and his people, something which the Hebrew text attributes to Mordecai's refusal to bow to Haman (see note on 3:2).

**A:17** *A Bougean:* the origin of this term is unknown; it may represent a garbled attempt to render the Hebrew "Agagite" (3:1). In the Greek additions Haman not only knows the plot to assassinate the king, but is apparently a co-conspirator.

**1:1** The Hebrew text opens with a portrait of the power and luxury of the Persian king Ahasuerus (Xerxes I, whose empire consisted of only about thirty provinces).

**1:2** Susa was the winter capital of the Persian empire. The "royal precinct" (sometimes translated "stronghold" or "citadel") was a well-fortified section of the city that included the king's residence. The Book of Esther depicts other citizens living in this section as well.

*

| | |
|---|---|
| **A:1** Est 2:5. | **A:9–10** Est F:3. |
| **A:3** Est 2:6; 2 Kgs 24:15; | **A:12–15** Est 2:21–23; 6:1–3. |
| 2 Chr 36:9–10; Jer | **A:16** Est 6:3. |
| 22:24–30; 24:1; | **A:17** Est 3:1–15; B:1–7; |
| 29:1–2. | E:13. |
| **A:4–10** Est F:2, 4–6. | **1:3** Jdt 1:16. |

was of porphyry, marble, mother-of-pearl, and colored stones. [7] Drinks were served in a variety of golden cups, and the royal wine flowed freely, as befitted the king's liberality. [8] By ordinance of the king the drinking was unstinted, for he had instructed all the stewards of his household to comply with the good pleasure of everyone. [9] Queen Vashti also gave a feast for the women in the royal palace of King Ahasuerus.

**Refusal of Vashti.** [10] On the seventh day, when the king was merry with wine, he instructed Mehuman, Biztha, Harbona, Bigtha, Abagtha, Zethar, and Carkas, the seven eunuchs who attended King Ahasuerus, * [11] to bring Queen Vashti into his presence wearing the royal crown, that he might display her beauty to the populace and the officials, for she was lovely to behold. [12] But Queen Vashti refused to come at the royal order issued through the eunuchs. At this the king's wrath flared up, and he burned with fury. [13] He conferred with the sages who understood the times, because the king's business was conducted in general consultation with lawyers and jurists. [14] He summoned Carshena, Shethar, Admatha, Tarshish, Meres, Marsena, and Memucan, the seven Persian and Median officials who were in the king's personal service and held first rank in the realm, * [15] and asked them, "What is to be done by law with Queen Vashti for disobeying the order of King Ahasuerus issued through the eunuchs?"

[16] In the presence of the king and of the officials, Memucan answered: "Queen Vashti has not wronged the king alone, but all the officials and the populace throughout the provinces of King Ahasuerus. [17] For the queen's conduct will become known to all the women, and they will look with disdain upon their husbands when it is reported, 'King Ahasuerus commanded that Queen Vashti be ushered into his presence, but she would not come.' [18] This very day the Persian and Median noblewomen who hear of the queen's conduct will recount it to all the royal officials, and disdain and rancor will abound. [19] If it please the king, let an irrevocable royal decree † be issued by him and inscribed among the laws of the Persians and Medes, forbidding Vashti to come into the presence of King Ahasuerus and authorizing the king to give her royal dignity to one more worthy than she. * [20] Thus, when the decree that the king will issue is published throughout his realm, vast as it is, all wives will honor their husbands, from the greatest to the least."

[21] This proposal pleased the king and the officials, and the king acted on the advice of Memucan. [22] He sent letters to all the royal provinces, to each province in its own script and to each people in its own language, to the effect that every man should be lord in his own home.

**2 The Search for a New Queen.** [1] After this, when King Ahasuerus' wrath had cooled, he thought over what Vashti had done and what had been decreed against her. [2] Then the king's personal attendants suggested: "Let beautiful young virgins be sought for the king. [3] Let the king appoint emissaries in all the provinces of his realm to gather all beautiful young virgins into the harem in the royal precinct of Susa. Under the care of the royal eunuch Hegai, guardian of the women, let cosmetics be given them. [4] Then the young woman who pleases the king shall reign in place of Vashti." This suggestion pleased the king, and he acted accordingly.

[5] There was in the royal precinct of Susa a certain Jew named Mordecai, † son of Jair, son of Shimei, son of Kish, a Benjaminite, [6] who had been exiled from Jerusalem with the captives taken with Jeconiah, king of Judah, whom Nebuchadnezzar, king of Babylon, had deported. * [7] He became foster father to his cousin Hadassah, that is, Esther, † when she lost both father and mother. The young

---

† **1:19** *An irrevocable royal decree:* the first of several in the book. In a satiric portrayal, even a minor domestic disagreement is resolved through a sweeping international edict. The irrevocable nature of the decree is intended to increase its force, but creates problems if the king needs to adapt to new information or conditions. See note on 8:8.

**2:5** *Mordecai:* a Babylonian name, deriving from the god Marduk. Like Esther, Mordecai may have had a Jewish name as well, although in his case we do not know what it is. The chronology of the book makes him well over one hundred

years old, since he was deported with Jehoiachin about 598 B.C.; cf. A:1.

**2:7** *Esther:* a Babylonian name, deriving from the goddess Ishtar. She is given a Hebrew name as well, "Hadassah," which means "myrtle."

---

| | |
|---|---|
| **1:10** Dn 5:1. | **2:6** Est A:3; 2 Kgs 24:15; |
| **1:14** 1 Chr 12:32; Ezr 7:14. | 2 Chr 36:9–10; Jer |
| **1:19** Est 8:5, 8; Dn 6:8–9. | 22:24–30; 24:1; |
| | 29:1–2. |

woman was beautifully formed and lovely to behold. On the death of her father and mother, Mordecai adopted her as his own daughter.*

⁸When the king's order and decree had been proclaimed and many young women brought together to the royal precinct of Susa under the care of Hegai, Esther also was brought in to the royal palace under the care of Hegai, guardian of the women. ⁹The young woman pleased him and won his favor. So he promptly furnished her with cosmetics and provisions. Then choosing seven maids for her from the royal palace, he transferred both her and her maids to the best place in the harem. ¹⁰Esther did not reveal her nationality or family, for Mordecai had commanded her not to do so.

¹¹Day by day Mordecai would walk about in front of the court of the harem to learn how Esther was faring and what was to become of her.

¹²After the twelve months' preparation decreed for the women, each one went in turn to visit King Ahasuerus. During this period of beautifying treatment, six months were spent with oil of myrrh, and the other six months with perfumes and cosmetics. ¹³Then, when each one was to visit the king, she was allowed to take with her from the harem to the royal palace whatever she chose. ¹⁴She would go in the evening and return in the morning to a second harem under the care of the royal eunuch Shaashgaz, guardian of the concubines. She could not return to the king unless he was pleased with her and had her summoned by name.* ¹⁵As for Esther, daughter of Abihail and adopted daughter of his nephew Mordecai, when her turn came to visit the king, she did not ask for anything but what the royal eunuch Hegai, guardian of the women, suggested. And she won the admiration of all who saw her.

**Ahasuerus Chooses Esther.** ¹⁶Esther was led to King Ahasuerus in his palace in the tenth month, Tebeth, in the seventh year of his reign. ¹⁷The king loved Esther more than all other women, and of all the virgins she won

his favor and good will. So he placed the royal crown on her head and made her queen in place of Vashti. ¹⁸Then the king gave a great feast in honor of Esther to all his officials and servants, granting a holiday to the provinces and bestowing gifts with royal generosity.

**Mordecai Thwarts an Assassination.**† ¹⁹* As was said, from the time the virgins had been brought together, and while Mordecai was passing his time at the king's gate, ²⁰Esther had not revealed her family or nationality, because Mordecai had told her not to; and Esther continued to follow Mordecai's instructions, just as she had when she was being brought up by him. ²¹* During the time that Mordecai spent at the king's gate, Bigthan and Teresh, two of the royal eunuchs who guarded the entrance, became angry and plotted to assassinate King Ahasuerus. ²²When the plot became known to Mordecai, he told Queen Esther, who in turn informed the king in Mordecai's name. ²³The matter was investigated and verified, and both of them were impaled on stakes.† This was written in the annals in the king's presence.

## III. HAMAN'S PLOT AGAINST THE JEWS

**3 Mordecai Refuses to Honor Haman.** ¹After these events King Ahasuerus promoted Haman, son of Hammedatha the Agagite, to high rank, seating him above all his fellow officials.* ²All the king's servants who were at the royal gate would kneel and bow down to Haman, for that is what the king had ordered in his regard.* Mordecai, however, would not kneel and bow down.† ³The king's servants who were at the royal gate said to Mordecai, "Why do you disobey the king's order?"* ⁴When they had reminded him day after day and he would not listen to them, they informed Haman, to see whether Mordecai's explanation would prevail, since he had told them that he was a Jew.

**Haman's Reprisal.** ⁵When Haman observed that Mordecai would not kneel and bow

---

† **2:19–23** This story is retold and placed at the beginning of the book in Greek addition A:12–17, with significant differences (see note). The Greek also has a translation of the account in 2:19–23 at this point in the narrative.

**2:23** *Impaled on stakes*: a method of execution used by the Persians, known from ancient records and reliefs.

**3:2** We are not told the reasons for Mordecai's refusal to bow.

It may be the result of a form of Jewish piety that refuses to offer such homage to any mortal; see also Greek addition C:5–7.

| | |
|---|---|
| **2:7** Est 2:15. | **3:1** Est B:3; 5:11; E:11. |
| **2:14** Est 2:19–20; 4:11, 16. | **3:2** Est C:5; 5:9, 13; 6:10, 12. |
| **2:19–20** Est 2:14. | |
| **2:21–23** Est A:12–15; 6:1–3. | **3:3** Est 4:16. |

EST (tab marker)

down to him, he was filled with anger. 6 But he thought it was beneath him to attack only Mordecai. Since they had told Haman of Mordecai's nationality, he sought to destroy all the Jews, Mordecai's people, throughout the realm of King Ahasuerus. 7 In the first month, Nisan, in the twelfth year of King Ahasuerus, the *pur*, or lot,† was cast in Haman's presence to determine the day and the month for the destruction of Mordecai's people on a single day, and the lot fell on the thirteenth day of the twelfth month, Adar.*

**Decree Against the Jews.** 8 Then Haman said to King Ahasuerus: "Dispersed among the nations throughout the provinces of your kingdom, there is a certain people living apart. Their laws differ from those of every other people and they do not obey the laws of the king; so it is not proper for the king to tolerate them.* 9 If it please the king, let a decree be issued to destroy them; and I will deliver to the procurators ten thousand silver talents for deposit in the royal treasury."* 10 The king took the signet ring† from his hand and gave it to Haman, son of Hammedatha the Agagite, the enemy of the Jews.* 11 The king said to Haman, "The silver is yours, as well as the people, to do with as you please."†

12 So the royal scribes were summoned on the thirteenth day of the first month, and they wrote, at the dictation of Haman, an order to the royal satraps, the governors of every province, and the officials of every people, to each province in its own script and to each people in its own language. It was written in the name of King Ahasuerus and sealed with the royal signet ring. 13 Letters were sent by couriers to all the royal provinces, to destroy, kill and annihilate all the Jews, young and old, including women and children in one day, the thirteenth day of the twelfth month, Adar, and to seize their goods as spoil.*

**B** 1 This is a copy of the letter:
"The great King Ahasuerus writes to the satraps of the hundred and twenty-seven provinces from India to Ethiopia, and the governors subordinate to them, as follows: 2 When I came to rule many peoples and to hold sway over the whole world, not being carried away by a sense of my own authority but always acting fairly and with mildness, I determined to provide for my subjects a life of lasting tranquility; and, by making my kingdom civilized and safe for travel to its farthest borders, to restore the peace desired by all people.* 3 When I consulted my counselors as to how this might be accomplished, Haman, who excels among us in discretion, who is outstanding for constant good will and steadfast loyalty, and who has gained a place in the kingdom second only to me,* 4 brought it to our attention that, mixed among all the nations throughout the world, there is one people of ill will, which by its laws is opposed to every other people and continually disregards the decrees of kings, so that the unity of empire blamelessly designed by us cannot be established.*

5 "Having noted, therefore, that this nation, and it alone, is continually at variance with all people, lives by divergent and alien laws, is inimical to our government, and does all the harm it can to undermine the stability of the kingdom, 6 we hereby decree that all those who are indicated to you in the letters of Haman, who is in charge of the administration and is a second father to us, shall, together with their wives and children, be utterly destroyed by the swords of their enemies, without any pity or mercy, on the fourteenth day† of the twelfth month, Adar, of the current year;* 7 so that when these people, whose present ill will is of long standing, have gone down into Hades by a violent death on a single day, they may leave our government completely stable and undisturbed for the future."

---

† **3:7** *The pur, or lot*: the Hebrew text preserves the Akkadian word *pur* because its plural, *purim*, became the name of the feast of Purim commemorating the deliverance of the Jews; cf. 9:24, 26. The lot functions as a kind of horoscope to determine the most favorable day for the pogrom.

**3:10** *Signet ring*: a ring containing a seal that was impressed on documents to authenticate them. With this ring, Haman can issue decrees in the king's name.

**3:11** Although Ahasuerus seems to refuse the bribe, this is probably a polite way of accepting it that makes him appear munificent (compare Gn 23:11–15, where Ephron tells Abraham that he "gives" him the field and, after a few more pleasantries, sets a very high price for it). Both 4:7 and 7:4 seem to assume

Ahasuerus has accepted the money.
**B:6** *Fourteenth day*: only the Greek text here names the fourteenth of Adar as the day set aside for the destruction of the Jews. The Hebrew text consistently gives the date as the thirteenth of Adar (e.g., 3:13) as does Greek addition E:20; see note on 9:17–19.

---

* **3:7** Est 9:24–32; F:10.
**3:8** Est 3:13; B:4; E:24; Wis 2:14–15; Dn 3:8–12.
**3:9** Est 7:4.
**3:10** Gn 41:42.
**3:13** Est B:6; 7:4.
**B:2** Est E:8–9.
**B:3** Est 3:1; 5:11; E:11.
**B:4** Est 3:8; E:24.
**B:6** Est 3:13; 7:4; E:11.

(**3**) ¹⁴ A copy of the decree to be promulgated as law in every province was published to all the peoples, that they might be prepared for that day. ¹⁵ The couriers set out in haste at the king's command; meanwhile, the decree was promulgated in the royal precinct of Susa. The king and Haman then sat down to drink, but the city of Susa was thrown into confusion.

## IV. ESTHER AND MORDECAI PLEAD FOR HELP

**4 Mordecai Exhorts Esther.** ¹ When Mordecai learned all that was happening, he tore his garments, put on sackcloth and ashes, and went through the city crying out loudly and bitterly,* ² till he came before the royal gate, which no one clothed in sackcloth might enter. ³ Likewise in each of the provinces, wherever the king's decree and law reached, the Jews went into deep mourning, with fasting, weeping, and lament; most of them lay on sackcloth and ashes.

⁴ Esther's maids and eunuchs came and told her. Overwhelmed with anguish, the queen sent garments for Mordecai to put on, so that he might take off his sackcloth; but he refused. ⁵ Esther then summoned Hathach, one of the king's eunuchs whom he had placed at her service, and commanded him to find out what this action of Mordecai meant and the reason for it. ⁶ So Hathach went out to Mordecai in the public square in front of the royal gate, ⁷ and Mordecai recounted all that had happened to him, as well as the exact amount of silver Haman had promised to pay to the royal treasury for the slaughter of the Jews. ⁸ He also gave him a copy of the written decree for their destruction that had been promulgated in Susa, to show and explain to Esther. Hathach was to instruct her to go to the king and to plead and intercede with him on behalf of her people.†

⁹ Hathach returned to Esther and told her what Mordecai had said. ¹⁰ Then Esther replied to Hathach and gave him this message for Mordecai: ¹¹ "All the servants of the king and the people of his provinces know that any man

or woman who goes to the king in the inner court without being summoned is subject to the same law—death. Only if the king extends the golden scepter will such a person live. Now as for me, I have not been summoned to the king for thirty days."*

¹² When Esther's words were reported to Mordecai, ¹³ he had this reply brought to her: "Do not imagine that you are safe in the king's palace, you alone of all the Jews. ¹⁴ Even if you now remain silent, relief and deliverance will come to the Jews from another source;† but you and your father's house will perish. Who knows—perhaps it was for a time like this that you became queen?"

¹⁵ Esther sent back to Mordecai the response: ¹⁶ "Go and assemble all the Jews who are in Susa; fast on my behalf, all of you, not eating or drinking night or day for three days. I and my maids will also fast in the same way. Thus prepared, I will go to the king, contrary to the law. If I perish, I perish!"* ¹⁷ Mordecai went away and did exactly as Esther had commanded.

**C Prayer of Mordecai.** ¹ Recalling all that the Lord had done, Mordecai prayed to the Lord ² and said: "Lord, Lord, King and Ruler of all, everything is in your power, and there is no one to oppose you when it is your will to save Israel. ³ You made heaven and earth and every wonderful thing under heaven. ⁴ You are Lord of all, and there is no one who can resist you, the Lord. ⁵* You know all things. You know, Lord, that it was not out of insolence or arrogance or desire for glory that I acted thus in not bowing down to the arrogant Haman. ⁶ I would have gladly kissed the soles of his feet for the salvation of Israel. ⁷ But I acted as I did so as not to place the honor of a mortal above that of God. I will not bow down to anyone but you, my Lord. It is not out of arrogance that I am acting thus. ⁸ And now, Lord God, King, God of Abraham, spare your people, for our enemies regard us with deadly envy and are bent upon destroying the inheritance that was yours from the beginning. ⁹ Do not spurn your portion, which you redeemed for yourself out of the land of Egypt. ¹⁰ Hear

---

**4:8** The Greek text adds the following to Mordecai's message to Esther: "Remember the days of your lowly estate, when you were brought up in my charge; for Haman, who is second to the king, has asked for our death. Invoke the Lord and speak to the king for us: save us from death."

**4:14** *From another source:* probably Mordecai refers to divine aid; the Greek additions (C) are explicit about this.

**4:1** Jdt 4:12.
**4:11** Est 2:14; 4:12; D:12.
**4:16** Est C:12–13.
**C:5–7** Est 3:2; 5:9.

my prayer; have pity on your inheritance and turn our mourning into feasting, that we may live to sing praise to your name, Lord. Do not silence the mouths of those who praise you."

[11] All Israel, too, cried out with all their strength, for death was staring them in the face.

**Prayer of Esther.** [12]* Queen Esther, seized with mortal anguish, fled to the Lord for refuge. [13] Taking off her splendid garments, she put on garments of distress and mourning. In place of her precious ointments she covered her head with dung and ashes. She afflicted her body severely and in place of her festive adornments, her tangled hair covered her.

[14] Then she prayed to the Lord, the God of Israel, saying: "My Lord, you alone are our King. Help me, who am alone and have no help but you, [15] for I am taking my life in my hand.* [16] From birth, I have heard among my people that you, Lord, chose Israel from among all nations, and our ancestors from among all their forebears, as a lasting inheritance, and that you fulfilled all your promises to them.* [17] But now we have sinned in your sight, and you have delivered us into the hands of our enemies, [18] because we worshiped their gods. You are just, O Lord. [19] But now they are not satisfied with our bitter servitude, but have sworn an oath to their idols [20] to do away with the decree you have pronounced, to destroy your inheritance, to close the mouths of those who praise you, to extinguish the glory of your house and your altar, [21] to open the mouths of the nations to acclaim their worthless gods, and to extol a mortal king forever.

[22] "Lord, do not relinquish your scepter to those who are nothing. Do not let our foes gloat over our ruin, but turn their own counsel against them and make an example of the one who began this against us. [23] Be mindful of us, Lord. Make yourself known in the time of our distress and give me courage, King of gods and Ruler of every power. [24] Put in my mouth persuasive words in the presence of the lion, and turn his heart to hatred for our enemy, so that he and his co-conspirators may perish. [25] Save

us by your power, and help me, who am alone and have no one but you, Lord.

[26] "You know all things. You know that I hate the pomp of the lawless, and abhor the bed of the uncircumcised or of any foreigner. [27] You know that I am under constraint, that I abhor the sign of grandeur that rests on my head when I appear in public. I abhor it like a polluted rag, and do not wear it in private. [28] I, your servant, have never eaten at the table of Haman, nor have I graced the banquet of the king or drunk the wine of libations.† [29] From the day I was brought here till now, your servant has had no joy except in you, Lord, God of Abraham. [30] O God, whose power is over all, hear the voice of those in despair. Save us from the power of the wicked, and deliver me from my fear."

**D**Esther Goes to Ahasuerus.† [1] On the third day, ending her prayers, she took off her prayer garments and arrayed herself in her splendid attire. [2] In making her appearance, after invoking the all-seeing God and savior, she took with her two maids; [3] on the one she leaned gently for support, [4] while the other followed her, bearing her train. [5] She glowed with perfect beauty and her face was as joyous as it was lovely, though her heart was pounding with fear. [6] She passed through all the portals till she stood before the king, who was seated on his royal throne, clothed in full robes of state, and covered with gold and precious stones, so that he inspired great awe. [7] As he looked up in extreme anger, his features fiery and majestic, the queen staggered, turned pale and fainted, collapsing against the maid in front of her. [8] But God changed the king's anger to gentleness. In great anxiety he sprang from his throne, held her in his arms until she recovered, and comforted her with reassuring words. [9] "What is it, Esther?" he said to her. "I am your brother.† Take courage! [10] You shall not die; this order of ours applies only to our subjects. [11] Come near!" [12] Raising the golden scepter, he touched her neck with it, embraced her, and said, "Speak to me."*

[13] She replied: "I saw you, my lord, as an

---

**C:28** *Wine of libations*: offered in sacrifice to the gods.
**D:1–16** Addition D expands on and replaces 5:1–2 of the Hebrew text.
**D:9** *Brother*: along with "sister," a common term of affection between lovers or husband and wife. See, e.g., Sg 4:9–12; 8:1; Tb 5:22; 7:11.

**C:12–13** Est 4:16.
**C:15** Est 4:16.
**C:16** Dt 4:20; 7:6; 9:29; 14:2; 26:18; 32:9.
**D:12** Est 4:11.

angel of God, and my heart was shaken by fear of your majesty. [14] For you are awesome, my lord, though your countenance is full of mercy." [15] As she said this, she fainted. [16] The king was shaken and all his attendants tried to revive her.

**5** [1]† [Now on the third day, Esther put on her royal garments and stood in the inner courtyard, looking toward the royal palace, while the king was seated on his royal throne in the audience chamber, facing the palace doorway. [2] When he saw Queen Esther standing in the courtyard, she won his favor and he extended toward her the golden scepter he held. She came up to him, and touched the top of the scepter.]

[3] Then the king said to her, "What is it, Queen Esther? What is your request? Even if it is half of my kingdom, it shall be granted you."* [4] Esther replied, "If it please your majesty, come today with Haman to a banquet I have prepared." [5] The king ordered, "Have Haman make haste to fulfill the wish of Esther."

## V. HAMAN'S DOWNFALL

**First Banquet of Esther.** So the king went with Haman to the banquet Esther had prepared. [6] During the drinking of the wine, the king said to Esther, "Whatever you ask for shall be granted, and whatever request you make shall be honored, even if it is for half my kingdom."* [7] Esther replied: "This is my petition and request: [8] if I have found favor with the king and if it pleases your majesty to grant my petition and honor my request, let the king come with Haman tomorrow to a banquet I will prepare; and tomorrow I will do as the king asks."

**Haman's Plot Against Mordecai.** [9] That day Haman left happy and in good spirits. But when he saw that Mordecai at the royal gate did not rise, and showed no fear of him, he was filled with anger toward him.* [10] Haman restrained himself, however, and went home, where he

summoned his friends and his wife Zeresh. [11] He recounted the greatness of his riches, the large number of his sons, and how the king had promoted him and placed him above the officials and royal servants.* [12] "Moreover," Haman added, "Queen Esther invited no one but me to come with the king to the banquet she prepared; again tomorrow I am to be her guest with the king. [13] Yet none of this satisfies me as long as I continue to see the Jew Mordecai sitting at the royal gate."* [14] His wife Zeresh and all his friends said to him, "Have a stake set up, fifty cubits in height, and in the morning ask the king to have Mordecai impaled on it. Then go to the banquet with the king in good spirits." This suggestion pleased Haman, and he had the stake erected.*

**6** **Mordecai's Reward from the King.** [1] That night the king, unable to sleep, asked that the chronicle of notable events be brought in. While this was being read to him, [2] the passage occurred in which Mordecai reported Bigthan and Teresh, two of the royal eunuchs who guarded the entrance, for seeking to assassinate King Ahasuerus.* [3] The king asked, "What was done to honor and exalt Mordecai for this?" The king's attendants replied, "Nothing was done for him."*

[4]† "Who is in the court?" the king asked. Now Haman had entered the outer court of the king's palace to suggest to the king that Mordecai should be impaled on the stake he had raised for him.* [5] The king's attendants answered him, "Haman is waiting in the court." The king said, "Let him come in." [6] When Haman entered, the king said to him, "What should be done for the man whom the king wishes to reward?" Now Haman thought to himself, "Whom would the king wish to honor more than me?" [7] So he replied to the king: "For the man whom the king wishes to honor [8] there should be brought the royal robe the king wore and the horse the king rode with the royal crest placed on its head. [9] The robe and the horse should be given to one of the noblest of the king's officials, who must clothe

---

† **5:1–2** The Hebrew text translated here is a short form of the account which is in Greek addition D.

**6:4–13** Haman's presumption that the king wants to honor him creates the irony that Haman himself prescribes and fulfills the elaborate terms of Mordecai's reward. This comic reversal mirrors the fatal reversal to come: Haman and those who hate the Jews find that their plot to destroy them recoils on their own head.

* **5:3** Est 5:6; 7:2; 9:12.
  **5:6** Est 5:3.
  **5:9** Est 3:2–3; C:5–7; 6:10, 12.
  **5:11** Est 3:1; B:3; E:11; 9:6–10.
  **5:13** Est 3:2–3; 6:10, 12.
  **5:14** Est 6:4; 7:9–10.
  **6:2** Est A:12–14; 2:21–23.
  **6:3** Est A:16.
  **6:4** Est 5:14; 7:9–10.

the man the king wishes to reward, have him ride on the horse in the public square of the city, and cry out before him, 'This is what is done for the man whom the king wishes to honor!'"* ¹⁰Then the king said to Haman: "Hurry! Take the robe and horse as you have proposed, and do this for the Jew Mordecai, who is sitting at the royal gate. Do not omit anything you proposed."* ¹¹So Haman took the robe and horse, clothed Mordecai, had him ride in the public square of the city, and cried out before him, "This is what is done for the man whom the king wishes to honor!"

¹²Mordecai then returned to the royal gate, while Haman hurried home grieving, with his head covered.* ¹³When he told his wife Zeresh and all his friends everything that had happened to him, his advisers and his wife Zeresh said to him, "If Mordecai, before whom you are beginning to fall, is of Jewish ancestry, you will not prevail against him, but will surely be defeated by him."

**Esther's Second Banquet.** ¹⁴While they were speaking with him, the king's eunuchs arrived and hurried Haman off to the banquet Esther had prepared.

**7** ¹So the king and Haman went to the banquet with Queen Esther. ²Again, on this second day, as they were drinking wine, the king said to Esther, "Whatever you ask, Queen Esther, shall be granted you. Whatever request you make, even for half the kingdom, shall be honored."* ³Queen Esther replied: "If I have found favor with you, O king, and if it pleases your majesty, I ask that my life be spared, and I beg that you spare the lives of my people. ⁴For we have been sold, I and my people, to be destroyed, killed, and annihilated. If we were only to be sold into slavery I would remain silent, for then our distress would not have been worth troubling the king."* ⁵King Ahasuerus said to Queen Esther, "Who and where is the man who has dared to do this?"* ⁶Esther replied, "The enemy oppressing us is this wicked Haman." At this, Haman was seized with dread of the king and queen.

⁷The king left the banquet in anger and went into the garden of the palace, but Haman stayed to beg Queen Esther for his life, since he saw that the king had decided on his doom. ⁸When the king returned from the palace garden to the banquet hall, Haman had thrown himself on the couch on which Esther was reclining; and the king exclaimed, "Will he also violate the queen while she is with me in my own house!" Scarcely had the king spoken when the face of Haman was covered over.

**Punishment of Haman.** ⁹* Harbona, one of the eunuchs who attended the king, said, "At the house of Haman stands a stake fifty cubits high. Haman made it for Mordecai, who gave the report that benefited the king." The king answered, "Impale him on it." ¹⁰So they impaled Haman on the stake he had set up for Mordecai, and the anger of the king abated.

**8** ¹That day King Ahasuerus gave the house of Haman, enemy of the Jews, to Queen Esther; and Mordecai was admitted to the king's presence, for Esther had revealed his relationship to her.* ²The king removed his signet ring that he had taken away from Haman, and gave it to Mordecai; and Esther put Mordecai in charge of the house of Haman.*

### VI. THE JEWISH VICTORY AND THE FEAST OF PURIM

**The Second Royal Decree.** ³Esther again spoke to the king. She fell at his feet and tearfully implored him to revoke the harm done by Haman the Agagite and the plan he had devised against the Jews. ⁴The king stretched forth the golden scepter to Esther. So she rose and, standing before him, ⁵said: "If it seems good to the king and if I have found favor with him, if the thing seems right to the king and I am pleasing in his eyes, let a document be issued to revoke the letters that the schemer Haman, son of Hammedatha the Agagite, wrote for the destruction of the Jews in all the royal provinces.* ⁶For how can I witness the evil that is to befall my people, and how can I behold the destruction of my kindred?"

⁷King Ahasuerus then said to Queen Esther and to the Jew Mordecai: "Now that I have given Esther the house of Haman, and they

---

**6:9** Gn 41:42–43; 1 Kgs 1:33; Dn 5:29.
**6:10** Est 2:21; 3:2–3; 5:9, 13.
**6:12** Est 2:21; 3:2–3; 5:9, 13.
**7:2** Est 5:3.
**7:4** Est 3:13; B:6.
**7:5** Est 3:8–9.
**7:9–10** Est 5:14; 6:4.
**8:1** Est 9:1; Prv 11:8; 26:27; Mt 7:2.
**8:2** Prv 13:22; Dn 2:48–49.
**8:5** Est 1:19.

E S T

have impaled him on the stake because he was going to attack the Jews, 8* you in turn may write in the king's name what you see fit concerning the Jews and seal the letter with the royal signet ring." For a decree written in the name of the king and sealed with the royal signet ring cannot be revoked.†

9 At that time, on the twenty-third day of the third month, Sivan, the royal scribes were summoned. Exactly as Mordecai dictated, they wrote to the Jews and to the satraps, governors, and officials of the hundred and twenty-seven provinces from India to Ethiopia: to each province in its own script and to each people in its own language, and to the Jews in their own script and language. 10 These letters, which he wrote in the name of King Ahasuerus and sealed with the royal signet ring, he sent by mounted couriers riding thoroughbred royal steeds. 11* In these letters the king authorized the Jews in each and every city to gather and defend their lives, to destroy, kill, and annihilate every armed group of any nation or province that might attack them, along with their wives and children, and to seize their goods as spoil 12 on a single day throughout the provinces of King Ahasuerus, the thirteenth day of the twelfth month, Adar.

E 1 The following is a copy of the letter: "The great King Ahasuerus to the governors of the provinces in the hundred and twenty-seven satrapies from India to Ethiopia, and to those who are loyal to our government: Greetings!

2 "Many have become more ambitious the more they were showered with honors through the bountiful generosity of their patrons. 3 Not only do they seek to do harm to our subjects but, incapable of dealing with such greatness, they even begin plotting against their own benefactors. 4 Not only do they drive out gratitude from among humankind but, with the arrogant boastfulness of those to whom

goodness has no meaning, they suppose they will escape the stern judgment of the all-seeing God.

5 "Often, too, the fair speech of friends entrusted with the administration of affairs has induced many placed in authority to become accomplices in the shedding of innocent blood, and has involved them in irreparable calamities 6 by deceiving with malicious slander the sincere good will of rulers. 7 This can be verified in the ancient stories that have been handed down to us, but more fully when you consider the wicked deeds perpetrated in your midst by the pestilential influence of those undeserving of authority. 8* We must provide for the future, so as to render the kingdom undisturbed and peaceful for all people, 9 taking advantage of changing conditions and always deciding matters coming to our attention with equitable treatment.

10 "For instance, Haman, son of Hammedatha, a Macedonian,† certainly not of Persian blood, and very different from us in generosity, was hospitably received by us. 11 He benefited so much from the good will we have toward all peoples that he was proclaimed 'our father,' before whom everyone was to bow down; and he attained a position second only to the royal throne.* 12 But, unable to control his arrogance, he strove to deprive us of kingdom and of life, 13 and by weaving intricate webs of deceit he demanded the destruction of Mordecai, our savior and constant benefactor, and of Esther, our blameless royal consort, together with their whole nation.* 14 For by such measures he hoped to catch us defenseless and to transfer the rule of the Persians to the Macedonians. 15 But we find that the Jews, who were doomed to extinction by this archcriminal, are not evildoers, but rather are governed by very just laws 16 and are the children of the Most High, the living God of majesty, who has maintained the kingdom in a flourishing condition for us and for our forebears.

---

† **8:8** *A decree written…cannot be revoked:* the king cannot directly grant Esther's request (v. 5) to revoke the previous decree against the Jews because of the irrevocable character of the laws of the Medes and Persians (see 1:19 and note). He can, however, empower Esther to issue another decree in his name to counteract the earlier one. The second decree authorizes the Jews to defend themselves against those who would kill them, which is what they do in 9:2. This is why the outcome of the two decrees is that the attackers are killed instead of the Jews, rather than a simple cancellation of all hostilities.

**E:10** *Macedonian:* throughout the book Haman is identified

with terms of contempt—in the Hebrew text as an Agagite (3:1, 10; 8:3, 5; 9:24; cf. note on A:17), thus making him a descendant of Agag, king of the Amalekites, a group hated by the Israelites; in the Greek additions Haman is identified as a Macedonian, reflecting the enmity between the Persians and the Macedonians after Macedonia's conquest of Persia in the fourth century B.C.

---

| | |
|---|---|
| **8:8** Est 1:19. | **E:11** Est B:3, 6. |
| **8:11–12** Est 9:1–4. | **E:13** Est A:17. |
| **E:8–9** Est B:2. | |

[17] "You will do well, then, to ignore the letter sent by Haman, son of Hammedatha, [18] for he who composed it has been impaled, together with his entire household, before the gates of Susa. Thus swiftly has God, who governs all, brought just punishment upon him.*

[19] "You shall exhibit a copy of this letter publicly in every place to certify that the Jews may follow their own laws [20] and that you may help them on the day set for their ruin, the thirteenth day of the twelfth month, Adar, to defend themselves against those who attack them. [21] For God, the ruler of all, has turned that day from one of destruction of the chosen people into one of joy for them. [22] Therefore, you too must celebrate this memorable day among your designated feasts with all rejoicing, [23] so that both now and in the future it may be a celebration of deliverance for us and for Persians of good will, but for those who plot against us a reminder of destruction.

[24] "Every city and province without exception that does not observe this decree shall be ruthlessly destroyed with fire and sword, so that it will be left not merely untrodden by people, but even shunned by wild beasts and birds forever."*

(8) [13] A copy of the letter to be promulgated as law in each and every province was published among all the peoples, so that the Jews might be prepared on that day to avenge themselves on their enemies. [14] Couriers mounted on royal steeds sped forth in haste at the king's order, and the decree was promulgated in the royal precinct of Susa.

[15] Mordecai left the king's presence clothed in a royal robe of violet and of white cotton, with a large crown of gold and a mantle of fine crimson linen. The city of Susa shouted with joy,* [16] and for the Jews there was splendor and gladness, joy and triumph. [17] In each and every province and in each and every city, wherever the king's order arrived, there was merriment and joy, banqueting and feasting for the Jews. And many of the peoples of the land identified themselves as Jews, for fear of the Jews fell upon them.*

9 **The Massacre Reversed.** [1]* When the day arrived on which the order decreed by the king was to be carried out, the thirteenth day of the twelfth month, Adar, on which the enemies of the Jews had expected to overpower them, the situation was reversed: the Jews overpowered those who hated them. [2] The Jews mustered in their cities throughout the provinces of King Ahasuerus to attack those who sought to do them harm, and no one could withstand them, for fear of them fell upon all the peoples. [3] Moreover, all the officials of the provinces, the satraps, governors, and royal procurators supported the Jews out of fear of Mordecai; [4] for Mordecai was powerful in the royal palace, and the report was spreading through all the provinces that he was continually growing in power.

[5] The Jews struck down all their enemies with the sword, killing and destroying them; they did to those who hated them as they pleased.* [6]* In the royal precinct of Susa, the Jews killed and destroyed five hundred people. [7] They also killed Parshandatha, Dalphon, Aspatha, [8] Poratha, Adalia, Aridatha, [9] Parmashta, Arisai, Aridai, and Vaizatha, [10]* the ten sons of Haman, son of Hammedatha, the foe of the Jews. However, they did not engage in plundering.

[11] On the same day, when the number of those killed in the royal precinct of Susa was reported to the king, [12] he said to Queen Esther: "In the royal precinct of Susa the Jews have killed and destroyed five hundred people, as well as the ten sons of Haman. What must they have done in the other royal provinces! You shall again be granted whatever you ask, and whatever you request shall be honored." [13] So Esther said, "If it pleases your majesty, let the Jews in Susa be permitted again tomorrow to act according to today's decree, and let the ten sons of Haman be impaled on stakes." [14] The king then gave an order that this be done, and the decree was published in Susa. So the ten sons of Haman were impaled,* [15] and the Jews in Susa mustered again on the fourteenth of the month of Adar and killed three hundred people in Susa. However, they did not engage in plundering.*

[16] The other Jews, who dwelt in the royal provinces, also mustered and defended themselves, and obtained rest from their enemies. They killed seventy-five thousand of those

**E:18** Est 7:10; 9:14.  
**E:24** Est 3:8–9; B:4.  
**8:15** Dn 5:7.  

**8:17** Est 9:27.  
**9:1–2** Est 8:11–12.  
**9:5** Jdt 15:6.  

**9:6–10** Est 5:11; B:3; E:11.  
**9:10** Est 9:15; Jdt 15:7, 11.  

**9:14** Est 7:10; E:18.  
**9:15** Est 9:10.

EST

who hated them, but they did not engage in plunder.* [17]This happened on the thirteenth day of the month of Adar.

### The Feast of Purim.†

On the fourteenth of the month they rested, and made it a day of feasting and rejoicing.

[18]The Jews in Susa, however, mustered on the thirteenth and fourteenth of the month. But on the fifteenth they rested, and made it a day of joyful banqueting. [19]That is why the rural Jews, who dwell in villages, celebrate the fourteenth of the month of Adar as a day of joyful banqueting, a holiday on which they send food to one another.

[20]Mordecai recorded these events and sent letters to all the Jews, both near and far, in all the provinces of King Ahasuerus. [21]† He ordered them to celebrate every year both the fourteenth and the fifteenth of the month of Adar [22]as the days on which the Jews obtained rest from their enemies and as the month which was turned for them from sorrow into joy, from mourning into celebration. They were to observe these days with joyful banqueting, sending food to one another and gifts to the poor. [23]† The Jews adopted as a custom what they had begun doing and what Mordecai had written to them.*

### VII. EPILOGUE: THE RISE OF MORDECAI

**Summary of the Story.** [24]* Haman, son of Hammedatha the Agagite, the foe of all the Jews, had planned to destroy them and had cast the *pur*, or lot, for the time of their defeat and destruction. [25]Yet, when the plot became known to the king, the king ordered in writing that the wicked plan Haman had devised against the Jews should instead be turned against Haman and that he and his sons should be impaled on stakes.* [26]And so these days have been named Purim after the word *pur*.

Thus, because of all that was contained in this letter, and because of what they had witnessed and experienced in this event, [27]the Jews established and adopted as a custom for themselves, their descendants, and all who should join them, the perpetual obligation of celebrating these two days every year in the manner prescribed by this letter, and at the time appointed.* [28]These days were to be commemorated and kept in every generation, by every clan, in every province, and in every city. These days of Purim were never to be neglected among the Jews, nor forgotten by their descendants.

### Esther and Mordecai Act in Concert.†

[29]Queen Esther, daughter of Abihail, and Mordecai the Jew, wrote to confirm with full authority this second letter about Purim, [30]and Mordecai sent documents concerning peace and security to all the Jews in the hundred and twenty-seven provinces of Ahasuerus' kingdom.* [31]Thus were established, for their appointed time, these days of Purim which Mordecai the Jew and Queen Esther had designated for the Jews, just as they had previously enjoined upon themselves and upon their descendants the duty of fasting and supplication. [32]The command of Esther confirmed these prescriptions for Purim and was recorded in the book.

# 10 The Rise of Mordecai Completed.

[1]King Ahasuerus levied a tax on the land and on the islands of the sea. [2]All the acts of his power and valor, as well as a detailed account of the greatness of Mordecai, whom the king promoted, are recorded in the chronicles of the kings of Media and Persia. [3]The Jew Mordecai was next in rank to King Ahasuerus, in high standing among the Jews, popular with many of his kindred, seeking the good of his people and speaking out on behalf of the welfare of all its descendants.*

---

†
**9:17–19** According to Esther, Jewish feasting on the day after the defeat of their enemies establishes the date of the holiday. Since in Susa the fighting lasts for two days, the Jews of that community initially celebrate Purim a day later than Jews elsewhere.
**9:21** Mordecai creates a compromise among the Jews by making Purim a two-day festival.
**9:23** According to the story, the two-day celebration has its roots in popular observance, which Mordecai's leadership reinforces and regularizes.
**9:29–32** In attempting to give the impression of concerted action between Esther and Mordecai, the Hebrew text here

presents several unresolved difficulties. Verse 29 makes Mordecai and Esther joint authors of a letter that is ascribed in v. 32 to Esther alone. Verse 31 makes Mordecai and Esther joint authors of a letter that is ascribed in vv. 20–22 to Mordecai alone. Finally, it is difficult to see the purpose of confirming a second letter in the second letter itself.

*
| | |
|---|---|
| **9:16** Jdt 15:6. | **9:27** Est 8:12, 17. |
| **9:23** Est 9:29. | **9:30** Est 9:23–26. |
| **9:24–26** Est 3:7; F:10. | **10:3** 2 Mc 15:14. |
| **9:25** Est 6:5–13. | |

**F** **Mordecai's Dream Fulfilled.** 1* Then Mordecai said: "This is the work of God. 2 I recall the dream I had about these very things, and not a single detail has been left unfulfilled— 3 the tiny spring that grew into a river, and there was light, and sun, and many waters. The river is Esther, whom the king married and made queen. 4 The two dragons are myself and Haman. 5 The nations are those who assembled to destroy the name of the Jews, 6 but my people is Israel, who cried to God and was saved.

"The Lord saved his people and delivered us from all these evils. God worked signs and great wonders, such as have not occurred among the nations. 7 For this purpose he arranged two lots:† one for the people of God, the second for all the other nations. 8 These two lots were fulfilled in the hour, the time, and the day of judgment before God and among all the nations. 9 God remembered his people and rendered justice to his inheritance.

10* "Gathering together with joy and happiness before God, they shall celebrate these days on the fourteenth and fifteenth of the month Adar throughout all future generations of his people Israel."

**Colophon.**† 11 In the fourth year of the reign of Ptolemy and Cleopatra, Dositheus, who said he was a priest and Levite, and his son Ptolemy brought the present letter of Purim, saying that it was genuine and that Lysimachus, son of Ptolemy, of the community of Jerusalem, had translated it.

---

† **F:7** *Two lots:* this passage of the Greek text gives an additional interpretation of the feast. The two lots are drawn by God to determine, respectively, the destiny of Israel and that of the nations; contrast with 3:7 of the Hebrew text.
**F:11** Several "Ptolemies" (Greek kings reigning in Egypt) had wives named Cleopatra. This postscript dates the Greek version somewhere between 116 B.C. and 48 B.C.

* F:1–6 Est A:4–10.  F:10 Est 3:7; 9:17–18, 21, 24–28.

# The First Book of

# Maccabees

## INTRODUCTION

### Patricia D. Ahearne-Kroll

For Jews living during the Hellenistic and early Roman periods, the Maccabean-led revolt and the rise of a somewhat autonomous Judean kingdom were phenomenal events. During the expansion of the Persian Empire (539–331 BCE), Judah was a province. Then, in an even more amazing demonstration of power, Alexander the Great swept through the Mediterranean region, conquering territory as far east as present-day Pakistan and swallowing up the Persian Empire.

After Alexander's premature death in 323 BCE, the ancient Mediterranean and Far East entered a new stage of imperial politics. In the Levant (the geographical territory along the eastern Mediterranean consisting of Phoenicia, Galilee, and Samaria in the north and Judea [roughly the region of Judah during the Persian period] and Idumea in the south, as well as territory to the east of the Jordan River and Dead Sea but west of the Arabian desert), and especially in Jerusalem, Jews now found themselves embedded in a conflict over the region between two post-Alexander empires, the Seleucids and the Ptolemies. When the Seleucid king, Antiochus III, took control of the land in 200 BCE, new challenges arose. However, after the Roman defeat of Antiochus in his western expansion across modern-day Turkey, the Seleucid Empire grew bankrupt and never fully recovered from this economic and political blow. During this decline in Seleucid history, Antiochus IV rose to power and the Maccabean revolt began.

Even though Seleucid rule was weakening in the Levant, despite the military exploits of Antiochus IV (see the initial introduction to 2 Maccabees), the ultimate victory of the Maccabees was nevertheless an incredible feat. For centuries, most Jews—like most conquered peoples—understood that their ancestral

## Outline of 1 Maccabees

I. Crisis and Response (1:1–2:70)

II. Leadership of Judas Maccabeus (3:1–9:22)

III. Leadership of Jonathan (9:23–12:53)

IV. Leadership of Simon (13:1–16:24)

kingdom was a reality of the distant past, and that far more powerful military complexes managed the course of events in their lifetime. But the Maccabean revolt changed this sentiment about the irretrievable nature of former sovereignty, and Jewish writers wanted to record the Maccabean success.

There are three books in the Roman Catholic Bible that were written about the Maccabean war against the Seleucid Empire: the books of Daniel, 1 Maccabees, and 2 Maccabees. All three narratives mention some of the same historical events, but each was written from a distinct perspective. In the book of Daniel, especially in Dn 7–12, military activity is reserved for the divine sphere (under the leadership of Gabriel and Michael), and the righteous are to resist the Seleucid persecution and faithfully wait for God's actions. Both 1 and 2 Maccabees promote active military engagement by Judeans and extensively describe particular battles and diplomatic actions of Seleucids and Maccabeans. Second Maccabees, however, is not a continuation of 1 Maccabees. It covers a shorter time period and concentrates on the Jerusalem Temple in its presentation of the causes for and direction of the revolt. For more on 2 Maccabees and on the historical chronology of Seleucid-Judean

1
M
C

relations, see the initial introduction to 2 Maccabees. This introduction will focus on the particular view of 1 Maccabees.

Initially, 1 Maccabees reads like a dense military and political history, beginning with Mattathias, a Judean and father of the Maccabees (1 Mc 2), and ending with the succession of Mattathias's grandson, John Hyrcanus, as the second ruler of Judea (ch. 16). First Maccabees is peppered with details about numerous battles (e.g., 3:38–41; 4:1–15; 5:17–44; 6:33–41; 7:39–46; 9:1–11; 10:67–85; 11:60–74; 12:24–34; 13:12–23, 43–48; 15:37–41; 16:4–10). Both the Seleucids and the Maccabeans fortify cities, and the citadel near the Temple Mount in Jerusalem is a focal point of the conflict between the two sides (1:33–35; 6:18–31; 9:52–53; 11:20–22, 41; 12:35–36; 13:49–52). The story includes much political intrigue, especially between competing factions among the Seleucids (such as between Alexander Balas and Demetrius II [chs. 10–11], Demetrius II and Trypho [chs. 11 and 14], and Antiochus VII and Trypho [ch. 14]). As the story unfolds, the Maccabeans conduct themselves like other Hellenistic rulers of their time; they forge alliances with other nations, especially with Rome (8:1–32; 12:1–4; 14:16–18, 24; 15:15–24), and they even engage in diplomatic friendships with Seleucid rulers (Alexander Balas [10:15–20; 88–89], and Demetrius II [11:24–37; 13:34–40]).

This narrative, however, is more than a description of military campaigns and the leaders who waged them. Like many ancient historiographies (e.g., the books of 1 and 2 Kings or Xenophon's *Cyropaedia*), 1 Maccabees is not simply a presentation of the past, but a narrative that persuades the audience to view a historical period or event in a specific way. First Maccabees seeks to convince the audience that the Maccabeans were the perfect choice to lead the revolt and ultimately rule over Judea. The book likely was written to promote the Hasmonean dynasty (the dynasty of the Maccabees) during or shortly after the reign of John Hyrcanus (ca. 134–104 BCE). The dramatic tone of the book—such as the sweeping characterizations of the Maccabees and even less believable portrayals of other figures (such as the deathbed repentance of Antiochus IV in

1 Mc 6:8–13)—reveal the author's intent. In modern historiography, the use of exaggeration and embellishment would raise suspicions about the historical accuracy of the account described, but in antiquity, writers used these techniques to persuade readers about their version of history.

First Maccabees utilizes two main strategies to sway the reader: first, the close association of biblical narratives and characters with the events and people of 1 Maccabees and, second, the oversimplified characterizations of those—many of them Jews—who opposed the Maccabean war and its leaders. As especially portrayed in Judas's campaigns, the Judean force imitates the behavior and achievements of the ancient Israelites as told by Deuteronomistic writers (the authors of the books of Deuteronomy–2 Kings; e.g., cf. Dt 20 with 1 Mc 3 and 5). Although God's activity in the Maccabean war is not mentioned explicitly, associating Maccabean success with stories about God's victory in ancient Israelite conflicts implies that God supported the Maccabees. Most striking are the frequent references to the Temple mount as Mount Zion (1 Mc 4:37, 60; 5:54; 6:48, 62; 7:33; 10:11; 14:26) and to the region or people of "Israel" (used sixty-three times); these terms allude to biblical concepts about the divine protection and power of God in Jerusalem (e.g., Pss 48, 76, 84) and to the territory of David's kingdom and its people (e.g., as romanticized by the book of Joshua and envisioned in Ez 33–48). Not surprisingly, the Maccabean leaders are always associated with these terms; they protect Mount Zion and fight for "Israel."

The people for whom the Maccabees actually fight, however, are technically "Judeans," inhabitants or descendants of the region of Judea (in the southern Levant), who are referred to in 1 Maccabees as *Ioudaios* (*Ioudaioi* in the plural). This word is often translated as "Jew," which today connotes a particular definition of ethnicity or kind of religious observance, meanings the writer of 1 Maccabees likely did not intend. In this narrative, *Ioudaios* is primarily an "ethnic-geographical" term that indicates an ancestral connection to Judea, but it does not explicitly refer to a particular understanding of Jewish religious practice.[1] The "Jewish people" referred to in the alliances with other nations (1 Mc 8, 12, 14), for example, are *Ioudaioi*, Judean inhabitants under Maccabean control and not Judeans who necessarily abided by a specified set of Jewish customs. For the author, then, *Ioudaioi* are not by definition Maccabean supporters; there are Judeans who did not join the revolt (like the Judean man of 2:23) and those who were opposed to it (such as the "renegades" discussed below). Judean supporters, however, are called "Israelites," and for the author, they are clearly on the side of the right (e.g., 4:59; 9:20–21; 12:52; 13:26).

This is not to say that *Ioudaioi* did not support the Temple or participate in other Jewish religious practices, but for the author of 1 Maccabees, the Maccabean leaders defined religious observance. Certainly the sanctity of the Jerusalem Temple is paramount (1 Mc 4:36–59 and 13:49–52), but the narrative ignores the negotiation of other religious practices that most Judeans likely lived out under the Seleucids. Although the Maccabees are justified to fight on the sabbath (2:41) and they ultimately become authorities over Jewish practices (10:20–21; 13:42; 14:38–47), the narrative does not consider how some Judeans may have feared the Seleucid response to circumcising their sons and instead portrays the Maccabees positively when they force circumcision upon these families (2:46). Likewise, without providing the reasons for the opposition, Judeans who oppose or do not follow the Maccabean leadership are defined as "transgressors of the law," "sinners," "the lawless," or "renegades" (e.g., 1:11; 2:44–48; 6:21–27; 7:5–7; 9:23–27, 58–61; 10:61; 11:21). Behind this rhetoric lies the historical likelihood that different factions existed in Judea, and non-Maccabeans who wanted power over the region worked closely with the Seleucids. So too, less influential Judeans had more immediate concerns that may have led them to engage in complex relationships with the Seleucid leadership. First Maccabees, though, does not tell the story this way; Judeans were either for or against the Maccabean cause, either right or wrong. For example, even though at one point there was a famine in the land and, in such occasions, military posts provided the local food supply, Judeans who sought assistance at Seleucid fortresses are said to "desert" Israel (9:23–24).[2] It is likely that most *Ioudaioi* or Judeans, then, engaged in Jewish religious practices, but 1 Maccabees clearly indicates that some of these Judeans practiced the "right" way and others did not.

The persuasive tone of this historical narrative is most profoundly demonstrated in the presentation of the persecution prescribed by Antiochus IV Epiphanes (1 Mc 1:20–61; 2:15–18) and in the unilateral opposition of the nations (the "Gentiles") to the Judeans (especially ch. 5). There is no doubt that Antiochus promulgated measures that persecuted Jewish practitioners in Judea, but the sources that discuss this catastrophe do not agree on the precise reasons for and details of the persecution (see the initial introduction to 2 Maccabees). First Maccabees embellishes when it states that Antiochus required all nations to conform to his religious practices (1 Mc 1:41–42), and the presentation of the persecution in 1 Maccabees serves to illustrate how the leadership of Mattathias and his sons best addressed the situation (as opposed to the Judeans who chose nonviolent resistance and were murdered as a result in 2:29–38). The uniform hatred of the nations portrayed in 1 Maccabees, and the Maccabean response to them, exaggerates what was likely a more varied and diverse relationship between non-Judeans and the Maccabees in the Levant, and the sweeping, negative portrayal of Gentiles opposed to Judeans casts a biblical light (in the fashion of the Deuteronomistic writers) onto the campaigns and the influence of the early Maccabees, especially of Judas. ∎

---

1. Shaye J. D. Cohen, *The Beginnings of Jewishness: Boundaries, Varieties, Uncertainties* (Berkeley, CA: University of California Press, 1999), 70–78, 87–89.

2. Jack Pastor, "The Famine in 1 Maccabees: History or Apology?" in *The Books of the Maccabees: History, Theology, Ideology*, ed. Géza G. Xeravits and József Zsengellér (Leiden: Brill, 2007), 31–43.

# THE FIRST BOOK OF MACCABEES

## New American Bible, Introduction

The name Maccabee, probably meaning "hammer," is actually applied in the Books of Maccabees to only one man, Judas, third son of the priest Mattathias and first leader of the revolt against the Seleucid kings who persecuted the Jews (1 Mc 2:4, 66; 2 Mc 8:5, 16; 10:1, 16). Traditionally the name has come to be extended to the brothers of Judas, his supporters, and even to other Jewish heroes of the period, such as the seven brothers (2 Mc 7).

The two Books of Maccabees contain independent accounts of events (in part identical) that accompanied the attempted suppression of Judaism in Palestine in the second century B.C. The vigorous reaction to this attempt established for a time the religious and political independence of the Jews.

First Maccabees was written about 100 B.C., in Hebrew, but the original has not come down to us. Instead, we have an early, pre-Christian, Greek translation full of Hebrew idioms. The author, probably a Palestinian Jew, is unknown. He was familiar with the traditions and sacred books of his people and had access to much reliable information on their recent history (from 175 to 134 B.C.). He may well have played some part in it himself in his youth. His purpose in writing is to record the deliverance of Israel that God worked through the family of Mattathias (5:62)—especially through his three sons, Judas, Jonathan, and Simon, and his grandson, John Hyrcanus. The writer compares their virtues and their exploits with those of Israel's ancient heroes, the Judges, Samuel, and David.

There are seven poetic sections in the book that imitate the style of classical Hebrew poetry: four laments (1:25–28, 36–40; 2:7–13; 3:45), and three hymns of praise of "our fathers" (2:51–64), of Judas (3:3–9), and of Simon (14:4–15). The doctrine expressed in the book is the customary belief of Israel, without the new developments which appear in 2 Maccabees and Daniel. The people of Israel have been specially chosen by the one true God as covenant-partner, and they alone are privileged to know and worship God, their eternal benefactor and unfailing source of help. The people, in turn, must worship the Lord alone and observe exactly the precepts of the law given to them. The rededication of the Jerusalem Temple described in 4:36–59 (see 2 Mc 10:1–8) is the origin of the Jewish feast of Hanukkah.

Unlike the Second Book of Maccabees, there is no doctrine of individual immortality except in the survival of one's name and fame, nor does the book express any messianic expectation, though messianic images are applied historically to "the days of Simon" (1 Mc 14:4–17). In true Deuteronomic tradition, the author insists on fidelity to the law as the expression of Israel's love for God. The contest which he describes is a struggle, not simply between Jew and Gentile, but between those who would uphold the law and those, Jews or Gentiles, who would destroy it. His severest condemnation goes, not to the Seleucid politicians, but to the lawless apostates among his own people, adversaries of Judas and his brothers, who are models of faith and loyalty.

The first and second Books of Maccabees, though regarded by Jews and Protestants as apocryphal, i.e., not inspired Scripture, because not contained in the Jewish list of books drawn up at the end of the first century A.D., have always been accepted by the Catholic Church as inspired and are called "deutero-canonical" to indicate that they are canonical even though disputed by some.

First Maccabees can be divided as follows:
I. Crisis and Response (1:1–2:70)
II. Leadership of Judas Maccabeus (3:1–9:22)
III. Leadership of Jonathan (9:23–12:53)
IV. Leadership of Simon (13:1–16:24) ■

# FIRST MACCABEES

## I. CRISIS AND RESPONSE

**1 From Alexander to Antiochus.** ¹* After Alexander the Macedonian, Philip's son, who came from the land of Kittim,† had defeated Darius, king of the Persians and Medes, he became king in his place, having first ruled in Greece. ² He fought many battles, captured fortresses, and put the kings of the earth to death. ³ He advanced to the ends of the earth, gathering plunder from many nations; the earth fell silent before him, and his heart became proud and arrogant. ⁴ He collected a very strong army and won dominion over provinces, nations, and rulers, and they paid him tribute.

⁵ But after all this he took to his bed, realizing that he was going to die. ⁶ So he summoned his noblest officers, who had been brought up with him from his youth, and divided his kingdom among them while he was still alive. ⁷ Alexander had reigned twelve years† when he died.

⁸ So his officers took over his kingdom, each in his own territory, ⁹ and after his death they all put on diadems,† and so did their sons after them for many years, multiplying evils on the earth.

¹⁰ There sprang from these a sinful offshoot, Antiochus Epiphanes, son of King Antiochus, once a hostage at Rome. He became king in the one hundred and thirty-seventh year† of the kingdom of the Greeks.

**Lawless Jews.** ¹¹* In those days there appeared in Israel transgressors of the law who seduced many, saying: "Let us go and make a covenant with the Gentiles all around us; since we separated from them, many evils have come upon us." ¹² The proposal was agreeable; ¹³ some from among the people promptly went to the king, and he authorized them to introduce the ordinances of the Gentiles. ¹⁴ Thereupon they built a gymnasium† in Jerusalem according to the Gentile custom. ¹⁵ They disguised their circumcision and abandoned the holy covenant; they allied themselves with the Gentiles and sold themselves to wrongdoing.

**Antiochus in Egypt.** ¹⁶* When his kingdom seemed secure, Antiochus undertook to become king of the land of Egypt and to rule over both kingdoms. ¹⁷ He invaded Egypt with a strong force, with chariots, elephants† and cavalry, and with a large fleet, ¹⁸ to make war on Ptolemy,† king of Egypt. Ptolemy was frightened at his presence and fled, and many were wounded and fell dead. ¹⁹ The fortified cities in the land of Egypt were captured, and Antiochus plundered the land of Egypt.

**Robbery of the Temple.** ²⁰* After Antiochus had defeated Egypt in the one hundred and forty-third year,† he returned and went up against Israel and against Jerusalem with a strong force. ²¹ He insolently entered the sanctuary† and took away the golden altar, the lampstand for the light with all its utensils, ²² the offering table, the cups and bowls, the golden censers, and the curtain. The cornices and the golden ornament on the facade of

---

**1:1** *Land of Kittim*: Greece. The name referred originally to inhabitants of Kiti, capital of the isle of Cyprus, then to any Cypriots (Is 23:1; Jer 2:10), later to Greeks in general, and finally even to Romans. See note on Dn 11:30. *Darius*: Darius III, Codoman (336–331 B.C.).

**1:7** *Twelve years*: 336–323 B.C. The division of the empire was not fully settled until 305 B.C.

**1:9** *Diadems*: decorated bands of white cloth worn around the head, symbolizing kingship. The Ptolemies, based in Egypt, controlled Judea until 198 B.C., when they were replaced by the Seleucids, based in Syria.

**1:10** *The one hundred and thirty-seventh year*: Antiochus IV seized the throne in September, 175 B.C. Dates are given in this book according to the beginning of the Seleucid era, which however was reckoned in two different ways. Antiochians considered this date to be October, 312 B.C. (Syrian calendar), while Babylonians and Jewish priests accepted April, 311 B.C. as the commencement of the era (Temple calendar). The author of 1 Maccabees dates political events by the Syrian calendar but religious events by the Temple calendar. Accordingly, the civil New Year occurred variously in September or October, the religious New Year in March or April.

**1:14** *Gymnasium*: symbol and center of Greek athletic and intellectual life, it was the chief instrument of Hellenistic culture. Jewish youth were attracted by sports and encouraged to join youth clubs. They received training in military skills and in the duties of citizens. Many were won over to paganism, and some even sought surgical correction of their circumcision (since physical exercise was carried out in nudity).

**1:17** *Elephants*: an important part of Seleucid armament (cf. 6:34–37).

**1:18** Ptolemy VI Philometor, a nephew of Antiochus.

**1:20** *Defeated Egypt in the one hundred and forty-third year*: 169 B.C. No mention is made in 1 Maccabees of the second expedition to Egypt a year later, described in 2 Mc 5:1, 11; Dn 11:25, 29 records both.

**1:21** *Entered the sanctuary*: to pay his soldiers, Antiochus seized the sacred vessels and the money deposited at the Temple (see 2 Mc 3:10–11).

---

**1:1–10** Dn 8:20–22; 11:3–4, 21.
**1:11–15** 2 Mc 4:12–17.
**1:16–19** 2 Mc 5:1–10; Dn 11:25–30.
**1:20–24** 2 Mc 5:11–21.

the temple—he stripped it all off. ²³ And he took away the silver and gold and the precious vessels; he also took all the hidden treasures he could find. ²⁴ Taking all this, he went back to his own country. He shed much blood and spoke with great arrogance.

²⁵     And there was great mourning
              throughout all Israel,
²⁶        and the rulers and the elders groaned.
       Young women and men languished,
       and the beauty of the women faded.
²⁷     Every bridegroom took up lamentation,
       while the bride sitting in her chamber
              mourned,
²⁸     And the land quaked on account of its
              inhabitants,
       and all the house of Jacob was clothed
              with shame.

**Attack and Occupation.** ²⁹* Two years later, the king sent the Mysian commander† to the cities of Judah, and he came to Jerusalem with a strong force. ³⁰ He spoke to them deceitfully in peaceful terms, and they believed him. Then he attacked the city suddenly, in a great on-slaught, and destroyed many of the people in Israel. ³¹ He plundered the city and set fire to it, demolished its houses and its surrounding walls. ³² And they took captive the women and children, and seized the animals. ³³ Then they built up the City of David with a high, strong wall and strong towers, and it became their citadel.† ³⁴ There they installed a sinful race, transgressors of the law, who fortified them-selves inside it. ³⁵ They stored up weapons and provisions, depositing there the plunder they had collected from Jerusalem, and they be-came a great snare.

³⁶     The citadel became an ambush against
              the sanctuary,
       and a wicked adversary to Israel at all
              times.
³⁷     They shed innocent blood around the
              sanctuary;
       they defiled the sanctuary.

³⁸     Because of them the inhabitants of
              Jerusalem fled away,
       she became the abode of strangers.
       She became a stranger to her own
              offspring,
       and her children forsook her.
³⁹*    Her sanctuary became desolate as a
              wilderness;
       her feasts were turned into mourning,
       Her sabbaths to shame,
       her honor to contempt.
⁴⁰     As her glory had been, so great was her
              dishonor:
       her exaltation was turned into
              mourning.

**Religious Persecution.** ⁴¹* Then the king wrote to his whole kingdom that all should be one people, ⁴² and abandon their particular customs. All the Gentiles conformed to the command of the king, ⁴³ and many Israelites delighted in his religion; they sacrificed to idols and profaned the sabbath.

⁴⁴ The king sent letters by messenger to Jerusa-lem and to the cities of Judah, ordering them to follow customs foreign to their land; ⁴⁵ to pro-hibit burnt offerings, sacrifices, and libations in the sanctuary, to profane the sabbaths and feast days, ⁴⁶ to desecrate the sanctuary and the sacred ministers, ⁴⁷ to build pagan altars and temples and shrines, to sacrifice swine and unclean an-imals, ⁴⁸ to leave their sons uncircumcised, and to defile themselves with every kind of impurity and abomination; ⁴⁹ so that they might forget the law and change all its ordinances. ⁵⁰ Who-ever refused to act according to the command of the king was to be put to death.*

⁵¹ In words such as these he wrote to his whole kingdom. He appointed inspectors over all the people, and he ordered the cities of Judah to offer sacrifices, each city in turn. ⁵² Many of the people, those who abandoned the law, joined them and committed evil in the land. ⁵³ They drove Israel into hiding, wherever places of refuge could be found.

⁵⁴ On the fifteenth day of the month Kis-lev, in the year one hundred and forty-five,†

---

† **1:29** *Mysian commander*: in 2 Mc 5:24 he is identified as "Apollonius, commander of the Mysians" (mercenaries from Asia Minor). The Greek text of 1 Mc 1:29 ("chief collector of tribute") reflects a misreading of the Hebrew original.
**1:33** *Citadel*: literally, *akra* means fortress. This was a garrison for foreign troops and renegade Jews that was estab-lished near the Temple area and fell to Simon only in 141 B.C. (13:49–50).

† **1:54** *Fifteenth day of the month Kislev, in the year one hun-dred and forty-five*: December 6, 167 B.C. *Desolating abomina-tion*: in the original Hebrew, a contemptuous pun on the title "Lord of heaven" given to the god to whom an image or perhaps

**1:29–40** 2 Mc 5:24–26.                    **1:50** 1 Mc 2:29–38; 2 Mc
**1:39–40** Am 8:10; Tb 2:6.                           6:18–7:42.
**1:41–64** 2 Mc 6:1–11.

the king erected the desolating abomination upon the altar of burnt offerings, and in the surrounding cities of Judah they built pagan altars.* ⁵⁵They also burned incense at the doors of houses and in the streets. ⁵⁶Any scrolls of the law† that they found they tore up and burned. ⁵⁷Whoever was found with a scroll of the covenant, and whoever observed the law, was condemned to death by royal decree. ⁵⁸So they used their power against Israel, against those who were caught, each month, in the cities. ⁵⁹On the twenty-fifth day of each month they sacrificed on the pagan altar that was over the altar of burnt offerings. ⁶⁰In keeping with the decree, they put to death women who had their children circumcised, ⁶¹and they hung their babies from their necks; their families also and those who had circumcised them were killed.

⁶²But many in Israel were determined and resolved in their hearts not to eat anything unclean; ⁶³they preferred to die rather than to be defiled with food or to profane the holy covenant; and they did die. ⁶⁴And very great wrath came upon Israel.

**2** **Mattathias and His Sons.** ¹In those days Mattathias, son of John, son of Simeon, a priest of the family of Joarib,* left Jerusalem and settled in Modein.† ²He had five sons: John, who was called Gaddi; ³Simon, who was called Thassi; ⁴Judas, who was called Maccabeus; ⁵Eleazar, who was called Avaran; and Jonathan, who was called Apphus. ⁶When he saw the sacrileges that were being committed in Judah and in Jerusalem, ⁷he said:

"Woe is me! Why was I born
　to see the ruin of my people,
　the ruin of the holy city—
To dwell there
　as it was given into the hands of
　　enemies,
　the sanctuary into the hands of
　　strangers?
⁸　Her temple has become like a man
　　disgraced,
⁹　　her glorious vessels carried off as spoils,

Her infants murdered in her streets,
　her youths by the sword of the
　　enemy.*
¹⁰　What nation has not taken its share of
　　her realm,
　and laid its hand on her spoils?
¹¹　All her adornment has been taken away.
　Once free, she has become a slave.
¹²　We see our sanctuary laid waste,
　our beauty, our glory.
　The Gentiles have defiled them!
¹³　Why are we still alive?"

¹⁴Then Mattathias and his sons tore their garments, put on sackcloth, and mourned bitterly.

**Pagan Worship Refused and Resisted.** ¹⁵The officers of the king in charge of enforcing the apostasy came to the city of Modein to make them sacrifice. ¹⁶Many of Israel joined them, but Mattathias and his sons drew together. ¹⁷Then the officers of the king addressed Mattathias: "You are a leader, an honorable and great man in this city, supported by sons and kindred. ¹⁸Come now, be the first to obey the king's command, as all the Gentiles and Judeans and those who are left in Jerusalem have done. Then you and your sons shall be numbered among the King's Friends,† and you and your sons shall be honored with silver and gold and many gifts."

¹⁹But Mattathias answered in a loud voice: "Although all the Gentiles in the king's realm obey him, so that they forsake the religion of their ancestors and consent to the king's orders, ²⁰yet I and my sons and my kindred will keep to the covenant of our ancestors. ²¹Heaven forbid that we should forsake the law and the commandments. ²²We will not obey the words of the king by departing from our religion in the slightest degree."

²³As he finished saying these words, a certain Jew came forward in the sight of all to offer sacrifice on the altar in Modein according to the king's order. ²⁴When Mattathias saw him, he was filled with zeal; his heart was moved and his just fury was aroused; he

---

† an altar was erected upon the altar of burnt offerings in the Temple of Jerusalem; cf. Dn 9:27; 11:31.

　**1:56** *Scrolls of the law*: one or more of the first five books of the Old Testament, the traditional law of Israel.

　**2:1** *Modein*: a village about twenty miles northwest of Jerusalem, the family's ancestral home (see 2:70; 9:19).

　**2:18** *The King's Friends*: a regular order of nobility at Hellenistic courts (see 10:65; 11:27).

**1:54** Dn 9:27; 11:31; Mk 13:14.　**2:1** 1 Chr 9:10; 24:7.　**2:9** Lam 2:11, 21.

sprang forward and killed him upon the altar. [25] At the same time, he also killed the messenger of the king who was forcing them to sacrifice, and he tore down the altar. [26] Thus he showed his zeal for the law, just as Phinehas did with Zimri, son of Salu.*

[27] Then Mattathias cried out in the city, "Let everyone who is zealous for the law and who stands by the covenant follow me!" [28] Then he and his sons fled to the mountains, leaving behind in the city all their possessions.*

[29] At that time many who sought righteousness and justice went out into the wilderness† to settle there, [30] they and their children, their wives and their animals, because misfortunes pressed so hard on them. [31] It was reported to the officers and soldiers of the king who were in the City of David, in Jerusalem, that those who had flouted the king's order had gone out to secret refuges in the wilderness. [32]* Many hurried out after them, and having caught up with them, camped opposite and prepared to attack them on the sabbath. [33] The pursuers said to them, "Enough of this! Come out and obey the king's command, and you will live." [34] But they replied, "We will not come out, nor will we obey the king's command to profane the sabbath." [35] Then the enemy attacked them at once. [36] But they did not retaliate; they neither threw stones, nor blocked up their secret refuges. [37] They said, "Let us all die in innocence; heaven and earth are our witnesses that you destroy us unjustly." [38] So the officers and soldiers attacked them on the sabbath, and they died with their wives, their children and their animals, to the number of a thousand persons.

[39] When Mattathias and his friends heard of it, they mourned deeply for them. [40] They said to one another, "If we all do as our kindred have done, and do not fight against the Gentiles for our lives and our laws, they will soon destroy us from the earth." [41] So on that day they came to this decision: "Let us fight against anyone who attacks us on the sabbath, so that we may not all die as our kindred died in their secret refuges."

[42] Then they were joined by a group of Hasideans,† mighty warriors of Israel, all of them devoted to the law. [43] And all those who were fleeing from the persecutions joined them and supported them. [44] They gathered an army and struck down sinners in their wrath and the lawless in their anger, and the survivors fled to the Gentiles for safety. [45] Mattathias and his friends went about and tore down the pagan altars; [46] they also forcibly circumcised any uncircumcised boys whom they found in the territory of Israel. [47] They put to flight the arrogant, and the work prospered in their hands. [48] They saved the law from the hands of the Gentiles and of the kings and did not let the sinner triumph.

**Farewell of Mattathias.** [49] When the time came for Mattathias to die, he said to his sons: "Arrogance and scorn have now grown strong; it is a time of disaster and violent wrath. [50] Therefore, my children, be zealous for the law and give your lives for the covenant of our ancestors.

[51]     "Remember the deeds that our ancestors
             did in their times,
         and you shall win great honor and an
             everlasting name.
[52]     Was not Abraham found faithful in trial,
         and it was credited to him as
             righteousness?*
[53]     Joseph, when in distress, kept the
             commandment,
         and he became master of Egypt.*
[54]     Phinehas our ancestor, for his burning
             zeal,
         received the covenant of an everlasting
             priesthood.*
[55]     Joshua, for executing his commission,
         became a judge in Israel.*
[56]     Caleb, for bearing witness before the
             assembly,
         received an inheritance in the land.*
[57]     David, for his loyalty,
         received as a heritage a throne of
             eternal kingship.*

---

† **2:29** *The wilderness*: the sparsely inhabited mountain country southward from Jerusalem and west of the Dead Sea, in the region where the Dead Sea Scrolls were found.

**2:42** *Hasideans*: in Hebrew *hasidim*, "pious ones," a militant religious group devoted to the strict observance of the law. They first supported the Maccabean movement, but subsequently opposed it, regarding it as too political (see 7:12–18).

* **2:26** Nm 25:6–15; Ps 106:28–31; Sir 45:23–24; 1 Mc 2:54.
**2:28** 2 Mc 5:27.
**2:32–38** 2 Mc 6:11.
**2:52** Gn 15:6; 22:1–18.
**2:53** Gn 39:7–10; 41:39–43.
**2:54** Nm 25:6–15.
**2:55** Jos 1, 2, 5.
**2:56** Nm 13:30; 14:6–9, 24; Jos 14:14.
**2:57** 2 Sm 2:4; 7:16.

1 M C

58 Elijah, for his burning zeal for the law,
    was taken up to heaven.*
59 Hananiah, Azariah and Mishael, for
    their faith,
    were saved from the fire.*
60 Daniel, for his innocence,
    was delivered from the mouths of
    lions.*
61 And so, consider this from generation to
    generation,
    that none who hope in Heaven shall
    fail in strength.
62 Do not fear the words of sinners,
    for their glory ends in corruption and
    worms.*
63 Today exalted, tomorrow not to be found,
    they have returned to dust,
    their schemes have perished.
64 Children! be courageous and strong in
    keeping the law,
    for by it you shall be honored.

65 "Here is your brother Simeon who I know
is a wise counselor; listen to him always, and
he will be a father to you. 66 And Judas Maccabeus, a mighty warrior from his youth, shall
be the leader of your army and wage the war
against the nations. 67 Gather about you all
who observe the law, and avenge your people.
68 Pay back the Gentiles what they deserve, and
observe the precepts of the law."

69 Then he blessed them, and he was gathered to his ancestors. 70 He died in the year one
hundred and forty-six,† and was buried in the
tombs of his ancestors in Modein, and all Israel mourned him greatly.

## II. LEADERSHIP OF JUDAS MACCABEUS

**3** **Judas and His Early Victories.** 1 Then his
son Judas, who was called Maccabeus,
took his place. 2 All his brothers and all who
had joined his father supported him, and they
gladly carried on Israel's war.

3    He spread abroad the glory of his
    people,

and put on his breastplate like a giant.
    He armed himself with weapons of war;
    he fought battles and protected the
    camp with his sword.
4 In his deeds he was like a lion,
    like a young lion roaring for prey.
5 He pursued the lawless, hunting them
    out,
    and those who troubled his people he
    destroyed by fire.
6 The lawless were cowed by fear of him,
    and all evildoers were dismayed.
    By his hand deliverance was happily
    achieved,
7    and he afflicted many kings.
    He gave joy to Jacob by his deeds,
    and his memory is blessed forever.
8 He went about the cities of Judah
    destroying the renegades there.
    He turned away wrath from Israel,
9    was renowned to the ends of the
    earth;
    and gathered together those who were
    perishing.

10 Then Apollonius† gathered together the
Gentiles, along with a large army from Samaria, to fight against Israel. 11 When Judas
learned of it, he went out to meet him and
struck and killed him. Many fell wounded,
and the rest fled. 12 They took their spoils,
and Judas took the sword of Apollonius and
fought with it the rest of his life.

13 But Seron, commander of the Syrian army,
heard that Judas had mustered an assembly of
faithful men ready for war. 14 So he said, "I will
make a name for myself and win honor in the
kingdom. I will wage war against Judas and
his followers, who have despised the king's
command." 15 And again a large company of
renegades advanced with him to help him take
revenge on the Israelites.

16 When he reached the ascent of Beth-horon,† Judas went out to meet him with a few
men. 17 But when they saw the army coming
against them, they said to Judas: "How can
we, few as we are, fight such a strong host as

---

† 2:70 In the year one hundred and forty-six: 166 B.C.
3:10 Apollonius: the Mysian commander mentioned in 1 Mc
1:29; 2 Mc 5:24.
3:16 Beth-horon: the famous pass leading up from the coastal
plain to the Judean hill country. Here Joshua won an important
battle (Jos 10:10–11), and in A.D. 66 a Roman force under Ces-
tius was trapped and massacred.

* 2:58 1 Kgs 19:10, 14; 2 Kgs     2:60 Dn 6:23.
2:11.     2:62 2 Mc 9:5–10, 28.
2:59 Dn 3:26.

this? Besides, we are weak since we have not eaten today." [18] But Judas said: "Many are easily hemmed in by a few; in the sight of Heaven there is no difference between deliverance by many or by few; [19] for victory in war does not depend upon the size of the army, but on strength that comes from Heaven.* [20] With great presumption and lawlessness they come against us to destroy us and our wives and children and to despoil us; [21] but we are fighting for our lives and our laws. [22] He† will crush them before us; so do not fear them." [23] When he finished speaking, he rushed suddenly upon Seron and his army, who were crushed before him. [24] He pursued Seron down the descent of Beth-horon into the plain. About eight hundred† of their men fell, and the rest fled to the land of the Philistines. [25] Then Judas and his brothers began to be feared, and dread fell upon the Gentiles about them. [26] His fame reached the king, and the Gentiles talked about the battles of Judas.

### The King's Strategy.
[27] When King Antiochus heard these reports, he was filled with rage; so he ordered that all the forces of his kingdom be gathered, a very strong army. [28] He opened his treasury, gave his soldiers a year's pay, and commanded them to be prepared for anything. [29] But then he saw that this exhausted the money in his treasury; moreover the tribute from the province was small because of the dissension and distress he had brought upon the land by abolishing the laws which had been in effect from of old. [30] He feared that, as had happened once or twice, he would not have enough for his expenses and for the gifts that he was accustomed to give with a lavish hand—more so than all previous kings. [31] Greatly perplexed, he decided to go to Persia and levy tribute on those provinces, and so raise a large sum of money.

[32] He left Lysias, a noble of royal descent, in charge of the king's affairs from the Euphrates River to the frontier of Egypt, [33] and commissioned him to take care of his son Antiochus

until his return. [34] He entrusted to him half of his forces, and the elephants, and gave him instructions concerning everything he wanted done. As for the inhabitants of Judea and Jerusalem, [35] Lysias was to send an army against them to crush and destroy the power of Israel and the remnant of Jerusalem and efface their memory from the place. [36] He was to settle foreigners in all their territory and distribute their land by lot. [37] † The king took the remaining half of the army and set out from Antioch, his capital, in the year one hundred and forty-seven; he crossed the Euphrates River and went through the provinces beyond.

### Preparations for Battle.
[38] * Lysias chose Ptolemy, son of Dorymenes, and Nicanor† and Gorgias, powerful men among the King's Friends, [39] and with them he sent forty thousand foot soldiers and seven thousand cavalry to invade and ravage the land of Judah according to the king's orders. [40] Setting out with their whole force, they came and pitched their camp near Emmaus† in the plain. [41] When the merchants of the region heard of their prowess, they came to the camp, bringing a huge sum of silver and gold, along with fetters, to buy the Israelites as slaves. A force from Edom and from Philistia joined with them.

[42] Judas and his brothers saw that evils had multiplied and that armies were encamped within their territory. They learned of the orders which the king had given to destroy and utterly wipe out the people. [43] So they said to one another, "Let us raise our people from their ruin and fight for them and for our sanctuary!" [44] The assembly gathered together to prepare for battle and to pray and ask for mercy and compassion.

[45]      Jerusalem was uninhabited, like a
                    wilderness;
             not one of her children came in or
                    went out.
         The sanctuary was trampled on,

---

† **3:22** *He*: out of reverence for God, the author of 1 Maccabees prefers to use the pronoun and other expressions, such as "Heaven," instead of the divine name. Cf. v. 50.

**3:24** *About eight hundred*: the figures given in this book for strength of armies and number of casualties are not always to be taken literally. In accordance with biblical usage, they indicate rather the importance of the battle described or the greatness of the victory.

**3:37** This expedition, in the spring of 165 B.C., resulted in failure; cf. chap. 6.

**3:38** *Nicanor*: perhaps the leader of another attack against the Jews four years later; he was finally killed by Judas; cf. 7:26–46.

**3:40** *Emmaus*: probably not the village mentioned in Lk 24:13 but a settlement about twenty miles west of Jerusalem at the edge of the hill country.

**3:19** 1 Sm 14:6.          **3:38–60** 2 Mc 8:9–23.

and foreigners were in the citadel;
    it was a habitation for Gentiles.
Joy had disappeared from Jacob,
    and the flute and the harp were silent.

46† Thus they assembled and went to Mizpah near Jerusalem, because formerly at Mizpah there was a place of prayer for Israel.* 47 That day they fasted and wore sackcloth; they sprinkled ashes on their heads and tore their garments. 48 They unrolled the scroll of the law, to learn about the things for which the Gentiles consulted the images of their idols.† 49 They brought with them the priestly garments, the first fruits, and the tithes; and they brought forward the nazirites†* who had completed the time of their vows. 50 And they cried aloud to Heaven: "What shall we do with these, and where shall we take them? 51 For your sanctuary has been trampled on and profaned, and your priests are in mourning and humbled. 52 Now the Gentiles are gathered together against us to destroy us. You know what they plot against us. 53 How shall we be able to resist them unless you help us?" 54 Then they blew the trumpets and cried out loudly.

55 After this Judas appointed officers for the people, over thousands, over hundreds, over fifties, and over tens. 56 He proclaimed that those who were building houses, or were just married, or were planting vineyards, and those who were afraid, could each return home, according to the law.* 57 Then the army moved off, and they camped to the south of Emmaus. 58 Judas said: "Arm yourselves and be brave; in the morning be ready to fight these Gentiles who have assembled against us to destroy us and our sanctuary. 59 It is better for us to die in battle than to witness the evils befalling our nation and our sanctuary. 60 Whatever is willed in heaven will be done."

**4** **Victory over Gorgias.** 1 Now Gorgias took five thousand infantry and a thousand picked cavalry, and this detachment set out at night 2 in order to fall upon the camp of the Jews in a surprise attack. Some from the citadel were his guides. 3 Judas heard of it and himself set out with his soldiers to attack the king's army at Emmaus 4 while these forces were still scattered away from the camp. 5 During the night Gorgias came into the camp of Judas, and found no one there; so he sought them in the mountains, saying, "They are fleeing from us."

6 But at daybreak Judas appeared in the plain with three thousand men; furthermore they lacked the helmets and swords they wanted. 7 They saw the army of the Gentiles,† strong, breastplated, and flanked with cavalry, and made up of experienced soldiers. 8* Judas said to the men with him: "Do not fear their numbers or dread their attack. 9 Remember how our ancestors were saved in the Red Sea, when Pharaoh pursued them with an army.* 10 So now let us cry to Heaven in the hope that he will favor us, remember the covenant with our ancestors, and destroy this army before us today. 11 All the Gentiles shall know that there is One who redeems and delivers Israel."

12 When the foreigners looked up and saw them marching toward them, 13 they came out of their camp for battle. The men with Judas blew the trumpet, and 14 joined the battle. They crushed the Gentiles, who fled toward the plain. 15 Their whole rear guard fell by the sword, and they were pursued as far as Gazara† and the plains of Idumaea, to Azotus and Jamnia. About three thousand of their men fell.

16 When Judas and the army returned from the pursuit, 17 he said to the people: "Do not be greedy for plunder; for there is a fight ahead of us, 18 and Gorgias and his army are near us on the mountain. But now stand firm against our enemies and fight them. Afterward you can freely take the plunder."

19 As Judas was finishing this speech, a detachment† appeared, looking down from the mountain. 20 They saw that their army had

---

**3:46** *Mizpah…a place of prayer for Israel*: a holy place of great antiquity eight miles north and slightly west of Jerusalem. It was here that Samuel began to judge the Israelites (1 Sm 7:5–11; 10:17).
**3:48** *To learn…idols*: favorable omens for the coming battle. A contrast is intended between the idol worship of the pagans and the consultation of the word of God by the Jews; cf. 2 Mc 8:23.
**3:49** *Nazirites*: see note on Nm 6:2–21.
**4:7** *Army of the Gentiles*: the main force; cf. 3:39–40; 4:1–2.

**4:15** *Gazara*: Gezer of the Hebrew Bible, five miles northwest of Emmaus; *Azotus*, Hebrew Ashdod, lay to the southwest; *and Jamnia*, Hebrew Jabneel (Jos 15:11) or Jabneh (2 Chr 26:6), to the west of Gazara.
**4:19** *A detachment*: i.e., Gorgias' force; cf. vv. 1–5.

**3:46** Jgs 20:1; 1 Sm 7:5–9; 10:17.
**3:49** Nm 6:1–21.
**3:56** Dt 20:5–8.
**4:8–11** Dt 20:3–4; Jgs 7:2–3.
**4:9** Ex 14:21–31.

been put to flight and their camp was burning. The smoke they saw revealed what had happened. 21 When they realized this, they completely lost heart; and when they also saw the army of Judas in the plain ready to attack, 22 they all fled to the land of the foreigners.†

23 Then Judas went back to plunder the camp, and they took much gold and silver, cloth dyed blue and marine purple, and great treasure. 24 As they returned, they were singing hymns and glorifying Heaven, "who is good, whose mercy endures forever."* 25 Thus Israel experienced a great deliverance that day.

**Victory over Lysias.** 26* But those of the foreigners who had escaped went and told Lysias all that had occurred. 27 When he heard it he was disturbed and discouraged, because things had not turned out in Israel as he intended and as the king had ordered.

28 So the following year he gathered together sixty thousand picked men and five thousand cavalry, to fight them. 29 They came into Idumea and camped at Beth-zur,† and Judas met them with ten thousand men. 30 Seeing that the army was strong, he prayed thus:

"Blessed are you, Savior of Israel, who crushed the attack of the mighty one by the hand of your servant David and delivered the foreign camp into the hand of Jonathan, the son of Saul, and his armor-bearer.* 31 Give this army into the hands of your people Israel; make them ashamed of their troops and their cavalry. 32 Strike them with cowardice, weaken the boldness of their strength, and let them tremble at their own destruction. 33 Strike them down by the sword of those who love you, that all who know your name may sing your praise."

34 Then they engaged in battle, and about five thousand of Lysias' army fell in hand-to-hand fighting. 35† When Lysias saw the tide of the battle turning, and the increased boldness of Judas, whose men were ready either to live or to die nobly, he withdrew to Antioch and

began to recruit mercenaries so as to return to Judea with greater numbers.*

**Purification and Rededication of the Temple.** 36* Then Judas and his brothers said, "Now that our enemies have been crushed, let us go up to purify the sanctuary† and rededicate it." 37 So the whole army assembled, and went up to Mount Zion. 38 They found the sanctuary desolate, the altar desecrated, the gates burnt, weeds growing in the courts as in a thicket or on some mountain, and the priests' chambers demolished.* 39 Then they tore their garments and made great lamentation; they sprinkled their heads with ashes 40 and prostrated themselves. And when the signal was given with trumpets, they cried out to Heaven.

41 Judas appointed men to attack those in the citadel, while he purified the sanctuary. 42 He chose blameless priests, devoted to the law; 43 these purified the sanctuary and carried away the stones of the defilement to an unclean place. 44 They deliberated what ought to be done with the altar for burnt offerings that had been desecrated.* 45 They decided it best to tear it down, lest it be a lasting shame to them that the Gentiles had defiled it; so they tore down the altar. 46 They stored the stones in a suitable place on the temple mount, until the coming of a prophet who could determine what to do with them.* 47 Then they took uncut stones, according to the law, and built a new altar like the former one.* 48 They also repaired the sanctuary and the interior of the temple and consecrated the courts. 49 They made new sacred vessels and brought the lampstand, the altar of incense, and the table into the temple.* 50 Then they burned incense on the altar and lighted the lamps on the lampstand, and these illuminated the temple. 51 They also put loaves on the table and hung up the curtains. Thus they finished all the work they had undertaken.

52 They rose early on the morning of the twenty-fifth day of the ninth month, that is,

---

4:22 *The land of the foreigners*: i.e., territory controlled by the Syrians. The Greek term used here is the same as that used throughout 1–2 Samuel in Greek for Philistine territory and intends to compare Maccabean victories to those of Saul and David.
4:29 *Beth-zur*: an important frontier city (between Judea and Idumea) in the mountain area, fifteen miles south of Jerusalem.
4:35 According to 2 Mc 11:13–15, peace negotiations followed between Lysias and Judas.
4:36 *The sanctuary*: the whole Temple area with its walls,

courts and outbuildings, to be distinguished from the Temple proper, the oblong edifice with porch, main room and inner shrine.

4:24 Ps 118:1–4, 29; 136.   4:38 Ps 74:2–7.
4:26–35 2 Mc 11:1–15.   4:44 1 Kgs 8:64.
4:30 1 Sm 17:48–58.   4:46 1 Mc 14:41; Dt 18:15.
4:35 1 Mc 6:28–31.   4:47 Ex 20:25.
4:36–61 2 Mc 10:1–8.   4:49 Ex 25:23–39; 30:1–6.

the month of Kislev, in the year one hundred and forty-eight,† ⁵³ and offered sacrifice according to the law on the new altar for burnt offerings that they had made.* ⁵⁴ On the anniversary of the day on which the Gentiles had desecrated it, on that very day it was rededicated with songs, harps, lyres, and cymbals. ⁵⁵ All the people prostrated themselves and adored and praised Heaven, who had given them success.

⁵⁶ For eight days they celebrated the dedication of the altar and joyfully offered burnt offerings and sacrifices of deliverance and praise. ⁵⁷ They ornamented the facade of the temple with gold crowns and shields; they repaired the gates and the priests' chambers and furnished them with doors. ⁵⁸ There was great joy among the people now that the disgrace brought by the Gentiles was removed. ⁵⁹ Then Judas and his brothers and the entire assembly of Israel decreed that every year for eight days, from the twenty-fifth day of the month Kislev,* the days of the dedication† of the altar should be observed with joy and gladness on the anniversary.

⁶⁰ At that time they built high walls and strong towers around Mount Zion, to prevent the Gentiles from coming and trampling it as they had done before. ⁶¹ Judas also placed a garrison there to protect it, and likewise fortified Beth-zur, that the people might have a stronghold facing Idumea.

# 5 Victories over Hostile Neighbors.†
¹* When the nations round about heard that the altar had been rebuilt and the sanctuary restored as before, they were enraged. ² So they decided to destroy the descendants of Jacob who were among them, and they began to kill and eradicate the people. ³* Then Judas attacked the Edomites† at Akrabattene in Idumea, because they were blockading Israel;

he dealt them a heavy blow, humbled and despoiled them. ⁴ He also remembered the malice of the Baeanites,† who had become a snare and a stumbling block to the people by ambushing them along the roads. ⁵ He forced them to take refuge in towers, which he besieged; he put them under the ban and burned down their towers along with all who were in them. ⁶†* Then he crossed over to the Ammonites, where he found a strong army and a large body of people with Timothy as their leader. ⁷ He fought many battles with them, routed them, and struck them down. ⁸ After seizing Jazer and its villages, he returned to Judea.

**Liberation of Jews in Galilee and Gilead.** ⁹ The Gentiles in Gilead assembled to destroy the Israelites who were in their territory; these then fled to the stronghold of Dathema.† ¹⁰ They sent a letter to Judas and his brothers saying: "The Gentiles around us have assembled against us to destroy us, ¹¹ and they are preparing to come and seize this stronghold to which we have fled. Timothy is the leader of their army. ¹² Come at once to rescue us from them, for many of us have fallen. ¹³ All our kindred who were in the territory of the Tobiads† have been killed; the Gentiles have captured their wives, their children and their goods, and they have slain there about a thousand men."*

¹⁴ While they were reading this letter, suddenly other messengers, with garments torn, arrived from Galilee to deliver a similar message: ¹⁵ that "the inhabitants of Ptolemais,† Tyre, and Sidon, and the whole of Gentile Galilee have joined forces to destroy us." ¹⁶ When Judas and the people heard this, a great assembly convened to consider what they should do for their kindred who were in distress and being attacked by enemies.

¹⁷ Judas said to his brother Simon: "Choose

---

**4:52** *Twenty-fifth day of the ninth month...in the year one hundred and forty-eight*: December 14, 164 B.C.
**4:59** *Days of the dedication*: institution of the feast of Hanukkah, also called the feast of Dedication (Jn 10:22). Josephus calls it the feast of Lights (*Ant.* 12:325).
**5:1** The events of this chapter occurred within the year 163 B.C.
**5:3** *Edomites*: lit., "sons of Esau"; here a pejorative term for the Idumeans. Cf. also 5:65. *Akrabattene*: either a district southwest of the Dead Sea or on the eastern border of Judea and Samaria.
**5:4** *Baeanites*: 2 Mc 10:15–23 calls them simply Idumeans.
**5:6–8** This summary anticipates the order of events and would fit better between vv. 36 and 37. It corresponds to 2 Mc 12:17–23. The action was probably a reprisal for the massacre

referred to in 1 Mc 5:13. Timothy may have been a local ruler, or the Seleucid governor of Transjordan. *Jazer*: a town on the road from the Jordan to Amman.
**5:9** *Dathema*: the exact location is uncertain; it was east of the Jordan (in Gilead) and a night's journey from Bozrah (v. 29).
**5:13** *Tobiads*: a prominent Jewish family that settled east of the Jordan.
**5:15** *Ptolemais*: Hebrew *Acco* (Jgs 1:31), modern Acre, on the coast north of Haifa.

---

| | |
|---|---|
| **4:53** Ex 30:10; Ez 43:18–27. | **5:3–5** 2 Mc 10:15–23. |
| **4:59** Jn 10:22. | **5:6–7** 2 Mc 8:30–33. |
| **5:1–2** 1 Mc 13:6. | **5:13** 2 Mc 12:17. |

men for yourself, and go, rescue your kindred in Galilee; my brother Jonathan and I will go to Gilead."

[18] He left Joseph, son of Zechariah, and Azariah, leader of the people, with the rest of the army in Judea to guard it. [19] He commanded them, "Take charge of these people, but do not join battle against the Gentiles until we return." [20] Three thousand men were allotted to Simon to go into Galilee, and eight thousand men to Judas, for Gilead.

[21] Simon went into Galilee and fought many battles with the Gentiles. They were crushed before him, [22] and he pursued them to the very gate of Ptolemais. About three thousand of the Gentiles fell, and he gathered their spoils. [23] He took with him the Jews who were in Galilee and in Arbatta,† with their wives and children and all that they had, and brought them to Judea with great rejoicing.

[24]* Judas Maccabeus and his brother Jonathan crossed the Jordan and marched for three days through the wilderness. [25] There they met some Nabateans,† who received them peaceably and told them all that had happened to their kindred in Gilead: [26] "Many of them are shut up in Bozrah, in Bosor near Alema, in Chaspho, Maked, and Carnaim"—all of these are large, fortified cities— [27] "and some are shut up in other cities of Gilead. Tomorrow their enemies plan to attack the strongholds and to seize and destroy all these people in one day."

[28] Thereupon Judas suddenly changed direction with his army, marched across the wilderness to Bozrah, and captured the city. He put every male to the sword, took all their spoils, and set fire to the city. [29]† He led his army from that place by night, and they marched toward the stronghold. [30] When morning came, they looked ahead and saw a countless multitude, with ladders and machines for capturing the stronghold, beginning to attack. [31] When Judas perceived that the struggle had begun and that the noise of the battle was resounding to heaven with trumpet blasts and loud shouting, [32] he said to the men of his army, "Fight

for our kindred today." [33] He came up behind them with three columns blowing their trumpets and crying out in prayer. [34] When the army of Timothy realized that it was Maccabeus, they fled before him, and he inflicted on them a great defeat. About eight thousand of their men fell that day.

[35] Then he turned toward Alema† and attacked and captured it; he killed every male, took spoils, and burned it down. [36] From there he moved on and took Chaspho, Maked, Bosor, and the other cities of Gilead.

[37]* After these events Timothy assembled another army and camped opposite Raphon, on the other side of the wadi. [38] Judas sent men to spy on the camp, and they reported to him: "All the Gentiles around us have rallied to him, making a very large force; [39] they have also hired Arabians to help them, and have camped beyond the wadi, ready to attack you." So Judas went forward to meet them.

[40] As Judas and his army were approaching the flowing wadi, Timothy said to the officers of his army: "If he crosses over to us first, we shall not be able to resist him; he will certainly defeat us.* [41] But if he is hesitant and camps on the other side of the river, we will cross over to him and defeat him." [42] But when Judas reached the flowing wadi, he stationed the officers of the people beside it and gave them this order: "Do not allow anyone to encamp; all must go into battle." [43] He was the first to cross to the attack, with all the people behind him, and all the Gentiles were crushed before them. They threw away their arms and fled to the temple enclosure at Carnaim. [44] But Judas' troops captured the city and burnt the temple enclosure with all who were in it. So Carnaim was subdued, and Judas met with no more resistance.

**Return to Jerusalem.** [45]* Then Judas assembled all the Israelites, great and small, who were in Gilead, with their wives and children and their goods, a very large company, to go into the land of Judah. [46] When they reached Ephron,† a large and strongly fortified city along the

5:23 *Arbatta*: (or, Narbatta), probably south of Mount Carmel.
5:25 *Nabateans*: an Arab people who acquired wealth and power as caravan merchants in the final two centuries B.C. They established Petra as their capital and for a time controlled all of Transjordan, even as far as Damascus. It was from a Nabatean governor of Damascus that Paul escaped (2 Cor 11:32–33).
5:29 Cf. v. 9.
5:35 *Alema*: see v. 26; other manuscripts read Maapha,

which may be Mizpah of Gilead (Jgs 11:29).
5:46 *Ephron*: a city in Transjordan opposite Beth-shan (v. 52), about nine miles east of the Jordan River. Situated on a height, it dominated the valleys of the two tributaries of the Jordan.

5:24–36 2 Mc 12:10–16.
5:37–44 2 Mc 12:17–25.
5:40 1 Sm 14:9–10.
5:45–54 2 Mc 12:26–31.

way, they found it impossible to go around it on either the right or the left; they would have to march right through it.* ⁴⁷But the people in the city shut them out and blocked up the gates with stones. ⁴⁸Then Judas sent them this peaceful message: "Let us cross your territory in order to reach our own; no one will harm you; we will only march through." But they would not open to him. ⁴⁹So Judas ordered a proclamation to be made in the camp that everyone should take up positions where they were. ⁵⁰When the men of the army took up their positions, he assaulted the city all that day and night, and it was delivered into his hand. ⁵¹He put every male to the sword, leveled the city, took spoils and passed through it over the slain.

⁵²Then they crossed the Jordan to the great plain in front of Beth-shan; ⁵³and Judas kept gathering the stragglers and encouraging the people the whole way, until he reached the land of Judah. ⁵⁴They ascended Mount Zion in joy and gladness and sacrificed burnt offerings, because not one of them had fallen; they had returned in safety.

**Joseph and Azariah Defeated.** ⁵⁵In those days when Judas and Jonathan were in the land of Gilead, and Simon his brother was in Galilee opposite Ptolemais, ⁵⁶Joseph, son of Zechariah, and Azariah, the leaders of the army, heard about the brave deeds and the fighting that they were doing. ⁵⁷They said, "Let us also make a name for ourselves by going out and fighting against the Gentiles around us." ⁵⁸They gave orders to those of their army who were with them, and marched against Jamnia.† ⁵⁹But Gorgias and his men came out of the city to meet them in battle. ⁶⁰Joseph and Azariah were routed and were pursued to the frontiers of Judea, and about two thousand Israelites fell that day. ⁶¹It was a great setback for the people, because they had not obeyed Judas and his brothers, thinking that they would do brave deeds. ⁶²But they were not of the family through whom Israel's deliverance was given.

**Victories at Hebron and Azotus.** ⁶³The valiant Judas and his brothers were greatly honored in all Israel and among all the Gentiles, wherever their name was heard; ⁶⁴and people gathered about them and praised them.

⁶⁵*Then Judas and his brothers went out and attacked the Edomites in the land toward the south; he took Hebron and its villages, and he destroyed its strongholds and burned the towers around it. ⁶⁶He then set out for the land of the foreigners and passed through Marisa. ⁶⁷On that day some priests fell in battle who had gone out rashly to fight in their desire to do brave deeds. ⁶⁸Judas then turned toward Azotus in the land of the foreigners. He destroyed their altars and burned the carved images of their gods; and after plundering their cities he returned to the land of Judah.

**6** ¹*As King Antiochus passed through the eastern provinces, he heard that in Persia there was a city, Elam,† famous for its wealth in silver and gold, ²and that its temple was very rich, containing gold helmets, breastplates, and weapons left there by the first king of the Greeks, Alexander, son of Philip, king of Macedon. ³He went therefore and tried to capture and loot the city. But he could not do so, because his plan became known to the people of the city ⁴who rose up in battle against him. So he fled and in great dismay withdrew from there to return to Babylon.

⁵While he was in Persia, a messenger brought him news that the armies that had gone into the land of Judah had been routed; ⁶that Lysias had gone at first with a strong army and been driven back; that the people of Judah had grown strong by reason of the arms, wealth, and abundant spoils taken from the armies they had cut down; ⁷that they had pulled down the abomination which he had built upon the altar in Jerusalem; and that they had surrounded with high walls both the sanctuary, as it had been before, and his city of Beth-zur.*

⁸When the king heard this news, he was astonished and very much shaken. Sick with grief because his designs had failed, he took to his bed. ⁹There he remained many days, assailed by waves of grief, for he thought he was

---

† **5:58** *Jamnia*: Yavneh (see 10:69), the capital of the province of Azotus (Ashdod).
**6:1** *Elam*: in fact, the mountainous region north of the Persian Gulf, rather than a city. The city may have been Persepolis. This section continues the story from 3:37 and pertains to events preceding those in 4:37–39.

* **5:46** Nm 20:17–21; 21:21–25.　**5:65–68** 2 Mc 12:36–46.　**6:1–13** 2 Mc 1:13–17; 9:1–29; Dn 11:40–45.　**6:7** 1 Mc 1:54; 4:41–61.

going to die. [10] So he called in all his Friends and said to them: "Sleep has departed from my eyes, and my heart sinks from anxiety. [11] I said to myself: 'Into what tribulation have I come, and in what floods of sorrow am I now! Yet I was kindly and beloved in my rule.' [12] But I now recall the evils I did in Jerusalem, when I carried away all the vessels of silver and gold that were in it, and for no cause gave orders that the inhabitants of Judah be destroyed. [13] I know that this is why these evils have overtaken me; and now I am dying, in bitter grief, in a foreign land."

[14] Then he summoned Philip, one of his Friends, and put him in charge of his whole kingdom. [15] He gave him his diadem, his robe, and his signet ring, so that he might guide the king's son Antiochus and bring him up to be king. [16] So King Antiochus died there in the one hundred and forty-ninth year. † [17] When Lysias learned that the king was dead, he set up the king's son Antiochus, † whom he had reared as a child, to be king in his place; and he gave him the title Eupator. *

**Siege of the Citadel.** [18] Those in the citadel were hemming Israel in around the sanctuary, continually trying to harm them and to strengthen the Gentiles. * [19] And so Judas planned to destroy them, and assembled the people to besiege them. [20] So in the one hundred and fiftieth year† they assembled and besieged the citadel, for which purpose he constructed platforms and siege engines. [21] But some of the besieged escaped, and some renegade Israelites joined them. [22] They went to the king and said: "How long will you fail to do justice and to avenge our kindred? [23] We agreed to serve your father and to follow his orders and obey his edicts. [24] And for this our own people have become our enemies; they have put to death as many of us as they could find and have seized our inheritances. [25] They have acted aggressively not only against us, but throughout their whole territory. [26] Look! Today they have besieged the citadel in Jerusalem

in order to capture it, and they have fortified the sanctuary and Beth-zur. [27] Unless you act quickly to prevent them, they will do even worse things than these, and you will not be able to stop them."

[28] * When the king heard this he was enraged, and he called together all his Friends, the officers of his army, and the commanders of the cavalry. [29] Mercenary forces also came to him from other kingdoms and from the islands of the seas. [30] His army numbered a hundred thousand footsoldiers, twenty thousand cavalry, and thirty-two elephants trained for war. [31] They passed through Idumea and camped before Beth-zur. For many days they attacked it; they constructed siege engines, but the besieged made a sortie and burned these, and they fought bravely.

**Battle of Beth-zechariah.** [32] Then Judas marched away from the citadel and moved his camp to Beth-zechariah, † opposite the king's camp. [33] The king, rising before dawn, moved his force hastily along the road to Beth-zechariah; and the troops prepared for battle and sounded the trumpet. [34] They made the elephants drunk on the juice of grapes and mulberries to get them ready to fight. [35] The beasts were distributed along the phalanxes, each elephant having assigned to it a thousand men in coats of mail, with bronze helmets on their heads, and five hundred picked cavalry. [36] These accompanied the beast wherever it was; wherever it moved, they moved too and never left it. [37] Each elephant was outfitted with a strong wooden tower, fastened to it by a harness; each tower held three soldiers who fought from it, besides the Indian driver. [38] The remaining cavalry were stationed on one or the other of the two flanks of the army, to harass the enemy and to be protected by the phalanxes. [39] When the sun shone on the gold and bronze shields, the mountains gleamed with their brightness and blazed like flaming torches. [40] Part of the king's army spread out along the heights, while some were on low

---

† **6:16** *The one hundred and forty-ninth year*: September 22, 164, to October 9, 163 B.C. A Babylonian list of the Seleucid kings indicates that Antiochus died in November or early December of 164, about the same time as the rededication of the Temple.
**6:17** *The king's son Antiochus*: Antiochus V Eupator ("of a good father"), then about nine years old. He was in Antioch, still in the charge of Lysias, who proceeded to govern and wage wars in his name. Both were put to death two years later, when Demetrius, brother of Antiochus IV, arrived to claim the kingship; cf. 7:1–3.
**6:20** *The one hundred and fiftieth year*: October, 163, to September, 162 B.C.
**6:32** *Beth-zechariah*: south of Jerusalem, and six miles north of Beth-zur.

**6:17** 2 Mc 10:10–11.   **6:28–54** 2 Mc 13:1–26.
**6:18** 1 Mc 1:33–36.

ground, and they marched forward steadily in good order. [41] All who heard the noise of their numbers, the tramp of their marching, and the clanging of the arms, trembled; for the army was very great and strong.

[42] Judas with his army advanced to fight, and six hundred men of the king's army fell. [43] Eleazar, called Avaran, saw one of the beasts covered with royal armor and bigger than any of the others, and so he thought the king was on it.* [44] He gave up his life to save his people and win an everlasting name for himself. [45] He dashed courageously up to it in the middle of the phalanx, killing men right and left, so that they parted before him. [46] He ran under the elephant, stabbed it and killed it. The beast fell to the ground on top of him, and he died there. [47] But when Judas' troops saw the strength of the royal army and the ardor of its forces, they retreated from them.

**The Siege of Jerusalem.** [48] Some of the king's army went up to Jerusalem to attack them, and the king established camps in Judea and at Mount Zion. [49] He made peace with the people of Beth-zur, and they evacuated the city, because they had no food there to enable them to withstand a siege, for that was a sabbath year in the land.†* [50] The king took Beth-zur and stationed a garrison there to hold it. [51] For many days he besieged the sanctuary, setting up platforms and siege engines, fire-throwers, catapults and mechanical bows for shooting arrows and projectiles. [52] The defenders countered by setting up siege engines of their own, and kept up the fight a long time. [53] But there were no provisions in the storerooms, because it was the seventh year, and the reserves had been eaten up by those who had been rescued from the Gentiles and brought to Judea. [54] Few men remained in the sanctuary because the famine was too much for them; the rest scattered, each to his own home.

**Peace Treaty.** [55]* Lysias heard that Philip, whom King Antiochus, before his death, had appointed to train his son Antiochus to be king, [56] had returned from Persia and Media with the army that accompanied the king, and that he was seeking to take over the government. [57] So he hastily decided to withdraw. He said to the king, the leaders of the army, and the soldiers: "We are growing weaker every day, our provisions are scanty, the place we are besieging is strong, and it is our duty to take care of the affairs of the kingdom.* [58] Therefore let us now come to terms with these people and make peace with them and all their nation. [59] Let us grant them freedom to live according to their own laws as formerly; it was on account of their laws, which we abolished, that they became enraged and did all these things."

[60] The proposal pleased the king and the leaders; he sent peace terms to the Jews, and they accepted. [61] So the king and the leaders swore an oath to them, and on these terms the Jews evacuated the fortification. [62] But when the king entered Mount Zion and saw how the place was fortified, he broke the oath he had sworn and gave orders to tear down the encircling wall. [63] Then he departed in haste and returned to Antioch, where he found Philip in control of the city. He fought against him and took the city by force.

# 7 Expedition of Bacchides and Alcimus.
[1]* In the one hundred and fifty-first year,† Demetrius, son of Seleucus, set out from Rome, arrived with a few men at a coastal city, and began to rule there. [2] As he was entering the royal palace of his ancestors, the soldiers seized Antiochus and Lysias to bring them to him. [3] When he was informed of this, he said, "Do not show me their faces." [4] So the soldiers killed them, and Demetrius assumed the royal throne.

[5] Then all the lawless men and renegades of Israel came to him. They were led by Alcimus,† who desired to be high priest. [6] They made this accusation to the king against the

---

**6:49** *A sabbath year in the land*: when sowing and reaping were prohibited (Ex 23:10–11; Lv 25:2–7). The year without a harvest (autumn of 164 to autumn of 163) was followed by a food shortage.
**7:1–3** *The one hundred and fifty-first year*: the spring of 161 B.C. Demetrius, son of Seleucus, was the lawful heir to the kingdom; but when only nine years old, he was taken as a hostage to Rome in place of his uncle, who ruled as Antiochus IV Epiphanes. At the age of twenty-five Demetrius fled secretly from Rome and, with the support of the Syrians, overcame his rival

Antiochus V and put him to death. *The royal palace*: at Antioch.
**7:5–6** *Alcimus*: a Jew hostile to the Maccabees, who became high priest after the death of Menelaus (2 Mc 14:3). He received confirmation in his office from the new king Demetrius (1 Mc 7:9), and brought malicious charges against Judas and his brothers and the people (1 Mc 7:6).

---

| | |
|---|---|
| **6:43** 2 Mc 13:15. | **6:57** 2 Mc 11:13–15. |
| **6:49** Lv 25:1–7. | **7:1–7** 2 Mc 14:1–11. |
| **6:55–63** 2 Mc 13:23–26. | |

people: "Judas and his brothers have destroyed all your friends and have driven us out of our land. [7] So now, send a man whom you trust to go and see all the destruction Judas has wrought on us and on the king's territory, and let him punish them and all their supporters."

[8] So the king chose Bacchides, one of the King's Friends, who ruled the province of West-of-Euphrates, a great man in the kingdom, and faithful to the king. [9] He sent him and the renegade Alcimus, to whom he granted the high priesthood, with orders to take revenge on the Israelites. [10] They set out and, on arriving in the land of Judah with a great army, sent messengers who spoke deceitfully to Judas and his brothers in peaceful terms. [11] But these paid no attention to their words, seeing that they had come with a great army.

[12] A group of scribes, however, gathered about Alcimus and Bacchides to ask for a just agreement. [13]* The Hasideans were the first among the Israelites to seek peace with them, [14] for they said, "A priest of the line of Aaron has come with the army, and he will not do us any wrong." [15] He spoke with them peacefully and swore to them, "We will not seek to injure you or your friends." [16] So they trusted him. But he arrested sixty of them and killed them in one day, according to the words that he wrote:†

[17]   "The flesh of your faithful,
         and their blood they have spilled all
            around about Jerusalem,
         and no one was left to bury them."*

[18] Then fear and dread of them came upon all the people, who said: "There is no truth or justice among them; they violated the agreement and the oath that they swore."

[19] Bacchides withdrew from Jerusalem and camped in Beth-zaith.† He had many of the men who deserted to him arrested and some of the people. He killed them and threw them into a great cistern. [20] He handed the province over to Alcimus, leaving troops to

help him, while he himself returned to the king.

[21] Alcimus struggled to maintain his high priesthood, [22] and all those who were troubling the people gathered about him. They took possession of the land of Judah and caused great distress in Israel. [23] When Judas saw all the evils that Alcimus and those with him were bringing upon the Israelites, even more than the Gentiles had, [24] he went about all the borders of Judea and took revenge on the men who had deserted, preventing them from going out into the country. [25] But when Alcimus saw that Judas and his followers were gaining strength and realized that he could not resist them, he returned to the king and accused them of grave crimes.

**Defeat of Nicanor.** [26]* Then the king sent Nicanor, one of his honored officers, who was a bitter enemy of Israel, with orders to destroy the people. [27] Nicanor came to Jerusalem with a large force and deceitfully sent to Judas† and his brothers this peaceable message: [28] "Let there be no fight between me and you. I will come with a few men to meet you face to face in peace."

[29] So he came to Judas, and they greeted one another peaceably. But Judas' enemies were prepared to seize him. [30] When he became aware that Nicanor had come to him with deceit in mind, Judas was afraid of him and would not meet him again.* [31] When Nicanor saw that his plan had been discovered, he went out to fight Judas near Capharsalama.† [32] About five hundred men of Nicanor's army fell; the rest fled to the City of David.†

[33]* After this, Nicanor went up to Mount Zion. Some of the priests from the sanctuary and some of the elders of the people came out to greet him peaceably and to show him the burnt offering that was being sacrificed for the king. [34] But he mocked and ridiculed them, defiled them,† and spoke arrogantly. [35] In a rage he swore: "If Judas and his army are not delivered to me at once, when I return victorious I

---

† **7:16** *The words that he wrote*: based on Ps 79:2–3. But who is "he"—David, Alcimus, Judas, or someone else?
**7:19** *Beth-zaith*: about three miles north of Beth-zur and twelve miles south of Jerusalem.
**7:27** *Nicanor...deceitfully sent to Judas*: a more favorable picture of Nicanor, as an honest man who became a personal friend of Judas, is given in 2 Mc 14:17–25. Their friendship was broken by the intrigues of Alcimus (2 Mc 14:26–30).
**7:31** *Capharsalama*: a village north of Jerusalem whose pre-

cise location is disputed.
**7:32** *City of David*: the citadel occupied by the Seleucid garrison in Jerusalem.
**7:34** *Defiled them*: spitting on the priests caused them to become legally defiled.

| | |
|---|---|
| **7:13–14** 1 Mc 2:42. | 2 Mc 8:9; 14:12–13. |
| **7:17** Ps 79:2–3. | **7:30** 2 Mc 14:30. |
| **7:26–27** 1 Mc 3:38; | **7:33–38** 2 Mc 14:31–36. |

1 MC

will burn this temple down." He went away in great anger. 36 * The priests, however, went in and stood before the altar and the sanctuary. They wept and said: 37 "You have chosen this house to bear your name, to be a house of prayer and supplication for your people. 38 Take revenge on this man and his army, and let them fall by the sword. Remember their blasphemies, and do not let them continue."

39 Nicanor left Jerusalem and camped at Beth-horon, where the Syrian army joined him. 40 But Judas camped in Adasa † with three thousand men. Here Judas uttered this prayer: 41 * "When they who were sent by the king † blasphemed, your angel went out and killed a hundred and eighty-five thousand of them. * 42 In the same way, crush this army before us today, and let the rest know that Nicanor spoke wickedly against your sanctuary; judge him according to his wickedness."

43 The armies met in battle on the thirteenth day of the month Adar. Nicanor's army was crushed, and he himself was the first to fall in the battle. * 44 When his army saw that Nicanor had fallen, they threw down their weapons and fled. 45 The Jews pursued them a day's journey from Adasa to near Gazara, blowing the trumpets behind them as signals. 46 From all the surrounding villages of Judea people came out and outflanked them. They turned them back, and all the enemies fell by the sword; not a single one escaped.

47 Then the Jews collected the spoils and the plunder; they cut off Nicanor's head and

his right arm, which he had lifted up so arrogantly. These they brought and displayed in the sight of Jerusalem. 48 The people rejoiced greatly, and observed that day as a day of much joy. 49 They decreed that it should be observed every year on the thirteenth of Adar. † 50 And so for a few days † the land of Judah was at rest.

# 8 Eulogy of the Romans. 1 † Judas had heard of the reputation of the Romans. They were valiant fighters and acted amiably to all who took their side. They established a friendly alliance with all who applied to them. 2 He was also told of their battles and the brave deeds that they performed against the Gauls, † conquering them and forcing them to pay tribute; 3 and what they did in Spain to get possession of the silver and gold mines there. 4 By planning and persistence they subjugated the whole region, although it was very remote from their own. They also subjugated the kings who had come against them from the far corners of the earth until they crushed them and inflicted on them severe defeat. The rest paid tribute to them every year. 5 Philip † and Perseus, king of the Macedonians, and the others who opposed them in battle they overwhelmed and subjugated. 6 Antiochus † the Great, king of Asia, who fought against them with a hundred and twenty elephants and with cavalry and chariots and a very great army, was defeated by them. 7 They took him alive and obliged him and the kings who succeeded him to pay a heavy tribute, to give

---

† **7:40** *Adasa*: a village between Jerusalem and Beth-horon.

**7:41** *They who were sent by the king*: 2 Kgs 18:19–25, 29–35; 19:10–13 recount in detail the boastful threats made by Sennacherib, the Assyrian king, through his emissaries. *Your angel*: a reference to 2 Kgs 19:35, which describes the fate of the Assyrian army which besieged Jerusalem in the days of Hezekiah, king of Judah.

**7:49** *The thirteenth of Adar*: March 27, 160 B.C. This day in the Jewish calendar was called the "Day of Nicanor" (2 Mc 15:36), but it was not long celebrated by the Jews.

**7:50** *For a few days*: about one month following the death of Nicanor. After that began the attack of Bacchides resulting in the death of Judas (9:1–18).

**8:1** This chapter contains the account of the embassy which Judas sent to Rome, probably before the death of Nicanor, to conclude a treaty of alliance between Rome and the Jewish nation. Without precise chronology, the pertinent data are gathered into a unified theme.

The image of the Roman Republic greatly impressed the smaller Eastern peoples seeking support against their overlords (vv. 1–16), because of Roman success in war (vv. 2–11) and effective aid to their allies (vv. 12–13). Numerous interventions by Rome in the politics of the Near East bear witness to its power and prestige in the second century B.C. See 1:10; 7:2; 12:3; 15:15–24; 2 Mc 11:34. With the increased Roman control of

Palestine after 63 B.C., the Republic and later the Empire became heartily detested. The eulogy of Rome in this chapter is one of the reasons why 1 Maccabees was not preserved by the Palestinian Jews of the century that followed.

**8:2** *Gauls*: probably the Celts of northern Italy and southern France, subdued by the Romans in 222 B.C., and again in 200–191 B.C.; but also those in Asia Minor (the Galatians), whom the Romans defeated in 189 B.C.

**8:5** *Philip*: Philip V of Macedonia, defeated by a Graeco-Roman alliance at Cynoscephalae in 197 B.C. Perseus, his son, was defeated at Pydna in 168 B.C., and died a prisoner. With this, the kingdom of Macedonia came to an end.

**8:6** *Antiochus*: Antiochus III, greatest of the Seleucid kings. He was defeated at Magnesia in 190 B.C. By the Treaty of Apamea in 189 B.C., he was obliged to pay Rome a crushing indemnity of 15,000 talents. The weakening of Antiochene power and the growing military and economic influence of Rome may have led Antiochus IV to adopt the policy of political, religious, and cultural unification of Syria and Palestine.

---

*    **7:36–38** 1 Kgs 8:29–30,      **7:41** 2 Kgs 19:35–36; Is
33–34, 43.             37:36–37.
**7:41–42** 2 Mc 8:19; 15:22–24.    **7:43** 2 Mc 15:25–36.

1
M
C

hostages and to cede [8] Lycia, Mysia, and Lydia †
from among their best provinces. The Romans
took these from him and gave them to King
Eumenes. [9] † When the Greeks planned to
come and destroy them, [10] the Romans discovered it, and sent against the Greeks a single
general who made war on them. Many were
wounded and fell, and the Romans took their
wives and children captive. They plundered
them, took possession of their land, tore down
their strongholds and reduced them to slavery even to this day. [11] All the other kingdoms
and islands that had ever opposed them they
destroyed and enslaved; with their friends,
however, and those who relied on them, they
maintained friendship. [12] They subjugated
kings both near and far, and all who heard of
their fame were afraid of them. [13] Those whom
they wish to help and to make kings, they
make kings; and those whom they wish, they
depose; and they were greatly exalted. [14] Yet
with all this, none of them put on a diadem
or wore purple as a display of grandeur. [15] But
they made for themselves a senate chamber,
and every day three hundred and twenty men
took counsel, deliberating on all that concerned the people and their well-being. [16] They
entrust their government to one man † every
year, to rule over their entire land, and they all
obey that one, and there is no envy or jealousy
among them.

**Treaty with the Romans.** [17] So Judas chose
Eupolemus, son of John, son of Accos, and Jason, son of Eleazar, and sent them to Rome to
establish friendship and alliance with them. *
[18] He did this to lift the yoke from Israel, for it
was obvious that the kingdom of the Greeks
was subjecting them to slavery. [19] After making a very long journey to Rome, the envoys
entered the senate chamber and spoke as
follows: [20] "Judas, called Maccabeus, and his
brothers, with the Jewish people, have sent
us to you to establish alliance and peace with

you, and to be enrolled among your allies and
friends." [21] The proposal pleased the Romans,
[22] and this is a copy of the reply they inscribed
on bronze tablets and sent to Jerusalem, † to
remain there with the Jews as a record of peace
and alliance: *

[23] "May it be well with the Romans and the
Jewish nation at sea and on land forever; may
sword and enemy be far from them. [24] But if
war is first made on Rome, or any of its allies
in any of their dominions, [25] the Jewish nation
will fight along with them wholeheartedly,
as the occasion shall demand; [26] and to those
who wage war they shall not give or provide
grain, weapons, money, or ships, as seems
best to Rome. They shall fulfill their obligations without receiving any recompense. [27] In
the same way, if war is made first on the Jewish nation, the Romans will fight along with
them willingly, as the occasion shall demand,
[28] and to those who attack them there shall not
be given grain, weapons, money, or ships, as
seems best to Rome. They shall fulfill their obligations without deception. [29] On these terms
the Romans have made an agreement with the
Jewish people. [30] But if both parties hereafter
agree to add or take away anything, they shall
do as they choose, and whatever they shall add
or take away shall be valid.

[31] "Moreover, concerning the wrongs that
King Demetrius is doing to them, we have
written to him thus: 'Why have you made your
yoke heavy upon our friends and allies the
Jews? [32] If they petition against you again, we
will enforce justice and make war on you by
sea and land.'"

**9** **Death of Judas.** [1] When Demetrius heard
that Nicanor and his army had fallen in
battle, he again sent Bacchides and Alcimus
into the land of Judah, along with the right
wing of his army. [2] They took the road to
Galilee, and camping opposite the ascent at
Arbela, they captured it † and killed many

---

† **8:8** *Lycia, Mysia, and Lydia*: regions in western Asia Minor.
"Lycia" and "Mysia" are restored here by conjectural emendation; the Greek text has "India, Media," most likely through scribal error. *Eumenes*: Eumenes II (197–158 B.C.), king of Pergamum,
an ally of Rome who benefited greatly from Antiochus' losses.
  **8:9–10** The revolt of the Achaean League, inserted here,
occurred in 146 B.C., after Judas' time. It was crushed by the
Roman consul Lucius Mummius and marked the end of Greek
independence.
  **8:16** *They entrust their government to one man*: actually the
Roman Republic had two consuls chosen yearly as joint heads
of the government.

**8:22** *The reply…on bronze tablets and sent to Jerusalem*: the
decree of the Senate would be inscribed on bronze and kept
in the Roman Capitol, with only a copy in letter form sent to
Jerusalem.
  **9:2** *They took the road…Arbela, they captured it*: this passage is restored, in part, by conjectural emendation. The present
Greek text could be translated, "They took the road to Gilgal,
and camping opposite Mesaloth at Arbela, they captured it."
But Arbela (modern Khirbet Irbid) was in Galilee, on a high hill

---

* **8:17** 1 Mc 12:1–4;        **8:22** 1 Mc 14:17–18.
  15:15–22.

people. ³ In the first month of the one hundred and fifty-second year,† they encamped against Jerusalem. ⁴ Then they set out for Berea with twenty thousand men and two thousand cavalry. ⁵ Judas, with three thousand picked men, had camped at Elasa. ⁶ When they saw the great number of the troops, they were very much afraid, and many slipped away from the camp, until only eight hundred of them remained.

⁷ When Judas saw that his army was melting away just as the battle was imminent, he was brokenhearted, because he had no time to gather them together. ⁸ In spite of his discouragement he said to those who remained: "Let us go forward to meet our enemies; perhaps we can put up a good fight against them." ⁹ They tried to dissuade him, saying: "We certainly cannot. Let us save our own lives now, and come back with our kindred, and then fight against them. Now we are too few." ¹⁰ But Judas said: "Far be it from me to do such a thing as to flee from them! If our time has come, let us die bravely for our kindred and not leave a stain upon our honor!"

¹¹ Then the army of Bacchides moved out of camp and took its position for combat. The cavalry were divided into two squadrons, and the slingers and the archers came on ahead of the army, and in the front line were all the best warriors. Bacchides was on the right wing. ¹² Flanked by the two squadrons, the phalanx attacked as they blew their trumpets. Those who were on Judas' side also blew their trumpets. ¹³ The earth shook with the noise of the armies, and the battle raged from morning until evening.

¹⁴ When Judas saw that Bacchides was on the right, with the main force of his army, all the most stouthearted rallied to him, ¹⁵ and the right wing was crushed; Judas pursued them as far as the mountain slopes.† ¹⁶ But when those on the left wing saw that the right wing was crushed, they closed in behind Judas and those with him. ¹⁷ The battle became intense, and many on both sides fell wounded. ¹⁸ Then Judas fell, and the rest fled.

¹⁹ Jonathan and Simon took their brother Judas and buried him in the tomb of their ancestors at Modein. ²⁰ All Israel wept for him with great lamentation. They mourned for him many days, and they said, ²¹ "How the mighty one has fallen, the savior of Israel!"* ²² The other acts of Judas, his battles, the brave deeds he performed, and his greatness have not been recorded; but they were very many.

## III. LEADERSHIP OF JONATHAN

**Jonathan Succeeds Judas.** ²³ After the death of Judas, the lawless raised their heads in every part of Israel, and all kinds of evildoers appeared. ²⁴ In those days there was a very great famine, and the country deserted to them. ²⁵ Bacchides chose renegades and made them masters of the country. ²⁶ These sought out and hunted down the friends of Judas and brought them to Bacchides, who punished and derided them. ²⁷ There was great tribulation in Israel, the like of which had not been since the time prophets ceased to appear among them.

²⁸ Then all the friends of Judas came together and said to Jonathan: ²⁹ "Ever since your brother Judas died, there has been no one like him to lead us against our enemies, both Bacchides and those of our nation who are hostile to us. ³⁰ Now therefore we have chosen you today to be our ruler and leader in his place, to fight our battle." ³¹ From that moment Jonathan accepted the leadership, and took the place of Judas his brother.

**Bacchides Pursues Jonathan.** ³² When Bacchides learned of it, he sought to kill him. ³³ But Jonathan and his brother Simon and all who were with him discovered this, and they fled to the wilderness of Tekoa† and camped by the waters of the pool of Asphar. [³⁴]†

³⁵ Jonathan sent his brother† as leader of the convoy to implore his friends, the Nabateans,

---

† overlooking the western shore of the Sea of Galilee. Gilgal, on the contrary, was in the Jordan valley near Jericho. "Mesaloth" is probably a corrupt form of a Hebrew word meaning "steps, ascent." It is possible, however, that all these terms referred to places in the Judean hills.
**9:3** *The first month of the one hundred and fifty-second year*: April/May 160 B.C., by the Temple calendar.
**9:15** *As far as the mountain slopes*: conjectural emendation. The Greek text has "as far as Mount Azotus"; this is most unlikely. Apparently the Greek translator mistook the Hebrew word *ash-*

dot, "slopes," for *ashdod*, "Azotus."
**9:33** *Tekoa*: home of the prophet Amos in the wild country above the Dead Sea, southeast of Jerusalem.
**9:34** Omitted, it is a dittography of v. 43.
**9:35** *Jonathan sent his brother*: this was John who was called Gaddi (2:2; cf. 9:36, 38).

---

**9:21** 2 Sm 1:19, 25, 27; Jgs 3:9.

to let them deposit with them their great quantity of baggage.* 36 But the tribe of Jambri from Medaba† made a raid and seized and carried off John and everything he had.

37 After this, word was brought to Jonathan and his brother Simon: "The tribe of Jambri are celebrating a great wedding, and with a large escort they are bringing the bride, the daughter of one of the great princes of Canaan, from Nadabath." 38 Remembering the blood of John their brother, they went up and hid themselves under cover of the mountain. 39 As they watched there appeared a noisy throng with much baggage; then the bridegroom and his friends and kinsmen had come out to meet them with tambourines and musicians with their instruments. 40 Jonathan and his party rose up against them from their ambush and killed them. Many fell wounded; the rest fled toward the mountain; all their spoils were taken. 41 Thus the wedding was turned into mourning, and the sound of their music into lamentation. 42 Having taken their revenge for the blood of their brother, they returned to the marshes of the Jordan.

43 When Bacchides heard of it, he came on the sabbath to the banks of the Jordan with a large force. 44 Then Jonathan said to his companions, "Let us rise up now and fight for our lives, for today is not like yesterday and the day before. 45 The battle is before us, behind us are the waters of the Jordan, on either side of us, marsh and thickets; there is no way of escape.† 46 Cry out now to Heaven so that you may be delivered from the hand of our enemies." 47 When they joined battle, Jonathan raised his hand to strike Bacchides, but Bacchides backed away from him. 48 Jonathan and those with him jumped into the Jordan and swam across to the other side, but the enemy did not pursue them across the Jordan. 49 About a thousand men on Bacchides' side fell that day.

50 On returning to Jerusalem, Bacchides built strongholds in Judea: the Jericho fortress, as well as Emmaus, Beth-horon, Bethel, Timnath, Pharathon, and Tephon, with high walls and gates and bars.† 51 In each he put a garrison to harass Israel. 52 He fortified the city of Beth-zur, Gazara and the citadel, and put troops in them and stores of provisions. 53 He took as hostages the sons of the leading people of the country and put them in custody in the citadel at Jerusalem.*

54 In the one hundred and fifty-third year, in the second month,† Alcimus ordered the wall of the inner court of the sanctuary to be torn down, thus destroying the work of the prophets. But he only began to tear it down. 55 Just at that time Alcimus was stricken, and his work was interrupted; his mouth was closed and he was paralyzed, so that he could no longer utter a word or give orders concerning his household. 56 Alcimus died in great agony at that time. 57 Seeing that Alcimus was dead, Bacchides returned to the king, and the land of Judah was at rest for two years.

58 Then all the lawless took counsel and said: "Jonathan and those with him are living in peace and security. Now then, let us have Bacchides return, and he will capture all of them in a single night." 59 So they went and took counsel with him. 60 When Bacchides was setting out with a large force, he sent letters secretly to all his allies in Judea, telling them to seize Jonathan and his companions. They were not able to do this, however, because their plan became known. 61 In fact, Jonathan's men seized about fifty of the men of the country who were leaders in the conspiracy and put them to death.

62 Then Jonathan and those with him, along with Simon, withdrew to Bethbasi† in the wilderness; he rebuilt its ruins and fortified it. 63 When Bacchides learned of this, he gathered together his whole force and sent word to those who were in Judea. 64 He came and camped before Bethbasi, and constructing siege engines, he fought against it for many days.

65 Leaving his brother Simon in the city, Jonathan, accompanied by a small group of men, went out into the countryside. 66 He struck down Odomera and his kindred and the tribe

---

† 9:36 *Medaba*: northeast of the Dead Sea.
  9:45 Jonathan's force may have been trapped in one of the many oxbows of the lower Jordan. Bacchides had crossed and caught them still on the east bank.
  9:50 These sites constitute a ring on the edges of the province of Judea.
  9:54 *In the one hundred and fifty-third year, in the second month*: May, 159 B.C. *The work of the prophets*: probably Haggai and Zechariah, who were instrumental in building the Second Temple after the Babylonian exile; cf. Hg 1:12–14; Zec 4:8–10; Ezr 5:1–2.
  9:62 *Bethbasi*: two miles east of Bethlehem and six miles north of Tekoa.

---

9:35 1 Mc 5:25.        9:53 1 Mc 10:9.

1 MC

of Phasiron in their encampment; these men had begun to attack and they were going up with their forces. [67] Simon and those with him then sallied forth from the city and set fire to the siege engines. [68] They fought against Bacchides, and he was crushed. They caused him great distress, because the enterprise he had planned was in vain. [69] He was enraged with the lawless men who had advised him to invade the province. He killed many of them and resolved to return to his own country.

[70] Jonathan learned of this and sent ambassadors to agree on peace with him and to obtain the release of the prisoners. [71] He agreed to do as Jonathan asked. He swore an oath to him that he would never try to do him any harm for the rest of his life; [72] and he released to him the prisoners he had previously taken from the land of Judah. Thereupon he returned to his own land and never came into their territory again. [73] Then the sword ceased from Israel. Jonathan settled in Michmash; † he began to judge the people and he eliminated the renegades from Israel.

# 10

**Jonathan Becomes High Priest.** [1] In the one hundred and sixtieth year, † Alexander Epiphanes, son of Antiochus, came up and took Ptolemais. They accepted him as king and he began to reign there. [2] When King Demetrius heard of it, he mustered a very large army and marched out to engage him in battle. [3] Demetrius sent a letter to Jonathan written in peaceful terms, to exalt him; [4] for he said: "Let us be the first to make peace with him, before he makes peace with Alexander against us, [5] since he will remember all the wrongs we have done to him, his brothers, and his nation."

[6] So Demetrius authorized him to gather an army and procure arms as his ally; and he ordered that the hostages in the citadel be released to him. [7] Accordingly Jonathan went to Jerusalem and read the letter to all the people

and to those who were in the citadel. [8] They were struck with fear when they heard that the king had given him authority to gather an army. [9] Those in the citadel released the hostages to Jonathan, and he gave them back to their parents. * [10] Thereafter Jonathan dwelt in Jerusalem, and began to build and restore the city. [11] He ordered those doing the work to build the walls and to encircle Mount Zion with square stones for its fortification, and they did so. [12] The foreigners in the strongholds that Bacchides had built took flight; [13] all of them left their places and returned to their own lands. [14] Only in Beth-zur did some remain of those who had abandoned the law and the commandments, for it was a place of refuge.

[15] King Alexander heard of the promises that Demetrius had made to Jonathan; he was also told of the battles and brave deeds of Jonathan and his brothers and of the troubles that they had endured. [16] He said, "Shall we ever find another man like him? Let us now make him our friend and ally." [17] So he sent Jonathan a letter written in these terms: [18] "King Alexander sends greetings to his brother Jonathan. [19] We have heard of you, that you are a mighty warrior and worthy to be our friend. [20] We have therefore appointed you today to be high priest of your nation; you are to be called the King's Friend, and you are to look after our interests and preserve friendship with us." He also sent him a purple robe and a crown of gold. * [21] Jonathan put on the sacred vestments in the seventh month of the one hundred and sixtieth year at the feast of Booths, † and he gathered an army and procured many weapons.

**A Letter from Demetrius to Jonathan.** [22] When Demetrius heard of these things, he was distressed and said: [23] "Why have we allowed Alexander to get ahead of us by gaining the friendship of the Jews and thus strengthening

---

† **9:73** *Michmash*, southeast of Bethel, famous for the exploits of Jonathan, son of Saul; see 1 Sm 14. It was Jonathan's base from 157 to 152 B.C. *Began to judge*: exercise the governing authority as in the Book of Judges. With Jerusalem and the garrison towns (v. 50) firmly in Seleucid hands, Jonathan's freedom of action was greatly restricted.

**10:1** *The one hundred and sixtieth year*: 152 B.C. *Alexander…Antiochus*: Alexander Balas claimed to be a son of Antiochus IV. He had the backing of the Romans, who had never forgiven Demetrius for becoming king without their permission. The latter meanwhile had become unpopular with his own people as well as with the Jews.

**10:21** *Jonathan…feast of Booths*: Jonathan began to discharge the office of high priest in October 152 B.C. For seven years after the death of Alcimus there had been no high priest in Jerusalem. It was taken for granted that the king, though a Gentile, had the power to appoint one (2 Mc 4:7, 23–24). The Maccabees, though a priestly family (1 Mc 2:1), were not of the line of Zadok, and some in Israel (perhaps the Qumran community) regarded Jonathan's tenure as a usurpation.

---

himself? ²⁴ I too will write them encouraging words and offer honors and gifts, so that they may support me." ²⁵ So he sent them this message: "King Demetrius sends greetings to the Jewish nation. ²⁶ We have heard how you have kept the treaty with us and continued in our friendship and not gone over to our enemies, and we are glad. ²⁷ Continue, therefore, to keep faith with us, and we will reward you with favors in return for what you do in our behalf. ²⁸ We will grant you many exemptions and will bestow gifts on you.

²⁹* "I now free you and exempt all the Jews from the tribute, the salt tax, and the crown levies. ³⁰ Instead of collecting the third of the grain and the half of the fruit of the trees that should be my share, I renounce the right from this day forward. Neither now nor in the future will I collect them from the land of Judah or from the three districts annexed from Samaria.† ³¹ Let Jerusalem and her territory, her tithes and her tolls, be sacred and free from tax. ³² I also yield my authority over the citadel in Jerusalem, and I transfer it to the high priest, that he may put in it such men as he shall choose to guard it. ³³ Every Jew who has been carried into captivity from the land of Judah into any part of my kingdom I set at liberty without ransom; and let all their taxes, even those on their cattle, be canceled.

³⁴ Let all feast days, sabbaths, new moon festivals, appointed days, and the three days that precede each feast day, and the three days that follow, be days of immunity and exemption for all Jews in my kingdom. ³⁵ No one will have authority to exact payment from them or to harass any of them in any matter.

³⁶ "Let thirty thousand Jews be enrolled in the king's army and allowances be given them, as is due to all the king's soldiers. ³⁷ Let some of them be stationed in the king's principal strongholds, and of these let some be given positions of trust in the affairs of the kingdom. Let their superiors and their rulers be chosen from among them, and let them follow their own laws, as the king has commanded in the land of Judah.

³⁸ "Let the three districts that have been added to Judea from the province of Samaria be annexed to Judea so that they may be under one rule and obey no other authority than the high priest. ³⁹ Ptolemais and its confines I give as a present to the sanctuary in Jerusalem for the necessary expenses of the sanctuary. ⁴⁰ I make a yearly personal grant of fifteen thousand silver shekels out of the royal revenues, taken from appropriate places. ⁴¹ All the additional funds that the officials did not hand over as they had done in the first years shall henceforth be handed over for the services of the temple. ⁴² Moreover, the dues of five thousand silver shekels that used to be taken from the revenue of the sanctuary every year shall be canceled, since these funds belong to the priests who perform the services. ⁴³ All who take refuge in the temple of Jerusalem or in any of its precincts, because of money they owe the king, or because of any other debt, shall be released, together with all the goods they possess in my kingdom. ⁴⁴ The cost of rebuilding and restoring the structures of the sanctuary shall be covered out of the royal revenue. ⁴⁵ Likewise the cost of building the walls of Jerusalem and fortifying it all around, and of building walls in Judea, shall be donated from the royal revenue."

⁴⁶ When Jonathan and the people heard these words, they neither believed nor accepted them, for they remembered the great evil that Demetrius had done in Israel, and the great tribulation he had brought upon them. ⁴⁷ They therefore decided in favor of Alexander, for he had been the first to address them peaceably, and they remained his allies for the rest of his life.

⁴⁸ Then King Alexander gathered together a large army and encamped opposite Demetrius. ⁴⁹ The two kings joined battle, and when the army of Demetrius fled, Alexander pursued him, and overpowered his soldiers. ⁵⁰ He pressed the battle hard until sunset, and Demetrius fell that day.

**Treaty of Ptolemy and Alexander.** ⁵¹ Alexander sent ambassadors to Ptolemy, king of Egypt, with this message: ⁵² "Now that I have returned to my realm, taken my seat on the throne of my ancestors, and established my rule by crushing Demetrius and gaining control of my country— ⁵³ for I engaged him in battle,

---

† **10:30** *The three districts annexed from Samaria:* mentioned by name in 11:34. The present Greek text, by a scribal error, has added "and Galilee" after "Samaria."

* **10:29–30** 1 Mc 11:28, 34.

he and his army were crushed by us, and we assumed his royal throne— ⁵⁴ let us now establish friendship with each other. Give me now your daughter for my wife; and as your son-in-law, I will give to you and to her gifts worthy of you."

⁵⁵ King Ptolemy answered in these words: "Happy the day on which you returned to the land of your ancestors and took your seat on their royal throne! ⁵⁶ I will do for you what you have written; but meet me in Ptolemais, so that we may see each other, and I will become your father-in-law as you have proposed."

⁵⁷ So Ptolemy with his daughter Cleopatra† set out from Egypt and came to Ptolemais in the one hundred and sixty-second year. ⁵⁸ There King Alexander met him, and Ptolemy gave him his daughter Cleopatra in marriage. Their wedding was celebrated at Ptolemais with great splendor according to the custom of kings.

⁵⁹ King Alexander also wrote to Jonathan to come and meet him. ⁶⁰ So he went with pomp to Ptolemais, where he met the two kings and gave them and their friends silver and gold and many gifts and thus won their favor. * ⁶¹ Some villainous men of Israel, transgressors of the law, united against him to accuse him, but the king paid no heed to them. ⁶² The king ordered Jonathan to be divested of his garments and to be clothed in royal purple; and so it was done. ⁶³ The king also had him seated at his side. He said to his magistrates: "Go with him to the center of the city and make a proclamation that no one is to bring charges against him on any grounds or be troublesome to him for any reason." ⁶⁴ * When his accusers saw the honor paid to him according to the king's proclamation, and him clothed in purple, they all fled. ⁶⁵ And so the king honored him, enrolling him among his Chief Friends, and he made him governor and chief of the province. ⁶⁶ So Jonathan returned in peace and happiness to Jerusalem.

**Jonathan Defeats Apollonius.** ⁶⁷ In the one hundred and sixty-fifth year,† Demetrius, son of Demetrius, came from Crete to the land of his ancestors. ⁶⁸ When King Alexander heard of it he was greatly troubled, and returned to Antioch. ⁶⁹ Demetrius set Apollonius over Coelesyria.† Having gathered a large army, Apollonius encamped at Jamnia. From there he sent this message to Jonathan the high priest:

⁷⁰ "You are the only one who resists us. I am laughed at and put to shame on your account. Why are you exercising authority against us in the mountains? ⁷¹ If you have confidence in your forces, come down now to us in the plain, and let us test each other's strength there; for the forces of the cities are on my side. ⁷² Inquire and find out who I am and who the others are who are helping me. People are saying that you cannot make a stand against us because your ancestors were twice put to flight† in their own land. ⁷³ Now you too will be unable to withstand our cavalry and such a force as this in the plain, where there is not a stone or a pebble or a place to flee."

⁷⁴ When Jonathan heard the message of Apollonius, he was provoked. Choosing ten thousand men, he set out from Jerusalem, and Simon his brother joined him to help him. ⁷⁵ He encamped near Joppa, but the people of the city shut him out because Apollonius had a garrison in Joppa. When they attacked it, ⁷⁶ the people of the city became afraid and opened the gates, and so Jonathan took possession of Joppa.†

⁷⁷ When Apollonius heard of it, he drew up three thousand cavalry and a large force of infantry. He marched toward Azotus as though he were going on through, but at the same time he was advancing into the plain, because he had such a large number of cavalry to rely on. ⁷⁸ Jonathan pursued him toward Azotus, and the armies engaged in battle. ⁷⁹ Apollonius, however, had left a thousand cavalry in hiding behind them. ⁸⁰ Jonathan discovered that there was an ambush behind him; his army was surrounded. From morning until evening they showered his troops with arrows. ⁸¹ But his troops held their ground, as

---

**10:57** *Cleopatra:* Cleopatra Thea, then about fifteen years old. She later married Demetrius II, and later still, his brother Antiochus VII. Ptolemais (Acco) on the coast of Palestine was a neutral site. *The one hundred and sixty-second year:* 151/150 B.C.
**10:67** *The one hundred and sixty-fifth year:* 147 B.C. *Demetrius:* Demetrius II Nicator.
**10:69** *Coelesyria:* originally the region between the Lebanon and anti-Lebanon mountains, it came later to refer to Palestine

also. *Jamnia:* on the coast, also known as Yavneh (5:58).
**10:72** *Twice put to flight:* the reference is unclear.
**10:76** *Joppa:* about forty miles northwest of Jerusalem. For the first time the Maccabees took possession of a seaport, though nominally it was on behalf of King Alexander.

---

**10:60** 1 Mc 2:18.      **10:64–65** 1 Mc 2:18; 11:27.

Jonathan had commanded, while the enemy's horses became tired out. 82 Then Simon brought forward his force, and engaged the phalanx in battle. Since the cavalry were exhausted, the phalanx was crushed by him and fled, 83 while the cavalry too were scattered over the plain. They fled to Azotus and entered Beth-dagon, the temple of their idol, to save themselves. 84 But Jonathan burned and plundered Azotus with its neighboring towns, and destroyed by fire both the temple of Dagon and those who had taken refuge in it. * 85 Those who fell by the sword, together with those who were burned alive, came to about eight thousand.

86 Then Jonathan left there and encamped at Askalon, and the people of that city came out to meet him with great pomp. 87 Jonathan and those with him then returned to Jerusalem, with much spoil. 88 When King Alexander heard of these events, he accorded new honors to Jonathan. 89 He sent him a gold buckle, such as is usually given to King's Kinsmen;† he also gave him Ekron and all its territory as a possession.

# 11 Alliance of Ptolemy and Demetrius II.
1 Then the king of Egypt gathered forces as numerous as the sands of the seashore, and many ships; and he sought by deceit to take Alexander's kingdom and add it to his own. 2 He set out for Syria with peaceful words, and the people in the cities opened their gates to welcome him, as King Alexander had ordered them to do, since Ptolemy was his father-in-law. 3 But when Ptolemy entered the cities, he stationed a garrison of troops in each one.

4 As they neared Azotus, they showed him the temple of Dagon destroyed by fire, Azotus and its suburbs demolished, corpses lying about, and the charred bodies of those burned in the war, for they had heaped them up along his route. * 5 They told the king what Jonathan had done in order to denigrate him; but the king said nothing. 6 Jonathan met the king with pomp at Joppa, and they greeted each other and spent the night there. 7 Jonathan

accompanied the king as far as the river called Eleutherus† and then returned to Jerusalem.

8 And so King Ptolemy took possession of the cities along the seacoast as far as Seleucia by the sea,† plotting evil schemes against Alexander all the while. 9 He sent ambassadors to King Demetrius, saying: "Come, let us make a covenant with each other; I will give you my daughter whom Alexander has married, and you shall reign over your father's kingdom. 10 I regret that I gave him my daughter, for he has sought to kill me."† 11 He was criticizing Alexander, however, because he coveted his kingdom. 12 After taking his daughter away, Ptolemy gave her to Demetrius and broke with Alexander; the enmity between them was now evident. 13 Then Ptolemy entered Antioch and assumed the crown† of Asia; thus he set upon his head two crowns, that of Egypt and that of Asia.

14 Now King Alexander was in Cilicia at that time, because the people of that region had revolted. 15 When Alexander heard the news, he came against Ptolemy in battle. Ptolemy marched out and met him with a strong force and routed him. 16 When Alexander fled to Arabia to seek protection, King Ptolemy was triumphant. 17 Zabdiel the Arabian cut off Alexander's head and sent it to Ptolemy. 18 But three days later King Ptolemy himself died, and his troops in the strongholds were killed by the inhabitants of the strongholds. 19 Thus Demetrius became king in the one hundred and sixty-seventh year.†

## Alliance of Jonathan and Demetrius II.
20 In those days Jonathan gathered together the people of Judea to attack the citadel in Jerusalem, and they set up many siege engines against it. 21 But some transgressors of the law, enemies of their own nation, went to the king and informed him that Jonathan was besieging the citadel. 22 When Demetrius heard this, he was enraged; and as soon as he heard it, he set out and came to Ptolemais. He wrote to Jonathan to discontinue the siege and to meet him for a conference at Ptolemais as soon as possible.

---

† **10:89** *Kinsmen*: a rank higher than Chief Friends.
**11:7** *Eleutherus*: two hundred miles north of Joppa, in the second century B.C. the northern limit of Coelesyria.
**11:8** *Seleucia by the sea*: at the mouth of the Orontes, the port city of Antioch.
**11:10** *I regret...to kill me*: according to Josephus, Ammonius, a friend of Alexander, had tried to assassinate Ptolemy, and the latter claimed that Alexander was the instigator, thus calumniat-

ing him to gain his kingdom (v. 11).
**11:13** *Crown*: lit., diadem.
**11:19** *The one hundred and sixty-seventh year*: 146/145 B.C. The two deaths (vv. 17–18) occurred in the summer of 145 B.C.

---

* **10:84** 1 Mc 11:4; 1 Sm 5:2–5.     **11:4** 1 Mc 10:84.

<sup>23</sup> On hearing this, Jonathan ordered the siege to continue. He selected some elders and priests of Israel and put himself at risk. <sup>24</sup> Taking with him silver, gold and apparel, and many other presents, he went to the king at Ptolemais, and found favor with him. <sup>25</sup> Although certain renegades of his own nation kept on bringing charges against him, <sup>26</sup> the king treated him just as his predecessors had done and exalted him in the presence of all his Friends. <sup>27</sup> He confirmed him in the high priesthood and in the other honors he had previously held, and had him enrolled among his Chief Friends.

<sup>28</sup> Jonathan asked the king to exempt Judea and the three districts of Samaria from tribute, promising him in return three hundred talents.* <sup>29</sup> The king agreed and wrote a letter to Jonathan about all these matters as follows:

<sup>30</sup>* "King Demetrius sends greetings to his brother† Jonathan and to the Jewish nation. <sup>31</sup> We are sending you, for your information, a copy of the letter that we wrote to Lasthenes† our Kinsman concerning you. <sup>32</sup> 'King Demetrius sends greetings to his father Lasthenes. <sup>33</sup> Upon the Jewish nation, who are our friends and observe their obligations to us, we have decided to bestow benefits because of the good will they show us. <sup>34</sup>* Therefore we confirm their possession, not only of the territory of Judea, but also of the three districts of Aphairema,† Lydda, and Ramathaim. These districts, together with all their dependencies, are hereby transferred from Samaria to Judea for those who offer sacrifices in Jerusalem in lieu of the royal taxes the king used to receive yearly from the produce of earth and trees. <sup>35</sup> From payment of the other things that would henceforth be due to us, namely, the tithes and taxes, as well as the salt tax, and the crown tax—from all these we grant them release. <sup>36</sup> Henceforth and forever not one of these provisions shall ever be revoked. <sup>37</sup> See to it, therefore, that a copy of these instructions be made and given to Jonathan. Let it be displayed on the holy mountain in a conspicuous place.'"

**The Intrigue of Trypho.** <sup>38</sup> When King Demetrius saw that the land was peaceful under his rule and that he had no opposition, he dismissed his entire army, each to his own home, except the foreign troops which he had hired from the islands of the nations. So all the soldiers who had served under his predecessors became hostile to him. <sup>39</sup> When a certain Trypho, who had previously supported Alexander, saw that all the troops were grumbling against Demetrius, he went to Imalkue the Arabian, who was raising Alexander's young son Antiochus.* <sup>40</sup> Trypho kept urging Imalkue to hand over the boy to him, so that he might succeed his father as king. He told him of all that Demetrius had done and of the hostility his soldiers had for him; and he remained there for many days.

**Jonathan Aids Demetrius II.** <sup>41</sup> Meanwhile Jonathan sent the request to King Demetrius to withdraw the troops in the citadel from Jerusalem and from the other strongholds, for they were constantly waging war on Israel. <sup>42</sup> Demetrius, in turn, sent this word to Jonathan: "I will do not only this for you and your nation, but I will greatly honor you and your nation when I find the opportunity. <sup>43</sup> Now, therefore, you will do well to send men to fight for me, because all my troops have revolted."

<sup>44</sup> So Jonathan sent three thousand good fighting men to him at Antioch. When they came to the king, he was delighted over their arrival. <sup>45</sup> The populace, one hundred and twenty thousand strong, massed in the center of the city in an attempt to kill the king. <sup>46</sup> So the king took refuge in the palace, while the populace gained control of the main streets of the city and prepared for battle. <sup>47</sup> Then the king called the Jewish force to his aid. They all rallied around him and spread out through the city. On that day they killed about a hundred thousand in the city. <sup>48</sup> At the same time, they set the city on fire and took much spoil. Thus they saved the king. <sup>49</sup> When the populace saw that the Jewish force controlled the city, they

---

† **11:30** *Brother*: this term and "father" in v. 32 are honorific expressions used of the Kinsmen.

**11:31** *Lasthenes*: leader of the mercenary troops who had come with Demetrius from Crete. He was now the young king's chief minister and was apparently responsible for the disastrous policy (v. 38) of disbanding the national army.

**11:34** *Aphairema*: the Ophrah of Jos 18:23; 1 Sm 13:17; the Ephron of 2 Chr 13:19; and the Ephraim of Jn 11:54—modern et-Taiyibeh, five miles northeast of Bethel. *Lydda*: the Lod of

the postexilic Jews (Ezr 2:33; Neh 11:35) and the hometown of Aeneas, who was cured by Peter (Acts 9:32–34). It is ten miles southeast of Joppa. *Ramathaim*: the Ramathaim-zophim of 1 Sm 1:1, and the Arimathea of Mt 27:57, modern Rentis, nine miles northeast of Lydda.

*

**11:28** 1 Mc 10:29;       **11:34–35** 1 Mc 10:29; 11:28.
    11:34–35.               **11:39** 1 Mc 12:39.
**11:30–37** 1 Mc 10:25–45.

lost courage and cried out to the king in supplication, [50] "Extend the hand of friendship to us, and make the Jews stop attacking us and the city." [51] So they threw down their weapons and made peace. The Jews thus gained honor in the eyes of the king and all his subjects, and they became renowned throughout his kingdom. Finally they returned to Jerusalem with much plunder.

[52] But when King Demetrius was sure of his royal throne, and the land was peaceful under his rule, [53] he broke all his promises and became estranged from Jonathan. Instead of repaying Jonathan for all the favors he had received from him, he caused him much distress.

**Alliance of Jonathan and Antiochus VI.** [54] After this, Trypho returned and brought with him the young boy Antiochus, who became king and put on the diadem.* [55] All the soldiers whom Demetrius had discharged rallied around Antiochus and fought against Demetrius, who was routed and fled. [56] Trypho captured the elephants and occupied Antioch. [57] Then young Antiochus wrote to Jonathan: "I confirm you in the high priesthood and appoint you ruler over the four districts, and to be one of the King's Friends." [58] He also sent him gold dishes and a table service, gave him the right to drink from gold cups, to dress in royal purple, and to wear a gold buckle.* [59] Likewise, he made Jonathan's brother Simon governor of the region from the Ladder of Tyre† to the borders of Egypt.

**Campaigns of Jonathan and Simon.** [60] Jonathan set out and traveled through the province of West-of-Euphrates† and its cities, and all the forces of Syria espoused his cause as allies. When he arrived at Askalon, the citizens welcomed him with pomp. [61] But when he set out for Gaza, the people of Gaza shut him out. So he besieged it, and burned and plundered its suburbs. [62] Then the people of Gaza appealed to Jonathan, and he granted them terms of peace. He took the sons of their leaders as hostages and sent them to Jerusalem. He then

traveled on through the province as far as Damascus.

[63] Jonathan heard that the generals of Demetrius had come with a strong force to Kadesh in Galilee, intending to remove him from office. [64] So he went to meet them, leaving his brother Simon in the province. [65]* Simon encamped against Beth-zur, attacked it for many days, and shut in the inhabitants. [66] They appealed to him, and he granted them terms of peace. He expelled them from the city, took possession of it, and put a garrison there.

[67] Meanwhile, Jonathan and his army pitched their camp near the waters of Gennesaret, and at daybreak they went to the plain of Hazor.† [68] There the army of the foreigners met him on the plain. Having first detached an ambush in the mountains, this army mounted a frontal attack. [69] Then those in ambush rose out of their places and joined in the battle. [70] All of Jonathan's men fled; no one stayed except the army commanders Mattathias, son of Absalom, and Judas, son of Chalphi. [71] Jonathan tore his clothes, threw dust on his head, and prayed. [72] Then he went back to the battle and routed them, and they fled. [73] Those of his men who were running away saw it and returned to him; and with him they pursued the enemy as far as their camp in Kadesh, and there they encamped. [74] About three thousand of the foreign troops fell on that day. Then Jonathan returned to Jerusalem.

# 12 Alliances with Rome and Sparta.
[1] When Jonathan saw that the time was right, he chose men and sent them to Rome to confirm and renew the friendship with the Romans.* [2] He also sent letters to the Spartans and other places to the same effect.

[3] After reaching Rome, the men entered the senate chamber and said, "The high priest Jonathan and the Jewish people have sent us to renew the friendship and alliance of earlier times with them." [4] The Romans gave them letters addressed to authorities in various places, with the request to provide them with safe conduct to the land of Judah.

[5] This is a copy of the letter that Jonathan

---

† **11:59** *Ladder of Tyre*: modern Ras en-Naqurah, where the mountains reach the sea, so that the coastal road must ascend in a series of steps. Thus the Maccabees controlled the coastal area from Syria to Egypt.
**11:60** *The province of West-of-Euphrates*: refers here to the territory of Palestine and Coelesyria, but not Upper Syria; cf. 7:8.

**11:67** *Plain of Hazor*: the site of the ancient Canaanite city (Jos 11:10), ten miles north of the Lake of Gennesaret.

* **11:54** 1 Mc 11:39; 12:39.    **11:65–66** 1 Mc 9:52; 10:14.
**11:58** 1 Mc 2:18.    **12:1** 1 Mc 8:17.

wrote to the Spartans: [6]"Jonathan the high priest, the senate of the nation, the priests, and the rest of the Jewish people send greetings to their brothers the Spartans. [7]Long ago a letter was sent† to the high priest Onias from Arius, who then reigned over you, stating that you are our brothers, as the attached copy shows.* [8]Onias welcomed the envoy with honor and received the letter, which spoke clearly of alliance and friendship. [9]Though we have no need of these things, since we have for our encouragement the holy books that are in our possession,†* [10]we have ventured to send word to you for the renewal of brotherhood and friendship, lest we become strangers to you; a long time has passed since you sent your message to us. [11]We, on our part, have unceasingly remembered you in the sacrifices and prayers that we offer on our feasts and other appropriate days, as it is right and proper to remember brothers. [12]We likewise rejoice in your renown. [13]But many tribulations and many wars have beset us, and the kings around us have attacked us. [14]We did not wish to be troublesome to you and to the rest of our allies and friends in these wars. [15]For we have the help of Heaven for our support, and we have been saved from our enemies, and our enemies have been humbled. [16]So we have chosen Numenius, son of Antiochus, and Antipater, son of Jason, and we have sent them to the Romans to renew with them the friendship and alliance of earlier times.* [17]We have also ordered them to come to you and greet you, and to deliver to you our letter concerning the renewal of our brotherhood. [18]Therefore kindly send us an answer on this matter."

[19]This is a copy of the letter that they sent to Onias: [20]* "Arius, king of the Spartans, sends greetings to Onias the high priest. [21]A document has been found stating that the Spartans and the Jews are brothers and that they are of the family of Abraham. [22]Now that we have learned this, kindly write to us about your welfare. [23]We, for our part, declare to you that your animals and your possessions are ours, and ours are yours. We have,

therefore, given orders that you should be told of this."

**More Campaigns of Jonathan and Simon.** [24]Then Jonathan heard that the officers of Demetrius had returned to attack him with a stronger army than before. [25]So he set out from Jerusalem and met them in the territory of Hamath,† giving them no opportunity to enter his province. [26]The spies he had sent into their camp came back and reported to him that the enemy were preparing to attack them that night. [27]Therefore, when the sun set, Jonathan ordered his men to keep watch, with their weapons at the ready for battle, throughout the night; and he set outposts around the camp. [28]When the enemy heard that Jonathan and his men were ready for battle, their hearts sank with fear and dread. They lighted fires in their camp and then withdrew. [29]But because Jonathan and his men were watching the campfires burning, they did not know until the morning what had happened. [30]Then Jonathan pursued them, but he could not overtake them, for they had crossed the river Eleutherus. [31]So Jonathan turned aside against the Arabians who are called Zabadeans, and he struck them down and plundered them. [32]Then he broke camp, marched on toward Damascus and traveled through the whole region.

[33]Simon also set out and traveled as far as Askalon and its neighboring strongholds. He then turned to Joppa and took it by surprise, [34]for he heard that its people intended to hand over the stronghold to the supporters of Demetrius. He left a garrison there to guard it.

[35]When Jonathan returned, he assembled the elders of the people, and with them he made plans for building strongholds in Judea, [36]for making the walls of Jerusalem still higher, and for erecting a high barrier between the citadel and the city, to separate it from the city and isolate it, so that its garrison could neither buy nor sell. [37]The people therefore gathered together to build up the city, for part of the wall of the eastern valley had collapsed. And Jonathan repaired the quarter

---

† **12:7** *Long ago a letter was sent*: i.e., a century and a half before. *Onias*: Onias I, high priest from 323 to 300 or 290 B.C. *Arius*: Arius I, king from 309 to 265 B.C.

**12:9** *The holy books…in our possession*: a reference to "the law, the prophets and other books," as mentioned in the Prologue to Sirach.

**12:25** *Territory of Hamath*: the Seleucid territory of Up-

per Syria northeast of Coelesyria and separated from it by the Eleutherus River. The latter territory was under the command of Jonathan (11:59–60).

* **12:7** 1 Mc 12:20–23.    **12:16** 1 Mc 14:22; 15:15.
**12:9** 2 Mc 2:14.    **12:20–23** 1 Mc 12:7.

called Chaphenatha. [38] Simon likewise built up Adida in the Shephelah, and fortified it by installing gates and bars.

**Capture of Jonathan.** [39] Then Trypho sought to become king of Asia, assume the diadem, and do violence to King Antiochus.* [40] But he was afraid that Jonathan would not permit him, but would fight against him. Looking for a way to seize and kill him, he set out and came to Beth-shan. [41] Jonathan marched out to meet him with forty thousand picked fighting men and came to Beth-shan. [42] But when Trypho saw that Jonathan had arrived with a large army he was afraid to do him violence. [43] Instead, he received him with honor, introduced him to all his friends, and gave him presents. He also ordered his friends and soldiers to obey him as they would himself. [44] Then he said to Jonathan: "Why have you put all these people to so much trouble when we are not at war? [45] Now pick out a few men to stay with you, send the rest to their homes, and then come with me to Ptolemais. I will hand it over to you together with other strongholds and the remaining troops, as well as all the officials; then I will turn back and go home. That is why I came here."

[46] Jonathan trusted him and did as he said. He dismissed his troops, and they returned to the land of Judah. [47] But he kept with him three thousand men, of whom he left two thousand in Galilee while one thousand accompanied him. [48] Then as soon as Jonathan entered Ptolemais, the people of Ptolemais closed the gates and seized him; all who had entered with him, they killed with the sword.*

[49] Then Trypho sent soldiers and cavalry to Galilee and the Great Plain† to destroy all Jonathan's men. [50] These, upon learning that Jonathan had been captured and killed along with his companions, encouraged one another and went out in close formation, ready to fight. [51] As their pursuers saw that they were ready to fight for their lives, they turned back. [52] Thus all Jonathan's men came safely into the land of Judah. They mourned Jonathan and those who were with him. They were in great fear, and all Israel fell into deep mourning. [53] All the nations round about sought to

crush them. They said, "Now that they have no leader or helper, let us make war on them and wipe out their memory from the earth."*

## IV. LEADERSHIP OF SIMON

**13** **Simon as Leader.** [1] When Simon heard that Trypho was gathering a large army to invade and ravage the land of Judah, [2] and saw that the people were trembling with terror, he went up to Jerusalem. There he assembled the people [3] and exhorted them in these words: "You know what I, my brothers, and my father's house have done for the laws and the sanctuary; what battles and hardships we have seen. [4] For the sake of this, for the sake of Israel, all my brothers have perished, and I alone am left. [5] Far be it from me, then, to save my own life in any time of distress, for I am not better than my brothers. [6] But I will avenge my nation and the sanctuary, as well as your wives and children, for out of hatred all the Gentiles have united to crush us."*

[7] As the people heard these words, their spirit was rekindled. [8] They shouted in reply: "You are our leader in place of your brothers Judas and Jonathan. [9] Fight our battles, and we will do everything that you tell us." [10] So Simon mustered all the men able to fight, and hastening to complete the walls of Jerusalem, fortified it on every side. [11] He sent Jonathan, son of Absalom, to Joppa with a strong force; Jonathan drove out the occupants and remained there.

**Trypho's Deceit.** [12] Then Trypho moved from Ptolemais with a large army to invade the land of Judah, bringing Jonathan with him as a prisoner. [13] Simon encamped at Adida, facing the plain. [14] When Trypho learned that Simon had succeeded his brother Jonathan, and that he intended to fight him, he sent ambassadors to him with this message: [15] "It was on account of the money your brother Jonathan owed the royal treasury in connection with the offices that he held, that we have detained him. [16] Now send a hundred talents of silver, and two of his sons as hostages to guarantee that when he is set free he will not revolt against us, and we will release him."

---

† **12:49** *The Great Plain*: of Beth-shan (v. 41), where Jonathan's disbanded troops remained.

**12:39** 1 Mc 11:39–40, 54–55.
**12:48** 1 Mc 5:15, 22, 55.
**12:53** 1 Mc 5:2; 13:6.
**13:6** 1 Mc 5:2; 12:53.

[17] Simon knew that they were speaking deceitfully to him. Nevertheless, for fear of provoking much hostility among the people, he sent for the money and the boys, [18] lest the people say "Jonathan perished because I would not send Trypho the money and the boys." [19] So he sent the boys and the hundred talents; but Trypho broke his promise and would not release Jonathan.

[20] † Next Trypho moved to invade and ravage the country. His troops went around by the road that leads to Adora, but Simon and his army moved along opposite him everywhere he went. [21] The people in the citadel kept sending emissaries to Trypho, pressing him to come to them by way of the wilderness, and to send them provisions. [22] Although Trypho got all his cavalry ready to go, there was a very heavy snowfall that night, and he could not go on account of the snow. So he left for Gilead. [23] When he was approaching Baskama, † he had Jonathan killed and buried him there. [24] Then Trypho returned to his own land.

**Jonathan's Tomb.** [25] Simon sent for the remains of his brother Jonathan, and buried him in Modein, the city of his ancestors. [26] All Israel bewailed him with solemn lamentation, mourning over him for many days. [27] Then Simon erected over the tomb of his father and his brothers a monument of stones, polished front and back, and raised high enough to be seen at a distance. [28] He set up seven pyramids facing one another for his father and his mother and his four brothers. * [29] For the pyramids he devised a setting of massive columns, which he adorned with suits of armor as a perpetual memorial, and next to the armor carved ships, which could be seen by all who sailed the sea. [30] This tomb which he built at Modein is there to the present day.

**Alliance of Simon and Demetrius II.** [31] Trypho dealt treacherously with the young King Antiochus. He killed him [32] and became king in his place, putting on the crown of Asia. Thus he brought much evil on the land. * [33] Simon,

for his part, built up the strongholds of Judea, fortifying them all around with high towers, thick walls, and gates with bars, and he stored up provisions in the strongholds. [34] Simon also chose men and sent them to King Demetrius to obtain for the land an exemption from taxation, since Trypho did nothing but plunder. [35] King Demetrius replied favorably and sent him the following letter:

[36] "King Demetrius sends greetings to Simon, high priest and friend of kings, and to the elders and the Jewish people. [37] We have received the gold crown and the palm branch that you sent. We are ready to make a lasting peace with you and to write to our officials to grant you exemption. [38] Whatever decrees we have made in your regard remain in force, and the strongholds that you have built you may keep. [39] We pardon any oversights and offenses committed up to now, as well as the crown tax that you owe. Any other tax that used to be collected in Jerusalem shall no longer be collected there. [40] Any of you qualified for enrollment in our service may be enrolled. Let there be peace between us."

[41] Thus in the one hundred and seventieth year, † the yoke of the Gentiles was removed from Israel, [42] and the people began to write in their records and contracts, "In the first year of Simon, great high priest, governor, and leader of the Jews."

**Simon Captures Gazara.** [43] * In those days Simon besieged Gazara † and surrounded it with troops. He made a siege machine, brought it up against the city, and attacked and captured one of the towers. [44] Those in the siege machine leaped down into the city and a great tumult arose there. [45] Those in the city, together with their wives and children, went up on the wall, with their garments rent, and cried out in loud voices, begging Simon to grant them terms of peace. [46] They said, "Treat us not according to our evil deeds but according to your mercy." [47] So Simon came to terms with them and did not attack them. He expelled them from the city, however, and he purified the

---

**13:20–21** The invaders made a wide flanking movement to invade Judea from the south (see 4:29; 6:31). Adora was a few miles southwest of Beth-zur. They would avoid Beth-zur itself and other strongholds of the Maccabees by following the way of the wilderness.
**13:23** *Baskama*: perhaps northeast of the Sea of Galilee.
**13:41** *The one hundred and seventieth year*: March, 142, to

April, 141 B.C., by the Temple calendar.
**13:43** *Gazara*: ancient Gezer, a key position in the Shephelah, fortified by Bacchides in 160 B.C.; cf. 9:52.

**13:28** 2 Sm 18:18.          **13:43–48** 2 Mc 10:32–38.
**13:32** 1 Mc 8:6.

houses in which there were idols. Then he entered the city with hymns and songs of praise. [48] After removing from it everything that was impure, he settled there people who observed the law. He improved its fortifications and built himself a residence.

**Simon Captures the Citadel.** [49] The people in the citadel in Jerusalem were prevented from going out into the country and back to buy or sell; they suffered greatly from hunger, and many of them died of starvation. [50] They finally cried out to Simon, and he gave them terms of peace. He expelled them from the citadel and cleansed it of impurities. [51] On the twenty-third day of the second month, † in the one hundred and seventy-first year, the Jews entered the citadel with shouts of praise, the waving of palm branches, the playing of harps and cymbals and lyres, and the singing of hymns and canticles, because a great enemy of Israel had been crushed. * [52] Simon decreed that this day should be celebrated every year with rejoicing. He also strengthened the fortifications of the temple mount alongside the citadel, and he and his people dwelt there. [53] Seeing that his son John † was now a grown man, Simon made him commander of all his soldiers, and he dwelt in Gazara.

# 14

**Capture of Demetrius II.** [1] In the one hundred and seventy-second year, † King Demetrius assembled his army and marched into Media to obtain help so that he could fight Trypho. [2] When Arsaces, † king of Persia and Media, heard that Demetrius had entered his territory, he sent one of his generals to take him alive. [3] The general went forth and attacked the army of Demetrius; he captured him and brought him to Arsaces, who put him under guard.

## Praise of Simon

[4]  The land was at rest all the days of
       Simon,

who sought the good of his nation.
His rule delighted his people
and his glory all his days. *

[5]  As his crowning glory he took Joppa for
       a port
and made it a gateway to the isles of
       the sea. *

[6]  He enlarged the borders of his nation
and gained control of the country.

[7]  He took many prisoners of war
and made himself master of Gazara,
       Beth-zur, and the citadel.
He cleansed the citadel of its impurities;
there was no one to withstand him.

[8]  The people cultivated their land in
       peace;
the land yielded its produce,
the trees of the field their fruit. *

[9]  Old men sat in the squares,
all talking about the good times,
while the young men put on the
       glorious raiment of war. *

[10] He supplied the cities with food
and equipped them with means of
       defense,
till his glorious name reached the
       ends of the earth.

[11] He brought peace to the land,
and Israel was filled with great joy. *

[12] Every one sat under his vine and fig tree,
with no one to disturb them. *

[13] No attacker was left in the land;
the kings in those days were crushed.

[14] He strengthened all the lowly among his
       people
and was zealous for the law;
he destroyed the lawless and the
       wicked.

[15] The sanctuary he made splendid
and multiplied its furnishings.

**Alliance with Rome and Sparta.** [16] When people in Rome and even in Sparta heard that Jonathan had died, they were deeply grieved. † [17] But when they heard that his brother Simon

---

† **13:51** *The twenty-third day of the second month*: June 3, 141 B.C.
**13:53** *John*: John Hyrcanus, who was to succeed his father as ruler and high priest; cf. 16:23–24.
**14:1** *The one hundred and seventy-second year*: 141/140 B.C. The expedition began most probably in the spring of 140.
**14:2** *Arsaces*: Arsaces VI, also called Mithridates I, the Parthian king (171–138 B.C.). Parthians had overrun Persia and now held Babylonia, both of which had hitherto belonged to the Seleucid empire. The Greeks and Macedonians in these countries

had appealed to Demetrius for help.
**14:16** The embassy to Rome and Sparta was sent soon after Simon's accession to power, and the replies were received before Demetrius' expedition (vv. 1–3), probably in 142 B.C.

---

**13:51** 1 Mc 1:36.         **14:9** Zec 8:4–5.
**14:4** 1 Mc 3:3–9.         **14:11** Lv 26:6.
**14:5** 1 Mc 12:33; 13:11.  **14:12** Mi 4:4; Zec 3:10.
**14:8** Lv 26:3–4; Zec 8:12.

had become high priest in his place and was master of the territory and its cities, [18] they sent him inscribed tablets of bronze to renew with him the friendship and alliance that they had established with his brothers Judas and Jonathan.* [19] These were read before the assembly in Jerusalem.

[20] This is a copy of the letter that the Spartans sent: "The rulers and the city of the Spartans send greetings to Simon the high priest, the elders, the priests, and the rest of the Jewish people, our brothers. [21] The ambassadors sent to our people have informed us of your glory and renown, and we rejoiced at their coming. [22] In accordance with what they said we have recorded the following in the public decrees: Numenius, son of Antiochus, and Antipater, son of Jason, ambassadors of the Jews, have come to us to renew their friendship with us.* [23] The people have resolved to receive these men with honor, and to deposit a copy of their words in the public archives, so that the people of Sparta may have a record of them. A copy of this decree has been made for Simon the high priest."

[24] After this, Simon sent Numenius to Rome with a large gold shield weighing a thousand minas, to confirm the alliance with the Romans.

**Official Honors for Simon.** [25] When the people heard of these things, they said, "How shall we thank Simon and his sons? [26] He and his brothers and his father's house have stood firm and repulsed Israel's enemies, and so have established its freedom." So they made an inscription on bronze tablets, which they affixed to pillars on Mount Zion.

[27] The following is a copy of the inscription: "On the eighteenth day of Elul,† in the one hundred and seventy-second year, that is, the third year under Simon the great high priest in Asaramel, [28] in a great assembly of priests, people, rulers of the nation, and elders of the region, the following proclamation was made to us:

[29] "'Since there have often been wars in our country, Simon, son of the priest Mattathias, descendant of Joarib, and his brothers have put themselves in danger and resisted the enemies of their nation, so that their sanctuary and law might be maintained, and they have thus brought great glory to their nation. [30] Jonathan rallied the nation, became their high priest, and was gathered to his people. [31] When their enemies sought to invade and ravage their country and to violate their sanctuary, [32] Simon rose up and fought for his nation, spending large sums of his own money to equip his nation's forces and give them their pay. [33] He fortified the cities of Judea, especially the border city of Beth-zur, formerly the site of the enemy's weaponry, and he stationed there a garrison of Jewish soldiers. [34] He also fortified Joppa by the sea and Gazara on the border of Azotus, a place previously occupied by the enemy; these cities he settled with Jews and furnished them with all that was necessary for their restoration. [35] When the people saw Simon's fidelity and the glory he planned to bring to his nation, they made him their leader and high priest because of all he had accomplished and the justice and fidelity he had shown his nation. In every way he sought to exalt his people.

[36] "'In his time and under his guidance they succeeded in driving the Gentiles out of their country and those in the City of David in Jerusalem, who had built for themselves a citadel from which they used to sally forth to defile the environs of the sanctuary and inflict grave injury on its purity. [37] In this citadel he stationed Jewish soldiers, and he strengthened its fortifications for the security of the land and the city, while he also built up the wall of Jerusalem to a greater height. [38] Consequently, King Demetrius confirmed him in the high priesthood, [39] made him one of his Friends, and conferred great honor on him.* [40] This was because he had heard that the Romans had addressed the Jews as friends, allies, and brothers, that they had received Simon's envoys with honor, [41] and that the Jewish people and their priests had decided the following: Simon shall be their leader and high priest forever until a trustworthy prophet arises.* [42] He shall act as governor over them, and shall have charge of the sanctuary, to make regulations concerning its functions and concerning the country, its weapons and strongholds. [43] He shall be

---

† **14:27** *Eighteenth day of Elul*: September 13, 140 B.C. *Asaramel*: perhaps a Hebrew name meaning "court of the people of God."

**14:18** 1 Mc 8:22.
**14:22** 1 Mc 12:16; 15:15.

**14:39** 1 Mc 2:18.
**14:41** 1 Mc 4:46; 9:27.

obeyed by all. All contracts in the country shall be written in his name, and he shall be clothed in purple and gold.* [44] It shall not be lawful for any of the people or priests to nullify any of these decisions, or to contradict the orders given by him, or to convene an assembly in the country without his consent, to be clothed in purple or wear a gold buckle. [45] Whoever acts otherwise or violates any of these prescriptions shall be liable to punishment.

[46] "Thus all the people approved of granting Simon the right to act in accord with these decisions, [47] and Simon accepted and agreed to be high priest, governor, and ethnarch† of the Jewish people and priests, and to have authority over all.'"

[48] It was decreed that this inscription should be engraved on bronze tablets, to be set up in a conspicuous place in the precincts of the sanctuary, [49] and that copies of it should be deposited in the treasury, where they would be available to Simon and his sons.

## 15 Letter of Antiochus VII.
[1] Antiochus,† son of King Demetrius, sent a letter from the islands of the sea to Simon, the priest and ethnarch of the Jews, and to all the nation, [2] which read as follows:

"King Antiochus sends greetings to Simon, the high priest and ethnarch, and to the Jewish nation. [3] Whereas certain villains have gained control of the kingdom of our ancestors, I intend to reclaim it, that I may restore it to its former state. I have recruited a large number of mercenary troops and equipped warships. [4] I intend to make a landing in the country so that I may take revenge on those who have ruined our country and laid waste many cities in my kingdom.

[5] "Now, therefore, I confirm to you all the tax exemptions that the kings before me granted you and whatever other privileges they conceded to you. [6] I authorize you to coin your own money, as legal tender in your country. [7] Jerusalem and its sanctuary shall be free. All the weapons you have prepared and all the strongholds you have built and now occupy shall remain in your possession. [8] All debts, present or future, due to the royal treasury shall be canceled for you, now and for all time. [9] When we establish our kingdom, we will greatly honor you and your nation and the temple, so that your glory will be manifest in all the earth."

[10] In the one hundred and seventy-fourth year† Antiochus invaded the land of his ancestors, and all the troops rallied to him, so that few were left with Trypho. [11] Pursued by Antiochus, Trypho fled to Dor, by the sea,† [12] realizing what troubles had come upon him now that his soldiers had deserted him. [13] Antiochus encamped before Dor with a hundred and twenty thousand infantry and eight thousand cavalry. [14] While he surrounded the city, his ships closed from the sea, so that he pressed it hard by land and sea and let no one go in or out.

**Roman Alliance Renewed.** [15] Meanwhile, Numenius and his companions came from Rome with letters containing this message to various kings and countries:* [16] "Lucius,† Consul of the Romans, sends greetings to King Ptolemy. [17] Ambassadors of the Jews, our friends and allies, have come to us to renew their earlier friendship and alliance. They had been sent by Simon the high priest and the Jewish people, [18] and they brought with them a gold shield of a thousand minas.* [19] Therefore we have decided to write to various kings and countries, that they are not to venture to harm them, or wage war against them or their cities or their country, and are not to assist those who fight against them. [20] We have also decided to accept the shield from them. [21] If, then, any troublemakers from their country take refuge with you, hand them over to Simon the high priest, so that he may punish them according to their law."

[22] The consul sent identical letters to Kings Demetrius, Attalus,† Ariarthes and Arsaces;

---

† 
**14:47** *Ethnarch:* a subordinate ruler over an ethnic group whose office needed confirmation by a higher authority within the empire.
**15:1** *Antiochus:* Antiochus VII Sidetes, son of Demetrius I, and younger brother of Demetrius II (now a prisoner of the Parthians). At the age of twenty he set out from the island of Rhodes to take his brother's place and drive out the usurper Trypho.
**15:10** *The one hundred and seventy-fourth year:* 138 B.C.
**15:11** *Dor, by the sea:* a fortress on the Palestinian coast, fifteen miles south of Carmel.

**15:16** *Lucius:* perhaps Lucius Caecilius Metellus, consul in 142 B.C., or Lucius Calpurnius Piso, consul in 140–139 B.C. This document pertains to Simon's first years as leader.
**15:22** *Attalus:* Attalus II of Pergamum, reigned 159–138 B.C. *Ariarthes:* Ariarthes V of Cappadocia, reigned 162–130 B.C. *Arsaces:* see note on 14:2.

---

**14:43** 1 Mc 10:20, 89.                    **14:22**, 24.
**15:15** 1 Mc 8:17; 12:16;                  **15:18** 1 Mc 14:24.

[23] to all the countries—Sampsames, the Spartans, Delos, Myndos, Sicyon, Caria, Samos, Pamphylia, Lycia, Halicarnassus, Rhodes, Phaselis, Cos, Side, Aradus, Gortyna, Cnidus, Cyprus, and Cyrene. [24] A copy of the letter was also sent to Simon the high priest.

**Hostility from Antiochus VII.** [25] When King Antiochus encamped before Dor, he assaulted it continuously both with troops and with the siege engines he had made. He blockaded Trypho by preventing anyone from going in or out. [26] Simon sent to Antiochus' support two thousand elite troops, together with silver and gold and much equipment. [27] But he refused to accept the aid; in fact, he broke all the agreements he had previously made with Simon and became hostile toward him. *

[28] He sent Athenobius, one of his Friends, to confer with Simon and say: "You are occupying Joppa and Gazara and the citadel of Jerusalem; these are cities of my kingdom. [29] You have laid waste their territories, done great harm to the land, and taken possession of many districts in my kingdom. [30] Now, therefore, give up the cities you have seized and the tribute money of the districts you control outside the territory of Judea; [31] or instead, pay me five hundred talents of silver for the devastation you have caused and five hundred talents more for the tribute money of the cities. If you do not do this, we will come and make war on you."

[32] So Athenobius, the king's Friend, came to Jerusalem and on seeing the splendor of Simon's court, the gold and silver plate on the sideboard, and his rich display, he was amazed. When he gave him the king's message, [33] Simon said to him in reply: "It is not foreign land we have taken nor have we seized the property of others, but only our ancestral heritage which for a time had been unjustly held by our enemies. [34] Now that we have the opportunity, we are holding on to the heritage of our ancestors. [35] As for Joppa and Gazara, which you demand, those cities were doing great harm to our people and our country. For these we will give you a hundred talents." Athenobius made no reply, [36] but returned to the king in anger. When he told him of Simon's words, of his splendor, and of all he had seen, the king fell into a violent rage.

**Victory over Cendebeus.** [37] Trypho had boarded a ship and escaped to Orthosia.† [38] Then the king appointed Cendebeus commander-in-chief of the seacoast, and gave him infantry and cavalry forces. [39] He ordered him to encamp against Judea and to fortify Kedron† and strengthen its gates, so that he could wage war on the people. Meanwhile the king went in pursuit of Trypho. [40] When Cendebeus came to Jamnia, he began to harass the people and to make incursions into Judea, where he took people captive and massacred them. [41] As the king ordered, he fortified Kedron and stationed cavalry and infantry there, so that they could go out and patrol the roads of Judea.

**16** [1] John then went up from Gazara and told his father Simon what Cendebeus was doing. * [2] Simon called his two oldest sons, Judas and John, and said to them: "I and my brothers and my father's house have fought the wars of Israel from our youth until today, and many times we succeeded in saving Israel. [3] I have now grown old, but you, by the mercy of Heaven, have come to maturity. Take my place and my brother's, and go out and fight for our nation; and may the help of Heaven be with you!"

[4] John then mustered in the land twenty thousand warriors and cavalry. Setting out against Cendebeus, they spent the night at Modein, [5] rose early, and marched into the plain. There, facing them, was an immense army of foot soldiers and cavalry, and between the two armies was a wadi. [6] John and his people took their position against the enemy. Seeing that his people were afraid to cross the wadi, John crossed first. When his men saw this, they crossed over after him. * [7] Then he divided his infantry and put his cavalry in the center, for the enemy's cavalry were very numerous. [8] They blew the trumpets, and Cendebeus and his army were routed; many of them fell wounded, and the

---

† 
**15:37** *Orthosia*: a port between Tripoli and the Eleutherus River.
**15:39** *Kedron*: a few miles southeast of Jamnia and facing the fortress of Gazara held by John Hyrcanus (13:53; 16:1).

*
**15:27** 1 Mc 15:5–9.      **16:6** 1 Mc 5:40–43.
**16:1** 1 Mc 13:53.

rest fled toward the stronghold. [9] It was then that John's brother Judas fell wounded; but John pursued them until Cendebeus reached Kedron, which he had fortified. [10] Some took refuge in the towers on the plain of Azotus, but John set fire to these, and about two thousand of the enemy perished. He then returned to Judea in peace.*

**Murder of Simon and His Sons.** [11] Ptolemy, son of Abubus, had been appointed governor of the plain of Jericho, and he had much silver and gold, [12] being the son-in-law of the high priest. [13] But his heart became proud and he was determined to get control of the country. So he made treacherous plans to do away with Simon and his sons. [14] As Simon was inspecting the cities of the country and providing for their needs, he and his sons Mattathias and Judas went down to Jericho in the one hundred and seventy-seventh year, in the eleventh month† (that is, the month Shebat). [15] The son of Abubus gave them a deceitful welcome in the little stronghold called Dok† which he had built. He served them a sumptuous banquet, but he had his men hidden there. [16] Then, when Simon and his sons were drunk, Ptolemy and his men sprang up, weapons in hand, rushed upon Simon in the banquet hall, and killed him, his two sons, and some of his servants. [17] By this vicious act of treachery he repaid good with evil.

[18] Then Ptolemy wrote a report and sent it to the king, asking him to send troops to help him and to turn over to him their country and its cities. [19] He sent other men to Gazara to do away with John. To the army officers he sent letters inviting them to come to him so that he might present them with silver, gold, and gifts. [20] He also sent others to seize Jerusalem and the temple mount. [21] But someone ran ahead and brought word to John at Gazara that his father and his brothers had perished, and "Ptolemy has sent men to kill you also." [22] On hearing this, John was utterly astounded. When the men came to kill him, he seized them and put them to death, for he knew that they sought to kill him.

[23]† Now the rest of the acts of John, his wars and the brave deeds he performed, his rebuilding of the walls, and all his achievements—* [24] these are recorded in the chronicle of his high priesthood, from the time that he succeeded his father as high priest.

---

† **16:14** *In the one hundred and seventy-seventh year, in the eleventh month*: January–February, 134 B.C., by the Temple calendar.

**16:15** *Dok*: a fortress built on a cliff three miles northwest of Jericho, near modern Ain Duq.

**16:23–24** John Hyrcanus was ruler and high priest from 134 B.C. till his death in 104 B.C. These verses suggest that the book was written, or at least completed, only after he died.

---

**16:10** 1 Mc 10:84.      **16:23** 1 Mc 9:22.

# The Second Book of

# Maccabees

## INTRODUCTION

Patricia D. Ahearne-Kroll

The Second Book of Maccabees is not a sequel to 1 Maccabees but is another narrative that tries to persuade the reader to understand the persecution of Antiochus IV Epiphanes (175–164 BCE) and the Maccabean revolt (167–140 BCE) in a particular way. First Maccabees narrates the Maccabean rise to power by concentrating on Maccabean leaders and the ways in which they defined Jewish religious practice, but 2 Maccabees describes the Maccabees' success in terms of how they and other Judeans defended "Judaism." Both 1 and 2 Maccabees (along with the book of Daniel, Dn 7–12) help scholars to reconstruct the historical chronology of events, but much like 1 Maccabees, 2 Maccabees emphasizes a specific view of this history. There remains much debate as to the sequence of events of the time period between 180 and 124 BCE in Judea because there is little documentation that exists outside of these books (e.g., we have no independent records about these Judean events from a Seleucid archive). But it is worth reviewing in the next two paragraphs the combination of factors that most scholars agree contributed to the Judean-Seleucid conflict so as better to understand 1 and 2 Maccabees. The remainder of this introduction will then discuss the distinct ways in which 2 Maccabees tells the story as opposed to 1 Maccabees.

Relations between Judean and Seleucid leaders became more intense after the Seleucid king Antiochus III (223–187 BCE) failed in his western expansion of the empire (through modern-day Turkey). Rome negotiated the terms of Antiochus's defeat, which included a hefty fine paid to Rome over the course of twelve years. As a result, Antiochus's successor, Seleucus IV (187–175 BCE), inherited a bankrupt empire, and much of his reign entailed collecting tribute to pay off the debt

## Outline of 2 Maccabees

(which explains Simon's motives and Heliodorus's mission in 2 Mc 3). When Antiochus IV succeeded Seleucus IV, he fulfilled the financial obligation with Rome and focused on controlling Egypt. After two wars with the Ptolemies (170–168 BCE), Antiochus was forced by the Romans to retreat from Egypt; he then concentrated his efforts on solidifying control over his eastern territories (e.g., Armenia and Persia).

In the midst of Antiochus's military campaigns, tensions arose between different leadership factions in Jerusalem. The actions of Jason (the brother of the high priest Onias III [2 Mc 3:1]) and Menelaus (the brother of Simon the superintendent of the temple [2 Mc 3:4]) reflect different ways in which some Judeans negotiated channels of influence so to maximize benefits under Seleucid rule (1 Mc 1:11–15; 2 Mc 4). Although it is difficult to ascertain the extent to which either person altered Jewish religious practice in Jerusalem (e.g., it is not clear if or how much Jason changed the traditional ritual practices in the

Temple), the Maccabean books clearly demonstrate that some Judeans considered the adaptations to be sacrilegious. The historical records are not clear about exactly when or why Antiochus promulgated decrees against Jewish ancestral practices, but his forced restrictions and violence against Judeans led some to support the Maccabean revolt. Not all Judeans agreed with the Maccabees' strategy, however, as both Maccabean narratives suggest; see, for example, the references to the "lawless" in 1 Maccabees (see the initial introduction to 1 Maccabees) and the counter-efforts of Menelaus and Alcimus in 2 Maccabees (respectively, 2 Mc 13:1–8 and 14:1–14).

As for the particular perspectives of the Maccabean books, important distinctions must be made. Although the Jerusalem Temple matters in 1 Maccabees, the Temple and the ritual activity associated with it play a more pivotal role in 2 Maccabees's historical account. The downward spiral of events in Judea begins with a series of profaning acts against the Temple: Heliodorus (chief minister of Seleucus IV) almost pollutes the holy space; Simon falsely accuses Onias III (the two are mentioned above), and afterward, Jason and then Menelaus wrongfully gain the high priesthood; Jason establishes non-Jewish customs that cause the neglect of the Temple; Lysimachus pillages the Temple treasuries; and Menelaus participates in the murder of Onias (2 Mc 3–4). Menelaus and Jason are blamed for creating the instability in Judea that causes Antiochus IV to attack, harass, and violently restrict Judeans (ch. 5), and the Temple becomes a primary target (5:15–17; 6:1–7). When the Maccabees regain control of the Temple and purify it, they facilitate the promulgation of a public decree that establishes the annual celebration of this victory (10:8), and 2 Maccabees begins with two letters to Egyptian Jews urging them to celebrate this holiday as well (1:1–2:18). Following the purification of the Temple, Judas appears to lead several battles from Jerusalem (implied: 10:16, 11:6–8; more explicitly stated: 10:25–27; 12:32), and he even interrupts a military campaign so as to return for ritual celebrations at the Temple (12:31–32). The last conflict in the book entails Nicanor's threat to permanently destroy the Temple (14:31–33), which the Judeans who fight against him understand (15:18), and Nicanor's defeat also becomes an annual holiday that celebrates the protection of the city and its temple (15:30–36).

In conjunction with this narrative's focus on the Temple, Judas and his companions engage in more religious activity than they do in 1 Maccabees. In 2 Maccabees, Judas's military strategy always entails prayer (2 Mc 8:2–4; 10:16, 25–29, 38; 11:6, 9; 12:6, 15, 28, 36; 13:10–12; 14:15; 15:21–24, 26–27) or other ritual actions (8:23; 10:25; 14:15; cf. 1 Mc 3:44–53; 4:30–33; and 7:40–41). Most interestingly, whereas Mattathias had no qualms about fighting on the sabbath (1 Mc 2:41), the Maccabeans are careful not to do so in 2 Maccabees (8:26–28; 12:38). Second Maccabees also incorporates Deuteronomistic ideas (that is, ideas promoted by the scribal school that produced the books of Deuteronomy, Joshua, Judges, 1 and 2 Samuel, and 1 and 2 Kings), but different from those promoted by 1 Maccabees (see the initial introduction to 1 Maccabees). Most prominent in 2 Maccabees is the author's interest (1) to assign military victory to God (or God's angelic agents) and not to Maccabean skill or weaponry (2 Mc 8:18, 24, 35; 9:5–6; 10:1, 29–30; 11:8, 10; 12:11, 16, 22; 15:7–8; cf. Dt 20 and Jos 6–11); and (2) indicate how God ensures the inviolability of the Temple *when* adherents are in right relationship with God (2 Mc 3:24–34 and implied by chs. 14–15, but see why Antiochus IV is able to enter the sanctuary in 5:18–20; cf. 2 Sm 7; 1 Kgs 9).

Although much of the book praises Judas's leadership, 2 Maccabees primarily extols faithful adherence to Jewish religious practices, and so the Maccabees are not the only heroes. First Maccabees asserts that actively engaging in warfare against the Seleucids *is* according to God's plan, not choosing innocent death as a form of faithful resistance (1 Mc 2:29–48). But 2 Maccabees adamantly disagrees. Eleazar and the mother with her seven sons (2 Mc 6:18–7:42) are the first to demonstrate great virtue, nobility, and courage (not the Maccabees), and Razis's death near the end of the book (and not Judas's leadership) serves as a counterpart to Alcimus's treachery (14:37–46).

Devotion to Jewish ancestral customs and ritual practice in the Temple are the key features of faithful adherence to God, whether or not one has fought in battle.

This point leads to another distinction between the two Maccabean narratives. Whereas in 1 Maccabees, being Jewish is defined mostly by Maccabean leadership (see the initial introduction to 1 Maccabees), 2 Maccabees describes Jewish religious practice in a broader way. The Maccabees do not define Judaism, but rather, there is an abstract understanding of what Judaism is—and the Maccabees and other faithful Judeans defend it. To make this point, the author several times refers to "Judaism" (*Ioudaismos*), assuming that the reader understands the essential aspects that this term entails. Thus the author asserts that God was behind the Judean fight for "Judaism" (2 Mc 2:21), and Judas's initial army consists of "others who had remained faithful to Judaism" (8:1). Second Maccabees is one of the first Greek texts to use this term, and it implies a uniformity of Jewish practice that was not the case in the Hellenistic and early Roman periods. The object of this narrative, however, is to convey how the righteous adherents of God reconciled the nation with God and helped to maintain Jewish ancestral practices in Judea, and the author summarizes this message as fighting on behalf of Judaism.

What is then seen to be a threat to this way of life is also drawn in simplistic, overarching terms: "Hellenism," "Greek way of life," or "Greek customs" (2 Mc 4:10, 13; 6:9; 11:24). Even within polytheistic cultures, families often were devoted to a particular god (not to the whole pantheon), and people's understanding of deities depended upon particular traditions about that god at particular locations. Apollo at Daphne near Antioch, for example, was not the same as Apollo at Delphi. Although these cultures could more easily add the gods of imperial leaders to their worldviews, it does not mean that they welcomed doing so or even found it meaningful. Likewise, as in Judea, the peoples of the Levant had their own ancestral traditions that for some (e.g., the Phoenicians) were centuries old, and they likely did not view themselves primarily as "Greek." Even the author's insistence that Jason's gymnasium and the activities there demonstrated his "craze for Hellenism" (4:12–15) is probably exaggerated. In the Hellenistic world, gymnasiums not only educated and trained elite boys but also connected them with the civic life of the city, which included religious practice. Although Jason introduced a foreign educational system to Jerusalem, it is not clear how much (if at all) he also prohibited Jewish religious practice. The fact that priests take part in some gymnasium activities (4:14) suggests that Jason's vision for Jerusalem may have supported Jewish religious practices more than what the author implies. At the very least, Jason's gymnasium is best understood as an example of the kind of negotiation that all local cultures engaged in after the conquest of Alexander the Great.

The defense of "Judaism" and the Jerusalem Temple in 2 Maccabees, rather than the defense of the Maccabees, makes it clear that this narrative was not written to defend the Hasmonean dynasty (as 1 Maccabees does). Second Maccabees praises the leadership of Judas, but it also extols the innocent suffering and death of those who upheld "Judaism." Eleazar, the mother and her seven sons, and Razis are models of faithful adherence to God, but 1 Maccabees disagrees about the place of such deaths in the fight against the Seleucids (1 Mc 2:29–48). For 2 Maccabees, the ultimate victory is the preservation of religious activity in the Temple, but for 1 Maccabees, it is the establishment of the Judean kingdom under Maccabean rule. ■

# THE SECOND BOOK OF MACCABEES

## New American Bible, Introduction

Although this book, like the preceding one, receives its title from its protagonist, Judas Maccabee (or Maccabeus), it is not a sequel to 1 Maccabees. The two differ in many respects. Whereas the first covers the period from the beginning of the reign of Antiochus IV (175 B.C.) to the accession of John Hyrcanus I (134 B.C.), this book treats of the events in Jewish history from the time of the high priest Onias III and King Seleucus IV (ca. 180 B.C.) to the defeat of Nicanor's army (161 B.C.).

The author of 2 Maccabees states (2:23) that this one-volume work is an abridgment of a five-volume work by Jason of Cyrene; but since this latter has not survived, it is difficult to determine its relationship to the present epitome. One does not know how freely the anonymous epitomizer may have rewritten the original composition or how closely the abridgment follows the wording of the original. Some parts of the text here clearly not derived from Jason's work are the preface (2:19–32), the epilogue (15:37–39), and probably also certain moralizing reflections (e.g., 5:17–20; 6:12–17). It is certain, however, that both works were written in Greek, which explains in part why 2 Maccabees was not included in the canon of the Hebrew Bible.

The book is not without genuine historical value in supplementing 1 Maccabees, and it contains some apparently authentic official documents (11:16–38). Its purpose, whether intended by Jason himself or read into it by the compiler, is to give a theological interpretation to the history of the period. The major concern is the Jerusalem Temple, whose defender is the God of Israel. There is less interest, therefore, in the military exploits of Judas Maccabeus and more in God's marvelous interventions on behalf of the Jews and their Temple. These divine actions direct the course of events, both to punish the sacrilegious and blasphemous pagans and to purify and restore the Temple. The author sometimes effects this purpose by transferring events from their proper chronological order, by giving exaggerated figures for the size of armies and the numbers killed in battle, by placing long, edifying discourses and prayers in the mouths of heroes, and by describing elaborate celestial apparitions (3:24–34; 5:2–4; 10:29–30; 15:11–16). The book is the earliest known source of stories that glorify God's holy martyrs (6:18–7:42; 14:37–46).

Of theological importance are the author's teachings on Israel's sufferings (5:17–20; 6:12–17), the resurrection of the just on the last day (7:9, 11, 14, 23; 14:46), the intercession of the saints in heaven for people living on earth (15:11–16), and the power of the living to offer prayers and sacrifices for the dead (12:39–46).

The beginning of 2 Maccabees consists of two letters sent by the Jews of Jerusalem to their coreligionists in Egypt. They deal with the observance of the feast commemorating the central event of the book, the purification of the Temple (Hanukkah). It is uncertain whether the author or a later scribe prefixed these letters to the narrative proper. If the author is responsible for their insertion, the book must have been written some time after 124 B.C., the date of the more recent of the two letters. A date of composition in the late second century B.C. is likely.

The main divisions of 2 Maccabees are:

I. Letters to the Jews in Egypt (1:1–2:18)
II. Compiler's Preface (2:19–32)
III. Heliodorus' Attempt to Profane the Temple (3:1–40)
IV. Profanation and Persecution (4:1–7:42)
V. Victories of Judas and Purification of the Temple (8:1–10:9)
VI. Renewed Persecution (10:10–15:36)
VII. Epilogue (15:37–39) ■

# SECOND MACCABEES

## I. LETTERS TO THE JEWS IN EGYPT

**1** **Letter 1: 124 B.C.** [1] The Jews in Jerusalem and in the land of Judea send greetings to their kindred, the Jews in Egypt, and wish them true peace! [2] May God do good to you and remember his covenant with his faithful servants, Abraham, Isaac and Jacob, [3] give to all of you a heart to worship him and to do his will wholeheartedly and with a willing spirit, [4] open your heart to his law and commandments and grant you peace, [5] hear your prayers, and be reconciled to you, and never forsake you in time of adversity. [6] Even now we are praying for you here.

[7] In the reign of Demetrius,† the one hundred and sixty-ninth year, we Jews wrote to you during the height of the distress that overtook us in those years after Jason and his followers revolted against the holy land and the kingdom,* [8] set fire to the gatehouse and shed innocent blood. But we prayed to the Lord, and our prayer was heard;† we offered sacrifices and fine flour; we lighted the lamps and set out the loaves of bread.* [9] We are now reminding you to celebrate the feast of Booths in the month of Kislev.† [10] Dated in the one hundred and eighty-eighth year.†

**Letter 2: 164 B.C.** The people of Jerusalem and Judea, the senate, and Judas send greetings and good wishes to Aristobulus, teacher of King Ptolemy and member of the family of the anointed priests, and to the Jews in Egypt. [11] Since we have been saved by God from grave dangers, we give him great thanks as befits those who fought against the king;† [12]* for it was God who drove out those who fought against the holy city. [13] When their leader arrived in Persia with his seemingly irresistible army, they were cut to pieces in the temple of the goddess Nanea† through a deceitful stratagem employed by Nanea's priests. [14]† On the pretext of marrying the goddess, Antiochus with his Friends had come to the place to get its great treasures as a dowry. [15] When the priests of Nanea's temple had displayed the treasures and Antiochus with a few attendants had come inside the wall of the temple precincts, the priests locked the temple as soon as he entered. [16] Then they opened a hidden trapdoor in the ceiling, and hurling stones at the leader and his companions, struck them down. They dismembered the bodies, cut off their heads and tossed them to the people outside. [17] Forever blessed be our God, who has thus punished the impious!

[18]† Since we shall be celebrating the purification of the temple on the twenty-fifth day of the month Kislev,* we thought it right to inform you, that you too may celebrate the feast of Booths and of the fire that appeared when Nehemiah, the rebuilder of the temple† and the altar, offered sacrifices. [19] For when our ancestors were being led into captivity in Persia,† devout priests at the time took some of the fire from the altar and hid it secretly in the hollow of a dry cistern, making sure that the place would be unknown to anyone. [20] Many years later, when it so pleased God, Nehemiah, commissioned by the king of Persia, sent the

---

† **1:7** *Demetrius*: Demetrius II, king of Syria (145–139, 129–125 B.C.). *The one hundred and sixty-ninth year*: i.e., of the Seleucid era, 143 B.C. Regarding the dates in 1 and 2 Maccabees, see note on 1 Mc 1:10. On the troubles caused by Jason and his revolt against the kingdom, i.e., the rule of the legitimate high priest, see 2 Mc 4:7–22.

**1:8** *Our prayer was heard*: in the victory of the Maccabees.

**1:9** *Feast of Booths in the month of Kislev*: really the feast of the Dedication of the Temple, Hanukkah (2 Mc 10:1–8), celebrated on the twenty-fifth of Kislev (Nov.–Dec.). Its solemnity resembles that of the actual feast of Booths (Lv 23:33–43), celebrated on the fifteenth of Tishri (Sept.–Oct.); cf. 2 Mc 1:18.

**1:10** *The one hundred and eighty-eighth year*: 124 B.C. The date pertains to the preceding, not the following letter. *Senate*: the council of Jewish elders of Jerusalem; cf. 1 Mc 12:6. *King Ptolemy*: Ptolemy VI Philometor, ruler of Egypt from 180 to 145 B.C.; he is mentioned also in 1 Mc 1:18; 10:51–59.

**1:11–12** *The king*: Antiochus IV of Syria, the bitter persecutor of the Jews, who, as leader of the Syrian army that invaded Persia, perished there in 164 B.C.

**1:13** *Nanea*: an oriental goddess comparable to Artemis of the Greeks.

**1:14–17** Differing accounts of the death of Antiochus IV are found in 2 Mc 9:1–29 and in 1 Mc 6:1–16 (see also Dn 11:40–45). The writer of this letter had probably heard a distorted rumor of the king's death. This and other indications suggest that the letter was written very soon after Antiochus IV died, perhaps in 164 B.C.

**1:18–36** This legendary account of Nehemiah's miraculous fire is incorporated in the letter because of its connection with the Temple and its rededication. *Booths*: see note on v. 9.

**1:18** *Nehemiah, the rebuilder of the temple*: he rebuilt the walls of Jerusalem, but the Temple had been rebuilt by Zerubbabel almost a century before.

**1:19** *Persia*: actually Babylonia, which later became part of the Persian empire.

---

**1:7** 2 Mc 4:7–20.
**1:8** 1 Mc 4:50–51.
**1:12–17** 2 Mc 9:1–29; 1 Mc

6:1–13; Dn 11:40–45.
**1:18** 2 Mc 6:7; 10:5; 1 Mc 1:59; 4:59.

descendants of the priests who had hidden the fire to look for it. [21] When they informed us that they could not find any fire, but only a thick liquid, he ordered them to scoop some out and bring it. After the material for the sacrifices had been prepared, Nehemiah ordered the priests to sprinkle the wood and what lay on it with the liquid. [22] This was done, and when at length the sun, which had been clouded over, began to shine, a great fire blazed up, so that everyone marveled. [23] While the sacrifice was being burned, the priests recited a prayer, and all present joined in with them. Jonathan led and the rest responded with Nehemiah.

[24] The prayer was as follows: "Lord, Lord God, creator of all things, awesome and strong, just and merciful, the only king and benefactor, [25] who alone are gracious, just, almighty, and eternal, Israel's savior from all evil, who chose our ancestors and sanctified them: [26] accept this sacrifice on behalf of all your people Israel and guard and sanctify your portion. [27] Gather together our scattered people, free those who are slaves among the Gentiles, look kindly on those who are despised and detested, and let the Gentiles know that you are our God. [28] Punish those who lord it over us and in their arrogance oppress us. [29] Plant your people in your holy place, as Moses said."*

[30] Then the priests sang hymns. [31] After the sacrifice was consumed, Nehemiah ordered the rest of the liquid to be poured upon large stones. [32] As soon as this was done, a flame blazed up, but its light was lost in the brilliance coming from the altar. [33] When the event became known and the king of the Persians was told that, in the very place where the exiled priests had hidden the fire, a liquid was found with which Nehemiah and his people had burned the sacrifices, [34] the king, after verifying the fact, fenced the place off and declared it sacred. [35] To those whom the king favored, he distributed many benefits he received. [36] Nehemiah and his companions

called the liquid nephthar, meaning purification, but most people named it naphtha.†*

**2** [1] In the records it will be found that Jeremiah the prophet ordered the deportees to take some of the fire with them as indicated, [2] and that the prophet, in giving them the law, directed the deportees not to forget the commandments of the Lord or be led astray in their thoughts, when seeing the gold and silver idols and their adornments.* [3] With other similar words he exhorted them that the law should not depart from their hearts.

[4] † The same document also tells how the prophet, in virtue of an oracle, ordered that the tent and the ark should accompany him, and how he went to the very mountain that Moses climbed to behold God's inheritance.* [5] When Jeremiah arrived there, he found a chamber in a cave in which he put the tent, the ark, and the altar of incense; then he sealed the entrance. [6] Some of those who followed him came up intending to mark the path, but they could not find it. [7] When Jeremiah heard of this, he reproved them: "The place is to remain unknown until God gathers his people together again and shows them mercy. [8] Then the Lord will disclose these things, and the glory of the Lord and the cloud will be seen, just as they appeared in the time of Moses and of Solomon when he prayed that the place† might be greatly sanctified."*

[9] It is also related how Solomon in his wisdom offered a sacrifice for the dedication and the completion of the temple. [10] Just as Moses prayed to the Lord and fire descended from the sky and consumed the sacrifices, so also Solomon prayed and fire came down and consumed the burnt offerings.* [11] † Moses had said, "Because it had not been eaten, the purification offering was consumed."* [12] Solomon also celebrated the feast in the same way for eight days.

[13] These same things are also told in the records and in Nehemiah's memoirs,† as well

---

† **1:36** By a play on words, the Greek term *naphtha* (petroleum) is assimilated to some Semitic word, perhaps *nephthar*, meaning "loosened."
  **2:4–5** This legendary account is given for the purpose of explaining why the postexilic Temple was the legitimate place of worship even without these sacred objects. *The very mountain*: Nebo; cf. Dt 32:49; 34:1.
  **2:8** *The place*: the Temple of Jerusalem.
  **2:11** The statement attributed here to Moses seems to be based on Lv 10:16–20.

**2:13** *Nehemiah's memoirs*: a lost apocryphal work, or perhaps Neh 1–7, 11–13.

*   **1:29** 2 Mc 2:18; Ex 15:17; Dt 30:3–5.
  **1:36** 2 Mc 2:18; 10:3; 14:36.
  **2:2** Bar 6:1–72.
  **2:4** Dt 32:49; 34:1;
  Rev 11:19.
  **2:8** Ex 40:34–35; 1 Kgs 8:11.
  **2:10** Lv 9:23–24; 2 Chr 7:1.
  **2:11** Lv 10:16–20.

as how he founded a library and collected the books about the kings and the prophets, the books of David, and the royal letters about votive offerings. [14] In like manner Judas also collected for us all the books that had been scattered because of the war, and we now have them in our possession. * [15] If you need them, send messengers to get them for you.

[16] As we are about to celebrate the purification, we are writing: you should celebrate the feast days. [17] It is God who has saved all his people and has restored to all of them their inheritance, the kingdom, the priesthood, and the sacred rites, [18] as he promised through the law. For we hope in God, that he will soon have mercy on us and gather us together from everywhere under the heavens to his holy place, for he has rescued us from great perils and has purified the place. *

## II. COMPILER'S PREFACE

[19] This is the story of Judas Maccabeus and his brothers, of the purification of the great temple, the dedication of the altar, [20] the campaigns against Antiochus Epiphanes and his son Eupator, † [21] and of the heavenly manifestations accorded to the heroes who fought bravely for the Jewish people. Few as they were, they plundered the whole land, put to flight the barbarian hordes, [22] regained possession of the temple renowned throughout the world, and liberated the city. They reestablished the laws that were in danger of being abolished, while the Lord favored them with every kindness. [23] All this, detailed by Jason of Cyrene in five volumes, we will try to condense into a single book.

[24] For in view of the flood of data, and the difficulties encountered, given such abundant material, by those who wish to plunge into accounts of the history, [25] we have aimed to please those who prefer simply to read, to make it easy for the studious who wish to commit things to memory, and to be helpful to all. [26] For us who have undertaken the labor of making this digest, the task, far from being easy, is one of sweat and of sleepless nights. [27] Just so, the preparation of a festive banquet is no light matter for one who seeks to give enjoyment to others. Similarly, to win the gratitude of many we will gladly endure this labor, [28] leaving the responsibility for exact details to the historian, and confining our efforts to presenting only a summary outline. [29] As the architect of a new house must pay attention to the whole structure, while the one who undertakes the decoration and the frescoes has to be concerned only with what is needed for ornamentation, so I think it is with us. * [30] To enter into questions and examine them from all sides and to be busy about details is the task of the historian; [31] but one who is making an adaptation should be allowed to aim at brevity of expression and to forgo complete treatment of the matter. [32] Here, then, let us begin our account without adding to what has already been said; it would be silly to lengthen the preface to the history and then cut short the history itself.

## III. HELIODORUS' ATTEMPT TO PROFANE THE TEMPLE†

**3** **Heliodorus' Arrival in Jerusalem.** [1] While the holy city lived in perfect peace and the laws were strictly observed because of the piety of the high priest Onias † and his hatred of evil, * [2] the kings themselves honored the place and glorified the temple with the most magnificent gifts. [3] Thus Seleucus, † king of Asia, defrayed from his own revenues all the expenses necessary for the liturgy of sacrifice.

[4] But a certain Simon, of the priestly clan of Bilgah, † who had been appointed superintendent of the temple, had a quarrel with the high priest about the administration of the city market. * [5] Since he could not prevail against Onias, he went to Apollonius of Tarsus, who at that time was governor of Coelesyria and Phoenicia, [6] and reported to him that the treasury in Jerusalem was full of such untold

---

† **2:20** For the account of the campaigns against Antiochus IV Epiphanes, see 4:7–10:9; and for the account of those against his son Antiochus V Eupator, see 10:10–13:26.

**3:1–40** This legendary episode about Heliodorus is recounted here for the purpose of stressing the inviolability of the Temple of Jerusalem; its later profanation was interpreted as owing to the sins of the people; cf. 5:17–18.

**3:1** *Onias*: Onias III was high priest from 196 to 175 B.C. and died in 171 B.C. He was the son of Simon, whose praises are sung in Sir 50:1–21.

**3:3** *Seleucus*: Seleucus IV Philopator, who reigned from 187 to 175 B.C.

**3:4** *Bilgah*: a priestly family mentioned in 1 Chr 24:14; Neh 12:5, 18.

*

**2:14** 1 Mc 1:57.
**2:18** Dt 30:3–5.
**2:29** 2 Mc 15:38–39.

**3:1** 2 Mc 5:19–20; 15:12.
**3:4** 2 Mc 4:23.

riches that the sum total of the assets was past counting and that since they did not belong to the account of the sacrifices, it would be possible for them to fall under the authority of the king. [7] When Apollonius had an audience with the king, he informed him about the riches that had been reported to him. The king chose his chief minister Heliodorus and sent him with instructions to seize those riches. [8] So Heliodorus immediately set out on his journey, ostensibly to visit the cities of Coelesyria and Phoenicia, but in reality to carry out the king's purpose.

[9] When he arrived in Jerusalem and had been graciously received by the high priest of the city, he told him about the information that had been given, and explained the reason for his presence, and he inquired if these things were really true. [10] The high priest explained that there were deposits for widows and orphans,* [11] and some was the property of Hyrcanus, son of Tobias,† a man who occupied a very high position. Contrary to the misrepresentations of the impious Simon, the total amounted only to four hundred talents of silver and two hundred of gold. [12] It was utterly unthinkable to defraud those who had placed their trust in the sanctity of the place and in the sacred inviolability of a temple venerated all over the world.

**Heliodorus' Plan To Rob the Temple.** [13] But Heliodorus, because of the orders he had from the king, said that in any case this money must be confiscated for the royal treasury. [14] So on the day he had set he went in to take an inventory of the funds. There was no little anguish throughout the city. [15] Priests prostrated themselves before the altar in their priestly robes, and called toward heaven for the one who had given the law about deposits to keep the deposits safe for those who had made them.* [16] Whoever saw the appearance of the high priest was pierced to the heart, for the changed complexion of his face revealed his mental anguish. [17] The terror and bodily trembling that had come over the man clearly showed those who saw him the pain that lodged in his heart. [18] People rushed out of their houses and crowded together making common supplication, because the place was in danger of being profaned. [19] Women, girded with sackcloth below their breasts, filled the streets. Young women secluded indoors all ran, some to the gates, some to the walls, others peered through the windows— [20] all of them with hands raised toward heaven, making supplication. [21] It was pitiful to see the populace prostrate everywhere and the high priest full of dread and anguish. [22] While they were imploring the almighty Lord to keep the deposits safe and secure for those who had placed them in trust, [23] Heliodorus went on with his plan.

**God Protects the Temple.** [24] But just as Heliodorus was arriving at the treasury with his bodyguards, the Lord of spirits and all authority produced an apparition so great that those who had been bold enough to accompany Heliodorus were panic-stricken at God's power and fainted away in terror. [25] There appeared to them a richly caparisoned horse, mounted by a fearsome rider. Charging furiously, the horse attacked Heliodorus with its front hooves. The rider was seen wearing golden armor. [26] Then two other young men, remarkably strong, strikingly handsome, and splendidly attired, appeared before him. Standing on each side of him, they flogged him unceasingly, inflicting innumerable blows. [27] Suddenly he fell to the ground, enveloped in great darkness. His men picked him up and laid him on a stretcher. [28] They carried away helpless the man who a moment before had entered that treasury under arms with a great retinue and his whole bodyguard. They clearly recognized the sovereign power of God.

**The Restoration and Testimony of Heliodorus.** [29] As Heliodorus lay speechless because of God's action and deprived of any hope of recovery, [30] the people praised the Lord who had marvelously glorified his own place; and the temple, charged so shortly before with fear and commotion, was filled with joy and gladness, now that the almighty Lord had appeared. [31] Quickly some of the companions of Heliodorus begged Onias to call upon the Most High to spare the life of one who was about to

---

† **3:11** *Hyrcanus, son of Tobias:* a member of the Tobiad family of Transjordan (Neh 2:10; 6:17–19; 13:4–8). Hyrcanus' father was Joseph, whose mother was the sister of the high priest Onias II.

* **3:10** Dt 14:29; 26:12.     **3:15** Ex 22:6–14.

breathe his last. ³²The high priest, suspecting that the king might think that Heliodorus had suffered some foul play at the hands of the Jews, offered a sacrifice for the man's recovery. ³³While the high priest was offering the sacrifice of atonement, the same young men dressed in the same clothing again appeared and stood before Heliodorus. "Be very grateful to the high priest Onias," they told him. "It is for his sake that the Lord has spared your life. ³⁴Since you have been scourged by Heaven, proclaim to all God's great power." When they had said this, they disappeared.

³⁵After Heliodorus had offered a sacrifice to the Lord and made most solemn vows to the one who had spared his life, he bade Onias farewell, and returned with his soldiers to the king. ³⁶Before all he gave witness to the deeds of the most high God that he had seen with his own eyes. ³⁷When the king asked Heliodorus what sort of person would be suitable to be sent to Jerusalem next, he answered: ³⁸"If you have an enemy or one who is plotting against the government, send him there, and you will get him back with a flogging, if indeed he survives at all; for there is certainly some divine power about the place. ³⁹The one whose dwelling is in heaven watches over that place and protects it, and strikes down and destroys those who come to harm it." ⁴⁰This was how the matter concerning Heliodorus and the preservation of the treasury turned out.

## IV. PROFANATION AND PERSECUTION

**4** **Simon Accuses Onias.** ¹The Simon mentioned above as the informer about the funds against his own country slandered Onias as the one who incited Heliodorus and instigated the whole miserable affair. ²He dared to brand as a schemer against the government the man who was the benefactor of the city, the protector of his compatriots, and a zealous defender of the laws. ³When Simon's hostility

reached such a pitch that murders were being committed by one of his henchmen, ⁴Onias saw that the opposition was serious and that Apollonius, son of Menestheus, the governor of Coelesyria and Phoenicia, was abetting Simon's wickedness. ⁵So he had recourse to the king, not as an accuser of his compatriots, but as one looking to the general and particular good of all the people. ⁶He saw that without royal attention it would be impossible to have a peaceful government, and that Simon would not desist from his folly.

**Jason as High Priest.** ⁷But Seleucus died,† and when Antiochus surnamed Epiphanes succeeded him on the throne, Onias' brother Jason obtained the high priesthood by corrupt means:* ⁸in an interview, he promised the king three hundred and sixty talents of silver, as well as eighty talents from another source of income. ⁹Besides this he would undertake to pay a hundred and fifty more, if he was given authority to establish a gymnasium and a youth center† for it and to enroll Jerusalemites as citizens of Antioch.

¹⁰When Jason received the king's approval and came into office, he immediately initiated his compatriots into the Greek way of life. ¹¹He set aside the royal concessions granted to the Jews through the mediation of John, father of Eupolemus† (that Eupolemus who would later go on an embassy to the Romans to establish friendship and alliance with them); he set aside the lawful practices and introduced customs contrary to the law.* ¹²*With perverse delight he established a gymnasium† at the very foot of the citadel, where he induced the noblest young men to wear the Greek hat. ¹³The craze for Hellenism and the adoption of foreign customs reached such a pitch, through the outrageous wickedness of Jason, the renegade and would-be high priest, ¹⁴that the priests no longer cared about the service of the altar. Disdaining the temple and neglecting

---

4:7 *Seleucus died*: he was murdered by Heliodorus. Antiochus Epiphanes was his younger brother. Onias' brother showed his enthusiasm for the Greek way of life (v. 10) by changing his Hebrew name Joshua, or Jesus, to the Greek name Jason.

4:9 *Youth center*: an educational institution in which young men were trained both in Greek intellectual culture and in physical fitness. *Citizens of Antioch*: honorary citizens of Antioch, a Hellenistic city of the Seleucid Kingdom that had a corporation of such Antiochians, who enjoyed certain political and commercial privileges.

4:11 *Eupolemus*: one of the two envoys sent to Rome by Ju-

das Maccabeus (1 Mc 8:17).

4:12 Since the *gymnasium*, where the youth exercised naked (Greek *gymnos*), lay in the Tyropoeon Valley to the east of the citadel, it was directly next to the Temple on its eastern side. *The Greek hat*: a wide-brimmed hat, traditional headgear of Hermes, the patron god of athletic contests; it formed part of the distinctive costume of the members of the "youth center."

4:7 2 Mc 1:7; 1 Mc 1:10.    4:12–17 1 Mc 1:11–15.
4:11 1 Mc 8:17.

the sacrifices, they hastened, at the signal for the games, to take part in the unlawful exercises at the arena. [15] What their ancestors had regarded as honors they despised; what the Greeks esteemed as glory they prized highly. [16] For this reason they found themselves in serious trouble: the very people whose manner of life they emulated, and whom they desired to imitate in everything, became their enemies and oppressors. [17] It is no light matter to flout the laws of God, as subsequent events will show.

[18] When the quinquennial games were held at Tyre in the presence of the king, [19] the vile Jason sent representatives of the Antiochians of Jerusalem, to bring three hundred silver drachmas for the sacrifice to Hercules. But the bearers themselves decided that the money should not be spent on a sacrifice, as that was not right, but should be used for some other purpose. [20] So the contribution meant for the sacrifice to Hercules by the sender, was in fact applied to the construction of triremes† by those who brought it.

[21] When Apollonius, son of Menestheus, was sent to Egypt for the coronation of King Philometor,† Antiochus learned from him that the king was opposed to his policies. He took measures for his own security; so after going to Joppa, he proceeded to Jerusalem. [22] There he was received with great pomp by Jason and the people of the city, who escorted him with torchlights and acclamations; following this, he led his army into Phoenicia.

**Menelaus as High Priest.** [23] Three years later Jason sent Menelaus,† brother of the aforementioned Simon, to deliver the money to the king, and to complete negotiations on urgent matters. [24] But after his introduction to the king, he flattered him with such an air of authority that he secured the high priesthood for himself, outbidding Jason by three hundred talents of silver. [25] He returned with the royal commission, but with nothing that made him worthy of the high priesthood; he had the temper of a cruel tyrant and the rage of a wild beast. [26] So Jason, who had cheated his own brother and now saw himself cheated by another man, was driven out as a fugitive to the country of the Ammonites. [27] But Menelaus, who obtained the office, paid nothing of the money he had promised to the king, [28] in spite of the demand of Sostratus, the commandant of the citadel, whose duty it was to collect the taxes. For this reason, both were summoned before the king. [29] Menelaus left his brother Lysimachus as his deputy in the high priesthood, while Sostratus left Crates, commander of the Cypriots.*

**Murder of Onias.** [30] While these things were taking place, the people of Tarsus and Mallus† rose in revolt, because their cities had been given as a gift to Antiochis, the king's concubine. [31] So the king hastened off to settle the affair, leaving Andronicus, one of his nobles, as his deputy. [32] Menelaus, for his part, thinking this a good opportunity, stole some gold vessels from the temple and presented them to Andronicus; he had already sold other vessels in Tyre and in the neighboring cities. [33] When Onias had clear evidence, he accused Menelaus publicly, after withdrawing to the inviolable sanctuary at Daphne, near Antioch. [34] Thereupon Menelaus approached Andronicus privately and urged him to seize Onias. So Andronicus went to Onias, treacherously reassuring him by offering his right hand in oath, and persuaded him, in spite of his suspicions, to leave the sanctuary. Then, with no regard for justice, he immediately put him to death.

[35] As a result, not only the Jews, but many people of other nations as well, were indignant and angry over the unjust murder of the man. [36] When the king returned from the region of Cilicia, the Jews of the city,† together with the Greeks who detested the crime, went to see him about the murder of Onias. [37] Antiochus was deeply grieved and full of pity; he wept as he recalled the prudence and noble conduct of the deceased. [38] Inflamed with anger, he immediately stripped Andronicus of his purple robe, tore off his garments, and had him led through the whole city to the very place where he had committed the outrage

---

† **4:20** *Triremes:* war vessels with three banks of oars.
**4:21** *Philometor:* Ptolemy VI, king of Egypt, ca. 172 to ca. 145 B.C.
**4:23** *Menelaus:* Jewish high priest from ca. 172 to his execution in 162 B.C. (13:3–8).
**4:30** *Mallus:* a city of Cilicia (v. 36) in southeastern Asia Mi-

nor, about thirty miles east of Tarsus.
**4:36** *The city:* Antioch. But some understand the Greek to mean "each city."

* **4:29** 2 Mc 4:39–42.

against Onias; and there he put the murderer to death. Thus the Lord rendered him the punishment he deserved.

**More Outrages.** 39 Many acts of sacrilege had been committed by Lysimachus in the city† with the connivance of Menelaus. When word spread, the people assembled in protest against Lysimachus, because a large number of gold vessels had been stolen. 40 As the crowds, now thoroughly enraged, began to riot, Lysimachus launched an unjustified attack against them with about three thousand armed men under the leadership of a certain Auranus, a man as advanced in folly as he was in years. 41 Seeing Lysimachus' attack, people picked up stones, pieces of wood or handfuls of the ashes lying there and threw them in wild confusion at Lysimachus and his men. 42 As a result, they wounded many of them and even killed a few, while they put all to flight. The temple robber himself they killed near the treasury.

43 Charges about this affair were brought against Menelaus. 44 When the king came to Tyre, three men sent by the senate pleaded the case before him. 45 But Menelaus, seeing himself on the losing side, promised Ptolemy, son of Dorymenes, a substantial sum of money if he would win the king over.* 46 So Ptolemy took the king aside into a colonnade, as if to get some fresh air, and persuaded him to change his mind. 47 Menelaus, who was the cause of all the trouble, the king acquitted of the charges, while he condemned to death those poor men who would have been declared innocent even if they had pleaded their case before Scythians. 48 Thus, those who had prosecuted the case on behalf of the city, the people, and the sacred vessels, quickly suffered unjust punishment. 49 For this reason, even Tyrians, detesting the crime, provided sumptuously for their burial. 50 But Menelaus, thanks to the greed of those in power, remained in office, where he grew in wickedness, scheming greatly against his fellow citizens.

**5 Jason's Revolt.** 1 About this time Antiochus sent his second expedition† into Egypt.* 2 * It then happened that all over the city, for nearly forty days, there appeared horsemen, clothed in garments of a golden weave, charging in midair—companies fully armed with lances and drawn swords; 3 squadrons of cavalry in battle array, charges and countercharges on this side and that, with brandished shields and bristling spears, flights of arrows and flashes of gold ornaments, together with armor of every sort. 4 Therefore all prayed that this vision might be a good omen.

5 But when a false rumor circulated that Antiochus was dead, Jason† gathered at least a thousand men and suddenly attacked the city. As the defenders on the walls were forced back and the city was finally being taken, Menelaus took refuge in the citadel. 6 For his part, Jason continued the merciless slaughter of his fellow citizens, not realizing that triumph over one's own kindred is the greatest calamity; he thought he was winning a victory over his enemies, not over his own people. 7 Even so, he did not gain control of the government, but in the end received only disgrace for his treachery, and once again took refuge in the country of the Ammonites. 8 At length he met a miserable end. Called to account before Aretas,† ruler of the Arabians, he fled from city to city, hunted by all, hated as an apostate from the laws, abhorred as the executioner of his country and his compatriots. Driven into Egypt, 9 he set out by sea for the Lacedaemonians, among whom he hoped to find protection because of his relations with them. He who had exiled so many from their country perished in exile; 10 and he who had cast out so many to lie unburied went unmourned and without a funeral of any kind, nor any place in the tomb of his ancestors.

**Revenge by Antiochus.** 11 *When these happenings were reported to the king, he thought that Judea was in revolt. Raging like a wild animal, he set out from Egypt and took

† **4:39** *The city*: Jerusalem. Menelaus was still in Syria.
**5:1** *Second expedition*: the first invasion of Egypt by Antiochus IV in 169 B.C. (1 Mc 1:16–20) is not mentioned in 2 Maccabees, unless the coming of the Syrian army to Palestine (2 Mc 4:21–22) is regarded as the first invasion. The author of 2 Maccabees apparently combines the first pillage of Jerusalem in 169 B.C. after Antiochus' first invasion of Egypt (1 Mc 1:20–28; cf. 2 Mc 5:5–7) with the second pillage of the city two years later (167 B.C.), following the king's second invasion of Egypt in 168

B.C. (1 Mc 1:29–35; cf. 2 Mc 5:24–26).
**5:5** *Jason*: brother of Onias III, claimant of the high priesthood (4:7–10). Later he was supplanted by Menelaus, who drove him into Transjordan (4:26).
**5:8** *Aretas*: King Aretas I of the Nabateans; cf. 1 Mc 5:25.

*
**4:45** 2 Mc 8:8; 1 Mc 3:38.     **5:2–3** 2 Mc 3:24–26;
**5:1–10** 1 Mc 1:16–19; Dn          10:29–30; 11:8.
11:25–30.                          **5:11–21** 1 Mc 1:20–24.

Jerusalem by storm. [12] He ordered his soldiers to cut down without mercy those whom they met and to slay those who took refuge in their houses. [13] There was a massacre of young and old, a killing of women and children, a slaughter of young women and infants. [14] In the space of three days, eighty thousand were lost, forty thousand meeting a violent death, and the same number being sold into slavery.

[15] Not satisfied with this, the king dared to enter the holiest temple in the world; Menelaus, that traitor both to the laws and to his country, served as guide. [16] He laid his impure hands on the sacred vessels and swept up with profane hands the votive offerings made by other kings for the advancement, the glory, and the honor of the place. [17] Antiochus became puffed up in spirit, not realizing that it was because of the sins of the city's inhabitants that the Sovereign Lord was angry for a little while: hence the disregard of the place.* [18] If they had not become entangled in so many sins, this man, like that Heliodorus sent by King Seleucus to inspect the treasury, would have been flogged and turned back from his presumptuous act as soon as he approached. [19] The Lord, however, had not chosen the nation for the sake of the place, but the place for the sake of the nation. [20] Therefore, the place itself, having shared in the nation's misfortunes, afterward participated in their good fortune; and what the Almighty had forsaken in wrath was restored in all its glory, once the great Sovereign Lord became reconciled.

[21]* Antiochus carried off eighteen hundred talents from the temple and hurried back to Antioch, thinking in his arrogance that he could make the land navigable and the sea passable on foot, so carried away was he with pride. [22] He left governors to harass the nation: at Jerusalem, Philip, a Phrygian by birth,† and in character more barbarous than the man who appointed him;* [23] at Mount Gerizim,† Andronicus; and besides these, Menelaus, who

lorded it over his fellow citizens more than the others. Out of hatred for the Jewish citizens, [24]* the king sent Apollonius,† commander of the Mysians, at the head of an army of twenty-two thousand, with orders to kill all the grown men and sell the women and children into slavery. [25] When this man arrived in Jerusalem, he pretended to be peacefully disposed and waited until the holy day of the sabbath; then, finding the Jews refraining from work, he ordered his men to parade fully armed. [26] All those who came out to watch, he massacred, and running through the city with armed men, he cut down a large number of people.

[27] But Judas Maccabeus and about nine others withdrew to the wilderness to avoid sharing in defilement; there he and his companions lived like the animals in the hills, eating what grew wild.*

## 6 Abolition of Judaism. [1]* Not long after this the king sent an Athenian senator† to force the Jews to abandon the laws of their ancestors and live no longer by the laws of God, [2] also to profane the temple in Jerusalem and dedicate it to Olympian Zeus,† and the one on Mount Gerizim to Zeus the Host to Strangers, as the local inhabitants were wont to be.* [3] This was a harsh and utterly intolerable evil. [4] The Gentiles filled the temple with debauchery and revelry; they amused themselves with prostitutes and had intercourse with women even in the sacred courts. They also brought forbidden things into the temple,* [5] so that the altar was covered with abominable offerings prohibited by the laws.

[6] No one could keep the sabbath or celebrate the traditional feasts, nor even admit to being a Jew. [7] Moreover, at the monthly celebration of the king's birthday the Jews, from bitter necessity, had to partake of the sacrifices, and when the festival of Dionysus† was celebrated, they were compelled to march in his procession, wearing wreaths of ivy.*

---

† 
**5:22** *Philip, a Phrygian by birth*: the Philip of 2 Mc 6:11 and 8:8, but probably not the same as Philip the regent of 2 Mc 9:29 and 1 Mc 6:14.
**5:23** *Mount Gerizim*: the sacred mountain of the Samaritans at Shechem; cf. 2 Mc 6:2.
**5:24** *Apollonius*: the Mysian commander of 1 Mc 1:29; mentioned also in 2 Mc 3:5; 4:4.
**6:1** *Athenian senator*: or, Geron the Athenian, since *geron* can also be a proper name.
**6:2** *Olympian Zeus*: equated with the Syrian Baal Shamen ("the lord of the heavens"), a term which the Jews mockingly

rendered as *shiqqus shomem*, "desolating abomination" (Dn 9:27; 11:31; 12:11; 1 Mc 1:54).
**6:7** *Dionysus*: also called Bacchus, the god of the grape harvest and of wine; ivy was one of his symbols.

**5:17** 2 Mc 6:12–16;
    7:16–19, 32–38.
**5:21** 1 Mc 1:23–24.
**5:22** 2 Mc 6:11; 8:8.
**5:24–26** 1 Mc 1:29–40.
**5:27** 2 Mc 8:1; 1 Mc 2:28.

**6:1** 1 Mc 1:41–63.
**6:2** 1 Mc 1:46, 54; Dn
    9:27; 11:31; 12:11.
**6:4** Ez 23:36–49; Dn
    11:31; Am 2:7.
**6:7** 1 Mc 1:58–59.

⁸ Following upon a vote of the citizens of Ptolemais, a decree was issued ordering the neighboring Greek cities to adopt the same measures, obliging the Jews to partake of the sacrifices ⁹ and putting to death those who would not consent to adopt the customs of the Greeks. It was obvious, therefore, that disaster had come upon them. ¹⁰ Thus, two women who were arrested for having circumcised their children were publicly paraded about the city with their babies hanging at their breasts and then thrown down from the top of the city wall.* ¹¹ Others, who had assembled in nearby caves to observe the seventh day in secret, were betrayed to Philip and all burned to death. In their respect for the holiness of that day, they refrained from defending themselves.*

**God's Purpose.** ¹²* Now I urge those who read this book not to be disheartened by these misfortunes, but to consider that these punishments were meant not for the ruin but for the correction of our nation. ¹³ It is, in fact, a sign of great kindness to punish the impious promptly instead of letting them go for long. ¹⁴* Thus, in dealing with other nations, the Sovereign Lord patiently waits until they reach the full measure of their sins before punishing them; but with us he has decided to deal differently, ¹⁵ in order that he may not have to punish us later, when our sins have reached their fullness. ¹⁶ Therefore he never withdraws his mercy from us. Although he disciplines us with misfortunes, he does not abandon his own people. ¹⁷ Let these words suffice for recalling this truth. Without further ado we must go on with our story.

**Martyrdom of Eleazar.** ¹⁸† Eleazar, one of the foremost scribes, a man advanced in age and of noble appearance, was being forced to open his mouth to eat pork.* ¹⁹ But preferring a glorious death to a life of defilement, he went forward of his own accord to the instrument of torture, ²⁰ spitting out the meat as they should do who have the courage to reject food unlawful to taste even for love of life.
²¹ Those in charge of that unlawful sacrifice took the man aside, because of their long

acquaintance with him, and privately urged him to bring his own provisions that he could legitimately eat, and only to pretend to eat the sacrificial meat prescribed by the king. ²² Thus he would escape death, and be treated kindly because of his old friendship with them. ²³ But he made up his mind in a noble manner, worthy of his years, the dignity of his advanced age, the merited distinction of his gray hair, and of the admirable life he had lived from childhood. Above all loyal to the holy laws given by God, he swiftly declared, "Send me to Hades!"
²⁴ "At our age it would be unbecoming to make such a pretense; many of the young would think the ninety-year-old Eleazar had gone over to an alien religion. ²⁵ If I dissemble to gain a brief moment of life, they would be led astray by me, while I would bring defilement and dishonor on my old age. ²⁶ Even if, for the time being, I avoid human punishment, I shall never, whether alive or dead, escape the hand of the Almighty. ²⁷ Therefore, by bravely giving up life now, I will prove myself worthy of my old age, ²⁸ and I will leave to the young a noble example of how to die willingly and nobly for the revered and holy laws."
He spoke thus, and went immediately to the instrument of torture. ²⁹ Those who shortly before had been kindly disposed, now became hostile toward him because what he had said seemed to them utter madness.* ³⁰ When he was about to die under the blows, he groaned, saying: "The Lord in his holy knowledge knows full well that, although I could have escaped death, I am not only enduring terrible pain in my body from this scourging, but also suffering it with joy in my soul because of my devotion to him." ³¹ This is how he died, leaving in his death a model of nobility and an unforgettable example of virtue not only for the young but for the whole nation.

**7 Martyrdom of a Mother and Her Seven Sons.** ¹ It also happened that seven brothers with their mother were arrested and tortured with whips and scourges by the king to force them to eat pork in violation of God's law.* ² One of the brothers, speaking for the

† **6:18–7:42** The stories of Eleazar and of the mother and her seven sons, among the earliest models of "martyrology," were understandably popular. Written to encourage God's people in times of persecution, they add gruesome details to the record of tortures, and place long speeches in the mouths of the martyrs.

**6:10** 1 Mc 1:60–61.
**6:11** 1 Mc 2:32–38.
**6:12–16** 2 Mc 5:17; 7:16–19, 32–38.
**6:14** Wis 11:9–10; 12:2, 22.
**6:18** Lv 11:6–8.
**6:29** Wis 3:1–4; 5:4.
**7:1** Jer 15:9.

others, said: "What do you expect to learn by questioning us? We are ready to die rather than transgress the laws of our ancestors."

³ At that the king, in a fury, gave orders to have pans and caldrons heated. ⁴ These were quickly heated, and he gave the order to cut out the tongue of the one who had spoken for the others, to scalp him and cut off his hands and feet, while the rest of his brothers and his mother looked on. ⁵ When he was completely maimed but still breathing, the king ordered them to carry him to the fire and fry him. As a cloud of smoke spread from the pan, the brothers and their mother encouraged one another to die nobly, with these words: ⁶ "The Lord God is looking on and truly has compassion on us, as Moses declared in his song, when he openly bore witness, saying, 'And God will have compassion on his servants.'" *

⁷ After the first brother had died in this manner, they brought the second to be made sport of. After tearing off the skin and hair of his head, they asked him, "Will you eat the pork rather than have your body tortured limb by limb?" ⁸ Answering in the language of his ancestors, he said, "Never!" So he in turn suffered the same tortures as the first. ⁹ With his last breath he said: "You accursed fiend, you are depriving us of this present life, but the King of the universe will raise us up† to live again forever, because we are dying for his laws." *

¹⁰ After him the third suffered their cruel sport. He put forth his tongue at once when told to do so, and bravely stretched out his hands, ¹¹ as he spoke these noble words: "It was from Heaven that I received these; for the sake of his laws I disregard them; from him I hope to receive them again." ¹² Even the king and his attendants marveled at the young man's spirit, because he regarded his sufferings as nothing.

¹³ After he had died, they tortured and maltreated the fourth brother in the same way. ¹⁴ When he was near death, he said, "It is my choice to die at the hands of mortals with the hope that God will restore me to life; but for you, there will be no resurrection to life."

¹⁵ They next brought forward the fifth brother and maltreated him. ¹⁶ Looking at the king, he said:* "Mortal though you are, you have power over human beings, so you do what you please. But do not think that our nation is forsaken by God. ¹⁷ Only wait, and you will see how his great power will torment you and your descendants."

¹⁸ After him they brought the sixth brother. When he was about to die, he said: "Have no vain illusions. We suffer these things on our own account, because we have sinned against our God; that is why such shocking things have happened. ¹⁹ Do not think, then, that you will go unpunished for having dared to fight against God."

²⁰ Most admirable and worthy of everlasting remembrance was the mother who, seeing her seven sons perish in a single day, bore it courageously because of her hope in the Lord. ²¹ Filled with a noble spirit that stirred her womanly reason with manly emotion, she exhorted each of them in the language of their ancestors with these words: ²² * "I do not know how you came to be in my womb; it was not I who gave you breath and life, nor was it I who arranged the elements you are made of. ²³ Therefore, since it is the Creator of the universe who shaped the beginning of humankind and brought about the origin of everything, he, in his mercy, will give you back both breath and life, because you now disregard yourselves for the sake of his law."

²⁴ Antiochus, suspecting insult in her words, thought he was being ridiculed. As the youngest brother was still alive, the king appealed to him, not with mere words, but with promises on oath, to make him rich and happy if he would abandon his ancestral customs: he would make him his Friend and entrust him with high office. ²⁵ When the youth paid no attention to him at all, the king appealed to the mother, urging her to advise her boy to save his life. ²⁶ After he had urged her for a long time, she agreed to persuade her son. ²⁷ She leaned over close to him and, in derision of the cruel tyrant, said in their native language: "Son, have pity on me, who carried you in my womb for nine months, nursed you for three years, brought you up, educated and supported you to your present age. ²⁸ I beg you, child, to look at the heavens and

† **7:9** *The King of the universe will raise us up*: here, and in vv. 11, 14, 23, 29, 36, belief in the future resurrection of the body, at least for the just, is clearly stated; cf. also 12:44; 14:46; Dn 12:2.

* **7:6** Dt 32:36–38.                                    **7:32**.
**7:9** 2 Mc 12:44; 14:46;          **7:22–23** 2 Mc 7:11, 28;
    Dn 12:1–3.                                Jb 1:10–12; Ps
**7:16–19** 2 Mc 5:17; 6:12–16;          139:13–16; Eccl 11:5.

the earth and see all that is in them; then you will know that God did not make them out of existing things.† In the same way humankind came into existence. 29 Do not be afraid of this executioner, but be worthy of your brothers and accept death, so that in the time of mercy I may receive you again with your brothers."

30 She had scarcely finished speaking when the youth said: "What is the delay? I will not obey the king's command. I obey the command of the law given to our ancestors through Moses. 31 But you, who have contrived every kind of evil for the Hebrews, will not escape the hands of God. 32 We, indeed, are suffering because of our sins.* 33 Though for a little while our living Lord has been angry, correcting and chastising us, he will again be reconciled with his servants. 34 But you, wretch, most vile of mortals, do not, in your insolence, buoy yourself up with unfounded hopes, as you raise your hand against the children of heaven. 35 You have not yet escaped the judgment of the almighty and all-seeing God. 36 Our brothers, after enduring brief pain, have drunk of never-failing life, under God's covenant. But you, by the judgment of God, shall receive just punishments for your arrogance. 37 Like my brothers, I offer up my body and my life for our ancestral laws, imploring God to show mercy soon to our nation, and by afflictions and blows to make you confess that he alone is God. 38 Through me and my brothers, may there be an end to the wrath of the Almighty that has justly fallen on our whole nation."

39 At that, the king became enraged and treated him even worse than the others, since he bitterly resented the boy's contempt. 40 Thus he too died undefiled, putting all his trust in the Lord. 41 Last of all, after her sons, the mother was put to death. 42 Enough has been said about the sacrificial meals and the excessive cruelties.

## V. VICTORIES OF JUDAS AND PURIFICATION OF THE TEMPLE

**8** **Resistance from Judas Maccabeus.** 1* Judas Maccabeus and his companions entered the villages secretly, summoned their kindred, and enlisted others who had remained faithful to Judaism. Thus they assembled about six thousand men. 2 They implored the Lord to look kindly upon this people, who were being oppressed by all; to have pity on the sanctuary, which was profaned by renegades; 3 to have mercy on the city, which was being destroyed and was about to be leveled to the ground; to listen to the blood that cried out to him; 4 to remember the criminal slaughter of innocent children and the blasphemies uttered against his name; and to manifest his hatred of evil.

5* Once Maccabeus got his men organized, the Gentiles could not withstand him, for the Lord's wrath had now changed to mercy. 6 Coming by surprise upon towns and villages, he set them on fire. He captured strategic positions, and put to flight not a few of the enemy. 7 He preferred the nights as being especially favorable for such attacks. Soon talk of his valor spread everywhere.

**First Victory over Nicanor.**† 8 When Philip saw that Judas was gaining ground little by little and that his successful advances were becoming more frequent, he wrote to Ptolemy, governor of Coelesyria and Phoenicia, to come to the aid of the king's interests.* 9* Ptolemy promptly selected Nicanor, son of Patroclus, one of the Chief Friends, and sent him at the head of at least twenty thousand armed men of various nations to wipe out the entire Jewish nation. With him he associated Gorgias, a general, experienced in the art of war.* 10 Nicanor planned to raise the two thousand talents of tribute owed by the king to the Romans† by selling captured Jews into slavery. 11 So he immediately sent word to the coastal cities, inviting them to buy Jewish slaves and promising to deliver ninety slaves for a talent† —little anticipating the punishment that was to fall upon him from the Almighty.

12 When Judas learned of Nicanor's advance and informed his companions about the approach of the army, 13 those who were fearful

---

† **7:28** *God did not make them out of existing things*: that is, all things were made solely by God's omnipotent will and creative word; cf. Heb 11:3. This statement has often been taken as a basis for "creation out of nothing" (Latin *creatio ex nihilo*).

**8:8–29, 34–35** This account of the campaign of Nicanor and Gorgias against Judas is paralleled, with certain differences, in 1 Mc 3:38–4:24.

**8:10** *Tribute owed by the king to the Romans*: the payment imposed on Antiochus III in 188 B.C. by the treaty of Apamea.

**8:11** *Ninety slaves for a talent*: a low price for so many slaves, thus expressing the opponents' contempt for the Jews.

| | |
|---|---|
| **7:32** 2 Mc 5:17; 6:12–16; 7:16–19. | **8:8** 2 Mc 4:45; 1 Mc 3:38. |
| **8:1–7** 2 Mc 5:27; 1 Mc 3:10–26. | **8:9–23** 1 Mc 3:38–59. |
| **8:5–7** 1 Mc 3:3–9. | **8:9** 1 Mc 7:26. |

and those who lacked faith in God's justice deserted and got away. [14] But the others sold everything they had left, and at the same time entreated the Lord to deliver those whom the ungodly Nicanor had sold before even capturing them. [15] They entreated the Lord to do this, if not for their sake, at least for the sake of the covenants made with their ancestors, and because they themselves invoked his holy and glorious name. [16] Maccabeus assembled his forces, six thousand strong, and exhorted them not to be panic-stricken before the enemy, nor to fear the very large number of Gentiles unjustly attacking them, but to fight nobly. [17] They were to keep before their eyes the lawless outrage perpetrated by the Gentiles against the holy place and the affliction of the humiliated city, as well as the subversion of their ancestral way of life. [18] He said, "They trust in weapons and acts of daring, but we trust in almighty God, who can by a mere nod destroy not only those who attack us but even the whole world." [19] He went on to tell them of the times when help had been given their ancestors: both the time of Sennacherib, when a hundred and eighty-five thousand of his men perished,* [20] and the time of the battle in Babylonia against the Galatians,† when only eight thousand Jews fought along with four thousand Macedonians; yet when the Macedonians were hard pressed, the eight thousand, by the help they received from Heaven, destroyed one hundred and twenty thousand and took a great quantity of spoils. [21]* With these words he encouraged them and made them ready to die for their laws and their country.

Then Judas divided his army into four, [22] placing his brothers, Simon, Joseph,† and Jonathan, each over a division, assigning them fifteen hundred men apiece.* [23] There was also Eleazar.† After reading to them from the holy book and giving them the watchword, "The help of God," Judas himself took charge of the first division and joined in battle with Nicanor.* [24] With the Almighty as their ally, they killed more than nine thousand of the enemy, wounded and disabled the greater part of Nicanor's army, and put all of them to flight. [25] They also seized the money of those who had come to buy them as slaves. When they had pursued the enemy for some time, they were obliged to return by reason of the late hour. [26] It was the day before the sabbath, and for that reason they could not continue the pursuit. [27] They collected the enemy's weapons and stripped them of their spoils, and then observed the sabbath with fervent praise and thanks to the Lord who kept them safe for that day on which he allotted them the beginning of his mercy. [28] After the sabbath, they gave a share of the spoils to those who were tortured and to widows and orphans; the rest they divided among themselves and their children.* [29] When this was done, they made supplication in common, imploring the merciful Lord to be completely reconciled with his servants.

**Other Victories.** [30] They also challenged the forces of Timothy and Bacchides, killed more than twenty thousand of them, and captured some very high fortresses. They divided the considerable plunder, allotting half to themselves and the rest to victims of torture, orphans, widows, and the aged. [31] They collected the enemies' weapons and carefully stored them in strategic places; the rest of the spoils they carried to Jerusalem. [32] They also killed the commander of Timothy's forces, a most wicked man, who had done great harm to the Jews. [33] While celebrating the victory in their ancestral city, they burned both those who had set fire to the sacred gates and Callisthenes, who had taken refuge in a little house; so he received the reward his wicked deeds deserved.

[34]* The thrice-accursed Nicanor, who had brought the thousand slave dealers to buy the Jews, [35] after being humbled through the Lord's help by those whom he had thought of no account, laid aside his fine clothes and fled alone across country like a runaway slave, until he reached Antioch. He was eminently successful in destroying his own army. [36] So he

---

† **8:20** *Galatians:* a mercenary force, defeated by Jews and Macedonians in Babylon. Nothing else is known about this battle.

**8:22** *Joseph:* called John in 1 Mc 2:2; 9:36, 38. This paragraph interrupts the story of Nicanor's defeat, which is resumed in v. 34. The purpose of the author apparently is to group together the defeats suffered by the Syrians on various occasions. Battles against Timothy are recounted in 1 Mc 5:37–44 and 2 Mc 12:10–25; against Bacchides, in 1 Mc 7:8–20.

**8:23** *Eleazar:* this parenthetical reference notes the existence of a fifth brother; cf. 1 Mc 2:5.

**8:19** 2 Mc 15:22; 2 Kgs 19:35–36; 1 Mc 7:41–42; Is 37:36–37.
**8:21–29** 1 Mc 4:1–25.
**8:22** 1 Mc 2:2–5; 5:18, 55–62.
**8:23** 1 Mc 3:48.
**8:28** Nm 31:25–47; Dt 26:12–13; 1 Sm 30:21–25.
**8:34–35** 2 Mc 8:23–24; 1 Mc 7:26.

who had promised to provide tribute for the Romans by the capture of the people of Jerusalem proclaimed that the Jews had a champion, and that because they followed the laws laid down by him, they were unharmed.

## 9 Punishment and Death of Antiochus IV.†

1* About that time Antiochus retreated in disgrace from the region of Persia. 2 He had entered the city called Persepolis and attempted to rob the temples and gain control of the city. Thereupon the people had swift recourse to arms, and Antiochus' forces were routed, so that in the end Antiochus was put to flight by the people of that region and forced to beat a shameful retreat. 3 On his arrival in Ecbatana, he learned what had happened to Nicanor and to Timothy's forces. 4 Overcome with anger, he planned to make the Jews suffer for the injury done by those who had put him to flight. Therefore he ordered his charioteer to drive without stopping until he finished the journey. Yet the condemnation of Heaven rode with him, because he said in his arrogance, "I will make Jerusalem the common graveyard of Jews as soon as I arrive there."

5 So the all-seeing Lord, the God of Israel, struck him down with an incurable and invisible blow; for scarcely had he uttered those words when he was seized with excruciating pains in his bowels and sharp internal torment,* 6 a fit punishment for him who had tortured the bowels of others with many barbarous torments. 7 Far from giving up his insolence, he was all the more filled with arrogance. Breathing fire in his rage against the Jews, he gave orders to drive even faster. As a result he hurtled from the speeding chariot, and every part of his body was racked by the violent fall. 8 Thus he who previously, in his superhuman presumption, thought he could command the waves of the sea, and imagined he could weigh the mountaintops in his scales, was now thrown to the ground and had to be carried on a litter, clearly manifesting to all the power of God. * 9 The body of this impious man swarmed with worms, and while he was still alive in hideous torments, his flesh rotted off, so that the entire army was sickened by the stench of his corruption. * 10 Shortly before, he had thought that he could reach the stars of heaven, and now, no one could endure to transport the man because of this intolerable stench.

11 At last, broken in spirit, he began to give up his excessive arrogance, and to gain some understanding, under the scourge of God, for he was racked with pain unceasingly. 12 When he could no longer bear his own stench, he said, "It is right to be subject to God, and not to think one's mortal self equal to God."* 13 Then this vile man vowed to him who would never again show him mercy, the Sovereign Lord, 14 that the holy city, toward which he had been hurrying with the intention of leveling it to the ground and making it a common graveyard, he would now set free; 15 that the Jews, whom he had judged not even worthy of burial, but fit only to be thrown out with their children to be eaten by vultures and wild animals—all of them he would make equal to the Athenians; 16 that he would adorn with the finest offerings the holy temple which he had previously despoiled, restore all the sacred vessels many times over, and provide from his own revenues the expenses required for the sacrifices. 17 Besides all this, he would become a Jew himself and visit every inhabited place to proclaim there the power of God. 18 But since his sufferings were not lessened, for God's just judgment had come upon him, he lost hope for himself and wrote the following letter to the Jews in the form of a supplication. It read thus:

19† "To the worthy Jewish citizens, Antiochus, king and general, sends hearty greetings and best wishes for their health and prosperity. 20 If you and your children are well and

9:1–29 In order to keep together the various accounts of God's punishment of the persecutors of his people, the author places here the stories of Antiochus' illness and death (in actuality the king died about the same time as the purification of the Temple, i.e., 164 B.C.; cf. 1 Mc 4:36–59; 6:1–16; 2 Mc 10:1–8); of Judas' campaigns in Idumea and Transjordan; cf. 1 Mc 5:1–51; 2 Mc 10:14–38; and of the first expedition of Lysias (1 Mc 4:26–35; 2 Mc 11:1–15).

9:19–27 Despite the statement in v. 18 this letter is not really a supplication. It is rather a notification to all the king's subjects of the appointment of his son as his successor and a request that they be loyal to the new king. Apparently the same letter, which has every appearance of being authentic, was sent to the various peoples throughout the kingdom, with only a few words of address changed for each group.

9:1–29 2 Mc 1:12–17; 1 Mc 6:1–13; Dn 11:40–45.
9:5 Acts 12:20–23.
9:8 Jb 38:8–11; Ps 65:6–7; Is 40:12.
9:9 Jdt 16:17; Sir 7:17; Is 14:11; 66:24; Acts 12:23.
9:12 Dn 4:31–34.

your affairs are going as you wish, I thank God very much, for my hopes are in heaven. [21] Now that I am ill, I recall with affection your esteem and goodwill. On returning from the regions of Persia, I fell victim to a troublesome illness; so I thought it necessary to form plans for the general security of all. [22] I do not despair about my health, since I have much hope of recovering from my illness. [23] Nevertheless, I know that my father, whenever he went on campaigns in the hinterland, would name his successor, [24] so that, if anything unexpected happened or any unwelcome news came, the people throughout the realm would know to whom the government had been entrusted, and so not be disturbed. [25] I am also bearing in mind that the neighboring rulers, especially those on the borders of our kingdom, are on the watch for opportunities and waiting to see what will happen. I have therefore appointed as king my son Antiochus, whom I have often before entrusted and commended to most of you, when I made hurried visits to the outlying provinces. I have written to him what is written here. [26] Therefore I beg and entreat each of you to remember the general and individual benefits you have received, and to continue to show goodwill toward me and my son. [27] I am confident that, following my policy, he will treat you with equity and kindness in his relations with you."

[28] So this murderer and blasphemer, after extreme sufferings, such as he had inflicted on others, died a miserable death in the mountains of a foreign land. [29] His foster brother† Philip brought the body home; but fearing Antiochus' son, he later withdrew into Egypt, to Ptolemy Philometor.*

# 10

**Purification of the Temple.** [1]* When Maccabeus and his companions, under the Lord's leadership, had recovered the temple and the city, [2] they destroyed the altars erected by the foreigners in the marketplace and the sacred shrines. [3] After purifying the temple, they made another altar. Then, with fire struck from flint, they offered sacrifice for the first time in two years,† burned incense, and lighted lamps. They also set out the showbread. [4] When they had done this, they prostrated themselves and begged the Lord that they might never again fall into such misfortunes, and that if they should sin at any time, he might chastise them with moderation and not hand them over to blasphemous and barbarous Gentiles. [5] On the anniversary of the day on which the temple had been profaned by the foreigners, that is, the twenty-fifth of the same month Kislev, the purification of the temple took place. [6] The Jews celebrated joyfully for eight days as on the feast of Booths, remembering how, a little while before, they had spent the feast of Booths living like wild animals in the mountains and in caves. [7] Carrying rods entwined with leaves,† beautiful branches and palms, they sang hymns of grateful praise to him who had successfully brought about the purification of his own place. [8] By public decree and vote they prescribed that the whole Jewish nation should celebrate these days every year. [9] Such was the end of Antiochus surnamed Epiphanes.

## VI. RENEWED PERSECUTION

**Accession of Antiochus V.** [10] Now we shall relate what happened under Antiochus Eupator, the son of that godless man, and shall give a summary of the chief evils caused by the wars. [11] When Eupator succeeded to the kingdom, he put a certain Lysias in charge of the government as commander-in-chief of Coelesyria and Phoenicia. [12] Ptolemy, called Macron,† had taken the lead in treating the Jews fairly because of the previous injustice that had been done them, and he endeavored to have peaceful relations with them. [13] As a result, he was accused before Eupator by the King's Friends. In fact, on all sides he heard himself called a traitor for having abandoned Cyprus, which Philometor had entrusted to him, and for having gone over to Antiochus Epiphanes. Since he could not command the respect due to his high office, he ended his life by taking poison.

---

† **9:29** *Foster brother:* an honorary title conferred by the king on prominent courtiers, whether or not they had been raised with him. Philip tried to seize control of Antioch from the young Antiochus V (1 Mc 6:55–56, 63) and fled to Egypt when he failed.

**10:3** *Two years:* three years according to 1 Mc 1:54 and 4:52.
**10:7** *Rods entwined with leaves:* the wreathed wands (*thyr-*

*soi*) carried in processions honoring Dionysus (6:7) were apparently not regarded as distinctively pagan.
**10:12** *Ptolemy, called Macron:* son of Dorymenes (4:45); he supported Antiochus IV in 168 B.C. during his invasion of Cyprus.

* **9:29** 1 Mc 6:55–56, 63.          **10:1–8** 1 Mc 4:36–61.

## Victory over the Idumeans.† [14]* When Gorgias became governor of the region, he employed foreign troops and used every opportunity to attack the Jews. [15] At the same time the Idumeans, who held some strategic strongholds, were harassing the Jews; they welcomed fugitives from Jerusalem and endeavored to continue the war. [16] Maccabeus and his companions, after public prayers asking God to be their ally, moved quickly against the strongholds of the Idumeans. [17] Attacking vigorously, they gained control of the places, drove back all who were fighting on the walls, and cut down those who opposed them, killing no fewer than twenty thousand. [18] When at least nine thousand took refuge in two very strong towers, well equipped to sustain a siege, [19] Maccabeus left Simon and Joseph, along with Zacchaeus and his forces, in sufficient numbers to besiege them, while he himself went off to places where he was more urgently needed. [20] But some of those in Simon's force who were lovers of money let themselves be bribed by some of those in the towers; on receiving seventy thousand drachmas, they allowed a number of them to escape. [21] When Maccabeus was told what had happened, he assembled the rulers of the people and accused those men of having sold their kindred for money by setting their enemies free to fight against them. [22] So he put them to death as traitors, and without delay captured the two towers. [23] As he was successful at arms in all his undertakings, he destroyed more than twenty thousand in the two strongholds.

## Victory over Timothy. [24] Timothy, who had previously been defeated by the Jews,† gathered a tremendous force of foreign troops and collected a large number of cavalry from Asia; then he appeared in Judea, ready to conquer it by force. [25] At his approach, Maccabeus and his companions made supplication to God, sprinkling earth upon their heads and girding their loins in sackcloth. [26] Lying prostrate at the foot of the altar, they begged him to be gracious to them, and to be an enemy to their enemies, and a foe to their foes, as the law declares.* [27] After the prayer, they took up their weapons and advanced a considerable distance from the city, halting when they were close to the enemy. [28] As soon as dawn broke,† the armies joined battle, the one having as pledge of success and victory not only their valor but also their reliance on the Lord, and the other taking fury as their leader in the fight.

[29]* In the midst of the fierce battle, there appeared to the enemy five majestic men from the heavens riding on golden-bridled horses, leading the Jews. [30] They surrounded Maccabeus, and shielding him with their own armor, kept him from being wounded. They shot arrows and hurled thunderbolts at the enemy, who were bewildered and blinded, routed in utter confusion. [31] Twenty thousand five hundred of their foot soldiers and six hundred cavalry were slain.

[32] Timothy, however, fled to a well-fortified stronghold called Gazara, where Chaereas was in command.* [33] For four days Maccabeus and his forces eagerly besieged the fortress. [34] Those inside, relying on the strength of the place, kept repeating outrageous blasphemies and uttering abominable words. [35] When the fifth day dawned, twenty young men in the army of Maccabeus, angered over such blasphemies, bravely stormed the wall and with savage fury cut down everyone they encountered. [36] Similarly, others climbed up and swung around on the defenders; they put the towers to the torch, spread the fire and burned the blasphemers alive. Still others broke down the gates and let in the rest of the troops, who took possession of the city. [37] Timothy had hidden in a cistern, but they killed† him, along with his brother Chaereas, and Apollophanes. [38] On completing these exploits, they blessed, with hymns of grateful praise, the Lord who shows great kindness to Israel and grants them victory.

# 11
## Defeat of Lysias.† [1]* Very soon afterward, Lysias, guardian and kinsman

---

†  **10:14–23** Probably the same campaign of Judas against the Idumeans that is mentioned in 1 Mc 5:1–3.
  **10:24** *Timothy, who had previously been defeated by the Jews:* as recounted in 8:30–33.
  **10:28** *As soon as dawn broke:* the same battle at dawn as in 1 Mc 5:30–34.
  **10:37** *Timothy…they killed:* apparently Timothy is still alive in 12:2, 18–25. Perhaps there was more than one Timothy. Or the present passage is not in chronological order. Gazara, v. 32

(Gezer), was not captured by the Jews until much later (cf. 1 Mc 9:50–52; 13:53). See 1 Mc 5:8 for the capture of Jazer.
  **11:1–12** The defeat of Lysias at Beth-zur probably occurred before the purification of the Temple; cf. 1 Mc 4:26–35.

*
**10:14** 1 Mc 5:3–5.                                    11:8.
**10:26** Ex 23:22.                        **10:32** 1 Mc 13:43–48.
**10:29–30** 2 Mc 3:24–26; 5:2–3;    **11:1–15** 1 Mc 4:26–35.

of the king and head of the government, being greatly displeased at what had happened, [2] mustered about eighty thousand infantry and all his cavalry and marched against the Jews. His plan was to make their city a Greek settlement; [3] to levy tribute on the temple, as he did on the shrines of the other nations; and to put the high priesthood up for sale every year.* [4] He did not take God's power into account at all, but felt exultant confidence in his myriads of foot soldiers, his thousands of cavalry, and his eighty elephants.* [5] So he invaded Judea, and when he reached Beth-zur, a fortified place about five stadia† from Jerusalem, launched a strong attack against it.

[6] When Maccabeus and his companions learned that Lysias was besieging the strongholds, they and all the people begged the Lord with lamentations and tears to send a good angel to save Israel.* [7] Maccabeus himself was the first to take up arms, and he exhorted the others to join him in risking their lives to help their kindred. Then they resolutely set out together. [8] Suddenly, while they were still near Jerusalem, a horseman appeared at their head, clothed in white garments and brandishing gold weapons.* [9] Then all of them together thanked the merciful God, and their hearts were filled with such courage that they were ready to assault not only human beings but even the most savage beasts, or even walls of iron. [10] Now that the Lord had shown mercy toward them, they advanced in battle order with the aid of their heavenly ally. [11] Hurling themselves upon the enemy like lions, they laid low eleven thousand foot soldiers and sixteen hundred cavalry, and put all the rest to flight. [12] Most of those who survived were wounded and disarmed, while Lysias himself escaped only by shameful flight.

**Peace Negotiations.** [13]* But Lysias was not a stupid man. He reflected on the defeat he had suffered, and came to realize that the Hebrews were invincible because the mighty God was their ally. He therefore sent a message [14] persuading them to settle everything on just terms, and promising to persuade the king also, and to induce him to become their friend. [15] Maccabeus, solicitous for the common good, agreed to all that Lysias proposed; and the king granted on behalf of the Jews all the written requests of Maccabeus to Lysias.

[16] These are the terms of the letter which Lysias wrote to the Jews: "Lysias sends greetings to the Jewish people. [17] John and Absalom, your envoys, have presented your signed communication and asked about the matters contained in it. [18] Whatever had to be referred to the king I called to his attention, and the things that were acceptable he has granted. [19] If you maintain your loyalty to the government, I will endeavor to further your interests in the future. [20] On the details of these matters I have authorized my representatives, as well as your envoys, to confer with you. [21] Farewell." The one hundred and forty-eighth year,† the twenty-fourth of Dioscorinthius.

[22] The king's letter read thus: "King Antiochus sends greetings to his brother Lysias. [23] Now that our father has taken his place among the gods, we wish the subjects of our kingdom to be undisturbed in conducting their own affairs. [24] We have heard that the Jews do not agree with our father's change to Greek customs but prefer their own way of life. They are petitioning us to let them retain their own customs. [25] Since we desire that this people too should be undisturbed, our decision is that their temple be restored to them and that they live in keeping with the customs of their ancestors. [26] Accordingly, please send them messengers to give them our assurances of friendship, so that, when they learn of our decision, they may have nothing to worry about but may contentedly go about their own business."

[27] The king's letter to the people was as follows: "King Antiochus sends greetings to the Jewish senate and to the rest of the Jews. [28] If you are well, it is what we desire. We too are in good health. [29] Menelaus has told us of your wish to return home and attend to your own affairs. [30] Therefore, those who return by the thirtieth of Xanthicus will have our assurance of full permission [31] to observe their dietary

---

† 11:5 *Five stadia*: one stadium is equal to about six hundred six feet. The actual distance to Beth-zur is about twenty miles.
11:21 *The one hundred and forty-eighth year*: 164 B.C. The reading of the name of the month and its position in the calendar are uncertain. The most likely chronological sequence of the four letters is vv. 16–21; vv. 34–38; vv. 27–33; vv. 22–26.

* 11:3 2 Mc 4:7–8, 23–24.
11:4 1 Mc 3:34.
11:6 Ex 23:20.
11:13–33 1 Mc 6:57–61.
11:8 2 Mc 3:24–26; 5:2–3; 10:29–30.

and other laws, just as before, and none of the Jews shall be molested in any way for faults committed through ignorance. [32] I have also sent Menelaus to reassure you. [33] Farewell." In the one hundred and forty-eighth year, the fifteenth of Xanthicus.†

[34] The Romans also sent them a letter as follows: "Quintus Memmius and Titus Manius, legates of the Romans, send greetings to the Jewish people. [35] What Lysias, kinsman of the king, has granted you, we also approve. [36] But for the matters that he decided should be submitted to the king, send someone to us immediately with your decisions so that we may present them to your advantage, for we are on our way to Antioch. [37] Make haste, then, to send us those who can inform us of your preference. [38] Farewell." In the one hundred and forty-eighth year, the fifteenth of Xanthicus.†

# 12 Incidents at Joppa and Jamnia.

[1] After these agreements were made, Lysias returned to the king, and the Jews went about their farming. [2] But some of the local governors, Timothy and Apollonius, son of Gennaeus,† as also Hieronymus and Demophon, to say nothing of Nicanor, the commander of the Cyprians, would not allow them to live in peace and quiet.

[3] Some people of Joppa also committed this outrage: they invited the Jews who lived among them, together with their wives and children, to embark on boats which they had provided. There was no hint of enmity toward them. [4] This was done by public vote of the city. When the Jews, wishing to live on friendly terms and not suspecting anything, accepted the invitation, the people of Joppa took them out to sea and drowned at least two hundred of them.

[5] As soon as Judas heard of the barbarous deed perpetrated against his compatriots, he summoned his men; [6] and after calling upon God, the just judge, he marched against the murderers of his kindred. In a night attack he set the harbor on fire, burned the boats,

and put to the sword those who had taken refuge there. [7] Because the gates of the town were shut, he withdrew, intending to come back later and wipe out the entire population of Joppa.

[8] On hearing that the people of Jamnia planned in the same way to wipe out the Jews who lived among them, [9] he attacked the Jamnians by night, setting fire to the harbor and the fleet, so that the glow of the flames was visible as far as Jerusalem, thirty miles away.

**More Victories by Judas.** [10]* When the Jews had gone about a mile from there† in the march against Timothy, they were attacked by Arabians numbering at least five thousand foot soldiers and five hundred cavalry. [11] After a hard fight, Judas and his companions, with God's help, were victorious. The defeated nomads begged Judas to give pledges of friendship, and they promised to supply the Jews with livestock and to be of service to them in any other way. [12] Realizing that they could indeed be useful in many respects, Judas agreed to make peace with them. After the pledges of friendship had been exchanged, the Arabians withdrew to their tents.

[13] He also attacked a certain city called Caspin, fortified with earthworks and walls and inhabited by a mixed population of Gentiles. [14] Relying on the strength of their walls and their supply of provisions, the besieged treated Judas and his men with contempt, insulting them and even uttering blasphemies and profanity. [15] But Judas and his men invoked the aid of the great Sovereign of the world, who, in the days of Joshua, overthrew Jericho without battering rams or siege engines; then they furiously stormed the walls.* [16] Capturing the city by the will of God, they inflicted such indescribable slaughter on it that the adjacent pool, which was about a quarter of a mile wide, seemed to be filled with the blood that flowed into it.

[17]* When they had gone on some ninety miles, they reached Charax, where there were

---

† **11:33** The date, which is the same as the date of the Romans' letter (v. 38), cannot be correct. The king's letter must be connected with the peace treaty of the one hundred forty-ninth year of the Seleucid era, i.e., 163 B.C. Perhaps the mention of the month of Xanthicus in the body of the letter (v. 30) caused the date of the Romans' letter to be transferred to this one.

**11:38** The date is March 12, 164 B.C.

**12:2** *Apollonius, son of Gennaeus*: not the Apollonius who was the son of Menestheus (4:21). *Nicanor*: probably distinct

from the Nicanor of 14:2.

**12:10** *From there*: not from Jamnia (vv. 8–9) or Joppa (vv. 3–7), but from a place in Transjordan; vv. 10–26 parallel the account given in 1 Mc 5:9–13, 24–54 of Judas' campaign in northern Transjordan.

---

**12:10–16** 1 Mc 5:24–36.     **12:17–26** 1 Mc 5:37–44.
**12:15** Jos 6:1–21.

certain Jews known as Toubians.†* [18] But they did not find Timothy in that region, for he had already departed from there without having done anything except to leave behind in one place a very strong garrison. [19] But Dositheus and Sosipater, two of Maccabeus' captains, marched out and destroyed the force of more than ten thousand men that Timothy had left in the stronghold. [20] Meanwhile, Maccabeus divided his army into cohorts, with a commander over each cohort, and went in pursuit of Timothy, who had a force of a hundred and twenty thousand foot soldiers and twenty-five hundred cavalry. [21] When Timothy learned of the approach of Judas, he sent on ahead of him the women and children, as well as the baggage, to a place called Karnion, which was hard to besiege and even hard to reach because of the difficult terrain of that region. [22] But when Judas' first cohort appeared, the enemy was overwhelmed with fear and terror at the manifestation of the all-seeing One. Scattering in every direction, they rushed away in such headlong flight that in many cases they wounded one another, pierced by the points of their own swords. [23] Judas pressed the pursuit vigorously, putting the sinners to the sword and destroying as many as thirty thousand men.

[24] Timothy himself fell into the hands of those under Dositheus and Sosipater; but with great cunning, he begged them to spare his life and let him go, because he had in his power the parents and relatives of many of them, and would show them no consideration. [25] When he had fully confirmed his solemn pledge to restore them unharmed, they let him go for the sake of saving their relatives.

[26]* Judas then marched to Karnion and the shrine of Atargatis,† where he killed twenty-five thousand people. [27] After the defeat and destruction of these, he moved his army to Ephron, a fortified city inhabited by Lysias and people of many nationalities. Robust young men took up their posts in defense of the walls, from which they fought valiantly; inside were large supplies of war machines and missiles. [28] But the Jews, invoking the Sovereign who powerfully shatters the might of enemies, got possession of the city and slaughtered twenty-five thousand of the people in it.

[29] Then they set out from there and hastened on to Scythopolis,† seventy-five miles from Jerusalem. [30] But when the Jews who lived there testified to the goodwill shown by the Scythopolitans and to their kind treatment even in times of adversity, [31] Judas and his men thanked them and exhorted them to be well disposed to their nation in the future also. Finally they arrived in Jerusalem, shortly before the feast of Weeks.

[32] After this feast, also called Pentecost, they lost no time in marching against Gorgias, governor of Idumea, [33] who opposed them with three thousand foot soldiers and four hundred cavalry. [34] In the ensuing battle, a few of the Jews were slain. [35] A man called Dositheus, a powerful horseman and one of Bacenor's men,† caught hold of Gorgias, grasped his military cloak and dragged him along by brute strength, intending to capture the vile wretch alive, when a Thracian horseman attacked Dositheus and cut off his arm at the shoulder. Then Gorgias fled to Marisa.

[36] After Esdris and his men had been fighting for a long time and were weary, Judas called upon the Lord to show himself their ally and leader in the battle. [37] Then, raising a battle cry in his ancestral language, and with hymns, he charged Gorgias' men when they were not expecting it and put them to flight.

**Expiation for the Dead.** [38] Judas rallied his army and went to the city of Adullam. As the seventh day was approaching, they purified themselves according to custom and kept the sabbath there. [39] On the following day, since the task had now become urgent, Judas and his companions went to gather up the bodies of the fallen and bury them with their kindred in their ancestral tombs. [40] But under the tunic of each of the dead they found amulets sacred to the idols of Jamnia, which the law forbids the Jews to wear. So it was clear to all that this was why these men had fallen.* [41] They all therefore praised the ways of the Lord, the

---

† **12:17** *Certain Jews known as Toubians*: because they lived "in the land of Tob" (1 Mc 5:13).

**12:26** *Atargatis*: a Syrian goddess, represented by the body of a fish, who in Hellenistic times was identified with Astarte and Artemis.

**12:29** *Scythopolis*: the Greek name of the city of Beth-shan;

cf. 1 Mc 5:52.

**12:35** *One of Bacenor's men*: certain ancient witnesses to the text have "one of the Toubians"; cf. v. 17.

* **12:17** 1 Mc 5:13.                    **12:40** Dt 7:25–26.
**12:26–31** 1 Mc 5:45–54.

just judge who brings to light the things that are hidden. [42]† Turning to supplication, they prayed that the sinful deed might be fully blotted out. The noble Judas exhorted the people to keep themselves free from sin, for they had seen with their own eyes what had happened because of the sin of those who had fallen.* [43] He then took up a collection among all his soldiers, amounting to two thousand silver drachmas, which he sent to Jerusalem to provide for an expiatory sacrifice. In doing this he acted in a very excellent and noble way, inasmuch as he had the resurrection in mind; [44] for if he were not expecting the fallen to rise again, it would have been superfluous and foolish to pray for the dead. [45] But if he did this with a view to the splendid reward that awaits those who had gone to rest in godliness, it was a holy and pious thought. [46] Thus he made atonement for the dead that they might be absolved from their sin.

# 13

**Death of Menelaus.** [1]* In the one hundred and forty-ninth year,† Judas and his men learned that Antiochus Eupator was invading Judea with a large force, [2] and that with him was Lysias, his guardian, who was in charge of the government. They led† a Greek army of one hundred and ten thousand foot soldiers, fifty-three hundred cavalry, twenty-two elephants, and three hundred chariots armed with scythes.

[3] Menelaus also joined them, and with great duplicity kept urging Antiochus on, not for the welfare of his country, but in the hope of being established in office. [4] But the King of kings* aroused the anger of Antiochus against the scoundrel. When the king was shown by Lysias that Menelaus was to blame for all the trouble, he ordered him to be taken to Beroea† and executed there in the customary local method. [5] There is at that place a tower seventy-five feet high, full of ashes,† with a circular rim sloping down steeply on all sides toward the ashes.

[6] Anyone guilty of sacrilege or notorious for certain other crimes is brought up there and then hurled down to destruction. [7] In such a manner was Menelaus, that transgressor of the law, fated to die, deprived even of burial. [8] It was altogether just that he who had committed so many sins against the altar with its pure fire and ashes, in ashes should meet his death.

**Battle near Modein.** [9] The king was advancing, his mind full of savage plans for inflicting on the Jews things worse than those they suffered in his father's time. [10] When Judas learned of this, he urged the people to call upon the Lord day and night, now more than ever, to help them when they were about to be deprived of their law, their country, and their holy temple; [11] and not to allow this people, which had just begun to revive, to be subjected again to blasphemous Gentiles. [12] When they had all joined in doing this, and had implored the merciful Lord continuously with weeping and fasting and prostrations for three days, Judas encouraged them and told them to stand ready.

[13] After a private meeting with the elders, he decided that, before the king's army could invade Judea and take possession of the city, the Jews should march out and settle the matter with God's help. [14] Leaving the outcome to the Creator of the world, and exhorting his followers to fight nobly to death for the laws, the temple, the city, the country, and the government, he encamped near Modein. [15] Giving his troops the battle cry "God's Victory," he made a night attack on the king's pavilion with a picked force of the bravest young men and killed about two thousand in the camp. He also stabbed the lead elephant and its rider.* [16] Finally they withdrew in triumph,† having filled the camp with terror and confusion. [17] Day was just breaking when this was accomplished with the help and protection of the Lord.

---

**12:42–45** This is the earliest statement of the doctrine that prayers (v. 42) and sacrifices (v. 43) for the dead are efficacious. Judas probably intended his purification offering to ward off punishment from the living. The author, however, uses the story to demonstrate belief in the resurrection of the just (7:9, 14, 23, 36), and in the possibility of expiation for the sins of otherwise good people who have died. This belief is similar to, but not quite the same as, the Catholic doctrine of purgatory.
**13:1** *In the one hundred and forty-ninth year:* 163/162 B.C.
**13:2** *They led:* the Greek means literally "each (of them) led," but it is unlikely that the author meant the already im-

mense numbers to be doubled; the numbers are similar to those in 1 Mc 6:30.
**13:4** *Beroea:* the Greek name of Aleppo in Syria.
**13:5** *Ashes:* probably smoldering ashes; the tower resembles the ancient Persian fire towers.
**13:16** *They withdrew in triumph:* according to 1 Mc 6:47 they fled.

*

**12:42** Jos 7:1–26.
**13:1–26** 1 Mc 6:28–54.
**13:4** 1 Tm 6:15; Rev 17:14; 19:16.
**13:15** 1 Mc 6:43–46.

**Treaty with Antiochus V.** ¹⁸* The king, having had a taste of the Jews' boldness, tried to take their positions by a stratagem. ¹⁹ So he marched against Beth-zur, a strong fortress of the Jews; but he was driven back, checked, and defeated. ²⁰ Judas sent supplies to the men inside, ²¹ but Rhodocus, of the Jewish army, betrayed military secrets† to the enemy. He was found out, arrested, and imprisoned. ²² The king made a second attempt by negotiating with the people of Beth-zur. After giving them his pledge and receiving theirs, he withdrew ²³ and attacked Judas' men. But he was defeated. Next he heard that Philip, who was left in charge of the government in Antioch, had rebelled. Dismayed, he negotiated with the Jews, submitted to their terms, and swore to observe all their rights. Having come to this agreement, he offered a sacrifice, and honored the sanctuary and the place with a generous donation. ²⁴ He received Maccabeus, and left Hegemonides as governor of the territory from Ptolemais to the region of the Gerrhenes.† ²⁵ When he came to Ptolemais, the people of Ptolemais were angered by the peace treaty; in fact they were so indignant that they wanted to annul its provisions. ²⁶ But Lysias took the platform, defended the treaty as well as he could and won them over by persuasion. After calming them and gaining their goodwill, he returned to Antioch. That is the story of the king's attack and withdrawal.

**14** ¹* Three years later,† Judas and his companions learned that Demetrius, son of Seleucus, had sailed into the port of Tripolis with a powerful army and a fleet, ² and that he had occupied the country, after doing away with Antiochus and his guardian Lysias.

³ A certain Alcimus, a former high priest,† who had willfully incurred defilement before the time of the revolt, realized that there was no way for him to be safe and regain access to the holy altar. ⁴ So he went to King Demetrius around the one hundred and fifty-first year and presented him with a gold crown and a palm branch, as well as some of the customary olive branches from the temple. On that day he kept quiet.* ⁵ But he found an opportunity to further his mad scheme when he was invited to the council by Demetrius and questioned about the dispositions and intentions of the Jews. He replied: ⁶ "Those Jews called Hasideans, led by Judas Maccabeus,† are warmongers, who stir up sedition and keep the kingdom from enjoying peace.* ⁷ For this reason, now that I am deprived of my ancestral dignity, that is to say, the high priesthood, I have come here, ⁸ first, out of my genuine concern for the king's interests, and second, out of consideration for my own compatriots, since our entire nation is suffering no little affliction from the rash conduct of the people just mentioned. ⁹ When you have informed yourself in detail on these matters, O king, provide for our country and its hard-pressed people with the same gracious consideration that you show toward all. ¹⁰ As long as Judas is around, it is impossible for the government to enjoy peace." ¹¹ When he had said this, the other Friends who were hostile to Judas quickly added fuel to Demetrius' indignation.

**Dealings with Nicanor.** ¹²* The king immediately chose Nicanor, who had been in command of the elephants, and appointed him governor of Judea. He sent him off ¹³ with orders to put Judas to death, to disperse his followers, and to set up Alcimus as high priest of the great temple. ¹⁴ The Gentiles from Judea, who had fled before Judas, flocked to Nicanor, thinking that the misfortunes and calamities of the Jews would mean prosperity for themselves.

¹⁵* When the Jews heard of Nicanor's coming, and that the Gentiles were rallying to him, they sprinkled themselves with earth and prayed to him who established his people forever, and who always comes to the aid of his heritage by manifesting himself. ¹⁶ At their leader's command, they set out at once from there and came upon the enemy at the village

---

† 13:21 *Military secrets:* probably about the lack of provisions in the besieged city; cf. 1 Mc 6:49.
  13:24 *Gerrhenes:* probably the inhabitants of Gerar, southeast of Gaza.
  14:1 *Three years later:* actually, Demetrius (I Soter), son of Seleucus (IV), landed at Tripolis in the year 151 of the Seleucid era (1 Mc 14:4), i.e., 162/161 B.C.; cf. 1 Mc 7:1–7.
  14:3 *Alcimus, a former high priest:* he was apparently appointed high priest by Antiochus V after Menelaus was executed,

and then deposed for collaborating with the Seleucids.
  14:6 *Hasideans, led by Judas Maccabeus:* according to 1 Mc 2:42 and 7:12–17, the Hasideans were a party separate from the Maccabees.

13:18–23 1 Mc 6:48–53.    14:12–13 2 Mc 8:9; 1 Mc 3:38;
14:1–11 1 Mc 7:1–7.                  7:26–27.
14:4 1 Mc 7:5–7, 25.      14:15–19 1 Mc 7:26–32.
14:6 1 Mc 2:42; 7:12–17.

of Adasa. [17] Judas' brother Simon had engaged Nicanor, but he suffered a slight setback because of the sudden appearance of the enemy. [18] However, when Nicanor heard of the valor of Judas and his companions, and the great courage with which they fought for their country, he shrank from deciding the issue by bloodshed. [19] So he sent Posidonius, Theodotus and Mattathias to exchange pledges of friendship. [20] After a long discussion of the terms, each leader communicated them to his troops; and when general agreement was expressed, they assented to the treaty. [21] A day was set on which the leaders would meet by themselves. From each side a chariot came forward, and thrones were set in place. [22] Judas had posted armed men in readiness at strategic points for fear that the enemy might suddenly commit some treachery. But the conference was held in the proper way.

[23] Nicanor stayed on in Jerusalem, where he did nothing out of place. He disbanded the throngs of people who gathered around him; [24] and he always kept Judas in his company, for he felt affection† for the man. [25] He urged him to marry and have children; so Judas married and settled into an ordinary life.

**Nicanor's Threat Against Judas.** [26] When Alcimus saw their mutual goodwill, he took the treaty that had been made, went to Demetrius, and said that Nicanor was plotting against the government, for he had appointed Judas, that conspirator against the kingdom, as his successor. [27] Stirred up by the villain's slander, the king became enraged. He wrote to Nicanor, stating that he was displeased with the treaty, and ordering him to send Maccabeus at once as a prisoner to Antioch. [28] When this message reached Nicanor he was dismayed and troubled at the thought of annulling his agreement with a man who had done no wrong. [29] However, there was no way of opposing the king, so he watched for an opportunity to carry out this order by a stratagem. [30] But Maccabeus, noticing that Nicanor was more harsh in his dealings with him, and acting with unaccustomed rudeness when they met, concluded that this

harshness was not a good sign. So he gathered together not a few of his men, and went into hiding from Nicanor.

[31]* When Nicanor realized that he had been cleverly outwitted by the man, he went to the great and holy temple, at a time when the priests were offering the customary sacrifices, and ordered them to surrender Judas. [32] As they declared under oath that they did not know where the man they sought was, [33] he stretched out his right arm toward the temple and swore this oath: "If you do not hand Judas over to me as prisoner, I will level this shrine of God to the ground; I will tear down the altar, and erect here a splendid temple to Dionysus."

[34] With these words he went away. The priests stretched out their hands toward heaven, calling upon the unfailing defender of our nation in these words: [35] "Lord of all, though you are in need of nothing, you were pleased to have a temple for your dwelling place among us. [36] Therefore, Holy One, Lord of all holiness, preserve forever undefiled this house, which has been so recently purified."*

**Martyrdom of Razis.**† [37] A certain Razis, one of the elders of Jerusalem, was denounced to Nicanor as a patriot. A man highly regarded, he was called a father of the Jews because of his goodwill toward them. [38] In the days before the revolt, he had been convicted of being a Jew, and had risked body and soul in his ardent zeal for Judaism. [39] Nicanor, to show his disdain for the Jews, sent more than five hundred soldiers to arrest him. [40] He thought that by arresting that man he would deal the Jews a hard blow.

[41] But when the troops, on the point of capturing the tower, were forcing the outer gate and calling for fire to set the door ablaze, Razis, now caught on all sides, turned his sword against himself, [42] preferring to die nobly† rather than fall into the hands of vile men and suffer outrages unworthy of his noble birth. [43] In the excitement of the struggle he failed to strike exactly. So while the troops rushed in through the doors, he gallantly ran up to the

---

† **14:24** *Affection*: compare 1 Mc 7:26–32, where there is no hint of this cordial relationship between Nicanor and Judas.

**14:37–46** The story of Razis belongs to the "martyrology" class of literature; it is similar to the stories in 6:18–7:42.

**14:42** *Die nobly*: Razis's willingness to die nobly rather than to fall into enemy hands had a precedent in Saul (1 Sm 31:4).

Razis took his life because he was convinced that God would restore his body in the resurrection of the dead (see 7:11, 22–23; 14:46).

*

**14:31–36** 1 Mc 7:30–38.          **14:36** 2 Mc 15:34.

top of the wall and courageously threw himself down into the crowd. **44** But as they quickly drew back and left an opening, he fell into the middle of the empty space. **45** Still breathing, and inflamed with anger, he got up and ran through the crowd, with blood gushing from his frightful wounds. Then, standing on a steep rock, **46** as he lost the last of his blood, he tore out his entrails and flung them with both hands into the crowd, calling upon the Lord of life and of spirit to give these back to him again. Such was the manner of his death.*

**15** **Nicanor's Arrogance.** **1** When Nicanor learned that Judas and his companions were in the territory of Samaria, he decided he could attack them in complete safety on the day of rest. **2** The Jews who were forced to accompany him pleaded, "Do not massacre them so savagely and barbarously, but show respect for the day which the All-seeing has exalted with holiness above all other days." **3** At this the thrice-accursed wretch asked if there was a ruler in heaven who prescribed the keeping of the sabbath day.* **4** They replied, "It is the living Lord, the ruler in heaven, who commands the observance of the sabbath day." **5** Then he said, "I, the ruler on earth, command you to take up arms and carry out the king's business." Nevertheless he did not succeed in carrying out his cruel plan.

**6** In his utter boastfulness and arrogance Nicanor had determined to erect a public victory monument† over Judas and his companions. **7** But Maccabeus remained confident, fully convinced that he would receive help from the Lord. **8** He urged his men not to fear the attack of the Gentiles, but mindful of the help they had received in the past from Heaven, to expect now the victory that would be given them by the Almighty. **9** By encouraging them with words from the law and the prophets,† and by reminding them of the battles they had already won, he filled them with fresh enthusiasm. **10** Having stirred up their courage, he gave his orders and pointed out at the same time the perfidy of the Gentiles and their violation of oaths. **11** When he had armed each of them, not so much with the security of shield and spear as with the encouragement of noble words, he cheered them all by relating a dream, a kind of waking vision, worthy of belief.

**12** What he saw was this: Onias, the former high priest,† a noble and good man, modest in bearing, gentle in manner, distinguished in speech, and trained from childhood in all that belongs to excellence, was praying with outstretched arms for the whole Jewish community.* **13** Then in the same way another man appeared, distinguished by his white hair and dignity, and with an air of wondrous and majestic authority. **14** Onias then said of him, "This is a man† who loves his fellow Jews and fervently prays for the people and the holy city—the prophet of God, Jeremiah." **15** Stretching out his right hand, Jeremiah presented a gold sword to Judas. As he gave it to him he said, **16** "Accept this holy sword as a gift from God; with it you shall shatter your adversaries."

**17** Encouraged by Judas' words, so noble and capable of instilling valor and stirring young hearts to courage, they determined not merely to march, but to charge gallantly and decide the issue by hand-to-hand combat with the utmost courage, since city, sanctuary and temple were in danger. **18** They were not so much concerned about wives and children, or family and relations; their first and foremost fear was for the consecrated sanctuary.* **19** Those who were left in the city suffered no less an agony, anxious as they were about the battle in the open country. **20** Everyone now awaited the decisive moment. The enemy were already drawing near with their troops drawn up in battle line, their beasts placed in strategic positions, and their cavalry stationed on the flanks.

**Defeat of Nicanor.** **21** Maccabeus, surveying the hosts before him, the variety of weaponry, and the fierceness of their beasts, stretched out

---

† **15:6** *Public victory monument*: a heap of stones covered with the arms and armor of the fallen enemy.

**15:9** *The law and the prophets*: the first of the three parts of the Hebrew Scriptures, called the sacred books (1 Mc 12:9; 2 Mc 2:14).

**15:12** *Onias, the former high priest*: Onias III (3:1–40). Evidently the author believed that departed just persons were in some way alive even before their resurrection.

**15:14** *A man*: regarded by the postexilic Jews as one of the greatest figures in their history; cf. 2:1; Mt 16:14. *Who...prays for the people*: Jeremiah's prayer in heaven has been taken in the Roman Catholic tradition as a biblical witness to the intercession of the saints.

* 14:46 2 Mc 7:9–11.      15:12 2 Mc 3:1–40.
15:3 1 Mc 7:34.      15:18 1 Mc 4:36.

his hands toward heaven and called upon the Lord who works wonders; for he knew that it is not weapons but the Lord's decision that brings victory to those who deserve it. <sup>22</sup> Calling upon God, he spoke in this manner: "You, master, sent your angel in the days of King Hezekiah of Judea, and he slew a hundred and eighty-five thousand men of Sennacherib's camp.* <sup>23</sup> And now, Sovereign of the heavens, send a good angel to spread fear and trembling ahead of us. <sup>24</sup> By the might of your arm may those be struck down who have blasphemously come against your holy people!" With these words he ended his prayer.

<sup>25</sup>* Nicanor and his troops advanced to the sound of trumpets and battle songs. <sup>26</sup> But Judas and his troops met the enemy with supplication and prayers. <sup>27</sup> Fighting with their hands and praying to God with their hearts, they laid low at least thirty-five thousand, and rejoiced greatly over this manifestation of God's power. <sup>28</sup> When the battle was over and they were joyfully departing, they discovered Nicanor fallen there in all his armor; <sup>29</sup> so they raised tumultuous shouts in their ancestral language in praise of the divine Sovereign.

<sup>30</sup> Then Judas, that man who was ever in body and soul the chief defender of his fellow citizens, and had maintained from youth his affection for his compatriots, ordered Nicanor's head and right arm up to the shoulder to be cut off and taken to Jerusalem. <sup>31</sup> When he arrived there, he assembled his compatriots, stationed the priests before the altar, and sent

for those in the citadel.† <sup>32</sup> He showed them the vile Nicanor's head and the wretched blasphemer's arm that had been boastfully stretched out against the holy dwelling of the Almighty. <sup>33</sup> He cut out the tongue of the godless Nicanor, saying he would feed it piecemeal to the birds and would hang up the other wages of his folly opposite the temple. <sup>34</sup> At this, everyone looked toward heaven and praised the Lord who manifests himself: "Blessed be the one who has preserved undefiled his own place!" <sup>35</sup> Judas hung Nicanor's head and arm on the wall of the citadel, a clear and evident sign to all of the Lord's help.* <sup>36</sup> By public vote it was unanimously decreed never to let this day pass unobserved, but to celebrate the thirteenth day of the twelfth month, called Adar in Aramaic, the eve of Mordecai's Day.†*

## VII. EPILOGUE

**Compiler's Apology.** <sup>37</sup> Since Nicanor's doings ended in this way, with the city remaining in the possession of the Hebrews from that time on, I will bring my story to an end here too. <sup>38</sup>* If it is well written and to the point, that is what I wanted; if it is poorly done and mediocre, that is the best I could do. <sup>39</sup> Just as it is unpleasant to drink wine by itself or just water, whereas wine mixed with water makes a delightful and pleasing drink, so a skillfully composed story delights the ears of those who read the work. Let this, then, be the end.

---

† **15:31** *Those in the citadel*: presumably Jewish soldiers; actually, the citadel was still in the possession of the Syrians (1 Mc 13:50).

**15:36** *Mordecai's Day*: the feast of Purim, celebrated on the fourteenth and fifteenth days of Adar (Est 3:7; 9:20–23; F:10).

**15:22–23** 2 Mc 8:19; 2 Kgs 19:35–36; 1 Mc 7:41–42; Is 37:36–37.
**15:25–36** 1 Mc 7:43.
**15:35** 1 Sm 31:9–10.
**15:36** 1 Mc 7:49.
**15:38–39** 2 Mc 2:19–32.

# Introduction to the Wisdom Books

## Andrew T. Glicksman

Have you ever wondered: What is life all about? How can I live a long, happy, and successful life? Why do liars and cheaters sometimes prosper while honest and innocent people occasionally suffer? If God allows evil to harm those who are good, then how can God be good or just? If you've pondered any of these issues, you're not alone. These are among life's transcendent questions, asked by humans in all places and times, and the ancient Israelites and Jews are no exception. We find them wrestling with such concerns in the Wisdom literature of the Old Testament.

In the Catholic tradition, the books that belong to the Wisdom corpus are Proverbs, Job, Ecclesiastes (also called Qoheleth), Ben Sira (also called the Wisdom of Ben Sira, Sirach, or Ecclesiasticus), and the book of Wisdom (also called the Wisdom of Solomon). The last two are among the seven deuterocanonical books (also called the Apocrypha) and are not part of the Jewish or Protestant canons. Although the book of Psalms is grouped with the Wisdom books in the Christian canon and some individual psalms exhibit wisdom characteristics (see especially Pss 1, 37, 49, 128), as a whole this collection of prayerful songs is not technically Wisdom literature. The same is true of the Song of Songs, which is Hebrew love poetry, placed in this part of the canon because of its association with Solomon (see Sg 1:1).

## Common Characteristics and Themes of Wisdom Texts

Each Old Testament Wisdom book exhibits at least a few of the following elements that help us categorize it as part of this literature: (1) Solomonic attribution, (2) personification of wisdom, (3) universalistic flavor, (4) practical and experiential matters, and (5) the belief in divine retribution.

## Solomonic Attribution

Of the five Wisdom books, three claim association with King Solomon on some level. In Proverbs, three collections bear Solomonic headings (see Prv 1:1; 10:1; 25:1). The opening verse of Ecclesiastes identifies its author as "David's son, Qoheleth, king in Jerusalem" (Eccl 1:1). Since Solomon was renowned for his wisdom and the only one of David's sons to succeed him to the throne in Jerusalem, the identification is clear. Like Ecclesiastes, the book of Wisdom never explicitly mentions Solomon by name but hints that he composed the work (Wis 9:7–8). The other two Wisdom books, Job and Ben Sira, make no claim of Solomonic authorship.

Even though many of the Wisdom books are attributed to Solomon, who lived in the tenth century BCE, scholars question whether he actually composed most of these texts. Ecclesiastes was written in a form of Hebrew with strong Aramaic influence, and its content displays possible contact with Greek modes of thinking. The book of Wisdom was composed in Greek and exhibits elements of Hellenistic philosophy and culture. These texts could not have been written by a tenth-century Israelite king, no matter how wise.

If the Old Testament contains works attributed to Solomon that he didn't actually write, then who wrote them? And why did these authors write under his name? The authors of these pseudonymous texts were most likely Jewish sages living in the mid- to late Second Temple period (roughly from the late fourth to late first centuries BCE), who engaged the thought and culture of their neighbors and confronted challenges to Jewish belief and identity. By claiming Solomonic authorship, these writers did not necessarily intend to trick their readers into thinking that Solomon actually wrote these works. Rather, they wrote in his name to show that their work was "in the tradition of" or "in the same line of thinking as" Solomon and deserved a similar level of attention; as if to say: "If Solomon were alive today, this is how he would respond to our present situation."

## Lady Wisdom

Aside from Solomon, another well-known character from Wisdom texts is wisdom personified as a female figure, often called "Lady" or "Woman" Wisdom. This abstract attribute of God is portrayed more concretely as a feminine figure because the words for wisdom in both Hebrew (*hokmah*) and Greek (*sophia*) are feminine nouns. She appears in every Wisdom book except Ecclesiastes and possibly Job. In Prv 1–9, she actively seeks her followers, describes her origins from God and her role in creation, and invites those who seek her to a sumptuous banquet where she grants them life. In addition to similar themes in Wis 6–10 and Sir 24, these later Wisdom texts add to our understanding of Lady Wisdom. Ben Sira presents Wisdom singing her own praises in God's heavenly court, dwelling in Israel (specifically, in the Temple), and being equivalent to the Torah. The book of Wisdom praises Lady Wisdom by closely identifying her with the Almighty, linking her to the idea of immortality, and depicting her as saving early biblical figures. No wonder scholars debate whether wisdom is personified in Jb 28, because in this passage wisdom does not exhibit any clear actions or human-like characteristics as in the Lady Wisdom passages mentioned above.

Scholars have also debated the exact background and nature of Lady Wisdom. Was she originally a goddess who was demoted once monotheism prevailed in Judaism? Is she merely a literary device? Could she be something more—perhaps an entity distinct from Yahweh or even a *hypostasis* (a person)? It is difficult to arrive at definite conclusions concerning these issues. Though Lady Wisdom is closely associated with the nature and activity of God in Wisdom texts, strict monotheistic belief among Second Temple Jews would militate against identifying this figure as a deity. Rather than being a separate entity or having distinct personhood, she appears to be a literary way of describing God's activity in the human realm while preserving God's transcendence. Nonetheless, it comes as no surprise that New Testament writers turned to language and imagery used for Lady Wisdom when making claims about Jesus' divine origins, activity, and identity (see Jn 1:1–18; Col 1:15–20).

## Universalistic Outlook

Since the Wisdom writings of the Old Testament seek to answer fundamental questions about life and how to master it, they often bear a distinctly universalistic flavor and reflect an approach to reality similar to that of surrounding ancient Near Eastern cultures (see "Historical Context" below). This universalistic tendency is further emphasized in earlier Wisdom texts (i.e., Proverbs, Job, and Ecclesiastes) by the lack of reference to events in Israelite history and the special covenantal relationship between God and his people as expressed in the Pentateuch, Historical Books, and Prophetic Literature. Proverbs presupposes that one must seek wisdom in the context of a proper relationship with the Israelite deity (often expressed as "fear of the LORD," cf. Prv 1:7; 9:10), but it is generally devoid of distinctly Israelite or Jewish material. Proverbs 30 and 31 are clearly attributed to non-Israelites, and Prv 22:17–24:22 most likely derives from an ancient Egyptian collection (see the discussion under "Historical Context"). Job and his companions are not Israelites and the book only mentions the divine name a handful of times, while Ecclesiastes opts for the generic Hebrew term for God (*Elohim*) throughout. The implicit message is that the Israelites and Jews do not have a monopoly on wise living.

The situation changes slightly in the two later Wisdom books. Ben Sira alludes to the Sinai covenant, equates Wisdom with the Torah, and claims that she dwells in Jerusalem's Temple. For Ben Sira, wisdom is clearly concentrated in Israel. Also Sir 44–50, often called the "Praise of the Ancestors," is a review of Israelite history in which various figures are either praised for their wisdom and righteousness or condemned for their foolishness and wickedness, and in some cases both (note the treatment of Solomon in Sir 47). The latter part of the book of Wisdom has a similar section. Through prominent wisdom themes, such as Lady Wisdom and the righteous versus the unrighteous, Wis 10 reviews early biblical figures and events from Adam to Moses. Wisdom 11–19 then reinterprets the Exodus and wilderness wanderings according to similar themes. Yet a universal element remains: the biblical figures in Wis 10 are not explicitly named, and their success is contingent upon their righteous pursuit of Wisdom and not whether they are Israelite. Some figures, such as Adam, Noah, and Lot, are not Israelites at all. So, while Israel is sometimes a focus in Wisdom texts, this literature is generally universalistic in outlook.

## Practical Instruction Based on Experience

Most of Old Testament Wisdom literature has a pragmatic objective: to instruct one how to live a long, happy, and successful earthly life. The keys to achieving these goals are proper behavior and maintaining good relationships. Proper behavior means living a righteous life and discerning the appropriate time to act and speak. For many Wisdom texts, knowing the right time to act is gained by experience and, especially, by observing the causes and effects of human actions and discerning the order inherent in creation. Even the smallest creatures, such as the ant, teach one how to behave correctly (Prv 6:6–11). Correct behavior is an essential part of maintaining quality relationships, which build and preserve one's reputation and therefore ensure happiness and success.

Of course, one's relationship with God is of highest importance in the pursuit of wisdom. Nearly every Old Testament Wisdom text mentions "fear of the LORD/God" as the prerequisite for attaining wisdom (Prv 1:7; 9:10; Jb 28:28; Eccl 12:13; Sir 1:11–28; 2:7–17). This phrase is best understood as awe, reverence, and, especially, obedience to God. In terms of human relationships, Proverbs and Ben Sira emphasize that one must have respect for one's elders and associate with the right kinds of people to build genuine friendships. Of these human relationships, special emphasis is placed on finding a good spouse as a lifelong companion.

## Divine Retribution and Wisdom in Crisis

The belief in divine retribution is closely associated with the practical aspect of Wisdom literature. This tenet, found especially in Proverbs and Ben Sira, maintains that during their earthly lives God rewards the righteous and wise but punishes the wicked and foolish. Or understood another way, since God ordered the world by imbuing it with wisdom, the wise recognize and conform their lives to this order and therefore prosper, while the foolish are ignorant of or reject this order to their own detriment. Many ancient Israelites and early Jews believed that all who died had a somber, shadowy existence in the netherworld, called Sheol. This meant that reward or punishment for behavior only occurred on earth; there would be no carryover into the next realm, for all had the same fate in death. So what was the incentive to live wisely in the present life, if you lost all earthly reward upon death?

Even more disconcerting was the frequent observation that the wicked could live a long, happy, and successful earthly life, while the righteous often suffered! Here we enter the realm of critical Wisdom texts such as Job and Ecclesiastes, which have been categorized as "wisdom in crisis" because, by drawing on human experience, they challenge the validity of the traditional view of retribution. Job is a righteous individual who suffers terribly for no apparent reason and demands that God account for this injustice against him. The author of Ecclesiastes is a wise skeptic who questions the point of life and the purpose for pursuing wisdom if humans cannot always determine the right time to act (Eccl 3:1–15). Although some of their objections are later softened by the understanding of reward in the afterlife (see Wis 3:1–9), these books raise difficult questions that may never be fully answered. They show us that in addition to passing along practical instructions, the sages critiqued traditional teachings to arrive at a deeper wisdom about reality, namely, that God's ways are often mysterious to us and there are no simple solutions to life's complexities.

# Literary Context

## Hebrew Poetry

Most Wisdom texts can be categorized as Hebrew poetry, which is often structured as groupings of two or three parallel lines (a bicolon and tricolon, respectively) and bound by poetic features such as wordplay, alliteration, and structural devices. One- or four-line constructions are also possible, but these are not as common. Those familiar with English poetry will recognize similar poetic features in the Hebrew variety, even in translation (naturally, you must be able to vocalize the Hebrew text to appreciate the alliterative features). Even though the primary texts of Ben Sira and the book of Wisdom have come down to us in the Septuagint, they both exhibit the parallelism characteristic of Hebrew poetry. Ben Sira was originally written in Hebrew and so the Greek translation made by the author's grandson reflects the underlying Hebrew poetic structure. The book of Wisdom was originally composed in Greek, but its Jewish author arranges his work according to Hebrew parallelism rather than Greek meter (of course, the wordplay in his work is based upon the Greek).

Hebrew poetry exhibits three types of parallelism: synonymous, antithetical, and synthetic. Synonymous parallelism is when the second line uses different words to restate and reinforce the message of the first line. Proverbs 19:5 states: "The false witness will not go unpunished, / and whoever utters lies will not escape." When lines are antithetical, the second states the opposite of the first while both convey the same basic message. As Prv 15:2 states: "The tongue of the wise pours out knowledge, / but the mouth of fools spews folly." Here the word-pair tongue/mouth are synonymous, while the word-pairs wise/fools and knowledge/folly are clearly antithetical. Overall, the two lines are antithetical in meaning, but together they communicate a unified message: speak wisely and not foolishly. You can often identify antithetical lines by the presence of the word "but" at the beginning of the second line. It is also helpful to note that parallelism can work on many levels, including between bicola. Consider Prv 5:3–4: "Indeed, the lips of the stranger drip honey, / and her mouth is smoother than oil; / But in the end she is as bitter as wormwood, / as sharp as a two-edged sword." In this case, there are two sets of bicola: each employs synonymous parallelism within itself, but antithetical parallelism in relationship to the other bicolon. Synthetic parallelism, the last type of parallelism, ultimately functions as a catchall, and most lines of Hebrew poetry fall into this category. It occurs when the second line completes the thought of the first. Proverbs 21:3 claims: "To do what is right and just / is more acceptable to the LORD than sacrifice." Another example several verses later warns: "Those who shut their ears to the cry of the poor / will themselves call out and not be answered" (Prv 21:13). This last case exhibits synonymous elements (shutting the ear/not being answered and cry/call out) between the lines that ultimately express a cause-and-effect relationship; the first is incomplete without the second, and therefore is synthetic.

In addition to parallelism, Hebrew poetry exhibits many other poetic features such as wordplay, alliteration, and structural devices. Some of these features can be appreciated in the compact statement from Eccl 7:1a. The transliteration of the Hebrew with English translation reads:

A B C B′ A′

*tob shem mishshemen tob*

"A good name is better than good ointment."

Here we have alliteration in the repetition of *sh*, *m*, *t*, and *b* consonants and *o* and *e* vowels. Furthermore, the ABCB′A′ chiastic structure (a crossing pattern) binds the line together. Also, notice the use of synecdoche (the part stands for the whole), where "good ointment" represents all of one's valuables. Not only did these poetic features make the saying pleasing to the ear, but they also facilitated memorization, recall, and application.

## Literary Genres

The *mashal* is the most basic literary form in Old Testament Wisdom literature. The Hebrew word derives from one of two roots meaning either (1) "to compare; to represent; to be like" or (2) "to govern; to rule." Thus, a *mashal* would be any statement or teaching that reflects or "is like" the truth found in the world around us, or it could be a wise teaching that "governs" reality. In either case the *mashal* is an insightful statement often meant to persuade the hearer, whether implicitly or explicitly, to pursue a specific way of living that will yield the most out of life. This Hebrew term is often rendered in English as "proverb," which we usually define as a relevant, pithy saying packed with insight into how the world works. While many *meshalim* (the plural of *mashal*) are indeed proverbs, other types of literature such as riddles (see Prv 1:6; Ez 17:2), parables (Ez 24:3), satires/taunt-songs (Prv 1:6; Is 14:4; Mi 2:4; Hb 2:6), and long instructions (see Prv 1–9) also fall under this general category.

To move beyond the ambiguous designation *mashal*, biblical scholar Roland Murphy categorizes Wisdom texts into (1) sayings, (2) admonitions, and (3) Wisdom poems. Each of these three categories takes a variety of forms, which cannot be treated here. However, it is at least helpful to look at some of the ways that they are expressed.

Sayings are often experiential and can also be didactic. The experiential type presents a general observation about the world or society (usually stated in the indicative), sometimes explicitly teaching a lesson or moral. Proverbs 22:7 observes, "The rich rule over the poor, / and the borrower is the slave of the lender." No overt lesson is taught here, but this general observation implies that to preserve financial freedom and high social standing one should avoid borrowing large sums of money. At the same time, the observation can be paired with an explicit didactic purpose, such as: "A slanderer reveals secrets; / so have nothing to do with a babbler!" (Prv 20:19). Other general sayings are primarily didactic in nature, teaching specific moral values. For example, Prv 21:6 instructs, "Trying to get rich by lying / is chasing a bubble over deadly snares," which encourages a life founded upon integrity by emphasizing the precarious position of one who attempts to gain wealth under false pretenses.

Admonitions are commands (in the imperative) that are clearly didactic and phrased as either positive or negative. The book of Wisdom opens with the positive variety, "Love righteousness, you who judge the earth; / think of the LORD in goodness, / and seek him in integrity of heart" (Wis 1:1). Beginning a long collection of negative commands, Ben Sira states, "Do no evil, and evil will not overtake you; / avoid wickedness, and it will turn away from you" (Sir 7:1–2).

Wisdom poems come in all kinds and are found in every Old Testament Wisdom book. In Proverbs, we encounter long instructions of a parent to his or her child (see especially Prv 1–9; 31:1–9). Much of the poetic middle section of Job (Jb 3–37) is a series of laments, disputations, and dialogues that address the problem of evil and the case of the righteous sufferer through subgenres such as lawsuit (Jb 31:35–37; 40:7–8) and parody (compare Jb 3 to Gn 1, and Jb 7:17–21 to Ps 8), among others. In Ecclesiastes, which is harder to categorize into specific genres, we have theologically reflective and tradition-critiquing Wisdom poems presented as a royal pseudo-autobiography. Ben Sira presents much of his wisdom in the form of extended instructions (Sir 2–23; 25–38), hymns (Sir 39:12–35; 42:15–43:33), and praises (Sir 1:11–30; 24; 44–50). In the book of Wisdom, the Wisdom poems are set within the framework of an exhortative discourse (*logos protreptikos*), which tries to persuade its audience to follow a particular course of action through a variety of subgenres including diatribe (Wis 2), praise (Wis 6–10), and comparison (Wis 10–19).

## Historical Context

Similar traditions in surrounding ancient Near Eastern cultures, especially in Egypt and Mesopotamia, shed light on the Old Testament Wisdom texts. Sapiential learning in Israel did not occur in complete isolation. In some cases the sages read, borrowed from, and critiqued the Wisdom traditions of their neighbors. The subject matter of these writings from other cultures and the setting within which they were produced provide insight into the themes and development of Old Testament Wisdom.

Egyptologists have discovered many collections of wise sayings, including 17 examples of instruction texts, the earliest dating to the mid- to late third millennium BCE (*The Instruction of Prince Hardjedef*) and the latest from the first century CE (*Papyrus Insinger*). In these instruction texts a pharaoh, leading official, or scribe draws on his own experience to pass along practical advice to his son or student. The most notable of these is *The Instruction of Amen-em-ope*, which dates to the late second millennium BCE (ca. 1200–1100 BCE). This text bears a striking resemblance in format and content to the short collection in Prv 22:17–24:22, and therefore, many scholars believe that the collection in Proverbs is in some way dependent on the Egyptian text. In Egypt, such texts would have emerged from the scribal schools associated with the royal court, instructing aspiring young scribes in basic literacy and successful living. Egyptian scribes were encouraged to live according to the principle of "order, truth, justice" known as *ma'at*, which was also understood to be an Egyptian goddess. If a scribe honored her and ordered his actions by constantly seeking her, he could expect a long and happy life. Scholars see a possible link between this Egyptian figure and the Israelite concept of Lady Wisdom.

Like that of Egypt, Mesopotamian cultures also provide many parallels to biblical Wisdom texts. The Sumerian scribal schools produced collections of proverbs, riddles, and fables dating to the third millennium BCE, some of which are similar to what we encounter in Prv 10:1–22:16, the oldest part of the book. In addition, a text called *Man and His God*, in which an individual complains about his suffering to his personal gods, could be considered a parallel to Job. The Old Babylonians (second millennium BCE) also had texts with themes similar to Job, including *The Babylonian Theodicy* and *I Will Praise the Lord of Wisdom*. Furthermore, the Babylonian *Dialogue of Pessimism* touches upon themes of skepticism found in Ecclesiastes. Another Wisdom collection, which may have Canaanite origins, is *The Words of Ahiqar* (eighth to seventh centuries

BCE). This text begins with a tale about a wise man who proves himself after being falsely accused by his nephew and concludes with a list of wise sayings reminiscent of material in Proverbs and Ben Sira. Not to say that all this Mesopotamian material directly influenced the Israelite and Jewish sages, but they may have been aware of some of these other works. Most importantly, we learn that similar modes of thinking were present among Israel's neighbors to the north and east.

How Wisdom traditions developed in Israel is much debated. We cannot assume that it was the same as in Egypt or Mesopotamia, though it was probably not too different. The difficulty is that, aside from what we read in the biblical text itself, there is not much evidence to reconstruct the environment in which wisdom was transmitted and developed. Most scholars now agree that Israel's Wisdom tradition began in a family setting where parents taught tribal values to their children. When the monarchy developed, the need for record-keeping necessitated professional scribes who, along with recording bureaucratic matters, preserved Israelite culture in the form of ancient stories, laws, and traditional practical advice. We assume that such a profession included schools where young men were trained, perhaps much like in Egypt and Mesopotamia. During the exile, when the monarchy no longer existed, such preservation of texts and traditions became even more important for the survival of Jewish culture and formation of Jewish identity. In the postexilic era, young men most likely learned the ways of Wisdom alongside the Torah in a school setting. Ben Sira 51:23 provides some evidence for such an environment since the wise man calls to prospective students to come learn at his "house of instruction." Some of these schools may have been associated with the Jerusalem Temple, but they undoubtedly existed in Jewish communities throughout Palestine and beyond.

# The Message and Role of Wisdom for Us

Though some of its language and imagery is initially foreign to us, Wisdom literature ultimately possesses a timeless quality. Here we encounter sage advice based on lived experience from those who, though from a culture long ago, share a common humanity. Like us, they strive to answer questions about how best to live life. On the surface, their overall message is straightforward: honor God and order your life according to the harmony he has set in the world around you. Following this seemingly simple directive can be more difficult than it sounds. Once we have acquired knowledge through observation we must still correctly apply what we've learned. There are no ready-made solutions or formulas that will work for every situation in life. Rather, careful discernment is needed in the proper application of knowledge. Also, as Job and Ecclesiastes poignantly teach, there are limits to human understanding, and we may never fully know the answers to some of life's most difficult questions. By reading and rereading these ancient Wisdom texts, we enter into an age-old conversation and continue the human quest to live a meaningful existence. ■

# THE WISDOM BOOKS

## New American Bible, Introduction

"Wisdom" is a convenient umbrella term to designate the Books of Job, Proverbs, Ecclesiastes (Qoheleth), Wisdom, and Sirach (Ecclesiasticus). Two other books are often associated with them: Psalms, a collection of mostly devotional lyrics, and the Song of Songs, a collection of love poems. All are marked by a skillful use of parallelism, or verses of balanced and symmetrical phrases. These works have been classified as wisdom or didactic literature, so called because their general purpose is instruction.

A striking feature of the wisdom books is the absence of references to the promises made to the patriarchs or to Moses, or to Sinai or typical items in Israelite tradition; Sirach (chaps. 44–50) and Wisdom (chaps. 10–19) are the exception. Biblical wisdom literature concentrates on daily human experience: how is life to be lived? In this respect it is comparable to other ancient Near Eastern compositions from Mesopotamia and Egypt that also reflect on the problems of everyday life. The literary style is wide-ranging: aphorisms, numerical sayings, paradoxes, instructions, alphabetical and acrostic poems, lively speeches, and so forth. Wisdom itself is an art: how to deal with various situations and achieve a good life. And it is also a teaching: the lessons garnered from experience were transmitted at various levels, from education in the home all the way to training in the court. Belief in the Lord and acceptance of the prevailing codes of conduct were presupposed; they fed into the training of youths. The task of wisdom is character formation: what is the wise path to follow? The lessons are conveyed by observations that challenge as well as by admonitions that warn. Although the need of discipline is underlined, the general approach is persuasion. The pursuit of wisdom demands more than human industry. Paradoxically, it remains also the gift of God (Prv 2:6). Its religious character is indicated by the steady identification of wisdom and virtue (e.g., Prv 10–15).

But wisdom is far more than a practical guide. The strongest personification in the Bible is Woman Wisdom, and she speaks somewhat mysteriously in divine accents about her origins and identity. Her appeal to humanity is sounded in several books: Prv 8; Sir 24; Wis 7–9; Bar 3:9–4:4. She offers "life" to her followers (Prv 8:35, "whoever finds me finds life"). This image of personified Wisdom is reflected in the Logos poem of Jn 1:1–18 and in Paul's reference to Jesus as "the wisdom of God" (1 Cor 1:24, 30). The bearing of wisdom literature on the New Testament is also exemplified in the sayings and parables of Jesus and in the practical admonitions in the Letter of James.

Each book has a distinctive character. Proverbs consists of long poems dealing with moral conduct (chaps. 1–9), which introduce collections of aphorisms (chaps. 10–29) reflecting on the experiences of life. The Book of Job is a literary presentation of the problem of the suffering of the innocent and god-fearing Job. Psalms, the book of prayer par excellence, derives from varied origins, especially liturgical celebrations; it contains personal cries of agony as well as of praise and thanksgiving. Some betray a wisdom influence (e.g., Ps 37), and the very first Psalm serves as an invitation to learn about the ways of the just and wicked in the rest of the psalter. Ecclesiastes examines the hard questions of life, and has become famous for the expressive phrase "vanity of vanities." The Song of Songs is a collection of poems that give meaning to human and divine love (Sg 8:6; Prv 30:18–19). Ben Sira is the only author who identifies himself (Sir 50:27), and circa 200 B.C. he writes a compendium of Jewish wisdom and creation theology. The Wisdom of Solomon was written in Greek against a Hellenistic background, affirming human immortality in terms of a continuing relationship with God. Except for Psalms (of which almost half are attributed to David), Job, and Sirach, the books are attributed to Solomon, but he is not the author. The Solomonic claim is doubtless due to his fame as a wise man, according to 1 Kgs 5:9–14; 10:1–10. Who were the sages? Some were found in ordinary families (father, mother, Prv 1:8; 10:1); others were scribes at court. All contributed, both men (the counselors of Absalom, 2 Sm 16–17; the men of King Hezekiah, Prv 25:1) and also women (the "wise woman" of Abel Beth-maacah, 2 Sm 20:16). The wisdom literature is predominantly a postexilic composition, but the dating is only approximate.

In Jewish tradition, *Megillot* (Scrolls) came to be the accepted term for the five books of Ruth, Song of Songs, Ecclesiastes, Lamentations, and Esther. In the Protestant tradition, Sirach and Wisdom are classified as apocrypha and not printed as a part of Scripture. The Orthodox tradition does accept them, along with other works, such as 3–4 Maccabees and the Prayer of Manasseh. ■

# The Book of

# Job

## INTRODUCTION

### Geoffrey Miller

The problem of evil poses the greatest challenge to belief in a benevolent God, and the book of Job addresses this thorny issue by means of a fictional story. The book's titular character is a righteous man who loses his children, wealth, and health in rapid succession. The ensuing grief drives him to the brink of despair, and his subsequent outbursts come close to blasphemy as he rails against the God who has allowed these calamities to befall him. Nevertheless that same God vindicates Job at the end of the tale and restores his fortune doubly.

This classic tale is profound yet enigmatic, and only a few aspects of the story are certain. The book consists of poetic musings about the vicissitudes of life and the causes of human suffering, all situated within a narrative framework. The prose prologue (Jb 1–2) and epilogue (42:7–17) introduce the story and its central dilemma (Job's plight) and provide some resolution at the end. But it is the poetic core of the book (3:1–42:6) that carries the greatest theological weight. Here Job and his three friends (Eliphaz, Bildad, and Zophar) wrangle cyclically over Job's predicament: Job speaks, and his friends respond in turn. Eventually Elihu joins the conversation, and finally Yahweh intervenes, bringing the discussion to a close with two mystifying speeches.

As the cycles of speeches progress, the author of the book introduces the extended metaphor of a lawsuit to tie them together. Job's laments become increasingly acerbic, and he decides to bring legal charges against the God who has afflicted him (Jb 9–10, 13). Job calls for an arbiter to settle the case in his favor (16:18–21; 19:21–29), and he submits testimony on his own behalf (chs. 29–30). Elihu enters the story as an arbiter (chs. 32–37) but does not give a verdict favorable to Job. Yahweh, who has been accused by Job of

---

## Outline of Job

I. **Prologue (1:1–2:13)**

II. **First Cycle of Speeches (3:1–14:22)**

III. **Second Cycle of Speeches (15:1–21:34)**

IV. **Third Cycle of Speeches (22:1–27:21)**

V. **The Poem on Wisdom (28:1–28)**

VI. **Job's Final Summary of His Cause (29:1–31:37)**

VII. **Elihu's Speeches (32:1–37:24)**

VIII. **The Lord and Job Meet (38:1–42:6)**

IX. **Epilogue (42:7–17)**

---

wrongdoing, finally emerges and challenges Job so severely that the latter retracts his litigation (38:1–42:6). Paradoxically, however, Yahweh exculpates Job at the end (42:7–9).

The vindication of the book's protagonist comes at the expense of most of the other characters in the story. After acknowledging that Job has spoken correctly about him, God bestows the honorific title of "servant" on Job and condemns his friends for speaking erroneously. These so-called friends fail Job in two ways. First, they do not respond to Job's duress properly. Instead of offering compassion, they offer theological disputations and arguments aimed at convincing Job that his anguish is justified. A healthier approach is exhibited later by Job's relatives and acquaintances who comfort him and ameliorate his poverty by providing him with financial support (Jb 42:11). Second, the friends' theological speculations about how God operates in human affairs are inaccurate. They assume that suffering is a consequence of sin, but as the prologue points out, the doctrine of retribution does not apply in Job's case. Job is a blameless man, and his hardship constitutes a test rather than punishment.

Job's successful completion of this test exposes the folly of the "satan," whose name means "adversary." He initially claimed that Job would curse God if he were to lose his fortune and health. To the uninformed reader, God's agreement with the satan might seem reprehensible, for God appears to be making a pact with the devil. However, the satan is not an evil figure at this point in the Bible, but a member of God's angelic host, assigned to patrol the earth and to test the righteous. In this role, the satan seeks to determine if Job reveres God for the right reasons. He contests that Job's prosperity is the sole reason for his pious behavior, and so God permits him to deprive Job of his material possessions, his children, and his physical well-being. After carrying out his orders, the satan vanishes from the story, but his prediction does not come true. Amid all the vociferous remarks that Job utters, he never curses God.

This much of the story is certain, but many other aspects remain unclear. Scholars are divided over the date and provenance of the book of Job, although many would place it some time between the seventh and fifth centuries BCE, possibly in Persia or Mesopotamia. As for the setting of the story, no date is supplied by the author, and the whereabouts of Uz (Jb 1:1) are unknown. Some scholars speculate that the story takes place outside of Israel since at least one of Job's friends comes from the neighboring nation of Edom (e.g., Eliphaz's hometown of Teman is in Edom; cf. Gn 36:11–16). However, the friends travel some distance to visit Job, which means his residence might not be in Edom but in Israel. Some also propose a setting closer to the patriarchal stories for the book, since a small number of details can also be found in the narratives of Genesis (e.g., the unit of currency mentioned in Jb 42:11 is a rare word, used only in reference to Jacob's purchase of a plot of land in Gn 33:19). Yet such clues are few and far between. This ambiguity about time and place, however, might be deliberate on the part of the author, who intends to give the book a timeless feel. The story deals with perennial issues such as the problem of evil and the inscrutability of God, and these matters are relevant for every generation from every region of the globe. Instead of limiting the text to a particular era or geographical locale, the author shows that these issues transcend the bounds of time and space.

These issues also transcend facile solutions, and it is not clear how the author seeks to resolve them, if at all. The question of theodicy is especially difficult, for it attempts to justify the goodness of God despite the presence of evil in the world. In commenting on Job's situation, the various interlocutors articulate different theodicies, but the author does not explicitly endorse any one of them. Least plausible is the doctrine of retribution, which affirms that suffering and hardship constitute divine punishment for sin. This simplistic way of thinking typifies the conventional wisdom of the day, and several Old Testament passages reflect this mindset, especially the Pentateuch and the Deuteronomistic History. In the book of Job, the three friends are the most outspoken advocates for this position as they reiterate the idea of retribution throughout the dialogues. Yet the reader is expected to dismiss their claims as unfounded, for the narrator had already attested to Job's innocence in the prologue. Hence, suffering is not always the result of iniquity. On the other hand, God's actions in the epilogue imply that the doctrine of retribution is correct. The three friends deserve to be punished for speaking improperly about God, whereas Job merits an abundance of wealth and children for speaking properly about God. This disparity is hard to explain, but at best, the book shows some ambivalence about the notion of divine retribution.

Oddly enough, neither the friends nor Job consider a more likely reason for Job's tribulation: probationary suffering. According to this theodicy, human suffering is the result of divine testing, at least occasionally (Gn 22:1–19; Tb 12:14; Jdt 8:25–27; Wis 3:5). God wants to ensure that the righteous are truly devoted to him, and so God tests them to see how they will respond in the face of adversity. This is precisely the scenario in the book of Job. God declares Job blameless and then allows the satan to carry out a series of tests to prove that Job's piety is genuine. Unbeknownst to Job, he passes these tests by the end of the story, proving that God's original estimation of him was correct.

However, the whole ordeal that Job is put through seems to damage God's integrity in the process. In other instances of divine testing, God or an angel divulges to the tested person why he has undergone such hardship (e.g., Gn 22:12, 16; Tb 12:14), but God does not show Job the same courtesy. To be sure, God speaks to Job at great length at the end of the story but says nothing about testing or the wager with the satan, opting instead to pontificate about the inner workings of the physical world. Moreover, God's willingness to subject a holy man to such torment undermines God's justice and goodness. God appears more concerned with proving the satan wrong than with the well-being of a virtuous man, and God shows little compassion when killing Job's ten children just to see how their father will react. The God of the prologue is so cavalier about the welfare of human beings that the narrator might be creating a caricature for readers to reject, hoping they will dismiss one theodicy in favor of another. This portrait of the deity is intolerable and meant to be supplanted by a more acceptable viewpoint expressed elsewhere in the book.

That viewpoint, however, is difficult to find. It is reasonable to suppose that God expresses the correct theodicy when speaking to Job, but God's statements are as nebulous as the whirlwind enveloping him. God bombards Job with a litany of rhetorical questions about the natural world, inquiring about various things such as the dimensions of the earth, the ferocity of sea monsters, and the birthing habits of mountain goats. This tour de force renders Job speechless and also leaves exegetes perplexed, for God never broaches the topic of Job's suffering. If Yahweh addresses the problem of evil, he does so implicitly, and several interpretations are possible.

The first has to do with divine mystery. God insinuates that Job is wrestling with things too difficult for him to fathom. Verse after verse, God poses questions that are impossible for Job to answer, forcing him to recognize that the only one with such knowledge is God himself. If Job cannot comprehend matters of zoology, meteorology, and cosmology, he certainly cannot understand the more difficult subject of divine providence. The only suitable response is to profess one's ignorance and to show humility before God, which Job does at the culmination of the divine speeches. But at the same time, such mystery should not lead to a crisis of belief, and God's references to the natural world serve another purpose here. God provides for everything in nature so that all creatures are taken care of. Job should find comfort in this fact, for he too lives in the natural world and therefore comes under God's providential care, even if he is oblivious to how that care is manifest in his life.

God's use of natural imagery could lead to another interpretation, however. Many of the animals in these speeches come from the remotest parts of nature, such as the lion, the mountain goat, and the ostrich. Eventually God speaks of enormous, foreboding beasts such as Behemoth and Leviathan, whom human beings could never hope to tame. These undomesticated animals represent the wildness that characterizes life beyond the city and countryside, where law and order do not prevail. Organization and structure instead give way to haphazardness and disarray, and God intimates that the same is true of life generally. Job and his friends presume that life is ordered and that everything is under control, but reality is often otherwise. The world does not run smoothly like a machine but contains an element of randomness. Sometimes life is unpredictable, as when bad things happen to morally upright people, and Job must accept the fact that his life will sometimes feel chaotic.

Fortunately, God does not forsake Job amidst the chaos. Job never receives a clear answer to why he has suffered, but perhaps God never intended to give him one. In fact, it is fitting that a book about one of life's most vexing problems should itself be shrouded in mystery. Nonetheless, the act of speaking is significant, for God shows Job that he cares about him. God does not turn a deaf ear to Job's misery but appears before him and engages him in conversation. When God praises Job at the conclusion of the story, readers of the story should likewise find consolation. They may experience tragedy in life just as Job has, but they can voice their frustration to God without fear of reprisal. They must also emulate Job by remaining steadfast in their faith, hoping one day for vindication from the Almighty. ■

# THE BOOK OF JOB

## New American Bible, Introduction

The Book of Job, named after its protagonist (apparently not an Israelite; cf. Ez 14:14, 20), is an exquisite dramatic treatment of the problem of the suffering of the innocent. The contents of the book, together with its artistic structure and elegant style, place it among the literary masterpieces of all time. This is a literary composition, and not a transcript of historical events and conversations.

The prologue (chaps. 1–2) provides the setting for Job's testing. When challenged by the satan's questioning of Job's sincerity, the Lord gives leave for a series of catastrophes to afflict Job. Three friends come to console him. Job breaks out in complaint (chap. 3), and a cycle of speeches begins. Job's friends insist that his plight can only be a punishment for personal wrongdoing and an invitation from God to repent. Job rejects their inadequate explanation and challenges God to respond (chaps. 3–31). A young bystander, Elihu, now delivers four speeches in support of the views of the three friends (chaps. 32–37). In response to Job's plea that he be allowed to see God and hear directly the reason for his suffering, the Lord answers (38:1–42:6), not by explaining divine justice, but by cataloguing the wonders of creation. Job is apparently content with this, and, in an epilogue (42:7–17), the Lord restores Job's fortune.

The author or authors of the book are unknown; it was probably composed some time between the seventh and fifth centuries B.C. Its literary pattern, with speeches, prologue and epilogue disposed according to a studied plan, indicates that the purpose of the writing is didactic. But the lessons that the book teaches are not transparent, and different interpretations of the divine speeches and of the final chapter are possible. The Book of Job does not definitively answer the problem of the suffering of the innocent, but challenges readers to come to their own understanding.

The Book of Job can be divided as follows:

# JOB

## I. PROLOGUE

**1** **Job's Piety.** ¹ In the land of Uz† there was a blameless and upright man named Job,* who feared God and avoided evil. ² Seven sons and three daughters were born to him; ³ and he had seven thousand sheep, three thousand camels, five hundred yoke of oxen, five hundred she-donkeys, and a very large household, so that he was greater than anyone in the East.† ⁴ His sons used to take turns giving feasts, sending invitations to their three sisters to eat and drink with them. ⁵ And when each feast had run its course, Job would send for them and sanctify them, rising early and offering sacrifices for every one of them. For Job said, "It may be that my children have sinned and cursed† God in their hearts." Job did this habitually.

**The Interview Between the Lord and the Satan.** ⁶ * One day, when the sons of God† came to present themselves before the LORD, the satan also came among them.* ⁷ The LORD said to the satan, "Where have you been?" Then the satan answered the LORD and said,* "Roaming the earth and patrolling it." ⁸ The LORD said to the satan, "Have you noticed my servant Job? There is no one on earth like him, blameless and upright, fearing God and avoiding evil." ⁹ The satan answered the LORD and said, "Is it for nothing that Job is God-fearing? ¹⁰ Have you not surrounded him and his family and all that he has with your protection? You have blessed the work of his hands, and his livestock are spread over the land. ¹¹ * But now put forth your hand and touch all that he has, and surely he will curse you to your face." ¹² The LORD said to the satan, "Very well, all that he has is in your power; only do not lay a hand on him." So the satan went forth from the presence of the LORD.

**The First Trial.** ¹³ One day, while his sons and daughters were eating and drinking wine in the house of their eldest brother, ¹⁴ a messenger came to Job and said, "The oxen were plowing and the donkeys grazing beside them, ¹⁵ and the Sabeans† carried them off in a raid. They put the servants to the sword, and I alone have escaped to tell you." ¹⁶ He was still speaking when another came and said, "God's fire has fallen from heaven and struck the sheep and the servants and consumed them; I alone have escaped to tell you." ¹⁷ He was still speaking when another came and said, "The Chaldeans† formed three columns, seized the camels, carried them off, and put the servants to the sword; I alone have escaped to tell you." ¹⁸ He was still speaking when another came and said, "Your sons and daughters were eating and drinking wine in the house of their eldest brother, ¹⁹ and suddenly a great wind came from across the desert and smashed the four corners of the house. It fell upon the young people and they are dead; I alone have escaped to tell you."

**Job's Reaction.** ²⁰ Then Job arose and tore his cloak and cut off his hair. He fell to the ground and worshiped. ²¹ He said,

> "Naked I came forth from my mother's
> womb,*
> and naked shall I go back there.†
> The LORD gave and the LORD has taken
> away;
> blessed be the name of the LORD!"

²² In all this Job did not sin,* nor did he charge God with wrong.

**2** **The Second Interview.** ¹ One day, when the sons of God* came to present themselves before the LORD, the satan also came with them. ² The LORD said to the satan, "Where have you been?" Then the satan answered the LORD and said, "Roaming the earth and patrolling it." ³ The LORD said to the satan, "Have you

---

**1:1** *Uz:* somewhere in Edom or Arabia; see Lam 4:21. *Job:* the name probably means "Where is the (divine) father?" In Hebrew it is almost a homonym with the word for "enemy" (see note on 13:24; cf. 33:10).
**1:3** *The East:* that is, east of Palestine.
**1:5** *Cursed:* lit., "blessed." So also in v. 11; 2:5, 9.
**1:6** *Sons of God:* members of the divine council; see Gn 6:1–4; Dt 32:8; Ps 82:1. *The satan:* lit., "adversary" (as in 1 Kgs 11:14). Here a member of the heavenly court, "the accuser" (Zec 3:1). In later biblical traditions this character will be developed as the devil (Gk. *diabolos,* "adversary").

**1:15** *Sabeans:* from southern Arabia.
**1:17** *Chaldeans:* from southern Mesopotamia; in the mid-first millennium B.C., synonymous with "Babylonians."
**1:21** *Go back there:* to the earth; cf. Gn 2:7; see note on Sir 40:1.

*
**1:1** Jb 2:3.
**1:6–8** Jb 2:1–3.
**1:6** Gn 6:2, 4; Zec 3:1; Lk 22:31; Rev 12:9.
**1:7** 1 Pt 5:8.
**1:11** Jb 2:5.
**1:21** Eccl 5:14; 1 Tm 6:7.
**1:22** Jb 2:10; Jas 5:11.
**2:1** Jb 1:6.

noticed my servant Job? There is no one on earth like him, blameless and upright, fearing God and avoiding evil.* He still holds fast to his innocence although you incited me against him to ruin him for nothing." [4] The satan answered the LORD and said, "Skin for skin!† All that a man has he will give for his life. [5]* But put forth your hand and touch his bone and his flesh. Then surely he will curse you to your face." [6] And the LORD said to the satan, "He is in your power; only spare his life."

**The Second Trial.** [7] So the satan went forth from the presence of the LORD and struck Job with severe boils from the soles of his feet to the crown of his head.

**Job's Reaction.** [8] He took a potsherd to scrape himself, as he sat among the ashes. [9] Then his wife said to him,* "Are you still holding to your innocence? Curse God and die!"† [10] But he said to her, "You speak as foolish women do. We accept good things from God; should we not accept evil?" Through all this, Job did not sin in what he said.*

**Job's Three Friends.** [11] Now when three of Job's friends heard of all the misfortune that had come upon him, they set out each one from his own place: Eliphaz from Teman,† Bildad from Shuh, and Zophar from Naamath. They met and journeyed together to give him sympathy and comfort. [12] But when, at a distance, they lifted up their eyes and did not recognize him, they began to weep aloud; they tore their cloaks and threw dust into the air over their heads. [13] Then they sat down upon the ground with him seven days and seven nights, but none of them spoke a word to him; for they saw how great was his suffering.

## II. FIRST CYCLE OF SPEECHES

**3** **Job's Complaint.** [1] After this, Job opened his mouth and cursed his day.† [2] Job spoke out and said:

3 Perish the day on which I was born,*
the night when they said, "The child is a boy!"

4 May that day be darkness:
may God† above not care for it,
may light not shine upon it!

5 May darkness and gloom claim it,
clouds settle upon it,
blackness of day† affright it!

6 May obscurity seize that night;
may it not be counted among the days of the year,
nor enter into the number of the months!

7 May that night be barren;
let no joyful outcry greet it!

8 Let them curse it who curse the Sea,
those skilled at disturbing Leviathan!†

9 May the stars of its twilight be darkened;
may it look for daylight, but have none,
nor gaze on the eyes of the dawn,

10 Because it did not keep shut the doors of the womb
to shield my eyes from trouble!

11 Why did I not die at birth,*
come forth from the womb and expire?

12 Why did knees receive me,
or breasts nurse me?

13 For then I should have lain down and been tranquil;
had I slept, I should then have been at rest

14 With kings and counselors of the earth
who rebuilt what were ruins

15 Or with princes who had gold
and filled their houses with silver.

16 Or why was I not buried away like a stillborn child,
like babies that have never seen the light?

17 There† the wicked cease from troubling,
there the weary are at rest.

18 The captives are at ease together,

---

† 2:4 *Skin for skin*: a proverbial expression derived perhaps from bartering; the precise meaning is unclear.
2:9 *Curse God and die*: the presupposition is that such blasphemy would be met with immediate death.
2:11 *Teman*: in Edom (see Gn 36:9–11). The Temanites (Jer 49:7; cf. Ob 8) enjoyed a reputation for wisdom. *Shuh* and *Naamath*: locations unknown.
3:1 *His day*: that is, the day of his birth.
3:4 *God*: in Heb. *'Eloah*, another name for the divinity, used frequently in Job.

**3:5** *Blackness of day*: that is, an eclipse.
**3:8** *Leviathan*: a mythological sea monster symbolizing primeval chaos. It is parallel to Sea, which was the opponent of Baal in the Ugaritic legends. Cf. 9:13; 26:13; 40:25–41:26; Ps 74:13–14; 104:26; Is 27:1.
**3:17** *There*: in death.

---

* 2:3 Jb 1:1.     2:10 Jb 1:22; Sir 2:4.
2:5 Jb 1:11.     3:3 Jer 20:14.
2:9 Jb 19:17.     3:11 Jb 10:18–19.

and hear no overseer's voice.

19 Small and great are there;
  the servant is free from the master.

20 Why is light given to the toilers,
  life to the bitter in spirit?

21 They wait for death and it does not
    come;
  they search for it more than for
    hidden treasures.

22 They rejoice in it exultingly,
  and are glad when they find the grave:

23 A man whose path is hidden from him,
  one whom God has hemmed in!†

24 For to me sighing comes more readily
    than food;
  my groans well forth like water.

25 For what I feared overtakes me;
  what I dreaded comes upon me.

26 I have no peace nor ease;
  I have no rest, for trouble has come!

## 4 Eliphaz's First Speech. ¹Then Eliphaz the Temanite answered and said:

2 If someone attempts a word with you,
    would you mind?
  How can anyone refrain from
    speaking?

3 Look, you have instructed many,
  and made firm their feeble hands.

4 Your words have upheld the stumbler;
  you have strengthened faltering knees.

5 But now that it comes to you, you are
    impatient;
  when it touches you, you are
    dismayed.

6 Is not your piety a source of confidence,
  and your integrity of life your hope?

7 Reflect now, what innocent person
    perishes?*
  Where are the upright destroyed?

8 As I see it, those who plow mischief
  and sow trouble will reap them.

9 By the breath of God they perish,*
  and by the blast of his wrath they are
    consumed.

10 Though the lion† roars, though the king
    of beasts cries out,
  yet the teeth of the young lions are
    broken;

11 The old lion perishes for lack of prey,
  and the cubs of the lioness are
    scattered.

12 A word was stealthily brought to me,†
  my ear caught a whisper of it.

13 In my thoughts during visions of the
    night,*
  when deep sleep falls on mortals,

14 Fear came upon me, and shuddering,
  that terrified me to the bone.

15 Then a spirit passed before me,
  and the hair of my body stood on
    end.

16 It paused, but its likeness I could not
    recognize;
  a figure was before my eyes,
  in silence I heard a voice:*

17 "Can anyone be more in the right than
    God?*
  Can mortals be more blameless than
    their Maker?

18 Look, he puts no trust in his servants,*
  and even with his messengers he finds
    fault.

19 How much more with those who dwell
    in houses of clay,
  whose foundation is in the dust,
  who are crushed more easily than a
    moth!

20 Morning or evening they may be
    shattered;
  unnoticed, they perish forever.

21 The pegs of their tent are plucked up;
  they die without knowing wisdom."

## 5 ¹Call now! Will anyone respond to you?
  To which of the holy ones† will you
    turn?

2 Surely impatience kills the fool
  and indignation slays the simpleton.

3 I have seen a fool spreading his roots,*
  but I cursed his household suddenly:

---

† **3:23** *Hemmed in:* contrast the same verb as used in 1:10.
  **4:10** *The lion:* used figuratively here for the violent, rapacious sinner who cannot prevail against God.
  **4:12–21** A dramatic presentation of the idea of human nothingness in contrast to God's greatness (v. 17). The message of the "private revelation" that stirs Eliphaz so deeply is in reality expressed countless times in the Bible. The statements of the friends are often "truths" that are insensitive or irrelevant to Job's questioning.

**5:1** *Holy ones:* members of the heavenly court; cf. 1:6 and note. They were viewed as heavenly intercessors.

**4:7** Ps 37:25.
**4:9** Ps 18:16; Is 11:4;
  2 Thes 2:8.
**4:13** Jb 33:15.
**4:16** 1 Kgs 19:12.
**4:17** Jb 9:2; 15:14–16;
  25:4; Ps 130:3; 143:2.
**4:18** Jb 15:15; 2 Pt 2:4;
  Jude 6.
**5:3** Ps 37:35–36.

4 May his children be far from safety;
 may they be crushed at the gate †
  without a rescuer.

5 What they have reaped may the hungry
  eat up,
 or God take away by blight,
 or the thirsty swallow their substance.

6 For not from dust does mischief come,
 nor from the soil does trouble sprout.

7 Human beings beget mischief
 as sparks † fly upward.

8 In your place, I would appeal to God,
 and to God I would state my plea.

9 † He does things great and unsearchable,
 things marvelous and innumerable.

10 He gives rain upon the earth
 and sends water upon the fields;

11 * He sets up the lowly on high,
 and those who mourn are raised to
  safety.

12 He frustrates the plans of the cunning,
 so that their hands achieve no
  success;

13 He catches the wise in their own ruses, *
 and the designs of the crafty are
  routed.

14 They meet with darkness in the daytime,
 at noonday they grope as though it
  were night.

15 But he saves the poor from the sword of
  their mouth, †
 from the hand of the mighty.

16 Thus the needy have hope,
 and iniquity closes its mouth.

17 Happy the one whom God reproves!
 The Almighty's † discipline do not
  reject.

18 For he wounds, but he binds up; *
 he strikes, but his hands give healing.

19 Out of six troubles he will deliver you,
 and at the seventh † no evil shall
  touch you.

20 In famine he will deliver you from
  death,
 and in war from the power of the
  sword;

21 From the scourge of the tongue you
  shall be hidden,
 and you shall not fear approaching
  ruin.

22 At ruin and want you shall laugh;
 the beasts of the earth, do not fear.

23 With the stones of the field shall your
  covenant be,
 and the wild beasts shall be at peace
  with you.

24 And you shall know that your tent is
  secure;
 taking stock of your household, you
  shall miss nothing.

25 You shall know that your descendants
  are many,
 and your offspring like the grass of the
  earth.

26 You shall approach the grave in full
  vigor,
 as a shock of grain comes in at its
  season.

27 See, this we have searched out; so it is!
 This we have heard, and you should
  know.

# 6 Job's First Reply. 1 Then Job answered and said:

2 Ah, could my anguish but be measured
 and my calamity laid with it in the
  scales,

3 They would now outweigh the sands of
  the sea!
 Because of this I speak without
  restraint.

4 For the arrows of the Almighty are in
  me, *
 and my spirit drinks in their poison;
 the terrors of God are arrayed against
  me.

5 Does the wild donkey bray when it has
  grass? †
 Does the ox low over its fodder?

6 Can anything insipid be eaten without
  salt?

---

5:4 *At the gate*: of the city, where justice was administered.
5:7 *Sparks*: in Hebrew, "sons of resheph," which the ancient versions took as the name of a bird. Resheph was an underworld deity of plague, but the word also means "flames" in Sg 8:6.
5:9 Perhaps to be omitted here; it is a duplicate of 9:10.
5:15 *From the sword of their mouth*: the Hebrew is obscure.
5:17 *Almighty*: standard translation of Heb. *Shaddai*.
5:19 *Six...the seventh*: proverbial expression for any large number; cf. Prv 24:16; Lk 17:4.

6:5–6 Job would not complain if his life were as pleasant to him as fodder to a hungry animal; but his life is as disagreeable as insipid food. *White of an egg*: thus the obscure Hebrew has been understood in Jewish tradition; some render it "mallow juice."

---

5:11 1 Sm 2:7–8; Ps 113:7;
 Lk 1:52.
5:13 1 Cor 3:19.
5:18 Hos 6:1–2.
6:4 Ps 88:17.

Is there flavor in the white of an egg?
7  I refuse to touch them;
they are like loathsome food to me.
8  Oh, that I might have my request,
and that God would grant what I long
for:
9  Even that God would decide to crush
me,
that he would put forth his hand and
cut me off!
10  Then I should still have consolation
and could exult through unremitting
pain,
because I have not transgressed the
commands of the Holy One.
11  What strength have I that I should
endure,
and what is my limit that I should be
patient?
12  Have I the strength of stones,
or is my flesh of bronze?
13  Have I no helper,*
and has my good sense deserted me?
14  A friend owes kindness to one in
despair,
though he has forsaken the fear of the
Almighty.
15  My companions are undependable as a
wadi,
as watercourses that run dry in the
wadies;
16  Though they may be black with ice,
and with snow heaped upon them,
17  Yet once they flow, they cease to be;
in the heat, they disappear from their
place.
18  Caravans wander from their routes;
they go into the wasteland and perish.
19  The caravans of Tema† search,
the companies of Sheba have hopes;
20  They are disappointed, though they were
confident;
they come there and are frustrated.
21  It is thus that you have now become for
me;†
you see a terrifying thing and are
afraid.

22  Have I said, "Give me something,
make a bribe on my behalf from your
possessions"?
23  Or "Deliver me from the hand of the
enemy,
redeem me from oppressors"?
24  Teach me, and I will be silent;
make me understand how I have
erred.
25  How painful honest words can be;
yet how unconvincing is your
argument!
26  Do you consider your words as proof,
but the sayings of a desperate man as
wind?
27  You would even cast lots for the orphan,
and would barter over your friend!
28  Come, now, give me your attention;
surely I will not lie to your face.
29  Think it over; let there be no injustice.
Think it over; I still am right.
30  Is there insincerity on my tongue,
or cannot my taste discern falsehood?

7  1*  Is not life on earth a drudgery,†
its days like those of a hireling?
2  Like a slave who longs for the shade,
a hireling who waits for wages,
3  So I have been assigned months of
futility,
and troubled nights have been
counted off for me.
4  When I lie down I say, "When shall I
arise?"
then the night drags on;
I am filled with restlessness until the
dawn.
5  My flesh is clothed with worms and
scabs;*
my skin cracks and festers;
6  My days are swifter than a weaver's
shuttle;
they come to an end without hope.
7  Remember that my life is like the wind;*
my eye will not see happiness again.
8  The eye that now sees me shall no more
behold me;

---

†  **6:19** *Tema:* in northwest Arabia. *Sheba:* home of the Sabeans;
see note on 1:15.
  **6:21** It is only at this point that the previous lines (vv. 1–20)
are clearly directed to the three friends. The style of replying in
these chapters (3–31) is often indirect. Job and the friends become mouthpieces through which the author presents current
views on divine retribution in dramatic fashion. In chap. 7, Job
will not even speak directly to the friends.
  **7:1** *Drudgery:* taken by some to refer to military service; cf.
also 14:14.

| 6:13 Jb 19:14–15. | 7:5 Jb 2:7–8. |
| 7:1 Jb 14:14. | 7:7 Ps 144:4. |

when your eye is on me, I shall be
    gone.

9 As a cloud dissolves and vanishes,*
    so whoever goes down to Sheol shall
       not come up.

10 They shall not return home again;
    their place shall know them no more.

11 My own utterance I will not restrain;
    I will speak in the anguish of my
       spirit;
    I will complain in the bitterness of my
       soul.

12† Am I the Sea, or the dragon,
    that you place a watch over me?†

13 When I say, "My bed shall comfort me,
    my couch shall ease my complaint,"

14 Then you frighten me with dreams
    and terrify me with visions.

15 So that I should prefer strangulation
    and death rather than my existence.†

16 I waste away: I will not live forever;*
    let me alone, for my days are but a
       breath.

17† What are human beings, that you make
    much of them,
    or pay them any heed?

18 You observe them every morning*
    and try them at every moment!

19 How long before you look away from me,
    and let me alone till I swallow my
       spit?

20 If I sin, what do I do to you,
    O watcher of mortals?
    Why have you made me your target?
    Why should I be a burden for you?

21 Why do you not pardon my offense,
    or take away my guilt?
    For soon I shall lie down in the dust;
    and should you seek me I shall be
       gone.

## 8 Bildad's First Speech. ¹ Bildad the Shuhite
answered and said:

2 How long will you utter such things?
    The words from your mouth are a
       mighty wind!

3 Does God pervert judgment,*
    does the Almighty pervert justice?

4 If your children have sinned against him
    and he has left them in the grip of
       their guilt,

5 Still, if you yourself have recourse to
       God
    and make supplication to the
       Almighty,

6 Should you be blameless and upright,
    surely now he will rouse himself for
       you
    and restore your rightful home.

7 Though your beginning was small,
    your future will flourish indeed.

8 Inquire of the former generations,
    pay attention to the experience of
       their ancestors—*

9 As we are but of yesterday and have no
       knowledge,
    because our days on earth are but a
       shadow—*

10 Will they not teach you and tell you
    and utter their words of
       understanding?

11† Can the papyrus grow up without mire?
    Can the reed grass flourish without
       water?

12 While it is yet green and uncut,
    it withers quicker than any grass.

13 So is the end of everyone who forgets
       God,
    and so shall the hope of the godless
       perish.

14 His confidence is but a gossamer thread,
    his trust is a spider's house.

15 He shall lean upon his house, but it
       shall not stand;
    he shall cling to it, but it shall not
       endure.

16 He thrives in full sun,
    and over his garden his shoots go
       forth;

17 About a heap of stones his roots are
       entwined;
    among the rocks he takes hold.

18 Yet if one tears him from his place,

J
B

---

† **7:12–21** Job now speaks not to his friends (who never speak
to God), but to God. He does this frequently; cf. 9:28; 10:2–22;
13:20–28; 14:13–22.

  **7:12** An allusion to the personification of primeval chaos as a
monstrous ocean vanquished by God; see note on 3:8.

  **7:15** *Existence*: lit., bones; the Hebrew is unclear.

  **7:17–18** An ironic allusion to Ps 8:5.

  **8:11–13** As marsh plants need water, so human beings need

God. These verses may be a quotation from the teaching of the
ancestors; cf. v. 10.

*  
| | |
|---|---|
| **7:9–10** Jb 10:21; 14:10–12; | **8:3** Jb 34:10–12. |
| 2 Sm 12:23; 14:14; | **8:8** Dt 4:32; 32:7. |
| Wis 2:1. | **8:9** Jb 14:2; Ps 102:12; |
| **7:16** Jb 14:1–2, 5. | 109:23; 144:4; Wis |
| **7:18** Ps 17:3. | 2:5. |

it will disown him: "I have never seen
you!"

19 There he lies rotting beside the road,
and out of the soil another sprouts.

20 Behold, God will not cast away the
upright;
neither will he take the hand of the
wicked.

21 Once more will he fill your mouth with
laughter
and your lips with rejoicing.

22 Those who hate you shall be clothed
with shame,
and the tent of the wicked shall be no
more.

## 9 Job's Second Reply.
¹Then Job answered
and said:

2 I know well that it is so;
but how can anyone be in the right
before God?

3 Should one wish to contend with
him, †
he could not answer him once in a
thousand times.

4 God is wise in heart and mighty in
strength;
who has withstood him and remained
whole?

5 He removes the mountains before they
know it;
he overturns them in his anger.

6 He shakes the earth out of its place, *
and the pillars beneath it tremble.

7 He commands the sun, and it does not
rise;
he seals up the stars.

8 He alone stretches out the heavens *
and treads upon the back of the sea.

9 He made the Bear and Orion,
the Pleiades and the constellations of
the south;

10 He does things great and unsearchable,
things marvelous and innumerable.

11 Should he come near me, I do not see
him;
should he pass by, I am not aware of
him;

12 Should he seize me forcibly, who can
resist?
Who can say to him, "What are you
doing?"

13 He is God and he does not relent;
the helpers of Rahab † bow beneath
him.

14 How then could I give him any answer,
or choose out arguments against him!

15 Even though I were right, I could not
answer, *
but should rather beg for what was
due me.

16 If I appealed to him and he answered
me,
I could not believe that he would
listen to me;

17 With a storm he might overwhelm me,
and multiply my wounds for nothing;

18 He would not allow me to draw breath,
but might fill me with bitter griefs.

19 If it be a question of strength, he is
mighty;
or of judgment, who will call him to
account?

20 Though I were right, my own mouth
might condemn me; *
were I innocent, it might put me in
the wrong.

21 I am innocent, but I cannot know it;
I despise my life.

22 It is all one! therefore I say:
Both the innocent and the wicked he
destroys. *

23 When the scourge slays suddenly,
he scoffs at the despair of the
innocent.

24 The earth is given into the hands of the
wicked;
he covers the faces of its judges.
If it is not he, who then is it?

25 My days are swifter than a runner,
they flee away; they see no
happiness; *

26 They shoot by like skiffs of reed,
like an eagle swooping upon its prey.

27 If I say: I will forget my complaining,
I will lay aside my sadness and be of
good cheer,

---

† **9:3** Job begins to explore the possibility of challenging God in a lawsuit, a theme that will recur (10:2), but he knows the odds are against him (vv. 12–20).

**9:13** *Rahab:* another name for the primeval sea-monster; see notes on 3:8 and Ps 89:11; cf. Jb 7:12; 26:12.

* **9:6** Jb 26:11.            **9:20** Jb 15:6.
**9:8** Ps 104:2; Is 40:22.    **9:22** Eccl 9:2.
**9:15** Jb 10:15.             **9:25** Jb 7:6.

28 Then I am in dread of all my pains;
    I know that you † will not hold me
        innocent.
29 It is I who will be accounted guilty;
    why then should I strive in vain?
30 If I should wash myself with soap
    and cleanse my hands with lye,
31 Yet you would plunge me in the ditch,
    so that my garments would abhor me.
32 For he is not a man like myself, that I
        should answer him,
    that we should come together in
        judgment.
33 Would that there were an arbiter
        between us,
    who could lay his hand upon us
        both
34     and withdraw his rod from me,
So that his terrors did not frighten me;
35     that I might speak without being
        afraid of him.
Since this is not the case with me,
10:1 †   I loathe my life. *

**10** I will give myself up to complaint;
    I will speak from the bitterness of my
        soul.
2 I will say to God: Do not put me in the
        wrong!
    Let me know why you oppose me.
3 † Is it a pleasure for you to oppress,
    to spurn the work of your hands,
    and shine on the plan of the wicked?
4 Have you eyes of flesh?
    Do you see as mortals see?
5 Are your days like the days of a mortal, *
    and are your years like a human
        lifetime,
6 That you seek for guilt in me
    and search after my sins,
7 Even though you know that I am not
        wicked, *
    and that none can deliver me out of
        your hand?
8 Your hands have formed me and
        fashioned me;
    will you then turn and destroy me?

9 Oh, remember that you fashioned me
        from clay! *
    Will you then bring me down to dust
        again?
10 Did you not pour me out like milk,
    and thicken me like cheese?
11 With skin and flesh you clothed me,
    with bones and sinews knit me
        together.
12 Life and love you granted me,
    and your providence has preserved my
        spirit.
13 Yet these things you have hidden in your
        heart;
    I know they are your purpose:
14 If I should sin, you would keep a watch
        on me,
    and from my guilt you would not
        absolve me.
15 If I should be wicked, alas for me!
    even if righteous, I dare not hold up
        my head,
    sated with shame, drenched in
        affliction!
16 Should it lift up, you hunt me like a
        lion:
    repeatedly you show your wondrous
        power against me,
17 You renew your attack † upon me
    and multiply your harassment of me;
    in waves your troops come against
        me.
18 Why then did you bring me forth from
        the womb? *
    I should have died and no eye have
        seen me.
19 I should be as though I had never
        lived;
    I should have been taken from the
        womb to the grave.
20 Are not my days few? Stop!
    Let me alone, that I may recover a
        little
21 Before I go whence I shall not return, *
    to the land of darkness and of gloom,
22 The dark, disordered land
    where darkness is the only light.

---

**9:28–31** You: refers to God.
**10:1** I loathe my life: these words complete the thought of 9:35.
**10:3–12** These lines are a delicate mixture of sarcasm and prayer; Job "reminds" God, challenging the divine providence. Note the piteous tone of the final request in vv. 20–22.

**10:17** Attack: or "witnesses," continuing the metaphor of lawsuit used in these chapters.

| | |
|---|---|
| **10:1** Jb 9:21. | **10:9** Jb 4:19; 33:6; Gn 2:7; |
| **10:5** Jb 36:26. | 3:19; Ps 146:4. |
| **10:7** Jb 2:3, 9; Dt 32:39; | **10:18** Jb 3:3, 11. |
| Wis 16:15. | **10:21** Jb 7:9–10; 16:22. |

# 11 Zophar's First Speech. [1]And Zophar the Naamathite answered and said:

2 Should not many words be answered,
  or must the garrulous man necessarily
    be right?

3 Shall your babblings keep others silent,
  and shall you deride and no one give
    rebuke?

4 Shall you say: "My teaching is pure,
  and I am clean in your sight"?

5 But oh, that God would speak,†
  and open his lips against you,

6 And tell you the secrets of wisdom,
  for good sense has two sides;
So you might learn that God
  overlooks some of your sinfulness.

7 Can you find out the depths of God?*
  or find out the perfection of the
    Almighty?

8 It is higher than the heavens; what can
    you do?
  It is deeper than Sheol; what can you
    know?

9 It is longer than the earth in measure,
  and broader than the sea.

10 If he should seize and imprison
  or call to judgment, who then could
    turn him back?

11 For he knows the worthless
  and sees iniquity; will he then ignore
    it?

12 An empty head will gain understanding,
  when a colt of a wild jackass* is born
    human.†

13 If you set your heart aright
  and stretch out your hands toward
    him,

14 If iniquity is in your hand, remove it,
  and do not let injustice dwell in your
    tent,

15 Surely then you may lift up your face in
    innocence;
  you may stand firm and unafraid.

16 For then you shall forget your misery,
  like water that has ebbed away you
    shall regard it.

17 Then your life shall be brighter than the
    noonday;
  its gloom shall become like the
    morning,

18 And you shall be secure, because there is
    hope;
  you shall look round you and lie
    down in safety;*

19 you shall lie down and no one will
    disturb you.
Many shall entreat your favor,

20 but the wicked, looking on, shall be
    consumed with envy.
Escape shall be cut off from them,
  their only hope their last breath.

# 12 Job's Third Reply. [1]† Then Job answered and said:

2 No doubt you are the people
  with whom wisdom shall die!

3 But I have intelligence as well as you;*
  I do not fall short of you;
  for who does not know such things as
    these?

4 I have become the sport of my
    neighbors:†
  "The one whom God answers when
    he calls upon him,
  The just, the perfect man," is a
    laughingstock;*

5 The undisturbed esteem my downfall a
    disgrace
  such as awaits unsteady feet;

6 Yet the tents of robbers are prosperous,
  and those who provoke God are
    secure,
  whom God has in his power.†

7 But now ask the beasts to teach you,
  the birds of the air to tell you;

8 Or speak to the earth to instruct you,

---

**11:5** This is another of many ironies (e.g., cf. 11:16–19) that occur throughout the book. Zophar does not know that God will speak (chaps. 38–42), but contrary to what he thinks.

**11:12** *A colt…is born human*: the Hebrew is obscure. As translated, it seems to be a proverb referring to an impossible event.

**12:1** Job begins his third and longest speech to the friends with sarcasm, and eventually he accuses them of falsehood (13:4–11). The dialogue between them becomes increasingly sharp. With the appeal to learning from beasts and birds (12:7), Job launches into what seems to be a bitter parody of the power of God.

**12:4–5** The Hebrew is somewhat obscure, but the general sense is that the wicked mock the pious when the latter appear to be abandoned by God; cf. Ps 22:7–9; Mt 27:39–43.

**12:6** *Whom God has in his power*: the Hebrew is obscure. The line may be a scribal error; some of the phrases occur in vv. 9, 10.

---

**11:7** Rom 11:33.  **12:3** Jb 13:2; 15:9.
**11:12** Jb 39:5–8.  **12:4** Jb 21:3; 30:1.
**11:18** Lv 26:6; Ps 4:9.

and the fish of the sea to inform you.

9 Which of all these does not know
   that the hand of God has done this?

10 In his hand is the soul of every living
   thing,*
   and the life breath of all mortal flesh.

11 Does not the ear judge words
   as the mouth tastes food?*

12 So with old age is wisdom,*
   and with length of days
   understanding.

13 With him are wisdom and might;
   his are counsel and understanding.

14 If he knocks a thing down, there is no
   rebuilding;*
   if he imprisons, there is no release.

15 He holds back the waters and there is
   drought;*
   he sends them forth and they
   overwhelm the land.

16 With him are strength and prudence;
   the misled and the misleaders are his.

17 He sends counselors away barefoot,
   makes fools of judges.

18 He loosens the belt of kings,
   ties a waistcloth on their loins.†

19 He sends priests away barefoot,
   leads the powerful astray.

20 He silences the trusted adviser,
   takes discretion from the elders.

21 He pours shame on nobles,*
   the waistband of the strong he
   loosens.

22 He uncovers deep things from the
   darkness,
   brings the gloom into the light.

23 He makes nations great and destroys
   them,
   spreads peoples abroad and abandons
   them.

24 He takes understanding from the leaders
   of the land,
   makes them wander in a pathless
   desert.

25 They grope in the darkness without light;
   he makes them wander like drunkards.

# 13

1 All this my eye has seen;
   my ear has heard and perceived it.

2 What you know, I also know;*
   I do not fall short of you.

3 But I would speak with the Almighty;*
   I want to argue with God.

4 But you gloss over falsehoods,
   you are worthless physicians, every
   one of you!

5 Oh, that you would be altogether silent;
   that for you would be wisdom!

6 Hear now my argument
   and listen to the accusations from my
   lips.

7 Is it for God that you speak falsehood?
   Is it for him that you utter deceit?

8 Is it for him that you show partiality?
   Do you make accusations on behalf of
   God?

9 Will it be well when he shall search you
   out?
   Can you deceive him as you do a
   mere human being?

10 He will openly rebuke you
   if in secret you show partiality.

11 Surely his majesty will frighten you
   and dread of him fall upon you.

12 Your reminders are ashy maxims,
   your fabrications mounds of clay.

13 Be silent! Let me alone that I may speak,
   no matter what happens to me.

14 I will carry my flesh between my teeth,
   and take my life in my hand.†

15 Slay me though he might,* I will wait
   for him;†
   I will defend my conduct before him.

16 This shall be my salvation:
   no impious man can come into his
   presence.

17 Pay close attention to my speech,
   give my statement a hearing.

18 Behold, I have prepared my case,*
   I know that I am in the right.

19 If anyone can make a case against me,
   then I shall be silent and expire.

20 Two things only do not use against me,†

---

† **12:18** He reduces kings to the condition of slaves, who wear only a cloth wrapped about the waist.

**13:14** The second half of the verse is a common biblical expression for risking one's life; cf. Jgs 12:3; 1 Sm 19:5; 28:21; Ps 119:109; the first half of the verse must have a similar meaning. Job is so confident of his innocence that he is willing to risk his life by going to judgment with God.

**13:15** Many translations adopt the Ketib reading, "I have no hope."

**13:20** In 13:20–14:22, Job directs his address to God; cf. 7:8–21; 9:28–10:22. His three friends never do this.

| | |
|---|---|
| **12:10** Acts 17:28. | **12:21** Ps 107:40. |
| **12:11** Jb 34:3. | **13:2** Jb 12:3; 15:9. |
| **12:12** Jb 32:7. | **13:3** Jb 23:4. |
| **12:14** Jer 1:10; Rev 3:7. | **13:15** Jb 27:5. |
| **12:15** Gn 7:11–24. | **13:18** Jb 33:9. |

then from your presence I need not
    hide:

21 Withdraw your hand far from me,
    do not let the terror of you frighten
     me.

22 Then call me, and I will respond;
    or let me speak first, and answer me.

23 What are my faults and my sins?
    My misdeed, my sin make known to
     me!

24 Why do you hide your face
    and consider me your enemy? †*

25 Will you harass a wind-driven leaf
    or pursue a withered straw?

26 For you draw up bitter indictments
    against me,
    and punish in me the faults of my
     youth.

27 You put my feet in the stocks;
    you watch all my paths
    and trace out all my footsteps,

28 Though I wear out like a leather bottle,
    like a garment the moth has
     consumed.

# 14

¹ Man born of woman
is short-lived and full of trouble, †*

2 Like a flower that springs up and fades, *
    swift as a shadow that does not abide.

3 Upon such a one will you set your eyes,
    bringing me into judgment before you?

4 Can anyone make the unclean clean? *
    No one can.

5 Since his days are determined—
    you know the number of his months;
    you have fixed the limit which he
     cannot pass—

6 Look away from him and let him be,
    while, like a hireling, he completes his
     day.

7 For a tree there is hope;
    if it is cut down, it will sprout again,
    its tender shoots will not cease.

8 Even though its root grow old in the
    earth

and its stump die in the dust,

9 Yet at the first whiff of water it sprouts
    and puts forth branches like a young
     plant.

10 But when a man dies, all vigor leaves
    him; *
    when a mortal expires, where then is
     he?

11 As when the waters of a lake fail,
    or a stream shrivels and dries up,

12 So mortals lie down, never to rise.
    Until the heavens are no more, they
     shall not awake,
    nor be roused out of their sleep. *

13 Oh, that you would hide me in Sheol,
    shelter me till your wrath is past,
    fix a time to remember me!

14 If a man were to die, and live again,
    all the days of my drudgery I would
     wait *
    for my relief to come.

15 You would call, and I would answer you;
    you would long for the work of your
     hands.

16 Surely then you would count my steps, *
    and not keep watch for sin in me.

17 My misdeeds would be sealed up in a
    pouch, †
    and you would cover over my guilt.

18 Mountains fall and crumble,
    rocks move from their place,

19 And water wears away stone,
    and floods wash away the soil of the
     land—
    so you destroy the hope of mortals!

20 You prevail once for all against them
    and they pass on;
    you dismiss them with changed
     appearance.

21 If their children are honored, they are
    not aware of it;
    or if disgraced, they do not know
     about them.

22 Only for themselves, their pain;
    only for themselves, their mourning.

---

† **13:24** The Hebrew word for "enemy" ('*oyeb*) is very close to the Hebrew form of Job's name ('*iyyob*). The play on the word implies that God has confused the two.

**14:1** The sorrowful lament of Job is that God should relent in view of the limited life of human beings. When compared to plant life, which dies but can revive, the death of human beings is final. Job's wild and "unthinkable" wish in vv. 13–17 is a bold stroke of imagination and desire: if only in Sheol he were protected till God would remember him! Were he to live again (v. 14), things would be different, but alas, God destroys

"the hope of mortals" (v. 19).

**14:17** *Sealed up in a pouch*: hidden away and forgotten.

**13:24** Jb 19:11; 33:10.
**14:1** Jb 10:20; 15:14; Ps 39:5–6; 89:46; Wis 2:1.
**14:2** Jb 8:9; Ps 90:6; 102:12; 103:15; 109:23; 144:4;
Is 40:6–7; Jas 1:10.
**14:4** Ps 51:4, 7.
**14:10** Jb 20:7.
**14:12** Jb 7:10.
**14:14** Jb 7:1.
**14:16** Jb 31:4; 34:21.

## III. SECOND CYCLE OF SPEECHES

# 15 Second Speech of Eliphaz. ¹† Then Eliphaz the Temanite answered and said:

2 Does a wise man answer with windy
    opinions,
    or puff himself up with the east wind?
3 Does he argue in speech that does not
    avail,
    and in words that are to no profit?
4 You in fact do away with piety,
    you lessen devotion toward God,
5 Because your wickedness instructs your
    mouth,
    and you choose to speak like the
    crafty.
6 Your own mouth condemns you, not I;*
    your own lips refute you.
7 Were you the first to be born?
    Were you brought forth before the
    hills?
8 Do you listen in on God's council*
    and restrict wisdom to yourself?
9 What do you know that we do not
    know,*
    or understand that we do not?
10 There are gray-haired old men among
    us,
    more advanced in years than your
    father.
11 Are the consolations of God not enough
    for you,
    and speech that deals gently with you?
12 Why does your heart carry you away,
    and why do your eyes flash,
13 So that you turn your anger against God
    and let such words escape your
    mouth!
14 How can any mortal be blameless,*
    anyone born of woman be
    righteous?*
15 If in his holy ones God places no
    confidence,*
    and if the heavens are not without
    blame in his sight,
16 How much less so is the abominable
    and corrupt:

people who drink in iniquity like
    water!
17 I will show you, if you listen to me;
    what I have seen I will tell—
18 What the wise relate
    and have not contradicted since the
    days of their ancestors,
19 To whom alone the land was given,
    when no foreigner moved among
    them:
20 The wicked is in torment all his days,
    and limited years are in store for the
    ruthless;
21 The sound of terrors is in his ears;
    when all is prosperous, a spoiler
    comes upon him.
22 He despairs of escaping the darkness,
    and looks ever for the sword;
23 A wanderer, food for vultures,
    he knows destruction is imminent.
24 A day of darkness fills him with dread;
    distress and anguish overpower him,
    like a king expecting an attack.
25 Because he has stretched out his hand
    against God
    and arrogantly challenged the Almighty,
26 Rushing defiantly against him,
    with the stout bosses of his shields.
27 Although he has covered his face with
    his crassness,
    padded his loins with blubber,
28 He shall dwell in ruined cities,
    in houses that are deserted,
    crumbling into rubble.
29 He shall not be rich, his possessions
    shall not endure;
    his property shall not spread over the
    land.
30 A flame shall sear his early growth,
    and with the wind his blossoms shall
    disappear.
31 Let him not trust in his height, misled,
    even though his height be like the
    palm tree.†
32 He shall wither before his time,
    his branches no longer green.
33 He shall be like a vine that sheds its
    grapes unripened,

---

† **15:1** The tone of Eliphaz's speech is now much rougher. In vv. 7–9 he ridicules Job's knowledge with a sarcastic question about whether he was a member of the divine council before creation and thus had unique wisdom (according to Prv 8:22–31, only Woman Wisdom existed before creation). Verses 20–35 are a typical description of the fate of the wicked.

**15:31** The translation is uncertain.

**15:6** Jb 9:20.
**15:8** Jb 11:7; Wis 9:13; Jer 23:18; Rom 11:34; 1 Cor 2:11, 16.
**15:9** Jb 12:3; 13:2.
**15:14–16** Jb 25:4–6.
**15:14** Jb 14:4.
**15:15** Jb 4:18–19.

like an olive tree casting off its
   blossom.

34 For the breed of the impious shall be
      sterile, *
   and fire shall consume the tents of
      extortioners.

35 They conceive malice, bring forth
      deceit, *
   give birth to fraud. †

# 16

**Job's Fourth Reply.** ¹ Then Job answered and said:

2 I have heard this sort of thing many
      times. *
   Troublesome comforters, all of you!

3 Is there no end to windy words?
   What sickness makes you rattle on?

4 I also could talk as you do,
   were you in my place.
   I could declaim over you,
   or wag my head at you;

5 I could strengthen you with talk,
   with mere chatter give relief.

6 If I speak, my pain is not relieved;
   if I stop speaking, nothing changes.

7 But now he has exhausted me;
   you have stunned all my companions.

8 You † have shriveled me up; it is a
      witness,
   my gauntness rises up to testify
      against me;

9 His wrath tears and assails me,
   he gnashes his teeth against me;
   My enemy looks daggers at me.

10 They gape at me with their mouths;
   They strike me on the cheek with
      insults;
   they are all enlisted against me.

11 God has given me over to the impious;
   into the hands of the wicked he has
      cast me.

12 I was in peace, but he dislodged me,
   seized me by the neck, dashed me to
      pieces.
   He has set me up for a target;

13 his arrows strike me from all
      directions.

He pierces my sides without mercy,
   pours out my gall upon the ground.

14 He pierces me, thrust upon thrust,
   rushes at me like a warrior.

15 I have sewn sackcloth on my skin,
   laid my horn low in the dust.

16 My face is inflamed with weeping,
   darkness covers my eyes,

17 Although my hands are free from
      violence,
   and my prayer sincere.

18 O earth, do not cover my blood,
   nor let my outcry come to rest! †

19 Even now my witness † is in heaven,
   my advocate is on high.

20 My friends it is who wrong me;
   before God my eyes shed tears,

21 That justice may be done for a mortal
      with God:
   as for a man with his neighbor.

22 For my years are numbered,
   and I go the road of no return.

# 17

¹ My spirit is broken, my days finished,
   my burial at hand.

2 Surely mockers surround me,
   at their provocation, my eyes grow
      dim.

3 Put up a pledge for me with you: †
   who is there to give surety for me?

4 You darken their minds to knowledge;
   therefore you will not exalt them.

5 For a share of property he informs on
      friends,
   while the eyes of his children grow
      dim.

6 I am made a byword of the people; *
   I am one at whom people spit.

7 My eyes are blind with anguish,
   and my whole frame is like a shadow.

8 The upright are astonished at this,
   the innocent aroused against the
      wicked.

9 The righteous holds to his way,
   the one with clean hands increases in
      strength.

10 But turn now, and come on again;
   I do not find a wise man among you!

---

† **15:35** The plans of the wicked yield nothing but futile results. Cf. Ps 7:15; Is 59:4.

**16:8** *You:* God. Job then describes in vv. 9–17 the savage treatment that he has received from God.

**16:18** As the exposed blood of those who were unjustly slain cries to heaven for vengeance (Gn 4:10; Ez 24:6–9), so Job's sufferings demand redress.

**16:19** *Witness:* refers perhaps to God (is Job appealing to God against God?), or to a mediator (cf. 9:33), or to a personification of Job's prayer.

**17:3** Addressed to God; v. 10 to Job's friends.

---

**15:34** Wis 3:11, 18.             **16:2** Jb 12:3.
**15:35** Ps 7:15; Is 59:4.         **17:6** Jb 30:9.

11 My days pass by, my plans are at an end,
  the yearning of my heart.

12 They would change the night into day;
  where there is darkness they talk of
    approaching light.

13 † If my only hope is dwelling in Sheol,
  and spreading my couch in darkness,

14 If I am to say to the pit, "You are my
    father,"
  and to the worm "my mother," "my
    sister,"

15 Where then is my hope,
  my happiness, who can see it?

16 Will they descend with me into Sheol?
  Shall we go down together into the
    dust?

# 18 Bildad's Second Speech. ¹ Then Bildad the Shuhite answered and said:

2 When will you put an end to words?
  Reflect, and then we can have
    discussion.

3 Why are we accounted like beasts,
  equal to them in your sight?

4 You who tear yourself in your anger—
  shall the earth be neglected on your
    account
  or the rock be moved out of its place?

5 Truly, the light of the wicked is
    extinguished;
  the flame of his fire casts no light.

6 In his tent light is darkness;
  the lamp above him goes out. *

7 His vigorous steps are hemmed in,
  his own counsel casts him down.

8 A net catches him by the feet,
  he wanders into a pitfall.

9 A trap seizes him by the heel,
  a snare lays hold of him.

10 A noose is hidden for him on the
    ground,
  a netting for him on the path.

11 On every side terrors frighten him; *
  they harry him at each step.

12 His strength is famished,
  disaster is ready at his side,

13 His skin is eaten to the limbs,

  the firstborn of Death † eats his limbs.

14 He is plucked from the security of his
    tent;
  and marched off to the king of
    terrors. †

15 Fire lodges in his tent,
  over his abode brimstone is scattered.

16 Below, his roots dry up,
  and above, his branches wither.

17 His memory perishes from the earth, *
  and he has no name in the
    countryside.

18 He is driven from light into darkness,
  and banished from the world.

19 He has neither offshoot nor offspring
    among his people,
  no survivor where once he dwelt.

20 Those who come after shall be appalled
    at his fate;
  those who went before are seized with
    horror.

21 So is it then with the dwelling of the
    impious;
  such is the place of the one who does
    not know God!

# 19 Job's Fifth Reply. ¹ † Then Job answered and said:

2 How long will you afflict my spirit,
  grind me down with words?

3 These ten times you have humiliated
    me,
  have assailed me without shame!

4 Even if it were true that I am at fault,
  my fault would remain with me;

5 If truly you exalt yourselves at my
    expense,
  and use my shame as an argument
    against me,

6 Know then that it is God who has dealt
    unfairly with me,
  and compassed me round with his
    net.

7 If I cry out "Violence!" I am not
    answered. *
  I shout for help, but there is no
    justice.

---

**17:13–16** Job elaborates another of the vivid descriptions of "life" in Sheol; cf. 3:13–23; 10:21–22.
  **18:13** *Firstborn of Death*: that is, disease, plague.
  **18:14** *The king of terrors*: of Sheol, of Death (cf. the "terrors" in v. 11). However, the Hebrew of this verse is obscure.
  **19:1** Job continues railing against his friends (vv. 2–5),

and describing God's savage attack in words reminiscent of 16:9–17.

---

| | |
|---|---|
| **18:6** Jb 21:17; Prv 13:9; 24:20. | **18:17** Ps 34:17; Prv 2:22; 10:7. |
| **18:11** Jb 15:20–24; 27:20. | **19:7** Jb 30:20. |

8   He has barred my way and I cannot
        pass;
      veiled my path in darkness;

9   He has stripped me of my glory,
      taken the diadem from my brow.

10  He breaks me down on every side, and I
        am gone;
      he has uprooted my hope like a tree.

11  He has kindled his wrath against me;
      he counts me one of his enemies.*

12  His troops advance as one;
      they build up their road to attack me,
      encamp around my tent.

13  My family has withdrawn from me,*
      my friends are wholly estranged.

14  My relatives and companions neglect
        me,
      my guests have forgotten me.

15  Even my maidservants consider me a
        stranger;
      I am a foreigner in their sight.

16  I call my servant, but he gives no answer,
      though I plead aloud with him.

17  My breath is abhorrent to my wife;*
      I am loathsome to my very children.

18  Even young children despise me;
      when I appear, they speak against me.

19  All my intimate friends hold me in
        horror;
      those whom I loved have turned
        against me!*

20  My bones cling to my skin,
      and I have escaped by the skin of my
        teeth.†

21  Pity me, pity me, you my friends,
      for the hand of God has struck me!

22  Why do you pursue me like God,
      and prey insatiably upon me?

23  Oh, would that my words were written
        down!*
      Would that they were inscribed in a
        record:†

24  That with an iron chisel and with lead
      they were cut in the rock forever!

25  As for me, I know that my vindicator
        lives,†

and that he will at last stand forth
    upon the dust.*

26  This will happen when my skin has
      been stripped off,
    and from my flesh I will see God:

27  I will see for myself,
      my own eyes, not another's, will
        behold him:
    my inmost being is consumed with
        longing.

28  But you who say, "How shall we
      persecute him,
    seeing that the root of the matter is
        found in him?"

29  Be afraid of the sword for yourselves,
    for your anger is a crime deserving the
        sword;
    that you may know that there is a
        judgment.

# 20

**Zophar's Second Speech.** 1 Then Zophar the Naamathite answered and said:

2   So now my thoughts provide an answer
      for me,
    because of the feelings within me.

3   A rebuke that puts me to shame I hear,
      and from my understanding a spirit
        gives me a reply.

4   Do you not know this: from of old,
      since human beings were placed upon
        the earth,

5   The triumph of the wicked is short
      and the joy of the impious but for a
        moment?*

6   Though his pride mount up to the
        heavens
      and his head reach to the clouds,

7   Yet he perishes forever like the dung he
        uses for fuel,
      and onlookers say, "Where is he?"*

8   Like a dream he takes flight and cannot
        be found;
      he fades away like a vision of the
        night.

---

† **19:20** *Skin of my teeth*: although the metaphor is not clear, this has become a proverbial expression for a narrow escape. It does not fit Job's situation here.

**19:23–24** What Job is about to say is so important that he wants it recorded in a permanent manner.

**19:25–27** The meaning of this passage is obscure because the original text has been poorly preserved and the ancient versions do not agree among themselves. Job asserts three times that he shall see a future vindicator (Hebrew *goel*), but he leaves

the time and manner of this vindication undefined. The Vulgate translation has Job indicating a belief in resurrection after death, but the Hebrew and the other ancient versions are less specific.

---

**19:11** Jb 13:24; 33:10.
**19:13** Jb 6:13.
**19:17** Jb 2:9.
**19:19** Sir 6:8.
**19:23** Jb 31:35.

**19:25–26** Phil 3:20; Ti 2:13.
**20:5** Jb 21:13; Ps
    37:35–36.
**20:7** Jb 14:10; Ps 37:10,
    36.

9 The eye which saw him does so no
			more;
		nor shall his dwelling again behold
			him.
10 His sons will restore to the poor,
		and his hands will yield up his
			riches. *
11 Though his bones are full of youthful
			vigor,
		it shall lie with him in the dust.
12 Though wickedness is sweet in his
			mouth,
		and he hides it under his tongue,
13 Though he retains it and will not let
			it go
		but keeps it still within his mouth,
14 Yet in his stomach the food shall turn;
		it shall be venom of asps inside him.
15 The riches he swallowed he shall vomit
			up;
		God shall make his belly disgorge
			them.
16 The poison of asps he shall drink in;
		the viper's fangs shall slay him.
17 He shall see no streams of oil, †
		no torrents of honey or milk.
18 He shall give back his gains, never used;
		like his profit from trade, never
			enjoyed.
19 Because he has oppressed and neglected
			the poor,
		and stolen a house he did not build;
20 For he has known no quiet in his greed,
		in his treasure he cannot save
			himself. *
21 None of his survivors will consume it,
		therefore his prosperity shall not
			endure.
22 * When he has more than enough, distress
			shall be his,
		every sort of trouble shall come upon
			him.
23 When he has filled his belly,
		God shall send against him the fury of
			his wrath
		and rain down his missiles upon him.
24 Should he escape an iron weapon,

		a bronze bow shall pierce him
			through;
25 The dart shall come out of his back,
		a shining point out of his gall-
			bladder:
		terrors fall upon him.
26 Complete darkness is in store for his
			treasured ones;
		a fire unfanned shall consume him; *
		any survivor in his tent shall be
			destroyed.
27 The heavens shall reveal his guilt,
		and the earth rise up against him.
28 The flood shall sweep away his house,
		torrents in the day of God's anger.
29 This is the portion of the wicked,
		the heritage appointed him by God. † *

# 21

**Job's Sixth Reply.** [1] Then Job answered
and said:

2 At least listen to my words, *
		and let that be the consolation you
			offer.
3 Bear with me while I speak;
		and after I have spoken, you can
			mock!
4 Is my complaint toward any human
			being?
		Why should I not be impatient?
5 Look at me and be appalled,
		put your hands over your mouths.
6 When I think of it, I am dismayed,
		and shuddering seizes my flesh.
7 † Why do the wicked keep on living,
		grow old, become mighty in power? *
8 Their progeny is secure in their sight;
		their offspring are before their eyes.
9 Their homes are safe, without fear,
		and the rod of God is not upon them.
10 Their bulls breed without fail;
		their cows calve and do not miscarry.
11 They let their young run free like sheep,
		their children skip about.
12 They sing along with drum and lyre,
		and make merry to the sound of the
			pipe.

---

† **20:17** *Oil*: olive oil, one of the main agricultural products of ancient Palestine, a land proverbially rich in honey and milk; see Ex 3:8; etc.

**20:29** Zophar ends his lecture in the style of Bildad (cf. 18:19) with a summary appraisal of what he has been saying about the fate of the wicked.

**21:7** In vv. 7–29 Job launches into a realistic description

of the fate of the wicked, contrary to the claims made by the friends.

**20:10** Jb 27:14.
**20:20** Eccl 5:9; Lk 12:20.
**20:22** Jb 15:20–35.
**20:26** Dt 32:22.
**20:29** Jb 27:13.

**21:2** Jb 13:17.
**21:7** Jb 12:6; Ps 37:35;
		73:3; Eccl 8:14; Jer
		12:1–2; Mal 3:14–15.

<sup>13</sup> They live out their days in prosperity,
and tranquilly go down to Sheol. *

<sup>14</sup> Yet they say to God, "Depart from us, *
for we have no desire to know your
ways!

<sup>15</sup> What is the Almighty that we should
serve him?
And what do we gain by praying to
him?" *

<sup>16</sup> Their happiness is not in their own
hands.
The designs of the wicked are far from
me! *

<sup>17</sup> How often is the lamp of the wicked put
out?
How often does destruction come
upon them,
the portion God allots in his anger?

<sup>18</sup> Let them be like straw before the wind,
like chaff the storm carries away!

<sup>19</sup> "God is storing up the man's misery for
his children"?—
let him requite the man himself so
that he knows it!

<sup>20</sup> Let his own eyes behold his calamity,
and the wrath of the Almighty let him
drink!

<sup>21</sup> For what interest has he in his family
after him,
when the number of his months is
finished?

<sup>22</sup> Can anyone teach God knowledge,
seeing that he judges those on high?†

<sup>23</sup> One dies in his full vigor,
wholly at ease and content;

<sup>24</sup> His figure is full and nourished,
his bones are moist with marrow.

<sup>25</sup> Another dies with a bitter spirit,
never having tasted happiness.

<sup>26</sup> Alike they lie down in the dust,
and worms cover them both.

<sup>27</sup> See, I know your thoughts,
and the arguments you plot against
me.

<sup>28</sup> For you say, "Where is the house of the
great,

and where the dwelling place of the
wicked?"

<sup>29</sup> Have you not asked the wayfarers
and do you not acknowledge the
witness they give?

<sup>30</sup> On the day of calamity the evil man is
spared,
on the day that wrath is released.

<sup>31</sup> Who will charge him to his face about
his conduct,
and for what he has done who will
repay him?

<sup>32</sup> He is carried to the grave
and at his tomb they keep watch.

<sup>33</sup> Sweet to him are the clods of the valley.
All humankind will follow after him,
and countless others before him.

<sup>34</sup> How empty the consolation you offer
me!
Your arguments remain a fraud.

## IV. THIRD CYCLE OF SPEECHES†

# 22

**Eliphaz's Third Speech.** <sup>1</sup> Then Eliphaz
the Temanite answered and said:

<sup>2</sup> Can a man be profitable to God? *
Can a wise man be profitable to him?

<sup>3</sup> Does it please the Almighty that you are
just? *
Does he gain if your ways are
perfect?†

<sup>4</sup> Is it because of your piety that he
reproves you—
that he enters into judgment with
you?

<sup>5</sup> Is not your wickedness great,
your iniquity endless?

<sup>6</sup> You keep your relatives' goods in pledge
unjustly, †
leave them stripped naked of their
clothing. *

<sup>7</sup> To the thirsty you give no water to drink,
and from the hungry you withhold
bread;

<sup>8</sup> As if the land belonged to the powerful,

---

**21:22** *Those on high*: the heavenly beings; cf. 1:6; Ps 82:1–8.
**21:1–27:23** The traditional three cycles of speeches breaks
down in chaps. 22–27, because Zophar does not appear. This
may be interpreted as a sign that the three friends see no point
in further dialogue, or that Job's replies have reduced them to silence, or that there has been a mistake in the transmission of the
text (hence various transferrals of verses have been proposed to
include Zophar, but without any textual evidence).
**22:3** Another irony: God will "gain," because he will have

been proved right in his claim to the satan that Job is "perfect."
**22:6–9** This criticism of Job by Eliphaz is untrue (cf. 31:19),
but he is driven to it by his belief that God always acts justly,
even when he causes someone to suffer; suffering is due to
wrongdoing (cf. v. 29).

**21:13** Jb 34:20.          **22:2** Jb 9:2.
**21:14** Jb 22:17.          **22:3** Jb 35:7.
**21:15** Mal 3:14.          **22:6** Jb 24:3; Dt 24:6, 17;
**21:16** Jb 22:18.                Ez 18:12, 16.

and only the privileged could dwell in
  it!

9 You sent widows away empty-handed,
  and the resources of orphans are
  destroyed.*

10 Therefore snares are round about you,*
  sudden terror makes you panic,

11 Or darkness—you cannot see!
  A deluge of waters covers you.

12 Does not God, in the heights of the
  heavens,*
  behold the top of the stars, high
  though they are?

13 Yet you say, "What does God know?*
  Can he judge through the thick
  darkness?

14 Clouds hide him so that he cannot see
  as he walks around the circuit of the
  heavens!"

15 Do you indeed keep to the ancient way
  trodden by the worthless?

16 They were snatched before their time;
  their foundations a river swept away.

17 They said to God, "Let us alone!"
  and, "What can the Almighty do to us?"

18 Yet he had filled their houses with good
  things.
  The designs of the wicked are far from
  me!†*

19 The just look on and are glad,
  and the innocent deride them:†*

20 "Truly our enemies are destroyed,
  and what was left to them, fire has
  consumed!"

21 Settle with him and have peace.
  That way good shall come to you:

22 Receive instruction from his mouth,
  and place his words in your heart.

23 If you return to the Almighty, you will
  be restored;
  if you put iniquity far from your tent,

24 And treat raw gold as dust,
  the fine gold of Ophir† as pebbles in
  the wadi,

25 Then the Almighty himself shall be your
  gold

and your sparkling silver.

26 For then you shall delight in the
  Almighty,
  you shall lift up your face toward
  God.

27 Entreat him and he will hear you,*
  and your vows you shall fulfill.

28 What you decide shall succeed for you,
  and upon your ways light shall shine.

29 For when they are brought low, you will
  say, "It is pride!"
  But downcast eyes he saves.*

30 He will deliver whoever is innocent;
  you shall be delivered if your hands
  are clean.*

# 23 Job's Seventh Reply. ¹Then Job an-
swered and said:

2 Today especially my complaint is bitter,
  his hand is heavy upon me in my
  groanings.

3 Would that I knew how to find him,
  that I might come to his dwelling!

4 I would set out my case before him,
  fill my mouth with arguments;

5 I would learn the words he would
  answer me,
  understand what he would say to me.

6 Would he contend against me with his
  great power?
  No, he himself would heed me!

7 There an upright man might argue with
  him,
  and I would once and for all be
  delivered from my judge.

8 But if I go east, he is not there;†
  or west, I cannot perceive him;

9 The north enfolds him, and I cannot
  catch sight of him;
  The south hides him, and I cannot see
  him.

10 Yet he knows my way;
  if he tested me, I should come forth
  like gold.*

11 My foot has always walked in his steps;

---

† **22:18** The second part of the verse repeats 21:16.
   **22:19** *Them*: the wicked. Eliphaz obviously thinks that the
just can be pleased by God's punishment of the wicked. Such
pleasure at the downfall of the wicked is expressed elsewhere,
e.g., Ps 58:11; 63:12.
   **22:24** *Ophir*: see note on Ps 45:10.
   **23:8** Job's confident desire to confront God (vv. 2–7, contrary
to his fears in 9:14–20 and 13:21–27) gives way to his dark night:
God's absence (vv. 8–9), which also terrifies (vv. 13–17).

**22:9** Jb 29:12–13; Dt
   24:17; 27:19.
**22:10** Jb 18:8–10.
**22:12** Jb 11:8.
**22:13–14** Ps 10:11; 73:11; 94:7;
   Is 29:15; Ez 8:12; 9:9.
**22:18** Jb 21:16.
**22:19** Ps 107:42.
**22:27** Jb 33:26.
**22:29** Ps 138:6; Prv 29:23;
   Mt 23:12; Lk 1:52; Jas
   4:10; 1 Pt 5:5.
**22:30** Jb 17:9; Ps 18:21, 25;
   24:4.
**23:10** Ps 66:10; Prv 17:3;
   Mal 3:3; 1 Pt 1:7.

I have kept his way and not turned
  aside.

12  From the commands of his lips I have
      not departed;
    the words of his mouth I have
      treasured in my heart.

13  But once he decides, who can contradict
      him?
    What he desires, that he does. *

14  For he will carry out what is appointed
      for me,
    and many such things he has in store.

15  Therefore I am terrified before him;
    when I take thought, I dread him.

16  For it is God who has made my heart
      faint, †
    the Almighty who has terrified me.

17  Yes, would that I had vanished in
      darkness,
    hidden by the thick gloom before me.

# 24

1  Why are times not set by the
    Almighty,
  and why do his friends not see his
    days? †

2  People remove landmarks;
    they steal herds and pasture them.

3  The donkeys of orphans they drive away;
    they take the widow's ox for a pledge.

4  They force the needy off the road;
    all the poor of the land are driven
      into hiding.

5  Like wild donkeys in the wilderness,
    they go forth to their task of seeking
      prey;
    the steppe provides food for their
      young;

6  They harvest fodder in the field,
    and glean in the vineyard of the
      wicked.

7  They pass the night naked, without
      clothing;
    they have no covering against the
      cold;

8  They are drenched with rain from the
      mountains,
    and for want of shelter they cling to
      the rock.

9  Orphans are snatched from the breast,
    infants of the needy are taken in
      pledge. †

10  They go about naked, without clothing,
    and famished, they carry the sheaves. †

11  Between the rows they press out the oil;
    they tread the wine presses, yet are
      thirsty.

12  In the city the dying groan,
    and the souls of the wounded cry out.
    Yet God does not treat it as a disgrace!

13  They are rebels against the light: *
    they do not recognize its ways;
    they do not stay in its paths.

14  When there is no light the murderer
      rises,
    to kill the poor and needy;
    in the night he acts like a thief.

15  The eye of the adulterer watches for the
      twilight; *
    he says, "No eye will see me."
  He puts a mask over his face;

16    in the dark he breaks into houses;
  By day they shut themselves in;
    they do not know the light.

17  Indeed, for all of them morning is deep
      darkness;
    then they recognize the terrors of deep
      darkness.

18  He is swift on the surface of the water: †
    their portion in the land is accursed,
    they do not turn aside by way of the
      vineyards.

19  Drought and heat snatch away the snow
      waters,
    Sheol, those who have sinned.

20  May the womb forget him,
    may the worm find him sweet,
    may he no longer be remembered;
  And may wickedness be broken like a
      tree.

21  May his companion be barren, unable
      to give birth,
    may his widow not prosper!

22  He † sustains the mighty by his strength,
    to him who rises without assurance of
      his life

23    he gives safety and support,

---

† **24:1** After his failure to find God, Job takes up the question:
Why does God not favor his friends by the speedy punishment
of his enemies?
  **24:9** This verse continues the description of the plight of the
poor in vv. 2–4, and may belong there.
  **24:10** This verse is a variant of v. 7, and may be an erroneous
scribal repetition.

**24:18–24** These verses are inconsistent with Job's views elsewhere. Moreover, they are in general poorly preserved, and in
some cases obscure.
  **24:22** *He:* God.

**23:13** Jb 42:2; Ps 115:3;       **24:13** Jn 3:19–20.
      135:6.                       **24:15** Prv 7:9–10.

and his eyes are on their ways.

24 They are exalted for a while, and then
are no more;
laid low, like everyone else they are
gathered up;
like ears of grain they shrivel.

25 If this be not so, who can make me a
liar,
and reduce my words to nothing?

# 25 Bildad's Third Speech. [1]† Then Bildad the Shuhite answered and said:

2 Dominion and dread are his
who brings about harmony in his
heavens.

3 Is there any numbering of his troops? †
Yet on which of them does his light
not rise?

4 How can anyone be in the right against
God, *
or how can any born of woman be
innocent?

5 Even the moon is not bright
and the stars are not clean in his eyes.

6 How much less a human being, who is
but a worm,
a mortal, who is only a maggot? *

# 26 Job's Reply. [1]Then Job answered and said:†

2 What help you give to the powerless,
what strength to the feeble arm!

3 How you give counsel to one without
wisdom;
how profuse is the advice you offer!

4 With whose help have you uttered those
words,
whose breath comes forth from you? *

5 The shades† beneath writhe in terror, *

the waters, and their inhabitants.

6 Naked before him is Sheol, †
and Abaddon has no covering. *

7 He stretches out Zaphon† over the void,
and suspends the earth over nothing
at all;

8 He binds up the waters in his clouds,
yet the cloud is not split by their
weight;

9 He holds back the appearance of the full
moon
by spreading his clouds before it.

10 He has marked out a circle† on the
surface of the deep *
as the boundary of light and darkness.

11 The pillars of the heavens tremble
and are stunned at his thunderous
rebuke; *

12 By his power he stilled Sea,
by his skill he crushed Rahab; †

13 By his wind the heavens were made
clear,
his hand pierced the fleeing
serpent. †*

14 Lo, these are but the outlines of his
ways,
and what a whisper of a word we hear
of him:
Who can comprehend the thunder of
his power?

# 27 Job's Reply. [1]Job took up his theme again and said:

2 As God lives, † who takes away my
right, *
the Almighty, who has made my life
bitter,

3 So long as I still have life breath in me,
the breath of God in my nostrils,

4 My lips shall not speak falsehood,

**25:1** At this point any structure in the dialogues disappears. Bildad's speech is very short, and there follow two speeches attributed to Job, with significantly different introductions in 27:1 and 29:1, and with no intervening third speech of Zophar.
**25:3** *His troops*: the heavenly host, or army, the stars (cf. Jgs 5:20), later understood as angels.
**26:1–14** Perhaps to be read as Job's reply to Bildad's short speech.
**26:5** *Shades*: the dead in Sheol, the nether world; cf. Ps 88:11; Is 26:14.
**26:6** *Sheol*: cf. note on Ps 6:6. *Abaddon*: Hebrew for "(place of) destruction," a synonym for nether world; cf. Jb 28:22; Rev 9:11.
**26:7** *Zaphon*: lit., "the north," used here as a synonym for the firmament, the heavens; cf. Is 14:13.
**26:10** *Circle*: the horizon of the ocean which serves as the boundary for the activity of light and darkness; cf. Prv 8:27.

**26:12** *Rahab*: another name for the primeval sea-monster; see notes on Jb 3:8 and Ps 89:11; cf. also Jb 7:12; 9:13.
**26:13** *The fleeing serpent*: the same term occurs in Is 27:1 in apposition to Leviathan; see note on Jb 3:8.
**27:2–6** *As God lives…far be it*: Job affirms two oaths about his innocence by the very God whom he has accused of violating his right. Such is the paradoxical situation of a tortured person who cannot give the lie to his personal justice, but also refuses to renounce God. He dares God to be "just" as he, Job, understands this.

25:4 Jb 4:17; 9:2; 35:2.        26:10 Jb 38:8–11; Prv 8:29.
25:6 Jb 4:19; 15:16.            26:11 Jb 9:6; Ps 18:16;
26:4 Gn 2:7.                          104:7.
26:5 Prv 9:18.                 26:13 Is 27:1.
26:6 Ps 139:7–12.              27:2 Jb 34:5.

nor my tongue utter deceit!

5 Far be it from me to account you right;
till I die I will not renounce my
innocence.*

6 My justice I maintain and I will not
relinquish it;
my heart does not reproach me for
any of my days.

7† Let my enemy be as the wicked
and my adversary as the unjust!

8 For what hope has the impious when he
is cut off,
when God requires his life?

9 Will God then listen to his cry
when distress comes upon him,

10 If he delights in the Almighty
and calls upon God constantly?

11 I will teach you what is in God's hand,
and the way of the Almighty I will not
conceal.

12 Look, you yourselves have all seen it;
why do you spend yourselves in
empty words!

13 This is the portion of the wicked with
God,
the heritage oppressors receive from
the Almighty:*

14 Though his children be many, the sword
awaits them.
His descendants shall want for bread.

15 His survivors shall be buried in death;
their widows shall not weep.

16 Though he heap up silver like dust
and store away mounds of clothing,

17 What he has stored the righteous shall
wear,
and the innocent shall divide the
silver.

18 He builds his house as of cobwebs,
or like a booth put up by a watchman.

19 He lies down a rich man, one last time;
he opens his eyes—nothing is there.*

20 Terrors flood over him like water,
at night the tempest carries him off.

21 The east wind seizes him and he is gone;
it sweeps him from his place;

22 It hurls itself at him without pity,
as he tries to flee from its power.

23 It claps its hands at him,
and whistles at him from its place.

## V. THE POEM ON WISDOM

### Where Is Wisdom to Be Found?

**28** ¹ There is indeed a mine for silver,†
and a place for refining gold.

2 Iron is taken from the earth,
and copper smelted out of stone.

3† He sets a boundary for the darkness;
the farthest confines he explores.

4 He breaks open a shaft far from
habitation,
unknown to human feet;
suspended, far from people, they
sway.

5 The earth, though out of it comes forth
bread,
is in fiery upheaval underneath.

6 Its stones are the source of lapis lazuli,
and there is gold in its dust.

7 The path no bird of prey knows,
nor has the hawk's eye seen it.

8 The proud beasts have not trodden it,
nor has the lion gone that way.

9 He sets his hand to the flinty rock,
and overturns the mountains at their
root.

10 He splits channels in the rocks;
his eyes behold all that is precious.

11 He dams up the sources of the streams,
and brings hidden things to light.

12 As for wisdom—where can she be
found?
Where is the place of understanding?*

13 Mortals do not know her path,
nor is she to be found in the land of
the living.

14 The Deep says, "She is not in me";

---

† **27:7–23** These verses are inconsistent with Job's views elsewhere, and may be part of a missing speech of Zophar; cf. notes
on 24:18–24 and 25:1. Or possibly they are an ironic description
of the fate of the three friends.
**28:1–28** This chapter contains a beautifully vivid description
of that Wisdom which is beyond the attainment of creatures and
known only to God. The pronouns referring to Wisdom may be
translated as either feminine or neuter; in view of Wisdom's role
as God's companion and partner in creation (see Prv 8:22–30;
Sir 24:1–21; Wis 9:9; Bar 3:9–4:4), the feminine is used here.
There is no consensus about the authorship of this poem; it may

originally have been an independent composition incorporated
into the Book of Job.
**28:3–4** The subject of the verbs in these verses has no clear
antecedent; the context of vv. 2–6 suggests miners. The Hebrew
of v. 4 is especially difficult. The general sense of vv. 1–11 is that
one can find minerals in the earth; in contrast, where is Wisdom
to be found (vv. 12, 20)?

**27:5** Jb 2:3, 9; 13:15; 33:9.    **28:12** Eccl 7:24–25; Bar
**27:13** Jb 20:4–29.            3:14–15, 29–33.
**27:19** Ps 49:18; 76:6.

and the Sea says, "She is not with
   me."
15 Solid gold cannot purchase her,
   nor can her price be paid with silver.*
16 She cannot be bought with gold of
   Ophir,†
   with precious onyx or lapis lazuli,
17 Gold or crystal cannot equal her,
   nor can golden vessels be exchanged
   for her.
18 Neither coral nor crystal should be
   thought of;
   the value of wisdom surpasses pearls.
19 Ethiopian topaz does not equal her,
   nor can she be weighed out for pure
   gold.
20 As for wisdom, where does she come
   from?
   Where is the place of understanding?
21 She is hidden from the eyes of every
   living thing;
   even from the birds of the air she is
   concealed.
22 Abaddon† and Death say,
   "Only by rumor have we heard of
   her."
23† But God understands the way to her;*
   it is he who knows her place.*
24 For he beholds the ends of the earth
   and sees all that is under the heavens.
25 When he weighed out the wind,
   and measured out the waters;
26 When he made a rule for the rain
   and a path for the thunderbolts,*
27 Then he saw wisdom and appraised her,
   established her, and searched her out.
28† And to mortals he said:
   See: the fear of the Lord is wisdom;
   and avoiding evil is understanding.*

## VI. JOB'S FINAL SUMMARY OF HIS CAUSE

**29** 1† Job took up his theme again and
said:

2 Oh, that I were as in the months past,
   as in the days when God watched over
   me:*
3 While he kept his lamp shining above
   my head,
   and by his light I walked through
   darkness;
4 As I was in my flourishing days,
   when God sheltered my tent;
5 When the Almighty was still with me,
   and my children were round about
   me;
6 When my footsteps were bathed in
   cream,
   and the rock flowed with streams of
   oil.†
7 Whenever I went out to the gate of the
   city
   and took my seat in the square,
8 The young men saw me and withdrew,
   and the elders rose up and stood;
9 Officials refrained from speaking
   and covered their mouths with their
   hands;*
10 The voice of the princes was silenced,
   and their tongues stuck to the roofs of
   their mouths.
11 The ear that heard blessed me;
   the eye that saw acclaimed me.
12 For I rescued the poor who cried out for
   help,
   the orphans, and the unassisted;
13 The blessing of those in extremity came
   upon me,
   and the heart of the widow I made
   joyful.
14 I wore my righteousness like a garment;
   justice was my robe and my turban.
15 I was eyes to the blind,
   and feet to the lame was I.
16 I was a father to the poor;
   the complaint of the stranger I
   pursued,
17 And I broke the jaws of the wicked man;

---

28:16 *Ophir*: cf. note on Ps 45:10.
28:22 *Abaddon*: cf. note on Jb 26:6.
28:23–27 In reply to the question of vv. 12, 20, these verses indicate that the creator (vv. 24–26) knows the "place" of wisdom and even "established" her, but the specifics are not given. For further development of this theme, cf. Sir 1:1–10 and Bar 3:9–4:4.
28:28 This verse may be a later addition expressing a commonplace of the wisdom tradition; see cross-references. The addition seems to tie the poem in with the description of Job as fearing God and avoiding evil (1:1, 8; 2:3).

29:1 This chapter begins Job's soliloquy, which will end in 31:40. He describes in florid and exaggerated terms his former lifestyle with all its blessings, a deliberate contrast to his current plight, which will be further described in chap. 30.
29:6 Hyperbole to express abundance; see note on 20:17.

28:15 Prv 3:14; 8:10–11, 19; 16:16; Wis 7:7–11.
28:23–27 Prv 8:22–31.
28:23 Prv 2:6; Sir 1:1; Jas 1:5.
28:26 Jb 38:25; Prv 3:20.
28:28 Ps 111:10; Prv 1:7; 9:10; Sir 1:13–21.
29:2 Jb 1:10.
29:9 Wis 8:10–12.

from his teeth I forced the prey.

18 I said: "In my own nest I shall grow old;
I shall multiply years like the
phoenix.†

19 My root is spread out to the waters;
the dew rests by night on my
branches.

20 My glory is fresh within me,
and my bow is renewed in my hand!"

21 For me they listened and waited;
they were silent for my counsel.

22 Once I spoke, they said no more,
but received my pronouncement drop
by drop.

23 They waited for me as for the rain;
they drank in my words like the
spring rains.

24 When I smiled on them they could not
believe it;
they would not let the light of my face
be dimmed.

25 I decided their course and sat at their
head,
I lived like a king among the troops,
like one who comforts mourners.

# 30

1 But now they hold me in derision
who are younger than I,*
Whose fathers I should have disdained
to rank with the dogs of my flock.

2 Such strength as they had meant
nothing to me;
their vigor had perished.

3 In want and emaciating hunger*
they fled to the parched lands:
to the desolate wasteland by night.

4 They plucked saltwort† and shrubs;
the roots of the broom plant were
their food.

5 They were banished from the
community,
with an outcry like that against a
thief—

6 To dwell on the slopes of the wadies,
in caves of sand and stone;

7 Among the bushes they brayed;

under the nettles they huddled
together.

8 Irresponsible, of no account,
they were driven out of the land.

9 Yet now they sing of me in mockery;
I have become a byword among
them.*

10 They abhor me, they stand aloof,
they do not hesitate to spit in my
face!

11† Because he has loosened my bowstring
and afflicted me,
they have thrown off restraint in my
presence.

12 On my right the young rabble rise up;
they trip my feet,
they build their approaches for my
ruin.

13 They tear up my path,
they promote my ruin,
no helper is there against them.

14 As through a wide breach they advance;
amid the uproar they come on in
waves;

15 terrors roll over me.
My dignity is driven off like the wind,
and my well-being vanishes like a
cloud.

16 And now my life ebbs away from me,
days of affliction have taken hold of
me.

17† At night he pierces my bones,
my sinews have no rest.

18 With great difficulty I change my
clothes,
the collar of my tunic fits around my
waist.

19 He has cast me into the mire;
I have become like dust and ashes.

20 I cry to you, but you do not answer me;*
I stand, but you take no notice.

21 You have turned into my tormentor,
and with your strong hand you attack
me.

22 You raise me up and drive me before the
wind;

---

† **29:18** *Phoenix*: a legendary bird which, after several centuries of life, consumed itself in fire, then rose from its ashes in youthful freshness.

**30:4** *Saltwort*: found in salt marshes and very sour to the taste; eaten by the extremely poor as a cooked vegetable. *Broom plant*: the juniper or brushwood; cf. Ps 120:4; a figure of bitterness and poverty, because of its bitter-tasting roots which are practically inedible.

**30:11** God is the subject of the verbs. *Loosened my bowstring*: i.e., disarmed and disabled me.

**30:17–23** Job here refers to God's harsh treatment of him. Cf. 16:9–17; 19:6–12.

**30:1** Jb 12:4; 19:18.          **30:9** Jb 17:6.
**30:3–8** Jb 24:5–6.             **30:20** Jb 19:7.

I am tossed about by the tempest.

23 Indeed I know that you will return me
to death
to the house destined for everyone
alive. *

24 Yet should not a hand be held out
to help a wretched person in distress?

25 Did I not weep for the hardships of
others;
was not my soul grieved for the
poor? *

26 Yet when I looked for good, evil came;
when I expected light, darkness came.

27 My inward parts seethe and will not be
stilled;
days of affliction have overtaken me.

28 I go about in gloom, without the sun;
I rise in the assembly and cry for help.

29 I have become a brother to jackals,
a companion to ostriches.

30 My blackened skin falls away from me;
my very frame is scorched by the heat.

31 My lyre is tuned to mourning,
and my reed pipe to sounds of
weeping.

# 31

1 I made a covenant with my eyes
not to gaze upon a virgin.

2 What portion comes from God above,
what heritage from the Almighty on
high?

3 Is it not calamity for the unrighteous,
and woe for evildoers?

4 Does he not see my ways,
and number all my steps? *

5 If I have walked in falsehood†
and my foot has hastened to deceit,

6 Let God weigh me in the scales of
justice;
thus will he know my innocence! *

7 If my steps have turned out of the way,
and my heart has followed my eyes,
or any stain clings to my hands,

8 Then may I sow, but another eat,
and may my produce be rooted up!

9 If my heart has been enticed toward a
woman,
and I have lain in wait at my
neighbor's door;

10 Then may my wife grind for another,
and may others kneel over her!

11 For that would be heinous,
a crime to be condemned, *

12 A fire that would consume down to
Abaddon†
till it uprooted all my crops. *

13 Had I refused justice to my manservant
or to my maidservant, when they had
a complaint against me,

14 What then should I do when God rises
up?
What could I answer when he
demands an account?

15 Did not he who made me in the belly
make him?
Did not the same One fashion us in
the womb?

16 If I have denied anything that the poor
desired, *
or allowed the eyes of the widow to
languish

17 While I ate my portion alone,
with no share in it for the fatherless,

18 Though like a father he† has reared me
from my youth,
guiding me even from my mother's
womb—

19 If I have seen a wanderer without
clothing,
or a poor man without covering,

20 Whose limbs have not blessed me
when warmed with the fleece of my
sheep;

21 If I have raised my hand against the
innocent
because I saw that I had supporters at
the gate—†

22 Then may my arm fall from the
shoulder,
my forearm be broken at the elbow!

23 For I dread calamity from God,
and his majesty will overpower me.

24 Had I put my trust in gold
or called fine gold my security;

25 Or had I rejoiced that my wealth was
great,
or that my hand had acquired
abundance—

---

† **31:5–34** In a series of purificatory oaths, Job protests his
innocence.
**31:12** *Abaddon*: see note on 26:6.
**31:18** *He*: presumably God.
**31:21** *Gate*: cf. notes on 5:4; Ru 4:1.

---

* 30:23 Heb 9:27.           31:11 Ex 20:14; Lv 20:10;
30:25 Jb 29:12–16.                 Dt 22:22.
31:4 Jb 14:16; 34:21; Ps    31:12 Sir 9:8–9.
  139:3; Prv 5:21.          31:16–23 Jb 29:12–16.
31:6 Jb 23:10.

<sup>26</sup> Had I looked upon the light† as it
        shone, *
      or the moon in the splendor of its
        progress,
<sup>27</sup> And had my heart been secretly enticed
      to blow them a kiss with my hand,
<sup>28</sup> This too would be a crime for
        condemnation,
      for I should have denied God above. *
<sup>29</sup> Had I rejoiced at the destruction of my
        enemy
      or exulted when evil came upon
        him, *
<sup>30</sup> Even though I had not allowed my
        mouth to sin
      by invoking a curse against his life—
<sup>31</sup> Had not the men of my tent exclaimed,
      "Who has not been filled with his
        meat!"†
<sup>32</sup> No stranger lodged in the street,
      for I opened my door to wayfarers—
<sup>33</sup>† Had I, all too human, hidden my sins
      and buried my guilt in my bosom
<sup>34</sup> Because I feared the great multitude
      and the scorn of the clans terrified
        me—
      then I should have remained silent,
      and not come out of doors!
<sup>35</sup>† Oh, that I had one to hear my case:
      here is my signature:† let the Almighty
        answer me!
      Let my accuser write out his
        indictment! *
<sup>36</sup> Surely, I should wear it on my shoulder†
      or put it on me like a diadem;
<sup>37</sup> Of all my steps I should give him an
        account;
      like a prince† I should present myself
        before him.
<sup>38</sup> If my land has cried out against me

      till its furrows wept together;
<sup>39</sup> If I have eaten its strength without
        payment
      and grieved the hearts of its tenants;
<sup>40</sup> Then let the thorns grow instead of
        wheat
      and stinkweed instead of barley!

The words of Job are ended.

## VII. ELIHU'S SPEECHES

**32** <sup>1</sup> Then the three men ceased to answer
Job, because in his own eyes he was in
the right. * <sup>2</sup> But the anger of Elihu,† son of
Barachel the Buzite, of the clan of Ram, was
kindled. He was angry with Job for considering himself rather than God to be in the right.
<sup>3</sup> * He was angry also with the three friends
because they had not found a good answer
and had not condemned Job. <sup>4</sup> But since these
men were older than he, Elihu bided his time
before addressing Job. <sup>5</sup> When, however, Elihu
saw that there was no reply in the mouths of
the three men, his wrath was inflamed. <sup>6</sup> So
Elihu, son of Barachel the Buzite, answered
and said:

      I am young and you are very old;
        therefore I held back and was afraid
        to declare to you my knowledge.
<sup>7</sup> I thought, days should speak,
        and many years teach wisdom! *
<sup>8</sup> But there is a spirit in human beings, *
        the breath of the Almighty, that gives
        them understanding.
<sup>9</sup> It is not those of many days who are
        wise,
        nor the aged who understand the
        right.

---

**31:26–28** *Light:* of the sun. Job never sinned by worshiping
the sun or the moon. *Blow them a kiss:* an act of idolatrous
worship.
   **31:31** The members of his extended family will testify to his
hospitality.
   **31:33–34** Job's present protest is made, not in spite of hidden
sins which he had been unwilling to disclose, but out of genuine
innocence. *All too human:* can also be translated "like Adam."
   **31:35–37** This concluding bravado fits better after v. 40a.
   **31:35** *My signature:* lit., "tau," the last letter of the Hebrew
alphabet, shaped like a cross. Job issues a subpoena to God, and
challenges him to follow proper legal procedure as well.
   **31:36** *On my shoulder:* i.e., boldly, proudly.
   **31:37** *Like a prince:* not as a frightened criminal.
   **32:2** *Elihu* means "My God is he." This speaker was from
Buz, which, according to Jer 25:23, was near Tema and Dedan. A young man, he impetuously and impatiently upbraids

Job for his boldness toward God, and the three friends for not
successfully answering Job. He undertakes to defend God's
absolute justice and to explain more clearly why there is suffering. While fundamentally his position is the same as that of the
three friends, he locates the place of suffering in the divine plan.
Because Elihu's four speeches (32:6–33:33; 34:2–37; 35:2–16;
36:2–37:24) repeat the substance of the earlier arguments of
the three friends and also anticipate the content of the divine
speeches (chaps. 39–41), many scholars consider them a later
addition to the book.

---

**31:26–27** Dt 4:19.             **32:2** Jb 13:18; 27:6; 34:5;
   **31:28** Dt 17:2–7.                35:2.
   **31:29** Prv 24:17.           **32:3** Jb 22:5.
   **31:35** Jb 19:23; 23:3–7.     **32:7** Jb 12:12.
   **32:1** Jb 33:9.             **32:8** Jb 33:4.

10 Therefore I say, listen to me;
   I also will declare my knowledge!
11 Behold, I have waited for your words,
   have given ear to your arguments,
   as you searched out what to say.
12 Yes, I followed you attentively:
   And look, none of you has convicted
      Job,
   not one could refute his statements.
13 So do not say, "We have met wisdom; †
   God can vanquish him but no
      mortal!"
14 For had he addressed his words to me,
   I would not then have answered him
      with your words.
15 They are dismayed, they make no more
      reply;
   words fail them.
16 Must I wait? Now that they speak no
      more,
   and have ceased to make reply,
17 I too will speak my part;
   I also will declare my knowledge!
18 For I am full of words;
   the spirit within me compels me.
19 My belly is like unopened wine,
   like wineskins ready to burst.
20 Let me speak and obtain relief;
   let me open my lips, and reply.
21 I would not be partial to anyone,
   nor give flattering titles to any.
22 For I know nothing of flattery;
   if I did, my Maker would soon take
      me away.

# 33

1 Therefore, O Job, hear my discourse;
   listen to all my words.
2 Behold, now I open my mouth;
   my tongue and voice form words.
3 I will state directly what is in my mind,
   my lips shall speak knowledge clearly;
4 For the spirit of God made me,
   the breath of the Almighty keeps me
      alive. *
5 If you are able, refute me;
   draw up your arguments and take
      your stand.

6 Look, I am like you before God,
   I too was pinched from clay. † *
7 Therefore fear of me should not dismay
      you,
   nor should I weigh heavily upon you.
8 But you have said in my hearing,
   as I listened to the sound of your
      words:
9 "I am clean, without transgression;
   I am innocent, there is no guilt in
      me. *
10 Yet he invents pretexts against me
   and counts me as an enemy. † *
11 He puts my feet in the stocks,
   watches all my paths!" *
12 In this you are not just, let me tell you;
   for God is greater than mortals.
13 Why, then, do you make complaint
      against him
   that he gives no reply to their words? *
14 For God does speak, once,
   even twice, though you do not see it: †
15 In a dream, in a vision of the night,
   when deep sleep falls upon mortals
   as they slumber in their beds.
16 It is then he opens their ears
   and with a warning, terrifies them,
17 By turning mortals from acting
   and keeping pride away from a man,
18 He holds his soul from the pit,
   his life from passing to the grave.
19 Or he is chastened on a bed of pain,
   suffering continually in his bones,
20 So that to his appetite food is repulsive,
   his throat rejects the choicest
      nourishment. *
21 His flesh is wasted, it cannot be seen;
   bones, once invisible, appear;
22 His soul draws near to the pit,
   his life to the place of the dead.
23 If then there be a divine messenger, †
   a mediator, one out of a thousand,
   to show him what is right,
24 He will take pity on him and say,
   "Deliver him from going down to the
      pit;
   I have found him a ransom."

---

32:13 *Met wisdom*: in Job's arguments.
33:6 *Pinched from clay*: a reference to the tradition that human beings were made from clay; cf. Gn 2:7; Jb 10:9; Is 64:7.
33:10 *Enemy*: see note on 1:1; cf. 13:24.
33:14 Elihu asserts that God speaks through warning in dream and also through pain. However, his presupposition is that the restored person admits sinfulness (v. 27). This of course is not relevant to Job's situation.

33:23 *Divine messenger*: or "angel," one of the thousands who serve as mediators.

---

33:4 Jb 32:8.              33:10 Jb 13:24; 19:11.
33:6 Jb 31:15.            33:11 Jb 13:27; 31:4.
33:9 Jb 10:7; 13:18;     33:13 Jb 31:35.
     27:5–6; 29:14; 32:1;   33:20 Jb 6:7.
     34:5.

25 Then his flesh shall become soft as a
     boy's;
   he shall be again as in the days of his
     youth.
26 He shall pray and God will favor him;
   he shall see God's face with rejoicing;*
   for he restores a person's
     righteousness.
27 He shall sing before all and say,
   "I sinned and did wrong,
   yet I was not punished accordingly.
28 He delivered me from passing to the pit,
   and my life sees light."
29 See, all these things God does,
   two, even three times, for a man,
30 Bringing back his soul from the pit
   to the light, in the light of the living.
31 Be attentive, Job, listen to me!
   Be silent and I will speak.
32 If you have anything to say, then answer
     me.
   Speak out! I should like to see you
     justified.
33 If not, then you listen to me;
   be silent, and I will teach you
     wisdom.

# 34

1 Then Elihu answered and said:†

2 Hear my discourse, you that are wise;
   you that have knowledge, listen to me!
3 For the ear tests words,
   as the palate tastes food.*
4 Let us choose what is right;
   let us determine among ourselves
     what is good.
5 For Job has said, "I am innocent,
   but God has taken away what is my
     right.*
6 I declare the judgment on me to be a lie;
   my arrow-wound is incurable, sinless
     though I am."*
7 What man is like Job?
   He drinks in blasphemies like water,
8 Keeps company with evildoers
   and goes along with the wicked,

9 When he says, "There is no profit
   in pleasing God."*
10 Therefore, you that have understanding,
     hear me:
   far be it from God to do wickedness;
   far from the Almighty to do wrong!*
11 Rather, he requites mortals for their
     conduct,
   and brings home to them their way of
     life.*
12 Surely, God cannot act wickedly,
   the Almighty cannot pervert justice.*
13 Who gave him charge over the earth,
   or who set all the world in its place?*
14 If he were to set his mind to it,
   gather to himself his spirit and breath,
15 All flesh would perish together,
   and mortals return to dust.*
16 Now you†—understand, hear this!
   Listen to the words I speak!
17 Can an enemy of justice be in control,
   will you condemn the supreme Just
     One,
18 Who says to a king, "You are worthless!"
   and to nobles, "You are wicked!"
19 Who neither favors the person of
     princes,
   nor respects the rich more than the
     poor?
   For they are all the work of his hands;*
20 in a moment they die, even at
     midnight.*
   People are shaken, and pass away,
   the powerful are removed without
     lifting a hand;
21 For his eyes are upon our ways,
   and all our steps he sees.
22 There is no darkness so dense
   that evildoers can hide in it.
23 For no one has God set a time
   to come before him in judgment.
24 Without inquiry he shatters the mighty,*
   and appoints others in their place,
25 Thus he discerns their works;
   overnight they are crushed.
26† Where the wicked are, he strikes them,

---

† **34:1** Elihu replies, although no one else has spoken. This connective phrase (see also 35:1 and 36:1) may indicate that these speeches of Elihu are a secondary addition to the book (see note on 32:2).
**34:16** *Now you:* Elihu turns to Job and addresses him directly.
**34:26, 29–30** The extant Hebrew text of these verses is obscure.

* **33:26** Jb 22:26–29.     **34:3** Jb 12:11.

**34:5** Jb 33:9–10.
**34:6** Jb 9:20.
**34:9** Jb 9:22–23, 30–31;
   21:15; 35:3.
**34:10** Jb 36:23.
**34:11** Ps 62:13; Prv 24:12;
   Mt 16:27; Rom 2:6;
   2 Cor 5:10; Rev
   22:12.

**34:12** Jb 8:3.
**34:13** Jb 38:4–7.
**34:15** Jb 10:9.
**34:19** Dt 10:17; 2 Chr 19:7;
   Wis 6:7; Acts 10:34;
   Rom 2:11; Eph 6:9;
   Col 3:25; 1 Pt 1:17.
**34:20** Jb 21:13.
**34:24** Ps 2:9.

in a place where all can see,

27 Because they turned away from him
    and did not understand his ways at all:

28 And made the cry of the poor reach him,
    so that he heard the cry of the
        afflicted.

29 If he is silent, who then can condemn?
    If he hides his face, who then can
        behold him,
    whether nation or individual?

30 Let an impious man not rule,
    nor those who ensnare their people.

31 Should anyone say to God,
    "I accept my punishment; I will
        offend no more;

32 What I cannot see, teach me:
    if I have done wrong, I will do so no
        more,"

33 Would you then say that God must
        punish,
    when you are disdainful?
    It is you who must choose, not I;
    speak, therefore, what you know.

34 Those who understand will say to me,
    all the wise who hear my views:

35 "Job speaks without knowledge,
    his words make no sense. *

36 Let Job be tested to the limit,
    since his answers are those of the
        impious;

37 For he is adding rebellion to his sin
    by brushing off our arguments
    and addressing many words to God."

# 35

1 † Then Elihu answered and said:

2 Do you think it right to say,
    "I am in the right, not God"? *

3 When you ask what it profits you,
    "What advantage do I have from not
        sinning?" *

4 I have words for a reply to you †
    and your friends as well.

5 Look up to the skies and see;
    behold the heavens high above you.

6 If you sin, what do you do to God?
    Even if your offenses are many, how
        do you affect him?

7 If you are righteous, what do you give
        him,
    or what does he receive from your
        hand? *

8 Your wickedness affects only someone
        like yourself,
    and your justice, only a fellow human
        being.

9 In great oppression people cry out;
    they call for help because of the
        power of the great,

10 No one says, "Where is God, my Maker,
    who gives songs in the night,

11 Teaches us more than the beasts of the
        earth,
    and makes us wiser than the birds of
        the heavens?"

12 Though thus they cry out, he does not
        answer
    because of the pride of the wicked.

13 But it is idle to say God does not hear
    or that the Almighty does not take
        notice.

14 Even though you say, "You take no
        notice of it," †
    the case is before him; with trembling
        wait upon him.

15 But now that you have done otherwise,
        God's anger punishes,
    nor does he show much concern over
        a life.

16 Yet Job to no purpose opens his mouth,
    multiplying words without
        knowledge. *

# 36

1 Elihu continued and said:

2 Wait a little and I will instruct you,
    for there are still words to be said for
        God.

3 I will assemble arguments from afar,
    and for my maker I will establish
        what is right.

4 For indeed, my words are not a lie;
    one perfect in knowledge is before
        you.

5 Look, God is great, not disdainful;
    his strength of purpose is great.

---

† 35:1 See note on 34:1.
35:4 *A reply to you*: Elihu refers to Job's statement that the innocent suffer as much as the wicked, and especially to Eliphaz's
words in 22:2–3.
35:14–15 The text here is uncertain. It seems to indicate
that Job should have realized God's indifference is only ap-

parent, and that, because he has not done so, God will punish
him.

---

34:35 Jb 35:16; 38:2; 42:3.       35:7 Jb 22:3; 41:2; Lk
35:2 Jb 32:2.                          17:10; Rom 11:35.
35:3 Jb 34:9.                      35:16 Jb 34:35; 38:2; 42:3.

He does not preserve the life of the
    wicked.

6 He establishes the right of the poor;*
    he does not divert his eyes from the
      just

7 But he seats them upon thrones
    with kings, exalted forever.*

8 If they are bound with fetters,
    held fast by bonds of affliction,

9 He lets them know what they have done,
    and how arrogant are their sins.

10 He opens their ears to correction
    and tells them to turn back from evil.

11 If they listen and serve him,
    they spend their days in prosperity,
    their years in happiness.

12 But if they do not listen, they pass to the
      grave,
    they perish for lack of knowledge.

13 The impious in heart lay up anger;
    they do not cry for help when he
      binds them;

14 They will die young—
    their life† among the reprobate.

15 But he saves the afflicted through their
      affliction,
    and opens their ears through
      oppression.

16† He entices you from distress,
    to a broad place without constraint;
    what rests on your table is rich food.

17 Though you are full of the judgment of
      the wicked,
    judgment and justice will be
      maintained.

18 Let not anger at abundance entice you,
    nor great bribery lead you astray.

19 Will your wealth equip you against
      distress,
    or all your exertions of strength?

20 Do not long for the night,
    when peoples vanish in their place.

21 Be careful; do not turn to evil;
    for this you have preferred to
      affliction.

22† Look, God is exalted in his power.
    What teacher is there like him?

23 Who prescribes for him his way?

Who says, "You have done wrong"?*

24 Remember, you should extol his work,
    which people have praised in song.

25 All humankind beholds it;
    everyone views it from afar.

26 See, God is great beyond our knowledge,
    the number of his years past searching
      out.

27 He holds in check the waterdrops
    that filter in rain from his flood,

28 Till the clouds flow with them
    and they rain down on all
      humankind.

29† Can anyone understand the spreading
      clouds,
    the thunderings from his tent?

30 Look, he spreads his light over it,
    it covers the roots of the sea.

31 For by these he judges the nations,
    and gives food in abundance.

32 In his hands he holds the lightning,
    and he commands it to strike the
      mark.

33 His thunder announces him
    and incites the fury of the storm.

# 37

1 At this my heart trembles
    and leaps out of its place.

2 Listen to his angry voice†
    and the rumble that comes forth from
      his mouth!

3 Everywhere under the heavens he sends
      it,
    with his light, to the ends of the earth.

4 Again his voice roars,
    his majestic voice thunders;
    he does not restrain them when his
      voice is heard.

5 God thunders forth marvels with his
      voice;
    he does great things beyond our
      knowing.

6 He says to the snow, "Fall to the earth";
    likewise to his heavy, drenching rain.

7 He shuts up all humankind indoors,
    so that all people may know his work.

8 The wild beasts take to cover
    and remain quiet in their dens.

---

† **36:14** *Life*: a miserable life before death or a shadowy existence in Sheol. *Reprobate*: cf. Dt 23:18–19.
   **36:16–20** The Hebrew text here is obscure. Although each
verse makes some sense, they do not constitute a logical sequence.
   **36:22–25** These verses serve as an introduction to the hymn
about the divine marvels, 36:26–37:24, which in some respects

anticipates the tone and content of the Lord's speeches in chaps.
38–41.
   **36:29–31** The translation of these verses is uncertain.
   **37:2** *Voice*: the thunder.

**36:6** Ps 72:4, 12–13.        **36:23** Jb 34:10; Is 40:13.
**36:7** Ps 113:7–8.

<sup>9</sup> Out of its chamber the tempest comes
      forth;
    from the north winds, the cold.
<sup>10</sup> With his breath God brings the frost,
    and the broad waters congeal.*
<sup>11</sup> The clouds too are laden with moisture,
    the storm-cloud scatters its light.
<sup>12†</sup> He it is who changes their rounds,
      according to his plans,
    to do all that he commands them
    across the inhabited world.
<sup>13</sup> Whether for punishment or mercy,
    he makes it happen.
<sup>14</sup> Listen to this, Job!
    Stand and consider the marvels of
      God!
<sup>15</sup> Do you know how God lays his
      command upon them,
    and makes the light shine forth from
      his clouds?
<sup>16</sup> Do you know how the clouds are
      banked,
    the marvels of him who is perfect in
      knowledge?
<sup>17</sup> You, who swelter in your clothes
    when calm lies over the land from the
      south,
<sup>18</sup> Can you with him spread out the
      firmament of the skies,
    hard as a molten mirror?†
<sup>19</sup> Teach us then what we shall say to him;
    we cannot, for the darkness, make our
      plea.
<sup>20</sup> Will he be told about it when I speak?
    Can anyone talk when he is being
      destroyed?
<sup>21</sup> Rather, it is as the light that cannot be
      seen
    while it is obscured by the clouds,
    till the wind comes by and sweeps
      them away.†
<sup>22</sup> From Zaphon† the golden splendor
    comes,

    surrounding God's awesome majesty!
<sup>23</sup> The Almighty! We cannot find him,
    preeminent in power and judgment,
    abundant in justice, who never
      oppresses.
<sup>24</sup> Therefore people fear him;
    none can see him, however wise their
      hearts.†

## VIII. THE LORD AND JOB MEET

**38** <sup>1</sup> Then the Lord† answered Job out of
the storm and said:

<sup>2</sup> Who is this who darkens counsel
    with words of ignorance?
<sup>3</sup> Gird up your loins† now, like a man;
    I will question you, and you tell me
      the answers!*
<sup>4</sup> Where were you when I founded the
      earth?
    Tell me, if you have understanding.
<sup>5</sup> Who determined its size? Surely you
      know?
    Who stretched out the measuring line
      for it?
<sup>6</sup> Into what were its pedestals sunk,
    and who laid its cornerstone,
<sup>7</sup> While the morning stars sang together
    and all the sons of God† shouted for
      joy?
<sup>8</sup> Who shut within doors the sea,
    when it burst forth from the womb,*
<sup>9</sup> When I made the clouds its garment
    and thick darkness its swaddling
      bands?
<sup>10</sup> When I set limits for it
    and fastened the bar of its door,
<sup>11</sup> And said: Thus far shall you come but
      no farther,
    and here shall your proud waves stop?
<sup>12</sup> Have you ever in your lifetime
    commanded the morning

---

† **37:12–13** The translation of these verses is uncertain.
**37:18** *The firmament...mirror*: the ancients thought of the sky as a ceiling above which were the "upper waters" (cf. Gn 1:6–7; 7:11); when this ceiling became as hard as metal, the usual rain failed to fall on the earth (cf. Lv 26:19; Dt 28:23).
**37:21** Elihu argues that even though God seems not to know our circumstances, he does know them, just as surely as the sun shines behind the clouds.
**37:22** *Zaphon*: the mythical mountain of the gods; cf. note on 26:7.
**37:24** The concluding remark of Elihu is ironic in view of the appearance of the Lord in the next chapter and Job's claim in 42:5.

**38:1** Now the Lord enters the debate and addresses two discourses (chaps. 38–39 and 40–41) to Job, speaking of divine wisdom and power. Such things are altogether beyond the capacity of Job. *Out of the storm*: frequently the background of the appearances of the Lord in the Old Testament; cf. Ps 18; 50; Na 1:3; Hb 3:2–15.
**38:3** *Gird up your loins*: prepare for combat—figuratively, be ready to defend yourself in debate.
**38:7** *Sons of God*: see note on 1:6.

---

**37:10** Ps 147:17.      **38:8** Gn 1:9.
**38:3** Jb 40:2.

and shown the dawn its place

13 For taking hold of the ends of the earth,
   till the wicked are shaken from it?

14 The earth is changed as clay by the seal,
   and dyed like a garment;

15 But from the wicked their light is
      withheld,
   and the arm of pride is shattered.

16 Have you entered into the sources of the
      sea,
   or walked about on the bottom of the
      deep?

17 Have the gates of death been shown to
      you,
   or have you seen the gates of
      darkness?

18 Have you comprehended the breadth of
      the earth?
   Tell me, if you know it all.

19 What is the way to the dwelling of light,
   and darkness—where is its place?

20 That you may take it to its territory
   and know the paths to its home?

21 You know, because you were born then,
   and the number of your days is
      great! †

22 Have you entered the storehouses of the
      snow,
   and seen the storehouses of the hail

23 Which I have reserved for times of
      distress,
   for a day of war and battle? *

24 What is the way to the parting of the
      winds,
   where the east wind spreads over the
      earth?

25 Who has laid out a channel for the
      downpour
   and a path for the thunderstorm

26 To bring rain to uninhabited land,
   the unpeopled wilderness;

27 To drench the desolate wasteland
   till the desert blooms with verdure?

28 Has the rain a father?
   Who has begotten the drops of dew?

29 Out of whose womb comes the ice,
   and who gives the hoarfrost its birth
      in the skies,

30 When the waters lie covered as though
      with stone

that holds captive the surface of the
      deep?

31 Have you tied cords to the Pleiades, †
   or loosened the bonds of Orion?

32 Can you bring forth the Mazzaroth in
      their season,
   or guide the Bear with her children?

33 Do you know the ordinances of the
      heavens;
   can you put into effect their plan on
      the earth?

34 Can you raise your voice to the clouds,
   for them to cover you with a deluge of
      waters?

35 Can you send forth the lightnings on
      their way,
   so that they say to you, "Here we are"?

36 Who gives wisdom to the ibis,
   and gives the rooster † understanding?

37 Who counts the clouds with wisdom?
   Who tilts the water jars of heaven

38 So that the dust of earth is fused into a
      mass
   and its clods stick together?

39 Do you hunt the prey for the lion
   or appease the hunger of young lions,

40 While they crouch in their dens,
   or lie in ambush in the thicket?

41 Who provides nourishment for the raven
   when its young cry out to God, *
   wandering about without food?

# 39

1 Do you know when mountain goats
      are born,
   or watch for the birth pangs of deer,

2 Number the months that they must
      fulfill,
   or know when they give birth,

3 When they crouch down and drop their
      young,
   when they deliver their progeny?

4 Their offspring thrive and grow in the
      open,
   they leave and do not return.

5 Who has given the wild donkey his
      freedom,
   and who has loosed the wild ass from
      bonds?

6 I have made the wilderness his home
   and the salt flats his dwelling.

---

† 38:21 Ironic, but not a harsh rebuke.
  38:31–32 *Pleiades...Orion...Bear*: cf. 9:9. *Mazzaroth*: it is
uncertain what astronomical group is meant by this Hebrew
word; perhaps a southern constellation.

38:36 *Ibis...rooster*: the translation is uncertain.

* ——————
38:23 Jos 10:11; Sir 46:5.          38:41 Ps 147:9.

| | |
|---|---|

7   He scoffs at the uproar of the city,
      hears no shouts of a driver.
8   He ranges the mountains for pasture,
      and seeks out every patch of green.
9   Will the wild ox consent to serve you,
      or pass the nights at your manger?
10  Will you bind the wild ox with a rope in
      the furrow,
      and will he plow the valleys after you?
11  Will you depend on him for his great
      strength
      and leave to him the fruits of your
      toil?
12  Can you rely on him to bring in your
      grain
      and gather in the yield of your
      threshing floor?
13  The wings of the ostrich† flap away;
      her plumage is lacking in feathers.
14  When she abandons her eggs on the
      ground†
      and lets them warm in the sand,
15  She forgets that a foot may crush them,
      that the wild beasts may trample
      them;
16  She cruelly disowns her young
      and her labor is useless; she has no
      fear.
17  For God has withheld wisdom from
      her
      and given her no share in
      understanding.
18  Yet when she spreads her wings high,
      she laughs at a horse and rider.
19  Do you give the horse his strength,†
      and clothe his neck with a mane?
20  Do you make him quiver like a locust,
      while his thunderous snorting spreads
      terror?
21  He paws the valley, he rejoices in his
      strength,
      and charges into battle.
22  He laughs at fear and cannot be
      terrified;
      he does not retreat from the sword.
23  Around him rattles the quiver,
      flashes the spear and the javelin.

24  Frenzied and trembling he devours the
      ground;
      he does not hold back at the sound of
      the trumpet;
25  at the trumpet's call he cries, "Aha!"
    Even from afar he scents the battle,
      the roar of the officers and the
      shouting.
26  Is it by your understanding that the
      hawk soars,
      that he spreads his wings toward the
      south?
27  Does the eagle fly up at your
      command
      to build his nest up high?
28  On a cliff he dwells and spends the
      night,
      on the spur of cliff or fortress.
29  From there he watches for his food;
      his eyes behold it afar off.
30  His young ones greedily drink blood;
      where the slain are, there is he. *

**40** ¹The LORD then answered Job and
      said:

2       Will one who argues with the Almighty
          be corrected?
        Let him who would instruct God give
          answer! *

³Then Job answered the LORD and said:

4†      Look, I am of little account; what can I
          answer you?
        I put my hand over my mouth.
5       I have spoken once, I will not reply;
          twice, but I will do so no more.

⁶Then the LORD answered Job out of the
storm and said:

7       Gird up your loins now, like a man.
          I will question you, and you tell me
          the answers!
8†      Would you refuse to acknowledge my
          right?

---

† **39:13** The wings of the ostrich cannot raise her from the
ground, but they help her to run swiftly.
  **39:14–16** People thought that, because the ostrich laid her
eggs on the sand, she was thereby cruelly abandoning them;
cf. Lam 4:3.
  **39:19–25** A classic description of a war horse.
  **40:4–5** Job's first reaction is humble, but also seemingly
cautious.

**40:8–14** The issue is joined in these verses, and the Lord
seems to challenge Job to play God and to bring down the proud
and wicked.

---

**39:30** Mt 24:28; Lk 17:37.       **40:2** Jb 38:3.

Would you condemn me that you
may be justified?

9 Have you an arm like that of God,
or can you thunder with a voice like
his?

10 Adorn yourself with grandeur and
majesty,
and clothe yourself with glory and
splendor.

11 Let loose the fury of your wrath;
look at everyone who is proud and
bring them down.

12 Look at everyone who is proud, and
humble them.
Tear down the wicked in their place,

13 bury them in the dust together;
in the hidden world imprison them.

14 Then will I too praise you,
for your own right hand can save you.

15 Look at Behemoth,† whom I made
along with you,
who feeds on grass like an ox.

16 See the strength in his loins,
the power in the sinews of his belly.

17 He carries his tail like a cedar;
the sinews of his thighs are like cables.

18 His bones are like tubes of bronze;
his limbs are like iron rods.

19 He is the first of God's ways,
only his maker can approach him
with a sword.

20 For the mountains bring him produce,
and all wild animals make sport there.

21 Under lotus trees he lies,
in coverts of the reedy swamp.

22 The lotus trees cover him with their
shade;
all about him are the poplars in the
wadi.

23 If the river grows violent, he is not
disturbed;
he is tranquil though the Jordan
surges about his mouth.

24 Who can capture him by his eyes,
or pierce his nose† with a trap?

25 Can you lead Leviathan† about with a
hook,
or tie down his tongue with a rope?

26 Can you put a ring into his nose,

or pierce through his cheek with a
gaff?

27 Will he then plead with you, time after
time,
or address you with tender words?

28 Will he make a covenant with you
that you may have him as a slave
forever?

29 Can you play with him, as with a bird?
Can you tie him up for your little
girls?

30 Will the traders bargain for him?
Will the merchants† divide him up?

31 Can you fill his hide with barbs,
or his head with fish spears?

32 Once you but lay a hand upon him,
no need to recall any other conflict!

# 41

1 Whoever might vainly hope to do so
need only see him to be overthrown.

2 No one is fierce enough to arouse him;
who then dares stand before me?

3 Whoever has assailed me, I will pay
back—
Everything under the heavens is mine.

4 I need hardly mention his limbs,
his strength, and the fitness of his
equipment.

5 Who can strip off his outer garment,
or penetrate his double armor?

6 Who can force open the doors of his
face,
close to his terrible teeth?

7 Rows of scales are on his back,
tightly sealed together;

8 They are fitted so close to each other
that no air can come between them;

9 So joined to one another
that they hold fast and cannot be
parted.

10 When he sneezes, light flashes forth;
his eyes are like the eyelids of the
dawn.

11 Out of his mouth go forth torches;
sparks of fire leap forth.

12 From his nostrils comes smoke
as from a seething pot or bowl.

13 His breath sets coals afire;
a flame comes from his mouth.

---

† **40:15** *Behemoth*: a primeval monster of chaos; identified by some scholars as the hippopotamus, on which the description of Behemoth is partially based. The point of the Behemoth-Leviathan passages is that only the Lord, not Job, can control the cosmic evil which these forces symbolize.

**40:24** *Eyes…nose*: the only exposed parts of the submerged beast.

**40:25** *Leviathan*: although identified by some scholars as the crocodile, it is more likely another chaos monster; see note on 3:8.

14 Strength abides in his neck,
   and power leaps before him.
15 The folds of his flesh stick together,
   it is cast over him and immovable.
16 His heart is cast as hard as stone;
   cast as the lower millstone.
17 When he rises up, the gods are afraid;
   when he crashes down, they fall back.
18 Should a sword reach him, it will not
   avail;
   nor will spear, dart, or javelin.
19 He regards iron as chaff,
   and bronze as rotten wood.
20 No arrow will put him to flight;
   slingstones used against him are but
   straw.
21 Clubs he regards as straw;
   he laughs at the crash of the spear.
22 Under him are sharp pottery fragments,
   spreading a threshing sledge upon the
   mire.
23 He makes the depths boil like a pot;
   he makes the sea like a perfume
   bottle.
24 Behind him he leaves a shining path;
   you would think the deep had white
   hair.
25 Upon the earth there is none like him,
   he was made fearless.
26 He looks over all who are haughty,
   he is king over all proud beasts.

42 ¹Then Job answered the Lord and
    said:

2 I know that you can do all things,†
   and that no purpose of yours can be
   hindered.
3 "Who is this who obscures counsel with
   ignorance?"
   I have spoken but did not understand;

things too marvelous for me, which I
   did not know.*
4 "Listen, and I will speak;
   I will question you, and you tell me the
   answers."
5 By hearsay I had heard of you,
   but now my eye has seen you.†
6 Therefore I disown what I have said,
   and repent in dust and ashes.†

## IX. EPILOGUE

**Job's Restoration.** ⁷And after the Lord had spoken these words to Job, the Lord said to Eliphaz the Temanite, "My anger blazes against you and your two friends!† You have not spoken rightly concerning me, as has my servant Job. ⁸So now take seven bulls and seven rams, and go to my servant Job, and sacrifice a burnt offering for yourselves, and let my servant Job pray for you.† To him I will show favor, and not punish your folly, for you have not spoken rightly concerning me, as has my servant Job." ⁹Then Eliphaz the Temanite, and Bildad the Shuhite, and Zophar the Naamathite, went and did as the Lord had commanded them. The Lord showed favor to Job.

¹⁰The Lord also restored the prosperity of Job, after he had prayed for his friends; the Lord even gave to Job twice† as much as he had before. ¹¹Then all his brothers and sisters came to him, and all his former acquaintances, and they dined with him in his house. They consoled and comforted him for all the evil the Lord had brought upon him, and each one gave him a piece of money† and a gold ring.

¹²*Thus the Lord blessed the later days of Job more than his earlier ones. Now he had fourteen thousand sheep, six thousand camels,

---

**40:30** *Merchants:* lit., "Canaanites," whose reputation for trading was so widespread that their name came to be used for merchants; cf. Prv 31:24.

**42:2–4** In his final speech, Job quotes God's own words (see 38:2–3; 40:7).

**42:5** In 19:25–27 Job had affirmed a hope to "see" (three times) his vindicator. Now he has seen the Lord about whom he had heard so much.

**42:6** A difficult verse. Some doubt, in view of God's commendation in v. 7, that Job does in fact express repentance, and alternative translations are often given. Along with v. 5, it describes a change in Job, which the encounter with the Lord has brought about. *Dust and ashes:* an ambiguous phrase. It can refer to the human condition (cf. Gn 18:27; Jb 30:19) or to Job's ash heap (2:8).

**42:7** The three friends of Job (Elihu is ignored in the epilogue) are criticized by the Lord because they had "not spoken rightly" (vv. 7–8).

**42:8** An ironic touch: Job becomes the intercessor for his friends.

**42:10** *Twice:* this is the fine for damage inflicted upon another; cf. Ex 22:3. The Lord pays up!

**42:11** *A piece of money:* lit., *qesitah,* value unknown; also used in Gn 33:19; Jos 24:32. *Gold ring:* for the nose or ear.

---

*
**42:3** Jb 34:35; 35:16; 38:2;            **42:12** Jb 1:3.
Ps 131:1; Prv 30:18.

a thousand yoke of oxen, and a thousand she-donkeys. ¹³ He also had seven sons and three daughters: ¹⁴ the first daughter he called Jemimah, the second Keziah, and the third Kerenhappuch.† ¹⁵ In all the land no other women were as beautiful as the daughters of Job; and

their father gave them an inheritance† among their brothers.

¹⁶ After this, Job lived a hundred and forty years; and he saw his children, his grandchildren, and even his great-grandchildren.* ¹⁷ Then Job died, old and full of years.

---

† **42:14** Job's daughters had names symbolic of their charms: *Jemimah*, dove; *Keziah*, precious perfume (cf. Ps 45:9); *Kerenhappuch*, cosmetic jar—more precisely, a container for a black powder used like modern mascara.

**42:15** Ordinarily daughters did not inherit property unless there were no sons; cf. Nm 27:1–11.

* 

**42:16** Jb 5:25–26.

# The Book of
# Psalms

## INTRODUCTION

### Harry P. Nasuti

For many interpreters, both ancient and modern, the book of Psalms occupies a distinctive place among the books of Scripture. In support of this view, one may point first of all to the comprehensive nature of this book, which has often been characterized as a Bible in miniature. The psalms recount and celebrate God's foundational actions in creation, as well as God's special history with Israel and wider relationship with the rest of humanity. They also contain praise of God's torah (instruction/law), prophetic oracles of judgment and salvation, and wisdom reflections on life, especially on the contrasting paths of the righteous and the wicked. For Christian interpreters, the psalms' comprehensiveness often includes the New Testament, with the psalms seen as bearing witness to the person and life of Jesus.

## As One's Own Words: The Power of Psalms

Also distinctive is the way that Jews and Christians make use of the book of Psalms. Only rarely has this book been approached primarily as a historical collection of liturgical texts from ancient Israel, what scholars have sometimes called the "hymnbook of the second Temple." Rather, the psalms have always played a much more immediate role in the ongoing prayer and liturgical life of the communities that have treasured them. As Saint Athanasius (fourth century CE) noted in his *Letter to Marcellinus*, the "remarkable" thing about the psalms is that the person reciting them utters them "as his own words, and each sings them as if they were written concerning him, and he accepts them and recites them not as if another were speaking, nor as if speaking about someone else. But he handles them as if he is speaking about himself. And the things spoken are such

that he lifts them up to God as himself acting and speaking them from himself."[1]

The psalms are able to become "one's own words," at least in part because of the way that they reflect the full range of human experience. The breadth and depth of the psalms is evident in the range of genres that one finds in this book, from individual and collective laments to hymns of praise and songs of thanksgiving. (See the NAB introduction to the book of Psalms for a more extended introduction to these genres.) This diversity has made it possible for later generations to use the psalms to express their own feelings and attitudes in a variety of settings that are similar (even if not identical) to those out of which the psalms originally arose. Those who use the psalms in this way are often able to come to a better understanding of both themselves and the world in which they live.

There is, however, another way in which the psalms become the words of those who use them, one that explains why these texts have always been seen to play a key role in such individuals' spiritual development. Rather than simply being a way to express already existent feelings, the psalms can also function as a "means of grace," capable of transforming those who use them into the type of individual described in the psalms themselves. Once again, Athanasius is representative of the tradition when he sees the psalms' power to "affect," "mold," and even "constrain" those who use them as that which distinguishes this book from the rest of Scripture.[2]

The transformative power of the psalms

---

1. Athanasius, "A Letter of Athanasius, Our Holy Father, Archbishop of Alexandria, to Marcellinus on the Interpretation of the Psalms," in *The Life of Antony and the Letter to Marcellinus*, trans., R. C. Gregg (New York: Paulist, 1980), p. 110.

2. Ibid., p. 108.

P
S

is particularly evident in their role in Jewish and Christian liturgy. By prescribing specific psalms for various liturgical occasions, these communities not only describe the appropriate attitudes for those occasions but also actually provide the effective means by which worshipers can come to adopt the proper stance before God—as, for example, in the use of such penitential psalms as Pss 130 and 51 for the days before Yom Kippur and for Ash Wednesday, respectively. In a similar way, the liturgical use of the psalms also enables later generations of Jews and Christians to participate in the defining events of their faith—as in the use of Pss 113–118 at Passover to commemorate the Exodus from Egypt and the use of Ps 22 on Palm Sunday in connection with the reading of the passion and the events of Holy Week.

Such required use of specific texts helps to bring about a shared communal identity that goes beyond individual needs and preferences. It can even support a certain solidarity between differently placed members of a community, as, for example, when more favorably situated members are asked to pray the same lament psalms as those who are truly suffering and in need. In all of these cases, the liturgical use of the psalms is to specify and shape the identity of the members of the community and have an impact upon the way they live their daily lives.

## Praying with David, Jesus, and the Psalms

Already depicted as a musician, singer, and composer in the historical books, the royal figure of David is closely associated with the psalms throughout this work. Seventy-three of the psalms have the superscription *ledawid* ("of" or "for David"), and one of the only purely editorial notations in the book (Ps 72:20) specifically refers to an earlier collection of Davidic psalms. In addition, thirteen psalms have detailed superscriptions that relate these texts to specific episodes of David's life. Given all of this, it is not surprising that Judaism and Christianity have long associated the psalms with this important biblical character, often attributing the authorship of all the psalms to David in some way.

A number of ancient and modern scholars have noted certain problems with this attribution, especially in light of the presence of other names in many superscriptions and the obvious references to such later events as the Babylonian exile (as in Ps 137). In spite of such difficulties, several recent scholars have argued for the continued interpretive fruitfulness of approaching the psalms in connection with David. Through such a connection, the psalms provide access to the inner life of this deeply human character and allow him to serve as a model of faith and repentance for later generations—as in the case of Ps 51, which is presented in the superscription as David's response to his sin with Bathsheba (2 Sm 11). Also important is the perception of David as a prophet in the Jewish tradition, which sees him not only as predicting later events of Jewish history but also as providing the appropriate prayerful responses to those events.

Christian tradition has associated the psalms not only with David but also with Jesus. Picking up on David's prophetic status, Christian interpreters from the New Testament on have found in the psalms predictions of the events of Jesus' life and confirmation of his Messianic status. In keeping with references such as Mk 15:34, Christian interpreters also saw Jesus as the one who speaks the psalms in the most authentic way, both with respect to himself and on behalf of the church, whose praying of the psalms becomes effective by praying them in union with the church's head. In both this case and in the case of David, those who imitate these figures by praying their prayers also are seen to become ever more shaped along the lines of these figures' paradigmatic relationships with God.

## Relationship and Metaphor in the Psalms

The relationship with God mediated by the psalms is characterized by a deep intimacy in which the one who prays has the freedom to complain bitterly about God's apparent absence and abandonment, while still relying on God as one's only hope and refuge in a world of adversity. Such a relationship is grounded in both the ebb and flow of daily life and the larger currents of Israel's history—from election, to exile, and beyond. The psalms celebrate God's presence in the Jerusalem Temple but also recognize the painful distance between real life and all that God's presence implies. As a result, these texts are filled with expressions of both trust and longing, affirming God's present faithfulness while eagerly looking forward to God's future deliverance. At the same time, they also contain ecstatic praise of a God who has acted and will act again on behalf of those who depend on God's justice and mercy.

In keeping with their status as poetry, the psalms render the dynamics of this relationship concrete and immediate through the vibrant use of metaphor. God is portrayed and addressed as king, judge, shepherd, teacher, healer, and rock, among other images. Such imagery for God implies corresponding imagery for those who through their use of these texts come to see themselves as subjects, plaintiffs or defendants, sheep, students, and individuals in need of healing and protection. The psalms use vivid metaphors to describe those who oppose and afflict the psalmist, at times depicting them as wild animals intent on devouring the speaker. They also contain anguished descriptions of the psalmist's suffering, which is described as an eruption of the realm of death into the individual's life and a descent into a watery pit far from God's presence. Attention to such imagery and the other poetic features of these texts (such as parallelism, terseness, and the repetition of sounds, words, and phrases) is necessary for a full appreciation of the psalms' power, but much of this is unfortunately lost in translation.

## The Psalms as a Literary and Theological Whole

Recent scholarship has paid considerable attention to the way the psalms work together as a larger literary and theological whole with an overarching structure and meaning. Like earlier interpreters, modern scholars have often seen Pss 1 and 2 as an introduction that sets forth the major themes of torah/wisdom, kingship, and covenant that resound throughout the book. Similarly, Pss 146–150 have been seen to conclude this work with an ever-wider and more exuberant outpouring of praise, as is fitting for a book whose Hebrew title is *tehillim* ("praises").

Also significant is the way that a series of doxologies (Pss 41:14; 72:18–19; 89:53; and 106:48) divide this work into five distinct units, apparently to suggest an analogy with the five books of the Torah or Pentateuch. Some of the psalms that begin and conclude these units (especially Pss 72, 73, 89, 90, and 107) seem to focus on the question of God's trustworthiness in the face of human suffering and the historical travails of God's covenant with Israel and the Davidic monarchy. So, for example, the description of the troubled state of the Davidic covenant that concludes book three (cf. Ps 89:39–52) is met with Ps 90, a communal request for God's mercy attributed to Moses, as well as with the celebration of divine kingship in the psalms that follow (especially Pss 93, 96–99).

Another aspect of this book's literary structure is the order in which the psalms now occur. While the present position of some psalms may simply reflect the book's historical development, other features of the psalms' sequence seem to have interpretive significance. So, for example, one sometimes finds consecutive psalms that either complement each other or constitute a theological dialogue (such as Pss 22–23, 105–106). Also of possible significance is the presence of particular types of psalms at certain points in the book. Along these lines, some scholars have suggested that the somewhat larger concentration of lament psalms in its first half implies a move from lament to praise for the book as a whole. Scholars have also seen a possible move toward a more communal orientation in the psalms of the second half of the book. This attempt to understand the psalms as a literary whole with a particular order is obviously a different approach from one that emphasizes the individual psalms and their settings in either ancient Israel or later liturgical usage. It is, however, an approach with an important place in Jewish and Christian tradition, which has clearly emphasized the necessity of engaging all of the psalms and the importance of maintaining their present sequence. Alongside their prescribing specific texts for particular occasions, both Judaism and Christianity have also seen praying and reflecting on all of the psalms in their canonical order as a means of spiritual growth and formation—as is perhaps most clearly seen in certain monastic approaches to the psalms, where some traditional arrangements of the Divine Office use all the psalms in a weekly arrangement.

# Multifaceted Text, Rich and Varied History

As is apparent from even this brief introduction, the psalms stand out in part because of the wide variety of ways in which they have been interpreted and used over the years. Both human words to God and God's word to humanity, the psalms have functioned as normative prayer and a rich source for theological reflection. In this dual capacity, they continue to be the means by which the rest of Scripture becomes concrete in the lives of believers, as well as the place of a living encounter between these believers and their God. ■

# THE BOOK OF PSALMS

## New American Bible, Introduction

The Hebrew Psalter numbers 150 songs. The corresponding number in the Septuagint differs because of a different division of certain Psalms. Hence the numbering in the Greek Psalter (which was followed by the Latin Vulgate) is usually one digit behind the Hebrew. In *The New American Bible* the numbering of the verses follows the Hebrew numbering; many of the traditional English translations are often a verse number behind the Hebrew because they do not count the superscriptions as a verse.

The superscriptions derive from pre-Christian Jewish tradition, and they contain technical terms, many of them apparently liturgical, which are no longer known to us. Seventy-three Psalms are attributed to David, but there is no sure way of dating any Psalm. Some are preexilic (before 587), and others are postexilic (after 539), but not as late as the Maccabean period (ca. 165). The Psalms are the product of many individual collections (e.g., Songs of Ascents, Ps 120–134), which were eventually combined into the present work in which one can detect five "books," because of the doxologies which occur at 41:14; 72:18–19; 89:53; 106:48.

Two important features of the Psalms deserve special notice. First, the majority were composed originally precisely for liturgical worship. This is shown by the frequent indication of liturgical leaders interacting with the community (e.g., Ps 118:1–4). Secondly, they follow certain distinct patterns or literary forms. Thus, the hymn is a song of praise, in which a community is urged joyfully to sing out the praise of God. Various reasons are given for this praise (often introduced by "for" or "because"): the divine work of creation and sustenance (Ps 135:1–12; 136). Some of the hymns have received a more specific classification, based on content. The "Songs of Zion" are so called because they exalt Zion, the city in which God dwells among the people (Ps 47; 96–99). Characteristic of the songs of praise is the joyful summons to get involved in the activity; Ps 104 is an exception to this, although it remains universal in its thrust.

Another type of Psalm is similar to the hymn: the thanksgiving Psalm. This too is a song of praise acknowledging the Lord as the rescuer of the psalmist from a desperate situation. Very often the psalmist will give a flashback, recounting the past distress, and the plea that was uttered (Ps 30; 116). The setting for such prayers seems to have been the offering of a *todah* (a "praise" sacrifice) with friends in the Temple.

There are more Psalms of lament than of any other type. They may be individual (e.g., Ps 3–7; 22) or communal (e.g., Ps 44). Although they usually begin with a cry for help, they develop in various ways. The description of the distress is couched in the broad imagery typical of the Bible (one is in Sheol, the Pit, or is afflicted by enemies or wild beasts, etc.)—in such a way that one cannot pinpoint the exact nature of the psalmist's plight. However, Ps 51 (cf. also Ps 130) seems to refer clearly to deliverance from sin. Several laments end on a note of certainty that the Lord has heard the prayer (cf. Ps 7, but contrast Ps 88), and the Psalter has been characterized as a movement from lament to praise. If this is somewhat of an exaggeration, it serves at least to emphasize the frequent expressions of trust which characterize the lament. In some cases it would seem as if the theme of trust has been lifted out to form a literary type all its own; cf. Ps 23, 62, 91. Among the communal laments can be counted Ps 74 and 79. They complain to the Lord about some national disaster, and try to motivate God to intervene in favor of the suffering people.

Other Psalms are clearly classified on account of content, and they may be in themselves laments or Psalms of thanksgiving. Among the "royal" Psalms that deal directly with the currently reigning king, are Ps 20, 21, and 72. Many of the royal Psalms were given a messianic interpretation by Christians. In Jewish tradition they were preserved, even after kingship had disappeared, because they were read in the light of the Davidic covenant reported in 2 Sm 7. Certain Psalms are called wisdom Psalms because they seem to betray the influence of the concerns of the ages (cf. Ps 37, 49), but there is no general agreement as to the number of these prayers. Somewhat related to the wisdom Psalms are the "torah" Psalms, in which the torah (instruction or law) of the Lord is glorified (Ps 1; 19:8–14; 119). Ps 78, 105, 106 can be considered as "historical" Psalms. Although the majority of the Psalms have a liturgical setting, there are

certain prayers that may be termed "liturgies," so clearly does their structure reflect a liturgical incident (e.g., Ps 15, 24).

It is obvious that not all of the Psalms can be pigeon-holed into neat classifications, but even a brief sketch of these types help us to catch the structure and spirit of the Psalms we read. It has been rightly said that the Psalms are "a school of prayer." They not only provide us with models to follow, but inspire us to voice our own deepest feelings and aspirations.

# PSALMS

## First Book—Psalms 1–41

## PSALM 1†

## True Happiness in God's Law

**I**

1 Blessed is the man who does not walk
   in the counsel of the wicked,
  Nor stand in the way† of sinners,
    nor sit in company with scoffers.*

2 Rather, the law of the LORD† is his joy;
    and on his law he meditates day and
      night.*

3 He is like a tree*
    planted near streams of water,
    that yields its fruit in season;
  Its leaves never wither;
    whatever he does prospers.

**II**

4 But not so are the wicked,† not so!
  They are like chaff driven by the wind.*

5 Therefore the wicked will not arise at the
      judgment,
    nor will sinners in the assembly of the
      just.

6 Because the LORD knows the way of the
      just,*
    but the way of the wicked leads to
      ruin.

## PSALM 2†

## A Psalm for a Royal Coronation

1 Why do the nations protest
    and the peoples conspire in vain?*

2 Kings on earth rise up
    and princes plot together
  against the LORD and against his
      anointed one:†*

3 "Let us break their shackles
    and cast off their chains from us!"*

4 The one enthroned in heaven laughs;
    the Lord derides them,*

5 Then he speaks to them in his anger,
    in his wrath he terrifies them:

6 "I myself have installed my king
    on Zion, my holy mountain."

7 I will proclaim the decree of the LORD,
    he said to me, "You are my son;
    today I have begotten you.*

8 Ask it of me,
    and I will give you the nations as your
      inheritance,
    and, as your possession, the ends of
      the earth.

9 With an iron rod you will shepherd
      them,
    like a potter's vessel you will shatter
      them."*

10 And now, kings, give heed;
    take warning, judges on earth.

11 Serve the LORD with fear;
    exult with trembling,
  Accept correction
    lest he become angry and you perish
      along the way
    when his anger suddenly blazes up.*
  Blessed are all who take refuge in
      him!

## PSALM 3†

## Threatened but Trusting

1 A psalm of David, when he fled from his son
      Absalom.†*

---

Psalm 1 A preface to the whole Book of Psalms, contrasting with striking similes the destiny of the good and the wicked. The Psalm views life as activity, as choosing either the good or the bad. Each "way" brings its inevitable consequences. The wise through their good actions will experience rootedness and life, and the wicked, rootlessness and death.
  1:1 *The way*: a common biblical term for manner of living or moral conduct (Ps 32:8; 101:2, 6; Prv 2:20; 1 Kgs 8:36).
  1:2 *The law of the LORD*: either the Torah, the first five books of the Bible, or, more probably, divine teaching or instruction.
  1:4 *The wicked*: those who by their actions distance themselves from God's life-giving presence.
  Psalm 2 A royal Psalm. To rebellious kings (Ps 2:1–3) God responds vigorously (Ps 2:4–6). A speaker proclaims the divine decree (in the legal adoption language of the day), making the Israelite king the earthly representative of God (Ps 2:7–9) and warning kings to obey (Ps 2:10–11). The Psalm has a messianic meaning for the Church; the New Testament understands it of

Christ (Acts 4:25–27; 13:33; Heb 1:5).
  2:2 *Anointed*: in Hebrew *mashiah*, "anointed"; in Greek *christos*, whence English Messiah and Christ. In Israel kings (Jgs 9:8; 1 Sm 9:16; 16:12–13) and high priests (Lv 8:12; Nm 3:3) received the power of their office through anointing.
  Psalm 3 An individual lament complaining of enemies who deny that God will come to the rescue (Ps 3:2–3). Despite such taunts the psalmist hopes for God's protection even in sleep (Ps

---

*
| 1:1 Ps 26:4–5; 40:5. | 2:3 Ps 149:8. |
| 1:2 Jos 1:8; Ps 119; Sir | 2:4 Ps 37:13; 59:9; Wis |
|   39:1. |   4:18. |
| 1:3 Ps 52:10; 92:13–15; | 2:7 Ps 89:27; 110:2–3; Is |
|   Jer 17:8. |   49:1. |
| 1:4 Ps 35:5; 83:14–16; Jb | 2:9 Rev 2:27; 12:5; 19:15. |
|   21:18. | 2:11 Ps 34:9; 146:5; Prv |
| 1:6 Ps 37:18. |   16:20. |
| 2:1 Rev 11:18. | 3:1 2 Sm 15:13ff. |
| 2:2 Ps 83:6. | |

P
S

**I**

2 How many are my foes, LORD!
  How many rise against me!
3† How many say of me,
  "There is no salvation for him in
    God."*                          *Selah*
4 But you, LORD, are a shield around me;
  my glory, you keep my head high.*

**II**

5 With my own voice I will call out to the
    LORD,
  and he will answer me from his holy
    mountain.                       *Selah*
6 I lie down and I fall asleep,
  [and] I will wake up, for the LORD
    sustains me.*
7 I do not fear, then, thousands of people
  arrayed against me on every side.

**III**

8 Arise, LORD! Save me, my God!
  For you strike the cheekbone of all my
    foes;
  you break the teeth of the wicked.*
9 Salvation is from the LORD!
  May your blessing be upon your
    people!*                        *Selah*

## PSALM 4†

### Trust in God

1 For the leader;† with stringed instruments.
  A psalm of David.

**I**

2 Answer me when I call, my saving God.
  When troubles hem me in, set me
    free;
  take pity on me, hear my prayer.*

**II**

3 How long, O people, will you be hard of
    heart?
  Why do you love what is worthless,
    chase after lies?† *            *Selah*
4 Know that the LORD works wonders for
    his faithful one;
  the LORD hears when I call out to him.
5 Tremble† and sin no more;
  weep bitterly† within your hearts,
  wail upon your beds,*
6 Offer fitting sacrifices
  and trust in the LORD.*

**III**

7 Many say, "May we see better times!
  LORD, show us the light of your
    face!"*                         *Selah*
8 But you have given my heart more joy
  than they have when grain and wine
    abound.
9*† In peace I will lie down and fall asleep,
  for you alone, LORD, make me
    secure.

## PSALM 5†

### Prayer for Divine Help

1 For the leader; with wind instruments.
  A psalm of David.

**I**

2 Give ear to my words, O LORD;
  understand my sighing.*
3 Attend to the sound of my cry,
  my king and my God!
  For to you I will pray, LORD;
4   in the morning you will hear my
    voice;

---

† 
**3:4–7).** The Psalm prays for an end to the enemies' power to speak maliciously (Ps 3:8) and closes peacefully with an expression of trust (Ps 3:9).

**3:1** The superscription, added later, relates the Psalm to an incident in the life of David.

**3:3, 3:5, 3:9** *Selah:* the term is generally considered a direction to the cantor or musicians but its exact meaning is not known. It occurs seventy-one times in thirty-nine Psalms.

**Psalm 4** An individual lament emphasizing trust in God. The petition is based upon the psalmist's vivid experience of God as savior (Ps 4:2). That experience of God is the basis for the warning to the wicked: revere God who intervenes on the side of the faithful (Ps 4:3–6). The faithful psalmist exemplifies the blessings given to the just (Ps 4:7–8).

**4:1** *For the leader:* many Psalm headings contain this rubric. Its exact meaning is unknown but may signify that such Psalms once stood together in a collection of "the choirmaster," cf. 1 Chr 15:21.

**4:3** *Love what is worthless…lies:* these expressions probably refer to false gods worshiped by those the psalmist is addressing.

**4:5** *Tremble:* be moved deeply with fear for failing to worship the true God. The Greek translation understood the emotion to

be anger, and it is so cited in Eph 4:26. *Weep bitterly…wail:* weeping within one's heart and wailing upon one's bed denote sincere repentance because these actions are not done in public or with the community but in the privacy of one's heart and one's home. The same idiom is found in Hos 7:14.

**4:9** *In peace I will…fall asleep:* the last verse repeats two themes in the Psalm. One is the security of one who trusts in the true God; the other is the interior peace of those who sincerely repent ("on [their] beds"), whose sleep is not disturbed by a guilty conscience.

**Psalm 5** A lament contrasting the security of the house of God (Ps 5:8–9, 12–13) with the danger of the company of evildoers (Ps 5:5–7, 10–11). The psalmist therefore prays that God will hear (Ps 5:2–4) and grant the protection and joy of the Temple.

---

**3:3** Ps 71:11.
**3:4** Ps 7:11; 18:3; 62:7–8;
  Dt 33:29; Is 60:19.
**3:6** Ps 4:9; Prv 3:24.
**3:8** Ps 58:7.
**3:9** Ps 28:9; Jon 2:10.
**4:2** Ps 118:5.
**4:3** Ps 62:4.
**4:5** Eph 4:26.
**4:6** Ps 51:19.
**4:7** Ps 31:17; 44:4; 67:1;
  80:4; Jb 13:24; Nm
  6:25; Dn 9:17.
**4:9** Ps 3:6.
**5:2** Ps 86:6; 130:1–2.

in the morning I will plead before you
    and wait.*

**II**

5   You are not a god who delights in evil;
        no wicked person finds refuge with
            you;
6   the arrogant cannot stand before your
            eyes.
    You hate all who do evil;
7       you destroy those who speak falsely.*
    A bloody and fraudulent man
        the LORD abhors.

**III**

8   But I, through the abundance of your
            mercy,†
    will enter into your house.
    I will bow down toward your holy
            sanctuary
        out of fear of you.*
9   LORD, guide me in your justice because
            of my foes;
        make straight your way before me.*

**IV**

10  For there is no sincerity in their mouth;
        their heart is corrupt.
    Their throat† is an open grave;*
        on their tongue are subtle lies.
11  Declare them guilty, God;
        make them fall by their own devices.*
    Drive them out for their many sins;
        for they have rebelled against you.

**V**

12  Then all who trust in you will be glad
        and forever shout for joy.*
    You will protect them and those will
            rejoice in you
        who love your name.
13  For you, LORD, bless the just one;

you surround him with favor like a
    shield.

## PSALM 6†

### Prayer in Distress

1   For the leader; with stringed instruments,
            "upon the eighth."†
    A psalm of David.

**I**

2   Do not reprove me in your anger, LORD,
        nor punish me in your wrath.*
3   Have pity on me, LORD, for I am weak;
        heal me, LORD, for my bones are
            shuddering.*
4   My soul too is shuddering greatly—
        and you, LORD, how long...?†*
5   Turn back, LORD, rescue my soul;
        save me because of your mercy.
6   For in death there is no remembrance of
            you.
    Who praises you in Sheol?†*

**II**

7   I am wearied with sighing;
        all night long I drench my bed with
            tears;
    I soak my couch with weeping.
8   My eyes are dimmed with sorrow,
        worn out because of all my foes.*

**III**

9   Away from me, all who do evil!*
    The LORD has heard the sound of my
            weeping.
10  The LORD has heard my plea;
        the LORD will receive my prayer.
11  My foes will all be disgraced and will
            shudder greatly;
        they will turn back in sudden disgrace.*

---

**5:8** *Mercy*: used to translate the Hebrew word, *hesed*. This term speaks to a relationship between persons. It is manifested in concrete actions to persons with some need or desire. The one who offers *hesed* has the ability to respond to that need of the other person. Other possible ways to translate *hesed* include "steadfast love" and "loving kindness."

**5:10** *Their throat*: their speech brings harm to their hearers (cf. Jer 5:16). The verse mentions four parts of the body, each a source of evil to the innocent.

**Psalm 6** The first of the seven Penitential Psalms (Ps 6, 32, 38, 51, 102, 130, 143), a designation dating from the seventh century A.D. for Psalms suitable to express repentance. The psalmist does not, as in many laments, claim to be innocent but appeals to God's mercy (Ps 6:5). Sin here, as often in the Bible, is both the sinful act and its injurious consequences; here it is physical sickness (Ps 6:3–4, 7–8) and the attacks of enemies (Ps 6:8, 9, 11). The psalmist prays that the effects of personal and social sin be taken away.

**6:1** *Upon the eighth*: apparently a musical notation, now lost.
**6:4** *How long?*: elliptical for "How long will it be before you

answer my prayer?" cf. Ps 13:2–3.

**6:6** A motive for God to preserve the psalmist from death: in the shadowy world of the dead no one offers you praise. Sheol is the biblical term for the underworld where the insubstantial souls of dead human beings dwelt. It was similar to the Hades of Greek and Latin literature. In the second century B.C., biblical books begin to speak positively of life with God after death (Dn 12:1–3; Wis 3).

| | |
|---|---|
| **5:4** Wis 16:28. | **6:4** Ps 13:2–3; 74:10; |
| **5:7** Ps 101:7; Wis 14:9; | 89:47. |
| Heb 1:13. | **6:6** Ps 30:10; 88:11; |
| **5:8** Ps 138:2; Jon 2:5. | 115:17; Is 38:18. |
| **5:9** Ps 23:3; Prv 4:11; Is | **6:8** Ps 31:10; 38:11; |
| 26:7. | 40:13. |
| **5:10** Rom 3:13. | **6:9** Ps 119:115; Mt 7:23; |
| **5:11** Ps 141:10. | Lk 13:27. |
| **5:12** Ps 64:11. | **6:11** Ps 35:4, 26; 40:15; |
| **6:2** Ps 38:2. | 71:13. |
| **6:3** Jer 17:14–15. | |

**P**
**S**

## PSALM 7†

### God the Vindicator

¹ A plaintive song of David, which he sang
    to the L{{ORD}} concerning Cush,
      the Benjaminite.

**I**

² L{{ORD}} my God, in you I trusted;
    save me; rescue me from all who
      pursue me,*

³ Lest someone maul me like a lion,
    tear my soul apart with no one to
      deliver.

**II**

⁴ L{{ORD}} my God, if I have done this,†
    if there is guilt on my hands,

⁵ If I have maltreated someone treating
    me equitably—
    or even despoiled my oppressor
      without cause—

⁶ Then let my enemy pursue and overtake
    my soul,
    trample my life to the ground,
    and lay my honor in the dust.*   *Selah*

**III**

⁷ Rise up, L{{ORD}}, in your anger;
    be aroused against the outrages of my
      oppressors.*
    Stir up the justice, my God, you have
      commanded.

⁸ Have the assembly of the peoples gather
    about you;
    and return on high above them,

⁹ the L{{ORD}} will pass judgment on the
    peoples.
    Judge me, L{{ORD}}, according to my
      righteousness,
    and my integrity.

¹⁰ Let the malice of the wicked end.
    Uphold the just one,

O just God,*
    who tries hearts and minds.

**IV**

¹¹ God is a shield above me
    saving the upright of heart.*

¹² God is a just judge, powerful and
    patient,†
    not exercising anger every day.

¹³ If one does not repent,
    God sharpens his sword,
    strings and readies the bow,*

¹⁴ Prepares his deadly shafts,
    makes arrows blazing thunderbolts.*

**V**

¹⁵ Consider how one conceives iniquity;
    is pregnant with mischief,
    and gives birth to deception.*

¹⁶ He digs a hole and bores it deep,
    but he falls into the pit he has made.*

¹⁷ His malice turns back upon his head;
    his violence falls on his own skull.

**VI**

¹⁸ I will thank the L{{ORD}} in accordance with
    his justice;
    I will sing the name of the L{{ORD}} Most
      High.*

## PSALM 8†

### Divine Majesty and Human Dignity

¹ For the leader; "upon the *gittith*."†
    A psalm of David.

² O L{{ORD}}, our Lord,
    how awesome is your name through
      all the earth!

I will sing of your majesty above the
    heavens

³ with the mouths of babes* and
    infants.†

---

† **Psalm 7** An individual lament. The psalmist flees to God's presence in the sanctuary for justice and protection (Ps 7:2–3) and takes an oath that only the innocent can swear (Ps 7:4–6). The innocent psalmist can thus hope for the just God's protection (Ps 7:7–14) and be confident that the actions of the wicked will come back upon their own heads (Ps 7:15–17). The justice of God leads the psalmist to praise (Ps 7:18).

**7:4** *Have done this*: in the accusation the enemies have made against the psalmist.

**7:12** *Powerful and patient*: the inclusion of these words is drawn from the Septuagint tradition concerning this verse.

**Psalm 8** While marvelling at the limitless grandeur of God (Ps 8:2–3), the psalmist is struck first by the smallness of human beings in creation (Ps 8:4–5), and then by the royal dignity and power that God has graciously bestowed upon them (Ps 8:6–9).

**8:1** *Upon the gittith*: probably the title of the melody to which the Psalm was to be sung or a musical instrument.

**8:3** *With the mouths of babes and infants*: the psalmist realizes that his attempts to praise such an awesome God are hopelessly inadequate and amount to little more than the sounds made by infants. *Established a bulwark*: an allusion to lost myth telling how God built a fortress for himself in the heavens in primordial times in his battle with the powers of chaos. This "bulwark" is the firmament. *Enemy and avenger*: probably cosmic enemies. The primeval powers of watery chaos are often personified in poetic texts (Ps 74:13–14; 89:11; Jb 9:13; 26:12–13; Is 51:9).

---

| | |
|---|---|
| **7:2** Ps 6:5; 22:21. | **7:14** Is 50:11. |
| **7:6** Ps 143:3. | **7:15** Jb 15:35; Is 59:4. |
| **7:7** Ps 9:4; 19:20. | **7:16** Ps 9:16; 35:8; 57:7; |
| **7:10** Ps 17:3; 26:2; 35:24; |     Prv 26:27; Eccl 10:8; |
|     43:1; 139:23; Jer |     Sir 27:26. |
|     17:10; 20:12. | **7:18** Ps 18:50; 30:5; 135:3; |
| **7:11** Ps 3:4. |     146:2. |
| **7:13** Ps 11:2. | **8:3** Mt 21:16; Wis 10:21. |

You have established a bulwark† against
    your foes,
    to silence enemy and avenger.†

4   When I see your heavens, the work of
    your fingers,
    the moon and stars that you set in
    place—

5†  What is man that you are mindful of
    him,*
    and a son of man that you care for
    him?*

6   Yet you have made him little less than a
    god,†
    crowned him with glory and honor.

7   You have given him rule over the works
    of your hands,*
    put all things at his feet:

8   All sheep and oxen,
    even the beasts of the field,

9   The birds of the air, the fish of the sea,
    and whatever swims the paths of the
    seas.

10  O LORD, our Lord,
    how awesome is your name through
    all the earth!

## PSALM 9†

### Thanksgiving for Victory and Prayer for Justice

¹ For the leader; according to *Muth Labben*.†
A psalm of David.

**I**

2   I will praise you, LORD, with all my
    heart;
    I will declare all your wondrous
    deeds.

3   I will delight and rejoice in you;
    I will sing hymns to your name, Most
    High.

4   When my enemies turn back,
    they stumble and perish before you.

**II**

5   For you upheld my right and my cause,
    seated on your throne, judging justly.

6   You rebuked the nations, you destroyed
    the wicked;
    their name you blotted out for all
    time.*

7   The enemies have been ruined forever;
    you destroyed their cities;
    their memory has perished.

**III**

8   The LORD rules forever,
    has set up his throne for judgment.

9   It is he who judges the world with
    justice,*
    who judges the peoples with fairness.

10  The LORD is a stronghold for the
    oppressed,
    a stronghold in times of trouble.*

11  Those who know your name trust in
    you;
    you never forsake those who seek you,
    LORD.

**IV**

12  Sing hymns to the LORD enthroned on
    Zion;
    proclaim his deeds among the
    nations!

13  For the avenger of bloodshed
    remembers,
    does not forget the cry of the
    afflicted.*

**V**

14  Be gracious to me, LORD;
    see how my foes afflict me!
    You alone can raise me from the gates
    of death.*

15  Then I will declare all your praises,
    sing joyously of your salvation
    in the gates of daughter Zion.†

P
S

---

**8:5** *Man...a son of man*: the emphasis is on the fragility and mortality of human beings to whom God has given great dignity.
**8:6** *Little less than a god*: Hebrew *'elohim*, the ordinary word for "God" or "the gods" or members of the heavenly court. The Greek version translated *'elohim* by "angel, messenger"; several ancient and modern versions so translate. The meaning seems to be that God created human beings almost at the level of the beings in the heavenly world. Heb 2:9, translating "for a little while," finds the eminent fulfillment of this verse in Jesus Christ, who was humbled before being glorified, cf. also 1 Cor 15:27 where St. Paul applies to Christ the closing words of Ps 8:7.
**Psalms 9–10** Ps 9 and Ps 10 in the Hebrew text have been transmitted as separate poems but they actually form a single acrostic poem and are so transmitted in the Greek and Latin tradition. Each verse of the two Psalms begins with a succes-

sive letter of the Hebrew alphabet (though several letters have no corresponding stanza). The Psalm states loosely connected themes: the rescue of the helpless poor from their enemies, God's worldwide judgment and rule over the nations, the psalmist's own concern for rescue (Ps 9:14–15).
**9:1** *Muth Labben*: probably the melodic accompaniment of the Psalm, now lost.
**9:15** *Daughter Zion*: an ancient Near Eastern city could sometimes be personified as a woman or a queen, the spouse of the god of the city.

---

**8:5** Ps 144:3; Jb 7:17.    **9:9** Ps 96:10; 98:9.
**8:5** Heb 2:6ff.    **9:10** Ps 37:39; Is 25:4.
**8:7ff** Gn 1:26, 28; Wis 9:2;    **9:13** Jb 16:18.
    1 Cor 15:27.    **9:14** Wis 16:13.
**9:6** Jb 18:17.

## VI

16 The nations fall into the pit they dig;
    in the snare they hide, their own foot
        is caught.

17† The LORD is revealed in making
        judgments:
    by the deeds they do the wicked are
        trapped.*                Higgaion. Selah†

## VII

18 To Sheol the wicked will depart,
    all the nations that forget God.

19 For the needy will never be forgotten,
    nor will the hope of the afflicted ever
        fade.*

20 Arise, LORD, let no mortal prevail;
    let the nations be judged in your
        presence.

21 Strike them with terror, LORD;
    show the nations they are only
        human.                          Selah

## PSALM 10

### I

1 Why, LORD, do you stand afar
    and pay no heed in times of trouble?

2 Arrogant scoundrels pursue the poor;
    they trap them by their cunning
        schemes.*

### II

3 The wicked even boast of their greed;
    these robbers curse and scorn the
        LORD.*

4 In their insolence the wicked boast:
    "God does not care; there is no God."*

5 Yet their affairs always succeed;
    they ignore your judgment on high;
    they sneer at all who oppose them.

6 They say in their hearts, "We will never
        fall;
    never will we see misfortune."

7 Their mouths are full of oaths, violence,
        and lies;
    discord and evil are under their
        tongues.*

8 They wait in ambush near towns;
    their eyes watch for the helpless

to murder the innocent in secret.*

9 They lurk in ambush like lions in a
        thicket,
    hide there to trap the poor,
    snare them and close the net.*

10 The helpless are crushed, laid low;
    they fall into the power of the wicked,

11 Who say in their hearts, "God has
        forgotten,
    shows no concern, never bothers to
        look."*

### III

12 Rise up, LORD! God, lift up your hand!
    Do not forget the poor!

13 Why should the wicked scorn God,
    say in their hearts, "God does not
        care"?

14 But you do see;
    you take note of misery and sorrow;*
    you take the matter in hand.
    To you the helpless can entrust their
        cause;
    you are the defender of orphans.*

15 Break the arm of the wicked and
        depraved;
    make them account for their crimes;
    let none of them survive.

### IV

16 The LORD is king forever;*
    the nations have vanished from his
        land.

17 You listen, LORD, to the needs of the
        poor;
    you strengthen their heart and incline
        your ear.

18 You win justice for the orphaned and
        oppressed;*
    no one on earth will cause terror again.

## PSALM 11†

### Confidence in the Presence of God

1 For the leader. Of David.

### I

In the LORD I take refuge;
    how can you say to me,

---

**9:17** The LORD is revealed in making judgments: God has so made the universe that the wicked are punished by the very actions they perform. Selah: see note on Ps 3:3.
    **Psalm 11** A song of trust. Though friends counsel flight to the mountain country (a traditional hideout) to escape trouble (Ps 11:1–3), the innocent psalmist reaffirms confidence in God, who protects those who seek asylum in the Temple (Ps 11:4–7).

**9:17** Ps 35:8; Sir 27:26.
**9:19** Prv 23:18.
**10:2** Is 32:7.
**10:3** Ps 36:2.
**10:4** Ps 14:1; Jb 22:13; Is 29:15; Jer 5:12; Zep 1:12.
**10:7** Is 32:7; Rom 3:14.
**10:8** Ps 11:2; Jb 24:14.
**10:9** Ps 17:12; Prv 1:11;

Jer 5:26.
**10:11** Ps 44:25; 64:6; 73:11; 94:7; Ez 9:9.
**10:14** Ps 31:8; 56:9; 2 Kgs 20:5; Is 25:8; Rev 7:17.
**10:14** Ex 22:21–22.
**10:16** Ps 145:13; Jer 10:10.
**10:18** Dt 10:18.

"Flee like a bird to the mountains!*

2 See how the wicked string their bows,
fit their arrows to the string
to shoot from the shadows at the
upright of heart.*

3† If foundations are destroyed,
what can the just one do?"

**II**

4 The Lord is in his holy temple;
the Lord's throne is in heaven.*
God's eyes keep careful watch;
they test the children of Adam.

5 The Lord tests the righteous and the
wicked,
hates those who love violence,

6 And rains upon the wicked
fiery coals and brimstone,
a scorching wind their allotted cup.†*

7 The Lord is just and loves just deeds;
the upright will see his face.

## PSALM 12†

### Prayer Against Evil Tongues

1 For the leader; "upon the eighth."
A psalm of David.

**I**

2 Help, Lord, for no one loyal remains;
the faithful have vanished from the
children of men.*

3 They tell lies to one another,
speak with deceiving lips and a
double heart.*

**II**

4 May the Lord cut off all deceiving lips,
and every boastful tongue,

5 Those who say, "By our tongues we
prevail;
when our lips speak, who can lord it
over us?"*

**III**

6 "Because they rob the weak, and the
needy groan,
I will now arise," says the Lord;
"I will grant safety to whoever longs
for it."*

**IV**

7 The promises of the Lord are sure,
silver refined in a crucible,†
silver purified seven times.*

8 You, O Lord, protect us always;
preserve us from this generation.

9 On every side the wicked roam;
the shameless are extolled by the
children of men.

## PSALM 13†

### Prayer for Help

1 For the leader. A psalm of David.

**I**

2 How long, Lord? Will you utterly forget
me?
How long will you hide your face
from me?*

3 How long must I carry sorrow in my
soul,
grief in my heart day after day?
How long will my enemy triumph
over me?

**II**

4 Look upon me, answer me, Lord, my
God!
Give light to my eyes lest I sleep in
death,

5 Lest my enemy say, "I have prevailed,"
lest my foes rejoice at my downfall.*

**III**

6 But I trust in your mercy.
Grant my heart joy in your salvation,

---

† **11:3** *Foundations*: usually understood of public order, cf. Ps 82:5.

**11:6** *Their allotted cup*: the cup that God gives people to drink is a common figure for their destiny, cf. Ps 16:5; 75:9; Mt 20:22; 26:39; Rev 14:10.

**Psalm 12** A lament. The psalmist, thrown into a world where lying and violent people persecute the just (Ps 12:2–3), prays that the wicked be punished (Ps 12:4–5). The prayer is not simply for vengeance but arises from a desire to see God's justice appear on earth. Ps 12:6 preserves the word of assurance spoken by the priest to the lamenter; it is not usually transmitted in such Psalms. In Ps 12:7–8 the psalmist affirms the intention to live by the word of assurance.

**12:7** *A crucible*: lit., "in a crucible in the ground." The crucible was placed in the ground for support.

**Psalm 13** A typical lament, in which the psalmist feels forgot-ten by God (Ps 13:2–3)—note the force of the repetition of "How long." The references to enemies may suggest some have wished evil on the psalmist. The heartfelt prayer (Ps 13:4–5) passes on to a statement of trust (Ps 13:6a), intended to reinforce the prayer, and a vow to thank God when deliverance has come (Ps 13:6b).

---

*

**11:1** Ps 55:7; 91:4.
**11:2** Ps 7:13; 37:14; 57:5; 64:4.
**11:4** Ps 14:2; 102:20; Hb 2:20; Dt 26:15; Is 66:1; Mt 5:34.
**11:6** Ps 120:4; 140:11; Prv 16:27; Ez 38:22; Rev 8:5; 20:10.
**12:2** Ps 14:3; 116:11; Is 59:15; Mi 7:2.

**12:3** Ps 28:3; 55:22; Is 59:3–4; Jer 9:7.
**12:5** Sir 5:3.
**12:6** Is 33:10.
**12:7** Ps 18:31; 19:8; Prv 30:5.
**13:2** Ps 6:4; 44:25; 77:8; 79:5; 89:47; 94:3; Lam 5:20.
**13:5** Ps 38:17.

I will sing to the LORD,
  for he has dealt bountifully
    with me!*

## PSALM 14†

### A Lament over Widespread Corruption

¹ For the leader. Of David.

**I**

The fool says in his heart,
  "There is no God."
Their deeds are loathsome and
    corrupt;
  not one does what is good.*

² The LORD looks down from heaven
  upon the children of men,*
To see if even one is wise,
  if even one seeks God.*

³ All have gone astray;
  all alike are perverse.
Not one does what is good,
  not even one.*

**II**

⁴ Will these evildoers never learn?
  They devour my people as they devour
    bread;*
  they do not call upon the LORD.*

⁵ They have good reason, then, to fear;
  God is with the company of the
    just.

⁶ They would crush the hopes of the
    poor,
  but the poor have the LORD as their
    refuge.

**III**

⁷* Oh, that from Zion might come
  the salvation of Israel!
Jacob would rejoice, and Israel be glad
  when the LORD restores his people!†

## PSALM 15†

### The Righteous Israelite

¹* A psalm of David.

**I**

LORD, who may abide in your tent?†
  Who may dwell on your holy
    mountain?†

**II**

² Whoever walks without blame,*
  doing what is right,
  speaking truth from the heart;

³ Who does not slander with his tongue,
  does no harm to a friend,
  never defames a neighbor;

⁴ Who disdains the wicked,
  but honors those who fear the LORD;
  Who keeps an oath despite the cost,

⁵ lends no money at interest,†
  accepts no bribe against the
    innocent.*

**III**

Whoever acts like this
  shall never be shaken.

## PSALM 16†

### God the Supreme Good

¹* A *miktam*† of David.

**I**

Keep me safe, O God;
  in you I take refuge.

² I say to the LORD,
  you are my Lord,
  you are my only good.

³ As for the holy ones who are in the
    land,
  they are noble,
  in whom is all my delight.

---

† **Psalm 14** The lament (duplicated in Ps 53) depicts the world as consisting of two types of people: "the fool" (equals the wicked, Ps 14:1–3) and "the company of the just" (Ps 14:4–6; also called "my people," and "the poor"). The wicked persecute the just, but the Psalm expresses the hope that God will punish the wicked and reward the good.

**14:7** *Jacob…Israel…his people*: the righteous poor are identified with God's people.

**Psalm 15** The Psalm records a liturgical scrutiny at the entrance to the Temple court (cf. Ps 24:3–6; Is 33:14b–16). The Israelite wishing to be admitted had to ask the Temple official what conduct was appropriate to God's precincts. Note the emphasis on virtues relating to one's neighbor.

**15:1** *Your tent*: the Temple could be referred to as "tent" (Ps 61:5; Is 33:20), a reference to the tent of the wilderness period and the tent of David (2 Sm 6:17; 7:2), predecessors of the Temple. *Holy mountain*: a venerable designation of the divine abode (Ps 2:6; 3:5; 43:3; 48:2, etc.).

**15:5** *Lends no money at interest*: lending money in the Old Testament was often seen as assistance to the poor in their distress, not as an investment; making money off the poor by charging interest was thus forbidden (Ex 22:24; Lv 25:36–37; Dt 23:20).

**Psalm 16** In the first section, the psalmist rejects the futile worship of false gods (Ps 16:2–5), preferring Israel's God (Ps 16:1), the giver of the land (Ps 16:6). The second section reflects on the wise and life-giving presence of God (Ps 16:7–11).

**16:1** *Miktam*: a term occurring six times in Psalm superscriptions, always with "David." Its meaning is unknown.

* —

| | |
|---|---|
| **13:6** Ps 116:7. | **14:4** Ps 79:6. |
| **14:1** Ps 10:4; 36:2; Is 32:6; | **14:7** Ps 85:2. |
| Jer 5:12. | **15:1** Is 56:7. |
| **14:2–3** Rom 3:11–12. | **15:2** Ps 119:1. |
| **14:2** Ps 11:4; 102:20. | **15:5** Ex 22:24; 23:8. |
| **14:3** Ps 12:1. | **16:1** Ps 25:20. |
| **14:4** Ps 27:2; Is 9:11. | |

4† They multiply their sorrows
      who court other gods.
  Blood libations to them I will not pour
      out,
      nor will I take their names upon my
      lips.
5 LORD, my allotted portion and my cup,
      you have made my destiny secure.*
6† Pleasant places were measured out for
      me;
      fair to me indeed is my inheritance.

**II**

7 I bless the LORD who counsels me;
      even at night my heart exhorts me.
8 I keep the LORD always before me;
      with him at my right hand, I shall
      never be shaken.*
9 Therefore my heart is glad, my soul
      rejoices;
      my body also dwells secure,
10 For you will not abandon my soul to
      Sheol,
      nor let your devout one see the pit.†*
11 You will show me the path to life,
      abounding joy in your presence,
      the delights at your right hand forever.

**PSALM 17†**

**Prayer for Rescue from Persecutors**

¹ A prayer of David.

**I**

  Hear, LORD, my plea for justice;
      pay heed to my cry;
  Listen to my prayer
      from lips without guile.
2 From you let my vindication come;
      your eyes see what is right.
3 You have tested my heart,
      searched it in the night.*
  You have tried me by fire,

  but find no malice in me.
  My mouth has not transgressed
4     as others often do.
  As your lips have instructed me,
      I have kept from the way of the lawless.
5 My steps have kept to your paths;
      my feet have not faltered.*

**II**

6 I call upon you; answer me, O God.
      Turn your ear to me; hear my speech.
7 Show your wonderful mercy,
      you who deliver with your right arm
      those who seek refuge from their foes.
8† Keep me as the apple of your eye;
      hide me in the shadow of your wings
9     from the wicked who despoil me.*

**III**

  My ravenous enemies press upon me;*
10†    they close their hearts,
      they fill their mouths with proud
      roaring.
11 Their steps even now encircle me;
      they watch closely, keeping low to the
      ground,
12 Like lions eager for prey,
      like a young lion lurking in ambush.
13 Rise, O LORD, confront and cast them
      down;
      rescue my soul from the wicked.
14 Slay them with your sword;
      with your hand, LORD, slay them;
      snatch them from the world in their
      prime.
  Their bellies are being filled with your
      friends;
      their children are satisfied too,
      for they share what is left with their
      young.
15 I am just—let me see your face;
      when I awake, let me be filled with
      your presence.*

---

† **16:4** *Take their names*: to use the gods' names in oaths and hence to affirm them as one's own gods.
  **16:6** *Pleasant places were measured out for me*: the psalmist is pleased with the plot of land measured out to the family, which was to be passed on to succeeding generations ("my inheritance").
  **16:10** *Nor let your devout one see the pit*: Hebrew *shahath* means here the pit, a synonym for Sheol, the underworld. The Greek translation derives the word here and elsewhere from the verb *shahath*, "to be corrupt." On the basis of the Greek, Acts 2:25–32; 13:35–37 apply the verse to Christ's resurrection, "Nor will you suffer your holy one to see corruption."
  **Psalm 17** A lament of an individual unjustly attacked. Confident of being found innocent, the psalmist cries out for God's just judgment (Ps 17:1–5) and requests divine help against enemies (Ps 17:6–9a). Those ravenous lions (Ps 17:9b–12) should be pun-

ished (Ps 17:13–14). The Psalm ends with a serene statement of praise (Ps 17:15). The Hebrew text of Ps 17:3–4, 14 is uncertain.
  **17:8** *Apple of your eye…shadow of your wings*: images of God's special care, cf. Dt 32:10; Prv 7:2; Is 49:2.
  **17:10–12, 14** An extended metaphor: the enemies are lions.

**16:5** Ps 23:5; 73:26; Nm 18:20; Lam 3:24.
**16:8** Ps 73:23; 121:5, 8–12; Acts 2:25–28.
**16:10** Ps 28:1; 30:4; 49:16; 86:13; Jon 2:7; Acts 13:35.
**17:3** Ps 26:2; 139:23.
**17:5** Ps 18:36; Jb 23:11–12.
**17:9–12** Ps 10:9; 22:14, 22; 35:17; 58:7; Jb 4:10–11.
**17:9** Ps 36:8; 57:2; 61:5; 63:8; 91:4; Dt 32:10; Ru 2:12; Zec 2:12; Mt 23:37.
**17:15** Ps 4:7; 31:17; 67:2; 80:4; Nm 6:25; Dn 9:17.

## PSALM 18†

### A King's Thanksgiving for Victory

¹ For the leader. Of David, the servant of the LORD, who sang to the LORD the words of this song after the LORD had rescued him from the clutches of all his enemies and from the hand of Saul. ² He said:*

**I**

I love you, LORD, my strength,
³    LORD, my rock, my fortress, my
         deliverer,
    My God, my rock of refuge,
         my shield, my saving horn,† my
         stronghold!*
⁴    Praised be the LORD, I exclaim!
    I have been delivered from my
         enemies.

**II**

⁵    The cords of death encompassed me;
    the torrents of destruction terrified
         me.
⁶    The cords† of Sheol encircled me;
    the snares of death lay in wait for
         me.*
⁷    In my distress I called out: LORD!
    I cried out to my God.*
    From his temple he heard my voice;
    my cry to him reached his ears.
⁸†    The earth rocked and shook;
    the foundations of the mountains
         trembled;
    they shook as his wrath flared up.*
⁹    Smoke rose from his nostrils,
    a devouring fire from his mouth;
    it kindled coals into flame.
¹⁰    He parted the heavens and came down,
    a dark cloud under his feet.*
¹¹    Mounted on a cherub† he flew,
    borne along on the wings of the wind.

¹²    He made darkness his cloak around
         him;
    his canopy, water-darkened
         stormclouds.
¹³    From the gleam before him, his clouds
         passed,
    hail and coals of fire.*
¹⁴    The LORD thundered from heaven;
    the Most High made his voice
         resound.*
¹⁵    He let fly his arrows† and scattered
         them;
    shot his lightning bolts and dispersed
         them.*
¹⁶    Then the bed of the sea appeared;
    the world's foundations lay bare,*
    At your rebuke, O LORD,
    at the storming breath of your nostrils.
¹⁷    He reached down from on high and
         seized me;
    drew me out of the deep waters.*
¹⁸    He rescued me from my mighty enemy,
    from foes too powerful for me.
¹⁹    They attacked me on my day of distress,
    but the LORD was my support.
²⁰    He set me free in the open;
    he rescued me because he loves me.

**III**

²¹    The LORD acknowledged my
         righteousness,
    rewarded my clean hands.*
²²    For I kept the ways of the LORD;
    I was not disloyal to my God.
²³    For his laws were all before me,
    his decrees I did not cast aside.
²⁴    I was honest toward him;
    I was on guard against sin.
²⁵    So the LORD rewarded my righteousness,
    the cleanness of my hands in his
         sight.

---

† **Psalm 18** A royal thanksgiving for a military victory, duplicated in 2 Sm 22. Thanksgiving Psalms are in essence reports of divine rescue. The Psalm has two parallel reports of rescue, the first told from a heavenly perspective (Ps 18:5–20), and the second from an earthly perspective (Ps 18:36–46). The first report adapts old mythic language of a cosmic battle between sea and rainstorm in order to depict God's rescue of the Israelite king from his enemies. Each report has a short hymnic introduction (Ps 18:2–4, 32–36) and conclusion (Ps 18:21–31, 47–50).

**18:3** *My saving horn*: my strong savior. The horn referred to is the weapon of a bull and the symbol of fertility, cf. 1 Sm 2:10; Ps 132:17; Lk 1:69.

**18:6** *Cords*: hunting imagery, the cords of a snare.

**18:8–16** God appears in the storm, which in Palestine comes from the west. The introduction to the theophany (Ps 18:8–9) is probably a description of a violent, hot, and dry east-wind storm. In the fall transition period from the rainless summer to

the rainy winter such storms regularly precede the rains, cf. Ex 14:21–22.

**18:11** *Cherub*: a winged creature, derived from myth, in the service of the deity (Gn 3:24; Ex 25:18–20; 37:6–9). Cherubim were the throne bearers of the deity (Ps 80:2; 99:1; 1 Kgs 6:23–28; 8:6–8).

**18:15** *Arrows*: lightning.

---

18:2–51 2 Sm 22:2–51.
    18:3 Ps 3:4; 31:3–4; 42:10;
         Gn 49:24; Dt 32:4.
    18:6 Ps 88:8; 93:3–4;
         116:3–4.
    18:7 Jon 2:3.
    18:8 Ps 97:3–4; 99:1; Jgs
         5:4–5; Is 64:1; Heb
         3:9–11.
18:10 Ps 104:3; 144:5; Is
         63:19.
18:13 Ex 13:21; 19:16.
18:14 Ps 29; 77:19; Ex
         19:19; Jb 37:3–4.
18:15 Ps 144:6; Wis 5:21.
18:16 Ps 77:17; Zec 9:14.
18:17 Ps 144:7.
18:21 Ps 26; 1 Sm 26:23.

26 Toward the faithful you are faithful;
to the honest man you are honest;*

27 Toward the pure, you are pure;
but to the perverse you are devious.

28 For humble people you save;
haughty eyes you bring low.*

29 For you, LORD, give light to my lamp;
my God brightens my darkness.*

30 With you I can rush an armed band,
with my God to help I can leap a
wall.

31 God's way is unerring;
the LORD's promise is refined;
he is a shield for all who take refuge
in him.*

### IV

32 Truly, who is God except the LORD?
Who but our God is the rock?*

33 This God who girded me with might,
kept my way unerring,

34 Who made my feet like a deer's,
and set me on the heights,*

35 Who trained my hands for war,
my arms to string a bow of bronze.†*

### V

36 You have given me your saving shield;
your right hand has upheld me;
your favor made me great.

37 You made room for my steps beneath
me;
my ankles never twisted.*

38 I pursued my enemies and overtook
them;
I did not turn back till I destroyed
them.

39 I decimated them; they could not rise;
they fell at my feet.

40 You girded me with valor for war,
subjugated my opponents beneath
me.

41 You made my foes expose their necks to
me;
those who hated me I silenced.

42 They cried for help, but no one saved
them;

cried to the LORD but received no
answer.

43 I ground them to dust before the wind;
I left them like mud in the streets.

44 You rescued me from the strife of
peoples;
you made me head over nations.
A people I had not known served me;

45 as soon as they heard of me they
obeyed.
Foreigners submitted before me;

46 foreigners cringed;
they came cowering from their
dungeons.*

### VI

47 The LORD lives! Blessed be my rock!*
Exalted be God, my savior!

48 O God who granted me vengeance,
made peoples subject to me,*

49 and saved me from my enemies,
Truly you have elevated me above my
opponents,
from a man of lawlessness you have
rescued me.

50 Thus I will praise you, LORD, among the
nations;
I will sing praises to your name.*

51 You have given great victories to your
king,
and shown mercy to his anointed,
to David and his posterity forever.*

## PSALM 19†

## God's Glory in the Heavens and in the Law

1 For the leader. A psalm of David.

### I

2 The heavens declare the glory of God;
the firmament proclaims the works of
his hands.*

3 Day unto day pours forth speech;
night unto night whispers knowledge.

4† There is no speech, no words;
their voice is not heard;

5 A report goes forth through all the earth,

---

† **18:35** *Bow of bronze*: hyperbole for a bow difficult to bend and therefore capable of propelling an arrow with great force.
**Psalm 19** The heavenly elements of the world, now beautifully arranged, bespeak the power and wisdom of their creator (Ps 19:2–7). The creator's wisdom is available to human beings in the law (Ps 19:8–11), toward which the psalmist prays to be open (Ps 19:12–14). The themes of light and speech unify the poem.
**19:4** *No speech, no words*: the regular functioning of the heavens and the alternation of day and night inform human beings without words of the creator's power and wisdom.

**18:26** Ps 125:4.
**18:28** Jb 22:29; Prv 3:34.
**18:29** Ps 27:1; 36:10; 43:3;
119:105; Jb 29:3; Mi
7:8.
**18:31** Ps 12:6; 77:13; Prv
30:5.
**18:32** Is 44:8; 45:21.
**18:34** Heb 3:19.
**18:35** Ps 144:1.
**18:37** Ps 17:5.
**18:46** Mi 7:17.
**18:47** Ps 144:1.
**18:48** Ps 144:2.
**18:50** Ps 7:18; 30:5; 57:9;
135:3; 146:2; Rom
15:9.
**18:51** Ps 89:28–37; 144:10;
1 Sm 2:10.
**19:2** Ps 8:1; 50:6; 97:6.

P
S

their messages, to the ends of the
world.
He has pitched in them a tent for the
sun;†

6    it comes forth like a bridegroom from
his canopy,
and like a hero joyfully runs its
course.

7    From one end of the heavens it comes
forth;
its course runs through to the other;
nothing escapes its heat.

**II**

8    The law of the LORD is perfect,
refreshing the soul.
The decree of the LORD is trustworthy,
giving wisdom to the simple.*

9    The precepts of the LORD are right,
rejoicing the heart.
The command of the LORD is clear,
enlightening the eye.

10   The fear of the LORD is pure,
enduring forever.
The statutes of the LORD are true,
all of them just;

11   More desirable than gold,
than a hoard of purest gold,
Sweeter also than honey
or drippings from the comb.*

12   By them your servant is warned;†
obeying them brings much reward.

**III**

13   Who can detect trespasses?
Cleanse me from my inadvertent sins.

14   Also from arrogant ones restrain your
servant;
let them never control me.
Then shall I be blameless,
innocent of grave sin.

15   Let the words of my mouth be acceptable,
the thoughts of my heart before you,
LORD, my rock and my redeemer.

## PSALM 20†

### Prayer for the King in Time of War

1 For the leader. A psalm of David.

**I**

2    The LORD answer you in time of distress;
the name of the God of Jacob defend
you!

3    May he send you help from the
sanctuary,
from Zion be your support.*

4    May he remember† your every offering,
graciously accept your burnt offering,
                       *Selah*

5    Grant what is in your heart,
fulfill your every plan.

6    May we shout for joy at your victory,†
raise the banners in the name of our
God.
The LORD grant your every petition!

**II**

7    Now I know the LORD gives victory
to his anointed.*
He will answer him from the holy
heavens
with a strong arm that brings victory.

8    Some rely on chariots, others on horses,
but we on the name of the LORD our
God.*

9    They collapse and fall,
but we stand strong and firm.*

10   LORD, grant victory to the king;
answer when we call upon you.

## PSALM 21†

### Thanksgiving and Assurances for the King

1 For the leader. A psalm of David.

**I**

2    LORD, the king finds joy in your power;*
in your victory how greatly he
rejoices!

---

† **19:5** *The sun*: in other religious literature the sun is a judge and lawgiver since it sees all in its daily course; Ps 19:5b–7 form a transition to the law in Ps 19:8–11. The six synonyms for God's revelation (Ps 19:8–11) are applied to the sun in comparable literature.

**19:12** *Warned*: the Hebrew verb means both to shine and to warn, cf. Dn 12:3.

**Psalm 20** The people pray for the king before battle. The people ask for divine help (Ps 20:2–6) and express confidence that such help will be given (Ps 20:7–10). A solemn assurance of divine help may well have been given between the two sections in the liturgy, something like the promises of Ps 12:6; 21:9–13. The final verse (Ps 20:10) echoes the opening verse.

**20:4** *Remember*: God's remembering implies readiness to act, cf. Gn 8:1; Ex 2:24.

**20:6** *Victory*: the Hebrew root is often translated "salvation,"

"to save;" but in military contexts it can have the specific meaning of "victory."

**Psalm 21** The first part of this royal Psalm is a thanksgiving (Ps 21:2–8), and the second is a promise that the king will triumph over his enemies (Ps 21:9–13). The king's confident prayer (Ps 21:3–5) and trust in God (Ps 21:8) enable him to receive the divine gifts of vitality, peace, and military success. Ps 21:14 reprises Ps 21:2. When kings ceased in Israel after the sixth century B.C., the Psalm was sung of a future Davidic king.

**19:8** Ps 12:7; 119.
**19:11** Sir 24:19.
**20:3** Ps 128:5; 134:3.
**20:7** Ps 18:51; 144:10;
    1 Sm 2:10.

**20:8** Ps 147:10–11; 2 Chr
    14:10; Prv 21:31;
    1 Sm 17:45; Is 31:1;
    36:9.
**20:9** Is 40:30.
**21:2** Ps 63:12.

PS

3  You have granted him his heart's
      desire;
   you did not refuse the request of his
      lips.                              *Selah*
4  For you welcomed him with goodly
      blessings;
   you placed on his head a crown of
      pure gold.
5  He asked life of you;
   you gave it to him,
      length of days forever.*
6  Great is his glory in your victory;
   majesty and splendor you confer
      upon him.
7  You make him the pattern of blessings
      forever,
   you gladden him with the joy of your
      face.
8  For the king trusts in the LORD,
   stands firm through the mercy of the
      Most High.

**II**

9  Your hand will find all your enemies;
   your right hand will find your foes!
10  At the time of your coming
   you will make them a fiery furnace.
   Then the LORD in his anger will consume
      them,
   devour them with fire.
11  Even their descendants you will wipe
      out from the earth,
   their offspring from the human
      race.
12  Though they intend evil against you,
   devising plots, they will not succeed,
13  For you will put them to flight;
   you will aim at their faces with your
      bow.

**III**

14  Arise, LORD, in your power!*
   We will sing and chant the praise of
      your might.

## PSALM 22†

### The Prayer of an Innocent Person

1 For the leader; according to "The deer of the
      dawn."† A psalm of David.

**I**

2  My God, my God, why have you
      abandoned me?
   Why so far from my call for help,
   from my cries of anguish?*
3  My God, I call by day, but you do not
      answer;
   by night, but I have no relief.*
4  Yet you are enthroned as the Holy One;
   you are the glory of Israel.*
5  In you our fathers trusted;
   they trusted and you rescued them.
6  To you they cried out and they escaped;
   in you they trusted and were not
      disappointed.*
7† But I am a worm, not a man,
   scorned by men, despised by the
      people.*
8  All who see me mock me;
   they curl their lips and jeer;
   they shake their heads at me:*
9  "He relied on the LORD—let him deliver
      him;
   if he loves him, let him rescue him."*
10  For you drew me forth from the womb,
   made me safe at my mother's breasts.
11  Upon you I was thrust from the womb;
   since my mother bore me you are my
      God.*
12  Do not stay far from me,
   for trouble is near,
   and there is no one to help.*

**II**

13  Many bulls† surround me;
   fierce bulls of Bashan† encircle me.
14  They open their mouths against me,
   lions that rend and roar.*

---

**Psalm 22** A lament unusual in structure and in intensity of feeling. The psalmist's present distress is contrasted with God's past mercy in Ps 22:2–12. In Ps 22:13–22 enemies surround the psalmist. The last third is an invitation to praise God (Ps 22:23–27), becoming a universal chorus of praise (Ps 22:28–31). The Psalm is important in the New Testament. Its opening words occur on the lips of the crucified Jesus (Mk 15:34; Mt 27:46), and several other verses are quoted, or at least alluded to, in the accounts of Jesus' passion (Mt 27:35, 43; Jn 19:24).

**22:1** *The deer of the dawn*: apparently the title of the melody.

**22:7** *I am a worm, not a man*: the psalmist's sense of isolation and dehumanization, an important motif of Ps 22, is vividly portrayed here.

**22:13–14** *Bulls*: the enemies of the psalmist are also por-

trayed in less-than-human form, as wild animals (cf. Ps 22:17, 21–22). *Bashan*: a grazing land northeast of the Sea of Galilee, famed for its cattle, cf. Dt 32:14; Ez 39:18; Am 4:1.

---

**21:5** 1 Kgs 3:14.
**21:14** Nm 10:35.
**22:2** Is 49:14; 54:7; Mt 27:46; Mk 15:34.
**22:3** Sir 2:10.
**22:4** Is 6:3.
**22:6** Ps 25:3; Is 49:23; Dn 3:40.
**22:7** Is 53:3.
**22:8** Ps 109:25; Mt 27:39; Mk 15:29; Lk 23:35.
**22:9** Ps 71:11; Wis 2:18–20; Mt 27:43.
**22:11** Ps 71:6; Is 44:2; 46:3.
**22:12** Ps 35:22; 38:22; 71:12.
**22:14** Ps 17:12; Jb 4:10; 1 Pt 5:8.

15　Like water my life drains away;
　　all my bones are disjointed.
　　My heart has become like wax,
　　it melts away within me.

16　As dry as a potsherd is my throat;
　　my tongue cleaves to my palate;
　　you lay me in the dust of death.†

17　Dogs surround me;
　　a pack of evildoers closes in on me.
　　They have pierced my hands and my feet

18　I can count all my bones.*
　　They stare at me and gloat;

19　they divide my garments among
　　　them;
　　for my clothing they cast lots.*

20　But you, LORD, do not stay far off;
　　my strength, come quickly to help me.

21　Deliver my soul from the sword,
　　my life from the grip of the dog.

22　Save me from the lion's mouth,
　　my poor life from the horns of wild
　　　bulls.*

### III

23　Then I will proclaim your name to my
　　　brethren;
　　in the assembly I will praise you:†*

24　"You who fear the LORD, give praise!
　　All descendants of Jacob, give honor;
　　show reverence, all descendants of
　　　Israel!

25　For he has not spurned or disdained
　　the misery of this poor wretch,
　　Did not turn away† from me,
　　but heard me when I cried out.

26　I will offer praise in the great assembly;
　　my vows I will fulfill before those
　　　who fear him.

27　The poor† will eat their fill;
　　those who seek the LORD will offer
　　　praise.
　　May your hearts enjoy life forever!"*

### IV

28　All the ends of the earth
　　will remember and turn to the LORD;
　　All the families of nations
　　will bow low before him.*

29　For kingship belongs to the LORD,
　　the ruler over the nations.*

30†　All who sleep in the earth
　　will bow low before God;
　　All who have gone down into the dust
　　will kneel in homage.

31　And I will live for the LORD;
　　my descendants will serve you.

32　The generation to come will be told of
　　　the Lord,
　　that they may proclaim to a people
　　　yet unborn
　　the deliverance you have brought.*

## PSALM 23†

### The Lord, Shepherd and Host

¹A psalm of David.

### I

　The LORD is my shepherd;†
　　there is nothing I lack.*

2　In green pastures he makes me lie down;
　　to still waters he leads me;

3*　he restores my soul.
　　He guides me along right paths†
　　for the sake of his name.

4　Even though I walk through the valley of
　　the shadow of death,*

---

† **22:16** *The dust of death*: the netherworld, the domain of the dead.

**22:23** *In the assembly I will praise you*: the person who offered a thanksgiving sacrifice in the Temple recounted to the other worshipers the favor received from God and invited them to share in the sacrificial banquet. The final section (Ps 22:24–32) may be a summary or a citation of the psalmist's poem of praise.

**22:25** *Turn away*: lit., "hides his face from me," an important metaphor for God withdrawing from someone, e.g., Mi 3:4; Is 8:17; Ps 27:9; 69:18; 88:15.

**22:27** *The poor*: originally the poor, who were dependent on God; the term ('anawim) came to include the religious sense of "humble, pious, devout."

**22:30** Hebrew unclear. The translation assumes that all on earth (Ps 22:27–28) and under the earth (Ps 22:29) will worship God.

**Psalm 23** God's loving care for the psalmist is portrayed under the figures of a shepherd for the flock (Ps 23:1–4) and a host's generosity toward a guest (Ps 23:5–6). The imagery of both sections is drawn from traditions of the exodus (Is 40:11; 49:10; Jer 31:10).

**23:1** *My shepherd*: God as good shepherd is common in both the Old Testament and the New Testament (Ez 34:11–16; Jn 10:11–18).

**23:3** *Right paths*: connotes "right way" and "way of righteousness."

**23:5** *You set a table before me*: this expression occurs in an exodus context in Ps 78:19. *In front of my enemies*: my enemies see that I am God's friend and guest. *Oil*: a perfumed ointment made from olive oil, used especially at banquets (Ps 104:15; Mt 26:7; Lk 7:37, 46; Jn 12:2).

**22:18** Ps 109:24.
**22:19** Mt 27:35; Mk 15:24; Lk 23:34; Jn 19:24.
**22:22** Ps 7:2–3; 17:12; 35:17; 57:5; 58:7; 2 Tm 4:17.
**22:23** Ps 26:12; 35:18; 40:10; 109:30; 149:1; 2 Sm 22:50; Heb 2:12.
**22:27** Ps 23:5; 69:33.
**22:28** Ps 86:9; Tb 13:11; Is 45:22; 52:10; Zec 14:16.
**22:29** Ps 103:19; Ob 21; Zec 14:9.
**22:32** Ps 48:14–15; 71:18; 78:6; 102:19; Is 53:10.
**23:1** Ps 80:2; 95:7; 100:3; Dt 2:7.
**23:3** Prv 4:11.
**23:4** Jb 10:21–22; Is 50:10.

I will fear no evil, for you are with me;
   your rod and your staff comfort me.

**II**

5†  You set a table before me
      in front of my enemies;†
   You anoint my head with oil;†*
      my cup overflows.*

6  Indeed, goodness and mercy† will
         pursue me
      all the days of my life;
   I will dwell in the house of the LORD*
      for endless days.

## PSALM 24†

### The Glory of God in Procession to Zion

¹ A psalm of David.

**I**

The earth is the LORD's and all it holds,*
   the world and those who dwell in it.

2  For he founded it on the seas,
      established it over the rivers.*

**II**

3  Who may go up the mountain of the
         LORD?*
   Who can stand in his holy place?

4†  "The clean of hand and pure of heart,
      who has not given his soul to useless
         things,
      what is vain.

5  He will receive blessings from the LORD,
      and justice from his saving God.

6  Such is the generation that seeks him,
      that seeks the face of the God of
         Jacob."                    *Selah*

**III**

7  Lift up your heads, O gates;†
      be lifted, you ancient portals,
      that the king of glory may enter.*

8  Who is this king of glory?
      The LORD, strong and mighty,

the LORD, mighty in war.

9  Lift up your heads, O gates;
      rise up, you ancient portals,
      that the king of glory may enter.

10  Who is this king of glory?
      The LORD of hosts, he is the king of
         glory.                    *Selah*

## PSALM 25†

### Confident Prayer for Forgiveness
### and Guidance

¹ Of David.

**I**

To you, O LORD, I lift up my soul,
2*      my God, in you I trust;
      do not let me be disgraced;*
      do not let my enemies gloat over me.

3  No one is disgraced who waits for you,*
      but only those who are treacherous
         without cause.

4  Make known to me your ways, LORD;
      teach me your paths.*

5  Guide me by your fidelity and teach me,
      for you are God my savior,
      for you I wait all the day long.

6  Remember your compassion and your
         mercy, O LORD,
      for they are ages old.*

7  Remember no more the sins of my
         youth;*
      remember me according to your
         mercy,
      because of your goodness, LORD.

**II**

8  Good and upright is the LORD,
      therefore he shows sinners the way,

9  He guides the humble in righteousness,
      and teaches the humble his way.

10  All the paths of the LORD are mercy and
         truth

---

**23:6** *Goodness and mercy*: the blessings of God's covenant with Israel.

**Psalm 24** The Psalm apparently accompanied a ceremony of the entry of God (invisibly enthroned upon the ark), followed by the people, into the Temple. The Temple commemorated the creation of the world (Ps 24:1–2). The people had to affirm their fidelity before being admitted into the sanctuary (Ps 24:3–6; cf. Ps 15). A choir identifies the approaching God and invites the very Temple gates to bow down in obeisance (Ps 24:7–10).

**24:4–5** Lit., "the one whose hands are clean." The singular is used for the entire class of worshipers.

**24:7, 9** *Lift up your heads, O gates…you ancient portals*: the literal meaning would involve disassembly of the gates, since the portcullis (a gate that moves up and down) was unknown in the ancient world. Extra-biblical parallels might also suggest a full personification of the circle of gate towers: they are like a

council of elders, bowed down and anxious, awaiting the return of the army and the great warrior gone to battle.

**Psalm 25** A lament. Each verse begins with a successive letter of the Hebrew alphabet. Such acrostic Psalms are often a series of statements only loosely connected. The psalmist mixes ardent pleas (Ps 25:1–2, 16–22) with expressions of confidence in God who forgives and guides.

---

23:5 Ps 92:11.
23:5 Ps 16:5.
23:6 Ps 27:4.
24:1 Ps 50:12; 89:12; Dt
   10:14; 1 Cor 10:26.
24:2 Ps 136:6; Is 42:5.
24:3 Ps 15:1.
24:7 Ps 118:19–20.
25:2 Ps 86:4; 143:8.

25:2 Ps 71:1.
25:3 Ps 22:6; Is 49:23; Dn
   3:40.
25:4 Ps 27:11; 86:11;
   119:12, 35; 143:8,
   10.
25:6 Sir 51:8.
25:7 Jb 13:26; Is 64:8.

toward those who honor his covenant
   and decrees.

11 For the sake of your name, LORD,
      pardon my guilt, though it is great.

12 Who is the one who fears the LORD?
      God shows him the way he should
         choose.*

13 He will abide in prosperity,
      and his descendants will inherit the
         land.*

14 The counsel of the LORD belongs to
         those who fear him;
      and his covenant instructs them.

15 My eyes are ever upon the LORD,
      who frees my feet from the snare.*

**III**

16 Look upon me, have pity on me,
      for I am alone and afflicted.*

17 Relieve the troubles of my heart;
      bring me out of my distress.

18 Look upon my affliction and suffering;
      take away all my sins.

19 See how many are my enemies,
      see how fiercely they hate me.

20 Preserve my soul and rescue me;
      do not let me be disgraced, for in you
         I seek refuge.

21 Let integrity and uprightness preserve me;
      I wait for you, O LORD.

22† Redeem Israel, O God,
      from all its distress!

## PSALM 26†

### Prayer of Innocence

¹ Of David.

**I**

Judge me, LORD!
   For I have walked in my integrity.*

In the LORD I trust;
   I do not falter.

2 Examine me, Lord, and test me;
      search my heart and mind.*

3 Your mercy is before my eyes;
      I walk guided by your faithfulness.*

**II**

4 I do not sit with worthless men,
      nor with hypocrites do I mingle.

5 I hate an evil assembly;
      with the wicked I do not sit.

6 I will wash my hands† in innocence*
      so that I may process around your
         altar, Lord,

7 To hear the sound of thanksgiving,
      and recount all your wondrous deeds.

8 Lord, I love the refuge of your house,
      the site of the dwelling-place of your
         glory.*

**III**

9 Do not take me away with sinners,
      nor my life with the men of blood,*

10 In whose hands there is a plot,
      their right hands full of bribery.

11 But I walk in my integrity;*
      redeem me, be gracious to me!*

12 My foot stands on level ground;†
      in assemblies I will bless the LORD.*

## PSALM 27†

### Trust in God

¹* Of David.

**A**

**I**

The LORD is my light and my salvation;
   whom should I fear?
The LORD is my life's refuge;
   of whom should I be afraid?

---

† **25:22** A final verse beginning with the Hebrew letter *pe* is added to the normal twenty-two-letter alphabet. Thus the letters *aleph, lamed,* and *pe* open the first, middle (Ps 25:11), and last lines of the Psalm. Together, they spell *aleph,* the first letter of the alphabet, from a Hebrew root that means "to learn."

**Psalm 26** Like a priest washing before approaching the altar (Ex 30:17–21), the psalmist seeks God's protection upon entering the Temple. Ps 26:1–3, matched by Ps 26:11–12, remind God of past integrity while asking for purification; Ps 26:4–5, matched by Ps 26:9–10, pray for inclusion among the just; Ps 26:6–8, the center of the poem, express the joy in God at the heart of all ritual.

**26:6** *I will wash my hands*: the washing of hands was a liturgical act (Ex 30:19, 21; 40:31–32), symbolic of inner as well as outer cleanness, cf. Is 1:16.

**26:12** *On level ground*: in safety, where there is no danger of tripping and falling. *In assemblies*: at the Temple. Having walked around the altar, the symbol of God's presence, the psalmist blesses God.

**Psalm 27** Tradition has handed down the two sections of the Psalm (Ps 27:1–6; 7–14) as one Psalm, though each part could be understood as complete in itself. Asserting boundless hope that God will bring rescue (Ps 27:1–3), the psalmist longs for the presence of God in the Temple, protection from all enemies (Ps 27:4–6). In part B there is a clear shift in tone (Ps 27:7–12); the climax of the poem comes with "I believe" (Ps 27:13), echoing "I trust" (Ps 27:3).

**25:12** Prv 19:23.
**25:13** Ps 37:9, 29.
**25:15** Ps 123:1, 2; 141:8.
**25:16** Ps 86:16; 119:132.
**26:1** Ps 7:9.
**26:2** Ps 17:3; 139:23.
**26:3** Ps 86:11.
**26:6** Ps 73:13.

**26:8** Ps 29:9; 63:3;
   Ex 24:16; 25:8.
**26:9** Ps 28:3.
**26:11** Ps 101:6.
**26:11** Ps 25:16.
**26:12** Ps 22:23; 35:18;
   149:1.
**27:1** Ps 18:29; 36:10; 43:3;
   Is 10:17; Mi 7:8.

2    When evildoers come at me
         to devour my flesh,†*
     These my enemies and foes
         themselves stumble and fall.
3    Though an army encamp against me,
         my heart does not fear;
     Though war be waged against me,
         even then do I trust.

**II**

4    One thing I ask of the LORD;
         this I seek:
     To dwell in the LORD's house
         all the days of my life,
     To gaze on the LORD's beauty,
         to visit his temple.*
5    For God will hide me in his shelter
         in time of trouble,*
     He will conceal me in the cover of his
         tent;
         and set me high upon a rock.
6    Even now my head is held high
         above my enemies on every side!
     I will offer in his tent
         sacrifices with shouts of joy;
         I will sing and chant praise to the
         LORD.

**B**
**I**

7    Hear my voice, LORD, when I call;
         have mercy on me and answer me.
8    "Come," says my heart, "seek his face";†
         your face, LORD, do I seek!*
9    Do not hide your face from me;
         do not repel your servant in anger.
     You are my salvation; do not cast me off;
         do not forsake me, God my savior!
10   Even if my father and mother forsake
         me,
         the LORD will take me in.*

**II**

11   LORD, show me your way;
         lead me on a level path

         because of my enemies.*
12   Do not abandon me to the desire of my
         foes;
     malicious and lying witnesses have
         risen against me.
13   I believe I shall see the LORD's goodness
         in the land of the living.†*
14   Wait for the LORD, take courage;
         be stouthearted, wait for the LORD!

## PSALM 28†

### Petition and Thanksgiving

¹ Of David.

**I**

     To you, LORD, I call;
         my Rock, do not be deaf to me,*
     Do not be silent toward me,
         so that I join those who go down to
         the pit.*
2    Hear the sound of my pleading when I
         cry to you for help
     when I lift up my hands toward your
         holy place.†*
3    Do not drag me off with the wicked,
         with those who do wrong,*
     Who speak peace to their neighbors
         though evil is in their hearts.*
4    Repay them for their deeds,
         for the evil that they do.
     For the work of their hands repay them;
         give them what they deserve.*
5    Because they do not understand the
         LORD's works,
         the work of his hands,*
     He will tear them down,
         never to rebuild them.

**II**

6†   Blessed be the LORD,
         who has heard the sound of my
         pleading.
7    The LORD is my strength and my shield,

---

**27:2** *To devour my flesh*: the psalmist's enemies are rapacious beasts (Ps 7:3; 17:12; 22:14, 17).

**27:8** *Seek his face*: to commune with God in the Temple. The idiom is derived from the practice of journeying to sacred places, cf. Hos 5:15; 2 Sm 21:1; Ps 24:6.

**27:13** *In the land of the living*: or "in the land of life," an epithet of the Jerusalem Temple (Ps 52:7; 116:9; Is 38:11), where the faithful had access to the life-giving presence of God.

**Psalm 28** A lament asking that the psalmist, who has taken refuge in the Temple (Ps 28:2), not be punished with the wicked, who are headed inevitably toward destruction (Ps 28:1, 3–5). The statement of praise is exceptionally lengthy and vigorous (Ps 28:6–7). The Psalm ends with a prayer (Ps 28:8–9).

**28:2** *Your holy place*: the innermost part of the Temple, the

holy of holies, containing the ark, cf. 1 Kgs 6:16, 19–23; 8:6–8.

**28:6** The psalmist shifts to fervent thanksgiving, probably responding to a priestly or prophetic oracle in Ps 28:5cd (not usually transmitted) assuring the worshiper that the prayer has been heard.

---

27:2 Ps 14:4.
27:4 Ps 23:6; 61:5.
27:5 Ps 31:21.
27:8 Ps 24:6; Hos 5:15.
27:10 Is 49:15.
27:11 Ps 25:4; 86:11.
27:13 Ps 116:9; Is 38:11.
28:1 Ps 18:2.

28:1 Ps 30:4; 88:5; 143:7;
     Prv 1:12.
28:2 Ps 134:2.
28:3 Ps 26:9.
28:3 Ps 12:2; 55:22; 62:5;
     Prv 26:24–28.
28:4 2 Sm 3:39.
28:5 Is 5:12.

in whom my heart trusts.
I am helped, so my heart rejoices;
with my song I praise him.

**III**

8†   LORD, you are a strength for your people,
the saving refuge of your anointed.

9   Save your people, bless your inheritance;
pasture and carry them forever!

## PSALM 29†

### The Lord of Majesty Acclaimed as King of the World

¹ A psalm of David.

**I**

Give to the LORD, you sons of God,†
give to the LORD glory and might;

2   Give to the LORD the glory due his name.
Bow down before the LORD's holy
splendor!*

**II**

3   The voice of the LORD† is over the
waters;
the God of glory thunders,
the LORD, over the mighty waters.

4   The voice of the LORD is power;
the voice of the LORD is splendor.*

5   The voice of the LORD cracks the cedars;
the LORD splinters the cedars of
Lebanon,

6   Makes Lebanon leap like a calf,
and Sirion† like a young bull.

7   The voice of the LORD strikes with fiery
flame;

8   the voice of the LORD shakes the
desert;

the LORD shakes the desert of Kadesh.

9†   The voice of the LORD makes the deer
dance
and strips the forests bare.
All in his Temple say, "Glory!"

**III**

10   The LORD sits enthroned above the
flood!†*
The LORD reigns as king forever!

11   May the LORD give might to his people;†
may the LORD bless his people with
peace!*

## PSALM 30†

### Thanksgiving for Deliverance

¹ A psalm. A song for the dedication of the
Temple.† Of David.

**I**

2   I praise you, LORD, for you raised me up
and did not let my enemies rejoice
over me.

3   O LORD, my God,
I cried out to you for help and you
healed† me.

4   LORD, you brought my soul up from
Sheol;
you let me live, from going down to
the pit.†*

**II**

5   Sing praise to the LORD, you faithful;
give thanks to his holy memory.

6   For his anger lasts but a moment;
his favor a lifetime.
At dusk weeping comes for the night;
but at dawn there is rejoicing.

---

**28:8** *Your people...your anointed*: salvation is more than individual, affecting all the people and their God-given leader.

**Psalm 29** The hymn invites the members of the heavenly court to acknowledge God's supremacy by ascribing glory and might to God alone (Ps 29:1–2a, 9b). Divine glory and might are dramatically visible in the storm (Ps 29:3–9a). The storm apparently comes from the Mediterranean onto the coast of Syria-Palestine and then moves inland. In Ps 29:10 the divine beings acclaim God's eternal kingship. The Psalm concludes with a prayer that God will impart the power just displayed to the Israelite king and through the king to Israel.

**29:1** *Sons of God*: members of the heavenly court who served Israel's God in a variety of capacities.

**29:3** *The voice of the LORD*: the sevenfold repetition of the phrase imitates the sound of crashing thunder and may allude to God's primordial slaying of Leviathan, the seven-headed sea monster of Canaanite mythology.

**29:6** *Sirion*: the Phoenician name for Mount Hermon, cf. Dt 3:9.

**29:9b–10** Having witnessed God's supreme power (Ps 29:3–9a), the gods acknowledge the glory that befits the king of the divine and human world.

**29:10** *The flood*: God defeated the primordial waters and made them part of the universe, cf. Ps 89:10–13; 93:3–4.

**29:11** *His people*: God's people, Israel.

**Psalm 30** An individual thanksgiving in four parts: praise and thanks for deliverance and restoration (Ps 30:2–4); an invitation to others to join in (Ps 30:5–6); a flashback to the time before deliverance (Ps 30:7–11); a return to praise and thanks (Ps 30:12). Two sets of images recur: 1) going down, death, silence; 2) coming up, life, praising. God has delivered the psalmist from one state to the other.

**30:1** *For the dedication of the Temple*: a later adaptation of the Psalm to celebrate the purification of the Temple in 164 B.C. during the Maccabean Revolt.

**30:3** *Healed*: for God as healer, see also Ps 103:3; 107:20; Hos 6:1; 7:1; 11:3; 14:5.

**30:4** *Sheol...pit*: the shadowy underworld residence of the spirits of the dead, here a metaphor for near-death.

---

**29:2** Ps 68:35; 96:7–9.
**29:4** Ps 46:7; 77:18–19; Jb 37:4; Is 30:30.
**29:10** Bar 3:3.
**29:11** Ps 68:36.
**30:4** Ps 28:1; Jon 2:7.

### III

7 Complacent,† I once said,
"I shall never be shaken."

8 LORD, you showed me favor,
established for me mountains of
virtue.
But when you hid your face
I was struck with terror.*

9 To you, LORD, I cried out;
with the Lord I pleaded for mercy:

10† "What gain is there from my
lifeblood,
from my going down to the grave?
Does dust give you thanks
or declare your faithfulness?

11 Hear, O LORD, have mercy on me;
LORD, be my helper."

### IV

12 You changed my mourning into
dancing;
you took off my sackcloth
and clothed me with gladness.*

13 So that my glory may praise you
and not be silent.
O LORD, my God,
forever will I give you thanks.

## PSALM 31†

### Prayer in Distress and Thanksgiving for Escape

1 For the leader. A psalm of David.

### I

2 In you, LORD, I take refuge;*
let me never be put to shame.
In your righteousness deliver me;

3 incline your ear to me;
make haste to rescue me!
Be my rock of refuge,
a stronghold to save me.

4 For you are my rock and my fortress;*
for your name's sake lead me and
guide me.

5 Free me from the net they have set for
me,
for you are my refuge.

6† Into your hands I commend my spirit;*
you will redeem me, LORD, God of
truth.

7 You hate those who serve worthless
idols,
but I trust in the LORD.

8 I will rejoice and be glad in your mercy,
once you have seen my misery,
[and] gotten to know the distress of
my soul.*

9 You will not abandon me into enemy
hands,
but will set my feet in a free and open
space.

### II

10† Be gracious to me, LORD, for I am in
distress;
affliction is wearing down my eyes,
my throat and my insides.

11 My life is worn out by sorrow,
and my years by sighing.
My strength fails in my affliction;
my bones are wearing down.*

12 To all my foes I am a thing of scorn,
and especially to my neighbors
a horror to my friends.
When they see me in public,
they quickly shy away.*

13 I am forgotten, out of mind like the
dead;
I am like a worn-out tool.†

14 I hear the whispers of the crowd;
terrors are all around me.†
They conspire together against me;
they plot to take my life.

15 But I trust in you, LORD;
I say, "You are my God."*

16 My destiny is in your hands;
rescue me from my enemies,
from the hands of my pursuers.

---

**30:7** *Complacent*: untroubled existence is often seen as a source of temptation to forget God, cf. Dt 8:10–18; Hos 13:6; Prv 30:9.

**30:10** In the stillness of Sheol no one gives you praise; let me live and be among your worshipers, cf. Ps 6:6; 88:11–13; 115:17; Is 38:18.

**Psalm 31** A lament (Ps 31:2–19) with a strong emphasis on trust (Ps 31:4, 6, 15–16), ending with an anticipatory thanksgiving (Ps 31:20–24). As is usual in laments, the affliction is couched in general terms. The psalmist feels overwhelmed by evil people but trusts in the "God of truth" (Ps 31:6).

**31:6** *Into your hands I commend my spirit*: in Lk 23:46 Jesus breathes his last with this Psalm verse. Stephen in Acts 7:59 al-

ludes to these words as he is attacked by enemies. The verse is used as an antiphon in the Divine Office at Compline, the last prayer of the day.

**31:13** *Like a worn-out tool*: a common comparison for something ruined and useless, cf. Is 30:14; Jer 19:11; 22:28.

**31:14** *Terrors are all around me*: a cry used in inescapable danger, cf. Jer 6:25; 20:10; 46:5; 49:29.

---

**30:8** Ps 104:29.      **31:8** Ps 10:14.
**30:12** Is 61:3; Jer 31:13.      **31:11** Ps 32:3; 38:10–11.
**31:2–4** Ps 71:1–3.      **31:12** Jb 19:13–19.
**31:4** Ps 18:2.      **31:15** Ps 140:7; Is 25:1.
**31:6** Lk 23:46; Acts 7:59.

17 Let your face shine on your servant; *
       save me in your mercy.
18 Do not let me be put to shame,
       for I have called to you, LORD.
   Put the wicked to shame;
       reduce them to silence in Sheol.
19 Strike dumb their lying lips,
       which speak arrogantly against the
           righteous
       in contempt and scorn. *

### III

20 How great is your goodness, Lord,
       stored up for those who fear you.
   You display it for those who trust you,
       in the sight of the children of Adam.
21 You hide them in the shelter of your
           presence,
       safe from scheming enemies.
   You conceal them in your tent,
       away from the strife of tongues. *
22 Blessed be the LORD,
       marvelously he showed to me
       his mercy in a fortified city.
23 Though I had said in my alarm,
       "I am cut off from your eyes." *
   Yet you heard my voice, my cry for
           mercy,
       when I pleaded with you for help.
24 Love the LORD, all you who are faithful
           to him.
   The LORD protects the loyal,
       but repays the arrogant in full.
25 Be strong and take heart,
       all who hope in the LORD.

## PSALM 32†

### Remission of Sin

1 *Of David. A *maskil.*

### I

   Blessed is the one whose fault is removed,
       whose sin is forgiven.
2 Blessed is the man to whom the LORD
           imputes no guilt,
       in whose spirit is no deceit.

### II

3 Because I kept silent, † my bones wasted
           away;
       I groaned all day long. *
4 For day and night your hand was heavy
           upon me;
       my strength withered as in dry
           summer heat.          *Selah*
5 Then I declared my sin to you;
       my guilt I did not hide. *
   I said, "I confess my transgression to the
       LORD,"
       and you took away the guilt of my sin.
                                       *Selah*
6 Therefore every loyal person should pray
           to you
       in time of distress.
   Though flood waters† threaten,
       they will never reach him. *
7 You are my shelter; you guard me from
           distress;
       with joyful shouts of deliverance you
           surround me.          *Selah*

### III

8 I will instruct you and show you the way
           you should walk,
       give you counsel with my eye upon you.
9 Do not be like a horse or mule, without
           understanding;
       with bit and bridle their temper is
           curbed,
       else they will not come to you.

### IV

10 Many are the sorrows of the wicked one,
       but mercy surrounds the one who
           trusts in the LORD.
11 Be glad in the LORD and rejoice, you
           righteous;
       exult, all you upright of heart. *

## PSALM 33†

### Praise of God's Power and Providence

### I

1   Rejoice, you righteous, in the LORD;

---

**Psalm 32** An individual thanksgiving and the second of the seven Penitential Psalms (cf. Ps 6). The opening declaration—the forgiven are blessed (Ps 32:1–2)—arises from the psalmist's own experience. At one time the psalmist was stubborn and closed, a victim of sin's power (Ps 32:3–4), and then became open to the forgiving God (Ps 32:5–7). Sin here, as often in the Bible, is not only the personal act of rebellion against God but also the consequences of that act—frustration and waning of vitality. Having been rescued, the psalmist can teach others the joys of justice and the folly of sin (Ps 32:8–11).

**32:3** *I kept silent*: did not confess the sin before God.

**32:6** *Flood waters*: the untamed waters surrounding the earth, a metaphor for danger.

**Psalm 33** A hymn in which the just are invited (Ps 33:1–3) to praise God, who by a mere word (Ps 33:4–5) created the three-tiered universe of the heavens, the cosmic waters, and the earth (Ps 33:6–9). Human words, in contrast, effect nothing

| 31:17 Ps 67:1; Nm 6:24. | Rom 4:7–8. |
| 31:19 Ps 12:4. | 32:3 Ps 31:11. |
| 31:21 Ps 27:5. | 32:5 Ps 38:19; 51:5. |
| 31:23 Jon 2:5. | 32:6 Ps 18:5. |
| 32:1 Is 1:18; Ps 65:3; | 32:11 Ps 33:1. |

praise from the upright is fitting. *

2 Give thanks to the LORD on the harp;
　　on the ten-stringed lyre offer praise. *

3 Sing to him a new song;
　　skillfully play with joyful chant.

4 For the LORD's word is upright;
　　all his works are trustworthy.

5 He loves justice and right.
　　The earth is full of the mercy of the
　　　LORD. *

## II

6 By the LORD's word the heavens were made;
　　by the breath of his mouth all their
　　　host. †*

7† He gathered the waters of the sea as a
　　　mound;
　　he sets the deep into storage vaults. *

## III

8 Let all the earth fear the LORD;
　　let all who dwell in the world show
　　　him reverence.

9 For he spoke, and it came to be,
　　commanded, and it stood in place. *

10 The LORD foils the plan of nations,
　　frustrates the designs of peoples.

11 But the plan of the LORD stands forever,
　　the designs of his heart through all
　　　generations. *

12 Blessed is the nation whose God is the
　　　LORD,
　　the people chosen as his inheritance. *

## IV

13 From heaven the LORD looks down
　　and observes the children of Adam, *

14 From his dwelling place he surveys
　　all who dwell on earth.

15 The One who fashioned together their
　　　hearts
　　is the One who knows all their works.

## V

16 A king is not saved by a great army,
　　nor a warrior delivered by great
　　　strength.

17 Useless is the horse for safety;
　　despite its great strength, it cannot be
　　　saved.

18 Behold, the eye of the LORD is upon
　　those who fear him,
　　upon those who count on his mercy,

19 To deliver their soul from death,
　　and to keep them alive through
　　　famine.

## VI

20 Our soul waits for the LORD,
　　he is our help and shield. *

21 For in him our hearts rejoice;
　　in his holy name we trust.

22 May your mercy, LORD, be upon us;
　　as we put our hope in you.

## PSALM 34†

### Thanksgiving to God Who Delivers the Just

1 Of David, when he feigned madness before
　Abimelech, † who drove him out and he
　　went away.

## I

2 I will bless the LORD at all times;
　　his praise shall be always in my
　　　mouth. *

3 My soul will glory in the LORD;
　　let the poor hear and be glad.

4 Magnify the LORD with me;
　　and let us exalt his name together.

## II

5 I sought the LORD, and he answered me,
　　delivered me from all my fears.

6 Look to him and be radiant,
　　and your faces may not blush for
　　　shame.

7 This poor one cried out and the LORD
　　　heard,
　　and from all his distress he saved him.

8 The angel of the LORD encamps
　　around those who fear him, and he
　　　saves them. *

---

† (Ps 33:10–11). The greatness of human beings consists in God's choosing them as a special people and their faithful response (Ps 33:12–22).

**33:6** *All their host:* the stars of the sky are commonly viewed as a vast army, e.g., Neh 9:6; Is 40:26; 45:12; Jer 33:22.

**33:7** *The waters…as a mound:* ancients sometimes attributed the power keeping the seas from overwhelming land to a primordial victory of the storm-god over personified Sea.

**Psalm 34** A thanksgiving in acrostic form, each line beginning with a successive letter of the Hebrew alphabet. In this Psalm one letter is missing and two are in reverse order. The psalmist, fresh from the experience of being rescued (Ps 34:5, 7), can teach the "poor," those who are defenseless, to trust in God

alone (Ps 34:4, 12). God will make them powerful (Ps 34:5–11) and give them protection (Ps 34:12–22).

**34:1** *Abimelech:* a scribal error for Achish. In 1 Sm 21:13–16, David feigned madness before Achish, not Abimelech.

---

**33:1** Ps 32:11; 147:1.
**33:2** Ps 92:4; 144:9.
**33:5** Ps 119:64.
**33:6** Gn 2:1.
**33:7** Ps 78:13; Gn 1:9–10;
　Ex 15:8; Jos 3:16.
**33:9** Ps 148:5; Gn 1:3f; Jdt
　16:14.
**33:11** Prv 19:21; Is 40:8.
**33:12** Ps 144:15; Ex 19:6; Dt
　7:6.
**33:13** Jb 34:21; Sir 15:19;
　Jer 16:17; 32:19.
**33:20** Ps 115:9.
**34:2** Ps 145:2.
**34:8** Ex 14:19.

9  Taste and see that the LORD is good;
   blessed is the stalwart one who takes
     refuge in him.*
10 Fear the LORD, you his holy ones;
   nothing is lacking to those who fear
     him.*
11 The rich grow poor and go hungry,
   but those who seek the LORD lack no
     good thing.

### III

12 Come, children,† listen to me;*
   I will teach you fear of the LORD.
13 Who is the man who delights in life,*
   who loves to see the good days?
14 Keep your tongue from evil,
   your lips from speaking lies.
15 Turn from evil and do good;*
   seek peace and pursue it.
16 The eyes of the LORD are directed toward
     the righteous*
   and his ears toward their cry.
17 The LORD's face is against evildoers
   to wipe out their memory from the
     earth.
18 The righteous cry out, the LORD hears
   and he rescues them from all their
     afflictions.
19 The LORD is close to the
     brokenhearted,
   saves those whose spirit is crushed.
20 Many are the troubles of the
     righteous,
   but the LORD delivers him from them
     all.
21 He watches over all his bones;
   not one of them shall be broken.*
22 Evil will slay the wicked;
   those who hate the righteous are
     condemned.
23 The LORD is the redeemer of the souls of
     his servants;
   and none are condemned who take
     refuge in him.

## PSALM 35†

### Prayer for Help Against Unjust Enemies

[1] Of David.

### I

†  Oppose, O LORD, those who oppose
     me;
   war upon those who make war upon
     me.
2  Take up the shield and buckler;
   rise up in my defense.
3  Brandish lance and battle-ax
   against my pursuers.
   Say to my soul,
     "I am your salvation."
4  Let those who seek my life
   be put to shame and disgrace.
   Let those who plot evil against me*
   be turned back and confounded.
5  Make them like chaff before the wind,*
   with the angel of the LORD driving
     them on.
6  Make their way slippery and dark,
   with the angel of the LORD pursuing
     them.

### II

7  Without cause they set their snare for me;
   without cause they dug a pit for me.
8  Let ruin overtake them unawares;
   let the snare they have set catch them;
   let them fall into the pit they have
     dug.*
9  Then I will rejoice in the LORD,
   exult in God's salvation.
10 My very bones shall say,
   "O LORD, who is like you,*
   Who rescue the afflicted from the
     powerful,
   the afflicted and needy from the
     despoiler?"

### III

11 Malicious witnesses rise up,
   accuse me of things I do not know.

---

† **34:12** *Children:* the customary term for students in wisdom literature.

**Psalm 35** A lament of a person betrayed by friends. The psalmist prays that the evildoers be publicly exposed as unjust (Ps 35:1–8), and gives thanks in anticipation of vindication (Ps 35:9–10). Old friends are the enemies (Ps 35:11–16). May their punishment come quickly (Ps 35:17–21)! The last part (Ps 35:22–26) echoes the opening in praying for the destruction of the psalmist's persecutors. The Psalm may appear vindictive, but one must keep in mind that the psalmist is praying for public redress now of a public injustice. There is at this time no belief in an afterlife in which justice will be redressed.

**35:1–6** The mixture of judicial, martial, and hunting images shows that the language is figurative. The actual injustice is false accusation of serious crimes (Ps 35:11, 15, 20–21). The psalmist seeks lost honor through a trial before God.

---

**34:9** Ps 2:12.
**34:10** Prv 3:7.
**34:12** Prv 1:8; 4:1.
**34:13–17** 1 Pt 3:10–12.
**34:15** Ps 37:27.
**34:16** Ps 33:18.
**34:21** Jn 19:36.
**35:4** Ps 40:15; 71:13.

**35:5** Ps 1:4; 83:14; Jb 21:18.
**35:8** Ps 7:16; 9:16; 57:7; Prv 26:27; Eccl 10:8; Sir 27:26.
**35:10** Ps 86:8; 89:7, 9; Ex 15:11.

12 They repay me evil for good;
    my soul is desolate.*
13† Yet I, when they were ill, put on
    sackcloth,
    afflicted myself with fasting,
    sobbed my prayers upon my bosom.
14 I went about in grief as for my brother,
    bent in mourning as for my mother.
15 Yet when I stumbled they gathered with
    glee,
    gathered against me and I did not
    know it.
    They slandered me without ceasing;
16    without respect they mocked me,
    gnashed their teeth against me.

### IV

17 O Lord, how long will you look on?
    Restore my soul from their
    destruction,
    my very life from lions!*
18 Then I will thank you in the great
    assembly;
    I will praise you before the mighty
    throng.*
19 Do not let lying foes rejoice over me,
    my undeserved enemies wink
    knowingly.*
20 They speak no words of peace,
    but against the quiet in the land
    they fashion deceitful speech.*
21 They open wide their mouths against
    me.
    They say, "Aha! Good!
    Our eyes have seen it!"*
22 You see this, Lord; do not be silent;*
    Lord, do not withdraw from me.
23 Awake, be vigilant in my defense,
    in my cause, my God and my Lord.
24 Defend me because you are just, Lord;
    my God, do not let them rejoice over
    me.
25 Do not let them say in their hearts,
    "Aha! Our soul!"†
    Do not let them say,

    "We have devoured that one!"
26 Put to shame and confound
    all who relish my misfortune.
    Clothe with shame and disgrace
    those who lord it over me.
27 But let those who favor my just cause
    shout for joy and be glad.
    May they ever say, "Exalted be the Lord
    who delights in the peace of his loyal
    servant."
28 Then my tongue shall recount your
    justice,
    declare your praise, all the day long.*

## PSALM 36†

### Human Wickedness and Divine Providence

1 For the leader. Of David, the servant of the Lord.

### I

2 Sin directs the heart of the wicked man;
    his eyes are closed to the fear of
    God.*
3 For he lives with the delusion:
    his guilt will not be known and
    hated.†
4 Empty and false are the words of his
    mouth;
    he has ceased to be wise and do good.
5 On his bed he hatches plots;
    he sets out on a wicked way;
    he does not reject evil.*

### II

6† Lord, your mercy reaches to heaven;
    your fidelity, to the clouds.*
7 Your justice is like the highest
    mountains;
    your judgments, like the mighty deep;
    human being and beast you sustain,
    Lord.
8 How precious is your mercy, O God!
    The children of Adam take refuge in
    the shadow of your wings.†*
9 They feast on the rich food of your
    house;

---

† **35:13, 15–17** The Hebrew is obscure.
  **35:25** *Aha! Our soul!*: an ancient idiomatic expression meaning that we have attained what we wanted.
  **Psalm 36** A Psalm with elements of wisdom (Ps 36:2–5), the hymn (Ps 36:6–10), and the lament (Ps 36:11–13). The rule of sin over the wicked (Ps 36:2–5) is contrasted with the rule of divine love and mercy over God's friends (Ps 36:6–10). The Psalm ends with a prayer that God's guidance never cease (Ps 36:11–12).
  **36:3** *Hated*: punished by God.
  **36:6–7** God actively controls the entire world.
  **36:8** *The shadow of your wings*: metaphor for divine pro-

tection. It probably refers to the winged cherubim in the holy of holies in the Temple, cf. 1 Kgs 6:23–28, 32; 2 Chr 3:10–13; Ez 1:4–9.

* **35:12** Ps 27:12; 38:20–21; 109:5; Jer 18:20.
**35:17** Ps 17:12; 22:22; 58:7.
**35:18** Ps 22:23; 26:12; 35:18; 40:10; 149:1.
**35:19** Ps 38:17.
**35:20** Ps 120:6–7.
**35:21** Ps 40:16; Lam 2:16.
**35:22** Ps 22:12; 38:21; 109:1.
**35:28** Ps 71:15–16.
**36:2** Rom 3:18.
**36:5** Mi 2:1.
**36:6** Ps 57:11; 71:19.
**36:8** Ps 17:8.

from your delightful stream* you give
them drink.

10 For with you is the fountain of life,*
and in your light we see light.*

11 Show mercy on those who know you,
your just defense to the upright of
heart.

12 Do not let the foot of the proud
overtake me,
nor the hand of the wicked disturb
me.

13 There make the evildoers fall;
thrust them down, unable to rise.

## PSALM 37†

### The Fate of Sinners and the Reward of the Just

¹ Of David.

**Aleph**

Do not be provoked by evildoers;
do not envy those who do wrong.*

2 Like grass they wither quickly;
like green plants they wilt away.*

**Beth**

3 Trust in the LORD and do good
that you may dwell in the land† and
live secure.*

4 Find your delight in the LORD
who will give you your heart's
desire.*

**Gimel**

5 Commit your way to the LORD;
trust in him and he will act*

6 And make your righteousness shine like
the dawn,
your justice like noonday.*

**Daleth**

7 Be still before the LORD;
wait for him.
Do not be provoked by the prosperous,
nor by malicious schemers.

**He**

8 Refrain from anger; abandon wrath;
do not be provoked; it brings only
harm.

9 Those who do evil will be cut off,
but those who wait for the LORD will
inherit the earth.*

**Waw**

10 Wait a little, and the wicked will be no
more;
look for them and they will not be
there.

11 But the poor will inherit the earth,*
will delight in great prosperity.

**Zayin**

12 The wicked plot against the righteous
and gnash their teeth at them;

13 But my Lord laughs at them,*
because he sees that their day is
coming.

**Heth**

14 The wicked unsheath their swords;
they string their bows
To fell the poor and oppressed,
to slaughter those whose way is
upright.*

15 Their swords will pierce their own
hearts;
their bows will be broken.

**Teth**

16 Better the meagerness of the righteous
one
than the plenty of the wicked.*

17 The arms of the wicked will be broken,
while the LORD will sustain the
righteous.

**Yodh**

18 The LORD knows the days of the
blameless;
their heritage lasts forever.

19 They will not be ashamed when times
are bad;

---

**Psalm 37** The Psalm responds to the problem of evil, which the Old Testament often expresses as a question: why do the wicked prosper and the good suffer? The Psalm answers that the situation is only temporary. God will reverse things, rewarding the good and punishing the wicked here on earth. The perspective is concrete and earthbound: people's very actions place them among the ranks of the good or wicked. Each group or "way" has its own inherent dynamism—eventual frustration for the wicked, eventual reward for the just. The Psalm is an acrostic, i.e., each section begins with a successive letter of the Hebrew alphabet. Each section has its own imagery and logic.

**37:3** *The land*: the promised land, Israel, which became for later interpreters a type or figure of heaven, cf. Heb 11:9–10, 13–16. The New Testament Beatitudes (Mt 5:3–12; Lk 6:20–26)

have been influenced by the Psalm, especially their total reversal of the present and their interpretation of the happy future as possession of the land.

**36:9** Gn 2:8, 10.
**36:10** Is 55:1; Jn 4:14.
**36:10** Ps 80:4, 8, 20.
**37:1** Prv 3:31; 23:17; 24:1, 19.
**37:2** Ps 90:5–6; 102:12; 103:15–16; Jb 14:2; Is 40:7.
**37:3** Ps 128:2.
**37:4** Prv 10:24.
**37:5** Ps 55:23; Prv 3:5; 16:3.
**37:6** Wis 5:6; Is 58:10.
**37:9** Ps 25:13; Prv 2:21; Is 57:13.
**37:11** Mt 5:4.
**37:13** Ps 2:4; 59:9; Wis 4:18.
**37:14** Ps 11:2; 57:5; 64:4.
**37:16** Prv 15:16; 16:8.

in days of famine they will be
    satisfied.

### Kaph

20 The wicked perish,
    enemies of the LORD;
They shall be consumed like fattened
    lambs;
    like smoke they disappear. *

### Lamedh

21 The wicked one borrows but does not
    repay;
    the righteous one is generous and
    gives.

22 For those blessed by the Lord will
    inherit the earth,
    but those accursed will be cut off.

### Mem

23 The valiant one whose steps are guided
    by the LORD,
    who will delight in his way, *

24 May stumble, but he will never fall,
    for the LORD holds his hand.

### Nun

25 Neither in my youth, nor now in old age
    have I seen the righteous one
    abandoned *
    or his offspring begging for bread.

26 All day long he is gracious and lends,
    and his offspring become a blessing.

### Samekh

27 Turn from evil and do good,
    that you may be settled forever. *

28 For the LORD loves justice
    and does not abandon the faithful.

### Ayin

When the unjust are destroyed,
    and the offspring of the wicked cut
    off,

29 The righteous will inherit the earth
    and dwell in it forever. *

### Pe

30 The mouth of the righteous utters
    wisdom; *
    his tongue speaks what is right.

31 God's teaching is in his heart; *
    his steps do not falter.

### Sadhe

32 The wicked spies on the righteous
    and seeks to kill him.

33 But the LORD does not abandon him in
    his power,
    nor let him be condemned when
    tried.

### Qoph

34 Wait eagerly for the LORD,
    and keep his way; *
He will raise you up to inherit the
    earth;
    you will see when the wicked are cut
    off.

### Resh

35 I have seen a ruthless scoundrel,
    spreading out like a green cedar. *

36 When I passed by again, he was gone;
    though I searched, he could not be
    found.

### Shin

37 Observe the person of integrity and
    mark the upright;
    Because there is a future for a man of
    peace. *

38 Sinners will be destroyed together;
    the future of the wicked will be cut
    off.

### Taw

39 The salvation of the righteous is from
    the LORD,
    their refuge in a time of distress. *

40 The LORD helps and rescues them,
    rescues and saves them from the
    wicked,
    because they take refuge in him.

## PSALM 38†

### Prayer of an Afflicted Sinner

1 A psalm of David. For remembrance.

#### I

2 LORD, do not punish me in your anger;
    in your wrath do not chastise me! *

3 Your arrows have sunk deep in me; *
    your hand has come down upon me.

---

† **Psalm 38** In this lament, one of the Penitential Psalms (cf. Ps 6), the psalmist acknowledges the sin that has brought physical and mental sickness and social ostracism. There is no one to turn to for help; only God can undo the past and restore the psalmist.

**37:20** Wis 5:14.
**37:23** Prv 20:24.
**37:25** Jb 4:7; Sir 2:10.
**37:27** Ps 34:14–15; Am 5:14.
**37:29** Ps 25:13; Prv 2:21; Is 57:13.
**37:30** Prv 10:31.
**37:31** Ps 40:9; Dt 6:6; Is

51:7; Jer 31:33.
**37:34** Ps 31:24.
**37:35** Ps 92:8–9; Is 2:13; Ez 31:10–11.
**37:37** Prv 23:18; 24:14.
**37:39** Ps 9:10; Is 25:4.
**38:2** Ps 6:2.
**38:3** Jb 6:4; Lam 3:12; Ps 31:11; 64:7.

4 There is no wholesomeness in my flesh
  because of your anger;
  there is no health in my bones
  because of my sin.*

5 My iniquities overwhelm me,
  a burden too heavy for me.*

**II**

6 Foul and festering are my sores
  because of my folly.

7 I am stooped and deeply bowed;*
  every day I go about mourning.

8 My loins burn with fever;
  there is no wholesomeness in my
  flesh.

9 I am numb and utterly crushed;
  I wail with anguish of heart.*

10 My Lord, my deepest yearning is before
  you;
  my groaning is not hidden from you.

11 My heart shudders, my strength forsakes
  me;
  the very light of my eyes has failed.*

12 Friends and companions shun my
  disease;
  my neighbors stand far off.

13 Those who seek my life lay snares for
  me;
  they seek my misfortune, they speak
  of ruin;
  they plot treachery every day.

**III**

14 But I am like the deaf, hearing nothing,
  like the mute, I do not open my
  mouth,

15 I am even like someone who does not
  hear,
  who has no answer ready.

16 LORD, it is for you that I wait;
  O Lord, my God, you respond.*

17 For I have said that they would gloat
  over me,
  exult over me if I stumble.

**IV**

18 I am very near to falling;
  my wounds are with me always.

19 I acknowledge my guilt
  and grieve over my sin.*

20 My enemies live and grow strong,
  those who hate me grow numerous
  fraudulently,

21 Repaying me evil for good,
  accusing me for pursuing good.*

22 Do not forsake me, O LORD;
  my God, be not far from me!*

23 Come quickly to help me,*
  my Lord and my salvation!

## PSALM 39†

### The Vanity of Life

1 For the leader, for Jeduthun.* A psalm of David.

**I**

2 I said, "I will watch my ways,
  lest I sin with my tongue;
  I will keep a muzzle on my mouth."

3 Mute and silent before the wicked,
  I refrain from good things.
  But my sorrow increases;
  my heart smolders within me.*
  In my sighing a fire blazes up,
  and I break into speech:

**II**

5 LORD, let me know my end, the number
  of my days,
  that I may learn how frail I am.

6 To be sure, you establish the expanse of
  my days;
  indeed, my life is as nothing before you.
  Every man is but a breath.*    Selah

**III**

7 Man goes about as a mere phantom;
  they hurry about, although in vain;
  he heaps up stores without knowing
  for whom.

8 And now, LORD, for what do I wait?
  You are my only hope.

9 From all my sins deliver me;
  let me not be the taunt of fools.

10 I am silent and do not open my mouth
  because you are the one who did this.

11 Take your plague away from me;
  I am ravaged by the touch of your
  hand.

---

† **Psalm 39** The lament of a mortally ill person who at first had resolved to remain silently submissive (Ps 39:2–4). But the grief was too much and now the psalmist laments the brevity and vanity of life (Ps 39:5–7), yet remaining hopeful (Ps 39:8–10). The psalmist continues to express both acceptance of the illness and hope for healing in Ps 39:11–13.

* **38:4** Is 1:5–6.
**38:5** Ps 40:13; Ezr 9:6.
**38:7** Ps 35:14.
**38:9** Ps 102:4–6.
**38:11** Ps 6:8; 31:10.
**38:16** Ps 13:4.
**38:19** Ps 32:5; 51:5.
**38:21** Ps 109:5.
**38:22** Ps 22:2, 12, 20;

35:22.
**38:23** Ps 40:14.
**39:1** 1 Chr 16:41; Ps 62:1; 77:1.
**39:4** Jer 20:9.
**39:6** Ps 62:10; 90:9–10; 144:4; Jb 7:6, 16; 14:1, 5; Eccl 6:12; Wis 2:5.

12   You chastise man with rebukes for sin;
     like a moth you consume his
       treasures.
     Every man is but a breath.     *Selah*

13   Listen to my prayer, LORD, hear my cry;
     do not be deaf to my weeping!
     For I am with you like a foreigner,
     a refugee, like my ancestors. *

14   Turn your gaze from me, that I may
       smile
     before I depart to be no more.

## PSALM 40†

### Gratitude and Prayer for Help

1 For the leader. A psalm of David.

**A**

2   Surely, I wait for the LORD;
     who bends down to me and hears my
       cry, *

3   Draws me up from the pit of
       destruction,
     out of the muddy clay, *
     Sets my feet upon rock,
       steadies my steps,

4   And puts a new song† in my mouth, *
     a hymn to our God.
     Many shall look on in fear
     and they shall trust in the LORD.

5   Blessed the man who sets
     his security in the LORD,
     who turns not to the arrogant
     or to those who stray after
       falsehood. *

6   You, yes you, O LORD, my God,
     have done many wondrous deeds!
     And in your plans for us
     there is none to equal you. *
     Should I wish to declare or tell them,
     too many are they to recount. *

7†   Sacrifice and offering you do not want; *
     you opened my ears.

     Holocaust and sin-offering you do not
       request;

8   so I said, "See; I come
     with an inscribed scroll written upon
       me.

9   I delight to do your will, my God;
     your law is in my inner being!" *

10   When I sing of your righteousness
     in a great assembly,
     See, I do not restrain my lips;
     as you, LORD, know. *

11   I do not conceal your righteousness
     within my heart;
     I speak of your loyalty and your
       salvation.
     I do not hide your mercy or
       faithfulness from a great assembly.

12   LORD, may you not withhold
     your compassion from me;
     May your mercy and your faithfulness
     continually protect me. *

**B**

13   But evils surround me
     until they cannot be counted.
     My sins overtake me,
     so that I can no longer see.
     They are more numerous than the hairs
       of my head;
     my courage fails me. *

14   LORD, graciously rescue me! *
     Come quickly to help me, LORD!

15   May those who seek to destroy my life
     be shamed and confounded.
     Turn back in disgrace
     those who desire my ruin. *

16   Let those who say to me "Aha!" *
     Be made desolate on account of their
       shame.

17   While those who seek you
     rejoice and be glad in you.
     May those who long for your salvation
     always say, "The LORD is great." *

---

**Psalm 40** A thanksgiving (Ps 40:2–13) has been combined with a lament (Ps 40:14–17) that appears also in Ps 70. The psalmist describes the rescue in spatial terms—being raised up from the swampy underworld to firm earth where one can praise God (Ps 40:2–4). All who trust God will experience like protection (Ps 40:5–6)! The Psalm stipulates the precise mode of thanksgiving: not animal sacrifice but open and enthusiastic proclamation of the salvation just experienced (Ps 40:7–11). A prayer for protection concludes (Ps 40:12–17).

**40:4** *A new song*: a song in response to the new action of God (cf. Ps 33:3; 96:1; 144:9; 149:1; Is 42:10). Giving thanks is not purely a human response but is itself a divine gift.

**40:7–9** Obedience is better than sacrifice (cf. 1 Sm 15:22; Is 1:10–20; Hos 6:6; Am 5:22–25; Mi 6:6–8; Acts 7:42–43 [quoting Am 5:25–26]). Heb 10:5–9 quotes the somewhat different Greek version and interprets it as Christ's self-oblation.

---

* 39:13 Ps 119:19; Gn 23:4; Heb 11:13; 1 Pt 2:11.
40:2 Lam 3:25.
40:3 Ps 28:1; 30:4; 69:3, 15–16; 88:5; Prv 1:12; Jon 2:7.
40:4 Ps 33:3.
40:5 Ps 1:1; Prv 16:20; Jer 17:7.
40:6 Ps 35:10.
40:6 Ps 71:15; 139:17–18.
40:7–9 Heb 10:5–7; Ps 51:18–19; Am 5:22; Hos 6:6; Is 1:11–15.
40:9 Ps 37:31.
40:10 Ps 22:23; 26:12; 35:18; 149:1.
40:12 Ps 89:34.
40:13 Ps 38:5, 11; Ezr 9:6.
40:14–18 Ps 70:2–6; 71:12.
40:15 Ps 35:4, 26.
40:16 Ps 35:21, 25.
40:17 Ps 35:27.

18 Though I am afflicted and poor,
        my Lord keeps me in mind.
    You are my help and deliverer;
        my God, do not delay!

## PSALM 41†

### Thanksgiving After Sickness

¹ For the leader. A psalm of David.

**I**

2   Blessed the one concerned for the poor;†
        on a day of misfortune, the LORD
            delivers him.*
3   The LORD keeps and preserves him,
        makes him blessed in the land,
        and does not betray him to his
            enemies.
4   The LORD sustains him on his sickbed,
        you turn down his bedding whenever
            he is ill.†

**II**

5   Even I have said, "LORD, take note of me;
        heal me, although I have sinned
            against you.
6   My enemies say bad things against me:
        'When will he die and his name be
            forgotten?'
7   When someone comes to visit me, he
            speaks without sincerity.
        His heart stores up malice;
        when he leaves, he gossips.*
8   All those who hate me whisper together
            against me;
        they imagine the worst about me:
9   'He has had ruin poured over him;
        that one lying down will never rise
            again.'

10† Even my trusted friend,
        who ate my bread,
        has raised his heel against me.*

**III**

11  "But you, LORD, take note of me to raise
            me up
        that I may repay them."†
12  By this I will know you are pleased with
            me,
        that my enemy no longer shouts in
            triumph over me.
13  In my integrity may you support me
        and let me stand in your presence
            forever.
14† Blessed be the LORD, the God of Israel,
        from all eternity and forever.
        Amen. Amen.*

### Second Book—Psalms 42–72

## PSALM 42†

### Longing for God's Presence in the Temple

¹ For the leader. A *maskil* of the Korahites.†

**I**

2   As the deer longs for streams of water,*
        so my soul longs for you, O God.
3   My soul thirsts for God, the living God.
        When can I enter and see the face of
            God?†*
4   My tears have been my bread day and
            night,*
        as they ask me every day, "Where is
            your God?"*
5   Those times I recall
        as I pour out my soul,*

---

**Psalm 41** A thanksgiving for rescue from illness (Ps 41:4, 5, 9). Many people, even friends, have interpreted the illness as a divine punishment for sin and have ostracized the psalmist (Ps 41:5–11). The healing shows the return of God's favor and rebukes the psalmist's detractors (Ps 41:12–13).

**41:2** *Blessed the one concerned for the poor:* cf. Ps 32:1–2; 34:9; 40:5; 65:5. The psalmist's statement about God's love of the poor is based on the experience of being rescued (Ps 41:1–3).

**41:4** *You turn down his bedding whenever he is ill:* the Hebrew is obscure. It suggests ongoing attentive care of the one who is sick.

**41:10** *Even my trusted friend…has raised his heel against me:* Jn 13:18 cites this verse to characterize Judas as a false friend. *Raised his heel against me:* an interpretation of the unclear Hebrew, "made great the heel against me."

**41:11** *That I may repay them:* the healing itself is an act of judgment through which God decides for the psalmist and against the false friends. The prayer is not necessarily for strength to punish enemies.

**41:14** The doxology, not part of the Psalm, marks the end of the first of the five books of the Psalter, cf. Ps 72:18–20; 89:53; 106:48.

**Psalms 42–43** Ps 42–43 form a single lament of three sections, each section ending in an identical refrain (Ps 42:6, 12; 43:5). The psalmist is far from Jerusalem, and longs for the divine presence that Israel experienced in the Temple liturgy. Despite sadness, the psalmist hopes once again to join the worshiping crowds.

**42:1** *The Korahites:* a major guild of Temple singers (2 Chr 20:19) whose name appears in the superscriptions of Ps 42; 44–49; 84–85; 87–88.

**42:3** *See the face of God:* "face" designates a personal presence (Gn 33:10; Ex 10:28–29; 2 Sm 17:11). The expressions "see God/God's face" occur elsewhere (Ps 11:7; 17:15; cf. Ex 24:10; 33:7–11; Jb 33:26) for the presence of God in the Temple.

---

**41:2** Tb 4:7–11.
**41:7** Ps 31:12; 38:12–13;
    88:8; Jb 19:13–19; Jer
    20:10.
**41:10** Ps 55:14–15; Jn
    13:18.
**41:14** Neh 9:5.

**42:2–3** Ps 63:2; 84:3; 143:6;
    Is 26:9.
**42:3** Ps 27:4.
**42:4** Ps 80:6; 102:10.
**42:4** Ps 79:10; Jl 2:17.
**42:5** Lam 3:20.

When I would cross over to the shrine of
the Mighty One,†
to the house of God,
Amid loud cries of thanksgiving,
with the multitude keeping festival.*

6 Why are you downcast, my soul;
why do you groan within me?
Wait for God, for I shall again praise him,
my savior and my God.

**II**

7 My soul is downcast within me;
therefore I remember you
From the land of the Jordan† and
Hermon,
from Mount Mizar,*

8† Deep calls to deep
in the roar of your torrents,
and all your waves and breakers
sweep over me.*

9 By day may the LORD send his mercy,
and by night may his righteousness be
with me!
I will pray† to the God of my life,

10 I will say to God, my rock:
"Why do you forget me?*
Why must I go about mourning
with the enemy oppressing me?"

11 It shatters my bones, when my
adversaries reproach me,
when they say to me every day:
"Where is your God?"

12 Why are you downcast, my soul,
why do you groan within me?
Wait for God, for I shall again praise him,
my savior and my God.

### PSALM 43

1 Grant me justice, O God;
defend me from a faithless people;

from the deceitful and unjust rescue
me.*

2 You, O God, are my strength.
Why then do you spurn me?
Why must I go about mourning,
with the enemy oppressing me?

3* Send your light and your fidelity,†
that they may be my guide;*
Let them bring me to your holy
mountain,
to the place of your dwelling,

4 That I may come to the altar of God,
to God, my joy, my delight.
Then I will praise you with the harp,
O God, my God.

5 Why are you downcast, my soul?
Why do you groan within me?
Wait for God, for I shall again praise
him,
my savior and my God.

## PSALM 44†

### God's Past Favor and Israel's Present Need

1 For the leader. A *maskil* of the Korahites.

**I**

2 O God, we have heard with our own
ears;
our ancestors have told us*
The deeds you did in their days,
with your own hand in days of old:

3 You rooted out nations to plant them,*
crushed peoples and expelled them.

4 Not with their own swords did they
conquer the land,*
nor did their own arms bring victory;
It was your right hand, your own arm,
the light of your face for you favored
them.*

5 You are my king and my God,*

---

† 
**42:5** *The shrine of the Mighty One*: this reading follows the
tradition of the Septuagint and the Vulgate.

**42:7** *From the land of the Jordan*: the sources of the Jordan
are in the foothills of Mount Hermon in present-day southern
Lebanon. Mount Mizar is presumed to be a mountain in the
same range.

**42:8** *Deep calls to deep*: to the psalmist, the waters arising in
the north are overwhelming and far from God's presence, like the
waters of chaos (Ps 18:5; 69:2–3, 15; Jon 2:3–6).

**42:9–10** *I will pray…I will say*: in the midst of his depression
the psalmist turns to prayer. Despite his situation he trusts the
Lord to deliver him from his sorrow so that he may enter the
Temple precincts and praise him once again (Ps 43:3–4, 5b).

**43:3** *Your light and your fidelity*: a pair of divine attributes
personified as guides for the pilgrimage. As in Ps 42:9 the psalmist prays that these divine attributes lead him back to Jerusalem
and ultimately to God's presence in the Temple.

**Psalm 44** In this lament the community reminds God of
past favors which it has always acknowledged (Ps 44:2–9).
But now God has abandoned Israel to defeat and humiliation
(Ps 44:10–17), though the people are not conscious of any sin
against the covenant (Ps 44:18–23). They struggle with being
God's special people amid divine silence; yet they continue to
pray (Ps 44:24–26).

---

*
**42:5** Ps 122:5.
**42:7** Ps 43:3.
**42:8** Ps 18:5; 32:6; 69:2;
88:8; Jon 2:4.
**42:10** Ps 18:2; 31:3–4.
**43:1** Ps 119:154.
**43:3** Ps 18:29; 27:1; 36:10;
Mi 7:8.

**43:3** Ps 122:1.
**44:2** Ps 78:3.
**44:3** Ps 78:55; 80:9f.
**44:4** Dt 8:17f; Jos 24:12.
**44:4** Ps 4:7; 31:17; 67:2;
80:4; Nm 6:25; Dn
9:17.
**44:5** Ps 145:1.

who bestows victories on Jacob.

6     Through you we batter our foes;
        through your name we trample our
          adversaries.

7     Not in my bow do I trust,
        nor does my sword bring me victory.

8     You have brought us victory over our
          enemies,
        shamed those who hate us.

9     In God we have boasted all the day long;
        your name we will praise forever.

                                        *Selah*

**II**

10 *   But now you have rejected and disgraced
          us;
        you do not march out with our
          armies.*

11    You make us retreat† before the foe;
        those who hate us plunder us at will.*

12    You hand us over like sheep to be
          slaughtered,
        scatter us among the nations.*

13    You sell your people for nothing;
        you make no profit from their sale.*

14    You make us the reproach of our
          neighbors,*
        the mockery and scorn of those
          around us.

15    You make us a byword among the
          nations;
        the peoples shake their heads at us.

16    All day long my disgrace is before me;
        shame has covered my face

17    At the sound of those who taunt and
          revile,
        at the sight of the enemy and avenger.

**III**

18    All this has come upon us,
        though we have not forgotten you,
        nor been disloyal to your covenant.

19 †   Our hearts have not turned back,

        nor have our steps strayed from your
          path.

20    Yet you have left us crushed,
        desolate in a place of jackals;†*
        you have covered us with a shadow of
          death.

21    If we had forgotten the name of our
          God,
        stretched out our hands to another
          god,

22    Would not God have discovered this,
        God who knows the secrets of the
          heart?

23    For you we are slain all the day long,
        considered only as sheep to be
          slaughtered.*

**IV**

24    Awake! Why do you sleep, O Lord?
        Rise up! Do not reject us forever!*

25    Why do you hide your face;*
        why forget our pain and misery?

26    For our soul has been humiliated in the
          dust;*
        our belly is pressed to the earth.

27    Rise up, help us!
        Redeem us in your mercy.

## PSALM 45†

### Song for a Royal Wedding

1 For the leader; according to "Lilies." A *maskil* of
        the Korahites. A love song.

**I**

2     My heart is stirred by a noble theme,
        as I sing my ode to the king.
        My tongue is the pen of a nimble
          scribe.

**II**

3     You are the most handsome of men;
        fair speech has graced your lips,
        for God has blessed you forever.*

---

† **44:11** *You make us retreat*: the corollary of Ps 44:3. Defeat,
like victory, is God's doing; neither Israel nor its enemies can
claim credit (Ps 44:23).
  **44:19** *Our hearts have not turned back*: Israel's defeat was
not caused by its lack of fidelity.
  **44:20** *A place of jackals*: following Israel's defeat and exile
(Ps 44:11–12), the land lies desolate, inhabited only by jackals,
cf. Is 13:22; Jer 9:10; 10:22. Others take *tannim* as "sea monster"
(cf. Ez 29:3; 32:2) and render: "you crushed us as you did the
sea monster."
  **Psalm 45** A song for the Davidic king's marriage to a foreign
princess from Tyre in Phoenicia. The court poet sings (Ps 45:2,
18) of God's choice of the king (Ps 45:3, 8), of his role in establishing divine rule (Ps 45:4–8), and of his splendor as he waits
for his bride (Ps 45:9–10). The woman is to forget her own house

when she becomes wife to the king (Ps 45:11–13). Her majestic
beauty today is a sign of the future prosperity of the royal house
(Ps 45:14–17). The Psalm was retained in the collection when
there was no reigning king, and came to be applied to the king
who was to come, the messiah.

---

**44:10–27** Ps 89:39–52.          **44:20** Jer 9:10.
   **44:10** Ps 60:12.             **44:23** Rom 8:36.
   **44:11** Lv 26:17; Dt 28:25.   **44:24** Ps 10:1; 74:1; 77:8;
   **44:12** Lv 26:33; Dt 28:64.        79:5; 83:2.
   **44:13** Dt 32:30; Is 52:3.    **44:25** Ps 10:11; 89:47; Jb
**44:14–17** Ps 79:4; 80:7;             13:24.
        123:3–4; Jb 12:4; Dn       **44:26** Ps 119:25.
        9:16.                      **45:3** Sg 5:10–16.

4    Gird your sword upon your hip, mighty
         warrior!
      In splendor and majesty ride on
         triumphant! *
5    In the cause of truth, meekness, and
         justice
      may your right hand show your
         wondrous deeds.
6    Your arrows are sharp;
      peoples will cower at your feet;
      the king's enemies will lose heart.
7    Your throne, O God, † stands forever; *
      your royal scepter is a scepter for
         justice.
8    You love justice and hate wrongdoing;
      therefore God, your God, has
         anointed you
      with the oil of gladness above your
         fellow kings.
9    With myrrh, aloes, and cassia
      your robes are fragrant.
      From ivory-paneled palaces †
      stringed instruments bring you joy.
10   Daughters of kings are your lovely wives;
      a princess arrayed in Ophir's gold †
      comes to stand at your right hand.

                      **III**
11   Listen, my daughter, and understand;
      pay me careful heed.
      Forget your people and your father's
         house, †
12   that the king might desire your
         beauty.
      He is your lord;
13 *    honor him, daughter of Tyre.
      Then the richest of the people
      will seek your favor with gifts.
14   All glorious is the king's daughter as she
         enters, *
      her raiment threaded with gold;

15   In embroidered apparel she is led to the
         king.
      The maids of her train are presented
         to the king.
16   They are led in with glad and joyous
         acclaim;
      they enter the palace of the king.

                      **IV**
17   The throne of your fathers your sons will
         have;
      you shall make them princes through
         all the land. *
18   I will make your name renowned
         through all generations;
      thus nations shall praise you forever. *

                   **PSALM 46**†

            **God, the Protector of Zion**

1 For the leader. A song of the Korahites.
            According to *alamoth*. †
                       **I**
2    God is our refuge and our strength,
      an ever-present help in distress. *
3 †  Thus we do not fear, though earth be
         shaken
      and mountains quake to the depths of
         the sea,
4    Though its waters rage and foam
      and mountains totter at its surging. *
                                      *Selah*

                      **II**
5 †  Streams of the river gladden the city of
         God,
      the holy dwelling of the Most High. *
6    God is in its midst; it shall not be
         shaken;
      God will help it at break of day. *
7    Though nations rage and kingdoms
         totter,

---

† **45:7** *O God:* the king, in courtly language, is called "god," i.e., more than human, representing God to the people. Heb 1:8–9 applies Ps 45:7–8 to Christ.
**45:9** *Ivory-paneled palaces:* lit., "palaces of ivory." Ivory paneling and furniture decoration have been found in Samaria and other ancient Near Eastern cities, cf. Am 3:15.
**45:10** *Ophir's gold:* uncertain location, possibly a region on the coast of southern Arabia or eastern Africa, famous for its gold, cf. 1 Kgs 9:28; 10:11; Jb 22:24.
**45:11** *Forget your people and your father's house:* the bride should no longer consider herself a daughter of her father's house, but the wife of the king—the queen.
**Psalm 46** A song of confidence in God's protection of Zion with close parallels to Ps 48. The dominant note in Ps 46 is sounded by the refrain, The LORD of hosts is with us (Ps 46:8, 12). The first strophe (Ps 46:2–4) sings of the security of God's presence even in utter chaos; the second (Ps 46:5–8), of divine

protection of the city from its enemies; the third (Ps 46:9–11), of God's imposition of imperial peace.
**46:1** *Alamoth:* the melody of the Psalm, now lost.
**46:3–4** Figurative ancient Near Eastern language to describe social and political upheavals.
**46:5** Jerusalem is not situated on a river. This description derives from mythological descriptions of the divine abode and symbolizes the divine presence as the source of all life (cf. Is 33:21; Ez 47:1–12; Jl 4:18; Zec 14:8; Rev 22:1–2).

---

**45:4** Ps 21:5.                    **46:2** Ps 48:4; Is 33:2.
**45:7–8** Heb 1:8–9.             **46:4** Ps 93:3–4; Jb 9:5–6; Is
**45:13** Ps 72:10–11; Is 60:5f.        24:18–20; 54:10.
**45:14–16** Ez 16:10–13.        **46:5** Ps 48:2–3; 76:3.
**45:17** Gn 17:6.                    **46:6** Is 7:14.
**45:18** Is 60:15.

he utters his voice and the earth
    melts.*
8† The LORD of hosts is with us;
    our stronghold is the God of Jacob.
                                                    *Selah*

### III

9  Come and see the works of the LORD,
    who has done fearsome deeds on
      earth;*
10 Who stops wars to the ends of the earth,
    breaks the bow, splinters the spear,
    and burns the shields with fire;*
11* "Be still and know that I am God!
    I am exalted among the nations,
    exalted on the earth."
12 The LORD of hosts is with us;
    our stronghold is the God of Jacob.
                                                    *Selah*

## PSALM 47†

### The Ruler of All the Nations

¹ For the leader. A psalm of the Korahites.

### I

2  All you peoples, clap your hands;
    shout to God with joyful cries.*
3  For the LORD, the Most High, is to be
      feared,
    the great king over all the earth,*
4  Who made people subject to us,
    nations under our feet,*
5† Who chose our heritage for us,
    the glory of Jacob, whom he loves.*
                                                    *Selah*

### II

6† God has gone up with a shout;
    the LORD, amid trumpet blasts.*

7  Sing praise to God, sing praise;
    sing praise to our king, sing praise.

### III

8  For God is king over all the earth;*
    sing hymns of praise.
9  God rules over the nations;
    God sits upon his holy throne.
10 The princes of the peoples assemble
    with the people of the God of
      Abraham.
    For the shields of the earth belong to
      God,
    highly exalted.*

## PSALM 48†

### The Splendor of the Invincible City

¹ A psalm of the Korahites.† A song.

### I

2  Great is the LORD and highly praised
    in the city of our God:*
    His holy mountain,
3     fairest of heights,
    the joy of all the earth,*
    Mount Zion, the heights of
      Zaphon,†*
    the city of the great king.

### II

4  God is in its citadel,
    renowned as a stronghold.
5  See! The kings assembled,
    together they advanced.
6† When they looked they were
      astounded;
    terrified, they were put to flight!*
7  Trembling seized them there,
    anguish, like a woman's labor,*

---

† **46:8** The first line of the refrain is similar in structure and meaning to Isaiah's name for the royal child, Emmanuel, With us is God (Is 7:14; 8:8, 10).

**Psalm 47** A hymn calling on the nations to acknowledge the universal rule of Israel's God (Ps 47:2–5) who is enthroned as king over Israel and the nations (Ps 47:6–9).

**47:5** *Our heritage…the glory*: the land of Israel (cf. Is 58:14), which God has given Israel in an act of sovereignty.

**47:6** *God has gone up*: Christian liturgical tradition has applied the verse to the Ascension of Christ.

**Psalm 48** A Zion hymn, praising the holy city as the invincible dwelling place of God. Unconquerable, it is an apt symbol of God who has defeated all enemies. After seven epithets describing the city (Ps 48:2–3), the Psalm describes the victory by the Divine Warrior over hostile kings (Ps 48:4–8). The second half proclaims the dominion of the God of Zion over all the earth (Ps 48:9–12) and invites pilgrims to announce that God is eternally invincible like Zion itself (Ps 48:13–14).

**48:1** *Korahites*: see note on Ps 42:1.

**48:3** *The heights of Zaphon*: the mountain abode of the Canaanite storm-god Baal in comparable texts. To speak of Zion as

if it were Zaphon was to claim for Israel's God what Canaanites claimed for Baal. Though topographically speaking Zion is only a hill, viewed religiously it towers over other mountains as the home of the supreme God (cf. Ps 68:16–17).

**48:6** *When they looked*: the kings are stunned by the sight of Zion, touched by divine splendor. The language is that of holy war, in which the enemy panics and flees at the sight of divine glory.

---

**46:7** Ps 2:1–5; 48:5–8;
  76:7–9; Is 17:12–14.
**46:9** Ps 48:9–10.
**46:10** Ps 76:4.
**46:11** Ps 48:11.
**47:2** Ps 89:16; Zep 3:14.
**47:3** Ps 95:3; Ex 15:18; Is
  24:23; 52:7.
**47:4** Ps 2:8.
**47:5** Is 58:14.

**47:6** Ps 24:8, 10;
  68:18–19; 98:6.
**47:8–9** Ps 72:11; 93:1; 96:10;
  97:1; 99:1; Jer 10:7.
**47:10** Ps 89:19; Ex 3:6; Is
  2:2–4.
**48:2** Ps 96:4; 145:3.
**48:3** Ps 50:2; Lam 2:15.
**48:3** Is 14:13.
**48:6** Jgs 5:19.
**48:7** Ex 15:14; Jer 4:31.

8   As when the east wind wrecks
       the ships of Tarshish!†

### III

9†  What we had heard we have now seen
       in the city of the LORD of hosts,
    In the city of our God,
       which God establishes forever.    *Selah*

10  We ponder, O God, your mercy
       within your temple

11  Like your name, O God,
       so is your praise to the ends of the
          earth.*
    Your right hand is fully victorious.

12     Mount Zion is glad!
    The daughters of Judah rejoice
       because of your judgments!*

### IV

13  Go about Zion, walk all around it,
       note the number of its towers.

14  Consider the ramparts, examine its
          citadels,
       that you may tell future generations:*

15  That this is God,
       our God for ever and ever.†
    He will lead us until death.

## PSALM 49†

### Confidence in God Rather than in Riches

1 For the leader. A psalm of the Korahites.†

2   Hear this, all you peoples!
       Give ear, all who inhabit the world,

3   You of lowly birth or high estate,
       rich and poor together.

4   My mouth shall speak words of wisdom,
       my heart shall offer insights.*

5   I will turn my ear to a riddle,†
       expound my question on a lyre.

6   Why should I fear in evil days,
       with the iniquity of my assailants
          surrounding me,

7   Of those who trust in their wealth
       and boast of their abundant riches?*

8†  No man can ransom even a brother,
       or pay to God his own ransom.*

9   The redemption of his soul is costly;
       and he will pass away forever.

10  Will he live on forever, then,
       and never see the Pit of Corruption?

11  Indeed, he will see that the wise die,
       and the fool will perish together with
          the senseless,*
       and they leave their wealth to others.*

12  Their tombs are their homes forever,
       their dwellings through all generations,
       "They named countries after
          themselves"

13  —but man does not abide in
          splendor.
    He is like the beasts—they perish.*

### II

14  This is the way of those who trust in
          themselves,
    and the end of those who take
       pleasure in their own mouth.    *Selah*

15  Like a herd of sheep they will be put
          into Sheol,
       and Death will shepherd them.
    Straight to the grave they descend,
       where their form will waste away,
    Sheol will be their palace.

16  But God will redeem my life,
       will take me† from the hand of
          Sheol.*    *Selah*

---

**48:8** *The ships of Tarshish*: large ships, named after the distant land or port of Tarshish, probably ancient Tartessus in southern Spain, although other identifications have been proposed, cf. Is 2:16; 60:9; Jon 1:3.

**48:9** *What we had heard we have now seen*: the glorious things that new pilgrims had heard about the holy city—its beauty and awesomeness—they now see with their own eyes. The seeing here contrasts with the seeing of the hostile kings in Ps 48:6.

**48:15** *Our God for ever and ever*: Israel's God is like Zion in being eternal and invincible. The holy city is therefore a kind of "sacrament" of God.

**Psalm 49** The Psalm affirms confidence in God (cf. Ps 23; 27:1–6; 62) in the face of the apparent good fortune of the unjust rich, cf. Ps 37; 73. Reliance on wealth is misplaced (Ps 49:8–10) for it is of no avail in the face of death (Ps 49:18–20). After inviting all to listen to this axiom of faith (Ps 49:2–5), the psalmist depicts the self-delusion of the ungodly (Ps 49:6–13), whose destiny is to die like ignorant beasts (Ps 49:13, 18; cf. Prv 7:21–23). Their wealth should occasion no alarm, for they will

come to nought, whereas God will save the just (Ps 49:14–20).

**49:1** *Korahites*: see note on Ps 42:1.

**49:5** *Riddle*: the psalmist's personal solution to the perennial biblical problem of the prosperity of the wicked. *Question*: parallel in meaning to problem; in wisdom literature it means the mysterious way of how the world works.

**49:8** *No man can ransom even a brother*: an axiom. For the practice of redemption, cf. Jb 6:21–23. A play on the first Hebrew word of Ps 49:8, 16 relates the two verses.

**49:16** *Will take me*: the same Hebrew verb is used of God "taking up" a favored servant: Enoch in Gn 5:24; Elijah in 2 Kgs 2:11–12; the righteous person in Ps 73:24. The verse apparently states the hope that God will rescue the faithful psalmist in the same manner.

---

| | |
|---|---|
| **48:11** Mal 1:11. | Ez 7:19; Mt 16:26. |
| **48:12** Ps 97:8. | **49:11** Eccl 2:16. |
| **48:14** Ps 22:31–32; 71:18. | **49:11** Ps 39:7; Sir 11:18–19. |
| **49:4** Ps 78:2; Mt 13:35. | **49:13** Eccl 3:18–21. |
| **49:7** Jb 31:24. | **49:16** Ps 16:10; 86:13; |
| **49:8** Prv 10:15; 11:4; | 103:4; 116:8. |

17 Do not fear when a man becomes rich,
when the wealth of his house grows
great.
18 At his death he will not take along
anything,
his glory will not go down after him. *
19 During his life his soul uttered blessings;
"They will praise you, for you do well
for yourself."
20 But he will join the company of his
fathers,
never again to see the light. *
21 In his prime, man does not understand.
He is like the beasts—they perish.

## PSALM 50†

### The Acceptable Sacrifice

¹ A psalm of Asaph.

**I**

The God of gods, the LORD,
has spoken and summoned the earth
from the rising of the sun to its
setting. *
2 From Zion, the perfection of beauty,
God shines forth. *
3 Our God comes and will not be silent!
Devouring fire precedes him,
it rages strongly around him. *
4 He calls to the heavens above
and to the earth to judge his people:
5 "Gather my loyal ones to me,
those who made a covenant with me
by sacrifice."
6 The heavens proclaim his righteousness,
for God himself is the judge. *    Selah

**II**

7 "Listen, my people, I will speak;
Israel, I will testify against you;
God, your God, am I.
8 Not for your sacrifices do I rebuke you,
your burnt offerings are always before
me.
9 I will not take a bullock from your
house,
or he-goats from your folds. *

10 For every animal of the forest is mine,
beasts by the thousands on my
mountains.
11 I know every bird in the heights;
whatever moves in the wild is mine.
12 Were I hungry, I would not tell you,
for mine is the world and all that fills
it. *
13 Do I eat the flesh of bulls
or drink the blood of he-goats?
14 Offer praise as your sacrifice to God; *
fulfill your vows to the Most High.
15 Then call on me on the day of
distress; *
I will rescue you, and you shall honor
me."

**III**

16 But to the wicked God says:
"Why do you recite my
commandments
and profess my covenant with your
mouth?
17 You hate discipline;
you cast my words behind you!
18 If you see a thief, you run with him;
with adulterers you throw in your
lot.
19 You give your mouth free rein for evil;
you yoke your tongue to deceit.
20 You sit and speak against your
brother,
slandering your mother's son.
21 When you do these things should I be
silent?
Do you think that I am like you?
I accuse you, I lay out the matter
before your eyes.

**IV**

22 "Now understand this, you who forget
God,
lest I start ripping apart and there be
no rescuer.
23 Those who offer praise as a sacrifice
honor me;
I will let him whose way is steadfast
look upon the salvation of God." *

---

† **Psalm 50** A covenant lawsuit stating that the sacrifice God really wants is the sacrifice of praise accompanied by genuine obedience (cf. Mi 6:1–8). It begins with a theophany and the summoning of the court (Ps 50:1–6). Then in direct address God explains what is required of the faithful (Ps 50:7–15), rebukes the hypocritical worshiper (Ps 50:16–21), and concludes with a threat and a promise (Ps 50:22–23; cf. Is 1:19–20).

**49:18** Sir 11:18–19; Eccl 5:15; 1 Tm 6:7.
**49:20** Jb 10:21–22.
**50:1** Dt 10:17; Jos 22:22.
**50:2** Ps 48:2.
**50:3** Ps 97:3; Dn 7:10.
**50:6** Ps 19:2; 97:6.
**50:9** Ps 69:32; Am 5:21–22.
**50:12** Ps 24:1; 89:12; Dt 10:14; 1 Cor 10:26.
**50:14** Heb 13:15.
**50:15** Ps 77:3.
**50:23** Ps 91:16.

## PSALM 51†

### The Miserere: Prayer of Repentance

¹ For the leader. A psalm of David, ² when Nathan the prophet came to him after he had gone in to Bathsheba.*

**I**

³ Have mercy on me, God, in accord with
    your merciful love;
  in your abundant compassion blot
    out my transgressions.

⁴ Thoroughly wash away my guilt;
  and from my sin cleanse me.

⁵ For I know my transgressions;
  my sin is always before me.*

⁶ Against you, you alone have I sinned;
  I have done what is evil in your eyes
So that you are just in your word,
  and without reproach in your
    judgment.*

⁷ Behold, I was born in guilt,
  in sin my mother conceived me.†*

⁸ Behold, you desire true sincerity;
  and secretly you teach me wisdom.

⁹ Cleanse me with hyssop,† that I may be
    pure;
  wash me, and I will be whiter than
    snow.*

¹⁰ You will let me hear gladness and joy;
  the bones you have crushed will rejoice.

**II**

¹¹ Turn away your face from my sins;
  blot out all my iniquities.

¹² A clean heart create for me, God;
  renew within me a steadfast spirit.*

¹³ Do not drive me from before your face,
  nor take from me your holy spirit.*

¹⁴ Restore to me the gladness of your
    salvation;
  uphold me with a willing spirit.

¹⁵ I will teach the wicked your ways,
  that sinners may return to you.

¹⁶ Rescue me from violent bloodshed,
    God, my saving God,
  and my tongue will sing joyfully of
    your justice.*

¹⁷ Lord, you will open my lips;
  and my mouth will proclaim your
    praise.

¹⁸ For you do not desire sacrifice† or I
    would give it;
  a burnt offering you would not accept.*

¹⁹ My sacrifice, O God, is a contrite spirit;
  a contrite, humbled heart, O God, you
    will not scorn.

**III**

²⁰† Treat Zion kindly according to your
    good will;
  build up the walls of Jerusalem.*

²¹ Then you will desire the sacrifices of the
    just,
  burnt offering and whole offerings;
  then they will offer up young bulls on
    your altar.

## PSALM 52†

### The Deceitful Tongue

¹ For the leader. A *maskil* of David, ² when Doeg the Edomite entered and reported to Saul,

---

**Psalm 51** A lament, the most famous of the seven Penitential Psalms, prays for the removal of the personal and social disorders that sin has brought. The poem has two parts of approximately equal length: Ps 51:3–10 and Ps 51:11–19, and a conclusion in Ps 51:20–21. The two parts interlock by repetition of "blot out" in the first verse of each section (Ps 51:3, 11), of "wash (away)" just after the first verse of each section (Ps 51:4) and just before the last verse (Ps 51:9) of the first section, and of "heart," "God," and "spirit" in Ps 51:12, 19. The first part (Ps 51:3–10) asks deliverance from sin, not just a past act but its emotional, physical, and social consequences. The second part (Ps 51:11–19) seeks something more profound than wiping the slate clean: nearness to God, living by the spirit of God (Ps 51:12–13), like the relation between God and people described in Jer 31:33–34. Nearness to God brings joy and the authority to teach sinners (Ps 51:15–16). Such proclamation is better than offering sacrifice (Ps 51:17–19). The last two verses express the hope that God's good will toward those who are cleansed and contrite will prompt him to look favorably on the acts of worship offered in the Jerusalem Temple (Ps 51:19 [20–21]).

**51:7** *In sin my mother conceived me:* lit., "In iniquity was I conceived," an instance of hyperbole: at no time was the psalmist ever without sin, cf. Ps 88:15, "I am mortally afflicted since youth," i.e., I have always been afflicted. The verse does not imply that the sexual act of conception is sinful.

**51:9** *Hyssop:* a small bush whose many woody twigs make a natural sprinkler. It was prescribed in the Mosaic law as an instrument for sprinkling sacrificial blood or lustral water for cleansing, cf. Ex 12:22; Lv 14:4; Nm 19:18.

**51:18** *For you do not desire sacrifice:* the mere offering of the ritual sacrifice apart from good dispositions is not acceptable to God, cf. Ps 50.

**51:20–21** Most scholars think that these verses were added to the Psalm some time after the destruction of the Temple in 587 B.C. The verses assume that the rebuilt Temple will be an ideal site for national reconciliation.

**Psalm 52** A condemnation of the powerful and arrogant (Ps 52:3–6), who bring down upon themselves God's judgment (Ps 52:7). The just, those who trust in God alone, are gladdened and strengthened by the downfall of their traditional enemies (Ps 52:8–9).

---

**51:2** 2 Sm 12.
**51:5** Ps 32:5; 38:19; Is 59:12.
**51:6** Rom 3:4.
**51:7** Jb 14:4.
**51:9** Jb 9:30; Is 1:18; Ez 36:25.
**51:12** Ez 11:19.
**51:13** Wis 1:5; 9:17; Is 63:11; Hg 2:5; Rom 8:9.
**51:16** Ps 30:10.
**51:18** Ps 40:7; 50:8; Am 5:21–22; Hos 6:6; Is 1:11–15; Heb 10:5–7.
**51:20** Jer 31:4; Ez 36:33.

saying to him: "David has entered the house of
     Ahimelech." *

**I**

3  Why do you glory in what is evil, you who
         are mighty by the mercy of God?
   All day long
4      you are thinking up intrigues;
         your tongue is like a sharpened razor,
         you worker of deceit. *
5  You love evil more than good,
         lying rather than saying what is right. *
                                         *Selah*
6  You love all the words that create
         confusion,
         you deceitful tongue. *

**II**

7  God too will strike you down forever,
         he will lay hold of you and pluck you
             from your tent,
         uproot you from the land of the
             living. *                          *Selah*
8  The righteous will see and they will fear;
         but they will laugh at him: *
9  "Behold the man! He did not take God
         as his refuge,
         but he trusted in the abundance of his
             wealth,
         and grew powerful through his
             wickedness." *

**III**

10 But I, like an olive tree† flourishing in
         the house of God, *
       I trust in God's mercy forever and ever.
11 I will thank you forever
         for what you have done.
       I will put my hope in your name—for it
         is good, *
       —in the presence of those devoted to
         you.

### PSALM 53†

### A Lament over Widespread Corruption

1 For the leader; according to *Mahalath*. A *maskil*
   of David.

2  The fool says in his heart, *
      "There is no God." *
   They act corruptly and practice injustice;
      there is none that does good.
3  God looks out from the heavens
      upon the children of Adam, *
   To see if there is a discerning person *
      who is seeking God.
4  All have gone astray;
      each one is altogether perverse.
   There is not one who does what is
      good, not even one. *

**II**

5 * Do they not know better, those who do
      evil,
      who feed upon my people as they
         feed upon bread? *
   Have they not called upon God?
6  They are going to fear his name with
      great fear,
      though they had not feared it before.
   For God will scatter the bones
      of those encamped against you.
   They will surely be put to shame,
      for God has rejected them.

**III**

7  Who will bring forth from Zion
      the salvation of Israel?
   When God reverses the captivity of his
      people
   Jacob will rejoice and Israel will be
      glad. *

### PSALM 54†

### Confident Prayer in Great Peril

1 For the leader. On stringed instruments. A *maskil*
   of David, 2 when the Ziphites came and said to
   Saul, "David is hiding among us." *

**I**

3  O God, by your name† save me.
      By your strength defend my cause.
4  O God, hear my prayer.
      Listen to the words of my mouth.

---

**52:10** *Like an olive tree*: the righteous will flourish in the
house of God like a well-watered olive tree, cf. Ps 92:14; 128:3.
   **Psalm 53** A lament of an individual, duplicated in Ps 14, except
that "God" is used for "the LORD," and Ps 53:6 is different, cf. Ps 14.
   **Psalm 54** A lament in which the person under attack calls
directly upon God for help (Ps 54:3–5). Refusing to despair, the
psalmist hopes in God, who is active in history and just (Ps 54:6–7).
The Psalm ends with a serene promise to return thanks (Ps 54:8–9).
   **54:3** *By your name*: one is present in one's name, hence God
as revealed to human beings.

**52:2** 1 Sm 21:8; 22:6ff.
**52:4** Ps 12:3; 59:8;
   120:2–3; Sir 51:3.
**52:5** Jer 4:22; Jn 3:19–20.
**52:6** Jer 9:4.
**52:7** Ps 27:13; 28:5; 56:14;
   Jb 18:14; Prv 2:22; Is
   38:11.
**52:8** Ps 44:14; 64:9.
**52:9** Jb 31:24; Prv 11:28.
**52:10** Ps 1:3; 92:12–14; Jer
   11:16; 17:8.

**52:11** Ps 22:23; 26:12;
   35:18; 149:1.
**53:2–6a** Ps 14:1–5a.
**53:2** Ps 10:4; 36:2; Is 32:6;
   Jer 5:12.
**53:2b–3** Rom 3:11–12.
**53:3** Ps 11:4; 102:20.
**53:4** Ps 12:2.
**53:5** Ps 79:6.
**53:5** Ps 27:2; Is 9:11.
**53:7** Ps 85:2.
**54:2** 1 Sm 23:19; 26:1.

5  Strangers have risen against me;
   the ruthless seek my life;
   they do not keep God before them. *
                                   Selah

**II**

6  God is present as my helper; *
   the Lord sustains my life.
7  Turn back the evil upon my foes;
   in your faithfulness, destroy them. *
8  Then I will offer you generous sacrifice
   and give thanks to your name, LORD,
   for it is good.
9  Because it has rescued me from every
   trouble,
   and my eyes look down on my foes. *

## PSALM 55†

### A Lament over Betrayal

1 For the leader. On stringed instruments. A *maskil*
   of David.

**I**

2  Listen, God, to my prayer; *
   do not hide from my pleading;
3  hear me and give answer.
   I rock with grief; I groan
4  at the uproar of the enemy,
   the clamor of the wicked.
   They heap trouble upon me,
   savagely accuse me.
5  My heart pounds within me;
   death's terrors fall upon me.
6  Fear and trembling overwhelm me;
   shuddering sweeps over me.
7  I say, "If only I had wings like a dove
   that I might fly away and find rest. *
8  Far away I would flee;
   I would stay in the desert. *        Selah
9  "I would soon find a shelter
   from the raging wind and storm."

**II**

10  Lord, check and confuse their tongues.
    For I see violence and strife in the city

11  making rounds on its walls day and
    night.
    Within are mischief and trouble;
12  treachery is in its midst;
    oppression and fraud never leave its
    streets. *
13  For it is not an enemy that reviled me—
    that I could bear—
    Not a foe who viewed me with
    contempt,
    from that I could hide.
14  But it was you, my other self,
    my comrade and friend, *
15  You, whose company I enjoyed,
    at whose side I walked
    in the house of God.

**III**

16  Let death take them;
    let them go down alive to Sheol, *
    for evil is in their homes and bellies.
17  But I will call upon God,
    and the LORD will save me.
18  At dusk, dawn, and noon
    I will grieve and complain,
    and my prayer will be heard. *
19  He will redeem my soul in peace
    from those who war against me,
    though there are many who oppose
    me.
20  God, who sits enthroned forever, *
    will hear me and afflict them.    Selah
    For they will not mend their ways;
    they have no fear of God.
21  He stretched out his hand at his friends
    and broke his covenant.
22  Softer than butter is his speech,
    but war is in his heart.
    Smoother than oil are his words,
    but they are unsheathed swords. *
23  Cast your care upon the LORD,
    who will give you support.
    He will never allow
    the righteous to stumble. *

---

† **Psalm 55** The psalmist, betrayed by intimate friends (Ps 55:14–15, 20–21), prays that God punish those oath breakers and thus be acknowledged as the protector of the wronged. The sufferings of the psalmist include both ostracism (Ps 55:4) and mental turmoil (Ps 55:5–6), culminating in the wish to flee society (Ps 55:7–9). The wish for a sudden death for one's enemies (Ps 55:16) occurs elsewhere in the Psalms; an example of such a death is the earth opening under the wicked Dathan and Abiram (Nm 16:31–32). The psalmist, confident of vindication, exhorts others to a like trust in the God of justice (Ps 55:23). The Psalm is not so much for personal vengeance as for a public vindication of God's righteousness now. There was no belief in an afterlife where such vindication could take place.

54:5 Ps 86:14.
54:6 Ps 118:7.
54:7 Ps 143:12.
54:9 Ps 59:11; 91:8; 92:12.
55:2–3 Ps 5:2–3; 86:6;
  130:1–2; Lam 3:56;
  Jon 2:3.
55:7 Ps 11:1.
55:8 Jer 9:1; Rev 12:6.
55:12 Jer 5:1; 6:6; Ez 22:2;
  Heb 1:3; Zep 3:1.
55:14 Ps 41:10; Jer 9:3; Mt
  26:21–24 par.
55:16 Ps 49:15; Nm 16:33;
  Prv 1:2; Is 5:14.
55:18 Dn 6:11.
55:20 Ps 29:10; 93:2; Bar
  3:3.
55:22 Ps 12:3; 28:3; 57:5;
  62:5; 64:4; Prv 26:24–
  28; Jer 9:7.
55:23 Ps 37:5; Prv 3:5; 16:3;
  1 Pt 5:7.

24 But you, God, will bring them down
 to the pit of destruction. *
These bloodthirsty liars
 will not live half their days,
 but I put my trust in you. *

## PSALM 56†

### Trust in God

¹ For the director. According to *Yonath elem rehoqim.*† A *miktam* of David, when the Philistines seized him at Gath. *

**I**

2 Have mercy on me, God,
 for I am treated harshly;
 attackers press me all the day.
3 My foes treat me harshly all the day;
 yes, many are my attackers.
O Most High, ⁴ when I am afraid,
 in you I place my trust.
5 I praise the word of God;
 I trust in God, I do not fear. *
 What can mere flesh do to me? *

**II**

6 All the day they foil my plans;
 their every thought is of evil against
 me.
7 They hide together in ambush;
 they watch my every step;
 they lie in wait for my life. *
8 They are evil; watch them, God!
 Cast the nations down in your anger!
9 My wanderings you have noted;
 are my tears not stored in your flask,†
 recorded in your book? *
10 My foes turn back when I call on you.
 This I know: God is on my side.
11 I praise the word of God,
 I praise the word of the LORD.
12 In God I trust, I do not fear.
 What can man do to me?

**III**

13 I have made vows to you, God;
 with offerings I will fulfill them, *
14 For you have snatched me from death,
 kept my feet from stumbling,
That I may walk before God
 in the light of the living.

## PSALM 57†

### Confident Prayer for Deliverance

¹ For the director. Do not destroy.† A *miktam* of David, when he fled from Saul into a cave. *

**I**

2 Have mercy on me, God,
 have mercy on me.
 In you I seek refuge.
In the shadow of your wings† I seek
 refuge
 till harm pass by. *
3 I call to God Most High,
 to God who provides for me.
4 May God send help from heaven to
 save me,
 shame those who trample upon me.
 May God send fidelity and mercy.
 *Selah*
5 I must lie down in the midst of lions
 hungry for human prey. *
Their teeth are spears and arrows;
 their tongue, a sharpened sword. *
6 Be exalted over the heavens, God;
 may your glory appear above all the
 earth. *

**II**

7 They have set a trap for my feet;
 my soul is bowed down;
They have dug a pit before me.
 May they fall into it themselves! *
 *Selah*

---

† **Psalm 56** Beset physically (Ps 56:2–3) and psychologically (Ps 56:6–7), the psalmist maintains a firm confidence in God (Ps 56:5, 9–10). Nothing will prevent the psalmist from keeping the vow to give thanks for God's gift of life (Ps 56:13). A refrain (Ps 56:5, 11–12) divides the Psalm in two equal parts.

**56:1** *Yonath elem rehoqim:* Hebrew words probably designating the melody to which the Psalm was to be sung.

**56:9** *Are my tears not stored in your flask:* a unique saying in the Old Testament. The context suggests that the tears are saved because they are precious; God puts a high value on each of the psalmist's troubles.

**Psalm 57** Each of the two equal strophes contains a prayer for rescue from enemies, accompanied by joyful trust in God (Ps 57:2–5, 7–11). The refrain prays that God be manifested as saving (Ps 57:6, 12). Ps 108 is nearly identical to part of this Psalm (cf. Ps 57:8–11, Ps 108:2–6).

**57:1** *Do not destroy:* probably the title of the melody to which the Psalm was to be sung.

**57:2** *The shadow of your wings:* probably refers to the wings of the cherubim (powerful winged animals) whose wings spread over the ark in the inner chamber of the Temple (1 Kgs 6:23–28).

---

**55:24** Ps 28:1; 30:4; 40:3; 88:5; 143:7; Prv 1:12; Jon 2:7.
**55:24** Ps 25:2; 56:4; 130:5.
**56:1** 1 Sm 21:10.
**56:5** Ps 130:5.
**56:5** Ps 118:6; Heb 13:6.
**56:7** Ps 140:5–6.
**56:9** Ps 10:14; 2 Kgs 20:5; Is 25:8; Rev 7:17.
**56:13** Nm 30:3.
**57:1** 1 Sm 22:1.
**57:2** Ps 17:8; 36:8.
**57:5** Ps 17:11–12; 22:22; 58:7.
**57:5** Ps 11:2; 64:4.
**57:6** Ps 72:19; Nm 14:21.
**57:7** Ps 7:15; 9:16–17; 140:5–6.

<sup>8</sup> My heart is steadfast, God,
  my heart is steadfast.
  I will sing and chant praise. *
<sup>9</sup> Awake, my soul;
  awake, lyre and harp!
  I will wake the dawn. † *
<sup>10</sup> I will praise you among the peoples,
  Lord;
  I will chant your praise among the
  nations. *
<sup>11</sup> For your mercy towers to the heavens;
  your faithfulness reaches to the skies. *
<sup>12</sup> Exalt yourself over the heavens, God;
  may your glory appear above all the
  earth.

## PSALM 58†

### The Dethroning of Unjust Rulers

<sup>1</sup> For the leader. Do not destroy. † A *miktam*
  of David.

**I**

<sup>2</sup> Do you indeed pronounce justice,
  O gods; †
  do you judge fairly you children of
  Adam? *
<sup>3</sup> No, you freely engage in crime;
  your hands dispense violence to the
  earth.

**II**

<sup>4</sup> The wicked have been corrupt since
  birth;
  liars from the womb, they have gone
  astray.
<sup>5</sup>† Their venom is like the venom of a
  snake,
  like that of a serpent stopping its
  ears, *

<sup>6</sup> So as not to hear the voice of the
  charmer
  or the enchanter with cunning spells.

**III**

<sup>7</sup> O God, smash the teeth in their mouths;
  break the fangs of these lions, LORD! *
<sup>8</sup> Make them vanish like water flowing
  away; *
  trodden down, let them wither like
  grass. *
<sup>9</sup> Let them dissolve like a snail that oozes
  away, †
  like an untimely birth that never sees
  the sun. *
<sup>10</sup> Suddenly, like brambles or thistles,
  have the whirlwind snatch them
  away. *
<sup>11</sup> Then the just shall rejoice to see the
  vengeance
  and bathe their feet in the blood of
  the wicked. *
<sup>12</sup> Then people will say:
  "Truly there is a reward for the just;
  there is a God who is judge on earth!"

## PSALM 59†

### Complaint Against Bloodthirsty Enemies

<sup>1</sup> For the director. Do not destroy. † A *miktam* of
David, when Saul sent people to watch his house
and kill him. *

**I**

<sup>2</sup> Rescue me from my enemies, my God;
  lift me out of reach of my foes.
<sup>3</sup> Deliver me from evildoers;
  from the bloodthirsty save me.
<sup>4</sup> They have set an ambush for my life;
  the powerful conspire against me.

---

**57:9** *I will wake the dawn:* by a bold figure the psalmist imagines the sound of music and singing will waken a new day.

**Psalm 58** A lament expressing trust in God's power to dethrone all powers obstructing divine rule of the world. First condemned are "the gods," the powers that were popularly imagined to control human destinies (Ps 58:2–3), then "the wicked," the human instruments of these forces (Ps 58:4–6). The psalmist prays God to prevent them from harming the just (Ps 58:7–10). The manifestation of justice will gladden the just; they will see that their God is with them (Ps 58:11). The Psalm is less concerned with personal vengeance than with public vindication of God's justice now.

**58:1** *Do not destroy:* probably the title of the melody to which the Psalm was to be sung.

**58:2** *Gods:* the Bible sometimes understands pagan gods to be lesser divine beings who are assigned by Israel's God to rule the foreign nations. Here they are accused of injustice, permitting the human judges under their patronage to abuse the righteous, cf. Ps 82.

**58:5–6** The image is that of a poisonous snake that is con-

trolled by the voice or piping of its trainer.

**58:9** *A snail that oozes away:* empty shells suggested to ancients that snails melted away as they left a slimy trail.

**Psalm 59** A lament in two parts (Ps 59:2–9, 11b–17), each ending in a refrain (Ps 59:10, 18). Both parts alternate prayer for vindication (Ps 59:2–3, 4b–5, 11b–14) with vivid depictions of the psalmist's enemies (Ps 59:4–5a, 7–8, 15–16). The near curse in Ps 59:12–13 is not a crude desire for revenge but a wish that God's just rule over human affairs be recognized now.

**59:1** *Do not destroy:* probably the title of the melody to which the Psalm was to be sung.

---

**57:8** Ps 108:2.
**57:9** Jb 38:12.
**57:10** Ps 9:12; 18:50.
**57:11** Ps 36:6; 71:19.
**58:2** Ps 82:2; Dt 16:19.
**58:5** Ps 64:4; 140:3; Rom 3:13.
**58:7** Ps 3:7.
**58:8** Wis 16:29.
**58:8** Ps 37:2.
**58:9** Jb 3:16.
**58:10** Jb 21:18; Hos 13:3; Na 1:10.
**58:11** Ps 68:24; Is 63:1–6.
**59:1** 1 Sm 19:11.

PS

For no offense or misdeed of mine, LORD,
<sup>5</sup> for no fault they hurry to take up arms.
Come near and see my plight!
<sup>6</sup> You, LORD God of hosts, are the God
of Israel!
Awake! Punish all the nations.
Have no mercy on these worthless
traitors. *Selah*
<sup>7</sup> Each evening they return,
growling like dogs, prowling the city.*
<sup>8</sup> Their mouths pour out insult,
sharp words are on their lips.
They say: "Who is there to hear?"†
<sup>9</sup> But you, LORD, laugh at them;
you deride all the nations.*
<sup>10</sup> My strength, for you I watch;
you, God, are my fortress,
<sup>11</sup> my loving God.

**II**

May God go before me,
and show me my fallen foes.
<sup>12</sup> Slay them, God,
lest they deceive my people.
Shake them by your power;
Lord, our shield, bring them down.
<sup>13</sup> For the sinful words of their mouths and
lips
let them be caught in their pride.
For the lies they have told under oath*
<sup>14</sup> destroy them in anger,
destroy till they are no more.
Then people will know God rules over
Jacob,
yes, even to the ends of the earth.*
*Selah*
<sup>15</sup> Each evening they return,
growling like dogs, prowling the city.
<sup>16</sup> They roam about as scavengers;
if they are not filled, they howl.

**III**

<sup>17</sup> But I shall sing of your strength,
extol your mercy at dawn,

For you are my fortress,
my refuge in time of trouble.
<sup>18</sup> My strength, your praise I will sing;
you, God, are my fortress, my loving
God.

## PSALM 60†

### Lament After Defeat in Battle

<sup>1</sup> For the leader; according to "The Lily of…."
A *miktam* of David (for teaching), <sup>2</sup> when he
fought against Aram-Naharaim and Aram-Zobah;
and Joab, coming back, killed twelve thousand
Edomites in the Valley of Salt.*

**I**

<sup>3</sup> O God, you rejected us, broke our
defenses;
you were angry but now revive us.
<sup>4</sup> You rocked the earth, split it open;*
repair the cracks for it totters.
<sup>5</sup> You made your people go through
hardship,
made us stagger from the wine you
gave us.*
<sup>6</sup> Raise up a banner for those who revere
you,
a refuge for them out of bow shot.
*Selah*
<sup>7</sup>† Help with your right hand and answer
us
that your loved ones may escape.

**II**

<sup>8</sup>† In the sanctuary God promised:
"I will exult, will apportion Shechem;
the valley of Succoth† I will measure
out.
<sup>9</sup> Gilead is mine, mine is Manasseh;
Ephraim is the helmet for my head,
Judah, my own scepter.†
<sup>10</sup>† Moab is my washbowl;
upon Edom I cast my sandal.†*
I will triumph over Philistia."

---

**59:8** *Who is there to hear?*: a sample of the enemies'
godless reflection. The answer is that God hears their blasphemies.
**Psalm 60** The community complains that God has let the
enemy win the battle (Ps 60:3–5) and asks for an assurance of
victory (Ps 60:6–7). In the oracle God affirms ownership of the
land; the invasion of other nations is not permanent and will
be reversed ultimately (Ps 60:8–10). With renewed confidence,
the community resolves to fight again (Ps 60:11). The opening
lament is picked up again (Ps 60:12), but this time with new
awareness of God's power and human limitation.
**60:7–12** These verses occur again as the second half of Ps
108.
**60:8** *I will…apportion…measure out*: God lays claim to these

places. *The valley of Succoth*: probably the lower stretch of the
Jabbok valley.
**60:9** *Judah, my own scepter*: an allusion to the Testament of
Jacob, Gn 49:10.
**60:10** *Moab is my washbowl*: Moab borders the Dead Sea,
hence a metaphor for the country. *Upon Edom I cast my sandal*:
an ancient legal gesture of taking possession of land.

---

| | |
|---|---|
| **59:7** Ps 55:11. | **60:2** 2 Sm 8:2, 3, 13; 1 Chr |
| **59:9** Ps 2:4; 37:13; Wis | 18:2, 3, 12. |
| 4:18. | **60:4** Ps 75:4; Is 24:19. |
| **59:13** Prv 12:13; 18:7. | **60:5** Ps 75:9; Is 51:17, |
| **59:14** Ps 83:18–19; Ez 5:13. | 21–22; Jer 25:15. |
| | **60:10** Ru 4:7–8. |

### III

11 Who will bring me to the fortified city?†
   Who will lead me into Edom?
12 Was it not you who rejected us, God?
   Do you no longer march with our
      armies?*
13 Give us aid against the foe;
   worthless is human help.
14 We will triumph with the help of God,
   who will trample down our foes.

## PSALM 61†

### Prayer of the King in Time of Danger

1 For the leader; with stringed instruments.
   Of David.

### I

2 Hear my cry, O God,
   listen to my prayer!
3 From the ends of the earth† I call;
   my heart grows faint.
   Raise me up, set me on a rock,
4    for you are my refuge,
   a tower of strength against the foe.*
5 Let me dwell in your tent forever,
   take refuge in the shelter of your
      wings.*          Selah

### II

6 For you, O God, have heard my
      vows,
   you have granted me the heritage of
      those who revere your name.
7 Add days to the life of the king;
   may his years be as from generation
      to generation;*
8* May he reign before God forever;
   send your love and fidelity† to
      preserve him—*
9 I will duly sing to your name forever,
   fulfill my vows day after day.

## PSALM 62†

### Trust in God Alone

1 For the leader; 'al Jeduthun.† A psalm of David.

### I

2 My soul rests in God alone,*
   from whom comes my salvation.
3 God alone is my rock and salvation,
   my fortress; I shall never fall.
4 How long will you set yourself against a
      man?
   You shall all be destroyed,
   Like a sagging wall
   or a tumbled down fence!
5 Even highly placed people
   plot to overthrow him.
   They delight in lies;
   they bless with their mouths,
   but inwardly they curse.*          Selah

### II

6 My soul, be at rest in God alone,
   from whom comes my hope.
7 God alone is my rock and my salvation,
   my fortress; I shall not fall.
8 My deliverance and honor are with
      God,*
   my strong rock;
   my refuge is with God.
9 Trust God at all times, my people!
   Pour out your hearts to God our
      refuge!          Selah

### III

10 Mortals are a mere breath,
   the sons of man but an illusion;*
   On a balance they rise;†
   together they weigh nothing.
11 Do not trust in extortion;
   in plunder put no empty hope.
   On wealth that increases,
   do not set your heart.*

---

**60:11** *The fortified city*: perhaps Bozrah, the fortified capital of Edom, cf. Is 34:6; 63:1; Am 1:12.
**Psalm 61** A lament of the king who feels himself at the brink of death (Ps 61:3) and cries out for the strong and saving presence of God (Ps 61:3b–5). The king cites the prayer being made for him (Ps 61:7–8), and promises to give thanks to God.
**61:3** *Ends of the earth*: "earth" being taken in its occasional meaning "the underworld," cf. Jon 2:3.
**61:8** *Send your love and fidelity*: as in Ps 43:3 the psalmist asks God to send these two divine attributes like angels to protect the king.
**Psalm 62** A song of trust displaying serenity from experiencing God's power (the refrains of Ps 62:2–3 and Ps 62:6–7) and anger toward unjust enemies (Ps 62:4–5). From the experience of being rescued, the psalmist can teach others to trust in God (Ps 62:9–12).

**62:1** *'Al Jeduthun*: apparently the Hebrew name for the melody.
**62:10** *On a balance they rise*: precious objects were weighed by balancing two pans suspended from a beam. The lighter pan rises.

---

60:12 Ps 44:10.
61:4 Ps 46:2.
61:5 Ps 17:8; 36:8; 57:2.
61:7 Ps 21:5.
61:8 Ps 72:5; 89:5, 30, 37.
61:8 Ps 85:11; 89:15, 25; Prv 20:28.
62:2–3, 6–7 Ps 18:3; 31:3–4; 42:10; 118:8; 146:3.
62:5 Ps 12:3; 28:3; 55:22; Prv 26:24–25.
62:8 Ps 3:3; Is 26:4; 60:19.
62:10 Ps 39:6–7; 144:4; Jb 7:16; Wis 2:5.
62:11 Jb 31:25; Eccl 5:9; Jer 17:11; Mt 6:19–21, 24.

12 † One thing God has said;
  two things I have heard: *
Strength belongs to God;

13  so too, my Lord, does mercy,
For you repay each man
  according to his deeds. *

## PSALM 63†

### Ardent Longing for God

¹ A psalm of David, when he was in the
  wilderness of Judah. *

**I**

2  O God, you are my God—
  it is you I seek!
For you my body yearns;
  for you my soul thirsts,
In a land parched, lifeless,
  and without water. *

3  I look to you in the sanctuary
  to see your power and glory.

4  For your love is better than life; †
  my lips shall ever praise you!

**II**

5  I will bless you as long as I live;
  I will lift up my hands, calling on
  your name.

6  My soul shall be sated as with choice
  food,
  with joyous lips my mouth shall
  praise you!

7  I think of you upon my bed,
  I remember you through the watches
  of the night

8  You indeed are my savior,
  and in the shadow of your wings I
  shout for joy. *

9  My soul clings fast to you;
  your right hand upholds me.

**III**

10  But those who seek my life will come to
  ruin;

they shall go down to the depths of
  the netherworld!

11  Those who would hand over my life
  to the sword shall
  become the prey of jackals!

12  But the king shall rejoice in God;
  all who swear by the Lord † shall exult,
  but the mouths of liars will be shut! *

## PSALM 64†

### Treacherous Conspirators Punished by God

¹ For the leader. A psalm of David.

**I**

2  O God, hear my anguished voice;
  from a dreadful foe protect my life.

3  Hide me from the malicious crowd,
  the mob of evildoers.

4  They sharpen their tongues like swords,
  bend their bows of poison words. *

5  They shoot at the innocent from ambush,
  they shoot him in a moment and do
  not fear.

6  They resolve on their wicked plan;
  they conspire to set snares;
  they say: "Who will see us?"

7  They devise wicked schemes,
  conceal the schemes they devise;
  the designs of their hearts are
  hidden. *

**II**

8  God shoots an arrow at them;
  in a moment they are struck down. *

9  They are brought down by their own
  tongues;
  all who see them flee. *

10  Every person fears and proclaims God's
  actions,
  they ponder his deeds.

11  The righteous rejoices and takes refuge
  in the LORD;
  all the upright give praise. *

---

† **62:12** *One thing…two things*: parallelism of numbers for the sake of variation, a common device in Semitic poetry. One should not literally add up the numbers, cf. Am 1:3; Prv 6:16–19; 30:15, 18, 21.
  **Psalm 63** A Psalm expressing the intimate relationship between God and the worshiper. Separated from God (Ps 63:2), the psalmist longs for the divine life given in the Temple (Ps 63:3–6), which is based on a close relationship with God (Ps 63:7–9). May all my enemies be destroyed and God's true worshipers continue in giving praise (Ps 63:10–11)!
  **63:4** *For your love is better than life*: only here in the Old Testament is anything prized above life—in this case God's love.
  **63:12** *All who swear by the Lord*: to swear by a particular god meant that one was a worshiper of that god (Is 45:23; 48:1; Zep 1:5).

**Psalm 64** A lament of a person overwhelmed by the malice of the wicked who are depicted in the Psalms as the enemies of the righteous (Ps 64:2–7). When people see God bringing upon the wicked the evil they intended against others, they will know who is the true ruler of the world (Ps 64:8–10). The final verse is a vow of praise (Ps 64:11).

* 

**62:12** Jb 40:5.
**62:13** Ps 28:4; 31:24; 2 Sm 3:39; Jb 34:11; Jer 17:10; Mt 16:27; Rom 2:6; 2 Tm 4:14.
**63:1** 1 Sm 24.
**63:2** Ps 42:2; 143:6; Is 26:9.
**63:8** Ps 17:8; 36:8.

**63:12** Ps 107:42.
**64:4** Ps 11:2; 37:14; 55:22; 57:5.
**64:7** Ps 140:3; Prv 6:14.
**64:8** Ps 7:13–14; 38:3; Dt 32:42.
**64:9** Ps 5:11; 44:14; 52:6.
**64:11** Ps 36:8; 57:2.

## PSALM 65†

### Thanksgiving for God's Blessings

[1] For the leader. A psalm of David. A song.

**I**

[2] To you we owe our hymn of praise,
    O God on Zion;
  To you our vows † must be fulfilled,
[3]†     you who hear our prayers.
  To you all flesh must come *
[4]     with its burden of wicked deeds.
  We are overcome by our sins;
    only you can pardon them. *
[5] Blessed the one whom you will choose
        and bring
    to dwell in your courts.
  May we be filled with the good things of
        your house,
    your holy temple!

**II**

[6] You answer us with awesome deeds † of
        justice,
    O God our savior,
  The hope of all the ends of the earth
    and of those far off across the sea. *
[7] You are robed in power,
    you set up the mountains by your
        might.
[8] You still the roaring of the seas, *
    the roaring of their waves,
    the tumult of the peoples. *
[9] Distant peoples stand in awe of your
        marvels;
    the places of morning and evening
        you make resound with joy.
[10]† You visit the earth and water it,
    make it abundantly fertile. *
  God's stream † is filled with water;
    you supply their grain.

Thus do you prepare it:
[11]   you drench its plowed furrows,
    and level its ridges.
  With showers you keep it soft,
    blessing its young sprouts.
[12] You adorn the year with your bounty;
    your paths † drip with fruitful rain.
[13] The meadows of the wilderness also
        drip;
    the hills are robed with joy.
[14] The pastures are clothed with flocks,
    the valleys blanketed with grain;
    they cheer and sing for joy. *

## PSALM 66†

### Praise of God, Israel's Deliverer

[1] For the leader. A song; a psalm.

**I**

[2] Shout joyfully to God, all the earth;
    sing of his glorious name;
    give him glorious praise. *
[3] Say to God: "How awesome your deeds!
    Before your great strength your
        enemies cringe.
[4] All the earth falls in worship before
        you; *
    they sing of you, sing of your name!"
                                    *Selah*

**II**

[5]† Come and see the works of God,
    awesome in deeds before the children
        of Adam.
[6] He changed the sea to dry land;
    through the river they passed on
        foot. *
  There we rejoiced in him,
[7]     who rules by his might forever,
  His eyes are fixed upon the nations.

---

† **Psalm 65** The community, aware of its unworthiness (Ps 65:3–4), gives thanks for divine bounty (Ps 65:5), a bounty resulting from God's creation victory (Ps 65:6–9). At God's touch the earth comes alive with vegetation and flocks (Ps 65:10–13).

**65:2** *Vows*: the Israelites were accustomed to promising sacrifices in the Temple if their prayers were heard.

**65:3** *To you all flesh must come*: all must have recourse to God's mercy.

**65:6** *Awesome deeds*: the acts of creating—installing mountains, taming seas, restraining nations (Ps 65:7–8)—that are visible worldwide (Ps 65:6, 9).

**65:10–14** Apparently a description of the agricultural year, beginning with the first fall rains that soften the hard sun-baked soil (Ps 65:9–10).

**65:10** *God's stream*: the fertile waters of the earth derive from God's fertile waters in the heavenly world.

**65:12** *Paths*: probably the tracks of God's storm chariot dropping rain upon earth.

**Psalm 66** In the first part (Ps 66:1–12), the community praises God for powerful acts for Israel, both in the past (the exodus from Egypt and the entry into the land [Ps 66:6]) and in the present (deliverance from a recent but unspecified calamity [Ps 66:8–12]). In the second part (Ps 66:13–20), an individual from the rescued community fulfills a vow to offer a sacrifice of thanksgiving. As often in thanksgivings, the rescued person steps forward to teach the community what God has done (Ps 66:16–20).

**66:5–6** cf. the events described in Ex 14:1–15, 21; Jos 3:11–4:24 and Ps 114.

---

**65:3** Is 66:23.
**65:4** Ps 32:1–2; 78:38; Is 1:18.
**65:6** Is 66:19.
**65:8** Ps 89:10; 107:29; Jb 38:11; Mt 8:26.
**65:8** Is 17:12.
**65:10** Lv 26:4; Is 30:23, 25; Jl 2:22–23.
**65:14** Is 44:23.
**66:2** Ps 65:14; Is 44:23.
**66:3–4** Ps 18:45; Mi 7:17.
**66:6** Ps 74:15; 114:3; Ex 14:21f; Jos 3:14ff; Is 44:27; 50:2.

Let no rebel rise to challenge! *Selah*

8 Bless our God, you peoples;
loudly sound his praise,
9 Who has kept us alive
and not allowed our feet to slip.*
10 You tested us, O God,
tried us as silver tried by fire.*
11 You led us into a snare;
you bound us at the waist as
captives.
12† You let captors set foot on our neck;
we went through fire and water;
then you led us out to freedom.*

**III**

13 I will bring burnt offerings† to your
house;
to you I will fulfill my vows,
14 Which my lips pronounced
and my mouth spoke in my distress.
15 Burnt offerings of fatlings I will offer
you
and sacrificial smoke of rams;
I will sacrifice oxen and goats. *Selah*
16 Come and hear, all you who fear God,
while I recount what has been done
for me.
17 I called to him with my mouth;
praise was upon my tongue.
18 Had I cherished evil in my heart,
the Lord would not have heard.
19 But God did hear
and listened to my voice in prayer.
20 Blessed be God, who did not reject my
prayer
and refuse his mercy.

**66:12** *You let captors set foot on our neck:* lit., "you let men mount our heads." Conquerors placed their feet on the neck of their enemies as a sign of complete defeat, cf. Jos 10:24. A ceremonial footstool of the Egyptian king Tutankhamen portrays bound and prostrate bodies of enemies ready for the king's feet on their heads, and one of Tutankhamen's ceremonial chariots depicts the king as a sphinx standing with paw atop the neck of an enemy.

**66:13** *Burnt offerings:* cf. Lv 1:3–13; 6:1–4; 22:17–20.

**Psalm 67** A petition for a bountiful harvest (Ps 67:7), made in the awareness that Israel's prosperity will persuade the nations to worship its God.

**67:2** *May God be gracious to us:* the people's petition echoes the blessing pronounced upon them by the priests, cf. Nm 6:22–27.

**Psalm 68** The Psalm is extremely difficult because the Hebrew text is badly preserved and the ceremony that it describes is uncertain. The translation assumes the Psalm accompanied the early autumn Feast of Tabernacles (Sukkoth), which included a procession of the tribes (Ps 68:25–28). Israel was being oppressed by a foreign power, perhaps Egypt (Ps 68:31–32)—unless Egypt stands for any oppressor. The Psalm may have been composed from segments of ancient poems, which would explain why the transitions are implied rather than explicitly stated. At

## PSALM 67†

### Harvest Thanks and Petition

1 For the leader; with stringed instruments. A
psalm; a song.

**I**

2 May God be gracious to us† and bless us;
may his face shine upon us.* *Selah*
3 So shall your way be known upon the
earth,
your victory among all the nations.*
4 May the peoples praise you, God;
may all the peoples praise you!

**II**

5 May the nations be glad and rejoice;
for you judge the peoples with fairness,
you guide the nations upon the
earth.* *Selah*
6 May the peoples praise you, God;
may all the peoples praise you!

**III**

7 The earth has yielded its harvest;
God, our God, blesses us.*
8 May God bless us still;
that the ends of the earth may revere
him.

## PSALM 68†

### The Exodus and Conquest, Pledge of Future Help

1 For the leader. A psalm of David; a song.

**I**

2† May God arise;
may his enemies be scattered;

any rate, Ps 68:2 is based on Nm 10:35–36, and Ps 68:8–9 are derived from Jgs 5:4–5. The argument develops in nine stanzas (each of three to five poetic lines): 1. confidence that God will destroy Israel's enemies (Ps 68:2–4); 2. call to praise God as savior (Ps 68:5–7); 3. God's initial rescue of Israel from Egypt (Ps 68:8), the Sinai encounter (Ps 68:9), and the settlement in Canaan (Ps 68:10–11); 4. the defeat of the Canaanite kings (Ps 68:12–15); 5. the taking of Jerusalem, where Israel's God will rule the world (Ps 68:16–19); 6. praise for God's past help and for the future interventions that will be modeled on the ancient exodus-conquest (Ps 68:20–24); 7. procession at the Feast of Tabernacles (Ps 68:25–28); 8. prayer that the defeated enemies bring tribute to the Temple (Ps 68:29–32); 9. invitation for all kingdoms to praise Israel's God (Ps 68:33–35).

**68:2** The opening line alluding to Nm 10:35 makes clear that God's assistance in the period of the exodus and conquest is the model and assurance of all future divine help.

66:9 Ps 91:12; 121:3; 1 Sm 2:9; Prv 3:23.
66:10 Is 48:10.
66:12 Is 43:2.
67:2 Ps 4:7; 31:17; 44:4;
80:4; Dn 9:17.
67:3 Jer 33:9.
67:5 Ps 98:9.
67:7 Ps 85:13; Lv 26:4; Ez 34:27; Hos 2:23–24.

may those who hate him flee before
　　him. *

3　As the smoke is dispersed, disperse
　　them;
　　as wax is melted by fire,
　　so may the wicked perish before
　　God. *

4　Then the just will be glad;
　　they will rejoice before God;
　　they will celebrate with great joy.

**II**

5　Sing to God, praise his name;
　　exalt the rider of the clouds. †
　　Rejoice before him
　　whose name is the LORD. *

6　Father of the fatherless, defender of
　　widows *—
　　God in his holy abode,

7　God gives a home to the forsaken,
　　who leads prisoners out to prosperity,
　　while rebels live in the desert. †

**III**

8　God, when you went forth before your
　　people, *
　　when you marched through the
　　desert,　　　　　　　　　　*Selah*

9　The earth quaked, the heavens poured,
　　before God, the One of Sinai,
　　before God, the God of Israel.

10　You poured abundant rains, God,
　　your inheritance was weak and you
　　repaired it.

11　Your creatures dwelt in it;
　　you will establish it in your goodness
　　for the poor, O God.

**IV**

12　The Lord announced:
　　"Those bringing news are a great Army.

13　The kings of the armies are in
　　desperate flight. *
　　Every household will share the spoil,

14　though you lie down among the
　　sheepfolds, *

you shall be covered with silver as the
　　wings of a dove,
　　her feathers bright as fine gold."

15　When the Almighty routs the kings
　　there,
　　it will be as when snow fell on
　　Zalmon. †

**V**

16　You mountain of God, mountain of
　　Bashan,
　　you rugged mountain, mountain of
　　Bashan,

17　You rugged mountains, why look with
　　envy
　　at the mountain† where God has
　　chosen to dwell,
　　where the LORD resides forever? *

18　God's chariots were myriad, thousands
　　upon thousands;
　　from Sinai the Lord entered the holy
　　place.

19　You went up to its lofty height;
　　you took captives, received slaves as
　　tribute, *
　　even rebels, for the LORD God to
　　dwell.

**VI**

20　Blessed be the Lord day by day,
　　God, our salvation, who carries us. *
　　　　　　　　　　　　　　*Selah*

21　Our God is a God who saves;
　　escape from death is the LORD God's.

22　God will crush the heads of his enemies,
　　the hairy scalp of the one who walks
　　in sin. *

23　The Lord has said:
　　"Even from Bashan I will fetch them,
　　fetch them even from the depths of
　　the sea. †

24　You will wash your feet in your enemy's
　　blood;
　　the tongues of your dogs will lap it
　　up." *

---

† **68:5** *Exalt the rider of the clouds*: God's intervention is in the imagery of Canaanite myth in which the storm-god mounted the storm clouds to ride to battle. Such theophanies occur throughout the Psalm: Ps 68:2–3, 8–10, 12–15, 18–19, 22–24, 29–32, 34–35. See Dt 33:26; Ps 18:8–16; Is 19:1.

**68:7** *While rebels live in the desert*: rebels must live in the arid desert, whereas God's people will live in the well-watered land (Ps 68:8–11).

**68:15** *Zalmon*: generally taken as the name of a mountain where snow is visible in winter, perhaps to be located in the Golan Heights or in the mountains of Bashan or Hauran east of the Sea of Galilee.

**68:17** *The mountain*: Mount Zion, the site of the Temple.

**68:23** *Even from Bashan...from the depths of the sea*: the heights and the depths, the farthest places where enemies might flee.

---

| | |
|---|---|
| **68:2** Nm 10:35. | **68:14** Jgs 5:16. |
| **68:3** Ps 97:5; Jdt 16:15; Wis 5:14; Mi 1:4. | **68:17** Ps 132:13–14; Ez 43:7. |
| **68:5** Ps 18:10; 104:3; Dt 33:26; Is 19:1. | **68:19** Ps 47:8; Eph 4:8–10. |
| **68:6–7** Ps 103:6; 146:7, 9; Ex 22:20–22; Bar 6:37. | **68:20** Ps 34:2; 145:2; Is 46:3–4; 63:9. |
| **68:8–9** Ps 44:10; 114:4, 7; Jgs 5:4–5; Heb 12:26. | **68:22** Dt 32:42. |
| **68:13** Jgs 5:19, 22. | **68:24** Ps 58:11; 1 Kgs 21:19; 22:38; Is 63:1–6. |

## VII

25 † Your procession comes into view,
O God,
your procession into the holy place,
my God and king.

26 The singers go first, the harpists follow;
in their midst girls sound the
timbrels. *

27 In your choirs, bless God;
LORD, Israel's fountain.

28 In the lead is Benjamin, few in number;
there the princes of Judah, a large
throng,
the princes of Zebulun, the princes of
Naphtali, too. *

## VIII

29 Summon again, O God, your power,
the divine power you once showed for
us,

30 From your temple on behalf of
Jerusalem,
that kings may bring you tribute.

31 Roar at the wild beast of the reeds, †
the herd of mighty bulls, the calves of
the peoples;
trampling those who lust after silver
scatter the peoples that delight in war.

32 Let bronze be brought from Egypt, *
Ethiopia hurry its hands to God. *

## IX

33 You kingdoms of the earth, sing to
God; *
chant the praises of the Lord,          *Selah*

34 Who rides the heights of the ancient
heavens,
Who sends forth his voice as a mighty
voice?

35 Confess the power of God,
whose majesty protects Israel,

whose power is in the sky.

36 Awesome is God in his holy place,
the God of Israel,
who gives power and strength to his
people. *
Blessed be God!

## PSALM 69 †

### A Cry of Anguish in Great Distress

1 For the leader; according to "Lilies." † Of David.

## I

2 Save me, God,
for the waters † have reached my
neck. *

3 I have sunk into the mire of the deep,
where there is no foothold.
I have gone down to the watery depths;
the flood overwhelms me. *

4 I am weary with crying out;
my throat is parched.
My eyes fail,
from looking for my God. *

5 More numerous than the hairs of my
head
are those who hate me without
cause. *
Those who would destroy me are
mighty,
my enemies without reason.
Must I now restore
what I did not steal? †

## II

6 God, you know my folly;
my faults are not hidden from you.

7 Let those who wait in hope for you,
LORD of hosts,
not be shamed because of me.
Let those who seek you, God of Israel, *

---

† **68:25–28** *Your procession*: the procession renews God's original taking up of residence on Zion, described in Ps 68:16–19.

**68:31** *The wild beast of the reeds*: probably the Nile crocodile, a symbol for Egypt; see Ps 68:32 and Ez 29:2–5.

**Psalm 69** A lament complaining of suffering in language both metaphorical (Ps 69:2–3, 15–16, the waters of chaos) and literal (Ps 69:4, 5, 9, 11–13, exhaustion, alienation from family and community, false accusation). In the second part the psalmist prays with special emphasis that the enemies be punished for all to see (Ps 69:23–29). Despite the pain, the psalmist does not lose hope that all be set right, and promises public praise (Ps 69:30–36). The Psalm, which depicts the suffering of the innocent just person vividly, is cited often by the New Testament especially in the passion accounts, e.g., Ps 69:5 in Jn 15:25; Ps 69:22 in Mk 15:23, 36 and parallels and in Jn 19:29. The Psalm prays not so much for personal vengeance as for public vindication of God's justice. There was, at this time, no belief in an afterlife where such vindi-

cation could take place. Redress had to take place now, in the sight of all.

**69:1** *"Lilies"*: apparently the name of the melody.

**69:2** *Waters*: the waters of chaos from which God created the world are a common metaphor for extreme distress, cf. Ps 18:5; 42:8; 88:8; Jon 2:3–6.

**69:5** *What I did not steal*: the psalmist, falsely accused of theft, is being forced to make restitution.

---

*

| | |
|---|---|
| **68:26** Ps 81:2–3; 87:7; 149:3; 150:3–5; 2 Sm 6:5. | **69:2** Ps 18:5; 93:3–4; Jb 22:11. |
| **68:28** Is 8:23. | **69:3** Ps 40:2; 124:4–5. |
| **68:32** Ez 29:2ff. | **69:4** Ps 25:15; 119:82; 123:2; 141:8; Is 38:14. |
| **68:32** Is 18:7; 45:14. | |
| **68:33** Ps 138:4. | **69:5** Ps 40:13; Lam 3:52; Jn 15:25. |
| **68:36** Ps 28:8; 29:11. | **69:7** Ps 40:17. |

not be disgraced because of me.

8 For it is on your account I bear insult,
  that disgrace covers my face. *

9 I have become an outcast to my kindred,
  a stranger to my mother's children. *

10 Because zeal for your house has
  consumed me, †
  I am scorned by those who scorn
  you. † *

11 When I humbled my spirit with fasting, *
  this led only to scorn.

12 When I clothed myself in sackcloth;
  I became a byword for them.

13 Those who sit in the gate gossip about
  me;
  drunkards make me the butt of songs.

### III

14 But I will pray to you, LORD,
  at a favorable time.
  God, in your abundant kindness,
    answer me
  with your sure deliverance. *

15 Rescue me from the mire, *
  and do not let me sink.
  Rescue me from those who hate me
  and from the watery depths.

16 Do not let the flood waters overwhelm
  me,
  nor the deep swallow me,
  nor the pit close its mouth over me.

17 Answer me, LORD, in your generous love;
  in your great mercy turn to me.

18 Do not hide your face from your servant;
  hasten to answer me, for I am in
  distress. *

19 Come and redeem my life;
  because of my enemies ransom me.

20 You know my reproach, my shame, my
  disgrace;
  before you stand all my foes.

21 Insult has broken my heart, and I
  despair;
  I looked for compassion, but there
  was none, *
  for comforters, but found none.

22 Instead they gave me poison for my
  food;
  and for my thirst they gave me
  vinegar. *

### IV

23 May their own table be a snare for them,
  and their communion offerings a
  trap. *

24 Make their eyes so dim they cannot see;
  keep their backs ever feeble.

25 Pour out your wrath upon them;
  let the fury of your anger overtake
  them.

26 Make their camp desolate,
  with none to dwell in their tents. *

27 For they pursued the one you struck,
  added to the pain of the one you
  wounded.

28 Heap punishment upon their
  punishment;
  let them gain from you no
  vindication.

29 May they be blotted from the book of
  life;
  not registered among the just! *

### V

30 But here I am miserable and in pain;
  let your saving help protect me, God,

31 † That I may praise God's name in song
  and glorify it with thanksgiving.

32 That will please the LORD more than
  oxen,
  more than bulls with horns and
  hooves: *

33 "See, you lowly ones, and be glad;
  you who seek God, take heart! *

34 For the LORD hears the poor,
  and does not spurn those in bondage.

35 Let the heaven and the earth praise him,
  the seas and whatever moves in
  them!"

### VI

36 For God will rescue Zion,
  and rebuild the cities of Judah. *
  They will dwell there and possess it;

---

† **69:10** *Zeal for your house has consumed me*: the psalmist's commitment to God's cause brings only opposition, cf. Jn 2:17. *I am scorned by those who scorn you*: Rom 15:3 uses the verse as an example of Jesus' unselfishness.

**69:31** *That I may praise God's name in song*: the actual song is cited in Ps 69:33–35, the word "praise" in Ps 69:35 referring back to "praise" in Ps 69:31.

**69:8** Jer 15:15.
**69:9** Jb 19:13–15.
**69:10** Ps 119:139; Jn 2:17; Rom 15:3.
**69:11–13** Ps 109:24–25; Jb 30:9; Lam 3:14.
**69:14** Is 49:8.
**69:15–16** Ps 28:1; 30:4; 32:6; 40:3; 88:5; Prv 1:12.
**69:18** Ps 102:3; 143:7.
**69:21** Lam 1:2.
**69:22** Lam 3:15; Mt 27:34,
48; Mk 15:23.
**69:23** Rom 11:9–10.
**69:26** Acts 1:20.
**69:29** Ps 139:16; Ex 32:32; Is 4:3; Dn 12:1; Mal 3:16; Rev 3:5.
**69:32** Ps 40:7; 50:8–9, 14; 51:18; Is 1:11–15; Hos 6:6; Am 5:21–22; Heb 10:5–8.
**69:33** Ps 22:27; 35:27; 70:5.
**69:36** Is 44:26; Ez 36:10.

37 the descendants of God's servants will
   inherit it;
     those who love God's name will dwell
   in it. *

## PSALM 70†

### Prayer for Divine Help

¹ For the leader; of David. For remembrance.

2 Graciously rescue me, God! *
     Come quickly to help me, LORD! *
3 Let those who seek my life
     be confused and put to shame. *
Let those who desire my ruin
     turn back in disgrace.
4 Let those who say "Aha!" *
     turn back in their shame.
5 But may all who seek you
     rejoice and be glad in you,
Those who long for your help
     always say, "God be glorified!" *
6 I am miserable and poor.
     God, come to me quickly!
You are my help and deliverer.
     LORD, do not delay!

## PSALM 71†

### Prayer in Time of Old Age

**I**

1 In you, LORD, I take refuge; *
     let me never be put to shame. *
2 In your justice rescue and deliver me;
     listen to me and save me!
3 Be my rock of refuge,
     my stronghold to give me safety;
     for you are my rock and fortress. *
4 My God, rescue me from the hand of
   the wicked,
     from the clutches of the evil and
   violent. *
5 You are my hope, Lord;
     my trust, GOD, from my youth.
6 On you I have depended since birth;

     from my mother's womb you are my
   strength; *
     my hope in you never wavers.
7† I have become a portent to many,
     but you are my strong refuge!
8 My mouth shall be filled with your
   praise,
     shall sing your glory every day.

**II**

9 Do not cast me aside in my old age;
     as my strength fails, do not forsake
   me.
10 For my enemies speak against me;
     they watch and plot against me. *
11 They say, "God has abandoned him.
     Pursue, and seize him!
     No one will come to the rescue!"
12 God, be not far from me;
     my God, hasten to help me. *
13 Bring to a shameful end
     those who attack me;
Cover with contempt and scorn
     those who seek my ruin. *
14 I will always hope in you
     and add to all your praise.
15 My mouth shall proclaim your just
   deeds,
     day after day your acts of deliverance,
     though I cannot number them all. *
16 I will speak of the mighty works of the
   Lord;
     O GOD, I will tell of your singular
   justice.

**III**

17 God, you have taught me from my
   youth;
     to this day I proclaim your wondrous
   deeds.
18 Now that I am old and gray, *
     do not forsake me, God,
That I may proclaim your might
     to all generations yet to come, *
Your power ¹⁹ and justice, God,
     to the highest heaven.

† **Psalm 70** A lament of a poor and afflicted person (Ps 70:6) who has no resource except God, and who cries out to be saved from the enemy. The Psalm is almost identical to Ps 40:14–17.

**Psalm 71** A lament of an old person (Ps 71:9, 18) whose afflictions are interpreted by enemies as a divine judgment (Ps 71:11). The first part of the Psalm pleads for help (Ps 71:1–4) on the basis of a hope learned from a lifetime's experience of God; the second part describes the menace (Ps 71:9–13) yet remains buoyant (Ps 71:14–16); the third develops the theme of hope and praise.

**71:7** *A portent to many*: the afflictions of the sufferer are taken as a manifestation of God's anger, cf. Dt 28:46; Ps 31:12.

* **69:37** Ps 102:29; Is 65:9.
**70:2–6** Ps 40:14–18.
  **70:2** Ps 71:12.
  **70:3** Ps 35:4, 26.
  **70:4** Ps 35:21, 25.
  **70:5** Ps 35:27.
**71:1–3** Ps 31:2–4.
  **71:1** Ps 25:2.
  **71:3** Ps 18:3.

**71:4** Ps 140:2.
**71:6** Ps 22:11.
**71:10** Ps 3:2; 22:8.
**71:12** Ps 22:20.
**71:13** Ps 35:4; 40:15; 70:3.
**71:15** Ps 35:28.
**71:18** Is 46:3–4.
**71:18** Ps 22:31–32;
  48:14–15; 145:4.

You have done great things; *
   O God, who is your equal? *
20 Whatever bitter afflictions you sent me,
   you would turn and revive me.
From the watery depths of the earth
   once more raise me up.
21 Restore my honor;
   turn and comfort me,
22 That I may praise you with the lyre
   for your faithfulness, my God,
And sing to you with the harp,
   O Holy One of Israel!
23 My lips will shout for joy as I sing your
   praise;
   my soul, too, which you have
   redeemed.
24 Yes, my tongue shall recount
   your justice day by day.
For those who sought my ruin
   have been shamed and disgraced.

## PSALM 72†

### A Prayer for the King

1 Of Solomon.

**I**

2 O God, give your judgment to the king;
   your justice to the king's son; †*
That he may govern your people with
   justice,
   your oppressed with right judgment, *
3 That the mountains may yield their
   bounty for the people,
   and the hills great abundance, *
4 That he may defend the oppressed
   among the people,
   save the children of the poor and
   crush the oppressor.

**II**

5 May they fear you with the sun,
   and before the moon, through all
   generations. *

6 May he be like rain coming down upon
   the fields,
   like showers watering the earth, *
7 That abundance may flourish in his
   days,
   great bounty, till the moon be no
   more.

**III**

8 † May he rule from sea to sea,
   from the river to the ends of the
   earth. *
9 May his foes kneel before him,
   his enemies lick the dust. *
10 May the kings of Tarshish and the
   islands † bring tribute,
   the kings of Sheba and Seba offer
   gifts. *
11 May all kings bow before him,
   all nations serve him. *
12 For he rescues the poor when they cry
   out,
   the oppressed who have no one to
   help.
13 He shows pity to the needy and the
   poor *
   and saves the lives of the poor.
14 From extortion and violence he redeems
   them,
   for precious is their blood † in his
   sight.

**IV**

15 Long may he live, receiving gold from
   Sheba,
   prayed for without cease, blessed day
   by day.
16 † May wheat abound in the land,
   flourish even on the mountain
   heights.
May his fruit be like that of Lebanon,
   and flourish in the city like the grasses
   of the land. *
17 May his name be forever;

---

**Psalm 72** A royal Psalm in which the Israelite king, as the representative of God, is the instrument of divine justice (Ps 72:1–4, 12–14) and blessing (Ps 72:5–7, 15–17) for the whole world. The king is human, giving only what he has received from God. Hence intercession must be made for him. The extravagant language is typical of oriental royal courts.

**72:2** *The king...the king's son*: the crown prince is the king's son; the prayer envisages the dynasty.

**72:8** *From sea to sea...the ends of the earth*: the boundaries of the civilized world known at the time: from the Mediterranean Sea (the western sea) to the Persian Gulf (the eastern sea), and from the Euphrates (the river) to the islands and lands of southwestern Europe, "the ends of the earth." The words may also have a mythic nuance—the earth surrounded by cosmic waters, hence everywhere.

**72:10** *Tarshish and the islands*: the far west (Ps 48:6); Arabia and Seba: the far south (1 Kgs 10:1).
**72:14** *Their blood*: cf. Ps 116:15.
**72:16** The translation of the difficult Hebrew is tentative.

---

**71:19** Ps 72:18.      **72:8** Dt 11:24; Zec 9:10.
**71:19** Ps 86:8.      **72:9** Is 49:23; Mi 7:17.
**72:2** Ps 99:4; Jer 23:5.      **72:10** Ps 68:30; Is 60:5–6;
**72:2** Prv 31:8–9.             1 Kgs 10:1ff.
**72:3** Is 52:7; 55:12.      **72:11** Ps 47:8.
**72:5** Ps 89:37–38; Jer      **72:13** Prv 31:9.
   31:35.      **72:16** Is 27:6; Hos 14:6–8;
**72:6** Dt 32:2; Is 45:8; Hos      Am 9:13.
   6:3.

**PS**

as long as the sun, may his name
    endure.*
May the tribes of the earth give blessings
    with his name;†
    may all the nations regard him as
    favored.*

18† Blessed be the Lord God, the God of
    Israel,
    who alone does wonderful deeds.*

19 Blessed be his glorious name forever;
    may he fill all the earth with his glory.*
    Amen and amen.

20 The end of the psalms of David, son of
Jesse.

### Third Book—Psalms 73–89

### PSALM 73†

### The Trial of the Just

¹ A psalm of Asaph.

How good God is to the upright,
    to those who are pure of heart!

**I**

2 But, as for me, my feet had almost
    stumbled;
    my steps had nearly slipped,

3 Because I was envious of the arrogant
    when I saw the prosperity of the
    wicked.*

4 For they suffer no pain;
    their bodies are healthy and sleek.

5 They are free of the burdens of life;
    they are not afflicted like others.

6 Thus pride adorns them as a necklace;
    violence clothes them as a robe.

7 Out of such blindness comes sin;
    evil thoughts flood their hearts.*

8 They scoff and spout their malice;

    from on high they utter threats.*

9† They set their mouths against the
    heavens,
    their tongues roam the earth.

10† So my people turn to them
    and drink deeply of their words.

11 They say, "Does God really know?"
    "Does the Most High have any
    knowledge?"*

12 Such, then, are the wicked,
    always carefree, increasing their
    wealth.

**II**

13 Is it in vain that I have kept my heart
    pure,
    washed my hands in innocence?*

14 For I am afflicted day after day,
    chastised every morning.

15 Had I thought, "I will speak as they do,"
    I would have betrayed this generation
    of your children.

16 Though I tried to understand all this,
    it was too difficult for me,

17 Till I entered the sanctuary of God
    and came to understand their end.†

**III**

18 You set them, indeed, on a slippery
    road;
    you hurl them down to ruin.

19 How suddenly they are devastated;
    utterly undone by disaster!

20 They are like a dream after waking, Lord,
    dismissed like shadows when you
    arise.*

**IV**

21 Since my heart was embittered
    and my soul deeply wounded,

22 I was stupid and could not understand;
    I was like a brute beast in your
    presence.

23 Yet I am always with you;

---

† **72:17** *May the tribes of the earth give blessings with his name*: an echo of the promise to the ancestors (Gn 12:3; 26:4; 28:14), suggesting that the monarchy in Israel fulfilled the promise to Abraham, Isaac, and Jacob.

**72:18–19** A doxology marking the end of Book II of the Psalter.

**Psalm 73** The opening verse of this probing poem (cf. Ps 37; 49) is actually the psalmist's hard-won conclusion from personal experience: God is just and good! The psalmist describes near loss of faith (Ps 73:2–3), occasioned by observing the wicked who blasphemed God with seeming impunity (Ps 73:4–12). Feeling abandoned despite personal righteousness, the psalmist could not bear the injustice until an experience of God's nearness in the Temple made clear how deluded the wicked were. Their sudden destruction shows their impermanence (Ps 73:13–20). The just can thus be confident, for, as the psalmist

now knows, their security is from God (Ps 73:1, 23–28).

**73:9** *They set their mouths against the heavens*: in an image probably derived from mythic stories of half-divine giants, the monstrous speech of the wicked is likened to enormous jaws gaping wide, devouring everything in sight.

**73:10** The Hebrew is obscure.

**73:17** *And came to understand their end*: the psalmist receives a double revelation in the Temple: 1) the end of the wicked comes unexpectedly (Ps 73:18–20); 2) God is with me.

*     **72:17** Ps 21:7.     **73:3** Ps 37:1; Jb 21:13.
    **72:17** Gn 12:3; 22:18; 26:4;     **73:7** Jb 15:27.
        Zec 8:13.     **73:8** Ps 17:10.
    **72:18** Ps 41:14; 89:53;     **73:11** Ps 10:11; Jb 22:13.
        106:48; 136:4.     **73:13** Ps 26:6; Mal 3:14.
    **72:19** Ps 57:5; Nm 14:21.     **73:20** Jb 20:8.

PS

you take hold of my right hand. *
24 With your counsel you guide me,
     and at the end receive me with
       honor. †
25 Whom else have I in the heavens?
     None beside you delights me on earth.
26 Though my flesh and my heart fail,
     God is the rock of my heart, my
       portion forever.
27 But those who are far from you perish;
     you destroy those unfaithful to you.
28 As for me, to be near God is my good,
     to make the Lord GOD my refuge.
   I shall declare all your works
     in the gates of daughter Zion. †

## PSALM 74†

### Prayer at the Destruction of the Temple

1 A *maskil* of Asaph.

**I**

Why, God, have you cast us off
     forever? †*
   Why does your anger burn against the
     sheep of your pasture? *
2 Remember your people, whom you
     acquired of old,
   the tribe you redeemed as your own
       heritage,
   Mount Zion where you dwell. *
3 Direct your steps toward the utter
     destruction,
   everything the enemy laid waste in the
       sanctuary.
4 Your foes roared triumphantly in the
     place of your assembly;

they set up their own tokens of
     victory.
5 They hacked away like a forester
     gathering boughs,
   swinging his ax in a thicket of trees.
6 They smashed all its engraved work,
     struck it with ax and pick.
7 They set your sanctuary on fire,
     profaned your name's abode by razing
       it to the ground. *
8 They said in their hearts, "We will
     destroy them all!
   Burn all the assembly-places of God
       in the land!"
9† Even so we have seen no signs for us,
     there is no prophet any more, *
   no one among us who knows for how
       long.
10 How long, O God, will the enemy jeer? *
     Will the enemy revile your name
       forever?
11 Why draw back your hand,
     why hold back your right hand within
       your bosom? †

**II**

12† Yet you, God, are my king from of old,
     winning victories throughout the
       earth.
13 You stirred up the sea by your might; *
     you smashed the heads of the dragons
       on the waters. *
14 You crushed the heads of Leviathan, *
     gave him as food to the sharks.
15 You opened up springs and torrents,
     brought dry land out of the primeval
       waters. †

**73:24** *And at the end receive me with honor*: a perhaps deliberately enigmatic verse. It is understood by some commentators as reception into heavenly glory, hence the traditional translation, "receive me into glory." The Hebrew verb can indeed refer to mysterious divine elevation of a righteous person into God's domain: Enoch in Gn 5:24; Elijah in 2 Kgs 2:11–12; the righteous psalmist in Ps 49:16. Personal resurrection in the Old Testament, however, is clearly attested only in the second century B.C. The verse is perhaps best left unspecified as a reference to God's nearness and protection.
**73:28** *In the gates of daughter Zion*: this reading follows the tradition of the Septuagint and Vulgate.
**Psalm 74** A communal lament sung when the enemy invaded the Temple; it would be especially appropriate at the destruction of Jerusalem in 587 B.C. Israel's God is urged to look upon the ruined sanctuary and remember the congregation who worshiped there (Ps 74:1–11). People and sanctuary are bound together; an attack on Zion is an attack on Israel. In the second half of the poem, the community brings before God the story of their origins—their creation (Ps 74:12–17)—in order to move God to reenact that deed of creation now. Will God allow a lesser power to destroy the divine project (Ps 74:18–23)?
**74:1** *Forever*: the word implies that the disaster is already of

long duration, cf. Ps 74:9 and note.
**74:9** *Even so we have seen no signs*…: ancients often asked prophets to say for how long a divine punishment was to last, cf. 2 Sm 24:13. Here no prophet has arisen to indicate the duration.
**74:11** *Why hold back…within your bosom*: i.e., idle beneath your cloak.
**74:12–17** Comparable Canaanite literature describes the storm-god's victory over all-encompassing Sea and its allies (dragons and Leviathan) and the subsequent peaceful arrangement of the universe, sometimes through the placement of paired cosmic elements (day and night, sun and moon), cf. Ps 89:12–13. The Psalm apparently equates the enemies attacking the Temple with the destructive cosmic forces already tamed by God. Why then are those forces now raging untamed against your own people?
**74:15** *Waters*: lit., "rivers" (cf. Ps 24:7; Isa 50:2) upon which, or from which, in primordial times the earth is created.

**73:23** Ps 121:5.           **74:7** Ps 79:1; Is 64:10.
**74:1** Ps 10:1; 44:24; 77:8.   **74:9** Lam 2:9.
**74:1** Ps 80:5.              **74:10** Ps 89:47.
**74:2** Ps 68:17; 132:13;     **74:13** Ps 89:10.
  Ex 15:17; Jer 10:16;        **74:13** Is 51:9–10.
  51:19.                      **74:14** Jb 3:8; 40:25; Is 27:1.

16 Yours the day and yours the night too;
    you set the moon and sun in place.
17 You fixed all the limits of the earth;
    summer and winter you made.*
18 Remember how the enemy has jeered,
    LORD,
    how a foolish people has reviled your
    name.
19 Do not surrender to wild animals those
    who praise you;
    do not forget forever the life of your
    afflicted.
20 Look to your covenant,
    for the recesses of the land
    are full of the haunts of violence.
21 Let not the oppressed turn back in
    shame;
    may the poor and needy praise your
    name.
22 Arise, God, defend your cause;
    remember the constant jeering of the
    fools.
23 Do not forget the clamor of your foes,
    the unceasing uproar of your
    enemies.

## PSALM 75†

### God the Judge of the World

1 For the leader. Do not destroy! A psalm of
    Asaph; a song.

    I

2 We thank you, God, we give thanks;
    we call upon your name,
    we declare your wonderful deeds.
    [You said:]†
3 "I will choose the time;
    I will judge fairly.
4 Though the earth and all its inhabitants
    quake,
    I make steady its pillars."*          Selah

5 So I say to the boastful: "Do not
    boast!"*
    to the wicked: "Do not raise your
    horns!†
6 Do not raise your horns against heaven!
    Do not speak with a stiff neck!"*
7 For judgment comes not from east or
    from west,
    not from the wilderness or the
    mountains,*
8 But from God who decides,
    who brings some low and raises
    others high.*
9 Yes, a cup† is in the LORD's hand,
    foaming wine, fully spiced.†
    When God pours it out,
    they will drain it even to the dregs;
    all the wicked of the earth will drink.*
10 But I will rejoice forever;
    I will sing praise to the God of Jacob,
11* [Who has said:]
    "I will cut off all the horns of the
    wicked,
    but the horns of the righteous will be
    exalted."

## PSALM 76†

### God Defends Zion

1 For the leader; a psalm with stringed
    instruments. A song of Asaph.

    I

2 Renowned in Judah is God,*
    whose name is great in Israel.
3 On Salem† is God's tent, his shelter on
    Zion.
4 There the flashing arrows were
    shattered,
    shield, sword, and weapons of war.*
                                          Selah

---

**Psalm 75** The psalmist gives thanks and rejoices (Ps 75:2, 10) for the direct intervention of God, which is promised in two oracles (Ps 75:3–4, 11). Expecting that divine intervention, the psalmist warns evildoers to repent (Ps 75:5–9).
**75:2** *You said:* supplied for clarity here and in Ps 75:11. The translation assumes in both places that the psalmist is citing an oracle of God.
**75:5** *Do not raise your horns!:* the horn is the symbol of strength; to raise one's horn is to exalt one's own power as Ps 75:5 explains.
**75:9** *A cup:* "the cup of God's wrath" is the punishment inflicted on the wicked, cf. Is 51:17; Jer 25:15–29; 49:12; Eze 23:31–33. *Spiced:* lit., "a mixed drink"; spices or drugs were added to wine, cf. Prv 9:2, 5.
**Psalm 76** A song glorifying Zion, the mountain of Jerusalem where God destroyed Israel's enemies. Zion is thus the appropri-

ate site to celebrate the victory (Ps 76:3–4), a victory described in parallel scenes (Ps 76:5–7, 8–11). Israel is invited to worship its powerful patron deity (Ps 76:12).
**76:3** *Salem:* an ancient name for Jerusalem, used here perhaps on account of its allusion to the Hebrew word for peace, *shalom*, cf. Gn 14:18; Heb 7:1–3.

---

74:16–17 Gn 1.                    75:8 Jb 5:11; 1 Sm 2:7.
    75:4 Ps 46:3; 60:4; 93:1;      75:9 Ps 60:5; Jb 21:20;
        96:10; 104:5; 1 Sm             Is 51:17, 21–22; Jer
        2:8; Is 24:19.                 25:15ff; Hb 2:16.
    75:5 1 Sm 2:3; Zec 2:1–4.      75:11 Ps 92:11.
    75:6 Jb 15:25.                 76:2 Hb 3:2.
    75:7 Mt 24:23–27.              76:4 Ps 46:10; 122:6–9.

**II**

5  Terrible and awesome are you,
     stronger than the ancient mountains.†
6  Despoiled are the stouthearted;
     they sank into sleep;
     the hands of all the men of valor have
         failed.*
7  At your roar, O God of Jacob,
     chariot and steed lay still.
8  You, terrible are you;
     who can stand before you and your
         great anger?*
9  From the heavens you pronounced
         sentence;
     the earth was terrified and reduced to
         silence,
10  When you arose, O God, for judgment
     to save the afflicted of the land.   *Selah*
11  Surely the wrath of man will give you
         thanks;
     the remnant of your furor will keep
         your feast.

**III**

12  Make and keep vows to the LORD your
         God.*
     May all around him bring gifts to the
         one to be feared,
13  Who checks the spirit of princes,
     who is fearful to the kings of earth.

### PSALM 77†

### Confidence in God During National Distress
[1] For the leader; According to *Jeduthun*. A psalm
         of Asaph.

**I**

2  I cry aloud to God,
     I cry to God to hear me.
3  On the day of my distress I seek the
         Lord;
     by night my hands are stretched out
         unceasingly;*

     I refuse to be consoled.
4  When I think of God, I groan;
     as I meditate, my spirit grows faint.*
                                    *Selah*
5  You have kept me from closing my eyes
         in sleep;
     I am troubled and cannot speak.
6  I consider the days of old;
     the years long past [7] I remember.*
   At night I ponder in my heart;
     and as I meditate, my spirit probes:
8  "Will the Lord reject us forever,*
     never again show favor?
9  Has God's mercy ceased forever?
     The promise to go unfulfilled for
         future ages?
10  Has God forgotten how to show mercy,
     in anger withheld his compassion?"
                                    *Selah*
11†  I conclude: "My sorrow is this,
     the right hand of the Most High has
         abandoned us."*

**II**

12†  I will recall the deeds of the LORD;
     yes, recall your wonders of old.*
13  I will ponder all your works;
     on your exploits I will meditate.
14  Your way, God, is holy;
     what god is as great as our God?*
15  You are the God who does wonders;
     among the peoples you have revealed
         your might.*
16  With your mighty arm you redeemed
         your people,
     the children of Jacob and Joseph.*
                                    *Selah*
17  The waters saw you, God;
     the waters saw you and lashed about,
     even the deeps of the sea† trembled.*
18  The clouds poured down their rains;
     the thunderheads rumbled;
     your arrows flashed back and forth.*

---

† **76:5** *Ancient mountains*: conjectural translation of a difficult Hebrew phrase on the basis of Gn 49:26. The mountains are part of the structure of the universe (Ps 89:12–13).
**Psalm 77** A community lament in which the speaker ("I") describes the anguish of Israel at God's silence when its very existence is at stake (Ps 77:2–11). In response the speaker recites the story of how God brought the people into existence (Ps 77:12–20). The question is thus posed to God: Will you allow the people you created to be destroyed?
**77:11** *I conclude*: lit., "I said." The psalmist, after pondering the present distress and God's promises to Israel, has decided that God has forgotten the people.
**77:12** *I will recall*: the verb sometimes means to make present the great deeds of Israel's past by reciting them, cf. Ps 78:42; 105:5; 106:7.

**77:17** *The deeps of the sea*: Heb. *tehom*; the same word is used in Gn 1:2, where it alludes to the primeval seas which in ancient Semitic cosmography are tamed by God in creation, cf. Ps 74:12–17; 89:12–13 and notes.

---

**76:6** 2 Kgs 19:35; Jer
    51:39; Na 3:18.
**76:8** Dt 7:21; 1 Sm 6:20;
    Na 1:6; Mal 3:2.
**76:12** Nm 30:3.
**77:3** Ps 50:15; 88:2.
**77:4** Jon 2:8.
**77:7** Ps 143:5; Dt 32:7.
**77:8–10** Ps 13:2; 44:24; 74:1;
    80:5; 89:47; Lam 3:31.
**77:11** Ps 17:7; 18:36;

Ex 15:6, 12.
**77:12** Ps 143:5.
**77:14** Ps 18:31; Ex 15:11.
**77:15** Ps 86:10; 89:6.
**77:16** Gn 46:26–27; Neh
    1:10.
**77:17** Ps 18:16; 114:3; Na 1:4.
**77:18** Ps 18:14–15; 29;
    144:6; Jb 37:3–4; Wis
    5:21; Hb 3:10–11;
    Zec 9:14.

**P**
**S**

19 The thunder of your chariot wheels
 resounded;
 your lightning lit up the world;
 the earth trembled and quaked. *
20 Through the sea was your way;
 your path, through the mighty waters,
 though your footsteps were unseen. *
21 You led your people like a flock
 by the hand of Moses and Aaron. *

## PSALM 78†

### A New Beginning in Zion and David

1 A *maskil* of Asaph.

#### I

Attend, my people, to my teaching;
 listen to the words of my mouth.
2 I will open my mouth in a parable, †
 unfold the puzzling events of the past. *
3 What we have heard and know;
 things our ancestors have recounted
  to us. *
4 We do not keep them from our children;
 we recount them to the next generation,
The praiseworthy deeds of the LORD and
 his strength,
 the wonders that he performed. *
5 God made a decree in Jacob,
 established a law in Israel: *
Which he commanded our ancestors,
 they were to teach their children;
6 That the next generation might come to
 know,
 children yet to be born. *
In turn they were to recount them to
 their children,

7 that they too might put their
 confidence in God,
And not forget God's deeds,
 but keep his commandments.
8 They were not to be like their ancestors,
 a rebellious and defiant generation, *
A generation whose heart was not
 constant, *
 and whose spirit was not faithful to
  God.
9 The ranks of Ephraimite archers, †
 retreated on the day of battle.
10 They did not keep God's covenant;
 they refused to walk according to his
  law.
11 They forgot his deeds,
 the wonders that he had shown them.

#### II
#### A

12 In the sight of their ancestors God did
 wonders,
 in the land of Egypt, the plain of
  Zoan. †*
13 He split the sea and led them across, *
 making the waters stand like walls. *
14 He led them with a cloud by day,
 all night with the light of fire. *
15 He split rocks in the desert,
 gave water to drink, abundant as the
  deeps of the sea. *
16 He made streams flow from crags,
 caused rivers of water to flow down.

#### B

17 But they went on sinning against him,
 rebelling against the Most High in the
  desert. *

---

† **Psalm 78** A recital of history to show that past generations did not respond to God's gracious deeds and were punished by God making the gift into a punishment. Will Israel fail to appreciate God's act—the choosing of Zion and of David? The tripartite introduction invites Israel to learn the lessons hidden in its traditions (Ps 78:1–4, 5–7, 8–11); each section ends with the mention of God's acts. There are two distinct narratives of approximately equal length: the wilderness events (Ps 78:12–39) and the movement from Egypt to Canaan (Ps 78:40–72). The structure of both is parallel: gracious act (Ps 78:12–16, 40–55), rebellion (Ps 78:17–20, 56–58), divine punishment (Ps 78:21–31, 59–64), God's readiness to forgive and begin anew (Ps 78:32–39, 65–72). While the Psalm has been thought to reflect the reunification program of either King Hezekiah (late eighth century) or King Josiah (late seventh century) in that the Northern Kingdom (Ephraim, Joseph) is especially invited to accept Zion and the Davidic king, a postexilic setting is also possible. Notable is the inclusion of the David-Zion tradition into the history of Israel recounted in the sources of the Pentateuch.

**78:2** *Parable*: Hebrew *mashal* literally refers to some sort of relationship of comparison and can signify a story whose didactic potential becomes clear in the telling, as here in the

retrospective examination of the history of Israel. Mt 13:35 cites the verse to explain Jesus' use of parables.

**78:9** *Ephraimite archers*: Ephraim was the most important tribe of the Northern Kingdom. Its military defeat (here unspecified) demonstrates its infidelity to God, who otherwise would have protected it.

**78:12, 43** *Zoan*: a city on the arm of the Nile, a former capital of Egypt.

---

* 77:19 Ps 18:8; 97:4; 99:1;
 Ex 19:16; Jgs 5:4–5.
77:20 Neh 9:11; Wis 14:3; Is
 51:10; Hb 3:15.
77:21 Ps 78:52; Is 63:11–14;
 Hos 12:14; Mi 6:4.
78:2 Ps 49:5; Mt 13:35.
78:3 Ps 44:2.
78:4 Ex 10:2; Dt 4:9; Jb
 8:8.
78:5 Ps 147:19; Dt 33:4.
78:6 Ps 22:31–32; Dt 4:9;
 6:7.

78:8 Dt 31:27; 32:5.
78:8b Ps 95:10.
78:12 Ps 106:7.
78:13–14 Ps 136:13; Ex 14–15.
78:13 Ex 14:22; 15:8.
78:14 Ps 105:39; Ex 13:21;
 Wis 18:3.
78:15 Ps 105:41; 114:8; Ex
 17:1–7; Nm 20:2–13;
 Dt 8:15; Wis 11:4; Is
 48:21.
78:17 Dt 9:7; Ez 20:13.

P S

18  They tested God in their hearts,
        demanding the food they craved. *
19  They spoke against God, and said,
        "Can God spread a table in the
            wilderness? *
20  True, when he struck the rock,
        water gushed forth,
        the wadies flooded.
    But can he also give bread,
        or provide meat to his people?"

### C

21  The LORD heard and grew angry; *
        fire blazed up against Jacob;
        anger flared up against Israel.
22  For they did not believe in God,
        did not trust in his saving power.
23 †  So he commanded the clouds above;
        and opened the doors of heaven.
24  God rained manna upon them for food;
        grain from heaven he gave them. *
25  Man ate the bread of the angels; †
        food he sent in abundance.
26  He stirred up the east wind in the skies;
        by his might God brought on the
            south wind.
27  He rained meat upon them like dust,
        winged fowl like the sands of the sea,
28  They fell down in the midst of their
            camp,
        all round their dwellings.
29  They ate and were well filled;
        he gave them what they had craved.
30  But while they still wanted more,
        and the food was still in their mouths,
31  God's anger flared up against them,
        and he made a slaughter of their
            strongest,
        laying low the youth of Israel. *
32  In spite of all this they went on sinning,
        they did not believe in his wonders.

### D

33  God ended their days abruptly,
        their years in sudden death.

34  When he slew them, they began to seek
            him;
        they again looked for God. *
35  They remembered † that God was their
            rock,
        God Most High, their redeemer.
36  But they deceived him with their
            mouths,
        lied to him with their tongues.
37  Their hearts were not constant toward
            him;
        they were not faithful to his
            covenant. *
38 †  But God being compassionate forgave
            their sin;
        he did not utterly destroy them.
    Time and again he turned back his
            anger,
        unwilling to unleash all his rage. *
39  He remembered that they were flesh,
        a breath that passes on and does not
            return.

### III

### A

40  How often they rebelled against God in
            the wilderness,
        grieved him in the wasteland.
41  Again and again they tested God,
        provoked the Holy One of Israel.
42  They did not remember his power,
        the day he redeemed them from the
            foe, *
43 †  When he performed his signs in Egypt,
        his wonders in the plain of Zoan. *
44  God turned their rivers to blood;
        their streams they could not drink.
45  He sent swarms of insects that devoured
            them, *
        frogs that destroyed them.
46  He gave their harvest to the caterpillar,
        the fruits of their labor to the locust.
47  He killed their vines with hail, *
        their sycamores with frost.

---

† **78:23–31** On the manna and the quail, see Ex 16 and Nm 11. Unlike Ex 16, here both manna and quail are instruments of punishment, showing that a divine gift can become deadly because of Israel's apostasy.

**78:25** *Bread of the angels*: the translation "angels" comports with the supernatural origin of the manna, though the Hebrew *lechem 'abbirim* is more literally translated as "bread of the strong ones" or "bread of the mighty." In the context of the manna event, this phrase cannot possibly mean the Israelites or any human being.

**78:35** *Remembered*: invoked God publicly in worship. Their words were insincere (Ps 78:36).

**78:38** God is always ready to forgive and begin anew, as in choosing Zion and David (Ps 78:65–72).

**78:43–55** Ex 7–12 records ten plagues. Here there are six divine attacks upon Egypt; the seventh climactic act is God's bringing Israel to the holy land.

---

**78:18** Ps 106:14; Ex 16:2–36.
**78:19** Ps 23:5.
**78:21f** Nm 11; Dt 32:22.
**78:24** Ps 105:40; Ex 16:4, 14; Dt 8:3; Wis 16:20; Jn 6:31.
**78:31** Nm 14:29.
**78:34** Dt 32:15, 18; Is 26:16.
**78:37** Ps 95:10; Is 29:13.
**78:38** Ps 85:4; Ex 32:14; Is 48:9; Ez 20:22.
**78:42** Ps 106:21.
**78:43f** Ps 105:27–36; 135:9; Ex 7:14–11:10; 12:29–36; Wis 16–18.
**78:45** Ex 8:17.
**78:47** Wis 16:16.

48 He exposed their cattle to plague,
     their flocks to pestilence.*
49 He let loose against them the heat of his
        anger,
     wrath, fury, and distress,
     a band of deadly messengers.
50 He cleared a path for his anger;
     he did not spare them from death,
     but delivered their animals to the
        plague.
51 He struck all the firstborn of Egypt,*
     the first fruits of their vigor in the
        tents of Ham.
52 Then God led forth his people like
        sheep,
     guided them like a flock through the
        wilderness.*
53 He led them on secure and unafraid,
     while the sea enveloped their
        enemies.*
54 And he brought them to his holy
        mountain,
     the hill his right hand had won.*
55 He drove out the nations before them,
     allotted them as their inherited
        portion,
     and settled in their tents the tribes of
        Israel.

                    B
56 But they tested and rebelled against God
        Most High,
     his decrees they did not observe.
57 They turned disloyal, faithless like their
        ancestors;
     they proved false like a slack bow.
58 They enraged him with their high places,
     and with their idols provoked him† to
        jealous anger.*

                    C
59 God heard and grew angry;
     he rejected Israel completely.
60 He forsook the shrine at Shiloh,†*

61 He gave up his might into captivity,
     his glorious ark into the hands of the
        foe.*
62 God delivered his people to the sword;
     he was enraged against his heritage.
63 Fire consumed their young men;
     their young women heard no wedding
        songs.*
64 Their priests fell by the sword;
     their widows made no lamentation.

                    D
65 Then the Lord awoke as from sleep,
     like a warrior shouting from the
        effects of wine.
66 He put his foes to flight;
     everlasting shame he dealt them.
67 He rejected the tent of Joseph,
     chose not the tribe of Ephraim.
68† God chose the tribe of Judah,
     Mount Zion which he loved.*
69 He built his shrine like the heavens,
     like the earth which he founded
        forever.
70 He chose David his servant,
     took him from the sheepfolds.*
71 From tending ewes God brought him,
     to shepherd Jacob, his people,
     Israel, his heritage.*
72 He shepherded them with a pure heart;
     with skilled hands he guided them.

## PSALM 79†

### A Prayer for Jerusalem

¹ A psalm of Asaph.
                    I
O God, the nations have invaded your
        inheritance;
     they have defiled your holy temple;
     they have laid Jerusalem in ruins.*

---

† **78:58** *Provoked him*: lit., "made him jealous."
**78:60** *Shiloh*: an important shrine in the north prior to Jerusalem. Despite its holy status, it was destroyed (Ps 78:60–64; cf. Jer 7:12, 14).
**78:68, 70** God's ultimate offer of mercy to the sinful, helpless people is Zion and the Davidic king.
**Psalm 79** A communal lament complaining that the nations have defiled the Temple and murdered the holy people, leaving their corpses unburied (Ps 79:1–4). The occasion is probably the destruction of Jerusalem by the Babylonian army in 587 B.C. The people ask how long the withdrawal of divine favor will last (Ps 79:5), pray for action now (Ps 79:6–7), and admit that their own sins have brought about the catastrophe (Ps 79:8–9). They seek to persuade God to act for reasons of honor: the nations who do

not call upon the Name are running amok (Ps 79:6); the divine honor is compromised (Ps 79:1, 10, 12); God's own servants suffer (Ps 79:2–4, 11).

---

**78:48** Ex 9:3.
**78:51** Ps 105:36; 136:10; Ex 12:29.
**78:52** Ps 77:21.
**78:53** Ex 14:26–28.
**78:54** Ex 15:17.
**78:58** Dt 32:16, 21.
**78:60** Jos 18:1; 1 Sm 1:3; Jer 7:12; 26:6.
**78:61** 1 Sm 4:11, 22.
**78:63** Dt 32:25; Jer 7:34.
**78:68** Ps 48:2; 50:2; Lam 2:15.
**78:70** Ps 89:21; Ez 34:23; 37:24; 2 Chr 6:6.
**78:71** 1 Sm 16:11–13; 2 Sm 7:8.
**79:1** 2 Kgs 25:9–10; Lam 1:10.

2 They have left the corpses of your servants
    as food for the birds of the sky,
  the flesh of those devoted to you for
    the beasts of the earth.*

3 They have poured out their blood like
    water
  all around Jerusalem,
  and no one is left to do the burying.*

4 We have become the reproach of our
    neighbors,
  the scorn and derision of those
    around us.*

**II**

5 How long, Lord? Will you be angry
    forever?
  Will your jealous anger keep burning
    like fire?*

6 Pour out your wrath on nations that do
    not recognize you,
  on kingdoms that do not call on your
    name,*

7 For they have devoured Jacob,
  laid waste his dwelling place.

8 Do not remember against us the
    iniquities of our forefathers;
  let your compassion move quickly
    ahead of us,
  for we have been brought very low.*

**III**

9 Help us, God our savior,
  on account of the glory of your name.
  Deliver us, pardon our sins
    for your name's sake.*

10 Why should the nations say,
  "Where is their God?"*
  Before our eyes make known to the
    nations
  that you avenge the blood of your
    servants which has been poured
    out.*

**IV**

11 Let the groaning of the imprisoned
  come in before you;

  in accord with the greatness of your
    arm
  preserve those doomed to die.*

12 Turn back sevenfold into the bosom of
    our neighbors
  the insult with which they insulted
    you, Lord.*

13 Then we, your people, the sheep of your
    pasture,
  will give thanks to you forever;
  from generation to generation
  we will recount your praise.

## PSALM 80†

### Prayer to Restore God's Vineyard

1 For the leader; according to "Lilies." *Eduth.*†
    A psalm of Asaph.

**I**

2 O Shepherd of Israel, lend an ear,
  you who guide Joseph like a flock!
  Seated upon the cherubim, shine forth*

3 upon Ephraim, Benjamin, and
    Manasseh.
  Stir up your power, and come to save us.

4* O God, restore us;
  light up your face and we shall be
    saved.

**II**

5 Lord of hosts,
  how long will you smolder in anger
  while your people pray?*

6 You have fed them the bread of tears,
  made them drink tears in great
    measure.†*

7 You have left us to be fought over by our
    neighbors;
  our enemies deride us.*

8 O God of hosts, restore us;
  light up your face and we shall be saved.

**III**

9 You brought a vine† out of Egypt;
  you drove out nations and planted it.

† **Psalm 80** A community lament in time of military defeat. Using the familiar image of Israel as a vineyard, the people complain that God has broken down the wall protecting the once splendid vine brought from Egypt (Ps 80:9–14). They pray that God will again turn to them and use the Davidic king to lead them to victory (Ps 80:15–19).

**80:1** *Lilies…. Eduth*: the first term is probably the title of the melody to which the Psalm was to be sung; the second is unexplained.

**80:6** Both the Septuagint and the Vulgate translate this verse in the first person, i.e., "You have fed us the bread of tears."

**80:9** *A vine*: a frequent metaphor for Israel, cf. Is 5:1–7; 27:2–5; Jer 2:21; Hos 10:1; Mt 21:33.

**79:2** Jer 7:33.
**79:3** 1 Mc 7:17; Jer 14:16.
**79:4** Ps 44:14; 80:7; 123:3–4; Jb 12:4; Dn 9:16; Zep 2:8.
**79:5** Ps 13:2; 44:24; 89:47; Dt 4:24.
**79:6** Ps 14:4; Jer 10:25.
**79:8** Ps 142:7.
**79:9** Ez 20:44; 36:22.
**79:10** Ps 42:4; 115:2; Jl 2:17.
**79:10** Jl 4:21.
**79:11** Ps 102:21.
**79:12** Ps 89:51–52.
**80:2** Ps 23:1–3; 95:7; 100:3; Gn 48:15; Ex 25:22; 1 Sm 4:4; 2 Sm 6:2; Mi 7:14.
**80:4, 8, 20** Ps 4:7; 31:17; 67:2; 85:5; Nm 6:25; Dn 9:17.
**80:5** Ps 13:2; 44:24; 74:1; 79:5; 89:47; Dt 4:24.
**80:6** Ps 42:4; 102:10.
**80:7** Ps 44:14; 79:4; 123:3–4; Jb 12:4; Dn 9:16; Zep 2:8.

<sup>10</sup> You cleared out what was before it;
    it took deep root and filled the land.
<sup>11</sup> The mountains were covered by its
       shadow,
    the cedars of God by its branches.
<sup>12</sup> It sent out its boughs as far as the sea,†
    its shoots as far as the river.†
<sup>13</sup> Why have you broken down its walls,
    so that all who pass along the way
       pluck its fruit?*
<sup>14</sup> The boar from the forest strips the vine;
    the beast of the field feeds upon it.*
<sup>15</sup> Turn back again, God of hosts;
    look down from heaven and see;
Visit this vine,
<sup>16</sup>     the stock your right hand has planted,
    and the son† whom you made strong
       for yourself.
<sup>17</sup> Those who would burn or cut it down—
    may they perish at your rebuke.
<sup>18</sup> May your hand be with the man on your
       right,†
    with the son of man whom you made
       strong for yourself.
<sup>19</sup> Then we will not withdraw from you;
    revive us, and we will call on your
       name.
<sup>20</sup> Lord God of hosts, restore us;
    light up your face and we shall be
       saved.

## PSALM 81†

### An Admonition to Fidelity

<sup>1</sup> For the leader; "upon the *gittith*."† Of Asaph.

### I

<sup>2</sup> Sing joyfully to God our strength;*
    raise loud shouts to the God of Jacob!
<sup>3</sup> Take up a melody, sound the timbrel,

    The pleasant lyre with a harp.
<sup>4</sup>† Blow the shofar at the new moon,
    at the full moon, on our solemn
       feast.*
<sup>5</sup> For this is a law for Israel,
    an edict of the God of Jacob,*
<sup>6</sup> He made it a decree for Joseph
    when he came out of the land of
       Egypt.

### II

<sup>7</sup>† I heard a tongue I did not know:
    "I removed his shoulder from the
       burden;†
    his hands moved away from the
       basket."†*
<sup>8</sup> In distress you called and I rescued you;
    I answered you in secret with thunder;
    At the waters of Meribah† I tested
       you:*         *Selah*
<sup>9</sup> "Listen, my people, I will testify against
       you
    If only you will listen to me, Israel!*
<sup>10</sup> There shall be no foreign god among
       you;†*
    you shall not bow down to an alien
       god.

<sup>11</sup> I am the Lord your God,
    who brought you up from the land of
       Egypt.
    Open wide your mouth that I may fill
       it."
<sup>12</sup> But my people did not listen to my
       words;
    Israel would not submit to me.
<sup>13</sup> So I thrust them away to the hardness of
       their heart;
    "Let them walk in their own
       machinations."*

---

**80:12** *The sea*: the Mediterranean. *The river*: the Euphrates, cf. Gn 15:18; 1 Kgs 5:1. The terms may also have a mythic nuance—the seas that surround the earth; sea and river are sometimes paralleled in poetry.

**80:16** The Vulgate and Septuagint use "son of man."

**80:18** *The man on your right*: the Davidic king who will lead the army in battle.

**Psalm 81** At a pilgrimage feast, probably harvest in the fall, the people assemble in the temple in accord with the Sinai ordinances (Ps 81:2–6). They hear a divine word (mediated by a temple speaker) telling how God rescued them from slavery in Egypt (Ps 81:7–9), gave them the fundamental commandment of fidelity (Ps 81:9–11), which would bring punishment if they refused to obey (Ps 81:12–13). But if Israel repents, God will be with them once again, bestowing protection and fertility (Ps 81:14–16).

**81:1** *Upon the gittith*: probably the title of the melody to which the psalm was to be sung or a musical instrument.

**81:4** *New moon…full moon*: the pilgrimage feast of harvest began with a great assembly (Lv 23:24; Nm 29:1), used the new

moon as a sign (Nm 29:6), and included trumpets (Lv 23:24).

**81:7** *I heard a tongue I did not know*: a Temple official speaks the word of God (Ps 81:5b–16), which is authoritative and unlike merely human words (cf. Nm 24:4, 16). *I removed his shoulders from the burden*: lit., "his [Israel's] shoulders," hence the pural translation. A reference to the liberation of Israel from slavery in Egypt. *The basket*: for carrying clay to make bricks, cf. Ex 1:14.

**81:8** *Meribah*: place of rebellion in the wilderness; cf. Ex 17:7; Nm 20:13.

**81:10** *There shall be no foreign god among you*: as in Psalm 50 and 95, Israel is challenged to obey the first commandment of fidelity to God after the proclamation of the exodus.

---

**80:13** Ps 89:41.
**80:14** Hos 2:14.
**81:2** Ps 43:4; 68:26; 149:3;
    150:3–4; Jdt 16:1.
**81:4** Lv 23:24; Nm 29:1.
**81:5** Ex 23:14ff.
**81:7** Ex 1:14; 6:6.

**81:8** Ps 95:8; Ex 2:23ff;
    17:7; 19:16; Nm
    20:13; 27:14.
**81:9** Ex 1:14; 6:6.
**81:10–11** Ex 20:2–6; Dt 5:6–10.
**81:13** Jer 3:17; 7:24.

14 O that my people would listen to me,
   that Israel would walk in my ways,*

15 In a moment I would humble their foes,
   and turn back my hand against their
      oppressors.*

16 Those who hate the LORD will try
      flattering him,
   but their fate is fixed forever.

17 But Israel I will feed with the finest
      wheat,
   I will satisfy them with honey from
      the rock."*

## PSALM 82†

### The Downfall of Unjust Gods

¹ A psalm of Asaph.

**I**

God takes a stand in the divine council,
   gives judgment in the midst of the
      gods.*

2 "How long will you judge unjustly
   and favor the cause of the wicked?*
                                    *Selah*

3 "Defend the lowly and fatherless;
   render justice to the afflicted and
      needy.

4 Rescue the lowly and poor;
   deliver them from the hand of the
      wicked."*

**II**

5† The gods neither know nor understand,
   wandering about in darkness,
   and all the world's foundations shake.

6 I declare: "Gods though you be,†*
   offspring of the Most High all of you,

7 Yet like any mortal you shall die;
   like any prince you shall fall."

8 Arise, O God, judge the earth,†
   for yours are all the nations.

## PSALM 83†

### Prayer Against a Hostile Alliance

¹ A song; a psalm of Asaph.

**I**

2 God, do not be silent;
   God, do not be deaf or remain
      unmoved!*

3 See how your enemies rage;
   your foes proudly raise their heads.

4 They conspire against your people,
   plot against those you protect.*

5 They say, "Come, let us wipe them out
      as a nation;
   let Israel's name be remembered no
      more!"

6 They scheme with one mind,
   they have entered into a covenant
      against you:*

7† The tents of Edom and the Ishmaelites,
   of Moab and the Hagrites,*

8 Gebal, Ammon, and Amalek,*
   Philistia and the inhabitants of Tyre.*

9 Assyria, too, in league with them,
   backs the descendants of Lot.      *Selah*

**II**

10† Deal with them as with Midian;
   as with Sisera and Jabin at the wadi
      Kishon,*

11 Those destroyed at Endor,
   who became dung for the ground.*

---

† **Psalm 82** As in Ps 58, the pagan gods are seen as subordinate divine beings to whom Israel's God had delegated oversight of the foreign countries in the beginning (Dt 32:8–9). Now God arises in the heavenly assembly (Ps 82:1) to rebuke the unjust "gods" (Ps 82:2–4), who are stripped of divine status and reduced in rank to mortals (Ps 82:5–7). They are accused of misruling the earth by not upholding the poor (Ps 82:8). A short prayer for universal justice concludes the Psalm (Ps 82:8).

**82:5** The gods are blind and unable to declare what is right. Their misrule shakes earth's foundations (cf. Ps 11:3; 75:4), which God made firm in creation (Ps 96:10).

**82:6** *I declare: "Gods though you be"*: in Jn 10:34 Jesus uses the verse to prove that those to whom the word of God is addressed can fittingly be called "gods."

**82:8** *Judge the earth*: according to Dt 32:8–9, Israel's God had originally assigned jurisdiction over the foreign nations to the subordinate deities, keeping Israel as a personal possession. Now God will directly take over the rulership of the whole world.

**Psalm 83** The community lament complains to God of the nations' attempts to wipe out the name of Israel (Ps 83:1–8). The psalmist sees all Israel's enemies throughout its history united in a conspiracy (Ps 83:2–8). May God destroy the current crop of enemies as the enemies of old were destroyed (Ps 83:9–12), and may they be pursued until they acknowledge the name of Israel's God (Ps 83:13–18).

**83:7–9** Apart from the Assyrians, all the nations listed here were neighbors of Israel. The Hagrites are a tribe of the desert regions east of Ammon and Moab (1 Chr 5:10, 19–22). Gebal is the Phoenician city of Byblos or perhaps a mountain region south of the Dead Sea. The descendants of Lot are Moab and Edom (Gn 19:36–38 and Dt 2:9). These nations were never united against Israel in the same period; the Psalm has lumped them all together.

**83:10–13** For the historical events, see Jgs 4–8.

---

* **81:14** Is 48:18.
**81:15** Lv 26:7–8.
**81:17** Ps 147:14; Dt 32:13–14.
**82:1** Is 3:13–14.
**82:2** Ps 58:2.
**82:4** Dt 1:17.
**82:6** 2 Pt 1:4.
**83:2** Ps 10:1; 44:24; 109:1.

**83:4** Jer 11:9.
**83:6** Ps 2:2.
**83:7** Nm 20:23; 1 Chr 5:10, 19.
**83:8** Ex 17:8.
**83:8** Jos 13:2.
**83:10** Ex 2:15; Is 9:3; 10:26.
**83:11** Jer 8:2.

12  Make their nobles like Oreb and Zeeb,
       all their princes like Zebah and
          Zalmunna,
13  Who made a plan together,
       "Let us take for ourselves the pastures
          of God."
14  My God, make them like tumbleweed,
       into chaff flying before the wind. *
15  As a fire raging through a forest,
       a flame setting mountains ablaze, *
16  Pursue them with your tempest;
       terrify them with your storm-wind.
17  Cover their faces with shame,
       till they seek your name, † LORD.
18  Let them be ashamed and terrified
          forever;
       let them perish in disgrace.
19  Let them know that your name is
          LORD,
       you alone are the Most High over all
          the earth. *

## PSALM 84†

### Prayer of a Pilgrim to Jerusalem

1 For the leader; "upon the *gittith*." A psalm of the
       Korahites.

**I**

2  How lovely your dwelling,
       O LORD of hosts! *
3  My soul yearns and pines
       for the courts of the LORD. *
   My heart and flesh cry out
       for the living God.
4 †  As the sparrow finds a home
       and the swallow a nest to settle her
          young,
   My home is by your altars,
       LORD of hosts, my king and my God! *

5  Blessed are those who dwell in your
          house!
       They never cease to praise you.    *Selah*

**II**

6  Blessed the man who finds refuge in
          you,
       in their hearts are pilgrim roads.
7  As they pass through the Baca valley, †
       they find spring water to drink.
   The early rain covers it with blessings.
8  They will go from strength to strength †
       and see the God of gods on Zion.

**III**

9  LORD God of hosts, hear my prayer;
       listen, God of Jacob.        *Selah*
10 †  O God, watch over our shield;
       look upon the face of your anointed. *

**IV**

11  Better one day in your courts
       than a thousand elsewhere.
   Better the threshold of the house of my
          God
       than a home in the tents of the
          wicked.
12  For a sun and shield is the LORD God,
       bestowing all grace and glory.
   The LORD withholds no good thing
       from those who walk without
          reproach.
13  O LORD of hosts,
       blessed the man who trusts in you!

## PSALM 85†

### Prayer for Divine Favor

1 For the leader. A psalm of the Korahites.

**I**

2  You once favored, LORD, your land,
       restored the captives of Jacob. *

---

**83:17** *Seek your name*: a variant of the more typical phrase "to seek the face of God" (Ps 24:6; 27:8; 105:4). Seeking the face of God refers to the worshiper having recourse to a temple or sanctuary where in non-Jewish contexts a statue embodies the physical presence of the Deity. In Israel's aniconic tradition no visible image or statue can represent God. This understanding is conveyed here concretely by use of the term "your name" rather than the more typical "your face."
**Psalm 84** Israelites celebrated three pilgrimage feasts in Jerusalem annually. The Psalm expresses the sentiments of the pilgrims eager to enjoy the divine presence.
**84:4** The desire of a restless bird for a secure home is an image of the desire of a pilgrim for the secure house of God, cf. Ps 42:2–3, where the image for the desire of the pilgrim is the thirst of the deer for water.
**84:7** *Baca valley*: Hebrew obscure; probably a valley on the way to Jerusalem.
**84:8** *Strength to strength*: pass through outer and inner wall.

**84:10** *Our shield…your anointed*: the king had a role in the liturgical celebration. For the king as shield, cf. Ps 89:19.
**Psalm 85** A national lament reminding God of past favors and forgiveness (Ps 85:2–4) and begging for forgiveness and grace now (Ps 85:5–8). A speaker represents the people who wait humbly with open hearts (Ps 85:9–10): God will be active on their behalf (Ps 85:11–13). The situation suggests the conditions of Judea during the early postexilic period, the fifth century B.C.; the thoughts are similar to those of postexilic prophets (Hg 1:5–11; 2:6–9).

---

**83:14** Ps 1:4; 35:5; 58:10;     **84:2** Ps 43:3–4; 122:1.
    Is 5:24; 10:17; 17:13;     **84:3** Ps 42:2–3; 63:2–3;
    29:5; Ez 21:3.                    143:6; Is 26:9.
**83:15** Ps 50:3.                 **84:4** Ps 5:3.
**83:19** Ps 97:9; Dt 4:39; Dn     **84:10** Ps 89:19.
    3:45.                          **85:2** Ps 14:7; 126:4.

3   You forgave the guilt of your people,
       pardoned all their sins.          *Selah*
4   You withdrew all your wrath,
       turned back from your burning
          anger. *

**II**

5   Restore us, God of our salvation;
       let go of your displeasure with us. *
6   Will you be angry with us forever,
       prolong your anger for all
          generations? *
7   Certainly you will again restore our life,
       that your people may rejoice in you.
8   Show us, LORD, your mercy;
       grant us your salvation.

**III**

9 †  I will listen for what God, the LORD, has
       to say;
    surely he will speak of peace
    To his people and to his faithful.
       May they not turn to foolishness!
10  Near indeed is his salvation for those
       who fear him;
       glory will dwell in our land.
11 †  Love and truth will meet;
       justice and peace will kiss. *
12  Truth will spring from the earth;
       justice will look down from heaven. *
13  Yes, the LORD will grant his bounty;
       our land will yield its produce. *
14  Justice will march before him,
       and make a way for his footsteps.

## PSALM 86 †

### Prayer in Time of Distress

¹ A prayer of David.

**I**

Incline your ear, LORD, and answer me,
    for I am poor and oppressed.
2   Preserve my life, for I am devoted;
       save your servant who trusts in you.
    You are my God; ³ be gracious to me,
       Lord;
       to you I call all the day.

4   Gladden the soul of your servant;
       to you, Lord, I lift up my soul. *
5   Lord, you are good and forgiving,
       most merciful to all who call on you. *
6   LORD, hear my prayer;
       listen to my cry for help. *
7   On the day of my distress I call to you,
       for you will answer me.

**II**

8   None among the gods can equal you,
          O Lord;
    nor can their deeds compare to yours. *
9   All the nations you have made shall
          come
       to bow before you, Lord,
       and give honor to your name. *
10  For you are great and do wondrous
          deeds;
       and you alone are God.

**III**

11  Teach me, LORD, your way
       that I may walk in your truth, *
       single-hearted and revering your
          name.
12  I will praise you with all my heart,
       glorify your name forever, Lord my
          God.
13  Your mercy to me is great;
       you have rescued me from the depths
          of Sheol. *
14  O God, the arrogant have risen against
          me;
       a ruthless band has sought my life;
       to you they pay no heed.
15  But you, Lord, are a compassionate and
          gracious God,
       slow to anger, abounding in mercy
          and truth. *
16  Turn to me, be gracious to me;
       give your strength to your servant;
       save the son of your handmaid. *
17  Give me a sign of your favor:
       make my enemies see, to their
          confusion,
       that you, LORD, help and comfort me.

† 85:9 The prophet listens to God's revelation, cf. Heb 2:1.
85:11–13 Divine activity is personified as pairs of virtues.
   Psalm 86 An individual lament. The psalmist, "poor and oppressed" (Ps 86:1), "devoted" (Ps 86:2), "your servant" (Ps 86:2,
4, 16), "rescued…from the depths of Sheol" (Ps 86:13), attacked
by the ruthless (Ps 86:14), desires only God's protection (Ps
86:1–7, 11–17).

85:4 Ps 78:38; Ex 32:14; Is
      48:9.
85:5 Ps 80:4.
85:6 Ps 79:5; 89:47.
85:11 Ps 89:15; 97:2.
85:12 Is 45:8.
85:13 Ps 67:7; Lv 26:4; Ez
      34:27; Hos 2:23–24;
      Zec 8:12.
86:4 Ps 25:1; 143:8.
86:5 Jl 2:13.
86:6 Ps 5:2; 130:1–2.

86:8 Ps 35:10; 89:9; Ex
      15:11; Dt 3:24; Jer
      10:6.
86:9 Ps 22:28; Zec 14:16;
      Rev 15:4.
86:11 Ps 25:4; 26:3; 27:11;
      119:12, 35; 143:8, 10.
86:13 Ps 30:4; 40:3; Jon 2:7.
86:15 Ps 103:8; 130:7;
      145:8; Ex 34:6.
86:16 Ps 25:16; 116:16; Wis
      9:5.

## PSALM 87†

### Zion the True Birthplace

¹*A psalm of the Korahites. A song.

**I**

His foundation is on holy mountains,
2 The LORD loves the gates† of Zion
   more than any dwelling in Jacob.
3 Glorious things are said of you,
   O city of God!                    *Selah*

**II**

4 Rahab and Babylon I count
   among those who know me.
   See, Philistia and Tyre, with Ethiopia,
   "This one was born there."
5† And of Zion it will be said:
   "Each one was born in it."*
   The Most High will establish it;*
6   the LORD notes in the register of the
       peoples:
   "This one was born there."*       *Selah*
7 So singers and dancers:
   "All my springs are in you."*

## PSALM 88†

### A Despairing Lament

¹A song; a psalm of the Korahites. For the leader;
according to *Mahalath*. For singing; a *maskil* of
   Heman the Ezrahite.

**I**

2 LORD, the God of my salvation, I call out
       by day;
   at night I cry aloud in your presence.*
3 Let my prayer come before you;
   incline your ear to my cry.*
4† For my soul is filled with troubles;*
   my life draws near to Sheol.
5 I am reckoned with those who go down
       to the pit;
   I am like a warrior without strength.
6 My couch is among the dead,
   like the slain who lie in the grave.

You remember them no more;
   they are cut off from your influence.
7 You plunge me into the bottom of the
       pit,
   into the darkness of the abyss.
8 Your wrath lies heavy upon me;
   all your waves crash over me.*      *Selah*

**II**

9 Because of you my acquaintances shun
       me;
   you make me loathsome to them;*
Caged in, I cannot escape;
10   my eyes grow dim from trouble.

All day I call on you, LORD;
   I stretch out my hands to you.
11† Do you work wonders for the dead?
   Do the shades arise and praise you?*
                                       *Selah*

**III**

12 Is your mercy proclaimed in the grave,
   your faithfulness among those who
       have perished?†
13 Are your marvels declared in the
       darkness,
   your righteous deeds in the land of
       oblivion?

**IV**

14 But I cry out to you, LORD;
   in the morning my prayer comes
       before you.
15 Why do you reject my soul, LORD,
   and hide your face from me?
16 I have been mortally afflicted since youth;
   I have borne your terrors and I am
       made numb.
17 Your wrath has swept over me;
   your terrors have destroyed me.*
18 All day they surge round like a flood;
   from every side they encircle me.
19 Because of you friend and neighbor
       shun me;*
   my only friend is darkness.

---

**Psalm 87** A song of Zion, like Ps 46; 48; 76; 132.
**87:2** *The gates:* the city itself, a common Hebrew idiom.
**87:5–6** The bond between the exile and the holy city was so
strong as to override the exile's citizenship of lesser cities.
**Psalm 88** A lament in which the psalmist prays for rescue
from the alienation of approaching death. Each of the three
stanzas begins with a call to God (Ps 88:2, 10, 14) and complains of the death that separates one from God. The tone is
persistently grim.
**88:4–8** In imagination the psalmist already experiences the
alienation of Sheol.
**88:11–13** The psalmist seeks to persuade God to act out of
concern for divine honor: the shades give you no worship, so

keep me alive to offer you praise.
**88:12** *Perished:* lit., "Abaddon," the deepest part of Sheol.

---

**87:1–2** Ps 76:2–3; 78:68–69.
**87:5** Gal 4:26.
**87:5** Ps 48:9.
**87:6** Is 4:3.
**87:7** Ps 68:26; 149:3.
**88:2** Ps 77:3.
**88:3** Ps 119:170.
**88:4–7** Ps 28:1; 30:4; 40:3;
   86:13; 143:7; Nm
   16:33; Jb 17:1;
   Jon 2:7.
**88:8** Ps 18:5; 32:6; 42:8;
   69:2; Jon 2:4.
**88:9** Ps 38:12; 79:4; 80:7;
   123:3–4; 142:8; Jb
   12:4; 19:13; Lam 3:7;
   Dn 9:16.
**88:11** Ps 6:6; 30:10; 38:18;
   115:17.
**88:17** Jb 6:4; 20:25.
**88:19** Jb 19:13.

## PSALM 89†

### A Lament over God's Promise to David

¹ A *maskil* of Ethan the Ezrahite.

**A**

**I**

2    I will sing of your mercy forever, LORD*
        proclaim your faithfulness through all
            ages.

³† For I said, "My mercy is established
        forever;
        my faithfulness will stand as long as
            the heavens.

4    I have made a covenant with my chosen
        one;
        I have sworn to David my servant:

5    I will make your dynasty stand forever
        and establish your throne through all
            ages."*                              *Selah*

**II**

6    The heavens praise your marvels,
        LORD,
        your loyalty in the assembly of the
            holy ones.*

7    Who in the skies ranks with the LORD?
        Who is like the LORD among the sons
            of the gods?†*

8    A God dreaded in the council of the
        holy ones,
        greater and more awesome than all
            those around him!

9    LORD, God of hosts, who is like you?
        Mighty LORD, your faithfulness
            surrounds you.

10   You rule the raging sea;*
        you still its swelling waves.

11   You crush Rahab† with a mortal blow;
        with your strong arm you scatter your
            foes.

12   Yours are the heavens, yours the earth;

you founded the world and everything
    in it.*

13†  Zaphon and Amanus you created;
        Tabor and Hermon rejoice in your
            name.

14   You have a mighty arm.
        Your hand is strong; your right hand
            is ever exalted.

15   Justice and judgment are the foundation
        of your throne;
        mercy and faithfulness march before
            you.*

16   Blessed the people who know the war
        cry,
        who walk in the radiance of your face,
            LORD.

17   In your name they sing joyfully all the
        day;
        they rejoice in your righteousness.*

18   You are their majestic strength;
        by your favor our horn† is exalted.*

19   Truly the LORD is our shield,
        the Holy One of Israel, our king!*

**III**

20   Then you spoke in vision;*
        to your faithful ones you said:
        "I have set a leader over the warriors;
        I have raised up a chosen one from
            the people.

21   I have chosen David, my servant;
        with my holy oil I have anointed
            him.

22   My hand will be with him;*
        my arm will make him strong.

23   No enemy shall outwit him,
        nor shall the wicked defeat him.

24   I will crush his foes before him,
        strike down those who hate him.

25   My faithfulness and mercy will be with
        him;

---

**Psalm 89** The community laments the defeat of the Davidic king, to whom God promised kingship as enduring as the heavens (Ps 89:2–5). The Psalm narrates how God became king of the divine beings (Ps 89:6–9) and how the Davidic king became king of earthly kings (Ps 89:20–38). Since the defeat of the king calls into question God's promise, the community ardently prays God to be faithful to the original promise to David (Ps 89:39–52).

**89:3–5** David's dynasty is to be as long-lasting as the heavens, a statement reinforced by using the same verbs (establish, stand) both of the divine love and loyalty and of the Davidic dynasty and throne, cf. Ps 89:29–30.

**89:7** *The sons of the gods:* "the holy ones" and "courtiers" of Ps 89:6, 8. These heavenly spirits are members of God's court.

**89:11** *Rahab:* a mythological sea monster whose name is used in the Bible mainly as a personification of primeval chaos, cf. Jb 9:13; 26:12; Ps 74:13–14; Is 51:9.

**89:13** *Zaphon and Amanus:* two sacred mountains in north-

ern Syria which came to designate the directions of north and south. *Tabor:* a high hill in the valley of Jezreel in northern Israel. *Hermon:* a mountain in Lebanon, forming the southern spur of the Anti-Lebanon range.

**89:18, 25** *Horn:* a concrete noun for an abstract quality; horn is a symbol of strength.

---

| | |
|---|---|
| **89:2** Is 63:7. | 10:14; 1 Cor 10:26. |
| **89:5** Ps 61:7–8; 132:11; | **89:15** Ps 85:11–12; 97:2. |
| 2 Sm 7:8–16. | **89:17** Ps 47:2; Zep 3:14. |
| **89:6** Ps 29:1; 82:1; Jb 1:6; | **89:18** Ps 112:9; 148:14. |
| 5:1. | **89:19** Ps 47:9; 96:10; 97:1; |
| **89:7–9** Ps 35:10; 86:8; 113:5; | 99:1; Is 6:3. |
| Ex 15:11; Jer 10:6. | **89:20–21** Ps 78:70; 132:11–12; |
| **89:10–11** Ps 65:8; 74:13–15; | 2 Sm 7:4, 8–16; 1 Chr |
| 107:29; Jb 7:12; Is | 17:3, 7–14; Is 42:1; |
| 51:9–10. | Acts 13:22. |
| **89:12** Ps 24:1–2; 50:12; Dt | **89:22–25** 1 Sm 2:9–10. |

through my name his horn will be
exalted.

26 † I will set his hand upon the sea,
his right hand upon the rivers.

27 He shall cry to me, 'You are my father, *
my God, the Rock of my salvation!'

28 I myself make him the firstborn,
Most High † over the kings of the earth.

29 Forever I will maintain my mercy for
him; *
my covenant with him stands firm.

30 I will establish his dynasty forever,
his throne as the days of the heavens.

31 If his descendants forsake my teaching, *
do not follow my decrees,

32 If they fail to observe my statutes,
do not keep my commandments,

33 I will punish their crime with a rod
and their guilt with blows.

34 But I will not take my mercy from him,
nor will I betray my bond of
faithfulness. *

35 I will not violate my covenant;
the promise of my lips I will not alter. *

36 By my holiness I swore once for all: *
I will never be false to David.

37 † His dynasty will continue forever, *
his throne, like the sun before me.

38 Like the moon it will stand eternal,
forever firm like the sky!"　　　Selah

**B**

**IV**

39 But now you have rejected and spurned, *
been enraged at your anointed.

40 You renounced the covenant with your
servant,
defiled his crown in the dust.

41 You broke down all city walls, *
left his strongholds in ruins.

42 All who pass through seize plunder;
his neighbors deride him.

43 You have exalted the right hand of his
foes,
have gladdened all his enemies. *

44 You turned back his sharp sword,
did not support him in battle.

45 You brought to an end his splendor,
hurled his throne to the ground.

46 You cut short the days of his youth,
covered him with shame.　　　Selah

**V**

47 How long, LORD? Will you hide forever?
Must your wrath smolder like fire? *

48 Remember how brief life is,
how frail the sons of man you have
created! *

49 What is man, that he should live and
not see death?
Who can deliver his soul from the
power of Sheol? *　　　Selah

**VI**

50 Where are your former mercies, Lord,
that you swore to David in your
faithfulness?

51 Remember, Lord, the insults to your
servants,
how I have borne in my bosom the
slander of the nations. *

52 Your enemies, LORD, insult;
they insult each step of your anointed.

53 † Blessed be the LORD forever! Amen and
amen! *

## Fourth Book—Psalms 90–106

## PSALM 90 †

## God's Eternity and Human Frailty

[1] A prayer of Moses, the man of God.

**I**

Lord, you have been our refuge
through all generations.

---

† **89:26** *The sea...the rivers*: geographically the limits of the Davidic empire (the Mediterranean and the Euphrates); mythologically, the traditional forces of chaos. See note on Ps 89:11.

**89:28** *Most High*: a divine title, which is here extended to David as God's own king, cf. Ps 2:7–9; Is 9:5. As God rules over the members of the heavenly council (Ps 89:6–9), so David, God's surrogate, rules over earthly kings.

**89:37–38** *Like the sun before me...like the sky*: as enduring as the heavenly lights, cf. Ps 89:2–5 and Ps 72:5, 17.

**89:53** The doxology at the end of the third book of the Psalms; it is not part of Ps 89.

**Psalm 90** A communal lament that describes only in general terms the cause of the community's distress. After confidently invoking God (Ps 90:1), the Psalm turns to a complaint contrasting God's eternity with the brevity of human life (Ps 90:2–6) and

sees in human suffering the punishment for sin (Ps 90:7–12). The Psalm concludes with a plea for God's intervention (Ps 90:13–17).

**89:27–28** Ps 2:7; 110:2–3; 2 Sm 7:9, 14; Col 1:15, 18; Rev 1:5.
**89:29–30** Ps 18:51; 61:8; 144:10; 2 Sm 7:11; Is 55:3.
**89:31–33** Lv 26:14–33.
**89:34** Ps 40:12; Sir 47:22.
**89:35** Jer 33:20–21.
**89:36** Am 4:2.
**89:37–38** Ps 61:8; 72:5; Sir 43:6.
**89:39–47** Ps 44:10–25.
**89:41–42** Ps 80:13–14.
**89:43** Lam 1:5.
**89:47** Ps 13:2; 44:25; 74:10; 79:5; Dt 4:24.
**89:48** Ps 39:5–6; 62:10; 90:9–10; 144:4; Jb 7:6, 16; 14:1, 5; Eccl 6:12; Wis 2:5.
**89:49** Ps 90:3.
**89:51** Ps 79:12.
**89:53** Ps 41:14; 72:18; 106:48.

2 Before the mountains were born,
    the earth and the world brought forth,
    from eternity to eternity you are
        God. *
3 You turn humanity back into dust, †
    saying, "Return, you children of
        Adam!" *
4 A thousand years in your eyes
    are merely a day gone by, *
    Before a watch passes in the night,
5† you wash them away; *
  They sleep,
    and in the morning they sprout again
        like an herb.
6 In the morning it blooms only to pass
        away;
    in the evening it is wilted and
        withered. †*

II

7 Truly we are consumed by your anger,
    filled with terror by your wrath.
8 You have kept our faults before you,
    our hidden sins in the light of your
        face. *
9 Our life ebbs away under your wrath; *
    our years end like a sigh.
10 Seventy is the sum of our years,
    or eighty, if we are strong;
  Most of them are toil and sorrow;
    they pass quickly, and we are gone.
11 Who comprehends the strength of your
        anger?
  Your wrath matches the fear it
        inspires.
12 Teach us to count our days aright,
    that we may gain wisdom of heart.

III

13 Relent, O LORD! How long?
    Have pity on your servants!

14 Fill us at daybreak with your mercy, *
    that all our days we may sing for joy.
15 Make us glad as many days as you
        humbled us,
    for as many years as we have seen
        trouble. *
16 Show your deeds to your servants,
    your glory to their children.
17 May the favor of the Lord our God be
        ours. *
  Prosper the work of our hands!
  Prosper the work of our hands!

## PSALM 91†

### Security Under God's Protection

I

1 You who dwell in the shelter of the Most
        High, †
    who abide in the shade of the
        Almighty, †
2 Say to the LORD, "My refuge and fortress,
    my God in whom I trust." *
3 He will rescue you from the fowler's
        snare,
    from the destroying plague,
4 He will shelter you with his pinions,
    and under his wings you may take
        refuge; *
    his faithfulness is a protecting shield.
5 You shall not fear the terror of the night
    nor the arrow that flies by day, *
6 Nor the pestilence that roams in
        darkness,
    nor the plague that ravages at noon. *
7 Though a thousand fall at your side,
    ten thousand at your right hand,
    near you it shall not come.
8 You need simply watch;

P
S

the punishment of the wicked you
will see.*

9 Because you have the LORD for your
refuge
and have made the Most High your
stronghold,

10 No evil shall befall you,
no affliction come near your tent.*

11† For he commands his angels with regard
to you,*
to guard you wherever you go.*

12 With their hands they shall support you,
lest you strike your foot against a
stone.*

13 You can tread upon the asp and the
viper,
trample the lion and the dragon.*

**II**

14 Because he clings to me I will deliver
him;
because he knows my name I will set
him on high.*

15 He will call upon me and I will answer;*
I will be with him in distress;*
I will deliver him and give him honor.

16 With length of days I will satisfy him,
and fill him with my saving power.*

## PSALM 92†

### A Hymn of Thanksgiving for God's Fidelity

1 A psalm. A sabbath song.

**I**

2 It is good to give thanks to the LORD,
to sing praise to your name, Most
High,*

3 To proclaim your love at daybreak,
your faithfulness in the night,

4 With the ten-stringed harp,
with melody upon the lyre.*

5 For you make me jubilant, LORD, by
your deeds;
at the works of your hands I shout for
joy.

**II**

6 How great are your works, LORD!*
How profound your designs!

7 A senseless person cannot know this;
a fool cannot comprehend.

8 Though the wicked flourish like grass*
and all sinners thrive,
They are destined for eternal destruction;

9 but you, LORD, are forever on high.

10 Indeed your enemies, LORD,
indeed your enemies shall perish;
all sinners shall be scattered.*

**III**

11 You have given me the strength of a wild
ox;*
you have poured rich oil upon me.*

12 My eyes look with glee on my wicked
enemies;
my ears shall hear what happens to
my wicked foes.*

13 The just shall flourish like the palm tree,
shall grow like a cedar of Lebanon.*

14† Planted in the house of the LORD,
they shall flourish in the courts of our
God.

15 They shall bear fruit even in old age,
they will stay fresh and green,

16 To proclaim: "The LORD is just;
my rock, in whom there is no
wrong."*

## PSALM 93†

### God Is a Mighty King

1 The LORD is king,† robed with majesty;
the LORD is robed, girded with might.*

---

**91:11–12** The words are cited in Lk 4:10–11; Mt 4:6, as Satan tempts Jesus in the desert.
**Psalm 92** A hymn of praise and thanks for God's faithful deeds (Ps 92:2–5). The wicked, deluded by their prosperity (Ps 92:6–9), are punished (Ps 92:10), whereas the psalmist has already experienced God's protection (Ps 92:11–15).
**92:14** *Planted*: the just are likened to trees growing in the sacred precincts of the Temple, which is often seen as the source of life and fertility because of God's presence, cf. Ps 36:9, 10; Ez 47:1–12.
**Psalm 93** A hymn celebrating the kingship of God, who created the world (Ps 93:1–2) by defeating the sea (Ps 93:3–4). In the ancient myth that is alluded to here, Sea completely covered the land, making it impossible for the human community to live. Sea, or Flood, roars in anger against God, who is personified in the storm. God's utterances or decrees are given authority by the victory over Sea (Ps 93:5).

**93:1** *The LORD is king*: lit., "the LORD reigns." This Psalm, and Ps 47; 96–99, are sometimes called enthronement Psalms. They may have been used in a special liturgy during which God's ascent to the throne was ritually reenacted. They have also been interpreted eschatologically, pointing to the coming of God as king at the end-time.

---

**91:8** Ps 92:12.
**91:10** Prv 12:21; Dt 7:15.
**91:11–12** Mt 4:6; Lk 4:10f.
**91:11** Heb 1:14.
**91:12** Ps 121:3; Prv 3:23.
**91:13** Is 11:8; Lk 10:19.
**91:14** Ps 9:11; 119:132.
**91:15** Jer 33:3; Zec 13:9.
**91:15** Is 43:2.
**91:16** Prv 3:2.
**92:2** Ps 33:1; 147:1.
**92:4** Ps 33:2; 144:9.

**92:6–7** Ps 131:1; 139:6, 17;
Wis 13:1; 17:1.
**92:8** Ps 37:35.
**92:10** Ps 68:1–2; 125:5.
**92:11** Ps 75:11; Dt 33:17.
**92:11** Ps 23:5.
**92:12** Ps 91:8.
**92:13** Ps 1:3; 52:10;
Jer 17:8.
**92:16** Dt 32:4.
**93:1** Ps 47:8; 96:10; 97:1;
99:1.

The world will surely stand in place,
  never to be moved.*

2  Your throne stands firm from of old;
     you are from everlasting.*

3† The flood has raised up, LORD;
     the flood has raised up its roar;
     the flood has raised its pounding
        waves.

4  More powerful than the roar of many
        waters,
     more powerful than the breakers of
        the sea,
     powerful in the heavens is the LORD.

5  Your decrees are firmly established;
     holiness befits your house, LORD,
     for all the length of days.

## PSALM 94†

### A Prayer for Deliverance from the Wicked

**I**

1  LORD, avenging God,
     avenging God, shine forth!*

2  Rise up, O judge of the earth;
     give the proud what they deserve!*

**II**

3  How long, LORD, shall the wicked,
     how long shall the wicked glory?*

4  How long will they mouth haughty
        speeches,
     go on boasting, all these evildoers?*

5  They crush your people, LORD,
     torment your very own.

6  They kill the widow and alien;
     the orphan they murder.*

7  They say, "The LORD does not see;
     the God of Jacob takes no notice."*

**III**

8  Understand, you stupid people!
     You fools, when will you be wise?*

9  Does the one who shaped the ear not
        hear?
     The one who formed the eye not
        see?*

10  Does the one who guides nations not
        rebuke?
     The one who teaches man not have
        knowledge?

11  The LORD knows the plans of man;
     they are like a fleeting breath.*

**IV**

12  Blessed the one whom you guide,
        LORD,*
     whom you teach by your instruction,

13  To give rest from evil days,
     while a pit is being dug for the
        wicked.

14  For the LORD will not forsake his
        people,
     nor abandon his inheritance.*

15  Judgment shall again be just,
     and all the upright of heart will follow
        it.

**V**

16  Who will rise up for me against the
        wicked?
     Who will stand up for me against
        evildoers?

17  If the LORD were not my help,
     I would long have been silent in the
        grave.*

18  When I say, "My foot is slipping,"
     your mercy, LORD, holds me up.*

19  When cares increase within me,
     your comfort gives me joy.

**VI**

20  Can unjust judges be your allies,
     those who create burdens by decree,

21  Those who conspire against the just
     and condemn the innocent to death?

22  No, the LORD is my secure height,
     my God, my rock of refuge,

23* Who will turn back their evil upon
        them*
     and destroy them for their
        wickedness.
     Surely the LORD our God will destroy
        them!

---

**P
S**

---

93:3 *The flood:* the primordial sea was tamed by God in the act of creation. It is a figure of chaos and rebellion, cf. Ps 46:4.

**Psalm 94** A lament of an individual who is threatened by wicked people. The danger affects the whole community. Calling upon God as judge (Ps 94:1–2), the Psalm complains about oppression of the holy community by people within (Ps 94:3–7). Bold declarations of faith follow: denunciation of evildoers (Ps 94:8–11) and assurance to the just (Ps 94:12–15). The Psalm continues with further lament (Ps 94:16–19) and ends with strong confidence in God's response (Ps 94:20–23).

93:1 Ps 75:2–3; 104:5.
93:2 Ps 55:20; 90:2;
  102:13; Heb 1:12.
94:1 Na 1:2.
94:2 Jer 51:56; Lam 3:64.
94:3 Ps 13:2; 75:5; Jer
  12:1.
94:4 Ps 73; Mal 2:17; 3:14.
94:6 Ex 22:21–22; Dt
  24:17–22.
94:7 Ps 10:11; 64:6; 73:11;
  Jb 22:13–14; Ez 9:9.

94:8 Prv 1:22; 8:5.
94:9 Ex 4:11; Prv 20:12.
94:11 Ps 33:15; 1 Cor 3:20.
94:12 Ps 119:71; Jb 5:17.
94:14 1 Sm 12:22; Sir 47:22.
94:17 Ps 6:6; 115:17.
94:18 Ps 145:14.
94:23 Ps 7:16; 9:16; 35:8;
  57:7; Prv 26:27; Eccl
  10:8; Sir 27:26.
94:23 Ps 107:42.

## PSALM 95†

### A Call to Praise and Obedience

#### I

1 Come, let us sing joyfully to the LORD;
   cry out to the rock of our salvation.*

2 Let us come before him with a song of
      praise,
   joyfully sing out our psalms.

3 For the LORD is the great God,
   the great king over all gods,*

4 Whose hand holds the depths of the
      earth;
   who owns the tops of the
      mountains.

5 The sea and dry land belong to God,
   who made them, formed them by
      hand.*

#### II

6 Enter, let us bow down in worship;
   let us kneel before the LORD who
      made us.

7 For he is our God,
   we are the people he shepherds,
   the sheep in his hands.*

#### III

   Oh, that today you would hear his
      voice:*

8 Do not harden your hearts as at
      Meribah,
   as on the day of Massah in the
      desert.†

9 There your ancestors tested me;
   they tried me though they had seen
      my works.*

10 Forty years I loathed that generation;
   I said: "This people's heart goes
      astray;
   they do not know my ways."*

11 Therefore I swore in my anger:
   "They shall never enter my rest."†

## PSALM 96†

### God of the Universe

#### I

1 Sing to the LORD a new song;*
   sing to the LORD, all the earth.

2 Sing to the LORD, bless his name;
   proclaim his salvation day after day.

3 Tell his glory among the nations;
   among all peoples, his marvelous
      deeds.*

#### II

4† For great is the LORD and highly to be
      praised,
   to be feared above all gods.*

5 For the gods of the nations are idols,
   but the LORD made the heavens.*

6 Splendor and power go before him;
   power and grandeur are in his holy
      place.

#### III

7 Give to the LORD, you families of
      nations,
   give to the LORD glory and might;

8 give to the LORD the glory due his
      name!*
   Bring gifts and enter his courts;

9 bow down to the LORD, splendid in
      holiness.
   Tremble before him, all the earth;

10* declare among the nations: The LORD
      is king.
   The world will surely stand fast, never to
      be shaken.
   He rules the peoples with fairness.

#### IV

11 Let the heavens be glad and the earth
      rejoice;
   let the sea and what fills it resound;*

12 let the plains be joyful and all that is
      in them.

---

† **Psalm 95** Twice the Psalm calls the people to praise and worship God (Ps 95:1–2, 6), the king of all creatures (Ps 95:3–5) and shepherd of the flock (Ps 95:7a, 7b). The last strophe warns the people to be more faithful than were their ancestors in the journey to the promised land (Ps 95:7c–11). This invitation to praise God regularly opens the Church's official prayer, the Liturgy of the Hours.

**95:8** *Meribah*: lit., "contention"; the place where the Israelites quarreled with God. *Massah*: "testing," the place where they put God to the trial, cf. Ex 17:7; Nm 20:13.

**95:11** *My rest*: the promised land as in Dt 12:9. Heb 4 applies the verse to the eternal rest of heaven.

**Psalm 96** A hymn inviting all humanity to praise the glories of Israel's God (Ps 96:1–3), who is the sole God (Ps 96:4–6). To the just ruler of all belongs worship (Ps 96:7–10); even inanimate creation is to offer praise (Ps 96:11–13). This Psalm has numerous verbal and thematic contacts with Is 40–55, as does Ps 98. Another version of the Psalm is 1 Chr 16:23–33.

**96:4** For references to other gods, see comments on Ps 58 and 82.

---

**95:1** Dt 32:15.
**95:3** Ps 47:2; 135:5.
**95:5** Ps 24:1–2.
**95:7–11** Ps 81:8; 106:32; Heb 3:7–11, 15; 4:3, 5, 7.
**95:7** Ps 23:1–3; 100:3; Mi 7:14.
**95:9** Nm 14:22; 20:2–13; Dt 6:16; 33:8.
**95:10** Ps 78:8; Nm 14:34; Dt 32:5.
**96:1** Ps 98:1; Is 42:10.
**96:3** Ps 98:4; 105:1.
**96:4** Ps 48:2; 95:3; 145:3.
**96:5** Ps 97:7; 115:4–8; Is 40:17; 1 Cor 8:4.
**96:8** Ps 29:2.
**96:10** Ps 75:4; 93:1.
**96:11** Ps 98:7.

Then let all the trees of the forest rejoice
13    before the LORD who comes,
      who comes to govern the earth,*
To govern the world with justice
      and the peoples with faithfulness.

## PSALM 97†

### The Divine Ruler of All

**I**

1  The LORD is king; let the earth rejoice;
      let the many islands be glad.*
2  Cloud and darkness surround him;
      justice and right are the foundation of
      his throne.*
3  Fire goes before him,
      consuming his foes on every side.
4  His lightening illumines the world;
      the earth sees and trembles.*
5  The mountains melt like wax before the
      LORD,
      before the Lord of all the earth.*
6  The heavens proclaim his justice;
      all peoples see his glory.*

**II**

7  All who serve idols are put to shame,
      who glory in worthless things;
      all gods† bow down before him.*
8  Zion hears and is glad,
      and the daughters of Judah rejoice
      because of your judgments, O LORD.*
9  For you, LORD, are the Most High over
      all the earth,*
      exalted far above all gods.
10  You who love the LORD, hate evil,
      he protects the souls of the faithful,*
      rescues them from the hand of the
      wicked.
11  Light dawns for the just,
      and gladness for the honest of
      heart.*

12  Rejoice in the LORD, you just,
      and give thanks at the remembrance
      of his holiness.*

## PSALM 98†

### The Coming of God

¹A psalm.

**I**

Sing a new song to the LORD,
      for he has done marvelous deeds.*
His right hand and holy arm
      have won the victory.†*
2  The LORD has made his victory known;
      has revealed his triumph in the sight
      of the nations,
3  He has remembered his mercy and
      faithfulness
      toward the house of Israel.
All the ends of the earth have seen
      the victory of our God.

**II**

4  Shout with joy to the LORD, all the
      earth;
      break into song; sing praise.
5  Sing praise to the LORD with the lyre,
      with the lyre and melodious song.
6  With trumpets and the sound of the
      horn
      shout with joy to the King, the LORD.*

**III**

7  Let the sea and what fills it resound,*
      the world and those who dwell
      there.
8  Let the rivers clap their hands,
      the mountains shout with them for
      joy,*
9* Before the LORD who comes,
      who comes to govern the earth,*
To govern the world with justice
      and the peoples with fairness.

---

**Psalm 97** The hymn begins with God appearing in a storm, a traditional picture of some ancient Near Eastern gods (Ps 97:1–6); cf. Ps 18:8–16; Mi 1:3–4; Heb 3:3–15. Israel rejoices in the overthrowing of idol worshipers and their gods (Ps 97:7–9) and the rewarding of the faithful righteous (Ps 97:10–12).

**97:7** *All gods*: divine beings thoroughly subordinate to Israel's God. The Greek translates "angels," an interpretation adopted by Heb 1:6.

**Psalm 98** A hymn, similar to Ps 96, extolling God for Israel's victory (Ps 98:1–3). All nations (Ps 98:4–6) and even inanimate nature (Ps 98:7–8) are summoned to welcome God's coming to rule over the world (Ps 98:9).

**98:1** *Marvelous deeds...victory*: the conquest of all threats to the peaceful existence of Israel, depicted in the Psalms variously

as a cosmic force such as sea, or nations bent on Israel's destruction, or evildoers seemingly triumphant. *His right hand and holy arm*: God is pictured as a powerful warrior.

**96:13** Ps 98:9.
**97:1** Ps 75:4; 93:1; 96:10.
**97:2** Ps 85:11; 89:15; Ex 19:6; Dt 4:11; 5:22; 1 Kgs 8:12.
**97:4** Ps 18:8; 50:3; 77:18; 99:1; Jgs 5:4–5.
**97:5** Jdt 16:15; Mi 1:4.
**97:6** Ps 50:6.
**97:7** Ps 96:5.
**97:8** Ps 48:12.
**97:9** Ps 83:19.
**97:10** Ps 121:7.
**97:11** Ps 112:4.
**97:12** Ps 30:5.
**98:1** Ps 96:1; Is 42:10.
**98:1** Is 59:16; 63:5.
**98:6** Ps 47:6–7.
**98:7** Ps 96:11.
**98:8** Is 44:23; 55:12.
**98:9** Ps 96:13.
**98:9** Ps 67:5.

# PSALM 99†

## The Holy King

### I

1 The LORD is king, the peoples tremble;
   he is enthroned on the cherubim,†
      the earth quakes.*
2 Great is the LORD in Zion,
   exalted above all the peoples.
3 Let them praise your great and awesome
      name:
   Holy is he!*

### II

4 O mighty king, lover of justice,
   you have established fairness;
   you have created just rule in Jacob.*
5 Exalt the LORD, our God;
   bow down before his footstool;†*
   holy is he!

### III

6 Moses and Aaron were among his
      priests,
   Samuel among those who called on
      his name;
   they called on the LORD, and he
      answered them.*
7 From the pillar of cloud he spoke to
      them;
   they kept his decrees, the law he had
      given them.*
8 O LORD, our God, you answered
      them;
   you were a forgiving God to them,
   though you punished their
      offenses.*
9 Exalt the LORD, our God;
   bow down before his holy
      mountain;
   holy is the LORD, our God.

# PSALM 100†

## Processional Hymn

1 A psalm of thanksgiving.

   Shout joyfully to the LORD, all you lands;
2    serve the LORD with gladness;
   come before him with joyful song.
3† Know that the LORD is God,
   he made us, we belong to him,
   we are his people, the flock he
      shepherds.*
4 Enter his gates with thanksgiving,
   his courts with praise.
   Give thanks to him, bless his name;*
5 good indeed is the LORD,
   His mercy endures forever,
   his faithfulness lasts through every
      generation.

# PSALM 101†

## Norm of Life for Rulers

1 A psalm of David.

### I

   I sing of mercy and justice;
   to you, LORD, I sing praise.
2 I study the way of integrity;*
   when will you come to me?
   I act with integrity of heart
   within my household.†*
3 I do not allow into my presence
      anything base.
   I hate wrongdoing;
   I will have no part of it.*
4 May the devious heart keep far from me;
   the wicked I will not acknowledge.
5 Whoever slanders a neighbor in secret
   I will reduce to silence.*

---

† **Psalm 99** A hymn to God as the king whose grandeur is most clearly seen on Mount Zion (Ps 99:2) and in the laws given to Israel (Ps 99:4). Israel is special because of God's word of justice, which was mediated by the revered speakers, Moses, Aaron, and Samuel (Ps 99:6–8). The poem is structured by the threefold statement that God is holy (Ps 99:3, 5, 9) and by the twice-repeated command to praise (Ps 99:5, 9).

**99:1** *Enthroned on the cherubim*: cherubim were composite beings with animal and human features, common in ancient Near Eastern art. Two cherubim were placed on the ark (or box) of the covenant in the holy of holies. Upon them God was believed to dwell invisibly, cf. Ex 25:20–22; 1 Sm 4:4; 2 Sm 6:2; Ps 80:2.

**99:5** *Footstool*: a reference to the ark, cf. 1 Chr 28:2; Ps 132:7.

**Psalm 100** A hymn inviting the people to enter the Temple courts with thank offerings for the God who created them.

**100:3** Although the people call on all the nations of the world

to join in their hymn, they are conscious of being the chosen people of God.

**Psalm 101** The king, grateful at being God's chosen (Ps 101:1), promises to be a ruler after God's own heart (Ps 101:2–3), allowing into the royal service only the God-fearing (Ps 101:3–8).

**101:2** *Within my household*: the king promises to make his own household, i.e., the royal court, a model for Israel, banning all officials who abuse their power.

---

**99:1** Ps 18:8–11; 80:2;
   93:1; Ex 25:22; 1 Sm
   4:4; 2 Sm 6:2.
**99:3** Is 6:3.
**99:4** Ps 72:1; Jer 23:5.
**99:5** Ps 132:7.
**99:6** Jer 15:1.
**99:7** Ex 33:9; Nm 12:5.
**99:8** Ex 32:11; Nm 20:12.

**100:3** Ps 23:1; 95:7; Mi
   7:14; Is 64:7.
**100:4–5** Ps 106:1; 107:1;
   118:1; 136:1; 138:8;
   Jer 33:11.
**101:2** Ps 26:11; Is 33:15.
**101:2** 1 Kgs 9:4.
**101:3** Prv 11:20.
**101:5** Prv 17:20; 30:10.

Haughty eyes and arrogant hearts*
  I cannot endure.

**II**

6 I look to the faithful of the land†
  to sit at my side.
Whoever follows the way of integrity*
  is the one to enter my service.
7 No one who practices deceit
  can remain within my house.
No one who speaks falsely
  can last in my presence.*
8† Morning after morning I clear all the
    wicked from the land,
  to rid the city of the Lord of all doers
    of evil.

## PSALM 102†

### Prayer in Time of Distress

1 The prayer of one afflicted and wasting away whose anguish is poured out before the Lord.

**I**

2 Lord, hear my prayer;
  let my cry come to you.
3 Do not hide your face from me
  in the day of my distress.*
Turn your ear to me;
  when I call, answer me quickly.
4 For my days vanish like smoke;*
  my bones burn away as in a furnace.
5 My heart is withered, dried up like grass,
  too wasted to eat my food.
6 From my loud groaning
  I become just skin and bones.
7 I am like a desert owl,
  like an owl among the ruins.
8 I lie awake and moan,
  like a lone sparrow on the roof.
9 All day long my enemies taunt me;
  in their rage, they make my name a
    curse.†

10 I eat ashes like bread,
  mingle my drink with tears.*
11 Because of your furious wrath,
  you lifted me up just to cast me down.
12* My days are like a lengthening
    shadow;*
  I wither like the grass.

**II**

13 But you, Lord, are enthroned forever;
  your renown is for all generations.*
14 You will again show mercy to Zion;
  now is the time for pity;
  the appointed time has come.
15 Its stones are dear to your servants;
  its dust moves them to pity.
16 The nations shall fear your name, Lord,
  all the kings of the earth, your glory,*
17 Once the Lord has rebuilt Zion
  and appeared in glory,
18 Heeding the plea of the lowly,
  not scorning their prayer.
19 Let this be written for the next
    generation,
  for a people not yet born,
  that they may praise the Lord:*
20† "The Lord looked down from the holy
    heights,
  viewed the earth from heaven,*
21 To attend to the groaning of the
    prisoners,
  to release those doomed to die."*
22 Then the Lord's name will be declared
    on Zion,
  his praise in Jerusalem,
23 When peoples and kingdoms gather
  to serve the Lord.*

**III**

24 He has shattered my strength in mid-
    course,
  has cut short my days.
25 I plead, O my God,

---

**101:6** *I look to the faithful of the land*: the king seeks companions only among those faithful to God.
**101:8** *Morning after morning*: the morning is the normal time for the administration of justice (2 Sm 15:2; Jer 21:12) and for the arrival of divine aid (Ps 59:17; 143:8; Is 33:2). *I clear all the wicked from the land*: the king, as God's servant, is responsible for seeing that divine justice is carried out.
**Psalm 102** A lament, one of the Penitential Psalms. The psalmist, experiencing psychological and bodily disintegration (Ps 102:4–12), cries out to God (Ps 102:1–3). In the Temple precincts where God has promised to be present, the psalmist recalls God's venerable promises to save the poor (Ps 102:13–23). The final part (Ps 102:24–28) restates the original complaint and prayer, and emphasizes God's eternity.
**102:9** *They make my name a curse*: enemies use the psalm-

ist's name in phrases such as, "May you be as wretched as this person!"
**102:20–23** Both Ps 102:20–21 and Ps 102:22–23 depend on Ps 102:19.

---

**101:5** Prv 21:4.
**101:6** Ps 26:11; Prv 20:7.
**101:7** Ps 5:5; Prv 25:5.
**102:3** Ps 69:18; 143:7.
**102:4–6** Ps 38:7–9.
**102:10** Ps 42:4; 80:6.
**102:12** Ps 109:23; 144:4; Jb 8:9; 14:2; Eccl 6:12; Wis 2:5.
**102:12** Ps 90:5–6.
**102:13** Ps 55:20; 90:2; 93:2; 135:13; 145:13; Lam 5:19; Heb 1:12.
**102:16** Is 59:19; 66:18.
**102:19** Ps 22:31–32.
**102:20** Ps 11:4; 14:2.
**102:21** Ps 79:11.
**102:23** Is 60:3–4; Zec 2:15; 8:22.

do not take me in the midst of my
    days.†*
Your years last through all
    generations.

26 Of old you laid the earth's foundations;*
    the heavens are the work of your
    hands.

27 They perish, but you remain;
    they all wear out like a garment;
Like clothing you change them and they
    are changed,

28 but you are the same, your years have
    no end.

29 May the children of your servants live on;
    may their descendants live in your
    presence.*

## PSALM 103†

### Praise of Divine Goodness

¹ Of David.

**I**

Bless the LORD, my soul;
    all my being, bless his holy name!

2 Bless the LORD, my soul;
    and do not forget all his gifts,

3 Who pardons all your sins,
    and heals all your ills,

4 Who redeems your life from the pit,*
    and crowns you with mercy and
    compassion,

5 Who fills your days with good things,
    so your youth is renewed like the
    eagle's.†

**II**

6 The LORD does righteous deeds,
    brings justice to all the oppressed.*

7 He made known his ways to Moses,
    to the Israelites his deeds.

8 Merciful and gracious is the LORD,
    slow to anger, abounding in mercy.*

9 He will not always accuse,
    and nurses no lasting anger;

10 He has not dealt with us as our sins
    merit,

nor requited us as our wrongs deserve.

**III**

11 For as the heavens tower over the earth,
    so his mercy towers over those who
    fear him.*

12 As far as the east is from the west,
    so far has he removed our sins from
    us.

13 As a father has compassion on his
    children,
so the LORD has compassion on those
    who fear him.

14 For he knows how we are formed,
    remembers that we are dust.*

15 As for man, his days are like the grass;
    he blossoms like a flower in the
    field.*

16 A wind sweeps over it and it is gone;
    its place knows it no more.

17 But the LORD's mercy is from age to age,
    toward those who fear him.
His salvation is for the children's
    children

18 of those who keep his covenant,
    and remember to carry out his
    precepts.

**IV**

19 The LORD has set his throne in heaven;
    his dominion extends over all.

20 Bless the LORD, all you his angels,*
    mighty in strength, acting at his
    behest,
obedient to his command.

21 Bless the LORD, all you his hosts,
    his ministers who carry out his will.

22 Bless the LORD, all his creatures,
    everywhere in his domain.
Bless the LORD, my soul!

## PSALM 104†

### Praise of God the Creator

**I**

1 Bless the LORD, my soul!
    LORD, my God, you are great indeed!

---

**102:25** *In the midst of my days*: when the normal span of life is but half completed, cf. Is 38:10; Jer 17:11.

**Psalm 103** The speaker in this hymn begins by praising God for personal benefits (Ps 103:1–5), then moves on to God's mercy toward all the people (Ps 103:6–18). Even sin cannot destroy that mercy (Ps 103:11–13), for the eternal God is well aware of the people's human fragility (Ps 103:14–18): The psalmist invites the heavenly beings to join in praise (Ps 103:19–22).

**103:5** *Your youth is renewed like the eagle's*: because of the eagle's long life it was a symbol of perennial youth and vigor, cf. Is 40:31.

**Psalm 104** A hymn praising God who easily and skillfully made rampaging waters and primordial night into a world vibrant with life. The psalmist describes God's splendor in the heavens (Ps

**102:25** Ps 39:5; 90:10; Jb 14:5.
**102:26–28** Heb 1:10–12.
**102:29** Ps 69:36–37.
**103:4** Ps 28:1; 30:4; 40:3; 69:16; 88:5; 143:7; Prv 1:12; Jon 2:7.
**103:6** Ps 146:6–7.

**103:8** Ps 86:15; 145:8; Ex 34:6–7; Nm 14:18; Jer 3:12; Jl 2:13; Jon 4:2.
**103:11** Is 55:9.
**103:14** Ps 90:3.
**103:15** Ps 37:2; 90:5–6; Is 40:7.
**103:20** Ps 148:2; Dn 3:58.

You are clothed with majesty and
    splendor,
2    robed in light as with a cloak.
You spread out the heavens like a tent;*
3    setting the beams of your chambers
       upon the waters.†
You make the clouds your chariot;
    traveling on the wings of the wind.
4  You make the winds your messengers;
    flaming fire, your ministers.*

**II**

5† You fixed the earth on its foundation,
    so it can never be shaken.
6  The deeps covered it like a garment;
    above the mountains stood the waters.
7  At your rebuke they took flight;
    at the sound of your thunder they
       fled.*
8  They rushed up the mountains, down
       the valleys
    to the place you had fixed for them.
9  You set a limit they cannot pass;
    never again will they cover the
       earth.*

**III**

10  You made springs flow in wadies
    that wind among the mountains.
11  They give drink to every beast of the
       field;*
    here wild asses quench their thirst.
12  Beside them the birds of heaven nest;
    among the branches they sing.
13  You water the mountains from your
       chambers;
    from the fruit of your labor the earth
       abounds.
14  You make the grass grow for the cattle
    and plants for people's work
    to bring forth food from the earth,
15    wine to gladden their hearts,
    oil to make their faces shine,
    and bread to sustain the human
       heart.

16† The trees of the LORD drink their fill,
    the cedars of Lebanon, which you
       planted.
17  There the birds build their nests;
    the stork in the junipers, its home.*
18  The high mountains are for wild
       goats;
    the rocky cliffs, a refuge for badgers.

**IV**

19  You made the moon to mark the
       seasons,*
    the sun that knows the hour of its
       setting.
20  You bring darkness and night falls,
    then all the animals of the forest
       wander about.
21  Young lions roar for prey;
    they seek their food from God.*
22  When the sun rises, they steal away
    and settle down in their dens.
23  People go out to their work,
    to their labor till evening falls.

**V**

24  How varied are your works, LORD!
    In wisdom you have made them all;
    the earth is full of your creatures.*
25  There is the sea, great and wide!
    It teems with countless beings,
    living things both large and small.*
26  There ships ply their course
    and Leviathan,† whom you formed to
       play with.*

**VI**

27  All of these look to you
    to give them food in due time.*
28  When you give it to them, they gather;
    when you open your hand, they are
       well filled.
29† When you hide your face, they panic.
    Take away their breath, they perish
    and return to the dust.*
30  Send forth your spirit, they are created
    and you renew the face of the earth.

---

104:1–4), how the chaotic waters were tamed to fertilize and feed
the world (Ps 104:5–18), and how primordial night was made into
a gentle time of refreshment (Ps 104:19–23). The picture is like Gn
1:1–2: a dark and watery chaos is made dry and lighted so that creatures might live. The psalmist reacts to the beauty of creation with
awe (Ps 104:24–34). May sin not deface God's work (Ps 104:35)!
   **104:3** *Your chambers upon the waters*: God's heavenly dwelling above the upper waters of the sky, cf. Gn 1:6–7; Ps 29:10.
   **104:5–9** God places the gigantic disk of the earth securely on
its foundation and then, as a warrior, chases away the enveloping
waters and confines them under, above, and around the earth.
   **104:16–18** Even the exotic flora and fauna of the high mountains of the Lebanon range receive adequate water.

   **104:26** *Leviathan*: a sea monster symbolizing primeval chaos,
cf. Ps 74:14; Is 27:1; Jb 40:25. God does not destroy chaos but
makes it part of the created order.
   **104:29–30** On one level, the spirit (or wind) of God is the fall

---

**104:2** Prv 8:27–28; Jb 9:8; Is
   40:22; Gn 1:6–7; Am
   9:6.
**104:4** Heb 1:7.
**104:7** Ps 29:3.
**104:9** Jer 5:22; Gn 9:11–15.
**104:11–14** Ps 147:8–9.
**104:17** Ez 31:6.
**104:19** Sir 43:6.
**104:21** Jb 38:39.
**104:24** Ps 92:6; Sir 39:16.
**104:25** Sir 43:26.
**104:26** Jb 3:8; 40:25, 29.
**104:27** Ps 136:25; 145:15–
   16.
**104:29** Ps 90:3; Jb 34:14–15;
   Eccl 3:20.

**VII**

31 May the glory of the Lord endure
   forever;
   may the Lord be glad in his works!

32 Who looks at the earth and it trembles,
   touches the mountains and they
   smoke!*

33 I will sing to the Lord all my life;
   I will sing praise to my God while I
   live.*

34 May my meditation be pleasing to him;
   I will rejoice in the Lord.

35 May sinners vanish from the earth,
   and the wicked be no more.
   Bless the Lord, my soul! Hallelujah!†

## PSALM 105†

### God's Fidelity to the Promise

**I**

1 Give thanks to the Lord, invoke his
   name;*
   make known among the peoples his
   deeds!*

2 Sing praise to him, play music;
   proclaim all his wondrous deeds!

3 Glory in his holy name;
   let hearts that seek the Lord rejoice!

4 Seek out the Lord and his might;
   constantly seek his face.*

5 Recall the wondrous deeds he has done,
   his wonders and words of judgment,

6 You descendants of Abraham his
   servant,
   offspring of Jacob the chosen one!

**II**

7 He the Lord, is our God
   whose judgments reach through all
   the earth.

8 He remembers forever his covenant,

the word he commanded for a
   thousand generations,

9 Which he made with Abraham,
   and swore to Isaac,*

10 And ratified in a statute for Jacob,
   an everlasting covenant for Israel:

11 "To you I give the land of Canaan,
   your own allotted inheritance."*

**III**

12 When they were few in number,*
   a handful, and strangers there,

13 Wandering from nation to nation,
   from one kingdom to another
   people,

14 He let no one oppress them;
   for their sake he rebuked kings:†

15† "Do not touch my anointed ones,
   to my prophets do no harm."

**IV**

16 Then he called down a famine on the
   land,
   destroyed the grain that sustained
   them.†*

17 He had sent a man ahead of them,
   Joseph, sold as a slave.*

18 They shackled his feet with chains;
   collared his neck in iron,*

19 Till his prediction came to pass,
   and the word of the Lord proved him
   true.*

20 The king sent and released him;
   the ruler of peoples set him free.*

21 He made him lord over his household,
   ruler over all his possessions,*

22 To instruct his princes as he desired,
   to teach his elders wisdom.

**V**

23 Then Israel entered Egypt;*
   Jacob sojourned in the land of Ham.†

24 God greatly increased his people,

---

and winter rains that provide food for all creatures. On another, it is the breath (or spirit) of God that makes beings live.

**104:35** *Hallelujah:* a frequent word in the last third of the Psalter. The word combines the plural imperative of praise (*hallelu*) with an abbreviated form of the divine name Yah(weh).

**Psalm 105** A hymn to God who promised the land of Canaan to the holy people, cf. Ps 78; 106; 136. Israel is invited to praise and seek the presence of God (Ps 105:1–6), who is faithful to the promise of land to the ancestors (Ps 105:7–11). In every phase of the national story—the ancestors in the land of Canaan (Ps 105:12–15), Joseph in Egypt (Ps 105:16–22), Israel in Egypt (Ps 105:23–38), Israel in the desert on the way to Canaan (Ps 105:39–45)—God remained faithful, reiterating the promise of the land to successive servants.

**105:14** *Kings:* Pharaoh and Abimelech of Gerar, cf. Gn 12:17; 20:6–7.

**105:15** *My anointed ones…my prophets:* the patriarchs

Abraham, Isaac, and Jacob, who were "anointed" in the sense of being consecrated and recipients of God's revelation.

**105:16** *The grain that sustained them:* lit., every "staff of bread."

**105:23, 27** *The land of Ham:* a synonym for Egypt, cf. Gn 10:6.

---

| | |
|---|---|
| **104:32** Ps 144:5. | **105:16** Gn 41:54, 57. |
| **104:33** Ps 146:2. | **105:17** Gn 37:28, 36; 45:5. |
| **105:1–15** 1 Chr 16:8–22. | **105:18** Gn 39:20. |
| **105:1** Ps 18:50; 96:3; 145:5; Is 12:4–5. | **105:19** Gn 40–41. |
| | **105:20** Gn 41:14. |
| **105:4** Ps 24:6; 27:8. | **105:21** Gn 41:41–44. |
| **105:9** Gn 15:1ff; 26:3. | **105:23** Gn 46:1–47:12; Acts 7:15. |
| **105:11** Gn 12:7; 15:18. | |
| **105:12–13** Dt 4:27; 26:5. | |

made them more numerous than their
    foes.*

25 He turned their hearts to hate his
    people,
    to treat his servants deceitfully.*

26 He sent his servant Moses,
    and Aaron whom he had chosen.*

27† They worked his signs in Egypt*
    and wonders in the land of Ham.

28 He sent darkness and it grew dark,
    but they rebelled against his word.

29 He turned their waters into blood
    and killed their fish.

30 Their land swarmed with frogs,
    even the chambers of their kings.

31 He spoke and there came swarms of
    flies,
    gnats through all their country.

32 For rain he gave them hail,
    flashes of lightning throughout their
    land.

33 He struck down their vines and fig trees,
    shattered the trees of their country.

34 He spoke and the locusts came,
    grasshoppers without number.*

35 They devoured every plant in the land;
    they devoured the crops of their
    fields.

36 He struck down every firstborn in the
    land,
    the first fruits of all their vigor.

37 He brought his people out,
    laden with silver and gold;*
    no one among the tribes stumbled.

38 Egypt rejoiced when they left,
    for fear had seized them.

**VI**

39 He spread a cloud out as a cover,
    and made a fire to light up the night.*

40 They asked and he brought them
    quail;
    with bread from heaven he filled
    them.*

41 He split the rock and water gushed
    forth;
    it flowed through the desert like a
    river.*

42 For he remembered his sacred promise
    to Abraham his servant.

43 He brought his people out with joy,
    his chosen ones with shouts of
    triumph.

44 He gave them the lands of the nations,
    they took possession of the wealth of
    the peoples,*

45 That they might keep his statutes
    and observe his teachings.*
Hallelujah!

## PSALM 106†

### Israel's Confession of Sin

1 Hallelujah!
    **A**
Give thanks to the LORD, who is good,
    whose mercy endures forever.*

2 Who can recount the mighty deeds of
    the LORD,
    proclaim in full God's praise?

3 Blessed those who do what is right,
    whose deeds are always just.*

4 Remember me, LORD, as you favor your
    people;
    come to me with your saving help,*

5 That I may see the prosperity of your
    chosen ones,
    rejoice in the joy of your people,
    and glory with your heritage.

**P**
**S**

---

† **105:27–38** This Psalm and Ps 78:43–51 have an account of the plagues differing in number or in order from Ex 7:14–12:30. Several versions of the exodus story were current.

**Psalm 106** Israel is invited to praise the God whose mercy has always tempered judgment of Israel (Ps 106:1–3). The speaker, on behalf of all, seeks solidarity with the people, who can always count on God's fidelity despite their sin (Ps 106:4–5). Confident of God's mercy, the speaker invites national repentance (Ps 106:6) by reciting from Israel's history eight instances of sin, judgment, and forgiveness. The sins are the rebellion at the Red Sea (Ps 106:6–12; see Ex 14–15), the craving for meat in the desert (Ps 106:13–15; see Nm 11), the challenge to Moses' authority (Ps 106:16–18; see Nm 16), the golden calf episode (Ps 106:19–23; see Ex 32–34), the refusal to take Canaan by the southern route (Ps 106:24–27; see Nm 13–14 and Dt 1–2), the rebellion at Baal-Peor (Ps 106:28–31; see Nm 25:1–10), the anger of Moses (Ps 106:32–33; see Nm 20:1–13), and mingling with the nations (Ps 106:34–47). The last, as suggested by its

length and generalized language, may be the sin that invites the repentance of the present generation. The text gives the site of each sin: Egypt (Ps 106:7), the desert (Ps 106:14), the camp (Ps 106:16), Horeb (Ps 106:19), in their tents (Ps 106:25), Baal-Peor (Ps 106:28), the waters of Meribah (Ps 106:32), Canaan (Ps 106:38).

---

**105:24** Ex 1:7; Acts 7:17.  
**105:25** Ex 1:8–14.  
**105:26** Ex 3:10; 4:27.  
**105:27–36** Ps 78:43–51; Ex 7–12.  
**105:34** Jl 1:4.  
**105:37** Ex 12:33–36.  
**105:39** Ps 78:14; Ex 13:21–22; Wis 18:3.  
**105:40** Ps 78:24–28; Ex 16:13–15; Nm 11:31ff;  

Wis 16:20.  
**105:41** Ps 78:15–16; Ex 17:1–7; Nm 20:11.  
**105:44** Dt 4:37–40.  
**105:45** Dt 6:20–25; 7:8–11.  
**106:1** Ps 100:5; 107:1; 1 Chr 16:34; Jer 33:11; Dn 3:89.  
**106:3** Is 56:1–2.  
**106:4** Ps 25:7; Neh 5:19.

### B

6 We have sinned like our ancestors;*
　　we have done wrong and are guilty.

### I

7 Our ancestors in Egypt
　　did not attend to your wonders.
　　They did not remember your manifold
　　　　mercy;
　　they defied the Most High at the Red
　　　　Sea.
8 Yet he saved them for his name's sake
　　to make his power known.*
9 He roared at the Red Sea and it dried up.
　　He led them through the deep as
　　　　through a desert.*
10 He rescued them from hostile hands,
　　freed them from the power of the
　　　　enemy.
11 The waters covered their oppressors;
　　not one of them survived.
12 Then they believed his words
　　and sang his praise.*

### II

13 But they soon forgot all he had done;
　　they had no patience for his plan.
14 In the desert they gave in to their
　　　　cravings,
　　tempted God in the wasteland.*
15 So he gave them what they asked
　　and sent a wasting disease against
　　　　them.*

### III

16 In the camp they challenged Moses*
　　and Aaron, the holy one of the LORD.
17 The earth opened and swallowed
　　　　Dathan,
　　it closed on the followers of Abiram.
18 Against their company the fire blazed;
　　flames consumed the wicked.

### IV

19 At Horeb they fashioned a calf,*
　　worshiped a metal statue.
20 They exchanged their glory†

for the image of a grass-eating bull.
21 They forgot the God who had saved
　　　　them,
　　who had done great deeds in Egypt,*
22 Amazing deeds in the land of Ham,
　　fearsome deeds at the Red Sea.
23 He would have decreed their
　　　　destruction,
　　had not Moses, his chosen one,
　　Withstood him in the breach†
　　to turn back his destroying anger.*

### V

24 Next they despised the beautiful land;*
　　they did not believe the promise.
25 In their tents they complained;
　　they did not heed the voice of the
　　　　LORD.
26 So with raised hand he swore
　　he would destroy them in the desert,
27 And scatter their descendants among the
　　　　nations,
　　disperse them in foreign lands.

### VI

28 They joined in the rites of Baal of Peor,*
　　ate food sacrificed to the dead.
29 They provoked him by their actions,
　　and a plague broke out among them.
30 Then Phinehas rose to intervene,
　　and the plague was brought to a halt.
31 This was counted for him as a righteous
　　　　deed
　　for all generations to come.

### VII

32 At the waters of Meribah they angered
　　　　God,*
　　and Moses suffered because of them.†
33 They so embittered his spirit
　　that rash words crossed his lips.

### VIII

34 They did not destroy the peoples
　　as the LORD had commanded them,*
35 But mingled with the nations
　　and imitated their ways.*

---

† **106:20** *Their glory*: meant as a reference to God.
**106:23** *Withstood him in the breach*: the image is that of Moses standing in a narrow break made in the wall to keep anyone from entering.
**106:32** *Moses suffered because of them*: Moses was not allowed to enter the promised land because of his rash words (Nm 20:12). According to Dt 1:37, Moses was not allowed to cross because of the people's sin, not his own.

---

* **106:6–7** Ps 78:11–17; Ex 14:11; Lv 26:40;　1 Kgs 8:47; Bar 2:12; Dn 9:5.

**106:8** Ez 36:20–22.
**106:9** Ex 14:21–31; Is 50:2; 63:11–14; Na 1:4.
**106:12** Ex 15:1–21.
**106:14** Ps 78:18; Ex 15:24; 16:3; Nm 11:1–6.
**106:15** Ps 78:26–31; Nm 11:33.
**106:16–18** Nm 16; Dt 11:6; Is 26:11.
**106:19–20** Ex 32; Dt 9:8–21; Jer 2:11; Acts 7:41; Rom 1:23.
**106:21** Ps 78:42–58;

Dt 32:18; Jer 2:32.
**106:23** Ex 32:11; Dt 9:25; Ez 22:30.
**106:24–27** Lv 26:33; Nm 14; 1:25–36; Ez 20:15, 23.
**106:28–31** Nm 25; Dt 26:14; Sir 45:23–24.
**106:32–33** Ps 95:8–9; Ex 17:1–7; Nm 20:2–13; Dt 6:16; 33:8.
**106:34** Dt 7:1; Jgs 2:1–5.
**106:35** Lv 18:3; Jgs 1:27–35; 3:5.

36  They served their idols
    and were ensnared by them.*
37  They sacrificed to demons†
    their own sons and daughters,
38  Shedding innocent blood,
    the blood of their own sons and
        daughters,
    Whom they sacrificed to the idols of
        Canaan,
    desecrating the land with bloodshed.
39  They defiled themselves by their actions,
    became adulterers by their conduct.
40  So the LORD grew angry with his
        people,
    abhorred his own heritage.
41  He handed them over to the nations,
    and their adversaries ruled over
        them.*
42  Their enemies oppressed them,
    kept them under subjection.
43  Many times did he rescue them,
    but they kept rebelling and scheming
    and were brought low by their own
        guilt.*
44  Still God had regard for their affliction
    when he heard their wailing.
45  For their sake he remembered his
        covenant
    and relented in his abundant mercy,*
46  Winning for them compassion
    from all who held them captive.

                    C
47  Save us, LORD, our God;
    gather us from among the nations
    That we may give thanks to your holy
        name
    and glory in praising you.*
48† Blessed be the LORD, the God of Israel,
    from everlasting to everlasting!
    Let all the people say, Amen!*
    Hallelujah!

## Fifth Book—Psalms 107–150

## PSALM 107†

### God the Savior of Those in Distress

1  "Give thanks to the LORD for he is good,
    his mercy endures forever!"*
2  Let that be the prayer of the LORD's
        redeemed,
    those redeemed from the hand of the
        foe,*
3  Those gathered from foreign lands,
    from east and west, from north and
        south.*

                    I
4  Some had lost their way in a barren
        desert;
    found no path toward a city to live in.
5  They were hungry and thirsty;
    their life was ebbing away.*
6  In their distress they cried to the LORD,
    who rescued them in their peril,
7* Guided them by a direct path
    so they reached a city to live in.*
8  Let them thank the LORD for his mercy,
    such wondrous deeds for the children
        of Adam.
9  For he satisfied the thirsty,
    filled the hungry with good things.*

                    II
10  Some lived in darkness and gloom,
    imprisoned in misery and chains.
11  Because they rebelled against God's
        word,
    and scorned the counsel of the Most
        High,*
12  He humbled their hearts through
        hardship;
    they stumbled with no one to help.*
13  In their distress they cried to the LORD,
    who saved them in their peril;

---

†
**106:37** *Demons:* Hebrew *shedim* occurs in parallelism with "gods" in an important inscription from Transjordan and hence can also be translated "the gods."

**106:48** A doxology ending Book IV of the Psalter. It is not part of the Psalm.

**Psalm 107** A hymn inviting those who have been rescued by God to give praise (Ps 107:1–3). Four archetypal divine rescues are described, each ending in thanksgiving: from the sterile desert (Ps 107:4–9), from imprisonment in gloom (Ps 107:10–16), from mortal illness (Ps 107:17–22), and from the angry sea (Ps 107:23–32). The number four connotes totality, all the possible varieties of rescue. The same saving activity of God is shown in Israel's history (Ps 107:33–41); whenever the people were endangered God rescued them. The last verses invite people to ponder the persistent saving acts of God (Ps 107:42–43).

*
**106:36–38** Lv 18:21; Nm 35:33; Dt 32:17; Jgs 2:11–13, 17, 19; 2 Kgs 16:3; Bar 4:7; 1 Cor 10:20.
**106:41** Jgs 2:14–23.
**106:43** Is 63:7–9.
**106:45** Lv 26:42.
**106:47** 1 Chr 16:35.
**106:48** Ps 41:14; 72:18; 89:53; 1 Chr 16:36; Neh 9:5.

**107:1** Ps 100:4–5; 106:1; Jer 33:11.
**107:2** Is 63:12.
**107:3** Is 43:5–6; 49:12; Zec 8:7.
**107:5** Dt 8:15; 32:10; Is 49:10.
**107:7** Is 35:8; 40:3; 43:19.
**107:7** Dt 6:10.
**107:9** Lk 1:53.
**107:11** Is 42:7, 22; Jb 36:8–9; Prv 1:25.
**107:12** Ps 106:43.

14 He brought them forth from darkness
    and the shadow of death
    and broke their chains asunder.*
15 Let them thank the LORD for his mercy,
    such wondrous deeds for the children
        of Adam.
16 For he broke down the gates of bronze
    and snapped the bars of iron.

**III**

17 Some fell sick from their wicked ways,
    afflicted because of their sins.
18 They loathed all manner of food;*
    they were at the gates of death.
19 In their distress they cried to the LORD,
    who saved them in their peril,
20 Sent forth his word to heal them,*
    and snatched them from the grave.
21 Let them thank the LORD for his mercy,
    such wondrous deeds for the children
        of Adam.
22 Let them offer a sacrifice in thanks,
    recount his works with shouts of joy.

**IV**

23 Some went off to sea in ships,
    plied their trade on the deep waters.*
24 They saw the works of the LORD,
    the wonders of God in the deep.
25 He commanded and roused a storm
        wind;
    it tossed the waves on high.*
26 They rose up to the heavens, sank to the
        depths;
    their hearts trembled at the danger.
27 They reeled, staggered like drunkards;
    their skill was of no avail.*
28 In their distress they cried to the LORD,
    who brought them out of their peril;
29 He hushed the storm to silence,
    the waves of the sea were stilled.*
30 They rejoiced that the sea grew calm,
    that God brought them to the harbor
        they longed for.
31 Let them thank the LORD for his mercy,
    such wondrous deeds for the children
        of Adam.

32 Let them extol him in the assembly of
        the people,
    and praise him in the council of the
        elders.

**V**

33† God changed rivers into desert,
    springs of water into thirsty ground,*
34 Fruitful land into a salty waste,
    because of the wickedness of its
        people.*
35 He changed the desert into pools of
        water,
    arid land into springs of water,*
36 And settled the hungry there;
    they built a city to live in.*
37 They sowed fields and planted vineyards,
    brought in an abundant harvest.*
38* God blessed them, and they increased
        greatly,
    and their livestock did not decrease.*
39 But he poured out contempt on princes,
    made them wander trackless wastes,
40 Where they were diminished and
        brought low
    through misery and cruel oppression.
41 While he released the poor man from
        affliction,
    and increased their families like flocks.*
42 The upright saw this and rejoiced;*
    all wickedness shut its mouth.
43 Whoever is wise will take note of these
        things,*
    and ponder the merciful deeds of the
        LORD.

## PSALM 108†

### Prayer for Victory

1 A song; a psalm of David.

**I**

2 My heart is steadfast, God;*
    my heart is steadfast.
    Let me sing and chant praise.
3 Awake, lyre and harp!
    I will wake the dawn.*

---

107:33–41 God destroyed Sodom and Gomorrah in Gn 18–19, which the Psalm sees as the destruction of the wicked inhabitants of Canaan to prepare the way for Israel (Ps 107:33–34). God then led Israel through the desert to give them a fertile land (Ps 107:35–38) and protected them from every danger (Ps 107:39–41).

Psalm 108 A prayer compiled from two other Psalms: Ps 108:2–6 are virtually the same as Ps 57:8–12; Ps 108:7–14 are the same as Ps 60:7–14. An old promise of salvation (Ps 108:8–10) is combined with a confident assurance (Ps 108:2–6, 13) and petition (Ps 108:7, 12–13).

107:14 Is 42:7; 49:9; 51:14.
107:18 Jb 6:6–7; 33:20.
107:20 Ps 147:15; Wis 16:12; Is 55:11; Mt 8:8.
107:23 Sir 43:25.
107:25 Jon 1:4.
107:27 Is 29:9.
107:29 Ps 65:8; 89:10; Mt 8:26 par.
107:33 Is 35:7; 42:15; 50:2.
107:34 Gn 19:23–28; Dt
29:22; Sir 39:23.
107:35 Ps 114:8; Is 41:8.
107:36 Ez 36:35.
107:37 Is 65:21; Jer 31:5.
107:38 Jb 12:23–25.
107:38 Dt 7:13–14.
107:41 Ps 113:7.
107:42 Ps 58:11; 63:12.
107:43 Hos 14:10.
108:2–6 Ps 57:8–12.
108:3 Jb 38:12.

4  I will praise you among the peoples,
       LORD;
   I will chant your praise among the
       nations.*
5  For your mercy is greater than the
       heavens;
   your faithfulness, to the skies.*

**II**

6  Appear on high over the heavens, God;
   your glory above all the earth.
7  Help with your right hand and
       answer us
   that your loved ones may escape.

8  God speaks in his holiness:†*
   "I will exult, I will apportion
       Shechem;
   the valley of Succoth I will measure
       out.
9  Gilead is mine, mine is Manasseh;
   Ephraim is the helmet for my head,
   Judah, my scepter.
10 Moab is my washbowl;
       upon Edom I cast my sandal;*
   I will shout in triumph over Philistia."

11 Who will bring me to the fortified city?
   Who will lead me into Edom?
12 Was it not you who rejected us, God?
   Do you no longer march with our
       armies?*
13 Give us aid against the foe;
   worthless is human help.
14 We will triumph with the help of God,
   who will trample down our foes.

## PSALM 109†

### Prayer of a Person Falsely Accused

1 For the leader. A psalm of David.

**I**

2  O God, whom I praise, do not be
       silent,*

for wicked and treacherous mouths
    attack me.
They speak against me with lying
    tongues;
3   with hateful words they surround me,
    attacking me without cause.
4   In return for my love they slander me,
    even though I prayed for them.
5   They repay me evil for good,
    hatred for my love.*

**II**

6   Appoint an evil one over him,
    an accuser† to stand at his right hand,
7   That he may be judged and found guilty,
    that his plea may be in vain.
8   May his days be few;
    may another take his office.*
9   May his children be fatherless,
    his wife, a widow.*
10  May his children wander and beg,
    driven from their hovels.
11  May the usurer snare all he owns,
    strangers plunder all he earns.
12  May no one treat him with mercy
    or pity his fatherless children.
13  May his posterity be destroyed,*
    their name rooted out in the next
    generation.
14  May his fathers' guilt be mentioned to
    the LORD;
    his mother's sin not rooted out.*
15  May their guilt be always before the
    LORD,*
    till their memory is banished from the
    earth,*
16  For he did not remember to show mercy,
    but hounded the wretched poor
    and brought death to the
    brokenhearted.
17  He loved cursing; may it come upon
    him;
    he hated blessing; may none come to
    him.

---

**108:8** *Holiness*: may also be translated as "sanctuary" or as referring to God's heavenly abode.
**Psalm 109** A lament notable for the length and vehemence of its prayer against evildoers (Ps 109:6–20); the cry to God (Ps 109:1) and the complaint (Ps 109:22–25) are brief in comparison. The psalmist is apparently the victim of a slander campaign, potentially devastating in a society where reputation and honor are paramount. In the emotional perspective of the Psalm, there are only two types of people: the wicked and their poor victims. The psalmist is a poor victim (Ps 109:22, 31) and by that fact a friend of God and enemy of the wicked. The psalmist seeks vindication not on the basis of personal virtue but because of God's promise to protect the poor.

**109:6** *An accuser*: Hebrew *satan*, a word occurring in Job 1–2 and Zec 3:1–2. In the latter passage Satan stands at the right hand of the high priest to bring false accusations against him before God. Here the accuser is human.

**108:4** Ps 9:12; 18:50; 148:13.
**108:5** Ps 36:6; 71:19.
**108:8–14** Ps 60:8–14.
**108:10** Ru 4:7–8.
**108:12** Ps 44:10.
**109:2** Ps 35:22; 83:1.
**109:5** Ps 35:12; 38:21; Prv 17:13; Jer 18:20.
**109:8** Acts 1:20.
**109:9** Ex 22:23; Jer 18:21.
**109:13** Ps 21:11; Prv 10:7.
**109:14** Ex 20:5.
**109:15** Ps 90:8.
**109:15** Ps 34:16.

18 May cursing clothe him like a robe;
may it enter his belly like water,
his bones like oil.

19 May it be near as the clothes he wears,
as the belt always around him.

20† May this be the reward for my accusers
from the LORD,
for those speaking evil against me.

### III

21 But you, LORD, are my Lord,
deal kindly with me for your name's
sake;
in your great mercy rescue me.

22 For I am poor and needy;
my heart is pierced within me.

23 Like a lengthening shadow I am gone,
I am shaken off like the locust.

24 My knees totter from fasting;*
my flesh has wasted away.

25 I have become a mockery to them;
when they see me, they shake their
heads.

26 Help me, LORD, my God;
save me in your mercy.

27 Make them know this is your hand,
that you, LORD, have done this.

28 Though they curse, may you bless;
arise, shame them, that your servant
may rejoice.

29 Clothe my accusers with disgrace;
make them wear their shame like a
mantle.

30 I will give fervent thanks to the LORD;
before a crowd I will praise him.*

31 For he stands at the right hand of the
poor
to save him from those who pass
judgment on him.

## PSALM 110†

### God Appoints the King both King and Priest

¹A psalm of David.

The LORD says to my lord:†
"Sit at my right hand,
while I make your enemies your
footstool."†*

2 The scepter of your might:
the LORD extends your strong scepter
from Zion.
Have dominion over your enemies!

3 Yours is princely power from the day of
your birth.
In holy splendor before the daystar,
like dew I begot you.*

4 The LORD has sworn and will not waver:
"You are a priest forever in the
manner of Melchizedek."†*

5 At your right hand is the Lord,
who crushes kings on the day of his
wrath,*

6 Who judges nations, heaps up corpses,
crushes heads across the wide earth,

7† Who drinks from the brook by the
wayside
and thus holds high his head.*

## PSALM 111†

### Praise of God for Goodness to Israel

¹Hallelujah!

I will praise the LORD with all my heart*
in the assembled congregation of the
upright.†

2 Great are the works of the LORD,
studied by all who delight in them.

---

† **109:20** *May this be the reward...from the LORD*: the psalmist
prays that God ratify the curses of Ps 109:6–19 and bring them
upon the wicked.
**Psalm 110** A royal Psalm in which a court singer recites
three oracles in which God assures the king that his enemies
are conquered (Ps 110:1–2), makes the king "son" in traditional
adoption language (Ps 110:3), gives priestly status to the king and
promises to be with him in future military ventures (Ps 110:4–7).
**110:1** *The LORD says to my lord*: a polite form of address of an
inferior to a superior, cf. 1 Sm 25:25; 2 Sm 1:10. The court singer
refers to the king. Jesus in the synoptic gospels (Mt 22:41–46 and
parallels) takes the psalmist to be David and hence "my lord"
refers to the messiah, who must be someone greater than David.
*Your footstool*: in ancient times victorious kings put their feet on
the prostrate bodies of their enemies.
**110:4** *Melchizedek*: Melchizedek was the ancient king of Salem (Jerusalem) who blessed Abraham (Gn 14:18–20); like other
kings of the time he performed priestly functions. Heb 7 sees in
Melchizedek a type of Christ.

**110:7** *Who drinks from the brook by the wayside*: the meaning is uncertain. Some see an allusion to a rite of royal consecration at the Gihon spring (cf. 1 Kgs 1:33, 38). Others find here
an image of the divine warrior (or king) pursuing enemies so
relentlessly that he does not stop long enough to eat and drink.
**Psalm 111** A Temple singer (Ps 111:1) tells how God is revealed in Israel's history (Ps 111:2–10). The deeds reveal God's
very self, powerful, merciful, faithful. The poem is an acrostic,
each verse beginning with a successive letter of the Hebrew
alphabet.
**111:1** *In the assembled congregation of the upright*: in the
Temple, cf. Ps 149:1.

---

109:24–25 Ps 69:11–13.
  109:30 Ps 111:1.
110:1 Mt 22:44; Acts
  2:34–35; 1 Cor
  15:25; Heb 1:13; 8:1;
  10:12–13; 1 Pt 3:22.
110:3 Ps 2:7; 89:27; Is 49:1.

110:4 Ps 89:35; 132:11; Gn
  14:18; Heb 5:6; 7:21.
110:5 Ps 2:9; Rev 2:27;
  12:5; 19:15.
110:7 Ps 3:4.
111:1 Ps 138:1.

3 Majestic and glorious is his work,
   his righteousness endures forever.
4 He won renown for his wondrous deeds;
   gracious and merciful is the LORD.*
5 He gives food to those who fear him,†
   he remembers his covenant forever.
6 He showed his powerful deeds to his
      people,
   giving them the inheritance of the
      nations.
7 The works of his hands are true and just,
   reliable all his decrees,
8 Established forever and ever,
   to be observed with truth and equity.
9 He sent release to his people,
   decreed his covenant forever;
   holy and fearsome is his name.
10† The fear of the LORD is the beginning of
      wisdom;*
   prudent are all who practice it.
   His praise endures forever.

## PSALM 112†

### The Blessings of the Just

¹ Hallelujah!

Blessed the man who fears the LORD,
   who greatly delights in his commands.*
2 His descendants shall be mighty in the
      land,
   a generation of the upright will be
      blessed.
3 Wealth and riches shall be in his house;
   his righteousness† shall endure
      forever.
4 Light shines through the darkness for
      the upright;*
   gracious, compassionate, and
      righteous.
5 It is good for the man gracious in
      lending,

who conducts his affairs with justice.
6 For he shall never be shaken;
   the righteous shall be remembered
      forever.*
7 He shall not fear an ill report;
   his heart is steadfast, trusting the
      LORD.
8 His heart is tranquil, without fear,
   till at last he looks down on his foes.
9 Lavishly he gives to the poor;
   his righteousness shall endure
      forever;*
   his horn† shall be exalted in honor.
10 The wicked sees and is angry;
   gnashes his teeth and wastes away;
   the desire of the wicked come to
      nothing.

## PSALM 113†

### Praise of God's Care for the Poor

¹ Hallelujah!

I

Praise, you servants of the LORD,
   praise the name of the LORD.*
2 Blessed be the name of the LORD
   both now and forever.
3 From the rising of the sun to its setting*
   let the name of the LORD be praised.

II

4 High above all nations is the LORD;
   above the heavens his glory.*
5 Who is like the LORD our God,
   enthroned on high,
6* looking down on heaven and earth?
7 He raises the needy from the dust,
   lifts the poor from the ash heap,*
8 Seats them with princes,
   the princes of the people,
9 Gives the childless wife a home,
   the joyful mother of children.*
Hallelujah!

---

**111:5** *Food to those who fear him*: probably a reference to the manna in the desert, which elsewhere is seen as a type of the Eucharist, cf. Jn 6:31–33, 49–51.
**111:10** *The fear of the LORD*: reverence for God.
**Psalm 112** An acrostic poem detailing the blessings received by those who remain close to God by obedience to the commandments. Among their blessings are children (Ps 112:2), wealth that enables them to be magnanimous (Ps 112:3, 5, 9), and virtue by which they encourage others (Ps 112:4). The just person is an affront to the wicked, whose hopes remain unfulfilled (Ps 112:10). The logic resembles Ps 1; 111.
**112:3** *Righteousness*: in the Second Temple period the word acquired the nuance of liberality and almsgiving, cf. Sir 3:30; 7:10; Mt 6:1–4.
**112:9** *His horn*: the symbol for vitality and honor.

**Psalm 113** A hymn exhorting the congregation to praise God's name, i.e., the way in which God is present in the world; the name is mentioned three times in Ps 113:1–3. The divine name is especially honored in the Temple (Ps 113:1) but its recognition is not limited by time (Ps 113:2) and space (Ps 113:3), for God is everywhere active (Ps 113:4–5) especially in rescuing the lowly faithful (Ps 113:7–9).

| | |
|---|---|
| **111:4** Ps 103:8; 112:4. | **112:9** Prv 22:9; 2 Cor 9:9. |
| **111:10** Prv 1:7; 9:10; Sir 1:16. | **113:1** Ps 135:1. |
| **112:1** Ps 1:1–2; 119:1–2; 128:1. | **113:3** Mal 1:11. |
| **112:4** Ps 37:6; 97:11; Prv 13:9; Is 58:10. | **113:4** Ps 148:13. |
| **112:6** Prv 10:7; Wis 8:13. | **113:6** Ps 89:7–9. |
| | **113:7** Ps 107:41; 1 Sm 2:7–8. |
| | **113:9** 1 Sm 2:5; Is 54:1. |

P
S

## PSALM 114†

### The Lord's Wonders at the Exodus

1 When Israel came forth from Egypt,
  the house of Jacob from an alien
    people,
2 Judah became God's sanctuary,
  Israel, God's domain.*
3† The sea saw and fled;
  the Jordan turned back.*
4 The mountains skipped like rams;
  the hills, like lambs.*
5 Why was it, sea, that you fled?
  Jordan, that you turned back?
6 Mountains, that you skipped like rams?
  You hills, like lambs?
7 Tremble, earth, before the Lord,*
  before the God of Jacob,
8† Who turned the rock into pools of water,
  flint into a flowing spring.*

## PSALM 115†

### The Greatness of the True God

#### I

1 Not to us, Lord, not to us
  but to your name give glory
  because of your mercy and
    faithfulness.*
2 Why should the nations say,
  "Where is their God?"†*
3 Our God is in heaven
  and does whatever he wills.*

#### II

4 Their idols are silver and gold,*
  the work of human hands.*

5 They have mouths but do not speak,
  eyes but do not see.
6 They have ears but do not hear,
  noses but do not smell.
7 They have hands but do not feel,
  feet but do not walk;
  they produce no sound from their
    throats.
8 Their makers will be like them,
  and anyone who trusts in them.

#### III

9† The house of Israel trusts in the Lord,*
  who is their help and shield.*
10 The house of Aaron trusts in the Lord,
  who is their help and shield.
11 Those who fear the Lord trust in the
    Lord,
  who is their help and shield.
12 The Lord remembers us and will bless
    us,
  will bless the house of Israel,
  will bless the house of Aaron,
13 Will bless those who fear the Lord,
  small and great alike.
14 May the Lord increase your number,
  yours and your descendants.
15 May you be blessed by the Lord,
  maker of heaven and earth.
16† The heavens belong to the Lord,
  but he has given the earth to the
    children of Adam.*
17† The dead do not praise the Lord,
  not all those go down into silence.*
18 It is we who bless the Lord,
  both now and forever.
  Hallelujah!

---

† **Psalm 114** A hymn celebrating Israel's escape from Egypt, journey through the wilderness, and entry into the promised land, and the miracles of nature that bore witness to God's presence in their midst. In the perspective of the Psalm, the people proceed directly from Egypt into the promised land (Ps 114:1–2). Sea and Jordan, which stood like soldiers barring the people from their battle, flee before the mighty God as the earth recoils from the battle (Ps 114:3–4). The poet taunts the natural elements as one taunts defeated enemies (Ps 114:5–6).

**114:3–4** Pairs of cosmic elements such as sea and rivers, mountains and hills, are sometimes mentioned in creation accounts. Personified here as warriors, the pairs tremble in fear before the Divine Warrior. The quaking also recalls the divine appearance in the storm at Sinai (Ex 19:16–19) and elsewhere (Jgs 5:4–5; Ps 18:7–15).

**114:8** The miracles of giving drink to the people in the arid desert, cf. Ex 17:1–7; Is 41:17–18.

**Psalm 115** A response to the enemy taunt, "Where is your God?" This hymn to the glory of Israel's God (Ps 115:1–3) ridicules the lifeless idols of the nations (Ps 115:4–8), expresses in a litany the trust of the various classes of the people in God (Ps 115:9–11), invokes God's blessing on them as they invoke the divine name (Ps 115:12–15), and concludes as it began with praise

of God. Ps 135:15–18 similarly mocks the Gentile gods and has a similar litany and hymn (Ps 135:19–21).

**115:2** *Where is their God?*: implies that God cannot help them.

**115:9–11** *The house of Israel...the house of Aaron...those who fear the Lord*: the laity of Israelite birth, the priests, and the converts to Judaism, cf. Ps 118:2–4; 135:19–21. In the New Testament likewise "those who fear the Lord" means converts to Judaism (cf. Acts 10:2, 22, 35; 13:16, 26).

**115:16** *The heavens*: the Septuagint reads here "the heaven of heavens" or "the highest heavens," i.e., above the firmament. See note on Ps 148:4.

**115:17** See note on Ps 6:5.

---

**114:2** Ex 19:6.
**114:3** Ps 66:6; 74:15; Ex 14:21f; Jos 3:14ff.
**114:4** Ps 29:6; Wis 19:9.
**114:7** Ps 68:9.
**114:8** Ex 17:6; Nm 20:11.
**115:1** Ez 36:22–23.
**115:2** Ps 79:10.
**115:3** Ps 135:6.

**115:4–10** Ps 135:15–19; Wis 15:15–16; Is 44:9f; Jer 10:1–5.
**115:4** Is 40:19.
**115:9** Ps 118:2–4.
**115:9** Ps 33:20.
**115:16** Gn 1:28.
**115:17** Ps 6:6; 88:11ff; Sir 17:22f; Is 38:18.

## PSALM 116†

### Thanksgiving to God Who Saves from Death

**I**

1 I love the LORD, who listened
   to my voice in supplication,

2 Who turned an ear to me
   on the day I called.

3 I was caught by the cords of death;†*
   the snares of Sheol had seized me;
   I felt agony and dread.

4 Then I called on the name of the LORD,
   "O LORD, save my life!"

**II**

5 Gracious is the LORD and righteous;
   yes, our God is merciful.*

6 The LORD protects the simple;
   I was helpless, but he saved me.

7 Return, my soul, to your rest;
   the LORD has been very good to
     you.*

8 For my soul has been freed from death,
   my eyes from tears, my feet from
     stumbling.*

9 I shall walk before the LORD
   in the land of the living.†*

**III**

10† I kept faith, even when I said,
   "I am greatly afflicted!"*

11 I said in my alarm,
   "All men are liars!"*

12 How can I repay the LORD
   for all the great good done for me?

13 I will raise the cup of salvation†
   and call on the name of the LORD.

14 I will pay my vows to the LORD
   in the presence of all his people.

15† Dear in the eyes of the LORD
   is the death of his devoted.*

16 LORD, I am your servant,
   your servant, the child of your
     maidservant;*
   you have loosed my bonds.

17 I will offer a sacrifice of praise
   and call on the name of the LORD.*

18 I will pay my vows to the LORD*
   in the presence of all his people,

19 In the courts of the house of the LORD,
   in your midst, O Jerusalem.
Hallelujah!

## PSALM 117†

### The Nations Called to Praise

1 Praise the LORD, all you nations!
   Extol him, all you peoples!*

2 His mercy for us is strong;
   the faithfulness of the LORD is
     forever.
Hallelujah!

## PSALM 118†

### Hymn of Thanksgiving

**I**

1 Give thanks to the LORD, for he is
     good,*
   his mercy endures forever.

2 Let Israel say:
   his mercy endures forever.

3 Let the house of Aaron say,
   his mercy endures forever.

4 Let those who fear the LORD say,*
   his mercy endures forever.

---

**Psalm 116** A thanksgiving in which the psalmist responds to divine rescue from mortal danger (Ps 116:3–4) and from near despair (Ps 116:10–11) with vows and Temple sacrifices (Ps 116:13–14, 17–19). The Greek and Latin versions divide the Psalm into two parts: Ps 116:1–9 and Ps 116:10–19, corresponding to its two major divisions.

**116:3** *The cords of death:* death is personified here; it attempts to capture the psalmist with snares and nets, cf. Ps 18:6.

**116:9** *The land of the living:* the phrase elsewhere is an epithet of the Jerusalem Temple (cf. Ps 27:13; 52:5; Is 38:11). Hence the psalmist probably refers to being present to God in the Temple.

**116:10** *I kept faith, even when I said:* even in the days of despair, the psalmist did not lose all hope.

**116:13** *The cup of salvation:* probably the libation of wine poured out in gratitude for rescue, cf. Ex 25:29; Nm 15:5, 7, 10.

**116:15** *Dear in the eyes of the LORD:* the meaning is that the death of God's faithful is grievous to God, not that God is pleased with the death, cf. Ps 72:14. In Wis 3:5–6, God accepts the death of the righteous as a sacrificial burnt offering.

**Psalm 117** This shortest of hymns calls on the nations to acknowledge God's supremacy. The supremacy of Israel's God has

been demonstrated to them by the people's secure existence, which is owed entirely to God's gracious fidelity.

**Psalm 118** A thanksgiving liturgy accompanying a procession of the king and the people into the Temple precincts. After an invocation in the form of a litany (Ps 118:1–4), the psalmist (very likely speaking in the name of the community) describes how the people confidently implored God's help (Ps 118:5–9) when hostile peoples threatened its life (Ps 118:10–14); vividly God's rescue is recounted (Ps 118:15–18). Then follows a possible dialogue at the Temple gates between the priests and the psalmist as the latter enters to offer the thanksgiving sacrifice (Ps 118:19–25). Finally, the priests impart their blessing (Ps 118:26–27), and the psalmist sings in gratitude (Ps 118:28–29).

**116:3** Ps 18:5; Jon 2:3.
**116:5** Ex 34:6.
**116:7** Ps 13:6.
**116:8** Ps 56:14; Is 25:8; Rev 21:4.
**116:9** Ps 27:13; 56:14; Is 38:11.
**116:10** 2 Cor 4:13.
**116:11** Ps 12:2.
**116:15** Ps 72:14; Is 43:4.
**116:16** Ps 86:16; 143:12; Wis 9:5.
**116:17** Lv 7:12ff.
**116:18** Jon 2:10.
**117:1** Rom 15:11.
**118:1** Ps 100:5; 136:1f.
**118:4** Ps 115:9–11.

**II**

5 In danger I called on the LORD;
     the LORD answered me and set me
         free.

6 The LORD is with me; I am not afraid;
     what can mortals do against me? *

7 The LORD is with me as my helper;
     I shall look in triumph on my foes.

8 Better to take refuge in the LORD *
     than to put one's trust in mortals.

9 Better to take refuge in the LORD
     than to put one's trust in princes.

**III**

10 All the nations surrounded me;
     in the LORD's name I cut them off.

11 They surrounded me on every side;
     in the LORD's name I cut them off.

12 They surrounded me like bees; *
     they burned up like fire among
         thorns;
     in the LORD's name I cut them off.

13 I was hard pressed and falling,
     but the LORD came to my help. *

14 The LORD, my strength and might,
     has become my savior. *

**IV**

15 The joyful shout of deliverance
     is heard in the tents of the righteous:
     "The LORD's right hand works valiantly;

16      the LORD's right hand is raised;
     the LORD's right hand works valiantly."

17 I shall not die but live
     and declare the deeds of the LORD.

18 The LORD chastised me harshly,
     but did not hand me over to death.

**V**

19 Open the gates of righteousness;
     I will enter and thank the LORD. *

20 This is the LORD's own gate,

through it the righteous enter.

21 I thank you for you answered me;
     you have been my savior.

22 † The stone the builders rejected
     has become the cornerstone. *

23 By the LORD has this been done;
     it is wonderful in our eyes.

24 This is the day the LORD has made;
     let us rejoice in it and be glad.

25 LORD, grant salvation! †
     LORD, grant good fortune!

**VI**

26 Blessed is he
     who comes in the name of the LORD. *
We bless you from the house of the
     LORD.

27      The LORD is God and has enlightened
     us.
Join in procession with leafy branches
     up to the horns of the altar.

**VII**

28 You are my God, I give you thanks;
     my God, I offer you praise.

29 Give thanks to the LORD, for he is good,
     his mercy endures forever.

## PSALM 119†

### A Prayer to God, the Lawgiver

### Aleph

1 Blessed those whose way is blameless,
     who walk by the law of the LORD. *

2 Blessed those who keep his testimonies,
     who seek him with all their heart. *

3 They do no wrong;
     they walk in his ways.

4 You have given them the command
     to observe your precepts with care.

5 May my ways be firm

---

**118:22** *The stone the builders rejected*: a proverb: what is insignificant to human beings has become great through divine election. The "stone" may originally have meant the foundation stone or capstone of the Temple. The New Testament interpreted the verse as referring to the death and resurrection of Christ (Mt 21:42; Acts 4:11; cf. Is 28:16 and Rom 9:33; 1 Pt 2:7).

**118:25** *Grant salvation*: the Hebrew for this cry has come into English as "Hosanna." This cry and the words in Ps 118:26 were used in the gospels to welcome Jesus entering the Temple on Palm Sunday (Mk 11:9–10).

**Psalm 119** This Psalm, the longest by far in the Psalter, praises God for giving such splendid laws and instruction for people to live by. The author glorifies and thanks God for the Torah, prays for protection from sinners enraged by others' fidelity to the law, laments the cost of obedience, delights in the law's consolations, begs for wisdom to understand the precepts, and asks for the rewards of keeping them. Several expected elements do not appear in the Psalm: Mount Sinai with its story of God's revelation and gift to Israel of instruction and commandments, the Temple

and other institutions related to revelation and laws (frequent in other Psalms). The Psalm is fascinated with God's word directing and guiding human life. The poem is an acrostic; its twenty-two stanzas (of eight verses each) are in the order of the Hebrew alphabet. Each of the eight verses within a stanza begins with the same letter. Each verse contains one word for "instruction." The translation here given attempts to translate each Hebrew word for "instruction" with the same English word. There are, however, nine words for "instruction," not eight, so the principle of a different word for "instruction" in each verse cannot be maintained with perfect consistency. The nine words for "instruction" in the translation are: law, statute, commandment, precept, testimony, word, judgment, way, and promise.

**118:6** Ps 27:1; Heb 13:6.
**118:8f** Ps 146:3.
**118:12** Dt 1:44.
**118:13** Ps 129:1–2.
**118:14** Ex 15:2; Is 12:2.
**118:19** Is 26:2.
**118:22** Mt 21:42; Lk 20:17;
     Acts 4:11; Rom 9:33;
     1 Pt 2:7.
**118:26** Mt 21:9; 23:39.
**119:1** Ps 1:1–2; 15:2; 112:1.
**119:2** Dt 4:29.

in the observance of your statutes!

6 Then I will not be ashamed
   to ponder all your commandments.
7 I will praise you with sincere heart
   as I study your righteous judgments.
8 I will observe your statutes;
   do not leave me all alone.

### Beth

9 How can the young keep his way
      without fault?
   Only by observing your words.
10 With all my heart I seek you;
   do not let me stray from your
      commandments.
11 In my heart I treasure your promise,
   that I may not sin against you.
12 Blessed are you, O LORD;
   teach me your statutes. *
13 With my lips I recite
   all the judgments you have spoken.
14 I find joy in the way of your testimonies
   more than in all riches.
15 I will ponder your precepts
   and consider your paths.
16 In your statutes I take delight;
   I will never forget your word.

### Gimel

17 Be kind to your servant that I may live,
   that I may keep your word.
18 Open my eyes to see clearly
   the wonders of your law.
19 I am a sojourner in the land; †*
   do not hide your commandments
      from me.
20 At all times my soul is stirred
   with longing for your judgments.
21 With a curse you rebuke the proud
   who stray from your commandments.
22 Free me from disgrace and contempt,
   for I keep your testimonies.
23 Though princes meet and talk against me,
   your servant meditates on your
      statutes.
24 Your testimonies are my delight;
   they are my counselors.

### Daleth

25 My soul clings to the dust; *
   give me life in accord with your word.
26 I disclosed my ways and you answered
      me;

teach me your statutes.

27 Make me understand the way of your
      precepts;
   I will ponder your wondrous deeds.
28 My soul is depressed;
   lift me up acccording to your word.
29 Lead me from the way of deceit;
   favor me with your law.
30 The way of loyalty I have chosen;
   I have kept your judgments.
31 I cling to your testimonies, LORD;
   do not let me come to shame.
32 I will run the way of your
      commandments,
   for you will broaden my heart.

### He

33 LORD, teach me the way of your statutes;
   I shall keep them with care. *
34 Give me understanding to keep your
      law,
   to observe it with all my heart.
35 Lead me in the path of your
      commandments, *
   for that is my delight.
36 Direct my heart toward your testimonies
   and away from gain.
37 Avert my eyes from what is worthless;
   by your way give me life.
38 For your servant, fulfill your promise
   made to those who fear you.
39 Turn away from me the taunts I dread,
   for your judgments are good.
40 See how I long for your precepts;
   in your righteousness give me life.

### Waw

41 Let your mercy come to me, LORD,
   salvation in accord with your promise.
42 Let me answer my taunters with a word,
   for I trust in your word.
43 Do not take the word of truth from my
      mouth,
   for in your judgments is my hope.
44 I will keep your law always,
   for all time and forever.
45 I will walk freely in an open space
   because I cherish your precepts.
46 I will speak openly of your testimonies
   without fear even before kings.
47 I delight in your commandments,
   which I dearly love.

---

† 119:19 A sojourner in the land: like someone without the legal protection of a native inhabitant, the psalmist has a special need for the guidance of God's teaching.

* 119:12 Ps 25:4; 27:11; 86:11;     119:33 Ps 19:12.
   143:8, 10.                        119:35 Ps 25:4; 27:11; 86:11;
119:19 Ps 39:13.                        143:8, 10.
119:25 Ps 44:26.

48† I lift up my hands to your
     commandments;
     I study your statutes, which I love.

### Zayin

49 Remember your word to your servant
     by which you give me hope.
50 This is my comfort in affliction,
     your promise that gives me life.
51 Though the arrogant utterly scorn me,
     I do not turn from your law.
52 When I recite your judgments of old
     I am comforted, LORD.
53 Rage seizes me because of the wicked;
     they forsake your law.
54 Your statutes become my songs
     wherever I make my home.
55 Even at night I remember your name
     in observance of your law, LORD.
56 This is my good fortune,
     for I have kept your precepts.

### Heth

57 My portion is the LORD;
     I promise to observe your words.
58 I entreat you with all my heart:
     have mercy on me in accord with your
       promise.
59 I have examined my ways
     and turned my steps to your
       testimonies.
60 I am prompt, I do not hesitate
     in observing your commandments.
61 Though the snares of the wicked
       surround me,
     your law I do not forget.
62 At midnight I rise to praise you
     because of your righteous judgments.
63 I am the friend of all who fear you,
     of all who observe your precepts.
64 The earth, LORD, is filled with your
       mercy;*
     teach me your statutes.

### Teth

65 You have treated your servant well,
     according to your word, O LORD.
66 Teach me wisdom and knowledge,
     for in your commandments I trust.
67 Before I was afflicted I went astray,
     but now I hold to your promise.
68 You are good and do what is good;
     teach me your statutes.

69 The arrogant smear me with lies,
     but I keep your precepts with all my
       heart.
70 Their hearts are gross and fat;*
     as for me, your law is my delight.
71 It was good for me to be afflicted,
     in order to learn your statutes.
72 The law of your mouth is more precious
       to me
     than heaps of silver and gold.

### Yodh

73 Your hands made me and fashioned me;
     give me understanding to learn your
       commandments.
74 Those who fear you rejoice to see me,
     because I hope in your word.
75 I know, LORD, that your judgments are
       righteous;
     though you afflict me, you are
       faithful.
76 May your mercy comfort me
     in accord with your promise to your
       servant.
77 Show me compassion that I may live,
     for your law is my delight.
78 Shame the proud for leading me astray
       with falsehood,
     that I may study your testimonies.
79 Let those who fear you turn to me,
     those who acknowledge your
       testimonies.
80 May I be wholehearted toward your
       statutes,
     that I may not be put to shame.

### Kaph

81 My soul longs for your salvation;
     I put my hope in your word.*
82 My eyes long to see your promise.*
     When will you comfort me?
83 I am like a wineskin shriveled by
       smoke,*
     but I have not forgotten your statutes.
84 How long can your servant survive?
     When will your judgment doom my
       foes?
85 The arrogant have dug pits for me;
     defying your law.
86 All your commandments are steadfast.
     Help me! I am pursued without
       cause.

---

† **119:48** *I lift up my hands to your commandments*: to lift up the hands was an ancient gesture of reverence to God. Here the picture is applied to God's law.

* **119:64** Ps 33:5.
**119:70** Ps 17:10; 73:7; Jb 15:27.
**119:81** Ps 130:6.
**119:82** Ps 25:15; 123:1–2; 141:8.
**119:83** Jb 30:30.

87  They have almost put an end to me on
        earth,
      but I do not forsake your precepts.
88  In your mercy give me life,
      to observe the testimonies of your
          mouth.

### Lamedh

89† Your word, LORD, stands forever;*
      it is firm as the heavens.
90  Through all generations your truth
        endures;
      fixed to stand firm like the earth.
91  By your judgments they stand firm to
        this day,
      for all things are your servants.
92  Had your law not been my delight,
      I would have perished in my
          affliction.
93  I will never forget your precepts;
      through them you give me life.
94  I am yours; save me,
      for I cherish your precepts.
95  The wicked hope to destroy me,
      but I seek to understand your
          testimonies.
96  I have seen the limits of all perfection,
      but your commandment is without
          bounds.

### Mem

97  How I love your law, Lord!†
      I study it all day long.
98  Your commandment makes me wiser
        than my foes,
      as it is forever with me.
99  I have more insight than all my teachers,
      because I ponder your testimonies.
100 I have more understanding than my
        elders,
      because I keep your precepts.*
101 I keep my steps from every evil path,
      that I may observe your word.
102 From your judgments I do not turn,
      for you have instructed me.
103 How sweet to my tongue is your
        promise,
      sweeter than honey to my mouth!*
104 Through your precepts I gain
        understanding;
      therefore I hate all false ways.

### Nun

105 Your word is a lamp for my feet,
      a light for my path.*
106 I make a solemn vow
      to observe your righteous judgments.
107 I am very much afflicted, LORD;
      give me life in accord with your word.
108 Accept my freely offered praise;*
      LORD, teach me your judgments.
109 My life is always at risk,
      but I do not forget your law.
110 The wicked have set snares for me,
      but from your precepts I do not stray.
111 Your testimonies are my heritage forever;
      they are the joy of my heart.
112 My heart is set on fulfilling your statutes;
      they are my reward forever.

### Samekh

113 I hate every hypocrite;
      your law I love.
114 You are my refuge and shield;
      in your word I hope.
115 Depart from me, you wicked,*
      that I may keep the commandments
          of my God.
116 Sustain me by your promise that I may
        live;
      do not disappoint me in my hope.
117 Strengthen me that I may be safe,
      ever to contemplate your statutes.
118 You reject all who stray from your statutes,
      for vain is their deceit.
119 Like dross you regard all the wicked on
        earth;
      therefore I love your testimonies.
120 My flesh shudders with dread of you;
      I fear your judgments.

### Ayin

121 I have fulfilled your righteous judgment;
      do not abandon me to my oppressors.
122 Guarantee your servant's welfare;
      do not let the arrogant oppress me.
123 My eyes long to see your salvation
      and the promise of your
          righteousness.
124 Act with mercy toward your servant;
      teach me your statutes.
125 I am your servant; give me discernment
      that I may know your testimonies.

---

† **119:89–91** God's word creates the world, which manifests
that word by its permanence and reliability.
  **119:97** *Lord*: the inclusion of "Lord" follows the tradition of
the Septuagint and the Vulgate.

**119:89** Is 40:8.
**119:100** Jb 32:6; Wis 4:8–9.
**119:103** Ps 19:11.
**119:105** Ps 18:29; Prv 6:23.
**119:108** Ps 50:14, 23; Heb
      13:15.
**119:115** Ps 6:9; 139:19; Jb
      21:14.

126 It is time for the LORD to act;
    they have disobeyed your law.
127 Truly I love your commandments
    more than gold, more than the finest
        gold.
128 Thus, I follow all your precepts;
    every wrong way I hate.

### Pe

129 Wonderful are your testimonies;
    therefore I keep them.
130 The revelation of your words sheds light,
    gives understanding to the simple.
131 I sigh with open mouth,
    yearning for your commandments.
132 Turn to me and be gracious, *
    according to your judgment for those
        who love your name.
133 Steady my feet in accord with your
        promise;
    do not let iniquity lead me.
134 Free me from human oppression,
    that I may observe your precepts.
135 Let your face shine upon your servant;
    teach me your statutes.
136 My eyes shed streams of tears
    because your law is not observed.

### Sadhe

137 You are righteous, LORD,
    and just are your judgments. *
138 You have given your testimonies in
        righteousness
    and in surpassing faithfulness.
139 I am consumed with rage,
    because my foes forget your words.
140 Your servant loves your promise;
    it has been proved by fire.
141 Though belittled and despised,
    I do not forget your precepts.
142 Your justice is forever right,
    your law true.
143 Though distress and anguish come upon
        me,
    your commandments are my delight.
144 Your testimonies are forever righteous;
    give me understanding that I may live.
145 I call with all my heart, O LORD;
    answer me that I may keep your
        statutes.
146 I call to you to save me
    that I may observe your testimonies.
147 I rise before dawn and cry out;

    I put my hope in your words.
148 My eyes greet the night watches
    as I meditate on your promise. *
149 Hear my voice in your mercy, O LORD;
    by your judgment give me life.
150 Malicious persecutors draw near me;
    they are far from your law.
151 You are near, O LORD;
    reliable are all your commandments.
152 Long have I known from your
        testimonies
    that you have established them
        forever.

### Resh

153 Look at my affliction and rescue me,
    for I have not forgotten your law.
154 Take up my cause and redeem me; *
    for the sake of your promise give me
        life.
155 Salvation is far from sinners
    because they do not cherish your
        statutes.
156 Your compassion is great, O LORD;
    in accord with your judgments, give
        me life.
157 Though my persecutors and foes are
        many,
    I do not turn from your testimonies.
158 I view the faithless with loathing *
    because they do not heed your
        promise.
159 See how I love your precepts, LORD;
    in your mercy give me life.
160 Your every word is enduring;
    all your righteous judgments are
        forever.

### Shin

161 Princes persecute me without reason,
    but my heart reveres only your word.
162 I rejoice at your promise,
    as one who has found rich spoil.
163 Falsehood I hate and abhor;
    your law I love.
164 Seven times a day I praise you
    because your judgments are righteous.
165 Lovers of your law have much peace; *
    for them there is no stumbling block.
166 I look for your salvation, LORD,
    and I fulfill your commandments.
167 I observe your testimonies;
    I love them very much.

---

119:132 Ps 25:16; 86:16.    119:148 Ps 63:7; 77:7.    119:158 Ps 139:22.    119:165 Ps 72:7.
119:137 Tb 3:2.    119:154 Ps 43:1.

168 I observe your precepts and testimonies;
    all my ways are before you.

### Taw

169 Let my cry come before you, LORD; *
    in keeping with your word, give me
      understanding.

170 Let my prayer come before you;
    rescue me according to your promise.

171 May my lips pour forth your praise,
    because you teach me your statutes.

172 May my tongue sing of your promise,
    for all your commandments are
      righteous.

173 Keep your hand ready to help me,
    for I have chosen your precepts.

174 I long for your salvation, LORD;
    your law is my delight.

175 Let my soul live to praise you;
    may your judgments give me help.

176 I have wandered like a lost sheep;
    seek out your servant,
    for I do not forget your
      commandments. *

## PSALM 120†

### Prayer of a Returned Exile

1 A song of ascents. †

The LORD answered me
    when I called in my distress: *

2 LORD, deliver my soul from lying lips,
    from a treacherous tongue. *

3 What will he inflict on you,
    O treacherous tongue,

and what more besides? †

4 A warrior's arrows
    sharpened with coals of brush
      wood! † *

5† Alas, I am a foreigner in Meshech,
    I live among the tents of Kedar!

6 Too long do I live
    among those who hate peace.

7 When I speak of peace,
    they are for war. *

## PSALM 121†

### The Lord My Guardian

1 A song of ascents.

I raise my eyes toward the mountains. †
    From whence shall come my help? *

2 My help comes from the LORD,
    the maker of heaven and earth. *

3 He will not allow your foot to slip; *
    or your guardian to sleep.

4 Behold, the guardian of Israel
    never slumbers nor sleeps.

5† The LORD is your guardian;
    the LORD is your shade
    at your right hand. *

6 By day the sun will not strike you,
    nor the moon by night. *

7 The LORD will guard you from all evil;
    he will guard your soul. *

8 The LORD will guard your coming and
      going
    both now and forever. *

---

† **Psalm 120** A thanksgiving, reporting divine rescue (Ps 120:1) yet with fervent prayer for further protection against lying attackers (Ps 120:2–4). The psalmist is acutely conscious of living away from God's own land where divine peace prevails (Ps 120:5–7).

**120:1** *A song of ascents*: Ps 120–134 all begin with this superscription. Most probably these fifteen Psalms once formed a collection of Psalms sung when pilgrims went to Jerusalem, since one "ascended" to Jerusalem (1 Kgs 12:28; Ps 24:3; 122:4; Lk 2:42) or to the house of God or to an altar (1 Kgs 12:33; 2 Kgs 23:2; Ps 24:3). Less probable is the explanation that these Psalms were sung by the exiles when they "ascended" to Jerusalem from Babylonia (cf. Ezr 7:9). The idea, found in the Mishnah, that the fifteen steps on which the Levites sang corresponded to these fifteen Psalms (Middot 2:5) must underlie the Vulgate translation *canticum graduum*, "song of the steps" or "gradual song."

**120:3** *More besides*: a common curse formula in Hebrew was "May the Lord do such and such evils to you [the evils being specified], and add still more to them," cf. 1 Sm 3:17; 14:44; 25:22. Here the psalmist is at a loss for a suitable malediction.

**120:4** *Coals of brush wood*: coals made from the stalk of the broom plant burn with intense heat. The psalmist thinks of lighted coals cast at his enemies.

**120:5** Meshech was in the far north (Gn 10:2) and Kedar was a tribe of the north Arabian desert (Gn 25:13). The psalmist may be thinking generally of all aliens living among inhospitable peoples.

**Psalm 121** A blessing given to someone embarking on a dangerous journey whether a soldier going on a campaign or a pilgrim returning home from the Temple. People look anxiously at the wooded hills. Will God protect them on their journey (Ps 121:1)? The speaker declares that God is not confined to a place or a time (Ps 121:2), that every step is guarded (Ps 121:3–4); night and day (Ps 121:5–6) God watches over their every movement (Ps 121:7–8).

**121:1** *The mountains*: possibly Mount Zion, the site of the Temple and hence of safety, but more probably mountains as a place of dangers, causing anxiety to the psalmist.

**121:5–6** The image of shade, a symbol of protection, is apt: God as shade protects from the harmful effects that ancients believed were caused by the sun and moon.

---

**119:169** Ps 88:3.
**119:176** Is 53:6; Jer 50:6; Lk 15:1–7.
**120:1** Jon 2:3.
**120:2** Ps 12:3–5; Sir 51:3.
**120:4** Ps 11:6; 140:11; Prv 16:27.
**120:7** Ps 35:20; 140:3–4.
**121:1** Jer 3:23.
**121:2** Ps 124:8; 146:6.
**121:3** Ps 66:9; 91:12; 1 Sm 2:9; Prv 3:23.
**121:5** Ps 16:8; 73:23.
**121:6** Wis 18:3; Is 25:4; 49:10.
**121:7** Ps 97:10.
**121:8** Dt 28:6.

P
S

## PSALM 122†

### A Pilgrim's Prayer for Jerusalem

¹ A song of ascents. Of David.

**I**

I rejoiced when they said to me,
  "Let us go to the house of the LORD."*

² And now our feet are standing
  within your gates, Jerusalem.

³ Jerusalem, built as a city,
  walled round about.†*

⁴ There the tribes go up,
  the tribes of the LORD,
As it was decreed for Israel,
  to give thanks to the name of the LORD.*

⁵ There are the thrones of justice,
  the thrones of the house of David.

**II**

⁶ For the peace of Jerusalem pray:
  "May those who love you prosper!

⁷ May peace be within your ramparts,
  prosperity within your towers."*

⁸ For the sake of my brothers and friends
  I say,
  "Peace be with you."*

⁹ For the sake of the house of the LORD,
  our God,
I pray for your good.

## PSALM 123†

### Reliance on the Lord

¹ A song of ascents.

To you I raise my eyes,
  to you enthroned in heaven.*

² Yes, like the eyes of servants
  on the hand of their masters,
Like the eyes of a maid
  on the hand of her mistress,

So our eyes are on the LORD our God,
  till we are shown favor.

³ Show us favor, LORD, show us favor,
  for we have our fill of contempt.*

⁴ Our souls are more than sated
  with mockery from the insolent,
  with contempt from the arrogant.

## PSALM 124†

### God, the Rescuer of the People

¹ A song of ascents. Of David.

Had not the LORD been with us,
  let Israel say,*

² Had not the LORD been with us,
  when people rose against us,

³ Then they would have swallowed us alive,*
  for their fury blazed against us.

⁴ Then the waters would have engulfed us,
  the torrent overwhelmed us;*

⁵ then seething water would have
  drowned us.

⁶ Blessed is the LORD, who did not leave us
  to be torn by their teeth.

⁷ We escaped with our lives like a bird
  from the fowler's snare;
  the snare was broken,
  and we escaped.

⁸† Our help is in the name of the LORD,
  the maker of heaven and earth.*

## PSALM 125†

### Israel's Protector

¹ A song of ascents.

Those trusting in the LORD are like
  Mount Zion,
  unshakable, forever enduring.*

---

**Psalm 122** A song of Zion, sung by pilgrims obeying the law to visit Jerusalem three times on a journey. The singer anticipates joining the procession into the city (Ps 122:1–3). Jerusalem is a place of encounter, where the people praise God (Ps 122:4) and hear the divine justice mediated by the king (Ps 122:5). The very buildings bespeak God's power (cf. Ps 48:13–15). May the grace of this place transform the people's lives (Ps 122:6–9)!

**122:3** *Walled round about*: lit., "which is joined to it," probably referring both to the density of the buildings and to the dense population.

**Psalm 123** A lament that begins as a prayer of an individual (Ps 123:1), who expresses by a touching comparison exemplary confidence in God (Ps 123:2). The Psalm ends in prayer that God relieve the people's humiliation at the hands of the arrogant (Ps 123:3–4).

**Psalm 124** A thanksgiving which teaches that Israel's very existence is owed to God who rescues them. In the first part Israel's enemies are compared to the mythic sea dragon (Ps 124:2b–3a;

cf. Jer 51:34) and Flood (Ps 124:3b–5; cf. Is 51:9–10). The Psalm heightens the malice of human enemies by linking them to the primordial enemies of God's creation. Israel is a bird freed from the trapper's snare (Ps 124:6–8)—freed originally from Pharaoh and now from the current danger.

**124:8** *Our help is in the name*: for the idiom, see Ex 18:4.

**Psalm 125** In response to exilic anxieties about the ancient promises of restoration, the Psalm expresses confidence that God will surround the people as the mountains surround Zion (Ps 125:1–2). The just will not be contaminated by the wicked (Ps 125:3). May God judge between the two groups (Ps 125:4–5).

---

**122:1** Ps 43:3–4; 84:2–5.
**122:3** Ps 48:13–14.
**122:4** Dt 16:16.
**122:7** Ps 128:5.
**122:8** Jn 20:19ff.
**123:1** Ps 25:15; 119:82; 141:8.

**123:3** Ps 44:13–14; Jb 12:4.
**124:1** Ps 129:1.
**124:3** Prv 1:12.
**124:4** Ps 18:5; 69:2.
**124:8** Ps 121:2; 146:6.
**125:1** Prv 10:25.

2 As mountains surround Jerusalem,
  the LORD surrounds his people
  both now and forever. *

3 The scepter of the wicked will not
    prevail
  in the land allotted to the just, †
Lest the just themselves
  turn their hands to evil.

4 Do good, LORD, to the good,
  to those who are upright of heart. *
5 But those who turn aside to crooked
    ways
  may the LORD send down with the
    evildoers. *
Peace upon Israel! *

## PSALM 126†

### The Reversal of Zion's Fortunes

¹ A song of ascents.

**I**

When the LORD restored the captives of
    Zion, *
  we thought we were dreaming.
2 Then our mouths were filled with
    laughter;
  our tongues sang for joy. *
Then it was said among the nations,
  "The LORD had done great things for
    them."
3 The LORD has done great things for us;
  Oh, how happy we were!
4 Restore our captives, LORD,
  like the dry stream beds of the
    Negeb. †

**II**

5 Those who sow in tears
  will reap with cries of joy. *

6 Those who go forth weeping,
  carrying sacks of seed,
Will return with cries of joy,
  carrying their bundled sheaves.

## PSALM 127†

### The Need of God's Blessing

¹ A song of ascents. Of Solomon.

**I**

Unless the LORD build the house,
  they labor in vain who build.
Unless the LORD guard the city,
  in vain does the guard keep watch.
2 It is vain for you to rise early
  and put off your rest at night,
To eat bread earned by hard toil—
  all this God gives to his beloved in
    sleep. *

**II**

3 Certainly sons are a gift from the LORD,
  the fruit of the womb, a reward. *
4 Like arrows in the hand of a warrior
  are the sons born in one's youth.
5 Blessed is the man who has filled his
    quiver with them.
He will never be shamed
  for he will destroy his foes at the
    gate. †

## PSALM 128†

### The Blessed Home of the Just

¹ A song of ascents.

**I**

Blessed are all who fear the LORD,
  and who walk in his ways. *
2 What your hands provide you will enjoy;
  you will be blessed and prosper: *
3 Your wife will be like a fruitful vine

---

125:3 *The land allotted to the just*: lit., "the lot of the righteous." The promised land was divided among the tribes of Israel by lot (Nm 26:55; Jos 18). The righteous are the members of the people who are obedient to God. If the domination of the wicked were to continue in the land, even the just would be infected by their evil attitudes.
  **Psalm 126** A lament probably sung shortly after Israel's return from exile. The people rejoice that they are in Zion (Ps 126:1–3) but mere presence in the holy city is not enough; they must pray for the prosperity and the fertility of the land (Ps 126:4). The last verses are probably an oracle of promise: the painful work of sowing will be crowned with life (Ps 126:5–6).
  126:4 *Like the dry stream beds of the Negeb*: the psalmist prays for rain in such abundance that the dry riverbeds will run.
  **Psalm 127** The Psalm puts together two proverbs (Ps 127:1–2, 3–5) on God establishing "houses" or families. The prosperity of human groups is not the work of human beings but the gift of God.

127:5 *At the gate*: the reference is not to enemies besieging the walls of a city but to adversaries in litigation. Law courts functioned in the open area near the main city gate. The more adult sons a man had, the more forceful he would appear in disputes, cf. Prv 31:23.
  **Psalm 128** A statement that the ever-reliable God will bless the reverent (Ps 128:1). God's blessing is concrete: satisfaction and prosperity, a fertile spouse and abundant children (Ps 128:2–4). The perspective is that of the adult male, ordinarily the ruler and representative of the household to the community. The last verses extend the blessing to all the people for generations to come (Ps 128:5–6).

---

125:2 Dt 32:11.                    126:5 Bar 4:23; Is 65:19.
125:4 Ps 18:25ff.                  127:2 Eccl 2:24.
125:5 Prv 3:32.                    127:3 Ps 115:14; 128:3; Dt
125:5 Ps 128:6.                        28:11; Prv 17:6.
126:1 Ps 14:7.                     128:1 Ps 112:1.
126:2 Jb 8:21.                     128:2 Ps 112:3.

**P**
**S**

within your home,
Your children like young olive plants
  around your table.*

4  Just so will the man be blessed
     who fears the LORD.

**II**

5  May the LORD bless you from Zion;
     may you see Jerusalem's prosperity
     all the days of your life,*
6  and live to see your children's
     children.*
   Peace upon Israel!*

## PSALM 129†

### Against Israel's Enemies

¹A song of ascents.

**I**

Viciously have they attacked me from
  my youth,
  let Israel say now.*
2  Viciously have they attacked me from
     my youth,*
     yet they have not prevailed against
     me.
3  Upon my back the plowers plowed,
     as they traced their long furrows.*
4  But the just LORD cut me free
     from the ropes of the wicked.†

**II**

5  May they recoil in disgrace,
     all who hate Zion.
6  May they be like grass on the
     rooftops†
     withered in early growth,*
7  Never to fill the reaper's hands,
     nor the arms of the binders of
     sheaves,
8  And with none passing by to call out:

"The blessing of the LORD be upon
  you!†
We bless you in the name of the
  LORD!"*

## PSALM 130†

### Prayer for Pardon and Mercy

¹A song of ascents.

**I**

Out of the depths† I call to you, LORD;
2    Lord, hear my cry!
   May your ears be attentive
     to my cry for mercy.*
3  If you, LORD, keep account of sins,
     Lord, who can stand?*
4  But with you is forgiveness
     and so you are revered.†

**II**

5  I wait for the LORD,
     my soul waits
     and I hope for his word.*
6  My soul looks for the Lord
     more than sentinels for daybreak.*
   More than sentinels for daybreak,
7    let Israel hope in the LORD,
   For with the LORD is mercy,
     with him is plenteous redemption,*
8  And he will redeem Israel
     from all its sins.*

## PSALM 131†

### Humble Trust in God

¹A song of ascents. Of David.

LORD, my heart is not proud;
  nor are my eyes haughty.
I do not busy myself with great matters,

---

† **Psalm 129** A Psalm giving thanks for God's many rescues of Israel over the long course of their history (Ps 129:1–4); the people pray that their oppressors never know the joy of harvest (Ps 129:5–8).

**129:4** *The ropes of the wicked*: usually understood as the rope for yoking animals to the plow. If it is severed, the plowing (cf. Ps 129:3) comes to a halt.

**129:6** *Like grass on the rooftops*: after the spring rains, grass would sprout from the coat of mud with which the flat roofs of simple houses were covered, but when the dry summer began there was no moisture in the thin roof-covering to sustain the grass.

**129:8** *The blessing of the LORD be upon you*: harvesters greeted one another with such blessings, cf. Ru 2:4.

**Psalm 130** This lament, a Penitential Psalm, is the *De profundis* used in liturgical prayers for the faithful departed. In deep sorrow the psalmist cries to God (Ps 130:1–2), asking for mercy (Ps 130:3–4). The psalmist's trust (Ps 130:5–6) becomes a model for the people (Ps 130:7–8).

**130:1** *The depths*: Sheol here is a metaphor of total misery. Deep anguish makes the psalmist feel "like those descending to the pit" (Ps 143:7).

**130:4** *And so you are revered*: the experience of God's mercy leads one to a greater sense of God.

**Psalm 131** A song of trust, in which the psalmist gives up self-sufficiency (Ps 131:1), like a babe enjoying the comfort of its mother's lap (Ps 131:2), thus providing a model for Israel's faith (Ps 131:3).

---

**128:3** Ps 144:12; Jb 29:5.
**128:5** Ps 20:3; 134:3.
**128:6** Jb 42:16; Prv 17:6.
**128:6** Ps 125:5.
**129:1** Ps 124:1.
**129:2** Ps 118:13.
**129:3** Is 51:23.
**129:6** Is 37:27.
**129:8** Ps 118:26.

**130:2** Ps 5:2–3; 55:2–3;
  86:6; Lam 3:55–56;
  Jon 2:3.
**130:3** Na 1:6.
**130:5** Ps 119:81.
**130:6** Is 21:11; 26:9.
**130:7** Ps 86:15; 100:5;
  103:8.
**130:8** Ps 25:22; Mt 1:21.

with things too sublime for me.*

2 Rather, I have stilled my soul,
 Like a weaned child to its mother,
 weaned is my soul.*

3 Israel, hope in the LORD,
 now and forever.

## PSALM 132†

## The Covenant Between David and God

¹ A song of ascents.

### I

Remember, O LORD, for David
 all his hardships;

2 How he swore an oath to the LORD,
 vowed to the Mighty One of Jacob:†

3 "I will not enter the house where I
 live,*
 nor lie on the couch where I sleep;

4 I will give my eyes no sleep,
 my eyelids no rest,

5 Till I find a place for the LORD,
 a dwelling for the Mighty One of
 Jacob."

6 "We have heard of it in Ephrathah;†
 we have found it in the fields of
 Jaar.†

7 Let us enter his dwelling;
 let us worship at his footstool."*

8 "Arise, LORD, come to your resting
 place,*
 you and your mighty ark.

9 Your priests will be clothed with
 justice;
 your devout will shout for joy."

10 For the sake of David your servant,
 do not reject your anointed.

### II

11 The LORD swore an oath to David in
 truth,
 he will never turn back from it:*
 "Your own offspring* I will set upon
 your throne.

12 If your sons observe my covenant,
 and my decrees I shall teach them,
 Their sons, in turn,
 shall sit forever on your throne."

13 Yes, the LORD has chosen Zion,
 desired it for a dwelling:

14 "This is my resting place forever;
 here I will dwell, for I desire it.

15 I will bless Zion with provisions;
 its poor I will fill with bread.

16 I will clothe its priests with salvation;
 its devout shall shout for joy.*

17 There I will make a horn sprout for
 David;†*
 I will set a lamp for my anointed.

18 His foes I will clothe with shame,
 but on him his crown shall shine."

## PSALM 133†

## A Vision of a Blessed Community

¹ A song of ascents. Of David.

How good and how pleasant it is,
 when brothers† dwell together as one!

2 Like fine oil on the head,†*
 running down upon the beard,
 Upon the beard of Aaron,
 upon the collar of his robe.

3 Like dew† of Hermon† coming down
 upon the mountains of Zion.*

---

**Psalm 132** A song for a liturgical ceremony in which the ark, the throne of Israel's God, was carried in procession to the Temple. The singer asks that David's care for the proper housing of the ark be regarded with favor (Ps 132:1–5), and tells how it was brought to Jerusalem (Ps 132:6–10). There follows God's promise of favor to the Davidic dynasty (Ps 132:11–12) and to Zion (Ps 132:13–17). The transfer of the ark to the tent in Jerusalem is described in 2 Sm 6.

**132:2, 132:5** *Mighty One of Jacob*: one of the titles of Israel's God, cf. Gn 49:24; Is 49:26; 60:16.

**132:6** *Ephrathah*: the homeland of David, cf. Ru 4:11. *The fields of Jaar*: poetic for Kiriath-jearim, a town west of Jerusalem, where the ark remained for several generations, cf. 1 Sm 7:1–2; 2 Sm 6:2; 1 Chr 13:5–6.

**132:17** *A horn sprout for David*: the image of the horn, a symbol of strength, is combined with that of a "sprout," a term used for the Davidic descendant (cf. Jer 23:5; 33:15; Zec 3:8; 6:12). Early Christians referred the latter designation to Christ as son of David (Lk 1:69).

**Psalm 133** A benediction over a peaceful community, most probably the people Israel, but appropriate too for Israelite families (Ps 133:1). The history of Israel, whether of its ancestors in the Book of Genesis or of later periods, was a history of distinct groups struggling to live in unity. Here that unity is declared blessed, like the holy oils upon the priest Aaron or the dew of the rainless summer that waters the crops (Ps 133:2–3).

**133:1** *Brothers*: in biblical Hebrew this word includes both the male and female members of a group united by blood relationships or by shared experiences and values. In this Psalm, the term could be applied most appropriately to the people of Israel, those privileged by God to be his chosen children.

**133:2** *Oil on the head*: oil was used at the consecration of the high priest (Ex 30:22–33).

**133:3** *Dew*: dew was an important source of moisture in the dry climate (Gn 27:28; Hos 14:6). *Hermon*: the majestic snow-capped mountain visible in the north of Palestine.

131:1 Ps 139:6.
131:2 Is 66:12–13.
132:3 2 Sm 7; 1 Chr 28:2.
132:7 Ps 99:5.
132:8–10 Ps 2:2; 89:21; 95:11; Nm 10:35; 2 Chr 6:41–42; Sir 24:7.
132:11–14 Ps 68:17;
1 Kgs 8:13; Sir 24:7.
132:11 Ps 110:4; 2 Sm 7:12.
132:16 2 Chr 6:41; Is 61:10.
132:17 Is 11:1; Jer 33:15; Ez 29:21; Zec 3:8; Lk 1:69.
133:2 Ex 30:25, 30.
133:3 Hos 14:6.

There the LORD has decreed a blessing,
life for evermore! *

## PSALM 134†

### Exhortation to the Night Watch to Bless God

¹A song of ascents.

O come, bless the LORD,
all you servants of the LORD †
You who stand in the house of the LORD
throughout the nights. *

2 Lift up your hands toward the sanctuary, *
and bless the LORD.

3 May the LORD bless you from Zion,
the Maker of heaven and earth. *

## PSALM 135†

### Praise of God, the Ruler and Benefactor of Israel

¹Hallelujah!

**I**

Praise the name of the LORD!
Praise, you servants of the LORD, *

2 Who stand in the house of the LORD,
in the courts of the house of our
God! *

3 Praise the LORD, for the LORD is good!
Sing to his name, for it brings joy!

4† For the LORD has chosen Jacob for
himself,
Israel as his treasured possession. *

**II**

5 For I know that the LORD is great,
that our Lord is greater than all gods. *

6 Whatever the LORD desires
he does in heaven and on earth,
in the seas and all the depths. *

7 It is he who raises storm clouds from
the end of the earth,

makes lightning for the rain,
and brings forth wind from his
storehouse. *

**III**

8 He struck down Egypt's firstborn, *
of human being and beast alike,

9 And sent signs and wonders against you,
Egypt,
against Pharaoh and all his servants.

10 It is he who struck down many
nations, *
and slew mighty kings—

11 Sihon, king of the Amorites,
and Og, king of Bashan,
all the kings of Canaan—

12 And made their land a heritage,
a heritage for Israel his people.

13 O LORD, your name is forever,
your renown, from generation to
generation! *

14 For the LORD defends his people,
shows mercy to his servants. *

**IV**

15 The idols of the nations are silver and
gold, *
the work of human hands.

16 They have mouths but do not speak;
they have eyes but do not see;

17 They have ears but do not hear;
nor is there breath in their mouths.

18 Their makers will become like them,
and anyone who trusts in them.

**V**

19 House of Israel, bless the LORD! *
House of Aaron, bless the LORD!

20 House of Levi, bless the LORD!
You who fear the LORD, bless the
LORD!

21 Blessed be the LORD from Zion,
who dwells in Jerusalem!
Hallelujah!

---

† **Psalm 134** A brief liturgy exhorting all those who serve in the Jerusalem Temple during the night (cf. Is 30:29) to praise God with words and gestures. Although he is the Creator of the whole universe, God's blessings emanate in a unique way from Zion, the city of Jerusalem.

**134:1** *Servants of the LORD*: priests and Levites, cf. Dt 10:8; Ps 113:1; 135:1; Dn 3:85.

**Psalm 135** The hymn begins and ends with an invitation to praise God (Ps 135:1–3, 19–20) for the great act of choosing Israel (Ps 135:4). The story of Israel's emergence as a people is told in Ps 135:5–14; God created and redeemed the people, easily conquering all opposition. God's defeat of hostile powers means that the powers themselves and their images are useless (Ps 135:15–18). The last three verses appear also in Ps 115:4–8.

**135:4** Though all nations are God's, Israel has a special status as God's "treasured" people: Ex 19:5; Dt 7:6; 14:2; 26:18; Mal 3:17.

**133:3** Dt 28:8; 30:20.
**134:1** Ps 135:1–2; 1 Chr 9:33.
**134:2** Ps 28:2; 141:2.
**134:3** Ps 20:3; 128:5; Nm 6:24.
**135:1** Ps 113:1.
**135:2** Ps 134:1.
**135:4** Ps 33:12; 144:15; Ex 19:6; Dt 7:6.
**135:5** Ps 95:3; Ex 18:11.
**135:6** Ps 115:3.
**135:7** Ps 148:8; Jer 10:13; 51:16; Jb 37:9.
**135:8–9** Ps 78:51; 105:27, 36; 136:10; Ex 12:29.
**135:10–12** Ps 136:17–22; Nm 21:21–35; Dt 2:24–3:17.
**135:13** Ps 102:13; Ex 3:15.
**135:14** Dt 32:36.
**135:15–18** Ps 115:4–6, 8.
**135:19–20** Ps 118:2–4.

## PSALM 136†

### Hymn of Thanksgiving for God's Everlasting Mercy

**I**

1   Praise the LORD, for he is good; *
    for his mercy endures forever;
2   Praise the God of gods;
    for his mercy endures forever;
3   Praise the Lord of lords;
    for his mercy endures forever;

**II**

4   Who alone has done great wonders, *
    for his mercy endures forever;
5   Who skillfully made the heavens, *
    for his mercy endures forever;
6   Who spread the earth upon the
        waters, *
    for his mercy endures forever;
7   Who made the great lights,
    for his mercy endures forever;
8   The sun to rule the day,
    for his mercy endures forever;
9   The moon and stars to rule the
        night, *
    for his mercy endures forever;

**III**

10  Who struck down the firstborn of
        Egypt, *
    for his mercy endures forever;
11  And led Israel from their midst,
    for his mercy endures forever;
12  With mighty hand and outstretched
        arm, *
    for his mercy endures forever;
13  Who split in two the Red Sea,
    for his mercy endures forever;
14  And led Israel through its midst,
    for his mercy endures forever;
15  But swept Pharaoh and his army into
        the Red Sea, *
    for his mercy endures forever;

16  Who led the people through the desert, *
    for his mercy endures forever;

**IV**

17  Who struck down great kings, *
    for his mercy endures forever;
18  Slew powerful kings,
    for his mercy endures forever;
19  Sihon, king of the Amorites,
    for his mercy endures forever;
20  Og, king of Bashan,
    for his mercy endures forever;
21  And made their lands a heritage,
    for his mercy endures forever;
22† A heritage for Israel, his servant,
    for his mercy endures forever.

**V**

23  The Lord remembered us in our low
        estate,
    for his mercy endures forever;
24  Freed us from our foes,
    for his mercy endures forever;
25  And gives bread to all flesh,
    for his mercy endures forever.

**VI**

26  Praise the God of heaven,
    for his mercy endures forever.

## PSALM 137†

### Sorrow and Hope in Exile

**I**

1   By the rivers of Babylon
    there we sat weeping
    when we remembered Zion. *
2   On the poplars in its midst
    we hung up our harps. *
3   For there our captors asked us
    for the words of a song;
    Our tormentors, for joy:
    "Sing for us a song of Zion!"
4   But how could we sing a song of the LORD
    in a foreign land?

† **Psalm 136** The hymn praises Israel's God ("the God of gods," Ps 136:2), who has created the world in which Israel lives. The refrain occurring after every line suggests that a speaker and chorus sang the Psalm in antiphonal fashion. A single act of God is described in Ps 136:4–25. God arranges the heavens and the earth as the environment for human community, and then creates the community by freeing them and giving them land. In the final section (Ps 136:23–25) God, who created the people and gave them land, continues to protect and nurture them.

**136:22** *A heritage for Israel*: the land was given to Israel by God to be handed on to future generations.

**Psalm 137** A singer refuses to sing the people's sacred songs in an alien land despite demands from Babylonian captors (Ps 137:1–4). The singer swears an oath by what is most dear to a musician—hands and tongue—to exalt Jerusalem always (Ps 137:5–6). The Psalm ends with a prayer that the old enemies of Jerusalem, Edom and Babylon, be destroyed (Ps 137:7–9).

**136:1** Ps 100:5; 118:1.
**136:4** Ps 72:18.
**136:5** Gn 1:9–19.
**136:6** Ps 24:2.
**136:9** Jer 31:35.
**136:10** Ex 12:29, 51; 14:22, 27; 15:22;
Ps 78:51–52; 135:8.
**136:12** Dt 4:34.
**136:15** Ex 14:21f.
**136:16** Dt 8:2, 15.
**136:17–22** Ps 135:10–12.
**137:1** Ez 3:15; Lam 3:48.
**137:2** Is 24:8; Lam 5:14.

**II**

5 If I forget you, Jerusalem,
   may my right hand forget.*
6 May my tongue stick to my palate
   if I do not remember you,
   If I do not exalt Jerusalem
   beyond all my delights.

**III**

7 Remember, LORD, against Edom
   that day at Jerusalem.
   They said: "Level it, level it
   down to its foundations!"*
8 Desolate Daughter Babylon, you shall be
   destroyed,
   blessed the one who pays you back
   what you have done us!*
9† Blessed the one who seizes your children
   and smashes them against the rock.*

## PSALM 138†

### Hymn of a Grateful Heart

¹ Of David.

**I**

I thank you, Lord, with all my heart;*
   in the presence of the angels† to you
   I sing.
2 I bow low toward your holy temple;
   I praise your name for your mercy and
   faithfulness.
   For you have exalted over all
   your name and your promise.
3 On the day I cried out, you answered;
   you strengthened my spirit.

**II**

4 All the kings of earth will praise you,
   LORD,
   when they hear the words of your
   mouth.
5 They will sing of the ways of the LORD:

"How great is the glory of the LORD!"
6 The LORD is on high, but cares for the
   lowly*
   and knows the proud from afar.
7 Though I walk in the midst of dangers,
   you guard my life when my enemies
   rage.
   You stretch out your hand;
   your right hand saves me.
8 The LORD is with me to the end.
   LORD, your mercy endures forever.
   Never forsake the work of your hands!

## PSALM 139†

### The All-knowing and Ever-present God

¹ For the leader. A psalm of David.

**I**

LORD, you have probed me, you know
   me:
2 you know when I sit and stand;† *
   you understand my thoughts from
   afar.
3 You sift through my travels and my rest;
   with all my ways you are familiar.
4 Even before a word is on my tongue,
   LORD, you know it all.
5 Behind and before you encircle me
   and rest your hand upon me.
6 Such knowledge is too wonderful for me,
   far too lofty for me to reach.*
7 Where can I go from your spirit?
   From your presence, where can I flee?
8 If I ascend to the heavens, you are there;
   if I lie down in Sheol, there you are.*
9 If I take the wings of dawn†
   and dwell beyond the sea,†
10 Even there your hand guides me,
   your right hand holds me fast.

---

† **137:9** *Blessed the one who seizes your children and smashes them against the rock*: the children represent the future generations, and so must be destroyed if the enemy is truly to be eradicated.

**Psalm 138** A thanksgiving to God, who came to the rescue of the psalmist. Divine rescue was not the result of the psalmist's virtues but of God's loving fidelity (Ps 138:1–3). The act is not a private transaction but a public act that stirs the surrounding nations to praise God's greatness and care for the people (Ps 138:4–6). The psalmist, having experienced salvation, trusts that God will always be there in moments of danger (Ps 138:7–8).

**138:1** *In the presence of the angels*: heavenly beings who were completely subordinate to Israel's God. The earthly Temple represents the heavenly palace of God.

**Psalm 139** A hymnic meditation on God's omnipresence and omniscience. The psalmist is keenly aware of God's all-knowing

gaze (Ps 139:1–6), of God's presence in every part of the universe (Ps 139:7–12), and of God's control over the psalmist's very self (Ps 139:13–16). Summing up Ps 139:1–16, 17–18 express wonder. There is only one place hostile to God's rule—wicked people. The psalmist prays to be removed from their company (Ps 139:19–24).

**139:2** *When I sit and stand*: in all my physical movement.

**139:9** *Take the wings of dawn*: go to the extremities of the east. *Beyond the sea*: uttermost bounds of the west; the sea is the Mediterranean.

---

* **137:5** Jer 51:50.
**137:7** Jer 49:7; Lam 4:21–22; Ez 25:12–14.
**137:8** Is 47:1–3; Jer 50–51.
**137:9** Hos 14:1.
**138:1** Ps 9:1.
**138:6** Lk 1:51–52.
**139:2** 2 Kgs 19:27; Jb 12:3.
**139:6** Ps 131:1.
**139:8** Jb 23:8–9; Jer 23:23–24.

11 If I say, "Surely darkness shall hide me,
    and night shall be my light"† —
12 Darkness is not dark for you,
    and night shines as the day.
    Darkness and light are but one.*

**II**

13 You formed my inmost being;
    you knit me in my mother's womb.*
14 I praise you, because I am wonderfully
        made;
    wonderful are your works!
    My very self you know.
15 My bones are not hidden from you,
    When I was being made in secret,
    fashioned in the depths of the earth.†
16 Your eyes saw me unformed;
    in your book all are written down;*
    my days were shaped, before one
        came to be.

**III**

17 How precious to me are your designs,
        O God;
    how vast the sum of them!
18 Were I to count them, they would
        outnumber the sands;
    when I complete them, still you are
        with me.*
19 When you would destroy the wicked,
        O God,
    the bloodthirsty depart from me!*
20 Your foes who conspire a plot against
        you
    are exalted in vain.

**IV**

21 Do I not hate, LORD, those who hate you?
    Those who rise against you, do I not
        loathe?*
22 With fierce hatred I hate them,
    enemies I count as my own.

23 Probe me, God, know my heart;
    try me, know my thoughts.*

24 See if there is a wicked path in me;
    lead me along an ancient path.†

## PSALM 140†

### Prayer for Deliverance from the Wicked

1 For the leader. A psalm of David.

**I**

2 Deliver me, LORD, from the wicked;
    preserve me from the violent,*
3 From those who plan evil in their hearts,
    who stir up conflicts every day,
4† Who sharpen their tongue like a serpent,
    venom of asps upon their lips.*   *Selah*

**II**

5 Keep me, LORD, from the clutches of the
        wicked;
    preserve me from the violent,
    who plot to trip me up.*
6† The arrogant have set a trap for me;
    they have spread out ropes for a net,
    laid snares for me by the wayside.
                                        *Selah*

7 I say to the LORD: You are my God;*
    listen, LORD, to the words of my pleas.
8 LORD, my master, my strong deliverer,
    you cover my head on the day of
        armed conflict.
9 LORD, do not grant the desires of the
        wicked one;
    do not let his plot succeed.   *Selah*

**III**

10 Those who surround me raise their heads;
    may the mischief they threaten
        overwhelm them.
11 Drop burning coals upon them;*
    cast them into the watery pit never
        more to rise.

12 Slanderers will not survive on earth;
    evil will hunt down the man of
        violence to overthrow him.

---

† **139:11** *Night shall be my light*: night to me is what day is to others.
    **139:15** *The depths of the earth*: figurative language for the womb, stressing the hidden and mysterious operations that occur there.
    **139:24** *Lead me along an ancient path*: the manner of living of our ancestors, who were faithful to God's will, cf. Jer 6:16.
    **Psalm 140** A lament seeking rescue from violent and treacherous foes (Ps 140:2–6). The psalmist remains trusting (Ps 140:7–8), vigorously praying that the plans of the wicked recoil upon themselves (Ps 140:9–12). A serene statement of praise ends the Psalm (Ps 140:13). The psalmist is content to be known as one of "the needy," "the poor," "the just," "the upright" (Ps 140:13), a class of people expecting divine protection.

**140:4** Similar metaphors for a wicked tongue are used in Ps 52:2; 55:20; 58:3.
    **140:6** *Have set a trap…have spread out ropes for a net*: the same figure, of hunters setting traps, occurs in Ps 9:16; 31:5; 35:7; 64:6, cf. Mt 22:15; Lk 11:54.

---

**139:12** Jb 12:22.
**139:13** Wis 7:1; Eccl 11:5; Jb 1:21.
**139:16** Mal 3:16.
**139:18** Jb 11:7.
**139:19** Jb 21:14.
**139:21** Ps 119:158.
**139:23** Ps 17:3; 26:2.

**140:2** Ps 71:4.
**140:4** Ps 64:4; Rom 3:13.
**140:5** Jer 18:22; Ps 56:7; 57:7.
**140:7** Ps 31:15.
**140:11** Ps 11:6; 120:4; Gn 19:24.

13 For I know the LORD will take up the
   cause of the needy,
   justice for the poor.
14 Then the righteous will give thanks to
   your name;
   the upright will dwell in your
   presence. *

## PSALM 141†

### Prayer for Deliverance from the Wicked

¹ A psalm of David.

LORD, I call to you; hasten to me;
   listen to my plea when I call.
2 Let my prayer be incense† before you;
   my uplifted hands† an evening
   offering. *
3 Set a guard, LORD, before my mouth,
   keep watch over the door of my lips. *
4 Do not let my heart incline to evil,
   to perform deeds in wickedness.
   On the delicacies of evildoers
   let me not feast.
5† Let a righteous person strike me; it is
   mercy if he reproves me.
   Do not withhold oil from my head *
   while my prayer opposes their evil
   deeds.
6 May their leaders be cast over the cliff,
   so that they hear that my speeches are
   pleasing.
7 Like the plowing and breaking up of the
   earth,
   our bones are strewn at the mouth of
   Sheol.
8 For my eyes are upon you, O LORD, my
   Lord; *
   in you I take refuge; do not take away
   my soul.
9 Guard me from the trap they have set
   for me,
   from the snares of evildoers. *

10 Let the wicked fall into their own nets,
   while only I pass over them safely.

## PSALM 142†

### A Prayer in Time of Trouble

¹ A maskil of David, when he was in the cave. †
   A prayer.

2 With my own voice I cry to the LORD;
   with my own voice I beseech the LORD.
3 Before him I pour out my complaint,
   tell of my distress in front of him.
4 When my spirit is faint within me, *
   you know my path. *
   As I go along this path,
   they have hidden a trap for me. *
5 I look to my right hand to see *
   that there is no one willing to
   acknowledge me.
   My escape has perished;
   no one cares for me.
6 I cry out to you, LORD,
   I say, You are my refuge, *
   my portion in the land of the living. *
7 Listen to my cry for help,
   for I am brought very low. *
   Rescue me from my pursuers,
   for they are too strong for me.
8 Lead my soul from prison,
   that I may give thanks to your name.
   Then the righteous shall gather around
   me†
   because you have been good to me.

## PSALM 143†

### A Prayer in Distress

¹ A psalm of David.

LORD, hear my prayer;
   in your faithfulness listen to my
   pleading;

---

† Psalm 141 A lament of an individual (Ps 141:1–2) who is keenly aware that only the righteous can worship God properly and who therefore prays to be protected from the doomed wicked (Ps 141:3–10).

141:2 Incense: lit., "smoke," i.e., the fragrant fumes arising from the altar at the burning of sacrificial animals or of aromatic spices; also used in Rev 5:8 as a symbol of prayer. My uplifted hands: the gesture of supplication, cf. Ps 28:2; 63:5; 88:10; 119:48; 134:2; 143:6.

141:5–7 The Hebrew text is obscure.

Psalm 142 In this lament imploring God for help (Ps 142:2–4), the psalmist tells how enemies have set a trap (Ps 142:4–5), and prays for rescue (Ps 142:6–8). The speaker feels utterly alone (Ps 142:5), exhausted (Ps 142:7), and may even be imprisoned

(Ps 142:7). Prison is possibly a metaphor for general distress. The last two verses are the vow of praise, made after receiving an assurance of divine help (Ps 142:7).

142:1 In the cave: cf. 1 Sm 22:1; 24:1–3; Ps 57:1.

142:8 Then the righteous shall gather around me: in the Temple, when the psalmist offers a thanksgiving sacrifice.

Psalm 143 One of the Church's seven Penitential Psalms,

---

140:14 Ps 11:7; 16:11; 17:15.
141:2 Ps 134:2; Ex 30:8.
141:3 Sir 22:27.
141:5 Prv 9:8; 25:12.
141:8 Ps 25:15; 123:1–2.
141:9 Ps 142:4.
142:4 Ps 143:4.
142:4 Ps 139:24.
142:4 Ps 141:9.
142:5 Ps 16:8; 73:23; 121:5.
142:6 Ps 91:2, 9.
142:6 Ps 16:5; 27:13; 116:9;
    Is 38:11.
142:7 Ps 79:8.

answer me in your righteousness.
2 Do not enter into judgment with your
servant;
before you no one can be just.*
3 The enemy has pursued my soul;
he has crushed my life to the
ground.*
He has made me dwell in darkness
like those long dead.*
4 My spirit is faint within me;
my heart despairs.*
5 I remember the days of old;
I ponder all your deeds;
the works of your hands I recall.*
6 I stretch out my hands toward you,
my soul to you like a parched land.*
*Selah*
7 Hasten to answer me, LORD;
for my spirit fails me.
Do not hide your face from me,
lest I become like those descending to
the pit.*
8 In the morning let me hear of your
mercy,
for in you I trust.
Show me the path I should walk,
for I entrust my life to you.*
9 Rescue me, LORD, from my foes,
for I seek refuge in you.
10 Teach me to do your will,
for you are my God.
May your kind spirit guide me
on ground that is level.
11 For your name's sake, LORD, give me life;
in your righteousness lead my soul
out of distress.
12 In your mercy put an end to my foes;
all those who are oppressing my soul,
for I am your servant.*

# PSALM 144†

## A Prayer for Victory and Prosperity

1 Of David.

### I

† Blessed be the LORD, my rock,
who trains my hands for battle,
my fingers for war;
2 My safeguard and my fortress,
my stronghold, my deliverer,
My shield, in whom I take refuge,
who subdues peoples under me.

### II

3† LORD, what is man that you take notice
of him;
the son of man, that you think of
him?*
4† Man is but a breath,
his days are like a passing shadow.*
5† LORD, incline your heavens and come
down;
touch the mountains and make them
smoke.*
6 Flash forth lightning and scatter my
foes;
shoot your arrows and rout them.
7 Reach out your hand from on high;
deliver me from the many waters;
rescue me from the hands of foreign
foes.
8 Their mouths speak untruth;
their right hands are raised in lying
oaths.†
9 O God, a new song I will sing to you;
on a ten-stringed lyre I will play for
you.*
10 You give victory to kings;
you delivered David your servant.*
From the menacing sword 11 deliver me;

---

this lament is a prayer to be freed from death-dealing enemies. The psalmist addresses God, aware that there is no equality between God and human beings; salvation is a gift (Ps 143:1–2). Victimized by evil people (Ps 143:3–4), the psalmist recites ("remembers") God's past actions on behalf of the innocent (Ps 143:5–6). The Psalm continues with fervent prayer (Ps 143:7–9) and a strong desire for guidance and protection (Ps 143:10–12).

**Psalm 144** The Psalm may reflect a ceremony in which the king, as leader of the army, asked God's help (Ps 144:1–8). In Ps 144:9 the poem shifts abruptly from pleading to thanksgiving, and (except for Ps 144:11) shifts again to prayer for the people. The first section (Ps 144:1–2) is a prayer of thanks for victory; the second (Ps 144:3–7a), a humble acknowledgment of human nothingness and a supplication that God show forth saving power; the third (Ps 144:9–11), a promise of future thanksgiving; the fourth (Ps 144:12–15), a wish for prosperity and peace. A prayer for deliverance from treacherous foes serves as a refrain after the second and third sections (Ps 144:7b–8, 11). Except for

its final section, the Psalm is made up almost entirely of verses from other Psalms.
**144:1–2** Composed of phrases from Ps 18:3, 35, 47–48.
**144:3** Similar to Ps 8:4.
**144:4** Composed of phrases from Ps 39:6; 102:12.
**144:5–7** Adapted in large part from Ps 18:10, 15, 17; 104:32.
**144:8b, 11b** *Their right hands are raised in lying oaths*: the psalmist's enemies give false testimony.

---

**143:2** Eccl 7:20; Jb 4:17; Rom 3:20.
**143:3** Ps 7:6.
**143:3** Lam 3:6.
**143:4** Ps 142:4; Jb 17:1.
**143:5** Ps 77:6, 12.
**143:6** Ps 42:2; 63:2.
**143:7** Ps 28:1; 30:4; 88:5; Prv 1:12.
**143:8** Ps 25:4; 27:11; 86:11; 119:12, 35.
**143:12** Ps 116:16.
**144:3** Jb 7:17.
**144:4** Ps 62:10; 90:9–10; Jb 7:16; Eccl 6:12; Wis 2:5.
**144:5** Is 63:19.
**144:9** Ps 33:2–3.
**144:10** Ps 18:51.

rescue me from the hands of foreign
foes.
Their mouths speak untruth;
their right hands are raised in lying
oaths.

**III**

12 May our sons be like plants *
well nurtured from their youth,
Our daughters, like carved columns,
shapely as those of the temple.
13 May our barns be full
with every kind of store.
May our sheep increase by thousands,
by tens of thousands in our fields;
may our oxen be well fattened.
14 May there be no breach in the walls,
no exile, no outcry in our streets. *
15 Blessed the people so fortunate;
blessed the people whose God is the
LORD. *

## PSALM 145†

### The Greatness and Goodness of God

1 Praise. Of David.

I will extol you, my God and king;
I will bless your name forever and
ever.
2 Every day I will bless you;
I will praise your name forever and
ever. *
3 Great is the LORD and worthy of much
praise, *
whose grandeur is beyond
understanding.
4 One generation praises your deeds to
the next
and proclaims your mighty works. *
5 They speak of the splendor of your
majestic glory,
tell of your wonderful deeds. *
6 They speak of the power of your
awesome acts

and recount your great deeds. *
7 They celebrate your abounding
goodness
and joyfully sing of your justice.
8 The LORD is gracious and merciful,
slow to anger and abounding in
mercy. *
9 The LORD is good to all,
compassionate toward all your
works. *
10 All your works give you thanks, LORD
and your faithful bless you. *
11 They speak of the glory of your reign
and tell of your mighty works,
12 Making known to the sons of men your
mighty acts,
the majestic glory of your rule.
13 Your reign is a reign for all ages,
your dominion for all generations. *
The LORD is trustworthy in all his words,
and loving in all his works.
14 The LORD supports all who are falling
and raises up all who are bowed
down. *
15 The eyes of all look hopefully to you;
you give them their food in due
season. *
16 You open wide your hand
and satisfy the desire of every living
thing.
17 The LORD is just in all his ways,
merciful in all his works. *
18 The LORD is near to all who call upon
him,
to all who call upon him in truth. *
19 He fulfills the desire of those who fear
him;
he hears their cry and saves them. *
20 The LORD watches over all who love him,
but all the wicked he destroys. *
21 My mouth will speak the praises of the
LORD;
all flesh will bless his holy name
forever and ever.

---

† **Psalm 145** A hymn in acrostic form; every verse begins with
a successive letter of the Hebrew alphabet. Acrostic poems
usually do not develop ideas but consist rather of loosely
connected statements. The singer invites all to praise God (Ps
145:1–3, 21). The "works of God" make God present and invite human praise (Ps 145:4–7); they climax in a confession
(Ps 145:8–9). God's mighty acts show forth divine kingship (Ps
145:10–20), a major theme in the literature of early Judaism
and in Christianity.

**144:12** Ps 128:3.
**144:14** Is 65:19.
**144:15** Ps 33:12.
**145:2** Ps 34:2.
**145:3** Ps 48:2; 95:3; 96:4; Jb
36:26.
**145:4** Ps 22:31–32;
48:14–15; 71:18;
78:4; Ex 10:2; Dt 4:9.
**145:5** Ps 96:3; 105:2.
**145:6** Ps 66:3.
**145:8** Ps 86:5, 15; 103:8; Ex
34:6; Sir 2:11.
**145:9** Ps 103:13; Wis 11:24.
**145:10** Dn 3:57.
**145:13** Ps 10:16; 102:13;
146:10; Lam 5:19; Dn
3:33; Rev 11:15.
**145:14** Ps 94:18; 146:8.
**145:15** Ps 136:25; 104:27–
28; Mt 6:25–26.
**145:17** Dt 32:4.
**145:18** Dt 4:7; Is 55:6; 58:9.
**145:19** Ps 34:18.
**145:20** Jgs 5:31.

## PSALM 146†

### Trust in God the Creator and Redeemer

¹ Hallelujah!

² Praise the LORD, my soul;
  I will praise the LORD all my life,
  sing praise to my God while I live. *

**I**

³ Put no trust in princes,
  in children of Adam powerless to save. *
⁴ Who breathing his last, returns to the
    earth;
  that day all his planning comes to
    nothing. *

**II**

⁵ Blessed the one whose help is the God
    of Jacob,
  whose hope is in the LORD, his God,
⁶ The maker of heaven and earth,
  the seas and all that is in them, *
  Who keeps faith forever,
⁷  secures justice for the oppressed, *
  who gives bread to the hungry.
  The LORD sets prisoners free; *
⁸  the LORD gives sight to the blind.
  The LORD raises up those who are bowed
    down; *
  the LORD loves the righteous.
⁹ The LORD protects the resident alien,
  comes to the aid of the orphan and
    the widow, *
  but thwarts the way of the wicked.
¹⁰ The LORD shall reign forever,
  your God, Zion, through all
    generations! *
  Hallelujah!

## PSALM 147†

### God's Word Restores Jerusalem

¹ Hallelujah!

**I**

How good to sing praise to our God;
  how pleasant to give fitting praise. *
² The LORD rebuilds Jerusalem,
  and gathers the dispersed of Israel, *
³ Healing the brokenhearted,
  and binding up their wounds. *
⁴ He numbers the stars,
  and gives to all of them their names. *
⁵ Great is our Lord, vast in power,
  with wisdom beyond measure. *
⁶ The LORD gives aid to the poor,
  but casts the wicked to the ground. *

**II**

⁷ Sing to the LORD with thanksgiving;
  with the lyre make music to our
    God, *
⁸† Who covers the heavens with clouds,
  provides rain for the earth,
  makes grass sprout on the
    mountains, *
⁹ Who gives animals their food
  and young ravens what they cry for. *
¹⁰† He takes no delight in the strength of
    horses,
  no pleasure in the runner's stride. *
¹¹ Rather the LORD takes pleasure in those
    who fear him,
  those who put their hope in his
    mercy.

**III**

¹² Glorify the LORD, Jerusalem;
  Zion, offer praise to your God,
¹³ For he has strengthened the bars of your
    gates,
  blessed your children within you. *
¹⁴ He brings peace to your borders,
  and satisfies you with finest wheat. *
¹⁵† He sends his command to earth;
  his word runs swiftly! *
¹⁶ Thus he makes the snow like wool,

---

**Psalm 146** A hymn of someone who has learned there is no other source of strength except the merciful God. Only God, not mortal human beings (Ps 146:3–4), can help vulnerable and oppressed people (Ps 146:5–9). The first of the five hymns that conclude the Psalter.
**Psalm 147** The hymn is divided into three sections by the calls to praise in Ps 147:1, 7, 12. The first section praises the powerful creator who restores exiled Judah (Ps 147:1–6); the second section, the creator who provides food to animals and human beings; the third and climactic section exhorts the holy city to recognize it has been re-created and made the place of disclosure for God's word, a word as life-giving as water.
**147:8–9** God clothes the fields and feeds the birds, cf. Mt 6:26, 30.
**147:10–11** Acknowledging one's dependence upon God rather than claiming self-sufficiency pleases God, cf. Ps 20:8; 33:16–19.

**147:15–19** God speaks through the thunder of nature and the word of revealed law, cf. Is 55:10–11. The weather phenomena

| | |
|---|---|
| **146:2** Ps 103:1; 104:33. | **147:2** Is 11:12; 56:8; Jer |
| **146:3** Ps 118:8–9. | 31:10. |
| **146:4** Ps 90:3; 104:29; 1 Mc | **147:3** Jb 5:18; Is 30:26; |
| 2:63; Jb 34:14–15; | 61:1; Jer 33:6. |
| Eccl 3:20; 12:7; Sir | **147:4** Is 40:26. |
| 40:11; Is 2:22. | **147:5** Jdt 16:13; Jer 51:15. |
| **146:6** Ps 121:2; 124:8; Ex | **147:6** Ps 146:9; 1 Sm 2:7–8. |
| 20:11; Acts 14:15; | **147:7** Ps 71:22. |
| Rev 14:7. | **147:8** Ps 104:13f; Jb 5:10; |
| **146:7** Ps 103:6. | Jer 14:22; Jl 2:23. |
| **146:7** Ps 68:7; Is 49:9; 61:1. | **147:9** Jb 38:41; Mt 6:26. |
| **146:8** Ps 145:14. | **147:10** Ps 20:8; 33:16–18. |
| **146:9** Ps 68:6; Dt 10:18. | **147:13** Ps 48:14. |
| **146:10** Ps 145:13; Lam 5:19. | **147:14** Ps 81:17. |
| **147:1** Ps 33:1; 92:2. | **147:15** Ps 33:9. |

and spreads the frost like ash; *
17  He disperses hail like crumbs.
    Who can withstand his cold?
18  Yet when again he issues his command,
        it melts them;
    he raises his winds and the waters
        flow.
19  He proclaims his word to Jacob,
        his statutes and laws to Israel. *
20  He has not done this for any other
            nation;
        of such laws they know nothing.
    Hallelujah!

## PSALM 148†

### All Creation Summoned to Praise
    ¹ Hallelujah!

**I**

    Praise the LORD from the heavens;
        praise him in the heights.
2   Praise him, all you his angels;
        give praise, all you his hosts. *
3   Praise him, sun and moon;
        praise him, all shining stars.
4   Praise him, highest heavens, †
        you waters above the heavens.
5   Let them all praise the LORD's name;
        for he commanded and they were
            created, *
6   Assigned them their station forever,
        set an order that will never change.

**II**

7   Praise the LORD from the earth,
        you sea monsters and all the deeps of
            the sea; *
8   Lightning and hail, snow and thick
            clouds,
        storm wind that fulfills his command;
9   Mountains and all hills,
        fruit trees and all cedars; *

10  Animals wild and tame,
        creatures that crawl and birds that
            fly; *
11  Kings of the earth and all peoples,
        princes and all who govern on earth;
12  Young men and women too,
        old and young alike.
13  Let them all praise the LORD's name,
        for his name alone is exalted,
        His majesty above earth and heaven. *
14† He has lifted high the horn of his
            people;
        to the praise of all his faithful,
        the Israelites, the people near to him.
    Hallelujah!

## PSALM 149†

### Praise God with Song and Sword
    ¹ Hallelujah!

    Sing to the LORD a new song,
        his praise in the assembly of the
            faithful. *
2   Let Israel be glad in its maker,
        the people of Zion rejoice in their
            king.
3   Let them praise his name in dance,
        make music with tambourine and
            lyre. † *
4   For the LORD takes delight in his people,
        honors the poor with victory.
5   Let the faithful rejoice in their glory,
        cry out for joy on their couches, †
6   With the praise of God in their mouths,
        and a two-edged sword in their
            hands, *
7   To bring retribution on the nations,
        punishment on the peoples, *
8   To bind their kings in shackles,
        their nobles in chains of iron,

---

† are well known in Jerusalem: a blizzard of snow and hail followed by a thunderstorm that melts the ice.
  **Psalm 148** A hymn inviting the beings of heaven (Ps 148:1–6) and of earth (Ps 148:7–14) to praise God. The hymn does not distinguish between inanimate and animate (and rational) nature.
  **148:4** *Highest heavens*: lit., "the heavens of the heavens," i.e., the space above the firmament, where the "upper waters" are stored, cf. Gn 1:6–7; Dt 10:14; 1 Kgs 8:27; Ps 104:3, 13.
  **148:14** *Has lifted high the horn of his people*: the horn symbolizes strength, the concrete noun for the abstract. Of all peoples, God has chosen Israel to return praise and thanks in a special way.
  **Psalm 149** A hymn inviting the people of Israel to celebrate their God in song and festive dance (Ps 149:1–3, 5) because God has chosen them and given them victory (Ps 149:4). The exodus and conquest are the defining acts of Israel; the people must be

ready to do again those acts in the future at the divine command (Ps 149:6–9).
  **149:3** *Make music with tambourine and lyre*: the verse recalls the great exodus hymn of Ex 15:20.
  **149:5** *On their couches*: the people reclined to banquet.

| | |
|---|---|
| **147:16** Jb 6:16; 37:10; 38:22. | Dt 4:7. |
| **147:19** Ps 78:5; Bar 3:37; Dt 4:7–8. | **148:13** Ps 30:5; Dt 4:7. |
| **148:2** Ps 103:20f; Dn 3:58–63. | **149:1** Ps 22:23; 26:12; 35:18; 40:10; Jdt 16:1. |
| **148:5** Ps 33:9; Gn 1:3f; Jdt 16:14. | **149:3** Ps 68:26; 81:2–3; 87:7; 150:3–4. |
| **148:7** Ps 135:6; Gn 1:21. | **149:6** Neh 4:10–12; 2 Mc 15:27. |
| **148:9** Is 44:23. | **149:7** Wis 3:8. |
| **148:10** Ps 30:5; Gn 1:21, 24f; | |

9 To execute the judgments decreed for
    them—
  such is the glory† of all God's faithful.
Hallelujah!

### PSALM 150†

### Final Doxology

¹ Hallelujah!

Praise God in his holy sanctuary; †*
  give praise in the mighty dome of
    heaven.

---

2 Give praise for his mighty deeds, *
  praise him for his great majesty.
3 Give praise with blasts upon the
    horn, *
  praise him with harp and lyre.
4 Give praise with tambourines and
    dance,
  praise him with strings and pipes. *
5 Give praise with crashing cymbals,
  praise him with sounding cymbals.
6 Let everything that has breath
  give praise to the LORD! *
Hallelujah!

# The Book of

# Proverbs

## INTRODUCTION

### Christine Roy Yoder

The book of Proverbs is for the ordinary of days. Proverb after proverb, page after page, it invites readers into an ancient and ongoing conversation about what is good and wise in life. How does one discern right from wrong in a world of fiercely competing claims? What values does one treasure and why? What makes for just communities and strong families? What characterizes a good neighbor, loving partner, or trusted friend? How does one understand money, the role of integrity, and the power of speech? And how do we teach all this to our children? Proverbs takes up such questions as part and parcel of the reverent life. It recognizes the ordinary as the arena in which people develop their moral character and work out their faithfulness. And it commends for the journey wisdom born of the experiences of generations who have gone before—poetry wrought and recited time and again by the people of God. Not all of the book's assumptions and insights will resonate as true for readers across centuries and different worldviews. But proverb after proverb, page after page, Proverbs inspires and requires fresh moral and theological reflection.

This collection of ancient Israel's wisdom is ascribed to Solomon (cf. Prv 1:1; 10:1; 25:1), the second and last king of the united monarchy (ca. 966–926 BCE) and the quintessential sage of Israel. Solomon's name lends authority to the book. Tradition tells that Solomon's wisdom was granted by God, surpassed that of all others, and was celebrated and sought by world leaders (1 Kgs 3–11). At the same time, Solomon's larger-than-life status as a patron and author of Wisdom cautions against interpreting claims of his authorship as historically reliable. Like David with the psalms and Moses with the law, Solomon is identified conventionally with wisdom. Other Wisdom texts are

## Outline of Proverbs

I.   Title and Introduction (1:1–7)

II.  Instructions of Parents and of Woman Wisdom (1:8–9:18)

III. First Solomonic Collection of Sayings (10:1–22:16)

IV.  Sayings of the Wise (22:17–24:22)

V.   Further Sayings of the Wise (24:23–34)

VI.  Second Solomonic Collection, Collected Under King Hezekiah (25:1–29:27)

VII. Sayings of Agur and Others (30:1–33)

VIII. Sayings of King Lemuel (31:1–9)

IX.  Poem on the Woman of Worth (31:10–31)

associated with him also, such as Ecclesiastes and the book of Wisdom.

Compilation of Proverbs occurred over centuries. Proverbs 10–30 is presumably the oldest section of the book, consisting largely of originally oral folk proverbs that "sages," namely, counselors and educators associated with the royal court, gathered and edited starting perhaps as early as the time of Solomon. Reference to "the servants of Hezekiah, king of Judah" (25:1) suggests this work continued in the late eighth to early seventh centuries BCE, possibly as part of Hezekiah's religious and political reforms. Finally, the framing units of Prv 1–9 and 31 were added in the early postexilic period (late sixth to early fifth centuries BCE) as the community struggled to rebuild in the aftermath of the Babylonian exile. The book thus reflects Israel's wisdom as interpreted and reinterpreted, often at significant moments when the community was claiming or reclaiming its values.

The book contains hundreds of proverbs. A "proverb" is a statement of an apparent truth that is based on human experience and endures in a community over time. The term encompasses a wide variety of speech, from one-line statements to extended poems. In Proverbs, the most prevalent form is the two-line proverb; the first line makes an observation or claim which the second line develops, contrasts, or motivates. Whereas a proverb's brevity and parallel structure convey precision, its details captivate and complicate. Vivid metaphors and similes are abundant, and frequent wordplay, alliteration (repetition of the same or similar consonant[s] in a line or group of lines), assonance (repetition of the same vowel sound), ambiguity, irony, humor, and so on typify proverbs. The artistry invites readers to linger and discover what the sages knew: proverbs teach moral imagination. Each proverb has several possible meanings and may "mean" differently depending on who says it and how, to whom, and in what circumstances. That is, proverbs are contingent claims, slices of truth—not static and universal maxims. The wise not only need to know the proverbs, but how to read the world so that they use the proverbs rightly ("one has joy from an apt response; a word in season, how good it is!" Prv 15:23; cf. 25:11).

Reading proverbs within the context of a collection invites additional interpretation. Features like catchwords, metaphors, or sounds that animate one proverb may extend to create units of two or more (e.g., reference to the "city" and "wicked" in Prv 11:10–11). Elsewhere thematic threads or *inclusios*, the repetition of a word or phrase at the beginning and ending of a unit, may invite reading a group of proverbs together. The word "happy," for example, frames one of the tributes to personified wisdom (3:13–18), and a string of proverbs about God's sovereignty (16:1–9) precedes a series that reflects on the king, the earthly representative of God in ancient Near Eastern thought (16:10–15). These connections highlight how proverbs may comment on one another and, as such, generate a larger conversation across the book.

The book may also be read as a literary whole. Remarkably similar portraits of two women, personified wisdom (Prv 1–9) and "a woman of worth" (31:10–31), frame the book, suggesting that the women should be identified with each other. Readers begin in the position of a silent son urged by his father to love wisdom and accept the invitation to her household (chs. 1–9) and ultimately become an esteemed adult who lives there (31:10–31). The sections of Proverbs in between—announced by superscriptions or titles along the way—contribute to this "growing up" in various ways, including a progression from Israelite to international wisdom, an increasing variety and complexity of literary forms, heightened debate and contradiction between proverbs, and an expanding moral purview from household to cosmos. Proverbs thus forms readers by its content *and* arrangement.

A prologue (Prv 1:2–7) announces that the book aims to impart wisdom. Thick with vocabulary critical to that endeavor, these opening verses highlight the relational nature of wisdom. Young and wise alike must accept discipline and listen to instruction. Wisdom is about "what is right, just and fair" (1:3b), terms that together refer comprehensively to ethical relationships between individuals and communities. And wisdom begins with and is most fully expressed as "fear of the LORD" (1:7), namely, reverence for and obedience to God that motivates virtuous behavior and fosters well-being. Found fourteen times (and twice as an imperative, "fear the LORD!" 3:7; 24:21), "fear of the LORD" is the book's refrain. The phrase is an *inclusio* to Prv 1–9 (1:7; 9:10) and to the book as a whole (1:7; 31:30).

Instruction begins in the household. Proverbs 1–9, like many ancient Near Eastern Wisdom texts, is a long didactic poem by a father to his son or sons (he refers to the mother twice but she evidently does not speak, cf. 1:8; 6:20). The father describes the world as marked by moral polarities: wisdom and foolishness, righteousness and wickedness. Choices have immediate, predictable, and often life-or-death consequences. And the youth must find the "way" or "path" of wisdom amid conflicting and compelling appeals for his attention by street gangs (1:8–19), wicked

P
R
V

people (e.g., 2:12–19), the "strange" woman (e.g., 7:13–20), and scoundrels and fools (e.g., 6:12–19). The father warns the youth repeatedly to stay away from such company lest they influence him, and implores the youth to seek the wisdom of God, family, community, and nature ("go to the ant!" 6:6–8) so that he might flourish.

Two women stand at the heart of the father's instruction: wisdom (Prv 1:20–33; 3:13–18; 4:5–9; 7:4–5; 8:1–9:6, 11) and the "strange" woman or folly (2:16–19; 5:1–14; 6:20–35; 7:1–27; 9:13–18). They stand literarily shoulder to shoulder; poems about them alternate across these opening chapters and culminate in an extended description of each that together form a diptych in Prv 7–9.

Wisdom personified as a woman is breathtakingly complex. Like the precious gems to which she is frequently compared, each poem about wisdom catches the light a bit differently, revealing new facets of her power and splendor. She speaks as God or a prophet, taking her stand in the busiest places of the city and calling out to the naive, scoffers, and fools to heed her instruction lest disaster befall them (Prv 1:20–33). She is a teacher who promises to reveal all that she knows and to provide generously for those who seek her (e.g., 1:23, 33). She is a "tree of life," a mythological image in the ancient Near East (3:18); in the Hebrew Bible, the tree is found elsewhere in Gn 2–3 where the cherubim and flaming sword guard it after Adam and Eve's expulsion from the garden. Here the tree of life is not "off limits," but may be grasped—not as a means to everlasting life, but for health, prosperity, and joy (Prv 3:13–18). Wisdom is a most desirable bride who bestows a garland and crown, signs of nobility and marriage, on her beloved (4:5–9). She speaks what is right and true. She empowers all who govern rightly (e.g., 8:15–16). And she prepares for everyone a feast and builds a seven-pillared house, a number that signifies wholeness (9:1–6).

Wisdom's authority springs from her existence prior to God's creation of the cosmos. This theme first appears in Prv 3:19–20, where the parent asserts that wisdom is the means by which God created the world. She is woven into God's handiwork. Wisdom then emphasizes the point herself in 8:22–31, the pinnacle of her self-revelation. There she is explicit and repetitive about her preeminence, using various prepositions (e.g., "before," 8:25), negative expressions (e.g., "when there were no," 8:24), and phrases (e.g., "the beginning," 8:22a) to indicate her existence before creation. She further asserts her presence during God's creative work: "there was I" (8:27). She was at God's side daily, "all the while" (8:30–31). From the beginning, she was. And she was always in the company of God.

Wisdom is mysterious about her origins, however. Wisdom's frequent use of obscure and debated verbs in Prv 8:22–31 (see the translation notes), especially when more precise verbs are available, suggests that the details of her beginning lie beyond words. The multiple metaphors she evokes—birthing, acquiring, anointing, creating—point variously to what is otherwise inexpressible. Wisdom's role in God's creative activity is likewise cloaked in mystery. Her announcement "Then was I beside him as 'āmôn" (8:30)—a child? an artisan or architect? a trusted one?—has confounded interpreters for millennia.

What is clear is that wisdom is joy personified. Her words bind God's delight in her with her delight in creation and humanity (Prv 8:30b–31). That her merriment is at once before God and in the world means that she is a vital bridge between God, humans, and the world. To love wisdom and to accept the invitation to her table is to awaken to the interconnectedness of God's creation, to align with and participate in God's ongoing work in the world and, as a result, to flourish. Learning so conceived is neither burdensome nor tedious. It is a joy-filled relationship with knowledge, God, and the world. And wisdom offers that relationship to everyone, not solely a privileged few (8:3).

Unlike the "strange" woman who for the most part exits the stage after Prv 1–9 (cf. 22:14; 23:26–28) and receives little attention in later Wisdom literature, personified wisdom strides with increasing boldness across time, texts, and testaments, captivating the imaginations of many and taking on a robust life of her own. She becomes identified in Judaism with Torah (Bar 3:9–4:4; Sir 24:23–34) and, in the book of Wisdom, she is the spirit of Sophia—the breath of the power of God (Wis 7:7–11:1). Kabbalistic writings of medieval Judaism drew from depictions of her to portray the *Shekinah*, the female element in divinity, as did the Talmud and midrash to depict *Knesseth Yisra'el*, the personification of the community of Israel. Early Christians described the person and work of Jesus Christ using language and imagery associated with wisdom (e.g., Jn 1:1–18; Col 1:15–20; Heb 1:1–3). And some theologians evoke her to describe the Holy Spirit. In short, she is a remarkable female figure who has been neglected or downplayed far too long in the religious life of Jews and Christians—despite such persistent and compelling testimony to her significance.

A new literary landscape begins at Prv 10:1. Proverbs 10:1–22:16 is comprised primarily of two-line proverbs—antithetical proverbs at first (esp. in 10:1–15:33) and then a greater diversity of wisdom genres, including synonymous and synthetic proverbs, "better than" proverbs, and rhetorical questions (esp. in 16:1–22:16). Each proverb stands on its own and appears, at least initially, disconnected to the proverbs around it. Disorienting at first, the arrangement fosters the development of moral imagination by shifting the responsibility for making sense of the proverbs from the father in chs. 1–9 to the reader. Lack of prioritization among the proverbs requires careful consideration of the meaning of each one and the context in which it might be applicable. And the increasing variety of genres requires dexterity from readers, and affords greater opportunity for nuance and the expression of relative values.

Topics from Prv 1–9 continue but, absent the father's firm mediation, readers discover that conflict and contradiction exist not only between the wise and foolish, but within the community's wisdom. Divergent proverbs occur side by side or nearly so without qualification. Some proverbs, for example, consider wealth to be an unqualified good (e.g., 10:15, 22; 14:20) while others regard it a liability (11:4, 28); some attribute poverty to laziness (e.g., 10:4; 20:13) while others attribute poverty to violence, extortion, and deceit (e.g., 11:1, 16; 13:23). The interweaving of countering claims, none of which the sages discount

or trivialize, teaches that wisdom does not have only one perspective on wealth or poverty or, for that matter, on many subjects.

From wisdom ascribed to Solomon (Prv 1:1; 10:1), readers move next to internationally-inspired instruction (22:17–24:22; 24:23–34). The first of these two sections attributed to the "wise" (22:17–24:22) is an artful adaptation of the Egyptian *Instruction of Amen-em-ope*, a late-second-millennium BCE text that presents thirty instructions of Amen-em-ope to his youngest son. That the transition to the section occurs seamlessly in the Hebrew suggests that movement between Israelite and foreign wisdom is rather ordinary. The sages assume that their work requires critical engagement with the wisdom of cultures. At the same time, because the sages rework *Amen-em-ope* in various ways, they teach that the borrowing of traditions and texts is not done mechanically but critically, mindful of one's context and purposes.

The wise address the reader not only as a child in the family home (much like Prv 1–9), but as a neighbor and a citizen, a young man responsible for building a household, a commoner, a messenger, a present or potential member of the royal court, and a military leader. The youth appears poised to assume new roles and responsibilities. Appeals for moral courage are also resonant. The sages point to God's attention to and investment in the human situation to motivate compassion and justice particularly for the sake of those in peril: the poor and afflicted for whom God pleads (22:22–23), the orphans for whom God is the redeemer (23:10–11), and those "being dragged off to death" for whom God looks for rescuers (24:10–12).

Proverbs 25–29 focuses on the royal court and government. Indeed, some interpreters argue that portions of this section were used to educate aspiring young men for royal office. Although the audience need not be so limited, many of the proverbs address how to navigate wisely in an increasingly complex moral arena that includes kings, nobles, bosses, enemies, gossips, sluggards, and liars. For the first time in Proverbs, the sages also speak about the precariousness of power. Injustice may be bought for a mere morsel of bread (28:21). The upright can be led astray (28:10). And what had been an idealistic portrait of the king to this point in the book (e.g., 16:10–15) yields to repeated caution about wicked rulers who, like roaring lions or charging bears, trample the poor (28:15), callously extort from their people (28:16; 29:4), and let transgressions go unchecked (29:16). The damage is extensive. The king who entertains lies emboldens wicked officials (29:12) and whole communities cry out and go into hiding (28:28; 29:2).

Two sections attributed to otherwise unknown foreigners stretch wisdom's horizons further (Prv 30; 31:1–9). An arguably feeble old sage named Agur first heralds God's power and mystery and insists that humanity's moral purview is the whole creation (ch. 30). He blurs distinctions between humans and the natural world by ascribing humanlike qualities to creatures (e.g., 30:15, 24–28), comparing himself and the king to animals (30:2, 31), animating the inanimate (30:15–16), and describing the natural world as swooping in to preserve human social order (30:17). Agur manifests wonder. He emphasizes how creaturely people are, and turns to the smallest and least powerful creatures for wisdom and instruction.

Next speaks a queen mother from Massa, a north Arabian tribe descended from Ishmael (Prv 31:1–9). Hers is the only instruction attributed to a queen mother known from the ancient Near East. Her rebuke and appeal to the mother-child relationship recalls the household setting of Prv 1–9; her voice near Proverbs' end balances that of the father at its beginning. At stake for her is Lemuel's self-restraint. He cannot allow indulgence to impair his good judgment and impede his commitment to justice.

Proverbs concludes with a hymn of praise for "a woman of worth" that is an alphabetic acrostic—a poem in which each line begins with the next letter of the Hebrew alphabet.

The poem features her many activities and attributes in no apparent order apart from an introduction (Prv 31:10–12), an enumeration of her qualities and deeds (31:13–27), and concluding praise (31:28–31). Rather the poem reads much like an impressionistic painting. Up close the brushstrokes seem haphazard but, from a step or two away, they merge into the cumulative image of a wise and valiant woman.

Numerous parallels in vocabulary and themes suggest that this woman is to be identified with personified wisdom in Prv 1–9. The two women who frame the book, that is, essentially coalesce as one. For example, both women are described as hard to find and more precious than jewels. Both have a house and a staff of young women. Both provide food and a life of security. Both are known at the city gates and bestow honor on their companions. Both are strong and loathe wickedness. They laugh. Both extend their hands to the needy. Both teach, and their identities and instructions are associated with "fear of the LORD." The nature and extent of these parallels indicate that readers encounter personified wisdom here one last time and glimpse life abundant in her household.

Thus readers of Proverbs mature in the quest for wisdom—from a silent, amenable son (Prv 1–9) to a king and respected companion of a "woman of worth" or wisdom (31:1–31). The sages urge the search onward, progressing from Israelite to international wisdom, introducing an increasing variety and complexity of literary forms, heightening debate and contradiction between proverbs, and expanding the moral purview from household to cosmos. Yet the end of Proverbs proves to be not the end. The palace is now home and the next generation of children embrace wisdom's teaching and stand up to praise her (31:28). Whether by old or young, royal or common, it seems, the search for wisdom continues. ■

# THE BOOK OF PROVERBS

## New American Bible, Introduction

Proverbs is an anthology of collections of sayings and instructions. Many of the sayings and perhaps some instructions were composed in the monarchic period (late eleventh to the early sixth centuries). Editing of the whole book was done in the early postexilic period, in the view of most scholars; at that time chaps. 1–9 would have been added as the introduction. Whether the material originated among royal scribes (as 25:1 seems to suggest) imitating common literary genres, or whether it arose among tribal elders inculcating traditional ways, is disputed. The origin of the material, however, need not be imagined in an either/or scenario. Folk wisdom and observations could surely have been elaborated and re-expressed by learned scribes: "What oft was thought but ne'er so well expressed" (Alexander Pope). There can be no doubt, however, that Proverbs is sophisticated literature by talented writers, winning readers with its compelling portrait of wisdom and inviting them to see life afresh, "wisely," through its wit, originality, and shrewd observation.

The primary purpose of the book is to teach wisdom, not only to the young and inexperienced (1:2–4) but also to the advanced (1:5–6). Wisdom in the ancient Near East was not theoretical knowledge but practical expertise. Jewelers who cut precious stones were wise; kings who made their dominion peaceful and prosperous were wise. One could be wise in daily life, too, in knowing how to live successfully (having a prosperous household and living a long and healthy life) and without trouble in God's universe. Ultimately wisdom, or "sound guidance" (1:5), aims at the formation of character.

In the ancient Near East, people assumed that wisdom belonged to the gods, who were wise by reason of their divinity; human beings needed to have wisdom granted them by the gods. Creation accounts of neighboring cultures depict creation in two stages. In the first stage, human beings lived an animal-like existence, without clothes, writing, or

kingship (proper governance). Over time, the gods came to realize that such a low grade of existence made the human race inadequate as their servants, so they endowed the race with "wisdom," which consisted of culture (e.g., kingship) and crafts (e.g., knowledge of farming, ability to weave). Such wisdom elevated the race to a "human" level and made them effective servants of the gods. Furthermore, divine wisdom was *mediated* to human beings through earthly institutions—the king, scribes (who produced wise writings), and heads of families (fathers, sometimes mothers). These traditional mediators appear in Proverbs: the book is credited to King Solomon, and kings are respectfully mentioned as pillars of society (e.g., 16:12–15); *writings* are a source of wisdom (1:1–7); the father instructing his son is the major paradigm of teaching. Proverbs differs, however, from other wisdom books in concentrating on wisdom itself, treating it as a virtually independent entity and personifying it as an attractive woman. Other books urge readers to perform wise acts, but Proverbs urges them to seek wisdom itself and portrays wisdom as a woman seeking human beings as disciples and companions.

Chapters 1–9 introduce the book, drawing attention to wisdom itself and its inherent value rather than exhorting to particular wise actions. The chapters personify wisdom as a woman and draw an extended analogy between finding a wife, or founding and maintaining a house(hold), and finding wisdom. The collections following chap. 9 consist largely of independent, two-line sayings, yielding their often indirect or paradoxical meaning only to readers willing to ponder them. To reflect on the sayings is perhaps what chaps. 1–9 mean by living with Wisdom and dwelling in her house.

The Book of Proverbs can make an important contribution to Christians and Jews today. First, it places the pursuit of wisdom over the performance of individual wise acts. To seek wisdom above all things is a fundamental option and a way of life. Second, it portrays the quest as filled with obstacles. There are men and women who offer a substitute for the real thing; discernment is required. Third, the book teaches that acquiring wisdom is both a human task and a divine gift. One can make oneself ready to receive by discipline, but one cannot take so divine a gift. Fourth, wisdom is in the world but it is not obvious to people entirely caught up with daily activities. The instructions and the aphorisms of the book can free the mind to see new things. Christians will see in personified Wisdom aspects of Jesus Christ, who they believe is divine wisdom sent to give human beings true and full life. Yet there is a universal dimension to Proverbs, for in its attention to human experience it creates a link to all people of good will.

The genres and themes of Proverbs continued on in Sirach, Wisdom of Solomon, and the later *Pirqe Abot* (The Sayings of the Fathers), a treatise in the Mishnah, which became the object of commentary in *Abot de Rabbi Nathan*. The New Testament saw Jesus as a wisdom teacher and employed the tradition of personified wisdom of chaps. 2 and 8 to express his incarnation. The Letter of James is an instruction resembling those in Proverbs. Wisdom traditions influenced the Gospels of Matthew and Luke through a common source (see, e.g., Mt 11:25–27 and Lk 10:21–22, which seem to derive their father-son language, at least in part, from the parental language of Proverbs). The Gospel of John regards Jesus as incarnate wisdom descended from on high to offer human beings life and truth and make disciples of them, a view largely reflected in Proverbs 1–9. In later Judaism, Hebrew ethical wills, in which

parents hand on to their children their wisdom, borrowed from the genre of instruction.

The original audience of the instructions and sayings seems to have been male. The father addresses his son, marriage is finding a wife, success often is serving the king or farming effectively. The book itself, however, expands the traditional audience of youths (1:4) to include older, more experienced, people (1:5). It broadens the father-son language by mentioning the mother, and incorporates sayings on human experience generally. The father teaching his son becomes a model for anyone teaching a way of life to another person. The canonical process furthered such inclusiveness, for Proverbs was made part of the Bible that addresses *all* Israel.

The Book of Proverbs has nine sections:

   I. Title and Introduction (1:1–7)
  II. Instructions of Parents and of Woman Wisdom (1:8–9:18)
 III. First Solomonic Collection of Sayings (10:1–22:16)
 IV. Sayings of the Wise (22:17–24:22)
  V. Further Sayings of the Wise (24:23–34)
 VI. Second Solomonic Collection, Collected Under King Hezekiah (25:1–29:27)
VII. Sayings of Agur and Others (30:1–33)
VIII. Sayings of King Lemuel (31:1–9)
 IX. Poem on the Woman of Worth (31:10–31)

Part II is judged by many scholars to contain ten instructions (1:8–19; chap. 2; 3:1–12, 21–35; 4:1–9, 10–19, 20–27; chap. 5; 6:20–35; chap. 7), three wisdom poems (1:20–33; chap. 8; 9:1–6 + 11, 13–18), and two interludes (3:13–20; 6:1–19). ∎

# PROVERBS

## I. TITLE AND INTRODUCTION

### Purpose of the Proverbs of Solomon†

1 ¹ The proverbs† of Solomon,* the son of
David,
 king of Israel:

² That people may know wisdom and
discipline,†
 may understand intelligent sayings;

³ May receive instruction in wise conduct,
 in what is right, just and fair;

⁴ That resourcefulness may be imparted to
the naive,†
 knowledge and discretion to the
young.

⁵ The wise by hearing them will advance
in learning,
 the intelligent will gain sound
guidance,

⁶ To comprehend proverb and byword,
 the words of the wise and their
riddles.

⁷ Fear of the LORD† is the beginning of
knowledge;*
 fools despise wisdom and discipline.

## II. INSTRUCTIONS OF PARENTS AND
## OF WOMAN WISDOM

### The Path of the Wicked:
### Greed and Violence†

⁸ Hear, my son, your father's instruction,
 and reject not your mother's teaching;

⁹ A graceful diadem will they be for your
head;
 a pendant for your neck.

¹⁰ My son, should sinners entice you,
¹¹ do not go if they say, "Come along
with us!
 Let us lie in wait for blood,
 unprovoked, let us trap the
innocent;

¹² Let us swallow them alive, like Sheol,
 whole, like those who go down to the
pit!

¹³ All kinds of precious wealth shall we
gain,
 we shall fill our houses with booty;

¹⁴ Cast in your lot with us,
 we shall all have one purse!"

¹⁵ My son, do not walk in the way with
them,
 hold back your foot from their
path!

¹⁶ [For their feet run to evil,
 they hasten to shed blood.*]

¹⁷ In vain a net is spread†
 right under the eyes of any bird—

¹⁸ They lie in wait for their own blood,
 they set a trap for their own lives.

¹⁹ This is the way of everyone greedy for
loot:
 it takes away their lives.

### Wisdom in Person Gives a Warning†

²⁰ Wisdom cries aloud in the street,
 in the open squares she raises her
voice;*

²¹ Down the crowded ways she calls out,
 at the city gates she utters her
words:

---

**1:1–7** The prologue explains the purpose of the book. The book has a sapiential, ethical, and religious dimension: to bring the inexperienced to knowledge and right conduct, to increase the facility of those already wise for interpreting proverbs, parables and riddles, and to encourage the fulfillment of one's duties to God.

**1:1** *Proverbs*: the Hebrew word *mashal* is broader than English "proverb," embracing the instructions of chaps. 1–9 and the sayings, observations, and comparisons of chaps. 10–31.

**1:2** *Discipline*: education or formation which dispels ignorance and corrects vice. Note the reprise of v. 2a in v. 7b.

**1:4** *Naive*: immature, inexperienced, sometimes the young, hence easily influenced for good or evil.

**1:7** *Fear of the LORD*: primarily a disposition rather than the emotion of fear; reverential awe and respect toward God combined with obedience to God's will.

**1:8–19** A parental warning to a young person leaving home, for them to avoid the company of the greedy and violent. Two ways lie before the hearer, a way that leads to death and a way that leads to life. The trap which the wicked set for the innocent

(v. 11) in the end takes away the lives of the wicked themselves (v. 19). This theme will recur especially in chaps. 1–9. A second theme introduced here is that of founding (or managing) a household and choosing a spouse. A third theme is the human obstacles to attaining wisdom. Here (and in 2:12–15 and 4:10–19), the obstacle is men (always in the plural); in 2:16–19; 5:1–6; 6:20–35; chap. 7; 9:13–18, the obstacle to the quest is the "foreign" woman (always in the singular).

**1:17** A difficult verse. The most probable interpretation is that no fowler lifts up the net so the bird can see it. The verse might be paraphrased: God does not let those who walk on evil paths see the net that will entrap them. The passive construction ("a net is spread") is sometimes used to express divine activity. Verse 16 is a later attempt to add clarity. It is a quotation from Is 59:7 and is not in the best Greek manuscripts.

**1:20–33** Wisdom is personified as in chaps. 8 and 9:1–6.

---

**1:1** Prv 10:1; 25:1; 1 Kgs      Ps 111:10; Sir 1:16.
     4:32.                  **1:16** Is 59:7.
**1:7** Prv 9:10; Jb 28:28;      **1:20** Prv 8:1–3; 9:3.

P
R
V

22† "How long, you naive ones, will you
　　　love naivete,

23　　How long will you turn away at my
　　　reproof?
　　[The arrogant delight in their arrogance,
　　　and fools hate knowledge.]
　　Lo! I will pour out to you my spirit,
　　I will acquaint you with my words:

24　　'Because I called and you refused,
　　　extended my hand and no one took
　　　　notice; *

25　　Because you disdained all my counsel,
　　　and my reproof you ignored—

26　　I, in my turn, will laugh at your doom;
　　　will mock when terror overtakes you;

27　　When terror comes upon you like a
　　　　storm,
　　　and your doom approaches like a
　　　　whirlwind;
　　　when distress and anguish befall you.'

28　　Then they will call me, but I will not
　　　answer;
　　　they will seek me, but will not find
　　　　me,

29　　Because they hated knowledge,
　　　and the fear of the LORD they did not
　　　　choose.

30　　They ignored my counsel,
　　　they spurned all my reproof;

31　　Well, then, they shall eat the fruit† of
　　　their own way,
　　　and with their own devices be glutted.

32　　For the straying of the naive kills them,
　　　the smugness of fools destroys them.

33　　But whoever obeys me dwells in security,
　　　in peace, without fear of harm." *

## The Blessings of Wisdom†

2 ¹ My son, if you receive my words
　　　and treasure my commands,

2　　Turning your ear to wisdom, †
　　　inclining your heart to understanding;

3　　Yes, if you call for intelligence,
　　　and to understanding raise your voice;

4　　If you seek her like silver,
　　　and like hidden treasures search her
　　　　out,

5　　Then will you understand the fear of the
　　　LORD;
　　　the knowledge of God you will find;

6　　For the LORD gives wisdom,
　　　from his mouth come knowledge and
　　　　understanding; *

7　　He has success in store for the upright,
　　　is the shield of those who walk
　　　　honestly,

8　　Guarding the paths of justice,
　　　protecting the way of his faithful ones,

9　　Then you will understand what is right
　　　and just,
　　　what is fair, every good path;

10　　For wisdom will enter your heart,
　　　knowledge will be at home in your
　　　　soul,

11　　Discretion will watch over you,
　　　understanding will guard you;

12†　Saving you from the way of the wicked,
　　　from those whose speech is perverse.

13　　From those who have left the straight
　　　paths
　　　to walk in the ways of darkness,

14　　Who delight in doing evil

---

† With divine authority she proclaims the moral order, threatening to leave to their own devices those who disregard her invitation. All three speeches of Woman Wisdom have common features: a setting in city streets; an audience of simple or naive people; a competing appeal (chap. 7 is the competing appeal for chap. 8); an invitation to a relationship that brings long life, riches, repute.

The structure of the speeches is: A: setting (vv. 20–21); B: Wisdom's withdrawal, rebuke and announcement (vv. 22–23); reason and rejection I (vv. 24–27); reason and rejection II (vv. 28–31); summary (v. 32); C: the effects of Wisdom's presence (v. 33). Wisdom's opening speech is an extended threat ending with a brief invitation (v. 33). Her second speech is an extended invitation ending with a brief threat (8:36). The surprisingly abrupt and harsh tone of her speech is perhaps to be explained as a response to the arrogant words of the men in the previous scene (1:8–19).

**1:22–23** There is textual confusion. Verse 22bc (in the third person) is an addition, interrupting vv. 22a and 23a (in the second person). The addition has been put in brackets, to separate it from the original poem. The original verses do not ask for a change of heart but begin to detail the consequences of disobedience to Wisdom.

**1:31** Eat the fruit: sinners are punished by the consequences of their sins. Wisdom's voice echoes that of the parents in vv. 8–19. The parents mediate wisdom in vv. 8–19, but here Wisdom herself speaks.

**2:1–22** Chapter 2 is a single poem, an acrostic of twenty-two lines, the number of consonants in the Hebrew alphabet. In vv. 1–11, the letter aleph, the first letter of the alphabet, predominates, and in vv. 12–22, the letter lamed, the first letter of the second half of the alphabet, A single structure runs through the whole: if (aleph) you search…then (aleph) the Lord/Wisdom will grant…saving (lamed) you from the wicked man/woman…thus (lamed) you can walk in the safe way….

**2:2–3** Wisdom…understanding…intelligence: various names or aspects of the same gift.

**2:12–15** As in 1:8–19, there is an obstacle to the quest for wisdom—deceitful and violent men. Cf. also 4:10–19. They offer a way of life that is opposed to the way of wisdom.

---

**1:24** Is 65:2, 12; 66:4; Jer 7:13.
**1:33** Prv 8:33–34.

**2:6** Jb 32:8; Wis 7:25; Sir 1:1; Jas 1:5.

and celebrate perversity;

15 Whose ways are crooked,
    whose paths are devious;

16 † Saving you from a stranger,
    from a foreign woman with her
        smooth words, *

17 One who forsakes the companion of her
        youth
    and forgets the covenant of her God;

18 For her path sinks down to death,
    and her footsteps lead to the
        shades. † *

19 None who enter there come back,
    or gain the paths of life.

20 Thus you may walk in the way of the
        good,
    and keep to the paths of the just.

21 † For the upright will dwell in the land, *
    people of integrity will remain in it;

22 But the wicked will be cut off from the
        land,
    the faithless will be rooted out of it.

## Confidence in God Leads to Prosperity†

**3** ¹ My son, do not forget † my teaching,
        take to heart my commands;

2 For many days, and years of life, *
    and peace, will they bring you.

3 Do not let love and fidelity forsake you;

bind them around your neck;
    write them on the tablet of your heart.

4 Then will you win favor and esteem
    before God and human beings.

5 Trust in the LORD with all your heart,
    on your own intelligence do not rely;

6 In all your ways be mindful of him,
    and he will make straight your paths.

7 Do not be wise in your own eyes, *
    fear the LORD and turn away from evil;

8 This will mean health for your flesh
    and vigor for your bones.

9 Honor the LORD with your wealth,
    with first fruits of all your produce; *

10 Then will your barns be filled with
        plenty,
    with new wine your vats will overflow.

11 The discipline of the LORD, my son, do
        not spurn; *
    do not disdain his reproof;

12 † For whom the LORD loves he reproves,
    as a father, the son he favors. *

## The Benefits of Finding Wisdom†

13 Happy the one who finds wisdom,
    the one who gains understanding! *

14 Her profit is better than profit in silver,
    and better than gold is her revenue;

15 She is more precious than corals,

---

† **2:16–19** A second obstacle and counter-figure to Wisdom, personified as an attractive woman, is the "stranger," or "foreigner," from outside the territory or kinship group, hence inappropriate as a marriage partner. In Proverbs she comes to be identified with Woman Folly, whose deceitful words promise life but lead to death. Woman Folly appears also in chap. 5, 6:20–35, chap. 7 and 9:13–18. *Covenant*: refers to the vow uttered with divine sanction at the woman's previous marriage, as the parallel verse suggests. She is already married and relations with her would be adulterous.

**2:18** *Shades*: the inhabitants of Sheol.

**2:21–22** Verses 21–22 echo the ending of Wisdom's speech in 1:32–33, in which refusing Wisdom's invitation meant death and obedience to her meant life. The same set of ideas is found in Ps 37 (especially vv. 3, 9, 11, 22, 29, 34, and 38): to live on (or inherit) the land and to be uprooted from the land are expressions of divine recompense.

**3:1–12** The instruction consists of a series of six four-line exhortations in which the second line of each exhortation mentions a reward or benefit. In the first five exhortations, the teacher promises a reward: long life, a good name, divine protection, health, abundant crops. The last exhortation, vv. 11–12, departs from the command-reward scheme, implying that being a disciple of the Lord does not guarantee unalloyed bliss: one must allow God freedom to "reprove" or educate. The process of education is like that described in chap. 2: the father first invites his son (or disciple) to memorize his teaching (v. 1), then to enter upon a relationship of trust with him (v. 3), and finally to place his trust in God, who takes up the parental task of education (v. 5). Education begun by the parent is brought to full completion by God.

**3:1** *Do not forget*: this word and several others in the sec-

tion such as "teaching," "commands," "years of life," and the custom of affixing written teaching to one's body, occur also in Deuteronomy. This vocabulary suggests that Proverbs and Deuteronomy had a common origin in the scribal class of Jerusalem. This section (and vv. 21–34) subtly elaborates Dt 6:5–9, "You shall love the LORD with all your heart (v. 5)…Take to heart these words when you are at home and when you are away (v. 23)…when you lie down (v. 24)…Bind them (v. 3) on your arm as a sign and let them be a pendant on your forehead" (v. 21).

**3:12** One might be tempted to judge the quality of one's relationship to God by one's prosperity. It is an inadequate criterion, for God as a teacher might go counter to student expectations. The discipline of God can involve suffering.

**3:13–20** An encomium of Wisdom through the listing of her benefits to the human race and the depiction of her role in creation. Wisdom, or understanding, is more valuable than silver and gold. Its fruit is long life, riches, honor and happiness (vv. 13–18). Even the creation of the universe and its adornment (Gn 1) were not done without wisdom (vv. 19–20). The praise of Wisdom foreshadows the praise of a noble wife in the final poem (31:10–31), even to the singling out of the hands extended in a helpful way toward human beings.

---

**2:16** Prv 5:3, 20; 6:24; 7:5;
      22:14.
**2:18** Prv 5:5; 7:27.
**2:21** Prv 10:7, 30; Jb
      18:17; Ps 21:9–13;
      37:22, 28.
**3:2** Prv 4:10; 9:11; 10:27.

**3:7** Rom 11:25; 12:16.
**3:9** Ex 34:26; Lv 27:30;
      Dt 26:2; Sir 7:31;
      35:7.
**3:11** Heb 12:5–6.
**3:12** Jdt 8:27; Rev 3:19.
**3:13** Prv 8:34–35.

and no treasure of yours can compare
with her.*

16 Long life is in her right hand,
in her left are riches and honor;

17 Her ways are pleasant ways,
and all her paths are peace;

18 She is a tree of life† to those who grasp
her,
and those who hold her fast are
happy.*

19 The LORD by wisdom founded the earth,
established the heavens by
understanding;

20 By his knowledge the depths† are split,
and the clouds drop down dew.

### Justice Toward One's Neighbor Brings Blessing†

21 My son, do not let these slip from your
sight:
hold to deliberation and planning;

22 So will they be life to your soul,†
and an adornment for your neck.

23 Then you may go your way securely;
your foot will never stumble;

24 When you lie down, you will not be
afraid,
when you rest, your sleep will be
sweet.

25 Do not be afraid of sudden terror,
of the ruin of the wicked when it
comes;

26 For the LORD will be your confidence,
and will keep your foot from the
snare.

27 Do not withhold any goods from the
owner
when it is in your power to act.

28 Say not to your neighbor, "Go, come
back tomorrow,
and I will give it to you," when all the
while you have it.

29 Do not plot evil against your neighbors,
when they live at peace with you.

30 Do not contend with someone without
cause,
with one who has done you no harm.

31 Do not envy the violent
and choose none of their ways:*

32 To the LORD the devious are an
abomination,
but the upright are close to him.

33 The curse of the LORD is on the house of
the wicked,
but the dwelling of the just he blesses;

34 Those who scoff, he scoffs at,*
but the lowly he favors.

35 The wise will possess glory,
but fools will bear shame.

### The Teacher as Model Disciple†

4 1 Hear, O children, a father's instruction,
be attentive, that you may gain
understanding!

---

**3:18** *A tree of life*: in the Old Testament this phrase occurs only in Proverbs (11:30; 13:12; 15:4) and Genesis (2:9; 3:22, 24). The origins of the concept are obscure; there is no explicit mention of it in ancient Near Eastern literature, though on ancient seals trees are sometimes identified as trees of life. When the man and the woman were expelled from the garden, the tree of life was put off limits to them, lest they "eat of it and live forever" (Gn 3:22). The quest for wisdom gives access to the previously sequestered tree of life. The tree of life is mentioned also in the apocryphal work 1 Enoch 25:4–5. Rev 2 and 22 mention the tree of life as a source of eternal life.

**3:20** *Depths*: for the Hebrews, the depths enclosed the great subterranean waters; the rain and dew descended from the waters above the firmament; cf. Gn 1:6–10; Jb 26:8, 12; Ps 18:15; 24:2. The cosmogony provides the reason why Wisdom offers such benefits to human beings: the world was created in wisdom so that all who live in accord with wisdom live in tune with the universe.

**3:21–35** As in other instructions, the father in vv. 21–26 urges the son to seek wisdom, which in this case means practicing the virtues of "deliberation and planning," a specification of wisdom. Practicing these virtues brings protection from violence (vv. 22–26) and friendship with God (vv. 32–35). The language is like Ps 91.

Verses 27–35 are arranged according to a clear order. Serving God requires serving one's neighbor through kindness (vv. 27–28), maintaining peace with the good (vv. 29–31), having no envy of the wicked (v. 31), because the Lord's friendship and kindness are with the just, not with the wicked. Matching the six exhortations of vv. 1–12, vv. 27–34 contain six prohibitions. The righteous/wicked contrast is progressively developed: in contrast to the wicked, the righteous are in God's inner circle, their houses are blessed, they deal with a merciful God, and obtain honor.

**3:22** *Your soul*: Heb. *nephesh* means "throat, esophagus; life; soul." The meanings are connected. The throat area is the moist, breathing center of the body, which stands for life and for self. The figure of speech is called metonymy, in which one word is substituted for another on the basis of a causal relation, e.g., eye for sight, arm for power, or, as here, "throat area" for life. Proverbs sometimes plays on this concrete meaning of life (e.g., 21:23).

**4:1–9** The teacher draws a parallel between his teaching the disciples now and his father's teaching him in his youth (vv. 3–4): what my father taught me about wisdom is what I am teaching you. The poem implies that the teacher has acquired wisdom and has in fact been protected and honored as his father promised long ago. Thus the teacher has the authority of someone who has been under wisdom's sway since earliest youth.

There are two sections, a call for attention and introduction of the speaker (vv. 1–3) and the father's quoting of his own father's

---

**3:15** Prv 8:11, 19; Wis 7:8–11.
**3:18** Prv 4:13; 8:35; 11:30; Gn 2:9; 3:22.
**3:31** Prv 23:17; 24:1, 19; Ps 37:1.
**3:34** Prv 1:26.

2   Yes, excellent advice I give you;
      my teaching do not forsake.
3   When I was my father's child,
      tender, the darling of my mother,
4   He taught me and said to me:
      "Let your heart hold fast my words: *
      keep my commands, and live!
5   Get wisdom, † get understanding!
      Do not forget or turn aside from the
      words of my mouth.
6   Do not forsake her, and she will preserve
      you;
      love her, and she will safeguard you;
7   The beginning of wisdom is: get
      wisdom;
      whatever else you get, get
      understanding.
8   Extol her, and she will exalt you;
      she will bring you honors if you
      embrace her;
9   She will put on your head a graceful
      diadem;
      a glorious crown will she bestow on
      you."

## The Two Ways†

10  Hear, my son, and receive my words,
      and the years of your life shall be
      many. *
11  On the way of wisdom I direct you,
      I lead you on straight paths.
12  When you walk, your step will not be
      impeded,
      and should you run, you will not
      stumble.

13  Hold fast to instruction, never let it go;
      keep it, for it is your life.
14 † The path of the wicked do not enter,
      nor walk in the way of the evil;
15  Shun it, do not cross it,
      turn aside from it, pass on.
16  For they cannot rest unless they have
      done evil;
      if they do not trip anyone they lose
      sleep.
17  For they eat the bread of wickedness
      and drink the wine of violence.
18  But the path of the just is like shining
      light,
      that grows in brilliance till perfect
      day. †
19  The way of the wicked is like darkness;
      they do not know on what they
      stumble.

## With Your Whole Being Heed My Words and Live†

20  My son, to my words be attentive,
      to my sayings incline your ear;
21  Let them not slip from your sight,
      keep them within your heart;
22  For they are life to those who find
      them, *
      bringing health to one's whole being.
23  With all vigilance guard your heart,
      for in it are the sources of life.
24 † Dishonest mouth put away from you,
      deceitful lips put far from you.
25  Let your eyes look straight ahead
      and your gaze be focused forward.

teaching (vv. 4–9). Beginning with v. 5, the father's words are no longer quoted, wisdom herself becoming the active agent; she becomes the subject, not the object, of the verbs. Three Hebrew verbs are repeated in the two parts, "to forsake" in vv. 2 and 6, "to keep/guard" in vv. 4 and 6, and "to give/bestow" in vv. 2 and 9. Each verb in its first appearance has the father's words as its object; in its second appearance each verb has wisdom as its subject or object. The teaching process is like that in 2:1–22 and 3:1–12: heeding the words of one's parent puts one in touch with wisdom, who completes the process and bestows her gifts.
**4:5, 7** *Get wisdom:* the same Hebrew word "to get" can mean to acquire merchandise and to acquire a wife (18:22; 31:10); both meanings are in keeping with Proverbs' metaphors of acquiring wisdom over gold and silver and of acquiring wisdom as a personified woman, a wife.
**4:10–19** A central metaphor of the poem is "the way." The way of wisdom leads directly to life (vv. 10–13); it is a light that grows brighter (v. 18). The wise are bound to shun (vv. 14–17) the dark and violent path of the wicked (v. 19). Singleness of purpose and right conduct proceed from the heart of the wise as from the source of life (vv. 23–26), saving them from destruction on evil paths (4:27; 5:21–23). As in 1:8–19 and 2:12–15, the obstacles to the quest are men and their way. Elsewhere in chaps. 1–9, the obstacle is the foreign woman (2:16–19; chap. 5; 6:20–35; chap. 7; 9:13–18).

**4:14–15** One is always free to choose. The righteous may choose to leave their path to walk on the wicked path and the wicked may choose the righteous path.
**4:18** *Till perfect day:* lit., "till the day is established"; this may refer to full daylight or to noonday.
**4:20–27** Acquiring wisdom brings life and health. The learning process involves two stages: (1) hearing the teacher's words and treasuring them in the heart; (2) speaking and acting in accord with the wisdom that one has stored in one's heart. Seven organs of the body are mentioned: ear, eyes, heart, mouth, lips, eyelids ("gaze," v. 25), feet. Each of the organs is to be strained to its limit as the disciple puts wisdom into practice. The physical organ stands for the faculty, e.g., the eye for sight, the foot for movement. The figure of speech is called metonymy; one word is substituted for another on the basis of a causal relation.
**4:24–27** In vv. 20–21 the faculties of hearing (ear) and seeing (eye) take in the teaching and the heart stores and ponders it, so in the second half of the poem, vv. 24–27, the faculties of speech, sight, and walking enable the disciple to put the teaching into practice.

**4:4** Dt 6:1–6.        **4:22** Prv 8:35.
**4:10** Prv 3:2.

26 Survey the path for your feet,
  and all your ways will be sure.
27 Turn neither to right nor to left,
  keep your foot far from evil.

## Warning Against Adultery†

**5** ¹ My son, to my wisdom be attentive,
  to understanding incline your ear,
² That you may act discreetly,
  and your lips guard what you know.
³ Indeed, the lips of the stranger drip
    honey,†
  and her mouth is smoother than oil;*
⁴ But in the end she is as bitter as
    wormwood,
  as sharp as a two-edged sword.
⁵ Her feet go down to death,
  her steps reach Sheol;*
⁶ Her paths ramble, you know not where,
  lest you see before you the road to
    life.
⁷ So now, children, listen to me,
  do not stray from the words of my
    mouth.
⁸ Keep your way far from her,*
  do not go near the door of her house,
⁹ Lest you give your honor† to others,*
  and your years to a merciless one;
¹⁰ Lest outsiders take their fill of your
    wealth,
  and your hard-won earnings go to
    another's house;
¹¹ And you groan in the end,
  when your flesh and your body are
    consumed;
¹² And you say, "Oh, why did I hate
    instruction,
  and my heart spurn reproof!

¹³ Why did I not listen to the voice of my
    teachers,
  incline my ear to my instructors!
¹⁴ I am all but ruined,
  in the midst of the public assembly!"
¹⁵ Drink water† from your own cistern,
  running water from your own well.
¹⁶ Should your water sources be dispersed
    abroad,
  streams of water in the streets?
¹⁷ Let them be yours alone,
  not shared with outsiders;
¹⁸ Let your fountain be blessed and have
    joy of the wife of your youth,
¹⁹ your lovely hind, your graceful doe.†
  Of whose love you will ever have your
    fill,
  and by her ardor always be
    intoxicated.
²⁰ Why then, my son, should you be
    intoxicated with a stranger,
  and embrace another woman?
²¹ Indeed, the ways of each person are
    plain to the LORD's sight;
  all their paths he surveys;*
²² By their own iniquities the wicked will
    be caught,
  in the meshes of their own sin they
    will be held fast;
²³ They will die from lack of discipline,
  lost because of their great folly.

## Miscellaneous Proverbs†

## Against Going Surety for One's Neighbor

**6** ¹† My son, if you have become surety to
    your neighbor,*
  given your hand in pledge to another,

---

**5:1–23** This is the first of three poems on the forbidden woman, the "stranger" outside the social boundaries (cf. 2:16–19); the other two are 6:20–35 and chap. 7. Understanding and discretion are necessary to avoid adultery, which leads astray and begets bitterness, bloodshed, and death (vv. 1–6). It destroys honor, wastes the years of life, despoils hard-earned wealth, and brings remorse in the end (vv. 7–14). Conjugal fidelity and love bring happiness and security (vv. 15–20). Cf. 6:20–7:27. The structure of the poem consists of a two-line introduction; part one consists of three stanzas of four lines each warning of the forbidden woman's effect on her lovers (vv. 3–14); part two consists of a stanza of twelve lines exhorting the disciple to marital fidelity (vv. 15–20); and a final stanza of six lines on the perils of the woman (vv. 21–23).

**5:3** A metaphorical level is established in the opening description of the forbidden woman: her lips drip honey and her feet lead to death. By her lies, she leads people away from the wisdom that gives life.

**5:9** *Honor:* the words "life" and "wealth" have also been read in this place. *A merciless one:* the offended husband; cf. 6:34–35.

**5:15–16** *Water:* water may have an erotic meaning as in Sg 4:15, "[You are] a garden fountain, a well of living water." Eating and drinking can be metaphors expressing the mutuality of love. The wife is the opposite of the adulterous woman; she is not an outsider, not unfeeling, not a destroyer of her husband's self and goods. The best defense against adultery is appreciating and loving one's spouse. The best defense against folly is to appreciate and love wisdom.

**5:19** *Lovely hind...graceful doe:* ancient Near Eastern symbols of feminine beauty and charm; cf. Sg 2:7, 9, 17.

**6:1–19** Four independent pieces akin to those in 30:1–5, 6–11, 12–15, and 16–19. Some judge the verses to be an ancient addition, but the fact that the pieces differ from the other material in chaps. 1–9 is not a strong argument against their originality. Ancient anthologies did not always have the symmetry of modern collections. An editor may have placed the four pieces in

---

5:3 Prv 7:5.                    5:21 Jb 14:16; 31:4; 34:21.
5:5 Prv 2:18; 7:27.             6:1 Prv 11:15; 22:26; Sir
5:8 Prv 7:25.                        8:13; 29:19.
5:9 Sir 9:6.

2    You have been snared by the utterance
         of your lips,
         caught by the words of your mouth;
3    So do this, my son, to free yourself,
         since you have fallen into your
             neighbor's power:
         Go, hurry, rouse your neighbor!
4    Give no sleep to your eyes,
         nor slumber to your eyelids;
5    Free yourself like a gazelle from the
             hunter,
         or like a bird from the hand of the
             fowler.

### The Ant and the Sluggard at Harvest

6†   Go to the ant,* O sluggard,
         study her ways and learn wisdom;
7    For though she has no chief,
         no commander or ruler,
8    She procures her food in the summer,
         stores up her provisions in the
             harvest.
9    How long, O sluggard, will you lie
             there?
         when will you rise from your sleep?
10   A little sleep, a little slumber,
         a little folding of the arms to rest—†
11   Then poverty will come upon you like a
             robber,
         and want like a brigand.

### The Scoundrel

12†  Scoundrels, villains, are they
         who deal in crooked talk.
13   Shifty of eye,
         feet ever moving,
         pointing with fingers,
14   They have perversity in their hearts,
         always plotting evil,
         sowing discord.
15   Therefore their doom comes suddenly;
         in an instant they are crushed beyond
             cure.

### What the Lord Rejects

16   There are six things the LORD hates,
         yes, seven† are an abomination to him;
17†  Haughty eyes, a lying tongue,
         hands that shed innocent blood,
18   A heart that plots wicked schemes,
         feet that are quick to run to evil,
19   The false witness who utters lies,
         and the one who sows discord among
             kindred.

### Warning Against Adultery†

20   Observe, my son, your father's
             command,
         and do not reject your mother's
             teaching;

---

† the midst of the three poems on the forbidden woman to shed light on some of their themes. Verses 1–5 warn against getting trapped by one's words to another person (the Hebrew word for "another" is the same used for the forbidden woman); vv. 6–11 proposes the ant as a model of forethought and diligence; vv. 12–15 describes the reprobate who bears some similarity to the seductive woman, especially as portrayed in chap. 7; vv. 16–19 depicts the typical enemy of God, underscoring the person's destructive words.

**6:1–5** Unlike other instructions that begin with "my son," this instruction does not urge the hearer to store up the father's words as a means to wisdom, but only to avoid one practice—going surety for one's neighbor. The warning is intensified by repetition of "neighbor" and "free yourself," the mention of bodily organs, and the imagery of hunting. *Given your hand in pledge*: lit., "struck your hands"; this was probably the legal method for closing a contract. To become surety meant intervening in favor of the insolvent debtor and assuming responsibility for the payment of the debt, either by obtaining it from the debtor or substituting oneself. Proverbs is strongly opposed to the practice (11:15; 17:18; 20:16; 22:26–27; 27:13) apparently because of the danger it poses to the freedom of the one providing surety.

**6:6–11** The sluggard or lazybones is a type in Proverbs, like the righteous and the wicked. Sometimes the opposite type to the sluggard is the diligent person. Other extended passages on the sluggard are 24:30–34 and 26:13–16. The malice of the type is not low physical energy but the refusal to act. To describe human types, Proverbs often uses comparisons from the animal world, e.g., 27:8 (bird); 28:1, 15 (lion); 30:18–19 (eagle, snake); 30:24–28 (ant, badger, locust, lizard).

**6:10** This verse may be regarded as the sluggard's reply or as a continuation of the remonstrance.

**6:12–15** Proverbs uses types to make the point that certain ways of acting have inherent consequences. The typifying intensifies the picture. All the physical organs—mouth, eyes, feet, fingers—are at the service of evil. Cf. Rom 6:12–13: "Therefore, sin must not reign over your mortal bodies so that you obey their desires. And do not present the parts of your bodies to sin as weapons for wickedness, but present yourselves to God as raised from the dead to life and the parts of your bodies to God as weapons of righteousness."

**6:16** *Six…seven*: this literary pattern (n, n + 1) occurs frequently; cf., e.g., Am 1–2; Prv 30:18–19.

**6:17–19** The seven vices, symbolized for the most part by bodily organs, are pride, lying, murder, intrigue, readiness to do evil, false witness, and the stirring up of discord.

**6:20–35** The second of three instructions on adultery (5:1–23; 6:20–35; and chap. 7). The instructions assume that wisdom will protect one from adultery and its consequences: loss of property and danger to one's person. In this poem, the father and the mother urge their son to keep their teaching constantly before his eyes. The teaching will light his way and make it a path to life (v. 23). The teaching will preserve him from the adulterous woman who is far more dangerous than a prostitute. Prostitutes may cost one money, but having an affair with someone else's wife puts one in grave danger. The poem bluntly urges self-interest as a motive to refrain from adultery.

The poem has three parts. I (vv. 20–24, ten lines), in which v. 23 repeats "command" and "teaching" of v. 20 and "keeping" in v. 24 completes the fixed pair initiated by "observe" in v. 20; II (vv. 25–29, ten lines) is a self-contained argument comparing the costs of a liaison with a prostitute and a married woman; III (vv.

* ——————————
**6:6** Prv 30:25.

21    Keep them fastened over your heart
      always,
      tie them around your neck.

22    When you lie down they† will watch
      over you,
      when you wake, they will share your
      concerns;
      wherever you turn, they will guide
      you.

23    For the command is a lamp, and the
      teaching a light,
      and a way to life are the reproofs that
      discipline,

24    Keeping you from another's wife,
      from the smooth tongue of the
      foreign woman. *

25    Do not lust in your heart after her
      beauty,
      do not let her captivate you with her
      glance! *

26    For the price of a harlot
      may be scarcely a loaf of bread,
      But a married woman
      is a trap for your precious life.

27 †   Can a man take embers into his
      bosom,
      and his garments not be burned?

28    Or can a man walk on live coals,
      and his feet not be scorched?

29    So with him who sleeps with another's
      wife—

      none who touches her shall go
      unpunished. *

30    Thieves are not despised
      if out of hunger they steal to satisfy
      their appetite.

31    Yet if caught they must pay back
      sevenfold,
      yield up all the wealth of their house.

32    But those who commit adultery have no
      sense;
      those who do it destroy themselves.

33 †   They will be beaten and disgraced,
      and their shame will not be wiped
      away;

34    For passion enrages the husband,
      he will have no pity on the day of
      vengeance;

35    He will not consider any restitution,
      nor be satisfied by your many bribes.

## The Seduction†

7 ¹ † My son, keep my words,
      and treasure my commands.

2    Keep my commands and live, †
      and my teaching as the apple of your
      eye;

3    Bind them on your fingers,
      write them on the tablet of your
      heart. *

4    Say to Wisdom, "You are my sister!" †
      Call Understanding, "Friend!"

---

† 30–35, twelve lines) draws conclusions from the comparison of adultery with theft: the latter involves property only but adultery destroys one's name and very self. The best protection against such a woman is heeding parental instruction, which is to be kept vividly before one's eyes like a written tablet.

**6:22** *They:* Heb. has "she." If this verse is not out of place, then the antecedent of "she" is command (v. 20), or perhaps wisdom.

**6:27–29** There is a play on three words of similar sound, *ʾîsh,* "man," *ʾishshâ,* "woman," and *ʾēsh,* "fire, embers." The question, "Can a man (*ʾîsh*) take embers (*ʾēsh*) into his bosom / and his garments not be burned?", has a double meaning. "Into his bosom" has an erotic meaning as in the phrase "wife of one's bosom" (Dt 13:6; 28:54; Sir 9:1). Hence one will destroy one's garments, which symbolize one's public position, by taking fire/another's wife into one's bosom.

**6:33–35** The nature of the husband's vengeance is disputed, some believing it is simply a physical beating whereas others hold it is public and involves the death penalty because Lv 20:20 and Dt 22:22 demand the death penalty.

**7:1–27** The third and climactic instruction on adultery and seduction is an example story, of the same type as the example story in 24:30–34. By its negative portrayal of the deceitful woman, who speaks in the night to a lone youth, it serves as a foil to trustworthy Wisdom in chap. 8, who speaks in broad daylight to all who pass in the street.

As in 6:20–24, the father warns his son to keep his teaching to protect him from the dangerous forbidden woman. The father's language in 7:4 ("Say to Wisdom, 'You are my sister,' and call Understanding 'Friend'") sets this admonition apart, however; it

is the language of courtship and love. If the son makes Woman Wisdom his companion and lover, she will protect him from the other woman. As in chap. 5, loving the right woman protects the man from the wrong woman.

As motivation, the father in vv. 6–23 tells his son of an incident he once observed while looking out his window—a young man went to the bed of an adulterous woman and wound up dead. As in chap. 5, the realistic details—the purposeful woman, the silent youth, the vow, the perfumed bed—have a metaphorical level. Ultimately the story is about two different kinds of love.

**7:1–3** Verses 1–3 are artistically constructed. "Keep" in v. 1a recurs in v. 2a; "commands" in v. 1b recurs in v. 2a; the imperative verb "live" occurs in the very center of the three lines; v. 3, on preserving the teaching upon one's very person, matches vv. 1–2, on preserving the teaching internally by memorizing it.

**7:2** *Live:* here as elsewhere (Gn 20:7; 42:18; 2 Kgs 18:32; Jer 27:12, 17; Ez 18:32), the imperative ("Live!") is uttered against the danger of death, e.g., "Do such and such and you will live (= survive the danger); why should you die?"

**7:4** *You are my sister:* "sister" and "brother" are examples of love language in the ancient Near East, occurring in Egyptian love poetry and Mesopotamian marriage songs. In Sg 4:9, 10, 12; 5:1, the man calls the woman, "my sister, my bride." Intimate friendship with Woman Wisdom saves one from false and dangerous relationships.

---

**6:24** Prv 2:16; 7:5.      **6:29** Sir 9:9.
**6:25** Ex 20:17; Dt 5:21; Sir    **7:3** Dt 6:8.
     9:8; 25:20; Mt 5:28.

5 That they may keep you from a
      stranger,
  from the foreign woman with her
      smooth words. *

6 For at the window of my house,
  through my lattice I looked out †

7 And I saw among the naive,
  I observed among the young men,
  a youth with no sense,

8 Crossing the street near the corner,
  then walking toward her house,

9 In the twilight, at dusk of day,
  in the very dark of night.

10 Then the woman comes to meet him,
  dressed like a harlot, with secret
      designs.

11 She is raucous and unruly,
  her feet cannot stay at home;

12 Now she is in the streets, now in the
      open squares,
  lurking in ambush at every corner.

13 Then she grabs him, kisses him,
  and with an impudent look says to
      him:

14 "I owed peace offerings,
  and today I have fulfilled my vows;

15 So I came out to meet you,
  to look for you, and I have found
      you!

16 With coverlets I have spread my couch,
  with brocaded cloths of Egyptian
      linen;

17 I have sprinkled my bed † with myrrh,
  with aloes, and with cinnamon.

18 Come, let us drink our fill of love,
  until morning, let us feast on love!

19 For my husband is not at home, †
  he has gone on a long journey;

20 A bag of money he took with him,
  he will not return home till the full
      moon."

21 She wins him over by repeated urging,
  with her smooth lips she leads him
      astray. † *

22 He follows her impulsively,
  like an ox that goes to slaughter;
  Like a stag that bounds toward the net,

23   till an arrow pierces its liver;
  Like a bird that rushes into a snare,
  unaware that his life is at stake.

24 So now, children, listen to me, †
  be attentive to the words of my
      mouth!

25 Do not let your heart turn to her ways,
  do not go astray in her paths;

26 For many are those she has struck down
      dead,
  numerous, those she has slain.

27 Her house is a highway to Sheol,
  leading down into the chambers of
      death. *

## The Discourse of Wisdom †

**8** 1 Does not Wisdom call,
  and Understanding raise her voice? *

2   On the top of the heights along the
      road,
  at the crossroads she takes her stand;

---

† **7:6–7** *I looked out…I saw…*: the perspective is unusual. The narrator looks through a window upon the drama in the street.

**7:17** *Bed*: a bed can designate a place of burial in Is 57:2; Ez 32:25; 2 Chr 16:14. *Myrrh…aloes*: the spices could be used for funerals as for weddings (Jn 19:39). It is possible that the language is ambivalent, speaking of death as it seems to speak of life. As the woman offers the youth a nuptial feast, she is in reality describing his funerary feast.

**7:19–20** *For my husband is not at home*: the woman is calculating. She knows exactly how long her husband will be gone.

**7:21** The verbs "to win over" (lit., "to lead astray") and "to lead off" can be used of leading animals such as a donkey (Nm 22:23) or sheep (Jer 23:2 and 50:17). The animal imagery continues as the youth is compared to an ox, a fallow deer, and a bird in the moment they are slaughtered. None of the animals are aware of their impending death.

**7:24–27** The father addresses "children," a larger audience than his own son; the story is typical, intended for others as an example. The story is a foil to the speech of the other woman in chap. 8.

**8:1–36** Chapter 8 is Wisdom's longest speech in the book. Wisdom is here personified as in 1:20–33. She exalts her grandeur and origin, and invites all (vv. 1–11) to be attentive to her salutary influence in human society (vv. 12–21), for she was privileged to be present at the creation of the world (vv. 22–31). Finally, she promises life and the favor of God to those who are devoted to her, death to those who reject her.

The poem has four sections, each (except the fourth) with two parts of five lines each:

|  |  |  |
|---|---|---|
| I. | A. vv. 1–5 | B. vv. 6–10 |
| II. | A. vv. 12–16 | B. vv. 17–21 |
| III. | A. vv. 22–26 | B. vv. 27–31 |
| IV. | vv. 32–36 |  |

Within chaps. 1–9, chap. 8 is the companion piece to Wisdom's first speech in 1:20–33. There she spoke harshly, giving a promise only in the last line; here she speaks invitingly, giving a threat only in the last line.

Chapter 8 is the best-known chapter in Proverbs and has profoundly influenced Jewish and Christian thought. The most explicit and lengthy biblical comment is in Sir 24; it too has thirty-five lines in seven five-line stanzas and develops the theme of Wisdom's intimacy with God and desire to be with human beings. The Gospel of John portrays Jesus in the language of wisdom in Proverbs: Jesus, like Wisdom, calls out to people to listen to him, promises to tell them the truth, seeks disciples, invites them to a banquet, and gives them life. Writers in the patristic period used the language of pre-existent wisdom to express the idea of the pre-existent Word with God.

---

* **7:5** Prv 2:16; 6:24.      **7:27** Prv 2:18–19; 5:5.
**7:21** Prv 5:3; 6:24.      **8:1** Prv 1:20–21; 9:3.

3 By the gates at the approaches of the
      city,
      in the entryways she cries aloud:

4 "To you, O people, I call;
      my appeal is to you mortals.

5 You naive ones, gain prudence,
      you fools,† gain sense.

6 Listen! for noble things I speak;
      my lips proclaim honest words.

7† Indeed, my mouth utters truth,
      and my lips abhor wickedness.

8 All the words of my mouth are sincere,
      none of them wily or crooked;

9 All of them are straightforward to the
      intelligent,
      and right to those who attain
      knowledge.

10 Take my instruction instead of silver,
      and knowledge rather than choice
      gold.

11 [For Wisdom is better than corals,
      and no treasures can compare with
      her.*]

12 I, Wisdom, dwell with prudence,
      and useful knowledge I have.

13 [The fear of the LORD is hatred of evil;]
  Pride, arrogance, the evil way,
      and the perverse mouth I hate.*

14 Mine are counsel and advice;
      Mine is strength; I am
      understanding.†

15 By me kings reign,
      and rulers enact justice;

16 By me princes govern,
      and nobles, all the judges of the earth.

17 Those who love me I also love,
      and those who seek me find me.

18 With me are riches and honor,*

19 wealth that endures, and righteousness.
  My fruit is better than gold, even pure
      gold,
      and my yield than choice silver.*

20 On the way of righteousness I walk,
      along the paths of justice,

21 Granting wealth to those who love me,
      and filling their treasuries.

22† "The LORD begot me, the beginning of
      his works,
      the forerunner of his deeds of long
      ago;*

23 From of old I was formed,†
      at the first, before the earth.*

24† When there were no deeps I was brought
      forth,
      when there were no fountains or
      springs of water;

25 Before the mountains were settled into
      place,
      before the hills, I was brought forth;

26 When the earth and the fields were not
      yet made,
      nor the first clods of the world.

27 When he established the heavens, there
      was I,*
      when he marked out the vault over
      the face of the deep;

28 When he made firm the skies above,
      when he fixed fast the springs of the
      deep;

29 When he set for the sea its limit,
      so that the waters should not
      transgress his command;
  When he fixed the foundations of earth,

30     then was I beside him as artisan;†*
  I was his delight day by day,

---

**8:5** *Naive ones…fools:* see note on 1:4.

**8:7–8** The truth and sincerity of wisdom are absolute because they are of divine origin. They can neither deceive nor tolerate deception. The intelligent understand and accept this. "Straight" and "crooked" in Hebrew and English are metaphors for true, trustworthy and false, deceitful.

**8:14** What is here predicated of Wisdom is elsewhere attributed to God (Jb 12:13–16).

**8:22–31** Wisdom is of divine origin. She is represented as existing before all things (vv. 22–26), when God planned and created the universe, adorning it with beauty and variety, and establishing its wonderful order (vv. 27–30). The purpose of the two cosmogonies (vv. 22–26 and 27–31) is to ground Wisdom's claims. The first cosmogony emphasizes that she was born before all else (and so deserving of honor) and the second underscores that she was with the Lord during the creation of the universe. The pre-existence of Woman Wisdom with God is developed in Sir 24 and in New Testament hymns to Christ, especially in Jn 1 and Col 1:15–20.

**8:23** *Formed:* since the other verbs of the origin of Wisdom in these verses describe birth, it is likely that the somewhat uncer-

tain verb is to be understood of birth as in Ps 139:13.

**8:24–26** Perhaps the formless mass from which God created the heavens and the earth; cf. Gn 1:1–2; 2:4–6.

**8:30** *Artisan:* the translation of the Hebrew word *'āmôn* has been controverted since antiquity. There have been three main opinions: (1) artisan; (2) trustworthy (friend); (3) ward, nursling. The most likely explanation is that *'āmôn* is artisan, related to Akkadian *ummānu,* legendary sages and heroes who brought divine gifts and culture to the human race. *I was his delight:* the chiastic or ABBA structure of vv. 30–31 unifies the four lines and underscores the analogy between Woman Wisdom's intimate relation to the Lord and her intimate relation to human beings, i.e., "delight" + "playing" parallels "playing" + "delight." She is God's friend and intimate and invites human beings to a similar relationship to God through her.

---

**8:11** Prv 3:15; Wis 7:8.
**8:13** Prv 6:16–17; 16:5.
**8:18** Prv 3:16.
**8:19** Prv 3:14.
**8:22** Wis 9:9; Sir 1:1; 24:9.
**8:23** Sir 1:4.
**8:27** Prv 3:19; Sir 24:4–5.
**8:30** Wis 9:9.

playing before him all the while,

31 Playing over the whole of his earth,
   having my delight with human beings.

32† Now, children, listen to me;
   happy are they who keep my ways.

33 Listen to instruction and grow wise,
   do not reject it!

34 Happy the one who listens to me,
   attending daily at my gates,
   keeping watch at my doorposts;

35 For whoever finds me finds life,*
   and wins favor from the LORD;

36 But those who pass me by do violence
   to themselves;
   all who hate me love death."

## The Two Women Invite Passersby to Their Banquets†

### Woman Wisdom Issues Her Invitation

**9** ¹ Wisdom has built her house,†
   she has set up her seven columns;

2 She has prepared her meat, mixed her
   wine,
   yes, she has spread her table.

3 She has sent out her maidservants; she
   calls†
   from the heights out over the city:*

4 "Let whoever is naive turn in here;
   to any who lack sense I say,

5 Come, eat of my food,

and drink of the wine I have mixed!

6 Forsake foolishness that you may live;†
   advance in the way of understanding."

### Miscellaneous Aphorisms

7 Whoever corrects the arrogant earns
   insults;
   and whoever reproves the wicked
   incurs opprobrium.

8 Do not reprove the arrogant, lest they
   hate you;
   reprove the wise, and they will love
   you.*

9 Instruct the wise, and they become still
   wiser;
   teach the just, and they advance in
   learning.

10 The beginning of wisdom is fear of the
   LORD,
   and knowledge of the Holy One is
   understanding.*

11 For by me your days will be multiplied
   and the years of your life increased.*

12 If you are wise, wisdom is to your
   advantage;
   if you are arrogant, you alone shall
   bear it.

### Woman Folly Issues Her Invitation

13† Woman Folly is raucous,*
   utterly foolish; she knows nothing.

---

**8:32–36** The final appeal of Woman Wisdom to her disciples is similar to the appeal of the father in 7:24–27.
**9:1–6, 13–18** Wisdom and folly are represented as women, each inviting people to her banquet. Wisdom's banquet symbolizes joy and closeness to God. Unstable and senseless Folly furnishes stolen bread and water of deceit and vice that bring death to her guests. The opposition between wisdom and folly was stated at the beginning of chaps. 1–9 (folly in 1:8–19 and wisdom in 1:20–33) and is maintained throughout, down to this last chapter.
In comparable literature, gods might celebrate their sovereign by building a palace and inviting the other gods to come to a banquet and celebrate with them. Presumably, Woman Wisdom is celebrating her grandeur (just described in chap. 8); her grand house is a symbol for her status as the Lord's friend. In order to enter the sacred building and take part in the banquet ("eat of my food"), guests must leave aside their old ways ("forsake foolishness").
Verses 7–12 are unrelated to the two invitations to the banquet. They appear to be based on chap. 1, especially on 1:1–7, 22. The Greek version has added a number of verses after v. 12 and v. 18. In the confusion, 9:11 seems to have been displaced from its original position after 9:6. It has been restored to its original place in the text.
**9:1** *House*: house has a symbolic meaning. Woman Wisdom encourages marital fidelity (2:16–19; 5; 6:20–35; 7), which builds up a household (cf. chap. 5). Some scholars propose that an actual seven-pillared house is referred to, but so far none have been unearthed by archaeologists. Seven may simply connote completeness—a great house.
Some scholars see a connection between the woman's house

here and the woman's house in the final poem (31:10–31). In chap. 9, she invites the young man to enter her house and feast, i.e., to marry her. Chapter 31 shows what happens to the man who marries her; he has a house and enjoys "life" understood as consisting of a suitable wife, children, wealth, and honor.
**9:3** *She calls*: i.e., invites; this is done indirectly through her maidservants, but the text could also mean that Wisdom herself publicly proclaims her invitation.
**9:6** *That you may live*: life in Proverbs is this-worldly, consisting in fearing God or doing one's duty toward God, enjoying health and long life, possessing wealth, good reputation, and a family. Such a life cannot be attained without God's help. Hence Wisdom speaks not of life simply but of life with her; the guest is to live in Wisdom's house.
**9:13–18** Woman Folly is the mirror image of Woman Wisdom. Both make identical invitations but only one of the offers is trustworthy. Their hearers must discern which is the true offer. She is depicted with traits of the adulterous woman in 2:16–19; chap. 5; 6:20–35; chap. 7. Woman Folly is restless (cf. 7:11), her path leads to the underworld (2:18; 5:5; 7:27), and she is ignorant (5:6). In this final scene, she appears in single combat with her great nemesis, Woman Wisdom. Though the invitations of the two women appear at first hearing to be the same, they differ profoundly. Wisdom demands that her guests reject their ignorance, whereas Woman Folly trades on their ignorance.

---

**8:35** Prv 3:13–18; 4:22.  Ps 111:10; Sir 1:16.
**9:3** Prv 8:1–2.  **9:11** Prv 3:2; 16:4, 10;
**9:8** Sir 10:27.  10:27.
**9:10** Prv 1:7; Jb 28:28;  **9:13–18** Prv 7:7–27.

PRV

14 　She sits at the door of her house
　　　　upon a seat on the city heights,
15 　Calling to passersby
　　　　as they go on their way straight ahead:
16 　"Let those who are naive turn in here,
　　　　to those who lack sense I say,
17 　Stolen water is sweet,
　　　　and bread taken secretly is pleasing!" †
18 　Little do they know that the shades are
　　　　there,
　　　　that her guests are in the depths of
　　　　Sheol! †

## III. FIRST SOLOMONIC COLLECTION OF SAYINGS†

**10** ¹The Proverbs of Solomon:
　　A wise son gives his father joy,
　　　　but a foolish son is a grief to his
　　　　mother. †*
2 　Ill-gotten treasures profit nothing,
　　　　but justice saves from death. †*
3 　The LORD does not let the just go hungry,
　　　　but the craving of the wicked he
　　　　thwarts. †
4 　The slack hand impoverishes,
　　　　but the busy hand brings riches. *
5 　A son who gathers in summer is a credit;
　　　　a son who slumbers during harvest, a
　　　　disgrace.

6 　Blessings are for the head of the just;
　　　　but the mouth of the wicked conceals
　　　　violence. †
7 　The memory of the just serves as
　　　　blessing,
　　　　but the name of the wicked will rot. †
8 　A wise heart accepts commands,
　　　　but a babbling fool will be
　　　　overthrown. †
9 　Whoever walks honestly walks securely,
　　　　but one whose ways are crooked will
　　　　fare badly.
10 　One who winks at a fault causes trouble,
　　　　but one who frankly reproves
　　　　promotes peace.
11 　The mouth of the just is a fountain of
　　　　life,
　　　　but the mouth of the wicked conceals
　　　　violence.
12 　Hatred stirs up disputes,
*　　　but love covers all offenses. †
13 　On the lips of the intelligent is found
　　　　wisdom,
　　　　but a rod for the back of one without
　　　　sense. †
14 　The wise store up knowledge,
　　　　but the mouth of a fool is imminent
　　　　ruin.
15 　The wealth of the rich is their strong city;
　　　　the ruin of the poor is their poverty. †

---

**9:17** "Stolen water" seems to refer to adultery, for "water" in 5:15–17 refers to the wife's sexuality; "stolen" refers to stealing the sexuality belonging to another's household. "Secret" evokes the furtive meeting of the wife and the youth in chap. 7.

**9:18** The banquet chamber of Folly is a tomb from which no one who enters it is released; cf. 7:27. *Shades*: the Rephaim, the inhabitants of the underworld.

**10:1–22:16** The Proverbs of Solomon are a collection of three hundred and seventy-five proverbs on a wide variety of subjects. No overall arrangement is discernible, but there are many clusters of sayings related by vocabulary and theme. One thread running through the whole is the relationship of the "son," the disciple, to the parents, and its effect upon the house(hold). In chaps. 10–14 almost all the proverbs are antithetical; "the righteous" and "the wicked" (ethical), "the wise" and "the foolish" (sapiential), and "the devout, the pious" and "the irreverent" (religious). Chapters 15–22 have fewer sharp antitheses. The sayings are generally witty, often indirect, and are rich in irony and paradox.

**10:1** The opening saying ties the whole collection to the first section, for "son," "father," and "mother" evoke the opening line of the first instruction, "Hear, my son, your father's instruction, and reject not your mother's teaching." The son is the subject of parental exhortation throughout chaps. 1–9. This is the first of many sayings on domestic happiness or unhappiness, between parents and children (e.g., 15:20; 17:21) and between husband and wife (e.g., 12:4; 14:1). Founding or maintaining a household is an important metaphor in the book.

Adult children represented the family (headed by the oldest married male) to the outside world. Foolishness, i.e., malicious ignorance, brought dishonor to the parents and the family.

**10:2** *Death*: untimely, premature, or sorrowful. The word "death" can have other overtones (see Wis 1:15).

**10:3** The last of the three introductory sayings in the collection, which emphasize, respectively, the sapiential (v. 1), ethical (v. 2), and religious (v. 3) dimensions of wisdom. In this saying, God will not allow the appetite of the righteous to go unfulfilled. The appetite of hunger is singled out; it stands for all the appetites.

**10:6** This saying, like several others in the chapter, plays on the different senses of the verb "to cover." As in English, "to cover" can mean to fill (as in Is 60:2) and to conceal (as in Jb 16:18). Colon B can be read either "violence *fills* the mouth (= head) of the wicked" or "the mouth of the wicked *conceals* violence." The ambiguity is intentional; the proverb is meant to be read both ways.

**10:7** The name of the righteous continues to be used after their death in blessings such as "May you be as blessed as Abraham," but the wicked, being enemies of God, do not live on in anyone's memory. Their names rot with their bodies.

**10:8** The wise take in instruction from their teachers but those who expel or pour out folly through their words will themselves be expelled.

**10:12** *Love covers all offenses*: a favorite maxim in the New Testament; cf. 1 Cor 13:7; Jas 5:20; 1 Pt 4:8. Cf. also Prv 17:9.

**10:13** An unusual juxtaposition of "lips" and "back." Those who have no wisdom on their lips (words) are fated to feel a punishing rod on their back.

**10:15** An observation rather than a moral evaluation of wealth and poverty; but cf. 18:10–11.

---

**10:1** Prv 1:1; 15:20; 17:25;　　　　**10:4** Prv 6:11; 12:24; 13:4;
　　19:13; 25:1; 29:15.　　　　　　　　20:13; 28:19.
**10:2** Prv 11:4, 6.　　　　　　　　　**10:12** 1 Cor 13:4–7; 1 Pt
　　　　　　　　　　　　　　　　　　　　4:8.

16 The labor of the just leads to life,
 the gains of the wicked, to futility.†*

17 Whoever follows instruction is in the
 path to life,
 but whoever disregards reproof goes
 astray.*

18 Whoever conceals hatred has lying lips,
 and whoever spreads slander is a fool.

19 Where words are many, sin is not
 wanting;
 but those who restrain their lips do
 well.*

20 Choice silver is the tongue of the just;
 the heart of the wicked is of little
 worth.

21 The lips of the just nourish many,
 but fools die for want of sense.†

22 It is the LORD's blessing that brings
 wealth,*
 and no effort can substitute for it.†

23 Crime is the entertainment of the fool;
 but wisdom is for the person of
 understanding.

24 What the wicked fear will befall them,
 but the desire of the just will be
 granted.

25 When the tempest passes, the wicked are
 no more;
 but the just are established forever.

26 As vinegar to the teeth, and smoke to
 the eyes,
 are sluggards to those who send them.

27 Fear of the LORD prolongs life,
 but the years of the wicked are cut
 short.*

28 The hope of the just brings joy,
 but the expectation of the wicked
 perishes.†

29 The LORD is a stronghold to those who
 walk honestly,
 downfall for evildoers.

30 The just will never be disturbed,
 but the wicked will not abide in the
 land.

31 The mouth of the just yields wisdom,
 but the perverse tongue will be cut off.

32 The lips of the just know favor,
 but the mouth of the wicked,
 perversion.†

# 11

1 False scales are an abomination to
 the LORD,
 but an honest weight, his delight.†*

2 When pride comes, disgrace comes;
 but with the humble is wisdom.†

3 The honesty of the upright guides them;
 the faithless are ruined by their
 duplicity.

4 Wealth is useless on a day of wrath,†*
 but justice saves from death.

5 The justice of the honest makes their
 way straight,
 but by their wickedness the wicked
 fall.†*

6 The justice of the upright saves them,
 but the faithless are caught in their
 own intrigue.

7 When a person dies, hope is destroyed;*
 expectation pinned on wealth is
 destroyed.†

PRV

---

†

**10:16** Wages are a metaphor for reward and punishment. The Hebrew word does not mean "sin" here but falling short, a meaning that is frequent in Proverbs. Cf. Rom 6:1: "But what profit did you get then from the things of which you are now ashamed? For the end of those things is death."

**10:21** The wise by their words maintain others in life whereas the foolish cannot keep themselves from sin that leads to premature death.

**10:22** Human industry is futile without divine approval; cf. Ps 127:1–2; Mt 6:25–34.

**10:28** The thought is elliptical. Joy comes from fulfillment of one's plans, which the righteous can count on. The opposite of joy thus is not sadness but unfulfillment ("perishes").

**10:32** The word used for "favor" is favor shown by an authority (God or the king), not favor shown by a peer. A righteous person's words create a climate of favor and acceptance, whereas crooked words will not gain acceptance. In Hebrew as in English, straight and crooked are metaphors for good and wicked.

**11:1** The word pair "abomination" and "delight" (= acceptable) to God is common in Proverbs. Originally the language of ritual, the words came to be applied to whatever pleases or displeases God (cf. also 11:20). False weights were a constant problem even though weights were standardized. Cf. 20:23; Hos 12:8; Am 8:5.

**11:2** Disgrace is the very opposite of what the proud so ardently want. Those who do not demand their due receive wisdom.

**11:4** Cf. note on 10:2. A day of wrath is an unforeseen disaster (even death). Only one's relationship to God, which makes one righteous, is of any help on such a day.

**11:5** In Hebrew as in English, "way" means the course of one's life; similarly, "straight" and "crooked" are metaphors for morally straightforward and for bad, deviant, perverted.

**11:7** An ancient scribe added "wicked" to person in colon A, for the statement that hope ends at death seemed to deny life after death. The saying, however, is not concerned with life after death but with the fact that in the face of death all hopes based on one's own resources are vain. The aphorism is the climax of the preceding six verses; human resources cannot overcome mortality (cf. Ps 49:13).

---

*

**10:16** Prv 11:18–19.   14:27.
**10:17** Prv 15:10.   **11:1** Prv 16:11; 20:10; Lv
**10:19** Prv 17:27; Sir 20:17;  19:35–36.
 Jas 1:19.   **11:4** Prv 10:2.
**10:22** Sir 11:22.   **11:5** Prv 28:18.
**10:27** Prv 3:2; 4:10; 9:11;  **11:7** Prv 10:28; Wis 3:18.

8 The just are rescued from a tight spot,
  but the wicked fall into it instead.
9 By a word the impious ruin their
    neighbors, *
  but through their knowledge the just
    are rescued. †
10 When the just prosper, the city rejoices; *
  when the wicked perish, there is
    jubilation.
11 Through the blessing of the upright the
    city is exalted,
  but through the mouth of the wicked
    it is overthrown.
12 Whoever reviles a neighbor lacks sense,
  but the intelligent keep silent.
13 One who slanders reveals secrets, *
  but a trustworthy person keeps a
    confidence.
14 For lack of guidance a people falls;
  security lies in many counselors. *
15 Harm will come to anyone going surety
    for another, *
  but whoever hates giving pledges is
    secure. †
16 A gracious woman gains esteem,
  and ruthless men gain wealth. †
17 Kindly people benefit themselves,
  but the merciless harm themselves.
18 The wicked make empty profits,
  but those who sow justice have a sure
    reward. *
19 Justice leads toward life,
  but pursuit of evil, toward death.
20 The crooked in heart are an
    abomination to the LORD,
  but those who walk blamelessly are
    his delight. †

21 Be assured, the wicked shall not go
    unpunished,
  but the offspring of the just shall
    escape.
22 Like a golden ring in a swine's snout
  is a beautiful woman without
    judgment. †
23 The desire of the just ends only in good;
  the expectation of the wicked is
    wrath.
24 One person is lavish yet grows still
    richer;
  another is too sparing, yet is the
    poorer. †
25 Whoever confers benefits will be amply
    enriched,
  and whoever refreshes others will be
    refreshed.
26 Whoever hoards grain, the people curse,
  but blessings are on the head of one
    who distributes it!
27 Those who seek the good seek favor,
  but those who pursue evil will have
    evil come upon them. †
28 Those who trust in their riches will fall,
  but like green leaves the just will
    flourish. *
29 Those who trouble their household
    inherit the wind,
  and fools become slaves to the wise of
    heart.
30 The fruit of justice is a tree of life,
  and one who takes lives is a sage. †
31 If the just are recompensed on the
    earth,
  how much more the wicked and the
    sinner! †*

---

† **11:9** What the wicked express harms others; what the righteous leave unsaid protects. Verses 9–14 are related in theme: the effect of good and bad people, especially their words, on their community.

**11:15** Proverbs is opposed to providing surety for another's loan (see note on 6:1–5) and expresses this view throughout the book.

**11:16** Wealth and esteem are good things in Proverbs, but the means for acquiring them are flawed. As precious gifts, they must be granted, not taken. The esteem of others that depends on beauty is as fleeting as beauty itself (cf. 31:30) and the wealth acquired by aggressive behavior lasts only as long as one has physical strength.

**11:20** The terminology of ritual (acceptable and unacceptable sacrifice, "abomination" and "delight") is applied to human conduct as in v. 1. The whole of human life is under divine scrutiny, not just ritual.

**11:22** Ear and nose rings were common jewelry for women. A humorous saying on the priority of wisdom over beauty in choosing a wife.

**11:24** A paradox: spending leads to more wealth.

**11:27** The saying is about seeking one thing and finding

another. Striving for good leads to acceptance by God; seeking evil means only that trouble will come. The same Hebrew word means evil and trouble.

**11:30** Most translations emend Hebrew "wise person" in colon B on the basis of the Greek and Syriac translations to "violence" (similar in spelling), because the verb "to take a life" is a Hebrew idiom for "to kill" (as also in English). The emendation is unnecessary, however, for the saying deliberately plays on the odd meaning: the one who takes lives is not the violent but the wise person, for the wise have a profound influence upon life. There is a similar wordplay in 29:10.

**11:31** The saying is not about life after death; "on the earth" means life in the present world. The meaning is that divine judgment is exercised on all human action, even the best. The thought should strike terror into the hearts of habitual wrongdoers.

---

**11:9** Prv 29:5.
**11:10** Prv 28:12; 29:2.
**11:13** Prv 20:19.
**11:14** Prv 15:22; 20:18;
24:6.
**11:15** Prv 6:1–2.
**11:18** Prv 10:16.
**11:28** Ps 52:9–10.
**11:31** 1 Pt 4:18.

# 12

¹ Whoever loves discipline loves knowledge,
  but whoever hates reproof is stupid. †*

2 A good person wins favor from the LORD,
  but the schemer he condemns. †

3 No one is made secure by wickedness,
  but the root of the just will never be disturbed. †

4 A woman of worth is the crown of her husband, *
  but a disgraceful one is like rot in his bones. †

5 The plans of the just are right;
  the designs of the wicked are deceit. †

6 The words of the wicked are a deadly ambush,
  but the speech of the upright saves them. †

7 Overthrow the wicked and they are no more,
  but the house of the just stands firm.

8 For their good sense people are praised,
  but the perverse of heart are despised. †

9 Better to be slighted and have a servant
  than put on airs and lack bread. *

10 The just take care of their livestock,
  but the compassion of the wicked is cruel. †

11 Those who till their own land have food in plenty,
  but those who engage in idle pursuits lack sense. †*

12 A wicked person desires the catch of evil people,
  but the root of the righteous will bear fruit. †

13 By the sin of their lips the wicked are ensnared,
  but the just escape from a tight spot.

14 From the fruit of their mouths people have their fill of good, *
  and the works of their hands come back upon them. †

15 The way of fools is right in their own eyes,
  but those who listen to advice are the wise.

16 Fools immediately show their anger,
  but the shrewd conceal contempt.

17 Whoever speaks honestly testifies truly,
  but the deceitful make lying witnesses. †*

18 The babble of some people is like sword thrusts,
  but the tongue of the wise is healing.

19 Truthful lips endure forever,
  the lying tongue, for only a moment. †

20 Deceit is in the heart of those who plot evil,
  but those who counsel peace have joy.

21 No harm befalls the just,
  but the wicked are overwhelmed with misfortune.

22 Lying lips are an abomination to the LORD, *
  but those who are truthful, his delight.

---

wicked will pay the price for their self-centeredness and cruelty.

**12:1** Discipline in Proverbs is both doctrine and training. The path to wisdom includes obedience to teachers and parents, acceptance of the community's traditions.

**12:2** The antithesis is between the good person who, by reason of that goodness, already has divine acceptance, and the wicked person who, despite great effort, gains only condemnation.

**12:3** Human beings are described as "made secure" in Jb 21:8; Ps 101:7; 102:29. "Root" in the context means enduring to succeeding generations, as in Mal 3:19 and Jb 8:17.

**12:4** In Proverbs a crown is the result and sign of wise conduct. A good wife is a public sign of the husband's shrewd judgment and divine blessing (crown), whereas a bad wife brings him inner pain (rot in the bones).

**12:5** The opposite of "just" is not injustice but "deceit." The wicked will be deceived in their plans in the sense that their planning will not succeed.

**12:6** Words are a favorite theme of Proverbs. The words of the wicked effect harm to others whereas the words of the righteous protect themselves.

**12:8** The heart, the seat of intelligence, will eventually be revealed in the actions that people do, either for praise or for blame.

**12:10** The righteous are sympathetically aware of the needs of their livestock and prosper from their herd's good health. The

**12:11** The second line clarifies the first: idleness will give one plenty of nothing. "Lacking sense" is a common phrase for fools.

**12:12** A difficult, possibly corrupt saying, but there is no good alternative to the Hebrew text. The wicked desire what the malevolent have captured or killed, but their actions will go for naught because they invite punishment. The righteous, on the other hand, will bear fruit.

**12:14** The saying contrasts words and deeds. "Fruit" here is not what one normally eats, as in 1:31; 8:19; 31:16, 31, but the consequences of one's actions. In the second line the things that issue from one's hands (one's deeds) come back to one in recompense or punishment. Prv 13:2a and 18:20 are variants. Cf. Mt 7:17; Gal 6:8.

**12:17** What is the rule of thumb for judging legal testimony? Look to the ordinary conduct and daily speech of a witness.

**12:19** The saying has a double meaning: lies are quickly found out whereas truthful statements endure; truth-tellers, being favored by God, live long lives, whereas liars invite punishment.

---

**12:1** Prv 15:5, 10; Sir 21:6.
**12:4** Prv 31:10; Sir 21:1, 16.
**12:9** Sir 10:26.
**12:11** Prv 28:19; Sir 20:27.
**12:14** Prv 13:2; 18:20.
**12:17** Prv 14:5.
**12:22** Prv 6:17.

23 The shrewd conceal knowledge,
   but the hearts of fools proclaim folly.†

24 The diligent hand will govern,
   but sloth makes for forced labor.*

25 Worry weighs down the heart,
   but a kind word gives it joy.*

26 The just act as guides to their neighbors,
   but the way of the wicked leads them
      astray.

27 Sloth does not catch its prey,
   but the wealth of the diligent is
      splendid.

28 In the path of justice is life,
   but the way of abomination leads to
      death.

# 13 1 A wise son loves correction,
   but the scoffer heeds no rebuke.†

2 From the fruit of the mouth one enjoys
      good things,*
   but from the throat of the treacherous
      comes violence.†

3 Those who guard their mouths preserve
      themselves;†
   those who open wide their lips bring
      ruin.*

4 The appetite of the sluggard craves but
      has nothing,
   but the appetite of the diligent is
      amply satisfied.

5 The just hate deceitful words,
   but the wicked are odious and
      disgraceful.

6 Justice guards one who walks honestly,

but sin leads the wicked astray.*

7 One acts rich but has nothing;
   another acts poor but has great
      wealth.†

8 People's riches serve as ransom for their
      lives,
   but the poor do not even hear a
      threat.†

9 The light of the just gives joy,
   but the lamp† of the wicked goes
      out.*

10 The stupid sow discord by their
      insolence,
   but wisdom is with those who take
      counsel.

11 Wealth won quickly dwindles away,
   but gathered little by little, it grows.*

12 Hope deferred makes the heart sick,
   but a wish fulfilled is a tree of life.†

13 Whoever despises the word must pay for
      it,†
   but whoever reveres the command
      will be rewarded.

14 The teaching of the wise is a fountain of
      life,
   turning one from the snares of death.

15 Good sense brings favor,
   but the way of the faithless is their
      ruin.†

16 The shrewd always act prudently
   but the foolish parade folly.†

17 A wicked messenger brings on disaster,
   but a trustworthy envoy is a healing
      remedy.

---

† 12:23 "Knowledge" here is "what one knows, has in one's heart," not knowledge in general. Fools reveal all they have stored in their heart and it naturally turns out to be folly. Revealing and concealing are constant themes in Proverbs.
13:1 Another in the series on the household, this one on the relation of parents and children. See under 10:1. The scoffer in Proverbs condemns discipline and thus can never become wise. Wise adult children advertise to the community what they received from their parents, for children become wise through a dialectical process involving the parents. A foolish adult child witnesses to foolish parents.
13:2 One's mouth normally eats food from outside, but in the moral life, things are reversed: one eats from the fruit of one's mouth, i.e., one experiences the consequences of one's own actions. Since the mouth of the treacherous is filled with violence, one must assume that they will some day endure violence.
13:3 Preserve themselves: in Hebrew, literally to preserve the throat area, the moist breathing center of one's body, thus "life," "soul," or "self." There is wordplay: if you guard your mouth (= words) you guard your "soul." Fools, on the other hand, do not guard but open their lips and disaster strikes. A near duplicate is 21:23.
13:7 Appearances can be deceiving; possessions do not always reveal the true state of a person.

13:8 Related to v. 7. Possessions enable the wealthy to pay ransom but the poor are "protected" by lack of possessions: they never hear the threat of the pursuer. Cf. the use of the word "threat" in Is 30:17.
13:9 Light...lamp: symbols of life and prosperity; cf. 4:18–19.
13:12 "Tree of life" occurs in Gn 2–3, Prv 3:18; 11:30; 13:12; 15:4, and Rev 2:7; 22:2, 14, 19. It provides food and healing.
13:13 Must pay for it: lit., "is pledge to it," i.e., just as one who has pledged or provided surety for another's loan is obligated to that pledge, so one is not free of a command until one performs it.
13:15 As the behavior of the wise wins them favor that increases their prosperity, like Abigail with David in 1 Sm 25, so the way (= conduct) of the faithless ruins their lives.
13:16 Like 12:23 and 15:2, 3, the saying is about revealing and concealing. The wise reveal their wisdom in their actions whereas fools "parade," spread out their folly for all to see. The verb is used of vendors spreading their wares and of birds spreading their wings.

---

* 12:24 Prv 10:4; 13:4.          13:6 Prv 11:3, 5–6.
12:25 Prv 15:13; 17:22.          13:9 Prv 24:20.
13:2 Prv 12:14; 18:20.           13:11 Prv 28:20, 22.
13:3 Prv 18:7; 21:23.

18 Poverty and shame befall those who let
    go of discipline,
    but those who hold on to reproof
    receive honor.†
19 Desire fulfilled delights the soul,
    but turning from evil is an
    abomination to fools.
20 Walk with the wise and you become wise,
    but the companion of fools fares
    badly.*
21 Misfortune pursues sinners,
    but the just shall be recompensed
    with good.
22 The good leave an inheritance to their
    children's children,
    but the wealth of the sinner is stored
    up for the just.
23 The tillage of the poor yields abundant
    food,
    but possessions are swept away for
    lack of justice.†
24 Whoever spares the rod hates the child,
    but whoever loves will apply
    discipline.*
25 When the just eat, their hunger is
    appeased;
    but the belly of the wicked suffers
    want.

14 ¹Wisdom builds her house,
    but Folly tears hers down with her
    own hands.†
2 Those who walk uprightly fear the LORD,
    but those who are devious in their
    ways spurn him.
3 In the mouth of the fool is a rod for
    pride,
    but the lips of the wise preserve them.
4 Where there are no oxen, the crib is
    clean;

but abundant crops come through the
    strength of the bull.†
5 A trustworthy witness does not lie,
    but one who spouts lies makes a lying
    witness.†*
6 The scoffer seeks wisdom in vain,
    but knowledge is easy for the
    intelligent.
7 Go from the face of the fool;
    you get no knowledge from such lips.
8 The wisdom of the shrewd enlightens
    their way,
    but the folly of fools is deceit.†
9 The wicked scorn a guilt offering,
    but the upright find acceptance.
10 The heart knows its own bitterness,
    and its joy no stranger shares.†
11 The house of the wicked will be
    destroyed,
    but the tent of the upright will
    flourish.†*
12 Sometimes a way seems right,
    but the end of it leads to death!*
13 Even in laughter the heart may be sad,
    and the end of joy may be sorrow.
14 From their own ways turncoats are
    sated,
    from their own actions, the loyal.
15 The naive believe everything,
    but the shrewd watch their steps.†
16 The wise person is cautious and turns
    from evil;
    the fool is reckless and gets
    embroiled.
17 The quick-tempered make fools of
    themselves,
    and schemers are hated.
18 The simple have folly as an adornment,
    but the shrewd wear knowledge as a
    crown.†

down retribution.

**13:18** The saying plays on letting go and holding on. Wisdom consists in not rejecting discipline and being open to the comments of others, even if they are reproving comments.
**13:23** An observation on the poor. The lands of the poor are as fertile as anyone's, for nature does not discriminate against them. Their problem is lack of justice, which puts their harvest at risk from unscrupulous human beings.
**14:1** The relationship between Wisdom, personified as a woman, and building a house is a constant theme. As elsewhere, the book here warns against the wrong woman and praises the right woman.
**14:4** If one has no animals, one does not have the burden of keeping the crib full, but without them one will have no crops to fill the barn. Colon B reverses the sense of colon A and also reverses the consonants of *bar* ("clean") to *rab* ("abundant").
**14:5** On discerning the truthfulness of witnesses; see 12:17.
**14:8** Wisdom enables the shrewd to know their path is right but folly leads fools on the wrong path ("deceit"), which calls

**14:10** The heart in Proverbs is where a person's sense impressions are stored and reflected upon. It is thus one's most personal and individual part. One's sorrows and joys (= the full range of emotions) cannot be shared fully with another. Verse 13 expresses the same individuality of the human person.
**14:11** The traditional fixed pair "house" and "tent" is used to express the paradox that a house can be less secure than a tent if there is no justice.
**14:15** The naive gullibly rely on others' words whereas the shrewd watch their own steps.
**14:18** The inner quality of a person, simple or wise, will eventually be revealed.

**13:20** Sir 6:34; 8:8, 17.      **14:5** Prv 12:17.
**13:24** Prv 19:18; 22:15;       **14:11** Prv 3:33; 12:7; 15:25.
23:13–14; 29:15; Sir             **14:12** Prv 16:25.
30:1, 8–13.

19 The malicious bow down before the
    good,
       and the wicked, at the gates of the
          just.
20 Even by their neighbors the poor are
    despised,
       but a rich person's friends are many.*
21 Whoever despises the hungry comes up
    short,
       but happy the one who is kind to the
          poor! †
22 Do not those who plan evil go astray?
       But those who plan good win
          steadfast loyalty.
23 In all labor there is profit,
       but mere talk tends only to loss.
24 The crown of the wise is wealth;
       the diadem of fools is folly.
25 The truthful witness saves lives,
       but whoever utters lies is a betrayer.
26 The fear of the LORD is a strong defense,
       a refuge even for one's children.
27 The fear of the LORD is a fountain of life,
       turning one from the snares of death.
28 A multitude of subjects is the glory of
    the king;
       but if his people are few, a prince is
          ruined.
29 Long-suffering results in great wisdom;
       a short temper raises folly high. † *
30 A tranquil mind gives life to the body,
       but jealousy rots the bones.
31 Those who oppress the poor revile their
    Maker,
       but those who are kind to the needy
          honor him. *
32 The wicked are overthrown by their
    wickedness,
       but the just find a refuge in their
          integrity.

33 Wisdom can remain silent in the
    discerning heart,
       but among fools she must make
          herself known. † *
34 Justice exalts a nation,
       but sin is a people's disgrace. †
35 The king favors the skillful servant,
       but the shameless one incurs his
          wrath.

# 15

1 † A mild answer turns back wrath, *
   but a harsh word stirs up anger. †
2 The tongue of the wise pours out
    knowledge,
       but the mouth of fools spews folly.
3 The eyes of the LORD are in every place,
       keeping watch on the evil and the
          good.
4 A soothing tongue is a tree of life,
       but a perverse one breaks the spirit.
5 The fool spurns a father's instruction,
       but whoever heeds reproof is
          prudent. † *
6 In the house of the just there are ample
    resources,
       but the harvest of the wicked is in
          peril.
7 The lips of the wise spread knowledge,
       but the heart of fools is not steadfast. †
8 The sacrifice of the wicked is an
    abomination to the LORD, *
       but the prayer of the upright is his
          delight.
9 The way of the wicked is an
    abomination to the LORD,
       but he loves one who pursues
          justice. *
10 Discipline seems bad to those going
    astray;
       one who hates reproof will die. †

---

†
**14:21** The paradox is that anyone who spurns the hungry will lack something, but anyone who shows mercy (presumably by giving to the poor) will gain prosperity.
**14:29** A series of puns on short and long; lit., "long of nostrils (idiom for "patient"), large in wisdom, / short in breath (idiom for "impatient"), makes folly tall."
**14:33** Wisdom can remain silent in a wise person as a welcome friend. But it must speak out among fools, for the dissonance is so strong.
**14:34** The rare noun "disgrace" occurs elsewhere only in Lv 20:17. In measuring the greatness of a nation, one is tempted to consider territory, wealth, history, but the most important criterion is its relationship to God ("justice").
**15:1–7** These verses form a section beginning and ending with the topic of words.
**15:1** Paradoxically, where words are concerned soft is powerful and hard is ineffective.

**15:5** One becomes wise by keeping and foolish by rejecting. One must accept the tradition of the community.
**15:7** "Lips" and "heart" are a fixed pair, in Proverbs signifying, respectively, expression and source. The wise disseminate what they have in their heart, but the wicked are unsound even in the source of their words, their hearts.
**15:10** Discipline, always a good thing in Proverbs, seems bad to those deliberately wandering from justice.

---

*
**14:20** Prv 19:4, 7; Sir 6:8,     **15:1** Prv 25:15; Sir 6:5.
      12.                           **15:5** Prv 12:1; 13:18.
**14:29** Prv 16:32; 19:11; Jas     **15:8** Prv 21:27; Eccl 4:17;
      1:19.                               Is 1:11–15.
**14:31** Prv 17:5.                 **15:9** Prv 11:20; 21:21.
**14:33** Prv 1:22; 8:1.

<sup>11</sup> Sheol and Abaddon† lie open before the
    LORD;
    how much more the hearts of
        mortals!
<sup>12</sup> Scoffers do not love reproof;
    to the wise they will not go.
<sup>13</sup> A glad heart lights up the face,
    but an anguished heart breaks the
        spirit. *
<sup>14</sup> The discerning heart seeks knowledge,
    but the mouth of fools feeds on
        folly. †
<sup>15</sup> All the days of the poor are evil,
    but a good heart is a continual feast. †
<sup>16</sup>† Better a little with fear of the LORD
    than a great fortune with anxiety.
<sup>17</sup> Better a dish of herbs where love is
    than a fatted ox and hatred with it.
<sup>18</sup> The ill-tempered stir up strife, *
    but the patient settle disputes.
<sup>19</sup> The way of the sluggard is like a thorn
        hedge,
    but the path of the diligent is a
        highway.
<sup>20</sup> A wise son gives his father joy,
    but a fool despises his mother. *
<sup>21</sup> Folly is joy† to the senseless,
    but the person of understanding goes
        the straight way.
<sup>22</sup> Plans fail when there is no counsel,
    but they succeed when advisers are
        many. †*
<sup>23</sup> One has joy from an apt response;
    a word in season, how good it is! †*
<sup>24</sup> The path of life leads upward for the
        prudent,

    turning them from Sheol below. †
<sup>25</sup> The LORD pulls down the house of the
        proud,
    but preserves intact the widow's
        landmark.
<sup>26</sup> The schemes of the wicked are an
        abomination to the LORD, *
    but gracious words are pure. †
<sup>27</sup> The greedy tear down their own house,
    but those who hate bribes will live. †
<sup>28</sup> The heart of the just ponders a response,
    but the mouth of the wicked spews
        evil.
<sup>29</sup> The LORD is far from the wicked,
    but hears the prayer of the just.
<sup>30</sup> A cheerful glance brings joy to the heart;
    good news invigorates the bones.
<sup>31</sup> The ear that listens to salutary reproof*
    is at home among the wise. †
<sup>32</sup> Those who disregard discipline hate
        themselves,
    but those who heed reproof acquire
        understanding.
<sup>33</sup> The fear of the LORD is training for
        wisdom,
    and humility goes before honors. *

**16** <sup>1</sup> Plans are made in human hearts,
    but from the LORD comes the tongue's
        response. †
<sup>2</sup> All one's ways are pure† in one's own
        eyes,
    but the measurer of motives is the
        LORD. *
<sup>3</sup> Entrust your works to the LORD,
    and your plans will succeed.

---

**15:11** *Sheol and Abaddon:* terms for the abode of the dead, signifying the profound obscurity which is open nevertheless to the sight and power of God; cf. 27:20.
**15:14** The contrasts include heart (organ of reflection) and mouth (organ of expression), and the wise and fools. One type feeds its mind with wisdom and the other feeds its face with folly.
**15:15** Good heart does not refer to good intentions but to an instructed mind. Wisdom makes poverty not only bearable but even joyful like the joy of feast days.
**15:16–17** The sages favor wealth over poverty—but not at any price; cf. Ps 37:16.
**15:21** The word "joy" occurs in the first line of vv. 20, 21, and 23. The state of folly is joy to a fool but the wise person is totally absorbed in keeping on the right or straight road.
**15:22** Failure to consult makes it likely a plan will not succeed. The point is nicely made by contrasting the singular number in the first line ("no counsel") with the plural number in the second line ("many advisors").
**15:23** Conversation is the art of saying the right thing at the right time. It gives pleasure to speaker and hearer alike.
**15:24** Death is personified as Sheol, the underworld. "Up" and "down" in Hebrew as in English are metaphors for success and failure (see Dt 28:43). One who stays on the path of life need

not fear the punishment that stalks sinners.
**15:26** "Pure" here means acceptable. The language of ritual (acceptable or pure) is applied to ordinary human actions. "Gracious words" are words that bring peace to the neighbor.
**15:27** The same lesson as the opening scene of Proverbs (1:8–19): one cannot build a house by unjust gain. Injustice will come back upon a house so built.
**15:31** To become wise, one must hear and integrate perspectives contrary to one's own, which means accepting "reproof." Wisdom does not isolate one but places one in the company of the wise.
**16:1** Words, like actions, often produce results different from those which were planned, and this comes under the agency of God.
**16:2** "Pure" in a moral sense for human action is found only in Job and Proverbs. As in v. 1, the contrast is between human intent and divine assessment.

| | |
|---|---|
| **15:13** Prv 12:25; 17:22; Sir 30:22. | **15:23** Prv 25:11; Sir 20:6. |
| **15:18** Prv 6:21; 29:22; Sir 28:11. | **15:26** Prv 6:18. |
| **15:20** Prv 10:1; 29:3. | **15:31** Prv 25:12. |
| **15:22** Prv 11:14. | **15:33** Prv 1:7; 19:12; Sir 1:24. |
| | **16:2** Prv 21:2. |

P R V

4 The LORD has made everything for a
    purpose,
  even the wicked for the evil day.†

5 Every proud heart† is an abomination to
    the LORD;*
  be assured that none will go
    unpunished.

6 By steadfast loyalty guilt is expiated,
  and by the fear of the LORD evil is
    avoided.†

7 When the LORD is pleased with
    someone's ways,
  he makes even enemies be at peace
    with them.

8 Better a little with justice,
  than a large income with injustice.

9 The human heart plans the way,
  but the LORD directs the steps.†*

10 An oracle is upon the king's lips,
  no judgment of his mouth is false.†

11 Balance and scales belong to the LORD;
  every weight in the sack is his
    concern.*

12 Wrongdoing is an abomination to kings,
  for by justice the throne endures.*

13 The king takes delight in honest lips,
  and whoever speaks what is right he
    loves.*

14 The king's wrath is a messenger of death,*
  but a wise person can pacify it.

15 A king's smile means life,
  and his favor is like a rain cloud in
    spring.†

16 How much better to get wisdom than
    gold!
  To get understanding is preferable to
    silver.†*

17 The path of the upright leads away from
    misfortune;

those who attend to their way guard
    their lives.†

18 Pride goes before disaster,
  and a haughty spirit before a fall.

19 It is better to be humble with the poor
  than to share plunder with the
    proud.*

20 Whoever ponders a matter will be
    successful;
  happy the one who trusts in the LORD!

21 The wise of heart is esteemed for
    discernment,
  and pleasing speech gains a reputation
    for learning.

22 Good sense is a fountain of life to those
    who have it,
  but folly is the training of fools.

23 The heart of the wise makes for eloquent
    speech,
  and increases the learning on their
    lips.

24 Pleasing words are a honeycomb,
  sweet to the taste and invigorating to
    the bones.

25 Sometimes a way seems right,
  but the end of it leads to death!*

26 The appetite of workers works for them,
  for their mouths urge them on.†*

27 Scoundrels are a furnace of evil,
  and their lips are like a scorching
    fire.

28 Perverse speech sows discord,
  and talebearing separates bosom
    friends.*

29 The violent deceive their neighbors,
  and lead them into a way that is not
    good.

30 Whoever winks an eye plans perversity;
  whoever purses the lips does evil.†

---

**16:4** Even the wicked do not lie outside God's plan.

**16:5** *Proud heart*: lit., "high of heart." To forget one is a fallible human being is so basic an error that one cannot escape exposure and punishment.

**16:6** As v. 5 used the language of worship to express what is acceptable or not to God, so this saying uses similar language to declare that lovingly loyal conduct undoes the effects of sin.

**16:9** As in vv. 1–3, the antithesis is between human plans and divine disposal. The saying uses the familiar metaphor of path for the course of life.

**16:10** Six sayings on the king and his divine authority begin here, following the series of sayings about the Lord's governance in 15:33–16:9, in which "LORD" was mentioned nine times.

**16:15** The last of six sayings about the king. In the previous verse, royal wrath means death; in this verse royal favor means life. It is significant that royal favor is compared to something not under human control—the clouds preceding the spring rains.

**16:16** The point of comparison is the superiority of the pursuit of wisdom and gold, not the relative merits of wealth and wisdom.

**16:17** In the metaphor of the two ways, the way of the righteous is protected and the way of the wicked is unprotected. Since the path of the righteous leads therefore away from trouble, one's task is to stay on it, to "attend to" it.

**16:26** The adage puzzled ancient and modern commentators. The meaning seems to state the paradox that a person does not toil to feed the gullet but that the gullet itself "toils" in the sense that it forces the person to work. As often in Proverbs, the sense organ stands for the faculty by metonymy. Cf. Eccl 6:7.

**16:30** A restless or twitching eye or lip betrays the condition of the heart (cf. 6:13).

---

16:5 Prv 6:16–17; 8:13.
16:9 Prv 19:21; 20:24; Jer
    10:23.
16:11 Prv 11:1.
16:12 Prv 25:5.
16:13 Prv 14:35; 22:11.
16:14 Prv 19:12; 20:2.

16:16 Prv 8:10–11.
16:19 Prv 11:2.
16:25 Prv 14:12.
16:26 Prv 10:4.
16:28 Prv 6:14, 19; 17:9;
    26:22; Sir 28:15.

31 Gray hair is a crown of glory;*
     it is gained by a life that is just.
32 The patient are better than warriors,
     and those who rule their temper,
         better than the conqueror of a
         city.*
33 Into the bag the lot is cast,
     but from the LORD comes every
         decision.†

17 ¹ Better a dry crust with quiet
     than a house full of feasting with
         strife.†
2 A wise servant will rule over an
     unworthy son,
     and will share the inheritance of the
         children.†
3 The crucible for silver, and the furnace
         for gold,
     but the tester of hearts is the LORD.
4 The evildoer gives heed to wicked lips,
     the liar, to a mischievous tongue.
5 Whoever mocks the poor reviles their
         Maker;
     whoever rejoices in their misfortune
         will not go unpunished.*
6 Children's children are the crown of the
         elderly,
     and the glory of children is their
         parentage.
7 Fine words ill fit a fool;
     how much more lying lips, a noble!
8 A bribe seems a charm to its user;
     at every turn it brings success.†
9 Whoever overlooks an offense fosters
         friendship,
     but whoever gossips about it separates
         friends.†

10 A single reprimand does more for a
         discerning person
     than a hundred lashes for a fool.†
11 The wicked pursue only rebellion,
     and a merciless messenger is sent
         against them.†
12 Face a bear robbed of her cubs,
     but never fools in their folly!†
13 If you return evil for good,
     evil will not depart from your
         house.†*
14 The start of strife is like the opening of a
         dam;
     check a quarrel before it bursts forth!
15 Whoever acquits the wicked,* whoever
         condemns the just—
     both are an abomination to the LORD.
16 Of what use is money in the hands of
         fools
     when they have no heart to acquire
         wisdom?†
17 A friend is a friend at all times,
     and a brother is born for the time of
         adversity.*
18 Those without sense give their hands in
         pledge,
     becoming surety for their neighbors.*
19 Those who love an offense love a fight;*
     those who build their gate high† court
         disaster.
20 The perverse in heart come to no good,
     and the double-tongued fall into
         trouble.†
21 Whoever conceives a fool has grief;
     the father of a numskull has no joy.
22 A joyful heart is the health of the body,
     but a depressed spirit dries up the
         bones.*

P
R
V

---

† 
**16:33** Dice were given meanings of "yes" or "no" and then cast for their answer. What came out was the decision. Here the saying interprets the sequence of actions: a human being puts the dice in the bag but what emerges from the bag is the Lord's decision.
**17:1** A "better than" saying, stating the circumstances when a dry crust is better than a banquet. Peace and fellowship give joy to a meal, not the richness of the food. For a similar thought, see 15:16 and 16:8.
**17:2** Ability is esteemed more highly than ties of blood.
**17:8** An observation on the effect of the bribe upon the bribe-giver: it gives an intoxicating feeling of power ("seems"). In v. 23 the evil effects of a bribe are noted.
**17:9** A paradox. One finds (love, friend) by concealing (an offense), one loses (a friend) by revealing (a secret). In 10:12 love also covers up a multitude of offenses.
**17:10** A wonderful comment on the openness and sensitivity of the wise and the foolish. One type learns from a single word and for the other one hundred blows are not enough.
**17:11** The irony is that such people will meet up with what they so energetically pursue—in the form of an unrelenting emis-

sary sent to them.
**17:12** Humorous hyperbole. An outraged dangerous beast poses less danger than a fool.
**17:13** The paradox is that to pay out evil for good means that the evil will never leave one's own house.
**17:16** The exhortation to acquire or purchase wisdom is common in Proverbs. Fools misunderstand the metaphor, assuming they can buy it with money. Their very misunderstanding shows they have no "heart" = mind, understanding. Money in the hand is no good without such a "heart" to store it in.
**17:19** *Build their gate high:* a symbol of arrogance.
**17:20** The saying employs the familiar metaphors of walking = conducting oneself ("fall into trouble"), and of straight and crooked = right and wrong ("perverse," "double-tongued").

---

*
| | |
|---|---|
| **16:31** Prv 20:29. | **17:15** Prv 24:24; Is 5:23. |
| **16:32** Prv 14:29. | **17:17** Prv 18:24. |
| **17:5** Prv 14:31. | **17:18** Prv 6:1–2; 11:15. |
| **17:13** Mt 5:39; Rom 12:17; | **17:19** Prv 15:18. |
| 1 Thes 5:15; 1 Pt 3:9. | **17:22** Prv 12:25; 15:13. |

**PRV**

23    A guilty person takes out a bribe from
      the pocket,
        thus perverting the course of justice.†
24    On the countenance of a discerning
      person is wisdom,*
        but the eyes of a fool are on the ends
          of the earth.†
25    A foolish son is vexation to his father,
        and bitter sorrow to her who bore
          him.*
26    It is wrong to fine an innocent person,
        but beyond reason to scourge nobles.
27    Those who spare their words are truly
      knowledgeable,
        and those who are discreet are
          intelligent.*
28    Even fools, keeping silent, are
      considered wise;
        if they keep their lips closed,
          intelligent.†

# 18

1 One who is alienated seeks a pretext,
   with all persistence picks a quarrel.
2    Fools take no delight in understanding,
      but only in displaying what they
        think.†
3    With wickedness comes contempt,
      and with disgrace, scorn.
4    The words of one's mouth are deep waters,
      the spring of wisdom, a running
        brook.†*
5    It is not good to favor the guilty,
      nor to reject the claim of the just.*
6    The lips of fools walk into a fight,
      and their mouths are asking for a
        beating.†

7    The mouths of fools are their ruin;
      their lips are a deadly snare.*
8    The words of a talebearer are like dainty
      morsels:
        they sink into one's inmost being.*
9    Those slack in their work
      are kin to the destroyer.
10†    The name of the LORD is a strong
      tower;
        the just run to it and are safe.
11    The wealth of the rich is their strong
      city;*
        they fancy it a high wall.
12    Before disaster the heart is haughty,*
      but before honor is humility.
13    Whoever answers before listening,*
      theirs is folly and shame.†
14    One's spirit supports one when ill,
      but a broken spirit who can bear?†
15    The heart of the intelligent acquires
      knowledge,
        and the ear of the wise seeks
         knowledge.†
16    Gifts clear the way for people,
      winning access to the great.*
17    Those who plead the case first seem to
      be in the right;
        then the opponent comes and cross-
         examines them.†
18    The lot puts an end to disputes,
      and decides a controversy between the
        mighty.†
19    A brother offended is more unyielding
      than a stronghold;
        such strife is more daunting than
         castle gates.†

---

**17:23** A sharp look at the sly withdrawing of a bribe from the pocket and a blunt judgment on its significance.

**17:24** Wisdom is visible on the countenance (i.e., mouth, lips, tongue) of the wise person; its ultimate source is the heart. Fools have no such source of wisdom within them, a point that is nicely made by referring to the eye of the fool, roving over the landscape.

**17:28** Related to v. 27. Words provide a glimpse into the heart. In the unlikely event that fools, who usually pour out words (15:2), were to say nothing, people would not be able to see their folly and would presume them intelligent. Alas, the saying is contrary to fact.

**18:2** One grows in wisdom by listening to others, but fools take delight in expounding the contents of their minds.

**18:4** Words express a person's thoughts ("deep waters"), which in turn become accessible to others. Cf. 20:5a.

**18:6** The bold personification of lips and mouth is similar to Ps 73:9, "They set their mouths against the heavens, their tongues roam the earth." Careless words can lead one into serious trouble.

**18:10–11** Contrast this judgment with the observation in 10:15.

**18:13** To speak without first listening is characteristic of a

fool; cf. 10:14; Sir 11:8.

**18:14** The paradox is that something as slight as a column of air offers protection against the encroachment of death. If it is stilled, nothing, no matter how powerful, can substitute for it.

**18:15** "Knowledge" here refers to what one knows, not knowledge in itself. The mind acquires and stores it, the ear strains toward it.

**18:17** A persuasive speech in court can easily make one forget there is another side to the question. When the other party speaks, people realize they made a premature judgment. The experience at court is a lesson for daily life: there are two sides to every question.

**18:18** See note on 16:33.

**18:19** The Greek version, followed by several ancient versions, has the opposite meaning: "A brother helped by a brother is like a strong and lofty city; it is strong like a well-founded pal-

---

17:24 Eccl 8:1.
17:25 Prv 10:1; 29:15.
17:27 Prv 10:19; Sir 1:21; Jas 1:19.
18:4 Prv 20:5; Jn 7:38.
18:5 Prv 24:23; 28:21.
18:7 Prv 10:14; 12:13;

13:3; Eccl 10:12.
18:8 Prv 26:22.
18:11 Prv 10:15.
18:12 Prv 11:2; 16:18; Sir 10:15.
18:13 Sir 11:8.
18:16 Prv 21:14.

20 With the fruit of one's mouth one's belly
   is filled,
     with the produce of one's lips one is
     sated.†*
21 Death and life are in the power of the
   tongue;*
     those who choose one shall eat its
     fruit.†
22 To find a wife is to find happiness,
     a favor granted by the LORD.*
23 The poor implore,
     but the rich answer harshly.
24 There are friends who bring ruin,
     but there are true friends more loyal
     than a brother.*

19 ¹Better to be poor and walk in
   integrity
     than rich and crooked in one's
     ways.*
2 Desire without knowledge is not good;
     and whoever acts hastily, blunders.†
3 Their own folly leads people astray;
     in their hearts they rage against the
     LORD.†
4 Wealth adds many friends,
     but the poor are left friendless.*
5 The false witness will not go
   unpunished,
     and whoever utters lies will not
     escape.†*
6 Many curry favor with a noble;
     everybody is a friend of a gift giver.
7 All the kin of the poor despise them;

how much more do their friends shun
them!†
8 Those who gain sense truly love
   themselves;
     those who preserve understanding
     will find success.†
9 The false witness will not go
   unpunished,
     and whoever utters lies will perish.
10 Luxury is not befitting a fool;
     much less should a slave rule over
     princes.
11 It is good sense to be slow to anger,
     and an honor to overlook an offense.†
12 The king's wrath is like the roar of a
   lion,
     but his favor, like dew on the grass.†*
13 The foolish son is ruin to his father,*
     and a quarrelsome wife is water
     constantly dripping.†
14 Home and possessions are an
     inheritance from parents,
     but a prudent wife is from the LORD.*
15 Laziness brings on deep sleep,
     and the sluggard goes hungry.*
16 Those who keep commands keep their
   lives,
     but those who despise these ways will
     die.*
17 Whoever cares for the poor lends to the
   LORD,*
     who will pay back the sum in full.
18 Discipline your son, for there is hope;
     but do not be intent on his death.†*

ace." The Greek is secondary as is shown by the need to supply
the phrase "by a brother"; further, the parallelism is inadequate.
The Hebrew is to be preferred.
   **18:20** Fruit from the earth is our ordinary sustenance, but "the
fruit of one's lips," i.e., our words, also affect our well-being. If
our words and our deeds are right, then we are blessed, our
"belly is filled."
   **18:21** This enigmatic saying has provoked many interpretations, e.g., judicious speech brings a reward; those who love the
tongue in the sense of rattling on must face the consequences of
their loquacity. This translation interprets the verb "love" in colon
B in its occasional sense of "choose" (e.g., 12:1; 20:13; Dt 4:37)
and interprets its pronominal object as referring to both death
and life in colon A. Death and life are set before every person
(cf. Dt 30:15–20) and we have the power to choose either one
by the quality of our deeds. Words (= "the tongue") are regarded
here as the defining actions of human beings.
   **19:2** When not guided by wisdom, appetite—or desire—is
not good. "Running feet" (so the Hebrew) miss the mark, i.e., do
not reach their destination.
   **19:3** One's own folly destroys one's life. It is an indication of
that folly that one blames God rather than oneself.
   **19:5** The punishment fits the crime: those who abuse the legal system will be punished by the same system. They will not
be acquitted.
   **19:7** Closely related to vv. 4 and 6. An observation, not with-

out sympathy, on the social isolation of poor people.
   **19:8** Wisdom benefits the one who practices it.
   **19:11** The paradox is that one obtains one thing by giving
up another.
   **19:12** An observation on the exercise of royal power. Both
images suggest royal attitudes are beyond human control. Colon
A is a variant of 20:2a and colon B of 16:15b.
   **19:13** One of many sayings about domestic happiness. The
perspective is male; the two greatest pains to a father is a malicious son and an unsuitable wife. The immediately following
saying is on the noble wife, perhaps to make a positive statement
about women.
   **19:18** The pain of disciplining the young cannot be compared
with the danger no discipline may bring. The chief reason for disciplining the young is their capacity to change; excluded thereby
are revenge and punishment.

**18:20** Prv 12:14; 13:2.          Dn 13:61.
**18:21** Sir 37:18.                **19:12** Prv 20:2.
**18:22** Prv 12:4; 19:14; Sir     **19:13** Prv 10:1; 17:25.
   7:26.                            **19:14** Prv 18:22.
**18:24** Prv 17:17.                **19:15** Prv 6:9–10.
**19:1** Prv 28:6.                  **19:16** Prv 13:13; 16:17.
**19:4** Prv 14:20; Sir            **19:17** Prv 14:21; 22:9;
   13:20–23.                           28:27.
**19:5** Dt 19:16–20;              **19:18** Prv 13:24; 23:13–14.

19 A wrathful person bears the penalty;
   after one rescue, you will have it to do
   again.
20 Listen to counsel and receive instruction,
   that you may eventually become wise.
21 Many are the plans of the human heart,
   but it is the decision of the LORD that
   endures.*
22 What is desired of a person is fidelity;
   rather be poor than a liar.†
23 The fear of the LORD leads to life;
   one eats and sleeps free from any
   harm.
24 The sluggard buries a hand in the dish;
   not even lifting it to the mouth.*
25 Beat a scoffer and the naive learn a
   lesson;
   rebuke the intelligent and they gain
   knowledge.*
26 Whoever mistreats a father or drives
   away a mother,
   is a shameless and disgraceful child.†*
27 My son, stop attending to correction;
   start straying from words of
   knowledge.†
28 An unprincipled witness scoffs at justice,
   and the mouth of the wicked pours
   out iniquity.
29 Rods are prepared for scoffers,
   and blows for the backs of fools.*

20 ¹ Wine is arrogant, strong drink is
   riotous;
   none who are intoxicated by them are
   wise.†*
2 The terror of a king is like the roar of a
   lion;*

   those who incur his anger forfeit their
   lives.
3 A person gains honor by avoiding strife,
   while every fool starts a quarrel.†
4 In seedtime sluggards do not plow;
   when they look for the harvest, it is
   not there.
5 The intention of the human heart is
   deep water,
   but the intelligent draw it forth.†*
6 Many say, "My loyal friend,"
   but who can find someone worthy of
   trust?
7 The just walk in integrity;
   happy are their children after them!
8 A king seated on the throne of judgment
   dispels all evil with his glance.†
9 Who can say, "I have made my heart
   clean,*
   I am cleansed of my sin"?†
10 Varying weights, varying measures,
   are both an abomination to the
   LORD.*
11 In their actions even children can
   playact
   though their deeds be blameless and
   right.†
12 The ear that hears, the eye that sees—
   the LORD has made them both.†
13 Do not love sleep lest you be reduced to
   poverty;
   keep your eyes open, have your fill of
   food.
14 "Bad, bad!" says the buyer,
   then goes away only to boast.†
15 One can put on gold and abundant
   jewels,

---

† —

**19:22** The proverb has been read in two ways: (1) "Desire (greed) is a shame to a person," which assumes the rare Hebrew word for "shame" is being used; (2) "What is desired in a person is fidelity." The second interpretation is preferable. The context may be the court: better to forego money (a bribe) than perjure oneself.

**19:26** Children who disgrace the family equivalently plunder their father's wealth and expel their mother from the home.

**19:27** The meaning was disputed even in antiquity. The interpretation that most respects the syntax is to take it as ironic advice as in 22:6: to stop (listening) is to go (wandering).

**20:1** The cause stands for its effect (wine, drunken behavior). In Proverbs wine is a sign of prosperity and a symbol of feasting (3:10; 4:17; 9:2, 5) but also a potential threat to wisdom as in 20:1; 21:17; 23:29–35.

**20:3** The honor that one might seek to gain from fighting comes of itself to the person who refrains from fighting.

**20:5** The heart is where human plans are made and stored; they remain "deep water" until words reveal them to others. The wise know how to draw up those waters, i.e., express them. Cf. 18:4.

**20:8** The royal throne is established in justice and the king is the agent of that justice.

**20:9** A claim to sinlessness can be merely self-deception; see 16:2; cf. also 15:11.

**20:11** The verb in colon A can mean either "to make oneself known" or "to play another person" (as in Gn 42:7 and 1 Kgs 14:5, 6). The second meaning makes a better parallel to colon B. The meaning is that if a child can playact, an adult can do so even more. Actions do not always reveal character.

**20:12** Human judgments are not ultimate; the Lord expects proper use of these faculties.

**20:14** Bartering invites playacting and masking one's true intent. The truth of words depends on their context.

---
*—

**19:21** Prv 16:9.
**19:24** Prv 26:15.
**19:25** Prv 17:10; 21:11.
**19:26** Sir 3:16.
**19:29** Prv 26:3.
**20:1** Prv 23:29–35.

**20:2** Prv 19:12.
**20:5** Prv 18:4.
**20:9** 1 Kgs 8:46; 2 Chr 6:36; Eccl 7:20; 1 Jn 1:8.
**20:10** Prv 11:1; 20:23.

but wise lips are the most precious
ornament.†

16 Take the garment of the one who
became surety for a stranger;*
if for foreigners, exact the pledge!†

17 Bread earned by deceit is sweet,
but afterward the mouth is filled with
gravel.

18 Plans made with advice succeed;
with wise direction wage your war.

19 A slanderer reveals secrets;
so have nothing to do with a babbler!

20 Those who curse father or mother—
their lamp will go out† in the dead of
night.*

21 Possessions greedily guarded at the
outset
will not be blessed in the end.†

22 Do not say, "I will repay evil!"
Wait for the LORD, who will help
you.†*

23 Varying weights are an abomination to
the LORD,
and false scales are not good.*

24 Our steps are from the LORD;*
how, then, can mortals understand
their way?†

25 It is a trap to pledge rashly a sacred gift,
and after a vow, then to reflect.†

26 A wise king winnows the wicked,
and threshes them under the
cartwheel.†

27 A lamp from the LORD is human life-
breath;
it searches through the inmost being.†

28 His steadfast loyalty safeguards the king,
and he upholds his throne by justice.*

29 The glory of the young is their strength,
and the dignity of the old is gray
hair.*

30 Evil is cleansed away by bloody lashes,
and a scourging to the inmost being.

# 21

1 A king's heart is channeled water in
the hand of the LORD;
God directs it where he pleases.†

2 All your ways may be straight in your
own eyes,
but it is the LORD who weighs hearts.*

3 To do what is right and just*
is more acceptable to the LORD than
sacrifice.†

4 Haughty eyes and a proud heart—
the lamp of the wicked will fail.†

5 The plans of the diligent end in profit,
but those of the hasty end in loss.†

6 Trying to get rich by lying
is chasing a bubble over deadly snares.

7 The violence of the wicked will sweep
them away,
because they refuse to do what is
right.

8 One's path may be winding and
unfamiliar,

---

**20:15** Wisdom is said to be preferable to gold in 3:14; 8:10, 19; 16:16. Colon B suggests that the gold and jewelry here are ornaments for the face (cf. Gn 24:53; Ex 3:22; Is 61:10). Wise lips are the most beautiful adornment, for they display the wisdom of the heart.

**20:16** The text is not clear. See 27:13. Caution in becoming surety is always advised (cf. 6:1–3), and it is especially advisable with strangers.

**20:20** *Their lamp will go out*: misfortune, even death, awaits them; cf. 13:9; Ex 21:17.

**20:21** By definition, an inheritance is not gained by one's own efforts but is received as a gift. If, when one first receives the inheritance, one drives everyone away, one treats it as if one acquired it by one's own efforts. In an agricultural society, an inheritance would often be a field that would require God's blessing to be fertile.

**20:22** Appointing oneself an agent of divine retribution is dangerous. Better to wait for God to effect justice. Cf. 24:17–18.

**20:24** An indication of the Lord's inscrutable providence; cf. Jer 10:23; see Prv 21:2; cf. also 14:12.

**20:25** This verse cautions against making vows without proper reflection; cf. Dt 23:22–25; Eccl 5:4–5.

**20:26** The king is responsible for effecting justice. Judgment is portrayed in agricultural imagery—exposing grain to a current of air so that the chaff is blown away, and passing a wheel over the cereal to break the husk. Winnowing as image for judgment is found throughout the Bible.

**20:27** A parallel is drawn between the life-breath that is God's gift (Jb 32:8; 33:2) coursing through the human body (Is

2:22) and the lamp of God, which can be a symbol of divine scrutiny. In Zep 1:12, God declares, "And in that day I will search through Jerusalem with lamps."

**21:1** "Channeled water" in Is 32:2 and Prv 5:16 is water that fertilizes arid land. It takes great skill to direct water, whether it be water to fertilize fields or cosmic floods harnessed at creation, for water is powerful and seems to have a mind of its own. It also requires great skill to direct the heart of a king, for it is inscrutable and beyond ordinary human control.

**21:3** External rites or sacrifices do not please God unless accompanied by internal worship and right moral conduct; cf. 15:8; 21:27; Is 1:11–15; Am 5:22; Mal 1:12.

**21:4** Heart and eyes depict, respectively, the inner and the outer person. "Haughty eyes" peering out from a "proud heart" show a thoroughly arrogant person. How can such a person flourish! Their lamp, which signifies life, will go out.

**21:5** The antitheses are diligent and impetuous. The metaphor characterizing each type is taken from the world of commerce. Planning is important; bustle leads to waste.

---

**20:16** Prv 27:13.
**20:20** Prv 30:11, 17; Ex 21:17; Lv 20:9; Mt 15:4.
**20:22** Prv 24:29; Sir 28:1; Mt 5:39; Rom 12:17, 19; 1 Thes 5:15;

1 Pt 3:9.
**20:23** Prv 11:1; 20:10.
**20:24** Prv 16:9.
**20:28** Prv 16:12.
**20:29** Prv 16:31.
**21:2** Prv 16:2.
**21:3** 1 Sm 15:22; Hos 6:6.

but one's conduct is blameless and
    right.†

9  It is better to dwell in a corner of the
    housetop
    than in a mansion with a quarrelsome
    woman.†*

10  The soul of the wicked desires evil;
    their neighbor finds no pity in their
    eyes.

11  When scoffers are punished the naive
    become wise;
    when the wise succeed, they gain
    knowledge.*

12  The Righteous One appraises the house
    of the wicked,
    bringing down the wicked to ruin.†

13  Those who shut their ears to the cry of
    the poor
    will themselves call out and not be
    answered.

14  A secret gift allays anger,
    and a present concealed, violent
    wrath.†

15  When justice is done it is a joy for the
    just,
    downfall for evildoers.†*

16  Whoever strays from the way of good
    sense
    will abide in the assembly of the
    shades.†

17  The lover of pleasure will suffer want;
    the lover of wine and perfume will
    never be rich.

18  The wicked serve as ransom for the just,
    and the faithless for the upright.†*

19  It is better to dwell in a wilderness

than with a quarrelsome wife and
    trouble.

20  Precious treasure and oil are in the
    house of the wise,
    but the fool consumes them.

21  Whoever pursues justice and kindness
    will find life and honor.†

22  The wise person storms the city of the
    mighty,
    and overthrows the stronghold in
    which they trust.

23  Those who guard mouth and tongue
    guard themselves† from trouble.*

24  Proud, boastful—scoffer is the name:
    those who act with overbearing
    pride.

25  The desire of sluggards will slay them,
    for their hands refuse to work.†

26  Some are consumed with avarice all the
    day,
    but the just give unsparingly.

27  The sacrifice of the wicked is an
    abomination,
    the more so when they offer it with
    bad intent.*

28  The false witness will perish,*
    but one who listens will give lasting
    testimony.

29  The face of the wicked hardens,
    but the upright maintains a straight
    course.†

30  No wisdom, no understanding,
    no counsel prevail against the LORD.

31  The horse is equipped for the day of
    battle,
    but victory is the LORD's.

---

**21:8** One cannot always read others' hearts from their behavior. Unconventional conduct need not indicate evil motives.

**21:9** In Proverbs, two great obstacles to a happy household are foolish children and quarrelsome spouses. The nagging wife is also mentioned in 19:13 and 27:15; 25:24 is a duplicate.

**21:12** It is difficult to ascertain the subject of the saying. Some hold it is the Lord, the "Righteous One," who is normally the executor of justice in Proverbs. Others believe it is the just person who is the agent of divine justice. "Righteous One" is a title for God in Is 24:16. The best argument for making God the subject of the verb is that elsewhere in Proverbs righteous human beings never do anything to the wicked; only God does.

**21:14** Proverbs offers several remedies for anger—a soft word (15:1), patience, and a bribe. The last remedy implies a certain disdain for the disordered passion of anger, for it can be so easily assuaged by a discreetly offered "gift."

**21:15** The second line is a duplicate of 10:29b.

**21:16** *Assembly of the shades:* those who dwell in Sheol.

**21:18** In this bold paradox, the ransom that protects the righteous is the wicked person who attracts, like a lightning rod, the divine wrath that might have been directed at the righteous.

**21:21** The paradox is that one comes upon something other

than what one pursued. The way to (long and healthy) life and honor is the vigorous pursuit of virtue.

**21:23** *Themselves:* see note on 13:3. To guard your "self" (lit., "throat," the moist and breathing center of the body, by metonymy, "life"), you must guard your tongue. Speech in Proverbs is the quintessential human activity and often has a meaning broader than speech alone; it can stand for all human activity. Acting rightly is the best way to protect yourself from evil.

**21:25** Desire, or appetite, is the impulse toward food and drink (see Ps 42:3) which spurs animals and human beings into action. But sluggards cannot lift hand to mouth; they bury their hand in the dish (19:24), and so their appetite is thwarted.

**21:29** The wicked cannot deter the righteous from walking the straight path, i.e., from practicing virtue.

---

**21:9** Prv 21:19; 25:24;
    27:15; Sir 25:23.
**21:11** Prv 19:25.
**21:15** Prv 10:29.
**21:18** Prv 11:8.

**21:23** Prv 13:3.
**21:27** Prv 15:8; Sir
    34:21–23.
**21:28** Prv 19:5, 9.

1023  Proverbs 22:17

# 22

¹A good name is more desirable than
  great riches,
and high esteem, than gold and
  silver. †*

² Rich and poor have a common bond:
  the LORD is the maker of them all. *

³ The astute see an evil and hide,
  while the naive continue on and pay
  the penalty. †*

⁴ The result of humility and fear of the
  LORD
  is riches, honor and life. †

⁵ Thorns and snares are on the path of the
  crooked;
  those who would safeguard their lives
  will avoid them.

⁶ Train the young in the way they should
  go;
  even when old, they will not swerve
  from it. †

⁷ The rich rule over the poor,
  and the borrower is the slave of the
  lender. †

⁸ Those who sow iniquity reap calamity, *
  and the rod used in anger will fail. †

⁹ The generous will be blessed,
  for they share their food with the poor.

¹⁰ Expel the arrogant and discord goes too;
  strife and insult cease.

¹¹ The LORD loves the pure of heart; *
  the person of winning speech has a
  king for a friend.

¹² The eyes of the LORD watch over the
  knowledgeable,
  but he defeats the projects of the
  faithless.

¹³ The sluggard says, "A lion is outside; *
  I might be slain in the street." †

¹⁴ The mouth of the foreign woman is a
  deep pit; *
  whoever incurs the LORD's anger will
  fall into it.

¹⁵ Folly is bound to the heart of a youth,
  but the rod of discipline will drive it
  out. †

¹⁶ Oppressing the poor for enrichment,
  giving to the rich: both are sheer loss. †

## IV. SAYINGS OF THE WISE†

¹⁷ The Words of the Wise: †
  Incline your ear, and hear my words, *
  and let your mind attend to my
  teaching;

---

**22:1** "Good name" (Heb. *shem*) and "high esteem" (Heb. *chen*) are declared to be of more value than great riches. Human beings belong to a community and without the acceptance of that community, which is built on esteem and trust, human life is grievously damaged. Riches are less essential to the human spirit.

**22:3** The wise see dangers before they are engulfed by them whereas fools, through dullness or boldness, march right on.

**22:4** Humiliation can be an occasion for knowing one's place in God's world. Such knowledge is part of fear (or revering) of the Lord. Revering the Lord brings the blessings of wealth, honor, and long life. The saying is perhaps meant to counter the view that humiliation is an unmixed evil; something good can come of it.

**22:6** One of the few exhortations in the collection (cf. 14:7; 16:3; 19:18, 20). "Way" in the first colon has been taken in two different senses: (1) the morally right way, "according to the way one ought to go"; (2) personal aptitude, i.e., the manner of life for which one is destined, as "the way of Egypt" (Is 10:24). Neither interpretation, however, accounts for the pronoun in the Hebrew phrase, lit., "his own way." The most natural solution is to take the whole as ironic advice (like 19:27): yes, go ahead and let the young do exactly what they want; they will become self-willed adults.

**22:7** An observation on money and power. One who borrows becomes poor in the sense of indebted, a slave to the lender.

**22:8** Agricultural metaphors express the failure of malicious actions. In the first line, bad actions are seeds yielding trouble. In the second line, "the rod" is a flail used to beat grains as in Is 28:27.

**22:13** To avoid the effort required for action, the sluggard exaggerates the difficulties that must be overcome.

**22:15** Folly is attached to children as the husk is attached to the grain. "Rod" here, as in v. 8, seems to be the flail. Discipline is the process of winnowing away the folly.

**22:16** A difficult saying. One possibility is to take it as a seemingly neutral observation on the plight of the poor: taking

money from the poor is relatively easy for the powerful but it is dangerous as the poor have the Lord as their defender (24:22–23), who will punish their oppressors. Giving to the rich, perhaps to win their favor by presents and bribes, is equally a waste of money, for the rich will always do what they please in any case.

**22:17–24:22** This collection consists of an introduction (22:17–21) urging openness and stating the purpose of the Words and diverse admonitions, aphorisms, and counsels. It is written with faith in the Lord, shrewdness, and a satirical eye. The first part seems aimed at young people intent on a career (22:22–23:11); the second is taken up with the concerns of youth (23:12–35); the third part is interested in the ultimate fate of the good and the wicked (24:1–22). The whole can be described as a guidebook of professional ethics. The aim is to inculcate trust in the Lord and to help readers avoid trouble and advance their careers by living according to wisdom. Its outlook is very practical: avoid bad companions because in time you will take on some of their qualities; do not post bond for others because you yourself will be encumbered; do not promote yourself too aggressively because such promotion is self-defeating; do not abuse sex or alcohol because they will harm you; do not emulate your peers if they are wicked (23:14; 24:1, 19) because such people have no future. Rather, trust the vocation of a sage (22:29–23:9).

The Egyptian *Instructions of Amenemope* (written ca. 1100 B.C.) was discovered in 1923. Scholars immediately recognized it as a source of Prv 22:17–23:11. The Egyptian work has thirty chapters (cf. Prv 22:20); its preface resembled Prv 22:17–21; its first two admonitions matched the first two in Proverbs (Prv 22:22–25). There are many other resemblances as well, some of which are pointed out in the notes. The instruction of a father to his son (or an administrator to his successor) was a well-known

---

**22:1** Eccl 7:1.
**22:2** Prv 29:13.
**22:3** Prv 27:12.
**22:8** Jb 4:8; Sir 7:3; Hos 8:7.
**22:11** Mt 5:8.
**22:13** Prv 26:13.
**22:14** Prv 23:27.
**22:17** Prv 5:1.

18 For it will be well if you hold them
     within you,
  if they all are ready on your lips.
19 That your trust may be in the LORD,
  I make them known to you today—
     yes, to you.
20 Have I not written for you thirty sayings,
  containing counsels and knowledge,
21 To teach you truly
  how to give a dependable report to
     one who sends you?
22 Do not rob the poor because they are
     poor,
  nor crush the needy at the gate;†
23 For the LORD will defend their cause,*
  and will plunder those who plunder
     them.
24 Do not be friendly with hotheads,
  nor associate with the wrathful,
25 Lest you learn their ways,
  and become ensnared.
26 Do not be one of those who give their
     hand in pledge,
  those who become surety for debts;*
27 For if you are unable to pay,
  your bed will be taken from under
     you.†

28 Do not remove the ancient landmark†
  that your ancestors set up.*
29 Do you see those skilled at their work?
  They will stand in the presence of
     kings,
  but not in the presence of the obscure.

# 23

1† When you sit down to dine with
     a ruler,
  mark well the one who is before you;
2 Stick the knife in your gullet†
  if you have a ravenous appetite.
3 Do not desire his delicacies;
  it is food that deceives.
4 Do not wear yourself out to gain wealth,
  cease to be worried about it;
5 When your glance flits to it, it is gone!
  For assuredly it grows wings,
  like the eagle that flies toward heaven.†
6† Do not take food with unwilling hosts,
  and do not desire their delicacies;
7 For like something stuck in the throat is
     that food.
  "Eat and drink," they say to you,
  but their hearts are not with you;
8 The little you have eaten you will vomit
     up,

---

genre in Egypt; seventeen works are extant, spanning the period from 2500 B.C. to the first century A.D. The instructions aimed to help a young person live a happy and prosperous life and avoid mistakes that cause difficulties. They make concrete and pragmatic suggestions rather than hold up abstract ideals. Pragmatic though they were, the instructions were religious; they assumed that the gods implanted an order in the world (Egyptian *maat*, which is found both in nature and in the human world. *Amenemope* represents a stage in the development of the Egyptian genre, displaying a new inwardness and quest for serenity while still assuming that the practice of virtue brings worldly success. Proverbs borrows from the Egyptian work with great freedom: it does not, for example, import as such the Egyptian concept of order; it engages the reader with its characteristic wit, irony, and paradox (e.g., 22:26–27; 23:1–3).

**22:17–23:35** The maxims warn against: robbing the poor and defenseless (22:22–23), anger (22:24–25), giving surety for debts (22:26–27), advancing oneself by socializing with rulers (23:1–2), anxiety for riches (23:4–5), forcing oneself on a grudging host (23:6–8), intemperance in food and drink (23:19–21, 29–35), and adultery (23:26–28). They exhort to: careful workmanship (22:29), respect for the rights of orphans (23:10–11), correction of the young (23:13–14), filial piety (23:15–16, 22–25), and fear of the Lord (23:17–18).

**22:22** *At the gate*: of the city, where justice was administered and public affairs discussed; cf. Ru 4:1. Cf. also Ps 69:13; 127:5; Prv 24:7; 31:23, 31. The Lord will personally avenge those who have no one to defend them.

**22:27** Providing surety for a debtor puts one in danger of having the very basics of one's life suddenly seized.

**22:28** *Landmark*: marks the boundary of property. To remove it is the equivalent of stealing land. A similar warning is contained in 23:10.

**23:1–9** Four admonitions for someone aspiring to be a sage: be careful about advancing your career by socializing with the

great (vv. 1–3); avoid greed (vv. 4–5); do not force yourself on an unwilling host (vv. 6–8); do not waste your wisdom on those who cannot profit from it (v. 9).

**23:2** *Stick the knife in your gullet*: a metaphor for self-restraint. The usual translation, "Put a knife to your throat," is misleading, for in English it is a death threat. The exhortation is humorously exaggerated: stick the table-knife in your own gullet rather than take too much food. It assumes that the young courtier is unused to opulent banquets and will be tempted to overindulgence.

**23:5** The frustration of covetous intent and elusiveness of wealth are portrayed by the sudden flight of an eagle. *Amenemope*, chap. 7, has a similar statement: "Do not set your heart on wealth. There is no ignoring Fate and Destiny; / Do not let your heart go straying." Proverbs imagines covetous intent as a flight of the eyes, whereas *Amenemope* imagines it as a straying of the heart.

**23:6–8** Some humorous advice on not trading on the courtesy of unwilling hosts who, for convention's sake, use the language of welcome. *Amenemope*, chap. 11, gives similar advice: "Do not intrude on a man in his house, / Enter when you have been called; / He may say 'Welcome' with his mouth, / Yet deride you in his thoughts." "Unwilling," lit., "evil of eye," is usually translated "stingy," but the context suggests unwilling. In v. 8, the unwanted guest vomits up the food, thus destroying the desired good impression. Proverbs regards the uninvited banqueters as thieves who will suffer the consequences of their theft. *Amenemope*, chap. 11, is relevant: "Do not covet a poor man's goods,…A poor man's goods are a block in the throat, / It makes the gullet vomit."

---

**22:23** Prv 23:11.     **22:28** Prv 23:10; Dt 19:14;
**22:26** Prv 6:1–2; 11:15;     27:17.
    17:18.

and you will have wasted your
        agreeable words.

9   Do not speak in the hearing of fools;
        they will despise the wisdom of your
        words.*

10  Do not remove the ancient landmark,*
        nor invade the fields of the
        fatherless;†

11  For their redeemer is strong;
        he will defend their cause against
        you.*

12  Apply your heart to instruction,
        and your ear to words of knowledge.

13† Do not withhold discipline from youths;
        if you beat them with the rod, they
        will not die.*

14  Beat them with the rod,*
        and you will save them from Sheol.

15  My son, if your heart is wise,
        my heart also will rejoice;

16  And my inmost being will exult,
        when your lips speak what is right.

17  Do not let your heart envy sinners,*
        but only those who always fear the
        Lord;†

18  For you will surely have a future,
        and your hope will not be cut off.*

19  Hear, my son, and be wise,
        and guide your heart in the right way.

20  Do not join with wine bibbers,
        nor with those who glut themselves
        on meat.

21  For drunkards and gluttons come to
        poverty,
        and lazing about clothes one in rags.

22† Listen to your father who begot you,
        do not despise your mother when she
        is old.

23  Buy truth and do not sell:

wisdom, instruction, understanding!

24  The father of a just person will exult
        greatly;
        whoever begets a wise son will rejoice
        in him.*

25  Let your father and mother rejoice;
        let her who bore you exult.

26† My son, give me your heart,
        and let your eyes keep to my ways,

27  For the harlot is a deep pit,
        and the foreign woman a narrow well;

28  Yes, she lies in wait like a robber,*
        and increases the number of the
        faithless.

29† Who scream? Who shout?
        Who have strife? Who have anxiety?
    Who have wounds for nothing?
        Who have bleary eyes?

30  Whoever linger long over wine,
        whoever go around quaffing wine.*

31  Do not look on the wine when it is red,
        when it sparkles in the cup.
    It goes down smoothly,

32      but in the end it bites like a serpent,
        and stings like an adder.

33  Your eyes behold strange sights,
        and your heart utters incoherent
        things;

34  You are like one sleeping on the high
        seas,
        sprawled at the top of the mast.

35  "They struck me, but it did not pain me;
        they beat me, but I did not feel it.
    When can I get up,
        when can I go out and get more?"†

# 24

1† Do not envy the wicked,
    nor desire to be with them;*

2   For their hearts plot violence,

---

† **23:10** In Israel ownership of property and other legal rights were vested mainly in the father as head of the family; thus the widow and fatherless child were vulnerable, left prey to those who would exploit them.

**23:13–14** The young will not die from instructional blows but from their absence, for (premature) death results from uncorrected folly. The sardonic humor means the exhortation is not to be taken literally, as an argument for corporal punishment. The next verses (vv. 15–16) are exceedingly tender toward the young.

**23:17** Those whom one admires or associates with exercise enormous influence. Do not join the wicked, who are a doomed group. The warning is repeated in 24:1–2, 19–20.

**23:22–23** Father and mother are associated with truth and wisdom. One should no more rid oneself of truth and wisdom than rid oneself of one's parents, who are their source.

**23:26–28** The exhortation is a condensed version of chap. 7 with its emotional appeal to "my son" to avoid the forbidden woman (7:1–5), her traps (7:21–23), and her intent to add the youth to her list of victims (7:24–27). As in 23:15, 19, 22, a trust-

ful and affectionate relationship between student and teacher is the basis of teaching. The danger of the woman is expressed in imagery that has sexual overtones (cf. 22:14).

**23:29–35** A vivid description of the evil effects, physical and psychological, of drunkenness. The emphasis is on the unwise behavior, the folly, caused by alcohol. Cf. 20:1.

**23:35** Drunkards become insensible to bodily and moral harm. Their one desire is to indulge again.

**24:1–22** A new section (24:1–14)—on the fates of the wicked and foolish—begins with a warning not to take the foolish as role models. The same admonition is repeated in 23:17–18 and 24:19–20. In 24:1, the verb means "to be jealous, zealous; to

---

**23:9** Prv 9:7.
**23:10** Prv 22:28.
**23:11** Prv 22:23.
**23:13** Prv 13:24; 19:18; Sir 30:1.
**23:14** Prv 29:15, 17.
**23:17** Prv 3:31; 24:1, 19.
**23:18** Prv 24:14.
**23:24** Prv 10:1.
**23:28** Prv 7:10–27.
**23:30** Prv 20:1; Sir 19:2; Hos 4:11.
**24:1** Prv 3:31; 23:17; Ps 37:1.

and their lips speak of foul play.

3 By wisdom a house is built,
    by understanding it is established;
4 And by knowledge its rooms are filled
    with every precious and pleasing
    possession.
5 The wise are more powerful than the
    strong,
    and the learned, than the mighty,*
6 For by strategy war is waged,
    and victory depends on many
    counselors.*
7† Wise words are beyond fools' reach,*
    in the assembly they do not open
    their mouth;
8 As they calculate how to do evil,
    people brand them troublemakers.
9 The scheme of a fool gains no
    acceptance,
    the scoffer is an abomination to the
    community.
10† Did you fail in a day of adversity,
    did your strength fall short?
11 Did you fail to rescue those who were
    being dragged off to death,†
    those tottering, those near death,
12 because you said, "We didn't know
    about it"?
    Surely, the Searcher of hearts knows
    and will repay all according to their
    deeds.*
13† If you eat honey, my son, because it is
    good,
    if pure honey is sweet to your taste,
14 Such, you must know, is wisdom to your
    soul.
    If you find it, you will have a future,
    and your hope will not be cut off.*

15† Do not lie in wait at the abode of the just,
    do not ravage their dwelling places;
16 Though the just fall seven times, they
    rise again,
    but the wicked stumble from only one
    mishap.
17† Do not rejoice when your enemies fall,
    and when they stumble, do not let
    your heart exult,
18 Lest the LORD see it, be displeased with
    you,
    and withdraw his wrath from your
    enemies.
19 Do not be provoked at evildoers,
    do not envy the wicked;
20 For the evil have no future,
    the lamp of the wicked will be put
    out.*
21 My son, fear the LORD and the king;
    have nothing to do with those who
    hate them;
22 For disaster will issue suddenly,
    and calamity from them both, who
    knows when?

## V. FURTHER SAYINGS OF THE WISE†

23 These also are Words of the Wise:
    To show partiality in judgment is not
    good.*
24 Whoever says to the guilty party, "You
    are innocent,"
    will be cursed by nations, scorned by
    peoples;
25 But those who render just verdicts will
    fare well,
    and on them will come the blessing
    of prosperity.

---

† emulate." The motive stated in the other passages—the wicked have no future—is indirectly stated here.

**24:7–9** The verses are unclear; most scholars take them as two or even three single sayings, but, taken singly, the verses are banal. They are best taken as a single statement. Just as vv. 3–6 described the advantages of wisdom, so vv. 7–9 describe the disadvantages of its opposite, folly: it alienates one from the community (v. 7), for fools become notorious (v. 8), dooming their plans and ostracizing themselves.

**24:10–12** Excuses for not coming to the aid of one's neighbor in serious trouble do not suffice before God, who sees through self-serving excuses.

**24:11** *Rescue...death*: perhaps refers to the legal rescue of those unjustly condemned to death.

**24:13–14** God's word is sometimes said to be sweeter than honey, e.g., Ps 119:101–103. Cf. also Ps 19:11; Prv 16:24; Ez 3:3; Sir 24:19–22.

**24:15–16** The just will overcome every misfortune that oppresses them. *Seven times* is an indefinite number.

**24:17–18** The admonition is linked to the previous by the

words "fall" and "stumble." Premature public celebration of the downfall of enemies equivalently preempts the retribution that belongs to God.

**24:23–34** A little collection between the thirty sayings of 22:17–24:22 and the Hezekiah collection in chaps. 25–29. Its title (v. 23) suggests that editors took it as an appendix. At this point, the Greek edition of Proverbs begins to arrange the later sections of the book in a different order than the Hebrew edition.

An editor has arranged originally separate sayings into two parallel groups.

| | I. | II. |
|---|---|---|
| Conduct in court: | Judges (vv. 24–25) | Witnesses (v. 28) |
| Speaking, thinking: | Good speech (v. 26) | Bad speech (v. 29) |
| Wisdom in work: | Positive (v. 27) | Negative (vv. 30–34) |

\* 
**24:5** Prv 21:22.      **24:14** Prv 23:18.
**24:6** Prv 20:18.      **24:20** Prv 13:9.
**24:7** Sir 6:21.      **24:23** Prv 18:5; 28:21; Lv
**24:12** Ps 62:13; Sir 16:12;           19:15; Dt 1:17; 16:19.
     Mt 16:27; Rom 2:6.

P
R
V

26 An honest reply—
   a kiss on the lips.†

27 Complete your outdoor tasks,
   and arrange your work in the field;
   afterward you can build your
   house.†

28 Do not testify falsely against your
   neighbor*
   and so deceive with your lips.

29 Do not say, "As they did to me, so will I
   do to them;*
   I will repay them according to their
   deeds."†

30† I passed by the field of a sluggard,
   by the vineyard of one with no
   sense;

31 It was all overgrown with thistles;
   its surface was covered with nettles,
   and its stone wall broken down.

32 As I gazed at it, I reflected;
   I saw and learned a lesson:

33 A little sleep, a little slumber,*
   a little folding of the arms to rest—

34 Then poverty will come upon you like a
   robber,
   and want like a brigand.

## VI. SECOND SOLOMONIC COLLECTION, COLLECTED UNDER KING HEZEKIAH†

**25** ¹These also are proverbs of Solomon.* The servants of Hezekiah,† king of Judah, transmitted them.

2† It is the glory of God to conceal a
   matter,
   and the glory of kings to fathom a
   matter.†

3 Like the heavens in height, and the earth
   in depth,
   the heart of kings is unfathomable.

4† Remove the dross from silver,
   and it comes forth perfectly purified;

5 Remove the wicked from the presence of
   the king,
   and his throne is made firm through
   justice.

6† Claim no honor in the king's presence,
   nor occupy the place of superiors;

7 For it is better to be told, "Come up
   closer!"
   than to be humbled before the
   prince.*

8 What your eyes have seen
   do not bring forth too quickly against
   an opponent;
   For what will you do later on
   when your neighbor puts you to
   shame?

9† Argue your own case with your
   neighbor,
   but the secrets of others do not
   disclose;

10 Lest, hearing it, they reproach you,
   and your ill repute never ceases.

11 Golden apples in silver settings
   are words spoken at the proper time.

---

**24:26** The kiss is a gesture of respect and affection. The greatest sign of affection and respect for another is to tell that person the truth.

**24:27** *House*: can refer to both the building and the family (cf. 2 Sm 7). In the context established by the placement noted above under 24:23, the saying means that neglect of one's field is a sign that one is not building the house properly. In an agricultural society especially, the concept of household includes fields for animals and crops. On the metaphorical level, one must lay a careful preparation before embarking on a great project. This verse is sometimes interpreted as advocating careful and practical preparation for marriage.

**24:29** Retribution is a long and complex process that belongs to the Lord, not to individuals. Cf. vv. 12d, 17–18.

**24:30–34** Neglect of one's fields through laziness ruins all plans to build a house (v. 27). This vignette is a teaching story, like those in 7:1–27; Ps 37:35–36.

**25:1–29:27** Chaps. 25–29 make up the fifth collection in the book, and the third longest. King Hezekiah reigned in Judah in 715–687 B.C. According to 2 Kgs 18–20 and 2 Chr 29–32, he initiated political and religious reforms after the destruction of the Northern Kingdom in 722 B.C. Such reforms probably included copying and editing sacred literature such as Proverbs. Prv 25:1 is an important piece of evidence about the composition of the book, suggesting this collection was added to an already-existing collection also attributed to Solomon. The older collection is probably 10:1–22:16 (or part of it). By the end of the

eighth century B.C., therefore, there existed in Israel two large collections of aphorisms.

Chap. 25 has two general themes: (1) social hierarchy, rank, or position; (2) social conflict and its resolution.

**25:1** *The servants of Hezekiah*: presumably scribes at the court of Hezekiah. *Transmitted*: lit., "to move, transfer from," hence "to collect," and perhaps also to arrange and compose.

**25:2–7** The topic is the king—who he is (vv. 2–3) and how one is to behave in his presence (vv. 4–7).

**25:2** God and king were closely related in the ancient world and in the Bible. The king had a special responsibility for divine justice. Hence, God would give him special wisdom to search it out.

**25:4–5** Wisdom involves virtue as well as knowledge. As in Ps 101 the king cannot tolerate any wickedness in the royal service.

**25:6–7** An admonition with a practical motive for putting the teaching into practice. Pragmatic shrewdness suggests that we not promote ourselves but let others do it for us. See Lk 14:7–11.

**25:9–10** Another admonition on the use of law courts to settle personal disputes. Speak privately with your opponent lest others' personal business become public and they resent you.

---

**24:28** Prv 19:5; 25:18.          **25:1** Prv 1:1.
**24:29** Prv 20:22.               **25:7** Lk 14:8–10.
**24:33** Prv 6:10–11.

12 A golden earring or a necklace of fine
        gold—
    one who gives wise reproof to a
        listening ear.

13 Like the coolness of snow in the heat of
        the harvest
    are faithful messengers for those who
        send them,
    lifting the spirits of their masters.

14 Clouds and wind but no rain—
    the one who boasts of a gift not given.

15 By patience is a ruler persuaded,*
    and a soft tongue can break a bone.

16† If you find honey, eat only what you
        need,
    lest you have your fill and vomit it up.

17 Let your foot be seldom in your
        neighbors' house,
    lest they have their fill of you—and
        hate you.

18 A club, sword, or sharp arrow—
    the one who bears false witness
        against a neighbor.*

19 A bad tooth or an unsteady foot—
    a trust betrayed in time of trouble.†

20 Like the removal of clothes on a cold
        day, or vinegar on soda,
    is the one who sings to a troubled
        heart.

21† If your enemies are hungry, give them
        food to eat,
    if thirsty, give something to drink;*

22 For live coals you will heap on their
        heads,
    and the LORD will vindicate you.

23 The north wind brings rain,
    and a backbiting tongue, angry looks.

24 It is better to dwell in a corner of the
        housetop
    than in a mansion with a quarrelsome
        wife.†*

25 Cool water to one faint from thirst
    is good news from a far country.

26 A trampled fountain or a polluted
        spring—†
    a just person fallen before the wicked.

27 To eat too much honey is not good;
    nor to seek honor after honor.†

28 A city breached and left defenseless
    are those who do not control their
        temper.

# 26

†1 Like snow in summer, like rain in
        harvest,
    honor for a fool is out of place.†

2 Like the sparrow in its flitting, like the
        swallow in its flight,
    a curse uncalled-for never lands.†

3 The whip for the horse, the bridle for
        the ass,
    and the rod for the back of fools.*

4† Do not answer fools according to their
        folly,
    lest you too become like them.

5 Answer fools according to their folly,
    lest they become wise in their own
        eyes.

6 Those who send messages by a fool
    cut off their feet; they drink down
        violence.

---

**25:16–17** The two admonitions are complementary, expressing nicely the need to restrain the inclination for delightful things, whether for honey or friendship.

**25:19** "A time of trouble" defeats all plans (cf. 10:2; 11:4). At such times human resources alone are like a tooth that falls out as one bites or a foot that goes suddenly lame.

**25:21–22** A memorable statement of humanity and moderation; such sentiments could be occasionally found even outside the Bible, e.g., "It is better to bless someone than to do harm to one who has insulted you" (Egyptian *Papyrus Insinger*). Cf. Ex 23:4 and Lv 19:17–18. Human beings should not take it upon themselves to exact vengeance, leaving it rather in God's hands. This saying has in view an enemy's vulnerability in time of need, in this case extreme hunger and thirst; such a need should not be an occasion for revenge. The motive for restraining oneself is to allow God's justice to take its own course, as in 20:22 and 24:17–19. *Live coals*: either remorse and embarrassment for the harm done, or increased punishment for refusing reconciliation. Cf. Mt 5:44. Rom 12:20 cites the Greek version and interprets it, "Do not be overcome by evil but overcome evil with good."

**25:24** A humorous saying about domestic unhappiness: better to live alone outdoors than indoors with an angry spouse. Prv 21:9 is identical and 21:19 is similar in thought.

**25:26** "Spring" is a common metaphor for source. The righ-

teous should be a source of life for others. When they fail, it is as if a spring became foul and its water undrinkable. It is not clear whether the righteous person yielded to a scoundrel out of cowardice or was simply defeated by evil. The latter seems more likely, for other proverbs say the just person will never "fall" (lit. "be moved," 10:30; 12:3). The fall, even temporary, of a righteous person is a loss of life for others.

**25:27** *Nor...honor*: the text is uncertain.

**26:1–28** Concrete images describe the vices of fools (vv. 1–12), of sluggards (vv. 13–16), of meddlers (vv. 17–19), of talebearers (vv. 20–22), and of flatterers (vv. 23–28).

**26:1** There is no fit ("out of place") between weather and agricultural season.

**26:2** The point is the similarity of actions: a hovering bird that never lands, a groundless curse that never "lands." It hangs in the air posing no threat to anyone.

**26:4–5** There is no contradiction between these two proverbs. In their answers, the wise must protect their own interests against fools. Or perhaps the juxtaposition of the two proverbs suggests that no single proverb can resolve every problem in life.

---

**25:15** Prv 15:1, 4.          **25:24** Prv 21:9.
**25:18** Ex 20:16.             **26:3** Prv 19:29; Sir 33:25.
**25:21** Rom 12:20.

7† A proverb in the mouth of a fool
    hangs limp, like crippled legs.
8  Giving honor to a fool
    is like entangling a stone in the sling.
9  A thorn stuck in the hand of a drunkard
    is a proverb in the mouth of fools.
10 An archer wounding all who pass by
    is anyone who hires a drunken fool.
11 As dogs return to their vomit,
    so fools repeat their folly.*
12 You see those who are wise in their own
    eyes?
    There is more hope for fools than for
    them.
13† The sluggard says, "There is a lion in the
    street,
    a lion in the middle of the square!"*
14 The door turns on its hinges
    and sluggards, on their beds.
15 The sluggard buries a hand in the dish,
    too weary to lift it to the mouth.*
16 In their own eyes sluggards are wiser
    than seven who answer with good
    judgment.
17 Whoever meddles in the quarrel of
    another
    is one who grabs a passing dog by the
    ears.
18 Like a crazed archer
    scattering firebrands and deadly
    arrows,
19 Such are those who deceive their
    neighbor,
    and then say, "I was only joking."
20† Without wood the fire dies out;
    without a talebearer strife subsides.
21 Charcoal for coals, wood for fire—
    such are the quarrelsome, enkindling
    strife.*

22 The words of a talebearer are like dainty
    morsels:
    they sink into one's inmost being.†*
23 Like a glazed finish on earthenware
    are smooth lips and a wicked heart.†
24 With their lips enemies pretend,
    but inwardly they maintain deceit;
25 When they speak graciously, do not trust
    them,*
    for seven abominations† are in their
    hearts.
26 Hatred can be concealed by pretense,
    but malice will be revealed in the
    assembly.†
27 Whoever digs a pit falls into it;
    and a stone comes back upon the one
    who rolls it.*
28 The lying tongue is its owner's enemy,
    and the flattering mouth works ruin.

27 ¹Do not boast about tomorrow,
    for you do not know what any day
    may bring forth.
2  Let another praise you, not your own
    mouth;
    a stranger, not your own lips.
3  Stone is heavy, and sand a burden,
    but a fool's provocation is heavier
    than both.*
4  Anger is cruel, and wrath overwhelming,
    but before jealousy who can stand?†
5† Better is an open rebuke
    than a love that remains hidden.
6  Trustworthy are the blows of a friend,
    dangerous, the kisses of an enemy.†
7  One who is full spurns honey;
    but to the hungry, any bitter thing is
    sweet.
8  Like a bird far from the nest

† 26:7–9 Fools either abuse or are unable to use whatever knowledge they have. *A thorn:* a proverb is "words spoken at the proper time" (25:11). Fools have no sense of the right time; their statements are like thorns that fasten on clothing randomly.

26:13–16 Each verse mentions the sluggard, whom Proverbs regards with derision. The criticism is not against low energy but failure to act and take responsibility. Proverbs' ideal is the active person who uses heart, lips, hands, feet to keep to the good path. The verses are examples of the sardonic humor of the book.

26:20–22 The three proverbs have a common theme—the destructive power of slanderous words. Certain words are repeated: wood and fire, talebearer.

26:22 Malicious gossip is compared to delicious food that is swallowed and lodges in the deepest recesses of one's body. Negative comments are seldom forgotten. Prv 18:8 is a duplicate.

26:23 Heart = what is within, and lips (words) = what is expressed, are compared to an earthenware jar covered with glaze.

26:25 *Seven abominations:* many evil intentions.

26:26 Hate may be concealed for a time, but it will eventually issue in a deed and become known in the public assembly. There is a play on words: the consonants of the word "hatred" (ś'n) are literally concealed in the word "pretense" (mś'n).

27:4 Anger generally subsides with time but jealousy coolly calculates and plots revenge.

27:5–6 Verses 5 and 6 are concerned with true friendship. "Better than" sayings often declare one thing superior to another in view of some value, e.g., 15:17, vegetables are better than meat in view of a milieu of love. In v. 5, a rebuke is better than an act of affection in view of discipline that imparts wisdom.

27:6 The present translation is conjectural. The meaning seems to be that a friend's rebuke can be life-giving and an enemy's kiss can be deadly (like the kiss of Judas in Mt 26:48).

* 
26:11 2 Pt 2:22.          26:25 Sir 12:10; 27:33.
26:13 Prv 22:13.          26:27 Eccl 10:8; Sir
26:15 Prv 19:24.              27:25–26.
26:21 Prv 15:18; 29:22.   27:3 Sir 22:14–15.
26:22 Prv 18:8.

so is anyone far from home.†

9 Perfume and incense bring joy to the
heart,
but by grief the soul is torn asunder.

10 Do not give up your own friend and
your father's friend;
do not resort to the house of your
kindred when trouble strikes.
Better a neighbor near than kin far
away.†

11 Be wise, my son, and bring joy to my
heart,
so that I can answer whoever taunts
me.†

12 The astute see an evil and hide;
the naive continue on and pay the
penalty.*

13 Take the garment of the one who
became surety for a stranger;*
if for a foreign woman, exact the
pledge!†

14 Those who greet their neighbor with a
loud voice† in the early
morning,
a curse can be laid to their charge.

15 For a persistent leak on a rainy day
the match is a quarrelsome wife;*

16 Whoever would hide her hides a
stormwind
and cannot tell north from south.

17 Iron is sharpened by iron;
one person sharpens another.†

18 Those who tend a fig tree eat its fruit;
so those attentive to their master will
be honored.

19 As face mirrors face in water,
so the heart reflects the person.

20 Sheol and Abaddon can never be
satisfied;*
so the eyes of mortals can never be
satisfied.†

21 The crucible for silver, the furnace for
gold,
so you must assay the praise you
receive.

22 Though you pound fools with a pestle,
their folly never leaves them.

23† Take good care of your flocks,
give careful attention to your herds;

24 For wealth does not last forever,
nor even a crown from age to age.

25 When the grass comes up and the new
growth appears,
and the mountain greens are gathered
in,

26 The lambs will provide you with
clothing,
and the goats, the price of a field,

27 And there will be ample goat's milk for
your food,
food for your house, sustenance for
your maidens.

# 28

1 The wicked flee though none
pursue;
but the just, like a lion, are confident.

2 If a land is rebellious, its princes will be
many;
but with an intelligent and wise ruler
there is stability.†

3 One who is poor and extorts from the
lowly
is a devastating rain that leaves no
food.†

---

27:8 The bird symbolizes vulnerability as it flees before danger as in Is 10:14; 16:2; and Ps 11:1. For the importance of place in human life, see Jb 20:8–9. People are defined by their place, but, tragically, war, poverty, or illness can force them from it.
27:10 The adage is about the difference between friends and kin in a crisis. Two admonitions are grounded in one maxim (colon C). The same Hebrew word means both "one who is near" and "friend." The whole proverb urges the reader to cultivate old family friends and neighbors and not to rely exclusively on kin in times of trouble, for kin may not be there for us.
27:11 A father's command to a son to be wise, another way of saying that sons or daughters bring joy or shame to their parents.
27:13 See note on 20:16.
27:14 One interpretation takes the proverb as humorous and the other takes it as serious: (1) an overly loud and ill-timed greeting (lit., "blessing") invites the response of a curse rather than a "blessing" (greeting); (2) the loud voice suggests hypocrisy in the greeting.
27:17 Iron sharpens the "face" (panim = surface, edge) of iron, and a human being sharpens the "face" (panim = face, words) of another. Human beings learn from each other and

grow in wisdom by conversing.
27:20 Sheol, the underworld abode of the dead, is personified as a force that is never satisfied and always desires more. Cf. Is 5:14 and Hos 13:14. The saying is applicable to modern consumerism.
27:23–27 A little treatise on farming in the form of admonitions. It proposes the advantages of field and flock over other forms of wealth. Herds are the most productive wealth, for their value does not diminish; they are a source of money, clothing, and food. The thought is conservative and traditional but the development is vivid and concrete.
28:2 The first line expresses the paradox that rebellion, far from doing away with rulers, actually multiplies them. The second line is corrupt.
28:3 The reference may be to tax farmers who collected taxes and took a commission. The collectors' lack of wealth was the cause of their oppression of poor farmers. They are like a rain too violent to allow crops to grow.

---

*
27:12 Prv 22:3.      27:15 Prv 21:9; 25:24.
27:13 Prv 20:16.      27:20 Prv 30:16; Eccl 4:8.

4 Those who abandon instruction† praise
     the wicked,
       but those who keep instruction
       oppose them.
5 The evil understand nothing of justice,†
     but those who seek the Lord
       understand everything.
6 Better to be poor and walk in integrity
     than rich and crooked in one's ways.*
7 Whoever heeds instruction is a wise son,
     but whoever joins with wastrels
       disgraces his father.
8 Whoever amasses wealth by interest and
     overcharge†
       gathers it for the one who is kind to
       the poor.
9 Those who turn their ears from hearing
     instruction,*
       even their prayer is an abomination.
10 Those who mislead the upright into an
     evil way
       will themselves fall into their own pit,
       but the blameless will attain
       prosperity.
11 The rich are wise in their own eyes,
     but the poor who are intelligent see
       through them.
12 When the just triumph, there is great
     glory;
       but when the wicked prevail, people
       hide.†
13 Those who conceal their sins do not
     prosper,
       but those who confess and forsake
       them obtain mercy.†
14 Happy those who always fear;†
     but those who harden their hearts fall
       into evil.
15 A roaring lion or a ravenous bear

     is a wicked ruler over a poor people.
16 The less prudent the rulers, the more
       oppressive their deeds.
     Those who hate ill-gotten gain
       prolong their days.
17 Though a person burdened with blood
       guilt is in flight even to the grave,
     let no one offer support.
18 Whoever walks blamelessly is safe,
     but one whose ways are crooked falls
       into a pit.
19 Those who cultivate their land will have
       plenty of food,
     but those who engage in idle pursuits
       will have plenty of want.*
20 The trustworthy will be richly blessed;
     but whoever hastens to be rich will
       not go unpunished.*
21 To show partiality is never good:*
     for even a morsel of bread one may
       do wrong.†
22 Misers hurry toward wealth,
     not knowing that want is coming
       toward them.†
23 Whoever rebukes another wins more
       favor
     than one who flatters with the tongue.
24 Whoever defrauds father or mother and
       says, "It is no sin,"*
     is a partner to a brigand.
25 The greedy person stirs up strife,
     but the one who trusts in the Lord
       will prosper.
26 Those who trust in themselves are fools,
     but those who walk in wisdom are safe.
27 Those who give to the poor have no
       lack,*
     but those who avert their eyes, many
       curses.

---

**28:4** *Instruction: torah*; the word is used both for the teaching of the wise and the law of Moses.

**28:5** *Understanding nothing of justice* plays on the twofold sense of justice as righteousness and as punishment that comes on the wicked. On the other hand, *those who seek the Lord understand everything*, i.e., that the Lord punishes the wicked and rewards the righteous (themselves).

**28:8** Interest and overcharge were strictly forbidden in the old law among Israelites because it was presumed that the borrower was in distress; cf. Ex 22:25; Lv 25:35–37; Dt 23:20; Ps 15:5; Ez 18:8. Divine providence will take the offender's wealth; cf. Eccl 2:26.

**28:12** People react in opposite ways to the triumph of good and evil. To the triumph of good, they react by public display, public celebration, and to the triumph of evil, by hiding.

**28:13** Concealing the faults of another is a good thing in Proverbs (17:9), but concealing one's own sins is not. Ps 32:1–5 expresses the anguish caused by concealing one's sins rather

than bringing them to light so they can be healed by God.

**28:14** *Fear* is a different verb than in the phrase "to fear (or revere) the Lord." In its only other biblical occurrence (Is 51:13), the verb means to dread an oppressor. The saying states a paradox: those who fear in the sense of being cautious are declared happy, whereas those who are fearless will fall into traps they did not "fear." In short, there is good fear and bad fear.

**28:21** Cf. 24:23. Verse 21b warns that even in a light matter one must remain impartial.

**28:22** "Bad of eye" is the Hebrew idiom for miserly. Misers fail to see that poverty is hurrying toward them because of their wrong attitude toward wealth. Because misers are "bad of eye," they do not see the danger.

---

28:6 Prv 19:1.
28:9 Prv 15:8; 21:27.
28:19 Prv 12:11.
28:20 Prv 13:11.

28:21 Prv 24:23.
28:24 Mk 7:11–13.
28:27 Prv 19:17; Sir 4:3–8.

28 When the wicked prevail, people hide;
but at their fall the just abound.*

# 29

1 Those stiff-necked in the face of
reproof
in an instant will be shattered beyond
cure.†

2 When the just flourish, the people
rejoice;
but when the wicked rule, the people
groan.†*

3 Whoever loves wisdom gives joy to his
father,
but whoever consorts with harlots
squanders his wealth.

4 By justice a king builds up the land;
but one who raises taxes tears it
down.†

5 Those who speak flattery to their
neighbor
cast a net at their feet.†

6 The sin of the wicked is a trap,
but the just run along joyfully.*

7 The just care for the cause of the poor;
the wicked do not understand such
care.†

8 Scoffers enflame the city,
but the wise calm the fury.*

9 If a wise person disputes with a fool,
there is railing and ridicule but no
resolution.

10 The bloodthirsty hate the blameless,
but the upright seek his life.†

11 Fools give vent to all their anger;
but the wise, biding their time,
control it.*

12 If rulers listen to lying words,
their servants all become wicked.

13 The poor and the oppressor meet:*
the LORD gives light to the eyes of
both.

14 If a king is honestly for the rights of the
poor,
his throne stands firm forever.*

15 The rod of correction gives wisdom,
but uncontrolled youths disgrace their
mothers.*

16 When the wicked increase, crime
increases;
but the just will behold their
downfall.†

17 Discipline your children, and they will
bring you comfort,
and give delight to your soul.

18 Without a vision the people lose
restraint;
but happy is the one who follows
instruction.†

19 Not by words alone can servants be
trained;*
for they understand but do not
respond.†

20 Do you see someone hasty in speech?*
There is more hope for a fool!

21 If servants are pampered from
childhood
they will turn out to be stubborn.

22 The ill-tempered stir up strife,
and the hotheaded cause many sins.*

23 Haughtiness brings humiliation,
but the humble of spirit acquire
honor.†*

---

† **29:1** The idiom "to stiffen one's neck" occurs in a context of not heeding a message in Dt 10:16 and 2 Kgs 17:14. To stiffen one's neck in this sense risks having it broken, as in 1 Sm 4:18.

**29:2** Popular response to a just or unjust ruler is expressed in sound—shouts of joy or groans of anguish. "Rejoice" can mean to express one's joy, i.e., joyous shouts.

**29:4** In Hebrew as in English high and low are metaphors for prosperity and depression. A king who is just "causes the land to stand up," i.e., to be prosperous, and one who makes taxes high brings a country low.

**29:5** When one addresses deceptive words to someone's face, one equivalently throws a net at their feet to snare them.

**29:7** As in 12:10 (on care for animals), the righteous care for those who are without a voice and often treated like animals. Colon B has a double meaning: the wicked have no such knowledge (care for the poor) and they have no knowledge (wisdom), for they are fools.

**29:10** An enigmatic saying in that "seek one's life" is a common idiom for killing. The saying probably plays on the idiom, interpreting "to seek the life of another" not as killing but as caring for another (as in 11:30).

**29:16** When the wicked grow numerous they sow the seeds of their own destruction, for there is a corresponding increase in offenses calling down divine retribution.

**29:18** This much-cited proverb has been interpreted in several different ways. "Vision" and "instruction" mean authoritative guidance for the community. People are demoralized without credible leadership, but any individual heeding traditional instruction can still find happiness. As in 15:15 wisdom enables an individual to surmount days of trouble.

**29:19** The give and take of reproving is not possible for servants or slaves. Ancient custom dictated silent acquiescence for them. There is no open and free dialogue, which is part of ancient discipline.

**29:23** One's prideful height brings one down and one's lowly state brings glory.

---

**28:28** Prv 28:12.
**29:2** Prv 11:10; 28:12, 28.
**29:6** Prv 12:13.
**29:8** Prv 11:11.
**29:11** Prv 12:16; 25:28; Sir 21:26.
**29:13** Prv 22:2.
**29:14** Prv 16:12; 20:28; 25:5.
**29:15** Prv 13:24; 22:15; 23:13–14; Sir 22:6; 30:1.
**29:19** Sir 33:25–30.
**29:20** Sir 9:18; Prv 26:12.
**29:22** Prv 15:18; 22:24.
**29:23** Prv 11:2; 16:18; 18:12.

24 Partners of a thief hate themselves;†
  they hear the imprecation but do not
  testify.

25 Fear of others becomes a snare,
  but the one who trusts in the LORD is
  safe.

26 Many curry favor with a ruler,
  but it is from the LORD that one
  receives justice.

27 An abomination to the just, the evildoer;
  an abomination to the wicked, one
  whose way is straight.

## VII. SAYINGS OF AGUR AND OTHERS

**30** ¹† The words of Agur, son of Jakeh the
  Massaite:

The pronouncement of mortal man: "I
  am weary, O God;
I am weary, O God, and I am
  exhausted.

2 I am more brute than human being,
  without even human intelligence;

3† Neither have I learned wisdom,
  nor have I the knowledge of the Holy
  One.

4 Who has gone up to heaven and come
  down again—
who has cupped the wind in the
  hollow of the hand?
Who has bound up the waters in a
  cloak—
who has established all the ends of
  the earth?

What is that person's name, or the name
  of his son?"†

5† Every word of God is tested;*
  he is a shield to those who take refuge
  in him.

6 Add nothing to his words,*
  lest he reprimand you, and you be
  proved a liar.

7† Two things I ask of you,
  do not deny them to me before I die:

8 Put falsehood and lying far from me,
  give me neither poverty nor riches;
  provide me only with the food I need;

9 Lest, being full, I deny you,
  saying, "Who is the LORD?"
Or, being in want, I steal,
  and profane the name of my God.

10 Do not criticize servants to their master,
  lest they curse you, and you have to
  pay the penalty.

11† There are some who curse their fathers,
  and do not bless their mothers.*

12 There are some pure in their own eyes,
  yet not cleansed of their filth.

13 There are some—how haughty their
  eyes!
  how overbearing their glance!

14 There are some—their teeth are swords,
  their teeth are knives,
Devouring the needy from the earth,
  and the poor from the human race.

15† The leech has two daughters:
  "Give," and "Give."

---

† **29:24** *Hate themselves*: because they not only incur guilt as accomplices but, by their silence, bring down on themselves the curse invoked on the unknown guilty partner. Such a case is envisioned in Lv 5:1. After a theft, a public proclamation was made, enforced by a curse. No one in a town or city could avoid hearing it. The curse hung over the accomplice. By doing nothing, neither directly stealing nor confessing, accomplices put themselves in serious danger.

**30:1–6** Scholars are divided on the original literary unit. Is it vv. 1–3, 1–4, 1–5, or 1–6? The unit is probably vv. 1–6, for a single contrast dominates: human fragility (and ignorance) and divine power (and knowledge). A similar contrast is found in Jb 28; Ps 73; Is 49:1–4. The language of self-abasement is hyperbolic; cf. 2 Sm 9:8; Ps 73:21–22; Jb 25:4–6. *Agur*: an unknown person. *Massaite*: from Massa in northern Arabia, elsewhere referred to as an encampment of the Ishmaelites (Gn 25:14). But Heb. *massa* may not be intended as a place name; it might signify "an oracle," "a prophecy," as in Is 15:1; 17:1; etc.

**30:3–4** Agur denies he has secret heavenly knowledge. The purpose of the denial is to underline that God directly gives wisdom to those who conduct themselves pleases him.

**30:4** The Hebrew text has the phrase "do you know?" at the end of v. 4, which is supported by the versions. The phrase, however, does not appear in the important Greek manuscripts Vaticanus and Sinaiticus and spoils the sense, for Agur, not God,

is the questioner. The phrase seems to be an addition to the Hebrew text, borrowed from Job 38:5, where it also follows a cosmic question.

**30:5–6** Verse 5, like the confession of the king in Ps 18:31 (and its parallel, 2 Sm 22:31), expresses total confidence in the one who rescues from death. Agur has refused a word from any other except God and makes an act of trust in God.

**30:7–9** A prayer against lying words and for sufficiency of goods, lest reaction to riches or destitution lead to offenses against God.

**30:11–14** Perverted people are here classified as unfilial (v. 11), self-righteous (v. 12), proud (v. 13) and rapacious (v. 14).

**30:15–16** Here begins a series of numerical sayings; the pattern is n, n + 1. The slight variation in number (two and three, three and four) is an example of parallelism applied to numbers. The poetic technique is attested even outside the Bible. *Two daughters: "Give," and "Give"*: the text is obscure; as the leech (a bloodsucking worm) is insatiable in its desire for blood (v. 15), so are the nether world for victims, the barren womb for offspring, the earth for water, and fire for fuel (v. 16). *Sheol*: here not so much the place of the dead as a force (death) that eventually draws all the living into it; cf. 27:20; Is 5:14; Hb 2:5. *Land...fire*:

---

* **30:5** Ps 12:7; 18:31.         **30:11** Prv 20:20.
**30:6** Dt 4:2; 13:1.

Three things never get their fill,
  four never say, "Enough!"
16 Sheol, a barren womb,*
  land that never gets its fill of water,
  and fire, which never says, "Enough!"
17 The eye that mocks a father,
  or scorns the homage due a mother,
  Will be plucked out by brook ravens;
  devoured by a brood of vultures.
18† Three things are too wonderful for me,
  yes, four I cannot understand:
19 The way of an eagle in the sky,
  the way of a serpent upon a rock,
  The way of a ship on the high seas,
  and the way of a man with a woman.
20 This is the way of an adulterous woman:
  she eats, wipes her mouth,
  and says, "I have done no wrong."†
21† Under three things the earth trembles,
  yes, under four it cannot bear up:
22 Under a slave who becomes king,
  and a fool who is glutted with food;*
23 Under an unloved woman who is wed,
  and a maidservant who displaces her
  mistress.
24† Four things are among the smallest on
  the earth,
  and yet are exceedingly wise:
25 Ants—a species not strong,
  yet they store up their food in the
  summer;
26 Badgers—a species not mighty,
  yet they make their home in the crags;
27 Locusts—they have no king,

  yet they march forth in formation;
28 Lizards—you can catch them with your
  hands,
  yet they find their way into kings'
  palaces.
29† Three things are stately in their stride,
  yes, four are stately in their carriage:
30 The lion, mightiest of beasts,
  retreats before nothing;
31 The strutting cock, and the he-goat,
  and the king at the head of his people.
32† If you have foolishly been proud
  or presumptuous—put your hand on
  your mouth;
33 For as the churning of milk produces
  curds,
  and the pressing of the nose produces
  blood,
  the churning of anger produces strife.

## VIII. SAYINGS OF KING LEMUEL†

**31** ¹ The words of Lemuel, king of Massa,†
  the instruction his mother taught him:

2 What are you doing, my son!†
  what are you doing, son of my womb;
  what are you doing, son of my vows!
3 Do not give your vigor to women,
  or your strength† to those who ruin
  kings.
4 It is not for kings, Lemuel,
  not for kings to drink wine;
  strong drink is not for princes,

---

† land (especially the dry land of Palestine) always absorbs more water; fire always requires more fuel.
**30:18–19** The soaring flight of the eagle, the mysterious movement upon a rock of the serpent which has no feet, the path of the ship through the trackless deep, and the marvelous attraction between the sexes; there is a mysterious way common to them all.
**30:20** This verse portrays the indifference of an adulterous woman who casually dismisses her guilt because it cannot be traced.
**30:21–23** Shaking heavens are part of general cosmic upheaval in Is 14:16; Jl 2:10; Am 8:8; Jb 9:6. Disturbances in nature mirror the disturbance of unworthy people attaining what they do not deserve. *Glutted with food:* someone unworthy ends up with the fulfillment that befits a wise person. *Unloved woman:* an older woman who, contrary to expectation, finds a husband.
**30:24–28** The creatures may be small, but they are wise in knowing how to govern themselves—the definition of wisdom. *Badgers:* the rock badger is able to live on rocky heights that provide security from its enemies. *Locusts:* though vulnerable individually their huge swarms are impossible to deflect.
**30:29–31** Four beings with an imperiousness visible in their walk. Only the lion is described in detail; the reader is expected to transpose its qualities to the others.
**30:32–33** The same Hebrew verb, "to churn, shake," is applied to milk, the nose (sometimes a symbol of anger), and wrath.

In each case something is eventually produced by the constant agitation. The wise make peace and avoid strife, for strife eventually harms those who provoke it.
**31:1–9** Though mothers are sources of wisdom in Proverbs (1:8; 6:20), the mother of Lemuel is special in being queen mother, which was an important position in the palace. Queen mothers played an important role in ancient palace life because of their longevity, knowledge of palace politics, and loyalty to their sons; they were in a good position to offer him sound counsel. The language of the poem contains Aramaisms, a sign of its non-Israelite origin.
  The first section, vv. 3–5, warns against abuse of sex and alcohol (wine, strong drink) lest the king *forget* the *poor*. The second section, vv. 6–9, urges the use of alcohol (strong drink, wine) so that the downtrodden *poor* can *forget* their poverty. The real subject of the poem is justice for the poor.
**31:1** *Massa:* see note on 30:1–6.
**31:2** *My son:* in the Septuagint, "my son, my firstborn."
**31:3** The Hebrew word here translated "strength" normally means "ways," but the context and a cognate language support "authority" or "strength" here.

---

*
**30:16** Prv 27:20.     **30:22** Prv 19:10; Eccl 10:6–7.

5　Lest in drinking they forget what has
　　　been decreed,
　　and violate the rights of any who are
　　　in need.
6　Give strong drink to anyone who is
　　　perishing,
　　and wine to the embittered;
7　When they drink, they will forget their
　　　misery,
　　and think no more of their troubles.
8　Open your mouth in behalf of the mute,
　　and for the rights of the destitute;
9　Open your mouth, judge justly,
　　defend the needy and the poor!

## IX. POEM ON THE WOMAN OF WORTH†

10　Who can find† a woman of worth?*
　　Far beyond jewels is her value.
11　Her husband trusts her judgment;
　　he does not lack income.
12　She brings him profit, not loss,†
　　all the days of her life.
13　She seeks out wool and flax
　　and weaves with skillful hands.
14　Like a merchant fleet,†
　　she secures her provisions from afar.
15　She rises while it is still night,
　　and distributes food to her
　　　household,
　　a portion to her maidservants.
16　She picks out a field and acquires it;
　　from her earnings she plants a
　　　vineyard.
17　She girds herself with strength;

she exerts her arms with vigor.†
18　She enjoys the profit from her dealings;
　　her lamp is never extinguished at
　　　night.†
19　She puts her hands to the distaff,
　　and her fingers ply the spindle.†
20　She reaches out her hands to the poor,
　　and extends her arms to the needy.
21　She is not concerned for her household
　　　when it snows—
　　all her charges are doubly clothed.
22　She makes her own coverlets;
　　fine linen and purple are her clothing.
23　Her husband is prominent at the city
　　　gates
　　as he sits with the elders of the land.†
24　She makes garments and sells them,
　　and stocks the merchants with belts.
25　She is clothed with strength and dignity,
　　and laughs at the days to come.†
26　She opens her mouth in wisdom;
　　kindly instruction is on her tongue.
27　She watches over† the affairs of her
　　　household,
　　and does not eat the bread of idleness.
28　Her children rise up and call her blessed;
　　her husband, too, praises her:
29　"Many are the women of proven worth,
　　but you have excelled them all."
30　Charm is deceptive and beauty fleeting;
　　the woman who fears the Lord is to
　　　be praised.†
31　Acclaim her for the work of her hands,
　　and let her deeds praise her at the city
　　　gates.

P
R
V

---

**31:10–31** An acrostic poem of twenty-two lines; each line begins with a successive letter of the Hebrew alphabet. As with many other acrostic poems in the Bible, the unity of the poem is largely extrinsic, coming not from the narrative logic but from the familiar sequence of letters. The topic is the ideal woman described through her activity as a wife. Some have suggested that the traditional hymn extolling the great deeds of a warrior has been transposed to extol a heroic wife; the focus is on her exploits. She runs a household distinguished by abundant food and clothing for all within, by its trade (import of raw materials and export of finished products), and by the renown of its head, her husband, in the community. At v. 28, the voice is no longer that of the narrator but of her children and husband as they praise her. The purpose of the poem has been interpreted variously: an encomium to offset the sometimes negative portrayal of women in the book, or, more symbolically (and more likely), a portrait of a household ruled by Woman Wisdom and a disciple of Woman Wisdom, i.e., he now has a worthy wife and children, a great household, renown in the community.
**31:10** *Who can find…?*: in 20:6 and Eccl 8:1 the question implies that finding such a person is well-nigh impossible.
**31:12** *Profit, not loss*: a commercial metaphor.
**31:14** *Like a merchant fleet*: she has her eye on the far horizon, like the ship of a merchant ready to bring supplies into her

larder. It is the only simile ("like") in the poem.
**31:17** The metaphor of clothing oneself is used to show the woman's readiness. One can gird on weapons of war and might and splendor (Ps 69:7; Is 52:9).
**31:18** *Her lamp is never extinguished at night*: indicates abundance of productive work and its accompanying prosperity; cf. 20:20; Jb 18:6.
**31:19** The wife weaves linen cloth from flax and wool from fleece, which she cultivated according to v. 13. *Distaff*: staff for holding the flax, tow, or wool, which in spinning was drawn out and twisted into yarn or thread by the spindle or round stick.
**31:23** The husband is mentioned for the first time since vv. 10–12 but as "her husband." He will not be mentioned again until v. 28, where he praises her.
**31:25** *Laughs at the days to come*: anticipates the future with joy, free of anxiety.
**31:27** *Watches over*: Hebrew *sopiyyâ*, perhaps a pun on the Greek *sophia* (= wisdom). *Bread of idleness*: she does not eat from the table of others but from her own labors.
**31:30** The true charm of this woman is her religious spirit, for she fears the Lord; cf. note on 1:7.

**31:10** Prv 12:4; Sir 26:1–4, 13–18.

# The Book of
# Ecclesiastes

## INTRODUCTION

Andrew T. Glicksman

Eat, drink, and be merry! Enjoy life while you can because you don't know when calamity will befall you or when you'll face the inevitability of death! These are basic themes in Ecclesiastes, whose author has been called a skeptic, a pessimist, a nihilist, a cynic, a philosopher, an existential thinker, a realist, and even an optimist. Such diverse judgments about the author reflect the various interpretations and applications of his Wisdom book, attesting to its rich and enduring nature.

The book's name in the Christian canon comes from its title in the Greek Septuagint, which is a translation of the Hebrew title, Qoheleth, deriving from the root qahal meaning "to assemble; to gather; to summon." The term probably refers to someone who has an important function at an assembly or gathering of people; in this case, that function is most likely to instruct individuals in the ways of wisdom. Alternatively, the title could refer to one who collects wise teachings. Perhaps both meanings were intended: "Qoheleth taught the people knowledge, and weighed, scrutinized and arranged many proverbs. Qoheleth sought to find appropriate sayings, and to write down true sayings with precision" (Eccl 12:9–10).

## Wisdom Characteristics in Ecclesiastes

Ecclesiastes is easily categorized as Wisdom literature since it exhibits most of the characteristics associated with the genre. To begin with, the work is attributed to King Solomon, who was known for his wisdom (1 Kgs 3, 5). Although the wise king's name is never explicitly mentioned in the book, the opening verse of the work identifies its contents as: "The words of David's son, Qoheleth, king in Jerusalem" (Eccl 1:1). A few verses later, the author

## Outline of Ecclesiastes

I. Qoheleth's Investigation of Life (1:12–6:9)

II. Qoheleth's Conclusions (6:10–12:14)

   A. No One Can Find Out the Best Way of Acting (7:1–8:17)

   B. No One Knows the Future (9:1–12:14)

asserts, "I, Qoheleth, was king over Israel in Jerusalem" (Eccl 1:12). Since Solomon was the only one of David's sons to reign as king over Israel, the identification is undeniable.

Another factor that makes Ecclesiastes a Wisdom work is its universalistic flavor. This feature is exhibited in its treatment of issues relevant to human beings in all times and places. Some of the terms that Qoheleth repeats throughout his work such as "all; all things" (kol; 38 times) and "under the sun" (tahat hashshamesh; 29 times) attest to this broad outlook. His opening assertions that "All things are vanity" (Eccl 1:2) and "Nothing is new under the sun" (1:9) contend that all humans experience absurdity and that life follows a cyclical pattern. A further universalistic element is that Qoheleth never uses the personal name of the Israelite deity (Yahweh) but rather opts for the generic term for God (Elohim) throughout.

At the heart of this book, as with most Wisdom texts, we encounter instructions for proper living founded upon Qoheleth's lived experience. However, in many cases Qoheleth's experience appears to contradict conventional Wisdom teaching, such as the traditional understanding of retribution (so prevalent in Proverbs and Ben Sira): "I have seen all manner of things in my vain days: the just perishing in their justice, and the wicked living long in their wickedness" (Eccl 7:15). Qoheleth admits that God has ordered creation and time itself, as evidenced in the famous poem in Eccl 3:1–8, which he summarizes in the first part of v. 11: "God has made everything appropriate to its time." Yet, in the rest of the verse, he questions whether humans are able to discern the appropriate time to act: "But [God] has put the timeless into their hearts so they cannot find out, from beginning to end, the work which God has done." Human access to wisdom within creation is limited, while the desire to seek wisdom never ends. Though wisdom is not personified in Ecclesiastes as in other Old Testament Wisdom texts (e.g., Prv 1; 8–9; Wis 6–10; Sir 24), the book is still concerned with the quest for wisdom, however limited and seemingly futile such a quest might be (Eccl 7:23–25). After all, Qoheleth's critique of wisdom is part of his search for it.

## Literary Context

There is no scholarly consensus on the exact genre of Ecclesiastes. Some have suggested that the work, and especially Eccl 1:12–2:26, reflects the style of a "royal testament" or a didactic autobiography by a king. Qoheleth is presented as the elderly King Solomon who looks back on life and teaches lessons that he has learned from experience. But this "royal testament" form is not sustained throughout the book. Others have proposed that the work has no specific overarching genre and is a collection of randomly arranged reflections and instructions. Ultimately the form of Ecclesiastes is unique, not falling into a specific genre (though it is clearly Wisdom literature). Unlike the majority of Wisdom texts, the book is primarily prose and not poetry, though some long Wisdom poems (3:1–8) and also short poetic sayings and admonitions (chs. 7, 10–11) are present throughout.

Just as the book's exact genre has puzzled scholars, so too has its structure. Topics are raised, quickly dropped, and taken up again later in the book. The main source of unity in the book is its constant repetition of catchwords and phrases. Some examples include

the repetition of *hebel*, "vanity" (37 times) and "under the sun" (29 times) and "a chase after wind" (7 times). The phrase "vanity of vanities," which is a superlative in Hebrew, expresses the absurdity and unpredictability of life. This phrase appears at the beginning and end of the book (Eccl 1:2 and 12:8), forming an *inclusio* or framing device for the work.

The majority of the book is presented in the first person, with third-person references to Qoheleth at the beginning (Eccl 1:1–2) and end (12:9–14). The latter passage, known as the epilogue, was most likely written by a disciple (or group of disciples) associated with the sage. The last verse of the book is especially surprising since it affirms the traditional understanding of retribution that Qoheleth frequently calls into question. The epilogue was probably added to make the challenging nature of the book more palatable and may be the reason it was eventually accepted as canonical by the Jewish and Christian communities.

## Historical Context

Although Ecclesiastes is attributed to Solomon, the wise king of Israel in the tenth century BCE, it was not actually written by him. Because the book shows heavy Aramaic influence and has Persian loanwords, some scholars believe it was composed in the late Persian period (mid-fifth to mid-fourth centuries BCE), though most assign a date in the early Hellenistic era (late fourth to late third centuries BCE). There are possible Greek influences, but no direct dependence upon a particular Greek philosophy has been demonstrated conclusively. For example, in the past, some scholars noted a striking similarity between Hellenistic Epicureanism and Qoheleth's stance on enjoying life (Eccl 9:7–10). However, such a view of life is already present thousands of years earlier in the Egyptian *Harper's Song* and the Old Babylonian *Epic of Gilgamesh*. In addition, Egyptian and Mesopotamian works address the absurdity and apparent randomness of life and the problem of human mortality. Examples include *An Argument between a Man and his Ba*, the *Babylonian Theodicy*, the *Dialogue of Pessimism*, and the *Epic of Gilgamesh*. Thus

Qoheleth is one voice in a long tradition of reflecting on such themes and the author may have been aware of these other texts.

# Themes of the Book

Five main themes pervade Ecclesiastes and assist in binding the work together despite its meandering style: (1) the absurdity and fleetingness of life, (2) the quest for wisdom, (3) critique of the traditional belief in divine retribution, (4) the toil of life and the inevitability of death, and (5) enjoying life while one is still able. For many of these closely related themes, Qoheleth presents both positive and negative evaluations. At times he seems to contradict himself, thereby reflecting life's complexity.

## Life is Incomprehensible and Ephemeral

Human existence is filled with uncertainty and inconsistency, which Qoheleth expresses through the Hebrew term *hebel*. This word has a wide range of meaning: "breath; vapor; fleetingness; absurdity; vanity," and the proper way to translate it differs depending on the context. It is often coupled with "a chase after wind." Running after the wind is pointless—you can never catch it because you don't know where it's blowing. Through these images, Qoheleth means to say that life is delicate and unpredictable. At times it is fleeting and absurd: rarely can we make any sense of it. No wonder so many have called this sage a pessimist!

## Pursuit of Wisdom

As a Wisdom book, Ecclesiastes is concerned with the pursuit of knowledge and truth. But Qoheleth acknowledges that this quest has its limits and at times can even seem utterly futile: "Yet when I applied my mind to know wisdom and knowledge, madness and folly, I learned that this also is a chase after wind" (Eccl 1:17). Unlike the traditional stance in Proverbs, which suggests that wisdom is readily accessible to humans (Prv 1:20–23; 8:1–11), Qoheleth claims that it is difficult to acquire. Wisdom is ultimately a gift from God—if and when he chooses to give it (Eccl 2:26; 7:24;

which is similar to Jb 28:20–28). Thus a major part of wisdom is to enjoy God's gifts while you still have them.

## Problems with the Traditional View of Retribution

In addition to questioning wisdom's accessibility, Qoheleth tackles another major traditional Wisdom teaching: divine retribution. The ancient Israelites and early Jews generally believed that God always rewarded the righteous and wise and punished the wicked and foolish. Yet Qoheleth observes: "There are those who are just but are treated as though they had done evil, and those who are wicked but are treated as though they had done justly" (Eccl 8:14). For the most part, the traditional view does not seem to be operative in the world. God may indeed reward the righteous and punish the wicked, but he does so as he sees fit and not according to any human expectation of divine justice. As a result of this human inability to understand God's ways in the world concerning retribution, Qoheleth recommends merriment: "There is nothing better for mortals under the sun than to eat and to drink and to be joyful" (8:15). Even this small consolation is overshadowed by human mortality and the lack of any real reward for working hard.

## Meaninglessness of Toil and Inevitability of Death

Qoheleth's view of toil is predominantly negative. He describes it as busywork: "A bad business God has given / to human beings to be busied with" (Eccl 1:13b; see also 3:9–10). We need something to keep us occupied until we die, and then we aren't even rewarded in the end. Here we encounter the ultimate problem in the book: the inevitability of death. Even though we are aware that we must die one day, we still don't know exactly when that will be, which adds to the "vanity" of life. These problems concerning death are further colored by a belief held by many ancient Israelites that one was only rewarded or punished in the here and now. Upon death the wise and foolish alike faced a shadowy, lifeless existence in the netherworld, known as Sheol. So, Qoheleth asks, what is the point of being wise and hardworking if everyone has the same fate in the end (2:15)? His only solution to this difficulty is to take the time to enjoy the fruit of one's labors.

## Enjoyment of Life

For Qoheleth, the answer to good living comes down to enjoying what you have while you have it. Though merrymaking is not altogether satisfying for Qoheleth, since it too lasts only a little while (Eccl 2:1–2), it is perhaps the only way to bear the uncertainties of life. Yet, as in any Wisdom book, Qoheleth recognizes appropriate limits to one's behavior: "Rejoice, O youth, while you are young / and let your heart be glad in the days of your youth. / Follow the ways of your heart, / the vision of your eyes; / Yet understand regarding all this / that God will bring you to judgment" (11:9). Qoheleth clarifies that he does not advocate an unbridled pursuit of pleasure. We should enjoy God's gift of life within reason since God is watching and at any point may choose to judge us according to our actions—shortening our already short life. While the unchecked pursuit of pleasure does not always appear to yield negative consequences, it is best to play it safe because irresponsible behavior can and often does result in calamity.

In the end, Qoheleth's basic message rings true even today. We must remember that striving for material wealth, power, and knowledge cannot ensure security and happiness. In the face of such human limitation and death's looming grip, we have no alternative but to treasure every moment of our existence as a divine gift. ∎

# THE BOOK OF ECCLESIASTES

## New American Bible, Introduction

The Hebrew name of this book and of its author, Qoheleth, is actually a title, and it perhaps means "assembler" (of students, listeners) or "collector" (of wisdom sayings). The book's more common name, Ecclesiastes, is an approximate translation into Greek of this Hebrew word. The book comprises an extended reflective essay employing autobiographical narrative, proverbs, parables, and allegories. An almost unrelenting skepticism characterizes the tone or outlook. The issues with which the author deals and the questions he raises are aimed at those who would claim any absolute values in this life, including possessions, fame, success, or pleasure. Wisdom itself is challenged, but folly is condemned.

The refrain which begins and ends the book, "Vanity of vanities" (1:1; 12:8), recurs at key points throughout. The Hebrew word, *hebel* ("vanity"), has the sense of "emptiness, futility, absurdity": "I have seen all things that are done under the sun, and behold, all is vanity and a chase after wind" (1:14; 2:11, 17, 26; etc.). Everything in human life is subject to change, to qualification, to loss: "What profit have we from all the toil which we toil at under the sun?" (1:3). The answer is in the negative: No absolute profit or gain is possible. Even if some temporary profit or gain is achieved, it will ultimately be cancelled out by death, the great leveller (2:14–15; 3:19–20). Wisdom has some advantage over foolishness, but even wisdom's advantage is only a temporary and qualified one.

Many would locate Ecclesiastes in the third century B.C., when Judea was under the oppressive domination of Hellenistic kings from Egypt. These kings were highly efficient in their ruthless exploitation of the land and people (4:1; 5:7). The average Jew would have felt a sense of powerlessness and inability to change things for the better. For Qoheleth, God seems remote and uncommunicative, and we cannot hope to understand, much less influence, God's activity in the world (3:11; 8:16–17).

The book's honest and blunt appraisal of the human condition provides a healthy corrective to the occasionally excessive self-assurance of other wisdom writers. Its radical skepticism is somewhat tempered by the resigned conclusions to rejoice in whatever gifts God may give (2:24; 3:12–13, 22; 5:17–18; 8:15; 9:7–9; 11:9).

The Book of Ecclesiastes is divided as follows:

I. Qoheleth's Investigation of Life (1:12–6:9)

II. Qoheleth's Conclusions (6:10–12:14)

   A. No One Can Find Out the Best Way of Acting (7:1–8:17)

   B. No One Knows the Future (9:1–12:14) ■

# ECCLESIASTES

**1** ¹ The words of David's son, Qoheleth, king in Jerusalem:†*

² 　Vanity of vanities,† says Qoheleth,
　　　vanity of vanities! All things are
　　　　vanity!*

### Vanity of Human Toil

³ 　What profit have we from all the toil
　　　which we toil at under the sun?†*

⁴ 　One generation departs and another
　　　generation comes,
　　but the world forever stays.

⁵ 　The sun rises and the sun sets;
　　　then it presses on to the place where it
　　　　rises.

⁶ 　Shifting south, then north,
　　　back and forth shifts the wind,
　　　　constantly shifting its course.

⁷ 　All rivers flow to the sea,
　　　yet never does the sea become full.
　　To the place where they flow,
　　　the rivers continue to flow.

⁸ 　All things are wearisome,†
　　　too wearisome for words.
　　The eye is not satisfied by seeing
　　　nor has the ear enough of hearing.*

⁹ What has been, that will be; what has been done, that will be done. Nothing is new under the sun!* ¹⁰ Even the thing of which we say, "See, this is new!" has already existed in the ages that preceded us.* ¹¹ There is no remembrance of past generations;* nor will future generations be remembered by those who come after them.†

## I. QOHELETH'S INVESTIGATION OF LIFE

**Twofold Introduction.** ¹² I, Qoheleth, was king over Israel in Jerusalem, ¹³ and I applied my mind to search and investigate in wisdom all things that are done under the sun.*

　　A bad business God has given
　　　to human beings to be busied with.

¹⁴ I have seen all things that are done under the sun, and behold, all is vanity and a chase after wind.†*

¹⁵ 　What is crooked cannot be made
　　　straight,
　　and you cannot count what is not
　　　there.†

¹⁶* Though I said to myself, "See, I have greatly increased my wisdom beyond all who were before me in Jerusalem, and my mind has broad experience of wisdom and knowledge," ¹⁷ yet when I applied my mind to know wisdom and knowledge, madness and folly, I learned that this also is a chase after wind.*

¹⁸ 　For in much wisdom there is much
　　　sorrow;
　　whoever increases knowledge
　　　increases grief.†

**2** **Study of Pleasure-seeking.** ¹ I said in my heart,† "Come, now, let me try you with pleasure and the enjoyment of good things." See, this too was vanity. ² Of laughter I said:

---

**1:1** *David's son...king in Jerusalem*: the intent of the author is to identify himself with Solomon. This is a literary device, by which the author hopes to commend his work to the public under the name of Israel's most famous sage (see 1 Kgs 5:9–14).
**1:2** *Vanity of vanities*: a Hebrew superlative expressing the supreme degree of futility and emptiness.
**1:3** *Under the sun*: used throughout this book to signify "on the earth."
**1:8** *All things are wearisome*: or, "All speech is wearisome."
**1:11** Movement in nature and human activity appears to result in change and progress. The author argues that this change and progress are an illusion: "Nothing is new under the sun."
**1:14** *A chase after wind*: an image of futile activity, like an attempt to corral the winds; cf. Hos 12:2. The ancient versions understood "affliction, dissipation of the spirit." This phrase concludes sections of the text as far as 6:9.
**1:15** *You cannot count what is not there*: perhaps originally a commercial metaphor alluding to loss or deficit in the accounts ledger.

**1:18** *Sorrow...grief*: these terms refer not just to a store of knowledge or to psychological or emotional pain. Corporal punishment, sometimes quite harsh, was also employed frequently by parents and teachers.
**2:1–11** The author here assumes the role of Solomon who, as king, would have had the wealth and resources at his disposal to acquire wisdom and engage in pleasurable pursuits. Verses 4–8 in particular, with their description of abundant wealth and physical gratifications, parallel the descriptions in 1 Kgs 4–11 of the extravagances of Solomon's reign.

---

*
**1:1** Eccl 1:12; 12:9–10.　　**1:10** Eccl 3:15.
**1:2** Eccl 2:8.　　**1:11** Eccl 2:16.
**1:3** Eccl 2:11, 22; 3:9;　　**1:13** Eccl 8:9.
　5:15.　　**1:14** Eccl 2:11, 17.
**1:8** Eccl 4:8; 5:9–11.　　**1:16** Eccl 2:9.
**1:9** Eccl 3:15; 6:10.　　**1:17** Eccl 1:3; 8:16.

"Mad!" and of mirth: "What good does this do?" ³Guided by wisdom,† I probed with my mind how to beguile my senses with wine and take up folly, until I should understand what is good for human beings to do under the heavens during the limited days of their lives.

⁴I undertook great works; I built myself houses and planted vineyards; ⁵I made gardens and parks, and in them set out fruit trees of all sorts. ⁶And I constructed for myself reservoirs to water a flourishing woodland. ⁷I acquired male and female slaves, and had slaves who were born in my house. I also owned vast herds of cattle and flocks of sheep, more than all who had been before me in Jerusalem. ⁸I amassed for myself silver and gold, and the treasures of kings and provinces. I provided for myself male and female singers and delights of men, many women.† ⁹I accumulated much more than all others before me in Jerusalem; my wisdom, too, stayed with me. ¹⁰Nothing that my eyes desired did I deny them, nor did I deprive myself of any joy; rather, my heart rejoiced in the fruit of all my toil. This was my share for all my toil. ¹¹*But when I turned to all the works that my hands had wrought, and to the fruit of the toil for which I had toiled so much, see! all was vanity and a chase after wind. There is no profit under the sun. ¹²What about one who succeeds a king? He can do only what has already been done.†

**Study of Wisdom and Folly.** I went on to the consideration of wisdom, madness and folly. ¹³And I saw that wisdom has as much profit over folly as light has over darkness.

¹⁴     Wise people have eyes in their heads,
       but fools walk in darkness.

Yet I knew that the same lot befalls both.†* ¹⁵So I said in my heart, if the fool's lot is to befall me also, why should I be wise? Where is the profit? And in my heart I decided that this too is vanity. ¹⁶*The wise person will have no more abiding remembrance than the fool; for in days to come both will have been forgotten. How is it that the wise person dies† like the fool! ¹⁷Therefore I detested life, since for me the work that is done under the sun is bad; for all is vanity and a chase after wind.

**Study of the Fruits of Toil**

**To Others the Profits.** ¹⁸And I detested all the fruits of my toil under the sun, because I must leave them to the one who is to come after me. ¹⁹And who knows whether that one will be wise or a fool? Yet that one will take control of all the fruits of my toil and wisdom under the sun. This also is vanity. ²⁰So my heart turned to despair over all the fruits of my toil under the sun. ²¹For here is one who has toiled with wisdom and knowledge and skill, and that one's legacy must be left to another who has not toiled for it. This also is vanity and a great evil. ²²*For what profit comes to mortals from all the toil and anxiety of heart with which they toil under the sun? ²³Every day sorrow and grief are their occupation; even at night their hearts are not at rest. This also is vanity.

²⁴†*There is nothing better for mortals than to eat and drink and provide themselves with good things from their toil. Even this, I saw, is from the hand of God. ²⁵For who can eat or drink apart from God? ²⁶†*For to the one who pleases God, he gives wisdom and knowledge and joy; but to the one who displeases, God gives the task of gathering possessions for

---

**2:3** *Guided by wisdom*: using all the means money can buy, the author sets out on a deliberate search to discover if pleasure constitutes true happiness.

**2:8** *Many women*: the final phrase of this verse is difficult to translate. One word, *shiddah*, which appears here in both singular and plural, is found nowhere else in the Hebrew Bible. A suggested meaning is "woman" or "concubine," as it is interpreted here: "many women." The rest of the section (2:1–12) seems to be a description of Solomon's kingdom, and the "many women" would represent his huge harem (1 Kgs 11:1–3). In rabbinic Hebrew the word comes to mean "chest" or "coffer."

**2:12** *What…been done*: the verse is difficult and elliptical. The words "He can do only" have been added for clarity. The two halves of the verse have been reversed. The author argues that it is useless to repeat the royal experiment described in vv. 1–11. The results would only be the same.

**2:14** *Yet I knew…befalls both*: the author quotes a traditional saying upholding the advantages of wisdom, but then qualifies

it. Nothing, not even wisdom itself, can give someone absolute control over their destiny and therefore guarantee any advantage.

**2:16** *The wise person dies*: death, until now only alluded to (vv. 14–15), takes center stage and will constantly appear in the author's reflections through the remainder of the book.

**2:24–26** The author is not advocating unrestrained indulgence. Rather he counsels acceptance of the good things God chooses to give. This is the first of seven similar conclusions that Qoheleth provides; see 3:12–13, 22; 5:17–18; 8:15; 9:7–9; 11:9.

**2:26** According to 7:15 and 9:1–3, God does not make an objective, evidential, moral distinction between saint and sinner. God "gives" as God pleases.

**2:11** Eccl 1:3, 17; Sir 44:9.
**2:14** Eccl 9:2–3.
**2:16** Eccl 1:11; Wis 2:4.
**2:22** Eccl 1:3.
**2:24** Eccl 3:12–13, 22; 5:17–19; 8:15.
**2:26** Eccl 7:26; Prv 13:22.

the one who pleases God. This also is vanity and a chase after wind.

## No One Can Determine the Right Time to Act

**3** [1]† There is an appointed time for everything,
and a time for every affair under the heavens.
[2] A time to give birth, and a time to die;
a time to plant, and a time to uproot the plant.
[3] A time to kill, and a time to heal;
a time to tear down, and a time to build.
[4] A time to weep, and a time to laugh;
a time to mourn, and a time to dance.
[5] A time to scatter stones, and a time to gather them;
a time to embrace, and a time to be far from embraces.
[6] A time to seek, and a time to lose;
a time to keep, and a time to cast away.
[7] A time to rend, and a time to sew;
a time to be silent, and a time to speak.
[8] A time to love, and a time to hate;
a time of war, and a time of peace.

[9]* What profit have workers from their toil? [10] I have seen the business that God has given to mortals to be busied about. [11]* God has made everything appropriate to its time, but has put the timeless† into their hearts so they cannot find out, from beginning to end, the work which God has done. [12]* I recognized that there is nothing better than to rejoice and to do well during life. [13] Moreover, that all can eat and drink and enjoy the good of all their toil—this is a gift of God. [14] I recognized that whatever God does will endure forever; there is no adding to it, or taking from it. Thus has God done that he may be revered. [15]†* What now is has already been; what is to be, already is: God retrieves what has gone by.

**The Problem of Retribution.** [16]* And still under the sun in the judgment place I saw wickedness, and wickedness also in the seat of justice. [17]* I said in my heart, both the just and the wicked God will judge, since a time is set for every affair and for every work.† [18] I said in my heart: As for human beings, it is God's way of testing them and of showing that they are in themselves like beasts. [19] For the lot of mortals and the lot of beasts is the same lot: The one dies as well as the other. Both have the same life breath. Human beings have no advantage over beasts, but all is vanity. [20]* Both go to the same place; both were made from the dust, and to the dust they both return. [21] Who knows† if the life breath of mortals goes upward and the life breath of beasts goes earthward? [22]* And I saw that there is nothing better for mortals than to rejoice in their work; for this is their lot. Who will let them see what is to come after them?*

**4** **Vanity of Toil.** [1] Again I saw all the oppressions that take place under the sun: the tears of the victims with none to comfort† them! From the hand of their oppressors comes violence, and there is none to comfort them!* [2] And those now dead, I declared more fortunate in death than are the living to be still alive.* [3] And better off than both is the yet unborn, who has not seen the wicked work that is done under the sun. [4] Then I saw that all toil and skillful work is the rivalry of one person with another. This also is vanity and a chase after wind.

---

† **3:1–8** The fourteen pairs of opposites describe various human activities. The poem affirms that God has determined the appropriate moment or "time" for each. Human beings cannot know that moment; further, the wider course of events and purposes fixed by God are beyond them as well.
**3:11** The timeless: others translate "eternity," "the world," or "darkness." The author credits God with keeping human beings ignorant about God's "work"—present and future.
**3:15** The verse is difficult. Literally it reads "and God seeks out what was pursued." It appears to be a variation of the theme in 1:9, "There is nothing new under the sun."
**3:17** A time is set…work: another possible reading would see this verse referring to a judgment in or after death: "a time for every affair and for every work there" (that is, in death or in Sheol).
**3:21** Who knows: the author presumes a negative answer:

"No one knows." In place of speculation on impossible questions, the author counsels enjoyment of what is possible (cf. v. 22; but see also 2:10–11).
**4:1** Oppressions…victims…none to comfort: the author obviously feels deeply about the plight of the oppressed, but he seems to feel powerless to do anything. The repetition of "none to comfort" is purposeful, and emphatic.

* 
**3:9** Eccl 1:3.
**3:11** Eccl 8:17; 11:5.
**3:12** Eccl 2:24.
**3:15** Eccl 1:9.
**3:16** Eccl 4:1.
**3:17** Eccl 8:6a; 11:9; 12:14.
**3:20** Eccl 12:7; Gn 3:19; Sir 17:2.
**3:22** Eccl 3:12–13; 5:17–18.
**3:22** Eccl 8:7; 10:14.
**4:1** Eccl 3:16; 5:7; 9:4–5.
**4:2** Eccl 6:3–5.

5   "Fools fold their arms
     and consume their own flesh"—†

6   Better is one handful with tranquility
     than two with toil and a chase after
     wind!

**Companions and Successors.** 7 Again I saw this vanity under the sun: 8 those all alone with no companion, with neither child nor sibling—with no end to all their toil, and no satisfaction from riches. For whom do I toil and deprive myself of good things? This also is vanity and a bad business. 9 Two are better than one: They get a good wage for their toil. 10 If the one falls, the other will help the fallen one. But woe to the solitary person! If that one should fall, there is no other to help. 11 So also, if two sleep together, they keep each other warm. How can one alone keep warm? 12 Where one alone may be overcome, two together can resist. A three-ply cord† is not easily broken.

13 † Better is a poor but wise youth than an old but foolish king who no longer knows caution; 14 for from a prison house he came forth to reign; despite his kingship he was born poor. 15 I saw all the living, those who move about under the sun, with the second youth who will succeed him.† 16 There is no end to all this people, to all who were before them; yet the later generations will not have joy in him. This also is vanity and a chase after wind.

**Vanity of Many Words.** 17 * Guard your step when you go to the house of God.† Draw near for obedience, rather than for the fools' offering of sacrifice; for they know not how to keep from doing evil.

5 1 † Be not hasty in your utterance and let not your heart be quick to utter a promise in God's presence. God is in heaven and you are on earth; therefore let your words be few. *

2   As dreams come along with many cares,
     so a fool's voice along with a
     multitude of words.

3 * When you make a vow to God, delay not its fulfillment. For God has no pleasure in fools; fulfill what you have vowed. 4 It is better not to make a vow than make it and not fulfill it. 5 Let not your utterances make you guilty, and say not before his representative, "It was a mistake." Why should God be angered by your words and destroy the works of your hands? 6 * Despite many dreams, futilities, and a multitude of words, fear God!

**Gain and Loss of Goods.** 7 * If you see oppression of the poor, and violation of rights and justice in the realm, do not be astonished by the fact, for the high official has another higher than he watching him and above these are others higher still—. 8 But profitable for a land in such circumstances is a king concerned about cultivation.†

9 * The covetous are never satisfied with money, nor lovers of wealth with their gain; so this too is vanity. 10 Where there are great riches, there are also many to devour them. Of what use are they to the owner except as a feast for the eyes alone? 11 Sleep is sweet to the laborer, whether there is little or much to eat; but the abundance of the rich allows them no sleep.

12 This is a grievous evil which I have seen under the sun: riches hoarded by their owners

---

**4:5** *Consume their own flesh*: an enigmatic statement. In the context of vv. 4 and 6 it seems to warn that those who refuse to work for the necessities of life will suffer hunger and impair their bodily health. But the verse could also be intended for the industrious: Even the lazy may manage to have "their own flesh," that is, have sufficient food to eat.

**4:12** *A three-ply cord*: an ancient proverb known centuries before biblical times. The progression ("two together...three-ply") seems to imply, "If two are good, three are even better."

**4:13–16** This passage deals with kingship and succession, but is obscure.

**4:15** The king is no sooner dead than the people transfer their allegiance to his successor.

**4:17** *The house of God*: the Temple in Jerusalem. *Obedience...sacrifice*: the Temple was the place not only for sacrifice but also for instruction in the Law. Sacrifice without obedience was unacceptable; cf. 1 Sm 15:22; Hos 6:6.

**5:1–6** Further counsels on prudence and circumspection in fulfilling one's religious obligations. It is not the multitude of words but one's sincerity that counts in the acknowledgment of God's sovereignty (v. 1), especially through obedience (4:17) and reverence (v. 6).

**5:8** *A king concerned about cultivation*: the Hebrew text is ambiguous and obscure. The author does not criticize the oppression he describes in v. 7. Now perhaps he expresses the hope that the king would use his power to upbuild agriculture in order to alleviate the hunger and suffering of the poor and oppressed.

**4:17** 1 Sm 15:22; Ps 40:7–9; Prv 15:8; 21:3; Hos 6:6.
**5:1** Ps 115:3, 16; Mt 6:7; Jas 1:19.
**5:3** Nm 30:3; Dt 23:22–24; Prv 20:25; Sir 18:22–23.
**5:6** Eccl 3:14.
**5:7** Eccl 3:16; 4:1.
**5:9** Eccl 4:8; Prv 28:22.

to their own hurt. [13] Should the riches be lost through some misfortune, they may have offspring when they have no means. [14]* As they came forth from their mother's womb, so again shall they return, naked as they came, having nothing from their toil to bring with them. [15] This too is a grievous evil, that they go just as they came. What then does it profit them to toil for the wind? [16] All their days they eat in gloom with great vexation, sickness and resentment.

[17]* Here is what I see as good: It is appropriate to eat and drink and prosper from all the toil one toils at under the sun during the limited days of life God gives us; for this is our lot. [18] Those to whom God gives riches and property, and grants power to partake of them, so that they receive their lot and find joy in the fruits of their toil: This is a gift from God. [19] For they will hardly dwell on the shortness of life, because God lets them busy themselves with the joy of their heart.†

**6** **Limited Worth of Enjoyment.** [1] There is another evil I have seen under the sun, and it weighs heavily upon humankind: [2]* There is one to whom God gives riches and property and honor, and who lacks nothing the heart could desire; yet God does not grant the power to partake of them, but a stranger devours them. This is vanity and a dire plague. [3] Should one have a hundred children and live many years, no matter to what great age, still if one has not the full benefit of those goods, I proclaim that the child born dead, even if left unburied, is more fortunate.† [4]* Though it came in vain and goes into darkness and its name is enveloped in darkness, [5] though it has not seen the sun or known anything, yet the dead child has more peace. [6] Should such a one live twice a thousand years and not enjoy those goods, do not both go to the same place?†

[7] All human toil is for the mouth,† yet the appetite is never satisfied. [8] What profit have the wise compared to fools, or what profit have the lowly in knowing how to conduct themselves in life? [9] "What the eyes see is better than what the desires wander after."† This also is vanity and a chase after wind.

## II. QOHELETH'S CONCLUSIONS

[10] Whatever is, was long ago given its name, and human nature is known; mortals cannot contend in judgment with One who is stronger.† [11] For the more words, the more vanity; what profit is there for anyone? [12]* For who knows what is good for mortals in life, the limited days of their vain life, spent like a shadow? Because who can tell them what will come afterward under the sun?*

### A. No One Can Find Out the Best Way of Acting

#### Critique of Sages on the Day of Adversity

**7** [1] A good name is better than good
　　　　ointment,†
　　　and the day of death than the day of
　　　　birth.*
[2]　It is better to go to the house of
　　　　mourning
　　　than to the house of feasting,
　　　For that is the end of every mortal,
　　　　and the living should take it to heart.*
[3]　Sorrow is better than laughter;
　　　when the face is sad, the heart grows
　　　　wise.
[4]　The heart of the wise is in the house of
　　　　mourning,
　　　but the heart of fools is in the house
　　　　of merriment.
[5]　It is better to listen to the rebuke of the
　　　　wise

---

**5:19** The joys of life, though temporary and never assured, keep one from dwelling on the ills which afflict mankind.

**6:3** Even a large family and exceptionally long life cannot compensate for the absence of good things and the joy which they bring.

**6:6** *Same place*: the grave; cf. 3:20; 12:7.

**6:7** *The mouth*: symbolic of human desires.

**6:9** Compare the English proverb, "A bird in the hand is worth two in the bush." However, it could also mean, "The seeing of the eyes is better than the wandering of the desire," with the emphasis on the actions of seeing and desiring. Seeing is a way of possessing whereas desire, by definition, can remain frustrated and unfulfilled.

**6:10–11** *One who is stronger* is, of course, God. *The more*

*vanity*: contending with God is futile.

**7:1** *Ointment*: a good name can be affirmed only with death, when one is normally anointed. The author dialogues in this section (vv. 1–14) with traditional wisdom, alternately affirming or countering its assertions. The real value of traditional wisdom lies in its ability to provoke one to thought and reflection, and not to absolve one from such activity.

---

| | |
|---|---|
| **5:14** Jb 1:21; 1 Tm 6:7. | **6:12** Jb 8:9; 14:2; Ps |
| **5:17** Eccl 2:24. | 102:12. |
| **6:2** Eccl 2:18–19. | **6:12** Eccl 3:22; 8:7. |
| **6:4** Eccl 4:2–3; Jb 3:11; | **7:1** Eccl 4:2; Prv 22:1. |
| 16. | **7:2** Eccl 12:1. |

than to listen to the song of fools;

6   For as the crackling of thorns under a
     pot,
     so is the fool's laughter.
     This also is vanity.

7   Extortion can make a fool out of the wise,
     and a bribe corrupts the heart.

8   Better is the end of a thing than its
     beginning;
     better is a patient spirit than a lofty
     one.

9   Do not let anger upset your spirit,
     for anger lodges in the bosom of a
     fool.

10 Do not say: How is it that former times were better than these? For it is not out of wisdom that you ask about this.

11   Wisdom is as good as an inheritance
     and profitable to those who see the
     sun.

12† For the protection of wisdom is as the protection of money; and knowledge is profitable because wisdom gives life to those who possess it.

13 Consider the work of God. Who can make straight what God has made crooked?* 14 On a good day enjoy good things, and on an evil day consider: Both the one and the other God has made, so that no one may find the least fault with him.

### Critique of Sages on Justice and Wickedness.
15† I have seen all manner of things in my vain days: the just perishing in their justice, and the wicked living long in their wickedness. 16 "Be not just to excess, and be not overwise. Why work your own ruin? 17 Be not wicked to excess, and be not foolish. Why should you die before your time?" 18 It is good to hold to this

rule, and not to let that one go; but the one who fears God will succeed with both.

19 Wisdom is a better defense for the wise than ten princes in the city, 20* yet there is no one on earth so just as to do good and never sin. 21 Do not give your heart to every word that is spoken; you may hear your servant cursing you, 22 for your heart knows that you have many times cursed others.

23 All these things I probed in wisdom. I said, "I will acquire wisdom"; but it was far beyond me. 24 What exists is far-reaching; it is deep, very deep:† Who can find it out? 25†* I turned my heart toward knowledge; I sought and pursued wisdom and its design, and I recognized that wickedness is foolishness and folly is madness.

### Critique of Advice on Women.
26* More bitter than death I find the woman† who is a hunter's trap, whose heart is a snare, whose hands are prison bonds. The one who pleases God will be delivered from her, but the one who displeases will be entrapped by her. 27 See, this have I found, says Qoheleth, adding one to one to find the sum. 28 What my soul still seeks and has yet to find is this: "One man out of a thousand have I found, but a woman among them all I have not found." 29 But this alone I have found: God made humankind honest, but they have pursued many designs.

### Critique of Advice to Heed Authority
**8** 1† Who is like the wise person,
     and who knows the explanation of
     things?
     Wisdom illumines the face
     and transforms a grim countenance.

2 Observe the command of the king, in view of your oath to God. 3 Be not hasty to withdraw from the king; do not persist in an

---

7:12 St. Jerome's translation of v. 12b gives an edge to wisdom over money: "But learning and wisdom excel in this, that they bestow life on the one who possesses them."

7:15–24 The author continues both to affirm and to counter traditional wisdom. He affirms a certain validity to wisdom, but challenges complacency and mindless optimism. His sense of life's uncertainty and insecurity finds expression, for example, in the irony evident when v. 16 is read in the light of vv. 20–24: How can one be "excessively" just or wise, when justice and wisdom may be out of reach to begin with? The only sure thing is to "fear God" (v. 18).

7:24 Far-reaching…deep: the spatial metaphor here emphasizes wisdom's inaccessibility, a frequent theme in wisdom literature; cf. Jb 28; Prv 30:1–4; Sir 24:28–29; Bar 3:14–23.

7:25–29 The emphasis is on the devious designs of human beings in general, reflecting the viewpoint of Genesis.

7:26 More bitter than death…the woman: warnings against the scheming, adulterous woman are common in ancient wisdom (e.g., Prv 2:16–19, etc.).

8:1–4 The author continues to quote traditional wisdom but then to counter and qualify it. He concedes wisdom's advantages (v. 1), but then describes the subservience and sometimes demeaning demands required of the sage in the court of the king (vv. 2–4).

7:13 Eccl 1:15.        7:25 Eccl 1:17.
7:20 Jb 9:2; 1 Kgs 8:46;      7:26 Prv 5:4.
     Rom 3:23.

unpleasant situation, for he does whatever he pleases. ⁴His word is sovereign, and who can say to him, "What are you doing?"

⁵†* "Whoever observes a command knows no harm, and the wise heart knows times and judgments." ⁶* Yes, there is a time and a judgment for everything. But it is a great evil for mortals ⁷* that they are ignorant of what is to come; for who will make known to them how it will be? ⁸No one is master of the breath of life so as to retain it, and none has mastery of the day of death. There is no exemption in wartime, nor does wickedness deliver those who practice it. ⁹All these things I saw and I applied my heart to every work that is done under the sun, while one person tyrannizes over another for harm.

**The Problem of Retribution.** ¹⁰Meanwhile I saw the wicked buried. They would come and go from the holy place. But those were forgotten in the city who had acted justly. This also is vanity.† ¹¹Because the sentence against an evil deed is not promptly executed, the human heart is filled with the desire to commit evil— ¹²† because the sinner does evil a hundred times and survives. Though indeed I know that it shall be well with those who fear God, for their reverence toward him; ¹³and that it shall not be well with the wicked, who shall not prolong their shadowy days, for their lack of reverence toward God.

¹⁴This is a vanity that occurs on earth: There are those who are just but are treated as though they had done evil, and those who are wicked but are treated as though they had done justly. This, too, I say is vanity. ¹⁵* Therefore I praised joy, because there is nothing better for mortals under the sun than to eat and to drink and to be joyful; this will accompany them in their toil through the limited days of life God gives them under the sun.

¹⁶I applied my heart to know wisdom and to see the business that is done on earth, though neither by day nor by night do one's eyes see sleep, ¹⁷* and I saw all the work of God: No mortal can find out the work that is done under the sun. However much mortals may toil in searching, no one finds it out; and even if the wise claim to know, they are unable to find it out.

### B. No One Knows the Future

**9** ¹All this I have kept in my heart and all this I examined: The just, the wise, and their deeds are in the hand of God. Love from hatred† mortals cannot tell; both are before them. ²* Everything is the same for everybody: the same lot for the just and the wicked, for the good, for the clean and the unclean, for the one who offers sacrifice and the one who does not. As it is for the good, so it is for the sinner; as it is for the one who takes an oath, so it is for the one who fears an oath. ³Among all the things that are done under the sun, this is the worst, that there is one lot for all. Hence the hearts of human beings are filled with evil, and madness is in their hearts during life; and afterward—to the dead! ⁴For whoever is chosen among all the living has hope: "A live dog† is better off than a dead lion." ⁵* For the living know that they are to die, but the dead no longer know anything. There is no further recompense for them, because all memory of them is lost. ⁶For them, love and hatred and rivalry have long since perished. Never again will they have part in anything that is done under the sun.

⁷* Go, eat your bread† with joy and drink

---

† **8:5–9** The wise exhibit keen insight about human nature and the course of events (vv. 5–6a). Yet their knowledge and wisdom confront certain limits, such as the mystery of evil and the time and inevitability of death (vv. 6b–9).

**8:10** This difficult verse seems to contrast the wicked, who die enjoying a good reputation as pious individuals, and the just, who are quietly forgotten.

**8:12–17** The author admits that traditional wisdom affirms the long life and success of the just and the short unhappy life of the wicked (vv. 12b–13). But he points out clear exceptions: the wicked who live long, and the just who suffer for no apparent reason (v. 14). His puzzlement and frustration prompt a twofold response: acceptance of whatever joy God chooses to give each day, and honest acknowledgment that no one can discover "the work of God" (cf. 3:11; 7:13; 11:5).

**9:1–3** Love from hatred…everything is the same: God seems to bestow divine favor or disfavor (love or hatred) indiscriminately on the just and wicked alike. More ominously, the arbitrariness and inevitability of death and adversity confront every human being, whether good or bad.

**9:4–6** A live dog…no further recompense: human reason and experience persuaded Qoheleth that death with its finality and annihilating power cruelly negates the supreme value—life, and with it, all possibilities (cf. v. 10). Faith in eternal life has its foundation only in hope and trust in God's promise and in God's love.

**9:7–10** Go, eat your bread…enjoy life: the author confesses his inability to imprison God in a fixed and predictable way of acting. Thus he ponders a practical and pragmatic solution: Seize whatever opportunity one has to find joy, if God grants it.

* 8:5 Prv 19:16.                5:17–18; 9:7.
8:6 Eccl 3:17; 9:12.           8:17 Eccl 3:11.
8:7 Eccl 3:22; 6:12;           9:2 Eccl 2:14; 3:15.
  10:14.                       9:5 Eccl 1:11; 2:16.
8:15 Eccl 2:24; 3:22;          9:7 Eccl 2:24; 8:15; 11:9.

your wine with a merry heart, because it is now that God favors your works. [8] At all times let your garments be white, and spare not the perfume for your head. [9] Enjoy life with the wife you love, all the days of the vain life granted you under the sun. This is your lot in life, for the toil of your labors under the sun. [10] Anything you can turn your hand to, do with what power you have; for there will be no work, no planning, no knowledge, no wisdom in Sheol where you are going.

**The Time of Misfortune Is Not Known.** [11] Again I saw under the sun that the race is not won by the swift, nor the battle by the valiant, nor a livelihood by the wise, nor riches by the shrewd, nor favor by the experts; for a time of misfortune comes to all alike. [12] Human beings no more know their own time than fish taken in the fatal net or birds trapped in the snare; like these, mortals are caught when an evil time suddenly falls upon them.

**The Uncertain Future and the Sages.** [13] On the other hand I saw this wise deed under the sun, which I thought magnificent. [14] Against a small city with few inhabitants advanced a mighty king, who surrounded it and threw up great siegeworks about it. [15] But in the city lived a man who, though poor, was wise, and he delivered it through his wisdom. Yet no one remembered this poor man. [16] * Though I had said, "Wisdom is better than force," yet the wisdom of the poor man is despised and his words go unheeded.

[17]     The quiet words of the wise are better
           heeded
       than the shout of a ruler of fools.
[18]     Wisdom is better than weapons of war,
           but one bungler destroys much good.

**10** [1] Dead flies corrupt and spoil the
           perfumer's oil;
       more weighty than wisdom or wealth
           is a little folly! †

[2]     The wise heart turns to the right;
           the foolish heart to the left. †

[3] Even when walking in the street the fool, lacking understanding, calls everyone a fool. †

[4] Should the anger of a ruler burst upon you, do not yield your place; for calmness† abates great offenses.

[5] I have seen under the sun another evil, like a mistake that proceeds from a tyrant: [6] a fool put in high position, while the great and the rich sit in lowly places. [7] I have seen slaves on horseback, while princes† went on foot like slaves.

[8]     Whoever digs a pit may fall into it,*
           and whoever breaks through a wall, a
               snake may bite.
[9]     Whoever quarries stones may be hurt by
               them,
           and whoever chops wood† is in
               danger from it.

[10] If the ax becomes dull, and the blade is not sharpened, then effort must be increased. But the advantage of wisdom is success.

[11]     If the snake bites before it is charmed,
           then there is no advantage in a
               charmer. †
[12]     Words from the mouth of the wise win
               favor,
           but the lips of fools consume them.
[13] *   The beginning of their words is folly,
           and the end of their talk is utter
               madness;

---

† 

**10:1** *Dead flies…a little folly*: wisdom is vulnerable to even the smallest amount of folly. The collection of proverbs and sayings in chaps. 10 and 11 demonstrates the author's sharp insight and strengthens his credentials as a sage. It thus adds weight to his critique of the wisdom tradition's tendencies to self-assurance and naive optimism.

**10:2** *Right…left*: the right hand is identified with power, moral goodness, favor; the left hand with ineptness and bad luck.

**10:3** *Calls everyone a fool*: or, "tells everyone that he (himself) is a fool."

**10:4** *Calmness*: a frequent motif of wisdom; silence and reserve characterize the wise, while boisterousness and impetuosity identify the fool.

**10:6–7** *A fool…the rich…slaves…princes*: another wisdom

motif: astonishment at the reversal of the usual order in the world and in human affairs.

**10:8–9** *A pit…a wall…stones…wood*: popular sayings reflecting the need for caution and alertness against the unexpected. Snakes could find a home in the stone walls of ancient Palestine; cf. Am 5:19.

**10:10–11** *Ax…success…snake…charmer*: possession of the proper skill (a form of "wisdom") can ensure success, as in the case of a sharpened ax; but one must use it before it is too late (v. 11). Cf. Sir 12:13.

---

**9:16** Prv 24:5.             Sir 27:29.
**10:8** Prv 26:27; Ps 7:16;      **10:13** Eccl 5:2; 6:11.

14  yet fools multiply words.
No one knows what is to come,
  for who can tell anyone what will
    be?*
15  The toil of fools wearies them,
  so they do not know even the way to
    town.

## No One Knows What Evil Will Come

16  Woe to you, O land, whose king is a
    youth,†
  and whose princes feast in the
    morning!
17  Happy are you, O land, whose king is of
    noble birth,
  and whose princes dine at the right
    time—
  for vigor† and not in drinking
    bouts.
18  Because of laziness, the rafters sag;
  when hands are slack, the house
    leaks.
19  A feast is made for merriment
  and wine gives joy to the living,
  but money answers† for everything.
20  Even in your thoughts do not curse the
    king,
  nor in the privacy of your bedroom
    curse the rich;
  For the birds of the air may carry your
    voice,
  a winged creature† may tell what you
    say.

**11** ¹† Send forth your bread upon the
    face of the waters;
  after a long time you may find it
    again.
2  Make seven, or even eight portions;
  you know not what misfortune may
    come upon the earth.

## No One Knows What Good Will Come

3†  When the clouds are full,
  they pour out rain upon the earth.
  Whether a tree falls to the south or to
    the north,
  wherever it falls, there shall it lie.
4  One who pays heed to the wind will
    never sow,
  and one who watches the clouds will
    never reap.
5  Just as you do not know how the life
    breath
  enters the human frame in the
    mother's womb,
  So you do not know the work of God,
  who is working in everything.*
6  In the morning sow your seed,
  and at evening do not let your hand
    be idle:
  For you do not know which of the two
    will be successful,
  or whether both alike will turn out well.

**Poem on Youth and Old Age.** 7† Light is sweet!
and it is pleasant for the eyes to see the sun.
8 However many years mortals may live, let
them, as they enjoy them all, remember that
the days of darkness will be many. All that is
to come is vanity.

9  Rejoice, O youth, while you are young
  and let your heart be glad in the days
    of your youth.
  Follow the ways of your heart,
  the vision of your eyes;
  Yet understand regarding all this
  that God will bring you to judgment.
10  Banish misery from your heart
  and remove pain from your body,
  for youth and black hair are fleeting.†

---

**10:16** *A youth*: thus too young and inexperienced to govern effectively. *Feast in the morning*: either concluding a whole night of revelry or beginning a new round of merrymaking.
**10:17** *For vigor*: or, "with self-control, restraint."
**10:19** *Money answers*: a stark reminder that such a life requires money. It could also be an affirmation of the power of wealth: "Money conquers all."
**10:20** *Birds of the air…winged creature*: a common motif in ancient literature, and a vivid reminder of the need for caution in dealing with the rich and powerful.
**11:1–2** These two sayings can be understood against a commercial background. They acknowledge the uncertainty and risk such activity involves. At the same time they encourage action and a spirit of adventure. The first (v. 1) speaks of trade and overseas investment: Export your grain ("bread") to foreign markets

and you may be surprised at the substantial profits. The second (v. 2) encourages diversification of investment (seven, or even eight shipments of grain) to insure against heavy losses.
**11:3–6** Verses 3, 4, and 6 expand on the theme of uncertainty and human inability to assess accurately every situation. Verse 4, however, comments on the disadvantages of too much caution: Only those willing to risk will enjoy success. But only the Creator knows the mystery of the "work of God" (v. 5).
**11:7–10** The concluding part of the book opens with a final bittersweet homage to life and an enthusiastic encouragement to rejoice in its gifts while they are within grasp.
**11:10** *Fleeting*: lit., "vanity."

---

**10:14** Eccl 3:22; 6:12;         **11:5** Eccl 3:11; 7:13; 8:17.
    10:14.

# 12

¹† Remember your Creator in the days
of your youth,
before the evil days come
And the years approach of which you
will say,
"I have no pleasure in them";
² Before the sun is darkened
and the light and the moon and the
stars
and the clouds return after the rain;
³† When the guardians of the house
tremble,
and the strong men are bent;
When the women who grind are idle
because they are few,
and those who look through the
windows grow blind;
⁴ When the doors to the street are shut,
and the sound of the mill is low;
When one rises at the call of a bird,
and all the daughters of song are
quiet;
⁵ When one is afraid of heights,
and perils in the street;
When the almond tree blooms,
and the locust grows sluggish
and the caper berry is without effect,
Because mortals go to their lasting
home,

and mourners go about the streets;
⁶† Before the silver cord is snapped
and the golden bowl is broken,
And the pitcher is shattered at the
spring,
and the pulley is broken at the well,
⁷ And the dust returns to the earth as it
once was,
and the life breath returns to God
who gave it.†*
⁸ Vanity of vanities, says Qoheleth,
all things are vanity!*

**Epilogue.** ⁹† Besides being wise, Qoheleth taught the people knowledge, and weighed, scrutinized and arranged many proverbs. ¹⁰ Qoheleth sought to find appropriate sayings, and to write down true sayings with precision. ¹¹ The sayings of the wise are like goads; like fixed spikes are the collected sayings given by one shepherd.† ¹²* As to more than these,† my son, beware. Of the making of many books there is no end, and in much study there is weariness for the flesh.

¹³†* The last word, when all is heard: Fear God and keep his commandments, for this concerns all humankind; ¹⁴* because God will bring to judgment every work, with all its hidden qualities, whether good or bad.

---

**12:1–7** The homage to life of 11:7–10 is deliberately balanced by the sombre yet shimmering radiance of this poem on old age and death. The poem's enigmatic imagery has often been interpreted allegorically, especially in vv. 3–5. Above all it seeks to evoke an atmosphere as well as an attitude toward death and old age.
**12:3–5** An allegorical reading of these verses sees references to the human body—"guardians": the arms; "strong men": the legs; "women who grind": the teeth; "those who look": the eyes; "the doors": the lips; "daughters of song": the voice; "the almond tree blooms": resembling the white hair of old age; "the locust… sluggish": the stiffness in movement of the aged; "the caper berry": a stimulant for appetite.
**12:6** The golden bowl suspended by the silver cord is a symbol of life; the snapping of the cord and the breaking of the bowl, a symbol of death. *The pitcher…the pulley*: another pair of metaphors for life and its ending.
**12:7** Death is portrayed in terms of the description of creation in Gn 2:7; the body corrupts in the grave, and the life breath (lit., "spirit"), or gift of life, returns to God who had breathed upon what he had formed.

**12:9** A disciple briefly describes and praises the master's skill and reputation as a sage.
**12:11** *One shepherd*: perhaps referring to the book's author, who gathers or "shepherds" together its contents. God could also be "the one shepherd," the ultimate depository and source of true wisdom.
**12:12** *As to more than these*: the words seem to refer to the writings of Ecclesiastes and other sages. They are adequate and sufficient; any more involves exhaustive labor.
**12:13–14** These words reaffirm traditional wisdom doctrine such as fear of God and faithful obedience, perhaps lest some of the more extreme statements of the author be misunderstood. Although the epilogue has been interpreted as a criticism of the book's author, it is really a summary that betrays the unruffled spirit of later sages, who were not shocked by Qoheleth's statements. They honored him as a *hakam* or sage (v. 9), even as they preserved his statements about the futility of life (v. 8), and the mystery of divine judgment (8:17; 11:5).

---

| | |
|---|---|
| **12:7** Eccl 3:20–21; Jb 34:14–15. | **12:12** Eccl 1:18. |
| **12:8** Eccl 1:2. | **12:13** Eccl 5:6. |
| | **12:14** Eccl 11:9. |

# INTRODUCTION

### Dianne Bergant, CSA

The Song of Songs has always been highly regarded. While there is general agreement about the erotic nature of this lyric poetry, considerable controversy has been generated regarding its literary integrity, its genre, and its interpretation. Some scholars maintain that it is really a collection of independent poems, but today most think that the eight chapters should be interpreted as a unit composed of several different poems.

Over the centuries, four ways of interpreting the Song of Songs have been advanced: an allegorical understanding of a love relationship with God; a liturgical reenactment of ancient Canaanite marriage rites; an ancient dramatic performance of courting ritual with a narrator and a chorus; and a literal reading of erotic wedding poetry. The book contains certain features that lend themselves to all these approaches. While the preferred method of interpreting most of the Bible traditionally has been some form of the literal approach, the opposite has been true with this book. Most ancient commentators read the poems allegorically, as a mystical love relationship between God and Israel, Christ and the Church, or Christ and the individual soul (see the NAB introduction to the Song of Songs). The great Christian biblical scholar Origen (ca. 184–253 CE) promoted the interpretation of the Song of Songs as an allegory of the relationship of an individual soul with God. Today, however, the literal reading of the poems has gained prominence among scholars.

Many scholars recognize the similarity between the poems in the Song of Songs and Egyptian wedding songs. While no direct links can be established, the influence of other ancient Near Eastern poetry can be seen in the Song of Song's use of the Arabic *wasf*, a form of Arabic poetry in which the physical charms of the loved one are extolled.

## Literary Elements

The opening words, "The Song of Songs, which is Solomon's" (Sg 1:1), identify the book's genre as a song and relate it to Solomon. Thus some think the man in the poems is King Solomon. However, the Hebrew for these introductory words can be understood in two quite different ways. Either this book actually originated from Solomon, or it is somehow associated with him. Since the poems report the woman's point of view, not the man's, the opening phrase probably serves to indicate Solomonic patronage in order to confer Solomonic authority on the message of the book.

The shift in the poems between second- and third-person speakers makes it difficult to divide the book into clear sections. However, different speakers can be identified: the woman, the man, and the daughters of Jerusalem. Watchmen and the woman's brothers are also identified, but they do not speak. The Song of Songs is unique in that it is the only book of the Bible that consists totally of poetic speeches; there is no straightforward narration. The material itself can be identified as: poems of yearning (Sg 2:6), self-descriptions (8:10), poems of admiration (4:9–15), accounts of an experience (5:2–8), the *wasf* (4:1–7), and invitations to a tryst (7:12–14).

## The Lovers

Some translations refer to the woman as a girl or a maiden in order to underscore her presumed unmarried state. However, the idea of immaturity conflicts with the book's depiction of her. She describes herself as fully developed (Sg 8:10). Furthermore, she is quite independent of gender-biased societal restraints. While she may be young, she is a mature woman, not a naive girl.

Although the Song is a tribute to mutual love, the principal frame of reference is the amorous disposition of the woman. Her words open (Sg 1:2–4) and close (8:14) the Song and her voice is dominant throughout it. Most of the poems of yearning are uttered by her. She is the one who is portrayed as lovesick, longing to follow her beloved should he bid her come with him, and she is the one who celebrates their mutual belonging. She is neither slow to speak erotically about their union (3:4) nor embarrassed by the titillating language that he uses to describe her body (4:5–6). It is clear that the woman depicted in the Song is driven by love, not inhibited by social opinion or by some narrow sense of sexual propriety.

The woman's description of the charms of her lover and the pleasures of their lovemaking is quite provocative. She characterizes him as comely and agile like a young stag, renowned for its sexual prowess. The beauty of his body is praised part by part from his head to his thighs (Sg 5:10–15). She rhapsodizes about the impassioned delights they experience that intoxicate like wine, and about those that can be savored like one savors luscious fruits. This woman is not intimidated by eroticism.

The words of the young man provide a glimpse of the woman as perceived by her companion in love. His first words acclaim her as beautiful, the fairest among women (Sg 1:8). No other woman can compare with her; her beauty is unblemished. The jewelry that adorns her makes her resplendence rival the most ornate of Pharaoh's chariots. Her eyes have enraptured him, even though they are as gentle and innocent as doves. He compares her to a garden that is fruitful yet inaccessible to all but him. This is a man who has been smitten by love. His interest in the woman is certainly erotic, but there is no indication that he desires her merely for his own pleasure. The desire described in these poems is mutual, seeking mutual fulfillment. The woman is not being used; she is being loved.

## The Trysts

The trysts take place in several locations: cultivated orchards, gardens, and vineyards; natural fertile settings; and enclosed chambers. Each natural site is lavish with fruits and the possibility of continuous fertility. In each case the reference to fertility has less to do with progeny than with ongoing sensual satisfaction. The rooms that lend themselves to lovemaking include a wine house and a room in the home of the woman's mother. The wine house promotes the image of the vineyard and the notion of intoxication. It denotes fruitfulness and maturity, two characteristics of these lovers that have sexual connotations. The room in her mother's home is described as the place where the woman's life began, an allusion to newness but also heavily laden with sexual significance. The description of the exchange that took place in her own sleeping chamber is quite provocative (Sg 5:1–6). It is his intent to enter and consummate their love. Some believe that the passage actually describes sexual union. Whether the reference is to a real room or is a euphemism for genitalia, the only thing that hinders his entry is her delay in opening to him.

Another feature of the Song that addresses the vibrant surging of the powers of nature is the season of the year suggested by the Song's vivid imagery. Near Eastern winter, the rainy season, is over; spring has arrived. An abundance of flowers appears; the vines are all in blossom (Sg 2:11–15). There is a freshness and innocence to nature, just as there is freshness and innocence to the love that has captivated this couple.

The passion of the woman is not indecent, but neither is she demure about it. It is clear that this couple has already experienced the pleasures of lovemaking. He has lain on her breast, been encircled in her embrace, and been aroused by her. The relationship between the woman and the man is one of mutual desire and enjoyment. They are fiercely committed to each other and to no one else. They have known some form of sexual union and have both relished the enjoyment that came from it (Sg 2:16; 6:3). Not only is this clearly stated throughout the Song, but it is implied by the use of metaphors of eating and drinking.

The titles of endearment employed in this book are telling. The woman uses straightforward language, consistently calling him "my love." Once she uses "friend" in a way that implies the same intimacy. He calls her "bride"

(Sg 4:8), "sister" (4:9), and "dove" (5:2). He further refers to her as "perfect one" (5:2) and "beautiful one" (2:10). These are all pet names that express the affection that he has for her. Since the poem itself contains no indication that the couple is married or planning to do so, the term "bride" is probably merely an expression of intimacy. "Sister" is also a term of endearment, while "dove" invokes the image of a lovebird.

While the book certainly rejoices in the glories of lovemaking, more importantly, it celebrates the depth of the commitment shared by the woman and man. Song 8:6–7 has been described as the highpoint of the entire Song. There the woman asks that her lover allow her to be for him a kind of seal, a sign of the love that they share. She maintains that their love possesses a force that rivals the power of death. No power from the netherworld and no treasure from this world can compare with the strength and the value of human love. Nothing in this portrayal of human love suggests impropriety or overindulgence. If anything, it characterizes sexual passion as noble and self-transcending. ■

# THE SONG OF SONGS

## New American Bible, Introduction

The Song of Songs (or Canticle of Canticles) is an exquisite collection of love lyrics, arranged to tell a dramatic tale of mutual desire and courtship. It presents an inspired portrayal of ideal human love, a resounding affirmation of the goodness of human sexuality that is applicable to the sacredness and the depth of married union.

Although the poem is attributed to Solomon in the traditional title (1:1), the language and style of the work, among other considerations, suggest a time after the end of the Babylonian exile (538 B.C.) when an unknown poet collected extant love poems, perhaps composing new material, and arranged the whole into the masterpiece we have before us. Some scholars argue the possibility of female authorship for at least portions of the Song.

The structure of the Song is difficult to analyze; this translation regards it as a lyric dialogue, with dramatic movement and interest. In both form and content, sections of the Song bear great similarity to the secular love songs of ancient Egypt and the "Sacred Marriage" cult songs of Mesopotamia which celebrate the union between divine partners.

While the lovers in the Song are clearly human figures, both Jewish and Christian traditions across the centuries have adopted "allegorical" interpretations. The Song is seen as a beautiful picture of the ideal Israel, the chosen people whom the Lord leads by degrees to a greater understanding and closer union in the bond of perfect love. Such readings of the Song build on Israel's covenant tradition. Isaiah (Is 5:1–7; 54:4–8; 62:5), Jeremiah (Jer 2:2, 3, 32), and Ezekiel (Ez 16; 23) all characterize the covenant between the Lord and Israel as a marriage. Hosea the prophet sees the idolatry of Israel in the adultery of Gomer (Hos 1–3). He also represents the Lord speaking to Israel's heart (Hos 2:16) and changing her into a new spiritual people, purified by the Babylonian captivity and betrothed anew to her divine Lover "in justice and uprightness, in love and mercy" (Hos 2:21). Similar imagery has also been used frequently in Jewish mystical texts. The Song offers a welcome corrective to negative applications of the theological metaphor of the marriage/covenant in some prophetic texts. It frequently proclaims a joyous reciprocity between the lovers and highlights the active role of the female partner, now a pure figure to be cherished rather than an adulterous woman to be punished and abused. See also Is 62:3–5.

Christian tradition has followed Israel's example in using marriage as an image for the relationship with God. This image is found extensively in the New Testament (Mt 9:15; 25:1–13; Jn 3:29; 2 Cor 11:2; Eph 5:23–32; Rev 19:7–9; 21:9–11). Thus the Song has been read as a sublime portrayal and praise of this mutual love of the Lord and his people. Christian writers have interpreted the Song in terms of the union between Christ and the Church and of the union between Christ and the individual soul, particularly in the writings of Origen and St. Bernard. ■

# SONG OF SONGS

## 1

¹ The Song of Songs,† which is Solomon's.

### The Woman Speaks of Her Lover

²†\* **W** Let him kiss me with kisses of his
        mouth,
    for your love is better than wine,†
³    better than the fragrance of your
        perfumes.†
    Your name is a flowing perfume—
    therefore young women love you.
⁴\*   Draw me after you! Let us run!†
    The king has brought me to his bed
        chambers.
    Let us exult and rejoice in you;
        let us celebrate your love: it is beyond
        wine!
    Rightly do they love you!

### Love's Boast

⁵    **W** I am black and beautiful,
        Daughters of Jerusalem†—
    Like the tents of Qedar,
        like the curtains of Solomon.
⁶    Do not stare at me because I am so
        black,†
    because the sun has burned me.

The sons of my mother were angry with
    me;
    they charged me with the care of the
        vineyards:
    my own vineyard I did not take care
        of.

### Love's Inquiry

⁷    **W** Tell me, you whom my soul loves,
    where you shepherd,† where you give
        rest at midday.
    Why should I be like one wandering
    after the flocks of your companions?
⁸    **M** If you do not know,
        most beautiful among women,
    Follow the tracks of the flock
    and pasture your lambs†
    near the shepherds' tents.

### Love's Vision

⁹    **M** To a mare among Pharaoh's
        chariotry†
    I compare you, my friend:
¹⁰   Your cheeks lovely in pendants,
        your neck in jewels.
¹¹   We will make pendants of gold for you,
        and ornaments of silver.

### How Near Is Love!

¹²   **W** While the king was upon his couch,
        my spikenard† gave forth its fragrance.
¹³   My lover† is to me a sachet of myrrh;

---

**1:1** *Song of Songs*: in Hebrew and Aramaic the idiom "the X of Xs" denotes the superlative (e.g., "king of kings" = "the highest king"; cf. Dt 10:17; Eccl 1:2; 12:8; Ezr 7:12; Dn 2:37). The ascription of authorship to Solomon is traditional. The heading may also mean "for Solomon" or "about Solomon."

**1:2–8:14** This translation augments the canonical text of the Song with the letters *W, M,* and *D,* placed in the margin, to indicate which of the characters in the Song is speaking: the woman, the man, or the "Daughters of Jerusalem." This interpretive gloss follows an early Christian scribal practice, attested in some Septuagint manuscripts from the first half of the first millennium A.D.

**1:2–7** The woman and her female chorus address the man, here viewed as king and shepherd (both are familiar metaphors for God; cf. Ps 23:1; Is 40:11; Jn 10:1–16). There is a wordplay between "kiss" (Hebrew *nashaq*) and "drink" (*shaqah*), anticipating 8:1–2. The change from third person ("let him kiss…") to second person ("…for your love …") is not uncommon in the Song and elsewhere (1:4; 2:4; 4:5, 6; etc.) and reflects the woman's move from interior monologue to direct address to her partner.

**1:3** *Your perfumes: shemen* (perfume) is a play on *shem* (name).

**1:4** Another change, but from second to third person (cf. 1:2). The "king" metaphor recurs in 1:12; 3:5–11; 7:6. *Let us exult:* perhaps she is addressing young women, calling on them to join in the praise of her lover.

**1:5** *Daughters of Jerusalem:* the woman contrasts herself with the elite city women, who act as her female "chorus" (5:9; 6:1). *Qedar:* a Syrian desert region whose name suggests darkness;

tents were often made of black goat hair. *Curtains:* tent coverings, or tapestries. *Solomon:* it could also be read Salma, a region close to Qedar.

**1:6** *So black:* tanned from working outdoors in her brothers' vineyards, unlike the city women she addresses. *My own vineyard:* perhaps the woman herself; see 8:8–10 for her relationship to her brothers.

**1:7** *Shepherd:* a common metaphor for kings. Here and elsewhere in the Song (3:1; 5:8; 6:1), the woman expresses her desire to be in the company of her lover. The search for the lover and her failure to find him create a degree of tension. Only at the end (8:5–14) do the lovers finally possess each other.

**1:8** *Pasture your lambs:* both the woman and the man act as shepherds in the Song.

**1:9–11** The man compares the woman's beauty to the rich adornment of the royal chariot of Pharaoh. *My friend:* a special feminine form of the word "friend," appearing only in the Song (1:15; 2:2, 10, 13; 4:1, 7; 5:2; 6:4) and used to express endearment and equality in love. Cf. Hos 3:1 for the use of the masculine form of the term in a context with sexual overtones.

**1:12** *Spikenard:* a precious perfumed ointment from India; in 4:13–14, a metaphor for the woman herself.

**1:13** *My lover:* the woman's favorite term for her partner (used twenty-seven times). *Myrrh:* an aromatic resin of balsam or roses used in cosmetics, incense, and medicines.

---

between my breasts he lies.

14 My lover is to me a cluster of henna†
   from the vineyards of En-gedi.

15* M How beautiful you are, my friend,
     how beautiful! your eyes are doves!†

16 W How beautiful you are, my lover—
     handsome indeed!

Verdant indeed is our couch;†

17   the beams of our house are cedars,
     our rafters, cypresses.

**2** ¹ W I am a flower of Sharon,†
       a lily of the valleys.

2  M Like a lily among thorns,
     so is my friend among women.

3  W Like an apple tree among the trees of
     the woods,
     so is my lover among men.

In his shadow† I delight to sit,
   and his fruit is sweet to my taste.

4* He brought me to the banquet hall†
   and his glance at me signaled love.

5* Strengthen me with raisin cakes,†
   refresh me with apples,
   for I am sick with love.

6* His left hand is under my head
   and his right arm embraces me.

7* I adjure you, Daughters of Jerusalem,†
   by the gazelles and the does of the
   field,

Do not awaken, or stir up love
   until it is ready.

### Her Lover's Visit Remembered

8  W The sound of my lover! here he
     comes†

springing across the mountains,
leaping across the hills.

9  My lover is like a gazelle†
   or a young stag.

See! He is standing behind our wall,
   gazing through the windows,
   peering through the lattices.

10 My lover speaks and says to me,
     M "Arise, my friend, my beautiful
       one,
     and come!

11 For see, the winter is past,
   the rains are over and gone.

12 The flowers appear on the earth,
   the time of pruning the vines has
     come,
   and the song of the turtledove is
     heard in our land.

13 The fig tree puts forth its figs,
   and the vines, in bloom, give forth
     fragrance.

Arise, my friend, my beautiful one,
   and come!

14 My dove in the clefts of the rock,†
   in the secret recesses of the cliff,

Let me see your face,
   let me hear your voice,

For your voice is sweet,
   and your face is lovely."

15 W Catch us the foxes,† the little foxes
     that damage the vineyards; for our
       vineyards are in bloom!

16* My lover belongs to me and I to him;
   he feeds among the lilies.

17* Until the day grows cool† and the
     shadows flee,

---

† **1:14** *Henna:* a plant which bears white scented flowers, used in cosmetics and medicines. *En-gedi:* a Judean desert oasis over-looking the Dead Sea.

**1:15** *Doves:* doves are pictured in the ancient world as messengers of love.

**1:16–17** Continuing the royal metaphor, the meeting place of the lovers, a shepherd's hut of green branches, becomes a palace with beams of cedar and rafters of cypress when adorned with their love.

**2:1** *Flower of Sharon:* probably the narcissus, which grows in the fertile Plain of Sharon lying between Mount Carmel and Jaffa on the Mediterranean coast. *Lily:* the lotus plant.

**2:3** *Shadow:* suggestive of protection (cf. Jgs 9:15; Ez 17:23; Ps 17:8; 121:5) and, here, of the woman's joy in the presence of her lover.

**2:4–6** *The banquet hall:* the sweet things of the table, the embrace of the woman and man, express the richness of their affection and the intimacy of their love.

**2:5** *Raisin cakes:* perhaps pastries used in the worship of the fertility goddess (cf. Hos 3:1; Jer 7:18; 44:19). *Apples:* this is the common translation of a fruit that cannot be identified (cf. 2:3; 8:5); it appears frequently in Sumerian love poetry associated with the worship of the goddess Inanna. *Sick:* love-sickness is a

popular motif in ancient love poetry.

**2:7** Cf. 3:5; 5:8; 8:4. *By the gazelles and the does:* perhaps a mitigated invocation of the divinity based on the assonance in Hebrew of the names of these animals with terms for God.

**2:8–13** In this sudden change of scene, the woman describes a rendezvous and pictures her lover hastening toward her dwelling until his voice is heard calling her to him.

**2:9** *Gazelle:* a frequent motif in ancient poems from Mesopotamia.

**2:14** The woman is addressed as though she were a dove in a mountain cleft out of sight and reach.

**2:15** A snatch of song in answer to the request of 2:14; cf. 8:13–14. *Foxes:* they threaten to disturb the security of vineyards. The vineyards are women sought after by young lovers, i.e., foxes.

**2:17** *Grows cool:* in the evening when the sun is going down. Cf. Gn 3:8. *Rugged:* Hebrew obscure; some interpret it as a geographical name; others, in the sense of spices (cf. 8:14); still others, of sacrifice (Gn 15:10); the image probably refers here to the woman herself.

---

**1:15** Sg 4:1, 7.          **2:7** Sg 3:5; 8:4.
**2:4** Sg 1:4.              **2:16** Sg 6:3; 7:10.
**2:5** Sg 5:8.              **2:17** Sg 4:6; 8:14.
**2:6** Sg 8:3.

SG

roam, my lover,
Like a gazelle or a young stag
   upon the rugged mountains.

## Loss and Discovery

**3** 1* **W** On my bed at night I sought him†
   whom my soul loves—
I sought him but I did not find him.
2 "Let me rise then and go about the city,†
   through the streets and squares;
Let me seek him whom my soul loves."
   I sought him but I did not find him.
3 The watchmen found me,
   as they made their rounds in the city:
"Him whom my soul loves—have you
   seen him?"
4* Hardly had I left them
   when I found him whom my soul
      loves.†
I held him and would not let him go
   until I had brought him to my
      mother's house,
to the chamber of her who conceived
      me.
5* I adjure you, Daughters of Jerusalem,
   by the gazelles and the does of the
      field,
Do not awaken or stir up love
   until it is ready.

## Solomon's Wedding Procession

6* **D** Who is this coming up from the
      desert,†
   like columns of smoke
Perfumed with myrrh and frankincense,
   with all kinds of exotic powders?
7 See! it is the litter of Solomon;
   sixty valiant men surround it,
   of the valiant men of Israel:
8 All of them expert with the sword,
   skilled in battle,

Each with his sword at his side
   against the terrors† of the night.
9 King Solomon made himself an
      enclosed litter
   of wood from Lebanon.
10 He made its columns of silver,
   its roof of gold,
Its seat of purple cloth,
   its interior lovingly fitted.†
Daughters of Jerusalem, 11 go out
   and look upon King Solomon
In the crown with which his mother has
      crowned him
on the day of his marriage,
   on the day of the joy of his heart.

## The Beauty of the Woman

**4** 1*,* **M** How beautiful you are, my friend,
   how beautiful you are!
Your eyes are doves
   behind your veil.
Your hair is like a flock of goats
   streaming down Mount Gilead.†
2 Your teeth† are like a flock of ewes to be
      shorn,
   that come up from the washing,
All of them big with twins,
   none of them barren.
3 Like a scarlet strand, your lips,
   and your mouth—lovely!
Like pomegranate† halves, your cheeks
   behind your veil.
4* Like a tower of David, your neck,
   built in courses,
A thousand shields hanging upon it,
   all the armor of warriors.†
5* Your breasts are like two fawns,
   twins of a gazelle
   feeding among the lilies.
6* Until the day grows cool
   and the shadows flee,

---

**3:1–5** See the parallel in 5:2–8.

**3:2** The motif of seeking/finding here and elsewhere is used by later Christian and Jewish mystics to speak of the soul's search for the divine.

**3:4** *Whom my soul loves*: the fourfold repetition of this phrase in vv. 1–4 highlights the depth of the woman's emotion and desire. *Mother's house*: cf. 8:2; a place of safety and intimacy, one which implicitly signifies approval of the lovers' relationship.

**3:6–11** This may be an independent poem. In context it portrays the lover as King Solomon, escorted by sixty armed men, coming in royal procession to meet a bride.

**3:8** *Terrors*: cf. Ps 91:5; perhaps bandits lying in wait, unidentified dangers lurking in darkness.

**3:10** *Lovingly fitted*: translation uncertain. The phrase "Daughters of Jerusalem" is read here with the following verse.

**4:1** This section (vv. 1–7) begins a *wasf*, a traditional poetic

form describing the physical attributes of one's partner in terms of the natural world (cf. 5:10–16; 6:5b–7; 7:1–7). *Veil*: women of the region customarily veiled their faces for some occasions (cf. 4:3; 6:7; Gn 24:65–67; 38:14–19).

**4:2** *Teeth*: praised for whiteness and evenness.

**4:3** *Pomegranate*: a fruit with a firm skin and deep red color. The woman's cheek (or perhaps her brow) is compared, in roundness and tint, to a half-pomegranate.

**4:4** The ornaments about her neck are compared to the trophies and armaments on the city walls. Cf. 1 Kgs 10:10; 14:26–28; Ez 27:10.

| | |
|---|---|
| **3:1–5** Sg 5:2–8. | **4:1** Sg 1:15. |
| **3:4** Sg 8:2. | **4:4** Sg 7:5. |
| **3:5** Sg 2:7; 8:4. | **4:5** Sg 7:4. |
| **3:6** Sg 6:10; 8:5. | **4:6** Sg 2:17. |
| **4:1–3** Sg 6:5–7. | |

I shall go to the mountain of myrrh,
   to the hill of frankincense.†

7 You are beautiful in every way, my
   friend,
   there is no flaw in you!†

8 With me from Lebanon, my bride!
   With me from Lebanon, come!
Descend from the peak of Amana,
   from the peak of Senir and Hermon,†
From the lairs of lions,
   from the leopards' heights.

9* You have ravished my heart, my sister,†
   my bride;
   you have ravished my heart with one
     glance of your eyes,
   with one bead of your necklace.

10* How beautiful is your love,
   my sister, my bride,
How much better is your love than wine,
   and the fragrance of your perfumes
     than any spice!

11 Your lips drip honey,† my bride,
   honey and milk are under your
     tongue;
And the fragrance of your garments
   is like the fragrance of Lebanon.

### The Lover's Garden

12* **M** A garden enclosed, my sister, my
   bride,
   a garden enclosed, a fountain sealed!†

13 Your branches are a grove of
   pomegranates,
   with fruits of choicest yield:
Henna with spikenard,

14 spikenard and saffron,
Sweet cane and cinnamon,
   with all kinds of frankincense;
Myrrh and aloes,
   with all the finest spices;†

15 A garden fountain, a well of living water,
   streams flowing from Lebanon.

16 Awake,† north wind!
   Come, south wind!
Blow upon my garden
   that its perfumes may spread abroad.
**W** Let my lover come to his garden
   and eat its fruits of choicest yield.

**5** 1* **M** I have come to my garden, my sister,
   my bride;
I gather my myrrh with my spices,
I eat my honeycomb with my honey,
I drink my wine with my milk.
**D?** Eat, friends; drink!
   Drink deeply, lovers!†

### A Fruitless Search

2* **W** I was sleeping, but my heart was
   awake.†
The sound of my lover knocking!
"Open to me, my sister, my friend,
   my dove, my perfect one!
For my head is wet with dew,
   my hair, with the moisture of the
     night."

3 I have taken off my robe,†
   am I then to put it on?
I have bathed my feet,
   am I then to soil them?

4 My lover put his hand in through the
   opening:
   my innermost being† trembled
     because of him.

5 I rose to open for my lover,
   my hands dripping myrrh:
My fingers, flowing myrrh
   upon the handles of the lock.

6 I opened for my lover—
   but my lover had turned and gone!

---

**4:6** *Mountain of myrrh … hill of frankincense*: spoken figuratively of the woman; cf. 8:14.

**4:7** Cf. the description of the church in Eph 5:27.

**4:8** *Amana … Senir and Hermon*: these rugged heights symbolize obstacles that would separate the lovers; cf. 2:14.

**4:9** *Sister*: a term of endearment; brother-sister language forms part of the conventional language of love used in this canticle, the Book of Tobit, and elsewhere in poetry from Egypt, Mesopotamia, and Syro-Palestine.

**4:11** *Honey*: sweet words (cf. Prv 5:3) or perhaps kisses (1:2–3). *Honey and milk*: familiar descriptions for the fertile promised land (Ex 3:8, 17; Lv 20:24; Nm 13:27; Dt 6:3).

**4:12** *Garden enclosed … fountain sealed*: reserved for the lover alone. Cf. Prv 5:15–19 for similar images used to describe fruitful, committed relationship.

**4:14** These plants are all known for their sweet fragrance.

**4:16** *Awake*: the same verb is used of love in 3:5. The woman

may be the speaker of 16a, as it is she who issues the invitation of 16b. *His garden*: the woman herself.

**5:1** *Eat … lovers*: the translation and meaning are uncertain.

**5:2–8** An experience of anticipation and loss similar to that in 3:1–5. The lover's abrupt appearance resembles that in 2:8–9.

**5:3** *Robe*: knee-length undergarment worn by men and women. *Am I then … ?*: the woman's refusal is a form of gentle teasing; that she does not really reject her lover is shown by her actions in vv. 5–6. See 1:7–8; 2:14–15, for other teasing interchanges.

**5:4** *My innermost being*: lit., "innards." In Gn 25:23, Is 49:1; Ps 71:6, the word appears to carry the meaning of "womb."

---

**4:9** Sg 6:5.       **5:1** Sg 6:2.
**4:10** Sg 1:2–3.     **5:2** Sg 3:1–2.
**4:12** Sg 6:2, 11.

At his leaving, my soul sank.
I sought him, but I did not find him;
   I called out after him, but he did not
      answer me.†

7   The watchmen† found me,
   as they made their rounds in the city;
They beat me, they wounded me,
   they tore off my mantle,
   the watchmen of the walls.

8*  I adjure you, Daughters of Jerusalem,
   if you find my lover
What shall you tell him?
   that I am sick with love.

### The Lost Lover Described

9   **D** How does your lover differ from any
      other lover,
   most beautiful among women?
How does your lover differ from any
     other,
   that you adjure us so?

10  **W** My lover is radiant and ruddy;†
   outstanding among thousands.

11  His head is gold, pure gold,
   his hair like palm fronds,
   as black as a raven.

12  His eyes are like doves
   beside streams of water,
Bathing in milk,
   sitting† by brimming pools.

13  His cheeks are like beds of spices
   yielding aromatic scents;
his lips are lilies
   that drip flowing myrrh.

14  His arms are rods of gold
   adorned with gems;
His loins, a work of ivory
   covered with sapphires.

15  His legs, pillars of alabaster,
   resting on golden pedestals.
His appearance, like the Lebanon,
   imposing as the cedars.

16  His mouth is sweetness itself;
   he is delightful in every way.
Such is my lover, and such my friend,
   Daughters of Jerusalem!

### The Lost Lover Found

**6**  1 **D** Where has your lover gone,
    most beautiful among women?
Where has your lover withdrawn
   that we may seek him with you?†

2*  **W** My lover has come down to his
      garden,†
   to the beds of spices,
To feed in the gardens
   and to gather lilies.

3*  I belong to my lover, and my lover
     belongs to me;
   he feeds among the lilies.

### The Beauty of the Woman

4   **M** Beautiful as Tirzah are you, my friend;†
   fair as Jerusalem,
   fearsome as celestial visions!

5*  Turn your eyes away from me,
   for they stir me up.
Your hair is like a flock of goats
   streaming down from Gilead.

6*  Your teeth are like a flock of ewes
   that come up from the washing,
All of them big with twins,
   none of them barren.

7   Like pomegranate halves,
   your cheeks behind your veil.

8   Sixty are the queens, eighty the
      concubines,
   and young women without number—

9   One alone† is my dove, my perfect one,
   her mother's special one,
   favorite of the one who bore her.
Daughters see her and call her happy,
   queens and concubines, and they
     praise her:

---

† **5:6** The motif of the locked-out lover is common in classical Greek and Latin poetry.

**5:7** *The watchmen*: they do not know the reason for the woman's appearance in the city streets; cf. 3:2–4.

**5:10–11** In answer to the question of 5:9 the woman sings her lover's praises (vv. 10–16). *Ruddy*: also used of David (1 Sm 16:12; 17:42). *Gold*: indicates how precious the lover is. *Palm fronds*: his thick, luxuriant growth of hair.

**5:12** *Sitting …*: the translation of this line is uncertain; it may continue the metaphor of the lover's eyes, or refer to another part of his anatomy (e.g., teeth) which has been omitted from the text.

**6:1** The Daughters of Jerusalem are won by this description of the lover and offer their aid in seeking him (cf. 5:6, 9).

**6:2–3** The woman implies here that she had never really lost her lover, for he has come down to his garden (cf. 2:16; 4:5).

*Feed … lilies*: the imagery here evokes both a shepherd pasturing his flocks and erotic play between the lovers (2:16; 4:5, 12, 16).

**6:4–9** The man again celebrates the woman's beauty. *Tirzah*: probably meaning "pleasant"; it was the early capital of the Northern Kingdom of Israel (1 Kgs 16). *Celestial visions*: the meaning is uncertain. Military images may be implied here, i.e., the "heavenly hosts" who fight along with God on Israel's behalf (cf. Jgs 5:20), or perhaps a reference to the awesome goddesses of the region who combined aspects of both fertility and war.

**6:9** *One alone*: the incomparability of the woman is a favorite motif in love poetry.

---

**5:8** Sg 2:7; 8:4.           **6:5** Sg 4:9.
**6:2** Sg 4:12; 5:1.        **6:6–7** Sg 4:1–3.
**6:3** Sg 2:16; 7:11.

10* "Who† is this that comes forth like the
    dawn,
  beautiful as the white moon, pure as
    the blazing sun,
  fearsome as celestial visions?"

### Love's Meeting

11* **W** To the walnut grove† I went down,
  to see the young growth of the valley;
  To see if the vines were in bloom,
    if the pomegranates had blossomed.
12 Before I knew it, my desire had
    made me
  the blessed one of the prince's
    people.†

### The Beauty of the Beloved

**7** 1 **D?** Turn, turn, O Shulammite!†
  turn, turn that we may gaze upon
    you!
  **W** How can you gaze upon the
    Shulammite
  as at the dance of the two camps?
2 **M** How beautiful are your feet in
    sandals,†
  O noble daughter!
  Your curving thighs like jewels,
    the product of skilled hands.
3 Your valley,† a round bowl
    that should never lack mixed wine.
  Your belly, a mound of wheat,
    encircled with lilies.
4* Your breasts are like two fawns,
    twins of a gazelle.
5* Your neck like a tower of ivory;

your eyes, pools in Heshbon
  by the gate of Bath-rabbim.
Your nose like the tower of Lebanon
  that looks toward Damascus.†
6 Your head rises upon you like Carmel;†
  your hair is like purple;
  a king is caught in its locks.

### Love's Desires

7 How beautiful you are, how fair,
  my love, daughter of delights!
8 Your very form resembles a date-palm,†
  and your breasts, clusters.
9 I thought, "Let me climb the date-palm!
  Let me take hold of its branches!
Let your breasts be like clusters of the
    vine
  and the fragrance of your breath like
    apples,
10 And your mouth like the best wine—
  **W** that flows down smoothly for my
    lover,
  gliding† over my lips and teeth.
11* I belong to my lover,†
  his yearning is for me.
12 Come, my lover! Let us go out to the
    fields,
  let us pass the night among the
    henna.
13* Let us go early to the vineyards, and see
    if the vines are in bloom,
If the buds have opened,
    if the pomegranates have blossomed;
There will I give you my love.
14 The mandrakes† give forth fragrance,

---

**6:10** *"Who … ":* the speakers may be the women of vv. 8–9. *Moon … sun:* lit., "the white" and "the hot," respectively (cf. Is 24:23; 30:26). *Fearsome:* see note on 6:4–9.

**6:11** *Walnut grove:* also a site of activity in a wedding hymn of the Syrian moon goddess Nikkal (cf. the woman compared to the moon in v. 10).

**6:12** The text is obscure in Hebrew and in the ancient versions. The Vulgate reads: "I did not know; my soul disturbed me because of the chariots of Aminadab." Based on a parallel in Jgs 5:24, "chariots" is here emended to "blessed one."

**7:1** *Shulammite:* the woman is so designated because she is considered to be from Shulam (or Shunem) in the plain of Esdraelon (cf. 1 Kgs 1:3), or because the name may mean "the peaceful one," and thus recall the name of Solomon. *Turn:* she is asked to face the speaker(s). *How …:* she refuses to be regarded as a spectacle ("the dance of the two camps" is unknown). Some interpret the episode as an invitation to her to dance.

**7:2–6** Another description of the woman's charms. *Sandals:* the woman's sandaled foot was apparently considered quite seductive (Jdt 16:9). *Noble:* a possible connection to the enigmatic "prince" of 6:12. *Curving … jewels:* the meaning of these Hebrew words is not certain. Wine and wheat suggest fertility.

**7:3** *Valley:* lit., navel; a discreet allusion to her sex.

**7:5** The comparison emphasizes the stateliness of her neck,

and the clarity of her eyes. *Bath-rabbim:* a proper name which occurs only here; there was a city of Rabbah northeast of Heshbon in Transjordan. Cf. Jer 49:3.

**7:6** *Carmel:* a prominent set of cliffs overlooking the Mediterranean.

**7:8–9** *Date-palm:* a figure of stateliness. The lover is eager to enjoy the possession of his beloved.

**7:10** *Gliding:* the beloved interrupts her partner's compliment by referring to the intoxication of their union. The translation rests on an emendation of the enigmatic "the lips of the sleepers."

**7:11–14** The woman's answer assures him of her love, and invites him to return with her to the rural delights associated with their love (cf. also 6:11–12). *Yearning:* used only here and in Gn 3:16; 4:7. The dependency and subordination of woman to man presented as a consequence of sin in the Genesis story is here transcended in the mutuality of true love.

**7:14** *Mandrakes:* herbs believed to have power to arouse love and promote fertility; cf. Gn 30:14–16.

\*———
**6:10** Sg 3:6; 8:5.     **7:5** Sg 4:4.
**6:11** Sg 4:12–5:1; 7:13.     **7:11** Sg 2:16; 6:3.
**7:4** Sg 4:5.     **7:13** Sg 6:11.

and over our doors are all choice
      fruits;
Fruits both fresh and dried, my lover,
      have I kept in store for you.

**8** <sup>1</sup> Would that you were a brother to me,
      nursed at my mother's breasts!
If I met you out of doors, I would kiss
      you
      and none would despise me.
2* I would lead you, bring you to my
      mother's house,
      where you would teach me,
Where I would give you to drink
      spiced wine, my pomegranate† juice.
3* His left hand is under my head,
      and his right arm embraces me.
4* I adjure you, Daughters of Jerusalem,
      do not awaken or stir up love
      until it is ready!

### The Return from the Desert

5* **D?** Who is this coming up from the
      desert,
      leaning upon her lover?
 **W** Beneath the apple tree I awakened
      you;†
      there your mother conceived you;
      there she who bore you conceived.

### True Love

6 Set me as a seal† upon your heart,
      as a seal upon your arm;
For Love is strong as Death,
      longing is fierce as Sheol.
Its arrows are arrows of fire,
      flames of the divine.
7* Deep waters† cannot quench love,
      nor rivers sweep it away.

Were one to offer all the wealth of his
      house for love,
      he would be utterly despised.

### An Answer to the Brothers

8 **W** "We have a little sister;†
      she has no breasts as yet.
What shall we do for our sister
      on the day she is spoken for?
9 If she is a wall,
      we will build upon her a silver turret;
But if she is a door,
      we will board her up with cedar
      planks."
10 I am a wall,†
      and my breasts are like towers.
I became in his eyes
      as one who brings peace.

### A Boast

11 **M?** Solomon had a vineyard at Baal-
      hamon;†
      he gave over the vineyard to caretakers.
For its fruit one would have to pay
      a thousand silver pieces.
12 My vineyard is at my own disposal;
      the thousand pieces are for you,
      Solomon,
      and two hundred for the caretakers of
      its fruit.

### The Lovers' Yearnings

13 **M** You who dwell in the gardens,†
      my companions are listening for your
      voice—
      let me hear it!
14* **W** Swiftly, my lover,
      be like a gazelle or a young stag
      upon the mountains of spices.

---

**8:2** *Wine ... pomegranate*: sexual connotations are implied, since the root "drink" (*shaqah*) is a wordplay on "kiss" (*nashaq*) in v. 1; cf. 1:2.
**8:5** *Awakened you*: the speakers in this verse are difficult to identify. Someone (the poet? Daughters?) hails the couple in v. 5a. According to the Masoretic vocalization, the woman is the speaker in v. 5b.
**8:6** *Seal*: this could be worn bound to the arm, as here, or suspended at the neck, or as a ring (Jer 22:24). It was used for identification and signatures. *Strong ... fierce*: in human experience, Death and Sheol are inevitable, unrelenting; in the end they always triumph. Love, which is just as certain of its victory, matches its strength against the natural enemies of life; waters cannot extinguish it nor floods carry it away. It is more priceless than all riches. *Flames of the divine*: the Hebrew is difficult: the short form (-Yah) of the divine name Yhwh found here may associate love with the Lord, or it may be acting as a superlative—i.e., god-sized flames.
**8:7** *Deep waters*: often used to designate chaos (Ps 93:4; 144:7; Is 17:12–13; Hb 3:15). The fires of love cannot be extin-

guished, even by waters of chaos. *Wealth*: love cannot be bought.
**8:8–9** The woman quotes the course of action her elder brothers had decided on. While she is yet immature, they will shelter her in view of eventual marriage. *Wall ... door*: if she is virtuous, she will be honored; if she is not, she will be kept under strict vigilance. *Silver turret*: a precious ornament.
**8:10** In reply to the officious and meddling attitude of the brothers, she answers with their terms: she is mature ("wall," "towers"). *Brings peace*: or, "finds peace."
**8:11–12** These enigmatic verses have been variously interpreted, depending on who is taken to be the speaker. In v. 11, if the woman, she boasts that she is a vineyard of great value. If the man, he boasts over his possession of her.
**8:13–14** As in 2:14, her lover asks for a word or a song and she replies in words similar to those found in 2:17.

---

| | |
|---|---|
| **8:2** Sg 3:4. | **8:5** Sg 3:6; 6:10. |
| **8:3** Sg 2:6. | **8:7** Prv 6:31. |
| **8:4** Sg 2:7; 3:5. | **8:14** Sg 2:9, 17; 4:6. |

# The Book of
# Wisdom

## INTRODUCTION

### Dianne Bergant, CSA

Many engaging passages from the book of Wisdom are quite well known. Chief among these are: "The spirit of the LORD fills the world" (Wis 1:7) and "The souls of the righteous are in the hand of God" (3:1). Despite this familiarity, the book itself is relatively unknown. Unlike the Prophets or the Psalms, Wisdom is seldom the focus of Bible study. This is unfortunate, because the book of Wisdom demonstrates something that few biblical books do. It demonstrates how believers reshape their religious traditions in order to make them relevant in a new cultural situation.

The conquest of Alexander the Great (ca. 333 BCE) was not merely military, it was cultural as well. This was particularly true in centers such as Alexandria, Egypt. The Jewish community living there was faced with a serious dilemma: How much of Hellenistic (Greek) culture could they accept without it undermining their religious principles (a challenge not unlike the one facing Christians living in society today)? How was one to be faithful to the precepts of the faith while living in a society that was not Jewish? The struggle these believers faced was twofold: they had to contend with the Hellenistic influences and also with those Jews who accepted Hellenization more than others.

The author of the book of Wisdom is referred to as Pseudo-Solomon because he assumed the identity of that wise king (Wis 7:7–12) though he wrote hundreds of years after Solomon's death (d. ca. 930 BCE). This teacher was a skillful theologian. Religiously he was Jewish, treating Jewish themes such as justice and the story of the Exodus; culturally he was a Hellenist, employing several Greek literary forms and ideas as he developed his theology. He, along with the author of Ben Sira, brought the religion of ancient Israel out of the confines of

## Outline of Wisdom

I. **The Reward of Righteousness (1:1–6:21).**

II. **Praise of Wisdom by Solomon (6:22–11:1).**

III. **Special Providence of God During the Exodus (11:2–16; 12:23–27; 15:18–19:22) with digressions on God's mercy (11:17–12:22) and on the folly and shame of idolatry (13:1–15:17).**

a strictly Israelite faith into the broader world of Hellenism. In his writing, religion met a foreign culture and both benefited from the encounter.

## Justice, Death, and Immortality

The first section of the book (Wis 1:1–6:21) treats three distinct yet interrelated themes: the justice of God, the inevitability of death, and the possibility of immortality. The first two themes are prominent in earlier Israelite teaching. Justice or righteousness is a divine characteristic. It describes how God acts toward us (Pss 119:138; 143:1; 145:17). The Israelites accepted the fact that death is the natural fate of all living things. They did not seem to be troubled by death if it followed a long and fruitful life. However, premature death, particularly the death of the righteous, presented a real problem. It was considered unfair. Furthermore, though they did not equate death with ultimate annihilation, they did not have a clear idea of life after death, whereas many other ancient Near Eastern religions did. The Israelites held that the dead went to Sheol, which was not a place of reward or punishment, but a shadowy existence where one could not even praise God (Ps 6:6). Finally, the Israelites viewed the human creature as an integral "living being" (Gn 2:7), not as a composite of an impermanent, material body and an eternal, spiritual soul, as many Greeks did.

The author of Wisdom championed three important concepts that were new to Jewish thinking: soul (Wis 1:11; 3:1; 4:11, 14; 9:15; 10:7, 16; 13:17; 15:11; 16:14; 17:8), immortality (3:4; 4:1; 8:13, 17; 15:3), and incorruptibility (6:18–19). Though the concepts are Greek, the author used them in ways that are faithful to ancient Jewish thinking. According to him, the basis of incorruptibility is not the immortal character of the soul, but one's relationship with wisdom (6:18–19). Furthermore, this author does not state that the soul is immortal. Rather, hope (3:4), memory (4:1; 8:13), kinship with wisdom (8:17), and knowledge of God (15:3) are immortal. It is clear that immortality is rooted in one's relationship with God.

An examination of a passage often read at funerals reveals just how the author employs Greek concepts to develop Jewish theology.

> The souls of the righteous are in the hand
> of God,
> and no torment shall touch them.
> They seemed, in the view of the foolish, to
> be dead;
> and their passing away was thought an
> affliction
> and their going forth from us, utter
> destruction.
> But they are in peace.
> For if to others, indeed, they seem punished
> yet is their hope full of immortality.
> (Wis 3:1–4)

According to Israelite thinking, what appears to be an untimely death, perhaps the result of violence, may actually be evidence that secretly those who died were sinners, and their passing away was really punishing affliction, and their going forth was truly destruction. However, this passage says that whoever thinks this way is, in truth, foolish. The dead are not destroyed; they are in peace. The theology has significantly changed.

To be in peace one must be in right relationship with God. According to the author of Wisdom, immortality and incorruptibility are also rooted in right relationship, a very Jewish idea. This means that it is this right relationship that assures peace, and those who die in such a relationship hope that not even death will sever the relationship. The author's discussion of justice, death, and immortality in this first section may best be understood from the perspective of this theological development. (Years later Paul will state, "For I am convinced that neither death, nor life . . . will be able to separate us from the love of God in Christ Jesus our Lord" [Rom 8:38–39]).

# In Praise of Wisdom

The second section of the book (Wis 6:22–11:1) advances the traditional understanding of Wisdom found in the book of Proverbs. Both books characterize Wisdom as a remarkable female figure, originating from God at the time of creation (Prv 8:22–31; Wis 9:6, 9). Woman Wisdom is given to human beings that they may live righteous lives (Prv 8:32–36; Wis 9:10–11). Further descriptions of Woman Wisdom are derived from Hellenistic culture. She is said to possess the cardinal virtues found in the writings of Plato—moderation, prudence, justice, and fortitude (Wis 8:7). A more extensive description of her consists of terms found in Hellenistic philosophy:

> For in her is a spirit
> intelligent, holy, unique,
> Manifold, subtle, agile,
> clear, unstained, certain,
> Never harmful, loving the good, keen,
> unhampered, beneficent, kindly,
> Firm, secure, tranquil,
> all-powerful, all-seeing,
> And pervading all spirits,
> though they be intelligent, pure and very
> subtle.
>
> For Wisdom is mobile beyond all motion,
> and she penetrates and pervades all
> things by reason of her purity.
> (Wis 7:22–24)

Some see a similarity in this depiction of Woman Wisdom with that of Isis, the Egyptian

W
I
S

goddess who personified wisdom and who was widely worshiped in Egypt and beyond at the time of the writing of this book. This would show how the author brought together elements of Jewish faith and aspects of Hellenistic culture, thus reinterpreting both.

Having stated that Woman Wisdom was with God at the time of creation (Wis 9:9), the author credits her with several interventions. According to this author, it was Wisdom who raised up the first human being after the fall, restored the earth after the flood, saved Lot from fiery destruction and Jacob from the wrath of Esau, rescued Joseph when he was sold into slavery by his brothers, and led the people through the Red Sea (10:1–21). The image of Woman Wisdom has been refined by this author, and the record of her accomplishments has been expanded.

## The Story of the Plagues

The third part of the book (Wis 11:2–19:22) provides another example of reinterpretation of the tradition for a new context. The overriding form employed is the Greek encomium or declaration of praise. Here God is praised for the protection shown the Israelites. The story of the plagues recounted in Exodus (Ex 7–12) is retold from a very different perspective. With the exception of two digressions on divine

mercy (Wis 11:17–12:22 and 13:1–15:17), this section contains a series of negative comparisons. By means of this Greek technique known as *syncrisis*, the author shows how nature acted to benefit the Israelites, but punished the Egyptians. The Israelites enjoyed water from the rock, while the Egyptians saw the water of the Nile turn to blood (Wis 11:6–14); the Egyptians, who engaged in a form of animal worship, were plagued by small animals, while the Israelites were fed by other small creatures (Wis 11:15–16); the heavens poured down both water and fire on the land of Egypt, but rained manna on the Israelites (Wis 16:16–29); the Egyptians were plagued with darkness, but the Israelites were led by a pillar of light (Wis 17:1–18:4); the Egyptians' decision to massacre the sons of the Hebrews reverted onto their own sons (Wis 18:5–19:21).

The purpose of this retelling was to demonstrate that God favors the faithful Israelites over the Egyptians, whether they are the original Egyptians or the Hellenists living in Alexandria at the time of Pseudo-Solomon. This preference can even be seen in the workings of nature.

Intended to reassure Jews who were struggling with their faith in a new context, the book of Wisdom assures Christians today that the essence of their faith is not limited to one cultural expression, but can take root in the soil of another worldview and thrive. ■

# THE BOOK OF WISDOM

## New American Bible, Introduction

The Book of Wisdom was written about fifty years before the coming of Christ. Its author, whose name is not known to us, was probably a member of the Jewish community at Alexandria, in Egypt. He wrote in Greek, in a style patterned on that of Hebrew verse. At times he speaks in the person of Solomon, placing his teachings on the lips of the wise king of Hebrew tradition in order to emphasize their value. His profound knowledge of the earlier Old Testament writings is reflected in almost every line of the book, and marks him, like Ben Sira, as an outstanding representative of religious devotion and learning among the sages of postexilic Judaism.

The primary purpose of the author was the edification of his co-religionists in a time when they had experienced suffering and oppression, in part at least at the hands of apostate fellow Jews. To convey his message he made use of the most popular religious themes of his time, namely the splendor and worth of divine wisdom (6:22–11:1), the glorious events of the exodus (11:2–16; 12:23–27; 15:18–19:22), God's mercy (11:17–12:22), the folly of idolatry (13:1–15:17), and the manner in which God's justice operates in rewarding or punishing the individual (1:1–6:21). The first ten chapters in particular provide background for the teaching of Jesus and for some New Testament theology about Jesus. Many passages from this section of the book, notably 3:1–8, are used by the church in the liturgy.

The principal divisions of the Book of Wisdom are:

   I. The Reward of Righteousness (1:1–6:21).

  II. Praise of Wisdom by Solomon (6:22–11:1).

 III. Special Providence of God During the Exodus (11:2–16; 12:23–27; 15:18–19:22) with digressions on God's mercy (11:17–12:22) and on the folly and shame of idolatry (13:1–15:17). ■

W
I
S

# WISDOM

## I. THE REWARD OF RIGHTEOUSNESS†

### Exhortation to Righteousness, the Key to Life

**1** ¹ Love righteousness,† you who judge the
          earth;*
   think of the Lord in goodness,
   and seek him in integrity of heart;*

² Because he is found by those who do
          not test him,
   and manifests himself to those who
          do not disbelieve him.*

³ For perverse counsels separate people
          from God,
   and his power, put to the proof,
          rebukes the foolhardy;*

⁴† Because into a soul that plots evil
          wisdom does not enter,
   nor does she dwell in a body under
          debt of sin.*

⁵ For the holy spirit of discipline† flees
          deceit
   and withdraws from senseless
          counsels
   and is rebuked when unrighteousness
          occurs.*

⁶ For wisdom is a kindly spirit,
   yet she does not acquit blasphemous
          lips;
   Because God is the witness of the
          inmost self*
   and the sure observer of the heart
   and the listener to the tongue.*

⁷ For the spirit of the Lord fills the
          world,*

is all-embracing, and knows whatever
          is said.

⁸ Therefore those who utter wicked things
          will not go unnoticed,
   nor will chastising condemnation pass
          them by.*

⁹ For the devices of the wicked shall be
          scrutinized,
   and the sound of their words shall
          reach the Lord,
   for the chastisement of their
          transgressions;

¹⁰ Because a jealous ear hearkens to
          everything,*
   and discordant grumblings are not
          secret.

¹¹ Therefore guard against profitless
          grumbling,
   and from calumny† withhold your
          tongues;
   For a stealthy utterance will not go
          unpunished,
   and a lying mouth destroys the
          soul.

¹² Do not court death† by your erring way
          of life,
   nor draw to yourselves destruction by
          the works of your hands.

¹³ Because God did not make death,*
   nor does he rejoice in the destruction
          of the living.

¹⁴ For he fashioned all things that they
          might have being,
   and the creatures of the world are
          wholesome;
   There is not a destructive drug among
          them
   nor any domain of Hades† on earth,

¹⁵ For righteousness is undying.†*

---

† **1:1–6:21** The reward is the gift of immortality, to the righteous (1:15; 3:1–3), but not to the wicked (5:1–13). Contrasts between these two groups dominate chaps. 1–5. The philosophy of the wicked and their persecution of the righteous are dramatically presented in 1:16–2:24. New light is shed on the suffering of the righteous (3:1–9), childlessness (3:13–15), and premature death (4:7–16)—in contrast to the fate of the wicked (3:10–12, 16–19; 4:3–6, 17–20).

**1:1** *Righteousness:* not merely the cardinal virtue of justice (cf. 8:7), but the universal moral quality which is the application of wisdom to moral conduct. *You who judge:* "judges" and "kings" (cf. 6:1) are addressed in accordance with the literary customs of the times and with the putative Solomonic authorship, but the real audience is the Jewish community.

**1:4** In these verses personified Wisdom is identified with the spirit of the Lord; so also in 9:17.

**1:5** *Discipline:* here and elsewhere, another name for Wisdom.

**1:11** *Calumny:* speech against God and divine providence is meant.

**1:12** *Death:* as will become clear, the author is not speaking of physical death but of spiritual death, the eternal separation from God.

**1:14** *Hades:* the Greek term for the Hebrew Sheol, the dwelling place of the dead.

**1:15** *Undying:* immortality is not seen as an innate quality of the soul but as a gift of God to the righteous.

---

**1:1** 1 Chr 29:17; Ps 2:10; Is 26:9.
**1:1–2** Sir 1:25.
**1:2** 1 Chr 28:9.
**1:3** Is 59:2.
**1:4** Sir 15:7–8; Rom 7:14.
**1:5** Is 63:10.
**1:6** Jer 17:10.
**1:6–7** Jer 23:24–25.
**1:7** Wis 12:1.
**1:8** Prv 19:5.
**1:10–11** Nm 14:27–28.
**1:13–14** Ez 18:32; 33:11; 2 Pt 3:9.
**1:15** Is 51:6–8.

## The Wicked Reject Immortality and Righteousness Alike

16 It was the wicked who with hands and
  words invited death,
    considered it a friend, and pined for
      it,
    and made a covenant with it,
  Because they deserve to be allied with
    it.*

**2** ¹ For, not thinking rightly, they said
    among themselves:†
  "Brief and troubled is our lifetime;*
    there is no remedy for our dying,
    nor is anyone known to have come
      back from Hades.
2 For by mere chance were we born,
    and hereafter we shall be as though
      we had not been;
  Because the breath in our nostrils is
    smoke,
    and reason a spark from the beating
      of our hearts,
3 And when this is quenched, our body
      will be ashes
    and our spirit will be poured abroad
      like empty air.*
4 Even our name will be forgotten in time,
    and no one will recall our deeds.
  So our life will pass away like the traces
      of a cloud,
    and will be dispersed like a mist
  Pursued by the sun's rays
    and overpowered by its heat.
5 For our lifetime is the passing of a
      shadow;
    and our dying cannot be deferred
    because it is fixed with a seal; and no
      one returns.*
6 Come, therefore, let us enjoy the good
      things that are here,
    and make use of creation with
      youthful zest.*
7 Let us have our fill of costly wine and
    perfumes,

and let no springtime blossom pass us
  by;
8 let us crown ourselves with rosebuds
    before they wither.
9 Let no meadow be free from our
    wantonness;
  everywhere let us leave tokens of our
    merriment,
  for this is our portion, and this our
    lot.*
10 Let us oppress the righteous poor;
    let us neither spare the widow
    nor revere the aged for hair grown
      white with time.*
11 But let our strength be our norm of
    righteousness;
    for weakness proves itself useless.
12† Let us lie in wait for the righteous one,
    because he is annoying to us;
  he opposes our actions,
  Reproaches us for transgressions of the
    law†
    and charges us with violations of our
      training.*
13 He professes to have knowledge of God
    and styles himself a child of the
      LORD.*
14 To us he is the censure of our thoughts;
    merely to see him is a hardship for us,*
15 Because his life is not like that of others,
    and different are his ways.
16 He judges us debased;
    he holds aloof from our paths as from
      things impure.
  He calls blest the destiny of the
    righteous
    and boasts that God is his Father.*
17 Let us see whether his words be true;
    let us find out what will happen to
      him in the end.*
18 For if the righteous one is the son of
    God, God will help him
    and deliver him from the hand of his
      foes.*

2:1–20 In this speech the wicked deny survival after death and indeed invite death by their evil deeds.
2:12–5:23 From 2:12 to 5:23 the author draws heavily on Is 52–62, setting forth his teaching in a series of characters or types taken from Isaiah and embellished with additional details from other texts. The description of the "righteous one" in 2:12–20 seems to undergird the New Testament passion narrative.
2:12 Law: the law of Moses; "training" has the same meaning.

1:16 Is 28:15.
2:1 Jb 14:1; 7:9.
2:3 Jb 7:9; Jas 4:14.
2:5 Ps 144:4.
2:6 Is 22:13; 1 Cor 15:32.
2:9 Jer 13:25.
2:10 Ex 22:21–23; Lv 19:32.
2:12 Hos 8:1.
2:13 Mt 27:43; Jn 8:55; 10:36–39.
2:14 Mt 9:4.
2:16 Jer 6:30.
2:17 Gn 37:20.
2:18 Ps 22:9; Is 42:1; Mt 27:43; Jn 5:18.

19 With violence and torture let us put him
　　to the test
　　that we may have proof of his
　　　gentleness
　　and try his patience.
20 Let us condemn him to a shameful
　　death;
　　for according to his own words, God
　　　will take care of him."*

21 These were their thoughts, but they
　　erred;
　　for their wickedness blinded them,*
22† And they did not know the hidden
　　counsels of God;
　　neither did they count on a
　　　recompense for holiness
　　nor discern the innocent souls'
　　　reward.*
23 For God formed us to be imperishable;
　　the image of his own nature he made
　　　us.*
24 But by the envy† of the devil, death
　　entered the world,
　　and they who are allied with him
　　　experience it.*

## The Hidden Counsels of God†

### A. ON SUFFERING†

**3** <sup>1</sup> The souls of the righteous are in the
　　hand of God,*
　　and no torment shall touch them.
2 They seemed, in the view of the foolish,
　　to be dead;
　　and their passing away was thought
　　　an affliction
3 and their going forth from us, utter
　　destruction.

But they are in peace.*
4 For if to others, indeed, they seem
　　punished,
　　yet is their hope full of immortality;
5 Chastised a little, they shall be greatly
　　blessed,
　　because God tried them
　　and found them worthy of himself.*
6 As gold in the furnace, he proved
　　them,
　　and as sacrificial offerings† he took
　　　them to himself.*
7 In the time of their judgment† they shall
　　shine
　　and dart about as sparks through
　　　stubble;*
8 They shall judge nations and rule over
　　peoples,
　　and the LORD shall be their King
　　　forever.*
9 Those who trust in him shall understand
　　truth,
　　and the faithful shall abide with him
　　　in love:
Because grace and mercy are with his
　　holy ones,*
　　and his care is with the elect.
10 But the wicked shall receive a
　　punishment to match their
　　　thoughts,†
　　since they neglected righteousness and
　　　forsook the LORD.
11 For those who despise wisdom and
　　instruction are doomed.*
Vain is their hope, fruitless their labors,
　　and worthless their works.*
12 Their wives are foolish and their
　　children wicked,
　　accursed their brood.*

---

† **2:22** This verse announces the subject of the next section.
**2:24** *Envy*: perhaps because Adam was in the image of God or because Adam had control over all creation. *Devil*: the first biblical text to equate the serpent of Gn 3 with the devil.
**3:1–4:19** The central section of chaps. 1–6. The author begins by stating that immortality is the reward of the righteous, and then in the light of that belief comments on three points of the traditional discussion of the problem of retribution (suffering, childlessness, early death) each of which was often seen as a divine punishment.
**3:1–12** The author affirms that, for the righteous, sufferings are not punishments but purification and opportunities to show fidelity, whereas for the wicked suffering is truly a punishment.
**3:6** *Offerings*: the image is that of the burnt offering, in which the victim is completely consumed by fire.
**3:7** *Judgment*: the Greek *episkopē* is God's loving judgment of those who have been faithful to him; the same word is used

in 14:11 for the punishment of the wicked at God's judgment. Cf. also v. 13.
**3:10** *To match their thoughts*: a fate as empty as that which they describe in 2:1–5.

*
**2:20** Jas 5:6.
**2:21** Rom 1:21.
**2:22** Ps 18:24–25; Prv 11:18; Mt 11:25.
**2:23** Gn 1:26–27; Is 54:16 LXX.
**2:24** Gn 3:1–24; Rom 5:12.
**3:1** Jb 12:10.
**3:3** Is 57:2.
**3:5** Tb 12:13; 2 Cor 4:17; 1 Pt 1:6–7.
**3:6** Ps 51:19; Prv 17:3; Sir 2:5; Is 48:10.
**3:7** Dn 12:3; Ob 18; Mal 3:3; Mt 13:43.
**3:8** Wis 8:14; Prv 8:16; Dn 7:22; 1 Cor 6:2; Rev 20:4.
**3:9** Wis 4:15; Jb 10:12; Jn 15:10.
**3:11** Prv 1:7.
**3:11–12** Sir 41:8.
**3:12** Dt 28:18.

## B. ON CHILDLESSNESS†

13 Yes, blessed is she who, childless and
      undefiled,
      never knew transgression of the
            marriage bed;
      for she shall bear fruit at the judgment
            of souls.†

14 So also the eunuch whose hand wrought
      no misdeed,
      who held no wicked thoughts against
            the LORD—
   For he shall be given fidelity's choice
            reward†
      and a more gratifying heritage in the
            LORD's temple.*

15 For the fruit of noble struggles is a
      glorious one;
      and unfailing is the root of
            understanding.†*

16 But the children of adulterers† will
      remain without issue,
      and the progeny of an unlawful bed
            will disappear.*

17 For should they attain long life, they will
      be held in no esteem,
      and dishonored will their old age be
            in the end;

18 Should they die abruptly, they will have
      no hope
      nor comfort in the day of scrutiny;

19   for dire is the end of the wicked
            generation.*

**4** ¹ Better is childlessness with virtue;
      for immortal is the memory of virtue,
      acknowledged both by God and
            human beings.*

2 When it is present people imitate it,
      and they long for it when it is gone;
   Forever it marches crowned in triumph,
      victorious in unsullied deeds of valor.

3 But the numerous progeny of the wicked
      shall be of no avail;
      their spurious offshoots shall not
            strike deep root
      nor take firm hold.*

4 For even though their branches flourish
      for a time,
      they are unsteady and shall be rocked
            by the wind
      and, by the violence of the winds,
            uprooted;*

5 Their twigs shall be broken off untimely,
      their fruit useless, unripe for eating,
      fit for nothing.

6 For children born of lawless unions
      give evidence of the wickedness of
            their parents, when they are
            examined.

## C. ON EARLY DEATH†

7 But the righteous one, though he die
      early, shall be at rest.*

8 For the age that is honorable comes not
      with the passing of time,*
      nor can it be measured in terms of
            years.

9 Rather, understanding passes for gray hair,
      and an unsullied life is the attainment
            of old age.

10† The one who pleased God was loved,*
      living among sinners, was
            transported—

11 Snatched away, lest wickedness pervert
      his mind
      or deceit beguile his soul;*

12 For the witchery of paltry things
      obscures what is right
      and the whirl of desire transforms the
            innocent mind.*

13 Having become perfect in a short while,
      he reached the fullness of a long
            career;

---

† **3:13–4:6** The true fruit of life is not children but virtue which leads to immortality. The many children of the wicked will be a disappointing fruit.

**3:13** See vv. 7–9.

**3:14** *Fidelity's choice reward*: cf. Is 56:1–8. *More gratifying*: better than sons and daughters; cf. Is 56:5.

**3:15** *Root of understanding*: the root that is understanding (wisdom).

**3:16** *Adulterers*: understood here as a type of sinners in general; cf. Is 57:3–5.

**4:7–19** Early death is not a punishment for the righteous because genuine old age is the attainment of perfection and early death is a preservation from corruption. The old age and death of the wicked, however, will not be honorable.

**4:10–11** There are allusions here to Enoch (Gn 5:21–24), who was young by patriarchal standards, and to Lot (Gn 19:10–11; 2 Pt 2:7–8). Cf. also Is 57:1–2.

* **3:14** Is 56:2–5.
**3:15** Sir 1:18.
**3:16** 2 Sm 12:14.
**3:19** Ps 34:22.
**4:1** Prv 3:3–4; Sir 16:1–3.
**4:3** Sir 23:25.
**4:4** Sir 40:15; Is 40:24.
**4:7** Wis 3:3.
**4:8** Jb 12:12; 32:9; Sir 25:4–6.
**4:10** Gn 5:24; Sir 44:16; Heb 11:5.
**4:11** Is 57:1–2.
**4:12** Wis 2:21; Dn 13:9.

14 for his soul was pleasing to the LORD,
    therefore he sped him out of the
    midst of wickedness.*
But the people saw and did not
    understand,
    nor did they take that consideration
    into account.†

16 Yes, the righteous one who has died will
    condemn
    the sinful who live;
And youth, swiftly completed, will
    condemn
    the many years of the unrighteous
    who have grown old.*

17 For they will see the death of the wise
    one
    and will not understand what the
    LORD intended,
    or why he kept him safe.

18 They will see, and hold him in
    contempt;
    but the LORD will laugh them to
    scorn.*

19 And they shall afterward become
    dishonored corpses*
    and an unceasing mockery among the
    dead.
For he shall strike them down speechless
    and prostrate*
    and rock them to their foundations;
They shall be utterly laid waste
    and shall be in grief
    and their memory shall perish.

### The Judgment of the Wicked

20 Fearful shall they come, at the counting
    up of their sins,
    and their lawless deeds shall convict
    them to their face.

5 ¹† Then shall the righteous one with great
    assurance confront*
    his oppressors who set at nought his
    labors.*

2 Seeing this, the wicked shall be shaken
    with dreadful fear,
    and be amazed at the unexpected
    salvation.

3 They shall say among themselves, rueful
    and groaning through anguish of
    spirit:

"This is the one whom once we held as
    a laughingstock
    and as a type for mockery,

4 fools that we were!
His life we accounted madness,
    and death dishonored.

5 See how he is accounted among the
    heavenly beings;†
    how his lot is with the holy ones!*

6 We, then, have strayed from the way of
    truth,*
    and the light of righteousness did not
    shine for us,
    and the sun did not rise for us.*

7 We were entangled in the thorns of
    mischief and of ruin;
    we journeyed through trackless deserts,
    but the way of the LORD we never
    knew.

8 What did our pride avail us?
    What have wealth and its boastfulness
    afforded us?*

9 All of them passed like a shadow
    and like a fleeting rumor;*

10 Like a ship traversing the heaving water:
    when it has passed, no trace can be
    found,
    no path of its keel in the waves.

11 Or like a bird flying through the air;
    no evidence of its course is to be
    found—
But the fluid air, lashed by the beating
    of pinions,
    and cleft by the rushing force
Of speeding wings, is traversed;
    and afterward no mark of passage can
    be found in it.

12 Or as, when an arrow has been shot at a
    mark,
    the parted air straightway flows
    together again

---

† **4:14** Verse 15 is omitted because it repeats the last two lines of 3:9.
**5:1–13** In contrast to their speech in chap. 2 the wicked now regret their assessment of life and righteousness.
**5:5** *Heavenly beings:* lit., "sons of God." These are the holy ones, members of the heavenly court, among whom the righteous are to be found. A bodily resurrection does not seem to be envisioned.

* **4:14** Gn 19:22, 29; 2 Pt 2:7.
**4:16** Mt 12:41–42.
**4:18** Ps 37:13.
**4:19** Neh 1:10 LXX; Ps 18:8; Is 14:19; Jer 23:39–40.
**4:19** 2 Mc 3:29.
**5:1–2** 2 Thes 1:6–7.
**5:1** Col 2:15.
**5:5** Acts 26:18; Col 1:12.
**5:6** Prv 4:18–19; Jn 12:35.
**5:8** Ps 49:7; Prv 10:2.
**5:6–7** Prv 22:5; Is 59:6–14.
**5:9–12** 1 Chr 20:15; Jb 9:25–26 LXX; Ps 144:4.

so that none discerns the way it
 went—

13 Even so, once born, we abruptly came to
 nought
 and held no sign of virtue to display,
 but were consumed in our
  wickedness."*

14† Yes, the hope of the wicked is like chaff
 borne by the wind,
 and like fine, storm-driven snow;
Like smoke scattered by the wind,
 and like the passing memory of the
  nomad camping for a single day.*

15 But the righteous live forever,
 and in the LORD is their recompense,
 and the thought of them is with the
  Most High.*

16 Therefore shall they receive the splendid
 crown,
 the beautiful diadem, from the hand
  of the LORD,
For he will shelter them with his right
 hand,
 and protect them with his arm.*

17 He shall take his zeal for armor*
 and arm creation to requite the
  enemy,

18 Shall put on righteousness for a
 breastplate,
 wear sure judgment for a helmet,

19 Shall take invincible holiness for a
 shield,*

20  and sharpen his sudden anger for a
  sword.
The universe will war with him against
 the foolhardy;

21 Well-aimed bolts of lightning will go
 forth
 and from the clouds will leap to the
  mark as from a well-drawn bow;*

22  and as from a sling, wrathful
  hailstones shall be hurled.
The waters of the sea will be enraged

and flooding rivers will overwhelm
 them;*

23 A mighty wind will confront them
 and winnow them like a tempest;
Thus lawlessness will lay waste the
 whole earth
 and evildoing overturn the thrones of
  the mighty.*

## Exhortation to Seek Wisdom†

**6** ¹ Hear, therefore, kings, and understand;*
learn, you magistrates† of the earth's
 expanse!

2 Give ear, you who have power over
 multitudes
 and lord it over throngs of peoples!

3 Because authority was given you by the
 Lord
 and sovereignty by the Most High,
who shall probe your works and
 scrutinize your counsels!*

4 Because, though you were ministers of
 his kingdom, you did not judge
 rightly,
 and did not keep the law,†
 nor walk according to the will of God,

5 Terribly and swiftly he shall come
 against you,
 because severe judgment awaits the
 exalted—

6 For the lowly may be pardoned out of
 mercy*
 but the mighty shall be mightily put
 to the test.

7 For the Ruler of all shows no partiality,
 nor does he fear greatness,*
Because he himself made the great as
 well as the small,
 and provides for all alike;

8 but for those in power a rigorous
 scrutiny impends.

9 To you, therefore, O princes, are my
 words addressed*

† 5:14–23 A picture of the reward of the righteous which develops into an apocalyptic description of the divine warrior's
destruction of evil. The author utilizes Is 59–62.
 6:1–21 The first part of the book closes with an exhortation
comparable to 1:1–15, and it leads into "Solomon's" personal
comments on wisdom in chaps. 7–9.
 6:1 Kings . . . magistrates: note the inclusion with v. 21
("kings"). The address to earthly powers is in accord with the
opening (1:1), but the true audience remains the Jewish community.
 6:4 Law: that of Moses; cf. 2:12; 6:10.

* 5:13 Ez 33:10.
5:14 Jb 21:18; Ps 1:4;
 37:20; Is 17:13.
5:15 Is 62:11; Ez 18:9.
5:16 Ex 33:22; Is 62:3;
 2 Tm 4:8; 1 Pt 5:4.
5:17 Is 59:17.
5:19–20 Dt 32:40–43.
5:21 Hb 3:9–11.
5:22 Dt 11:4.

5:23 Wis 11:20; Sir
 10:13–14.
6:1–2 Wis 1:1; Ps 2:10; Sir
 33:19; Mi 3:1, 9.
6:3 2 Chr 36:23; Prv
 8:15–16; Jn 19:11;
 Rom 13:1.
6:6–7 Lk 12:48.
6:7 Dt 1:17; Prv 22:2.
6:9–11 Dt 4:10; Ps 2:12; Sir
 32:14; 1 Jn 3:7.

that you may learn wisdom and that
you may not fall away.

10 For those who keep the holy precepts
hallowed will be found holy,
and those learned in them will have
ready a response.†

11 Desire therefore my words;
long for them and you will be
instructed.

12 Resplendent and unfading is Wisdom,
and she is readily perceived by those
who love her,
and found by those who seek her.*

13 She hastens to make herself known to
those who desire her;*

14 one who watches for her at dawn will
not be disappointed,
for she will be found sitting at the
gate.

15 For setting your heart on her is the
perfection of prudence,
and whoever keeps vigil for her is
quickly free from care;

16 Because she makes her rounds, seeking
those worthy of her,
and graciously appears to them on the
way,
and goes to meet them with full
attention.*

17† For the first step toward Wisdom is an
earnest desire for discipline;*

18 then, care for discipline is love of
her;
love means the keeping of her laws;
To observe her laws is the basis for
incorruptibility;

19 and incorruptibility makes one close
to God;

20 thus the desire for Wisdom leads to a
kingdom.

21 If, then, you find pleasure in throne and
scepter, you princes of peoples,

honor Wisdom, that you may reign as
kings forever.

## II. PRAISE OF WISDOM BY SOLOMON†

### Introduction

22 Now what wisdom is, and how she
came to be I shall proclaim;
and I shall conceal no secrets from
you,
But from the very beginning I shall
search out
and bring to light knowledge of her;
I shall not diverge from the truth.*

23 Neither shall I admit consuming
jealousy to my company,
because that can have no fellowship
with Wisdom.*

24 A multitude of the wise is the safety of
the world,
and a prudent king, the stability of the
people;*

25 so take instruction from my words, to
your profit.

### Solomon Is Like All Others

7 1 I too am a mortal, the same as all the
rest,*
and a descendant of the first one
formed of earth.†
And in my mother's womb I was
molded into flesh

2 in a ten-month period†—body and
blood,
from the seed of a man, and the
pleasure that accompanies
marriage.

3 And I too, when born, inhaled the
common air,
and fell upon the kindred earth;
wailing, I uttered that first sound
common to all.

4 In swaddling clothes and with constant
care I was nurtured.

---

**6:10** *Response:* a suitable plea before the great Judge. Cf. Prv 22:21; Jb 31:14; Hb 2:1; Sir 8:9.

**6:17–20** This type of reasoning approximates the rhetorical sorites, a series of statements in which the predicate of each becomes the subject of the next. Cf. Rom 5:3–5.

**6:22–9:18** In these verses the author identifies with Solomon (without mentioning that name anywhere), and praises the beauty of Wisdom, describing how he sought her out. Thus the readers of the book can find a model in their search for Wisdom.

**7:1** *First one formed of earth:* Adam. The author omits throughout the book the proper names of the characters in sacred history of whom he speaks; see especially chap. 10.

**7:2** *In a ten-month period:* ten lunar months.

---

| | |
|---|---|
| **6:12** Wis 7:10; Prv 8:17; Jer 29:13. | **6:22** Tb 12:7, 11; Mt 13:11; Jn 15:15. |
| **6:13–16** Prv 8:3, 17, 34. | **6:23** Wis 7:13; Jas 3:14–15. |
| **6:16** Prv 8:20–21; Sir 15:1–5. | **6:24** Prv 11:14; 24:6; 29:4; Sir 10:1–5. |
| **6:17–21** Ps 2:10–12; Prv 4:4–9; 7:1–4; 8:15–16; Dn 7:27; Jn 14:15, 21; 1 Jn 5:3. | **7:1–2** Wis 10:1; Gn 2:7; Jb 10:9–12; 33:6; 1 Cor 15:47–49. |

5   For no king has any different origin or
        birth;
6       one is the entry into life for all,
        and in one same way they leave it.*

### Solomon Prayed and Wisdom and Riches Came to Him

7   Therefore I prayed, and prudence was
        given me;
        I pleaded and the spirit of Wisdom
        came to me.*
8   I preferred her to scepter and throne,*
    And deemed riches nothing in
        comparison with her,
9       nor did I liken any priceless gem to her;
    Because all gold, in view of her, is a bit
        of sand,
        and before her, silver is to be
        accounted mire.
10  Beyond health and beauty I loved her,
    And I chose to have her rather than the
        light,
        because her radiance never ceases.*
11  Yet all good things together came to me
        with her,*
        and countless riches at her hands;
12  I rejoiced in them all, because Wisdom
        is their leader,
        though I had not known that she is
        their mother.†*

### Solomon Prays for Help to Speak Worthily of Wisdom

13  Sincerely I learned about her, and
        ungrudgingly do I share—
        her riches I do not hide away;*
14  For she is an unfailing treasure;
        those who gain this treasure win the
        friendship of God,
        being commended by the gifts that
        come from her discipline.†
15  Now God grant I speak suitably
        and value these endowments at their
        worth:

    For he is the guide of Wisdom
        and the director of the wise.
16  For both we and our words are in his
        hand,
        as well as all prudence and knowledge
        of crafts.*
17† For he gave me sound knowledge of
        what exists,
        that I might know the structure of
        the universe and the force of its
        elements,
18  The beginning and the end and the
        midpoint of times,
        the changes in the sun's course and
        the variations of the seasons,
19  Cycles of years, positions of stars,
20      natures of living things, tempers of
        beasts,
    Powers of the winds and thoughts of
        human beings,
        uses of plants and virtues of roots—
21  Whatever is hidden or plain I learned,
22      for Wisdom, the artisan of all, taught
        me.*

### Nature and Incomparable Dignity of Wisdom

†   For in her is a spirit
        intelligent, holy, unique,
    Manifold, subtle, agile,
        clear, unstained, certain,
    Never harmful, loving the good, keen,*
23      unhampered, beneficent, kindly,
    Firm, secure, tranquil,
        all-powerful, all-seeing,
    And pervading all spirits,
        though they be intelligent, pure and
        very subtle.

24  For Wisdom is mobile beyond all motion,
        and she penetrates and pervades all
        things by reason of her purity.*
25† For she is a breath of the might of God
        and a pure emanation of the glory of
        the Almighty;

---

**7:12** *Mother:* lit., "she who begets." Although Wisdom her-self is begotten of God (Prv 8:22–24), she is here the one who brings into being.

**7:14** *Discipline:* cf. note on 1:5.

**7:17–22a** Wisdom teaches not only righteousness and friend-ship with God but also sound knowledge of the world, the uni-verse, plants, animals and human beings. See also 1 Kgs 5:9–14; these specialties reflect Hellenistic culture.

**7:22b–23** The twenty-one (7 × 3) attributes of the spirit in Wisdom reflect the influence of contemporary philosophy, espe-cially the Stoa, but the personification rests also on Prv 8:22–31 and Sir 24.

**7:25–26** Five strong metaphors underline the origins and closeness of Wisdom with God. See the use of this language in Heb 1:3; Col 1:15.

---

**7:6** Jb 1:21; Lk 2:12; 1 Tm 6:7–8.
**7:7** 1 Kgs 3:5–15; Prv 2:3–11.
**7:8–9** Wis 8:5; 1 Kgs 10:21; Jb 28:15–19; Prv 3:14–16; 8:10, 18–19.
**7:10** Prv 6:23.
**7:11** Prv 8:21.
**7:12** Prv 8:14–15.
**7:13** Wis 6:23.
**7:16** Wis 3:1.
**7:22** Wis 14:2; Prv 8:30.
**7:22–23** Heb 4:12–13; Jas 3:17.
**7:24** Wis 8:1.

W
I
S

therefore nothing defiled can enter
into her.

26 For she is the reflection of eternal light,
the spotless mirror of the power of
God,
the image of his goodness.*

27 Although she is one, she can do all
things,
and she renews everything while
herself perduring;
Passing into holy souls from age to age,
she produces friends of God and
prophets.*

28 For God loves nothing so much as the
one who dwells with Wisdom.

29 For she is fairer than the sun*
and surpasses every constellation of
the stars.
Compared to light, she is found more
radiant;

30 though night supplants light,
wickedness does not prevail over
Wisdom.

# 8

1 Indeed, she spans the world from end to
end mightily
and governs all things well.*

## Wisdom, the Source of Blessings

2 Her I loved and sought after from my
youth;
I sought to take her for my bride†
and was enamored of her beauty.*

3 She adds to nobility the splendor of
companionship with God;
even the Ruler of all loved her.

4 For she leads into the understanding of
God,
and chooses his works.*

5 If riches are desirable in life,
what is richer than Wisdom, who
produces all things?*

6 And if prudence is at work,*
who in the world is a better artisan
than she?

7 Or if one loves righteousness,

whose works are virtues,
She teaches moderation and prudence,
righteousness and fortitude,†
and nothing in life is more useful
than these.

8 Or again, if one yearns for wide
experience,
she knows the things of old, and
infers the things to come.
She understands the turns of phrases
and the solutions of riddles;
signs and wonders she knows in
advance
and the outcome of times and ages.*

## Wisdom as Solomon's Counselor and Comfort

9 So I determined to take her to live with
me,
knowing that she would be my
counselor while all was well,
and my comfort in care and grief.

10 Because of her I have glory among the
multitudes,*
and esteem from the elders, though I
am but a youth.

11 I shall become keen in judgment,
and shall be a marvel before rulers.

12 They will wait while I am silent and
listen when I speak;
and when I shall speak the more,
they will put their hands upon their
mouths.†

13 Because of her I shall have immortality
and leave to those after me an
everlasting memory.*

14 I shall govern peoples, and nations will
be my subjects—*

15 tyrannical princes, hearing of me, will
be afraid;
in the assembly I shall appear noble,
and in war courageous.

16 Entering my house, I shall take my
repose beside her;
For association with her involves no
bitterness

---

**8:2** *I loved . . . my bride*: the erotic quality in the pursuit of and living with Woman Wisdom, who is the Lord's consort (9:4) and loved by him, continues throughout this chapter (vv. 16, 18). It is reflected already in Prv 4:5–9; 7:4–5. See also Sir 15:2–5; 51:13–21.

**8:7** *Moderation . . . fortitude*: known also as the cardinal virtues, and recognized in Greek philosophy (Plato).

**8:12** *Hands upon their mouths*: a sign of respect for unanswerable wisdom; cf. Jb 40:4.

---

**7:26** 2 Cor 4:4; Col 1:15; Heb 1:3.
**7:27** Ex 33:11; Jb 42:2; Ps 104:29; Jl 3:1.
**7:29–30** Sg 6:3, 9.
**8:1** Wis 7:24; 15:1.
**8:2** Prv 5:13–18; 8:17.
**8:4** Prv 8:27–31.
**8:5** Prv 8:18–19.
**8:6–7** Prv 8:14–15.
**8:8** Prv 1:6; Sir 39:1–3; 42:19–20; Dn 2:21.
**8:10–12** 1 Kgs 3:28; Jb 29:8–10, 21–22.
**8:13** Sir 15:6; 41:12–13; Is 56:5.
**8:14** Wis 3:8; Ps 18:48; 47:4.

and living with her no grief,
  but rather joy and gladness.*

## Wisdom Is a Gift of God

17 Reflecting on these things,
  and considering in my heart
  That immortality lies in kinship with
    Wisdom,*
18   great delight in love of her,
  and unfailing riches in the works of
    her hands;
  And that in associating with her there is
    prudence,
  and fair renown in sharing her
    discourses,
  I went about seeking to take her for
    my own.
19† Now, I was a well-favored child,
  and I came by a noble nature;
20   or rather, being noble, I attained an
    unblemished body.
21 And knowing that I could not otherwise
    possess her unless God gave it—
  and this, too, was prudence, to know
    whose gift she is—
  I went to the LORD and besought
    him,*
  and said with all my heart:

## Solomon's Prayer†

9 1† God of my ancestors, Lord of mercy,*
  you who have made all things by your
    word*
2 And in your wisdom have established
    humankind
  to rule the creatures produced by
    you,*
3 And to govern the world in holiness and
    righteousness,
  and to render judgment in integrity of
    heart:*

4 Give me Wisdom, the consort at your
    throne,
  and do not reject me from among
    your children;*
5 For I am your servant, the child of your
    maidservant,
  a man weak and short-lived
  and lacking in comprehension of
    judgment and of laws.*
6 Indeed, though one be perfect among
    mortals,
  if Wisdom, who comes from you, be
    lacking,
  that one will count for nothing.*
7 You have chosen me king over your
    people
  and magistrate over your sons and
    daughters.*
8 You have bid me build a temple on your
    holy mountain
  and an altar in the city that is your
    dwelling place,
  a copy of the holy tabernacle which
    you had established from of
    old.*
9 Now with you is Wisdom, who knows
    your works
  and was present when you made the
    world;
  Who understands what is pleasing in
    your eyes
  and what is conformable with your
    commands.*
10 Send her forth from your holy heavens
  and from your glorious throne
    dispatch her
  That she may be with me and work with
    me,
  that I may know what is pleasing to
    you.*

---

**8:19–20** Here the author mentions first bodily, then spiritual, excellence. To make it plain that the latter is the governing factor in the harmonious development of the human person, he then reverses the order. The Platonic doctrine of the pre-existence of the soul is often read into these lines, but such an anthropology does not seem to be the intent of the author (cf. 7:1–6). Verse 20 appears to rule out any misunderstanding of v. 19. Verse 21 emphasizes that he did not bring talent to his "birth"; his wisdom is the gift of God.
  **9:1–18** The author presents his version of Solomon's prayer (1 Kgs 3:6–9; 2 Chr 1:8–10).
  **9:1–2** The author identifies Wisdom with the word of God just as he again identifies Wisdom with the spirit of God in v. 17. All three are alternate ways of expressing God's activity in relationship with the world and its inhabitants.

**8:16** Prv 29:6; Sir 15:6; Bar 3:38.
**8:17** Prv 3:18.
**8:21** 1 Kgs 3:9; 1 Kgs 5:9; Prv 2:6; Jas 1:5.
**9:1–2** Ps 86:15.
**9:1** Gn 1; Ps 33:6; Prv 3:19; Jer 10:12; Jn 1:3, 10.
**9:2** Ps 8:7–9; Sir 17:3–4.
**9:3** 1 Kgs 3:6; 9:4–5; Ps 9:8–9.
**9:4** 2 Chr 1:10.
**9:5** 1 Kgs 3:7; Ps 116:16.
**9:6** Wis 3:17; 1 Kgs 11:4; 1 Cor 3:18–21.
**9:7** 1 Chr 28:5.
**9:8** Ex 25:8–9; 2 Sm 7:13; 1 Chr 28:5; 2 Chr 6:1–2; 7:7; Tb 1:4; Ps 15:1; 48:2–3.
**9:9** Dt 6:17–18; Prv 8:22–31; Jn 1:1–3, 10.
**9:10** Wis 18:15; Mt 5:34; Jn 3:17; 20:21.

11 For she knows and understands all
    things,
    and will guide me prudently in my
      affairs
    and safeguard me by her glory;*
12 Thus my deeds will be acceptable,
    and I will judge your people justly
    and be worthy of my father's throne.*

13 For who knows God's counsel,
    or who can conceive what the Lord
      intends?*
14 For the deliberations of mortals are timid,
    and uncertain our plans.
15† For the corruptible body burdens the
    soul
    and the earthly tent weighs down the
      mind with its many concerns.*
16 Scarcely can we guess the things on
    earth,
    and only with difficulty grasp what is
      at hand;
    but things in heaven, who can search
      them out?*
17 Or who can know your counsel, unless
    you give Wisdom
    and send your holy spirit from on
      high?*
18† Thus were the paths of those on earth
    made straight,
    and people learned what pleases you,
    and were saved by Wisdom.*

**Wisdom Preserves Her Followers**

**10** †1 She preserved the first-formed
    father† of the world*
    when he alone had been created;*
    And she raised him up from his fall,
2     and gave him power to rule all
      things.*
3 But when an unrighteous man†
    withdrew from her in his anger,

    he perished through his fratricidal
      wrath.*
4 When on his account the earth was
    flooded, Wisdom again saved it,
    piloting the righteous man† on
      frailest wood.*
5 She, when the nations were sunk in
    universal wickedness,
    knew the righteous man,† kept him
      blameless before God,
    and preserved him resolute against
      pity for his child.*
6 She rescued a righteous man† from
    among the wicked who were
      being destroyed,*
    when he fled as fire descended upon
      the Pentapolis—
7 Where as a testimony to its wickedness,
    even yet there remain a smoking
      desert,
    Plants bearing fruit that never ripens,
    and the tomb of a disbelieving soul,†
      a standing pillar of salt.*
8 For those who forsook Wisdom
    not only were deprived of knowledge
      of the good,
    But also left the world a memorial of
      their folly,
    so that they could not even be hidden
      in their fall.
9 But Wisdom rescued from tribulations
    those who served her.*
10 She, when a righteous man† fled from
    his brother's anger,*
    guided him in right ways,
    Showed him the kingdom of God
    and gave him knowledge of holy
      things;
    She prospered him in his labors

W
I
S

---

**9:15–17** Although the expressions in v. 15 draw on the language of Plato concerning the human condition, the conclusion is very biblical: God remains a mystery (Jb 38–39; Eccl 8:17; Is 40:12–14; Rom 11:33–34). The plight of humankind is clearly one of ignorance, unless the "holy spirit" is sent from God.

**9:18** An announcement of the next section.

**10:1–21** This chapter prepares for the following section (Wis 11:2–19:22) on the history of Israel in the exodus, by reviewing the dealings of Wisdom with the patriarchs. It has a parallel in Sir 44–50; cf. also Wis 18:9.

**10:1–2** Adam.
**10:3** Cain.
**10:4** Noah.
**10:5** Abraham.

**10:6** Lot. *Pentapolis*: the five cities, including Sodom; cf. Gn 14:2.
**10:7** *Disbelieving soul*: Lot's wife; cf. Gn 19:26.
**10:10–12** Jacob.

---

**9:11** Wis 8:8.
**9:12** 1 Kgs 3:6–9.
**9:13** Is 40:13; Bar 3:31.
**9:15** Jb 4:19.
**9:16** Sir 1:3; Jn 3:12.
**9:17** Jn 14:26.
**9:18** Wis 10:9; Prv 28:26.
**10:1–16** Heb 11:17–27.
**10:1** Wis 7:1.
**10:2** Gn 1:28.

**10:3** Gn 4:1–16.
**10:4** Wis 14:5–6; Gn 6:5–9.
**10:5** Gn 22:7–10.
**10:6** Gn 18:22–33; 19:15–25; 2 Pt 2:6–7.
**10:7** Gn 19:26; Lk 17:32.
**10:9** Wis 16:8.
**10:10** Gn 27:43–45; 28:12–15.

and made abundant the fruit of his
        works,

11 Stood by him against the greed of his
        defrauders,
    and enriched him;*

12 She preserved him from foes,
    and secured him against ambush,
    And she gave him the prize for his hard
        struggle
    that he might know that devotion to
        God† is mightier than all else.*

13 She did not abandon a righteous man†
        when he was sold,*
    but rescued him from sin.*

14 She went down with him into the
        dungeon,
    and did not desert him in his bonds,
    Until she brought him the scepter of
        royalty
    and authority over his oppressors,
    Proved false those who had defamed
        **him**,
    and gave him eternal glory.

15 The holy people and their blameless
        descendants—it was she
    who rescued them from the nation
        that oppressed them.*

16 She entered the soul of the Lord's
        servant,†
    and withstood fearsome kings with
        signs and wonders;*

17 she gave the holy ones the reward of
        their labors,*
    Conducted them by a wondrous road,
    became a shelter for them by day
    a starry flame by night.

18 She took them across the Red Sea
    and brought them through the deep
        waters.

19 Their enemies she overwhelmed,

and churned them up† from the
        bottom of the depths.

20 Therefore the righteous despoiled the
        wicked;
    and they sang of your holy name,
        Lord,
    and praised in unison your
        conquering hand,*

21 Because Wisdom opened the mouths of
        the mute,
    and gave ready speech to infants.*

**11** ¹ She prospered their affairs through
        the holy prophet.*

## III. SPECIAL PROVIDENCE OF GOD DURING THE EXODUS†

### Introduction

2 They journeyed through the uninhabited
        desert,
    and in lonely places they pitched their
        tents;*

3 they withstood enemies and warded
        off their foes.*

4 When they thirsted, they called upon you,
    and water was given them from the
        sheer rock,
    a quenching of their thirst from the
        hard stone.

5 For by the things through which their
        foes were punished
    they in their need were benefited.*

### First Example: Water Punishes the Egyptians and Benefits the Israelites

6 Instead of a river's† perennial source,
    troubled with impure blood*

7 as a rebuke to the decree for the
        slaying of infants,
    You gave them abundant water beyond
        their hope,

---

**10:12** *Devotion to God*: in the Greek this signifies "piety" or "religion," and is the equivalent of the Hebrew "fear of the Lord"; cf. Prv 1:7.
**10:13–14** Joseph.
**10:16** Moses.
**10:19** *Churned them up*: casting their bodies on the shore.
**11:2–19:22** Few verses in chaps. 11–19 can be fully understood without consulting the passages in the Pentateuch which are indicated in the cross-references. The theme of this part of the book is expressed in v. 5 and is illustrated in the following chapters by five examples drawn from Exodus events.
**11:6–8** *River*: the Nile; the contrast is between the first plague of Egypt (Ex 7:17–24) and the water drawn from the rock in Horeb (Ex 17:5–7; Nm 20:8–11).

**10:11** Gn 30:29–30; 31:5–12.
**10:12** Gn 32:24–29; 1 Tm 4:8.
**10:13–14** Gn 37–45.
**10:13** Gn 39:7–10.
**10:15** Ex 3:9; 14:30; 19:6.
**10:16** Wis 1:4; 7:27; Ex 4:10; Ps 76:13.
**10:17–19** Wis 14:3; 19:7; Ex 13:21–22; Ex 14–15; Ps 77:20–21; 78:13, 53; Is 4:5–6.

**10:20** Ex 12:35–36; 15:1–21.
**10:21** Ex 4:10–15; Ps 8:3; Mt 11:25.
**11:1** Dt 2:7; Hos 12:14.
**11:2–5** Ex 17:2–6; Nm 20:1–13; Ps 63:2; 107:4–7; Jer 2:6.
**11:3** Ex 17:8–16; Nm 21:1–3, 21–35; 31:1–12; Ps 118:10–12.
**11:5** Wis 16:1–2.
**11:6–8** Wis 18:5; Ex 1:22; 7:17–24.

WIS

8    after you had shown by the thirst they
experienced
how you punished their
adversaries.

9    For when they had been tried, though
only mildly chastised,*
they recognized how the wicked,
condemned in anger, were being
tormented.

10    You tested your own people,
admonishing them as a father;
but as a stern king you probed and
condemned the wicked.

11    Those near and far were equally
afflicted:*

12    for a twofold grief† took hold of
them*
and a groaning at the remembrance of
the ones who had departed.

13    For when they heard that the cause of
their own torments
was a benefit to these others, they
recognized the Lord.

14    For though they had mocked and
rejected him who had been cast
out and abandoned long ago,
in the final outcome, they marveled at
him,
since their thirst proved unlike that of
the righteous.*

## Second Example: Animals Punish the Egyptians and Benefit the Israelites

15    In return for their senseless, wicked
thoughts,
which misled them into worshiping
dumb† serpents and worthless
insects,
You sent upon them swarms of dumb
creatures for vengeance;*

16    that they might recognize that one
is punished by the very things
through which one sins.*

## Digression on God's Mercy

17    For not without means was your
almighty hand,*
that had fashioned the universe from
formless matter,†
to send upon them many bears or
fierce lions,

18    Or newly created, wrathful, unknown
beasts
breathing forth fiery breath,
Or pouring out roaring smoke,
or flashing terrible sparks from their
eyes.

19    Not only could these attack and
completely destroy them;
even their frightful appearance itself
could slay.

20    Even without these, they could have
been killed at a single blast,
pursued by justice
and winnowed by your mighty spirit.
But you have disposed all things by
measure and number and
weight.*

21    For great strength is always present with
you;
who can resist the might of your
arm?*

22    Indeed, before you the whole universe is
like a grain from a balance,†
or a drop of morning dew come down
upon the earth.*

23†    But you have mercy on all, because you
can do all things;
and you overlook sins for the sake of
repentance.*

24    For you love all things that are
and loathe nothing that you have
made;
for you would not fashion what you
hate.*

---

† **11:12** *Twofold grief:* the double distress described in vv. 13–14.

**11:15** *Dumb:* that is, irrational.

**11:17** *Formless matter:* a Greek philosophical concept is used to interpret the chaos of Gn 1:2.

**11:22** *Grain from a balance:* a tiny particle used for weighing on sensitive scales.

**11:23** The combination of divine mercy and power is an unusual paradox, but cf. 12:15–18; Ps 62:12–13; Sir 2:18. The main emphasis is on a creating that is motivated by love; the divine "imperishable spirit" (either Wisdom as in 1:4, 7, or perhaps the breath of life as in Gn 2:7) is in everything (12:1).

* **11:9–11** Wis 3:5; 16:3–4; Dt 8:2–5; 2 Mc 6:12–16; Ps 6:2; Prv 3:12.
**11:11** Ps 6:2.
**11:12–13** Wis 16:8; Ex 14:4, 18.
**11:14** Ex 2:3.
**11:15** Wis 12:23–24; 15:18–16:1; Ex 7:26–8:11.
**11:16** Wis 12:23, 27; Ex 10:16; Prv 1:31–32; 26:27.
**11:17–19** Wis 12:8–9; 16:1, 5; Gn 1:1–2; Dt 32:24; 2 Kgs 17:25–26; Hos 13:4–8.
**11:20** Jb 4:9.
**11:21** Wis 12:12; 2 Chr 20:6.
**11:22** Hos 13:3.
**11:23** Wis 12:10; Dt 9:27; Acts 17:30; Rom 2:4; 11:32; 2 Pt 3:9.
**11:24** Ps 145:9.

WIS

25 How could a thing remain, unless you
  willed it;
    or be preserved, had it not been called
    forth by you?*
26 But you spare all things, because they
  are yours,
    O Ruler and Lover of souls,*
12:1 for your imperishable spirit is in all
  things!*

# 12

2 Therefore you rebuke offenders little
  by little,
  warn them, and remind them of the
    sins they are committing,
  that they may abandon their
    wickedness and believe in you,
    Lord!

3 For truly, the ancient inhabitants of your
  holy land,*
4   whom you hated for deeds most
    odious—
  works of sorcery and impious
    sacrifices;
5 These merciless murderers of children,
  devourers of human flesh,†
  and initiates engaged in a blood
    ritual,
6   and parents who took with their own
    hands defenseless lives,*
  You willed to destroy by the hands of
    our ancestors,
7   that the land that is dearest of all to
    you
  might receive a worthy colony of
    God's servants.*
8 But even these you spared, since they
    were but mortals
  and sent wasps as forerunners of your
    army
  that they might exterminate them by
    degrees.*

9 Not that you were without power to
    have the wicked vanquished in
    battle by the righteous,

  or wiped out at once by terrible beasts
    or by one decisive word;*
10 But condemning them by degrees, you
    gave them space for repentance.
  You were not unaware that their origins
    were wicked
  and their malice ingrained,*
  And that their dispositions would never
    change;
11   for they were a people accursed from
    the beginning.
  Neither out of fear for anyone
    did you grant release from their sins.*
12 For who can say to you, "What have you
    done?"
    or who can oppose your decree?
  Or when peoples perish, who can
    challenge you, their maker;
    or who can come into your presence
    to vindicate the unrighteous?*
13 For neither is there any god besides you
    who have the care of all,
    that you need show you have not
    unjustly condemned;*
14 Nor can any king or prince confront
    you on behalf of those you have
    punished.*

15 But as you are righteous, you govern all
    things righteously;
  you regard it as unworthy of your
    power
    to punish one who has incurred no
    blame.*
16 For your might is the source of
    righteousness;
  your mastery over all things makes
    you lenient to all.*
17 For you show your might when the
    perfection of your power is
    disbelieved;
  and in those who know you, you
    rebuke insolence.†*
18 But though you are master of might, you
    judge with clemency,
  and with much lenience you govern us;

---

12:5 The horrible crimes here attributed to the Canaanites (cf. also 14:23) were not unheard of in the ancient world.
  12:17 The brunt of divine anger and justice is borne by those who know God but defy divine authority and might. Cf. 1:2; 15:2, but also 12:27; 18:13.

---

11:25 Is 41:4.
11:26 Wis 12:16; Is 63:9.
12:1 Wis 1:7.

12:3–6 Wis 14:23; Dt 18:9–12; Ps 5:6; 106:28, 34–39; Jer 19:4–5; Ez 16:3, 20–21, 36.
12:6 Nm 33:52.
12:7 Dt 11:12.
12:8 Ex 23:28–30; Dt 7:17–24.
12:9 Wis 11:18; 18:15; Nm 16:21.
12:10 Wis 11:23; Ps 55:20; Sir 16:9.
12:11 Gn 9:25.

12:12 2 Sm 16:10; Eccl 8:4; Sir 46:19; Is 45:9; Dn 4:32; Rom 9:19–21.
12:13 Wis 6:7; Dt 3:24; 32:39; Is 44:6, 8.
12:14 Jer 49:19; 50:44.
12:15 Gn 18:23–32; Dt 32:4.
12:16 Wis 2:11; 11:26; Ps 103:19.
12:17 Wis 15:2–3; Ex 9:16.

WIS

for power, whenever you will, attends
you.

19 You taught your people, by these deeds,*
that those who are righteous must be
kind;
And you gave your children reason to
hope
that you would allow them to repent
for their sins.

20 For these were enemies of your servants,
doomed to death;
yet, while you punished them with
such solicitude and indulgence,
granting time and opportunity to
abandon wickedness,

21 With what exactitude you judged your
children,
to whose ancestors you gave the
sworn covenants of goodly
promises!*

22 Therefore to give us a lesson you punish
our enemies with measured
deliberation
so that we may think earnestly of your
goodness when we judge,
and, when being judged, we may look
for mercy.

### Second Example Resumed

23 Hence those unrighteous who lived a
life of folly,
you tormented through their own
abominations.*

24 For they went far astray in the paths of
error,
taking for gods the worthless and
disgusting among beasts,
being deceived like senseless infants.*

25 Therefore as though upon unreasoning
children,
you sent your judgment on them as a
mockery;*

26 But they who took no heed of a
punishment which was but
child's play
were to experience a condemnation
worthy of God.

27 For by the things through which they
suffered distress,
being tortured by the very things they
deemed gods,
They saw and recognized the true God
whom formerly they had refused
to know;
with this, their final condemnation†
came upon them.*

### Digression on False Worship

### A. NATURE WORSHIP†

**13** ¹ Foolish by nature were all who were
in ignorance of God,
and who from the good things seen
did not succeed in knowing the
one who is,†
and from studying the works did not
discern the artisan;*

2 Instead either fire, or wind, or the swift
air,
or the circuit of the stars, or the
mighty water,
or the luminaries of heaven, the
governors† of the world, they
considered gods.*

3 Now if out of joy in their beauty they
thought them gods,
let them know how far more excellent
is the Lord than these;
for the original source of beauty
fashioned them.*

4 Or if they were struck by their might and
energy,
let them realize from these things how
much more powerful is the one
who made them.*

**12:27** *Condemnation*: the death of Egyptian firstborn and the destruction of their army in the sea.

**13:1–9** The author holds a relatively benign view of the efforts of the philosophers to come to know God from various natural phenomena. This is not a question of proving the existence of God in scholastic style. The author thinks that the beauty and might of the world should have pointed by analogy (v. 5) to the Maker. Instead, those "in ignorance of God" remained fixed on the elements (v. 2, three named, along with the stars). His Greek counterparts are not totally blameless; they should have gone further and acknowledged the creator of nature's wonders (vv. 4–5). Cf. Rom 1:18–23; Acts 17:27–28.

**13:1** *One who is*: this follows the Greek translation of the sacred name for God in Hebrew; cf. Ex 3:14.
**13:2** *Governors*: the sun and moon (cf. Gn 1:16).

**12:19–20** Wis 11:23; Sir 17:24.
**12:21** Wis 18:22; Gn 50:24; Dt 7:6–14; Ps 105:8–11.
**12:23** Wis 11:16; 16:1.
**12:24** Dt 11:28; Jer 5:28; Rom 1:23.
**12:25** Jer 4:22.
**12:27** Wis 16:16; Ex 14:4, 28.
**13:1** Acts 14:17; Eph 4:17–19.
**13:2** Gn 1:14–19; Dt 4:19; Jb 31:26–28.
**13:3** Ps 8:4.
**13:4** Jer 10:2; Bar 6:39.

5 For from the greatness and the beauty of
   created things
  their original author, by analogy, is
   seen.
6 But yet, for these the blame is less;†
  For they have gone astray perhaps,
   though they seek God and wish to
   find him.
7 For they search busily among his works,
   but are distracted by what they see,
    because the things seen are fair.
8 But again, not even these are
   pardonable.
9 For if they so far succeeded in
   knowledge
   that they could speculate about the
    world,
   how did they not more quickly find
    its Lord?

## B. IDOLATRY†

10 But wretched are they, and in dead
    things are their hopes,
   who termed gods things made by
    human hands:
   Gold and silver, the product of art, and
    images of beasts,
   or useless stone, the work of an
    ancient hand.*

### The Carpenter and Wooden Idols

11 A carpenter may cut down a suitable
    tree*
   and skillfully scrape off all its bark,
   And deftly plying his art
    produce something fit for daily use,*
12 And use the scraps from his handiwork
    in preparing his food, and have his
    fill;
13 Then the good-for-nothing refuse from
    these remnants,
   crooked wood grown full of knots,
   he takes and carves to occupy his
    spare time.*
   This wood he models with mindless
    skill,

and patterns it on the image of a
  human being
14 or makes it resemble some worthless
   beast.
  When he has daubed it with red and
   crimsoned its surface with red
   stain,
   and daubed over every blemish in it,*
15 He makes a fitting shrine for it
   and puts it on the wall, fastening it
    with a nail.*
16 Thus he provides for it lest it fall down,
   knowing that it cannot help itself;
   for, truly, it is an image and needs
    help.*
17 But when he prays about his goods or
   marriage or children,*
  he is not ashamed to address the
   thing without a soul.
  For vigor he invokes the powerless;
18  for life he entreats the dead;
  For aid he beseeches the wholly
   incompetent;
  for travel, something that cannot even
   walk;
19 For profit in business and success with
   his hands
  he asks power of a thing with hands
   utterly powerless.

14 ¹Again, one preparing for a voyage
     and about to traverse the wild
      waves
    cries out to wood more unsound than
     the boat that bears him.*
2  For the urge for profits devised this latter,
   and Wisdom the artisan produced it.

3† But your providence, O Father! guides it,
   for you have furnished even in the sea
    a road,
   and through the waves a steady path,*
4  Showing that you can save from any
    danger,
   so that even one without skill may
    embark.*

---

† **13:6** *The blame is less:* the greater blame is incurred by those
mentioned in v. 10; 15:14–16.
  **13:10–19** The second digression is an example of the polemic against idolatry (cf. Is 44:9–20; Jer 10:3–9; Ps 135:15–18).
Whether the idols be of wood or clay, they were made by human
beings and have become the source of evil.
  **14:3–6** The wooden ship mentioned in vv. 1–2 prompts a
short meditation on the providence of God, who in fact has
watched over boats in their dangerous courses. The wood as

described in v. 7 became a favorite patristic type for the wood
of the cross.

---
*

**13:10** Wis 3:11; 15:5, 17; Dt       **13:14** Jer 10:9.
   4:25–28; 7:25; 27:15;               **13:15** Is 40:20; 41:7; 44:13.
   Ps 115:4; Hos 14:4;                 **13:16** 1 Sm 5:3–5; Bar 6:57.
   Acts 17:29.                         **13:17–19** Wis 15:15.
**13:11–19** Is 44:9–20.               **14:1** Is 46:7.
   **13:11** Wis 15:7; Bar 6:58.       **14:3** Ps 107:23–30; Is 43:16.
   **13:13** Dt 4:16.                  **14:4** Wis 16:8.

5    But you will that the products of your
        Wisdom be not idle;
     therefore people trust their lives even
        to most frail wood,
     and were safe crossing the waves on a
        raft.*

6    For of old, when the proud giants were
        being destroyed,
     the hope of the universe, who took
        refuge on a raft,†
     left to the world a future for the
        human family, under the
        guidance of your hand.

7    For blest is the wood through which
        righteousness comes about;

8    but the handmade idol is accursed,
        and its maker as well:
     he for having produced it, and the
        corruptible thing, because it was
        termed a god.*

9    Equally odious to God are the evildoer
        and the evil deed;

10   and the thing made will be punished
        with its maker.

11   Therefore upon even the idols of the
        nations shall a judgment come,
     since they became abominable among
        God's works,
     Snares for human souls
        and a trap for the feet of the
        senseless.*

### The Origin and Evils of Idolatry

12   For the source of wantonness is the
        devising of idols;
     and their invention, a corruption of
        life.*

13   For in the beginning they were not,
        nor can they ever continue;*

14   for from human emptiness they came
        into the world,
     and therefore a sudden end is devised
        for them.

15†  For a father, afflicted with untimely
        mourning,

made an image of the child so quickly
        taken from him,
     And now honored as a god what once
        was dead
     and handed down to his household
        mysteries and sacrifices.

16   Then, in the course of time, the impious
        practice gained strength and was
        observed as law,
     and graven things were worshiped by
        royal decrees.*

17   People who lived so far away that they
        could not honor him in his
        presence
     copied the appearance of the distant
        king
     And made a public image of him they
        wished to honor,
     out of zeal to flatter the absent one as
        though present.

18   And to promote this observance among
        those to whom it was strange,
     the artisan's ambition provided a
        stimulus.

19   For he, perhaps in his determination to
        please the ruler,
     labored over the likeness† to the best
        of his skill;*

20   And the masses, drawn by the charm of
        the workmanship,
     soon took as an object of worship
     the one who shortly before was
        honored as a human being.*

21   And this became a snare for the world,
     that people enslaved to either grief or
        tyranny
     conferred the incommunicable Name
        on stones and wood.

22   Then it was not enough for them to err
        in their knowledge of God;*
     but even though they live in a great
        war resulting from ignorance,
     they call such evils peace.*

23   For while they practice either child
        sacrifices or occult mysteries,
     or frenzied carousing in exotic rites,*

---

†
**14:6** Noah.
**14:15–21** The author develops two examples of idolatry: cult of the dead, and cult of the king.
**14:19** *Likeness*: he made this more flattering than the reality.

---

Ps 115:4; Jer 6:15;
10:15; 46:25; Hos
9:15.
**14:12** Rom 1:23–32.
**14:13** Is 2:18.
**14:16** 1 Mc 1:47–50; Dn
3:4–7.
**14:19** Is 44:12–13 LXX.
**14:20** Wis 15:4.

**14:22–31** Jer 2:20; 3:1–25;
Hos 4:1–2, 9–19;
Rom 1:26–31; Gal
5:19–21; 1 Tm
1:9–10.
**14:22** Jer 6:14; Ez 13:10.
**14:23** Wis 12:4–5; 14:15; Is
57:5.

---

**14:5** Wis 10:4.                    **14:11** Wis 3:7; Nm 33:4;
**14:8** Rom 1:23.                         Jos 23:13;

24 They no longer respect either lives or
        purity of marriage;
    but they either waylay and kill each
        other, or aggrieve each other by
        adultery.
25 And all is confusion—blood and
        murder, theft and guile,*
    corruption, faithlessness, turmoil,
        perjury,
26 Disturbance of good people, neglect of
        gratitude,
    besmirching of souls, unnatural lust,
    disorder in marriage, adultery and
        shamelessness.
27 For the worship of infamous idols
    is the reason and source and extreme
        of all evil.*

28 For they either go mad with enjoyment,
        or prophesy lies,
    or live lawlessly or lightly perjure
        themselves.*
29 For as their trust is in lifeless idols,
    they expect no harm when they have
        sworn falsely.
30 But on both counts justice shall overtake
        them:
    because they thought perversely of God
        by devoting themselves to idols,*
    and because they deliberately swore
        false oaths, despising piety.†
31 For it is not the might of those by whom
        they swear,
    but the just retribution of sinners,
    that ever follows upon the
        transgression of the wicked.†

15 ¹† But you, our God, are good and
        true,
    slow to anger, and governing all with
        mercy.*
2 For even if we sin, we are yours, and
        know your might;
    but we will not sin, knowing that we
        belong to you.*

3 For to know you well is complete
        righteousness,
    and to know your might is the root of
        immortality.*
4 For the evil creation of human fancy did
        not deceive us,
    nor the fruitless labor of painters,*
    A form smeared with varied colors,
5 the sight of which arouses yearning in
        a fool,
    till he longs for the inanimate form of
        a dead image.
6 Lovers of evil things, and worthy of such
        hopes
    are they who make them and long for
        them and worship them.*

**The Potter's Clay Idols**

7 For the potter, laboriously working the
        soft earth,
    molds for our service each single
        article:
    He fashions out of the same clay
    both the vessels that serve for clean
        purposes
    and their opposites, all alike;
    As to what shall be the use of each
        vessel of either class
    the worker in clay is the judge.*
8† With misspent toil he molds a
        meaningless god from the
        selfsame clay,
    though he himself shortly before was
        made from the earth,
    And is soon to go whence he was
        taken,
    when the life that was lent him is
        demanded back.*
9 But his concern is not that he is to die
    nor that his span of life is brief;
    Rather, he vies with goldsmiths and
        silversmiths
    and emulates molders of bronze,
    and takes pride in fashioning
        counterfeits.*

10 Ashes his heart is!† more worthless than
    earth is his hope,*
    more ignoble than clay his life;

11 Because he knew not the one who
    fashioned him,
    and breathed into him a quickening
      soul,
    and infused a vital spirit.*

12 Instead, he esteemed our life a mere
    game,
    and our span of life a holiday for
      gain;
    "For one must," says he, "make a profit
    in every way, be it even from
    evil."*

13 For more than anyone else he knows
    that he is sinning,
    when out of earthen stuff he creates
    fragile vessels and idols alike.

14 But most stupid of all and worse than
    senseless in mind,
    are the enemies of your people who
    enslaved them.*

15 For they esteemed all the idols of the
    nations as gods,
    which cannot use their eyes to see,
    nor nostrils to breathe the air,
    Nor ears to hear,
    nor fingers on their hands for
      feeling;
    even their feet are useless to walk
    with.*

16 For it was a mere human being who
    made them;*
    one living on borrowed breath who
    fashioned them.
    For no one is able to fashion a god like
    himself;

17 he is mortal, and what he makes with
    lawless hands is dead.
    For he is better than the things he
    worships;
    he at least lives, but never his idols.

**Second Example Resumed**

18† Besides, they worship the most
    loathsome beasts—*
    as regards stupidity, these are worse
    than the rest,†

19 For beasts are neither good-looking nor
    desirable;
    they have escaped both the approval
    of God and his blessing.*

**16** ¹Therefore they† were fittingly
    punished by similar creatures,
    and were tormented by a swarm of
    insects.*

2 Instead of this punishment, you
    benefited your people
    with a novel dish, the delight they
    craved,
    by providing quail for their food,*

3 So that those others, when they desired
    food,
    should lose their appetite even for
    necessities,
    since the creatures sent to plague
    them were so loathsome,
    While these, after a brief period of privation,
    partook of a novel dish.*

4 For inexorable want had to come upon
    those oppressors;
    but these needed only to be shown
    how their enemies were being
    tormented.*

5 For when the dire venom of beasts came
    upon them*
    and they were dying from the bite of
    crooked serpents,
    your anger endured not to the end.

6 But as a warning, for a short time they
    were terrorized,
    though they had a sign† of salvation,
    to remind them of the precept of
    your law.

---

**15:10** *Ashes his heart is!*: the words of this cry are taken from Is 44:20 (the Septuagint).

**15:18–19** The author here returns (11:15; 12:23–27) to the main theme of chaps. 11–19, which was interrupted by the digression of 13:1–15:17.

**15:18** *Worse than the rest*: this may mean that the creatures worshiped by the Egyptians (e.g., crocodiles, serpents, scarabs, etc.) were less intelligent than the general run of beasts.

**16:1** *They*: the Egyptian idolaters, who are punished according to the principle laid down in 11:5, 15–16.

**16:6** *Sign*: the brazen serpent, as related in Numbers 21, but the author deliberately avoids any misunderstanding by addressing

the Lord as responsible for the healing, since he is "the savior of all" (v. 7; see also vv. 12 and 26 for the role of the "word" of God).

---

**15:10** Jb 13:12 LXX.
**15:11** Gn 2:7; Zec 12:1.
**15:12** Jas 4:13–14.
**15:14** Ex 1:13.
**15:15** Wis 14:11; Dt 4:28; Ps 115:4–7; 135:15–18.
**15:16–17** Wis 13:10.
**15:18** Wis 11:15; 12:24.
**15:19** Gn 1:25; 3:14.

**16:1** Wis 11:15–16; 12:23, 27; Ex 7:27; 8:12, 17.
**16:2** Wis 11:13; 19:11–12; Ex 16:13; Nm 11:31–32; Ps 105:40.
**16:3** Wis 11:15; Ex 8:10; 16:3.
**16:4** Wis 11:8–9.
**16:5–6** Nm 21:4–9; Dt 32:24; Jer 8:17 LXX.

7  For the one who turned toward it was
       saved,
     not by what was seen,
     but by you, the savior of all.
8  By this also you convinced our foes
     that you are the one who delivers
       from all evil.*
9  For the bites of locusts and of flies slew
       them,
     and no remedy was found to save
       their lives
     because they deserved to be punished
       by such means;*
10 But not even the fangs of poisonous
       reptiles overcame your children,
     for your mercy came forth and healed
       them.*
11 For as a reminder of your injunctions,
       they were stung,
     and swiftly they were saved,
   Lest they should fall into deep
       forgetfulness
     and become unresponsive to your
       beneficence.*
12 For indeed, neither herb nor application
       cured them,
     but your all-healing word, O Lord!*
13† For you have dominion over life and
       death;*
     you lead down to the gates of Hades
       and lead back.
14 Human beings, however, may kill
       another with malice,
     but they cannot bring back the
       departed spirit,
     or release the soul that death has
       confined.
15 Your hand no one can escape.

### Third Example: A Rain of Manna for Israel Instead of the Plague of Storms

16 For the wicked who refused to know
       you
     were punished by the might of your
       arm,

Were pursued by unusual rains and
       hailstorms and unremitting
       downpours,
     and were consumed by fire.*
17 For against all expectation, in water
       which quenches everything,
     the fire grew more active;
   For the universe fights on behalf of the
       righteous.*
18 Then the flame was tempered*
     so that the beasts that were sent upon
       the wicked might not be burnt
       up,
     but that these might see and know
       that they were struck by the
       judgment of God;
19 And again, even in the water, fire blazed
       beyond its strength
     so as to consume the produce of the
       wicked land.
20 Instead of this, you nourished your
       people with food of angels†
     and furnished them bread from
       heaven, ready to hand, untoiled-
       for,
     endowed with all delights and
       conforming to every taste.*
21 For this substance of yours revealed
       your sweetness toward your
       children,
     and serving the desire of the one who
       received it,
     was changed to whatever flavor each
       one wished.*
22 Yet snow and ice† withstood fire and
       were not melted,
     so that they might know that their
       enemies' fruits
   Were consumed by a fire that blazed in
       the hail
     and flashed lightning in the rain.*
23 But this fire, again, in order that the
       righteous might be nourished,
     forgot even its proper strength;*

---

† **16:13–14** The author recognizes the power of the Lord over life and death, as expressed in 1 Sm 2:6; Tb 13:2. The traditional imagery of Sheol (gates and confinement) colors the passage.

**16:20** *Food of angels*: the famous phrase (cf. the hymn "Panis Angelicus") is taken from Ps 78:24 as rendered by the Septuagint. The "bread from heaven" (cf. Ex 16:4; Ps 105:40) with its marvelous "sweetness" becomes a type of the "bread come down from heaven" in Jn 6:32–51, and plays a large role in later Christian devotion.

**16:22** *Snow and ice*: the manna; cf. v. 27; 19:21.

**16:8** Gn 48:16; 2 Mc 1:24–25.
**16:9** Ex 8:16–28; 10:4–19; Ps 78:45–46; 105:31, 34; Rev 9:1–11.
**16:10** Dt 32:33.
**16:11** Ps 78:11.
**16:12** Ex 15:26.
**16:13–15** Dt 32:39; 1 Sm 2:6; Tb 13:2; 2 Mc 6:26; 7:23; Ps 78:34, 39; Eccl 8:8; Dn 5:19.
**16:16** Wis 11:21; 12:27; Ex 5:2; 9:29–34.
**16:17** Wis 10:20; 19:20; Ex 9:23–28; 2 Mc 8:36; 14:34.
**16:18–19** Wis 19:20–21.
**16:20** Ex 16:4; Nm 11:8; Ps 78:24–25; Jn 6:31.
**16:21** Ps 34:9.
**16:22** Ex 9:25–31; 10:12; Ps 148:8.
**16:23** Wis 19:21.

WIS

24 For your creation, serving you, its
maker,
grows tense for punishment against
the wicked,
but is relaxed in benefit for those who
trust in you.*

25 Therefore at that very time, transformed
in all sorts of ways,
it was serving your all-nourishing
bounty
according to what they needed and
desired;

26 That your children whom you loved
might learn, O LORD,
that it is not the various kinds of fruits
that nourish,
but your word that preserves those
who believe you!*

27 For what was not destroyed by fire,
melted when merely warmed by a
momentary sunbeam;*

28 To make known that one must give you
thanks before sunrise,
and turn to you at daybreak.*

29 For the hope of the ungrateful melts like
a wintry frost
and runs off like useless water.*

## Fourth Example: Darkness Afflicts the Egyptians, While the Israelites Have Light†

**17** 1 For great are your judgments, and
hard to describe;
therefore the unruly souls went
astray.*

2 For when the lawless thought to enslave
the holy nation,
they themselves lay shackled with
darkness, fettered by the long
night,
confined beneath their own roofs
as exiles from the eternal
providence.*

3 For they, who supposed their secret sins
were hid*

under the dark veil of oblivion,
Were scattered in fearful trembling,
terrified by apparitions.

4 For not even their inner chambers kept
them unafraid,
for crashing sounds on all sides
terrified them,
and mute phantoms with somber
looks appeared.

5 No fire had force enough to give light,
nor did the flaming brilliance of the
stars
succeed in lighting up that gloomy
night.*

6 But only intermittent, fearful fires
flashed through upon them;
And in their terror they thought
beholding these was worse
than the times when that sight was no
longer to be seen.*

7 And mockeries of their magic art†
failed,
and there was a humiliating refutation
of their vaunted shrewdness.*

8 For they who undertook to banish fears
and terrors from the sick soul
themselves sickened with ridiculous
fear.

9 For even though no monstrous thing
frightened them,
they shook at the passing of insects
and the hissing of reptiles,*

10 And perished trembling,
reluctant to face even the air that they
could nowhere escape.

11 For wickedness, of its nature cowardly,
testifies in its own condemnation,
and because of a distressed
conscience, always magnifies
misfortunes.*

12 For fear is nought but the surrender of
the helps that come from reason;

13 and the more one's expectation is of
itself uncertain,

---

† **17:1–18:4** The description of the darkness of the ninth plague is a very creative development of Ex 10:21–29. It betrays a wide knowledge of contemporary thought. For the first and only time in the Septuagint the Greek word for "conscience" occurs, in 17:11. There is no Hebrew word that is equivalent; the idea is expressed indirectly. The horrendous darkness is illumined by "fires" (v. 6), i.e., lightnings that only contributed to the terror.

**17:7** *Magic art*: the Egyptian magicians who were successful at first (Ex 7:11, 22) and then failed (Ex 8:14; 9:11) are now powerless against the darkness and the phantoms and are totally discredited.

**16:24** Wis 5:17, 20; 19:6;
Sir 39:25–27.
**16:26** Dt 8:3; Mt 4:4.
**16:27** Ex 16:21.
**16:28** Ps 57:9–10; 92:3.
**16:29** Wis 5:14; 2 Sm 14:14.
**17:1** Ex 6:6 LXX.
**17:2** Wis 18:4; Ex 1:13–14;
9:6; 10:21–23.
**17:3–4** Wis 1:7–8; 10:8;
18:17.

**17:5** Wis 10:17; Jer 23:24
LXX.
**17:6** Ex 9:23–24.
**17:7** Wis 12:25–26; Ex
7:11–12, 22; 8:3;
9:11; 10:2.
**17:9** Wis 16:1; Jer 26:22
LXX.
**17:11** Wis 4:6; 10:7; Rom
2:15.

the more one makes of not knowing
    the cause that brings on torment.
14  So they, during that night, powerless
        though it was,
    since it had come upon them from the
        recesses of a powerless† Hades,
    while all sleeping the same sleep,
15    Were partly smitten by fearsome
        apparitions
    and partly stricken by their souls'
        surrender;
    for fear overwhelmed them, sudden
        and unexpected.*
16  Thus, then, whoever was there fell
    into that prison without bars and was
        kept confined.*
17  For whether one was a farmer, or a
        shepherd,
    or a worker at tasks in the wasteland,
    Taken unawares, each served out the
        inescapable sentence;
18    for all were bound by the one bond of
        darkness.*
    And were it only the whistling wind,
    or the melodious song of birds in the
        spreading branches,
    Or the steady sound of rushing water,
19    or the rude crash of overthrown rocks,
    Or the unseen gallop of bounding
        animals,
    or the roaring cry of the fiercest
        beasts,
    Or an echo resounding from the hollow
        of the hills—
    these sounds, inspiring terror,
        paralyzed them.
20  For the whole world shone with brilliant
        light*
    and continued its works without
        interruption;
21  But over them alone was spread
        oppressive night,
    an image of the darkness† that was
        about to come upon them.
    Yet they were more a burden to
        themselves than was the darkness.

# 18

1  But your holy ones had very great
        light;
    And those others, who heard their voices
        but did not see their forms,
    counted them blest for not having
        suffered;
2  And because they who formerly had
        been wronged did not harm
        them, they thanked them,
    and because of the difference between
        them,† pleaded with them.
3  Instead of this, you furnished the
        flaming pillar,
    a guide on the unknown way,
    and the mild sun for an honorable
        migration.*
4† For they deserved to be deprived of light
    and imprisoned by darkness,
    they had kept your children
        confined,
    through whom the imperishable light
        of the law was to be given to the
        world.*

## Fifth Example: Death of the Egyptian Firstborn; the Israelites Are Spared

5  When they determined to put to death
        the infants of the holy ones,
    and when a single boy† had been cast
        forth and then saved,
    As a reproof you carried off a multitude
        of their children
    and made them perish all at once in
        the mighty water.*
6  That night was known beforehand to
        our ancestors,
    so that, with sure knowledge of the
        oaths in which they put their
        faith, they might have courage.*
7  The expectation of your people
    was the salvation of the righteous and
        the destruction of their foes.*
8  For by the same means with which you
        punished our adversaries,
    you glorified us whom you had
        summoned.*

WIS

---

† 17:14 *Powerless*: Hades (or Sheol), i.e., the nether world, is often portrayed in the Old Testament as a hostile power, since all must die (Ps 49:8–13), but it has no power against God.
    17:21 *Darkness*: of Hades or Sheol; see note on 16:13–14.
    18:2 *The difference between them*: God's distinctive manner of treating the Israelites and the Egyptians according to their respective deeds. *Pleaded*: perhaps, for their departure.
    18:4 The discussion of physical light climaxes with a reference to the "imperishable light" of the torah.

18:5 *Single boy*: Moses.

17:15 Ex 11:9–10.              18:5 Wis 11:7, 14; Ex 1:16,
17:16 Wis 18:4; Ex 10:23.          22; 2:3, 6–10; 15:10;
17:18–19 Lv 26:36.                 Neh 9:11.
17:20–21 Ex 10:23; Is 9:1;     18:6 Wis 12:21; Ex 6:8;
    60:1–3; 2 Pt 2:17.             13:5.
18:3 Ex 13:21.                  18:7 Ex 14:13.
18:4 Wis 17:2; Ps 119:105;     18:8 Wis 19:22; Ex 3:18; Is
    Is 2:3, 5.                     43:3–4.

9 For in secret the holy children of the
    good were offering sacrifice
and carried out with one mind the
    divine institution,†
So that your holy ones should share
    alike the same blessings and
    dangers,
    once they had sung the ancestral
    hymns of praise.*

10 But the discordant cry of their enemies
    echoed back,
    and the piteous wail of mourning for
    children was borne to them.*

11 And the slave was smitten with the same
    retribution as the master;
    even the commoner suffered the same
    as the king.*

12 And all alike by one common form of
    death
    had countless dead;
For the living were not even sufficient
    for the burial,
    since at a single instant their most
    valued offspring had been
    destroyed.*

13 For though they disbelieved at every
    turn on account of sorceries,
    at the destruction of the firstborn they
    acknowledged that this people†
    was God's son.*

14† For when peaceful stillness encompassed
    everything
    and the night in its swift course was
    half spent,

15 Your all-powerful word from heaven's
    royal throne
    leapt into the doomed land,*

16 a fierce warrior bearing the sharp
    sword of your inexorable
    decree,
And alighted, and filled every place with
    death,
    and touched heaven, while standing
    upon the earth.*

17 Then, at once, visions in horrible dreams
    perturbed them*
    and unexpected fears assailed them;

18 And cast half-dead, one here, another
    there,
    they revealed why they were dying.

19 For the dreams that disturbed them had
    proclaimed this beforehand,
    lest they perish unaware of why they
    endured such evil.

20 The trial of death touched even the
    righteous,
    and in the desert a plague struck the
    multitude;
Yet not for long did the anger last.*

21 For the blameless man† hastened to be
    their champion,
    bearing the weapon of his special
    office,
    prayer and the propitiation of incense;
He withstood the wrath and put a stop
    to the calamity,
    showing that he was your servant.

22 He overcame the bitterness
    not by bodily strength, not by force of
    arms;
But by word he overcame the smiter,†
    recalling the sworn covenants with
    their ancestors.*

23 For when corpses had already fallen one
    on another in heaps,
    he stood in the midst and checked the
    anger,
    and cut off its way to the living.*

24 For on his full-length robe was the
    whole world,
    and ancestral glories were carved on
    the four rows of stones,
    and your grandeur† was on the crown
    upon his head.*

25 To these the destroyer yielded, these he
    feared;
    for this sole trial of anger sufficed.*

---

**18:9** *Divine institution*: the Passover. *Ancestral hymns of praise*: possibly the Hallel psalms, the psalms sung at the end of the Passover meal; cf. Mt 26:30; Mk 14:26.
**18:13** *People*: the Israelites (cf. Ex 4:22).
**18:14–16** These verses attribute to the personified "word" the actions of the Lord mentioned in Ex 12:13–17 (note the role of the "destroyer" in Ex 12:23 and compare Wis 18:22, 25).
**18:21** *Blameless man*: Aaron, acting according to his office of high priest and intercessor (cf. Nm 17:9–15; Ex 28:15–21, 31–38).
**18:22** *Smiter*: the destroying angel; cf. v. 25.
**18:24** *Glories . . . grandeur*: the name of God and the names

of the tribes were inscribed on the high priest's apparel.

**18:9** Ex 12:21–28; Sir
    44–50.
**18:10** Ex 12:30; Jer 9:17, 19.
**18:11** Ex 11:5; 12:29.
**18:12** Nm 33:4.
**18:13** Wis 17:7; Ex 4:22–23;
    12:12, 29; 13:2, 13,
    15.
**18:15** Wis 9:10; Ex 15:3.
**18:16** 1 Chr 21:16; Heb
    4:12; Rev 1:16.
**18:17–19** Wis 17:3–4.
**18:20** Wis 16:5; Nm
    17:9–15.
**18:22** Wis 12:21; Ex
    32:12–13; Ps 20:8.
**18:23** Nm 14:29–30.
**18:24** Ex 28:15–21, 31–38;
    Sir 45:8–12; 50:11.
**18:25** 1 Chr 21:15.

# 19

¹ But merciless wrath assailed the
    wicked until the end,
  for God knew beforehand what they
    were yet to do:*

² That though they themselves had agreed
    to the departure
  and had anxiously sent them on their
    way,
  they would regret it and pursue
    them.*

³ For while they were still engaged in
    funeral rites
  and mourning at the burials of the
    dead,
  They adopted another senseless plan:
    those whom they had driven out with
      entreaties
    they now pursued as fugitives.*

⁴ For a compulsion appropriate to this
    ending drew them on,
  and made them forget what had
    befallen them,
  That they might complete the torments
    of their punishment,

⁵ and your people might experience a
    glorious† journey
  while those others met an
    extraordinary death.

⁶† For all creation, in its several kinds, was
    being made over anew,
  serving your commands, that your
    children might be preserved
    unharmed.*

⁷ The cloud overshadowed their camp;
  and out of what had been water, dry
    land was seen emerging:
  Out of the Red Sea an unimpeded road,
  and a grassy plain out of the mighty
    flood.*

⁸ Over this crossed the whole nation
    sheltered by your hand,
  and they beheld stupendous
    wonders.

⁹ For they ranged about like horses,
  and leapt like lambs,
  praising you, LORD, their deliverer.*

¹⁰ For they were still mindful of what had
    happened in their sojourn:
  how instead of the young of animals
    the land brought forth gnats,
  and instead of fishes the river
    swarmed with countless frogs.*

¹¹ And later they saw also a new kind of
    bird*
  when, prompted by desire, they asked
    for pleasant foods;

¹² For to appease them quail came to them
    from the sea.

¹³ And the punishments came upon the
    sinners
  not without forewarnings from the
    violence of the thunderbolts.

  For they justly suffered for their own
    misdeeds,
  since they treated their guests with the
    more grievous† hatred.*

¹⁴ For those others† did not receive
    unfamiliar visitors,*
  but these were enslaving beneficent
    guests.

¹⁵ And not that only; but what punishment
    was to be theirs†
  since they received strangers
    unwillingly!

¹⁶ Yet these,† after welcoming them with
    festivities,
  oppressed with awful toils
  those who had shared with them the
    same rights.*

¹⁷ And they were struck with blindness,†
  as those others had been at the doors
    of the righteous man—
  When, surrounded by yawning
    darkness,
  each sought the entrance of his own
    door.*

---

† **19:5** *Glorious*: more precisely, "wondrous," but the word reflects "glorified" in 18:8 and 19:22.

  **19:6** The cooperation of creation in Israel's deliverance (vv. 7–12) under the direction of the Lord is a favorite theme; cf. 16:24–25.

  **19:13** *More grievous*: than that of the people of Sodom (Gn 19) with whom the Egyptians are compared.

  **19:14** *Others*: the people of Sodom refused to receive strangers. *Beneficent*: because of the services rendered by Joseph.

  **19:15** *Theirs*: the people of Sodom.

  **19:16** *These*: the Egyptians.

**19:17** *Blindness*: the plague of darkness. *Righteous man*: Lot (Gn 19:11).

**19:1** Ex 14:4.
**19:2** Ex 12:33; 14:5, 8.
**19:3** Wis 18:10, 12; Ex 12:30–36.
**19:6** Wis 5:17; 16:24.
**19:7** Ex 14:21–29.
**19:9** Wis 10:20; 16:8; Ex 15:1–18; Ps 114:4–6.
**19:10** Ex 7:27–8:3; 8:12–15; Ps 105:30–31.
**19:11–12** Wis 16:2; Ps 78:18.
**19:13** 2 Mc 7:18, 32.
**19:14–15** Gn 15:13; Ex 2:22.
**19:16** Gn 45:17–20; 47:4–6; Ex 1:11.
**19:17** Wis 17:2; Gn 19:11.

18 For the elements, in ever-changing
      harmony,
   like strings of the harp, produce new
      melody,
   while the flow of music steadily persists.
   And this can be perceived exactly from a
      review of what took place.
19 For land creatures were changed into
      water creatures,
   and those that swam went over on land.
20 Fire in water maintained its own
      strength,*

and water forgot its quenching
      nature;
21 Flames, by contrast, neither consumed
      the flesh
   of the perishable animals that went
      about in them,
   nor melted the icelike, quick-melting
      kind of ambrosial food.
22 For every way, LORD! you magnified and
      glorified your people;
   unfailing, you stood by them in every
      time and circumstance.*

---

**19:20–21** Wis 16:17–19, 22–23, 27.   **19:22** Wis 18:8; Lv 26:44; Ps 126:3.

# The Book of
# Ben Sira

## INTRODUCTION

### Dianne Bergant, CSA

By the time the author, Ben Sira, put his teachings into writing (ca. 200–175 BCE), the educated upper classes of the Near East, including Israel, had already embraced the Greek (Hellenic) culture. It appears that many Jews were wondering whether their ancient traditions could match the breadth and depth of Greek thought. As a well-traveled man, Ben Sira would have witnessed the widespread decline in fervor that had overtaken his coreligionists. As an observant Jew, he would have been greatly troubled by this. It seems clear that his object in writing was to convince contemporary Jews that real wisdom was to be found in the traditions of Israel and not in the Greek philosophy of the day.

The book—also known as Sirach, the Wisdom of Ben Sira, and Ecclesiasticus—highlights two crucial theological issues, issues dealt with in the book of Wisdom as well: the enduring significance of the biblical tradition; and the inherent merit of other cultures as settings within which the revelation of God can take root and flourish. His work showed that the religious value of the Bible was not lost when translated into a different language and cultural expression. In fact, the Greek language and the new cultural insights of Hellenism enhanced the understanding of the word of God.

In content, basic structure, and choice of literary forms, Ben Sira was particularly influenced by the book of Proverbs. However, not content with merely citing a specific proverb, he joined individual sayings by means of common words or themes. Thus he developed a specific topic and explained its implications for his own day. The book itself cannot be easily divided into identifiable sections. Nonetheless, a basic division of the work helps one to understand its teaching. A foreword written by Ben Sira's grandson opens the book. This foreword includes the grandson's evaluation of Ben Sira's teaching, as well as interesting religious-cultural information. Like Proverbs, the teaching begins with a hymn to Woman Wisdom (Prv 1–9; Sir 1:1–20) and ends with an acrostic or alphabetic poem (Prv 31:10–31; Sir 51:13–20). The bulk of the book (Sir 2–43) consists of moral instruction. The final section (Sir 44–50) highlights the role of Wisdom in the lives of Israel's heroes.

New Testament writers seem to have preferred the Greek version of their religious traditions. This explains the influence of Ben Sira detected in some of their writings. For example, the Letter of James addresses questions of pride (Jas 4:6; see Sir 10:7) and humility (Jas 1:9–10; see Sir 3:18), respect for the poor (Jas 2:1–5; see Sir 10:22), and true wisdom (Jas 3:13–17; see Sir 19:18–21). There are also obvious parallels between directives found in Ben Sira and those found in the Gospels. These include teaching on forgiveness (Mk 11:25; see Sir 28:2) and against placing false hope in possessions (Lk 12:16–21; see Sir 11:18–19).

## Foreword

Ben Sira is the only book in the Bible that provides a foreword explaining its origin and purpose. In it, the grandson of Ben Sira states that he translated his grandfather's work "for those living abroad who wish to acquire learning and are disposed to live their lives according to the Law." Both Ben Sira and his grandson can surely be considered wisdom teachers, for they reinterpreted the received wisdom tradition for people living in a very different time.

The grandson makes a bold claim. He argues that his grandfather's teaching deserves the same respect as that given to the earlier wisdom teaching. He also takes a courageous step, translating from Hebrew, the language considered the vehicle through which God revealed the sacred tradition, into Greek, the language of unbelievers.

Finally, this foreword tells us that by Ben Sira's time (ca. 132 BCE) the Hebrew Bible had taken the tripartite form that it has today, namely, "the Law," "the prophets" (Prophets), and "the rest of the books" (Writings).

# In Praise of Wisdom

The book of Ben Sira begins with a hymn praising Wisdom. Like Proverbs (Prv 8:22–31) and Wisdom (Wis 9:9) before it, Ben Sira places Wisdom at the beginning of creation (Sir 1:4–10). It then insists: "The beginning of wisdom is to fear the Lord" (1:14). This "fear of the Lord" (1:11–30) is an attitude of profound awe in the face of God's power and splendor. "Fear of the Lord," a prominent wisdom theme, is more an attitude of profound religious awe than of disquieting terror. It "rejoices the heart, giving gladness, joy, and long life" (Sir 1:12).

It is this same Wisdom, now personified, who sings her own praises later in the book (Sir 24). She recounts how she came forth from God and enjoys a place of honor in the heavens. She held sway over the cosmic forces of chaos: the abyss and the sea. This is an important point, because only the Creator-God controls the forces of chaos. Wisdom also exercises jurisdiction over all nations, having the freedom to roam throughout the world looking for a place to establish her permanent dwelling. It was God who told her to set up her dwelling in Jacob/Israel, in Zion/Jerusalem (24:8–12). Now she can be found there, in the holy tent (the Temple). Ben Sira creatively argues that true wisdom is found in the Israelite tradition and not in Greek philosophy.

Comparing herself to various luxurious trees and plants, Lady Wisdom describes her own desirability (Sir 24:13–22). She invites those who seek her to fill themselves with her sweet fruits. However, their hunger will never be satisfied, for one taste of these fruits will only produce the desire for more. Thus the search for wisdom becomes an ongoing adventure.

Finally, Ben Sira boldly links this wisdom with the instruction found in the book of the covenant, the Law of Moses, yet another argument for the superiority of Israel's tradition over Greek thought (Sir 24:23–33). He compares the blessings of wisdom to the rivers found in the story of the garden in Eden. Along with the Nile and the Jordan, these rivers flow through the entire world, carrying the life-giving blessings of paradise to all. Ben Sira believes that as a teacher of wisdom he himself is a channel of this life-giving water.

# Moral Instruction

The major part of the book (Sir 2–23; 25–43) contains instruction for living the kind of ethical life that flows from the "fear of the Lord." According to Ben Sira, this attitude of awe and reverence prompts the wise person to obey the law, a point important to this biblical writer. In his instruction, Ben Sira discusses religious duties (ch. 2), duties towards parents (ch. 3), diligence in raising children (30:1–13), conduct in public life (7:1–17), virtues like humility (3:17–29), and responsibility toward the poor (3:30–4:10). He is attentive to interaction with other people (7:18–14:19) and is particularly concerned with friendship (6:14–17; 9:10–16; 11:29–13:26; 22:19–26; 37:1–6). He holds the traditional view on retribution (4:11–19; 16:1–21). Finally, like every teacher of wisdom, he cautions the reader about the improper use of speech (5:11–6:4; 19:5–16).

There is probably no biblical writer who compares with Ben Sira in his disparagement of women. They are often portrayed as lacking in merit and trustworthiness. He warns young men against women who appear to be unguarded and sexually available (Sir 9:1–9). He maintains that wives are only acceptable if they are willing and able to serve their husbands and give them comfort and happiness (26:1–18). If they fail in this, they are considered querulous, even evil. Employing a numerical proverb, Ben Sira lists three serious social evils, but insists that a jealous wife is worse than any of them (26:5–6). He condemns wives who might be wicked, drunken, or unchaste. Nothing is said about similar characteristics in husbands. Daughters are not exempt from Ben Sira's sharp criticism. He admonishes fathers to exercise vigilance over their daughters lest they cause shame by their stubbornness, impertinence, or wanton behavior (42:9–14). One half verse summarizes Ben Sira's bias against women: "There is hardly an evil like that in a woman" (25:19).

Unlike most of the Wisdom writings, the book of Ben Sira demonstrates interest in the cult and support for the priesthood (Sir 7:29–31; 45:15; 50:1). Though the Sadducees did not exist as an identifiable group until after the Maccabean period (167 BCE), many of the theological ideas found in Ben Sira were eventually taken up by that group.

Finally, in a long lyric poem Ben Sira extols the works of God in the natural world (Sir 42:15–43:33). While all creatures show forth the glory of God, the most mysterious of God's creations is the human heart. Still the wisdom of God can plumb even its depths. God's wisdom is seen in the order of and balance within the universe. The sun, the most splendid of the heavenly bodies, proclaims the glory of God even as its force parches the land and burns human beings; the moon controls the seasons and the festivals dependent upon them; the stars continuously stand watch over the earth; the rainbow encircles the sky with its brilliant colors. All these heavenly creatures praise God. Even the chaotic waters of the deep are under God's control.

## The Heroes of Israel

The unifying theme of this section (Sir 44–50) is the praise of the major heroes of Israelite history. Some are explicitly remembered; the names of others have been lost. These heroes appear to be arranged in three categories: (1) those involved in the establishment of covenants and the settlement in the land, (2) several prophets and the kings, and (3) Simon the high priest at the time of Ben Sira. This survey of history begins with mention of the covenants that God made through Noah with all of creation and the one made with Abraham and his descendants (44:17–21). It is then traced through the ancestors (44:22–23), the leaders of the Exodus and wilderness period

(ch. 45), the judges (ch. 46), the kings (47:1–49:12), and ends with Nehemiah, who rebuilt the walls of Jerusalem (49:13).

This recital of heroes is meant to remind Ben Sira's contemporaries that those who fashioned their history were men of integrity and courage, ancestors of whom they could be proud, individuals after whom they could model their own lives.

Praise of the heroes of the past leads into praise of Simon the high priest, the "greatest of his family, the glory of his people" (Sir 50:1). Like several of the heroes before him, Simon organized building projects that strengthened the city of Jerusalem and the Temple within it. Through the use of striking metaphors taken from the natural world, he is portrayed participating in the Temple liturgy. He is surrounded by all of the priests, and the entire assembly of Israel is present. The service concludes with the high priest's blessing (Nm 6:24–26) and the people's veneration. Ben Sira paints a spectacular liturgical scene.

The book ends with a prayer of thanksgiving and a poem (Sir 51:13–30). Ben Sira thanks God for having delivered him from slander and false accusation. Surrounded by peril on every side, he had no human recourse. His confidence that God would hear his prayer is based on remembrance of God's earlier favors to Israel's past heroes. In the original Hebrew, the poem is an acrostic or alphabetic in which the first verse begins with the first letter of the alphabet and each following verse begins with the successive letter of the alphabet. Besides acting as an aid to memory, the very structure of this poem suggests comprehensiveness; it includes everything from A to Z.

This final poem describes Ben Sira's prayerful search for and discovery of wisdom. Good teacher that he is, he invites others to discover the lessons of wisdom by learning them from him. His instruction ends with a prayer for his prospective students and a promise that those who work diligently to discover wisdom will eventually receive the reward that was promised. Though not explicitly mentioned, the reward for seeking wisdom is Wisdom herself. ■

# THE WISDOM OF BEN SIRA (ECCLESIASTICUS)

## New American Bible, Introduction

The Wisdom of Ben Sira derives its title from the author, "Yeshua [Jesus], son of Eleazar, son of Sira" (50:27). This seems to be the earliest title of the book. The designation "Liber Ecclesiasticus," meaning "Church Book," appended to some Greek and Latin manuscripts, is perhaps due to the extensive use the church made of this book in presenting moral teaching to catechumens and to the faithful. The title "Sirach" comes from the Greek form of the author's name.

The author, a sage who lived in Jerusalem, was thoroughly imbued with love for the wisdom tradition, and also for the law, priesthood, Temple, and divine worship. As a wise and experienced observer of life he addressed himself to his contemporaries with the motive of helping them to maintain religious faith and integrity through study of the books sacred to the Jewish tradition.

The book contains numerous well-crafted maxims, grouped by affinity, and dealing with a variety of subjects such as the individual, the family, and the community in their relations with one another and with God. It treats of friendship, education, poverty and wealth, laws, religious worship, and many other matters that reflect the religious and social customs of the time.

Written in Hebrew in the early years of the second century B.C., the book was finished by ca. 175. The text was translated into Greek by the author's grandson after 117 B.C. He also wrote a foreword which contains valuable information about the book, its author, and himself as translator. Until the close of the nineteenth century the Wisdom of Ben Sira was known to Christians in translations, of which the Greek rendering was the most important. From it the Latin version was made. Between 1896 and 1900, again in 1931, and several times since 1956, incomplete manuscripts were discovered, so that more than two thirds of the book in Hebrew is available; these Hebrew texts agree substantially with the Greek. One such text, from Masada, is pre-Christian in date. *The New American Bible* provides a critical translation based on the evidence of all the ancient texts.

Though not included in the Jewish Bible after the first century A.D., nor, therefore, accepted by Protestants, the Wisdom of Ben Sira has been recognized by the Catholic Church as inspired and canonical. The Foreword, though not properly part of the book, is always included with it because of its antiquity and importance.

The contents of the Wisdom of Ben Sira are of a discursive nature, not easily divided into separate parts. Chapters 1–43 deal largely with moral instruction; 44:1–50:24 contain a eulogy of the heroes of Israel. There are two appendixes in which the author expresses his gratitude to God (51:1–12), and invites the unschooled to acquire true wisdom (51:13–30).

# BEN SIRA

## FOREWORD

Inasmuch as many and great truths have been given to us through the Law, the prophets, and the authors who followed them,† for which the instruction and wisdom of Israel merit praise, it is the duty of those who read the scriptures not only to become knowledgeable themselves but also to use their love of learning in speech and in writing to help others less familiar. So my grandfather Jesus, who had long devoted himself to the study of the law, the prophets, and the rest of the books of our ancestors, and had acquired great familiarity with them, was moved to write something himself regarding instruction and wisdom. He did this so that those who love learning might, by accepting what he had written, make even greater progress in living according to the Law.

You are invited therefore to read it with good will and attention, with indulgence for any failure on our part, despite earnest efforts, in the interpretation of particular passages. For words spoken originally in Hebrew do not have the same effect when they are translated into another language. That is true not only of this book but of the Law itself, the prophecies, and the rest of the books, which differ no little when they are read in the original.

I arrived in Egypt in the thirty-eighth year of the reign of King Euergetes, and while there, I had access to no little learning. I therefore considered it my duty to devote some diligence and industry to the translation of this book. During this time I applied my skill for many sleepless hours to complete the book and publish it for those living abroad who wish to acquire learning and are disposed to live their lives according to the Law.

## THE WISDOM OF BEN SIRA

### God's Gift of Wisdom†

1 ¹ All wisdom† is from the Lord
   and remains with him forever.*
² The sands of the sea, the drops of rain,
   the days of eternity—who can count
   them?
³ Heaven's height, earth's extent,
   the abyss and wisdom—who can
   explore them?
⁴ Before all other things wisdom was
   created;
   and prudent understanding, from
   eternity.‡
⁶ The root of wisdom—to whom has it
   been revealed?
   Her subtleties—who knows them?‡*
⁸† There is but one, wise and truly awesome,
   seated upon his throne—the Lord.
⁹ It is he who created her,
   saw her and measured her,*
   Poured her forth upon all his works,
¹⁰ upon every living thing according to
   his bounty,
   lavished her upon those who love him.

### Fear of the Lord Is Wisdom†

¹¹ The fear of the Lord† is glory and
   exultation,

---

† **Foreword** *The Law, the prophets, and the authors who followed them*: an indication of the eventual tripartite division of the Hebrew Scriptures: Law (*torah*), Prophets (*nebi'im*), and Writings (*ketubim*), shortened in the acronym Tanak. *Thirty-eighth… Euergetes*: 132 B.C. The reference is to Ptolemy VII, Physkon Euergetes II (170–163; 145–117 B.C.).

**1:1–10** This brief poem serves as an introduction to the book. The Lord is the source and preserver of all wisdom, which he pours out upon all. See Jb 28:20–28; Prv 2:6; 8:22–31; Wis 7:25–27.

**1:1** *Wisdom*: throughout the book Ben Sira describes in great detail just what wisdom is: sometimes divine (1:6, 8), sometimes a synonym for God's law (24:22–23). Ben Sira makes clear that all wisdom comes from God.

**‡1:4** Other ancient texts read as v. 5:
The wellspring of wisdom is the word of God in the heights,
   and its runlets are the ageless commandments.
**‡1:6** Other ancient texts read as v. 7:

An understanding of wisdom—to whom has this been disclosed?
   her resourcefulness, who has known?

**1:8–10** In contrast to Jb 28, wisdom is not only with God, but given to all, especially Israel; see Bar 3:9; 4:4.

**1:11–30** This is one of several poems of twenty-two bicola, or poetic lines, corresponding to the number of letters in the Hebrew alphabet. Ben Sira uses the expression "fear of the Lord" twelve times and the noun "wisdom" seven times to emphasize the connection between the two ideas. He describes the blessings that come to those who fear the Lord, i.e., those who practice true religion by loving and serving God and keeping the Law (2:7–10, 15–17; 4:11–16; see Dt 6:1–5, 24). Such blessings recur throughout the book.

**1:11** *Fear of the Lord*: Ben Sira identifies wisdom with the fear of the Lord (vv. 26–27).

---

**1:1** 1 Kgs 3:9.          Jb 28:10, 20.
**1:6** Bar 3:15;          **1:9** Jb 28:27.

gladness and a festive crown.

12 The fear of the Lord rejoices the heart,
giving gladness, joy, and long life.‡

13 Those who fear the Lord will be happy
at the end,
even on the day of death they will be
blessed.

14 The beginning of wisdom is to fear the
Lord;
she is created with the faithful in the
womb.*

15 With the godly she was created from of
old,
and with their descendants she will
keep faith.

16 The fullness of wisdom is to fear the
Lord;
she inebriates them with her fruits.*

17 Their entire house she fills with choice
foods,
their granaries with her produce.

18 The crown of wisdom is the fear of the
Lord,
flowering with peace and perfect
health.‡

19 Knowledge and full understanding she
rains down;
she heightens the glory of those who
possess her.

20 The root of wisdom is to fear the Lord;
her branches are long life.

21 The fear of the Lord drives away sins;
where it abides it turns back all anger.

22 Unjust anger can never be justified;
anger pulls a person to utter ruin.

23† Until the right time, the patient remain
calm,
then cheerfulness comes back to
them.

24 Until the right time they hold back their
words;
then the lips of many will tell of their
good sense.

25 Among wisdom's treasures is the model
for knowledge;
but godliness is an abomination to
the sinner.

26 If you desire wisdom, keep the
commandments,
and the Lord will bestow her upon
you;

27 For the fear of the Lord is wisdom and
discipline;
faithfulness and humility are his
delight.

28 Do not disobey the fear of the Lord,†
do not approach it with duplicity of
heart.*

29 Do not be a hypocrite before others;
over your lips keep watch.

30 Do not exalt yourself lest you fall
and bring dishonor upon yourself;

For then the Lord will reveal your
secrets
and cast you down in the midst of the
assembly.
Because you did not approach the fear
of the Lord,
and your heart was full of deceit.

## Trust in God

2 ¹ My child, when you come to serve the
Lord,†
prepare yourself for trials.*

2 Be sincere of heart and steadfast,
and do not be impetuous in time of
adversity.

3 Cling to him, do not leave him,
that you may prosper in your last
days.

---

† ‡1:12 Other ancient texts read as v. 12cd:
Fear of the Lord is the Lord's gift;
also for love he makes firm paths.
‡1:18 Other ancient texts read as v. 18cd:
Both are gifts of God toward peace;
splendor opens out for those who love him.
1:23–24 Ben Sira pays close attention to *kairos*, the right time,
occurring some sixty times in his book.
1:28–30 Attempting to serve the Lord with duplicity of heart
is hypocrisy and self-exaltation, deserving of public disgrace.
2:1–11 Serving the Lord is not without its trials (v. 1); but no

matter what happens, the genuine believer will remain sincere,
steadfast, and faithful (vv. 2–3). Misfortune and humiliation are
means of purification to prove one's worth (vv. 4–5). Ben Sira believed that patience and unwavering trust in God are ultimately
rewarded with the benefits of God's mercy and of lasting joy
(vv. 6–11).

---

*
| | |
|---|---|
| 1:14 Jb 28:28; Ps 111:10; | 1:28 Jas 1:8; 2:8. |
| Prv 1:7; 9:10. | 2:1 2 Tm 3:10–12. |
| 1:16 Eccl 12:13. | |

4 Accept whatever happens to you;
   in periods of humiliation be patient.
5 For in fire gold is tested,
   and the chosen, in the crucible of
      humiliation.*
6 Trust in God, and he will help you;
   make your ways straight and hope in
      him.

7 You that fear the Lord, wait for his
      mercy,
   do not stray lest you fall.
8 You that fear the Lord, trust in him,
   and your reward will not be lost.
9 You that fear the Lord, hope for good
      things,
   for lasting joy and mercy.

10 Consider the generations long past and
      see:
   has anyone trusted in the Lord and
      been disappointed?
   Has anyone persevered in his fear and
      been forsaken?
   has anyone called upon him and been
      ignored?*
11 For the Lord is compassionate and
      merciful;
   forgives sins and saves in time of
      trouble.

12 Woe to timid hearts and drooping
      hands,†
   to the sinner who walks a double
      path!
13 Woe to the faint of heart! For they do
      not trust,
   and therefore have no shelter!
14 Woe to you that have lost hope!
   what will you do at the Lord's
      visitation?

15 Those who fear the Lord do not disobey
      his words;
   those who love him keep his ways.*

16 Those who fear the Lord seek to please
      him;
   those who love him are filled with his
      law.
17 Those who fear the Lord prepare their
      hearts
   and humble themselves before him.

18 Let us fall into the hands of the Lord
   and not into the hands of mortals,
   For equal to his majesty is his mercy;
   and equal to his name are his
      works.*

### Responsibilities to Parents†

**3** 1 Children, listen to me, your father;
   act accordingly, that you may be safe.
2 For the Lord sets a father in honor over
      his children
   and confirms a mother's authority
      over her sons.
3 Those who honor their father atone for
      sins;
4 they store up riches who respect their
      mother.
5 Those who honor their father will have
      joy in their own children,
   and when they pray they are heard.
6 Those who respect their father will live a
      long life;
   those who obey the Lord honor their
      mother.
7 Those who fear the Lord honor their
      father,
   and serve their parents as masters.
8 In word and deed honor your father,
   that all blessings may come to you.*
9 A father's blessing gives a person firm
      roots,
   but a mother's curse uproots the
      growing plant.*
10 Do not glory in your father's disgrace,
   for that is no glory to you!
11 A father's glory is glory also for oneself;

SIR

---
**2:12–18** A stern warning to those who compromise their faith
in time of affliction; they fail in courage and trust and therefore
have no security (vv. 12–14). But those who fear the Lord through
obedience, reverence, love, and humility find his "mercy equal
to his majesty" (vv. 15–18).
   **3:1–16** Besides the virtues that must characterize our conduct
toward God, special duties are enjoined, such as honor and respect toward parents, with corresponding blessings (vv. 1–9). By
showing such respect especially to old and infirm parents (vv.
10–13), the sins of children are pardoned (vv. 14–15). Failure to
honor father and mother is blasphemy and merits a curse from
God (v. 16). Cf. Ex 20:12; Eph 6:2–3.

---
**2:5** Prv 17:3; Wis 3:6; Is        **3:8** Ex 20:12; Dt 5:16;
   48:10; 1 Pt 1:7.                      Mt 15:4; 19:19; Mk
**2:10** Ps 31:2; 145:18–20.            7:10; 10:19; Lk 18:20;
**2:15** Jn 14:23.                      Eph 6:2–3.
**2:18** Sir 17:29.                  **3:9** Gn 27:27–29;
                                        49:2–27.

they multiply sin who demean their
   mother. *

12 My son, be steadfast in honoring your
      father;
   do not grieve him as long as he lives. *
13 Even if his mind fails, be considerate of
      him;
   do not revile him because you are in
      your prime.
14 Kindness to a father will not be
      forgotten;
   it will serve as a sin offering—it will
      take lasting root.
15 In time of trouble it will be recalled to
      your advantage,
   like warmth upon frost it will melt
      away your sins.
16 Those who neglect their father are like
      blasphemers;
   those who provoke their mother are
      accursed by their Creator. *

## Humility†

17 My son, conduct your affairs with
      humility,
   and you will be loved more than a
      giver of gifts.
18 Humble yourself the more, the greater
      you are,
   and you will find mercy in the sight of
      God. ‡*
20 For great is the power of the Lord;
   by the humble he is glorified.
21 What is too sublime for you, do not seek;
   do not reach into things that are
      hidden from you. *
22 What is committed to you, pay heed to;
   what is hidden is not your concern.
23 In matters that are beyond you do not
      meddle,
   when you have been shown more
      than you can understand.
24 Indeed, many are the conceits of human
      beings;
   evil imaginations lead them astray.

## Docility†

25 Without the pupil of the eye, light is
      missing;
   without knowledge, wisdom is
      missing.
26 A stubborn heart will fare badly in the
      end;
   those who love danger will perish in
      it.
27 A stubborn heart will have many a
      hurt;
   adding sin to sin is madness.
28 When the proud are afflicted, there is no
      cure;
   for they are offshoots of an evil
      plant. *
29 The mind of the wise appreciates
      proverbs,
   and the ear that listens to wisdom
      rejoices.

## Alms for the Poor

30 As water quenches a flaming fire,
   so almsgiving atones for sins. *
31 The kindness people have done crosses
      their paths later on;
   should they stumble, they will find
      support.

4 ¹ My child, do not mock the life of the
      poor;
   do not keep needy eyes† waiting. *
2 Do not grieve the hungry,
   nor anger the needy.
3 Do not aggravate a heart already angry,
   nor delay giving to the needy.
4 A beggar's request do not reject;
   do not turn your face away from the
      poor.
5 From the needy do not turn your eyes;
   do not give them reason to curse
      you.
6 If in their pain they cry out bitterly,
   their Rock will hear the sound of their
      cry.

---

† **3:17–24** Humility gives you a true estimate of yourself (vv. 17–20; cf. 10:28), so that you will do what should be done, and avoid what is beyond your understanding and strength (vv. 21–23). Intellectual pride, however, leads you astray (v. 24). Ben Sira is perhaps warning his students against the perils of Greek philosophy.
   ‡ **3:18** Other ancient texts read as v. 19:
      Many are the lofty and famous,
      but to the humble he reveals his plan.

**3:25–29** The antidote for stubbornness is to be found in the search for knowledge and wisdom.
   **4:1** *Needy eyes*: when the poor look for help; cf. 18:18.

**3:11** Prv 17:6.
**3:12** Prv 23:22.
**3:16** Prv 19:26; 30:11, 14, 17.
**3:18** Mt 23:12; Lk 1:52; 14:11; 18:14.
**3:21** Ps 131:1.
**3:28** Dt 32:32; Wis 12:10.
**3:30** Sir 7:32–36; 29:8–13; Dt 15:7–11; Tb 12:9; Dn 4:24.
**4:1** Tb 4:7–11.

SIR

## Social Conduct

7  Endear yourself to the assembly;
     before the city's ruler bow your head.
8  Give a hearing to the poor,
     and return their greeting with
       deference;
9  Deliver the oppressed from their
       oppressors;*
     right judgment should not be
       repugnant to you.
10 Be like a father to orphans,
     and take the place of a husband to
       widows.
   Then God will call you his child,
     and he will be merciful to you and
       deliver you from the pit.

## The Rewards of Wisdom†

11 Wisdom teaches her children
     and admonishes all who can
       understand her.
12 Those who love her love life;
     those who seek her out win the LORD's
       favor.
13 Those who hold her fast will attain
       glory,
     and they shall abide in the blessing of
       the LORD.
14 Those who serve her serve the Holy One;
     those who love her the Lord loves.*
15 "Whoever obeys me will judge nations;
     whoever listens to me will dwell in
       my inmost chambers.
16 If they remain faithful, they will possess
       me;
     their descendants too will inherit me.
17 "I will walk with them in disguise,
     and at first I will test them with trials.
   Fear and dread I will bring upon them
     and I will discipline them with my
       constraints.
   When their hearts are fully with me,

18   then I will set them again on the
       straight path
     and reveal my secrets to them.
19   But if they turn away from me, I will
       abandon them
     and deliver them over to robbers."

## Sincerity and Justice†

20   My son, watch for the right time; fear
       what is evil;
     do not bring shame upon yourself.
21   There is a shame heavy with guilt,
     and a shame that brings glory and
       respect.
22   Show no favoritism to your own
       discredit;
     let no one intimidate you to your own
       downfall.
23   Do not refrain from speaking at the
       proper time,
     and do not hide your wisdom;
24   For wisdom becomes known through
       speech,
     and knowledge through the tongue's
       response.

25   Never speak against the truth,
     but of your own ignorance be
       ashamed.
26   Do not be ashamed to acknowledge
       your sins,
     and do not struggle against a rushing
       stream.
27   Do not abase yourself before a fool;
     do not refuse to do so before rulers.
28   Even to the death, fight for what is right,
     and the LORD will do battle for you.

29   Do not be haughty in your speech,
     or lazy and slack in your deeds.
30   Do not be like a lion at home,
     or sly and suspicious with your
       servants.
31   Do not let your hand be open to receive,
     but clenched when it is time to give.

---

† **4:11–19** The Hebrew text in vv. 15–19 presents wisdom speaking in the first person, as in chap. 24. The precious fruits of wisdom—life, favor, glory, blessings, God's love—arouse desire for her (vv. 11–14). Her disciples are like ministers (v. 14) and judges (v. 15), whose descendants have her for their heritage (v. 16). They enjoy happiness and learn her secrets after surviving her tests (vv. 17–18). Those who fail her are abandoned to destruction (v. 19).
   **4:20–31** The student of wisdom is warned about interior

trials of discipline and external dangers to sincerity and justice, namely evil, human respect (vv. 20–22), compromise of liberty in speech and action (vv. 23–25), false shame (v. 26). The student must fight for the truth (vv. 25, 28), avoiding cynicism and laziness (v. 29), and inconsistency (v. 30).

---

**4:9** Jb 29:12, 17.          **4:14** Wis 7:28.

## Against Presumption†

**5** ¹ Do not rely on your wealth,
    or say, "I have the power."*

² Do not rely on your strength
    in following the desires of your heart.

³ Do not say, "Who can prevail against
    me?"
    for the LORD will exact punishment.

⁴ Do not say, "I have sinned, yet what has
    happened to me?"
    for the LORD is slow to anger!

⁵ Do not be so confident of forgiveness
    that you add sin upon sin.

⁶ Do not say, "His mercy is great;
    my many sins he will forgive."
For mercy and anger alike are with him;
    his wrath comes to rest on the wicked.

⁷ Do not delay turning back to the LORD,
    do not put it off day after day.
For suddenly his wrath will come forth;
    at the time of vengeance, you will
    perish.

⁸ Do not rely on deceitful wealth,
    for it will be no help on the day of
    wrath.*

## Use and Abuse of the Tongue†

⁹ Do not winnow in every wind,
    nor walk in every path.†

¹⁰ Be steadfast regarding your knowledge,
    and let your speech be consistent.

¹¹ Be swift to hear,
    but slow to answer.*

¹² If you can, answer your neighbor;
    if not, place your hand over your
    mouth!

¹³ Honor and dishonor through speaking!
    The tongue can be your downfall.

¹⁴ Do not be called double-tongued;
    and with your tongue do not slander
    a neighbor.
For shame has been created for the thief,
    and sore disgrace for the double-
    tongued.

¹⁵ In little or in much, do not act corruptly;

**6** ¹ Do not be a foe instead of a friend.
A bad name, disgrace, and dishonor you
    will inherit.
Thus the wicked, the double-
    tongued!†

## Unruly Passions

² Do not fall into the grip of your
    passion,*
    lest like fire it consume your strength.

³ It will eat your leaves and destroy your
    fruits,
    and you will be left like a dry tree.

⁴ For fierce passion destroys its owner
    and makes him the sport of his
    enemies.

## True Friendship†

⁵ Pleasant speech multiplies friends,
    and gracious lips, friendly greetings.

⁶ Let those who are friendly to you be
    many,
    but one in a thousand your
    confidant.

⁷ When you gain friends, gain them
    through testing,*
    and do not be quick to trust them.

⁸ For there are friends when it suits them,
    but they will not be around in time of
    trouble.

⁹ Another is a friend who turns into an
    enemy,
    and tells of the quarrel to your
    disgrace.

¹⁰ Others are friends, table companions,
    but they cannot be found in time of
    affliction.

¹¹ When things go well, they are your other
    self,

---

**5:1–8** The vices of the rich are pride and independence (vv. 1–2), presumption (v. 3), false security (vv. 4–6), and impenitence (v. 7), which cannot escape the divine wrath (vv. 7–8). Cf. Prv 18:23; 19:1; 28:6.

**5:9–6:1** Proper use of the tongue requires constancy in speech (v. 10), prudence (vv. 11–12), good judgment (v. 13), charity (5:15; 6:1); detraction, calumny (v. 14), and double-talk bring shame and disgrace (5:14; 6:1).

**5:9** The metaphors indicate careless behavior.

**6:1** *Thus...double-tongued!*: people will say this against those disgraced by lying and double-talk.

**6:5–17** One of several poems Ben Sira wrote on friendship;

see also 9:10–16; 12:8–18; 13:1–23; 19:13–17; 22:19–26; 27:16–21. True friends are discerned not by prosperity (v. 11), but through the trials of adversity: distress, quarrels (v. 9), sorrow (v. 10) and misfortune (v. 12). Such friends are rare, a gift from God (vv. 14–17).

**5:1** Sir 11:24; Prv 27:1; Lk
    12:19; 1 Tm 6:17.
**5:8** Prv 10:2; 11:4, 28; Ps
    52:9.
**5:11** Prv 29:20; Eccl 5:1;

Jas 1:19.
**6:2–3** Sir 9:8; 23:16; 25:21;
    41:20, 22; Jb 31:12.
**6:7–9** Sir 12:8–9; 37:1–5;
    Prv 19:4.

S
I
R

and lord it over your servants.

12 If disaster comes upon you, they turn
against you
and hide themselves.
13 Stay away from your enemies,
and be on guard with your friends.
14 Faithful friends are a sturdy shelter;
whoever finds one finds a treasure.
15 Faithful friends are beyond price,
no amount can balance their worth.
16 Faithful friends are life-saving
medicine;
those who fear God will find them.
17 Those who fear the Lord enjoy stable
friendship,
for as they are, so will their
neighbors be.

### Blessings of Wisdom†

18 My child, from your youth choose
discipline;
and when you have gray hair you will
find wisdom.
19 As though plowing and sowing, draw
close to her;
then wait for her bountiful crops.
For in cultivating her you will work but
little,
and soon you will eat her fruit.
20 She is rough ground to the fool!
The stupid cannot abide her.
21 She will be like a burdensome stone to
them,
and they will not delay in casting her
aside.
22 For discipline† is like her name,
she is not accessible to many.

23 Listen, my child, and take my advice;
do not refuse my counsel.
24 Put your feet into her fetters,
and your neck under her yoke.
25 Bend your shoulders and carry her
and do not be irked at her bonds.

26 With all your soul draw close to her;
and with all your strength keep her
ways.
27 Inquire and search, seek and find;
when you get hold of her, do not let
her go.
28 Thus at last you will find rest in her,
and she will become your joy.

29 Her fetters will be a place of strength;
her snare, a robe of spun gold.
30 Her yoke will be a gold ornament;*
her bonds, a purple cord.
31 You will wear her as a robe of glory,
and bear her as a splendid crown.

32 If you wish, my son, you can be wise;
if you apply yourself, you can be
shrewd.
33 If you are willing to listen, you can
learn;
if you pay attention, you can be
instructed.

34 Stand in the company of the elders;
stay close to whoever is wise.
35 Be eager to hear every discourse;
let no insightful saying escape you.*
36 If you see the intelligent, seek them out;
let your feet wear away their
doorsteps!

37 Reflect on the law of the Most High,
and let his commandments be your
constant study.
Then he will enlighten your mind,
and make you wise as you desire.*

### Conduct Toward God and Neighbor†

**7** 1 Do no evil, and evil will not overtake
you;†
2 avoid wickedness, and it will turn
away from you.
3 Do not sow in the furrows of injustice,
lest you harvest it sevenfold.*

---

† **6:18–37** The various figures in each of the eight stanzas urge the search for wisdom through patience (vv. 18–19), persistence (vv. 20–22), docility and perseverance (vv. 23–28). Wisdom bestows rich rewards (vv. 29–31) on those who apply themselves and learn from the wise (vv. 32–36). Although one must strive for wisdom, it is God who grants it (v. 37). Cf. 4:11–19.
**6:22** *Discipline: musar* (in the sense of wisdom) is a perfect homonym for *musar,* "removed, withdrawn"; thus the path of discipline is not accessible to many.
**7:1–17** In the conduct of social relations wisdom forbids evil

and injustice (vv. 1–3), pride (vv. 5, 15–17), ambition and partiality (vv. 4, 6), public disorder (v. 7), presumption and impatience toward God (vv. 9–10), ridicule (v. 11), mischief and deceit toward one's neighbor (vv. 8, 12–13). See the several wisdom poems in Prv 1–9.
**7:1** There is a play on "evil" which means both moral wrong and material calamity.

---

**6:30** Is 62:3.     **7:3** Jb 4:8; Prv 22:8; Hos
**6:35** Sir 8:8–9.                8:7.
**6:37** Ps 1:2.

4 Do not seek from God authority
　　or from the king a place of honor.
5 Do not parade your righteousness before
　　　the LORD,
　　and before the king do not flaunt
　　　your wisdom.*
6 Do not seek to become a judge
　　if you do not have the strength to root
　　　out crime,
　　Lest you show fear in the presence of the
　　　prominent
　　and mar your integrity.
7 Do not be guilty of any evil before the
　　　city court
　　or disgrace yourself before the
　　　assembly.
8 Do not plot to repeat a sin;
　　even for one, you will not go
　　　unpunished.
9 Do not say, "He will appreciate my
　　　many gifts;
　　the Most High God will accept my
　　　offerings."*
10 Do not be impatient in prayer
　　or neglect almsgiving.
11 Do not ridicule the embittered;
　　Remember: there is One who exalts
　　　and humbles.†
12 Do not plot mischief against your
　　　relative
　　or against your friend and
　　　companion.
13 Refuse to tell lie after lie,
　　for it never results in good.
14 Do not babble in the assembly of the
　　　elders
　　or repeat the words of your prayer.†*
15 Do not hate hard work;
　　work was assigned by God.*
16 Do not esteem yourself more than your
　　　compatriots;
　　remember, his wrath will not delay.

17 More and more, humble your pride;
　　what awaits mortals is worms.†*

## Duties of Family Life, Religion and Charity†

18 Do not barter a friend for money,
　　or a true brother for the gold of
　　　Ophir.†
19 Do not reject a sensible wife;
　　a gracious wife is more precious than
　　　pearls.
20 Do not mistreat a servant who works
　　　faithfully,
　　or laborers who devote themselves to
　　　their task.*
21 Love wise servants as yourself;
　　do not refuse them freedom.†
22 Do you have livestock? Look after them;
　　if they are dependable, keep them.
23 Do you have sons? Correct them
　　and cure their stubbornness† in their
　　　early youth.*
24 Do you have daughters? Keep them
　　　chaste,
　　and do not be indulgent to them.*
25 Give your daughter in marriage, and a
　　　worry comes to an end;
　　but give her to a sensible man.
26 Do you have a wife? Do not mistreat her,
　　but do not trust the wife you hate.
27 With your whole heart honor your
　　　father;
　　your mother's birth pangs do not
　　　forget.*
28 Remember, of these parents you were
　　　born;
　　what can you give them for all they
　　　gave you?
29 With all your soul fear God
　　and revere his priests.

---

† 7:11 *One who exalts and humbles*: God; cf. 1 Sm 2:7; Ps 75:8; Lk 1:52.

7:14 *Repeat...prayer*: brevity of speech is a wisdom ideal; toward superiors and God it is a sign of respect; cf. Eccl 5:1; Mt 6:7.

7:17 *Worms*: i.e., corruption; the Septuagint adds "fire."

7:18–36 Respect and appreciation, justice and kindness should characterize relations toward members of the household (vv. 18–28), God and the priests (vv. 29–31), the poor and afflicted, the living and the dead (vv. 32–35).

7:18 *Ophir*: the port, at present unidentified, to which the ships of Solomon sailed and from which they brought back gold and silver; cf. note on Ps 45:10.

7:21 After six years of service a Hebrew slave was entitled to

freedom; cf. Ex 21:2; Dt 15:12–15.

7:23 *Cure their stubbornness*: keep them from rebellious pride; so with the Greek. Cf. 30:1–13. The Hebrew text, probably not original here, reads: "Choose wives for them while they are young."

* 7:5 Jb 9:2; Ps 143:2; Prv 25:6; 1 Cor 4:4.
7:9 Sir 34:21–24; 35:14–15.
7:14 Sir 32:7–10; Mt 6:7.
7:15 Gn 2:15; 3:17.
7:17 Sir 10:11; Jb 17:14; Is 66:24.
7:20 Lv 19:13; Dt 24:14–15; Jas 5:4.
7:23 Sir 30:1–13; Prv 13:24; 19:18; 23:13–14; 29:15, 17.
7:24 Sir 42:9–12.
7:27 Sir 3:1–16; Ex 20:12; Dt 5:16; Tb 4:3–4; Prv 23:22.

**S**
**I**
**R**

30 With all your strength love your Maker
   and do not neglect his ministers.
31 Honor God and respect the priest;
   give him his portion as you have been
      commanded: *
   First fruits and contributions,
   his portion of victims and holy
      offerings. †
32 To the poor also extend your hand,
   that your blessing may be complete.
33 Give your gift to all the living,
   and do not withhold your kindness
      from the dead. †
34 Do not avoid those who weep,
   but mourn with those who mourn. *
35 Do not hesitate to visit the sick,
   because for such things you will be
      loved. *

36 In whatever you do, remember your last
      days,
   and you will never sin. †

## Prudence in Dealing with Others†

8 ¹ Do not contend with the mighty,
   lest you fall into their power.
2 Do not quarrel with the rich,
   lest they pay out the price of your
      downfall.
   For gold has unsettled many,
   and wealth perverts the character of
      princes. *

3 Do not quarrel with loud-mouths,
   or heap wood upon their fire. † *
4 Do not associate with the senseless,
   lest your ancestors be insulted.

5 Do not reproach one who turns away
      from sin; *
   remember, we all are guilty. †
6 Do not insult one who is old,

7 for some of us will also grow old.
   Do not rejoice when someone dies;
   remember, we are all to be gathered in.

8 Do not neglect the discourse of the
      wise, *
   but busy yourself with their proverbs;
   For in this way you will acquire the
      training
   to stand in the presence of princes.
9 Do not reject the tradition of the elders
   which they have heard from their
      ancestors;
   For from it you will learn
   how to answer when the need arises.

10 Do not kindle the coals of sinners,
   lest you be burned in their flaming
      fire.
11 Do not give ground before scoundrels;
   it will set them in ambush against
      you. †
12 Do not lend to one more powerful than
      yourself;
   or if you lend, count it as lost. *

13 Do not give collateral beyond your
      means;
   consider any collateral a debt you
      must pay.

14 Do not go to court against a judge,
   for the case will be settled in his favor.
15 Do not travel with the ruthless
   lest they weigh you down with
      calamity;
   For they will only go their own way,
   and through their folly you will also
      perish.
16 Do not defy the quick-tempered,
   or ride with them through the desert.
   For bloodshed is nothing to them;
   when there is no one to help, they
      will destroy you.

---

**7:31** *First fruits…holy offerings*: cf. Ex 29:27; Lv 7:31–34; Nm 18:8–20; Dt 18:1–5.
**7:33** This seems to refer to the observances ordained toward the dead, that is, proper mourning and burial. Cf. 2 Sm 21:12–14; Tb 1:17–18; 12:12.
**7:36** *Never sin*: because the last days of the sinner, it was presumed, would be troubled.
**8:1–19** The prudent will be circumspect, avoiding conflict with the powerful, the rich and insolent, the impious, the irascible, and judges (vv. 1–3, 10–12, 14, 16). They will not associate with the undisciplined (v. 4) or the ruthless (v. 15), with fools or strangers (vv. 17–19), but with the wise and the elders of the people (vv. 8–9). Caution is a recurring theme in Ben Sira.

**8:3** One should avoid increasing the ire of those who are hotheaded; cf. vv. 10, 16.
**8:5** *We all are guilty*: cf. 1 Kgs 8:46; 2 Chr 6:36; Jb 25:4; Eccl 7:20; Rom 3:9–10; 5:12; 1 Jn 1:8.
**8:11** Giving in to the wicked only encourages them to take advantage.

---

**7:31** Lv 7:31; Nm 18:18.            **8:3** Prv 26:20–21.
**7:34** Rom 12:15.                     **8:5** 1 Kgs 8:46; 1 Jn 1:8.
**7:35** Mt 25:36.                      **8:8–9** Sir 6:34–36.
**8:2** Sir 31:5–6; Dt 16:19.          **8:12** Sir 29:4–7; Prv 17:18.

<sup>17</sup> Do not take counsel with simpletons,
    for they cannot keep a confidence.

<sup>18</sup> Before a stranger do nothing that should
    be kept secret,
    for you do not know what it will
    produce later on.†*

<sup>19</sup> Open your heart to no one,
    do not banish your happiness.

## Advice Concerning Women†

**9** <sup>1</sup> Do not be jealous of the wife of your
    bosom,
    lest you teach her to do evil against
    you.†

<sup>2</sup> Do not give a woman power over you
    to trample on your dignity.*

<sup>3</sup> Do not go near a strange woman,
    lest you fall into her snares.

<sup>4</sup> Do not dally with a singer,
    lest you be captivated by her charms.

<sup>5</sup> Do not entertain any thoughts about a
    virgin,
    lest you be enmeshed in damages for
    her.†

<sup>6</sup> Do not give yourself to a prostitute
    lest you lose your inheritance.*

<sup>7</sup> Do not look around the streets of the city
    or wander through its squares.

<sup>8</sup> Avert your eyes from a shapely woman;
    do not gaze upon beauty that is not
    yours;
    Through woman's beauty many have
    been ruined,
    for love of it burns like fire.*

<sup>9</sup> Never recline at table with a married
    woman,
    or drink intoxicants with her,
    Lest your heart be drawn to her
    and you go down in blood† to the
    grave.

## Choice of Friends†

<sup>10</sup> Do not abandon old friends;
    new ones cannot equal them.

A new friend is like new wine—
    when it has aged, you drink it with
    pleasure.

<sup>11</sup> Do not envy the wicked
    for you do not know when their day
    will come.

<sup>12</sup> Do not delight in the pleasures of the
    ungodly;
    remember, they will not die
    unpunished.

<sup>13</sup> Keep away from those who have power
    to kill,
    and you will not be filled with the
    dread of death.
    But if you come near them, do not
    offend them,
    lest they take away your life.
    Know that you are stepping among
    snares
    and walking over a net.

<sup>14</sup> As best you can, answer your neighbor,
    and associate with the wise.

<sup>15</sup> With the learned exchange ideas;
    and let all your conversation be about
    the law of the Most High.

<sup>16</sup> Take the righteous for your table
    companions;
    and let your glory be in the fear of
    God.

## Concerning Rulers†

<sup>17</sup> Work by skilled hands will earn praise;
    but the people's leader is proved wise
    by his words.

<sup>18</sup> Loud mouths are feared in their city,
    and whoever is reckless in speech is
    hated.

**10** <sup>1</sup> A wise magistrate gives stability to
    his people,
    and government by the intelligent is
    well ordered.*

---

**8:18** To keep a secret, or a confidence, is a major concern of Ben Sira; cf. 1:30; 22:22; 27:16–21; 37:10; 42:1.
**9:1–9** Ben Sira writes about women only from the androcentric viewpoint of his culture. Cf. 25:13–26:27.
**9:1** Jealousy may lead to suspicion and may prompt a wife to those actions her husband fears.
**9:5** Cf. Ex 22:15–16; Dt 22:28–29; Jb 31:1. Cf. note on Ex 22:16.
**9:9** *In blood*: perhaps refers to blood revenge; cf. Lv 20:10.
**9:10–16** The second of Ben Sira's poems on friendship; cf. note on 6:5–17. In choosing friends, adherence to the law of the

Lord should serve as a guide (v. 15), with the righteous and the learned (vv. 14–16); avoid the company of the mighty and of sinners (vv. 11–13). Cf. 8:1–19.
**9:17–10:5** Public office as conducted justly or unjustly benefits or destroys the people, according to the axiom, "as the prince, so the people." God, however, has sovereignty over both.

---

**8:18** Prv 25:9–10.
**9:2** Sir 25:21.
**9:6** Prv 5:1–14; 6:24; 29:3.
**9:8** Sir 25:20; 41:21; Prv 6:25–29.
**10:1** Prv 29:4; Wis 6:24.

2   As the people's judge, so the officials;*
      as the head of a city, so the
      inhabitants.
3   A reckless king destroys his people,
      but a city grows through the
      intelligence of its princes.*
4   Sovereignty over the earth is in the hand
      of God,
      who appoints the right person for the
      right time.
5   Sovereignty over everyone is in the hand
      of God,
      who imparts his majesty to the ruler.

### The Sin of Pride

6   No matter what the wrong, never harm
      your neighbor
      or go the way of arrogance.*
7   Odious to the Lord and to mortals is
      pride,
      and for both oppression is a crime.
8   Sovereignty is transferred from one
      people to another
      because of the lawlessness of the
      proud.
9   Why are dust and ashes proud?†
      Even during life the body decays.
10  A slight illness—the doctor jests;
      a king today—tomorrow he is dead.
11  When a people die,
      they inherit corruption and worms,
      gnats and maggots.*

12  The beginning of pride is stubbornness
      in withdrawing the heart from one's
      Maker.
13  For sin is a reservoir of insolence,
      a source which runs over with vice;
      Because of it God sends unheard-of
      afflictions
      and strikes people with utter ruin.*
14  God overturns the thrones of the proud
      and enthrones the lowly in their place.
15  God plucks up the roots of the proud,
      and plants the lowly in their place.
16  The Lord lays waste the lands of the
      nations,

and destroys them to the very
      foundations of the earth.
17  He removes them from the earth,
      destroying them,
      erasing their memory from the world.
18  Insolence does not befit mortals,
      nor impudent anger those born of
      women.

### True Glory†

19  Whose offspring can be honorable?
      Human offspring.
      Those who fear the LORD are
      honorable offspring.
      Whose offspring can be disgraceful?
      Human offspring.
      Those who transgress the
      commandment are disgraceful
      offspring.
20  Among relatives their leader is honored;
      but whoever fears God is honored
      among God's people.‡
22  Resident alien, stranger, foreigner,
      pauper—
      their glory is the fear of the LORD.
23  It is not right to despise anyone wise but
      poor,
      nor proper to honor the lawless.*

24  The prince, the ruler, the judge are in
      honor;
      but none is greater than the one who
      fears God.
25  When the free serve a wise slave,
      the wise will not complain.*
26  Do not flaunt your wisdom in managing
      your affairs,
      or boast in your time of need.
27  Better the worker who has goods in
      plenty
      than the boaster who has no food.*

28  My son, with humility have self-esteem;
      and give yourself the esteem you
      deserve.
29  Who will acquit those who condemn
      themselves?

---

† **10:9–10** The general implication is that a slight illness today may be followed by death tomorrow. The uncertainty of life leaves no room for pride.
  **10:19–11:6** Genuine honor comes not from one's place in society but from fear of the Lord and a true estimate of oneself. The Lord exalts the lowly and oppressed; transgressors of the commandment merit dishonor and disgrace.
  ‡**10:20** Other ancient texts read as v. 21:

The beginning of acceptance is the fear of the Lord;
  the beginning of rejection, effrontery and pride.

---

*  **10:2–3** Ez 16:44; Prv 29:12.    **10:13** Prv 11:2; 16:18;
   **10:3** Prv 29:4–8.                         18:12.
   **10:6** Lv 19:18.                  **10:23** Jas 2:1–4.
   **10:11** Sir 7:17; Jb 17:14; Is    **10:25** Prv 17:2.
         66:24.                        **10:27** Prv 12:9.

Who will honor those who disgrace
   themselves?

30   The poor are honored for their
        wisdom;
     the rich are honored for their wealth.
31   Honored in poverty, how much more so
        in wealth!
     Disgraced in wealth, in poverty how
        much the more!

# 11

¹ The wisdom of the poor lifts their
        head high
   and sets them among princes.
2   Do not praise anyone for good looks;
     or despise anyone because of
        appearance.
3   The bee is least among winged
        creatures,
     but it reaps the choicest of harvests.
4   Do not mock the one who wears only a
        loin-cloth,
     or scoff at a person's bitter day.
   For strange are the deeds of the LORD,
     hidden from mortals his work.†
5   Many are the oppressed who rise to the
        throne;
     some that none would consider wear
        a crown.†
6   Many are the exalted who fall into utter
        disgrace,
     many the honored who are given into
        the power of the few.

## Moderation and Patience†

7   Before investigating, do not find fault;
     examine first, then criticize.
8   Before listening, do not say a word,
     interrupt no one in the midst of
        speaking.*
9   Do not dispute about what is not your
        concern;
     in the quarrels of the arrogant do not
        take part.

10   My son, why increase your anxiety,
     since whoever is greedy for wealth will
        not be blameless?
   Even if you chase after it, you will never
        overtake it;
     and by fleeing you will not escape.
11   One may work and struggle and drive,
     and fall short all the same.*
12   Others go their way broken-down
        drifters,
     with little strength and great misery—
   Yet the eye of the LORD looks favorably
        upon them,
     shaking them free of the stinking
        mire.
13   He lifts up their heads and exalts them
     to the amazement of the many.

14†   Good and evil, life and death,*
     poverty and riches—all are from the
        LORD.‡
17   The Lord's gift remains with the devout;
     his favor brings lasting success.
18   Some become rich through a miser's life,
     and this is their allotted reward:
19   When they say: "I have found rest,*
     now I will feast on my goods,"
   They do not know how long it will be
     till they die and leave them to others.†

20   My child, stand by your agreement and
        attend to it,
     grow old while doing your work.
21   Do not marvel at the works of a sinner,
     but trust in the LORD and wait for his
        light;
   For it is easy in the eyes of the LORD
     suddenly, in an instant, to make the
        poor rich.

22   God's blessing is the lot of the righteous,
     and in due time their hope bears fruit.
23   Do not say: "What do I need?
     What further benefits can be mine?"
24   Do not say: "I am self-sufficient.

---

**11:4** The implication is similar to Eccl 7:13; 8:17: the mysterious work of God.
   **11:5** Cf. 1 Sm 2:8; Ps 75:8; 105:17–22; Lk 1:52.
   **11:7–28** Discretion should regulate conduct toward others (vv. 7–9); as regards personal interests, one should avoid solicitude for the passing external benefits of life and property (vv. 10–14, 18–19, 21, 23–25) and cultivate the lasting inward gifts of wisdom, virtue (vv. 20, 22), and patience (vv. 25–28).
   **11:14** In mysterious ways God ultimately governs the lives of men and women.
   ‡**11:14** Other ancient texts read as vv. 15–16:

¹⁵ Wisdom and understanding and knowledge of the Law,
     love and virtuous paths, are from the Lord.
¹⁶ Error and darkness were formed with sinners from their
        birth,
     and evil grows old with those who exult in evil.
**11:19** Cf. the parable of the rich man, Lk 12:16–21.

---

**11:8** Prv 18:13.                **11:19** Eccl 4:8; 6:2; Lk
**11:11** Ps 127:2; Eccl 4:8.           12:19.
**11:14** Jb 1:21; 2:10.

What harm can come to me now?"

25  The day of prosperity makes one forget
      adversity;
    the day of adversity makes one forget
      prosperity.*

26  For it is easy for the Lord on the day of
      death†
    to repay mortals according to their
      conduct.

27  A time of affliction brings forgetfulness
      of past delights;
    at the end of life one's deeds are
      revealed.

28  Call none happy before death,
    for how they end, they are known.

## Care in Choosing Friends

29  Not everyone should be brought into
      your house,
    for many are the snares of the crafty.

30  Like a decoy partridge in a cage, so is the
      heart of the proud,
    and like a spy they will pick out the
      weak spots.

31  For they lie in wait to turn good into
      evil,
    and to praiseworthy deeds they attach
      blame.

32  One spark kindles many coals;
    a sinner lies in wait for blood.

33  Beware of scoundrels, for they breed
      only evil,
    and they may give you a lasting stain.

34  Admit strangers into your home, and
      they will stir up trouble
    and make you a stranger to your own
      family.

**12** ¹ If you do good, know for whom you
      are doing it,†
    and your kindness will have its effect.

2   Do good to the righteous and reward
      will be yours,
    if not from them, from the LORD.*

3   No good comes to those who give
      comfort to the wicked,

    nor is it an act of mercy that they do.

4   Give to the good but refuse the sinner;

5   refresh the downtrodden but give
      nothing to the proud.
    No arms for combat should you give
      them,
    lest they use these against you;
    Twofold evil you will obtain for every
      good deed you do for them.

6   For God also hates sinners,
    and takes vengeance on evildoers.†

8   In prosperity we cannot know our
      friends;†
    in adversity an enemy will not remain
      concealed.*

9   When one is successful even an enemy is
      friendly;
    but in adversity even a friend
      disappears.*

10  Never trust your enemies,
    for their wickedness is like corrosion
      in bronze.

11  Even though they act deferentially and
      peaceably toward you,
    take care to be on your guard against
      them.*
    Treat them as those who reveal secrets,†
    and be certain that in the end there
      will still be envy.

12  Do not let them stand near you,
    lest they push you aside and take your
      place.
    Do not let them sit at your right hand,
    or they will demand your seat,
    And in the end you will appreciate my
      advice,
    when you groan with regret, as I
      warned.

13  Who pities a snake charmer when he is
      bitten,†
    or anyone who goes near a wild
      beast?

14  So it is with the companion of the
      proud,
    who is involved in their sins:

† **11:26–28** Ben Sira thought that divine retribution took place
only in the present life, and even at the end of life; cf. 9:12;
14:16–17.
**12:1** The import of this verse is brought out in vv. 4–5.
**12:6** Verse 7 is a variant of verse 4 and is omitted.
**12:8–18** Adversity distinguishes friends from enemies; to trust
the latter or permit them intimacy is to invite disaster. Cf. note
on 6:5–17.

**12:11** Ben Sira has harsh words for those who reveal secrets;
see also 8:18; 27:16–21; 42:1; Prv 11:13; 20:19.
**12:13** For v. 13a, see especially Eccl 10:11.

**11:25** Sir 18:24–25.                    **12:9** Prv 19:4–7.
**12:2** Dt 14:29.                          **12:11** Prv 26:24–26.
**12:8** Prv 17:17.

15 While you stand firm, they make no
     move;
    but if you slip, they cannot hold back.

16 With their lips enemies speak sweetly,
    but in their heart they scheme to
     plunge you into the abyss.
    Though enemies have tears in their eyes,
    given the chance, they will never have
     enough of your blood.*

17 If evil comes upon you, you will find
     them at hand;
    pretending to help, they will trip you
     up,

18 Then they will shake their heads and
     clap their hands
    and hiss repeatedly, and show their
     true faces.

## Caution Regarding Associates†

# 13

1 Touch pitch and you blacken your
     hand;
    associate with scoundrels and you
     learn their ways.

2 Do not lift a weight too heavy for you,
    or associate with anyone wealthier
     than you.
    How can the clay pot go with the metal
     cauldron?
    When they knock together, the pot
     will be smashed:

3 The rich do wrong and boast of it,
    while the poor are wronged and beg
     forgiveness.

4 As long as the rich can use you they will
     enslave you,
    but when you are down and out they
     will abandon you.

5 As long as you have anything they will
     live with you,
    but they will drain you dry without
     remorse.

6 When they need you they will deceive
     you
    and smile at you and raise your
     hopes;
    they will speak kindly to you and say,
     "What do you need?"

7 They will embarrass you at their dinner
     parties,
    and finally laugh at you.
    Afterwards, when they see you, they will
     pass you by,
    and shake their heads at you.

8 Be on guard: do not act too boldly;
    do not be like those who lack sense.

9 When the influential draw near, keep
     your distance;
    then they will urge you all the more.

10 Do not draw too close, lest you be
     rebuffed,
    but do not keep too far away lest you
     be regarded as an enemy.

11 Do not venture to be free with them,
    do not trust their many words;
    For by prolonged talk they will test you,
    and though smiling they will probe
     you.

12 Mercilessly they will make you a
     laughingstock,
    and will not refrain from injury or
     chains.

13 Be on your guard and take care
    never to accompany lawless people.‡

15 Every living thing loves its own kind,
    and we all love someone like
     ourselves.

16 Every living being keeps close to its own
     kind;
    and people associate with their own
     kind.

17 Is a wolf ever allied with a lamb?
    So the sinner with the righteous.*

18 Can there be peace between the hyena
     and the dog?
    Or peace between the rich and the
     poor?†

19 Wild donkeys of the desert are lion's
     prey;
    likewise the poor are feeding grounds
     for the rich.

20 Humility is an abomination to the
     proud;

---

† **13:1–14:2** By means of various images, most of them unfavorable to the rich, Ben Sira indicates the practical impossibility
of genuine and sincere companionship between the poor and
the rich. He lays down a principle of associating with equals
(13:6–19).
‡**13:13** Other ancient texts read as v. 14:
    If you hear these things in your sleep, wake up!

With your whole life, love the Lord
  and call on him for your salvation.
  **13:18** The hostility between the dogs which guard the flocks
(Jb 30:1) and the rapacious hyenas (Jer 12:9) is proverbial in
Palestine.

**12:16** Jer 9:7.      **13:17** 2 Cor 6:14–17.

and the poor are an abomination to
the rich.

21 When the rich stumble they are
supported by friends;
when the poor trip they are pushed
down by friends.

22 When the rich speak they have many
supporters;
though what they say is repugnant, it
wins approval.
When the poor speak people say,
"Come, come, speak up!"
though they are talking sense, they get
no hearing.

23 When the rich speak all are silent,
their wisdom people extol to the
clouds.
When the poor speak people say: "Who
is that?"
If they stumble, people knock them
down. *

24 Wealth is good where there is no sin; †
but poverty is evil by the standards of
the proud.

25 The heart changes one's face,
either for good or for evil. *

26 The sign of a good heart is a radiant
face;
withdrawn and perplexed is the
toiling schemer.

# 14

1 † Happy those whose mouth causes
them no grief,
those who are not stung by remorse
for sin. *

2 Happy are those whose conscience does
not reproach them,
those who have not lost hope.

### The Use of Wealth

3 Wealth is not appropriate for the mean-
spirited; †

to misers, what use is gold?

4 What they deny themselves they collect
for someone else,
and strangers will live sumptuously
on their possessions. *

5 To whom will they be generous that are
stingy with themselves
and do not enjoy what is their own?

6 None are worse than those who are
stingy with themselves;
they punish their own avarice.

7 If ever they do good, it is by mistake;
in the end they reveal their meanness.

8 Misers are evil people,
they turn away and disregard others.

9 The greedy see their share as not
enough;
greedy injustice dries up the soul.

10 The eye of the miserly is rapacious for
food,
but there is none of it on their own
table.

11 † My son, if you have the means, treat
yourself well,
and enjoy life as best you can. *

12 Remember that death does not delay,
and you have not been told the grave's
appointed time.

13 Before you die, be good to your friends;
give them a share in what you
possess. *

14 Do not deprive yourself of good things
now
or let a choice portion escape you.

15 Will you not leave your riches to others,
and your earnings to be divided by
lot?

16 Give and take, treat yourself well,
for in Sheol there are no joys to seek.

17 All flesh grows old like a garment;
the age-old law is: everyone must
die. *

---

**13:24** Ben Sira allows that the rich can be virtuous—but with
difficulty; cf. 31:1–11.
**14:1–2** A clear conscience, the result of honoring personal
commitments and responsibilities, brings contentment and
peace.
**14:3–10** Ben Sira offers a case study about the miserable life
of the "small-hearted" (Heb. *leb qaṭan*) to verify vv. 1–2. They
are evil because they do not use their wealth properly to benefit
themselves or others. While they are never satisfied that they
have enough, they ignore their own needs and hospitality itself,
feeding on the generosity of others, in order to protect their own
resources. Ironically, after their death, strangers, with no obligation to keep their memory alive, enjoy their wealth.

**14:11–19** Three realities govern Ben Sira's attitude toward a
proper use of wealth: the inevitability and uncertainty of death,
the ephemeral nature of human accomplishments, the lack of reward or punishment after death. He advises generous enjoyment
of God's gift of wealth before death.

---

**13:21–23** Prv 14:20; 19:4, 7.　　　**14:11–12** Eccl 5:17–19.
**13:25** Prv 15:13.　　　　　　　　**14:13** Prv 3:27–28; Tb 4:7.
**14:1** Sir 5:13–14; 19:16;　　　　　**14:17** Ps 103:14–16; Jb
　25:8; Jas 1:26; 3:2.　　　　　　　　14:1–2; Is 40:6; Jas
**14:4** Eccl 2:18–19; 6:2.　　　　　　1:10; 1 Pt 1:24.

18 As with the leaves growing on a
        luxuriant tree—
    one falls off and another sprouts—
    So with the generations of flesh and
        blood:
    one dies and another flourishes.*
19 All human deeds surely perish;
    the works they do follow after them.

## The Search for Wisdom and Her Blessings†

20 Happy those who meditate on Wisdom,
    and fix their gaze on knowledge;*
21 Who ponder her ways in their heart,
    and understand her paths;
22 Who pursue her like a scout,
    and watch at her entry way;
23 Who peep through her windows,
    and listen at her doors;
24 Who encamp near her house
    and fasten their tent pegs next to her
        walls;
25 Who pitch their tent beside her,
    and dwell in a good place;†
26† Who build their nest in her leaves,
    and lodge in her branches;
27 Who take refuge from the heat in her
        shade
    and dwell in her home.

**15** ¹ Whoever fears the Lord will do this;
    whoever is practiced in the Law will
        come to Wisdom.
2 She will meet him like a mother;
    like a young bride she will receive
        him,
3† She will feed him with the bread of
        learning,
    and give him the water of
        understanding to drink.*
4 He will lean upon her and not fall;
    he will trust in her and not be put to
        shame.
5 She will exalt him above his neighbors,

    and in the assembly she will make
        him eloquent.
6 Joy and gladness he will find,
    and an everlasting name he will
        inherit.*
7 The worthless will not attain her,
    and the haughty will not behold her.
8 She is far from the impious;
    liars never think of her.
9† Praise is unseemly on the lips of sinners,
    for it has not been allotted to them by
        God.
10 But praise is uttered by the mouth of the
        wise,
    and its rightful owner teaches it.

## Free Will†

11 Do not say: "It was God's doing that I
        fell away,"
    for what he hates he does not do.
12 Do not say: "He himself has led me
        astray,"
    for he has no need of the wicked.*
13 Abominable wickedness the Lord hates
    and he does not let it happen to those
        who fear him.
14 God in the beginning created human
        beings
    and made them subject to their own
        free choice.*
15 If you choose, you can keep the
        commandments;
    loyalty is doing the will of God.
16 Set before you are fire and water;
    to whatever you choose, stretch out
        your hand.
17 Before everyone are life and death,
    whichever they choose will be given
        them.*
18 Immense is the wisdom of the Lord;
    mighty in power, he sees all things.

---

**14:20–15:10** This poem charts the growing intimacy between those seeking Wisdom and Wisdom herself. They move from static reflection to playful pursuit, from camping outside the walls of her house to nesting inside her leafy shade. Ben Sira portrays Wisdom as both mother and bride, a feminine figure who is the fullness of womanhood according to his androcentric society.

**14:25** *In a good place*: i.e., where Wisdom dwells.

**14:26–27** The shift in imagery creates a more intimate relationship. Those seeking Wisdom dwell within her as a bird nests within a leafy tree.

**15:3–6** In this role reversal Woman Wisdom teaches, nourishes, supports, and protects the vulnerable man. For similar imagery cf. Prv 8:4–21, 34–35; 9:1–5; 31:10–31.

**15:9–10** There is an intimate association between wisdom and praise of the Lord.

**15:11–20** Here Ben Sira links freedom of the will with human responsibility. God, who sees everything, is neither the cause nor the occasion of sin. We have the power to choose our behavior and we are responsible for both the good and the evil we do (vv. 15–17).

---

**14:18** Eccl 1:4.          **15:12** Jas 1:13.
**14:20** Ps 1:2.           **15:14** Gn 1:27.
**15:3** Jn 4:10; 6:31–33.  **15:17** Dt 30:15–20.
**15:6** Sir 6:28–33.

19 The eyes of God behold his works,
   and he understands every human
      deed.*

20 He never commands anyone to sin,
   nor shows leniency toward deceivers.†

## God's Punishment of Sinners†

# 16

1 Do not yearn for worthless children,
   or rejoice in wicked offspring.

2 Even if they be many, do not rejoice in
      them
   if they do not have fear of the LORD.

3 Do not count on long life for them,*
   or have any hope for their future.
   For one can be better than a thousand;
      rather die childless than have impious
         children!

4 Through one wise person a city can be
      peopled;
   but through a clan of rebels it
      becomes desolate.

5 Many such things my eye has seen,
   and even more than these my ear has
      heard.

6 Against a sinful band fire is kindled,*
   upon a godless people wrath blazes.†

7 He did not forgive the princes of old†
   who rebelled long ago in their
      might.*

8 He did not spare the neighbors of Lot,†*
   abominable in their pride.

9 He did not spare the doomed people,†
   dispossessed because of their sin;

10 Nor the six hundred thousand foot
      soldiers,†*
   sent to their graves for the arrogance
      of their hearts.

11 Had there been but one stiff-necked†
      person,
   it would be a wonder had he gone
      unpunished.
   For mercy and anger alike are with him;
      he remits and forgives, but also pours
         out wrath.

12 Great as his mercy is his punishment;
   he judges people, each according to
      their deeds.

13 Criminals do not escape with their
      plunder;
   the hope of the righteous, God never
      leaves unfulfilled.

14 Whoever does good has a reward;
   each receives according to their deeds.‡

17 Do not say: "I am hidden from God;
   and on high who remembers me?
   Among so many people I am unknown;
   what am I in the world of spirits?

18 Look, the heavens and the highest
      heavens,
   the abyss and the earth tremble at his
      visitation.

19 The roots of the mountains and the
      earth's foundations—
   at his mere glance they quiver and
      quake.

20 Of me, therefore, he will take no notice;
   with my ways who will be concerned?

21 If I sin, no eye will see me;
   if all in secret I act deceitfully, who is
      to know?*

22 Who tells him about just deeds?
   What can I expect for doing my duty?"

23 Such the thoughts of the senseless;
   only the foolish entertain them.

---

† **15:20** *Deceivers*: those who hold the Lord responsible for their sins.

**16:1–23** One child who does God's will is a greater blessing than many sinful offspring (vv. 1–4), for history and experience show that God punishes sin (vv. 5–10). God judges everyone according to their deeds (vv. 11–14); no one can hide from God or escape retribution at his hand (vv. 17–23).

**16:6** For Korah and his band (v. 6a), see 45:18–19; Nm 16:1–35; Ps 106:18; for the disgruntled Israelites (v. 6b), Ps 78:21–22.

**16:7** *The princes of old*: e.g., the mighty destroyed in the flood (Gn 6:1–4; Wis 14:6; Bar 3:26–28), as well as the king of Babylon (Is 14:4–21) and Nebuchadnezzar (Dn 4:7–30).

**16:8** *Neighbors of Lot*: the people of Sodom and Gomorrah, condemned elsewhere for their sexual violence (Gn 19:24–25) and failure at hospitality (Ez 16:49–50).

**16:9** *Doomed people*: the Canaanite tribes whose aberrant religious practices, at least in Israelite opinion, caused their downfall: Ex 23:23–24, 27–33; 33:2; 34:11–16; Dt 7:1–2; Wis 12:3–7.

**16:10** *Six hundred thousand foot soldiers*: the number given for those rescued by Moses, who murmured against the Lord in the wilderness and died there: 46:1, 7–8; Nm 11:20; 14:1–12, 22–24, 29, 36–38; 26:65; Dt 1:35–38.

**16:11** *Stiff-necked*: sinful Israelites; cf. Ex 32:9; 33:3, 5. Not even one Israelite would have gone unpunished for insolence or pride.

‡**16:14** Other ancient texts read as vv. 15–16:
   15 The LORD hardened the heart of Pharaoh so that he did not
         recognize him
      whose acts were manifest under the heavens;
   16 His mercy was seen by all his creatures,
      and his light and his darkness he apportioned to
         humankind.

---

* **15:19** Ps 33:18; 34:16; Heb 4:13.
**16:3–4** Wis 4:1–2.
**16:6** Sir 21:9.
**16:7** Gn 6:4; Wis 14:6; Bar 3:26–28.
**16:8** Gn 19:24–25.
**16:10** Nm 14:29.
**16:21** Sir 23:18–20.

## Divine Wisdom Seen in Creation†

24 Listen to me, my son, and take my
    advice,
        and apply your mind to my words,

25 While I pour out my spirit by measure
        and impart knowledge with care.

26 When at the first God created his works
    and, as he made them, assigned their
        tasks,*

27 He arranged for all time what they were
        to do,
    their domains from generation to
        generation.
    They were not to go hungry or grow
        weary,
        or ever cease from their tasks.

28 Never does a single one crowd its
        neighbor,
        or do any ever disobey his word.

29 Then the Lord looked upon the earth,
        and filled it with his blessings.*

30 Its surface he covered with every kind of
        living creature
    which must return into it again.

## Creation of Human Beings

# 17

1 The Lord created human beings from
        the earth,
    and makes them return to earth
        again.*

2 A limited number of days he gave
        them,*
    but granted them authority over
        everything on earth.

3 He endowed them with strength like his
        own,
    and made them in his image.

4 He put fear of them in all flesh,

and gave them dominion over beasts
        and birds.‡

6 Discernment, tongues, and eyes,
    ears, and a mind for thinking he gave
        them.

7 With knowledge and understanding he
        filled them;
    good and evil he showed them.

8 He put fear of him into their hearts
    to show them the grandeur of his
        works,

9 That they might describe the wonders of
        his deeds

10 and praise his holy name.

11 He set before them knowledge,
    and allotted to them the law of life.

12 An everlasting covenant he made with
        them,
    and his commandments† he revealed
        to them.

13 His majestic glory their eyes beheld,
    his glorious voice their ears heard.

14 He said to them, "Avoid all evil";
    to each of them he gave precepts
        about their neighbor.

15 Their ways are ever known to him,
    they cannot be hidden from his eyes.‡

17 Over every nation he appointed a ruler,†
    but Israel is the Lord's own portion.‡*

19 All their works are clear as the sun to
        him,
    and his eyes are ever upon their ways.

20 Their iniquities cannot be hidden from
        him;
    all their sins are before the Lord.‡

22 Human goodness is like a signet ring
        with God,
    and virtue he keeps like the apple of
        his eye.

---

† **16:24–17:23** In harmony with Gn 1–2, the author describes God's wisdom in creating the universe and everything in it (vv. 24–30), endowing human beings with a moral nature, with wisdom, knowledge, and freedom of will (cf. 15:14) according to his own image (17:1–3, 7). Now they can govern the earth (vv. 3–4), praise God's name (vv. 9–10), obey his law (vv. 11–14), and render to him an account of their deeds (v. 23). Cf. Ps 19; 104.

‡ **17:4** Other ancient texts read as v. 5:
They received the use of the Lord's five faculties;
    of mind, the sixth, he granted them a share,
    as also of speech, the seventh, the interpreter of his
        actions.

**17:12** *An everlasting covenant…his commandments*: God made several covenants, e.g., Gn 9:8–17; 15:17–21; 17:1–22, entered into with humankind, especially on Mount Sinai, where the people saw God's glory and heard his voice (v. 13; cf. Ex 19:16–24:18).

‡ **17:15** Other ancient texts read as v. 16:

Their ways are directed toward evils from their youth,
    and they are unable to make their hearts flesh rather
        than stone.

**17:17** *Ruler*: this may refer to civil officials or to heavenly beings placed over nations as guardians; see note on Dt 32:8, and the cross-references.

‡ **17:17** Other ancient texts read as v. 18:
Israel, as his firstborn, he cares for with chastisement;
    the light of his love he shares with him without neglect.

‡ **17:20** Other ancient texts read as v. 21:
But the Lord, being good and knowing how they are
        formed,
    neither neglected them nor ceased to spare them.

---

**16:26** Gn 1:3–30.
**16:29** Gn 1:11–31.
**17:1** Gn 2:7; 3:19.
**17:2–4** Gn 1:26–28; Ps 8:4–9.
**17:17** Ex 19:5; Dt 4:19–20;
        32:8–9; Dn 10:13–21;
        12:1.

S
I
R

23 Later he will rise up and repay them,
   requiting each one as they deserve.*

### Appeal for a Return to God†

24 But to the penitent he provides a way
   back
   and encourages those who are losing
   hope!

25 Turn back to the Lord and give up your
   sins,
   pray before him and make your
   offenses few.

26 Turn again to the Most High and away
   from iniquity,
   and hate intensely what he loathes.

27† Who in Sheol can glorify the Most
   High*
   in place of the living who offer their
   praise?

28 The dead can no more give praise than
   those who have never lived;
   they who are alive and well glorify the
   Lord.

29 How great is the mercy of the Lord,
   and his forgiveness for those who
   return to him!

30 For not everything is within human
   reach,
   since human beings are not immortal.

31 Is anything brighter than the sun? Yet it
   can be eclipsed.
   How worthless† then the thoughts of
   flesh and blood!

32 God holds accountable the hosts of
   highest heaven,
   while all mortals are dust and ashes.

### The Divine Power and Mercy†

# 18
1 He who lives forever created the
   whole universe;
2 the LORD alone is just.‡

4 To whom has he given power to describe
   his works,
   and who can search out his mighty
   deeds?

5 Who can measure his majestic power,
   or fully recount his mercies?

6 No one can lessen, increase,
   or fathom the wonders of the Lord.

7 When mortals finish, they are only
   beginning,
   and when they stop they are still
   bewildered.

8 What are mortals? What are they worth?
   What is good in them, and what is
   evil?

9 The number of their days seems great
   if it reaches a hundred years.*

10 Like a drop of water from the sea and a
   grain of sand,
   so are these few years among the days
   of eternity.

11 That is why the Lord is patient with
   them
   and pours out his mercy on them.

12 He sees and understands that their death
   is wretched,
   and so he forgives them all the more.

13 Their compassion is for their neighbor,
   but the Lord's compassion reaches all
   flesh,
   Reproving, admonishing, teaching,
   and turning them back, as a shepherd
   his flock.*

14 He has compassion on those who accept
   his discipline,
   who are eager for his precepts.

### The Need for Prudence

15 My child, add no reproach to your
   charity,†
   or spoil any gift by harsh words.

---

† **17:24–32** Ben Sira opens this poem with a prophetic summons to repent, urging sinners to give up their sins and to pray for forgiveness (vv. 24–26, 29). Ben Sira reflects the belief of his day that there was no life after death (vv. 27–28, 30; see note on 11:26–28). Cf. Ez 18:23, 30–32; 33:11–16. See note on Ps 6:6.

**17:27–28** True life consists in praise of God; this is not possible in Sheol.

**17:31** *Worthless:* cf. Gn 6:5. Though moral fault is not excluded, the thought here is the inability to understand the designs of God. Cf. Wis 9:14–18.

**18:1–14** Not only are God's justice and power beyond human understanding (vv. 1–7), his mercy also is boundless and surpasses all human compassion (vv. 8–14); he pities human frailty and mortality.

‡**18:2** Other ancient texts read as v. 3:

He controls the world within the span of his hand,
   and everything obeys his will;
For he in his might is the King of all,
   separating what is holy among them from what is
   profane.

**18:15–27** The practice of charity, especially almsgiving, is an art which avoids every offense to another (vv. 15–18). Prudence directs the changing circumstances of daily life in view of the time of scrutiny (i.e., the day of reckoning, or death, v. 24).

---

* **17:23** Ps 7:17; Jl 4:4, 7; Jer
  23:19; Ez 22:31.
**17:27–28** Ps 6:6; 88:4–7;
  115:17; Is 38:18.
**18:9** Ps 90:10.

**18:13** Ps 23:1–4; Is 40:11;
  49:9–10; Jn 10:11–16;
  Heb 13:20–21; Rev
  7:17.

16 Does not the dew give relief from the
      scorching heat?
   So a word can be better than a gift.
17 Indeed does not a word count more
      than a good gift?
   But both are offered by a kind person.
18 The fool is ungracious and abusive,
   and a grudging gift makes the eyes
      smart.*

19 Before you speak, learn;
   before you get sick, prepare the cure.
20 Before you are judged, examine yourself,
   and at the time of scrutiny you will
      have forgiveness.
21 Before you fall ill, humble yourself;
   and when you have sinned, show
      repentance.†
   Do not delay forsaking your sins;
   do not neglect to do so until you are
      in distress.

22 Let nothing prevent the prompt payment
      of your vows;
   do not wait until death to fulfill
      them.*
23 Before making a vow prepare yourself;
   do not be like one who puts the Lord
      to the test.
24 Think of wrath on the day of death,
   the time of vengeance when he will
      hide his face.*
25 Think of the time of hunger in the time
      of plenty,
   poverty and need in the day of
      wealth.*
26 Between morning and evening there is a
      change of time;
   before the Lord all things are fleeting.

27 The wise are discreet in all things;
   where sin is rife they keep themselves
      from wrongdoing.
28 Every wise person teaches wisdom,†

and those who know her declare her
      praise;
29 Those skilled in words become wise
      themselves,
   and pour forth apt proverbs.

### Self-Control†

30 Do not let your passions be your guide,*
   but keep your desires in check.
31 If you allow yourself to satisfy your
      passions,
   they will make you the laughingstock
      of your enemies.
32 Take no pleasure in too much luxury
   which brings on poverty redoubled.
33 Do not become a glutton and a
      drunkard
   with nothing in your purse.

19 ¹Whoever does this grows no richer;
   those who waste the little they have
      will be stripped bare.
2 Wine and women make the heart
      lustful,
   and the companion of prostitutes
      becomes reckless.*
3 Rottenness and worms will possess
      him,
   and the reckless will be snatched
      away.*
4 Whoever trusts others too quickly has a
      shallow mind,
   and those who sin wrong themselves.

### The Proper Use of Speech†

5 Whoever gloats over evil will be
      destroyed,
6 and whoever repeats gossip has no
      sense.
7 Never repeat gossip,
   and no one will reproach you.*
8 Tell nothing to friend or foe;
   and unless it be a sin for you, do not
      reveal a thing.*

---

18:21 Sickness was often viewed as a punishment for sin;
hence, the need for repentance. Cf. 38:9–10; Jb 15:20–24.
   18:28–29 A general statement on the teaching of wisdom,
serving either as a conclusion to the preceding section or as an
introduction to the following one.
   18:30–19:4 Inordinate gratification of the senses makes people unreasonable, slaves of passion, the laughingstock of their
enemies, and it leads to an untimely death.
   19:5–17 An excellent commentary on bearing false witness
(Ex 20:16; Dt 5:20). Ben Sira speaks harshly about calumny, rash
judgment, and detraction (vv. 5–7), and urges discreet silence

(vv. 8–12). Justice requires that an accused neighbor be given a
hearing, and charity urges fraternal correction; both together fulfill the law of the Most High (vv. 13–17); cf. Mt 7:1–2; 18:15–16.

18:18 Sir 20:14–15.          18:30 Rom 6:12; 13:14;
18:22 Nm 30:3; Dt 23:22;          2 Tm 2:22; Jas
      Ps 50:14; Prv 20:25;          1:14–15.
      Eccl 5:4.                19:2 Prv 20:1; 23:20–28.
18:24 Sir 7:16.              19:3 Gal 6:8.
18:25 Sir 11:25–27.          19:7 Prv 25:10.
                             19:8 Sir 8:18–19.

9  For someone may have heard you and
       watched you,
   and in time come to hate you.
10 Let anything you hear die with you;
   never fear, it will not make you burst!
11 Having heard something, the fool goes
       into labor,
   like a woman giving birth to a child.
12 Like an arrow stuck in a fool's thigh,
   so is gossip in the belly of a fool.
13 Admonish your friend—he may not
       have done it;
   and if he did, that he may not do it
       again.*
14 Admonish your neighbor—he may not
       have said it;
   and if he did, that he may not say it
       again.
15 Admonish your friend—often it may be
       slander;
   do not believe every story.
16 Then, too, a person can slip and not
       mean it;
   who has not sinned with his tongue?*
17 Admonish your neighbor before you
       break with him;
   and give due place to the Law of the
       Most High.‡*

### How to Recognize True Wisdom†

20 All wisdom is fear of the LORD;
   and in all wisdom, the observance of
       the Law.‡*
22 The knowledge of wickedness is not
       wisdom,
   nor is there prudence in the counsel
       of sinners.
23 There is a shrewdness that is detestable,
   while the fool may be free from sin.
24 Better are the God-fearing who have
       little understanding
   than those of great intelligence who
       violate the Law.

25 There is a shrewdness keen but
       dishonest,
   and there are those who are
       duplicitous to win a judgment.
26 There is the villain bowed in grief,
   but full of deceit within.
27 He hides his face and pretends not to
       hear,
   but when not observed, he will take
       advantage of you:
28 Even if his lack of strength keeps him
       from sinning,
   when he finds the right time he will
       do harm.
29 People are known by their appearance;
   the sensible are recognized as such
       when first met.
30 One's attire, hearty laughter, and gait
   proclaim him for what he is.

### Conduct of the Wise and the Foolish

20 ¹There is an admonition that is
       untimely,†
   but the silent person is the wise one.
2 It is much better to admonish than to
       lose one's temper;
3 one who admits a fault will be kept
       from disgrace.
4 Like a eunuch lusting to violate a young
       woman
   is the one who does right under
       compulsion.†
5 One is silent and is thought wise;
   another, for being talkative, is disliked.
6 One is silent, having nothing to say;
   another is silent, biding his time.*
7 The wise remain silent till the right time
       comes,
   but a boasting fool misses the proper
       time.
8 Whoever talks too much is detested;
   whoever pretends to authority is
       hated.

---

‡19:17 Other ancient texts read as vv. 18–19:
18 Fear of the Lord is the beginning of acceptance;
   and wisdom from him obtains love.
19 Knowledge of the Lord's commandments is life-giving
   instruction;
   those who do what pleases him will harvest the fruit of
   the tree of immortality.
19:20–30 True wisdom is contrasted with a dishonest shrewdness.
‡19:20 Other ancient texts read as v. 21:
   The slave who says to his master, "What pleases you I will
   not do"—
   even if he does it later, provokes the one who feeds him.

20:1–8 The wise know the proper times for speech and silence, that is, the occasions when the most benefit can be gained
from them. On the ambiguity of silences, see Prv 17:27–28.
20:4 Force can prevent an external act of sin or compel a
good deed, but it does not eliminate the internal sin or desire
of wrongdoing.

19:13 Lv 19:17; Mt 18:15;        19:20 Sir 1:1, 12, 14; Jb
   Lk 17:3.                          28:28; Ps 111:10; Prv
19:16 Sir 14:1; Jas 3:2.             1:7; 9:10.
19:17 Lv 19:17.                   20:5–6 Prv 17:27–28.

9  There is the misfortune that brings
       success;†
   and there is the gain that turns into
       loss.
10 There is the gift that profits you nothing,
   and there is the gift that must be paid
       back double.
11 There is the loss for the sake of glory,
   and there is the one who rises above
       humble circumstances.
12 There is one who buys much for little,
   but pays for it seven times over.
13 The wise make themselves beloved by a
       few words,
   but the courtesies of fools are wasted.
14 A gift from a fool will do you no good,
   for in his eyes this one gift is equal to
       many.
15 He gives little, criticizes often,
   and opens his mouth like a town
       crier.
   He lends today and asks for it
       tomorrow;
   such a person is hateful.
16 A fool says, "I have no friends
   nor thanks for my generosity."
   Those who eat his bread have a mocking
       tongue.
17 How many will ridicule him, and how
       often!

18 A slip on the floor is better than a slip of
       the tongue;†
   in like manner the downfall of the
       wicked comes quickly.
19 A coarse person, an untimely story;
   the ignorant are always ready to offer
       it.
20 A proverb spoken by a fool is
       unwelcome,
   for he does not tell it at the proper
       time.

21 There is a person whose poverty prevents
       him from sinning,
   but when he takes his rest he has no
       regrets.
22 There is a person who is destroyed
       through shame,
   and ruined by foolish posturing.
23 There is one who promises a friend out
       of shame,
   and so makes an enemy needlessly.

24 A lie is a foul blot in a person,
   yet it is always on the lips of the
       ignorant.
25 A thief is better than an inveterate liar,
   yet both will suffer ruin.
26 A liar's way leads to dishonor,
   and his shame remains ever with
       him.

27 The wise gain promotion with few
       words,†
   the prudent please the great.
28 Those who work the land have
       abundant crops,
   and those who please the great are
       pardoned their faults.
29 Favors and gifts blind the eyes;
   like a muzzle over the mouth they
       silence reproofs.*
30 Hidden wisdom and unseen treasure—
   what value has either?
31 Better are those who hide their folly
   than those who hide their wisdom.‡

## Dangers from Sin†

**21** ¹ My child, if you have sinned, do so
       no more,
   and for your past sins pray to be
       forgiven.
2  Flee from sin as from a serpent
   that will bite you if you go near it;
   Its teeth, lion's teeth,
       destroying human lives.
3  All lawlessness is like a two-edged
       sword;
   when it cuts, there is no healing.*

---

† **20:9–17** In a series of paradoxes the author indicates how much true and lasting values differ from apparent ones.
**20:18–26** The ill-timed speech brings disaster (vv. 18–20); human respect may lead to rash promises and enmity (vv. 22–23); lies bring dishonor and lasting disgrace (vv. 24–26).
**20:27–31** Through prudent speech the wise gain honor and esteem among the great (vv. 27–28). They must beware, however, of accepting bribes, lest they share in evil through silence when they should reprove (vv. 29–31).
‡**20:31** Other ancient texts read as v. 32:

It is better to await the inevitable while serving the Lord than to be the ungoverned helmsman for the careening of one's life.
**21:1–10** Under various figures, the consequences of sin are described as destructive of wealth, and even of life, deserving of death (vv. 2–4, 6a, 8–10). Fear of the Lord motivates repentance (vv. 5, 6b).

---

* **20:29** Ex 23:8; Dt 16:19.          **21:3** Prv 5:4.

S
I
R

4 Panic and pride wipe out wealth;
    so too the house of the proud is
    uprooted.
5 Prayer from the lips of the poor is heard
    at once,
    and justice is quickly granted them.
6 Whoever hates correction walks the
    sinner's path,*
    but whoever fears the Lord repents in
    his heart.
7 Glib speakers are widely known,
    but when they slip the sensible
    perceive it.
8 Those who build their houses with
    someone else's money
    are like those who collect stones for
    their funeral mounds.
9 A band of criminals is like a bundle of
    tow;
    they will end in a flaming fire.*
10 The path of sinners is smooth stones,
    but its end is the pit of Sheol.†

## The Wise and Foolish: A Contrast†

11 Those who keep the Law control their
    thoughts;
    perfect fear of the Lord is wisdom.
12 One who is not clever can never be
    taught,
    but there is a cleverness filled with
    bitterness.

13 The knowledge of the wise wells up like
    a flood,
    and their counsel like a living
    spring.*
14 A fool's mind is like a broken jar:
    it cannot hold any knowledge at all.

15 When the intelligent hear a wise
    saying,
    they praise it and add to it.
    The wanton hear it with distaste
    and cast it behind their back.

16 A fool's chatter is like a load on a
    journey,
    but delight is to be found on the lips
    of the intelligent.
17 The views of the prudent are sought in
    an assembly,
    and their words are taken to heart.

18 Like a house in ruins is wisdom to a
    fool;
    to the stupid, knowledge is
    incomprehensible chatter.
19 To the senseless, education is fetters on
    the feet,
    like manacles on the right hand.
20 Fools raise their voice in laughter,
    but the prudent at most smile
    quietly.*
21 Like a gold ornament is education to the
    wise,
    like a bracelet on the right arm.

22 A fool steps boldly into a house,
    while the well-bred are slow to make
    an entrance.*
23 A boor peeps through the doorway of a
    house,
    but the educated stay outside.
24 It is rude for one to listen at a door;
    the discreet person would be
    overwhelmed by the disgrace.

25 The lips of the arrogant talk of what is
    not their concern,
    but the discreet carefully weigh their
    words.
26 The mind of fools is in their mouths,
    but the mouth of the wise is in their
    mind.†
27 When the godless curse their
    adversary,†
    they really curse themselves.
28 Slanderers sully themselves,
    and are hated by their neighbors.

---

† **21:10** *The path of sinners…Sheol*: Ben Sira refers to the death that awaits unrepentant sinners; see notes on 11:26–28; 17:24–32.
**21:11–28** The mind of the wise is a fountain of knowledge (vv. 13, 15); their will is trained to keep the Law (v. 11); their words are gracious, valued, carefully weighed, sincere (vv. 16–17, 25–26); their conduct is respectful, cultured and restrained (vv. 20, 22–24). The mind of the foolish is devoid of knowledge and impenetrable to it (vv. 12, 14, 18–19); their will rejects it (v. 15); their talk is burdensome (v. 16), their laughter unrestrained (v. 20), their conversation shallow and meddlesome (vv. 25–26);

their conduct is bold and rude (vv. 22–24); their abuse of others redounds on themselves (vv. 27–28).
**21:26** A clever play on words.
**21:27** *Curse their adversary*: the curse of the godless often recoils on their own head; cf. Gn 27:29; Nm 24:9.

**21:6** Prv 12:1.                            18:4.
**21:9** Sir 16:6; Ps 21:10.        **21:20** Eccl 7:6.
**21:13** Prv 13:14; 16:22;        **21:22** Prv 25:17.

## On Laziness and Foolishness

**22** ¹† The sluggard is like a filthy stone;† everyone hisses at his disgrace.

² The sluggard is like a lump of dung;
   whoever touches it shakes it off the
      hands.

³ An undisciplined child is a disgrace to
      its father;
   if it be a daughter, she brings him to
      poverty.*

⁴ A thoughtful daughter obtains a
      husband of her own;
   a shameless one is her father's grief.

⁵ A hussy shames her father and her
      husband;
   she is despised by both.

⁶ Like music at the time of mourning is
      ill-timed talk,†
   but lashes and discipline are at all
      times wisdom.‡

⁹ Teaching a fool is like gluing a broken
      pot,*
   or rousing another from deep sleep.

¹⁰ Whoever talks with a fool talks to
      someone asleep;
   when it is over, he says, "What was
      that?"

¹¹ Weep over the dead, for their light has
      gone out;
   weep over the fool, for sense has left
      him.
   Weep but less bitterly over the dead, for
      they are at rest;
   worse than death is the life of a fool.

¹² Mourning for the dead, seven days—*
   but for the wicked fool, a whole
      lifetime.

¹³ Do not talk much with the stupid,
   or visit the unintelligent.
   Beware of them lest you have trouble
   and be spattered when they shake
      themselves off.
   Avoid them and you will find rest
   and not be wearied by their lack of
      sense.

¹⁴ What is heavier than lead?
   What is its name but "Fool"?

¹⁵ Sand, salt, and an iron weight
   are easier to bear than the stupid
      person.*

¹⁶ A wooden beam firmly bonded into a
      building†
   is not loosened by an earthquake;
   So the mind firmly resolved after careful
      deliberation
   will not be afraid at any time.

¹⁷ The mind solidly backed by intelligent
      thought
   is like a stucco decoration on a
      smooth wall.

¹⁸ Small stones lying on an open height
   will not remain when the wind
      blows;
   So a timid mind based on foolish plans
   cannot stand up to fear of any kind.

### The Preservation of Friendship†

¹⁹ Whoever jabs the eye brings tears;
   whoever pierces the heart bares its
      feelings.

²⁰ Whoever throws a stone at birds drives
      them away;
   whoever insults a friend breaks up the
      friendship.

²¹ Should you draw a sword against a
      friend,
   do not despair, for it can be undone.

---

**22:1–15** To Ben Sira, a lazy person and an unruly child are a cause of shame and disgrace; everyone wishes to be rid of them (vv. 1–5). Speaking with a wicked fool is as senseless as talking with someone who is asleep or dead (v. 10). The fool is an intolerable burden that merits a lifetime of mourning (v. 12). Seven days was the usual mourning period. Cf. Gn 50:10; Jdt 16:24.

**22:1** *Stone*: used then and even today for wiping oneself after a bowel movement.

**22:6** As a joyful song is out of place among mourners so a rebuke may be insufficient when corporal punishment is called for.

‡**22:6** Other ancient texts read as vv. 7–8:
  ⁷ Children whose upbringing leads to a wholesome life
     veil over the lowly origins of their parents.
  ⁸ Children whose pride is in scornful misconduct
     besmirch the nobility of their own family.

**22:16–18** A prudent mind firmly resolved is undisturbed by violent and conflicting thoughts, whereas a foolish person is tossed about by the winds of fear, like small stones whipped about by high winds.

**22:19–26** Disputes and violence weaken friendship, and disloyalty and abuse of confidence destroy it utterly (vv. 19–22, 24, 26); but kindness to a poor person in time of poverty and adversity builds up friendship and merits a share in his prosperity and inheritance (vv. 23, 25).

---

**22:3** Prv 10:1; 17:21, 25;
   19:13.
**22:9–12** Prv 23:9.
**22:12** Gn 50:10; Jdt 16:24.
**22:15** Prv 27:3.

22 Should you open your mouth against a
        friend,
    do not worry, for you can be
        reconciled.
    But a contemptuous insult, a confidence
        broken,
    or a treacherous attack will drive any
        friend away.

23 Win your neighbor's trust while he is
        poor,
    so that you may rejoice with him in
        his prosperity.
    In time of trouble remain true to him,
        so that you may share in his
        inheritance when it comes.

24 The billowing smoke of a furnace
        precedes the fire,
    so insults precede bloodshed.

25 I am not ashamed to shelter a friend,
    and I will not hide from him.

26 But if harm should come to me because
        of him,
    all who hear of it will beware of him.

### Prayer†

27 Who will set a guard over my mouth,
    an effective seal on my lips,
    That I may not fail through them,
    and my tongue may not destroy me?*

# 23

1 Lord, Father and Master of my life,†
    do not abandon me to their designs,
    do not let me fall because of them!

2 Who will apply the lash to my thoughts,
    and to my mind the rod of discipline,
    That my failings may not be spared
    or the sins of my heart overlooked?

3 Otherwise my failings may increase,
    and my sins be multiplied;
    And I fall before my adversaries,
    and my enemy rejoice over me?

4 Lord, Father and God of my life,
    do not give me haughty eyes;

5 remove evil desire from my heart.

6 Let neither gluttony nor lust overcome
        me;
    do not give me up to shameless
        desires.*

### Proper Use of the Tongue†

7 Listen, my children, to instruction
        concerning the mouth,
    for whoever keeps it will not be
        ensnared.

8 Through the lips the sinner is caught;
    by them the reviler and the arrogant
        are tripped up.

9 Do not accustom your mouth to oaths,
    or habitually utter the Holy Name.*

10 Just as a servant constantly under
        scrutiny
    will not be without bruises,
    So one who swears continually by the
        Holy Name
    will never remain free from sin.

11 Those who swear many oaths heap up
        offenses;
    and the scourge will never be far from
        their houses.
    If they swear in error, guilt is incurred;
    if they neglect their obligation, the sin
        is doubly great.*
    If they swear without reason they cannot
        be declared innocent,
    for their households will be filled
        with calamities.

12 There are words comparable to death;
    may they never be heard in the
        inheritance of Jacob.
    To the devout all such words are foreign;
    they do not wallow in sin.

13 Do not accustom your mouth to coarse
        talk,
    for it involves sinful speech.

14 Keep your father and mother in mind
        when you sit among the mighty,*
    Lest you forget yourself in their presence

---

**22:27–23:6** Ben Sira implores the divine assistance to preserve him through stern discipline from sins of the tongue
(22:27; 23:1), from ignorance of mind and weakness of will (vv.
2–3), and from inclinations of the senses and the flesh, lest he
fall into the hands of his enemies or become a prey of shameful
desires (vv. 4–6).

**23:1–6** *Lord, Father and Master of my life*: these words express the tender personal relationship Ben Sira experiences with
God, and introduce his prayer for divine assistance and providence in avoiding sins of pride and lust.

**23:7–15** A warning against sins of the tongue through misuse
of the sacred Name, against thoughtless swearing (vv. 7–11),
blasphemy (v. 12), coarse talk (vv. 13–14), and abusive language
(v. 15).

---

22:27 Ps 141:3.              Mt 5:33–37; Jas 5:12.
23:6 Rom 13:13.              23:11 Lv 5:4–10.
23:9 Ex 20:7; Lv 19:12;      23:14 Sir 7:27; Ex 20:12; Dt
    24:16; Dt 5:11;              5:16.

and disgrace your upbringing.
Then you will wish you had never been
    born
and will curse the day of your birth.

15 Those accustomed to using abusive
        language
    will never acquire discipline as long as
        they live.

### Sins of the Flesh†

16 Two types of people multiply sins,
    and a third† draws down wrath:
    Burning passion is like a blazing fire,
        not to be quenched till it burns itself
        out;
    One unchaste with his kindred
        never stops until fire breaks forth.
17 To the unchaste all bread is sweet;
    he is never through till he dies.*

18 The man who dishonors his marriage
        bed
    says to himself, "Who can see me?
    Darkness surrounds me, walls hide me,
        no one sees me. Who can stop me
        from sinning?"*
    He is not mindful of the Most High,
19    fearing only human eyes.
    He does not realize that the eyes of the
        Lord,
    ten thousand times brighter than the
        sun,
    Observe every step taken
        and peer into hidden corners.
20 The one who knows all things before
        they exist
    still knows them all after they are
        made.
21 Such a man will be denounced in the
        streets of the city;*
    and where he least suspects it, he will
        be apprehended.

22 So it is with the woman unfaithful to
        her husband,
    who offers him an heir by another
        man.
23 First of all, she has disobeyed the law of
        the Most High;
    second, she has wronged her
        husband;
    Third, through her wanton adultery
        she has brought forth children by
        another man.
24 Such a woman will be dragged before
        the assembly,†
    and her punishment will extend to
        her children.
25 Her children will not take root;
    her branches will not bring forth fruit.
26 She will leave behind an accursed
        memory;
    her disgrace will never be blotted out.

27 Thus all who dwell on the earth shall
        know,
    all who remain in the world shall
        understand,
    That nothing is better than the fear of
        the Lord,
    nothing sweeter than obeying the
        commandments of the Lord.* ‡

### Praise of Wisdom

24 ¹ Wisdom sings her own praises,†
    among her own people she proclaims
        her glory.
2 In the assembly of the Most High she
        opens her mouth,
    in the presence of his host she tells of
        her glory:

3 "From the mouth of the Most High I
        came forth,*
    and covered the earth like a mist.

---

† **23:16–27** Ben Sira treats sexual sins and their consequences. Lust destroys its victims (vv. 16–17, 22–26). A false sense of security aggravates the adulterer's inevitable fate (vv. 18–21).

**23:16** *Two types…a third*: a numerical proverb, as in 25:1–2, 7–11; 26:5–6, 28; 50:25–26; Prv 6:16–19; 30:15b–16, 18–19, 21–23, 29–31. Ben Sira condemns three kinds of sexual sin: incest (v. 16), fornication (v. 17), and adultery (vv. 18–26).

**23:24–25** The judgment of the assembly determined the illegitimacy of children born of adultery or incest and excluded them from the "community of the Lord" (Dt 23:3). Cf. Wis 3:16–19; 4:3–6.

‡**23:27** Other ancient texts read as v. 28:
    It is a great glory to follow after God,
    and for you to be received by him is length of days.

**24:1–29** Wisdom speaks in the first person, describing her origin, her dwelling place in Israel, and the reward she gives her followers. As in Proverbs 8, Wisdom is personified as coming from God, yet distinct from him. This description is reflected in the Johannine *logos*, or Word (Jn 1:1–14). It is used extensively in the Roman liturgy.

**23:17** Prv 9:17.
**23:18–19** Jb 24:15; Prv 15:3, 11; 17:3; 24:12; Is 29:15; Ez 8:12.
**23:21–22** Lv 18:20; 20:10; Dt 22:21–22.
**23:27** Sir 1:11–30; Prv 3:1–2.
**24:3–6** Sir 1:1–4; Prv 2:6; 8:22–36; Wis 7:24–25.

<sup>4</sup> In the heights of heaven I dwelt,
and my throne was in a pillar of
cloud.
<sup>5</sup> The vault of heaven I compassed alone,
and walked through the deep abyss.
<sup>6</sup> Over waves of the sea, over all the land,
over every people and nation I held
sway.
<sup>7</sup> Among all these I sought a resting place.
In whose inheritance should I abide?

<sup>8</sup> "Then the Creator of all gave me his
command,
and my Creator chose the spot for my
tent.
He said, 'In Jacob make your dwelling,
in Israel your inheritance.'
<sup>9</sup> Before all ages, from the beginning, he
created me,
and through all ages I shall not cease
to be.
<sup>10</sup> In the holy tent I ministered before him,
and so I was established in Zion.
<sup>11</sup> In the city he loves as he loves me, he
gave me rest;
in Jerusalem, my domain.
<sup>12</sup> I struck root among the glorious people,
in the portion of the Lord, his
heritage.

<sup>13</sup> "Like a cedar in Lebanon I grew tall,
like a cypress on Mount Hermon;
<sup>14</sup> I grew tall like a palm tree in Engedi,
like rosebushes in Jericho;
Like a fair olive tree in the field,
like a plane tree beside water I grew
tall.
<sup>15</sup> Like cinnamon and fragrant cane,
like precious myrrh I gave forth
perfume;
Like galbanum and onycha and mastic,*
like the odor of incense in the holy
tent.†

<sup>16</sup> "I spread out my branches like a terebinth,
my branches so glorious and so
graceful.
<sup>17</sup> I bud forth delights like a vine;
my blossoms are glorious and rich
fruit.‡
<sup>19</sup> Come to me, all who desire me,
and be filled with my fruits.†
<sup>20</sup> You will remember me as sweeter than
honey,
better to have than the honeycomb.
<sup>21</sup> Those who eat of me will hunger still,†
those who drink of me will thirst for
more.*
<sup>22</sup> Whoever obeys me will not be put to
shame,
and those who serve me will never go
astray."

<sup>23</sup> All this is the book of the covenant of
the Most High God,*
the Law which Moses commanded us†
as a heritage for the community of
Jacob.‡
<sup>25</sup> It overflows, like the Pishon, with
wisdom,*
and like the Tigris at the time of first
fruits.
<sup>26</sup> It runs over, like the Euphrates, with
understanding,
and like the Jordan at harvest time.
<sup>27</sup> It floods like the Nile with instruction,
like the Gihon† at vintage time.
<sup>28</sup> The first human being never finished
comprehending wisdom,
nor will the last succeed in fathoming
her.
<sup>29</sup> For deeper than the sea are her thoughts,
and her counsels, than the great abyss.

<sup>30</sup> Now I, like a stream from a river,†
and like water channeling into a
garden—

---

**24:15** These substances, associated with worship, are mentioned in Ex 30:23–28, 34–35 as the ingredients of the anointing oil and the sacred incense. Israel was a priestly nation (Ex 19:6; Is 61:6).
‡**24:17** Other ancient texts read as v. 18:
I am the mother of fair love, of reverence,
of knowledge, and of holy hope;
To all my children I give
to be everlasting: to those named by Him.
**24:19** Mt 11:28–30 contains a similar invitation.
**24:21** The paradox of wisdom is that, far from being satiated, those who partake of her will always desire more.
**24:23** Ben Sira now identifies Wisdom and the law of Moses; see also Bar 4:1.

‡**24:23** Other ancient texts read as v. 24:
Do not grow weary of striving with the Lord's help,
but cling to him that he may reinforce you.
The Lord Almighty alone is God,
and apart from him there is no savior.
**24:27** *Gihon*: understood by some to have been a name for the Nile; cf. Gn 2:13.
**24:30–33** Ben Sira again speaks about himself. He had at first drawn a small portion of the water of wisdom for his own

---

24:15 Ex 30:23–28, 34–35.          24:23 Ex 24:7.
24:21 Is 55:1; Jn 4:10–14;          24:23–27 Gn 2:11–14.
6:35.

31 I said, "I will water my plants,
   I will drench my flower beds."
Then suddenly this stream of mine
   became a river,
   and this river of mine became a sea.
32 Again I will make my teachings shine
   forth like the dawn;
   I will spread their brightness afar off.
33 Again I will pour out instruction like
   prophecy
   and bestow it on generations yet to
   come.

### Those Who Are Worthy of Praise

**25** 1† With three things I am delighted,
   for they are pleasing to the Lord and
   to human beings:
Harmony among relatives, friendship
   among neighbors,
   and a wife and a husband living
   happily together.
2 Three kinds of people I hate,
   and I loathe their manner of life:
A proud pauper, a rich liar,
   and a lecherous old fool.

3 In your youth you did not gather.
   How will you find anything in your
   old age?
4 How appropriate is sound judgment in
   the gray-haired,
   and good counsel in the elderly!
5 How appropriate is wisdom in the aged,
   understanding and counsel in the
   venerable!
6 The crown of the elderly, wide
   experience;
   their glory, the fear of the Lord.

7 There are nine who come to mind as
   blessed,
   a tenth whom my tongue proclaims:†
The man who finds joy in his children,
   and the one who lives to see the
   downfall of his enemies.

8 Happy the man who lives with a
   sensible woman,
   and the one who does not plow with
   an ox and a donkey combined.†
Happy the one who does not sin with
   the tongue,
   who does not serve an inferior.
9 Happy the one who finds a friend,
   who speaks to attentive ears.
10 How great is the one who finds wisdom,
   but none is greater than the one who
   fears the Lord.
11 Fear of the Lord surpasses all else.
   To whom can we compare the one
   who has it?‡

### Wicked and Virtuous Women†

13 Any wound, but not a wound of the
   heart!
Any wickedness, but not the
   wickedness of a woman!
14 Any suffering, but not suffering from
   one's foes!
Any vengeance, but not the vengeance
   of one's enemies!
15 There is no poison worse than that of a
   serpent,
   no venom greater than that of a
   woman.
16 I would rather live with a dragon or a
   lion
   than live with a wicked woman.*
17 A woman's wicked disposition changes
   her appearance,
   and makes her face as dark as a bear.
18 When her husband sits among his
   neighbors,
   a bitter sigh escapes him unawares.
19 There is hardly an evil like that in a
   woman;
   may she fall to the lot of the sinner!
20 Like a sandy hill to aged feet
   is a garrulous wife to a quiet husband.
21 Do not be enticed by a woman's beauty,

---

† private benefit, but finding it so useful, he soon began to let others share in this boon by teaching them the lessons of wisdom. Like the words of the prophets, Ben Sira's instruction is valuable for all generations (v. 33). The comparison to prophecy is bold and unique.
**25:1–2** A numerical saying in threes.
**25:7–11** A numerical proverb (9 + 1), in which the tenth element, "the one who fears the Lord," is the most important.
**25:8** *An ox and a donkey combined*: the reference is to a man married to two incompatible women (cf. 37:11a); the imagery derives from Dt 22:10.

‡**25:11** Other ancient texts read as v. 12:
   Fear of the Lord is the beginning of loving him,
      and fidelity is the beginning of clinging to him.
**25:13–26** The harsh statements Ben Sira makes about women reflect the kind of instruction young Jewish males were exposed to in the early second century B.C. His patriarchal perspective is as unfair as it is one-sided.

**25:16** Prv 21:9, 19; 25:24; 27:15.

S
I
R

or be greedy for her wealth.

22 Harsh is the slavery and great the shame
   when a wife supports her husband.

23 Depressed mind, gloomy face,
   and a wounded heart—a wicked
   woman.
   Drooping hands and quaking knees,
   any wife who does not make her
   husband happy.

24 With a woman sin had a beginning,
   and because of her we all die.†

25 Allow water no outlet,
   and no boldness of speech to a
   wicked woman.

26 If she does not go along as you direct,
   cut her away from you.

# 26

1 Happy the husband of a good wife;†
the number of his days will be
doubled.*

2 A loyal wife brings joy to her husband,
   and he will finish his years in peace.

3 A good wife is a generous gift
   bestowed upon him who fears the
   Lord.*

4 Whether rich or poor, his heart is content,
   a smile ever on his face.

5 There are three things I dread,
   and a fourth which terrifies me:
   Public slander, the gathering of a mob,
   and false accusation—all harder to
   bear than death.

6 A wife jealous of another wife is
   heartache and mourning;†
   everyone feels the lash of her tongue.

7 A wicked wife is a chafing yoke;
   taking hold of her is like grasping a
   scorpion.

8 A drunken wife arouses great anger,
   for she does not hide her shame.

9 By her haughty stare and her eyelids
   an unchaste wife can be recognized.

10 Keep a strict watch over an unruly wife,
   lest, finding an opportunity, she use
   it;*

11 Watch out for her impudent eye,
   and do not be surprised if she betrays
   you:

12 As a thirsty traveler opens his mouth
   and drinks from any water nearby,
   So she sits down before every tent peg
   and opens her quiver for every
   arrow.

13 A gracious wife delights her husband;
   her thoughtfulness puts flesh on his
   bones.

14 A silent wife is a gift from the Lord;
   nothing is worth more than her self-
   discipline.

15 A modest wife is a supreme blessing;
   no scales can weigh the worth of her
   chastity.

16 The sun rising in the Lord's heavens—
   the beauty of a good wife in her well-
   ordered home.

17 The light which shines above the holy
   lampstand—†
   a beautiful face on a stately figure.

18 Golden columns on silver bases—
   so her shapely legs and steady feet.‡

---

† **25:24** Ben Sira refers to the story of the first sin in Gn 3:1–6.
Cf. 2 Cor 11:3 and 1 Tm 2:14. St. Paul, however, singles out
Adam; cf. Rom 5:12–19; 1 Cor 15:22.
**26:1–4, 13–18** A good wife is as a gift from God, bringing
joy and peace, happiness and contentment to her husband (vv.
1–4) through her thoughtfulness, reserve, modesty and chastity,
beauty, grace, and virtue (vv. 13–18).
**26:6–12** A repetition of the thought expressed in
25:13–26.
**26:17–18** The lampstand and the columns were located in
the holy place of the ancient tabernacle (Ex 25:31–40; 26:32).
‡**26:18** Other ancient texts read as vv. 19–27:
¹⁹My child, keep intact the bloom of your youth,
   and do not give your strength to strangers.
²⁰Seek out a fertile field from all the land,
   and sow it with your own seed, confident in your fine
   stock.
²¹So shall your offspring prosper,
   and grow great, confident in their good descent.
²²A woman for hire is regarded as spittle,
   but a married woman is a deadly snare for her lovers.

²³A godless wife will be given to the lawless man as his portion,
   but a godly wife will be given to the man who fears the
   Lord.
²⁴A shameless woman wears out reproach,
   but a virtuous daughter will be modest even before her
   husband.
²⁵A headstrong wife is regarded as a bitch,
   but the one with a sense of shame fears the Lord.
²⁶The wife who honors her husband will seem wise to
   everyone,
   but if she dishonors him in her pride, she will be
   known to everyone as ungodly.
   Happy is the husband of a good wife,
   for the number of his years will be doubled.
²⁷A loud-mouthed and garrulous wife will be regarded
   as a trumpet sounding the charge,
   And every person who lives like this
   will spend his life in the anarchy of war.

---

**26:1** Sir 25:8; Prv 18:22.          **26:10** Sir 42:11.
**26:3** Sir 36:27–29.

### Dangers to Integrity and Friendship

28† Two things bring grief to my heart,
   and a third arouses my anger:
The wealthy reduced to want,
   the intelligent held in contempt,
And those who pass from righteousness
      to sin—
   the Lord prepares them for the
      sword.*

29 A merchant can hardly keep from
      wrongdoing,
   nor can a shopkeeper stay free from
      sin;

# 27

¹ For the sake of profit many sin,
   and the struggle for wealth blinds the
      eyes.*

² A stake will be driven between fitted
      stones—
   sin will be wedged in between buying
      and selling.

³ Unless one holds fast to the fear of the
      Lord,
   with sudden swiftness will one's
      house be thrown down.

⁴ When a sieve is shaken, the husks appear;
   so do people's faults when they
      speak.†

⁵ The furnace tests the potter's vessels;
   the test of a person is in
      conversation.*

⁶ The fruit of a tree shows the care it has
      had;
   so speech discloses the bent of a
      person's heart.*

⁷ Praise no one before he speaks,
   for it is then that people are tested.

⁸ If you strive after justice, you will attain it,
   and wear it like a splendid robe.

⁹ Birds nest with their own kind,
   and honesty comes to those who
      work at it.

¹⁰ A lion lies in wait for prey,
   so does sin for evildoers.

¹¹ The conversation of the godly is always
      wisdom,
   but the fool changes like the moon.

¹² Limit the time you spend among the
      stupid,
   but frequent the company of the
      thoughtful.

¹³ The conversation of fools is offensive,
   and their laughter is wanton sin.

¹⁴ Their oath-filled talk makes the hair
      stand on end,
   and their brawls make one stop the
      ears.

¹⁵ The wrangling of the proud ends in
      bloodshed,
   and their cursing is painful to hear.*

¹⁶ Whoever betrays a secret destroys
      confidence,†
   and will never find a congenial
      friend.*

¹⁷ Cherish your friend, keep faith with him;
   but if you betray his secrets, do not go
      after him;

¹⁸ For as one might kill another,
   you have killed your neighbor's
      friendship.

¹⁹ Like a bird released from your hand,
   you have let your friend go and
      cannot recapture him.

²⁰ Do not go after him, for he is far away,
   and has escaped like a gazelle from a
      snare.

²¹ For a wound can be bandaged, and an
      insult forgiven,
   but whoever betrays secrets does
      hopeless damage.*

---

† **26:28–27:15** From proper conduct in family life, Ben Sira proceeds to social morality, warning especially against injustice in business (26:29–27:3), and perversity of speech in daily life (27:4–7). The pursuit of justice in these matters is all the more meritorious as it is difficult (27:8–10). The discourses of the godly are marked with wisdom, but the conversations of the wicked with offense, swearing, cursing, quarrels, and even bloodshed (27:11–15).
**27:4–7, 11–15** The importance of effective speech is a favorite wisdom topic; e.g., cf. 20:1–8, 18–20; 22:27–23:15.
**27:16–28:11** Betrayal of confidence through indiscretion destroys friendship and does irreparable harm (27:16–21); cf. 22:22. False friendship based on hypocrisy and deceit is hateful

to Ben Sira and, he adds, to God as well (27:22–24); it soon becomes a victim of its own treachery (27:25–27). The same fate awaits the malicious and vengeful (27:28–28:1). They can obtain mercy and forgiveness only by first forgiving their neighbor, being mindful of death and of the commandments of the Most High (28:2–7). And they must avoid quarrels and strife (28:8–11).

---

* 
**26:28** Ez 18:24–29.        **27:6** Mt 7:20.
**27:1** Sir 7:18; 31:5–6; Prv   **27:15** Sir 23:8–15.
   30:7–9.                       **27:16** Prv 11:13; 20:19.
**27:5** 1 Pt 1:7.             **27:21** Sir 22:20.

S
I
R

## Malice, Anger and Vengeance

22 Whoever has shifty eyes plots mischief
   and those who know him will keep
      their distance;

23 In your presence he uses honeyed talk,
      and admires your words,
   But later he changes his tone
      and twists the words to your ruin.*

24 I have hated many things but not as
      much as him,
   and the Lord hates him as well.*

25 A stone falls back on the head of the
      one who throws it high,*
   and a treacherous blow causes many
      wounds.

26 Whoever digs a pit falls into it,
   and whoever lays a snare is caught in
      it.†

27 The evil anyone does will recoil on
      him
   without knowing how it came upon
      him.

28 Mockery and abuse will befall the
      arrogant,
   and vengeance lies in wait for them
      like a lion.

29 Those who rejoice in the downfall of the
      godly will be caught in a snare,
   and pain will consume them before
      they die.

30 Wrath and anger, these also are
      abominations,
   yet a sinner holds on to them.

# 28

1 The vengeful will face the Lord's
      vengeance;
   indeed he remembers their sins in
      detail.*

2 Forgive your neighbor the wrong done
      to you;
   then when you pray, your own sins
      will be forgiven.*

3 Does anyone nourish anger against
      another
   and expect healing from the LORD?*

4 Can one refuse mercy to a sinner like
      oneself,
   yet seek pardon for one's own sins?

5 If a mere mortal cherishes wrath,
   who will forgive his sins?

6 Remember your last days and set enmity
      aside;
   remember death and decay, and cease
      from sin!*

7 Remember the commandments and do
      not be angry with your neighbor;
   remember the covenant of the Most
      High, and overlook faults.

8 Avoid strife and your sins will be fewer,
   for the hot-tempered kindle strife;

9 The sinner disrupts friendships
   and sows discord among those who
      are at peace.*

10 The more the wood, the greater the fire,*
   the more the cruelty, the fiercer the
      strife;
   The greater the strength, the sterner the
      anger,
   the greater the wealth, the greater the
      wrath.

11 Pitch and resin make fire flare up,
   and a hasty quarrel provokes
      bloodshed.

## The Evil Tongue†

12 If you blow on a spark, it turns into
      flame,
   if you spit on it, it dies out;
   yet both you do with your mouth!

13 Cursed be gossips and the double-
      tongued,
   for they destroy the peace of many.*

14 A meddlesome tongue subverts many,
   and makes them refugees among
      peoples.
   It destroys strong cities,

S
I
R

---

† **27:26** This expresses a popular idea of act and consequence;
an evil (or good) deed is repaid by an evil (or good) result. The
frequent metaphor is the digging of a hole for another to fall into;
cf. Prv 26:27; Ps 7:14; 9:16; Eccl 10:8.

**28:12–26** Further treatment of sins of the tongue and the
havoc that results; cf. 5:9–6:1; 19:5–17; 20:18–26; 23:7–15.
Gossips and the double-tongued destroy domestic peace (vv.
12–16). The whip, the sword, chains, even Sheol, are not so
cruel as the suffering inflicted by an evil tongue (vv. 17–21). Not
the godly but those who forsake the Lord are victims of their evil

tongues (vv. 22–23). Therefore, guard your mouth and tongue as
you would guard treasure against an enemy (vv. 24–26).

* ————————————————
  **27:23** Prv 26:24–28.            **28:3** Mt 18:23–35.
  **27:24** Prv 6:16–19.             **28:6** Sir 7:36; 38:20.
  **27:25–27** Ps 7:16–17; Prv       **28:9** Prv 15:18.
     26:27; Eccl 10:8.               **28:10–11** Prv 26:20–21.
  **28:1** Dt 32:35; Rom 12:19.      **28:13** Sir 5:13–6:1.
  **28:2** Mt 6:14.

and overthrows the houses of the
    great.

15  A meddlesome tongue drives virtuous
        women from their homes,
    and robs them of the fruit of their
        toil.

16  Whoever heed it will find no rest,
    nor will they dwell in peace.

17  A blow from a whip raises a welt,
    but a blow from the tongue will break
        bones.

18  Many have fallen by the edge of the
        sword,
    but not as many as by the tongue.*

19  Happy the one who is sheltered from it,
    and has not endured its wrath;
    Who has not borne its yoke
    nor been bound with its chains.

20  For its yoke is a yoke of iron,
    and its chains are chains of bronze;

21  The death it inflicts is an evil death,
    even Sheol is preferable to it.

22  It will have no power over the godly,
    nor will they be burned in its flame.

23  But those who forsake the Lord will fall
        victim to it,
    as it burns among them
        unquenchably;
    It will hurl itself against them like a lion,
    and like a leopard, it will tear them to
        pieces.

24  As you fence in your property with
        thorns,
    so make a door and a bolt for your
        mouth.*

25  As you lock up your silver and gold,
    so make balances and scales for your
        words.

26  Take care not to slip by your tongue
    and fall victim to one lying in
        ambush.

### Loans, Alms and Surety†

**29** ¹The merciful lend to their neighbor,
    by holding out a helping hand, they
        keep the commandments.*

2   Lend to your neighbor in his time of
        need,
    and pay back your neighbor in time.*

3   Keep your promise and be honest with
        him,
    and at all times you will find what
        you need.

4   Many borrowers ask for a loan
    and cause trouble for those who help
        them.

5   Till he gets a loan, he kisses the lender's
        hand
    and speaks softly of his creditor's
        money,
    But at time of payment, delays,
    makes excuses, and finds fault with
        the timing.

6   If he can pay, the lender will recover
        barely half,
    and will consider that a windfall.
    If he cannot pay, the lender is cheated of
        his money
    and acquires an enemy at no extra
        charge;
    With curses and insults the borrower
        will repay,
    and instead of honor will repay with
        abuse.

7   Many refuse to lend, not out of meanness,
    but from fear of being cheated
        needlessly.

8   But with those in humble circumstances
        be patient;
    do not keep them waiting for your
        alms.

9   Because of the commandment, help the
        poor,
    and in their need, do not send them
        away empty-handed.*

10  Lose your money for relative or friend;
    do not hide it under a stone to rot.

11  Dispose of your treasure according to
        the commandments of the Most
        High,
    and that will profit you more than the
        gold.*

---

**29:1–20** Some practical maxims concerning the use of
wealth. Give to the poor (vv. 8–9), lend to a needy neighbor, but
repay when a loan falls due lest the lender's burden be increased
(vv. 1–5) and his kindness abused (vv. 6–7); through charity
build up defense against evil (vv. 10–13). Help your neighbor
according to your means, but take care not to fall (v. 20), for the
shameless play false and bring their protectors and themselves to
misfortune and ruin (vv. 14–19).

**28:18** Jas 3:5–12.
**28:24** Sir 22:27; Ps 141:3.
**29:1** Dt 15:8; Ps 112:5; Prv
    19:17.
**29:2** Ex 22:24–26; Lv

25:36; Mt 5:42.
**29:9** Sir 4:1–6; Lv 19:9–10;
    23:22.
**29:11** Sir 17:22–23; Tb
    4:7–11.

12† Store up almsgiving in your treasury,
and it will save you from every evil.

13 Better than a mighty shield and a sturdy
spear
it will fight for you against the enemy.

14† A good person will be surety for a
neighbor,
but whoever has lost a sense of shame
will fail him.*

15 Do not forget the kindness of your
backer,
for he has given his very life for you.

16 A sinner will turn the favor of a pledge
into misfortune,

17 and the ungrateful will abandon his
rescuer.

18 Going surety has ruined many who were
prosperous
and tossed them about like waves of
the sea;*
It has exiled the prominent
and sent them wandering through
foreign lands.

19 The sinner will come to grief through
surety,
and whoever undertakes too much
will fall into lawsuits.

20 Help your neighbor according to your
means,
but take care lest you fall yourself.

### Frugality and Its Rewards†

21 Life's prime needs are water, bread, and
clothing,
and also a house for decent privacy.*

22 Better is the life of the poor under the
shadow of their own roof
than sumptuous banquets among
strangers.*

23 Whether little or much, be content with
what you have:
then you will hear no reproach as a
parasite.

24 It is a miserable life to go from house to
house,
for where you are a guest you dare not
open your mouth.

25 You will entertain and provide drink
without being thanked;
besides, you will hear these bitter
words:

26 "Come here, you parasite, set the table,
let me eat the food you have there!

27 Go away, you parasite, for one more
worthy;
for my relative's visit I need the
room!"

28 Painful things to a sensitive person
are rebuke as a parasite and insults
from creditors.

### The Training of Children†

30 ¹ Whoever loves a son will chastise
him often,
that he may be his joy when he grows
up.*

2 Whoever disciplines a son will benefit
from him,
and boast of him among
acquaintances.

3 Whoever educates a son will make his
enemy jealous,
and rejoice in him among his friends.

4 At the father's death, he will seem not
dead,
for he leaves after him one like
himself,

5 Whom he looked upon through life
with joy,
and in death, without regret.

6 Against his enemies he has left an
avenger,
and one to repay his friends with
kindness.

7 Whoever spoils a son will have wounds
to bandage,

---

**29:12–13** In Ben Sira's day, almsgiving and righteousness were practically identified.
**29:14–17** Ben Sira is more lenient on going surety than earlier sages; cf. Prv 6:1–5.
**29:21–28** Those who provide their own basic needs of food, clothing and dwelling, and are content with what they have, preserve their freedom and self-respect (vv. 21–23). But if they live as guests, even among the rich, they expose themselves to insult and rebuke (vv. 24–28).
**30:1–13** Sound discipline (which would include physical beating) and careful education of children correct self-indul-

gence and stubbornness, prevent remorse and humiliation, and bring to parents lasting joy and delight, prestige among friends, jealousy of enemies, perpetuation and vindication of themselves through their offspring (vv. 1–6). Lack of discipline and overindulgence of children bring sorrow and disappointment, terror and grief (vv. 7–13).

**29:14** Sir 8:13.    **30:1** Prv 13:24; 19:18;
**29:18** Prv 6:1–2; 11:15.      22:15; 23:13; 29:15;
**29:21** Sir 39:26.      Heb 12:7.
**29:22** Sir 40:29.

and will suffer heartache at every cry.

8 An untamed horse turns out stubborn;
  and a son left to himself grows up
  unruly.

9 Pamper a child and he will be a terror
  for you,
  indulge him, and he will bring you
  grief.

10 Do not laugh with him lest you share
   sorrow with him,
   and in the end you will gnash your
   teeth.

11 Do not give him his own way in his
   youth,
   and do not ignore his follies.

12 Bow down his head in his youth,
   beat his sides while he is still young,
   Lest he become stubborn and disobey
   you,
   and leave you disconsolate.*

13 Discipline your son and make heavy his
   yoke,
   lest you be offended by his
   shamelessness.

## Health and Cheerfulness†

14 Better the poor in vigorous health
   than the rich with bodily ills.

15 I would rather have bodily health than
   any gold,
   and contentment of spirit than pearls.

16 No riches are greater than a healthy
   body;
   and no happiness than a joyful heart.

17 Better is death than a wretched life,*
   everlasting sleep than constant illness.

18 Good things set before one who cannot
   eat
   are like food offerings placed before a
   tomb.†*

19 What good is an offering to an idol
   that can neither eat nor smell?
   So it is with the one being punished by
   the Lord,

20 who groans at what his eyes behold.

21 Do not give in to sadness,
   or torment yourself deliberately.*

22 Gladness of heart is the very life of a
   person,
   and cheerfulness prolongs his days.

23 Distract yourself and renew your
   courage,
   drive resentment far away from you;
   For grief has killed many,*
   and nothing is to be gained from
   resentment.

24 Envy and anger shorten one's days,
   and anxiety brings on premature old
   age.

25 Those who are cheerful and merry at
   table
   benefit from their food.†*

## The Proper Attitude Toward Riches†

31 [1] Wakefulness over wealth wastes away
   the flesh,
   and anxiety over it drives away sleep.

2 Wakeful anxiety banishes slumber;
  more than a serious illness it disturbs
  repose.

3 The rich labor to pile up wealth,
  and if they rest, it is to enjoy pleasure;

4 The poor labor for a meager living,
  and if they ever rest, they become
  needy.

5 The lover of gold will not be free from
  sin;
  whoever pursues money will be led
  astray by it.

6 Many have come to ruin for the sake of
  gold,
  yet destruction lay before their very
  eyes;*

7 It is a stumbling block for fools;
  any simpleton will be ensnared by it.

8 Happy the rich person found without
  fault,
  who does not turn aside after wealth.*

9 Who is he, that we may praise him?

---

**30:14–25** Health of mind and body and joy of heart Ben Sira judges to be more precious than wealth (vv. 14–16), whereas bitterness, constant illness, and affliction are more difficult to bear than death (vv. 17–20). Sadness, resentment, anxiety, envy, and anger shorten days; they should be dispelled by cheerfulness and gladness of heart, which help to prolong one's days (vv. 21–25).
**30:18** The saying ridicules the practice of putting food and drink on the tombs of the dead.
**30:25(27)** Because of the dislocation of the Greek text, the numbering of this verse follows Ziegler's edition. There are no verses 25–26.

**31:1–11** Solicitude for acquiring wealth and anxiety over preserving it disturb repose and easily lead to sin and ruin (vv. 1–7). Cf. Mt 6:25–34. The rich who have not sinned or been seduced by wealth are worthy of highest praise (vv. 8–11).

**30:12** Sir 7:23; Prv 23:14.
**30:17** Sir 41:2.
**30:18** Tb 4:17.
**30:21** Prv 12:25; 15:13; 17:22.
**30:23** Sir 38:18–19.
**30:25** Prv 15:15.
**31:6** Sir 8:2.
**31:8** Sir 5:1, 8.

For he has done wonders among his
    people.
10 Who has been tested by gold and been
    found perfect?
Let it be for him his glory;
Who could have sinned but did not,
    and could have done evil but did not?
11 So his good fortune is secure,
    and the assembly will recount his
    praises.*

### Table Etiquette†

12 Are you seated at the table of the great?
    Bring to it no greedy gullet,
Nor say, "How much food there is
    here!"
13 Remember that the greedy eye is evil.
What has been created more greedy than
    the eye?
    Therefore, it weeps for any cause.*
15 Recognize that your neighbor feels as
    you do,
    and keep in mind everything you
    dislike.
14 Toward what he looks at, do not put out
    a hand;
    nor reach for the same dish when he
    does.
16 Eat, like anyone else, what is set before
    you,
    but do not eat greedily, lest you be
    despised.
17 Be the first to stop, as befits good
    manners;
    and do not gorge yourself, lest you
    give offense.*
18 If there are many with you at table,
    do not be the first to stretch out your
    hand.
19 Does not a little suffice for a well-bred
    person?
    When he lies down, he does not
    wheeze.*
20 Moderate eating ensures sound slumber
    and a clear mind on rising the next
    day.

The distress of sleeplessness and of
    nausea
    and colic are with the glutton!
21 Should you have eaten too much,
    get up to vomit† and you will have
    relief.
22 Listen to me, my child, and do not scorn
    me;
    later you will find my advice good.
In whatever you do, be moderate,
    and no sickness will befall you.
23 People bless one who is generous with
    food,
    and this testimony to his goodness is
    lasting.*
24 The city complains about one who is
    stingy with food,
    and this testimony to his stinginess is
    lasting.
25 Let not wine be the proof of your
    strength,
    for wine has been the ruin of many.
26 As the furnace tests the work of the
    smith,
    so does wine the hearts of the insolent.
27 Wine is very life to anyone,
    if taken in moderation.
Does anyone really live who lacks the
    wine
    which from the beginning was created
    for joy?*
28 Joy of heart, good cheer, and delight
    is wine enough, drunk at the proper
    time.
29 Headache, bitterness, and disgrace
    is wine drunk amid anger and strife.
30 Wine in excess is a snare for the fool;
    it lessens strength and multiplies
    wounds.
31 Do not wrangle with your neighbor
    when wine is served,
    nor despise him while he is having a
    good time;
Say no harsh words to him
    nor distress him by making demands.

---

† **31:12–32:13** Whoever observes etiquette at table avoids greed and selfishness (31:12–13), is considerate of a neighbor's likes and dislikes and is generous toward him (31:15, 14, 23, 24), observes proper manners (31:16–18), is moderate in eating and drinking (31:19–20, 25–30). A good host is solicitous for the guests (32:1–2), provides conversation and diversion (32:3–6), is modest in speech (32:7, 8, 10), is respectful of elders (32:9), polite in comportment and grateful to God for his favors (32:11–13).

**31:21** *Get up to vomit*: the practice of induced vomiting, well-known among Romans, and less well-known among the Jews, seems to be referred to here.

**31:11** Prv 29:14.          **31:19** Eccl 5:11.
**31:13** Prv 23:1–2.       **31:23** Prv 22:9.
**31:17** Sir 37:27–31.    **31:27** Ps 104:15; 1 Tm 5:23.

# 32

¹ If you are chosen to preside at a
dinner, do not be puffed up,
but with the guests be as one of them;
Take care of them first and then sit
down;

² see to their needs, and then take your
place,
To share in their joy
and receive a wreath for a job well
done.

³ You who are older, it is your right to
speak,
but temper your knowledge and do
not interrupt the singing.

⁴ Where there is entertainment, do not
pour out discourse,
and do not display your wisdom at
the wrong time.

⁵ Like a seal of carnelian in a setting of
gold:
a concert of music at a banquet of
wine.

⁶ A seal of emerald in a work of gold:
the melody of music with delicious
wine.

⁷ Speak, young man, only when necessary,*
when they have asked you more than
once.

⁸ Be brief, say much in few words;
be knowledgeable and yet quiet.

⁹ When among elders do not be forward,
and with officials do not be too
insistent.

¹⁰ The lightning that flashes before a
hailstorm:
the esteem that shines on modesty.

¹¹ Leave in good time and do not be the
last;
go home quickly without delay.

¹² There enjoy doing as you wish,
but do not sin through words of
pride.

¹³ Above all, bless your Maker,
who showers his favors upon you.

### The Providence of God

¹⁴ Whoever seeks God must accept
discipline;†

and whoever resorts to him obtains
an answer.*

¹⁵ Whoever seeks the law will master it,
but the hypocrite will be ensnared
by it.*

¹⁶ Whoever fears the LORD will understand
what is right,
and out of obscurity he will draw
forth a course of action.*

¹⁷ The lawless turn aside warnings
and distort the law to suit their
purpose.*

¹⁸ The sensible will not neglect direction;
the proud and insolent are deterred by
no fear.

¹⁹ Do nothing without deliberation;
then once you have acted, have no
regrets.*

²⁰ Do not go on a way set with snares,
and do not stumble on the same
thing twice.

²¹ Do not trust the road, because of bandits;
²² be careful on your paths.

²³ Whatever you do, be on your guard,
for whoever does so keeps the
commandments.

²⁴ Whoever keeps the law preserves
himself;
and whoever trusts in the LORD shall
not be put to shame.

# 33

¹ No evil can harm the one who fears
the LORD;
through trials, again and again he is
rescued.*

² Whoever hates the law is without
wisdom,
and is tossed about like a boat in a
storm.

³ The prudent trust in the word of the
LORD,
and the law is dependable for them as
a divine oracle.†

⁴ Prepare your words and then you will be
listened to;
draw upon your training, and give
your answer.

---

† **32:14–33:4** God is shown to reveal himself through the discipline of his law, a clear and safe plan of life for the pious. Direction and deliberation are aids in following it (32:14–16, 18–24; 33:1, 3–4). Sinners and hypocrites, hating the law or distorting it, fail in wisdom and are devoid of security (32:15b, 17, 18b; 33:2).
   **33:3** *Oracle*: as the answer given through the Urim and

Thummim to the high priest is true, so the law proves itself true to those who obey it. Cf. Ex 28:30; Nm 27:21.

---

**32:7–10** Sir 7:14.     **32:17** Sir 21:6; Prv 12:1.
**32:14** Sir 4:13.       **32:19** Sir 37:16; Tb 4:18.
**32:15** Sir 2:16.       **33:1** Ps 91:10–13; Mt 4:6;
**32:16** Ps 37:6.            Lk 4:10–11.

S I R

5  Like the wheel of a cart is the mind of a
       fool,
   and his thoughts like a turning axle.
6  A mocking friend is like a stallion
   that neighs, no matter who the rider
       may be.

7†  Why is one day more important than
       another,
   when the same sun lights up every day
       of the year?
8  By the LORD's knowledge they are kept
       distinct;
   and he designates the seasons and
       feasts.*
9  Some he exalts and sanctifies,
   and others he lists as ordinary days.*
10  Likewise, all people are of clay,
   and from earth humankind was
       formed;*
11  In the fullness of his knowledge the
       Lord distinguished them,
   and he designated their different ways.
12  Some he blessed and exalted,
   and some he sanctified and drew to
       himself.
   Others he cursed and brought low,
   and expelled them from their place.
13  Like clay in the hands of a potter,
   to be molded according to his
       pleasure,
   So are people in the hands of their
       Maker,
   to be dealt with as he decides.*
14  As evil contrasts with good, and death
       with life,
   so are sinners in contrast with the
       godly.*
15  See now all the works of the Most High:
   they come in pairs, one the opposite
       of the other.

16  Now I am the last to keep vigil,†
   like a gleaner following the grape-
       pickers;

17  Since by the Lord's blessing I have made
       progress
   till like a grape-picker I have filled my
       wine press,
18  Consider that not for myself only have I
       labored,
   but for all who seek instruction.

## Property and Servants†

19  Listen to me, leaders of the people;
   rulers of the congregation, pay heed!*
20a  Let neither son nor wife, neither brother
       nor friend,
   have power over you as long as you
       live.
21  While breath of life is still in you,
   let no one take your place.
20b  Do not give your wealth to another,
   lest you must plead for support
       yourself.
22  Far better that your children plead with
       you
   than that you should look for a
       handout from them.
23  Keep control over all your affairs;
   bring no stain on your honor.
24  When your few days reach their limit,
   at the time of death distribute your
       inheritance.

25  Fodder and whip and loads for a
       donkey;
   food, correction and work for a slave.
26  Make a slave work, and he will look for
       rest;
   let his hands be idle and he will seek
       to be free.*
27  The yoke and harness will bow the neck;
   and for a wicked slave, punishment in
       the stocks.
28  Force him to work that he be not idle,
29      for idleness teaches much mischief.
30  Put him to work, as is fitting for him;
   and if he does not obey, load him
       with chains.

---

† **33:7–15** An important doctrine of Ben Sira is his view of the polarities in creation and history; cf. v. 15; 42:24. Contrasts observable in the physical universe as well as in the moral order serve the purposes of divine wisdom (vv. 5–9). All creatures are like clay in the hands of their Maker—the fool and the wise, the sinner and the just (vv. 10–15). This does not imply that some are created to be sinners: God is not the author of wickedness. Divine determinism and human freedom are a mysterious mix.

**33:16–18** Ben Sira refers to himself as the most recent of the biblical writers who have endeavored to present true wisdom to their readers.

**33:19–33** Public officials should reject every influence that would restrict their freedom in the management of their affairs. They must make their own household subservient to them rather than be subservient to it (vv. 19–24). Slaves are to be given food and work and correction but never to be treated unjustly (vv. 25–30). Great care should be taken of good slaves (vv. 31–33).

---

*
| **33:8** Gn 1:14. | Rom 9:20–21. |
| **33:9** Ex 20:11; Dt 5:13–14. | **33:14** Sir 42:25. |
| **33:10** Gn 2:7. | **33:19** Wis 6:1–2. |
| **33:13** Wis 15:7; Jer 18:1–6; | **33:26** Prv 29:19. |

But never lord it over any human being,
and do nothing unjust.
31 If you have but one slave, treat him like
yourself,
for you have acquired him with your
life's blood;
If you have but one slave, deal with him
as a brother,
for you need him as you need your
life.*
32 If you mistreat him and he runs away,
33 in what direction will you look for
him?

## Trust in the Lord and Not in Dreams†

# 34

1 Empty and false are the hopes of the
senseless,
and dreams give wings to fools.
2 Like one grasping at shadows or chasing
the wind,
so anyone who believes in dreams.
3 What is seen in dreams is a reflection,
the likeness of a face looking at itself.
4 How can the unclean produce what is
clean?
How can the false produce what is
true?*
5 Divination, omens, and dreams are
unreal;
what you already expect, the mind
fantasizes.
6 Unless they are specially sent by the
Most High,
do not fix your heart on them.
7 For dreams have led many astray,
and those who put their hope in them
have perished.
8 Without such deceptions the Law will be
fulfilled,
and in the mouth of the faithful is
complete wisdom.
9 A much-traveled person knows many
things;
and one with much experience speaks
sense.

10 An inexperienced person knows little,
11 whereas with travel one adds to
resourcefulness.
12 I have seen much in my travels,
and learned more than I could ever
say.
13 Often I was in danger of death,
but by these experiences I was saved.
14 Living is the spirit of those who fear the
Lord,
15 for their hope is in their savior.
16 Whoever fear the Lord are afraid of
nothing
and are never discouraged, for he is
their hope.*
17 Happy the soul that fears the Lord!
18 In whom does he trust, and who is his
support?
19 The eyes of the Lord are upon those who
love him;
he is their mighty shield and strong
support,
A shelter from the heat, a shade from
the noonday sun,
a guard against stumbling, a help
against falling.*
20 He lifts up spirits, brings a sparkle to the
eyes,
gives health and life and blessing.

## True Worship of God†

21 Ill-gotten goods offered in sacrifice are
tainted.
22 Presents from the lawless do not win
God's favor.*
23 The Most High is not pleased with the
gifts of the godless,
nor for their many sacrifices does he
forgive their sins.
24 One who slays a son in his father's
presence—
whoever offers sacrifice from the
holdings of the poor.
25 The bread of charity is life itself for the
needy;*

† **34:1–20** Confidence placed in dreams, divinations, and omens is false because these are devoid of reality (vv. 1–8). True confidence is founded on knowledge and experience (vv. 9–13), and above all on the fear of the Lord, with its accompanying blessings of divine assistance and protection (vv. 14–20).
**34:21–31** To be acts of true religion, sacrifice and penance must be accompanied by the proper moral dispositions. To offer to God goods taken from the poor (vv. 21–27), or to practice penance without interior reform, is a mockery, worthless in the sight of God (vv. 28–31). Cf. Mt 15:4–7; Mk 7:9–13.

33:31 Sir 7:20–21.　　34:22 Sir 35:14–15; Prv
34:4 Jb 14:4.　　　　　21:27.
34:16 Ps 23:4; 112:7–8; Prv　34:25–27 Lv 19:13; Dt
　3:23–24; 28:1.　　　24:14–15; Tb 4:14.
34:19 Ps 33:18–19; 34:16.

whoever withholds it is a murderer.

26 To take away a neighbor's living is to
commit murder;

27    to deny a laborer wages is to shed
blood.

28 If one builds up and another tears
down,
what do they gain but trouble?

29 If one prays and another curses,
whose voice will God hear?

30 If one again touches a corpse after
bathing,
what does he gain by the
purification?*

31 So one who fasts for sins,
but goes and commits them again:
Who will hear his prayer,
what is gained by mortification?

# 35 †1 To keep the law is to make many
offerings;*

2    whoever observes the commandments
sacrifices a peace offering.

3 By works of charity one offers fine
flour,†

4    and one who gives alms presents a
sacrifice of praise.

5 To refrain from evil pleases the Lord,
and to avoid injustice is atonement.

6 Do not appear before the Lord empty-
handed,

7    for all that you offer is in fulfillment
of the precepts.*

8 The offering of the just enriches the
altar:
a sweet odor before the Most High.

9 The sacrifice of the just is accepted,
never to be forgotten.

10 With a generous spirit pay homage to
the Lord,
and do not spare your freewill gifts.*

11 With each contribution show a cheerful
countenance,
and pay your tithes in a spirit of joy.*

12 Give to the Most High as he has given to
you,
generously, according to your means.

13 For he is a God who always repays
and will give back to you sevenfold.*

14 But offer no bribes; these he does not
accept!

15 Do not trust in sacrifice of the fruits of
extortion,*
For he is a God of justice,
who shows no partiality.*

16 He shows no partiality to the weak
but hears the grievance of the
oppressed.†

17 He does not forsake the cry of the
orphan,*
nor the widow when she pours out
her complaint.

18 Do not the tears that stream down her
cheek

19    cry out against the one that causes
them to fall?

20 Those who serve God to please him are
accepted;
their petition reaches the clouds.

21 The prayer of the lowly pierces the
clouds;
it does not rest till it reaches its goal;
Nor will it withdraw till the Most High
responds,

22    judges justly and affirms the right.*

God indeed will not delay,
and like a warrior, will not be still*
Till he breaks the backs of the merciless

23    and wreaks vengeance upon the
nations;
Till he destroys the scepter of the proud,
and cuts off the staff of the wicked;

---

† **35:1–26** Keeping the commandments of the law and avoiding injustice constitute sacrifice pleasing and acceptable to God
(vv. 1–5). Offerings also should be made to him, cheerfully and
generously; these he repays sevenfold (vv. 6–13). Extortion from
widows and orphans is injustice, and God will hear their cries
(vv. 14–22a). Punishing the proud and the merciless and coming
to the aid of the distressed, he requites everyone according to
their deeds (vv. 22b–26).

**35:3** *Fine flour,* together with oil and frankincense, was a
prescribed offering to God; cf. Lv 2:1–3.

**35:16** Cf. Lv 19:15; Dt 1:17. The divine impartiality is paradoxical, for it is tilted toward the poor.

* 34:30 Nm 19:11–12; Prv
26:11; 2 Pt 2:22.
**35:1–5** 1 Sm 15:22; Ps
51:18–19; Is 1:11–18;
Hos 6:6; Am 5:21–24.
**35:7** Ex 23:15; 34:20; Dt
16:16.
**35:10** Sir 7:31.
**35:11** Dt 14:22; 2 Cor 9:7.
**35:13** Prv 19:17;

Mt 25:34–40.
**35:15** Sir 34:21–23; Prv
15:8; 21:27.
**35:15** Dt 10:17; 2 Chr 19:7;
Jb 34:19; Wis 6:7;
Acts 10:34; Rom 2:11;
Gal 2:6; 1 Pt 1:17.
**35:17–19** Ex 22:22.
**35:22** Lk 18:7.
**35:22** Is 42:13–16; 2 Pt 3:9.

24   Till he requites everyone according to
their deeds,
and repays them according to their
thoughts;

25   Till he defends the cause of his people,
and makes them glad by his salvation.

26   Welcome is his mercy in time of distress
as rain clouds in time of drought.

### A Prayer for God's People†

**36** ¹Come to our aid, O God of the
universe,

2   and put all the nations in dread of
you!

3   Raise your hand against the foreign
people,
that they may see your mighty deeds.

4   As you have used us to show them your
holiness,†
so now use them to show us your
glory.

5   Thus they will know, as we know,
that there is no God but you.

6   Give new signs and work new wonders;

7   show forth the splendor of your right
hand and arm.

8   Rouse your anger, pour out wrath;

9   humble the enemy, scatter the foe.*

10   Hasten the ending, appoint the time,
and let people proclaim your mighty
deeds.

11   Let raging fire consume the fugitive,
and your people's oppressors meet
destruction.

12   Crush the heads of the hostile rulers
who say, "There is no one besides
me."

13   Gather all the tribes of Jacob,†

16   that they may inherit the land as in
days of old.

17   Show mercy to the people called by your
name:
Israel, whom you named your
firstborn.*

18   Take pity on your holy city:
Jerusalem, your dwelling place.*

19   Fill Zion with your majesty,
your temple with your glory.

20   Give evidence of your deeds of old;
fulfill the prophecies spoken in your
name.

21   Reward those who have hoped in you,
and let your prophets be proved true.

22   Hear the prayer of your servants,
according to your good will toward
your people.
Thus all the ends of the earth will know
that you are the eternal God.

### Choice of Associates†

23   The throat can swallow any food,
yet some foods are more agreeable
than others.

24   The palate tests delicacies put forward as
gifts,
so does a keen mind test deceitful
tidbits.

25   One with a tortuous heart brings about
grief,
but an experienced person can turn
the tables on him.

26   A woman will accept any man as
husband,
but one woman will be preferable to
another.

27   A woman's beauty makes her husband's
face light up,
for it surpasses all else that delights
the eye.*

28   And if, besides, her speech is soothing,

---

**36:1–22** A prayer that God hasten the day for the gathering of the tribes of Israel, and Zion once more be filled with the divine glory. All the earth will then know that the Lord is the eternal God.

**36:4** *Show…holiness:* this cultic language is used to indicate God's liberation of his people; cf. Ez 20:41; 28:25.

**36:13** This verse marks the end of a major dislocation in the Greek text of Sirach (which is followed here) at the head of chap. 33. The verse numbers 1–13 come from the placement of these verses in Greek. Verse 13 here is the first half of a bicolon, the matching half of which is numbered in the Greek 36:16b. Thus although the numbering for vv. 14–15 is not used, none of the text is missing.

**36:23–37:15** In the choice of wife, friend, or associate,

experience is a discerner of character (36:23–26). Beauty and soothing speech make a woman desirable as wife (36:27–28). The good wife becomes her husband's richest treasure, his help in establishing his household (36:29–31). Good friends fight for comrades and share the spoils with them (37:5–6); false friends deceive and abandon in time of need (37:1–4). A true counselor and associate should be sought among those who keep the commandments, not among those who break them and seek their own advantage (37:7–12). In all things one should pray to God for light and follow conscience (37:13–15).

**36:9** Ps 79:6; Jer 10:25.      Mi 4:1–3.
**36:17** Ex 4:22.      **36:26–28** Sir 26:13–18; Prv
**36:18** 2 Chr 6:41; Ps 132:8,      12:4; 18:22; 19:14.
14; Is 2:1–3;

her husband's lot is beyond that of
    mortal men.
29 A wife is her husband's richest treasure,
    a help like himself and a staunch
        support.*
30 A vineyard with no hedge will be
    overrun;
    and a man with no wife becomes a
        homeless wanderer.
31 Who will trust an armed band
    that shifts from city to city?
    Or a man who has no nest,
    who lodges wherever night overtakes
        him?*

# 37

1 Every friend declares friendship,
    but there are friends who are friends
    in name only.*
2 Is it not a sorrow unto death
    when your other self becomes your
        enemy?
3 "Alas, my companion! Why were you
    created
    to fill the earth with deceit?"
4 A harmful friend will look to your table,
    but in time of trouble he stands aloof.
5 A good friend will fight with you against
    the foe,
    and against your enemies he will hold
        up your shield.
6 Do not forget your comrade during the
    battle,
    and do not neglect him when you
        distribute your spoils.
7 Every counselor points out a way,
    but some counsel ways of their own.
8 Watch out when one offers advice;
    find out first of all what he wants.
    For he also may be thinking of
        himself—
    Why should the opportunity fall to
        him?
9 He may tell you how good your way will
    be,
    and then stand by to see you
        impoverished.

10 Seek no advice from your father-in-law,
    and from one who is envious of you,
    keep your intentions hidden.
11 Seek no advice from a woman about her
    rival,
    from a coward about war,
    from a merchant about business,
    from a buyer about value,
    from a miser about generosity,
    from a cruel person about well-being,
    from a worthless worker about his
        work,
    from a seasonal laborer about the
        harvest,
    from an idle slave about a great task—
    pay no attention to any advice they
        give.
12 Instead, associate with a religious
    person,
    who you know keeps the
        commandments;
    Who is like-minded with yourself
    and will grieve for you if you fall.
13 Then, too, heed your own heart's
    counsel;
    for there is nothing you can depend
        on more.
14 The heart can reveal your situation
    better than seven sentinels on a tower.
15 Then with all this, pray to God
    to make your steps firm in the true
        path.

## Wisdom and Temperance

16 A word is the source of every deed;†
    a thought, of every act.*
17 The root of all conduct is the heart;
18     four branches it shoots forth:
    Good and evil, death and life,
    and their absolute mistress is the
        tongue.*
19 One may be wise and benefit many,
    yet appear foolish to himself.
20 One may be wise, but if his words are
    rejected,
    he will be deprived of all enjoyment.†

---

37:16–26 Thoughts determine action. Wisdom is the source of good and life; folly, of evil and death (vv. 16–18). If the fruits of a person's wisdom benefit himself, he may be praised in his own lifetime; if they benefit others, the praise endures after him, in their lives (vv. 19–26).

37:20 Verse 21 appears only in Greek, but not in the Hebrew, which is the basis for the translation here.

36:29 Gn 2:18.         37:16 Sir 32:19.
36:31 Prv 27:8.        37:18 Prv 18:21.
37:1 Sir 6:7–17.

22 When one is wise to his own advantage,
    the fruits of knowledge are seen in his
        own person.

23 When one is wise to the advantage of
    people,
    the fruits of knowledge are lasting.*

24 One wise for himself has full enjoyment,
    and all who see him praise him.

25 The days of one's life are numbered,
    but the life of Israel, days without
        number.

26 One wise among the people wins a
    heritage of glory,
    and his name lives on and on.*

27 My son, while you are well, govern your
    appetite,†
    and see that you do not allow it what
        is bad for you.

28 For not everything is good for everyone,
    nor is everything suited to every
        taste.*

29 Do not go to excess with any
    enjoyment,*
    neither become a glutton for choice
        foods;

30 For sickness comes with overeating,
    and gluttony brings on nausea.

31 Through lack of self-control many have
    died,
    but the abstemious one prolongs life.

### Sickness and Death

**38** 1 Make friends with the doctor, for he
    is essential to you;†
    God has also established him in his
        profession.

2 From God the doctor has wisdom,
    and from the king he receives
        sustenance.

3 Knowledge makes the doctor
    distinguished,
    and gives access to those in authority.

4 God makes the earth yield healing herbs
    which the prudent should not neglect;

5 Was not the water sweetened by a twig,
    so that all might learn his power?*

6 He endows people with knowledge,
    to glory in his mighty works,

7 Through which the doctor eases pain,

8     and the druggist prepares his
        medicines.
Thus God's work continues without
    cease
    in its efficacy on the surface of the
        earth.

9 My son, when you are ill, do not delay,
    but pray to God, for it is he who
        heals.*

10 Flee wickedness and purify your hands;
    cleanse your heart of every sin.

11 Offer your sweet-smelling oblation and
    memorial,
    a generous offering according to your
        means.*

12 Then give the doctor his place
    lest he leave; you need him too,

13 For there are times when recovery is in
    his hands.

14     He too prays to God
That his diagnosis may be correct
    and his treatment bring about a cure.

15 Whoever is a sinner before his Maker
    will be defiant toward the doctor.

16 My son, shed tears for one who is dead†
    with wailing and bitter lament;
As is only proper, prepare the body,
    and do not absent yourself from the
        burial.

17 Weeping bitterly, mourning fully,
    pay your tribute of sorrow, as
        deserved:
A day or two, to prevent gossip;
    then compose yourself after your grief.

18 For grief can bring on death,
    and heartache can sap one's strength.*

19 When a person is carried away, sorrow is
    over;

---

**37:27–31** Temperance and self-control should govern appetite for food, which is intended not to destroy but to preserve life.
    **38:1–15** The profession of medicine comes from God, who makes the earth yield healing herbs and gives the physician knowledge of their power (vv. 1–8). In illness the sick should cleanse their soul from sin and petition God for help through an offering of sacrifice; the physician, too, does well to invoke God that he may understand the illness and apply the proper remedy (vv. 9–14). The sinner, in contrast, defies both his Maker and the doctor (v. 15).

**38:16–23** A period of mourning for the deceased and care for their burial are proper (vv. 16–17). But grief should not be excessive, for it cannot help the dead, who will not return, and may do harm to the living. The mourner should be realistic (vv. 18–23).

---

**37:23** Sir 39:10–11.
**37:26** Sir 39:9; 44:13–16.
**37:28** 1 Cor 6:12; 10:23.
**37:29–31** Sir 31:13, 16–21.
**38:5** Ex 15:25.
**38:9** Is 38:1–3.
**38:11** Lv 2:1–3.
**38:18** Prv 12:25; 15:13; 17:22.

and the life of the poor one is
grievous to the heart.

20 Do not turn your thoughts to him again;
cease to recall him; think rather of the
end.*

21 Do not recall him, for there is no hope
of his return;
you do him no good, and you harm
yourself.*

22 Remember that his fate will also be
yours;
for him it was yesterday, for you
today.*

23 With the dead at rest, let memory cease;
be consoled, once the spirit has gone.

## Vocations of the Skilled Worker and the Scribe†

24 The scribe's wisdom increases wisdom;
whoever is free from toil can become
wise.

25 How can one become learned who
guides the plow,
and thrills in wielding the goad like a
lance,
Who guides the ox and urges on the
bullock,
and whose every concern is for cattle?

26 His concern is to plow furrows,
and he is careful to fatten the
livestock.

27 So with every engraver and designer
who, laboring night and day,
Fashions carved seals,
and whose concern is to vary the
pattern.
His determination is to produce a
lifelike impression,
and he is careful to finish the work.

28 So too the smith sitting by the anvil,
intent on the iron he forges.
The flame from the fire sears his flesh,
yet he toils away in the furnace heat.
The clang of the hammer deafens his
ears;

his eyes are on the object he is
shaping.
His determination is to finish the work,
and he is careful to perfect it in
detail.

29 So also the potter sitting at his labor,
revolving the wheel with his feet.
He is always concerned for his products,
and turns them out in quantity.

30 With his hands he molds the clay,
and with his feet softens it.
His determination is to complete the
glazing,
and he is careful to fire the kiln.

31 All these are skilled with their hands,
each one an expert at his own work;

32 Without them no city could be lived in,
and wherever they stay, they do not go
hungry.
But they are not sought out for the
council of the people,

33 nor are they prominent in the
assembly.
They do not sit on the judge's bench,
nor can they understand law and
justice.
They cannot expound discipline or
judgment,
nor are they found among the rulers.

34 Yet they maintain the fabric of the
world,
and their concern is for exercise of
their skill.

**39** How different the person who
devotes himself
to the study of the law of the Most
High!

1 He explores the wisdom of all the
ancients
and is occupied with the prophecies;

2 He preserves the discourses of the
famous,
and goes to the heart of involved
sayings;

† 38:24–39:11 Ben Sira has a balanced view of the various vocations of skilled laborers—the farmer, engraver, smith and potter—but the profession of scribe is more excellent (38:24–34). He studies and meditates on the law of the Most High, seeks him in prayer of thanksgiving, petition and repentance for sin (39:1, 5, 7), explores the wisdom of the past and present, travels abroad to observe the conduct of many peoples, and attends rulers and great men. Through the spirit of understanding granted by God, he will show forth his wisdom to the glory of God's law, gaining renown for generations to come (39:2–4, 6–11).

* 38:20 Sir 7:36; 18:24; 30:21.    38:21 2 Sm 12:23; Wis 2:1. 38:22 Jas 4:13–15.

3 He seeks out the hidden meaning of
        proverbs,
    and is busied with the enigmas found
        in parables.

4 He is in attendance on the great,
    and appears before rulers.
  He travels among the peoples of foreign
        lands
    to test what is good and evil among
        people.

5 His care is to rise early
    to seek the Lord his Maker,
    to petition the Most High,
  To open his mouth in prayer,
    to ask pardon for his sins.

6 If it pleases the Lord Almighty,
    he will be filled with the spirit of
        understanding;
  He will pour forth his words of wisdom
    and in prayer give praise to the Lord.

7 He will direct his knowledge and his
        counsel,
    as he meditates upon God's
        mysteries.

8 He will show the wisdom of what he
        has learned
    and glory in the Law of the Lord's
        covenant.

9 Many will praise his understanding;
    his name can never be blotted out;
  Unfading will be his memory,
    through all generations his name will
        live; *

10 Peoples will speak of his wisdom,
    and the assembly will declare his
        praise.

11 While he lives he is one out of a
        thousand,
    and when he dies he leaves a good
        name.

### Praise of God the Creator†

12 Once more I will set forth my theme
    to shine like the moon in its fullness!

13 Listen to me, my faithful children: open
        up your petals,
    like roses planted near running
        waters;

14 Send up the sweet odor of incense,
    break forth in blossoms like the lily.
  Raise your voices in a chorus of praise;
    bless the Lord for all his works!

15 Proclaim the greatness of his name,
    loudly sing his praises,
  With music on the harp and all stringed
        instruments;
    sing out with joy as you proclaim:

16 The works of God are all of them good;
    he supplies for every need in its own
        time. *

17 At his word the waters become still as in
        a flask;
    he had but to speak and the reservoirs
        were made. *

18 He has but to command and his will is
        done;
    nothing can limit his saving action.

19 The works of all humankind are present
        to him;
    nothing is hidden from his eyes. *

20 His gaze spans all the ages:
    is there any limit to his saving action?
  To him, nothing is small or
        insignificant,
    and nothing too wonderful or hard
        for him.

21 No cause then to say: "What is the
        purpose of this?"
    Everything is chosen to satisfy a need.

22 His blessing overflows like the Nile;
    like the Euphrates it enriches the
        surface of the earth.

23 Even so, his wrath dispossesses the
        nations
    and turns fertile land into a salt
        marsh. *

24 For the virtuous his paths are level,
    to the haughty they are clogged with
        stones.

---

† **39:12–35** Ben Sira invites his disciples to join him in joyfully proclaiming his favorite theme: The works of God are all good; God supplies for every need in its own time (vv. 12–16, 32–35). The sage describes God's omniscience, supreme power and wisdom, whereby all created things, good in themselves, are ever present to him, obey him, and fulfill their intended purpose (vv. 17–21), bringing blessing to the virtuous, but evil and pun-

ishment to the wicked who misuse them (vv. 22–31). Cf. similar hymns of praise, 36:1–22; 42:15–43:33.

**39:9** Sir 37:26; 44:14.
**39:16** Sir 39:33; Gn
        1:29–31; Eccl 3:11.
**39:17** Gn 1:6–10; Ex 14:21–
        22; Jos 3:15–16.
**39:19** Sir 15:18–19;
        42:18–20.
**39:23** Gn 13:10; 19:24–28;
        Dt 29:22; Jos 1:2–6;
        Ps 107:34; Wis 10:7.

25　Good things for the good he provided
　　　from the beginning,
　　but for the wicked good things and
　　　bad.

26　Chief of all needs for human life
　　are water and fire, iron and salt,
　　The heart of the wheat, milk and honey,
　　　the blood of the grape, and oil, and
　　　clothing.*

27　For the good all these are good,
　　but for the wicked they turn out evil.

28　There are stormwinds created to
　　　punish;
　　in their fury they can dislodge
　　　mountains.
　　In a time of destruction they hurl their
　　　force
　　and calm the anger of their Maker.

29　Fire and hail, famine and disease:
　　　these too were created for
　　　punishment.

30　Ravenous beasts, scorpions, vipers,
　　　and the avenging sword to
　　　exterminate the wicked:
　　All these were created to meet a need,
　　　and are kept in his storehouse for the
　　　proper time.

31　When he commands them, they rejoice,
　　　in their assigned tasks they do not
　　　disobey his command.

32　That is why from the first I took my
　　　stand,
　　and wrote down as my theme:

33　The works of God are all of them good;
　　　he supplies for every need in its own
　　　time.*

34　There is no cause then to say: "This is
　　　not as good as that";
　　for each shows its worth at the proper
　　　time.

35　So now with full heart and voice
　　　proclaim
　　and bless his name!

## Joys and Miseries of Life

**40** [1] A great anxiety has God allotted,†
　　　and a heavy yoke, to the children of
　　　Adam,*
　From the day they leave their mother's
　　　womb
　　until the day they return to the
　　　mother of all the living.†

2　Troubled thoughts and fear of heart are
　　　theirs
　　and anxious foreboding until death.

3　Whether one sits on a lofty throne
　　or grovels in dust and ashes,

4　Whether one wears a splendid crown
　　or is clothed in the coarsest of
　　　garments—

5　There is wrath and envy, trouble and
　　　dread,
　　terror of death, fury and strife.
　Even when one lies on his bed to rest,
　　his cares disturb his sleep at night.

6　So short is his rest it seems like none,
　　till in his dreams he struggles as he
　　　did by day,
　Troubled by the visions of his mind,
　　like a fugitive fleeing from the
　　　pursuer.

7　As he reaches safety, he wakes up,
　　astonished that there was nothing to
　　　fear.

8　To all flesh, human being and beast,
　　but for sinners seven times more,

9　Come plague and bloodshed, fiery heat
　　　and drought,
　　plunder and ruin, famine and death.*

10　For the wicked evil was created,
　　and because of them destruction
　　　hastens.

11　All that is of earth returns to earth,
　　and what is from above returns
　　　above.†

12　All that comes from bribes or injustice
　　will be wiped out,

---

40:1–17 The former idyllic description of the universe is contrasted with the picture of the evils afflicting humanity. Every person, high or low, is burdened from birth to death with fears, anxieties, and troubles, by day and often by night, the time appointed for rest (vv. 1–7). For sinners, the suffering is much greater (vv. 8–10). What they gained by violence and injustice is quickly destroyed; but righteousness will prevail (vv. 14–17).
40:1 *Mother of all the living*: the earth from which human beings were taken. Cf. Gn 2:7; 3:19–20; Jb 1:21; Ps 139:15.

40:11 *All that is of earth…returns above*: a reference to bodily mortality and to the divine origin of life. Cf. 41:10; Gn 2:7; 3:19; Jb 34:14–15; Ps 104:29–30; 146:4; Eccl 12:7. The Greek and the Latin render the second half of the verse: "all waters shall return to the sea."

**39:26** Sir 29:21.
**39:33** Sir 39:16; Gn 1:29–31; Eccl 3:11.
**40:1** Gn 3:17–19; Jb 7:1; 14:1–2; Eccl 2:23.
**40:9** Sir 39:28–31.

13 but loyalty remains forever.
Wealth from injustice is like a flooding
wadi,
like a mighty stream with lightning
and thunder,

14 Which, in its rising, rolls along the
stones,
but suddenly, once and for all, comes
to an end.*

15 The offshoot of violence will not
flourish,
for the root of the godless is on sheer
rock.

16 They are like reeds on riverbanks,
withered before all other plants;

17 But goodness, like eternity, will never be
cut off,
and righteousness endures forever.

18 Wealth or wages can make life sweet,†
but better than either, finding a
treasure.

19 A child or a city will preserve one's
name,
but better than either, finding
wisdom.
Cattle and orchards make a person
flourish;
but better than either, a devoted
wife.*

20 Wine and strong drink delight the soul,
but better than either, love of friends.*

21 Flute and harp offer sweet melody,
but better than either, a pure tongue.

22 Grace and beauty delight the eye,
but better than either, the produce of
the field.

23 A friend and a neighbor are timely
guides,
but better than either, a sensible wife.

24 Relatives and helpers for times of stress;
but better than either, charity that
rescues.

25 Gold and silver make one's way secure,
but better than either, sound
judgment.

26 Wealth and vigor make the heart exult,
but better than either, fear of God.
In the fear of the Lord there is no want;
whoever has it need seek no other
support.

27 The fear of God is a paradise of
blessings;
its canopy is over all that is glorious.*

28 My son, do not live the life of a beggar;†
better to die than to beg.

29 When one has to look to a stranger's
table,
life is not worth living.
The delicacies offered bring revulsion of
spirit,
and to the intelligent, inward torture.*

30 In the mouth of the shameless begging
is sweet,
but within him it burns like fire.

**41** ¹ O death! How bitter is the thought
of you†
for the one at peace in his home,
For the one who is serene and always
successful,
who can still enjoy life's pleasures.

2 O death! How welcome is your sentence
to the weak, failing in strength,
Stumbling and tripping on everything,
with sight gone and hope lost.*

3 Do not fear death's decree for you;
remember, it embraces those before
you and those to come.*

4 This decree for all flesh is from God;
why then should you reject a law of
the Most High?
Whether one has lived a thousand years,
a hundred, or ten,
in Sheol there are no arguments about
life.

5 The children of sinners are a reprobate
line,*
and witless offspring are in the homes
of the wicked.

---

† **40:18–27** Of the many treasures making life sweet, such as children, friends, music, vigor, the best are called true married love, wisdom, and above all, fear of God; cf. 25:6–11.
**40:28–30** Among the Jews, begging was considered degrading to human dignity; it was agreeable only to the shameless, who had lost their sense of honor. Cf. 29:22–23.
**41:1–13** Whether death seems bitter to one who enjoys peace, success, and pleasure, or welcome to one who is weak and in despair, it comes to all and must be accepted as the will

of God (vv. 1–4). The human body passes away (v. 11). Sinners as well as their offspring pass away as if they had never been (vv. 5–10). Only the good name of the virtuous endures (vv. 11–13).

**40:14** Sir 23:25–26; Wis 4:3–6.
**40:19** Prv 18:22; 19:14.
**40:20** Ps 104:15.
**40:27** Is 4:5–6.
**40:29** Sir 29:24.
**41:2** Sir 30:17.
**41:3** Sir 38:20–22.
**41:5–10** Sir 3:9–11; Wis 3:16–19.

S
I
R

6　The inheritance of children of sinners
　　　will perish,
　　　and on their offspring will be
　　　　perpetual disgrace.

7　Children curse their wicked father,
　　　for they suffer disgrace because of
　　　　him.

8　Woe to you, O wicked people,
　　　who forsake the Law of the Most
　　　　High.

9　If you have children, calamity will be
　　　theirs;
　　　and if you beget them, it will be only
　　　　for groaning.
　　When you stumble, there is lasting joy;
　　　and when you die, you become a
　　　　curse.

10　All that is nought returns to nought,
　　　so too the godless—from void to
　　　　void.*

11　The human body is a fleeting thing,
　　　but a virtuous name will never be
　　　　annihilated.*

12　Have respect for your name, for it will
　　　stand by you
　　　more than thousands of precious
　　　　treasures.*

13　The good things of life last a number of
　　　days,
　　　but a good name, for days without
　　　　number.

### True and False Shame†

14b　Hidden wisdom and concealed treasure,
　　　of what value is either?

15　Better is the person who hides his folly
　　　than the one who hides his wisdom.

14a　My children, listen to instruction about
　　　shame;

16a　judge of disgrace according to my
　　　rules,

16b　Not every kind of shame is shameful,
　　　nor is every kind of disgrace to be
　　　　recognized.

17　Before father and mother be ashamed of
　　　immorality,
　　　before prince and ruler, of falsehood;

18　Before master and mistress, of deceit;

before the public assembly, of crime;
Before associate and friend, of disloyalty,

19　and in the place where you settle, of
　　　theft.
Be ashamed of breaking an oath or a
　　　covenant,
　　　and of stretching your elbow at
　　　　dinner;
Of refusing to give when asked,

21　of rebuffing your own relatives;
Of defrauding another of his appointed
　　　share,

20a　of failing to return a greeting;

21c　Of gazing at a man's wife,

20b　of entertaining thoughts about
　　　another woman;*

22　Of trifling with a servant girl you have,
　　　of violating her bed;
Of using harsh words with friends,
　　　of following up your gifts with
　　　　insults;*

**42** ¹Of repeating what you hear,
　　　of betraying any secret.*
Be ashamed of the right things,
　　　and you will find favor in the sight of
　　　　all.

But of these things do not be ashamed,
　　　lest you sin to save face:*

2　Of the Law of the Most High and his
　　　precepts,
　　　or of justice that acquits the ungodly;

3　Of sharing the expenses of a business or
　　　a journey,
　　　of dividing an inheritance or property;

4　Of accuracy of scales and balances,
　　　of tested measures and weights;*

Of acquiring much or little,

5　of bargaining in dealing with a
　　　merchant;
Of constant training of children,
　　　of beating the sides of a wicked
　　　　servant;*

6　Of a seal to keep a foolish wife at home,
　　　of a key where there are many hands;

7　Of numbering every deposit,
　　　of recording all that is taken in and
　　　　given out;

† **41:14—42:8** Ben Sira illustrates the subject of true and false shame with numerous and detailed examples of wrongdoing (41:14–22) and virtue (42:1–8), following the norm of the commandments.

* **41:10** Sir 40:11; Wis 4:19.
**41:11** Prv 10:7.
**41:12** Prv 22:1; Eccl 7:1.
**41:20** Sir 9:8; Mt 5:28.
**41:22** Sir 18:15; 20:14.
**42:1** Sir 27:16.
**42:1** Prv 24:23; Jas 2:1.
**42:4** Lv 19:35; Prv 11:1;
　　16:11; 20:10.
**42:5** Sir 30:1–13;
　　33:25–33.

8      Of chastisement for the silly and the
           foolish,
         for the aged and infirm answering for
           wanton conduct.
       Thus you will be truly refined
         and recognized by all as discreet.

## A Father's Care for His Daughter†

9      A daughter is a treasure that keeps her
           father wakeful,
         and worry over her drives away sleep:*
       Lest in her youth she remain unmarried,
         or when she is married, lest she be
           childless;
10     While unmarried, lest she be defiled,
         or in her husband's house, lest she
           prove unfaithful;
       Lest she become pregnant in her father's
           house,
         or be sterile in that of her husband.
11     My son, keep a close watch on your
           daughter,
         lest she make you a laughingstock for
           your enemies,
       A byword in the city and the assembly
           of the people,
         an object of derision in public
           gatherings.*
       See that there is no lattice in her room,
         or spot that overlooks the approaches
           to the house.
12     Do not let her reveal her beauty to any
           male,*
         or spend her time with married women;
13     For just as moths come from garments,
         so a woman's wickedness comes from
           a woman.
14     Better a man's harshness than a woman's
           indulgence,
         a frightened daughter than any disgrace.

## The Works of God in Nature†

15     Now will I recall God's works;
         what I have seen, I will describe.

       By the LORD's word his works were
           brought into being;
         he accepts the one who does his
           will.*
16     As the shining sun is clear to all,
         so the glory of the LORD fills all his
           works;
17     Yet even God's holy ones must fail
         in recounting the wonders of the
           LORD,
       Though God has given his hosts the
           strength
         to stand firm before his glory.
18     He searches out the abyss and penetrates
           the heart;
         their secrets he understands.
       For the Most High possesses all
           knowledge,
         and sees from of old the things that
           are to come.
19     He makes known the past and the
           future,
         and reveals the deepest secrets.
20     He lacks no understanding;
         no single thing escapes him.*
21     He regulates the mighty deeds of his
           wisdom;
         he is from all eternity one and the
           same,
       With nothing added, nothing taken
           away;
         no need of a counselor for him!*
22     How beautiful are all his works,
         delightful to gaze upon and a joy to
           behold!
23     Everything lives and abides forever;
         and to meet each need all things are
           preserved.
24     All of them differ, one from another,
         yet none of them has he made in
           vain;
25     For each in turn, as it comes, is good;
         can one ever see enough of their
           splendor?*

---

† **42:9–14** Ben Sira considers a daughter to be a source of anxiety to her father, lest she fail to marry, or be defiled, or lest, marrying, she be childless, prove unfaithful, or find herself sterile (vv. 9–10). He is advised to keep a close watch on her and on her companions, lest he suffer on her account among the people (vv. 11–12). The exhortations, which take into account only a father's concern, are quite unflattering to young women. The concluding statements (vv. 13–14) show the limitations of Ben Sira's perspective in the male-oriented society of his day.

**42:15–43:33** These verses comprise another hymn; cf. 16:24–18:14. In them Ben Sira contemplates God's power, beauty, and goodness as manifested in the mighty work of creating and preserving the universe (42:15–17, 22–25; 43:1–26), his omniscience (42:18–20), perfect wisdom and eternity (42:21). The conclusion is a fervent hymn of praise (43:27–31).

---

*
**42:9** Sir 7:24–25.
**42:11** Dt 22:20–21.
**42:12–13** Sir 9:1–9.
**42:15** Ps 77:12–13.
**42:20** Sir 39:19; Wis 1:6–9.

**42:21** Wis 9:13; Is 40:13;
     Rom 11:34; 1 Cor
     2:11.
**42:25** Sir 33:15.

SIR

# 43

1 The beauty of the celestial height
     and the pure firmament,*
heaven itself manifests its glory.

2 The sun at its rising shines at its fullest,
     a wonderful instrument, the work of
     the Most High!

3 At noon it scorches the earth,
     and who can bear its fiery heat?

4 Like a blazing furnace of solid metal,
     the sun's rays set the mountains
     aflame;
Its fiery tongue consumes the world;
     the eyes are burned by its fire.

5 Great indeed is the LORD who made it,
     at whose orders it urges on its steeds.

6 It is the moon that marks the changing
     seasons,
governing the times, their lasting
     sign.*

7 By it we know the sacred seasons and
     pilgrimage feasts,
     a light which wanes in its course:

8 The new moon like its name† renews
     itself;
     how wondrous it is when it changes:
A military signal for the waterskins on
     high,
     it paves the firmament with its
     brilliance,

9 The beauty of the heavens and the glory
     of the stars,
     a shining ornament in the heights of
     God.*

10 By the LORD's command the moon keeps
     its appointed place,
     and does not fade as the stars keep
     watch.

11 Behold the rainbow! Then bless its
     Maker,
     for majestic indeed is its splendor;*

12 It spans the heavens with its glory,
     the hand of God has stretched it out
     in power.

13 His rebuke marks out the path for the
     hail,
     and makes the flashes of his judgment
     shine forth.

14 For his own purposes he opens the
     storehouse
     and makes the rain clouds fly like
     vultures.

15 His might gives the clouds their
     strength,
     and breaks off the hailstones.

16 The thunder of his voice makes the earth
     writhe;
     by his power he shakes the mountains.

17 A word from him drives on the south
     wind,
     whirlwind, hurricane, and stormwind.
He makes the snow fly like birds;
     it settles down like swarms of locusts.

18 Its shining whiteness blinds the eyes,
     the mind marvels at its steady fall.

19 He scatters frost like salt;
     it shines like blossoms on the
     thornbush.

20 He sends cold northern blasts
     that harden the ponds like solid
     ground,
Spreads a crust over every body of water,
     and clothes each pool with a coat of
     armor.

21 When mountain growth is scorched by
     heat,
     and flowering plains as by fire,

22 The dripping clouds restore them all,
     and the scattered dew enriches the
     parched land.

23 His is the plan that calms the deep,
     and plants the islands in the sea.

24 Those who go down to the sea recount
     its extent,
     and when we hear them we are
     thunderstruck;*

25 In it are his creatures, stupendous,
     amazing,
     all kinds of life, and the monsters of
     the deep.

26 For him each messenger succeeds,
     and at his bidding accomplishes his
     will.*

27 More than this we need not add;
     let the last word be, he is the all!†

S
I
R

---

† **43:8** *Like its name*: there is a play in the Hebrew text on the words for moon and renewal. *Waterskins*: clouds as source of rain.
     **43:27** *The all*: the perfections reflected in creation are found in a transcendent way in God, who alone is their source.

* **43:1–12** Ps 19:2–5.         **43:11** Gn 9:13.
   **43:6** Lv 23:5; Nm         **43:24–25** Ps 104:25–26.
      28:11–14; Ps 81:4–6.     **43:26** Ps 33:6.
   **43:9** Ps 8:4.

28 Let us praise him the more, since we
       cannot fathom him,
    for greater is he than all his works;
29 Awesome indeed is the LORD,
       and wonderful his power.
30 Lift up your voices to glorify the LORD
       as much as you can, for there is still
       more.
    Extol him with renewed strength,
       do not grow weary, for you cannot
       fathom him.
31 For who has seen him and can describe
       him?
    Who can praise him as he is?*
32 Beyond these, many things lie hidden;
       only a few of his works have I seen.
33 It is the LORD who has made all things;
       to those who fear him he gives
       wisdom.*

## Praise of Israel's Great Ancestors†

**44** ¹I will now praise the godly,
       our ancestors, in their own time,†
2 The abounding glory of the Most High's
       portion,
    his own part, since the days of old.*
3 Subduers of the land in kingly fashion,
       renowned for their might,
    Counselors in their prudence,
       seers of all things in prophecy,*
4 Resolute princes of the flock,
       lawgivers and their rules,
    Sages skilled in composition,
       authors of sharp proverbs,
5 Composers of melodious psalms,
       writers of lyric poems;
6 Stalwart, solidly established,
       at peace in their own estates—
7 All these were glorious in their time,
       illustrious in their day.
8 Some of them left behind a name
       so that people recount their praises.

9 Of others no memory remains,
       for when they perished, they perished,
    As if they had never lived,
       they and their children after them.
10 Yet these also were godly;
       their virtues have not been forgotten.
11 Their wealth remains in their families,
       their heritage with their descendants.
12 Through God's covenant their family
       endures,
    and their offspring for their sake.
13 And for all time their progeny will
       endure,
    their glory will never be blotted out;
14 Their bodies are buried in peace,
       but their name lives on and on.*
15 At gatherings their wisdom is retold,
       and the assembly proclaims their
       praises.

## The Early Ancestors

16 [ENOCH† walked with the LORD and was
       taken,*
    that succeeding generations might
       learn by his example.]
17 NOAH, found just and perfect,
       renewed the race in the time of
       devastation.*
    Because of his worth there were
       survivors,
    and with a sign to him the deluge
       ended.
18 A lasting covenant was made with him,
       that never again would all flesh be
       destroyed.
19 ABRAHAM, father of many peoples,
       kept his glory without stain:*
20 He observed the Most High's command,
       and entered into a covenant with him;
    In his own flesh he incised the
       ordinance,†
    and when tested was found loyal.*

---

**44:1–50:24** As in the previous section God's glory shone forth in the works of nature, so in these chapters it is revealed through the history of God's people as seen in the lives of their ancestors, prophets, priests, and rulers. The example of these great people, whose virtues are recalled here, constitutes a high point of Ben Sira's teaching.
**44:1–15** The reader is here introduced to those people of Israel, later mentioned by name, who through various achievements and beneficial social activities have acquired great renown (vv. 1–8, 14–15); and also to those who, though forgotten, endure through the fruit of their virtues and through their families because of God's covenant with them (vv. 9–15).
**44:16** *Enoch*: because of his friendship with God and his unusual disappearance from the earth, this prophet's renown was great among the chosen people, particularly in the two centuries

just before the coming of Christ; cf. Gn 5:21–24; Heb 11:5. The present verse is an expansion of the original text; cf. 49:14.
**44:20** *In his own flesh…ordinance*: the covenant of circumcision; cf. Gn 17:10–14. *And when tested…loyal*: Abraham's willingness to sacrifice his son Isaac at the Lord's command; cf. Gn 22:1–12.

**43:31** Ps 106:2.
**43:33** Sir 1:10.
**44:2** Dt 32:8–9.
**44:3** Sir 39:1.
**44:14** Wis 3:2–3.
**44:16** Sir 49:14; Gn 5:18–24; Heb 11:5.
**44:17** Gn 6:8–9:29; Heb 11:7.
**44:19** Gn 12:1–25:10; Rom 4:3; Gal 3:6; Heb 11:8–19; Jas 2:23.
**44:20** Gn 17:10–14; 22:1–12.

21 For this reason, God promised him with
   an oath
   to bless the nations through his
   descendants,
To make him numerous as grains of
   dust,
   and to exalt his posterity like the stars,
Giving them an inheritance from sea to
   sea,
   and from the River† to the ends of the
   earth.

22 For ISAAC, too, he renewed the same
   promise
   because of Abraham, his father.
The covenant with all his forebears was
   confirmed,
23    and the blessing rested upon the head
   of ISRAEL.*
God acknowledged him as the firstborn,
   and gave him his inheritance.
He fixed the boundaries for his tribes
   and their division into twelve.

### Praise of Moses, Aaron, and Phinehas

45 1 From him came the man†
   who would win the favor of all the
   living:*
Dear to God and human beings,
   MOSES, whose memory is a blessing.
2 God made him like the angels in honor,
   and strengthened him with fearful
   powers.*
3 At his words God performed signs
   and sustained him in the king's
   presence.
He gave him the commandments for his
   people,
   and revealed to him his glory.*
4 Because of his trustworthiness and
   meekness
   God selected him from all flesh;*
5 He let him hear his voice,
   and led him into the cloud,

Where he handed over the
   commandments,
   the law of life and understanding,†
That he might teach his precepts to
   Jacob,
   his judgments and decrees to Israel.

6 He also raised up, like Moses in
   holiness,†
   his brother AARON, of the tribe of Levi.*
7 He made his office perpetual
   and bestowed on him priesthood for
   his people;
He established him in honor
   and crowned him with lofty majesty.
8 He clothed him in splendid garments,
   and adorned him with glorious
   vestments:
Breeches, tunic, and robe
9    with pomegranates at the hem
And a rustle of bells round about,
   whose pleasing sound at each step
Would make him heard within the
   sanctuary,
   a reminder for the people;
10 The sacred vestments of gold, violet,
   and crimson, worked with
   embroidery;
The breastpiece for decision, the ephod
   and cincture
11    with scarlet yarn, the work of the
   weaver;
Precious stones with seal engravings
   in golden settings, the work of the
   jeweler,
To commemorate in incised letters
   each of the tribes of Israel;
12 On his turban a diadem of gold,
   its plate engraved with the sacred
   inscription—
Majestic, glorious, renowned for
   splendor,
   a delight to the eyes, supremely
   beautiful.

---

† **44:21** *The River*: the Euphrates; cf. Gn 2:14.
   **44:23(end)–45:5** Moses manifested God's power through marvels (vv. 1–3), God's authority through the commandments and the Law (v. 5), and God's mercy through the intimacy granted him by the Lord for his own faithfulness and meekness (v. 4).
   **45:5** On God's intimacy with Moses, see Ex 33:11; Nm 12:8; Dt 34:10.
   **45:6–25** Ben Sira here expresses his reverence and esteem for the priesthood of the old covenant. He recalls God's choice of Aaron and his sons for this sublime office (vv. 6–7), and describes in detail the beauty of the high priest's vestments (vv. 8–13). He relates the ordination of Aaron at the hands of Moses (v. 15), and

describes the priestly functions, namely, offering sacrifice to God (v. 16), and blessing (v. 15), teaching, governing, and judging the people (v. 17); the inheritance of the high priest (vv. 20–22); the punishment of those who were jealous of Aaron (vv. 18–19); and the confirmation of the covenant of the priesthood with Aaron's descendants through Phinehas (vv. 23–25).

---

* **44:22–23** Gn 26:3–5, 24;
   27:28–29; 28:13–15.
   **45:1** Ex 2:2; 11:3; 33:11;
   Nm 12:7.
   **45:2–5** Ex 7–Dt 34.

   **45:3** Ex 7:1–7; 20:2–17; Dt
   5:6–21.
   **45:4** Nm 12:3, 7.
   **45:6–22** Ex 28–29; Wis 18:24.

SIR

13 Before him, no one had been adorned
with these,
nor may they ever be worn by any
other
Except his sons and them alone,
generation after generation, for all
time.

14 His grain offering is wholly burnt
as an established offering twice each
day;

15 For Moses ordained him
and anointed him with the holy oil,
In a lasting covenant with him and his
family,
as permanent as the heavens,
That he should serve God in the
priesthood
and bless the people in his name.

16 He chose him from all the living
to sacrifice burnt offerings and choice
portions,
To burn incense, sweet odor as a
memorial,
and to atone for the people of Israel.

17 He gave to him the laws,
and authority to prescribe and to
judge:
To teach precepts to the people,
and judgments to the Israelites.

18 Strangers rose in anger against him,
grew jealous of him in the desert—
The followers of Dathan and Abiram,
and the band of Korah in their
defiance.*

19 When the LORD saw this he became
angry,
and destroyed them in his burning
wrath.
He brought against them a marvel,
and consumed them in flaming fire.

20 Then he increased the glory of Aaron*
and bestowed upon him his
inheritance:
The sacred offerings he allotted to him,
with the showbread† as his portion;

21 The oblations of the LORD are his food,
a gift to him and his descendants.

22 But he holds no land among the people
nor shares with them their heritage;
For the LORD himself is his portion and
inheritance
among the Israelites.

23 PHINEHAS too, the son of Eleazar,
was the courageous third of his line
When, zealous for the God of all,
he met the crisis of his people*
And, at the prompting of his noble
heart,
atoned for the children of Israel.

24 Therefore, on him also God conferred
the right,
in a covenant of friendship, to provide
for the sanctuary,
So that he and his descendants
should possess the high priesthood
forever.

25 For even his covenant with David,
the son of Jesse of the tribe of Judah,
Was an individual heritage through one
son alone;*
but the heritage of Aaron is for all his
descendants.

So now bless† the LORD
who has crowned you with glory!

26 May he grant you wisdom of heart
to govern his people in justice,
Lest the benefits you confer should be
forgotten,
or your authority, throughout all time.

## Joshua, Caleb, the Judges, and Samuel

# 46

1 Valiant warrior was JOSHUA,† son of
Nun,
aide to Moses in the prophetic office,
Formed to be, as his name implies,
the great savior of God's chosen ones,
To punish the enemy
and to give to Israel their heritage.*

2 What glory was his when he raised his
hand,
to brandish his sword against the
city!*

---

† 
**45:20** *Showbread:* cf. note on Ex 25:29–30.
**45:25–26** *So now bless:* Ben Sira addresses the whole line of high priests, especially Simon II; cf. 50:1.
**46:1–6** *Joshua:* whose name means "the lord is savior" (v. 1), was the instrument through which God delivered his people in marvelous ways (vv. 2–6) by destroying their enemies, whose land he gave to the Israelites as a heritage (v. 1).

**45:18** Nm 16:1–35.
**45:20–21** Nm 18:11–24; Dt 10:9.
**45:23** Nm 25:7–13; 1 Mc 2:26, 54; Ps 106:30–31.
**45:25** 2 Sm 7:12–16.
**46:1** Ex 17:9; Nm 27:18–23; Dt 34:9; Jos 1:1–9.
**46:2** Jos 8:18–19.

3 Who could withstand him
    when he fought the battles of the
       Lᴏʀᴅ?†
4 Was it not by that same hand the sun
    stopped,
    so that one day became two?*
5 He called upon the Most High God
    when his enemies beset him on all
       sides,
    And God Most High answered him
       with hailstones of tremendous power,
6 That rained down upon the hostile army
    till on the slope he destroyed the foe;
    That all the doomed nations might
       know
      the Lᴏʀᴅ was watching over his
       people's battles.
    He was indeed a devoted follower of
       God
7   and showed himself loyal in Moses'
       lifetime.
    He and Cᴀʟᴇʙ,† son of Jephunneh,
    when they opposed the rebel
       assembly,
    Averted God's anger from the people
    and suppressed the wicked
       complaint.*
8 Because of this, these two alone were
    spared
      from the six hundred thousand
       infantry,
    To lead the people into their heritage,
    the land flowing with milk and
       honey.*
9 The strength God gave to Caleb
    remained with him even in old age
    Till he won his way onto the summits of
       the land;
    his family too received a heritage,*
10 That all the offspring of Jacob might
    know
      how good it is to be a devoted
       follower of the Lᴏʀᴅ.

11 The Jᴜᴅɢᴇs,† each one of them,
    whose hearts were not deceived,

    Who did not abandon God—
      may their memory be ever blessed!*
12 May their bones flourish with new life
    where they lie,
    and their names receive fresh luster in
       their children!
13 Beloved of his people, dear to his Maker,
    pledged in a vow from his mother's
       womb,
    As one consecrated to the Lᴏʀᴅ in the
       prophetic office,
    was Sᴀᴍᴜᴇʟ, the judge who offered
       sacrifice.
    At God's word he established the
       kingdom
    and anointed princes to rule the
       people.*
14 By the law of the Lᴏʀᴅ he judged the
    congregation,
    and visited the encampments of
       Jacob.
15 As a trustworthy prophet he was sought
    out
      and his words proved him to be a true
       seer.
16 He, too, called upon the mighty Lord
    when his enemies pressed him on
       every side,
    and offered up a suckling lamb.*
17 Then the Lᴏʀᴅ thundered from heaven,
    and the tremendous roar of his voice
       was heard.*
18 He brought low the rulers of the enemy
    and destroyed all the lords of the
       Philistines.
19 When Samuel neared the end of life,
    he testified before the Lᴏʀᴅ and his
       anointed prince,
    "No bribe or secret gift have I taken
      from anyone!"
    and no one could accuse him.*
20 Even after death his guidance was
    sought;
      he made known to the king his fate.
    From the grave he spoke in prophecy
      to put an end to wickedness.*

---

† **46:3** *The battles of the Lord*: cf. Jos 6–11.
  **46:7–10** *Caleb*: with Joshua he advised Moses to enter Canaan, despite the counsel of their companion scouts and the rebellion of the people. He led the next generation of Israelites into the promised land. He received a portion of land which he himself had conquered; cf. Jos 15:13–14.
  **46:11–20** Of the judges praised and blessed for their fidelity to God in opposing idolatry, Samuel was the greatest (vv. 11–13, 19). He was judge, prophet, and priest. Through his sacrificial

offering he obtained victory over the Philistines. He established the kingdom, anointed kings (vv. 13–18), and even after his death foretold the king's fate (v. 20).

---

**46:4** Jos 10:12–13.
**46:7** Nm 13:30; 14:1–3.
**46:8** Nm 14:22–38.
**46:9** Jos 14:6–13; 15:13.
**46:11** Jgs 1:1–16:31.

**46:13** 1 Sm 1:10–20;
        8:4–10:1; 16:12–13.
**46:16** 1 Sm 7:9.
**46:17** 1 Sm 7:10–13.
**46:19** 1 Sm 12:3.
**46:20** 1 Sm 28:14–19.

## Nathan, David, and Solomon

**47** [1] After him came NATHAN†
who served in David's presence.*

[2] Like the choice fat of sacred offerings,
so was DAVID in Israel.*

[3] He played with lions as though they
were young goats,
and with bears, like lambs of the flock.*

[4] As a youth he struck down the giant
and wiped out the people's disgrace;
His hand let fly the slingstone
that shattered the pride of Goliath.*

[5] For he had called upon the Most High
God,
who gave strength to his right arm
To defeat the skilled warrior
and establish the might of his people.

[6] Therefore the women sang his praises
and honored him for "the tens of
thousands."
When he received the royal crown, he
battled*

[7] and subdued the enemy on every side.
He campaigned against the hostile
Philistines
and shattered their power till our own
day.*

[8] With his every deed he offered thanks
to God Most High, in words of praise.
With his whole heart he loved his Maker

[9] and daily had his praises sung;

[10] He added beauty to the feasts
and solemnized the seasons of each
year

[9b] With string music before the altar,
providing sweet melody for the psalms*

[10b] So that when the Holy Name was
praised,
before daybreak the sanctuary would
resound.

[11] The LORD forgave him his sins
and exalted his strength forever;
He conferred on him the rights of
royalty
and established his throne in Israel.*

[12] Because of his merits he had as
successor†
a wise son, who lived in security:*

[13] SOLOMON reigned during an era of peace,
for God brought rest to all his
borders.
He built a house to the name of God,
and established a lasting sanctuary.*

[14] How wise you were when you were
young,
overflowing with instruction, like the
Nile in flood!*

[15] Your understanding covered the whole
earth,
and, like a sea, filled it with
knowledge.

[16] Your fame reached distant coasts,
and you were beloved for your
peaceful reign.

[17] With song and proverb and riddle,
and with your answers, you astounded
the nations.

[18] You were called by that glorious name
which was conferred upon Israel.†
Gold you gathered like so much iron;
you heaped up silver as though it were
lead.

[19] But you abandoned yourself to women
and gave them dominion over your
body.*

[20] You brought a stain upon your glory,
shame upon your marriage bed,
Wrath upon your descendants,
and groaning upon your deathbed.

[21] Thus two governments came into being,
when in Ephraim kingship was
usurped.*

[22] But God does not withdraw his mercy,
nor permit even one of his promises
to fail.
He does not uproot the posterity of the
chosen,
nor destroy the offspring of his
friends.
So he gave to Jacob a remnant,
to David a root from his own family.*

---

**47:1–11** An idealized portrait of David; cf. 1 Chronicles.
**47:12–24** The standard view of Solomon is echoed by Ben Sira, but he affirms the divine promise (v. 22) to David's line.
**47:18** Cf. 2 Sm 12:25, where Solomon is called Jedidiah, "beloved of the Lord." A similar term is used of Israel in Jer 11:15.

**47:1** 2 Sm 7:2–17.
**47:2** 1 Sm 16:11–13.
**47:3** 1 Sm 17:34–36.
**47:4** 1 Sm 17:49.
**47:6** 1 Sm 18:7.
**47:7** 2 Sm 5:6–25.
**47:9** 1 Chr 16:4–37; 23:5; 25:1–7.
**47:11** 2 Sm 12:13; 7:12–16.
**47:12** 1 Kgs 2:12.
**47:13** 1 Kgs 5:1, 5; 6:2–38.
**47:14–18** 1 Kgs 5:9–14; 10:14–29.
**47:19** 1 Kgs 11:1–10.
**47:21** 1 Kgs 12:1–25.
**47:22** 2 Sm 7:15; Ps 89:34–38.

## Rehoboam and Jeroboam

23 Solomon finally slept with his ancestors,
   and left behind him one of his sons,
   Broad† in folly, narrow in sense,
   whose policy made the people rebel.
   Then arose the one who should not be
   remembered,
   the sinner who led Israel into sin,*
   Who brought ruin to Ephraim
24   and caused them to be exiled from
   their land.

## Elijah and Elisha

25 Their sinfulness grew more and more,
   and they gave themselves to every
   evil†

**48** ¹ Until like fire a prophet appeared,
   his words a flaming furnace.*
2  The staff of life, their bread, he
   shattered,
   and in his zeal he made them few in
   number.
3  By God's word he shut up the heavens
   and three times brought down fire.*
4  How awesome are you, ELIJAH!
   Whose glory is equal to yours?
5  You brought a dead body back to life
   from Sheol, by the will of the LORD.*
6  You sent kings down to destruction,
   and nobles, from their beds of
   sickness.*
7  You heard threats at Sinai,
   at Horeb avenging judgments.*
8  You anointed the agent of these
   punishments,
   the prophet to succeed in your
   place.*

9  You were taken aloft in a whirlwind,
   in a chariot with fiery horses.*
10 You are destined, it is written, in time to
   come
   to put an end to wrath before the day
   of the LORD,
   To turn back the hearts of parents
   toward their children,
   and to re-establish the tribes of
   Israel.*
11 Blessed is the one who shall have seen
   you before he dies!†

12    When Elijah was enveloped in the
   whirlwind,
   ELISHA was filled with his spirit;†
   He worked twice as many marvels,*
   and every utterance of his mouth was
   wonderful.
   During his lifetime he feared no one,
   nor was anyone able to intimidate his
   will.
13 Nothing was beyond his power;*
   and from where he lay buried, his
   body prophesied.†
14 In life he performed wonders,
   and after death, marvelous deeds.
15 Despite all this the people did not
   repent,
   nor did they give up their sins,
   Until they were uprooted from their
   land
   and scattered all over the earth.

## Judah

   But Judah remained, a tiny people,
   with its ruler from the house of
   David.*
16 Some of them did what was right,
   but others were extremely sinful.

---

**47:23** *Broad*: the name Rehoboam means "the people is broad, or expansive," that is, widespread. *The sinner*: Jeroboam; cf. 1 Kgs 12:1, 20, 26–32.

**47:25–48:11** The prophetic ministry of Elijah amid widespread idolatry is here described as a judgment by fire (48:1). Through his preaching, marvels, and acts of vengeance against God's enemies, he succeeded for a time in restoring faith in and worship of the Lord (vv. 2–8). His mysterious departure from this life gave rise to the belief that he did not die but would return before the day of the Lord. Cf. Mal 3:23–24; Mt 17:9–13.

**48:11** Verse 11b is not extant in the Hebrew; it is represented in the Greek tradition by "for we too shall certainly live." But this can hardly be the original reading.

**48:12–16** Elisha continued Elijah's work (vv. 12–14), but the obstinacy of the people eventually brought on the destruction of the kingdom of Israel and the dispersion of its subjects. Judah,

however, survived under the rule of Davidic kings, both good and bad (vv. 15–16).

**48:13** The reference in v. 13b seems to be to 2 Kgs 13:21 where it is related that a dead man, thrown into Elisha's grave, came back to life.

---

**47:23** 1 Kgs 11:43; 12:13,
   21; 13:34; 2 Kgs
   17:6–22.
**48:1** 1 Kgs 17:1.
**48:3** 2 Kgs 1:9–14.
**48:5** 1 Kgs 17:17–23.
**48:6** 1 Kgs 21:19; 2 Kgs
   1:17.
**48:7** 1 Kgs 19:8–15.

**48:8** 1 Kgs 19:16–17.
**48:9** 2 Kgs 2:11.
**48:10** Mal 3:23–24; Mt
   17:10.
**48:12** 2 Kgs 2:9–12.
**48:13–14** 2 Kgs 13:21.
**48:15** 2 Kgs 15:29;
   18:11–12.

## Hezekiah and Isaiah†

17 HEZEKIAH fortified his city
　　and had water brought into it;*
　With bronze tools he cut through the
　　rocks
　　and dammed up a mountain site for
　　water.†

18 During his reign Sennacherib led an
　　invasion
　　and sent his adjutant;
　He shook his fist at Zion
　　and blasphemed God in his pride.*

19 The people's hearts melted within them,
　　and they were in anguish like that of
　　childbirth.

20 But they called upon the Most High God
　　and lifted up their hands to him;
　He heard the prayer they uttered,
　　and saved them through ISAIAH.*

21 God struck the camp of the Assyrians
　　and routed them with a plague.*

22 For Hezekiah did what was right
　　and held fast to the paths of David,
　As ordered by the illustrious prophet
　　Isaiah, who saw truth in visions.

23 In his lifetime he turned back the sun
　　and prolonged the life of the king.*

24 By his powerful spirit he looked into the
　　future*
　　and consoled the mourners of Zion;

25 He foretold what would happen till the
　　end of time,
　　hidden things yet to be fulfilled.

## Josiah and the Prophets†

49 ¹The name JOSIAH is like blended
　　incense,
　　made lasting by a skilled perfumer.*
　Precious is his memory, like honey to
　　the taste,
　　like music at a banquet.

2 For he grieved over our betrayals,

3 and destroyed the abominable idols.
　He kept his heart fixed on God,
　　and in times of lawlessness practiced
　　virtue.

4 Except for David, Hezekiah, and Josiah,
　　they all were wicked;
　They abandoned the Law of the Most High,
　　these kings of Judah, right to the very
　　end.

5 So he gave over their power to others,
　　their glory to a foreign nation

6 Who burned the holy city
　　and left its streets desolate,

7 As foretold by JEREMIAH.* They
　　mistreated him
　who even in the womb had been
　　made a prophet,
　To root out, pull down, and destroy,
　　and then to build and to plant.*

8 EZEKIEL beheld a vision
　　and described the different creatures
　　of the chariot;*

9 He also referred to JOB,
　　who always persevered in the right
　　path.*

10 Then, too, the TWELVE PROPHETS—
　　may their bones flourish with new life
　　where they lie!—
　They gave new strength to Jacob
　　and saved him with steadfast hope.

## The Heroes After the Exile

11 How to extol ZERUBBABEL?†
　　He was like a signet ring on the right
　　hand,*

12 And JESHUA, Jozadak's son?
　　In their time they rebuilt the altar
　And erected the holy temple,
　　destined for everlasting glory.

13 Exalted be the memory of NEHEMIAH!
　　He rebuilt our ruined walls,
　Restored our shattered defenses,
　　and set up gates and bars.*

---

† **48:17–25** The fidelity of King Hezekiah (vv. 17, 22), the zeal of the prophet Isaiah, and the prayer of the people (v. 20) were effective. The Assyrian oppressors under Sennacherib withdrew (vv. 18–19, 21). The king's life was prolonged. The people were consoled by Isaiah's words about the future (vv. 23–25); the "consolations" refer to Is 40–66.
**48:17** The reference is to the famous Siloam tunnel in present-day Jerusalem.
**49:1–10** Ben Sira's praise of King Josiah (vv. 1–3) and of the prophets Jeremiah and Ezekiel and the minor prophets (vv. 7–10) derives from their spirit of fidelity to the Lord and his Law (vv. 4–6, 10).
**49:11–13** The rebuilding of the Temple and the repair of the

walls of the Holy City led to a restoration of religious worship and civil authority.

|  |  |
|---|---|
| **48:17** 2 Kgs 20:20; 2 Chr 32:30. | **49:1–2** 2 Kgs 22:1–2, 10–13, 19; 23:4–15, 19–20, 24; 2 Chr 34:1–7. |
| **48:18** 2 Kgs 18:13–37; Is 36:1–22. | **49:7** 2 Kgs 25:9; 2 Chr 36:19. |
| **48:20** 2 Kgs 19:20. | **49:7** Jer 1:5, 10. |
| **48:21** 2 Kgs 19:35; Is 37:36. | **49:8** Ez 1:4–21. |
| **48:23** 2 Kgs 20:11; Is 38:8. | **49:9** Ez 14:14, 20. |
| **48:24–25** 2 Kgs 20:17; Is 40:1–11; 42:9; 46:10; 48:6; 61:2–3. | **49:11–12** Ezr 3:2; Hg 1:12; Zec 3:1. |
|  | **49:13** Neh 1:1–3:32. |

## The Earliest Patriarchs

14  Few on earth have been created like
    ENOCH;†
        he also was taken up bodily.*
15  Was ever a man born like JOSEPH?
        Even his dead body was provided
        for.*
16  Glorious, too, were SHEM and SETH and
    ENOSH;
        but beyond that of any living being
        was the splendor of ADAM.*

## Simeon, Son of Jochanan

**50**  ¹ Greatest of his family, the glory of
        his people,
    was SIMEON the priest, son of
    Jochanan,†
    In whose time the house of God was
        renovated,
        in whose days the temple was
        reinforced.
2   In his time also the retaining wall was
        built
        with powerful turrets for the temple
        precincts.
3   In his time the reservoir was dug,
        a pool as vast as the sea.
4   He protected the people against
        brigands
        and strengthened the city against the
        enemy.
5   How splendid he was as he looked out
        from the tent,
        as he came from behind the veil!
6   Like a star shining among the clouds,
        like the full moon at the festal season;
7   Like sun shining upon the temple of the
        King,
        like a rainbow appearing in the
        cloudy sky;
8   Like blossoms on the branches in
        springtime,
        like a lily by running waters;
    Like a green shoot on Lebanon in
        summer,
9       like the fire of incense at sacrifice;

Like a vessel of hammered gold,
    studded with all kinds of precious
    stones;
10  Like a luxuriant olive tree heavy with
    fruit,
    a plant with branches abounding in
    oil;
11  Wearing his glorious robes,
    and vested in sublime magnificence,*
As he ascended the glorious altar
    and lent majesty to the court of the
    sanctuary.
12  When he received the portions from the
    priests
    while he stood before the sacrificial
    wood,
His sons stood round him like a
    garland,
    like young cedars on Lebanon;
And like poplars by the brook they
    surrounded him,
13  all the sons of Aaron in their glory,
With the offerings to the LORD in their
    hands,
    in the presence of the whole assembly
    of Israel.
14  Once he had completed the service at
    the altar
    and arranged the sacrificial hearth for
    the Most High,
15  And had stretched forth his hand for the
    cup,
    to offer blood of the grape,
And poured it out at the foot of the
    altar,
    a sweet-smelling odor to God the
    Most High,*
16  Then the sons of Aaron would sound a
    blast,
    the priests, on their trumpets of
    beaten metal;
A blast to resound mightily
    as a reminder before the Most High.*
17  All the people with one accord
    would fall with face to the ground
In adoration before the Most High,
    before the Holy One of Israel.

---

† **49:14–16** The patriarchs here mentioned were glorious because of their spirit of religion, i.e., their profound reverence for God and obedience to him. *The splendor of Adam*: suggests his direct origin from God (Gn 1:26–27; 2:7).
  **50:1–21** *Son of Jochanan*: Simeon II, in whose time as high priest (219–196 B.C.) great works were accomplished for the benefit of public worship and welfare (vv. 1–4). Ben Sira, a con-

temporary, describes detailed liturgical action, perhaps pertaining to the Day of Atonement (Yom Kippur, cf. Lv 16).

**49:14** Sir 44:16; Gn                4:25–26.
    5:18–24.                      **50:11** Sir 45:8–13; Ex
**49:15** Gn 37; 39–50; Ex          28:2–43; 39:1–31.
    13:19; Jos 24:32.             **50:15** Nm 15:5; 28:7.
**49:16** Gn 1:26–30; 2:7;          **50:16** Nm 10:10.

S
I
R

18 Then hymns would re-echo,
   and over the throng sweet strains of
      praise resound.
19 All the people of the land would shout
      for joy,
   praying to the Merciful One,
   As the high priest completed the service
      at the altar
   by presenting to God the fitting
      sacrifice.
20 Then coming down he would raise his
      hands
   over all the congregation of Israel;
   The blessing of the Lord would be upon
      his lips,
   the name of the Lord would be his
      glory.*
21 The people would again fall down
   to receive the blessing of the Most
      High.

22 And now, bless the God of all,†
   who has done wonders on earth;
   Who fosters growth from the womb,
   fashioning it according to his will!
23 May he grant you a wise heart
   and abide with you in peace;
24 May his goodness toward Simeon last
      forever;
   may he fulfill for him the covenant
      with Phinehas
   So that it may not be abrogated for him
   or his descendants while the heavens
      last.

### Epilogue

25 My whole being loathes two nations,
   the third is not even a people:†
26 The inhabitants of Seir† and Philistia,
   and the foolish people who dwell in
      Shechem.*

27 Wise instruction, appropriate proverbs,†
   I have written in this book—
   I, Yeshua Ben Eleazar Ben Sira—

as they poured forth from my heart's
   understanding.
28 Happy those who meditate upon these
      things;
   wise those who take them to heart!
29 If they put them into practice, they can
      cope with anything,
   for the fear of the Lord is their lamp.

### A Prayer of Thanksgiving

**51** ¹ I give you thanks, Lord and King,†
   I praise you, God my savior!
   I declare your name, refuge of my life,*
2    because you have ransomed my life
      from death;
   You held back my body from the pit,
   and delivered my foot from the power
      of Sheol.*

   You have preserved me from the scourge
      of the slanderous tongue,
   and from the lips of those who went
      over to falsehood.
   You were with me against those who rise
      up against me;
3    You have rescued me according to
      your abundant mercy*
   From the snare of those who look for
      my downfall,
   and from the power of those who seek
      my life.

   From many dangers you have saved me,
4    from flames that beset me on every
      side,*
   From the midst of fire till there was not
      a whiff of it,†
5    from the deep belly of Sheol,
   From deceiving lips and painters of lies,
6    from the arrows of a treacherous
      tongue.

   I was at the point of death,
   my life was nearing the depths of
      Sheol;*

---

**50:22–24** Ben Sira urges the reader to praise and bless God for his wondrous works and then invokes a blessing on all that they may enjoy peace and gladness of heart and the abiding goodness of the Most High.

**50:25** *Not even a people*: the Samaritans.

**50:26** *Seir*: Mount Seir in the territory of the Edomites. *Shechem*: a city in Samaria.

**50:27** This colophon may have been the original ending of the book. It is unusual for a biblical writer to append his name.

**51:1–30** This chapter contains two appendixes: a prayer

(vv. 1–12) and an autobiographical poem praising wisdom (vv. 13–30).

**51:4** So complete is the deliverance from fire that even the smell of smoke cannot be detected. Cf. Dn 3:27.

---

**50:20** Nm 6:23–27.
**50:26** 2 Kgs 17:24; Jn 4:9.
**51:1** Ps 138:1.
**51:2** Ps 91:3.
**51:3** Ps 56:10–12; 124:2.
**51:4** Ps 66:12.
**51:6** Ps 88:4; 94:17.

7 I turned every way, but there was no one
　　to help;
　I looked for support but there was
　　none. *

8 Then I remembered the mercies of the
　　LORD,
　his acts of kindness through ages past;
　For he saves those who take refuge in
　　him,
　　and rescues them from every evil.

9 So I raised my voice from the grave;
　　from the gates of Sheol I cried for
　　help.

10 I called out: LORD, you are my Father,
　　my champion, my savior!
　Do not abandon me in time of trouble,
　　in the midst of storms and dangers. *

11 I will always praise your name
　　and remember you in prayer!

Then the LORD heard my voice,
　　and listened to my appeal.

12 He saved me from every evil
　　and preserved me in time of trouble.
　For this reason I thank and praise him;
　　I bless the name of the LORD. †

### Ben Sira's Pursuit of Wisdom

13 † When I was young and innocent,
　　I sought wisdom. *

14 She came to me in her beauty,
　　and until the end I will cultivate her.

15 As the blossoms yielded to ripening
　　grapes,
　　the heart's joy,

My feet kept to the level path
　　because from earliest youth I was
　　familiar with her.

16 In the short time I paid heed,
　　I met with great instruction.

17 Since in this way I have profited,
　　I will give my Teacher grateful praise.

18 I resolved to tread her paths;
　　I have been jealous for the good and
　　will not turn back.

19 I burned with desire for her,
　　never relenting.
　I became preoccupied with her,
　　never weary of extolling her.

I spread out my hands to the heavens
　　and I came to know her secrets.

20 For her I purified my hands;
　　in cleanness I attained to her.

At first acquaintance with her, I gained
　　understanding
　such that I will never forsake her. *

21 My whole being was stirred to seek her;
　　therefore I have made her my prize
　　possession.

22 The LORD has rewarded me with lips,
　　with a tongue for praising him.

23 Come aside to me, you untutored,
　　and take up lodging in the house of
　　instruction; † *

24 How long will you deprive yourself of
　　wisdom's food,
　how long endure such bitter thirst?

SIR

---

† **51:12** After this verse the Hebrew text gives the litany of praise contained below. It is similar to Ps 136. Though not found in any versions, and therefore of doubtful authenticity, the litany seems from internal evidence to go back to the time of Ben Sira.

Give praise to the LORD, for he is good, for God's love endures forever;
Give praise to the God of glory, for God's love endures forever;
Give praise to the Guardian of Israel, for God's love endures forever;
Give praise to the creator of all things, for God's love endures forever;
Give praise to the redeemer of Israel, for God's love endures forever;
Give praise to God who gathers the dispersed of Israel, for God's love endures forever;
Give praise to God who builds the city and sanctuary, for God's love endures forever;
Give praise to God who makes a horn sprout forth for the house of David, for God's love endures forever;
Give praise to God who has chosen the sons of Zadok as priests, for God's love endures forever;

Give praise to the Shield of Abraham, for God's love endures forever;
Give praise to the Rock of Isaac, for God's love endures forever;
Give praise to the Mighty One of Jacob, for God's love endures forever;
Give praise to God who has chosen Zion, for God's love endures forever;
Give praise to the King, the king of kings, for God's love endures forever;
He has lifted up the horn of his people! Let this be his praise from all the faithful,
From Israel, the people near to him. Hallelujah! (Cf. Ps 148:14.)

**51:13–30** A Hebrew manuscript from Qumran demonstrates the acrostic style of vv. 13–20. This is an elegant twenty-three-line alphabetic acrostic hymn that describes Ben Sira's relationship to wisdom: (a) his approach to wisdom through prayer,

---

**51:7** Ps 22:12; 142:5. 　　　　　**51:20** Prv 4:6.
**51:10** Ps 89:27; 95:1. 　　　　　**51:23** Prv 8:5.
**51:13** Sir 34:9–13; Prv 8:17.

25    I open my mouth and speak of her:
          gain wisdom for yourselves at no cost.*

26    Take her yoke upon your neck;
          that your mind may receive her
              teaching.
       For she is close to those who seek her,
          and the one who is in earnest finds
              her.*

27    See for yourselves! I have labored only a
          little,

                                 but have found much.

28    Acquire but a little instruction,
          and you will win silver and gold
              through her.

29    May your soul rejoice in God's
              mercy;
       do not be ashamed to give him
              praise.

30    Work at your tasks in due season,
          and in his own time God will give you
              your reward.*

---

persistent study, and instruction (vv. 13–17); (b) his purification from sin, his enlightenment, and ardent desire to possess wisdom (vv. 18–22). Ben Sira concludes with an urgent invitation to his students to receive instruction in wisdom from him, and to live by it, because wisdom gives herself to those who seek her (vv. 23–26); and for their labor, God will reward them in his own time (vv. 27–30). Cf. Mt 11:28; Eccl 12:14.

**51:23** *House of instruction*: this may be a metaphor for Ben Sira's teaching.

---

**51:25** Sir 6:19; Is 55:1–3.         **51:30** Sir 2:8; Jb 34:11;
**51:26** Sir 6:26–28.                     Jn 9:4.

# Introduction to the Prophets

## Carol J. Dempsey, OP

In the Hebrew canon of the Bible, one of the most dynamic, engaging, and imaginative sets of books is the Prophets. These texts include the Major Prophets: Isaiah, Jeremiah, and Ezekiel, and the Minor Prophets, otherwise known as the Book of the Twelve: Hosea, Joel, Amos, Obadiah, Jonah, Micah, Nahum, Habakkuk, Zephaniah, Haggai, Zechariah, and Malachi. Written in both prose and poetry, these books present the struggles, pain, and hope of the people of Israel living in the northern kingdom of Israel and the southern kingdom of Judah. The historical time span covered in these books, from the perspective of their poetic storylines, is roughly from the eighth century BCE to the fourth century BCE—from the years leading up to the fall of Jerusalem and the Temple (preexilic times), to the exile (exilic times), and finally to the time when some of the people resettled in the land after their experiences of trauma and devastation (postexilic times). Israel's prophets were not the first people to exercise the charism of prophecy that enjoys a rich and long history that began in the ancient Near East.

## Prophecy in the Ancient Near East

The earliest records of prophetic activity come from the city of Mari, located in upper Mesopotamia on the Euphrates River. In this region and specifically in the royal archives of Mari, letters have been found from the reign of Zimri-lin (ca. 1775–1761 BCE). Zimri-lin was the last Mari ruler before the people were defeated by Hammurapi, a Babylonian king. Evidence shows that these letters were written by officials and administrators and contained communications from intermediaries delivering divine messages intended for the king. In essence, a message was given from a god to an intermediary or prophet who, in turn, told the message to a letter writer who wrote it down and then gave it to the king. The intermediaries were both professional and non-professional men and women who received the messages in dreams and visions, often at the temple and sometimes during sacrificial rites. Interestingly, none of the Mari texts show that prophecy was associated with any one individual in particular. Most of the messages sent to the king concerned military, political, and religious matters; some even warned the king about various undertakings yet to occur. Most of the messages served to support the king in his role of leadership. Thus the Mari texts provide evidence that shows that prophecy was and is not restricted to the Bible and is part of a much larger religious tradition. Additionally, the Mari texts show that divine communication happened through intuitive divination that took the form of a verbal message. Prophecy, then, is an example of intuitive divination also found in Israel.

Finally, another set of texts has also been found. These texts reflect prophetic activity in the Neo-Assyrian period, roughly the eighth to seventh centuries BCE. These less well known tablets preserve the proclamations of nine women and four men known as prophets.

## Prophecy in Ancient Israel

Although prophecy in Israel seems to share some similarities with ancient Near Eastern prophecy, the Israelite prophetic tradition had its own distinctive character. For instance, ancient Near Eastern prophecy often made no distinction between a prophet and a priest, which was not the case for Israel. Some of those who were later recognized as prophets may have been priests, as in the cases of Jeremiah and Ezekiel, but others were not priests, such as Hosea and Micah, among others.

In ancient Israel, various types of prophets existed. One type was the shamanistic prophets who were known for their ecstatic activity. They were often itinerant and usually prophesied in groups. Other types included cultic or temple prophets who were often associated with the priesthood and were sometimes found proclaiming in the Temple like Jeremiah. Some were court prophets who often advised the king, as in the case of Daniel, who is both a prophetic and wisdom figure. Others were free prophets, who began their work around the mid-eighth century BCE. These prophets included Amos, Hosea, Micah, and Isaiah. For them, their primary authority was God. They often stood on the periphery of Israelite society and worked to provoke social and religious change. Israel's prophets are typically divided into two major divisions known as the Former Prophets, which include Elijah and Elisha, and the Latter Prophets: Isaiah, Jeremiah, Ezekiel, and the Book of the Twelve. The bulk of Israel's prophetic literature comes from the Latter Prophets, whose texts have been preserved in the Old Testament canon.

## Early Israelite Pre-Monarchic and Early Monarchic Prophets

In Israel's pre-monarchic period, there are three individuals designated by the biblical text as "prophets": Moses, Miriam, and Deborah. The prophets who are most remembered from Israel's monarchic times are Samuel, Nathan, Gad, Ahijah, Elijah, Elisha, and Micaiah. Other prophets active during the later years of Israel's monarchic period included Jonah, Huldah, Hananiah, and Uriah.

Samuel's prophetic activity began at an early age when he was under the mentorship of the priest Eli (1 Sm 3). Samuel emerged as a major religious force, and he was responsible for anointing Israel's earliest kings (1 Sm 9:27–10:8; 16:1–13). Nathan was a prophet during King David's time. Most notably, he mediated God's dynastic promise to David (2 Sm 7:1–17) and confronted David about his adulterous relationship with Bathsheba and his sin against Uriah (2 Sm 12:1–25). Ahijah, a prophet from Shiloh, tore his garments into twelve pieces to symbolize the coming division of Israel's united kingdom (1 Kgs 11:29–31; 12:15; 2 Chr 10:15) and also predicted Jeroboam's accession to power in the

northern kingdom of Israel. Elijah, one of the greatest prophets, was active during the ninth century BCE during the reign of King Ahab. Elijah appeared on the scene as Israel struggled between worship of Yahweh and worship of Baal and between fidelity and idolatry. Elijah had a marvelous encounter with God at Horeb (1 Kgs 19:9–18) and later cursed King Ahab and his house (1 Kgs 21). According to the biblical text, he was taken up to heaven by a whirlwind as chariots of fire appeared between him and his successor, Elisha (2 Kgs 2:1–18). Elisha, the "man of God," ministered to Elijah and succeeded him. He performed miracles and made many visionary proclamations.

## Later Monarchic and Post-Monarchic Prophets (before 587 BCE to ca. 333 BCE)

Following the death of Solomon, Israel's united kingdom split in two: the northern kingdom, Israel, with Samaria as its capital, and the southern kingdom, Judah, with Jerusalem as its capital. The period leading up to the destruction of Israel by the Assyrians and Judah by the Babylonians is known as preexilic times, from around 922 BCE to 587 BCE. These times were most difficult for the prophets because some people enjoyed prosperity and peace while others at the bottom of the economic pyramid suffered many hardships to which the prophets drew attention. Within Israel and Judah, religious apostasy and idolatry were rampant, and injustices and transgressions were many. Israel's political, social, and religious institutions were sunk in the mire of sin and corruption. Civil war raged intermittently, poor alliances were made, and ineffective coalitions were formed.

On the world scene, Assyria rose to its zenith of power during this time only to be defeated by Babylon, which later succumbed to Persia. Preexilic times lasted until around 587 BCE when the southern kingdom of Judah collapsed, the capital city of Jerusalem burned, and the Temple was destroyed by the Babylonians. The prophetic literature that describes the events of these times includes the books of Amos, Hosea, First Isaiah, Micah, Zephaniah,

Nahum, Habakkuk, and Jeremiah. Many of the prophets of this time warned against alliances and coalitions; they upbraided kings, large landowners, and other political and social leaders and powerbrokers, because they had become corrupt and had blatantly disregarded torah. These prophets also addressed the religious leaders of their day, many of whom had become hypocrites (e.g., Mi 1–3). Further, the prophets passed judgment on the ordinary folk of their day who were not faithful to covenant and the law. Nations who took advantage of Israel and other peoples were also put on notice (e.g., Is 13–23; Am 1–2). Despite their harsh words and warnings, these prophets saw the reign of God dawning on the horizon, which would be a time when all nations, all peoples would come together in peace on God's holy mountain (e.g., Is 2:1–4; Mi 4:1–5), but that day would not arrive until all corruption and wickedness had been rooted out. Hence, turmoil, chaos, and devastation were the forerunners to restoration, renewal, and transformation.

The preexilic period ended with the inhabitants of Judah being exiled to either Babylon or Egypt. This event ushered in the exilic period from around 587 BCE to about 539 BCE. During these years the Israelite people struggled because they were now without land, a king and monarchy, and a temple. They wondered if their God had abandoned them completely. Life in Babylon, however, was not a terrible experience for the Israelites and in fact, when they were freed from exile, many chose to stay in Babylon rather than start the hard work of rebuilding and re-establishing themselves as a people and a community. These exilic times, though, did bring a certain degree of sadness, despair, and lamentation to the Israelites. They had lost so much! The prophetic texts that describe the events and situations of these times include Obadiah, Ezekiel, and Second Isaiah. The message of the prophets in these texts was often one of comfort (e.g., Is 40:1–2; 43–44). God would redeem the people; the Temple would be rebuilt; the people would be re-established on their land; and the land and community would flourish.

When Cyrus, king of Persia, defeated the Babylonians, he issued an edict that essentially ended the Israelites' exile. The people were now free to return to their land. Some did; some did not. This edict began the postexilic period in Israel's history and took place around 539 BCE to about 333 BCE. This period was also known as the Restoration Period. The texts that describe these times include Third Isaiah, Joel, Jonah, Haggai, Zechariah, and Malachi. In these texts, the focus of the prophets' messages was on shoring up life in the community, on re-building the Temple, or as in the case of Malachi, discerning whether the Temple could be re-built at all. Malachi thought that the Temple service and personnel were hopelessly corrupt. The messages in these texts were a mixture of encouragement and warning.

## The Books of Baruch, Lamentations, and Daniel and Their Place in Prophetic Literature

Three other books often associated with the prophetic corpus but which are not part of the block of material known as the Major or Minor Prophets are the books of Baruch, Lamentations, and Daniel. The book of Baruch has as its backdrop both the fall of Jerusalem in 587 BCE and the exile. This book is not part of the Hebrew or Palestinian canon of sacred texts but is found in the Greek Septuagint. Therefore Baruch is known to both the Roman Catholic and Greek Orthodox traditions and is one of the seven deuterocanonical books. For Protestants, the book of Baruch appears in the apocryphal texts of the Bible.

Like the book of Baruch, the book of Lamentations has as its historical backdrop the fall of Jerusalem in 587 BCE. The inspiration and canonicity of Lamentations has been acknowledged but its location in the canon varies: the Hebrew tradition places the book among the Writings; the Greek and Latin traditions place Lamentations among the Prophets.

A similar situation exists for the book of Daniel. This book portrays the Judahites in exile. The two prayers in Dn 3 and the stories of Susanna and Bel and the Dragon, chs. 13 and 14 respectively, are found in the Greek and Latin versions of the text but not in the Hebrew canon. The Roman Catholic tradition accepts these passages as canonical, but Protestant tradition rejects them, viewing them as apocryphal. The Hebrew text places Daniel among the Writings, but the Greek, Catholic, and Protestant canons place Daniel among the Prophets.

# The "Prophetic Persona" in the Books of the Major and Minor Prophets

Whether or not all of Israel's prophets were actual historical persons is debated among biblical scholars today. Despite such historical questions, the prophetic books of the Bible do offer a comprehensive picture of the "prophetic persona." Based on the literature of the books of the Prophets, Israel's prophets seem to be, for the most part, common people but based on the form and style of the prophetic texts, scholarly arguments have been made to suggest that some prophets were very well educated. Some may have been priests; many were not. Israel's prophets were the keepers of the covenant and the guardians of justice, righteousness, and lovingkindness. Their message is both time-bound and timeless. What the prophets proclaimed was often colored by and reflective of the historical, cultural, social, political, and theological setting and thought of their day. The prophets were persons of deep feeling and were passionate about issues concerning justice (Am 5:21–24; 8:4–6). They frequently challenged what some held "sacred," which included institutions, systems, structures, attitudes, and mindsets (Is 1:10–20; 58:1–14; Jer 7:1–15).

## The Vocation of the Prophet

Prophecy was not only a charism but also a vocation that called Israel's prophets to remain faithful to Israel's God, faithful to himself or herself, faithful to the vocation, and faithful to the task to be done and the mission to be accomplished. As one divinely inspired, the prophet was called to comfort (Is 40:1–2), confront (Hos 4:1–3), offer hope (Jl 2:21–27), proclaim (Mi 1), envision (Jer 31:31–34), energize (Is 25), challenge (Am 6:1–8), exhort (Hos

6:1–3), intercede (Hb 3:1–16), and keep alive the gift of imagination (Ez 1).

## The Mission of the Prophet

The mission of Israel's prophets was multi-faceted; some announced judgment (Hos 4:1–3), others proclaimed salvation (Is 62), and others offered words of comfort and hope (Jer 30:31–34). The prophets had an ethical mission. They were to help liberate creation from pain and suffering, which included both the victims and the perpetrators of injustice (e.g., Jl 2:21–22; Is 42:1–4; 52:13–53:12). They also had a theological mission, which was to make known who Israel's God was, namely, a God of justice and compassion (Mi 7:18–20). Their mission was also political insofar as they had to advise political, social, and religious leaders of the day (Jer 38:14–28). Finally, the prophet was to be forever in dialogue with his or her God, who would reveal what needed to be said and done (Mi 6:6–8). As keepers of the covenant, Israel's prophets were heralds of good news, calling people back to right relationship with God and with each other (Is 1:16–17).

## The Experience of the Prophet

The biblical texts of the prophets suggest that the experience of Israel's prophets was an intuitive one, as exemplified by the opening words of Jeremiah's call narrative: "The word of the LORD came to me . . ." (Jer 1:4). Israel's God also revealed to the prophets what needed to be done in relation to their prophetic vocation and mission (Jer 13:1–11). When first called to serve as a prophet, some were initially reluctant (see Jer 1:4–10 and Is 6:1–9), but the gifts needed for this vocation were divinely and freely bestowed (Jer 1:6–10), enabling them to say, "Here I am, . . . send me!" (Is 6:8).

Israel's prophets were people who lived life with passion, and they felt deeply all sorts of emotions related to their vocation (Hb 1). They felt joy, delight, fear, frustration, pain, and most importantly, righteous anger over the people's apostasy, idolatry, and other transgressions (Mi 3). Perhaps the best example of a passion-filled prophet can be found in the book of Jeremiah, where the prophet complains to his God (Jer

15:10–18), expresses utter frustration yet not without a sense of confidence and hope (Jer 20:7–18), and then prays to his God for understanding (Jer 32:16–25). Through the person of Hosea, Israel came to know the struggle within the heart of the God of Israel, depicted as vacillating between love, remembrance, frustration, fidelity, and compassion (Hos 11:1–9). Because of an inner compulsion that often welled up inside of them, the prophets had to speak; the spirited and Spirit-filled word of God had to go forth even when the prophet would rather not speak (Jer 20:9). Israel's prophets were both in touch with God's Spirit and filled with this Spirit, which was the source of their proclamation and the inspiration behind their mission (e.g., Mi 3:8).

## The Word of the Prophet

According to the prophetic corpus, Israel's prophets either delivered their God's word (Ez 21) or they proclaimed a message related to their divine mission, as in the case of Micah, who upbraided the political, social, and religious leaders of his day because they had acted unjustly and the priests and prophets had corrupted their religious offices (Mi 3:1–7, 9–12). Although the word of Israel's prophets is often harsh and foreboding, this word is always the graced word inviting people to change their ways and to be transformed into the holy and godly human beings they are meant to be (Gn 1:27; Lv 20:26). It is important to remember that the word that the prophets proclaimed was oftentimes historically, socially, culturally, politically, and theologically conditioned and reflected the times and the specific agenda of the biblical writers and final editors of the biblical text. For example, the prophets often spoke out against idolatry. This emphasis not only supported torah but also firmly established the sovereignty of Israel's God over all other gods. Often the prophets began their proclamations with the phrase "Thus says the Lord," a typical prophetic messenger formula and later addition to the message. The phrase was added to lend both authority and credence to the prophets' words.

The prophets' word was also delivered symbolically. Often the prophets would perform some sort of symbolic action, the meaning of which only came to light much later in the life of the community. For example, Micah lamented, wailed, and went barefoot and naked to draw attention to the community's sinfulness (Mi 1:8). Jeremiah sported the yoke of oxen to symbolize and indicate to his people that they were about to go into Babylonian captivity (Jer 27). Thus, Israel's prophets delivered their God's message through spoken word and symbolic action.

## The Vision of the Prophet

The prophetic books make clear that Israel's prophets read the signs of the time. They studied their community and world events and circumstances and knew what was about to befall Israel and Judah. Hence the prophets warned their communities and the surrounding nations what their fate was going to be if they did not chart a new course. The prophets were also graced with intuitive vision—of seeing God's vision for the world, which was and continues to be a vision of unity and peace for all creation, so beautifully expressed in Is 2:1–4; 65:17–25; Mi 4:1–5. The prophets also heralded a vision of a new kind of leadership that would help to usher in the reign of God and a new world order (Is 9:1–6; 11:1–9; 32:1). Israel's prophets were double-visioned: they saw what was and they saw what could be, and thus they gave both sight and insight to their listeners. The entire prophetic experience is "vision," so wondrously captured by this next phrase: "The vision which Isaiah, son of Amoz, saw concerning Judah and Jerusalem in the days of Uzziah, Jotham, Ahaz and Hezekiah, kings of Judah" (Is 1:1).

# True and False Prophets

Not all who made proclamations in God's name were considered true prophets. In ancient Israel, false prophets co-existed with true prophets. The criterion for deciding whether a prophet was true or false was whether the word proclaimed was fulfilled or not. For this reason, many people within the Israelite community recognized those gifted "seers" as poets and they were only later acknowledged as prophets. Like the true prophets, the false prophets engaged in ecstatic activities (1 Kgs 18:19–40; 22:5–23); they also experienced dreams and delivered their contents to the people, but these dreams were later condemned (Dt 13:1–4; Jer 23:25–40; Ez 13:9). Unlike the true prophets, the false prophets led the people astray especially when they spoke in the name of Baal (e.g., 1 Kgs 18:19–40). The false prophets often gave the people a false sense of confidence (Jer 4:10; 6:14; Ez 13:10) that served to undermine the message of the true prophets, thereby creating conflict. Only true prophets stood in the council of God, and only true prophets were called and sent by God (Is 6:1–13; Jer 1:4–10). Jeremiah 28 describes an exchange between Jeremiah and Hananiah and provides an example of the conflict and opposition that also existed among the prophets.

## The Prophets, God, and the Expression of Violence

Central to the message of the prophets is their portrayal of God. They portray a God who forewarns the people about impending disasters because of the people's transgressions (e.g., Is 24). Using metaphorical language influenced by the social setting of the day, the prophets depict God as a warrior judge (Am 1:3–2:16), an agonized parent (Is 1:2–9), a teacher (Is 48:17–19), an artist and creator (Is 44:24–28), a designer and crafter of symbols (Jer 11:11–19), a weaver of visions and maker of dreams (Am 7:1–3). God is one who raises up prophets (Jer 1:4–10), replaces stony hearts (Ez 36:22–26), acts as a shepherd (Ez 34:11–16), is sovereign over all nations (Is 25:1–10), sustains, redeems, heals, renews, restores, and transforms life (Is 43:1–13, 25; Hos 14:4–9), and God desires to be one with humankind (Jer 31:31–34; Hos 6:4–6).

Often the prophets portray God as a violent God, inflicting chastisements upon a wayward people. This violence seems to reflect the culture of the prophets' times as well as a belief in a theology of retribution (e.g., Dt 28). Additionally, in attempting to proclaim Israel's God as the sovereign one who is more powerful than all other gods and earthly rulers and forces at work in the culture, the prophets have to depict this God in human ways—as a God of unsurpassable power and might, larger than life, and capable of leveling peoples, nations, and lands (e.g., Mi 1:2–7; see also the proclamations to the nations in Is 13–23; cf. Jer 46–51; Am 1:2–2:16). One point is certain: the prophets are trying to put those in power "on notice," warning them that one more powerful is going to establish justice by toppling abusive, domineering, controlling, unjust leaders. The prophets and later biblical authors and editors assert that Israel's God is Lord of creation and Lord of history. Interestingly, the biblical text and evolving history have shown that such violent and aggressive use of power either on God's or Israel's or the nations' part has not succeeded in hastening the reign of God or ushering in peace. Violence begets violence. In this way, the prophetic texts remain prophetic, beckoning people to turn their swords into plowshares and their spears into pruning hooks for the sake of a new world order. For the prophets, God is, ultimately, a God of compassion, which is the deepest expression of justice (Mi 7:7–20). This point, however, does not preclude constructive consequences for wrongdoing.

## The Literature of the Prophetic Books

Composed of prose and poetry, the writings of Israel's prophets are literary masterpieces that include many forms and use many techniques. Some of these forms are: symbolic action reports (Is 20:1–6), commissioning reports (Jer 1:4–10), vision reports (Am 7:1), biographies (Jer 37–44), woe proclamations (Mi 2:1–5), dirges (Ez 32:17–19), laments (Am 5:1–3), judgment speeches (Mi 1:2–7), *rîb* or courtroom scenes (Mi 6:1–5; Hos 4:1–3), parables (Is 5:1–7; Jer 18:1–11), disputation speeches (Mi 2:6–11), complaints (Hb 1:2–17), prayers (Hb 3:1–16), and taunt songs (Is 14:3–21), among other forms. The most prominent literary techniques employed are metaphors, similes, and metaphorical language along with anthropomorphism, which ascribes human qualities to God. The main feature of the poetry of the prophets is parallelism, which includes reversed word-pairs (Mi 3:1–2), numerical word-pairs (Am 1–2), and chiastic structures (Is 24:18). Other rhetorical elements used include imagery, hyperbole, irony, and personification.

## The Literature of the Prophetic Books and the New Testament

Perhaps no other body of Old Testament writings appears more often in the New Testament than the literature of the Prophets. Both the Synoptic Gospels and the Gospel of John contain references and allusions to the Prophets. For example, in Mt 12:15–21, one finds a reference to Is 42:1–4. Was the Gospel writer simply excerpting pieces of prophetic literature to argue the point that the Old Testament prophecy comes to fulfillment in the New Testament? One might assume that this was the case, but a closer look at the context presents a different scenario.

What the writers of the New Testament seem to be doing is re-reading the Prophets in light of who Jesus was and in relation to his mission and ministry.[1] The life of Jesus brought some of the writings of the Prophets to a deeper sense of fulfillment, and that fulfillment is ongoing as the texts continue to take on a life of their own in new contexts. The Gospel writers in particular recognized this point of deeper fulfillment and wrote accordingly. Having the memories of the community and the writings and preaching of Paul, they were most likely able to see the "connections" between Jesus' life and mission and the texts of the Prophets; they did not merely "apply" the texts to Jesus' life or use the prophetic texts in a manner that resembles

"prooftexting." For example, in Is 42:1–4, justice will be proclaimed to the "nations." The "nations" are a central point and play a major role in the times of the prophets, and specifically in the world and times of Isaiah. In Matthew, however, justice will be proclaimed to the "Gentiles." The change in wording is significant because Matthew's concern is with the Gentiles. He focuses on proclaiming the good news to them, namely, that they too have a place in the reign of God.

In Lk 4:16–30, one finds an allusion to Is 61:1–2a. Again, the Gospel writer is re-reading the Isaiah text in light of the person of Jesus and his mission, which included proclaiming the year of the Lord's favor—the jubilee year—when all debts were to be cancelled. For Luke, the cancellation of debts—the year of the Lord's favor—included the forgiveness of sin. Interestingly, Luke makes no mention of Isaiah's reference to proclaiming the vengeance of God, which appears in the last part of Is 61:2. For Luke as a Gospel writer and in his portrait of Jesus, the preaching to be done was the work of evangelization—sharing the good news of God's love for all—and not the proclamation of God's vengeance.

Re-readings of the prophetic texts also appear in Epistles (see, e.g., Heb 8:8–12; 10:16–17; cf. Jer 31:31–34). Finally, Isaiah's vision of a new heavens and a new earth (see Is 65:17–25) finds an echo in Rev 21:1–4. This vision, shared by Isaiah and the book of Revelation, remains prophetic today, for God's people have yet to embrace the kind of justice, righteousness, and lovingkindness that would bring the vision to fruition and fulfillment.

## In Sum

Israel's prophetic literature is rich in form, content, and style, and its main characters—Israel's God and the prophets—are all colorful figures who reveal the struggle to remain faithful in the face of rejection, adversity, and disappointment. Israel's prophets offer a vision for the good life and a new world order that will dawn when the earth's peoples act justly, love tenderly, and walk humbly with their God. ∎

---

1. For further study on the method of re-reading texts and the relationships between the Old Testament and the New Testament, see the Pontifical Biblical Commission's document on "The Interpretation of the Bible in the Church," *Origins* (Jan. 6, 1994), vol. 23; No. 29, pp. 513–515. Also available at http://catholic-resources.org/ChurchDocs/PBC_Interp.htm.

# THE PROPHETIC BOOKS
## New American Bible, Introduction

The prophetic books bear the names of the four major and twelve minor prophets, in addition to Lamentations and Baruch. The terms "major" and "minor" refer to the length of the respective compositions and not to their relative importance. Jonah is a story about a prophet rather than a collection of prophetic pronouncements. In the Hebrew Bible, Lamentations and Daniel are listed among the Writings (Hagiographa), not among the prophetic books. The former contains a series of laments over the destruction of Jerusalem by the Babylonians. The latter is considered to be a prophetic book, though it consists of a collection of six edifying diaspora tales (chaps. 1–6) and four apocalyptic visions about the end time (chaps. 7–12). Baruch is not included in the Hebrew canon, but is in the Septuagint or Old Greek version of the Bible, and the Church has from the beginning acknowledged its sacred and inspired character.

The prophetic books contain a deposit of prophetic preaching, and several of them in addition are filled out with narrative about prophets (e.g., Is 7; 36–39; Jer 26–29; 36–45; Am 7:10–17). In ancient Israel a prophet was understood to be an intermediary between God and the community, someone called to proclaim the word of God. Prophets received such communications through various means, including visions and dreams, often in a state of transformed consciousness, and transmitted them to the people as God's messengers through oracular utterances, sermons, writings, and symbolic actions.

It would be misleading to think of these works as books in our sense of the term. While some prophecies originated as written material, prophetic activity more commonly took the form of public speaking. Prophetic discourse addressed to different audiences in different situations would, typically, be committed first to memory, then to writing, often by the prophet's followers, sometimes by the prophet himself (e.g., Is 8:1–4, 16; Jer 36:1–2; Hb 2:2). Small compilations of such pronouncements and discourses would be put together, arranged according to subject matter (e.g., pronouncements against foreign nations), audience (e.g., Jeremiah to King Zedekiah, Jer 21:1–24:10), chronological sequence (e.g., in Ezekiel generally), or by verbal association (e.g., catchwords). These units would be circulated, edited, expanded and interpreted as the need arose to bring out the contemporary relevance of older prophecies, and eventually integrated into larger collections. The titles would have been added at a later date, in some instances centuries after the time of the prophet in question.

The office of the prophet came about as the result of a direct call from God. Unlike that of the priest, the prophetic function was not hereditary and did not correspond to a fixed office. In Israel as elsewhere in the ancient Near East and Levant, there were, however, prophets (*nĕbî'îm* in Hebrew) who were employed in temples and at royal courts, and some of the canonical prophets may have started out as "professionals" of this kind. Prophecy also differed from priesthood in ancient Israel in that there were both male and female prophets. Though none of the prophetic books is named for a female prophet, Miriam (Ex 15:20) and Deborah (Jgs 4:4) played important roles at the beginning of Israel's history and Huldah (2 Kgs 22:14) toward the end. The Bible gives great importance to the call or commissioning of the prophet, which was often accompanied by visionary or other extraordinary experiences (e.g., Jer 23:21–22; Ez 1–2). In these accounts the prophetic intermediary can be represented as a messenger commissioned by the Lord as king (e.g., Micaiah in 1 Kgs 22:19–23, and Isaiah in Is 6:1–13), and therefore prophetic speech is often introduced with the form used in the delivery of a message: "thus says the Lord" or some similar formula. Sometimes the prophetic calling could be expected to involve struggle, persecution, and suffering.

While prophetic messages sometimes bore on the future, their primary concern was with contemporary events in the public sphere of social life and politics, national and international. They focus on public morality, the treatment of the poor and disadvantaged, and the abuse of power, especially of the judicial system. They pass judgment in the strongest terms on the moral conduct of rulers and the ruling class, in the belief that a society that does not practice justice and righteousness will not survive. With equal rigor, they also condemn a religious formalism that would legitimate such a society (e.g., Is 1:10–17; Jer 7:1–15; Am 5:21–24). They view international affairs, the rise and fall of the great empires, in the light of their own passionate belief in the God of Israel and the destiny of Israel. The prophets never take political and military power as absolutes. They do not preach a new morality. They are radicals only in the sense of a radical commitment to and interpretation of the religious, legal, and moral traditions inherited from Israel's past.

Prophetic speech is not, however, confined to judgment and condemnation. The prophets also exhort, cajole, encourage; they announce salvation and a good prognosis for the future. Sometimes present realities and situations shade off into, or are taken up into, a panorama of a more distant future. In many instances, too, prophetic pronouncements are developed by a cumulative and incremental editorial process into a more inclusive and total vision of a final salvation and a final judgment, with or without the presence of a messianic figure. This process is particularly evident throughout the Book of Isaiah, and played an important part in the self-understanding of early Christian churches and their interpretation of the person and mission of Jesus. For early Christianity, therefore, prophetic texts were used to describe the new reality of Christ and the church (e.g., Mt 1:23; Acts 2:14–21; Gal 4:27). ∎

# The Book of

# Isaiah

## INTRODUCTION

### Carol J. Dempsey, OP

Stunning in its breadth, depth, scope, and literary artistry is the book of Isaiah, whose historical time period spans from the latter half of the eighth century BCE to approximately the fourth century BCE. This vast span is indicated by the two names that appear in the book: Uzziah (Is 1:1), a Judahite king who reigned from 783 to 742 BCE, and Cyrus (45:1), a Persian emperor who reigned from 539 to 530 BCE. Various other clues in the text also help to determine the time frame for the book of Isaiah. For example, in chs. 1–39, Jerusalem, the capital of the southern kingdom of Judah, is described as a city engaged in sinful deeds. The prophet Isaiah delivers stinging messages to the city that is now threatened with punishment (e.g., Is 3; 10:11). In chs. 40–55, the city has been destroyed (e.g., 40:1–2) and its reconstruction is greatly anticipated (44:26; 49:13–26). In chs. 56–66, the city and the Temple have been rebuilt (e.g., 56:1–8). The rebuilt Temple was dedicated in 515 BCE. Thus, Isaiah seems to span from around 735 to about 480 BCE.

Consisting of sixty-six chapters, the book of Isaiah imaginatively describes the major events that occurred in both the northern kingdom of Israel and the southern kingdom of Judah, the latter being the poet's primary focus. Some of these events included the fall of Israel to the Assyrians and the deportation of the Israelites to Assyria in 722/721 BCE; the time of the exile after the southern kingdom of Judah fell to the Babylonians after Jerusalem was destroyed around 587 BCE; and the liberation of the people by King Cyrus of Persia in 539 BCE, which paved the way for the Israelites to resettle in their land. Thus, Isaiah focuses on three different historical periods: preexilic times, around 740–700 BCE (Is 1–39, also known as First Isaiah); exilic days, around 550–515 BCE (Is 40–55, also known as Second Isaiah);

## Outline of Isaiah

I. Isaiah 1–39

  A. Indictment of Israel and Judah (1:1–5:30)

  B. The Book of Emmanuel (6:1–12:6)

  C. Oracles Against the Foreign Nations (13:1–23:18)

  D. Apocalypse of Isaiah (24:1–27:13)

  E. The Lord Alone, Israel's and Judah's Salvation (28:1–33:24)

  F. The Lord, Zion's Avenger (34:1–35:10)

  G. Historical Appendix (36:1–39:8)

II. Isaiah 40–55

  A. The Lord's Glory in Israel's Liberation (40:1–48:22)

  B. Expiation of Sin, Spiritual Liberation of Israel (49:1–55:13)

III. Isaiah 56–66

and postexilic times, around 515–480 BCE (Is 56–66, also known as Third Isaiah).

## The Historical Times and Social World of Isaiah

The entire book of Isaiah describes some of the most gruesome, unjust and yet remarkably visionary times in the life of the Israelite community. First Isaiah opens with a superscription (Is 1:1) that provides a historical context for the prophet and the text. The drama begins in the last days of Uzziah, king of Judah, who reigned from 783 to 742 BCE. During this time, Judah's main threat and primary enemy was Assyria, which had reached its zenith of power in the mid-eighth to mid-seventh century. Assyria met its demise in 605 BCE. During the years 740–700 BCE, several significant events took place. The first was the Syro-Ephraimite crisis that posed a great threat to Judah (734–732 BCE). Tiglath-Pileser III ruled Assyria. This king was noted for his inordinate spirit of expansion at grave cost to other countries.

In response to Tiglath-Pileser III's advances and abuse of power, the kings of Syria (Aram) and Ephraim (Israel) made a joint defense alliance against the king of Assyria. They wanted Ahaz, king of Judah, to join them but he refused. Syria's King Rezin and Israel's King Pekah feared that Judah would ally itself with Assyria. In order to pressure Ahaz into joining the Syro-Ephraimite alliance, Rezin and Pekah planned to attack Jerusalem, depose Ahaz, and replace him with a person known as "the son of Tabeel." Fearing the advances of Syria and Israel, Ahaz sought the help of Assyrian ruler Tiglath-Pileser III who, in turn, invaded and subdued Syria and Israel. Rezin was killed in the crisis. Tiglath-Pileser III then appointed Hoshea (732–723 BCE) to be Israel's new king. Judah survived all of these events but not without cost. Ahaz paid a large indemnity to Assyria (see 2 Kgs 16:8), and Judah became a vassal state of Assyria.

The second major event was the northern kingdom of Israel's rebellion against Assyria in 722/721 BCE. In 725 BCE, Hoshea rebelled against Assyria, thinking that Egypt would come to the aid of the Israelites. This bold move on Israel's part caused Shalmaneser V (726–722 BCE) of Assyria to lay siege to Samaria, Israel's capital. The siege lasted for three years during which time Shalmaneser V died and was succeeded by Sargon II, who eventually destroyed Samaria in 721 BCE. Following Samaria's destruction, approximately 27,290 Israelites were deported to Assyria. With these two dramatic events, the northern kingdom of Israel collapsed, leaving only the kingdom of Judah in the south.

The third major event was the siege of Jerusalem in 701 BCE. The ruler of Judah at the time of this event was Hezekiah, the son of Ahaz, who reigned from 715 to 687 BCE.

During his reign, Hezekiah initiated a spirit of religious reform. The death of Sargon II in 705 BCE ignited Hezekiah's and others' desire for rebellion against Assyria. Once again, Egypt had pledged its support to assist Judah and its neighbors. Sargon II's successor, King Sennacherib, stopped the revolt in 701 BCE and led a campaign that destroyed forty-six of Judah's cities. Assyria then plundered a large number of Judah's and the cities' inhabitants. Jerusalem was not captured and so Sennacherib sent one of his officials, Rabshakeh, to meet with Hezekiah (Is 36:2). Rabshakeh tried to convince Hezekiah to submit to Assyria, arguing that assistance from Egypt, Jerusalem's military strength, or the people's belief in God would not be sufficient to ward off an Assyrian invasion (see 36:4–20).

Hezekiah then implored the prophet Isaiah to intercede on behalf of the people of Jerusalem. Isaiah responded favorably to the king's request, delivered him a message that the Assyrians would retreat, and assured him that Jerusalem would not be taken captive (Is 37:33–35; 38:4–6). According to the Isaian biblical story, with its imaginative and highly metaphorical language and images, an angel of God struck down the Assyrian soldiers and Jerusalem was not destroyed. Before Sennacherib withdrew from Jerusalem, however, he imposed a large indemnity on Hezekiah, turned the city into vassalage, and forced him to pay a greater annual tribute. These historical events of 740–700 BCE shaped the first book of Isaiah and laid the foundation for Second Isaiah (Is 40–55), a time of exile and bewilderment for the Israelite community.

The event that led up to the exile was the Babylonian invasion of the southern kingdom of Judah. The Babylonians destroyed the Temple, burned Jerusalem, and in 587 BCE the entire southern kingdom of Judah collapsed. The people were exiled to Babylon and Egypt. Without land, a king, a Temple, and the holy city of Jerusalem, the people felt completely abandoned. Little did they realize that their God had not abandoned them but was present through the prophet who remained in their midst. In Is 40–55, the prophet delivered words of comfort. Not until the Babylonian Empire collapsed during the time of the Persian Empire did the people of Israel experience a new kind of freedom under Persian King Cyrus, who allowed the Jews to return to their homeland if they so desired.

Isaiah 56–66 tells of a new era for the Jewish people. Cyrus, king of Persia, decreed in 539 BCE that the exile was ended. Life in Babylon did afford the Jews some good opportunities, and so not all of the people chose to return to their homeland. Ezra 2:64–65 records that a group of about 50,000 Jews did return to Judah. They were not greeted warmly, however, by the descendants of those who had been left behind in the land. The returnees began work on the second Temple but struggled with disillusionment, their sense of identity, and their self-understanding. Bitter strife and circumstances that alienated one person from another soon characterized the fabric of Jewish life in Judah, but times were not all grim. New visions of a new heaven and a new earth emerged, offering a renewed sense of hope (e.g., Is 65:17–25). Thus Third Isaiah focuses on resettlement in the land amid uncertainties, judgment, promise, and hope.

# The Literary Dimensions of the Book of Isaiah

The typical subdivisions of the book are Is 1–39, 40–55, and 56–66, though recently many scholars have subdivided the text into two parts, Is 1–39 and 40–66, and have been trying to discover links between the divisions. With respect to authorship, Isaiah is the work of multiple authors, editors, and later redactors. As a whole, it depicts an extraordinary poet-prophet who walks by the light of God.

Many themes emerge from the book of Isaiah. One theme focuses on the sovereignty of God, who is a God of justice and compassion, a healer, restorer, savior, liberator, and redeemer. This God works through history, e.g., the Persian King Cyrus, a non-Jew who liberates the Jews from exile. Other themes center on transgression, the abuse of power, apostasy, idolatry, inordinate pride and arrogance, and the violation of right relationship that affects the good of the community. Both Israel and the other nations are called to act justly. Transformed by God, all the nations, and not just Israel, will

have a place in the reign of God (Is 2:2–4), and foreigners will be "at home" in God's house (56:3–8). Another theme is promise—of a new type of governor for Israel and for the world, of a new world order, of a new heavens and a new earth, of covenant renewal, redemption, restoration, and transformation, of a rebuilt Jerusalem and Temple, and lastly, of peace for all peoples and nations. Finally, throughout the book of Isaiah, Jerusalem/Daughter Zion is a prominent motif. A city condemned and scorned by her God (1:8, 21–23; 29:1–6) will one day become a glorious crown in the hand of her God (62:3; see also vv. 1–12). These are just a few of the book's many themes.

The book of Isaiah is a poetic vision that features multiple voices, proclamations to the nations (Is 13–23), judgment speeches (5:8–25), summons (1:2), apostrophes (26:8, 11–13), symbolic actions (8:1–10), a call narrative (ch. 6), prayers (33:2–6), songs (5:1–7), visions (2:2–4), confessions (25:1–5), exhortations (1:16), instructions (30:8–14), and promises of peace (11:1–9; 32:1–8), among other literary forms. Perhaps the best known of all the Isaian passages are the Servant Songs. Later some of these verses would be key passages for the interpretation of the identity and mission of Jesus by a variety of New Testament writers; see, e.g., Is 42:1 for the baptism and transfiguration scenes of the Synoptic Gospels (Mt 3:17//Mk 1:11//Lk 3:22; Mt 17:5//Mk 9:7//Lk 9:35) and Is 50:5–7 for the abuse Christ endured during his passion (Mt 27:30–31//Mk 15:19). In 1 Pt 2:21–25, slaves unjustly abused by their masters are encouraged to see in their suffering the example of Christ, an allusion to the suffering servant of Is 53. Thus the book of Isaiah is a marvelous poem sprinkled with prose, all of which was sung by poets who dared to proclaim the shortcomings, hardships, hopes, and joys of a people who were struggling to be in right relationship with one another and with their God.

# Theological Dimensions of the Book of Isaiah

The book's rich theological message is embedded in its literary content. In many places, both the poetic storyline of the text and its theological message reflect the theologies of the ancient biblical world and culture, namely, the Deuteronomic theology of retribution (see Dt 28) and the Deuteronomic theology of love (Dt 6:1–9; 7:6–11; 10:12–22). For example, because the inhabitants of Israel did not follow the ways of their God, divine judgment would befall them (Is 9:7–14; cf. Dt 28:20). The final word, however, is not divine chastisement but hope because Israel's God remains faithful to the people (see Is 60; 65:17–25; cf. Dt 7:6–11). The poet's primary audience is the political, social, and religious leaders of his day. In addressing this group, the theological theme of justice and injustice emerges. The poet calls the Israelite and Judahite leaders, as well as the leaders of the other nations, to right relationships. Because many of the Israelites have not followed the law and have forgotten their God or gone after other gods, injustice prevails. Thus the people experience God's indignation and anger and live under the threat of severe chastisement. Repeatedly the poet calls the people to (re)turn to their God (e.g., Is 44:22; 55:7).

A second theological theme is leadership. The poet presents a new picture of a new kind of leader. Instead of the hierarchical, patriarchal model that was dominant in the ancient world, the author presents a model of leadership whereby the leader is the servant of God and God's people, whose mission and work is to liberate the people from injustice—and not

only those who are victims of injustice but also the perpetrators of injustice who are caught in their own pain, greed, and web of violence. Unlike the leaders of the day, this new leader will accomplish the mission of transformation nonviolently (e.g., Is 9:1–7; 11:1–9; 42:1–4 [5–9]).[1] This new leader will be a light to all nations (see 49:1–7), giving all nations a new transformative and divine vision.

Hope is another theological theme of the book of Isaiah. Jerusalem, a city once devastated, will be re-built and transformed from desolation to delight, and so will God's people (Is 60–62). Justice will prevail; the new heavens and new earth will be the lived reality (65:17–25). Worship and ethical praxis will be intertwined (58:1–14). As people are redeemed from their sin so will the natural world be freed from the effects of human transgression. The entire cosmos will rejoice (44:23). Thus Isaiah's theological vision is broad, deep, expansive, and inclusive. Finally, embedded in the Isaiah text is a timeless vision of a new world order that waits to be discovered and lived out (e.g., 2:2–4; 56:1–8; 65:17–25). ■

---

1. In Is 49:2 the servant of the Lord is described as a "sharp-edged sword" and a "sharpened arrow." Although these images reflect the language of warfare and the culture of the day, they are applied to the servant metaphorically to indicate the kind of strength and power that his person embodies. Ultimately, the power that the servant has and uses is the power of the word divinely given to him (cf. Is 11:1–5).

# THE BOOK OF ISAIAH

## New American Bible, Introduction

Isaiah, one of the greatest of the prophets, appeared at a critical moment in Israel's history. The Northern Kingdom collapsed, under the hammerlike blows of Assyria, in 722/721 B.C., and in 701 Jerusalem itself saw the army of Sennacherib drawn up before its walls. In the year that Uzziah, king of Judah, died (742), Isaiah received his call to the prophetic office in the Temple of Jerusalem. Close attention should be given to chap. 6, where this divine summons to be the ambassador of the Most High is circumstantially described.

The vision of the Lord enthroned in glory stamps an indelible character on Isaiah's ministry and provides a key to the understanding of his message. The majesty, holiness and glory of the Lord took possession of his spirit and, at the same time, he gained a new awareness of human pettiness and sinfulness. The enormous abyss between God's sovereign holiness and human sinfulness overwhelmed the prophet. Only the purifying coal of the seraphim could cleanse his lips and prepare him for acceptance of the call: "Here I am, send me!"

The ministry of Isaiah extended from the death of Uzziah in 742 B.C. to Sennacherib's siege of Jerusalem in 701 B.C., and it may have continued even longer, until after the death of Hezekiah in 687 B.C. Later legend (the Martyrdom and Ascension of Isaiah) claims that Hezekiah's son, Manasseh, executed Isaiah by having him sawed in two; cf. Heb 11:37. During this long ministry, the prophet returned again and again to the same themes, and there are indications that he may have sometimes re-edited his older prophecies to fit new occasions. There is no evidence that the present arrangement of the oracles in the book reflects a chronological order. Indeed, it appears that there were originally separate smaller collections of oracles (note especially chaps. 6–12), each with its own logic for ordering, that were preserved fairly intact as blocks when the material was finally put together as a single literary work.

Isaiah's oracles cluster around several key historical events of the late eighth century: the Syro-Ephraimite War (735–732 B.C.), the accession of Hezekiah (715 B.C.), the revolt of Ashdod (714–711 B.C.), the death of Sargon (705 B.C.), and the revolt against Sennacherib (705–701 B.C.). In 738 B.C., with the Assyrian defeat of Calno/Calneh (Is 10:9; Am 6:2), the anti-Assyrian league, of which Judah may have been the ringleader, collapsed, and both Israel and the Arameans of Damascus paid tribute to Assyria. By 735 B.C., however, Rezin of Damascus had created a new anti-Assyrian league, and when Ahaz refused to join, the league attempted to remove Ahaz from the throne of Judah. The resulting Syro-Ephraimite War was the original occasion for many of Isaiah's oracles (cf. chaps. 7–8), in which he tried to reassure Ahaz of God's protection and dissuade him from seeking protection by an alliance with Assyria. Ahaz refused Isaiah's message, however.

When Hezekiah came to the throne in 715 B.C., Isaiah appears to have put great hopes in this new scion of David, and he undoubtedly supported the religious reform that Hezekiah undertook. But the old intrigues began again, and the king was sorely tempted to join with neighboring states in an alliance sponsored by Egypt against Assyria. Isaiah succeeded in keeping Hezekiah out of Ashdod's abortive revolt against Assyria, but when Sargon died in 705 B.C., with both Egypt and Babylon encouraging revolt, Hezekiah was won over to the pro-Egyptian party. Isaiah denounced this "covenant with death" (28:15, 18), and again summoned Judah to faith in the Lord as the only hope. But it was too late; the revolt had already begun. Assyria acted quickly and its army, after ravaging Judah, laid siege to Jerusalem (701). "I shut up Hezekiah like a bird in his cage," boasts the famous inscription of Sennacherib. The city was spared but at the cost of paying a huge indemnity to Assyria. Isaiah may have lived and prophesied for another dozen years after 701. There is material in the book that may plausibly be associated with

Sennacherib's campaign against Babylon and its Arabian allies in 694–689 B.C.

For Isaiah, the vision of God's majesty was so overwhelming that military and political power faded into insignificance. He constantly called his people back to a reliance on God's promises and away from vain attempts to find security in human plans and intrigues. This vision also led him to insist on the ethical behavior that was required of human beings who wished to live in the presence of such a holy God. Isaiah couched this message in oracles of singular poetic beauty and power, oracles in which surprising shifts in syntax, audacious puns, and double- or triple-entendre are a constant feature.

The complete Book of Isaiah is an anthology of poems composed chiefly by the great prophet, but also by disciples, some of whom came many years after Isaiah. In 1–39 most of the oracles come from Isaiah and reflect the situation in eighth-century Judah. Sections such as the Apocalypse of Isaiah (24–27), the oracles against Babylon (13–14), and probably the poems of 34–35 were written by followers deeply influenced by the prophet, in some cases reusing earlier Isaianic material; cf., e.g., 27:2–8 with 5:1–7.

Chapters 40–55 (Second Isaiah, or Deutero-Isaiah) are generally attributed to an anonymous poet who prophesied toward the end of the Babylonian exile. From this section come the great oracles known as the Servant Songs, which are reflected in the New Testament understanding of the passion and glorification of Christ. Chapters 56–66 (Third Isaiah, or Trito-Isaiah) contain oracles from the postexilic period and were composed by writers imbued with the spirit of Isaiah who continued his work.

The principal divisions of the Book of Isaiah are the following:

I. Isaiah 1–39
   A. Indictment of Israel and Judah (1:1–5:30)
   B. The Book of Emmanuel (6:1–12:6)
   C. Oracles Against the Foreign Nations (13:1–23:18)
   D. Apocalypse of Isaiah (24:1–27:13)
   E. The Lord Alone, Israel's and Judah's Salvation (28:1–33:24)
   F. The Lord, Zion's Avenger (34:1–35:10)
   G. Historical Appendix (36:1–39:8)
II. Isaiah 40–55
   A. The Lord's Glory in Israel's Liberation (40:1–48:22)
   B. Expiation of Sin, Spiritual Liberation of Israel (49:1–55:13)
III. Isaiah 56–66

# ISAIAH

## I. ISAIAH 1—39

### A. Indictment of Israel and Judah

**1** ¹† The vision which Isaiah, son of Amoz, saw concerning Judah and Jerusalem in the days of Uzziah, Jotham, Ahaz and Hezekiah, kings of Judah.

### Accusation and Appeal

²†    Hear, O heavens, and listen, O earth,
     for the LORD speaks:
     Sons have I raised and reared,
      but they have rebelled against me! *

³     An ox knows its owner,
     and an ass,† its master's manger;
     But Israel does not know,
      my people has not understood. *

⁴     Ah!† Sinful nation, people laden with
      wickedness,
     evil offspring, corrupt children!
     They have forsaken the LORD,
      spurned the Holy One of Israel,
     apostatized, *

⁵     Why† would you yet be struck,
     that you continue to rebel?
     The whole head is sick,
      the whole heart faint.

⁶     From the sole of the foot to the head
     there is no sound spot in it;

     Just bruise and welt and oozing wound,
      not drained, or bandaged,
      or eased with salve.

⁷     Your country is waste,
     your cities burnt with fire;
     Your land—before your eyes
     strangers devour it,
     a waste, like the devastation of
      Sodom.†*

⁸     And daughter Zion† is left
     like a hut in a vineyard,
     Like a shed in a melon patch,
     like a city blockaded.

⁹     If the LORD of hosts† had not
     left us a small remnant,
    We would have become as Sodom,
     would have resembled Gomorrah. *

¹⁰†   Hear the word of the LORD,
     princes of Sodom!
    Listen to the instruction of our God,
     people of Gomorrah!

¹¹    What do I care for the multitude of your
     sacrifices?
    says the LORD.
    I have had enough of whole-burnt
     rams
     and fat of fatlings;
    In the blood of calves, lambs, and goats
     I find no pleasure. *

¹²    When you come to appear before me,
     who asks these things of you?

¹³    Trample my courts no more!
     To bring offerings is useless;
     incense is an abomination to me.

---

**1:1** The title, or inscription, of the book is an editorial addition to identify the prophet and the circumstances of his ministry. *Isaiah:* meaning "the salvation of the Lord," or "the Lord is salvation." *Amoz:* not Amos the prophet. *Judah:* the Southern Kingdom of the tribes of Judah and Benjamin. *Uzziah:* also called Azariah; cf. 2 Kgs 15:1; 2 Chr 26:1.

**1:2–31** This chapter is widely considered to be a collection of oracles from various periods in Isaiah's ministry, chosen by the editor as a compendium of his most characteristic teachings.

**1:3** *Ox...ass:* Isaiah uses animals proverbial for their stupidity and stubbornness to underline Israel's failure to respond to God. *Israel:* a term Isaiah (and other prophets) frequently applies to Judah, especially after the fall of the Northern Kingdom (which Isaiah normally calls Ephraim, as in 7:2, 9, 17; 9:8), but sometimes applies to the entire chosen people, as in 8:14.

**1:4** *Ah:* see note on 5:8–24. *Holy One of Israel:* a title used frequently in the Book of Isaiah, rarely elsewhere in the Old Testament (see 5:19, 24; 10:20; 12:6; 17:7; 29:19; 30:11, 12, 15; 31:1; 37:23; 41:14, 16, 20; 43:3, 14; 45:11; 47:4; 48:17; 49:7; 54:5; 55:5; 60:9, 14).

**1:5–6** The Hebrew expression translated "Why?" may also be translated "Where?" The ambiguity is probably intentional: "Why, O Israel, would you still be beaten, and where on your bruised body do you want the next blow?" The bruised body is a metaphor for the historical disaster that has overtaken Israel (see

v. 7) because of its sins.

**1:7** *Sodom:* Sodom and Gomorrah (see vv. 9–10; cf. Gn 19) were proverbial as wicked cities completely overthrown and destroyed by God. Judah, more fortunate, survives at least as a remnant. The devastation of the land and the isolation of Jerusalem suggest the time of Sennacherib's invasion of 701.

**1:8** *Daughter Zion:* Jerusalem, as isolated as a little hut erected in a field for the shelter of watchmen and laborers.

**1:9** *LORD of hosts:* God, who is the Creator and Ruler of the armies of Israel, the angels, stars, etc.

**1:10–17** A powerful indictment of the religious hypocrisy of rulers and others who neglect just judgment and oppress the weaker members, yet believe they can please God with sacrifices and other external forms of worship. The long list of observances suggests the Lord's tedium with such attempts. *Sodom...Gomorrah:* the names are picked up from v. 9, but now to emphasize their wickedness rather than the good fortune of escaping total destruction.

---

*
**1:2** Dt 32:1, 5–6, 18.        Am 4:11.
**1:3** Jer 8:7; Lk 2:12.       **1:9** Rom 9:29.
**1:4** Is 5:24; Dt 32:15.      **1:11** Ps 50:8–13; Sir 34:23;
**1:7** Is 13:19; Dt 29:22; Jer     Mi 6:7.
49:18; 50:40;

New moon and sabbath, calling
    assemblies—
  festive convocations with wickedness—
  these I cannot bear. *

14  Your new moons and festivals I detest; *
  they weigh me down, I tire of the load.

15  When you spread out your hands,
  I will close my eyes to you;
  Though you pray the more,
  I will not listen.
  Your hands are full of blood!†*

16    Wash yourselves clean!
  Put away your misdeeds from before my
    eyes;
  cease doing evil;

17    learn to do good.
  Make justice your aim: redress the
    wronged,
  hear the orphan's plea, defend the
    widow. *

18  Come now, let us set things right, †
  says the LORD:
  Though your sins be like scarlet,
  they may become white as snow;
  Though they be red like crimson,
  they may become white as wool. *

19  If you are willing, and obey,
  you shall eat the good things of the
    land;

20  But if you refuse and resist,
  you shall be eaten by the sword:
  for the mouth of the LORD has spoken!

### The Purification of Jerusalem

21  How she has become a prostitute,
  the faithful city, † so upright!
  Justice used to lodge within her,

  but now, murderers. *

22  Your silver is turned to dross,
  your wine is mixed with water.

23  Your princes are rebels
  and comrades of thieves;
  Each one of them loves a bribe
  and looks for gifts.
  The fatherless they do not defend,
  the widow's plea does not reach them. *

24  Now, therefore, says the Lord,
  the LORD of hosts, the Mighty One of
    Israel:
  Ah! I will take vengeance on my foes
  and fully repay my enemies! *

25  I will turn my hand against you,
  and refine your dross in the furnace,
  removing all your alloy.

26  I will restore your judges† as at first,
  and your counselors as in the
    beginning;
  After that you shall be called
  city of justice, faithful city. *

27 †  Zion shall be redeemed by justice,
  and her repentant ones by
    righteousness.

28  Rebels and sinners together shall be
    crushed,
  those who desert the LORD shall be
    consumed.

### Judgment on the Sacred Groves

29 †  You shall be ashamed of the terebinths
  which you desired,
  and blush on account of the gardens
  which you chose.

30  You shall become like a terebinth whose
    leaves wither,
  like a garden that has no water.

---

† **1:15–16** *Hands…blood*: oppression of the poor is likened to violence that bloodies the hands, which explains why the hands spread out in prayer (v. 15) are not regarded by the Lord. This climax of the accusations is followed by positive admonitions for reversing the evil situation.

**1:18–20** *Let us set things right*: the Hebrew word refers to the arbitration of legal disputes (Jb 23:7). God offers to settle his case with Israel on the basis of the change of behavior demanded above. For Israel it is a life or death choice; life in conformity with God's will or death for continued disobedience.

**1:21–28** *Faithful city*: the phrase, found in v. 21 and v. 28, forms an *inclusio* which marks off the passage and also suggests three chronological periods: the city's former ideal state, its present wicked condition (described in vv. 21b–23), and the future ideal conditions intended by God. This will be brought about by a purging judgment directed primarily against the leaders ("judges…counselors").

**1:26** *Judges*: the reference must be to royal judges appointed by David and his successors, not to the tribal judges of the Book of Judges, since the "beginning" of Jerusalem as an Israelite city

dates only to the time of David. The Davidic era is idealized here; obtaining justice in the historical Jerusalem of David's time was more problematic (see 2 Sm 15:1–6).

**1:27–28** These verses expand the oracle that originally ended at v. 26. The expansion correctly interprets the preceding text as proclaiming a purifying judgment on Zion in which the righteous are saved while the wicked perish. The meaning of "by justice" and "by righteousness" is ambiguous. Do these terms refer to God's judgment or to the justice and righteousness of Zion's surviving inhabitants? Is 33:14–16 suggests the latter interpretation.

**1:29–31** These verses were secondarily inserted here on the catchword principle; like v. 28 they pronounce judgment on certain parties "together" (v. 31). The terebinths and gardens re-

---

**1:13** Prv 15:8; Jer 6:20.        Am 5:14–15; Zec
**1:14** Am 5:21–24.                     7:9–10.
**1:15** Prv 1:28; Sir              **1:18** Ps 51:9.
      34:25–31.                    **1:21** Jer 3:8; Hos 2:7.
**1:17** Ex 23:6; Dt 24:17; Sir    **1:23** Ex 23:8; Dt 16:19.
      4:9–10; Jer 22:3;           **1:24** Dt 32:41.
      Ez 22:7;                    **1:26** Jer 33:7–11; Zec 8:8.

31  The strong tree shall turn to tinder,
and the one who tends it shall
    become a spark;
Both of them shall burn together,
and there shall be none to quench
    them.

**2** <sup>1</sup>† This is what Isaiah, son of Amoz, saw
concerning Judah and Jerusalem.

## Zion, the Royal City of God

2†    In days to come,
The mountain of the LORD's house
    shall be established as the highest
        mountain
    and raised above the hills.
All nations shall stream toward it.*
3      Many peoples shall come and say:
"Come, let us go up to the LORD's
    mountain,
    to the house of the God of Jacob,
That he may instruct us in his ways,
    and we may walk in his paths."*
For from Zion shall go forth instruction,
    and the word of the LORD from
        Jerusalem.
4†    He shall judge between the nations,
    and set terms for many peoples.
They shall beat their swords into
        plowshares
    and their spears into pruning hooks;*
One nation shall not raise the sword
        against another,
    nor shall they train for war again.*
5†    House of Jacob, come,
    let us walk in the light of the LORD!

## The Lord's Day of Judgment on Pride

6    You have abandoned your people,
    the house of Jacob!
Because they are filled with diviners,
    and soothsayers, like the Philistines;
    with foreigners they clasp hands.*
7    Their land is full of silver and gold,
    there is no end to their treasures;
Their land is full of horses,
    there is no end to their chariots.
8    Their land is full of idols;
    they bow down to the works of their
        hands,
    what their fingers have made.*
9    So all shall be abased,
    each one brought low.†
    Do not pardon them!
10    Get behind the rocks,
    hide in the dust,
From the terror of the LORD
    and the splendor of his majesty!
11    The eyes of human pride shall be
        lowered,
    the arrogance of mortals shall be
        abased,
    and the LORD alone will be exalted, on
        that day.†
12    For the LORD of hosts will have his day
    against all that is proud and arrogant,
    against all that is high, and it will be
        brought low;
13    Yes, against all the cedars of Lebanon†
    and against all the oaks of Bashan,
14    Against all the lofty mountains
    and all the high hills,

---

† fer to the sacred groves or asherahs that functioned as idolatrous cultic symbols at the popular shrines or high places (1 Kgs 14:23; 2 Kgs 18:4); Hezekiah cut down these groves during his reform (2 Kgs 18:4); they were a religious issue during Isaiah's ministry (cf. Is 17:7–11). Isaiah threatens those who cultivate these symbols with the same fate that befalls trees when deprived of water.
**2:1** This editorial heading probably introduced the collection of chaps. 2–12, to which chap. 1 with its introduction was added later (see note on 1:2–31).
**2:2–22** These verses contain two very important oracles, one on the pilgrimage of nations to Mount Zion (vv. 2–4—completed with an invitation to the "house of Jacob," v. 5), the other on the day of the Lord (see note on Am 5:18), which was probably composed from at least two earlier pieces. Whereas vv. 6–8 indict Judah for trust in superstitious practices and human resources rather than in the Lord, the following verses are directed against humankind in general and emphasize the effect of the "day of the Lord," the humbling of human pride. This may be taken as a precondition for the glorious vision of vv. 2–4. This vision of Zion's glorious future, which is also found in a slightly variant form in Mi 4:1–4, is rooted in the early Zion tradition, cultivated in the royal cult in Jerusalem. It celebrated God's choice of Jerusalem as the divine dwelling place, along with God's choice of

the Davidic dynasty (Ps 68:16–17; 78:67–72; 132:13–18). *Highest mountain*: the Zion tradition followed earlier mythological conceptions that associate the abode of deities with very high mountains (Ps 48:2–3). The lifting of Mount Zion is a metaphor for universal recognition of the Lord's authority.
**2:4** Once the nations acknowledge God as sovereign, they go up to Jerusalem to settle their disputes, rather than having recourse to war.
**2:5** This verse is added as a conclusion to vv. 2–4; cf. Mi 4:4–5, where a quite different conclusion is provided for the parallel version of this oracle.
**2:9** Bowing down to idols will not bring deliverance to Israel, but rather total abasement. *Do not pardon them*: this line is so abrupt that it is almost certainly an intrusion in the text.
**2:11** *That day*: i.e., the day of the Lord; cf. note on Am 5:18.
**2:13** *Lebanon*: Mount Lebanon in Syria, famed for its cedars. *Bashan*: the fertile uplands east of the Sea of Galilee.

---

*
**2:2–4** Mi 4:1–4.
**2:3** Is 56:7; 2 Kgs 17:26–
    28; Jer 31:6–14; Zec
    8:20–23.
**2:4** Jl 4:10.

**2:4** Is 9:7; 11:4; Ps 46:10;
    Zec 9:10.
**2:6** Is 10:32.
**2:8** Is 17:7–8; 31:1–3.

15 Against every lofty tower
  and every fortified wall,
16 Against all the ships of Tarshish
  and all stately vessels.
17 Then human pride shall be abased,
  the arrogance of mortals brought low,
  And the LORD alone will be exalted on
    that day.
18 The idols will vanish completely.
19 People will go into caves in the rocks
  and into holes in the earth,
  At the terror of the LORD
  and the splendor of his majesty,
  as he rises to overawe the earth.
20 On that day people shall throw to moles
    and bats
  their idols of silver and their idols of
    gold
  which they made for themselves to
    worship.
21 And they shall go into caverns in the
    rocks
  and into crevices in the cliffs,
  At the terror of the LORD
  and the splendor of his majesty,
  as he rises to overawe the earth.
22† As for you, stop worrying about mortals,
  in whose nostrils is but a breath;
  for of what worth are they?

## Judgment on Jerusalem and Judah

3 ¹† The Lord, the LORD of hosts,
    will take away from Jerusalem and
      from Judah
  Support and staff—
    all support of bread,
    all support of water:*
2 Hero and warrior,
  judge and prophet, diviner and elder,
3 The captain of fifty and the nobleman,
  counselor, skilled magician, and
    expert charmer.
4 I will place boys as their princes;
  the fickle will govern them,*

5 And the people will oppress one
    another,
  yes, each one the neighbor.
  The child will be insolent toward the
    elder,
  and the base toward the honorable.*
6 When anyone seizes a brother
  in their father's house, saying,
  "You have clothes! Be our ruler,
  and take in hand this ruin!"—
7 He will cry out in that day:
  "I cannot be a healer,*
  when there is neither bread nor
    clothing in my own house!
  You will not make me a ruler of the
    people!"
8 Jerusalem has stumbled, Judah has
    fallen;
  for their speech and deeds affront the
    LORD,
  a provocation in the sight of his
    majesty.
9 Their very look bears witness against
    them;*
  they boast of their sin like Sodom,*
  They do not hide it.
    Woe to them!
  They deal out evil to themselves.
10 Happy the just, for it will go well with
    them,
  the fruit of their works they will eat.
11 Woe to the wicked! It will go ill with
    them,
  with the work of their hands they will
    be repaid.
12 My people—infants oppress them,
  women rule over them!
  My people, your leaders deceive you,*
  they confuse the paths you should
    follow.

13† The LORD rises to accuse,
  stands to try his people.
14 The Lord enters into judgment

---

2:22 The meaning of this verse, certainly a later addition, is not clear. It is not addressed to God but to a plural subject.
  3:1–12 These verses suggest deportation, with resulting social upheaval, and thus may date to sometime after Ahaz submitted as vassal to Assyria. The deportation practiced by Assyria, as later by Babylon, exiled the leading elements of society, such as those named in vv. 2–3; cf. 2 Kgs 24:12, 14–16 for a similar list of those exiled by the Babylonians. Denuding society of its leaders opens the way to near anarchy and a situation in which leadership is seized by or thrust upon those unqualified for it (vv. 5–7). The situation has been provoked by sinfully inept leadership (vv. 4, 8–9, 12). Some suggest that vv. 4 and 12 refer to Ahaz, who may

have come to the throne at an early age. Verses 10–11 form a wisdom couplet that was inserted later.
  3:13–15 The princes and the elders, here accused of despoiling the poor, are the very ones who should be their defenders. Loot: by the Hebrew term (gazela) Isaiah conveys the idea of violent seizure, though 10:1–4 suggests the poor could be plundered by legal means.

---

*
| 3:1 Lv 26:26; Ez 4:16. | 3:9 Jer 3:3. |
| 3:4 Eccl 10:16. | 3:9 Is 1:10. |
| 3:5 Mi 7:5–6. | 3:12 Mi 3:5. |
| 3:7 Is 1:6. | |

with the people's elders and princes:
You, you who have devoured the
　　vineyard;
　the loot wrested from the poor is in
　　your houses.
15　What do you mean by crushing my
　　people,
　and grinding down the faces of the
　　poor?
　says the Lord, the GOD of hosts.

### The Haughty Women of Zion†

16　The LORD said:*
　Because the daughters of Zion are
　　haughty,
　and walk with necks outstretched,
Ogling and mincing as they go,
　their anklets tinkling with every step,
17　The Lord shall cover the scalps of Zion's
　　daughters with scabs,
　and the LORD shall lay bare their
　　heads.†*

18† On that day the LORD will do away with
the finery of the anklets, sunbursts, and crescents; 19 the pendants, bracelets, and veils;
20 the headdresses, bangles, cinctures, perfume
boxes, and amulets; 21 the signet rings, and the
nose rings; 22 the court dresses, wraps, cloaks,
and purses; 23 the lace gowns, linen tunics, turbans, and shawls.

24　Instead of perfume there will be stench,
　　instead of a girdle, a rope,
　And instead of elaborate coiffure,
　　baldness;
　　instead of a rich gown, a sackcloth
　　skirt.
　Then, instead of beauty, shame.
25　Your men will fall by the sword,
　　and your champions,† in war;*
26　Her gates will lament and mourn,

as the city sits desolate on the
　　ground.*

**4**　¹ Seven women will take hold of one
　　man†
　on that day, saying:
"We will eat our own food
　and wear our own clothing;
Only let your name be given us,
　put an end to our disgrace!"

### Jerusalem Purified

2†　On that day,
The branch† of the LORD will be beauty
　　and glory,
　and the fruit of the land will be honor
　　and splendor
　for the survivors of Israel.
3　Everyone who remains in Zion,
　everyone left in Jerusalem
Will be called holy:
　everyone inscribed for life† in
　　Jerusalem.*
4　When the Lord washes away
　the filth of the daughters of Zion,
And purges Jerusalem's blood from her
　　midst
　with a blast of judgment, a searing
　　blast,*
5　Then will the LORD create,
　over the whole site of Mount Zion
　and over her place of assembly,
A smoking cloud by day
　and a light of flaming fire by night.*
6　For over all, his glory will be shelter and
　　protection:
　shade from the parching heat of day,
　refuge and cover from storm and rain.*

### The Song of the Vineyard†

**5**　¹ Now let me sing of my friend,
　　my beloved's song about his vineyard.

---

**3:16–4:1** Here and again in 32:9–14 Isaiah condemns the
women of the ruling class for their part in Jerusalem's plight.
　**3:17** A shaven head is a mark of social disgrace; cf. Nm 5:18.
　**3:18–23** The long list of women's apparel in these verses suggests luxury and vanity; it contains a number of rare words, and
the precise meaning of many of the terms is uncertain.
　**3:25** *Your men...your champions*: the second person feminine singular pronoun here shows that the prophet has shifted his
attention from the women of Zion to the personified city of Zion.
　**4:1** *Seven women...one man*: deportation (cf. note on 3:1–
12) would result in a disproportion of the sexes and leave the
female population without enough male partners. The women
are willing to marry, not for support, but to avoid disgrace.
　**4:2–6** Usually judged a later addition to the oracles of Isaiah.
It relieves the threatening tone of the surrounding chaps. 3 and 5.

**4:2** *Branch*: the term (Heb. *semah*) that is sometimes used of
the ideal Davidic king of the future (cf. Jer 23:5; 33:15; Zec 3:8;
6:12). However, the parallel "fruit of the land" does not favor
that usage here.
　**4:3** *Inscribed for life*: in God's list of the elect; cf. Ex 32:32.
　**5:1–7** *Vineyard*: although the term is sometimes used in an
erotic context (Sg 1:6; 8:12), "vineyard" or "vine" is used more
frequently as a metaphor for God's people (27:2; Ps 80:9, 14, 15;
Jer 2:21; 12:10; Ez 17:7; Hos 10:1; Na 2:2). The terms translated
"friend" (*yadid*) and "beloved" (*dod*) suggest the Lord's favor (Dt

---

**3:16** Is 32:9–14; Ez 16:50;　　　**4:3** Is 6:13; Ob 17; Mal
　　　Am 4:1–3.　　　　　　　　　　3:16.
**3:17** Jer 13:26; Ez 16:37.　　　**4:4** Is 1:21–28.
**3:25** Hos 14:1.　　　　　　　　**4:5** Ex 13:21.
**3:26** Is 47:1; Lam 2:10.　　　　**4:6** Is 32:1–2.

My friend had a vineyard
  on a fertile hillside;
2 He spaded it, cleared it of stones,
  and planted the choicest vines;
Within it he built a watchtower,
  and hewed out a wine press.
Then he waited for the crop of grapes,
  but it yielded rotten grapes. *
3 Now, inhabitants of Jerusalem, people
  of Judah,
  judge between me and my vineyard:
4 What more could be done for my
  vineyard
  that I did not do? *
Why, when I waited for the crop of
  grapes,
  did it yield rotten grapes?
5 Now, I will let you know
  what I am going to do to my
  vineyard:
Take away its hedge, give it to grazing,
  break through its wall, let it be
  trampled! †
6 Yes, I will make it a ruin:
  it shall not be pruned or hoed,
  but will be overgrown with thorns
  and briers;
I will command the clouds
  not to rain upon it.
7 The vineyard of the LORD of hosts is the
  house of Israel,
  the people of Judah, his cherished
  plant;
He waited for judgment, but see,
  bloodshed!
  for justice, but hark, the outcry! †

### Oracles of Reproach †

8 † Ah! Those who join house to house,
  who connect field with field,

Until no space remains, and you alone
  dwell
  in the midst of the land! *
9 In my hearing the LORD of hosts has
  sworn: *
Many houses shall be in ruins,
  houses large and fine, with nobody
  living there. *
10 Ten acres of vineyard
  shall yield but one bath, †
And a homer of seed
  shall yield but an ephah.
11 † Ah! Those who rise early in the morning
  in pursuit of strong drink,
lingering late
  inflamed by wine,
12 Banqueting on wine with harp and lyre,
  timbrel and flute, *
But the deed of the LORD they do not
  regard,
  the work of his hands they do not
  see! *
13 Therefore my people go into exile
  for lack of understanding, *
Its nobles starving,
  its masses parched with thirst.
14 Therefore Sheol enlarges its throat
  and opens its mouth beyond
  measure; *
Down into it go nobility and masses,
  tumult and revelry.
15 All shall be abased, each one brought
  low,
  and the eyes of the haughty lowered, *
16 But the LORD of hosts shall be exalted by
  judgment,
  by justice the Holy God shown holy. *
17 Lambs shall graze as at pasture,
  young goats shall eat in the ruins of
  the rich.

---

† 33:12; 2 Sm 12:25; Ps 127:2) and familial background rather than introducing the piece as a "love song," as is sometimes suggested. The prophet disguises the real theme (the people's infidelity) so that the hearers will participate in the unfavorable judgment called for (vv. 3–4). Cf. the reversal of this parable in 27:2–6.

**5:5–6** Trampled...thorns and briers: this judgment is echoed in the description of the devastated land in 7:23–25.

**5:7** Judgment...bloodshed...justice...outcry: in Hebrew there is an impressive play on words: mishpat parallels mispah, sedaqah parallels se'aqah. See also the threefold "waited for" in vv. 2, 4, 7.

**5:8–24** These verses contain a series of short oracles introduced by the Hebrew particle hoy ("Ah!"), an emphatic exclamation, sometimes translated "Woe!"

**5:8–10** An oracle against land-grabbers (v. 8); they will be impoverished instead of enriched (vv. 9–10).

**5:10** Ten acres: a field with ten times the surface area a yoke of oxen could plow in one day. Bath: a liquid measure equal to about twelve gallons. Homer: a dry measure equal to what a donkey can carry, calculated to be about ten bushels. Ephah: a dry measure of about one bushel. So small a harvest is the fruit of the land-grabbers' greed.

**5:11–13** An oracle against debauchery and indifference. Strong drink: the Hebrew word shekar means either beer or a type of wine, perhaps date wine, not distilled liquor.

**5:2** Dt 32:32.
**5:4** Mi 6:3–5.
**5:8** Mi 2:1–3.
**5:9** Is 22:14.
**5:9** Is 6:12.
**5:12** Is 5:22; Am 6:1–7.
**5:12** Is 5:19; 10:12; 14:24–27; 19:12, 17; 23:9; 28:21; 30:1.
**5:13** Hos 4:6.
**5:14** Hb 2:5.
**5:15** Is 2:9, 11, 17.
**5:16** Is 1:27.

18 Ah! Those who tug at guilt with cords of
    perversity,
    and at sin as if with cart ropes!

19† Who say, "Let him make haste,
    let him speed his work, that we may
      see it;
On with the plan of the Holy One of
    Israel!
    let it come to pass, that we may know
      it!"*

20 Ah! Those who call evil good, and good
    evil,
    who change darkness to light, and
      light into darkness,
    who change bitter to sweet, and sweet
      into bitter!*

21 Ah! Those who are wise in their own
    eyes,
    prudent in their own view!*

22 Ah! Those who are champions at
    drinking wine,
    masters at mixing drink!

23 Those who acquit the guilty for bribes,
    and deprive the innocent of justice!*

24 Therefore, as the tongue of fire licks up
    stubble,
    as dry grass shrivels in the flame,
Their root shall rot
    and their blossom scatter like dust;
For they have rejected the instruction of
    the Lord of hosts,
    and scorned the word of the Holy
      One of Israel.

25† Therefore the wrath of the Lord blazes
    against his people,
    he stretches out his hand to strike
      them;
The mountains quake,*

their corpses shall be like refuse in the
    streets.
For all this, his wrath is not turned back,
    his hand is still outstretched.

### Invasion†

26 He will raise a signal to a far-off nation,
    and whistle for it from the ends of the
      earth.*
Then speedily and promptly they will
    come.

27 None among them is weary, none
    stumbles,
    none will slumber, none will sleep.
None with waist belt loose,
    none with sandal thong broken.

28 Their arrows are sharp,
    and all their bows are bent,
The hooves of their horses like flint,
    and their chariot wheels like the
      whirlwind.

29 They roar like the lion,
    like young lions, they roar;
They growl and seize the prey,
    they carry it off and none can rescue.

30 They will growl over it, on that day,
    like the growling of the sea,
Look to the land—
    darkness closing in,
    the light dark with clouds!*

## B. The Book of Emmanuel

**6** **The Sending of Isaiah.** ¹In the year King Uzziah died,† I saw the Lord seated on a high and lofty throne,* with the train of his garment filling the temple. ²Seraphim† were stationed above; each of them had six wings: with two they covered their faces, with two

---

**5:19** An indication that some, presumably of the ruling class, scoff at Isaiah's teaching on the Lord's "plan" and "work" (cf. v. 12; 14:26–27; 28:9–14; 30:10–11).

**5:25–30** These verses do not suit their present context. Apparently v. 25 was originally the conclusion of the poem of 9:7–20 directed against the Northern Kingdom; the refrain that occurs here and in 9:11, 16, and 20. Verses 26–30 look to an invasion by Assyria and might originally have come immediately after the poem of 9:1–20 plus 5:25. The insertion of chaps. 6–8 may have occasioned the dislocation, as well as that of 10:1–4a, which may have originally belonged with the "reproach" oracles of 5:8–23.

**5:26–30** This oracle threatens a future judgment, an invasion of the Assyrian army, God's instrument for punishing Judah (10:5, 15).

**6:1** *In the year King Uzziah died*: probably 742 B.C., although the chronology of this period is disputed. *A high and lofty throne*: within the holy of holies of the Jerusalem Temple stood two cherubim, or winged sphinxes, whose outstretched wings

served as the divine throne (1 Kgs 6:23–28; Ez 1:4–28; 10:1, 20). The ark of the covenant was God's footstool (Ps 132:7–8; 1 Chr 28:2), placed under the cherubim (1 Kgs 8:6–7). *Temple*: the holy place, just in front of the holy of holies.

**6:2** *Seraphim*: the plural of *saraph* ("to burn"), a term used to designate the "fiery" serpents of the wilderness (Nm 21:8; Dt 8:15), and to refer to "winged" serpents (Is 14:29; 30:6). Here, however, it is used adjectivally of the cherubim, who are not serpent-like, as seen in the fact that they have faces and sexual parts ("feet"). See the adaptation of these figures by Ezekiel (Ez 1:10–12; 10:4–15).

---

**5:19** Jer 17:15; 2 Pt 3:3–4.
**5:20** Is 32:4–5.
**5:21** Prv 3:7; 26:12; Rom 11:25; 12:16.
**5:23** Ex 23:8; Prv 17:15.
**5:25** Am 1:1; Zec 14:5; cf.

Is 9:18a.
**5:26** Is 7:18; 11:12; Jer 4:6; 50:2.
**5:30** Is 8:22.
**6:1** 1 Kgs 22:19–23; Jn 12:41.

they covered their feet, and with two they hovered.* ³One cried out to the other:

> "Holy, holy, holy† is the LORD of hosts!
> All the earth is filled with his glory!"

⁴At the sound of that cry, the frame of the door shook and the house was filled with smoke.†* ⁵Then I said, "Woe is me, I am doomed!† For I am a man of unclean lips, living among a people of unclean lips,* and my eyes have seen the King, the LORD of hosts!" ⁶Then one of the seraphim flew to me, holding an ember which he had taken with tongs from the altar. ⁷He touched my mouth with it. "See," he said, "now that this has touched your lips,† your wickedness is removed, your sin purged."*

⁸Then I heard the voice of the Lord saying, "Whom shall I send? Who will go for us?" "Here I am," I said; "send me!" ⁹† And he replied: Go and say to this people:

> Listen carefully, but do not understand!
> Look intently, but do not perceive!*
> 10 Make the heart of this people sluggish,
>     dull their ears and close their eyes;
> Lest they see with their eyes, and hear
>     with their ears,
>     and their heart understand,
>     and they turn and be healed.*

¹¹"How long, O Lord?" I asked. And he replied:

> †  Until the cities are desolate,
>     without inhabitants,
>     Houses, without people,
>     and the land is a desolate waste.
> 12  Until the LORD sends the people far
>     away,
>     and great is the desolation in the
>     midst of the land.
> 13  If there remain a tenth part in it,
>     then this in turn shall be laid waste;
>     As with a terebinth or an oak
>     whose trunk remains when its leaves
>     have fallen.†*
>     Holy offspring is the trunk.

### The Syro-Ephraimite War†

**7 Crisis in Judah.** ¹In the days of Ahaz,† king of Judah, son of Jotham, son of Uzziah, Rezin, king of Aram, and Pekah, king of Israel, son of Remaliah, went up to attack Jerusalem, but they were not able to conquer it.* ²When word came to the house of David that Aram had allied itself with Ephraim, the heart of the king and heart of the people trembled, as the trees of the forest tremble in the wind.

³Then the LORD said to Isaiah: Go out to meet Ahaz, you and your son Shear-jashub,† at the end of the conduit of the upper pool,

---

† **6:3** *Holy, holy, holy*: these words have been used in Christian liturgy from the earliest times.

**6:4** *Smoke*: reminiscent of the clouds which indicated God's presence at Mount Sinai (Ex 19:16–19; Dt 4:11) and which filled the tabernacle (Ex 40:34–38) and the Temple (1 Kgs 8:10–11) at their dedication.

**6:5** *Doomed*: there are two roots from which the verb here could be derived; one means "to perish, be doomed," the other "to become silent," and given Isaiah's delight in puns and double entendre, he probably intended to sound both notes. "I am doomed!" is suggested by the popular belief that to see God would lead to one's death; cf. Gn 32:31; Ex 33:20; Jgs 13:22. "I am struck silent!" is suggested by the emphasis on the lips in vv. 5–6, and such silence is attested elsewhere as the appropriate response to the vision of the Lord in the Temple (Hb 2:20).

**6:7** *Touched your lips*: Isaiah is thus symbolically purified of sin in preparation for his mission as God's prophet.

**6:9–10** Isaiah's words give evidence that he attempted in every way, through admonition, threat, and promise, to bring the people to conversion (cf. 1:18–20), so it is unlikely that this charge to "harden" is to be understood as Isaiah's task; more probably it reflects the refusal of the people, more particularly the leaders, who were supposed to "see," "hear," and "understand," a refusal which would then lead to a disastrous outcome (vv. 11–12).

**6:11–12** The desolation described would be the result of the sort of deportation practiced by the Assyrians and later by the Babylonians. Isaiah seems to expect this as an eventual consequence of Judah's submission as vassal to the Assyrians;

cf. 3:1–3; 5:13.

**6:13** *When its leaves have fallen*: the meaning of the Hebrew is uncertain, and the text may be corrupt. *Holy offspring*: part of the phrase is missing from the Septuagint and may be a later addition; it provides a basis for hope for the future.

**7:1–8:18** These verses (often termed Isaiah's "Memoirs") contain a series of oracles and narratives (some in first person), all closely related to the Syro-Ephraimite war of 735–732 B.C. Several passages feature three children whose symbolic names refer to the Lord's purposes: Shear-jashub (7:3), Emmanuel (7:10–17; 8:8–10), and Maher-shalal-hash-baz (8:1–4). Judah and its Davidic dynasty should trust God's promises and not fear the combined armies of Israel and Syria; within a very short time these two enemy states will be destroyed, and David's dynasty will continue.

**7:1** *Days of Ahaz*: who ruled from 735 to 715 B.C. This attack against Jerusalem by the kings of Aram (Syria) and Israel in 735 B.C. was occasioned by the refusal of Ahaz to enter with them into an anti-Assyrian alliance; cf. 2 Kgs 16.

**7:3** *Shear-jashub*: this name means "a remnant will return" (cf. 10:20–22).

---

**6:2** Rev 4:8.
**6:4** Rev 15:8.
**6:5** Is 29:13; Mt 15:1–11;
    Mk 7:1–13; Col
    2:20–23.
**6:7** Jer 1:9; Dn 10:16.

**6:9** Mt 13:10–17; Mk
    4:10–12; Lk 8:9–10;
    Acts 28:25–28.
**6:10** Jer 5:21; Jn 12:40.
**6:13** Is 10:22.
**7:1** 2 Kgs 16:5; 2 Chr
    28:5–15.

on the highway to the fuller's field, [4] and say to him: Take care you remain calm and do not fear; do not let your courage fail before these two stumps of smoldering brands,* the blazing anger of Rezin and the Arameans and of the son of Remaliah— [5] because Aram, with Ephraim and the son of Remaliah, has planned† evil against you. They say, [6] "Let us go up against Judah, tear it apart, make it our own by force, and appoint the son of Tabeel† king there."

[7]        Thus says the Lord GOD:
        It shall not stand, it shall not be!*
[8]†      The head of Aram is Damascus,
            and the head of Damascus is Rezin;
[9]       The head of Ephraim is Samaria,
            and the head of Samaria is the son of
                Remaliah.
        Within sixty-five years,
            Ephraim shall be crushed, no longer a
                nation.
        Unless your faith is firm,
            you shall not be firm!*

**Emmanuel.** [10] Again the LORD spoke to Ahaz: [11] Ask for a sign from the LORD, your God; let it be deep as Sheol, or high as the sky!† [12] But Ahaz answered, "I will not ask! I will not tempt the LORD!"† [13] Then he said: Listen, house of David! Is it not enough that you weary human beings? Must you also weary my God? [14] Therefore the Lord himself will give you a sign;† the young woman, pregnant

and about to bear a son, shall name him Emmanuel. [15] Curds and honey† he will eat so that he may learn to reject evil and choose good; [16] for before the child learns to reject evil and choose good, the land of those two kings whom you dread shall be deserted.

[17] The LORD shall bring upon you and your people and your father's house such days as have not come since Ephraim seceded† from Judah (the king of Assyria). [18] On that day

        The LORD shall whistle
            for the fly in the farthest streams of
                Egypt,
            and for the bee in the land of
                Assyria.*
[19]      All of them shall come and settle
            in the steep ravines and in the rocky
                clefts,
            on all thornbushes and in all pastures.

[20]† On that day the Lord shall shave with the razor hired from across the River (the king of Assyria) the head, and the hair of the feet; it shall also shave off the beard.*

[21] On that day a man shall keep alive a young cow or a couple of sheep, [22] and from their abundant yield of milk he shall eat curds; curds and honey shall be the food of all who are left in the land. [23]† On that day every place where there were a thousand vines worth a thousand pieces of silver shall become briers and thorns. [24] One shall have to go there with bow and arrows, for all the country shall be

---

† **7:5** *Planned*: the plans of those who plot against Ahaz shall not be accomplished (v. 7). What the Lord plans will unfailingly come to pass, whereas human plans contrary to those of the Lord are doomed to frustration; cf. 8:10; 14:24–27; 19:11–14; 29:15; 30:1. See further the note on 14:24–27.

**7:6** *Son of Tabeel*: a puppet of Jerusalem's enemies. His appointment would interrupt the lawful succession from David.

**7:8–9** God had chosen and made a commitment to David's dynasty and his capital city Jerusalem, not to Rezin and his capital Damascus, nor to the son of Remaliah and his capital Samaria (2 Sm 7:12–16; Ps 2:6; 78:68–72; 132:11–18). *Within sixty-five years...nation*: this text occurs at the end of v. 8 in the Hebrew. Ahaz would not have been reassured by so distant a promise; the phrase is probably a later addition.

**7:11** *Deep...sky*: an extraordinary or miraculous sign that would prove God's firm will to save the royal house of David from its oppressors.

**7:12** *Tempt the LORD*: Ahaz prefers to depend upon the might of Assyria rather than the might of God.

**7:14** Isaiah's sign seeks to reassure Ahaz that he need not fear the invading armies of Syria and Israel in the light of God's promise to David (2 Sm 7:12–16). The oracle follows a traditional announcement formula by which the birth and sometimes naming of a child is promised to particular individuals (Gn 16:11; Jgs 13:3). *The young woman*: Hebrew *'almah* designates a young

woman of marriageable age without specific reference to virginity. The Septuagint translated the Hebrew term as *parthenos*, which normally does mean virgin, and this translation underlies Mt 1:23. *Emmanuel*: the name means "with us is God." Since for the Christian the incarnation is the ultimate expression of God's willingness to "be with us," it is understandable that this text was interpreted to refer to the birth of Christ.

**7:15–16** *Curds and honey*: the only diet available to those who are left after the devastation of the land; cf. vv. 21–25.

**7:17** *Such days as have not come since Ephraim seceded*: the days of the kingdom prior to the secession of Ephraim and the other northern tribes (1 Kgs 12). *The king of Assyria*: the final comment appears to be a later editorial gloss indicating days worse than any since the secession.

**7:20** God will use the Assyrians from across the River (the Euphrates) as his instrument ("razor") to inflict disgrace and suffering upon his people. Ahaz paid tribute to the Assyrian king Tiglath-pileser III, who decimated Syria and Israel in his campaigns of 734–732 B.C. (cf. 2 Kgs 16:7–9). *The feet*: euphemism for sexual parts; cf. Is 6:2.

**7:23–25** Cf. note on 5:5–6.

---

| | |
|---|---|
| **7:4** Is 8:12; 30:15. | **7:18** Is 5:26. |
| **7:7** Is 8:10; Ps 33:10. | **7:20** Is 3:24; 2 Sm 10:4–6; |
| **7:9** 2 Chr 20:20. | Ez 5:1. |

briers and thorns.* ²⁵But as for all the hills which were hoed with a mattock, for fear of briers and thorns you will not go there; they shall become a place for cattle to roam and sheep to trample.*

**8** **A Son of Isaiah.** ¹The LORD said to me: Take a large tablet, and inscribe on it with an ordinary stylus,† "belonging to Maher-shalal-hash-baz,"* ²and call reliable witnesses† for me, Uriah the priest, and Zechariah, son of Jeberechiah.

³Then I went to the prophetess and she conceived and bore a son. The LORD said to me: Name him Maher-shalal-hash-baz, ⁴for before the child learns to say, "My father, my mother," the wealth of Damascus and the spoils of Samaria shall be carried off by the king of Assyria.

**The Choice: The Lord or Assyria.** ⁵Again the LORD spoke to me:

6    Because this people† has rejected
         the waters of Shiloah that flow gently,
     And melts with fear at the display of
         Rezin and Remaliah's son,
7    Therefore the Lord is bringing up against
         them
     the waters of the River, great and
         mighty,
     the king of Assyria and all his glory.
     It shall rise above all its channels,
         and overflow all its banks.
8    It shall roll on into Judah,
         it shall rage and pass on—
     up to the neck it shall reach.*
     But his outspread wings will fill

the width of your land, Emmanuel!
9    Band together, O peoples, but be
         shattered!
     Give ear, all you distant lands!
     Arm yourselves, but be shattered! Arm
         yourselves, but be shattered!
10   Form a plan, it shall be thwarted;
         make a resolve, it shall not be carried
         out,
     for "With us is God!"†*

**Disciples of Isaiah.** ¹¹For thus said the LORD—his hand strong upon me—warning me not to walk in the way of this people:

12†  Do not call conspiracy what this people
         calls conspiracy,
         nor fear what they fear, nor feel dread.
13   But conspire with the LORD of hosts;
         he shall be your fear, he shall be your
         dread.*
14   He shall be a snare,
         a stone for injury,
     A rock for stumbling
         to both the houses of Israel,
     A trap and a snare
         to those who dwell in Jerusalem;*
15   And many among them shall stumble;
         fallen and broken;
         snared and captured.*

¹⁶Bind up my testimony, seal the instruction with my disciples.† ¹⁷I will trust in the LORD, who is hiding his face from the house of Jacob; yes, I will wait for him. ¹⁸Here am I and the children whom the LORD has given me: we are signs† and portents in Israel from the LORD of hosts, who dwells on Mount Zion.*

---

† **8:1** *Ordinary stylus*: lit., "stylus of men." *Maher-shalal-hash-baz*: a symbolic name to be given to another son of Isaiah (v. 3); it means "quick spoils; speedy plunder," and describes what the Assyrians will do to Syria and Israel.
**8:2** *Reliable witnesses*: who would testify that Isaiah had indeed prophesied the future destruction. *Uriah the priest*: cf. 2 Kgs 16:10.
**8:6–8** *This people*: Judah. *Waters of Shiloah*: the stream that flows from the Gihon spring into the pool of Shiloah in Jerusalem and provides a sure supply in time of siege; here it symbolizes the divine protection which Judah has rejected by seeking Assyrian support, symbolized by "the River" (i.e., the Euphrates). Ultimately Assyrian power will devastate Judah. *His outspread wings*: the Lord's wings, a recurring symbol for divine protection (Ps 17:8; 36:8; 57:2; 61:5; 91:4; Ru 2:12). Some understand the image to refer to the sides of the flooding river, but this use of the Hebrew word for "wings" is unparalleled elsewhere in classical Hebrew.
**8:10** The plan of Israel's enemies will be thwarted because, as the name "Emmanuel" signifies, "with us is God."

**8:12–14** Because Isaiah and his followers resisted the official policy of seeking help from Assyria they were labeled "conspirators"; Isaiah uses the term to express what is really the case, cooperating with the Lord.
**8:16** *Bind...seal...with my disciples*: because the prophet's message was not well received at the time, he wanted to preserve it until the future had vindicated him as God's true prophet (cf. 30:8–9).
**8:18** *Signs*: in the meantime, while awaiting the vindication of his message, Isaiah and his children with their symbolic names stood as a reminder of God's message to Israel.

---

7:24 Is 32:13.                    8:14 Lk 2:34; Rom
7:25 Is 5:5; 32:14.                   9:32–33; 1 Pt 2:7–8.
8:1 Is 10:6.                      8:15 Mt 21:44.
8:8 Is 30:28.                     8:18 Is 2:2–5; 4:5; 11:9;
8:10 Is 7:7; 17:12–14.                14:32; 28:16; 31:9;
8:13 Is 29:23; 1 Pt                   33:5.
    3:14–15.

¹⁹ And when they say to you, "Inquire of ghosts and soothsayers who chirp and mutter;†* should not a people inquire of their gods, consulting the dead on behalf of the living, ²⁰ for instruction and testimony?" Surely, those who speak like this are the ones for whom there is no dawn.†

21  He will pass through it hard-pressed and
        hungry,
      and when hungry, shall become
          enraged,
      and curse king and gods.
      He will look upward,
22    and will gaze at the earth,
      But will see only distress and darkness,
          oppressive gloom,
          murky, without light.†

**The Promise of Salvation Under a New Davidic King.†** ²³ There is no gloom where there had been distress. Where once he degraded the land of Zebulun and the land of Naphtali, now he has glorified the way of the Sea, the land across the Jordan, Galilee of the Nations.†

**9** ¹ The people who walked in darkness
          have seen a great light;
        Upon those who lived in a land of
            gloom
          a light has shone.*
2      You have brought them abundant joy
          and great rejoicing;

They rejoice before you as people rejoice
    at harvest,
  as they exult when dividing the spoils.
3  For the yoke that burdened them,
      the pole on their shoulder,
    The rod of their taskmaster,
      you have smashed, as on the day of
          Midian.†*
4  For every boot that tramped in battle,
      every cloak rolled in blood,
      will be burned as fuel for fire.*
5  For a child† is born to us, a son is given
      to us;
    upon his shoulder dominion rests.
  They name him Wonder-Counselor,
      God-Hero,*
      Father-Forever, Prince of Peace.
6  His dominion is vast
      and forever peaceful,
    Upon David's throne, and over his
        kingdom,
      which he confirms and sustains
    By judgment and justice,
      both now and forever.*
  The zeal of the LORD of hosts will do this!

**Judgment on the Northern Kingdom†**
7  The Lord has sent a word against Jacob,
      and it falls upon Israel;
8  And all the people know it—
      Ephraim and those who dwell in
          Samaria—
      those who say in arrogance and pride
          of heart,

---

**8:19** *Chirp and mutter*: a mocking reference to necromancers.

**8:20** *Surely…no dawn*: reliance on necromancy brings futility.

**8:22** *Oppressive gloom…without light*: the meaning of the Hebrew here is quite uncertain.

**8:23–9:6** The meaning of 8:23 is somewhat uncertain, for example, whether the expressions translated "once" and "now" refer to times or to individuals, and also whether the verbs speak of degrading and glorifying the territories. If this traditional translation is correct, the passage would seem to promise the former Northern Kingdom of Israel deliverance from the Assyrians and might relate to Hezekiah's program of trying to reincorporate the northern territories into the kingdom of Judah and thus restore the boundaries of the country as it was under David.

**8:23** The territories mentioned in this verse are those which the Assyrian king Tiglath-pileser III took from Israel and incorporated into the Assyrian provincial system as a result of the Syro-Ephraimite War of 735–732 B.C. (2 Kgs 15:29). *Zebulun… Naphtali*: regions of the former Northern Kingdom of Israel. *The way of the Sea*: the area along the Mediterranean coast south of Mount Carmel which became the Assyrian province of Dor. *Land across the Jordan*: the province of Gilead east of the Jordan. *Galilee of the Nations*: the territory north of Mount Carmel which was incorporated into the Assyrian province of Megiddo. Galilee apparently had a large non-Israelite population. Mt 4:15–16

cites this verse in the context of the beginning of Jesus' public mission in Galilee.

**9:3** *Day of Midian*: when God used the judge Gideon to deliver these northern territories from Midianite oppression (Jgs 6–7).

**9:5** *A child*: perhaps to be identified with the Emmanuel of 7:14 and 8:8; cf. 11:1–2, 9. This verse may reflect a coronation rather than a birth. *Upon his shoulder*: the reference may be to a particular act in the ritual in which a symbol of the king's authority was placed on his shoulder (cf. 2 Kgs 11:12; Is 22:22).

**9:7–20 + 5:25–30** These verses describe a series of judgments God sent against the Northern Kingdom of Israel because of its sins. Despite the judgments, however, Israel continued to rebel, and God's anger remained unabated, as the recurring refrain emphasizes (9:11, 16, 20). The refrain ties Is 9:7–20 together as a unit, but 9:20 is far too abrupt to be the original conclusion to the oracle. With its series of past judgments and repeated refrain, the oracle resembles Am 4:6–12; by analogy with that model one expects a conclusion in which the prophet turns from the narration of past judgments to the announcement of a future judgment. Is 5:25–30 fits the pattern found in 9:7–20 and provides a suitable and possibly original conclusion for the whole oracle.

**8:19** Is 29:4.    **9:4** Ps 46:10.
**9:1** Mt 4:15–16.    **9:5** Is 10:21.
**9:3** Is 10:26; Jgs 7:22–25.    **9:6** Jer 23:5; Lk 1:32–33.

9 "Bricks have fallen,
    but we will rebuild with cut stone;
  Sycamores have been felled,
    but we will replace them with
      cedars."*
10 So the LORD raises up their foes against
      them
    and stirs up their enemies to action—
11 Aram† from the east and the Philistines
      from the west—
    they devour Israel with open mouth.
  For all this, his wrath is not turned
      back,
    and his hand is still outstretched!
12 The people do not turn back to the one
      who struck them,
    nor do they seek the LORD of hosts.
13 So the LORD cuts off from Israel head
      and tail,
    palm branch and reed in one day.*
14 (The elder and the noble are the head,
    the prophet who teaches falsehood is
      the tail.)*
15 Those who lead this people lead them
      astray,
    and those who are led are swallowed
      up.*
16 That is why the Lord does not spare
      their young men,
    and their orphans and widows he
      does not pity;
  For they are totally impious and wicked,
    and every mouth speaks folly.
  For all this, his wrath is not turned back,
    his hand is still outstretched!
17 For wickedness burns like fire,
    devouring brier and thorn;
  It kindles the forest thickets,
    which go up in columns of smoke.*
18 At the wrath of the LORD of hosts the
      land quakes,
    and the people are like fuel for fire;
    no one spares his brother.*

19 They hack on the right, but remain
      hungry;
    they devour on the left, but are not
      filled.
  Each devours the flesh of the
      neighbor;
20 Manasseh devours Ephraim,† and
      Ephraim Manasseh,
  together they turn on Judah.
  For all this, his wrath is not turned back,
    his hand is still outstretched!

## Perversion of Justice

**10** ¹† Ah! Those who enact unjust
      statutes,
    who write oppressive decrees,*
2 Depriving the needy of judgment,
    robbing my people's poor of justice,
  Making widows their plunder,
    and orphans their prey!*
3 What will you do on the day of
      punishment,
    when the storm comes from afar?
  To whom will you flee for help?
    Where will you leave your wealth,
4 Lest it sink beneath the captive
    or fall beneath the slain?
  For all this, his wrath is not turned back,
    his hand is still outstretched!†

## Judgment on Assyria

5† Ah! Assyria, the rod of my wrath,
    the staff I wield in anger.*
6 Against an impious nation† I send him,
    and against a people under my wrath
      I order him
  To seize plunder, carry off loot,
    and to trample them like the mud of
      the street.
7 But this is not what he intends,
    nor does he have this in mind;
  Rather, it is in his heart to destroy,
    to make an end of not a few nations.

---

† 9:11 *Aram*: the Syrian kingdom, with its capital at Damascus.
9:20 *Manasseh...Ephraim*: two of the leading tribes of the
Northern Kingdom. The reference is to the civil wars that marked
the final decades of the Northern Kingdom (2 Kgs 15:10, 14–16,
25; cf. Hos 7:3–7).
10:1–4 This is another *hoy*-oracle; cf. note on 5:8–24. It may
originally have been part of the collection at 5:8–24.
10:4 *For all this...outstretched!*: this refrain appears to be out
of place here; cf. 9:11, 16, 20.
10:5–34 These verses contain a series of oracles directed
against Assyria. Verses 5–15 portray Assyria as simply the rod
God uses to punish Israel, though Assyria does not realize
this. The original conclusion to this unit may be the judg-

ment found in vv. 24–27a, which continues the imagery and
motifs found in vv. 5–15. Verses 16–23, because of the quite
different imagery and motifs, may originally have been an
insertion directed against Aram and Israel at the time of the
Syro-Ephraimite War.
10:6 *Impious nation*: Judah. It was God's intention to use Assyria merely to punish, not to destroy, the nation.

---

9:9 Mal 1:4.                          9:17 Is 5:24; 33:11–12.
9:13 Is 19:15; Dt 28:13,              9:18 Is 3:5.
    44.                               10:1 Jer 8:8.
9:14 Is 28:7.                         10:2 Is 1:23; 3:14–15.
9:15 Is 3:12.                         10:5 Jer 51:20–23.

8 For he says, "Are not my commanders all
     kings?"
9† "Is not Calno like Carchemish,
     Or Hamath like Arpad,
         or Samaria like Damascus?
10 Just as my hand reached out to
     idolatrous kingdoms
     that had more images than Jerusalem
         and Samaria—
11 Just as I treated Samaria and her idols,
     shall I not do to Jerusalem and her
         graven images?"

12 But when the LORD has brought to an end
all his work on Mount Zion and in Jerusalem,

     I will punish the utterance
         of the king of Assyria's proud heart,
         and the boastfulness of his haughty
             eyes.
13 For he says:
     "By my own power I have done it,
         and by my wisdom, for I am shrewd.
     I have moved the boundaries of peoples,
         their treasures I have pillaged,
         and, like a mighty one, I have brought
             down the enthroned.
14 My hand has seized, like a nest,
     the wealth of nations.
     As one takes eggs left alone,
         so I took in all the earth;
     No one fluttered a wing,
         or opened a mouth, or chirped!"
15 Will the ax boast against the one who
     hews with it?
     Will the saw exalt itself above the one
         who wields it?
     As if a rod could sway the one who lifts it,
         or a staff could lift the one who is not
             wood!
16 Therefore the Lord, the LORD of hosts,
     will send leanness among his fat
         ones,†
     And under his glory there will be a
         kindling
     like the kindling of fire. *

17 The Light of Israel will become a fire,
     the Holy One, a flame,
     That burns and consumes its briers
         and its thorns in a single day. *
18 And the glory of its forests and orchards
     will be consumed, soul and body,
     and it will be like a sick man who
         wastes away.
19 And the remnant of the trees in his
         forest
     will be so few,
         that any child can record them.
20 On that day
     The remnant of Israel,
         the survivors of the house of Jacob,
         will no more lean upon the one who
             struck them;
     But they will lean upon the LORD,
         the Holy One of Israel, in truth.
21 A remnant will return,† the remnant of
         Jacob,
     to the mighty God.
22 Though your people, O Israel,
     were like the sand of the sea, *
     Only a remnant of them will return;
         their destruction is decreed,
         as overflowing justice demands. *

23 For the Lord, the GOD of hosts, is about to
carry out the destruction decreed in the midst
of the whole land. *
24† Therefore thus says the Lord, the GOD of
hosts: My people, who dwell in Zion, do not
fear the Assyrian, though he strikes you with a
rod, and raises his staff against you as did the
Egyptians. 25 For just a brief moment more,
and my wrath shall be over, and my anger
shall be set for their destruction. 26 Then the
LORD of hosts will raise against them a scourge
such as struck Midian at the rock of Oreb; *
and he will raise his staff over the sea as he did
in Egypt. * 27 On that day,

     His burden shall be taken from your
         shoulder,
     and his yoke shattered from your neck. *

---

**10:9–10** The cities mentioned were all cities captured, some
more than once, by the Assyrians in the eighth century B.C. Verse
9 suggests a certain historical order in the fall of these cities, and
v. 10 suggests that all of them had fallen before Samaria (cf. Am
6:2). That implies that one should think primarily of events during the reign of Tiglath-pileser III (745–727).
**10:16** *His fat ones:* the strong men of the enemy army.
**10:21** *A remnant will return:* in Hebrew, *shear-jashub*, an allusion to the name of Isaiah's son, Shear-jashub; cf. 7:3.

**10:24** This verse with its reference to Assyria's rod may introduce the original conclusion to vv. 5–15.

**10:16** Is 17:4.
**10:17** Is 9:17–18; 30:27–33;
     31:9; 33:14.
**10:22** Hos 2:1; Rom
     9:27–28.
**10:22** Is 28:16–18.
**10:23** Is 28:22.
**10:26** Is 9:3; Jgs 7:25.
**10:26** Ex 14:16.
**10:27** Is 9:3.

## The March of an Enemy Army†

He has come up from Rimmon,
28    he has reached Aiath, passed through
        Migron,
    at Michmash he has stored his
        supplies.
29    He has crossed the ravine,
    at Geba he has camped for the night.
    Ramah trembles,
        Gibeah of Saul has fled.
30    Cry and shriek, Bath-Gallim!
        Hearken, Laishah! Answer her,
        Anathoth!
31    Madmenah is in flight,
        the inhabitants of Gebim seek refuge.
32    Even today he will halt at Nob,
        he will shake his fist at the mount of
            daughter Zion,
        the hill of Jerusalem!
33†  Now the Lord, the LORD of hosts,
        is about to lop off the boughs with
            terrible violence;
    The tall of stature shall be felled,
        and the lofty ones shall be brought
            low;
34    He shall hack down the forest thickets
        with an ax,
    and Lebanon in its splendor shall fall.

## The Ideal Davidic King†

**11**† ¹But a shoot shall sprout from the
        stump† of Jesse,
    and from his roots a bud shall
        blossom.*

2†  The spirit of the LORD shall rest upon
        him:*
    a spirit of wisdom and of
        understanding,
    A spirit of counsel and of strength,
    a spirit of knowledge and of fear of
        the LORD,
3    and his delight shall be the fear of the
        LORD.
    Not by appearance shall he judge,
        nor by hearsay shall he decide,
4    But he shall judge the poor with justice,
        and decide fairly for the land's
            afflicted.*
    He shall strike the ruthless with the rod
        of his mouth,
    and with the breath of his lips he
        shall slay the wicked.*
5    Justice shall be the band around his
        waist,
    and faithfulness a belt upon his
        hips.*
6†  Then the wolf shall be a guest of the
        lamb,
    and the leopard shall lie down with
        the young goat;
    The calf and the young lion shall browse
        together,
    with a little child to guide them.*
7    The cow and the bear shall graze,
        together their young shall lie down;
    the lion shall eat hay like the ox.*
8    The baby shall play by the viper's den,
    and the child lay his hand on the
        adder's lair.

---

† **10:27b–32** A poetic description of the march of an enemy army from the north, advancing south to the very gates of Jerusalem, where the enemy waves his hand in a gesture of derision against the city. Though Sennacherib's troops took a different route, advancing down the coast and then approaching Jerusalem from the southeast, the arrogant attitude toward God's chosen city was the same. *Aiath:* the Ai of Jos 7:22–8:29. *Migron:* modern Makrun north of Michmash. *The ravine:* the deep valley between Michmash and Geba (cf. 1 Sm 14:1–5). *Ramah…Gibeah…Bath-Gallim…Laishah…Anathoth…Madmenah…Gebim:* cities north of Jerusalem threatened by the sudden appearance of this enemy army. *Nob:* probably to be identified with the present Mount Scopus from where one has a clear view of Jerusalem.

**10:33–34** Just when the enemy is about to capture Jerusalem, God intervenes and destroys the hostile army. Cf. 29:1–8; 31:4–9.

**11:1–16** Isaiah 11 contains a prophecy of the rise of a new Davidic king who will embody the ancient ideal of Davidic kingship (vv. 1–9), an elaboration of that prophecy in a further description of that king's rule (v. 10), and a prophecy of God's deliverance of the chosen people from exile and cessation of enmities (vv. 11–16).

**11:1–9 (10)** Here Isaiah looks forward to a new Davidide

who will realize the ancient ideals (see Ps 72). The oracle does not seem to have a particular historical person in mind.

**11:1** *Shoot…stump:* the imagery suggests the bankruptcy of the monarchy as embodied in the historical kings, along with the need for a new beginning, to spring from the very origin from which David and his dynasty arose. *Jesse:* David's father (cf. 1 Sm 16:1–13).

**11:2–3** The source of the traditional names of the gifts of the Holy Spirit. The Septuagint and the Vulgate read "piety" for "fear of the Lord" in its first occurrence, thus listing seven gifts.

**11:6–9** This picture of the idyllic harmony of paradise is a dramatic symbol of universal peace and justice under the rule of the new Davidic king. The peace and harmony even among carnivores and their natural prey in this description suggest a paradisiac aspect of the reign of the new king.

---

**11:1** Is 4:2; 53:2; Jer        Jn 1:32.
    23:5–6; 33:14–16;   **11:4** Ps 72:2, 4; 98:9.
    Zec 3:8; 6:12; Rev   **11:4** 2 Thes 2:8; Rev 2:16.
    22:16.               **11:5** Eph 6:14.
**11:2** Is 42:1; 1 Sm 16:13; **11:6** Hos 2:20.
    Mt 3:16; Mk 1:10;   **11:7** Is 65:25.

IS

9  They shall not harm or destroy on all
      my holy mountain;
   for the earth shall be filled with
      knowledge of the LORD,
   as water covers the sea.

### Restoration†

10  On that day,
   The root of Jesse,
      set up as a signal for the peoples—
   Him the nations will seek out;
      his dwelling shall be glorious.*
11  On that day,
   The Lord shall again take it in hand
      to reclaim the remnant of his people
      that is left from Assyria and Egypt,
   Pathros, Ethiopia, and Elam,
      Shinar, Hamath, and the isles of the
         sea.*
12  He shall raise a signal to the nations*
      and gather the outcasts of Israel;
   The dispersed of Judah he shall
         assemble
      from the four corners of the earth.
13  The envy of Ephraim shall pass away,
      and those hostile to Judah shall be cut
         off;
   Ephraim shall not envy Judah,
      and Judah shall not be hostile to
         Ephraim;
14  But they shall swoop down on the
         foothills
      of the Philistines to the west,
      together they shall plunder the people
         of the east;†
   Edom and Moab shall be their
         possessions,
      and the Ammonites their subjects.
15  The LORD shall dry up the tongue† of
         the Sea of Egypt,
      and wave his hand over the Euphrates
         with his fierce wind,

And divide it into seven streamlets,
      so that it can be crossed in sandals.*
16  There shall be a highway for the
         remnant of his people
      that is left from Assyria,
   As there was for Israel
      when it came up from the land of
         Egypt.*

### Song of Thanksgiving†

**12** 1  On that day, you will say:
   I give you thanks, O LORD;
      though you have been angry with
         me,
      your anger has abated, and you have
         consoled me.
2  God indeed is my salvation;
      I am confident and unafraid.
   For the LORD is my strength and my
         might,
      and he has been my salvation.*
3  With joy you will draw water
      from the fountains of salvation,*
4  And you will say on that day:
      give thanks to the LORD, acclaim his
         name;
   Among the nations make known his
         deeds,
      proclaim how exalted is his name.*
5  Sing praise to the LORD for he has done
         glorious things;
      let this be known throughout all the
         earth.*
6  Shout with exultation, City of Zion,
      for great in your midst
   is the Holy One of Israel!*

### C. Oracles Against the Foreign Nations†

**13** Babylon.† 1 An oracle† concerning Babylon; a vision of Isaiah, son of Amoz.

---

**11:10–16** This passage, with its reference to God's people in
widely scattered lands, is probably from a much later period.
God will restore them to their own land. The reconciliation of
Ephraim (i.e., the Northern Kingdom) and Judah reverses what
Isaiah saw as a disastrous event of the past (cf. 7:17). God's
action is likened to a new exodus, analogous to the time God
first acquired Israel in bringing them out of the land of Egypt.
*Pathros*: upper Egypt. *Elam*: east of Babylonia. *Shinar*: Babylonia.
*Hamath*: on the Orontes River in Syria. *Isles*: or coastlands, in
the Mediterranean.
**11:14** *People of the east*: tribes in the Arabian Desert (cf. Jgs
6:3, 33; 7:12).
**11:15** *Tongue*: perhaps to be identified with the Gulf of Suez.
**12:1–6** Israel's thanksgiving to the Lord, expressed in language like that of the Psalms.

**13:1–23:18** These chapters, which probably existed at one
time as an independent collection, consist primarily of oracles
from various sources against foreign nations. While some of the
material is Isaianic, in many cases it has been reworked by later
editors or writers.
**13:1–22** Although attributed to Isaiah (v. 1), this oracle does
not reflect conditions of Isaiah's time. Babylon did not achieve
imperial status until a century later, after its victory over Assyria

---

**11:10** Is 2:2–4; Rom 15:12.
**11:11** Ex 3:20; Jer 23:7–8;
  31:1–22; Zec 10:10.
**11:12** Is 18:3.
**11:15** Zec 10:11; Rev 16:12.
**11:16** Is 51:10; Ex 14:29.
**12:2** Ex 15:2; Ps 118:14.

**12:3** Jgs 5:11; Jer 2:13; Jn
  4:10, 14.
**12:4** Ps 105:1; 148:13.
**12:5** Is 11:9; Ex 15:1.
**12:6** Is 52:8–9; 54:1; Zep
  3:14–15.

2   Upon the bare mountains set up a
      signal;
    cry out to them,†
  Beckon for them to enter
    the gates of the nobles.*

3   I have commanded my consecrated
      ones,†
    I have summoned my warriors,
    eager and bold to carry out my
      anger.*

4   Listen! the rumble on the mountains:
    that of an immense throng!
  Listen! the noise of kingdoms, nations
    assembled!
  The Lord of hosts is mustering
    an army for battle.*

5   They come from a far-off country,
    and from the end of the heavens,
  The Lord and the instruments of his
      wrath,
    to destroy all the land.

6   Howl, for the day of the Lord† is near;
    as destruction from the Almighty it
      comes.*

7   Therefore all hands fall helpless,*
    every human heart melts,

8   and they are terrified,
  Pangs and sorrows take hold of them,
    like a woman in labor they writhe;
  They look aghast at each other,
    their faces aflame.*

9   Indeed, the day of the Lord comes,
    cruel, with wrath and burning anger;
  To lay waste the land
    and destroy the sinners within it!*

10   The stars of the heavens and their
      constellations
    will send forth no light;
  The sun will be dark at its rising,
    and the moon will not give its light.*

11   Thus I will punish the world for its evil
    and the wicked for their guilt.
  I will put an end to the pride of the
      arrogant,
    the insolence of tyrants I will humble.*

12   I will make mortals more rare than pure
      gold,
    human beings, than the gold of
      Ophir.†*

13   For this I will make the heavens tremble
    and the earth shall be shaken from its
      place,
  At the wrath of the Lord of hosts
    on the day of his burning anger.*

14   Like a hunted gazelle,
    or a flock that no one gathers,
  They shall turn each to their own people
    and flee each to their own land.*

15   Everyone who is taken shall be run
      through;
    and everyone who is caught shall fall
      by the sword.

16   Their infants shall be dashed to pieces in
      their sight;
    their houses shall be plundered
    and their wives ravished.*

17   I am stirring up against them the Medes,
    who think nothing of silver
    and take no delight in gold.*

18   With their bows they shall shatter the
      young men,
  And the fruit of the womb they shall not
      spare,
    nor shall their eye take pity on
      children.

19   And Babylon, the jewel of kingdoms,
    the glory and pride of the Chaldeans,
  Shall become like Sodom and
      Gomorrah,
    overthrown by God.*

---

† in 609 B.C. The mention of the Medes (v. 17) rather than Persia suggests a date prior to 550 B.C., when the Median empire of Astyages fell to Cyrus the Persian. Tension is created in that the attackers are not named until v. 17 and the foe to be attacked until v. 19.

**13:1** *Oracle:* Heb. *massaʾ;* used eight more times in this collection.

**13:2** *To them:* the Medes (v. 17), who are being summoned to destroy Babylon. *Gates of the nobles:* the reference is apparently to the gates of Babylon and involves a wordplay on the city name (Babylon = *bab ilani,* "gate of the gods").

**13:3** *Consecrated ones:* in the sense that they will wage a "holy war" and carry out God's plan.

**13:6–8** *Day of the Lord:* described often in prophetic writings, it generally signified the coming of the Lord in power and majesty to destroy his enemies. The figures used convey the idea of horror and destruction (Am 5:18–20). *The Almighty:* Heb.

*shaddai;* there is a play on words between destruction (*shod*) and Shaddai, a title for God traditionally rendered as "the Almighty" (cf. Gn 17:1; Ex 6:3).

**13:12** *Ophir:* cf. note on Ps 45:10.

---

* 
| | |
|---|---|
| **13:2** Is 5:26; Jer 50:2. | Zep 1:15; Mt 24:29. |
| **13:3** Jl 4:9. | **13:11** Is 2:17; Jer 50:32. |
| **13:4** Jer 50:9. | **13:12** 1 Kgs 9:28; Jb 22:24. |
| **13:6** Is 2:12–21; Jer 46:10; | **13:13** Hg 2:6; Lam 1:12. |
|     Am 5:18–20; Jl 1:15; | **13:14** 1 Kgs 22:17; Jer |
|     Zep 1:7; Rev 6:17. |     50:16; 51:9. |
| **13:7** Jer 6:24; Ez 7:17. | **13:16** 2 Kgs 8:12; Ps 137:9; |
| **13:8** Is 21:3; Ps 48:7; Mi |     Na 3:10. |
|     4:9. | **13:17** Is 21:2; Jer 51:11, 28. |
| **13:9** Jer 4:7; 18:16; Mal | **13:19** Dt 29:22; Is 1:7; Jer |
|     3:19. |     49:18; 50:40; Am |
| **13:10** Is 24:23; Jer 4:23; |     4:11. |

IS

20 It shall never be inhabited,
     nor dwelt in, from age to age;
   Arabians shall not pitch their tents there,
     nor shepherds rest their flocks there.*
21 But desert demons shall rest there
     and owls shall fill the houses;
   There ostriches shall dwell,
     and satyrs† shall dance.*
22 Wild dogs shall dwell in its castles,
     and jackals in its luxurious palaces.
   Its time is near at hand
     and its days shall not be prolonged.*

**14** **Restoration of Israel.** ¹ But the LORD will take pity on Jacob and again choose Israel, and will settle them on their own land; foreigners will join them and attach themselves to the house of Jacob.* ² The nations will take them and bring them to their place, and the house of Israel will possess them† as male and female slaves on the Lord's land; they will take captive their captors and rule over their oppressors.*

**Downfall of the King of Babylon.** ³ On the day when the LORD gives you rest from your sorrow and turmoil, from the hard service with which you served,* ⁴ you will take up this taunt-song† against the king of Babylon:*

   How the oppressor has come to an end!
     how the turmoil has ended!
5  The LORD has broken the rod of the
     wicked,
     the staff of the tyrants*
6  That struck the peoples in wrath
     with relentless blows;
   That ruled the nations in anger,

with boundless persecution.*
7  The whole earth rests peacefully,
     song breaks forth;
8  The very cypresses rejoice over you,
     the cedars of Lebanon:
   "Now that you are laid to rest,
     no one comes to cut us down."*
9  Below, Sheol is all astir
     preparing for your coming;
   Awakening the shades to greet you,
     all the leaders of the earth;
   Making all the kings of the nations
     rise from their thrones.
10 All of them speak out
     and say to you,
   "You too have become weak like us,
     you are just like us!
11 Down to Sheol your pomp is brought,
     the sound of your harps.
   Maggots are the couch beneath you,
     worms your blanket."*
12 How you have fallen from the heavens,
     O Morning Star,† son of the dawn!
   How you have been cut down to the
     earth,
     you who conquered nations!*
13 In your heart you said:
   "I will scale the heavens;
   Above the stars of God†
     I will set up my throne;
   I will take my seat on the Mount of
     Assembly,
     on the heights of Zaphon.*
14 I will ascend above the tops of the
     clouds;
   I will be like the Most High!"*
15 No! Down to Sheol you will be brought
     to the depths of the pit!*

---

**13:21** *Satyrs*: in the popular mind, demons of goatlike form dwelling in ruins, symbols of immorality; cf. Lv 17:7; Is 34:14.
**14:2** *Possess them*: Israel will make slaves of the nations who escort it back to its land.
**14:4–21** This taunt-song, a satirical funeral lament, is a beautiful example of classical Hebrew poetry. According to the prose introduction and the prosaic conclusion (vv. 22–23), it is directed against the king of Babylon, though Babylon is mentioned nowhere in the song itself. If the reference to Babylon is accurate, the piece was composed long after the time of Isaiah, for Babylon was not a threat to Judah in the eighth century. Some have argued that Isaiah wrote it at the death of an Assyrian king and the references to Babylon were made by a later editor, but this is far from certain.
**14:12** *Morning Star*: term addressed to the king of Babylon. The Vulgate translates as "Lucifer," a name applied by the church Fathers to Satan. *Son of the dawn*: Heb., *ben shahar*, may reflect the name of a pagan deity.
**14:13–15** *God*: not Elohim, the common word for God, but El, the name of the head of the pantheon in Canaanite mythol-

ogy, a god who was early identified with the Lord in Israelite thought. *Mount of Assembly*: mountain where the council of the gods met, according to Canaanite mythology. *Zaphon*: the sacred mountain of Baal, originally the Jebel el-Aqra north of Ugarit, but other mountains have been identified with it, including Mount Zion in Jerusalem (Ps 48:3). The attempt to usurp the place of God (v. 14), coupled with the dramatic reversal ("above the stars of God" to "the depths of the pit") occasioned the interpretation that saw here the rebellion and fall of Satan.

---

**13:20** Jer 51:62.
**13:21** Is 34:13–14; 35:7.
**13:22** Ez 32:23.
**14:1** Is 56:3; 60:4; Ps 102:14; Jer 24:6; Zec 1:17.
**14:2** Is 49:22–23; 60:14; 66:20.
**14:3** Ex 33:14; Jos 1:13; Jer 30:10.
**14:4** Hb 2:6.
**14:5** Is 10:24–27.
**14:6** Is 10:5–7.
**14:8** Is 37:24; 44:23; 55:12; Ez 31:16.
**14:11** Sir 10:11.
**14:12** Jb 14:10.
**14:13** Jer 51:53; Am 9:2.
**14:14** Ez 28:2; Zep 2:15; 2 Thes 2:4.
**14:15** Ez 28:8–9; 32:23; Mt 11:23; Acts 12:23.

16 When they see you they will stare,
     pondering over you:
  "Is this the man who made the earth
       tremble,
     who shook kingdoms?
17 Who made the world a wilderness,
     razed its cities,
     and gave captives no release?"
18 All the kings of the nations lie in glory,
     each in his own tomb; *
19 But you are cast forth without burial,
     like loathsome carrion,
  Covered with the slain, with those struck
       by the sword,
     a trampled corpse,
  Going down to the very stones of the pit. *
20   You will never be together with them
       in the grave,
  For you have ruined your land,
     you have slain your people!
  Let him never be named,
     that offshoot of evil!
21 Make ready to slaughter his sons
     for the guilt of their fathers; *
  Lest they rise and possess the earth,
     and fill the breadth of the world with
       cities. †

22 I will rise up against them, says the LORD of
hosts, and cut off from Babylon name and remnant, progeny and offspring, says the LORD. *
23 I will make it a haunt of hoot owls and a
marshland; I will sweep it with the broom of
destruction, oracle of the LORD of hosts.

### God's Plan for Assyria†

24   The LORD of hosts has sworn:
     As I have resolved,

  so shall it be;
  As I have planned,
     so shall it stand:
25 To break the Assyrian in my land
     and trample him on my mountains;
  Then his yoke shall be removed from
       them,
     and his burden from their shoulder. *
26 This is the plan proposed for the whole
       earth,
     and this the hand outstretched over
       all the nations. †
27 The LORD of hosts has planned;
     who can thwart him?
  His hand is stretched out;
     who can turn it back? *

**Philistia.** † 28 In the year that King Ahaz died, †
there came this oracle:

29 † Do not rejoice, Philistia, not one of you,
     that the rod which struck you is broken;
  For out of the serpent's root shall come
       an adder,
     its offspring shall be a flying saraph.
30 In my pastures the poor shall graze,
     and the needy lie down in safety;
  But I will kill your root with famine
     that shall slay even your remnant.
31 Howl, O gate; cry out, O city!
     Philistia, all of you melts away!
  For there comes a smoke from the north, †
     without a straggler in its ranks.
32 What will one answer the messengers of
       the nations? †
  "The LORD has established Zion,
     and in her the afflicted of his people
       find refuge."

---

14:21 *Cities*: if the text is correct, it presumably refers to cities as expressions of human pride, authority, and oppression (cf. Gn 11:1–9; Na 3:1–4).

14:24–27 The motif of God's plan or work is a recurring thread running through Isaiah's oracles. The plans of Judah's enemies will not come to pass (7:5–7; 8:9–10; 10:7), but God's plan for his work of disciplining his own people (5:12, 19; 28:21), and then for punishing the foreign agents God used to administer that discipline (10:12) will come to pass.

14:26 *Hand outstretched over all the nations*: as it was once outstretched over Israel (9:11, 16, 20; 5:25).

14:28–31 This oracle seems to reflect the political situation soon after the death of Ahaz in 715 B.C., when Ashdod and the other Philistine cities were trying to create a united front to rebel against Assyria. Ahaz had refused to join the rebels in 735 B.C. and remained loyal to Assyria during the rest of his reign, but the Philistines may have had higher hopes for his son Hezekiah. Judah, however, did not join in Ashdod's disastrous revolt in 713–711 B.C. (cf. 20:1).

14:28 *The year that King Ahaz died*: 715 B.C.

14:29 The occasion for this oracle is usually taken to be the death of an Assyrian king; the Philistines were vassals of Assyria, whereas no victories of Ahaz over the Philistines are recorded. The chronological notice (*in the year that King Ahaz died*) may be incorrect, for no Assyrian king died around 715, the date usually assigned for the death of Ahaz. *Flying saraph*: a winged cobra, often portrayed in Egyptian art and on Israelite seals. The Hebrew *saraph* means "to burn" and perhaps is applied to the cobra because of the burning sensation of its bite.

14:31 *Smoke from the north*: the dust raised from the approach of the Assyrian army.

14:32 *Messengers of the nations*: envoys from Philistia, and from Egypt and Ethiopia, the real powers behind the Philistine revolt (20:1–6; cf. 18:1–2).

---

14:18 Jb 3:14–15.
14:19 Is 66:24.
14:21 Ex 20:5; Mt 23:35.
14:22 Jer 51:62; Jb 18:19.
14:25 Is 9:3; 10:27a.
14:27 Is 23:8–9; Jb 40:8; Jer
4:28.

### Moab†

**15** ¹   Oracle on Moab:
Laid waste in a night,
  Ar of Moab is destroyed;
Laid waste in a night,
  Kir of Moab is destroyed.

²   Daughter Dibon has gone up
    to the high places to weep;
Over Nebo and over Medeba
    Moab is wailing.
Every head is shaved,
    every beard sheared off.†*

³   In the streets they wear sackcloth,
    and on the rooftops;
In the squares
    everyone wails, streaming with
      tears.*

⁴   Heshbon and Elealeh cry out,
    they are heard as far as Jahaz.
At this the loins of Moab tremble,
    his soul quivers within him;*

⁵   My heart cries out for Moab,
    his fugitives reach Zoar,
    Eglath-shelishiyah:
The ascent of Luhith
    they ascend weeping;
On the way to Horonaim
    they utter rending cries;*

⁶   The waters of Nimrim
    have become a waste,
The grass is withered,
    new growth is gone,
    nothing is green.

⁷   So now whatever they have acquired or
    stored away
    they carry across the Wadi of the
      Poplars.

⁸   The cry has gone round
    the territory of Moab;
As far as Eglaim his wailing,
    even at Beer-elim his wailing.

⁹†   The waters of Dimon are filled with
    blood,
    but I will bring still more upon Dimon:
Lions for those who are fleeing from
    Moab
    and for those who remain in the land!

**16** ¹ Send them forth,† hugging the earth
    like reptiles,
    from Sela across the desert,
    to the mount of daughter Zion.

²   Like flushed birds,
    like scattered nestlings,
Are the daughters of Moab
    at the fords of the Arnon.†*

³†   Offer counsel, take their part;
    at high noon make your shade like
      the night;
Hide the outcasts,
    do not betray the fugitives.

⁴   Let the outcasts of Moab live with you,
    be their shelter from the destroyer.
When there is an end to the oppressor,
    when destruction has ceased,
    and the marauders have vanished
      from the land,

⁵   A throne shall be set up in mercy,
    and on it shall sit in fidelity,
    in David's tent,
A judge upholding right,
    prompt to do justice.*

⁶   We have heard of the pride of Moab,
    how very proud he is,
Of his haughtiness, pride, and arrogance
    that his empty words do not match.*

⁷†   Therefore let Moab wail,
    let everyone wail for Moab;
For the raisin cakes† of Kir-hareseth
    let them sigh, stricken with grief.

⁸   The terraced slopes of Heshbon languish,
    the vines of Sibmah,
Whose clusters once overpowered

---

**15:1–16:14** Both the historical situation reflected in this oracle against Moab and the date of composition are uncertain. Variants of the same poem are found in Jer 48, and there are connections with Nm 21:27–30 as well.

**15:2** *Shaved…sheared off:* traditional signs of grief.

**15:9** There is a play on words between "Dimon" and *dam,* the Hebrew word for blood.

**16:1** *Send them forth:* the Hebrew text is disturbed; it could also be understood to refer to tribute (a lamb) sent from Moab to Zion, presumably to encourage the king to receive the Moabite refugees.

**16:2** *The Arnon:* principal river of Moab.

**16:3–5** Directed to Jerusalem, which should receive the suffering Moabites with mercy, as befits the city of David's family,

who were partly descended from Ruth the Moabite; and cf. 1 Sm 22:3–4. This would be a gracious act on Judah's part, since its relations with Moab were strained at best.

**16:7–14** Moab had been prosperous; now it has become a desert.

**16:7** *Raisin cakes:* masses of dried compressed grapes used as food (cf. 2 Sm 6:19; 1 Chr 16:3; Sg 2:5), and also in the worship of other gods (Hos 3:1).

*

**15:2** Jer 48:37; Ez 7:18; Am 8:10.
**15:3** Is 22:12; Jer 48:38.
**15:4** Jer 48:34.
**15:5** Jer 48:5, 34.

**16:2** Nm 21:13.
**16:5** Is 9:6; 11:3–4; 32:1; Jer 23:5; Ps 89:14; Prv 20:28.
**16:6** Jer 48:29–30.

the lords of nations,
Reaching as far as Jazer
  winding through the wilderness,†
Whose branches spread forth,
  crossing over the sea.

9   Therefore I weep with Jazer
      for the vines of Sibmah;
    I drench you with my tears,
      Heshbon and Elealeh;
    For on your summer fruits and harvests
      the battle cry† has fallen.*

10  From the orchards are taken away
      joy and gladness,
    In the vineyards there is no singing,
      no shout of joy;
    In the wine presses no one treads grapes,
      the vintage shout is stilled.*

11  Therefore for Moab
      my heart moans like a lyre,
      my inmost being for Kir-hareseth.*

12† When Moab wears himself out on the
      high places,
    and enters his sanctuary to pray,
      it shall avail him nothing.*

13† That is the word the LORD spoke against
Moab in times past. 14 But now the LORD
speaks: In three years, like the years of a hired
laborer, the glory of Moab shall be empty despite all its great multitude; and the remnant
shall be very small and weak.*

## Damascus

**17** 1   Oracle on Damascus:†
        See, Damascus shall cease to be a city
          and become a pile of ruins;*

2   Her cities shall be forever abandoned,
      for flocks to lie in undisturbed.

3   The fortress shall vanish from Ephraim†

and dominion from Damascus;
The remnant of Aram shall become like
  the glory
  of the Israelites—
  oracle of the LORD of hosts.

4   On that day
    The glory of Jacob shall fade,
      and his full body shall grow thin.*

5   Like the reaper's mere armful of stalks,
      when he gathers the standing grain;
    Or as when one gleans the ears
      in the Valley of Rephaim.†

6†  Only gleanings shall be left in it,
      as when an olive tree has been
      beaten—
    Two or three olives at the very top,
      four or five on its most fruitful
      branches—
      oracle of the LORD, the God of Israel.*

7   On that day people shall turn to their
      maker,
    their eyes shall look to the Holy One
      of Israel.*

8   They shall not turn to the altars, the
      work of their hands,
    nor shall they look to what their
      fingers have made:
    the asherahs† or the incense stands.

9   On that day his strong cities shall be
      like those abandoned by the Hivites
      and Amorites
    When faced with the Israelites;
      and there shall be desolation.*

10  Truly, you have forgotten the God who
      saves you,
    the Rock, your refuge, you have not
      remembered.*
    Therefore, though you plant plants for
      the Pleasant One,†

---

**16:8** *Wilderness*: i.e., eastward. *Sea*: i.e., westward.
**16:9–10** *Battle cry…shout of joy*: the same Hebrew word
(*hedad*), which normally refers to the joyful shout of those
treading the grapes (cf. Jer 25:30), here is used both for the triumphant shout of the enemy (v. 9) and for the vintagers' shout,
which has ceased.
**16:12** In vain do the Moabites appeal to their god Chemosh.
**16:13–14** A prose application of the preceding poetic oracle
against Moab (15:1–16:12); cf. Jer 4:8. *Like the years of a hired
laborer*: the fixed period of time for which the hired laborer
contracted his services; cf. Is 21:16.
**17:1** *Damascus*: capital of Aram or Syria, conquered by
Tiglath-pileser III at the end of the Syro-Ephraimite War in 732 B.C.
**17:3** *Ephraim*: Israel, leagued with Aram against Judah in
the Syro-Ephraimite War. Assyria ravaged and captured most of
Israelite territory in 734–733 B.C. *Like the glory of the Israelites*:
the remnant of Aram will be no more impressive than the pitiful
remnant of the Northern Kingdom.

**17:5** *Valley of Rephaim*: a fertile plain just to the southwest
of Jerusalem (cf. Jos 15:8; 2 Sm 5:18). Since it was near a large
population center, the fields there would be thoroughly gleaned
by the poor after the harvest, leaving very few ears of grain.
**17:6** Olives not easily picked by hand were knocked from the
tree by means of a long stick; cf. 24:13.
**17:8** *Asherahs*: see note on Ex 34:13. *Incense stands*: small
altars on which incense was burned; cf. Is 27:9; Lv 26:30.
**17:10** *The Pleasant One*: an epithet for a foreign god of
fertility, probably Adonis, in whose honor saplings were planted.

---

* 
**16:9** Is 15:5; Jer 48:32.        **17:4** Is 10:16.
**16:10** Is 24:8.                   **17:6** Is 24:13.
**16:11** Is 15:5; Jer 48:36.        **17:7** Is 5:12.
**16:12** Jer 48:13.                 **17:9** Is 27:10.
**16:14** Dt 15:18.                  **17:10** Ps 106:13, 21; Jer
**17:1** 2 Kgs 16:9; Jer 49:23;        2:32; Hos 8:14.
Am 1:3; Zec 9:1.

and set out cuttings for a foreign
         one, *
11    Though you make them grow the day
         you plant them
      and make them blossom the morning
         you set them out,
      The harvest shall disappear on a day of
         sickness
      and incurable pain.
12    Ah! the roaring of many peoples—†
      a roar like the roar of the seas!
      The thundering of nations—
         thunder like the thundering of mighty
         waters! *
13 †  But God shall rebuke them,
      and they shall flee far away,
      Driven like chaff on the mountains
         before a wind,
      like tumbleweed before a storm. *
14    At evening, there is terror,
      but before morning, they are gone!
      Such is the portion of those who despoil
         us,
      the lot of those who plunder us. *

## Ethiopia

# 18
¹ Ah! Land of buzzing insects, †
beyond the rivers of Ethiopia, *
2    Sending ambassadors by sea,
      in papyrus boats on the waters!
      Go, swift messengers,
      to a nation tall and bronzed,
      To a people dreaded near and far,
      a nation strong and conquering,
      whose land is washed by rivers. *
3 †  All you who inhabit the world,
      who dwell on earth,
      When the signal is raised on the
         mountain, look!
      When the trumpet blows, listen!
4    For thus says the LORD to me:
      I will be quiet, looking on from where
      I dwell, *

Like the shimmering heat in sunshine,
   like a cloud of dew at harvest time.
5    Before the vintage, when the flowering
         has ended,
      and the blooms are succeeded by
         ripening grapes,
      Then comes the cutting of branches with
         pruning hooks,
      and the discarding of the lopped-off
         shoots.
6    They shall all be left to the mountain
         vultures
      and to the beasts of the earth;
      The vultures shall summer on them,
      all the beasts of the earth shall winter
         on them.

⁷ Then will gifts be brought to the LORD of
hosts—to the place of the name of the LORD
of hosts, Mount Zion—from a people tall and
bronzed, from a people dreaded near and far,
a nation strong and conquering, whose land is
washed by rivers. *

## Egypt

# 19
¹ Oracle on Egypt:
See, the LORD is riding on a swift
         cloud
      on his way to Egypt;
      The idols of Egypt tremble before him,
      the hearts of the Egyptians melt
         within them. *
2    I will stir up Egypt against Egypt:
      brother will war against brother,
      Neighbor against neighbor,
      city against city, kingdom against
         kingdom.
3    The courage of the Egyptians shall ebb
         away within them,
      and I will bring their counsel to
         nought;
      They shall consult idols and charmers,
      ghosts and clairvoyants. *

---

**17:12** *Many peoples:* the hordes that accompanied the invading Assyrians, whom God repels just as he vanquished the
primeval waters of chaos; see notes on Jb 3:8; 7:12; Ps 89:11.
   **17:13–14** The passage seems to evoke the motif of invincibil-
ity, part of the early Zion tradition that Jerusalem could not be
conquered because God protected it (Ps 48:1–8).
   **18:1–2** *Land of buzzing insects:* the region of the Upper Nile
where these multiplied with great rapidity. *Ethiopia:* in Hebrew,
*Kush.* The center of this ancient kingdom corresponds geographically to the modern Sudan, Roman Nubia. *Papyrus boats:* light
and serviceable vessels made of bundles of papyrus stalks and
sealed with pitch. Egypt, ruled by a dynasty from Ethiopia, had
invited Judah to join a coalition against Assyria, but Isaiah told

the ambassadors to return to their own people.
   **18:3–6** A more general address but probably relating to the
same topic. The Lord will not act at once, but later there will
be a "harvest" of terrible destruction, probably directed against
Assyria (cf. 14:24–27).

* ——
17:10 Is 1:29–31.          18:4 Is 8:18; 18:7; 2 Chr
17:12 Ps 46:3–7; 93:3–4.          6:30; Ps 33:14.
17:13 Ps 76:7; 83:14.          18:7 Is 45:14; Ps 68:30;
17:14 Is 29:8.                Zep 3:10; Mal 1:11.
18:1 Zep 3:10.          19:1 Is 13:7.
18:2 Is 18:7.          19:3 Is 8:19; 44:25; Lv
                        19:31.

⁴ I will deliver Egypt
  into the power of a cruel master,
 A harsh king† who shall rule over
        them—
     oracle of the Lord, the LORD of hosts.*
⁵ The waters shall be drained from the
        sea,
     the river shall parch and dry up;*
⁶ Its streams shall become foul,
     and the canals of Egypt shall dwindle
        and parch.*
 Reeds and rushes shall wither away,
     and bulrushes on the bank of the
        Nile;*
 All the sown land along the Nile
     shall dry up and blow away, and be
        no more.
⁸ The fishermen shall mourn and lament,
     all who cast hook in the Nile;
 Those who spread their nets in the water
     shall pine away.
⁹ The linen-workers shall be disappointed,
     the combers and weavers shall turn
        pale;*
¹⁰ The spinners shall be crushed,
     all the hired laborers shall be
        despondent.
¹¹ Utter fools are the princes of Zoan!†
     the wisest of Pharaoh's advisers give
        stupid counsel.
 How can you say to Pharaoh,
     "I am a descendant of wise men, of
        ancient kings"?
¹² Where then are your wise men?
     Let them tell you and make known
 What the LORD of hosts has planned
     against Egypt.*
¹³ The princes of Zoan have become fools,
     the princes of Memphis have been
        deceived.
 The chiefs of its tribes
     have led Egypt astray.*
¹⁴ The LORD has prepared among them
     a spirit of dizziness,

 And they have made Egypt stagger in
     whatever she does,
     as a drunkard staggers in his vomit.*
¹⁵ Egypt shall accomplish nothing—
     neither head nor tail, palm branch
     nor reed,† shall accomplish
        anything.

¹⁶ On that day the Egyptians shall be like women, trembling with fear, because of the LORD of hosts shaking his fist at them.* ¹⁷ And the land of Judah shall be a terror to the Egyptians. Every time they think of Judah, they shall stand in dread because of the plan the LORD of hosts has in mind for them.

¹⁸ On that day there shall be five cities† in the land of Egypt that speak the language of Canaan and swear by the LORD of hosts; one shall be called "City of the Sun."

¹⁹ On that day there shall be an altar to the LORD at the center of Egypt, and a sacred pillar to the LORD near its boundary. ²⁰ This will be a sign and witness to the LORD of hosts in the land of Egypt, so that when they cry out to the LORD because of their oppressors, he will send them a savior to defend and deliver them.* ²¹ The LORD shall make himself known to Egypt, and the Egyptians shall know the LORD in that day; they shall offer sacrifices and oblations, make vows to the LORD and fulfill them.* ²² Although the LORD shall smite Egypt severely, he shall heal them; they shall turn to the LORD and he shall be moved by their entreaty and heal them.*

²³ On that day there shall be a highway from Egypt to Assyria; the Assyrians shall enter Egypt, and the Egyptians enter Assyria, and the Egyptians shall worship with the Assyrians.

²⁴ On that day Israel shall be a third party with Egypt and Assyria, a blessing in the midst of the earth,* ²⁵ when the LORD of hosts gives this blessing: "Blessed be my people Egypt, and the work of my hands Assyria, and my heritage, Israel."

---

  **19:4** *Cruel master...harsh king*: possibly the Nubian (Ethiopian) Shabaka who gained control of all of Egypt around 712 B.C.
  **19:11, 13** *Zoan*, later known as Tanis, and *Memphis* (Hebrew *Noph*) were key cities in the Nile Delta.
  **19:15** *Head...reed*: the leaders and the people; cf. 9:13–14.
  **19:18** *Five cities*: colonies of Jews living together and speaking their native language; cf. Jer 43. *City of the Sun*: the meaning is uncertain, but the reference seems to be to the city known later as Heliopolis.

**19:4** Ez 29:19; 30:10.
**19:5** Jer 51:36; Ez 30:12;
    32:2.
**19:6** 2 Kgs 19:24.
**19:7** Jb 8:11.
**19:9** Ez 27:7.
**19:12** Is 14:26; 41:22–23.

**19:13** Jer 2:16; Hos 9:6.
**19:14** Is 28:7; Jer 48:26.
**19:16** Na 3:13.
**19:20** Ex 2:23; Jgs 2:18.
**19:21** Zec 14:16, 18.
**19:22** Hos 6:1.
**19:24** Gn 12:2; Zec 8:13.

# 20 Isaiah's Warning Against Trust in Egypt and Ethiopia.

¹In the year the general sent by Sargon, king of Assyria, came to Ashdod,† fought against it, and captured it— ²† at that time the LORD had spoken through Isaiah, the son of Amoz: Go and take off the sackcloth from your waist, and remove the sandals from your feet. This he did, walking naked and barefoot.* ³Then the LORD said: Just as my servant Isaiah has gone naked and barefoot for three years as a sign and portent against Egypt and Ethiopia,* ⁴so shall the king of Assyria lead away captives from Egypt, and exiles from Ethiopia, young and old, naked and barefoot, with buttocks uncovered, the shame of Egypt.* ⁵They shall be dismayed and ashamed because of Ethiopia, their hope, and because of Egypt, their boast.* ⁶The inhabitants of this coastland shall say on that day, "See what has happened to those we hoped in, to whom we fled for help and deliverance from the king of Assyria! What escape is there for us now?"*

## Fall of Babylon†

# 21
¹    Oracle on the wastelands by the
        sea:†
Like whirlwinds sweeping through the
        Negeb,
    it comes from the desert,
    from the fearful land.*
²    A harsh vision has been announced to me:
    "The traitor betrays,
        the despoiler spoils.*
    Go up, O Elam; besiege, O Media;†
        put an end to all its groaning!"*
³    Therefore my loins are filled with
        anguish,
        pangs have seized me like those of a
        woman in labor;

    I am too bewildered to hear,
        too dismayed to look.*
⁴    My mind reels,
        shuddering assails me;
    The twilight I yearned for
        he has turned into dread.*
⁵    They set the table,
        spread out the rugs;
        they eat, they drink.†*
    Rise up, O princes,
        oil the shield!
⁶    For thus my Lord said to me:
        Go, station a watchman,
        let him tell what he sees.
⁷    If he sees a chariot,
        a pair of horses,
    Someone riding a donkey,
        someone riding a camel,
    Then let him pay heed,
        very close heed.
⁸    Then the watchman cried,
    "On the watchtower, my Lord,
        I stand constantly by day;
    And I stay at my post
        through all the watches of the
        night.*
⁹    Here he comes—
        a single chariot,
        a pair of horses—
    He calls out and says,
        'Fallen, fallen is Babylon!
    All the images of her gods
        are smashed to the ground!'"*
¹⁰    To you, who have been threshed,
        beaten on my threshing floor,
    What I have heard
        from the LORD of hosts,
    The God of Israel,
        I have announced to you.*

---

† **20:1** *Ashdod*: a city of Philistia. In 713 B.C., Azuri, the king of Ashdod was deposed by Sargon for plotting rebellion, but the citizens of Ashdod rejected the ruler installed by the Assyrian king and followed a certain Yamani, who in 712 B.C., with the protection of Egypt, attempted to draw Edom, Moab, and Judah into a coalition against Assyria. In 711 B.C., Sargon's general marched against Ashdod, and Yamani fled to Ethiopia. Ashdod was captured, and a short time later Ethiopia handed Yamani over to the Assyrians for punishment.

**20:2–6** Isaiah's nakedness is a symbolic act to convey the message that Assyria would lead the Egyptians and Ethiopians away as captives. The Judeans and their allies would then realize the folly of having trusted in them. The purpose of the oracle was to dissuade Hezekiah, the Judean king, from being drawn into Ashdod's anti-Assyrian coalition (14:28–32).

**21:1–10** This oracle against Babylon is probably to be dated to the period just before the fall of Babylon to the Persians in 539 B.C. (v. 9).

**21:1** *Wastelands by the sea*: Babylonia. *Negeb*: the wilderness south of Judah.

**21:2** *Elam…Media*: nations which, under the leadership of Cyrus, captured Babylon in 539 B.C. *End to all its groaning*: those who were captive of Babylon will be freed.

**21:5** Babylon is destroyed while its leaders are feasting; cf. Dn 5. *Oil the shield*: shields were oiled and greased so as to divert blows more easily; cf. 2 Sm 1:21.

---

*

**20:2** 1 Sm 19:24.
**20:3** Is 8:18.
**20:4** 2 Sm 10:4.
**20:5** Is 30:3, 5.
**20:6** Is 31:3; 36:6.
**21:1** Is 30:6; Dt 1:19; Jer 2:6.
**21:2** Is 24:16; 33:1.
**21:2** Is 13:17; Jer 49:34.
**21:3** Is 16:11; Ps 38:8.
**21:4** Dt 28:67.
**21:5** Dn 5:5.
**21:8** Hb 2:1.
**21:9** Is 46:1; Jer 50:2; 51:8; Rev 14:8; 18:2.
**21:10** Is 51:23; Jer 51:33; Mi 4:13; Hb 3:12.

### Dumah

11 Oracle on Dumah:†
They call to me from Seir,
"Watchman, how much longer the
    night?
Watchman, how much longer the
    night?"
12 The watchman replies,
"Morning has come, and again night.
    If you will ask, ask; come back again."

### In the Steppe

13 Oracle: in the steppe:†
In the thicket in the steppe you will
    spend the night,
caravans of Dedanites.
14 Meet the thirsty, bring them water,
inhabitants of the land of Tema,
    greet the fugitives with bread.*
15 For they have fled from the sword,
    from the drawn sword;
From the taut bow,
    from the thick of battle.

16 For thus the Lord has said to me: In another
year, like the years of a hired laborer,† all the
glory of Kedar shall come to an end. 17 Few of
Kedar's stalwart archers shall remain, for the
Lord, the God of Israel, has spoken.

### The Valley of Vision

**22** 1 Oracle on the Valley of Vision:†*
What is the matter with you now,
    that you have gone up,
all of you, to the housetops,
2† You who were full of noise,
    tumultuous city,
    exultant town?*
Your slain are not slain with the sword,
    nor killed in battle.
3 All your leaders fled away together,
    they were captured without use of
        bow;
All who were found were captured
        together,
    though they had fled afar off.
4 That is why I say: Turn away from me,
    let me weep bitterly;
Do not try to comfort me
    for the ruin of the daughter of my
        people.*
5 It is a day of panic, rout and confusion,
    from the Lord, the God of hosts, in
        the Valley of Vision†
Walls crash;
    a cry for help to the mountains.
6 Elam takes up the quiver,
    Aram mounts the horses
    and Kir† uncovers the shields.
7 Your choice valleys are filled with
        chariots,
    horses are posted at the gates—
8 and shelter over Judah is removed.†

On that day you looked to the weapons in
the House of the Forest; 9† you saw that the
breaches in the City of David were many; you
collected the water of the lower pool. 10 You
numbered the houses of Jerusalem, tearing

---

† **21:11–12** *Dumah*: an oasis in north Arabia (cf. Gn 25:14 and
1 Chr 1:30), may be identified with the north Arabian Adum-
matu mentioned in Assyrian records of Sennacherib's campaign
against north Arabia. *Seir*: a site in Edom. The Edomites ask the
prophet how much longer they must suffer ("the night" of suffering); he answers ambiguously: "Liberation ("morning") and
further suffering ("night")," but perhaps they will later receive a
more encouraging answer ("ask; come back again").
   **21:13–14** *In the steppe*: the north Arabian steppe where the
oases referred to were located. *Dedanites*: a north Arabian tribe
associated with the oasis of Tema; cf. Gn 10:7; 25:3; Jer 25:23.
   **21:16** *Year...of a hired laborer*: see note on 16:13–14. *Kedar*:
a nomadic tribe in Arabia; cf. 42:11; 60:7; Ps 120:5.
   **22:1–14** The title "oracle on the valley of vision," like the
other oracle headings in chaps. 13–23, was supplied by an editor
and is taken from v. 5. In all probability it relates to the events of
701, the lifting of Sennacherib's siege of Jerusalem. The
death of the Assyrian king Sargon II in 705 occasioned the revolt of many
of the vassal nations subject to Assyria, a revolt in which Hezekiah joined, over Isaiah's bitter opposition. The biblical and other
data concerning the outcome of this adventure are conflicting
and confusing. While 2 Kgs 19 (Is 37) tells of a miraculous deliverance of the city after the siege had been renewed, Assyrian
documents and 2 Kgs 18:13–16 report that Sennacherib, Sargon II's successor, devastated Judah (the destruction of 46 cities

is mentioned in Assyrian records); Hezekiah had to surrender
and paid Sennacherib a heavy indemnity, taken from the Temple
treasury and adornments. The inhabitants of Jerusalem apparently took the lifting of the siege as occasion for great rejoicing,
a response that Isaiah condemns. They should be mourning the
dead and learning that their confidence in allies rather than in
the Lord leads to disaster.
   **22:2–3** The retreat of Judah's soldiers is a further reason that
rejoicing is not in order.
   **22:5** *Valley of Vision*: frequently identified as the Hinnom
Valley, west of Jerusalem.
   **22:6** *Elam...Kir*: the Assyrian forces presumably included
auxiliary troops from various places.
   **22:8** *Shelter over Judah is removed*: the reference is obscure;
it has been suggested that Judah's protection was Jerusalem itself,
and with the fall of the city the country was exposed. *House of
the Forest*: an armory built by Solomon; its columns of wood
suggested the trees of a forest; cf. 1 Kgs 7:2; 10:17.
   **22:9–11** Frenetic efforts made to fortify the city before the
impending siege; cf. 2 Kgs 20:20; 2 Chr 32:3–4, 30. Some suggest that the description of these preparations comes from the
time of Nebuchadnezzar's assault on Jerusalem in 588. *You did*

---

*
**21:14** Jb 6:19.              **22:2** Is 32:13.
**22:1** Is 21:2.              **22:4** Jer 6:26; 9:1; 14:17.

IS

some down to strengthen the wall; <sup>11</sup>you
made a reservoir between the two walls for the
water of the old pool. But you did not look
to the city's Maker, nor consider the one who
fashioned it long ago.

<sup>12</sup>     On that day the Lord,
         the GOD of hosts, called
    For weeping and mourning,
         for shaving the head and wearing
             sackcloth.
<sup>13</sup>    But look! instead, there was celebration
         and joy,
         slaughtering cattle and butchering
             sheep,
    Eating meat and drinking wine:
         "Eat and drink, for tomorrow we
             die!"*

<sup>14</sup>This message was revealed in my hearing
from the LORD of hosts:

         This iniquity will not be forgiven you
             until you die,
         says the Lord, the GOD of hosts.

### Shebna and Eliakim

<sup>15</sup>    Thus says the Lord, the GOD of hosts:
         Up, go to that official,
         Shebna,† master of the palace,
<sup>16</sup>†   "What have you here? Whom have you
             here,
         that you have hewn for yourself a
             tomb here,
         Hewing a tomb on high,
             carving a resting place in the rock?"
<sup>17</sup>    The LORD shall hurl you down headlong,
             mortal man!
         He shall grip you firmly,
<sup>18</sup>    And roll you up and toss you like a ball
             into a broad land.

         There you will die, there with the
             chariots you glory in,
         you disgrace to your master's house!
<sup>19</sup>    I will thrust you from your office
         and pull you down from your station.
<sup>20</sup>    On that day I will summon my servant
         Eliakim,† son of Hilkiah;*
<sup>21</sup>    I will clothe him with your robe,
         gird him with your sash,
         confer on him your authority.
    He shall be a father to the inhabitants of
         Jerusalem,
         and to the house of Judah.*
<sup>22</sup>    I will place the key† of the House of
             David on his shoulder;
         what he opens, no one will shut,
         what he shuts, no one will open.*
<sup>23</sup>    I will fix him as a peg in a firm place,
         a seat of honor for his ancestral
             house;
<sup>24</sup>    On him shall hang all the glory of his
             ancestral house:†
         descendants and offspring,
         all the little dishes, from bowls to
             jugs.

<sup>25</sup>On that day, says the LORD of hosts, the
peg fixed in a firm place shall give way, break
off and fall, and the weight that hung on it
shall be done away with; for the LORD has
spoken.

### Tyre and Sidon

**23** <sup>1</sup>† Oracle on Tyre:
         Wail, ships of Tarshish,
         for your port is destroyed;
    From the land of the Kittim†
         the news reaches them.*
<sup>2</sup>    Silence! you who dwell on the coast,
         you merchants of Sidon,
    Whose messengers crossed the sea

---

† *not look to the city's Maker*: Isaiah here makes the crucial point. Jerusalem's safety lay not in military forces nor in alliances with other nations nor in playing power politics but in the Lord, here presented as the creator and founder of the city. Isaiah may be alluding to the belief that the city was inviolable.

**22:15** *Shebna*: by the time of the siege of Jerusalem in 36:3, Shebna, the scribe, no longer held the office of master of the palace.

**22:16** What is probably Shebna's inscribed tomb has been discovered in the village of Silwan on the eastern slope of Jerusalem.

**22:20** *Eliakim*: by the time of the events described in 36:3, Eliakim had replaced Shebna as master of the palace.

**22:22** *Key*: symbol of authority; cf. Mt 16:19; Rev 3:7.

**22:24–25** Apparently Eliakim proved to be a disappointment,

so an oracle of judgment was added to the originally positive oracle to Eliakim.

**23:1–17** This oracle, a satire directed against the Phoenician cities of Tyre and Sidon, is perhaps to be situated at the time of Sennacherib's campaign against the Phoenician cities in 701 B.C., following his subjugation of their Babylonian allies in 703 B.C.

**23:1** *Kittim*: Cyprus. The Hebrew word is derived from the term for the well-known city of Cyprus, Kition. In later centuries the term Kittim is used for the Greeks, the Romans, and other distant peoples.

**22:13** Is 56:12; Wis 2:6; 1 Cor 15:32. **22:20** 2 Kgs 18:18, 37. **22:21** Jb 29:16. **22:22** Rev 3:7. **23:1** Jer 25:22; Ez 26; Am 1:9; Zec 9:2, 4.

3       over the deep waters,
        Whose revenue was the grain of Shihor,†
            the harvest of the Nile,
        you who were the merchant among
            the nations. *

4       Be ashamed, Sidon, fortress on the sea,
            for the sea† has spoken,
        "I have not been in labor, nor given birth,
            nor raised young men,
            nor reared young women."

5       When the report reaches Egypt
            they shall be in anguish at the report
                about Tyre.

6       Pass over to Tarshish,†
            wail, you who dwell on the coast!

7       Is this your exultant city,
            whose origin is from old,
        Whose feet have taken her
            to dwell in distant lands?

8       Who has planned such a thing
            against Tyre, the bestower of crowns,
        Whose merchants are princes,
            whose traders are the earth's honored
                men?

9       The LORD of hosts has planned it,
            to disgrace the height of all beauty,
            to degrade all the honored of the earth. *

10      Cross to your own land,
            ship of Tarshish;
            the harbor is no more.

11      His hand he stretches out over the sea,
            he shakes kingdoms;
        The LORD commanded the destruction
            of Canaan's strongholds:†*

12      Crushed, you shall exult no more,
            virgin daughter Sidon.
        Arise, pass over to the Kittim,

        even there you shall find no rest. *

13†     Look at the land of the Chaldeans,
            the people that has ceased to be.
        Assyria founded it for ships,
            raised its towers,
        Only to tear down its palaces,
            and turn it into a ruin. *

14      Lament, ships of Tarshish,
            for your stronghold is destroyed.

15 On that day, Tyre shall be forgotten for seventy years,† the lifetime of one king. At the end of seventy years, the song about the prostitute will be Tyre's song:

16      Take a harp, go about the city,
            forgotten prostitute;
        Pluck the strings skillfully, sing many
            songs,
            that you may be remembered.

17 At the end of the seventy years the LORD shall visit Tyre. She shall return to her hire and serve as prostitute† with all the world's kingdoms on the face of the earth. * 18 But her merchandise and her hire shall be sacred to the LORD. It shall not be stored up or laid away; instead, her merchandise shall belong to those who dwell before the LORD, to eat their fill and clothe themselves in choice attire.

### D. Apocalypse of Isaiah†

#### Judgment upon the World and the Lord's Enthronement on Mount Zion†

24  ¹ See! The LORD is about to empty the earth and lay it waste;

---

23:3 Shihor: a synonym for the Nile.

23:4 The sea: here personified, it brings to distant coasts the news that Sidon must disown her children; her people are dispersed.

23:6–7 Tarshish: perhaps Tartessus in Spain. Distant lands: the reference is to the far-flung colonies established by the Phoenicians throughout the Mediterranean, including North Africa, Spain, and Sardinia. Oceangoing vessels were therefore called Tarshish ships.

23:11 Canaan's strongholds: the fortresses of Phoenicia.

23:13 The reference here seems to be to Assyria's subjugation of Babylon in 703 B.C., which left the coastal cities of Phoenicia as well as Judah open to Sennacherib's invasion in 701 B.C. Founded it...its palaces...turn it: the city of Babylon.

23:15 Seventy years: a conventional expression for a long period of time; cf. Jer 25:11 and 29:10.

23:17–18 Her hire...prostitute: the international trade engaged in by Tyre will become a source of wealth to God's people (cf. 45:14; 60:4–14; Zec 14:14).

24:1–27:13 Although it has become traditional to call these chapters "Apocalypse of Isaiah," and although they do contain some apocalyptic traits, many others are lacking, so that the title

is imprecise as a designation. These chapters are not a unified composition and their growth into their present form was a long, complicated process. They echo many themes from chaps. 13–23, "Oracles Against the Foreign Nations," as well as from earlier parts of Isaiah (e.g., the reversal of the "vineyard song," 5:1–7, in 27:2–5). Of particular interest is an unnamed city (24:10–13; 25:2; 26:5–6; 27:10–11), a wicked city, doomed to destruction; to the extent that it is identifiable, it may be Babylon, but more generally it symbolizes all forces hostile to God. And it stands in contrast to another city, also unnamed but no doubt to be identified with Jerusalem (26:1–2).

24:1–23 The world is about to be shaken by a devastating judgment that will overthrow both the human and divine enemies of the Lord, who will then reign in glory over his people on Mount Zion.

---

23:3 Ez 27:3.
23:9 Is 14:24–27; 22:11; Ez 28:7.
23:11 Is 14:27; Ps 65:8.
23:12 Ez 28:21–22.
23:13 Is 13:21; 34:14; Jer 50:39.
23:17 Rev 17:5; 18:3, 11, 13.

he will twist its surface,
and scatter its inhabitants:*
2 People and priest shall fare alike:
servant and master,
Maid and mistress,
buyer and seller,
Lender and borrower,
creditor and debtor.*
3 The earth shall be utterly laid waste,
utterly stripped,
for the LORD has decreed this word.
4 The earth mourns and fades,
the world languishes and fades;
both heaven and earth languish.*
5 The earth is polluted because of its
inhabitants,
for they have transgressed laws,
violated statutes,
broken the ancient covenant.†*
6 Therefore a curse devours the earth,
and its inhabitants pay for their
guilt;
Therefore they who dwell on earth have
dwindled,
and only a few are left.*
7 The new wine mourns, the vine
languishes,
all the merry-hearted groan.*
8 Stilled are the cheerful timbrels,
ended the shouts of the jubilant,
stilled the cheerful harp.*
9 They no longer drink wine and sing;
strong brew is bitter to those who
drink it.*
10 Broken down is the city of chaos,†
every house is shut against entry.*
11 In the streets they cry out for lack of
wine;
all joy has grown dim,
cheer is exiled from the land.*
12 In the city nothing remains but
desolation,
gates battered into ruins.
13 For thus it shall be in the midst of the
earth,
among the peoples,

As when an olive tree has been beaten,
as with a gleaning when the vintage is
done.*
14 These† shall lift up their voice,
they shall sing for joy in the majesty
of the LORD,
they shall shout from the western sea:
15 "Therefore, in the east
give glory to the LORD!
In the coastlands of the sea,
to the name of the LORD, the God of
Israel!"*
16 From the end of the earth we hear
songs:
"Splendor to the Just One!"
But I said, "I am wasted, wasted away.
Woe is me! The traitors betray;
with treachery have the traitors
betrayed!*
17 Terror, pit, and trap
for you, inhabitant of the earth!*
18 One who flees at the sound of terror
will fall into the pit;
One who climbs out of the pit
will be caught in the trap.
For the windows on high are open
and the foundations of the earth
shake.*
19 The earth will burst asunder,
the earth will be shaken apart,
the earth will be convulsed.
20 The earth will reel like a drunkard,
sway like a hut;
Its rebellion will weigh it down;
it will fall, never to rise again."*
21 On that day the LORD will punish
the host of the heavens† in the
heavens,
and the kings of the earth on the
earth.
22 They will be gathered together
like prisoners into a pit;
They will be shut up in a dungeon,
and after many days they will be
punished.*
23 Then the moon will blush

---

† **24:5** *Ancient covenant*: God's commandments to all human-kind (cf. Gn 9:4–6).
**24:10** *City of chaos*: a godless city which appears several times in chaps. 24–27; see note on 24:1–27:13.
**24:14** *These*: the saved.
**24:21** *Host of the heavens*: the stars, which were often re-garded as gods; cf. Dt 4:19; Jer 8:2.

* **24:1** Is 13:9; Na 2:3, 11.
**24:2** Hos 4:9.
**24:4** Is 33:9.
**24:5** Nm 35:33; Hos 4:2–3.
**24:6** Lv 26:15–16.
**24:7** Jl 1:10–12.
**24:8** Jer 7:34; Hos 2:13.
**24:9** Am 6:5–7.
**24:10** Is 25:2.
**24:11** Jer 48:33; Lam 5:14–15.
**24:13** Is 17:6; Mi 7:1.
**24:15** Is 42:10, 12; Zep 2:11.
**24:16** Is 21:2; 33:1.
**24:17** Jer 48:43.
**24:18** Gn 7:11; Am 5:19.
**24:20** Am 5:2.
**24:22** 2 Pt 2:4; Jude 6.

and the sun be ashamed,*
For the LORD of hosts will reign
  on Mount Zion and in Jerusalem,
  glorious in the sight of the elders.†*

## Praise for God's Deliverance and the Celebration in Zion†

**25** [1] O LORD, you are my God,
  I extol you, I praise your name;
For you have carried out your wonderful
      plans of old,
  faithful and true.*

[2] For you have made the city a heap,
  the fortified city a ruin,
The castle of the insolent, a city no
      more,
  not ever to be rebuilt.*

[3] Therefore a strong people will honor
      you,
  ruthless nations will fear you.

[4] For you have been a refuge to the poor,
  a refuge to the needy in their distress;
Shelter from the rain,
  shade from the heat.*
When the blast of the ruthless was like a
      winter rain,

[5] the roar of strangers like heat in the
      desert,
You subdued the heat with the shade of
      a cloud,
  the rain of the tyrants was
      vanquished.

[6] On this mountain† the LORD of hosts
      will provide for all peoples
A feast of rich food and choice wines,
  juicy, rich food and pure, choice
      wines.

[7] On this mountain he will destroy
  the veil that veils all peoples,
The web that is woven over all nations.

[8] He will destroy death forever.
The Lord GOD will wipe away
  the tears from all faces;

The reproach of his people he will
      remove
  from the whole earth; for the LORD
      has spoken.*

[9] On that day it will be said:
"Indeed, this is our God; we looked to
      him, and he saved us!
This is the LORD to whom we looked;
  let us rejoice and be glad that he has
      saved us!"*

### Judgment on Moab†

[10] For the hand of the LORD will rest on
      this mountain,
  but Moab will be trodden down
  as straw is trodden down in the mire.*

[11] He will spread out his hands in its
      midst,
  as a swimmer spreads out his hands
      to swim;
His pride will be brought low
  despite his strokes.*

[12] The high-walled fortress he will raze,
  bringing it low, leveling it to the
      ground, to the very dust.*

**26** Judah's Praise and Prayer for Deliverance.† [1] On that day this song shall be sung in the land of Judah:

"A strong city† have we;
  he sets up victory as our walls and
      ramparts.*

[2] Open up the gates
  that a righteous nation may enter,
  one that keeps faith.*

[3] With firm purpose you maintain peace;
  in peace, because of our trust in
      you."*

[4] Trust in the LORD forever!
  For the LORD is an eternal Rock.*

[5] He humbles those who dwell on high,
  the lofty city he brings down,

---

**24:23** *The elders*: the tradition in Ex 24:9–11 suggests that this refers to the people of God who are to share in the banquet on Mount Zion (Is 25:6–8).
**25:1–9** These verses praise God for carrying out his plan to destroy the enemy and to save the poor of his people in Zion (14:32), and they announce the victory banquet to be celebrated in the Lord's city.
**25:6** *This mountain*: i.e., Jerusalem's mountain, Zion.
**25:10–12** *Moab*: one of Israel's bitterest enemies.
**26:1–19** This text is a mixture of praise for the salvation that will take place, a confession of Judah's inability to achieve deliverance on its own, and earnest prayer that God may quickly bring about the longed-for salvation.

**26:1** *Strong city*: Jerusalem, the antithesis of the "city of chaos" (24:10); see note on 24:1–27:13.

**24:23** Is 13:10; Jl 3:3–4; 4:15.
**24:23** Is 4:5; 60:1–3; Ex 24:9–11; Mi 4:7; Rev 19:4–6.
**25:1** Is 12:1, 4; 22:11; 28:29; 37:26.
**25:2** Is 17:1; Jer 51:37.
**25:4** Is 14:32; 32:2; Na 1:7.
**25:8** Is 60:1, 3; 1 Cor 15:53–55; Rev 7:17; 21:4.
**25:9** Is 30:18–19.
**25:10** Zep 2:9–10.
**25:11** Is 16:6–7, 14.
**25:12** Is 26:5.
**26:1** Is 60:18.
**26:2** Ps 118:19–20.
**26:3** Is 32:17–18; Ps 112:7.
**26:4** Is 17:10; 30:29; Ps 62:8.

Brings it down to the ground,
   levels it to the dust.*

6 The feet of the needy trample on it—
   the feet of the poor.

7 The way of the just is smooth;
   the path of the just you make level.*

8 The course of your judgments, LORD, we
   await;
     your name and your memory are the
     desire of our souls.

9 My soul yearns for you at night,
   yes, my spirit within me seeks you at
   dawn;
When your judgment comes upon the
   earth,
     the world's inhabitants learn justice.*

10 The wicked, when spared, do not learn
   justice;
     in an upright land they act perversely,
     and do not see the majesty of the
     LORD.*

11 LORD, your hand is raised high,
   but they do not perceive it;
Let them be put to shame when they see
   your zeal for your people:
     let the fire prepared for your enemies
     consume them.*

12 LORD, you will decree peace for us,
   for you have accomplished all we have
   done.*

13 LORD, our God, lords other than you
   have ruled us;
     only because of you can we call upon
     your name.

14 Dead they are, they cannot live,
   shades that cannot rise;
Indeed, you have punished and
   destroyed them,
     and wiped out all memory of them.

15 You have increased the nation, LORD,
   you have increased the nation, have
   added to your glory,
     you have extended far all the
     boundaries of the land.*

16 LORD, oppressed by your punishment,
   we cried out in anguish under your
   discipline.*

17 As a woman about to give birth
   writhes and cries out in pain,
     so were we before you, LORD.*

18 We conceived and writhed in pain,
   giving birth only to wind;
Salvation we have not achieved for the
   earth,
     no inhabitants for the world were
     born.*

19† But your dead shall live, their corpses
   shall rise!
Awake and sing, you who lie in the
   dust!
For your dew is a dew of light,
   and you cause the land of shades to
   give birth.*

## The Lord's Response†

20 Go, my people, enter your chambers,
   and close the doors behind you;
Hide yourselves for a brief moment,
   until the wrath is past.*

21 See, the LORD goes forth from his place,
   to punish the wickedness of the
   earth's inhabitants;
The earth will reveal the blood shed
   upon it,
     and no longer conceal the slain.*

## The Judgment and Deliverance of Israel

**27** ¹ On that day,
   The LORD will punish with his
   sword
     that is cruel, great, and strong,
Leviathan the fleeing serpent,
Leviathan the coiled serpent;
   he will slay the dragon† in the sea.*

---

**26:19** This verse refers not to resurrection of the dead, but to the restoration of the people; cf. Ez 37. The population of Judah was radically reduced by the slaughter and deportations that the historical disasters of the late eighth and seventh centuries B.C. brought upon the country. In this context, a major concern for the future was for an increase in the population, a rebirth of the nation's life.

**26:20–21** The time of wrath for Judah would soon be over, and the just punishment of its enemies would begin (cf. Hb 2:1–3).

**27:1** *Leviathan…dragon:* the description of Leviathan is almost identical to a passage from a much earlier Ugaritic text. The sea dragon became a symbol of the forces of evil which

God vanquishes even as he overcame primeval chaos; cf. notes on 30:7; 51:9–10; Jb 3:8; 7:12; no power can challenge God. Leviathan is even spoken of playfully in Ps 104:26.

**26:5** Is 25:11–12; 32:19.
**26:7** Ps 23:3–4; Prv 11:3,
  5.
**26:9** Ps 63:2.
**26:10** Is 5:12; Eccl 8:11.
**26:11** Is 9:6; 30:27; 37:32.
**26:12** Jer 29:11; Phil 2:13.
**26:15** Is 54:2–3.
**26:16** Hos 5:15.
**26:17** Mi 4:10.
**26:18** Is 37:3.
**26:19** Ez 37:5–14; Dn 12:2;
  Hos 6:2.
**26:20** Is 10:25.
**26:21** Gn 4:10; Jb 16:18; Ps
  106:38; Mi 1:3.
**27:1** Jb 40:25–32; Ps
  74:12–14; Ez 32:2.

2†     On that day—
     The pleasant vineyard, sing about it! *
3      I, the LORD, am its keeper,
     I water it every moment;
     Lest anyone harm it,
     night and day I guard it. *
4      I am not angry.
     But if I were to find briers and thorns,
     In battle I would march against it;
     I would burn it all. *
5      But if it holds fast to my refuge,
     it shall have peace with me; *
     it shall have peace with me.

6      In days to come Jacob shall take root,
     Israel shall sprout and blossom,
     covering all the world with fruit. *
7†     Was he smitten as his smiter was
     smitten?
     Was he slain as his slayer was slain?
8      Driving out and expelling, he struggled
     against it,
     carrying it off with his cruel wind on a
     day of storm. *
9      This, then, shall be the expiation of
     Jacob's guilt,
     this the result of removing his sin:
     He shall pulverize all the stones of the
     altars
     like pieces of chalk;
     no asherahs or incense altars shall
     stand.
10      For the fortified city shall be desolate,
     an abandoned pasture, a forsaken
     wilderness;
     There calves shall graze, there they shall
     lie down,
     and consume its branches.
11      When its boughs wither, they shall be
     broken off;

     and women shall come to kindle fires
     with them.
     For this is not an understanding
     people;
     therefore their maker shall not spare
     them;
     their creator shall not be gracious to
     them. *
12      On that day,
     The LORD shall beat out grain
     from the channel of the Euphrates to
     the Wadi of Egypt,
     and you shall be gleaned† one by one,
     children of Israel.
13      On that day,†
     A great trumpet shall blow,
     and the lost in the land of Assyria
     and the outcasts in the land of Egypt
     Shall come and worship the LORD
     on the holy mountain, in Jerusalem. *

## E. The Lord Alone, Israel's and Judah's Salvation

### The Fate of Samaria†

**28** ¹ Ah! majestic garland
     of the drunkards of Ephraim,†
     Fading blooms of his glorious beauty,
     at the head of the fertile valley,
     upon those stupefied with wine. *
2      See, the LORD has a strong one, a mighty
     one,†
     who, like an onslaught of hail, a
     destructive storm,
     Like a flood of water, great and
     overflowing,
     levels to the ground with violence; *
3      With feet that will trample
     the majestic garland of the drunkards
     of Ephraim.

IS

---

**27:2–5** This passage mitigates the harsh words on Israel as the Lord's vineyard in 5:1–7; here is given the rain there withheld, though Israel's welfare is still made dependent on fidelity.

**27:7–9** Israel was not treated as sternly as were its enemies whom God used to punish it. God did, however, drive Israel from its land, and if it wants to make peace with God, it must change its former cultic practices, destroying its altars and sacred groves (cf. 17:7–11).

**27:12** *Gleaned*: God will harvest his people who have been scattered from Assyria to Egypt. Note the same language of gleaning to describe the remnant of the Northern Kingdom in 17:5–6.

**27:13** The remnant of Israel will return to Jerusalem for worship; cf. 11:10–16.

**28:1–6** These verses once constituted an independent oracle against the Northern Kingdom, probably originally spoken during the time between its overthrow by Assyria in 732 and its

destruction in 722/721. Isaiah has reused them as an introduction to his oracle against Judah (vv. 7–22), because the leaders of Judah were guilty of the same excesses that had once marked Ephraim's leadership.

**28:1** *Ephraim*: the Northern Kingdom. Its capital, Samaria, was built upon a hill, suggestive of a majestic garland adorning a human head. The characterization of the leadership of Ephraim as drunken underscores its inattention to justice and good government (cf. 5:11–13; Am 6:1–6).

**28:2** *A strong one, a mighty one*: Assyria (cf. 8:7–8).

---

**27:2** Is 5:1; Am 5:11.
**27:3** Is 5:2–7.
**27:4** Is 10:17.
**27:5** Jb 22:21.
**27:6** Is 37:31–32; Hos 14:5–6.
**27:8** Jer 18:17.
**27:11** Is 1:3; 5:13; Jer 4:22.
**27:13** Is 11:11–16.
**28:1** Hos 7:5; Am 6:1–6.
**28:2** Is 25:4–5; 28:17–18; 30:30.

4  The fading blooms of his glorious
         beauty
      at the head of the fertile valley
   Will be like an early fig before summer:
      whoever sees it,
      swallows it as soon as it is in hand.*

5  On that day the LORD of hosts
      will be a glorious crown
   And a brilliant diadem
      for the remnant of his people,

6  A spirit of judgment
      for the one who sits in judgment,
   And strength for those
      who turn back the battle at the gate.

## Against Judah

7  But these also stagger from wine
      and stumble from strong drink:
   Priest and prophet stagger from strong
         drink,
      overpowered by wine;
   They are confused by strong drink,
      they stagger in their visions,
      they totter when giving judgment.*

8  Yes, all the tables
      are covered with vomit,
      with filth, and no place left clean.

9†  "To whom would he impart knowledge?
   To whom would he convey the message?
   To those just weaned from milk,
      those weaned from the breast?

10  For he says,
   'Command on command, command on
         command,
      rule on rule, rule on rule,
      here a little, there a little!'"

11†  Yes, with stammering lips and in a
         strange language

12  he will speak to this people,*
   to whom he said:
   "This is the resting place,
      give rest to the weary;
   And this is the place of repose"—
      but they refused to hear.*

13  So for them the word of the LORD shall
         be:
   "Command on command, command
         on command,
   Rule on rule, rule on rule,
      here a little, there a little!"
   So that when they walk, they shall
         stumble backward,
      broken, ensnared, and captured.*

14  Therefore, hear the word of the LORD,
         you scoffers,
      who rule† this people in Jerusalem:*

15  You have declared, "We have made a
         covenant with death,
      with Sheol† we have made a pact;
   When the raging flood passes through,
      it will not reach us;
   For we have made lies our refuge,
      and in falsehood we have found a
         hiding place,"—*

16  Therefore, thus says the Lord GOD:
      See, I am laying a stone in Zion,†
      a stone that has been tested,
   A precious cornerstone as a sure
         foundation;
      whoever puts faith in it will not
         waver.*

17  I will make judgment a measuring line,
      and justice a level.—†
   Hail shall sweep away the refuge of lies,
      and waters shall flood the hiding
         place.

---

28:9–10 The words of those who ridicule Isaiah. The Hebrew of v. 10, by its very sound, conveys the idea of mocking imitation of what the prophet says, as though he spoke like a stammering child: "sau lasau, sau lasau, kau lakau, kau lakau, ze'er sham, ze'er sham." But in v. 13 God repeats these words in deadly earnest, putting them in the mouth of the victorious Assyrian army.

28:11 God will answer the mockers and defend Isaiah. *Strange language*: spoken by the invading army.

28:14 *Who rule*: there is a play on words; the same expression could also mean, "Proverb makers," that is, scoffers of this people.

28:15, 18 *A covenant with death, with Sheol*: an alliance with foreign powers, such as Egypt and Babylon. *Have made lies…a hiding place*: this confidence in human aid will prove to be false and deceitful, incapable of averting the dreaded disaster. *Raging flood*: the Assyrian invasion; cf. 8:7–8.

28:16 *A stone in Zion*: the true and sure foundation of salvation, i.e., the presence of God, who had chosen and founded Zion as his city (Ps 78:68–69; Is 14:32) and had chosen the Davidic dynasty to rule over his people (Ps 78:70–72; Is 9:1–6;

11:1–10). *Cornerstone*: the assurance of salvation, rejected by the people of Judah in the prophet's time, is picked up in Ps 118:22 and later applied to Christ; cf. Mt 21:42; Lk 20:17; Acts 4:11; Rom 9:33; 1 Pt 2:7. Chapters 28–31 alternate between threats of the danger of rebelling against Assyria (with implied trust in Egypt) with assurances of the power and protection of the Lord.

28:17 *Line…level*: instruments used in constructing a building, to keep it true. They are used metaphorically here to refer to the qualities that Zion, the city of God, must manifest, judgment and justice, not bloodshed (Mi 3:10), nor deceit and violence, which would result in a bulging unstable wall doomed to destruction (Is 30:12–14). Cf. 1 Cor 3:10–17.

---

*
**28:4** Is 17:6; Na 3:12.          **28:14** Is 3:1–4; 5:18–21.
**28:7** Is 5:11–12; Mi 2:11.      **28:15** Wis 1:16; Jer 5:12.
**28:11** Jer 5:15; 1 Cor 14:21;   **28:16** Ps 118:22; Mt 21:42;
    Dt 28:49; Bar 4:15.              Acts 4:11; Rom 9:33;
**28:12** Is 30:9.                   1 Pt 2:6.
**28:13** Is 8:15.

IS

18  Your covenant with death shall be
        canceled
    and your pact with Sheol shall not
        stand.
    When the raging flood passes through,
        you shall be beaten down by it. *
19  Whenever it passes, it shall seize you;
        morning after morning it shall pass,
        by day and by night.
    Sheer terror
        to impart the message!
20  For the bed shall be too short to stretch
        out in,
    and the cover too narrow to wrap in.
21  For the LORD shall rise up as on Mount
        Perazim,
    bestir himself as in the Valley of
        Gibeon, †
    To carry out his work—strange his work!
        to perform his deed—alien his deed!
22  Now, cease scoffing,
        lest your bonds be tightened,
    For I have heard a decree of destruction
        from the Lord, the GOD of hosts,
        for the whole land. *

### The Parable of the Farmer

23 †  Give ear and hear my voice,
        pay attention and hear my word:
24  Is the plowman forever plowing in order
        to sow,
    always loosening and harrowing the
        field?
25  When he has leveled the surface,
        does he not scatter caraway and sow
        cumin, †
    Put in wheat and barley,
        with spelt as its border?
26  His God has taught him this rule,
        he has instructed him.
27  For caraway is not threshed with a
        sledge,
        nor does a cartwheel roll over cumin.

But caraway is beaten out with a staff,
        and cumin with a rod.
28  Grain is crushed for bread, but not
        forever;
    though he thresh it thoroughly,
        and drive his cartwheel and horses
        over it,
    he does not pulverize it.
29  This too comes from the LORD of hosts;
        wonderful is his counsel and great his
        wisdom. *

### Judgment and Deliverance of Jerusalem

**29** ¹Ah! Ariel, Ariel, †
        city where David encamped!
    Let year follow year,
        and feast follow feast, *
2   But I will bring distress upon Ariel,
        and there will be mourning and
        moaning.
    You shall be to me like Ariel: *
3       I will encamp like David against you;
    I will circle you with outposts
        and set up siege works against you. *
4   You shall speak from beneath the earth,
        and from the dust below, your words
        shall come.
    Your voice shall be that of a ghost from
        the earth,
        and your words shall whisper from
        the dust. *
5   The horde of your arrogant shall be like
        fine dust,
        a horde of tyrants like flying chaff. *
    Then suddenly, in an instant,
6       you shall be visited by the LORD of
            hosts,
    With thunder, earthquake, and great
        noise,
        whirlwind, storm, and the flame of
        consuming fire. *
7 †    Then like a dream,
        a vision of the night,

---

**28:21** *Mount Perazim...Valley of Gibeon:* where David defeated the Philistines; cf. 2 Sm 5:20, 25; 1 Chr 14:11, 16. God's new work will be strange, because instead of fighting for Judah as the Lord did in David's time, God will now fight against Jerusalem (see 29:1–4).
**28:23–29** The practical variation of the farmer's work reflects the way God deals with his people, wisely adapted to circumstances; he does not altogether crush them in their weakness.
**28:25** *Caraway...cumin:* herbs used in seasoning food. *Spelt:* a variety of wheat.
**29:1–2** *Ariel:* a poetic name for Jerusalem. It has been variously interpreted to mean "lion of God," "altar hearth of God" (Ez 43:15–16), "city of God," or "foundation of God." In v. 2 the term

refers to "altar hearth," i.e., a place of burning for its people (cf. 30:33; 31:9). God will attack Jerusalem, as David did long ago.
**29:7–8** Just when the attackers think their capture of Jerusalem is certain, the Lord will snatch victory from their hands and save the city. The sudden shift from the Lord's attack on the city to its deliverance by him is surprising and unexplained; it may reflect the account related in 37:36.

---

**28:18** Is 28:2–3.
**28:22** Is 5:18–19; 10:23.
**28:29** Rom 11:33.
**29:1** 2 Sm 5:6–9.
**29:2** Is 33:7.
**29:3** 2 Kgs 25:1; Ez 4:2.
**29:4** Is 8:19; 1 Sm 28:14.
**29:5** Is 17:13; Ps 18:43; Jb 21:18.
**29:6** Is 30:27, 30.

I
S

Shall be the horde of all the nations
  who make war against Ariel:
All the outposts, the siege works against
  it,
  all who distress it.

8 As when a hungry man dreams he is
  eating
  and awakens with an empty stomach,
Or when a thirsty man dreams he is
  drinking
  and awakens faint, his throat parched,
So shall the horde of all the nations be,
  who make war against Mount Zion.

### Blindness and Perversity

9† Stupefy yourselves and stay stupid;
  blind yourselves and stay blind!
You who are drunk, but not from wine,
  who stagger, but not from strong
  drink!*
10 For the LORD has poured out on you
  a spirit of deep sleep.
He has shut your eyes (the prophets)
  and covered your heads (the seers).†*

11 For you the vision of all this has become
like the words of a sealed scroll. When it is
handed to one who can read, with the request,
"Read this," the reply is, "I cannot, because
it is sealed." 12 When the scroll is handed to
one who cannot read, with the request, "Read
this," the reply is, "I cannot read."

13        The Lord said:
Since this people draws near with words
  only
  and honors me with their lips alone,
  though their hearts are far from me,
And fear of me has become
  mere precept of human teaching,*
14 Therefore I will again deal with this
  people
  in surprising and wondrous fashion:
The wisdom of the wise shall perish,

the prudence of the prudent shall
  vanish.*
15 Ah! You who would hide a plan
  too deep for the LORD!
Who work in the dark, saying,
  "Who sees us, who knows us?"*
16 Your perversity is as though the potter
  were taken to be the clay:
As though what is made should say of
  its maker,
  "He did not make me!"
Or the vessel should say of the potter,
  "He does not understand."*

### Redemption†

17 Surely, in a very little while,
  Lebanon shall be changed into an
  orchard,
  and the orchard be considered a
  forest!*
18 On that day the deaf shall hear
  the words of a scroll;
And out of gloom and darkness,
  the eyes of the blind shall see.*
19 The lowly shall again find joy in the
  LORD,
  the poorest rejoice in the Holy One of
  Israel.*
20 For the tyrant shall be no more,
  the scoffer shall cease to be;
All who are ready for evil shall be cut
  off,*
21 those who condemn with a mere
  word,
Who ensnare the defender at the gate,
  and leave the just with an empty
  claim.*
22 Therefore thus says the LORD,
  the God of the house of Jacob,
  who redeemed Abraham:†
No longer shall Jacob be ashamed,
  no longer shall his face grow pale.*
23 For when his children see
  the work of my hands in his midst,

---

† **29:9–16** Despite their show of piety, Judah's leaders refused
to accept the prophet's words of assurance. They rejected prophetic advice (cf. 30:10–11), did not consult the prophetic oracle
in forming their political plans (30:1–2; 31:1), and tried to hide
their plans even from God's prophet (v. 15), who, they thought,
simply did not understand military and political reality.

**29:10** *Prophets…seers*: interpretive glosses.

**29:17–24** The prophet presents the positive aspects of God's
plan in terms of a series of reversals: an end to pride, ignorance,
and injustice. Cf. 32:3–5.

**29:22** *Who redeemed Abraham*: perhaps by revealing him-

self and delivering Abraham from idolatrous worship; cf. Gn
12:1–3; 17:1; Jos 24:2–3.

---

| | |
|---|---|
| **29:9** Is 19:14; 28:7–8. | Rom 9:20. |
| **29:10** Is 6:10; Rom 11:8. | **29:17** Is 32:15. |
| **29:13** Ez 33:31; Mt 15:8–9; | **29:18** Is 35:5; 42:6–7. |
| Mk 7:6–7. | **29:19** Is 61:1–2. |
| **29:14** Jer 49:7; 1 Cor 1:19. | **29:20** Is 28:22. |
| **29:15** Is 30:1–2; 31:1; Ez | **29:21** Is 5:23; 10:1–2; Am |
| 8:12; Jn 3:19–20. | 5:10, 12. |
| **29:16** Is 45:9; Jer 18:6; | **29:22** Is 45:17. |

They shall sanctify my name;
  they shall sanctify the Holy One of
    Jacob,
  be in awe of the God of Israel.*
24 Those who err in spirit shall acquire
    understanding,
  those who find fault shall receive
    instruction.

## Oracle on the Futility of an Alliance with Egypt†

**30** 1 Ah! Rebellious children,
    oracle of the LORD,
  Who carry out a plan that is not mine,
    who make an alliance† I did not inspire,
    thus adding sin upon sin;*
2 They go down to Egypt,
    without asking my counsel,†
  To seek strength in Pharaoh's protection
    and take refuge in Egypt's shadow.*
3 Pharaoh's protection shall become your
    shame,
  refuge in Egypt's shadow your
    disgrace.*
4 When his princes are at Zoan
    and his messengers reach Hanes,*
5 All shall be ashamed
    of a people that gain them nothing,
  Neither help nor benefit,
    but only shame and reproach.*
6 Oracle on the Beasts of the Negeb.
  Through the distressed and troubled
    land†
  of the lioness and roaring lion,
  of the viper and flying saraph,
  They carry their riches on the backs of
    donkeys
  and their treasures on the humps of
    camels

To a people good for nothing,
  to Egypt whose help is futile and vain.
7 Therefore I call her
  "Rahab† Sit-still."
8† Now come, write it on a tablet they can
    keep,
  inscribe it on a scroll;
  That in time to come it may be
    an eternal witness.*
9 For this is a rebellious people,
    deceitful children,
  Children who refuse
    to listen to the instruction of the LORD;*
10 Who say to the seers, "Do not see";
  to the prophets,† "Do not prophesy
    truth for us;
  speak smooth things to us, see visions
    that deceive!*
11 Turn aside from the way! Get out of the
    path!
  Let us hear no more
    of the Holy One of Israel!"*
12 Therefore, thus says the Holy One of
    Israel:
  Because you reject this word,
  And put your trust in oppression and
    deceit,
    and depend on them,*
13 This iniquity of yours shall be
    like a descending rift
  Bulging out in a high wall
    whose crash comes suddenly, in an
      instant,*
14 Crashing like a potter's jar
    smashed beyond rescue,
  And among its fragments cannot be
    found
  a sherd to scoop fire from the hearth
    or dip water from the cistern.*

---

**30:1–17** Several independent oracles against making an alliance with Egypt have been strung together in this chapter: vv. 1–5, vv. 6–7, and vv. 8–17. That these were originally separate oracles is indicated by the fact that the oracle in vv. 6–7 is still introduced by its own heading: Oracle on the Beasts of the Negeb.
**30:1** Make an alliance: lit., "pour out a libation," namely, as part of the ritual of treaty making.
**30:2** Without asking my counsel: it was a practice to consult God through the prophets or through the priestly oracle before making a major political decision (1 Sm 23:1–12; 1 Kgs 22:5), but Judah's leadership, in its concern for security, was apparently trying to keep its plan for a treaty with Egypt secret even from the prophets, thus implicitly from God (29:15).
**30:6** Distressed…land: the wilderness between Judah and Egypt, through which Judahite messengers had to pass, carrying their tribute to Egypt to buy assistance in the struggle against Assyria. Flying saraph: see notes on 6:2; 14:29.
**30:7** Here as elsewhere (cf. Ps 87:4) Egypt is compared to Rahab, the raging, destructive sea monster (cf. Is 51:9; Jb 26:12;

Ps 89:11); yet Egypt, when asked for aid by Judah, becomes silent and "sits still."
**30:8** Isaiah will write down his condemnation of the foolish policy pursued so that the truth of his warning of its dire consequences (vv. 12–17) may afterward be recognized.
**30:10** Seers…prophets: the two terms are synonyms for prophetic figures such as Isaiah (1:1; 2:1; 6:1, 5). There is wordplay between the nouns and their cognate verbs, both of which mean "to see." The authorities are depicted as forbidding prophets to contradict their secret political and military policies.

---

29:23 Is 8:12–13.
30:1 Is 1:4; 5:21; 28:15;
  29:15.
30:2 Is 31:1; 36:6.
30:3 Is 20:5; Jer 2:36–37.
30:4 Is 19:11.
30:5 Is 36:6.
30:8 Is 8:1, 16; Jer 36:2;

Hb 2:2.
30:9 Is 1:4; 28:12; Jer 7:28.
30:10 Is 29:10; Jer 5:31;
  11:21; Am 2:12.
30:11 Jb 21:14–15.
30:12 Is 28:15; Ps 62:11.
30:13 Is 28:17; Ez 13:14.
30:14 Jer 19:11.

15 For thus said the Lord GOD,
   the Holy One of Israel:
By waiting and by calm you shall be
      saved,
   in quiet and in trust shall be your
      strength.
   But this you did not will.*

16 "No," you said,
   "Upon horses we will flee."
   Very well, you shall flee!
"Upon swift steeds we will ride."
   Very well, swift shall be your
      pursuers!*

17 A thousand shall tremble at the threat of
      one—
   if five threaten, you shall flee.
You will then be left like a flagstaff on a
      mountaintop,
   like a flag on a hill.*

### Zion's Future Deliverance

18 Truly, the LORD is waiting to be gracious
      to you,
   truly, he shall rise to show you
      mercy;
For the LORD is a God of justice:
   happy are all who wait for him!*

19 Yes, people of Zion, dwelling in
      Jerusalem,
   you shall no longer weep;
He will be most gracious to you when
      you cry out;
   as soon as he hears he will answer
      you.*

20 The Lord will give you bread in adversity
      and water in affliction.
No longer will your Teacher† hide
      himself,
   but with your own eyes you shall see
      your Teacher,*

21 And your ears shall hear a word behind
      you:
   "This is the way; walk in it,"
   when you would turn to the right or
      the left.

22 You shall defile your silver-plated idols
   and your gold-covered images;

You shall throw them away like filthy
      rags,
   you shall say, "Get out!"*

23 He will give rain for the seed
      you sow in the ground,
And the bread that the soil produces
   will be rich and abundant.
On that day your cattle will graze
   in broad meadows;*

24 The oxen and the donkeys that till the
      ground
   will eat silage tossed to them
   with shovel and pitchfork.

25 Upon every high mountain and lofty
      hill
   there will be streams of running water.
On the day of the great slaughter,
   when the towers fall,

26 The light of the moon will be like the
      light of the sun,
   and the light of the sun will be seven
      times greater,
   like the light of seven days,
On the day the LORD binds up the
      wounds of his people
   and heals the bruises left by his
      blows.*

### Divine Judgment on Assyria†

27 See, the name of the LORD is coming
      from afar,
   burning with anger, heavy with threat,
His lips filled with fury,
   tongue like a consuming fire,*

28 Breath like an overflowing torrent
   that reaches up to the neck!
He will winnow the nations with a
      destructive winnowing
   and bridle the jaws of the peoples to
      send them astray.*

29 For you, there will be singing
   as on a night when a feast is observed,
And joy of heart
   as when one marches along with a
      flute
Going to the mountain of the LORD,
   to the Rock of Israel.

---

† **30:20** *Teacher:* God, who in the past made the people blind and deaf through the prophetic message (6:9–10) and who in his anger hid his face from the house of Jacob (8:17), shall in the future help them to understand his teaching clearly (cf. Jer 31:34).
   **30:27–33** *God's punishment of Assyria. The name of the LORD:* here, God himself; cf. Ps 20:2.

* **30:15** Is 7:4; 8:6; 28:12.  ⸳ 29:18.
**30:16** Is 31:3.   **30:22** Is 2:20; 27:9; 31:7.
**30:17** Is 11:10; Dt 32:30.   **30:23** Lv 26:3–5.
**30:18** Ex 34:6; Ps 34:9; Jer   **30:26** Is 1:6; Jer 30:17; Hos
   17:7.      6:1.
**30:19** Is 25:8; 58:9; 65:24.   **30:27** Is 10:17; 29:6.
**30:20** Is 6:9–10; 8:17;   **30:28** Is 8:7–8; 37:29.

30 The LORD will make his glorious voice
        heard,
   and reveal his arm coming down
In raging fury and flame of consuming
        fire,
   in tempest, and rainstorm, and hail.*
31 For at the voice of the LORD, Assyria will
        be shattered,
   as he strikes with the rod;
32 And every sweep of the rod of his
        punishment,
   which the LORD will bring down on
        him,
Will be accompanied by timbrels and
        lyres,
   while he wages war against him.*
33 For his tophet† has long been ready,
   truly it is prepared for the king;
His firepit made both deep and wide,
   with fire and firewood in abundance,
And the breath of the LORD, like a
        stream of sulfur,
   setting it afire.*

## Against the Egyptian Alliance

**31** ¹ Ah! Those who go down to Egypt
        for help,
   who rely on horses;
Who put their trust in chariots because
        of their number,
   and in horsemen because of their
        combined power,
But look not to the Holy One of Israel
   nor seek the LORD!†*
2 Yet he too is wise and will bring disaster;
   he will not turn from his threats.
He will rise up against the house of the
        wicked
   and against those who help
        evildoers.*
3 The Egyptians are human beings, not
        God,
   their horses flesh, not spirit;

When the LORD stretches forth his hand,
   the helper shall stumble, the one
        helped shall fall,
   and both of them shall perish
        together.*
4 For thus says the LORD to me:
As a lion or its young
   growling over the prey,
With a band of shepherds
   assembled against it,
Is neither dismayed by their shouts
   nor cowed by their noise,
So shall the LORD of hosts come down
   to wage war upon Mount Zion, upon
        its height.*
5 Like hovering birds, so the LORD of hosts
   shall shield Jerusalem,
To shield and deliver,
   to spare and rescue.*

⁶ Return, O Israelites, to him whom you
have utterly deserted.* ⁷ On that day each one
of you shall reject his idols of silver and gold,
which your hands have made.*

8 Assyria shall fall by a sword, not wielded
        by human being,
   no mortal sword shall devour him;
He shall flee before the sword,
   and his young men shall be impressed
        as laborers.*
9 He shall rush past his crag† in panic,
   and his princes desert the standard in
        terror,
Says the LORD who has a fire in Zion
   and a furnace in Jerusalem.*

## The Kingdom of Justice

**32** ¹ See, a king will reign justly
        and princes will rule rightly.*
2 Each of them will be like a shelter from
        the wind,
   a refuge from the rain.

---

† **30:33** *Tophet:* a site, near Jerusalem, where children were sacrificed by fire to Molech (2 Kgs 23:10), and where, probably, Ahaz sacrificed his son (2 Kgs 16:3). Here, Isaiah speaks of "his tophet," the site prepared for burning up the king of Assyria. *King:* there seems to be a play on words between the Heb. word for king (*melek*) and the name Molech. This defeat of Assyria becomes the occasion for Israel's festal rejoicing (v. 32).

 **31:1** *Seek the LORD:* a technical expression for seeking a prophetic or priestly oracle, similar to the expression "asking my counsel" in 30:2. The prophet complains that Judah has decided on its policy of alliance with Egypt without first consulting the Lord.

 **31:9** *Crag:* the king as the rallying point of the princes. *Panic:*

terror is an element of Israel's holy war tradition, in which defeat of the enemy is accomplished by the Lord rather than by human means (cf. v. 8).

---

**30:30** Is 10:17; 28:2; 29:6.
**30:32** Is 10:24–26;
   14:24–27.
**30:33** Gn 19:24; Ez 38:22.
**31:1** Is 5:12, 24; 18:2;
   22:11; 29:15; 30:2;
   36:6.
**31:2** Is 28:21.
**31:3** Ps 146:3–5.
**31:4** Hos 5:14;

Am 1:2; 3:8, 12.
**31:5** Is 37:35; Dt 32:11; Ps
   91:4.
**31:6** Is 1:2–4; Jer 3:12.
**31:7** Is 2:20; 30:22.
**31:8** Is 27:1; 34:5–6;
   37:36.
**31:9** Is 30:17, 33.
**32:1** Is 9:6; 11:4; 16:5; Ps
   72:1–4; Jer 23:5–6.

I
S

They will be like streams of water in a
    dry country,
  like the shade of a great rock in a
      parched land.*

3   The eyes of those who see will not be
      closed;
    the ears of those who hear will be
      attentive.*

4   The hasty of heart shall take thought to
      know,
    and tongues of stutterers shall speak
      readily and clearly.

5   No more will the fool be called noble,
    nor the deceiver be considered
      honorable.*

6   For the fool speaks folly,
    his heart plans evil:
  Godless actions,
    perverse speech against the LORD,
  Letting the hungry go empty
    and the thirsty without drink.*

7   The deceits of the deceiver are evil,
    he plans devious schemes:
  To ruin the poor with lies,
    and the needy when they plead their
      case.*

8   But the noble plan noble deeds,
    and in noble deeds they persist.

### The Women of Jerusalem

9   You women so complacent, rise up and
      hear my voice,
    daughters so confident, give heed to
      my words.*

10  In a little more than a year
    your confidence will be shaken;
  For the vintage will fail,
    no fruit harvest will come in.*

11  Tremble, you who are so complacent!
    Shudder, you who are so confident!
  Strip yourselves bare,
    with only a loincloth for cover.*

12  Beat your breasts

  for the pleasant fields,
  for the fruitful vine;*

13  For the soil of my people,
    overgrown with thorns and briers;
  For all the joyful houses,
    the exultant city.*

14  The castle† will be forsaken,
    the noisy city deserted;
  Citadel and tower will become
      wasteland forever,
    the joy of wild donkeys, the pasture of
      flocks;*

15† Until the spirit from on high
    is poured out on us.
  And the wilderness becomes a garden
      land
    and the garden land seems as
      common as forest.*

16  Then judgment will dwell in the
      wilderness
    and justice abide in the garden land.

17  The work of justice will be peace;
    the effect of justice, calm and security
      forever.*

18  My people will live in peaceful country,
    in secure dwellings and quiet resting
      places.*

19  And the forest will come down
      completely,
    the city will be utterly laid low.†*

20  Happy are you who sow beside every
      stream,
    and let the ox and the donkey go
      freely!*

### Overthrow of Assyria†

**33** ¹ Ah! You destroyer never destroyed,
    betrayer never betrayed!
  When you have finished destroying, you
      will be destroyed;
    when you have stopped betraying, you
      will be betrayed.*

2     LORD, be gracious to us; for you we wait.

---

**32:14** *The castle*: the fortified royal palace in Jerusalem. *Cita-del*: Ophel, the fortified hill, with its stronghold called "the great projecting tower" (Neh 3:27).
   **32:15–18, 20** Extraordinary peace and prosperity will come to Israel under just rulers.
   **32:19** Probably from a different context, perhaps after v. 14a.
   **33:1–24** After an introductory address to Assyria (v. 1), there follows a prayer on behalf of Jerusalem which recalls what God had done in the past (vv. 2–6) and a description of the present situation (vv. 7–9). In response, the Lord announces a judgment on Assyria (vv. 10–12) that will lead to the purification of Jerusalem's inhabitants (vv. 13–16). The text ends with an idealized portrait of the redeemed Jerusalem of the future (vv. 17–24).

**32:2** Is 4:6; 16:4; 25:4.
**32:3** Is 6:10; 29:18; 35:5.
**32:5** Is 5:20.
**32:6** Prv 15:2.
**32:7** Is 29:20–21; Mi 2:1.
**32:9** Is 3:16–24; Am 6:1.
**32:10** Zep 1:13.
**32:11** Is 20:2; Jer 4:8; Mi 1:8.
**32:12** Is 16:9.
**32:13** Is 5:6; 7:23–25; 22:2; 34:13.
**32:14** Is 7:25; 24:10–11.
**32:15** Is 44:3; Ps 104:30; Ez 37:9–10; Jl 3:1–2.
**32:17** Is 9:6; 30:15; 33:15–16; Ps 72:2–3, 7; Jas 3:18.
**32:18** Jer 23:6; Mi 4:4.
**32:19** Is 10:33–34; 26:5.
**32:20** Is 7:25; 30:18, 23.
**33:1** Is 10:12; 16:4; 21:2; 24:16.

Be our strength every morning,
our salvation in time of trouble!*

3 At the roaring sound, peoples flee;
when you rise in your majesty, nations
are scattered.*

4 Spoil is gathered up as caterpillars
gather,
an onrush like the rush of locusts.*

5 The Lord is exalted, enthroned on high;
he fills Zion with right and justice.*

6 That which makes her seasons certain,
her wealth, salvation, wisdom, and
knowledge,
is the fear of the Lord, her treasure.*

7 See, the men of Ariel cry out in the
streets,
the messengers of Shalem† weep
bitterly.

8 The highways are desolate,
travelers have quit the paths,
Covenants are broken, witnesses
spurned;
yet no one gives it a thought.*

9 The country languishes in mourning,
Lebanon withers with shame;
Sharon† is like the Arabah,
Bashan and Carmel are stripped
bare.*

10 Now I will rise up, says the Lord,
now exalt myself,
now lift myself up.*

11 You conceive dry grass, bring forth
stubble;
my spirit shall consume you like fire.

12 The peoples shall be burned to lime,
thorns cut down to burn in fire.*

13 Hear, you who are far off, what I have
done;
you who are near, acknowledge my
might.

14 In Zion sinners are in dread,
trembling grips the impious:
"Who of us can live with consuming
fire?

who of us can live with everlasting
flames?"*

15 Whoever walks righteously and speaks
honestly,
who spurns what is gained by
oppression,
Who waves off contact with a bribe,
who stops his ears so as not to hear of
bloodshed,
who closes his eyes so as not to look
on evil—*

16 That one shall dwell on the heights,
with fortresses of rock for stronghold,
food and drink in steady supply.

17 Your eyes will see a king† in his
splendor,
they will look upon a vast land.*

18 Your mind will dwell on the terror:
"Where is the one who counted,
where the one who weighed?
Where the one who counted the
towers?"*

19 You shall no longer see a defiant people,
a people of speech too obscure to
comprehend,
stammering in a tongue not
understood.*

20 Look to Zion, the city of our festivals;
your eyes shall see Jerusalem
as a quiet abode, a tent not to be
struck,
Whose pegs will never be pulled up,
nor any of its ropes severed.*

21 Indeed the Lord in majesty will be there
for us
a place of rivers and wide streams
on which no galley may go,
where no majestic ship† may pass.*

22 For the Lord is our judge,
the Lord is our lawgiver,
the Lord is our king;
he it is who will save us.

23 The rigging hangs slack;
it cannot hold the mast in place,

† **33:7** *Ariel…Shalem*: Jerusalem; cf. 29:1; Gn 14:18; Ps 76:3.
There is a play on words between "Shalem," the city name, and
*shalom*, Heb. for "peace."
**33:9** *Sharon*: the fertile plain near the Mediterranean.
**33:17** *King*: either the ideal Davidic king or God; cf. v. 22.
**33:21–23** *Galley…majestic ship*: of a foreign oppressor.
Though the broad streams of the future Jerusalem will make it
accessible by boat, no foreign invader will succeed in a naval
attack on the city, for the Lord will protect it, the enemy fleet will
be disabled, and even the weakest inhabitants will gather much
plunder from the defeated enemy.

* **33:2** Is 25:9; 30:18–19.      **33:12** Is 10:17.
**33:3** Is 17:13; Nm 10:35;      **33:14** Is 30:27, 30, 32; 31:9.
Ps 68:2.                           **33:15** Ps 15:2–6; 24:4–5.
**33:4** Is 9:2; 33:23.            **33:17** Is 26:15.
**33:5** Is 1:26–27; 2:11, 17;     **33:18** Ps 48:13–14.
32:1; 33:16.                       **33:19** Is 28:11.
**33:6** Is 11:2; 13:22; 60:22.    **33:20** Is 32:18; Ps 46:6;
**33:8** Is 24:5; Jgs 5:6.         122:1–4.
**33:9** Na 1:4.                   **33:21** Ez 47:1–12; Ps 46:5;
**33:10** Ps 12:6; Zep 3:8.        48:7.

nor keep the sail spread out.
Then the blind will divide great spoils
and the lame will carry off the loot.*

24 No one who dwells there will say, "I am
sick";
the people who live there will be
forgiven their guilt.*

### F. The Lord, Zion's Avenger†

### Judgment upon Edom

**34** ¹Come near, nations, and listen;
be attentive, you peoples!
Let the earth and what fills it listen,
the world and all it produces.*

2 The LORD is angry with all the nations,
enraged against all their host;
He has placed them under the ban,
given them up to slaughter.*

3 Their slain shall be cast out,
their corpses shall send up a stench;
the mountains shall run with their
blood,*

4 All the host of heaven shall rot;
the heavens shall be rolled up like a
scroll.
All their host shall wither away,
as the leaf wilts on the vine,
or as the fig withers on the tree.*

5 When my sword has drunk its fill in the
heavens,
it shall come down upon Edom for
judgment,
upon a people under my ban.*

6 The LORD has a sword sated with
blood,
greasy with fat,
With the blood of lambs and goats,
with the fat of rams' kidneys;
For the LORD has a sacrifice in Bozrah,
a great slaughter in the land of
Edom.*

7 Wild oxen shall be struck down with
fatlings,
and bullocks with bulls;
Their land shall be soaked with blood,
and their soil greasy with fat.

8† For the LORD has a day of vengeance,
a year of requital for the cause of
Zion.*

9 Edom's streams shall be changed into
pitch,
its soil into sulfur,
and its land shall become burning
pitch;

10 Night and day it shall not be quenched,
its smoke shall rise forever.
From generation to generation it shall
lie waste,
never again shall anyone pass through
it.*

11 But the desert owl and hoot owl shall
possess it,
the screech owl and raven shall dwell
in it.
The LORD will stretch over it the
measuring line of chaos,
the plumb line of confusion.†*

12 Its nobles shall be no more,
nor shall kings be proclaimed there;
all its princes are gone.*

13 Its castles shall be overgrown with
thorns,
its fortresses with thistles and briers.
It shall become an abode for jackals,
a haunt for ostriches.*

14 Wildcats shall meet with desert beasts,
satyrs† shall call to one another;
There shall the lilith repose,
and find for herself a place to rest.

15 There the hoot owl shall nest and lay
eggs,
hatch them out and gather them in
her shadow;

---

† **34:1–35:10** These two chapters form a small collection which looks forward to the vindication of Zion, first by defeat of its enemies (chap. 34), then by its restoration (chap. 35). They are generally judged to be later than the time of Isaiah (eighth century), perhaps during the Babylonian exile or thereafter; they are strongly influenced by Deutero-Isaiah (sixth century). In places they reflect themes from other parts of the Isaian collection.

**34:8–17** The extreme hostility against Edom in this passage is reflected in a number of other prophetic texts from the seventh and sixth centuries B.C. (cf. e.g., 63:1–6; Jer 49:7–22; Ez 25:12–14). The animus was probably prompted by Edomite infiltration of the southern territories of Judah, especially after the Babylonian conquest of Judah.

**34:11** *Chaos...confusion:* tohu...bohu in Hebrew, the terms used to describe the primeval chaos in Gn 1:2.
**34:14** *Satyrs:* see note on 13:21. *The lilith:* a female demon thought to roam about the desert.

**33:23** 2 Sm 8:6–7.
**33:24** Mi 7:18–19.
**34:1** Mi 1:2.
**34:2** Is 24:21.
**34:3** Ez 32:4, 6.
**34:4** Is 13:10; 24:23; Ez 32:7; Jl 3:3–4; Mt 24:29; 2 Pt 3:10; Rev 6:12–14.
**34:5** Jer 46:10.
**34:6** Is 63:1; Lv 3:4; 2 Sm 1:22; Jer 49:12–13; Zep 1:7.
**34:8** Is 13:9; 63:4.
**34:10** Mal 1:4; Rev 14:11; 18:18.
**34:11** Is 14:23; 28:17; 2 Kgs 21:13; Zep 2:14.
**34:12** Ob 18.
**34:13** Is 13:21; Hos 9:6.

There shall the kites assemble,
    each with its mate.

16 Search through the book of the LORD†
        and read:
    not one of these shall be lacking,
    For the mouth of the LORD has ordered
        it,
        and his spirit gathers them there.

17 It is he who casts the lot for them;
        his hand measures off† their portions;
    They shall possess it forever,
        and dwell in it from generation to
        generation. *

## Israel's Deliverance†

**35** ¹ The wilderness and the parched
        land will exult;
    the Arabah will rejoice and bloom; *

2 Like the crocus it shall bloom
        abundantly,
    and rejoice with joyful song.
    The glory of Lebanon will be given to it,
        the splendor of Carmel and Sharon;
    They will see the glory of the LORD,
        the splendor of our God. *

3 Strengthen hands that are feeble,
    make firm knees that are weak, *

4 Say to the fearful of heart:
    Be strong, do not fear!
    Here is your God,
        he comes with vindication;
    With divine recompense
        he comes to save you. *

5 Then the eyes of the blind shall see,
        and the ears of the deaf be opened; *

6 Then the lame shall leap like a stag,
        and the mute tongue sing for joy.
    For waters will burst forth in the
        wilderness,

7 and streams in the Arabah. *
    The burning sands will become pools,
        and the thirsty ground, springs of
        water;
    The abode where jackals crouch
        will be a marsh for the reed and
        papyrus.

8 A highway will be there,
        called the holy way;
    No one unclean may pass over it,
        but it will be for his people;
    no traveler, not even fools, shall go
        astray on it. *

9 No lion shall be there,
        nor any beast of prey approach,
        nor be found.
    But there the redeemed shall walk, *

10 And the ransomed of the LORD shall
        return,
    and enter Zion singing,
        crowned with everlasting joy;
    They meet with joy and gladness,
        sorrow and mourning flee away. *

## G. Historical Appendix†

**36** **Invasion of Sennacherib.** ¹ In the
        fourteenth year of King Hezekiah,
Sennacherib, king of Assyria, went up against
all the fortified cities of Judah and captured
them.†* ² From Lachish the king of Assyria sent his commander with a great army
to King Hezekiah in Jerusalem. When he
stopped at the conduit of the upper pool, on
the highway of the fuller's field, ³ there came
out to him the master of the palace, Eliakim, son of Hilkiah, and Shebna the scribe,
and the chancellor, Joah, son of Asaph. ⁴ The
commander said to them, "Tell Hezekiah:

---

**34:16** *Book of the LORD*: a list of God's creatures; cf. Ex 32:32–33; Ps 69:29, "the book of the living"; Ps 139:16, "your book."

**34:17** *Casts the lot…measures off*: an ironic reference to how land might be distributed to new possessors (cf. Jos 14–21; Mi 2:5).

**35:1–10** This chapter contains a number of themes similar to those in Deutero-Isaiah (chaps. 40–55), for example, the blossoming of the wilderness (vv. 1–2; cf. 41:18–19), which is now well-irrigated (v. 7; cf. 43:19–20); sight to the blind (vv. 5–6; cf. 42:7, 16); a highway in the wilderness (v. 8; cf. 41:3); and the return of the redeemed/ransomed to Zion (vv. 9–10; cf. 51:11). Nevertheless, it forms a unit with chap. 34 (see note on 34:1–35:10) and reflects, along with that chapter, themes found in chaps. 1–33.

**36:1–39:8** Except for 38:9–20 (Hezekiah's prayer of thanks-giving), this historical appendix describing the siege, etc., is par-alleled in 2 Kgs 18:13–20:19, which, however, has certain details

proper to itself. The events are also reflected in the cuneiform inscriptions of Sennacherib.

**36:1** The occasion for this Assyrian attack was Hezekiah's at-tempt to reject Judah's status as vassal to Assyria, relying on help from Egypt, a course of action condemned by Isaiah (see notes on 28:15, 18; 28:16; 29:7–8; 30:1–17; etc.). 2 Kgs 19:14–16 reports that Hezekiah surrendered to the Assyrians and paid the tribute imposed on him—a report omitted in the Isaiah text.

---

**34:17** Jos 18:10; Ps 78:55.
**35:1** Is 41:18–19;
    55:12–13.
**35:2** Is 40:5; 60:13.
**35:3** Is 40:29–30; Jb 4:3–4;
    Heb 12:12.
**35:4** Is 41:10; Zec 8:13.
**35:5** Is 29:18; 32:3.

**35:6** Is 32:3–4; 41:18;
    43:19–20; 44:3; Mt
    11:5.
**35:8** Is 11:16; 43:19;
    49:11.
**35:9** Is 62:10; Lv 26:6.
**35:10** Is 51:11.
**36:1** 2 Kgs 18:13; 2 Chr
    32:1.

Thus says the great king, the king of Assyria: On what do you base this trust of yours? ⁵ Do you think mere words substitute for strategy and might in war? In whom, then, do you place your trust, that you rebel against me? ⁶ Do you trust in Egypt, that broken reed of a staff which pierces the hand of anyone who leans on it? That is what Pharaoh, king of Egypt, is to all who trust in him.* ⁷ Or do you say to me: It is in the LORD, our God, we trust? Is it not he whose high places and altars Hezekiah has removed,† commanding Judah and Jerusalem, 'Worship before this altar'?*

⁸ "Now, make a wager with my lord, the king of Assyria: I will give you two thousand horses, if you are able to put riders on them. ⁹ How then can you turn back even a captain, one of the least servants of my lord, trusting, as you do, in Egypt for chariots and horses? ¹⁰ Did I come up to destroy this land without the LORD? The LORD himself said to me, Go up and destroy that land!"*

¹¹ Then Eliakim and Shebna and Joah said to the commander, "Please speak to your servants in Aramaic; we understand it. Do not speak to us in the language of Judah within earshot of the people who are on the wall."†

¹² But the commander replied, "Was it to your lord and to you that my lord sent me to speak these words? Was it not rather to those sitting on the wall, who, with you, will have to eat their own excrement and drink their own urine?" ¹³ Then the commander stepped forward and cried out in a loud voice in the language of Judah, "Listen to the words of the great king, the king of Assyria. ¹⁴ Thus says the king: Do not let Hezekiah deceive you, for he cannot rescue you. ¹⁵ And do not let Hezekiah induce you to trust in the LORD, saying, 'The LORD will surely rescue us, and this city will not be handed over to the king of Assyria.' ¹⁶ Do not listen to Hezekiah, for thus says the king of Assyria:

> Make peace with me
>   and surrender to me!
> Eat, each of you, from your vine,
>   each from your own fig tree.
> Drink water, each from your own
>   well,*

¹⁷
> until I arrive and take you
>   to a land like your own,
> A land of grain and wine,
>   a land of bread and vineyards.

¹⁸ Do not let Hezekiah seduce you by saying, 'The LORD will rescue us.' Has any of the gods of the nations rescued his land from the power of the king of Assyria?* ¹⁹ Where are the gods of Hamath and Arpad? Where are the gods of Sepharvaim? Where are the gods of Samaria? Have they saved Samaria from my power?* ²⁰ Who among all the gods of these lands ever rescued their land from my power, that the LORD should save Jerusalem from my power?" ²¹ But they remained silent and did not answer at all, for the king's command was, "Do not answer him."

²² Then the master of the palace, Eliakim, son of Hilkiah, Shebna the scribe, and the chancellor Joah, son of Asaph, came to Hezekiah with their garments torn, and reported to him the words of the commander.

# 37

¹† When King Hezekiah heard this, he tore his garments, covered himself with sackcloth, and went into the house of the LORD. ² He sent Eliakim, the master of the palace, and Shebna the scribe, and the elders of the priests, covered with sackcloth, to tell the prophet Isaiah, son of Amoz,

³
> "Thus says Hezekiah:
> A day of distress and rebuke,
>   a day of disgrace is this day!
> Children are due to come forth,
>   but the strength to give birth is
>     lacking.†*

---

**36:7** The Assyrians assert that Hezekiah's removal of the high places and altars (unofficial sanctuaries) was taken by the Lord as an insult. They declare to Jerusalem's emissaries that the city therefore no longer has a right to the Lord's protection and that they are the ones who truly carry out his will (cf. v. 10).

**36:11** The emissaries of King Hezekiah ask that the conversation be carried on in Aramaic, not in Hebrew, for they fear the effect of the Assyrian claims upon the morale of the people.

**37:1–35** There appear to be parallel accounts of Hezekiah's appeal and the response received (vv. 1–7 and vv. 14–35): in each, Hezekiah goes to the Temple, refers to the Assyrian boasts

(found in 36:15–20; 37:10–14), and receives a favorable response from Isaiah.

**37:3** A proverbial expression. In the Bible the pangs of childbirth often typify extreme anguish; cf. 13:8; Jer 6:24; Mi 4:9–10. In this instance there is reference to the desperate situation of Hezekiah from which he would scarcely be able to free himself.

**36:6** Is 30:2–3, 7.     **36:18** Is 37:11.
**36:7** 2 Kgs 18:4.     **36:19** Is 10:9; 37:13.
**36:10** Is 10:5–6.     **37:3** Is 26:18.
**36:16** 1 Kgs 5:5; Zec 3:10.

⁴Perhaps the LORD, your God, will hear the words of the commander, whom his lord, the king of Assyria, sent to taunt the living God, and will rebuke him for the words which the LORD, your God, has heard. So lift up a prayer for the remnant that is here."

⁵When the servants of King Hezekiah had come to Isaiah, ⁶he said to them: "Tell this to your lord: Thus says the LORD: Do not be frightened by the words you have heard, by which the deputies of the king of Assyria have blasphemed me.*

⁷    I am putting in him such a spirit
        that when he hears a report
        he will return to his land.
    I will make him fall by the sword in
        his land."

⁸When the commander, on his return, heard that the king of Assyria had withdrawn from Lachish, he found him besieging Libnah. ⁹The king of Assyria heard a report: "Tirhakah,† king of Ethiopia, has come out to fight against you." Again he sent messengers to Hezekiah to say: ¹⁰"Thus shall you say to Hezekiah, king of Judah: Do not let your God in whom you trust deceive you by saying, 'Jerusalem will not be handed over to the king of Assyria.'* ¹¹You, certainly, have heard what the kings of Assyria have done to all the lands: they put them under the ban! And are you to be delivered? ¹²Did the gods of the nations whom my fathers destroyed deliver them—Gozan, Haran, Rezeph, and the Edenites in Telassar? ¹³Where are the king of Hamath, the king of Arpad, or a king of the cities Sepharvaim, Hena or Ivvah?"

¹⁴Hezekiah took the letter from the hand of the messengers and read it; then he went up to the house of the LORD, and spreading it out before the LORD, ¹⁵Hezekiah prayed to the LORD:

¹⁶    "LORD of hosts, God of Israel,
        enthroned on the cherubim!
    You alone are God
        over all the kingdoms of the earth.

    It is you who made
        the heavens and the earth.†

¹⁷    Incline your ear, LORD, and listen!
        open your eyes, LORD, and see!
    Hear all the words Sennacherib has sent
        to taunt the living God.

¹⁸    Truly, O LORD,
        the kings of Assyria have laid waste
        the nations and their lands.

¹⁹    They gave their gods to the fire
        —they were not gods at all,
        but the work of human hands—
    Wood and stone, they destroyed them.*

²⁰    Therefore, LORD, our God,
        save us from this man's power,
    That all the kingdoms of the earth may
        know
        that you alone, LORD, are God."

²¹† Then Isaiah, son of Amoz, sent this message to Hezekiah: "Thus says the LORD, the God of Israel, to whom you have prayed concerning Sennacherib, king of Assyria: I have listened! ²²This is the word the LORD has spoken concerning him:*

    She despises you, laughs you to scorn,
        the virgin daughter Zion;
    Behind you she wags her head,
        daughter Jerusalem.

²³    Whom have you insulted and
            blasphemed,
        at whom have you raised your voice
    And lifted up your eyes on high?
        At the Holy One of Israel!*

²⁴    Through the mouths of your messengers
        you have insulted the Lord when you
            said:
    'With my many chariots I went up
        to the tops of the peaks,
        to the recesses of Lebanon,
    To cut down its lofty cedars,
        its choice cypresses;
    I reached the farthest shelter,
        the forest ranges.

²⁵    I myself dug wells

---

† **37:9** *Tirhakah*: may have been general of the Egyptian army in 701 B.C.; later he became pharaoh, one of the Ethiopian dynasty of Egyptian kings (ca. 690–664 B.C.). Many consider that this account in Isaiah combines features of two originally distinct sieges of Jerusalem by Sennacherib.
**37:16** In contrast to the empty boasting of the Assyrians, Hezekiah proclaims the Lord as "God over all the kingdoms of the earth."
**37:21–37** The reversal of Isaiah's attitude toward Hezekiah's

revolt (see note on 36:1) and a wonderful deliverance after Hezekiah had already submitted and paid tribute raise questions difficult to answer. See note on 22:1–14. Some have postulated that chaps. 36–37 combine accounts of two different Assyrian invasions.

**37:6** Is 7:4; 10:24.        **37:22** 2 Kgs 19:21.
**37:10** Is 36:14.           **37:23** Is 10:12.
**37:19** Jer 16:20.

and drank foreign water;
Drying up all the rivers of Egypt
 beneath the soles of my feet.'
26 Have you not heard?
 A long time ago I prepared it,
 from days of old I planned it,
Now I have brought it about:
 You are here to reduce
 fortified cities to heaps of ruins, *
27 Their people powerless,
 dismayed and distraught,
They are plants of the field,
 green growth,
thatch on the rooftops,
Grain scorched by the east wind.
28 I know when you stand or sit,
 when you come or go,
 and how you rage against me.
29 Because you rage against me
 and your smugness has reached my
  ears,
I will put my hook in your nose
 and my bit in your mouth,
And make you leave by the way you
  came. *
30 This shall be a sign† for you:
This year you shall eat the aftergrowth,
 next year, what grows of itself;
But in the third year, sow and reap,
 plant vineyards and eat their fruit!
31 The remaining survivors of the house of
  Judah
 shall again strike root below
 and bear fruit above. *
32 For out of Jerusalem shall come a remnant,
 and from Mount Zion, survivors.
The zeal of the LORD of hosts shall do
  this. *

33 Therefore, thus says the LORD about the
king of Assyria:

He shall not come as far as this city,
 nor shoot there an arrow,

nor confront it with a shield,
Nor cast up a siege-work against it.
34 By the way he came he shall leave,
 never coming as far as this city,
  oracle of the LORD.
35 I will shield and save this city
 for my own sake and the sake of
  David my servant." *

36 Then the angel of the LORD went forth and struck down one hundred and eighty-five thousand in the Assyrian camp. Early the next morning, there they were, all those corpses, dead! †* 37 So Sennacherib, the king of Assyria, broke camp, departed, returned home, and stayed in Nineveh.

38 When he was worshiping in the temple of his god Nisroch, his sons Adrammelech and Sharezer struck him down with the sword and fled into the land of Ararat. † His son Esarhaddon reigned in his place.

# 38 Sickness and Recovery of Hezekiah.

1 † In those days, † when Hezekiah was mortally ill, the prophet Isaiah, son of Amoz, came and said to him: "Thus says the LORD: Put your house in order, for you are about to die; you shall not recover." * 2 Hezekiah turned his face to the wall and prayed to the LORD:

3 "Ah, LORD, remember how faithfully and wholeheartedly I conducted myself in your presence, doing what was good in your sight!" And Hezekiah wept bitterly. *

4 Then the word of the LORD came to Isaiah: 5 Go, tell Hezekiah:† Thus says the LORD, the God of your father David: I have heard your prayer; I have seen your tears. Now I will add fifteen years to your life. 6 I will rescue you and this city from the hand of the king of Assyria; I will be a shield to this city. *

7 This will be the sign for you from the LORD that the LORD will carry out the word he has spoken: 8 See, I will make the shadow cast by

---

**37:30** *A sign*: sets a time limit. After two years the normal conditions of life will be resumed. See the similar use of time limits as signs in 7:15–16; 8:4; 16:14; and 21:16. *You*: Hezekiah.

**37:36** The destruction of Sennacherib's army is also recorded by Herodotus, a Greek historian of the fifth century B.C. It was possibly owing to a plague, which the author interprets as God's activity.

**37:38** The violent death of Sennacherib (681 B.C.) is also mentioned in non-biblical sources. It occurred twenty years after his invasion of Judah. *Ararat*: the land of Urartu in the mountains north of Assyria.

**38:1–39:8** The events of this section—sickness and recovery

of Hezekiah, embassy of Merodach-baladan—anticipate the rise of Babylon (chaps. 40–66). They occurred prior to the events of 36:1–37:38, which point back to Assyria (1:1–35:10).

**38:1** *In those days*: before the siege of Jerusalem in 701 B.C.

**38:5** Since Hezekiah died in 687 B.C., his sickness may have occurred in 702 B.C., that is, fifteen years before.

| | |
|---|---|
| **37:26** Is 10:6, 15. | **37:36** Is 10:12; 17:14. |
| **37:29** Is 30:28. | **38:1** 2 Kgs 20:1. |
| **37:31** Is 27:6. | **38:2** 2 Kgs 18:5–6. |
| **37:32** Is 9:6. | **38:6** Is 37:35. |
| **37:35** Is 31:5; 1 Kgs 15:4. | |

the sun on the stairway to the terrace of Ahaz†
go back the ten steps it has advanced. So the
sun came back the ten steps it had advanced. *

### Hezekiah's Hymn of Thanksgiving. ⁹The song
of Hezekiah, king of Judah, after he had been
sick and had recovered from his illness:

10    In the noontime of life† I said,
        I must depart!
    To the gates of Sheol I have been
        consigned
        for the rest of my years. *
11    I said, I shall see the LORD† no more
        in the land of the living.
    Nor look on any mortals
        among those who dwell in the world.
12    My dwelling, like a shepherd's tent,
        is struck down and borne away from
        me;
    You have folded up my life, like a weaver
        who severs me from the last thread.†*
    From morning to night you make an
        end of me;
13    I cry out even until the dawn.
    Like a lion he breaks all my bones;
        from morning to night you make an
        end of me. *
14    Like a swallow I chirp;
        I moan like a dove.
    My eyes grow weary looking
        heavenward:
        Lord, I am overwhelmed; go security
        for me!
15†   What am I to say or tell him?
        He is the one who has done it!
    All my sleep has fled,
        because of the bitterness of my soul.
16    Those live whom the LORD protects;
        yours is the life of my spirit.

    You have given me health and restored
        my life!
17    Peace in place of bitterness!
    You have preserved my life
        from the pit of destruction;
    Behind your back
        you cast all my sins.†
18†   For it is not Sheol that gives you thanks,
        nor death that praises you;
    Neither do those who go down into the
        pit
        await your kindness. *
19    The living, the living give you thanks,
        as I do today.
    Parents declare to their children,
        O God, your faithfulness.
20    The LORD is there to save us.
        We shall play our music
    In the house of the LORD
        all the days of our life.

21† Then Isaiah said, "Bring a poultice of figs
and apply it to the boil for his recovery."
22 Hezekiah asked, "What is the sign that I
shall go up to the house of the LORD?"

## 39 Embassy from Merodach-baladan. ¹At
that time Merodach-baladan,† son of
Baladan, king of Babylon, sent letters and
gifts to Hezekiah, when he heard that he had
been sick and had recovered. * ²Hezekiah was
pleased at their coming, and then showed the
messengers his treasury, the silver and gold,
the spices and perfumed oil, his whole armory,
and everything in his storerooms; there was
nothing in his house or in all his realm that
Hezekiah did not show them. *

³Then Isaiah the prophet came to King Hezekiah and asked him, "What did these men say
to you? Where did they come from?" Hezekiah

---

**38:8** *Stairway to the terrace of Ahaz:* this interpretation is
based on a reading of the Hebrew text revised according to
the Dead Sea Scroll of Isaiah; cf. 2 Kgs 23:12. Many translate
the phrase as "steps of Ahaz" and understand this as referring
to a sundial.
**38:10** *In the noontime of life:* long before the end of a full
span of life; cf. Ps 55:24; 102:25.
**38:11** *See the LORD:* go to the Temple and take part in its
service.
**38:12** These two metaphors emphasize the suddenness and
finality of death.
**38:15–16** The Hebrew text is very problematic and its meaning uncertain.
**38:17** *Behind your back you cast all my sins:* figurative language to express the divine forgiveness of sins, as if God no
longer saw or cared about them.
**38:18–19** See note on Ps 6:6.

**38:21–22** These verses are clearly out of place. Logically they
should come after v. 6, as they do in the parallel account in 2 Kgs
20, but the two accounts are not identical, and it appears that the
version in Isaiah is abbreviated from that in Kings. If that is so, Is
38:21–22 would be a secondary addition from Kings, inserted by
a later reader who thought the account incomplete.
**39:1** *Merodach-baladan:* twice king of Babylon, probably
from 721 to 710 B.C., and again for nine months, in 704–703.
This visit of his messengers, certainly before 701, was in reality a political one. Babylon hoped to lead an anti-Assyrian
confederation composed of neighboring states and wanted
Judah to join.

---

**38:8** 2 Kgs 20:9–11.      **38:13** Jb 23:14.
**38:10** Jb 17:11–13; Ps      **38:18** Ps 6:6; 88:11–13.
      102:25.                  **39:1** 2 Kgs 20:12.
**38:12** Jb 7:6.             **39:2** 2 Chr 32:25–31.

I
S

replied, "They came to me from a distant land, from Babylon." [4] He asked, "What did they see in your house?" Hezekiah answered, "They saw everything in my house. There is nothing in my storerooms that I did not show them." [5] Then Isaiah said to Hezekiah, "Hear the word of the LORD of hosts: [6] The time is coming when all that is in your house, everything that your ancestors have stored up until this day, shall be carried off to Babylon;† nothing shall be left, says the LORD.* [7] Some of your own descendants, your progeny, shall be taken and made attendants in the palace of the king of Babylon."* [8] Hezekiah replied to Isaiah, "The word of the LORD which you have spoken is good."† For he thought, "There will be peace and stability in my lifetime."

## II. ISAIAH 40—55†

### A. The Lord's Glory in Israel's Liberation

### Promise of Salvation

# 40

[1]† Comfort, give comfort to my people,
   says your God.
[2] Speak to the heart of Jerusalem, and proclaim to her
   that her service† has ended,
   that her guilt is expiated,
That she has received from the hand of the LORD
   double for all her sins.

[3] A voice proclaims:†
In the wilderness prepare the way of the LORD!
   Make straight in the wasteland a highway for our God!*
[4] Every valley shall be lifted up,
   every mountain and hill made low;
The rugged land shall be a plain,
   the rough country, a broad valley.
[5] Then the glory of the LORD shall be revealed,
   and all flesh shall see it together;
   for the mouth of the LORD has spoken.

[6] A voice says, "Proclaim!"
   I answer, "What shall I proclaim?"
   "All flesh is grass,
   and all their loyalty like the flower of the field.*
[7] The grass withers, the flower wilts,
   when the breath of the LORD blows upon it."
   "Yes, the people is grass!
[8] The grass withers, the flower wilts,
   but the word of our God stands forever."

[9] Go up onto a high mountain,
   Zion, herald of good news!†
Cry out at the top of your voice,
   Jerusalem, herald of good news!
Cry out, do not fear!
   Say to the cities of Judah:

---

† **39:6** Because Judah preferred to follow a pro-Babylonian policy, instead of trusting in the Lord, it would later be exiled to Babylon.
**39:8** Hezekiah was relieved that the disaster would not occur in his lifetime.
**40:1–55:13** Chapters 40–55 are usually designated Second Isaiah (or Deutero-Isaiah) and are believed to have been written by an anonymous prophet toward the end of the Babylonian exile. Isaiah, who is named frequently in chaps. 1–39, does not appear here; the Assyrians, the great threat during the eighth century, hardly appear; the Judeans are in Babylon, having been taken there by the victorious Babylonians; Cyrus, the Persian king, is named; he will defeat Babylon and release the captives. Second Isaiah, who sees this not as a happy circumstance but as part of God's age-old plan, exhorts the Judeans to resist the temptations of Babylonian religion and stirs up hopes of an imminent return to Judah, where the Lord will again be acknowledged as King (52:7). Because the prophet proclaimed the triumph of Persia over Babylon, his message would have been considered seditious, and it is very likely for this reason that the collection would have circulated anonymously. At some point it was appended to Is 1–39 and consequently was long considered the work of Isaiah of Jerusalem of the eighth century. But the fact that it is addressed to Judean exiles in Babylon indicates a sixth-century date. Nevertheless, this eloquent prophet in many ways works within the tradition of Isaiah and develops themes found in the earlier chapters, such as the holiness of the Lord (cf. note on 1:4)

and his lordship of history. Second Isaiah also develops other Old Testament themes, such as the Lord as Israel's redeemer or deliverer (cf. Ex 3:8; 6:6; 15:13; 18:8).
**40:1** The "voices" of vv. 3, 6 are members of the heavenly court addressing the prophet; then v. 1 can be understood as the Lord addressing them. It is also possible to translate, with the Vulgate, "Comfort, give comfort, O my people" (i.e., the exiles are called to comfort Jerusalem). The juxtaposition of "my people" and "your God" recalls the covenant formulary.
**40:2** *Service*: servitude (cf. Jb 7:1) and exile.
**40:3–5** A description of the return of the exiles from Babylon to Jerusalem (Zion). The language used here figuratively describes the way the exiles will take. The Lord leads them, so their way lies straight across the wilderness rather than along the well-watered routes usually followed from Mesopotamia to Israel. Mt 3:3 and gospel parallels adapt these verses to the witness of John the Baptizer to Jesus.
**40:9** *Herald of good news*: i.e., of the imminent restoration of the people to their land. This theme of the proclamation of the good news occurs elsewhere in Second Isaiah; cf. also 41:27; 52:7.

---

* **39:6** 2 Kgs 24:13; 25:13–17.
**39:7** Dn 1:3–19.
**40:3** Mt 3:3; Mk 1:3;
Lk 2:27; Jn 1:23.
**40:6** Jb 8:12; 14:2; Ps 37:2; Sir 14:18; Jas 1:10; 1 Pt 1:24.

Here is your God!
10    Here comes with power
      the Lord GOD,
      who rules by his strong arm;
      Here is his reward with him,
      his recompense before him.
11    Like a shepherd he feeds his flock;
      in his arms he gathers the lambs,
      Carrying them in his bosom,
      leading the ewes with care.*

### Power of God and the Vanity of Idols

12    Who has measured with his palm the
          waters,
      marked off the heavens with a span,
      held in his fingers the dust of the
          earth,
      weighed the mountains in scales
      and the hills in a balance?†
13    Who has directed the spirit of the LORD,
      or instructed him as his counselor?*
14    Whom did he consult to gain
          knowledge?
      Who taught him the path of
          judgment,
      or showed him the way of
          understanding?

15    See, the nations count as a drop in the
          bucket,
      as a wisp of cloud on the scales;
      the coastlands weigh no more than a
          speck.†
16    Lebanon would not suffice for fuel,†
      nor its animals be enough for burnt
          offerings.
17    Before him all the nations are as nought,
      as nothing and void he counts them.

18    To whom can you liken God?*
      With what likeness can you confront
          him?
19    An idol? An artisan casts it,
      the smith plates it with gold,

fits it with silver chains.†*
20    Is mulberry wood the offering?
      A skilled artisan picks out
      a wood that will not rot,
      Seeks to set up for himself
      an idol that will not totter.*

21    Do you not know? Have you not heard?
      Was it not told you from the
          beginning?
      Have you not understood from the
          founding of the earth?
22    The one who is enthroned above the
          vault of the earth,
      its inhabitants like grasshoppers,
      Who stretches out the heavens like a veil
      and spreads them out like a tent to
          dwell in,*
23    Who brings princes to nought
      and makes the rulers of the earth as
          nothing.
24    Scarcely are they planted, scarcely sown,
      scarcely their stem rooted in the earth,
      When he breathes upon them and they
          wither,
      and the stormwind carries them away
          like straw.

25    To whom can you liken me as an equal?
      says the Holy One.
26    Lift up your eyes on high
      and see who created† these:
      He leads out their army and numbers
          them,
      calling them all by name.
      By his great might and the strength of
          his power
      not one of them is missing!*
27    Why, O Jacob, do you say,†
      and declare, O Israel,
      "My way is hidden from the LORD,
      and my right is disregarded by my
          God"?
28    Do you not know?

---

40:12 The implicit answer is "the hand of the LORD" (v. 2). *Waters...heavens...earth*: together form the universe; cf. Gn 1:1–2. *Span*: the distance between the extended little finger and the thumb. *Fingers*: lit., "three fingers" (i.e., thumb, index, and middle).

40:15 *Drop...wisp of cloud...a speck*: the smallest constituent parts of the cosmic waters, heavens, and earth mentioned in v. 12.

40:16 *Lebanon...fuel*: the famed cedars would not be enough to keep the fires of sacrifice burning.

40:19 *Chains*: needed to hold the idol steady when carried in processions; cf. v. 20; Jer 10:4.

40:26 *Created*: see note on Gn 1:1–2:3. *By name*: for he is their Creator.

40:27–28 The exiles, here called Jacob-Israel (Gn 32:29), must not give way to discouragement: their Lord is the eternal God.

---

| 40:11 Is 49:9–10; 63:11; | 40:18–19 Acts 17:29. |
| Ez 34:23; 37:24; Jn | 40:19 Ps 115:4–7; Jer 10:4. |
| 10:11. | 40:20 Is 44:13. |
| 40:13 Wis 9:13; Rom | 40:22 Ps 104:2. |
| 11:34; 1 Cor 2:16; Jb | 40:26 Ps 147:4–5. |
| 38:1–11. | |

IS

Have you not heard?
The LORD is God from of old,
   creator of the ends of the earth.
He does not faint or grow weary,
   and his knowledge is beyond scrutiny.
29 He gives power to the faint,
   abundant strength to the weak.
30 Though young men faint and grow weary,
   and youths stagger and fall,
31 They that hope in the LORD will renew
     their strength,
   they will soar on eagles' wings;
They will run and not grow weary,
   walk and not grow faint.

## The Liberator of Israel

**41** ¹ Keep silence before me,
   O coastlands;†
   let the nations renew their strength.
Let them draw near and speak;
   let us come together for judgment.
2 Who has stirred up from the East the
     champion of justice,
   and summoned him to be his
     attendant?
To him he delivers nations
   and subdues kings;
With his sword he reduces them to dust,
   with his bow, to driven straw.
3 He pursues them, passing on without
     loss,
   by a path his feet scarcely touch.
4 Who has performed these deeds?
   Who has called forth the generations
     from the beginning?*
I, the LORD, am the first,
   and at the last† I am he.
5 The coastlands see, and fear;
   the ends of the earth tremble:
   they approach, they come on.

6 Each one helps his neighbor,
   one says to the other, "Courage!"
7 The woodworker encourages the
     goldsmith,

the one who beats with the hammer,
   him who strikes on the anvil,
Saying of the soldering, "It is good!"
   then fastening it with nails so it will
     not totter.

8 But you, Israel, my servant,*
   Jacob, whom I have chosen,
   offspring of Abraham my friend—
9 You whom I have taken from the ends
     of the earth
   and summoned from its far-off places,
To whom I have said, You are my
     servant;
   I chose you, I have not rejected you—
10 Do not fear: I am with you;
   do not be anxious: I am your God.
I will strengthen you, I will help you,
   I will uphold you with my victorious
     right hand.

11 Yes, all shall be put to shame and
     disgrace
   who vent their anger against you;
Those shall be as nothing and perish
   who offer resistance.
12 You shall seek but not find
   those who strive against you;
They shall be as nothing at all
   who do battle with you.

13 For I am the LORD, your God,
   who grasp your right hand;
It is I who say to you, Do not fear,
   I will help you.
14 Do not fear, you worm Jacob,
   you maggot Israel;
I will help you—oracle of the LORD;
   the Holy One of Israel is your
     redeemer.†
15 I will make of you a threshing sledge,
   sharp, new, full of teeth,
To thresh the mountains and crush
     them,
   to make the hills like chaff.

---

† **41:1–4** Earlier prophets had spoken of the Assyrians and Babylonians as the Lord's instruments for the punishment of Israel's sins; here the Lord is described as raising up and giving victory to a foreign ruler in order to deliver Israel from the Babylonian exile. The ruler is Cyrus (44:28; 45:1), king of Anshan in Persia, a vassal of the Babylonians. He rebelled against the Babylonian overlords in 556 B.C., and after a series of victories, entered Babylon as victor in 539; the following year he issued a decree which allowed the Jewish captives to return to their homeland (2 Chr 36:22–23; Ezr 1:1–4). For Second Isaiah, the meteoric success of Cyrus was the work of the Lord to accomplish the deliverance promised by earlier prophets.

**41:4** *The first…the last*: God as the beginning and end encompasses all reality. The same designation is used in 44:6 and 48:12.

**41:14** *Redeemer*: in Hebrew, *go'el*, one who frees others from slavery and avenges their sufferings; cf. Lv 25:48; Dt 19:6, 12. Cf. note on Ru 2:20.

**41:4** Is 44:7; 46:10.          **41:8–9** Is 44:1–2, 21; 45:4.

16 When you winnow them, the wind shall
        carry them off,
    the storm shall scatter them.
    But you shall rejoice in the LORD;
        in the Holy One of Israel you shall
        glory.

17 The afflicted and the needy seek water in
        vain,
    their tongues are parched with thirst.
    I, the LORD, will answer them;
        I, the God of Israel, will not forsake
        them.
18 I will open up rivers on the bare heights,
        and fountains in the broad valleys;
    I will turn the wilderness into a
        marshland,
        and the dry ground into springs of
        water.
19 In the wilderness I will plant the cedar,
        acacia, myrtle, and olive;
    In the wasteland I will set the cypress,
        together with the plane tree and the
        pine,
20 That all may see and know,
        observe and understand,
    That the hand of the LORD has done this,
        the Holy One of Israel has created it.

21 Present your case, says the LORD;†
        bring forward your arguments, says
        the King of Jacob.
22 Let them draw near and foretell to us
        what it is that shall happen!
    What are the things of long ago?
        Tell us, that we may reflect on them
        and know their outcome;
    Or declare to us the things to come,†
23     tell what is to be in the future,
        that we may know that you are gods!
    Do something, good or evil,
        that will put us in awe and in fear.

24 Why, you are nothing
        and your work is nought;
    to choose you is an abomination!

25 I have stirred up one from the north,
        and he comes;
    from the east I summon him† by
        name;
    He shall trample the rulers down like
        mud,
        like a potter treading clay.
26 Who announced this from the
        beginning, that we might know;
    beforehand, that we might say,
        "True"?
    Not one of you foretold it, not one
        spoke;
        not one heard you say,
27 "The first news for Zion: here they
        come,"
    or, "I will give Jerusalem a herald of
        good news."
28 When I look, there is not one,
        not one of them to give counsel,
    to make an answer when I question
        them.
29 Ah, all of them are nothing,
        their works are nought,
        their idols, empty wind!

## The Servant of the Lord

42 ¹ Here is my servant† whom I uphold,
    my chosen one with whom I am
        pleased.
    Upon him I have put my spirit;
        he shall bring forth justice to the
        nations.*
2 He will not cry out, nor shout,
        nor make his voice heard in the street.
3 A bruised reed† he will not break,
        and a dimly burning wick he will not
        quench.

---

**41:21–29** This indictment of Babylonian gods is patterned on a legal trial, in which they are challenged to prove power over events of history and so justify their status as gods (vv. 21–24). Israel's God, on the other hand, has foretold and now brings to pass Israel's deliverance (vv. 25–27). The accused are unable to respond (vv. 28–29). By such polemics (see also 43:12) the prophet declares that all gods other than the Lord are nonexistent; this implicit claim of monotheism later becomes explicit (see 43:10–11; 45:5–7, 14, 18, 21–22; 46:9; and note on 44:6).
**41:22** *Things of long ago…things to come*: there are no predictions attributed to idols that have since been fulfilled. Second Isaiah makes frequent reference to "things of long ago," sometimes in conjunction with "things to come" or "new things" in connection with the Lord's activity (cf. 42:9; 43:9, 18; 46:9–10; 48:3–8); both the old things (e.g., creation, exodus) and the

new things (release from exile) God brings to pass (cf. 51:9–11), which is why he can declare them beforehand.
**41:25** *I summon him*: Cyrus.
**42:1–4** *Servant*: three other passages have been popularly called "servant of the Lord" poems: 49:1–7; 50:4–11; 52:13–53:12. Whether the servant is an individual or a collectivity is not clear (e.g., contrast 49:3 with 49:5). More important is the description of the mission of the servant. In the early Church and throughout Christian tradition, these poems have been applied to Christ; cf. Mt 12:18–21.
**42:3** *Bruised reed…*: images to express the gentle manner of the servant's mission.

---

*
    **42:1** Is 45:6; 49:6.

He will faithfully bring forth justice.

4 He will not grow dim or be bruised
   until he establishes justice on the earth;
   the coastlands† will wait for his
      teaching.

5 Thus says God, the LORD,
   who created the heavens and stretched
      them out,
   who spread out the earth and its
      produce,
   Who gives breath to its people
   and spirit to those who walk on it:
6 I, the LORD, have called you for justice,
   I have grasped you by the hand;
   I formed you, and set you
   as a covenant for the people,
   a light for the nations,*
7 To open the eyes of the blind,
   to bring out prisoners from
      confinement,
   and from the dungeon, those who live
      in darkness.
8 I am the LORD, LORD is my name;
   my glory I give to no other,
   nor my praise to idols.
9 See, the earlier things have come to pass,
   new ones I now declare;
   Before they spring forth
   I announce them to you.

## The Lord's Purpose for Israel

10 Sing to the LORD a new song,
   his praise from the ends of the earth:
   Let the sea and what fills it resound,
   the coastlands, and those who dwell
      in them.
11 Let the wilderness and its cities cry out,
   the villages where Kedar† dwells;
   Let the inhabitants of Sela exult,
   and shout from the top of the
      mountains.
12 Let them give glory to the LORD,
   and utter his praise in the coastlands.

13 The LORD goes forth like a warrior,
   like a man of war he stirs up his fury;

He shouts out his battle cry,
   against his enemies he shows his
      might:*
14 For a long time I have kept silent,
   I have said nothing, holding myself
      back;
   Now I cry out like a woman in labor,
   gasping and panting.
15† I will lay waste mountains and hills,
   all their undergrowth I will dry up;
   I will turn the rivers into marshes,
   and the marshes I will dry up.*
16 I will lead the blind on a way they do
      not know;
   by paths they do not know I will
      guide them.
   I will turn darkness into light before
      them,
   and make crooked ways straight.
   These are my promises:
   I made them, I will not forsake them.*

17 They shall be turned back in utter shame
   who trust in idols;
   Who say to molten images,
   "You are our gods."
18 You deaf ones, listen,†
   you blind ones, look and see!
19 Who is blind but my servant,
   or deaf like the messenger I send?
   Who is blind like the one I restore,
   blind like the servant of the LORD?
20 You see many things but do not observe;
   ears open, but do not hear.
21 It was the LORD's will for the sake of his
      justice
   to make his teaching great and
      glorious.

22 This is a people† plundered and
      despoiled,
   all of them trapped in holes,
   hidden away in prisons.
   They are taken as plunder, with no one
      to rescue them,
   as spoil, with no one to say, "Give
      back!"

---

**42:4** *Coastlands*: for Israel, the world to the west: the islands and coastal nations of the Mediterranean.
**42:11** *Kedar*: cf. note on 21:16. *Sela*: Petra, the capital of Edom.
**42:15–16** Active once more, God will remove the obstacles that hinder the exiles' return, and will lead them by new roads to Jerusalem; cf. 40:3–4.
**42:18–20** The Lord rebukes his people for their failures, but

their role and their mission endure: they remain his servant, his messenger to the nations.
**42:22** *A people*: Israel in exile.

---

**42:6** Is 45:13.
**42:13** Ex 14:3.

**42:15** Ex 9:25; 10:15; 14:21;
   Ps 105:33–35.
**42:16** Ex 13:21.

23 Who among you will give ear to this,
    listen and pay attention from now on?
24 Who was it that gave Jacob to be
        despoiled,
    Israel to the plunderers?†
    Was it not the LORD, against whom we
        have sinned?
    In his ways they refused to walk,
    his teaching they would not heed.
25 So he poured out wrath upon them,
    his anger, and the fury of battle;
    It blazed all around them, yet they did
        not realize,
    it burned them, but they did not take
        it to heart.

## Promises of Redemption and Restoration

**43** ¹ But now, thus says the LORD,
    who created you, Jacob, and formed
        you, Israel:
    Do not fear, for I have redeemed you;
    I have called you by name: you are
        mine.
2 When you pass through waters, I will be
        with you;
    through rivers, you shall not be swept
        away.
    When you walk through fire, you shall
        not be burned,
    nor will flames consume you.
3 For I, the LORD, am your God,
    the Holy One of Israel, your savior.
    I give Egypt as ransom for you,
    Ethiopia and Seba† in exchange for you.
4 Because you are precious in my eyes
    and honored, and I love you,
    I give people in return for you
    and nations in exchange for your life.*
5 Fear not, for I am with you;
    from the east I will bring back your
        offspring,
    from the west I will gather you.

6 I will say to the north: Give them up!
    and to the south: Do not hold them!
    Bring back my sons from afar,
    and my daughters from the ends of
        the earth:*
7 All who are called by my name
    I created for my glory;
    I formed them, made them.
8 Lead out the people, blind though they
        have eyes,
    deaf though they have ears.

9 Let all the nations gather together,
    let the peoples assemble!
    Who among them could have declared
        this,
    or announced to us the earlier things?†
    Let them produce witnesses to prove
        themselves right,
    that one may hear and say, "It is true!"
10 You are my witnesses†—oracle of the
        LORD—
    my servant whom I have chosen
    To know and believe in me
    and understand that I am he.
    Before me no god was formed,
    and after me there shall be none.
11 I, I am the LORD;
    there is no savior but me.
12 It is I who declared, who saved,
    who announced, not some strange
        god among you;
    You are my witnesses—oracle of the
        LORD.
    I am God,
13 yes, from eternity I am he;
    There is none who can deliver from my
        hand:
    I act and who can cancel it?*

14 Thus says the LORD, your redeemer,†
    the Holy One of Israel:

---

**42:24** *Plunderers*: the Assyrians and Babylonians. *We...they*: the switch from first- to third-person speech, though puzzling, does not obscure the fact that "the people" is meant.

**43:3–4** *Egypt...Ethiopia and Seba*: countries which God permitted the Persians to conquer in return for having given Israel its freedom.

**43:9** *Who among them...?*: God, and only God, can foretell the future because it is he who brings it to pass. The argument from prediction is an important theme in Second Isaiah and occurs also in 41:22; 43:10; 44:7–8, 26.

**43:10** *You are my witnesses*: Israel's role as chosen people now takes a new turn as they are given the active role of bearing witness before humankind to the Lord's role in history by proclaiming events beforehand and bringing them to pass; see

also 44:8. The false gods, on the other hand, cannot produce such witnesses (v. 9; cf. 44:9). *I am he*: this formula of self-identification, repeated in vv. 13 and 25, is used here to support the assertion that the Lord alone is God; see also 41:4; 46:4; 48:12; 51:12; 52:6. This expression in part may be behind the self-identification formula used by Jesus in John's gospel (cf. Jn 8:58). *Before...after*: another example of the same assertion, that the Lord alone is God; see also note on 44:6.

**43:14–17** The destruction of Babylon is described in language that recalls the drowning of the Egyptian army in the Red Sea (Ex 14–15).

---

**43:4** Dt 4:37; Hos 11:1.          **43:13** Is 41:4.
**43:6** Is 49:22; Ez 16:20.

For your sake I send to Babylon;
  I will bring down all her defenses,
  and the Chaldeans shall cry out in
    lamentation.

15 I am the LORD, your Holy One,
  the creator of Israel, your King.

16 Thus says the LORD,
  who opens a way in the sea,
  a path in the mighty waters,*

17 Who leads out chariots and horsemen,
  a powerful army,
Till they lie prostrate together, never to
    rise,
  snuffed out, quenched like a wick.*

18 Remember not† the events of the past,
  the things of long ago consider not;

19 See, I am doing something new!
  Now it springs forth, do you not
    perceive it?
In the wilderness I make a way,
  in the wasteland, rivers.

20 Wild beasts honor me,
  jackals and ostriches,
For I put water in the wilderness
  and rivers in the wasteland
  for my chosen people to drink,

21 The people whom I formed for myself,
  that they might recount my praise.

22 Yet you did not call upon me, Jacob,†
  for you grew weary of me, Israel.

23 You did not bring me sheep for your
    burnt offerings,
  nor honor me with your sacrifices.
I did not exact from you the service of
    offerings,
  nor weary you for frankincense.*

24 You did not buy me sweet cane,†
  nor did you fill me with the fat of
    your sacrifices;
Instead, you burdened me with your sins,
  wearied me with your crimes.

25 It is I, I, who wipe out,
  for my own sake, your offenses;
  your sins I remember no more.

26 Would you have me remember, have us
    come to trial?
  Speak up, prove your innocence!

27 Your first father† sinned;
  your spokesmen rebelled against me

28 Till I repudiated the holy princes,
  put Jacob under the ban,
  exposed Israel to scorn.

# 44

1 Hear then, Jacob, my servant,
  Israel, whom I have chosen.

2 Thus says the LORD who made you,
  your help, who formed you from the
    womb:
Do not fear, Jacob, my servant,
  Jeshurun,† whom I have chosen.

3 I will pour out water upon the thirsty
    ground,
  streams upon the dry land;
I will pour out my spirit upon your
    offspring,
  my blessing upon your descendants.

4 They shall spring forth amid grass
  like poplars beside flowing waters.*

5 One shall say, "I am the LORD's,"
  another shall be named after Jacob,
And this one shall write on his hand,†
    "The LORD's,"
  and receive the name Israel.*

## The True God and False Gods

6† Thus says the LORD, Israel's king,
  its redeemer, the LORD of hosts:
I am the first, I am the last;
  there is no God but me.†*

7 Who is like me? Let him stand up and
    declare,
  make it evident, and confront me
    with it.

---

**43:18** *Remember not*: God's new act of delivering Israel from the Babylonian captivity is presented as so great a marvel as to eclipse even the memory of the exodus from Egypt. This comparison of the return from Babylon to the exodus from Egypt recurs throughout Second Isaiah (cf. 41:17–20; 43:18–21; 48:20–21; 49:8–13; 51:9–11).

**43:22–28** The reason for the liberation of the Israelites is not their constancy but rather God's faithfulness to his promise (cf. 40:6–8).

**43:24** *Sweet cane*: a fragrant substance used in making incense and the sacred anointing oil; cf. Ex 30:23; Jer 6:20.

**43:27** *First father*: Jacob. *Spokesmen*: leaders, priests, prophets.

**44:2** *Jeshurun*: see note on Dt 32:15; cf. also Dt 33:5, 26.

**44:5** *Write on his hand*: an allusion to the Babylonian custom

of tattooing the owner's name on the hand of his slave.

**44:6–8** Prediction and fulfillment are here seen as the hallmarks of true divinity. See note on 43:9.

**44:6** *No god but me*: with Second Isaiah, Israel's faith is declared to be explicitly monotheistic. However implicit it may have been, earlier formulas did not exclude the existence of other gods, not even that of the first commandment: "You shall not have other gods besides me" (Ex 20:3). Cf. also note on 41:21–29.

---

**43:16** Is 51:10–11; Ex 14:21.
**43:17** Ex 15:4.
**43:23** Jer 6:20.
**44:4** Is 54:1–3.
**44:5** Is 43:7; 45:14.
**44:6** Is 41:4; 43:15; 45:21; 48:3, 12; 51:15; 54:5.

Who of old announced future events?
    Let them foretell to us the things to
      come.
8  Do not fear or be troubled.
    Did I not announce it to you long ago?
      I declared it, and you are my
        witnesses.
    Is there any God but me?
      There is no other Rock,† I know of
        none!*

9†  Those who fashion idols are all nothing;
    their precious works are of no avail.
    They are their witnesses:†
      they see nothing, know nothing,
      and so they are put to shame.*
10  Who would fashion a god or cast an idol,
    that is of no use?
11  Look, all its company will be shamed;
    they are artisans, mere human beings!
    They all assemble and stand there,
      only to cower in shame.
12  The ironsmith fashions a likeness,
    he works it over the coals,
    Shaping it with hammers,
      working it with his strong arm.
    With hunger his strength wanes,
      without water, he grows faint.*
13  The woodworker stretches a line,
    and marks out a shape with a stylus.
    He shapes it with scraping tools,
      with a compass measures it off,
    Making it the copy of a man,†
      human display, enthroned in a shrine.
14  He goes out to cut down cedars,
    takes a holm tree or an oak.
    He picks out for himself trees of the
      forest,
    plants a fir, and the rain makes it grow.
15  It is used for fuel:
    with some of the wood he warms
      himself,
    makes a fire and bakes bread.
    Yet he makes a god and worships it,
    turns it into an idol and adores it!
16  Half of it he burns in the fire,
    on its embers he roasts meat;

he eats the roast and is full.
He warms himself and says, "Ah!
    I am warm! I see the flames!"
17  The rest of it he makes into a god,
    an image to worship and adore.
    He prays to it and says,
      "Help me! You are my god!"
18  They do not know, do not understand;
    their eyes are too clouded to see,
    their minds, to perceive.
19  He does not think clearly;
    he lacks the wit and knowledge to say,
  "Half the wood I burned in the fire,
    on its embers I baked bread,
    I roasted meat and ate.
  Shall I turn the rest into an
    abomination?
    Shall I worship a block of wood?"
20  He is chasing ashes!†
  A deluded mind has led him astray;
    He cannot save himself,
    does not say, "This thing in my right
      hand—is it not a fraud?"

21  Remember these things, Jacob,
    Israel, for you are my servant!
  I formed you, a servant to me;
    Israel, you shall never be forgotten by
      me:
22  I have brushed away your offenses like a
    cloud,
    your sins like a mist;
    return to me, for I have redeemed you.

23  Raise a glad cry, you heavens—the LORD
    has acted!
    Shout, you depths of the earth.
  Break forth, mountains, into song,
    forest, with all your trees.
  For the LORD has redeemed Jacob,
    shows his glory through Israel.

### Cyrus, Anointed of the Lord, Agent of Israel's Liberation

24  Thus says the LORD, your redeemer,
    who formed you from the womb:
    I am the LORD, who made all things,

---

**44:8** *Rock*: place of refuge, a title here used of God; cf., e.g., Dt 32:4, 18; 1 Sm 2:2; Ps 18:3.
    **44:9–20** A satire on the makers and worshipers of idols.
    **44:9** *Their witnesses*: Israel has been called to bear witness to the awesome power of God (cf. 43:10, 12; 44:8), but idol makers cannot testify in support of their creations, for idols cannot act (Dt 4:28; Ps 135:15–18).

**44:13** *Copy of a man*: in the biblical view human beings are made in the image of God; here gods are made in the image of human beings.
    **44:20** *Chasing ashes*: an exercise in futility.

**44:8** Is 43:10, 12; Dt 32:4.    **44:12** Wis 13:11–16.
**44:9** Is 48:5, 7.

who alone stretched out the heavens,
I spread out the earth by myself.*

25 I bring to nought the omens of babblers,
make fools of diviners,
Turn back the wise
and make their knowledge foolish.

26 I confirm the words of my servant,
carry out the plan my messengers
announce.
I say to Jerusalem, Be inhabited!
To the cities of Judah, Be rebuilt!
I will raise up their ruins.

27 I say to the deep, Be dry!
I will dry up your rivers.*

28 I say of Cyrus,† My shepherd!
He carries out my every wish,
Saying of Jerusalem, "Let it be rebuilt,"
and of the temple, "Lay its
foundations."*

# 45

¹Thus says the LORD to his anointed,†
Cyrus,
whose right hand I grasp,
Subduing nations before him,
stripping kings of their strength,
Opening doors before him,
leaving the gates unbarred:

2 I will go before you
and level the mountains;
Bronze doors† I will shatter,
iron bars I will snap.*

3 I will give you treasures of darkness,
riches hidden away,
That you may know I am the LORD,
the God of Israel, who calls you by
name.

4 For the sake of Jacob, my servant,
of Israel my chosen one,
I have called you by name,
giving you a title, though you do not
know me.*

5 I am the LORD, there is no other,
there is no God besides me.

It is I who arm you, though you do not
know me,

6 so that all may know, from the rising
of the sun
to its setting, that there is none
besides me.†
I am the LORD, there is no other.

7 I form the light, and create the
darkness,
I make weal and create woe;†
I, the LORD, do all these things.

8 Let justice descend, you heavens, like
dew from above,
like gentle rain let the clouds drop it
down.
Let the earth open and salvation bud
forth;
let righteousness spring up with
them!†
I, the LORD, have created this.*

9 Woe to anyone who contends with their
Maker;*
a potsherd among potsherds of the
earth!†
Shall the clay say to the potter, "What
are you doing?"
or, "What you are making has no
handles"?

10 Woe to anyone who asks a father, "What
are you begetting?"
or a woman, "What are you giving
birth to?"

11 Thus says the LORD,
the Holy One of Israel, his maker:
Do you question me about my children,
tell me how to treat the work of my
hands?

12 It was I who made the earth
and created the people upon it;
It was my hands that stretched out the
heavens;
I gave the order to all their host.

13 It was I who stirred him† up for justice;
all his ways I make level.

---

**44:28** *Cyrus:* king of Persia (559–529 B.C.); cf. note on 41:1–4.

**45:1** *Anointed:* in Hebrew, *mashiah,* from which the word "Messiah" is derived; from its Greek translation, *Christos,* we have the title "Christ." Applied to kings, "anointed" originally referred only to those of Israel, but it is here given to Cyrus because he is the agent of the Lord.

**45:2** *Bronze doors:* those defending the city gates of Babylon.

**45:6** The nations will come to know that Israel's God is the only God; cf. also vv. 20–25.

**45:7** *Create woe:* God created and controls all aspects of creation (light and darkness, order and chaos).

**45:8** The Vulgate rendering gave a messianic sense to this verse, using "just one" and "savior" in place of "justice" and "salvation," phraseology taken over in the Advent liturgy, e.g., the "Rorate coeli."

**45:9** No one may challenge God's freedom of action, exemplified here by the selection of Cyrus as his anointed.

**45:13** *Him:* Cyrus, called by God for the deliverance and restoration of Israel. *Justice:* the Hebrew word (*sedeq*) has mul-

**44:24** Is 40:22; Jb 9:8.
**44:27** Is 42:15; 51:10.
**44:28** Jer 3:15; Ez 34:23.
**45:2** Ps 107:16.
**45:4** Is 40:26; 44:5.
**45:8** Ps 72:6; 85:11.
**45:9** Jer 18:6; Rom 9:20.

IS

He shall rebuild my city
  and let my exiles go free
Without price or payment,
  says the LORD of hosts.

14   Thus says the LORD:
The earnings of Egypt, the gain of
      Ethiopia,
  and the Sabeans,† tall of stature,
Shall come over to you and belong to
      you;
  they shall follow you, coming in
      chains.
Before you they shall bow down,
  saying in prayer:
"With you alone is God; and there is
      none other,
  no other god!*

15   Truly with you God is hidden,†
  the God of Israel, the savior!*
16   They are put to shame and disgrace, all
      of them;
  they go in disgrace who carve images.
17   Israel has been saved by the LORD,
  saved forever!
You shall never be put to shame or
      disgrace
  in any future age."

18   For thus says the LORD,
The creator of the heavens,
  who is God,
The designer and maker of the earth
  who established it,
Not as an empty waste† did he create it,
  but designing it to be lived in:
I am the LORD, and there is no other.
19   I have not spoken in secret
  from some place in the land of
      darkness,
I have not said to the descendants of
      Jacob,
  "Look for me in an empty waste."

I, the LORD, promise justice,
  I declare what is right.
20   Come and assemble, gather together,
  you fugitives from among the nations!
They are without knowledge who bear
      wooden idols†
  and pray to gods that cannot save.
21   Come close and declare;
  let them take counsel together:
Who announced this from the
      beginning,
  declared it from of old?
Was it not I, the LORD,
  besides whom there is no other God?
There is no just and saving God but
      me.
22   Turn to me and be safe,
  all you ends of the earth,
  for I am God; there is no other!
23   By myself I swear,
  uttering my just decree,
  a word that will not return:
To me every knee shall bend;
  by me every tongue shall swear,*
24   Saying, "Only in the LORD
  are just deeds and power.
Before him in shame shall come
  all who vent their anger against him.
25   In the LORD all the descendants of
      Israel
  shall have vindication and glory."

## The Gods of Babylon

46  ¹ Bel bows down, Nebo† stoops,
  their idols set upon beasts and cattle;
They must be borne upon shoulders,
  a load for weary animals.
2   They stoop and bow down together;
  unable to deliver those who bear
      them,
  they too go into captivity.

---

tiple connotations; here it relates to the saving victory that the
Lord will give to Cyrus for the deliverance of his people Israel.
This word and others from the same root frequently have this
connotation in Second Isaiah, occurring as a parallel term with
"deliverance," "salvation," etc. Cf. its use in 41:10 (rendered
"victorious") and 51:5 (rendered "victory").
   **45:14** *Egypt…Ethiopia…Sabeans:* the Egyptians and their allies who, when conquered by Cyrus, are seen as acknowledging
the God of Israel; cf. 43:3.
   **45:15** *God is hidden:* i.e., the one known only to Israel, who
cannot be represented by wooden or molten images. The concept of the "Deus absconditus," "the hidden God," becomes an
important theme in later theology.

**45:18** *Empty waste:* an allusion to Gn 1:2, where the earth is
waste and void; the same Hebrew word, *tohu,* is used in both
passages. Here it points to devastated Judah and Jerusalem,
where God wishes to resettle the returning exiles.
   **45:20** *Who bear wooden idols:* in their religious processions.
Such idols have feet but cannot walk; cf. Ps 115:7; Bar 6:25.
   **46:1–4** *Bel…Nebo:* gods of Babylon; their complete help-
lessness is here contrasted with God's omnipotence; whereas
they must be carried about, the Lord carries Israel as a parent
does a child.

45:14 Is 43:3.                        45:23 Rom 14:11; Phil 2:10.
45:15 Is 55:8; Prv 25:2.

3    Hear me, O house of Jacob,
       all the remnant of the house of Israel,
     My burden from the womb,
       whom I have carried since birth.*
4    Even to your old age I am he,
       even when your hair is gray I will
         carry you;
     I have done this, and I will lift you up,
       I will carry you to safety.

5    To whom would you liken me as an
         equal,
       compare me, as though we were
         alike?
6    There are those who pour out gold from
         a purse
       and weigh out silver on the scales;
     They hire a goldsmith to make it into a
         god
       before which they bow down in
         worship.
7    They lift it to their shoulders to carry;
       when they set it down, it stays,
       and does not move from the place.
     They cry out to it, but it cannot answer;
       it delivers no one from distress.

8    Remember this and be firm,
       take it to heart, you rebels;
9    remember the former things, those
         long ago:
     I am God, there is no other;
       I am God, there is none like me.
10   At the beginning I declare the outcome;
       from of old, things not yet done.
     I say that my plan shall stand,
       I accomplish my every desire.
11   I summon from the east a bird of prey,†
       from a distant land, one to carry out
         my plan.
     Yes, I have spoken, I will accomplish it;
       I have planned it, and I will do it.
12   Listen to me, you fainthearted,
       far from the victory of justice:
13   I am bringing on that victory, it is not
         far off,
       my salvation shall not tarry;

     I will put salvation within Zion,
       give to Israel my glory.

## The Fall of Babylon†

**47** ¹Come down, sit in the dust,
       virgin daughter Babylon;
     Sit on the ground, dethroned,
       daughter of the Chaldeans.
     No longer shall you be called
       dainty and delicate.*
2    Take the millstone and grind flour,
       remove your veil;
     Strip off your skirt, bare your legs,
       cross through the streams.
3    Your nakedness shall be uncovered,
       and your shame be seen;
     I will take vengeance,
       I will yield to no entreaty,
       says ⁴our redeemer,
     Whose name is the LORD of hosts,
       the Holy One of Israel.

5    Go into darkness and sit in silence,
       daughter of the Chaldeans,
     No longer shall you be called
       sovereign mistress of kingdoms.
6    Angry at my people,
       I profaned my heritage
     And gave them into your power;
       but you showed them no mercy;
     Upon the aged
       you laid a very heavy yoke.
7    You said, "I shall remain always,
       a sovereign mistress forever!"
     You did not take these things to heart,
       but disregarded their outcome.*
8    Now hear this, voluptuous one,
       enthroned securely,
     Saying in your heart,
       "I, and no one else!†
     I shall never be a widow,
       bereft of my children"—*
9    Both these things shall come to you
       suddenly, in a single day:
     Complete bereavement and widowhood
       shall come upon you
     Despite your many sorceries
       and the full power of your spells;†

---

**46:11** *From the east a bird of prey*: Cyrus; cf. 41:2–4.
**47:1–15** A taunt-song, mocking Babylon, once queen of the
nations, now a mere slave.
**47:8, 10** *I, and no one else*: Babylon is mockingly presented
as making the same claim as the Lord (cf. 45:6, 14, 22; 46:9), a
claim that events will soon prove to be false and foolish (v. 11).

**47:9–13, 15** Babylon was known for its sorcery and astrol-
ogy.

**46:3** Is 44:2.                    **47:7** Is 14:13–14.
**47:1** Dt 28:56.                   **47:8** Zep 2:15; Rev 18:7.

10 Secure in your wickedness,
    you said, "No one sees me."
Your wisdom and your knowledge
    led you astray,
And you said in your heart,
    "I, and no one else!"
11 But upon you shall come an evil
    you will not be able to charm away;
Upon you shall fall a disaster
    you cannot ward off.
Upon you shall suddenly come
    a ruin you cannot imagine.

12 Keep on with your spells
    and your many sorceries,
    at which you toiled from your youth.
Perhaps you can prevail,
    perhaps you can strike terror!
13 You wore yourself out with so many
        consultations!
    Let the astrologers stand forth to save
        you,
The stargazers who forecast at each new
        moon
    what would happen to you.
14 See, they are like stubble,
    fire consumes them;
They cannot deliver themselves
    from the spreading flames.
This is no warming ember,
    no fire to sit before!
15 Thus do your wizards serve you
    with whom you have toiled from your
        youth;
They wander their separate ways,
    with none to save you.

### Exhortations to the Exiles

48 ¹ Hear this, house of Jacob
    called by the name Israel,
    sprung from the stock of Judah,
You who swear by the name of the LORD
    and invoke the God of Israel
    without sincerity, without justice,
² Though you are named after the holy
        city
    and rely on the God of Israel,
    whose name is the LORD of hosts.
³ Things of the past I declared long ago,
    they went forth from my mouth, I
        announced them;

then suddenly I took action and they
        came to be.
⁴ Because I know that you are stubborn
    and that your neck is an iron sinew
    and your forehead bronze,
⁵ I declared them to you of old;
    before they took place I informed
        you,
That you might not say, "My idol did
        them,
    my statue, my molten image
        commanded them."
⁶ Now that you have heard, look at all
        this;
    must you not admit it?*
From now on I announce new things to
        you,
    hidden events you never knew.
⁷ Now, not from of old, they are created,
    before today you did not hear of
        them,
    so that you cannot claim, "I have
        known them."
⁸ You never heard, you never knew,
    they never reached your ears
        beforehand.
Yes, I know you are utterly treacherous,
    a rebel you were named from the
        womb.*
⁹ For the sake of my name I restrain my
        anger,
    for the sake of my renown I hold it
        back from you,
    lest I destroy you.
10 See, I refined you, but not like silver;
    I tested you in the furnace of
        affliction.*
11 For my sake, for my own sake, I do this;
    why should my name be profaned?
    My glory I will not give to another.

12 Listen to me, Jacob,
    Israel, whom I called!
I, it is I who am the first,
    and am I the last.*
13 Yes, my hand laid the foundations of the
        earth;
    my right hand spread out the
        heavens.
When I summon them,
    they stand forth at once.*

14 All of you assemble and listen:
    Who among you declared these
        things?
    The one the Lord loves† shall do his
        will
    against Babylon and the offspring of
        Chaldea.
15 I myself have spoken, I have summoned
        him,
    I have brought him, and his way
        succeeds!
16 Come near to me and hear this!
    From the beginning I did not speak in
        secret;
    At the time it happens, I am there:
    "Now the Lord God has sent me, and
        his spirit."†

17 Thus says the Lord, your redeemer,
        the Holy One of Israel:
    I am the Lord, your God,
        teaching you how to prevail,
        leading you on the way you should go.
18 If only you would attend to my
        commandments,
        your peace would be like a river,
        your vindication like the waves of the
            sea,
19 Your descendants like the sand,
        the offspring of your loins like its
            grains,
    Their name never cut off
        or blotted out from my presence.
20 Go forth from Babylon, flee from
        Chaldea!
    With shouts of joy declare this,
        announce it;
    Make it known to the ends of the earth,
        Say: "The Lord has redeemed his
            servant Jacob.
21 They did not thirst
        when he led them through dry lands;
    Water from the rock he set flowing for
        them;

he cleft the rock, and waters welled
    forth."*

22 There is no peace† for the wicked,
    says the Lord.

## B. Expiation of Sin, Spiritual Liberation of Israel

### The Servant of the Lord†

**49** ¹ Hear me, coastlands,
    listen, distant peoples.*
    Before birth the Lord called me,
        from my mother's womb he gave me
            my name.†
2 He made my mouth like a sharp-edged
        sword,
        concealed me, shielded by his hand.
    He made me a sharpened arrow,
        in his quiver he hid me.
3 He said to me, You are my servant,
        in you, Israel,† I show my glory.

4 Though I thought I had toiled in vain,
        for nothing and for naught spent my
            strength,
    Yet my right is with the Lord,
        my recompense is with my God.*
5 For now the Lord has spoken
        who formed me as his servant from
            the womb,
    That Jacob may be brought back to him
        and Israel gathered to him;
    I am honored in the sight of the Lord,
        and my God is now my strength!
6 It is too little, he says, for you to be my
        servant,
        to raise up the tribes of Jacob,
        and restore the survivors of Israel;*
    I will make you a light to the nations,
        that my salvation may reach to the
            ends of the earth.†
7 Thus says the Lord,
        the redeemer, the Holy One of Israel,

---

**48:14** *The one the* Lord *loves*: the reference is no doubt to Cyrus, who does the Lord's will by overcoming Babylon and releasing Israel from captivity.
**48:16** *"Now the Lord…spirit"*: said by Cyrus; cf. v. 14.
**48:22** *No peace*: while the good news proclaimed by the prophet is directed to the people as a whole, "peace," which can represent the fullness of God's blessings and which would here include deliverance from exile, is not extended to all regardless of disposition.
**49:1–7** The second of the four "servant of the Lord" oracles (cf. note on 42:1–4).
**49:1** *Gave me my name*: designated me for a special task or

mission (cf. Jer 1:5).
**49:3** *Israel*: the servant is identified with the people of Israel as their ideal representative; however, vv. 5–6 seem to distinguish the servant from Israel.
**49:6** The servant's vocation extends beyond the restoration of Israel in order to bring the knowledge of Israel's God to the rest of the earth; cf. Lk 2:32.

---

48:21 Ex 17:6; Nm 20:11.
49:1 Is 41:9; 43:1; 44:2,
    24; 46:3.
49:4 Is 40:27.

49:6 Is 42:1–6; 44:5;
    45:14; Lk 2:32; Acts
    13:46–47.

To the one despised, abhorred by the
      nations,
   the slave of rulers:
When kings see you, they shall stand up,
   and princes shall bow down
Because of the Lord who is faithful,
   the Holy One of Israel who has
      chosen you.*

## The Liberation and Restoration of Zion

8   Thus says the Lord:
   In a time of favor I answer you,†
      on the day of salvation I help you;
   I form you and set you
      as a covenant for the people,
   To restore the land
      and allot the devastated heritages,*
9   To say to the prisoners: Come out!
   To those in darkness: Show
      yourselves!
   Along the roadways they shall find
      pasture,
      on every barren height shall their
         pastures be.*
10   They shall not hunger or thirst;
      nor shall scorching wind or sun strike
         them;
   For he who pities them leads them
      and guides them beside springs of
         water.*
11   I will turn all my mountains into
         roadway,
      and make my highways level.*
12   See, these shall come from afar:
      some from the north and the west,
      others from the land of Syene.†

13   Sing out, heavens, and rejoice, earth,
      break forth into song, you mountains,
   For the Lord comforts his people
      and shows mercy to his afflicted.

14   But Zion said, "The Lord has forsaken
         me;
      my Lord has forgotten me."*
15   Can a mother forget her infant,
      be without tenderness for the child of
         her womb?

Even should she forget,
   I will never forget you.*
16   See, upon the palms of my hands I have
         engraved you;†
      your walls are ever before me.
17   Your children hasten—
      your levelers, your destroyers
         go forth from you;
18   Look about and see,
      they are all gathering and coming to
         you.
   As I live—oracle of the Lord—
      you shall don them as jewels,
      bedeck yourself like a bride.

19   Though you were waste and desolate,
      a land of ruins,
   Now you shall be too narrow for your
         inhabitants,
      while those who swallowed you up
         will be far away.
20   The children of whom you were bereft
      shall yet say in your hearing,
   "This place is too narrow for me,
      make room for me to live in."
21   You shall ask yourself:
   "Who has borne me these,
      when I was bereft and barren?
   Exiled and repudiated,
      who has reared them?
   I was left all alone;
      where then do these come from?"*
22   Thus says the Lord God:
   See, I will lift up my hand to the
         nations,
      and to the peoples raise my signal;
   They shall bring your sons in their arms,
      your daughters shall be carried on
         their shoulders.*
23   Kings shall be your guardians,
      their princesses your nursemaids;
   Face to the ground, they shall bow down
         before you
      and lick the dust at your feet.
   Then you shall know that I am the Lord,
      none who hope in me shall be
         ashamed.
24   Can plunder be taken from a warrior,

49:8 You: the individual is not named; perhaps Cyrus or the
prophet.
49:12 Syene: now called Aswan, at the first cataract of the
Nile in southern Egypt.
49:16 Upon the palms…you: for continual remembrance; cf.
Ex 13:9, 16; Dt 6:6–9.

49:7 Is 49:23; 55:5.              49:14 Is 40:27.
49:8 2 Cor 6:2.                  49:15 Is 43:4; 44:21;
49:9 Is 42:7, 18–20.                46:3–4.
49:10 Is 51:14; Rev 7:16.        49:21 Is 54:1–3.
49:11 Is 40:3–4.                 49:22 Is 5:26; 13:2.

or captives rescued from a tyrant?

25 Thus says the LORD:
Yes, captives can be taken from a warrior,
    and plunder rescued from a tyrant;
Those who oppose you I will oppose,
    and your sons I will save.
26 I will make your oppressors eat their
        own flesh,
    and they shall be drunk with their
        own blood
    as though with new wine.
All flesh shall know
    that I, the LORD, am your savior,
    your redeemer, the Mighty One of
        Jacob.*

## Salvation Through the Lord's Servant

**50** ¹ Thus says the LORD:
Where is the bill of divorce
with which I dismissed your mother?†
Or to which of my creditors
    have I sold you?
It was for your sins you were sold,
    for your rebellions your mother was
        dismissed.*

2 Why was no one there when I came?
Why did no one answer when I
        called?†
Is my hand too short to ransom?
    Have I not the strength to deliver?
See, with my rebuke I dry up the sea,
    I turn rivers into wilderness;
Their fish rot for lack of water,
    and die of thirst.*

3 I clothe the heavens in black,
    and make sackcloth their covering.

4† The Lord GOD has given me
    a well-trained tongue,
That I might know how to answer the
        weary
    a word that will waken them.
Morning after morning

he wakens my ear to hear as disciples
        do;
5 The Lord GOD opened my ear;
    I did not refuse,
    did not turn away.†
6 I gave my back to those who beat me,
    my cheeks to those who tore out my
        beard;†
My face I did not hide
    from insults and spitting.*

7 The Lord GOD is my help,
    therefore I am not disgraced;
Therefore I have set my face like flint,
    knowing that I shall not be put to
        shame.*
8 He who declares my innocence is near.
    Who will oppose me?
    Let us appear together.
Who will dispute my right?
    Let them confront me.
9 See, the Lord GOD is my help;
    who will declare me guilty?
See, they will all wear out like a garment,
    consumed by moths.*
10 Who among you fears the LORD,†
    heeds his servant's voice?
Whoever walk in darkness,
    without any light,
Yet trust in the name of the LORD
    and rely upon their God!*
11 All you who kindle flames
    and set flares alight,
Walk by the light of your own fire
    and by the flares you have burnt!
This is your fate from my hand:
    you shall lie down in a place of
        torment.

## Exhortation to Trust in the Lord

**51** ¹ Listen to me, you who pursue justice,
    who seek the LORD;
Look to the rock from which you were
        hewn,

---

† **50:1** Responding to the people's complaint of utter abandonment by God, the prophet asserts that their sins were responsible for their banishment. Since there was no bill of divorce, the bond between the Lord and his people still exists and he has the power to deliver them (v. 2).

**50:2** Israel's faith in God is weak; the people do not answer God's call, nor believe promises of deliverance.

**50:4–11** The third of the four "servant of the Lord" oracles (cf. note on 42:1–4); in vv. 4–9 the servant speaks; in vv. 10–11 God addresses the people directly.

**50:5** The servant, like a well-trained disciple, does not refuse

the divine vocation.

**50:6** He willingly submits to insults and beatings. *Tore out my beard*: a grave and painful insult.

**50:10–11** The Lord offers a choice to those who walk in darkness: either trust in the true light (v. 10), or walk in their false light and suffer the consequences.

**49:26** Is 19:2; Ez 38:21; Zec 14:13.
**50:1** Is 54:6–8; Dt 24:1–4; Mt 19:3; Mk 10:2–4.
**50:2** Ex 7:18; Ps 105:29.
**50:6** 2 Sm 10:4–6; Mt 26:67; 27:30.
**50:7** Ez 3:9.
**50:9** Is 51:6–8; Ps 102:27.
**50:10** Is 43:1–2; 44:1–2.

to the quarry† from which you were
    taken;*
2 Look to Abraham, your father,
    and to Sarah, who gave you birth;
Though he was but one when I called
    him,
    I blessed him and made him many.*
3 Yes, the LORD shall comfort Zion,
    shall comfort all her ruins;
Her wilderness he shall make like Eden,
    her wasteland like the garden of the
    LORD;
Joy and gladness shall be found in her,
    thanksgiving and the sound of song.

4 Be attentive to me, my people;†
    my nation, give ear to me.
For teaching shall go forth from me,
    and my judgment, as light to the
    peoples.*
5 I will make my victory come swiftly;
    my salvation shall go forth
    and my arm shall judge the nations;
In me the coastlands shall hope,
    and my arm they shall await.

6 Raise your eyes to the heavens,
    look at the earth below;
Though the heavens vanish like smoke,
    the earth wear out like a garment
    and its inhabitants die like flies,
My salvation shall remain forever
    and my victory shall always be firm.†
7 Hear me, you who know justice,
    you people who have my teaching at
    heart:
Do not fear the reproach of others;
    remain firm at their revilings.
8 They shall be like a garment eaten by
    moths,
    like wool consumed by grubs;
But my victory shall remain forever,
    my salvation, for all generations.*

9 Awake, awake, put on strength,
    arm of the LORD!
Awake as in the days of old,

    in ages long ago!
Was it not you who crushed Rahab,†
    you who pierced the dragon?*
10 Was it not you who dried up the sea,
    the waters of the great deep,†
You who made the depths of the sea
    into a way
    for the redeemed to pass through?
11 Those whom the LORD has ransomed
    will return
    and enter Zion singing,
    crowned with everlasting joy;
They will meet with joy and gladness,
    sorrow and mourning will flee.

12 I, it is I who comfort you.
    Can you then fear mortals who die,
    human beings who are just grass,
13 And forget the LORD, your maker,
    who stretched out the heavens
    and laid the foundations of earth?
All the day you are in constant dread
    of the fury of the oppressor
When he prepares himself to destroy;
    but where is the oppressor's fury?
14 The captives shall soon be released;
    they shall not die and go down into
    the pit,
    nor shall they want for bread.
15 For I am the LORD, your God,
    who stirs up the sea so that its waves
    roar;
    the LORD of hosts by name.*
16 I have put my words into your mouth,
    I covered you, shielded by my hand,
Stretching out the heavens,
    laying the foundations of the earth,
    saying to Zion: You are my people.

### The Cup of the Lord

17 Wake up, wake up!
    Arise, Jerusalem,
You who drank at the LORD's hand
    the cup of his wrath;
Who drained to the dregs
    the bowl of staggering!*

---

† **51:1** *Rock…quarry:* your glorious ancestry.
**51:4–5** The conversion of the nations.
**51:6** While the heavens and the earth appear eternal and change-
less, they are not so firm and lasting as God's saving will for Israel.
**51:9** *Rahab:* see note on 30:7. *The dragon:* see notes on 27:1;
Ps 74:12–17.
**51:10** *Great deep:* a reference to the primeval chaos (cf. Gn
1:2; 7:11; 49:25; Jb 28:14; Ps 36:7; Jon 2:4).

* **51:1** Rom 9:30–31.
**51:2** Ez 33:24; Gn 12:2–4;
  22:17.
**51:4** Is 2:3.
**51:8** Is 50:9.
**51:9** Ex 15:16; Jb 9:13;
  26:12; Ps 74:13;
  89:11.
**51:15** Jer 31:35.
**51:17** Jer 25:15–17; Ez
  23:32–34.

18 She has no one to guide her
    of all the children she bore;
She has no one to take her by the hand,
    of all the children she reared!—

19 Your misfortunes are double;
    who is there to grieve with you?
Desolation and destruction, famine and
        sword!
    Who is there to comfort you?

20 Your children lie helpless
    at every street corner
    like antelopes in a net.
They are filled with the wrath of the LORD,
    the rebuke of your God.

21 But now, hear this, afflicted one,
    drunk, but not with wine,*

22 Thus says the LORD, your Master,
    your God, who defends his people:
See, I am taking from your hand
    the cup of staggering;
The bowl of my wrath
    you shall no longer drink.

23 I will put it into the hands of your
        tormentors,
    those who said to you,
    "Bow down, that we may walk over
        you."
So you offered your back like the ground,
    like the street for them to walk on.

### Let Zion Rejoice

# 52
1 Awake, awake!
    Put on your strength, Zion;
Put on your glorious garments,
    Jerusalem, holy city.
Never again shall the uncircumcised
    or the unclean enter you.

2 Arise, shake off the dust,
    sit enthroned, Jerusalem;
Loose the bonds from your neck,
    captive daughter Zion!

3 For thus says the LORD:
For nothing you were sold,
    without money you shall be redeemed.

4 For thus says the Lord GOD:
To Egypt long ago my people went down,

to sojourn there;
    Assyria, too, oppressed them for
        nought.

5 But now, what am I to do here?
    —oracle of the LORD.
My people have been taken away for
        nothing;
    their rulers mock, oracle of the LORD;
    constantly, every day, my name is
        reviled.

6 Therefore my people shall know my name
    on that day, that it is I who speaks:
    Here I am!

7 How beautiful upon the mountains†
    are the feet of the one bringing good
        news,
Announcing peace, bearing good news,
    announcing salvation, saying to Zion,
    "Your God is King!"*

8 Listen! Your sentinels raise a cry,
    together they shout for joy,
For they see directly, before their eyes,
    the LORD's return to Zion.*

9 Break out together in song,
    O ruins of Jerusalem!
For the LORD has comforted his people,
    has redeemed Jerusalem.

10 The LORD has bared his holy arm
    in the sight of all the nations;
All the ends of the earth can see
    the salvation of our God.

11 Depart, depart, go out from there,
    touch nothing unclean!
Out from there!† Purify yourselves,
    you who carry the vessels of the LORD.

12 But not in hurried flight will you go out,
    nor leave in headlong haste,
For the LORD goes before you,
    and your rear guard is the God of
        Israel.*

### Suffering and Triumph of the Servant of the Lord†

13 See, my servant shall prosper,
    he shall be raised high and greatly
        exalted.

---

52:7–10 God leads the people back from Babylon to Zion, from whose ruined walls sentinels greet the returning exiles.
52:11 *From there*: from Babylon. *Vessels of the LORD*: taken to Babylon by Nebuchadnezzar, now carried back by the exiles returning in procession to Zion; cf. Ezr 1:7.
52:13–53:12 The last of the "servant of the Lord" oracles (see

note on 42:1–4). Taken together, these oracles depict a figure of one called by God for a vocation to Israel and the nations (42:4; 49:5–6); the servant's exaltation both opens and closes the pas-

---

51:21 Is 29:9.          52:8 Is 62:6.
52:7 Is 40:9; Rom 10:15.   52:12 Ex 12:11.

14 Even as many were amazed at him—
   so marred were his features,
   beyond that of mortals
   his appearance, beyond that of human
      beings—*

15 So shall he startle many nations,
   kings shall stand speechless;
   For those who have not been told shall
      see,
   those who have not heard shall
      ponder it.*

# 53

1 Who would believe what we have
   heard?†
To whom has the arm of the LORD
   been revealed?*

2 He grew up like a sapling before him,*
   like a shoot from the parched earth;
   He had no majestic bearing to catch our
      eye,
   no beauty to draw us to him.

3 He was spurned and avoided by men,
   a man of suffering, knowing pain,
   Like one from whom you turn your face,
   spurned, and we held him in no
      esteem.*

4 Yet it was our pain that he bore,
   our sufferings he endured.
   We thought of him as stricken,
   struck down by God† and afflicted,*

5 But he was pierced for our sins,
   crushed for our iniquity.
   He bore the punishment that makes us
      whole,

      by his wounds we were healed.*

6 We had all gone astray like sheep,
   all following our own way;
   But the LORD laid upon him†
   the guilt of us all.*

7 Though harshly treated, he submitted
   and did not open his mouth;
   Like a lamb led to slaughter
   or a sheep silent before shearers,
   he did not open his mouth.*

8 Seized and condemned, he was taken
      away.
   Who would have thought any more of
      his destiny?
   For he was cut off from the land of the
      living,
   struck for the sins of his people.

9 He was given a grave among the
      wicked,
   a burial place with evildoers,
   Though he had done no wrong,
   nor was deceit found in his mouth.*

10 But it was the LORD's will to crush him
      with pain.
   By making his life as a reparation
      offering,†
   he shall see his offspring, shall
      lengthen his days,
   and the LORD's will shall be
      accomplished through him.

11 Because of his anguish he shall see the
      light;
   because of his knowledge he shall be
      content;

---

sage (52:13; 53:12). The servant responded in fidelity but has suffered opposition (50:4–6). In this fourth oracle the servant is characterized as "a man of suffering" (53:3) and appears to be unjustly put to death (53:8–9). Those who have witnessed his career somehow recognize that he is innocent, has undergone suffering for their sins (53:4–6), and his death is referred to as a reparation offering (see note on 53:10–11). The servant is described in ways that identify him with Israel (which is frequently referred to as "servant" in the context of Second Isaiah—e.g., 41:8, 9; 44:2, 21; 43:4) and is designated as "Israel" in 49:3; yet Israel outside the "servant of the Lord" oracles is not presented as sinless, but rather in exile because of sin (40:2; 42:21–25) and even as servant as deaf and blind (42:18–19). The servant is thus both identified with Israel and distinguished from it. As with the previous servant poems, this chapter helped the followers of Jesus to interpret his suffering, death, and resurrection; see especially the passion narratives.

**53:1–10** *What we have heard*: this fourth servant oracle is introduced by words of the Lord (52:13–15) but is now continued by speakers who are not identified, perhaps those referred to in 52:15, perhaps Israel (cf. "struck for the sins of his people"—v. 8). The Lord is again the speaker in vv. 11–13.

**53:4** *Struck down by God*: the Bible often sees suffering as a punishment for sin (e.g., Ps 6:2; 32:1–5), yet sin sometimes

appears to go unpunished and the innocent often suffer (cf. Ps 73; the Book of Job). In the case of the servant, the onlookers initially judge him guilty because of his suffering but, in some way not explained, they come to understand that his sufferings are for the sins of others. One notes the element of surprise, for such vicarious suffering, in the form described here, is without parallel in the Old Testament.

**53:6** *The LORD laid upon him*: the servant's suffering is no accidental or casual matter, but part of God's plan; see v. 10. The bystanders' speculation of v. 4 is verified, but not in the sense intended by them.

**53:10–11** *Reparation offering*: the Hebrew term *'asham* is used of a particular kind of sacrifice, one that is intended as compensation for that which is due because of guilt. See Lv 5:14–26 and note. *Justify*: the verb means "to be acquitted," "declared innocent," but since the servant bears "their iniquity," an effective rather than simply legal action is suggested.

---

52:14 Ps 69:8.                     Ps 31:11–13; Mk 9:11.
52:15 Mi 7:16.                     53:4 Jer 10:19; Mt 8:17.
53:1 Is 52:10; Jn 12:38;          53:5 1 Cor 15:3; 1 Pt 2:24.
      Rom 10:16.                   53:6 Lv 16:21–22.
53:2 Is 11:1.                      53:7 Mt 26:63; Acts 8:32.
53:3 Jb 19:18;                     53:9 1 Pt 2:22–23; 1 Jn 3:5.

IS

My servant, the just one, shall justify the
    many,
    their iniquity he shall bear.

12 Therefore I will give him his portion
    among the many,
and he shall divide the spoils with the
    mighty,
Because he surrendered himself to
    death,
    was counted among the transgressors,
Bore the sins of many,
    and interceded for the transgressors. *

## The New Zion

**54** ¹ Raise a glad cry, you barren one †
    who never bore a child,
break forth in jubilant song, you who
    have never been in labor,
For more numerous are the children of
    the deserted wife
than the children of her who has a
    husband,
    says the LORD. *

2 Enlarge the space for your tent,
    spread out your tent cloths
      unsparingly;
lengthen your ropes and make firm
    your pegs. *

3 For you shall spread abroad to the right
    and left;
your descendants shall dispossess the
    nations
and shall people the deserted cities. †

4 † Do not fear, you shall not be put to
    shame;
do not be discouraged, you shall not
    be disgraced.
For the shame of your youth you shall
    forget,
the reproach of your widowhood no
    longer remember.

5 For your husband is your Maker;
    the LORD of hosts is his name,
Your redeemer, † the Holy One of Israel,
    called God of all the earth.

6 The LORD calls you back,
    like a wife forsaken and grieved in
      spirit,
A wife married in youth and then cast
    off,
    says your God. *

7 For a brief moment I abandoned you,
    but with great tenderness I will take
      you back.

8 In an outburst of wrath, for a moment
    I hid my face from you;
But with enduring love I take pity on
    you,
    says the LORD, your redeemer.

9 This is for me like the days of Noah:
As I swore then that the waters of Noah
    should never again flood the earth,
So I have sworn now not to be angry
    with you,
    or to rebuke you. *

10 Though the mountains fall away
    and the hills be shaken,
My love shall never fall away from you
    nor my covenant of peace † be shaken,
    says the LORD, who has mercy on
      you. *

11 O afflicted one, † storm-battered and
    unconsoled,
I lay your pavements in carnelians,
    your foundations in sapphires; *

12 I will make your battlements of rubies,
    your gates of jewels,
    and all your walls of precious stones.

13 All your children shall be taught by the
    LORD;

---

**54:1** Jerusalem, pictured as a wife who had been barren and deserted, now suddenly finds herself with innumerable children (the returning exiles); cf. Gal 4:27 for an application to a new context.

**54:3** Those who had taken advantage of the exile to encroach on Jerusalem's territory will be driven out, and the returning exiles will repopulate the cities of Judah.

**54:4–8** As with some other Old Testament themes, Second Isaiah uses that of Israel as the Lord's bride in a new manner. Whereas Hosea and Jeremiah had depicted Israel as the Lord's spouse to emphasize both Israel's infidelity and the Lord's continued love (Hos 1–3; Jer 2:2; 3:1–15) and Ezekiel to accuse Israel unsparingly (Ez 16; 23), Second Isaiah speaks only of the love with which the Lord restores the people, speaking tender words

with no hint of reproach.

**54:5** *Redeemer:* cf. note on 41:14.

**54:10** *Covenant of peace:* this whole section, vv. 9–17, is given to various assurances of God's love for Israel and of safety from various possible threats; the phrase sums up both the positive aspects of *shalom,* which implies a fullness of blessing, and protection from all that might harm. Cf. also 55:3; Nm 25:12; Ez 34:25; 37:26; Mal 2:5.

**54:11** *Afflicted one:* Jerusalem.

**53:12** Mk 15:28; Lk 22:37.      **54:9** Gn 9:15.
**54:1** Gal 4:27.      **54:10** Ps 46:3; 76:5.
**54:2** Is 49:20.      **54:11** Rev 21:18–21.
**54:6** Mal 2:14–15.

great shall be the peace of your
children.

14   In justice shall you be established,
far from oppression, you shall not
fear,
from destruction, it cannot come
near.

15   If there be an attack, it is not my doing;
whoever attacks shall fall before you.

16   See, I have created the smith
who blows on the burning coals
and forges weapons as his work;
It is I also who have created
the destroyer to work havoc.

17   Every weapon fashioned against you
shall fail;
every tongue that brings you to trial
you shall prove false.

This is the lot of the servants of the
LORD,
their vindication from me—oracle of
the LORD.

## An Invitation to Grace

# 55
¹ All you who are thirsty,†
come to the water!
You who have no money,
come, buy grain and eat;
Come, buy grain without money,
wine and milk without cost!*

2   Why spend your money for what is not
bread;
your wages for what does not satisfy?
Only listen to me, and you shall eat
well,
you shall delight in rich fare.

3   Pay attention and come to me;
listen, that you may have life.
I will make with you an everlasting
covenant,
the steadfast loyalty promised to
David.*

4   As I made him a witness to peoples,
a leader and commander of peoples,

5   So shall you summon a nation you
knew not,
and a nation† that knew you not shall
run to you,
Because of the LORD, your God,
the Holy One of Israel, who has
glorified you.*

6†  Seek the LORD while he may be found,
call upon him while he is near.

7   Let the wicked forsake their way,
and sinners their thoughts;
Let them turn to the LORD to find mercy;
to our God, who is generous in
forgiving.

8   For my thoughts are not your thoughts,
nor are your ways my ways—oracle of
the LORD.

9   For as the heavens are higher than the
earth,
so are my ways higher than your ways,
my thoughts higher than your
thoughts.

10† Yet just as from the heavens
the rain and snow come down
And do not return there
till they have watered the earth,
making it fertile and fruitful,
Giving seed to the one who sows
and bread to the one who eats,

11   So shall my word be
that goes forth from my mouth;
It shall not return to me empty,
but shall do what pleases me,
achieving the end for which I sent it.

12   Yes, in joy you shall go forth,
in peace you shall be brought home;
Mountains and hills shall break out in
song before you,
all trees of the field shall clap their
hands.

13   In place of the thornbush, the cypress
shall grow,
instead of nettles,† the myrtle.

---

55:1–3 The prophet invites all to return, under the figure of a banquet; cf. the covenant banquet in Ex 24:9–11 and wisdom's banquet in Prv 9:1–6. The Lord's covenant with David (2 Sm 7) is now to be extended beyond his dynasty.
55:5 The "nation" is Persia under Cyrus, but the perspective is worldwide.
55:6–9 The invitation to seek the Lord is motivated by the mercy of a God whose "ways" are completely mysterious.
55:10–11 The efficacy of the word of God recalls 40:5, 8.

55:13 Thornbush…nettles: suggestive of the desert and therefore symbolic of suffering and hardship; cypress…myrtle: suggestive of fertile land and therefore symbolic of joy and strength. To the LORD's renown: lit., "to the name of the Lord."

---

55:1 Jn 4:10–15; 6:35;
7:37–39; Rev 21:6;
22:17.

55:3 2 Sm 7:12–16.
55:5 Acts 13:34.

This shall be to the LORD's renown,
as an everlasting sign that shall not
fail.

## III. ISAIAH 56—66

### Salvation for the Just†

**56** [1]† Thus says the LORD:
Observe what is right, do what is
just,
for my salvation is about to come,
my justice, about to be revealed.*

[2] Happy is the one who does this,
whoever holds fast to it:
Keeping the sabbath without profaning
it,
keeping one's hand from doing any
evil.*

### Obligations and Promises to Share in the Covenant

[3]† The foreigner joined to the LORD should
not say,
"The LORD will surely exclude me
from his people";
Nor should the eunuch say,
"See, I am a dry tree."*

[4] For thus says the LORD:
To the eunuchs who keep my sabbaths,
who choose what pleases me,
and who hold fast to my covenant,*

[5] I will give them, in my house
and within my walls, a monument
and a name†
Better than sons and daughters;
an eternal name, which shall not be
cut off, will I give them.

[6] And foreigners who join themselves to
the LORD,
to minister to him,
To love the name of the LORD,
to become his servants—
All who keep the sabbath without
profaning it
and hold fast to my covenant,

[7]† Them I will bring to my holy mountain
and make them joyful in my house of
prayer;
Their burnt offerings and their
sacrifices
will be acceptable on my altar,
For my house shall be called
a house of prayer for all peoples.*

[8]† Oracle of the Lord GOD,
who gathers the dispersed of Israel—
Others will I gather to them
besides those already gathered.*

### Unworthy Shepherds†

[9] All you beasts of the field, †
come to devour,
all you beasts in the forest!*

---

**56:1–8** This poem inaugurates the final section of the Book of Isaiah, often referred to as Third or Trito-Isaiah. While Second or Deutero-Isaiah (Is 40–55) gave numerous references to the hopes of the community of Israel during the Babylonian exile (ca. 587–538 B.C.), Third Isaiah witnesses to the struggles and hoped-for blessings of the postexilic community now back in the home-land of Israel. In this opening poem, the references to "keeping the sabbath" (vv. 2, 4, 6), "holding fast to the covenant" (vv. 4, 6) and "God's holy mountain" as a house of prayer (v. 7), all tell of the postexilic community that was establishing itself again in the land according to the pattern of God's word given through the prophet. The poem can be classified as a "prophetic exhortation" in which the prophet gives instruction for those who wish to live according to God's word and covenant. What is important to note are the conditions placed upon the people of God; while Is 40–55 show an unconditional promise of redemption, these final chapters delineate clear expectations for receiving God's salvific promises. Both the expectations and the great promises of God will unfold in the succeeding chapters of Third Isaiah.

**56:1** This opening verse echoes themes that are well known throughout the Book of Isaiah: justice and right judgment (1:27; 5:7, 16; 9:6; 16:5; 26:9; 28:17; 32:1, 16; 33:5; 42:1, 4, 6; 45:8, 13, 19), salvation and deliverance (12:3; 26:18; 33:2; 45:8, 21; 46:13; 51:5, 6, 8). These themes will be developed also through-out Third Isaiah.

**56:3** Eunuchs had originally been excluded from the commu-nity of the Lord; cf. Dt 23:2; Neh 13:1–3; Wis 3:14.

**56:5** *A monument and a name*: literally in Hebrew, "a hand and a name"; a memorial inscription to prevent oblivion for one who had no children; cf. 2 Sm 18:18; Neh 7:5; 13:14.

**56:7** This verse continues the theme of universalism found in Is 49:6. As Israel was to be "a light to the nations" so that God's "salvation may reach to the ends of the earth," so now does that come to pass as foreigners, faithful to the divine commands, are brought to the Temple by God and joined to the covenant com-munity of Israel.

**56:8** For the gathering of the dispersed people of Israel, cf. Jer 23:3; 31:8–9; Ez 11:17. Here the Lord not only gathers the displaced of Israel, but also unites other peoples to them. Cf. Is 60:3–10; 66:18–21.

**56:9–57:21** This section is made up of two pronouncements of judgment (56:9–57:2; 57:3–13) and an oracle of salvation (57:14–21), each of which ends with a reversal of imagery and language. While there are harsh indictments against the corrupt leaders of Israel (56:9–12), a promise of peace is offered to those who are just (57:1–2). Then the judgment and its subsequent punishment for idolaters (57:3–13a) change to an announce-ment of reward for those who place their trust in God (57:13c). And the promises of salvation (57:14–19) then shift to a word of warning to the wicked (57:20–21).

**56:9** *Beasts of the field*: foreign nations, which are invited to come and ravage Israel.

---

**56:1** Is 59:9, 14, 19–20.
**56:2** Is 1:13; 58:13–14; Ex 23:12.
**56:3** Dt 23:3–5; Neh 13:1–3.
**56:4** Wis 3:14.
**56:7** 1 Kgs 8:29–30, 41; Mt 21:13.
**56:8** Ps 147:2.
**56:9** Jer 12:9–10; Ez 34:5.

10 † All the sentinels of Israel are blind,
    they are without knowledge;
  They are all mute dogs,
    unable to bark;
  Dreaming, reclining,
    loving their sleep.
11 Yes, the dogs have a ravenous appetite;
    they never know satiety,
  Shepherds who have no understanding;
    all have turned their own way,
    each one covetous for gain:
12 "Come, let me bring wine;
    let us fill ourselves with strong drink,
  And tomorrow will be like today,
    or even greater."*

# 57

1 The just have perished,
  but no one takes it to heart;
The steadfast are swept away,
  while no one understands.
Yet the just are taken away from the
    presence of evil,
2 †  and enter into peace;
They rest upon their couches,
  the sincere, who walk in integrity.*

### An Idolatrous People†

3 But you, draw near,
  you children of a sorceress,
  offspring of an adulterer and a
    prostitute!†
4 Against whom do you make sport,
  against whom do you open wide your
    mouth,
  and stick out your tongue?
Are you not rebellious children,
  deceitful offspring—
5 You who burn with lust among the
    oaks,

  under every green tree;
You who immolate children in the
    wadies,
  among the clefts of the rocks?†*
6 Among the smooth stones† of the wadi
    is your portion,
  they, they are your allotment;
Indeed, you poured out a drink offering
    to them,
  and brought up grain offerings.
With these things, should I be
    appeased?
7 Upon a towering and lofty mountain
  you set up your bed,
  and there you went up to offer
    sacrifice.*
8 Behind the door and the doorpost
  you set up your symbol.
Yes, deserting me, you carried up your
    bedding;
  and spread it wide.
You entered an agreement with them,
  you loved their couch, you gazed
    upon nakedness.†
9 You approached the king† with oil,
  and multiplied your perfumes;
You sent your ambassadors far away,
  down even to deepest Sheol.
10 Though worn out with the length of
    your journey,
  you never said, "It is hopeless";
You found your strength revived,
  and so you did not weaken.
11 Whom did you dread and fear,
  that you told lies,
And me you did not remember
  nor take to heart?
Am I to keep silent and conceal,
  while you show no fear of me?

---

**56:10–11** These shepherds of Israel are without "knowledge," a theme developed earlier in the Isaian corpus; cf. 1:3; 6:9–10. Ezekiel 34 has similar condemnatory words against the unfaithful shepherds of Israel.

**57:2** Despite their sad fate, the just will ultimately attain peace (most likely in this world); cf. v. 13.

**57:3–13** In this courtroom imagery, the idolaters are summoned before the judge (v. 3), their crimes are graphically described (vv. 4–11), their guilt is established, and condemnation is carried out (vv. 12–13b). In contrast to this, v. 13c describes the inheritance of God's land and holy mountain given to those who place their confidence in God instead of in idols.

**57:3** Language of sexual infidelity is often used in a figurative way to describe idolatry. Cf. Ez 16:15–22; Hos 2:4–7; Col 3:5.

**57:5** Child sacrifice is also attested in 2 Kgs 23:10; Jer 7:31; Ez 16:20; 20:28, 31; 23:37–39.

**57:6** *Smooth stones*: the Hebrew word for this expression has the same consonants as the word for "portion"; instead of mak-

ing the Lord their portion (cf. Ps 16:5), the people adored slabs of stone which they took from the streambeds in valleys and set up as idols; cf. Jer 3:9. Therefore, it is implied, they will be swept away as by a sudden torrent of waters carrying them down the rocky-bottomed gorge to destruction and death without burial.

**57:8** *Nakedness*: literally in Hebrew, "hand." In this context, it may euphemistically refer to a phallus.

**57:9** *The king*: in Hebrew, the word for king is *melek*, similar in sound to the Canaanite god Molech, to whom children were offered as a sacrifice in pagan ritual. The expression "your ambassadors" could be a figurative expression for the children whose death served as an offering to this deity.

**56:12** Is 22:13; 28:7; Wis 2:7.
**57:2** Wis 3:1–3.
**57:5** Dt 12:2; 2 Kgs 17:10;

Jer 7:31; 19:5; Ez 20:28, 31.
**57:7** Jer 2:20; Ez 6:13; Hos 4:13.

**12** I will proclaim your justice†
 and your works;
 but they shall not help you.
**13†** When you cry out,
 let your collection of idols save you.
 All these the wind shall carry off,
 a mere breath shall bear them away;
 But whoever takes refuge in me shall
 inherit the land,
 and possess my holy mountain.

### The Way to Peace for God's People

**14** And I say:
 Build up, build up, prepare the way,
 remove every obstacle from my
 people's way.†*
**15†** For thus says the high and lofty One,
 the One who dwells forever, whose
 name is holy:
 I dwell in a high and holy place,
 but also with the contrite and lowly of
 spirit,
 To revive the spirit of the lowly,
 to revive the heart of the crushed.
**16** For I will not accuse forever,
 nor always be angry;
 For without me their spirit fails,
 the life breath that I have given.*
**17** Because of their wicked avarice I grew
 angry;
 I struck them, hiding myself from
 them in wrath.
 But they turned back, following the way
 of their own heart.*
**18** I saw their ways,
 but I will heal them.
 I will lead them and restore full comfort
 to them
 and to those who mourn for them,*
**19** creating words of comfort.†

Peace! Peace to those who are far and
 near,
 says the Lord; and I will heal them.
**20** But the wicked are like the tossing sea
 which cannot be still,
 Its waters cast up mire and mud.*
**21** There is no peace for the wicked!
 says my God.*

### Reasons for Judgment†

# 58
**1** Cry out full-throated and
 unsparingly,
 lift up your voice like a trumpet blast;
 Proclaim to my people their
 transgression,
 to the house of Jacob their sins.*
**2** They seek me day after day,
 and desire to know my ways,
 Like a nation that has done what is just
 and not abandoned the judgment of
 their God;
 They ask of me just judgments,
 they desire to draw near to God.
**3** "Why do we fast, but you do not see it?
 afflict ourselves, but you take no
 note?"
 See, on your fast day you carry out your
 own pursuits,
 and drive all your laborers.*
**4** See, you fast only to quarrel and fight
 and to strike with a wicked fist!
 Do not fast as you do today
 to make your voice heard on high!
**5** Is this the manner of fasting I would
 choose,
 a day to afflict oneself?
 To bow one's head like a reed,
 and lie upon sackcloth and ashes?
 Is this what you call a fast,
 a day acceptable to the Lord?*

**57:12** *Justice:* here used sarcastically. The activity described in these verses is far from the justice which God demands of those who are aligned with the covenant (cf. 56:1, 4, 6). In the larger context of Third Isaiah and the whole of the Isaian tradition, justice is a key theological motif. The justice to which God calls Israel will eventually come to its fulfillment in an act of divine intervention (cf. 60:21; 61:3c). Until then, the people of God must strive to live in the ways of justice and right judgment (56:1).

**57:13** In v. 6, the smooth stones of the valley are the portion which the unfaithful will receive as their due reward (cf. note on v. 6); while in v. 13c, an inheritance of the land and possession of God's holy mountain will be the portion of the upright.

**57:14** *The way...my people's way:* the language and imagery are reminiscent of 40:1–2, but in this context, when the people have already returned, the physical road through the desert is replaced by the spiritual way that leads to redemption.

**57:15** The God of Israel is presented in both a transcendent and an immanent manner. God's holiness is the transcendent quality; the immanence is shown in the choice of dwelling among the downtrodden and humble.

**57:19** *Creating words of comfort:* lit., "fruit of the lips," perhaps referring to praise and thanksgiving for the divine healing; cf. Hos 14:3.

**58:1–5** The prophet is commanded to condemn the formalism of the people, specifically their hypocritical fasting.

**57:14** Is 40:3–4.
**57:16** Gn 2:7.
**57:17** Is 56:11.
**57:18** Is 61:2.
**57:20** Jon 2:3–7.
**57:21** Is 48:22.

**58:1** Lv 25:9.
**58:3** 1 Sm 7:6; 1 Kgs 21:12; 1 Mc 3:47; Jl 1:1–2:17.
**58:5** Zec 7:5.

## Authentic Fasting That Leads to Blessing†

6   Is this not, rather, the fast that I choose:
       releasing those bound unjustly,
       untying the thongs of the yoke;
    Setting free the oppressed,
       breaking off every yoke?*
7   Is it not sharing your bread with the
          hungry,
       bringing the afflicted and the
          homeless into your house;
    Clothing the naked when you see them,
       and not turning your back on your
          own flesh?*
8   Then your light shall break forth like the
          dawn,
       and your wound shall quickly be
          healed;
    Your vindication shall go before you,
       and the glory of the LORD shall be
          your rear guard.
9   Then you shall call, and the LORD will
          answer,
       you shall cry for help, and he will say:
          "Here I am!"
    If you remove the yoke from among you,
       the accusing finger, and malicious
          speech;*
10  If you lavish your food on the hungry
       and satisfy the afflicted;
    Then your light shall rise in the
          darkness,
       and your gloom shall become like
          midday;
11  Then the LORD will guide you always
       and satisfy your thirst in parched
          places,
       will give strength to your bones
    And you shall be like a watered garden,
       like a flowing spring whose waters
          never fail.*
12  Your people shall rebuild the ancient
          ruins;
       the foundations from ages past you
          shall raise up;

"Repairer of the breach," they shall call
       you,
    "Restorer of ruined dwellings."*

## Authentic Sabbath Observance
## That Leads to Blessing†

13  If you refrain from trampling the
          sabbath,
       from following your own pursuits on
          my holy day;
    If you call the sabbath a delight,
       the LORD's holy day glorious;
    If you glorify it by not following your
          ways,
       seeking your own interests, or
          pursuing your own affairs—
14  Then you shall delight in the LORD,
       and I will make you ride upon the
          heights of the earth;
    I will nourish you with the heritage of
          Jacob, your father,
       for the mouth of the LORD has
          spoken.*

## Salvation Delayed

59  1† No, the hand of the LORD is not
          too short to save,
       nor his ear too dull to hear.*
2   Rather, it is your crimes
       that separate you from your God,
    It is your sins that make him hide his
          face
       so that he does not hear you.
3   For your hands are defiled with blood,
       and your fingers with crime;
    Your lips speak falsehood,
       and your tongue utters deceit.*
4   No one brings suit justly,
       no one pleads truthfully;
    They trust an empty plea and tell lies;
       they conceive mischief and bring forth
          malice.
5†  They hatch adders' eggs,
       and weave spiders' webs:
    Whoever eats the eggs will die,

---

† **58:6–12** Fasting is not genuine without reforming one's way of life. A true social morality will ensure prosperity.
   **58:13–14** Sabbath observance becomes a cornerstone of postexilic piety; cf. 56:2, 4, 6.
   **59:1–20** This poem brings together a lament of the postexilic community and a harsh word of judgment from the prophet. After the opening rhetorical question, each of the stanzas begins with a reference to the justice and right judgment which are lacking among the people (vv. 4, 9, 14). Toward the end of the poem, God is depicted as a Divine Warrior (vv. 16–20) who is

the only one who can intervene in order to bring redemption. This same Divine Warrior imagery is repeated in a similar fashion in 63:1–6.
   **59:5–6** The eggs signify evil works, doing positive harm; the webs are devices that serve no useful purpose.

---

*
**58:6** Is 35:5–6.                    **58:12** Is 61:4.
**58:7** Ez 18:7, 16; Mt 25:35.        **58:14** Hb 3:19.
**58:9** Am 5:7.                        **59:1** Is 50:2; Nm 11:23.
**58:11** Is 51:3; Ps 24.              **59:3** Is 1:15.

if one of them is crushed, it will hatch
    a viper;*

6 Their webs cannot serve as clothing,
    nor can they cover themselves with
        their works.
Their works are evil works,
    and deeds of violence are in their
        hands.

7 Their feet run to evil,
    and they hasten to shed innocent
        blood;
Their thoughts are thoughts of
    wickedness,
    violence and destruction are on their
        highways.*

8 The way of peace they know not,
    and there is no justice on their paths;
Their roads they have made crooked,
    no one who walks in them knows
        peace.

## Acknowledgment of Transgressions

9† That is why judgment is far from us
    and justice does not reach us.
We look for light, but there is darkness;
    for brightness, and we walk in
        gloom!*

10 Like those who are blind we grope along
    the wall,
    like people without eyes we feel our
        way.
We stumble at midday as if at twilight,
    among the vigorous, we are like the
        dead.

11 Like bears we all growl,
    like doves we moan without ceasing.
We cry out for justice, but it is not there;
    for salvation, but it is far from us.*

12 For our transgressions before you are
    many,
    our sins bear witness against us.
Our transgressions are present to us,
    and our crimes we acknowledge:

13 Transgressing, and denying the LORD,
    turning back from following our God,
Planning fraud and treachery,
    uttering lying words conceived in the
        heart.

14 Judgment is turned away,
    and justice stands far off;
For truth stumbles in the public square,
    and uprightness cannot enter.*

15 Fidelity is lacking,
    and whoever turns from evil is
        despoiled.

## Divine Intervention

The LORD saw this, and was aggrieved
    that there was no justice.

16 He saw that there was no one,
    was appalled that there was none to
        intervene;
Then his own arm brought about the
    victory,
    and his justice sustained him.

17 He put on justice as his breastplate,
    victory as a helmet on his head;
He clothed himself with garments of
    vengeance,
    wrapped himself in a mantle of zeal.*

18 According to their deeds he repays his
    enemies
    and requites his foes with wrath;
    to the coastlands he renders
        recompense.

19 Those in the west shall fear the name of
    the LORD,
    and those in the east, his glory,
Coming like a pent-up stream
    driven on by the breath of the LORD.

20 Then for Zion shall come a redeemer,
    to those in Jacob who turn from
        transgression—oracle of the
        LORD.*

21† This is my covenant with them,
    which I myself have made, says the
        LORD:
My spirit which is upon you
    and my words that I have put in your
        mouth
Shall not depart from your mouth,
    nor from the mouths of your children
Nor the mouths of your children's
    children
    from this time forth and forever, says
        the LORD.*

---

† **59:9–15** The turning point in the poem comes when the people acknowledge their transgressions and describe the horror of their present state. Light is a metaphor for salvation (cf. 9:1; 42:16; 60:1–3, 19–20) and darkness represents sin and disaster.
**59:21** This verse makes the transition from chaps. 56–59 to chaps. 60–62. Oracles of judgment yield to oracles about God's redemptive action.

**59:5** Jb 20:12–16.
**59:7** Prv 1:15, 19; 2:8–9, 12–13, 15, 18–19; Rom 3:15.
**59:9** Am 5:18–19.
**59:11** Is 38:14.
**59:14** Jb 28:28.
**59:17** Wis 5:17–20; Eph 6:14–16; 1 Thes 5:8.
**59:20** Is 35:4; Rom 11:26–27.
**59:21** Is 1:27.

## The Dawning of Divine Glory for Zion

**60** ¹† Arise! Shine, for your light has
come,
the glory of the LORD has dawned
upon you.*
² Though darkness covers the earth,
and thick clouds, the peoples,
Upon you the LORD will dawn,
and over you his glory will be seen.
³ Nations shall walk by your light,
kings by the radiance of your
dawning.*

## The Nations Come to Zion

⁴ Raise your eyes and look about;
they all gather and come to you—
Your sons from afar,
your daughters in the arms of their
nurses.*
⁵ Then you shall see and be radiant,
your heart shall throb and overflow.
For the riches of the sea shall be poured
out before you,
the wealth of nations shall come to
you.
⁶ Caravans of camels shall cover you,
dromedaries of Midian and Ephah;
All from Sheba shall come
bearing gold and frankincense,
and heralding the praises of the LORD.
⁷ All the flocks of Kedar shall be gathered
for you,
the rams of Nebaioth shall serve your
needs;
They will be acceptable offerings on my
altar,
and I will glorify my glorious house.
⁸ Who are these that fly along like a
cloud,
like doves to their cotes?
⁹ The vessels of the coastlands are
gathering,
with the ships of Tarshish in the lead,
To bring your children from afar,
their silver and gold with them—
For the name of the LORD, your God,

for the Holy One of Israel who has
glorified you.

## Honor and Service for Zion†

¹⁰ Foreigners shall rebuild your walls,
their kings shall minister to you;
Though in my wrath I struck you,
yet in my good will I have shown you
mercy.*
¹¹ Your gates shall stand open constantly;
day and night they shall not be closed
So that they may bring you the wealth of
nations,
with their kings in the vanguard.*
¹² For the nation or kingdom that will not
serve you shall perish;
such nations shall be utterly
destroyed!*
¹³ The glory of Lebanon shall come to you—
the juniper, the fir, and the cypress all
together—
To bring beauty to my sanctuary,
and glory to the place where I stand.*
¹⁴ The children of your oppressors shall
come,
bowing before you;
All those who despised you,
shall bow low at your feet.
They shall call you "City of the LORD,"
"Zion of the Holy One of Israel."
¹⁵ No longer forsaken and hated,
with no one passing through,
Now I will make you the pride of the
ages,
a joy from generation to generation.
¹⁶ You shall suck the milk of nations,
and be nursed at royal breasts;
And you shall know that I, the LORD, am
your savior,
your redeemer, the Mighty One of
Jacob.
¹⁷ Instead of bronze I will bring gold,
instead of iron I will bring silver;
Instead of wood, bronze;
instead of stones, iron.
I will appoint peace your governor,
and justice your ruler.*

---

† **60:1–9** The light the prophet proclaims to Zion symbolizes the blessing to come to her: the glory of the Lord, the return of her children, the wealth of nations who themselves will walk by her light. The passage is famous from its use in the Latin liturgy for the feast of Epiphany.

**60:10–18** The glorious promises for the future continue: the wealth of the nations (vv. 5, 10), tribute from kings, glorification of the Temple, peace and justice (cf. Ps 85:11).

* **60:1** Is 40:5; 49:14–26; 51:17–23.
**60:3** Is 42:6; 45:14; 49:6.
**60:4** Is 49:18.
**60:10** Is 54:11–12.
**60:11** Rev 21:25.
**60:12** Is 61:2.
**60:13** Is 35:2; 66:1.
**60:17** Ps 85:11.

18 No longer shall violence be heard of in
    your land,
  or plunder and ruin within your
    borders.
You shall call your walls "Salvation"
  and your gates "Praise."

## Eternal Light for Zion

19† No longer shall the sun
  be your light by day,
Nor shall the brightness of the moon
  give you light by night;
Rather, the LORD will be your light
  forever,
  your God will be your glory.*
20 No longer will your sun set,
  or your moon wane;
For the LORD will be your light forever,
  and the days of your grieving will be
    over.
21 Your people will all be just;
  for all time they will possess the land;
They are the shoot that I planted,
  the work of my hands, that I might be
    glorified.*
22 The least one shall become a clan,
  the smallest, a mighty nation;
I, the LORD, will swiftly accomplish
  these things when the time comes.*

## The Anointed Bearer of Glad Tidings

**61** ¹† The spirit of the Lord GOD is
    upon me,
  because the LORD has anointed me;
He has sent me to bring good news to
    the afflicted,
  to bind up the brokenhearted,
To proclaim liberty to the captives,
  release to the prisoners,*
2 To announce a year of favor from the
    LORD
  and a day of vindication by our God;
To comfort all who mourn;*
3   to place on those who mourn in Zion
  a diadem instead of ashes,

To give them oil of gladness instead of
    mourning,
  a glorious mantle instead of a faint
    spirit.

## Restoration and Blessing

They will be called oaks of justice,
  the planting of the LORD to show his
    glory.
4 They shall rebuild the ancient ruins,
  the former wastes they shall raise up
And restore the desolate cities,
  devastations of generation upon
    generation.*
5 Strangers shall stand ready to pasture
    your flocks,
  foreigners shall be your farmers and
    vinedressers.
6† You yourselves shall be called "Priests of
    the LORD,"
  "Ministers of our God" you shall be
    called.
You shall eat the wealth of the nations
  and in their riches you will boast.*
7 Because their shame was twofold†
  and disgrace was proclaimed their
    portion,
They will possess twofold in their own
    land;
  everlasting joy shall be theirs.*

## God's Word of Promise

8 For I, the LORD, love justice,
  I hate robbery and wrongdoing;
I will faithfully give them their
    recompense,
  an everlasting covenant I will make
    with them.*
9 Their offspring shall be renowned
    among the nations,
  and their descendants in the midst of
    the peoples;
All who see them shall acknowledge them:
  "They are offspring the LORD has
    blessed."

---

**60:19–20** The theme of light is taken up again, but in an apocalyptic vein: the Lord's radiant presence replaces physical light.

**61:1–2** The prophet proclaims that he has been anointed by the Lord to bring good news (cf. 40:9) to the afflicted and to comfort Zion. The background to the "year of favor" is the jubilee year of release from debts (Lv 25:10–11; Is 49:8).

**61:6** The bestowal of a new name suggests a new identity and mission. The whole people will be priests (cf. Ex 19:6), even ministering to nations who will serve God's people.

**61:7** *Twofold*: Israel was punished double for infidelity (40:2); the blessings of its restoration will also be double.

**60:19** Is 2:5; Rev 21:23; 22:5.
**60:21** Is 57:13c.
**60:22** Gn 12:2; 17:6.
**61:1** Is 40:9; 42:1; 48:16; 52:7; 58:7; Lk 4:18–19.
**61:2** Mt 5:4.
**61:4** Is 58:12.
**61:6** Ex 19:6; 1 Pt 2:9.
**61:7** Is 40:2.
**61:8** Is 55:3; 54:9–10; 59:21.

## Thanksgiving for God's Deliverance

10† I will rejoice heartily in the LORD,
     my being exults in my God;
   For he has clothed me with garments of
        salvation,
     and wrapped me in a robe of justice,
   Like a bridegroom adorned with a
        diadem,
     as a bride adorns herself with her
        jewels.*
11 As the earth brings forth its shoots,
     and a garden makes its seeds spring up,
   So will the Lord GOD make justice spring
        up,
     and praise before all the nations.

## A New Name for Zion

**62** ¹† For Zion's sake I will not be silent,
       for Jerusalem's sake I will not keep
        still,
   Until her vindication shines forth like
        the dawn
     and her salvation like a burning
        torch.*
2  Nations shall behold your vindication,
     and all kings your glory;
   You shall be called by a new name
     bestowed by the mouth of the LORD.*
3  You shall be a glorious crown in the
        hand of the LORD,
     a royal diadem in the hand of your
        God.
4  No more shall you be called "Forsaken,"
     nor your land called "Desolate,"
   But you shall be called "My Delight is in
        her,"
     and your land "Espoused."
   For the LORD delights in you,
     and your land shall be espoused.*
5  For as a young man marries a virgin,
     your Builder shall marry you;
   And as a bridegroom rejoices in his
        bride
     so shall your God rejoice in you.

6  Upon your walls, Jerusalem,
     I have stationed sentinels;
   By day and by night,
     they shall never be silent.
   You who are to remind the LORD,
     take no rest,
7  And give him no rest,
     until he re-establishes Jerusalem
   And makes it the praise of the earth.

## The Blessings of Salvation for God's People

8† The LORD has sworn by his right hand
     and by his mighty arm:
   No more will I give your grain
     as food to your enemies;
   Nor shall foreigners drink the wine,
     for which you toiled.*
9  But those who harvest shall eat,
     and praise the LORD;
   Those who gather shall drink
     in my holy courts.*
10† Pass through, pass through the gates,
     prepare a way for the people;*
   Build up, build up the highway, clear it
        of stones,
     raise up a standard over the nations.
11 The LORD has proclaimed
     to the ends of the earth:
   Say to daughter Zion,
     "See, your savior comes!
   See, his reward is with him,
     his recompense before him."*
12 They shall be called "The Holy People,"
     "The Redeemed of the LORD."
   And you shall be called "Cared For,"
     "A City Not Forsaken."*

## The Divine Warrior†

**63** ¹Who is this that comes from Edom,
       in crimsoned garments, from Bozrah?
   Who is this, glorious in his apparel,
     striding in the greatness of his
        strength?
   "It is I, I who announce vindication,
     mighty to save."*

---

**61:10–11** The new life of the restored Zion is expressed in nuptial (cf. also 62:5) and agricultural (cf. v. 3; 60:21) imagery.
**62:1–12** As in chap. 60, the prophet addresses Zion, announcing the reversal of her fortune. Several motifs reappear: light and glory (60:1–3, 19–20), tribute of nations (60:11), and especially the marriage (61:10; cf. also 54:5–8).
**62:8–9** Peace and prosperity are indicated by the absence of invaders who would live off the land.
**62:10–11** The gates of Babylon are to be opened for the exiles to return, led by the Lord, as in 40:3–5, 10.

**63:1–6** Two questions are raised at the approach of a majestic figure coming from Edom. It is the Lord, his garments red with the blood from the judgment battle. Edom (its capital Bozrah) plundered Judah after the fall of Jerusalem; cf. 34:5–17. *Wine press*: here a symbol of a bloody judgment; cf. Lam 1:15; Jl 4:13.

**61:10** 1 Sm 2:1; Ps 138:1–2.
**62:1** Is 42:14; 64:11.
**62:2** Rev 2:17; 3:12.
**62:4** Is 49:15–16; 54:7–8.
**62:8** Is 52:10.
**62:9** Dt 12:17–18; 14:23.
**62:10** Is 58:14.
**62:11** Is 40:10.
**62:12** Is 62:4.
**63:1** Is 34:6; 49:19.

2     Why is your apparel red,
      and your garments like one who
        treads the wine press?*

3     "The wine press I have trodden alone,
      and from the peoples no one was
        with me.
    I trod them in my anger,
      and trampled them down in my wrath;
    Their blood spurted on my garments,
      all my apparel I stained.

4     For a day of vindication was in my heart,
      my year for redeeming had come.*

5     I looked about, but there was no one to
      help,
    I was appalled that there was no one
      to lend support;
    So my own arm brought me victory
      and my own wrath lent me support.*

6     I trampled down the peoples in my
      anger,
    I made them drunk in my wrath,
    and I poured out their blood upon
      the ground."

### Prayer for the Return of God's Favor

7†   The loving deeds of the LORD I will recall,
      the glorious acts of the LORD,
    Because of all the LORD has done for us,
      the immense goodness to the house
        of Israel,
    Which he has granted according to his
      mercy
      and his many loving deeds.*

8     He said: "They are indeed my people,
      children who are not disloyal."
    So he became their savior

9     in their every affliction.
    It was not an envoy or a messenger,
      but his presence that saved them.
    Because of his love and pity
      the LORD redeemed them,
    Lifting them up and carrying them
      all the days of old.*

10    But they rebelled
      and grieved his holy spirit;
    So he turned to become their enemy,
      and warred against them.*

11 Then they remembered the days of old, of
Moses, his servant:
    Where is the one who brought up out of
      the sea
      the shepherd of his flock?
    Where is the one who placed in their
      midst
      his holy spirit,*

12    Who guided Moses by the hand,
      with his glorious arm?
    Where is the one who divided the waters
      before them—
      winning for himself an everlasting
        renown—

13    Who guided them through the depths,
      like horses in open country?

14    As cattle going down into the valley,
      they did not stumble.
    The spirit of the LORD guided them.
    Thus you led your people,
      to make for yourself a glorious name.

15    Look down from heaven and regard us
      from your holy and glorious palace!
    Where is your zealous care and your
      might,
      your surge of pity?*
    Your mercy hold not back!

16    For you are our father.
    Were Abraham not to know us,
      nor Israel to acknowledge us,
    You, LORD, are our father,
      our redeemer you are named from of
       old.

17    Why do you make us wander, LORD,
      from your ways,
      and harden our hearts so that we do
       not fear you?†
    Return for the sake of your servants,
      the tribes of your heritage.

18    Why have the wicked invaded your holy
      place,
      why have our enemies trampled your
       sanctuary?

19†   Too long have we been like those you do
      not rule,
      on whom your name is not invoked.

---

63:7–64:11 This lament of the exilic community recalls God's protection, and especially the memories of the exodus (vv. 7–14), before begging the Lord to come once more to their aid (63:15–64:3), as they confess their sins (64:4–11). The prayer is marked by God's "holy spirit" (63:10–11, 14) and fatherhood (63:8, 9, 16; 64:7).

63:17 The hardening of the heart (Ex 4:21; 7:3) serves to explain Israel's sins—a motif to induce the Lord to relent.

63:19–64:3 A new theophany, like Sinai of old, is invoked so that Israel's enemies will be humbled by God's intervention.

---

63:2 Rev 19:13.
63:4 Is 34:8; 61:2.
63:5 Is 59:16.
63:7 Is 26:15.
63:9 Dt 4:37–40.
63:10 Dt 32:15; Ps 51:12.
63:11 Heb 13:20.
63:15 Dt 26:15; Bar 2:16.

Oh, that you would rend the heavens
    and come down,
    with the mountains quaking before
        you, *

**64** ¹As when brushwood is set ablaze,
    or fire makes the water boil!
Then your name would be made known
        to your enemies
    and the nations would tremble before
        you,
² While you worked awesome deeds we
        could not hope for, †
³     such as had not been heard of from of
        old.
No ear has ever heard, no eye ever seen,
    any God but you
    working such deeds for those who
        wait for him. *
⁴ Would that you might meet us doing
        right,
    that we might be mindful of you in
        our ways!
Indeed, you are angry; we have sinned,
    we have acted wickedly.
⁵ We have all become like something
        unclean,
    all our just deeds are like polluted
        rags;
We have all withered like leaves,
    and our crimes carry us away like the
        wind. *
⁶ There are none who call upon your
        name,
    none who rouse themselves to take
        hold of you;
For you have hidden your face from us
    and have delivered us up to our
        crimes.

### A Final Plea

⁷† Yet, LORD, you are our father;
    we are the clay and you our potter:
    we are all the work of your hand.
⁸ Do not be so very angry, LORD,

do not remember our crimes forever;
    look upon us, who are all your
        people!
⁹ Your holy cities have become a
        wilderness;
    Zion has become wilderness,
        Jerusalem desolation! *
¹⁰ Our holy and glorious house
        in which our ancestors praised you
Has been burned with fire;
    all that was dear to us is laid waste.
¹¹ Can you hold back, LORD, after all this?
    Can you remain silent, and afflict us
        so severely?

**65** ¹† I was ready to respond to those
        who did not ask,
    to be found by those who did not
        seek me.
I said: Here I am! Here I am!
    To a nation that did not invoke my
        name. *
² I have stretched out my hands all day
        to a rebellious people,
Who walk in a way that is not good,
    following their own designs; *
³ A people who provoke me
        continually to my face,
Offering sacrifices in gardens
    and burning incense on bricks,
⁴ Sitting in tombs
    and spending the night in caves,
Eating the flesh of pigs,
    with broth of unclean meat in their
        dishes;
⁵ Crying out, "Hold back,
    do not come near me, lest I render
        you holy!" †
These things are smoke in my nostrils,
    a fire that burns all the day.
⁶ See, it stands written before me;
    I will not remain quiet until I have
        repaid in full
⁷ Your crimes and the crimes of your
        ancestors as well,

---

**64:2** The translation here omits some words repeated in the Hebrew from 63:19 ("would that you would come down, with the mountains trembling before you").

**64:7–11** The motifs of father (63:16) and creator (clay and potter, 29:16; 45:9) are adduced to move the Lord to action in view of the damage done to his "holy cities" and "glorious house."

**65:1–7** These verses serve as a response to the preceding questions about God's inaction (64:6, 11). It is not God who has been absent, but the people who have walked away from God

by idolatrous acts and rituals (vv. 3–4). That is the reason for their punishment (vv. 6–7).

**65:5** *Render you holy*: unclean food is what these people claim has made them sacred! The prophet ridicules them. Sacredness was understood as something communicable (cf. Ex 19:9–15).

* ————————
63:19 Ps 144:5; Mk 1:10.        64:9 Ps 79:1; Lam 1.
64:3 1 Cor 2:9.                 65:1 Rom 10:20.
64:5 Is 1:30; 34:4.             65:2 Rom 10:21.

I
S

says the LORD.
Since they burned incense on the
  mountains,
and insulted me on the hills,
I will at once pour out in full measure
  their recompense into their laps.

### Fate of the Just and Unjust in Israel

8†     Thus says the LORD:
As when the juice is pressed from a cluster,
  and someone says, "Do not destroy it,
  for there is still good in it,"
So will I do for the sake of my servants:
  I will not destroy them all.

9   From Jacob I will bring forth offspring,
  from Judah, those who are to possess
    my mountains;
My chosen ones shall possess the land,
  my servants shall dwell there.

10   Sharon shall become a pasture for the
    flocks,
  the Valley of Achor a resting place for
    the cattle,
  for my people who have sought me.*

11   But you who forsake the LORD,
  who forget my holy mountain,
Who spread a table for Fortune
  and fill cups of mixed wine for
    Destiny,†

12   You I will destine for the sword;
  you shall all bow down for slaughter;
Because I called and you did not answer,
  I spoke and you did not listen,
But did what is evil in my sight
  and things I do not delight in, you
    chose,*

13   therefore thus says the Lord GOD:
My servants shall eat,
  but you shall go hungry;
My servants shall drink,
  but you shall be thirsty;
My servants shall rejoice,
  but you shall be put to shame;

14   My servants shall shout
  for joy of heart,
But you shall cry out for grief of heart,
  and howl for anguish of spirit.

15   You will leave your name for a curse to
    my chosen ones
  when the Lord GOD slays you,
  and calls his servants by another
    name.

16   Whoever invokes a blessing in the land
    shall bless by the God of truth;†
Whoever takes an oath in the land
    shall swear by the God of truth;
For the hardships of the past shall be
    forgotten
  and hidden from my eyes.

### A World Renewed

17†   See, I am creating new heavens
    and a new earth;
The former things shall not be
    remembered
  nor come to mind.*

18   Instead, shout for joy and be glad
    forever
  in what I am creating.
Indeed, I am creating Jerusalem to be a
    joy
  and its people to be a delight;

19   I will rejoice in Jerusalem
  and exult in my people.
No longer shall the sound of weeping be
    heard there,
  or the sound of crying;

20   No longer shall there be in it
    an infant who lives but a few days,
  nor anyone who does not live a full
    lifetime;
One who dies at a hundred years shall
    be considered a youth,
  and one who falls short of a hundred
    shall be thought accursed.*

21   They shall build houses and live in
    them,
  they shall plant vineyards and eat
    their fruit;

22   They shall not build and others live
    there;
  they shall not plant and others eat.
As the years of a tree, so the years of my
    people;

---

† **65:8** This verse reflects the remnant theology found elsewhere in the Book of Isaiah: 1:8–9; 4:3; 6:11–13; etc.
    **65:11–12** *Destiny:* the play on words is found in the Hebrew, in which "destiny" and "destine" are *menî* and *manîthî.*
    **65:16** *God of truth:* lit., "God of Amen," i.e., the one who keeps his word.
    **65:17–18** The new creation (cf. 66:22) is described with

apocalyptic exuberance: long life, material prosperity, and so forth. As the former events in 43:18 are to be forgotten, so also the new creation wipes out memory of the first creation.

---

*

| | |
|---|---|
| **65:10** Hos 2:17. | **65:17** Is 66:22; Rev 21:1. |
| **65:12** Is 66:4; Prv 1:24; Jer 7:13. | **65:20** Dt 4:40. |

and my chosen ones shall long enjoy
   the work of their hands.
23 They shall not toil in vain,
   nor beget children for sudden
      destruction;
   For they shall be a people blessed by the
      LORD
   and their descendants with them.
24 Before they call, I will answer;
   while they are yet speaking, I will
      hear.
25† The wolf and the lamb shall pasture
      together,
   and the lion shall eat hay like the
      ox—
   but the serpent's food shall be dust.*
None shall harm or destroy
   on all my holy mountain, says the
      LORD.

### True and False Worship

**66** ¹† Thus says the LORD:
The heavens are my throne,
   the earth, my footstool.
What house can you build for me?
   Where is the place of my rest?*
2 My hand made all these things
   when all of them came to be—oracle
      of the LORD.
This is the one whom I approve:
   the afflicted one, crushed in spirit,
   who trembles at my word.*
3† The one slaughtering an ox, striking a
      man,
   sacrificing a lamb, breaking a dog's
      neck,
Making an offering of pig's blood,
   burning incense, honoring an idol—
These have chosen their own ways,
   and taken pleasure in their own
      abominations.*
4 I in turn will choose affliction for them
   and bring upon them what they fear.
Because when I called, no one answered,

when I spoke, no one listened.
Because they did what was evil in my
      sight,
   and things I do not delight in they
      chose,*
5 Hear the word of the LORD,
   you who tremble at his word!
Your kin who hate you
   and cast you out because of my name
      say,
"May the LORD show his glory,
   that we may see your joy";
   but they shall be put to shame.
6 A voice roaring from the city,
   a voice from the temple;
The voice of the LORD
   rendering recompense to his
      enemies!*

### Blessings of Prosperity and Consolation

7† Before she is in labor,
   she gives birth;*
Before her pangs come upon her,
   she delivers a male child.
8 Who ever heard of such a thing,
   or who ever saw the like?
Can a land be brought forth in one day,
   or a nation be born in a single
      moment?
Yet Zion was scarcely in labor
   when she bore her children.
9 Shall I bring a mother to the point of
      birth,
   and yet not let her child be born? says
      the LORD.
Or shall I who bring to birth
   yet close her womb? says your God.
10† Rejoice with Jerusalem and be glad
      because of her,
   all you who love her;
Rejoice with her in her joy,
   all you who mourn over her—*
11 So that you may nurse and be satisfied
   from her consoling breast;

---

† **65:25** The imagery reflects the ideal era described in 11:6–9; see note there.
**66:1–2** The Lord rejects the abuses associated with Temple worship in order to emphasize his concern for the sincere worshiper.
**66:3–6** The sacrificial abuses listed will only merit punishment. The true worshipers, the downtrodden, are those who "tremble" (vv. 2, 5) at God's word. Although they are ridiculed by those who reject them (v. 5), the latter will be afflicted with divine punishment; their "choice" will be met by the Lord's choice (v. 4).
**66:7–9** The renewal of Zion is pictured in terms of a miracu-

lous, instantaneous birth, facilitated by God's intervention.
**66:10–16** The poet addresses the children born of Jerusalem, their mother. In v. 13 the metaphor switches to the Lord as mother (cf. 49:15), comforting her charges but destroying the enemies.

---

**65:25** Is 11:6–9.
**66:1** 2 Sm 7:4–7; 1 Kgs 8:27; Acts 7:49; 17:24.
**66:2** Ps 24:1–2.
**66:3** Lv 11:7.
**66:4** Is 65:12; Prv 1:24; Jer 7:13.
**66:6** Jl 4:16; Am 1:2.
**66:7–9** Is 49:18–21; 54:1.
**66:10** Tb 13:14.

I
S

That you may drink with delight
    at her abundant breasts!
12    For thus says the LORD:
I will spread prosperity over her like a
    river,
    like an overflowing torrent,
    the wealth of nations.
You shall nurse, carried in her arms,
    cradled upon her knees;
13    As a mother comforts her child,
    so I will comfort you;
    in Jerusalem you shall find your
      comfort.*
14    You will see and your heart shall exult,
    and your bodies shall flourish like the
      grass;
The LORD's power shall be revealed to
    his servants,
    but to his enemies, his wrath.
15    For see, the LORD will come in fire,
    his chariots like the stormwind;
To wreak his anger in burning rage
    and his rebuke in fiery flames.
16    For with fire the LORD shall enter into
      judgment,
    and, with his sword, against all flesh;
    Those slain by the LORD shall be
      many.*

17† Those who sanctify and purify themselves to go into the gardens, following one
who stands within, eating pig's flesh, abominable things, and mice, shall all together come
to an end, with their deeds and purposes—oracle of the LORD.

---

66:17 This verse seems to have some connection with
65:2–3.

**66:18–21** God summons the neighboring nations to Zion and
from among them will send some to far distant lands to proclaim
the divine glory. *All your kin*: Jews in exile. The "gathering of the
people and the nations" is an eschatological motif common in
the prophetic tradition; cf. 56:8.

**God Gathers the Nations.** 18† I am coming
to gather all nations and tongues; they shall
come and see my glory.* 19 I will place a sign
among them; from them I will send survivors to the nations: to Tarshish, Put and Lud,
Mosoch, Tubal and Javan, to the distant coastlands which have never heard of my fame, or
seen my glory; and they shall proclaim my
glory among the nations. 20 They shall bring
all your kin from all the nations as an offering to the LORD, on horses and in chariots, in
carts, upon mules and dromedaries, to Jerusalem, my holy mountain, says the LORD, just
as the Israelites bring their grain offering in a
clean vessel to the house of the LORD. 21 Some
of these I will take as priests and Levites, says
the LORD.

22    Just as the new heavens and the new
      earth
    which I am making
    Shall endure before me—oracle of the
      LORD—
    so shall your descendants and your
      name endure.*
23    From new moon to new moon,
    and from sabbath to sabbath,
All flesh shall come to worship
    before me, says the LORD.*
24†    They shall go out and see the corpses*
    of the people who rebelled against me;
For their worm shall not die,
    their fire shall not be extinguished;
    and they shall be an abhorrence to all
      flesh.

---

**66:24** God's enemies lie dead outside the walls of the New Jerusalem; just as in the past, corpses, filth and refuse lay in the Valley of Hinnom (Gehenna) outside the city; cf. 34:1–4; 2 Kgs 23:10.

**66:13** Is 40:1; 49:13.     **66:22** Is 65:17; Rev 21:1.
**66:16** Lv 11:29.     **66:23** Is 1:13.
**66:18** Is 56:1, 8; 59:20.     **66:24** Is 1:27–28; Mk 9:45.

IS

# The Book of

# Jeremiah

## INTRODUCTION

Carol J. Dempsey, OP

One of the most complex and engaging books of the Old Testament is the book of Jeremiah. Jeremiah, one of the book's main characters, is appointed by God to be a prophet to the nations (Jer 1:4–10), a divinely initiated vocation that, according to the biblical story, occurs at the time of his conception (1:5). Though reluctant at first (1:6), he eventually fulfills the role of his office. His mission is challenging, and he often complains to God (e.g., 12:1–4) and wonders why he came forth from the womb to see sorrow and shame and end his days in pain (20:18; see also vv. 7–17). Yet he remains a prophet of hope. In the final words of his call narrative, he is commissioned "to build and to plant" (1:10), and anticipating a return to the land and a resettlement on it after his people are freed from exile, Jeremiah buys a field (32:1–15). Although the fall of Jerusalem does happen and the collapse of Judah does occur, destruction and devastation will not be the final words for the Judahites.

## Historical, Religious, and Social World of Jeremiah

According to the book's superscription, Jeremiah was called to be a prophet in the days of Josiah, Jehoiakim, and Zedekiah (Jer 1:2–3). Supposedly Jeremiah lived during the period between 627 BCE and approximately 581 BCE, a time plagued by much social and political upheaval and religious unrest. Although many important international events occurred during Jeremiah's lifetime, perhaps the three most important events were the religious reforms of Josiah in 622 BCE, the destruction of Jerusalem and the collapse of Judah in 587 BCE, and the exile of many of Judah's leaders and citizens before and after 587 BCE.

On the geopolitical scale, Jeremiah began

## Outline of Jeremiah

I.   Oracles in the Days of Josiah (1:1–6:30)

II.  Oracles Primarily from the Days of Jehoiakim (7:1–20:18)

III. Oracles in the Last Years of Jerusalem (21:1–25:38)

IV.  The Temple Sermon (26:1–24; cf. 7:1–15)

V.   Controversies with the False Prophets (27:1–29:32)

VI.  Oracles of the Restoration of Israel and Judah (30:1–35:19)

VII. Jeremiah and the Fall of Jerusalem (36:1–45:5)

VIII. Oracles Against the Nations (46:1–51:64)

IX.  Historical Appendix (52:1–34)

preaching when Assyria was declining and Egypt and Babylon were in conflict with each other over the control of Syria-Palestine. After Ashurbanipal, Assyria's last great king, died in 627 BCE, Assyria was no longer able to resist the Babylonians, who became the dominant power in the region. This loss of Assyrian control in Syria-Palestine allowed Judah to have a slightly more independent stance.

On the home front of Judah, the end of the seventh century BCE was a perilous time. Josiah reigned from 640 to 609 BCE. By this time, the political and religious atmosphere in Judah had changed significantly. Many of the people had become engaged in non-Yahwistic cults and practices in both the Temple and at the high places or shrines, to the point that the essential distinction between Israel's God and the pagan gods had been obscured (Jer 2:20; 3:1, 6, 8). Covenant had been violated (11:1–7); idolatry and apostasy were on the rise. Socially, the decay of the national religion brought contempt for the law along with violence and injustice (2:1–28; 5:26–28; 6:13–15; 7:9; 9:1–8; 32:30–35). Ironically, despite all of their wrongdoings, the people maintained their innocence (8:6), which caused Israel's God to become infuriated (8:4–17). Such conditions caused Josiah to attempt a complete religious reform (see 2 Kgs 22:8–23:3). Though extensive and far-reaching, the reform was short-lived. As a prophet, Jeremiah would probably have supported these reforms, though his book makes no mention of them.

After the death of Josiah, a series of incompetent kings, especially Jehoiakim, led the people of Judah into deeper ruin and depravity. Jeremiah tried to advise Jehoiakim but to no avail (see Jer 36). In 601 BCE Jehoiakim rebelled against Babylonian rule, and in response Babylon advanced against Jerusalem. Jehoiakim died in the siege, and his son, Jehoiachin, who reigned only for three months before Jerusalem fell, was exiled to Babylon, along with many of Judah's leading citizens (22:24–30).

Following the exile of Jehoiachin, the Babylonians set up Zedekiah as Judah's ruler. Zedekiah was also one of Josiah's sons and uncle to Jehoiachin. As king, Zedekiah was not successful in maintaining an effective relationship with Babylon. According to the biblical story, Zedekiah was the only king with whom Jeremiah had had personal contact. He consistently advised Zedekiah to submit to the yoke of Babylon (Jer 21:1–14; 27:12; 32:1–5; 34:1–7; 37–38), but the king refused to heed such advice and rebelled against Babylon (52:3). In the end, Babylon attacked Jerusalem, destroyed the Temple and city, killed Zedekiah's sons and Judah's officers, blinded and bound the king, and exiled him to Babylon where he was put in prison until he died (52:6–11). Finally, Nebuchadrezzar appointed Gedaliah, a prominent Judean citizen, as head over Judah. Jeremiah was not exiled to Babylon because he did not rebel against the Babylonians. Instead, he became involved with advising those

Judeans who were left in the land. Gedaliah eventually died at the hands of a group of anti-Babylonian zealots, which resulted in the further exile of more Judeans around 582 BCE.

These were the conditions under which the prophet Jeremiah delivered his stinging judgment proclamations (e.g., Jer 17:1–4). His speeches, however, were not all foreboding. Persistently he pleaded with the people to repent and return to their God and to re-establish right relationship (15:19–21; 26:12–13). He also announced promises of eventual restoration (31:1–26, 31–34, 38–40) that became a source of hope for those living in exile.

# Literary Dimensions of Jeremiah

One interesting literary feature about the book of Jeremiah is the fact that it has been preserved in two significantly different versions, namely the Hebrew version found in the Masoretic Text (MT) and the Greek version found in the Septuagint (LXX). The ancient Greek version is about three thousand words shorter than the Hebrew text, and the ordering of the texts is quite different from version to version. For example, the proclamations to the nations occur in Jer 46–51 in the MT but in the LXX they follow the first half of 25:13 and occur in chs. 25–31. Additionally, in the LXX the list of nations being addressed is ordered differently from the MT. Both the MT and the LXX have the same number of chapters, and even though the LXX is shorter, it has approximately 307 words that the MT does not have and has less repeated material than does the MT. The LXX version was not fully appreciated until the discovery and analysis of the Dead Sea Scrolls, which revealed that several Hebrew scrolls of Jeremiah were the same length as the LXX version. Scholars who once thought that the brevity of the LXX was the result of vagaries of translation now had to give greater credence to the LXX in their research and analysis of the book of Jeremiah.

The structure of the book of Jeremiah has raised many questions. The text is not arranged chronologically. For example, ch. 25 seems to reflect events during the reign of Jehoiakim in 605 BCE, and the events in ch. 26 seem to be from around 609 BCE, an earlier time in Jehoiakim's reign. Furthermore, ch. 28 reflects the time around 594 BCE when Zedekiah was king. The seemingly random arrangements of events may reflect decisions of editors to highlight various periods instead of giving a historical sequence of events in Jeremiah's life. The book as a whole seems to fall neatly into two parts: chs. 2–24 and 26–51. Chapter 25 functions as a hinge between the two parts; ch. 1 is an introductory chapter, and ch. 52 is an epilogue. Thus the book is a collection of materials that emerged at various times and places, which makes the dating of the book virtually impossible. Finally, scholars generally agree that the book's present form took shape over an extended period of time.

Another interesting literary aspect of the book of Jeremiah is the presence of the character Baruch, a scribe and son of Neriah (Jer 32:16). Jeremiah 36:4 and 45:1 refer to Jeremiah dictating a large collection of his proclamations to Baruch, who supposedly wrote them on a scroll. This event may have been the starting point for the preservation and written transmission of Jeremiah's proclamations. Chapters 26–45 contain biographical or historical narratives that indicate that Baruch may have recorded other events in Jeremiah's life. Scholars today debate how much of the text is authentic to Jeremiah. Parts of the book present the words of Jeremiah in first person; other parts consist of third-person narratives about Jeremiah. What is clear, however, is that the text contains many editorial reflections, some of which bear strong resemblance to the style, vocabulary, and perspective of the book of Deuteronomy, the Deuteronomistic History (Joshua, Judges, 1–2 Samuel, and 1–2 Kings), and the Deuteronomists, who were active during this time. Hence quite possibly editors who had been at work on the texts of Deuteronomy and the Deuteronomistic History may have had some role in editing Jeremiah as well.

Composed of both poetry and prose, the book contains many literary forms, such as the famous Temple Sermon (Jer 7 and 26) and the so-called "confessions" or laments in which Jeremiah pours out his heart to God (e.g., 12:1–6; 15:15, 16–21; 17:14–18; 18:19–23;

20:7–18). In these laments, the persona of the prophet comes to life. The text also contains a parable (18:1–12), prayers (32:16–25), a vision report (1:11–13; 24:1–10), disputations (2:23–25; 3:1–5; 8:8–9), letters (ch. 29), and proclamations of disaster (4:1–18) and salvation (chs. 30–31), among other literary forms. Some prominent topics include conflicts among prophets (chs. 27–28) and Jeremiah's persecutions (20:1–6; 38:1–6). Additionally, the book contains multiple voices and dialogues between God and Jeremiah, as well as several stories laden with symbolic actions that point to Judah's impending devastation and the eventual restoration of Israel as a whole (e.g., 13:1–11; 16:1–13; 19:1–15; 25:15–29; 27:1–22; and 32:1–15). Israel's God will make a new covenant and give the people a new law to be written on their hearts (31:31–34). The book as a whole tells the story of a people struggling to live life under the peril of threat and the hope of promise.

## Theological Themes

Much of the book of Jeremiah consists of announcements of doom and proclamations of hope. Jeremiah's theological perspective reflects the influence of both the Exodus and Wisdom traditions as well as many of the other concerns voiced by earlier prophets. The God in whom Jeremiah believes is the God of creation, who "knows" people, events, what is to come, who "remembers" (Jer 2:2; 14:10), who not only sees but also acts. This God is perceived to be a righteous judge (11:20), one who is merciful (3:12), but who can also be overpowering (20:7).

For Jeremiah, God's "word" is central to his vocation, mission, and ministry as a preacher. The divine word moves Jeremiah to proclaim weal and woe, hope and comfort. The word brings him to a deeper awareness of what is and what can be. This word is all-consuming (Jer 20:9).

Two major themes running through the book are sin-judgment and repentance-redemption-salvation, both of which entail a theology of suffering. Jeremiah's community suffers because of its estrangement from God and its own powerlessness in the face of three powerful nations: Egypt, Assyria, and Babylon. Jeremiah suffers because he sees what is to befall his people on account of their choices. He experiences pain from having done the "right thing" demanded by his vocation, and he feels deeply the pain and pathos of God, who agonizes over the people's infidelities, transgressions, and lack of love.

Despite all of these hardships, however, the book of Jeremiah presents a theology of hope first expressed in Jer 1:10. This message of hope is at the heart of many of Jeremiah's symbolic actions such as buying a patch of land (32:1–15), which will come to symbolize the people's resettlement in the land. Finally, the vision of the new covenant anticipates the time when Israel will once again be a united nation in right relationship with God and with one another.

The book of Jeremiah also provides an insight into the role of prayer in relation to the prophetic vocation. Jeremiah is a person of profound prayer who prays to God and makes intercession on behalf of his wayward community. God, however, is completely disgusted with the people's actions and instructs Jeremiah not to pray for the people (Jer 7:16–20; 11:14), but rather to lament on behalf of the community (14:17–22). Jeremiah also offers a prayer of trust to God (16:19–21) and asks for understanding (32:16–25). For Jeremiah, prayer is a simple yet dynamic conversation with God. Jeremiah draws God into his pain and suffering throughout his prophetic ministry (4:19–26; 6:10–11; 8:18–23; 10:19–25; 11:18–12:6; 15:15–21; 17:14–18; 18:18–23; 20:7–18). Jeremiah shows people then and now how to let go to God.

In sum, the book of Jeremiah is a rich text that draws its readers into the heart of a prophet, the heart of the prophetic vocation, and essentially, into the heart of God. ■

# THE BOOK OF JEREMIAH

## New American Bible, Introduction

The Book of Jeremiah combines history, biography, and prophecy. It portrays a nation in crisis and introduces the reader to an extraordinary person whom the Lord called to prophesy under the trying circumstances of the final days of the kingdom of Judah. Jeremiah was born, perhaps about 650 B.C., of a priestly family from the village of Anathoth, two and a half miles northeast of Jerusalem. He was called to his task in the thirteenth year of King Josiah (Jer 1:2). Josiah's reform, begun with enthusiasm and hope, ended with his death on the battlefield of Megiddo (609 B.C.) as he attempted to stop the northward march of the Egyptian Pharaoh Neco, who was going to provide assistance to the Assyrians who were in retreat before the Babylonians.

Nineveh, the capital of Assyria, fell in 612 B.C., preparing the way for the new colossus, Babylon, which was soon to put an end to the independence of Judah.

The prophet supported the reform of King Josiah (2 Kgs 22–23), but after the death of Josiah the old idolatry returned. Jeremiah opposed this as well as royal policy toward Babylon. Arrest, imprisonment, and public disgrace were his lot. In the nation's apostasy Jeremiah saw the sealing of its doom. Nebuchadnezzar captured Jerusalem (598 B.C.) and carried King Jehoiachin into exile (Jer 22:24).

During the years 598–587, Jeremiah counseled Zedekiah in the face of bitter opposition. The false prophet Hananiah proclaimed that the yoke of Babylon was broken and a strong pro-Egyptian party in Jerusalem induced Zedekiah to revolt. Nebuchadnezzar took swift vengeance; Jerusalem was destroyed in 587 and its leading citizens sent into exile.

The prophet remained in Jerusalem, but was later forced into Egyptian exile. We do not know the details of his death. The influence of Jeremiah was greater after his death than before. The exiled community read and meditated on the lessons of the prophet; his influence is evident in Ezekiel, some of the psalms, Is 40–66, and Daniel. In the postexilic period, the Book of Jeremiah circulated in various editions.

The book may be divided as follows:
I. Oracles in the Days of Josiah (1:1–6:30)
II. Oracles Primarily from the Days of Jehoiakim (7:1–20:18)
III. Oracles in the Last Years of Jerusalem (21:1–25:38)
IV. The Temple Sermon (26:1–24; cf. 7:1–15)
V. Controversies with the False Prophets (27:1–29:32)
VI. Oracles of the Restoration of Israel and Judah (30:1–35:19)
VII. Jeremiah and the Fall of Jerusalem (36:1–45:5)
VIII. Oracles Against the Nations (46:1–51:64)
IX. Historical Appendix (52:1–34) ■

# JEREMIAH

## I. ORACLES IN THE DAYS OF JOSIAH

**1** ¹The words of Jeremiah, son of Hilkiah, one of the priests from Anathoth,† in the land of Benjamin. ²The word of the LORD came to him in the days of Josiah, son of Amon, king of Judah, in the thirteenth year of his reign,* ³and again in the days of Jehoiakim, son of Josiah, king of Judah, until the end of the eleventh year of Zedekiah, son of Josiah, king of Judah—down to the exile of Jerusalem, in the fifth month.*

### Call of Jeremiah

4    The word of the LORD came to me:
5    Before I formed you in the womb I
          knew you,
        before you were born I dedicated you,
        a prophet to the nations I appointed
          you.†*
6    "Ah, Lord GOD!" I said,
        "I do not know how to speak. I am
          too young!"†
7    But the LORD answered me,
     Do not say, "I am too young."
        To whomever I send you, you shall go;
        whatever I command you, you shall
          speak.
8    Do not be afraid of them,
        for I am with you to deliver you—
          oracle of the LORD.

⁹Then the LORD extended his hand and touched my mouth, saying to me,

        See, I place my words in your mouth!*
10       Today I appoint you
          over nations and over kingdoms,

To uproot and to tear down,
        to destroy and to demolish,
        to build and to plant.

¹¹The word of the LORD came to me: What do you see, Jeremiah? "I see a branch of the almond tree,"† I replied. ¹²Then the LORD said to me: You have seen well, for I am watching over my word to carry it out. ¹³* A second time the word of the LORD came to me: What do you see? I replied, "I see a boiling kettle whose mouth is tipped away from the north."†

¹⁴The LORD said to me, And from the north evil will pour out over all who dwell in the land.*

15       Look, I am summoning
          all the kingdoms of the north—oracle
            of the LORD—
        Each king shall come and set up his
          throne
          in the gateways of Jerusalem,
        Against all its surrounding walls
          and against all the cities of Judah.*
16       I will pronounce my sentence against
          them
          for all their wickedness in forsaking
            me,
        In burning incense to other gods,
          in bowing down to the works of their
            hands.*
17       But you, prepare yourself;
          stand up and tell them
          all that I command you.
        Do not be terrified on account of
            them,
          or I will terrify you before them;
18       For I am the one who today
          makes you a fortified city,
        A pillar of iron, a wall of bronze,
          against the whole land:
        Against Judah's kings and princes,
          its priests and the people of the land.*

---

† **1:1** *Anathoth*: a village about three miles northeast of Jerusalem, to which Solomon had exiled Abiathar the priest (1 Kgs 2:26–27); it is likely that Jeremiah belonged to that priestly family.

**1:5** Jeremiah was destined to become a prophet before his birth; cf. Is 49:1, 5; Lk 1:15; Gal 1:15–16. *I knew you*: I loved you and chose you. *I dedicated you*: I set you apart to be a prophet. *The nations*: the neighbors of Judah, along with Assyria, Babylonia, and Egypt.

**1:6** *I am too young*: like Moses (Ex 3:11, 13; 4:10), Jeremiah at first resists God's call. This narrative is perhaps patterned after the story of Moses' call in order to identify Jeremiah as the prophet "like me" in Dt 18:15.

**1:11** There is wordplay between the Hebrew noun *shaqed*, "almond tree," and the Hebrew verb *shoqed*, "watcher/watching." Because the almond tree begins to bloom in late winter in Palestine, it is called "the watcher" for the coming of spring. God is also "watcher," observing the fulfillment of the prophetic word.

**1:13** *Kettle...the north*: symbol of an invasion from the north; cf. vv. 14–15.

*

**1:2** Jer 25:3.　　　　**1:14** Jer 4:6; 6:1.
**1:3** Jer 25:1.　　　　**1:15** Jer 6:22.
**1:5** Jer 49:1; Gal 1:15–16.　**1:16** Is 2:8.
**1:9** Dt 18:18; Is 6:7.　　**1:18** Jer 6:27; 15:20; Ez
**1:13** Ez 11:3, 7; 24:3.　　　　3:8.

19     They will fight against you, but not
            prevail over you,
        for I am with you to deliver you—
            oracle of the LORD.

# 2 Infidelity of Israel.†

¹The word of the LORD came to me: ²Go, cry out this message for Jerusalem to hear!

I remember the devotion† of your
            youth,
        how you loved me as a bride,
    Following me in the wilderness,
        in a land unsown.*
3   Israel was dedicated to the LORD,
        the first fruits† of his harvest;
    All who ate of it were held guilty,
        evil befell them—oracle of the LORD.*
4   Listen to the word of the LORD, house of
            Jacob!
        All you clans of the house of Israel,
5           thus says the LORD:
    What fault did your ancestors find in me
        that they withdrew from me,
    Went after emptiness,
        and became empty themselves?*
6   They did not ask, "Where is the LORD
        who brought us up from the land of
            Egypt,
    Who led us through the wilderness,
        through a land of wastes and ravines,
    A land of drought and darkness,
        a land which no one crosses,
        where no one dwells?"*
7   I brought you into the garden land
        to eat its fine fruits,
    But you entered and defiled my land,
        you turned my heritage into an
            abomination.*
8   The priests did not ask,

        "Where is the LORD?"
    The experts in the law† did not know
            me:
        the shepherds rebelled against me.
    The prophets prophesied by Baal,
        and went after useless idols.*
9   Therefore I will again accuse you—oracle
            of the LORD—
        even your children's children I will
            accuse.*
10  Cross to the coast of Cyprus and see,
        send to Kedar† and carefully inquire:
    Where has anything like this been
            done?
11  Does any other nation change its
            gods?—
        even though they are not gods at all!
    But my people have changed their glory
        for useless things.*
12  Be horrified at this, heavens;
        shudder, be appalled—oracle of the
            LORD.
13  Two evils my people have done:
        they have forsaken me, the source of
            living waters;
    They have dug themselves cisterns,
        broken cisterns that cannot hold
            water.*
14  Is Israel a slave, a house-born servant?†
        Why then has he become plunder?
15  Against him lions roar,
        they raise their voices.
    They have turned his land into a waste;
        his cities are charred ruins, without an
            inhabitant.*
16  Yes, the people of Memphis† and
            Tahpanhes
        shave the crown of your head.
17  Has not forsaking the LORD, your God,
        done this to you?*

---

† **2:1–3:5** These chapters may contain some of Jeremiah's early preaching. He portrays Israel as the wife of the Lord, faithful only in the beginning, when she walked behind him (2:2–3, 5; 3:1). Consistent with the marriage metaphor, he describes her present unfaithfulness as adultery (2:20; 3:2–3); now she walks behind the Baals.

**2:2** *Devotion*: Heb. *hesed*; Israel's gratitude, fidelity, and love for God.

**2:3** *First fruits*: the first yield of a harvest offered as a sign of dependence on and gratitude toward the Lord of the land, thus divine property. Israel, then, is a gift made to God, set apart for his use; cf. Ex 23:19.

**2:8** *Experts in the law*: the priests. *The shepherds*: the kings and nobles.

**2:10** *Kedar*: a nomadic tribe in north Arabia. Cyprus and Kedar represent west and east.

**2:14** *House-born servant*: one born in the master's house,

in contrast to a slave acquired by purchase or as a captive; cf. Lv 22:11.

**2:16** *Memphis*: the capital of Lower Egypt. *Tahpanhes*: a frontier city of Egypt, east of the Delta. *Shave the crown of your head*: an image for Egypt plundering Judah; perhaps a reference to the capture of King Jehoahaz in 609 B.C. (2 Kgs 23:34).

**2:2** Dt 2:7; 32:9–12; Mi 6:4.
**2:3** Jer 12:14; Ex 4:22; Dt 7:6; 14:2.
**2:5** 2 Kgs 17:15; Is 5:4; Mi 6:3.
**2:6** Ex 20:2–3; Dt 8:14; Is 63:11–14.
**2:7** Lv 18:24–25; Dt 8:7–10; 32:13–14.
**2:8** Jer 8:8–9; 23:1, 13.
**2:9** Ex 20:5.
**2:11** Jer 16:20; Ps 106:20.
**2:13** Jer 17:13; Ps 36:9; Is 1:4.
**2:15** Jer 9:11.
**2:17** Jer 4:18; 30:15.

JER

18 And now, why go to Egypt,†
    to drink the waters of the Nile?
Why go to Assyria,
    to drink the waters of the River?

19 Your own wickedness chastises you,
    your own infidelities punish you.
Know then, and see, how evil and bitter
    is your forsaking the LORD, your God,
And your showing no fear of me,
    oracle of the Lord, the GOD of hosts. *

20 Long ago you broke your yoke, *
    you tore off your bonds.
You said, "I will not serve."
On every high hill, under every green
        tree,
    you sprawled and served as a
        prostitute.†

21 But I had planted you as a choice vine,
    all pedigreed stock;
How could you turn out so obnoxious
        to me,
    a spurious vine? *

22 Even if you scour it with lye,
    and use much soap,
The stain of your guilt is still before me,
    oracle of the Lord GOD. *

23 How can you say, "I am not defiled,
    I have not pursued the Baals"?
Consider your conduct in the Valley,†
    recall what you have done:
A skittish young camel,
    running back and forth,

24 a wild donkey bred in the wilderness,
Sniffing the wind in her desire—
    who can restrain her lust?
None seeking her need tire themselves;
    in her time they will find her.

25 Stop wearing out your feet
    and parching your throat!
But you say, "No use! No!
    How I love these strangers,
    after them I must go." *

26 As the thief is shamed when caught,
    so shall the house of Israel be
        shamed:
They, their kings, their princes,
    their priests and their prophets; *

27 They say to a piece of wood, "You are
        my father,"
    and to a stone, "You gave me birth."
They turn their backs to me, not their
        faces;
    yet in their time of trouble they cry
        out,
    "Rise up and save us!"

28 Where are the gods you made for
        yourselves?
    Let them rise up!
Will they save you in your time of
        trouble?
For as numerous as your cities
    are your gods, O Judah!
And as many as the streets of Jerusalem
    are the altars you have set up for
        Baal. *

29 Why are you arguing with me?
    You have all rebelled against me—
        oracle of the LORD.

30 In vain I struck your children;
    correction they did not take.
Your sword devoured your prophets
    like a ravening lion. *

31 You people of this generation,
    consider the word of the Lord:
Have I become a wilderness to Israel,
    a land of gloom?
Why then do my people say, "We have
        moved on,
    we will not come to you any more"?

32 Does a young woman forget her jewelry,
    a bride her sash?
Yet my people have forgotten me
    days without number. *

33 How well you pick your way
    when seeking love!
In your wickedness,
    you have gone by ways unclean!

34 On your clothing is
    the life-blood of the innocent,
    you did not find them committing
        burglary;

35 Nonetheless you say, "I am innocent;
    at least, his anger is turned away from
        me."

---

† **2:18** Egypt and Assyria were the competing foreign powers favored by rival parties within Judah. The desire for such foreign alliances is a further desertion of the Lord, the source of living waters (v. 13), in favor of the above-named powers, symbolized by the waters of the Nile and the Euphrates rivers.
**2:20** *Served as a prostitute*: idolatry (because Israel is the "bride" of God); cf. vv. 2–3.
**2:23** *The Valley*: probably Ben-hinnom, south of Jerusalem,

site of the sanctuary of Topheth, where children were sacrificed to Molech; cf. 7:31.

* **2:19** Prv 5:22; Hos 5:5.
**2:20** Jer 3:6, 13; Jgs 10:6.
**2:21** Ex 15:17; Ps 80:9; Is 5:4.
**2:22** Jb 9:30.
**2:25** Jer 18:12.
**2:26** Jer 48:27; Rom 6:21.
**2:28** Jer 11:13; Dt 32:38; Jgs 10:14.
**2:30** Jer 5:3; Neh 9:26.
**2:32** Jer 13:25; Dt 32:18.

JER

Listen! I will judge you
    on that word of yours, "I have not
        sinned."
36  How frivolous you have become
        in changing your course!
    By Egypt you will be shamed,
        just as you were shamed by Assyria.*
37  From there too you will go out,
        your hands upon your head;
    For the LORD has rejected those in whom
        you trust,
        with them you will have no success.*

# 3

1  If a man divorces his wife*
    and she leaves him
    and then becomes the wife of another,
Can she return to the first?†
    Would not this land be wholly
        defiled?
But you have played the prostitute with
    many lovers,
    and yet you would return to me!—
        oracle of the LORD.
2  Raise your eyes to the heights, and look,
        where have men not lain with you?
    Along the roadways you waited for them
        like an Arabian† in the wilderness.
    You defiled the land
        by your wicked prostitution.*
3  Therefore the showers were withheld,
        the spring rain did not fall.
    But because you have a prostitute's brow,
        you refused to be ashamed.*
4  Even now do you not call me, "My
        father,
        you are the bridegroom of my youth?
5  Will he keep his wrath forever,
        will he hold his grudge to the end?"
    This is what you say; yet you do
        all the evil you can.

**Judah and Israel.** 6 The LORD said to me in the days of King Josiah: Do you see what rebellious Israel has done? She has gone up every high mountain, and under every green tree

she has played the prostitute.* 7 And I thought: After she has done all this, she will return to me. But she did not return. Then, even though that traitor her sister Judah, saw 8 that, in response to all the adulteries rebel Israel had committed, I sent her away and gave her a bill of divorce, nevertheless Judah, the traitor, her sister, was not frightened; she too went off and played the prostitute.* 9 With her casual prostitution, she polluted the land, committing adultery with stone and wood.* 10 In spite of all this, Judah, the traitor, her sister, did not return to me wholeheartedly, but insincerely— oracle of the LORD.

**Restoration of Israel.** 11 Then the LORD said to me: Rebel Israel is more just than traitor Judah.* 12 Go, proclaim these words toward the north, and say:

Return, rebel Israel—oracle of the
    LORD—
    I will not remain angry with you;
For I am merciful, oracle of the LORD,
    I will not keep my anger forever.*
13  Only admit your guilt:
        how you have rebelled against the
            LORD, your God,
    How you ran here and there to strangers
        under every green tree
        and would not listen to my voice—
            oracle of the LORD.*
14  Return, rebellious children—oracle of
        the LORD—†
        for I am your master;
    I will take you, one from a city, two
            from a clan,
        and bring you to Zion.*
15  I will appoint for you shepherds after
            my own heart,
        who will shepherd you wisely and
            prudently.*
16  When you increase in number and are
            fruitful in the land—
        oracle of the LORD—

---

3:1 *Can she return to the first?*: i.e., her first husband. Here the Hebrew is emended in light of the Septuagint and Dt 24:1–4, which forbids a man to take back a woman once he has divorced her. The prophet uses this analogy to illustrate the presumption of Judah, the unfaithful wife, who assumes she can easily return to the Lord after worshiping other gods.
    3:2 *An Arabian*: here depicted as a marauder lying in wait for caravans.
    3:14–18 A remnant of Israel (v. 14) will reunite with Judah (v. 18). The former Israelite community, represented by the ark of

the covenant, will be replaced by a universal alliance, symbolized by Jerusalem, the Lord's throne, to which all nations will be gathered (v. 17).

* 
2:36 2 Chr 28:16–21.              Ez 23:11.
2:37 2 Sm 13:19.              3:9 Jer 2:27.
3:1 Dt 24:1–4.              3:11 Ez 16:51; 23:11.
3:2 Ex 16:24–25.              3:12 Dt 4:29–31.
3:3 Jer 6:15; 8:12.              3:13 Jer 2:20, 25; Lv 26:40.
3:6 Jer 2:20; Dt 12:2.              3:14 Jer 23:3; Is 10:21–22.
3:8 2 Kgs 17:6, 18–23;              3:15 Ez 34:23; Jn 21:15.

They will in those days no longer say,
  "The ark of the covenant of the LORD!"
They will no longer think of it, or
    remember it,
  or miss it, or make another one.

17 At that time they will call Jerusalem "the
LORD's throne." All nations will gather together there to honor the name of the LORD at
Jerusalem, and they will no longer stubbornly
follow their wicked heart.* 18 In those days the
house of Judah will walk alongside the house
of Israel; together they will come from the
land of the north to the land which I gave your
ancestors as a heritage.*

## Conditions for Forgiveness

19  I thought:
      How I would like to make you my
        children!
    So I gave you a pleasant land,
      the most beautiful heritage among the
        nations!
    You would call me, "My Father," I
        thought,
      and you would never turn away from
        me.*
20  But like a woman faithless to her lover,
      thus have you been faithless to me,
      house of Israel—oracle of the LORD.*
21  A cry is heard on the heights!
      the plaintive weeping of Israel's
        children,
    Because they have perverted their way,
      they have forgotten the LORD, their
        God.
22  Return, rebellious children!
      I will heal your rebellions.
    "Here we are! We belong to you,
      for you are the LORD, our God.*
23  Deceptive indeed are the hills,
      the mountains, clamorous;
    Only in the LORD our God
      is Israel's salvation.*
24  The shameful thing† has devoured

our ancestors' worth from our youth,
    Their sheep and cattle,
      their sons and daughters.
25  Let us lie down in our shame,
      let our disgrace cover us,
    for we have sinned against the LORD,
        our God,
    We and our ancestors, from our youth to
        this day;
      we did not listen to the voice of the
        LORD, our God."*

**4** 1 If you return, Israel—oracle of the
        LORD—
      return to me.
    If you put your detestable things out of
        my sight,
      and do not stray,*
2   And swear, "As the LORD lives,"†
      in truth, in judgment, and in justice,
    Then the nations shall bless themselves
        in him
      and in him glory.*

3 For to the people of Judah and Jerusalem,
thus says the LORD:

    Till your untilled ground,
      and do not sow among thorns.*
4   Be circumcised for the LORD,†
      remove the foreskins of your hearts,
      people of Judah and inhabitants of
        Jerusalem;
    Or else my anger will break out like
        fire,
      and burn so that no one can quench
        it,
      because of your evil deeds.*

## The Invasion from the North

5   Proclaim it in Judah,
      in Jerusalem announce it;
    Blow the trumpet throughout the land,
      call out, "Fill the ranks!"
    Say, "Assemble, let us march

---

**3:24** *The shameful thing*: Heb. *bosheth* ("shame"), a term often substituted for the name of Baal, a Canaanite god worshiped
at local shrines.
  **4:2** *As the LORD lives*: this oath, made sincerely, implies
Israel's return and loyal adherence to God. Thus the ancient
promises are fulfilled; cf. Gn 12:3; 18:18; 22:18; 26:4; Ps 72:17.
  **4:4** The external rite of circumcision accomplishes nothing
unless it is accompanied by the removal of blindness and obstinacy of heart. Jeremiah's view is reflected in Rom 2:25, 29; 1 Cor
7:19; Gal 5:6; 6:13, 15.

**3:17** Is 2:2.                          **4:1** Jer 25:5.
**3:18** Jer 30:3; 31:8.                  **4:2** Jer 12:16; Dt 10:20; Is
**3:19** Jer 31:9, 20; Is 63:16.              65:16.
**3:20** Jer 5:11.                        **4:3** Hos 10:12; Mt 13:7,
**3:22** Hos 3:5.                             22.
**3:23** Jer 14:8.                        **4:4** Jer 9:24.
**3:25** Jer 16:11–12; 22:21.

to the fortified cities."

6 Raise the signal—to Zion!
  Seek refuge! Don't stand there!
  Disaster I bring from the north,
  and great destruction.

7 Up comes the lion from its lair,
  the destroyer of nations has set out,
  has left its place,
  To turn your land into a desolation,
  your cities into an uninhabited
  waste.*

8 So put on sackcloth,
  mourn and wail:
  "The blazing anger of the LORD
  has not turned away from us."*

9 In that day—oracle of the LORD—
  The king will lose heart, and the
  princes;
  the priests will be horrified,
  and the prophets stunned.

10 "Ah! Lord GOD," they will say,
   "You really did deceive† us
   When you said: You shall have peace,
   while the sword was at our very
   throats."*

11 At that time it will be said
   to this people and to Jerusalem,
   A scorching wind from the bare heights
   comes
   through the wilderness toward my
   daughter, the people.†
   Not to winnow, not to cleanse,

12 a strong wind from there comes at my
   bidding.
   Now I too pronounce
   sentence upon them.*

13 See! like storm clouds he advances,
   like a whirlwind, his chariots;
   Swifter than eagles, his horses:
   "Woe to us! we are ruined."

14 Cleanse your heart of evil, Jerusalem,
   that you may be saved.
   How long will you entertain
   wicked schemes?

15 A voice proclaims it from Dan,
   announces wickedness from Mount
   Ephraim:

16 "Make this known to the nations,
   announce it against Jerusalem:
   Besiegers are coming from the distant
   land,
   shouting their war cry against the
   cities of Judah."*

17 Like watchers in the fields they surround
   her,
   for she has rebelled against me—
   oracle of the LORD.*

18 Your conduct, your deeds, have done
   this to you;
   how bitter is this evil of yours,
   how it reaches to your very heart!*

19 My body! my body! how I writhe!†
   The walls of my heart!
   My heart beats wildly,
   I cannot be still;
   For I myself have heard the blast of the
   horn,
   the battle cry.

20 Ruin upon ruin is reported;
   the whole land is laid waste.
   In an instant my tents are ravaged;
   in a flash, my shelters.*

21 How long must I see the signal,
   hear the blast of the horn!

22 My people are fools,
   they do not know me;
   They are senseless children,
   without understanding;
   They are wise at evil,
   but they do not know how to do
   good.*

23 I looked at the earth—it was waste and
   void;
   at the heavens—their light had gone
   out!*

24 I looked at the mountains—they were
   quaking!
   All the hills were crumbling!

25 I looked—there was no one;
   even the birds of the air had flown
   away!

26 I looked—the garden land was a
   wilderness,
   with all its cities destroyed

---

† **4:10** *You really did deceive*: Jeremiah complains that the Lord misled the people by fostering their complacency, leaving them unprepared and unrepentant as judgment approaches.

**4:11** *My daughter, the people*: the covenant people personified as a young woman. Ezekiel 16 presents Israel and Judah as female infants whom the Lord adopts and then abandons and punishes because they desire other lords.

**4:19–21** Probably the prophet's own anguish at the coming destruction of Judah.

**4:7** Jer 2:15; 5:6.          **4:17** Jer 6:3.
**4:8** Jer 6:26; Is 5:25.      **4:18** Jer 2:17, 19.
**4:10** Jer 6:14.              **4:20** Jer 10:20.
**4:12** Jer 1:16.              **4:22** Dt 32:5–6, 28.
**4:16** Jer 5:15.              **4:23** Is 24:1, 3.

before the Lord, before his blazing
    anger.*
27 For thus says the Lord:
The whole earth shall be waste,
    but I will not wholly destroy it.*
28 Because of this the earth shall mourn,
    the heavens above shall darken;
I have spoken, I will not change my
    mind,
    I have decided, I will not turn back.*
29 At the shout of rider and archer
    each city takes to flight;
They shrink into the thickets,
    they scale the rocks:
All the cities are abandoned,
    no one lives in them.
30 You now who are doomed, what are you
    doing
    dressing in purple,
    bedecking yourself with gold,
Enlarging your eyes with kohl?
    You beautify yourself in vain!
Your lovers reject you,
    they seek your life.
31 Yes, I hear the cry, like that of a woman
    in labor,
    like the anguish of a mother bearing
    her first child—
The cry of daughter Zion gasping,
    as she stretches out her hands:
"Ah, woe is me! I sink exhausted
    before my killers!"*

## Universal Corruption

5 ¹ Roam the streets of Jerusalem,
    look about and observe,
Search through her squares,
    to find even one
Who acts justly
    and seeks honesty,
    and I will pardon her!
2 They say, "As the Lord lives,"
    but in fact they swear falsely.
3 Lord, do your eyes not search for
    honesty?
You struck them, but they did not flinch;
    you laid them low, but they refused
    correction;

They set their faces harder than stone,
    and refused to return.*
4 I thought: These are only the lowly,
    they behave foolishly;
For they do not know the way of the
    Lord,
    the justice of their God.*
5 Let me go to the leaders
    and speak with them;
For they must know the way of the
    Lord,
    the justice of their God.
But, one and all, they have broken the
    yoke,
    torn off the harness.*
6 Therefore, lions from the forest slay
    them,
    wolves of the desert ravage them,
Leopards keep watch round their cities:
    all who come out are torn to pieces,
For their crimes are many,
    their rebellions numerous.
7 Why should I pardon you?
    Your children have forsaken me,
    they swear by gods that are no gods.
I fed them, but they commit adultery;
    to the prostitute's house they throng.
8 They are lustful stallions,
    each neighs after the other's wife.*
9 Should I not punish them for this?—
    oracle of the Lord;
    on a nation like this should I not take
    vengeance?
10 Climb her terraces, and ravage them,
    destroy them completely.
Tear away her tendrils,
    they do not belong to the Lord.*
11 For they have openly rebelled against
    me,
    both the house of Israel and the
    house of Judah—
    oracle of the Lord.*
12 They denied the Lord,†
    saying, "He is nothing,
No evil shall come to us,
    neither sword nor famine shall we
    see.*
13 The prophets are wind,

---

† **5:12** *They denied the Lord:* the people act as though God does not matter and will not interfere.

4:26 Lv 26:31.
4:27 Jer 5:18.
4:28 Is 24:4.
4:31 Jer 6:24.
5:3 Jer 2:30.
5:4 Jer 8:7.
5:5 Jer 6:13.
5:8 Jer 13:27.
5:10 Jer 2:21.
5:11 Jer 3:20.
5:12 Jer 14:13; Is 28:15.

JER

and the word is not with them.
  Let it be done to them!"

14 Therefore, thus says the LORD, the God
      of hosts,
    because you have said this—
    See! I make my words
      a fire in your mouth,
    And this people the wood
      that it shall devour!—

15 Beware! I will bring against you
      a nation from far away,
    O House of Israel—oracle of the
      LORD;
    A long-lived nation, an ancient nation,
      a people whose language you do not
      know,
    whose speech you cannot
      understand.*

16 Their quivers are like open graves;
    all of them are warriors.

17 They will devour your harvest and your
      bread,
    devour your sons and your daughters,
    Devour your sheep and cattle,
      devour your vines and fig trees;
    With their swords they will beat down
      the fortified cities in which you trust.*

18 Yet even in those days—oracle of the
LORD—I will not completely destroy you.*
19 And when they ask, "Why has the LORD our
God done all these things to us?" say to them,
"As you have abandoned me to serve foreign
gods in your own land, so shall you serve foreigners in a land not your own."

20 Announce this to the house of Jacob,
    proclaim it in Judah:

21 Pay attention to this,
    you foolish and senseless people,
    Who have eyes and do not see,
    who have ears and do not hear.*

22 Should you not fear me—oracle of the
      LORD—
    should you not tremble before me?
    I made the sandy shore the sea's limit,
      which by eternal decree it may not
      overstep.
    Toss though it may, it is to no avail;

though its billows roar, they cannot
  overstep.*

23 But this people's heart is stubborn and
      rebellious;
    they turn and go away,

24 And do not say in their hearts,
    "Let us fear the LORD, our God,
    Who gives us rain
      early and late,† in its time;
    Who watches for us
      over the appointed weeks of
      harvest."*

25 Your crimes have prevented these
      things,
    your sins have turned these blessings
      away from you.*

26 For criminals lurk among my people;
    like fowlers they set traps,
    but it is human beings they catch.*

27 Their houses are as full of treachery
    as a bird-cage is of birds;
    Therefore they grow powerful and rich,

28 fat and sleek.
    They pass over wicked deeds;
      justice they do not defend
    By advancing the claim of the orphan
      or judging the cause of the poor.*

29 Shall I not punish these things?—oracle
      of the LORD;
    on a nation such as this shall I not
      take vengeance?

30 Something shocking and horrible
    has happened in the land:

31 The prophets prophesy falsely,
      and the priests teach on their own
      authority;
    Yet my people like it this way;
      what will you do when the end
      comes?*

## The Enemy at the Gates

**6** 1 Seek refuge, Benjaminites,
      from the midst of Jerusalem!
    Blow the trumpet in Tekoa,
      raise a signal over Beth-haccherem;
    For disaster threatens from the north,
      and mighty destruction.*

2 Lovely and delicate
    daughter Zion, you are ruined!

† 5:24 *Rain early and late*: autumn and spring rains respectively. *Appointed weeks of harvest*: the seven weeks between the
Passover (Dt 16:9–10) and the feast of Weeks (Pentecost), when
it did not ordinarily rain.

5:15 Dt 28:49.          5:25 Jer 2:17, 19.
5:17 Dt 28:31.          5:26 Prv 1:11.
5:18 Jer 4:27.          5:28 Jer 12:1; Is 1:23.
5:21 Is 6:9.            5:31 Jer 14:14; Mi 2:11.
5:22 Jb 38:10–11.       6:1 Jer 1:14–15.
5:24 Gn 8:22; Dt 11:14.

3    Against her, shepherds come with their
       flocks;†
     all around, they pitch their tents
       against her;
     each one grazes his portion.*

4    "Prepare for war against her,
       Up! let us rush upon her at midday!"
     "Woe to us! the day is waning,
       evening shadows lengthen!"

5    "Up! let us rush upon her by night,
       destroy her palaces!"*

6    For thus says the LORD of hosts:
     Hew down her trees,
       throw up a siege mound against
       Jerusalem.
     Woe to the city marked for punishment;
       there is nothing but oppression
       within her!*

7    As a well keeps its waters fresh,
       so she keeps fresh her wickedness.
     Violence and destruction resound in her;
       ever before me are wounds and blows.*

8    Be warned, Jerusalem,
       or I will be estranged from you,
     And I will turn you into a wilderness,
       a land where no one dwells.

9    Thus says the LORD of hosts:
     Glean, glean like a vine
       the remnant of Israel;
     Pass your hand, like a vintager,
       repeatedly over the tendrils.

10    To whom shall I speak?
       whom shall I warn, and be heard?
     See! their ears are uncircumcised,
       they cannot pay attention;
     See, the word of the LORD has become
       for them
       an object of scorn, for which they
       have no taste.*

11    But the wrath of the LORD brims up
       within me,
     I am weary of holding it in.
     I will pour it out upon the child in the
       street,
       upon the young men gathered together.
     Yes, husband and wife will be taken,
       elder with ancient.*

12    Their houses will fall to others,

     their fields and their wives as well;
     For I will stretch forth my hand
       against those who dwell in the land—
       oracle of the LORD.*

13    Small and great alike, all are greedy for
       gain;
     prophet and priest, all practice fraud.*

14    They have treated lightly
       the injury to my people:
     "Peace, peace!" they say,
       though there is no peace.*

15    They have acted shamefully, committing
       abominations,
       yet they are not at all ashamed,
       they do not know how to blush.
     Therefore they will fall among the fallen;
       in the time of their punishment they
       shall stumble,
       says the LORD.*

16    Thus says the LORD:
     Stand by the earliest roads,
       ask the pathways of old,†
     "Which is the way to good?" and walk it;
       thus you will find rest for yourselves.
     But they said, "We will not walk it."*

17    I raised up watchmen† for them:
     "Pay attention to the sound of the
       trumpet!"
     But they said, "We will not pay
       attention!"

18    Therefore hear, O nations,
       and know, O earth,
       what I will do with them:

19    See, I bring evil upon this people,
       the fruit of their own schemes,
     Because they did not pay attention to
       my words,
       because they rejected my law.*

20    Of what use to me is incense that comes
       from Sheba,
       or sweet cane from far-off lands?
     Your burnt offerings find no favor with
       me,
       your sacrifices do not please me.*

21    Therefore, thus says the LORD:
     See, I will place before this people
       obstacles to trip them up;
     Parents and children alike,

---

**6:3** *Shepherds come with their flocks*: foreign invaders with their armies.

**6:16** *Pathways of old*: history and the lessons to be learned from it.

**6:17** *Watchmen*: the prophets who, like Jeremiah, had upheld God's moral law.

**6:3** Jer 4:17.
**6:5** 2 Chr 36:19.
**6:6** Jer 32:24; Zep 3:1–4.
**6:7** Is 57:20.
**6:10** Jer 7:26; 20:8.
**6:11** Ez 9:6.
**6:12** Jer 8:10; Dt 28:30–32.
**6:13** Jer 8:10; 23:11.
**6:14** Jer 8:11.
**6:15** Jer 3:3; 8:12.
**6:16** Jer 7:23–24; 18:15.
**6:19** Prv 1:31.
**6:20** Is 1:11; 43:24.

neighbors and friends shall perish.*

22      Thus says the LORD:
        See, a people comes from the land of
            the north,
        a great nation, rising from the very
            ends of the earth.*

23      Bow and javelin they wield;
            cruel and pitiless are they.
        They sound like the roaring sea
            as they ride forth on horses,
        Each in his place for battle
            against you, daughter Zion.

24      We hear news of them;
            our hands hang helpless,
        Anguish takes hold of us,
            pangs like a woman in childbirth.*

25      Do not go out into the field,
            do not step into the street,
        For the enemy has a sword;
            terror on every side!

26      Daughter of my people, dress in sackcloth,
            roll in the ashes.
        Mourn as for an only child
            with bitter wailing:
        "How suddenly the destroyer
            comes upon us!"*

27†     A tester for my people I have appointed
            you,
        to search and test their way.*

28      Arch-rebels are they all,
            dealers in slander,
        bronze and iron, all of them,
            destroyers they are.

29      The bellows are scorched,
            the lead is consumed by the fire;
        In vain has the refiner refined,
            the wicked are not drawn off.

30      "Silver rejected" they shall be called,
            for the LORD has rejected them.

## II. ORACLES PRIMARILY FROM THE DAYS OF JEHOIAKIM

**7** **The Temple Sermon.**† ¹The word came
to Jeremiah from the LORD: ²Stand at the

gate of the house of the LORD and proclaim
this message there: Hear the word of the
LORD, all you of Judah who enter these gates
to worship the LORD! ³Thus says the LORD of
hosts, the God of Israel: Reform your ways
and your deeds so that I may dwell with you
in this place.* ⁴Do not put your trust in these
deceptive words: "The temple of the LORD! The
temple of the LORD! The temple of the LORD!"*
⁵Only if you thoroughly reform your ways and
your deeds; if each of you deals justly with
your neighbor; ⁶if you no longer oppress the
alien,† the orphan, and the widow; if you no
longer shed innocent blood in this place or
follow after other gods to your own harm,*
⁷only then will I let you continue to dwell in
this place, in the land I gave your ancestors
long ago and forever.*

⁸But look at you! You put your trust in
deceptive words to your own loss! ⁹Do you
think you can steal and murder, commit adultery and perjury, sacrifice to Baal, follow other
gods that you do not know,* ¹⁰and then come
and stand in my presence in this house, which
bears my name, and say: "We are safe! We
can commit all these abominations again!"?*
¹¹Has this house which bears my name become in your eyes a den of thieves? I have seen
it for myself!—oracle of the LORD.* ¹²Go to
my place at Shiloh,† where I made my name
dwell in the beginning. See what I did to it because of the wickedness of my people Israel.*
¹³And now, because you have committed all
these deeds—oracle of the LORD—because you
did not listen, though I spoke to you untiringly, and because you did not answer, though
I called you, ¹⁴I will do to this house, which
bears my name, in which you trust, and to the
place which I gave you and your ancestors,
exactly what I did to Shiloh.* ¹⁵I will cast you
out of my sight, as I cast away all your kindred,
all the offspring of Ephraim.*

**Abuses in Worship.** ¹⁶You, now, must not
intercede for this people! Do not raise a cry

---

**6:27–30** God appoints Jeremiah to be a "tester" of his people.
The passage uses the metaphor of the refining of silver: the silver
was extracted from lead ore, but the process in ancient times was
inexact, so that sometimes all that was left was a scummy mess,
to be thrown out.

**7:1–15** The Temple of the Lord will not guarantee safety
against enemy invasion or any other misfortune.

**7:6** *The alien*: specially protected within Israelite society; cf.
Ex 22:20; Nm 9:14; 15:14; Dt 5:14; 28:43.

**7:12** *Shiloh*: an important sanctuary where the ark of the covenant was kept, according to the Books of Joshua, Judges, and

1 Samuel. In response to the corrupt behavior of the priests serving there, God allows the Philistines to destroy Shiloh and take
the ark of the covenant. Cf. 1 Sm 1:9; 4:3–4; Ps 78:60, 68–69.

| | |
|---|---|
| **6:21** Is 8:14–15. | **7:7** Dt 4:40. |
| **6:22** Jer 1:15; 5:15. | **7:9** Jer 44:17. |
| **6:24** Jer 4:31. | **7:10** Jer 32:34. |
| **6:26** Jer 25:34; Am 8:10. | **7:11** Mt 21:13. |
| **6:27** Jer 1:18. | **7:12** Jos 18:1. |
| **7:3** Jer 18:11; 26:13. | **7:14** Jer 26:9. |
| **7:4** Mi 3:11. | **7:15** 1 Kgs 9:7; 2 Kgs |
| **7:6** Ex 22:21–24. |     17:23. |

or prayer in their behalf!* Do not press me, for I will not listen to you! 17 Do you not see what they are doing in the cities of Judah, in the streets of Jerusalem? 18 The children gather wood, their fathers light the fire, and the women knead dough to make cakes for the Queen of Heaven,† while libations are poured out to other gods—all to offend me!* 19 Are they really offending me—oracle of the LORD—or rather themselves, to their own disgrace?* 20 Therefore, thus says the Lord GOD: my anger and my wrath will pour out upon this place, upon human being and beast, upon the trees of the field and the fruits of the earth; it will burn and not be quenched.*

21 Thus says the LORD of hosts, the God of Israel: Heap your burnt offerings upon your sacrifices; eat up the meat! 22 In speaking to your ancestors on the day I brought them out of the land of Egypt, I gave them no command† concerning burnt offering or sacrifice. 23 This rather is what I commanded them: Listen to my voice; then I will be your God and you shall be my people. Walk exactly in the way I command you, so that you may prosper.*

24 But they did not listen to me, nor did they pay attention. They walked in the stubbornness of their evil hearts and turned their backs, not their faces, to me.* 25 From the day that your ancestors left the land of Egypt even to this day, I kept on sending all my servants the prophets to you.* 26 Yet they have not listened to me nor have they paid attention; they have stiffened their necks and done worse than their ancestors.* 27 When you speak all these words to them, they will not listen to you either. When you call to them, they will not answer you. 28 Say to them: This is the nation which does not listen to the voice of the LORD, its God, or take correction. Faithfulness has disappeared; the word itself is banished from their speech.

29 * Cut off your hair† and throw it away!
on the heights raise a lament;
The LORD has indeed rejected and cast off
the generation that draws down his wrath.

30 The people of Judah have done what is evil in my eyes—oracle of the LORD. They have set up their detestable things in the house which bears my name, thereby defiling it.* 31 In the Valley of Ben-hinnom† they go on building the high places of Topheth to sacrifice their sons and daughters by fire, something I never commanded or considered. 32 Be assured! Days are coming—oracle of the LORD—when they will no longer say "Topheth" or "Valley of Ben-hinnom" but "Valley of Slaughter." For want of space, Topheth will become burial ground.* 33 The corpses of this people will be food for the birds of the sky and beasts of the earth, which no one will drive away.* 34 I will silence the cry of joy, the cry of gladness, the voice of the bridegroom and the voice of the bride, in the cities of Judah and in the streets of Jerusalem; for the land will be turned to rubble.*

**8** 1 At that time—oracle of the LORD—the bones of the kings and princes of Judah, the bones of the priests and the prophets, and the bones of the inhabitants of Jerusalem will be brought out of their graves* 2 and spread out before the sun, the moon, and the whole host of heaven,† which they loved and served, which they followed, consulted, and worshiped. They will not be gathered up for burial, but will lie like dung upon the ground.* 3 Death will be preferred to life by all the survivors of this wicked people who remain in any of the places to which I banish them—oracle of the LORD of hosts.

---

† **7:18** *Queen of Heaven*: probably Astarte, goddess of fertility (cf. 1 Sm 31:10; 1 Kgs 11:5), worshiped particularly by women (cf. Jer 44:15–19). Such worship was evidently reinforced during the reign of King Manasseh (2 Kgs 21:3–7) and was revived after Josiah's death.

**7:22** *I gave them no command*: right conduct rather than formal ritual was God's will concerning his people (v. 23).

**7:29** *Hair*: the unshorn hair of the nazirite, regarded as sacred because of a vow, temporary or permanent, to abstain from cutting or shaving the hair; nazirites also avoided contact with a corpse and with all products of the vine; cf. Nm 6:4–8. The cutting of this hair was a sign of extreme mourning.

**7:31** *Valley of Ben-hinnom*: this valley was probably south of

Jerusalem. *Topheth*: perhaps, "fire pit."

**8:2** *Host of heaven*: the stars, worshiped by other nations and even by the inhabitants of Jerusalem, particularly during the reigns of Manasseh and Amon.

| | |
|---|---|
| **7:16** Jer 11:14; 14:11. | **7:26** Jer 19:15; 2 Chr 30:8. |
| **7:18** Jer 44:17, 19. | **7:29** Jer 9:17–21. |
| **7:19** Jb 35:6. | **7:30** Jer 32:34. |
| **7:20** Jer 36:29; 2 Kgs 22:17. | **7:32** Jer 19:6; 32:35. |
| | **7:33** Jer 16:4; 34:20. |
| **7:23** Jer 11:4; Lv 26:3, 12. | **7:34** Jer 16:9. |
| **7:24** Jer 17:23. | **8:1** Bar 2:24. |
| **7:25** 2 Chr 36:15–16; Bar 1:19. | **8:2** Dt 4:19. |

## Israel's Conduct Incomprehensible

4  Tell them: Thus says the LORD:
   When someone falls, do they not rise
      again?
      if they turn away, do they not turn
         back?
5  Why then do these people resist
      with persistent rebellion?
   Why do they cling to deception,
      refuse to turn back?*
6  I have listened closely:
      they speak what is not true;
   No one regrets wickedness,
      saying, "What have I done?"
   Everyone keeps on running their course,
      like a horse dashing into battle.*
7  Even the stork in the sky
      knows its seasons;
   Turtledove, swift, and thrush
      observe the time of their return,
   But my people do not know
      the order of the LORD.*
8  How can you say, "We are wise,*
      we have the law of the LORD"?
   See, that has been changed into
         falsehood
      by the lying pen of the scribes! †
9  The wise are put to shame,
      terrified, and trapped;
   Since they have rejected the word of the
         LORD,
      what sort of wisdom do they have?*

## Shameless in Their Crimes

10  Therefore, I will give their wives to other
         men,
      their fields to new owners.
   Small and great alike, all are greedy for
         gain,
      prophet and priest, all practice fraud.*
11  They have treated lightly
      the injury to the daughter of my
         people:†
   "Peace, peace!" they say,
      though there is no peace.*
12  They have acted shamefully; they have
         done abominable things,
      yet they are not at all ashamed,

they do not know how to blush.
   Hence they shall be among those who
      fall;
   in their time of punishment they shall
      stumble,
   says the LORD. *

## Threats of Punishment

13  I will gather them all in—oracle of the
      LORD:
      no grapes on the vine,
   No figs on the fig trees,
      foliage withered!
   Whatever I have given them is gone.
14  Why do we remain here?
      Let us assemble and flee to the
         fortified cities,
      where we will meet our doom;
   For the LORD our God has doomed us,
      he has given us poisoned water to
         drink,
      because we have sinned against the
         LORD.*
15  We wait for peace to no avail;
      for a time of healing, but terror comes
         instead.*
16  From Dan is heard
      the snorting of horses;
   The neighing of stallions
      shakes the whole land.
   They come to devour the land and
         everything in it,
      the city and its inhabitants.
17  Yes, I will send against you
      poisonous snakes.
   Against them no charm will work
      when they bite you—oracle of the
         LORD.*

## The Prophet's Grief over the People's Suffering

18  My joy is gone,
      grief is upon me,
      my heart is sick.
19  Listen! the cry of the daughter of my
         people,
      far and wide in the land!
   "Is the LORD no longer in Zion,
      is her King no longer in her midst?"

---

**8:8** *Lying pen of the scribes*: because the teachings and interpretations of the scribes ran counter to the word of the Lord.
   **8:11** *Daughter of my people*: see note on 4:11.

**8:5** Jer 5:3; 7:24, 26.                 **8:6** Jb 34:31–32.

**8:7** Is 1:3.                    **8:11** Jer 6:14.
**8:8** Mal 2:8; Rom          **8:12** Jer 6:15.
   2:17–23.                    **8:14** Jer 9:14; 23:15.
**8:9** 1 Cor 3:20.             **8:15** Jer 14:19.
**8:10** Jer 6:13; Dt 28:30.   **8:17** Dt 32:24.

Why do they provoke me with their
  idols,
  with their foreign nonentities?*

20 "The harvest is over, the summer ended,
  but we have not yet been saved!"

21 I am broken by the injury of the
  daughter of my people.
  I am in mourning; horror has seized
  me.*

22 Is there no balm in Gilead,†
  no healer there?
  Why does new flesh not grow
  over the wound of the daughter of my
  people?*

23 Oh, that my head were a spring of water,
  my eyes a fountain of tears,
  That I might weep day and night
  over the slain from the daughter of
  my people!

### The Corruption of the People

**9** ¹ Oh, that I had in the wilderness
  a travelers' lodging!
  That I might leave my people
  and depart from them.
  They are all adulterers,
  a band of traitors.

2 They ready their tongues like a drawn
  bow;
  with lying, and not with truth,
  they are powerful in the land.
  They go from evil to evil,
  and me they do not know—oracle of
  the LORD.

3 Be on your guard, everyone against his
  neighbor;
  put no trust in any brother.
  Every brother imitates Jacob, the
  supplanter,†
  every neighbor is guilty of slander.

4 Each one deceives the other,
  no one speaks the truth.
  They have accustomed their tongues to
  lying,
  they are perverse and cannot repent.*

5 Violence upon violence,
  deceit upon deceit:
  They refuse to know me—

oracle of the LORD.

6 Therefore, thus says the LORD of hosts:
  I will refine them and test them;
  how else should I deal with the
  daughter of my people?

7 A murderous arrow is their tongue,
  their mouths utter deceit;
  They speak peaceably with their
  neighbors,
  but in their hearts they lay an
  ambush!*

8 Should I not punish them for these
  deeds—oracle of the LORD;
  on a nation such as this should I not
  take vengeance?*

### Dirge over the Ravaged Land

9 Over the mountains I shall break out in
  cries of lamentation,
  over the pastures in the wilderness, in
  a dirge:
  They are scorched, and no one crosses
  them,
  no sound of lowing cattle;
  Birds of the air as well as beasts,
  all have fled and are gone.*

10 I will turn Jerusalem into a heap of
  ruins,
  a haunt of jackals;
  The cities of Judah I will make a waste,
  where no one dwells.*

¹¹ Who is wise enough to understand this?
To whom has the mouth of the LORD spoken?
Let him declare it!

  Why is the land ravaged,
    scorched like a wilderness no one
    crosses?*

¹² The LORD said: Because they have abandoned my law, which I set before them, and
did not listen to me or follow it, ¹³ but followed instead their stubborn hearts and the
Baals, as their ancestors had taught them,*
¹⁴ therefore, thus says the LORD of hosts, the
God of Israel: See now, I will give this people wormwood to eat and poisoned water to

---

**8:22** *Gilead:* a region southeast of the Sea of Galilee noted
for its healing balm.
  **9:3** *Jacob, the supplanter:* in Hebrew, a play on words. In the
popular etymology given in Gn 25:26, the name Jacob means
"he supplants," for he deprived his brother Esau of his birthright
(cf. Gn 25:33).

**8:19** Dt 32:21; Mi 4:9.
**8:21** Jer 14:17.
**8:22** Jer 46:11.
**9:4** Jer 12:6.
**9:7** Ps 28:3; 62:4.
**9:8** Jer 5:9, 29.
**9:9** Jer 4:25; 12:4.
**9:10** Is 13:22.
**9:11** Ps 107:43; Hos 14:10.
**9:13** Jer 7:24; 19:4–5.

drink.* ¹⁵ I will scatter them among nations whom neither they nor their ancestors have known; I will send the sword to pursue them until I have completely destroyed them.*

¹⁶ Thus says the LORD of hosts:
Inquire, and call the wailing women to
    come;
    summon the most skilled of them.
¹⁷ Let them come quickly
    and raise for us a dirge,
That our eyes may run with tears,
    our pupils flow with water.*
¹⁸ The sound of the dirge is heard from
    Zion:
    We are ruined and greatly ashamed;
We have left the land,
    given up our dwellings!
¹⁹ Hear, you women, the word of the LORD,
    let your ears receive the word of his
        mouth.
Teach your daughters a dirge,
    and each other a lament:
²⁰ Death has come up through our
    windows,
    has entered our citadels,
To cut down children in the street,
    young people in the squares.*
²¹ Corpses shall fall
    like dung in the open field,
Like sheaves behind the harvester,
    with no one to gather them.

### True Glory

²² Thus says the LORD:
Let not the wise boast of his wisdom,
    nor the strong boast of his strength,
    nor the rich man boast of his riches;
²³ But rather, let those who boast, boast of
    this,
    that in their prudence they know me,*
Know that I, the LORD, act with fidelity,
    justice, and integrity on earth.
How I take delight in these—oracle of
    the LORD.

**False Circumcision.** ²⁴ See, days are coming—oracle of the LORD—when I will demand an account of all those circumcised in the fore-skin:* ²⁵ Egypt and Judah, Edom and the Am-monites, Moab, and those who live in the wilderness and shave their temples.† For all the nations are uncircumcised, even the whole house of Israel is uncircumcised at heart.

# 10

**The Folly of Idolatry.** ¹ Hear the word the LORD speaks to you, house of Israel. ² Thus says the LORD:

Do not learn the ways of the nations,
    and have no fear of the signs in the
        heavens,†
    even though the nations fear them.*
³ For the carvings of the nations are
        nonentities,
    wood cut from the forest,
Fashioned by artisans with the adze,*
⁴     adorned with silver and gold.
With nails and hammers they are
        fastened,
    so they do not fall.*
⁵ Like a scarecrow in a cucumber field are
    they,
    they cannot speak;
They must be carried about,
    for they cannot walk.
Do not fear them, they can do no harm,
    neither can they do good.*
⁶ No one is like you, LORD,
    you are great,
    great and mighty is your name.*
⁷ Who would not fear you,
    King of the nations,
    for it is your due!
Among all the wisest of the nations,
    and in all their domains,
    there is none like you.*
⁸ One and all they are stupid and
        senseless,
    the instruction from nonentities—
        only wood!
⁹ Silver plates brought from Tarshish,
    and gold from Ophir,
The work of the artisan
    and the handiwork of the smelter,
Clothed with violet and purple—

---

† 
   **9:25** *Shave their temples*: some Arabian tribes practiced this custom. None of the nations who practice circumcision under-stand the meaning of their action, not even Israel; no one con-forms to life under the covenant.
   **10:2** *Signs in the heavens*: phenomena in the sky, such as eclipses or comets, used to predict disasters.

* 
**9:14** Jer 23:15.
**9:15** Lv 26:33; Dt 28:36, 64.
**9:17** Jer 14:17.
**9:20** Jer 14:16.
**9:23** Prv 21:30.
**9:24** Jer 4:4.
**10:2** Bar 6:6.
**10:3** Wis 13:11; Is 44:9.
**10:4** Is 40:19; 41:7.
**10:5** Ps 115:4–8; Bar 6:15.
**10:6** Ps 86:8–10.
**10:7** Jer 5:22; Ps 47:2, 8.

all of them the work of skilled workers.

10 The LORD is truly God,
he is the living God, the eternal King,
Before whose anger the earth quakes,
whose wrath the nations cannot
endure.*

11 Thus shall you say of them: The gods that did not make heaven and earth—let these perish from earth and from beneath heaven!†*

12 The one who made the earth by his
power,
established the world by his wisdom,
and by his skill stretched out the
heavens.*

13 When he thunders, the waters in the
heavens roar,
and he brings up clouds from the end
of the earth,
Makes lightning flash in the rain,
and brings forth the wind from his
storehouses.

14 Everyone is too stupid to know;
every artisan is put to shame by his
idol:
He has molded a fraud,
without breath of life.*

15 They are nothing, objects of ridicule;
they will perish in their time of
punishment.

16 Jacob's portion is nothing like them:
for he is the maker of everything!
Israel is his very own tribe,
LORD of hosts is his name.*

### Abandonment of Judah

17 Gather up your bundle from the land,
City living under siege!

18 For thus says the LORD:
Now, at this time
I will sling away the inhabitants of the
land;
I will hem them in,
that they may be taken.

19 Woe is me! I am undone,
my wound is beyond healing.
Yet I had thought:
if I make light of my sickness, I can
bear it.

20 My tent is ruined,
all its cords are severed.
My children have left me, they are no
more:
no one to pitch my tent,
no one to raise its curtains.*

21 How stupid are the shepherds!
The LORD they have not sought;
For this reason they have failed,
and all their flocks scattered.*

22 Listen! a rumor! here it comes,
a great commotion from the land of
the north:
To make the cities of Judah a desolation,
the haunt of jackals.

### Prayer of Jeremiah

23 I know, LORD,
that no one chooses their way,
Nor determines their course
nor directs their own step.

24 Correct me, LORD, but with equity,
not in anger, lest you diminish me.

25 Pour out your wrath on the nations that
do not know you,
on the tribes that do not call your
name;
For they have utterly devoured Jacob,
and laid waste his home.*

**11** **Plea for Fidelity to the Covenant.** ¹ The word that came to Jeremiah from the LORD: ² Speak to the people of Judah and the inhabitants of Jerusalem, ³ and say to them: Thus says the LORD, the God of Israel: Cursed be anyone who does not observe the words of this covenant,* ⁴ which I commanded your ancestors the day I brought them up out of the land of Egypt, that iron furnace, saying: Listen to my voice and do all that I command you. Then you shall be my people, and I will be your God.* ⁵ Thus I will fulfill the oath I swore to your ancestors, to give them a land flowing with milk and honey, the one you have today. "Amen, LORD," I answered.

⁶ Then the LORD said to me: Proclaim all these words in the cities of Judah and in the streets of Jerusalem: Hear the words of this covenant and obey them. ⁷ I warned your ancestors unceasingly from the day I brought

---

† **10:11** This verse is in Aramaic.

* **10:10** Ps 10:16.  **10:11** Ps 96:5.

**10:12** Ps 104:5.  **10:21** Jer 23:1; Ez 34:5–6.
**10:14** Rom 1:22–23.  **10:25** Ps 79:6–7.
**10:16** Ps 33:12; Jer 31:35.  **11:3** Dt 27:26.
**10:20** Jer 4:20.  **11:4** Dt 4:20; 1 Kgs 8:51.

them up out of the land of Egypt even to this day: obey my voice. 8 But they did not listen or obey. They each walked in the stubbornness of their evil hearts, till I brought upon them all the threats of this covenant which they had failed to observe as I commanded them.*

9 A conspiracy has been found, the LORD said to me, among the people of Judah and the inhabitants of Jerusalem: 10 They have returned to the crimes of their ancestors who refused to obey my words. They also have followed and served other gods; the house of Israel and the house of Judah have broken the covenant I made with their ancestors.* 11 Therefore, thus says the LORD: See, I am bringing upon them a disaster they cannot escape. Though they cry out to me, I will not listen to them.* 12 Then the cities of Judah and the inhabitants of Jerusalem will go and cry out to the gods to whom they have been offering incense. But these gods will give them no help whatever in the time of their disaster.*

13 For as many as your cities
    are your gods, O Judah!
As many as the streets of Jerusalem
    are the altars for sacrifice to Baal.*

14 Now, you must not intercede for this people; do not raise on their behalf a cry or prayer! I will not listen when they call to me in the time of their disaster.*

### Sacrifices of No Avail

15 What right has my beloved in my house,
    while she devises her plots?
Can vows and sacred meat turn away
    your disaster from you?
Will you still be jubilant
16 when you hear the great tumult?
The LORD has named you
    "a spreading olive tree, a pleasure to
        behold";
Now he sets fire to it,
    its branches burn.

17 The LORD of hosts who planted you has decreed disaster for you because of the evil done by the house of Israel and by the house of Judah, who provoked me by sacrificing to Baal.*

**The Plot Against Jeremiah.** 18 I knew it because the LORD informed me: at that time you showed me their doings.

19 Yet I was like a trusting lamb led to slaughter, not knowing that they were hatching plots against me: "Let us destroy the tree in its vigor; let us cut him off from the land of the living, so that his name will no longer be remembered."*

20 But, you, LORD of hosts, just Judge,
    searcher of mind and heart,
Let me witness the vengeance you take
    on them,
    for to you I have entrusted my cause!*

21 Therefore, thus says the LORD concerning the men of Anathoth who seek your life and say, "Do not prophesy in the name of the LORD; otherwise you shall die by our hand."* 22 Therefore, thus says the LORD of hosts: I am going to punish them. The young men shall die by the sword; their sons and daughters shall die by famine.* 23 None shall be spared among them, for I will bring disaster upon the men of Anathoth, the year of their punishment.*

**12** 1 You would be in the right, O LORD,
    if I should dispute with you;
    even so, I must lay out the case
        against you.
Why does the way of the wicked prosper,
    why do all the treacherous live in
        contentment?*
2 You planted them; they have taken root,
    they flourish and bear fruit as well.
You are upon their lips,
    but far from their thoughts.*
3 LORD, you know me, you see me,
    you have found that my heart is with
        you.*
Pick them out like sheep for the butcher,
    set them apart for the day of
        slaughter.†

12:3 Jeremiah calls the Lord to account for allowing the wicked to flourish while he himself is persecuted for his fidelity to the Lord's mission; cf. 20:12. See Jesus' judgment, Mk 9:42. The metaphors indicate that Jeremiah has even greater trials ahead of him.

11:8 2 Kgs 17:14.  11:10 Dt 31:16;

Ez 20:21–30.
11:11 Jer 14:12; Mi 3:4.
11:12 Dt 32:37–38.
11:13 Jer 2:28; Hos 10:1.
11:14 Jer 7:16; 14:11.
11:17 Is 5:2.
11:19 Jer 18:18; 20:10; Wis 2:20.
11:20 Jer 15:15.
11:21 Am 7:13, 16.
11:22 Jer 18:21–22.
11:23 Jer 23:12.
12:1 Jb 21:7; Mal 3:15.
12:2 Is 29:13.
12:3 Jer 17:18; Jb 23:10.

4    How long must the land mourn,
        the grass of the whole countryside
            wither?
     Because of the wickedness of those who
            dwell in it
        beasts and birds disappear,
        for they say, "God does not care about
            our future."

5    If running against men has wearied you,
        how will you race against horses?
     And if you are safe only on a level
            stretch,
        what will you do in the jungle of the
            Jordan?

⁶ Your kindred and your father's house, even
they betray you; they have recruited a force
against you. Do not believe them, even when
they speak fair words to you. *

## The Lord's Complaint

7    I have abandoned my house,
        cast off my heritage;
     The beloved of my soul I have delivered
        into the hand of her foes. *
8    My heritage has become for me
        like a lion in the thicket;
     She has raised her voice against me,
        therefore she has incurred my hatred. *
9    My heritage is a prey for hyenas,
        is surrounded by vultures;
     Come, gather together, all you wild
            animals,
        come and eat! *
10   Many shepherds have ravaged my
            vineyard,
        have trampled down my heritage;
     My delightful portion they have turned
        into a desert waste. *
11   They have made it a mournful waste,
        desolate before me,
     Desolate, the whole land,
        because no one takes it to heart.
12   Upon every height in the wilderness
        marauders have appeared.
     The LORD has a sword that consumes

the land from end to end:
    no peace for any living thing. *
13   They have sown wheat and reaped
            thorns,
     they have tired themselves out for no
            purpose;
     They are shamed by their harvest,
        the burning anger of the LORD.

**Judah's Neighbors.** ¹⁴ Thus says the LORD,
against all my evil neighbors† who plunder
the heritage I gave my people Israel as their
own: See, I will uproot them from their land;
the house of Judah I will uproot in their
midst. * ¹⁵ But after uprooting them, I will have compassion on them again and bring them back,
each to their heritage, each to their land. *
¹⁶ And if they truly learn my people's custom
of swearing by my name, "As the LORD lives,"
just as they taught my people to swear by Baal,
then they shall be built up in the midst of my
people. * ¹⁷ But if they do not obey, I will uproot and destroy that nation entirely—oracle
of the LORD. *

**13** **Judah's Corruption.**† ¹ The LORD said
to me: Go buy yourself a linen loincloth; wear it on your loins, but do not put it
in water. ² I bought the loincloth, as the LORD
commanded, and put it on. ³ A second time
the word of the LORD came to me thus: ⁴ Take
the loincloth which you bought and are wearing, and go at once to the Perath; hide it there
in a cleft of the rock. ⁵ Obedient to the LORD's
command, I went to the Perath and buried
the loincloth. ⁶ After a long time, the LORD
said to me: Go now to the Perath and fetch
the loincloth which I told you to hide there.
⁷ So I went to the Perath, looked for the loincloth and took it from the place I had hidden
it. But it was rotted, good for nothing! ⁸ Then
the word came to me from the LORD: ⁹ Thus
says the LORD: So also I will allow the pride
of Judah to rot, the great pride of Jerusalem. *
¹⁰ This wicked people who refuse to obey my
words, who walk in the stubbornness of their

---

**12:14** *My evil neighbors*: nations surrounding Israel, the land
belonging to the Lord; cf. Is 8:8.

**13:1–11** In this symbolic action, Jeremiah probably went to
the village and spring of Parah, two and a half miles northeast of
Anathoth, whose name closely resembled the Hebrew name of
the river Euphrates (*Perath*), in order to dramatize the religious
corruption of Judah at the hands of the Babylonians.

---

**12:6** Jer 9:4.
**12:7** Ps 78:62; Lam 2:1–2.
**12:8** Ps 106:40.
**12:9** 2 Kgs 24:2; Is 56:9.
**12:10** Jer 6:3; Is 63:18.
**12:12** Is 42:25; 57:21.
**12:14** 2 Kgs 24:2.
**12:15** Am 9:14.
**12:16** Dt 6:13.
**12:17** Is 60:12.
**13:9** Prv 16:18.

hearts and follow other gods, serving and worshiping them, will be like this loincloth, good for nothing.* ¹¹ For, as the loincloth clings to a man's loins, so I made the whole house of Israel and the whole house of Judah cling to me—oracle of the LORD—to be my people, my fame, my praise, my glory. But they did not listen.*

**The Broken Wineflask.** ¹² Now speak to them this word: Thus says the LORD, the God of Israel: Every wineflask should be filled with wine. If they reply, "Do we not know that every wineflask should be filled with wine?" ¹³ say to them: Thus says the LORD: Beware! I am making all the inhabitants of this land drunk, the kings who sit on David's throne, the priests and prophets, and all the inhabitants of Jerusalem.* ¹⁴ I will smash them against each other, parents and children together—oracle of the LORD—showing no compassion, I will neither spare nor pity, but I will destroy them.*

### A Last Warning

15  Listen and give ear, do not be arrogant,
    for the LORD speaks.
16  Give glory to the LORD, your God,
    before he brings darkness;
  Before your feet stumble
    on mountains at twilight;
  Before the light you look for turns to
    darkness,
    changes into black clouds.*
17  If you do not listen to this in your pride,
    I will weep many tears in secret;
  My eyes will run with tears
    for the LORD's flock, led away to
    exile.*

### Exile

18  Say to the king and to the queen
    mother:
  come down from your throne;
  From your heads
    your splendid crowns will fall.*
19  The cities of the Negeb are besieged,
    with no one to relieve them;

Judah is taken into exile—all of it—
    in total exile.

### Jerusalem's Disgrace

20  Lift up your eyes and see
    those coming in from the north.
  Where is the flock entrusted to you,
    your splendid sheep?*
21  What will you say when rulers are
    appointed over you,
    those you taught to be allies?
  Will not pains seize you
    like those of a woman giving birth?*
22  If you say to yourself:
    "Why have these things happened to
    me?"
  For your great guilt your skirts are
    stripped away
    and you are violated.*
23  Can Ethiopians change their skin,
    leopards their spots?
  As easily would you be able to do good,
    accustomed to evil as you are.*
24  I will scatter them like chaff that flies
    on the desert wind.*
25  This is your lot, the portion I have
    measured out to you—
    oracle of the LORD.
  Because you have forgotten me,
    and trusted in deception,†*
26  I now will strip away your skirts,
    so that your shame is visible.*
27  Your adulteries, your neighings,
    your shameless prostitutions:
  On the hills, in the fields
    I see your detestable crimes.
  Woe to you, Jerusalem! How long will
    it be
    before you are clean?*

**14** **The Great Drought.** ¹ The word of the LORD that came to Jeremiah concerning the drought:*

2  Judah mourns,
    her gates are lifeless;
  They are bowed to the ground,
    and the outcry of Jerusalem goes up.*

---

† **13:25** Heb. *sheqer*: lit., "deception," often used to designate an idol.

**13:10** Jer 2:20; 7:24; 16:11.
**13:11** Ex 19:5; Dt 26:18–19.
**13:13** Jer 25:15–18;
    Is 51:17.
**13:14** Jer 19:10–11.
**13:16** Prv 4:18–19; Is 5:30;

    Am 8:9.
**13:17** Jer 14:17; Ps 119:136.
**13:18** Jer 22:26; 2 Kgs
    24:12, 15.
**13:20** Jer 6:22–23.
**13:21** 2 Kgs 16:7.
**13:22** Is 47:2–3.
**13:23** Ps 55:20.
**13:24** Ps 1:4; 83:14.
**13:25** Jb 20:29.
**13:26** Ez 16:32.
**13:27** Jer 2:20.
**14:1** Lv 26:19–20.
**14:2** Is 3:26.

3    The nobles send their servants for water,
         but when they come to the cisterns
     They find no water
         and return with empty jars.*
     Confounded, despairing, they cover
         their heads
4        because of the ruined soil;
     Because there is no rain in the land
         the farmers are confounded, they
             cover their heads.*
5    Even the doe in the field deserts her
             young
         because there is no grass.
6    The wild donkeys stand on the bare
             heights,
         gasping for breath like jackals;
     Their eyes grow dim;
         there is no grass.
7    Even though our crimes bear witness
             against us,
         act, LORD, for your name's sake—
     Even though our rebellions are many,
         and we have sinned against you.*
8    Hope of Israel, LORD,
         our savior in time of need!
     Why should you be a stranger in the
             land,
         like a traveler stopping only for a
             night?
9    Why are you like someone bewildered,
         a champion who cannot save?
     You are in our midst, LORD,
         your name we bear:
         do not forsake us!*
10       Thus says the LORD about this people:
     They so love to wander
         that they cannot restrain their feet.
     The LORD takes no pleasure in them;
         now he remembers their guilt,
         and will punish their sins.*

11 Then the LORD said to me: Do not intercede for the well-being of this people.* 12 If
they fast, I will not listen to their supplication.
If they sacrifice burnt offerings or grain offerings, I will take no pleasure in them. Rather, I
will destroy them with the sword, famine, and
plague.* 13 "Ah! Lord GOD," I replied, "it is the prophets who say to them, 'You shall not see the

sword; famine shall not befall you. Indeed, I
will give you lasting peace in this place.'"* 14 These prophets utter lies in my name, the
LORD said to me: I did not send them; I gave
them no command, nor did I speak to them.
They prophesy to you lying visions, foolish
divination, deceptions from their own imagination.* 15 Therefore, thus says the LORD:
Concerning the prophets who prophesy in
my name, though I did not send them, and
who say, "Sword and famine shall not befall
this land": by sword and famine shall these
prophets meet their end.* 16 The people to
whom they prophesy shall be thrown out into
the streets of Jerusalem because of famine
and the sword. No one shall bury them, their
wives, their sons, or their daughters, for I will
pour out upon them their own wickedness.* 17 Speak to them this word:

     Let my eyes stream with tears
         night and day, without rest,
     Over the great destruction which
             overwhelms
         the virgin daughter of my people,
         over her incurable wound.*
18   If I walk out into the field,
         look! those slain by the sword;
     If I enter the city,
         look! victims of famine.
     Both prophet and priest ply their trade
         in a land they do not know.
19   Have you really cast Judah off?
         Is Zion loathsome to you?
     Why have you struck us a blow
         that cannot be healed?
     We wait for peace, to no avail;
         for a time of healing, but terror comes
             instead.*
20   We recognize our wickedness, LORD,
         the guilt of our ancestors:
         we have sinned against you.*
21   Do not reject us, for your name's sake,
         do not disgrace your glorious throne.
         Remember! Do not break your
             covenant with us.*
22   Among the idols of the nations are there
             any that give rain?
         Or can the mere heavens send
             showers?

**14:3** Am 4:8.
**14:4** Dt 28:23.
**14:7** Dn 9:4–14.
**14:9** Is 59:1–2; 63:19.

**14:10** Jer 2:25.
**14:11** Jer 11:14; Ex 32:10.
**14:12** Jer 6:20; Is 1:11, 13.
**14:13** Jer 4:10; 5:12.

**14:14** Jer 5:31; 23:16.
**14:15** Jer 5:12–13.
**14:16** Jer 7:33; 19:7.
**14:17** Jer 9:17.

**14:19** Jer 8:15; 2 Chr 36:16.
**14:20** Ps 106:6; Dn 9:5, 8.
**14:21** Jer 14:7; Lv 26:44; Ps 25:11.

Is it not you, LORD,
>> our God, to whom we look?
>> You alone do all these things.*

**15** ¹The LORD said to me: Even if Moses and Samuel stood before me, my heart would not turn toward this people. Send them away from me and let them go.* ²If they ask you, "Where should we go?" tell them, Thus says the LORD: Whoever is marked for death, to death; whoever is marked for the sword, to the sword; whoever is marked for famine, to famine; whoever is marked for captivity, to captivity.* ³Four kinds of scourge I have decreed against them—oracle of the LORD—the sword to kill them; dogs to drag them off; the birds of the sky and the beasts of the earth to devour and destroy them.* ⁴And I will make them an object of horror to all the kingdoms of the earth because of what Manasseh, son of Hezekiah, king of Judah, did in Jerusalem.*

### Scene of Tragedy

5 Who will pity you, Jerusalem,
>> who will grieve for you?
>> Who will stop to ask
>> about your welfare?*
6 It is you who have disowned me—oracle
>> of the LORD—
>> turned your back upon me;
>> I stretched out my hand to destroy you,
>> because I was weary of relenting.*
7 I winnowed them with a winnowing
>> fork
>> at the gates of the land;
>> I have bereaved, destroyed my people;
>> they have not turned from their evil
>> ways.*
8 Their widows were more numerous
>> before me
>> than the sands of the sea.
>> I brought against the mother of youths
>> the destroyer at midday;
>> Suddenly I struck her
>> with anguish and terror.
9 The mother of seven faints away,
>> breathing out her life;

Her sun sets in full day,
>> she is ashamed, abashed.
>> Their survivors I will give to the sword
>> in the presence of their enemies—
>> oracle of the LORD.*

### Jeremiah's Complaint

10 Woe to me, my mother, that you gave
>> me birth!
>> a man of strife and contention to all
>> the land!
>> I neither borrow nor lend,
>> yet everyone curses me.*
11 Tell me, LORD, have I not served you for
>> their good?
>> Have I not interceded with you
>> in time of misfortune and anguish?*
12 Can one break iron,
>> iron from the north, and bronze?
13† Your wealth and your treasures
>> I give as plunder, demanding no
>> payment,
>> because of all your sins, throughout
>> all your territory.
14 And I shall enslave you to your enemies
>> in a land you do not know,
>> For fire has broken out from my anger,
>> it is kindled against you.
15 You know, LORD:
>> Remember me and take care of me,
>> avenge me on my persecutors.
>> Because you are slow to anger, do not
>> banish me;
>> know that for you I have borne
>> insult.*
16 When I found your words, I devoured
>> them;
>> your words were my joy, the
>> happiness of my heart,
>> Because I bear your name,
>> LORD, God of hosts.
17 I did not sit celebrating
>> in the circle of merrymakers;
>> Under the weight of your hand I sat
>> alone
>> because you filled me with rage.*
18 Why is my pain continuous,

† **15:13–14** Though the wording of these verses is close to that in 17:3–4, the present passage is evidently God's word to Jeremiah, whereas 17:3–4 is evidently a word of judgment on Judah. It is noteworthy that the references to "you" in the present passage are singular, until a shift to plural in "against you" in the last line; this "you" is then doubtless a reference to both the prophet and his enemies.

14:22 Jer 5:24; Zec 10:1.    15:6 Am 7:8.
15:1 Ps 99:6; Ez 14:14, 16.    15:7 Is 41:16.
15:2 Jer 14:12; Ez 5:12.    15:9 1 Sm 2:5.
15:3 Ez 14:21.    15:10 Jer 20:14.
15:4 Jer 24:9; 2 Kgs    15:11 Jer 39:11–14.
21:11–16; 23:26;    15:15 Jer 11:20; 12:3; Ps
24:3–4.    69:8.
15:5 Is 51:19.    15:17 Ps 25:4.

my wound incurable, refusing to be
 healed?
To me you are like a deceptive brook,
 waters that cannot be relied on!*

19     Thus the LORD answered me:
If you come back and I take you back,
 in my presence you shall stand;
If you utter what is precious and not
 what is worthless,
 you shall be my mouth.
Then they will be the ones who turn to
 you,
 not you who turn to them.

20     And I will make you toward this people
 a fortified wall of bronze.
Though they fight against you,
 they shall not prevail,
For I am with you,
 to save and rescue you—oracle of the
 LORD.*

21     I will rescue you from the hand of the
 wicked,
 and ransom you from the power of
 the violent.

# 16

**Jeremiah's Life a Warning.** ¹This word
came to me from the LORD: ²Do not
take a wife and do not have sons and daughters in this place, ³for thus says the LORD concerning the sons and daughters born in this
place, the mothers who give them birth, the fathers who beget them in this land: ⁴Of deadly
disease they shall die. Unlamented and unburied they will lie like dung on the ground.
Sword and famine will make an end of them,
and their corpses will become food for the
birds of the sky and the beasts of the earth.*

⁵Thus says the LORD: Do not go into a house
of mourning; do not go there to lament or
grieve for them. For I have withdrawn my
peace from this people—oracle of the LORD—
my love and my compassion.* ⁶They shall die,
the great and the lowly, in this land, unburied
and unlamented.† No one will gash themselves or shave their heads for them.* ⁷They
will not break bread with the bereaved to offer
consolation for the dead; they will not give
them the cup of consolation to drink over the
death of father or mother.*

⁸Do not enter a house of feasting to sit eating and drinking with them. ⁹For thus says the
LORD of hosts, the God of Israel: Before your
eyes and in your lifetime, I will silence in this
place the song of joy and the song of gladness,
the song of the bridegroom and the song of
the bride.*

¹⁰When you proclaim all these words to this
people and they ask you: "Why has the LORD
pronounced all this great disaster against us?
What is our crime? What sin have we committed against the LORD, our God?"—* ¹¹*you
shall answer them: It is because your ancestors
have forsaken me—oracle of the LORD—and
followed other gods that they served and worshiped; but me they have forsaken, and my
law they did not keep. ¹²And you have done
worse than your ancestors. Here you are, every
one of you, walking in the stubbornness of
your evil heart instead of listening to me.* ¹³I
will throw you out of this land into a land that
neither you nor your ancestors have known;
there you can serve other gods day and night
because I will not show you mercy.

**Return from Exile.** ¹⁴Therefore, days are coming—oracle of the LORD—when it will no longer
be said, "As the LORD lives, who brought the
Israelites out of Egypt";* ¹⁵but rather, "As the
LORD lives, who brought the Israelites out of
the land of the north and out of all the countries
to which he had banished them." I will bring
them back to the land I gave their ancestors.*

**Double Punishment.** ¹⁶Look!—oracle of the
LORD—I will send many fishermen to catch
them. After that, I will send many hunters to
hunt them out from every mountain and hill
and rocky crevice.* ¹⁷For my eyes are upon all
their ways; they are not hidden from me, nor
does their guilt escape my sight.* ¹⁸I will at
once repay them double for their crime and
their sin because they profaned my land with
the corpses of their detestable idols, and filled
my heritage with their abominations.*

## Conversion of the Nations

19     LORD, my strength, my fortress,
 my refuge in the day of distress!

---

† 
**16:6–7** These verses refer to popular mourning practices in
the land; cf. Dt 14:1–2.

*

**15:18** Jer 14:19; 30:15.
**15:20** Jer 1:18; 6:27.

**16:4** Jer 7:33; 22:18.
**16:5** Ez 24:16–17.

**16:6** Lv 19:28; Dt 14:1.
**16:7** Ez 24:17.
**16:9** Jer 7:34; 25:10.
**16:10** Jer 2:35; 5:19; 13:22.
**16:11** Jer 22:9; Dt 29:25.
**16:12** Jer 7:24–26.

**16:14** Jer 23:7–8.
**16:15** Jer 24:6.
**16:16** 2 Kgs 24:2; Lam 4:19.
**16:17** Jer 32:19; Jb 34:21.
**16:18** Is 40:2.

To you nations will come
  from the ends of the earth, and say,
"Our ancestors inherited mere frauds,
  empty, worthless."*
20 Can human beings make for themselves
      gods?
   But these are not gods at all!*
21 Therefore, I will indeed give them
      knowledge;
   this time I will make them
      acknowledge
My strength and my power:
  they shall know that my name is
  LORD.*

## The Sin of Judah and Its Punishment

**17** ¹ The sin of Judah is written
  with an iron stylus,
Engraved with a diamond point
  upon the tablets of their hearts,*

And the horns of their altars, ² when their children remember their altars and their asherahs,
beside the green trees, on the high hills, ³ the
peaks in the country.

Your wealth and all your treasures
  I give as plunder,
As payment for all your sins
  throughout your territory,
4 You will relinquish your hold on your
      heritage
   which I have given you.
I will enslave you to your enemies
  in a land you do not know:
For a fire has broken out from my anger,
  burning forever.*

### True Wisdom

5      Thus says the LORD:
Cursed is the man who trusts in human
      beings,
   who makes flesh his strength,
   whose heart turns away from the
      LORD.*
6 He is like a barren bush in the wasteland
      that enjoys no change of season,
   But stands in lava beds in the
      wilderness,
   a land, salty and uninhabited.

7 Blessed are those who trust in the LORD;
   the LORD will be their trust.*
8 They are like a tree planted beside the
      waters
   that stretches out its roots to the
      stream:
It does not fear heat when it comes,
  its leaves stay green;
In the year of drought it shows no
      distress,
   but still produces fruit.*
9 More tortuous than anything is the
      human heart,
   beyond remedy; who can understand
      it?
10 I, the LORD, explore the mind
   and test the heart,
Giving to all according to their ways,
  according to the fruit of their deeds.*
11 A partridge that broods but does not
      hatch
   are those who acquire wealth unjustly:
In midlife it will desert them;
  in the end they are only fools.*

### The Source of Life

12 A throne of glory, exalted from the
      beginning,
   such is our holy place.*
13 O Hope of Israel, LORD!
   all who forsake you shall be put to
      shame;
The rebels shall be enrolled in the
      netherworld;
   they have forsaken the LORD, source of
      living waters.*

### Prayer for Vengeance

14 Heal me, LORD, that I may be healed;
   save me, that I may be saved,
   for you are my praise.
15 See how they say to me,
   "Where is the word of the LORD?
   Let it come to pass!"*
16 Yet I did not press you to send disaster;
   the day without remedy I have not
      desired.
   You know what passed my lips;
   it is present before you.
17 Do not become a terror to me,

**16:19** Jer 2:11; Is 2:2–3.
**16:20** Jer 2:11; Gal 4:8.
**16:21** Am 5:8.
**17:1** Jb 19:24.
**17:4** Jer 5:19; Dt 32:22.
**17:5** Ps 146:2–3.
**17:7** Ps 1:3.
**17:8** Is 58:11.
**17:10** Jer 32:19; 1 Sm 16:7; Eccl 12:14.
**17:11** Prv 13:11; Lk 12:20.
**17:12** Jer 14:21.
**17:13** Jer 2:13.
**17:15** Is 5:19; 2 Pt 3:4.

JER

you are my refuge in the day of
disaster.*
18 Let my persecutors be confounded—not
me!
let them be terrified—not me!
Bring upon them the day of disaster,
crush them with double destruction.*

**Observance of the Sabbath.** ¹⁹Thus said the
LORD to me: Go, stand at the Gate of Benjamin,† where the kings of Judah enter and
leave, and at the other gates of Jerusalem.*
²⁰There say to them: Hear the word of the
LORD, you kings of Judah, and all Judah, and
all you inhabitants of Jerusalem who enter
these gates! ²¹Thus says the LORD: As you love
your lives, take care not to carry burdens on
the sabbath, to bring them in through the
gates of Jerusalem.* ²²Bring no burden from
your homes on the sabbath. Do no work whatever, but keep holy the sabbath day, as I commanded your ancestors,* ²³though they did
not listen or give ear, but stiffened their necks
so they could not hear or take correction.* ²⁴If
you truly obey me—oracle of the LORD—and
carry no burden through the gates of this city
on the sabbath, keeping the sabbath day holy
and abstaining from all work on it,* ²⁵then,
through the gates of this city, kings who sit
upon the throne of David will continue to
enter, riding in their chariots or upon their
horses, along with their princes, and the people of Judah, and the inhabitants of Jerusalem.
This city will remain inhabited forever.* ²⁶To it
people will come from the cities of Judah and
the neighborhood of Jerusalem, from the land
of Benjamin and from the Shephelah, from
the hill country and the Negeb, to bring burnt
offerings and sacrifices, grain offerings, incense, and thank offerings to the house of the
LORD.* ²⁷But if you do not obey me and keep
holy the sabbath day, if you carry burdens and
come through the gates of Jerusalem on the
sabbath, I will set fire to its gates—a fire never
to be extinguished—and it will consume the
palaces of Jerusalem.*

**18 The Potter's Vessel.†** ¹This word came
to Jeremiah from the LORD: ²Arise and
go down to the potter's house; there you will
hear my word. ³I went down to the potter's
house and there he was, working at the wheel.
⁴Whenever the vessel of clay he was making
turned out badly in his hand, he tried again,
making another vessel of whatever sort he
pleased.* ⁵Then the word of the LORD came
to me: ⁶Can I not do to you, house of Israel,
as this potter has done?—oracle of the LORD.
Indeed, like clay in the hand of the potter, so
are you in my hand, house of Israel.* ⁷*At one
moment I may decree concerning a nation or
kingdom that I will uproot and tear down and
destroy it; ⁸but if that nation against whom
I have decreed turns from its evil, then I will
have a change of heart regarding the evil which
I have decreed.* ⁹At another moment, I may
decree concerning a nation or kingdom that I
will build up and plant it; ¹⁰but if that nation
does what is evil in my eyes, refusing to obey
my voice, then I will have a change of heart
regarding the good with which I planned to
bless it.*

¹¹And now, tell this to the people of Judah
and the inhabitants of Jerusalem: Thus says
the LORD: Look, I am fashioning evil against
you and making a plan. Return, all of you,
from your evil way; reform your ways and your
deeds.* ¹²But they will say, "No use! We will
follow our own devices; each one of us will
behave according to the stubbornness of our
evil hearts!"*

**Unnatural Apostasy**

13     Therefore thus says the LORD:
Ask among the nations—
who has ever heard the like?
Truly horrible things
virgin Israel has done!*
14     Does the snow of Lebanon†
desert the rocky heights?
Do the gushing waters dry up
that flow fresh down the mountains?
15     Yet my people have forgotten me:

17:19 *The Gate of Benjamin*: this gate, probably part of the
Temple area, is otherwise unknown.
18:1–12 The lesson of the potter is that God has the power
to destroy or restore, changing his plans accordingly as these
nations disobey him or fulfill his will. Cf. Jon 3:10.
18:14 *Lebanon*: here apparently including Mount Hermon,
whose snow-capped peak can be seen from parts of Palestine all
year round. The prophet contrasts the certainties of nature with
Israel's unnatural desertion of the Lord for idols (v. 15).

17:17 Jer 16:19.
17:18 Jer 15:15; 18:20–23; Ps 35:5–6.
17:19 Jer 7:2.
17:21 Neh 13:15–19.
17:22 Ex 20:8; 23:12.
17:23 Jer 5:3; 7:24.
17:24 Is 58:14.
17:25 Jer 22:4.
17:26 Jer 32:44.
17:27 Ez 22:8.
18:4 Rom 9:20–21.
18:6 Wis 15:7; Is 45:9.
18:7 Jer 1:10.
18:8 Jer 26:3; Is 55:7; Ez 18:21, 27; Jon 3:10.
18:10 Nm 14:22–23.
18:11 Jer 7:3; 25:5; 35:15.
18:12 Jer 2:25; 7:24.
18:13 Jer 2:10–11; 5:30.

they offer incense in vain.
They stumble off their paths,
    the ways of old,
Traveling on bypaths,
    not the beaten track.*

16 Their land shall be made a waste,
        an object of endless hissing:†
    All passersby will be horrified,
        shaking their heads.*

17 Like the east wind, I will scatter them
        before their enemies;
    I will show them my back, not my face,
        in their day of disaster.*

**Another Prayer for Vengeance.** 18 "Come," they said, "let us devise a plot against Jeremiah, for instruction will not perish from the priests, nor counsel from the wise, nor the word from the prophets. Come, let us destroy him by his own tongue. Let us pay careful attention to his every word."*

19 Pay attention to me, O LORD,
        and listen to what my adversaries say.

20 Must good be repaid with evil
        that they should dig a pit to take my
            life?
    Remember that I stood before you
        to speak on their behalf,
        to turn your wrath away from them.*

21 So now, give their children† to famine,*
        deliver them to the power of the sword.
    Let their wives be childless and widows;
        let their husbands die of pestilence,
        their youths be struck down by the
            sword in battle.

22 May cries be heard from their homes,
        when suddenly you send plunderers
            against them.
    For they have dug a pit to capture me,
        they have hidden snares for my feet;

23 But you, LORD, know
        all their planning for my death.
    Do not forgive their crime,
        and their sin do not blot out from
            your sight!

**19** **Symbol of the Potter's Flask.** 1 Thus said the LORD: Go, buy a potter's earthenware flask. Take along some of the elders of the people and some of the priests, 2 and go out toward the Valley of Ben-hinnom, at the entrance of the Potsherd Gate;† there proclaim the words which I will speak to you: 3 You shall say, Listen to the word of the LORD, kings of Judah and inhabitants of Jerusalem: Thus says the LORD of hosts, the God of Israel: I am going to bring such evil upon this place that the ears of all who hear of it will ring. 4 All because they have forsaken me and profaned this place by burning incense to other gods which neither they nor their ancestors knew; and because the kings of Judah have filled this place with innocent blood,* 5 building high places for Baal to burn their children in fire as offerings to Baal—something I never considered or said or commanded.* 6† Therefore, days are coming—oracle of the LORD—when this place will no longer be called Topheth, or the Valley of Ben-hinnom, but rather, the Valley of Slaughter.* 7 In this place I will foil the plan of Judah and Jerusalem; I will make them fall by the sword before their enemies, at the hand of those who seek their lives. Their corpses I will give as food to the birds of the sky and the beasts of the earth.* 8 I will make this city a waste and an object of hissing. Because of all its wounds, every passerby will be horrified and hiss. 9 I will have them eat the flesh of their sons and daughters; they shall eat one another's flesh during the harsh siege under which their enemies and those who seek their lives will confine them.*

10 And you shall break the flask in the sight of the men who went with you, 11 and say to them: Thus says the LORD of hosts: Thus will I smash this people and this city, as one smashes a clay pot so that it cannot be repaired. And

---

† **18:16** *Hissing*: in some ancient Near Eastern cultures hissing was not only a sign of derision but a magical means of keeping demons away; people hissed in order to ward off danger, like whistling in a cemetery.
    **18:21** *Give their children*: often an extended family is meant, to be rewarded or punished as a unit.
    **19:2** *Potsherd Gate*: perhaps in the south wall of Jerusalem, through which potsherds and other refuse were thrown into the Valley of Ben-hinnom.

**19:6** Cf. note on 7:31.

**18:15** Jer 2:13, 32.
**18:16** Jer 19:8; Lv 26:32;
        1 Kgs 9:8.
**18:17** Prv 1:24–31.
**18:18** Jer 11:19; Ps
        35:15–16.
**18:20** Ps 35:12.
**18:21** Ps 109:9–10.

**18:23** Neh 4:5; Ps 35:4;
        37:32–33.
**19:4** Jer 1:16; 2 Kgs 21:16;
        24:4.
**19:5** Jer 7:31–32; 32:35.
**19:6** Jer 7:32.
**19:7** Jer 7:33.
**19:9** Lv 26:29.

JER

Topheth shall be its burial place, for there will be no other place for burial.* <sup>12</sup>Thus I will do to this place and to its inhabitants—oracle of the Lord; I will make this city like Topheth.* <sup>13</sup>And the houses of Jerusalem and the houses of the kings of Judah shall be defiled like the place of Topheth, all the houses upon whose roofs they burnt incense to the whole host of heaven and poured out libations to other gods.*

<sup>14</sup>When Jeremiah returned from Topheth, where the Lord had sent him to prophesy, he stood in the court of the house of the Lord and said to all the people:* <sup>15</sup>Thus says the Lord of hosts, the God of Israel: I will bring upon this city all the evil I have spoken against it, because they have become stubborn and have not obeyed my words.*

**20** <sup>1</sup>Now the priest Pashhur,* son of Immer, chief officer in the house of the Lord,† heard Jeremiah prophesying these things. <sup>2</sup>So he struck the prophet and put him in the stocks at the upper Gate of Benjamin in the house of the Lord.* <sup>3</sup>The next morning, after Pashhur had released Jeremiah from the stocks, the prophet said to him:* "Instead of Pashhur, the Lord names you 'Terror on every side.'† <sup>4</sup>For thus says the Lord: Indeed, I will hand you over to terror, you and all your friends. Your own eyes shall see them fall by the sword of their enemies. All Judah I will hand over to the power of the king of Babylon,† who shall take them captive to Babylon or strike them down with the sword. <sup>5</sup>All the wealth of this city, all its resources and its valuables, all the treasures of the kings of Judah, I will hand over to their enemies, who will plunder it and carry it away to Babylon.* <sup>6</sup>You, Pashhur, and all the members of your household shall go into exile. To Babylon you shall go; there you shall die and be buried, you and all your friends, because you have prophesied lies to them."*

## Jeremiah's Interior Crisis

<sup>7</sup> You seduced me,† Lord, and I let myself
   be seduced;
  you were too strong for me, and you
   prevailed.
All day long I am an object of laughter;
  everyone mocks me.
<sup>8</sup> Whenever I speak, I must cry out,
  violence and outrage I proclaim;
The word of the Lord has brought me
  reproach and derision all day long.
<sup>9</sup> I say I will not mention him,
  I will no longer speak in his name.
But then it is as if fire is burning in my
   heart,
  imprisoned in my bones;
I grow weary holding back,
  I cannot!*
<sup>10</sup> Yes, I hear the whisperings of many:
  "Terror on every side!
  Denounce! let us denounce him!"
All those who were my friends
  are on the watch for any misstep of
   mine.
"Perhaps he can be tricked; then we will
   prevail,
  and take our revenge on him."*
<sup>11</sup> But the Lord is with me, like a mighty
   champion:
  my persecutors will stumble, they will
   not prevail.
In their failure they will be put to utter
   shame,
  to lasting, unforgettable confusion.*
<sup>12</sup> Lord of hosts, you test the just,
  you see mind and heart,
Let me see the vengeance you take on
   them,
  for to you I have entrusted my cause.*
<sup>13</sup> Sing to the Lord,
  praise the Lord,
For he has rescued the life of the poor
  from the power of the evildoers!*

---

**20:1** *Chief officer in the house of the Lord:* head of the Temple police; cf. 29:26. By entering the Temple court (19:14), Jeremiah had put himself under Pashhur's jurisdiction.

**20:3** *Terror on every side:* the name indicates the siege that will beset Jerusalem.

**20:4** *Babylon:* mentioned here for the first time in Jeremiah as the land of exile. The prophecy dates from after 605 B.C., when Nebuchadnezzar defeated Egypt and made the Babylonian (Chaldean) empire dominant in Syria and Palestine.

**20:7** *You seduced me:* Jeremiah accuses the Lord of having deceived him; cf. 15:18.

**19:11** Jer 7:32.
**19:12** 2 Kgs 23:10.
**19:13** Jer 32:29.
**19:14** Jer 26:2.
**19:15** Jer 7:26; Prv 29:1.
**20:1** Jer 21:1.
**20:2** Jer 29:26.
**20:3** Jer 6:25.
**20:5** 2 Kgs 20:17;
24:12–16.
**20:6** Jer 14:13–14; 28:15.
**20:9** Jer 6:11; Jb 32:18.
**20:10** Jb 19:19; Ps 31:13; Lk 20:20.
**20:11** Jer 1:8; 15:20.
**20:12** Jer 11:20.
**20:13** Ps 35:9–10; 109:30–31.

14  Cursed be the day†
       on which I was born!
    May the day my mother gave me birth
       never be blessed!*
15  Cursed be the one who brought the
          news
       to my father,
    "A child, a son, has been born to you!"
       filling him with great joy.
16  Let that man be like the cities
       which the LORD relentlessly overthrew;
    Let him hear war cries in the morning,
       battle alarms at noonday,*
17     because he did not kill me in the
          womb!
    Then my mother would have been my
          grave,
       her womb confining me forever.*
18  Why did I come forth from the womb,
       to see sorrow and pain,
       to end my days in shame?*

## III. ORACLES IN THE LAST YEARS OF JERUSALEM

**21 Fate of Zedekiah and Jerusalem.** ¹The word which came to Jeremiah from the LORD when King Zedekiah† sent Pashhur, son of Malchiah, and the priest Zephaniah, son of Maaseiah, to him with this request: ²Inquire for us of the LORD, because Nebuchadnezzar, king of Babylon, is attacking us. Perhaps the LORD will act for us in accord with his wonderful works by making him withdraw from us. ³But Jeremiah answered them: This is what you shall report to Zedekiah: ⁴Thus says the LORD, the God of Israel: I will turn against you the weapons with which you are fighting the king of Babylon and the Chaldeans who besiege you outside the walls. These weapons I will pile up in the midst of this city,* ⁵and I myself will fight against you with outstretched

hand and mighty arm, in anger, wrath, and great rage!* ⁶I will strike down the inhabitants of this city, human being and beast; they shall die in a great pestilence.* ⁷After that—oracle of the LORD—I will hand over Zedekiah, king of Judah, and his ministers and the people in this city who survive pestilence, sword, and famine, to Nebuchadnezzar, king of Babylon, to their enemies and those who seek their lives. He shall strike them down with the edge of the sword, without quarter, without mercy or compassion.* ⁸And to this people you shall say: Thus says the LORD: See, I am giving you a choice between the way to life and the way to death.* ⁹Whoever remains in this city shall die by the sword or famine or pestilence. But whoever leaves and surrenders to the Chaldeans who are besieging you shall live and escape with his life. ¹⁰I have set my face against this city, for evil and not for good—oracle of the LORD. It shall be given into the power of the king of Babylon who shall set it on fire.†

### Oracles Regarding the Kings†

11  To the royal house of Judah:
    Hear the word of the LORD,
12        house of David!
    Thus says the LORD:
    Each morning dispense justice,
       rescue the oppressed from the hand of
          the oppressor,
    Or my fury will break out like fire
       and burn with no one to quench it
       because of your evil deeds.*
13  Beware! I am against you, Ruler of the
          Valley,
       Rock of the Plain†—oracle of the
          LORD.
    You say, "Who will attack us,
       who can storm our defenses?"
14  I will punish you—oracle of the LORD—
       as your deeds deserve!

---

**20:14–18** Deception, sorrow and terror have brought the prophet to the point of despair; nevertheless he maintains confidence in God (vv. 11–13); cf. Jb 3:3–12.

**21:1** Zedekiah: brother of Jehoiakim, appointed king by Nebuchadnezzar after he had carried Jehoiachin away to captivity (2 Kgs 24:17). Pashhur: different from the one in 20:1–3 but also one of Jeremiah's enemies; cf. 38:1, 4.

**21:10** Jeremiah consistently pointed out the uselessness of resistance to Babylon, since the Lord had delivered Judah to Nebuchadnezzar (27:6). Because of this the prophet was denounced and imprisoned (37:13–14).

**21:11–23:8** This section contains an editor's collection of Jeremiah's oracles against the kings of Judah. They are placed in the chronological order of the kings, and are prefaced by oracles

against the kings of Judah in general (21:11–22:9).

**21:13** Ruler of the Valley, Rock of the Plain: Mount Zion, surrounded by valleys, was regarded by the royal house as impregnable. Despite this natural fortification, God derides it as no more than a rock rising from the plain, useless against the attack of his fury.

| | |
|---|---|
| **20:14** Jer 15:10; Jb 3:1–10; 10:18. | **21:5** Is 63:10; Lam 2:4–5. |
| **20:16** Gn 19:25; Is 13:19. | **21:6** Jer 16:4. |
| **20:17** Jb 3:10–11; 10:19. | **21:7** Jer 24:8–10; Dt 28:49–50. |
| **20:18** Jb 14:1. | **21:8** Jer 21:9; Dt 30:15, 19. |
| **21:4** Jer 37:8–10. | **21:12** Jer 4:4; 22:3; Zec 7:9. |

I will kindle a fire in its forest†
　　that shall devour all its surroundings.*

**22** ¹Thus says the LORD: Go down to the palace of the king of Judah and there deliver this word: ²You shall say: Listen to the word of the LORD, king of Judah, who sit on the throne of David, you, your ministers, and your people who enter by these gates!* ³Thus says the LORD: Do what is right and just. Rescue the victims from the hand of their oppressors. Do not wrong or oppress the resident alien, the orphan, or the widow, and do not shed innocent blood in this place.* ⁴If you carry out these commands, kings who succeed to the throne of David will continue to enter the gates of this house, riding in chariots or mounted on horses, with their ministers, and their people. ⁵But if you do not obey these commands, I swear by myself—oracle of the LORD: this house shall become rubble. ⁶For thus says the LORD concerning the house of the king of Judah:

Though you be to me like Gilead,
　　like the peak of Lebanon,
I swear I shall turn you into a waste,
　　with cities uninhabited.
⁷Against you I will send destroyers,
　　each with their tools:
They shall cut down your choice cedars,
　　and cast them into the fire.*

⁸Many nations will pass by this city and ask one another: "Why has the LORD done this to so great a city?"* ⁹And they will be told: "Because they have deserted their covenant with the LORD, their God, by worshiping and serving other gods."*

### Jehoahaz

¹⁰ Do not weep for him who is dead,†
　　nor mourn for him!

Weep rather for him who is going away;
　　never again to see
　　the land of his birth.*

¹¹Thus says the LORD concerning Shallum,† son of Josiah, king of Judah, his father's successor, who left this place: He shall never return, ¹²but in the place where they exiled him, there he shall die; he shall never see this land again.

### Jehoiakim

¹³ Woe to him who builds his house on wrongdoing,
　　his roof-chambers on injustice;
Who works his neighbors without pay,†
　　and gives them no wages.*
¹⁴ Who says, "I will build myself a spacious house,
　　with airy rooms,"
Who cuts out windows for it,
　　panels it with cedar,
　　and paints it with vermilion.
¹⁵ Must you prove your rank among kings†
　　by competing with them in cedar?
Did not your father eat and drink,
　　And act justly and righteously?
　　Then he prospered.*
¹⁶ Because he dispensed justice to the weak and the poor,
　　he prospered.
Is this not to know me?—
　　oracle of the LORD.*
¹⁷ But your eyes and heart are set on nothing
　　except your own gain,
On shedding innocent blood
　　and practicing oppression and extortion.*

¹⁸Therefore, thus says the LORD concerning Jehoiakim, son of Josiah, king of Judah:

---

†

**21:14** *Its forest*: probably the royal palace, built of cedar wood; cf. 22:14; in 1 Kgs 7:2 the palace is called "the house of the forest of Lebanon."
**22:10** *Him who is dead*: Josiah. His successor, Jehoahaz, was deported by Pharaoh Neco to Egypt, where he died (2 Kgs 23:33–34).
**22:11** *Shallum*: i.e., Jehoahaz; cf. 1 Chr 3:15. This may have been his name at birth, in which case Jehoahaz would have been his throne name.
**22:13** *Without pay*: either by forced labor in public works, or by defrauding the workers. Despite the impoverishment caused in Judah by the payment of foreign tribute, Jehoiakim embarked on a building program in Jerusalem (v. 14); cedar was an expensive building material which had to be imported. Social

injustice is the cause of much of the prophetic condemnation of the kings (v. 17).
**22:15–16** The rule of Josiah, Jehoiakim's father, shows that authentic kingship is rooted in knowledge of the Lord and creates a society in which the most disadvantaged can expect and receive justice.

---

**21:14** 2 Kgs 25:9; 2 Chr 36:19.
**22:2** Jer 17:20.
**22:3** Jer 21:12; Ex 22:21–24; Dt 24:17.
**22:7** Jer 21:14.
**22:8** Dt 29:24–27.
**22:9** Jer 19:4; 40:2–3.
**22:10** 2 Chr 35:23–25.
**22:13** Lv 19:13; Dt 24:14; Hb 2:9, 12.
**22:15** 2 Sm 5:11; 7:2; 2 Kgs 23:25.
**22:16** Prv 31:9.
**22:17** Ez 22:13, 27.

They shall not lament him,
 "Alas! my brother"; "Alas! sister."†
They shall not lament him,
 "Alas, Lord! alas, Majesty!"*
19 The burial of a donkey† he shall be
 given,
  dragged forth and cast out
 beyond the gates of Jerusalem.*

### Jeconiah

20 Climb Lebanon and cry out,†
 in Bashan lift up your voice;
 Cry out from Abarim,
  for all your lovers are crushed.*
21 I spoke to you when you were secure,
 but you answered, "I will not listen."
 This has been your way from your
  youth,
 not to listen to my voice.
22 The wind shall shepherd all your
  shepherds,
 your lovers shall go into exile.
 Surely then you shall be ashamed and
  confounded
 because of all your wickedness.
23 You who dwell on Lebanon,
 who nest in the cedars,
 How you shall groan when pains come
  upon you,
 like the pangs of a woman in
  childbirth!

24 As I live—oracle of the LORD—even if you,
Coniah,† son of Jehoiakim, king of Judah,

were a signet ring* on my right hand, I would
snatch you off. 25 I will hand you over to those
who seek your life, to those you dread: Nebuchadnezzar, king of Babylon, and the Chaldeans.* 26 I will cast you out, you and the mother
who bore you,† into a land different from the
land of your birth; and there you will die;*
27 Neither shall return to the land for which
they yearn.*

28 Is this man Coniah a thing despised, to
  be broken,
 a vessel that no one wants?
 Why are he and his offspring cast out?
 why thrown into a land they do not
  know?
29 O land, land, land,
 hear the word of the LORD—
30 Thus says the LORD:
* Write this man down as childless,†
 a man who will never prosper in his
  life!
 Nor shall any of his descendants
  prosper,
 to sit upon the throne of David,
 to rule again over Judah.

## 23

**A Just Shepherd.**† 1* Woe to the shepherds who destroy and scatter the flock
of my pasture—oracle of the LORD. 2 Therefore,
thus says the LORD, the God of Israel, against
the shepherds who shepherd my people: You
have scattered my sheep and driven them
away. You have not cared for them, but I will

---

**22:18** *"Alas! my brother"; "Alas! sister":* customary cries of mourning.
**22:19** *The burial of a donkey:* no burial at all, except to be cast outside the city as refuse. This prophecy describes the popular feeling toward Jehoiakim rather than the actual circumstances of his burial. According to 2 Kgs 24:5 he was buried with his ancestors in Jerusalem.
**22:20–23** The prophet first bids Jerusalem to scale Lebanon, Bashan, and Abarim, i.e., the highest surrounding mountains to the north, northeast, and southeast, and gaze on the ruin of its lovers, i.e., the false leaders of Judah, called its shepherds (v. 22); cf. 2:8. Jerusalem still stands (v. 23), apparently as secure as the heights of Lebanon, but destruction is to follow (cf. v. 6).
**22:24** *Coniah:* a shortened form of Jeconiah, the name Jeremiah gives King Jehoiachin (cf. 24:1). *A signet ring:* the seal used by kings and other powerful figures—a symbol of their power and status—mounted in a ring worn constantly on the hand. The Lord says that even were Jehoiachin such a precious possession, he would reject him. Hg 2:23 uses the same imagery to signal the restoration of Zerubbabel. The words in Jer 22:24–30 date from the short three-month reign of Jehoiachin, before he was deported by Nebuchadnezzar.
**22:26** *You and the mother who bore you:* the queen mother held a special position in the monarchy of Judah, and in the Books of Kings she is invariably mentioned by name along with the king

(1 Kgs 15:2; 2 Kgs 18:2). Jehoiachin did indeed die in Babylon.
**22:30** *Childless:* Jehoiachin is considered childless because none of his seven sons became king. His grandson Zerubbabel presided for a time over the Judahite community after the return from exile, but not as king. According to Ezekiel, whose oracles are dated by Jehoiachin's fictitious regnal years, the people expected Jehoiachin to return. Jeremiah's prophecy dispels this hope, despite the words of Hananiah (28:4).
**23:1–8** With the false rulers (shepherds) who have governed his people the Lord contrasts himself, the true shepherd, who will in the times of restoration appoint worthy rulers (vv. 1–4). He will provide a new king from David's line who will rule justly, fulfilling royal ideals (vv. 5, 6). "The Lord our justice" is an ironic wordplay on the name of the weak King Zedekiah ("The Lord is justice"). Unlike Zedekiah, the future king will be true to the name he bears. Verses 7–8 may have been added during the exile.

---

**22:18** Jer 16:4–7; 1 Kgs
  13:30.
**22:19** Jer 36:30.
**22:20** Jer 30:14–15; Dt
  32:49.
**22:24** Hg 2:23.
**22:25** Jer 21:7; 34:20.
**22:26** 2 Kgs 24:15.
**22:27** Jer 44:14.
**22:30** Jer 36:30; 1 Chr
  3:16–17; Mt 1:12.
**23:1** Jer 22:22.

JER

take care to punish your evil deeds.* ³I my-self will gather the remnant of my flock from all the lands to which I have banished them and bring them back to their folds; there they shall be fruitful and multiply.* ⁴I will raise up shepherds for them who will shepherd them so that they need no longer fear or be terrified; none shall be missing—oracle of the LORD.*

<sup></sup>

⁵ See, days are coming—oracle of the
LORD—
when I will raise up a righteous
branch for David;
As king he shall reign and govern wisely,
he shall do what is just and right in
the land.*
⁶ In his days Judah shall be saved,
Israel shall dwell in security.
This is the name to be given him:
"The LORD our justice."*

⁷* Therefore, the days are coming—oracle of the LORD—when they shall no longer say, "As the LORD lives, who brought the Israelites out of the land of Egypt"; ⁸but rather, "As the LORD lives, who brought the descendants of the house of Israel up from the land of the north"—and from all the lands to which I banished them; they shall again live on their own soil.

### The False Prophets†

⁹ Concerning the prophets:
My heart is broken within me,
all my bones tremble;
I am like a drunk,
like one overcome by wine,
Because of the LORD,
because of his holy words.
¹⁰ The land is filled with adulterers;
because of the curse the land mourns,
the pastures of the wilderness are
withered.*
Theirs is an evil course,
theirs is unjust power.

¹¹ Both prophet and priest are godless!
In my very house I find their
wickedness—
oracle of the LORD.*
¹² Hence their way shall become for them
slippery ground.
Into the darkness they shall be driven,
and fall headlong;
For I will bring disaster upon them,
the year of their punishment—oracle
of the LORD.*
¹³ Among Samaria's prophets
I saw something unseemly:
They prophesied by Baal
and led my people Israel astray.*
¹⁴ But among Jerusalem's prophets
I saw something more shocking:
Adultery, walking in deception,†
strengthening the power of the
wicked,
so that no one turns from evil;
To me they are all like Sodom,
its inhabitants like Gomorrah.*

¹⁵Therefore, thus says the LORD of hosts against the prophets:

Look, I will give them wormwood to
eat,
and poisoned water to drink;
For from Jerusalem's prophets
ungodliness has gone forth into the
whole land.*
¹⁶ Thus says the LORD of hosts:
Do not listen to the words of your
prophets,
who fill you with emptiness;
They speak visions from their own fancy,
not from the mouth of the LORD.*
¹⁷ They say to those who despise the word
of the LORD,†
"Peace shall be yours";
And to everyone who walks in hardness
of heart,
"No evil shall overtake you."*

† **23:9–40** After the collection of oracles against the kings, the editor of the book placed this collection of oracles against the false prophets. With them are associated the priests, for both have betrayed their trust as instructors in the ways of the Lord; cf. 2:8; 4:9; 6:13–14.
**23:14** Cf. note on 13:25.
**23:17–20** Not only are the false prophets personally immoral, but they encourage immorality by prophesying good for evil-doers. The true prophet, on the other hand, sees the inevitable consequences of evil behavior.

* **23:2** Ez 34:4–10; Zec 11:16–17.
**23:3** Jer 29:14; 32:37.
**23:4** Jer 3:15; Ez 34:11–12.
**23:5** Jer 33:14–16; Is 4:2; 9:5–6; 11:1–5.
**23:6** Dn 9:24.
**23:7–8** Jer 16:14–15.
**23:10** Jer 4:22; 5:7–8; 9:2, 10.
**23:11** Jer 6:13.
**23:12** Ps 35:6.
**23:13** 1 Kgs 18:19.
**23:14** Jer 29:21–23; Is 1:9–10.
**23:15** Jer 8:14; 9:14.
**23:16** Jer 14:14.
**23:17** Jer 5:12; Ez 13:10; Mi 3:11; Zec 10:2.

18 Now, who has stood in the council of
   the LORD,
     to see him and to hear his word?
   Who has heeded his word so as to
     announce it?*
19 See, the storm of the LORD!
   His wrath breaks forth
   In a whirling storm
     that bursts upon the heads of the
       wicked.*
20 The anger of the LORD shall not abate
     until he has carried out completely
     the decisions of his heart.
   In days to come
     you will understand fully.
21 I did not send these prophets,
     yet they ran;
   I did not speak to them,
     yet they prophesied.*
22 Had they stood in my council,
     they would have proclaimed my
       words to my people,
   They would have brought them back
       from their evil ways
     and from their wicked deeds.
23 Am I a God near at hand only—oracle
       of the LORD—*
     and not a God far off?†
24 Can anyone hide in secret
     without my seeing them?—oracle of
       the LORD.
   Do I not fill
     heaven and earth?—oracle of the
       LORD.

25 I have heard the prophets who prophesy lies in my name say, "I had a dream! I had a dream!" 26 How long? Will the hearts of the prophets who prophesy lies and their own deceitful fancies ever turn back? 27 By the dreams they tell each other, they plan to make my people forget my name, just as their ancestors forgot my name for Baal.* 28 Let the prophets who have dreams tell their dreams; let those who have my word speak my word truthfully!

   What has straw to do with wheat?†
     —oracle of the LORD.*
29 Is not my word like fire—oracle of the
       LORD—
     like a hammer shattering rock?

30 Therefore I am against the prophets—oracle of the LORD—those who steal my words from each other.* 31 Yes, I am against the prophets—oracle of the LORD—those who compose their own speeches and call them oracles. 32 Yes, I am against the prophets who tell lying dreams—oracle of the LORD—those who lead my people astray by recounting their reckless lies. It was not I who sent them or commanded them; they do this people no good at all—oracle of the LORD.*

33† And when this people or a prophet or a priest asks you, "What is the burden of the LORD?" you shall answer, "You are the burden, and I cast you off"—oracle of the LORD. 34 If a prophet or a priest or anyone else mentions "the burden of the LORD," I will punish that man and his household. 35 Thus you shall ask, when speaking to one another, "What answer did the LORD give?" or "What did the LORD say?" 36 But "the burden of the LORD" you shall mention no more. For each of you, your own word becomes the burden so that you pervert the words of the living God, the LORD of hosts, our God. 37 Thus shall you ask the prophet, "What answer did the LORD give?" or "What did the LORD say?" 38 But if you ask about "the burden of the LORD," then thus says the LORD: Because you use this phrase, "the burden of the LORD," though I forbade you to use it, 39 therefore I will lift you on high and cast you from my presence, you and the city which I gave to you and your ancestors. 40 And I will bring upon you eternal reproach, eternal shame, never to be forgotten.*

## 24 The Two Baskets of Figs.†
1 The LORD showed me two baskets of figs placed before the temple of the LORD.* This was after Nebuchadnezzar, king of Babylon, had exiled

---

† 23:23–24 *Near at hand only...far off*: a divine claim that no one can hide from God and that God is aware of all that happens.
23:28–29 *Straw...wheat*: a contrast between false and true prophecy. True prophecy is also like fire (cf. 5:14; 20:9), producing violent results (v. 29); Jeremiah's own life is a testimony of this.
23:33–40 A wordplay on *massa'*, which means both "oracle" (usually of woe) and "burden." In vv. 34–40 the word *massa'* itself is forbidden to the people under the meaning of a divine oracle.

24:1–10 For Jeremiah, as for Ezekiel, no good could be expected from the people who had been left in Judah under Zedekiah or who had fled into Egypt; a future might be expected only for those who would pass through the purifying experience of the exile to form the new Israel.

---

23:18 Jb 15:8; Is 40:13; 1 Cor 2:16.
23:19 Jer 30:23.
23:21 Jer 29:9.
23:23 Jer 16:17; Ps 139:8.
23:27 Jgs 3:7; 8:33.
23:28 Nm 12:6.
23:30 Dt 18:20.
23:32 Jer 28:15–17.
23:40 Jer 20:11.
24:1 Am 8:1–2.

from Jerusalem Jeconiah,† son of Jehoiakim, king of Judah, and the princes of Judah, the artisans and smiths, and brought them to Babylon. ²One basket contained excellent figs, those that ripen early. But the other basket contained very bad figs, so bad they could not be eaten. ³Then the LORD said to me: What do you see, Jeremiah?* "Figs," I replied; "the good ones are very good, but the bad ones very bad, so bad they cannot be eaten." ⁴Thereupon this word of the LORD came to me: ⁵Thus says the LORD, the God of Israel: Like these good figs, I will also regard with favor Judah's exiles whom I sent away from this place into the land of the Chaldeans.* ⁶I will look after them for good and bring them back to this land, to build them up, not tear them down; to plant them, not uproot them.* ⁷I will give them a heart to know me, that I am the LORD. They shall be my people and I will be their God, for they shall return to me with their whole heart.* ⁸But like the figs that are bad, so bad they cannot be eaten—yes, thus says the LORD—even so will I treat Zedekiah, king of Judah, and his princes, the remnant of Jerusalem remaining in this land and those who have settled in the land of Egypt.* ⁹I will make them an object of horror to all the kingdoms of the earth, a reproach and a byword, a taunt and a curse, in all the places to which I will drive them.* ¹⁰I will send upon them sword, famine, and pestilence, until they have disappeared from the land which I gave them and their ancestors.*

## 25 Seventy Years of Exile.

¹The word that came to Jeremiah concerning all the people of Judah, in the fourth year of Jehoiakim,† son of Josiah, king of Judah (the first year of Nebuchadnezzar, king of Babylon).* ²This word the prophet Jeremiah spoke to all the people of Judah and all the inhabitants of Jerusalem: ³Since the thirteenth year of Josiah, son of Amon, king of Judah, to this day—that is, twenty-three years—the word of the LORD

has come to me and I spoke to you untiringly, but you would not listen.* ⁴The LORD kept sending you all his servants the prophets,* but you refused to listen or pay attention ⁵to this message: Turn back, each of you, from your evil way and from your evil deeds; then you shall remain in the land which the LORD gave you and your ancestors, from of old and forever. ⁶Do not follow other gods to serve and bow down to them; do not provoke me with the works of your hands, or I will bring evil upon you.* ⁷But you would not listen to me—oracle of the LORD—and so you provoked me with the works of your hands to your own harm.* ⁸Hence, thus says the LORD of hosts: Since you would not listen to my words, ⁹I am about to send for and fetch all the tribes from the north—oracle of the LORD—and I will send for Nebuchadnezzar, king of Babylon, my servant; I will bring them against this land, its inhabitants, and all these neighboring nations. I will doom them, making them an object of horror, of hissing, of everlasting reproach.* ¹⁰Among them I will put to an end the song of joy and the song of gladness, the voice of the bridegroom and the voice of the bride, the sound of the millstone and the light of the lamp. ¹¹This whole land shall be a ruin and a waste. Seventy years these nations shall serve the king of Babylon;* ¹²but when the seventy years have elapsed, I will punish the king of Babylon and that nation and the land of the Chaldeans for their guilt—oracle of the LORD. Their land I will turn into everlasting waste.* ¹³Against that land I will fulfill all the words I have spoken against it, all that is written in this book, which Jeremiah prophesied against all the nations. ¹⁴They also shall serve many nations and great kings, and thus I will repay them according to their own deeds and according to the works of their hands.*

**The Cup of Judgment on the Nations.** ¹⁵† For thus said the LORD, the God of Israel, to me:

---

**24:1** *Jeconiah*: alternative form of Jehoiachin (cf. note on 22:24).
**25:1–14** *The fourth year of Jehoiakim*: 605 B.C. Officially, the first year of Nebuchadnezzar began the following year; but as early as his victory over Egypt at Carchemish in 605, Nebuchadnezzar wielded dominant power in the Near East. Jeremiah saw in him the fulfillment of his prophecy of the enemy to come from the north (cf. 1:13; 6:22–24). In vv. 11–12 the prophecy of the seventy years' exile occurs for the first time; cf. 29:10. This number signifies that the present generation must die out; cf. forty in the exodus tradition (Nm 14:20–23).
**25:15–17** Jeremiah is a prophet to the nations (cf. 1:5) as well as to his own people. All the nations mentioned here ap-

pear again in the more extensive collection of Jeremiah's oracles against the nations in chaps. 46–51.

**24:3** Jer 1:11.
**24:5** Jer 29:11; Lv 26:44–45.
**24:6** Jer 12:15; Am 9:15.
**24:7** Jer 30:22; 31:1; 32:37; Bar 2:31.
**24:8** Jer 29:18.
**24:9** Jer 15:4; Dt 28:37.
**24:10** Jer 14:12.
**25:1** Jer 36:1.
**25:3** Jer 1:2.
**25:4** 2 Chr 36:15.
**25:6** Jer 7:6–7.
**25:7** Jer 7:17–19.
**25:9** Jer 1:15; 43:10.
**25:11** Lv 26:32–35.
**25:12** Is 13:20–22.
**25:14** Jer 27:7; 50:9, 41–42; 51:6, 24.

Take this cup of the wine of wrath† from my hand and have all the nations to whom I will send you drink it.* ¹⁶They shall drink, and retch, and go mad, because of the sword I will send among them.* ¹⁷I took the cup from the hand of the LORD and gave it as drink to all the nations to whom the LORD sent me: ¹⁸to Jerusalem, the cities of Judah, its kings and princes, to make them a ruin and a waste, an object of hissing and cursing, as they are today; ¹⁹to Pharaoh, king of Egypt, and his servants, princes, all his people ²⁰and those of mixed ancestry; all the kings of the land of Uz;† all the kings of the land of the Philistines: Ashkelon, Gaza, Ekron, and the remnant of Ashdod; ²¹Edom, Moab, and the Ammonites; ²²all the kings of Tyre, of Sidon, and of the shores beyond the sea;† ²³Dedan and Tema and Buz,† all the desert dwellers who shave their temples; ²⁴all the kings of Arabia; ²⁵all the kings of Zimri, of Elam, of the Medes; ²⁶all the kings of the north, near and far, one after the other; all the kingdoms upon the face of the earth and after them the king of Sheshach† shall drink.

²⁷Tell them: Thus says the LORD of hosts, the God of Israel: Drink! Get drunk and vomit! Fall, never to rise, before the sword that I will send among you!* ²⁸If they refuse to take the cup from your hand and drink, say to them: Thus says the LORD of hosts: You must drink!* ²⁹Now that I am inflicting evil on this city, called by my name, how can you possibly escape? You shall not escape! I am calling down the sword upon all the inhabitants of the earth—oracle of the LORD of hosts. ³⁰As for you, prophesy against them all these words and say to them:

> The LORD roars from on high,
>     from his holy dwelling he raises his
>         voice;
> Mightily he roars over his sheepfold,
>     a shout like that of vintagers echoes*
>         over all the inhabitants of the earth.

³¹     The uproar spreads
>         to the end of the earth;
>     For the LORD has an indictment against
>         the nations,
>     he enters into judgment against all
>         flesh:
>     The wicked shall be given to the sword—
>         oracle of the LORD.
³²     Thus says the LORD of hosts:
>     Look! disaster stalks
>         nation after nation;
>     A violent storm surges
>         from the recesses of the earth.

³³On that day, those whom the LORD has slain will be strewn from one end of the earth to the other. They will not be mourned, they will not be gathered, they will not be buried; they shall lie like dung upon the ground.*

³⁴     Howl, you shepherds, and wail!
>         roll on the ground, leaders of the
>             flock!
>     The time for your slaughter has come;
>         like choice rams you shall fall.
³⁵     There is no flight for the shepherds,
>         no escape for the leaders of the flock.*
³⁶     Listen! Wailing from the shepherds,
>         howling from the leaders of the flock!
>     For the LORD lays waste their grazing
>         place;
³⁷     desolate are the peaceful pastures,
>         from the burning wrath of the LORD.
³⁸     Like a lion he leaves his lair,
>         and their land is made desolate
>     By the sweeping sword,
>         and the burning wrath of the LORD.*

## IV. THE TEMPLE SERMON

# 26

**Jeremiah Threatened with Death.** ¹In the beginning of the reign† of Jehoiakim, son of Josiah, king of Judah, this word came from the LORD: ²Thus says the LORD: Stand in the court of the house of the LORD

---

† **25:15** *Cup...wrath:* a metaphor for destruction that occurs often in the Old Testament (cf. Ps 11:6; 75:9; Hb 2:15–16; Ez 23:31–33, etc.).
**25:20** *Uz:* the homeland of legendary Job, in Edomite or Arabian territory.
**25:22** *The shores beyond the sea:* Phoenician commercial colonies located throughout the Mediterranean world.
**25:23** *Dedan and Tema and Buz:* North Arabian tribes.
**25:26** *Sheshach:* a contrived word from the Hebrew letters of Babylon.

**26:1** *The beginning of the reign:* a technical expression for the time between a king's accession to the throne and the beginning of his first official (calendar) year as king. Jehoiakim's first regnal year was 608 B.C.

---

| | |
|---|---|
| **25:15** Rev 14:10. | **25:30** Jer 51:14. |
| **25:16** Jer 51:7. | **25:33** Jer 8:2; 16:4, 6. |
| **25:27** Ob 16. | **25:35** Jer 32:4. |
| **25:28** Jer 49:12. | **25:38** Jer 4:7. |

and speak to the inhabitants of all the cities of Judah who come to worship in the house of the LORD; whatever I command you, tell them, and hold nothing back.* ³Perhaps they will listen and turn, all of them from their evil way, so that I may repent of the evil I plan to inflict upon them for their evil deeds.* ⁴Say to them: Thus says the LORD: If you do not obey me, by walking according to the law I set before you ⁵and listening to the words of my servants the prophets, whom I kept sending you, even though you do not listen to them,* ⁶I will treat this house like Shiloh, and make this city a curse for all the nations of the earth.*

⁷Now the priests, the prophets, and all the people heard Jeremiah speaking these words in the house of the LORD. ⁸When Jeremiah finished speaking all that the LORD commanded him to speak to all the people, then the priests, the prophets, and all the people laid hold of him, crying, "You must die! ⁹Why do you prophesy in the name of the LORD: 'This house shall become like Shiloh,' and 'This city shall be desolate, without inhabitant'?" And all the people crowded around Jeremiah in the house of the LORD.

¹⁰When the princes of Judah heard about these things, they came up from the house of the king to the house of the LORD and convened at the New Gate of the house of the LORD. ¹¹The priests and prophets said to the princes and to all the people, "Sentence this man to death! He has prophesied against this city! You heard it with your own ears."* ¹²Jeremiah said to the princes and all the people: "It was the LORD who sent me to prophesy against this house and city everything you have heard. ¹³Now, therefore, reform your ways and your deeds; listen to the voice of the LORD your God, so that the LORD will have a change of heart regarding the evil he has spoken against you.* ¹⁴As for me, I am in your hands; do with me what is good and right in your eyes. ¹⁵But you should certainly know that by putting me to death, you bring innocent blood on yourselves, on this city and its inhabitants. For in truth it was the LORD who sent me to you, to speak all these words for you to hear."

¹⁶Then the princes and all the people said to the priests and the prophets, "This man does not deserve a death sentence; it is in the name of the LORD, our God, that he speaks to us." ¹⁷At this, some of the elders of the land arose and said to the whole assembly of the people, ¹⁸"Micah of Moresheth† used to prophesy in the days of Hezekiah, king of Judah, and he said to all the people of Judah: Thus says the LORD of hosts:

Zion shall be plowed as a field,
  Jerusalem, a heap of ruins,
  and the temple mount,
  a forest ridge.*

¹⁹Did Hezekiah, king of Judah, and all Judah condemn him to death? Did he not fear the LORD and entreat the favor of the LORD, so that the LORD had a change of heart regarding the evil he had spoken against them? We, however, are about to do great evil against ourselves."*

**The Fate of Uriah.** ²⁰There was another man who used to prophesy in the name of the LORD, Uriah, son of Shemaiah, from Kiriath-jearim; he prophesied against this city and this land the same message as Jeremiah. ²¹When King Jehoiakim and all his officers and princes heard his words, the king sought to have him killed. But Uriah heard of it and fled in fear to Egypt. ²²Then King Jehoiakim sent Elnathan, son of Achbor, and others with him into Egypt, ²³and they brought Uriah out of Egypt and took him to Jehoiakim the king, who struck him down with the sword and threw his corpse into the common burial ground. ²⁴But the hand of Ahikam, son of Shaphan,† protected Jeremiah, so they did not hand him over to the people to be put to death.

## V. CONTROVERSIES WITH THE FALSE PROPHETS†

**27** **Serve Babylon or Perish.** ¹In the beginning of the reign of Zedekiah,† son of Josiah, king of Judah, this word came to Jeremiah from the LORD: ²The LORD said to

26:18 *Micah of Moresheth:* the prophet Micah, who appears among the canonical minor prophets (cf. Mi 1:1).
26:24 *Ahikam, son of Shaphan:* one of Josiah's officials (2 Kgs 22:12) and Jeremiah's friend. He was the father of Gedaliah, who was governor of Judah after Zedekiah's deportation (cf. Jer 39:14; 40:5–7).

27:1–29:32 A special collection of Jeremiah's prophecies dealing with false prophets. Stylistic peculiarities evident in the

26:2 Jer 7:2.          26:11 Jer 38:4.
26:3 Jer 18:3.         26:13 Jer 7:3.
26:5 Jer 25:4.         26:18 Mi 1:1; 3:12.
26:6 Jer 7:12, 14.     26:19 2 Chr 32:26.

me: Make for yourself thongs and yoke bars and put them on your shoulders. ³ Send them to the kings of Edom, Moab, the Ammonites, Tyre, and Sidon, through the ambassadors who have come to Jerusalem to Zedekiah, king of Judah,† ⁴ and command them to tell their lords: Thus says the LORD of hosts, the God of Israel, Thus shall you say to your lords: ⁵ It was I who made the earth, human being and beast on the face of the earth, by my great power, with my outstretched arm; and I can give them to whomever I think fit.* ⁶ Now I have given all these lands into the hand of Nebuchadnezzar, king of Babylon, my servant; even the wild animals I have given him to serve him.* ⁷ All nations shall serve him and his son and his grandson, until the time comes for him and his land; then many nations and great kings will enslave him.* ⁸ Meanwhile, the nation or the kingdom that will not serve him, Nebuchadnezzar, king of Babylon, or bend its neck under the yoke of the king of Babylon, I will punish that nation with sword, famine, and pestilence—oracle of the LORD—until I finish them by his hand.*

⁹ You, however, must not listen to your prophets,† to your diviners and dreamers, to your soothsayers and sorcerers, who say to you, "Do not serve the king of Babylon."* ¹⁰ For they prophesy lies to you, so as to drive you far from your land, making me banish you so that you perish.* ¹¹ The people that bends the neck to the yoke of the king of Babylon to serve him, I will leave in peace on its own land—oracle of the LORD—to cultivate it and dwell on it.*

¹² To Zedekiah, king of Judah, I spoke the same words: Bend your necks to the yoke of the king of Babylon; serve him and his people, so that you may live.* ¹³ Why should you and your people die by sword, famine, and pestilence, in accordance with the word the LORD has spoken to the nation that will not serve the king of Babylon?* ¹⁴ Do not listen to the words of the prophets who say to you, "Do not serve the king of Babylon." They prophesy lies

to you!* ¹⁵ I did not send them—oracle of the LORD—but they prophesy falsely in my name. As a result I must banish you, and you will perish, you and the prophets who are prophesying to you.*

¹⁶* To the priests and to all the people I said: Thus says the LORD: Do not listen to the words of your prophets who prophesy to you: "The vessels of the house of the LORD will soon be brought back from Babylon," for they prophesy lies to you. ¹⁷ Do not listen to them! Serve the king of Babylon that you may live. Why should this city become rubble? ¹⁸ If they were prophets, if the word of the LORD were with them, then they would intercede with the LORD of hosts, that the vessels remaining in the house of the LORD and in the house of the king of Judah and in Jerusalem should not also go to Babylon. ¹⁹ For thus says the LORD of hosts concerning the pillars, the sea, the stands, and the rest of the vessels remaining in this city, ²⁰ which Nebuchadnezzar, king of Babylon, did not take when he exiled Jeconiah, son of Jehoiakim, king of Judah, from Jerusalem to Babylon, along with all the nobles of Judah and Jerusalem— ²¹ thus says the LORD of hosts, the God of Israel, concerning the vessels remaining in the house of the LORD, in the house of the king of Judah, and in Jerusalem:* ²² To Babylon they shall go, and there they shall remain, until the day I look for them— oracle of the LORD; then I will bring them back and restore them to this place.

# 28 The Two Yokes.
¹ That same year, in the beginning of the reign of Zedekiah, king of Judah, in the fifth month of the fourth year, Hananiah the prophet, son of Azzur, from Gibeon, said to me in the house of the LORD in the sight of the priests and all the people: ² "Thus says the LORD of hosts, the God of Israel: I have broken the yoke of the king of Babylon. ³ Within two years I will restore to this place all the vessels of the house of the LORD which Nebuchadnezzar, king of Babylon, took from this place and carried

---

† Hebrew suggest that these three chapters once existed as an independent work.

**27:1** *Zedekiah:* The Hebrew text actually has "Jehoiakim," but the content of the chapter indicates that Zedekiah is intended.

**27:3** The time is the fourth year of Zedekiah, 594 B.C., the occasion of a delegation from the neighboring states, doubtless for the purpose of laying plans against Nebuchadnezzar.

**27:9** *Your prophets:* seers and diviners served non-Israelite kings just as the professional prophets served the kings of Judah.

**27:5** Jer 32:17.
**27:6** Jer 25:9; 43:10; Ez 30:21, 25.
**27:7** Jer 25:11; 2 Chr 36:20.
**27:8** Jer 25:9; Bar 2:22.
**27:9** Jer 29:8.
**27:10** Jer 14:13–16.
**27:11** Bar 2:21.
**27:12** Jer 38:17.
**27:13** Jer 24:8–10.
**27:14** Jer 14:14; 23:21.
**27:15** Jer 20:6.
**27:16** Jer 28:3; 2 Chr 36:7, 10, 18.
**27:21–22** 2 Kgs 25:13–17; 2 Chr 36:18, 22.

away to Babylon. ⁴And Jeconiah, son of Jehoiakim, king of Judah, and all the exiles of Judah who went to Babylon, I will bring back to this place—oracle of the LORD—for I will break the yoke of the king of Babylon."

⁵Jeremiah the prophet answered the prophet Hananiah in the sight of the priests and all the people standing in the house of the LORD, ⁶and said: Amen! thus may the LORD do! May the LORD fulfill your words that you have prophesied, by bringing back the vessels of the house of the LORD and all the exiles from Babylon to this place! ⁷But now, listen to the word I am about to speak in your hearing and the hearing of all the people. ⁸In the past, the prophets who came before you and me prophesied war, disaster, and pestilence against many lands and mighty kingdoms. ⁹But the prophet who prophesies peace is recognized as the prophet whom the LORD has truly sent only when his word comes to pass.*

¹⁰Thereupon Hananiah the prophet took the yoke bar from the neck of Jeremiah the prophet and broke it. ¹¹He said in the sight of all the people: "Thus says the LORD: Like this, within two years I will break the yoke of Nebuchadnezzar, king of Babylon, from the neck of all the nations." At that, the prophet Jeremiah went on his way.

¹²After Hananiah the prophet had broken the yoke bar off the neck of the prophet Jeremiah, the word of the LORD came to Jeremiah: ¹³Go tell Hananiah this: Thus says the LORD: By breaking a wooden yoke bar, you make an iron yoke! ¹⁴For thus says the LORD of hosts, the God of Israel: A yoke of iron I have placed on the necks of all these nations serving Nebuchadnezzar, king of Babylon, and they shall serve him; even the wild animals I have given him.* ¹⁵And Jeremiah the prophet said to Hananiah the prophet: Listen to this, Hananiah! The LORD has not sent you, and you have led this people to rely on deception. ¹⁶For this, says the LORD, I am sending you from the face of the earth; this very year you shall die, because you have preached rebellion against the LORD.* ¹⁷Hananiah the prophet died in that year, in the seventh month.

**29** **Letter to the Exiles in Babylon.** ¹These are the words of the scroll which Jeremiah the prophet sent from Jerusalem to the remaining elders among the exiles, to the priests, the prophets, and all the people whom Nebuchadnezzar exiled from Jerusalem to Babylon. ²This was after King Jeconiah and the queen mother, the court officials, the princes of Judah and Jerusalem, the artisans and smiths had left Jerusalem.* ³Delivered in Babylon by Elasah,† son of Shaphan, and by Gemariah, son of Hilkiah, whom Zedekiah, king of Judah, sent to the king of Babylon, the letter read:

⁴Thus says the LORD of hosts, the God of Israel, to all the exiles whom I exiled from Jerusalem to Babylon: ⁵Build houses and live in them; plant gardens and eat their fruits. ⁶Take wives and have sons and daughters; find wives for your sons and give your daughters to husbands, so that they may bear sons and daughters. Increase there; do not decrease. ⁷Seek the welfare of the city to which I have exiled you; pray for it to the LORD, for upon its welfare your own depends.* ⁸For thus says the LORD of hosts, the God of Israel: Do not be deceived by the prophets and diviners who are among you; do not listen to those among you who dream dreams,* ⁹for they prophesy lies to you in my name; I did not send them—oracle of the LORD.*

¹⁰For thus says the LORD: Only after seventy years have elapsed for Babylon will I deal with you and fulfill for you my promise to bring you back to this place.* ¹¹For I know well the plans I have in mind for you—oracle of the LORD—plans for your welfare and not for woe, so as to give you a future of hope. ¹²When you call me, and come and pray to me, I will listen to you.* ¹³When you look for me, you will find me. Yes, when you seek me with all your heart, ¹⁴I will let you find me—oracle of the LORD—and I will change your lot; I will gather you together from all the nations and all the places to which I have banished you—oracle of the LORD—and bring you back to the place from which I have exiled you.* ¹⁵As for your saying, "The LORD has raised up for us prophets here in Babylon"—

---

† **29:3** *Elasah*: probably the brother of Ahikam (cf. 26:24). *Gemariah*: probably the son of the high priest Hilkiah; cf. 2 Kgs 22:4. Zedekiah had dispatched these men to Nebuchadnezzar for some other purpose, possibly the payment of tribute, but Jeremiah took advantage of their mission to send his letter with them.

**28:9** Dt 18:22.
**28:14** Jer 27:6–7; Dt 28:48.
**28:16** Dt 13:6.
**29:2** 2 Kgs 24:15.
**29:7** 1 Tm 2:1–2.
**29:8** Jer 27:9, 14.
**29:9** Jer 5:31.
**29:10** Jer 25:11; 2 Chr 36:21–22; Ezr 1:1; Dn 9:2; Zec 1:12; 7:5.
**29:12** Jer 33:3.
**29:14** Jer 23:3, 8.

[16] Thus says the LORD concerning the king sitting on David's throne and all the people living in this city, your kinsmen who did not go with you into exile; [17] thus says the LORD of hosts: I am sending against them sword, famine, and pestilence. I will make them like rotten figs, so spoiled that they cannot be eaten. [18] I will pursue them with sword, famine, and pestilence, and make them an object of horror to all the kingdoms of the earth, a curse, a desolation, a hissing, and a reproach to all the nations among which I have banished them,* [19] because they did not listen to my words—oracle of the LORD—even though I kept sending them my servants the prophets, but they would not listen to them—oracle of the LORD.*

[20] As for you, listen to the word of the LORD, all you exiles whom I sent away from Jerusalem to Babylon. [21] This is what the LORD of hosts, the God of Israel, says about Ahab, son of Kolaiah, and Zedekiah, son of Maaseiah, who prophesy lies to you in my name: I am handing them over to Nebuchadnezzar, king of Babylon, who will kill them before your eyes.* [22] And because of them this curse will be used by all the exiles of Judah in Babylon: "May the LORD make you like Zedekiah and Ahab, whom the king of Babylon roasted in fire," [23] because they have committed an outrage in Israel, committing adultery with their neighbors' wives, and alleging in my name things I did not command. I know, I am witness—oracle of the LORD.*

**The False Prophet Shemaiah.** [24] To Shemaiah, the Nehelamite, say: [25] Thus says the LORD of hosts, the God of Israel: Because you sent documents in your own name to all the people in Jerusalem, to Zephaniah, the priest, son of Maaseiah, and to all the priests saying: [26]† "It is the LORD who has appointed you priest in place of the priest Jehoiada, to provide officers for the house of the LORD, that you may confine in stocks or pillory any madman who

poses as a prophet. [27] Why, then, have you not rebuked Jeremiah of Anathoth who poses as a prophet among you? [28] For he sent this message to us in Babylon: It will be a long time; build houses to live in; plant gardens and eat their fruit. . . ."

[29] When the priest Zephaniah read this letter to Jeremiah the prophet, [30] the word of the LORD came to Jeremiah: [31] Send to all the exiles: Thus says the LORD concerning Shemaiah, the Nehelamite: Because Shemaiah prophesies to you, although I did not send him, and has led you to rely on a lie, [32] therefore thus says the LORD, I will punish Shemaiah, the Nehelamite, and his descendants. None of them shall dwell among this people to see the good I will do for this people—oracle of the LORD—because he preached rebellion against the LORD.

## VI. ORACLES OF THE RESTORATION OF ISRAEL AND JUDAH

**30** **The Restoration.**† [1] This word came to Jeremiah from the LORD: [2] Thus says the LORD, the God of Israel: Write down on a scroll all the words I have spoken to you.* [3] For indeed, the days are coming—oracle of the LORD—when I will restore the fortunes of my people Israel and Judah—oracle of the LORD. I will bring them back to the land which I gave to their ancestors, and they shall take possession of it.*

[4] These are the words the LORD spoke to Israel and to Judah: [5] Thus says the LORD:

> We hear a cry of fear:
>     terror, not peace.
> [6] Inquire and see:
>     does a male give birth?
> Why, then, do I see all these men,
>     their hands on their loins
> Like women in labor,
>     all their faces drained of color?*
> [7] Ah! How mighty is that day—

---

† **29:26–29** Jeremiah's message to Shemaiah is not completely preserved in the current Hebrew text, hence the incomplete sentence in vv. 25–28.

**30:1–31:40** These two chapters contain salvation oracles that originally expressed the double expectation that the Lord would return the exiled survivors of the Northern Kingdom of Israel and reunite Israel and Judah as one kingdom under a just Davidic king. They were probably composed early in Josiah's reign (the reference of v. 9), when he took advantage of Assyria's internal disintegration and asserted control over northern Israel (cf. 2 Kgs

23:15–17). With the destruction of Jerusalem, the oracles were re-worked to include Judah and their fulfillment along with the renewal of the Davidic dynasty became associated with the eschatological "day of the Lord."

* **29:18** Jer 15:4; 24:9; 34:17–18.
**29:19** Jer 25:4.
**29:21** Jer 14:14.
**29:23** Jer 23:14.
**30:2** Jer 36:2; Hb 2:2; Rev 1:11.
**30:3** Jer 29:14; 31:8, 10, 23; 32:37, 44; Ez 39:25; Am 9:14.
**30:6** Jer 6:24; 50:43.

there is none like it!
A time of distress for Jacob,
though he shall be saved from it.*

⁸ On that day—oracle of the LORD of hosts—
I will break his yoke off your neck and snap
your bonds. Strangers shall no longer enslave
them;* ⁹ instead, they shall serve the LORD,
their God, and David, their king,† whom I will
raise up for them.*

10    But you, my servant Jacob, do not
                fear!—oracle of the LORD—
        do not be dismayed, Israel!
    For I will soon deliver you from places
                far away,
        your offspring from the land of their
                exile;
    Jacob shall again find rest,
        secure, with none to frighten him,*
11    for I am with you—oracle of the
                LORD—to save you.
    I will bring to an end all the nations
        among whom I have scattered you;
    but you I will not bring to an end.
    I will chastise you as you deserve,
        I will not let you go unpunished.*
12    For thus says the LORD:
    Incurable is your wound,
        grievous your injury;*
13    There is none to plead your case,
        no remedy for your running sore,
        no healing for you.
14    All your lovers have forgotten you,
        they do not seek you out.
    I struck you as an enemy would strike,
        punishing you cruelly.*
15    Why cry out over your wound?
        There is no relief for your pain.
    Because of your great guilt,
        your numerous sins,
    I have done this to you.*
16    Yet all who devour you shall be
                devoured,
        all your enemies shall go into exile.

All who plunder you shall become
                plunder,
    all who pillage you I will hand over to
                be pillaged.*
17    For I will restore your health;
        I will heal your injuries—oracle of the
                LORD.
    "The outcast" they have called you,
        "whom no one looks for."*
18    Thus says the LORD:
    See! I will restore the fortunes of Jacob's
                tents,
        on his dwellings I will have
                compassion;
    A city shall be rebuilt upon its own
                ruins,
        a citadel restored where it
                should be.*
19    From them will come praise,
        the sound of people rejoicing.
    I will increase them, they will not
                decrease,
    I will glorify them, they will not be
                insignificant.*
20    His children shall be as of old,
        his assembly shall stand firm in my
                presence,
    I will punish all his oppressors.*
21    His leader† shall be one of his own,
        and his ruler shall emerge from his
                ranks.
    He shall approach me when I summon
                him;
        Why else would he dare
        approach me?—oracle of the LORD.
22    You shall be my people,
        and I will be your God.*
23    Look! The storm of the LORD!
        His wrath breaks out
    In a whirling storm
        that bursts upon the heads of the
                wicked.*
24    The anger of the LORD will not abate
        until he has carried out completely
        the decisions of his heart.

---

**30:9** *David, their king*: a descendant of David ("his leader" in
v. 21) who, like his ancestor, would rule a unified kingdom and
"walk in the ways of the Lord," as the Deuteronomistic historians
claimed David did. Other prophets also refer to this idealized
ruler as "David"; cf. Ez 34:23–24; 37:24–25; Hos 3:5.
    **30:21** *His leader*: cf. v. 9. *Approach me*: i.e., in the sanctuary
of the Temple for worship. This new David is given a priestly
function to perform on behalf of the assembly. To approach God
on one's own brings death; cf. Lv 16:1–2.

**30:7** Am 5:18; Zep
    1:14–15.
**30:8** Is 14:5–6; Ez 34:27.
**30:9** Ez 34:23; 37:24; Hos
    3:5; Lk 1:69.
**30:10** Jer 46:27; Is 43:5.
**30:11** Jer 46:28; Ez
    11:16–17; Am 9:8–9.
**30:12** Jer 10:19; 14:17;
    15:18.
**30:14** Jer 22:22; Lam 1:19.

**30:15** Jer 15:18.
**30:16** Jer 2:3.
**30:17** Jer 33:6.
**30:18** Jer 33:7, 11; Ezr
    6:3–15; Ez 36:10.
**30:19** Is 35:10; 51:11.
**30:20** Is 49:26.
**30:22** Jer 24:7; 31:1, 33;
    32:38; Lv 26:12; Ez
    11:20; 36:28.
**30:23** Jer 23:19.

In days to come
　　you will fully understand it.*

## Good News of the Return

**31** ¹At that time—oracle of the LORD—
I will be the God of all the families
　　of Israel,
and they shall be my people.*

²† Thus says the LORD:
The people who escaped the sword
　　find favor in the wilderness.
As Israel comes forward to receive rest,
³　　from afar the LORD appears:
With age-old love I have loved you;
　　so I have kept my mercy toward you.*

⁴ Again I will build you, and you shall
　　stay built,
　　virgin Israel;
Carrying your festive tambourines,
　　you shall go forth dancing with
　　merrymakers.

⁵ You shall again plant vineyards
　　on the mountains of Samaria;
　　those who plant them shall enjoy
　　their fruits.*

⁶ Yes, a day will come when the
　　watchmen
　　call out on Mount Ephraim:
"Come, let us go up to Zion,
　　to the LORD, our God."*

## The Road of Return

⁷ For thus says the LORD:
Shout with joy for Jacob,
　　exult at the head of the nations;
　　proclaim your praise and say:
The LORD has saved his people,
　　the remnant of Israel.*

⁸ Look! I will bring them back
　　from the land of the north;
I will gather them from the ends of the
　　earth,
　　the blind and the lame in their midst,
Pregnant women, together with those in
　　labor—

an immense throng—they shall
　　return.*

⁹ With weeping they shall come,
　　but with compassion I will guide
　　them;
I will lead them to streams of water,
　　on a level road, without stumbling.
For I am a father to Israel,
　　Ephraim is my firstborn.*

¹⁰ Hear the word of the LORD, you nations,
　　proclaim it on distant coasts, and say:
The One who scattered Israel, now
　　gathers them;
　　he guards them as a shepherd his
　　flock.

¹¹ The LORD shall ransom Jacob,
　　he shall redeem him from a hand too
　　strong for him.*

¹² Shouting, they shall mount the heights
　　of Zion,
　　they shall come streaming to the
　　LORD's blessings:
The grain, the wine, and the oil,
　　flocks of sheep and cattle;
They themselves shall be like watered
　　gardens,
　　never again neglected.*

¹³ Then young women shall make merry
　　and dance,
　　young men and old as well.
I will turn their mourning into joy,
　　I will show them compassion and
　　have them rejoice after their
　　sorrows.

¹⁴ I will lavish choice portions on the
　　priests,
　　and my people shall be filled with my
　　blessings—
oracle of the LORD.

## End of Rachel's Mourning

¹⁵ Thus says the LORD:
In Ramah† is heard the sound of
　　sobbing,
　　bitter weeping!

† **31:2–3** Jeremiah describes the exiles of the Northern Kingdom on their way home from the nations where the Assyrians had resettled them (722/721 B.C.). The favor they discover in the wilderness is the appearance of the Lord to guide them to Jerusalem. Implicit in these verses is the presentation of the people's return from captivity as a second exodus, a unifying theme in Second Isaiah (chaps. 40–55).
**31:15** *Ramah*: a village about five miles north of Jerusalem, where one tradition locates Rachel's tomb (1 Sm 10:2). The wife of Jacob/Israel, Rachel is the matriarchal ancestor of Ephraim, chief among the northern tribes. She personified Israel as a

mother whose grief for her lost children is especially poignant because she had to wait a long time to bear them. Mt 2:18 applies this verse to Herod's slaughter of the innocents.

* **30:24** Jer 23:20.
**31:1** Jer 30:22.
**31:3** Dt 7:8; 10:15; Is 43:4; 63:9; Hos 11:1, 4.
**31:5** Dt 28:30; Is 65:21; Am 9:14.
**31:6** Is 2:3; 27:13; Mi 4:2.
**31:7** Is 12:6.
**31:8** Jer 3:18; 23:3, 8; Is 35:5–6.
**31:9** Ex 4:22.
**31:11** Is 44:23; 48:20.
**31:12** Is 58:11.

Rachel mourns for her children,
  she refuses to be consoled
  for her children—they are no more!*
16 Thus says the LORD:
Cease your cries of weeping,
  hold back your tears!
There is compensation for your labor—
  oracle of the LORD—
  they shall return from the enemy's
    land.
17 There is hope for your future—oracle of
    the LORD—
  your children shall return to their own
    territory.*
18 Indeed, I heard Ephraim rocking in grief:
  You chastised me, and I was chastised;
    I was like an untamed calf.
  Bring me back, let me come back,
    for you are the LORD, my God.*
19 For after I turned away, I repented;
  after I came to myself, I struck my
    thigh;†
  I was ashamed, even humiliated,
    because I bore the disgrace of my
    youth.*
20 Is Ephraim not my favored son,
    the child in whom I delight?
  Even though I threaten him,
    I must still remember him!
  My heart stirs for him,
    I must show him compassion!—
    oracle of the LORD.*

### Summons to Return Home

21 Set up road markers,
    put up signposts;
  Turn your attention to the highway,
    the road you walked.
  Turn back, virgin Israel,
    turn back to these your cities.

22 How long will you continue to hesitate,
    rebellious daughter?
  The LORD has created a new thing upon
    the earth:
  woman encompasses man.†

23 Thus says the LORD of hosts, the God of Israel: When I restore their fortunes in the land of Judah and in its cities, they shall again use this greeting: "May the LORD bless you, Tent of Justice, Holy Mountain!"* 24 Judah and all its cities, the farmers and those who lead the flock shall dwell there together. 25 For I will slake the thirst of the faint; the appetite of all the weary I will satisfy. 26 At this I awoke and opened my eyes; my sleep was satisfying.†

27 See, days are coming—oracle of the LORD—when I will sow the house of Israel and the house of Judah with the seed of human beings and the seed of animals. 28 As I once watched over them to uproot and tear down, to demolish, to destroy, and to harm, so I will watch over them to build and to plant—oracle of the LORD.* 29 In those days they shall no longer say,

"The parents ate unripe grapes,*
  and the children's teeth are set on
    edge,"†

30 but all shall die because of their own iniquity: the teeth of anyone who eats unripe grapes shall be set on edge.

**The New Covenant.**† 31 See, days are coming—oracle of the LORD—when I will make a new covenant with the house of Israel and the house of Judah.* 32 It will not be like the covenant I made with their ancestors the day I took them by the hand to lead them out of the land of Egypt. They broke my covenant,

---

† **31:19** *Struck my thigh*: a gesture signifying grief and dread (cf. Ez 21:17).
**31:22** No satisfactory explanation has been given for this text. Jerome, for example, saw the image as a reference to the infant Jesus enclosed in Mary's womb. Since Jeremiah often uses marital imagery in his description of a restored Israel, the phrase may refer to a wedding custom, perhaps women circling the groom in a dance. It may also be a metaphor describing the security of a new Israel, a security so complete that it defies the imagination and must be expressed as hyperbolic role reversal: any danger will be so insignificant that women can protect their men.
**31:26** *I awoke...satisfying*: an intrusive comment.
**31:29** *"The parents...on edge"*: Jeremiah's opponents use this proverb to complain that they are being punished for sins of their ancestors. Jeremiah, however, insists that the Lord knows the depth of their wickedness and holds them accountable for their actions.

**31:31–34** The new covenant is an occasional prophetic theme, beginning with Hosea. According to Jeremiah, (a) it lasts forever; (b) its law (*torah*) is written in human hearts; (c) it gives everyone true knowledge of God, making additional instruction (*torah*) unnecessary. The Dead Sea Scroll community claimed they were partners in a "new covenant." The New Testament presents the death and resurrection of Jesus of Nazareth as inaugurating a new covenant open to anyone who professes faith in Jesus the Christ. Cf. Lk 22:20; 1 Cor 11:25; Heb 8:8–12. *Know the LORD*: cf. note on 22:15–16.

**31:15** Mt 2:18.
**31:17** Jer 29:10–14.
**31:18** Lv 26:40–42.
**31:19** Dt 30:1–3.
**31:20** Hos 11:8.
**31:23** Jer 30:3; Ps 122:8.
**31:28** Jer 1:10; 18:7.
**31:29** Dt 24:16; Ez 18:2.
**31:31** Jer 32:40; Heb 9:15.

though I was their master—oracle of the LORD.* ³³But this is the covenant I will make with the house of Israel after those days—oracle of the LORD. I will place my law within them, and write it upon their hearts; I will be their God, and they shall be my people.* ³⁴They will no longer teach their friends and relatives, "Know the LORD!" Everyone, from least to greatest, shall know me—oracle of the LORD—for I will forgive their iniquity and no longer remember their sin.*

### Certainty of God's Promise

35    Thus says the LORD,
Who gives the sun to light the day,
    moon and stars to light the night;
Who stirs up the sea so that its waves
        roar,
    whose name is LORD of hosts:*
36    If ever this fixed order gives way
        before me—oracle of the LORD—
    Then would the offspring of Israel cease
        as a people before me forever.*
37    Thus says the LORD:
    If the heavens on high could be
        measured,
    or the foundations below the earth be
        explored,
    Then would I reject all the offspring of
        Israel
    because of all they have done—oracle
        of the LORD.

### Jerusalem Rebuilt.†

³⁸See, days are coming— oracle of the LORD—when the city shall be rebuilt as the LORD's,* from the Tower of Hananel to the Corner Gate. ³⁹A measuring line shall be stretched from there straight to the hill Gareb and then turn to Goah. ⁴⁰The whole valley of corpses and ashes, all the terraced

slopes toward the Wadi Kidron, as far as the corner of the Horse Gate at the east, shall be holy to the LORD. Never again shall the city be uprooted or demolished.

## 32 Pledge of Restoration.†

¹The word came to Jeremiah from the LORD in the tenth year of Zedekiah,† king of Judah, the eighteenth year of Nebuchadnezzar. ²At that time the army of the king of Babylon was besieging Jerusalem, while Jeremiah the prophet was confined to the court of the guard, in the house of the king of Judah.* ³Zedekiah, king of Judah, had confined him there, saying: "How dare you prophesy: Thus says the LORD: I am handing this city over to the king of Babylon that he may capture it.* ⁴Zedekiah, king of Judah, shall not escape the hands of the Chaldeans: he shall indeed be handed over to the king of Babylon. He shall speak with him face to face and see him eye to eye.* ⁵He shall take Zedekiah to Babylon. There he shall remain, until I attend to him—oracle of the LORD. If you fight against the Chaldeans, you cannot win!"*

⁶†Jeremiah said, This word came to me from the LORD: ⁷Hanamel, son of your uncle Shallum, will come to you with the offer:* "Purchase my field in Anathoth, since you, as nearest relative, have the first right of purchase."† ⁸And, just as the LORD had said, my cousin Hanamel came to me in the court of the guard and said, "Please purchase my field in Anathoth, in the territory of Benjamin; as nearest relative, you have the first right of possession—purchase it for yourself." Then I knew this was the word of the LORD. ⁹So I bought the field in Anathoth from my cousin Hanamel, weighing out for him the silver, seventeen shekels of silver.

---

† **31:38–40** The landmarks in these verses outline the borders of Jerusalem during the time of Nehemiah: the Tower of Hananel (Neh 3:1; 12:39) in the northeast and the Corner Gate (2 Kgs 14:13) in the northwest; Goah in the southeast and Gareb Hill in the southwest; the Valley of Ben-hinnom ("the Valley of corpses and ashes"), which met the Wadi Kidron in the southeast, and the Horse Gate in the eastern wall at the southeast corner of the Temple area.

**32:1–44** This chapter recounts a prophecy "in action." At the Lord's command, Jeremiah fulfills his family duty to purchase the land of his cousin, carrying out all the legal details, even putting the deed away for safekeeping against the day he will have to produce it to verify his ownership of the land. The Lord defines the meaning of this symbolic action: In the future, Judah will be restored and daily life will return to normal.

**32:1** *The tenth year of Zedekiah:* 588 B.C. *The eighteenth year of Nebuchadnezzar:* dating his reign from his victory at

Carchemish; see note on 25:1–14.

**32:6–9** Jeremiah's imprisonment by the weak-willed Zedekiah was a technical custody that did not deprive him of all freedom of action.

**32:7** *The first right of purchase:* the obligation of the closest relative to redeem the property of a family member in economic distress so that the ancestral land remains within the family (Lv 25:25–28); see note on Ru 2:20.

---

**31:32** Ex 24:7–8; Dt 5:2.
**31:33** Jer 32:40; Ez 37:26; Heb 10:16.
**31:34** Is 54:13.
**31:35** Gn 1:14–18.
**31:36** Jer 33:20–21.
**31:38** Neh 12:38; Zec 14:10–11.
**32:2** Jer 33:1; 37:20; 38:6; 39:14.
**32:3** Jer 26:9; 34:2; 37:6–10.
**32:4** Jer 34:3; 38:18, 23; 39:4–7.
**32:5** Jer 39:7; 52:11.
**32:7** Lv 25:24–34; Ru 4:4.

¹⁰When I had written and sealed the deed, called witnesses and weighed out the silver on the scales, ¹¹I accepted the deed of purchase, both the sealed copy, containing title and conditions, and the open copy.† ¹²I gave this deed of purchase to Baruch, son of Neriah, son of Mahseiah, in the presence of my cousin Hanamel and the witnesses who had signed the deed of purchase and before all the Judahites sitting around in the court of the guard.*

¹³In their presence I gave Baruch this charge: ¹⁴Thus says the LORD of hosts, the God of Israel: Take these deeds of purchase, both the sealed and the open deeds, and put them in an earthenware jar,† so they can last a long time. ¹⁵For thus says the LORD of hosts, the God of Israel: They shall again purchase houses and fields and vineyards in this land.

¹⁶After I had given the deed of purchase to Baruch, son of Neriah, I prayed to the LORD: ¹⁷Ah, my Lord GOD! You made the heavens and the earth with your great power and your outstretched arm; nothing is too difficult for you.* ¹⁸You continue your kindness through a thousand generations; but you repay the ancestors' guilt upon their children who follow them. Great and mighty God, whose name is LORD of hosts,* ¹⁹great in counsel, mighty in deed, whose eyes are fixed on all the ways of mortals, giving to all according to their ways, according to the fruit of their deeds:* ²⁰you performed signs and wonders in the land of Egypt and to this day, in Israel and among all peoples, you have made a name for yourself as on this day.* ²¹You brought your people Israel out of the land of Egypt with signs and wonders, with a strong hand and an outstretched arm, and great terror. ²²And you gave them this land, as you had sworn to their ancestors to give them, a land flowing with milk and honey.* ²³They went in and took possession of it, but they did not listen to your voice. They did not live by your law; they did not do anything you commanded them to do.

Then you made all this evil fall upon them.* ²⁴See, the siegeworks have arrived at this city to capture it; the city is handed over to the Chaldeans who are attacking it, with sword, starvation, and disease. What you threatened has happened—you can see it for yourself.* ²⁵Yet you told me, my Lord GOD: Purchase the field with silver and summon witnesses, when the city has already been handed over to the Chaldeans!

²⁶Then this word of the LORD came to Jeremiah: ²⁷I am the LORD, the God of all the living! Is anything too difficult for me? ²⁸Therefore the LORD says: I am handing over this city to the Chaldeans and to Nebuchadnezzar, king of Babylon, and he shall capture it. ²⁹The Chaldeans who are attacking this city shall go in and set the city on fire, burning it and the houses, on whose roofs incense was burned to Baal and libations were poured out to other gods in order to provoke me.* ³⁰From their youth the Israelites and the Judahites have been doing only what is evil in my eyes; the Israelites have been provoking me with the works of their hands—oracle of the LORD.* ³¹This city has so stirred my anger and wrath, from the day it was built to this day, that I must put it out of my sight, ³²for all the evil the Israelites and Judahites have done to provoke me—they, their kings, their princes, their priests, and their prophets, the people of Judah and the inhabitants of Jerusalem.* ³³They turned their backs to me, not their faces; though I taught them persistently, they would not listen or accept correction.* ³⁴Instead they set up their abominations in the house which bears my name in order to defile it.* ³⁵They built high places to Baal in the Valley of Ben-hinnom to sacrifice their sons and daughters to Molech;† I never commanded them to do this, nor did it even enter my mind that they would practice this abomination, so as to bring sin upon Judah.*

³⁶Now, therefore, thus says the LORD, the

---

**32:11** *The sealed copy…and the open copy:* the legal deed of sale was written on a scroll, which was then rolled up and sealed; a second scroll containing a copy of the legal deed was then rolled around it and left unsealed so the contents of the legal deed would be accessible without destroying the original seal.

**32:14** *In an earthenware jar:* to protect the scroll from drying out and disintegrating. Some of the Dead Sea Scrolls were found in such jars.

**32:35** *Molech:* a god to whom human sacrifice was offered in the Valley of Ben-hinnom. Here, as in 19:5, he is called "Baal"; see note on Lv 18:21.

---

**32:12** Jer 36:4.
**32:17** 2 Kgs 19:15; Jb 42:2.
**32:18** Ex 20:5–6; 34:6; Dt 5:9.
**32:19** Jb 34:21; Ps 33:13–15.
**32:20** Ex 6:6; Dt 4:34; Ps 135:9.
**32:22** Jer 11:5; Gn 15:18; 17:8; 26:3.
**32:23** Jer 7:24–26; Dn 9:10–14.
**32:24** Jer 21:5; 33:4.
**32:29** Jer 21:10; 37:8–10.
**32:30** Jer 3:25; 44:8.
**32:32** Jer 2:26; Is 3:8.
**32:33** Jer 7:24.
**32:34** Jer 7:30; 2 Kgs 21:4–5.
**32:35** Jer 7:31; 19:5; Ps 106:37–38.

JER

God of Israel, concerning this city, which you say is being handed over to the king of Babylon by means of the sword, starvation, and disease: ³⁷See, I am gathering them from all the lands to which I drove them in my rising fury and great anger; I will bring them back to this place and settle them here in safety.* ³⁸They shall be my people, and I will be their God.* ³⁹I will give them one heart and one way, that they may fear me always, for their own good and the good of their children after them. ⁴⁰With them I will make an everlasting covenant, never to cease doing good to them; I will put fear of me in their hearts so that they never turn away from me.* ⁴¹I will take delight in doing good to them: I will plant them firmly in this land, with all my heart and soul.*

⁴²For thus says the LORD: Just as I have brought upon this people all this great evil, so I will bring upon them all the good I have promised them.* ⁴³Fields shall be purchased in this land, about which you say, "It is a wasteland, without human beings or animals, handed over to the Chaldeans."* ⁴⁴They will purchase fields with silver, write up deeds, seal them, and have them witnessed in the land of Benjamin, in the neighborhood of Jerusalem, in the cities of Judah and of the hill country, in the cities of the Shephelah and the Negeb, when I restore their fortunes—oracle of the LORD.*

# 33 Restoration of Jerusalem.

¹The word of the LORD came to Jeremiah a second time while he was still confined in the court of the guard: ²Thus says the LORD who made the earth, giving it shape and stability, LORD is his name: ³Call to me, and I will answer you; I will tell you great things beyond the reach of your knowledge.* ⁴Thus says the LORD, the God of Israel, concerning the houses of this city and the houses of the kings of Judah, which are being torn down because of the siegeworks and the sword:* ⁵men come to battle the Chaldeans, and to fill these houses with the corpses of those whom I have struck down in my raging anger, when I hid my face from this city because of all their wickedness.*

⁶Look! I am bringing the city recovery and healing; I will heal them and reveal to them an abundance of lasting peace.* ⁷I will restore the fortunes of Judah and Israel, and rebuild them as they were in the beginning.* ⁸I will purify them of all the guilt they incurred by sinning against me; I will forgive all their offenses by which they sinned and rebelled against me.* ⁹Then this city shall become joy for me, a name of praise and pride, before all the nations of the earth, as they hear of all the good I am doing for them. They shall fear and tremble because of all the prosperity I give it.

¹⁰Thus says the LORD: In this place, about which you say: "It is a waste without people or animals!" and in the cities of Judah, in the streets of Jerusalem now deserted, without people, without inhabitant, without animal, there shall yet be heard* ¹¹the song of joy, the song of gladness, the song of the bridegroom, the song of the bride, the song of those bringing thank offerings to the house of the LORD: "Give thanks to the LORD of hosts, for the LORD is good; God's love endures forever." For I will restore the fortunes of this land as they were in the beginning, says the LORD.*

¹²Thus says the LORD of hosts: In this place, now a waste, without people or animals, and in all its cities there shall again be sheepfolds for the shepherds to rest their flocks. ¹³In the cities of the hill country, of the Shephelah and the Negeb, in the land of Benjamin and the neighborhood of Jerusalem, and in the cities of Judah, flocks will again pass under the hands of the one who counts them, says the LORD.

¹⁴†The days are coming—oracle of the LORD—when I will fulfill the promise I made to the house of Israel and the house of Judah. ¹⁵In those days, at that time, I will make a just shoot spring up for David; he shall do what is right and just in the land.* ¹⁶In those days Judah shall be saved and Jerusalem shall

---

**33:14–26** This is the longest continuous passage in the Hebrew text of Jeremiah that is missing from the Greek text of Jeremiah. It is probably the work of a postexilic writer who applied parts of Jeremiah's prophecies to new situations. The hope for an eternal Davidic dynasty (vv. 14–17; cf. 2 Sm 7:11–16) and for a perpetual priesthood and sacrificial system (v. 18) was not realized after the exile. On the canonical authority of the Septuagint, see note on Dn 13:1–14:42.

**32:37** Jer 23:3; 29:14; Is 11:12; Ez 11:17.
**32:38** Jer 24:7; 31:33.
**32:40** Jer 31:31–33.
**32:41** Dt 30:9.
**32:42** Jer 33:10–14; Zec 8:13.
**32:43** Jer 33:10.
**32:44** Jer 17:26; 33:7.
**33:3** Is 48:6.

**33:4** Jer 32:24.
**33:5** Jer 21:4–6.
**33:6** Is 57:18.
**33:7** Jer 30:3; 32:44.
**33:8** Ez 36:25.
**33:10** Jer 32:43.
**33:11** 1 Chr 16:34; Ezr 3:11; Ps 136:1.
**33:15** Jer 23:5; Ps 72:1–4, 12–14; Is 11:1.

dwell safely; this is the name they shall call her: "The LORD our justice." [17] For thus says the LORD: David shall never lack a successor on the throne of the house of Israel,* [18] nor shall the priests of Levi ever be lacking before me, to sacrifice burnt offerings, to burn cereal offerings, and to make sacrifices.*

[19] This word of the LORD also came to Jeremiah: [20] Thus says the LORD: If you can break my covenant with day* and my covenant with night so that day and night no longer appear in their proper time, [21] only then can my covenant with my servant David be broken, so that he will not have a descendant to act as king upon his throne, and my covenant with the priests of Levi who minister to me. [22] Just as the host of heaven cannot be numbered and the sands of the sea cannot be counted, so I will multiply the descendants of David my servant and the Levites who minister to me.

[23] This word of the LORD came to Jeremiah: [24] Have you not noticed what these people are saying: "The LORD has rejected the two tribes he had chosen"? They hold my people in contempt as if it were no longer a nation in their eyes.* [25] * Thus says the LORD: If I have no covenant with day and night, if I did not establish statutes for heaven and earth, [26] then I will also reject the descendants of Jacob and of David my servant, no longer selecting from his descendants rulers for the offspring of Abraham, Isaac, and Jacob. Yes, I will restore their fortunes and show them mercy.

# 34 Fate of Zedekiah.
[1] The word which came to Jeremiah from the LORD while Nebuchadnezzar, king of Babylon, and all his army and all the earth's kingdoms under his rule, and all the peoples were attacking Jerusalem and all her cities:* [2] Thus says the LORD, the God of Israel: Go to Zedekiah, king of Judah, and tell him: Thus says the LORD: I am handing this city over to the king of Babylon; he will burn it with fire.* [3] You yourself shall

not escape his hand; rather you will be captured and fall into his hand. You shall see the king of Babylon eye to eye and speak to him face to face. Then you shall go to Babylon.*

[4] Just hear the word of the LORD, Zedekiah, king of Judah! Then, says the LORD concerning you, you shall not die by the sword. [5] You shall die in peace, and they will burn spices for you as they did for your ancestors, the earlier kings who preceded you, and they shall make lament over you, "Alas, Lord." I myself make this promise—oracle of the LORD.

[6] Jeremiah the prophet told all these things to Zedekiah, king of Judah, in Jerusalem, [7] while the army of the king of Babylon was attacking Jerusalem and the remaining cities of Judah, Lachish, and Azekah.† Only these fortified cities were left standing out of all the cities of Judah!

**The Pact Broken.**† [8] This is the word that came to Jeremiah from the LORD after King Zedekiah had made a covenant with all the people in Jerusalem to proclaim freedom: [9] Everyone must free their Hebrew slaves, male and female, so that no one should hold another Judahite in servitude.* [10] All the princes and the people who entered this covenant agreed to set free their slaves, their male and female servants, so that they should no longer be in servitude. But even though they agreed and freed them, [11] afterward they took back their male and female servants whom they had set free and again forced them into servitude.

[12] Then this word of the LORD came to Jeremiah: [13] Thus says the LORD, the God of Israel: I myself made a covenant with your ancestors the day I brought them out of the land of Egypt, out of the house of slavery: [14] Every seventh year each of you must set free all Hebrews who have sold themselves to you; six years they shall serve you, but then you shall let them go free. Your ancestors, however, did not listen to me or obey me. [15] As for you, today

---

**34:7** *Lachish, and Azekah:* fortress towns southwest of Jerusalem which Nebuchadnezzar besieged to prevent any help coming to Jerusalem from Egypt. At Lachish, archaeologists found several letters written on ostraca (pottery fragments) dated to 598 or 588 B.C., which mention both Lachish and Azekah.

**34:8–22** During the siege of Jerusalem, its citizens made a covenant at Zedekiah's instigation to free Judahites they held in servitude, thus providing additional defenders for the city, leaving slave owners with fewer mouths to feed, and making reparation for past violations of the law, which dictated that Hebrew slaves should serve no longer than six years (Dt 15:12–15).

But when the siege was temporarily lifted, when the assistance promised by Pharaoh Hophra arrived (cf. Jer 37:5), the inhabitants of Jerusalem broke the covenant and once more pressed their fellow citizens into slavery (v. 11).

**33:17** 2 Sm 7:16; 1 Kgs 2:4; Ps 89:4–5, 29, 36–37.
**33:18** Ez 44:15–16.
**33:20–21** Jer 31:36–37; Ps 89:37–38.
**33:24** Rom 11:1–2.
**33:25–26** Jer 31:36–37; 32:44.
**34:1** Jer 52:4; 2 Kgs 25:1.
**34:2** Jer 21:10; 32:3, 28.
**34:3** Jer 32:4; 52:11.
**34:9** Ex 21:2–4; Lv 25:39, 46; Dt 15:12–15.

you repented and did what is right in my eyes by proclaiming freedom for your neighbor and making a covenant before me in the house which bears my name. 16 But then you again profaned my name by taking back your male and female slaves whom you had just set free for life; you forced them to become your slaves again.* 17 Therefore, thus says the LORD: You for your part did not obey me by proclaiming freedom for your families and neighbors. So I now proclaim freedom for you—oracle of the LORD—for the sword, starvation, and disease. I will make you an object of horror to all the kingdoms of the earth. 18 † Those who violated my covenant and did not observe the terms of the covenant they made in my presence—I will make them like the calf which they cut in two so they could pass between its parts— 19 the princes of Judah and of Jerusalem, the court officials, the priests, and all the people of the land, who passed between the parts of the calf. 20 These I will hand over to their enemies, to those who seek their lives: their corpses shall become food for the birds of the air and the beasts of the field.*

21 Zedekiah, king of Judah, and his princes, I will hand also over to their enemies, to those who seek their lives, to the army of the king of Babylon which is now withdrawing from you.* 22 I am giving the command—oracle of the LORD—to bring them back to this city. They shall attack and capture it, and burn it with fire; the cities of Judah I will turn into a waste, where no one dwells.*

**35** **The Faithful Rechabites.** 1 The word that came to Jeremiah from the LORD in the days of Jehoiakim,† son of Josiah, king of Judah: 2 Go to the house† of the Rechabites,

speak to them, and bring them to the house of the LORD, to one of the rooms there, and give them wine to drink. 3 So I took Jaazaniah, son of Jeremiah, son of Habazziniah, his brothers and all his sons—the whole house of the Rechabites— 4 and I brought them to the house of the LORD, to the room of the sons of Hanan,† son of Igdaliah, the man of God, next to the room of the princes above the room of Maaseiah, son of Shallum, the guard at the entrance. 5 I set before the Rechabites bowls full of wine, and cups, and said to them, "Drink some wine."

6 "We do not drink wine," they said to me; "Jonadab,† Rechab's son, our father, commanded us, 'Neither you nor your children shall ever drink wine.* 7 Build no house and sow no seed; do not plant vineyards or own any. You must dwell in tents all your lives, so that you may live long on the land where you live as resident aliens.' 8 We have obeyed Jonadab, Rechab's son, our father, in everything that he commanded us: not drinking wine as long as we live—neither we nor our wives nor our sons nor our daughters; 9 not building houses to live in; not owning vineyards or fields or crops. 10 We live in tents, doing everything our father Jonadab commanded us. 11 But when Nebuchadnezzar, king of Babylon, invaded this land, we said, 'Come, let us go into Jerusalem to escape the army of the Chaldeans and the army of the Arameans.'† That is why we are now living in Jerusalem."*

12 Then the word of the LORD came to Jeremiah: 13 Thus says the LORD of hosts, the God of Israel: Go, say to the people of Judah and to the inhabitants of Jerusalem: Will you not take correction and obey my words?—oracle of the LORD.* 14 The words of Jonadab, Rechab's son,

† **34:18–19** Both the Old Testament (Gn 15:10–17) and the eighth century B.C. Sefire inscription indicate that sometimes contracting parties ratified an agreement by walking between dismembered animals, invoking upon themselves the animals' fate if they failed to keep their word. *The covenant:* that mentioned in vv. 10, 15.
**35:1** *In the days of Jehoiakim:* probably in 599 or 598 B.C. (cf. 2 Kgs 24:1–2).
**35:2** *House:* both members of the family of Rechab (cf. v. 3) and the place where they live; cf. note on v. 11. *The Rechabites:* traditionalists who rejected the settled agricultural and urban cultures to which other Israelites had assimilated, maintaining their loyalty to the Lord by perpetuating the semi-nomadic life of their distant ancestors (cf. 2 Kgs 10:15–17). Jeremiah contrasts their adherence to their vows with the Judahites' disregard for divine commands.
**35:4** *The sons of Hanan:* probably disciples of Hanan. *Man of God:* occurring only here in Jeremiah, the title frequently is applied to prophets: e.g., Samuel (1 Sm 9:6–10), Elijah (2 Kgs

1:9–13), Elisha (2 Kgs 4–13). Whatever the function of the sons of Hanan, they encourage Jeremiah by lending him their room. *Maaseiah:* perhaps the father of the priest Zephaniah (29:25; 37:3). *Guard at the entrance:* an important priestly responsibility (cf. 52:24).
**35:6** *Jonadab:* another spelling of Jehonadab, a contemporary of King Jehu; cf. 2 Kgs 10:15–17.
**35:11** *The army of the Arameans:* Nebuchadnezzar enlisted the help of Judah's neighbors in his assault on Jerusalem. *Living in Jerusalem:* the current military threat and the prospect of being killed or captured as plunder drove the Rechabites into the city and away from their tents.

**34:16** Lv 19:12.
**34:20** Jer 7:33; 16:4; 19:7.
**34:21** Jer 37:5, 11.
**34:22** Jer 37:8; 52:7–13; 2 Chr 36:17, 19.
**35:6** Jgs 4:17, 24; 1 Sm 15:6; 2 Kgs 10:15–17.
**35:11** 2 Kgs 24:1–2.
**35:13** Jer 32:33.

by which he commanded his children not to drink wine, have been upheld: to this day they have not drunk wine; they obeyed their ancestor's command. I, however, have spoken to you time and again. But you did not obey me! * 15 Time and again I sent you all my servants the prophets, saying: Turn away, each of you, from your evil way and reform your actions! Do not follow other gods to serve them that you may remain in the land which I gave you and your ancestors. But you did not pay attention. You did not obey me. * 16 Yes, the children of Jonadab, Rechab's son, upheld the command which their father laid on them. But this people has not obeyed me! 17 Now, therefore, says the LORD God of hosts, the God of Israel: I will soon bring upon Judah and all the inhabitants of Jerusalem every evil with which I threatened them because I spoke but they did not obey, I called but they did not answer. *

18 But to the house of the Rechabites Jeremiah said: Thus says the LORD of hosts, the God of Israel: Since you have obeyed the command of Jonadab, your father, kept all his commands and done everything he commanded you, 19 therefore, thus says the LORD of hosts, the God of Israel: Never shall there fail to be a descendant of Jonadab, Rechab's son, standing in my presence.

## VII. JEREMIAH AND THE FALL OF JERUSALEM

# 36

**Baruch, the Scribe of Jeremiah.** 1 In the fourth year of Jehoiakim, son of Josiah, king of Judah, this word came to Jeremiah from the LORD: 2 Take a scroll and write on it all the words I have spoken to you about Israel, Judah, and all the nations, from the day I first spoke to you, from the days of Josiah, until today. 3 Perhaps, if the house of Judah hears all the evil I have in mind to do to them, so that all of them turn from their evil way, then I can forgive their wickedness and their sin. * 4 So Jeremiah called Baruch, son of Neriah, and he wrote down on a scroll what Jeremiah said, all the words which the LORD had

spoken to him. 5 Then Jeremiah commanded Baruch: "I cannot enter the house of the LORD; I am barred † from it. 6 So you yourself must go. On a fast day in the hearing of the people in the LORD's house, read the words of the LORD from the scroll you wrote at my dictation; read them also to all the people of Judah who come up from their cities. 7 Perhaps they will present their supplication before the LORD and will all turn back from their evil way; for great is the anger and wrath with which the LORD has threatened this people." *

8 Baruch, son of Neriah, did everything Jeremiah the prophet commanded; from the scroll he read the LORD's words in the LORD's house. 9 In the ninth month, in the fifth year of Jehoiakim, son of Josiah, king of Judah, all the people of Jerusalem and all those who came from Judah's cities to Jerusalem proclaimed a fast before the LORD. 10 So Baruch read the words of Jeremiah from the scroll in the room of Gemariah, † son of the scribe Shaphan, in the upper court of the LORD's house, at the entrance of the New Temple Gate, in the hearing of all the people.

11 Now Micaiah, son of Gemariah, son of Shaphan, heard all the words of the LORD read from the scroll. 12 So he went down to the house of the king, into the scribe's chamber, † where the princes were meeting in session: Elishama, the scribe; Delaiah, son of Shemaiah; Elnathan, son of Achbor; Gemariah, son of Shaphan; Zedekiah, son of Hananiah; and the other princes. 13 Micaiah reported to them all that he had heard Baruch read from his scroll in the hearing of the people. 14 The princes immediately sent Jehudi, son of Nethaniah, son of Shelemiah, son of Cushi, to Baruch with the order: "The scroll you read in the hearing of the people—bring it with you and come." Scroll in hand, Baruch, son of Neriah, went to them. 15 "Sit down," they said to him, "and read it in our hearing." Baruch read it in their hearing, 16 and when they had heard all its words, they turned to each other in alarm and said to Baruch, "We have to tell the king all these things." 17 Then they asked

---

Baruch: "Tell us, please, how did you come to write down all these words? Was it at his dictation?" ¹⁸"Yes, he would dictate all these words to me," Baruch answered them, "while I wrote them down with ink in the scroll." ¹⁹The princes said to Baruch, "Go into hiding, you and Jeremiah; do not let anyone know where you are."

²⁰They went in to the king, into the courtyard; they had deposited the scroll in the room of Elishama the scribe. When they told the king everything that had happened, ²¹the king sent Jehudi to get the scroll. Jehudi brought it from the room of Elishama the scribe, and read it to the king and to all the princes who were attending the king. ²²Now the king was sitting in his winter house, since it was the ninth month, and a fire was burning in the brazier before him. ²³Each time Jehudi finished reading three or four columns, he would cut off the piece with a scribe's knife† and throw it into the fire in the brazier, until the entire scroll was consumed in the fire in the brazier. ²⁴As they were listening to all these words the king and all his officials did not become alarmed, nor did they tear their garments. ²⁵And though Elnathan, Delaiah, and Gemariah urged the king not to burn the scroll, he would not listen to them. ²⁶He commanded Jerahmeel, a royal prince, and Seraiah, son of Azriel, and Shelemiah, son of Abdeel, to arrest Baruch, the scribe, and Jeremiah the prophet. But the LORD had hidden them away.

²⁷The word of the LORD came to Jeremiah, after the king burned the scroll and the words Jeremiah had dictated to Baruch: ²⁸Take another scroll, and write on it all the words in the first scroll, which Jehoiakim, king of Judah, burned. ²⁹And against Jehoiakim, king of Judah, say this: Thus says the LORD: You are the one who burned that scroll, saying, "Why did you write on it: Babylon's king shall surely come and ravage this land, emptying it of every living thing"? ³⁰The LORD now says of Jehoiakim, king of Judah:* No descendant of his shall sit on David's throne; his corpse shall be thrown out, exposed to heat by day, frost by night.† ³¹I

will punish him and his descendants and his officials for their wickedness; upon them, the inhabitants of Jerusalem, and the people of Judah I will bring all the evil threats to which they did not listen.

³²Then Jeremiah took another scroll and gave it to his scribe, Baruch, son of Neriah, who wrote on it at Jeremiah's dictation all the words contained in the scroll which Jehoiakim, king of Judah, had burned in the fire, adding many words like them.

# 37 Jeremiah in the Dungeon. ¹Zedekiah, son of Josiah, became king, succeeding Coniah, son of Jehoiakim; Nebuchadnezzar, king of Babylon, appointed him king over the land of Judah.* ²Neither he, nor his officials, nor the people of the land would listen to the words which the LORD spoke through Jeremiah the prophet. ³Yet King Zedekiah sent Jehucal, son of Shelemiah, and Zephaniah, son of Maaseiah the priest, to Jeremiah the prophet with this request: "Please appeal to the LORD, our God, for us."* ⁴At this time Jeremiah still came and went freely among the people; he had not yet been put into prison.† ⁵Meanwhile, Pharaoh's army† had set out from Egypt, and when the Chaldeans who were besieging Jerusalem heard this report, they withdrew from the city.*

⁶Then the word of the LORD came to Jeremiah the prophet: ⁷Thus says the LORD, the God of Israel: Thus you must say to the king of Judah who sent you to consult me: Listen! Pharaoh's army, which has set out to help you, will return to Egypt, its own land.* ⁸The Chaldeans shall return and attack this city; they shall capture it and destroy it by fire.*

⁹Thus says the LORD: Do not deceive yourselves, saying: "The Chaldeans are surely leaving us forever." They are not! ¹⁰Even if you could defeat the whole Chaldean army that is now attacking you, and only the wounded remained, each in his tent, these would rise up and destroy the city with fire.*

¹¹Now when the Chaldean army withdrew from Jerusalem because of the army of

---

† **36:23** *A scribe's knife*: used to sharpen reed pens.
**36:30** Jehoiakim's son Jehoiachin was named king, but reigned only three months; he was better known for his long exile in Babylon. *His corpse shall be thrown out*: just as Jehoiakim had thrown pieces of the scroll into the fire (cf. 22:19).
**37:4** *Put into prison*: as described in 32:1–3. Chronologically, the present episode follows 34:1–7.
**37:5** *Pharaoh's army*: the force sent by Pharaoh Hophra;

when they arrived, the Chaldeans temporarily lifted the siege against Jerusalem (cf. 34:21).

* **36:30** Jer 22:19.
**37:1** Jer 52:1; 2 Kgs 24:17; 2 Chr 36:10.
**37:3** Jer 21:1.
**37:5** Ez 17:15; 29:6–7.
**37:7** Ez 17:17.
**37:8** Jer 34:22.
**37:10** Jer 21:4.

Pharaoh.* <sup>12</sup>Jeremiah set out from Jerusalem to go to the territory of Benjamin, to receive his share of property among the people. <sup>13</sup>But at the Gate of Benjamin, the captain of the guard, by the name of Irijah, son of Shelemiah, son of Hananiah, arrested Jeremiah the prophet, saying, "You are deserting to the Chaldeans!" <sup>14</sup>"That is a lie!" Jeremiah answered, "I am not deserting to the Chaldeans." Without listening to him, Irijah kept Jeremiah in custody and brought him to the princes.

<sup>15</sup>The princes were enraged at Jeremiah and had Jeremiah beaten and imprisoned in the house of Jonathan the scribe, for they were using it as a jail.* <sup>16</sup>And so Jeremiah went into a room in the dungeon, where he remained many days.

<sup>17</sup>Then King Zedekiah had him brought to his palace, and he asked him secretly, "Is there any word from the LORD?" "There is!" Jeremiah answered: "You shall be handed over to the king of Babylon."* <sup>18</sup>Jeremiah then asked King Zedekiah: "How have I wronged you or your officials or this people, that you should put me in prison?* <sup>19</sup>Where are your own prophets who prophesied for you, saying: 'The King of Babylon will not attack you or this land'? <sup>20</sup>Please hear me, my lord king! Grant my petition: do not send me back into the house of Jonathan the scribe, or I shall die there."

<sup>21</sup>So King Zedekiah ordered that Jeremiah be confined in the court of the guard and given a ration of bread every day from the bakers' street until all the bread in the city was eaten up. Thus Jeremiah remained in the court of the guard.*

# 38 Jeremiah in the Muddy Cistern.

<sup>1</sup>Shephatiah, son of Mattan, Gedaliah, son of Pashhur, Jucal, son of Shelemiah, and Pashhur, son of Malchiah, heard the words Jeremiah was speaking to all the people:† <sup>2</sup>Thus says the LORD: Those who remain in this city shall die by means of the sword, starvation, and disease; but those who go out to the Chaldeans shall live. Their lives shall

be spared them as spoils of war that they may live.* <sup>3</sup>Thus says the LORD: This city shall certainly be handed over to the army of the king of Babylon; he shall capture it.

<sup>4</sup>Then the princes said to the king, "This man ought to be put to death. He is weakening the resolve† of the soldiers left in this city and of all the people, by saying such things to them; he is not seeking the welfare of our people, but their ruin."* <sup>5</sup>King Zedekiah answered: "He is in your hands," for the king could do nothing with them. <sup>6</sup>And so they took Jeremiah and threw him into the cistern of Prince Malchiah, in the court of the guard, letting him down by rope. There was no water in the cistern, only mud, and Jeremiah sank down into the mud.*

<sup>7</sup>Now Ebed-melech, an Ethiopian, a court official in the king's house, heard that they had put Jeremiah in the cistern. The king happened to be sitting at the Gate of Benjamin, <sup>8</sup>and Ebed-melech went there from the house of the king and said to him, <sup>9</sup>"My lord king, these men have done wrong in all their treatment of Jeremiah the prophet, throwing him into the cistern. He will starve to death on the spot, for there is no more bread in the city."* <sup>10</sup>Then the king ordered Ebed-melech the Ethiopian: "Take three men with you, and get Jeremiah the prophet out of the cistern before he dies." <sup>11</sup>Ebed-melech took the men with him, and went first to the linen closet in the house of the king. He took some old, tattered rags and lowered them by rope to Jeremiah in the cistern. <sup>12</sup>Then he said to Jeremiah, "Put these old, tattered rags between your armpits and the ropes." Jeremiah did so, <sup>13</sup>and they pulled him up by rope out of the cistern. But Jeremiah remained in the court of the guard.

<sup>14</sup>King Zedekiah summoned Jeremiah the prophet to meet him at the third entrance of the house of the LORD. "I have a question to ask you," the king said to Jeremiah. "Do not hide anything from me."* <sup>15</sup>Jeremiah answered Zedekiah: "If I tell you anything, will you not have me put to death? If I counsel you, you will not listen to me!"* <sup>16</sup>But King

---

**38:1** Jeremiah enjoyed sufficient liberty in the court of the guard (37:21) to speak to the people; cf. 32:6–9. *Gedaliah, son of Pashhur:* the latter is possibly the Pashhur of 20:1. *Pashhur, son of Malchiah:* mentioned in 21:1.

**38:4** *He is weakening the resolve:* lit., "he weakens the hands." One of the Lachish ostraca (cf. note on 34:7) makes the same claim against the princes in Jerusalem.

**37:11** Zec 14:10.
**37:15** Jer 38:6–13.
**37:17** Jer 21:7; 32:3; 34:21.
**37:18** Jer 26:19.
**37:21** Jer 32:2; 38:28.
**38:2** Jer 21:9–10; 39:18;

45:5.
**38:4** Jer 26:11.
**38:6** Jer 37:14–15.
**38:9** Jer 52:6.
**38:14** Jer 37:16.
**38:15** Lk 22:67–68.

Zedekiah swore to Jeremiah secretly: "As the LORD lives who gave us our lives, I will not kill you, nor will I hand you over to those men who seek your life."

17 Jeremiah then said to Zedekiah: "Thus says the LORD God of hosts, the God of Israel: If you will only surrender to the princes of Babylon's king, you shall save your life; this city shall not be destroyed by fire, and you and your household shall live. * 18 But if you do not surrender to the princes of Babylon's king, this city shall fall into the hand of the Chaldeans, who shall destroy it by fire, and you shall not escape their hand." *

19 King Zedekiah said to Jeremiah, "I am afraid of the Judahites who have deserted to the Chaldeans; I could be handed over to them, and they will mistreat me." * 20 "You will not be handed over to them," Jeremiah answered. "I beg you! Please listen to the voice of the LORD regarding what I tell you so that it may go well with you and your life be spared. * 21 But if you refuse to surrender, this is what the LORD has shown: 22 I see all the women who remain in the house of Judah's king being brought out to the princes of Babylon's king, and they are crying:

'They betrayed you, outdid you,
    your good friends!
Now that your feet are sunk in mud,
    they slink away.' *

23 All your wives and children shall be brought out to the Chaldeans, and you shall not escape their hands; you shall be handed over to the king of Babylon, and this city shall be destroyed by fire." *

24 Then Zedekiah said to Jeremiah, "Let no one know about this conversation, or you shall die. 25 If the princes should hear I spoke with you and if they should come and ask you, 'Tell us what you said to the king; do not hide it from us, or we will kill you,' or, 'What did the king say to you?' 26 then give them this answer: 'I petitioned the king not to send me back to Jonathan's house lest I die there.'" 27 When all the princes came to Jeremiah and questioned him, he answered them with the very words the king had commanded. They said no more to him, for nothing had been overheard of the conversation. 28 Thus Jeremiah stayed in the court of the guard until the day Jerusalem was taken. *

**39** **The Capture of Jerusalem.** When Jerusalem was taken, 1 in the ninth year of Zedekiah, * king of Judah, in the tenth month,† Nebuchadnezzar, king of Babylon, and all his army marched against Jerusalem and placed it under siege. 2 In the eleventh year of Zedekiah, on the ninth day of the fourth month,† the city wall was breached. 3 All the princes of the king of Babylon came and took their seats at the middle gate: Nergal-sharezer of Simmagir, a chief officer; Nebushazban, a high dignitary; and all the rest of the princes of the king of Babylon.† 4 When Zedekiah, king of Judah, and all his warriors saw this, they fled, leaving the city at night by way of the king's garden,† through a gate between the two walls. He went in the direction of the Arabah, * 5 but the Chaldean army pursued them; they caught up with Zedekiah in the wilderness near Jericho and took him prisoner. They brought him to Nebuchadnezzar, king of Babylon, in Riblah,† in the land of Hamath, and he pronounced sentence upon him. * 6 The king of Babylon executed the sons of Zedekiah at Riblah before his very eyes; the king of Babylon also executed all the nobles of Judah. * 7 He then blinded Zedekiah and bound him in chains to bring him to Babylon. *

8 The Chaldeans set fire to the king's house and the houses of the people and tore down the walls of Jerusalem. * 9 Nebuzaradan,

**39:1** In the ninth year…in the tenth month: the month Tebet (mid-December to mid-January) of the year 589/588 B.C., according to the Babylonian calendar, whose New Year began in March/April.
**39:2** In the eleventh year…the ninth day of the fourth month: in July, 587 B.C.
**39:3** The Babylonian officers act as a military tribunal or government, headed by Nergal-sharezer, Nebuchadnezzar's son and successor.
**39:4** By way of the king's garden: along the southeast side of the city; the royal garden was in the Kidron Valley. A gate between the two walls: the southernmost city gate, at the end of the Tyropoeon Valley. The Arabah: the southern Jordan Valley.

Zedekiah was perhaps trying to escape across the Jordan when he was captured near Jericho.
**39:5** Riblah: Nebuchadnezzar's headquarters north of Damascus; Pharaoh Neco had once used the town as a military post (2 Kgs 23:33).

38:17 Jer 27:12–13; 2 Kgs 24:12.
38:18 Jer 32:4.
38:19 1 Sm 31:4.
38:20 2 Chr 20:20.
38:22 Jb 6:15; 19:13–14, 19.
38:23 Jer 41:10.
38:28 Jer 39:14.
39:1–2 Jer 52:4–16; 2 Kgs 25:1–12; Ez 24:1.
39:4 Jer 52:7.
39:5 Jer 32:4–5; 38:18.
39:6 Jer 34:21.
39:7 Jer 32:4–5; Ez 12:13.
39:8 Jer 21:10; 34:2; 52:13.

captain of the bodyguard, deported to Babylon the rest of the people left in the city, those who had deserted to him, and the rest of the workers.* ¹⁰But Nebuzaradan, captain of the bodyguard, left in the land of Judah some of the poor who had nothing and at the same time gave them vineyards and farms.*

**Jeremiah Released to Gedaliah's Custody.**
¹¹Concerning Jeremiah, Nebuchadnezzar, king of Babylon, gave these orders through Nebuzaradan, captain of the bodyguard: ¹²"Take him and look after him; do not let anything happen to him. Whatever he may ask, you must do for him."* ¹³Thereupon Nebuzaradan, captain of the bodyguard, and Nebushazban, a high dignitary, and Nergal-sharezer, a chief officer, and all the nobles of the king of Babylon, ¹⁴had Jeremiah taken out of the courtyard of the guard and entrusted to Gedaliah, son of Ahikam, son of Shaphan, to bring him home. And so he remained among the people.*

**A Word of Comfort for Ebed-melech.** ¹⁵While Jeremiah was still imprisoned in the court of the guard, the word of the Lord came to him: ¹⁶Go, tell this to Ebed-melech the Ethiopian: Thus says the Lord of hosts, the God of Israel: See, I am now carrying out my words against this city, for evil and not for good; this will happen in your presence on that day.* ¹⁷But on that day I will deliver you—oracle of the Lord; you shall not be handed over to the men you dread. ¹⁸I will make certain that you escape and do not fall by the sword. Your life will be your spoils of war because you trusted in me—oracle of the Lord.*

**40** **Jeremiah Still in Judah.** ¹The word† which came to Jeremiah from the Lord, after Nebuzaradan, captain of the bodyguard, had released him in Ramah, where he found him a prisoner in chains among the captives of Jerusalem and Judah being exiled to Babylon.* ²The captain of the bodyguard took charge of Jeremiah and said to him, "The

Lord, your God, decreed ruin for this place. ³Now he has made it happen, accomplishing what he decreed; because you sinned against the Lord and did not listen to his voice, this decree has been realized against you. ⁴Now, I release you today from the chains upon your hands; if you want to come with me to Babylon, then come: I will look out for you. But if you do not want to come to Babylon, very well. See, the whole land lies before you; go wherever you think good and proper.* ⁵Or go to Gedaliah, son of Ahikam, son of Shaphan, whom the king of Babylon has set over the cities of Judah. Stay with him among the people. Or go wherever you want!" The captain of the bodyguard gave him food and gifts and let him go.* ⁶So Jeremiah went to Gedaliah, son of Ahikam, in Mizpah,† and dwelt with him among the people left in the land.*

⁷When the military leaders still in the field with their soldiers heard that the king of Babylon had set Gedaliah, son of Ahikam, over the land and had put him in charge of men, women, and children, from the poor of the land who had not been deported to Babylon, ⁸they and their soldiers came to Gedaliah in Mizpah: Ishmael, son of Nethaniah; Johanan, son of Kareah; Seraiah, son of Tanhumeth; the sons of Ephai of Netophah; and Jezaniah of Beth-maacah. ⁹Gedaliah, son of Ahikam, son of Shaphan, swore an oath to them and their men: "Do not be afraid to serve the Chaldeans. Stay in the land and serve the king of Babylon, so that everything may go well with you.* ¹⁰As for me, I will remain in Mizpah, as your representative before the Chaldeans when they come to us. You, for your part, harvest the wine, the fruit, and the oil, store them in jars, and remain in the cities you occupied." ¹¹Then all the Judahites in Moab, in Ammon, in Edom, and those in all other lands heard that the king of Babylon had left a remnant in Judah and had set over them Gedaliah, son of Ahikam, son of Shaphan. ¹²They all returned to the land of Judah from the places to which they had scattered. They went to Gedaliah at Mizpah and had a rich harvest of wine and fruit.

---

40:1 *The word*: this "word" does not actually appear until 42:7.
40:6 While Jerusalem had suffered a great deal of damage, the Babylonian leaders' selection of Mizpah as their local headquarters was probably as much a symbolic statement as it was a utilitarian move: Jerusalem and its political and religious worldview had given way to disorder and no longer existed as a symbol of order.

39:9 2 Kgs 25:11.
39:10 2 Kgs 25:12, 22.
39:12 Jer 40:4.
39:14 Jer 26:24; 38:28.
39:16 Jer 21:10; Dn 9:12.
39:18 Jer 45:5; Ps 25:3; 37:40.
40:1 Jer 39:14.
40:4 Jer 39:12.
40:5 Jer 39:14; 2 Kgs 25:22.
40:6 Jer 39:14.
40:9 Jer 27:12–13; 2 Kgs 25:24.

**Assassination of Gedaliah.** ¹³ Now Johanan, son of Kareah, and all the military leaders in the field came to Gedaliah in Mizpah ¹⁴ and said to him, "Surely you are aware that Baalis, the Ammonite king,† has sent Ishmael, son of Nethaniah, to assassinate you?"* But Gedaliah, son of Ahikam, would not believe them. ¹⁵ Then Johanan, son of Kareah, said secretly to Gedaliah in Mizpah: "Please let me go and kill Ishmael, son of Nethaniah; no one will know it. What if he assassinates you? All the Judahites who have now rallied behind you would scatter and the remnant of Judah would perish." ¹⁶ Gedaliah, son of Ahikam, answered Johanan, son of Kareah, "You must not do that. What you are saying about Ishmael is a lie!"

**41** ¹ In the seventh month, Ishmael, son of Nethaniah, son of Elishama, of royal descent, one of the king's nobles, came with ten men to Gedaliah, son of Ahikam, at Mizpah.* While they were together at table in Mizpah, ² Ishmael, son of Nethaniah, and the ten with him, stood up and struck down Gedaliah, son of Ahikam, son of Shaphan, with swords. They killed him, since the king of Babylon had set him over the land; ³ Ishmael also killed all the Judahites of military age who were with Gedaliah and the Chaldean soldiers stationed there.

⁴ The day after the murder of Gedaliah, before anyone learned about it, ⁵ eighty men, in ragged clothes, with beards shaved off and gashes on their bodies, came from Shechem, Shiloh, and Samaria, bringing grain offerings and incense for the house of the LORD. ⁶ Weeping as he went, Ishmael son of Nethaniah, set out from Mizpah to meet them. "Come to Gedaliah, son of Ahikam," he said as he met them. ⁷ Once they were inside the city, Ishmael, son of Nethaniah, and his men slaughtered them and threw them into the cistern. ⁸ Ten of them said to Ishmael: "Do not kill us! We have stores of wheat and barley, oil and honey hidden in the field." So he spared them and did not kill them as he had killed their companions. ⁹ The cistern into which Ishmael threw all the bodies of the men he had killed was the large one King Asa made to defend himself against Baasha, king of Israel; Ishmael, son of Nethaniah, filled this cistern with the slain.*

¹⁰ Ishmael led away the rest of the people left in Mizpah, including the princesses,† whom Nebuzaradan, captain of the bodyguard, had consigned to Gedaliah, son of Ahikam. With these captives, Ishmael, son of Nethaniah, set out to cross over to the Ammonites.

**Flight to Egypt.** ¹¹ But when Johanan, son of Kareah, and the other army leaders with him heard about the crimes Ishmael, son of Nethaniah, had committed, ¹² they took all their men and set out to attack Ishmael, son of Nethaniah. They overtook him at the great pool in Gibeon.† ¹³ At the sight of Johanan, son of Kareah, and the other army leaders, the people with Ishmael rejoiced; ¹⁴ all of those whom Ishmael had taken captive from Mizpah went back to Johanan, son of Kareah. ¹⁵ But Ishmael, son of Nethaniah, escaped from Johanan with eight men and fled to the Ammonites. ¹⁶ Then Johanan, son of Kareah, and all the military leaders took charge of all the rest of the people whom Ishmael, son of Nethaniah, had taken away from Mizpah after he killed Gedaliah, son of Ahikam—the soldiers, the women with children, and court officials, whom he brought back from Gibeon. ¹⁷ They set out and stopped at Geruth Chimham near Bethlehem, intending to go into Egypt. ¹⁸ They were afraid of the Chaldeans, because Ishmael, son of Nethaniah, had slain Gedaliah, son of Ahikam, whom the king of Babylon had set over the land.

**42** ¹ Then all the military leaders, including Johanan, son of Kareah, Azariah, son of Hoshaiah, and all the people, from the least to the greatest, ² approached Jeremiah the prophet and said, "Please grant our petition; pray for us to the LORD, your God, for all this remnant. As you see, only a few of us remain, but once we were many. ³ May the LORD, your God, show us the way we should take and what we should do." ⁴ "Very well!" Jeremiah

---

† **40:14** In an attempt, perhaps, to weaken Babylon's hold on the area and to add Judah to the Ammonite kingdom, Baalis supported Ishmael's claim to the throne of David (cf. 41:1 for Ishmael's genealogy).
**41:10** *The princesses*: the women of Judah's royal house.
**41:12** *Gibeon*: modern El-Jib; northwest of Jerusalem. A huge

pit carved into limestone provided water in time of siege, here called the great pool, lit., "many waters"; cf. 2 Sm 2:12–14.

**40:14** Jer 41:1–3, 10.         **41:9** 1 Kgs 15:16; 2 Chr
**41:1** Jer 40:14–16; 2 Kgs        16:6.
25:25.

the prophet answered them: "I will pray to the LORD, your God, as you desire; whatever the LORD answers, I will tell you; I will withhold nothing from you."* [5]And they said to Jeremiah, "May the LORD be a true and faithful witness against us if we do not follow all the instructions the LORD, your God, sends us through you.* [6]Whether we like it or not, we will obey the command of the LORD, our God, to whom we are sending you, so that it may go well with us for obeying the command of the LORD, our God."*

[7]Ten days passed before the word of the LORD came to Jeremiah. [8]Then he called Johanan, son of Kareah, his army leaders, and all the people, from the least to the greatest, [9]and said to them: Thus says the LORD, the God of Israel, to whom you sent me to offer your petition: [10]If indeed you will remain in this land, I will build you up, and not tear you down; I will plant you, not uproot you; for I repent of the evil I have done you.* [11]Do not fear the king of Babylon, as you do now. Do not fear him—oracle of the LORD—for I am with you to save you, to rescue you from his power.* [12]I will take pity on you, so that he will have pity on you and let you return to your land.* [13]But if you keep saying, "We will not stay in this land," thus disobeying the voice of the LORD, your God, [14]and saying, "No, we will go to the land of Egypt, where we will not see war, nor hear the trumpet alarm, nor hunger for bread. There we will live!"* [15]then listen to the word of the LORD, remnant of Judah: Thus says the LORD of hosts, the God of Israel: If you are set on going to Egypt and settling down there once you arrive, [16]the sword you fear shall overtake you in the land of Egypt; the hunger you dread shall pursue you to Egypt and there you shall die.* [17]All those determined to go to Egypt to live shall die by the sword, famine, and disease: not one shall survive or escape the evil that I am bringing upon them.* [18]For thus says the LORD of hosts, the God of Israel: Just as my furious wrath was poured out upon the inhabitants of Jerusalem, so shall my anger be poured out on you when you reach Egypt. You shall become a malediction and a horror, a curse and a reproach, and you shall never see this place again.*

[19]The LORD has spoken to you, remnant of Judah. Do not go to Egypt! Mark well that I am warning you this day. [20]At the cost of your lives you have been deceitful, for you yourselves sent me to the LORD, your God, saying, "Pray for us to the LORD, our God; whatever the LORD, our God, shall say, tell us and we will do it." [21]Today I have told you, but you have not listened to the voice of the LORD your God, in anything that he has sent me to tell you.* [22]Have no doubt about this: you shall die by the sword, famine, and disease in the place where you want to go and live.*

[1]When Jeremiah finished telling the people all the words the LORD, their God, sent to them, [2]Azariah, son of Hoshaiah, Johanan, son of Kareah, and all the others had the insolence to say to Jeremiah: "You lie; the LORD, our God, did not send you to tell us, 'Do not to go to Egypt to live there.' [3]Baruch, son of Neriah, is inciting you against us, to hand us over to the Chaldeans to be killed or exiled to Babylon."*

[4]So Johanan, son of Kareah, and the rest of the leaders and the people did not listen to the voice of the LORD to stay in the land of Judah.* [5]Instead, Johanan, son of Kareah, and the military leaders took along all the remnant of Judah who had been dispersed among the nations and then had returned to dwell in the land of Judah: [6]men, women, and children, the princesses and everyone whom Nebuzaradan, captain of the bodyguard, had consigned to Gedaliah, son of Ahikam, son of Shaphan; also Jeremiah, the prophet, and Baruch, son of Neriah.* [7]They went to Egypt—they did not listen to the voice of the LORD—and came to Tahpanhes.*

**Jeremiah in Egypt.** [8]The word of the LORD came to Jeremiah in Tahpanhes: [9]Take some large stones in your hand and set them in mortar in the terrace at the entrance to the house of Pharaoh in Tahpanhes, while the Judahites watch. [10]Then say to them: Thus says the LORD of hosts, the God of Israel: I will send for my servant Nebuchadnezzar, king of Babylon. He will place his throne upon these stones which

42:4 1 Sm 3:18.
42:5 Jgs 11:10.
42:6 Jer 7:23; Dt 5:33; 6:3.
42:10 Jer 31:28; 32:41.
42:11 Jer 30:10–11.
42:12 Ps 106:45–46; Prv 16:7.
42:14 Dt 28:68.
42:16 Jer 44:13–14, 27.
42:17 Jer 29:17–18;
44:14, 28.
42:18 Jer 44:12.
42:21 Zec 7:11–12.
42:22 Jer 42:12; Hos 9:6.
43:3 Jer 38:4.
43:4 Jer 41:16.
43:6 Jer 41:10.
43:7 Jer 42:13–14; 44:1.

I, Jeremiah, have set up, and stretch his canopy above them.* [11] He shall come and strike the land of Egypt: with death, those marked for death; with exile, those marked for exile; with the sword, those marked for the sword.* [12] He shall set fire to the temples of Egypt's gods, burn the gods and carry them off. He shall pick the land of Egypt clean, as a shepherd picks lice off his cloak, and then depart victorious.* [13] He shall smash the obelisks at the Temple of the Sun in the land of Egypt and destroy with fire the temples of the Egyptian gods.

**44** [1] The word that came to Jeremiah for all the Judahites who were living in Egypt, those living in Migdol, Tahpanhes, and Memphis, and in Upper Egypt: [2] † Thus says the LORD of hosts, the God of Israel: You yourselves have seen all the evil I brought upon Jerusalem and the other cities of Judah. Today they lie in ruins uninhabited,* [3] because of the evil they did to provoke me, going after other gods, offering incense and serving other gods they did not know, neither they, nor you, nor your ancestors.* [4] Though I repeatedly sent you all my servants the prophets, saying: "You must not commit this abominable deed I hate," [5] they did not listen or incline their ears in order to turn from their evil, no longer offering incense to other gods.* [6] Therefore the fury of my anger poured forth and kindled fire in the cities of Judah and the streets of Jerusalem, to turn them into the ruined wasteland they are today.

[7] Now thus says the LORD God of hosts, the God of Israel: Why inflict so great an evil upon yourselves, cutting off from Judah man and woman, child and infant, not leaving yourselves even a remnant? [8] Why do you provoke me with the works of your hands, offering sacrifice to other gods here in the land of Egypt where you have come to live? Will you cut yourselves off and become a curse, a reproach among all the nations of the earth?* [9] Have you forgotten the evil of your ancestors, the evil of the kings of Judah, the evil of their wives, and your own evil and the evil of your wives—all that they did in the land of Judah and in the streets of Jerusalem?* [10] To this day they have not been crushed down, nor have they shown fear. They have not followed my law and my statutes that I set before you and your ancestors.*

[11] Therefore, thus says the LORD of hosts, the God of Israel: I have set my face against you for evil, to cut off all Judah. [12] I will take away the remnant of Judah who insisted on going to the land of Egypt to live there; in the land of Egypt they shall meet their end. They shall fall by the sword or be consumed by hunger. From the least to the greatest, they shall die by sword or hunger; they shall become a malediction, a horror, a curse, a reproach.* [13] Thus I will punish those who live in Egypt, just as I punished Jerusalem, with sword, hunger, and disease, [14] so that none of the remnant of Judah who came to live in the land of Egypt shall escape or survive.* No one shall return to the land of Judah. Even though they long to return and live there, they shall not return except as refugees.

[15] They answered Jeremiah—all the men who knew that their wives were offering sacrifices to other gods, all the women standing there in the immense crowd, and all the people who lived in Lower and Upper Egypt: [16] "Regarding the word you have spoken to us in the name of the LORD, we are not listening to you.* [17] Rather we will go on doing what we proposed; we will offer incense to the Queen of Heaven and pour out libations to her, just as we have done, along with our ancestors, our kings and princes, in the cities of Judah and in the streets of Jerusalem. Then we had plenty to eat, we prospered, and we suffered no misfortune.* [18] But ever since we stopped offering sacrifices to the Queen of Heaven and pouring out libations to her, we lack everything and are being destroyed by sword and hunger." [19] And the women said, "When we offered sacrifices to the Queen of Heaven and poured out libations to her, did we bake cakes in her image and pour out

---

† **44:2–30** Chronologically, these are the last of Jeremiah's words to his people. As the narrative ends, Jeremiah meets with rejection. According to tradition, recorded in a much later work, he was murdered in Egypt by fellow Judahites.

---

**43:10** Jer 27:6; Ez 29:19.          **43:11** Jer 46:13; Ez 30:10.

**43:12** Jer 46:25; Ez 30:13–14.
**44:2** Jer 34:22; Lv 26:32–33.
**44:3** Jer 11:17; Dt 32:17.
**44:5** Jer 7:24, 26; 19:4.
**44:8** Jer 25:6–7.

**44:9** 1 Kgs 11:1, 8; Ezr 9:7, 14.
**44:10** Jer 7:24.
**44:12** Jer 42:15, 18, 22.
**44:14** Jer 43:11.
**44:16** Jer 6:16–17.
**44:17** Jer 5:3; 7:18.

libations to her without our husbands' consent?"*

20 To all the people, men and women, who gave him this answer, Jeremiah said: 21 As for the sacrifices you offered in the cities of Judah and in the streets of Jerusalem—you, your ancestors, your kings and princes, and the people of the land—did not the LORD remember them? Did it not enter his mind?* 22 The LORD could no longer bear the evil of your deeds, the abominations you were doing; then your land became a waste, a horror, a curse, without even one inhabitant, as it is today.* 23 Because you offered sacrifice and sinned against the LORD, not listening to the voice of the LORD, not following his law, his statutes, and his decrees, therefore this evil has overtaken you, as it is today.*

24 Jeremiah said to all the people and to all the women: Hear the word of the LORD, all you Judahites in the land of Egypt: 25 Thus says the LORD of hosts, the God of Israel: You and your wives have carried out with your hands what your mouths have spoken: "We will go on fulfilling the vows we have made to offer sacrifice to the Queen of Heaven and to pour out libations to her." Very well! keep your vows, fulfill your vows! 26 And then listen to the word of the LORD, all you Judahites living in Egypt; I swear by my own great name, says the LORD: in the whole land of Egypt, my name shall no longer be pronounced by the lips of any Judahite, saying, "As the Lord GOD lives." 27 I am watching over them for evil, not for good. All the Judahites in Egypt shall come to an end by sword or famine until they are completely destroyed.* 28 Those who escape the sword to return from the land of Egypt to the land of Judah shall be few in number. The whole remnant of Judah who came to Egypt to live shall know whose word stands, mine or theirs.*

29 And this shall be a sign to you—oracle of the LORD—I will punish you in this place so that you will know that my words stand solidly against you for evil. 30 Thus says the LORD: See! I will hand over Pharaoh Hophra,† king of Egypt, to his enemies, to those seeking his life, just as I handed over Zedekiah, king of Judah, to his enemy Nebuchadrezzar, king of Babylon, to the one seeking his life.*

## 45 A Message to Baruch.†

1 The word that Jeremiah the prophet spoke to Baruch, son of Neriah, when he wrote on a scroll words from Jeremiah's own mouth in the fourth year of Jehoiakim, son of Josiah, king of Judah:* 2 Thus says the LORD, God of Israel, to you, Baruch. 3 You said, "Woe is me! the LORD has added grief to my pain.* I have worn myself out with groaning; rest eludes me." 4 You must say this to him. Thus says the LORD: What I have built, I am tearing down; what I have planted, I am uprooting: all this land.* 5 And you, do you seek great things for yourself? Do not seek them! I am bringing evil on all flesh—oracle of the LORD—but I will grant you your life as spoils of war, wherever you may go.*

## VIII. ORACLES AGAINST THE NATIONS†

## 46 

1 The word of the LORD that came to Jeremiah the prophet concerning the nations.

**Against Egypt.** 2 Concerning Egypt. Against the army of Pharaoh Neco, king of Egypt, defeated at Carchemish on the Euphrates† by Nebuchadrezzar, king of Babylon, in the fourth year of Jehoiakim, son of Josiah, king of Judah:

3    Prepare buckler and shield!
        move forward to battle!
4    Harness the horses,
        charioteers, mount up!
     Fall in, with helmets on;

---

† 44:30 *Hophra:* killed by his own people. Hophra's successor, Amasis, ruled Egypt when Nebuchadnezzar took control of the country.
45:1–5 At the conclusion of his narrative, Baruch appends a message Jeremiah had given him when he first wrote down Jeremiah's words (cf. 36:4). The future revealed by the prophet overwhelmed Baruch; now he learns his own safety is assured, even though the Lord will destroy Judah.
46:1–51:64 A collection of oracles against foreign nations constitutes the final section of the Hebrew text of Jeremiah; in the Greek text they follow 25:13. The oracles here appear to be arranged in loose chronological order: 46:2 mentions the fourth year of Jehoiakim; the oracles in 50:1–51:64 are evidently from

the end of Jeremiah's life.
46:2 *Carchemish on the Euphrates:* the western terminus of the Mesopotamian trade route, where Nebuchadnezzar defeated Pharaoh Neco in 605 B.C., thus gaining undisputed control of Syria and Palestine.

---

| | |
|---|---|
| **44:19** Jer 7:18. | **44:30** Jer 39:5–7; 46:25–26; |
| **44:21** Jer 11:13. | Ez 29:3–4; 30:21. |
| **44:22** Jer 15:6. | **45:1** Jer 36:4, 18, 32. |
| **44:23** 2 Kgs 17:15; Dn | **45:3** Lam 1:3; 5:5. |
| 9:11–12. | **45:4** Jer 18:7; Is 5:5–6. |
| **44:27** Ezr 7:3–7. | **45:5** Jer 25:26–29. |
| **44:28** Dt 28:62; Is 10:22. | |

polish your spears, put on your armor.

5   What do I see?
    Are they panicking, falling apart?
    Their warriors are hammered back,
They flee headlong
    never making a stand.
Terror on every side—
    oracle of the LORD! *
6   The swift cannot flee,
    nor the warrior escape:
There up north, on the banks of the
    Euphrates
    they stumble and fall.
7   Who is this? Like the Nile, it rears up;
    like rivers, its waters surge.
8   Egypt rears up like the Nile,
    like rivers, its waters surge.
"I will rear up," it says, "and cover the
    earth,
    destroying the city and its people. *
9   Forward, horses!
    charge, chariots!
March forth, warriors,
    Cush and Put, bearing shields,
    Archers of Lud, stretching bows!"
10  Today belongs to the Lord GOD of hosts,
    a day of vengeance, vengeance on his
    foes!
The sword devours and is sated, drunk
    with their blood:
    for the Lord GOD of hosts holds a
    sacrifice
    in the land of the north, on the River
    Euphrates. *
11  Go up to Gilead, procure balm,
    Virgin daughter Egypt!
No use to multiply remedies;
    for you there is no healing. *
12  The nations hear your cries,
    your screaming fills the earth.
Warrior stumbles against warrior,
    both collapse together. *

13 * The word that the LORD spoke to Jeremiah the prophet when Nebuchadrezzar, king of Babylon, came to attack the land of Egypt: †

14  Proclaim in Egypt, announce in Migdol,
    announce in Memphis and
    Tahpanhes!
Say: Fall in, get ready,
    the sword has devoured your
    neighbors. *
15  Why has Apis † fled?
    Your champion did not stand,
Because the LORD thrust him down;
    he stumbled repeatedly then collapsed.
16  They said to each other,
    "Get up! We must return to our own
    people,
To the land of our birth,
    away from the destroying sword." *
17  Give Pharaoh, king of Egypt, the name
    "Braggart-missed-his-chance." †
18  As I live, says the King
    whose name is LORD of hosts,
Like Tabor above mountains,
    like Carmel † above the sea, he comes.
19  Pack your bags for exile,
    enthroned daughter Egypt;
Memphis shall become a wasteland,
    an empty ruin.
20  Egypt is a beautiful heifer,
    a horsefly from the north keeps
    coming.
21  Even the mercenaries in her ranks
    are like fattened calves;
They too turn and flee together—
    they do not stand their ground,
For their day of ruin comes upon them,
    their time of punishment.
22  Her voice is like a snake!
    Yes, they come in force;
They attack her with axes,
    like those who fell trees.
23  They cut down her forest—oracle of the
    LORD—
    impenetrable though it be;
More numerous than locusts,
    they cannot be counted.
24  Shamed is daughter Egypt,
    handed over to a people from the
    north.

---

46:13 In 601 B.C. Nebuchadnezzar advanced into Egypt itself, but finally had to withdraw to Syria.
46:15 *Apis:* the chief god of Memphis; the black bull honored as an incarnation of the god Ptah and, later, of the god Osiris.
46:17 *"Braggart-missed-his-chance":* the Hebrew phrase may contain a pun on the Pharaoh's name or royal title.
46:18 *Tabor…Carmel:* mountains in Palestine that seem to tower over their surroundings as Nebuchadnezzar towers over the nations in his path as he makes his way toward Egypt.

46:5 Jer 6:25; 49:29.
46:8 Ez 29:3; 32:2.
46:10 Dt 32:42; Is 13:9; Ez 39:17–20.
46:11 Jer 8:22; 51:8; Ez 30:21–22.
46:12 Ez 32:9–12.
46:13 Jer 43:10–11; 44:30; Is 19:1.
46:14 Jer 44:1.
46:16 Lv 26:37.

25 The LORD of hosts, the God of Israel, has said: See! I will punish Amon† of Thebes and Egypt, gods, kings, Pharaoh, and those who trust in him.* 26 I will hand them over to those who seek their lives, to Nebuchadrezzar, king of Babylon, and to his officers. But later, Egypt shall be inhabited again, as in days of old—oracle of the LORD.*

27 But you, my servant Jacob, do not
        fear;
    do not be dismayed, Israel!
Listen! I will deliver you from far-off
        lands;
        your offspring, from the land of their
            exile.
Jacob shall again find rest,
    secure, with none to frighten him.*
28 You, Jacob my servant, must not fear—
            oracle of the LORD—
    for I am with you;
I will make an end of all the nations
    to which I have driven you,
But of you I will not make an end:
    I will chastise you as you deserve,
    I cannot let you go unpunished.*

# 47

**Against the Philistines.** 1 The word of the LORD that came to Jeremiah the prophet concerning the Philistines, before Pharaoh attacked Gaza:*

2 Thus says the LORD:
†   See: waters are rising from the north,
        to become a torrent in flood;
    They shall flood the land and all it
        contains,
        the cities and their inhabitants.
    People will howl and wail,
        every inhabitant of the land.
3 At the noise of the pounding hooves of
        his steeds,

the clanking chariots, the rumbling
            wheels,
    Parents do not turn back for their
            children;
        their hands hang helpless,
4 Because of the day that is coming
        to destroy all the Philistines
    And cut off from Tyre and Sidon†
        the last of their allies.
    Yes, the LORD is destroying the
            Philistines,
        the remnant from the coasts of
            Caphtor.*
5 Baldness is visited upon Gaza,*
        Ashkelon is reduced to silence;
    Ashdod, remnant of their strength,
        how long will you gash yourself?†
6 Ah! Sword of the LORD!
        When will you find rest?
    Return to your scabbard;
        stop, be still!
7 How can it find rest
        when the LORD has commanded it?
    Against Ashkelon and the seacoast,
        there he has appointed it.*

# 48

**Against Moab.**† 1 Concerning Moab. Thus says the LORD of hosts, the God of Israel:

Ah, Nebo! it is ravaged;
        Kiriathaim is disgraced, captured;
    Disgraced and overthrown is the
            stronghold:
2       Moab's glory is no more.
    In Heshbon they plot evil against her:
        "Come! We will put an end to her as a
            nation."
    You, too, Madmen,† shall be silenced;
        you the sword stalks!
3   Listen! an outcry from Horonaim,*
        "Ruin and great destruction!"

**46:25** *Amon:* the sun-god worshiped at Thebes in Upper Egypt.

**47:2–7** Nebuchadnezzar's military campaign against Ashkelon in 604 B.C. may provide some historical background for this poem.

**47:4** *Tyre and Sidon:* Phoenician seaports allied commercially with the Philistines and often rebelling against Nebuchadnezzar; cf. 27:1–4. After the capture of Jerusalem, Nebuchadnezzar carried out a partially successful thirteen-year siege of Tyre. *Caphtor:* Crete and other Aegean islands, points of origin for the Philistines and other sea peoples; cf. Am 9:7.

**47:5** *Baldness...gash yourself:* close-cropped hair, silence, and ritual slashing of the body express mourning and grief and here represent the mourner's awareness that chaos has overcome order (cf. 41:5).

**48:1–47** Moab, located east of the Dead Sea, was one of Israel's bitter enemies (cf., e.g., Is 15–16; Am 2:1–3). According to Flavius Josephus, Nebuchadnezzar conquered Moab and Ammon in his twenty-third year (582 B.C.), five years after the destruction of Jerusalem. This chapter is full of local place names in Moab.

**48:2** *Madmen:* a place name, not mentioned elsewhere in the Old Testament.

**46:25** Ez 30:15–16.
**46:26** Jer 44:30; Ez 30:4;
        32:11–12.
**46:27** Jer 30:10; 43:5.
**46:28** Jer 30:11.
**47:1** Ez 25:15–16; Zep 2:4.
**47:4** Jer 25:22; Ez
        25:16–17; Am 1:8;
        9:7.
**47:5** Am 1:7.
**47:7** Zep 2:5–6.
**48:3–5** Is 15:5.

4   "Moab is crushed!"
   their outcry is heard in Zoar.
5   Up the ascent of Luhith
   they go weeping;
  At the descent to Horonaim
   they hear cries of anguish:
6   "Flee, save your lives!
   Be like a wild donkey in the
     wilderness!"
7   Because you trusted in your works and
     your treasures,
   you also shall be captured.
  Chemosh† shall go into exile,
   his priests and princes with him.*
8   The destroyer comes upon every city,
   not a city escapes;
  Ruined is the valley,
   wasted the plateau—oracle of the
     LORD.
9   Set up a tombstone for Moab;
   it will soon become a complete
     wasteland,
  Its cities turned into ruins
   where no one dwells.
10  Cursed are they who do the LORD's work
     carelessly,
  cursed those who keep their sword
   from shedding blood.
11† Moab has been resting from its youth,
   suspended above its dregs,
  Never poured from flask to flask,
   never driven into exile.
  Thus it retained its flavor,
   its bouquet is not lost.*

12 Be assured! The days are coming—oracle of the LORD—when I will send him wine-makers to decant the wine; they shall empty its flasks and smash its jars. 13 Chemosh shall disappoint Moab, just as the house of Israel was disappointed by Bethel, in which they trusted.*

14  How can you say, "We are heroes,
   mighty warriors"?
15  The one who ravages Moab and its cities
     comes up,
  the best of its youth go down to
     slaughter—

   oracle of the King, whose name is
     LORD of hosts.
16  Moab's ruin is near at hand,
   its disaster approaches swiftly.
17  Mourn, all you neighbors,
   all you who know its name!
  Say: How the mighty scepter is broken,
   the glorious staff!
18  Come down from glory, sit on the
     parched ground,
   enthroned daughter Dibon;†
  Moab's destroyer has fallen upon you,
   has shattered your strongholds.*
19  Stand along the road, keep watch,
   enthroned Aroer;
  Ask the fleeing man, the escaping woman:
   ask them what has happened.*
20  "Moab is put to shame, destroyed."
   Wail and cry out,
  Proclaim it at the Arnon:
   "Moab is destroyed!"*

21 Judgment has come upon the plateau: on Holon, Jahzah, and Mephaath,* 22 on Dibon, Nebo, and Beth-diblathaim, 23 on Kiriathaim, Beth-gamul, and Beth-meon, 24 on Kerioth and on Bozrah: on all the cities of the land of Moab, far and near.

25  The horn of Moab is cut off,
   its arm is broken—oracle of the LORD.

26 Make him drunk because he set himself over against the LORD; let Moab swim in his vomit and become a laughingstock. 27 Has Israel not been a laughingstock to you? Was he caught among thieves that you wag your heads whenever you speak of him?*

28  Abandon the cities, take shelter in the
     crags,
   inhabitants of Moab.
  Be like the dove that nests
   in the walls of a gorge.
29  We have heard of the pride of Moab,*
   pride beyond bounds:
  His loftiness, his pride, his scorn,
   his insolent heart.

J
E
R

---

**48:7** *Chemosh*: chief god of Moab (cf. Nm 21:29).
  **48:11–12** Moabite wine was known for its high quality. Here the wine is a metaphor for Moab's complacency.
  **48:18** Dibon, the capital of Moab at that time, is situated on a height. The prophet here offers a personification of the city, pictured as a confident ruler.

**48:7** Nm 21:29.       **48:20** Is 16:7.
**48:11** Zep 1:12.     **48:21** Is 15:4.
**48:13** Is 16:12.     **48:27** Zep 2:8–10.
**48:18** Nm 21:30.    **48:29–30** Is 16:6.
**48:19** Dt 2:36.

30 I myself know his arrogance—oracle of
      the LORD—
   liar in word, liar in deed.
31 And so I wail over Moab,
      over all Moab I cry,
   over the people of Kir-heres I moan. *
32 More than for Jazer I weep for you,
      vine of Sibmah.
   Your tendrils trailed down to the sea,
      as far as Jazer they stretched.
   Upon your summer harvest and your
      vintage,
   the destroyer has fallen. *
33 Joy and gladness are taken away
      from the garden land, the land of
      Moab.
   I dry up the wine from the wine vats,
      the treader treads no more,
   the vintage shout is stilled.

³⁴ The cry of Heshbon and Elealeh is heard as
far as Jahaz; they call from Zoar to Horonaim
and to Eglath-shelishiyah; even the waters of
Nimrim turn into a wasteland. * ³⁵ I will leave
no one in Moab—oracle of the LORD—to offer
burnt offerings on the high place or to make
sacrifices to their gods. ³⁶ Hence my heart wails
like a flute for Moab; my heart wails like a flute
for the people of Kir-heres: the wealth they
accumulated has perished. * ³⁷ Every head has
been shaved bald, every beard cut off; every
hand gashed, and all their loins are draped
in sackcloth. * ³⁸ On all the rooftops of Moab
and in all its squares there is mourning. I have
shattered Moab like a pot that no one wants—
oracle of the LORD. ³⁹ How terrified they are,
how they wail! How Moab turns its back in
shame! Moab has become a laughingstock
and a horror to all its neighbors!

40 For thus says the LORD:
   Look there! Like an eagle he swoops,
      spreading his wings over Moab. *
41 Cities are captured,
      strongholds seized:
   On that day the hearts of Moab's warriors
      become like the heart of a woman in
      labor. *

42 Moab shall be wiped out, a people no
      more,
   because it set itself over against the
      LORD. *
43 Terror, pit, and trap be upon you,
      enthroned Moab—oracle of the
      LORD. *
44 Those fleeing the terror
      fall into the pit;
   Those climbing out of the pit
      are caught in the trap;
   Ah, yes! I will bring these things upon
      Moab
   in the year of their punishment—
      oracle of the LORD.
45 In Heshbon's shadow the fugitives
      stop short, exhausted;
   For fire blazes up from Heshbon,
      and flames up from the house of
      Sihon:
   It consumes the forehead of Moab,
      the scalp of the noisemakers. *
46 Woe to you, Moab!
      You are finished, people of Chemosh!
   Your sons are taken into exile,
      your daughters into captivity.
47 Yet I will restore the fortunes of Moab
      in the days to come—oracle of the
      LORD. *

Thus far the judgment on Moab.

# 49 Against the Ammonites. ¹ Concerning the Ammonites. Thus says the LORD:

   Has Israel no sons?
      none to inherit?
   Why has Milcom † disinherited Gad,
      why are his people living in its cities?
2  Therefore the days are coming—oracle
      of the LORD—
   when I will sound the battle alarm
      against Rabbah of the Ammonites;
   It shall become a mound of ruins,
      and its villages destroyed by fire.
   Israel shall then inherit those who
      disinherited it—
      oracle of the LORD. *

---

† 49:1 *Milcom*: chief god of the Ammonites (cf. 1 Kgs 11:5).
The Ammonites shared a border with Gad, an Israelite tribe in
Transjordan (Jos 13:8–10); the Ammonites occupied its territory
after the collapse of the Northern Kingdom.

* 48:31 Is 16:7.
48:32 Is 16:8–9.
48:34 Is 15:4–5.
48:36 Is 16:11.
48:37 Jer 47:5; Is 15:2–3; Ez 7:18.
48:40 Jer 49:22.
48:41 Jer 6:24; 30:6.
48:42 Zep 2:9–10.
48:43 Is 24:17–18.
48:45 Nm 21:28–29.
48:47 Jer 49:39.
49:2 Am 1:14.

3  Wail, Heshbon, "The ruin is destroyed!"
       shriek, villages of Rabbah!
   Put on sackcloth and lament!
       Run back and forth in the sheepfolds.
   For Milcom is going into exile,
       taking priest and prince with him. *
4  Why boast in your strength,
       your ebbing strength, rebellious
           daughter?
   Why trust in your treasures, saying,
       "Who would dare attack me?"
5  See, I am bringing terror upon you—
       oracle of the Lord GOD of hosts—
       from all around you;
   You shall be scattered, each in headlong
           flight,
       with no one to gather the fugitives. *
6  But afterward I will restore the fortunes
       of the Ammonites—oracle of the
           LORD.

**Against Edom.** † 7 Concerning Edom. Thus says
the LORD of hosts:

   Is there no more wisdom in Teman, †
       has counsel perished from the
           prudent,
       is their wisdom gone?
8  Flee, retreat, hide deep for lodging,
       inhabitants of Dedan:
   For I bring disaster upon Esau †
       when I come to punish them. *
9  If vintagers came upon you,
       they would leave no gleanings;
   If thieves by night,
       they would destroy as they pleased. *
10 So I myself will strip Esau;
       I will uncover his lairs so he cannot
           hide.
   Offspring and family are destroyed,
       neighbors, too; he is no more. *
11 Leave your orphans behind, I will keep
           them alive;
       your widows, let them trust in me. *

12 For thus says the LORD: Look, even those
not sentenced to drink the cup must drink it!

Shall you then go unpunished? You shall not!
You shall drink every bit of it! * 13 By myself
I have sworn—oracle of the LORD—Bozrah †
shall become an object of horror, a disgrace,
a desolation, and a curse. Bozrah and all its
cities shall become ruins forever. *

14 I have heard a report from the LORD,
       a herald has been sent among the
           nations:
   "Gather together, move against it,
       get ready for battle!"
15 I will make you the least among the
           nations,
       despised by all people! *
16 The terror you spread,
       the pride of your heart, beguiled you.
   You denizens of rocks and crevices,
       occupying towering peaks:
   Though you build your nest high as the
           eagle,
       from there I will bring you down—
           oracle of the LORD. *

17 Edom shall become an object of horror.
Passersby recoil in terror, hissing at all its
wounds. 18 As when Sodom, Gomorrah, and
their neighbors were overthrown—oracle of
the LORD—no one shall live in it, nor anyone
settle there. *

19 As when a lion comes up from a thicket
           of the Jordan
       to a permanent pasture,
   So in an instant, I will chase them off;
       I will establish there whomever I
           choose.
   For who is like me? Who holds me
           accountable?
       What shepherd can stand against
           me? *
20 Therefore, listen to the strategy
       the LORD devised for Edom;
   The plans he has drawn up
       against the inhabitants of Teman:
   They shall be dragged away, even the
           smallest of the flock;

---

† **49:7–22** *Edom*: southeast of the Dead Sea, a traditional enemy who profited from Judah's downfall; cf. Ps 137:7; Lam 4:21–22; Ob 11–12.

**49:7** Teman, a district of Edom (cf. Jb 2:11), represents the whole country, which was famous for the wisdom of its sages.

**49:8** *Esau*: Jacob's brother, the traditional ancestor of the Edomites; cf. Gn 36:1.

**49:13** *Bozrah*: capital of Edom.

* **49:3** Is 15:2–5.
**49:5** Jer 48:47.
**49:8** Ez 25:13.
**49:9** Ob 5.
**49:10** Mal 1:3.
**49:11** Dt 10:18; Ps 68:6.
**49:12** Jer 25:15, 28; Lam 4:21–22.
**49:13** Is 34:6; Ez 35:3–9; Ob 16.
**49:15** Ob 2.
**49:16** Jer 48:29–30.
**49:18** Jer 50:40; Dt 29:23.
**49:19** Jer 12:5; 25:9; 50:44–45.

JER

their pasture shall be aghast because
        of them.
21  With the din of their collapse the earth
        quakes,
    to the Red Sea the outcry is heard!
22  Look! like an eagle he soars aloft,
        and spreads his wings over Bozrah;
    On that day the hearts of Edom's
            warriors become
    like the heart of a woman in labor.*

**Against Damascus.** 23 Concerning Damascus.

    Hamath and Arpad† are shamed,
        for they have heard bad news;
    Anxious, they surge like the sea
        which cannot calm down.*
24  Damascus loses heart, turns to flee;
        panic has seized it.
    Distress and pangs take hold,
        like the pain of a woman in labor.
25  How can the glorious city be
            abandoned,
        the town of joy!
26  But now its young men shall fall in its
            squares,
    all the warriors destroyed on that
            day—
        oracle of the LORD of hosts.
27  I will set fire to the wall of Damascus;
        it shall devour the palaces of
            Ben-hadad.†

**Against Arabia.** 28 About Kedar and the kingdoms of Hazor, which Nebuchadnezzar, king
of Babylon, defeated.

    Thus says the LORD:
    Rise up, attack Kedar,
        destroy the people from the east.*
29  Their tents and flocks shall be taken
            away,
        their tent curtains and all their
            goods;
    Their camels they carry off,
        they shout over them, "Terror on every
            side!"*
30  Flee! wander about, hide deep for
        lodging,

inhabitants of Hazor—oracle of the
        LORD;
For Nebuchadnezzar, king of Babylon,
        has devised a strategy against you,
        drawn up a plan against you,
31  Get up! set out against a tranquil nation,
        living in security—oracle of the
            LORD—
    Without gates or bars,
        dwelling alone.
32  Their camels shall become spoils,
        their hordes of cattle, plunder;
    I will scatter to the winds those who
            shave their temples;
        from every side I will bring their
            ruin—
        oracle of the LORD.*
33  Hazor shall become a haunt for jackals,
        a wasteland forever,
    Where no one lives,
        no mortal stays.

**Against Elam.** 34 The word of the LORD that
came to Jeremiah the prophet concerning
Elam† at the beginning of the reign of Zedekiah, king of Judah:

35  Thus says the LORD of hosts:
    Look! I will break the bow of Elam,
        the mainstay of their might.
36  I will bring upon Elam the four winds
        from the four ends of the heavens:
    I will scatter them to all these winds,
            until there is no nation
        to which the outcasts of Elam have
            not gone.
37  I will terrify Elam before their foes,
        those seeking their life;
    I will bring evil upon them,
        my burning wrath—oracle of the LORD.
    I will send sword after them
        until I have finished them off;
38  I will set up my throne in Elam
        and destroy from there king and
            princes—
        oracle of the LORD.
39  But at the end of days I will restore
        the fortunes of Elam—oracle of the
            LORD.

---

**49:23** *Hamath and Arpad:* independent Aramean states north
of Damascus, the direction from which the invasion is coming.
Cf. Is 10:9–10.
    **49:27** *Ben-hadad:* a dynastic name for some of the kings who
ruled in Damascus; cf. 1 Kgs 15:18, 20.

**49:34** *Elam:* an ancient kingdom east of Babylonia.

---

| | |
|---|---|
| **49:22** Jer 4:13. | **49:29** Jer 4:20. |
| **49:23** Is 36:19; 37:13. | **49:32** Jer 9:25. |
| **49:28** Is 21:16. | |

# 50 The First Oracle Against Babylon.

¹The word the LORD spoke against Babylon,† against the land of the Chaldeans, through Jeremiah the prophet:*

2   Proclaim this among the nations,
        announce it!
    Announce it, do not hide it, but say:
    Babylon is captured, Bel† put to shame,
        Marduk terrified;
        its images are put to shame, its idols
            shattered.

3   A nation from the north advances
        against it,
    making the land desolate
    So that no one can live there;
        human beings and animals have
            fled.*

4   In those days and at that time—oracle of
        the LORD—
    Israelite and Judahite shall come
        together,
    Weeping as they come, to seek the LORD,
        their God;*

5   They shall ask for Zion,
        seeking out the way.
    "Come, let us join ourselves to the LORD
        in an everlasting covenant, never to be
            forgotten."*

6   Lost sheep were my people,
        their shepherds misled them,
        leading them astray on the
            mountains;
    From mountain to hill they wandered,
        forgetting their fold.*

7   Whoever happened upon them
        devoured them;
        their enemies said, "We are not guilty,
    Because they sinned against the LORD,
        the abode of justice, the hope of their
            ancestors."*

8   Flee from the midst of Babylon,
        leave the land of the Chaldeans,
        be like rams at the head of the flock.*

9   See, I am stirring up against Babylon
        a band of great nations from the land
            of the north;

They are arrayed against her,
    from there she shall be taken.
Their arrows are like the arrows of a
        skilled warrior
    who never returns empty-handed.*

10  Chaldea shall become plunder;
        all its plunderers shall be enriched—
        oracle of the LORD.

11  Yes, rejoice and exult,
        you that plunder my heritage;
    Frisk like calves on the grass,
        neigh like stallions!

12  Your mother will indeed be put to
        shame,
        she that bore you shall be abashed;
    See, the last of the nations,
        a wilderness, a dry wasteland.*

13  Because of the LORD's wrath it shall be
        uninhabited,
        become an utter wasteland;
    Everyone who passes by Babylon will be
        appalled
        and hiss at all its wounds.*

14  Take your posts encircling Babylon,
        you who bend the bow;
    Shoot at it, do not spare your arrows,*

15  raise the war cry against it on every
        side.
    It surrenders, its bastions fall,
        its walls are torn down;†
    This is retribution from the LORD! Take
        retribution on her,
        as she has done, do to her;
        for she sinned against the LORD.*

16  Cut off the sower from Babylon
        and those who wield sickles at harvest
            time!
    Before the destroying sword,
        all of them turn back to their own
            people,
        all flee to their own land.*

17  Israel was a stray sheep
        that lions pursued;
    The king of Assyria once devoured
        him;
        now Nebuchadnezzar of Babylon
            gnaws his bones.*

---

**50:1–51:58** A collection of miscellaneous oracles against Babylon introducing the story in 51:59–64.
**50:2** Bel: originally the title of the god of Nippur in Mesopotamia, later associated with Merodach (Marduk), chief god of Babylon (cf. Is 46:1).
**50:15** Its walls are torn down: the prophet describes the downfall of Babylon in conventional language. Babylon surrendered peacefully to the Persians in 539 B.C.

**50:1** Jer 51:1; Is 13:1–14; 21:1–10.
**50:3** Jer 51:48; Is 13:17.
**50:4** Jer 3:18; Ps 126:6.
**50:5** Jer 31:31; 32:40.
**50:6** Is 53:6; 1 Pt 2:25.
**50:7** Jer 31:23.
**50:8** Jer 51:6, 45; Is 48:20.
**50:9** Jer 51:27.
**50:12** Jer 51:43; Is 13:20–22.
**50:13** Jer 25:12.
**50:14** Jer 51:11; Is 21:2.
**50:15** Jer 51:11, 44, 58; Ps 137:8.
**50:16** Is 13:14.
**50:17** 2 Kgs 17:24; 18:14.

JER

18 Therefore, thus says the LORD of hosts,
    the God of Israel:
I will punish the king of Babylon and
    his land,
  as I once punished the king of
    Assyria; *

19 But I will bring Israel back to its pasture,
    to feed on Carmel and Bashan,
And on Mount Ephraim and Gilead,
    until they have their fill. *

20 In those days, at that time—oracle of the
LORD:

The guilt of Israel may be sought, but it
    no longer exists,
  the sin of Judah, but it can no longer
    be found;
  for I will forgive the remnant I
    preserve. *

21 Attack the land of Merathaim,
    and those who live in Pekod; †
Slaughter and put them under the ban—
    oracle of the LORD—
  do all I have commanded you.

22 Battle alarm in the land,
    great destruction!

23 How the hammer of the whole earth
    has been cut off and broken!
What an object of horror
    Babylon has become among the
    nations! *

24 You ensnared yourself and were caught,
    Babylon, before you knew it!
You were discovered and seized,
    because you challenged the LORD. *

25 The LORD opens his armory,
    brings out the weapons of his wrath;
The Lord GOD of hosts has work to do
    in the land of the Chaldeans. *

26 Come upon them from every side,
    open their granaries,
Pile them up in heaps and put them
    under the ban;
  do not leave a remnant.

27 Slay all the oxen,
    take them down to slaughter;
Woe to them! their day has come,
    the time of their punishment.

28 Listen! the fugitives, the refugees
    from the land of Babylon:
They announce in Zion
    the retribution of the LORD, our God. *

29 Call archers out against Babylon,
    all who bend the bow;
Encamp around them;
    let no one escape.
Repay them for their deeds;
    what they have done, do to them,
For they insulted the LORD,
    the Holy One of Israel. *

30 Therefore their young men shall fall in
    the squares,
  all their warriors shall be stilled on
    that day—
  oracle of the LORD. *

31 I am against you, O Insolence—
    oracle of the Lord GOD of hosts;
For your day has come,
    the time for me to punish you.

32 Insolence stumbles and falls;
    there is no one to raise him up.
I will kindle a fire in his cities
    to devour everything around him.

33 Thus says the LORD of hosts:
Oppressed are the people of Israel,
    together with the people of Judah;
All their captors hold them fast
    and refuse to let them go.

34 Strong is their Redeemer,
    whose name is LORD of hosts,
The sure defender of their cause,
    who gives rest to their land,
    but unrest to those who live in
    Babylon. *

35 A sword upon the Chaldeans—oracle of
    the LORD—
  upon the inhabitants of Babylon, her
    princes and sages!

36 A sword upon the soothsayers,
    and they become fools!
A sword upon the warriors,
    and they tremble;

37 A sword upon their motley throng,
    and they become women!
A sword upon their treasures,
    and they are plundered; *

38 A drought upon the waters,

---

† **50:21** *Merathaim…Pekod*: "twice bitter," "punishment," symbolic terms for Babylon that recall the names of regions in the country.

**50:18** Is 10:12; 14:24–25.
**50:19** Jer 23:3; Ez 34:13–14.
**50:20** Jer 31:34; Is 43:25; Mi 7:19.
**50:23** Jer 51:20; Is 14:6.
**50:24** Jer 51:57.
**50:25** Jer 51:11–12; Is 13:5.
**50:28** Jer 51:10–11.
**50:29** Jer 51:56.
**50:30** Jer 49:26; 51:4.
**50:34** Jer 51:36.
**50:37** Jer 51:30; Na 3:13.

JER

and they dry up!
For it is a land of idols,
    soon made frantic by phantoms. *

39 Hence, wildcats shall dwell there with
    hyenas,
    and ostriches occupy it;
Never again shall it be inhabited or
    settled,
    from age to age. *

40 As happened when God overturned
    Sodom
    and Gomorrah and their neighbors—
    oracle of the LORD—
No one shall dwell there,
    no mortal shall settle there. *

41 See, a people comes from the north,
    a great nation, and mighty kings
    rising from the ends of the earth. *

42 Bow and javelin they wield,
    cruel and pitiless are they;
They sound like the roaring sea,
    as they ride forth on horses,
Each in place for battle
    against you, daughter Babylon.

43 The king of Babylon hears news of them,
    and his hands hang helpless;
Anguish takes hold of him,
    like the pangs of a woman giving
    birth. *

44 As happens when a lion comes up from
    a thicket of the Jordan
    to permanent pasture,
So I, in an instant, will chase them off,
    and establish there whomever I
    choose!
For who is like me? Who can call me to
    account?
    What shepherd can stand against me? *

45 Therefore, hear the strategy of the LORD,
    which he has devised against Babylon;
Hear the plans drawn up
    against the land of the Chaldeans:
They shall be dragged away, even the
    smallest sheep;
    their own pasture aghast because of
    them. *

46 At the cry "Babylon is captured!" the
    earth quakes;

the outcry is heard among the
    nations. *

## The Second Oracle Against Babylon

**51** ¹ Thus says the LORD:
    See! I rouse against Babylon,
    and the inhabitants of Chaldea,
    a destroyer wind. †

2 To Babylon I will send winnowers
    to winnow and lay waste the land;
They shall besiege it on every side
    on the day of affliction. *

3 How can the archers draw back their
    bows,
    lift their armor?
Do not spare her young men,
    put the entire army under the ban. *

4 The slain shall fall in the land of Chaldea,
    the wounded, in its streets; *

5 For Israel and Judah are not left
    widowed
    by their God, the LORD of hosts,
Even though the land is full of guilt
    against the Holy One of Israel.

6 Flee from Babylon;
    each of you save your own life,
    do not perish because of her guilt;
This is a time of retribution from the
    LORD,
    who pays out her due. *

7 Babylon was a golden cup in the hand
    of the LORD
    making the whole earth drunk;
The nations drank its wine,
    thus they have gone mad. *

8 Babylon suddenly falls and is broken:
    wail over her!
Bring balm for her wounds,
    in case she can be healed. *

9 "We have tried to heal Babylon,
    but she cannot be healed.
    Leave her, each of us must go to our
    own land."
The judgment against her reaches the
    heavens,
    it touches the clouds. *

10 The LORD has brought forth our
    vindication;

---

† **51:1** The destroyer wind is the fierce dry wind from the east (cf. 4:11).

**50:38** Jer 51:32, 36.
**50:39** Jer 51:37;
    Is 13:21–22.
**50:40** Jer 51:43.
**50:41** Jer 51:27–28.
**50:43** Is 13:7.
**50:44** Jer 49:19.
**50:45** Jer 51:12, 29.
**50:46** Jer 51:29.
**51:2** Jer 15:7; Is 41:16.
**51:3** Jer 50:14, 29.
**51:4** Jer 50:30.
**51:7** Jer 50:8, 15, 29; Is 48:20.
**51:7** Rev 14:8; 17:4.
**51:8** Rev 18:9–18.
**51:9** Is 13:14; Rev 18:5.

come, let us tell in Zion
what the LORD, our God, has done.*

11 Sharpen the arrows,
fill the quivers;
The LORD has stirred up the spirit of the
kings of the Medes,†
for his resolve is Babylon's
destruction.
Yes, it is retribution from the LORD,
retribution for his temple.*

12 Over the walls of Babylon raise a signal,
reinforce the watch;
Post sentries,
arrange ambushes!
For the LORD has both planned and
carried out
what he spoke against the inhabitants
of Babylon.

13 You who dwell by mighty waters,
rich in treasure,
Your end has come,
the time at which you shall be cut
off!*

14 The LORD of hosts has sworn by himself:
I will fill you with people as
numerous as locusts,
who shall raise over you a joyous
shout!

15 He made the earth by his power,
established the world by wisdom,
and by his skill stretched out the
heavens.*

16 When he thunders, the waters in the
heavens roar,
he summons clouds from the ends of
the earth,
Makes lightning flash in the rain,
and brings out winds from their
storehouses.

17 Every man is stupid, ignorant;
every artisan is put to shame by his
idol;
He molds a fraud,
without life-breath.

18 They are nothing, a ridiculous work,
that will perish at the time of
punishment.

19 Jacob's portion is nothing like them:

he is the creator of all things.
Israel is his very own tribe;
LORD of hosts is his name.

20 You are my hammer,
a weapon for war;
With you I shatter nations,
with you I destroy kingdoms.

21 With you I shatter horse and rider,
with you I shatter chariot and driver.*

22 With you I shatter man and woman,
with you I shatter old and young,
with you I shatter the young man and
young woman.*

23 With you I shatter shepherd and flock,
with you I shatter farmer and team,
with you I shatter governors and
officers.

24 Thus I will repay Babylon,
all the inhabitants of Chaldea,
For all the evil they committed against
Zion,
before your very eyes—oracle of the
LORD.*

25 Beware! I am against you,
destroying mountain—oracle of the
LORD—
destroyer of the entire earth,
I will stretch forth my hand against
you,
roll you down over the cliffs,
and make you a burnt mountain:*

26 They will not take from you a
cornerstone,
or a foundation stone;
You shall remain ruins forever—
oracle of the LORD.*

27 Raise a signal in the land,
sound the trumpet among the
nations;
Dedicate nations for war against her,
summon against her the kingdoms:
Ararat, Minni, and Ashkenaz;†
Appoint a recruiting officer against her,
dispatch horses like bristling locusts.*

28 Dedicate nations for war against her:
the king of the Medes,
Its governors and all its officers,
every land in its domain.

---

† 51:11 Kings of the Medes: the Medes and the Persians lived
in the area known today as Iran.
51:27 Ararat, Minni, and Ashkenaz: regions in eastern Asia
Minor under the control of the Medes.

* 51:10 Jer 50:28.
51:11 2 Kgs 17:6; Is 13:17.
51:13 Na 2:1.
51:15 Jer 10:12.
51:21 Dn 7:7, 19, 23.
51:22 Is 13:16, 18.
51:24 Jer 25:14; 50:29; Ps
137:8.
51:25 Rev 8:7; 18:8–9.
51:26 Jer 25:12; Ps 118:22.
51:27 Na 3:17.

29 The earth quakes and writhes,
   the LORD's plan against Babylon is
      carried out,
Turning the land of Babylon
   into a wasteland without inhabitants.
30 Babylon's warriors have ceased to fight,
   they remain in their strongholds;
Dried up is their strength,
   they have become women.
Burned down are their homes,
   broken their gates.
31 One runner meets another,
   herald meets herald,
Telling the king of Babylon
   that his entire city has been taken.*
32 The fords have been seized,
   marshes set on fire,
   warriors panic.

33 For thus says the LORD of hosts, the God
of Israel:

   Daughter Babylon is like a threshing
      floor
   at the time of treading;
   Yet a little while,
      and the harvest time will come for
         her.*
34 "He consumed me, defeated me,
   Nebuchadnezzar, king of Babylon;
   he left me like an empty vessel,
   Swallowed me like a sea monster,
      filled his belly with my delicacies and
         cast me out.
35 Let my torn flesh be visited upon
      Babylon,"
   says enthroned Zion;
"My blood upon the inhabitants of
      Chaldea,"
   says Jerusalem.
36 But now, thus says the LORD:
   I will certainly defend your cause,
   I will certainly avenge you;
   I will dry up her sea,
      and drain her fountain.
37 Babylon shall become a heap of ruins,
   a haunt of jackals;
A place of horror and hissing,
   without inhabitants.*
38 They roar like lions,
   growl like lion cubs.*

39 When they are parched, I will set drink
      before them
   to make them drunk, that they may
      be overcome
   with everlasting sleep, never to
      awaken—
   oracle of the LORD.
40 I will bring them down like lambs to
      slaughter,
   like rams and goats.
41 How she has been seized, taken captive,
   the glory of the whole world!
What a horror Babylon has become
   among the nations:*
42 against Babylon the sea rises,
   she is overwhelmed by roaring waves!
43 Her cities have become wasteland,
   a parched and arid land
Where no one lives,
   no one passes through.
44 I will punish Bel in Babylon,
   and make him vomit up what he
      swallowed;
   nations shall no longer stream to him.
Even the wall of Babylon falls!
45 Leave her, my people; each of you save
   your own life
   from the burning wrath of the LORD.

46 Do not be discouraged when rumors
spread through the land; this year one rumor
comes, next year another: "Violence in the
land!" or "Ruler against ruler!"* 47 Realize that
the days are coming when I will punish the
idols of Babylon; the whole land shall be put
to shame, all her slain shall fall in her midst.
48 Then heaven and earth and everything in
them shall shout over Babylon with joy, when
the destroyers come against her from the
north—oracle of the LORD.* 49 Babylon, too,
must fall, you slain of Israel, because by the
hand of Babylon the slain of all the earth have
fallen.

50 You who have escaped the sword,
   go, do not stand idle;
Remember the LORD from far away,
   let Jerusalem come to mind.
51 We are ashamed because we have heard
      taunts,
   disgrace covers our faces;

J
E
R

strangers have entered sanctuaries in
　　the Lord's house. *

52　Therefore see, the days are coming—
　　　oracle of the Lord—
　　when I will punish her idols,
　　and throughout the land the wounded
　　　will groan.

53　Though Babylon scale the heavens,
　　and make her strong heights
　　　inaccessible,
　　my destroyers shall reach her—oracle
　　　of the Lord. *

54　A sound of crying from Babylon,
　　great destruction from the land of the
　　　Chaldeans;

55　For the Lord lays Babylon waste,
　　silences her loud cry,
　　Waves roaring like mighty waters,
　　a clamor resounding.

56　For the destroyer comes upon her, upon
　　　Babylon;
　　warriors are captured, their bows
　　　broken;
　　The Lord is a God of recompense,
　　he will surely repay. *

⁵⁷ I will make her princes and sages drunk,
with her governors, officers, and warriors, so
that they sleep an everlasting sleep, never to
awaken—oracle of the King, whose name is
Lord of hosts.

58　Thus says the Lord of hosts:
　　The walls of spacious Babylon shall be
　　　leveled to the ground,
　　its lofty gates destroyed by fire.
　　The toil of the peoples is for nothing;
　　the nations weary themselves for what
　　　the flames consume. *

**The Prophecy Sent to Babylon.** ⁵⁹ The mission Jeremiah the prophet gave to Seraiah, † son of Neriah, son of Mahseiah, when he went to Babylon with King Zedekiah, king of Judah, in the fourth year of his reign;

Seraiah was chief quartermaster. ⁶⁰ Jeremiah wrote down on one scroll the disaster that would befall Babylon; † all these words were written against Babylon. ⁶¹ And Jeremiah said to Seraiah: "When you reach Babylon, see that you read all these words aloud, * ⁶² and then say: Lord, you yourself spoke against this place in order to cut it down so that nothing, human being or beast, could live in it, because it is to remain a wasteland forever. ⁶³ When you have finished reading this scroll, tie a stone to it and throw it into the Euphrates, * ⁶⁴ and say: Thus Babylon shall sink. It will never rise, because of the disaster I am bringing upon it." Thus far the words of Jeremiah.

## IX. HISTORICAL APPENDIX†

**52** **Capture of Jerusalem.** ¹ Zedekiah was twenty-one years old when he became king; he reigned eleven years in Jerusalem. * His mother's name was Hamutal, daughter of Jeremiah from Libnah. ² He did what was evil in the sight of the Lord, just as Jehoiakim had done. ³ Indeed, the things done in Jerusalem and in Judah so angered the Lord that he cast them out from his presence. Thus Zedekiah rebelled against the king of Babylon. ⁴ * In the tenth month of the ninth year of his reign, on the tenth day of the month, † Nebuchadnezzar, king of Babylon, and his entire army advanced against Jerusalem, encamped around it, and built siege walls on every side. ⁵ The siege of the city continued until the eleventh year of King Zedekiah.

⁶ On the ninth day of the fourth month, when famine had gripped the city and the people had no more bread, ⁷ the city walls were breached. All the soldiers fled and left the city by night through the gate between the two walls which was near the king's garden. With the Chaldeans surrounding the city, they went in the direction of the Arabah. ⁸ But the Chaldean army pursued the king and overtook

**51:59** *Seraiah*: the brother of Baruch; cf. 32:12. He may have gone to Babylon to explain away the presence of foreign ambassadors in Jerusalem that same year; cf. 27:3.
**51:60** Jeremiah prophesied against Babylon, even as he foretold Judah's release from Babylon's power (3:14–18; 32:15; 33:6–9, 12–13); but his scroll against Babylon was thrown in the Euphrates (v. 63). Some of the preceding oracles may have been composed by later writers; see note on 50:1–51:58.
**52:1–34** One of the editors of the Book of Jeremiah took most of this supplement from 2 Kgs 24:18–25:30 and placed it here

to show the fulfillment of Jeremiah's prophecies. The supplement repeats part of the history given in Jeremiah 39–41, but omits the history of Gedaliah in 2 Kgs 25:22–26.
**52:4** *In the tenth month of the ninth year of his reign, on the tenth day of the month*: January 15, 588 B.C. Cf. 39:1.

**51:51** Ps 44:16–17; 78:1–4.　**51:61** Jer 50:1–51.
**51:53** Is 14:13.　**51:63** Rev 18:21.
**51:56** Na 1:2.　**52:1–27** 2 Kgs 24:18–25:21.
**51:58** Hb 2:13.　**52:4–16** Jer 39:1–10.

Zedekiah in the wilderness near Jericho; his whole army fled from him.

⁹ The king, therefore, was arrested and brought to Riblah, in the land of Hamath, to the king of Babylon, who pronounced judgment on him. ¹⁰ As Zedekiah looked on, the king of Babylon slaughtered his sons before his eyes! All the nobles of Judah were slaughtered at Riblah. ¹¹ And the eyes of Zedekiah he then blinded, bound him with chains, and the King of Babylon brought him to Babylon and kept him in prison until the day he died.

**Destruction of Jerusalem.** ¹² On the tenth day of the fifth month, this was in the nineteenth year† of Nebuchadnezzar, king of Babylon, Nebuzaradan, captain of the bodyguard, came to Jerusalem as the representative of the king of Babylon. ¹³ He burned the house of the LORD, the palace of the king, and all the houses of Jerusalem; every large building he destroyed with fire. ¹⁴ Then the Chaldean troops with the captain of the guard tore down all the walls that surrounded Jerusalem.

¹⁵ Nebuzaradan, captain of the guard, led into exile the remnant of people left in the city, those who had deserted to the king of Babylon, and the rest of the artisans. ¹⁶ But Nebuzaradan, captain of the guard, left behind some of the country's poor as vinedressers and farmers.

¹⁷ The bronze pillars that belonged to the house of the LORD, and the wheeled carts and the bronze sea in the house of the LORD, the Chaldeans broke into pieces; they carried away all the bronze to Babylon. ¹⁸ They also took the pots, shovels, snuffers, bowls, pans, and all the bronze vessels used for service; ¹⁹ the basins, fire holders, bowls, pots, lampstands, pans, the sacrificial bowls made of gold or silver. Along with these furnishings the captain of the guard carried off ²⁰ the two pillars, the one sea and its base of twelve oxen cast in bronze, and the wheeled carts King Solomon had commissioned for the house of the LORD. The bronze from all these furnishings was impossible to weigh.

²¹ As for the pillars, each of them was eighteen cubits high and twelve cubits in diameter; each was four fingers thick and hollow inside. ²² A bronze capital five cubits high crowned the one pillar, and a network with pomegranates encircled the capital, all of bronze; and so for the other pillar, with pomegranates. ²³ There were ninety-six pomegranates on the sides, a hundred pomegranates surrounding the network.

²⁴ The captain of the guard also took Seraiah the high priest, Zephaniah the second priest, and the three keepers of the entrance. ²⁵ From the city he took one courtier, a commander of soldiers, and seven men in the personal service of the king still in the city, the scribe of the army commander who mustered the people of the land, and sixty of the common people remaining in the city. ²⁶ The captain of the guard, Nebuzaradan, arrested them and brought them to the king of Babylon at Riblah, ²⁷ who had them struck down and executed in Riblah, in the land of Hamath.

Thus Judah was exiled from the land. ²⁸ † This is the number of people Nebuchadnezzar led away captive: in his seventh year, three thousand twenty-three people of Judah; ²⁹ in the eighteenth year of Nebuchadnezzar, eight hundred thirty-two persons from Jerusalem; ³⁰ in the twenty-third year of Nebuchadnezzar, Nebuzaradan, captain of the guard, deported seven hundred forty-five Judahites: four thousand six hundred persons in all.

**Favor Shown to Jehoiachin.** † ³¹ * In the thirty-seventh year of the exile of Jehoiachin, king of Judah, on the twenty-fifth day of the twelfth month, Evil-merodach, king of Babylon, in the inaugural year of his reign, raised up Jehoiachin, king of Judah, and released him from prison. ³² He spoke kindly to him and gave him a throne higher than the thrones of the other kings † who were with him in Babylon. ³³ Jehoiachin took off his prison garb and ate at the king's table as long as he lived. ³⁴ The allowance given him by the king of Babylon was a perpetual allowance, in fixed daily amounts, all the days of his life until the day of his death.

---

† **52:12** *On the tenth day of the fifth month…nineteenth year:* the tenth of Ab—July/August in 587/586 B.C.

**52:28–30** These verses, missing in the Greek text, do not come from 2 Kgs 25 but from a source using a different chronology. Besides the deportations of 598 and 587 B.C., this passage mentions a final deportation in 582/581, possibly a response to the murder of Gedaliah; cf. Jer 41:2.

**52:31–34** In the year 561/560 B.C., Nebuchadnezzar's successor Awel-Marduk (Evil-merodach), who reigned only two years, released Jehoiachin. Babylonian records confirm that Jehoiachin and his family were supported at public expense.

**52:32** *The other kings:* heads of state brought as captives to Babylon.

* **52:31–34** 2 Kgs 25:27–30.

# The Book of

# Lamentations

## INTRODUCTION

Carol J. Dempsey, OP

The book of Lamentations is both a magnificent work of art and a theological enigma that captures the raw sentiments of loss, pain, and grief over the destruction of Jerusalem by the Babylonians in 587 BCE. The book is a collection of five laments that bewail the fall of Jerusalem. The text functions as a dirge for fallen Jerusalem. It announces Jerusalem's death, describes how that death occurred, calls for commemoration, and invites mourning. Written in exquisite poetry, the text contains many images, uses a variety of literary techniques to communicate its message, and contains multiple voices.

## Historical Considerations

The backdrop to the poems found in the book of Lamentations is the period of Babylonian control (597–537 BCE), which was a time of tremendous turmoil and tragedy for the people of Judah and Jerusalem. Previously Jerusalem had been attacked three times and now both Egypt and Babylon struggled to gain control of the southern kingdom, Judah. Eventually Babylon defeated Egypt and in 597 BCE the Babylonians invaded Jerusalem and deported many of its prominent citizens to Babylon. For ten years, the people of Judah and Jerusalem lived in uneasiness, until Judah's King Zedekiah rebelled, an event that led to the devastating Babylonian invasion of Jerusalem in 587 BCE (see 2 Kgs 24:18–25:26; 2 Chr 36:11–20; Jer 39:1–10; 52:1–30). This invasion brought the demise of the Holy City and the further exile of many peoples. When the survivors of the Judean royal family assassinated Gedaliah, the Babylonian-appointed governor (see Jer 40–41), the Babylonians invaded Judah again in 582 BCE and once again exiled many people. Thus the political, social, and religious climate

## Outline of Lamentations

I.   The Desolation of Jerusalem (1:1–22).

II.  The Lord's Wrath and Zion's Ruin (2:1–22).

III. The Voice of a Suffering Individual (3:1–66).

IV.  Miseries of the Besieged City (4:1–22).

V.   The Community's Lament to the Lord (5:1–22).

of the day was not only chaotic but also grief-ridden, with the people undoubtedly benumbed by all that had happened to them. The book of Lamentations expresses the people's fury, grief, and disorientation in the face of horrific tragedy. Furthermore, even though the book is thought to have been composed in Palestine in response to the defeat of the people of Judah and their central city of Jerusalem, the beauty and power of the book's metaphorical language allows the text to speak to other trials and tribulations endured throughout history.

## Authorship, Versions, Place in the Canon

Until recently, scholars maintained that Jeremiah wrote all the poems in the book of Lamentations. Interestingly, neither the Hebrew nor the Masoretic Text (MT) assigns an author to Lamentations, but the later Septuagint (LXX) version adds an interpretative opening line: "Jeremiah sat weeping and lamented this lamentation over Jerusalem" (Lam 1:1). Thus Jeremiah has become the symbolic author of the text even though scholarly evidence now supports otherwise. Today most scholars think that an anonymous author composed the poems; in fact, multiple authors may have been responsible for the text as it now appears in the Bible

The book of Lamentations appears both in Hebrew and Greek. The Masoretic Text (MT) places Lamentations among the writings, though its position varies in Jewish liturgical practice, which places it among the *Megillot*, or five liturgical scrolls. There the book appears between Ruth and Ecclesiastes. Because the Septuagint (LXX) assumes Jeremiah authored Lamentations, the book is placed after the prophetic books, either right after the book of Jeremiah or after the book of Baruch (when Baruch follows Jeremiah). A later Aramaic version of Lamentations also exists, known as a targum.

## Literary Considerations

Chapters 1–4 of Lamentations are arranged in the form of an acrostic, a pattern based on the 22-letter Hebrew alphabet. Although ch. 5 is not a true acrostic, it continues the acrostic theme. The poetry of Lamentations consists primarily of individual and communal laments. The book opens with a cry of desolation (Lam 1:1) that bewails the desolation of Jerusalem (1:2–22). What follows is a vivid description of divine wrath aimed at "daughter Zion," which results in her demise (ch. 2). Embedded in ch. 2 is a direct call to lament addressed to the people (2:19) and to God (2:20). Clearly such a state of affairs has caused uncontrollable anguish (2:11; 3–4). The book closes with a communal lament addressed to Israel's God (ch. 5) that poignantly describes the people's pain and anguish but which also puts their God "on notice" (5:19–22). A devastated people acknowledge the regal existence of their God. They question, however, why their God continues to be silent and inactive in the face of such horrendous devastation. The entire book closes on a note of hope couched in the deep

awareness of the present situation. The people beckon their God to bring them back into divine relationship (5:21) while at the same time they acknowledge that they have truly fallen out of divine favor (5:25). Thus, the tone of all the poems is somber, as the people wait for their God (3:21–33) while trying to come to grips with the traumas they have experienced.

Besides being highly metaphorical in its language, with personification being one of its main literary techniques, the book of Lamentations also contains multiple voices. For example, within the book one hears the voice of the narrator (e.g., Lam 1–2 and most of 3–4), which may also be the voice of the poet; the voice of daughter Zion (e.g., 1:6); the voice of a "man" (3:1, translated "one" in the NABRE) in ch. 3 who has traditionally been identified as the prophet Jeremiah, largely because the pain expressed corresponds to Jeremiah's pain (cf. Jer 9:1; 15:10–18; 20:7–18); and the voice of the community heard largely throughout Lam 3–5. The voice of Israel's God is never heard, which brings increased anguish to a people already so devastated (Lam 5:22).

## Theological Considerations

Clearly the book of Lamentations reflects the Deuteronomic theology of retribution. Jerusalem, and particularly its political and religious leaders, has fallen out of right relationship with the God of Israel because of idolatry, apostasy, trust in ill-made political alliances, and a host of other transgressions. Covenant and law have been broken, and divine chastisement comes in the form of divine wrath that purges and humiliates in an attempt to purify and eventually transform (cf. Is 60–62). The book of Lamentations makes clear that the experience of the people is bitter and their experience of their God is equally as bitter. Yet, hope and faith prevail (Lam 3:21–33) as a devastated people struggle to carry on (5:19–22). ■

# THE BOOK OF LAMENTATIONS

## New American Bible, Introduction

The Book of Lamentations is a collection of five poems that serve as an anguished response to the destruction of Jerusalem in 587 B.C., after a long siege by the invading Babylonian army. (See 2 Kgs 25 for a prose account of the fall of Jerusalem.) Although the poems are traditionally ascribed to the prophet Jeremiah, this is unlikely. The Hebrew text of the book does not mention Jeremiah at all, and it is difficult to square some of the content of the poetry with what one finds in the Book of Jeremiah itself (cf. Lam 1:10; 2:9; 4:17, 20). While there are connections in theme and vocabulary among all five chapters (and especially between chaps. 1 and 2), the poems may have been composed separately and grouped together later. In any case, they are anonymous compositions probably used by survivors of the catastrophe of 587 B.C. in a communal expression of grief and mourning.

Jewish liturgical tradition considers the book one of the "scrolls" (*megillot*); it is read once a year on the ninth of Av (August–September), a fast day commemorating the destruction of both the first Temple in 587 B.C. and the second Temple in A.D. 70. While passages from chap. 3 are often incorporated into Christian services for Holy Thursday or Good Friday, the Church has otherwise tended to neglect the book. It is not hard to see why; a more anguished piece of writing is scarcely imaginable: from its portrayal of Jerusalem in chaps. 1 and 2 as an abandoned widow exposed to endless dangers, to the broken man of chap. 3, to the bleak description in chap. 4 of the inhabitants of the devastated city, to the final unanswered communal lament of chap. 5, the reader is not so much engaged by the Book of Lamentations as assaulted by it. But with its unsparing focus on destruction, pain, and suffering the book serves an invaluable function as part of Scripture, witnessing to a biblical faith determined to express honestly the harsh realities of a violent world and providing contemporary readers the language to do the same.

As a literary work, the Book of Lamentations combines elements of communal and individual laments (in which the speakers attempt to persuade God to intervene in the face of an acute crisis), funeral dirges (in which a death is mourned), and ancient Near Eastern city-laments (in which the destruction of a city is mourned). The meter is called *Qinah* (lament), that is, each verse normally has three beats followed by two. The poems are acrostics: in chaps. 1–4, the separate stanzas begin with successive letters of the Hebrew alphabet from the first to the last. The last chapter, while not strictly an acrostic, nevertheless partially conforms to the pattern in its use of 22 lines, the number of letters in the Hebrew alphabet. Far from destroying the spontaneous pathos of the songs, this feature conveys the expression of a profound grief that might otherwise seem to be without limit (cf. 2:13).

The book may be divided as follows:

I. The Desolation of Jerusalem (1:1–22).

II. The Lord's Wrath and Zion's Ruin (2:1–22).

III. The Voice of a Suffering Individual (3:1–66).

IV. Miseries of the Besieged City (4:1–22).

V. The Community's Lament to the Lord (5:1–22). ■

# LAMENTATIONS

## The Desolation of Jerusalem†

**1** ¹ How solitary sits the city,
    once filled with people.
She who was great among the nations
    is now like a widow.
Once a princess among the provinces,
    now a toiling slave.

² She weeps incessantly in the night,
    her cheeks damp with tears.
She has no one to comfort her
    from all her lovers;†
Her friends have all betrayed her,
    and become her enemies.*

³ Judah has gone into exile,
    after oppression and harsh labor;
She dwells among the nations,
    yet finds no rest:*
All her pursuers overtake her
    in the narrow straits.

⁴ The roads to Zion mourn,
    empty of pilgrims to her feasts.
All her gateways are desolate,
    her priests groan,
Her young women grieve;
    her lot is bitter.*

⁵ Her foes have come out on top,
    her enemies are secure;
Because the LORD has afflicted her
    for her many rebellions.
Her children have gone away,
    captive before the foe.

⁶ From daughter Zion has gone
    all her glory:
Her princes have become like rams

that find no pasture.
They have gone off exhausted
    before their pursuers.

⁷ Jerusalem remembers
    in days of wretched homelessness,
All the precious things she once had
    in days gone by.
But when her people fell into the hands
        of the foe,
    and she had no help,
Her foes looked on and laughed
    at her collapse.

⁸ Jerusalem has sinned grievously,
    therefore she has become a mockery;
Those who honored her now demean
        her,
    for they saw her nakedness;
She herself groans out loud,
    and turns away.*

⁹ Her uncleanness is on her skirt;
    she has no thought of her future.
Her downfall is astonishing,
    with no one to comfort her.
"Look, O LORD, at my misery;
    how the enemy triumphs!"†

¹⁰ The foe stretched out his hands
    to all her precious things;
She has seen the nations
    enter her sanctuary,
Those you forbade to come
    into your assembly.*

¹¹ All her people groan,
    searching for bread;
They give their precious things for food,
    to retain the breath of life.
"Look, O LORD, and pay attention
    to how I have been demeaned!

¹² Come, all who pass by the way,
    pay attention and see:

---

† **1:1–22** In this poem the poet first takes on the persona of an observer describing Jerusalem's abject state after the destruction wrought by the Babylonian army (vv. 1–11a); but the detached tone gives way to a more impassioned appeal when the city itself—personified as the grieving widow and mother Zion—abruptly intrudes upon this description (vv. 9c, 11c–16, 18–22) to demand that God look squarely at her misery.
**1:2** *Lovers*: language of love was typically used to describe the relationship between treaty partners, thus here it connotes

Judah's allies (see v. 19).
**1:9** Zion breaks in on the poet's description in v. 9c, albeit briefly, to demand that the Lord face squarely her misery. She takes up the lament in a more sustained fashion in v. 11c.

*

**1:2** Jer 30:14; Ez 16:37.
**1:3** Dt 28:65; Jer 45:3.
**1:4** Is 33:8–9; Jer 14:2.
**1:8** Is 47:2–3; Jer 13:22,

26; Na 3:5.
**1:10** Dt 23:3–6; Ps 74:4–8;
Is 56:6; 66:20–21; Jer
51:51.

L
A
M

Is there any pain like my pain,
  which has been ruthlessly inflicted
      upon me,
With which the Lord has tormented me
  on the day of his blazing wrath?

13  From on high he hurled fire down
      into my very bones;
  He spread out a net for my feet,
      and turned me back.
  He has left me desolate,
      in misery all day long.*

14  The yoke of my rebellions is bound
        together,
      fastened by his hand.
  His yoke is upon my neck;
      he has made my strength fail.
  The Lord has delivered me into the grip
      of those I cannot resist.

15  All my valiant warriors
      my Lord has cast away;
  He proclaimed a feast against me
      to crush my young men;
  My Lord has trodden in the wine press
      virgin daughter Judah.

16  For these things I weep—My eyes!
      My eyes!
  They stream with tears!
  How far from me is anyone to comfort,
      anyone to restore my life.
  My children are desolate;
      the enemy has prevailed."*

17  Zion stretches out her hands,
      with no one to comfort her;
  The Lord has ordered against Jacob
      his foes all around;
  Jerusalem has become in their midst
      a thing unclean.

18  "The Lord is in the right;
      I had defied his command.

Listen, all you peoples,
  and see my pain:
My young women and young men
  have gone into captivity.*

19  I cried out to my lovers,
      but they failed me.*
  My priests and my elders
      perished in the city;
  How desperately they searched for
        food,
      to save their lives!

20  Look, O Lord, at the anguish I suffer!
      My stomach churns,
  And my heart recoils within me:
      How bitter I am!
  Outside the sword bereaves—
      indoors, there is death.*

21  Hear how I am groaning;
      there is no one to comfort me.
  All my enemies hear of my misery and
        rejoice
      over what you have done.
  Bring on the day you proclaimed,
      and let them become like me!

22  Let all their evil come before you
      and deal with them
  As you have so ruthlessly dealt with me
      for all my rebellions.
  My groans are many,
      my heart is sick."*

## The Lord's Wrath and Zion's Ruin†

2  ¹ How the Lord in his wrath
      has abhorred daughter Zion,
  Casting down from heaven to earth
      the glory of Israel,†
  Not remembering his footstool
      on the day of his wrath!

2  The Lord has devoured without pity
      all of Jacob's dwellings;

---

†  **2:1–22** This chapter continues to move between the voice of the poet (vv. 1–20) and that of personified Zion (vv. 20–22). The persona of the poet, first portrayed in chap. 1 as a detached observer recounting both the desolation as well as the sins of the city, becomes in this chapter an advocate for Zion in her appeal to the Lord and never once mentions her sins.
  **2:1** *The glory of Israel*: the Temple. *His footstool*: the ark of the covenant (1 Chr 28:2; Ps 99:5; 132:7); or again, the Temple (Ez 43:7).

**2:3** *Horn*: a symbol of power and strength; cf. v. 17; 1 Sm 2:1, 10; Ps 89:18, 25; 92:11; 112:9.

**1:13** Ez 12:13.                    **1:19** Jer 30:14.
**1:16** Ps 69:21; Eccl 4:1; Jer      **1:20** Lam 2:11.
     13:17; 14:17; Na 3:7.            **1:22** Lam 3:64.
**1:18** Dt 28:41.

In his fury he has razed
    daughter Judah's defenses,
Has brought to the ground in
      dishonor
    a kingdom and its princes.

3 In blazing wrath, he cut down
      entirely
    the horn† of Israel;
He withdrew the support of his right
      hand
    when the enemy approached;
He burned against Jacob like a blazing
      fire
    that consumes everything in its
      path.

4 He bent his bow like an enemy;
    the arrow in his right hand
Like a foe, he killed
    all those held precious;
On the tent of daughter Zion
    he poured out his wrath like fire.

5 The Lord has become the enemy,
    he has devoured Israel:
Devoured all its strongholds,
    destroyed its defenses,
Multiplied moaning and groaning
    throughout daughter Judah.

6 He laid waste his booth like a garden,
    destroyed his shrine;†
The LORD has blotted out in Zion
    feast day and sabbath,
Has scorned in fierce wrath
    king and priest.*

7 The Lord has rejected his altar,
    spurned his sanctuary;
He has handed over to the enemy
    the walls of its strongholds.

They shout in the house of the LORD
    as on a feast day.*

8 The LORD was bent on destroying
    the wall of daughter Zion:
He stretched out the measuring line;†
    did not hesitate to devour,
Brought grief on rampart and wall
    till both succumbed.*

9 Her gates sank into the ground;
    he smashed her bars to bits.
Her king and her princes are among
      the nations;
    instruction is wanting,
Even her prophets do not obtain
    any vision from the LORD.*

10 The elders of daughter Zion
    sit silently on the ground;
They cast dust† on their heads
    and dress in sackcloth;
The young women of Jerusalem
    bow their heads to the ground.*

11 My eyes are spent with tears,
    my stomach churns;†
My bile is poured out on the ground
    at the brokenness of the daughter of
      my people,
As children and infants collapse
    in the streets of the town.*

12 They cry out to their mothers,
    "Where is bread and wine?"
As they faint away like the wounded
    in the streets of the city,
As their life is poured out
    in their mothers' arms.

13 To what can I compare you†—to what
    can I liken you—

---

**2:6** *Booth…shrine:* synonyms for the Temple; cf. Ps 27:5; 74:4, 8. The term for "shrine" in Hebrew (*mo'ed*) figures prominently in the pentateuchal expression "tent of meeting" (*'ohel mo'ed*).

**2:8** *The measuring line:* normally used for building, here employed ironically as an instrument of destruction; cf. Is 34:11; 2 Kgs 21:13.

**2:10** *They cast dust:* as a sign of mourning; cf. Jos 7:6; Jb 2:12; Ez 27:30.

**2:11** *My eyes are spent with tears, my stomach churns:* the poet appropriates the emotional language used by Zion in 1:16 and 1:20 to express a progressively stronger commitment to her cause. After describing the systematic dismantling of the city

in vv. 5–9, the poet turns to the plight of the inhabitants in vv. 10–12. It is the description of children dying in the streets that finally brings about the poet's emotional breakdown, even as it did for Zion in 1:16.

**2:13** *To what can I compare you…?:* the author calls attention to the poetic task: to find language that speaks adequately of the atrocities and incomparable suffering experienced by Zion, and thus to attempt to offer comfort.

**2:6** Is 1:13; 5:5.
**2:7** Ez 24:21.
**2:8** Jer 52:12–14.
**2:9** Dt 28:36.
**2:10** Is 3:26.
**2:11** Lam 1:16, 20; 3:48;
    Jer 8:18.

O daughter Jerusalem?
What example can I give in order to
comfort you,
virgin daughter Zion?
For your breach is vast as the sea;
who could heal you?*

14 Your prophets provided you visions
of whitewashed illusion;
They did not lay bare your guilt,
in order to restore your fortunes;
They saw for you only oracles
of empty deceit.*

15 All who pass by on the road,
clap their hands at you;
They hiss and wag their heads
over daughter Jerusalem:
"Is this the city they used to call
perfect in beauty and joy of all the
earth?"*

16 They open their mouths against you,
all your enemies;
They hiss and gnash their teeth,
saying, "We have devoured her!
How we have waited for this day—
we have lived to see it!"*

17 The LORD has done what he
planned.
He has fulfilled the threat
Decreed from days of old,
destroying without pity!
He let the enemy gloat over you
and exalted the horn of your foes.*

18 Cry out to the Lord from your heart,
wall of daughter Zion!
Let your tears flow like a torrent
day and night;

Give yourself no rest,
no relief for your eyes.

19 Rise up! Wail in the night,
at the start of every watch;
Pour out your heart like water
before the Lord;
Lift up your hands to him
for the lives of your children,
Who collapse from hunger
at the corner of every street.†

20 "Look, O LORD, and pay attention:
to whom have you been so
ruthless?
Must women eat their own offspring,†
the very children they have borne?
Are priest and prophet to be slain
in the sanctuary of the Lord?*

21 They lie on the ground in the streets,
young and old alike;
Both my young women and young
men
are cut down by the sword;
You killed them on the day of your
wrath,
slaughtered without pity.*

22 You summoned as to a feast day
terrors on every side;
On the day of the LORD's wrath,
none survived or escaped.
Those I have borne and nurtured,
my enemy has utterly destroyed."*

## The Voice of a Suffering Individual†

3 1 I am one who has known affliction
under the rod of God's anger,*
2 One whom he has driven and forced to
walk

---

† **2:19** The poet urges Zion to appeal to the Lord once more on behalf of her dying children. The image of Zion's children effectively condenses the metaphorical sense of all residents of the city (young and old alike) into the more poignant picture of actual children at the point of death. It was precisely this image, no doubt well known to survivors of besieged cities, that led to the emotional breakdown of both Zion (1:16) and the poet (2:11). The hope is that the Lord will be similarly affected by such a poignant image and respond with mercy.

**2:20** *Must women eat their own offspring*: extreme famine in a besieged city sometimes led to cannibalism; this becomes a stereotypical way of expressing the nearly unthinkable horrors of war; cf. Lam 4:10; Dt 28:53; 2 Kgs 6:28–29; Bar 2:3; Ez 5:10.

**3:1–66** This chapter is focused less on the destruction of Jerusalem than are chaps. 1 and 2 and more on the suffering of an individual. The identity of the individual is never given, and one probably should not search for a specific identification of the speaker. The figure of the representative sufferer makes concrete the pain of the people in a way similar to the personification of Zion as a woman in chaps. 1 and 2. Indeed, in vv. 40–48 the individual voice gives way to a communal voice, returning in vv. 49–66 to the individual sufferer.

---

**2:13** Lam 1:12; Jer 8:21.
**2:14** Is 58:1; Jer 2:8; 23:16; Ez 13:9; 22:28.
**2:15** Ps 48:3; 50:12; Jer 18:16.
**2:16** Lam 3:46.
**2:17** Dt 28:15.
**2:20** Lam 4:10.
**2:21** Lam 3:43; 2 Chr 36:17; Jer 6:11.
**2:22** Jer 42:17.
**3:1** Jer 20:18.

in darkness, not in light;
3    Against me alone he turns his hand—
    again and again all day long.

4    He has worn away my flesh and my
    skin,
    he has broken my bones;*
5    He has besieged me all around
    with poverty and hardship;
6    He has left me to dwell in dark places
    like those long dead.*

7    He has hemmed me in with no escape,
    weighed me down with chains;
8    Even when I cry for help,
    he stops my prayer;*
9    He has hemmed in my ways with fitted
    stones,
    and made my paths crooked.

10   He has been a bear lying in wait
    for me,
    a lion in hiding!*
11   He turned me aside and tore me apart,
    leaving me ravaged.*
12   He bent his bow, and set me up
    as a target for his arrow.*

13   He pierced my kidneys
    with shafts from his quiver.*
14   I have become a laughingstock to all
    my people,
    their taunt all day long;*
15   He has sated me with bitterness,
    filled me with wormwood.*

16   He has made me eat gravel,
    trampled me into the dust;
17   My life is deprived of peace,
    I have forgotten what happiness is;
18   My enduring hope, I said,
    has perished before the LORD.

19   The thought of my wretched
    homelessness

is wormwood and poison;
20   Remembering it over and over,
    my soul is downcast.
21   But this I will call to mind;†
    therefore I will hope:

22   The LORD's acts of mercy are not
    exhausted,
    his compassion is not spent;*
23   They are renewed each morning—
    great is your faithfulness!
24   The LORD is my portion, I tell
    myself,
    therefore I will hope in him.*

25   The LORD is good to those who trust
    in him,
    to the one that seeks him;*
26   It is good to hope in silence
    for the LORD's deliverance.
27   It is good for a person, when young,
    to bear the yoke,

28   To sit alone and in silence,
    when its weight lies heavy,
29   To put one's mouth in the dust—†
    there may yet be hope—
30   To offer one's cheek to be struck,
    to be filled with disgrace.*

31   For the Lord does not
    reject forever;*
32   Though he brings grief, he takes
    pity,
    according to the abundance of his
    mercy;*
33   He does not willingly afflict
    or bring grief to human beings.*

34   That someone tramples underfoot
    all the prisoners in the land,
35   Or denies justice to anyone
    in the very sight of the Most High,
36   Or subverts a person's lawsuit—
    does the Lord not see?

---

† **3:21–24** In the midst of a description of suffering, the speaker offers this brief but compelling statement of hope in God's ultimate mercy. It is a hard-won and precarious hope, nearly submerged by the volume and intensity of the surrounding lament, but it is hope nonetheless.

**3:29** *To put one's mouth in the dust*: a sign of humiliation and submission; cf. v. 16; Ps 72:9.

**3:4** Jb 30:30; Is 38:13.
**3:6** Ps 143:3.
**3:8** Ps 18:41; 22:2; 88:14–15.
**3:10** Jb 10:16; Hos 13:8.
**3:11** Lam 1:13.
**3:12** Lam 2:4; Jb 16:12.
**3:13** Jb 6:4; Ps 38:3.
**3:14** Jb 30:9; Ps 69:13.
**3:15** Jer 9:14; 23:15.
**3:22** 1 Sm 20:15; Neh 9:31.
**3:24** Ps 16:5; 73:26.
**3:25** Ps 130:6; Is 30:18.
**3:30** Is 50:6; Mt 5:39.
**3:31** Ps 85:6; 103:9.
**3:32** 1 Sm 2:6–7; Tb 13:2; Is 54:8.
**3:33** Ex 34:6–7.

**L A M**

37 Who speaks so that it comes to pass,
    unless the Lord commands it?
38 Is it not at the word of the Most High
    that both good and bad take place?*
39 What should the living complain
        about?
    about their sins!

40† Let us search and examine our ways,
    and return to the LORD!*
41 Let us lift up our hearts as well as our
        hands
    toward God in heaven!
42 We have rebelled and been obstinate;
    you have not forgiven us.

43 You wrapped yourself in wrath and
        pursued us,
    killing without pity;*
44 You wrapped yourself in a cloud,
    which no prayer could pierce.
45 You have made us filth and rubbish
    among the peoples.*

46 They have opened their mouths
        against us,
    all our enemies;
47 Panic and the pit have been our lot,
    desolation and destruction;*
48† My eyes stream with tears over the
        destruction
    of the daughter of my people.*

49 My eyes will flow without ceasing,
    without rest,
50 Until the LORD from heaven
    looks down and sees.
51 I am tormented by the sight
    of all the daughters of my city.

52 Without cause, my enemies snared me
    as though I were a bird;

53 They tried to end my life in the pit,
    pelting me with stones.
54 The waters flowed over my head:
    and I said, "I am lost!"*

55 I have called upon your name,
       O LORD,*
    from the bottom of the pit;
56 You heard me call, "Do not let your ear
       be deaf
    to my cry for help."
57 You drew near on the day I called you;
    you said, "Do not fear!"

58 You pleaded my case, Lord,
    you redeemed my life.
59 You see, LORD, how I am wronged;
    do me justice!*
60 You see all their vindictiveness,
    all their plots against me.

61 You hear their reproach, LORD,
    all their plots against me,
62 The whispered murmurings of my
       adversaries,
    against me all day long;
63 Look! Whether they sit or stand,
    I am the butt of their taunt.

64 Give them what they deserve, LORD,
    according to their deeds;
65 Give them hardness of heart;
    your curse be upon them;*
66 Pursue them in wrath and destroy
       them
    from under the LORD's heaven!

## Miseries of the Besieged City†

**4** ¹ How the gold has lost its luster,
    the noble metal changed;
Jewels† lie scattered
    at the corner of every street.

---

3:40–66 The plural voice in this lament suggests that a communal lament begins here; it then continues in the singular voice in vv. 55–66.

3:48–51 These verses are more appropriate on the lips of the poet, who speaks of "my city" (v. 51). *Daughters of my city*: here as elsewhere "daughter" may refer to villages dependent on a larger city.

4:1–22 This chapter returns to the focus of chaps. 1 and 2, namely the horrors of a siege. Unlike chaps. 1 and 2, however, the character of personified Zion never interrupts the voice of the poet to protest her abject state. As a result, the emotion of the poem is less intense, while at the same time seeming more grim on account of its lack of petition to the Lord.

4:1–2 *Jewels*: lit., "holy stones." These precious things designate the children who are abandoned, starving, and killed in the siege of Jerusalem (cf. Zec 9:16). Another explanation is that these are the stones of the destroyed Temple.

3:38 Is 45:7.
3:40 Jl 2:12–13.
3:43 Lam 2:21.
3:45 1 Cor 4:13.
3:47 Is 24:17–18; Jer
  48:43–44.
3:48 Lam 1:16; 2:11;

Jer 8:23; 9:17.
3:54 Ps 69:2–3; 88:8; Jon
  2:4.
3:55–56 Ps 130:1–2.
3:58–59 Ps 35:23–24; 43:1;
  119:154.
3:65 Jer 11:20; 2 Tm 4:14.

2 And Zion's precious children,
    worth their weight in gold—
How they are treated like clay jugs,
    the work of any potter! *

3 Even jackals offer their breasts
    to nurse their young;
But the daughter of my people is as
      cruel
    as the ostrich † in the wilderness. *

4 The tongue of the infant cleaves
    to the roof of its mouth in thirst;
Children beg for bread,
    but no one gives them a piece.

5 Those who feasted on delicacies
    are abandoned in the streets;
Those who reclined on crimson †
    now embrace dung heaps. *

6 The punishment of the daughter of my
      people
    surpassed the penalty of Sodom,
Which was overthrown in an instant
    with no hand laid on it. *

7 Her princes were brighter than snow,
    whiter than milk,
Their bodies more ruddy than coral,
    their beauty like the sapphire.

8 Now their appearance is blacker than
      soot,
    they go unrecognized in the streets;
Their skin has shrunk on their bones,
    and become dry as wood. *

9 Better for those pierced by the sword
    than for those pierced by hunger,
Better for those who bleed from
      wounds
    than for those who lack food.

10 The hands of compassionate women
    have boiled their own children!

    They became their food
    when the daughter of my people was
      shattered. *

11 The LORD has exhausted his anger,
    poured out his blazing wrath;
He has kindled a fire in Zion
    that has consumed her
      foundations. *

12 The kings of the earth did not believe,
    nor any of the world's inhabitants,
That foe or enemy could enter
    the gates of Jerusalem.

13 Except for the sins of her prophets
    and the crimes of her priests,
Who poured out in her midst
    the blood of the just. *

14 They staggered blindly in the streets,
    defiled with blood,
So that people could not touch
    even their garments: *

15 "Go away! Unclean!" they cried to
      them,
    "Away, away, do not touch!"
If they went away and wandered,
    it would be said among the nations,
    "They can no longer live here!"

16 The presence of the LORD was their
      portion,
    but he no longer looks upon them.
The priests are shown no regard,
    the elders, no mercy.

17 Even now our eyes are worn out,
    searching in vain for help;
From our watchtower we have
      watched
    for a nation † unable to save.

18 They dogged our every step,
    we could not walk in our squares;

---

**4:3** *Cruel as the ostrich*: see note on Jb 39:14–16. Jerusalem, in her distress, has abandoned her children.

**4:5** *Crimson*: a sign of luxury. Tyrian purple, a red-purple or blue-purple dye produced from shellfish, was very expensive and the only colorfast dye in the ancient Near East. Thus purple or crimson cloth was available only to the wealthy.

**4:17** *A nation*: probably Egypt, which failed to give effective aid against Babylon.

**4:2** Jer 19:11.
**4:3** Jb 39:16.
**4:5** Dt 28:56.
**4:6** Gn 19:23–29; 2 Pt 2:6; Jude 7.
**4:8** Lam 3:4.
**4:10** Lam 2:20; Dt 28:56–57; 2 Kgs 6:29.
**4:11** Jer 7:20; Ez 5:13.
**4:13** Jer 6:13.
**4:14** Dt 28:29; Is 59:10.

Our end drew near, our time was up;
   yes, our end had come.

19 Our pursuers were swifter
   than eagles in the sky,
In the mountains they were hot on
   our trail,
   they ambushed us in the
     wilderness.*

20 The LORD's anointed—our very
   lifebreath!—†
   was caught in their snares,
He in whose shade we thought
   to live among the nations.*

21 Rejoice and gloat, daughter Edom,
   dwelling in the land of Uz,†
The cup will pass to you as well;
   you shall become drunk and strip
     yourself naked!*

22 Your punishment is completed,
   daughter Zion,
   the Lord will not prolong your
     exile;
The Lord will punish your iniquity,
   daughter Edom,
   will lay bare your sins.*

### The Community's Lament to the Lord

**5** ¹ Remember, LORD, what has happened
   to us,
   pay attention, and see our disgrace:
2 Our heritage is turned over to
   strangers,
   our homes, to foreigners.*
3 We have become orphans, without
   fathers;
   our mothers are like widows.
4 We pay money to drink our own water,

5   our own wood comes at a price.
With a yoke on our necks, we are
   driven;
   we are worn out, but allowed no
     rest.

6 We extended a hand to Egypt and
   Assyria,
   to satisfy our need of bread.†

7 Our ancestors, who sinned, are no
   more;
   but now we bear their guilt.

8 Servants† rule over us,
   with no one to tear us from their
     hands.

9 We risk our lives just to get bread,
   exposed to the desert heat;*

10 Our skin heats up like an oven,
   from the searing blasts of famine.*

11 Women are raped in Zion,
   young women in the cities of
     Judah;*

12 Princes have been hanged by them,
   elders shown no respect.*

13 Young men carry millstones,
   boys stagger under loads of wood;

14 The elders have abandoned the gate,†
   the young men their music.

15 The joy of our hearts has ceased,
   dancing has turned into mourning;*

16 The crown has fallen from our head:
   woe to us that we sinned!

17 Because of this our hearts grow sick,
   at this our eyes grow dim:

18 Because of Mount Zion, lying desolate,
   and the jackals roaming there!

19 But you, LORD, are enthroned forever;
   your throne stands from age to age.*

---

† **4:20** *Our very lifebreath*: lit., "the breath of our nostrils," that is, the king. This expression occurs in Egyptian texts of the late second millennium B.C., and may have survived as a royal epithet in the Jerusalem court. After the disaster of 598 B.C. (2 Kgs 24:1–17), Jerusalem could have hoped to live in peace amidst her neighbors; but they (vv. 21–22) as well as Babylon turned against her to ensure her total devastation in 587 B.C.

**4:21** *Rejoice*: the address is sarcastic, since Edom (where Uz may have been located) ravaged the land after the fall of Jerusalem (cf. Ps 137).

**5:6** *Extended a hand*: that is, made an alliance. In its state of abjection, Judah was forced to depend on the major powers to the west and the east for subsistence.

**5:8** *Servants*: the Hebrew word for "servant" is also the word

used for an official of relatively high status (servant of the ruler; cf. 2 Kgs 25:24, where the term is used to refer to Babylonian rulers over occupied Jerusalem); the author doubtless intends the double meaning here.

**5:14** *The gate*: a place of assembly, where city decisions were made and judgment given by the elders and other community leaders; see note on Ru 4:1.

| | |
|---|---|
| **4:19** Jer 4:13; Hb 1:8. | **5:11** Zec 14:2. |
| **4:20** Lam 2:9; Ez 19:4, 8. | **5:12** Lam 4:16. |
| **4:21** Lam 1:21; Jer 25:15. | **5:15** Jer 16:9; 25:10; Am |
| **4:22** Is 40:2. |    8:10. |
| **5:2** Ps 79:1. | **5:19** Ps 9:8; 45:7; 102:13, |
| **5:9** Lam 1:11. |    27. |
| **5:10** Lam 4:8. | |

20 † Why have you utterly forgotten us,
　　forsaken us for so long? *
21 Bring us back to you, LORD, that we may
　　return:

22 renew our days as of old. *
　　For now you have indeed rejected us
　　and utterly turned your wrath
　　against us. *

---

† **5:20–22** Unlike most of the laments found in the Book of Psalms, the Book of Lamentations never moves from lament to thanksgiving. It ends with this question still unanswered by God: "Why have you utterly forgotten us?"

* **5:20** Ps 13:2; 42:10; Is 49:14.　　**5:21** Ps 80:19–20.
**5:22** Jer 14:19.

# The Book of
# Baruch

## INTRODUCTION

### Michael D. Guinan, OFM

The book of Baruch is a compilation of four separate compositions: (1) a prose confession of guilt and prayer for deliverance (Bar 1:15–3:8), (2) a poetic praise of wisdom (3:9–4:4), (3) a poetic lamentation and consolation (4:5–5:9), and (4) a prose letter of Jeremiah (6:1–72). A short narrative introduction (1:1–14) sets the scene. For a variety of reasons (e.g., dependence on earlier biblical texts), the book is often dated to the second century BCE.

The book survives only in Greek; other ancient translations (e.g., Latin, Syriac) are based on it. Many scholars, however, see evidence that each section was originally composed in Hebrew. The book appears in neither the Jewish nor the Protestant canon (where it is considered part of the Apocrypha and therefore noncanonical); it is accepted in the Roman Catholic community as well as in Eastern Christianity.

Baruch, a scribe in Jerusalem just before its destruction by Babylon in 587 BCE, appears only in the book of Jeremiah. He performs scribal duties for Jeremiah (Jer 32:12–16; 36:1–32) and suffers with him (Jer 36:19; 43:3). Assured by God that he will survive Jerusalem's destruction (Jer 45:1–5), Baruch, along with Jeremiah, is taken down into Egypt (Jer 43:5–7) and nothing more is heard of him. Later Jewish tradition will attribute to him several additional works: *2* and *3 Baruch* (visionary apocalypses), and *4 Baruch* (also called *Paraleipomena Jeremiou* [Things Left Out of Jeremiah]).

## Outline of Baruch

I. **Letter to Jerusalem (1:1–3:8)**

  A. **Historical Setting (1:1–9)**

  B. **Confession of Guilt (1:10–2:10)**

  C. **Prayer for Deliverance (2:11–3:8)**

II. **Praise of Wisdom (3:9–4:4)**

  A. **Importance of Wisdom (3:9–23)**

  B. **Inaccessibility of Wisdom (3:24–36)**

  C. **Wisdom Contained in the Law (3:37–4:4)**

III. **Baruch's Poem of Consolation (4:5–5:9)**

  A. **Baruch Addresses Diaspora (4:5–9a)**

  B. **Jerusalem Addresses Neighbors (4:9b–16)**

  C. **Jerusalem Addresses Diaspora (4:17–29)**

  D. **Baruch Addresses Jerusalem (4:30–5:9)**

IV. **Letter of Jeremiah (6:1–72)**

## Narrative Introduction (Bar 1:1–14)

According to Jer 43:6, Baruch is placed among the exiles in Babylon, where he writes this scroll and reads it out before them. While some historical inaccuracies appear, this preface serves to place the following compositions in the context of the exiles' recognition of their own sinfulness and their prayers for God's mercy.

## Confession of Guilt and Prayer for Deliverance (Bar 1:15–3:8)

The exiles begin (Bar 1:15–2:10), speaking in the first person of their sinfulness and in the third person of God who is just (1:15; 2:6).

They are punished because they did not listen to the voice of the Lord (i.e., were disobedient; 1:17–18) and did not heed the Lord's warnings (2:1). In the second part of the prayer (2:11–26), the Lord is addressed in the second person and asked to show mercy. In the context of this prayer, two oracles of the Lord appear (2:21–23, 29–35), the first expressing a threat and the second, a hope beyond the present punishment. The conclusion (3:1–8) furthers this prayer for mercy and forgiveness. This composition speaks mostly of and to "the Lord" (i.e., Yahweh), and echoes the language and theology of Deuteronomy, Jeremiah, and Daniel 9.

## Praise of Wisdom (Bar 3:9–4:4)

This poem begins with an introduction (Bar 3:9–14): Why is Israel suffering in exile? It is because they have forsaken the "fountain of wisdom" (3:12). But just where is wisdom to be found? The body of the poem (3:15–4:1) addresses this question, first negatively (3:16–31): wisdom is not to be found in the ancient generations and lands with a reputation for wisdom; and then positively (3:32–4:1): wisdom can be found with God who created the universe and has given wisdom to Israel. Wisdom has appeared on earth and is the book of the Torah (i.e., the Pentateuch, 3:38). (There is an ambiguity in the Greek here; the subject is not expressed, and so might be either feminine, i.e., Wisdom, or masculine. Early Christian writers assumed a masculine subject and saw here a reference to the Incarnation of Jesus as the Wisdom of God, i.e., "He has appeared on earth"). The conclusion (4:2–4) urges Israel to turn (repent) and live in the light of wisdom. This poem speaks of "God" and echoes the language of Deuteronomy, Proverbs, and Job (e.g., Jb 28).

## Poetic Lamentation and Consolation (Bar 4:5–5:9)

This poetic "scene" has two speakers: Baruch (not named but implied) and Jerusalem. Baruch first addresses the exiles (Bar 4:5–9) who have grieved Jerusalem, their "mother" city. Jerusalem then speaks (4:12–29). She is bereft of her children because they turned from God's law (4:12–13); she calls them to turn back to him (4:28), and God will bring them lasting joy (4:29). Baruch concludes by consoling Jerusalem with a vision of joyful hope (4:30–5:9). This composition speaks often of "the Eternal One," and echoes the language of Is 40–66, and Lamentations.

## Letter of Jeremiah (Bar 6:1–72)

In many ancient manuscripts, this letter stands apart with a heading of its own, but in the Latin Vulgate it is attached to Baruch as ch. 6. It purports to be a letter from Jeremiah to the exiles in Babylon (see Jer 29) but is really a sermon attacking the folly of idolatry. The God of Israel is all powerful; the gods of the nations are nothing; so "better the just [one] who has no idols" (Bar 6:72). It echoes other biblical polemics against idols (e.g., Ps 135:15–18; Is 40:18–20; 44:9–20; 46:1–7; Jer 10:1–11). ∎

# THE BOOK OF BARUCH

## New American Bible, Introduction

The opening verses ascribe the book to the well-known assistant to Jeremiah (Jer 32:12; 36:4, 32; 45:1). It is a collection of four very different compositions, ending with a work entitled "The Letter of Jeremiah," which circulated separately in major manuscripts of the Greek tradition. The original language may have been Hebrew, but only the Greek and other versions have been preserved. The fictional setting is Babylon, where Baruch reads his scroll to King Jechoniah (Jehoiachin) and the exiles; they react by sending gifts and the scroll to Jerusalem (1:1–14), presumably by the hand of Baruch (1:7). No certain date can be given for the book, but it may have been edited in final form during the last two centuries B.C. The work attempts to explain the trauma of the exile in terms of a Deuteronomic cycle: sin (of Israel), punishment, repentance, and return (cf. Jgs 2; also Dt 28–33).

The prayer of the exiles (2:11–3:8) is a confession of sin and a request for mercy, and has remarkable similarities to Dn 9 and to parts of Jeremiah. The poem on personified Wisdom is concerned with three themes: the importance of Wisdom, the elusive character of Wisdom (cf. Jb 28), and the identification of Wisdom with Torah (cf. Sir 24:23). Baruch's Poem of Consolation resembles parts of Is 40–66, and

it offers encouragement to the exiles in view of their eventual return; there are two addresses by personified Zion. The Letter of Jeremiah, unlike the letter in Jer 29, is a polemic against idolatry, a well-known theme (cf. Jer 10:2–11; Ps 115:4–8; 135:15–18; Is 44:9–20; Wis 13:10–15:17). It contains ten warnings that end in a kind of refrain that the idols are not gods and are not to be feared (vv. 14, 22, 28, 39, 44, 51, 56, 64, 68).

The book can be divided thus:

# BARUCH

## I. LETTER TO JERUSALEM

### A. Historical Setting

**1** ¹ Now these are the words of the scroll which Baruch, son of Neriah, son of Mahseiah, son of Zedekiah, son of Hasadiah, son of Hilkiah, wrote in Babylon,* ² in the fifth year, on the seventh day of the month,† at the time the Chaldeans took Jerusalem and destroyed it with fire.* ³ * Baruch read the words of this scroll in the hearing of Jeconiah, son of Jehoiakim, king of Judah, and all the people who came to the reading:* ⁴ the nobles, kings' sons, elders, and all the people, small and great—all who lived in Babylon by the river Sud.†

⁵ They wept, fasted, and prayed before the Lord, ⁶ and collected such funds as each could afford.* ⁷ These they sent to Jerusalem, to Jehoiakim the priest, son of Hilkiah, son of Shallum, and to the priests and the whole people who were with him in Jerusalem. ⁸ (At the same time he† received the vessels of the house of the LORD that had been removed from the temple, to restore them to the land of Judah, on the tenth of Sivan. These silver vessels Zedekiah, son of Josiah, king of Judah, had had made ⁹ * after Nebuchadnezzar, king of Babylon, carried off as captives Jeconiah and the princes, the skilled workers, the nobles, and the people of the land from Jerusalem, and brought them to Babylon.)

### B. Confession of Guilt

¹⁰ The message was: "We send you funds, with which you are to procure burnt offerings, sin offerings, and frankincense, and to prepare grain offerings; offer these† on the altar of the LORD our God,* ¹¹ and pray for the life of Nebuchadnezzar, king of Babylon, and of Belshazzar, his son,† that their lifetimes may be as the days of the heavens above the earth.* ¹² Pray that the LORD may give us strength, and light to our eyes, that we may live under the protective shadow of Nebuchadnezzar, king of Babylon, and of Belshazzar, his son, to serve them many days, and find favor in their sight. ¹³ Pray for us to the LORD, our God, for we have sinned against the LORD, our God. Even to this day the wrath of the LORD and his anger have not turned away from us. ¹⁴ On the feast day and during the days of assembly, read aloud in the house of the LORD this scroll that we send you:*

¹⁵ † "To the Lord our God belongs justice; to us, people of Judah and inhabitants of Jerusalem, to be shamefaced, as on this day—* ¹⁶ to us, our kings, rulers, priests, and prophets, and our ancestors. ¹⁷ We have sinned in the LORD's sight ¹⁸ and disobeyed him. We have not listened to the voice of the LORD, our God, so as to follow the precepts the LORD set before us. ¹⁹ From the day the LORD led our ancestors out of the land of Egypt until the present day, we have been disobedient to the LORD, our God, and neglected to listen to his voice. ²⁰ Even today evils cling to us, the curse the LORD pronounced to Moses, his servant, at the time he led our ancestors out of the land of Egypt to give us a land flowing with milk and honey.*

---

**1:2** *In the fifth year, on the seventh day of the month*: Jerusalem fell on the seventh day of the fifth month in 587 B.C.; cf. 2 Kgs 25:8; Jer 52:12. Either the text read originally "the fifth month," or it refers to the observance of an anniversary of the fall of Jerusalem.

**1:4** *The river Sud*: probably one of the Babylonian canals, not otherwise identified; or possibly a misreading of Ahava; cf. Ezr 8:21, 31.

**1:8–9** *He*: apparently Baruch; less likely Jehoiakim the priest (v. 7). The silver vessels here described are distinct from the vessels referred to in 2 Kgs 25:14 and Ezr 1:7–9. The author of this note may have thought of the fifth year (v. 1) of Zedekiah, in view of Jer 28:1; 29:1–3. A "fifth year," again with no month mentioned, is given in Ez 1:2 for the inaugural vision of Ezekiel's prophetic career.

**1:10** *Offer these*: since 2:26 suggests that the Temple is destroyed, the mention of sacrifices here may be an anachronism. Nevertheless, Jer 41:5 indicates that some people continued to worship at the Temple site after Nebuchadnezzar's destruction of the Temple.

**1:11** *Nebuchadnezzar...Belshazzar, his son*: Belshazzar was the son of Nabonidus, the last king of Babylon, not of Nebuchadnezzar, the destroyer of Jerusalem. Belshazzar was co-regent for a few years while his father was away in Arabia. Later Jewish tradition seems to have simplified the end of the Babylonian empire (cf. Dn 5:1–2), for three kings came between Nebuchadnezzar and Nabonidus.

**1:15–2:10** This confession of sin is similar to Dn 9:7–14, and echoes ideas from Deuteronomy and Jeremiah; cf. also Neh 9.

---

**1:1** Jer 32:12; 36:4; 45:1–5.
**1:2** 2 Kgs 25:8–10.
**1:3–4** 2 Kgs 23:1–2.
**1:3** 2 Kgs 24:8–17; Jer 22:24–30; 27:20; 51:59–64.
**1:6** Dt 16:17.
**1:9** Jer 24:1.
**1:10** Jer 17:26; 41:5.
**1:11** Dt 11:21; Ps 89:30; Jer 29:7; Dn 5:1–2; 1 Tm 2:1–2.
**1:14** Ex 23:14–17; Lv 23:35–36; Sir 50:6; Hos 9:5.
**1:15** Bar 2:6; 3:8; Ezr 9:6–15; Neh 9:6–37; Dn 9:4–19.
**1:20** Lv 26:14–39; Dt 28:15–68.

21 For we did not listen to the voice of the LORD, our God, in all the words of the prophets he sent us, 22 but each of us has followed the inclinations of our wicked hearts, served other gods, and done evil in the sight of the LORD, our God.

2 1 "So the LORD carried out the warning he had uttered against us: against our judges, who governed Israel, against our kings and princes, and against the people of Israel and Judah. 2 Nowhere under heaven has anything been done like what he did in Jerusalem, as was written in the law of Moses:†* 3 that we would each eat† the flesh of our sons, each the flesh of our daughters. 4 He has made us subject to all the kingdoms around us, an object of reproach and horror among all the peoples around us, where the LORD has scattered us.* 5 We are brought low, not raised high,* because we sinned against the LORD, our God, not listening to his voice.

6 "To the LORD, our God, belongs justice; to us and to our ancestors, to be shamefaced, as on this day.* 7 All the evils of which the LORD had warned us have come upon us. 8 We did not entreat the favor of the LORD by turning, each one, from the designs of our evil hearts. 9 The LORD kept watch over the evils, and brought them home to us; for the LORD is just in all the works he commanded us to do,* 10 but we did not listen to his voice, or follow the precepts of the LORD which he had set before us.

### C. Prayer for Deliverance

11† "And now, LORD, God of Israel, who led your people out of the land of Egypt with a strong hand, with signs and wonders and great might, and with an upraised arm, so that you have made for yourself a name to the present day:* 12 we have sinned, we have committed sacrilege, we have violated all your statutes, LORD, our God.* 13 Withdraw your anger from us, for we are left few in number among the nations where you have scattered us. 14 Hear, LORD, our prayer of supplication, and deliver us for your own sake: grant us favor in the sight of those who brought us into exile, 15 that the whole earth may know that you are the LORD, our God, and that Israel† and his descendants bear your name.* 16 LORD, look down from your holy dwelling and take thought of us; LORD, incline your ear to hear us.* 17 Open your eyes and see: it is not the dead in Hades,† whose breath has been taken from within them, who will declare the glory and vindication to the LORD.* 18 The person who is deeply grieved, who walks bowed and feeble, with failing eyes and famished soul, will declare your glory and justice, LORD!*

19 "Not on the just deeds of our ancestors and our kings do we base our plea for mercy in your sight, LORD, our God. 20 You have sent your wrath and anger upon us, as you had warned us through your servants the prophets: 21 Thus says the LORD: Bend your necks and serve the king of Babylon, that you may continue in the land I gave your ancestors;* 22† for if you do not listen to the LORD's voice so as to serve the king of Babylon, 23 I will silence from the cities of Judah and from the streets of Jerusalem the cry of joy and the cry of gladness, the voice of the bridegroom and the voice of the bride; and all the land shall be deserted, without inhabitants.* 24 But we did not listen to your voice, or serve the king of Babylon, and you carried out the threats you had made through your servants the prophets, that the bones of our kings and the bones of our ancestors would be brought out from their burial places.* 25 And indeed, they lie exposed† to the heat of day and the frost of night. They died in great suffering, by famine and sword and plague.* 26 And you reduced the house which bears your name† to what it is today,

---

† 2:2 Law of Moses: cf. Dt 28:53–57.

2:3 We would each eat: such dreadful events were the result of the prolonged siege of Jerusalem; cf. Lam 2:20.

2:11–35 An earnest appeal for divine mercy, along with confession of sin; cf. Dn 9:15–19.

2:15 Israel: the Israelites claimed descent from the patriarch Jacob, who had received the name Israel in a mysterious encounter with God (Gn 32:29). Thus the Deity was sometimes referred to as "the God of Israel" (Gn 33:20; Ex 5:1).

2:17 Hades: this is the Greek translation of Hebrew sheol, the nether world.

2:22–24 These words are very similar to Jer 7:34; 27:9, 12.

2:25 They lie exposed: Jeremiah's words threatened Jehoiakim with being left unburied (Jer 22:19; 36:30).

2:26 The house which bears your name: the Temple of Jerusalem; cf. Dt 12:11; Jer 7:11. What is today: during the exile it lay in ruins.

| | |
|---|---|
| 2:2–3 Dt 28:52–57; 2 Kgs 6:28–29; Jer 19:9; Lam 2:20; 4:10; Ez 5:10; Dn 9:12. | 2:12 Ps 106:6. |
| | 2:15 Gn 33:20; Sir 36:11; Jer 14:9; 35:17. |
| 2:4 Jer 29:18; Dn 9:16. | 2:16 Dt 26:15. |
| 2:5 Dt 28:13, 43–44. | 2:17 Ps 6:6; Is 38:18. |
| 2:6 Bar 1:15; Dn 9:7. | 2:18 Zep 2:3. |
| 2:9 Jer 1:12; 31:28; 44:27; Dn 9:14. | 2:21 Jer 27:12. |
| | 2:23 Jer 7:34. |
| 2:11 Dt 6:21–22. | 2:24 Jer 8:1–2. |
| | 2:25 Jer 7:34; 14:12; 31:30. |

because of the wickedness of the house of Israel and the house of Judah.*

**God's Promises Recalled.** 27 "But with us, Lord, our God, you have dealt in all your clemency and in all your great mercy. 28† Thus you spoke through your servant Moses, the day you ordered him to write down your law in the presence of the Israelites: 29 'If you do not listen to my voice, surely this great and numerous throng will dwindle away among the nations to which I will scatter them.* 30 For I know they will not listen to me, because they are a stiff-necked people. But in the land of their exile they shall have a change of heart;* 31 they shall know that I, the Lord, am their God. I will give them a heart and ears that listen;* 32 and they shall praise me in the land of their exile, and shall remember my name.* 33 Then they shall turn back from their stiff-necked stubbornness, and from their evil deeds, because they shall remember the ways of their ancestors, who sinned against the Lord.* 34 And I will bring them back to the land I promised on oath to their ancestors, to Abraham, Isaac, and Jacob; and they shall rule it. I will make them increase; they shall not be few. 35 And I will establish for them an eternal covenant: I will be their God, and they shall be my people; and I will never again remove my people Israel from the land I gave them.'*

3 1 "Lord Almighty, God of Israel, the anguished soul, the dismayed spirit cries out to you. 2 Hear, Lord, and have mercy, for you are a merciful God; have mercy on us, who have sinned against you: 3 for you are enthroned forever, while we are perishing forever.* 4 Lord Almighty, God of Israel, hear the prayer of the dead of Israel, children who sinned against you; they did not listen to the voice of the Lord, their God, and their evils cling to us.* 5 Do not remember the wicked deeds of our ancestors, but remember at this time your power and your name, 6 for you are the Lord our God; and you, Lord, we will

praise! 7 This is why you put into our hearts the fear of you: that we may call upon your name, and praise you in our exile, when we have removed from our hearts all the wickedness of our ancestors who sinned against you.* 8 See, today we are in exile, where you have scattered us, an object of reproach and cursing and punishment for all the wicked deeds of our ancestors, who withdrew from the Lord, our God."

## II. PRAISE OF WISDOM†

### A. Importance of Wisdom

9  Hear, Israel, the commandments of life:
     listen, and know prudence!*
10  How is it, Israel,
     that you are in the land of your foes,
     grown old in a foreign land,
11  Defiled with the dead,
     counted among those destined for
       Hades?*
12  You have forsaken the fountain of
       wisdom!*
13  Had you walked in the way of God,
     you would have dwelt in enduring
       peace.*

14  Learn where prudence is,
     where strength, where understanding;
  That you may know also
     where are length of days, and life,
     where light of the eyes, and peace.*
15  Who has found the place of wisdom?*
     Who has entered into her treasuries?
16  Where are the rulers of the nations,
     who lorded it over the wild beasts of
       the earth,*
17  made sport of the birds in the
       heavens,
  Who heaped up the silver,
     the gold in which people trust,
     whose possessions were unlimited,
18  Who schemed anxiously for money,
     their doings beyond discovery?
19  They have vanished, gone down to
       Hades,

† **2:28–35** These words do not actually quote anything Moses is recorded as having said, but they present the substance of a passage such as Dt 30:1–10, which envisions exile, repentance, and restoration.
**3:9–4:4** This poem in praise of personified Wisdom utilizes the theme of Jb 28 (where is wisdom to be found?) and it identifies wisdom and law, as in Sir 24:22–23.

**2:26** Jer 7:10–15; 11:17.    **2:29** Lv 26:39.

**2:30** Dt 30:1–2; 31:27.    **3:7** Jer 31:33.
**2:31** Ps 40:7; Jer 24:7; Ez 36:26.    **3:9** Dt 6:4–5; Prv 4:20–22.
**2:32** Tb 13:6.    **3:11** Ps 88:5.
**2:33–35** Lv 26:42–45; Dt 30:1–10.    **3:12** Jer 2:13; Jn 4:10; 14.
**2:35** Jer 31:31; Lam 4:22.    **3:13** Is 48:18.
**3:3** Ps 29:10; 102:12–13.    **3:14** Prv 3:2; 8:14.
**3:4** Jer 31:29.    **3:15–37** Jb 28:1–28.
      **3:16** Jer 27:6; 1 Cor 1:20.

and others have risen up in their
    stead.

20 Later generations have seen the light of
    day,
    have dwelt on the earth,
    But the way to understanding they have
        not known,

21     they have not perceived her paths or
        reached her;
    their children remain far from the way
        to her.

22 She has not been heard of in Canaan,†
    nor seen in Teman.*

23 The descendants of Hagar who seek
        knowledge on earth,
    the merchants of Medan and Tema,*
    the storytellers and those seeking
        knowledge—
  These have not known the way to
        wisdom,
    nor have they kept her paths in mind.

### B. Inaccessibility of Wisdom

24 O Israel, how vast is the dwelling of
    God,†
    how broad the scope of his dominion:

25 Vast and endless,
    high and immeasurable!

26 In it were born the giants,†
    renowned at the first,
    huge in stature, skilled in war.*

27 These God did not choose,
    nor did he give them the way of
        understanding;*

28 They perished for lack of prudence,
    perished through their own folly.*

29 Who has gone up to the heavens and
        taken her,
    bringing her down from the clouds?*

30 Who has crossed the sea and found her,
    bearing her away rather than choice
        gold?

31 None knows the way to her,

---

    nor has at heart her path.

32 But the one who knows all things knows
        her;
    he has probed her by his knowledge—
  The one who established the earth for
        all time,
    and filled it with four-footed animals,

33 Who sends out the lightning, and it
        goes,
    calls it, and trembling it obeys him;

34 Before whom the stars at their posts
    shine and rejoice.

35 When he calls them, they answer, "Here
        we are!"
    shining with joy for their Maker.*

36 Such is our God;
    no other is to be compared to him:

### C. Wisdom Contained in the Law

37† He has uncovered the whole way of
        understanding,
    and has given her to Jacob, his
        servant,
    to Israel, his beloved.*

38 Thus she has appeared on earth,
    is at home with mortals.*

4 1† She is the book of the precepts of God,
    the law that endures forever;
  All who cling to her will live,
    but those will die who forsake her.*

2 Turn, O Jacob, and receive her:
    walk by her light toward splendor.*

3 Do not give your glory to another,
    your privileges to an alien nation.

4 Blessed are we, O Israel;
    for what pleases God is known to us!*

### III. BARUCH'S POEM OF CONSOLATION†

### A. Baruch Addresses Diaspora

5 Take courage, my people!
    Remember, O Israel,

---

**3:22–23** Despite the renown for wisdom of the peoples of
Canaan and Phoenicia (Ez 28:3–4), of Teman (Jer 49:7), of the
descendants of Hagar or the Arabians of Medan and Tema, they
did not possess true wisdom, which is found only in the law of
God (Bar 4:1).
  **3:24** *The dwelling of God*: here, the whole universe; cf. Is 66:1.
  **3:26** *The giants*: Gn 6:1–4 reflects a tradition about giants
who existed before the flood; this was developed in the noncanonical Book of Enoch.
  **3:37–38** As in Sir 24:8, Wisdom is given to Israel but also is
said to live with all human beings (Prv 8:31).
  **4:1–4** The poem ends with the identification of Wisdom and

Torah, as in Sir 24:22–23; cf. also Dt 4:5–8.
  **4:5–5:9** The poet addresses the exiles (vv. 5–9a), and then

---

**3:22** Jb 2:11; Jer 49:7; Ez
  28:4–5; Zec 9:2.
**3:23** Gn 25:2, 15; Jb 6:19;
  Jer 25:23.
**3:26** Gn 6:4; Wis 14:6; Sir
  16:7.
**3:27** 1 Sm 16:7–10.
**3:28** Sir 10:8.
**3:29** Dt 30:12–13; Sir 24:4;
  Rom 10:6–7.

**3:35** Jb 38:7; Ps 147:4; Is
  40:26.
**3:37** Ps 147:19; Sir
  24:8–12.
**3:38** Wis 9:18; Jn 1:14.
**4:1** Dt 4:6–8; Prv
  8:35–36; Sir 24:22.
**4:2** Prv 4:13, 19.
**4:4** Dt 4:32–37; 33:29.

6 You were sold to the nations
  not for destruction;
It was because you angered God
  that you were handed over to your
    foes.*

7 For you provoked your Maker*
  with sacrifices to demons and not to
    God;

8 You forgot the eternal God who
  nourished you,
and you grieved Jerusalem who
  nurtured you.

9 She indeed saw coming upon you
  the wrath of God; and she said:

## B. Jerusalem Addresses Neighbors

"Hear, you neighbors of Zion!
  God has brought great mourning
    upon me,

10 For I have seen the captivity
  that the Eternal One has brought
  upon my sons and daughters.

11 With joy I nurtured them;
  but with mourning and lament I sent
    them away.

12 Let no one gloat over me,
  a widow, bereft of many;
For the sins of my children I am left
  desolate,
  because they turned from the law of
    God,*

13 and did not acknowledge his statutes;
In the ways of God's commandments
  they did not walk,
  nor did they tread the disciplined
    paths of his justice.

14 "Let Zion's neighbors come—
  Remember the captivity of my sons
    and daughters,
  brought upon them by the Eternal
    One.

15 He has brought against them a nation
    from afar,
  a nation ruthless and of alien speech,
That has neither reverence for old age
  nor pity for the child;*

16 They have led away this widow's beloved
    sons,
  have left me solitary, without
    daughters.

## C. Jerusalem Addresses Diaspora

17 What can I do to help you?

18 The one who has brought this evil
    upon you
  must himself deliver you from your
    enemies' hands.*

19 Farewell, my children, farewell;
  I am left desolate.

20 I have taken off the garment of peace,
  have put on sackcloth for my prayer of
    supplication;
  while I live I will cry out to the Eternal
    One.*

21 "Take courage, my children; call upon
    God;
  he will deliver you from oppression,
    from enemy hands.*

22 I have put my hope for your deliverance
    in the Eternal One,
  and joy has come to me from the
    Holy One
Because of the mercy that will swiftly
    reach you
  from your eternal Savior.

23 With mourning and lament I sent you
    away,
  but God will give you back to me
    with gladness and joy forever.*

24 As Zion's neighbors lately saw you taken
    captive,
  so shall they soon see God's salvation
    come to you,
  with great glory and the splendor of
    the Eternal One.*

25 "My children, bear patiently the wrath*
  that has come upon you from God;
Your enemies have persecuted you,
  but you will soon see their
    destruction
  and trample upon their necks.†

---

† Zion personified is introduced, speaking to the nations and mourning the loss of her children (vv. 9b–16). She then addresses the exiles (vv. 17–29). Finally (4:30–5:9) the poet issues three calls to Jerusalem (4:30, 36; 5:5): she will see her children returning (4:22, 36–37; 5:5).

4:25 *Trample upon their necks*: a sign of victory over the enemy (cf. Ps 44:6; Is 14:25). The Israelites considered their enemies to be God's enemies as well.

4:6 Jgs 2:14; Is 50:1; 52:3.
4:7–8 Dt 32:13–18; 1 Cor 10:20.
4:12 Lam 1:1, 2, 7.
4:15 Dt 28:49–50; Jer 5:15; 6:22–23.
4:18 Jer 32:42.
4:20 Jdt 9:1; Est 4:16.
4:21 Jer 51:5.
4:23 Jer 31:12–13.
4:24 Is 60:1–7.
4:25 Is 51:23.

**BAR**

<sup>26</sup> My pampered children have trodden
    rough roads,
    carried off by their enemies like sheep
    in a raid. *
<sup>27</sup> Take courage, my children; call out to
    God!
    The one who brought this upon you
    will remember you. *
<sup>28</sup> As your hearts have been disposed to
    stray from God,
    so turn now ten times the more to
    seek him;
<sup>29</sup> For the one who has brought disaster
    upon you
    will, in saving you, bring you eternal
    joy." *

### D. Baruch Addresses Jerusalem

<sup>30</sup> Take courage, Jerusalem!
    The one who gave you your name will
    console you. *
<sup>31</sup> Wretched shall be those who harmed
    you,
    who rejoiced at your downfall;
<sup>32</sup> Wretched shall be the cities where your
    children were enslaved,
    wretched the city that received your
    children. *
<sup>33</sup> As that city rejoiced at your collapse, *
    and made merry at your downfall,
    so shall she grieve over her own
    desolation.
<sup>34</sup> I will take from her the rejoicing crowds,
    and her exultation shall be turned to
    mourning:
<sup>35</sup> For fire shall come upon her *
    from the Eternal One, for many a
    day,
    to be inhabited by demons for a long
    time. †
<sup>36</sup> Look to the east, Jerusalem;
    see the joy that comes to you from
    God! *
<sup>37</sup> Here come your children whom you
    sent away,
    gathered in from east to west
    By the word of the Holy One,
    rejoicing in the glory of God.

**5** <sup>1</sup> Jerusalem, take off your robe of
    mourning and misery;
    put on forever the splendor of glory
    from God: *
<sup>2</sup> Wrapped in the mantle of justice from
    God,
    place on your head the diadem
    of the glory of the Eternal One. *
<sup>3</sup> For God will show your splendor to all
    under the heavens;
<sup>4</sup> you will be named by God forever:
    the peace of justice, the glory of God's
    worship. *

<sup>5</sup> Rise up, Jerusalem! stand upon the
    heights;
    look to the east and see your children
Gathered from east to west
    at the word of the Holy One,
    rejoicing that they are remembered by
    God.
<sup>6</sup> Led away on foot by their enemies they
    left you:
    but God will bring them back to you
    carried high in glory as on royal
    thrones. *
<sup>7</sup> For God has commanded
    that every lofty mountain
    and the age-old hills be made low,
That the valleys be filled to make level
    ground,
    that Israel may advance securely in the
    glory of God. *
<sup>8</sup> The forests and every kind of fragrant
    tree
    have overshadowed Israel at God's
    command; *
<sup>9</sup> For God is leading Israel in joy
    by the light of his glory,
    with the mercy and justice that are
    his.

### IV. LETTER OF JEREMIAH

**6** <sup>1</sup> A copy of the letter which Jeremiah sent
    to those led captive to Babylon by the king
of the Babylonians, to tell them what God had
commanded him: *

---

† **4:35** Deserts and desolate places were looked upon as the habitation of demons; cf. Tb 8:3; Lk 11:24.

---

* **4:26** Lam 2:22.
**4:27** Is 40:1.
**4:29** Is 35:10.
**4:30** Ps 46:5; Is 60:14.

**4:32** Jer 51:43.
**4:33–34** Is 13:20–22; 47:1–11;
Jer 50:13.
**4:35** Is 34:9–14.
**4:36** Is 60:4–5.
**5:1** Is 52:1.
**5:2** Ex 39:30; Wis 18:24;

Is 61:10; 62:3.
**5:4** Is 1:26; 32:17; Jer
33:16.
**5:6** Is 49:22.
**5:7** Is 40:3–4.
**5:8** Is 41:19.
**6:1** Jer 29:1.

For the sins you committed before God, you are being led captive to Babylon by Nebuchadnezzar, king of the Babylonians. ²When you reach Babylon you will be there many years, a long time—seven generations;† after that I will bring you back from there in peace. ³And now in Babylon you will see gods of silver and gold and wood, carried shoulder high, to cast fear upon the nations.* ⁴†Take care that you yourselves do not become like these foreigners and let not such fear possess you. ⁵When you see the crowd before them and behind worshiping them, say in your hearts, "You, Lord, are the one to be worshiped!"* ⁶For my angel† is with you, and he will keep watch on you.*

⁷Their tongues are smoothed by woodworkers; they are covered with gold and silver—but they are frauds, and cannot speak.* ⁸People bring gold, as though for a girl fond of dressing up, ⁹and prepare crowns for the heads of their gods. Then sometimes the priests filch the gold and silver from their gods and spend it on themselves, ¹⁰or give part of it to harlots† in the brothel. They dress them up in clothes like human beings, these gods of silver and gold and wood. ¹¹Though they are wrapped in purple clothing, they are not safe from rust and corrosion. ¹²Their faces are wiped clean of the cloud of dust which is thick upon them. ¹³Each has a scepter, like the human ruler of a district, but none can do away with those that offend against it. ¹⁴Each has in its right hand an ax or dagger, but it cannot save itself from war or pillage. Thus it is known they are not gods; do not fear them.

¹⁵As useless as a broken pot* ¹⁶are their gods, set up in their temples, their eyes full of dust from the feet of those who enter. ¹⁷Their courtyards are walled in like those of someone brought to execution for a crime against the king; the priests reinforce their temples with gates and bars and bolts, so they will not be carried off by robbers. ¹⁸They light more lamps for them than for themselves, yet not one of these can they see. ¹⁹They are like any timber in the temple; their hearts, it is said, are eaten away. Though crawling creatures from the ground consume them and their garments, they do not feel it. ²⁰Their faces become sooty from the smoke in the temple. ²¹Bats and swallows alight on their bodies and heads—any bird, and cats as well. ²²Know, therefore, that they are not gods; do not fear them.

²³Gold adorns them, but unless someone wipes away the corrosion, they do not shine; they felt nothing when they were molded. ²⁴They are bought at whatever price, but there is no spirit in them. ²⁵Since they have no feet, they are carried shoulder high, displaying to all how worthless they are; even those who worship them are put to shame* ²⁶because, if they fall to the ground, the worshipers must pick them up. They neither move of themselves if one sets them upright, nor come upright if they are tipped over; offerings are set out for them as for the dead.* ²⁷†Their priests sell their sacrifices for their own advantage. Likewise their wives cure some of the meat, but they do not share it with the poor and the weak;* ²⁸women ritually unclean or at childbirth handle their sacrifices. From such things, know that they are not gods; do not fear them.

²⁹How can they be called gods? Women set out the offerings for these gods of silver and gold and wood, ³⁰and in their temples the priests squat with torn tunic and with shaven hair and beard, and with their heads uncovered.* ³¹They shout and wail before their gods as others do at a funeral banquet. ³²The priests take some of the clothing from their gods and

---

† 

**6:2** *Seven generations:* this number may be symbolic. If it is not, it may indicate the date of this composition by an author writing for his contemporaries for whom the conditions of the exile were still realities. He has multiplied the seventy years of Jer 29:10 by three or four.
**6:4–72** This whole chapter is a sustained argument against the temptation to worship Babylonian gods. A pattern is repeated throughout the chapter: various reasons are set forth to prove that the idols in the Babylonian temples are not gods (e.g., they are weak, helpless, attended by unworthy ministers); each section is followed by an exhortation not to be deceived, not to worship them. Note the refrain at vv. 14, 22, 28, 39, 44, 51, 56, 64. Israelite religion was aniconic, i.e., it prohibited images; as elsewhere in the Old Testament (e.g., Is 42:17; 44:9–20), the polemic against idols here oversimplifies by identifying the god worshiped with the image that represents it.

**6:6** *My angel:* the prophet assures the people that God's watchful care is with them, just as he was with their ancestors during their journey to the promised land (Ex 23:20).
**6:10** *Harlots:* cult prostitutes, common in some religions of the ancient Near East.
**6:27–31** From the viewpoint of Jewish ritual law, the practices named here were grotesque and depraved; cf. Lv 12:2–8; 15:19–23.

---

*

| | |
|---|---|
| **6:3** Is 46:7; Jer 10:1–16. | **6:25** Wis 13:16. |
| **6:5** Dt 6:13; 10:20; Mt | **6:26** Sir 30:18–19. |
| 4:10; Lk 4:8. | **6:27** Lv 12:4; 15:19–20; Dt |
| **6:6** Ex 23:20. | 14:28–29. |
| **6:7** Ps 135:16. | **6:30** Lv 10:6; 21:5, 10. |
| **6:15** Jer 22:28. | |

put it on their wives and children. [33]† Whether these gods are treated well or badly by anyone, they cannot repay it. They can neither set up nor remove a king.* [34]They cannot give anyone riches or pennies; if one fails to fulfill a vow to them, they will not exact it. [35]They neither save anyone from death, nor deliver the weak from the strong,* [36]nor do they restore sight to the blind, or rescue anyone in distress. [37]The widow they do not pity, the orphan they do not help. [38]These gilded and silvered wooden statues are no better than stones from the mountains; their worshipers will be put to shame. [39]How then can it be thought or claimed that they are gods?

[40]Even the Chaldeans themselves have no respect for them; for when they see a deaf mute, unable to speak, they bring forward Bel† and expect him to make a sound, as though he could hear. [41]They themselves are unable to reflect and abandon these gods, for they have no sense. [42]† And the women, with cords around them, sit by the roads, burning chaff for incense;* [43]and whenever one of them is taken aside by some passerby who lies with her, she mocks her neighbor who has not been thought thus worthy, and has not had her cord broken. [44]All that is done for these gods is a fraud; how then can it be thought or claimed that they are gods?

[45]They are produced by woodworkers and goldsmiths; they are nothing other than what these artisans wish them to be. [46]Even those who produce them are not long-lived; [47]how then can the things they have produced be gods? They have left frauds and disgrace to their successors. [48]For when war or disaster comes upon them, the priests deliberate among themselves where they can hide with them. [49]How then can one not understand that these are not gods, who save themselves neither from war nor from disaster? [50]Beings that are wooden, gilded and silvered, they will later be known for frauds. To all nations and kings it will be clear that they are not gods,

but human handiwork; and that God's work is not in them. [51]Is it not obvious that they are not gods?

[52]† They set no king over the land, nor do they give rain. [53]They neither vindicate their own rights, nor do they rescue anyone wronged, for they are powerless. [54]They are like crows in midair. For when fire breaks out in the temple of these wooden or gilded or silvered gods, though the priests flee and are safe, they themselves are burned up in the fire like timbers. [55]They cannot resist a king or enemy forces. [56]How then can it be admitted or thought that they are gods?

They are safe from neither thieves nor bandits, these wooden and silvered and gilded gods. [57]Anyone who can will strip off the gold and the silver, and go away with the clothing that was on them; they cannot help themselves. [58]How much better to be a king displaying his valor, or a handy tool in a house, the joy of its owner, than these false gods; better the door of a house, protecting whatever is within, than these false gods; better a wooden post in a palace, than these false gods!* [59]† The sun and moon and stars are bright, obedient in the task for which they are sent. [60]Likewise the lightning, when it flashes, is a great sight; and the one wind blows over every land. [61]The clouds, too, when commanded by God to proceed across the whole world, fulfill the command; [62]and fire, sent from on high to burn up the mountains and the forests, carries out its command. But these false gods are not their equal, whether in appearance or in power. [63]So it is unthinkable, and cannot be claimed that they are gods. They can neither execute judgment, nor benefit anyone. [64]Know, therefore, that they are not gods; do not fear them.

[65]Kings they can neither curse nor bless. [66]They show the nations no signs in the heavens, nor do they shine like the sun, nor give light like the moon. [67]The beasts are better than they—beasts can help themselves by

---

† **6:33–39** All that the Babylonian gods cannot do, the true God does; they have neither power nor inclination to save those in need, unlike the God of Israel, who champions the cause of the weak over the strong, and who defends the widow and the orphan. Cf. 1 Sm 2:7; Ps 68:6; 146:7–9; Is 35:4–5.

**6:40** *Bel*: cf. note on Jer 50:2.

**6:42–43** Perhaps a reference to the Babylonian practice of cultic prostitution mentioned by Herodotus, the fifth-century Greek historian. The unbroken cord was a sign that this service had not yet been rendered.

**6:52–53** Unlike the God of Israel, the Babylonian gods are unable to set up and depose kings, or to provide life-giving rain.

**6:59–62** The elements of nature, obedient to God's orders and accomplishing the divine purpose, are better than the Babylonian gods.

*

**6:33** Dn 2:21.  
**6:35** Ps 68:6; 146:7–9.  
**6:42–43** Jer 3:2.  
**6:58** Wis 13:10–15; 15:7–17.

fleeing to shelter. [68] Thus is it in no way apparent to us that they are gods; so do not fear them.

[69] For like a scarecrow in a cucumber patch,* providing no protection, are their wooden, gilded, silvered gods. [70] Just like a thornbush in a garden on which perches every kind of bird,

or like a corpse hurled into darkness, are their wooden, gilded, silvered gods. [71] From the rotting of the purple and the linen upon them, you can know that they are not gods; they themselves will in the end be consumed, and be a disgrace in the land. [72] Better the just who has no idols; such shall be far from disgrace!

---

**6:69** Jer 10:5.

# The Book of

# Ezekiel

## INTRODUCTION

Jerome Walsh

## The Historical Setting

In 597 BCE, Babylonian forces under the leadership of Nebuchadnezzar conquered Judah and occupied Jerusalem. King Jehoiachin and the royal family of Judah were taken into exile in Babylonia along with many of the leading citizens of Jerusalem. Among them was a young man from a priestly family: Ezekiel, son of Buzi. If, as is likely, the cryptic opening words of the book ("In the thirtieth year") refer to Ezekiel's age, at the age when he would have begun to fulfill priestly duties in the Temple (see Nm 4:3, though 8:24 disagrees), Ezekiel is called to a different service of his people: he is commissioned as a prophet—the first we know of since Moses to have received such a commission while outside of the land of Israel. An introductory editorial note tells us that this took place in 592 BCE (Ez 1:2).

The exiles of Judah were allowed to form strong, cohesive communities in Babylon and elsewhere, communities that, a thousand years later, would produce one of the greatest intellectual achievements of ancient Judaism, the Babylonian Talmud. In general, prophets are those who speak God's word to their contemporaries, commenting on events of their own day and on the implications of those events for the immediate future. It was Ezekiel's calling to speak God's word to his exiled compatriots, living in sorrow "by the rivers of Babylon" (Ps 137:1).

Ezekiel lived during some of the most decisive events in the history of ancient Israel: the Babylonian exile, the destruction of the first Temple of Yahweh, and the obliteration of the Judahite state as a political entity. How did his message address and interpret those catastrophes? In a word, counterculturally. Between the first exile to Babylon (597 BCE) and the destruction of Jerusalem and its Temple a

## Outline of Ezekiel

I. Call of the Prophet (1:1–3:27)

II. Before the Siege of Jerusalem (4:1–24:27)

III. Prophecies Against Foreign Nations (25:1–32:32)

IV. Hope for the Future (33:1–39:29)

V. The New Israel (40:1–48:35)

decade later (587 BCE), there seems to have been an optimism among those in exile that by permitting the exile of 597 Yahweh had punished his people for their sins. The next step would be restoration. Ezekiel's message was the opposite: the punishment has only begun! See Ez 13:10–16. (Jeremiah, Ezekiel's contemporary, preached similarly; see Jer 29.) Once the full catastrophe was realized and the city and Temple lay in ruins, many Israelites in Babylon began to despair of returning to Jerusalem. Thereupon Ezekiel's message changed: *now* the punishment is complete, and Yahweh will act to save and restore his people.

Prophets proclaim the divine message not only by word but by deed as well. In what are called "symbolic acts," often but not always accompanied by a verbal interpretation, the prophet performs some pregnant gesture that embodies the core of the divine message he has been given. Since the divine word is understood as a word of power, the prophetic proclamation of that word, whether by spoken oracle or symbolic act, unleashes that divine power into the world to accomplish what it announces. Ezekiel's career seems to have been particularly rich in striking symbolic acts (see, for instance, Ez 4 and 5), one of them so shocking that it scandalized even Ezekiel himself (4:12–15).

Some of the prophets (most notably Ezekiel's older contemporary, Jeremiah) appear to have been more than preachers of the divine word and performers of symbolic acts. Their very lives can be seen as symbolic of the divine message they were entrusted to deliver. This is true of Ezekiel as well. Jeremiah was unmarried and childless by God's command, in order to indicate that his people had no future (Jer 16:1–9); Ezekiel lost his wife (the "delight of [his] eyes," Ez 24:16) by God's decree and was forbidden to mourn, as a living sign that God would allow his chosen place, the Temple, to be leveled (Ez 24:15–24).

Ezekiel's role as symbol, however, is not exhausted by his prophetic behavior as a widower. His call narrative (Ez 1–3) is a bizarre and florid elaboration of Isaiah's commissioning in Is 6, with significant variations. Where Isaiah's categories were cultic—he was called in the Temple in Jerusalem, witnessed a heavenly liturgy, realized his ritual impurity, and underwent a ritual purification—Ezekiel's categories are cosmic and creational. He is called while exiled from the sacred soil of Israel ("by the river Chebar," an irrigation channel in Babylonia); he is addressed as "human being" (NABRE's "son of man" is, literally, "son of Adam," Ez 2:1); he experiences his own nothingness before the creator-God ("I fell on my face," 1:28); he is re-created by infusion of the divine spirit ("the spirit entered into me and set me on my feet," 2:2); and he is sent out to a plain where again he falls upon his face before the divine glory and is re-created by the spirit (3:22–24).

Later (Ez 37:1–10) the book describes the future re-creation of the people of Israel in language that closely parallels that of Ezekiel's call. Indeed, the re-created prophet becomes himself the agent of Israel's re-creation. Judah has been reduced to dry bones strewn across the face of a plain (37:1; despite the NABRE's translation "valley," the word is the same as in 3:22). Ezekiel himself, at God's behest, prophesies to the spirit (37:9; again, despite the NABRE's translation "breath," the word is the same as that translated "spirit" in 2:2 and 3:24), which re-creates the people: it "entered

them" and they "stood on their feet, a vast army" (37:10). (Once more, the echo is much closer in the Hebrew than in the NABRE. In both 2:2 and 37:10, the spirit/breath enters *into* Ezekiel/Israel, and in both cases the verb "to stand" describes the result: 2:2 reads, literally, that the spirit *stood* me on my feet.")

Since the last dated oracle in the book is from 571 BCE (Ez 29:17–21), some twenty years or so after his call, we have no indication of how Ezekiel might have greeted the release of King Jehoiachin from detention in Babylon, which 2 Kgs 25:27 dates to nearly eleven years later. Would he have seen this as a gauge of God's determination to bring his people back from exile? Eventually the return from exile would take place (beginning in 538 or 537 BCE), though the restored nation and Temple would not live up to the glorious picture of them Ezekiel foresaw and painted in Ez 40–48.

## The Book

In its present form the book of Ezekiel is a later compilation of Ezekiel's prophetic words and deeds; the editor has organized the work clearly and coherently. The oracles are often precisely dated and, with few exceptions, the dated oracles are in chronological order. The first half of the book (Ez 1–24) contains Ezekiel's preaching of judgment against Judah before the catastrophe of 587 BCE. These chapters reach their tragic climax at the midpoint of the book (24:15–27) with the death of Ezekiel's wife and his explanation to his hearers that her death portends the destruction of the Temple and his grief foreshadows their grief. In the second half of the book (chs. 25–48) Ezekiel proclaims that God will act to save and restore his people. This half begins with several chapters of oracles against foreign nations perceived as enemies of Yahweh's people (chs. 25–32); disaster for Israel's enemies, of course, implies salvation for Israel. These judgment oracles move from nations closest to Judah (Ammon, Moab, Edom, and the Philistines: ch. 25) to Tyre and Sidon to the north (chs. 26–28) and Egypt to the south (chs. 29–32). Then comes a loose collection of more oracles against foreign nations along with oracles of restoration (chs. 33–39), including the famous "dry bones" passage mentioned above (37:1–14). Finally, chs. 40–48 describe in glowing and almost obsessive detail the new Temple that will be built, God's return to the land of Israel and the Temple (reversing his departure in ch. 10), and the new organization of the land and the people upon their return. Because of its preoccupation with architectural, liturgical, legal, and territorial particulars, this section is sometimes referred to as the "Torah of Ezekiel."

Like the prophets before him, Ezekiel was first and foremost a preacher to his contemporaries. Recording his proclamations in written form, gathering them into collections, and compiling those collections into a book were most likely the work of followers, as seems to have been the case with most of the other prophets as well. The effort to preserve the prophets' preaching demonstrates their followers' conviction that the prophetic word held lasting relevance for Israel. And the continued transmission of the prophetic word is to be attributed not to mere antiquarian curiosity but to the common conviction of Jewish and Christian traditions alike that the prophetic word transcends the historical context in which it was first uttered and continues to speak anew to people and situations far removed from the prophet's addressees and concerns.

Two unusual characteristics of the book of Ezekiel make it stand out among the other prophetic books of the Old Testament. First, despite its probable origin in the work of followers, the book presents itself almost entirely as Ezekiel's own first-person account of his prophetic experiences. First-person passages are rare in other prophetic books, where most often an anonymous narrator tells us that "The word of the Lord came to" Jeremiah, or Isaiah, or some other prophet; in Ezekiel, rather, we consistently find, "The word of the Lord came to me." In fact, were it not for the editor's

remark in 1:3 and Ezekiel's self-reference in 24:24, we would not even know the prophet's name. It is perhaps not a coincidence that Is 6, the Isaian commission narrative of which Ezekiel's call narrative is such a baroque embroidery, is also cast in the first person.

Second, also unlike other prophetic collections, the majority of narratives in the book depict God addressing the prophet but do not narrate the prophet actually carrying out divine commands. His obedience, if it is mentioned at all, is usually reduced to something like a simple "I spoke [or I did] as I was commanded"; often it is simply and silently assumed (e.g., Ez 11:13, 25). As a matter of fact, though we see Ezekiel himself speak six times in the book, five of those times he speaks to God! The only time we actually witness him deliver a prophetic word to those around him is on the occasion of the pivotal event at the midpoint of the book, the death of his wife, when he explains the national meaning of his personal tragedy (24:19–27). Doubtless this silence is due, at least in terms of the book's plot, to the muteness imposed upon the prophet in 3:26–27, whose release, prophesied at the precise middle of the book (24:26–27), is not effected until after the fall of Jerusalem in 587 BCE (33:21–22). Whatever the reason, the book's emphasis consistently falls upon the prophet's reception of the divine command rather than his performance of it.

These two unique characteristics of the book—the first-person perspective and the emphasis on the prophet's experience of receiving God's word—combine to focus the reader at least as strongly on the prophet as person as on the prophet's ministry of proclaiming a divine message. Thus the prophet's role as embodiment of the word comes to the fore. As Ezekiel says at the crux of the book: "Ezekiel shall be a sign for you" (Ez 24:24). ∎

# THE BOOK OF EZEKIEL

## New American Bible, Introduction

In response to the rebellion of Jehoiakim of Judah in 601 B.C., Nebuchadnezzar, the Babylonian ruler, besieged Jerusalem. When Jehoiakim's successor, Jehoiachin, surrendered in 597, Nebuchadnezzar appointed Zedekiah king and deported to Babylon Jehoiachin and the royal family, along with members of the upper class, including Ezekiel the priest. Five years later, as Zedekiah planned his own revolt against Babylon, Ezekiel became the first prophet to be commissioned outside Judah or Israel (chaps. 1–3). Before Jerusalem is destroyed (587 B.C.), Ezekiel is concerned to convince his audience that they are responsible for the punishment of exile and to justify the Lord's decision to destroy their city and Temple. Later, Ezekiel argues that the Judahites who embrace his preaching are the people whom the Lord has chosen as a new Israel, enlivened by a new heart, imbued with new breath (chaps. 36–37), and restored to a re-created land, Temple, and covenant relationship (chaps. 40–48). Ezekiel is clear on one point: the Lord punishes and restores for one reason—for the sake of his name, in order to demonstrate once and for all that he is Lord.

Ezekiel's symbolic actions or performances foreshadow the inevitable destruction of Jerusalem (4:1–5:4; 12:1–20; 24:15–24). The closely related judgment oracles are directed against increasingly larger groups: the inhabitants of Jerusalem (5:5–17); refugees who have fled into the mountains (6:1–14); Judah's total population, "the four corners of the land" (7:1–27). Particularly chilling is Ez 8–11, the prophet's vision of the violent injustice and idolatrous worship that fills Jerusalem. When Ezekiel protests the Lord's order to slaughter Jerusalem's wicked inhabitants, the Lord refuses to relent; the Lord's glory leaves the Temple, affirming his judgment on Jerusalem (11:22–25), whom Ezekiel portrays as a promiscuous woman, rebel from the beginning, more violent and sinful than Sodom (chap. 16). Appeals for a speedy end to the exile on the basis of a past relationship with the Lord or of Jerusalem's privileged status are futile gestures.

Ezekiel uses stereotypic oracles against the nations (chaps. 25–32) to claim universal sovereignty for Israel's God, to exemplify the consequences of arrogant national pride, and to set the stage for Israel's restoration. In order to demonstrate to all the nations that "I am the Lord," God becomes Israel's just shepherd (34:15) under whose rule a restored people (37:1–14) enjoy prosperity in a restored land. God again acts "for the sake of my name" when the mysterious forces of Gog attack Israel (chaps. 38–39). Their defeat is prelude to Ezekiel's vision of a new Israel whose source of life and prosperity is a well-ordered cult in a new Temple, where the divine glory again dwells (chaps. 40–48).

The Book of Ezekiel has the following divisions:

# EZEKIEL

## I. CALL OF THE PROPHET

**1** **The Vision: God on the Cherubim.** ¹ In the thirtieth year,† on the fifth day of the fourth month, while I was among the exiles by the river Chebar, the heavens opened, and I saw divine visions.*— ² On the fifth day of the month—this was the fifth year† of King Jehoiachin's exile*— ³ the word of the LORD came to the priest Ezekiel, the son of Buzi, in the land of the Chaldeans by the river Chebar. There the hand of the LORD came upon him.*

⁴ As I watched, a great stormwind came from the North,† a large cloud with flashing fire, a bright glow all around it, and something like polished metal gleamed at the center of the fire.* ⁵ From within it figures in the likeness of four living creatures† appeared. This is what they looked like:* ⁶ They were in human form, but each had four faces and four wings,* ⁷ and their legs were straight, the soles of their feet like the hooves of a bull, gleaming like polished brass.* ⁸ Human hands were under their wings, and the wings of one touched those of another.* ⁹ Their faces and their wings looked out on all their four sides; they did not turn when they moved, but each went straight ahead.*

¹⁰† Their faces were like this:* each of the four had a human face, and on the right the face of a lion, and on the left, the face of an ox, and each had the face of an eagle. ¹¹ Such were their faces. Their wings were spread out above. On each one, two wings touched one another, and the other two wings covered the body.* ¹² Each went straight ahead. Wherever the spirit would go, they went; they did not change direction when they moved.* ¹³† And the appearance of the living creatures seemed like burning coals of fire. Something indeed like torches moved back and forth among the living creatures. The fire gleamed intensely, and from it lightning flashed. ¹⁴ The creatures darting back and forth flashed like lightning.

¹⁵† As I looked at the living creatures, I saw wheels on the ground, one alongside each of the four living creatures.* ¹⁶ The wheels and their construction sparkled like yellow topaz, and all four of them looked the same: their construction seemed as though one wheel was inside the other. ¹⁷ When they moved, they went in any of the four directions without veering as they moved. ¹⁸* The four of them had rims, high and fearsome—eyes filled the four rims all around. ¹⁹ When the living creatures moved, the wheels moved with them; and when the living creatures were raised from the ground, the wheels also were raised. ²⁰ Wherever the spirit would go, they went. And they were raised up together with the living creatures, for the spirit of the living creatures was in the wheels. ²¹ Wherever the living creatures moved, the wheels moved; when they stood still, the wheels stood still. When they were lifted up from the earth, the wheels were lifted up with them.* For the spirit of the living creatures was in the wheels.

²²† Above the heads of the living creatures was a likeness of the firmament; it was

---

† **1:1** *The thirtieth year,* which corresponds to the fifth year of exile (v. 2), has never been satisfactorily explained; possibly it refers to the prophet's age, or the anniversary of the finding of the book of the law in the Temple during Josiah's reform of 622 (2 Kgs 22:1–13). *The river Chebar:* probably a canal near Nippur, southeast of Babylon, one of the sites on which the Jewish exiles were settled.

**1:2** *The fifth day…the fifth year:* the end of July, 593 B.C.; cf. v. 1.

**1:4** *The North:* Zaphon, the traditional abode of the gods; see notes on Jb 37:22; Ps 48:3; Is 14:13–15.

**1:5** *Four living creatures:* identified as cherubim in 10:1–2, 20. Known from Assyrian religion as minor guardian deities of palaces and temples, the cherubim were usually portrayed in gigantic sculpture with the bodies of bulls or lions, wings like an eagle and a human head. In the Jerusalem Temple, the Lord was enthroned above in the holy of holies (Is 6:1–2).

**1:10** The four faces together represent animate creation: wild animals, domesticated livestock, birds, human beings. Christian tradition associates them with the four evangelists: the lion with Mark, the ox with Luke, the eagle with John, and the man with Matthew.

**1:13–14** The coals and flashing lightning moving among the four creatures and yet coming from them identify this vision as a theophany. See note on 10:2–13.

**1:15–21** The repetitions and inconsistencies in the description of the wheels and the direction of their movements evoke the vision's mysterious quality and emphasize the difficulty of describing the divine world in human language.

**1:22–23, 26** This symbolic description of God's throne is similar to that in Ex 24:9–10.

---

**1:1** Ez 10:20; 11:24–25; 43:3; Ps 137:1.
**1:2** 2 Kgs 24:15.
**1:3** Ez 3:14, 22; 8:1; 33:22; 37:1; 40:1; 2 Kgs 3:15; Is 8:11.
**1:4** Ez 8:2; Jb 38:1.
**1:5** Is 6:2.
**1:6** Ez 10:14.
**1:7** Rev 1:15.
**1:8** Ez 10:8.
**1:9** Ez 10:22.
**1:10** Ez 10:14; Rev 4:6–7.
**1:11** Is 6:2.
**1:12** Ez 10:16–19.
**1:15** Ez 10:2.
**1:18** Ez 10:12; Rev 4:6, 8.
**1:21** Ez 10:9–12.

awesome, stretching upwards like shining crystal over their heads.* ²³Beneath the firmament their wings stretched out toward one another; each had two wings covering the body. ²⁴Then I heard the sound of their wings, like the roaring of mighty waters, like the voice of the Almighty. When they moved, the sound of the tumult was like the din of an army. And when they stood still, they lowered their wings.* ²⁵While they stood with their wings lowered, a voice came from above the firmament over their heads.

²⁶Above the firmament over their heads was the likeness of a throne that looked like sapphire; and upon this likeness of a throne was seated, up above, a figure that looked like a human being.†* ²⁷And I saw something like polished metal, like the appearance of fire enclosed on all sides, from what looked like the waist up; and from what looked like the waist down, I saw something like the appearance of fire and brilliant light surrounding him.* ²⁸Just like the appearance of the rainbow in the clouds on a rainy day so was the appearance of brilliance that surrounded him. Such was the appearance of the likeness of the glory of the LORD. And when I saw it, I fell on my face and heard a voice speak.*

The prophet describes "four living creatures" (Ez 1:5); these are identified as cherubim in 10:1–2, 20. Pictured above, a sculpture of a cherubim-like creature, a bull with wings and a human face, in the palace of King Sargon II of Assur (722–705 BCE) in the ancient Assyrian city of Khorsabad.

## 2 Eating of the Scroll.

¹The voice said to me: Son of man,† stand up! I wish to speak to you. ²As he spoke to me, the spirit† entered into me and set me on my feet, and I heard the one who was speaking* ³say to me: Son of man, I am sending you to the Israelites, a nation of rebels who have rebelled against me; they and their ancestors have been in revolt against me to this very day.* ⁴Their children are bold of face and stubborn of heart—to them I am sending you. You shall say to them: Thus says the Lord GOD.* ⁵And whether they hear or resist—they are a rebellious house—they shall know that a prophet has been among them.* ⁶But as for you, son of man, do not fear them or their words. Do not fear, even though there are briers or thorns and you sit among scorpions.† Do not be afraid of their words or be terrified by their looks for they are a rebellious house.* ⁷You must speak my words to them, whether they hear or resist, because they are rebellious.* ⁸But you, son of man, hear me when I speak to you and do not rebel like this rebellious house. Open your mouth and eat what I am giving you.*

⁹*It was then I saw a hand stretched out to me; in it was a written scroll. ¹⁰He unrolled it before me; it was covered with writing front and back. Written on it was: Lamentation, wailing, woe!*

---

† **1:26** *Looked like a human being*: the God who transcends the powers of the human imagination is pictured here in the likeness of an enthroned human king.

**2:1** *Son of man*: in Hebrew, "son/daughter of…" is a common idiom expressing affiliation in a group; in this case, "a human being." The title is God's habitual way of addressing the prophet throughout this book, probably used to emphasize the separation of the divine and the human.

**2:2** *The spirit*: lit., wind, breath; a vital power, coming from God, which enables the prophet to hear the divine word; cf. 8:3; 11:1, 24.

**2:6** *And you sit among scorpions*: the prophet must be prepared for bitter opposition.

**1:22** Ez 10:1; Gn 1:6.
**1:24** Ez 3:13; 10:5; 43:2; Rev 1:15.
**1:26** Rev 1:13.
**1:27** Ez 8:2.
**1:28** Rev 4:2–3.
**2:2** Ez 3:24; Dn 8:18.
**2:3** Ez 20:8, 13.
**2:4** Ex 32:9.
**2:5** Ez 3:11, 27; 33:33.
**2:6** Dt 31:6.
**2:7** Ez 3:10–11; Jer 7:27.
**2:8** Jer 15:16.
**2:9** Ez 8:3; Rev 10:2.
**2:10** Zec 5:3; Rev 5:1.

# 3

¹ He said to me: Son of man, eat what you find here: eat this scroll, then go, speak to the house of Israel. ² So I opened my mouth, and he gave me the scroll to eat. ³* Son of man, he said to me, feed your stomach and fill your belly with this scroll I am giving you. I ate it, and it was as sweet as honey† in my mouth. ⁴ Then he said to me, Son of man, go now to the house of Israel, and speak my words to them.

⁵ Not to a people with obscure speech and difficult language am I sending you, but to the house of Israel.* ⁶ Nor to many nations of obscure speech and difficult language whose words you cannot understand. For if I were to send you to these, they would listen to you.* ⁷ But the house of Israel will refuse to listen to you, since they refuse to listen to me. For the whole house of Israel is stubborn of brow and hard of heart.* ⁸† Look! I make your face as hard as theirs, and your brow as stubborn as theirs.* ⁹ Like diamond, harder than flint, I make your brow. Do not be afraid of them, or be terrified by their looks, for they are a rebellious house.*

¹⁰ Then he said to me, Son of man, take into your heart all my words that I speak to you; hear them well. ¹¹ Now go to the exiles, to your own people, and speak to them. Say to them, whether they hear or refuse to hear: Thus says the LORD God!

¹² Then the spirit lifted me up, and I heard behind me a loud rumbling noise as the glory of the LORD† rose from its place:* ¹³ the noise of the wings of the living creatures beating against one another, and the noise of the wheels alongside them, a loud rumbling.* ¹⁴ And the spirit lifted me up and took me away, and I went off, my spirit angry and bitter, for the hand of the LORD pressed hard on me. ¹⁵ Thus I came to the exiles who lived at Tel-abib† by the river Chebar; and there where they dwelt, I stayed among them distraught for seven days. ¹⁶* At the end of the seven days, the word of the LORD came to me:

**The Prophet as Sentinel.**† ¹⁷ Son of man, I have appointed you a sentinel for the house of Israel.* When you hear a word from my mouth, you shall warn them for me.

¹⁸ If I say to the wicked, You shall surely die—and you do not warn them or speak out to dissuade the wicked from their evil conduct in order to save their lives—then they shall die for their sin, but I will hold you responsible for their blood. ¹⁹ If, however, you warn the wicked and they still do not turn from their wickedness and evil conduct, they shall die for their sin, but you shall save your life.

²⁰ But if the just turn away from their right conduct and do evil when I place a stumbling block before them, then they shall die. Even if you warned them about their sin, they shall still die, and the just deeds that they performed will not be remembered on their behalf. I will, however, hold you responsible for their blood.* ²¹ If, on the other hand, you warn the just to avoid sin, and they do not sin, they will surely live because of the warning, and you in turn shall save your own life.

**Ezekiel Mute.** ²² The hand of the LORD came upon me there and he said to me: Get up and go out into the plain, where I will speak with you.* ²³* So I got up and went out into the plain. There it was! The glory of the LORD was standing there like the glory I had seen by the river Chebar. Then I fell on my face, ²⁴ but the spirit entered into me, set me on my feet; he spoke to me, and said: Go, shut yourself in your house. ²⁵ As for you, son of man, know that they will put ropes on you and bind you with them, so that you cannot go out among them.* ²⁶ And I will make your tongue stick to the roof of your mouth so that you will be mute,† no longer one who rebukes them for being a rebellious house.* ²⁷ Only when I

---

† **3:3** *As sweet as honey*: though the prophet must foretell terrible things, the word of God is sweet to the one who receives it.
**3:8** Cf. Jer 1:18. The prophet must face fierce opposition with the determination and resistance shown by his opponents.
**3:12** *The glory of the LORD*: the divine presence, manifested here in audible form. Cf. Ex 40:34; Lk 2:9.
**3:15** *Tel-abib*: one of the sites where the exiles were settled, probably near Nippur.
**3:17–21** This passage refers to the prophet's role as sentinel, placed here and in chap. 33 as introductions to sections containing judgment oracles and salvation oracles respectively; cf. Hb 2:1.

**3:26–27** *Mute*: here the prophet's inability to speak to the people in exile while Jerusalem was being besieged is seen as a consequence of God's direct intervention (cf. 24:27).

---

| | |
|---|---|
| **3:3** Jer 15:16; Rev 10:9–10. | **3:16** Ez 33:7–9; cf. 18:5–18. |
| **3:5** Is 28:11. | **3:17** Is 52:8; Jer 1:17; Hb 2:1. |
| **3:6** cf. Mt 11:21. | |
| **3:7** Jer 7:27. | **3:20** Is 8:14. |
| **3:8** Jer 1:18. | **3:22** Ez 1:3; 8:4. |
| **3:9** Is 48:4. | **3:23** Ez 10:15; 40:3. |
| **3:12** Ez 8:3; 43:5. | **3:25** Ez 4:8. |
| **3:13** Ez 10:16–17. | **3:26** Ps 22:15. |

speak to you and open your mouth, shall you say to them: Thus says the LORD God: Let those who hear, hear! Let those who resist, resist! They are truly a rebellious house.

## II. BEFORE THE SIEGE OF JERUSALEM

**4** **Acts Symbolic of Siege and Exile.** ¹† You, son of man, take a clay tablet; place it in front of you, and draw on it a city, Jerusalem. ² Lay siege to it: build up siege works, raise a ramp against it, pitch camps and set up battering rams all around it. ³ Then take an iron pan and set it up as an iron wall between you and the city. Set your face toward it and put it under siege. So you must lay siege to it as a sign for the house of Israel.* ⁴ Then lie down on your left side, while I place the guilt of the house of Israel upon you. As many days as you lie like this, you shall bear their guilt. ⁵ I allot you three hundred and ninety days† during which you must bear the guilt of the house of Israel, the same number of years they sinned. ⁶ When you have completed this, you shall lie down a second time, on your right side to bear the guilt of the house of Judah forty days; I allot you one day for each year.* ⁷ Turning your face toward the siege of Jerusalem, with bared arm† you shall prophesy against it. ⁸ See, I bind you with ropes so that you cannot turn from one side to the other until you have completed the days of your siege.*

⁹† Then take wheat and barley, beans and lentils, millet and spelt; put them into a single pot and make them into bread. Eat it for as many days as you lie upon your side, three hundred and ninety days. ¹⁰ The food you eat shall be twenty shekels a day by weight; each day you shall eat it. ¹¹ And the water you drink shall be the sixth of a hin† by measure; each day you shall drink it. ¹² And the barley cake you eat you must bake on human excrement

in the sight of all. ¹³ The LORD said: Thus the Israelites shall eat their food, unclean, among the nations where I drive them.* ¹⁴ "Oh no, Lord GOD," I protested. "Never have I defiled myself nor have I eaten carrion flesh or flesh torn by wild beasts, nor from my youth till now has any unclean meat entered my mouth."* ¹⁵ Very well, he replied, I will let you use cow manure in place of human dung. You can bake your bread on that. ¹⁶ Then he said to me: Son of man, I am about to break the staff of bread† in Jerusalem so they shall eat bread which they have weighed out anxiously and drink water which they have measured out fearfully.* ¹⁷ Because they lack bread and water they shall be devastated; each and every one will waste away because of their guilt.*

**5** ¹ Now you, son of man, take a sharp sword and use it like a barber's razor, to shave your head and your beard. Then take a balance scale for weighing and divide the hair.* ² Set a third on fire within the city,† when the days of your siege are completed; place another third around the city and strike it with the sword; the final third scatter to the wind and then unsheathe the sword after it.* ³ But take a few of the hairs and tie them in the hem of your garment. ⁴ Take some of these and throw them into the fire and burn them in the fire. Because of this, fire will flash out against the whole house of Israel.

⁵ Thus says the Lord GOD: This is Jerusalem! I placed it in the midst of the nations, surrounded by foreign lands. ⁶ But it rebelled against my ordinances more wickedly than the nations, and against my statutes more than the foreign lands around it; they rejected my ordinances and did not walk in my statutes.* ⁷ Therefore, thus says the Lord GOD: Because you have caused more uproar than the nations surrounding you, not living by my statutes nor

---

† **4:1–5:4** The symbolic actions in this section prepare for the series of oracles that follow in 5:5–7:27.

**4:5–6** *Three hundred and ninety days…forty days:* a symbol to represent the respective lengths of exile for the Northern Kingdom of Israel and the Southern Kingdom of Judah. Israel had already fallen to Assyria in 722/721 B.C. The numerical value of the Hebrew consonants in the phrase translated "the days of your siege" (v. 8) is three hundred and ninety. Forty years conventionally represents one generation.

**4:7** *Bared arm:* a symbol of unrestrained power.

**4:9–13** This action represents the scarcity of food during the siege of Jerusalem, and the consequent need to eat whatever is at hand. *Twenty shekels:* about nine ounces. *The sixth of a hin:* about one quart.

**4:11** *Hin:* see note on 45:24.

**4:16** *Break the staff of bread:* reducing the supply of bread that supports life as the walking staff supports a traveler; cf. 5:16; 14:13; Lv 26:26; Ps 105:16; Is 3:1.

**5:2** *The city:* the one drawn on the tablet (4:1).

---

*
| | |
|---|---|
| **4:3** Is 8:18. | **4:16** Ez 5:16; Lv 26:26. |
| **4:6** Dn 9:24–25; | **4:17** Lv 26:39. |
| 12:11–12. | **5:1** Is 7:20. |
| **4:8** Ez 3:25. | **5:2** Jer 13:24. |
| **4:13** Hos 9:4. | **5:6** Ez 16:47–51. |
| **4:14** Dn 1:8. | |

carrying out my judgments, nor even living by the ordinances of the surrounding nations; [8] therefore, thus says the Lord GOD: See, I am coming against you!† I will carry out judgments among you while the nations look on.* [9] Because of all your abominations I will do to you what I have never done before, the like of which I will never do again. [10] Therefore, parents will eat their children in your midst, and children will eat their parents.† I will inflict punishments upon you and scatter all who remain to the winds.*

[11] Therefore, as I live, says the Lord GOD, because you have defiled my sanctuary with all your atrocities and all your abominations, I will surely withdraw and not look upon you with pity nor spare you.* [12] A third of your people shall die of disease or starve to death within you; another third shall fall by the sword all around you; a third I will scatter to the winds and pursue them with the sword.*

[13] Thus my anger will spend itself; I will vent my wrath against them until I am satisfied. Then they will know that I the LORD spoke in my passion when I spend my wrath upon them.* [14] I will make you a desolation and a reproach among the nations around you, in the sight of every passerby.* [15] And you will be a reproach and a taunt, a warning and a horror to the nations around you when I execute judgments against you in angry wrath, with furious chastisements. I, the LORD, have spoken! [16] When I loose against you the deadly arrows of starvation that I am sending to destroy you, I will increase starvation and will break your staff of bread.* [17] I will send against you starvation and wild beasts who will leave you childless, while disease and bloodshed sweep through you. I will bring the sword against you. I, the LORD, have spoken.*

## 6 Against the Mountains of Israel.

[1] The word of the LORD came to me: [2] Son of man, set your face toward the mountains of Israel and prophesy against them:* [3] You shall say: Mountains of Israel, hear the word of the Lord GOD. Thus says the Lord GOD to the mountains and hills, to the ravines and valleys:* Pay attention! I am bringing a sword against you, and I will destroy your high places.† [4] Your altars shall be laid waste, your incense stands smashed, and I will throw your slain down in front of your idols. [5] Yes, I will lay the corpses of the Israelites in front of their idols, and scatter your bones around your altars.†* [6] Wherever you live, cities shall be ruined and high places laid waste, in order that your altars be laid waste and devastated, your idols broken and smashed, your incense altars hacked to pieces, and whatever you have made wiped out.* [7] The slain shall fall in your midst, and you shall know that I am the LORD.†* [8] But I will spare some of you from the sword to live as refugees among the nations when you are scattered to foreign lands. [9] Then your refugees will remember me among the nations to which they have been exiled, after I have broken their lusting hearts that turned away from me and their eyes that lusted after idols. They will loathe themselves for all the evil they have done, for all their abominations.* [10] Then they shall know that I the LORD did not threaten in vain to inflict this evil on them.

[11] Thus says the Lord GOD: Clap your hands, stamp your feet,† and cry "Alas!" for all the evil abominations of the house of Israel! They shall fall by the sword, starvation, and disease.* [12] Those far off shall die of disease, those nearby shall fall by the sword, and those who survive and are spared shall perish by starvation; thus will I spend my fury upon them.

---

**5:8** *I am coming against you:* an expression borrowed from the language of warfare in which an enemy attacked another with the sword. "You" in vv. 8–17 is Jerusalem.

**5:10** *Parents will eat their children…parents:* the prophet describes the consequences of the prolonged Babylonian siege of Jerusalem in 587/586 B.C. See note on Lam 2:20.

**6:3** *High places:* raised platforms usually built on hills outside towns for making sacrifices to the Lord or to Canaanite deities. They became synonymous with places of idolatry after the centralization of worship in the Jerusalem Temple.

**6:5** *Scatter your bones…altars:* the bones of the dead defiled a place; cf. 2 Kgs 23:14.

**6:7** *You shall know that I am the LORD:* this formula is repeated after most of Ezekiel's oracles from this point on. Whatever happens to Israel happens at the Lord's command; because the Lord uses the nations to punish or reward Israel for its behav-

ior, Israel will learn that its God has sole rule over the nations and the universe, and will acknowledge that rule in obedience.

**6:11** *Clap your hands, stamp your feet:* these gestures may express grief, even horror, at Israel's infidelities; in 25:6, they are signs of gloating.

---

| | |
|---|---|
| **5:8** Jer 21:5. | **5:17** Lv 26:25. |
| **5:10** Lv 26:29, 33; Dt 28:53; Jer 19:9. | **6:2** Ez 36:1. |
| | **6:3** Ez 36:4; Lv 26:30. |
| **5:11** Ez 7:4, 9; 8:18. | **6:5** Lv 26:30; Jer 8:12. |
| **5:12** Ez 6:11–12; Rev 6:8. | **6:6** Lv 26:30. |
| **5:13** Ez 16:42. | **6:7** Ez 11:10–12. |
| **5:14** Ez 26:32. | **6:9** Ez 20:7, 24; Ps 137:1. |
| **5:16** Ez 4:16; 14:13; Lv 26:26. | **6:11** Ez 21:14–17. |

<sup>13</sup>They shall know that I am the LORD, when their slain lie among their idols, all around their altars, on every high hill and mountaintop, beneath every green tree and leafy oak†—any place they offer sweet-smelling oblations to all their idols.* <sup>14</sup>I will stretch out my hand against them; I will make the land a desolate waste, from the wilderness to Riblah,† wherever they live. Thus they shall know that I am the LORD.*

**7** **The End Has Come.** <sup>1</sup>The word of the LORD came to me: <sup>2</sup>Son of man, now say: Thus says the Lord GOD to the land of Israel: An end! The end comes upon the four corners of the land!* <sup>3</sup>Now the end is upon you; I will unleash my anger against you, judge you according to your ways, and hold against you all your abominations. <sup>4</sup>My eye will not spare you, nor will I have pity; but I will hold your conduct against you, since your abominations remain within you; then shall you know that I am the LORD.*

<sup>5</sup>Thus says the Lord GOD: Evil upon evil! See it coming! <sup>6</sup>An end is coming, the end is coming; it is ripe for you! See it coming! <sup>7</sup>The crisis has come for you who dwell in the land! The time has come, near is the day: panic, no rejoicing on the mountains.* <sup>8</sup>Soon now I will pour out my fury upon you and spend my anger against you; I will judge you according to your ways and hold against you all your abominations.* <sup>9</sup>My eye will not spare, nor will I take pity; I will hold your conduct against you since your abominations remain within you, then you shall know that it is I, the LORD, who strikes.*

<sup>10</sup>The day is here! Look! it is coming! The crisis has come! Lawlessness is blooming, insolence budding; <sup>11</sup>the violent have risen up to wield a scepter of wickedness. But none of them shall remain; none of their crowd, none of their wealth, for none of them are innocent. <sup>12</sup>†The time has come, the day dawns. The buyer must not rejoice, nor the seller mourn, for wrath is coming upon all the throng.* <sup>13</sup>Assuredly, the seller shall not regain what was sold, as long as they all live; for the vision is for the whole crowd: it shall not be revoked! Yes, because of their guilt, they shall not hold on to life. <sup>14</sup>They will sound the trumpet and get everything ready, but no one will go out to battle, for my wrath weighs upon all the crowd.

<sup>15</sup>The sword is outside; disease and hunger are within. Whoever is in the fields will die by the sword; whoever is in the city disease and hunger will devour.* <sup>16</sup>If their survivors flee, they will die on the mountains, moaning like doves of the valley on account of their guilt. <sup>17</sup>All their hands will hang limp, and all their knees† turn to water.* <sup>18</sup>*They put on sackcloth, horror clothes them; shame is on all their faces, all their heads are shaved bald.† <sup>19</sup>They fling their silver into the streets, and their gold is considered unclean.* Their silver and gold cannot save them on the day of the LORD's wrath. They cannot satisfy their hunger or fill their bellies, for it has been the occasion of their sin. <sup>20</sup>†In their beautiful ornaments they took pride; out of them they made their abominable images, their detestable things. For this reason I will make them unclean.* <sup>21</sup>I will hand them over as spoils to foreigners, as plunder to the wicked of the earth, so that they may defile them. <sup>22</sup>I will turn my face away from them. My treasure will be defiled; the violent will enter and defile it.* <sup>23</sup>They will wreak slaughter, for the land is filled with bloodshed and the city with violence.* <sup>24</sup>I will bring in the worst of the nations to take possession of their houses. I will put an end to their proud strength,† and their sanctuaries will be defiled.* <sup>25</sup>When anguish comes, they

---

† **6:13** *Every green tree and leafy oak*: trees often identified with fertility deities and the "tree of life"; sacred groves had a long history in Palestine and throughout the Mediterranean basin as places of worship; cf. Dt 12:2.
**6:14** *From the wilderness to Riblah*: the whole land, from the far south to the far north.
**7:12–13** Normal affairs will cease to have any meaning in view of the disaster that is to come.
**7:17** *Hands…knees*: image of profound terror; loss of control of body movement and functions.
**7:18** *Shaved bald*: shaving the head was a sign of mourning.
**7:20** Assyrian wall paintings show that statues of deities were often cast in precious metals and then decorated with jewelry. Cf. Is 40:19–20; 41:6–7; 44:9–20.

**7:24** *Proud strength*: misplaced trust in the might and power of their kings and army. Cf. v. 22; 33:28 and related ideas in Is 2:12; 10:12; 13:11; Jer 48:29; Ez 24:21; 30:18.

---

| | |
|---|---|
| **6:13** Ez 20:28; Lv 26:30. | **7:15** Dt 32:25. |
| **6:14** Jer 48:22. | **7:17** Jer 47:3. |
| **7:2** Rev 7:1; 20:8. | **7:18** Is 15:2–3; Jer 4:8; |
| **7:4** Ez 5:11; Jer 13:14. | 48:3. |
| **7:7** Ez 12:23; 30:3; Am | **7:19** Zep 1:7, 18; 2:2. |
| 5:18–19; Zep 1:14. | **7:20** Jer 10:3–4. |
| **7:8** Ez 20:8, 13, 21. | **7:22** Ps 74:7–8. |
| **7:9** Ez 22:31; Jer 21:7. | **7:23** Ez 22:9; 24:6. |
| **7:12** Is 24:2; cf. Mt | **7:24** Lam 2:7. |
| 24:17–18. | |

will seek peace, but there is none.* ²⁶ Disaster after disaster, rumor upon rumor. They keep seeking a vision from the prophet; instruction from the priest is missing, and counsel from the elders.* ²⁷ The king mourns, the prince is terror-stricken, the hands of the common people tremble. I will deal with them according to their ways, and according to their judgments I will judge them. They shall know that I am the Lord.

**8** ¹ In the sixth year, on the fifth day of the sixth month,† as I was sitting in my house, with the elders of Judah sitting before me, the hand of the Lord God fell upon me there.* ² I looked up and there was a figure that looked like a man.† Downward from what looked like his waist, there was fire; from his waist upward, like the brilliance of polished bronze.*

**Vision of Abominations in the Temple.** ³ He stretched out the form of a hand and seized me by the hair of my head. The spirit lifted me up† between earth and heaven and brought me in divine vision to Jerusalem* to the entrance of the inner gate facing north where the statue of jealousy that provokes jealousy stood. ⁴ There I saw the glory of the God of Israel, like the vision I had seen in the plain.* ⁵ He said to me: Son of man, lift your eyes to the north! I looked to the north and there in the entry north of the altar gate was this statue of jealousy.* ⁶ He asked, Son of man, do you see what they are doing? Do you see the great abominations that the house of Israel is practicing here, so that I must depart from my sanctuary? You shall see even greater abominations!*

⁷ Then he brought me to the entrance of the courtyard, and there I saw a hole in the wall. ⁸ Son of man, he ordered, dig through the wall. I dug through the wall—there was a doorway. ⁹ Go in, he said to me, and see the evil abominations they are doing here. ¹⁰ I went in and looked—figures of all kinds of creeping things and loathsome beasts,† all the idols of the house of Israel,* pictured around the wall. ¹¹ Before them stood seventy of the elders of the house of Israel. Among them stood Jaazaniah, son of Shaphan, each with censer in hand; a cloud of incense drifted upward.* ¹² Then he said to me: Do you see, son of man, what the elders of the house of Israel are doing in the dark, each in his idol chamber? They think: "The Lord cannot see us; the Lord has forsaken the land."* ¹³ He said: You will see them practicing even greater abominations.

¹⁴ Then he brought me to the entrance of the north gate of the house of the Lord. There women sat and wept for Tammuz.†* ¹⁵ He said to me: Do you see this, son of man? You will see other abominations, greater than these!

¹⁶ Then he brought me into the inner court of the house of the Lord. There at the door of the Lord's temple, between the porch and the altar, were about twenty-five men with their backs to the Lord's temple and their faces toward the east; they were bowing eastward† to the sun.* ¹⁷ He said: Do you see, son of man? Are the abominable things the house of Judah has done here so slight that they should also fill the land with violence, provoking me again and again? Now they are putting the branch to my nose!† ¹⁸ Therefore I in turn will act furiously: my eye will not spare, nor will I take pity. Even if they cry out in a loud voice for me to hear, I shall not listen to them.

---

**8:1** *In the sixth year, on the fifth day of the sixth month*: September, 592 B.C.

**8:2** *Looked like a man*: the divine presence which accompanies Ezekiel in these visions. Cf. 40:3–4.

**8:3** *The spirit lifted me up*: the prophet is transported in vision from Babylon to Jerusalem. Ezekiel may be drawing on his memory of the Temple from before his exile in 598 B.C. *The statue of jealousy*: the statue which provokes the Lord's outrage against the insults of his own people; perhaps the statue of the goddess Asherah set up by Manasseh, king of Judah (cf. 2 Kgs 21:7; 2 Chr 33:7, 15). Although his successor, Josiah, had removed it (2 Kgs 23:6), the statue may have been set up again after his death.

**8:10** *Creeping things and loathsome beasts*: perhaps images of Egyptian deities, often represented in animal form. During the last days of Jerusalem Zedekiah, king of Judah, was allied with Egypt, hoping for protection against the Babylonians.

**8:14** *Wept for Tammuz*: the withering of trees and plants that began in late spring was attributed to the descent of Tammuz, the Mesopotamian god of fertility, to the world of the dead beneath the earth. During the fourth month of the year,

female worshipers of Tammuz would wail and mourn the god's disappearance.

**8:16** *Bowing eastward*: sun worship was perhaps introduced as a condition of alliance with other nations. While Josiah removed some elements of this worship (2 Kgs 23:11), Manasseh, for example, built altars to all the "hosts of heaven" in two Temple courtyards (2 Kgs 21:5).

**8:17** *Putting the branch to my nose*: the meaning is uncertain. It may be connected with the social injustice mentioned in v. 17b and in 9:9, e.g., "with their violence they tweak my nose," i.e., "goad my fury." The Masoretic text reads "their noses" as a euphemism for "my nose," thus avoiding the impropriety of these idolaters coming into contact with God even figuratively.

---

| | |
|---|---|
| **7:25** Jer 6:1. | **8:6** Ps 78:60. |
| **7:26** Jer 18:18; Mi 3:6–7. | **8:10** Ez 23:14. |
| **8:1** Ez 14:1; 33:31. | **8:11** Nm 11:16. |
| **8:2** Ez 1:4, 26–27. | **8:12** Is 29:15. |
| **8:3** Ez 2:9; 3:12; Dn 14:6. | **8:14** cf. Dn 11:37. |
| **8:4** Ez 3:22. | **8:16** Jb 31:26–28. |
| **8:5** Ps 78:58. | |

# 9

**Slaughter of the Idolaters.** [1] Then he cried aloud for me to hear: Come, you scourges of the city! [2] And there were six men coming from the direction of the upper gate which faces north, each with a weapon of destruction in his hand. In their midst was a man dressed in linen, with a scribe's case at his waist. They entered and stood beside the bronze altar.*
[3] Then the glory of the God of Israel moved off the cherub and went up to the threshold of the temple. He called to the man dressed in linen with the scribe's case at his waist,* [4]* and the LORD said to him:† Pass through the city, through the midst of Jerusalem, and mark an X on the foreheads of those who grieve and lament over all the abominations practiced within it. [5] To the others he said in my hearing: Pass through the city after him and strike! Do not let your eyes spare; do not take pity. [6] Old and young, male and female, women and children—wipe them out! But do not touch anyone marked with the X. Begin at my sanctuary. So they began with the elders who were in front of the temple.* [7] Defile the temple, he said to them, fill its courts with the slain. Then go out and strike in the city.

[8] As they were striking, I was left alone. I fell on my face, crying out, "Alas, Lord GOD! Will you destroy all that is left of Israel when you pour out your fury on Jerusalem?" [9] He answered me: The guilt of the house of Israel and the house of Judah is too great to measure; the land is filled with bloodshed, the city with lawlessness. They think that the LORD has abandoned the land, that he does not see them. [10] My eye, however, will not spare, nor shall I take pity, but I will bring their conduct down upon their heads.

[11] Just then the man dressed in linen with the scribe's case at his waist made his report: "I have done as you commanded!"

# 10

[1] Then I looked and there above the firmament over the heads of the cherubim was something like a sapphire, something that looked like a throne.* [2]† And he said to the man dressed in linen: Go within the wheelwork under the cherubim; fill both your hands with burning coals from the place among the cherubim, then scatter them over the city. As I watched, he entered.* [3] Now the cherubim were standing to the south of the temple when the man went in and a cloud filled the inner court. [4] The glory of the LORD had moved off the cherubim to the threshold of the temple; the temple was filled with the cloud, the whole court brilliant with the glory of the LORD. [5] The sound of the wings of the cherubim could be heard as far as the outer court; it was like the voice of God Almighty speaking.* [6] He commanded the man dressed in linen: Take fire from within the wheelwork among the cherubim. The man entered and stood by one of the wheels. [7] Thereupon a cherub stretched out a hand from among the cherubim toward the fire in the midst of the cherubim, took some, and put it in the hands of the one dressed in linen. He took it and came out. [8] Something like a human hand was visible under the wings of the cherubim.
[9] I also saw four wheels beside the cherubim, one wheel beside each cherub, and the wheels appeared to have the sparkle of yellow topaz. [10] And the appearance of the four all seemed alike, as though one wheel were inside the other. [11] When they moved, they went in any of the four directions without veering as they moved; in whatever direction the first cherub faced, the others followed without veering as they went. [12] Their entire bodies—backs, hands, and wings—and wheels were covered with eyes all around like the four wheels.* [13] I heard the wheels called "wheelwork." [14] Each living creature had four faces: the first a cherub, the second a human being, the third a lion, the fourth an eagle.* [15]† When the cherubim rose up, they were indeed the living creatures I had seen by the river Chebar.* [16] When the cherubim moved, the wheels went beside them; when the cherubim lifted up their wings

---

† **9:4** Ezekiel emphasizes personal accountability; the innocent inhabitants of Jerusalem are spared while the idolatrous are punished. *An X:* lit., the Hebrew letter *taw.*

**10:2–13** The burning coals, a sign of the divine presence (cf. 28:14; Ps 18:9), represent the judgment of destruction that God is visiting upon the city; they may also represent the judgment of purification that prepares the land to become the Lord's sanctuary (cf. Is 6:6–7).

**10:15–19** The throne represents God's presence as ruler and protector of the land. In chap. 1, God is revealed as the lord of

the world who can appear even in a far-off land; here God is about to abandon the Temple, that is, hand the city over to its enemies. God and the throne return again in 43:1–3.

| | |
|---|---|
| **9:2** Ez 10:2; Dn 10:5; 12:6; Rev 8:2; 15:6. | **10:2** Rev 8:2. |
| **9:3** Ez 11:22. | **10:5** Jb 40:9. |
| **9:4** Ex 12:7; Rev 7:2–4; 13:16. | **10:12** Ez 1:15–20; Rev 4:6–8. |
| **9:6** Gn 4:15; Ex 12:7. | **10:14** cf. Gn 3:24. |
| **10:1** Ex 24:10; Rev 4:2. | **10:15** Ps 137:1. |

to rise from the earth, even then the wheels did not leave their sides. 17 When they stood still, the wheels stood still; when they rose up, the wheels rose up with them, for the spirit of the living creatures was in them. 18 Then the glory of the LORD left the threshold of the temple and took its place upon the cherubim. 19 The cherubim lifted their wings and rose up from the earth before my eyes as they departed with the wheels beside them. They stopped at the entrance of the eastern gate of the LORD's house, and the glory of the God of Israel was up above them.* 20 † These were the living creatures I had seen beneath the God of Israel by the river Chebar. Now I knew they were cherubim.* 21 Each of them had four faces and four wings, and something like human hands under their wings. 22 Their faces looked just like the faces I had seen by the river Chebar; and each one went straight ahead.

# 11 Death for the Remnant in Jerusalem.

1 The spirit lifted me up and brought me to the east gate of the house of the LORD facing east. There at the entrance of the gate were twenty-five men; among them I saw the public officials Jaazaniah, son of Azzur, and Pelatiah, son of Benaiah. 2 The LORD said to me: Son of man, these are the men who are planning evil and giving wicked counsel in this city. 3 They are saying, "No need to build houses! The city is the pot, and we are the meat."† * 4 Therefore prophesy against them, son of man, prophesy! 5 Then the spirit of the LORD fell upon me and told me to say: Thus says the LORD: This is how you talk, house of Israel. I know the things that come into your mind! 6 You have slain many in this city, filled its streets with the slain. 7 Therefore thus says the Lord GOD: The slain whom you piled up in it, that is the meat, the pot is the city. But you I will bring out of it.* 8 You fear the sword— that sword I will bring upon you—oracle of

the Lord GOD.* 9 I will bring you out of the city, hand you over to foreigners, and execute judgments against you. 10 By the sword you shall fall. At the borders of Israel I will judge you so that you will know that I am the LORD. 11 The city shall not be a pot for you, nor shall you be meat within it. At the borders of Israel I will judge you,* 12 so you shall know that I am the LORD, whose statutes you did not follow, whose ordinances you did not keep. Instead, you acted according to the ordinances of the nations around you.

13 While I was prophesying, Pelatiah, the son of Benaiah, dropped dead. I fell down on my face and cried out in a loud voice: "Alas, Lord GOD! You are finishing off what remains of Israel!"† *

**Restoration for the Exiles.** 14 The word of the LORD came to me: 15 † Son of man, the inhabitants of Jerusalem are saying about all your relatives, the other exiles, and all the house of Israel, "They are far away from the LORD. The land is given to us as a possession."* 16 Therefore say: Thus says the Lord GOD: I have indeed sent them far away among the nations, scattered them over the lands, and have been but little sanctuary for them in the lands to which they have gone. 17 Therefore, thus says the Lord GOD, I will gather you from the nations and collect you from the lands through which you were scattered, so I can give you the land of Israel.* 18 They will enter it and remove all its atrocities and abominations. 19 * And I will give them another heart and a new spirit I will put within them. From their bodies I will remove the hearts of stone, and give them hearts of flesh, 20 so that they walk according to my statutes, taking care to keep my ordinances. Thus they will be my people, and I will be their God.* 21 But as for those whose hearts are devoted to their atrocities and abominations, I will bring their conduct

---

†

**10:20–22** The repetition of description from the preceding verses is a device intended to suggest the rapid, constantly changing motion of the vision and the difficulty of describing the divine in human language.

**11:3** *No need to build houses…meat:* this advice is based on the conviction that invincible Jerusalem will protect its citizens from further danger just as a pot shields the meat inside from the fire. The poorer citizens of Jerusalem and the refugees from nearby villages can now appropriate the property abandoned by the city's wealthier upper class when they were deported (v. 15). The metaphor of the pot and its contents reappears in chap. 24.

**11:13** In Ezekiel's vision Pelatiah represents the people left in Jerusalem, "the remnant of Israel." His sudden death in the

vision, but not in reality, is a figure for the judgment described in vv. 8–10 and prompts Ezekiel's anguished question about the survival of the people left in the land after the deportations in 597.

**11:15–21** Ezekiel insists that those who remained in Judah are doomed; the exiles, under a new covenant, will constitute a new Israel. Cf. chap. 36; Jer 24:7; 29.

---

**10:19** Ez 43:4.
**10:20** Ez 1:1.
**11:3** Ez 24:3; Jer 1:13.
**11:7** Mi 3:2–3.
**11:8** Lv 26:25.
**11:11** 2 Kgs 25:20–21.
**11:13** Ez 9:8.

**11:15** Ez 33:24.
**11:17** Ez 34:13; 36:28.
**11:19** Ez 18:31; 36:26;
  2 Cor 3:3.
**11:20** Ex 6:7; Jer 31:33;
  32:38.

down upon their heads—oracle of the Lord God.

22 Then the cherubim lifted their wings and the wheels alongside them, with the glory of the God of Israel above them.* 23† The glory of the LORD rose up from the middle of the city and came to rest on the mountain east of the city.* 24 In a vision, the spirit lifted me up and brought me back to the exiles in Chaldea, by the spirit of God. The vision I had seen left me,* 25 and I told the exiles everything the LORD had shown me.*

# 12 Acts Symbolic of the Exile. 
1 The word of the LORD came to me: 2 Son of man, you live in the midst of a rebellious house; they have eyes to see, but do not see, and ears to hear but do not hear. They are such a rebellious house!* 3 Now, son of man, during the day while they watch, pack a bag for exile,† and again while they watch, go into exile from your place to another place; perhaps they will see that they are a rebellious house. 4 During the day, while they watch, bring out your bag, an exile's bag. In the evening, again while they watch, go out as if into exile.* 5 While they watch, dig a hole through the wall† and go out through it. 6 While they watch, shoulder your load and go out in darkness. Cover your face so you cannot see the land, for I am making you a sign for the house of Israel!*

7 I did just as I was commanded. During the day I brought out my bag, an exile's bag. In the evening while they watched, I dug a hole through the wall with my hands and set out in darkness, shouldering my load.

8 In the morning, the word of the LORD came to me: 9 Son of man, did not the house of Israel, that house of rebels, say, "What are you doing?"* 10 Tell them: Thus says the Lord GOD: This load is the prince in Jerusalem and the whole house of Israel within it. 11 Say, I am a sign for you: just as I have done, so it shall be done to them; into exile, as captives they shall go.* 12 The prince among them shall shoulder his load in darkness and go out through the hole they dug in the wall to bring him out. His face shall be covered so that he cannot even see the ground.* 13* I will spread my net over him and he shall be caught in my snare. I will bring him into Babylon, to the land of the Chaldeans, though he shall not see it,† and there he shall die. 14 All his retinue, his aides and all his troops, I will scatter to the winds and pursue them with the sword.* 15 Then they shall know that I am the LORD, when I disperse them among the nations and scatter them throughout the lands.* 16 But I will let a few of them escape the sword, starvation, and plague, so that they may recount all their abominations among the nations to which they go. Thus they may know that I am the LORD.†

17 The word of the LORD came to me: 18 Son of man, eat your bread trembling and drink your water shaking with fear.* 19 And say to the people of the land:† Thus says the Lord GOD about the inhabitants of Jerusalem in the land of Israel: they shall eat their bread in fear and drink their water in horror, because the land will be emptied of what fills it—the lawlessness of all its inhabitants. 20 Inhabited cities shall be in ruins, the land a desolate place. Then you shall know that I am the LORD.

## Prophecy Ridiculed. 
21 The word of the LORD came to me: 22 Son of man, what is this proverb you have in the land of Israel: "The days drag on, and every vision fails"?†* 23 Say to them therefore: Thus says the Lord GOD: I will put an end to that proverb; they shall never use it again in Israel. Say to them instead: "The days are at hand and every vision fulfilled."*

---

† **11:23** The glory of the Lord departs toward the east, to the exiles in Babylon; it will return once the Temple is rebuilt (43:1–3).
**12:3–10** An exile's bag contains bare necessities, probably no more than a bowl, a mat, and a waterskin. The prophet's action foreshadows the fate of ruler and people (vv. 11–14).
**12:5** *Through the wall*: mud-brick outer wall of a private home. In this symbolic action, Ezekiel represents the enemy forces, and the house wall, the city wall of Jerusalem breached by the Babylonian army.
**12:13** *Though he shall not see it*: according to a Targum, an allusion to Nebuchadnezzar having Zedekiah blinded before deporting him to Babylonia (cf. 2 Kgs 25:7); according to the Septuagint, the king is ashamed of his flight from the city and disguises himself so others will not recognize him.
**12:16** Both exiles and nations shall know that the exile is divine punishment for Israel's betrayal of the Lord and the cov-

enant, not evidence that the Lord is too weak to fight off the Babylonian deity.
**12:19** *The people of the land*: the exiles in Babylon who, ironically, are now outside the land.
**12:22–28** This proverb conveys the skepticism the people of Jerusalem have; cf. Jer 20:7–9.

**11:22** Ex 24:16.
**11:23** Zec 14:4.
**11:24** Ez 37:1.
**11:25** Ez 3:4, 11.
**12:2** Is 6:9–10; Jer 5:21; cf. Mt 13:15; Mk 4:12; 8:18.
**12:4** 2 Kgs 25:4.
**12:6** Is 8:18.
**12:9** Ez 20:49; 24:19.
**12:11** 2 Kgs 25:7; Jer 52:15.
**12:12** Jer 23:33; 52:7.
**12:13** Ez 17:20; 19:8; 32:3.
**12:14** 2 Kgs 25:5; Jer 21:7.
**12:15** Lv 26:33.
**12:18** Lam 5:9.
**12:22** Ps 49:4.
**12:23** Ez 7:7.

24 No longer shall there be any false visions or deceitful divinations within the house of Israel,* 25 for whatever word I speak shall happen without delay. In your days, rebellious house, whatever I speak I will bring about—oracle of the Lord GOD.*

26 The word of the LORD came to me: 27 Son of man, listen! The house of Israel is saying, "The vision he sees is a long time off; he prophesies for distant times!"* 28 Say to them therefore: Thus says the Lord GOD: None of my words shall be delayed any longer. Whatever I say is final; it shall be done—oracle of the Lord GOD.

# 13 Against the Prophets of Peace.

1 The word of the LORD came to me: 2 Son of man, prophesy against the prophets of Israel, prophesy! Say to those who prophesy their own thoughts: Hear the word of the LORD!* 3 Thus says the Lord GOD: Woe to those prophets, the fools who follow their own spirit and see nothing.* 4 Like foxes among ruins are your prophets, Israel! 5 You did not step into the breach, nor repair the wall around the house of Israel so it would stand firm against attack on the day of the LORD. 6 False visions! Lying divinations! They say, "The oracle of the LORD," even though the LORD did not send them. Then they expect their word to be confirmed!* 7 Was not the vision you saw false? Did you not report a lying divination when you said, "Oracle of the LORD," even though I never spoke? 8 Therefore thus says the Lord GOD: Because you have spoken falsehood and seen lying visions, therefore, for certain I am coming at you—oracle of the Lord GOD. 9 My hand is against the prophets who see false visions and who make lying divinations. They shall not belong to the community of my people. They shall not be written in the register of the house of Israel, nor shall they enter the land of Israel. Thus you shall know that I am the LORD.*

10 Because they led my people astray, saying, "Peace!" when there is no peace, and when a wall is built, they cover it with whitewash,† 11 say then to the whitewashers: I will bring down a flooding rain; hailstones shall fall, and a stormwind shall break forth.* 12 When the wall has fallen, will you not be asked: "Where is the whitewash you spread on it?"

13 Therefore thus says the Lord GOD: In my fury I will let loose stormwinds; because of my anger there will be flooding rain, and hailstones will fall with destructive wrath.* 14 I will tear down the wall you whitewashed and level it to the ground, laying bare its foundations. When it falls, you shall be crushed beneath it. Thus you shall know that I am the LORD. 15 When I have poured out my fury on the wall and its whitewashers, it will fall. Then I will say to you: No wall! No whitewashers— 16 the prophets of Israel who prophesy to Jerusalem and see visions of peace for it when there is no peace—oracle of the Lord GOD.*

**Against Witches.** 17 As for you, son of man, now set your face against the daughters of your people who play the prophet from their own thoughts, and prophesy against them.* 18 You shall say, Thus says the Lord GOD: Woe to those who sew amulets for the wrists of every arm and make veils† for every head size to snare lives! You ensnare the lives of my people, even as you preserve your own lives! 19 You have profaned me among my people for handfuls of barley and crumbs of bread,† slaying those who should not be slain, and keeping alive those who should not live, lying to my people, who listen to lies. 20 Therefore thus says the Lord GOD: See! I am coming after your amulets by which you ensnare lives like prey. I will tear them from your arms and set free the lives of those you have ensnared like prey.* 21 I will tear off your veils and deliver my people from your power, so that they shall never again be ensnared by your hands. Thus you shall know that I am the LORD. 22 Because you discourage the righteous with lies when I

† **13:10** The false prophets contributed to popular illusions of security by predictions of peace, like those who whitewash a wall to conceal its defects.
**13:18** *Sew amulets…make veils*: used by sorcerers to mark individuals for life or for death. For a small price (v. 19), these women promised protection for the wicked, who, in the Lord's estimation, "should not live" (v. 19), and death for the righteous, "who should not be slain" (v. 19). Both decisions belong to the Lord.
**13:19** *Handfuls of barley and crumbs of bread*: payment for the amulets and scarves.

* **12:24** Ez 13:23; Jer 14:14; Zec 13:2–4.
**12:25** Hb 2:3.
**12:27** cf. Mt 24:48; 2 Pt 3:4.
**13:2** Jer 23:16, 21–22; 28:15.
**13:3** Ez 14:9; Nm 16:28; Is 32:6; Jer 23:1, 16, 25–40; Mi 2:11.
**13:6** cf. Is 30:10.
**13:9** Ex 32:32.
**13:11** cf. Ps 18:7–15; 77:17–18.
**13:13** Rev 11:19; 16:21.
**13:16** Jer 6:14.
**13:17** Rev 2:20.
**13:20** Ps 124:7.

did not want them to be distressed, and encourage the wicked so they do not turn from their evil ways and save their lives,* ²³ therefore you shall no longer see false visions or practice divination again. I will deliver my people from your hand. Thus you shall know that I am the LORD.

# 14 Idolatry and Unfaithfulness. ¹ Some elders of Israel came and sat down before me.* ² Then the word of the LORD came to me: ³ Son of man, these men keep the memory of their idols alive in their hearts, setting the stumbling block of their sin before them. Should I allow myself to be consulted by them? ⁴ Therefore say to them: Thus says the Lord GOD: If any of the house of Israel who keep the memory of their idols in their hearts, setting the stumbling block of their sin before them, come to a prophet, I the LORD will answer in person because of their many idols, ⁵ in order to catch the hearts of the house of Israel, estranged from me because of all their idols.

⁶ Therefore say to the house of Israel: Thus says the Lord GOD: Return, turn away from your idols; from all your abominations, turn your faces.* ⁷ For if anyone of the house of Israel or any alien residing in Israel who are estranged from me and who keep their idols in their hearts, setting the stumbling block of their sin before them, come to ask a prophet to consult me on their behalf, I the LORD will answer them in person. ⁸ I will set my face against them and make them a sign and a byword, and cut them off from the midst of my people. Thus you shall know that I am the LORD.

⁹* As for the prophet, if he speaks a deceiving word, I the LORD am the one who deceives that prophet.† I will stretch out my hand against him and destroy him from the midst of my people Israel. ¹⁰ They will be punished for their own sins, the inquirer and the prophet alike, ¹¹ so that the house of Israel may no longer stray from me, no longer defile themselves by all their sins. Then they shall be my people, and I shall be their God—oracle of the Lord GOD.

**Just Cause.**† ¹² The word of the LORD came to me: ¹³* Son of man, if a land sins against me by breaking faith, and I stretch out my hand against it, breaking its staff of bread and setting famine loose upon it, cutting off from it human being and beast alike— ¹⁴ even if these three were in it, Noah, Daniel, and Job,† they could only save themselves by their righteousness—oracle of the Lord GOD.* ¹⁵ If I summoned wild beasts to prowl the land, depopulating it so that it became a wasteland which no one would cross because of the wild beasts,* ¹⁶ and these three were in it, as I live— oracle of the Lord GOD—I swear they could save neither sons nor daughters; they alone would be saved, but the land would become a wasteland.* ¹⁷ Or if I bring the sword upon this land, commanding the sword to pass through the land cutting off from it human being and beast alike,* ¹⁸ and these three were in it, as I live—oracle of the Lord GOD—they could save neither sons nor daughters; they alone would be saved. ¹⁹ Or if I send plague into this land, pouring out upon it my bloody wrath, cutting off from it human being and beast alike, ²⁰ even if Noah, Daniel, and Job were in it, as I live—oracle of the Lord GOD—they could save neither son nor daughter; they would save only themselves by their righteousness.

²¹ Thus says the Lord GOD: Even though I send against Jerusalem my four evil punishments— sword, famine, wild beasts, and plague—to cut off from it human being and beast alike,* ²² there will still be some survivors in it who will bring out sons and daughters. When they come out to you and you see their ways and their deeds, you shall be consoled regarding the evil I brought on Jerusalem, everything I brought upon it. ²³ They shall console you when you see their ways and their deeds, and you shall know that not without reason did I do to it everything I did—oracle of the Lord GOD.*

---

† **14:9** The ancient Israelites thought that God could use deception as a means of promoting divine justice; cf. 2 Sm 24:1–3; 1 Kgs 22:19–23.

**14:12–23** According to Ezekiel, the people in Jerusalem deserve destruction because they are corrupt. Yet he admits an exception to the principle of individual responsibility when he affirms that some of those deserving death will survive and be reunited with family in exile. The depravity of Jerusalem testifies that the punishment of Jerusalem was just and necessary.

**14:14** *Noah, Daniel, and Job:* righteous folk heroes whom Israel shared with other ancient Near Eastern cultures. Daniel was the just judge celebrated in Ugaritic literature, perhaps the model for the hero of Dn 13.

---

* 
**13:22** Ez 18:21; 33:14–16.
**14:1** Ez 8:1; 20:1.
**14:6** Is 2:20; cf. Ez 18:30; 33:11.
**14:9** cf. 1 Kgs 22:23; 2 Chr 18:22.
**14:13** Lv 26:26.

**14:14** Ez 28:3; Dn 1:6; cf. Gn 6:9; Jb 1:1.
**14:15** cf. Lv 26:22.
**14:16** cf. Ez 18:20.
**14:17** Lv 26:25.
**14:21** cf. Rev 6:8.
**14:23** Jer 22:8–9.

# 15

**Parable of the Vine.** [1]† The word of the LORD came to me:

[2]
Son of man,
what makes the wood of the vine
Better than the wood of branches
found on the trees in the forest?*

[3]
Can wood be taken from it
to make something useful?
Can someone make even a peg out of it
on which to hang a vessel?

[4]
Of course not! If it is fed to the fire for
fuel,
and the fire devours both ends of it,
Leaving the middle charred,
is it useful for anything then?

[5]
Even when it is whole
it cannot be used for anything;
So when fire has devoured and charred it,
how useful can it be?

[6]
Therefore, thus says the Lord GOD:
Like vine wood among forest trees,
which I have given as fuel for fire,
So I will give the inhabitants of
Jerusalem.

[7]
I will set my face against them:
Although they have escaped the fire,
the fire will still devour them;
You shall know that I am the LORD,
when I set my face against them.*

[8]
Yes, I will make the land desolate,
because they are so unfaithful—
oracle of the Lord GOD.

# 16

**A Parable of Infidelity.** [1]The word of the LORD came to me: [2]Son of man, make known to Jerusalem her abominations.* [3]You shall say, Thus says the Lord GOD to Jerusalem: By origin and birth you belong to the land of the Canaanites; your father was an Amorite, your mother a Hittite.†* [4]† As for your birth, on the day you were born your navel cord was not cut; you were not washed with water or anointed; you were not rubbed with salt or wrapped in swaddling clothes.* [5]No eye looked on you with pity or compassion to do any of these things for you. Rather, on the day you were born you were left out in the field, rejected.

[6]Then I passed by and saw you struggling in your blood, and I said to you in your blood, "Live!" [7]I helped you grow up like a field plant, so that you grew, maturing into a woman with breasts developed and hair grown; but still you were stark naked. [8]I passed by you again and saw that you were now old enough for love. So I spread the corner of my cloak† over you to cover your nakedness; I swore an oath to you and entered into covenant with you—oracle of the Lord GOD—and you became mine.* [9]Then I bathed you with water, washed away your blood, and anointed you with oil.* [10]I clothed you with an embroidered gown, put leather sandals on your feet; I gave you a fine linen sash and silk robes to wear.* [11]I adorned you with jewelry, putting bracelets on your arms, a necklace about your neck,* [12]a ring in your nose, earrings in your ears, and a beautiful crown on your head. [13]Thus you were adorned with gold and silver; your garments made of fine linen, silk, and embroidered cloth. Fine flour, honey, and olive oil were your food. You were very, very beautiful, fit for royalty.* [14]You were renowned among the nations for your beauty, perfected by the splendor I showered on you—oracle of the Lord GOD.

[15]But you trusted in your own beauty and used your renown to serve as a prostitute. You poured out your prostitution on every passerby—let it be his.* [16]† You took some of

---

**15:1–8** Verses 2–5 point out that the wood of the vinestock may be burned for fuel, fit only for destruction. In vv. 6–8 Ezekiel asserts that Jerusalem has the same destiny.

**16:3–4** *By origin and birth…Hittite*: Jerusalem's pre-Israelite origins are the breeding ground for its inability to respond faithfully to the Lord's generosity.

**16:4–5** In this chapter, Ezekiel represents Jerusalem and Samaria as unwanted, abandoned sisters whom the Lord rescues and cares for. Here the prophet depicts Jerusalem as a newborn female, abandoned and left to die, an accepted practice in antiquity for females, who were considered financial liabilities by their families. That the infant has no one, not even her mother, to tie off her umbilical cord, wash her clean, and wrap her in swaddling clothes emphasizes Jerusalem's death-like isolation and accentuates the Lord's gracious action in her behalf. The practice of rubbing the skin of newborns with salt is an attested Palestinian custom that survived into the twentieth century.

**16:8** *I spread the corner of my cloak*: one way to acquire a woman for marriage; cf. Ru 3:9. In Dt 23:1 a son's illicit sexual relations with his father's wife is described as "uncovering the edge of the father's garment."

**16:16** In the allegory of this chapter the viewpoint often shifts from the figure (prostitution) to the reality (idolatry). A symbol of the woman's depravity supersedes her parents' cruel abandonment when she was an infant. It overrides the loyalty she owes her covenant partner and the care she owes their children.

---

| | |
|---|---|
| **15:2** cf. Ps 80; Is 5:1–7. | **16:8** cf. Ez 16:59; Ru 3:9. |
| **15:7** Is 24:18; Am 9:1–4. | **16:9** cf. Ru 3:3. |
| **16:2** cf. Ez 8:17. | **16:10** cf. Ps 45:14. |
| **16:3** cf. Dt 26:5; Gn 23:10; | **16:11** cf. Ez 23:40–42. |
| 48:22. | **16:13** Dt 32:13–14; Hos 2:8. |
| **16:4** cf. Lk 2:2. | **16:15** Is 57:7–8. |

your garments and made for yourself gaudy high places, where you served as a prostitute. It has never happened before, nor will it happen again!* 17 You took the splendid gold and silver ornaments that I had given you and made for yourself male images and served as a prostitute with them. 18 You took your embroidered garments to cover them; my oil and my incense you set before them; 19 the food I had given you, the fine flour, the oil, and the honey with which I fed you, you set before them as a pleasant odor, says the Lord God.* 20†* The sons and daughters you bore for me you took and offered as sacrifices for them to devour! Was it not enough that you had become a prostitute? 21* You slaughtered and immolated my children to them, making them pass through fire. 22 In all your abominations and prostitutions you did not remember the days of your youth when you were stark naked, struggling in your blood.*

23 Then after all your evildoing—woe, woe to you! oracle of the Lord God— 24 you built yourself a platform and raised up a dais† in every public place.* 25* At every intersection you built yourself a dais so that you could degrade your beauty by spreading your legs for every passerby, multiplying your prostitutions. 26 You served as a prostitute with the Egyptians, your big-membered neighbors, and multiplied your prostitutions to provoke me. 27 Therefore I stretched out my hand against you and reduced your allotment, and delivered you over to the whim of your enemies, the Philistines,† who were revolted by your depraved conduct.* 28 You also served as a prostitute for the Assyrians, because you were not satisfied. Even after serving as a prostitute for them, you were still not satisfied.* 29 You increased your prostitutions again, now going to Chaldea, the land of traders; but despite this, you were still not satisfied.*

30 How wild your lust!—oracle of the Lord God—that you did all these works of a shameless prostitute, 31 when you built your platform at every intersection and set up your high place in every public square. But unlike a prostitute, you disdained payment. 32 Adulterous wife, taking strangers in place of her husband! 33 Prostitutes usually receive gifts. But you bestowed gifts on all your lovers, bribing them to come to you for prostitution from every side.* 34 Thus in your prostitution you were different from any other woman. No one solicited you for prostitution. Instead, you yourself offered payment; what a reversal!

35 Therefore, prostitute, hear the word of the Lord! 36 Thus says the Lord God: Because you poured out your lust and exposed your nakedness in your prostitution with your lovers and your abominable idols, because you gave the life-blood of your children to them, 37* therefore, I will now gather together all your lovers with whom you found pleasure, both those you loved and those you hated; I will gather them against you from all sides and expose you naked for them to see. 38† I will inflict on you the sentence of adultery and murder; I will bring on you bloody wrath and jealous anger.* 39 I will hand you over to them to tear down your platform and demolish your high place, to strip you of your garments and take away your splendid ornaments, leaving you stark naked.* 40 They shall lead an assembly against you to stone you and hack you to pieces with their swords.* 41* They shall set fire to your homes and inflict punishments on you while many women watch. Thus I will put an end to your prostitution, and you shall never again offer payment. 42 When I have spent my fury upon you I will stop being jealous about you, and calm down, no longer angry. 43 Because you did not remember the days of your youth but enraged me with all these things, see, I am bringing down your ways upon your head— oracle of the Lord God. Have you not added depravity to your other abominations?

44 See, everyone who makes proverbs will

† 16:20–21 Also a reference to the practice of child sacrifice introduced under Judah's impious kings; cf. 2 Kgs 16:3; 17:17; Jer 7:31; 19:5; 32:35.
16:24 A platform…a dais: associated with rituals borrowed from the Canaanites.
16:27 Philistines: lit., "daughters of the Philistines," a common expression when referring to the various towns that make up a territory.
16:38 As a jealous husband, Yhwh severely punishes Jerusalem for her adultery: i.e., her worship of idols. Adultery was considered a capital crime in ancient Israel; cf. Lv 20:10–14; Nm 5:11–28; Dt 22:22.

16:16 cf. 2 Kgs 23:7.
16:19 Hos 2:13.
16:20 Jer 7:31; cf. Lv 18:21; Dt 18:10; 2 Kgs 21:6; 23:10.
16:21 2 Kgs 16:3; 17:17.
16:22 Jer 2:2; Hos 2:15; 11:1.
16:24 Is 57:7.
16:25 Jer 2:20; 3:2; 5:7; Hos 2:4.
16:27 cf. 2 Chr 28:18.
16:28 2 Kgs 16:7.
16:29 cf. Ez 23:14–17.
16:33 Hos 8:9–10.
16:37 cf. Ez 23:10, 22; Is 47:3; Rev 17:16.
16:38 Lv 20:10; Dt 22:22.
16:39 cf. 2 Kgs 18:11.
16:40 cf. Ez 23:47; Jn 8:5, 7.
16:41 2 Kgs 25:9; cf. Jgs 12:1; 15:6.

make this proverb about you, "Like mother, like daughter." [45] Yes, you are truly the daughter of your mother† who rejected her husband and children: you are truly a sister to your sisters who rejected their husbands and children—your mother was a Hittite and your father an Amorite.* [46]† Your elder sister was Samaria with her daughters to the north of you; and your younger sister was Sodom and her daughters, south of you.* [47] Not only did you walk in their ways and act as abominably as they did, but in a very short time you became more corrupt in all your ways than they were.* [48] As I live—oracle of the Lord GOD—I swear that your sister Sodom with her daughters have not done the things you and your daughters have done!* [49]* Now look at the guilt of your sister Sodom: she and her daughters were proud, sated with food, complacent in prosperity. They did not give any help to the poor and needy. [50] Instead, they became arrogant and committed abominations before me; then, as you have seen, I removed them.* [51] Samaria did not commit half the sins you did. You have done more abominable things than they did. You even made your sisters look righteous, with all the abominations you have done. [52] You, then, must bear your disgrace, for you have made a case for your sisters! Because your sins are more abominable than theirs, they seem righteous compared to you. Blush for shame, and bear the disgrace of having made your sisters appear righteous.

[53] I will restore their fortunes, the fortunes of Sodom and her daughters, the fortunes of Samaria and her daughters—and your fortunes along with them. [54] Thus you must bear your disgrace and be ashamed of all you have done to bring them comfort. [55] Yes, your sisters, Sodom and her daughters, Samaria and her daughters, shall return to the way they were,* and you and your daughters shall return to the way you were. [56] Did you not hold your sister Sodom in bad repute while you felt proud of yourself, [57] before your evil was exposed? Now you are like her, reproached by the Arameans and all their neighbors, despised on all sides by the Philistines.* [58] The penalty of your depravity and your abominations—you must bear it all—oracle of the LORD.

[59] For thus says the Lord GOD: I will deal with you for what you did; you despised an oath by breaking a covenant.* [60] But I will remember the covenant I made with you when you were young; I will set up an everlasting covenant† with you.* [61] Then you shall remember your ways and be ashamed when you receive your sisters, those older and younger than you; I give them to you as daughters, but not by reason of your covenant. [62] For I will re-establish my covenant with you, that you may know that I am the LORD,* [63] that you may remember and be ashamed, and never again open your mouth because of your disgrace, when I pardon you for all you have done—oracle of the Lord GOD.*

# 17

**The Eagles and the Vine.** [1] The word of the LORD came to me: [2] Son of man, propose a riddle, and tell this proverb to the house of Israel: [3] Thus says the Lord GOD:

> The great eagle, with wide wingspan
>     and long feathers, with thick plumage,
>     many-hued, came to Lebanon.
> He plucked the crest of the cedar,*
[4]     broke off its topmost branch,
> And brought it to a land of merchants,
>     set it in a city of traders.
[5]     Then he took some native seed
>     and planted it in fertile soil;
> A shoot beside plentiful waters,
>     like a willow he planted it,*
[6]     That it might sprout and become a vine,
>     dense and low-lying,
> With its branches turned toward him,
>     its roots beneath it.
> Thus it became a vine, produced branches,

---

† **16:45** *Truly the daughter of your mother*: Jerusalem's depraved behavior follows from the bad behavior of its non-Israelite forebears; cf. v. 3.

**16:46–47** Jerusalem is so much more corrupt than Samaria, the elder sister in size, and the smaller Sodom that both now appear just and righteous. Ezekiel's reference to Sodom indicates that the city's identification with wickedness and evil was already an established tradition in fifth century B.C. Judah.

**16:60** *Everlasting covenant*: Ezekiel foresees God renewing the covenant of Sinai in a new and spirit-empowered way that will not be fatally broken as in the present exile or force God to abandon Israel again; cf. 11:19–21; 36:25–27; 37:26–28.

**16:45** cf. Ez 23:2.
**16:46** Jer 3:8–11; Rev 11:8.
**16:47** cf. Dt 29:23; 32:32; Is 1:9–10.
**16:48** cf. Gn 19:25; Mt 10:15; 11:23–24.
**16:49** cf. Is 1:10; cf. Gn 49:24.
**16:50** cf. Gn 18:20–21.
**16:55** cf. Ez 36:11.
**16:57** cf. Ez 25:12–14; 35:1–15; 2 Kgs 16:6.
**16:59** cf. Ez 17:19.
**16:60** cf. Ez 37:26; Is 55:3; Jer 32:40.
**16:62** Dt 29:14.
**16:63** Dn 9:7–8.
**17:3** Dt 28:49; Jer 49:22; Dn 7:4.
**17:5** cf. 2 Kgs 24:17.

and put forth shoots.
7 Then another great eagle appeared,
    with wide wingspan, rich in plumage,
And see! This vine bent its roots to him,
    sent out branches for him to water.
From the bed where it was planted,*
8     it was transplanted to a fertile field
By abundant waters, to produce
    branches,
    to bear fruit, to become a majestic
    vine.
9 Say: Thus says the Lord GOD: Can it
    thrive?
Will he not tear up its roots
    and strip its fruit?
Then all its green leaves will wither—
    neither strong arm nor mighty nation
    is needed to uproot it.
10 True, it is planted; but will it thrive?
Will it not wither up
When the east wind strikes it,
    wither in the very bed where it
    sprouted?*

11† The word of the LORD came to me:

12     Now say to the rebellious house:
    Do you not understand this? Tell
    them!
The king of Babylon came to Jerusalem
    and took away its king and officials
    and brought them to him in
    Babylon.*
13 After removing the nobles from the
    land,
    he then took one of the royal line
And made a covenant with him,
    binding him under oath,*
14 To be a humble kingdom,
    without high aspirations,
    to keep his covenant and so survive.
15 But this one rebelled against him
    by sending envoys to Egypt
To obtain horses and a mighty army.
    Can he thrive?
Can he escape if he does this?

Can he break a covenant and go
    free?*
16 As I live—oracle of the Lord GOD—
    in the house of the king who set him
    up to rule,
Whose oath he ignored and whose
    covenant he broke,
    there in Babylon I swear he shall die!*
17 Pharaoh shall not help him on the day
    of battle,
    with a great force and mighty horde,
When ramps are thrown up and siege
    works built
    for the cutting down of many lives.
18 He ignored his oath, breaking his
    covenant;
    even though he gave his hand, he did
    all these things—
    he shall not escape!*
19 Therefore, thus says the Lord GOD:
    As I live, my oath which he spurned,
And my covenant which he broke,
    I will bring down on his head.
20 I will spread my net over him,
    and he will be caught in my snare.
I will bring him to Babylon
    to judge him there
    because he broke faith with me.*
21 Any among his forces who escape
    will fall by the sword,
And whoever might survive
    will be scattered to the winds.*
Thus you will know that I the LORD have
    spoken.
22 Thus says the Lord GOD:
I, too, will pluck from the crest of the
    cedar
    the highest branch.
From the top a tender shoot
    I will break off and transplant†
    on a high, lofty mountain.
23 On the mountain height of Israel
    I will plant it.
It shall put forth branches and bear
    fruit,
    and become a majestic cedar.

---

**17:11–21** These verses explain the allegory in vv. 3–10. In 597 B.C., Nebuchadnezzar removed Jehoiachin from the throne and took him into exile; in his place he set Zedekiah, Jehoiachin's uncle, on the throne and received from him the oath of loyalty. But Zedekiah was persuaded to rebel by Pharaoh Hophra of Egypt and thus deserved punishment; cf. 2 Kgs 24:10–25:7.
**17:22–23** The Lord will undo the actions of the Babylonian king by rebuilding the Davidic dynasty so the nations realize that only Israel's God can restore a people's destiny.

**17:7** cf. Ez 31:4–5; Jer 37:5; 44:30.
**17:10** cf. Ez 19:12.
**17:12** 2 Kgs 24:15.
**17:13** 2 Chr 36:13.
**17:15** Jer 52:3.
**17:16** 2 Kgs 24:17; 25:7; Jer 52:11.
**17:18** cf. 2 Kgs 10:15.
**17:20** cf. Ez 12:13; 32:3.
**17:21** Lv 26:33; 2 Kgs 25:5.

Every small bird will nest under it,
     all kinds of winged birds will dwell
     in the shade of its branches. *

24 Every tree of the field will know
     that I am the LORD.
I bring low the high tree,
     lift high the lowly tree,
Wither up the green tree,
     and make the dry tree bloom. *
As I, the LORD, have spoken, so will I do!

# 18 Personal Responsibility.

1 The word of the LORD came to me: Son of man, 2 what is the meaning of this proverb you recite in the land of Israel:

"Parents eat sour grapes, *
     but the children's teeth are set on
       edge"? †

3 As I live—oracle of the Lord GOD: I swear that none of you will ever repeat this proverb in Israel. 4 For all life is mine: the life of the parent is like the life of the child, both are mine. Only the one who sins shall die!

5 If a man is just—if he does what is right, 6 if he does not eat on the mountains, † or raise his eyes to the idols of the house of Israel; if he does not defile a neighbor's wife, or have relations with a woman during her period; * 7 * if he oppresses no one, gives back the pledge received for a debt, commits no robbery; gives food to the hungry and clothes the naked; 8 if he does not lend at interest or exact usury; if he refrains from evildoing and makes a fair judgment between two opponents; * 9 if he walks by my statutes and is careful to observe my ordinances, that man is just—he shall surely live—oracle of the Lord GOD. *

10 But if he begets a son who is violent and commits murder, or does any of these things, * 11 even though the father does none of them— a son who eats on the mountains, defiles the wife of his neighbor, 12 oppresses the poor and needy, commits robbery, does not give back a pledge, raises his eyes to idols, does

abominable things, 13 lends at interest and exacts usury—this son certainly shall not live. Because he practiced all these abominations, he shall surely be put to death; his own blood shall be on him. *

14 But, in turn, if he begets a son who sees all the sins his father commits, yet fears and does not imitate him— 15 a son who does not eat on the mountains, or raise his eyes to the idols of the house of Israel, or defile a neighbor's wife; 16 who does not oppress anyone, or exact a pledge, or commit robbery; who gives his food to the hungry and clothes the naked; * 17 who refrains from evildoing, accepts no interest or usury, but keeps my ordinances and walks in my statutes—this one shall not die for the sins of his father. He shall surely live! 18 Only the father, since he committed extortion and robbed his brother, and did what was not good among his people—he will die because of his sin! 19 You ask: "Why is not the son charged with the guilt of his father?" Because the son has done what is just and right and has been careful to observe all my statutes—he shall surely live! 20 * Only the one who sins shall die. The son shall not be charged with the guilt of his father, nor shall the father be charged with the guilt of his son. Justice belongs to the just, and wickedness to the wicked.

21 But if the wicked man turns away from all the sins he has committed, if he keeps all my statutes and does what is just and right, he shall surely live. He shall not die! 22 None of the crimes he has committed shall be remembered against him; he shall live because of the justice he has shown. 23 * Do I find pleasure in the death of the wicked—oracle of the Lord GOD? Do I not rejoice when they turn from their evil way and live?

24 And if the just turn from justice and do evil, like all the abominations the wicked do, can they do this evil and still live? None of the justice they did shall be remembered, because they acted treacherously and committed these sins; because of this, they shall die. * 25 * You say, "The LORD's way is not fair!" † Hear now,

---

**18:2** *Parents…on edge:* a proverb the people quoted to complain that they were being punished for their ancestors' sins; cf. Jer 31:29.

**18:6** *Eat on the mountains:* take part in meals after sacrifice at the high places.

**18:25** *The LORD's way is not fair:* this chapter rejects the idea that punishment is transferred from one generation to the next and emphasizes individual responsibility and accountability.

**17:23** Dn 4:12; Hos 14:5–7.
**17:24** Dn 5:21.
**18:2** Jer 31:29; cf. Ez 21:19.
**18:6** Lv 15:19–24; cf. Hos 4:13.
**18:7** Ex 22:26; Is 58:7; Mt 25:35.
**18:8** Ex 22:25; Lv 25:35–37; Dt 23:19–20.
**18:9** Lv 18:5.
**18:10** cf. Ez 22:6–9.
**18:13** Ex 22:25; Lv 20:9–11.
**18:16** cf. Ez 16:49; Is 58:7–10.
**18:20** Dt 24:16; 2 Kgs 14:6; cf. Mt 16:27; Jn 9:2.
**18:23** cf. Ez 33:11; 2 Pt 3:9.
**18:24** cf. 2 Pt 2:20–22.
**18:25** cf. Ez 33:20.

house of Israel: Is it my way that is unfair? Are not your ways unfair? ²⁶When the just turn away from justice to do evil and die, on account of the evil they did they must die. ²⁷But if the wicked turn from the wickedness they did and do what is right and just, they save their lives; ²⁸since they turned away from all the sins they committed, they shall live; they shall not die. ²⁹But the house of Israel says, "The Lord's way is not fair!" Is it my way that is not fair, house of Israel? Is it not your ways that are not fair?

³⁰*Therefore I will judge you, house of Israel, all of you according to your ways—oracle of the Lord GOD. Turn, turn back from all your crimes, that they may not be a cause of sin for you ever again. ³¹Cast away from you all the crimes you have committed, and make for yourselves a new heart and a new spirit. Why should you die, house of Israel?* ³²*For I find no pleasure in the death of anyone who dies—oracle of the Lord GOD. Turn back and live!

## Allegory of the Lions†

**19** ¹As for you, raise a lamentation over the princes of Israel, ²and say:

What a lioness was your mother,
  a lion among lions!
She made her lair among young lions,
  to raise her cubs;
³ One cub she raised up,
  a young lion he became;
He learned to tear apart prey,
  he devoured people.*
⁴ Nations heard about him;
  in their pit he was caught;
They took him away with hooks
  to the land of Egypt.†*
⁵ When she realized she had waited in
    vain,
  she lost hope.
She took another of her cubs,
  and made him a young lion.

⁶ He prowled among the lions,
  became a young lion;
He learned to tear apart prey,
  he devoured people.*
⁷ He ravaged their strongholds,
  laid waste their cities.
The earth and everything in it were
    terrified
  at the sound of his roar.
⁸ Nations laid out against him
  snares all around;
They spread their net for him,
  in their pit he was caught.*
⁹ They put him in fetters and took him
    away
  to the king of Babylon,
So his roar would no longer be heard
  on the mountains of Israel.

## Allegory of the Vine Branch

¹⁰ Your mother was like a leafy vine†
  planted by water,
Fruitful and full of branches
  because of abundant water.
¹¹ One strong branch grew
  into a royal scepter.
So tall it towered among the clouds,
  conspicuous in height,
  with dense foliage.*
¹² But she was torn out in fury
  and flung to the ground;
The east wind withered her up,
  her fruit was plucked away;
Her strongest branch dried up,
  fire devoured it.*
¹³ Now she is planted in a wilderness,
  in a dry, parched land.*
¹⁴ Fire flashed from her branch,
  and devoured her shoots;
Now she does not have a strong branch,
  a royal scepter!

This is a lamentation and serves as a lamentation.

---

† **19:1–9** Some commentators identify Jehoahaz and Zedekiah, sons of the same mother, as the "two young lions"; they were deported to Egypt and Babylon respectively. Cf. 2 Kgs 23:31–34; 24:18–20.

**19:4** A common fate for royal prisoners: e.g., Assurbanipal claims he put a ring in the jaw of a captive king and a dog collar around his neck (cf. v. 9). A wall relief shows Esarhaddon holding two royal captives with ropes tied to rings in their lips.

**19:10–14** *Vine*: Judah. *One strong branch*: the Davidic king. This allegory describes the deportation of the Davidic dynasty to Babylon and laments the destruction of the house of David. From

Ezekiel's perspective, the arrogance of Judah's kings leads to this tragedy (vv. 12–14).

---

18:30 Jer 35:15; cf. Mt 3:2;
  Lk 3:3.
18:31 cf. Ez 11:19; 36:26.
18:32 cf. Ez 18:23; 33:11.
19:3 2 Kgs 23:31–34.
19:4 2 Chr 36:4.
19:6 2 Kgs 24:9.
19:8 2 Kgs 24:2–15.
19:11 Dn 4:11.
19:12 Hos 13:15.
19:13 cf. Ez 20:35.

EZ

# 20

**Israel's History of Infidelity.** ¹In the seventh year, on the tenth day of the fifth month,† some of the elders of Israel came to consult the LORD and sat down before me.* ²Then the word of the LORD came to me: ³Son of man, speak to the elders of Israel and say to them: Thus says the Lord GOD: Have you come to consult me? As I live, I will not allow myself to be consulted by you!—oracle of the Lord GOD.

⁴Will you judge them? Will you judge, son of man? Tell them about the abominations of their ancestors,* ⁵and say to them: Thus says the Lord GOD: The day I chose Israel, I swore to the descendants of the house of Jacob; I revealed myself to them in the land of Egypt and swore to them, saying: I am the LORD, your God. ⁶That day I swore to bring them out of the land of Egypt to the land I had searched out for them, a land flowing with milk and honey, a jewel among all lands.* ⁷Then I said to them: Throw away, each of you, the detestable things† that held your eyes; do not defile yourselves with the idols of Egypt: I am the LORD, your God.*

⁸But they rebelled and refused to listen to me; none of them threw away the detestable things that held their eyes, nor did they abandon the idols of Egypt. Then I considered pouring out my fury and spending my anger against them there in the land of Egypt.* ⁹I acted for the sake of my name, that it should not be desecrated in the eyes of the nations among whom they were: in the eyes of the nations I had made myself known to them, to bring them out of the land of Egypt.* ¹⁰Therefore I led them out of the land of Egypt and brought them into the wilderness. ¹¹* Then I gave them my statutes and made known to them my ordinances, so that everyone who keeps them has life through them. ¹²* I also gave them my sabbaths to be a sign between me and them, to show that it is I, the LORD, who makes them holy.

¹³But the house of Israel rebelled against me in the wilderness. They did not observe my statutes, and they rejected my ordinances that bring life to those who keep them. My sabbaths, too, they desecrated grievously. Then I considered pouring out my fury on them in the wilderness to put an end to them,* ¹⁴but I acted for the sake of my name, so it would not be desecrated in the eyes of the nations in whose sight I had brought them out.* ¹⁵Nevertheless in the wilderness I swore to them that I would not bring them into the land I had given them—a land flowing with milk and honey, a jewel among all the lands. ¹⁶Their hearts followed after their idols so closely that they did not live by my statutes, but rejected my ordinances and desecrated my sabbaths. ¹⁷But I looked on them with pity, not wanting to destroy them, so I did not put an end to them in the wilderness.

¹⁸Then I said to their children in the wilderness: Do not follow the statutes of your parents. Do not keep their ordinances. Do not defile yourselves with their idols. ¹⁹I am the LORD, your God: follow my statutes and be careful to observe my ordinances; ²⁰keep holy my sabbaths as a sign between me and you so that you may know that I am the LORD, your God.* ²¹But their children rebelled against me: they did not follow my statutes or keep my ordinances that bring life to those who observe them; my sabbaths they desecrated. Then I considered pouring out my fury on them, spending my anger against them in the wilderness; ²²but I stayed my hand, acting for the sake of my name, lest it be desecrated in the eyes of the nations, in whose sight I had brought them out. ²³Nevertheless I swore to them in the wilderness that I would disperse them among the nations and scatter them in other lands, ²⁴because they did not carry out my ordinances, but rejected my statutes and desecrated my sabbaths, having eyes only for the idols of their ancestors. ²⁵Therefore I gave them statutes that were not good,† and ordinances through which they could not have

---

† **20:1** *The seventh year...the fifth month*: August 14, 591 B.C.
**20:7** *Detestable things*: in the Book of Ezekiel, Israel's continued worship of idols in Egypt and in the wilderness, despite the Lord's powerful deeds on their behalf, is the reason God punishes them so severely; they must learn and acknowledge that he is their only Lord. Cf., e.g., Exodus (5:1–6:9; 14:10–30; 16:1–36) and Numbers (11:1–15; 14:1–12; 20:1–9), where the people's failure to trust Moses and the Lord brings punishment.
**20:25–26** *I gave them statutes that were not good*: because Israel rejected the Lord's life-giving laws, he "gave" laws (e.g., the sacrifice of every firstborn) that would lead only to death and de-

struction. Dt 12:29–31; Jer 7:31; 19:4–5 may address a popular assumption that the Lord accepted and perhaps required child sacrifice, especially as evidence of great trust during national emergencies (2 Kgs 3:27; Mi 6:7). By combining language from

* 
| | |
|---|---|
| **20:1** cf. Ez 8:1. | **20:11** Lv 18:5; Dt 4:7–8; |
| **20:4** cf. Ez 16:2; Mt 23:32. | Rom 10:5. |
| **20:6** Ex 3:8; 6:8; Dt | **20:12** Ex 20:8; 31:13; Dt |
| 8:7–10. | 5:12; Neh 13:17–18. |
| **20:7** Ex 20:2–4. | **20:13** Jer 11:7–8; 17:21–23. |
| **20:8** cf. Ez 16:26; Ex 32:7. | **20:14** Is 48:11. |
| **20:9** cf. Ez 36:22. | **20:20** Ex 31:13. |

life.* [26] I let them become defiled by their offerings, by having them make a fiery offering of every womb's firstborn, in order to ruin them so they might know that I am the LORD.*

[27] Therefore speak to the house of Israel, son of man, and tell them: Thus says the Lord GOD: In this way also your ancestors blasphemed me, breaking faith with me. [28] When I brought them to the land I had sworn to give them, and they saw all its high hills and leafy trees, there they offered sacrifices, there they made offerings to provoke me, there they sent up sweet-smelling oblations, there they poured out their libations.* [29] So I said to them, "What is this high place† to which you go?" Thus its name became "high place" even to this day.* [30] Therefore say to the house of Israel: Thus says the Lord GOD: Will you defile yourselves in the way your ancestors did? Will you lust after their detestable idols? [31] By offering your gifts, by making your children pass through the fire, you defile yourselves with all your idols even to this day. Shall I let myself be consulted by you, house of Israel? As I live—oracle of the Lord GOD—I swear I will not let myself be consulted by you!*

[32] What has entered your mind shall never happen: You are thinking, "We shall be like the nations, like the peoples of foreign lands, serving wood and stone." [33] As I live—oracle of the Lord GOD—with mighty hand and outstretched arm, with wrath poured out, I swear I will be king over you!* [34] With mighty hand and outstretched arm, with wrath poured out, I will bring you out from the nations and gather you from the countries over which you are scattered;* [35] † I will lead you to the wilderness of the peoples and enter into judgment with you face to face. [36] Just as I entered into judgment with your ancestors in the wilderness of the land of Egypt, so will I enter into judgment with you—oracle of the Lord GOD. [37] Thus I will make you pass under the staff† and will impose on you the terms of the covenant.* [38] I will sort out from you those who defied me and rebelled against me; from the land where they resided as aliens I will bring them out, but they shall not return to the land of Israel. Thus you shall know that I am the LORD.

[39] As for you, house of Israel, thus says the Lord GOD: Go! each of you, and worship your idols. Listen to me! You shall never again desecrate my holy name with your offerings and your idols!* [40] For on my holy mountain,† on the highest mountain in Israel—oracle of the Lord GOD—there the whole house of Israel shall worship me; there in the land I will accept them all, there I will claim your tributes, the best of your offerings, from all your holy things.* [41] As a sweet-smelling oblation I will accept you, when I bring you from among the nations and gather you out of the lands over which you were scattered; and through you I will manifest my holiness in the sight of the nations.* [42] Thus you shall know that I am the LORD, when I bring you back to the soil of Israel, the land I swore to give your ancestors. [43] There you shall remember your ways, all the deeds by which you defiled yourselves; and you shall loathe yourselves because of all the evil you did.* [44] And you shall know that I am the LORD when I deal with you thus, for the sake of my name, not according to your evil ways and wanton deeds, house of Israel—oracle of the Lord GOD.*

# 21 The Sword of the Lord. [1] The word of the LORD came to me: [2] † Son of man, turn your face to the south: preach against

---

Ex 22:28 with the vocabulary of child sacrifice, Ezekiel suggests that firstborn sons were regularly sacrificed in Israel.

20:29 *High place*: a cultic site, originally a hilltop, but often a raised platform in a sacred area. Until Deuteronomy's insistence that official and legitimate worship of the Lord take place only in Jerusalem, these local shrines were popular places for worship (e.g., 1 Sm 9–10) or for consulting the Lord (1 Kgs 3:4–5). In order to unite the Kingdom of Judah politically and religiously, Dt 12:2 demands destruction of the high places. Ezekiel, like other prophets, condemns Israelite worship at these places and identifies this illegitimate worship as one reason for the punishment of exile.

20:35–38 Exile among other lands occasions a new exodus and a new wilderness journey back to Israel. The Lord will eliminate the rebellious, as he did on the first journey, and use the surviving remnant to reveal his power to the nations.

20:37 *Pass under the staff*: in Lv 27:32–33, a method of counting off animals to select those to be dedicated for the tithe. In Ezekiel, on the other hand, those who survive the selection process are marked for destruction for violating the covenant.

20:40 *Holy mountain*: the Temple mount and Jerusalem in contrast to "every high hill" in v. 28 (cf. the royal Zion theology in Ps 48:2). Acceptable worship takes place here among a restored people, a theme taken up in chaps. 40–48 (cf. 40:2).

21:2–4 In Babylon Ezekiel looks toward Judah, pictured as a forest about to be destroyed by fire.

20:25 cf. Rom 1:28.
20:26 Lv 18:21.
20:28 Ps 78:57–58.
20:29 cf. Ez 16:16.
20:31 Ps 106:37–39.
20:33 Dt 4:34; 5:1.
20:34 Ps 106:47.
20:37 Lv 27:3; Jer 33:13.
20:39 Ex 20:7.
20:40 cf. Ps 2:6; Is 11:9; 56:7.
20:41 cf. 2 Cor 2:14.
20:43 Lv 26:41.
20:44 cf. Ez 36:22.

the south, prophesy against the forest land in the south. ³ Say to the forest in the south: Hear the word of the LORD! Thus says the Lord GOD: See! I am kindling a fire in you that shall devour every green tree as well as every dry tree. The blazing flame shall not be quenched so that from south to north every face shall be scorched by it. ⁴ All flesh shall see that I, the LORD, have kindled it; it shall not be quenched.*

⁵ But I said, "Ah! Lord GOD, they are saying about me, 'Is not this the one who is forever spinning parables?'" ⁶ Then the word of the LORD came to me: ⁷ Son of man, turn your face toward Jerusalem: preach against its sanctuary, prophesy against the land of Israel.* ⁸ Say to the land of Israel: Thus says the LORD: See! I am coming against you; I will draw my sword from its scabbard and cut off from you the righteous and the wicked.† ⁹ Thus my sword shall come out from its scabbard against all flesh from south to north ¹⁰ and all flesh shall know that I, the LORD, have drawn my sword from its scabbard. It cannot return again.*

**Act Symbolic of the City's Fall.** ¹¹ As for you, son of man, groan! with shattered loins and bitter grief, groan in their sight. ¹² When they ask you, "Why are you groaning?" you shall say: Because of what I heard!† When it comes every heart shall melt, every hand fall helpless; every spirit will grow faint, and every knee run with water. See, it is coming, it is here!—oracle of the Lord GOD.

**Song of the Sword.** ¹³ The word of the LORD came to me:* ¹⁴ Son of man, prophesy! say: Thus says the LORD:

A sword, a sword has been sharpened,
   a sword, a sword has been
      burnished:*
¹⁵   Sharpened to make a slaughter,
      burnished to flash lightning!
   Why should I stop now?

You have rejected the rod and every
   judgment!
¹⁶ I have given it over to the burnisher
   that he might hold it in his hand,
A sword sharpened and burnished
   to be put in the hands of an
      executioner.
¹⁷ Cry out and howl, son of man,
   for it is destined for my people,
For all the princes of Israel,
   victims of the sword with my people.
Therefore, slap your thigh,†
¹⁸   for it is tested, and why not?
Since you rejected my staff,
   should it not happen?—
      oracle of the Lord GOD.
¹⁹ As for you, son of man, prophesy,
   and clap your hands!
Let the sword strike twice, a third time.
   It is a sword of slaughter,
A sword for slaughtering,
   whirling around them all,
²⁰ That every heart may tremble;
   for many will be made to stumble.
At all their gates
   I have stationed the sword for
      slaughter,
Made it flash lightning,
   drawn for slaughter.
²¹ Slash to the right!
   turn to the left,
   Wherever your edge is directed!*
²² Then I, too, shall clap my hands,†
   and spend my fury.
   I, the LORD, have spoken.

**Nebuchadnezzar at the Crossroads.** ²³ The word of the LORD came to me: ²⁴ Son of man, make for yourself two roads over which the sword of the king of Babylon can come. Both roads shall start out from the same land. Then put a signpost at the head of each road ²⁵ so the sword can come to Rabbah of the Ammonites or to Judah and its fortress, Jerusalem. ²⁶ For the king of Babylon is standing at the fork of the two roads to read the omens:†

---

† **21:8** *Cut off from you the righteous and the wicked*: a more complete devastation of Jerusalem than that described in 9:6.
  **21:12** *What I heard*: the news of the fall of Jerusalem; cf. 33:21–22.
  **21:17** *Slap your thigh*: a gesture signifying grief and dread; cf. Jer 31:19.
  **21:22** *Clap my hands*: the Lord declares himself no longer responsible for Judah; cf. 22:13; Nm 24:10; Jb 27:23; Lam 2:15.
  **21:26** Three forms of divination are mentioned: arrow div-

ination, consisting in the use of differently marked arrows extracted or shaken from a case at random; the consultation of the teraphim or household idols; and liver divination, scrutiny of the configurations of the livers of newly slaughtered animals, a common form of divination in Mesopotamia.

* **21:4** Lv 26:25.      **21:13** Gn 49:10.
  **21:7** Lv 26:36.      **21:14** cf. 2 Kgs 13:18–19.
  **21:10** Is 34:5–6.    **21:21** Prv 16:33; Zec 10:2.

he shakes out the arrows, inquires of the teraphim, inspects the liver.* 27 Into his right hand has fallen the lot marked "Jerusalem":† to order the slaughter, to raise the battle cry, to set the battering rams against the gates, to throw up a ramp, to build siege works. 28 In the eyes of those bound by oath this seems like a false omen; yet the lot taken in hand exposes the wickedness for which they, still bound by oath, will be taken in hand.

29 Therefore thus says the Lord GOD: Because your guilt has been exposed, your crimes laid bare, your sinfulness revealed in all your deeds—because you have been exposed, you shall be taken in hand.* 30 And as for you, depraved and wicked prince of Israel, a day is coming to end your life of crime.* 31 Thus says the Lord GOD: Off with the turban and away with the crown! Nothing shall be as it was! Exalt the lowly and bring the exalted low! 32 A ruin, a ruin, a ruin, I shall make it! Nothing will be the same until the one comes to whom I have given it for judgment.*

**To the Ammonites.**† 33 As for you, son of man, prophesy: Thus says the Lord GOD to the Ammonites and their insults:

O sword, sword drawn for slaughter,
   burnished to consume, to flash
      lightning!
34 Your false visions and lying omens,
   Set you over the necks of the slain,
      the wicked whose day had come—
   an end to their life of crime.
35 Return to your scabbard!
   In the place you were created,
In the land of your origin,
   I will judge you.
36 I will pour out my anger upon you,
   breathing my fiery wrath against you;
I will hand you over to ravagers,
   artisans of destruction!

37 You shall be fuel for the fire,
   your blood shall flow throughout the
      land;
You shall not be remembered,
   for I, the LORD, have spoken.

## 22 Crimes of Jerusalem.

1 The word of the LORD came to me: 2 You,† son of man, will you judge? will you judge the city of bloodshed? Then make known all its abominations, 3 and say: Thus says the Lord GOD: O city that sheds blood within itself so that its time has come, that has made idols for its own defilement: 4 By the blood you shed you have become guilty, and by the idols you made you have become defiled. You have brought on your day, you have come to the end of your years. Therefore I make you an object of scorn for the nations and a laughingstock for all lands.* 5 Those near and those far off will mock you: "Defiled of Name! Queen of Tumult!" 6 See! the princes of Israel within you use their power to shed blood.† 7 Within you, father and mother are dishonored; they extort the resident alien in your midst; within you, they oppress orphans and widows.* 8 What I consider holy you have rejected, and my sabbaths you have desecrated. 9 † In you are those who slander to cause bloodshed; within you are those who feast on the mountains; in your midst are those whose actions are depraved.* 10 In you are those who uncover the nakedness of their fathers; in you those who coerce women to intercourse during their period.* 11 * There are those in you who do abominable things with their neighbors' wives, men who defile their daughters-in-law by incest, men who coerce their sisters to intercourse, the daughters of their own fathers. 12 There are those in you who take bribes to shed blood. You exact interest and usury; you extort profit from your neighbor by violence. But me you have forgotten—oracle of the Lord GOD.*

---

† **21:27–28** A lot marked "Jerusalem" falls out, which marks the guilt of the city's inhabitants.
**21:33–37** In vv. 23–32 Ezekiel imagines Nebuchadnezzar deciding whether to attack Jerusalem or Rabbath-Ammon. As it happened, the Babylonians decided to attack Jerusalem first. Here (vv. 33–37) Ezekiel prophesies to the Ammonites that a nation which serves as an instrument of the Lord's judgment will itself be judged.
**22:2–16** This first oracle focuses on Jerusalem as a "city of bloodshed" (cf. Na 3:1). Here transgressions involving blood, the oppression of the poor, and improper cultic practices are seen as interrelated, for blood as the carrier of life is fundamental to both the cultic and social spheres of life.

**22:6** *To shed blood*: a very serious charge in light of the solemn command of God to Noah in Gn 9:6 against human bloodshed.
**22:9–11** The charges against Jerusalem echo the commandments of Lv 20:10–18.

21:26 Is 28:5; Ps 75:8.        22:9 cf. Ez 18:11.
21:29 Jer 8:11–12; 27:9–10.    22:10 Lv 18:7–8, 19.
21:30 cf. Ez 16:3.             22:11 Lv 18:7–20; 20:10–
21:32 Mal 3:19.                   21; Dt 23:1–30; Jer
22:4 Ps 44:13–14.                 5:8.
22:7 Ex 22:21–22; 23:9; Dt     22:12 Ez 18:8; Dt 27:25; Am
   5:16.                          5:12.

13 See, I am clapping my hands because of the profits you extorted and the blood shed in your midst. 14 Will your heart remain firm, will your hands be strong, in the days when I deal with you? I am the LORD; I have spoken, and I will act! 15 I will disperse you among the nations and scatter you over other lands, so that I may purge your filth. 16 In you I will allow myself to be desecrated in the eyes of the nations; thus you shall know that I am the LORD.

17 The word of the LORD came to me: 18† Son of man, the house of Israel has become dross to me. All of them are copper, tin, iron, and lead within a furnace; they have become the dross from silver.* 19 Therefore thus says the Lord GOD: Because all of you have become dross, See! I am gathering you within Jerusalem. 20 Just as silver, copper, iron, lead, and tin are gathered within a furnace to be blasted with fire to smelt it, so I will gather you together in my furious wrath, put you in, and smelt you.* 21 When I have assembled you, I will blast you with the fire of my anger and smelt you with it. 22 Just as silver is smelted in a furnace, so you shall be smelted in it. Thus you shall know that I, the LORD, have poured out my fury on you.

23 The word of the LORD came to me: 24† Son of man, say to her: You are an unclean land receiving no rain at the time of my fury. 25 A conspiracy of its princes is like a roaring lion tearing prey; they devour people, seizing their wealth and precious things, making many widows within her.* 26 Her priests violate my law and desecrate what I consider holy; they do not distinguish between holy and common, nor teach the difference between unclean and clean; they pay no attention to my sabbaths, so that I have been desecrated in their midst.* 27* Within her, her officials are like wolves tearing prey, shedding blood and destroying lives to extort profit. 28* And her prophets cover them with whitewash, seeing false visions and performing lying divinations, saying, "Thus says the Lord GOD," although the LORD has not spoken. 29 The people of the land practice extortion and commit robbery; they wrong the poor and the needy, and oppress the resident alien without justice. 30 Thus I have searched among them for someone who would build a wall or stand in the breach before me to keep me from destroying the land; but I found no one. 31 Therefore I have poured out my fury upon them; with my fiery wrath I have consumed them, bringing down their ways upon their heads—oracle of the Lord GOD.

# 23 The Two Sisters.

1* The word of the LORD came to me: 2 Son of man, there were two women, daughters of the same mother.* 3 Even as young girls, they were prostitutes, serving as prostitutes in Egypt. There the Egyptians fondled their breasts and caressed their virgin nipples.* 4 Oholah was the name of the elder, and the name of her sister was Oholibah.† They became mine and gave birth to sons and daughters.* As for their names: Samaria was Oholah and Jerusalem, Oholibah. 5* Oholah became a prostitute while married to me and lusted after her lovers, the Assyrians: warriors 6 dressed in purple, governors and officers, all of them handsome young soldiers, mounted on horses. 7 She gave herself as a prostitute to them, to all the Assyrian elite; with all those for whom she lusted, she also defiled herself with their idols. 8 She did not abandon the prostitution she had begun with the Egyptians, who had lain with her when she was young, fondling her virgin breasts and pouring out their lust upon her.* 9 Therefore I handed her over to her lovers, to the Assyrians for whom she lusted. 10* They exposed her nakedness; her sons and daughters they took away, and her they killed with the sword. She became a byword for women because of the sentence carried out against her.

11 Although her sister Oholibah saw all this, her lust was more depraved than her sister's; she outdid her in prostitution.* 12 She too lusted after the Assyrians, governors and officers, warriors impeccably clothed, mounted

† 22:18–22 The image of smelting metals for purifying the people by the attacks of their enemies is common among the prophets; cf. Is 1:22, 25; Jer 6:27–30.
22:24–31 For a similar oracle, cf. Zep 3:1–8.
23:4 Oholah…Oholibah: symbolic names for Samaria, "her own tent," and Jerusalem, "my tent is in her." Cf. Ps 15:1 where "tent" is a synonym for "holy mountain." The names refer to the temple set up in the Northern Kingdom of Samaria (1 Kgs 12:28–29) and the Jerusalem Temple.

* 22:18 Is 1:21–26; 48:10; Jer 6:27–30.
22:20 Hos 8:10; Mal 3:2.
22:25 Jer 15:8.
22:26 Lv 20:25; Hg 2:11–14.
22:27 Mi 3:11; Zep 3:3.
22:28–29 cf. Ez 13:2–10.

23:1 cf. Ez 16.
23:2 Jer 3:7.
23:3 Is 1:21.
23:4 Jer 3:6–12.
23:5 Hos 5:3; 8:9.
23:8 cf. Ez 20:5–8.
23:10 cf. Ez 16:37.
23:11 Jer 3:8–11.

on horses, all of them handsome young soldiers. * [13] I saw that she had defiled herself—now both had gone down the same path. [14] She went further in her prostitution: She saw male figures drawn on the wall, images of Chaldeans drawn with vermilion, [15] with sashes tied about their waists, flowing turbans on their heads, all looking like chariot warriors, images of Babylonians, natives of Chaldea. [16] As soon as she set eyes on them she lusted for them, and she sent messengers to them in Chaldea. * [17] The Babylonians came to her, to her love couch; they defiled her with their impurities. But as soon as they had defiled her, she recoiled from them. [18] When her prostitution was discovered and her shame revealed, I recoiled from her as I had recoiled from her sister. [19] But she increased her prostitution, recalling the days of her youth when she had served as a prostitute in the land of Egypt. [20] She lusted for the lechers of Egypt, whose members are like those of donkeys, whose thrusts are like those of stallions.

[21] You reverted to the depravity of your youth, when Egyptians fondled your breasts, caressing your young nipples. [22] Therefore, Oholibah, thus says the Lord GOD: I will now stir up your lovers against you, those from whom you recoiled, and I will bring them against you from every side: [23] the men of Babylon and all of Chaldea, Pekod, Shoa and Koa, † along with all the Assyrians, handsome young soldiers, all of them governors and officers, charioteers and warriors, all of them horsemen. [24] They shall invade you with armor, chariots and wagons, a horde of peoples; they will array against you on every side bucklers and shields and helmets. I will give them the right of judgment, and they will judge you according to their standards. * [25] I will direct my jealousy against you, so that they deal with you in fury, cutting off your nose and ears; what is left of you shall fall by the sword. They shall take away your sons and daughters, and what is left of you shall be devoured by fire. [26] They shall strip off your clothes and seize your splendid jewelry. [27] I will put an end to your depravity and to your prostitution from the land of Egypt; you shall no longer look to them, nor even remember Egypt again.

[28] For thus says the Lord GOD: I am now handing you over to those whom you hate, to those from whom you recoil. [29] They shall treat you with hatred, seizing all that you worked for and leaving you stark naked, so that your indecent nakedness is exposed. * Your depravity and prostitution [30] brought these things upon you because you served as a prostitute for the nations, defiling yourself with their idols. *

[31] Because you followed your sister's path, I will put her cup into your hand. †*

[32] Thus says the Lord GOD: *
    The cup of your sister you shall drink,
        deep and wide;
    It brings ridicule and mockery,
        it holds so much;
[33] You will be filled with drunkenness and
        grief—
    A cup of horror and devastation,
        the cup of your sister Samaria;
[34] You shall drink it dry,
        its very sherds you will gnaw;
    And you shall tear out your breasts;
        for I have spoken—oracle of the Lord
        GOD.

[35] Therefore thus says the Lord GOD: You have forgotten me and cast me behind your back; now suffer for your depravity and prostitution.

[36] † Then the LORD said to me: Son of man, would you judge Oholah and Oholibah? Then make known to them their abominations. * [37] For they committed adultery, and blood covers their hands. They committed adultery with their idols; even the children they bore for me they burnt as food for them. [38] And they also did this to me: on that day, they defiled my sanctuary and desecrated my sabbaths. [39] On the very day they slaughtered their children for their idols, they entered my sanctuary

---

† **23:23** *Pekod, Shoa and Koa*: nations along the Tigris River, part of "greater Babylonia."
**23:31** The cup is a metaphor for divine punishment, the lot of all who rebel against the Lord (cf. Ps 75:9; Jer 25:15–16; 51:7; Is 51:21–23; Lam 4:21; Hb 2:15–16).
**23:36–49** Unlike vv. 1–35, this short poem juxtaposes the careers of the two sisters and looks to a future punishment. The male lovers of the first poem become the sisters' executioners, and the guests at the love feast a lynch mob. So corrupt and

depraved are the two sisters that their executioners win the esteemed title "righteous," for they have acted appropriately as agents of the Lord's judgment.

**23:12** 2 Kgs 16:7–15; 2 Chr 28:16.
**23:16** Is 57:8–9.
**23:24** Jer 30:5–6.
**23:29** Jer 13:27; Mi 1:11.
**23:30** Ps 106:37–38.
**23:31** Ps 75:8; Ob 16; Mt 20:22; Rev 14:10.
**23:32–33** Jer 25:15–16.
**23:36** Is 58:1; Mi 3:8.

to desecrate it. Thus they acted within my house!* ⁴⁰Moreover, they sent for men who had to come from afar; when a messenger was sent to them, they came. On their account you bathed, painted your eyes, and put on jewelry.* ⁴¹You sat on a magnificent couch, set before it a table, on which to lay my incense and oil. ⁴²The cries of a mob! The shouts of men coming in from the wilderness! They put bracelets on the women's arms and splendid crowns on their heads. ⁴³I said: "That worn-out one still has adulteries in her! Now they engage her as a prostitute and she …" ⁴⁴And indeed they did come in to her as men come in to a prostitute. Thus they came to Oholah and Oholibah, the depraved women. ⁴⁵The righteous shall certainly punish them with sentences given to adulterers and murderers, for they committed adultery, and blood is on their hands.*

⁴⁶Indeed, thus says the Lord GOD: Raise up an army against them and hand them over to terror and plunder. ⁴⁷The army will stone them and hack them to pieces with their swords. They will kill their sons and daughters and set fire to their houses. ⁴⁸Thus I will put an end to depravity in the land, and all women will be warned not to imitate your depravity. ⁴⁹They shall inflict on you the penalty of your depravity, and you shall pay for your sins of idolatry. Then you shall know that I am the Lord GOD.*

# 24 Allegory of the Pot.† ¹On the tenth day of the tenth month, in the ninth year,† the word of the LORD came to me:* ²Son of man, write down today's date this very day, for on this very day the king of Babylon lays siege to Jerusalem. ³* Propose this parable to the rebellious house and say to them: Thus says the Lord GOD:

Put the pot on, put it on!
    Pour in some water;

⁴    Add to it pieces of meat,
        all choice pieces;
    With thigh and shoulder,
        with choice cuts fill it.
⁵    Choose the pick of the flock,
        then pile logs beneath it;
    Bring it to a boil,
        cook all the pieces in it.*
⁶    Therefore thus says the Lord GOD:
        Woe to the city full of blood!*
    A pot containing filth,
        whose filth cannot be removed!
    Take out its pieces one by one,
        for no lot has fallen on their behalf.
⁷    For her blood is still in her midst;
        on a bare rock she left it;
    She did not pour it on the ground
        to be covered with dirt.†
⁸    To arouse wrath, to exact vengeance,
        I have left her blood on bare rock
        not to be covered.
⁹    Therefore, thus says the Lord GOD:
    Woe to the city full of blood!
        I will make the pyre great!
¹⁰    Pile on the wood, kindle the fire.
    Cook the meat, stir the spicy mixture,
        char the bones!
¹¹    Then set it empty on the coals,
        to heat up until its copper glows,
    So its impurities melt,
        its filth disappears.
¹²†    The toil is exhausting,
        but the great filth will not come out—
    Filth, even with fire.
¹³    Even in defiling yourself with depravity
        I would still have cleansed you,
        but you would not have your impurity
            cleansed.
    You will not be cleansed now
        until I wreak my fury on you.*
¹⁴    I, the LORD, have spoken;
        it will happen!
    I will do it and not hold back!
    I will not have pity or relent.

---

**24:1–14** As the Babylonian siege of Jerusalem begins (588 B.C.), Ezekiel uses allegory to depict Jerusalem and its over-confident inhabitants as a pot of meat set on the fire for boiling (vv. 3–5; cf. 11:3) and left there until only burnt bones remain (v. 10). In vv. 6–8, the innocent blood shed by Jerusalem's inhabitants is the rust that, despite efforts to remove it, coats the interior of the pot filled with meat. Once emptied (v. 8), the rust-encrusted pot is set on hot coals (v. 11), but the rust remains (v. 12). Only the brunt of the Lord's fury can cleanse Jerusalem of its guilt (vv. 13–14).
**24:1** *The tenth day…the ninth year*: January 15, 588 B.C. The same wording appears in 2 Kgs 25:1 (Jer 52:4).

**24:7** *Blood…to be covered with dirt*: since blood was sacred to God, it had to be covered with earth (Gn 37:26; Lv 17:13); the blood of innocent victims left uncovered cried out for vengeance; cf. Gn 4:10; Jb 16:18; Is 26:21.
**24:12** A cryptic line in Hebrew.

---

**23:39** 2 Kgs 21:4.          **24:3–6** cf. Ez 11:3–12.
**23:40** Jer 27:3.             **24:5** Jer 52:24–27.
**23:45** Lv 20:10.            **24:6** Na 3:1; Hb 2:12.
**23:49** cf. Ez 24:13.        **24:13** Is 22:14; Jer 6:28–30.
**24:1** cf. Ez 8:1.

By your conduct and deeds you shall be
judged—
oracle of the Lord GOD.

**Ezekiel as a Sign for the Exiles.** <sup>15</sup>The word of the LORD came to me: <sup>16</sup>Son of man, with a sudden blow I am taking away from you the delight of your eyes, but do not mourn or weep or shed any tears.* <sup>17</sup>Groan, moan for the dead, but make no public lament; bind on your turban, put your sandals on your feet, but do not cover your beard or eat the bread of mourners.† <sup>18</sup>I spoke to the people in the morning. In the evening my wife died. The next morning I did as I had been commanded.* <sup>19</sup>Then the people asked me, "Will you not tell us what all these things you are doing mean for us?" <sup>20</sup>I said to them, The word of the LORD came to me: <sup>21</sup>Say to the house of Israel: Thus says the Lord GOD: I will now desecrate my sanctuary, the pride of your strength, the delight of your eyes, the concern of your soul. The sons and daughters you left behind shall fall by the sword.* <sup>22</sup>† Then you shall do as I have done, not covering your beards nor eating the bread of mourning. <sup>23</sup>* Your turbans shall remain on your heads, your sandals on your feet. You shall not mourn or weep, but you shall waste away because of your sins and groan to one another. <sup>24</sup>Ezekiel shall be a sign for you: everything he did, you shall do. When it happens, you shall know that I am the Lord GOD.

**End of Ezekiel's Muteness.** <sup>25</sup>* As for you, son of man, truly, on the very day I take away from them their strength, their glorious joy, the delight of their eyes, the desire of their soul, the pride of their hearts, their sons and daughters, <sup>26</sup>on that day a survivor will come to you so

that you may hear it with your own ears.* <sup>27</sup>On that day, with the survivor, your mouth shall be opened; you shall speak and be mute† no longer. You shall be a sign to them, and they shall know that I am the LORD.

## III. PROPHECIES AGAINST FOREIGN NATIONS†

# 25

†**Against Ammon.** <sup>1</sup>The word of the LORD came to me: <sup>2</sup>Son of man, turn toward the Ammonites and prophesy against them.* <sup>3</sup>Say to the Ammonites: Hear the word of the LORD! Thus says the Lord GOD: Because you jeered at my sanctuary when it was desecrated, at the land of Israel when it was destroyed, and at the house of Judah when they went into exile, <sup>4</sup>therefore I am giving you to people from the east† as a possession. They shall set up their encampments among you and pitch their tents in your midst; they shall eat your produce and drink your milk.* <sup>5</sup>And I will turn Rabbah into a pasture for camels and all of Ammon into a grazing place for flocks. Then you shall know that I am the LORD.

<sup>6</sup>For thus says the Lord GOD: Because you rejoiced over the land of Israel with scorn in your heart, clapping your hands and stamping your feet, <sup>7</sup>therefore, see, I am stretching out my hand against you and giving you up as plunder to the nations. I will cut you off from the peoples and wipe you out of the lands. I will destroy you, and you shall know that I am the LORD.*

**Against Moab.** <sup>8</sup>* Thus says the Lord GOD: Because Moab said, "See! the house of Judah is like all the other nations," <sup>9</sup>therefore, I am exposing the whole flank of Moab† with its cities, the jewels of its land: Beth-jesimoth,

---

† **24:17** *The bread of mourners*: a post-burial meal that mourners shared to comfort one another; cf. 2 Sm 3:35; Jer 16:7. The other gestures mentioned here were also popular mourning customs. Because Ezekiel does not observe any of the mourning customs mentioned, the people are puzzled and ask him to explain.
**24:22–24** The fall of the city will be so sudden and final that the exiles will have no time to go into mourning.
**24:27** *Mute*: unable to preach anything but the Lord's judgment against Judah and Jerusalem; cf. 3:27 and note on 33:21–22.
**25:1–32:32** These chapters form a body of oracles directed against foreign nations. They follow the prophet's condemnation of Judah and oracles announcing its destruction. The unit precedes the announcement of Judah's salvation in chaps. 33–48.
**25:1–17** Ezekiel condemns four nations for their reactions to Judah's destruction and exile: Ammon to the east (vv. 2–7); Moab to the southeast (vv. 8–11); Edom to the south (vv. 12–14); Philis-

tia to the west (vv. 15–17). Their hostility was not unprovoked; at one time or another, each one either lost territory to Israel or had been under Israelite control.
**25:4** *People from the east*: nomadic tribes from the desert east of Ammon and Moab (cf. Is 11:14; Jer 49:28), often a threat to outlying towns and villages.
**25:9** *The whole flank of Moab*: the eastern edge of the Moabite plateau, perhaps lightly fortified because the vast desert to the east provided a natural barrier to invasion.

---

**24:16** Jer 16:5–7.
**24:18** cf. Ez 12:9.
**24:21** Lv 26:31.
**24:23–24** Is 20:2–3.
**24:25** cf. Ez 3:22–27.
**24:26** cf. Ez 33:22.

**25:2** Jer 49:1–6; Am 1:13–15; Zep 2:8–11.
**25:4** Dt 28:33, 51.
**25:7** Am 1:14–15.
**25:8** Sir 50:26; Is 15–16; Jer 48; Am 2:1–3.

Baalmeon, and Kiriathaim. <sup>10</sup>I will hand it over, along with the Ammonites, to the people from the east that it may not be remembered among the nations. <sup>11</sup>I will execute judgment upon Moab that they may know that I am the LORD. *

**Against Edom.** <sup>12</sup> * Thus says the Lord GOD: Because Edom took vengeance on the house of Judah and incurred terrible guilt by taking vengeance on them, <sup>13</sup>therefore thus says the Lord GOD: I will stretch out my hand against Edom and cut off from it human being and beast alike. I will turn it into ruins from Teman to Dedan; they shall fall by the sword. * <sup>14</sup>I will put my vengeance against Edom into the hands of my people Israel; they will deal with Edom in accord with my furious anger. Thus they shall know my vengeance!—oracle of the Lord GOD. *

**Against the Philistines.** <sup>15</sup>Thus says the Lord GOD: Because the Philistines acted vengefully and exacted vengeance with intentional malice, destroying with undying hostility, * <sup>16</sup>therefore thus says the Lord GOD: See! I am stretching out my hand against the Philistines, and I will cut off the Cherethites † and wipe out the remnant on the seacoast. <sup>17</sup>Thus I will execute great acts of vengeance on them, punishing them furiously. Then they shall know that I am the LORD, when I wreak my vengeance on them.

# 26 **Against the City of Tyre.** <sup>1</sup> † On the first day of the eleventh month of the eleventh year, the word of the LORD came to me:

<sup>2</sup> †   Son of man, because Tyre said of
       Jerusalem:
    "Aha! The gateway of the peoples is
       smashed!
    It has been turned over to me;
    I will be enriched by its ruin!" *

<sup>3</sup>   therefore thus says the Lord GOD:
    See! I am coming against you, Tyre;
      I will churn up against you many
       nations,
      just as the sea churns up its waves.
<sup>4</sup>   They will destroy the walls of Tyre
      and tear down its towers;
    I will scrape off its debris
      and leave it a bare rock. †
<sup>5</sup>   It will become a place for drying nets
      in the midst of the sea.
    For I have spoken—oracle of the Lord
      GOD:
    she will become plunder for the
      nations.
<sup>6</sup>   Her daughter cities † on the mainland
      will be slaughtered by the sword;
    then they shall know that I am the
      LORD.
<sup>7</sup>   Indeed thus says the Lord GOD:
    I am bringing up against Tyre
      from the north, Nebuchadnezzar,
    King of Babylon, king of kings,
      with horses and chariots, with cavalry,
      and a mighty horde of troops. *
<sup>8</sup>   Your daughter cities on the mainland
      he shall slay with the sword.
    He shall build a siege wall around you,
      throw up a ramp against you,
      and raise his shields about you.
<sup>9</sup>   He shall pound your walls with
       battering-rams
      and break down your towers with his
       axes.
<sup>10</sup>   From the surging of his horses
      he will cover you with dust;
      from the noise of warhorses,
      wheels and chariots.
    Your walls will shake
      when he enters your gates,
      even as one enters a city that is
       breached.
<sup>11</sup>   With the hooves of his horses
      he will trample all your streets;

---

† **25:16** *Cherethites*: people from the island of Crete in the Aegean, the Philistines' point of origin. In Zep 2:5, the terms "Philistines," "Cherethites," and "seacoast people" describe the same group of people.

**26:1** The Hebrew text does not give a number with the month. This translation assumes a scribal error, the omission of the second occurrence of the number eleven.

**26:2** Tyre is pictured rejoicing over Jerusalem's fall to Babylon because now the wealth from caravans and other trade will go to Tyrian merchants.

**26:4–5** *A bare rock*: the Tyre of Ezekiel's time was situated on a rocky island just off the Phoenician coast. During the time of Alexander the Great a causeway was built to connect it to the mainland.

**26:6** *Daughter cities*: tributary towns and villages on the mainland.

**25:11** Am 2:1–3.
**25:12** 2 Sm 8:13–14; 2 Chr 28:17; Ob 11–14.
**25:13** cf. Ez 35; Is 34:5–17; 63:1–6; Jer 49:7–11.
**25:14** cf. Ez 35:11.
**25:15** Is 14:29–31; Jer 47:1–7; Am 1:6–8; Zep 2:4–7.
**26:2** Is 23:1–18; Jl 3:4–5; Am 1:9–10; Zec 9:2–4.
**26:7** Jer 27:6; Na 2:3–4.

Your people he will slay by the sword;
    your mighty pillars will collapse. *
12  They shall plunder your wealth
    and pillage your goods;
They will tear down your walls
    and demolish your splendid houses.
Your stones, timbers, and debris
    they will cast into the sea.
13  I will bring an end to the noise of your
        songs;
    the music of your lyres will be heard
        no more.
14  I will turn you into bare rock,
    you will become a place for drying
        nets.
You shall never be rebuilt,
    for I the LORD have spoken—
    oracle of the Lord GOD.
15  Thus says the Lord GOD to Tyre:
At the sound of your downfall,
    at the groaning of the wounded,
When victims are slain within you,
    will the islands not quake?
16  All the princes of the sea †
    will step down from their thrones,
Lay aside their robes,
    and strip off their embroidered
        garments.
Clothed in mourning,
    they will sit on the ground
And tremble, horror-struck
    and appalled at you. *
17  They will raise lament † over you
    and say to you:
How you have perished,
    gone from the seas,
    Renowned City!
Once she was mighty on the sea,
    she and her inhabitants,
Those who spread their terror
    to all who dwelt nearby. *
18  On this, the day of your fall,
    the islands quake!
The islands in the sea
    are terrified at your passing.
19  Indeed thus says the Lord GOD:

When I make you a ruined city
    like cities no longer inhabited,
When I churn up the deep
    and its mighty waters cover you,
20  Then I will thrust you down
    with those who go down to the pit, †
    to those of the bygone age;
I will make you dwell in the
        netherworld,
    in the everlasting ruins,
    with those who have gone down to
        the pit,
So you will never return
    or have a place in the land of the
        living. *
21  I will make you a horror,
    and you shall be no more;
You shall be sought for,
    but never found again—
    oracle of the Lord GOD.

# 27 The Ship Tyre. [1] The word of the LORD came to me: [2] You, son of man, raise a lament over Tyre, [3] and say to Tyre, who sits at the entrance to the sea, trader to peoples on many coastlands, Thus says the Lord GOD:

Tyre, you said, "I am a ship,
    perfect in beauty"; *
4  In the heart of the sea was your
        territory;
    your builders perfected your beauty. *
5  With juniper wood from Senir †
    they built all your decks;
A cedar from Lebanon they took
    to make you a mast.
6  With oaks of Bashan †
    they fashioned your oars,
Your bridge, of ivory-inlaid cypress
        wood
    from the coasts of Kittim.
7  Fine embroidered linen from Egypt
    became your sail;
Your awnings were made of purple and
        scarlet
    from the coasts of Elishah. † *

---

**26:16** *The princes of the sea*: the rulers of the islands and coastal cities leagued commercially with Tyre.

**26:17** *Lament*: the princes sing a funeral dirge at the burial of the personified Tyre; cf. the similar lamentation over Egypt in 32:3–8.

**26:20** *Those who go down to the pit*: the dead, pictured as dwelling in Sheol, a place or cave of darkness. Cf. 32:17–32; Is 14:4–21 for other examples.

**27:5** *Senir*: another name for Mount Hermon; cf. Dt 3:9.

**27:6** *Bashan*: an area in northern Transjordan, noted for its lush growth and great forests (cf. Is 2:13). *Kittim*: here, probably Cyprus.

**27:7** *Elishah*: perhaps another term for Cyprus.

---

**26:11** Na 3:11.                       24, 30.
**26:16** cf. Ez 32:10.                   **27:3** Is 23:9.
**26:17** cf. Ez 19:1.                    **27:4** cf. Ez 28:1.
**26:20** cf. Ez 31:14; 32:18,           **27:7** Is 19:9–10.

8   Inhabitants of Sidon† and Arvad
      were your oarsmen;
  Your own sages, Tyre, were on board,
      serving as your sailors.*

9   The elders and sages of Gebal
      were with you to caulk your seams.
  Every ship and sailor on the sea
      came to you to carry on trade.*

10   Persia and Lud and Put
      were warriors in your army;
  Shield and helmet they hung on you
      to enhance your splendor.

11   The men of Arvad and Helech†
      were on your walls all around
  And Gamadites on your towers;
      they hung their shields around your
        walls,
      they made your beauty perfect.

12   Tarshish traded with you,
      so great was your wealth,
  Exchanging for your wares
      silver, iron, tin, and lead.

13   Javan, Tubal, and Meshech
      also traded with you,
  Exchanging slaves and bronze vessels
      for your merchandise.*

14   Horses, steeds, and mules from Beth-
      togarmah
      were exchanged for your wares.

15   Men of Rhodes trafficked with you;
      many coastlands were your agents;
  Ivory tusks and ebony wood
      they brought back as your payment.

16   Edom traded with you for your many
      wares:
      garnets, purple dye, embroidered cloth,
  Fine linen, coral, and rubies
      they gave you as merchandise.

17   Judah and the land of Israel
      trafficked with you:
  Minnith wheat, grain,† honey, oil, and
      balm*
      they gave you as merchandise.

18   Damascus traded with you for your
      many wares,
      so great was your wealth,
      exchanging Helbon wine and Zahar
      wool.

19   Javan exchanged wrought iron, cassia,
      and aromatic cane
      from Uzal for your wares.

20   Dedan traded with you for riding gear.*

21   Arabia and the sheikhs of Kedar were
      your agents,
      dealing in lambs, rams, and goats.*

22   The merchants of Sheba and Raamah
      also traded with you,
      exchanging for your wares the very
        best spices,
      all kinds of precious stones, and gold.

23   Haran, Canneh, and Eden,
      the merchants of Sheba, Asshur, and
        Chilmad,

24   Traded with you, marketing rich
      garments,
      purple cloth, embroidered fabric,
      varicolored carpets, and braided cords.

25   The ships of Tarshish sailed for you with
      your goods;
  You were full and heavily laden
      in the heart of the sea.

26   Out into deep waters
      your oarsmen brought you;
  The east wind shattered you
      in the heart of the sea.*

27   Your wealth, your goods, your wares,
      your sailors, your crew,
  The caulkers of your seams,
      those who traded for your goods,
  All the warriors with you,
      the whole crowd with you
  Sank into the heart of the sea
      on the day of your downfall.*

28   At the sound of your sailors' shouts
      the waves shudder,*

29   Down from their ships
      come all who ply the oars;
  Sailors, all the seafaring crew,
      stand on the shore.

30   They raise their voices over you
      and shout their bitter cries;
  They pour dust on their heads
      and cover themselves with ashes.

31   For you they shave their heads bald
      and put on sackcloth;
  For you they weep bitterly,

---

27:8–9 *Sidon…Gebal*: Phoenician cities in Tyre's orbit of influence; Gebal is classical Byblos.
  27:11 *Helech*: perhaps in Asia Minor; otherwise unknown.
  27:17 *Grain*: most commentators have read "figs," but Hebrew *panag* more properly describes milled grains or prepared meal.

27:8 cf. Ez 28:20–23.
27:9 Ps 104:26.
27:13 cf. Ez 38:2; 39:1.
27:17 1 Kgs 5:9.
27:20 Is 21:13.
27:21 Is 21:17; Jer 49:28.
27:26 Ps 48:7; Jer 18:17.
27:27 cf. Ez 28:8.
27:28 Jer 49:21.

in anguished lament.*

32 They raise a lament for you;
    they wail over you:
"Who was ever destroyed like Tyre
    in the midst of the sea?"*

33 By exporting your goods by sea
    you satisfied many peoples,
With your great wealth and merchandise
    you enriched the kings of the earth.*

34 Now you are wrecked in the sea,
    in the watery depths;
Your wares and all your crew
    have fallen down with you.

35 All who dwell on the coastlands
    are aghast over you;
Their kings are terrified,
    their faces distorted.

36 The traders among the peoples
    now hiss at you;
You have become a horror,
    you shall be no more.

# 28 The Prince of Tyre. [1]† The word of the LORD came to me: [2] Son of man, say to the prince of Tyre: Thus says the Lord GOD:

Because you are haughty of heart,
    you say, "I am a god!
I sit on a god's throne
    in the heart of the sea!"
But you are a man, not a god;
    yet you pretend
    you are a god at heart!

3 Oh yes, you are wiser than Daniel,†
    nothing secret is too obscure for you!*

4 By your wisdom and intelligence
    you made yourself rich,
    filling your treasuries with gold and
        silver.

5 Through your great wisdom in trading
    you heaped up riches for yourself—
    your heart is haughty because of your
        riches.

6 Therefore thus says the Lord GOD:
Because you pretend you are a god at
    heart,

7 Therefore, I will bring against you
    strangers, the most bloodthirsty of
        nations.
They shall draw their swords
    against your splendid wisdom,
    and violate your radiance.*

8 They shall thrust you down into the pit:
    you shall die a violent death
    in the heart of the sea.

9 Then, face to face with your killers,
    will you still say, "I am a god"?
No, you are a man, not a god,
    handed over to those who slay you.

10 You shall die the death of the
        uncircumcised
    handed over to strangers,
    for I have spoken—oracle of the Lord
        GOD.*

[11] The word of the LORD came to me: [12] Son of man, raise a lament over the king of Tyre, and say to him: Thus says the Lord GOD:

† You were a seal of perfection,
    full of wisdom, perfect in beauty.*

13 In Eden, the garden of God, you lived;
    precious stones of every kind were
        your covering:
Carnelian, topaz, and beryl,
    chrysolite, onyx, and jasper,
    sapphire, garnet, and emerald.
Their mounts and settings
    were wrought in gold,
    fashioned for you the day you were
        created.*

14 With a cherub I placed you;
    I put you on the holy mountain of
        God,†
    where you walked among fiery stones.

15 Blameless were you in your ways
    from the day you were created,
Until evil was found in you.

16 Your commerce was full of
        lawlessness, and you sinned.
Therefore I banished you from the
        mountain of God;

---

† **28:1–10** Ezekiel mocks the arrogance of Tyre's leader, who mistakes the city's commercial success for evidence of his divinity. At the hands of a foreign army, commissioned by the only God worthy of the name, this leader dies a humiliating, unceremonious death.
    **28:3** *Wiser than Daniel:* see note on 14:14.
    **28:12–19** Ezekiel describes the leader of Tyre in language that recalls the imagery of Gn 2–3.
    **28:14** *The holy mountain of God:* the residence of gods in

Israelite and non-Israelite myth; cf. Is 14:13. *Fiery stones:* associated with the divine presence; cf. Ez 1:13; Ps 18:13.

---

**27:31** Is 15:2; Jer 48:37.
**27:32** Is 23:1–6.
**27:33** cf. Ez 28:4–5.
**28:3** cf. Ez 14:14; Dn 1:20;
    2:20–23.

**28:7** cf. Ez 30:11; 31:12;
    32:12.
**28:10** cf. Ez 32:19, 24.
**28:12** Is 14:12–15.
**28:13** cf. Ez 31:8–9; Gn 2:8,
    15.

the cherub drove you out
from among the fiery stones. *

17 Your heart had grown haughty
because of your beauty;
You corrupted your wisdom
because of your splendor.
I cast you to the ground,
I made you a spectacle
in the sight of kings. *

18 Because of the enormity of your guilt,
and the perversity of your trade,
you defiled your sanctuary.
I brought fire out of you;
it devoured you;
I made you ashes on the ground
in the eyes of all who see you. *

19 All the nations who knew you
are appalled on account of you;
You have become a horror,
never to be again. *

**Against Sidon.** 20 The word of the LORD came
to me: 21 Son of man, turn your face toward
Sidon and prophesy against it. 22 Thus says the
Lord GOD:

Watch out! I am against you, Sidon;
I will win glory for myself in your
midst.
They shall know that I am the LORD,
when I deliver judgment upon it
and manifest my holiness in it.

23 I will send disease into it;
blood will fill its streets,
Within it shall fall
those slain by the sword
raised against it on every side.
Then they shall know that I am the
LORD.

24 No longer will there be a thorn that
tears
or a brier that scratches for the house
of Israel
From the surrounding neighbors
who despise them;

thus they shall know that I am the
LORD. *

25 Thus says the Lord GOD: When I gather the
house of Israel from the peoples among whom
they are scattered, and I manifest my holiness
through them in the sight of the nations, then
they shall live on the land I gave my servant Jacob. * 26 They shall dwell on it securely, building houses and planting vineyards. They shall
dwell securely while I execute judgment on all
their neighbors who treated them with contempt; then they shall know that I, the LORD,
am their God. *

# 29 Egypt the Crocodile. 
1 In the tenth
year, on the twelfth day of the tenth
month, † the word of the LORD came to me:
2 Son of man, turn your face toward Pharaoh,
king of Egypt, and prophesy against him and
against all Egypt. † * 3 Say to him: Thus says the
Lord GOD:

Pay attention! I am against you,
Pharaoh, king of Egypt,
Great dragon † crouching
in the midst of the Nile,
Who says, "The Nile belongs to me;
I made it myself!" *

4 † I will put hooks in your jaws
and make all the fish of your Nile
Cling to your scales;
I will drag you up from your Nile,
With all the fish of your Nile
clinging to your scales. *

5 I will hurl you into the wilderness,
you and all the fish of your Nile.
You will fall into an open field,
you will not be picked up or gathered
together.
To the beasts of the earth
and the birds of the sky
I give you as food. *

6 * Then all the inhabitants of Egypt
will know that I am the LORD.

---

**29:1** The date is calculated to be January 7, 587 B.C. The
siege of Jerusalem had begun a year earlier; cf. 24:1.
**29:2** Egypt was allied with Judah against the Babylonians.
**29:3** *Dragon:* Hebrew reads *tannim,* usually translated "jackals," here a byform of *tannin,* the mythical dragon, or sea monster, representing chaos (cf. Is 27:1; 51:9; Jer 51:34; Ps 91:13;
Jb 7:12), and the crocodile native to the Nile. *Nile:* the many
rivulets of the Nile that branch out into the Delta.
**29:4–5** Ezekiel's repetition of detail creates a vivid picture of
Egypt's destruction: God hauls the crocodile (Pharaoh) and the
fish clinging to it for protection (the Egyptian populace) out of

the Nile and lands them in an open field, where their corpses
are torn apart by wildlife rather than being properly buried (cf.
Dt 28:26; 2 Kgs 9:36–37; Jer 34:20; Ez 39:17–20).

---

**28:16** Gn 3:24.
**28:17** Is 10:12.
**28:18** Ob 18.
**28:19** Lv 26:12.
**28:24** Nm 33:55.
**28:25** cf. Ez 20:41.
**28:26** Lv 25:18–19; Jer 23:6.
**29:2** Is 19:1–17; Jer 25:19.
**29:3** cf. Ez 32:2.
**29:4** Is 19:5.
**29:5** Jer 7:33.
**29:6–7** 2 Kgs 18:21; Is 36:6.

Because you were a staff of reeds †
    for the house of Israel:
7 When they took hold of you, you would
    splinter,
    throwing shoulders out of joint.
When they leaned on you, you would
    break,
    pitching them down headlong.
8 Therefore thus says the Lord GOD:
Look! I am bringing the sword against
    you
    to cut off from you people and
    animals.
9 The land of Egypt shall become a
    desolate waste;
    then they shall know that I am the
    LORD.
Because you said, "The Nile belongs to
    me;
    I made it!"
10 Beware! I am against you
    and against your Nile.
I will turn the land of Egypt into ruins,
    into a dry, desolate waste,
From Migdol to Syene, †
    up to the border of Ethiopia. *
11 No foot shall pass through it,
    no human being or beast cross it;
    it will remain uninhabited for forty
    years.
12 I will make the land of Egypt the most
    desolate
    among desolate lands;
Its cities, the most deserted
    among deserted cities for forty
    years;
I will scatter the Egyptians among the
    nations
    and disperse them throughout other
    lands. *
13 But thus says the Lord GOD:

At the end of forty years
    I will gather the Egyptians
    from among the peoples
    where they are scattered;
14 I will restore Egypt's fortunes,
    bringing them back to the land of
    Pathros, †
    the land of their origin.
But there it will be a lowly kingdom,
15     lower than any other kingdom,
    no longer able to set itself above the
    nations.
I will make them few in number,
    so they cannot rule other nations.
16 No longer shall they be security
    for the house of Israel,
But a reminder of its iniquity
    in turning away to follow them.
Then they shall know that I am the Lord
    GOD. *

**Wages for Nebuchadnezzar.** 17 In the twenty-seventh year on the first day of the first month, † the word of the LORD came to me: 18 Son of man, Nebuchadnezzar, the king of Babylon, has made his army wage a hard campaign against Tyre; † their heads grew bald, their shoulders rubbed raw, yet neither he nor his army received compensation from Tyre for all the effort they expended against it. * 19 Therefore thus says the Lord GOD: * See! I am giving to Nebuchadnezzar, king of Babylon, the land of Egypt! He will carry off its wealth, plundering and pillaging whatever he can find to provide pay for his army. 20 As payment for his toil I give him the land of Egypt—oracle of the Lord GOD.

21 On that day I will make a horn † sprout for the house of Israel, and I will let you again open your mouth in their midst; then they shall know that I am the LORD. *

---

**29:6** *Staff of reeds:* Pharaoh is like a reed that looks sturdy but breaks under pressure. For a similar image, cf. 2 Kgs 18:21 (Is 36:6).

**29:10** *From Migdol to Syene:* from the northeastern to the southern limits of Egypt. Syene is the modern Aswan, at the first cataract of the Nile; Ethiopia (Heb. *kush*) is the territory south of Aswan.

**29:14** *Pathros:* an Egyptian word for upper, i.e., southern, Egypt, above Memphis/Thebes. As silt filled the Delta region and richer land became available there, the population spread north, creating the tradition of a migration from the south (Is 11:11; Jer 44:1, 15).

**29:17** *In the twenty-seventh year on the first day of the first month:* April 26, 571 B.C. This is the latest date attached to any of Ezekiel's prophecies.

**29:18–19** Nebuchadnezzar's thirteen-year siege (587–574 B.C.) ended with Tyre's surrender on the condition that the Babylonian army would not loot and pillage (*pace* 26:3–14). According to Ezekiel, Nebuchadnezzar and his army should collect their wages for serving as God's instrument in Tyre's punishment, by plundering and controlling Egypt.

**29:21** *A horn:* God will give Israel renewed strength. For horn as a symbol of strength, cf. Dt 33:17; Ps 92:11; 132:17. Ezekiel suggests that the Babylonian conquest of Egypt precedes Israel's restoration, an event he expects to witness and acknowledge when God removes his muteness.

---

**29:10** cf. Ez 30:4, 6.
**29:12** Jer 46:19.
**29:16** Ps 40:5; Is 20:5.

**29:18** Is 26:7–14.
**29:19** Is 19:4.
**29:21** Ps 132:17; Lk 1:69.

# 30 The Day of the Lord Against Egypt.

[1] The word of the LORD came to me: [2] Son of man, prophesy and say: Thus says the Lord GOD:

Wail: "Alas the day!"
[3] Yes, a day approaches,
   a day of the Lord approaches:
A day of dark cloud,
   a time appointed for the nations.*
[4] A sword will come against Egypt,
   there will be anguish in Ethiopia,
When the slain fall in Egypt
   when its hordes are seized,
   its foundations razed.*
[5] Ethiopia, Put, and Lud,
   all the mixed rabble† and Kub,
and the people of allied lands
   shall fall by the sword with them.
[6] Thus says the LORD:
The pillars of Egypt shall fall,
   and its proud strength sink;
From Migdol to Syene,
   its people will fall by the sword—
   oracle of the Lord GOD.*
[7] It shall be the most desolate
   among desolate lands,
Its cities the most ruined
   among ruined cities.
[8] They shall know that I am the LORD,
   when I set fire to Egypt,
   and all its allies are shattered.*
[9] On that day, messengers from me
   will go forth in ships
   to terrorize confident Ethiopia.
Anguish will be among them
   on Egypt's day—it is certainly coming!†
[10] Thus says the Lord GOD:
I will put an end to Egypt's hordes
   by the hand of Nebuchadnezzar, king
      of Babylon:
[11] He and his army with him,
   the most ruthless of nations,
   will be brought in to devastate the
      land.

They will draw their swords against
      Egypt
   and fill the land with the slain.
[12] Then I will dry up the streams of the
      Nile,
   and sell the land into evil hands;
By the hand of foreigners I will devastate
   the land and everything in it.
I, the LORD, have spoken.*
[13]† Thus says the Lord GOD:
I will destroy idols,
   and put an end to images in
      Memphis.
There will never again be a prince
   over the land of Egypt.
Instead, I will spread fear
   throughout the land of Egypt.*
[14] I will devastate Pathros,
   set fire to Zoan,
   and execute judgment against
      Thebes.*
[15] I will pour out my wrath on Pelusium,
   the fortress of Egypt,
   and cut off the troops of Thebes.
[16] I will set fire to Egypt;
   Pelusium will writhe in anguish,
Thebes will be breached,
   and Memphis besieged in daylight.
[17] The warriors of On and Pi-beseth
   will fall by the sword,
   the cities taken captive.
[18] In Tahpanhes, the day will turn dark
   when I break the scepter of Egypt
      there
   and put an end to its proud strength.
Dark clouds will cover it,
   and its women will go into captivity.*
[19] I will execute judgment against Egypt
   that they may know that I am the
      LORD.

**Pharaoh's Broken Arm.** [20] On the seventh day of the first month in the eleventh year,† the word of the LORD came to me: [21]† Son of man, I have broken the arm of Pharaoh, king

---

**30:5** *Mixed rabble*: mercenaries.
**30:9** God spreads panic throughout Ethiopia, ancient Cush, by sending messengers with news of Egypt's fall. Rivers at its borders insulated Ethiopia and made it inaccessible except by boat.
**30:13–19** The prophet enumerates a list of major Egyptian cities that shall each bear the judgment proclaimed in the previous oracle, vv. 1–12.
**30:20** *The seventh day of the first month in the eleventh year*: April 29, 587 B.C.
**30:21–26** This oracle was delivered more than a year into the siege of Jerusalem (24:1). When Pharaoh Hophra came to help

Jerusalem, the Babylonians temporarily lifted the siege; cf. Jer 34:21; 37:6–7. In Ezekiel's eyes, Hophra was interfering with the punishment God intended the Babylonians to inflict on Judah. The Babylonians routed the Egyptians, who could not offer Jerusalem any more help; cf. chap. 31.

---

| | |
|---|---|
| **30:3** cf. Ez 7:7; Is 13:6. | **30:13** Is 19:13. |
| **30:4** Jer 25:19–20. | **30:14** Is 19:11, 13; Jer |
| **30:6** cf. Ez 29:10. | 46:25. |
| **30:8** Jer 49:27. | **30:18** Jer 43:4–7. |
| **30:12** Is 19:6. | |

of Egypt. See! It has not been immobilized for healing, nor set with a splint to make it strong enough to grasp a sword.* ²²Therefore thus says the Lord GOD: See! I am coming against Pharaoh, king of Egypt. I will break both his arms, the strong one and the broken one, making the sword fall from his hand. ²³I will scatter the Egyptians among the nations and disperse them throughout other lands. ²⁴I will, however, strengthen the arms of the king of Babylon and put my sword in his hand so he can bring it against Egypt for plunder and pillage.* ²⁵When I strengthen the arms of the king of Babylon, and the arms of Pharaoh collapse, they shall know that I am the LORD, because I put my sword into the hand of the king of Babylon to wield against the land of Egypt. ²⁶When I scatter the Egyptians among the nations and disperse them throughout other lands, they shall know that I am the LORD.

# 31

**Allegory of the Cedar.** ¹On the first day of the third month in the eleventh year,† the word of the LORD came to me: ²Son of man, say to Pharaoh, the king of Egypt, and to his hordes: In your greatness, whom do you resemble?

3      Assyria! It is Assyria!†
           A cedar of Lebanon—
       Beautiful branches,
           thick shade,
       Towering heights,
           its crown in the clouds!*
4      The waters made it grow,
           the deep made it tall,
       Letting its currents flow
           around the place it was planted,
       Then sending its channels
           to all the other trees of the field.*
5      Thereupon it towered in height
           above all the trees in the field;
       Its branches were numerous
           and its boughs long,
       Because of the many waters
           sent to its shoots.

6      In its branches nested
           all the birds of the sky;
       Under its boughs all the wild animals
           gave birth,
       And in its shade† dwelt
           all the mighty nations.*
7      It was magnificent in size
           and in the length of its branches,
       For its roots reached down
           to the many waters.
8      In the garden of God,
           no cedars could rival it,
       No juniper could equal its branches,
           no plane tree match its boughs.
       No tree in the garden of God
           could match its beauty.*
9      I made it beautiful
           with abundant foliage,
       So that all the trees in Eden
           were envious of it.†
10     Therefore, thus says the Lord GOD:
       Because it was arrogant about its height,
           lifting its crown among the clouds
           and exalting itself because of its size,*
11     I handed it over to a ruler of nations
           to deal with it according to its evil.
       I have cast it off,
12         and foreigners have cut it down,
       The most ruthless nations,
           have hurled it on the mountains.
       Its boughs fell into every valley
           and its branches lay broken
           in every ravine in the land.
       All the peoples of the earth
           departed from its shade
           when it was hurled down.*
13     On its fallen trunk
           sit all the birds of the sky;
       Beside its fallen branches,
           are found all the beasts of the field.
14     This has happened so no well-watered tree
           will gain such lofty height,
           or lift its crown to the clouds.
       Not one of those fed by water
           will tower in height over the rest.
       For all of them are destined for death,

---

**31:1** *The first day of the third month in the eleventh year:* June 21, 587 B.C.

**31:3** *Assyria:* this translates *te'ashshur,* which some interpret as "cypress tree." The oracle, however, compares the fate of Pharaoh to the terrible demise of Assyria because of its arrogant pride (cf. Na 1–3). Ezekiel may have drawn on an ancient myth of a cosmic tree of life to emphasize the greatness of Egypt's fall.

**31:6** *Shade:* a metaphor for protection (cf. Lam 4:20).

**31:9** Here Israel's God is responsible for Assyria's splendor, whereas in Is 10:13 Assyria claims to have created its own might.

**30:21** Jer 37:10; 44:30;          **31:6** Dn 4:12; cf. Mt 13:32.
       48:25.                         **31:8** Ps 80:10.
**30:24** cf. Ez 21:14.               **31:10** Is 2:11.
**31:3** Ps 92:12; Jer 50:18.         **31:12** Dn 4:14.
**31:4** Dn 4:10.

for the underworld, among mere
　　mortals,
　with those who go down to the pit.

15　Thus says the Lord GOD:
　On the day it went down to Sheol,
　　I made the deep close up
　　in mourning for it.
　I restrained the currents of the deep,
　　and held back the many waters.
　I darkened Lebanon because of it,
　　and all the trees of the field
　　languished because of it.

16　At the sound of its fall,
　　I made nations shudder,
　When I cast it down to Sheol
　　with those who go down to the pit.
　In the underworld
　　all the trees of Eden took comfort:
　Lebanon's choicest and best,
　　all that were fed by the waters. *

17　They too will go down to Sheol,
　　to those slain by the sword,
　Its allies † who dwelt
　　in its shade among the nations.

18　To whom among the trees of Eden
　　do you compare in glory and
　　　greatness?
　You will be brought down
　　with the trees of Eden to the
　　　underworld,
　And lie among the uncircumcised,
　　with those slain by the sword.
　Such is Pharaoh and all his hordes—
　　oracle of the Lord GOD.

# 32 Lament over Pharaoh. ¹On the first day of the twelfth month in the twelfth year, † the word of the LORD came to me: ²Son of man, utter a lament over Pharaoh, the king of Egypt, and say to him:

　You liken yourself to a lion among
　　nations,
　　but you are like the monster in the
　　　sea!
　Thrashing about in your streams,
　　churning the water with your feet,
　　polluting the streams. *

3　Thus says the Lord GOD:
　I will cast my net over you

　by assembling many armies,
　　and I will hoist you up in my mesh.

4　I will hurl you onto the land,
　　cast you into an open field.
　I will make all the birds of the sky
　　roost upon you,
　The beasts of the whole earth
　　gorge themselves on you.

5　I will strew your flesh on the mountains,
　　and fill the valleys with your corpse. *

6　I will drench the land,
　　pouring out your blood on the
　　　mountain;
　　filling up the ravines with you.

7　When I extinguish you,
　　I will cover the heavens
　　and darken all its stars.
　The sun I will cover with clouds;
　　the moon will not give light. *

8　All the shining lights in the heavens
　　I will darken over you;
　I will spread darkness over your land—
　　oracle of the Lord GOD.

9　I will trouble the hearts
　　of many peoples,
　When I bring you captive
　　among the nations,
　　to lands you do not know.

10　I will fill many nations with horror;
　　their kings will shudder at you,
　　when I brandish my sword in their
　　　faces.
　They will tremble violently
　　fearing for their lives on the day of
　　　your fall. *

11　For thus says the Lord GOD:
　The sword of the king of Babylon
　　will come against you.

12　I will cut down your hordes
　　with the swords of warriors,
　　all of them, ruthless nations;
　They will lay waste the glory of Egypt,
　　and all its hordes will be destroyed. *

13　I will wipe out all the livestock
　　from the banks of its many waters;
　No human foot will disturb them again,
　　no animal hoof stir them up.

14　Then I will make their waters clear
　　and their streams flow like oil—
　　oracle of the Lord GOD.

---

**31:17** *Allies*: lit., "arm."
**32:1** *The first day of the twelfth month in the twelfth year*:
March 3, 585 B.C.

**31:16** Is 14:8, 15.　　　　**32:7** Is 3:10.
**32:2** cf. Ez 19:1; 20:3.　　**32:10** Rev 18:9–10.
**32:5** Is 34:3.　　　　　　**32:12** cf. Ez 31:11–12.

EZ

15 When I make Egypt a wasteland
    and the land destitute of everything,
   When I strike down all its inhabitants
    they shall know that I am the LORD.
16 This is the lamentation
    women of all nations will chant;
   They will raise it over Egypt;
    over all its hordes they will chant it—
    oracle of the Lord GOD.

**Another Lament over Egypt.** 17 † On the fifteenth day of that month in the twelfth year,
the word of the LORD came to me:

18 Son of man, wail over the hordes of
        Egypt—
    you and the women of mighty
        nations—
   Send them down to the underworld,
    with those who go down into the pit.
19 Whom do you excel in beauty? Go
        down!
    Be laid to rest with the uncircumcised!
20 Among those slain by the sword they
        will fall,
    for the sword has been appointed!
   Seize Egypt and all its hordes. *
21 Out of Sheol the mighty warriors
    will speak to him and his allies:
   Let them descend and lie down among
        the uncircumcised,
    those slain by the sword! *
22 There is Assyria and all its company,
    around it are its graves,
    all of them slain, fallen by the sword.
23 The graves are set
    in the recesses of the pit;
   Its company is assembled
    around its grave,
   All of them slain, fallen by the sword,
    those who spread terror in the land of
        the living. *
24 There is Elam and all its horde
    around its grave,
   All of them slain, fallen by the sword;
    they descended uncircumcised
    into the underworld,
   Those who spread their terror
    in the land of the living.

They bear their disgrace
    with those who go down into the pit.
25 Among the slain is set its bed,
    with all its horde around its grave;
   All of them uncircumcised,
    slain by the sword
   Because of the terror they spread
    in the land of the living.
   They bear their disgrace
    with those who go down into the pit.
    Among the slain it is set!
26 There is Meshech and Tubal † and all the
        hordes
    surrounding it with their graves.
   All of them uncircumcised,
    slain by the sword
   Because they spread their terror
    in the land of the living. *
27 They do not rest with the warriors
    who fell in ancient times,
    who went down to Sheol fully armed.
   Their swords were placed under their
        heads
    and their shields laid over their bones;
   For there was terror of these warriors
    in the land of the living.
28 But as for you, among the uncircumcised
    you will be broken and laid to rest
    with those slain by the sword.
29 There is Edom, all its kings and princes,
    who, despite their might,
    are put with those slain by the sword.
   They lie among the uncircumcised,
    with those who go down into the
        pit. *
30 There are the generals of the north
    and all the Sidonians
   Who have gone down with the slain,
    because of the terror their might
        inspired.
   They lie uncircumcised
    with those slain by the sword,
   And bear their shame with those
    who have gone down into the pit. *
31 When Pharaoh sees them,
    he will be consoled on behalf of all
        his hordes,
    slain by the sword—
   Pharaoh and all his army—

---

**32:17–32** The description of Pharaoh in Sheol shifts rapidly
between the single individual and the collective body, between
corpses speaking and corpses lying inert, between singular (his,
hers, its) and plural (them, theirs) pronouns to emphasize that all
the enemies of Israel come to the same end.

---

**32:26** *Meshech and Tubal*: see note on 38:2.

---

**32:20** cf. Ez 31:17–18.  **32:26** cf. Ez 27:13.
**32:21** Is 14:9.          **32:29** Is 34:5–15.
**32:23** Is 14:15.         **32:30** Jer 25:26.

oracle of the Lord GOD.
32 I spread terror of him
    in the land of the living;
Now he is laid among the uncircumcised,
    with those slain by the sword—
Pharaoh and all his horde—
    oracle of the Lord GOD.

## IV. HOPE FOR THE FUTURE

**33** **The Prophet as Sentinel.** [1]The word of the LORD came to me: [2]Son of man, speak to your people and tell them: When I bring the sword against a land, if the people of that land select one of their number as a sentinel† for them,* [3]and the sentinel sees the sword coming against the land, he should blow the trumpet to warn the people.* [4]If they hear the trumpet but do not take the warning and a sword attacks and kills them, their blood will be on their own heads.* [5]They heard the trumpet blast but ignored the warning; their blood is on them. If they had heeded the warning, they could have escaped with their lives. [6]If, however, the sentinel sees the sword coming and does not blow the trumpet, so that the sword attacks and takes someone's life, his life will be taken for his own sin, but I will hold the sentinel responsible for his blood.

[7]*You, son of man—I have appointed you as a sentinel for the house of Israel; when you hear a word from my mouth, you must warn them for me. [8]When I say to the wicked, "You wicked, you must die," and you do not speak up to warn the wicked about their ways, they shall die in their sins, but I will hold you responsible for their blood. [9]If, however, you warn the wicked to turn from their ways, but they do not, then they shall die in their sins, but you shall save your life.

**Individual Retribution.** [10]As for you, son of man, speak to the house of Israel: You people say, "Our crimes and our sins weigh us down;

we are rotting away because of them. How can we survive?"* [11]*Answer them: As I live—oracle of the Lord GOD—I swear I take no pleasure in the death of the wicked, but rather that they turn from their ways and live. Turn, turn from your evil ways! Why should you die, house of Israel?

[12]As for you, son of man, say to your people: The justice of the just will not save them on the day they sin; the wickedness of the wicked will not bring about their downfall on the day they turn from their wickedness. No, the just cannot save their lives on the day they sin.* [13]Even though I say to the just that they shall surely live, if they, relying on their justice, do wrong, none of their just deeds shall be remembered; because of the wrong they have done, they shall die.* [14]And though I say to the wicked that they shall die, if they turn away from sin and do what is just and right— [15]returning pledges, restoring stolen goods, walking by statutes that bring life, doing nothing wrong—they shall surely live; they shall not die.* [16]None of the sins they committed shall be remembered against them. If they do what is right and just, they shall surely live.

[17]Your people say, "The way of the LORD is not fair!" But it is their way that is not fair. [18]When the just turn away from justice and do wrong, they shall die for it.* [19]When the wicked turn away from wickedness and do what is right and just, because of this they shall live. [20]But still you say, "The way of the LORD is not fair!" I will judge each of you according to your ways, house of Israel.

**The Survivor from Jerusalem.** [21]On the fifth day of the tenth month,† in the twelfth year of our exile, the survivor came to me from Jerusalem and said, "The city is taken!"* [22]The hand of the LORD had come upon me the evening before the survivor arrived and opened my mouth when he reached me in the morning. My mouth was opened, and I was mute no longer.*

---

† **33:2** *Sentinel:* the theme of the sentinel's duty initiates a new commission to announce salvation (chaps. 33–48), just as the same command (3:17–21) opened Ezekiel's ministry to announce judgment (chaps. 3–24).

**33:21–22** *The fifth day of the tenth month:* January 8, 585 B.C. According to Jeremiah (39:2), Jerusalem was taken in July, 587. Some manuscripts read "eleventh" for "twelfth" year (January, 586); even so, there was ample time between the fall of Jerusalem and the arrival of the survivor from that city to journey to Babylon. However, this is the survivor sent to fulfill the promise

of Ez 24:25–27, the eyewitness whose arrival would release Ezekiel from his muteness; cf. 3:26–27.

**33:2** Lv 26:25.
**33:3** Hos 5:8; 8:1.
**33:4** Lv 20:9; Jer 6:17.
**33:7** Jer 1:17.
**33:10** Lv 26:16, 39.
**33:11** Jer 44:7–8; cf. Ez 18:23.
**33:12** cf. Ez 3:20.
**33:13** Heb 10:38.
**33:15** Ex 22:1–4, 26.
**33:18** Jer 18:7–10.
**33:21** 2 Kgs 25:4, 10; Is 39:1–2.
**33:22** cf. Ez 3:26–27.

**Those Left in Judah.**† ²³ The word of the LORD came to me: ²⁴ Son of man, these who live among the ruins in the land of Israel are saying: "Abraham was only one person, yet he was given possession of the land. Since we are many, the land must be given to us as our possession."* ²⁵ Therefore say to them: Thus says the Lord GOD: You eat on the mountains, you raise your eyes to your idols, you shed blood— yet you would keep possession of the land?* ²⁶ You rely on your swords, you commit abominations, each defiles his neighbor's wife—yet you would keep possession of the land? ²⁷ Say this to them: Thus says the Lord GOD: As I live, those among the ruins shall fall by the sword; those in the open field I have made food for the wild beasts; and those in rocky hideouts and caves shall die by the plague. ²⁸ I will make the land a desolate waste, so that its proud strength will come to an end, and the mountains of Israel shall be so desolate that no one will cross them. ²⁹ Thus they shall know that I am the LORD, when I make the land a desolate waste because of all the abominations they committed.

**Popular Misunderstanding.** ³⁰ As for you, son of man, your people are talking about you beside the walls and in the doorways of houses. They say to one another, "Let's go hear the latest word that comes from the LORD." ³¹ My people come to you, gathering as a crowd and sitting in front of you to hear your words, but they will not act on them. Love songs are on their lips, but in their hearts they pursue dishonest gain.* ³² For them you are only a singer† of love songs, with a pleasant voice and a clever touch. They listen to your words, but they do not obey them. ³³ But when it comes—and it is surely coming!—they shall know that there was a prophet among them.

**34** **Parable of the Shepherds.** ¹ The word of the LORD came to me: ² Son of man, prophesy against the shepherds† of Israel.

Prophesy and say to them: To the shepherds, thus says the Lord GOD: Woe to the shepherds of Israel who have been pasturing themselves!* Should not shepherds pasture the flock? ³ You consumed milk, wore wool, and slaughtered fatlings, but the flock you did not pasture.* ⁴ You did not strengthen the weak nor heal the sick nor bind up the injured. You did not bring back the stray or seek the lost but ruled them harshly and brutally.* ⁵ So they were scattered for lack of a shepherd, and became food for all the wild beasts. They were scattered* ⁶ and wandered over all the mountains and high hills; over the entire surface of the earth my sheep were scattered. No one looked after them or searched for them.

⁷ Therefore, shepherds, hear the word of the LORD: ⁸ As I live—oracle of the Lord GOD—because my sheep became plunder, because my sheep became food for wild beasts, for lack of a shepherd, because my shepherds did not look after my sheep, but pastured themselves and did not pasture my sheep,* ⁹ therefore, shepherds, hear the word of the LORD: ¹⁰ Thus says the Lord GOD: Look! I am coming against these shepherds. I will take my sheep out of their hand and put a stop to their shepherding my flock, so that these shepherds will no longer pasture them. I will deliver my flock from their mouths so it will not become their food.*

¹¹ For thus says the Lord GOD: Look! I myself will search for my sheep and examine them. ¹² As a shepherd examines his flock while he himself is among his scattered sheep, so will I examine my sheep. I will deliver them from every place where they were scattered on the day of dark clouds.* ¹³ I will lead them out from among the peoples and gather them from the lands; I will bring them back to their own country and pasture them upon the mountains of Israel, in the ravines and every inhabited place in the land.* ¹⁴ In good pastures I will pasture them; on the mountain heights of Israel will be their grazing land. There they

---

† **33:23–29** News brought by the survivor furnished the occasion for this prophecy. Like Jeremiah, Ezekiel rejects the idea that those left in Judah have any claim to the land. The new Israel is to be formed from the exiles.

**33:32** *Singer*: perhaps the term indicates an entertainer whom one enjoys and then forgets.

**34:2** *Shepherds*: the leaders of the people. A frequent title for kings and deities in the ancient Near East; the ideal ruler took care of his subjects and anticipated their needs. Ezekiel's oracle broadens the reference to include the whole class of Jerusalem's leaders (v. 17). The prophet assures his audience, the exiles in

Babylon, that God holds these leaders responsible for what has happened to Jerusalem and will give Israel a new shepherd worthy of the title.

**33:24** Is 51:2.
**33:25** Gn 9:4; Jer 7:9–10.
**33:31** cf. Ez 8:1; Mt 13:22.
**34:2** Ps 78:70–72; Jn 10:11.
**34:3** Is 56:11.
**34:4** Ex 1:13; Zec 11:15–17; Mt 18:12–14.
**34:5** cf. Mk 6:34.
**34:8** Jude 12.
**34:10** Ps 72:14.
**34:12** Is 40:11; Lk 19:10.
**34:13** cf. Ez 36:24, 29–30.

will lie down on good grazing ground; in rich pastures they will be pastured on the mountains of Israel. * ¹⁵ I myself will pasture my sheep; I myself will give them rest—oracle of the Lord GOD. ¹⁶ The lost I will search out, the strays I will bring back, the injured I will bind up, and the sick I will heal; but the sleek and the strong I will destroy. I will shepherd them in judgment.

**Separation of the Sheep.** ¹⁷ As for you, my flock, thus says the Lord GOD: I will judge between one sheep and another, between rams and goats. * ¹⁸ Was it not enough for you to graze on the best pasture, that you had to trample the rest of your pastures with your hooves? Or to drink the clearest water, that you had to pollute the rest with your hooves? ¹⁹ Thus my flock had to graze on what your hooves had trampled and drink what your hooves had polluted. ²⁰ Therefore thus says the Lord GOD: Now I will judge between the fat and the lean. ²¹ Because you push with flank and shoulder, and butt all the weak sheep with your horns until you drive them off, ²² I will save my flock so they can no longer be plundered; I will judge between one sheep and another. ²³ * I will appoint one shepherd † over them to pasture them, my servant David; he shall pasture them and be their shepherd. ²⁴ I, the LORD, will be their God, and my servant David will be prince in their midst. I, the LORD, have spoken. *

²⁵ I will make a covenant of peace with them and rid the country of wild beasts so they will dwell securely in the wilderness and sleep in the forests. * ²⁶ I will settle them around my hill and send rain in its season, the blessing of abundant rain. ²⁷ The trees of the field shall bear their fruits, and the land its crops, and they shall dwell securely on their own soil. They shall know that I am the LORD when I break the bars of their yoke and deliver them

from the power of those who enslaved them. * ²⁸ They shall no longer be plundered by the nations nor will wild beasts devour them, but they shall dwell securely, with no one to frighten them. * ²⁹ I will prepare for them peaceful fields for planting so they are never again swept away by famine in the land or bear taunts from the nations. ³⁰ Thus they shall know that I, the LORD, their God, am with them, and that they are my people, the house of Israel—oracle of the Lord GOD. * ³¹ Yes, you are my flock: you people are the flock of my pasture, and I am your God—oracle of the Lord GOD. *

**35 Against Edom.** † ¹ The word of the LORD came to me: ² Son of man, set your face against Mount Seir and prophesy against it. ³ Say to it: Thus says the Lord GOD: Watch out! I am against you, Mount Seir. I will stretch out my hand against you and turn you into a desolate waste. * ⁴ Your cities I will turn into ruins, and you shall be a desolation; then you shall know that I am the LORD. *

⁵ Because you nursed a long-standing hatred and handed the Israelites over to the sword at the time of their collapse, at the time of their final punishment, † * ⁶ therefore, as I live—oracle of the Lord GOD—you are guilty of blood, and blood, I swear, shall pursue you. ⁷ I will make Mount Seir a desolate waste and cut off from it anyone who travels across it and back. * ⁸ I will fill its mountains with the slain; those slain by the sword shall fall on your hills, into your valleys and all your ravines.

⁹     I will make you a desolation forever,
      your cities will not be inhabited,
      and you shall know that I am the
      LORD. *

¹⁰ Because you said: The two nations and the two lands † belong to me; let us take

---

† **34:23** *One shepherd*: a future king to rule over a unified, restored Israel, in the image of the idealized David present in the Book of Kings (cf., e.g., 1 Kgs 3:3; 11:38; 2 Kgs 14:3; 22:2). *My servant David*: a common characterization of David; e.g., 1 Kgs 11:34, 36, 38; 2 Kgs 8:19; Ps 36:1; 78:70. See Ez 37:25.

**35:1–15** After the fall of Jerusalem, Edom assisted the Babylonians in devastating the land and subduing the population in order to occupy part of Judah's former territory. For this reason these oracles against Edom are found in the context of the city's fall.

**35:5** *Final punishment*: throughout this oracle the prophet echoes the threat against the mountains of Israel found in chaps. 6–7.

**35:10** *The two nations and the two lands*: by presenting Edom's excursion into the southern territory of Judah as its claim to both kingdoms, Ezekiel exaggerates Edom's greed and arrogance. LORD *was there*: Edom's betrayal of Judah becomes

---

| | |
|---|---|
| **34:14** Ps 23:2; Is 40:11. | **34:28** Jer 30:10. |
| **34:17** Mt 25:32–33. | **34:30** Ex 6:7. |
| **34:23** Ps 89:4, 20; Jer 23:5–6. | **34:31** Ps 28:9. |
| **34:24** cf. Ez 36:28; Ps 89:49; Jn 10:16. | **35:3** cf. Ez 25:12–14. |
| | **35:4** Ob 13. |
| **34:25** Is 11:6–9. | **35:5** Ob 11–15. |
| **34:27** Lv 26:13; Ps 72:16; Jer 28:10–13. | **35:7** Jer 46:19. |
| | **35:9** Is 34:5–6; Ob 10. |

possession of them—although the Lord was there— [11] therefore, as I live—oracle of the Lord God—I will deal with you according to the anger and envy you dealt out to them in your hatred, and I will make myself known to them when I execute judgment on you,* [12] then you shall know that I am the Lord.

I have heard all the insults you spoke against the mountains of Israel, saying: They are desolate; they have been given to us to devour. [13] You boasted against me with your mouths and used insolent words against me. I heard everything! [14] Thus says the Lord God: Because you rejoiced that the whole land was desolate, so I will do to you. [15] As you rejoiced over the devastation of the heritage of the house of Israel, the same I will do to you: you will become a ruin, Mount Seir, and the whole of Edom, all of it! Then they shall know that I am the Lord.*

# 36 Regeneration of the Land.

[1] As for you, son of man, prophesy to the mountains of Israel and say: Mountains of Israel, hear the word of the Lord! [2] Thus says the Lord God: Because the enemy said about you, "Ha! the ancient heights have become our possession," [3] therefore prophesy and say: Thus says the Lord God: because you have been ridiculed and hounded on all sides for becoming a possession for the remaining nations and have become a byword and a popular jeer,* [4] therefore, mountains of Israel, hear the word of the Lord God: Thus says the Lord God to the mountains and hills, to the ravines and valleys, to the desolate ruins and abandoned cities, plundered and mocked by the nations remaining around you:* [5] therefore thus says the Lord God: Truly, with burning jealousy I speak against the remaining nations and against Edom; they all took possession of my land for plunder with wholehearted joy and utter contempt. [6] Therefore, prophesy concerning the land of Israel and say to the mountains and hills, to the ravines and valleys: Thus says

the Lord God: See! in my jealous fury I speak, because you endured the reproach of the nations. [7] Therefore, thus says the Lord God: I raise my hand and swear: the nations around you shall bear their own reproach.

[8] But you, mountains of Israel, you will sprout branches and bear fruit for my people Israel, for they are coming soon.* [9] Look! I am for you! I will turn my face toward you; you will be plowed and planted.* [10] Upon you I will multiply the whole house of Israel; cities shall be resettled and ruins rebuilt.* [11] Upon you I will multiply people and animals so they can multiply and be fruitful. I will resettle you as in the past, and make you more prosperous than at your beginning; then you shall know that I am the Lord.*

[12] Upon you I will have them walk, my people Israel. They shall possess you, and you shall be their heritage. Never again shall you rob them of their children.

[13] Thus says the Lord God: Because they say of you, "You devour your own people,† you rob your nation of its children,"* [14] therefore, you shall never again devour your people or rob your nation of its children—oracle of the Lord God. [15] I will no longer make you listen to the reproach of nations. You will never again endure insults from the peoples. Never again shall you rob your nation of its children—oracle of the Lord God.

## Regeneration of the People.

[16] The word of the Lord came to me: [17] Son of man, when the house of Israel lived in its land, they defiled it with their behavior and their deeds. In my sight their behavior was like the impurity of a woman in menstruation.* [18] So I poured out my fury upon them for the blood they poured out on the ground and for the idols with which they defiled it. [19] I scattered them among the nations, and they were dispersed through other lands; according to their behavior and their deeds I carried out judgment against them.* [20]† But when they came to the

† an attack on Judah's God, the land's sovereign. In 11:15 and 33:24, Ezekiel condemns Judahites who annex land that does not belong to them. Now the exiles in Babylon learn that even though God had left Jerusalem (chap. 11), he witnesses Edom's insolence and pronounces judgment against it. Cf. 48:35, "The Lord is there!"

**36:13** *You devour your own people*: i.e., the land destroys its own population; this phrase also occurs in Nm 13:32, where Israelite spies describe Canaan as "a land that devours its inhabitants."

**36:20–24** These verses make clear that Israel's restoration is

God's initiative, independent of the people's shame and repentance (v. 31). By their wickedness, Israel provoked the exile; its presence among the nations gave the impression that God could not protect his people. God's gracious return of Israel to its land will restore his honor among these same nations.

| | |
|---|---|
| **35:11** Ob 15. | **36:10** Is 49:8, 17–23. |
| **35:15** Is 34:11; Ob 12. | **36:11** cf. Gn 1:22, 28. |
| **36:3** Ob 13. | **36:13** Nm 13:32. |
| **36:4** cf. Ez 6:3. | **36:17** Ps 106:37–38. |
| **36:8** Lv 26:3–5. | **36:19** Lv 18:24–28. |
| **36:9** Lv 26:9. | |

nations, where they went, they desecrated my holy name, for people said of them: "These are the people of the LORD, yet they had to leave their land." [21] So I relented because of my holy name which the house of Israel desecrated among the nations to which they came. [22] Therefore say to the house of Israel: Thus says the Lord GOD: Not for your sake do I act, house of Israel, but for the sake of my holy name, which you desecrated among the nations to which you came.* [23] But I will show the holiness of my great name, desecrated among the nations, in whose midst you desecrated it. Then the nations shall know that I am the LORD—oracle of the Lord GOD—when through you I show my holiness before their very eyes.* [24] I will take you away from among the nations, gather you from all the lands, and bring you back to your own soil. [25]†* I will sprinkle clean water over you to make you clean; from all your impurities and from all your idols I will cleanse you. [26]* I will give you a new heart, and a new spirit I will put within you. I will remove the heart of stone from your flesh and give you a heart of flesh.* [27] I will put my spirit within you so that you walk in my statutes, observe my ordinances, and keep them.* [28] You will live in the land I gave to your ancestors; you will be my people, and I will be your God.* [29] I will deliver you from all your impurities. I will summon the grain and make it plentiful; I will not send famine against you. [30] I will increase the fruit on your trees and the crops in your fields so that you no longer endure reproach from the nations because of famine.* [31] Then you will remember your evil behavior and your deeds that were not good; you will loathe yourselves for your sins and your abominations. [32] Not for your sake do I act—oracle of the Lord GOD. Let this be known to you! Be ashamed and humbled because of your behavior, house of Israel.

[33] Thus says the Lord GOD: When I cleanse you of all your guilt, I will resettle the cities and the ruins will be rebuilt.* [34] The desolate land will be tilled—once a wasteland in the eyes of every passerby. [35] They will say, "This once-desolate land has become like the garden of Eden. The cities once ruined, laid waste and destroyed, are now resettled and fortified."* [36] Then the surrounding nations that remain shall know that I, the LORD, have rebuilt what was destroyed and replanted what was desolate. I, the LORD, have spoken: I will do it. [37] Thus says the Lord GOD: This also I will be persuaded to do for the house of Israel: to multiply them like sheep. [38] Like sheep for sacrifice, like the sheep of Jerusalem on its feast days, the ruined cities shall be filled with flocks of people; then they shall know that I am the LORD.*

# 37 Vision of the Dry Bones.†

[1] The hand of the LORD came upon me, and he led me out in the spirit of the LORD and set me in the center of the broad valley. It was filled with bones. [2] He made me walk among them in every direction. So many lay on the surface of the valley! How dry they were! [3] He asked me: Son of man, can these bones come back to life? "Lord GOD," I answered, "you alone know that."* [4] Then he said to me: Prophesy over these bones, and say to them: Dry bones, hear the word of the LORD! [5] Thus says the Lord GOD to these bones: Listen! I will make breath enter you so you may come to life. [6] I will put sinews on you, make flesh grow over you, cover you with skin, and put breath into you so you may come to life. Then you shall know that I am the LORD. [7] I prophesied as I had been commanded. A sound started up, as I was prophesying, rattling like thunder. The bones came together, bone joining to bone. [8] As I watched, sinews appeared on them, flesh grew over them, skin covered them on top, but there was no breath in them. [9] Then he said to me:

---

† **36:25–26** God's initiative to cleanse Israel (cf. 24:13–14) is the first act in the creation of a new people, no longer disposed to repeating Israel's wicked past (chap. 20). To make this restoration permanent, God replaces Israel's rebellious and obdurate interiority ("heart of stone") with an interiority ("heart of flesh") susceptible to and animated by God's intentions ("my spirit," v. 27).

**37:1–14** This account is a figurative description of God's creation of a new Israel. Even though that creation begins with the remains of the old Israel, the exiles under the image of dry bones, depicting a totally hopeless situation, the new Israel is radically different: it is an ideal people, shaped by God's spirit to live the covenant faithfully, something the old Israel, exiles included,

were unable to do. While this passage in its present context is not about the doctrine of individual or communal resurrection, many Jewish and Christian commentators suggest that the doctrine is foreshadowed here.

*

| | |
|---|---|
| **36:22** cf. Ez 20:44; Dt 9:4–6; Is 37:35. | **36:28** Jer 30:22; 31:33. |
| **36:23** cf. Ez 20:41; Is 37:23. | **36:30** Lv 26:4–5. |
| **36:25** Ezr 6:21; Ps 51:2–7. | **36:33** Lv 26:31. |
| **36:26–27** Jer 31:33–34. | **36:35** cf. Ez 28:13; 31:9. |
| **36:26** cf. Rom 8:5–8. | **36:38** 1 Kgs 8:63. |
| **36:27** Ps 51:7–11. | **37:3** Is 26:19. |

Prophesy to the breath, prophesy, son of man! Say to the breath: Thus says the Lord GOD: From the four winds come, O breath, and breathe into these slain that they may come to life.†* 10 I prophesied as he commanded me, and the breath entered them; they came to life and stood on their feet, a vast army.* 11 He said to me: Son of man, these bones are the whole house of Israel! They are saying, "Our bones are dried up, our hope is lost, and we are cut off." 12 Therefore, prophesy and say to them: Thus says the Lord GOD: Look! I am going to open your graves; I will make you come up out of your graves, my people, and bring you back to the land of Israel.* 13 You shall know that I am the LORD, when I open your graves and make you come up out of them, my people! 14 I will put my spirit in you that you may come to life, and I will settle you in your land. Then you shall know that I am the LORD. I have spoken; I will do it—oracle of the LORD.*

**The Two Sticks.** 15 † Thus the word of the LORD came to me: 16 As for you, son of man, take one stick and write on it, "Judah and those Israelites associated with it." Then take another stick and write on it: "Joseph, Ephraim's stick, and the whole house of Israel associated with it." 17 Join the two sticks together so they become one stick in your hand. 18 When your people ask you, "Will you not tell us what you mean by all this?" 19 answer them: Thus says the Lord GOD: I will take the stick of Joseph, now in Ephraim's hand, and the tribes of Israel associated with it, and join to it the stick of Judah, making them one stick; they shall become one in my hand.* 20 The sticks on which you write, you must hold in your hand in their sight. 21 Say to them: Thus says the Lord GOD: I will soon take the Israelites from among the nations to which they have gone and gather them from all around to bring them back to their land. 22 I will make them one nation in the land, upon the mountains of Israel, and there shall be one king for them all. They shall never again be two nations, never again be divided into two kingdoms.*

23 No longer shall they defile themselves with their idols, their abominations, and all their transgressions. I will deliver them from all their apostasy through which they sinned. I will cleanse them so that they will be my people, and I will be their God.* 24 * David my servant shall be king over them; they shall all have one shepherd. They shall walk in my ordinances, observe my statutes, and keep them. 25 They shall live on the land I gave to Jacob my servant, the land where their ancestors lived; they shall live on it always, they, their children, and their children's children, with David my servant as their prince forever. 26 * I will make a covenant of peace with them; it shall be an everlasting covenant with them. I will multiply them and put my sanctuary among them forever. 27 My dwelling shall be with them; I will be their God, and they will be my people.* 28 Then the nations shall know that I, the LORD, make Israel holy, by putting my sanctuary among them forever.

**38 First Prophecy Against Gog.** 1 The word of the LORD came to me:† 2 Son of man, turn your face against Gog† of the land of Magog, the chief prince of Meshech and Tubal, and prophesy against him.* 3 Say: Thus says the Lord GOD: See! I am coming against you, Gog, chief prince of Meshech and Tubal. 4 I will turn you around and put hooks in your jaws to lead you out with all your army, horses and riders, all well armed, a great company,

---

† **37:9** The Hebrew word *rûah* has multiple related meanings expressed by different English words: wind, spirit, breath. In this translation, *rûah* is rendered "spirit," a powerful force that creates vision and insight (v. 1); "breath," physical energy that quickens and enlivens (vv. 5–6); "wind," invisible physical energy, sometimes destructive, sometimes invigorating (e.g., the rain-bearing winter winds), also a metaphor for restoration and new life (vv. 9–10); "my spirit," a share in God's power so the people observe the law that assures them life in the land (v. 14).

**37:15–22** The symbolic action of joining two sticks into one continues Ezekiel's description of God's future saving action: the unification of Judah and Israel under an ideal ruler.

**38:1–39:20** These three oracles against Gog (38:2–13; 14–23; 39:1–20) describe a mythic attack of God against a final enemy of his people sometime in the future. Like the oracles against the nations, their purpose is to strengthen Israel's hope in God, since they end with God's triumph on behalf of the people.

**38:2** *Gog*: the name is symbolic, probably derived from Gyges, king of Lydia. The gloss Magog may be an Akkadian expression, *mat-Gog*, "the land of Gog." Meshech and Tubal, as well as Gomer and Beth-togarmah (v. 6), were countries around the Black Sea, the northernmost countries known to the Israelites. The north was the traditional direction from which invasion was expected; cf. Jer 1:13–15.

---

**37:9** Ps 104:30; Is 32:15; Dn 7:2.
**37:10** cf. Rev 11:11.
**37:12** Is 26:19; Jer 19:14.
**37:14** cf. Ez 36:27–28; Jer 43:2; Jl 3:1–2.
**37:19** Zec 10:6.
**37:22** cf. Ez 17:22;
**37:23** cf. Ez 11:18; 36:28; Na 2:2.
**37:24** Ps 78:70–71; Is 55:4.
**37:26** Gn 9:16; Nm 25:12; Heb 13:20.
**37:27** Lv 26:11.
**38:2** cf. Gn 10:2; Ez 27:13.

EZ

all of them with bucklers and shields, carrying swords: 5* Persia, Cush, and Put with them, all with shields and helmets; 6 Gomer and all its troops, Beth-togarmah from the recesses of Zaphon and all its troops—many nations will accompany you. 7 Prepare and get ready, you and the company mobilized for you, but in my service. 8 After many days you will be called to battle; in the last years you will invade a land that has survived the sword—a people gathered from many nations back to the long-deserted mountains of Israel, brought forth from the nations to dwell securely.* 9 You shall come up like a sudden storm, covering the land like a cloud, you and all your troops and the many nations with you.*

10 Thus says the Lord GOD: On that day thoughts shall cross your mind, and you shall devise an evil plan. 11 You will say, "I will invade a land of open villages and attack a peaceful people who live in security—all of them living without city walls, bars, or gates"—* 12 in order to plunder and pillage, turning your hand against resettled ruins, against a people gathered from the nations, a people whose concern is cattle and goods, dwelling at the center† of the earth. 13 Sheba and Dedan, the merchants of Tarshish and all its "young lions" shall ask you: "Have you come here to plunder? Have you summoned your army for pillage, to carry off silver and gold, to take away cattle and goods, to seize much plunder?"*

**Second Prophecy Against Gog.** 14 Therefore, prophesy, son of man, and say to Gog: Thus says the Lord GOD: On that day, when my people Israel dwell securely, will you not take action, 15 leaving your base in the recesses of Zaphon,† you and many nations with you, all mounted on horses, a great company, a mighty army?* 16 You shall rise up over my people Israel like a cloud covering the land. In those last days, I will let you invade my land so that the nations acknowledge me, when in their sight I show my holiness through you, Gog.

17 Thus says the Lord GOD: About you I spoke in earlier times through my servants, the prophets of Israel, who prophesied at that time that I would let you invade them. 18 But on that day, the day Gog invades the land of Israel—oracle of the Lord GOD—my fury will flare up in my anger, 19 and in my jealousy, with fiery wrath, I swear on that day there will be a great earthquake in the land of Israel.* 20 Before me will tremble the fish of the sea and the birds of the air, the beasts of the field and everything that crawls on the ground, and everyone on the face of the earth. Mountains will be overturned, terraces will collapse, and every wall will fall to the ground.* 21 Against him I will summon every terror—oracle of the Lord GOD; every man's sword will be raised against his brother.* 22 I will execute judgment on him: disease and bloodshed; flooding rain and hailstones, fire and brimstone, I will rain down on him, on his troops and on the many nations with him.* 23 And so I will show my greatness and holiness and make myself known in the sight of many nations. Then they shall know that I am the LORD.*

# 39

**Third Prophecy Against Gog.** 1 You, son of man, prophesy against Gog, saying: Thus says the Lord GOD: Here I am, Gog, coming at you, chief prince of Meshech and Tubal. 2 I will turn you around, even though I urged you on and brought you up from the recesses of Zaphon and let you attack the mountains of Israel.* 3 Then I will strike the bow from your left hand and make the arrows drop from your right. 4 Upon the mountains of Israel you shall fall, you and all your troops and the peoples with you. I will give you as food to birds of prey of every kind and to wild beasts to be eaten. 5 In the open field you shall fall, for I have spoken—oracle of the Lord GOD.*

6 I will send fire against Magog and against those who live securely on the seacoast, and they will know that I am the LORD.* 7 I will reveal my holy name among my people Israel, and I will never again allow my holy name to be defiled. Then the nations shall know that I am the LORD, the Holy One of Israel.* 8 Yes, it is coming! It shall happen—oracle of the Lord GOD. This is the day I decreed.

† **38:12** *Center:* lit., "navel." Many ancient peoples spoke of their own homelands as "the navel," that is, the center of the earth.
**38:15** *Zaphon:* cf. note on Jb 37:22.

**38:5–6** Gn 10:2–3, 6.    **38:8** Is 24:22.

**38:9** Is 25:4; Jer 4:13; Rev 20:8.
**38:11** Zec 2:4–5.
**38:13** Gn 10:4, 7.
**38:15** cf. Ez 39:2.
**38:19** Is 24:18; Rev 6:12.
**38:20** Is 42:15.
**38:21** Is 34:5–6; 66:16.
**38:22** cf. Rev 9:17; 16:21.
**38:23** Rev 20:8.
**39:2** cf. Ez 32:30; 38:6, 15.
**39:5** cf. Ez 32:4.
**39:6** Rev 20:9.
**39:7** Is 12:6.

⁹Everyone living in the cities of Israel shall go out and set fire to the weapons, buckler and shield, bows and arrows, clubs and spears; for seven years they shall make fires with them.* ¹⁰They will not need to bring in wood from the fields or cut down trees in the forests, for they will make fires with the weapons, plundering those who plundered them, pillaging those who pillaged them—oracle of the Lord GOD.

¹¹On that day I will give Gog a place for his tomb in Israel, the Valley of Abarim,† east of the sea. It will block the way of travelers. There Gog shall be buried with all his horde; it shall be called "Valley of Hamon-Gog."* ¹²For seven months the house of Israel shall bury them in order to cleanse the land. ¹³All the people of the land shall take part in the burials, making a name for themselves on the day I am glorified—oracle of the Lord GOD. ¹⁴Men shall be permanently assigned to pass through the land, burying those who lie unburied in order to cleanse the land. For seven months they shall keep searching. ¹⁵When these pass through the land and see a human bone, they must set up a marker beside it, until the gravediggers bury it in the Valley of Hamon-Gog. ¹⁶Also the name of the city is Hamonah. Thus the land will be cleansed.

¹⁷As for you, son of man, thus says the Lord GOD: Say to birds of every kind and to every wild beast: "Assemble! Come from all sides for the sacrifice I am making for you, a great slaughter on the mountains of Israel. You shall eat flesh and drink blood! ¹⁸You shall eat the flesh of warriors and drink the blood of the princes of the earth: rams, lambs, and goats, bulls and fatlings from Bashan, all of them.* ¹⁹From the sacrifice I slaughtered for you, you shall eat fat until you are sated and drink blood until you are drunk. ²⁰At my table you shall be sated with horse and rider, with warrior and soldier of every kind—oracle of the Lord GOD.

**Israel's Return.** ²¹Then I will display my glory among the nations, and all the nations will see the judgment I executed, the hand I laid upon them. ²²From that day forward the house of Israel shall know that I am the LORD, their God. ²³The nations shall know that the house of Israel went into exile because of its sins. Because they betrayed me, I hid my face from them, handing them over to their foes, so they all fell by the sword.* ²⁴According to their defilement and their crimes I dealt with them, hiding my face from them.*

²⁵Therefore, thus says the Lord GOD: Now I will restore the fortunes of Jacob and take pity on the whole house of Israel; I am zealous for my holy name.* ²⁶They will forget their shame and all the infidelities they committed against me when they live securely on their own land with no one to frighten them. ²⁷When I bring them back from the nations and gather them from the lands of their enemies, I will show my holiness through them in the sight of many nations.* ²⁸Thus they shall know that I, the LORD, am their God, since I who exiled them among the nations will gather them back to their land, not leaving any of them behind. ²⁹I will no longer hide my face from them once I pour out my spirit upon the house of Israel—oracle of the Lord GOD.*

## V. THE NEW ISRAEL†

### The New Temple

**40** **The Man with a Measure.** ¹In the twenty-fifth year of our exile, at the beginning of the year, on the tenth day of the month, fourteen years after the city had been captured, on that very day the hand of the LORD came upon me and brought me back there.* ²In a divine vision he brought me to the land of Israel, where he set me down on a very high mountain. In front of me, there was something like a city built on it.* ³He

---

† **39:11** *The Valley of Abarim:* in the Abarim mountains, east of the Jordan. "Abarim" plays on the word *'oberim,* "travelers." *Hamon-Gog:* "the horde of Gog."

**40:1–48:35** This lengthy vision of a new Temple and a restored Israel is dated in v. 1 to April 28, 573 B.C. The literary form of the vision is sometimes compared to a mandala, a sacred model through which one can move symbolically to reach the world of the divine. Ezekiel describes the Temple through its boundaries, entrances, and exits in chaps. 40–43; by its sacred and profane use and space in 44–46; and by its central place within the land itself in 47–48. The prophet could not have ex-

pected a literal fulfillment of much of what he described. The passage doubtless went through several editorial stages, both from the prophet and from later writers.

---

**39:9** Ps 46:9; 76:3.
**39:11** cf. Ez 38:2.
**39:18** Jer 51:40; Rev 19:17–21.
**39:23** Ps 30:7; Is 54:8.
**39:24** 2 Kgs 17:23.
**39:25** Is 27:13.
**39:27** cf. Ez 20:41.
**39:29** cf. Ez 37:9; Is 11:2.
**40:1** 2 Kgs 25:7; Jer 39:1–10; 52:4–11.
**40:2** Is 2:2; Mi 4:1; Zec 14:10; cf. Rev 21:10.

brought me there, and there standing in the gateway was a man whose appearance was like bronze! He held in his hand a linen cord and a measuring rod.* [4]The man said to me, "Son of man, look carefully and listen intently. Pay strict attention to everything I show you, for you have been brought here so that I might show it to you. Then you must tell the house of Israel everything you see." [5]There an outer wall completely surrounded the temple. The measuring rod in the man's hand was six cubits long, each cubit being a cubit plus a handbreadth;† he measured the width of the structure, one rod, and its height, one rod.

## The East Gate.† [6]Going to the gate facing east, he climbed its steps and measured the threshold of the outer gateway as one rod wide.* [7]Each cell was one rod long and one rod wide, and there were five cubits between the cells; the threshold of the inner gateway adjoining the vestibule of the gate facing the temple was one rod wide. [8]He also measured the vestibule of the inner gate, [9]eight cubits, and its posts, two cubits each. The vestibule faced the inside. [10]On each side of the east gatehouse were three cells, all the same size; their posts were all the same size. [11]He measured the width of the gate's entryway, ten cubits, and the length of the gate itself, thirteen cubits. [12]The borders in front of the cells on both sides were one cubit, while the cells themselves measured six cubits by six cubits from one opening to the next. [13]Next he measured the gatehouse from the back wall of one cell to the back wall of the cell on the opposite side through the openings facing each other, a width of twenty-five cubits. [14]All around the courtyard of the gatehouse were posts six cubits high. [15]From the front of the gatehouse at its outer entry to the gateway of the porch facing inward, the length was fifty cubits. [16]There were recessed windows in the cells on all sides and in the posts on the inner side of the gate. Posts and windows were all around the inside, with palm trees decorating the posts.*

## The Outer Court. [17]Then he brought me to the outer court,† where there were chambers and pavement laid all around the courtyard: thirty chambers facing the pavement.* [18]The pavement lay alongside the gatehouses, the same length as the gates; this was the lower pavement. [19]He measured the length of the pavement from the front of the lower gate to the outside of the inner gate, one hundred cubits. He then moved from the east to the north side.

## The North Gate. [20]He measured the length and width of the north gate of the outer courtyard. [21]Its cells, three on each side, its posts, and its vestibule had the same measurements as those of the first gate, fifty cubits long and twenty-five cubits wide. [22]Its windows, its vestibule, and its palm decorations had the same proportions as those of the gate facing east. Seven steps led up to it, and its vestibule faced the inside. [23]The inner court had a gate opposite the north gate, just as at the east gate; he measured one hundred cubits from one gate to the other.

## The South Gate. [24]Then he led me to the south. There, too, facing south, was a gate! He measured its posts and vestibule; they were the same size as the others. [25]The gate and its vestibule had windows on both sides, like the other windows, fifty cubits long and twenty-five cubits wide. [26]Seven steps led up to it, its vestibule faced inside; and palms decorated each of the posts opposite one another. [27]The inner court also had a gate facing south. He measured it from gate to gate, facing south, one hundred cubits.

## Gates of the Inner Court.† [28]Then he brought me to the inner courtyard by the south gate, where he measured the south gateway; its measurements were the same as the others.

---

† 

**40:5** *A cubit plus a handbreadth*: a great cubit. The ordinary cubit consisted of six handbreadths; the great cubit, of seven. In measuring the Temple, a rod six great cubits long was used. The ordinary cubit was about one and a half feet, or, more exactly, 17.5 inches; the large cubit, 20.4 inches.
**40:6–16** The gate facing east, leading into the outer court of the Temple, is described more fully than the north and south gates, which, however, have the same dimensions. On the west side of the outer court there is a large building instead of a gate (cf. 41:12).

**40:17** *The outer court*: the court outside the Temple area proper, which had its own inner court (vv. 28–37).
**40:28–37** The gates leading into the inner court of the Temple area correspond to the gates leading into the outer court, with the exception that their vestibules are on the outer rather than the inner side.

* 

**40:3** Zec 2:1–2; Rev 1:15; 11:1; 21:15.
**40:6** cf. Ez 8:16.
**40:16** 1 Kgs 6:29, 32, 35.
**40:17** cf. Ez 41:6; 42:1.

[29] Its cells, posts, and vestibule were the same size as the others, fifty cubits long and twenty-five cubits wide. [30]† The vestibules all around were twenty-five cubits long and five cubits wide. [31] Its vestibule faced the outer court; palms decorated its posts, and its stairway had eight steps. [32] Then he brought me to the inner courtyard on the east and measured the gate there; its dimensions were the same as the others. [33] Its cells, posts, and vestibule were the same size as the others. The gate and its vestibule had windows on both sides, fifty cubits long and twenty-five cubits wide. [34] Its vestibule faced the outer court, palms decorated the posts opposite each other, and it had a stairway of eight steps. [35] Then he brought me to the north gate,* where he measured the dimensions [36] of its cells, posts, and vestibule; they were the same. The gate and its vestibule had windows on both sides, fifty cubits long and twenty-five cubits wide. [37] Its vestibule faced the outer court; palm trees decorated its posts opposite each other, and it had a stairway of eight steps.

**Side Rooms.** [38] There was a chamber opening off the vestibule of the gate where burnt offerings were washed.* [39] In the vestibule of the gate there were two tables on either side for slaughtering the burnt offerings, purification offerings, and reparation offerings.* [40] Two more tables stood along the wall of the vestibule by the entrance of the north gate, and two tables on the other side of the vestibule of the gate. [41] There were thus four tables on one side of the gate and four tables on the other side, eight tables in all, for slaughtering. [42] The four tables for burnt offerings were made of cut stone, one and a half cubits long, one and a half cubits wide, and one cubit high; the instruments used for slaughtering burnt offerings and other sacrifices were kept [43] on shelves the width of one hand, fixed all around the room; but on the tables themselves was the meat for the sacrifices. [44] Outside the inner gatehouse there were two rooms on the inner courtyard, one beside the north gate, facing south, and the other beside the south gate, facing north. [45] He said to me, "This chamber facing south is reserved for the priests who have charge of the temple area, [46] while this chamber facing north is reserved for the priests who have charge of the altar; they are the sons of Zadok,† the only Levites who may come near to minister to the LORD." [47] He measured the courtyard, a square one hundred cubits long and a hundred cubits wide, with the altar standing in front of the temple.*

**The Temple Building.**† [48]* Then he brought me into the vestibule of the temple and measured the posts, five cubits on each side. The gateway was fourteen cubits wide, its side walls three cubits. [49] The vestibule was twenty cubits long and twelve cubits wide; ten steps led up to it, and there were columns by the posts, one on each side.

**41** [1] Then he brought me to the nave and measured the posts; each was six cubits wide.* [2] The width of the entrance was ten cubits, and the walls on either side measured five cubits. He measured the nave, forty cubits long and twenty cubits wide.

[3] Then he went inside and measured the posts at the other entrance, two cubits wide. The entrance was six cubits wide, with walls seven cubits long on each side. [4] Next he measured the length and width of the room beyond the nave, twenty cubits long and twenty cubits wide. He said to me, "This is the holy of holies."†*

[5] Then he measured the wall of the temple, six cubits wide, and the width of the side chambers stretching all around the temple, four cubits each. [6]† There were thirty side chambers, chamber upon chamber in three stories; terraces on the outside wall of the temple enclosing the side chambers provided support, but there were no supports for the

---

†
  **40:30** The reference to vestibules all around is uncertain, and the verse may have arisen as a partial repetition of v. 29.
  **40:46** *Sons of Zadok:* descendants of the priestly line of Zadok; cf. 2 Sm 15:24–29; 1 Kgs 1:32–34; 2:35.
  **40:48–41:15** The description of Ezekiel's visionary Temple closely follows the description of the Temple of Solomon (1 Kgs 6), along with some crucial differences.
  **40:49–41:4** *Vestibule...nave...holy of holies:* the three divisions of the Temple building in progressing order of sanctity. The last is called "the inner sanctuary" in 1 Kgs 6.

  **41:6** The description of the three stories of rooms surrounding the Temple building can be compared with Solomon's Temple in 1 Kgs 6:6; there a step-like or terraced retaining wall supported the Temple building so no beams or nails from these chambers would enter the Temple wall itself.

*
  **40:35** cf. Ez 44:4; 47:2.
  **40:38** 2 Chr 4:6.
  **40:39** cf. Ez 46:2.
  **40:47** cf. Ez 41:13–14; 43:14–17.
  **40:48** 1 Kgs 6:2.
  **41:1** 1 Kgs 6:3–5.
  **41:4** 1 Kgs 6:20; cf. Ex 26:33; Heb 9:3–8.

temple wall itself. ⁷A broad passageway led up the side chambers, for the house was enclosed all the way up and all the way around. Thus the temple was widened by the ascent that went from the lowest story through the middle one to the highest story.* ⁸I saw a raised platform all around the temple, the foundation for the side chambers; the width of this terrace was a full rod, six cubits. ⁹The width of the outside wall enclosing the side chambers was five cubits. There was an open space between the side chambers of the temple ¹⁰and the other chambers that measured twenty cubits around the temple on all sides. ¹¹The side chambers had entrances to the open space, one entrance on the north and the other on the south. The width of the wall surrounding the open space was five cubits. ¹²The building† opposite the restricted area on the west side was seventy cubits long and ninety cubits wide, with walls five cubits thick all around it. ¹³Thus he measured the temple, one hundred cubits long. The restricted area, its building and walls, measured a hundred cubits in length. ¹⁴The temple facade, along with the restricted area to the east, was also one hundred cubits wide. ¹⁵He then measured the building opposite the restricted area which was behind it, together with its terraces on both sides, one hundred cubits.

**Interior of the Temple.** The inner nave and the outer vestibule ¹⁶were paneled; the windows had recesses and precious wood trim around all three sides except the sill. Paneling covered the walls from the floor up to the windows and even the window sections.* ¹⁷Even above the doorway and in the inner part of the temple and outside as well, around all the walls inside and out, ¹⁸were figures of cherubim and palm trees: a palm tree between each pair of cherubim. Each cherub had two faces:* ¹⁹the face of a human being looked toward one palm tree and the face of a lion looked toward the other palm tree. Thus the figures covered all the walls around the temple. ²⁰From the floor to the lintel of the door, cherubim and

palm trees decorated the walls. ²¹The nave had a square door frame, and inside facing the holy place was something that looked like ²²a wooden altar,† three cubits high, two cubits long, and two cubits wide. It had corners and a wooden base and sides. He said to me, "This is the table that stands before the LORD."* ²³The nave had a double door,* and the holy place ²⁴also had a double door; each door had two sections that could move; two sections on one door, and two on the other.* ²⁵Cherubim and palm trees decorated the doors of the nave like the decoration on the walls. Outside a wooden lattice faced the vestibule. ²⁶There were recessed windows and palm trees on the side walls of the vestibule. The side chambers of the temple also had latticework.

# 42 Other Structures. ¹Then he led me north to the outer court, bringing me to some chambers on the north side opposite the restricted area and the north building.* ²They were a hundred cubits long on the north side and fifty cubits wide. ³Built in rows at three different levels, they stood between the twenty cubits of the inner court and the pavement of the outer court. ⁴In front of the chambers was a walkway ten cubits wide on the inside of a wall one cubit wide. The doorways faced north. ⁵† The upper chambers were shorter because they lost space to the lower and middle tiers of the building. ⁶Because they were in three tiers, they did not have foundations like the court, but were set back from the lower and middle levels from the ground up. ⁷The outside walls ran parallel to the chambers along the outer court, a length of fifty cubits. ⁸The chambers facing the outer court were fifty cubits long; thus the wall along the nave was a hundred cubits. ⁹At the base of these chambers, there was an entryway from the east so that one could enter from the outer court ¹⁰where the wall of the court began.

To the south along the side of the restricted area and the building there were also chambers ¹¹with a walkway in front of them. They looked like the chambers on the north side in

---

† **41:12** *The building*: the function of this structure behind the Temple is never specified.

**41:22** *A wooden altar*: the altar of incense, standing in the nave at the entrance to the holy of holies.

**42:5–6** The three rows of identical chambers, on different ground levels, necessarily had roofs on correspondingly different levels.

length and width, in their exits, their design, and their doorways. [12] At the base of the chambers on the south side there was an entry at the end of a walkway in front of the protective wall by which one could enter from the east. [13] He said to me, "The north and south chambers facing the restricted area are the chambers of the holy place where the priests who approach the LORD shall eat the most holy meals. Here they shall place the most holy offerings: the grain offerings, the purification offerings, and the reparation offerings; for the place is holy.†* [14] When the priests have entered, they must not go out again from the holy place into the outer court without leaving the garments in which they ministered because they are holy. They shall put on other garments before approaching the area for the people."*

**Measuring the Outer Court.** [15] When he finished measuring the interior of the temple area, he brought me out by way of the gate facing east and measured all around it. [16] He measured the east side, five hundred cubits by his measuring rod. Then he turned [17] and measured the north side: five hundred cubits by his measuring rod. He turned [18] and measured the south side, five hundred cubits by his measuring rod. [19] He turned and measured the west side, also five hundred cubits by his measuring rod. [20] Thus he measured it on the four sides. It was surrounded by a wall five hundred cubits long and five hundred cubits wide, to separate the sacred from the profane.

### Restoration of the Temple

# 43

**The Glory of the Lord Returns.** [1] Then he led me to the gate facing east,* [2] and there was the glory of the God of Israel coming from the east! His voice was like the roar of many waters, and the earth shone with his glory. [3] The vision I saw was like the vision I had seen when he came to destroy the city and like the vision I had seen by the river

Chebar—I fell on my face. [4] The glory of the LORD entered the temple by way of the gate facing east.* [5] Then the spirit lifted me up and brought me to the inner court. And there the glory of the LORD filled the temple!* [6] I heard someone speaking to me from the temple, but the man was standing beside me. [7] The voice said to me: Son of man, do you see the place for my throne, and the place for the soles of my feet? Here I will dwell among the Israelites forever. The house of Israel, neither they nor their kings, will never again defile my holy name, with their prostitutions and the corpses of their kings at their death.* [8] When they placed their threshold against my threshold† and their doorpost next to mine, with only a wall between me and them, they defiled my holy name by the abominations they committed, and I devoured them in my wrath.* [9] From now on, let them put their prostitution and the corpses of their kings far from me, and I will dwell in their midst forever.*

**The Law of the Temple.** [10] As for you, son of man, describe the temple to the house of Israel so they are ashamed for their sins. Let them measure its layout. [11] If they are ashamed for all they have done, tell them about the layout and design of the temple, its exits and entrances, with all its regulations and instructions; write it down for them to see, that they may carefully observe all its laws and statutes. [12] This is the law for the temple: the entire area on top of the mountain all around will be a most holy place. This is the law for the temple.

**The Altar.** [13] These were the dimensions of the altar† in cubits, a cubit being one cubit plus a handbreadth. The channel was one cubit deep by one cubit wide, and its rim had a lip one span wide all around it.* The height of the altar itself was as follows: [14] from the channel at floor level up to the lower ledge was two cubits, with the ledge one cubit wide; from the lower ledge to the upper ledge, four cubits,

---

† **42:13** The function of these chambers is explained again in 46:19–20.

**43:8** *They placed their threshold against my threshold*: in preexilic Jerusalem, the Temple and the palace belonged to the same complex of buildings; kings like Ahaz and Manasseh treated it as their private chapel for the religious practices Ezekiel condemns. In the new Israel the Temple is free, even spatially, from civil jurisdiction; cf. 45:7–8. This is an instance of Ezekiel's broader program to separate the sacred from the secular.

**43:13–17** *The altar*: like altars from Assyria and other parts of

the ancient Near East, this altar has three parts: a base, a pedestal, and an upper block with a channel cut into the surface on all sides. The rim around the upper block (v. 17) stopped blood and other sacrificial material from falling to the ground.

*

**42:13** Lv 10:12–13, 17.
**42:14** Ex 29:9; Lv 8:7–9.
**43:1** 1 Chr 9:18.
**43:4** cf. Ez 10:19.
**43:5** cf. Ez 11:24.
**43:7** 1 Chr 28:2; Ps 132:7; Is 6:1; Jer 3:17.
**43:8** 1 Kgs 7:1–12.
**43:9** cf. Ez 37:26–28.
**43:13** cf. Ex 20:24.

with the ledge one cubit wide. ¹⁵The altar hearth was four cubits high, and extending up from the top of the hearth were four horns. ¹⁶The hearth was twelve cubits long and twelve cubits wide, a square with four equal sides. ¹⁷The upper ledge was fourteen cubits long and fourteen cubits wide on all four sides. The rim around it was half a cubit, with a channel one cubit all around. The steps faced east.*

¹⁸Then he said to me: Son of man, thus says the Lord GOD: These are the statutes for the altar when it is set up for sacrificing burnt offerings and splashing blood on it.* ¹⁹A young bull must be brought as a purification offering to the priests, the Levites descended from Zadok, who come near to serve me—oracle of the Lord GOD.* ²⁰You shall take some of its blood and smear it on the four horns of the altar, and on the four corners of the ledge, and all around its rim. Thus you shall purify and purge it.* ²¹Then take the bull as purification offering and burn it in the appointed place outside the sanctuary.* ²²On the second day present an unblemished male goat as a purification offering, to purify the altar as you did with the bull. ²³When you have completed the purification,* you must bring an unblemished young bull and an unblemished ram from the flock ²⁴and present them before the LORD. The priests shall throw salt on them and sacrifice them as burnt offerings to the LORD. ²⁵Daily for seven days you shall give a male goat as a purification offering; and a young bull and a ram from the flock, all unblemished,* shall be offered ²⁶for seven days. Thus they shall purge the altar, in order to cleanse and dedicate it. ²⁷And when these days are over, from the eighth day on, the priests shall sacrifice your burnt offerings and communion offerings on the altar. Then I will be pleased with you—oracle of the Lord GOD.

# 44 The Closed Gate. ¹Then he brought me back to the outer gate of the sanctuary facing east, but it was closed. ²The LORD

said to me: This gate must remain closed; it must not be opened, and no one should come through it. Because the LORD, the God of Israel, came through it, it must remain closed. ³Only the prince may sit in it to eat a meal in the presence of the LORD; he must enter through the vestibule of the gate and leave the same way.†*

## The New Law

**Admission to the Temple.** ⁴Then he brought me by way of the north gate to the facade of the temple. I looked—and the glory of the LORD filled the LORD's house! I fell on my face.* ⁵The LORD said to me: Son of man, pay close attention, look carefully, and listen intently to everything I tell you about all the statutes and laws of the LORD's house. Pay close attention to the entrance into the temple and all the exits of the sanctuary. ⁶Say to that rebellious house, the house of Israel: Thus says the Lord GOD: Enough of all your abominations, house of Israel! ⁷You have admitted foreigners, uncircumcised in heart and flesh, into my sanctuary to profane it when you offered me food, the fat and blood.† Thus you have broken my covenant by all your abominations.* ⁸Instead of caring for the service of my sanctuary, you appointed these foreigners to care for the service of my sanctuary. ⁹Thus says the Lord GOD: No foreigners, uncircumcised in heart and flesh, shall ever enter my sanctuary: not even any of the foreigners who live among the Israelites.*

**Levites.** ¹⁰As for the Levites who went far away from me when Israel strayed from me after their idols, they will bear the consequences of their sin. ¹¹They will serve in my sanctuary only as gatekeepers and temple servants; they will slaughter burnt offerings and sacrifices for the people. They will stand before the people to serve them.* ¹²Because they used to serve them before their idols, thus becoming a

† **44:3** Ezekiel imagines a scene like this: The prince stands at the eastern gate of the inner court while his sacrifice is being offered (46:2); he then goes to the vestibule of the outer court to eat the sacrificial meal. The closed outer gate on the eastern side signifies that the Lord has entered the Temple permanently, not to depart again.

**44:7–14** According to Ezekiel, the Levites' priestly role is reduced to the performance of menial tasks as punishment for their misdeeds (cf. vv. 10–14). This demotion was enforced during the restoration of Temple worship under Ezra and Nehemiah;

this may explain the small number of Levites willing to return to Jerusalem after the exile.

| | |
|---|---|
| **43:17** Ex 20:26. | **43:25** Ex 29:37; Lv 8:33. |
| **43:18** Ex 29:16; Lv 4:6; 5:9. | **44:3** Ex 24:9–11; 2 Chr |
| **43:19** Lv 4:3. | 26:16–20. |
| **43:20** Lv 4:7. | **44:4** Is 6:4; Rev 15:8. |
| **43:21** Ex 29:14; Lv 4:12; | **44:7** Lv 26:41. |
| 8:17; cf. Heb | **44:9** Jl 4:17; Neh 13:8. |
| 13:11–13. | **44:11** Nm 3:5–37; 1 Chr |
| **43:23** Ex 29:1. | 26:12–19. |

stumbling block to the house of Israel, therefore I have sworn an oath against them, says the Lord GOD, and they will bear the consequences of their sin. [13] They shall no longer come near to serve as my priests, nor shall they touch any of my sacred things or my most sacred offerings, for they must bear their shame, the abominations they committed. [14] Instead I will make them responsible for the service of the temple and all its work, for everything that must be done in it.*

**Priests.** [15] As for the levitical priests, sons of Zadok, who took charge of my sanctuary when the Israelites strayed from me, they may approach me to serve me and stand before me to offer the fat and the blood—oracle of the Lord GOD.* [16] They may enter my sanctuary; they may approach my table to serve me and carry out my service.* [17] Whenever they enter the gates of the inner court, they shall wear linen garments; they shall not put on anything woolen when they serve at the gates of the inner court or within the temple. [18]* They shall have linen turbans on their heads and linen undergarments on their loins; they shall not gird themselves with anything that causes sweat. [19]* And when they go out to the people in the outer court, they shall take off the garments in which they served and leave them in the rooms of the sanctuary, and put on other garments so they do not transmit holiness to the people† by their garments.

[20]* They shall not shave their heads nor let their hair hang loose, but they shall keep their hair carefully trimmed. [21] No priest shall drink wine before he enters the inner court. [22]* They shall not take as wives either widows or divorced women, but only unmarried women from the line of Israel; however, they may take as wives widows who are widows of priests. [23]* They shall teach my people to distinguish between sacred and profane and make known to them the difference between clean and unclean. [24]* In legal cases they shall stand as judges, judging according to my ordinances. They shall observe all my laws and statutes

regarding all my appointed feasts, and they shall keep my sabbaths holy.

[25]* They shall not make themselves unclean by going near a dead body; only for their father, mother, son, daughter, brother, or unmarried sister may they make themselves unclean. [26] After he is again clean, he must wait an additional seven days; [27] on the day he enters the inner court to serve in the sanctuary, he shall present a purification offering for himself—oracle of the Lord GOD. [28]* I will be their heritage: I am their heritage! You shall not give them any property in Israel, for I am their property! [29]* They shall eat grain offerings, purification offerings, and reparation offerings; anything under the ban† in Israel belongs to them; [30]* all the choicest first fruits of every kind and all the best of your offerings of every kind shall belong to the priests; the best of your dough you shall also give to the priests to bring a blessing upon your house. [31]* The priests shall not eat anything, whether bird or animal, that died naturally or was killed by wild beasts.

## 45 The Holy Portion.

[1] When you apportion the land heritage by heritage, you shall set apart a holy portion for the LORD, holier than the rest of the land—twenty-five thousand cubits long and twenty thousand cubits wide; the entire area shall be holy. [2] Of this land a square plot, five hundred by five hundred cubits, shall be assigned to the sanctuary, with fifty cubits of free space around it. [3] From this tract also measure off a length of twenty-five thousand cubits and a width of ten thousand cubits; on it the sanctuary, the holy of holies, shall stand. [4] This shall be the sacred part of the land belonging to the priests, the ministers of the sanctuary, who draw near to minister to the LORD; it shall be a place for their homes and an area set apart for the sanctuary. [5] There shall also be a strip twenty-five thousand cubits long and ten thousand wide for the Levites, the ministers of the temple, so they have cities to live in. [6] You shall assign a strip five thousand cubits wide and twenty-five

---

† **44:19** *Transmit holiness to the people:* holiness was considered to have a physical quality that could be communicated from person to person. It is a danger to those who have not prepared themselves to be in God's presence. The priests remove their ceremonial garments out of concern for the people.

**44:29** *Under the ban:* dedicated to the Lord.

**44:14** 1 Chr 23:28–32.
**44:15** 1 Chr 6:50–53.
**44:16** Lv 3:16–17.
**44:18** Ex 28:39, 42.
**44:19** Ex 39:27–29; Lv 6:10–11.
**44:20** Lv 21:5.
**44:22** Lv 21:7.
**44:23** Hg 2:10–13.
**44:24** Dt 17:8–9.
**44:25** Lv 21:1–4.
**44:28** Nm 18:23–24; Dt 18:1–2.
**44:29** Lv 6:16; 27:28.
**44:30** Nm 15:18–21; 18:12–13.
**44:31** Lv 11:39.

thousand long as the property of the city parallel to the sacred tract; this shall belong to the whole house of Israel. [7] A section shall belong to the prince, bordering both sides of the sacred tract and city combined, extending westward on the west side and eastward on the east side, corresponding in length to one of the tribal portions from the west boundary to the east boundary [8] of the land. This shall be his property in Israel so that my princes will no longer oppress my people, but will leave the land to the house of Israel according to its tribes. [9] Thus says the Lord GOD: Enough, you princes of Israel! Put away violence and oppression, and do what is just and right! Stop evicting my people!—oracle of the Lord GOD.

**Weights and Measures.**[†] [10][*] You shall have honest scales, an honest ephah, and an honest bath. [11] The ephah and the bath shall be the same size: the bath equal to one tenth of a homer, and the ephah equal to one tenth of a homer; their capacity is based on the homer. [12] The shekel shall be twenty gerahs. Twenty shekels plus twenty-five shekels plus fifteen shekels make up a mina[†] for you.

**Offerings.** [13] This is the offering you must make: one sixth of an ephah from each homer of wheat and one sixth of an ephah from each homer of barley. [14] This is the regulation for oil: for every bath of oil, one tenth of a bath, computed by the kor,[†] made up of ten baths, that is, a homer, for ten baths make a homer. [15] Also, one sheep from the flock for every two hundred from the pasture land of Israel, for the grain offering, the burnt offering, and communion offerings, to make atonement on their behalf—oracle of the Lord GOD.[*] [16] All the people of the land shall be responsible for these offerings to the prince in Israel. [17] It shall be the duty of the prince to provide burnt offerings, grain offerings, and libations on feast days, new moons, and sabbaths, on all the festivals of the house of Israel. He shall provide the purification offering, grain offering, burnt offering, and communion offerings, to make atonement on behalf of the house of Israel.[*]

**The Passover.** [18] Thus says the Lord GOD: On the first day of the first month you shall take an unblemished young bull to purify the sanctuary.[*] [19] The priest shall take some of the blood from the purification offering and smear it on the doorposts of the house, on the four corners of the ledge of the altar, and on the doorposts of the gates of the inner courtyard.[*] [20] You shall repeat this on the seventh day of the month for those who have sinned inadvertently or out of ignorance; thus you shall purge the temple.[*] [21] On the fourteenth day of the first month you shall observe the feast of Passover; for seven days unleavened bread must be eaten. [22] On that day the prince shall sacrifice, on his own behalf and on behalf of all the people of the land, a bull as a purification offering. [23] On each of the seven days of the feast he shall sacrifice, as a burnt offering to the LORD, seven bulls and seven rams without blemish, and as a purification offering he shall sacrifice one male goat each day.[*] [24] As a grain offering he shall offer one ephah for each bull and one ephah for each ram and one hin[†] of oil for each ephah.[*]

**The Feast of Booths.** [25] In the seventh month, on the fifteenth day of the seventh month, on the feast day and for the next seven days, he shall make the same offerings: the same purification offerings, burnt offerings, grain offerings, and offerings of oil.[*]

# 46

**Sabbaths.** [1] Thus says the Lord GOD: The gate of the inner court facing east shall remain closed throughout the six working days, but on the sabbath and on the day of the new moon it shall be open. [2][†] Then the

---

[45:10–12] Besides the land monopoly fostered by royal greed and collusion with the wealthy (Mi 2:2; Is 3:12–15; 5:8–10), one grave social evil of preexilic Israel was dishonesty in business; cf. Hos 12:8; Am 8:5. *Ephah, bath*: see note on Is 5:10.

[45:12] *Mina*: before the exile, a mina was worth fifty shekels; later, in imitation of Babylonian practice, its value increased to sixty shekels. A shekel weighed slightly less than half an ounce. A shekel's monetary value depended on whether it was gold or silver.

[45:14] *Kor*: a liquid and a dry measure, equal to a homer.

[45:24] *Hin*: one sixth of the liquid measure known as a bath.

[46:2–12] The prophet describes the inner eastern gateway opening on the inner court of the priests in front of the Temple itself where the altar of sacrifice stands. The people may watch the priests making offerings on sabbaths and feast days only by looking through the open gate; the prince, however, may stand inside the gate, in the vestibule on the edge of the inner court, to observe the offerings. Only priests could stand in the court itself.

---

[45:10] Lv 19:35–36; Dt 25:13–16; Mi 6:10–12.
[45:15] Lv 1:4; 6:23.
[45:17] cf. Ez 46:4–12.
[45:18] Lv 16:33.
[45:19] Lv 16:18–19.
[45:20] Lv 4:27.
[45:23] Nm 22:40; 28:16–25.
[45:24] Nm 28:12–13.
[45:25] Ex 23:16; 34:22; Lv 23:34–43; Nm 29:12–38.

prince shall enter from outside by way of the vestibule of the gate and remain standing at the doorpost of the gateway while the priests sacrifice his burnt offerings and communion offerings; then he shall bow down in worship at the opening of the gate and leave. But the gate shall not be closed until evening. ³The people of the land also shall bow down in worship before the LORD at the opening of this gate on the sabbaths and new moons. ⁴The burnt offerings which the prince sacrifices to the LORD on the sabbath shall consist of six unblemished lambs and an unblemished ram, ⁵together with a grain offering of one ephah for the ram and whatever he pleases for the lambs, and a hin of oil for each ephah. ⁶* On the day of the new moon, he shall provide an unblemished young bull, six lambs, and a ram without blemish, ⁷with a grain offering of one ephah for the bull and an ephah for the ram, and for the lambs whatever he can, and for each ephah a hin of oil.*

**Ritual Laws.** ⁸When the prince enters, he shall always enter and depart by the vestibule of the gate. ⁹When the people of the land come before the LORD to bow down on the festivals, if they enter by the north gate they shall leave by the south gate, and if they enter by the south gate they shall leave by the north gate. They shall not go back by the gate through which they entered; everyone shall leave by the opposite gate. ¹⁰When they come in, the prince shall be with them; he shall also leave with them. ¹¹On feasts and festivals, the grain offering shall be an ephah for a bull, an ephah for a ram, but for the lambs whatever they please, and a hin of oil with each ephah. ¹²When the prince makes a freewill offering to the LORD, whether a burnt offering or communion offering, the gate facing east shall be opened for him, and he shall bring his burnt offering or peace offering as he does on the sabbath. Then he shall leave, and the gate shall be closed after his departure. ¹³* Every day you shall bring as a burnt offering to the LORD an unblemished year-old lamb; you shall offer it every morning, ¹⁴and with it every morning a

grain offering of one sixth of an ephah, with a third of a hin of oil to moisten the fine flour. This grain offering for the LORD is a perpetual statute. ¹⁵* The lamb, the grain offering, and the oil you must bring every morning as a perpetual burnt offering.

**The Prince and the Land.** ¹⁶Thus says the Lord GOD: If the prince makes a gift of part of his heritage to any of his sons, it belongs to his sons; that property is their heritage. ¹⁷But if he makes a gift of part of his heritage to one of his servants, it belongs to him until the year of release;† then it reverts to the prince. Only the heritage given to his sons belongs to him.* ¹⁸The prince shall not seize any part of the heritage of the people by forcing them off their property. From his own property he shall provide heritage for his sons, so that none of my people will be driven off their property.

**The Temple Kitchens.** ¹⁹Then he brought me through the entrance at the side of the gateway to the chambers reserved for the priests, which faced north. There I saw a place at the far west end, ²⁰about which he said to me, "This is the place where the priests cook the reparation offerings and the purification offerings and bake the grain offerings, so they do not have to bring them into the outer court and so transmit holiness to the people."†* ²¹Then he led me into the outer court and had me cross to the four corners of the court, and there, in each corner, was another court! ²²In all four corners of the courtyard there were courts set off, each forty cubits long by thirty cubits wide, all four of them the same size. ²³A stone wall surrounded them on four sides, and ovens were built along the bottom of the walls all the way around. ²⁴He said to me, "These are the kitchens where the temple ministers cook the sacrifices of the people."

**47** **The Wonderful Stream.**† ¹Then he brought me back to the entrance of the temple, and there! I saw water flowing out from under the threshold of the temple toward the east, for the front of the temple faced

---

† **46:17** *The year of release*: the jubilee year; cf. Lv 25:23–55.
**46:20** Cf. note on 44:19.
**47:1–12** The life and refreshment produced wherever the Temple stream flows evoke the order and abundance of paradise (cf. Gn 1:20–22; 2:10–14; Ps 46:5) and represent the coming transformation Ezekiel envisions for the exiles and their land.

Water signifies great blessings and evidence of the Lord's presence (cf. Jl 2:14).

**46:6** Lv 22:20.      **46:15** Ex 29:42; Nm 28:5–6.
**46:7** cf. Nm 28:12.      **46:17** Lv 25:8–17.
**46:13** Ex 29:38; Nm 28:3–8.      **46:20** Lv 6:20.

east. The water flowed out toward the right side of the temple to the south of the altar.* ² He brought me by way of the north gate and around the outside to the outer gate facing east; there I saw water trickling from the southern side. ³ When he continued eastward with a measuring cord in his hand, he measured off a thousand cubits and had me wade through the water; it was ankle-deep. ⁴ He measured off another thousand cubits and once more had me wade through the water; it was up to the knees. He measured another thousand cubits and had me wade through the water; it was up to my waist. ⁵ Once more he measured off a thousand cubits. Now it was a river I could not wade across. The water had risen so high, I would have to swim—a river that was impassable. ⁶ Then he asked me, "Do you see this, son of man?" He brought me to the bank of the river and had me sit down. ⁷ As I was returning, I saw along the bank of the river a great many trees on each side.* ⁸ He said to me, "This water flows out into the eastern district, runs down into the Arabah and empties into the polluted waters of the sea† to freshen them.* ⁹ Wherever it flows, the river teems with every kind of living creature; fish will abound. Where these waters flow they refresh; everything lives where the river goes. ¹⁰ Fishermen will stand along its shore from En-gedi to En-eglaim;† it will become a place for drying nets, and it will abound with as many kinds of fish as the Great Sea.* ¹¹ Its marshes and swamps shall not be made fresh, but will be left for salt. ¹² Along each bank of the river every kind of fruit tree will grow; their leaves will not wither, nor will their fruit fail. Every month they will bear fresh fruit because the waters of the river flow out from the sanctuary. Their fruit is used for food, and their leaves for healing."*

## The New Israel

**Boundaries of the Land.†** ¹³ Thus says the Lord GOD: These are the boundaries of the land which you shall apportion among the twelve tribes of Israel, with Joseph having two portions.* ¹⁴ You shall apportion it equally because I swore to give it to your ancestors as a heritage; this land, then, is your heritage.* ¹⁵* These are the borders of the land: on the northern side, from the Great Sea in the direction of Hethlon, Lebo-hamath to Zedad, ¹⁶ Berothah, and Sibraim, along the frontiers of Damascus and Hamath, to Hazar-enon, on the border of Hauran.* ¹⁷ Thus the border extends from the sea to Hazar-enon, north of the border of Damascus, the frontier of Hamath to the north. This is the northern boundary. ¹⁸ The eastern border shall be between Damascus and Hauran, while the Jordan will form the border between Gilead and the land of Israel down to the eastern sea as far as Tamar. This is the eastern boundary. ¹⁹ The southern border shall go southward from Tamar to the waters of Meribath-kadesh, on to the Wadi of Egypt, and into the Great Sea. This is the southern boundary.* ²⁰ The western border shall have the Great Sea as a boundary as far as a point opposite Lebo-hamath. This is the western boundary.

**The Northern Portions.** ²¹ You shall divide this land according to the tribes of Israel. ²²* You shall allot it as heritage for yourselves and for the resident aliens in your midst who have fathered children among you. You shall treat them like native Israelites; along with you they shall receive a heritage among the tribes of Israel. ²³ In whatever tribe the resident alien lives, there you shall assign his heritage—oracle of the Lord GOD.

**48** ¹ These are the names† of the tribes: At the northern end, along the side of the way to Hethlon, Lebo-hamath, and Hazar-enon, the border of Damascus, and northward up to the frontier with Hamath, from the eastern border to the western: Dan, one portion. ² Along the territory of Dan from

---

47:8 *The sea:* the Dead Sea, in which nothing can live. This vision of the Temple stream which transforms places of death into places of life is similar in purpose to the oracle of dry bones in 37:1–14: it offers the exiles hope for the future.

47:10 *From En-gedi to En-eglaim:* En-gedi is about halfway down the western shore of the Dead Sea; En-eglaim may have been at its northern end.

47:13–20 These boundaries for a restored Israel correspond to the boundaries of the Davidic kingdom at its fullest extent; they are the "ideal boundaries" of the promised land; cf. Nm 34:3–12.

48:1–29 This distribution of the land among the tribes does not correspond to the geographical realities of Palestine. It is another idealizing element in Ezekiel's representation of a restored and transformed Israel.

*

| | |
|---|---|
| **47:1** cf. Gn 2:10; Ps 46:4; Rev 22:1. | 34:2–12. |
| **47:7** Rev 22:2. | **47:14** Gn 12:7; 15:9–21. |
| **47:8** Zec 14:8. | **47:15** Nm 34:1–12. |
| **47:10** Ps 104:25. | **47:16** 2 Sm 8:8. |
| **47:12** Ps 1:3; Jer 17:8. | **47:19** Nm 34:4; Dt 32:51. |
| **47:13** Gn 48:16; Nm | **47:22** Lv 24:22; Nm 15:29; 26:55–56; Is 56:6–7. |

the eastern border to the western border: Asher, one portion.* ³Along the territory of Asher from the eastern border to the western border: Naphtali, one portion.* ⁴Along the territory of Naphtali from the eastern border to the western border: Manasseh, one portion.* ⁵Along the territory of Manasseh from the eastern border to the western border: Ephraim, one portion.* ⁶Along the territory of Ephraim from the eastern border to the western border: Reuben, one portion.* ⁷Along the territory of Reuben from the eastern border to the western border: Judah, one portion.*

**The Sacred Tract.** ⁸Along the territory of Judah from the eastern border to the western border is the tract you shall set apart, twenty-five thousand cubits wide and as long as one of the portions from the eastern border to the western border. The sanctuary shall stand in the center of the tract. ⁹The tract you set apart for the LORD shall be twenty-five thousand cubits long by twenty thousand wide. ¹⁰The sacred tract will be given to the following: the priests shall have twenty-five thousand cubits on the north, ten thousand on the west, ten thousand on the east, and twenty-five thousand on the south. The sanctuary of the LORD shall be in its center. ¹¹The consecrated priests, the Zadokites, who fulfilled my service and did not stray with the Israelites as the Levites did, ¹²shall have their own tract set apart, next to the territory of the Levites, separate from the most holy tract. ¹³The Levites shall have territory corresponding to that of the priests, twenty-five thousand cubits long and ten thousand cubits wide. The whole tract shall be twenty-five thousand cubits long and twenty thousand wide. ¹⁴They may not sell or exchange or transfer any of it, the best part of the land, for it is sacred to the LORD. ¹⁵The remaining section, five thousand cubits long and twenty-five thousand cubits wide, is profane land, assigned to the city for dwellings and pasture. The city is at its center. ¹⁶These are the dimensions of the city: the north side, forty-five hundred cubits; the south side, forty-five hundred cubits; the east side, forty-five hundred cubits; and the west side, forty-five hundred cubits.* ¹⁷The pasture land for the city extends north two hundred fifty cubits, south two hundred fifty cubits, east two hundred fifty cubits, and west two hundred fifty cubits. ¹⁸The remaining section runs eastward along the sacred tract for ten thousand cubits and westward ten thousand cubits. Its produce shall provide food for the workers of the city. ¹⁹The workers of the city, from all the tribes of Israel, shall cultivate it. ²⁰The entire sacred tract measures twenty-five thousand by twenty-five thousand cubits; as a square you shall set apart the sacred tract together with the city property.

²¹The remaining land on both sides of the sacred tract and the property of the city shall belong to the prince, extending eastward twenty-five thousand cubits up to the eastern boundary, and westward twenty-five thousand cubits to the western boundary. This portion belongs to the prince and corresponds to the tribal portions. The sacred tract and the sanctuary of the temple shall be in the middle. ²²Except for the Levites' property and the city's property, which are in the middle of the prince's property, the territory between the portion of Judah and the portion of Benjamin shall belong to the prince.

**The Southern Portions.** ²³These are the remaining tribes:

From the eastern border to the western border: Benjamin, one portion.* ²⁴Along the territory of Benjamin from the eastern border to the western border: Simeon, one portion.* ²⁵Along the territory of Simeon from the eastern border to the western border: Issachar, one portion.* ²⁶Along the territory of Issachar from the eastern border to the western border: Zebulun, one portion.* ²⁷Along the territory of Zebulun from the eastern border to the western border: Gad, one portion.* ²⁸Along the territory of Gad shall be the southern border. This boundary shall extend from Tamar to the waters of Meribath-kadesh, and along the Wadi of Egypt to the Great Sea. ²⁹This is the land you shall apportion as a heritage among the tribes of Israel, and these are their portions—oracle of the Lord GOD.

**The Gates of the City.** ³⁰These are the exits from the city: On the north side, measuring

---

**48:2** Jos 19:24–31.　　**48:5** Jos 16:5–9.　　**48:16** Rev 21:16.　　**48:25** Jos 19:17–23.
**48:3** Jos 19:32–39.　　**48:6** Jos 13:15–21.　　**48:23** Jos 18:11–28.　　**48:26** Jos 19:10–16.
**48:4** Jos 17:1–11.　　**48:7** Jos 15:1–63.　　**48:24** Jos 19:1–9.　　**48:27** Jos 13:24–28.

forty-five hundred cubits— [31] the gates are named after the tribes of Israel—on the north, three gates: the gate of Reuben, one; the gate of Judah, one; and the gate of Levi, one. [32] On the east side, measuring forty-five hundred cubits, three gates: the gate of Joseph, one; the gate of Benjamin, one; and the gate of Dan, one. [33] On the south side, measuring forty-five hundred cubits, three gates: the gate of Simeon, one; the gate of Issachar, one; and the gate of Zebulun, one. [34] On the west side, measuring forty-five hundred cubits, three gates: the gate of Gad, one; the gate of Asher, one; and the gate of Naphtali, one.* [35] The circuit of the city shall be eighteen thousand cubits. From now on the name of the city is "The Lord is there."*

---

**48:34** Rev 21:12–13.          **48:35** Is 2:6; Rev 3:12; 21:3.

# The Book of

# Daniel

## INTRODUCTION

Jerome Walsh

## Contents of the Book

The book of Daniel is a complicated work. In the Hebrew text tradition, which is followed by Jewish congregations and most Protestant churches, it comprises two parts, Dn 1–6 and 7–12, and is written in two languages, Hebrew and Aramaic—though the two languages do not coincide precisely with the two parts. In the text tradition followed by Roman Catholic and Orthodox churches, which goes back to the Septuagint (a translation of the Hebrew Scriptures into Greek made by Jewish scholars in the third to first centuries BCE), there are three parts and three languages. Both text traditions present quite divergent pictures of the hero, Daniel, in the different parts of the book.

The first part of the book, Dn 1–6, collects five stories about Daniel's career at the royal court of Babylon. (Daniel himself does not appear in Dn 3, but his three associates do.) Daniel is first introduced as a young man exiled from Judah at the time of the Babylonian conquest of Jerusalem.[1] These stories describe Daniel in glowing terms that recall the ideal wise man. Like Joseph in Egypt (Gn 37–50), Daniel is utterly faithful to Israel's God and to the Torah (Dn 1, 6). God blesses him with wisdom that enables him to surpass the Babylonian sages in the interpretation of the king's dreams (Dn 2 and 4) and other portents (Dn 5), and he becomes a high official in the realm (Dn 2:48; 6:1–3).

---

1. Daniel 1:1 misdates that event. Nebuchadnezzar's siege of Jerusalem was in the eleventh year of Jehoiakim, not the third, and the first deportation into Babylonian exile occurred in 598/597 BCE. The error is possibly due to a misreading of 2 Kgs 24:1, which says that "Jehoiakim became [Nebuchadnezzar's] vassal for three years. Then Jehoiakim turned and rebelled against him." What Dn 1:1 overlooks is that Jehoiakim became Nebuchadnezzar's vassal in the eighth year of Jehoiakim's reign. According to 1:21, Daniel was still at court nearly sixty years later, in 539 BCE; 10:1 will extend the latter date to 537 BCE.

## Outline of Daniel

I. **Daniel and the Kings of Babylon (1:1–6:29)**

II. **Daniel's Visions (7:1–12:13)**

III. **Appendix: Susanna, Bel, and the Dragon (13:1–14:42)**

The main anomaly in this part of the book is its linguistic divide. In Dn 2:4, the text shifts from Hebrew to Aramaic when it begins to quote the Chaldeans, and it remains in Aramaic through the end of ch. 7. No one has proposed a completely satisfactory explanation of this peculiarity, though the appearance of Aramaic passages in the midst of Hebrew is not unprecedented (one word in Gn 31:47; one verse in Jer 10:11; and two extended passages in Ezra). Nor can it be decisively determined whether Hebrew or Aramaic was the original language of the various stories.

The second part of the book, Dn 7–12, recounts four symbolic visions or dreams that Daniel experienced (chs. 10–12 report a single vision). In these chapters, then, he is less a sage, a wise courtier, and interpreter of dreams along the lines of Joseph in Egypt, and more an apocalyptic visionary along the lines of such late figures as the author of the book of *Enoch* or John the Seer of the book of Revelation. The symbolism of all four visions points to historical events that take place in the early second century BCE, but its allegorical character requires that each vision be interpreted to Daniel by a heavenly figure. This sort of interpreter is a common element in apocalyptic writing.

The third part of the book, found in the

Roman Catholic and Orthodox canons, comprises material found in Greek in the Septuagint but not in the Hebrew Bible, though it is likely that all of this material too was originally composed in Hebrew or Aramaic. It includes two poems and a brief intervening prose passage that have been incorporated into ch. 3 (Dn 3:24–90; 3:91–100 in Roman Catholic Bibles corresponds to 3:24–33 in Protestant and Jewish Bibles), and three prose stories appended to the book as chs. 13 and 14 ("Susanna," "Bel," and "The Dragon"). Daniel is absent from the poetic material, which is ascribed to his three associates. The two poems contain no explicit references to their narrative context, and they have strong stylistic and theological similarities to the Psalms. It seems likely, therefore, that they were originally independent poems (perhaps liturgical) that have been used secondarily to elaborate the story of ch. 3. In the appended stories Daniel appears again as a sage, not an apocalyptic visionary. In "Susanna" he is a young man with no apparent standing, whom God unexpectedly seizes in the manner of some of the early prophets (see Am 7:14–15), or in the manner of the Phoenician lad in the Egyptian *Story of Wen-Amun*, to avert a miscarriage of justice and to punish perjury and misuse of power by authorities in the Jewish community. In "Bel" he proves that a god is false because it does not eat, and in "The Dragon" he proves that a god is false because it *does* eat. These three stories seem representative of a more extensive number of noncanonical Daniel stories extant in Jewish (and Christian?) circles near the turn of the era, a few of which have been found in fragmentary form among the Dead Sea Scrolls at Qumran.

# History and Composition

Discussing the historical aspects of the book of Daniel is no less complicated than discussing its content and organization. We must distinguish between the historical settings of the events described and the historical settings of the stories' composition and compilation. Beyond that, there are questions to be asked about the figure of Daniel himself.

## The Events

Each of the stories and visions in the first two parts of the book is set during the reign of a particular king of Babylonia and, usually, during a specific year of that reign. One would expect that to enable precise dating. Problems, however, abound. Not only would Daniel's career as a court sage have spanned an unlikely six decades and more, but the historical framework assumed by the book also does not square with what we know of history. For example, a king named "Darius the Mede" (who, according to chs. 6 and 9, reigned between Belshazzar and Cyrus) is attested nowhere in the reasonably complete records we have of the day, nor was there a Median hegemony over Babylonia; Cyrus of Persia had already conquered Media before he conquered Babylon. As for the appendices, the story of "Susanna" is set in Babylon, but there is nothing in the story that situates it chronologically. "Bel" is set in Babylonia during Cyrus's reign, therefore not before 539 BCE; and "The Dragon," though not explicitly dated, takes place apparently under the same king. In sum, the Daniel traditions seem to be set geographically in Babylonia, and mostly in the city of Babylon, but they are spread chronologically across a partially fictional reconstruction of the whole period of the Babylonian exile, that is, the first sixty years or so of the sixth century BCE.

## The Composition

The composition of the stories, as well as their compilation into the collection we now have, is quite a different matter. Aside from Dn 2, the narratives in chs. 1–6 are difficult to date on the basis of content, though the Aramaic in chs. 3–6 seems most at home during the late Persian and early Hellenistic periods. Chapter 2, however, uses the "four kingdom" allegory: the component parts of the statue in Nebuchadnezzar's dream represent, respectively, the successive kingdoms of Babylonia, Media, Persia, and the Hellenistic kingdom that arose after the division of the realm. This section dates, therefore, to after the death of Alexander the Great (323 BCE). It does not, however, reflect any awareness of the depredations of Antiochus IV Epiphanes or of the ensuing Maccabean rebellion, and so it is unlikely to have been composed as late as 170 BCE.

By contrast, each of the four visions clearly alludes to the persecution by Antiochus IV that began around 170 BCE, though none is aware of the circumstances of his death (164 BCE) or of the success of the Maccabean rebellion. The vision accounts, then, at least in their present form, date from the early 160s BCE, and the compilation of Dn 1–12 cannot be any earlier.

The poetry and stories in the Greek text resist precise dating, although the postexilic period is most likely. It is entirely possible that the Semitic originals of some of the Greek additions are older than parts of Dn 1–12, though their attachment to that material is, no doubt, subsequent to its compilation.

One clue to the composition history of the book may be the chiastic (A B C C′ B′ A′) organization of the Aramaic section. Daniel 2 and 7 both use the four-kingdom allegory to recount history; chs. 3 and 6 recount the miraculous deliverance of their Jewish protagonists from mortal danger; chs. 4 and 5 describe the divine punishment of royal arrogance. This arrangement may point to an intermediate stage in the growth of the book, to which ch. 1 was subsequently added as a preface and chs. 8–12 to fill out the portrait of Daniel the visionary.

In its final form, the book of Daniel is an example of Jewish apocalyptic literature, of which many other examples, not contained in the biblical canon, were composed between 300 BCE and 100 CE. One of the strategies common to much apocalyptic writing is to situate the apocalyptic visionary in the distant past and to describe events of the more recent past as if the visionary were predicting them. Another is the introduction of a heavenly intermediary to explain the vision authoritatively to the visionary.

The book of Daniel uses both strategies. Such traits can help distinguish apocalyptic writings like Daniel from writings the Hebrew Bible recognizes as "prophetic." Other traditions, however, notably at Qumran, in the Septuagint, and among New Testament and Christian authors, number Daniel among the prophets.

## Daniel

But who was "Daniel"? Was he a historical figure among the Jewish exiles in Babylon? Was he a second-century BCE apocalyptic visionary who retrojected his visions literarily to the Babylonian period? Was he a legendary figure around whom tradition constructed an apocalyptic persona (as occurred in works like the *Apocalypse of Adam* or the book of *Enoch*), or even a historical figure used in the same way (as in the *Ascension of Isaiah*)? With no helpful evidence outside the book of Daniel itself, we are reduced to conjecture and surmise. The most likely starting point for speculation is three passing references in Ezekiel (Ez 14:14, 20; 28:3), where a "Daniel" or "Dan'el" is mentioned. (The name is not exactly the same as the name of the hero of the book of Daniel, but the difference may simply reflect a spelling variation.) In the first two passages, "Dan'el" is proverbial for his righteousness; in the last, he is exemplary for his wisdom. Both qualities, of course, are prominent in our Daniel as well. Perhaps most striking, however, is Ezekiel's association of this proverbial figure with Noah and Job, both famous for their righteousness, but both also non-Israelites! This raises the question of whether the biblical Daniel may have non-Jewish blood in his literary veins, so to speak.

It also throws a light on another relevant figure lurking in the shadows. In the literature of ancient Ugarit, a thousand years and more before the compilation of our book of Daniel, there is a judge, Dan'el, renowned for his righteous judgments (*dan-'el* means "El [a deity's name] is Judge"). It seems possible, then, that the Daniel of the biblical book is a Jewish literary avatar of a legendary ancient Near Eastern figure of wisdom and righteous authority whose career spanned multiple literary incarnations over more than a millennium. ■

# THE BOOK OF DANIEL

## New American Bible, Introduction

This book takes its name not from the author, who is actually unknown, but from its hero, who was allegedly among the first Jews deported to Babylon, where he lived at least until 538 B.C. Strictly speaking, the book does not belong to the prophetic writings but rather to a distinctive type of literature known as "apocalyptic," of which it is an early specimen. Apocalyptic writing first appears about 200 B.C. and flourished among Jews and Christians down to the Middle Ages, especially in times of persecution. Apocalyptic literature has its roots in the older teaching of the prophets, who often pointed ahead to the day of the Lord, the consummation of history. For both prophet and apocalyptist there was one Lord of history, who would ultimately vindicate the chosen people. Apocalyptic also has roots in the wisdom tradition. Daniel has the gift of discernment from God. Greek wisdom (represented by the Babylonian "magicians and enchanters") is ridiculed (see especially chaps. 2 and 5), whereas God reveals hidden things to faithful servants.

This work was composed during the bitter persecution carried on by Antiochus IV Epiphanes (167–164 B.C.) and was written to strengthen and comfort the Jewish people in their ordeal. The persecution was occasioned by Antiochus's efforts to unify his kingdom, in face of the rising power of Rome, by continuing the hellenization begun by Alexander the Great; Antiochus tried to force Jews to adopt Greek ways, including religious practices. Severe penalties, including death, were exacted against those who refused (cf., e.g., 1 Mc 1:41–63).

The book contains traditional stories (chaps. 1–6), which tell of the trials and triumphs of the wise Daniel and his three companions. The moral is that people of faith can resist temptation and conquer adversity. The stories bristle with historical problems and have the character of historical novels rather than factual records. What is more important than the question of historicity, and closer to the intention of the author, is the fact that persecuted Jews of the second century B.C. would quickly see the application of these stories to their own plight.

There follows in chaps. 7–12 a series of visions promising deliverance and glory to the Jews in the days to come. The great nations of the ancient world have risen in vain against the Lord; his kingdom shall overthrow existing powers and last forever; in the end the dead will be raised for reward or punishment. Under this apocalyptic imagery some of the best elements of prophetic and sapiential teaching are synthesized: the insistence on right conduct, the divine control over events, the certainty that the kingdom of God will ultimately triumph and humanity attain the goal intended for it at the beginning of creation. The arrival of the kingdom is a central theme of the gospels, where Jesus is identified as the human figure (or "Son of Man") who appears in Daniel's vision in chap. 7. The message in both parts of the first twelve chapters (i.e., chaps. 1–6 and chaps. 7–12) is that history unrolls under the watchful eye of God, who does not abandon those who trust in him and will finally deliver and re-establish them. Moreover, it can be pointed out that chaps. 2 and 7 present the same teaching in different symbolism; 2:31 even describes the king's dream as a "vision."

The added episodes of Susanna, Bel, and the Dragon, found only in the Greek version, are edifying short stories with a didactic purpose (chaps. 13–14). The Greek version also adds a long prayer, numbered in the NAB and the Greek, 3:24–90, between 3:23–24 in the Hebrew text.

These three sections constitute the divisions of the Book of Daniel:

   I. Daniel and the Kings of Babylon (1:1–6:29)

  II. Daniel's Visions (7:1–12:13)

 III. Appendix: Susanna, Bel, and the Dragon (13:1–14:42) ■

DN

# DANIEL

## I. DANIEL AND THE KINGS OF BABYLON

**1** **The Food Test.** ¹In the third year of the reign of Jehoiakim,† king of Judah, King Nebuchadnezzar of Babylon came and laid siege to Jerusalem.* ²* The Lord handed over to him Jehoiakim, king of Judah, and some of the vessels of the temple of God, which he carried off to the land of Shinar† and placed in the temple treasury of his god.

³ The king told Ashpenaz,† his chief chamberlain, to bring in some of the Israelites, some of the royal line and of the nobility. ⁴They should be young men without any defect, handsome, proficient in wisdom, well informed, and insightful, such as could take their place in the king's palace; he was to teach them the language and literature of the Chaldeans. ⁵The king allotted them a daily portion of food and wine from the royal table. After three years' training they were to enter the king's service. ⁶Among these were Judeans, Daniel, Hananiah, Mishael, and Azariah. ⁷† The chief chamberlain changed their names: Daniel to Belteshazzar, Hananiah to Shadrach, Mishael to Meshach, and Azariah to Abednego.

⁸ But Daniel was resolved not to defile himself with the king's food or wine; so he begged the chief chamberlain to spare him this defilement.† ⁹Though God had given Daniel the favor and sympathy of the chief chamberlain, ¹⁰he said to Daniel, "I am afraid of my lord the king, who allotted your food and drink. If he sees that you look thinner in comparison to the other young men of your age, you will endanger my life with the king." ¹¹Then Daniel said to the guardian whom the chief chamberlain had put in charge of Daniel, Hananiah, Mishael, and Azariah, ¹²"Please test your servants for ten days. Let us be given vegetables to eat and water to drink. ¹³Then see how we look in comparison with the other young men who eat from the royal table, and treat your servants according to what you see." ¹⁴He agreed to this request, and tested them for ten days; ¹⁵after ten days they looked healthier and better fed than any of the young men who ate from the royal table. ¹⁶So the steward continued to take away the food and wine they were to receive, and gave them vegetables.

¹⁷ To these four young men God gave knowledge and proficiency in all literature and wisdom, and to Daniel the understanding of all visions and dreams. ¹⁸At the end of the time the king had specified for their preparation, the chief chamberlain brought them before Nebuchadnezzar. ¹⁹When the king had spoken with all of them, none was found equal to Daniel, Hananiah, Mishael, and Azariah; and so they entered the king's service. ²⁰In any question of wisdom or understanding which the king put to them, he found them ten times better than any of the magicians and enchanters in his kingdom. ²¹* Daniel remained there until the first year of King Cyrus.†

**2** **Nebuchadnezzar's Dream.**† ¹In the second year of his reign, King Nebuchadnezzar had a dream which left his spirit no rest and robbed him of his sleep. ²So he ordered that the magicians, enchanters, sorcerers, and Chaldeans† be summoned to interpret the dream for him. When they came and presented themselves to the king, ³he said to them, "I had a dream which will allow my

---

† **1:1** According to 2 Kgs 24, the siege of Jerusalem took place after the death of Jehoiakim, but 2 Chr 36:5–8 says that Jehoiakim was taken to Babylon.

**1:2** *Shinar:* ancient name for Babylonia, a deliberate archaism in this text; cf. Gn 10:10; 11:2.

**1:3** The proper name Ashpenaz is sometimes taken as a title, major-domo.

**1:7** Other prominent Jews with Babylonian names include Sheshbazzar and Zerubbabel, who were leaders of the postexilic community.

**1:8** *This defilement:* the bread, meat, and wine of the Gentiles were unclean (Hos 9:3; Tb 1:12; Jdt 10:5; 12:1–2) because they might have been offered to idols; and the meat may not have been drained of blood, as Jewish dietary law requires. This test relates to the attempt of Antiochus to force Jews to eat forbidden foods in contempt of their religion (1 Mc 1:62–63;

2 Mc 6:18; 7:1).

**1:21** *The first year of King Cyrus:* the year of this Persian king's conquest of Babylon, 539/538 B.C.

**2:1–49** The chronology of v. 1 is in conflict with that of 1:5, 18, and in 2:25 Daniel appears to be introduced to the king for the first time. It seems that the story of this chapter was originally entirely independent of chap. 1 and later retouched slightly to fit its present setting. The Septuagint (Papyrus 967) reads the twelfth year instead of the second.

**2:2** *Chaldeans:* because the Babylonians gave serious study to the stars and planets, "Chaldeans" were identified with astrologers throughout the Hellenistic world.

---

* **1:1** 2 Kgs 24:1; 2 Chr 36:6; Jer 25:1.
**1:21** Dn 6:29.
**1:2** Dn 5:2; 2 Chr 36:7; Gn 10:10.

spirit no rest until I know what it means." ⁴The Chaldeans answered the king in Aramaic:† "O king, live forever! Tell your servants the dream and we will give its meaning." ⁵The king answered the Chaldeans, "This is what I have decided: unless you tell me the dream and its meaning, you shall be cut to pieces and your houses made into a refuse heap. ⁶But if you tell me the dream and its meaning, you shall receive from me gifts and presents and great honors. Therefore tell me the dream and its meaning."

⁷Again they answered, "Let the king tell his servants the dream and we will give its meaning." ⁸But the king replied: "I know for certain that you are bargaining for time, since you know what I have decided. ⁹If you do not tell me the dream, there can be but one decree for you. You have conspired to present a false and deceitful interpretation to me until the crisis is past. Tell me the dream, therefore, that I may be sure that you can also give its correct interpretation."

¹⁰The Chaldeans answered the king: "There is not a man on earth who can do what you ask, O king; never has any king, however great and mighty, asked such a thing of any magician, enchanter, or Chaldean. ¹¹What you demand, O king, is too difficult; there is no one who can tell it to the king except the gods, who do not dwell among people of flesh." ¹²At this the king became violently angry and ordered all the wise men† of Babylon to be put to death. ¹³When the decree was issued that the wise men should be slain, Daniel and his companions were also sought out.

¹⁴Then Daniel prudently took counsel with Arioch, the chief of the king's guard, who had set out to kill the wise men of Babylon. ¹⁵He asked Arioch, the officer of the king, "What is the reason for this harsh order from the king?" When Arioch told him, ¹⁶Daniel went and asked for time from the king, that he might give him the interpretation.

¹⁷Daniel went home and informed his companions Hananiah, Mishael, and Azariah, ¹⁸that they might implore the mercy of the God of heaven in regard to this mystery, so that Daniel and his companions might not perish with the rest of the wise men of Babylon. ¹⁹During the night the mystery was revealed to Daniel in a vision, and he blessed the God of heaven:

²⁰ "Blessed be the name of God forever
　　　and ever,
　　for wisdom and power are his.
²¹ He causes the changes of the times and
　　　seasons,
　　establishes kings and deposes them.
　　He gives wisdom to the wise
　　　and knowledge to those who
　　　understand.
²² He reveals deep and hidden things
　　and knows what is in the darkness,
　　for the light dwells with him.*
²³ To you, God of my ancestors,
　　I give thanks and praise,
　　because you have given me wisdom
　　　and power.
　　Now you have shown me what we asked
　　　of you,
　　you have made known to us the king's
　　　dream."

²⁴So Daniel went to Arioch, whom the king had appointed to destroy the wise men of Babylon, and said to him, "Do not put the wise men of Babylon to death. Bring me before the king, and I will tell him the interpretation of the dream." Arioch quickly brought Daniel to the king and said, ²⁵"I have found a man among the Judean exiles who can give the interpretation to the king." ²⁶The king asked Daniel, whose name was Belteshazzar, "Can you tell me the dream that I had and its meaning?" ²⁷In the king's presence Daniel made this reply:

"The mystery about which the king has inquired, the wise men, enchanters, magicians, and diviners could not explain to the king. ²⁸But there is a God in heaven who reveals mysteries, and he has shown King Nebuchadnezzar what is to happen in the last days; this was your dream, the visions† you saw as you lay in bed. ²⁹To you in your bed there came

---

2:4 *Aramaic*: a gloss to indicate that at this point the text switches from Hebrew to Aramaic, which continues through the end of chap. 7; at 8:1, the text switches back to Hebrew.
2:12 *Wise men*: the satire, although directed against the Babylonian diviners in the text, refers to the Hellenistic Greeks, who made special claims to wisdom; the assertion here is that

true wisdom comes from God and resides with the Jews. Cf. also chap. 5.
2:28 *The visions*: lit., "the visions of your head," a phrasing which distinguishes visionary experiences that are personal from

2:22 Jn 1:9; 8:12; 1 Cor 4:5; 1 Jn 1:6.

thoughts about what should happen in the future, and he who reveals mysteries showed you what is to be. [30] To me also this mystery has been revealed; not that I am wiser than any other living person, but in order that its meaning may be made known to the king, that you may understand the thoughts of your own mind.

[31] "In your vision, O king, you saw a statue, very large and exceedingly bright, terrifying in appearance as it stood before you. [32] Its head was pure gold, its chest and arms were silver, its belly and thighs bronze, [33] its legs iron, its feet partly iron and partly clay.† [34] While you watched, a stone was hewn from a mountain without a hand being put to it, and it struck its iron and clay feet, breaking them in pieces. [35] The iron, clay, bronze, silver, and gold all crumbled at once, fine as the chaff on the threshing floor in summer, and the wind blew them away without leaving a trace. But the stone that struck the statue became a great mountain and filled the whole earth.

[36] † "This was the dream; the interpretation we shall also give in the king's presence. [37] You, O king, are the king of kings; to you the God of heaven has given dominion and strength, power and glory; [38] human beings, wild beasts, and birds of the air, wherever they may dwell, he has handed over to you, making you ruler over them all; you are the head of gold. [39] Another kingdom shall take your place, inferior to yours, then a third kingdom, of bronze, which shall rule over the whole earth. [40] There shall be a fourth kingdom, strong as iron; it shall break in pieces and subdue all these others, just as iron breaks in pieces and crushes everything else. [41] The feet and toes you saw, partly of clay and partly of iron, mean that it shall be a divided kingdom, but yet have some of the hardness of iron. As you saw the iron mixed with clay tile, [42] and the toes partly iron

and partly clay, the kingdom shall be partly strong and partly fragile. [43] The iron mixed with clay means that they shall seal their alliances by intermarriage, but they shall not stay united, any more than iron mixes with clay. [44] In the lifetime of those kings the God of heaven will set up a kingdom that shall never be destroyed or delivered up to another people; rather, it shall break in pieces all these kingdoms and put an end to them, and it shall stand forever. [45] * That is the meaning of the stone you saw hewn from the mountain without a hand being put to it, which broke in pieces the iron, bronze, clay, silver, and gold. The great God has revealed to the king what shall be in the future; this is exactly what you dreamed, and its meaning is sure."

[46] Then King Nebuchadnezzar fell down and worshiped Daniel and ordered sacrifice and incense offered to him. [47] To Daniel the king said, "Truly your God is the God of gods and Lord of kings and a revealer of mysteries; that is why you were able to reveal this mystery." [48] He advanced Daniel to a high post, gave him many generous presents, made him ruler of the whole province of Babylon and chief prefect over all the wise men of Babylon. [49] At Daniel's request the king made Shadrach, Meshach, and Abednego administrators of the province of Babylon, while Daniel himself remained at the king's court.

**3** **The Fiery Furnace.** [1] King Nebuchadnezzar had a golden statue made, sixty cubits high and six cubits wide, which he set up in the plain of Dura† in the province of Babylon. [2] He then ordered the satraps,† prefects, and governors, the counselors, treasurers, judges, magistrates and all the officials of the provinces to be summoned to the dedication of the statue which he had set up. [3] The satraps, prefects, and governors, the counselors, treasurers,

---

† those that are observable by others (see 4:2, 7, 10). That Daniel, unlike the Chaldeans, has access to these visions testifies to his God-given wisdom. Actually, this "dream" is more properly an apocalyptic vision; cf. the very similar message in Daniel's vision of chap. 7.

**2:33** *Clay:* it has been suggested that the motif of iron mixed with clay implies a hollow metal statue packed with clay to stabilize it. In the interpretation of the dream, however, the mixture is taken as a sign of weakness.

**2:36–45** The four successive kingdoms in this apocalyptic perspective are the Babylonian (gold), the Median (silver), the Persian (bronze), and the Hellenistic (iron). The last, after Alexander's death, was divided among his generals (vv. 41–42). Of the kingdoms which emerged from this partitioning, the two that

most affected the Jews were the dynasties of the Ptolemies in Egypt and the Seleucids in Syria. They tried in vain, by war and through intermarriage, to restore the unity of Alexander's empire (v. 43). The stone hewn from the mountain is the kingdom of God awaited by the Jews (vv. 44–45). Compare the image of the stone applied to Jesus in Lk 20:17–18.

**3:1** *Dura:* several places in Babylonia bore this name. Probably the present reference is to one located close to Babylon. Giant statues of the type mentioned here were not uncommon in antiquity; a cubit was about a foot and a half. The unrealistic proportions of this statue suggest a comic effect.

**3:2** *Satraps:* Persian provincial governors.

**2:45** Mt 21:44; Lk 20:18.

judges, magistrates and all the officials of the provinces came together for the dedication and stood before the statue which King Nebuchadnezzar had set up. [4]A herald cried out: "Nations and peoples of every language, [5]† when you hear the sound of the horn, pipe, zither, dulcimer, harp, double-flute, and all the other musical instruments, you must fall down and worship the golden statue which King Nebuchadnezzar has set up. [6]Whoever does not fall down and worship shall be instantly cast into a white-hot furnace." [7]Therefore, as soon as they heard the sound of the horn, pipe, zither, dulcimer, harp, double-flute, and all the other musical instruments, the nations and peoples of every language all fell down and worshiped the golden statue which King Nebuchadnezzar had set up.

[8]At that point, some of the Chaldeans came and accused the Jews [9]to King Nebuchadnezzar: "O king, live forever! [10]O king, you issued a decree that everyone who heard the sound of the horn, pipe, zither, dulcimer, harp, and double-flute, and all the other musical instruments should fall down and worship the golden statue; [11]whoever did not was to be cast into a white-hot furnace. [12]There are certain Jews whom you have made administrators of the province of Babylon: Shadrach, Meshach, and Abednego; these men, O king, have paid no attention to you; they will not serve your god or worship the golden statue which you set up."

[13]Nebuchadnezzar flew into a rage and sent for Shadrach, Meshach, and Abednego, who were promptly brought before the king. [14]King Nebuchadnezzar questioned them: "Is it true, Shadrach, Meshach, and Abednego, that you will not serve my god, or worship the golden statue that I set up? [15]Now, if you are ready to fall down and worship the statue I made, whenever you hear the sound of the horn, pipe, zither, dulcimer, harp, double-flute, and all the other musical instruments, then all will be well;† if not, you shall be instantly cast into the white-hot furnace; and who is the God who can deliver you out of my hands?" [16]Shadrach, Meshach, and Abednego answered King Nebuchadnezzar, "There is no need for us to defend ourselves before you in this matter. [17]If our God, whom we serve, can save us† from the white-hot furnace and from your hands, O king, may he save us! [18]But even if he will not, you should know, O king, that we will not serve your god or worship the golden statue which you set up."

[19]Nebuchadnezzar's face became livid with utter rage against Shadrach, Meshach, and Abednego. He ordered the furnace to be heated seven times more than usual [20]and had some of the strongest men in his army bind Shadrach, Meshach, and Abednego and cast them into the white-hot furnace. [21]They were bound and cast into the white-hot furnace with their trousers, shirts, hats and other garments, [22]for the king's order was urgent. So huge a fire was kindled in the furnace that the flames devoured the men who threw Shadrach, Meshach, and Abednego into it. [23]But these three fell, bound, into the midst of the white-hot furnace.

## Prayer of Azariah.†

[24]They walked about in the flames, singing to God and blessing the Lord. [25]Azariah† stood up in the midst of the fire and prayed aloud:

[26]    "Blessed are you, and praiseworthy,
        O Lord, the God of our ancestors,
        and glorious forever is your name.
[27]    For you are just in all you have done;
        all your deeds are faultless, all your
            ways right,
        and all your judgments proper.
[28]    You have executed proper judgments
        in all that you have brought upon us
        and upon Jerusalem, the holy city of
            our ancestors.
        By a proper judgment you have done all
            this
        because of our sins;
[29]    For we have sinned and transgressed
        by departing from you,
        and we have done every kind of evil.

---

3:5 The precise identification of the instruments is disputed. Several of the names are Greek.

3:15 *Then all will be well:* lacking in Aramaic; this phrase is supplied from the context.

3:17 *If our God...can save us:* the youths do not question the efficacy of the divine power, but whether it will be exercised (v. 18).

3:24–90 These verses are additions to the Aramaic text of Daniel, translated from the Greek form of the book. They were probably first composed in Hebrew or Aramaic, but are no longer extant in the original language. The Roman Catholic Church has always regarded them as part of the canonical Scriptures.

3:25 *Azariah:* i.e., Abednego; cf. Dn 1:7.

30 Your commandments we have not
        heeded or observed,
   nor have we done as you ordered us
        for our good.
31 Therefore all you have brought upon us,
   all you have done to us,
   you have done by a proper judgment.
32 You have handed us over to our
        enemies,
   lawless and hateful rebels;
   to an unjust king, the worst in all the
        world.
33 Now we cannot open our mouths;
   shame and reproach have come upon
        us,
   your servants, who revere you.
34 For your name's sake, do not deliver us
        up forever,
   or make void your covenant.
35 Do not take away your mercy from us,
   for the sake of Abraham, your
        beloved,
   Isaac your servant, and Israel your
        holy one,
36 To whom you promised to multiply
        their offspring
   like the stars of heaven,
   or the sand on the shore of the sea.
37 For we are reduced, O Lord, beyond any
        other nation,
   brought low everywhere in the world
        this day
   because of our sins.
38 We have in our day no prince, prophet,
        or leader,
   no burnt offering, sacrifice, oblation,
        or incense,
   no place to offer first fruits, to find
        favor with you.
39 But with contrite heart and humble
        spirit
   let us be received;
   As though it were burnt offerings of
        rams and bulls,
   or tens of thousands of fat lambs,
40 So let our sacrifice be in your presence
        today
   and find favor before you;
   for those who trust in you cannot be
        put to shame.
41 And now we follow you with our whole
        heart,
   we fear you and we seek your face.

   Do not put us to shame,
42 but deal with us in your kindness and
        great mercy.
43 Deliver us in accord with your wonders,
   and bring glory to your name, O Lord:
44 Let all those be put to shame
   who inflict evils on your servants;
   Let them be shamed and powerless,
   and their strength broken;
45 Let them know that you alone are the
        Lord God,
   glorious over the whole world."

46 Now the king's servants who had thrown them in continued to stoke the furnace with naphtha, pitch, tow, and brush. 47 The flames rose forty-nine cubits above the furnace, 48 and spread out, burning the Chaldeans that it caught around the furnace. 49 But the angel of the Lord went down into the furnace with Azariah and his companions, drove the fiery flames out of the furnace, 50 and made the inside of the furnace as though a dew-laden breeze were blowing through it. The fire in no way touched them or caused them pain or harm. 51 Then these three in the furnace with one voice sang, glorifying and blessing God:

52 "Blessed are you, O Lord, the God of
        our ancestors,
   praiseworthy and exalted above all
        forever;
   And blessed is your holy and glorious
        name,
   praiseworthy and exalted above all for
        all ages.
53 Blessed are you in the temple of your
        holy glory,
   praiseworthy and glorious above all
        forever.
54 Blessed are you on the throne of your
        kingdom,
   praiseworthy and exalted above all
        forever.
55 Blessed are you who look into the
        depths
   from your throne upon the
        cherubim,
   praiseworthy and exalted above all
        forever.
56 Blessed are you in the firmament of
        heaven,
   praiseworthy and glorious forever.

57 Bless the Lord, all you works of the
    Lord,
      praise and exalt him above all forever.
58 Angels of the Lord, bless the Lord,
      praise and exalt him above all forever.
59 You heavens, bless the Lord,
      praise and exalt him above all
    forever. *
60 All you waters above the heavens, bless
    the Lord,
      praise and exalt him above all forever.
61 All you powers, bless the Lord;
      praise and exalt him above all forever.
62 Sun and moon, bless the Lord;
      praise and exalt him above all forever.
63 Stars of heaven, bless the Lord;
      praise and exalt him above all forever.
64 Every shower and dew, bless the Lord;
      praise and exalt him above all forever.
65 All you winds, bless the Lord;
      praise and exalt him above all forever.
66 Fire and heat, bless the Lord;
      praise and exalt him above all forever.
67 Cold and chill, bless the Lord;
      praise and exalt him above all forever.
68 Dew and rain, bless the Lord;
      praise and exalt him above all forever.
69 Frost and chill, bless the Lord;
      praise and exalt him above all forever.
70 Hoarfrost and snow, bless the Lord;
      praise and exalt him above all forever.
71 Nights and days, bless the Lord;
      praise and exalt him above all forever.
72 Light and darkness, bless the Lord;
      praise and exalt him above all forever.
73 Lightnings and clouds, bless the Lord;
      praise and exalt him above all forever.
74 Let the earth bless the Lord,
      praise and exalt him above all forever.
75 Mountains and hills, bless the Lord;
      praise and exalt him above all forever.
76 Everything growing on earth, bless the
    Lord;
      praise and exalt him above all forever.
77 You springs, bless the Lord;
      praise and exalt him above all forever.
78 Seas and rivers, bless the Lord;
      praise and exalt him above all forever.
79 You sea monsters and all water creatures,
    bless the Lord;
      praise and exalt him above all forever.
80 All you birds of the air, bless the Lord;

      praise and exalt him above all forever.
81 All you beasts, wild and tame, bless the
    Lord;
      praise and exalt him above all forever.
82 All you mortals, bless the Lord;
      praise and exalt him above all forever.
83 O Israel, bless the Lord;
      praise and exalt him above all forever.
84 Priests of the Lord, bless the Lord;
      praise and exalt him above all forever.
85 Servants of the Lord, bless the Lord;
      praise and exalt him above all forever.
86 Spirits and souls of the just, bless the
    Lord;
      praise and exalt him above all forever.
87 Holy and humble of heart, bless the
    Lord;
      praise and exalt him above all forever.
88 Hananiah, Azariah, Mishael, bless the
    Lord;
      praise and exalt him above all forever.
For he has delivered us from Sheol,
    and saved us from the power of death;
He has freed us from the raging flame
    and delivered us from the fire.
89 Give thanks to the Lord, who is good,
    whose mercy endures forever.
90 Bless the God of gods, all you who fear
    the Lord;
    praise and give thanks,
    for his mercy endures forever."

**Deliverance from the Furnace.** 91 Then King Nebuchadnezzar was startled and rose in haste, asking his counselors, "Did we not cast three men bound into the fire?" "Certainly, O king," they answered. 92 "But," he replied, "I see four men unbound and unhurt, walking in the fire, and the fourth looks like a son of God." 93 Then Nebuchadnezzar came to the opening of the white-hot furnace and called: "Shadrach, Meshach, and Abednego, servants of the Most High God, come out." Thereupon Shadrach, Meshach, and Abednego came out of the fire. 94 When the satraps, prefects, governors, and counselors of the king came together, they saw that the fire had had no power over the bodies of these men; not a hair of their heads had been singed, nor were their garments altered; there was not even a smell of fire about them. 95 Nebuchadnezzar exclaimed, "Blessed be the God of Shadrach,

Meshach, and Abednego, who sent his angel to deliver the servants that trusted in him; they disobeyed the royal command and yielded their bodies rather than serve or worship any god except their own God. 96 Therefore I decree for nations and peoples of every language that whoever blasphemes the God of Shadrach, Meshach, and Abednego shall be cut to pieces and his house made into a refuse heap. For there is no other God who can rescue like this." 97 Then the king promoted Shadrach, Meshach, and Abednego in the province of Babylon.

98† King Nebuchadnezzar to the nations and peoples of every language, wherever they dwell on earth: May your peace abound! 99 It has seemed good to me to publish the signs and wonders which the Most High God has accomplished in my regard.

100    How great are his signs, how mighty his
            wonders;
        his kingship is an everlasting kingship,
        and his dominion endures through all
            generations. *

**4** **Nebuchadnezzar's Madness.** 1 I, Nebuchadnezzar, was at home in my palace, content and prosperous. 2 I had a terrifying dream as I lay in bed, and the images and my visions frightened me. 3 So I issued a decree that all the wise men of Babylon should be brought before me to give the interpretation of the dream. 4 When the magicians, enchanters, Chaldeans, and diviners had come in, I related the dream before them; but none of them could tell me its meaning. 5 Finally there came before me Daniel, whose name is Belteshazzar after the name of my god,† and in whom is a spirit of the holy gods.* I repeated the dream to him: 6 "Belteshazzar, chief of the magicians, I know that a spirit of the holy gods is in you and no mystery is too difficult for you; this is the dream that I saw, tell me its meaning.

7 "These were the visions I saw while in bed: I saw a tree of great height at the center of the earth. 8 It was large and strong, with its top

touching the heavens, and it could be seen to the ends of the earth. 9 Its leaves were beautiful, its fruit abundant, providing food for all. Under it the wild beasts found shade, in its branches the birds of the air nested; all flesh ate of it. 10 In the vision I saw while in bed, a holy watcher† came down from heaven 11 and cried aloud in these words:

'Cut down the tree and lop off its
        branches,
    strip off its leaves and scatter its fruit;
    Let the beasts flee from beneath it, and
        the birds from its branches,
12      but leave its stump in the earth.
    Bound with iron and bronze,
        let him be fed with the grass of the
            field
    and bathed with the dew of heaven;
        let his lot be with the beasts in the
            grass of the earth.
13  Let his mind be changed from a human
        one;
    let the mind of a beast be given him,
        till seven years pass over him.
14  By decree of the watchers is this
        proclamation,
    by order of the holy ones, this
        sentence;
    That all who live may know
        that the Most High is sovereign over
            human kingship,
    Giving it to whom he wills,
        and setting it over the lowliest of
            mortals.' *

15 "This is the dream that I, King Nebuchadnezzar, had. Now, Belteshazzar, tell me its meaning. None of the wise men in my kingdom can tell me the meaning, but you can, because the spirit of the holy gods is in you."

16 Then Daniel, whose name was Belteshazzar, was appalled for a time, dismayed by his thoughts. "Belteshazzar," the king said to him, "do not let the dream or its meaning dismay you." "My lord," Belteshazzar replied, "may this dream be for your enemies, and its

† 3:98–4:34 This section has the form of a letter written by Nebuchadnezzar to his subjects.
4:5 *After the name of my god:* Belteshazzar, the Babylonian name given to Daniel at the king's orders (1:7), is *Balāṭ-šu-uṣur,* "protect his life." This passage implies a name connected with Bel, a Babylonian god. *A spirit of the holy gods:* or a holy divine spirit; or spirit of a holy God. See also vv. 6, 15; 5:11–12, 14; 6:4.

4:10 *A holy watcher:* lit., "a watcher and a holy one." Two terms for angels. The term watcher is found in the Bible only in this chapter of Daniel, but it is common in extra-canonical Jewish literature. In 1 Enoch, the fallen angels are called watchers.

3:100 Dn 4:31; 7:14.        4:14 1 Sm 2:8.
4:5 Gn 41:38.

meaning for your foes. [17] The tree that you saw, large and strong, its top touching the heavens, that could be seen by the whole earth, [18] its leaves beautiful, its fruit abundant, providing food for all, under which the wild beasts lived, and in whose branches the birds of the air dwelt— [19] you are that tree, O king, large and strong! Your majesty has become so great as to touch the heavens, and your rule reaches to the ends of the earth. [20] As for the king's vision of a holy watcher, who came down from heaven and proclaimed: 'Cut down the tree and destroy it, but leave its stump in the earth. Bound with iron and bronze, let him be fed with the grass of the field, and bathed with the dew of heaven; let his lot be with wild beasts till seven years pass over him'— [21] here is its meaning, O king, here is the sentence that the Most High has passed upon my lord king: [22]* You shall be cast out from human society and dwell with wild beasts; you shall be given grass to eat like an ox; you shall be bathed with the dew of heaven; seven years shall pass over you, until you know that the Most High is sovereign over human kingship and gives it to whom he will. [23] The command that the stump of the tree is to be left means that your kingdom shall be preserved for you, once you have learned that heaven is sovereign. [24] Therefore, O king, may my advice be acceptable to you; atone for your sins by good deeds,† and for your misdeeds by kindness to the poor; then your contentment will be long lasting."

[25] All this happened to King Nebuchadnezzar. [26] Twelve months later, as he was walking on the roof of the royal palace in Babylon, [27] the king said, "Babylon the great! Was it not I, with my great strength, who built it as a royal residence for my splendor and majesty?" [28] While these words were still on the king's lips, a voice spoke from heaven, "It has been decreed for you, King Nebuchadnezzar, that your kingship is taken from you! [29] You shall be cast out from human society, and shall dwell with wild beasts; you shall be given grass to eat like an ox, and seven years shall pass

over you, until you learn that the Most High is sovereign over human kingship and gives it to whom he will." [30]† At once this was fulfilled. Nebuchadnezzar was cast out from human society, he ate grass like an ox, and his body was bathed with the dew of heaven, until his hair grew like the feathers of an eagle, and his nails like the claws of a bird.

[31] When this period was over, I, Nebuchadnezzar, raised my eyes to heaven; my reason was restored to me, and I blessed the Most High, I praised and glorified the One who lives forever,

> Whose dominion is an everlasting dominion,
> and whose kingdom endures through all generations.*
> [32] All who live on the earth are counted as nothing;
> he does as he wills with the powers of heaven
> and with those who live on the earth.
> There is no one who can stay his hand
> or say to him, "What have you done?"

[33] At the same time my reason returned to me, and for the glory of my kingdom, my majesty and my splendor returned to me. My counselors and nobles sought me out; I was restored to my kingdom and became much greater than before. [34] Now, I, Nebuchadnezzar, praise and exalt and glorify the King of heaven, all of whose works are right and ways just; and who is able to humble those who walk in pride.

## 5 The Writing on the Wall.
[1] King Belshazzar gave a great banquet for a thousand of his nobles, with whom he drank. [2] Under the influence of the wine, he ordered the gold and silver vessels which Nebuchadnezzar, his father,† had taken from the temple in Jerusalem, to be brought in so that the king, his nobles, his consorts, and his concubines might drink from them. [3] When the gold vessels taken from

---

† **4:24** *Good deeds*: the Aramaic word ṣidqâ has the root meaning of "righteousness," but in a late text such as this could mean "almsgiving."

**4:30–32** There is no historical record that these events happened to Nebuchadnezzar. Scholars have long suspected that the story originally involved Nabonidus, the father of Belshazzar, who was absent from Babylon and lived at Teima in the Arabian desert for a number of years. This suggestion is now strengthened by the Prayer of Nabonidus, found at Qumran, which is closely

related to chap. 4. The biblical author's chief interest was not in the historicity of this popular tale, but in the object lesson it contained for the proud "divine" kings of the Seleucid dynasty.

**5:2** *Nebuchadnezzar, his father*: between Nebuchadnezzar and Belshazzar several kings ruled in Babylon. Belshazzar was the son of Nabonidus, and he acted as regent in Babylon during his father's absence.

---

the temple, the house of God in Jerusalem, had been brought in, and while the king, his nobles, his consorts, and his concubines were drinking [4] wine from them, they praised their gods of gold and silver, bronze and iron, wood and stone.

[5] Suddenly, opposite the lampstand, the fingers of a human hand appeared, writing on the plaster of the wall in the king's palace. When the king saw the hand that wrote, [6] his face became pale; his thoughts terrified him, his hip joints shook, and his knees knocked. [7] The king shouted for the enchanters, Chaldeans, and diviners to be brought in. "Whoever reads this writing and tells me what it means," he said to the wise men of Babylon, "shall be clothed in purple, wear a chain of gold around his neck, and be third in governing the kingdom." [8] But though all the king's wise men came in, none of them could either read the writing or tell the king what it meant. [9] Then King Belshazzar was greatly terrified; his face became pale, and his nobles were thrown into confusion.

[10] When the queen heard of the discussion between the king and his nobles, she entered the banquet hall and said, "O king, live forever! Do not let your thoughts terrify you, or your face become so pale! [11] There is a man in your kingdom in whom is a spirit of the holy gods; during the lifetime of your father he showed brilliant insight and god-like wisdom. King Nebuchadnezzar, your father, made him chief of the magicians, enchanters, Chaldeans, and diviners. [12] Because this Daniel, whom the king named Belteshazzar, has shown an extraordinary spirit, knowledge, and insight in interpreting dreams, explaining riddles and solving problems, let him now be summoned to tell you what this means."

[13] Then Daniel was brought into the presence of the king. The king asked him, "Are you the Daniel, one of the Jewish exiles, whom my father, the king, brought from Judah? [14] I have heard that the spirit of the gods is in you, that you have shown brilliant insight and extraordinary wisdom. [15] The wise men and enchanters were brought in to me to read this writing and tell me its meaning, but they could not

say what the words meant. [16] But I have heard that you can give interpretations and solve problems; now, if you are able to read the writing and tell me what it means, you shall be clothed in purple, wear a chain of gold around your neck, and be third in governing the kingdom."

[17] Daniel answered the king: "You may keep your gifts, or give your presents to someone else; but the writing I will read for the king, and tell what it means. [18] The Most High God gave your father Nebuchadnezzar kingship, greatness, splendor, and majesty. [19] Because he made him so great, the nations and peoples of every language dreaded and feared him. Whomever he willed, he would kill or let live; whomever he willed, he would exalt or humble. [20] But when his heart became proud and his spirit hardened by insolence, he was put down from his royal throne and deprived of his glory; [21]* he was cast out from human society and his heart was made like that of a beast; · he lived with wild asses, and ate grass like an ox; his body was bathed with the dew of heaven, until he learned that the Most High God is sovereign over human kingship and sets over it whom he will. [22] You, his son, Belshazzar, have not humbled your heart, though you knew all this; [23] you have rebelled against the Lord of heaven. You had the vessels of his temple brought before you, so that you and your nobles, your consorts and your concubines, might drink wine from them; and you praised the gods of silver and gold, bronze and iron, wood and stone, that neither see nor hear nor have intelligence. But the God in whose hand is your very breath and the whole course of your life, you did not glorify. [24] By him was the hand sent, and the writing set down.

[25] "This is the writing that was inscribed: MENE, TEKEL, and PERES.† These words mean: [26]† MENE, God has numbered your kingdom and put an end to it; [27] TEKEL, you have been weighed on the scales and found wanting; [28] PERES, your kingdom has been divided and given to the Medes and Persians."

[29] Then by order of Belshazzar they clothed Daniel in purple, with a chain of gold around his neck, and proclaimed him third in

---

**5:25** MENE, TEKEL, and PERES: these seem to be the Aramaic names of weights and monetary values: the mina, the shekel (the sixtieth part of a mina), and the parsu (a half-mina).
**5:26–28** Daniel interprets these three terms by a play on the words: MENE, connected with the verb meaning to number; TEKEL,

with the verb meaning to weigh; PERES, with the verb meaning to divide. There is also a play on the last term with the word for Persians.

**5:21** Dn 4:22.

governing the kingdom. [30] That very night Belshazzar, the Chaldean king, was slain:

# 6

[1] And Darius the Mede† succeeded to the kingdom at the age of sixty-two.

**The Lions' Den.** [2] Darius decided to appoint over his entire kingdom one hundred and twenty satraps. [3] These were accountable to three ministers, one of whom was Daniel; the satraps reported to them, so that the king should suffer no loss. [4] Daniel outshone all the ministers and satraps because an extraordinary spirit was in him, and the king considered setting him over the entire kingdom. [5] Then the ministers and satraps tried to find grounds for accusation against Daniel regarding the kingdom. But they could not accuse him of any corruption. Because he was trustworthy, no fault or corruption was to be found in him. [6] Then these men said to themselves, "We shall find no grounds for accusation against this Daniel except in connection with the law of his God." [7] So these ministers and satraps stormed in to the king and said to him, "King Darius, live forever! [8]†* All the ministers of the kingdom, the prefects, satraps, counselors, and governors agree that the following prohibition ought to be put in force by royal decree: for thirty days, whoever makes a petition to anyone, divine or human, except to you, O king, shall be thrown into a den of lions. [9] Now, O king, let the prohibition be issued over your signature, immutable and irrevocable† according to the law of the Medes and Persians." [10] So King Darius signed the prohibition into law.

[11] Even after Daniel heard that this law had been signed, he continued his custom of going home to kneel in prayer and give thanks to his God in the upper chamber three times a day, with the windows open toward Jerusalem. [12] So these men stormed in and found Daniel praying and pleading before his God. [13] Then they went to remind the king about the prohibition: "Did you not sign a decree, O king, that for thirty days, whoever makes a petition to anyone, divine or human, except to you, O king, shall be cast into a den of lions?" The king answered them, "The decree is absolute, irrevocable under the law of the Medes and Persians." [14] To this they replied, "Daniel, one of the Jewish exiles, has paid no attention to you, O king, or to the prohibition you signed; three times a day he offers his prayer." [15] The king was deeply grieved at this news and he made up his mind to save Daniel; he worked till sunset to rescue him. [16] But these men pressed the king. "Keep in mind, O king," they said, "that under the law of the Medes and Persians every royal prohibition or decree is irrevocable." [17] So the king ordered Daniel to be brought and cast into the lions' den.† To Daniel he said, "Your God, whom you serve so constantly, must save you." [18] To forestall any tampering, the king sealed with his own ring and the rings of the lords the stone that had been brought to block the opening of the den.

[19] Then the king returned to his palace for the night; he refused to eat and he dismissed the entertainers. Since sleep was impossible for him, [20] the king rose very early the next morning and hastened to the lions' den. [21] As he drew near, he cried out to Daniel sorrowfully, "Daniel, servant of the living God, has your God whom you serve so constantly been able to save you from the lions?" [22] Daniel answered the king: "O king, live forever! [23] My God sent his angel and closed the lions' mouths so that they have not hurt me.* For I have been found innocent before him; neither have I done you any harm, O king!" [24] This gave the king great joy. At his order Daniel was brought up from the den; he was found to be unharmed because he trusted in his God. [25] The king then ordered the men who had accused Daniel, along with their children and their wives, to be cast into the lions' den.

---

† **6:1** *Darius the Mede*: unknown outside of the Book of Daniel. The Median kingdom did not exist at this time because it had already been conquered by Cyrus the Persian. Apparently the author of Daniel is following an apocalyptic view of history, linked to prophecy (cf. Is 13:17–19; Jer 51:11, 28–30), according to which the Medes formed the second of four world kingdoms preceding the messianic times; see note on Dn 2:36–45. The character of Darius the Mede has probably been modeled on that of the Persian king Darius the Great (522–486 B.C.), the second successor of Cyrus. The Persian Darius did appoint satraps over his empire.

**6:8–11** The Jews of the second century B.C. could relate

the king's attempt to force upon them, under pain of death, the worship of a foreign deity to the decrees of Antiochus IV; cf. 1 Mc 1:41–50.

**6:9** *Immutable and irrevocable*: Est 1:19 and 8:8 also refer to the immutability of Medo-Persian laws. The same idea is found in the historian Diodorus Siculus with reference to the time of Darius III (335–331 B.C.), the last of the Persian kings. Cf. Dn 6:13, 16.

**6:17** *The lions' den*: a pit too deep to be easily scaled; its opening was blocked with a stone (v. 18).

---

**6:8** Est 1:19.          **6:23** 1 Mc 2:60.

Before they reached the bottom of the den, the lions overpowered them and crushed all their bones.

²⁶Then King Darius wrote to the nations and peoples of every language, wherever they dwell on the earth: "May your peace abound! ²⁷I decree that throughout my royal domain the God of Daniel is to be reverenced and feared:

"For he is the living God, enduring
  forever,
whose kingdom shall not be
  destroyed,
whose dominion shall be without
  end,
28  A savior and deliverer,
  working signs and wonders in heaven
    and on earth,
  who saved Daniel from the lions'
    power."

²⁹So Daniel fared well during the reign of Darius and the reign of Cyrus the Persian.*

## II. DANIEL'S VISIONS

**7 The Beasts and the Judgment.†** ¹In the first year of King Belshazzar of Babylon, as Daniel lay in bed he had a dream, visions in his head. Then he wrote down the dream; the account began: ²In the vision I saw during the night, suddenly the four winds of heaven stirred up the great sea,† ³from which emerged four immense beasts,* each different from the others. ⁴The first was like a lion, but with eagle's wings.† While I watched, the wings were plucked; it was raised from the ground to stand on two feet like a human being, and given a human mind. ⁵The second beast was like a bear;† it was raised up on one side, and among the teeth in its mouth were three tusks. It was given the order, "Arise, devour much flesh." ⁶After this I looked and saw another beast, like a leopard;† on its back were four wings like those of a bird, and it had four heads. To this beast dominion was given. ⁷† After this, in the visions of the night I saw a fourth beast, terrifying, horrible, and of extraordinary strength; it had great iron teeth with which it devoured and crushed, and it trampled with its feet what was left. It differed from the beasts that preceded it. It had ten horns. ⁸I was considering the ten horns it had, when suddenly another, a little horn, sprang out of their midst, and three of the previous horns were torn away to make room for it. This horn had eyes like human eyes, and a mouth that spoke arrogantly. ⁹† As I watched,

Thrones were set up
  and the Ancient of Days took his
    throne.
His clothing was white as snow,
  the hair on his head like pure wool;
His throne was flames of fire,
  with wheels of burning fire.
10  A river of fire surged forth,
    flowing from where he sat;
  Thousands upon thousands were
    ministering to him,
  and myriads upon myriads stood
    before him.*

The court was convened, and the books were opened. ¹¹I watched, then, from the first

**7:1–27** This vision continues the motif of the four kingdoms from chap. 2; see note on 2:36–45. To the four succeeding world kingdoms, Babylonian, Median, Persian, and Greek, is opposed the heavenly kingdom of God and the kingdom of God's people on earth. The beast imagery of this chapter has been used extensively in the Book of Revelation, where it is applied to the Roman empire, the persecutor of the Church.
**7:2** *The great sea*: the primordial ocean beneath the earth, according to ancient Near Eastern cosmology (Gn 7:11; 49:25). It was thought to contain various monsters (Is 27:1; Jb 7:12), and in particular mythological monsters symbolizing the chaos which God had vanquished in primordial times (Jb 9:13; 26:12; Is 51:9–10; etc.).
**7:4** In ancient times the Babylonian empire was commonly represented as a winged lion, in the rampant position (raised up on one side). The two wings that were plucked may represent Nebuchadnezzar and Belshazzar. *On two feet like a human being…a human mind*: contrasts with what is said in 4:13, 30.
**7:5** *A bear*: represents the Median empire, its three tusks symbolizing its destructive nature; hence, the command: "Arise,

**7:6** *A leopard*: used to symbolize the swiftness with which Cyrus the Persian established his kingdom. *Four heads*: corresponding to the four Persian kings of 11:2.
**7:7–8** Alexander's empire was different from all the others in that it was Western rather than Eastern in inspiration, and far exceeded the others in power. The ten horns represent the kings of the Seleucid dynasty, the only part of the Hellenistic empire that concerned the author. The little horn is Antiochus IV Epiphanes (175–164 B.C.), who usurped the throne and persecuted the Jews.
**7:9–10** A vision of the heavenly throne of God (the Ancient of Days), who sits in judgment over the nations. Some of the details of the vision, depicting the divine majesty and omnipotence, are to be found in Ezekiel 1. Others are paralleled in 1 Enoch, a contemporary Jewish apocalypse.

devour much flesh."

of the arrogant words which the horn spoke, until the beast was slain and its body destroyed and thrown into the burning fire. [12] As for the other beasts, their dominion was taken away, but they were granted a prolongation of life for a time and a season. [13] As the visions during the night continued, I saw coming with the clouds of heaven*

> One like a son of man.†
> When he reached the Ancient of Days
>     and was presented before him,
> [14]     He received dominion, splendor, and
>     kingship;
>     all nations, peoples and tongues will
>     serve him.
> His dominion is an everlasting dominion
>     that shall not pass away,
>     his kingship, one that shall not be
>     destroyed.*

[15] Because of this, my spirit was anguished and I, Daniel, was terrified by my visions. [16] I approached one of those present and asked him the truth of all this; in answer, he made known to me its meaning: [17] "These four great beasts stand for four kings which shall arise on the earth. [18] But the holy ones† of the Most High shall receive the kingship, to possess it forever and ever."

[19] Then I wished to make certain about the fourth beast, so very terrible and different from the others, devouring and crushing with its iron teeth and bronze claws, and trampling with its feet what was left; [20] and about the ten horns on its head, and the other one that sprang up, before which three horns fell; and about the horn with the eyes and the mouth that spoke arrogantly, which appeared greater than its fellows. [21] For, as I watched, that horn made war against the holy ones and was victorious [22] until the Ancient of Days came, and judgment was pronounced in favor of the holy ones of the Most High, and the time arrived for the holy ones to possess the kingship. [23] He answered me thus:

> "The fourth beast shall be a fourth
>     kingdom on earth,
>     different from all the others;
> The whole earth it shall devour,
>     trample down and crush.
> [24]  The ten horns shall be ten kings
>     rising out of that kingdom;
>     another shall rise up after them,
> Different from those before him,
>     who shall lay low three kings.
> [25]  He shall speak against the Most High
>     and wear down the holy ones of the
>     Most High,
>     intending to change the feast days and
>     the law.†
> They shall be handed over to him
>     for a time, two times, and half a time.
> [26]  But when the court is convened,
>     and his dominion is taken away
>     to be abolished and completely
>     destroyed,
> [27]  Then the kingship and dominion and
>     majesty
>     of all the kingdoms under the heavens
>     shall be given to the people of the
>     holy ones of the Most High,
> Whose kingship shall be an everlasting
>     kingship,
>     whom all dominions shall serve and
>     obey."

[28] This is the end of the report. I, Daniel, was greatly terrified by my thoughts, and my face became pale, but I kept the matter to myself.†

## 8  The Ram and the He-goat.† 

[1] After this first vision, I, Daniel, had another, in the third

---

† **7:13–14** *One like a son of man*: In contrast to the worldly kingdoms opposed to God, which are represented as grotesque beasts, the coming Kingdom of God is represented by a human figure. Scholars disagree as to whether this figure should be taken as a collective symbol for the people of God (cf. 7:27) or identified as a particular individual, e.g., the archangel Michael (cf. 12:1) or the messiah. The phrase "Son of Man" becomes a title for Jesus in the gospels, especially in passages dealing with the Second Coming (Mk 13 and parallels).

**7:18** "Holy ones" in Hebrew and Aramaic literature are nearly always members of the heavenly court or angels (cf. 4:10, 14, 20; 8:13), though here the term is commonly taken to refer to Israel.

**7:25** The reference is to the persecution of Antiochus IV and specifically to the disruption of the Temple cult (1 Mc 1:41–64).

*A time, two times, and half a time*: an indefinite, evil period of time. Probably here, three and a half years, which becomes the standard period of tribulation in apocalyptic literature (Rev 11:2; 13:5 [in months]; 11:3 [in days]; and cf. 12:14). As seven is the Jewish "perfect" number, half of it signifies great imperfection. Actually, the Temple was desecrated for three years (1 Mc 4:52–54). The duration of the persecution was a little longer, since it was already under way before the Temple was desecrated.

**7:28** This verse ends the Aramaic part of the Book of Daniel.

**8:1–27** This vision continues images of the preceding one, and develops it in more detail. As explained in vv. 20–22 the two-horned ram represents the combined kingdom of the Medes and Persians, destroyed by Alexander's Hellenistic empire origi-

**7:13** Mk 13:26; 14:62.          **7:14** Dn 3:33; 4:31.

year of the reign of King Belshazzar. ²In my vision I saw myself in the fortress of Susa† in the province of Elam; I was beside the river Ulai. ³I looked up and saw standing by the river a ram with two great horns, the one larger and newer than the other. ⁴I saw the ram butting toward the west, north, and south. No beast could withstand it or be rescued from its power; it did what it pleased and grew powerful.

⁵As I was reflecting, a he-goat with a prominent horn on its forehead suddenly came from the west across the whole earth without touching the ground. ⁶It came to the two-horned ram I had seen standing by the river, and rushed toward it with savage force. ⁷I saw it reach the ram; enraged, the he-goat attacked and shattered both its horns. The ram did not have the strength to withstand it; the he-goat threw the ram to the ground and trampled upon it. No one could rescue the ram from its power.

⁸The he-goat grew very powerful, but at the height of its strength the great horn was shattered, and in its place came up four others, facing the four winds of heaven. ⁹Out of one of them came a little horn† which grew and grew toward the south, the east, and the glorious land. ¹⁰It grew even to the host of heaven,† so that it cast down to earth some of the host and some of the stars and trampled on them. ¹¹It grew even to the Prince of the host, from whom the daily sacrifice was removed, and whose sanctuary was cast down. ¹²The host was given over together with the daily sacrifice in the course of transgression. It cast truth to the ground, and was succeeding in its undertaking.

¹³I heard a holy one speaking, and another said to whichever one it was that spoke, "How long shall the events of this vision last concerning the daily sacrifice, the desolating sin,† the giving over of the sanctuary and the host

for trampling?" ¹⁴He answered him, "For two thousand three hundred evenings and mornings; then the sanctuary shall be set right."

¹⁵While I, Daniel, sought the meaning of the vision I had seen, one who looked like a man stood before me, ¹⁶and on the Ulai I heard a human voice that cried out, "Gabriel,† explain the vision to this man." ¹⁷When he came near where I was standing, I fell prostrate in terror. But he said to me, "Understand, O son of man, that the vision refers to the end time."† ¹⁸As he spoke to me, I fell forward unconscious; he touched me and made me stand up. ¹⁹"I will show you," he said, "what is to happen in the last days of wrath; for it is for the appointed time of the end.

²⁰"The two-horned ram you saw represents the kings of the Medes and Persians.† ²¹The he-goat is the king of the Greeks, and the great horn on its forehead is the first king. ²²The four that rose in its place when it was shattered are four kingdoms that will issue from his nation, but without his strength.

23    "At the end of their reign,
          when sinners have reached their
              measure,
      There shall arise a king,
          impudent, and skilled in intrigue.
24    He shall be strong and powerful,
          bring about fearful ruin,
          and succeed in his undertaking.
      He shall destroy powerful peoples;
25        his cunning shall be against the holy
              ones,
          his treacherous conduct shall succeed.
      He shall be proud of heart
          and destroy many by stealth.
      But when he rises against the Prince of
              princes,
          he shall be broken without a hand
              being raised.

---

† nating in the west. Once again the author is interested only in the Seleucid dynasty, which emerged from the dissolution of Alexander's empire after his death in 323 B.C.

**8:2** *The fortress of Susa*: the royal palace of the Persian kings in the ancient territory of Elam, east of Babylonia. *The river Ulai*: a canal along the northern side of Susa. Some scholars argue that the Hebrew word understood as "river" here should instead be translated "gate."

**8:9** *A little horn*: as in chap. 7, Antiochus IV. *The glorious land*: Israel.

**8:10–12** *The host of heaven*: the angelic host, symbolized by the stars. *The Prince of the host*: the Most High God, whose worship Antiochus suppressed (1 Mc 1:45).

**8:13** *The desolating sin*: the Hebrew contains a wordplay (*shomem*) on the name Baal Shamem ("lord of the heavens,"

identified by some as the Greek Zeus Olympios). The reference is to some object with which Antiochus profaned the Temple of Jerusalem (2 Mc 6:2), most probably a pagan altar.

**8:16** The angel Gabriel is mentioned here for the first time in the Bible. There is wordplay in the preceding verse on *geber*, "manlike figure."

**8:17** *The end time*: the time when God sits in judgment on the wicked (v. 19).

**8:20** *The Medes and Persians*: the Medes had been allies of the Babylonians in destroying the Assyrian empire (late seventh century B.C.), and Cyrus the Persian defeated the Medes en route to conquering the Babylonians; The Book of Daniel, however, treats the Medes and Persians as a dual kingdom; cf. also 5:28; 6:9; and note on 6:1.

26 As for the vision of the evenings and the
         mornings,
      what was spoken is true.
      But you, keep this vision secret:
         it is for the distant future."

27 I, Daniel, was weak and ill for some days;
then I arose and took care of the king's affairs.
But the vision left me desolate, without understanding.

**9** **The Seventy Weeks of Years.** ¹It was the
first year that Darius,† son of Ahasuerus,
of the race of the Medes, reigned over the kingdom of the Chaldeans; ²* in the first year of
his reign, I, Daniel, perceived in the books the
number of years the LORD had decreed to the
prophet Jeremiah: Jerusalem was to lie in ruins
for seventy years.†

³I turned to the Lord God, to seek help, in
prayer and petition, with fasting, sackcloth,
and ashes. ⁴* I prayed to the LORD, my God,
and confessed, "Ah, Lord, great and awesome
God, you who keep your covenant and show
mercy toward those who love you and keep
your commandments and your precepts! ⁵We
have sinned, been wicked and done evil; we
have rebelled and turned from your commandments and your laws. ⁶We have not
obeyed your servants the prophets, who spoke
in your name to our kings, our princes, our ancestors, and all the people of the land. ⁷Justice,
O Lord, is on your side; we are shamefaced
even to this day: the men of Judah, the residents of Jerusalem, and all Israel, near and far,
in all the lands to which you have scattered
them because of their treachery toward you.
⁸O LORD, we are ashamed, like our kings, our
princes, and our ancestors, for having sinned
against you. ⁹But to the Lord, our God, belong compassion and forgiveness, though we
rebelled against him ¹⁰and did not hear the
voice of the LORD, our God, by walking in his
laws given through his servants the prophets.
¹¹* The curse and the oath written in the law
of Moses, the servant of God, were poured out

over us for our sins, because all Israel transgressed your law and turned aside, refusing to
hear your voice. ¹²He fulfilled the words he
spoke against us and against those who ruled
us, by bringing upon us an evil—no evil so
great has happened under heaven as happened
in Jerusalem. ¹³As it is written† in the law of
Moses, this evil has come upon us. We did not
appease the LORD, our God, by turning back
from our wickedness and acting according to
your truth, ¹⁴so the LORD kept watch over the
evil and brought it upon us. The LORD, our
God, is just in all that he has done: we did not
listen to his voice.

¹⁵"Now, Lord, our God, who led your people out of the land of Egypt with a strong
hand, and made a name for yourself even to
this day, we have sinned, we are guilty. ¹⁶Lord,
in keeping with all your just deeds, let your
anger and your wrath be turned away from
your city Jerusalem, your holy mountain. On
account of our sins and the crimes of our
ancestors, Jerusalem and your people have
become the reproach of all our neighbors.
¹⁷Now, our God, hear the prayer and petition
of your servant; and for your own sake, Lord,
let your face shine upon your desolate sanctuary. ¹⁸Give ear, my God, and listen; open your
eyes and look upon our desolate city upon
which your name is invoked. When we present
our petition before you, we rely not on our
just deeds, but on your great mercy. ¹⁹Lord,
hear! Lord, pardon! Lord, be attentive and act
without delay, for your own sake, my God,
because your name is invoked upon your city
and your people!"

²⁰I was still praying to the LORD, my God,
confessing my sin and the sin of my people
Israel, presenting my petition concerning the
holy mountain of my God— ²¹I was still praying, when the man, Gabriel, whom I had seen
in vision before, came to me in flight at the
time of the evening offering.† ²²He instructed
me in these words: "Daniel, I have now come
to give you understanding. ²³When you began
your petition, an answer was given which I

---

† **9:1** *Darius:* see note on 6:1.
**9:2** *Seventy years:* Jeremiah was understood to prophesy a
Babylonian captivity of seventy years, a round number signifying
the complete passing away of the existing generation (Jer 25:11;
29:10). On this view Jeremiah's prophecy was seen to be fulfilled
in the capture of Babylon by Cyrus and the subsequent return of
the Jews to Palestine. However, the author of Daniel, living during the persecution of Antiochus, extends Jeremiah's number to
seventy weeks of years (Dn 9:24), i.e., seven times seventy years,

to encompass the period of Seleucid persecution.
**9:13** *As it is written:* the first time that this formula of Scriptural citation is used in the Bible. The reference (v. 11) is to the
sanctions of Lv 26:14–16; Dt 28:15–17.
**9:21** *At the time of the evening offering:* between three and
four in the afternoon.

---

**9:2** Jer 25:11; 29:10.                  9:6–37.
**9:4** Ezr 9:6–14; Neh                    **9:11** Dt 27:15.

have come to announce, because you are beloved. Therefore, mark the answer and understand the vision.

24 "Seventy weeks† are decreed
   for your people and for your holy city:
Then transgression will stop and sin will
   end,
   guilt will be expiated,
Everlasting justice will be introduced,
   vision and prophecy ratified,
   and a holy of holies will be anointed.
25 Know and understand:
From the utterance of the word
   that Jerusalem was to be rebuilt†
Until there is an anointed ruler,
   there shall be seven weeks.
In the course of sixty-two weeks
   it shall be rebuilt,
With squares and trenches,
   in time of affliction.
26 After the sixty-two weeks
   an anointed one† shall be cut down
   with no one to help him.
And the people of a leader who will
   come
   shall destroy the city and the
   sanctuary.
His end shall come in a flood;
   until the end of the war, which is
   decreed,
   there will be desolation.
27 For one week† he shall make
   a firm covenant with the many;
Half the week
   he shall abolish sacrifice and offering;
In their place shall be the desolating
   abomination

until the ruin that is decreed
is poured out upon the desolator."*

## 10 An Angelic Vision.† 

1 In the third year of Cyrus, king of Persia, a revelation was given to Daniel, who had been named Belteshazzar. The revelation was certain: a great war;† he understood this from the vision. 2 In those days, I, Daniel, mourned three full weeks. 3 I ate no savory food, took no meat or wine, and did not anoint myself at all until the end of the three weeks.

4 On the twenty-fourth day of the first month† I was on the bank of the great river, the Tigris. 5 As I looked up, I saw a man† dressed in linen with a belt of fine gold around his waist.* 6 His body was like chrysolite, his face shone like lightning, his eyes were like fiery torches, his arms and feet looked like burnished bronze, and the sound of his voice was like the roar of a multitude. 7 I alone, Daniel, saw the vision; but great fear seized those who were with me; they fled and hid themselves, although they did not see the vision. 8 So I was left alone to see this great vision. No strength remained in me; I turned the color of death and was powerless. 9 When I heard the sound of his voice, I fell face forward unconscious.

10 But then a hand touched me, raising me to my hands and knees. 11 "Daniel, beloved," he said to me, "understand the words which I am speaking to you; stand up, for my mission now is to you." When he said this to me, I stood up trembling. 12 "Do not fear, Daniel," he continued; "from the first day you made up your mind to acquire understanding and humble yourself before God, your prayer was heard.

---

9:24 Seventy weeks: i.e., of years. Just as Jeremiah's seventy years was an approximation (see note on v. 2), the four hundred and ninety years here is not to be taken literally. Similarly, the distribution of the "weeks" in the following verses indicates only relative proportions of the total figure. A holy of holies: or "most holy"; could be understood as a place (e.g., the Jerusalem Temple) or a person (cf. 1 Chr 23:13).
9:25 From the utterance...to be rebuilt: from the time of Jeremiah's prophecy. Anointed ruler: either Cyrus, who was called the anointed of the Lord to end the exile (Is 45:1), or the high priest Jeshua who presided over the rebuilding of the altar of sacrifice after the exile (Ezr 3:2). Seven weeks: forty-nine years, an approximation of the time of the exile. In the course of sixty-two weeks...rebuilt: a period of four hundred thirty-four years, roughly approximating the interval between the rebuilding of Jerusalem after the exile and the beginning of the Seleucid persecution.
9:26 An anointed one: the high priest Onias III, murdered in 171 B.C., from which the author dates the beginning of the persecution. Onias was in exile when he was killed. A leader: Antiochus IV.

9:27 One week: the final phase of the period in view, the time of Antiochus' persecution. He: Antiochus himself. The many: the faithless Jews who allied themselves with the Seleucids; cf. 1 Mc 1:11–13. Half the week: three and a half years; the Temple was desecrated by Antiochus from 167 to 164 B.C. The desolating abomination: see note on 8:13; probably a pagan altar. Jesus refers to this passage in his prediction of the destruction of Jerusalem in Mt 24:15.
10:1–12:13 This final vision is concerned with history from the time of Cyrus to the death of Antiochus Epiphanes.
10:1 A great war: or "the service was great," or "a mighty host." The Hebrew is ambiguous.
10:4 The first month: the month Nisan (mid-March to mid-April).
10:5–6 The heavenly person of the vision is probably the angel Gabriel, as in 9:21. Chrysolite: or topaz, a yellowish precious stone. Cf. the visions in Ez 1 and 8.

9:27 Mt 24:15; 1 Mc 1:54.  10:5 Ez 10:2.

Because of it I started out, 13 but the prince of the kingdom of Persia† stood in my way for twenty-one days, until finally Michael, one of the chief princes, came to help me. I left him there with the prince of the kingdom of Persia, 14 and came to make you understand what shall happen to your people in the last days; for there is yet a vision concerning those days."

15 While he was speaking thus to me, I fell forward and kept silent. 16 Then something like a hand touched my lips; I opened my mouth and said to the one standing before me, "My lord, I was seized with pangs at the vision and I was powerless. 17 How can my lord's servant speak with you, my lord? For now no strength or even breath is left in me." 18 The one who looked like a man touched me again and strengthened me, saying, 19 "Do not fear, beloved. Peace! Take courage and be strong." When he spoke to me, I grew strong and said, "Speak, my lord, for you have strengthened me." 20 "Do you know," he asked, "why I have come to you? Soon I must fight the prince of Persia again. When I leave, the prince of Greece will come; 21 but I shall tell you what is written in the book of truth.† No one supports me against these except Michael,* your prince, 11:1 and in the first year of Darius the Mede I stood to strengthen him and be his refuge.

# 11 The Hellenistic Age. 2 "Now I shall tell you the truth.

"Three kings of Persia† are yet to appear; and a fourth shall acquire the greatest riches of all. Strengthened by his riches, he shall stir up all kingdoms, even that of Greece. 3 But a powerful king† shall appear and rule with great might, doing as he wills. 4 No sooner shall he appear than his kingdom shall be broken and divided in four directions under heaven; but not among his descendants or in keeping with

his mighty rule, for his kingdom shall be torn to pieces and belong to others.

5 † "The king of the south shall grow strong, but one of his princes shall grow stronger still and govern a domain greater than his. 6 † After some years they shall become allies: the daughter of the king of the south shall come to the king of the north to carry out the alliance. But she shall not retain power: and his offspring shall not survive, and she shall be given up, together with those who brought her, her son, and her supporter in due time. 7 A descendant of her line shall succeed to his place, and shall come against the army, enter the stronghold of the king of the north, attack and conquer them. 8 Even their gods, with their molten images and their precious vessels of silver and gold, he shall carry away as spoils of war into Egypt. For years he shall have nothing to do with the king of the north. 9 Then the latter shall invade the land of the king of the south, and return to his own country.

10 "But his sons shall be aroused and assemble a great armed host, which shall pass through like a flood and again surge around the stronghold. 11 † The king of the south, enraged, shall go out to fight against the king of the north, who shall field a great host, but the host shall be given into his hand. 12 When the host is carried off, in the pride of his heart he shall bring down tens of thousands, but he shall not triumph. 13 † For the king of the north shall raise another army, greater than before; after some years he shall attack with this large army and great resources. 14 In those times many shall resist the king of the south, and violent ones among your people shall rise up in fulfillment of vision, but they shall stumble. 15 † When the king of the north comes, he shall set up siegeworks and take the fortified city by storm. The forces of the south shall not withstand him, and not even his picked troops

---

† **10:13** *The prince of the kingdom of Persia*: the angelic guardian of Persia. Where older texts speak of the gods of various countries (Dt 32:8), Daniel speaks of "princes." *Michael*: the patron angel of Israel (v. 21).
**10:21** *The book of truth*: a heavenly book in which future events are already recorded; cf. 7:10; 12:1.
**11:2** *Three kings of Persia*: it is unclear which kings are intended because there were more than three Persian kings between Cyrus and the dissolution of the kingdom. The fourth is Xerxes I (486–465 B.C.), the great campaigner against Greece.
**11:3** *A powerful king*: Alexander the Great, who broke Persian dominance by his victory at Issus in 333 B.C.
**11:5–45** These verses describe the dynastic histories of the Ptolemies in Egypt (the king of the south) and the Seleucids in

Syria (the king of the north), the two divisions of the Hellenistic empire that were of interest to the author (v. 6). Verses 10–20 describe the struggle between the two kingdoms for the control of Palestine; the Seleucids were eventually victorious.
**11:6** The marriage of Antiochus II Theos and Berenice of Egypt about 250 B.C., which ended in tragedy.
**11:11** The battle of Raphia (217 B.C.), in which Egypt defeated Syria.
**11:13** Syria defeated Egypt at the battle of Paneas in 200 B.C. Judea then passed under Syrian rule.
**11:15** The siege of Sidon after the battle of Paneas.

**10:21** Rev 12:7.

shall have the strength to withstand. ¹⁶The invader shall do as he wills, with no one to withstand him. He shall stop in the glorious land, and it shall all be in his power. ¹⁷† He shall resolve to come with the entire strength of his kingdom. He shall make an alliance with him and give him a daughter in marriage in order to destroy him, but this shall not stand. ¹⁸† He shall turn to the coastland and take many prisoners, but a commander shall put an end to his shameful conduct, so that he cannot retaliate. ¹⁹He shall turn to the strongholds of his own land, but shall stumble and fall, to be found no more. ²⁰† In his stead one shall arise who will send a collector of tribute through the glorious kingdom, but he shall soon be destroyed, though not in conflict or in battle.

²¹† "There shall arise in his place a despicable person, to whom the royal insignia shall not be given. He shall enter by stealth and seize the kingdom by fraud. ²²Armed forces shall be completely overwhelmed by him and crushed, even the prince of the covenant.† ²³After making alliances, he shall treacherously rise to power with only a few supporters. ²⁴By stealth he shall enter prosperous provinces and do that which his fathers or grandfathers never did; he shall distribute spoil, plunder, and riches among them and devise plots against their strongholds. ²⁵He shall rouse his strength and courage to meet the king of the south with a great army; the king of the south shall go into battle with a very large and strong army, but he shall not stand because of the plots devised against him. ²⁶Even his table companions shall seek to destroy him, his army shall be overwhelmed, and many shall be struck down. ²⁷The two kings, resolved on evil, shall sit at table together and exchange lies, but they shall have no success, because the appointed end is not yet.

²⁸"He† shall turn back toward his land with great riches, his mind set against the holy covenant; he shall take action and return to his land. ²⁹At the time appointed he shall come again to the south, but this time it shall not be as before. ³⁰When ships of the Kittim† confront him, he shall lose heart and retreat. Then he shall rage against the holy covenant and take action; he shall again favor those who forsake the holy covenant. ³¹Armed forces shall rise at his command and defile the sanctuary stronghold, abolishing the daily sacrifice and setting up the desolating abomination. ³²By his deceit he shall make some who were disloyal forsake the covenant; but those who remain loyal to their God shall take strong action. ³³Those with insight among the people shall instruct the many; though for a time the sword, flames, exile, and plunder will cause them to stumble. ³⁴When they stumble, they will be helped,† but only a little; many shall join them, but out of treachery. ³⁵Some of those with insight shall stumble so that they may be tested, refined, and purified, until the end time which is still appointed to come.

³⁶"The king shall do as he wills, exalting himself and making himself greater than any god; he shall utter dreadful blasphemies against the God of gods. He shall prosper only till the wrath is finished, for what is determined must take place. ³⁷He shall have no regard for the gods of his ancestors or for the one in whom women delight;† for no god shall he have regard, because he shall make himself greater than all. ³⁸Instead, he shall give glory to the god of strongholds;† a god unknown to his ancestors he shall glorify with gold, silver, precious stones, and other treasures. ³⁹He shall act for those who fortify strongholds, a people of a foreign god, whom he has recognized. He shall greatly honor them; he shall make them rule over the many and distribute the land as a reward.

⁴⁰† "At the end time the king of the south

**11:17** Antiochus III, the Great, betrothed his daughter to Ptolemy Epiphanes in 197 B.C.
**11:18** The Roman general Scipio defeated Antiochus at Magnesia in 190 B.C.
**11:20** Seleucus IV, who sent Heliodorus to Jerusalem (cf. 2 Mc 3).
**11:21** Here begins the career of Antiochus IV Epiphanes.
**11:22** *The prince of the covenant*: the high priest Onias III, who was murdered.
**11:28** *He*: the king of the north, probably Antiochus IV.
**11:30** *Kittim*: originally this word meant Cypriots or other westerners. It is sometimes used for the Greeks (1 Mc 1:1). Here it refers to the Romans, who forced Antiochus to withdraw from Egypt during his second campaign there.
**11:34** *Helped*: this may be a reference to the Maccabean re-

volt. The apocalyptic author expects deliverance from God and has little regard for human efforts. In fact, the Maccabees routed the Syrian troops, recaptured Jerusalem, purified and rededicated the Temple, and brought to an end the Syrian persecution.
**11:37** *The one in whom women delight*: Tammuz. Daniel takes this to imply the neglect of all other gods, although this does not appear to have been the case.
**11:38** *The god of strongholds*: the god worshiped in the fortress Akra, which Antiochus established in Jerusalem.
**11:40–45** In these concluding verses, the events described no longer correspond to the history of the Maccabean period. Daniel imagines the death of Antiochus on the model of Gog in Ez 38–39. Antiochus actually died in Persia.

shall engage him in battle but the king of the north shall overwhelm him with chariots and horsemen and a great fleet, passing through the lands like a flood. [41] He shall enter the glorious land and many shall fall, except Edom, Moab, and the chief part of Ammon, which shall escape his power. [42] He shall extend his power over the land, and not even Egypt shall escape. [43] He shall control the riches of gold and silver and all the treasures of Egypt; Libya and Ethiopia shall be in his entourage. [44] When reports from the east and the north disturb him, he shall set out with great fury to destroy many, putting them under the ban. [45] He shall pitch the tents of his royal pavilion between the sea and the glorious holy mountain, but he shall come to his end with none to help him.

## The Resurrection

**12** [1] "At that time there shall arise
    Michael,*
    the great prince,
    guardian of your people;
It shall be a time unsurpassed in distress
    since the nation began until that time.
At that time your people shall escape,
    everyone who is found written in the
    book.†
[2]     Many of those who sleep†
    in the dust of the earth shall awake;
Some to everlasting life,
    others to reproach and everlasting
    disgrace.*
[3]     But those with insight shall shine
    brightly
    like the splendor of the firmament,
And those who lead the many to justice
    shall be like the stars† forever.*

[4] "As for you, Daniel, keep secret the message and seal the book until the end time;

many shall wander aimlessly and evil shall increase."

[5] I, Daniel, looked and saw two others, one standing on either bank of the river. [6] One of them said to the man clothed in linen, who was upstream, "How long shall it be to the end of these appalling things?" [7] The man clothed in linen,* who was upstream, lifted his hands to heaven; and I heard him swear by him who lives forever that it should be for a time, two times, and half a time;† and that, when the power of the destroyer of the holy people was brought to an end, all these things should end. [8] I heard, but I did not understand; so I asked, "My lord, what follows this?" [9] "Go, Daniel," he said, "because the words are to be kept secret and sealed until the end time. [10] Many shall be refined, purified, and tested, but the wicked shall prove wicked; the wicked shall have no understanding, but those with insight shall. [11]† From the time that the daily sacrifice is abolished and the desolating abomination is set up, there shall be one thousand two hundred and ninety days. [12] Blessed are they who have patience and persevere for the one thousand three hundred and thirty-five days. [13] Go, take your rest, you shall rise for your reward at the end of days."

## III. APPENDIX: SUSANNA, BEL, AND THE DRAGON†

**13** **Susanna.** [1] In Babylon there lived a man named Joakim, [2] who married a very beautiful and God-fearing woman, Susanna, the daughter of Hilkiah; [3] her parents were righteous and had trained their daughter according to the law of Moses. [4] Joakim was very rich and he had a garden near his house. The Jews had recourse to him often because he was the most respected of them all.

[5] That year, two elders of the people were

---

† **12:1** *Written in the book*: cf. 10:21.
  **12:2** *Many of those who sleep*: Daniel does not envisage the universal resurrection as later developed. Two groups are distinguished, one that rises to eternal life, the other to reproach and disgrace. Then "those with insight" (11:33–35) are singled out for special honor.
  **12:3** *Like the stars*: like the heavenly host, or angels. Cf. Mt 22:30.
  **12:7** *A time, two times, and half a time*: see note on 7:25.
  **12:11** The specific numbers of days given in vv. 11–12 represent attempts to calculate the precise duration of the three and a half years. Most probably, when the first date (1,290 days) passed, the author attempted another calculation. Another, earlier calculation is preserved in 8:14. It is noteworthy, however, that the contradictory numbers were allowed to stand in the text;

this is a reminder that it is not possible to calculate a precise date for God's judgment; cf. Mk 13:32.
  **13:1–14:42** The short stories in these two chapters exist now only in Greek and other translations, but probably were first composed in Hebrew or Aramaic. They were never part of the Hebrew-Aramaic Book of Daniel, or of the Hebrew Bible. They are excluded from the Protestant canon of Scripture, but the Catholic Church has always included them among the inspired writings; they existed in the Septuagint, which was used as its Bible by the early church.

---

**12:1** Rev 12:7.      **12:3** Wis 3:7.
**12:2** Is 66:24; Mt 25:46; Jn    **12:7** Rev 10:5–6.
    5:29.

appointed judges, of whom the Lord said, "Lawlessness has come out of Babylon, that is, from the elders who were to govern the people as judges." 6These men, to whom all brought their cases, frequented the house of Joakim. 7When the people left at noon, Susanna used to enter her husband's garden for a walk. 8When the elders saw her enter every day for her walk, they began to lust for her. 9They perverted their thinking; they would not allow their eyes to look to heaven, and did not keep in mind just judgments. 10Though both were enamored of her, they did not tell each other their trouble, 11for they were ashamed to reveal their lustful desire to have her. 12Day by day they watched eagerly for her. 13One day they said to each other, "Let us be off for home, it is time for the noon meal." So they went their separate ways. 14But both turned back and arrived at the same spot. When they asked each other the reason, they admitted their lust, and then they agreed to look for an occasion when they could find her alone.

15One day, while they were waiting for the right moment, she entered as usual, with two maids only, wanting to bathe in the garden, for the weather was warm. 16Nobody else was there except the two elders, who had hidden themselves and were watching her. 17"Bring me oil and soap," she said to the maids, "and shut the garden gates while I bathe." 18They did as she said; they shut the garden gates and left by the side gate to fetch what she had ordered, unaware that the elders were hidden inside.

19As soon as the maids had left, the two old men got up and ran to her. 20"Look," they said, "the garden doors are shut, no one can see us, and we want you. So give in to our desire, and lie with us. 21If you refuse, we will testify against you that a young man was here with you and that is why you sent your maids away."

22"I am completely trapped," Susanna groaned. "If I yield, it will be my death; if I refuse, I cannot escape your power. 23Yet it is better for me not to do it and to fall into your power than to sin before the Lord." 24Then Susanna screamed, and the two old men also shouted at her, 25as one of them ran to open the garden gates. 26When the people in the house heard the cries from the garden, they rushed in by the side gate to see what had

happened to her. 27At the accusations of the old men, the servants felt very much ashamed, for never had any such thing been said about Susanna.

28When the people came to her husband Joakim the next day, the two wicked old men also came, full of lawless intent to put Susanna to death. 29Before the people they ordered: "Send for Susanna, the daughter of Hilkiah, the wife of Joakim." When she was sent for, 30she came with her parents, children and all her relatives. 31Susanna, very delicate and beautiful, 32was veiled; but those transgressors of the law ordered that she be exposed so as to sate themselves with her beauty. 33All her companions and the onlookers were weeping.

34In the midst of the people the two old men rose up and laid their hands on her head. 35As she wept she looked up to heaven, for she trusted in the Lord wholeheartedly. 36The old men said, "As we were walking in the garden alone, this woman entered with two servant girls, shut the garden gates and sent the servant girls away. 37A young man, who was hidden there, came and lay with her. 38When we, in a corner of the garden, saw this lawlessness, we ran toward them. 39We saw them lying together, but the man we could not hold, because he was stronger than we; he opened the gates and ran off. 40Then we seized this one and asked who the young man was, 41but she refused to tell us. We testify to this." The assembly believed them, since they were elders and judges of the people, and they condemned her to death.

42But Susanna cried aloud: "Eternal God, you know what is hidden and are aware of all things before they come to be: 43you know that they have testified falsely against me. Here I am about to die, though I have done none of the things for which these men have condemned me."

44The Lord heard her prayer. 45As she was being led to execution, God stirred up the holy spirit of a young boy named Daniel, 46and he cried aloud: "I am innocent of this woman's blood." 47All the people turned and asked him, "What are you saying?" 48He stood in their midst and said, "Are you such fools, you Israelites, to condemn a daughter of Israel without investigation and without clear evidence? 49Return to court, for they have testified falsely against her."

⁵⁰Then all the people returned in haste. To Daniel the elders said, "Come, sit with us and inform us, since God has given you the prestige of old age." ⁵¹But he replied, "Separate these two far from one another, and I will examine them."

⁵²After they were separated from each other, he called one of them and said: "How you have grown evil with age! Now have your past sins come to term: ⁵³passing unjust sentences, condemning the innocent, and freeing the guilty,* although the Lord says, 'The innocent and the just you shall not put to death.' ⁵⁴Now, then, if you were a witness, tell me under what tree you saw them together." ⁵⁵"Under a mastic tree,"† he answered. "Your fine lie has cost you your head," said Daniel; "for the angel of God has already received the sentence from God and shall split you in two." ⁵⁶Putting him to one side, he ordered the other one to be brought. "Offspring of Canaan, not of Judah," Daniel said to him, "beauty has seduced you, lust has perverted your heart. ⁵⁷This is how you acted with the daughters of Israel, and in their fear they yielded to you; but a daughter of Judah did not tolerate your lawlessness. ⁵⁸Now, then, tell me under what tree you surprised them together." ⁵⁹"Under an oak," he said. "Your fine lie has cost you also your head," said Daniel; "for the angel of God waits with a sword to cut you in two so as to destroy you both."

⁶⁰The whole assembly cried aloud, blessing God who saves those who hope in him. ⁶¹They rose up against the two old men, for by their own words Daniel had convicted them of bearing false witness.* They condemned them to the fate they had planned for their neighbor: ⁶²in accordance with the law of Moses they put them to death. Thus was innocent blood spared that day.

⁶³Hilkiah and his wife praised God for their daughter Susanna, with Joakim her husband and all her relatives, because she was found innocent of any shameful deed. ⁶⁴And from that day onward Daniel was greatly esteemed by the people.

# 14

**Bel and the Dragon.**† ¹After King Astyages† was gathered to his ancestors, Cyrus the Persian succeeded to his kingdom. ²Daniel was a companion of the king and was held in higher honor than any of the Friends of the King. ³The Babylonians had an idol called Bel,† and every day they provided for it six bushels of fine flour, forty sheep, and six measures of wine. ⁴The king revered it and went every day to worship it; but Daniel worshiped only his God. ⁵When the king asked him, "Why do you not worship Bel?" Daniel replied, "Because I do not revere idols made with hands, but only the living God who made heaven and earth and has dominion over all flesh." ⁶Then the king continued, "You do not think Bel is a living god? Do you not see how much he eats and drinks every day?" ⁷Daniel began to laugh. "Do not be deceived, O king," he said; "it is only clay inside and bronze outside; it has never eaten or drunk anything." ⁸Enraged, the king called his priests and said to them, "Unless you tell me who it is that consumes these provisions, you shall die. But if you can show that Bel consumes them, Daniel shall die for blaspheming Bel." ⁹Daniel said to the king, "Let it be as you say!"

There were seventy priests of Bel, besides their wives and children. ¹⁰†When the king went with Daniel into the temple of Bel, ¹¹the priests of Bel said, "See, we are going to leave. You, O king, set out the food and prepare the wine; then shut the door and seal it with your

---

**13:55–59** The contrast between the mastic tree, which is small, and the majestic oak emphasizes the contradiction between the statements of the two elders. In the Greek text there is a play on words between the names of these two trees and the mortal punishment decreed by Daniel for the elders. The mastic tree (*schinon*) sounds like the verb "to split" (*schisai*). The oak tree (*prinon*) suggests a play on *poisai* (to saw).

**14:1–22** In chap. 14, readings in the Septuagint differ markedly from those in Theodotion, which is followed here. See individual notes on 1–3a, 10–11, 12–14, 15–17 and 21–22; the translation is that of Collins, *Daniel*, pp. 405ff, with brackets indicating additions to the Septuagint according to Collins.

**14:1–3a** These verses in the Septuagint Greek text read: "From the prophecy of Habakkuk, son of Joshua, of the tribe of Levi. ² There was a certain man, a priest, whose name was Daniel, son of Abal, a companion of the king of Babylon. ³ There

was an idol, Bel, which the Babylonians revered,..." This may represent an earlier form of the story, before it was attached to the Book of Daniel. *King Astyages*: the last of the Median kings, defeated by Cyrus in 550 B.C. This story preserves the fiction of a successive Median and Persian rule of Babylon.

**14:3** *Bel*: see note on 4:5.

**14:10–11** These verses in the Septuagint Greek text read: "(Now, there were seventy priests of Bel, apart from women and children.) They led the king to the idol shrine. ¹¹ The food was set out in the presence of the king and of Daniel, and mixed wine was brought in and set before Bel. Daniel said, 'You yourself see that these things are laid out, O king. You, therefore, seal the door of temple when it is closed.' [The word pleased the king.]"

---

**13:53** Ex 23:7.          **13:61** Dt 19:18–19.

ring. **12**† If you do not find that Bel has eaten it all when you return in the morning, we are to die; otherwise Daniel shall die for his lies against us." **13** They were not perturbed, because under the table they had made a secret entrance through which they always came in to consume the food. **14** After they departed the king set the food before Bel, while Daniel ordered his servants to bring some ashes, which they scattered through the whole temple; the king alone was present. Then they went outside, sealed the closed door with the king's ring, and departed. **15**† The priests entered that night as usual, with their wives and children, and they ate and drank everything.

**16** Early the next morning, the king came with Daniel. **17** "Are the seals unbroken, Daniel?" he asked. And Daniel answered, "They are unbroken, O king." **18** As soon as he had opened the door, the king looked at the table and cried aloud, "You are great, O Bel; there is no deceit in you." **19**† But Daniel laughed and kept the king from entering. He said, "Look at the floor and consider whose footprints these are." **20** "I see the footprints of men, women, and children!" said the king. **21**† In his wrath the king arrested the priests, their wives, and their children. They showed him the secret door by which they used to enter to consume what was on the table. **22** The king put them to death, and handed Bel over to Daniel, who destroyed it and its temple.

**23** There was a great dragon† which the Babylonians revered. **24** The king said to Daniel, "You cannot deny that this is a living god, so worship it." **25** But Daniel answered, "I worship the Lord, my God, for he is the living God. **26** Give me permission, O king, and I will kill this dragon without sword or club." "I give you permission," the king said. **27** Then Daniel took some pitch, fat, and hair; these he boiled together and made into cakes. He put them into the mouth of the dragon, and when the dragon ate them, he burst. "This," he said, "is what you revered."

**28** When the Babylonians heard this, they were angry and turned against the king. "The king has become a Jew," they said; "he has destroyed Bel, killed the dragon, and put the priests to death." **29** They went to the king and demanded: "Hand Daniel over to us, or we will kill you and your family." **30** When he saw himself threatened with violence, the king was forced to hand Daniel over to them. **31** They threw Daniel into a lions' den,† where he remained six days. **32** In the den were seven lions. Two carcasses and two sheep had been given to them daily, but now they were given nothing, so that they would devour Daniel.

**33** The prophet Habakkuk was in Judea. He mixed some bread in a bowl with the stew he had boiled, and was going to bring it to the reapers in the field, **34** when an angel of the Lord told him, "Take the meal you have to Daniel in the lions' den at Babylon." **35** But Habakkuk answered, "Sir, I have never seen Babylon, and I do not know the den!" **36** The angel of the Lord seized him by the crown of his head and carried him by the hair;* with the speed of the wind, he set him down in Babylon above the den. **37** "Daniel, Daniel," cried Habakkuk, "take the meal God has sent you." **38** "You have remembered me, O God," said Daniel; "you have not forsaken those who love you." **39** So Daniel ate, but the angel of God at once brought Habakkuk back to his own place.

**40** On the seventh day the king came to mourn for Daniel. As he came to the den and looked in, there was Daniel, sitting there. **41** The king cried aloud, "You are great, O Lord, the God of Daniel, and there is no other besides you!" **42** He brought Daniel out, but those who had tried to destroy him he threw into the den, and they were devoured in a moment before his eyes.

---

**14:12–14** Theodotion's vv. 12–13 and 14's "After they departed the king set the food before Bel" are lacking in the Septuagint Greek text, which continues vv. 15–17 from v. 11 as follows: "Then Daniel commanded his attendants to make everyone go out from the temple and sprinkle the whole temple with ashes, unknown to anyone outside. Then he ordered them to apply the seal with the king's ring [and the seals of certain illustrious priests, and so it was done]."

**14:15–17** These verses in the Septuagint Greek text read: "15 On the next day they came to the place. But the priests of Bel had entered through false doors and had eaten all that was set forth for Bel and drunk the wine. Daniel said, 'See whether your seals remain, O priests, and you, O king, see that nothing has happened that seems improper to you.' They found the seal as it had been, and they removed the seal."

**14:19** Note that here the king seems unaware of Daniel's ruse.

**14:21–22** These verses in the Septuagint Greek text read: "21 And he went to the house where the priests had come, and he found Bel's food and the wine, and Daniel showed the king the false doors through which the priests entered and consumed what had been set before Bel. 22 The king led them out of the temple of Bel and gave them over to Daniel. He gave Daniel what was expended on him and destroyed Bel."

**14:23** *Dragon*: or "serpent," and see v. 27. Sacred snakes are well attested in the ancient world (e.g., in the temple of the god of healing Asclepius at Epidaurus), though evidence for their veneration in Babylon is doubtful.

**14:31** *A lions' den*: this story provides a different account from chap. 6 as to why Daniel was associated with the lions' den.

**14:36** Ez 8:3.

# The Book of

# Hosea

## INTRODUCTION

### Dale Launderville, OSB

Hosea is aptly described as the prophet of love. He envisions the good life for the Israelites as unfolding in a household in which Yahweh is married to the Israelites and the land on which they live. The Lord passionately loves the Israelites, but the Israelites do not respond in kind. The Lord does not abandon the Israelites but disciplines them so that their love might be rightly ordered toward the well-being of his household. The anger and anguish that the Lord feels toward the Israelites offers an explanation for the suffering and trauma that the Israelite nation would undergo as divine punishment at the hands of the Assyrians. The individual Israelites were victims of their collective waywardness. Hosea calls the Israelites to accept responsibility for their shared life as the family of God. Priests, prophets, and kings fail to promote collective responsibility and instead further fragment the community because they do not know the Lord. In the midst of the crushing events that led to the deportation of the Israelites and the devastation of their homeland, Hosea offers hope for the Israelites who would turn back to the Lord and be faithful.

Hosea delivers the Lord's message to Israel by actions as well as by words. Hosea recognizes that the nation of Israel consists literally of both women and men, but figuratively he imagines its collective existence as feminine. He is commanded to marry a promiscuous woman who will in turn give birth to illegitimate children. The point of this sign action is to communicate the Israelites' infidelity toward Yahweh. As a nation, the Israelites do not trust in the Lord as the one who provides them with their material needs and protection. Instead, they turn to other gods and peoples to manage their vulnerability. Hosea's wife Gomer acts on her previous patterns and has relations

## Outline of Hosea

I. The Prophet's Marriage and Its Symbolism (1:2–3:5)

II. Israel's Guilt, Punishment, and Restoration (4:1–14:9)

with other lovers instead of focusing her love on her husband. She gives birth to three children to whom the Lord gives names that point to their illegitimacy: the son Jezreel ("God will sow"), the daughter Lo' Ruhama ("not pitied"), and the son Lo' 'Ammi ("not my people"). In response to her infidelity, the Lord/Hosea punishes Israel/Gomer by depriving her of her material goods and bringing her lovers against her. Such imagery reflects the violence suffered by Israel in the eighth century and emphasizes the centrality of exclusive fidelity to the Lord, but runs the risk of scapegoating the woman as the troubled partner in the divine-human relationship and as the source of the nation's woes.

Israel did not "know" the Lord as the one who provided her with grain, wine, oil, silver, and gold (Hos 2:9). Such knowledge was not only informational but also interpersonal in character. Knowledge of the Lord could not be secured as a commodity but demanded personal engagement. The Lord instructs Israel by depriving her of access to the material goods she thinks are commodities delivered by her lovers. The Lord then "allures her" into the wilderness to persuade her that he is the one who has given her the land and the goods it produces (2:16–17). The exile from the land that the Israelites were to suffer at the hands of the Assyrians would not be the end of the people of Israel. Rather it was to be a traumatic

HOS

instructional experience in which the Israelites would come to know of the Lord's passionate love for them (2:21) and his sovereign power over heaven and earth, particularly the fertility essential to successful agriculture (2:23–25). How to love above all the giver of this power of fertility rather than his tangible gifts would be a harsh lesson that Israel would have to learn through deprivation and pain.

Hosea condemns the Israelite priests for depriving the people of knowledge of the Lord (Hos 4:4–14). Because the priests ignore the instruction or "law" (torah) of the Lord, they open the way for syncretism: i.e., foreign religious practices are adopted in the Israelite sanctuaries that distract from the exclusive worship of the Lord. They practice divination (4:12), and they prostitute themselves by serving other deities (4:9–11, 13). The priests' infidelity cascades through the Israelite community: the people imitate the priests (4:9); the men engage in prostitution by sacrificing to other gods (4:13–14), and their daughters and daughters-in-law follow suit and thus prostitute themselves (4:14). Even if sexual acts are not being enacted in the sanctuary as part of this perverted worship, the power of sexuality is being seized upon as a more important source of fertility than the Lord who gives the gift of sexuality in the first place. This overestimation of the power of sexuality is being imported into Yahwistic worship from the Baal cult (2:15; 4:17–19). Such baalistic worship deprives the Israelites of knowledge of the Lord and fosters addictive religious practices from which they cannot escape (4:14, 17–19; 5:4). Hosea charges the priests—and the kings who appointed them—with fostering syncretism (5:1–2). The Israelites will try to worship the Lord (5:6–7) but will be unsuccessful, because they are "defiled" (5:3) and the Lord has withdrawn from them (5:6).

Hosea criticizes the royal establishment not only for introducing idolatrous practices into Israelite worship but also for fostering international trade and foreign alliances that distort the way of life of traditional Yahwistic households. The commodities of wine and oil were well-suited for international trade. According to a number of scholars, the king and urban elite in eighth-century Israel collected agricultural goods for the purposes of trade and thereby encouraged the production of these commodities at the expense of the local households. Such goods became a more important concern for the Israelites than the Lord who gave the gifts in the first place (Hos 2:10–15).

As Assyria expanded its empire westward to the Mediterranean under Tiglath-Pileser III (745–727 BCE), kings of small nations such as Israel were forced to pay tribute or see their nation be swallowed up into the Assyrian provincial system. The only real choice for the Israelites was either to cooperate (pro-Assyrian) or to rebel (anti-Assyrian). Each alternative called for entering into foreign alliances, on the one hand, with Assyria or, on the other, with Aram or Egypt. The alliance with Aram resulted in Aram-Israel going to war against Judah in an effort to get Judah to join the resistance against the Assyrians (Hos 5:8–10; cf. Is 7:1–9). But Ahaz, king of Judah (735–715 BCE), refused and followed the previous example of Menahem of Israel (745–737 BCE), who had sided with the Assyrian king by paying tribute (Hos 5:13). Such maneuvering by way of international alliances was insufficient to keep the Assyrians at bay, however, and contributed to political instability at home. Of the six kings to reign in Israel from 746 to 721 BCE, four were assassinated by their successors; only Menahem and Hoshea (732–724 BCE) avoided that fate. Hosea characterizes the Israelites in their domestic turmoil as ones who "are all like heated ovens . . . [that] consume their rulers" (7:7). Because the Israelites believe they, rather than Yahweh, control the office of kingship (8:4; 13:11), they have allowed idolatry to bewitch them on the political and economic fronts but will wake up later and see how they have been blinded by such self-centered choices (8:8–10).

Hosea warns of a greater disaster on the horizon as a consequence of Israel's lack of knowledge of the Lord. When Israel seeks protection from Assyria, they do not seem to know that it is the Lord who is fighting against them. Hosea challenges the Israelites to see their sufferings as punishment from the Lord. He pictures the Lord as a judge who is "like a moth for Ephraim, like rot for the house of Judah" (Hos 5:12); "like a lion to Ephraim, like a young lion to the house of Judah" (5:14; cf. 11:10; 13:7–8). When they go to Egypt or Assyria for assistance, they are "like a dove, silly and senseless" (7:11). Thus the Lord warns them: "When they go I will spread my net around them, like birds in the air I will bring them down" (7:12). On a number of occasions, Hosea warns that the Lord intends to "return" them "to Egypt" (8:13; 9:3; 11:5): i.e., they will be exiled to another land where they will serve an earthly ruler. One of the ways the Israelites were not relying on the Lord was their construction of palaces and city fortifications. But the Lord warns that he will bring fire on the cities of Israel and Judah (8:14). Because of their worship of Baal, the Lord warns that in Ephraim there will be "no birth, no pregnancy, no conception" (9:11). Hosea, recognizing the Lord as the source of fertility who can bestow or withhold it, even goes so far as to invoke a curse against the Israelites: "Give them a miscarrying womb, and dry breasts" (9:14). Foretelling that military forces will come against Israel, the Lord warns: "Even though they bring up their children, I will make them childless, until no one is left. . . . Were they to bear children, I would slay the beloved of their womb" (9:12, 16). To make innocent children the victims in a divine punishment seems excessive and inappropriate for a divine judge. However, Hosea is making the case that the Assyrians' overrunning the cities of Israel is an event overseen by the Lord; it did not come about by chance but rather was provoked by the Lord.

Hosea's prophetic stance does not gloss over the harshness of historical reality. Although Hosea supports the sovereign power of the Lord, he raises questions about the justice of the Lord's rule. Fortunately, Hosea does not completely overwhelm his audience with the dark side of the Lord's rule, but counters it at strategic points with the Lord's desire to heal and be compassionate (Hos 7:1; 14:4). Probably the most profound passage in Hosea's prophecy pictures the Lord as a parent who is torn up inside over the need to exercise "tough love" toward rebellious Israel. The Lord recalls how he had called Israel from Egypt and loved him as a child; but the more he cared for Israel, the further Israel strayed from him (11:1–4). Israel's refusal to repent left the Lord no choice but to punish severely (11:5–7). But then Hosea gives us a unique view into the heart of the Lord as the Lord says, "How could I give you up, Ephraim, or deliver you up, Israel? How could I treat you as Admah, or make you like Zeboiim?[1] My heart is overwhelmed, my pity is stirred. I will not give vent to my blazing anger, I will not destroy Ephraim again; for I am God and not a man, the Holy One present among you; I will not come in wrath" (11:8–9). Here Hosea seems to have the Lord call into question the justice of the Lord's punishment that he announced in other parts of his prophecy. These harsh punishments may be just, but the Lord, like a loving parent, would prefer to exercise more compassion. This loving, parental compassion gives hope for Israel's future. What goes on in the heart of God indicates why the covenant between the Lord and Israel is resilient.

Hosea refers to the ancestor Jacob as a deceitful one who contended with human and divine beings but also encountered the Lord at Bethel. Hosea then exhorts his Israelite audience: "You must return to your God. Maintain loyalty and justice and always hope in your God" (Hos 12:7). Later, after condemning Israel for its infidelity and idolatry and warning of divine punishment for such behavior, Hosea gives Israel the words that they should speak to the Lord in order to be forgiven: "Assyria will not save us, nor will we mount horses; we will never again say, 'Our god,' to the work of our hands; for in you the orphan finds compassion" (14:4). In such a confession, the Israelites acknowledge that foreign powers, their own military power, and the idols that they manufacture are illusory sources of security; they thus turn away from three temptations to which they had repeatedly succumbed. They now turn to the God who is distinguished by compassion for the vulnerable. ∎

---

1. Cities near the Dead Sea destroyed along with Sodom and Gomorrah (Gn 14:2, 8; 19:24–25).

# THE BOOK OF HOSEA

## New American Bible, Introduction

Hosea, a prophet from the Northern Kingdom, preached in his homeland, which he addresses as Israel, Jacob or, frequently, Ephraim. Hosea began his mission in a period of prosperity, the last years of Jeroboam II (783–743 B.C.). This was followed by a period of internal instability, with intrigues at the royal court leading to the assassination of several kings. Hosea witnessed the revival of Assyria, the Syro-Ephraimite war, and the numerous treaties the Israelite kings made with Egypt and Assyria to survive. Hosea's long ministry (ca. 750–725) seems to have ended before the capture of Samaria in 722/721.

The only information the text provides us about the life of Hosea concerns his marriage. Even if we cannot reconstruct what happened exactly, the text as it now stands speaks of three moments in the relationship: first love, separation, reunion. This marriage is a symbol of the covenant between the Lord and Israel. Hosea speaks about the first love, the short period of Israel's loyalty in the desert, which was then followed by a long history of unfaithfulness lasting until his day. Hosea accuses Israel of three crimes in particular. Instead of putting their trust in the Lord alone, the people break the covenant: (1) by counting on their own military strength, (2) by making treaties with foreign powers (Assyria and Egypt), and (3) by running after the Baals, the gods of fertility. Israel thus forgets that the Lord is its strength, its covenant partner, and giver of fertility. This unfaithful behavior will lead to Israel's destruction by Assyria, but God's love will have the last word. The back and forth movement from doom to salvation is typical of the Book of Hosea.

Hosea began the Old Testament tradition of describing the relation between the Lord and Israel in terms of marriage (e.g., Jer 3:1; Ez 16:23; Is 50:1). The New Testament uses the marriage imagery to describe the union between Christ and the Church (e.g., Mk 2:19–20; Eph 5:25).

The Hebrew of the Book of Hosea is challenging to translate, possibly because the text is corrupt or because it is written in a nonstandard dialect of Hebrew. As a result, the English translations of the book sometimes offer very different readings of the same passage.

The book, which opens with a superscription (1:1) and ends with a final challenge (14:10), is divided into two major parts:

I. The Prophet's Marriage and Its Symbolism (1:2–3:5)
II. Israel's Guilt, Punishment, and Restoration (4:1–14:9) ◼

# HOSEA

**1** ¹ † The word of the LORD that came to Hosea son of Beeri, in the days of Uzziah, Jotham, Ahaz, Hezekiah, kings of Judah, and in the days of Jeroboam, son of Joash, king of Israel. †

## I. THE PROPHET'S MARRIAGE AND ITS SYMBOLISM

**Marriage of Hosea and Gomer.** ²When the LORD began to speak with Hosea, the LORD said to Hosea: Go, get for yourself a woman of prostitution † and children of prostitution, for the land prostitutes itself, * turning away from the LORD.

³So he went and took Gomer, daughter of Diblaim; and she conceived and bore him a son. ⁴Then the LORD said to him: Give him the name "Jezreel," † for in a little while I will punish the house of Jehu for the bloodshed at Jezreel and bring to an end the kingdom of the house of Israel; ⁵on that day I will break the bow of Israel in the valley of Jezreel.

⁶She conceived again and bore a daughter. The LORD said to him: Give her the name "Not-Pitied," † for I will no longer feel pity for the house of Israel: rather, I will utterly abhor them. ⁷ † Yet for the house of Judah I will feel pity; I will save them by the LORD, their God; but I will not save them by bow or sword, by warfare, by horses or horsemen. *

⁸After she weaned Not-Pitied, she conceived and bore a son. ⁹Then the LORD said: Give him the name "Not-My-People," † for you are not my people, and I am not "I am" for you.

**2** ¹ †The number of the Israelites
　　will be like the sand of the sea,
　which can be neither measured nor
　　counted. *
Instead of being told,
　"You are Not-My-People,"
They will be called,
　"Children of the living God." *

² Then the people of Judah and of Israel
　　will gather together;
They will appoint for themselves one
　　head
　and rise up from the land;
　great indeed shall be the day of
　　Jezreel!

³ Say to your brothers, "My People,"
　and to your sisters, "Pitied."

### The Lord and Israel His Spouse†

⁴ Accuse your mother, accuse!
　for she is not my wife,
　and I am not her husband. †
Let her remove her prostitution from her
　　face,
　her adultery from between her breasts,

⁵ Or I will strip her naked, †
　leaving her as on the day of her birth;
I will make her like the wilderness,
　make her like an arid land,

---

and let her die of thirst.
6 I will have no pity on her children,
    for they are children of prostitution.
7 Yes, their mother has prostituted herself;
    she who conceived them has acted
        shamefully.
    For she said, "I will go after my lovers,†
        who give me my bread and my water,
        my wool and my flax, my oil and my
        drink."*
8† Therefore, I will hedge in her way with
        thorns
    and erect a wall against her,
    so that she cannot find her paths.
9 If she runs after her lovers, she will not
        overtake them;
    if she seeks them she will not find
        them.
    Then she will say,
    "I will go back to my first husband,
        for I was better off then than now."*
10 She did not know
    that it was I who gave her
    the grain, the wine, and the oil,
    I who lavished upon her silver,
        and gold, which they used for Baal,†
11 Therefore I will take back my grain in its
        time,
    and my wine in its season;
    I will snatch away my wool and my flax,
    which were to cover her nakedness.
12 Now I will lay bare her shame
    in full view of her lovers,*
    and no one can deliver her out of my
        hand.*
13 I will put an end to all her joy,
    her festivals, her new moons, her
        sabbaths—
    all her seasonal feasts.
14 I will lay waste her vines and fig trees,

of which she said, "These are the fees
    my lovers have given me";
I will turn them into rank growth
    and wild animals shall devour them.
15 I will punish her for the days of the
        Baals,†
    for whom she burnt incense,
When she decked herself out with her
        rings and her jewelry,
    and went after her lovers—
but me she forgot—oracle of the
        LORD.*
16 Therefore,† I will allure her now;
    I will lead her into the wilderness*
    and speak persuasively to her.
17 Then I will give her the vineyards she had,
    and the valley of Achor† as a door of
        hope.*
There she will respond as in the days of
        her youth,
    as on the day when she came up from
        the land of Egypt.
18 On that day—oracle of the LORD—
You shall call me "My husband,"
    and you shall never again call me "My
        baal."†
19 I will remove from her mouth the
        names of the Baals;
    they shall no longer be mentioned by
        their name.
20 I will make a covenant for them on that
        day,*
    with the wild animals,
With the birds of the air,
    and with the things that crawl on the
        ground.
Bow and sword and warfare
    I will destroy from the land,
    and I will give them rest in safety.

H
O
S

---

**2:7** *My lovers*: even though Israel had experienced the Lord as the God of the desert, covenant and conquest, the people were inclined to turn to the local fertility deities, the Baals, who were believed to be responsible for agricultural success. They easily forgot that the Lord provides them with everything (v. 10; cf. Dt 7:13), and thus prostituted themselves by worshiping other gods.
**2:8** The crop failures sent by the Lord are meant to make Israel see the folly of its ways.
**2:10** *For Baal*: as an offering to Baal or to make statues of Baal.
**2:15** *The days of the Baals*: feast days of the Baal cult (v. 13), or the whole period of Israel's apostasy.
**2:16** *Therefore*: this word in Hebrew normally introduces an oracle of doom; here, surprisingly, it leads to hope. *Allure*: as though seducing a virgin (Ex 22:15–16). Ordinarily this word

connotes deception (Jgs 14:15; 16:5; 1 Kgs 22:20–22).
**2:17** *Valley of Achor*: lit., valley of trouble (Jos 7:26). Here this valley becomes a valley of hope, a new entry into the promised land.
**2:18–19** *Baal*: the word means "lord, master." It was commonly used by women of their husbands, but it is to be shunned as a title for the Lord because of its association with the fertility gods, the Baals. Many Israelites saw little if any difference between the worship of the Lord and the worship of the Baals, thereby dishonoring the true source of the land's fertility.

---

* 
**2:7** Jer 2:25.
**2:9** Lk 15:17–18.
**2:12** Ez 16:37.
**2:12** Jn 10:29.
**2:15** Jer 2:32.

**2:16** Jer 2:2–7.
**2:17** Jos 7:24–26.
**2:20** Gn 9:8–11; Ez 34:25;
    Jb 5:23.

<sup>21</sup> I will betroth you to me forever:
  I will betroth you to me with† justice
   and with judgment,
  with loyalty and with compassion;
<sup>22</sup> I will betroth you to me with fidelity,
  and you shall know the LORD.
<sup>23</sup> On that day I will respond—oracle of
   the LORD—
  I will respond to the heavens,
  and they will respond to the earth;
<sup>24</sup> The earth will respond to the grain, and
   wine, and oil,
  and these will respond to Jezreel.
<sup>25</sup> I will sow her for myself in the land,
  and I will have pity on Not-Pitied.
  I will say to Not-My-People, "You are my
   people,"*
  and he will say, "My God!"

# 3 Hosea and His Wife Reunited† <sup>1</sup>Again the LORD said to me:

Go, love a woman
  who is loved by her spouse but
   commits adultery;
Just as the LORD loves the Israelites,
  though they turn to other gods
  and love raisin cakes.†

<sup>2</sup>† So I acquired her for myself for fifteen pieces of silver and a homer and a lethech of barley. <sup>3</sup>Then I said to her:

"You will wait for me for many days;
  you will not prostitute yourself
Or belong to any man;

I in turn will wait for you."
<sup>4</sup>† For the Israelites will remain many days
  without king or prince,
  Without sacrifice or sacred pillar,
  without ephod or household gods.
<sup>5</sup> Afterward the Israelites will turn back
  and seek the LORD, their God,
  and David, their king;†*
  They will come trembling to the LORD
  and to his bounty, in the last days.

## II. ISRAEL'S GUILT, PUNISHMENT, AND RESTORATION

### Indictment of Israel†

# 4 <sup>1</sup>Hear the word of the LORD, Israelites,
  for the LORD has a dispute
  with the inhabitants of the land:*
  There is no fidelity, no loyalty,
  no knowledge of God in the land.
<sup>2</sup> Swearing, lying, murder,
  stealing and adultery break out;†
  bloodshed follows bloodshed.*
<sup>3</sup> Therefore the land dries up,
  and everything that dwells in it
   languishes:
  The beasts of the field,
   the birds of the air,
  and even the fish of the sea perish.*

### Guilt of Priest and of People

<sup>4</sup> But let no one accuse, let no one rebuke;
  with you is my dispute, priest!†
<sup>5</sup> You will stumble in the day,
  and the prophet will stumble with
   you at night;

---

† **2:21–22** *Betroth...with:* the betrothal was the legal moment before cohabitation when the dowry was paid to the father of the bride. In this remarriage the Lord gives the bride price to Israel herself "forever." *Justice...judgment:* refer to equity and fairness of conduct. The next two terms, "loyalty" (*hesed*), the steadfast love between the covenant partners, and "compassion," maternal love (cf. 1:6; 2:3, 25) are characteristic of Hosea. *You shall know:* not an abstract but a practical knowledge which means acknowledgment of God's will and obedience to his law (4:1; 5:4; 6:3, 6).

**3:1–5** Just as the Lord is ready to take Israel back, Hosea takes his wife back. She must undergo a period of purification, just as Israel must experience purification before the restoration of the covenant relationship.

**3:1** *Raisin cakes:* offerings to the fertility goddess Asherah, the female counterpart of Baal, cf. Jer 7:18; 44:19; Dn 14:5–8.

**3:2** Just as the Lord offered a new bride price to Israel (2:21–22), so Hosea offers a new bride price to his wife. He returns to her what he has taken away from her (2:5): "fifteen (shekels) of silver"; "a homer of barley," a unit of dry measurement, which according to the etymology means "a mule load"; and "a lethech of barley," which is a half-homer.

**3:4** Israel will lose its political and cultic institutions. *Sa-*

*cred pillar:* originally perhaps a phallic symbol, representing Baal. These were also used in Israelite worship (cf. notes on Gn 28:18; Ex 34:13). *Ephod:* an instrument used in consulting the deity (1 Sm 23:6–12; 30:7; cf. notes on Ex 28:6, 15–30). *Household gods:* in Hebrew, *teraphim;* images regarded as the tutelary deities of the household (Gn 31:19; Jgs 17:5; 18:14, 17–18).

**3:5** *David, their king:* the king belonging to the line of David who will restore the Israelite nation (Jer 23:5; Ez 34:23, 24). *The last days:* a future time of transformation.

**4:1–3** The introduction to the oracles (chaps. 4–11) which begin with "Hear the word of the Lord" (4:1) and end with "oracle of the Lord" (11:11).

**4:2** Similar to the decalogue (Ex 20:1–17; cf. Jer 7:9).

**4:4–6** Hosea is particularly severe with the priests in the Northern Kingdom who had led the way in the general apostasy from God's law. The prophets here associated with the priests (v. 5) were doubtless cult prophets; cf. Jer 2:8; 4:9–10; 6:13–14; 23:9–40.

---

**2:25** Rom 9:25–26; 1 Pt 2:10.
**3:5** Jer 30:9; Ez 34:23.
**4:1** Is 3:10–15; Mi 6:1–5.
**4:2** Ex 20:13–17.
**4:3** Is 24:4–7; Zep 1:2–3.

I will make an end of your mother.†

6 My people are ruined for lack of
    knowledge!
    Since you have rejected knowledge,
    I will reject you from serving as my
        priest;
    Since you have forgotten the law of your
        God,
    I will also forget your children.

7 The more they multiplied, the more they
        sinned against me,
    I will change their glory† into
        shame.*

8 They feed on the sin of my people,
    and are greedy for their iniquity.†

9 Like people, like priest:*
    I will punish them for their ways,
    and repay them for their deeds.

10 They will eat but not be satisfied,*
    they will promote prostitution† but
        not increase,
    Because they have abandoned the Lord,
        devoting themselves

11     to prostitution.
    Aged wine and new wine
        take away understanding.*

12 My people consult their piece of wood,†
    and their wand makes
        pronouncements for them,
    For the spirit of prostitution has led
        them astray;
    they prostitute themselves, forsaking
        their God.

13 On the mountaintops they offer sacrifice
    and on the hills they burn incense,

Beneath oak and poplar and terebinth,
    because of their pleasant shade.†
Therefore your daughters prostitute
    themselves,
    and your daughters-in-law commit
        adultery.

14 I will not punish your daughters for
    their prostitution,
    nor your daughters-in-law for their
        adultery,
    Because the men themselves consort
        with prostitutes,
    and with temple women† they offer
        sacrifice!
Thus a people without understanding
    comes to ruin.

15 Though you prostitute yourself, Israel,
    do not let Judah become guilty!
Do not come to Gilgal,†
    do not go up to Beth-aven,*
    do not swear, "As the Lord lives!"*

16 For like a stubborn cow,
    Israel is stubborn;
Will the Lord now pasture them,
    like lambs in a broad meadow?

17 Ephraim† is bound to idols,
    let him alone!

18† When their drinking is over,
    they give themselves to prostitution;*
    they love shame more than their
        honor.

19 A wind† has bound them up in its
    wings;*
    they shall be ashamed because of
        their altars.*

---

**4:5** *Your mother:* the one who gave life to the priest, understood here as an extension of the punishment to his whole family (Am 7:17), or "mother" taken as a metaphor for the community of Israel, of which the priest is a member (Hos 2:4).

**4:7** *Their glory:* possibly connoting "their children." See 9:11; Is 22:24. Or "Glory" may refer to the Lord in contrast to Ba'al. The Hebrew word for shame, *bosheth*, is often substituted for Ba'al in biblical names. See Ishbaal (Heb. *Ishbosheth,* 2 Sm 2:8, 10, 12, 15) and Meribaal (Heb. *Mephibosheth,* 2 Sm 9:6, 10–13).

**4:8** The priest receives part of the sacrifice (Lv 6:19; 7:7).

**4:10–11** *Prostitution:* often a synonym for idolatry. The covenant bond was symbolized as the relationship between husband and wife (see chaps. 1–2). Thus, abandoning the Lord for a foreign god was called prostitution or adultery.

**4:12** *Piece of wood:* a derogatory term for an idol. *Wand:* a sacred wooden object, perhaps some kind of staff, used for divination.

**4:13** The shrines on the "high places" typically had an altar, a grove of trees, and a stone pillar representing a god (Dt 12:2; Jer 2:20).

**4:14** *Temple women:* plural of Heb. *qedesha;* the exact import of the term is disputed. See notes on Gn 38:21 and Dt 23:18–19.

**4:15** *Gilgal:* close to Jericho (Jos 4:19–20; 5:2–9). *Beth-aven:* (lit., "house of iniquity") Hosea's derogatory term for the sanctuary of Bethel (lit., "house of God"), the major shrine of the Northern Kingdom (10:5, 8; cf. Am 5:5). *As the Lord lives:* a legitimate oath formula (1 Sm 26:10, 16), but unacceptable here because Israel is guilty of religious syncretism and the idolatrous worship of other gods.

**4:17** *Ephraim:* the name of one of the sons of Joseph, son of Jacob (Gn 41:52), also used to designate one of the tribes living in the heartland of the Northern Kingdom. Hosea often uses the name Ephraim to refer to the whole Northern Kingdom of Israel. During the latter part of his ministry, after the Assyrians occupied Galilee, Ephraim was all that remained of Israel.

**4:18** Cf. v. 11.

**4:19** *A wind:* (Heb. *ruah*), a metaphor for Israel's addiction to the Baal cult, which is nothing but wind, a "spirit (*ruah*) of prostitution" (v. 12).

---

4:7 Jer 2:11; Ps 106:20.      4:15 Am 8:14.
4:9 Is 24:2.      4:18 Am 2:8.
4:10 Mi 6:14.      4:19 Jer 4:11–12.
4:11 Is 28:7.      4:19 Is 1:29.
4:15 Am 4:4.

## Guilt of the Religious and Political Leaders

**5** [1] Hear this, priests,
   Pay attention, house of Israel,
Household of the king, give ear!*
   For you are responsible for
      judgment.†
But you have been a snare at Mizpah,†
   a net spread upon Tabor,
[2] a pit dug deep in Shittim.
   Now I will discipline them all.

[3] I know Ephraim,
   and Israel is not hidden from me:
Now, Ephraim, you have practiced
      prostitution,
   Israel is defiled.
[4] Their deeds do not allow them
   to return to their God;*
For the spirit of prostitution is in them,
   and they do not know the LORD.

[5] The arrogance of Israel bears witness
      against him;
   Israel and Ephraim stumble because
      of their iniquity,
   and Judah stumbles with them.
[6] With their flocks and herds they will go
   to seek the LORD, but will not find him;*
   he has withdrawn from them.
[7] They have betrayed the LORD,
   for they have borne illegitimate
      children;
Now the new moon† will devour them
   together with their fields.

## Political Upheavals†

[8] Blow the ram's horn in Gibeah,
   the trumpet in Ramah!

[9] Sound the alarm in Beth-aven:*
   "Look behind you, Benjamin!"†
Ephraim shall become a wasteland
   on the day of punishment:
Among the tribes of Israel
   I announce what is sure to be.
[10] The princes of Judah have become
   like those who move a boundary
      line;†*
Upon them I will pour out
   my wrath like water.
[11] Ephraim is oppressed, crushed by
      judgment,
   for he has willingly gone after filth!†
[12] I am like a moth for Ephraim,*
   like rot for the house of Judah.
[13] When Ephraim saw his infirmity,
   and Judah his sore,
Ephraim went to Assyria,
   and sent to the great king.†*
But he cannot heal you,
   nor take away your sore.
[14] For I am like a lion to Ephraim,
   like a young lion to the house of
      Judah;*
It is I who tear the prey and depart,
   I carry it away and no one can
      save it.*

## Insincere Conversion

[15] I will go back to my place
   until they make reparation
   and seek my presence.
In their affliction, they shall look
      for me.*

**6** [1] "Come, let us return to the LORD,*
For it is he who has torn, but he will
      heal us;

---

† **5:1** *For you...judgment*: possibly "for you are called to judgment."

**5:1–2** *Mizpah*: several places bear this name; the best known is in Benjamin (1 Sm 7:6, 16; 10:17). Perhaps this is a wordplay on *mishpat*, "justice," "judgment." *Tabor*: the mountain that dominates the valley of Jezreel. *Shittim*: in Transjordan, where Israel committed its first act of idolatry with the Baal of Peor (9:10; cf. Nm 25). At these three places the leaders had misled the people by an idolatrous cult or by an abuse of justice.

**5:7** *New moon*: normally a feast day of joy (2:13), but, because of infidelity, it will be a day of destruction.

**5:8–14** This passage describes political and military conflict between Judah and Israel. Perhaps some allusion is made to the Syro-Ephraimite war of 735–734 B.C., when a coalition of Arameans and Israelites attempted to dethrone the king of Judah (2 Kgs 16:5; Is 7:1–9). Judah repulsed the attempt with the aid of Assyria, and the latter devastated both Aram and Israel.

**5:8** A vision of invasion, from Gibeah and Ramah in northern Judah, into Israel.

**5:10** *Move a boundary line*: invasion by Judah (v. 8) is compared to a case of social injustice (Dt 19:14; 27:17; Prv 23:10–11).

**5:11** *Filth*: Ephraim's reliance on foreign nations and their gods.

**5:13** *Ephraim went...king*: in 738 the Israelite king Menahem had to pay tribute to the Assyrian king Tiglath-pileser III, whose vassal he became (2 Kgs 15:19–20). Under the threat of the Syro-Ephraimite invasion King Ahaz of Judah also submitted to Tiglath-pileser (2 Kgs 16:7–9). *Great king*: Heb. *melek-yarev*; may be a proper name: King Yarev, but unknown; or "the defender king": irony about the great king of Assyria (see note on 10:6).

---

**5:1** Mi 3:1.
**5:4** Jer 13:23.
**5:6** Is 55:6; Jer 29:13; Am 5:4–6; 8:12; Jn 7:34.
**5:8** Jer 4:5; Jl 2:1.
**5:10** Dt 19:14; 27:17.
**5:12** Is 50:9.
**5:13** 2 Kgs 15:19–20; 16:7–9.
**5:14** Is 5:29; Am 1:2; 3:12.
**5:14** Dt 32:39.
**5:15** Jer 29:13; Ps 78:34.
**6:1** Lam 3:40.

he has struck down, but he will bind
    our wounds.
2 He will revive us after two days;
    on the third day† he will raise us up,*
    to live in his presence.
3 Let us know, let us strive to know the
    LORD;
    as certain as the dawn is his coming.
He will come to us like the rain,
    like spring rain that waters the earth."*

4 What can I do with you, Ephraim?
    What can I do with you, Judah?
Your loyalty is like morning mist,
    like the dew that disappears early.
5 For this reason I struck them down
    through the prophets,
    I killed them by the words of my
    mouth;†*
    my judgment shines forth like the light.
6 For it is loyalty that I desire, not sacrifice,
    and knowledge of God rather than
    burnt offerings.*

## Further Crimes of Israel

7 But they, at Adam,† violated the covenant;
    there they betrayed me.

8 Gilead† is a city of evildoers,
    tracked with blood.
9 Like brigands lying in wait
    is the band of priests.
They murder on the road to Shechem,†
    indeed they commit a monstrous
    crime.
10 In the house of Israel I have seen a
    horrible thing:
    there is found Ephraim's prostitution,
    Israel is defiled.
11 For you also, Judah,
    a harvest† has been appointed!

**7** When I would have restored the fortunes
    of my people,
1 when I would have healed Israel,
The guilt of Ephraim was revealed,
    the wickedness of Samaria:
    They practiced falsehood.
Thieves break in,
    bandits roam outside.
2 Yet they do not call to mind
    that I remember all their
    wickedness.*
Now their crimes surround them,
    present to my sight.*

## Israel's Domestic Politics†

3 With their wickedness they make the
    king rejoice,
    the princes too, with their treacherous
    deeds.
4 They are all adulterers,†
    like a blazing oven,
Which the baker quits stoking,
    after the dough's kneading until its
    rising.
5 On the day of our king,
    they made the princes sick with
    poisoned wine;
    he extended his hand to the scoffers.
6 For they draw near in ambush
    with their hearts like an oven.
All the night their anger sleeps;
    in the morning it flares like a blazing
    fire.
7 They are all heated like ovens,
    and consume their rulers.
All their kings have fallen;
    none of them calls upon me.

## Israel's Foreign Politics

8 Ephraim is mixed with the nations,†
    Ephraim is an unturned cake.

---

6:2 *After two days; on the third day*: presumptuous Israel expects that soon God will renew them (cf. Ez 37).
6:5 The word of God proclaimed by the prophets is effective, it accomplished what it promised: punishment.
6:7 *At Adam*: the violation of the covenant at Adam is mentioned nowhere else in the Bible. The place Adam, the location of which is unknown, may be referred to in Jos 3:16.
6:8 *Gilead*: city in Transjordan (Gn 31:46–48; 2 Kgs 15:25).
6:9 *Shechem*: an important ancient religious and political center (Jos 24).
6:11 *Harvest*: God's judgment, when Judah will reap what it has sown.
7:3–7 This passage perhaps refers to a conspiracy at the royal court. Between the death of Jeroboam II (743 B.C.) and the fall of Samaria (722/721), nearly all the kings were murdered (2 Kgs 15:10, 14, 25, 30).

7:4 *Adulterers*: the unfaithful nobles who kill the king. Their passion is compared to the fire of the oven. The point of the metaphor is that, like this oven whose fire is always ready to blaze up again, the conspirators are always ready for rebellion.
7:8 *Is mixed with the nations*: the people reject exclusive allegiance to the Lord, and they now try to find their salvation in alliances with foreign nations. *An unturned cake*: burnt on one side, but not baked at all on the other, and thus worthless.

---

6:2 Lk 24:7, 46; 1 Cor
    15:4.
6:3 Dt 11:14; Ps 72:6.
6:5 Is 11:4; 49:2; Jer 5:14;
    Heb 4:12–13.
6:6 1 Sm 15:22; Am
    5:22–24; Mi 6:6–8;
    12:7.
    Eccl 4:17; Mt 9:13;
7:2 Ps 10:11.
7:2 Prv 5:21–22.

9    Strangers have consumed his strength,
        but he does not know it;*
     Gray hairs are strewn on his head,
        but he takes no notice of it.
10   The arrogance of Israel bears witness
        against him;
     yet they do not return to the LORD,
        their God,
     nor seek him, despite all this.*
11   Ephraim is like a dove,
        silly and senseless;
     They call upon Egypt,
        they go to Assyria.
12   When they go I will spread my net
        around them,
     like birds in the air I will bring them
        down.*
     I will chastise them when I hear of
        their assembly.
13   Woe to them, for they have strayed from
        me!
     Ruin to them, for they have rebelled
        against me!
     Though I wished to redeem them,
        they spoke lies against me.
14   They have not cried to me from their
        hearts
     when they wailed upon their beds;
     For wheat and wine they lacerated
        themselves;†
     they rebelled against me.
15   Though I trained and strengthened their
        arms,
     yet they devised evil against me.
16   They have again become useless,
        they have been like a treacherous
        bow.*
     Their princes shall fall by the sword
        because of the insolence of their
        tongues;
     thus they shall be mocked in the land
        of Egypt.

## Corruption of Cult, Domestic and Foreign Politics

**8** 1 Put the trumpet to your lips!*
     One like an eagle† is over the house
        of the LORD!
     Because they have violated my covenant,
        and rebelled against my law,
2    They cry out to me,
        "My God! We know you!"
3    But Israel has rejected what is good;
        the enemy† shall pursue him.

4†   They made kings, but not by my
        authority;
     they established princes, but without
        my knowledge.
     With their silver and gold
        they made idols for themselves,
        to their own destruction.
5    He has rejected your calf,† Samaria!*
     My wrath is kindled against them;
     How long will they be incapable of
        innocence
        in Israel?
6    An artisan made it,
        it is no god at all.*
     The calf of Samaria
        will be dashed to pieces.

7    When they sow the wind,
        they will reap the whirlwind;*
     The stalk of grain that forms no head
        can yield no flour;
     Even if it could,
        strangers would swallow it.
8    Israel is swallowed up;
        now they are among the nations,
        like a useless vessel.
9    For they went up to Assyria—†
        a wild ass off on its own—
        Ephraim bargained for lovers.*

---

† **7:14** *Lacerated themselves*: a ritual to obtain a good harvest from Baal (2:7–10; 1 Kgs 18:28; Jer 16:6; 41:5). This practice was forbidden (Lv 19:28; Dt 14:1).

**8:1** *Eagle*: perhaps an image for Tiglath-pileser III of Assyria, who overran the land of Israel in 733 B.C. (Jer 48:40; 49:22; Ez 17:3).

**8:3** *Enemy*: Assyria.

**8:4** Hosea is not against the monarchy, but against the conspiracies at the royal court (see note on 7:3–7). The king should be chosen by God (1 Kgs 19:15–16).

**8:5** *Calf*: a cultic object introduced by Jeroboam I after the separation of the Northern Kingdom from the Southern Kingdom (1 Kgs 12:26–30; cf. Ex 32).

**8:9** *They went up to Assyria*: a reference to the politics of appealing to Assyria (cf. 5:13; 7:11). There is a play on the Hebrew word for "wild ass" (*pere*) and "Ephraim."

---

**7:9** Jer 5:3; Rev 3:17.
**7:10** Is 9:12; Am 4:6.
**7:12** Ez 12:13; 32:3.
**7:16** Ps 78:57.
**8:1** Jl 2:1.
**8:5** 1 Kgs 12:28.

**8:6** Ex 20:4; 34:17; Is 40:19–20; 44:9–20; Jer 10:1–16.
**8:7** Jb 4:8; Prv 22:8; 2 Cor 9:6; Gal 6:7–8.
**8:9** Ez 16:32–34.

10 Even though they bargain with the
        nations,
     I will now gather them† together;
   They will soon succumb
        under the burden of king and princes.

11† When Ephraim made many altars to
        expiate sin,
     they became altars for sinning.
12 Though I write for him my many
        instructions,
     they are considered like a stranger's.
13 They love sacrifice,
     they sacrifice meat and eat it,
     but the LORD is not pleased with them.*
   Now he will remember their guilt
     and punish their sins;*
     they shall return to Egypt.†*
14 Israel has forgotten his maker*
     and has built palaces.
   Judah, too, has fortified many cities,
     but I will send fire upon his cities,
     to devour their strongholds.*

### From Days of Celebration to Days of Punishment

**9** ¹ Do not rejoice, Israel,
        do not exult like the nations!
   For you have prostituted yourself,
        abandoning your God,
        loving a prostitute's fee
        upon every threshing floor.†
2 Threshing floor and wine press will not
        nourish them,
     the new wine will fail them.

3 They will not dwell in the LORD's land;
     Ephraim will return to Egypt,
     and in Assyria they will eat unclean
        food.

4 They will not pour libations of wine to
        the LORD,
     and their sacrifices will not please
        him.
   Their bread will be like mourners'
        bread,†*
     that makes unclean all who eat of it;
   Their food will be for their own
        appetites;
     it cannot enter the house of the
        LORD.

5 What will you do on the festival day,
     the day of the LORD's feast?†
6† When they flee from the devastation,
     Egypt will gather them, Memphis will
        bury them.
   Weeds will overgrow their silver
        treasures,
     and thorns, their tents.

7 They have come, the days of
        punishment!
     they have come, the days of
        recompense!
   Let Israel know it!
     "The prophet is a fool,*
     the man of the spirit is mad!"
   Because your iniquity is great,
     great, too, is your hostility.
8† The watchman of Ephraim, the people
        of my God, is the prophet;*
     yet a fowler's snare is on all his
        ways,
     hostility in the house of his God.
9 They have sunk to the depths of
        corruption,
     as in the days of Gibeah;†*
   God will remember their iniquity
     and punish their sins.

---

†
**8:10** *I will now gather them*: for judgment and for deportation.

**8:11** The altars had become places of self-serving worship (cf. v. 13).

**8:13** *Return to Egypt*: to punish their violation of the covenant they will experience a reversal of the exodus.

**9:1** *Threshing floor*: an allusion to harvest festivals in honor of Baal, to whom the Israelites had attributed the fertility of the land; cf. 2:7.

**9:4** *Mourners' bread*: bread eaten at funeral rites (Dt 26:14). The presence of a corpse also made all food prepared in that house unclean (Jer 16:5–7).

**9:5** *The LORD's feast*: probably the important autumn feast of Booths, the most important of the Israelite public celebrations (Lv 23:34).

**9:6** Instead of gathering for celebration (v. 5), they will be

gathered for death. *Memphis*: known for the monumental pyramid tombs. *Silver treasures*: the silver statues of Baal (8:4).

**9:8** Prophets, like Hosea himself, are called to be sentinels for Israel, warning Israel of God's coming wrath (see Ez 3:17; 33:7), but often meet rejection.

**9:9** *The days of Gibeah*: the precise allusion is not clear. Perhaps it is a reference to the outrage committed at Gibeah in the days of the judges (Jgs 19–21), or to questions surrounding Saul's kingship at Gibeah (1 Sm 10:26; 14:2; 22:6).

---

*
| | |
|---|---|
| **8:13** Am 5:22. | 2:2, 5. |
| **8:13** Jer 14:10. | **9:4** Dt 26:14. |
| **8:13** Dt 28:68. | **9:7** 2 Kgs 9:11; Jn 10:20. |
| **8:14** Dt 32:15, 18; Is | **9:8** Jer 6:17; Ez 3:17; |
| 51:13. | 33:2, 6, 7. |
| **8:14** Am 1:7, 10, 12, 14; | **9:9** Jgs 19–21. |

HOS

## From Former Glory to a History of Corruption

10 Like grapes in the desert,
　I found Israel;
Like the first fruits of the fig tree, its first
　　to ripen,*
　I looked on your ancestors.
But when they came to Baal-peor† *
　and consecrated themselves to the
　　Shameful One,
　they became as abhorrent as the thing
　　they loved.

11 Ephraim is like a bird:
　their glory flies away—
no birth, no pregnancy, no
　　conception.*

12 Even though they bring up their children,
　I will make them childless, until no
　　one is left.
Indeed, woe to them
　when I turn away from them!

13 Ephraim, as I saw, was a tree
　planted in a meadow;
But now Ephraim will bring out
　his children to the slaughterer!

14 Give them, Lord!
　give them what?
Give them a miscarrying womb,
　and dry breasts!*

15 All their misfortune began in Gilgal;†
　yes, there I rejected them.
Because of their wicked deeds
　I will drive them out of my house.
I will love them no longer;
　all their princes are rebels.

16† Ephraim is stricken,
　their root is dried up;*
　they will bear no fruit.*
Were they to bear children,
　I would slay the beloved of their
　　womb.

17 My God will disown them
　because they have not listened to
　　him;
　they will be wanderers among the
　　nations.*

## Destruction of Idolatrous Cultic Objects

**10** 1* Israel is a luxuriant vine
　whose fruit matches its growth.
The more abundant his fruit,
　the more altars he built;
The more productive his land,
　the more sacred pillars† he set up.

2 Their heart is false!
　Now they will pay for their guilt:
God will break down their altars
　and destroy their sacred pillars.

3 For now they will say,
　"We have no king!†
Since we do not fear the Lord,
　the king—what could he do for us?"

4 They make promises,
　swear false oaths, and make
　　covenants,
While lawsuits sprout
　like poisonous weeds† in the furrows
　　of a field!

5 The inhabitants of Samaria are afraid
　for the calf of Beth-aven;†
Its people mourn for it
　and its idolatrous priests wail over it,
　—over its glory which has departed
　　from it.*

6 It too will be carried to Assyria,
　as an offering to the great king.† *
Ephraim will be put to shame,
　Israel will be shamed by his
　　schemes.

7 Samaria and her king will disappear,
　like a twig upon the waters.

---

† **9:10** *Baal-peor:* where the Israelites consecrated themselves for the first time to Baal (Nm 25; see note on Hos 5:1–2). Baal is here called the Shameful One.
**9:15** *Gilgal:* possibly a reference to Saul's disobedience to Samuel (1 Sm 13:7–14; 15), or to the idolatry practiced in that place (see note on Hos 4:15).
**9:16** Wordplay on the Hebrew word for "fruit" (*peri*) and Ephraim (see note on 8:9). The whole passage (vv. 10–17) presents a reversal of Ephraim's name (Gn 41:52). He will have no fruit, a condition which will result in extinction.
**10:1** *Sacred pillars:* see note on 3:4.
**10:3** *No king:* the instability of the monarchy (7:3–7) and its vassalage to foreign kings (7:8–16) render the monarchy ineffective. The kings do the opposite of what they are supposed

to do (10:4).
**10:4** *Lawsuits…like poisonous weeds:* the administration of justice, which should have been the mainstay of the people, has in corrupt hands become another instrument of oppression; cf. Am 6:12.
**10:5** *The calf of Beth-aven:* see note on 4:15.
**10:6** *The great king:* a title used by the Assyrian kings. See also note on 5:13.

---

| | |
|---|---|
| **9:10** Is 28:4; Jer 2:2. | **9:17** Gn 4:12, 14; Dt |
| **9:10** Nm 25. | 28:64–65. |
| **9:11** Dt 28:18. | **10:1** Is 5:1–7. |
| **9:14** Jb 3:11–12; Lk 23:29. | **10:5** 1 Sm 4:21–22. |
| **9:16** Am 2:9. | **10:6** Am 5:27. |
| **9:16** Mt 21:19. | |

8 The high places of Aven† will be
   destroyed,
      the sin of Israel;
   thorns and thistles will overgrow their
      altars.
   Then they will cry out to the mountains,
      "Cover us!"
   and to the hills, "Fall upon us!"*

## War Because of Israel's Wickedness

9 Since the days of Gibeah*
      you have sinned, Israel.
   There they took their stand;
      will war not reach them in Gibeah?
   Against a perverse people
10    I came and I chastised them;
   Peoples will be gathered against them
      when I bind them to their two crimes.†
11 Ephraim was a trained heifer,
      that loved to thresh;
   I myself laid a yoke
      upon her beautiful neck;
   I will make Ephraim break ground,
         Judah must plow,
      Jacob must harrow for himself:
12 "Sow for yourselves justice,
      reap the reward of loyalty;
   Break up for yourselves a new field,*
      for it is time to seek the LORD,
      till he comes and rains justice upon
         you."*
13 But you have plowed wickedness,
      reaped perversity,
      and eaten the fruit of falsehood.
   Because you have trusted in your own
         power,
      and in your many warriors,*
14 The clamor of war shall break out
         among your people
      and all your fortresses shall be ravaged
   As Salman ravaged Beth-arbel† on the
         day of war,

smashing mothers along with their
      children.*
15 So it will be done to you, Bethel,
      because of your utter wickedness:
   At dawn† the king of Israel
      will utterly disappear.

## The Disappointment of a Parent

# 11

¹† When Israel was a child I loved
      him,*
   out of Egypt† I called my son.*
2 The more I called them,
      the farther they went from me,
   Sacrificing to the Baals
      and burning incense to idols.
3 Yet it was I who taught Ephraim to walk,
      who took them in my arms;*
      but they did not know that I cared for
         them.
4 I drew them with human cords,
      with bands of love;†
   I fostered them like those
      who raise an infant to their cheeks;
      I bent down to feed them.*
5 He shall return to the land of Egypt,*
      Assyria shall be his king,
      because they have refused to repent.
6 The sword shall rage in his cities:
      it shall destroy his diviners,
      and devour them because of their
         schemings.
7 My people have their mind set on
         apostasy;
      though they call on God in unison,
      he shall not raise them up.

## But Love Is Stronger and Restores

8 How could I give you up, Ephraim,
      or deliver you up, Israel?
   How could I treat you as Admah,
      or make you like Zeboiim?†*

---

**10:8** *Aven:* wickedness, first of all at Bethel (v. 5), but also at all the high places.
**10:10** *Two crimes:* the allusion is not clear; a possible reference is the outrage described in Jgs 19.
**10:14** *As Salman ravaged Beth-arbel:* perhaps Salamanu, king of Moab, mentioned in an inscription of Tiglath-pileser III, after an invasion in Gilead (Transjordan), where there was a Beth-arbel, close to present Irbid.
**10:15** *At dawn:* normally the moment of God's victory over Israel's enemies, and thus his salvation (Is 17:14; Ps 46:6). Here it is a reversal of this expectation.
**11:1–3** After the image of husband-wife (chaps. 1–3), Hosea uses the image of parent-child (chaps. 11; 3:19).
**11:1** *Out of Egypt:* Hosea dates the real beginning of Israel from the time of the exodus. Mt 2:15 applies this text to the re-

turn of Jesus from Egypt.
**11:4** *I drew them…with bands of love:* perhaps a reversal of the yoke imagery of the previous chapter, i.e., not forcing them like draft animals, but drawing them with kindness and affection.
**11:8** *Admah…Zeboiim:* cities in the vicinity of Sodom and Gomorrah (Gn 14:2, 8) and destroyed with them (Gn 19:24–25; Dt 29:22).

---

* —
**10:8** Is 2:10, 19; Lk 23:30;          **11:1** Dt 7:8; 10:15; Jer
   Rev 6:16.                                   2:1–9.
**10:9** Jgs 19–21.                      **11:1** Ex 4:22; Mt 2:15.
**10:12** Jer 4:3.                        **11:3** Dt 1:31; 8:5.
**10:12** Is 45:8; Jl 2:23.               **11:4** Dt 8:16.
**10:13** Is 31:1.                        **11:5** Dt 17:16.
**10:14** Ps 137:9; Am 1:13.              **11:8** Dt 29:22.

My heart is overwhelmed,
    my pity is stirred.
9   I will not give vent to my blazing anger,
        I will not destroy Ephraim again;
    For I am God and not a man,*
        the Holy One present among you;
    I will not come in wrath.
10  They shall follow the LORD,
        who roars like a lion;*
    When he roars,
        his children shall come frightened
            from the west,
11  Out of Egypt they shall come trembling,
        like birds,
    like doves, from the land of Assyria;
    And I will resettle them in their homes,
        oracle of the LORD.

### Infidelity of Israel†

**12** ¹Ephraim has surrounded me with
        lies,
    the house of Israel, with deceit;
    Judah still wanders about with gods,
        and is faithful to holy ones.†
²†  Ephraim shepherds the wind,
        and pursues the east wind all day
            long.
    He multiplies lies and violence:
        They make a covenant with Assyria,
        and oil is carried to Egypt.

³   The LORD has a dispute with Judah,
        and will punish Jacob† for his
            conduct,
    and repay him for his deeds.
4   In the womb he supplanted his
        brother,*
    and in his vigor he contended with a
        divine being;
5   He contended with an angel and
        prevailed,*
    he wept and entreated him.
    At Bethel he met with him,
        and there he spoke with him.*

6   The LORD is the God of hosts,
        the LORD is his name!*
7   You must return to your God.
    Maintain loyalty and justice
        and always hope in your God.

8   A merchant who holds a false balance,
        he loves to extort!
9   Ephraim has said,
        "How rich I have become;
        I have made a fortune!"*
    All his gain will not suffice
        for the guilt of his sin.
10  I the LORD have been your God,
        since the land of Egypt;*
    I will again have you live in tents,
        as on feast days.
11  I spoke to the prophets,
        I granted many visions,*
    and through the prophets I told
        parables.
12  In Gilead is falsehood, they have come
        to nothing;
    in Gilgal they sacrifice bulls,
    But their altars are like heaps of stones*
        in the furrows of the field.

13  Jacob fled to the land of Aram,
        and Israel served for a wife;
    for a wife he tended sheep.*
14  But by a prophet† the LORD brought
        Israel out of Egypt,
    and by a prophet Israel was tended.*
15  Ephraim has aroused bitter anger,
        so his Lord shall cast his bloodguilt
            upon him
    and repay him for his scorn.

### The Death of Ephraim

**13** ¹When Ephraim spoke there was
        terror;
    he was exalted in Israel;†
    but he became guilty through Baal
        and died.

---

† **12:1–15** This chapter draws a parallel between the history of Israel and events in the life of Jacob-Israel, the ancestor.
**12:1** An attack on the idolatry of both kingdoms, Israel and Judah. *Holy ones*: subordinate gods, members of the divine council.
**12:2** Hosea frequently condemns the alliances with Assyria and Egypt, the two world powers (7:8–16).
**12:3** *Jacob*: whose name was changed to Israel (Gn 35:10).
**12:14** *A prophet*: Moses.
**13:1** *Exalted in Israel*: Ephraim enjoyed a privileged position in Israel (Gn 48:14–19).

**11:9** Nm 23:19; Is 31:3; Ez 28:2.
**11:10** Jl 4:16; Am 1:2; Jer 25:30.
**12:4** Gn 25:26; 27:35–36.
**12:5** Gn 32:25–30.
**12:5** Gn 28:12–19; 35:15.
**12:6** Ex 3:15; Am 4:13.
**12:9** Rev 3:17.
**12:10** Ex 20:2.
**12:11** Ps 74:9.
**12:12** Gn 31:45–54; Jos 4–5.
**12:13** Gn 28:5; 29:15–30; 30:31.
**12:14** Ex 3:7–10; Dt 18:18.

2 Now they continue to sin,
   making for themselves molten images,
Silver idols according to their skill,*
   all of them the work of artisans.
"To these, offer sacrifice," they say.
   People kiss calves!†*
3 Therefore, they will be like a morning
      cloud
   or like the dew that vanishes with the
      dawn,
Like chaff storm-driven from the
      threshing floor*
   or like smoke out of the window.

4 I, the LORD, am your God,
   since the land of Egypt;†*
Gods apart from me you do not know;
   there is no savior but me.*
5 I fed you in the wilderness,
   in the parched land.
6 When I fed them, they were satisfied;
   when satisfied, they became proud,
   therefore they forgot me.
7 So, I will be like a lion to them,
   like a leopard by the road I will keep
      watch.
8* I will attack them like a bear robbed of
      its young,
   and tear their hearts from their breasts;
I will devour them on the spot like a
      lion,
   as a wild animal would rip them
      open.

9† I destroy you, Israel!
   who is there to help you?
10 Where now is your king,
   that he may rescue you?
And all your princes,
   that they may defend you?

Of whom you said,
   "Give me a king and princes"?*
11 I give you a king in my anger,
   and I take him away in my wrath.†
12 The guilt of Ephraim is wrapped up,
   his sin is stored away.
13† The birth pangs will come for him,*
   but this is an unwise child,
Who, when it is time, does not present
      himself
   at the mouth of the womb.*
14† Shall I deliver them from the power of
      Sheol?
   shall I redeem them from death?
Where are your plagues, O death!
   where is your sting, Sheol!*
   Compassion is hidden from my eyes.

15 Though Ephraim† may flourish among
      his brothers,
   an east wind* will come, a wind from
      the LORD,
   rising from the wilderness,
That will dry up his spring,
   and leave his fountain dry.
It will loot his treasury
   of every precious thing.

# 14
1 Samaria† has become guilty,
for she has rebelled against her God.
They shall fall by the sword,
   their infants shall be dashed to pieces,*
   their pregnant women shall be ripped
      open.*

## Sincere Conversion and New Life

2 Return, Israel, to the LORD, your God;
   you have stumbled because of your
      iniquity.

---

**13:2** *Kiss calves:* apparently a reference to a ritual gesture associated with the worship of Baal represented as a calf (1 Kgs 19:18).

**13:4** *I, the* LORD…*land of Egypt:* according to 1 Kgs 12:28, Jeroboam introduced the calves used in the worship at the sanctuaries in Bethel and Dan with the words: "Here are your gods, O Israel, who brought you up from the land of Egypt."

**13:9–10** Only God can save Israel, not the king, whom Israel had requested from the Lord (1 Sm 8:1–9).

**13:11** *I give you a king…in my wrath:* the Lord punished the people of the Northern Kingdom by giving them kings who were soon deposed (see notes on 7:3–7 and 8:4).

**13:13** Ephraim will die along with its stored-up sin, just as a mother dies along with a child that she cannot deliver.

**13:14** God calls upon "death" and "Sheol" to send their auxiliaries, "plagues" and "sting," to punish Israel (Hb 3:5; Ps 91:6). Paul uses this text in a different way to speak about the victory

over death (1 Cor 15:54–55).

**13:15** Although "Ephraim" is not explicitly mentioned in the text (the Hebrew text has the word "he"), the wordplay with the Hebrew word for "flourish" (*yaphri*) suggests the use of "Ephraim" in the translation. *Wind:* possibly Assyria.

**14:1** *Samaria:* the capital of the Northern Kingdom will fall; this is the punishment predicted for Ephraim, the Northern Kingdom.

---

**13:2** Is 40:19–20; 44:9–20.    **13:13** Is 26:17–18; Jer 6:24;
**13:2** 1 Kgs 19:18.                                 22:23.
**13:3** Is 17:13; Zep 2:2; Ps    **13:13** Is 37:3.
      1:4.                            **13:14** 1 Cor 15:55.
**13:4** Ex 20:2.                **13:15** Ez 19:12.
**13:4** Is 43:11.              **14:1** Ps 137:9.
**13:8** 2 Sm 17:8.            **14:1** Am 1:13.
**13:10** 1 Sm 8:5.

HOS

3     Take with you words,
        and return to the LORD;
      Say to him, "Forgive all iniquity,
        and take what is good.
      Let us offer the fruit of our lips.*

4†    Assyria will not save us,
        nor will we mount horses;*
      We will never again say, 'Our god,'
        to the work of our hands;
      for in you the orphan finds
          compassion."*

5     I will heal their apostasy,
      I will love them freely;
        for my anger is turned away from
          them.

6     I will be like the dew for Israel:*
        he will blossom like the lily;
      He will strike root like the Lebanon
          cedar,

7        and his shoots will go forth.*
      His splendor will be like the olive tree
        and his fragrance like Lebanon cedar.*

8     Again they will live in his shade;
        they will raise grain,
      They will blossom like the vine,
        and his renown will be like the wine
          of Lebanon.

9     Ephraim! What more have I to do with
          idols?*
      I have humbled him, but I will take
          note of him.
      I am like a verdant cypress tree.†
      From me fruit will be found for
          you!

## Epilogue

10†   Who is wise enough to understand these
          things?*
      Who is intelligent enough to know
          them?
      Straight are the paths of the LORD,*
        the just walk in them,*
      but sinners stumble in them.

---

† **14:4** These good intentions promise a reversal of Israel's sins: no more reliance on "Assyria," i.e., on foreign alliances (see notes on 8:9 and 12:2), on "horses," i.e., on human power (10:13), and on idolatry (8:4–6; 13:2). Israel will trust in the Lord alone.

**14:9** *Verdant cypress tree*: the symbol of lasting life, the opposite of the sacred trees of the Baal cult (4:13). The Lord provides the "fruit" (*peri*) to Israel (2:7, 10), another instance of the wordplay on Ephraim (see notes on 9:16 and 13:15).

**14:10** A challenge to the reader in the style of the wisdom literature.

---

* 
| | |
|---|---|
| **14:3** Heb 13:15. | **14:9** 2 Cor 6:16. |
| **14:4** Is 31:1. | **14:10** Ps 107:43; Jer 9:11; |
| **14:4** Lam 5:3. | Eccl 8:1. |
| **14:6** Is 26:19. | **14:10** Dt 32:4. |
| **14:7** Is 27:6. | **14:10** Dt 8:6; 11:22; Mi 6:8. |
| **14:7** Sg 4:11. | |

# The Book of

# Joel

## INTRODUCTION

### Michael D. Guinan, OFM

Joel appears as the second of the Minor (i.e., shorter) Prophets (also known as the Book of the Twelve). The name "Joel" (Hebrew: "Yahweh is God") is common in the Old Testament, appearing more than a dozen times. The prophet is the "son of Pethuel" (Jl 1:1) and that is all that is known about him. Because the author shows deep concern for and appreciation of the Temple, its priests, and its worship (e.g., 1:8–9, 13–14; 2:12–13, 17; 4:18), some scholars conjecture that Joel may have been a priest or other cultic functionary.

In the Hebrew tradition, the book is divided into four chapters, but in the Greek tradition, only three. The five verses that make up ch. 3 in the Hebrew are attached to the end of ch. 2 as Jl 2:28–32. Chapter 3 in the Greek is identical to chapter 4 in the Hebrew. The NABRE reflects the Hebrew text and divides the book into four chapters.

The message of the book falls into two sections, Jl 1:2–2:17 and 2:18–4:21. Part one describes a major locust plague that has devastated the land of Judah. There are lamentations and calls to repentance. Part two describes how God responds with assurances of restoration and vindication for Judah before its enemies. More concisely, the book presents disaster followed by hope. Earlier scholars tended to view the book as a collection of diverse pieces, but more recently, scholars see it as presenting a unity of language, style, and theology.

## Part One: Disaster (Jl 1:2–2:17)

**Joel 1:2–14.** The prophet calls on "elders" (leaders) and all the people to remember the dire calamity brought by the locusts. The four terms for locusts (1:4) could represent different

### Outline of Joel

I. **Announcement of Unprecedented Disaster (1:2–20)**

II. **The Day of the Lord (2:1–27)**

III. **The Lord's Final Judgment (3:1–4:21)**

species or successive waves of locusts. These are compared to invading armies or ravening lions (1:6–7). Different groups are called to lament: drunkards (1:5), priests (1:9, 14), farmers (1:10–11), and vinedressers (1:11). In the literary form known as a "lament," the speaker cries out to God, describes the situation, and asks for God's help. In this example, the four groups that Joel addresses are repeatedly urged to wail (Hebrew: *helil*) and to fast (1:5, 8, 11, 13–14). The farmlands and the vineyards are devastated; food and drink necessary both for life and for offerings in the Temple are gone (1:7, 9–12). Such great suffering would easily be seen as punishment for sin; this is not explicit here, but will be in what follows (2:12–14). Nowhere, however, is any explicit sin mentioned.

**Joel 1:15–20.** The description of the suffering merges with imagery of the day of the Lord. This important theme appears five times in the book (1:15; 2:1, 11; 3:4; 4:14). The day of the Lord seems to have originally referred to the day in which Yahweh gives Israel victory over its enemies. However, beginning with Amos (Am 5:18–20), Israel and Judah themselves can become enemies of Yahweh and therefore suffer punishment and defeat. The animals too add their voices and groan (lament) and cry out to God (Jl 1:18, 20).

**Joel 2:1–11.** The description of the day of

the Lord, heightened in language reminiscent of the storm theophany motif, which sees the presence of God in darkness, thick clouds, and thunder (the voice of the Lord), forms a frame or *inclusio* around this section (2:2, 10–11). In between, the locust invasion is described as God's army bringing ruin and devastation.

**Joel 2:12–17.** The previous terrifying scene is followed immediately by the Lord ("oracle of the LORD," 2:12) calling the people to repent ("return to me") with fasting, weeping, and mourning. Joel reminds the people, in words recalling Ex 34:6, that God is indeed gracious and merciful (Jl 2:13–14). A great fast is proclaimed (this text is now part of the liturgy for Ash Wednesday). Even those usually excused from worship assemblies—the elderly, infants, and the newly married—are called to gather and pray that God forgive them (2:16–17). Why should they become a disgrace so that the nations will make fun of both them and their God (2:17)? In the ancient world of the Bible, experience of shame was a source of great suffering.

# Part Two: Hope (Jl 2:18–4:21)

**Joel 2:18–27.** The Lord relents and removes their disgrace. The dead locusts, with their stench (2:20), will be removed; the land, animals, and the children of Zion will again rejoice (2:21–24). The work of the locusts (compare 2:25 and 1:4) will be reversed. Instead of wailing (*helil*), the people will praise (*hillel*) (2:26). Twice it is said, "my people will never again be put to shame" (2:26–27).

**Joel 3:1–2.** The scene shifts to the distant future. The gift of God's spirit, previously reserved to special leaders or prophets, will be poured out (using water imagery) on all flesh (weak human beings) with no distinctions of gender, age, or class (3:1–2). The early church will see this fulfilled at Pentecost (Acts 2:17–21).

**Joel 3:3–4:27.** The cosmic day of the Lord returns, but with a double aspect: vindication for Judah and punishment for the nations. The day of the Lord, with its cosmic dimensions, appears in 3:3–5 and 4:15–21 (another *inclusio*) and assures Judah of restoration and safety. In between, Judah's enemies are gathered in the Valley of Jehoshaphat ("Yahweh judges") and the Valley of Decision, symbolic places (4:2, 12, 14), for judgment and punishment. Their weapons will be useless against God (4:10). The Lord dwells in Zion and that is the basis of Judah's hope. The language and imagery of chs. 3–4 are moving in the direction of apocalyptic literature.

Most scholars today, for a variety of reasons, see the book of Joel as coming from the postexilic period, perhaps between 450 and 350 BCE. It is now located, however, between Hosea and Amos, both eighth-century prophets who preached in and to the northern kingdom of Israel. In this context, the sin, unnamed in Joel, could be the infidelities manifested in Hosea, and the punishment of the nations, which ends Joel, would be continued in Am 1:3–2:16. And Jl 4:16 appears almost verbatim in Am 1:2. Coming near the beginning of the Book of the Twelve, Joel's call to repentance, the stress on the day of the Lord, and the promises of restoration and the removal of foreign enemies will echo throughout the rest of the books. ∎

# THE BOOK OF JOEL

## New American Bible, Introduction

In the two speeches that make up this book, Joel uses an agricultural crisis to measure his audience's knowledge of its God, warn them of a worse disaster if they ignore his preaching, and express his conviction that all faithful Judahites would someday enjoy a secure future. Although the superscription, or title (1:1), does not place Joel's preaching or the book's composition in a specific historical context, internal evidence favors a postexilic date for its composition, probably 450–400 B.C. This evidence includes: Joel's reliance on an established, possibly written, prophetic tradition; the existence of an organized temple liturgy; the dominance of priests and the absence of a king; and vocabulary characteristic of later material like Chronicles and Zechariah.

Inadequate winter rains and a spring locust infestation have devastated Judah's grain fields, vineyards, and orchards. Because the people carry on with business as usual, unaware that this crisis is the work of the Lord in their midst, Joel fears that the Lord may soon deliver a death blow by withholding the rains that normally fall in the late autumn. However, Joel's efforts to avert this crisis are successful. The first speech ends with Joel's assurance that at the end of the next agricultural year the people will enjoy a superabundant harvest.

The second speech begins with a summary description (chap. 3) of the prophet's hope that Judah's God will one day destroy its enemies and make Jerusalem secure once and for all. This divine intervention will create a more inclusive community, cutting across boundaries of gender, class, and age. In Peter's first public speech at Pentecost (Acts 2:16–21), the author uses Jl 3:1–5 to announce the formation of such a community among Christians in Jerusalem and the proximity of the day of the Lord. The rest of Joel's second speech (chap. 4) uses the imagery of drought and locusts from the first speech and introduces the metaphor of a grape harvest and wine making to describe the attack of the Lord's heavenly army on Judah's enemies. In the renewal of Judah's hillsides by the winter rains, the prophet sees the revitalization of the people because the Lord dwells with them.

The Book of Joel may be divided as follows:
I. Announcement of Unprecedented Disaster (1:2–20)
II. The Day of the Lord (2:1–27)
III. The Lord's Final Judgment (3:1–4:21) ∎

# JOEL

**1** ¹ The word of the LORD which came to Joel, the son of Pethuel.

## I. ANNOUNCEMENT OF UNPRECEDENTED DISASTER

2    Listen to this, you elders!
     Pay attention, all who dwell in the
       land!
   Has anything like this ever happened in
       your lifetime,
     or in the lifetime of your ancestors?
3    Report it to your children.
     Have your children report it to their
       children,
   and their children to the next
       generation.
4    What the cutter left,
     the swarming locust has devoured;
   What the swarming locust left,
     the hopper has devoured;
   What the hopper left,
     the consuming locust† has devoured.
5    Wake up, you drunkards,† and weep;
     wail, all you wine drinkers,
   Over the new wine,
     taken away from your mouths.
6    For a nation† invaded my land,
     powerful and past counting,
   With teeth like a lion's,
     fangs like those of a lioness.
7    It has stripped bare my vines,
     splintered my fig tree,
   Shearing off its bark and throwing it
       away,
     until its branches turn white.

8    Wail like a young woman† dressed in
       sackcloth
     for the husband of her youth.
9    Grain offering and libation are cut off
     from the house of the LORD;
   In mourning are the priests,
     the ministers of the LORD.
10    The field is devastated;
     the farmland mourns,†
   Because the grain is devastated,
     the wine has dried up,
     the oil has failed.
11    Be appalled, you farmers!
     wail, you vinedressers,
   Over the wheat and the barley,
     because the harvest in the field is
       ruined.
12    The vine has dried up,
     the fig tree has withered;
   The pomegranate, even the date palm
       and the apple—
   every tree in the field has dried up.
   Joy itself has dried up
     among the people.

### Cry Out to the Lord

13†    Gird yourselves and lament, you priests!
     wail, ministers of the altar!
   Come, spend the night in sackcloth,
     ministers of my God!
   For the grain offering and the libation
     are withheld from the house of your
       God.*
14    Proclaim a holy fast!
     Call an assembly!
   Gather the elders,
     all who dwell in the land,
   To the house of the LORD, your God,
     and cry out to the LORD!*
15    O! The day!†
     For near is the day of the LORD,

---

† **1:4** *Cutter...swarming locust...hopper...consuming locust*: these names may refer to various species of locusts, or to some phases in the insect's life cycle, or to successive waves of locusts ravaging the countryside.

**1:5** *Drunkards*: this metaphor expresses both the urgency behind Joel's preaching and his ironic assessment of his audience. There are no grapes to process into new wine, yet people view their situation as just another agricultural crisis. Joel argues that the problems they now face are lessons the Lord is using to provide the knowledge they lack.

**1:6** *A nation*: the locusts are compared to an invading army, whose numbers are overwhelming. The ravaged landscape resembles the wasteland left behind by marauding troops; the order and peace associated with agricultural productivity (1 Kgs 5:5; Mi 4:4) has been destroyed.

**1:8** *Like a young woman*: this simile personifies Jerusalem as

a youthful widow, left unprotected and without resources by her husband's sudden death.

**1:10** *The farmland mourns*: or "the farmland is dried up."

**1:13** Judah's situation is so grave and the day of the Lord so imminent that priests must lament day and night if they hope to reverse the divine punishment.

**1:15** As in Am 5:18–20, the day of the Lord in Joel's first speech brings punishment, not victory, for Judah. In his second speech, this event means victory for those faithful to the Lord and death for the nations who are the Lord's enemies. *Almighty*: Hebrew *shaddai*. There is wordplay between *shod* ("destruction") and *shaddai*.

---

**1:13** Jer 4:8.          **1:14** Jl 2:15.

like destruction from the Almighty it
    is coming!*

16 Before our very eyes†
    has not food been cut off?
And from the house of our God,
    joy and gladness?

17 The seed lies shriveled beneath clods of
    dirt;†
    the storehouses are emptied.
The granaries are broken down,
    for the grain is dried up.

18† How the animals groan!
    The herds of cattle are bewildered!
Because they have no pasture,
    even the flocks of sheep are starving.

19 To you, LORD, I cry!
    for fire has devoured the wilderness
      pastures,
    flame has scorched all the trees in the
      field.

20 Even the animals in the wild
    cry out to you;
For the streams of water have run dry,
    and fire has devoured the wilderness
      pastures.*

## II. THE DAY OF THE LORD

### The Day Approaches

2 1† Blow the horn in Zion,
    sound the alarm on my holy
      mountain!
Let all the inhabitants of the land
    tremble,
    for the day of the LORD is coming!*
Yes, it approaches,

2     a day of darkness and gloom,
    a day of thick clouds!
Like dawn† spreading over the
    mountains,
    a vast and mighty army!

Nothing like it has ever happened in
    ages past,
    nor will the future hold anything like
      it,
    even to the most distant generations.*

3 Before it,† fire devours,
    behind it flame scorches.
The land before it is like the garden of
    Eden,
    and behind it, a desolate wilderness;
    from it nothing escapes.*

4 Their appearance is that of horses;
    like war horses they run.

5 Like the rumble of chariots
    they hurtle across mountaintops;
Like the crackling of fiery flames
    devouring stubble;
Like a massive army
    in battle formation.*

6 Before them peoples tremble,
    every face turns pale.*

7 Like warriors they run,
    like soldiers they scale walls,
Each advancing in line,
    without swerving from the course.

8 No one crowds the other;
    each advances in its own track;
They plunge through the weapons;
    they are not checked.

9 They charge the city,
    they run upon the wall,
    they climb into the houses;
Through the windows
    they enter like thieves.

10 Before them the earth trembles;
    the heavens shake;
Sun and moon are darkened,
    and the stars withhold their
      brightness.*

11 The LORD raises his voice

---

**1:16** *Before our very eyes:* Joel's audience should have discerned the significance of the winter drought and the locust
invasion they witnessed. *Joy and gladness:* the loss of field crops
has reduced Joel's audience to subsistence living, with no means
for liturgical or personal celebration, as in v. 12.
  **1:17** *The seed…clods of dirt:* the meaning of the Hebrew is
uncertain. Most commentators use the translation given here,
since it fits the prophet's description of an agricultural year
plagued by winter drought and a spring locust infestation.
  **1:18–19** In figurative language, Joel describes how the insufficient winter rain, the locust invasions, and summer's heat on
pasture lands and water sources drive domestic and wild animals
to cry out for rain.
  **2:1–11** Joel warns the people about the destruction he sees
galloping toward Jerusalem. He combines the imagery of the locust invasion (chap. 1) with language from the holy war tradition

in order to describe the Lord leading a heavenly army against the
enemy, in this case, Jerusalem.
  **2:2** *Like dawn:* from the east comes dark destruction rather
than a new day's light.
  **2:3** *Before it:* fire precedes and follows the army's advance.
Even the ravaged landscape of chap. 1 looks like a lush garden
compared to the devastation this army leaves behind.

---

**1:15** Is 13:6; Ez 30:2–3; Ob
   15; Zep 1:7.
**1:20** Ps 42:2.
**2:1** Is 13:9; Jer 4:5; 6:1;
   51:27; Hos 5:8; Zep
   1:16.
**2:2** Is 13:14; Zep 1:4–15.

**2:3** Is 13:9; 51:3; Ez
   36:35.
**2:5** Jer 6:23.
**2:6** Na 2:11.
**2:10** Jl 4:15; Is 13:10,
   13; Ez 32:7–8; Mt
   24:29; Mk 13:24; Lk
   21:25–26.

at the head of his army;
How immense is his host!
　How numerous those who carry out
　　his command!
How great is the day of the LORD!
　Utterly terrifying! Who can survive
　　it? *

### Return to the Lord

12　Yet even now—oracle of the LORD—
　　return to me with your whole heart,
　　with fasting, weeping, and mourning.
13　Rend your hearts, not your garments,
　　and return to the LORD, your God,
　For he is gracious and merciful,
　　slow to anger, abounding in steadfast
　　　love,
　　and relenting in punishment. *
14　Perhaps he will again relent
　　and leave behind a blessing, †
　Grain offering and libation
　　for the LORD, your God. *
15　Blow the horn in Zion!
　　Proclaim a fast,
　　call an assembly! *
16　Gather the people,
　　sanctify the congregation;
　Assemble the elderly;
　　gather the children,
　　even infants nursing at the breast;
　Let the bridegroom leave his room,
　　and the bride † her bridal tent.
17　Between the porch and the altar †
　　let the priests weep,
　　let the ministers of the LORD weep and
　　　say:
　"Spare your people, LORD!
　　do not let your heritage become a
　　　disgrace,

a byword among the nations!
Why should they say among the
　peoples,
　'Where is their God?'" *

**The Lord Relents.** 18 Then the LORD grew jealous† for his land and took pity on his people. 19 In response the LORD said to his people:

I am sending you
　grain, new wine, and oil,
　and you will be satisfied by them;
Never again will I make you
　a disgrace among the nations.
20　The northerner† I will remove far from
　　　you,
　　driving them out into a dry and
　　　desolate land,
　Their vanguard to the eastern sea,
　　their rearguard to the western sea,
　And their stench will rise,
　　their stink will ascend,
　What great deeds the Lord has done!
21　Do not fear, O land!
　　delight and rejoice,
　　for the LORD has done great things! *
22　Do not fear, you animals in the wild,
　　for the wilderness pastures sprout
　　　green grass.
　The trees bear fruit,
　　the fig tree and the vine produce their
　　　harvest.
23　Children of Zion, delight
　　and rejoice in the LORD, your God!
　For he has faithfully given you the early
　　　rain, †
　　sending rain down on you,
　　the early and the late rains as before. *
24　The threshing floors will be full of grain,

---

**2:14** *Blessing*: the rain that makes possible the grapes and grain (v. 19) that workers will process into Temple offerings.

**2:16** *Elderly...infants...bridegroom...bride*: Jerusalem is in such great danger that even those normally excused from fasting or working are called upon to participate in activities to ward off the imminent catastrophe.

**2:17** *Between the porch and the altar*: the priests stood in the open space between the outdoor altar for burnt offerings and the Temple building.

**2:18** *Jealous*: the Hebrew word describes the passionate empathetic bond the Lord has with Israel. The people's wholehearted participation in Joel's call for fasting and prayer sparks the Lord's longing to protect and love his people Israel. This desire moves him to withhold punishment and to send the blessing of v. 14 instead.

**2:20** *The northerner*: the locusts, pictured as an invading army, which traditionally came from the north (Jer 1:14–15; Ez 26:7; 38:6, 15). Locusts are not usually an annual threat in

Palestine, nor are they often associated with the north. However, to demonstrate the extent of the Lord's care for Judah and control over what happens within its borders, Joel assures his audience that the Lord will quickly drive the locusts out of Judah the coming spring, should they reappear. Dead locusts will litter the shores of the "eastern" (the Dead Sea) and the "western" (the Mediterranean) seas.

**2:23** This autumn rain teaches the people to recognize God's compassionate presence in nature and history. There is a play on the double meaning of the Hebrew word *moreh*: "early rain" and "teacher." In the Dead Sea Scrolls, the word is used in the phrase "teacher (= *moreh*) of righteousness."

---

| | |
|---|---|
| **2:11** Jer 30:7; Am 5:18; Zep 1:15. | **2:15** Jl 1:14. |
| **2:13** Ex 34:6; Ps 86:5; Jon 4:2. | **2:17** Ps 42:4, 11; 79:10; 115:2. |
| **2:14** Jon 3:9. | **2:21** Ps 126:3. |
| | **2:23** Hos 10:12. |

the vats spilling over with new wine
   and oil.
25 I will repay you double
   what the swarming locust has eaten,
The hopper, the consuming locust, and
   the cutter,
   my great army I sent against you.*
26 You will eat until you are fully satisfied,
   then you will praise the name of the
   LORD, your God,
Who acts so wondrously on your behalf!
   My people will never again be put to
   shame.
27 Then you will know that I am in the
   midst of Israel:
   I, the LORD, am your God, and there is
   no other;
   my people will never again be put to
   shame.*

## III. THE LORD'S FINAL JUDGMENT

### The Day of the Lord*

3 ¹† It shall come to pass
   I will pour out my spirit upon all
   flesh.
Your sons and daughters will prophesy,
   your old men will dream dreams,
   your young men will see visions.
2 Even upon your male and female
   servants,
   in those days, I will pour out my
   spirit.
3 I will set signs in the heavens and on the
   earth,
   blood, fire, and columns of smoke;
4 The sun will darken,
   the moon turn blood-red,
Before the day of the LORD arrives,
   that great and terrible day.*
5 Then everyone who calls upon the name
   of the LORD

will escape harm.
For on Mount Zion there will be a
   remnant,
   as the LORD has said,
And in Jerusalem survivors
   whom the LORD will summon.*

### The Lord's Case Against the Nations

4 ¹ For see, in those days and at that time,*
   when I restore the fortunes
   of Judah and Jerusalem,
2 I will gather all the nations
   and bring them down to the Valley of
   Jehoshaphat.†
There I will enter into judgment with
   them
   on behalf of my people, my heritage,
   Israel;
Because they scattered them among the
   nations,
   they divided up my land.*
3 For my people they cast lots,
   trading a young boy for the price of a
   prostitute,
   exchanging a young girl for the wine
   they drank.*

⁴† Moreover, what are you doing to me, Tyre
and Sidon, and all the regions of Philistia? Are
you paying me back for something? If you are,
I will very quickly turn your deeds back upon
your own head.* ⁵ You took my silver and my
gold and brought my priceless treasures into
your temples! ⁶ You sold the people of Judah
and Jerusalem to the Greeks, taking them far
from their own country! ⁷ Look! I am rousing
them from the place to which you sold them,
and I will turn your deeds back upon your
own head. ⁸ I will sell your sons and daughters to the Judahites who will sell them to
the Sabeans,† a distant nation. The LORD has
spoken!

---

**3:1–5** In many places in the Old Testament, Hebrew *ruah*
is God's power, or spirit, bestowed on chosen individuals. The
word can also mean "breath" or "wind." In this summary introduction to his second speech, Joel anticipates that the Lord will
someday renew faithful Judahites with the divine spirit. In Acts
2:17–21 the author has Peter cite Joel's words to suggest that the
newly constituted Christian community, filled with divine life
and power, inaugurates the Lord's Day, understood as salvation
for all who believe that Jesus of Nazareth is the Christ.

**4:2** *Valley of Jehoshaphat*: one of the symbolic names of the
place of punishment for Judah's enemies; the other is "Valley
of Decision" (v. 14). The name Jehoshaphat means "the Lord
judges." If the popular identification of this place as the Kidron
Valley is accurate, Joel may imagine the Lord seated above the
valley on Mount Zion directing his troops in the destruction of

nations in the valley below.

**4:4–8** This prose material may be a later addition to the book.
It illustrates a common biblical theme (cf. Ps 7:16; 9:16; 35:8;
37:14–15; 57:7), having one's evil deed (selling Judahites into
slavery) turned into one's own punishment (being sold into slavery by the Judahites).

**4:8** *Sabeans*: traders from the southwestern tip of the Arabian peninsula, present-day Yemen (cf. 1 Kgs 10:1–2; Ps 72:10;
Jer 6:20).

---

**2:25** Jer 5:17.
**2:27** Is 45:5–6, 18; 46:9.
**3:1** Is 44:3; Ez 39:28–29;
    Acts 2:17–21.
**3:4** Jl 2:10; Mal 3:23.
**3:5** Ob 17–18; Rom
    10:13.
**4:1** Jer 33:15; 50:4, 20.
**4:2** Is 66:18; Zec 14:2.
**4:3** Ob 11, 16.
**4:4** Ob 15.

J
L

## The Nations Destroyed

9 Announce this to the nations:
    Proclaim a holy war!
    Alert the warriors!
    Let all the soldiers
        report and march! *

10 † Beat your plowshares into swords,
    and your pruning knives into spears;
    let the weakling boast, "I am a
        warrior!" *

11 Hurry and come, all you neighboring
        peoples,
    assemble there!
    Bring down, LORD, your warriors!

12 Let the nations rouse themselves and
        come up
    to the Valley of Jehoshaphat;
    For there I will sit in judgment
    upon all the neighboring nations.

13 Wield the sickle, *
    for the harvest is ripe;
    Come and tread,
    for the wine press is full;
    The vats overflow,
    for their crimes are numerous. †

14 Crowds upon crowds
    in the Valley of Decision;
    For near is the day of the LORD
    in the Valley of Decision. *

15 Sun and moon are darkened,
    and the stars withhold their brightness, *

16 The LORD roars from Zion,
    and from Jerusalem raises his voice, *
    The heavens and the earth quake,
    but the LORD will be a shelter for his
        people,
    a fortress for the people of Israel.

## A Secure Future for Judah

17 Then you will know † that I the LORD am
        your God, *
    dwelling on Zion, my holy
        mountain;
    Jerusalem will be holy,
    and strangers will never again travel
        through her.

18 † On that day
    the mountains will drip new wine,
    and the hills flow with milk,
    All the streams of Judah
    will flow with water.
    A spring will rise from the house of the
        LORD,
    watering the Valley of Shittim. *

19 Egypt will be a waste,
    Edom a desolate wilderness,
    Because of violence done to the
        Judahites,
    because they shed innocent blood in
        their land. *

20 But Judah will be inhabited forever,
    and Jerusalem for all generations.

21 I will avenge their blood,
    and I will not acquit the guilt.
    The LORD dwells in Zion.

---

**4:10** The Lord directs the troops to forge military weapons out of the agricultural tools necessary for life during peacetime. In Is 2:4 and Mi 4:3, both in contexts presuming the defeat of Israel's enemies, this imagery is reversed.

**4:13** *Their crimes are numerous*: the nations are ripe for punishment. Joel uses the vocabulary of the autumn grape harvest to describe the assault of the Lord's army against these nations. In Is 63:1–6, grape harvest imagery also controls the description of the Lord's return from Edom with blood-spattered clothing after having trod his enemies into the ground as if they were grapes (cf. Jer 25:30).

**4:17** *Then you will know*: this verse further develops the motif of knowledge introduced in 2:27. The Judahites will learn that the Lord is present in their economic prosperity and political autonomy, even though they did not associate God's presence with their crop failure.

**4:18** Images of agricultural abundance illustrate the harmony and order Joel expects the Lord to establish in Judah; like 2:18–27, this section reverses the deprivation and drought of chap. 1. *A spring…house of the LORD*: streams of water flowing from the Temple of an ideal Jerusalem also appear in Ez 47:1. *The Valley of Shittim*: or "the ravine of the acacia trees"; while there is a Shittim east of the Jordan, the reference here is probably to that rocky part of the Kidron Valley southeast of Jerusalem, an arid region where acacia trees flourished.

---

4:9 Jer 6:4.
4:10 Is 2:4; Mi 4:3.
4:13 Is 63:1–6; Rev 14:15.
4:14 Ob 15.
4:15 Jl 2:10; 3:4.
4:16 Jer 25:30; Am 1:2.
4:17 Ob 17; Na 2:1.
4:18 Ez 47:1–12; Am 9:13;
Zec 14:8.
4:19 Ob 10.

# The Book of
# Amos

## INTRODUCTION

### Michael D. Guinan, OFM

Amos is the first of Israel's prophets to have a book, a collection of writings, associated with him. It now appears as the third book of the Book of the Twelve. The superscription (Am 1:1) places his activity in the days of Uzziah of Judah (783–742 BCE) and Jeroboam II of Israel (786–746 BCE). The reference to the earthquake, known from archaeology, would place him earlier in this period, about 760 BCE.

The length of the reigns of both Uzziah and Jeroboam II indicate that this was a time of unusual peace and prosperity. The larger kingdoms of Egypt and Assyria were in decline so the smaller kingdoms in between could flourish. In 745 BCE, Tiglath-Pileser III assumed power in Assyria and began to expand his kingdom. Judah became a vassal of Assyria in 732 BCE, and the territory of the Israelite kingdom was incorporated into the Assyrian provincial system in 722 BCE.

In his confrontation with Amaziah, the priest of Bethel (Am 7:10–15), Amos denies being a prophet or belonging to a prophetic guild ("company of prophets"), insisting rather that he is a herdsman, a dresser of sycamores (7:14), and a sheepbreeder (1:1). While there is some uncertainty regarding the precise meaning of the Hebrew terms used, he was at least a well-off owner of livestock and orchards. He was from Tekoa, a town near Bethlehem, about ten miles southeast of Jerusalem, well within the kingdom of Judah. God called him from this place and this occupation to go and prophesy to the kingdom of Israel.

Evidence suggests that Israel's ruling and elite classes lived lives of leisure and luxury. Archaeological finds at Samaria, the capital of Israel, as well as other northern cities, provide interesting support for this, e.g., carved ivories that could have been part of the "beds of ivory"

## Outline of Amos

I. **Editorial Introduction (1:1–2)**

II. **Oracles Against the Nations (1:3–2:16)**

III. **Threefold Summons to Hear the Word of the Lord (3:1–5:9)**

IV. **Three Woes (5:7–6:14)**

V. **Symbolic Visions (7:1–9:10)**

VI. **Epilogue: Restoration Under a Davidic King (9:11–15)**

(Am 6:4). The poorer classes of the peasants, on the other hand, suffered greatly.

## The Message of Amos

The book of Amos is the end product of a process of transmission. The oracles of Amos were handed on and supplemented over time by his followers. Scholars have discerned various layers in this process. Perhaps the clearest example of a late addition is the epilogue (Am 9:11–15), which contains the only clear message of hope in the book and shows striking similarities to later postexilic prophets, such as Haggai and Zechariah.

The book can be conveniently divided as follows: between the introduction (Am 1:1–2) and the epilogue (9:11–15), chs. 1–2, the oracles against the nations, clearly form a unit. At the end, chs. 7–9, with five visions from the Lord, also are a clear unit. The chapters in between, 3–6, seem to fall into two sets, three calls to "hear this word" of the Lord (3:1; 4:1; 5:1) and three "woes" (5:7, 18; 6:1).

The overall message of the book can be organized under several headings.

## Yahweh is a Universal God

The book of Joel ends with a scene of the judgment of the nations (Jl 4); however, "the LORD roars from Zion" (Jl 4:16) and God's people will be safe. Amos opens by citing verbatim the first part of this verse (Am 1:2), but now the threat will be a threat against God's people, too. But first comes a series of six "oracles against the nations," the first such in the Book of the Twelve (Am 1:3–2:3). The nations mentioned (Aram, Philistia, Tyre, Edom, Ammon, and Moab) are the smaller nation states surrounding Israel with which both Israel and Judah would have had dealings at this time. While these oracles were spoken in the hearing of Israel, they reflect the belief that Yahweh, their God, is in fact a God over all the nations who holds them accountable for their behavior. The climactic last position in the list would have shocked its original hearers. It is directed squarely against them, Judah and Israel!

God also cares for the nations, having brought the Philistines from Caphtor (Crete) and the Arameans from Kir (locale in eastern Mesopotamia; see also Am 1:5), just as he brought Israel from Egypt (9:7).

What is more, Yahweh is also a God of all creation: the heavens, the earth, the stars and constellations, the waters, the light, and the darkness. This is affirmed in three hymnic doxologies (Am 4:13; 5:8–9; 9:5–6) that show affinities with creation passages in the Psalms. Some scholars consider these later additions to the book.

## Yahweh and Israel

The relationship of Yahweh and Israel was, however, special. "You alone have I known, among all the families of the earth" (Am 3:2). Israel had a special experience of Yahweh in its collective life. Yahweh had brought them up from Egypt, led them through the wilderness, and brought them into the land (2:10–11; 3:1). On this basis, Israel expected special care and protection. Amos turns this upside down; because of this special relationship, "therefore I will punish you for all your iniquities" (3:2).

## Covenant Obligations

Though Amos does not use the terms "election" or "covenant," he was well aware of Israel's special position and that it brought with it special obligations and responsibilities. The two basic areas of covenant obligation were: right worship of Yahweh and right behavior, i.e., for the Israelites to deal justly with each other. These are not two separate areas but are in fact flip sides of the same coin; they go together. In these areas, Israel had failed completely.

## Worship

Judah's ancestors had been led astray by the "lies" (false gods) that they followed (Am 2:4). Israel does go to its shrines in Bethel and Gilgal in the southern part of the kingdom, which seems to be the area where Amos was most active (e.g., 7:10–15), to make their sacrifices, but God spurns these offerings (4:4–5; 5:4–6). They are empty. Why?

## Social Behavior

While Amos mentions Israel's worship, his primary focus is clearly on their social behavior. It is the lack of justice in their lives that makes their worship hollow (Am 5:21–24). In denouncing these abuses, Amos emerges as one of the most eloquent prophetic voices on behalf of social justice; almost every chapter contains some indictment (2:6–8; 3:9–10; 4:1–3; 5:7–13, 21–24; 6:3; 8:4–6). The powerful trample on the heads of the poor (2:7; 4:1; 8:4) and fill Samaria (their capital city) with injustice ("violence") and oppression (3:9–10). They live luxurious lives (4:1; 6:4–6) and are oblivious to the sufferings of the people (6:6b, "the collapse of Joseph [the northern tribes]").

What concrete shape does this abuse and injustice take? They keep garments taken in pledge (Am 2:8); they pervert justice "at the gate" (5:10), the place where legal proceedings took place; they impose heavy taxes on the poor (5:11); and they cheat the poor in economic activities of buying and selling (8:5–6). The main areas of concern are the abuses by the rich and powerful of the judicial and economic systems at the expense of the poorest and weakest in the society. With good cause, God spurns their feasts and tells them, "Rather let justice surge like waters, and righteousness like an unfailing stream" (5:24).

## Punishment

Israel has forsaken Yahweh; therefore they will be punished. Typical of the prophetic judgment oracle, the charge is mentioned first, and the judgment and punishment flow from that. Woe oracles (Am 5:7, 18; 6:1) often expressed both anger and grief. Israel is as good as dead!

But God was not eager to punish them. Repeatedly—five times are mentioned—Israel was warned, but they "did not return" to God (Am 4:6, 8, 9, 10, 11). In his first two visions (7:1–3, 4–6) Amos saw images of destruction (locusts and a rain of fire from the great abyss) and pleaded with God, interceding for Israel. Twice God changed his mind and relented, but the third time was it. At the fourth God announces, "The end has come for my people Israel" (8:2). A series of oracles follows, promising judgment "on that day," "days are coming" (8:9, 11, 13).

## Day of the Lord

What day is that? The "day of the LORD" seems to have referred to a day on which the Lord protected Israel's life by giving them victory over their enemies. At those times when Israel felt under attack or threatened, they could look to the future with hope that God would protect them and give them similar victories. It had therefore very positive and happy connotations. However, here too, Amos will surprise his hearers. Just as he has done with the oracles against the nations and with the idea of Israel's special relationship with God, he will turn things upside down.

> Woe [grief, not happiness] to those who yearn
> for the day of the LORD!
> What will the day of the LORD mean for you?
> It will be darkness, not light! (Am 5:18).

Up to this point, Israel had thought in social and ethnic terms: they were the Lord's people; the Lord was on their side. But Amos shifts to moral grounds, in effect questioning whether they really were on the Lord's side. By their behavior and failure to live by the covenant, they too could become enemies of God.

Since Amos was the first, historically, of the classical prophets, this was the first time the image of the day of the Lord appeared, and it would have threatening implications for Israel. "That day" would be one of punishment and judgment. Israel would be conquered by Assyria and scattered throughout that empire; Judah would be led into exile by Babylon. When the Persians came to power, some exiles would return to Judah and rebuild their Temple but would still chafe under foreign rule and domination. In this context, they began to look to a more distant future, known to God, when the "day of the LORD" would be a cosmic event and mean decisive defeat for the enemies of God and full restoration for Israel.

In the present Book of the Twelve, the day of the Lord appears clearly first in the book of Joel. There it can be both a day of judgment upon Israel (Jl 2:1–11) and the future day of hope and restoration (Jl 3:3–4:21). The image and theme of the "day of the LORD" is an important one that will recur often throughout the Book of the Twelve (e.g., Jl 2:1–11; 3:3–4:21; Am 5:18–20; Ob 15; Mi 2:4; Hb 3:16; Hg 2:23; Zec 14:1–21; Mal 3:1–2).

## Word of Hope

One more instance of "on that day" and "days are coming" appears in the book of Amos (Am 9:11, 13). After citing the word of the Lord, "I will not destroy the house of Jacob completely" (9:8b), the epilogue (9:11–15) gives a clear message of hope. The "fallen hut" (the defeated dynasty and city) of David will be raised up once again. It will conquer its enemy Edom (see 1:11–13), and nature itself will be transformed with abundant fertility of fields and vineyards. God's people will dwell securely: "Never again shall they be plucked from the land that I have given them—the LORD, your God, has spoken" (9:15). This is probably a late, postexilic addition to the book enabling it to end with a vision of far-off restoration and peace.

As mentioned above, in the Book of the

Twelve, the book of Amos is connected with Joel, the book before it, by the quotation of the Lord roaring from Zion (Jl 4:16; Am 1:2). The reference to Edom (Am 9:12) provides a link to the book of Obadiah, which follows with its oracle against Edom. ■

# THE BOOK OF AMOS

## New American Bible, Introduction

Amos was a sheepbreeder of Tekoa in Judah, who delivered his oracles in the Northern Kingdom during the prosperous reign of Jeroboam II (786–746 B.C.). He prophesied in Israel at the great cult center of Bethel, from which he was finally expelled by the priest in charge of this royal sanctuary (7:10–17). The poetry of Amos, who denounces the hollow prosperity of the Northern Kingdom, is filled with imagery and language taken from his own pastoral background. The book is an anthology of his oracles and was compiled either by the prophet or by some of his disciples.

The prophecy begins with a sweeping indictment of Damascus, Philistia, Tyre, and Edom; but the forthright herdsman saves his climactic denunciation for Israel, whose injustice and idolatry are sins against the light granted to her. Israel could indeed expect the day of the Lord, but it would be a day of darkness and not light (5:18). When Amos prophesied the overthrow of the sanctuary, the fall of the royal house, and the captivity of the people, it was more than Israelite officialdom could bear. The priest of Bethel drove Amos from the shrine—but not before hearing a terrible sentence pronounced upon himself.

Amos is a prophet of divine judgment, and the sovereignty of the Lord in nature and history dominates his thought. But he was no innovator; his conservatism was in keeping with the whole prophetic tradition calling the people back to the high moral and religious demands of the Lord's revelation.

Amos's message stands as one of the most powerful voices ever to challenge hypocrisy and injustice. He boldly indicts kings, priests, and leaders (6:1; 7:9, 16–17). He stresses the importance and the divine origin of the prophetic word (3:3–8); one must either heed that word in its entirety or suffer its disappearance (8:11–12). Religion without justice is an affront to the God of Israel and, far from appeasing God, can only provoke divine wrath (5:21–27; 8:4–10). The Lord is not some petty national god but the sovereign creator of the cosmos (4:13; 5:8; 9:5–6). Amos alludes to historical forces at work through which God would exercise judgment on Israel (6:14). Several times he mentions deportation as the fate that awaits the people and their corrupt leaders (4:3; 5:5, 27; 7:17), a standard tactic of Assyrian foreign policy during this period. Through the prophetic word and various natural disasters (4:6–12) the Lord has tried to bring Israel to repentance, but to no avail. Israel's rebelliousness has exhausted the divine patience and the destruction of Israel as a nation and as God's people is inevitable (2:4, 13–16; 7:8–9). As it is presented in this book, Amos's message is one of almost unrelieved gloom (but see 5:14–15). A later appendix (9:11–15), however, ends the book on a hopeful note, looking beyond the judgment that had already taken place in fulfillment of Amos's word.

The Book of Amos may be divided as follows:

I. Editorial Introduction (1:1–2)
II. Oracles against the Nations (1:3–2:16)
III. Threefold Summons to Hear the Word of the Lord (3:1–5:9)
IV. Three Woes (5:7–6:14)
V. Symbolic Visions (7:1–9:10)
VI. Epilogue: Restoration Under a Davidic King (9:11–15) ■

# AMOS

## I. EDITORIAL INTRODUCTION

**1** ¹The words of Amos, who was one of the sheepbreeders from Tekoa,* which he received in a vision concerning Israel in the days of Uzziah, king of Judah, and in the days of Jeroboam, son of Joash, king of Israel, two years before the earthquake.† ²He said:

The LORD roars from Zion,†
 and raises his voice from Jerusalem;
The pastures of the shepherds languish,
 and the summit of Carmel withers.*

## II. ORACLES AGAINST THE NATIONS†

### Aram

³Thus says the LORD:

For three crimes of Damascus, and now
 four—†
I will not take it back—
Because they threshed Gilead
 with sledges of iron,
⁴ I will send fire upon the house of
 Hazael,
 and it will devour the strongholds of
 Ben-hadad.†*
⁵ I will break the barred gate of Damascus;
 From the Valley of Aven† I will cut off
 the one enthroned,
And the sceptered ruler from Beth-eden;
 the people of Aram shall be exiled to
 Kir,* says the LORD.

### Philistia

⁶Thus says the LORD:

For three crimes of Gaza, and now
 four—
 I will not take it back—
Because they exiled an entire
 population,
 handing them over to Edom,
⁷ I will send fire upon the wall of Gaza,
 and it will devour its strongholds;
⁸ From Ashdod I will cut off the one
 enthroned
 and the sceptered ruler from
 Ashkelon;
I will turn my hand against Ekron,
 and the last of the Philistines shall
 perish,
 says the Lord GOD.

### Tyre

⁹Thus says the LORD:

For three crimes of Tyre, and now four—
 I will not take it back—
Because they handed over an entire
 population to Edom,
 and did not remember their covenant
 of brotherhood,†
¹⁰ I will send fire upon the wall of Tyre,
 and it will devour its strongholds.

### Edom

¹¹Thus says the LORD:

For three crimes of Edom, and now
 four—
 I will not take it back—

---

**1:1** *The earthquake*: a major earthquake during the reign of Uzziah (ca. 783–742 B.C.), so devastating that it was remembered long afterwards (cf. Zec 14:5). See the description of an earthquake in Amos's final vision (9:1).

**1:2** Significantly, the roar comes to the Northern Kingdom from Jerusalem. This verse, perhaps an editorial remark, sets the tone of Amos's message.

**1:3–2:16** All the nations mentioned here may have been part of the ideal empire of David-Solomon (cf. 1 Kgs 5:1; 2 Kgs 14:25). Certain standards of conduct were expected not only in their relations with Israel but also with one another.

**1:3** *For three crimes…and now four*: this formula (n, n + 1) is frequent in poetry (e.g., Prv 6:16–19; 30:18–19). The progression "three" followed by "four" here suggests a climax. The fourth crime is one too many and exhausts the Lord's forbearance.

**1:4** *Hazael…Ben-hadad*: kings of the Arameans whose capital was Damascus (v. 5); they fought against Israel (2 Kgs 13:3) and had long occupied the region of Gilead (v. 3) in Transjordan.

**1:5** *Valley of Aven*: lit., "valley of wickedness," perhaps a distortion of a place name in Aramean territory, identity unknown. *Beth-eden*: an Aramean city-state on the Euphrates, about two hundred miles northeast of Damascus, called *Bit-adini* in Assyro-Babylonian texts. *Kir*: cf. 9:7; probably to be identified with the city of Emar on the Euphrates, a major Aramean center in the Late Bronze Age. One text from this site calls the king of Emar "the king of the people of the land of Kir."

**1:9** *Did not remember their covenant of brotherhood*: standard diplomatic language of this period, meaning "violated the treaty." The violation may not have been against Israel itself but against a fellow "subject" nation of the ideal Davidic-Solomonic empire (cf. 2:1).

---

**1:1** Zec 14:5.
**1:2** Jer 25:30; Jl 4:16.
**1:4** 2 Kgs 13:3–7; Hos 8:14.
**1:5** 2 Kgs 16:9.

Because he pursued his brother† with
the sword,
    suppressing all pity,
Persisting in his anger,
    his wrath raging without end,
12 I will send fire upon Teman,
    and it will devour the strongholds of
Bozrah.†

### Ammon

13 Thus says the LORD:

For three crimes of the Ammonites, and
now four—
    I will not take it back—
Because they ripped open pregnant
women in Gilead,*
    in order to extend their territory,
14 I will kindle a fire upon the wall of
Rabbah,†
    and it will devour its strongholds
Amid war cries on the day of battle,
    amid stormwind on the day of
tempest.
15 Their king shall go into exile,
    he and his princes with him, says the
LORD.

### Moab

2 ¹ Thus says the LORD:

For three crimes of Moab, and now
four—
    I will not take it back—
Because he burned to ashes†
    the bones of Edom's king,
2 I will send fire upon Moab,
    and it will devour the strongholds of
Kerioth;

Moab shall meet death amid uproar,
    battle cries and blasts of the ram's
horn.
3 I will cut off the ruler from its midst,
    and all the princes I will slay with
him, says the LORD.

### Judah

4† Thus says the LORD:

For three crimes of Judah, and now
four—
    I will not take it back—
Because they spurned the instruction of
the LORD,*
    and did not keep his statutes;
Because the lies† which their ancestors
followed
    have led them astray,
5 I will send fire upon Judah,
    and it will devour the strongholds of
Jerusalem.

### Israel

6 Thus says the LORD:

For three crimes of Israel,† and now
four—
    I will not take it back—
Because they hand over the just for
silver,
    and the poor for a pair of sandals;*
7 They trample the heads of the destitute
    into the dust of the earth,
    and force the lowly out of the way.
Son and father sleep with the same girl,†
    profaning my holy name.
8 Upon garments taken in pledge
    they recline beside any altar.†*

---

**1:11** *Pursued his brother:* "brother" here may denote a fellow
vassal or subject of Israel.
**1:12** *Teman…Bozrah:* two of the chief cities of Edom; cf.
Jer 49:20.
**1:14** *Rabbah:* now called Amman, the modern capital of Jordan.
**2:1** *He burned to ashes:* to the peoples of the Near East,
burning the bones of the dead was a particularly heinous crime,
as it was believed to cause the spirits of these dead to wander
without any hope of interment in their graves, where they could
rest in peace.
**2:4–8, 12** Unlike the crimes of the nations detailed in this
section, which are wrongs against other nations, those of Judah
and Israel named here are violations of the Lord's demands.
**2:4** *The lies:* false gods worshiped by the Judahites.
**2:6** *Israel:* Amos's audience would applaud his condemnation
of foreign kingdoms in the foregoing seven oracles, especially of
Judah. But now he adds an eighth, unexpected oracle—against
Israel itself. This is the real "punch line" of this whole section, to

which the preceding oracles serve mainly as introduction.
**2:7** *Son and father sleep with the same girl:* the crime condemned here may be the misuse of power by the rich who take
unfair advantage of young women from the ranks of the poor
and force themselves on them, thus adding oppression to the
sin of impurity.
**2:8** *Upon garments…any altar:* creditors kept the garments
taken as pledges from the poor instead of returning them to their
owners before nightfall as the law commanded (Ex 22:25; cf. Dt
24:12). *Wine…in their temples:* lavish feasts for the rich, serving
the finest wines in great abundance (see 6:4–7) and funded by
the treasuries of local temples (e.g., at Dan and Bethel). The Hebrew in this verse is difficult. Another possible translation would
be: "And the wine of those who have been fined / they drink in
the house of their god."

---

**1:13** 2 Kgs 8:12; 15:16.      **2:6** Am 8:6; Sir 46:19.
**2:4** Is 5:24.      **2:8** Dt 24:12–13.

A
M

Wine at treasury expense
    they drink in their temples.

9 Yet it was I who destroyed the Amorites
    before them,
    who were as tall as cedars,
    and as strong as oak trees.
I destroyed their fruit above
    and their roots beneath.*

10 It was I who brought you up from the
    land of Egypt,
    and who led you through the desert
    for forty years,
    to occupy the land of the Amorites;

11 I who raised up prophets among your
    children,
    and nazirites† among your young
    men.
Is this not so, Israelites?—
    oracle of the LORD.

12 But you made the nazirites drink wine,
    and commanded the prophets, "Do
    not prophesy!"*

13 Look, I am groaning beneath you,
    as a wagon groans when laden with
    sheaves.

14 Flight shall elude the swift,
    and the strong shall not retain
    strength;*
The warrior shall not save his life,

15     nor shall the archer stand his ground;
The swift of foot shall not escape,
    nor shall the horseman save his life.

16 And the most stouthearted of warriors
    shall flee naked on that day—
    oracle of the LORD.

## III. THREEFOLD SUMMONS TO HEAR THE WORD OF THE LORD

### First Summons

**3** ¹ Hear this word, Israelites, that the LORD
    speaks concerning you,
    concerning the whole family I brought
    up from the land of Egypt:

2 You alone I have known,†
    among all the families of the earth;*
Therefore I will punish you
    for all your iniquities.

3† Do two journey together
    unless they have agreed?

4 Does a lion roar in the forest
    when it has no prey?
Does a young lion cry out from its den
    unless it has seized something?

5 Does a bird swoop down on a trap on
    the ground
    when there is no lure for it?
Does a snare spring up from the ground
    without catching anything?

6 Does the ram's horn sound in a city
    without the people becoming
    frightened?
Does disaster befall a city
    unless the LORD has caused it?*

7 (Indeed, the Lord GOD does nothing without revealing his plan to his servants the prophets.)

8 The lion has roared,
    who would not fear?*
The Lord GOD has spoken,
    who would not prophesy?

9 Proclaim this in the strongholds of
    Assyria,†
    in the strongholds of the land of
    Egypt:
"Gather on the mount of Samaria,
    and see the great disorders within it,
    the oppressions within its midst."†

10 They do not know how to do what is
    right—
    oracle of the LORD—
Storing up in their strongholds
    violence and destruction.

11 Therefore thus says the Lord GOD:

---

† **2:11** *Nazirites:* see note on Nm 6:2–21. *Oracle of the LORD:* a phrase used extensively in prophetic books to indicate divine speech.

**3:2** *You alone I have known:* precisely because Israel enjoyed a special status among the nations of the world in the eyes of the Lord (but see 9:7) it was called to a high degree of fidelity to God. Because Israel has failed in this expectation, it must experience God's punishment.

**3:3–8** The metaphors in these sayings illustrate the principle of cause and effect, and lead up to the conclusion in v. 8.

**3:9** *Assyria:* following the Greek version, the Hebrew text has "Ashod." It is supposed that this was a copyist's error: "Assyria"

seems intended, in order to parallel "Egypt" in the next line.

**3:9** With a keen sense of irony, Amos invites the most powerful oppressors in Israel's memory, past and present—Egypt and Assyria—to see and marvel at the great oppression and injustice being wrought within Samaria by the people of Israel.

---

| | |
|---|---|
| **2:9** Nm 21:21–32; Dt | **2:14** Ps 33:16. |
| 2:24–37; Jb 18:16; | **3:2** Gn 18:19; Dt 7:6. |
| Hos 9:16. | **3:6** Jl 2:1. |
| **2:12** Am 7:13; Nm 6:1–4; | **3:8** Am 1:2. |
| Is 30:10; Jer 11:21. | |

An enemy shall surround the land,
  tear down your fortresses,
  and pillage your strongholds.
12 Thus says the LORD:
As the shepherd rescues from the mouth
    of the lion
  a pair of sheep's legs or the tip of an
    ear,
So shall the Israelites escape,
  those who dwell in Samaria,
With the corner of a couch
  or a piece of a cot.†

13 Hear and bear witness against the house
    of Jacob—
  an oracle of the Lord GOD, the God of
    hosts:
14 On the day when I punish Israel for its
    crimes,
  I will also punish the altars of Bethel;
The horns of the altar shall be broken
    off
  and fall to the ground.†*
15 I will strike the winter house
  and the summer house;
The houses of ivory shall lie in ruin,
  and their many rooms shall be no
    more—
  oracle of the LORD.

**Second Summons**

4 ¹Hear this word, you cows of Bashan,†
  who live on the mount of Samaria:
Who oppress the destitute
  and abuse the needy;
Who say to your husbands,
  "Bring us a drink!"
2 The Lord GOD has sworn by his
    holiness:
Truly days are coming upon you
  when they shall drag you away with
    ropes,
  your children with fishhooks;
3 You shall go out through the breached
    walls
  one in front of the other,

And you shall be exiled to Harmon—†
  oracle of the LORD.
4 Come to Bethel† and sin,
  to Gilgal and sin all the more!
Each morning bring your sacrifices,
  every third day your tithes;
5 Burn leavened bread as a thanksgiving
    sacrifice,
  proclaim publicly your voluntary
    offerings,
For so you love to do, Israelites—
  oracle of the Lord GOD.

6 Though I made your teeth
  clean of food in all your cities,
  and made bread scarce in all your
    dwellings,
Yet you did not return to me—
  oracle of the LORD.*
7* And I withheld the rain from you
  when the harvest was still three
    months away;
I sent rain upon one city
  but not upon another;
One field was watered by rain,
  but the one I did not water dried up;
8 Two or three cities staggered to another
    to drink water
  but were not satisfied;
Yet you did not return to me—
  oracle of the LORD.
9 I struck you with blight and mildew;
  locusts devoured your gardens and
    vineyards,
  the caterpillar consumed your fig trees
    and olive trees;
Yet you did not return to me—
  oracle of the LORD.*
10 I sent upon you pestilence like that of
    Egypt;*
  with the sword I killed your young
    men and your captured horses,
  and to your nostrils I brought the
    stench of your camps;
Yet you did not return to me—

---

† **3:12** The "escape" is clearly a disaster, not a deliverance.
  **3:14** On Bethel, see also 4:4; 5:5–6; and 7:13. The prophet is condemning the religiosity and formalism of the worship by Israel's leaders.
  **4:1** *Cows of Bashan*: the pampered women of Samaria; Bashan was a region east of the Sea of Galilee, famous for its rich pasture and fattened herds.
  **4:3** *Harmon*: or perhaps "Mount Mon"; an unidentified site, probably far to the north of Israel, under the control of Assyria.

**4:4** *Come to Bethel*: Amos's invitation to the people to come and "sin" at two of the major religious centers in Samaria is sarcastic. His point is that sacrifice and worship without justice is an abomination to the God of Israel; cf. 5:21–24.

  **3:14** Am 9:1; 1 Kgs 13:1–5.        **4:9** Dt 28:22; Jl 1:4; 2:25;
  **4:6** Wis 12:2, 10.                          Hg 2:17.
  **4:7** Jer 14:1–6.                             **4:10** Dt 7:15; 28:27.

oracle of the LORD.

11 I overthrew you
as when God overthrew Sodom and
Gomorrah;
you were like a brand plucked from
the fire,*
Yet you did not return to me—
oracle of the LORD.

12 Therefore thus I will do to you,† Israel:
and since I will deal thus with you,
prepare to meet your God, O Israel!

13 The one who forms mountains and
creates winds,
and declares to mortals their thoughts;
Who makes dawn into darkness
and strides upon the heights of the
earth,
the LORD, the God of hosts, is his
name!

## Third Summons†

**5** 1 Hear this word which I utter concerning
you,
this dirge, house of Israel:

2 She is fallen, to rise no more,
virgin Israel;
She lies abandoned on her land,
with no one to raise her up.*

3 For thus says the Lord GOD
to the house of Israel:
The city that marched out with a
thousand
shall be left with a hundred,
Another that marched out with a
hundred
shall be left with ten.

4 For thus says the LORD†
to the house of Israel:
Seek me, that you may live,*

5 but do not seek Bethel;
Do not come to Gilgal,
and do not cross over to Beer-sheba;
For Gilgal shall be led into exile

and Bethel shall be no more.

6† Seek the LORD, that you may live,
lest he flare up against the house of
Joseph† like a fire
that shall consume the house of Israel,
with no one to quench it.

8 The one who made the Pleiades and
Orion,
who turns darkness into dawn,
and darkens day into night;
Who summons the waters of the sea,
and pours them out on the surface of
the earth;*

9 Who makes destruction fall suddenly
upon the stronghold
and brings ruin upon the fortress,
the LORD is his name.

## IV. THREE WOES

### First Woe

7 Woe to those who turn justice into
wormwood
and cast righteousness to the ground,

10 They hate those who reprove at the gate
and abhor those who speak with
integrity;

11 Therefore, because you tax the destitute
and exact from them levies of grain,
Though you have built houses of hewn
stone,
you shall not live in them;
Though you have planted choice
vineyards,
you shall not drink their wine.*

12 Yes, I know how many are your crimes,
how grievous your sins:
Oppressing the just, accepting bribes,
turning away the needy at the gate.

13 (Therefore at this time the wise are
struck dumb
for it is an evil time.)

---

**4:12** *Therefore thus I will do to you*: this climax of vv. 6–12, announcing the sentence the Lord intends to pass on Israel, is open-ended.

**5:1–17** These verses form a chiastic section beginning and ending with a lament over Israel (vv. 2, 16–17) and containing a double appeal to "seek" the Lord (vv. 4, 14). This editorial arrangement gives the whole section a negative cast, in effect nullifying the only hopeful verse in Amos (v. 15). Israel is as good as dead.

**5:4–5** *For thus says the LORD…Bethel shall be no more*: these two verses continue the sarcasm of 4:4–5, verses in which Amos invites the people to come and "sin" at Bethel and Gilgal. The cult cities of Samaria should have been places where God could

be "sought" but, because of the sins of the Northern Kingdom, these cities would cease to exist.

**5:6** These verses have been rearranged to achieve the proper sequence according to the best possible manuscript tradition. Cf. the Textual Notes accompanying the translation.

**5:6** *House of Joseph*: the kingdom of Israel or Northern Kingdom, the chief tribes of which were descended from Ephraim and Manasseh, the sons of Joseph; cf. 5:15; 6:6.

---

4:11 Gn 19:24–25; Zec  
3:2.  
5:2 Am 8:13.  
5:4 Hos 5:6; 10:12.  

5:8 Am 9:6; Jb 9:9; 38:31.  
5:11 Am 9:14; Dt 28:30;  
Zep 1:13.

<sup>14</sup> Seek good and not evil,
     that you may live;
Then truly the LORD, the God of hosts,
     will be with you as you claim.
<sup>15</sup> Hate evil and love good,
     and let justice prevail at the gate;
Then it may be that the LORD, the God
          of hosts,
     will have pity on the remnant of
          Joseph.*

<sup>16</sup> Therefore, thus says the LORD,
     the God of hosts, the Lord:
In every square there shall be
          lamentation,
     and in every street they shall cry, "Oh,
          no!"
They shall summon the farmers to wail
     and the professional mourners to
          lament.
<sup>17</sup> And in every vineyard there shall be
          lamentation
     when I pass through your midst, says
          the LORD.

## Second Woe

<sup>18</sup> Woe to those who yearn
     for the day of the LORD!†
What will the day of the LORD mean for
          you?
     It will be darkness, not light!*
<sup>19</sup> As if someone fled from a lion
     and a bear met him;
Or as if on entering the house
     he rested his hand against the wall,
     and a snake bit it.
<sup>20</sup> Truly, the day of the LORD will be
          darkness, not light,
     gloom without any brightness!

<sup>21</sup>†* I hate, I despise your feasts,
     I take no pleasure in your solemnities.
<sup>22</sup> Even though you bring me your burnt
          offerings and grain offerings
     I will not accept them;
Your stall-fed communion offerings,
     I will not look upon them.
<sup>23</sup> Take away from me
     your noisy songs;
The melodies of your harps,
     I will not listen to them.
<sup>24</sup> Rather let justice surge like waters,
     and righteousness like an unfailing
          stream.
<sup>25</sup>* Did you bring me sacrifices and grain
          offerings
     for forty years in the desert, O house
          of Israel?*
<sup>26</sup> Yet you will carry away Sukuth,† your
          king,
     and Kaiwan, your star-image,
     your gods that you have made for
          yourselves,*
<sup>27</sup> As I exile you beyond Damascus,
     says the LORD,
     whose name is the God of hosts.

## Third Woe

**6** <sup>1</sup> Woe to those who are complacent in
          Zion,
     secure on the mount of Samaria,
Leaders of the first among nations,
     to whom the people of Israel turn.
<sup>2</sup> Pass over to Calneh and see,
     go from there to Hamath the great,
     and down to Gath† of the Philistines.
Are you better than these kingdoms,
     or is your territory greater than
          theirs?

---

**5:18** *The day of the LORD*: first mentioned in Amos, this refers to a specific time in the future, known to the Lord alone,
when God's enemies would be decisively defeated. The common assumption among Israelites was that the Lord's foes and
Israel's foes were one and the same. But Amos makes it clear
that because the people have become God's enemies by refusing to heed the prophetic word, they too would experience
the divine wrath on that fateful day. However, during the exile
this expression comes to mean a time when God would avenge
Israel against its oppressors and bring about its restoration (Jer
50:27; Ez 30:3–5).
**5:21–27** The prophet does not condemn cultic activity as
such but rather the people's attempt to offer worship with hands
unclean from oppression of their fellow Israelites (cf. Ps 15:2–5;
24:3–4). But worship from those who disregard justice and
righteousness (v. 24) is never acceptable to the God of Israel.
Through the Sinai covenant the love of God and the love of
neighbor are inextricably bound together.

**5:26** *Sukuth*: probably a hebraized form of Assyro-Babylonian *Shukudu* ("the Arrow"), a name of Sirius, the brightest star
in the night sky. It was associated with the god Ninurta, who was
widely worshiped in Mesopotamia. According to 2 Kgs 17:30
the cult of Sirius was introduced into Samaria by deportees from
Babylonia. *Kaiwan*: a hebraized form of an Akkadian name for
the planet Saturn, also worshiped as a deity in Mesopotamia.
**6:2** *Calneh…Hamath…Gath*: city-states overcome by the Assyrians in the eighth century B.C., whose fate should be a lesson
to the Israelites. The prophet castigates the leaders for being more
intent on pursuing a luxurious lifestyle (vv. 1, 4–6) than reading
the signs of the times.

---

**5:15** Jl 2:14; Rom 12:9.          **5:25–26** Acts 7:42–43.
**5:18** Jer 14:16; Jl 2:1–2, 11;    **5:25** Jer 7:21–26.
     Zep 1:14–18.                    **5:26** 2 Kgs 17:30; Jer 2:28.
**5:21–24** Is 1:10–17; Jer 6:20.

A
M

3  You who would put off the day of
        disaster,
    yet hasten the time of violence!
4  Those who lie on beds of ivory,
        and lounge upon their couches;
    Eating lambs taken from the flock,
        and calves from the stall;
5  Who improvise to the music of the harp,
        composing on musical instruments
            like David,
6  Who drink wine from bowls,
        and anoint themselves with the best
            oils,
    but are not made ill by the collapse of
        Joseph;
7  Therefore, now they shall be the first to
        go into exile,
    and the carousing of those who
        lounged shall cease.

8  The Lord GOD has sworn by his very
        self—
    an oracle of the LORD, the God of
        hosts:
    I abhor the pride of Jacob,
    I hate his strongholds,
    and I will hand over the city with
        everything in it;*
9  Should there remain ten people
        in a single house, these shall die.
10  When a relative or one who prepares the
        body picks up the remains
    to carry them out of the house,
    If he says to someone in the recesses of
        the house,
    "Is anyone with you?" and the answer
        is, "No one,"
    Then he shall say, "Silence!"
        for no one must mention the name of
            the LORD.†*
11  Indeed, the LORD has given the
        command
    to shatter the great house to bits,
        and reduce the small house to rubble.
12  Can horses run over rock,
        or can one plow the sea with oxen?

Yet you have turned justice into gall,
    and the fruit of righteousness into
        wormwood,*
13  You who rejoice in Lodebar,
    and say, "Have we not, by our own
        strength,
    seized Karnaim† for ourselves?"
14  Look, I am raising up against you, house
        of Israel—
    oracle of the LORD, the God of hosts—
    A nation† that shall oppress you
        from Lebo-hamath even to the Wadi
            Arabah.

## V. SYMBOLIC VISIONS

### First Vision: The Locust Swarm

**7** [1] This is what the Lord GOD showed me:
He was forming a locust swarm when the
late growth began to come up (the late growth
after the king's mowing†). [2] When they had
finished eating the grass in the land, I said:

Forgive, O Lord GOD!
    Who will raise up Jacob?
        He is so small!

[3] The LORD relented concerning this. "This
shall not be," said the Lord GOD.

### Second Vision: The Rain of Fire

[4] This is what the Lord GOD showed me: He
was summoning a rain of fire. It had devoured
the great abyss and was consuming the fields.
[5] Then I said:

Cease, O Lord GOD!
    Who will raise up Jacob?
        He is so small!

[6] The LORD relented concerning this. "This
also shall not be," said the Lord GOD.

### Third Vision: The Plummet

[7]* This is what the Lord GOD showed me:
He was standing, plummet in hand, by a

---

**6:10** In this desperate situation there seems to be a profound
fear of the Lord, who is the cause of the deaths (cf. 3:6).
  **6:13** *Lodebar…Karnaim*: two towns recaptured from Judah
by Israelite forces during the reign of Jeroboam II (see 2 Kgs
14:25). Some mockery of at least the first of these victories is
probably intended by the prophet here, as Lodebar can be translated "nothing."
  **6:14** *A nation*: Assyria. *Lebo-hamath…Wadi Arabah*: the terri-

torial limits of Solomon's kingdom, north and south respectively,
as re-established by Jeroboam II (see 2 Kgs 14:25).
  **7:1** *The king's mowing*: the first harvesting of the crops apparently belonged to the king as a kind of tax.

**6:8** Is 28:1–4; Jer 51:14.          **6:12** Am 5:7.
**6:10** Zep 1:7.                        **7:7–8** Jer 1:11–14.

wall built with a plummet.† ⁸The Lord GOD asked me, "What do you see, Amos?" And I answered, "A plummet." Then the LORD said:

> See, I am laying the plummet
>     in the midst of my people Israel;
>     I will forgive them no longer.
> ⁹  The high places of Isaac shall be laid
>         waste,
>     and the sanctuaries of Israel made
>         desolate;
>     and I will attack the house of
>         Jeroboam with the sword.

### Biographical Interlude: Amos and Amaziah

¹⁰Amaziah, the priest of Bethel, sent word to Jeroboam, king of Israel: "Amos has conspired against you within the house of Israel; the country cannot endure all his words. ¹¹For this is what Amos says:

> 'Jeroboam shall die by the sword,
>     and Israel shall surely be exiled from
>         its land.'"

¹²To Amos, Amaziah said: "Off with you, seer, flee to the land of Judah and there earn your bread by prophesying! ¹³But never again prophesy in Bethel;* for it is the king's sanctuary and a royal temple." ¹⁴Amos answered Amaziah, "I am not a prophet,† nor do I belong to a company of prophets. I am a herdsman and a dresser of sycamores,* ¹⁵but the LORD took me from following the flock, and the LORD said to me, 'Go, prophesy to my people Israel.'* ¹⁶Now hear the word of the LORD:

> You say: 'Do not prophesy against
>         Israel,
>     do not preach against the house of
>         Isaac.'
> ¹⁷  Therefore thus says the LORD:
>     Your wife shall become a prostitute in
>         the city,

and your sons and daughters shall fall
        by the sword.
Your land shall be parcelled out by
        measuring line,
    and you yourself shall die in an
        unclean land;
    and Israel shall be exiled from its
        land."

### Fourth Vision: The Summer Fruit

**8** ¹This is what the Lord GOD showed me: a basket of end-of-summer fruit.† ²He asked, "What do you see, Amos?" And I answered, "A basket of end-of-summer fruit." And the LORD said to me:

> The end has come for my people Israel;
>     I will forgive them no longer.
> ³  The temple singers will wail on that
>         day—
>     oracle of the Lord GOD.
> Many shall be the corpses,
>     strewn everywhere—Silence!*
>
> ⁴  Hear this, you who trample upon the
>         needy
>     and destroy the poor of the land:
> ⁵  "When will the new moon be over," you
>         ask,
>     "that we may sell our grain,
> And the sabbath,
>     that we may open the grain-bins?
> We will diminish the ephah,†
>     add to the shekel,
>     and fix our scales for cheating!*
> ⁶  We will buy the destitute for silver,
>     and the poor for a pair of sandals;*
>     even the worthless grain we will sell!"
> ⁷  The LORD has sworn by the pride of
>         Jacob:
>     Never will I forget a thing they have
>         done!
> ⁸  Shall not the land tremble because of
>         this,

---

**7:7** *A plummet*: with this vision, the pleas of the prophet (vv. 1–6) disappear, and disaster is announced. One use of the plummet in ancient times was to see how far out of line a wall or building had become, to determine whether it could be repaired or would have to be torn down. Like a structure that had become architecturally unsound, Israel was unsalvageable and would have to be demolished (cf. 2 Kgs 21:13; Is 34:11; Lam 2:8).

**7:14** *I am not a prophet*: Amos reacts strongly to Amaziah's attempt to classify him as a "prophet-for-hire" who "earns [his] bread" by giving oracles in exchange for payment (cf. 1 Sm 9:3–10; Mi 3:5). To disassociate himself from this kind of "professional" prophet, Amos rejects outright the title of *nabi'*

("prophet"). By profession he is a herdsman/sheepbreeder and a dresser of sycamore trees, but God's call has commissioned him to prophesy to Israel.

**8:1–2** *End-of-summer fruit...the end has come*: the English translation attempts to capture the wordplay of the Hebrew. The Hebrew word for "fruit picked late in the season" is *qayis*, while the word for "end" is *qes*.

**8:5** *Ephah*: see note on Is 5:10.

---

| | |
|---|---|
| 7:13 Am 2:12. | 8:3 Am 6:10. |
| 7:14 Am 1:1; 2 Sm 7:8. | 8:5 Dt 25:13; Hos 12:8. |
| 7:15 Am 3:8. | 8:6 Am 2:6. |

and all who dwell in it mourn?
It will all rise up and toss like the Nile,
  and subside like the river of Egypt.*

9 On that day—oracle of the Lord GOD—
I will make the sun set at midday
  and in broad daylight cover the land
    with darkness.

10 I will turn your feasts into mourning
  and all your songs into dirges.
I will cover the loins of all with
    sackcloth
  and make every head bald.
I will make it like the time of mourning
    for an only child,
  and its outcome like a day of bitter
    weeping.*

11 See, days are coming—oracle of the Lord
    GOD—
  when I will send a famine upon the
    land:
Not a hunger for bread, or a thirst for
    water,
  but for hearing the word of the LORD.

12 They shall stagger from sea to sea
  and wander from north to east
In search of the word of the LORD,
  but they shall not find it.*

13 On that day, beautiful young women
      and young men
  shall faint from thirst,

14 Those who swear by Ashima of
    Samaria,†*
  and who say, "By the life of your god,
    O Dan,"
"By the life of the Power of Beer-sheba!"
  They shall fall, never to rise again.

### Fifth Vision: The Destruction of the Sanctuary

**9** ¹ I saw the Lord standing beside the altar.
And he said:

Strike the capitals
  so that the threshold shakes!
Break them off on the heads of them
    all!
Those who are left I will slay with the
    sword.
Not one shall get away,
  no survivor shall escape.†*

2 Though they dig down to Sheol,
  even from there my hand shall take
    them;
Though they climb to the heavens,
  even from there I shall bring them
    down.*

3 Though they hide on the summit of
    Carmel,
  there too I will hunt them down and
    take them;
Though they hide from my gaze at the
    bottom of the sea,
  there I will command the serpent† to
    bite them.*

4 Though they go into captivity before
    their enemies,
  there I will command the sword to
    slay them.
I will fix my gaze upon them
  for evil and not for good.

5 The Lord GOD of hosts,
Who melts the earth with his touch,
  so that all who dwell on it mourn,
So that it will all rise up like the Nile,
  and subside like the river of
    Egypt;*

6 Who has built his upper chamber in
    heaven,
  and established his vault over the
    earth;
Who summons the waters of the sea
  and pours them upon the surface of
    the earth—
  the LORD is his name.*

---

**8:14** *Ashima of Samaria*: a high-ranking goddess worshiped in Hamath, whose cult was transplanted by the people of that city when they were deported to Samaria by the Assyrians (2 Kgs 17:30). *The Power of Beer-sheba*: possibly an epithet of a deity worshiped in Beer-sheba, either a syncretistic form of the worship of Israel's God or of another god. *Dan…Beer-sheba*: the traditional designation for the northern and southern limits of Israel to which the Israelites made pilgrimages.

**9:1** This vision may describe the destruction of the temple at Bethel and the fulfillment of the oracle in 3:14, linking God's judgment upon Israel with the "punishment" of the altars of Bethel. This dramatic event (perhaps to be identified with the earthquake mentioned in 1:1) symbolizes the end of the North-

ern Kingdom as the Lord's people, the consequence of their steadfast refusal to heed the prophetic word and return to the God of Israel.

**9:3** *The serpent*: a name for the primeval chaos monster, vanquished by God at the time of creation but not annihilated. He was a personification of the sea, another primary archetype of chaos in the ancient Near East.

8:8 Am 1:1; 9:1, 5.          9:2 Ps 139:7–12; Jb 20:6.
8:10 Tb 2:6; Zec 12:10.      9:3 Jb 7:12; Is 27:1.
8:12 Hos 5:6.                9:5 Am 8:8.
8:14 2 Kgs 17:30.            9:6 Am 5:8.
9:1 Am 2:13–16.

7    Are you not like the Ethiopians to me,
       O Israelites?—oracle of the LORD—
     Did I not bring the Israelites from the
         land of Egypt
       as I brought the Philistines from
         Caphtor
       and the Arameans† from Kir?
8    See, the eyes of the Lord GOD are on this
         sinful kingdom,
       and I will destroy it from the face of
         the earth—
     But I will not destroy the house of Jacob
         completely—
       oracle of the LORD.
9    For see, I have given the command
       to sift the house of Israel among all
         the nations,
     As one sifts with a sieve,
       letting no pebble fall to the ground.
10   All sinners among my people shall die
         by the sword,
       those who say, "Disaster will not reach
         or overtake us."*

## VI. EPILOGUE: RESTORATION UNDER A
## DAVIDIC KING

11†   On that day I will raise up
        the fallen hut of David;

     I will wall up its breaches,
       raise up its ruins,
       and rebuild it as in the days of
         old,*
12   That they may possess the remnant of
         Edom,
       and all nations claimed in my
         name—
       oracle of the LORD, the one who does
         this.
13   Yes, days are coming—
       oracle of the LORD—
     When the one who plows shall overtake
         the one who reaps
       and the vintager, the sower of the
         seed;
     The mountains shall drip with the juice
         of grapes,
       and all the hills shall run with it.*
14   I will restore my people Israel,
       they shall rebuild and inhabit their
         ruined cities,
     Plant vineyards and drink† the wine,
       set out gardens and eat the fruits.*
15   I will plant them upon their own
         ground;
       never again shall they be plucked
     From the land I have given them—
       the LORD, your God, has spoken.

A
M

---

† **9:7** *The Ethiopians…the Philistines…the Arameans*: although Israel's relationship to the Lord was special, even unique in some respects (3:2), Israel was not the only people on earth that God cared for. Striking here is the reference to divine intervention in the history of the Philistines and Arameans, not unlike the Lord's saving intervention to bring Israel out of Egypt. *Caphtor*: the island of Crete.

**9:11–15** These verses are most likely an editorial supplement to Amos, added to bring the book into harmony with the positive thrust of the prophetic books in general, especially those written after the exile, when the final edition of Amos was probably completed. The editors would have seen the destruction of Samaria in 722/721 B.C. as the fulfillment of Amos's prophecies,

but in this epilogue they express the view that destruction was not the Lord's final word for Israel. In Acts 15:15–17, James interprets this passage in a messianic sense. *The fallen hut of David*: the Davidic kingdom, which included what later became the divided Northern and Southern Kingdoms. *All nations claimed in my name*: lit., "all nations over whom my name has been pronounced." This idiom denotes ownership.

**9:14** *Rebuild…inhabit…plant…drink*: in this era of restoration, the Lord nullifies the curse of 5:11, which uses these same four verbs, and turns it into a blessing for Israel.

---

**9:10** Jer 5:12; 23:17.        **9:13** Jl 4:18.
**9:11** Acts 15:16–17.         **9:14** Is 65:21–22.

# The Book of
# Obadiah

## INTRODUCTION

### Dale Launderville, OSB

The book of Obadiah predicts that Edom will be invaded and depopulated (Ob 9) as punishment for its betrayal of Judah and Israel at the time of the fall of Jerusalem (587 BCE; vv. 10–11). Edom, a small, mountainous land to the southeast of the Dead Sea, was a nation whom the Israelite tradition regarded as a sibling of Israel/Judah (Gn 25:23–34; 27:1–45; 36:1), but Edom did not align itself with Judah/Jerusalem at the time of the Babylonian invasions in the sixth century. This betrayal gave rise to a fierce desire for vengeance (cf. Ps 137:7). Obadiah predicts that justice will be done on the day of the Lord (Ob 8, 15).

Obadiah, whose name means "one who serves Yahweh," reports on a "vision" (Ob 1) he has received concerning Edom. He describes both what he saw and heard from the Lord concerning the punishment of Edom and the restoration of Judah/Jerusalem. In times of crisis between nations in the ancient Near East, prophets were typically called upon to offer words of warning or encouragement from the divine world (Is 13–23; Jer 46–51; Ez 25–32; Am 1:3–2:16). The Israelites wanted a statement on how the Lord was going to act in international affairs. The need to know the divine will became particularly strong when animosity between peoples reached warlike proportions and the parties involved felt particularly vulnerable (1 Sm 10:10–13; 14:37; 1 Kgs 22:5–28).

The traditional stories of Jacob's stealing the birthright and the patriarchal blessing from Esau reflected the conviction that the younger nation (Israel) had reversed usual expectations and had become stronger than the older nation (Edom). In the tenth to the ninth centuries BCE, when the kingdoms of David and Omri were strong, Edom was a vassal of Israel. Edom revolted in the ninth century to be free of this

## Outline of Obadiah

I.  **Edom's Fall Decreed (1–7)**

II. **Edom's Betrayal of Judah (8–14)**

III. **Edom's Fall and Judah's Restoration (15–21)**

burden. In the sixth century, Judah entered into a parity treaty with Edom and other neighboring nations to revolt against the Babylonian overlord (Jer 27:3). When Babylon retaliated with the destruction of Jerusalem and Judah, Edom did not stand with the Judeans in their time of trouble (Ob 11). Obadiah charges that Edom was not only indifferent but actually rejoiced in Judah's misfortune. Obadiah's judgment against Edom becomes most pointed in the series of eight negative prohibitions in vv. 12–14, in which he accents crimes that brother Esau committed against brother Jacob in the time of his vulnerability. The righteous anger expressed in these second-person-singular commands leaves no room for the condemned Edomite to defend his behavior. Obadiah charges that not only were the Edomites indifferent to the plight of the Judeans (v. 11), they actually gloated over the fall of Jerusalem (vv. 12–13). Then the Edomites not only took over Judean possessions (v. 13) but also killed the Judean fugitives (v. 14). Perhaps only specific local groups of Edomites were killing Judeans, for there were places in Edom in which Judeans found refuge (Jer 40:11). Those Edomites who Obadiah claims participated in the plundering of Jerusalem not only took over moveable property but also settled into the southern parts of Judah.

The confiscation of Judean land is the crime

that Obadiah predicts will be reversed on the day of the Lord (Ob 8, 15). The agents who will restore Judah in this future event of divine intervention are Yahweh (vv. 1–8), those identified as "the house of Jacob/Joseph" (vv. 17–18), and the exiles in Zarephath in Phoenicia and Sepharad in Asia Minor or Assyria (v. 20). Obadiah builds upon Jer 49:9–10, 14–18 in predicting that Edom will be plundered and brought low but goes beyond it by claiming that Israelite/Judean exiles will be agents of this retribution (Ob 18, 20; cf. Ob 5). Obadiah summarizes his charges against Edom by claiming: "As you have done, so will it be done to you, your conduct will come back upon your own head" (Ob 15b). In his reworking of Jer 49:7–22, Obadiah emphasizes that Edom has been arrogant and has deceived itself in thinking that it could not be conquered

(Ob 3–4). Obadiah notes that on the day of the Lord's intervention (Ob 2, 4–9), Edom will be brought low and will suffer the same injuries as it inflicted on Judah: plundering (Ob 5–6), betrayal by covenant partners (Ob 7), widespread devastation, and depopulation (Ob 9–10).

Edom suffered the invasions of the Babylonian king Nabonidus (553–539 BCE), and then in the fourth to the third centuries BCE, Kedarite and Nabatean tribes moved in and took over Edom. Such population movements resulted in more Edomite refugees in the southern parts of Judah, a process of immigration that was already under way in the seventh century BCE. The prophecy of Obadiah held out promise to the Judeans that a fuller resolution of its conflicts with the Edomites over land rights would be resolved in their favor. ■

# THE BOOK OF OBADIAH

## New American Bible, Introduction

This book, the shortest among the twelve minor prophets, is a single twenty-one-verse oracle against Edom. Nothing is known of the author, although his prophecy against Edom, a neighbor and rival of Israel, indicates a date of composition sometime after the Babylonian destruction of Jerusalem in 587 B.C., when the Edomites apparently took advantage of the helpless people of Judah and Jerusalem (v. 11; Ps 137:7). The relations and rivalries between Israel and Edom are reflected in oracles against Edom (Is 34; Ez 35) and in the stories of their ancestors, the brothers Jacob and Esau (Gn 25–33).

The prophecy is a bitter cry for vengeance against Edom for its pride and its crimes. Mount Esau in Edom will be occupied and ravaged by the enemy, while Mount Zion will be restored to its former sanctity and security. The triumphant refrain of Israelite eschatology will be heard once more: "The kingdom is the Lord's!" The opening verses of this prophecy (vv. 1–5) are very similar to part of an oracle against Edom in Jer 49 (vv. 9, 14–16), suggesting that Israel's prophets drew upon traditional language and idioms in the composition of prophetic speech.

The book may be divided as follows:

I. Edom's Fall Decreed (1–7)
II. Edom's Betrayal of Judah (8–14)
III. Edom's Fall and Judah's Restoration (15–21) ∎

O
B

# OBADIAH

## Edom's Fall Decreed

1 The vision of Obadiah.
Thus says the Lord GOD concerning
   Edom:
We have heard a message from the LORD,
   and a herald has been sent among the
      nations:
   "Rise up, so we may go to war against
      it!"*

2 Now I make you least among the
      nations;
   you are utterly contemptible.

3 The pride of your heart has deceived
      you—
   you who dwell in mountain crevices,
   in your lofty home,†
Who say in your heart,
   "Who will bring me down to earth?"

4 Though you soar like the eagle,
   and your nest is set among the stars,
From there I will bring you down—
   oracle of the LORD.

5 If thieves came to you, robbers by night
   —how you have been destroyed!—
   would they not steal merely till they
      had enough?
If grape pickers came to you,
   would they not leave some
      gleanings?†*

6† How Esau has been searched out,
   his treasures hunted down!

7 To the border they have driven you—
   all your allies;
Your partners have deceived you,
   they have overpowered you;

Those who eat your bread†
   will replace you with foreigners,
   who have no understanding.

## Edom's Betrayal of Judah

8 On that day—oracle of the LORD—will I
      not
   make the wise disappear from Edom,
   and understanding from Mount
      Esau?*

9 Teman,† your warriors will be terror-
      stricken,
   so that everyone on Mount Esau will
      be cut down.

10 Because of violence to your brother†
      Jacob,
   disgrace will cover you,
   you will be done away with forever!*

11 On the day you stood by,
   the day strangers carried off his
      possessions,
And foreigners entered his gates
   and cast lots for Jerusalem,
   you too were like one of them.†*

12† Do not gloat over the day of your
      brother,
   the day of his disaster;
Do not exult over the people of Judah
   on the day of their ruin;
Do not speak haughtily
   on the day of distress!

13 Do not enter the gate of my people
   on the day of their calamity;
Do not gloat—especially you—over his
      misfortune
   on the day of his calamity;
Do not lay hands upon his possessions
   on the day of his calamity!

14 Do not stand at the crossroads
   to cut down his survivors;

---

**3** Edom occupied the mountains southeast of Israel and the Dead Sea.

**5** Something of value may escape the thief, and the grape picker always leaves something for the gleaners, but God's devastation of Edom will be complete.

**6** With the past tense in vv. 5–7, the prophet presents a future event as if it had already happened.

**7** *Those who eat your bread*: alliances were often established by covenant meals (cf. Gn 31:44–46). When Edom is destroyed, foreigners will replace the Edomites, who were known for wisdom (cf. v. 8; Jer 49:7; Jb 2:11).

**9** *Teman*: a synonym for Edom; perhaps the name of a region or a city, the part representing the whole. *Mount Esau*: whatever its geographic reference, the phrase is an effective representation of Edom's arrogance.

**10** *Your brother*: used with a double meaning referring to the

common lineage of Israel and Edom, in which their ancestors were brothers, Jacob and Esau (Gn 25:19–26), and referring also to their political alliance, in which allies were called brothers (cf. Am 1:9, 11).

**11** In 587 B.C., Edomites joined the invading Babylonian forces (v. 13) and captured escaping Judahites. The destruction of Jerusalem strengthened and expanded Edom's hold on Judah's southern territory.

**12–14** The commands in vv. 12–14 are not to be understood as future prohibitions but as descriptions of crimes Edom in fact already committed on the day of Jerusalem's fall described in v. 11.

---

**1–4** Jer 49:14–16.          **10** Gn 27:41–45; Ez
**5** Jer 49:9.                      25:12–14.
**8** Is 29:14; 1 Cor 1:19.   **11** Ps 137:7.

Do not hand over his fugitives
   on the day of distress!

### Edom's Fall and Judah's Restoration

15 Near is the day of the LORD *
   against all the nations!
As you have done, so will it be done to
   you,
      your conduct will come back upon
         your own head;
16 As you drank† upon my holy
     mountain,
   so will all the nations drink
     continually.
Yes, they will drink and swallow,
   and will become as though they had
     not been.
17 But on Mount Zion there will be some
   who escape;†
   the mountain will be holy,

And the house of Jacob will take
     possession
   of those who dispossessed them. *
18 The house of Jacob will be a fire,
   the house of Joseph a flame,
   and the house of Esau stubble.
They will set it ablaze and devour it;
   none will survive of the house of Esau,
   for the LORD has spoken.

19 They will take possession of the Negeb,† Mount Esau, the Shephelah, and Philistia, possess the countryside of Ephraim, the countryside of Samaria, Benjamin, and Gilead. * 20 The exiles of this Israelite army will possess the Canaanite land as far as Zarephath,† and the exiles of Jerusalem who are in Sepharad will possess the cities of the Negeb. 21 And deliverers† will ascend Mount Zion to rule Mount Esau, and the kingship shall be the LORD's.

---

† **16** *As you drank*: i.e., Judah has suffered the punishment of divine wrath in 587 B.C. The oracle promises a similar fate for the nations, especially Edom (v. 18). The metaphor "drinking the cup of God's wrath" occurs often in the Bible; cf. Jb 21:20; Is 51:17–23; Jer 25:15–16; Rev 14:10.

**17–19** The Israelites will be restored and will occupy the lands of those who oppressed them. The survivors of Judah will be rejoined by the returned exiles from northern Israel.

**19** *Negeb*: the area south of Judah and west of Edom. *Gilead*:

east of the Jordan River.

**20** *Zarephath*: a town in Phoenicia, north of Tyre; cf. 1 Kgs 17:10. *Sepharad*: perhaps Sardis in western Asia Minor. The later rabbis thought it was Spain.

**21** *Deliverers*: the victorious Israelites who will rule over their enemies, as the ancient judges did; cf. Jgs 3:9, 15, 31; 10:1.

---

* **15** Jl 4:11–12, 14.          **19** Jer 50:19.
     **17** Jer 49:2.

O
B

## INTRODUCTION

### Garrett Galvin, OFM

At just four chapters, Jonah is one of the shorter books of the Old Testament, but its importance far exceeds its length. Jonah is one of the few "prophets" directly mentioned by Jesus in the Gospels, and the Hebrew Bible places the book of Jonah among the Minor Prophets. And yet one hesitates to use the term "prophet" to describe Jonah, as he is most atypical.

The book of Jonah is a narrative, whereas most other prophetic books are primarily poetry, and some are poetry exclusively. The divine message usually stands at the center of a prophetic book, but the center of the book of Jonah consists of a conversation between the Lord and Jonah. But what makes the book of Jonah truly unique is its highly satiric nature. Elements of satire are found in other books of the Bible, but Jonah is a sustained satire on a number of levels. The sustained satiric nature makes it similar to some parables, and serves to alert the reader that, in this book, one is not dealing with sober history, but with something more akin to legend or fable. The Hebrew word for parable (*mashal*) can imply the idea of puzzle, and this multi-layered satire certainly contains a number of puzzles. Parables often exaggerate and puzzle the reader with their strangeness, as does Jonah. Recent studies have highlighted the important structure of the Book of the Twelve in which the book of Jonah is located. Micah serves as the chiastic[1] center of the Book of the Twelve and Jonah is just before it. The books immediately before Micah all have a strong focus on hope and salvation, whereas the books immediately after focus more on woe and tribulation.

---

1. Chiasm is a rhetorical inversion of two parallel structures.

## Outline of Jonah

I.  **Jonah's Disobedience and Flight (1:1–16)**

II. **Jonah's Prayer (2:1–11)**

III. **Jonah's Obedience and the Ninevites' Repentance (3:1–10)**

IV. **Jonah's Anger and God's Reproof (4:1–11)**

## Background to the Book of Jonah

Like other figures such as Enoch (Gn 4:17) and Solomon, who have later literature attached to their names, so too does Jonah. Jonah, son of Amittai, first appears in 2 Kgs 14:25. While the character in 2 Kings has the same name and social role (prophet), he appears to be quite different. The character in Kings served under Jeroboam II (785–745 BCE) and prophesied the successful restoration of the boundaries of Israel under this evil king. We find none of this information in the book of Jonah. In fact, very little biographical information exists about Jonah within the book.

The dating of the book of Jonah is a conundrum. While the role of Nineveh is in accordance with the time of the prophet Jonah mentioned in Kings, this allusion seems to be satirical as a later audience would know that Nineveh had been completely destroyed in 612 BCE. This fact also suggests the ironic nature of the book. Deuteronomy 18:22 says that prophets are false if their words do not come true. From a historical perspective Jonah's words do come true, but not within the story itself. The issues that the book addresses reflect the exilic experience of Israel. God is depicted with unusual freedom and, compared to the volcanic theophanies of the Exodus (Ex 34:6) or the triumphs of Elijah (1 Kgs 18:40), his actions are more subtle. Non-Israelites understand God's desire better than Jonah does at times.

The book of Jonah is highly structured around two journeys. We begin with the sea journey, which ends in Jon 2 with a lament asking for deliverance and God's response. Jonah 3 then has a journey across land to Nineveh, which is followed by another prayer from Jonah with a more nuanced response from God. There is a strong formal correspondence between chs. 1–2 and 3–4. Many similarities in vocabulary and syntax appear in these two settings, but the interactions between Jonah and God become much more complicated in the course of the second journey.

## The First Journey

The book starts abruptly. In the second verse, God tells Jonah to go to Nineveh and preach against it. Jonah does exactly the opposite; he goes to the port of Joppa and sets out for Tarshish. The location of Tarshish is debated: perhaps in Spain, Cyprus, or Asia Minor. The importance of Tarshish may be that it seems to be the exact opposite direction of where God told Jonah to go. The strange thing about these introductory verses is that we are given no reason for Jonah's actions. Reasons will emerge only gradually in the course of the story. For now, he remains a mysterious figure and his motivations are hard to fathom. He is more like Elijah or Elisha, about whom narratives are written, rather than a prophet producing oracles of woe and salvation—quite different from the figure of Jonah in the book of Kings. But unlike Elijah or Elisha, who are not depicted as doubting God's destiny for them, ambiguity surrounds Jonah.

Three more parts complete the first chapter: the ship (Jon 1:4–5), the discovery of Jonah (1:6–11), and Jonah's submission (1:12–16). Irony has already been introduced into the story by Jonah's reaction to God's call to preach to Nineveh. The irony increases when the story introduces the reader to the ship. The Lord hurls a great "wind" upon the sea,

reminiscent of the wind sweeping over the waters of primordial chaos (Gn 1:2). Subsequently we see the faithful reaction of the sailors to this "wind" as "each one cried to his god" (Jon 1:5a). Ironically, the prophet Jonah heads down to the hold of the ship and falls asleep. The word used for sleep is unusual; such sleep appears to be controlled by God in Dn 8:18 and 10:9. As God awakens Daniel, the pagan sailors awaken Jonah. This discovery of Jonah leads to the fulfillment of God's will for him; ironically, the pagan sailors will not allow Jonah to flee from God.

The discovery of Jonah leads to his faith statement, which some consider to be the chiastic center of the first chapter. Jonah states in 1:9: "I am a Hebrew. . . . I fear the LORD, the God of heaven, who made the sea and the dry land." Jonah speaks for the first time and identifies himself in the same manner as Abraham, Joseph, and Moses. The Diaspora community would have resonated with these individuals, all of whom lived outside the promised land for extended periods. Jonah continues his faith statement by saying that he fears the Lord, meaning that he worships the Lord. The faith statement concludes with language that recalls the chaos imagery of the chapter's beginning: the Lord is the God "who made the sea and the dry land" (cf. Gn 1:10). Jonah's allusions to Gn 1 and Abraham speak to the essentials of biblical faith within the book of Jonah.

Jonah 1 concludes with men desperately trying to get to God's dry land (Jon 1:13), but the chaos increases. In a sense both Jonah and the sailors must submit to God. Jonah's submission is obvious in v. 12 as he instructs the men to throw him into the water. The men ultimately give up trying to get to dry land by their effort alone. They cry to the Lord (1:14), fear the Lord (1:16), and obey Jonah, to whom the word of the Lord came (1:1).

The lament in Jonah 2 is reminiscent of a number of psalms. It acknowledges the hardships currently being experienced, but also places enormous trust in the Lord. Although the language of lament at times emphasizes the overwhelming and hopeless, the form of the lament almost always highlights trust and hope in the end. We see this clearly in Jon 2 where the imagery of chaos, drowning, and desperation characterize the greater part of the lament. The poem moves from desperation to the precipice of death in v. 7 where Jonah becomes faint and Sheol is very near, but abundant faith then enters the poem, and the poet seems assured of deliverance in the end (2:10). The fish cooperates by vomiting Jonah on the dry land (2:11).

The fish stands out as the most memorable aspect of the Jonah story. It appears at the beginning and conclusion of the chapter, thus forming an *inclusio*. Later translators equate the fish with Leviathan and other signs of evil and chaos, but the language of Jon 2 is clear: it is simply a big fish. Animals play important roles in a number of biblical stories; they generally influence the flow of the narrative— e.g., Balaam's ass (Nm 22:22–35)—rather than functioning as symbols. Part of the ongoing importance of Jonah for the New Testament is the three days and nights that Jonah spent in the belly of the fish. "The sign of Jonah" is understood in a number of different ways, but Mt 12:38–42 seems to understand it as a foreshadowing of the three days before Christ's Resurrection. Luke sees "the sign" as the prophet's mission of calling the Ninevites to repentance (Lk 11:30). These differing interpretations point once again to the parabolic nature of the book of Jonah. Because the book is an artistic creation, rather than objective history with a definitive interpretation, two Gospel writers can understand the sign quite differently.

## The Second Journey

Jonah's second journey quickly transpires at the beginning of Jon 3. The directions for Jonah are even more terse here than in ch. 1, but this time Jonah is obedient. The atypical prophet has become a typical prophet, but the satire of the book now comes into full relief as the response of the people becomes atypical. Like the pagan sailors before them, the ironic contrast between Jonah and the people of Nineveh could not be greater. The people of Nineveh do not hesitate; the word of God affects them instantly. We are accustomed to prophets being

met with antipathy (Jeremiah being thrown into a well [Jer 38:6]) or having to go to extraordinary lengths (Isaiah going naked through the streets of Jerusalem [Is 20:3]), but none of this seems necessary for Nineveh. The atypical prophet has met atypical people.

The people's response leads to frustration and prayer on the part of Jonah. This prayer is much shorter than that of Jon 2, but full of irony. He states that he knows God is "gracious and merciful" (4:2), but he resents the application of grace and mercy to the people of Nineveh. No scholarly consensus exists concerning our understanding of Jonah's motivations here. Some see it as quite limited and having nothing to do with universalistic impulses found in other postexilic biblical books. Others find a universalistic impulse behind this episode, arguing that God here rebukes the prophet for his narrow-mindedness and ethnocentrism.[2] As in the book of Ruth, foreigners have something to teach Israel, and Israel can live among foreigners.

Jonah 4 ties in nicely to the larger themes of the book. We see the recurrent use of the Hebrew word for "great" throughout the book and here again in Jon 4:1, 6, and 11. Irony seems never far from this word, especially in 4:6 where we see how a plant elicits far more joy in Jonah than the conversion of the people. As in ch. 2, Jonah is punished here as well. First it was the great fish; now it is the plant, the worm, and the east wind. Although the English does not reflect it, the narrator uses the same verb (*manah*) to send all these punishments on Jonah. Jonah resists God's universal salvific will, and the ultimate irony of this book is that the prophet, not the foreigners, keeps on getting punished. In a time of great change in Judah, perhaps this book warns ethnocentric religious figures not to put limits on the love of God.∎

---

2. The references to God as creator of all in ch. 1 are also sometimes cited as evidence of a universalistic tendency in the book of Jonah.

# THE BOOK OF JONAH

## New American Bible, Introduction

The story of Jonah has great theological import. It concerns a disobedient prophet who rejected his divine commission, was cast overboard in a storm and swallowed by a great fish, rescued in a marvelous manner, and returned to his starting point. Now he obeys and goes to Nineveh, the capital of Israel's ancient enemy. The Ninevites listen to his message of doom and repent immediately. All, from king to lowliest subject, humble themselves in sackcloth and ashes. Seeing their repentance, God does not carry out the punishment planned for them. At this, Jonah complains, angry because the Lord spares them. This fascinating story caricatures a narrow mentality which would see God's interest extending only to Israel, whereas God is presented as concerned with and merciful to even the inhabitants of Nineveh (4:11), the capital of the Assyrian empire which brought the Northern Kingdom of Israel to an end and devastated Jerusalem in 701 B.C. The Lord is free to "repent" and change his mind. Jonah seems to realize this possibility and wants no part in it (4:2; cf. Ex 34:6). But the story also conveys something of the ineluctable character of the prophetic calling.

The book is replete with irony, wherein much of its humor lies. The name "Jonah" means "dove" in Hebrew, but Jonah's character is anything but dove-like. Jonah is commanded to go east to Nineveh but flees toward the westernmost possible point (1:2–3), only to be swallowed by a great fish and dumped back at this starting point (2:1, 11). The sailors pray to their gods, but Jonah is asleep in the hold (1:5–6). The prophet's preaching is a minimum message of destruction, while it is the king of Nineveh who calls for repentance and conversion (3:4–10); the instant conversion of the Ninevites is greeted by Jonah with anger and sulking (4:1). He reproaches the Lord in words that echo Israel's traditional praise of his mercy (4:2; cf. Ex 34:6–7). Jonah is concerned about the loss of the gourd but not about the possible destruction of 120,000 Ninevites (4:10–11).

Unlike other prophetic books, this is not a collection of oracles but the story of a disobedient, narrow-minded prophet who is angry at the outcome of the sole message he delivers (3:4). It is difficult to date but almost certainly is postexilic and may reflect the somewhat narrow, nationalistic reforms of Ezra and Nehemiah. As to genre, it has been classified in various ways, such as parable or satire. The "sign" of Jonah is interpreted in two ways in the New Testament: His experience of three days and nights in the fish is a "type" of the experience of the Son of Man (Mt 12:39–40), and the Ninevites' reaction to the preaching of Jonah is contrasted with the failure of Jesus' generation to obey the preaching of one who is "greater than Jonah" (Mt 12:41–42; Lk 11:29–32).

The Book of Jonah may be divided as follows:

I. Jonah's Disobedience and Flight (1:1–16)

II. Jonah's Prayer (2:1–11)

III. Jonah's Obedience and the Ninevites' Repentance (3:1–10)

IV. Jonah's Anger and God's Reproof (4:1–11) ■

# JONAH

**Jonah's Disobedience and Flight.** ¹The word of the LORD came to Jonah,* son of Amittai:† ²Set out for the great city† of Nineveh, and preach against it; for their wickedness has come before me.* ³But Jonah made ready to flee to Tarshish,† away from the LORD. He went down to Joppa, found a ship going to Tarshish, paid the fare, and went down in it to go with them to Tarshish, away from the LORD.

⁴*The LORD, however, hurled a great wind upon the sea, and the storm was so great that the ship was about to break up. ⁵Then the sailors were afraid and each one cried to his god. To lighten the ship for themselves, they threw its cargo into the sea. Meanwhile, Jonah had gone down into the hold of the ship, and lay there fast asleep. ⁶The captain approached him and said, "What are you doing asleep? Get up, call on your god! Perhaps this god will be mindful of us so that we will not perish."

⁷Then they said to one another, "Come, let us cast lots to discover on whose account this evil has come to us." So they cast lots, and the lot fell on Jonah.* ⁸They said to him, "Tell us why this evil has come to us! What is your business? Where do you come from? What is your country, and to what people do you belong?" ⁹"I am a Hebrew," he replied; "I fear the LORD, the God of heaven, who made the sea and the dry land."

¹⁰Now the men were seized with great fear and said to him, "How could you do such a thing!"—They knew that he was fleeing from the LORD, because he had told them. ¹¹They asked, "What shall we do with you, that the sea may calm down for us?" For the sea was growing more and more stormy. ¹²Jonah responded, "Pick me up and hurl me into the sea and then the sea will calm down for you. For I know that this great storm has come upon you because of me."

¹³Still the men rowed hard to return to dry land, but they could not, for the sea grew more and more stormy. ¹⁴Then they cried to the LORD: "Please, O LORD, do not let us perish for taking this man's life; do not charge us with shedding innocent blood, for you, LORD, have accomplished what you desired."† ¹⁵Then they picked up Jonah and hurled him into the sea, and the sea stopped raging. ¹⁶Seized with great fear of the LORD, the men offered sacrifice to the LORD and made vows.

**Jonah's Prayer.** ¹But the LORD sent a great fish to swallow Jonah, and he remained in the belly of the fish three days and three nights.* ²Jonah prayed to the LORD, his God, from the belly of the fish:

³† Out of my distress I called to the LORD,
  and he answered me;
From the womb of Sheol† I cried for
  help,
  and you heard my voice.*
⁴ You cast me into the deep, into the heart
  of the sea,
  and the flood enveloped me;
All your breakers and your billows
  passed over me.*
⁵ Then I said, "I am banished from your
  sight!
  How will I again look upon your holy
  temple?"*
⁶ The waters surged around me up to my
  neck;
  the deep enveloped me;
  seaweed wrapped around my head.*
⁷ I went down to the roots of the
  mountains;
  to the land whose bars closed behind
  me forever,

**1:1** *Jonah, son of Amittai*: a prophet of this name lived at the time of Jeroboam II (786–746 B.C.). 
**1:2** *Great city*: exaggeration is characteristic of this book; the word "great" (Heb. *gadol*) occurs fourteen times. 
**1:3** *Tarshish*: identified by many with Tartessus, an ancient Phoenician colony in southwest Spain; precise identification with any particular Phoenician center in the western Mediterranean is uncertain. To the Israelites it stood for the far west. 
**1:14** Aware that this disaster is a divine punishment on Jonah, the sailors ask that in ridding themselves of him they not be charged with the crime of murder. 
**2:3–10** These verses, which may have originally been an independent composition, are a typical example of a song of thanksgiving, a common psalm genre (e.g., Ps 116; Is 38:9–20). Such a song is relevant here, since Jonah has not drowned, and the imagery of vv. 4, 6 is appropriate. 
**2:3** *Sheol*: c.f. note on Ps 6:6.

**1:1** 2 Kgs 14:25.
**1:2** Jon 3:3; 4:11.
**1:4–6** Mk 4:37–38.
**1:7** Jos 7:16–18; 1 Sm 14:40–42.
**2:1** Mt 12:40; 16:4; Lk 11:30; 1 Cor 15:4.
**2:3** Ps 18:7; 120:1.
**2:4** Ps 42:8.
**2:5** Ps 31:23; Is 38:11.
**2:6** Ps 18:5; 69:2.

But you brought my life up from the pit,
O LORD, my God.*

8  When I became faint,
I remembered the LORD;
My prayer came to you
in your holy temple.*

9  Those who worship worthless idols
abandon their hope for mercy.*

10  But I, with thankful voice,
will sacrifice to you;
What I have vowed I will pay:
deliverance is from the LORD.*

11 Then the LORD commanded the fish to vomit Jonah upon dry land.

### 3 Jonah's Obedience and the Ninevites' Repentance.

1 The word of the LORD came to Jonah a second time: 2 Set out for the great city of Nineveh, and announce to it the message that I will tell you. 3 So Jonah set out for Nineveh, in accord with the word of the LORD. Now Nineveh was an awesomely great city; it took three days to walk through it. 4 Jonah began his journey through the city, and when he had gone only a single day's walk announcing, "Forty days more and Nineveh shall be overthrown," 5 the people of Nineveh believed God; they proclaimed a fast and all of them, great and small,† put on sackcloth.*

6 When the news reached the king of Nineveh, he rose from his throne, laid aside his robe, covered himself with sackcloth, and sat in ashes. 7 Then he had this proclaimed throughout Nineveh:† "By decree of the king and his nobles, no man or beast, no cattle or sheep, shall taste anything; they shall not eat, nor shall they drink water. 8 Man and beast alike must be covered with sackcloth and call loudly to God; they all must turn from their evil way and from the violence of their hands. 9† Who knows? God may again repent and turn from his blazing wrath, so that we will not perish."* 10 When God saw by their actions how they turned from their evil way, he repented of the evil he had threatened to do to them; he did not carry it out.

### 4 Jonah's Anger and God's Reproof.

1 But this greatly displeased Jonah, and he became angry.† 2 He prayed to the LORD, "O LORD, is this not what I said while I was still in my own country? This is why I fled at first toward Tarshish. I knew that you are a gracious and merciful God, slow to anger, abounding in kindness, repenting of punishment.†* 3 So now, LORD, please take my life from me; for it is better for me to die than to live."* 4 But the LORD asked, "Are you right to be angry?"†

5 Jonah then left the city for a place to the east of it, where he built himself a hut and waited† under it in the shade, to see what would happen to the city. 6 Then the LORD God provided a gourd plant.† And when it grew up over Jonah's head, giving shade that relieved him of any discomfort, Jonah was greatly delighted with the plant. 7 But the next morning at dawn God provided a worm that attacked the plant, so that it withered. 8 And when the sun arose, God provided a scorching east wind; and the sun beat upon Jonah's head till he became faint. Then he wished for death, saying, "It is better for me to die than to live."

9 But God said to Jonah, "Do you have a right to be angry over the gourd plant?" Jonah answered, "I have a right to be angry—angry enough to die." 10 Then the LORD said, "You are concerned† over the gourd plant which cost

---

**3:5** *Great and small*: the contrast can refer to distinctions of social class (prominent citizens and the poor).

**3:7–8** Fasting and wearing sackcloth are signs of human repentance; here they are legislated even for the animals—a humorous touch, perhaps anticipating 4:11.

**3:9–10** Scripture frequently presents the Lord as repenting (or, changing his mind) of the evil that he threatens; e.g., Gn 6:6–7; Jer 18:8.

**4:1** *He became angry*: because of his narrow vindictiveness, Jonah did not wish the Lord to forgive the Ninevites.

**4:2** *Punishment*: lit., "evil"; see 1:2, 7, 8; 3:8, 10; 4:1.

**4:4** The Lord's question is as unexpected as it is pithy. It is also a mysterious reply to Jonah's wish to die; perhaps it serves to invite Jonah to think over his situation. However, it goes unanswered, and the request and reply will be repeated in vv. 8–9.

**4:5** *Waited*: Jonah still hopes his threat of doom will be fulfilled.

**4:6** *Gourd plant*: the Hebrew word, *qiqayon*, means here a wide-leafed plant of the cucumber or castor-bean variety.

**4:10** *Concerned*: the meaning of the Hebrew verb suggests "pity, care for," and this appears in the Lord's attitude to Nineveh in v. 11. Jonah has shown only a selfish concern over the plant in contrast to the Lord's true "concern" for his creatures.

---

**2:7** Ps 16:10; 30:4.
**2:8** Ps 5:8; 18:7; 88:3.
**2:9** Ps 31:7.
**2:10** Ps 50:14.
**3:5** Mt 12:41; Lk 11:32.
**3:9** Jl 2:14.
**4:2** Ex 34:6–7; Ps 86:5; Jl 2:13.
**4:3** 1 Kgs 19:4.

you no effort and which you did not grow; it came up in one night and in one night it perished. ¹¹And should I not be concerned over the great city of Nineveh, in which there are more than a hundred and twenty thousand persons who cannot know their right hand from their left, not to mention all the animals?"†

---

**4:11** A selfish Jonah bemoans his personal loss of a gourd plant for shade without any concern over the threat of loss of life to the Ninevites through the destruction of their city. If a solicitous God provided the plant for a prophet without the latter's effort or merit, how much more is God disposed to show love and mercy toward all people, Jew and Gentile, when they repent of their sins and implore divine pardon. God's care goes beyond human beings to all creation, as in Job 38.

# The Book of
# Micah

## INTRODUCTION

### Garrett Galvin, OFM

Along with Isaiah, Hosea, and Amos, Micah belongs to the small group of eighth-century prophets. Whereas Amos and Hosea prophesied in the northern kingdom of Israel and Isaiah worked primarily in Jerusalem, Micah represented the people living outside of Jerusalem in Judah. Micah, whose name is short for "who is like you (O God)" (Mi 7:18), speaks for the Judean countryside with his strident and uncompromising voice. No prophet criticizes the oppression of the poor as severely as Micah (3:2–3). Yet Micah's voice is not one of unrelenting doom, as he also preaches hope and returns to it frequently (chs. 4–5; 7:7–20). Like Isaiah, the book shows many signs of editorial structuring as well as signs of revisions during the Babylonian exile (587–535 BCE). These revisions leave the reader with a highly structured book, but a book that can be quite complicated at times.

Most scholars see three "books" within the seven chapters of Micah. Chapters 1–3 are known as the Book of Doom, but a high note of salvation is heard at the end of the second chapter (Mi 2:12–13). Micah 4–5 consists of oracles of salvation. Many understand this section to be a response to the oracles of woe that make up the first three chapters. The third book (chs. 6–7) returns to the negative tone of the Book of Doom; however, it ends with salvation in 7:7–20.

No scholarly consensus exists around the dating of the book. Jeremiah 26:18 makes reference to a Micah of Moresheth who prophesied during the reign of King Hezekiah (715–687 BCE). This is the same and only description we find of Micah in his book at Mi 1:1. Unlike the rest of the book, this superscription is not written in poetry and could easily come from a much later period. In this description Micah also prophecies during the reign of Hezekiah

### Outline of Micah

I. **Oracles of Punishment (1:2–3:12)**

II. **Oracles of Salvation (4:1–5:14)**

III. **Announcement of Judgment (6:1–7:6)**

IV. **Confidence in God's Future (7:7–20)**

as well as Jotham (ca. 750–732) and Ahaz (ca. 732–715). Many consider the first three chapters to be reflective of the historical Micah as they consist almost entirely of oracles of doom. The oracles of salvation in chs. 4–5 offer a strong contrast to this earlier material. Some have argued that, like the second section of Isaiah (Is 40–55), this second section of Micah represents much later material. The viewpoint is intriguing, but it has not garnered the same consensus found around Is 40–55. Nonetheless, the attentive reader will compare a striking difference between the first two sections of Micah (Mi 1–3 and 4–5) with a similar difference between the first two sections of Isaiah (Is 1–39 and 40–55). Micah 6–7 returns to many of the themes found in the original Book of Doom with an oracle of salvation as conclusion.

The beginning and end of the book would seem to reflect the devastation visited upon the countryside of Judah. Whereas the capital of Jerusalem managed to withstand the Assyrian onslaught visited upon Israel and Judah, this was not the case for the countryside. The destruction of a city like Lachish reflects this Judean devastation. Micah seems to imply that too much was sacrificed for Jerusalem. He decries the arrogance of the leaders in Mi 3:11, who appear to think Jerusalem is invulnerable and argue that no evil can come upon it. Micah sees all the evil that has been foisted upon the rest of Judah and argues that the same lies in store for Jerusalem if it does not change its ways. In 2:4 Micah seems to speak for a people who know mockery and ruin, who have seen their fields divided and given to their captors as he warns Jerusalem that the same is in store for it. While the oracles of salvation may represent a later age, many parts of Mi 1–3 and 6–7 would appear to reflect the crushing circumstances following the Assyrian assault on Judah.

# Micah 1–3: Oracles of Woe

The Book of Doom (Mi 1–3) can be divided into nine poems. The first poem (1:2–7) is a warning to the two capital cities of Israel and Judah: Samaria and Jerusalem. Samaria serves as a precursor to Jerusalem; both cities can expect the same fate. The second poem (1:8–9) is a lament that uses the image of jackals and ostriches familiar from the psalms and other laments to signal the plight of Judah and the hardships that await Jerusalem. Like many other images in Micah, this pairing is familiar from Isaiah (Is 34:13; 43:20). The mourning continues and escalates in the next poem (Mi 1:10–16). We hear the horrendous fate of the cities southwest of Jerusalem, including the winter capital of Lachish. This poem concludes with a line reminiscent of Hos 8:1; here, the vulture watches the sad fate of those taken into exile, perhaps as the prophet has. Micah 2 continues the strident tone found in Mi 1. In language reminiscent of Am 6:4, we hear of the evil being done while the wicked relax in bed (Mi 2:1). The fourth poem (2:1–5) warns of a reversal of fortune for the wicked. The fifth poem (2:6–11) may allude to the criticisms Micah heard. We hear someone told not to preach (2:6) and how the peaceful are mistreated by the arrogant (2:8). The sixth poem (2:12–13) offers a respite from all the woes previously heard. The Lord will reverse the evils and restore the remnant of Israel "like a herd in its pasture" (2:12). This poem gives us a foretaste of the hope that will be found in Mi 4–5 and at the end of the book (7:7–20).

Chapter 3 includes three poems that attack the leadership of Israel and Judah. The seventh poem (Mi 3:1–4) addresses the leaders in general, but the eighth poem (3:5–8) narrows in on prophets, and the ninth poem (3:9–12) broadens its scope to leaders again while explicitly mentioning both priests and prophets. The seventh poem includes what some scholars consider to be the sharpest denunciation of the exploitation of the powerless in all of biblical literature (3:2–3). At times the tone seems reminiscent of the Deuteronomic reform movement. The same word for leadership is used in Dt 1:15 and Mi 3:1. Deuteronomy 15:11 and 24:12–15 display the same concern for the plight of the poor as is found in this seventh poem. The eighth poem levels its attack upon the prophets. Micah appears to understand the prophets as central cult prophets. He wants nothing to do with this institution and shuns the title "prophet." Prophets simply seem to be at the service of the highest bidder in the time of Micah. The ninth and final poem of the Book of Doom sharpens its focus on Jerusalem. Justice is a commodity in Jerusalem that priests and prophets sell (Mi 3:11). Their hypocritical and specious faith in the Lord ultimately gives reason for the destruction of the city. Jeremiah 26:18 reports Micah using almost the exact same language as found in Mi 3:12 about the fate of Jerusalem.

# Micah 4–5: Oracles of Salvation

Micah 4–5 returns to the hope first articulated in 2:12–13. These two chapters consist of nine, or possibly ten, poems. The book of Micah seems to follow a pattern of descriptions of disaster followed by hope. Micah 4–5 is the second and longest of three descriptions of hope. In some respects, it may be considered the chiastic center (a rhetorical inversion of two parallel structures) of the book of Micah, in a book that is considered the chiastic center of the Book of the Twelve (i.e., the Minor Prophets). The beginning of these two chapters is almost exactly the same as Is 2:2–4. While

M
I

many consider it to be derivative of Isaiah, we cannot be certain. Isaiah's and Micah's oracles of salvation share much in common and there is no definitive answer as to which was written first.

Micah 4–5 moves from the dystopian vision of the Book of Doom to a utopian vision. Apart from 6:6–8 these chapters may be the best known parts of the book. They are often heard during Advent because of Matthew's use of Mi 5:1–3 (Mt 2:6); this messianic interpretation is most explicit and familiar in regard to the reference to Bethlehem in Mi 5:1. We hear that a ruler will come from Bethlehem. This ruler will deliver Israel and Judah from their foreign oppressors and be associated with peace (Mi 5:5). This all seems to happen within the context of exile.

The language of exile dominates these two chapters, particularly Mi 5. The oppressor here seems to be both Babylon (4:10) and Assyria (5:4). Micah 5:6 offers a beautiful and stirring description of the remnant. A strong argument can be made that these chapters come from the time of the Babylonian exile rather than the eighth century BCE. Babylon would not be seen as an oppressor in the eighth century. Micah 4:10 speaks of redemption, language much more characteristic of Is 40–55 and other material later than the eighth-century prophets.

## Micah 6–7: The Concluding Oracles

The final section, Mi 6–7, consists of between four and six poems, depending on how one divides them. This is the most balanced of the sections, with oracles characterized by despair and concluding with hope. We begin Mi 6 with language characteristic of the eighth-century prophets: we hear that the Lord has a case (rîb) against Israel. We hear the familiar rehearsal of Israel's deliverance from the land of Egypt so common throughout the Old Testament. All these events are rehearsed in order to remind Israel of how disloyal it has been to the Lord. This also serves to highlight what the Lord truly wants in 6:8b: "Only to do justice and to love goodness, and to walk humbly with your God." Many commentators would see this as the central plea of Micah and perhaps the most memorable of all biblical imperatives. This is placed in a northern (i.e., Israelite) context at the end of Mi 6, as the evildoers are accused of following Omri (886–875 BCE) and Ahab (875–854 BCE).

Micah 7 contains a great contrast between the initial lament (7:1–6) of a chaotic time in which no one can be trusted and the mending of a relationship (7:7–20) in which the Lord's faithfulness/mercy (hesed: 6:8; 7:18, 20) will be known again. The initial lament concludes the negative material of chs. 6–7 that decries the evils of Jerusalem. Here we have a devastating picture of civil and familial corruption in which neither judges nor children can be trusted. A four-part poem of two laments (7:7–10; 7:14–17) followed by two oracles of salvation (7:11–13; 7:18–20) conclude this book. This poem prophesies a reversal of fortune in which a resurgent Zion/Jerusalem will know the saving acts of God. Verses 7–10 chronicle the shame that Jerusalem currently knows, but the verses also place trust in the Lord to bring about a reversal. This reversal begins in v. 11 as we hear of the boundaries of Israel increasing. The nations will now stream to Israel as its boundaries and power increase (7:12). Before this reversal happens, there must be devastation. We have an eschatological description in v. 13 without any apocalyptic language, as Israel wishes to return to the "days of old" (7:14) when God shepherded them. Beginning in v. 14, Micah's supplication recalls the deliverance from Egypt again, but this time it is a warning to the other nations (7:15). The shame that Zion felt in vv. 7–10 will now be felt by the nations. As the Lord has delivered Israel in times past and as the Lord was loyal to Abraham (7:20), so will Jacob/Israel (7:20) know this faithfulness/mercy again. God is responsible for Zion's resurgence, but God is known not only through power but also mercy/faithfulness. Verse 18 returns to the meaning of the name Micah: "Who is a God like you?" Peoples expect either power or mercy from their gods, but Israel's God is a God of both power and mercy. ∎

# THE BOOK OF MICAH

## New American Bible, Introduction

This book consists of a collection of speeches, proclamations of punishment and of salvation, attributed to the prophet Micah. Following its superscription (1:1), the book has two major sections, each with two parts. The organization of the material is thematic, moving from judgment to salvation in both major sections. In the first section (Mi 1–5), chaps. 1–3 consist almost entirely of prophecies of punishment, and chaps. 4–5 of prophecies of salvation. The second section (chaps. 6–7) also moves from prophecies of punishment (6:1–7:6) to confidence in God's salvation (7:7–20).

Micah was a contemporary of the prophet Isaiah. The book's superscription (1:1) places his prophetic activity during the reigns of three kings of Judah: Jotham, Ahaz, and Hezekiah. It identifies him as a resident of Moresheth, a village in the Judean foothills. The solitary reference to Micah outside the book (Jer 26:17–18) places him in the reign of Hezekiah and reports that he went from his small town to proclaim the word of the Lord in the capital, and asserts that his announcements of judgment against Jerusalem moved the king and the people to repentance. Unlike Isaiah, who was a native of the holy city, Micah was an outsider from the countryside and must have been a controversial figure. He would have been unpopular with the leaders whom he condemned (3:1–4) and the wealthy whom he criticized (2:1–5). He was quick to separate himself from priests and other prophets, whom he considered to be corrupt (3:5–8).

Just how much of the Book of Micah can be traced to the eighth-century prophet is uncertain. Tradition considers all of the words

to be the recorded speeches of Micah, and some contemporary commentators agree. On the other hand, some modern scholars have thought of Micah as exclusively a prophet of doom, and therefore attributed as few as three of the seven chapters to him. The style, content, theological viewpoint, and historical perspective of some of the material reflect not the period of the Assyrian threat to Judah in the eighth century but the Babylonian exile in the sixth century B.C. and later. This is particularly evident in chap. 7, but also at other points in the book. The composition of this book, like most other prophetic texts, involved a complex editorial process. This is apparent from the fact that the stirring prophecy of peace and justice in 4:1–5 is virtually identical to Is 2:2–5.

Like Is 1–39, the Book of Micah is focused on Jerusalem, Zion, and the Judean leadership. The Micah who speaks in this prophetic book knows the tradition that Zion is the Lord's chosen place, but he is critical of the popular view that this election ensures the city's security (2:6–13; 3:9–12). Through the prophetic voice, the Lord announces the impending punishment of God's people by means of military defeat and exile because of their failure to establish justice. After that punishment God will bring the people back to their land and establish perpetual peace. The will of God for human beings is that they do justice, love goodness, and walk humbly with God (6:6–8).

The Book of Micah is divided as follows:

# MICAH

**1** [1] The word of the LORD which came to Micah of Moresheth in the days of Jotham, Ahaz, and Hezekiah, kings of Judah, which he saw concerning Samaria and Jerusalem.

## I. ORACLES OF PUNISHMENT

[2] Hear, O peoples, all of you,
    give heed, O earth, and all that is in
        it!*
Let the Lord GOD be witness against you,
    the Lord from his holy temple!†
[3] For see, the LORD goes out from his
        place*
    and descending, treads upon the
        heights of the earth.†
[4] The mountains melt under him
    and the valleys split open,
Like wax before the fire,
    like water poured down a slope.
[5] All this is for the crime of Jacob,
    for the sins of the house of Israel.†
What is the crime of Jacob? Is it not
        Samaria?
And what is the sin of the house of
        Judah?
    Is it not Jerusalem?
[6] So I will make Samaria a ruin in the
        field,
    a place to plant vineyards;
I will throw its stones into the valley,
    and lay bare its foundations.†
[7] All its carved figures shall be broken to
        pieces,*

all its wages shall be burned in the
        fire,
    and all its idols I will destroy.
As the wages of a prostitute† it gathered
        them,
    and to the wages of a prostitute they
        shall return.
[8]† For this I will lament and wail,
    go barefoot and naked;
I will utter lamentation like the jackals,
    mourning like the ostriches,*
[9] For her wound is incurable;
    it has come even to Judah.
It has reached to the gate of my people,
    even to Jerusalem.
[10]† Do not announce it in Gath,
    do not weep at all;
In Beth-leaphrah
    roll in the dust.*
[11] Pass by,
    you who dwell in Shaphir!
The inhabitants of Zaanan
    do not come forth from their city.
There is lamentation in Beth-ezel.
    It will withdraw its support from you.
[12] The inhabitants of Maroth
    hope for good,
But evil has come down from the LORD
    to the gate of Jerusalem.
[13] Harness steeds to the chariots,
    inhabitants of Lachish;
You are the beginning of sin
    for daughter Zion,
For in you were found
    the crimes of Israel.
[14] Therefore you must give back the dowry
    to Moresheth-gath;

---

**1:2** The prophet summons all the peoples to hear the divine accusations against them. What follows in 1:2–3:12 is a series of prophecies of punishment addressed to the capital cities of both the Northern and Southern Kingdoms, Samaria and Jerusalem. The prophecies indict the leaders and main officials, including prophets. Because of the corruption and selfishness of their leaders, Samaria and Jerusalem will fall to their enemies.
**1:3** The Lord comes in a theophany which has devastating effects on the natural world (1:4).
**1:5** Although the summons (1:2) had been addressed to all people, the Lord speaks against Israel and Judah, identifying their crimes with the respective capital cities of Samaria and Jerusalem. Only Samaria, however, is scheduled for destruction in the announcement of punishment (vv. 6–7).
**1:6** The punishment of Samaria will be a military disaster such as the one that actually came at the hands of the Assyrian army in 722/721 B.C.
**1:7** *The wages of a prostitute*: as often in the prophets, prostitution is a metaphor for idolatry (Hos 1–3; 4:14). *They shall re-*

turn: i.e., Samaria's idols shall come to nothing just as the wages of a prostitute are counted as nothing.
**1:8–16** The prophet laments and wails, singing a funeral song or dirge over the city of Jerusalem. Finally (1:16) he calls upon the people of Jerusalem to join in the mourning.
**1:10–15** Not all of the cities and villages in this long list can be located with certainty. However, those which can be identified, including the prophet's hometown, lie southwest of Jerusalem. In the Hebrew, wordplays on the names of these cities abound. The territory involved corresponds to that decimated by the Assyrian king Sennacherib in 701 B.C., during the reign of Hezekiah. *Do not weep at all*: some commentators and translators understand the Hebrew differently. They argue that the translation "in (unknown place name) weep!" fits the context better.

---

**1:2** Dt 32:1; Is 1:2.  **1:7** Hos 9:1.
**1:3–4** Is 26:21; Na 1:5; Hb  **1:8** Jb 30:29.
3:10.  **1:10** 2 Sm 1:20.

The houses of Achzib† are a dry stream
    bed
  to the kings of Israel.

15 Again I will bring the conqueror to you,
    inhabitants of Mareshah;
The glory of Israel shall come
    even to Adullam.

16 Make yourself bald, cut off your hair,
    for the children whom you cherish;
Make yourself bald as a vulture,
    for they are taken from you into
    exile.†

**2** ¹† Ah! you plotters of iniquity,
    who work out evil on your beds!
In the morning light you carry it out
    for it lies within your power.

2† You covet fields, and seize them;
    houses, and take them;
You cheat owners of their houses,
    people of their inheritance.

3    Therefore thus says the LORD:
Look, I am planning against this family
    an evil
  from which you cannot free your
    necks;
Nor shall you walk with head held high,
    for it will be an evil time.

4 On that day you shall be mocked,
  and there will be bitter lament:
"Our ruin is complete,
  our fields are divided among our
    captors,
The fields of my people are measured
    out,
  and no one can get them back!"†

5 Thus you shall have no one
  in the assembly of the LORD
  to allot to you a share of land.

6† "Do not preach," they preach,
  "no one should preach of these things!
  Shame will not overtake us."

7 How can it be said, house of Jacob,
  "Is the LORD short of patience;
  are these the Lord's deeds?"
Do not my words promise good
  to the one who walks in justice?

8 But you rise up against my people as an
    enemy:
  you have stripped off the garment
    from the peaceful,
From those who go their way in
    confidence,
  as though it were spoils of war.

9 The women of my people you drive out
  from their pleasant houses;
From their children you take away
  forever the honor I gave them.

10† "Get up! Leave,
  this is no place to rest";
Because of uncleanness that destroys
  with terrible destruction.

11 If one possessed of a lying spirit*
  speaks deceitfully, saying,
"I will preach to you wine and strong
    drink,"
  that one would be the preacher for
    this people.

12† I will gather you, Jacob, each and every
    one,

---

**1:14** *The houses of Achzib*: there is a wordplay here. In the Hebrew, the word translated here as "dry stream bed" is *'achzab*; this word is sometimes translated as "deception" or "disappointment."

**1:16** Shaving the head was a sign of mourning; cf. Is 3:24; Am 8:10.

**2:1–5** The cry "Ah" (*hoy*) begins a typical prophetic speech that is usually continued, as here (vv. 1–2), by a description of the addressees in terms of their unrighteous activities. This description is an indictment which gives the reasons for punishment announced to a particular group of people (vv. 3–5). The prophet spells out the crimes; the Lord announces the punishment, which corresponds to the crime: those who take the land of others will have their own land taken.

Those who plot iniquity and have the power to do it are wealthy landowners. The evil which they do consists in coveting the fields and houses of others and taking them.

**2:2** To covet the "house" and other property of the neighbor was a violation of the Decalogue (Ex 20:17; 34:24; Dt 5:21).

The Lord, as owner of the earth, allotted the land by tribes and families to the people of Israel (Jos 13–19). Losing one's inheritance diminished one's place in the community and threatened

the family's economic viability and existence. According to Micah, those who used their power to expand their estates at the expense of weaker Israelites took more than land from them: they were tampering with the divine order.

**2:4** Those who take land from the less powerful will in turn have their land taken away by invaders.

**2:6–11** This unit is a disputation, an argument in which the prophet is debating with his opponents. The words of the opponents are given to us only as the prophet quotes them. The opponents accuse Micah of being a false prophet, and he reacts by accusing them of injustice and of preferring prophets and preachers who speak lies (v. 11).

**2:10** The meaning of the Hebrew is uncertain.

**2:12–13** This announcement of salvation to the "remnant of Israel" stands out dramatically in the context, and is probably a later addition to the words of Micah, coming from the time of the Babylonian exile. The content of the promise and the images are similar to those found in Second Isaiah, the great poet of Israel's salvation and restoration (see Is 40:11; 43:5).

---

**2:11** 1 Kgs 22:22–23.

I will assemble all the remnant of
    Israel;
I will group them like a flock in the fold,
    like a herd in its pasture;
    the noise of the people will resound.

13 The one who makes a breach goes up
    before them;
    they make a breach and pass through
      the gate;
Their king shall go through before them,
    the LORD at their head.

**3** ¹† And I said:
Hear, you leaders of Jacob,
    rulers of the house of Israel!
Is it not your duty to know what is right,
2     you who hate what is good, and love
      evil?
You who tear their skin from them,
    and their flesh from their bones;*
3 Who eat the flesh of my people,
    flay their skin from them,
    and break their bones;
Who chop them in pieces like flesh in a
    kettle,
    like meat in a pot.
4 When they cry to the LORD,
    he will not answer them;
He will hide his face from them at that
    time,
    because of the evil they have done.

5† Thus says the LORD regarding the
    prophets:
O you who lead my people astray,
When your teeth have something to bite
    you announce peace,
But proclaim war against the one
    who fails to put something in your
      mouth.*

6 Therefore you shall have night, not
    vision,
    darkness, not divination;
The sun shall go down upon the
    prophets,
    and the day shall be dark for them.*
7 Then the seers shall be put to shame,
    and the diviners confounded;
They shall all cover their lips,
    because there is no answer from God.
8 But as for me, I am filled with power,
    with the spirit of the LORD,
    with justice and with might;
To declare to Jacob his crimes
    and to Israel his sins.

9† Hear this, you leaders of the house of
    Jacob,
    you rulers of the house of Israel!
You who abhor justice,
    and pervert all that is right;
10 Who build up Zion with bloodshed,
    and Jerusalem with wickedness!
11 Its leaders render judgment for a bribe,
    the priests teach for pay,
    the prophets divine for money,
While they rely on the LORD, saying,
    "Is not the LORD in the midst of us?
    No evil can come upon us!"*
12 Therefore, because of you,
    Zion shall be plowed like a field,
    and Jerusalem reduced to rubble,
And the mount of the temple
    to a forest ridge.*

## II. ORACLES OF SALVATION

**4** ¹† In days to come
    the mount of the LORD's house
Shall be established as the highest
    mountain;

---

**3:1–4** This prophecy of punishment has an introductory call to hear (v. 1a–b) and two major parts, the indictment or reasons for punishment (vv. 1c–3) and the announcement of judgment (v. 4). The prophet accuses the leaders and rulers of Israel of treating the people so badly that their actions are comparable to cannibalism. Those who, above all, should know and maintain justice are the most corrupt of all. In the time of trouble the Lord will withdraw (v. 4); that is, God will abandon the leaders to their fate and refuse to answer their prayers.
**3:5–8** This prophecy of punishment concerns and is addressed to false prophets. The prophets in Jerusalem who mislead the people are corrupt because their word can be bought (v. 5). Therefore such prophets, seers, and diviners shall be disgraced, put to shame, left in the dark without vision or answer (vv. 6–7). But Micah is convinced that he is filled with power and the spirit of the Lord, which corresponds to justice and might (v. 8).

**3:9–12** This is the most comprehensive of Micah's prophecies of punishment concerning the leaders in Jerusalem. The indictment (vv. 9–11) includes all political and religious leaders. They combine corruption and greed with a false confidence that the Lord is on their side. But the announcement of judgment (v. 12) is not limited to the punishment of the leaders but includes Mount Zion where the Temple stands and the entire city, thus encompassing the entire population.
**4:1–4** This magnificent prophecy of salvation is almost identical to Is 2:2–5, with the exception of its last verse. See also Jl 4:9–10, which transforms the promise into a call to war. It is not known if Micah or an editor of the book picked up the an-

---

**3:2** Am 2:7.                   Zec 13:3.
**3:5** Ez 13:10.           **3:11** Ez 22:27; Zep 3:3.
**3:6** Jer 15:9; Am 8:9;     **3:12** Jer 26:18.

it shall be raised above the hills,
And peoples shall stream to it:\*
2   Many nations shall come, and say,
"Come, let us climb the LORD's
mountain,
to the house of the God of Jacob,
That he may instruct us in his ways,
that we may walk in his paths."
For from Zion shall go forth instruction,
and the word of the LORD from
Jerusalem.
3   He shall judge between many peoples
and set terms for strong and distant
nations;
They shall beat their swords into
plowshares,
and their spears into pruning hooks;
One nation shall not raise the sword
against another,
nor shall they train for war again.
4   They shall all sit under their own vines,
under their own fig trees, undisturbed;
for the LORD of hosts has spoken.\*
5   Though all the peoples walk,
each in the name of its god,
We will walk in the name of the LORD,
our God, forever and ever.

6†  On that day—oracle of the LORD—
I will gather the lame,
And I will assemble the outcasts,
and those whom I have afflicted.
7   I will make of the lame a remnant,
and of the weak a strong nation;
The LORD shall be king over them on
Mount Zion,
from now on and forever.\*

8   And you, O tower of the flock,†
hill of daughter Zion!
To you it shall come:

the former dominion shall be
restored,
the reign of daughter Jerusalem.

9   Now why do you cry out so?
Are you without a king?
Or has your adviser perished,
That you are seized with pains
like a woman in labor?
10† Writhe, go into labor,
O daughter Zion,
like a woman giving birth;
For now you shall leave the city
and camp in the fields;
To Babylon you shall go,
there you shall be rescued.
There the LORD shall redeem you
from the hand of your enemies.

11† And now many nations are gathered
against you!
They say, "Let her be profaned,
let our eyes see Zion's downfall!"
12  But they do not know the thoughts of
the LORD,
nor understand his plan:
He has gathered them
like sheaves to the threshing floor.
13  Arise and thresh, O daughter Zion;
your horn I will make iron
And your hoofs I will make bronze,
that you may crush many peoples;
You shall devote their spoils to the
LORD,†
their riches to the Lord of the whole
earth.\*

14  Now grieve, O grieving daughter!†
"They have laid siege against us!"
With the rod they strike on the cheek
the ruler of Israel.

---

† nouncement from his contemporary Isaiah or if Isaiah borrowed it from Micah. Perhaps both Isaiah and Micah depended upon another, more ancient tradition. The ground of the prophetic hope voiced here is the justice and grace of the God who has chosen Israel. The basis for peace shall be a just order where all are obedient to the divine will. While the vision is a universal one, including all peoples and nations (vv. 3–4), its center and wellspring is the Temple of the Lord of Israel on Mount Zion in Jerusalem.
**4:6–8** An announcement of salvation proclaiming that the Lord will restore the lame and afflicted people of God as a nation on Mount Zion. *Oracle of the LORD*: a phrase used extensively in prophetic books to indicate divine speech.
**4:8** *Tower of the flock*: in Hebrew *migdal-eder,* a place name in Gn 35:21.

**4:10** Frequently the prophets personify the city of Jerusalem as a woman, and here as a woman in labor.
**4:11–13** The nations who have ridiculed Zion (v. 11) will be threshed like grain (v. 13).
**4:13** *Devote their spoils to the LORD*: the fulfillment of the ancient ordinance of the holy war in which all plunder taken in the war was "put under the ban," i.e., belonged to the Lord.
**4:14** *Grieve, O grieving daughter!*: the Hebrew actually reflects the ancient Near Eastern mourning practice of afflicting oneself with cuts and gashes, as evidence of grief. A literal rendering would be "gash yourself, O woman who gashes."

4:1–3 Is 2:2–4.            4:7 Is 6:13; Dn 7:14; Zep
4:4 Hos 14:8; Am 9:14.          3:19; Lk 1:32.
                                4:13 Is 41:15; Hos 10:11.

**5** ¹† But you, Bethlehem-Ephrathah*
    least among the clans of Judah,
From you shall come forth for me
    one who is to be ruler in Israel;
Whose origin is from of old,
    from ancient times.

² Therefore the Lord will give them up,
    until the time
    when she who is to give birth has
      borne,†
Then the rest of his kindred shall return
    to the children of Israel.*

³ He shall take his place as shepherd
    by the strength of the LORD,
    by the majestic name of the LORD, his
      God;
And they shall dwell securely, for now
    his greatness
    shall reach to the ends of the earth:

⁴ he shall be peace.†
If Assyria invades our country
    and treads upon our land,
We shall raise against it seven shepherds,
    eight of royal standing;

⁵ They shall tend the land of Assyria with
    the sword,
    and the land of Nimrod† with the
      drawn sword;
They will deliver us from Assyria,
    when it invades our land,
    when it treads upon our borders.

⁶ The remnant of Jacob shall be
    in the midst of many peoples,
Like dew coming from the LORD,
    like showers on the grass,
Which wait for no one,
    delay for no human being.

⁷ And the remnant of Jacob shall be
    among the nations,
    in the midst of many peoples,
Like a lion among beasts of the forest,
    like a young lion among flocks of
      sheep;
When it passes through it tramples;
    it tears and no one can rescue.

⁸ Your hand shall be lifted above your foes,
    and all your enemies shall be cut
      down.

⁹†     On that day—oracle of the LORD—
I will destroy the horses from your midst
    and ruin your chariots;

¹⁰ I will destroy the cities of your land
    and tear down all your fortresses.

¹¹ I will destroy the sorcery you practice,
    and there shall no longer be
    soothsayers among you.

¹² I will destroy your carved figures
    and the sacred stones† from your
      midst;
And you shall no longer worship
    the works of your hands.*

¹³ I will tear out the asherahs from your
      midst,
    and destroy your cities.

¹⁴ I will wreak vengeance in anger and
      wrath
    upon the nations that have not
      listened.

## III. ANNOUNCEMENT OF JUDGMENT

**6** ¹† Hear, then, what the LORD says:
Arise, plead your case before the
      mountains,
    and let the hills hear your voice!*

² Hear, O mountains, the LORD's case,
    pay attention, O foundations of the
      earth!
For the LORD has a case against his
      people;

---

†

**5:1–6** Salvation will come through a "messiah," an anointed ruler. The Book of Micah shares with Isaiah the expectation that God will deliver Israel through a king in the line of David. Bethlehem-Ephrathah is the home of the Davidic line.

**5:2** These words are sometimes understood as a reference to Isaiah's Emmanuel oracle, given some thirty years earlier (Is 7:14). The Gospel of Matthew reports that the chief priests and scribes cite this passage as the ancient promise of a messiah in the line of David to be born in Bethlehem (Mt 2:5–6).

**5:4** *Peace:* he will not only symbolize but also bring about harmony and wholeness.

**5:5** *Nimrod:* the legendary ancestor of the Mesopotamians; cf. Gn 10:10–12.

**5:9–13** The Lord will destroy all those features of the nation's life that have stood between the people and their God. These false supports include horses, chariots, fortifications, and forbid-

den practices such as sorcery and idolatry.

**5:12–13** *Sacred stones...asherahs:* the Hebrew *asherah* is a sacred pole. All forms of idolatry (standing stones and sacred poles were part of forbidden cult practices) were violations of Israel's covenant with the Lord.

**6:1–5** The Lord, through the prophet, initiates a legal case against the people. The initial calls (vv. 1–2) signal the beginning of a trial, and the proclamation that the Lord intends to enter into a legal dispute with Israel. One would expect accusations to follow such an introduction, but instead the Lord speaks in self-defense, reciting mighty acts done in behalf of Israel (vv. 3–5).

---

**5:1** Ru 1:2; 1 Sm 17:12;      **5:12** Hos 3:4; 10:1–2.
    Mt 2:6; Jn 7:42.           **6:1** Is 6:2; Ob 1.
**5:2–3** Is 7:14; 11:1–2.

> he enters into trial with Israel.

3 My people, what have I done to you?
how have I wearied you? Answer me!*

4 I brought you up from the land of
Egypt,
from the place of slavery I ransomed
you;
And I sent before you Moses,
Aaron, and Miriam.*

5† My people, remember what Moab's King
Balak planned,
and how Balaam, the son of Beor,
answered him.
Recall the passage from Shittim to
Gilgal,
that you may know the just deeds of
the LORD.*

6† With what shall I come before the
LORD,
and bow before God most high?
Shall I come before him with burnt
offerings,
with calves a year old?*

7 Will the LORD be pleased with thousands
of rams,
with myriad streams of oil?

† Shall I give my firstborn for my crime,
the fruit of my body for the sin of my
soul?

8† You have been told, O mortal, what is
good,
and what the LORD requires of you:
Only to do justice and to love
goodness,
and to walk humbly with your God.*

9† The LORD cries aloud to the city
(It is prudent to fear your name!):
Hear, O tribe and city assembly,

10 Am I to bear criminal hoarding
and the accursed short ephah?†

11 Shall I acquit crooked scales,
bags of false weights?

12 You whose wealthy are full of violence,
whose inhabitants speak falsehood
with deceitful tongues in their
mouths!

13 I have begun to strike you
with devastation because of your
sins.

14 You shall eat, without being satisfied,
food that will leave you empty;
What you acquire, you cannot save;
what you do save, I will deliver up to
the sword.*

15 You shall sow, yet not reap,
tread out the olive, yet pour no oil,
crush the grapes, yet drink no
wine.*

16 You have kept the decrees of Omri,
and all the works of the house of
Ahab,
and you have walked in their
counsels;
Therefore I will deliver you up to ruin,
and your citizens to derision;
and you shall bear the reproach of the
nations.

## 7

1 Woe is me! I am like the one who
gathers summer fruit,
when the vines have been gleaned;
There is no cluster to eat,
no early fig that I crave.

2 The faithful have vanished from the
earth,
no mortal is just!

---

† **6:5** The Lord calls for the people to remember the saving events of the past, from the encounters with Balak and Balaam (Nm 22:23) during the wandering in the wilderness to the entrance into the promised land ("from Shittim to Gilgal," Jos 3–5).

**6:6–8** These verses continue the previous unit (6:1–5), the dialogue between the Lord and the people in the pattern of a trial. The Lord has initiated proceedings against them, and they ask how to re-establish the broken relationship with God (vv. 6–7), and are given an answer (v. 8). The form of the passage borrows from a priestly liturgical pattern. When worshipers came to the temple, they inquired of the priest concerning the appropriate offering or sacrifice, and the priest answered them (see Ps 15; 24; Is 1:10–17; Am 5:21–24).

**6:7** The questions reach their climax with the possibility of child sacrifice, a practice known in antiquity (cf. 2 Kgs 16:3; 21:6).

**6:8** *To do justice* refers to human behavior in relationship to others. *To love goodness* refers to the kind of love and concern which is at the heart of the covenant between the Lord and Israel;

it is persistently faithful. *To walk humbly with your God* means to listen carefully to the revealed will of God.

**6:9–16** The language of the trial resumes as the Lord accuses the people of their sins (vv. 9–12, 16a) and announces their punishment (vv. 13–15, 16b). The city is Jerusalem, and those addressed are its inhabitants. Their wickedness includes cheating in business with false weights and measures, violence, lies, and following the practices of the Israelite kings Omri and Ahab (v. 16a), whose reigns came to symbolize a time of syncretistic worship. The punishment, which has already begun, will include a series of disasters. Finally, the Lord will destroy the city and see that its inhabitants are ridiculed (v. 16b).

**6:10** *Ephah*: see note on Is 5:10.

---

**6:3** Jer 2:5.
**6:4** Ex 15:20.
**6:5** Nm 22:23; Jos 3–5.
**6:6–7** Hos 6:6; 8:13; Am 5:21.
**6:8** Dt 26:16; Zec 7:9; Mt 23:23.
**6:14** Dt 28:38; Am 5:11; Hg 1:6.
**6:15** Hos 4:10.

They all lie in wait to shed blood,
  each one ensnares the other.*

3 Their hands succeed at evil;
    the prince makes demands,
  The judge is bought for a price,
    the powerful speak as they please.*

4 The best of them is like a brier,
    the most honest like a thorn hedge.
  The day announced by your sentinels!
    Your punishment has come;
    now is the time of your confusion.

5 Put no faith in a friend,
    do not trust a companion;
  With her who lies in your embrace
    watch what you say.*

6 For the son belittles his father,
    the daughter rises up against her
      mother,
  The daughter-in-law against her mother-
      in-law,
    and your enemies are members of
      your household.*

## IV. CONFIDENCE IN GOD'S FUTURE

7 But as for me, I will look to the LORD,
    I will wait for God my savior;
    my God will hear me!*

8† Do not rejoice over me, my enemy!†
    though I have fallen, I will arise;
    though I sit in darkness, the LORD is
      my light.

9 I will endure the wrath of the LORD
    because I have sinned against him,
  Until he pleads my case,
    and establishes my right.
  He will bring me forth to the light;
    I will see his righteousness.

10 When my enemy sees this,
    shame shall cover her:
  She who said to me,

"Where is the LORD, your God?"
  My eyes shall see her downfall;
    now she will be trampled†
      underfoot,
    like mud in the streets.

11† It is the day for building your walls;
    on that day your boundaries shall be
      enlarged.

12 It is the day when those from Assyria to
      Egypt
    shall come to you,
  And from Tyre even to the River,
    from sea to sea, and from mountain
      to mountain;*

13 And the earth shall be a waste
    because of its inhabitants,
    as a result of their deeds.

14† Shepherd your people with your staff,
    the flock of your heritage,
  That lives apart* in a woodland,
    in the midst of an orchard.
  Let them feed in Bashan and Gilead,
    as in the days of old;

15 As in the days when you came from the
      land of Egypt,
    show us wonderful signs.

16 The nations will see and will be put to
      shame,
    in spite of all their strength;
  They will put their hands over their
      mouths;
    their ears will become deaf.

17 They will lick the dust like a snake,
    like crawling things on the ground;
  They will come quaking from their
      strongholds;
    they will tremble in fear of you, the
      LORD, our God.

18† Who is a God like you, who removes
      guilt

---

**7:8–20** The book concludes with a collection of confident prayers for deliverance, affirmations of faith, and announcements of salvation. Most of these verses bear the marks of use in worship, and probably arose in the exilic or postexilic periods.

**7:8–10** An individual, possibly personified Jerusalem, expresses confidence that the Lord will deliver her from her enemy (cf. Ps 23).

**7:10** *She who said…she will be trampled*: in the Old Testament, cities are often personified as women. Here, the prophet is speaking of the enemies' cities.

**7:11–13** An announcement of salvation to Zion. The walls of Jerusalem will be rebuilt, its inhabitants who are now scattered from Assyria to Egypt shall return, but the other peoples will suffer for their evil deeds.

**7:14–17** A prayer that God will care for the people as in ancient days (v. 14) is answered (vv. 15–17) when the Lord promises to do marvelous things. The nations shall be afraid and turn to the Lord.

**7:18–20** The final lines of the book contain a hymn of praise for the incomparable God, who pardons sin and delights in mercy. Thus the remnant, those left after the exile, is confident in God's compassion and in the ancient promises sworn to the ancestors.

7:2 Is 1:21; Hos 4:2.          7:7 Is 8:17.
7:3 Is 1:23.                    7:12 Zec 14:16.
7:5 Jer 9:3.                    7:14 Nm 23:9.
7:6 Mt 10:35–36.

and pardons sin for the remnant of
   his inheritance;
Who does not persist in anger forever,
   but instead delights in mercy,*

19 And will again have compassion on us,
   treading underfoot our iniquities?

You will cast into the depths of the sea
   all our sins;
20 You will show faithfulness to Jacob,
   and loyalty to Abraham,
As you have sworn to our ancestors
   from days of old.*

---

7:18 Jer 10:6; Acts 10:43.     7:20 Ps 105:6; Is 41:8; 63:16.

# The Book of
# Nahum

N
A

## INTRODUCTION

Dale Launderville, OSB

Nahum, prophesying in Jerusalem in the latter part of the seventh century BCE, announces the end of the Assyrian Empire. For more than a century, the Assyrians had imposed their rule on Judah not only by political and economic measures but also through cultural and religious innovations. The Assyrian military machine worked in tandem with the Assyrian imperial bureaucracy to reshape local cultures into extensions of the culture of Nineveh. Nahum seems to have predicted the fall of Nineveh sometime between the death of Ashurbanipal in 627 BCE and the destruction of Nineveh by a coalition of Medes and Babylonians in 612 BCE. After laboring for more than a century in the shadow of the imperial culture of Assyria, some Judeans during the reign of their king Josiah (640–609 BCE) began to proclaim their own values and traditions. Nahum makes his case that Nineveh and its king will fall at the hands of Israel's God, the divine warrior Yahweh. Nahum's words are testimony to the resilience of the Yahwistic faith.

According to the superscription (Na 1:1), Nahum's prophecy takes the form of an oracle against the nations in accord with the "vision" of Nahum as articulated in the book bearing his name. Although words spoken to a live audience would probably have been Nahum's primary way of communicating God's message, he also worked with written prophecy and traditions about the Lord. The opening divine warrior hymn (1:2–8) begins each verse with a successive letter of the Hebrew alphabet, a distinctive feature that would be noticed only by a literate audience. Through this traditional hymn, Nahum makes the claim that Yahweh is the sovereign ruler over nature and history, who executes justice patiently but does not clear the guilty. This view of Yahweh's divine justice steadily working itself

---

## Outline of Nahum

I.  God's Terrifying Appearance (1:2–8)

II. Nineveh's Judgment and Judah's Restoration (1:9–2:1)

III. The Attack on Nineveh (2:2–3:7)

IV. Nineveh's Inescapable Fate (3:8–19)

---

out is supported in Nahum's interpretation of the lifting of the Assyrian siege of Jerusalem in 701 BCE (1:11–12; cf. Is 37:36–37). Although Assyrian control of Judah would persist for at least another eighty years, Nahum saw this event as the beginning of the end of Assyrian rule because the rule of Yahweh was patiently guiding the course of events (Na 1:14). Nahum sees a pattern in Yahweh's rule of history and argues that Yahweh protects those who trust in him (Na 1:7).

Three characters can be dimly perceived in Nahum's prophecy: a feminine character who is Judah (Na 1:11–13), a masculine character who is the king of Assyria (1:14; 3:18–19), and another feminine character who is the city of Nineveh (2:2, 8; 3:7). Nahum addresses each of these characters, but they do not speak. In fact, the actual audience probably consisted only of Judeans. When Nahum addresses the Assyrians and their king with words of judgment, the Judeans overhear this message as one of salvation. It may be that Nahum spoke his prophecy to a delegation of Judean officials just as Isaiah is reported to have done at the time of the siege in 701 BCE (Is 37:2–7).

Although a few words of salvation are directly addressed to the Judeans in the first part of the book (Na 2:1, 3), the primary source of consolation for the Judeans is the just but vengeful judgment that Yahweh metes out to the Assyrians. The city of Nineveh was established by Sennacherib (705–681 BCE) as the Assyrian capital. This strongly fortified 1800-acre site would have had streets wide enough for chariots to maneuver within them. Nahum provides a unique description of a battle raging within the streets of Nineveh (2:4–11; 3:2–7). The moats used as a defense for the city have been taken over by the enemy, who uses this water system to flood the city (2:7). Nahum predicts that just as the Egyptian capital of Thebes with its use of water as part of its fortifications (3:8) was conquered by the Assyrians in 663 BCE, so also will the city of Nineveh be taken by its foes (3:10–13).

Assyrian kings identified themselves as lions. They conducted lion hunts in the royal gardens of Nineveh to symbolize the king's prowess in defending the kingdom from threatening forces. Nahum uses this imagery to condemn the predatory behavior of the Assyrian kings toward Judah and other small kingdoms in the region (Na 2:12–14). The Assyrian king was a strong lion who provided a secure lair (2:12) and abundant food for his young ones (2:13), but now the Lord will confront him and bring to an end his political and economic exploitation of the eastern Mediterranean region.

According to traditional practice in ancient Mesopotamia and Israel, the city of Nineveh is personified as a woman. Therefore, when the city is attacked and breached, the imagery ready-to-hand to describe such a violent military activity is that of rape. As in Jer 13:22–27, Yahweh is described as one who lifts the skirts of Nineveh and exposes her nakedness, which probably means that the divine warrior has raped the city. Such violent, abusive behavior was part of ancient Near Eastern warfare. Nevertheless, it is shocking to see such vengeful human behavior predicated of God (Na 3:5–6). This hunger for vengeance on the part of Judah is as troubling as the expectation that Nineveh's infants will be "dashed to pieces at the corner of every street" (3:10). It would seem that the Judeans' memory of Assyrian atrocities toward them was passed on through the generations (3:19).

In addressing the Assyrians and their king as if they were present before him, Nahum concludes his message of doom by emphasizing that resistance to Yahweh as the divine warrior is useless (Na 3:13–19). He claims that the Assyrians can make bricks—as if in imitation of the Hebrew slaves in Egypt—to try to strengthen their fortifications (3:14), but fire and an army as numerous as grasshoppers will consume them (3:15). The traders, scribes, and sentries who had played important roles in the imperial government will vanish suddenly (3:16–17). Likewise, the king and his nobles will fall asleep and not protect the people (3:18); the Assyrian king himself is mortally wounded (3:19).

Nahum consoles his Judean audience by emphasizing that Yahweh has a plan for establishing justice in the world. Yahweh brought Assyria to humble Judah (Na 1:12), but Assyria's violent tactics gave rise to injustices that called for the destruction of Nineveh (3:7). ■

# THE BOOK OF NAHUM

## New American Bible, Introduction

Shortly before the fall of Nineveh, the capital of Assyria, in 612 B.C., Nahum uttered his prophecy against the hated city. To understand the prophet's exultant outburst of joy over the impending destruction it is necessary to recall the savage cruelty of Assyria, which had made it the scourge of the ancient Near East for almost three centuries. The royal inscriptions of Assyria afford the best commentary on Nahum's burning denunciation of "the bloody city." In the wake of their conquests, mounds of heads, impaled bodies, enslaved citizens, and avaricious looters testified to the ruthlessness of the Assyrians. Just such a conquest was suffered by Israel, when its capital Samaria fell to the Assyrians in 722/721 B.C., and by Judah, when its capital Jerusalem nearly fell to invading Assyrian armies twenty years later. Little wonder that in 3:19 Judah is shown as joining in the general outburst of joy over the destruction of Nineveh!

But Nahum is not a prophet of unrestrained revenge. He asserts God's moral government of the world. Nineveh's doom is evidence that God stands against oppression and the abuse of power. As an ancient Near Eastern superpower, Assyria had terrorized its smaller and weaker neighbors, exploiting their economies and subjugating their people for its own ends. Thus Nineveh's demise is viewed as an act of divine justice, and it is greeted by the small, oppressed countries as a time of deliverance, as a moment of renewal, and as a message of peace (2:1; 3:19).

The book is divided as follows:

I. God's Terrifying Appearance (1:2–8)
II. Nineveh's Judgment and Judah's Restoration (1:9–2:1)
III. The Attack on Nineveh (2:2–3:7)
IV. Nineveh's Inescapable Fate (3:8–19) ■

# NAHUM

**1** ¹Oracle† concerning Nineveh. The book of the vision of Nahum of Elkosh.

## God's Terrifying Appearance

²† A jealous and avenging God† is the
   LORD,
      an avenger is the LORD, full of wrath;
   The LORD takes vengeance on his
      adversaries,
      and rages against his enemies;
³ The LORD is slow to anger, yet great in
      power;
      the LORD will not leave the guilty
         unpunished.*
   In stormwind† and tempest he comes,
      and clouds are the dust at his feet;
⁴ He roars at the sea and leaves it dry,
      and all the rivers he dries up.
   Laid low are Bashan and Carmel,
      and the bloom of Lebanon withers;†
⁵ The mountains quake before him,
      and the hills dissolve;
   The earth is laid waste before him,
      the world and all who dwell in it.
⁶† Before his wrath, who can stand firm,
      and who can face his blazing
         anger?*
   His fury is poured out like fire,
      and boulders break apart before him.
⁷ The LORD is good to those who wait for
      him,
      a refuge on the day of distress,
   Taking care of those who look to him
      for protection,
⁸    when the flood rages;
   He makes an end of his opponents,

and pursues his enemies into
      darkness.

## Nineveh's Judgment and Judah's Restoration

⁹    What do you plot against the LORD,
      the one about to bring total
         destruction?
      No opponent rises a second time!
¹⁰† Like a thorny thicket, they are tangled,
      and like drunkards, they are drunk;
      like dry stubble, they are utterly
         consumed.
¹¹ From you has come
      one plotting evil against the LORD,
      one giving sinister counsel.†
¹² Thus says the LORD:
      though fully intact and so numerous,
      they† shall be mown down and
         disappear.
   Though I have humbled you,
      I will humble you no more.
¹³ Now I will break his yoke off of you,
      and tear off your bonds.*

¹⁴ The LORD has commanded regarding
      you:†
      no descendant will again bear your
         name;
   From the house of your gods I will abolish
      the carved and the molten image;
      I will make your grave a dung heap.

**2** ¹At this moment on the mountains
      the footsteps of one bearing good
         news,
      of one announcing peace!*
   Celebrate your feasts, Judah,
      fulfill your vows!
   For never again will destroyers invade
      you;†
      they are completely cut off.

---

† **1:1** *Oracle*: (Heb. *Massaʾ*) a word used frequently to describe a prophetic statement against a foreign nation or occasionally Israel; it is used favorably for Israel in Zec 12:1 and Mal 1:1. *Nahum of Elkosh*: Nahum means "comfort." Elkosh is a clan or village of unknown location, perhaps in southern Judah.
**1:2–8** A poem written in the style of the alphabetic psalms (cf. Ps 9; 25; 111; 119) in which each verse unit begins with a successive letter of the Hebrew alphabet. The second half of the alphabet is not represented here.
**1:2** *A jealous…God*: see note on Ex 20:5.
**1:3–6** *In stormwind*: the power of God is often pictured by natural forces and cosmic disruption (Ex 19:9–25; Ps 18:8–16; 104:1–9).
**1:4** Bashan, Carmel, and Lebanon were famous for their mountainous terrain and lush forests.
**1:6–7** When God comes in judgment those who oppose God

will be destroyed, and those who trust in God will be saved.
**1:10** Thorns (Is 34:13), drunkenness (Lam 4:21; Na 3:11), and burning stubble (Ob 18) are all images of the judgment of God's enemies.
**1:11** *From you…giving sinister counsel*: addressed to Nineveh, the capital city of Sennacherib, king of Assyria, who besieged Jerusalem ca. 700 B.C.
**1:12–13** *They*: the enemies of Judah. *You*: Judah. *His yoke*: the dominion of the Assyrian king over Judah.
**1:14** *You*: the king of Assyria.
**2:1** *For never again will destroyers invade you*: prophets are not always absolutely accurate in the things they foresee. Nin-

---

*
**1:3** Ex 34:6–7; Jl 2:13.        **1:13** Is 9:4; 10:27.
**1:6** Is 30:27–28; Zep          **2:1** Is 52:7; Rom 10:15.
      1:15.

## The Attack on Nineveh

2 One who scatters has come up against
  you;†
    guard the rampart,
  Watch the road, brace yourselves,
    marshal all your strength!
3† The LORD will restore the vine of Jacob,
    the honor of Israel,
  Because ravagers have ravaged them
    and ruined their branches.
4 The shields of his warriors are
    crimsoned,
    the soldiers clad in scarlet;
  Like fire are the trappings of the chariots
    on the day he prepares for war;
    the cavalry is agitated!
5 The chariots dash madly through the
    streets
    and wheel in the squares,
  Looking like torches,
    bolting like lightning.
6 His picked troops are called,
    ranks break at their charge;
  To the wall they rush,
    their screen† is set up.
7 The river gates† are opened,
    the palace is washed away.
8 The mistress is led forth captive,
    and her maidservants† led away,
  Moaning like doves,
    beating their breasts.
9 Nineveh is like a pool
    whose waters escape;
  "Stop! Stop!"
    but none turns back. *
10 "Plunder the silver, plunder the gold!"
    There is no end to the treasure,
    to wealth in every precious thing!

11 Emptiness, desolation, waste;
    melting hearts and trembling knees,

Churning in every stomach,
    every face turning pale! *
12 Where is the lionesses' den,
    the young lions' cave,
  Where the lion† went in and out,
    and the cub, with no one to disturb
      them? *
13 The lion tore apart enough for his cubs,
    and strangled for his lionesses;
  He filled his lairs with prey,
    and his dens with torn flesh.
14 I now come against you—
    oracle of the LORD of hosts—
  I will consume your chariots in smoke,
    and the sword will devour your young
      lions;
  Your preying on the land I will bring to
    an end,
    the cry of your lionesses will be heard
      no more.

3 ¹ Ah! The bloody city,
    all lies,
  Full of plunder,
    whose looting never stops! *
2 The crack of the whip,
    the rumbling of wheels;
  Horses galloping,
    chariots bounding,
3 Cavalry charging,
    the flash of the sword,
    the gleam of the spear;
  A multitude of slain,
    a mass of corpses,
  Endless bodies
    to stumble upon!
4 For the many debaucheries of the
    prostitute,
    a charming mistress of witchcraft,
  Who enslaved nations with her
    prostitution,
    and peoples by her witchcraft: *

---

† eveh was destroyed, as Nahum expected, but Judah was later invaded by the Babylonians and (much later) by the Romans. The prophets were convinced that Israel held a key place in God's plan and looked for the people to survive all catastrophes, always blessed by the Lord, though the manner was not always as they expected; the "fallen hut of David" was not rebuilt as Am 9:11 suggests, except in the coming of Jesus, and in a way far different than the prophet expected. Often the prophet speaks in hyperbole, as when Second Isaiah speaks of the restored Jerusalem being built with precious stones (Is 54:12) as a way of indicating a glorious future.
  **2:2** *One who scatters has come up against you*: the enemy is about to crush Nineveh, dispersing and deporting its people (v. 8; 3:18).
  **2:3** This verse does not fit its context well; it may have been

the conclusion for the preceding section and have once followed v. 1, or it may be a later scribal addition.
  **2:6** *Their screen*: that is, a mantelet, a movable military shelter protecting the besiegers.
  **2:7** *River gates*: a network of canals brought water into Nineveh from the Tigris and Khosr Rivers on which the city was located.
  **2:8** *Mistress…and her maidservants*: either the queen of Nineveh with the ladies of her court, or the city of Nineveh itself, pictured as a noblewoman (3:4).
  **2:12** *The lion*: the king of Assyria.

---

**2:9** Is 8:7–8.
**2:11** Jl 2:6.
**2:12** Ez 19:2–7.
**3:1** Is 10:13–14; Hb 2:12.
**3:4** Mi 1:7; Rev 17:1.

5 † I now come against you—
      oracle of the LORD of hosts—
      and I will lift your skirt above your
           face;
      I will show your nakedness to the
           nations,
      to the kingdoms your shame! *
6     I will cast filth upon you,
      disgrace you and make you a
           spectacle;
7     Until everyone who sees you
      runs from you saying,
      "Nineveh is destroyed;
      who can pity her?
      Where can I find
      any to console you?"

### Nineveh's Inescapable Fate

8     Are you better than No-amon † *
      that was set among the Nile's canals,
      Surrounded by waters,
      with the river for her rampart
      and water for her wall?
9     Ethiopia was her strength,
      and Egypt without end;
      Put † and the Libyans
      were her allies.
10    Yet even she became an exile,
      and went into captivity;
      Even her little ones were dashed to
           pieces
      at the corner of every street;
      For her nobles they cast lots,
      and all her great ones were put into
           chains.
11    You, too, will drink of this;
      you will be overcome; *
      You, too, will seek
      a refuge from the foe.
12    But all your fortresses are fig trees,
      bearing early figs; †
      When shaken, they fall
      into the devourer's mouth.

13    Indeed your troops
      are women in your midst;
      To your foes are open wide
      the gates of your land,
      fire has consumed their bars.
14    Draw water for the siege, †
      strengthen your fortresses;
      Go down into the mud
      and tread the clay,
      take hold of the brick mold!
15    There the fire will consume you,
      the sword will cut you down;
      it will consume you like the
           grasshoppers.

      Multiply like the grasshoppers,
      multiply like the locusts! *
16    You have made your traders † more
           numerous
      than the stars of the heavens;
      like grasshoppers that shed their skins
      and fly away.
17    Your sentries are like locusts,
      and your scribes like locust swarms
      Gathered on the rubble fences
      on a cold day!
      Yet when the sun rises, they vanish,
      and no one knows where they have
           gone.

18    Your shepherds slumber,
      O king of Assyria,
      your nobles have gone to rest;
      Your people are scattered upon the
           mountains,
      with none to gather them.
19    There is no healing for your hurt,
      your wound is fatal.
      All who hear this news of you
      clap their hands over you;
      For who has not suffered
      under your endless malice?

---

† 
**3:5–6** The punishment for adulterous women.
**3:8** No-amon: "No" was the Egyptian name of the capital of Upper Egypt, called Thebes by the Greeks; its patron deity was Amon. This great city was destroyed by the Assyrians in 663 B.C.
**3:9** Put: a North African people often associated with Egypt and Ethiopia (Jer 46:8–9).
**3:12** Early figs: the refugees from Nineveh who escape to presumably secure fortresses.

**3:14** An ironic exhortation to prepare the city for a futile defense. Go down…brick mold: make bricks for the city walls.
**3:16** Traders: agents of the economic exploitation that sustained and enriched the Assyrian empire.

---

* 
**3:5** Is 47:3; Jer 13:26.          **3:11** Jer 25:15–16; Ob 16.
**3:8** Jer 46:25.                     **3:15** Jer 46:23.

# The Book of
# Habakkuk

## INTRODUCTION

### Michael D. Guinan, OFM

Habakkuk is the eighth of the Book of the Twelve. We know nothing of the prophet except his name, which is most likely related to an Akkadian word for a type of garden plant. The only clue that provides a date and context is the mention of the Chaldeans (Hb 1:6), the Neo-Babylonian dynasty that overthrew Assyria in 612 BCE, defeated the Egyptians in 605, and annexed the kingdom of Judah as a vassal. There is no mention of the siege of Jerusalem in 597 BCE, so most scholars would locate Habakkuk in the seven years between 605 and 598 BCE.

Within the book, three different literary forms appear: (1) a dialogue/dispute between the prophet and God (Hb 1:2–2:4; (2) a series of "woes" in a taunt song (2:5–20), and (3) a victory psalm (3:1–19). However, two headings (an "oracle," 1:1 and a "prayer," 3:1) appear in the text. Consequently, some scholars divide the book into three sections, others into two.

## Dialogue/Dispute between Habakkuk and God (Hb 1:2-2:20)

The issue being disputed is the justice of God in the face of rampant injustice and suffering in the world, i.e., the problem of theodicy. The prophet has two complaints (Hb 1:2–4; 1:12–2:1), each one followed by a response from God (1:5–11; 2:2–4).

**The first complaint (Hb 1:2–4).** The questions "how long?" and "why?" followed by descriptions of "violence" (i.e., social injustice) and "iniquity" resemble a typical psalm of lament. The identity of "the wicked" (1:4b) is not clear. Some scholars argue that these are Judeans, especially the rich and powerful. This would fit what is known of the

## Outline of Habakkuk

I. Habakkuk's First Complaint (1:2–4)

II. God's Response (1:5–11)

III. Habakkuk's Second Complaint (1:12–2:1)

IV. God's Response (2:2–4)

V. Sayings Against Tyrants (2:5–20)

VI. Hymn About God's Reign (3:1–19)

reign of Jehoiakim (609–597 BCE; see 2 Kgs 23:34–24:7). Others see a consistent reference to the Babylonians running throughout chs. 1 and 2. In any event, the concern for social justice and the ability to argue with God are typical characteristics of biblical faith.

**God's first response (Hb 1:5–11).** God addresses the Judeans (the imperatives are plural). He will raise up the Chaldeans to come and bring punishment (1:6). Their destructive march is described, but also their serious error: "they make their own strength their god" (1:11).

**The second complaint (Hb 1:12–2:1).** The prophet is not satisfied with God's response so he presses further. How can God tolerate the evil being done by the Babylonians (1:13)? The enemy treats humans as mere fish in the sea (1:15–17). The prophet will stand as a watchman and wait for God's answer to his "reproof" (2:1, a more literal translation than the NABRE's "complaint").

**God's second response (Hb 2:2–4).** The prophet is told to write the vision down so that he (the one who reads it) may run to deliver it. The Hebrew text is difficult in these verses, and it is not clear if they contain an account of the vision or simply the urging to wait for it. Verse 4, the most famous in the book, presents a contrast between two types, the "rash" or "puffed up and proud" (here, Babylon) and the "righteous" who are suffering and questioning. The latter will live, survive "because of faith." This is not "faith" in the sense of belief in doctrines but in the more biblical sense of fidelity to God and steadfast endurance. Later, in the New Testament, Paul will cite this verse (Rom 1:16–17; Gal 3:11) but take it in a different direction to make it a cornerstone of his argument that faith in Christ is superior to observance of the Law.

**Taunt Song (Hb 2:5–20).** The taunt song, with its five "Woe/Alas" (the NABRE translation "Ah!" is a little weak; 2:6b, 9, 12, 15, 19), is the speech of everyone on whom Babylon has brought so much suffering by its accumulation of wealth (2:6b–8), search for security (2:9–11), use of violence (2:12–14), pursuit of fame and honor (2:15–17), and trust in idols (2:18–20). Babylon will suffer reversal and be destroyed, but "the LORD is in his holy temple" (2:20).

# Hymn About God's Reign (Hb 3:1–19)

**Victory Psalm (Hb 3:2–19).** Like other psalms prayed in the Temple, this one includes words whose precise meaning is no longer clear ("shigyonot," v. 1; "selah," v. 9); the final line (3:19b) seems to be liturgical instructions. It begins and ends with the prophet speaking in the first person (a prayer, 3:2, a response, 3:16–19a). Between these lies a depiction of an appearance of God, drawing on traditional language of the appearance of the storm god known from Canaanite mythology. God is depicted as a warrior before whose coming nature itself quakes; the forces of chaos (depicted as "rivers"/"sea") are defeated (3:4–15). The prophet concludes with his own reaction to this awesome experience and ends with rejoicing in the Lord.

The book of Job wrestles with similar questions. Why do the innocent suffer? Job receives no answers but does have an experience of God (Jb 38:1–42:6) that enables him to get on with his life. Habakkuk likewise receives no answers, but is able to live because of his fidelity (Hb 2:4). ■

# THE BOOK OF HABAKKUK

## New American Bible, Introduction

Habakkuk is the only prophet to devote his entire work to the question of the justice of God's government of the world. In the Bible as a whole, only Job delivers a more pointed challenge to divine rule. Habakkuk's challenge is set up as a dialogue between the prophet and God, in which Habakkuk's opening complaint about injustices in Judean society (1:2–4) is followed in 1:5–11 by God's promise that the perpetrators will be punished by invading Chaldeans, i.e., Babylonians. Habakkuk's second complaint about the violence of the Chaldeans themselves (1:12–2:1) is followed by a second divine response assuring the prophet of the reliability of God's rule and calling for human faithfulness (2:2–4).

This dialogue is followed by a series of observations on the disastrous nature of tyranny (2:5–20), and by a vivid description in chap. 3 of God's appearance to save the people. Chapter 3 may be the prophet's prayer that God fulfill the promises made earlier to Habakkuk, or a hymn praising God's power added to Habakkuk's speeches by editors. In either case, the description of the theophany draws heavily upon ancient traditions in which God establishes order by defeating chaos, symbolized by rebellious waters (see Jb 7:12; Ps 74:13–14; 77:17–21; 89:10–11; Is 51:9).

Two important events frame Habakkuk's prophecy: the great Babylonian (Chaldean) victory over the Egyptians at Carchemish (605 B.C.) and the second Babylonian invasion of Judah (587 B.C.), which ended with the destruction of Jerusalem. The desperate conditions in Judah during these years, arising from internal and external threats, provoked Habakkuk's struggle with difficult and important theological questions about divine justice.

The book may be divided as follows:
   I. Habakkuk's First Complaint (1:2–4)
  II. God's Response (1:5–11)
 III. Habakkuk's Second Complaint (1:12–2:1)
  IV. God's Response (2:2–4)
   V. Sayings Against Tyrants (2:5–20)
  VI. Hymn About God's Reign (3:1–19) ∎

# HABAKKUK

**1** ¹ The oracle which Habakkuk the prophet received in a vision.

## Habakkuk's First Complaint

2  How long, O Lord, must I cry for help†
   and you do not listen?*
  Or cry out to you, "Violence!"
   and you do not intervene?
3  Why do you let me see iniquity?
   why do you simply gaze at evil?
  Destruction and violence are before me;*
   there is strife and discord.
4  This is why the law is numb†
   and justice never comes,
  For the wicked surround the just;*
   this is why justice comes forth
    perverted.

## God's Response

5†  Look over the nations and see!
   Be utterly amazed!
  For a work is being done in your days
   that you would not believe, were it
    told.*
6  For now I am raising up the Chaldeans,*
   that bitter and impulsive people,
  Who march the breadth of the land
   to take dwellings not their own.
7  They are terrifying and dreadful;
   their right and their exalted position
    are of their own making.
8  Swifter than leopards are their horses,
   and faster than desert wolves.
  Their horses spring forward;
   they come from far away;

they fly like an eagle hastening to
   devour.
9  All of them come for violence,
   their combined onslaught, a
    stormwind
  to gather up captives like sand.
10  They scoff at kings,
   ridicule princes;
  They laugh at any fortress,
   heap up an earthen ramp, and
    conquer it.
11  Then they sweep through like the wind
   and vanish—
  they make their own strength their
    god!†

## Habakkuk's Second Complaint

12  Are you not from of old, O Lord,
   my holy God, immortal?*
  Lord, you have appointed them for
    judgment,†
  O Rock,† you have set them in place
    to punish!
13  Your eyes are too pure to look upon
    wickedness,
  and the sight of evil you cannot
    endure.
  Why, then, do you gaze on the faithless
    in silence
  while the wicked devour those more
    just than themselves?
14  You have made mortals like the fish in
    the sea,
  like creeping things without a leader.
15  He† brings them all up with a hook,
   and hauls them away with his net;
  He gathers them in his fishing net,
   and then rejoices and exults.
16  Therefore he makes sacrifices to his
    net,†

---

† **1:2–4** The prophet complains about God's apparent disregard for Judah's internal evils in language that echoes the preaching of prophets like Amos, Isaiah, and Jeremiah.

**1:4** *The law is numb*: because the Lord has been silent, the Law, whether in the form of the scroll found in the Temple in the time of Josiah (2 Kgs 22) or in the form of divine instruction given by priests and prophets, has proved ineffective and so appeared to be cold, unreceptive, and powerless. For the Law to be credible, the Lord must see to it that the wicked are punished and the just rewarded.

**1:5–7** Habakkuk interprets the Babylonian defeat of Egypt at Carchemish (605 B.C.) as the answer to his complaint: the Lord will send the Chaldean empire against Judah as punishment for their sins.

**1:11** The primary aim of military campaigns by ancient Near Eastern rulers was usually the gathering of spoils and the collection of tribute rather than the annexation of territory. However, in the eighth century B.C., the Assyrians began to administer many conquered territories as provinces.

**1:12–2:1** *Appointed them for judgment*: this complaint is directed against the violent Babylonians, the very nation God chose to punish Judah.

**1:12** *Rock*: an ancient title celebrating the Lord's power and fidelity; cf. Dt 32:4; Is 26:4; 30:29; Ps 18:3, 32, 47; 95:1.

**1:15** *He*: the Babylonian king (cf. vv. 6, 13), who easily conquers other nations and treats them as objects for his entertainment and enrichment.

**1:16** *He makes sacrifices to his net*: the leader attributes victory to the military weapons he wields; he and his weapons have won victory, not any god.

\*
**1:2** Ps 13:2.     **1:5** Acts 13:41.
**1:3** Ez 45:9.     **1:6** Jer 32:28.
**1:4** Is 29:20–21.   **1:12** Ps 90:2.

and burns incense to his fishing net;
For thanks to them his portion is rich,
and his meal lavish.
17 Shall they, then, keep on drawing his
sword
to slaughter nations without mercy?

**2** ¹ I will stand at my guard post,
and station myself upon the rampart; *
I will keep watch to see what he will say
to me,
and what answer he will give to my
complaint.

### God's Response

2 Then the LORD answered me and said:
Write down the vision; † *
Make it plain upon tablets,
so that the one who reads it may run.
3 For the vision is a witness for the
appointed time,
a testimony to the end; it will not
disappoint.
If it delays, wait for it,
it will surely come, it will not be late.
4 See, the rash have no integrity;
but the just one who is righteous
because of faith shall live. † *

### Sayings Against Tyrants

5† Indeed wealth is treacherous;
a proud man does not succeed.
He who opens wide his throat like
Sheol,
and is insatiable as death,
Who gathers to himself all the nations,
and collects for himself all the
peoples—
6 Shall not all these take up a taunt
against him, *
and make a riddle about him, saying:

Ah! you who store up what is not
yours
—how long can it last!—
you who load yourself down with
collateral.
7 Will your debtors† not rise suddenly?
Will they not awake, those who make
you tremble?
You will become their spoil!
8 Because you plundered many nations,
the remaining peoples shall plunder
you;
Because of the shedding of human
blood,
and violence done to the land,
to the city and to all who live in it.

9 Ah! you who pursue evil gain for your
household,
setting your nest on high
to escape the reach of misfortune!
10 You have devised shame for your
household,
cutting off many peoples, forfeiting
your own life;
11 For the stone in the wall shall cry out,†
and the beam in the frame shall
answer it!

12 Ah! you who build a city by
bloodshed,
and who establish a town with
injustice! *
13 Is this not from the LORD of hosts:
peoples toil† for what the flames
consume,
and nations grow weary for nothing!
14 But the earth shall be filled
with the knowledge of the LORD's
glory,
just as the water covers the sea. *

**2:2** *Write down the vision*: the vision is written down for two reasons: so that a herald may carry and proclaim its contents to the people, and so that the reception of the vision and its truth can be verified by its fulfillment (v. 3).
**2:4** *The just one who is righteous because of faith shall live*: the faithful survive the impending doom because they trust in God's justice and wait patiently for God to carry it out. Several New Testament passages cite these words (Rom 1:17; Gal 3:11; cf. Heb 10:38) to confirm the teaching that people receive justification and supernatural life through faith in Christ.
**2:5** This verse describes any tyrant who, like the Babylonians, possesses insatiable greed.
**2:7** *Debtors*: the Hebrew term can mean either debtors or creditors, and this double meaning is likely intended: the debtor nations rise up against their creditor nation and become its creditors in the reversal of affairs described here.
**2:11–12** The palaces, built at the expense of gross injustice (vv. 6–10), call down vengeance on their builders. This is typical prophetic language for the condemnation of social crimes within Israel and Judah.
**2:13** *Peoples toil*: those oppressed by the Babylonians do not benefit from their work. Verses 13–14 break the pattern of reversal in the oracles that precede and may have been added by an editor.

**2:1** Is 21:8.
**2:2** Is 30:8.
**2:4** Rom 1:17; Gal 3:11; Heb 10:38.
**2:6** Is 14:4.
**2:12** Ez 24:6; Mi 3:10; Na 3:1.
**2:14** Is 11:9.

15 Ah! you who give your neighbors
    the cup of your wrath to drink, and
      make them drunk,
    until their nakedness is seen! *
16 You are filled with shame instead of
      glory;
    drink, you too, and stagger!
The cup from the LORD's right hand shall
      come around to you,
    and utter shame shall cover your
      glory.
17 For the violence done to Lebanon† shall
      cover you, *
    and the destruction of the animals
      shall terrify you;
Because of the shedding of human
      blood,
    and violence done to the land,
    to the city and to all who live in it.

18 Of what use is the carved image,†
    that its maker should carve it?
Or the molten image, the lying oracle,
    that its very maker should trust in it,
    and make mute idols?
19 Ah! you who say to wood, "Awake!"
    to silent stone, "Arise!"
    Can any such thing give oracles? *
It is only overlaid with gold and silver,
    there is no breath in it at all.
20 But the LORD is in his holy temple;
    silence before him, all the earth! *

## Hymn About God's Reign

3 ¹Prayer of Habakkuk, the prophet. According to Shigyonot.†

2 O LORD, I have heard your renown,
    and am in awe, O LORD, of your work.
In the course of years revive it,†
    in the course of years make yourself
      known;
    in your wrath remember compassion!

3† God came from Teman,†
    the Holy One from Mount Paran. *
             *Selah*

His glory covered the heavens,
    and his praise filled the earth;
4   his splendor spread like the light.
He raised his horns high, *
    he rejoiced on the day of his strength.
5 Before him went pestilence,
    and plague† followed in his steps.
6 He stood and shook the earth;
    he looked and made the nations
      tremble.
Ancient mountains were shattered,
    the age-old hills bowed low,
    age-old orbits† collapsed.

7 The tents of Cushan trembled,
    the pavilions of the land of Midian.†
8 Was your anger against the rivers,
      O LORD?
    your wrath against the rivers,
    your rage against the sea,†*
That you mounted your steeds,
    your victorious chariot?
9 You readied your bow,
    you filled your bowstring with arrows.
             *Selah*

---

**2:17** *The violence done to Lebanon*: the destruction of the cedar forests of Lebanon, used in lavish building projects by the great conquerors; cf. Is 14:8; 37:24. *The destruction of the animals*: the killing off of the wild animals through excessive hunting by the same conquerors; cf. Bar 3:16.

**2:18–20** Idolatrous worship is here shown to be folly by contrasting idols with the majesty of the one true God. Verse 18 may originally have followed v. 19, since the term "Ah!" begins each new saying in this section.

**3:1** *Shigyonot*: a Hebrew technical term no longer understood, but probably a musical notation regarding the following hymn. This term, the references to the leader and stringed instruments at the end of the hymn (v. 19), and the use of the term *selah* in vv. 3, 9, and 13 are found elsewhere in the Bible only in the Psalter, and they indicate that, like the psalms, this poem was once used in worship.

**3:2** *In the course of years revive it*: a plea for God to renew the works of the past.

**3:3–15** Cf. the theophanies in Dt 33:2–3; Jgs 5:4–5; Ps 18:8–16; 68:8–9; 77:17–21; 97:1–5; Na 1:3–6, etc. Conventional language is employed to describe the appearance of the Lord, as in Ex 19:16–19.

**3:3** *Teman*: a region in Edom. *Mount Paran*: in the territory of Edom, or the northern part of the Sinai peninsula.

**3:5** *Pestilence...plague*: these may be figures who are part of the heavenly armies God leads into battle.

**3:6** *Age-old orbits*: the regular paths through the skies of heavenly bodies are disrupted at the appearance of the divine warrior, as are the ancient mountains on earth. Such cosmic disruption is typical of divine appearances (Ps 18:8; Na 1:5).

**3:7** *Cushan...Midian*: the inhabitants of the area southeast of Judah where the divine march originates (Teman, Mount Paran), who are shaken, together with the cosmos, at God's appearance.

**3:8** *Rivers...sea*: the forces of chaos personified as *yam* (Sea) and *nahar* (River) try to destroy the order God imposed at creation by sweeping past their boundaries and covering the earth. Their mention here and in v. 15 emphasizes that God is both creator and deliverer, subduing historical enemies and cosmic forces.

---

| | |
|---|---|
| 2:15 Jer 51:7; Lam 4:21. | 3:3 Dt 33:2. |
| 2:17 Is 14:8. | 3:4 Ps 18:3. |
| 2:19 Is 44:18–19. | 3:8 Ps 74:13; 89:11; Is |
| 2:20 Ps 11:4. | 51:9; Na 1:4. |

You split the earth with rivers;
10    at the sight of you the mountains
        writhed.
The clouds poured down water;
    the deep roared loudly.
The sun† forgot to rise,
11    the moon left its lofty station,*
At the light of your flying arrows,
    at the gleam of your flashing spear.

12    In wrath you marched on the earth,
        in fury you trampled the nations.
13    You came forth to save your people,
        to save your anointed one.†
    You crushed the back of the wicked,
        you laid him bare, bottom to neck.

                                    *Selah*

14†    You pierced his head with your shafts;
        his princes you scattered with your
            stormwind,
        as food for the poor in unknown
            places.
15    You trampled the sea with your horses
        amid the churning of the deep waters.

16    I hear, and my body trembles;
        at the sound, my lips quiver.
    Decay invades my bones,
        my legs tremble beneath me.
    I await the day of distress
        that will come upon the people who
            attack us.

17    For though the fig tree does not
            blossom,
        and no fruit appears on the vine,
    Though the yield of the olive fails
        and the terraces produce no
            nourishment,
    Though the flocks disappear from the fold
        and there is no herd in the stalls,
18    Yet I will rejoice in the LORD
        and exult in my saving God.
19    GOD, my Lord, is my strength;
        he makes my feet swift as those of
            deer
        and enables me to tread upon the
            heights.†*

For the leader; with stringed instruments.

---

**3:10–11** *Sun…moon:* heavenly figures who, like pestilence and plague (v. 5), serve in God's army, or are startled at God's appearance, as are the ancient constellations (v. 6).

**3:13** *Your anointed one:* the theocratic king, the head of God's people. *The back of the wicked:* this may refer both to God's cosmic enemy, River/Sea, and to the leader of Israel's historical enemy.

**3:14** The last two lines of this verse are obscure in Hebrew and difficult to translate.

**3:19** *The heights:* this term can also mean "backs" and may be an image of conquest over the poet's foes.

---

**3:11** Jos 10:12–13.    **3:19** Ps 18:32–34.

# The Book of
# Zephaniah

## INTRODUCTION

### Garrett Galvin, OFM

The book of Zephaniah focuses on Jerusalem in a manner not seen since Isaiah and Micah. It combines the concerns of Jerusalem with the larger vision of a prophet like Amos as it catalogues the adversaries of Jerusalem. It touches on a wide scope of biblical traditions as it includes both creation and Deuteronomic themes. Like many of the other prophets, it is generally written in poetry with a superscription (Zep 1:1) that tries to give it some context. The poetic nature of this prophetic text is seen through the predominance of oracles of judgment or woe followed by the renewal found in oracles of salvation.

The book of Zephaniah shares many characteristics with the eighth-century BCE prophets, but there are clear signs of a different social setting. One finds an increasing concern with the Cushites (Cush is the area south of Egypt), perhaps because Taharqa—biblical Tirhakah (Is 37:9; 2 Kgs 19:9)—was a Cushite pharaoh (reign 690–664 BCE) who may have invaded Jerusalem and who certainly fought with the Assyrians. Cush or Cushites are referred to in all three chapters of Zephaniah. Although Zephaniah, a name found in the ruins of Lachish, is overshadowed by the likes of Jeremiah, his career represents a new understanding of the spiritual importance of poverty in the Old Testament. Zephaniah associates with the "humble of the land" (Zep 2:3; 3:12) and portrays them as fulfilling the mandate of Mi 6:8. He elevates the poor, who have complete dependence on God, and offers their attitude as one to emulate. They will receive refuge (Zep 3:12) and enjoy a restored Jerusalem (Zep 3:19). Jerusalem is the setting of this book and receives a focused description that at times even includes its smaller neighborhoods (Maktesh) (Zep 1:10–11).

The 53 verses of Zephaniah start in an

## Outline of Zephaniah

I. The Day of the Lord: Judgment on Judah (1:2–2:3)

II. Judgment on the Nations (2:4–15)

III. Jerusalem Reproached (3:1–7)

IV. The Nations Punished and Jerusalem Restored (3:8–20)

unusual manner. The book begins with a genealogy—an unprecedented step for this type of literature. Zephaniah's roots are traced back four generations to Hezekiah (Zep 1:1). Most scholars assume that this refers to the king. Since this book has no sharp denunciations of the monarchy, Zephaniah is understood to be sympathetic to it. Like other prophets, he is associated with a king: Josiah in this case. All of this appears in the prose inscription, which easily could have been written by a later editor as none of these figures are mentioned in the rest of the book.

Two themes characterize the rest of Zep 1: creation and the "day of the Lord." The creation language resonates with the book of Genesis, but it reverses Genesis. Instead of populating the earth, the Lord announces judgment on humans, beasts, and the fish. Like Gn 1, cultic concerns also appear here as the prophet condemns idolatrous priests and worshipers of Baal and Milcom (the Ammonite god). The chapter concludes with a theme first met in Am 5:18: the day of the Lord. "The day of the LORD" seems to refer to earth-shattering occasions in Israel's past and future. Many other prophets develop this theme. Zephaniah 1 also has an international focus reminiscent of Amos as many nations are mentioned and condemned here. Finally the chapter shares some of Amos's concerns for social justice as it condemns absentee landlords in Zep 1:13 in language resonating with Am 5:11.

Zephaniah 2 intensifies the condemnation of evildoers. Developing the theme of fire from 1:18, God's blazing anger will drive away the shameless on the day of punishment (2:2). The first glimmers of hope appear after this announcement as the Lord inspires the "humble of the land" to seek justice and humility. The rest of the chapter turns to the nations. We have many nations mentioned in these oracles against the nations. Jerusalem was first threatened in 1:10–12 and afforded some relief in 2:3. Now the nations receive equally strong threats without the hope of redemption. The language of Genesis emerges again in 2:9 as the Transjordan's fate is compared to that of Sodom and Gomorrah. Special disdain is reserved for the cities of Philistia to the southwest of Jerusalem (2:4–7). This disdain expands

to include the whole region of the ancient Near East, from the southwest in Cush (2:12) to the northeast in Assyria (2:13). Unlike the oracles against Jerusalem, no hope is held out to them except to be the plunder of the humble remnant (2:9).

The woe ("Ah!" Zep 2:5; 3:1) announced to the nations in ch. 2 is now turned to Jerusalem in more muted tones without ever actually naming the city in the woe oracle. We are told its officials, judges, priests, and prophets are corrupt. The Lord has devastated the city (3:6), but the Lord will make it pure again (3:9). The theme of punishment followed by salvation is reminiscent of Genesis. Elements of speech in Zep 3:9 and 3:13 recall the Tower of Babel. Unlike the nations, the judgment on Jerusalem is quickly followed by salvation. In 3:19 Jerusalem, which has been named in 3:16, is promised praise and renown, not unlike Is 56:5 where Israel is promised a name and memorial. ■

# THE BOOK OF ZEPHANIAH

## New American Bible, Introduction

Zephaniah's prophecy of judgment on Judah and Jerusalem emphasizes, perhaps more than any other prophecy, the devastation and death that divine judgment will bring. Described as the day of the Lord, the day of judgment is pictured as a time of darkness, of anguish and distress, of destruction and plunder of cities, and of threat to all life, human and animal alike. The major sins motivating this judgment, in Zephaniah's view, are Judah's worship of other deities (1:4–9) and its unjust and abusive leadership (3:1–4).

The title of the prophecy informs us that the ministry of Zephaniah took place during the reign of Josiah (640–609 B.C.), not long before the fall of Jerusalem in 587 B.C. The protest against the worship of false gods and the condemnation of foreign practices (1:8–9) may indicate that Zephaniah spoke during the height of Assyrian influence in the early years of Josiah's reign, before Josiah launched the religious reforms praised by Israel's historians (2 Kgs 22:1–23:30). If so, the prophecy of Zephaniah would be contemporary with the early prophecy of Jeremiah, with which it shares both language and ideas.

Following are the book's four sections:

 I. The Day of the Lord: Judgment on Judah (1:2–2:3)
 II. Judgment on the Nations (2:4–15)
 III. Jerusalem Reproached (3:1–7)
 IV. The Nations Punished and Jerusalem Restored (3:8–20) ■

# ZEPHANIAH

**1** ¹The word of the LORD which came to Zephaniah, the son of Cushi, the son of Gedaliah, the son of Amariah, the son of Hezekiah,† in the days of Josiah, the son of Amon, king of Judah.

## The Day of the Lord: Judgment on Judah

2     I will completely sweep away all things
        from the face of the land—oracle of
           the LORD.
3     I will sweep away human being and
        beast alike,
    I will sweep away the birds of the sky,
    and the fish of the sea.
    I will make the wicked stumble;
    I will eliminate the people
        from the face of the land—oracle of
           the LORD.*
4     I will stretch out my hand against Judah,
        and against all the inhabitants of
           Jerusalem;
    I will eliminate from this place
        the last vestige of Baal,
        the name of the idolatrous priests.
5     And those who bow down on the roofs
        to the host of heaven,†
    And those who bow down to the LORD
        but swear by Milcom;*
6     And those who have turned away from
        the LORD,
        and those who have not sought the
           LORD,
        who have not inquired of him.

7     Silence in the presence of the Lord GOD!
        for near is the day of the LORD,
    Yes, the LORD has prepared a sacrifice,
        he has consecrated his guests.†*
8     On the day of the LORD's sacrifice

I will punish the officials and the king's
        sons,
    and all who dress in foreign apparel.
9     I will punish, on that day,
        all who leap over the threshold,†
    Who fill the house of their master
        with violence and deceit.
10     On that day—oracle of the LORD—
    A cry will be heard from the Fish Gate,
        a wail from the Second Quarter,†
        loud crashing from the hills.
11     Wail, O inhabitants of Maktesh!
        for all the merchants are destroyed,
        all who weigh out silver, done away
           with.

12     At that time,
    I will search Jerusalem with lamps,
        I will punish the people
        who settle like dregs in wine,†
    Who say in their hearts,
        "The Lord will not do good,
        nor will he do harm."
13     Their wealth shall be given to plunder
        and their houses to devastation;
    They will build houses,
        but not dwell in them;
    They will plant vineyards,
        but not drink their wine.*
14     Near is the great day of the LORD,
        near and very swiftly coming.
    The sound of the day of the LORD!
        Piercing—
        there a warrior shrieks!
15     A day of wrath is that day,
        a day of distress and anguish,
        a day of ruin and desolation,
    A day of darkness and gloom,
        a day of thick black clouds,*
16     A day of trumpet blasts and battle cries
        against fortified cities,
        against lofty battlements.*
17     I will hem the people in
        till they walk like the blind,

---

† **1:1** *Hezekiah:* it is possible, but not certain, that Zephaniah's ancestor was King Hezekiah who reigned in Judah from 715 to 687 B.C. (2 Kgs 18–20).

**1:5** *The host of heaven:* the sun, moon, planets, and stars, the worship of which became widespread in Judah under Assyrian influence. *Milcom:* the god of the Ammonites; cf. 1 Kgs 11:5, 7, 33; 2 Kgs 23:13.

**1:7** *He has consecrated his guests:* God has consecrated the troops, presumably foreign, who have been invited to share in the spoil on the day of slaughter.

**1:9** *Leap over the threshold:* the reference may be to a religious ritual like that practiced by the priests of the Philistine deity

Dagon (1 Sm 5:5).

**1:10–11** *The Second Quarter...Maktesh:* sections of Jerusalem (cf. 2 Kgs 22:14).

**1:12** *Settle like dregs in wine:* those who are overconfident because, like the sediment that settles to the bottom of a bottle of wine, they have remained at peace and undisturbed for a long time.

---

**1:3** Hos 4:3.         **1:13** Am 5:11.
**1:5** Jer 8:2; 2 Kgs 23:13.   **1:15** Is 13:9; Jl 2:1–2.
**1:7** Is 34:6; Am 5:18.     **1:16** Am 2:2.

because they have sinned against the
    LORD;
And their blood shall be poured out like
    dust,
    and their bowels like dung.
18 Neither their silver nor their gold
    will be able to save them.
On the day of the LORD's wrath,
    in the fire of his passion,
    all the earth will be consumed.
For he will make an end, yes, a sudden
    end,
    of all who live on the earth.*

2 ¹† Gather, gather yourselves together,
    O nation without shame!
² Before you are driven away,
    like chaff that disappears;
Before there comes upon you
    the blazing anger of the LORD;
Before there comes upon you
    the day of the LORD's anger.
³ Seek the LORD,
    all you humble of the land,
    who have observed his law;
Seek justice,
    seek humility;
Perhaps you will be sheltered
    on the day of the LORD's anger.*

### Judgment on the Nations

⁴ For Gaza shall be forsaken,
    and Ashkelon shall be a waste,
Ashdod they shall drive out at midday,
    and Ekron† shall be uprooted.*
⁵ Ah! You who dwell by the seacoast,
    the nation of Cherethites,†
    the word of the LORD is against you!
O Canaan, land of the Philistines,
    I will leave you to perish without an
    inhabitant!
⁶ You shall become fields for shepherds,
    and folds for flocks.
⁷ The seacoast shall belong
    to the remnant of the house of Judah;
    by the sea they shall pasture.
In the houses of Ashkelon

they shall lie down in the evening.
For the LORD their God will take care of
    them,
    and bring about their restoration.
⁸ I have heard the taunts uttered by Moab,
    and the insults of the Ammonites,†
When they taunted my people
    and made boasts against their
    territory.*
⁹ Therefore, as I live—
    oracle of the LORD of hosts—
    the God of Israel,
Moab shall become like Sodom,
    the Ammonites like Gomorrah:
A field of weeds,
    a salt pit,
    a waste forever.
The remnant of my people shall plunder
    them,
    the survivors of my nation dispossess
    them.
¹⁰ This will be the recompense for their
    pride,
    because they taunted and boasted
    against
    the people of the LORD of hosts.
¹¹ The LORD shall inspire them with terror
    when he makes all the gods of earth
    waste away;
Then the distant shores of the nations,
    each from its own place,
    shall bow down to him.
¹² You too, O Cushites,†
    shall be slain by the sword of the
    LORD.*
¹³ He will stretch out his hand against the
    north,
    to destroy Assyria;
He will make Nineveh a waste,
    dry as the desert.*
¹⁴ In her midst flocks shall lie down,
    all the wild life of the hollows;
The screech owl and the desert owl
    shall roost in her columns;
The owl shall hoot from the window,

**2:1–3** This oracle is a classic description of the day of the Lord as an overwhelming disaster, concluding with a call for repentance and reform. *Nation without shame:* Judah.
**2:4** *Gaza...Ashkelon...Ashdod...Ekron:* cities of the Philistine confederation.
**2:5** *Cherethites:* a synonym for, or subgroup of, the Philistines, which may be associated with Crete, a part of the larger Aegean area from which the Philistines came.

**2:8** *Moab...Ammonites:* Judah's neighbors to the East across the Jordan.
**2:12** *Cushites:* the Ethiopians, who had ruled Egypt a generation before Zephaniah's career.

**1:18** Zep 3:8; Jer 4:26–27.    **2:8** Jer 48:1; 49:1.
**2:3** Am 5:14–15.    **2:12** 2 Chr 14:7–14.
**2:4** Jer 47:5; Am 1:6–8.    **2:13** Na 3:7.

the raven croak from the doorway.*

15 Is this the exultant city†
   that dwelt secure,
That told itself,
   "I and there is no one else"?
How it has become a waste,
   a lair for wild animals!
Those who pass by it
   hiss, and shake their fists!

## Jerusalem Reproached

**3** 1 Ah! Rebellious and polluted,
   the tyrannical city!†
2 It listens to no voice,
   accepts no correction;
In the LORD it has not trusted,
   nor drawn near to its God.*
3 Its officials within it
   are roaring lions;
Its judges are desert wolves
   that have no bones to gnaw by
      morning.*
4 Its prophets are reckless,
   treacherous people;
Its priests profane what is holy,
   and do violence to the law.*
5 But the LORD in its midst is just,
   doing no wrong;
Morning after morning rendering judgment
   unfailingly, at dawn;
   the wicked, however, know no shame.

6 I have cut down nations,
   their battlements are laid waste;
I have made their streets deserted,
   with no one passing through;
Their cities are devastated,
   with no one dwelling in them.*
7 I said, "Surely now you will fear me,
   you will accept correction;
They cannot fail to see
   all I have brought upon them."
Yet the more eagerly they have done
   all their corrupt deeds.

## The Nations Punished and Jerusalem Restored

8 Therefore, wait for me—oracle of the
   LORD—

until the day when I arise as accuser;
For it is my decision to gather nations,
   to assemble kingdoms,
In order to pour out upon them my
      wrath,
   all my blazing anger;
For in the fire of my passion
   all the earth will be consumed.*

9 For then I will make pure
   the speech of the peoples,
That they all may call upon the name of
      the LORD,
   to serve him with one accord;
10 From beyond the rivers of Ethiopia
   and as far as the recesses of the North,
   they shall bring me offerings.

11    On that day
You will not be ashamed
   of all your deeds,
   when you rebelled against me;
For then I will remove from your midst
   the proud braggarts,
And you shall no longer exalt yourself
   on my holy mountain.
12 But I will leave as a remnant in your
      midst
   a people humble and lowly,
Who shall take refuge in the name of
      the LORD—*
13    the remnant of Israel.
They shall do no wrong
   and speak no lies;
Nor shall there be found in their
      mouths
   a deceitful tongue;
They shall pasture and lie down
   with none to disturb them.*
14 Shout for joy, daughter Zion!
   sing joyfully, Israel!
Be glad and exult with all your heart,
   daughter Jerusalem!*
15 The LORD has removed the judgment
      against you,
   he has turned away your enemies;
The King of Israel, the LORD, is in your
      midst,
   you have no further misfortune to fear.

---

† **2:15** *The exultant city*: Nineveh. *Hiss, and shake their fists*: gestures of derision.
  **3:1** *The tyrannical city*: Jerusalem.

* **2:14** Is 34:11.
**3:2** Jer 2:30; 7:28.
**3:3** Ez 22:27; Mi 3:11.
**3:4** Ez 22:26; Hb 1:4.
**3:6** Jer 2:15.
**3:8** Zep 1:18; Jl 4:2.
**3:12** Is 57:13; Ob 17.
**3:13** Mi 4:4.
**3:14** Zec 9:9.

16     On that day, it shall be said to
            Jerusalem:
         Do not fear, Zion,
            do not be discouraged!
17     The LORD, your God, is in your midst,
            a mighty savior,
         Who will rejoice over you with gladness,
            and renew you in his love,
         Who will sing joyfully because of you, *
18         as on festival days.

         I will remove disaster from among you,
            so that no one may recount your
            disgrace.

19     At that time I will deal
            with all who oppress you;
         I will save the lame,
            and assemble the outcasts;
         I will give them praise and renown
            in every land where they were
            shamed. *
20     At that time I will bring you home,
            and at that time I will gather you;
         For I will give you renown and praise,
            among all the peoples of the earth,
         When I bring about your restoration
            before your very eyes, says the
            LORD. *

---

**3:17** Jl 2:27.                          **3:20** Jl 4:1.
**3:19** Mi 4:6.

Z
E
P

# The Book of

# Haggai

## INTRODUCTION

Garrett Galvin, OFM

## Historical Setting

The book of Haggai exemplifies the postexilic interest in the Temple. Haggai's concerns and prophecies mark a very different world from that of many of his predecessors. Unlike many of the other classical prophets, he appears to be a prophet supporting the Temple cult. This lends an optimistic nature to the book not found in many of the other Prophets. The book of Haggai chronicles three and a half months of progress on the reconstruction of the Temple. The book moves from despair and frustration with the current state of affairs in August 520 BCE to hope and a sense of restoration by December of the same year. The book reflects Deuteronomic theological perspectives, specifically that well-being is the result of obedience to God, and hardship is the result of disobedience. In ancient Near Eastern understanding, temples housed gods who sanctioned laws through which taxes were levied, armies raised, and justice administered. The Lord caused suffering because the Temple was in ruins (Hg 1:9–10). The Lord restored blessings on the people three and a half months later when much progress had been made on the Temple (2:18–19) and promised even greater blessings in the future. True prosperity and blessings were not possible without the Temple.

Although the book of Ezra mentions Haggai twice (Ezr 5:1; 6:14), not much is known of his background. Did he return with Ezra from Babylon to Jerusalem or did he remain in Judah during the Babylonian exile? His concern with "the remnant" (Hg 1:12, 14; 2:2) may suggest that he returned with them, but no scholarly consensus exists. The book of Ezra closely associates him with Zechariah. The book of Zechariah continues to chronicle the construction of the Temple after the conclusion

## Outline of Haggai

I. The Restoration of the Temple (1:1–15)

II. Oracles of Encouragement (2:1–23)

of the book of Haggai in December 520 into the years 519–518 BCE. Haggai and Zec 1–8 seem to have been compiled as a single work chronicling the reconstruction of the Temple. They both share some characteristics with the Chronicler, especially an interest in the cult. The book of Haggai does not seem to have the broad social justice concerns of other Jerusalem prophets like Isaiah and Zephaniah; rather it focuses on cultic issues. The Temple is the central and overwhelming concern. The poor state of the Temple explains the suffering of the people.

## Structure

Most scholars break the book of Haggai into five sections: Hg 1:1–11; 1:12–15; 2:1–9; 2:10–19; and 2:20–23. Although scholars have previously treated this book as primarily poetic, recent studies suggest it is more of an elevated prose. Haggai 1:1–11 has many characteristics of an oracle of woe. The first two verses establish a familiar diarchic model of leadership from before the exile, consisting of a high priest (Joshua) and a political leader (Zerubbabel). The central concern of this section and the book is announced: "rebuild the house of the LORD." The word "house" appears seven times in this section, rivaling the intense focus upon the Temple in the final section of Ezekiel (Ez 40–48). This section chronicles the economic and social misery of Jerusalem in 520 BCE. While some enjoyed prosperity in their "paneled houses," (Hg 1:4) the great majority suffered and the common good was neglected as symbolized by the Temple, "which lies in ruins" (Hg 1:9). Many other signs of the neglected common good are also manifest: infertility of fields as well as poor clothing and work supplies (Hg 1:6), drought (Hg 1:10), and a devastating heat wave (Hg 1:11). Haggai argues that the restoration of the Temple is the only way to bring relief.

The chapter ends on a hopeful note in the second section (Hg 1:12–15), as Haggai's words are met with action by September 520. His critique was aimed broadly and the response was likewise broad as Zerubbabel, Joshua, and the remnant obeyed the word of the Lord. Haggai describes the people's response in language typical of the prophets: the Lord stirs up their spirit (1:14) and remedies the postexilic malaise of the first section of the chapter.

Chapter 2 resounds with encouraging words. Haggai does not overlook reality; he acknowledges that much work remains for the Temple to match its former glory (Hg 2:3). Nevertheless, hope and optimism resonate throughout the chapter as the Lord promises: "I am with you" (2:4). In the third section (2:1–9), dating from October 520 BCE, the prophet recalls the commitment of the Lord to their ancestors in Egypt (2:5). As the Lord provided for them in former times, the Lord will alter the balance of power and riches among the nations to the advantage of Israel once again. In language reminiscent of Is 66:12, the Lord will provide for Israel from the nations (Hg 2:6–7) and also bring peace (2:9).

The fourth section (Hg 2:10–19), dating from December 520, is unique as it consists of a prophetic interpretation of a priestly concern. The stature of the priesthood will continue to grow throughout the postexilic period. The prophet feels compelled to comment on priestly concerns of defilement before returning to the hopeful rebuilding of the Temple.

The fifth section (Hg 2:20–23) concludes with eschatological hope: kingdoms will be overthrown through heavenly power and Zerubbabel will be made like the Lord's signet ring. The restored Temple leads to the hope of the restoration of former glories and the fulfillment of God's plan now that the Lord is dwelling among them. ■

# THE BOOK OF HAGGAI

## New American Bible, Introduction

Haggai's words concern conditions in the Persian province of Judah at the beginning of the postexilic period during the reign of the Persian king Darius I (522–486 B.C.). The community in Judah is struggling with its identity in light of the loss of its statehood through the demise of the monarchy and the destruction of the Temple. Haggai's oracles address both these problems. First, the provincial government, despite its subordination to Persian hegemony, is seen as the legitimate heir to the Davidic monarchy; the governor Zerubbabel, himself a descendant of the Davidic line, and the high priest Joshua together provide political, economic, and religious leadership for the survivors of the Babylonian destruction and the returnees from the Babylonian exile who live together in Judah. Still, the possibility for restoration of Davidic rule is not relinquished but rather is shifted to the eschatological future. Second, the Temple's ruined state is addressed by a rebuilding program. The prophet links the well-being of the community to the work of Temple restoration, and his exhortations to the leaders and the people to begin work on this project are apparently heeded. The brief period of Haggai's ministry (August to December 520 B.C.) marks the resumption of work on the Temple, the symbol of divine presence among the people.

Six date formulas (1:1, 15; 2:1, 10, 18, 20) are an important feature of the Book of Haggai. In their specificity and in their link to the reign of a foreign king (Darius), the dates underscore God's control over history, as do similar chronological references in Zechariah, a prophetic book connected in literary and thematic ways to Haggai.

The prophecies of Haggai can be divided into two major parts:

I. The Restoration of the Temple (1:1–15)

II. Oracles of Encouragement (2:1–23) ■

# HAGGAI

## 1 Prophetic Call to Work on the Temple.
¹ On the first day of the sixth month in the second year† of Darius the king, the word of the LORD came through Haggai the prophet to the governor of Judah, Zerubbabel,* son of Shealtiel, and to the high priest Joshua, son of Jehozadak:* ² Thus says the LORD of hosts: This people has said: "Now is not the time to rebuild the house of the LORD."

³ Then the word of the LORD came through Haggai the prophet: ⁴ Is it time for you to dwell in your paneled houses while this house lies in ruins?†*

5   Now thus says the LORD of hosts:
      Reflect on your experience!†
6   You have sown much, but have brought
        in little;
      you have eaten, but have not been
        satisfied;*
    You have drunk, but have not become
        intoxicated;
      you have clothed yourselves, but have
        not been warmed;
    And the hired worker labors for a bag
        full of holes.

7 Thus says the LORD of hosts:

    Reflect on your experience!
8   Go up into the hill country;
      bring timber, and build the house
      that I may be pleased with it,

and that I may be glorified,† says the LORD.
9   You expected much, but it came to little;
      and what you brought home, I blew
        away.
    Why is this?—oracle of the LORD† of
        hosts—
      Because my house is the one which
        lies in ruins,
      while each of you runs to your own
        house.
10  Therefore, the heavens withheld the dew,
      and the earth its yield.
11  And I have proclaimed a devastating
        heat†
      upon the land and upon the
        mountains,
    Upon the grain, the new wine, and the
        olive oil,
      upon all that the ground brings forth;
    Upon human being and beast alike,
      and upon all they produce.

**Response of Leaders and People.** ¹² Then Zerubbabel, son of Shealtiel, and the high priest Joshua, son of Jehozadak, and all the remnant of the people† obeyed the LORD their God, and the words of Haggai the prophet, since the LORD their God had sent him; thus the people feared the LORD. ¹³ Then Haggai, the messenger of the LORD, proclaimed to the people as the message of the LORD: I am with you!—oracle of the LORD.

¹⁴ And so the LORD stirred up the spirit of the governor of Judah, Zerubbabel, son of Shealtiel, and the spirit of the high priest Joshua, son of Jehozadak, and the spirit of all the remnant of the people,* so that they came to do the work in the house of the LORD of hosts,

---

**1:1** First day of the sixth month in the second year: August 29, 520 B.C. This is the first of six chronological indicators in Haggai. Darius: Darius I, emperor of Persia from 522 to 486 B.C. Governor: term used for local rulers of provinces in the Persian imperial structure. Zerubbabel: grandson of King Jehoiachin (cf. 2 Kgs 24:8–17).
**1:4** Your paneled houses...house lies in ruins: the contrast here is between the unfinished Temple and the completed houses of the Judeans.
**1:5** Reflect on your experience: the prophet exhorts the people to consider the futility of their efforts as a result of their neglecting work on the Temple. The following verses call attention to harsh conditions in Judah after the return from exile and the preoccupation of the people with their personal concerns.
**1:8** That I may be glorified: for the prophet, the rebuilding of the Temple restores the glory God had lost in the eyes of the nations by the Temple's destruction.

**1:9** Oracle of the LORD: a phrase used extensively in prophetic books to indicate divine speech.
**1:11** Devastating heat: this pronouncement of natural disaster, which functions as a warning to the people for their failure to rebuild the Temple, concludes the opening oracular section of Haggai.
**1:12** The remnant of the people: here the phrase appears to refer to the prophet's audience, but the "remnant" theme, though often in different Hebrew terminology, suggesting especially those whom the Lord will call back from exile and re-establish as his people, is important in the prophets (cf. Is 4:3; 37:31–32; Jl 3:5; Mi 4:7; Ob 17) and in the New Testament (cf. Rom 11:1–10).

**1:1** Zec 4:6–10.
**1:1** Zec 3:1–10.
**1:4** 2 Sm 7:2.
**1:6** Lv 26:26; Hos 4:10.
**1:14** Ezr 1:5; 5:1–2.

their God, ¹⁵ on the twenty-fourth day of the sixth month in the second year† of Darius the king.

# 2 Assurance of God's Presence.
¹ On the twenty-first day of the seventh month,† the word of the LORD came through Haggai the prophet: ² Speak to the governor of Judah, Zerubbabel, son of Shealtiel, and to the high priest Joshua, son of Jehozadak, and to the remnant of the people:

3    Who is left among you†
        who saw this house in its former
            glory?
     And how do you see it now?
        Does it not seem like nothing in your
            eyes? *
4    Now be strong, Zerubbabel—oracle of
            the LORD—
        be strong, Joshua, son of Jehozadak,
            high priest,
     Be strong, all you people of the land—
            oracle of the LORD—
        and work! For I am with you—oracle
            of the LORD of hosts.
5    This is the commitment I made to you
            when you came out of Egypt.
     My spirit remains in your midst;
        do not fear!

⁶ For thus says the LORD of hosts: †

     In just a little while,
        I will shake the heavens and the
            earth, *

the sea and the dry land.
7    I will shake all the nations,
        so that the treasures of all the nations
            will come in.
     And I will fill this house with glory—
        says the LORD of hosts. *

⁸ Mine is the silver and mine the gold—oracle of the LORD of hosts.

9    Greater will be the glory of this house *
        the latter more than the former—says
            the LORD of hosts;
     And in this place I will give you
            peace— †
        oracle of the LORD of hosts.

## Priestly Ruling with Prophetic Interpretation. †
¹⁰ On the twenty-fourth day of the ninth month in the second year† of Darius, the word of the LORD came to Haggai the prophet: ¹¹ Thus says the LORD of hosts: Ask the priests for a ruling:† ¹² If someone carries sanctified meat in the fold of a garment and the fold touches bread, soup, wine, oil, or any other food, do they become sanctified? "No," the priests answered. ¹³ Then Haggai asked: "If a person defiled from contact with a corpse touches any of these, do they become defiled?" The priests answered, "They become defiled." * ¹⁴ Then Haggai replied:

     So is this people, † and so is this nation
        in my sight—oracle of the LORD—
     And so is all the work of their hands;
        what they offer there is defiled.

---

† **1:15** *Twenty-fourth day of the sixth month in the second year*: September 21, 520 B.C. The resumption of work on the Temple occurred twenty-three days from the beginning of Haggai's prophecy. This date formula repeats in reverse order the formula of v. 1, thereby bringing to conclusion chap. 1; it also initiates the next unit in 2:1.

**2:1** *Twenty-first day of the seventh month*: October 17, 520 B.C.

**2:3** *Who is left among you*: i.e., who is old enough to have seen the first Temple prior to its destruction in 587 B.C.? Compare the reaction of priests who were alive then (Ezr 3:12–13).

**2:6–9** These verses emphasize that the total fulfillment of God's promises to Israel is on the horizon. Such an eschatological event, which will shake the nations (v. 6; cf. v. 21), finds an echo not only in the political revolts in the Persian empire in 521 but also in the formative events of Israel's history (Ex 19:18; Jgs 5:4; Ps 68:8–9) when God intervened on behalf of the Israelites. The bringing of treasures of all the nations (v. 7) to Jerusalem recalls the visionary passages of Isaiah of the pilgrimage of all nations to Jerusalem (Is 2:2–4; 60:6–9).

**2:9** *Peace*: after God's presence or glory has returned to the Temple, Jerusalem will receive the treasures from the nations, making the Temple more glorious than ever; and from that place

God will extend *shalom*, a peace which embraces prosperity, well-being, harmony.

**2:10–14** A request for a priestly ruling (Heb. *torah*) is made in the form of a dialogue between Haggai and the priests. Explicit examples where such priestly rulings are quoted are rare in prophetic books. The interchange illustrates an essential role of the priesthood: the interpretation of God's law (cf. Lv 10:9–11).

**2:10** *Twenty-fourth day of the ninth month in the second year*: December 18, 520 B.C.

**2:11** *Ask the priests for a ruling*: i.e., a determination on whether defilement and sanctity can be physically transmitted. The priests are expected to make a legal decision. The answer is that sanctity cannot be transmitted (v. 12) but defilement can (v. 13). Priestly duties are enumerated in Lv 10:10–20.

**2:14** *So is this people*: the prophet's interpretation is that the restored sacrifices were not acceptable because the people's behavior was tainted.

---

**2:3** Ezr 3:10–13.       **2:9** 1 Kgs 8:11.
**2:6** Heb 12:26.          **2:13** Lv 22:4–7.
**2:7** Is 60:7–11.

<sup>15</sup> Now reflect, † from this day forward—before you set stone to stone in the temple of the LORD, <sup>16</sup> what was your experience?

> When one went to a heap of grain for
> 　twenty ephahs,
> there were only ten;
> When one went to a vat to draw fifty
> 　ephahs, †
> there were only twenty. *

<sup>17</sup>　I struck you, and all the work of your
> 　hands,
> with searing wind, blight, and hail,
> yet you did not return to me—oracle
> 　of the LORD. *

<sup>18</sup> Reflect from this day forward, from the twenty-fourth day of the ninth month. † From the day on which the temple of the LORD was founded, reflect!

<sup>19</sup>　Is there still seed in the storehouse?
> 　Have the vine, the fig, the pomegranate,

> and the olive tree still not borne fruit?
> From this day, I will bless you. †

**Future Hope.** † <sup>20</sup> The word of the LORD came a second time to Haggai on the twenty-fourth day of the month: † <sup>21</sup> Speak to Zerubbabel, the governor of Judah:

> I will shake the heavens and the earth;

<sup>22</sup>　I will overthrow the thrones of
> 　kingdoms,
> and destroy the power of the
> 　kingdoms of the nations.
> I will overthrow the chariots and their
> 　riders,
> and the riders with their horses
> will fall by each other's swords. *

<sup>23</sup> On that day—oracle of the LORD of hosts—I will take you, my servant, Zerubbabel, son of Shealtiel—oracle of the LORD—and I will make you like a signet ring, † for I have chosen you—oracle of the LORD of hosts. *

---

†
**2:15–19** This prophecy is retrospective and should be read with 1:5–11, a description of the conditions of economic deprivation before the rebuilding of the Temple.
**2:16** *Ephahs:* see note on Is 5:10.
**2:18** *Twenty-fourth day of the ninth month:* December 18, 520 B.C., the date of the refounding of the Temple (vv. 10, 20), the central date in Haggai.
**2:19** *I will bless you:* from the day of the refounding of the Temple, agricultural plenty and fertility are assured. This link between temple and prosperity is part of the ancient Near Eastern temple ideology that underlies Haggai and Zec 1–8.
**2:20–23** This final oracle of hope is uttered on the day of the refounding of the Temple. Unlike the other oracles it is addressed to Zerubbabel alone, who, as a Davidic descendant, will have a

servant role in God's future Israelite kingdom to be established when God intervenes to overthrow the nations.
**2:20** *Twenty-fourth day of the month:* December 18, 520 B.C. (as in v. 18).
**2:23** *Like a signet ring:* this promise to Zerubbabel reverses the punishment of his grandfather (Jer 22:23–25). A signet is a ring or other instrument used to mark documents or materials with the equivalent of an official signature. A lower official could thus be authorized to act on behalf of a higher official. Like a signet ring, Zerubbabel represents the Lord.

---

| * | |
|---|---|
| **2:16** Hos 4:3a. | **2:22** Sir 49:11. |
| **2:17** Am 4:9. | **2:23** Zec 6:12–13. |

# The Book of
# Zechariah

## INTRODUCTION

### Michael D. Guinan, OFM

Zechariah ("The Lord remembers") prophesied in Jerusalem in the sixth century BCE. The Persians conquered Babylon in 539 BCE and would rule the ancient Near East until themselves being conquered by the Greek Alexander the Great in 333. In 538 BCE, the exiles (which may have included Zechariah) were allowed to return from Babylon to Judah where they faced a number of obstacles. The rebuilding of the Temple began and then stalled, and Haggai and his contemporary Zechariah addressed this crisis. Three time indications in Zechariah suggest 520–518 BCE as the date range of activity (1:1—Oct/Nov 520 BCE; 1:7—Feb 519 BCE; 7:1—Dec 518 BCE). The Temple was complete and dedicated in 516 BCE.

Chapters 9–14 of the book differ quite a bit from chs. 1–8 in content, style, and vocabulary and are considered later additions. The earlier chapters are often designated "Proto- [First] Zechariah," and the later ones, "Deutero- [Second] Zechariah." (Some would divide further and call chs. 12–14, "Trito- [Third] Zechariah.") Many scholars would place Deutero-Zechariah perhaps a century or more after Proto-Zechariah, in the late Persian or early Greek period.

## Proto-Zechariah (Zec 1–8)

The time indications divide Proto-Zechariah into three parts: (1) Zec 1:1–6; (2) 1:7–6:15; (3) 7:1–8:23.

### Part One: Call to Repentance (Zec 1:1–6)

Like the prophets before the exile, Zechariah calls the people to repent, i.e., return to God. The primary task of the prophet is to speak the words and statutes (i.e., covenant law) which the Lord charges the people to obey. At issue is the renewal of the covenant relationship.

### Part Two: Visions and Exhortations (Zec 1:7–6:15)

The bulk of the book consists of a series of night visions. Some (e.g., the NABRE) count seven visions, others see eight. The difference is whether to include the cleansing of Joshua (Zec 3:1–10) as a separate vision. It was not unusual for prophets to have visions—an alternate word for "prophet" was "seer" (e.g., Is 1:1; Am 1:1)—but Zechariah's visions are unusual. The imagery and symbolism are more complicated and strange, and he has need of an angel (literally "messenger") interpreter from God to understand them. Both of these features would be developed further in later apocalyptic literature. Two sections of exhortations also appear (Zec 2:10–17; 6:9–15), one after the third vision and the other after the last.

**First Vision: Four Horses (Zec 1:7–17).** Four horses of different colors are sent by God to patrol the earth; they bring back a message of peace but Judah and Jerusalem are still suffering. God replies to the angel's lament (1:12) that he will indeed restore Jerusalem.

**Second Vision: Four Horns and Four Smiths (Zec 2:1–4).** If Judah/Jerusalem is to be restored, the nations which have oppressed them, Assyria and Babylon (the four horns = two animals), must be removed.

**Third Vision: A Man Measuring Jerusalem (Zec 2:5–9).** As a man goes out to measure Jerusalem, he is interrupted and told that the city will be unwalled; both people and animals will be abundant in the city. Instead of walls, the Lord will be its protection (2:9). The "glory" (2:9b) is a standard priestly image for the presence of God.

**First Exhortation (Zec 2:10–17).** After the

vision of restored prosperity, several short oracles urge those still in Babylon to return to Jerusalem and rejoice there, for the Lord will dwell in their midst.

**The Cleansing of Joshua (Zec 3:1–10).** Attention now turns to leadership in the restored community. Joshua, the high priest, is accused in the heavenly court by an adversary (Hebrew: *satan*), a kind of prosecuting attorney. His possible ritual contamination from living in Babylon is removed by God. This is expressed symbolically by exchanging filthy clothes for clean ones. In the restored community, centered on the Jerusalem Temple, the high priest would come to play an increasingly important leadership role. The reference to "the Branch" (3:8b) refers to a second, civil leader of the line of David (see Jer 23:5; 33:15); here probably Zerubbabel is meant. Many scholars consider this section to be a separate vision, the fourth in the series.

**Fourth Vision: The Lampstand and Two Olive Trees (Zec 4:1–14).** The prophet sees a lampstand with a bowl on top, and seven lamps, each with seven spouts. Two olive trees stand next to it, one on the right and the other on the left. In response to the prophet's questions, the angel explains that the seven (symbol of fullness and perfection) represent the all-seeing eyes of God, and the olive trees are two anointed ones who represent the high priest descended from Aaron and a royal figure descended from David. In between the vision and its explanation (4:6–10a), an oracle is addressed to Zerubbabel, who has laid the foundations of the new Temple, to remind him that he rules "not by might, and not by power, but by [God's] spirit" (4:6).

**Fifth Vision: The Flying Scroll (Zec 5:1–4).** The flying scroll of great size (approximately 30 feet x 15 feet) represents the curse that will affect those in the restored community who continue to violate the covenant. The thief and the perjurer (who swears falsely by God's name) recall the Ten Commandments, theft being a sin against neighbor and perjury a sin against God.

**Sixth Vision: The Basket of Wickedness (Zec 5:5–11).** In what is surely the strangest of his visions, the prophet now sees a basket with a lead lid inside of which is a woman personifying wickedness. It is flown back to Babylon

("Shinar"). In the Bible, the great sin is idolatry; it seems some returnees have brought worship of Babylonian gods with them. This wicked practice will be sent back where it belongs. The figure of the woman is perhaps suggested by the popular Babylonian goddess Ishtar.

**Seventh Vision: Four Chariots (Zec 6:1–8).** The four horses of Vision One return (forming an *inclusio*), but this time drawing chariots, as if for war. They represent the four winds (God's messengers, Ps 104:4) from the corners of the earth (i.e., the whole world). They come out from the Temple (the bronze mountains). Even the "land of the north," the traditional direction from which enemies come, will now know rest since Babylon will be punished.

**Second Exhortation (Zec 6:9–15).** The night visions conclude with an oracle from God. A group of exiled returnees will bring contributions of silver and gold. From these, two crowns will be made, one for Joshua, the high priest, and one for "the Branch." This partnership between the royal and priestly groups should lead to "peaceful understanding" (6:13).

## Part Three: A Series of Oracles (Zec 7:1–8:23)

In these oracles, Zechariah begins to sound more like a traditional prophet, speaking oracles from the Lord and calling the people to covenant fidelity.

**Zechariah 7:1–14.** Some men come and ask the priests and prophets for instruction (i.e., *torah*, as in 7:12). In view of the restored community, do they need to continue to weep and fast in the fifth (the destruction of the Temple, 2 Kgs 25:8–9) and seventh (the murder of Gedaliah, 2 Kgs 25:25; Jer 41:1–3) months? Instead of an answer (which will come in Zec 8:19), they are rebuked for self-centered practices. God then calls them to just and compassionate behavior (Zec 7:8–14). To be hardhearted (Zec 7:12) is a serious condition; the heart should be soft (of flesh) so that the word of God can enter in and change the person (Ez 36:26; Ps 95:7b–8). This then is manifested in covenant behavior.

**Zechariah 8:1–23.** The ten short oracles fall into two sets, seven (Zec 8:1–17) and three (8:18–23). The first set focuses on the Lord's care and concern to restore Jerusalem and the temple. People will live to ripe old ages, and there will be many children (Zec 8:4–5). God will gather the scattered people back from east and west (Zec 8:7–8). Instead of being a curse among the nations, Israel and Judah will be a blessing, recalling the promise to Abraham (Gn 12:3). They are admonished to be faithful to their covenant life (Zec 8:14–17).

The question of Zec 7:3 is answered: the sad feasts are turned to joy. The prosperity and joy of Judah will attract peoples and nations from all around who will come to implore the favor of the Lord. Proto-Zechariah ends with a universalist vision of joy and peace.

# Deutero-Zechariah (Zec 9–14)

The six chapters of Deutero-Zechariah fall into two sections, each marked with the word "an oracle" (*massa'*) (Zec 9–11, 12–14). They are among the most obscure and difficult texts in the Old Testament. Several factors contribute to this. (1) These chapters borrow heavily from other prophets, especially Jeremiah, Ezekiel, Joel, and Amos. These allusions, however, fail to clarify the author's meaning; it is not always clear exactly what point the writer is making. (2) There are allusions and references to people and events that are completely unknown to us. For example, who is the one "they have thrust through" for whom they mourn (12:10)?[1] Scholarly guesses vary widely. (3) The prophet looks to a decisive intervention of God in the far future. The phrase "on that day" occurs often (19 times, 17 of them in chs. 12–14). In describing that day, often highly symbolic language is used, having its roots in Canaanite mythology. It is not to be taken literally. The intended meanings may have been more obvious to the immediate audience, but they can be quite obscure for readers today.

## The Lord as Divine Warrior and King

In Canaanite mythology, Baal, the storm god, rides out on his dark storm clouds, utters

his thundering war cry, defeats the forces of chaos (sea/rivers), establishes creation with the life-giving rain, and is proclaimed king. For Israel, it is the Lord who does this (Zec 10:1; 12:1). Among the forces of chaos are historical enemies. The day of the Lord will mean, on the one hand, defeat for all Israel's enemies (e.g., 9:1–8; 10:11–12; 12:1–6, 9), and on the other, the secure, definitive establishment of the Lord's dwelling in Zion in the midst of the re-gathered Israel (Ephraim/Joseph) and Judah (9:13; 10:6). The Lord will become king over all the earth (14:9). The human representative of God as king will come humbly and with peace (9:9–10; 12:8).[2]

## Shepherd Imagery

In the ancient world, the king was often described with shepherd imagery. The Lord is the true shepherd who will remove false shepherds, leaders who fail in their duties (Zec 10:3; 11:17; 13:7–8). The almost allegorical "shepherd narrative" (11:4–16) would be an example of references that almost completely elude us.

For the struggling community, recently returned from exile in Babylon, Zec 1–8 offered visions of hope for a restored community with Temple, leadership, and worship. Their enemies are defeated. Zechariah 9–14 projects this vision into a far future time and a cosmic context when the day of the Lord will bring the complete defeat of all enemies and the establishment of God's throne and rule in Jerusalem. At that time, "everyone who is left of all the nations . . . will go up year after year to bow down to the King, the Lord of hosts, and to celebrate the feast of Booths" (14:16), a major festival celebrated in the fall. The three factors that make Deutero-Zechariah difficult—biblical allusions, obscure references, mythological language—mark a significant step beyond Proto-Zechariah in the direction of full-blown apocalyptic literature. ■

---

1. John 19:37 sees this Scripture fulfilled when Jesus was pierced with a spear during his crucifixion.

2. Matthew 21:5 and Jn 12:15 apply Zec 9:9 to Jesus' entry into Jerusalem, "humble, and riding on a donkey."

# THE BOOK OF ZECHARIAH

## New American Bible, Introduction

The Book of Zechariah, because of its great variation in style, content, and language, is widely believed to be a composite work. Made up of First Zechariah (chaps. 1–8) and Second Zechariah (chaps. 9–14), the book has been attributed to at least two different prophets. The prophecies of First Zechariah can be dated to the late sixth century B.C., contemporary with those of Haggai; the oracles of Second Zechariah are somewhat later.

The most striking feature of First Zechariah is a series of visions in which the prophet describes the centrality of Jerusalem, its Temple, and its leaders, who function both in the politics of the region and of the Persian empire and in God's universal rule. These visions clearly relate to the Temple restoration begun in 520 B.C.

The prophecies of First Zechariah can be divided into three literary units. A brief introductory unit (1:1–6) links the prophecies of chaps. 1–8 with those of Haggai. The visionary unit (1:7–6:15) consists of seven visionary images plus an associated vision dealing with the high priest Joshua. The third unit (7:1–8:23) consists of two parts: (1) an address (7:1–14) to a delegation sent from Bethel in anticipation of the end of the seventy years of exile; (2) a series of oracles (8:1–23): seven oracles dealing with

the restoration of Judah and Zion (vv. 1–17), followed by three oracles of hope concerning Judah and the nations (vv. 18–23).

Coming nearly a century later, the prophecies of Second Zechariah are extraordinarily diverse. A complex assortment of literary genres appears in these six chapters, which consist of two distinct parts (chaps. 9–11 and chaps. 12–14), each introduced by an unusual Hebrew word for "oracle." Despite the diversity of materials, the structural links among the chapters along with verbal and thematic connections point to an overall integrity for Zec 9–14.

Second Zechariah draws heavily on the words and ideas of earlier biblical prophets. The prophet is acutely aware of the devastation that comes from disobedience to God's word, as had been spoken by God's prophetic emissaries. Yet, it was now clear in this century after the rebuilding of the Temple and the repatriation of many of the exiles, that Judah would not soon regain political autonomy and a Davidic king. So the various poems, narratives, oracles, and parables of Second Zechariah maintain the hope of previous prophets by depicting a glorious eschatological restoration. At that time all nations will recognize Jerusalem's centrality and acknowledge God's universal sovereignty. ■

# ZECHARIAH

**1** **Call for Obedience.** ¹In the second year of Darius,† in the eighth month, the word of the Lord came to the prophet Zechariah, son of Berechiah, son of Iddo: ²The Lord was very angry with your ancestors.†* ³Say to them: Thus says the Lord of hosts, Return to me—oracle of the Lord† of hosts—and I will return to you, says the Lord of hosts. ⁴Do not be like your ancestors to whom the earlier prophets† proclaimed: Thus says the Lord of hosts: Turn from your evil ways and from your wicked deeds.* But they did not listen or pay attention to me*—oracle of the Lord.— ⁵Your ancestors, where are they? And the prophets, can they live forever? ⁶But my words and my statutes, with which I charged my servants the prophets, did these not overtake your ancestors?* Then they repented† and admitted: "Just as the Lord of hosts intended to treat us according to our ways and deeds, so the Lord has done."

**First Vision: Horses Patrolling the Earth.*** ⁷In the second year of Darius, on the twenty-fourth day of Shebat, the eleventh month,† the word of the Lord came to the prophet Zechariah, son of Berechiah, son of Iddo:

⁸† I looked out in the night,† and there was a man mounted on a red horse standing in the shadows among myrtle trees; and behind him were red, sorrel, and white horses. ⁹I asked, "What are these, my lord?"† Then the angel who spoke with me answered, "I will show you what these are." ¹⁰Then the man who was standing among the myrtle trees spoke up and said, "These are the ones whom the Lord has sent to patrol the earth."* ¹¹And they answered the angel of the Lord,† who was standing among the myrtle trees: "We have been patrolling the earth, and now the whole earth rests quietly." ¹²Then the angel of the Lord replied, "Lord of hosts, how long will you be without mercy for Jerusalem and the cities of Judah that have felt your anger these seventy years?"†* ¹³To the angel who spoke with me, the Lord replied favorably, with comforting words.

**Oracular Response.** ¹⁴The angel who spoke with me then said to me, Proclaim: Thus says the Lord of hosts:

I am jealous for Jerusalem
　　and for Zion† intensely jealous.*
¹⁵　I am consumed with anger
　　toward the complacent nations;†
　When I was only a little angry,
　　they compounded the disaster.*
¹⁶　Therefore, thus says the Lord:

---

**1:1** *Darius*: Darius I, emperor of Persia from 522 to 486 B.C. *The second year…eighth month*: October/November 520 B.C., i.e., prior to the latest date in Haggai (Dec. 18, 520 B.C., Hg 2:10). Unlike other prophets, Haggai and Zechariah 1–8 contain specific chronological information, probably because they were sensitive to the imminent end of the expected seventy years of exile. See note on Zec 1:12.
**1:2** *Your ancestors*: refers to the preexilic people of Judah, who were subjected to Babylonian destruction and exile.
**1:3** *Oracle of the Lord*: a phrase used extensively in prophetic books to indicate divine speech.
**1:4** *Earlier prophets*: preexilic prophets of the Lord. There are many allusions to them in Zechariah, indicating their influence on the postexilic community (see 7:7, 12).
**1:6** *Repented*: the Hebrew word *shub* literally means "turn back." This term is often used to speak of repentance as a return to the covenantal relationship between Israel and the Lord.
**1:7** *The second year…eleventh month*: February 15, 519 B.C. The largest set of visions (1:7–6:15) is dated to a time just prior to the beginning of the new year in the spring.
**1:8–11** Four riders on horses of three different colors are sent by God to patrol the four corners of the earth. Compare the four chariots of the seventh vision, 6:1–8.
**1:8** *In the night*: nighttime, or this night. This setting of darkness is meant only for the first vision.
**1:9** *My lord*: this expression in Hebrew (ʼadoni) is used as a polite form of address. *Angel who spoke with me*: angelic being

(not identical to the angel of the Lord who is one of the four horsemen) who serves as an interpreter, bringing a message from God to the prophet, who himself is a messenger of God.
**1:11** *Angel of the Lord*: chief angelic figure in God's heavenly court, and perhaps the "man" of 1:8.
**1:12** *These seventy years*: allusion to the period of divine anger mentioned in Jer 25:11–12 and 29:10. Here the symbolic number seventy is understood to mark the period without a Temple in Jerusalem. Since these seventy years would have been almost over at this point, this symbolic number would have provided motivation for rebuilding the Temple as a sign of the end of the exile.
**1:14** *For Jerusalem and for Zion*: rather than the usual order, Zion and Jerusalem, elsewhere in the Bible. The reversal highlights the centrality of Jerusalem, which is mentioned in all three of the brief oracles of 1:14–17.
**1:15** *Complacent nations*: probably a reference to the Persian empire, which in its imperial extent included many national groups that maintained separate identities. *Compounded the disaster*: the surrounding nations took advantage of the Lord's anger against Judah to further their own interests.

**1:2** Mi 3:7.
**1:4** Is 55:7.
**1:4** Lk 20:15.
**1:6** Zec 7:7–14.
**1:7** Zec 6:1–7; Rev 5:6; 6:1–9.
**1:10** Zec 7:5; Jer 25:11–12; 29:10.
**1:12** Rev 6:10.
**1:14** Zec 8:2.
**1:15** Is 47:6.

I return to Jerusalem in mercy;*
my house† will be rebuilt there*—
    oracle of the LORD of hosts—
and a measuring line will be stretched
    over Jerusalem.

17 Proclaim further: Thus says the LORD of
    hosts:
My cities will again overflow with
    prosperity;
the LORD will again comfort Zion,
and will again choose Jerusalem.*

## 2 Second Vision: The Four Horns and the Four Smiths.

¹ I raised my eyes and looked and there were four horns.† ² Then I asked the angel who spoke with me, "What are those?" He answered, "Those are the horns that scattered† Judah, Israel, and Jerusalem."*

³ Then the LORD showed me four workmen.† ⁴ And I said, "What are these coming to do?" And the LORD said, "Those are the horns that scattered Judah, so that none could raise their heads any more;* and these have come to terrify them—to cut down the horns of the nations that raised their horns to scatter the land of Judah."

### Third Vision: The Man with the Measuring Cord.

⁵ I raised my eyes and looked, and there was a man with a measuring cord† in his hand.* ⁶ I asked, "Where are you going?" And he said, "To measure Jerusalem—to see how great its width is and how great its length."

⁷ Then the angel who spoke with me advanced as another angel came out to meet him

⁸ and he said to the latter, "Run, speak to that official:† Jerusalem will be unwalled, because of the abundance of people and beasts in its midst.* ⁹ I will be an encircling wall of fire† for it—oracle of the LORD—and I will be the glory in its midst."*

### Expansion on the Themes of the First Three Visions.

¹⁰ Up! Up! Flee from the land of the north†—oracle of the LORD;—For like the four winds of heaven I have dispersed you—oracle of the LORD.* ¹¹ Up, Zion! Escape, you who dwell in daughter Babylon! ¹² For thus says the LORD of hosts after the LORD's glory had sent me, concerning the nations that have plundered you: Whoever strikes you strikes me directly in the eye.* ¹³ Now I wave my hand over them, and they become plunder for their own servants.* Thus you shall know that the LORD of hosts has sent me. ¹⁴ Sing and rejoice, daughter Zion! Now, I am coming to dwell in your midst—oracle of the LORD. ¹⁵ Many nations will bind themselves to the LORD on that day.* They will be my people,† and I will dwell in your midst. Then you shall know that the LORD of hosts has sent me to you. ¹⁶ The LORD will inherit Judah* as his portion of the holy land,† and the LORD will again choose Jerusalem. ¹⁷ Silence, all people, in the presence of the LORD, who stirs forth from his holy dwelling.*

## 3 Prophetic Vision: Joshua the High Priest.

¹ Then he showed me Joshua the high priest standing before the angel of the LORD, while the adversary† stood at his right side to

---

**1:16** *My house*: the Temple. See note on Hg 1:4. *Measuring line*: a builder's string, not for devastation, as in Is 34:11, but for reconstruction.

**2:1** *Four horns*: symbols of the total political and military might of Judah's imperial adversaries, probably representing Assyria, Babylonia, and Persia. The number four represents universality rather than any specific number of foes.

**2:2** *Scattered*: sent part of the population into exile. This was standard imperial policy initiated in the ancient Near East by the Assyrians for dealing with a conquered state.

**2:3** *Four workmen*: four agents of God's power. The imagery follows that of four horns: the workers cut down, or make ineffectual, the horns, i.e., enemy.

**2:5** *Measuring cord*: a string for measuring, as opposed to a builder's string, 1:16.

**2:8** *That official*: probably the man with the measuring cord of v. 5.

**2:9** *Encircling wall of fire*: divine protection for an unwalled Jerusalem. Urban centers were generally walled, and Jerusalem's walls were eventually rebuilt in the late fifth century B.C. (Neh 2:17–20).

**2:10** *Land of the north*: refers to Babylon (v. 11), in a geographic rather than a political sense, as the place from which exiles will return. The designation is "north" because imperial invaders historically entered Palestine from that direction (see Jer 3:18; 23:8).

**2:15** *Many nations…my people*: a way of expressing God's relationship to people in covenant language. The covenant between God and Israel (see Jer 31:33; 32:38) is here universalized to include all nations.

**2:16** *The holy land*: the Lord's earthly territory, a designation found only rarely in the Old Testament.

**3:1** *Adversary*: Hebrew *satan*, here, the prosecuting attorney, a figure in the Lord's heavenly courtroom. Cf. Jb 1:6–2:7. Later tradition understands this figure to be Satan.

---

**1:16** Is 54:6–10.
**1:16** Zec 2:5–9.
**1:17** Zec 2:15; 13:9.
**2:2** Dt 33:17; Dn 7:8.
**2:4** Jer 48:25.
**2:5** Jer 31:38–39; Ez 41:13; Rev 11:1; 21:15.
**2:8** Is 49:19–20; 54:2–3; Jer 31:27; Ez 38:11.
**2:9** Rev 21:23; 22:3–5.
**2:10** Zec 6:5; Is 48:20; Jer 50:8; 51:6.
**2:12** Dt 32:10; Ps 17:8.
**2:13** Is 14:2; Zep 3:15.
**2:15** Is 56:6; 66:18.
**2:16** Zec 1:17.
**2:17** Hb 2:20; Zep 1:7; Rev 8:1a.

ZEC

accuse him.* ²And the angel of the LORD said to the adversary, "May the LORD rebuke you, O adversary; may the LORD who has chosen Jerusalem rebuke you!* Is this not a brand plucked from the fire?"*

³† Now Joshua was standing before the angel, clad in filthy garments. ⁴Then the angel said to those standing before him, "Remove his filthy garments."* And to him he said, "Look, I have taken your guilt from you,* and I am clothing you in stately robes." ⁵Then he said, "Let them put a clean turban on his head." And they put a clean turban on his head and clothed him with the garments while the angel of the LORD was standing by. ⁶Then the angel of the LORD charged Joshua: ⁷"Thus says the LORD of hosts: If you walk in my ways and carry out my charge, you will administer my house and watch over my courts;† and I will give you access to those standing here."

**Supplementary Oracle.** ⁸"Hear, O Joshua, high priest! You and your associates who sit before you! For they are signs of things to come!†* I will surely bring my servant the Branch. ⁹Look at the stone* that I have placed before Joshua. On this one stone with seven facets†* I will engrave its inscription—oracle of the LORD of hosts—and I will take away the guilt of that land in one day. ¹⁰On that day—oracle of the LORD of hosts—you will invite one another under your vines and fig trees."*

**4 Fourth Vision: The Lampstand and the Two Olive Trees.** ¹Then the angel who spoke with me returned and aroused me, like one awakened from sleep. ²He said to me, "What do you see?" I replied, "I see a lampstand† all of gold,* with a bowl on top of it. There are seven lamps on it, with seven spouts on each of the lamps that are on top of it. ³And beside it are two olive trees,† one on the right of the bowl and one to its left." ⁴Then I said to the angel who spoke with me, "What are these things, my lord?" ⁵And the angel who spoke with me replied, "Do you not know what these things are?" I said, "No, my lord."

**An Oracle.** ⁶Then he said to me: "This is the word of the LORD to Zerubbabel: Not by might, and not by power, but by my spirit,†* says the LORD of hosts. ⁷Who are you, O great mountain?† Before Zerubbabel you become a plain. He will bring forth the first stone amid shouts of 'Favor, favor be upon it!'"

⁸Then the word of the LORD came to me: ⁹The hands of Zerubbabel have laid the foundations of this house, and his hands will finish it. Thus you shall know that the LORD of hosts has sent me to you. ¹⁰For whoever has scorned such a day of small things will rejoice to see the capstone† in the hand of Zerubbabel.

**Resumption of the Vision: Explanation of Lamps and Trees.** "These seven are the eyes of

---

**3:3–4** The filthy garments of Joshua symbolized the guilt of the Israelite people who have become unclean by going into exile. The angel of the Lord purifies the high priest by the removal of his garments.

**3:7** *If you walk…watch over my courts:* four components of priestly activity: (1) following God's commandments and teaching them to the people, (2) carrying out cultic functions, (3) participating in the judicial system in certain difficult cases, and (4) administering the laborers and lands in the Temple's domain.

**3:8** *Signs of things to come:* the restoration of the priesthood is a sign of the expected restoration of the Davidic line. *The Branch:* a tree metaphor for the expected future ruler as a descendant of the Davidic dynasty. This imagery also appears in Is 11:1, 10; Jer 23:5; 33:15; and Zec 6:12.

**3:9** *Stone with seven facets:* represents both the precious stones that were part of the high priest's apparel and the building stone (see 4:7, 10) that initiated a major construction project. The seven lamps (or "eyes") indicate the totality of its role as an instrument of God's vigilance and action. *Inscription:* can refer both to words engraved on the high priest's apparel (Ex 28:9, 11) and to words chiseled on a cornerstone.

**4:2** *Lampstand:* receptacle for lamps and one of the furnishings of the main room of the Temple. This visionary object does not correspond to the biblical descriptions of the menorah in either the tabernacle (Ex 25:31–40) or the Solomonic Temple (1 Kgs 7:49) but rather has properties of both. *Seven lamps… seven spouts:* seven lamps, each with seven pinched wick holes. Such objects were part of the repertoire of cultic vessels throughout the Old Testament period. Here they symbolize God's eyes,

i.e., divine omniscience; see v. 10.

**4:3** *Olive trees:* visionary image that picks up the botanical language describing the Israelite cultic lampstands, with the olive trees specifically connoting fertility, permanence, and righteousness.

**4:6** *Not by might…my spirit:* one of the most quoted verses from the Old Testament, particularly in Jewish tradition, which connects it with the theme of Hanukkah, sometimes called the Festival of Lights.

**4:7** *Great mountain:* part of symbolic imagery for the Temple on Mount Zion, as embodiment of the cosmic mountain where heaven and earth connect. *Plain:* leveled ground serving as the foundation area for the construction of the Temple, and symbolizing the foundation of the cosmos. *First stone:* foundation stone of a major public building. Such stones were laid with great ceremony in foundation rituals when monumental buildings were newly built or rebuilt in the biblical world.

**4:10** *Capstone:* topmost stone of a structure, which finishes the construction. This translation is based on the context. Other translations read: "stone of distinction," "plummet," "tin-stone."

---

| | |
|---|---|
| **3:1** Jb 1:6–2:7; 1 Chr 21:1. | **3:8** Is 8:18. |
| **3:2** Jude 9. | **3:9** Zec 4:7, 10; Is 28:16. |
| **3:2** Am 4:11. | **3:9** Rev 5:6. |
| **3:4** Lk 15:22; Rev 19:8. | **3:10** 1 Kgs 5:5; Mi 4:4. |
| **3:4** Is 6:7; Jer 31:34; Ez 36:33. | **4:2** Ex 25:31–40; 1 Kgs 7:49; Rev 11:4. |
| | **4:6** Hos 1:7. |

the LORD that range over the whole earth."* [11] I then asked him, "What are these two olive trees, on the right of the lampstand and on its left?" [12] A second time I asked, "What are the two streams from the olive trees that pour out golden oil through two taps of gold?" [13] He said to me, "Do you not know what these are?" I answered, "No, my lord." [14] Then he said, "These are the two anointed ones† who stand by the Lord of the whole earth."*

## 5 Fifth Vision: The Flying Scroll. [1] Then I raised my eyes again and saw a flying scroll. [2] He asked me, "What do you see?" I answered, "I see a flying scroll, twenty cubits long and ten cubits wide."†* [3] Then he said to me: "This is the curse which is to go forth over the whole land. According to it, every thief and every perjurer† will be expelled. [4] I will send it forth—oracle of the LORD of hosts—so that it will come to the house of the thief, and into the house of the one who swears falsely by my name.* It shall lodge within each house, consuming it, timber and stones."

**Sixth Vision: The Basket of Wickedness.** [5] Then the angel who spoke with me came forward and said to me, "Raise your eyes and look. What is this that comes forth?" [6] I said, "What is it?" And he answered, "This is the basket† that is coming." And he said, "This is their guilt in all the land." [7] Then a leaden cover was lifted, and there was a woman sitting inside the basket.† [8] He said, "This is Wickedness," and he thrust her inside the basket, pushing the leaden weight into the opening.

[9] Then I raised my eyes and saw two women coming forth with wind under their wings† — they had wings like the wings of a stork—and they lifted the basket into the air. [10] I said to the angel who spoke with me, "Where are they taking the basket?" [11] He replied, "To build a temple for it in the land of Shinar.† When the temple is constructed, they will set it there on its base."

## 6 Seventh Vision: Four Chariots.* [1] Again I raised my eyes and saw four chariots† coming out from between two mountains; and the mountains were of bronze. [2] The first chariot had red horses, the second chariot black horses, [3] the third chariot white horses, and the fourth chariot dappled horses—all of them strong horses. [4] I asked the angel who spoke with me, "What are these, my lord?" [5] The angel answered me, "These are the four winds of the heavens,† which are coming forth after presenting themselves before the LORD of all the earth.* [6] The one with the black horses is going toward the land of the north, and the white horses go toward the west, and the dappled ones go toward the land of the south." [7] These strong horses went out, eager to set about patrolling the earth, for he said, "Go, patrol the earth!" So they patrolled the earth. [8] Then he cried out to me and said, "See, those who go forth to the land of the north provide rest for my spirit in the land of the north."†

**The Crowning.** [9] Then the word of the LORD came to me: [10] Take from the exiles—Heldai, Tobijah, Jedaiah—and go the same day to the house of Josiah, son of Zephaniah. (These had come from Babylon.) [11] You will take silver

---

**4:14** *Two anointed ones*: two leadership positions in the ideal restored nation. The concept of a state headed by both priestly and political leaders harks back to premonarchic traditions (Aaron and Moses) and finds an echo in the two messianic figures—a Davidic and a levitical messiah—in the Dead Sea Scrolls and in apocryphal literature. See also the two crowns of 6:11–14.

**5:2** *Twenty cubits long and ten cubits wide*: ca. thirty feet by fifteen feet. These dimensions may represent the ratio of height to width in the exposed portion of a scroll being opened for liturgical reading; at the same time it may symbolize the approach to God's presence since the entryway to the Temple has the same measurements (1 Kgs 6:3). The scroll itself may represent God's covenant with the people, insofar as it contains curses against those who break the law.

**5:3** *Thief...perjurer*: a pair of miscreants representing all those who disobey God's covenant (see note on v. 2) and who must therefore be punished according to covenant curses.

**5:6** *Basket*: literally, ephah, a dry measure; see note on Is 5:10.

**5:7** *Woman sitting inside the basket*: figure representing wickedness or foreign idolatry being transported back to Babylonia (vv. 1–11). Returning exiles were apparently worshiping deities

they had learned to accept in Babylonia, and that "wickedness" (v. 8) must be removed.

**5:9** *Two women...wings*: composite beings, part human and part animal, similar to the cherubim flanking the holy ark (Ex 25:18–22; 1 Kgs 6:23–28; Ez 10:18–22). Such creatures accompany foreign deities as here, or the biblical God.

**5:11** *Shinar*: land of Babylonia; this name for Babylonia is found also in Gn 10:10; 11:2; 14:1; Is 11:11; and Dn 1:2.

**6:1** *Four chariots*: vehicles with horses of four different colors (vv. 2–3) represent God's presence throughout the world and correspond to the four horses of 1:7–11.

**6:5** *Four winds of the heavens*: four compass directions and therefore the whole world.

**6:8** *Land of the north*: the enemy (cf. 2:10). This emphasis on the land of the north refers to the fact that God will deal with Israel's foes and order will be re-established.

---

| | |
|---|---|
| **4:10** Zec 1:11; 6:7; Rev 5:6. | **5:2** Ez 2:9–10; Rev 10:9–11. |
| **4:14** Jos 3:11; Mi 4:13; Rev 11:4. | **5:4** Ex 20:7, 16. |
| | **6:1** Rev 6:2–8. |
| | **6:5** Rev 7:1. |

ZEC

and gold, and make crowns;† place one on the head of Joshua, son of Jehozadak, the high priest. ¹²And say to him: Thus says the LORD of hosts: There is a man whose name is Branch†*—and from his place he will branch out and he will build the temple of the LORD. ¹³He will build the temple of the LORD, and taking up the royal insignia, he will sit as ruler upon his throne. The priest will be at his right hand, and between the two of them there will be peaceful understanding.†* ¹⁴The other crown will be in the temple of the LORD as a gracious reminder to Heldai, Tobijah, Jedaiah, and the son of Zephaniah. ¹⁵And they who are from afar will come and build the temple of the LORD, and you will know that the LORD of hosts has sent me to you. This will happen if you truly obey the LORD your God.*

**7** **A Question About Fasting.** ¹In the fourth year of Darius the king, the word of the LORD came to Zechariah, on the fourth day of the ninth month, Kislev.† ²Bethelsarezer sent Regem-melech and his men to implore the favor of the LORD ³and to ask the priests of the house of the LORD of hosts, and the prophets, "Must I weep and abstain in the fifth month† as I have been doing these many years?" ⁴Then the word of the LORD of hosts came to me: ⁵Say to all the people of the land and to the priests: When you fasted and lamented in the fifth and in the seventh month† these seventy years, was it really for me that you fasted?* ⁶When you were eating and drinking, was it not for yourselves that you ate and for yourselves that you drank?

⁷Are these not the words which the LORD proclaimed through the earlier prophets,† when Jerusalem and its surrounding cities were inhabited and secure, when the Negeb and the Shephelah were inhabited? ⁸The word of the LORD came to Zechariah: ⁹Thus says the LORD of hosts: Judge with true justice, and show kindness and compassion toward each other.* ¹⁰Do not oppress the widow or the orphan, the resident alien or the poor;† do not plot evil against one another in your hearts.* ¹¹But they refused to listen; they stubbornly turned their backs and stopped their ears so as not to hear.* ¹²And they made their hearts as hard as diamond* so as not to hear the instruction and the words that the LORD of hosts had sent by his spirit through the earlier prophets. So great anger came from the LORD of hosts: ¹³Just as when I called out and they did not listen, so they will call out and I will not listen, says the LORD of hosts. ¹⁴And I will scatter them among all the nations that they do not know.* So the land was left desolate behind them with no one moving about, and they made a pleasant land into a wasteland.

**8** **Seven Oracles: Judah and Zion Restored.** ¹Then the word of the LORD of hosts came: ²Thus says the LORD of hosts:

I am intensely jealous for Zion,*
  stirred to jealous wrath for her.

³Thus says the LORD:

I have returned to Zion,
  and I will dwell within Jerusalem;
Jerusalem will be called the faithful city,†*

---

†
  **6:11** *Crowns*: two crowns made of precious metals and representing two high offices (compare the symbolism of the two olive trees in 4:14). One crown is for the high priest Joshua, who, with the governor Zerubbabel, was one of the recognized rulers of the Persian province of Judah. The other crown would have been for a royal ruler, a Davidic descendant. Zerubbabel was a Davidide but could not be king because the Persians would not allow such autonomy. The second crown was thus put in storage in the Temple (v. 14) for the crowning of a future king, or "branch" (see 3:8), from the house of David.
  **6:12** *Branch*: future Davidic ruler. See note on 3:8.
  **6:13** *Peaceful understanding*: harmonious rule of both the high priest and the king.
  **7:1** *The fourth year of Darius…the ninth month, Kislev*: December 7, 518 B.C., the last chronological heading in Zechariah.
  **7:3** *Weep…fifth month*: a mourning ritual commemorating the destruction of Jerusalem and the Temple on the seventh day of the fifth month in the nineteenth year of Nebuchadnezzar's reign (ca. 587/586 B.C.; see 2 Kgs 25:8).
  **7:5** *Seventh month*: the time of a fast in memory of the murder of Gedaliah, the governor installed by the Babylonians after

they conquered Jerusalem (see 2 Kgs 25:25; Jer 41:1–3). *Seventy years*: see note on 1:12.
  **7:7, 12** *Earlier prophets*: see note on 1:4.
  **7:10** *Widow…orphan…resident alien…poor*: four categories of socially and economically marginalized persons. Concern for their well-being is commanded in both pentateuchal and prophetic literature.
  **8:3** *Faithful city*: a unique biblical epithet for Jerusalem, signaling the importance of the holy city and its leaders for establishing justice in society (see also vv. 8, 16, 19). *Holy mountain*: Jerusalem and its Temple, the sacred center of the holy land (2:16) and of the whole world.

---

| | |
|---|---|
| **6:12** Zec 3:8; Jer 23:5. | Jer 5:28; Mi 2:1. |
| **6:13** Zec 4:14. | **7:11** Ex 32:9; Is 48:4. |
| **6:15** Dt 28:1. | **7:12** Ez 11:19. |
| **7:5** Am 5:21. | **7:14** Dt 4:27. |
| **7:9** Is 1:17; 58:6. | **8:2** Zec 1:14. |
| **7:10** Ex 22:20–24; Dt 24:17; | **8:3** Is 1:26. |

and the mountain of the LORD of
   hosts, the holy mountain.

[4] Thus says the LORD of hosts:
Old men and old women will again sit in
the streets of Jerusalem, each with staff in
hand because of old age.* [5] The city will be
filled with boys and girls playing in its streets.
   [6] Thus says the LORD of hosts:
Even if this should seem impossible in the
eyes of the remnant of this people in those
days, should it seem impossible in my eyes
also?*—oracle of the LORD of hosts.
   [7] Thus says the LORD of hosts:
I am going to rescue my people from the
land of the rising sun, and from the land of the
setting sun. [8] I will bring them back to dwell
within Jerusalem. They will be my people, and
I will be their God,* in faithfulness and justice.
   [9] Thus says the LORD of hosts:
Let your hands be strong, you who now hear
these words which were spoken by the prophets when the foundation of the house of the
LORD of hosts was laid† for the building of the
temple.* [10] For before those days, there were
no wages for people, nor hire for animals.
Those who came and went were not safe from
the enemy, for I set neighbor against neighbor.
[11] But now I will not deal with the remnant of
this people as in former days—oracle of the
LORD of hosts.

[12]    For there will be a sowing of peace:
      the vine will yield its fruit,
      the land will yield its crops,
      and the heavens† will yield their dew.

I will give all these things to the remnant of
this people to possess. [13] Just as you became
a curse among the nations, O house of Judah
and house of Israel, so will I save you that you

may be a blessing.* Do not fear; let your hands
be strong.
   [14] Thus says the LORD of hosts:
Just as I intended to harm you when your ancestors angered me—says the LORD of hosts—
and I did not relent, [15] so again in these days
I intend to favor Jerusalem and the house of
Judah; do not fear! [16] These then are the things
you must do: Speak the truth to one another;*
judge with honesty and complete justice in
your gates.†* [17] Let none of you plot evil against
another in your heart, nor love a false oath. For
all these things I hate—oracle of the LORD.

**Three Oracles: Judah and the Nations.** [18] The
word of the LORD of hosts came to me:
   [19] Thus says the LORD of hosts:
The fast days of the fourth, the fifth, the
seventh, and the tenth months†* will become
occasions of joy and gladness, and happy festivals for the house of Judah.* So love faithfulness and peace!
   [20] Thus says the LORD of hosts:
There will yet come peoples and inhabitants
of many cities;* [21] and the inhabitants of one
city will approach those of another, and say,
"Come! let us go to implore the favor of the
LORD and to seek the LORD of hosts. I too am
going." [22] Many peoples and strong nations
will come to seek the LORD of hosts in Jerusalem and to implore the favor of the LORD.
   [23] Thus says the LORD of hosts:
In those days ten people from nations of
every language will take hold,* yes, will take
hold of the cloak of every Judahite and say,
"Let us go with you, for we have heard that
God is with you."

**Restoration of the Land of Israel†**

**9** [1] An oracle:† the word of the LORD is
        against the land of Hadrach,

---

---

and Damascus is its destination,
For the cities of Aram are the LORD's,
    as are all the tribes of Israel.

2 Hamath also on its border,
    Tyre too, and Sidon, no matter how
       clever they be.

3 Tyre built itself a stronghold,
    and heaped up silver like dust,
    and gold like the mud of the streets.

4 But now the Lord will dispossess it,
    and cast its wealth into the sea,
    and it will be devoured by fire.

5 Ashkelon will see it and be afraid;
    Gaza too will be in great anguish;
    Ekron also, for its hope will wither.
The king will disappear from Gaza,
    Ashkelon will not be inhabited,

6 and the illegitimate will rule in
      Ashdod.
I will destroy the pride of the Philistines

7 and take from their mouths their
      bloody prey,
    their disgusting meat from between
      their teeth.
They will become merely a remnant for
      our God,*
    and will be like a clan in Judah;
Ekron will be like the Jebusites.†

8 I will encamp at my house,
    a garrison against invaders;
No oppressor will overrun them again,
    for now I have seen their affliction.

### The King's Entry into Jerusalem†

9 Exult greatly, O daughter Zion!
    Shout for joy, O daughter Jerusalem!
Behold: your king† is coming to you,
    a just savior is he,
Humble, and riding on a donkey,
    on a colt, the foal of a donkey.*

10 He shall banish the chariot from
      Ephraim,*
    and the horse from Jerusalem;
The warrior's bow will be banished,
    and he will proclaim peace to the
      nations.*
His dominion will be from sea to sea,
    and from the River† to the ends of the
      earth.*

### Restoration of the People

11 As for you, by the blood of your
      covenant,†*
I have freed your prisoners from a
      waterless pit.

12 Return to a fortress,†
    O prisoners of hope;
This very day, I announce
I am restoring double to you.

13 For I have bent Judah as my bow,
    I have set Ephraim as its arrow;
I will arouse your sons, O Zion,
    against your sons, O Yavan,†
and I will use you as a warrior's
      sword.

14 The LORD will appear over them,
    God's arrow will shoot forth as
      lightning;
The Lord GOD will sound the ram's horn,
    and come in a storm from the south.*

15 The LORD of hosts will protect them;
    they will devour and conquer with
      sling stones,
    they will drink and become heated as
      with wine;
    they will be full like bowls—like the
      corners of the altar.*

16 And the LORD their God will save them:
    the people, like a flock on that day;*
For like gemstones of a crown†

---

**9:7** *The Jebusites:* the pre-Israelite inhabitants of Jerusalem, conquered by David and incorporated into Israel.

**9:9–10** These two verses form the centerpiece of chap. 9. The restoration of a royal figure connects the first part of the chapter (vv. 1–8), which depicts the restored land of Israel, with the second part (vv. 11–17), which concerns the restoration of the people Israel.

**9:9** *Your king:* a just savior, a figure of humble demeanor, but riding on a donkey like royalty in the ancient Near East (Gn 49:11; Jgs 5:10; 10:4). The announcement of the coming of such a king marks a departure from the view of the royal figure as a conquering warrior. This depiction is in keeping with the tone of First Zechariah (3:8; 4:6–10; 6:12) but contrasts with Haggai (2:20–23). New Testament authors apply this prophecy to Jesus' triumphant entry into Jerusalem (Mt 21:4–5; Jn 12:14–15).

**9:10** *The River:* probably the Euphrates; see note on Ps 72:8.

**9:11** *The blood of your covenant:* the covenant between the Lord and Israel sealed with sacrificial blood (Ex 24:8).

**9:12** *Fortress:* the Hebrew word for "fortress" (*bissaron*) plays upon the Hebrew word for Zion (*siyyon*). Those who return to Zion will be protected by the Lord. *O prisoners of hope:* imagery of exile, conveying a sense that the future in Israel will be better.

**9:13** *Your sons, O Yavan:* the reference is to the Greeks and their struggle with the Persians for control of Syria-Palestine and the eastern Mediterranean in the mid-fifth century B.C.

**9:16** *Like gemstones of a crown:* imagery reminiscent of First Zechariah (3:9; 4:7, 10; 6:11, 14) and evocative of the Temple and the priestly headgear (cf. Ex 29:6 and Lv 8:9).

**9:7** Is 4:3.
**9:9** Is 9:6; 62:11; Jer 23:5; Mt 21:5; Jn 12:15.
**9:10** Mi 5:9.
**9:10** Is 2:4; 11:6; Hos 2:20; Eph 2:17.
**9:10** Ps 72:8.
**9:11** Ex 24:4–8; Mt 26:28; Heb 13:20.
**9:14** Dt 33:2; Ps 18:14; Hb 3:4.
**9:15** Ex 27:3; 38:3; Nm 4:14.
**9:16** Ez 34:11.

they will shine on the land.

17 Then how good and how lovely!
    Grain will make the young men
        flourish,
    and new wine the young women.*

## The Lord Strengthens Judah and Rescues Ephraim

**10** ¹ Ask the LORD for rain in the spring season,*
    the LORD who brings storm clouds,
        and heavy rains,*
    who gives to everyone grain in the
        fields.

2 For the teraphim† have spoken
        nonsense,*
    the diviners have seen false visions;
    Deceitful dreams they have told,
        empty comfort they have offered.
    This is why they wandered like sheep,
        wretched, for they have no
        shepherd.*

3 My wrath is kindled against the
        shepherds,†
    and I will punish the leaders.
    For the LORD of hosts attends to the
        flock, the house of Judah,
    and will make them like a splendid
        horse in battle.

4 From them will come the tower,
    from them the tent peg,
    from them the bow of war,
    from them every officer.

5 Together they will be like warriors,
    trampling the mud of the streets in
        battle.
    They will wage war because the LORD is
        with them,
    and will put the horsemen to shame.

6 I will strengthen the house of Judah,*
    the house of Joseph† I will save;
    I will bring them back, because I have
        mercy on them;
    they will be as if I had never cast them
        off,

for I am the LORD their God, and I
        will answer them.*

7 Then Ephraim will be like a hero,
    and their hearts will be cheered as by
        wine.*
    Their children will see and rejoice—
        their hearts will exult in the LORD.

8 I will whistle for them and gather them in;
    for I will redeem them
    and they will be as numerous as
        before.†

9 I sowed them among the nations,
    yet in distant lands they will
        remember me;
    they will bear their children and
        return.*

10 I will bring them back from the land of
        Egypt,
    and gather them from Assyria.
    To the land of Gilead and to Lebanon I
        will bring them,
    until no room is found for them.

11 I will cross over to Egypt
    and smite the waves of the sea,
    and all the depths of the Nile will
        dry up.
    The pride of Assyria will be cast down,
    and the scepter of Egypt disappear.

12 I will strengthen them in the LORD,*
    in whose name they will walk—oracle
        of the LORD.

## The Cry of Trees, Shepherds, and Lions

**11** ¹ Open your doors, Lebanon,
    that fire may devour your cedars!

2 Wail, cypress trees,
    for the cedars are fallen,
        the mighty are destroyed!
    Wail, oaks of Bashan,
        for the dense forest is cut down!

3 Listen! the wailing of shepherds,
    their glory has been destroyed.
    Listen! the roaring of young lions,
        the thickets of the Jordan are
        destroyed.

**ZEC**

---

**10:2** *Teraphim*: household idols or cult objects (see Gn 31:19, 30–35; Jgs 17:5; 1 Sm 19:11–17), or ancestor statuettes (see 2 Kgs 23:24; Hos 3:4).
**10:3** *Against the shepherds*: bad leaders or false prophets.
**10:6** *The house of Joseph*: represents the Northern Kingdom (Israel), as does Ephraim in v. 7 below.
**10:8** *Gather them in…be as numerous as before*: God's intention is to bring back the exiles and redeem them as at the time of the exodus. This image, resumed in vv. 10–11, anticipates an expanded population, echoes the ancestral promise

(Gn 1:22, 28; 9:1, 7; 35:11), and also suggests an awareness of the acute demographic decline of Jews in Palestine in the Persian period.

**9:17** Jer 31:12–13.
**10:1** Dt 11:14.
**10:1** Ps 135:7.
**10:2** 1 Sm 15:23.
**10:2** Ez 34:5; Mt 9:36.
**10:6** Zec 12:5.
**10:6** Is 41:17.
**10:7** Ps 104:15.
**10:9** Dt 30:1–3; Bar 2:30–32.
**10:12** Zec 12:5.

**The Shepherd Narrative.**†* ⁴Thus says the LORD, my God: Shepherd the flock to be slaughtered.* ⁵For they who buy them slay them and are not held accountable; while those who sell them say, "Blessed be the LORD, I have become rich!" Even their own shepherds will not pity them. ⁶For I will no longer pity the inhabitants of the earth—oracle of the LORD.—Yes, I will deliver them into each other's power, or into the power of their kings; they will crush the earth, and I will not deliver it out of their power.

⁷So I shepherded the flock to be slaughtered for the merchants of the flock. I took two staffs: one I called Delight, and the other Union. Thus I shepherded the flock. ⁸In a single month, I did away with the three shepherds, for I wearied of them, and they disdained me. ⁹"I will not shepherd you," I said. "Whoever is to die shall die; whoever is to be done away with shall be done away with; and those who are left shall devour one another's flesh."

¹⁰Then I took my staff Delight and snapped it in two, breaking my covenant which I had made with all peoples. ¹¹So it was broken on that day. The merchants of the flock, who were watching me, understood that this was the word of the LORD. ¹²Then I said to them, "If it seems good to you, give me my wages; but if not, withhold them."* And they counted out my wages,* thirty pieces of silver. ¹³Then the LORD said to me, Throw it in the treasury—the handsome price at which they valued me. So I took the thirty pieces of silver and threw them into the treasury in the house of the LORD. ¹⁴Then I snapped in two my second staff, Union, breaking the kinship between Judah and Israel.

¹⁵The LORD said to me: This time take the gear of a foolish shepherd.* ¹⁶For I am raising up a shepherd in the land who will take no note of those that disappear, nor seek the strays, nor heal the injured,* nor feed the exhausted; but he will eat the flesh of the fat ones and tear off their hoofs!

### Oracle to the Worthless Shepherd

17    Ah! my worthless shepherd
    who forsakes the flock!*
May the sword fall upon his arm
    and upon his right eye;
His arm will surely wither,
    and his right eye surely go blind!

**12** **Oracles Concerning the Nations and Judah.**† ¹An oracle:† The word of the LORD concerning Israel—oracle of the LORD, who spreads out the heavens, lays the foundations of the earth, and fashions the human spirit within:* ²See, I will make Jerusalem a cup of reeling† for all peoples round about.* Judah will be besieged, even Jerusalem. ³On that day I will make Jerusalem a heavy stone for all peoples. All who attempt to lift it will injure themselves badly, though all the nations of the earth will gather against it. ⁴On that day—oracle of the LORD—I will strike every horse with fright, and its rider with madness. But over the house of Judah I will keep watch, while I strike blind all the horses of the peoples. ⁵Then the clans of Judah will say to themselves, "The inhabitants of Jerusalem have their strength in the LORD of hosts, their God."* ⁶On that day I will make the clans of Judah like a brazier of fire in the woodland and like a burning torch among sheaves, and

---

† **11:4–17** This narrative has features of an allegory, a parable, and a commissioning narrative. The use of a symbolic action (vv. 7, 10, 14), however, places this text squarely in the tradition of classical prophecy. For example, the staff "Delight" signifies the Mosaic covenant, and the staff "Union" signifies the union of Israel and Judah. Breaking the staffs signifies the breaking of the Mosaic covenant (resulting in the destruction of Jerusalem and the exile) and the historical schism between north and south. In this narrative the prophet is the "shepherd" of God's flock, which is to be slaughtered. The "three shepherds" of v. 8 represent either leaders responsible for the decay in Israelite society or false prophets (cf. vv. 15, 17 and 13:2–6). The service of the good shepherd is contemptuously valued at thirty pieces of silver, the legal indemnity for a gored slave (Ex 21:32). The prophet throws the money into the Temple treasury, showing how poorly God's love is requited (cf. Mt 26:14–16; 27:5). With great rhetorical irony, payment is rejected. The entire wage-payment scenario may be regarded as another symbolic action, embedded within the primary action.

**12:1–10** The oracles deal with (1) the status of Judah in re-

lation to other political powers in the world that threaten its existence and (2) the reordering of Judah's internal structures so that its future can be realized. That future is linked to the fortunes of the house of David, which is mentioned five times between 12:7 and 13:1 (12:7, 8, 10, 12; 13:1).

**12:1** *An oracle*: part two of Second Zechariah begins with the same heading as that of part one (9:1; also Mal 1:1), suggesting two distinct blocks of material. The unusual cluster of introductory terms that follow the heading greatly intensifies the claim of prophetic authority, apparently an issue in postexilic prophecy.

**12:2** *Cup of reeling*: like a cup filled with intoxicating drink, Jerusalem will cause the nations to stumble and fall (cf. Is 51:17, 22; Jer 25:15; 49:12; Lam 4:21).

*                                   
**11:4** Ez 34:1.               **11:16** Is 42:3; Mt 12:20.
**11:4** Jer 12:3.               **11:17** Jer 23:1; Jn 10:12–13.
**11:12** Mt 27:3–10.          **12:1** Gn 2:7; Is 42:5.
**11:12** 2 Kgs 12:11; 22:4.    **12:2** Is 51:17.
**11:15** Ez 34:1–10.           **12:5** Zec 10:6, 12.

they will devour right and left all the surrounding peoples; but Jerusalem will again inhabit its own place.*

⁷The LORD will save the tents of Judah first, that the glory of the house of David and the glory of the inhabitants of Jerusalem may not be exalted over Judah. ⁸On that day the LORD will shield the inhabitants of Jerusalem, so that the weakest among them will be like David on that day; and the house of David will be like God, like the angel of the LORD before them.

⁹On that day I will seek the destruction of all nations that come against Jerusalem.* ¹⁰I will pour out on the house of David and on the inhabitants of Jerusalem a spirit of mercy and supplication, so that when they look on him whom they have thrust through,†* they will mourn for him as one mourns for an only child, and they will grieve for him as one grieves over a firstborn.*

**Catalogue of Mourners.** ¹¹On that day the mourning in Jerusalem will be as great as the mourning for Hadadrimmon in the plain of Megiddo.† ¹²And the land shall mourn, each family apart: the family of the house of David, and their women; the family of the house of Nathan, and their women; ¹³the family of the house of Levi, and their women; the family of Shimei, and their women; ¹⁴and all the rest of the families, each family apart, and the women apart.

# 13 Oracles Concerning the End of False Prophecy.† ¹On that day a fountain

will be opened for the house of David† and the inhabitants of Jerusalem, to purify from sin and uncleanness.*

²On that day—oracle of the LORD of hosts—I will destroy the names of the idols from the land, so that they will be mentioned no more; I will also remove the prophets and the spirit of uncleanness from the land. ³If any still prophesy, their father and mother who bore them will say, "You will not live, because you have spoken a lie in the name of the LORD." Their father and mother who bore them will thrust them through when they prophesy.*

⁴On that day, all prophets will be ashamed of the visions they prophesy; and they will not put on the hairy mantle† to mislead,* ⁵but each will say, "I am not a prophet. I am a tiller of the soil, for I have owned land since my youth."* ⁶And if anyone asks, "What are these wounds on your chest?"† each will answer, "I received these wounds in the house of my friends."*

## The Song of the Sword

7    Awake, O sword, against my shepherd,
      against the one who is my associate
      —oracle of the LORD of hosts.
    Strike the shepherd
      that the sheep may be scattered;†*
      I will turn my hand against the little
        ones.
8    In all the land—oracle of the LORD—
      two thirds of them will be cut off and
        perish,
      and one third will be left.

---

† **12:10** *They look on him…thrust through:* another possible rendering is "they shall look to me concerning him…thrust through." In either case, the victim is an enigmatic figure, perhaps referring to a Davidic descendant, a priestly leader, or even a true prophet. Some historical event, unknown to us from any surviving source, may underlie this reference. The Gospel of John applies this text to the piercing of Christ's side after his death (19:37).

**12:11** The mourning for the pierced victim in Jerusalem is compared to the annual ritual mourning in the plain of Megiddo over the death of the Phoenician fertility god, Hadadrimmon. According to others, Hadadrimmon is the name of a place near Megiddo, and the reference would then be to the mourning over the death of King Josiah at the hands of Pharaoh Neco in 609 B.C.; cf. 2 Kgs 23:29–30; 2 Chr 35:22–25.

**13:1–6** False prophecy is a major theme of Second Zechariah (chaps. 9–14) and figures in many other passages (10:1–2; 11; 12:10). Problems of idolatry and false prophecy occurred in postexilic Judah as they had in preexilic times. The understanding of the role of the prophet as an intermediary was challenged because (1) there was no king in Jerusalem, and (2) the texts of earlier prophets were beginning to be accorded the authority of prophetic tradition.

**13:1** *For the house of David:* anticipation that a cleansed leadership will enable the re-established monarchy to be rid of the misdeeds of its past.

**13:4** *Hairy mantle:* worn by prophets as a sign of their calling, for example, Elijah (1 Kgs 19:13; 2 Kgs 1:8) and John the Baptist (Mt 3:4).

**13:6** *Wounds on your chest:* lit., "wounds between your hands." The false prophets, like the prophets of Baal (1 Kgs 18:28), apparently inflicted wounds on themselves. Here it seems that persons accused of false prophecy deny having inflicted wounds on themselves and instead claim that they have received them at the houses of their friends.

**13:7** *Strike the shepherd…may be scattered:* in Matthew's Gospel (26:31) Jesus makes use of this text before his arrest in the Garden of Gethsemane and the flight of the disciples.

---

* **12:6** Zec 14:10.    **13:3** Jn 19:34.
**12:9** Zec 14:3.    **13:4** 2 Kgs 1:8; Mt 3:4.
**12:10** Jn 19:37; Rev 1:7.    **13:5** Am 7:14.
**12:10** Am 8:10.    **13:6** 1 Kgs 18:28.
**13:1** Ez 36:25; 47:1; Jn    **13:7** Ez 34:1–8; Mt 26:31.
    7:38.

ZEC

9 I will bring the one third through the
fire;
I will refine them as one refines
silver, *
and I will test them as one tests gold.
They will call upon my name, and I will
answer them; *
I will say, "They are my people," *
and they will say, "The Lord is my
God."

## 14 Devastation and Rescue of Jerusalem.
1 † A day is coming for the Lord when
the spoils taken from you will be divided in
your midst. 2 And I will gather all the nations
against Jerusalem for battle: The city will
be taken, houses will be plundered, women
raped; half the city will go into exile, but the
rest of the people will not be removed from
the city. 3 Then the Lord will go forth and fight
against those nations, fighting as on a day of
battle. * 4 On that day God's feet will stand † on
the Mount of Olives, which is opposite Jerusalem to the east. The Mount of Olives will be
split in two from east to west by a very deep
valley, * and half of the mountain will move to
the north and half of it to the south. 5 You will
flee by the valley between the mountains, for
the valley between the mountains will reach
to Azal. Thus you will flee as you fled because
of the earthquake † in the days of Uzziah king
of Judah. * Then the Lord, my God, will come,
and all his holy ones with him. *

### Jerusalem Restored.
6 On that day there will
no longer be cold or frost. 7 There will be one
continuous day—it is known to the Lord—not
day and night, for in the evening there will be
light. 8 On that day, fresh water will flow from
Jerusalem, * half to the eastern sea, and half
to the western sea. This will be so in summer
and in winter. 9 The Lord will be king over the
whole earth; * on that day the Lord will be the
only one, and the Lord's name the only one.
10 All the land will turn into a plain, from Geba
to Rimmon, south of Jerusalem, which will
stand exalted in its place—from the Gate of
Benjamin to the place of the first gate, to the
Corner Gate and from the Tower of Hananel
to the king's wine presses. 11 The city will be
inhabited; never again will it be doomed. Jerusalem will dwell securely. *

### The Fate of Jerusalem's Foes.
12 And this will
be the plague with which the Lord will strike
all the peoples that have fought against Jerusalem: their flesh will rot while they stand on
their feet, and their eyes will rot in their sock-
ets, and their tongues will rot in their mouths. *
13 On that day a great panic from the Lord will
be upon them. * They will seize each other's
hands, and their hands will be raised against
each other. 14 Even Judah will fight against
Jerusalem. The riches of all the surrounding
nations will be gathered together—gold, silver,
and garments—in great abundance. 15 Like the
plague on human beings will be the plague
upon the horses, mules, camels, donkeys, and
upon all the beasts that are in those camps.

### The Future: Jerusalem, Judah, and the Na-
tions.
16 Everyone who is left of all the nations
that came against Jerusalem will go up year after year to bow down to the King, the Lord of
hosts, and to celebrate the feast of Booths. † *
17 Should any of the families of the earth * not
go up to Jerusalem to bow down to the King,
the Lord of hosts, then there will be no rain

---

† **14:1–21** The marked eschatological thrust of Zec 9–14 culminates in this apocalyptic description, with its astonishing images
of the day of the Lord. This last and longest chapter focuses
on the restoration of Jerusalem and the return of the people of
Zion so that the rest of the world will acknowledge God's sovereignty. Four units constitute this chapter: vv. 1–5 concentrate
on the destruction and rescue of Jerusalem and the escape of
a remnant; vv. 6–11 describe the transformation of the climate
and the topography of Jerusalem; vv. 12–15 depict the defeat of
Jerusalem's enemies; and vv. 16–21 outline a vision for the end
time, in which even foreign nations will make the pilgrimage to
Jerusalem to acknowledge God's universal reign.

**14:4** *God's feet will stand*: a remarkable anthropomorphic
image adds emphasis to the traditional Old Testament scene of
God appearing on a mountain and causing extreme reactions
such as quaking, melting, shattering (see Ex 19:18; Ps 97:5; Hb
3:6). The Mount of Olives is split, which opens a way for those
fleeing from the Lord's appearance to escape from Jerusalem.

**14:5** *Earthquake*: Amos 1:1 mentions an earthquake in the
time of King Uzziah (cf. Is 6:4).

**14:16** *Feast of Booths*: fall harvest festival, also known as
the "festival of Ingathering" (Ex 23:16; 34:22) or "Booths" (Lv
23:33–36; Dt 16:13–15; 31:9–13). The singling out of this festival
indicates its special status in the sacred calendar; it is frequently
referred to as "the feast" (1 Kgs 8:1–2; 2 Chr 5:3; Ez 45:25).

* 
**13:9** Is 1:25; 48:10.
**13:9** Ps 91:15; Is 65:24.
**13:9** Zec 8:8; Jer 31:31.
**14:3** Is 31:4.
**14:4** Mi 1:4.
**14:5** Am 1:1.
**14:5** Dt 33:2–3; Mt 16:27;
1 Thes 3:13.
**14:8** Zec 13:1; Ez 47:1–8;
Jl 4:18.
**14:9** Ps 96:7–10; 97:1;
98:4–6; Rev 11:15.
**14:11** Dt 33:28; Jer 31:40;
Rev 22:3.
**14:12** Is 66:24.
**14:13** 1 Sm 5:9, 11;
14:18–20; Is 22:5.
**14:16** Lv 23:33–36; Dt
16:13–15.
**14:17** Zec 8:20–23; Is 2:1–4;
Mi 4:1–3.

for them. [18] And if the family of Egypt does not go up or enter, upon them will fall the plague,* with which the LORD strikes the nations that do not go up to celebrate the feast of Booths. [19] This will be the punishment of Egypt and the punishment of all the nations that do not go up to celebrate the feast of Booths.

[20] On that day, "Holy to the LORD"* will be written on the horses' bells.† The pots in the house of the LORD will be as the basins before the altar. [21] Every pot† in Jerusalem and in Judah will be holy to the LORD of hosts. All who come to sacrifice will take them and cook in them. No longer will there be merchants in the house of the LORD of hosts on that day.

---

† **14:20** *Horses' bells*: even these bells, part of the trappings of animals used for war, will become holy in the end time, like the bells of the high priest's garb (cf. Ex 28:34).
**14:21** *Every pot*: vessels used for mundane food preparation will, in the end time, be as holy as Temple vessels.

---

**14:18** Ex 5:3; 9:15.            **14:20** Lv 23:20; 27:30, 32.

ZEC

# Introduction to
# Malachi

## INTRODUCTION

### Dale Launderville, OSB

Malachi is the final book of the scroll known as the Book of the Twelve. Malachi shares a number of themes with the other books in this collection assembled from the seventh to the fifth centuries BCE, including covenant and election, fidelity and infidelity, the justice and mercy of God, and Yahweh as king dwelling on Zion. The book of Malachi, composed in the late sixth or early fifth century, addresses a postexilic community that has become disillusioned over the drawn-out process of restoration of the kingdom and has compromised its observance of the Torah. Two groups—the priests and the people at large—are exhorted to repent and reform.

The Persian Empire was locked in a struggle with the Greek world headed by Athens in the fifth century BCE. Both of these political powers were trying to extend their influence into Egypt. For Persia, Judah was strategically located on the way to Egypt and thus a stronger, more loyal Judah was in Persia's interests.

The Persian Empire not only subsidized the reconstruction of the Temple in 515 but also encouraged the Judean people to codify their ancestral laws. This officially-backed codification occurred under the leadership of Ezra, who returned to Judah from Babylonia in 458 BCE. Prior to this time in Judah, cultic regulations contained in the Pentateuch were known to the people but not linked as closely with imperial politics. In this pre-Ezra period, Malachi aimed to persuade the priests and the people that their dismal situation would improve if they were more committed to honoring Yahweh by obeying the ancestral laws.

The superscription in Mal 1:1 identifies the material as "an oracle" (massa'). This term appears repeatedly in the prophetic books, most recently in Zec 9:1 and 12:1. Although the more precise meaning of massa' is disputed,

## Outline of Malachi

I. Israel Preferred to Edom (1:2–5)

II. Offense in Sacrifice and Priestly Duty (1:6–2:9)

III. Marriage and Divorce (2:10–16)

IV. Purification and Just Judgment (2:17)

V. The Messenger of the Covenant (3:1–5)

VI. Gifts for God, Blessings for the People (3:6–12)

VII. The Need to Serve God (3:13–21)

VIII. Moses and Elijah (3:22–24)

it refers to oracular material emphasizing Yahweh's characteristic ways of acting in Israel's history. These patterns of divine activity are to be discerned by examining Israel's traditions so as to create a vision for the future. Malachi not only draws attention to the priestly role of preserving and teaching cultic regulations but also envisions an eschatological future based on the prophetic announcement of the day of the Lord. This convergence of the role of the priestly teacher with that of prophetic visionary threads its way through the book and is recapitulated in the concluding verses with their emphasis upon the Torah of Moses and the return of Elijah as a sign of the nearness of the day of the Lord (Mal 3:22–24). The diagnosis of the past and present undergirds the vision for the future; such an explanation urges repentance and reform.

In the opening disputation (Mal 1:2–5), Malachi uses a three-step rhetorical pattern to confront those Judeans who feel Yahweh has abandoned them. First, Malachi states a truth: the Lord loves the Judeans (1:2a). Second, he quotes the objection by the Judeans: "How do you love us?" (1:2b). Third, Malachi makes his case by arguing that the Judeans as the descendants of Jacob are in much better shape than the Edomites as descendants of Esau. Echoing Gn 25:21–23, Malachi reports that the Lord says: "I loved Jacob, but rejected Esau" (Mal 1:3). Such divine rejection was believed to be manifest in the series of invasions of Edom by the Babylonians around 550 BCE and then continued by Arab tribes in the fifth and fourth centuries. According to Malachi, Edom's resolve to rebuild is futile, for future invasions will follow. By contrast, the Judeans are the chosen ones of the Lord. The challenge for them is to embrace their covenantal status and obligations.

In the second speech (Mal 1:6–2:9), Malachi uses the same three-part pattern to challenge the priests for dishonoring Yahweh by compromising on their cultic service. First, he states a truth: "A son honors his father, and a servant fears his master" (1:6) and charges that the Judeans do not honor Yahweh. Second, Malachi quotes the Judeans' objection: "How have we disdained your name? . . . How have we defiled [your altar]?" (1:6d–7a). Third, Malachi makes his case that the priests have offered blind, lame, and sick animals instead of wholesome ones. He emphasizes that the priests would not dare to offer such defective gifts to the governor (1:8). How then can they cheat the Lord of the universe (1:11–14)? Such behavior will bring a curse (1:14). Malachi extends his argument by reminding the priests of the covenant the Lord made with Levi and warns that they have not followed the example of their ancestor in giving proper instruction and serving as a messenger of the Lord (2:8). Such negative behavior has brought them contempt (2:9) and will continue to do so (2:3).

In the third speech (Mal 2:10–16), Malachi challenges the people for their practices of intermarriage with foreign wives and of divorce. First, he argues that they have broken the ancestral covenant by marrying foreign wives who bring their deities into the Judean households (2:10–11) and by divorcing their Judean wives (2:14–15). These practices make their offerings unacceptable to Yahweh. Second,

Malachi quotes their objection in one word: "Why?" (2:14). Third, Malachi then explains that such intermarriage with foreigners and divorce of Judeans leads to illegitimate offspring. Divorce itself was allowed in ancient Israel (Dt 24:1–4). But in this context, divorce was undercutting the fabric of the Judean household and allowing foreign cultural influences to rule in this basic unit of Judean society.

In the fourth speech (Mal 2:17–3:5), Malachi shifts his attention from priestly tradition to prophetic prediction as he condemns the people's unethical attitudes and practices. First, he charges them with burdening the Lord with their claim that the evil prosper under his watch (2:17). Second, he quotes their objection: "How have we wearied him?" (2:17). Third, Malachi announces that the Lord is sending his messenger ahead of him and that the terrible day of the Lord is imminent (3:1–2; cf. Mt. 11:10, which identifies John the Baptist as the predicted "messenger"). The Lord will purify the Levites and refine them so that they might bring proper offerings (Mal 3:3). He will bring into judgment the sinners among the people, ranging from the sorcerers to those who mistreat the vulnerable in the community (3:5).

In the fifth speech (Mal 3:6–12), Malachi urges the people to be generous in giving to the Lord and to expect that they will receive much more in return. First, he claims that Yahweh is constant in his fidelity to the covenant but that the Judeans, like their ancestors, have repeatedly strayed. Second, Malachi quotes their objection to his exhortation to repent: "Why should we return?" (3:7). Third, Malachi explains that the failure of the people to bring the expected tithes and offerings to the Lord is simply a form of robbery (3:8). He then urges them to put the Lord's fidelity to the test. If they wager that being generous toward the Lord will pay off, Malachi promises that they will prosper (3:10–11).

In the sixth speech (Mal 3:13–21), Malachi exhorts the people to let go of their disillusionment with the injustices of their time and to trust the Lord. First, he charges that the objections of the people to the way that the Lord is overseeing events in their time are beginning to frustrate the Lord (3:13). Second, Malachi quotes some of the complaints that the people are lodging against the Lord: "It is useless to serve God. . . . For evildoers not only prosper but even test God and escape" (3:14–15). Third, Malachi counters their objections by explaining how those who fear the Lord are held in remembrance by the Lord: i.e., their names are recorded in his book (3:16). In other words, those who patiently bear with the inequities of their present circumstances and trust in the Lord will be rewarded according to God's timetable. On the day of the Lord, God will separate the just from the wicked (3:18–21). Purifying fire will wipe out the roots of the wicked (3:19)[1] and the illuminating sun will heal and energize the just (3:20–21; cf. Ps 19).

In the concluding three verses (Mal 3:22–24), Elijah—the prophet like Moses who will come to announce the day of the Lord—is aligned with the healing and enlightening

1. Chapter 3:19–24 is numbered 4:1–6 in the Latin Vulgate and in some modern translations.

power of the Mosaic Torah. (In Mt 11:14, Jesus identifies John the Baptist as having fulfilled the prophecy that Elijah would return.) Malachi's efforts to persuade the disillusioned Judeans to repent and return to the Lord are summed up in these priestly, prophetic figures who instruct and exhort the people to recognize their covenantal solidarity.

Just as Moses is revered as the promulgator of the Torah (Mal 3:22) and Elijah as the eschatological messenger (3:1, 23–24), so also Malachi is identified as a divine messenger in the superscription, which says: "the word of the LORD to Israel through Malachi" (1:1). The written medium of this prophetic book records Yahweh's characteristic ways of acting in Israel's past and appeals to its readers to fear the Lord (3:16–18). The book of Malachi forms a fitting conclusion to the Book of the Twelve and serves as a bridge to the Gospels by urging readers to trust in the Lord who is faithful to his covenant promises. ■

# THE BOOK OF MALACHI

## New American Bible, Introduction

This short book may have been written before Nehemiah's first return to Jerusalem in 445 B.C.; it is also possible that it was written while Nehemiah was there, or even later. What seems to be the author's name, *mal'ākî*, is found in 1:1 ("the word of the Lord to Israel through Malachi"), but many believe that this is a pseudonym based on *mal'ākî*, "my messenger," in 3:1 and that the author's real name is unknown. In any case, he shows us attitudes and behaviors characteristic of the Jewish community a few generations after the end of the Babylonian exile, and describes God's response.

God loves Israel (1:2–5), but the people return that love poorly. Taking advantage of the negligent attitude of the priests, they withhold tithes and sacrificial contributions (3:6–11) and cheat God by providing defective goods for sacrifice (1:6–14). People divorce their spouses and marry worshipers of other gods (2:10–16). Sorcerers, adulterers, perjurers, and people who take advantage of workers and the needy abound (3:5). Priests, who could strengthen discipline by their instruction, connive with the people, telling them what they want to hear (2:1–9). Underlying all this is a weary attitude, a cynical notion that nothing is to be gained by doing what God wants and that wrongdoers prosper (2:17; 3:14–15). God condemns the wrongdoing and the underlying attitude, issuing a challenge to immediate reform (3:10–12), but also announcing a general reckoning at a future moment (3:16–21).

The Book of Malachi may be divided as follows:

I. Israel Preferred to Edom (1:2–5)
II. Offense in Sacrifice and Priestly Duty (1:6–2:9)
III. Marriage and Divorce (2:10–16)
IV. Purification and Just Judgment (2:17)
V. The Messenger of the Covenant (3:1–5)
VI. Gifts for God, Blessings for the People (3:6–12)
VII. The Need to Serve God (3:13–21)
VIII. Moses and Elijah (3:22–24) ∎

M
A
L

# MALACHI

**1** ¹† An oracle. The word of the LORD to Israel through Malachi.

### Israel Preferred to Edom

²* I love you, says the LORD;
  but you say, "How do you love us?"
³†* Was not Esau Jacob's brother?—oracle of
  the LORD.
  I loved Jacob, but rejected Esau;
  I made his mountains a waste,
    his heritage a desert for jackals.
⁴* If Edom says, "We have been crushed,
  but we will rebuild the ruins,"
  Thus says the LORD of hosts:
    They indeed may build, but I will tear
      down,
  And they shall be called "territory of
    wickedness,"
    the people with whom the LORD is
      angry forever.
⁵* Your own eyes will see it, and you will
    say,
    "Great is the LORD, even beyond the
      territory of Israel."

### Offense in Sacrifice and Priestly Duty

⁶* A son honors his father,
  and a servant fears his master;
  If, then, I am a father,
    where is the honor due to me?
  And if I am a master,
    where is the fear due to me?
  So says the LORD of hosts to you,
    O priests,
    who disdain my name.
  But you ask, "How have we disdained
    your name?"

⁷ By offering defiled food on my altar!
  You ask, "How have we defiled it?"
    By saying that the table of the LORD
      may be disdained!
⁸†* When you offer a blind animal for
    sacrifice,
    is there no wrong in that?
  When you offer a lame or sick animal,
    is there no wrong in that?
  Present it to your governor!
    Will he be pleased with you—or show
      you favor?
    says the LORD of hosts.
⁹ So now implore God's favor, that he
    may have mercy on us!
  You are the ones who have done this;
  Will he show favor to any of you?
    says the LORD of hosts.
¹⁰† Oh, that one of you would just shut the
    temple gates
    to keep you from kindling fire on my
      altar in vain!
  I take no pleasure in you, says the LORD
    of hosts;
    and I will not accept any offering
      from your hands!
¹¹* From the rising of the sun to its setting,
    my name is great among the nations;
  Incense offerings are made to my name
    everywhere,
    and a pure offering;
  For my name is great among the
    nations,
    says the LORD of hosts.
¹² But you profane it by saying
    that the LORD's table is defiled,
    and its food may be disdained.
¹³ You say, "See what a burden this is!"
    and you exasperate me, says the LORD
      of hosts;
  You bring in what is mutilated, or lame,
    or sick;

---

† **1:1** See note on Zec 9:1.

**1:3–5** The thought passes from the person Esau to his descendants, Edom, and from the person Jacob to his descendants, Israel; cf. Gn 25:21–23. In the New Testament, Paul uses this passage as an example of God's freedom of choice in calling the Gentiles to faith (Rom 9:13).

**1:8** The sacrificial offering of a lame, sick, or blind animal was forbidden in the law (Lv 22:17–25; Dt 17:1).

**1:10–11** The imperfect sacrifices offered by the people of Judah are displeasing to the Lord. *Kindling fire on my altar:* kindle the altar fire for sacrifice. In contrast, the Lord is pleased with the sacrifices offered by other peoples in other places (*the rising of the sun:* the far east; *its setting:* the far west). Since the people of other nations could not be expected to know the Lord's name as

did the people of Judah, the rhetorical purpose of this statement is to shame the latter. *Incense offerings:* in the ancient world, the hallmark of an offering made to a god was the smoke it produced on an altar. In the Old Testament, this was true not only of animals (Lv 8:20–21) but also of incense (Ex 30:7), suet (Lv 3:11), and grain offerings (Lv 6:8). In a Christian interpretation of Mal 1:10–11, the "pure offering" of Mal 1:11 is seen as a reference to sacrifice in the Messianic Age. The Council of Trent endorsed this interpretation (DS 1724).

*
**1:2** Dt 7:8; Ez 16; Hos     **1:5** Is 60.
    11:1; Am 1:11.               **1:6** Prv 1:7; Is 29:13.
**1:3** Gn 25:23; Rom 9:13.     **1:8** Lv 22:17–25; Dt
**1:4** Is 34:2–15; 63:1–6;         15:21; 17:1.
    Jer 49:7–22; Ob 21.         **1:11** Ps 113:3; Is 59:19.

MAL

you bring it as an offering!
Will I accept it from your hands?
   says the LORD.

14 Cursed is the cheat who has in his flock
   an intact male,
   and vows it, but sacrifices to the LORD
   a defective one instead;
For a great king am I, says the LORD of
   hosts,
   and my name is feared among the
   nations.

**2** 1 And now, priests, this commandment is
for you:
   If you do not listen,
2 * And if you do not take to heart
   giving honor to my name, says the
   LORD of hosts,
I will send a curse upon you
   and your blessing I will curse.
In fact, I have already cursed it,
   because you do not take it to heart.
3 I will rebuke your offspring;
   I will spread dung on your faces,
Dung from your feasts,
   and will carry you to it.
4 You should know that I sent you this
   commandment
   so that my covenant with Levi might
   endure,
   says the LORD of hosts.
5 * My covenant with him was the life and
   peace which I gave him,
   and the fear he had for me,
   standing in awe of my name.
6 * Reliable instruction was in his mouth,
   no perversity was found upon his lips;
He walked with me in integrity and
   uprightness,
   and turned many away from evil.
7 * For a priest's lips preserve knowledge,
   and instruction is to be sought from
   his mouth,

because he is the messenger of the
   LORD of hosts.
8 But you have turned aside from the way,
   and have caused many to stumble by
   your instruction;
You have corrupted the covenant of
   Levi, †
   says the LORD of hosts.
9 I, therefore, have made you
   contemptible
   and base before all the people,
For you do not keep my ways,
   but show partiality in your
   instruction.

### Marriage and Divorce

10 †* Have we not all one father?
   Has not one God created us?
Why, then, do we break faith with each
   other,
   profaning the covenant of our
   ancestors?
11 * Judah has broken faith; an abominable
   thing
   has been done in Israel and in
   Jerusalem.
Judah has profaned the LORD's holy
   place, which he loves,
   and has married a daughter of a
   foreign god. †
12 May the LORD cut off from the man who
   does this
   both witness and advocate from the
   tents of Jacob,
   and anyone to bring an offering to the
   LORD of hosts!
13 This also you do: the altar of the LORD
   you cover
   with tears, weeping, and groaning,
Because the Lord no longer takes note of
   your offering
   or accepts it favorably from your
   hand.

---

**2:8** *The covenant of Levi*: not mentioned elsewhere in the Bible. The covenant with Phinehas the grandson of Aaron (Nm 25:11–13) and the Blessing of Levi (Dt 33:8–11) may lie in the background.

**2:10–16** Intermarriage of Israelites with foreigners was forbidden according to Dt 7:1–4. After the exile, attempts were made to enforce this law (Ezr 9–10). Foreign marriages are here portrayed as a covenantal violation (v. 10). They were all the more reprehensible when they were accompanied by the divorce of Israelite wives (vv. 14–16), and God finds their sacrifices unacceptable (vv. 13–14). In Mk 10:2–12, Jesus forbids divorce; in Mt 19:3–12, this ideal is maintained with the provision that unlawful marriage may be grounds for divorce (see 1 Cor 7:10–16). *You*

*should be on guard, then, for your life*: a warning of punishment for failure to obey God (cf. Dt 4:9; Jos 23:11; Jer 17:21).

**2:11** *Daughter of a foreign god*: this unusual phrase connotes a woman who does not share the same father/creator (v. 10), since she does not share the same covenant.

**2:2** Lv 26:14–45; Dt 28:15.
**2:5** Ez 37:26.
**2:6** Dt 33:8–11.
**2:7** Lv 10:10–11; Dt 17:9–10; Hg 2:11–13.
**2:10** Dt 32:6; Jb 31:15; Mt 23:9; Eph 4:6.
**2:11** Ezr 9:2; Neh 13:25.

MAL

14* And you say, "Why?"—
　　Because the LORD is witness
　　between you and the wife of your youth
　With whom you have broken faith,
　　though she is your companion, your
　　covenanted wife.†

15* Did he not make them one, with flesh
　　and spirit?
　　And what does the One require?
　　Godly offspring!
　You should be on guard, then, for your
　　life,
　　and do not break faith with the wife
　　of your youth.

16 For I hate divorce,
　　says the LORD, the God of Israel,
　And the one who covers his garment
　　with violence,
　　says the LORD of hosts.
　You should be on guard, then, for your
　　life,
　　and you must not break faith.

### Purification and Just Judgment

17 You have wearied the LORD with your
　　words,
　　yet you say, "How have we wearied
　　him?"
　By saying, "All evildoers
　　are good in the sight of the LORD,
　And he is pleased with them,"
　　or "Where is the just God?"

### The Messenger of the Covenant

3 1* Now I am sending my messenger—
　　he will prepare the way before me;†
　And the lord whom you seek will come
　　suddenly to his temple;
　The messenger of the covenant whom
　　you desire—
　　see, he is coming! says the LORD of
　　hosts.

2 But who can endure the day of his
　　coming?

Who can stand firm when he appears?
　For he will be like a refiner's fire,
　　like fullers' lye.

3* He will sit refining and purifying silver,
　　and he will purify the Levites,
　Refining them like gold or silver,
　　that they may bring offerings to the
　　LORD in righteousness.

4 Then the offering of Judah and
　　Jerusalem
　　will please the LORD,
　　as in ancient days, as in years gone by.

5 I will draw near to you for judgment,
　　and I will be swift to bear witness
　Against sorcerers, adulterers, and
　　perjurers,
　　those who deprive a laborer of wages,
　Oppress a widow or an orphan,
　　or turn aside a resident alien,
　　without fearing me, says the LORD of
　　hosts.

### Gifts for God, Blessings for the People

6 For I, the LORD, do not change,†
　　and you, sons of Jacob, do not cease
　　to be.

7* Since the days of your ancestors you
　　have turned aside
　　from my statutes and have not kept
　　them.
　Return to me, that I may return to you,
　　says the LORD of hosts.
　But you say, "Why should we return?"

8* Can anyone rob God? But you are
　　robbing me!
　And you say, "How have we robbed you?"
　　Of tithes and contributions!

9 You are indeed accursed,
　　for you, the whole nation, rob me.

10* Bring the whole tithe
　　into the storehouse,†
　That there may be food in my house.
　　Put me to the test, says the LORD of
　　hosts,

---

† **2:14** *Companion...covenanted wife*: the Hebrew word *habe-ret* signifies an equal, a partner. This woman, in contrast to the daughter of a foreign god, shares with her husband the same covenant with the Lord.

**3:1** *My messenger...before me*: Mt 11:10 applies these words to John the Baptist; Mt 11:14 further identifies John as Elijah (see Mal 3:23). Some take God's messenger in v. 1a to be a person distinct from "the lord" and "the messenger of the covenant" in v. 1b; others hold that they are one and the same person. Some consider "the lord" and "the messenger of the covenant" to be divine, while others hold that in the text's literal sense he is a

messianic earthly ruler.

**3:6–7** *Not change*: God remains faithful to the covenant even when the human partners break it.

**3:10** *Storehouse*: the temple treasury.

**2:14** Gn 31:49–50; Prv 5:18–19.
**2:15** Gn 2:7, 22–24.
**3:1** Ex 23:20–22; Is 40:3; Mt 11:10; Mk 1:2; Lk 1:17; 7:27.
**3:3** Is 1:25; Zec 13:9.
**3:7** Zec 1:3–4; Acts 7:51.
**3:8** Neh 13:10–14.
**3:10** Dt 28:2, 12; 2 Chr 31:10–11; Neh 10:38; 13:12; Prv 3:9–10.

And see if I do not open the floodgates
    of heaven for you,
    and pour down upon you blessing
       without measure!

11 I will rebuke the locust for you
    so that it will not destroy your crops,
    And the vine in the field will not be
       barren,
    says the LORD of hosts.

12* All the nations will call you blessed,
    for you will be a delightful land,
    says the LORD of hosts.

### The Need to Serve God

13 Your words are too much for me, says
    the LORD.
    You ask, "What have we spoken
       against you?"

14* You have said, "It is useless to serve
       God;
    what do we gain by observing God's
       requirements,
    And by going about as mourners†
    before the LORD of hosts?

15 But we call the arrogant blessed;
    for evildoers not only prosper
    but even test God and escape."

16* Then those who fear the LORD spoke
    with one another,
    and the LORD listened attentively;
    A record book† was written before
       him
    of those who fear the LORD and
       esteem his name.

17* They shall be mine, says the LORD of
       hosts,
    my own special possession, on the
       day when I take action.
    And I will have compassion on them,

    as a man has compassion on his son
       who serves him.

18 Then you will again distinguish
    between the just and the wicked,
    Between the person who serves God,
    and the one who does not.

19* For the day is coming, blazing like an
       oven,
    when all the arrogant and all evildoers
       will be stubble,
    And the day that is coming will set them
       on fire,
    leaving them neither root nor branch,
    says the LORD of hosts.

20* But for you who fear my name, the sun
       of justice
    will arise with healing in its wings;†
    And you will go out leaping like calves
       from the stall

21     and tread down the wicked;
    They will become dust under the soles
       of your feet,
    on the day when I take action, says
       the LORD of hosts.

### Moses and Elijah

22* Remember the law of Moses my servant,
    whom I charged at Horeb
    With statutes and ordinances
    for all Israel.

23* Now I am sending to you
    Elijah† the prophet,
    Before the day of the LORD comes,
    the great and terrible day;

24 He will turn the heart of fathers to their
       sons,
    and the heart of sons to their fathers,
    Lest I come and strike
    the land with utter destruction.

---

**3:14** *As mourners*: the adverb translated "as mourners" means something like "with a long face."

**3:16** *Record book*: see note on Ex 32:32.

**3:20** *Wings*: a common symbol of the manifestation of a god in the ancient Near East is the winged sun disk found, for example, on premonarchic jar handles. Cf. Nm 6:25; Ps 4:7; 31:17; 34:6; 84:12.

**3:23** *Elijah*: taken up in a whirlwind, according to 2 Kgs 2:11. Here his return seems to be foretold. A Jewish tradition interpreted this literally; the gospels saw Elijah in the person of John the Baptist (Mt 11:13–14; 17:10–13; Mk 9:9–13).

**3:12** Dt 28:10; Is 61:9.
**3:14** Jb 21:14–15; 22:17; Ps 73:11–12; Is 58:3; Zec 7:2–7.
**3:16** Rev 20:12.
**3:17** Ex 19:5; Dt 7:6; Ps 103:13; 135:4.
**3:19** Is 13:9; 34:8; Jl 3:3;
Zep 1:18; 2 Pt 3:7.
**3:20** Lk 1:78–79.
**3:22** Ex 20; Lv 26; Dt 4:1, 5–6.
**3:23** 2 Kgs 2:10–12; Sir 48:10; Mt 11:13–14; 17:10–13; Mk 9:9–13; Lk 1:17.

MAL

# New Testament

# PREFACE TO THE NEW AMERICAN BIBLE
## FIRST EDITION OF THE NEW TESTAMENT

The New Testament translation has been approached with essentially the same fidelity to the thought and individual style of the biblical writers as was applied in the Old Testament. In some cases, however, the problem of marked literary peculiarities had to be met. What by any Western standard are the limited vocabularies and stylistic infelicities of the evangelists cannot be retained in the exact form in which they appear in the originals without displeasing the modern ear. A compromise is here attempted whereby some measure of the poverty of the evangelists' expression is kept and placed at the service of their message in its richness. Similarly, the syntactical shortcomings of Paul, his frequent lapses into anacoluthon, and the like, are rendered as they occur in his epistles rather than "smoothed out." Only thus, the translators suppose, will contemporary readers have some adequate idea of the kind of writing they have before them. When the prose of the original flows more smoothly, as in Luke, Acts, and Hebrews, it is reflected in the translation.

The Gospel according to John comprises a special case. Absolute fidelity to his technique of reiterated phrasing would result in an assault on the English ear, yet the softening of the vocal effect by substitution of other words and phrases would destroy the effectiveness of his poetry. Again, resort is had to compromise. This is not an easy matter when the very repetitiousness which the author deliberately employed is at the same time regarded by those who read and speak English to be a serious stylistic defect. Only those familiar with the Greek originals can know what a relentless tattoo Johannine poetry can produce. A similar observation could be made regarding other New Testament books as well. Matthew and Mark are given to identical phrasing twice and three times in the same sentence. As for the rhetorical overgrowth and mixed figures of speech in the letters of Peter, James, and Jude, the translator must resist a powerful compulsion to tidy them up if only to render these letters intelligibly.

Without seeking refuge in complaints against the inspired authors, however, the translators of *The New American Bible* here state that what they have attempted is a translation rather than a paraphrase. To be sure, all translation can be called paraphrase by definition. Any striving for complete fidelity will shortly end in infidelity. Nonetheless, it must be pointed out that the temptation to improve overladen sentences by the consolidation or elimination of multiplied adjectives, or the simplification of clumsy hendiadys, has been resisted here. For the most part, rhetorically ineffective words and phrases are retained in this translation in some form, even when it is clear that a Western contemporary writer would never have employed them.

The spelling of proper names in *The New American Bible* follows the customary forms found in most English Bibles since the Authorized Version.

Despite the arbitrary character of the divisions into numbered verses (a scheme which in its present form is only four centuries old), the translators have made a constant effort to keep within an English verse the whole verbal content of the Greek verse. At times the effort has not seemed worth the result since it often does violence to the original author's flow of expression, which preceded it by so many centuries. If this translation had been prepared for purposes of public reading only, the editors would have forgone the effort at an early stage. But since they never departed from the threefold objective of preparing a translation suitable for liturgical use, private reading, and the purposes of students, the last-named consideration prevailed. Those familiar with Greek should be able to discover how the translators of the New Testament have rendered any given original verse of scripture, if their exegetical or theological tasks require them to know this. At the same time, the fact should be set down here that the editors did not commit themselves in the synoptic gospels to rendering repeated words or phrases identically.

This leads to a final consideration: the Greek text used for the New Testament. Here, punctuation and verse division are at least as important as variant readings. In general, Nestle-Aland's *Novum Testamentum Graece* (25th edition, 1963) was followed. Additional help was derived from *The Greek New Testament* (Aland, Black, Metzger, Wikgren), produced for the use of translators by the United Bible Societies in 1966. However, the editors did not confine themselves strictly to these texts; at times, they inclined toward readings otherwise attested. The omission of alternative translations does not mean that the translators think them without merit, but only that in every case they had to make a choice.

Poorly attested readings do not occur in this translation. Doubtful readings of some merit appear within brackets; public readers may include such words or phrases, or omit them entirely without any damage to sense. Parentheses are used, as ordinarily in English, as a punctuation device. Material they enclose is in no sense textually doubtful. It is simply thought to be parenthetical in the intention of the biblical author, even though there is no such punctuation mark in Greek. The difficulty in dealing with quotation marks is well known. Since they do not appear in any form in the original text, wherever they occur here they constitute an editorial decision.

# PREFACE TO
# THE REVISED EDITION

The New Testament of *The New American Bible*, a fresh translation from the Greek text, was first published in complete form in 1970, together with the Old Testament translation that had been completed the previous year. Portions of the New Testament had appeared earlier, in somewhat different form, in the provisional Mass lectionary of 1964 and in the *Lectionary for Mass* of 1970.

Since 1970 many different printings of the New Testament have been issued by a number of publishers, both separately and in complete bibles, and the text has become widely known both in the United States and in other English-speaking countries. Most American Catholics have been influenced by it because of its widespread use in the liturgy, and it has received a generally favorable reception from many other Christians as well. It has taken its place among the standard contemporary translations of the New Testament, respected for its fidelity to the original and its attempt to render this into current American English.

Although the scriptures themselves are timeless, translations and explanations of them quickly become dated in an era marked by rapid cultural change to a degree never previously experienced. The explosion of biblical studies that has taken place in our century and the changing nature of our language itself require periodic adjustment both in translations and in the accompanying explanatory materials. The experience of actual use of the New Testament of *The New American Bible*, especially in oral proclamation, has provided a basis for further improvement. Accordingly, it was decided in 1978 to proceed with a thorough revision of the New Testament to reflect advances in scholarship and to satisfy needs identified through pastoral experience.

For this purpose a steering committee was formed to plan, organize, and direct the work of revision, to engage collaborators, and to serve as an editorial board to coordinate the work of the various revisers and to determine the final form of the text and the explanatory materials. Guidelines were drawn up and collaborators selected in 1978 and early 1979, and November of 1980 was established as the deadline for manuscripts. From December 1980 through September 1986 the editorial board met a total of fifty times and carefully reviewed and revised all the material in order to ensure accuracy and consistency of approach. The editors also worked together with the bishops' ad hoc committee that was appointed by the National Conference of Catholic Bishops in 1982 to oversee the revision.

The threefold purpose of the translation that was expressed in the preface to the first edition has been maintained in the revision: to provide a version suitable for liturgical proclamation, for private reading, and for purposes of study. Special attention has been given to the first of these purposes, since oral proclamation demands special qualities in a translation, and experience had provided insights and suggestions that could lead to improvement in this area. Efforts have also been made, however, to facilitate devotional reading by providing suitable notes and introductory materials, and to assist the student by achieving greater accuracy and consistency in the translation and supplying more abundant information in the introductions and notes.

The primary aim of the revision is to produce a version as accurate and faithful to the meaning of the Greek original as is possible for a translation. The editors have consequently moved in the direction of a formal-equivalence approach to translation, matching the vocabulary, structure, and even word order of the original as closely as possible in the receptor language. Some other contemporary biblical versions have adopted, in varying degrees, a dynamic-equivalence approach, which attempts to respect the individuality of each language by expressing the meaning of the original in a linguistic structure suited to English, even though this may be very different from the corresponding Greek structure. While this approach often results in fresh and brilliant renderings, it has the disadvantages of more or less radically abandoning traditional biblical and liturgical terminology and phraseology, of expanding the text to include what more properly belongs in notes, commentaries, or preaching, and of tending toward paraphrase. A more formal approach seems better suited to the specific purposes intended for this translation.

At the same time, the editors have wished to produce a version in English that reflects contemporary American usage and is readily understandable to ordinary educated people, but one that will be recognized as dignified speech, on the level of formal rather than colloquial usage. These aims are not in fact contradictory, for there are different levels of language in current use: the language of formal situations as not that of colloquial conversation, though people understand both and may pass from one to the other without adverting to the transition. The liturgy is a formal situation that requires a level of discourse more dignified, formal, and hieratic than the world of business, sport, or informal communication. People readily understand this more formal level even though they may not often use it; our passive vocabulary is much larger than our active vocabulary. Hence this revision, while avoiding archaisms, does not shrink from traditional biblical terms that are easily understood even though not in common use in everyday speech. The level of language consciously aimed at is one appropriate for liturgical proclamation; this may also permit the translation to serve the purposes of devotional reading and serious study.

A particular effort has been made to insure consistency of vocabulary. Always to translate a given Greek word by the same English equivalent would lead to ludicrous results and to infidelity to the meaning of the text. But in passages where a particular Greek term retains the same meaning, it has been rendered in the same way insofar as this has been feasible; this is particularly significant in the case of terms that have a specific theological meaning. The synoptic gospels have been carefully translated so as to reveal both the similarities and the differences of the Greek.

An especially sensitive problem today is the question of discrimination in language. In recent years there has been much discussion about allegations of anti-Jewish expressions in the New Testament and of language that discriminates against various minorities. Above all, however, the question of discrimination against women affects the largest number of people and arouses the greatest degree of interest and concern. At present there is little agreement about these problems or about the best way to deal with them. In all these areas the present translation attempts to display a sensitivity appropriate to the present state of the questions under discussion, which are not yet resolved and in regard to which it is impossible to please everyone, since intelligent and sincere participants in the debate hold mutually contradictory views.

The primary concern in this revision is fidelity to what the text says. When the meaning of the Greek is inclusive of both sexes, the translation seeks to reproduce such inclusivity insofar as this is possible in normal English usage, without resort to inelegant circumlocutions or neologisms that would offend against the dignity of the language. Although the generic sense of *man* is traditional in English, many today reject it; its use has therefore generally been avoided, though it is retained in cases where no fully satisfactory equivalent could be found. English does not possess a gender-inclusive third personal pronoun in the singular, and this translation continues to use the masculine resumptive pronoun after *everyone* or *anyone*, in the traditional way, where this cannot be avoided without infidelity to the meaning.

The translation of the Greek word *adelphos*, particularly in the plural form *adelphoi*, poses an especially delicate problem. While the term literally means brothers or other male blood relatives, even in profane Greek the plural can designate two persons, one of either sex, who were born of the same parents. It was adopted by the early Christians to designate, in a figurative sense, the members of the Christian community, who were conscious of a new familial relationship to one another by reason of their adoption as children of God. They are consequently addressed as *adelphoi*. This has traditionally been rendered into English by *brothers* or, more archaically, *brethren*. There has never been any doubt that this designation includes *all* the members of the Christian community, both male and female. Given the absence in English of a corresponding term that explicitly includes both sexes, this translation retains the usage of *brothers*, with the inclusive meaning that has been traditionally attached to it in this biblical context.

Since the New Testament is the product of a particular time and culture, the views expressed in it and the language in which they are expressed reflect a particular cultural conditioning, which sometimes makes them quite different from contemporary ideas and concerns. Discriminatory language should be eliminated insofar as possible whenever it is unfaithful to the meaning of the New Testament, but the text should not be altered in order to adjust it to contemporary concerns. This translation does not introduce any changes, expansions, additions to, or subtractions from the text of scripture. It further retains the traditional biblical ways of speaking about God and about Christ, including the use of masculine nouns and pronouns.

The Greek text followed in this translation is that of the third edition of *The Greek New Testament*, edited by Kurt Aland, Matthew Black, Carlo Martini, Bruce Metzger, and Allen Wikgren, and published by the United Bible Societies in 1975. The same text, with a different critical apparatus and variations in punctuation and typography, was published as the twenty-sixth edition of the Nestle-Aland *Novum Testamentum Graece* in 1979 by the Deutsche Bibelstiftung, Stuttgart. This edition has also been consulted. When variant readings occur, the translation, with few exceptions, follows the reading that was placed in the text of these Greek editions, though the occurrence of the principal variants is pointed out in the notes.

The editors of the Greek text placed square brackets around words or portions of words of which the authenticity is questionable because the evidence of textual witnesses is inconclusive. The same has been done in the translation insofar as it is possible to reproduce this convention in English. It should be possible to read the text either with or without the disputed words, but in English it is not always feasible to provide this alternative, and in some passages the bracketed words must be included to make sense. As in the first edition, parentheses do not indicate textual uncertainty, but are simply a punctuation device to indicate a passage that in the editors' judgment appears parenthetical to the thought of the author.

Citations from the Old Testament are placed within quotation marks; longer citations are set off as block quotations in a separate indented paragraph. The sources of such citations, as well as those of many more or less subtle allusions to the Old Testament, are identified in the biblical cross-reference section at the bottom of each page. Insofar as possible, the translation of such Old Testament citations agrees with that of *The New American Bible* Old Testament whenever the underlying Greek agrees with the Hebrew (or, in some cases, the Aramaic or Greek) text from which the Old Testament translation was made. But citations in the New Testament frequently follow the Septuagint or some other version, or were made from memory, hence, in many cases the translation in the New Testament passage will not agree with what appears in the Old Testament. Some of these cases are explained in the notes.

It is a further aim of the revised edition to supply explanatory materials more abundantly than in the first edition. In most cases the introductions and notes have been entirely rewritten and expanded, and the cross-references checked and revised. It is intended that these materials should reflect the present state of sound biblical scholarship and should be presented in such a form that they can be assimilated by the ordinary intelligent reader without specialized biblical training. While they have been written with the ordinary educated Christian in mind, not all technical vocabulary can be entirely dispensed with in approaching the Bible, any more than in any other field. It is the hope of the editors that these materials, even if they sometimes demand an effort, will help the reader to a fuller and more intelligent understanding of the New Testament and a fruitful appropriation of its meaning for personal spiritual growth.

*The New American Bible* is a Roman

Catholic translation. This revision, however, like the first edition, has been accomplished with the collaboration of scholars from other Christian churches, both among the revisers and on the editorial board, in response to the encouragement of Vatican Council II (*Dei Verbum*, 22). The editorial board expresses gratitude to all who have collaborated in the revision: to all the revisers, consultants, and bishops who contributed to it, to reviewers of the first edition, and to those who voluntarily submitted suggestions. May this translation fulfill its threefold purpose, "so that the word of the Lord may speed forward and be glorified" (2 Thes 3:1).

*The Feast of St. Jerome*
*September 30, 1986*

# Introduction to the Gospels

## Susan Calef

The twenty-seven documents that comprise the New Testament all reflect upon the significance of Jesus for Christian faith. Of those documents, only the four that stand at the head of the collection—the Gospels of Matthew, Mark, Luke, and John—narrate Jesus' life and work. While the arrangement of the New Testament canon does not reflect the chronological order in which the texts were composed, placement of the Gospels at the front of the collection serves to affirm the historical priority of Jesus of Nazareth for Christian faith and the theological primacy of his story.

Texts are composed and interpreted according to conventions of form and content that determine their nature; familiarity with the conventions associated with a particular genre is necessary for proper interpretation of a piece of literature. Serious study of the Gospels therefore requires that one consider what type of writing they are. The nature of the canonical Gospels has been illumined by biblical scholars in two ways: by comparison of the Gospels to ancient text-types or genres known to us from roughly contemporaneous literatures, and by means of close examination and comparison of the Gospels themselves. Both procedures clarify the nature of canonical Gospel literature, and so, too, how these texts ought to be read and interpreted.

## The Nature of the Gospels

### Literary Genre: The Search for Parallels

Present-day readers often view the Gospels as a uniquely Christian genre, but would these texts have been viewed so by ancient audiences? In seeking to understand biblical texts in relation to their original historical and cultural contexts, biblical scholarship has sought to illumine the nature of the canonical Gospels by comparison to various genres known to us from ancient Greek, Roman, and Jewish literature. Since at least the time of Aristotle the

study of literature has classified literary works in three principal literary categories—narrative, drama, and poetry—each of which includes various subgenres based on differences of form or content. In their focus on the life, death, and Resurrection of Jesus, the Gospels may be classified as a form of narrative literature. But what is the precise nature of these narratives? Are they strictly accurate historical accounts? Are they fictional? A combination of the two? To clarify their nature further, scholars have compared them to subgenres of ancient narrative, e.g., aretalogies, epics, biographies, and novels, and in so doing, have revealed resemblances. There are obvious similarities, for example, to aretalogies, which told of humans who possessed a divine power confirmed by their miracle-working activity, some aretalogies even including a physical union between a mortal and a deity, hence, their alternate designation "divine man stories."

To persons in the ancient world familiar with the literary culture of the times, the Gospels probably looked more like biographies than anything else. The various types of biography (Greek *bios*, Latin *vita*) written in the centuries immediately before and after Christ afford fruitful comparisons: Diogenes Laertius's *Lives of the Ancient Philosophers*, Plutarch's *Lives of Famous Greeks and Romans*, and Suetonius's *Lives of the Caesars*, among others. These works present an overarching narrative of a life, beginning with the subject's birth or arrival on the public scene and ending with his death. Within this narrative framework a variety of shorter forms—anecdotes, speeches, maxims—conveyed the character of the subject. Similarly, the narrative frame of the Gospels extends from Jesus' birth or emergence on the public scene (his baptism) to his death, with a variety of short forms—sayings, genealogies, pronouncement stories, parables, miracle stories, etc.—filling the frame. This resemblance to the biographical genre does not mean, however, that the Gospels provide the degree of historical accuracy required by the canons of modern historiography. The ancient *bios* may be considered a subgenre of historical narrative, but while modern biography tends to emphasize the subject's individuality and historical particularity, the ancient form treated its subjects as stylized types (e.g., philosophers, statesmen, emperors), presenting them in terms of a typecast role and attributing to them the stereotypical virtues and vices associated with that role. The resemblance of the Gospels to the ancient biographical genre, then, does not ensure the historical accuracy of the Gospels in their entirety.

Moreover, these comparisons reveal that the Gospels are not an exact match to the ancient biographies. The most obvious difference is that Greco-Roman biographies, in addressing a social and literary elite, were written with literary pretensions and an appropriately high stylistic level; this is lacking in the Gospels. In this regard, the Gospels more closely resemble the biographical aspects of prophetic literature, which feature a simpler Hebraic style and share many elements with the Gospels. The book of Jeremiah, for example, opens with a report of the prophet's call that includes reference to God's plan before he was born (Jer 1:4–5), followed by an account of his speeches and prophetic actions, including words and acts in the Temple (Jer 7), warning of impending doom for Jerusalem, and reports of the prophet's suffering (Jer 26, 37–38). Similarly, in the Gospel of Mark, Jesus' baptismal call in accord with God's plan (Mk 1:2–11) is followed by an account of a public ministry of proclamation and mighty deeds (Mk 1:14–10:52), culminating in Jerusalem with critical words and actions in the Temple (Mk 11:15–18), warnings of trials and tribulations to come (Mk 13), and the events of Jesus' passion, death, and burial (Mk 14–15). The frequent use of Old Testament quotations and allusions in all four Gospels suggests a conscious effort to set the story of Jesus in relation to the story of God's relationship with ancient Israel; therefore, it is likely that the biographical elements of the prophetic books exerted a more direct influence on the Gospel portrayal of Jesus than did Greco-Roman biographies of emperors, philosophers, and orators.

The search for generic parallels has demonstrated that the Gospels are similar to ancient biographies but not an exact match. Given that this is the case, most scholars grant that the Gospel narratives are unique and may be classified as a singularly Christian subtype of biographical narrative. A fuller understanding of these narratives and their unique nature and purpose is gained by close comparison of the four Gospels and by investigation of the process by which they came to be written.

## Comparison of the Gospels

Those who take the time to read all four Gospels in their entirety, not piecemeal as in liturgy, soon discover that while the basic outline of the story of Jesus is similar, many of the episodes, figures, and details in the Gospel accounts are quite different. Close inspection of their contents reveals that some traditions about Jesus are found in three Gospels (the "triple tradition"), others in only two (the "double tradition"), and others in only one (the "single tradition"). The three Gospels that are most similar—Matthew, Mark, and Luke—tell the same general story in much the same way with more or less the same chronology, and so are referred to as the "Synoptic Gospels," from the Greek *synoptikos*, meaning "seen together." Indeed, reading any one of them with an eye to the other two proves enlightening in the process of interpretation. That these Gospels repeat many of the same stories in nearly identical wording suggests some kind of literary interdependence, even actual copying. But who copied from whom? Was the shortest Gospel, Mark, written first, and then copied and expanded by Matthew and Luke? Or was the shorter Mark an abridged version of Matthew or Luke? Were Matthew and Luke written independently of each other, or was one of them used in writing the other?

The problem of accounting for the multiple similarities and differences among the three Synoptic Gospels is known as "the Synoptic Problem." Based on centuries of painstaking analysis, scholarship has proposed two basic solutions to the problem. The first, offered by J. J. Griesbach in the late eighteenth century, is a variation of Augustine's view. Augustine argued that Matthew was written first, then abbreviated by Mark, then Luke drew upon them both in the writing of his Gospel. Griesbach agreed that Matthew was composed first (what scholars refer to as "Matthean Priority"), but concluded that Luke came next, and Mark used and abridged both. Despite the strengths of this "Two Gospel Hypothesis," its proponents find it difficult to explain satisfactorily why Mark left out so much of the other two. Because it is much easier to explain why Matthew and Luke would expand Mark than why Mark would delete so much of Matthew and Luke, the majority of scholars subscribe to the second solution, the "Two Source Theory," also known as the "Two Document Hypothesis."

According to this theory, Mark was composed first, then the authors of Matthew and Luke, independently of each other, incorporated most of Mark into their own compositions. Noting that Matthew and Luke also contain nearly identical sayings and parables not found in Mark (e.g., the temptation of Jesus, the Beatitudes, the Lord's Prayer, the parable of the Lost Sheep), scholars further hypothesize that both borrowed from a second source, which they designate "Q" (from the German *Quelle*, "source"). The discovery in 1945 of the *Gospel of Thomas*, a collection of sayings that includes some overlaps with the Q material, added plausibility to the Q theory. To explain the material found solely in Matthew or solely in Luke, some scholars posit the existence of two additional documents, designated "M" (for Matthean) and "L" (for Lukan) respectively.

The Gospel of John is not included in this theory, since it is by far the most distinctive of the Gospels. Although John resembles the Synoptics in telling of Jesus' ministry with the same basic elements—preaching, teaching, and healing that provokes controversy and culminates in his passion, death, and Resurrection—the material of which it is constructed differs in striking ways from that contained in the Synoptics. Some of those differences are chronological: in John Jesus' ministry spans roughly three years rather than one as in the Synoptics; his disruption of Temple commerce occurs near the start of his ministry (Jn 2:13–16), not in his final days; and Jesus dies a day

earlier, on Preparation Day. Other differences involve striking absences: Jesus' birth and baptism, his temptation and transfiguration, the institution of the Eucharist and the agony in Gethsemane, are all missing in John, as are his exorcisms and parables of the kingdom. These differences are compounded by the considerable amount of material unique to John: e.g., the signs and "I am" sayings; the foot washing, farewell, and final prayer; and revelatory conversations with figures either missing from the Synoptics (e.g., Nicodemus, the Samaritan woman at the well) or barely glimpsed there (Mary Magdalene). Due to these and other differences between the content of John and the Synoptics, scholars generally agree that the author of John seems not to have had access to the Synoptic Gospels, at least not in written form, but apparently was familiar with some of the traditions that were incorporated into the Synoptics (cleansing of the Temple, multiplication of the loaves, walking on the sea, entry into Jerusalem).

The similarities and differences between the Gospels, then, are best explained by concluding that, in the case of the Synoptics, a later Gospel develops an earlier one—that is, Matthew and Luke develop Mark and additional sources—while John develops a stream of tradition and set of sources that is for the most part quite different from that reflected in the Synoptics. Readers of the Gospels can discover this development for themselves by using a synopsis or "Gospel parallels," a tool of biblical research that aligns the Synoptic Gospels (sometimes John also) in parallel columns for ease of comparison. Viewing the Gospels laid out side by side discloses how Matthew and Luke develop their source Mark by means of additions, deletions, or simply changing the placement or wording of a particular pericope (a complete thought unit in the Gospels).[1]

---

1. Those interested in undertaking an examination of the evidence for Gospel development can work with Throckmorton's *Gospel Parallels* or access an on-line Synopsis at *http://www.utoronto.ca/religion/synopsis/*. The accounts of two significant Gospel episodes, Jesus' baptism (Mk 1:9–11//Mt 3:13–17//Lk 3:21–22) and his death (Mk 15:33–41; Mt 27:45–56; Lk 23:44–49), are especially useful places to examine the differences between them and to discover the kinds of questions that these differences raise for interpreters.

# Stages of Gospel Tradition

In addition to studying the literary interrelationship among the Gospels, modern biblical scholarship has also addressed the triple question: How, when, and why were the Gospels composed? There is general agreement that the Gospels are the end product of a three-stage process of formation, spanning roughly seventy years, in which material about Jesus was passed on and developed by the earliest generations of Christians in light of the Resurrection. This broad consensus on the history of the Gospel tradition is widely accepted by Christian interpreters of various confessional backgrounds, including the Roman Catholic Church. The Pontifical Biblical Commission made explicit use of the three stages of Gospel tradition in its *Instruction on the Historical Truth of the Gospels* (VI–X), issued in 1964. That endorsement, by Catholic biblical scholars, of the scholarly consensus was reaffirmed by Vatican Council II in its dogmatic constitution on "Divine Revelation" (*Dei Verbum* 19).

## Stage 1: The Public Activity of Jesus of Nazareth and His Disciples

The origin of the Gospel tradition may be traced to the public activity of Jesus of Nazareth late in the first third of the first century CE. That public activity, which focused on the renewal of his people Israel by proclamation of the nearness of the reign of God, was witnessed by a band of disciples who saw what Jesus said and did: what and whom he taught, how he responded to people in need, how he came to be arrested and crucified. The first stage of tradition, then, consists of the words and deeds of Jesus, living on in the memories of the disciples, becoming the raw Jesus material that was passed on and developed in subsequent stages.

## Stage 2: Christian Preaching about Jesus

The second stage of Gospel tradition consists of what Christians preached about Jesus in roughly 30–65 CE. It begins shortly after the death of Jesus, when the disciples' experience of post-Resurrection appearances (1 Cor 15:5–7) led to the conviction on which Christian faith is based: that Jesus had been raised from death and was now their living Lord. Because this original generation of preachers understood themselves as sent forth by the risen Christ, they are referred to as "apostolic," from the Greek *apostellein*, "to send forth." Initially the apostolic preaching focused not on what Jesus said and did during his public ministry but on what is known as the primitive *kerygma* (the Greek word for "proclamation"): the good news of Jesus' death and Resurrection in which his followers perceived the fulfillment of God's promise of salvation. Gradually, as the mission expanded and a network of Christian communities spread throughout the Mediterranean, memories of Jesus' words and deeds and his conflicts with opponents (stage one material) were utilized to address the emerging needs of Christians and the struggles that arose in community and mission. Thus, in the decades of oral transmission that stretched from Jesus' death to the composition of the Gospels, the raw Jesus material of stage one was shaped by preaching, catechetical needs, worship practices, and internal and external controversies.

## Stage 3: Composition of the Gospels by the Evangelists

The third stage of Gospel tradition consists of the four narratives about Jesus that were written about 65–100 CE, some forty to seventy years after the death of Jesus. As in the preceding stage of oral transmission, their composition involved a process of selection, editing, and enhancement of tradition, guided by the community's needs and the continuing presence of the risen Christ. Each of the four Gospel writers, known as "evangelists," gathered the traditions that had developed in the preceding decades, some of which had been committed to writing but are now lost (e.g., Q), then selected, shaped, and arranged them within an overall narrative framework of the life of Jesus. The scholarly consensus is that Mark was composed first, just before or after 70 CE, Matthew and Luke in the eighties, and

John in the nineties. The striking differences between the four suggest that the purpose of the evangelists in composing these quasi-biographical narratives was not simply to report the verifiable "facts" of Jesus' past historical existence, but to express the meaning and significance of Jesus for their present lives of faith (Lk 1:1–4; Jn 20:30–31).

The Gospels, then, are a composite of materials from all three stages: the words and deeds of Jesus as witnessed and remembered by his disciples (stage one), which were subsequently reflected upon and developed in the preaching, catechesis, and worship of Christian communities in the decades after his death and Resurrection (stage two), then further developed by the Gospel writers (stage three). Thus they contain earlier and later layers of material: the original Jesus layer, the layer of early Christian preaching, and the layer of the evangelists. Or to put it differently, the Gospels contain multiple voices: the remembered voice of Jesus, the voices of apostolic preachers, and the voices of the evangelists. Together they preserve for future generations the original disciples' *past* experience of Jesus of Nazareth and early Christians' *present* experience of him as their risen Lord. Reading and interpreting the Gospels properly, then, requires an appreciation of this combination of memory and testimony, of history and faith.

## The Question of Authorship

Christians generally assume that the authorship of the Gospels is indicated by their traditional titles, "Gospel According to Matthew," "Gospel According to Mark," and so on. However, because the original manuscripts of the Gospels (i.e., the *autographs* or signature copies) no longer exist, it is difficult to ascertain whether the texts originally bore these titles. Based on intensive study of the ancient manuscripts, scholars conclude that the Gospels get their traditional names from the headings of the Greek manuscripts, the oldest of which are dated to around 200 CE, more than a hundred years after the writing of the latest Gospel, John. The earliest titles in these manuscripts

consisted of just two words, *kata*, "according to," followed by the name of the evangelist. In the absence of such a naming convention (*kata* + author's name) for ancient literary works, it seems unlikely that four authors would have arrived, independently, at the exact same mode of designation; therefore, most scholars conclude that these stereotypical titles were affixed to them only after all four had been collected together and accepted as authoritative.

Similarly, the early tradition that attributes two Gospels to apostles who were eyewitnesses of Jesus' ministry (Matthew and John) and the other two to "apostolic men" (i.e., companions of apostles, with Mark thought to be a companion of Peter, and Luke a companion of Paul) now appears dubious. The striking differences among the Gospels and the evidence for borrowing among them suggest that the Gospels are not eyewitness reports. New Testament scholarship generally holds that the four Gospels were written anonymously.

## Use of the Word "Gospel"

The word "gospel," derived from the Anglo-Saxon *godspell*, meaning "good news," translates the New Testament Greek noun *euangelion* (Latin *evangelium*), which still survives in "evangelist" and related English words. For most Christians, "gospel" is, first and foremost, a designation for the four canonical texts that bear the names Matthew, Mark, Luke, and John, and so, a familiar genre of canonical Christian literature. Use of the word "gospel" (*euangelion*) for a written text, however, represents a late and secondary development in Christian usage of the term. The original and primary use of "gospel" by Christians reflects their cultural matrix, where it refers to various forms of messages. In the Greek translation of the Hebrew Bible (the Septuagint), for example, the noun *euangelion* was used in the plural to translate the Hebrew term for "good news" (e.g., 2 Sm 4:10). Especially pertinent, in view of its later usage in the New Testament, the related Greek verb, *euangelizesthai* ("to proclaim good news"), occurs multiple times in Isaiah in reference to the good news of the advent of God's reign (e.g., Is 40:9–11; 52:7–10; 61:1). Similarly, textual evidence from the early Roman Empire indicates that *euangelion* was part of the vocabulary of Roman propaganda, referring, for example, to public proclamation of significant imperial events such as the emperor's birthday, a Roman military victory, or the ascent of a new emperor to the throne. Thus, in the cultural context from which the New Testament comes, the noun *euangelion* is used for various forms of public good news.

The term first appears in Christian literature in the letters of Paul, who uses it in formulaic phrases such as "the gospel of God" (Rom 1:1; 15:16), "the gospel of Christ" (Rom 15:19; 1 Cor 9:12; 1 Thes 3:2), and "the gospel of his Son" (Rom 1:9). In Paul both "gospel" (*euangelion*) and the related verb "to proclaim the gospel" (*euangelizethai*) are technical terms for the Christian message of salvation that focused on the death, Resurrection, and exaltation of Jesus (Rom 1:2–4; 1 Cor 15:2–5) and for its proclamation. Only two of the canonical Gospels use the noun "gospel" (Mark and Matthew). Mark introduces his account, "The beginning of the gospel (*euangelion*) of Jesus Christ [the Son of God]" (Mk 1:1). Here the term *euangelion* does not designate the literary genre of Mark's work, but the primary message of his narrative, namely, that Jesus is the Christ, the Son of God. Similar to Paul, in Mark, "gospel" refers both to the message Jesus preached as the "gospel of God" (Mk 1:14–15) and to the message that disciples must preach to all the nations (Mk 8:35; 13:10). Although Matthew

qualifies the noun, most often as "the gospel of the kingdom" (Mt 4:23; 9:35; 24:14), his use of *euangelion* is consistent with Mark's, referring to the good news of salvation preached first by Jesus, then by the church. It was not until the mid-second century that the noun "gospel" was used for a literary work, when Justin Martyr writes that "the Apostles in their memoirs, which are called gospels, have handed down what Jesus ordered them to do" (*1 Apol.* 66.3).

From this point onward the narratives about Jesus became known as "the Gospel according to Matthew," "the Gospel according to Mark," and so on. Recent discoveries, however, reveal that several writings not in the biblical canon, some of a totally different content and text-type, were also designated as "gospels," such as *Gospel of Thomas*, *Gospel of Mary*, and *Gospel of Philip*. Unlike the canonical Gospels, these extracanonical or "apocryphal" gospels come in a variety of forms: *Gospel of Thomas*, for example, is a collection of sayings, while *Gospel of Mary* narrates post-Resurrection conversations between the risen Christ and his disciples. (See the article "Deuterocanonical and Noncanonical Scriptures.") The fact that writings of such diverse text-types were all designated "Gospels" suggests that even at this later stage of usage, the term retained its original and primary referent, i.e., the message of salvation associated with Jesus, and that Christian writers of the first four centuries chose to convey that message for their communities in various forms or genres. ∎

# THE GOSPELS

## New American Bible, Introduction

The collection of writings that constitutes the New Testament begins with four gospels. Next comes the Acts of the Apostles, followed by twenty-one letters that are attributed to Paul, James, Peter, John, and Jude. Finally, at the end of the early church's scriptures stands the Revelation to John. Virtually all Christians agree that these twenty-seven books constitute the "canon," a term that means "rule" and designates the list of writings that are regarded as authoritative for Christian faith and life.

It is the purpose of this Introduction to describe those features that are common to the four gospels. A similar treatment of the letters of the New Testament is provided in the two Introductions that appear before the Letter to the Romans and before the Letter of James, respectively. The Acts of the Apostles, a work that is both historical and theological, and Revelation, an apocalyptic work, have no counterparts in the New Testament; the special Introductions prefixed to these books treat of the literary characteristics proper to each of them.

While the New Testament contains four writings called "gospels," there is in reality only one gospel running through all of the Christian scriptures, the gospel of and about Jesus Christ. Our English word "gospel" translates the Greek term *euangelion*, meaning "good news." This noun was used in the plural by the Greek translators of the Old Testament to render the Hebrew term for "good news" (2 Sm 4:10; possibly also 2 Sm 18:20, 25). But it is the corresponding verb *euangelizomai*, "to proclaim good news," that was especially significant in preparing for the New Testament idea of "gospel," since this term is used by Deutero-Isaiah of announcing the great victory of God that was to establish his universal kingship and inaugurate the new age (Is 40:9; 52:7; 61:1).

Paul used the word *euangelion* to designate the message that he and the other apostles proclaimed, the "gospel of God" (Rom 1:1; 15:16; 2 Cor 11:7; 1 Thes 2:2, 8–9). He often referred to it simply as "the gospel" (Rom 1:16; 10:16; 11:28; etc) or, because of its content and origin, as "the gospel of Christ" (Rom 15:19; 1 Cor 9:12; 1 Thes 3:2; etc). Because of its personal meaning for him and his own particular manner of telling the story about Jesus Christ and of explaining the significance of his cross and resurrection, Paul also referred to this message as "my gospel" (Rom 2:16; cf. Gal 1:11; 2:2) or "our gospel" (2 Cor 4:3; 1 Thes 1:5; 2 Thes 2:14).

It was Mark, as far as we know, who first applied the term "gospel" to a book telling the story of Jesus; see Mk 1:1 and the note there. This form of presenting Jesus' life, works, teachings, passion, and resurrection was developed further by the other evangelists; see the Introduction to each gospel. The first three of the canonical gospels, Matthew, Mark, and Luke, are so similar at many points when viewed together, particularly when arranged in parallel columns or lines, that they are called "synoptic" gospels, from the Greek word for such a general view. The fourth gospel, John, often differs significantly from the synoptics in outline and approach. This work never uses the word "gospel" or its corresponding verb; nevertheless, its message concerns the same Jesus, and the reader is urged to believe in him as the Messiah, "that through this belief you may have life in his name" (Jn 20:31).

From the second century onward, the practice arose of designating each of these four books as a "gospel," understood as a title, and of adding a phrase with a name that identified the traditional author, e.g., "The Gospel according to Matthew." The arrangement of the canon that was adopted, with the four gospels grouped together at the beginning followed by Acts, provides a massive focus upon Jesus and allows Acts to serve as a framework for the letters of the New Testament. This order, however, conceals the fact that Luke's two volumes, a gospel and Acts, were intended by their author to go together. It further obscures the point that Paul's letters were written before any of our gospels, though the sayings and deeds of Jesus stand behind all the New Testament writings.

**ROMAN EMPIRE IN FIRST CENTURY CE**

© 2013 ANSELM ACADEMIC

ARMENIA

MEDIA

MESOPOTAMIA

ARABIAN DESERT

Damascus

SYRIA

JUDEA

Jerusalem

Red Sea

Black Sea

CRIMEA

CAPPADOCIA

CILICIA

LYCIA

CYPRUS

EGYPT

Alexandria

ASIA MINOR

Ephesus

THRACE

Byzantium

MACEDONIA

Athens

CRETE

LIBYA

Cyrene

Mediterranean Sea

DACIA

DALMATIA

Adriatic Sea

Baltic Sea

Rome

Milan

CORSICA

SARDINIA

SICILY

Syracuse

Carthage

NUMIDIA

SAHARA DESERT

North Sea

JUTLAND

GERMANY

Cologne

BELGIUM

GAUL

Lyons

Massilia

BRITAIN

ATLANTIC OCEAN

SPAIN

MAURETANIA

Gades

500 miles

500 kilometers

250

250

0

0

## INTRODUCTION

Warren Carter

## Author

The Gospel of Matthew twice mentions a disciple of Jesus named Matthew (Mt 9:9; 10:3). We commonly think of this Matthew as the Gospel's author, but this is probably not so. This disciple plays a minor role in the Gospel, and his name is not linked with the Gospel until late in the second century, some one hundred years after it was written.

How, then, are we to understand the linking of the name "Matthew" with this Gospel? One possibility is that a person named "Matthew," possibly a Jewish follower of Jesus, was significant in founding or leading the community of Jesus-followers from which the Gospel later emerged. Or perhaps he was an important teacher in shaping the message about Jesus that is reflected in the Gospel. Or perhaps the name is symbolic, pointing not so much to the Gospel's source as to its reception. The name "Matthew" is similar to two Greek words, one meaning "disciple," the other meaning "learn." Perhaps the name symbolizes the Gospel's ideal reader as one who is a disciple or follower of Jesus who wants to learn about following Jesus from this Gospel story.

## Date and Place of Writing

The Gospel was written in the last few decades of the first century CE. Several times it refers to the Romans destroying Jerusalem and its Temple at the end of the Jewish war of 66–70 CE (Mt 21:41; 22:7; 24:2, 15–16). In addition, several writings by Jesus-followers early in the second century refer to content in this Gospel (e.g., *Didache*, letters of Ignatius). These references establish a window of ca. 80–ca.100 CE for the Gospel's composition. It was written perhaps in Galilee or in Syria, possibly in the city of Antioch.

## Outline of Matthew

I.   **The Infancy Narrative (1:1–2:23)**

II.  **The Proclamation of the Kingdom (3:1–7:29)**

III. **Ministry and Mission in Galilee (8:1–11:1)**

IV.  **Opposition from Israel (11:2–13:53)**

V.   **Jesus, the Kingdom, and the Church (13:54–18:35)**

VI.  **Ministry in Judea and Jerusalem (19:1–25:46)**

VII. **The Passion and Resurrection (26:1–28:20)**

This means that some fifty years separate the ministry and crucifixion of Jesus (around 30 CE) from the writing of the Gospel (80–100 CE). The Gospel, then, is not an eyewitness account of Jesus' ministry. Rather, it appears to draw upon other sources, including the Gospel of Mark and a collection of sayings Jesus scholars have labeled "Q." It is not a day-by-day record of what Jesus said and did, but reflects an understanding about Jesus' significance that developed among his followers during the fifty intervening years. In learning to read the Gospel, it is important to recognize the geographical and temporal distance between this account of Jesus' activity and his ministry in the twenties and thirties.

## Type of Writing (Genre)

Also important for our reading of the Gospel is recognizing what type of literature it is. Its genre most closely resembles that of an ancient biography. Modern biographies often

MT

"dish the dirt" with juicy details about the subject's lifestyle and upbringing. Ancient biographies, however, were different.

Usually written for the small percentage of wealthy, powerful, and high-status people in the Roman Empire who could read, ancient biographies typically had as their subjects similar sorts of people. Mostly these were men, typically political or military leaders such as an emperor, though some biographies of philosophers were also written. Biographies described actions and qualities typical of the power and privilege of this ruling group. They usually used a chronological framework and episodic structure to narrate their subject's birth, actions, teaching, and death. Biographies were concerned not just with "facts" but with presenting the person either positively, as one who upheld societal virtues and practices, or negatively, as one who violated those values. Commonly they honored the person's memory, describing noble actions and virtuous teachings, instructing and entertaining readers, eliciting praise and providing a noble role model to shape how their readers might live.

Matthew's Gospel displays some of these features. It employs a chronological sequence, beginning with Jesus' conception and birth (Mt 1:1–4:16). It narrates his public ministry in Galilee as a Jewish man (4:17–16:20), his repeated predictions of his death and journey to Jerusalem (16:21–20:34), his death there (chs. 21–27), and his Resurrection by God (ch. 28). The Gospel uses an episodic structure to narrate his actions and teaching. It presents Jesus positively in terms of his central mission or destiny to manifest God's saving presence among people (1:21–23). It seeks to shape how readers live as followers of Jesus, with short scenes that describe his actions and with five lengthy accounts of his teaching (see chs. 5–7, 10, 13, 18, 24–25).

But there is one huge difference between the Gospel and ancient biographies. Jesus was not one of the elite and powerful "great men" of his time. He was not a political leader, military commander, or famous philosopher from an important city. On the contrary, he was one of the little people. He came from "nowhere" places like Bethlehem, Nazareth, and Capernaum (Mt 2:1, 22–23; 4:13). He had no

illustrious teachers, political allies, or military power. He challenged societal values with his teaching about the "reign" or "empire" of God (4:17). He shaped a community of followers to live with different values, practices, and structures (20:24–28). He died on a cross because he challenged the powerful leaders, both the Roman governor Pilate and his allies, the Jerusalem leaders based in the Temple. But the Gospel shows that their power was limited and contrary to God's purposes: they could not keep him dead. God raised him from the dead and gave him a share in "all power in heaven and on earth" (28:18), power that belongs to God, not to the Roman Empire.

In this way, the Gospel takes a genre that usually upholds the hierarchical structures and commitments of the ruling elite in Rome's empire and subverts it. In telling the story of Jesus, it shows that God is not allied with the powerful. God is at work in the world not to uphold the structures of the Roman Empire, but to transform them.

This biography addresses followers of Jesus living some fifty years after his time. From the way the story is told, we can surmise that the Gospel addresses circumstances that were difficult for two reasons. One difficulty involved conflict within the synagogue, the other negotiating Roman power on a daily basis.

# Difficult Circumstances

## Conflict within the Synagogue

One set of difficult circumstances concerns conflict with other members of the synagogue or synagogues of which these followers of Jesus were members. The tragic destruction of the Temple and Jerusalem in 70 CE by the Roman army reverberated among Jewish communities. This devastation raised significant theological issues and questions about the identity, way of life, and future of Jewish communities in the Roman Empire. What was God doing? Had God withdrawn God's presence and blessing? Was the event punishment? If so, was there forgiveness? How should they live in the future so as to prevent such a terrible thing happening again?

Through the telling of the story of Jesus,

Matthew's Gospel presents its interpretation of this post-70 CE situation and the issues that it raised. First, the Gospel explains the destruction of Jerusalem and its Temple as punishment on the rulers of Galilee and Judea for rejecting Jesus (Mt 22:1–10). So after Jesus enters Jerusalem for the first time, he goes straight to the Temple (the seat of their power), drives out money changers, and, quoting Jer 7:11, declares the Temple leadership to be "thieves" or brigands whose rule attacks and harms the people's well-being (Mt 21:12–13). He then tells several parables in which a landowner and a king (representing God, 21:33; 22:2) send "his son" and "servants" (Jesus, 21:37; 22:3, 4, 6, 8) to leaders who reject them (21:38–39; 22:6). The parables narrate the tragic consequences, which include their death and the burning of their city (21:41; 22:7). This destruction interprets Jerusalem's fall to the Romans in 70 CE as God's judgment on the leaders for rejecting Jesus (21:45–46).

But second, the Gospel declares that this judgment on the leaders is not the end. The Gospel presents Jesus as God's representative and revealer of God's will. It identifies Jesus, God's chosen agent, as "Christ" (Mt 1:1), a Greek equivalent to the Hebrew "Messiah." Both words mean "anointed," referring to an action that shows someone to be commissioned to be God's representative. Jesus is likewise identified as God's "Son" (3:17), another way of saying God has chosen him to be the agent of God's purposes.

So the Gospel begins with a genealogy for Jesus, thereby setting him in the context of Israel's history and showing him to be God's agent (Mt 1:1–17). Then it makes a big deal about naming him "Jesus" ("God saves") as a way of showing what his special commission or role is to be (1:18–25). Jesus is commissioned to save from sin and manifest God's presence (1:21–23).

Subsequently the Gospel shows Jesus carrying out his mission of manifesting God's saving presence in various ways. He calls disciples to form a new community (Mt 4:18–22) and teaches them (e.g., chs. 5–7, the Sermon on the Mount). He casts out demons and heals the sick (e.g., 8:28–9:8). He forgives sin (9:1–8; 26:26–29). He also declares that he represents God's presence wherever his followers gather (18:20) and when they engage in mission to the rest of the world (28:18–20). In presenting Jesus' identity as God's commissioned agent, and in showing him at work, the Gospel offers reassurance that God has not abandoned the people; God is present with them, forgives them, and is at work to transform their world.

Moreover, in five big blocks of teaching material, the Gospel shows Jesus teaching God's will and revealing God's purposes, shaping the identity and way of life of his followers (chs. 5–7, 10, 13, 18, 24–25). Jesus' teaching includes the surprising announcement of situations in which God's blessing is encountered: among the poor (most of the population), whose poverty corrodes their very being or spirit; among those who work for justice and show mercy; among those whose hearts and lives are committed to God's purposes of wholeness ("peace"), whatever the price (5:3–12). Jesus also interprets Israel's Scriptures to declare what is central to God's will for how people are to live (5:21–48). Twice, for example, he quotes from the prophet Hosea to declare that in the post-Temple world it is not sacrifice that God desires (Hos 6:6; Mt 9:13; 12:7). Mercy is an important value in the Gospel, defining how people are to treat each other (5:7; 9:13; 12:7; 18:21–35). In 25:31–46, Jesus explains that mercy is not just a feeling but is demonstrated in actions that relieve the harsh conditions of many in his society: feeding the hungry, giving drink to the thirsty, welcoming the stranger, clothing the naked, caring for the sick, visiting those in prison. Quoting from Dt 6:5 and Lv 19:18, he declares that at the heart of God's will is the double command to love God and neighbor (Mt 22:34–40).

Through this presentation of Jesus' actions and teaching, Matthew's Gospel reassures people after the terrible events of the destruction of Jerusalem and the Temple in 70 CE that God has not abandoned them or withdrawn God's presence and blessing. God's agent, Jesus, provides the way ahead. God has commissioned or chosen Jesus to reveal God's purposes in his actions and teaching, shaping the identity and way of life of God's people.

It is clear, though, from the Gospel's presentation that other members of the synagogue did

M
T

not accept the message of Jesus as recounted in this Gospel. The Gospel indicates considerable tension between Jesus-followers and the rest of the synagogue communities. Though Jesus is active in synagogues (Mt 4:23; 9:35), things do not go well for him there. The Gospel presents synagogues as places of conflict and rejection (12:9–14; 13:54–58). The Gospel describes the synagogues as being full of hypocrites (6:2, 5) and perpetrators of violence toward Jesus' followers (10:17). Throughout the narrative, Jesus constantly conflicts with leaders such as scribes, Pharisees, and chief priests (9:2–8; 12:1–14; 16:1–12; 26:57–68). They clash over how to interpret the Scriptures and over how God's will is to be practiced in matters such as observing the sabbath (12:1–14), caring for the elderly (15:1–9), divorce (19:3–12), and paying taxes (22:15–22). Those who oppose Jesus think he is a blasphemer (9:3), an agent not of God but of the devil (9:34; 12:24), without authority for his actions and teaching (21:23–27). In turn, Jesus declares them disqualified from God's purposes (15:7–9), warns against their teaching (16:9–12), and in the terrible ch. 23 he curses them. At the heart of this conflict is the issue of Jesus' identity. They reject his identity and authority as God's agent chosen to manifest God's will, presence, forgiveness, and purposes.

It seems, then, that the Gospel tells the story of Jesus in such a way as to address the circumstances at the time the Gospel was composed in the eighties CE. This situation is marked in part by struggles among synagogue members to make sense of the events of 70 CE and to discern a faithful way ahead. The Gospel sees Jesus as the key figure; others in the synagogue do not. The Gospel inscribes this bitter conflict in its story of Jesus.

## A Warning

This Gospel is harsh in presenting the conflict between Jesus, synagogues, and Jewish leaders. Jesus says some nasty things that are problematic for contemporary readers of the Gospel (e.g., ch. 23). The history of reading this Gospel over the last two millennia shows that its language can easily become a source of hostile anti-Jewish thought, rhetoric, and

action for Christians. The Gospel provides absolutely no warrant for such responses by contemporary readers, yet many have misread it nonetheless.

It is important to understand the specific circumstances from which the Gospel emerged. The particular conflictual circumstances that shaped this rhetoric are in no way binding on Christians for all times. The Gospel reflects a particular situation that is no longer our situation. The Gospel offers no lasting judgment on or rejection of Jewish people or institutions. In fact, strange as it may seem after such historical misreading, the Gospel presents Jesus declaring that God is merciful to everyone on Earth and that Jesus' followers are to imitate this mercy in order to be God's children (Mt 5:45).

## Daily Life in the Roman Empire

The Gospel addresses a second set of difficult circumstances for Jesus-followers. The destruction of Jerusalem and its Temple in 70 CE raised not only religious issues, but had political and military implications as well. It was a fresh assertion of Roman power. It made an example out of the Jewish people, some of whom had wanted freedom from Roman rule. It was a reminder to people living anywhere in the empire that Roman power was not to be challenged, and a warning of the drastic consequences that would follow if it was.

The challenge of living in this Roman world was especially acute for Jesus-followers. After all, they followed one whom Roman authorities had put to death on a cross. Rome used crucifixion, a cruel form of the death penalty, as punishment for runaway slaves, for bandits who attacked elite personnel and their property, and for insurrectionists who revolted against Roman rule. Crucifixion thus functioned as a deterrent, a means of keeping people in line. Jesus' death by crucifixion places him in such company. It attests that an alliance comprising the Roman governor Pilate, the face of Roman power in Judea, and the Jerusalem leaders with whom Pilate shared power, viewed Jesus as a threat. This alliance was typical of the way Rome ruled. Jesus' critique of the Jewish leaders and the Temple that was the basis for their power threatened not only them but also their allies, the Romans, who sanctioned their rule.

Matthew's Gospel explains the nature of Jesus' challenge to the ruling powers. In part Jesus dies because he announces and enacts God's empire or kingdom (Mt 4:17). God's ways are not Roman ways as Jesus teaches and demonstrates in his healings, feedings, and exorcisms. Many sick people occupy the world of the Gospel (4:23; 9:35) because Rome's imperial structures ensure that the ruling elite have plenty to eat while most of the rest struggle for daily sustenance. In such conditions, diseases of deprivation and contagion are rife. Jesus' healings and feedings (cf. 14:13–21; 15:32–39) anticipate the physical wholeness and abundant fertility that the prophets picture when God's reign or empire is established in full (Is 35:1–7).

The Gospel presents this Roman-ruled, sinful world as being in the hands of the devil. In the temptation story, the devil claims that he controls all the empires of the world and offers them to Jesus if Jesus would bow down to him (Mt 4:8–9). Jesus' exorcisms, or casting out of the devil's agents (known as demons), show his victory over the devil's control as Jesus sets people free (8:28–34). The Gospel also shows that Rome's empire is under judgment. Jesus declares that when he returns in the last days to establish God's empire or reign in full, God will destroy Rome's empire (24:27–34).

The nations, such as the Roman Empire, will be condemned because they have not cared for the broken and powerless (25:31–46). In fact, their sinful structures of power that rule for the benefit of the elite at the expense of the rest have created these unjust and harmful circumstances.

How, then, are followers of Jesus, who was crucified by Rome, to live in this world? The Gospel provides several guidelines. Those who follow Jesus are to understand God's perspective on the empire as controlled by the devil and under God's judgment. But they are also to understand that its power is not ultimate. The empire could not keep Jesus dead. God raised him from the dead (Mt 28). Disciples are not to "offer . . . [violent] resistance" but are to find active, non-violent ways of negotiating Roman power (5:39–42). They are to pay taxes but to do so recognizing that the earth belongs to God, not to Rome (17:24–27; 22:15–22). They are to pray for God's will and rule to be established (6:9–13). They are to reject hierarchical structures of power over people as contrary to God's will (20:20–28). They are to care for and support one another with practices marked by practical mercy, love, and forgiveness (5:42; 6:9–13; ch. 18; 22:34–40; 25:34–36).

The Gospel thus continues to shape the identity and way of living of those who follow Jesus in a world often not structured according to God's purposes of abundant life for all people. ■

# THE GOSPEL ACCORDING TO MATTHEW

## New American Bible, Introduction

The position of the Gospel according to Matthew as the first of the four gospels in the New Testament reflects both the view that it was the first to be written, a view that goes back to the late second century A.D., and the esteem in which it was held by the church; no other was so frequently quoted in the noncanonical literature of earliest Christianity. Although the majority of scholars now reject the opinion about the time of its composition, the high estimation of this work remains. The reason for that becomes clear upon study of the way in which Matthew presents his story of Jesus, the demands of Christian discipleship, and the breaking-in of the new and final age through the ministry but particularly through the death and resurrection of Jesus.

The gospel begins with a narrative prologue (Mt 1:1–2:23), the first part of which is a genealogy of Jesus starting with Abraham, the father of Israel (Mt 1:1–17). Yet at the beginning of that genealogy Jesus is designated as "the son of David, the son of Abraham" (Mt 1:1). The kingly ancestor who lived about a thousand years after Abraham is named first, for this is the genealogy of Jesus Christ, the Messiah, the royal anointed one (Mt 1:16). In the first of the episodes of the infancy narrative that follow the genealogy, the mystery of Jesus' person is declared. He is conceived of a virgin by the power of the Spirit of God (Mt 1:18–25). The first of the gospel's fulfillment citations, whose purpose it is to show that he was the one to whom the prophecies of Israel were pointing, occurs here (Mt 1:23): he shall be named Emmanuel, for in him God is with us.

The announcement of the birth of this newborn king of the Jews greatly troubles not only King Herod but all Jerusalem (Mt 2:1–3), yet the Gentile magi are overjoyed to find him and offer him their homage and their gifts (Mt 2:10–11). Thus his ultimate rejection by the mass of his own people and his acceptance by the Gentile nations is foreshadowed. He must be taken to Egypt to escape the murderous plan of Herod. By his sojourn there and

his subsequent return after the king's death he relives the Exodus experience of Israel. The words of the Lord spoken through the prophet Hosea, "Out of Egypt I called my son," are fulfilled in him (Mt 2:15); if Israel was God's son, Jesus is so in a way far surpassing the dignity of that nation, as his marvelous birth and the unfolding of his story show (see Mt 3:17; 4:1–11; 11:27; 14:33; 16:16; 27:54). Back in the land of Israel, he must be taken to Nazareth in Galilee because of the danger to his life in Judea, where Herod's son Archelaus is now ruling (Mt 2:22–23). The sufferings of Jesus in the infancy narrative anticipate those of his passion, and if his life is spared in spite of the dangers, it is because his destiny is finally to give it on the cross as "a ransom for many" (Mt 20:28). Thus the word of the angel will be fulfilled, ". . . he will save his people from their sins" (Mt 1:21; cf. Mt 26:28).

In Mt 4:12 Matthew begins his account of the ministry of Jesus, introducing it by the preparatory preaching of John the Baptist (Mt 3:1–12), the baptism of Jesus that culminates in God's proclaiming him his "beloved Son" (Mt 3:13–17), and the temptation in which he proves his true sonship by his victory over the devil's attempt to deflect him from the way of obedience to the Father (Mt 4:1–11). The central message of Jesus' preaching is the coming of the kingdom of heaven and the need for repentance, a complete change of heart and conduct, on the part of those who are to receive this great gift of God (Mt 4:17). Galilee is the setting for most of his ministry; he leaves there for Judea only in Mt 19:1, and his ministry in Jerusalem, the goal of his journey, is limited to a few days (Mt 21:1–25:46).

In this extensive material there are five great discourses of Jesus, each concluding with the formula "When Jesus finished these words" or one closely similar (Mt 7:28; 11:1; 13:53; 19:1; 26:1). These are an important structure of the gospel. In every case the discourse is preceded by a narrative section, each narrative and discourse together constituting a "book" of the gospel. The discourses are, respectively, the "Sermon on the Mount" (Mt 5:3–7:27), the missionary discourse (Mt 10:5–42), the parable discourse (Mt 13:3–52), the "church order" discourse (Mt 18:3–35), and the eschatological discourse (Mt 24:4–25:46). In large measure the material of these discourses came to Matthew from his tradition, but his work in modifying and adding to what he had received is abundantly evident. No other evangelist gives the teaching of Jesus with such elegance and order as he.

In the "Sermon on the Mount" the theme of righteousness is prominent, and even at this early stage of the ministry the note of opposition is struck between Jesus and the Pharisees, who are designated as "the hypocrites" (Mt 6:2, 5, 16). The righteousness of his disciples must surpass that of the scribes and Pharisees; otherwise, in spite of their alleged following of Jesus, they will not enter into the kingdom of heaven (Mt 5:20). Righteousness means doing the will of the heavenly Father (Mt 7:21), and his will is proclaimed in a manner that is startling to all who have identified it with the law of Moses. The antitheses of the Sermon (Mt 5:21–48) both accept (Mt 5:21–30, 43–48) and reject (Mt 5:31–42) elements of that law, and in the former case the understanding of the law's demands is deepened and extended. The antitheses are the best commentary on the meaning of Jesus' claim that he has come not to abolish but to fulfill the law (Mt 5:17). What is meant by fulfillment of the law is not the demand to keep it exactly as it stood before the coming of Jesus, but rather his bringing the law to be a lasting expression of the will of God, and in that fulfillment there is much that will pass away. Should this appear contradictory to his saying that "until heaven and earth pass away" not even the smallest part of the law will pass (Mt 5:18), that time of fulfillment is not the dissolution of the universe but the coming of the new age, which will occur with Jesus' death and resurrection. While righteousness in the new age will continue to mean conduct that is in accordance with the law, it will be conduct in accordance with the law as expounded and interpreted by Jesus (cf. Mt 28:20, ". . . all that I have commanded you").

Though Jesus speaks harshly about the Pharisees in the Sermon, his judgment is not solely a condemnation of them. The Pharisees are portrayed as a negative example for his disciples, and his condemnation of those who claim to belong to him while disobeying his word is no less severe (Mt 7:21–23, 26–27).

In Mt 4:23 a summary statement of Jesus' activity speaks not only of his teaching and proclaiming the gospel but of his "curing every disease and illness among the people"; this is repeated almost verbatim in Mt 9:35. The narrative section that follows the Sermon on the Mount (Mt 8:1–9:38) is composed principally of accounts of those merciful deeds of Jesus, but it is far from being simply a collection of stories about miraculous cures. The nature of the community that Jesus will establish is shown; it will always be under the protection of him whose power can deal with all dangers (Mt 8:23–27), but it is only for those who are prepared to follow him at whatever cost (Mt 8:16–22), not only believing Israelites but Gentiles who have come to faith in him (Mt 8:10–12). The disciples begin to have some insight, however imperfect, into the mystery of Jesus' person. They wonder about him whom "the winds and the sea obey" (Mt 8:27), and they witness his bold declaration of the forgiveness of the paralytic's sins (Mt 9:2). That episode of the narrative moves on two levels. When the crowd sees the cure that testifies to the authority of Jesus, the Son of Man, to forgive sins (Mt 9:6), they glorify God "who had given such authority to human beings" (Mt 9:8). The forgiveness of sins is now not the prerogative of Jesus alone but of "human beings," that is, of the disciples who constitute the community of Jesus, the church. The ecclesial character of this narrative section could hardly be more plainly indicated.

The end of the section prepares for the discourse on the church's mission (Mt 10:5–42). Jesus is moved to pity at the sight of the crowds who are like sheep without a shepherd (Mt 9:36), and he sends out the twelve disciples to make the proclamation with which his own ministry began, "The kingdom of heaven is at hand" (Mt 10:7; cf. Mt 4:17), and to drive out demons and cure the sick as he has done (Mt 10:1). Their mission is limited to Israel (Mt 10:5–6) as Jesus' own was (Mt 15:24), yet in

Mt 15:16 that perspective broadens and the discourse begins to speak of the mission that the disciples will have after the resurrection and of the severe persecution that will attend it (Mt 10:18). Again, the discourse moves on two levels: that of the time of Jesus and that of the time of the church.

The narrative section of the third book (Mt 11:2–12:50) deals with the growing opposition to Jesus. Hostility toward him has already been manifested (Mt 8:10; 9:3, 10–13, 34), but here it becomes more intense. The rejection of Jesus comes, as before, from Pharisees, who take "counsel against him to put him to death" (Mt 12:14) and repeat their earlier accusation that he drives out demons because he is in league with demonic power (Mt 12:22–24). But they are not alone in their rejection. Jesus complains of the lack of faith of "this generation" of Israelites (Mt 11:16–19) and reproaches the towns "where most of his mighty deeds had been done" for not heeding his call to repentance (Mt 11:20–24). This dark picture is relieved by Jesus' praise of the Father who has enabled "the childlike" to accept him (Mt 11:25–27), but on the whole the story is one of opposition to his word and blindness to the meaning of his deeds. The whole section ends with his declaring that not even the most intimate blood relationship with him counts for anything; his only true relatives are those who do the will of his heavenly Father (Mt 12:48–50).

The narrative of rejection leads up to the parable discourse (Mt 13:3–52). The reason given for Jesus' speaking to the crowds in parables is that they have hardened themselves against his clear teaching, unlike the disciples to whom knowledge of "the mysteries of the kingdom has been granted" (Mt 13:10–16). In Mt 13:36 he dismisses the crowds and continues the discourse to his disciples alone, who claim, at the end, to have understood all that he has said (Mt 13:51). But, lest the impression be given that the church of Jesus is made up only of true disciples, the explanation of the parable of the weeds among the wheat (Mt 13:37–43), as well as the parable of the net thrown into the sea "which collects fish of every kind" (Mt 13:47–49), shows that it is composed of both the righteous and the wicked,

and that separation between the two will be made only at the time of the final judgment.

In the narrative that constitutes the first part of the fourth book of the gospel (Mt 13:54–17:27), Jesus is shown preparing for the establishment of his church with its teaching authority that will supplant the blind guidance of the Pharisees (Mt 15:13–14), whose teaching, curiously said to be that of the Sadducees also, is repudiated by Jesus as the norm for his disciples (Mt 16:6, 11–12). The church of Jesus will be built on Peter (Mt 16:18), who will be given authority to bind and loose on earth, an authority whose exercise will be confirmed in heaven (Mt 16:19). The metaphor of binding and loosing has a variety of meanings, among them that of giving authoritative teaching. This promise is made to Peter directly after he has confessed Jesus to be the Messiah, the Son of the living God (Mt 16:16), a confession that he has made as the result of revelation given to him by the heavenly Father (Mt 16:17); Matthew's ecclesiology is based on his high christology.

Directly after that confession Jesus begins to instruct his disciples about how he must go the way of suffering and death (Mt 16:21). Peter, who has been praised for his confession, protests against this and receives from Jesus the sharpest of rebukes for attempting to deflect Jesus from his God-appointed destiny. The future rock upon whom the church will be built is still a man of "little faith" (see Mt 14:31). Both he and the other disciples must know not only that Jesus will have to suffer and die but that they too will have to follow him on the way of the cross if they are truly to be his disciples (Mt 16:24–25).

The discourse following this narrative (Mt 18:1–35) is often called the "church order" discourse, although that title is perhaps misleading since the emphasis is not on the structure of the church but on the care that the disciples must have for one another in respect to guarding each other's faith in Jesus (Mt 18:6–7), to seeking out those who have wandered from the fold (Mt 18:10–14), and to repeated forgiving of their fellow disciples who have offended them (Mt 18:21–35). But there is also the obligation to correct the sinful fellow Christian and, should one refuse to be corrected, separation from the community is demanded (Mt 18:15–18).

The narrative of the fifth book (Mt 19:1–23:39) begins with the departure of Jesus and his disciples from Galilee for Jerusalem. In the course of their journey Jesus for the third time predicts the passion that awaits him at Jerusalem and also his resurrection (Mt 20:17–19). At his entrance into the city he is hailed as the Son of David by the crowds accompanying him (Mt 21:9). He cleanses the temple (Mt 21:12–17), and in the few days of his Jerusalem ministry he engages in a series of controversies with the Jewish religious leaders (Mt 21:23–27; 22:15–22, 23–33, 34–40, 41–46), meanwhile speaking parables against them (Mt 21:28–32, 33–46), against all those Israelites who have rejected God's invitation to the messianic banquet (Mt 22:1–10), and against all, Jew and Gentile, who have accepted but have shown themselves unworthy of it (Mt 22:11–14). Once again, the perspective of the evangelist includes not only the time of Jesus' ministry but that of the preaching of the gospel after his resurrection. The narrative culminates in Jesus' denunciation of the scribes and Pharisees, reflecting not only his own opposition to them but that of Matthew's church (Mt 23:1–36), and in Jesus' lament over Jerusalem (Mt 23:37–39).

In the discourse of the fifth book (Mt 24:1–25:46), the last of the great structural discourses of the gospel, Jesus predicts the destruction of the temple and his own final coming. The time of the latter is unknown (Mt 24:36, 44), and the disciples are exhorted in various parables to live in readiness for it, a readiness that entails faithful attention to the duties of the interim period (Mt 24:45–25:30). The coming of Jesus will bring with it the great judgment by which the everlasting destiny of all will be determined (Mt 25:31–46).

The story of Jesus' passion and resurrection (Mt 26:1–28:20), the climax of the gospel, throws light on all that has preceded. In Matthew "righteousness" means both the faithful response to the will of God demanded of all to whom that will is announced and also the saving activity of God for his people (see Mt 3:15; 5:6; 6:33). The passion supremely exemplifies both meanings of that central Matthean word.

In Jesus' absolute faithfulness to the Father's will that he drink the cup of suffering (Mt 26:39), the incomparable model for Christian obedience is given; in his death "for the forgiveness of sins" (Mt 26:28), the saving power of God is manifested as never before.

Matthew's portrayal of Jesus in his passion combines both the majestic serenity of the obedient Son who goes his destined way in fulfillment of the scriptures (Mt 26:52–54), confident of his ultimate vindication by God, and the depths of fear and abandonment that he feels in face of death (Mt 26:38–39; 27:46). These two aspects are expressed by an Old Testament theme that occurs often in the narrative, i.e., the portrait of the suffering Righteous One who complains to God in his misery, but is certain of eventual deliverance from his terrible ordeal.

The passion-resurrection of God's Son means nothing less than the turn of the ages, a new stage of history, the coming of the Son of Man in his kingdom (Mt 28:18; cf. Mt 16:28). That is the sense of the apocalyptic signs that accompany Jesus' death (Mt 27:51–53) and resurrection (Mt 28:2). Although the old age continues, as it will until the manifestation of Jesus' triumph at his parousia, the final age has now begun. This is known only to those who have seen the Risen One and to those, both Jews and Gentiles, who have believed in their announcement of Jesus' triumph and have themselves become his disciples (cf. Mt 28:19). To them he is constantly, though invisibly, present (Mt 28:20), verifying the name Emmanuel, "God is with us" (cf. Mt 1:23).

The questions of authorship, sources, and the time of composition of this gospel have received many answers, none of which can claim more than a greater or lesser degree of probability. The one now favored by the majority of scholars is the following.

The ancient tradition that the author was the disciple and apostle of Jesus named Matthew (see Mt 10:3) is untenable because the gospel is based, in large part, on the Gospel according to Mark (almost all the verses of that gospel have been utilized in this), and it is hardly likely that a companion of Jesus would have followed so extensively an account that came from one who admittedly never had such an association rather than rely on his own memories. The attribution of the gospel to the disciple Matthew may have been due to his having been responsible for some of the traditions found in it, but that is far from certain.

The unknown author, whom we shall continue to call Matthew for the sake of convenience, drew not only upon the Gospel according to Mark but upon a large body of material (principally, sayings of Jesus) not found in Mark that corresponds, sometimes exactly, to material found also in the Gospel according to Luke. This material, called "Q" (probably from the first letter of the German word Quelle, meaning "source"), represents traditions, written and oral, used by both Matthew and Luke. Mark and Q are sources common to the two other synoptic gospels; hence the name the "Two-Source Theory" given to this explanation of the relation among the synoptics.

In addition to what Matthew drew from Mark and Q, his gospel contains material that is found only there. This is often designated "M," written or oral tradition that was available to the author. Since Mark was written shortly before or shortly after A.D. 70 (see the NAB introduction to Mark), Matthew was composed certainly after that date, which marks the fall of Jerusalem to the Romans at the time of the First Jewish Revolt (A.D. 66–70), and probably at least a decade later since Matthew's use of Mark presupposes a wide diffusion of that gospel. The post-A.D. 70 date is confirmed

within the text by Mt 22:7, which refers to the destruction of Jerusalem.

As for the place where the gospel was composed, a plausible suggestion is that it was Antioch, the capital of the Roman province of Syria. That large and important city had a mixed population of Greek-speaking Gentiles and Jews. The tensions between Jewish and Gentile Christians there in the time of Paul (see Gal 2:1–14) in respect to Christian obligation to observe Mosaic law are partially similar to tensions that can be seen between the two groups in Matthew's gospel. The church of Matthew, originally strongly Jewish Christian, had become one in which Gentile Christians were predominant. His gospel answers the question how obedience to the will of God is to be expressed by those who live after the "turn of the ages," the death and resurrection of Jesus.

The principal divisions of the Gospel according to Matthew are the following:

   I. The Infancy Narrative (1:1–2:23)
  II. The Proclamation of the Kingdom (3:1–7:29)
 III. Ministry and Mission in Galilee (8:1–11:1)
 IV. Opposition from Israel (11:2–13:53)
  V. Jesus, the Kingdom, and the Church (13:54–18:35)
 VI. Ministry in Judea and Jerusalem (19:1–25:46)
VII. The Passion and Resurrection (26:1–28:20) ∎

# Matthew

## I. THE INFANCY NARRATIVE

**1** **The Genealogy of Jesus.**† 1* The book of the genealogy of Jesus Christ, the son of David, the son of Abraham.†

2* Abraham became the father of Isaac, Isaac the father of Jacob, Jacob the father of Judah and his brothers.* 3 Judah became the father of Perez and Zerah, whose mother was Tamar.* Perez became the father of Hezron, Hezron the father of Ram, 4* Ram the father of Amminadab. Amminadab became the father of Nahshon, Nahshon the father of Salmon, 5* Salmon the father of Boaz, whose mother was Rahab. Boaz became the father of Obed, whose mother was Ruth. Obed became the father of Jesse, 6* Jesse the father of David the king.

David became the father of Solomon, whose mother had been the wife of Uriah. 7†* Solomon became the father of Rehoboam, Rehoboam the father of Abijah, Abijah the father of Asaph. 8 Asaph became the father of Jehoshaphat, Jehoshaphat the father of Joram, Joram the father of Uzziah. 9 Uzziah became the father of Jotham, Jotham the father of Ahaz, Ahaz the father of Hezekiah. 10 Hezekiah became the father of Manasseh, Manasseh the father of Amos,† Amos the father of Josiah. 11 Josiah became the father of Jechoniah and his brothers at the time of the Babylonian exile.

12* After the Babylonian exile, Jechoniah became the father of Shealtiel, Shealtiel the father of Zerubbabel, 13 Zerubbabel the father of Abiud. Abiud became the father of Eliakim, Eliakim the father of Azor, 14 Azor the father of Zadok. Zadok became the father of Achim, Achim the father of Eliud, 15 Eliud the father of Eleazar. Eleazar became the father of Matthan, Matthan the father of Jacob, 16 Jacob the father of Joseph, the husband of Mary. Of her was born Jesus who is called the Messiah.

17 Thus the total number of generations from Abraham to David is fourteen generations; from David to the Babylonian exile, fourteen generations; from the Babylonian exile to the Messiah, fourteen generations.†

**The Birth of Jesus.**† 18 Now this is how the birth of Jesus Christ came about. When his

---

1:1–2:23 The infancy narrative forms the prologue of the gospel. Consisting of a genealogy and five stories, it presents the coming of Jesus as the climax of Israel's history, and the events of his conception, birth, and early childhood as the fulfillment of Old Testament prophecy. The genealogy is probably traditional material that Matthew edited. In its first two sections (Mt 1:2–11) it was drawn from Ru 4:18–22; 1 Chr 1–3. Except for Jechoniah, Shealtiel, and Zerubbabel, none of the names in the third section (Mt 1:12–16) is found in any Old Testament genealogy. While the genealogy shows the continuity of God's providential plan from Abraham on, discontinuity is also present. The women Tamar (Mt 1:3), Rahab and Ruth (Mt 1:5), and the wife of Uriah, Bathsheba (Mt 1:6), bore their sons through unions that were in varying degrees strange and unexpected. These "irregularities" culminate in the supreme "irregularity" of the Messiah's birth of a virgin mother; the age of fulfillment is inaugurated by a creative act of God.

Drawing upon both biblical tradition and Jewish stories, Matthew portrays Jesus as reliving the Exodus experience of Israel and the persecutions of Moses. His rejection by his own people and his passion are foreshadowed by the troubled reaction of "all Jerusalem" to the question of the magi who are seeking the "newborn king of the Jews" (Mt 2:2–3), and by Herod's attempt to have him killed. The magi who do him homage prefigure the Gentiles who will accept the preaching of the gospel. The infancy narrative proclaims who Jesus is, the savior of his people from their sins (Mt 1:21), Emmanuel in whom "God is with us" (Mt 1:23), and the Son of God (Mt 2:15).

1:1 The Son of David, the son of Abraham: two links of the genealogical chain are singled out. Although the later, David is placed first in order to emphasize that Jesus is the royal Messiah. The mention of Abraham may be due not only to his being the father of the nation Israel but to Matthew's interest in the universal scope of Jesus' mission; cf. Gn 22:18 "…in your descendants all the nations of the earth shall find blessing."

1:7 The successor of Abijah was not Asaph but Asa (see 1 Chr 3:10). Some textual witnesses read the latter name; however, Asaph is better attested. Matthew may have deliberately introduced the psalmist Asaph into the genealogy (and in Mt 1:10 the prophet Amos) in order to show that Jesus is the fulfillment not only of the promises made to David (see 2 Sm 7) but of all the Old Testament.

1:10 Amos: some textual witnesses read Amon, who was the actual successor of Manasseh (see 1 Chr 3:14).

1:17 Matthew is concerned with fourteen generations, probably because fourteen is the numerical value of the Hebrew letters forming the name of David. In the second section of the genealogy (Mt 1:6b–11), three kings of Judah, Ahaziah, Joash, and Amaziah, have been omitted (see 1 Chr 3:11–12), so that there are fourteen generations in that section. Yet the third (Mt 1:12–16) apparently has only thirteen. Since Matthew here emphasizes that each section has fourteen, it is unlikely that the thirteen of the last was due to his oversight. Some scholars suggest that Jesus who is called the Messiah (Mt 1:16b) doubles the final member of the chain: Jesus, born within the family of David, opens up the new age as Messiah, so that in fact there are fourteen generations in the third section. This is perhaps too subtle, and the hypothesis of a slip not on the part of Matthew but of a later scribe seems likely. On Messiah, see note on Lk 2:11.

1:18–25 This first story of the infancy narrative spells out

---

**1:1** Gn 5:1; 1 Chr 17:11; Gn 22:18.
**1:2–17** Lk 3:23–38.
**1:2** Gn 21:3; 25:26; 29:35; 1 Chr 2:1.
**1:3** Gn 38:29–30; Ru 4:18; 1 Chr 2:4–9.
**1:4** Ru 4:19–20;

1 Chr 2:10–11.
**1:5** Ru 4:21–22; 1 Chr 2:11–12.
**1:6** 2 Sm 12:24; 1 Chr 2:15; 3:5.
**1:7–11** 2 Kgs 25:1–21; 1 Chr 3:10–15.
**1:12–16** 1 Chr 3:16–19.

mother Mary was betrothed to Joseph,† but before they lived together, she was found with child through the holy Spirit. ¹⁹ Joseph her husband, since he was a righteous man,† yet unwilling to expose her to shame, decided to divorce her quietly. ²⁰* Such was his intention when, behold, the angel of the Lord† appeared to him in a dream and said, "Joseph, son of David, do not be afraid to take Mary your wife into your home. For it is through the holy Spirit that this child has been conceived in her. ²¹ She will bear a son and you are to name him Jesus,† because he will save his people from their sins." ²² All this took place to fulfill what the Lord had said through the prophet:

²³†* "Behold, the virgin shall be with child
        and bear a son,
   and they shall name him Emmanuel,"

which means "God is with us." ²⁴ When Joseph awoke, he did as the angel of the Lord had commanded him and took his wife into his home. ²⁵ He had no relations with her until she bore a son,† and he named him Jesus.*

**2 The Visit of the Magi.**† ¹ When Jesus was born in Bethlehem of Judea, in the days of King Herod,† behold, magi from the east arrived in Jerusalem, ² saying, "Where is the newborn king of the Jews? We saw his star† at its rising and have come to do him homage."* ³ When King Herod heard this, he was greatly troubled, and all Jerusalem with him. ⁴ Assembling all the chief priests and the scribes of the people, he inquired of them where the Messiah was to be born.† ⁵* They said to him, "In Bethlehem of Judea, for thus it has been written through the prophet:

⁶      'And you, Bethlehem, land of Judah,
          are by no means least among the
             rulers of Judah;
       since from you shall come a ruler,
          who is to shepherd my people Israel.'"

⁷ Then Herod called the magi secretly and ascertained from them the time of the star's appearance. ⁸ He sent them to Bethlehem and said, "Go and search diligently for the child. When you have found him, bring me word, that I too may go and do him homage." ⁹ After their audience with the king they set out. And behold, the star that they had seen at its rising preceded them, until it came and stopped over the place where the child was. ¹⁰ They were overjoyed at seeing the star, ¹¹†* and on entering the house they saw the child with Mary his

---

**MT**

what is summarily indicated in Mt 1:16. The virginal conception of Jesus is the work of the Spirit of God. Joseph's decision to divorce Mary is overcome by the heavenly command that he take her into his home and accept the child as his own. The natural genealogical line is broken but the promises to David are fulfilled; through Joseph's adoption the child belongs to the family of David. Matthew sees the virginal conception as the fulfillment of Is 7:14.

**1:18** *Betrothed to Joseph*: betrothal was the first part of the marriage, constituting a man and woman as husband and wife. Subsequent infidelity was considered adultery. The betrothal was followed some months later by the husband's taking his wife into his home, at which time normal married life began.

**1:19** *A righteous man*: as a devout observer of the Mosaic law, Joseph wished to break his union with someone whom he suspected of gross violation of the law. It is commonly said that the law required him to do so, but the texts usually given in support of that view, e.g., Dt 22:20–21 do not clearly pertain to Joseph's situation. *Unwilling to expose her to shame*: the penalty for proved adultery was death by stoning; cf. Dt 22:21–23.

**1:20** *The angel of the Lord*: in the Old Testament a common designation of God in communication with a human being. *In a dream*: see Mt 2:13, 19, 22. These dreams may be meant to recall the dreams of Joseph, son of Jacob the patriarch (Gn 37:5–11, 19). A closer parallel is the dream of Amram, father of Moses, related by Josephus (*Antiquities* 2:212, 215–16).

**1:21** *Jesus*: in first-century Judaism the Hebrew name Joshua (Greek *Iēsous*) meaning "Yahweh helps" was interpreted as "Yahweh saves."

**1:23** *God is with us*: God's promise of deliverance to Judah in Isaiah's time is seen by Matthew as fulfilled in the birth of Jesus, in whom God is with his people. The name Emmanuel is alluded

to at the end of the gospel where the risen Jesus assures his disciples of his continued presence, "…I am with you always, until the end of the age" (Mt 28:20).

**1:25** *Until she bore a son*: the evangelist is concerned to emphasize that Joseph was not responsible for the conception of Jesus. The Greek word translated "until" does not imply normal marital conduct after Jesus' birth, nor does it exclude it.

**2:1–12** The future rejection of Jesus by Israel and his acceptance by the Gentiles are retrojected into this scene of the narrative.

**2:1** *In the days of King Herod*: Herod reigned from 37 to 4 B.C. *Magi*: originally a designation of the Persian priestly caste, the word became used of those who were regarded as having more than human knowledge. Matthew's magi are astrologers.

**2:2** *We saw his star*: it was a common ancient belief that a new star appeared at the time of a ruler's birth. Matthew also draws upon the Old Testament story of Balaam, who had prophesied that "A star shall advance from Jacob" (Nm 24:17), though there the star means not an astral phenomenon but the king himself.

**2:4** Herod's consultation with the chief priests and scribes has some similarity to a Jewish legend about the child Moses in which the "sacred scribes" warn Pharaoh about the imminent birth of one who will deliver Israel from Egypt and the king makes plans to destroy him.

**2:11** Cf. Ps 72:10, 15; Is 60:6. These Old Testament texts led to the interpretation of the magi as kings.

---

**1:20** 2:13, 19; Lk 1:35.
**1:23** Is 7:14 LXX.
**1:25** Lk 2:7.
**2:2** Nm 24:17.

**2:5–6** Mi 5:1; 2 Sm 5:2.
**2:11** Ps 72:10–11, 15; Is 60:6.

mother. They prostrated themselves and did him homage. Then they opened their treasures and offered him gifts of gold, frankincense, and myrrh. ¹²And having been warned in a dream not to return to Herod, they departed for their country by another way.

**The Flight to Egypt.** ¹³† When they had departed, behold, the angel of the Lord appeared to Joseph in a dream and said, "Rise, take the child and his mother, flee to Egypt,† and stay there until I tell you. Herod is going to search for the child to destroy him." ¹⁴Joseph rose and took the child and his mother by night and departed for Egypt. ¹⁵† He stayed there until the death of Herod, that what the Lord had said through the prophet* might be fulfilled, "Out of Egypt I called my son."

**The Massacre of the Infants.** ¹⁶When Herod realized that he had been deceived by the magi, he became furious. He ordered the massacre of all the boys in Bethlehem and its vicinity two years old and under, in accordance with the time he had ascertained from the magi. ¹⁷Then was fulfilled what had been said through Jeremiah the prophet:

¹⁸†* "A voice was heard in Ramah,
       sobbing and loud lamentation;

Rachel weeping for her children,
    and she would not be consoled,
    since they were no more."

**The Return from Egypt.** ¹⁹When Herod had died, behold, the angel of the Lord appeared in a dream to Joseph in Egypt ²⁰and said,* "Rise, take the child and his mother and go to the land of Israel, for those who sought the child's life are dead."† ²¹He rose, took the child and his mother, and went to the land of Israel. ²²But when he heard that Archelaus was ruling over Judea in place of his father Herod,† he was afraid to go back there. And because he had been warned in a dream, he departed for the region of Galilee. ²³†* He went and dwelt in a town called Nazareth, so that what had been spoken through the prophets might be fulfilled, "He shall be called a Nazorean."

## II. THE PROCLAMATION OF THE KINGDOM

**3** **The Preaching of John the Baptist.**†* ¹In those days John the Baptist appeared, preaching in the desert of Judea† ²[and] saying, "Repent,† for the kingdom of heaven is at hand!"* ³† It was of him that the prophet Isaiah* had spoken when he said:

---

**2:13–23** Biblical and nonbiblical traditions about Moses are here applied to the child Jesus, though the dominant Old Testament type is not Moses but Israel (Mt 2:15).

**2:13** *Flee to Egypt:* Egypt was a traditional place of refuge for those fleeing from danger in Palestine (see 1 Kgs 11:40; Jer 26:21), but the main reason why the child is to be taken to Egypt is that he may relive the Exodus experience of Israel.

**2:15** The fulfillment citation is taken from Hos 11:1. Israel, God's son, was called out of Egypt at the time of the Exodus; Jesus, the Son of God, will similarly be called out of that land in a new exodus. The father-son relationship between God and the nation is set in a higher key. Here the son is not a group adopted as "son of God," but the child who, as conceived by the holy Spirit, stands in unique relation to God. He is son of David and of Abraham, of Mary and of Joseph, but, above all, of God.

**2:18** Jer 31:15 portrays Rachel, wife of the patriarch Jacob, weeping for her children taken into exile at the time of the Assyrian invasion of the northern kingdom (722–21 B.C.). Bethlehem was traditionally identified with Ephrath, the place near which Rachel was buried (see Gn 35:19; 48:7), and the mourning of Rachel is here applied to her lost children of a later age. *Ramah:* about six miles north of Jerusalem. The lamentation of Rachel is so great as to be heard at a far distance.

**2:20** *For those who sought the child's life are dead:* Moses, who had fled from Egypt because the Pharaoh sought to kill him (see Ex 2:15), was told to return there, "for all the men who sought your life are dead" (Ex 4:19).

**2:22** With the agreement of the emperor Augustus, Archelaus received half of his father's kingdom, including Judea, after Herod's death. He had the title "ethnarch" (i.e., "ruler of a nation") and reigned from 4 B.C. to A.D. 6.

**2:23** *Nazareth...he shall be called a Nazorean:* the tradition

of Jesus' residence in Nazareth was firmly established, and Matthew sees it as being in accordance with the foreannounced plan of God. The town of Nazareth is not mentioned in the Old Testament, and no such prophecy can be found there. The vague expression "through the prophets" may be due to Matthew's seeing a connection between Nazareth and certain texts in which there are words with a remote similarity to the name of that town. Some such Old Testament texts are Is 11:1 where the Davidic king of the future is called "a bud" (*nēṣer*) that shall blossom from the roots of Jesse, and Jgs 13:5, 7 where Samson, the future deliverer of Israel from the Philistines, is called one who shall be consecrated (a *nāzîr*) to God.

**3:1–12** Here Matthew takes up the order of Jesus' ministry found in the gospel of Mark, beginning with the preparatory preaching of John the Baptist.

**3:1** Unlike Luke, Matthew says nothing of the Baptist's origins and does not make him a relative of Jesus. *The desert of Judea:* the barren region west of the Dead Sea extending up the Jordan valley.

**3:2** *Repent:* the Baptist calls for a change of heart and conduct, a turning of one's life from rebellion to obedience towards God. *The kingdom of heaven is at hand:* "heaven" (lit., "the heavens") is a substitute for the name "God" that was avoided by devout Jews of the time out of reverence. The expression "the kingdom of heaven" occurs only in the gospel of Matthew. It means the effective rule of God over his people. In its fullness it includes not only human obedience to God's word, but the triumph of God over physical evils, supremely over death. In

---

| | |
|---|---|
| **2:15** Hos 11:1. | Lk 2:39; 4:34; Jn 19:19. |
| **2:18** Jer 31:15. | **3:1–12** Mk 1:2–8; Lk 3:2–17. |
| **2:20** Ex 4:19. | **3:2** 4:17; 10:7. |
| **2:23** 13:54; Mk 1:9; | **3:3** Is 40:3. |

## PALESTINE AT THE TIME OF JESUS

| | A | B | C | D | E | F | |
|---|---|---|---|---|---|---|---|
| 1 | | | • Sidon | | | • Damascus | 1 |

SYRIA

+ Mt. Hermon

Tyre

PHOENICIA

• Caesarea Philippi

GAULANITIS

The Great Sea
(Mediterranean Sea)

BATANEA

TRACHONITIS

GALILEE

• Bethsaida

Capernaum •

Cana •   Magdala   *Lake of Galilee*

Mt. Carmel +

Tiberias

AURANITIS

Sepphoris •

Nazareth •

+ Mt. Tabor

CARMEL

Caesarea Maritima •

DECAPOLIS

SAMARIA

*Jordan River*

Mt. Gerizim +   • Sychar

• Gerasa

Joppa •

• Arimathea?

PEREA

• Philadelphia

Lydda •

JUDEA

Emmaus? •   Jericho •

Jerusalem •   + Mt. Olives

Bethany •   • Qumran

• Medeba

Salt
Sea
(Dead
Sea)

•••• Greatest extent of
Herod's Kingdom

Hebron •

• En Gedi

Beersheba •

IDUMEA

| 0 | 20 | 40 miles |
| 0 | 20 | 40 kilometers |

"A voice of one crying out in the desert,
'Prepare the way of the Lord,
    make straight his paths.'"

[4] †* John wore clothing made of camel's hair and had a leather belt around his waist. His food was locusts and wild honey. [5] At that time Jerusalem, all Judea, and the whole region around the Jordan were going out to him [6] and were being baptized by him in the Jordan River as they acknowledged their sins. †

[7] When he saw many of the Pharisees and Sadducees† coming to his baptism, he said to them, "You brood of vipers! Who warned you to flee from the coming wrath? * [8] Produce good fruit as evidence of your repentance, [9] And do not presume to say to yourselves, 'We have Abraham as our father.' For I tell you, God can raise up children to Abraham from these stones. * [10] Even now the ax lies at the root of the trees. Therefore every tree that does not bear good fruit will be cut down and thrown into the fire. [11] * I am baptizing you with water, for repentance, but the one who is coming after me is mightier than I. I am not worthy to carry his sandals. He will baptize you with the holy Spirit and fire. † [12] †* His winnowing fan is in his hand. He will clear his threshing floor and gather his wheat into his barn, but the chaff he will burn with unquenchable fire."

## The Baptism of Jesus. † [13] * Then Jesus came from Galilee to John at the Jordan to be baptized by him. [14] † John tried to prevent him, saying, "I need to be baptized by you, and yet you are coming to me?" [15] Jesus said to him in reply, "Allow it now, for thus it is fitting for us to fulfill all righteousness." Then he allowed him. [16] †* After Jesus was baptized, he came up from the water and behold, the heavens were opened [for him], and he saw the Spirit of God descending like a dove [and] coming upon him. [17] And a voice came from the heavens, saying, "This is my beloved Son, † with whom I am well pleased." *

## 4 The Temptation of Jesus. [1] †* Then Jesus was led by the Spirit into the desert to be tempted by the devil. [2] * He fasted for forty

---

the expectation found in Jewish apocalyptic, the kingdom was to be ushered in by a judgment in which sinners would be condemned and perish, an expectation shared by the Baptist. This was modified in Christian understanding where the kingdom was seen as being established in stages, culminating with the parousia of Jesus.

**3:3** See note on Jn 1:23.

**3:4** The clothing of John recalls the austere dress of the prophet Elijah (2 Kgs 1:8). The expectation of the return of Elijah from heaven to prepare Israel for the final manifestation of God's kingdom was widespread, and according to Matthew this expectation was fulfilled in the Baptist's ministry (Mt 11:14; 17:11–13).

**3:6** Ritual washing was practiced by various groups in Palestine between 150 B.C. and A.D. 250. John's baptism may have been related to the purificatory washings of the Essenes at Qumran.

**3:7** *Pharisees and Sadducees*: the former were marked by devotion to the law, written and oral, and the scribes, experts in the law, belonged predominantly to this group. The Sadducees were the priestly aristocratic party, centered in Jerusalem. They accepted as scripture only the first five books of the Old Testament, followed only the letter of the law, rejected the oral legal traditions, and were opposed to teachings not found in the Pentateuch, such as the resurrection of the dead. Matthew links both of these groups together as enemies of Jesus (Mt 16:1, 6, 11, 12; cf. Mk 8:11–13, 15). The threatening words that follow are addressed to them rather than to "the crowds" as in Lk 3:7. *The coming wrath*: the judgment that will bring about the destruction of unrepentant sinners.

**3:11** *Baptize you with the holy Spirit and fire*: the water baptism of John will be followed by an "immersion" of the repentant in the cleansing power of the Spirit of God, and of the unrepentant in the destroying power of God's judgment. However, some see *the holy Spirit* and *fire* as synonymous, and the effect of this "baptism" as either purification or destruction. See note on Mt 3:16.

**3:12** The discrimination between the good and the bad is compared to the procedure by which a farmer separates wheat and chaff. The *winnowing fan* was a forklike shovel with which

the threshed wheat was thrown into the air. The kernels fell to the ground; the light chaff, blown off by the wind, was gathered and burned up.

**3:13–17** The baptism of Jesus is the occasion on which he is equipped for his ministry by the holy Spirit and proclaimed to be the Son of God.

**3:14–15** This dialogue, peculiar to Matthew, reveals John's awareness of Jesus' superiority to him as the mightier one who is coming and who will baptize with the holy Spirit (Mt 3:11). His reluctance to admit Jesus among the sinners whom he is baptizing with water is overcome by Jesus' response. *To fulfill all righteousness*: in this gospel to *fulfill* usually refers to fulfillment of prophecy, and *righteousness* to moral conduct in conformity with God's will. Here, however, as in Mt 5:6; 6:33, *righteousness* seems to mean the saving activity of God. *To fulfill all righteousness* is to submit to the plan of God for the salvation of the human race. This involves Jesus' identification with sinners; hence the propriety of his accepting John's baptism.

**3:16** *The Spirit…coming upon him*: cf. Is 42:1.

**3:17** *This is my beloved Son*: the Marcan address to Jesus (Mk 1:11) is changed into a proclamation. The Father's voice speaks in terms that reflect Is 42:1; Ps 2:7; Gn 22:2.

**4:1–11** Jesus, proclaimed Son of God at his baptism, is subjected to a triple temptation. Obedience to the Father is a characteristic of true sonship, and Jesus is tempted by the devil to rebel against God, overtly in the third case, more subtly in the first two. Each refusal of Jesus is expressed in language taken from the Book of Deuteronomy (Dt 8:3; 6:13, 16). The testings of Jesus resemble those of Israel during the wandering in the desert and later in Canaan, and the victory of Jesus, the true

---

**3:4** 11:7–8; 2 Kgs 1:8;
  Zec 13:4.
**3:7** 12:34; 23:33; Is 59:5.
**3:9** Jn 8:33, 39; Rom
  9:7–8; Gal 4:21–31.
**3:11** Jn 1:26–27, 33; Acts
  1:5.
**3:12** 13:30; Is 41:16; Jer
  15:7.

**3:13–17** Mk 1:9–11; Lk
  3:21–22; Jn 1:31–34.
**3:16** Is 42:1.
**3:17** 12:18; 17:5; Gn 22:2;
  Ps 2:7; Is 42:1.
**4:1–11** Mk 1:12–13; Lk
  4:1–13.
**4:2** Ex 24:18; Dt 8:2.

days and forty nights,† and afterwards he was hungry. ³ The tempter approached and said to him, "If you are the Son of God, command that these stones become loaves of bread." ⁴† He said in reply, "It is written:*

> 'One does not live by bread alone,
>> but by every word that comes forth
>>> from the mouth of God.'"

⁵† Then the devil took him to the holy city, and made him stand on the parapet of the temple, ⁶ and said to him, "If you are the Son of God, throw yourself down. For it is written:

> 'He will command his angels concerning you'
>> and 'with their hands they will support you,
>>> lest you dash your foot against a stone.'"*

⁷ Jesus answered him, "Again it is written, 'You shall not put the Lord, your God, to the test.'"* ⁸ Then the devil took him up to a very high mountain, and showed him all the kingdoms of the world in their magnificence, ⁹ and he said to him, "All these I shall give to you, if you will prostrate yourself and worship me."† ¹⁰ At this, Jesus said to him, "Get away, Satan! It is written:

> 'The Lord, your God, shall you worship
>> and him alone shall you serve.'"*

¹¹ Then the devil left him and, behold, angels came and ministered to him.

## The Beginning of the Galilean Ministry.†

¹²* When he heard that John had been arrested, he withdrew to Galilee. ¹³ He left Nazareth and went to live in Capernaum by the sea, in the region of Zebulun and Naphtali,* ¹⁴ that what had been said through Isaiah the prophet might be fulfilled:

¹⁵     "Land of Zebulun and land of
>> Naphtali,*
> the way to the sea, beyond the
>> Jordan,
> Galilee of the Gentiles,
¹⁶     the people who sit in darkness
>> have seen a great light,
> on those dwelling in a land
>> overshadowed by death
> light has arisen."*

¹⁷† From that time on, Jesus began to preach and say,* "Repent, for the kingdom of heaven is at hand."

## The Call of the First Disciples.†

¹⁸* As he was walking by the Sea of Galilee, he saw two brothers, Simon who is called Peter, and his brother Andrew, casting a net into the sea; they were fishermen. ¹⁹ He said to them, "Come after me, and I will make you fishers of men." ²⁰† At once they left their nets and followed him. ²¹ He walked along from there and saw two other brothers, James, the son of Zebedee, and his brother John. They were in a boat, with their father Zebedee, mending their nets. He called them, ²² and immediately they left their boat and their father and followed him.

---

† Israel and the true Son, contrasts with the failure of the ancient and disobedient "son," the old Israel. In the temptation account Matthew is almost identical with Luke; both seem to have drawn upon the same source.

**4:2** *Forty days and forty nights:* the same time as that during which Moses remained on Sinai (Ex 24:18). The time reference, however, seems primarily intended to recall the forty years during which Israel was tempted in the desert (Dt 8:2).

**4:4** Cf. Dt 8:3. Jesus refuses to use his power for his own benefit and accepts whatever God wills.

**4:5–7** The devil supports his proposal by an appeal to the scriptures, Ps 91:11a, 12. Unlike Israel (Dt 6:16), Jesus refuses to "test" God by demanding from him an extraordinary show of power.

**4:9** The worship of Satan to which Jesus is tempted is probably intended to recall Israel's worship of false gods. His refusal is expressed in the words of Dt 6:13.

**4:12–17** Isaiah's prophecy of the light rising upon Zebulun and Naphtali (Is 8:22–9:1) is fulfilled in Jesus' residence at Capernaum. The territory of these two tribes was the first to be devastated (733–32 B.C.) at the time of the Assyrian invasion. In order to accommodate Jesus' move to Capernaum to the prophecy, Matthew speaks of that town as being "in the region

of Zebulun and Naphtali" (Mt 4:13), whereas it was only in the territory of the latter, and he understands the sea of the prophecy, the Mediterranean, as the sea of Galilee.

**4:17** At the beginning of his preaching Jesus takes up the words of John the Baptist (Mt 3:2) although with a different meaning; in his ministry the kingdom of heaven has already begun to be present (Mt 12:28).

**4:18–22** The call of the first disciples promises them a share in Jesus' work and entails abandonment of family and former way of life. Three of the four, Simon, James, and John, are distinguished among the disciples by a closer relation with Jesus (Mt 17:1; 26:37).

**4:20** Here and in Mt 4:22, as in Mark (Mk 1:16–20) and unlike the Lucan account (Lk 5:1–11), the disciples' response is motivated only by Jesus' invitation, an element that emphasizes his mysterious power.

---

**4:4** Dt 8:3.
**4:6** Ps 91:11–12.
**4:7** Dt 6:16.
**4:10** 16:23; Dt 6:13.
**4:12–13** Mk 1:14–15; Lk 4:14, 31.
**4:13** Jn 2:12.
**4:15–16** Is 8:23 LXX; 9:1.
**4:16** Lk 1:79.
**4:17** 3:2.
**4:18–22** Mk 1:16–20; Lk 5:1–11.

**Ministering to a Great Multitude.†** <sup>23</sup> He went around all of Galilee, teaching in their synagogues,† proclaiming the gospel of the kingdom, and curing every disease and illness among the people.* <sup>24</sup>† His fame spread to all of Syria, and they brought to him all who were sick with various diseases and racked with pain, those who were possessed, lunatics, and paralytics, and he cured them. <sup>25</sup>* And great crowds from Galilee, the Decapolis,† Jerusalem, and Judea, and from beyond the Jordan followed him.

**5** **The Sermon on the Mount.** <sup>1</sup>† When he saw the crowds,† he went up the mountain, and after he had sat down, his disciples came to him. <sup>2</sup> He began to teach them, saying:

### The Beatitudes†

3    "Blessed are the poor in spirit,†
       for theirs is the kingdom of heaven.*

4†   Blessed are they who mourn,*
       for they will be comforted.

5†   Blessed are the meek,*
       for they will inherit the land.

6    Blessed are they who hunger and thirst
       for righteousness,†
     for they will be satisfied.

7    Blessed are the merciful,
       for they will be shown mercy.*

8†   Blessed are the clean of heart,*
       for they will see God.

9    Blessed are the peacemakers,
       for they will be called children of
         God.

10   Blessed are they who are persecuted for
       the sake of righteousness,†
     for theirs is the kingdom of heaven.*

<sup>11</sup> Blessed are you when they insult you and persecute you and utter every kind of evil against you [falsely] because of me.* <sup>12</sup>† Rejoice and be glad, for your reward will be great in heaven.* Thus they persecuted the prophets who were before you.

### The Similes of Salt and Light.†

<sup>13</sup>* "You are the salt of the earth. But if salt loses its taste, with what can it be seasoned? It is no longer good for anything but to be thrown out and

---

**4:23–25** This summary of Jesus' ministry concludes the narrative part of the first book of Matthew's gospel (Mt 3–4). The activities of his ministry are teaching, proclaiming the gospel, and healing; cf. Mt 9:35.

**4:23** *Their synagogues*: Matthew usually designates the Jewish synagogues as *their synagogue(s)* (Mt 9:35; 10:17; 12:9; 13:54) or, in address to Jews, *your synagogues* (Mt 23:34), an indication that he wrote after the break between church and synagogue.

**4:24** *Syria*: the Roman province to which Palestine belonged.

**4:25** *The Decapolis*: a federation of Greek cities in Palestine, originally ten in number, all but one east of the Jordan.

**5:1–7:29** The first of the five discourses that are a central part of the structure of this gospel. It is the discourse section of the first book and contains sayings of Jesus derived from Q and from M. The Lucan parallel is in that gospel's "Sermon on the Plain" (Lk 6:20–49), although some of the sayings in Matthew's "Sermon on the Mount" have their parallels in other parts of Luke. The careful topical arrangement of the sermon is probably not due only to Matthew's editing; he seems to have had a structured discourse of Jesus as one of his sources. The form of that source may have been as follows: four beatitudes (Mt 5:3–4, 6, 11–12), a section on the new righteousness with illustrations (Mt 5:17, 20–24, 27–28, 33–48), a section on good works (Mt 6:1–6, 16–18), and three warnings (Mt 7:1–2, 15–21, 24–27).

**5:1–2** Unlike Luke's sermon, this is addressed not only to the disciples but to the crowds (see Mt 7:28).

**5:3–12** The form *Blessed are (is)* occurs frequently in the Old Testament in the Wisdom literature and in the psalms. Although modified by Matthew, the first, second, fourth, and ninth beatitudes have Lucan parallels (Mt 5:3 // Lk 6:20; Mt 5:4 // Lk 6:21b; Mt 5:6 // Lk 6:21a; Mt 5:11–12 // Lk 5:22–23). The others were added by the evangelist and are probably his own composition. A few manuscripts, Western and Alexandrian, and many versions and patristic quotations give the second and third beatitudes in inverted order.

**5:3** *The poor in spirit*: in the Old Testament, the poor (*'anāwîm*) are those who are without material possessions and whose confidence is in God (see Is 61:1; Zep 2:3; in the NAB

the word is translated *lowly* and *humble*, respectively, in those texts). Matthew added *in spirit* in order either to indicate that only the devout poor were meant or to extend the beatitude to all, of whatever social rank, who recognized their complete dependence on God. The same phrase *poor in spirit* is found in the Qumran literature (1QM 14:7).

**5:4** Cf. Is 61:2, "(The Lord has sent me)…to comfort all who mourn." *They will be comforted*: here the passive is a "theological passive" equivalent to the active "God will comfort them"; so also in Mt 5:6, 7.

**5:5** Cf. Ps 37:11, "…the meek shall possess the land." In the psalm "the land" means the land of Palestine; here it means the kingdom.

**5:6** *For righteousness*: a Matthean addition. For the meaning of *righteousness* here, see note on Mt 3:14–15.

**5:8** Cf. Ps 24:4. Only one "whose heart is clean" can take part in the temple worship. To be with God in the temple is described in Ps 42:3 as "beholding his face," but here the promise to *the clean of heart* is that they will *see God* not in the temple but in the coming kingdom.

**5:10** *Righteousness* here, as usually in Matthew, means conduct in conformity with God's will.

**5:12** *The prophets who were before you*: the disciples of Jesus stand in the line of the persecuted prophets of Israel. Some would see the expression as indicating also that Matthew considered all Christian disciples as prophets.

**5:13–16** By their deeds the disciples are to influence the world for good. They can no more escape notice than *a city set on a mountain*. If they fail in good works, they are as useless as flavorless salt or as a lamp whose light is concealed.

---

**4:23** 9:35; Mk 1:39; Lk 4:15, 44.
**4:25** Mk 3:7–8; Lk 6:17–19.
**5:3–12** Lk 6:20–23.
**5:4** Is 61:2–3; Rev 21:4.
**5:5** Gn 13:15; Ps 37:11.
**5:7** 18:33; Jas 2:13.
**5:8** Ps 24:4–5; 73:1.
**5:10** 1 Pt 2:20; 3:14; 4:14.
**5:11** 10:22; Acts 5:41.
**5:12** 2 Chr 36:16; Heb 11:32–38; Jas 5:10.
**5:13** Mk 9:50; Lk 14:34–35.

MT

trampled underfoot.† [14] You are the light of the world. A city set on a mountain cannot be hidden. * [15] Nor do they light a lamp and then put it under a bushel basket; it is set on a lampstand, where it gives light to all in the house. * [16] Just so, your light must shine before others, that they may see your good deeds and glorify your heavenly Father. *

**Teaching About the Law.** [17] † "Do not think that I have come to abolish the law or the prophets. I have come not to abolish but to fulfill. [18] Amen, I say to you, until heaven and earth pass away, not the smallest letter or the smallest part of a letter will pass from the law, until all things have taken place. * [19] Therefore, whoever breaks one of the least of these commandments and teaches others to do so will be called least in the kingdom of heaven. But whoever obeys and teaches these commandments will be called greatest in the kingdom of heaven. † [20] I tell you, unless your righteousness surpasses that of the scribes and Pharisees, you will not enter into the kingdom of heaven.

**Teaching About Anger.** † [21] "You have heard that it was said to your ancestors, * 'You shall not kill; and whoever kills will be liable to

judgment.'† [22] † But I say to you, whoever is angry† with his brother will be liable to judgment, * and whoever says to his brother, 'Raqa,' will be answerable to the Sanhedrin, and whoever says, 'You fool,' will be liable to fiery Gehenna. [23] Therefore, if you bring your gift to the altar, and there recall that your brother has anything against you, * [24] leave your gift there at the altar, go first and be reconciled with your brother, and then come and offer your gift. [25] Settle with your opponent quickly while on the way to court with him. * Otherwise your opponent will hand you over to the judge, and the judge will hand you over to the guard, and you will be thrown into prison. [26] Amen, I say to you, you will not be released until you have paid the last penny.

**Teaching About Adultery.** [27] † "You have heard that it was said, * 'You shall not commit adultery.' [28] But I say to you, everyone who looks at a woman with lust has already committed adultery with her in his heart. [29] † If your right eye causes you to sin, tear it out and throw it away. * It is better for you to lose one of your members than to have your whole body thrown into Gehenna. [30] And if your right hand causes you to sin, cut it off and throw it away. It is better for you to lose one of your

† 
**5:13** The unusual supposition of salt losing its flavor has led some to suppose that the saying refers to the salt of the Dead Sea that, because chemically impure, could lose its taste.

**5:17–20** This statement of Jesus' position concerning the Mosaic law is composed of traditional material from Matthew's sermon documentation (see note on Mt 5:1–7:29), other Q material (cf. Mt 18; Lk 16:17), and the evangelist's own editorial touches. *To fulfill* the law appears at first to mean a literal enforcement of the law in the least detail: *until heaven and earth pass away* nothing of the law *will pass* (Mt 5:18). Yet the "passing away" of heaven and earth is not necessarily the end of the world understood, as in much apocalyptic literature, as the dissolution of the existing universe. The "turning of the ages" comes with the apocalyptic event of Jesus' death and resurrection, and those to whom this gospel is addressed are living in the new and final age, prophesied by Isaiah as the time of "new heavens and a new earth" (Is 65:17; 66:22). Meanwhile, during Jesus' ministry when the kingdom is already breaking in, his mission remains within the framework of the law, though with significant anticipation of the age to come, as the following antitheses (Mt 5:21–48) show.

**5:19** Probably *these commandments* means those of the Mosaic law. But this is an interim ethic "until heaven and earth pass away."

**5:21–48** Six examples of the conduct demanded of the Christian disciple. Each deals with a commandment of the law, introduced by *You have heard that it was said to your ancestors* or an equivalent formula, followed by Jesus' teaching in respect to that commandment, *But I say to you*; thus their designation as "antitheses." Three of them accept the Mosaic law but extend or deepen it (Mt 5:21–22; 27–28; 43–44); three reject it as a standard of conduct for the disciples (Mt 5:31–32; 33–37; 38–39).

**5:21** Cf. Ex 20:13; Dt 5:17. The second part of the verse is not an exact quotation from the Old Testament, but cf. Ex 21:12.

**5:22–26** Reconciliation with an offended brother is urged in the admonition of Mt 5:23–24 and the parable of Mt 5:25–26 (// Lk 12:58–59). The severity of the judge in the parable is a warning of the fate of unrepentant sinners in the coming judgment by God.

**5:22** Anger is the motive behind murder, as the insulting epithets are steps that may lead to it. They, as well as the deed, are all forbidden. *Raqa:* an Aramaic word *rēqā'* or *rēqâ* probably meaning "imbecile," "blockhead," a term of abuse. The ascending order of punishment, *judgment* (by a local council?), trial before *the Sanhedrin*, condemnation to *Gehenna*, points to a higher degree of seriousness in each of the offenses. *Sanhedrin:* the highest judicial body of Judaism. *Gehenna:* in Hebrew *gê-hinnōm,* "Valley of Hinnom," or *gê ben-hinnōm,* "Valley of the son of Hinnom," southwest of Jerusalem, the center of an idolatrous cult during the monarchy in which children were offered in sacrifice (see 2 Kgs 23:10; Jer 7:31). In Jos 18:16 (Septuagint, Codex Vaticanus) the Hebrew is transliterated into Greek as *gaienna,* which appears in the New Testament as *geenna.* The concept of punishment of sinners by fire either after death or after the final judgment is found in Jewish apocalyptic literature (e.g., Enoch 90:26) but the name *geenna* is first given to the place of punishment in the New Testament.

**5:27** See Ex 20:14; Dt 5:18.

**5:29–30** No sacrifice is too great to avoid total destruction in *Gehenna.*

**5:14** Jn 8:12.
**5:15** Mk 4:21; Lk 8:16; 11:33.
**5:16** Jn 3:21.
**5:18** Lk 16:17.
**5:21** Ex 20:13; Dt 5:17.
**5:22** Jas 1:19–20.
**5:23** Mk 11:25.
**5:25–26** 18:34–35; Lk 12:58–59.
**5:27** Ex 20:14; Dt 5:18.
**5:29–30** 18:8–9; Mk 9:43–47.

members than to have your whole body go into Gehenna.

**Teaching About Divorce.** 31† "It was also said, 'Whoever divorces his wife must give her a bill of divorce.'* 32 But I say to you, whoever divorces his wife (unless the marriage is unlawful) causes her to commit adultery, and whoever marries a divorced woman commits adultery.*

**Teaching About Oaths.** 33†* "Again you have heard that it was said to your ancestors, 'Do not take a false oath, but make good to the Lord all that you vow.' 34* But I say to you, do not swear at all;† not by heaven, for it is God's throne; 35 nor by the earth, for it is his footstool; nor by Jerusalem, for it is the city of the great King. 36 Do not swear by your head, for you cannot make a single hair white or black. 37† Let your 'Yes' mean 'Yes,' and your 'No' mean 'No.' Anything more is from the evil one.

**Teaching About Retaliation.** 38† "You have heard that it was said,* 'An eye for an eye and a tooth for a tooth.' 39* But I say to you, offer no resistance to one who is evil. When someone strikes you on [your] right cheek, turn the other one to him as well. 40 If anyone wants to go to law with you over your tunic, hand him your cloak as well. 41 Should anyone press you into service for one mile,† go with him for two miles.* 42 Give to the one who asks of you, and do not turn your back on one who wants to borrow.*

**Love of Enemies.**† 43* "You have heard that it was said, 'You shall love your neighbor and hate your enemy.'* 44 But I say to you, love your enemies, and pray for those who persecute you, 45 that you may be children of your heavenly Father, for he makes his sun rise on the bad and the good, and causes rain to fall on the just and the unjust. 46 For if you love those who love you, what recompense will you have? Do not the tax collectors† do the same? 47 And if you greet your brothers only, what is unusual about that? Do not the pagans do the same?† 48 So be perfect,† just as your heavenly Father is perfect.*

**6** **Teaching About Almsgiving.**† 1 "[But] take care not to perform righteous deeds in order that people may see them;* otherwise, you will have no recompense from your heavenly

---

† **5:31–32** See Dt 24:1–5. The Old Testament commandment that a bill of divorce be given to the woman assumes the legitimacy of divorce itself. It is this that Jesus denies. *(Unless the marriage is unlawful):* this "exceptive clause," as it is often called, occurs also in Mt 19:9, where the Greek is slightly different. There are other sayings of Jesus about divorce that prohibit it absolutely (see Mk 10:11–12; Lk 16:18; cf. 1 Cor 7:10, 11b), and most scholars agree that they represent the stand of Jesus. Matthew's "exceptive clauses" are understood by some as a modification of the absolute prohibition. It seems, however, that the unlawfulness that Matthew gives as a reason why a marriage must be broken refers to a situation peculiar to his community: the violation of Mosaic law forbidding marriage between persons of certain blood and/or legal relationship (Lv 18:6–18). Marriages of that sort were regarded as incest (*porneia*), but some rabbis allowed Gentile converts to Judaism who had contracted such marriages to remain in them. Matthew's "exceptive clause" is against such permissiveness for Gentile converts to Christianity; cf. the similar prohibition of *porneia* in Acts 15:20, 29. In this interpretation, the clause constitutes no exception to the absolute prohibition of divorce when the marriage is lawful.

**5:33** This is not an exact quotation of any Old Testament text, but see Ex 20:7; Dt 5:11; Lv 19:12. The purpose of an oath was to guarantee truthfulness by one's calling on God as witness.

**5:34–36** The use of these oath formularies that avoid the divine name is in fact equivalent to swearing by it, for all the things sworn by are related to God.

**5:37** *Let your 'Yes' mean 'Yes,' and your 'No' mean 'No':* literally, "let your speech be 'Yes, yes,' 'No, no.'" Some have understood this as a milder form of oath, permitted by Jesus. In view of Mt 5:34, "Do not swear at all," that is unlikely. *From the evil one:* i.e., from the devil. Oath-taking presupposes a sinful weakness of the human race, namely, the tendency to lie. Jesus demands of his disciples a truthfulness that makes oaths unnecessary.

**5:38–42** See Lv 24:20. The Old Testament commandment was meant to moderate vengeance; the punishment should not exceed the injury done. Jesus forbids even this proportionate retaliation. Of the five examples that follow, only the first deals directly with retaliation for evil; the others speak of liberality.

**5:41** Roman garrisons in Palestine had the right to requisition the property and services of the native population.

**5:43–48** See Lv 19:18. There is no Old Testament commandment demanding hatred of one's enemy, but the "neighbor" of the love commandment was understood as one's fellow countryman. Both in the Old Testament (Ps 139:19–22) and at Qumran (1QS 9:21) hatred of evil persons is assumed to be right. Jesus extends the love commandment to the enemy and the persecutor. His disciples, as children of God, must imitate the example of their Father, who grants his gifts of sun and rain to both the good and the bad.

**5:46** *Tax collectors:* Jews who were engaged in the collection of indirect taxes such as tolls and customs. See note on Mk 2:14.

**5:47** Jesus' disciples must not be content with merely usual standards of conduct; see Mt 5:20 where the verb "surpass" (Greek *perisseuō*) is cognate with the *unusual* (*perisson*) of this verse.

**5:48** *Perfect:* in the gospels this word occurs only in Matthew, here and in Mt 19:21. The Lucan parallel (Lk 6:36) demands that the disciples be *merciful.*

**6:1–18** The sermon continues with a warning against doing good in order to be seen and gives three examples, almsgiving (Mt 6:2–4), prayer (Mt 6:5–15), and fasting (Mt 6:16–18). In each, the conduct of the hypocrites (Mt 6:2) is contrasted with that

| | |
|---|---|
| **5:31** 19:3–9; Dt 24:1. | **5:41** Lam 3:30. |
| **5:32** Lk 16:18; 1 Cor 7:10–11. | **5:42** Dt 15:7–8. |
| **5:33** Lv 19:12; Nm 30:3. | **5:43–48** Lv 19:18. |
| **5:34–37** Ps 48:3; Sir 23:9; Is 66:1; Jas 5:12. | **5:48** Lv 11:44; 19:2; Dt 18:13; Jas 1:4; 1 Pt 1:16; 1 Jn 3:3. |
| **5:38** Ex 21:24; Lv 24:19–20. | **6:1** 23:5. |
| **5:39–42** Lk 6:29–30. | |

Father. [2] When you give alms, do not blow a trumpet before you, as the hypocrites† do in the synagogues and in the streets to win the praise of others. Amen, I say to you, they have received their reward.* [3] But when you give alms, do not let your left hand know what your right is doing, [4] so that your almsgiving may be secret. And your Father who sees in secret will repay you.

**Teaching About Prayer.** [5] "When you pray, do not be like the hypocrites, who love to stand and pray in the synagogues and on street corners so that others may see them. Amen, I say to you, they have received their reward. [6] But when you pray, go to your inner room, close the door, and pray to your Father in secret. And your Father who sees in secret will repay you. [7]† In praying, do not babble like the pagans, who think that they will be heard because of their many words.† [8] Do not be like them. Your Father knows what you need before you ask him.

**The Lord's Prayer.** [9]† "This is how you are to pray:*

Our Father in heaven,†
    hallowed be your name,
[10]    your kingdom come,†
    your will be done,
     on earth as in heaven.*
[11]†* Give us today our daily bread;
[12]    and forgive us our debts,†
    as we forgive our debtors;*
[13]    and do not subject us to the final test,†
    but deliver us from the evil one.*

[14]† If you forgive others their transgressions, your heavenly Father will forgive you.* [15] But if you do not forgive others, neither will your Father forgive your transgressions.*

**Teaching About Fasting.** [16] "When you fast,† do not look gloomy like the hypocrites. They neglect their appearance, so that they may appear to others to be fasting. Amen, I say to you, they have received their reward. [17] But when you fast, anoint your head and wash your face, [18] so that you may not appear to others to be fasting, except to your Father who is hidden. And your Father who sees what is hidden will repay you.

---

†

demanded of the disciples. The sayings about reward found here and elsewhere (Mt 5:12, 46; 10:41–42) show that this is a genuine element of Christian moral exhortation. Possibly to underline the difference between the Christian idea of reward and that of the hypocrites, the evangelist uses two different Greek verbs to express the rewarding of the disciples and that of the hypocrites; in the latter case it is the verb *apechō*, a commercial term for giving a receipt for what has been paid in full (Mt 6:2, 5, 16).

**6:2** *The hypocrites*: the scribes and Pharisees, see Mt 23:13, 15, 23, 25, 27, 29. The designation reflects an attitude resulting not only from the controversies at the time of Jesus' ministry but from the opposition between Pharisaic Judaism and the church of Matthew. *They have received their reward*: they desire praise and have received what they were looking for.

**6:7–15** Matthew inserts into his basic traditional material an expansion of the material on prayer that includes the model prayer, the "Our Father." That prayer is found in Lk 11:2–4 in a different context and in a different form.

**6:7** The example of what Christian prayer should be like contrasts it now not with the prayer of the hypocrites but with that of *the pagans*. Their babbling probably means their reciting a long list of divine names, hoping that one of them will force a response from the deity.

**6:9–13** Matthew's form of the "Our Father" follows the liturgical tradition of his church. Luke's less developed form also represents the liturgical tradition known to him, but it is probably closer than Matthew's to the original words of Jesus.

**6:9** *Our Father in heaven*: this invocation is found in many rabbinic prayers of the post-New Testament period. *Hallowed be your name*: though the "hallowing" of the divine name could be understood as reverence done to God by human praise and by obedience to his will, this is more probably a petition that God hallow his own name, i.e., that he manifest his glory by an act of power (cf. Ez 36:23), in this case, by the establishment of his kingdom in its fullness.

**6:10** *Your kingdom come*: this petition sets the tone of the

prayer, and inclines the balance toward divine rather than human action in the petitions that immediately precede and follow it. *Your will be done, on earth as in heaven*: a petition that the divine purpose to establish the kingdom, a purpose present now in heaven, be executed *on earth*.

**6:11** *Give us today our daily bread*: the rare Greek word *epiousios*, here *daily*, occurs in the New Testament only here and in Lk 11:3. A single occurrence of the word outside of these texts and of literature dependent on them has been claimed, but the claim is highly doubtful. The word may mean *daily* or "future" (other meanings have also been proposed). The latter would conform better to the eschatological tone of the whole prayer. So understood, the petition would be for a speedy coming of the kingdom (*today*), which is often portrayed in both the Old Testament and the New under the image of a feast (Is 25:6; Mt 8:11; 22:1–10; Lk 13:29; 14:15–24).

**6:12** *Forgive us our debts*: the word *debts* is used metaphorically of sins, "debts" owed to God (see Lk 11:4). The request is probably for forgiveness at the final judgment.

**6:13** Jewish apocalyptic writings speak of a period of severe trial before the end of the age, sometimes called the "messianic woes." This petition asks that the disciples be spared that *final test*.

**6:14–15** These verses reflect a set pattern called "Principles of Holy Law." Human action now will be met by a corresponding action of God at the final judgment.

**6:16** The only fast prescribed in the Mosaic law was that of the Day of Atonement (Lv 16:31), but the practice of regular fasting was common in later Judaism; cf. *Didache* 9:1.

---

*

**6:2** Jn 12:43.
**6:9–13** Lk 11:2–4.
**6:10** 26:42.
**6:11** Prv 30:8–9.
**6:12** 18:21–22; Sir 28:2.
**6:13** Jn 17:15; 2 Thes 3:3.
**6:14** 18:35; Sir 28:1–5; Mk 11:25.
**6:15** Jas 2:13.

**Treasure in Heaven.** 19† "Do not store up for yourselves treasures on earth, where moth and decay destroy, and thieves break in and steal.* 20 But store up treasures in heaven, where neither moth nor decay destroys, nor thieves break in and steal. 21 For where your treasure is, there also will your heart be.*

**The Light of the Body.**† 22 "The lamp of the body is the eye. If your eye is sound, your whole body will be filled with light; 23 but if your eye is bad, your whole body will be in darkness. And if the light in you is darkness, how great will the darkness be.*

**God and Money.** 24† "No one can serve two masters.* He will either hate one and love the other, or be devoted to one and despise the other. You cannot serve God and mammon.

**Dependence on God.**† 25* "Therefore I tell you, do not worry about your life, what you will eat [or drink], or about your body, what you will wear. Is not life more than food and the body more than clothing? 26 Look at the birds in the sky; they do not sow or reap, they gather nothing into barns, yet your heavenly Father feeds them. Are not you more important than they?* 27 Can any of you by worrying add a single moment to your life-span?† 28 Why are you anxious about clothes? Learn from the way the wild flowers grow. They do not work or spin. 29 But I tell you that not even Solomon in all his splendor was clothed like one of them. 30† If God so clothes the grass

of the field, which grows today and is thrown into the oven tomorrow, will he not much more provide for you, O you of little faith? 31 So do not worry and say, 'What are we to eat?' or 'What are we to drink?' or 'What are we to wear?' 32 All these things the pagans seek. Your heavenly Father knows that you need them all. 33 But seek first the kingdom [of God] and his righteousness,† and all these things will be given you besides. 34 Do not worry about tomorrow; tomorrow will take care of itself. Sufficient for a day is its own evil.

**7 Judging Others.** 1†* "Stop judging,† that you may not be judged.* 2 For as you judge, so will you be judged, and the measure with which you measure will be measured out to you.* 3 Why do you notice the splinter in your brother's eye, but do not perceive the wooden beam in your own eye? 4 How can you say to your brother, 'Let me remove that splinter from your eye,' while the wooden beam is in your eye? 5 You hypocrite,† remove the wooden beam from your eye first; then you will see clearly to remove the splinter from your brother's eye.

**Pearls Before Swine.** 6 "Do not give what is holy to dogs,† or throw your pearls before swine, lest they trample them underfoot, and turn and tear you to pieces.*

**The Answer to Prayers.** 7* "Ask and it will be given to you; seek and you will find; knock and the door will be opened to you.* 8 For

**6:19–34** The remaining material of this chapter is taken almost entirely from Q. It deals principally with worldly possessions, and the controlling thought is summed up in Mt 6:24: the disciple can serve only one master and must choose between God and wealth (*mammon*). See further the note on Lk 16:9.

**6:22–23** In this context the parable probably points to the need for the disciple to be enlightened by Jesus' teaching on the transitory nature of earthly riches.

**6:24** *Mammon*: an Aramaic word meaning wealth or property.

**6:25–34** Jesus does not deny the reality of human needs (Mt 6:32), but forbids making them the object of anxious care and, in effect, becoming their slave.

**6:27** *Life-span*: the Greek word can also mean "stature." If it is taken in that sense, the word here translated *moment* (literally, "cubit") must be translated literally as a unit not of time but of spatial measure. The cubit is about eighteen inches.

**6:30** *Of little faith*: except for the parallel in Lk 12:28, the word translated *of little faith* is found in the New Testament only in Matthew. It is used by him of those who are disciples of Jesus but whose faith in him is not as deep as it should be (see Mt 8:26; 14:31; 16:8 and the cognate noun in Mt 17:20).

**6:33** *Righteousness*: see note on Mt 3:14–15.

**7:1–12** In Mt 7:1 Matthew returns to the basic traditional material of the sermon (Lk 6:37–38, 41–42). The governing thought is the correspondence between conduct toward one's fellows and God's conduct toward the one so acting.

**7:1** This is not a prohibition against recognizing the faults of others, which would be hardly compatible with Mt 7:5, 6 but against passing judgment in a spirit of arrogance, forgetful of one's own faults.

**7:5** *Hypocrite*: the designation previously given to the scribes and Pharisees is here given to the Christian disciple who is concerned with the faults of another and ignores his own more serious offenses.

**7:6** *Dogs* and *swine* were Jewish terms of contempt for Gentiles. This saying may originally have derived from a Jewish Christian community opposed to preaching the gospel (*what is holy, pearls*) to Gentiles. In the light of Mt 28:19 that can hardly be Matthew's meaning. He may have taken the saying as applying to a Christian dealing with an obstinately impenitent fellow Christian (Mt 18:17).

| | |
|---|---|
| **6:19** Jas 5:2–3. | **7:1–5** Lk 6:37–38, 41–42. |
| **6:20–21** Lk 12:33–34. | **7:1** Rom 2:1–2; 1 Cor 4:5. |
| **6:22–23** Lk 11:34–36. | **7:2** Wis 12:22; Mk 4:24. |
| **6:24** Lk 16:13. | **7:6** Prv 23:9. |
| **6:25–33** Lk 12:22–31. | **7:7–11** Mk 11:24; Lk 11:9–13. |
| **6:26** Ps 145:15–16; 147:9. | **7:7** 18:19. |

everyone who asks, receives; and the one who seeks, finds; and to the one who knocks, the door will be opened.* ⁹Which one of you would hand his son a stone when he asks for a loaf of bread,† ¹⁰or a snake when he asks for a fish? ¹¹If you then, who are wicked, know how to give good gifts to your children, how much more will your heavenly Father give good things to those who ask him.*

**The Golden Rule.** ¹²† "Do to others whatever you would have them do to you.* This is the law and the prophets.

**The Narrow Gate.** ¹³† "Enter through the narrow gate;† for the gate is wide and the road broad that leads to destruction, and those who enter through it are many.* ¹⁴How narrow the gate and constricted the road that leads to life. And those who find it are few.

**False Prophets.†** ¹⁵"Beware of false prophets, who come to you in sheep's clothing, but underneath are ravenous wolves.* ¹⁶* By their fruits you will know them. Do people pick grapes from thornbushes, or figs from thistles? ¹⁷Just so, every good tree bears good fruit, and a rotten tree bears bad fruit. ¹⁸A good tree cannot bear bad fruit, nor can a rotten tree bear good fruit. ¹⁹Every tree that does not bear good fruit will be cut down and thrown into the fire. ²⁰So by their fruits you will know them.*

**The True Disciple.** ²¹"Not everyone who says to me, 'Lord, Lord,' will enter the kingdom of heaven,† but only the one who does the will of my Father in heaven.* ²²Many will say to me on that day,* 'Lord, Lord, did we not prophesy in your name? Did we not drive out demons in your name? Did we not do mighty deeds in your name?'* ²³Then I will declare to them solemnly, 'I never knew you.† Depart from me, you evildoers.'*

**The Two Foundations.** ²⁴† "Everyone who listens to these words of mine and acts on them will be like a wise man who built his house on rock.* ²⁵The rain fell, the floods came, and the winds blew and buffeted the house.* But it did not collapse; it had been set solidly on rock. ²⁶And everyone who listens to these words of mine but does not act on them will be like a fool who built his house on sand. ²⁷The rain fell, the floods came, and the winds blew and buffeted the house. And it collapsed and was completely ruined."

²⁸† When Jesus finished these words, the crowds were astonished at his teaching, ²⁹†* for he taught them as one having authority, and not as their scribes.

## III. MINISTRY AND MISSION IN GALILEE†

**8** **The Cleansing of a Leper.** ¹* When Jesus came down from the mountain, great

---

**7:9–10** There is a resemblance between a stone and a round loaf of bread and between a serpent and the scaleless fish called *barbut.*

**7:12** See Lk 6:31. This saying, known since the eighteenth century as the "Golden Rule," is found in both positive and negative form in pagan and Jewish sources, both earlier and later than the gospel. *This is the law and the prophets* is an addition probably due to the evangelist.

**7:13–28** The final section of the discourse is composed of a series of antitheses, contrasting two kinds of life within the Christian community, that of those who obey the words of Jesus and that of those who do not. Most of the sayings are from Q and are found also in Luke.

**7:13–14** The metaphor of the "two ways" was common in pagan philosophy and in the Old Testament. In Christian literature it is found also in the *Didache* (1–6) and the *Epistle of Barnabas* (18–20).

**7:15–20** Christian disciples who claimed to speak in the name of God are called *prophets* (Mt 7:15) in Mt 10:41; Mt 23:34. They were presumably an important group within the church of Matthew. As in the case of the Old Testament prophets, there were both true and false ones, and for Matthew the difference could be recognized by the quality of their deeds, the *fruits* (Mt 7:16). The mention of *fruits* leads to the comparison with trees, some producing good fruit, others bad.

**7:21–23** The attack on the false prophets is continued, but is broadened to include those disciples who perform works of healing and exorcism in the name of Jesus (*Lord*) but live evil

lives. Entrance into the kingdom is only for those who do the will of the Father. On the day of judgment (*on that day*) the morally corrupt prophets and miracle workers will be rejected by Jesus.

**7:23** *I never knew you:* cf. Mt 10:33. *Depart from me, you evildoers:* cf. Ps 6:9.

**7:24–27** The conclusion of the discourse (cf. Lk 6:47–49). Here the relation is not between saying and doing as in Mt 7:15–23 but between hearing and doing, and the words of Jesus are applied to every Christian (*everyone who listens*).

**7:28–29** *When Jesus finished these words:* this or a similar formula is used by Matthew to conclude each of the five great discourses of Jesus (cf. Mt 11:1; 13:53; 19:1; 26:1).

**7:29** *Not as their scribes:* scribal instruction was a faithful handing down of the traditions of earlier teachers; Jesus' teaching is based on his own authority. *Their scribes:* for the implications of *their,* see note on Mt 4:23.

**8:1–9:38** This narrative section of the second book of the gospel is composed of nine miracle stories, most of which are found in Mark, although Matthew does not follow the Marcan order and abbreviates the stories radically. The stories are arranged in

---

| | |
|---|---|
| **7:8** Lk 18:1–8; Jn 14:13. | **7:22–23** Lk 13:26–27. |
| **7:11** 1 Jn 5:14–15. | **7:22** 25:11–12. |
| **7:12** Lk 6:31. | **7:23** Ps 5:5; 6:9. |
| **7:13** Lk 13:24. | **7:24–27** Lk 6:47–49. |
| **7:15** 2 Pt 2:1. | **7:25–26** Prv 10:25. |
| **7:16–17** 12:33; Lk 6:43–44. | **7:29** Mk 1:22; Lk 4:32. |
| **7:20** 3:10. | **8:1–4** Mk 1:40–44; Lk |
| **7:21** Is 29:13; Lk 6:46. | 5:12–14. |

MT

crowds followed him. ²And then a leper† approached, did him homage, and said, "Lord, if you wish, you can make me clean." ³He stretched out his hand, touched him, and said, "I will do it. Be made clean." His leprosy was cleansed immediately. ⁴†Then Jesus said to him, "See that you tell no one, but go show yourself to the priest, and offer the gift that Moses prescribed;* that will be proof for them."

## The Healing of a Centurion's Servant.†

⁵*When he entered Capernaum,† a centurion approached him and appealed to him, ⁶saying, "Lord, my servant is lying at home paralyzed, suffering dreadfully." ⁷He said to him, "I will come and cure him." ⁸The centurion said in reply,† "Lord, I am not worthy to have you enter under my roof; only say the word and my servant will be healed. ⁹For I too am a person subject to authority, with soldiers subject to me. And I say to one, 'Go,' and he goes; and to another, 'Come here,' and he comes; and to my slave, 'Do this,' and he does it." ¹⁰When Jesus heard this, he was amazed and said to those following him, "Amen, I say to you, in no one in Israel† have I found such faith. ¹¹*I say to you,† many will come from the east and the west, and will recline with Abraham, Isaac, and Jacob at the banquet in the kingdom of heaven, ¹²but the children of the kingdom will be driven out into the outer darkness, where there will be wailing and grinding of teeth." ¹³And Jesus said to the centurion, "You may go; as you have believed, let it be done for you." And at that very hour [his] servant was healed.

## The Cure of Peter's Mother-in-Law.† ¹⁴*

Jesus entered the house of Peter, and saw his mother-in-law lying in bed with a fever. ¹⁵He touched her hand, the fever left her, and she rose and waited on him.*

## Other Healings.

¹⁶When it was evening, they brought him many who were possessed by demons, and he drove out the spirits by a word† and cured all the sick, ¹⁷to fulfill what had been said by Isaiah the prophet:†*

> "He took away our infirmities
> and bore our diseases."

## The Would-be Followers of Jesus.†

¹⁸*When Jesus saw a crowd around him, he gave orders to cross to the other side.† ¹⁹*A scribe approached and said to him, "Teacher,† I will follow you wherever you go." ²⁰Jesus answered him, "Foxes have dens and birds of the sky

---

† three groups of three, each group followed by a section composed principally of sayings of Jesus about discipleship. Mt 9:35 is an almost verbatim repetition of Mt 4:23. Each speaks of Jesus' teaching, preaching, and healing. The teaching and preaching form the content of Mt 5–7; the healing, that of Mt 8–9. Some scholars speak of a portrayal of Jesus as "Messiah of the Word" in Mt 5–7 and "Messiah of the Deed" in Mt 8–9. That is accurate so far as it goes, but there is also a strong emphasis on discipleship in Mt 8–9; these chapters have not only christological but ecclesiological import.

**8:2** *A leper:* see note on Mk 1:40.

**8:4** Cf. Lv 14:2–9. *That will be proof for them:* the Greek can also mean "that will be proof against them." It is not clear whether *them* refers to the priests or the people.

**8:5–13** This story comes from Q (see Lk 7:1–10) and is also reflected in Jn 4:46–54. The similarity between the Q story and the Johannine is due to a common oral tradition, not to a common literary source. As in the later story of the daughter of the Canaanite woman (Mt 15:21–28) Jesus here breaks with his usual procedure of ministering only to Israelites and anticipates the mission to the Gentiles.

**8:5** *A centurion:* a military officer commanding a hundred men. He was probably in the service of Herod Antipas, tetrarch of Galilee; see note on Mt 14:1.

**8:8–9** Acquainted by his position with the force of a command, the centurion expresses faith in the power of Jesus' mere word.

**8:10** *In no one in Israel:* there is good textual attestation (e.g., Codex Sinaiticus) for a reading identical with that of Lk 7:9, "not even in Israel." But that seems to be due to a harmonization of Matthew with Luke.

**8:11–12** Matthew inserts into the story a Q saying (see Lk 13:28–29) about the entrance of Gentiles into the kingdom and the exclusion of those Israelites who, though descended from the patriarchs and members of the chosen nation (*the children of the kingdom*), refused to believe in Jesus. *There will be wailing and grinding of teeth:* the first occurrence of a phrase used frequently in this gospel to describe final condemnation (Mt 13:42, 50; 22:13; 24:51; 25:30). It is found elsewhere in the New Testament only in Lk 13:28.

**8:14–15** Cf. Mk 1:29–31. Unlike Mark, Matthew has no implied request by others for the woman's cure. Jesus acts on his own initiative, and the cured woman rises and waits not on "them" (Mk 1:31) but on *him*.

**8:16** *By a word:* a Matthean addition to Mk 1:34; cf. 8:8.

**8:17** This fulfillment citation from Is 53:4 follows the MT, not the LXX. The prophet speaks of the Servant of the Lord who suffers vicariously for the sins ("infirmities") of others; Matthew takes the *infirmities* as physical afflictions.

**8:18–22** This passage between the first and second series of miracles about following Jesus is taken from Q (see Lk 9:57–62). The third of the three sayings found in the source is absent from Matthew.

**8:18** *The other side:* i.e., of the Sea of Galilee.

**8:19** *Teacher:* for Matthew, this designation of Jesus is true, for he has Jesus using it of himself (Mt 10:24, 25; 23:8; 26:18), yet when it is used of him by others they are either his opponents (Mt 9:11; 12:38; 17:24; 22:16, 24, 36) or, as here and in Mt 19:16, well-disposed persons who cannot see more deeply. Thus it reveals an inadequate recognition of who Jesus is.

*
| | |
|---|---|
| **8:4** Lv 14:2–32; Lk 17:14. | **8:14–16** Mk 1:29–34; Lk |
| **8:5–13** Lk 7:1–10; Jn | 4:38–41. |
| 4:46–53. | **8:15** 9:25. |
| **8:11–12** 13:42, 50; 22:13; | **8:17** Is 53:4. |
| 24:51; 25:30; Lk | **8:18** Mk 4:35. |
| 13:28–29. | **8:19–22** Lk 9:57–60. |

MT

have nests, but the Son of Man† has nowhere to rest his head." 21 Another of [his] disciples said to him, "Lord, let me go first and bury my father." 22† But Jesus answered him, "Follow me, and let the dead bury their dead."

### The Calming of the Storm at Sea.

23†* He got into a boat and his disciples followed him. 24 Suddenly a violent storm† came up on the sea, so that the boat was being swamped by waves; but he was asleep. 25* They came and woke him, saying, "Lord, save us!† We are perishing!" 26 He said to them, "Why are you terrified, O you of little faith?"† Then he got up, rebuked the winds and the sea, and there was great calm. 27 The men were amazed and said, "What sort of man is this, whom even the winds and the sea obey?"

### The Healing of the Gadarene Demoniacs.

28* When he came to the other side, to the territory of the Gadarenes,† two demoniacs who were coming from the tombs met him. They were so savage that no one could travel by that road. 29 They cried out, "What have you to do with us,† Son of God? Have you come here to torment us before the appointed time?" 30 Some distance away a herd of many swine was feeding.† 31 The demons pleaded with him, "If you drive us out, send us into the herd of swine."* 32 And he said to them, "Go then!" They came out and entered the swine, and the whole herd rushed down the steep bank into the sea where they drowned. 33 The swineherds ran away, and when they came to the town they reported everything, including what had happened to the demoniacs. 34 Thereupon the whole town came out to meet Jesus, and when they saw him they begged him to leave their district.

## 9 The Healing of a Paralytic.

1†* He entered a boat, made the crossing, and came into his own town. 2 And there people brought to him a paralytic lying on a stretcher. When Jesus saw their faith, he said to the paralytic, "Courage, child, your sins are forgiven."* 3 At that, some of the scribes† said to themselves, "This man is blaspheming." 4 Jesus knew what they were thinking, and said, "Why do you harbor evil thoughts? 5 Which is easier, to say, 'Your sins are forgiven,' or to say, 'Rise and walk'? 6† But that you may know that the Son of Man has authority on earth to forgive sins"—he then said to the paralytic, "Rise, pick up your stretcher, and go home."* 7 He rose and went home. 8† When the crowds saw this they were struck with awe and glorified God who had given such authority to human beings.

---

**8:20** *Son of Man:* see note on Mk 8:31. This is the first occurrence in Matthew of a term that appears in the New Testament only in sayings of Jesus, except for Acts 7:56 and possibly Mt 9:6 (// Mk 2:10; Lk 5:24). In Matthew it refers to Jesus in his ministry (seven times, as here), in his passion and resurrection (nine times, e.g., Mt 17:22), and in his glorious coming at the end of the age (thirteen times, e.g., Mt 24:30).

**8:22** *Let the dead bury their dead:* the demand of Jesus overrides what both the Jewish and the Hellenistic world regarded as a filial obligation of the highest importance. See note on Lk 9:60.

**8:23** *His disciples followed him:* the first miracle in the second group (Mt 8:23–9:8) is introduced by a verse that links it with the preceding sayings by the catchword "follow." In Mark the initiative in entering the boat is taken by the disciples (Mk 4:35–41); here, Jesus enters first and the disciples follow.

**8:24** *Storm:* literally, "earthquake," a word commonly used in apocalyptic literature for the shaking of the old world when God brings in his kingdom. All the synoptics use it in depicting the events preceding the parousia of the Son of Man (Mt 24:7; Mk 13:8; Lk 21:11). Matthew has introduced it here and in his account of the death and resurrection of Jesus (Mt 27:51–54; 28:2).

**8:25** The reverent plea of the disciples contrasts sharply with their reproach of Jesus in Mk 4:38.

**8:26** *You of little faith:* see note on Mt 6:30. *Great calm:* Jesus' calming the sea may be meant to recall the Old Testament theme of God's control over the chaotic waters (Ps 65:8; 89:10; 93:3–4; 107:29).

**8:28** *Gadarenes:* this is the reading of Codex Vaticanus, supported by other important textual witnesses. The original reading of Codex Sinaiticus was Gazarenes, later changed to Gergesenes, and a few versions have Gerasenes. Each of these readings points to a different territory connected, respectively, with the

cities Gadara, Gergesa, and Gerasa (modern Jerash). There is the same confusion of readings in the parallel texts, Mk 5:1 and Lk 8:26; there the best reading seems to be "Gerasenes," whereas "Gadarenes" is probably the original reading in Matthew. The town of Gadara was about five miles southeast of the Sea of Galilee, and Josephus (*Life* 9:42) refers to it as possessing territory that lay on that sea. *Two demoniacs:* Mark (5:1–20) has one.

**8:29** *What have you to do with us?:* see note on Jn 2:4. *Before the appointed time:* the notion that evil spirits were allowed by God to afflict human beings until the time of the final judgment is found in Enoch 16:1 and Jubilees 10:7–10.

**8:30** The tending of pigs, animals considered unclean by Mosaic law (Lv 11:6–7), indicates that the population was Gentile.

**9:1** *His own town:* Capernaum; see Mt 4:13.

**9:3** *Scribes:* see note on Mk 2:6. Matthew omits the reason given in the Marcan story for the charge of blasphemy: "Who but God alone can forgive sins?" (Mk 2:7).

**9:6** It is not clear whether *But that you may know…to forgive sins* is intended to be a continuation of the words of Jesus or a parenthetical comment of the evangelist to those who would hear or read this gospel. In any case, Matthew here follows the Marcan text.

**9:8** *Who had given such authority to human beings:* a significant difference from Mk 2:12 ("They…glorified God, saying, 'We have never seen anything like this'"). Matthew's extension to *human beings* of the authority to forgive sins points to the belief that such authority was being claimed by Matthew's church.

---

8:23–27 Mk 4:35–40; Lk 8:22–25.
8:25–26 Ps 107:28–29.
8:28–34 Mk 5:1–17; Lk 8:26–37.
8:31 Lk 4:34, 41.
9:1–8 Mk 2:3–12; Lk 5:18–26.
9:2 Lk 7:48.
9:6 Jn 5:27.

**The Call of Matthew.†** ⁹As Jesus passed on from there,* he saw a man named Matthew† sitting at the customs post. He said to him, "Follow me." And he got up and followed him. ¹⁰While he was at table in his house,† many tax collectors and sinners came and sat with Jesus and his disciples.* ¹¹The Pharisees saw this and said to his disciples, "Why does your teacher† eat with tax collectors and sinners?" ¹²He heard this and said, "Those who are well do not need a physician, but the sick do.† ¹³Go and learn the meaning of the words,* 'I desire mercy, not sacrifice.'† I did not come to call the righteous but sinners."

**The Question About Fasting.** ¹⁴*Then the disciples of John approached him and said, "Why do we and the Pharisees fast [much], but your disciples do not fast?" ¹⁵Jesus answered them, "Can the wedding guests mourn as long as the bridegroom is with them? The days will come when the bridegroom is taken away from them, and then they will fast.† ¹⁶No one patches an old cloak with a piece of unshrunken cloth,† for its fullness pulls away from the cloak and the tear gets worse. ¹⁷People do not put new wine into old wineskins. Otherwise the skins burst, the wine spills out, and the skins are ruined. Rather, they pour new wine into fresh wineskins, and both are preserved."

**The Official's Daughter and the Woman with a Hemorrhage.** ¹⁸†While he was saying these things to them,* an official† came forward, knelt down before him, and said, "My daughter has just died. But come, lay your hand on her, and she will live." ¹⁹Jesus rose and followed him, and so did his disciples. ²⁰A woman suffering hemorrhages for twelve years came up behind him and touched the tassel† on his cloak. ²¹She said to herself, "If only I can touch his cloak, I shall be cured."* ²²Jesus turned around and saw her, and said, "Courage, daughter! Your faith has saved you." And from that hour the woman was cured.

²³When Jesus arrived at the official's house and saw the flute players and the crowd who were making a commotion, ²⁴he said, "Go away! The girl is not dead but sleeping."† And they ridiculed him. ²⁵When the crowd was put out, he came and took her by the hand, and the little girl arose. ²⁶And news of this spread throughout all that land.

**The Healing of Two Blind Men.†** ²⁷*And as Jesus passed on from there, two blind men

**9:9–17** In this section the order is the same as that of Mk 2:13–22.

**9:9** *A man named Matthew*: Mark names this tax collector Levi (Mk 2:14). No such name appears in the four lists of the twelve who were the closest companions of Jesus (Mt 10:2–4; Mk 3:16–19; Lk 6:14–16; Acts 1:13 [eleven, because of the defection of Judas Iscariot]), whereas all four list a Matthew, designated in Mt 10:3 as "the tax collector." The evangelist may have changed the "Levi" of his source to *Matthew* so that this man, whose call is given special notice, like that of the first four disciples (Mt 4:18–22), might be included among the twelve. Another reason for the change may be that the disciple Matthew was the source of traditions peculiar to the church for which the evangelist was writing.

**9:10** *His house*: it is not clear whether *his* refers to Jesus or Matthew. *Tax collectors*: see note on Mt 5:46. Table association with such persons would cause ritual impurity.

**9:11** *Teacher*: see note on Mt 8:19.

**9:12** See note on Mk 2:17.

**9:13** *Go and learn…not sacrifice*: Matthew adds the prophetic statement of Hos 6:6 to the Marcan account (see also Mt 12:7). If mercy is superior to the temple sacrifices, how much more to the laws of ritual impurity.

**9:15** Fasting is a sign of mourning and would be as inappropriate at this time of joy, when Jesus is proclaiming the kingdom, as it would be at a marriage feast. Yet the saying looks forward to the time when Jesus will no longer be with the disciples visibly, the time of Matthew's church. *Then they will fast*: see *Didache* 8:1.

**9:16–17** Each of these parables speaks of the unsuitability of attempting to combine the old and the new. Jesus' teaching is not a patching up of Judaism, nor can the gospel be contained within the limits of Mosaic law.

**9:18–34** In this third group of miracles, the first (Mt 9:18–26)

is clearly dependent on Mark (Mk 5:21–43). Though it tells of two miracles, the cure of the woman had already been included within the story of the raising of the official's daughter, so that the two were probably regarded as a single unit. The other miracles seem to have been derived from Mark and Q, respectively, though there Matthew's own editing is much more evident.

**9:18** *Official*: literally, "ruler." Mark calls him "one of the synagogue officials" (Mk 5:22). *My daughter has just died*: Matthew heightens the Marcan "my daughter is at the point of death" (Mk 5:23).

**9:20** *Tassel*: possibly "fringe." The Mosaic law prescribed that tassels be worn on the corners of one's garment as a reminder to keep the commandments (see Nm 15:37–39; Dt 22:12).

**9:24** *Sleeping*: sleep is a biblical metaphor for death (see Ps 87:6 LXX; Dn 12:2; 1 Thes 5:10). Jesus' statement is not a denial of the child's real death, but an assurance that she will be roused from her sleep of death.

**9:27–31** This story was probably composed by Matthew out of Mark's story of the healing of a blind man named Bartimaeus (Mk 10:46–52). Mark places the event late in Jesus' ministry, just before his entrance into Jerusalem, and Matthew has followed his Marcan source at that point in his gospel also (see Mt 20:29–34). In each of the Matthean stories the single blind man of Mark becomes two. The reason why Matthew would have given a double version of the Marcan story and placed the earlier one here may be that he wished to add a story of Jesus' curing the blind at this point in order to prepare for Jesus' answer to the emissaries of the Baptist (Mt 11:4–6) in which Jesus, recounting his works, begins with his giving sight to the blind.

followed [him], crying out, "Son of David,† have pity on us!"* 28 When he entered the house, the blind men approached him and Jesus said to them, "Do you believe that I can do this?" "Yes, Lord," they said to him. 29 Then he touched their eyes and said, "Let it be done for you according to your faith." 30 And their eyes were opened. Jesus warned them sternly, "See that no one knows about this." 31 But they went out and spread word of him through all that land.

**The Healing of a Mute Person.** 32 * As they were going out,† a demoniac who could not speak was brought to him, 33 and when the demon was driven out the mute person spoke. The crowds were amazed and said, "Nothing like this has ever been seen in Israel."* 34 † But the Pharisees said,* "He drives out demons by the prince of demons."

**The Compassion of Jesus.** 35 † * Jesus went around to all the towns and villages, teaching in their synagogues, proclaiming the gospel of the kingdom, and curing every disease and illness. 36 * At the sight of the crowds, his heart was moved with pity for them because they were troubled and abandoned,† like sheep without a shepherd. 37 † * Then he said to his disciples, "The harvest is abundant but the laborers are few; 38 so ask the master of the harvest to send out laborers for his harvest."

# 10 The Mission of the Twelve. 1 † Then he summoned his twelve disciples† and gave them authority over unclean spirits to drive them out and to cure every disease and every illness.* 2 The names of the twelve apostles† are these: first, Simon called Peter, and his brother Andrew; James, the son of Zebedee, and his brother John; 3 Philip and Bartholomew, Thomas and Matthew the tax collector; James, the son of Alphaeus, and Thaddeus; 4 Simon the Cananean, and Judas Iscariot who betrayed him.

**The Commissioning of the Twelve.** 5 * Jesus sent out these twelve† after instructing them thus, "Do not go into pagan territory or enter a Samaritan town. 6 * Go rather to the lost sheep of the house of Israel. 7 As you go, make this proclamation: 'The kingdom of heaven is at hand.'* 8 † Cure the sick, raise the dead, cleanse lepers, drive out demons. Without cost you have received; without cost you are to give. 9 * Do not take gold or silver or copper for your belts; 10 * no sack for the journey, or a second tunic, or sandals, or walking stick. The

---

**9:27** *Son of David*: this messianic title is connected once with the healing power of Jesus in Mark (Mk 10:47–48) and Luke (Lk 18:38–39) but more frequently in Matthew (see also Mt 12:23; 15:22; 20:30–31).

**9:32–34** The source of this story seems to be Q (see Lk 11:14–15). As in the preceding healing of the blind, Matthew has two versions of this healing, the later in Mt 12:22–24 and the earlier here.

**9:34** This spiteful accusation foreshadows the growing opposition to Jesus in Mt 11 and 12.

**9:35** See notes on Mt 4:23–25; Mt 8:1–9:38.

**9:36** See Mk 6:34; Nm 27:17; 1 Kgs 22:17.

**9:37–38** This Q saying (see Lk 10:2) is only imperfectly related to this context. It presupposes that only God (*the master of the harvest*) can take the initiative in sending out preachers of the gospel, whereas in Matthew's setting it leads into Mt 10 where Jesus does so.

**10:1–11:1** After an introductory narrative (Mt 10:1–4), the second of the discourses of the gospel. It deals with the mission now to be undertaken by the disciples (Mt 10:5–39), but the perspective broadens and includes the missionary activity of the church between the time of the resurrection and the parousia.

**10:1** *His twelve disciples*: although, unlike Mark (Mk 3:13–14) and Luke (Lk 6:12–16), Matthew has no story of Jesus' choosing the Twelve, he assumes that the group is known to the reader. The earliest New Testament text to speak of it is 1 Cor 15:5. The number probably is meant to recall the twelve tribes of Israel and implies Jesus' authority to call all Israel into the kingdom. While Luke (Lk 6:13) and probably Mark (Mk 4:10, 34) distinguish between the Twelve and a larger group also termed disciples, Matthew tends to identify the disciples and the Twelve. *Authority... every illness*: activities the same as those of Jesus; see Mt 4:23; Mt 9:35; 10:8. The Twelve also share in his proclamation of the

kingdom (Mt 10:7). But although he teaches (Mt 4:23; 7:28; 9:35), they do not. Their commission to teach comes only after Jesus' resurrection, after they have been fully instructed by him (Mt 28:20).

**10:2–4** Here, for the only time in Matthew, the Twelve are designated *apostles*. The word *apostle* means "one who is sent," and therefore fits the situation here described. In the Pauline letters, the place where the term occurs most frequently in the New Testament, it means primarily one who has seen the risen Lord and has been commissioned to proclaim the resurrection. With slight variants in Luke and Acts, the names of those who belong to this group are the same in the four lists given in the New Testament (see note on Mt 9:9). *Cananean*: this represents an Aramaic word meaning "zealot." The meaning of that designation is unclear (see note on Lk 6:15).

**10:5–6** Like Jesus (Mt 15:24), the Twelve are sent only to Israel. This saying may reflect an original Jewish Christian refusal of the mission to the Gentiles, but for Matthew it expresses rather the limitation that Jesus himself observed during his ministry.

**10:8–11** The Twelve have received their own call and mission through God's gift, and the benefits they confer are likewise to be given freely. They are not to take with them money, provisions, or unnecessary clothing; their lodging and food will be provided by those who receive them.

---

| | |
|---|---|
| **9:27** 15:22. | **10:1–4** Mk 3:14–19; Lk |
| **9:32–34** 12:22–24; Lk | 6:13–16; Acts 1:13. |
| 11:14–15. | **10:5–15** Mk 6:7–13; Lk 9:1–6. |
| **9:33** Mk 2:12; 7:37. | **10:6** 15:24. |
| **9:34** 10:25; Mk 3:22. | **10:7** 3:2; 4:17. |
| **9:35** 4:23; Lk 8:1. | **10:9–10** Mk 6:8–9; Lk 9:3; |
| **9:36** Nm 27:17; 1 Kgs | 10:4. |
| 22:17; Jer 50:6; Ez | **10:10** Lk 10:7; 1 Cor 9:14; |
| 34:5; Mk 6:34. | 1 Tm 5:18. |
| **9:37–38** Lk 10:2; Jn 4:35. | |

laborer deserves his keep. [11]* Whatever town or village you enter, look for a worthy person in it, and stay there until you leave. [12] As you enter a house, wish it peace. [13] If the house is worthy, let your peace come upon it; if not, let your peace return to you.† [14]†* Whoever will not receive you or listen to your words—go outside that house or town and shake the dust from your feet. [15] Amen, I say to you, it will be more tolerable for the land of Sodom and Gomorrah on the day of judgment than for that town.*

**Coming Persecutions.** [16]* "Behold, I am sending you like sheep in the midst of wolves; so be shrewd as serpents and simple as doves. [17]† But beware of people,* for they will hand you over to courts and scourge you in their synagogues,* [18] and you will be led before governors and kings for my sake as a witness before them and the pagans. [19] When they hand you over, do not worry about how you are to speak or what you are to say. You will be given at that moment what you are to say.* [20] For it will not be you who speak but the Spirit of your Father speaking through you. [21]†* Brother will hand over brother to death, and the father his child; children will rise up against parents and have them put to death. [22] You will be hated by all because of my name, but whoever endures to the end† will be saved. [23] When they persecute you in one town, flee to another. Amen, I say to you, you will not finish the towns of Israel before the Son of Man comes.† [24]* No disciple is above his teacher, no slave above his master. [25] It is enough for the disciple that he become like his teacher, for the slave that he become like his master. If they have called the master of the house Beelzebul,† how much more those of his household!

**Courage Under Persecution.** [26]* "Therefore do not be afraid of them. Nothing is concealed that will not be revealed, nor secret that will not be known.†* [27] What I say to you in the darkness, speak in the light; what you hear whispered, proclaim on the housetops. [28] And do not be afraid of those who kill the body but cannot kill the soul; rather, be afraid of the one who can destroy both soul and body in Gehenna.* [29] Are not two sparrows sold for a small coin? Yet not one of them falls to the ground without your Father's knowledge. [30] Even all the hairs of your head are counted. [31] So do not be afraid; you are worth more than many sparrows. [32]† Everyone who acknowledges me before others I will acknowledge before my heavenly Father. [33] But whoever denies me before others, I will deny before my heavenly Father.*

**Jesus: A Cause of Division.** [34]* "Do not think that I have come to bring peace upon the earth. I have come to bring not peace but the sword. [35] For I have come to set

a man 'against his father,
　　a daughter against her mother,
　and a daughter-in-law against her
　　　　mother-in-law;
36　　and one's enemies will be those of his
　　　　household.'

---

† **10:13** The greeting of peace is conceived of not merely as a salutation but as an effective word. If it finds no worthy recipient, it will return to the speaker.

**10:14** *Shake the dust from your feet:* this gesture indicates a complete disassociation from such unbelievers.

**10:17** The persecutions attendant upon the post-resurrection mission now begin to be spoken of. Here Matthew brings into the discourse sayings found in Mk 13 which deals with events preceding the parousia.

**10:21** See Mi 7:6 which is cited in Mt 10:35, 36.

**10:22** *To the end:* the original meaning was probably "until the parousia." But it is not likely that Matthew expected no missionary disciples to suffer death before then, since he envisages the martyrdom of other Christians (Mt 10:21). For him, *the end* is probably that of the individual's life (see Mt 10:28).

**10:23** *Before the Son of Man comes:* since the coming of the Son of Man at the end of the age had not taken place when this gospel was written, much less during the mission of the Twelve during Jesus' ministry, Matthew cannot have meant the coming to refer to the parousia. It is difficult to know what he understood it to be: perhaps the "proleptic parousia" of Mt 28:16–20, or the destruction of the temple in A.D. 70, viewed as a coming of Jesus in judgment on unbelieving Israel.

**10:25** *Beelzebul:* see Mt 9:34 for the charge linking Jesus with "the prince of demons," who is named *Beelzebul* in Mt 12:24. The meaning of the name is uncertain; possibly, "lord of the house."

**10:26** The *concealed* and *secret* coming of the kingdom is to be proclaimed by them, and no fear must be allowed to deter them from that proclamation.

**10:32–33** In the Q parallel (Lk 12:8–9), the Son of Man will acknowledge those who have acknowledged Jesus, and those who deny him will be denied (by the Son of Man) before the angels of God at the judgment. Here Jesus and the Son of Man are identified, and the acknowledgment or denial will be before his heavenly Father.

---

**10:11–15** Mk 6:10–11; Lk 9:4–5; 10:5–12.
**10:14** Acts 13:51; 18:6.
**10:15** 11:24; Gn 19:1–29; Jude 7.
**10:16** Lk 10:3.
**10:17–22** Mk 13:9–13; Lk 21:12–19.
**10:17** Acts 5:40.
**10:19** Ex 4:11–12; Jer 1:6–10; Lk 12:11–12.
**10:21–22** 24:9, 13.
**10:24–25** Lk 6:40; Jn 13:16; 15:20.
**10:26–33** Lk 12:2–9.
**10:26** Mk 4:22; Lk 8:17; 1 Tm 5:25.
**10:28** Jas 4:12.
**10:33** Mk 8:38; Lk 9:26; 2 Tm 2:12; Rev 3:5.
**10:34–35** Lk 12:51–53.

MT

**The Conditions of Discipleship.** 37* "Whoever loves father or mother more than me is not worthy of me, and whoever loves son or daughter more than me is not worthy of me; 38 and whoever does not take up his cross† and follow after me is not worthy of me. 39†* Whoever finds his life will lose it, and whoever loses his life for my sake will find it.

**Rewards.** 40 "Whoever receives you receives me,† and whoever receives me receives the one who sent me.* 41† Whoever receives a prophet because he is a prophet will receive a prophet's reward, and whoever receives a righteous man because he is righteous will receive a righteous man's reward. 42 And whoever gives only a cup of cold water to one of these little ones to drink because he is a disciple—amen, I say to you, he will surely not lose his reward."*

**11** 1 When Jesus finished giving these commands to his twelve disciples,† he went away from that place to teach and to preach in their towns.

## IV. OPPOSITION FROM ISRAEL

**The Messengers from John the Baptist.** 2†* When John heard in prison† of the works of the Messiah, he sent his disciples to him 3† with this question, "Are you the one who is to come, or should we look for another?" 4 Jesus said to them in reply, "Go and tell John what you hear and see: 5† the blind regain their sight, the lame walk, lepers are cleansed, the deaf hear, the dead are raised, and the poor have the good news proclaimed to them.* 6 And blessed is the one who takes no offense at me."

**Jesus' Testimony to John.**† 7 As they were going off, Jesus began to speak to the crowds about John, "What did you go out to the desert to see? A reed swayed by the wind?* 8 Then what did you go out to see? Someone dressed in fine clothing? Those who wear fine clothing are in royal palaces. 9 Then why did you go out? To see a prophet?† Yes, I tell you, and more than a prophet. 10 This is the one about whom it is written:

'Behold, I am sending my messenger
        ahead of you;
    he will prepare your way before you.'*

11 Amen, I say to you, among those born of women there has been none greater than John the Baptist; yet the least in the kingdom of heaven is greater than he.† 12 From the days of John the Baptist until now, the kingdom of heaven suffers violence,† and the violent

---

**10:38** The first mention of the cross in Matthew, explicitly that of the disciple, but implicitly that of Jesus (*and follow after me*). Crucifixion was a form of capital punishment used by the Romans for offenders who were not Roman citizens.

**10:39** One who denies Jesus in order to save one's earthly life will be condemned to everlasting destruction; loss of earthly life for Jesus' sake will be rewarded by everlasting life in the kingdom.

**10:40–42** All who receive the disciples of Jesus receive him, and God who sent him, and will be rewarded accordingly.

**10:41** *A prophet:* one who speaks in the name of God; here, the Christian prophets who proclaim the gospel. *Righteous man:* since righteousness is demanded of all the disciples, it is difficult to take the *righteous man* of this verse and *one of these little ones* (Mt 10:42) as indicating different groups within the followers of Jesus. Probably all three designations are used here of Christian missionaries as such.

**11:1** The closing formula of the discourse refers back to the original addressees, the Twelve.

**11:2–12:50** The narrative section of the third book deals with the growing opposition to Jesus. It is largely devoted to disputes and attacks relating to faith and discipleship and thus contains much sayings-material, drawn in large part from Q.

**11:2** *In prison:* see Mt 4:12; 14:1–12. *The works of the Messiah:* the deeds of Mt 8–9.

**11:3** The question probably expresses a doubt of the Baptist that Jesus is *the one who is to come* (cf. Mal 3:1) because his mission has not been one of fiery judgment as John had expected (Mt 3:2).

**11:5–6** Jesus' response is taken from passages of Isaiah (Is 26:19; 29:18–19; 35:5–6; 61:1) that picture the time of salva-

tion as marked by deeds such as those that Jesus is doing. The beatitude is a warning to the Baptist not to disbelieve because his expectations have not been met.

**11:7–19** Jesus' rebuke of John is counterbalanced by a reminder of the greatness of the Baptist's function (Mt 11:7–15) that is followed by a complaint about those who have heeded neither John nor Jesus (Mt 11:16–19).

**11:9–10** In common Jewish belief there had been no prophecy in Israel since the last of the Old Testament prophets, Malachi. The coming of a new prophet was eagerly awaited, and Jesus agrees that John was such. Yet he was *more than a prophet*, for he was the precursor of the one who would bring in the new and final age. The Old Testament quotation is a combination of Mal 3:1; Ex 23:20 with the significant change that the *before me* of Malachi becomes *before you*. The messenger now precedes not God, as in the original, but Jesus.

**11:11** John's preeminent greatness lies in his function of announcing the imminence of the kingdom (Mt 3:1). But to be in the kingdom is so great a privilege that the least who has it is greater than the Baptist.

**11:12** The meaning of this difficult saying is probably that the opponents of Jesus are trying to prevent people from accepting the kingdom and to snatch it away from those who have received it.

---

**10:37–39** 16:24–25; Lk 14:26–27.
**10:39** Mk 8:35; Lk 9:24; Jn 12:25.
**10:40** Lk 10:16; Jn 12:44; 13:20.
**10:42** 25:40; Mk 9:41.
**11:2–11** Lk 7:18–28.
**11:5** Is 26:19; 29:18–19; 35:5–6; 61:1.
**11:7** 3:3, 5.
**11:10** Ex 23:20; Mal 3:1; Mk 1:2; Lk 1:76.

are taking it by force.* ¹³All the prophets and the law† prophesied up to the time of John. ¹⁴And if you are willing to accept it, he is Elijah, the one who is to come.* ¹⁵Whoever has ears ought to hear.

¹⁶* "To what shall I compare this generation?† It is like children who sit in marketplaces and call to one another, ¹⁷'We played the flute for you, but you did not dance, we sang a dirge but you did not mourn.' ¹⁸For John came neither eating nor drinking, and they said, 'He is possessed by a demon.'* ¹⁹The Son of Man came eating and drinking and they said, 'Look, he is a glutton and a drunkard, a friend of tax collectors and sinners.' But wisdom is vindicated by her works."*

**Reproaches to Unrepentant Towns.** ²⁰* Then he began to reproach the towns where most of his mighty deeds had been done, since they had not repented. ²¹"Woe to you, Chorazin! Woe to you, Bethsaida! For if the mighty deeds done in your midst had been done in Tyre and Sidon,† they would long ago have repented in sackcloth and ashes.* ²²But I tell you, it will be more tolerable for Tyre and Sidon on the day of judgment than for you. ²³† And as for you, Capernaum:

'Will you be exalted to heaven?*
You will go down to the netherworld.'

For if the mighty deeds done in your midst had been done in Sodom, it would have remained until this day. ²⁴But I tell you, it will be more tolerable for the land of Sodom on the day of judgment than for you."*

**The Praise of the Father.** ²⁵* At that time Jesus said in reply,† "I give praise to you, Father, Lord of heaven and earth, for although you have hidden these things from the wise and the learned you have revealed them to the childlike. ²⁶Yes, Father, such has been your gracious will. ²⁷All things have been handed over to me by my Father. No one knows the Son except the Father, and no one knows the Father except the Son and anyone to whom the Son wishes to reveal him.*

**The Gentle Mastery of Christ.** ²⁸† "Come to me, all you who labor and are burdened,† and I will give you rest. ²⁹†* Take my yoke upon you and learn from me, for I am meek and humble of heart; and you will find rest for yourselves. ³⁰For my yoke is easy, and my burden light."

**12** **Picking Grain on the Sabbath.** ¹† At that time Jesus was going through a field of grain on the sabbath.* His disciples were hungry and began to pick the heads† of grain and eat them.* ²When the Pharisees saw

---

† **11:13** *All the prophets and the law*: Matthew inverts the usual order, "law and prophets," and says that both have *prophesied*. This emphasis on the prophetic character of the law points to its fulfillment in the teaching of Jesus and to the transitory nature of some of its commandments (see note on Mt 5:17–20).

**11:16–19** See Lk 7:31–35. The meaning of the parable (Mt 11:16–17) and its explanation (Mt 11:18–19b) is much disputed. A plausible view is that the *children* of the parable are two groups, one of which proposes different entertainments to the other that will not agree with either proposal. The first represents John, Jesus, and their disciples; the second those who reject John for his asceticism and Jesus for his table association with those despised by the religiously observant. Mt 11:19c (*her works*) forms an inclusion with Mt 11:2 ("the works of the Messiah"). The original form of the saying is better preserved in Lk 7:35 "… wisdom is vindicated by all her children." There John and Jesus are the children of Wisdom; here the works of Jesus the Messiah are those of divine Wisdom, of which he is the embodiment. Some important textual witnesses, however, have essentially the same reading as in Luke.

**11:21** Tyre and Sidon were pagan cities denounced for their wickedness in the Old Testament; cf. Jl 4:4–7.

**11:23** Capernaum's pride and punishment are described in language taken from the taunt song against the king of Babylon (Is 14:13–15).

**11:25–27** This Q saying, identical with Lk 10:21–22 except for minor variations, introduces a joyous note into this section, so dominated by the theme of unbelief. *While the wise and the learned*, the scribes and Pharisees, have rejected Jesus' preaching and the significance of his mighty deeds, *the childlike* have ac-

cepted them. Acceptance depends upon the Father's revelation, but this is granted to those who are open to receive it and refused to the arrogant. Jesus can speak of all mysteries because he is *the Son* and there is perfect reciprocity of knowledge between him and the Father; what has been *handed over* to him is revealed only to those whom he wishes.

**11:28–29** These verses are peculiar to Matthew and are similar to Ben Sirach's invitation to learn wisdom and submit to her yoke (Sir 51:23, 26).

**11:28** *Who labor and are burdened*: burdened by the law as expounded by the scribes and Pharisees (Mt 23:4).

**11:29** In place of the yoke of the law, complicated by scribal interpretation, Jesus invites the burdened to take the yoke of obedience to his word, under which they *will find rest*; cf. Jer 6:16.

**12:1–14** Matthew here returns to the Marcan order that he left in Mt 9:18. The two stories depend on Mk 2:23–28; 3:1–6, respectively, and are the only places in either gospel that deal explicitly with Jesus' attitude toward sabbath observance.

**12:1–2** The picking of the heads of grain is here equated with reaping, which was forbidden on the sabbath (Ex 34:21).

---

**11:12** Lk 16:16.
**11:14** 17:10–13; Mal 3:23; Lk 1:17.
**11:16–19** Lk 7:31–35.
**11:18** Lk 1:15.
**11:19** 9:10–11.
**11:20–24** Lk 10:12–15.
**11:21** Jl 4:4–7.
**11:23** Is 14:13–15.
**11:24** 10:15.
**11:25–27** Lk 10:21–22.
**11:27** Jn 3:35; 6:46; 7:28; 10:15.
**11:29** Sir 51:26; Jer 6:16.
**12:1–8** Mk 2:23–28; Lk 6:1–5.
**12:1** Dt 23:26.

this, they said to him, "See, your disciples are doing what is unlawful to do on the sabbath." ³He said to them,† "Have you not read what David* did when he and his companions were hungry, ⁴how he went into the house of God and ate the bread of offering,* which neither he nor his companions but only the priests could lawfully eat? ⁵† Or have you not read in the law that on the sabbath the priests serving in the temple violate the sabbath and are innocent?* ⁶I say to you, something greater than the temple is here. ⁷† If you knew what this meant, 'I desire mercy, not sacrifice,'* you would not have condemned these innocent men. ⁸†* For the Son of Man is Lord of the sabbath."

**The Man with a Withered Hand.** ⁹* Moving on from there, he went into their synagogue. ¹⁰And behold, there was a man there who had a withered hand. They questioned him, "Is it lawful to cure on the sabbath?"† so that they might accuse him. ¹¹† He said to them, "Which one of you who has a sheep that falls into a pit on the sabbath will not take hold of it and lift it out? ¹²How much more valuable a person is than a sheep. So it is lawful to do good on the sabbath." ¹³Then he said to the man, "Stretch out your hand." He stretched it out, and it was restored as sound as the other. ¹⁴But the Pharisees† went out and took counsel against him to put him to death.*

**The Chosen Servant.**† ¹⁵When Jesus realized this, he withdrew from that place. Many [people] followed him, and he cured them all,† ¹⁶but he warned them not to make him known. ¹⁷This was to fulfill what had been spoken through Isaiah the prophet:

18    "Behold, my servant whom I have
          chosen,*
       my beloved in whom I delight;
     I shall place my spirit upon him,
       and he will proclaim justice to the
          Gentiles.
19    He will not contend† or cry out,
       nor will anyone hear his voice in the
          streets.
20    A bruised reed he will not break,
       a smoldering wick he will not quench,
     until he brings justice to victory.
21       And in his name the Gentiles will
          hope."†

**Jesus and Beelzebul.**† ²²* Then they brought to him a demoniac who was blind and mute. He cured the mute person so that he could speak and see. ²³†* All the crowd was astounded, and said, "Could this perhaps be the Son of David?" ²⁴†* But when the Pharisees heard this, they said, "This man drives out demons only by the power of Beelzebul, the prince of demons." ²⁵* But he knew what they were thinking and said to them,† "Every

---

**12:3–4** See 1 Sm 21:2–7. In the Marcan parallel (Mk 2:25–26) the high priest is called Abiathar, although in 1 Samuel this action is attributed to Ahimelech. The Old Testament story is not about a violation of the sabbath rest; its pertinence to this dispute is that a violation of the law was permissible because of David's men being without food.

**12:5–6** This and the following argument (Mt 12:7) are peculiar to Matthew. The temple service seems to be the changing of the showbread on the sabbath (Lv 24:8) and the doubling on the sabbath of the usual daily holocausts (Nm 28:9–10). The argument is that the law itself requires work that breaks the sabbath rest, because of the higher duty of temple service. If temple duties outweigh the sabbath law, how much more does the presence of Jesus, with his proclamation of the kingdom (*something greater than the temple*), justify the conduct of his disciples.

**12:7** See note on Mt 9:13.

**12:8** The ultimate justification for the disciples' violation of the sabbath rest is that Jesus, the Son of Man, has supreme authority over the law.

**12:10** Rabbinic tradition later than the gospels allowed relief to be given to a sufferer on the sabbath if life was in danger. This may also have been the view of Jesus' Pharisaic contemporaries. But the case here is not about one in danger of death.

**12:11** Matthew omits the question posed by Jesus in Mk 3:4 and substitutes one about rescuing a sheep on the sabbath, similar to that in Lk 14:5.

**12:14** See Mk 3:6. Here the plan to bring about Jesus' death is attributed to the Pharisees only. This is probably due to the situation of Matthew's church, when the sole opponents were the Pharisees.

**12:15–21** Matthew follows Mk 3:7–12 but summarizes his source in two verses (Mt 12:15, 16) that pick up the withdrawal, the healings, and the command for silence. To this he adds a fulfillment citation from the first Servant Song (Is 42:1–4) that does not correspond exactly to either the Hebrew or the LXX of that passage. It is the longest Old Testament citation in this gospel, emphasizing the meekness of Jesus, the Servant of the Lord, and foretelling the extension of his mission to the Gentiles.

**12:15** Jesus' knowledge of the Pharisees' plot and his healing all are peculiar to Matthew.

**12:19** The servant's not contending is seen as fulfilled in Jesus' withdrawal from the disputes narrated in Mt 12:1–14.

**12:21** Except for a minor detail, Matthew here follows the LXX, although the meaning of the Hebrew ("the coastlands will wait for his teaching") is similar.

**12:22–32** For the exorcism, see note on Mt 9:32–34. The long discussion combines Marcan and Q material (Mk 3:22–30; Lk 11:19–20, 23; 12:10). Mk 3:20–21 is omitted, with a consequent lessening of the sharpness of Mt 12:48.

**12:23** See note on Mt 9:27.

**12:24** See note on Mt 10:25.

**12:25–26** Jesus' first response to the Pharisees' charge is that

---

12:3–4 1 Sm 21:2–7.              12:18–21 Is 42:1–4.
12:4 Lv 24:5–9.                   12:22–24 9:32–34; Lk
12:5 Lv 24:8; Nm 28:9–10.          11:14–15.
12:7 Hos 6:6.                     12:23 9:27.
12:8 Jn 5:16–17.                  12:24 10:25; Mk 3:22.
12:9–15 Mk 3:1–6; Lk 6:6–11.      12:25–29 Mk 3:23–27; Lk
12:14 Jn 5:18.                     11:17–22.

kingdom divided against itself will be laid waste, and no town or house divided against itself will stand. 26 And if Satan drives out Satan, he is divided against himself; how, then, will his kingdom stand? 27 And if I drive out demons by Beelzebul, by whom do your own people† drive them out? Therefore they will be your judges. 28†* But if it is by the Spirit of God that I drive out demons, then the kingdom of God has come upon you. 29† How can anyone enter a strong man's house and steal his property, unless he first ties up the strong man? Then he can plunder his house. 30†* Whoever is not with me is against me, and whoever does not gather with me scatters. 31* Therefore, I say to you, every sin and blasphemy will be forgiven people, but blasphemy against the Spirit† will not be forgiven. 32 And whoever speaks a word against the Son of Man will be forgiven; but whoever speaks against the holy Spirit will not be forgiven, either in this age or in the age to come.

**A Tree and Its Fruits.** 33* "Either declare† the tree good and its fruit is good, or declare the tree rotten and its fruit is rotten, for a tree is known by its fruit. 34†* You brood of vipers, how can you say good things when you are

evil? For from the fullness of the heart the mouth speaks. 35 A good person brings forth good out of a store of goodness, but an evil person brings forth evil out of a store of evil. 36†* I tell you, on the day of judgment people will render an account for every careless word they speak. 37 By your words you will be acquitted, and by your words you will be condemned."

**The Demand for a Sign.** † 38 Then some of the scribes and Pharisees said to him, "Teacher,† we wish to see a sign from you."* 39 He said to them in reply, "An evil and unfaithful† generation seeks a sign, but no sign will be given it except the sign of Jonah the prophet. 40 Just as Jonah was in the belly of the whale three days and three nights,† so will the Son of Man be in the heart of the earth three days and three nights. 41† At the judgment, the men of Nineveh will arise with this generation and condemn it, because they repented at the preaching of Jonah; and there is something greater than Jonah here. 42 At the judgment the queen of the south will arise with this generation and condemn it, because she came from the ends of the earth to hear the wisdom of Solomon; and there is something greater than Solomon here.*

---

† if it were true, Satan would be destroying his own kingdom.

**12:27** Besides pointing out the absurdity of the charge, Jesus asks how the work of Jewish exorcists (*your own people*) is to be interpreted. Are they, too, to be charged with collusion with Beelzebul? For an example of Jewish exorcism see Josephus, *Antiquities* 8:42–49.

**12:28** The Q parallel (Lk 11:20) speaks of the "finger" rather than of the "spirit" of God. While the difference is probably due to Matthew's editing, he retains *the kingdom of God* rather than changing it to his usual "kingdom of heaven." *Has come upon you*: see Mt 4:17.

**12:29** A short parable illustrates what Jesus is doing. The *strong man* is Satan, whom Jesus has tied up and whose *house* he is plundering. Jewish expectation was that Satan would be chained up in the last days (Rev 20:2); Jesus' exorcisms indicate that those days have begun.

**12:30** This saying, already attached to the preceding verses in Q (see Lk 11:23), warns that there can be no neutrality where Jesus is concerned. Its pertinence in a context where Jesus is addressing not the neutral but the bitterly opposed is not clear. The accusation of scattering, however, does fit the situation. Jesus is the shepherd of God's people (Mt 2:6), his mission is to the lost sheep of Israel (Mt 15:24); the Pharisees, who oppose him, are guilty of scattering the sheep.

**12:31** *Blasphemy against the Spirit*: the sin of attributing to Satan (Mt 12:24) what is the work of the Spirit of God (Mt 12:28).

**12:33** *Declare*: literally, "make." The meaning of this verse is obscure. Possibly it is a challenge to the Pharisees either to declare Jesus and his exorcisms good or both of them bad. A tree is known by its fruit; if the fruit is good, so must the tree be. If the driving out of demons is good, so must its source be.

**12:34** The admission of Jesus' goodness cannot be made by the Pharisees, for they are evil, and the words that proceed from their evil hearts cannot be good.

**12:36–37** If on the day of judgment people will be held accountable for even their *careless* words, the vicious accusations of the Pharisees will surely lead to their condemnation.

**12:38–42** This section is mainly from Q (see Lk 11:29–32). Mk 8:11–12, which Matthew has followed in Mt 16:1–4, has a similar demand for a sign. The scribes and Pharisees refuse to accept the exorcisms of Jesus as authentication of his claims and demand a sign that will end all possibility of doubt. Jesus' response is that no such sign will be given. Because his opponents are evil and see him as an agent of Satan, nothing will convince them.

**12:38** *Teacher*: see note on Mt 8:19. In Mt 16:1 the request is for a sign "from heaven" (Mk 8:11).

**12:39** *Unfaithful*: literally, "adulterous." The covenant between God and Israel was portrayed as a marriage bond, and unfaithfulness to the covenant as adultery; cf. Hos 2:4–14; Jer 3:6–10.

**12:40** See Jon 2:1. While in Q the sign was simply Jonah's preaching to the Ninevites (Lk 11:30, 32), Matthew here adds Jonah's sojourn *in the belly of the whale* for *three days and three nights*, a prefiguration of Jesus' sojourn in the abode of the dead and, implicitly, of his resurrection.

**12:41–42** The Ninevites who *repented* (see Jon 3:1–10) and *the queen of the south* (i.e., of Sheba; see 1 Kgs 10:1–13) were pagans who responded to lesser opportunities than have been offered to Israel in the ministry of Jesus, *something greater than Jonah* or *Solomon*. At the final judgment they will condemn the faithless *generation* that has rejected him.

---

*
**12:28** Lk 11:20.
**12:30** Lk 11:23.
**12:31–32** Mk 3:28–30; Lk 12:10.
**12:33–35** Lk 6:43–45.
**12:34** 3:7; 23:33; 15:11–12;

Lk 3:7.
**12:36–37** Jas 3:1–2.
**12:38–42** 16:1–4; Jon 2:1; 3:1–10; Mk 8:11–12; Lk 11:29–32.
**12:42** 1 Kgs 10:1–10.

M T

**The Return of the Unclean Spirit.**† ⁴³* "When an unclean spirit goes out of a person it roams through arid regions searching for rest but finds none. ⁴⁴Then it says, 'I will return to my home from which I came.' But upon returning, it finds it empty, swept clean, and put in order. ⁴⁵Then it goes and brings back with itself seven other spirits more evil than itself, and they move in and dwell there; and the last condition of that person is worse than the first. Thus it will be with this evil generation."

**The True Family of Jesus.**† ⁴⁶* While he was still speaking to the crowds, his mother and his brothers appeared outside, wishing to speak with him. ⁴⁷[Someone told him, "Your mother and your brothers are standing outside, asking to speak with you."]† ⁴⁸But he said in reply to the one who told him, "Who is my mother? Who are my brothers?" ⁴⁹And stretching out his hand toward his disciples, he said, "Here are my mother and my brothers. ⁵⁰For whoever does the will of my heavenly Father is my brother, and sister, and mother."

**13** **The Parable of the Sower.** ¹† On that day, Jesus went out of the house and sat down by the sea.* ²Such large crowds gathered around him that he got into a boat and sat down, and the whole crowd stood along the shore. ³† And he spoke to them at length in parables,† saying: "A sower went out to sow. ⁴And as he sowed, some seed fell on the path, and birds came and ate it up. ⁵Some fell on rocky ground, where it had little soil. It sprang up at once because the soil was not deep, ⁶and when the sun rose it was scorched, and it withered for lack of roots. ⁷Some seed fell among thorns, and the thorns grew up and choked it. ⁸But some seed fell on rich soil, and produced fruit, a hundred or sixty or thirtyfold. ⁹Whoever has ears ought to hear."

**The Purpose of Parables.** ¹⁰The disciples approached him and said, "Why do you speak to them in parables?" ¹¹† He said to them in reply, "Because knowledge of the mysteries of the kingdom of heaven has been granted to you, but to them it has not been granted. ¹²* To anyone who has, more will be given† and he will grow rich; from anyone who has not, even what he has will be taken away. ¹³† * This is why I speak to them in parables, because 'they look but do not see and hear

---

† **12:43–45** Another Q passage; cf. Mt 11:24–26. Jesus' ministry has broken Satan's hold over Israel, but the refusal of *this evil generation* to accept him will lead to a worse situation than what preceded his coming.

**12:46–50** See Mk 3:31–35. Matthew has omitted Mk 3:20–21 which is taken up in Mk 3:31 (see note on Mt 12:22–32), yet the point of the story is the same in both gospels: natural kinship with Jesus counts for nothing; only one who *does the will* of his *heavenly Father* belongs to his true family.

**12:47** This verse is omitted in some important textual witnesses, including Codex Sinaiticus (original reading) and Codex Vaticanus.

**13:1–53** The discourse in parables is the third great discourse of Jesus in Matthew and constitutes the second part of the third book of the gospel. Matthew follows the Marcan outline (Mk 4:1–35) but has only two of Mark's parables, the five others being from Q and M. In addition to the seven parables, the discourse gives the reason why Jesus uses this type of speech (Mt 13:10–15), declares the blessedness of those who understand his teaching (Mt 13:16–17), explains the parable of the sower (Mt 13:18–23) and of the weeds (Mt 13:36–43), and ends with a concluding statement to the disciples (Mt 13:51–52).

**13:3–8** Since in Palestine sowing often preceded plowing, much of the seed is scattered on ground that is unsuitable. Yet while much is wasted, the seed that falls on good ground bears fruit in extraordinarily large measure. The point of the parable is that, in spite of some failure because of opposition and indifference, the message of Jesus about the coming of the kingdom will have enormous success.

**13:3** *In parables*: the word "parable" (Greek *parabolē*) is used in the LXX to translate the Hebrew *māshāl*, a designation covering a wide variety of literary forms such as axioms, proverbs, similitudes, and allegories. In the New Testament the same breadth of meaning of the word is found, but there it primarily designates stories that are illustrative comparisons between Christian truths and events of everyday life. Sometimes the event has a strange element that is quite different from usual experience (e.g., in Mt 13:33 the enormous amount of dough in the parable of the yeast); this is meant to sharpen the curiosity of the hearer. If each detail of such a story is given a figurative meaning, the story is an allegory. Those who maintain a sharp distinction between parable and allegory insist that a parable has only one point of comparison, and that while parables were characteristic of Jesus' teaching, to see allegorical details in them is to introduce meanings that go beyond their original intention and even falsify it. However, to exclude any allegorical elements from a parable is an excessively rigid mode of interpretation, now abandoned by many scholars.

**13:11** Since a parable is figurative speech that demands reflection for understanding, only those who are prepared to explore its meaning can come to know it. To understand is a gift of God, granted to the disciples but not to the crowds. In Semitic fashion, both the disciples' understanding and the crowd's obtuseness are attributed to God. The question of human responsibility for the obtuseness is not dealt with, although it is asserted in Mt 13:13. *The mysteries*: as in Lk 8:10; Mk 4:11 has "the mystery." The word is used in Dn 2:18, 19, 27 and in the Qumran literature (1QpHab 7:8; 1QS 3:23; 1QM 3:9) to designate a divine plan or decree affecting the course of history that can be known only when revealed. *Knowledge of the mysteries of the kingdom of heaven* means recognition that the kingdom has become present in the ministry of Jesus.

**13:12** In the New Testament use of this axiom of practical "wisdom" (see Mt 25:29; Mk 4:25; Lk 8:18; 19:26), the reference transcends the original level. God gives further understanding to one who accepts the revealed mystery; from the one who does not, he will take it away (note the "theological passive," *more will be given, what he has will be taken away*).

**13:13** *Because 'they look…or understand'*: Matthew softens

---

* **12:43–45** Lk 11:24–26.
**12:46–50** Mk 3:31–35; Lk 8:19–21.
**13:1–15** Mk 4:1–12;

Lk 8:4–10.
**13:12** 25:29; Mk 4:25; Lk 8:18; 19:26.
**13:13** Jn 9:39.

but do not listen or understand.' 14* Isaiah's prophecy is fulfilled in them, which says:

> 'You shall indeed hear but not
>     understand,
> you shall indeed look but never see.
> 15     Gross is the heart of this people,
>     they will hardly hear with their ears,
>     they have closed their eyes,
>     lest they see with their eyes
>     and hear with their ears
>     and understand with their heart and be
>         converted,
>     and I heal them.'

**The Privilege of Discipleship.†** 16* "But blessed are your eyes, because they see, and your ears, because they hear. 17 Amen, I say to you, many prophets and righteous people longed to see what you see but did not see it, and to hear what you hear but did not hear it.

**The Explanation of the Parable of the Sower.†** 18* "Hear then the parable of the sower. 19 The seed sown on the path is the one who hears the word of the kingdom without understanding it, and the evil one comes and steals away what was sown in his heart. 20 The seed sown on rocky ground is the one who hears the word and receives it at once with joy. 21 But he has no root and lasts only for a time. When some tribulation or persecution comes because of the word, he immediately falls away.

22 The seed sown among thorns is the one who hears the word, but then worldly anxiety and the lure of riches choke the word and it bears no fruit. 23 But the seed sown on rich soil is the one who hears the word and understands it, who indeed bears fruit and yields a hundred or sixty or thirtyfold."

**The Parable of the Weeds Among the Wheat.** 24 He proposed another parable to them.† "The kingdom of heaven may be likened to a man who sowed good seed in his field. 25 While everyone was asleep his enemy came and sowed weeds† all through the wheat, and then went off. 26 When the crop grew and bore fruit, the weeds appeared as well. 27 The slaves of the householder came to him and said, 'Master, did you not sow good seed in your field? Where have the weeds come from?' 28 He answered, 'An enemy has done this.' His slaves said to him, 'Do you want us to go and pull them up?' 29 He replied, 'No, if you pull up the weeds you might uproot the wheat along with them. 30 Let them grow together until harvest;† then at harvest time I will say to the harvesters, "First collect the weeds and tie them in bundles for burning; but gather the wheat into my barn."'"*

**The Parable of the Mustard Seed.†** 31* He proposed another parable to them. "The kingdom of heaven is like a mustard seed that a person took and sowed in a field. 32†* It is the

---

his Marcan source, which states that Jesus speaks in parables so that the crowds may not understand (Mk 4:12), and makes such speaking a punishment given *because* they have not accepted his previous clear teaching. However, his citation of Is 6:9–10 in Mt 13:14 supports the harsher Marcan view.

**13:16–17** Unlike the unbelieving crowds, the disciples have seen that which the *prophets* and the *righteous* of the Old Testament *longed to see* without having their longing fulfilled.

**13:18–23** See Mk 4:14–20; Lk 8:11–15. In this explanation of the parable the emphasis is on the various types of soil on which the seed falls, i.e., on the dispositions with which the preaching of Jesus is received. The second and third types particularly are explained in such a way as to support the view held by many scholars that the explanation derives not from Jesus but from early Christian reflection upon apostasy from the faith that was the consequence of persecution and worldliness, respectively. Others, however, hold that the explanation may come basically from Jesus even though it was developed in the light of later Christian experience. The four types of persons envisaged are (1) those who never accept *the word of the kingdom* (Mt 13:19); (2) those who believe for a while but fall away because of *persecution* (Mt 13:20–21); (3) those who believe, but in whom *the word* is choked by *worldly anxiety* and the seduction of *riches* (Mt 13:22); (4) those who respond to *the word* and produce *fruit* abundantly (Mt 13:23).

**13:24–30** This parable is peculiar to Matthew. The comparison in Mt 13:24 does not mean that *the kingdom of heaven may*

*be likened* simply to the person in question but to the situation narrated in the whole story. The refusal of the *householder* to allow his *slaves* to separate *the wheat* from *the weeds* while they are still growing is a warning to the disciples not to attempt to anticipate the final judgment of God by a definitive exclusion of sinners from the kingdom. In its present stage it is composed of the good and the bad. The judgment of God alone will eliminate the sinful. Until then there must be patience and the preaching of repentance.

**13:25** *Weeds:* darnel, a poisonous weed that in its first stage of growth resembles wheat.

**13:30** *Harvest:* a common biblical metaphor for the time of God's judgment; cf. Jer 51:33; Jl 4:13; Hos 6:11.

**13:31–33** See Mk 4:30–32; Lk 13:18–21. The parables of the mustard seed and the yeast illustrate the same point: the amazing contrast between the small beginnings of the kingdom and its marvelous expansion.

**13:32** See Dn 4:7–9, 17–19 where the birds nesting in the tree represent the people of Nebuchadnezzar's kingdom. See also Ez 17:23; 31:6.

---

| | |
|---|---|
| **13:14–15** Is 6:9–10; Jn 12:40; | Lk 8:11–15. |
| Acts 28:26–27; Rom | **13:30** 3:12. |
| 11:8. | **13:31–32** Mk 4:30–32; Lk |
| **13:16–17** Lk 10:23–24; 1 Pt | 13:18–19. |
| 1:10–12. | **13:32** Ez 17:23; 31:6; Dn |
| **13:18–23** Mk 4:13–20; | 4:7–9, 17–19. |

smallest of all the seeds, yet when full-grown it is the largest of plants. It becomes a large bush, and the 'birds of the sky come and dwell in its branches.'"

**The Parable of the Yeast.** [33] He spoke to them another parable. "The kingdom of heaven is like yeast† that a woman took and mixed with three measures of wheat flour until the whole batch was leavened."*

**The Use of Parables.** [34]†* All these things Jesus spoke to the crowds in parables. He spoke to them only in parables, [35] to fulfill what had been said through the prophet:†

> "I will open my mouth in parables,
> I will announce what has lain hidden
>     from the foundation [of the
>     world]."*

**The Explanation of the Parable of the Weeds.** [36] Then, dismissing the crowds,† he went into the house. His disciples approached him and said, "Explain to us the parable of the weeds in the field." [37]† He said in reply, "He who sows good seed is the Son of Man, [38] the field is the world,† the good seed the children of the kingdom. The weeds are the children of the evil one, [39] and the enemy who sows them is the devil. The harvest is the end of the age,† and the harvesters are angels. [40] Just as weeds are

collected and burned [up] with fire, so will it be at the end of the age. [41] The Son of Man will send his angels, and they will collect out of his kingdom† all who cause others to sin and all evildoers. [42]* They will throw them into the fiery furnace, where there will be wailing and grinding of teeth. [43]†* Then the righteous will shine like the sun in the kingdom of their Father. Whoever has ears ought to hear.

**More Parables.**† [44]* "The kingdom of heaven is like a treasure buried in a field,† which a person finds and hides again, and out of joy goes and sells all that he has and buys that field. [45] Again, the kingdom of heaven is like a merchant searching for fine pearls. [46] When he finds a pearl of great price, he goes and sells all that he has and buys it. [47] Again, the kingdom of heaven is like a net thrown into the sea, which collects fish of every kind. [48] When it is full they haul it ashore and sit down to put what is good into buckets. What is bad they throw away. [49] Thus it will be at the end of the age. The angels will go out and separate the wicked from the righteous [50] and throw them into the fiery furnace, where there will be wailing and grinding of teeth.

**Treasures New and Old.** [51] "Do you understand† all these things?" They answered, "Yes." [52]† And he replied, "Then every scribe who has been instructed in the kingdom of heaven is

---

**13:33** Except in this Q parable and in Mt 16:12, *yeast* (or "leaven") is, in New Testament usage, a symbol of corruption (see Mt 16:6, 11–12; Mk 8:15; Lk 12:1; 1 Cor 5:6–8; Gal 5:9). *Three measures:* an enormous amount, enough to feed a hundred people. The exaggeration of this element of the parable points to the greatness of the kingdom's effect.

**13:34** *Only in parables:* see Mt 13:10–15.

**13:35** *The prophet:* some textual witnesses read "Isaiah the prophet." The quotation is actually from Ps 78:2; the first line corresponds to the LXX text of the psalm. The psalm's title ascribes it to Asaph, the founder of one of the guilds of temple musicians. He is called "the prophet" (NAB "the seer") in 2 Chr 29:30, but it is doubtful that Matthew averted to that; for him, any Old Testament text that could be seen as fulfilled in Jesus was prophetic.

**13:36** *Dismissing the crowds:* the return of Jesus to the house marks a break with the crowds, who represent unbelieving Israel. From now on his attention is directed more and more to his disciples and to their instruction. The rest of the discourse is addressed to them alone.

**13:37–43** In the explanation of the parable of the weeds emphasis lies on the fearful end of the wicked, whereas the parable itself concentrates on patience with them until judgment time.

**13:38** *The field is the world:* this presupposes the resurrection of Jesus and the granting to him of "all power in heaven and on earth" (Mt 28:18).

**13:39** *The end of the age:* this phrase is found only in Matthew (13:40, 49; 24:3; 28:20).

**13:41** *His kingdom:* the *kingdom* of the *Son of Man* is distin-

guished from that of the Father (Mt 13:43); see 1 Cor 15:24–25. The church is the place where Jesus' kingdom is manifested, but his royal authority embraces the entire world; see note on Mt 13:38.

**13:43** See Dn 12:3.

**13:44–50** The first two of the last three parables of the discourse have the same point. The *person* who *finds* a buried *treasure* and the *merchant* who finds a *pearl of great price* sell *all* that they have to acquire these finds; similarly, the one who understands the supreme value of the kingdom gives up whatever he must to obtain it. The *joy* with which this is done is made explicit in the first parable, but it may be presumed in the second also. The concluding parable of the fishnet resembles the explanation of the parable of the weeds with its stress upon the final exclusion of evil persons from the kingdom.

**13:44** In the unsettled conditions of Palestine in Jesus' time, it was not unusual to guard valuables by burying them in the ground.

**13:51** Matthew typically speaks of the understanding of the disciples.

**13:52** Since Matthew tends to identify the disciples and the Twelve (see note on Mt 10:1), this saying about the Christian *scribe* cannot be taken as applicable to all who accept the message of Jesus. While the Twelve are in many ways representative of all who

---

**13:33** Lk 13:20–21.  
**13:34–35** Mk 4:33–34.  
**13:35** Ps 78:2.  
**13:42** 8:12; Rev 21:8.  
**13:43** Dn 12:3.  
**13:44–45** Prv 2:4; 4:7.

like the head of a household who brings from his storeroom both the new and the old." [53] When Jesus finished these parables, he went away from there.

## V. JESUS, THE KINGDOM, AND THE CHURCH

**The Rejection at Nazareth.** [54]† He came to his native place and taught the people in their synagogue.* They were astonished† and said, "Where did this man get such wisdom and mighty deeds?* [55] Is he not the carpenter's son? Is not his mother named Mary and his brothers James, Joseph, Simon, and Judas?* [56] Are not his sisters all with us? Where did this man get all this?" [57] And they took offense at him. But Jesus said to them, "A prophet is not without honor except in his native place and in his own house."* [58] And he did not work many mighty deeds there because of their lack of faith.

**14** **Herod's Opinion of Jesus.** [1]†* At that time Herod the tetrarch†* heard of the reputation of Jesus* [2] and said to his servants, "This man is John the Baptist. He has been raised from the dead; that is why mighty powers are at work in him."

**The Death of John the Baptist.** [3]* Now Herod had arrested John, bound [him], and put him in prison on account of Herodias,† the wife of his brother Philip, [4]* for John had said to him, "It is not lawful for you to have her." [5]* Although he wanted to kill him, he feared the people, for they regarded him as a prophet. [6] But at a birthday celebration for Herod, the daughter of Herodias performed a dance before the guests and delighted Herod [7] so much that he swore to give her whatever she might ask for. [8] Prompted by her mother, she said, "Give me here on a platter the head of John the Baptist." [9] The king was distressed, but because of his oaths and the guests who were present, he ordered that it be given, [10] and he had John beheaded in the prison. [11] His head was brought in on a platter and given to the girl, who took it to her mother. [12] His disciples came and took away the corpse and buried him; and they went and told Jesus.

**The Return of the Twelve and the Feeding of the Five Thousand.** † [13]* When Jesus heard of it, he withdrew in a boat to a deserted place by himself. The crowds heard of this and followed him on foot from their towns. [14] When he disembarked and saw the vast crowd, his heart was moved with pity for them, and he cured their sick. [15] When it was evening, the disciples approached him and said, "This is a deserted place and it is already late; dismiss the crowds so that they can go to the villages and buy food for themselves." [16] [Jesus] said to

---

† believe in him, they are also distinguished from them in certain respects. The church of Matthew has leaders among whom are a group designated as "scribes" (Mt 23:34). Like the scribes of Israel, they are teachers. It is the Twelve and these their later counterparts to whom this verse applies. *The scribe…instructed in the kingdom of heaven* knows both the teaching of Jesus (*the new*) and the law and prophets (*the old*) and provides in his own teaching *both the new and the old* as interpreted and fulfilled by *the new*. On the translation *head of a household* (for the same Greek word translated *householder* in Mt 13:27), see note on Mt 24:45–51.

**13:54–17:27** This section is the narrative part of the fourth book of the gospel.

**13:54–58** After the Sermon on the Mount the crowds are in admiring astonishment at Jesus' teaching (Mt 7:28); here the astonishment is of those who take *offense at him*. Familiarity with his background and family leads them to regard him as pretentious. Matthew modifies his Marcan source (Mt 6:1–6). Jesus is not the carpenter but *the carpenter's son* (Mt 13:55), "and among his own kin" is omitted (Mt 13:57), *he did not work many mighty deeds* in face of such unbelief (Mt 13:58) rather than the Marcan "…he was not able to perform any mighty deed there" (Mt 6:5), and there is no mention of his amazement at his townspeople's lack of faith.

**14:1–12** The murder of the Baptist by Herod Antipas prefigures the death of Jesus (see Mt 17:12). The Marcan source (Mk 6:14–29) is much reduced and in some points changed. In Mark Herod reveres John as a holy man and the desire to kill him is attributed to Herodias (Mk 6:19, 20), whereas here that desire is Herod's from the beginning (Mt 14:5).

**14:1** *Herod the tetrarch*: Herod Antipas, son of Herod the

Great. When the latter died, his territory was divided among three of his surviving sons, Archelaus who received half of it (Mt 2:23), Herod Antipas who became ruler of Galilee and Perea, and Philip who became ruler of northern Transjordan. Since he received a quarter of his father's domain, Antipas is accurately designated *tetrarch* ("ruler of a fourth [part]"), although in Mt 14:9 Matthew repeats the "king" of his Marcan source (Mk 6:26).

**14:3** Herodias was not the wife of Herod's half-brother Philip but of another half-brother, Herod Boethus. The union prohibited by Lv 18:16; 20:21. According to Josephus (*Antiquities* 18:116–19), Herod imprisoned and then executed John because he feared that the Baptist's influence over the people might enable him to lead a rebellion.

**14:13–21** The feeding of the five thousand is the only miracle of Jesus that is recounted in all four gospels. The principal reason for that may be that it was seen as anticipating the Eucharist and the final banquet in the kingdom (Mt 8:11; 26:29), but it looks not only forward but backward, to the feeding of Israel with manna in the desert at the time of the Exodus (Ex 16), a miracle that in some contemporary Jewish expectation would be repeated in the messianic age (2 Bar 29:8). It may also be meant to recall Elisha's feeding a hundred men with small provisions (2 Kgs 4:42–44).

---

*

| | |
|---|---|
| **13:54–58** Mk 6:1–6; Lk 4:16–30. | **14:1** Lk 3:1. |
| **13:54** 2:23; Jn 1:46; 7:15. | **14:3–4** Lk 3:19–20. |
| **13:55** 12:46; 27:56; Jn 6:42. | **14:4** Lv 18:16; 20:21. |
| **13:57** Jn 4:44. | **14:5** 21:26. |
| **14:1–12** Mk 6:14–29. | **14:13–21** 15:32–38; Mk 6:32–44; Lk 9:10–17; Jn 6:1–13. |
| **14:1–2** Lk 9:7–9. | |

them, "There is no need for them to go away; give them some food yourselves." [17] But they said to him, "Five loaves and two fish are all we have here." [18] Then he said, "Bring them here to me," [19] and he ordered the crowds to sit down on the grass. Taking† the five loaves and the two fish, and looking up to heaven, he said the blessing, broke the loaves, and gave them to the disciples, who in turn gave them to the crowds. [20] They all ate and were satisfied, and they picked up the fragments left over†— twelve wicker baskets full. [21] Those who ate were about five thousand men, not counting women and children.

**The Walking on the Water.**† [22]* Then he made the disciples get into the boat and precede him to the other side, while he dismissed the crowds. [23]* After doing so, he went up on the mountain by himself to pray. When it was evening he was there alone. [24] Meanwhile the boat, already a few miles offshore, was being tossed about by the waves, for the wind was against it. [25] During the fourth watch of the night,† he came toward them, walking on the sea. [26] When the disciples saw him walking on the sea they were terrified. "It is a ghost," they said, and they cried out in fear. [27] At once [Jesus] spoke to them, "Take courage, it is I;† do not be afraid." [28] Peter said to him in reply,

"Lord, if it is you, command me to come to you on the water." [29] He said, "Come." Peter got out of the boat and began to walk on the water toward Jesus. [30]* But when he saw how [strong] the wind was he became frightened; and, beginning to sink, he cried out, "Lord, save me!" [31] Immediately Jesus stretched out his hand and caught him, and said to him, "O you of little faith,† why did you doubt?" [32] After they got into the boat, the wind died down. [33]†* Those who were in the boat did him homage, saying, "Truly, you are the Son of God."

**The Healings at Gennesaret.** [34]* After making the crossing, they came to land at Gennesaret. [35] When the men of that place recognized him, they sent word to all the surrounding country. People brought to him all those who were sick [36]* and begged him that they might touch only the tassel on his cloak, and as many as touched it were healed.

# 15

**The Tradition of the Elders.**† [1]* Then Pharisees and scribes came to Jesus from Jerusalem and said, [2]* "Why do your disciples break the tradition of the elders?† They do not wash [their] hands when they eat a meal." [3] He said to them in reply, "And why do you break the commandment of God† for the

---

**14:19** The *taking*, saying the blessing, breaking, and giving to the disciples correspond to the actions of Jesus over the bread at the Last Supper (Mt 26:26). Since they were usual at any Jewish meal, that correspondence does not necessarily indicate a eucharistic reference here. Matthew's silence about Jesus' dividing the fish among the people (Mk 6:41) is perhaps more significant in that regard.

**14:20** *The fragments left over*: as in Elisha's miracle, food was *left over* after all had been fed. The word *fragments* (Greek *klasmata*) is used, in the singular, of the broken bread of the Eucharist in *Didache* 9:3–4.

**14:22–33** The disciples, laboring against the turbulent sea, are saved by Jesus. For his power over the waters, see note on Mt 8:26. Here that power is expressed also by his *walking on the sea* (Mt 14:25; cf. Ps 77:20; Jb 9:8). Matthew has inserted into the Marcan material (Mk 6:45–52) that belongs to his special traditions on Peter (Mt 14:28–31).

**14:25** *The fourth watch of the night*: between 3 a.m. and 6 a.m. The Romans divided the twelve hours between 6 p.m. and 6 a.m. into four equal parts called "watches."

**14:27** *It is I*: see note on Mk 6:50.

**14:31** *You of little faith*: see note on Mt 6:30. *Why did you doubt?*: the verb is peculiar to Matthew and occurs elsewhere only in Mt 28:17.

**14:33** This confession is in striking contrast to the Marcan parallel (Mk 6:51) where the disciples are "completely astounded."

**15:1–20** This dispute begins with the question of the Pharisees and scribes why Jesus' disciples are breaking *the tradition of the elders* about washing one's hands before eating (Mt 15:2). Jesus' counterquestion accuses his opponents of breaking the

*commandment of God for the sake of* their *tradition* (Mt 15:3) and illustrates this by their interpretation of the commandment of the Decalogue concerning parents (Mt 15:4–6). Denouncing them as hypocrites, he applies to them a derogatory prophecy of Isaiah (Mt 15:7–8). Then with a wider audience (*the crowd*, Mt 15:10) he goes beyond the violation of tradition with which the dispute has started. The parable (Mt 15:11) is an attack on the Mosaic law concerning clean and unclean foods, similar to those antitheses that abrogate the law (Mt 5:31–32, 33–34, 38–39). After a warning to his disciples not to follow the moral guidance of the Pharisees (Mt 15:13–14), he explains the *parable* (Mt 15:15) to them, saying that defilement comes not from what *enters the mouth* (Mt 15:17) but from the evil thoughts and deeds that rise from within, *from the heart* (Mt 15:18–20). The last verse returns to the starting point of the dispute (eating *with unwashed hands*). Because of Matthew's omission of Mk 7:19b, some scholars think that Matthew has weakened the Marcan repudiation of the Mosaic food laws. But that half verse is ambiguous in the Greek, which may be the reason for its omission here.

**15:2** *The tradition of the elders*: see note on Mk 7:5. The purpose of the handwashing was to remove defilement caused by contact with what was ritually unclean.

**15:3–4** For the commandment see Ex 20:12 (// Dt 5:16); 21:17. The honoring of one's parents had to do with supporting them in their needs.

---

| | |
|---|---|
| **14:22–33** Mk 6:45–52; Jn 6:16–21. | **14:33** 16:16. |
| **14:23** Mk 1:35; Lk 5:16; | **14:34–36** Mk 6:53–56. |
| 6:12. | **14:36** 9:20–22. |
| **14:30–31** 8:25–26. | **15:1–20** Mk 7:1–23. |
| | **15:2** Lk 11:38. |

sake of your tradition? 4 * For God said, 'Honor your father and your mother,' and 'Whoever curses father or mother shall die.' 5 † But you say, 'Whoever says to father or mother, "Any support you might have had from me is dedicated to God,"' 6 need not honor his father.' You have nullified the word of God for the sake of your tradition. 7 Hypocrites, well did Isaiah prophesy about you when he said:

8 *     'This people honors me with their lips, †
          but their hearts are far from me;
9 *     in vain do they worship me,
          teaching as doctrines human precepts.'"

10 * He summoned the crowd and said to them, "Hear and understand. 11 It is not what enters one's mouth that defiles that person; but what comes out of the mouth is what defiles one." 12 Then his disciples approached and said to him, "Do you know that the Pharisees took offense when they heard what you said?" 13 He said in reply, † "Every plant that my heavenly Father has not planted will be uprooted. 14 * Let them alone; they are blind guides [of the blind]. If a blind person leads a blind person, both will fall into a pit." 15 Then Peter † said to him in reply, "Explain [this] parable to us." 16 He said to them, "Are even you still without understanding? 17 Do you not realize that everything that enters the mouth passes into the stomach and is expelled into the latrine? 18 * But the things that come out of the mouth come from the heart, and they defile. 19 † For from the heart come evil thoughts, murder, adultery, unchastity, theft, false witness, blasphemy. 20 These are what defile a person, but to eat with unwashed hands does not defile."

**The Canaanite Woman's Faith.** † 21 * Then Jesus went from that place and withdrew to the region of Tyre and Sidon. 22 And behold, a Canaanite woman of that district came and called out, "Have pity on me, Lord, Son of David! My daughter is tormented by a demon." 23 But he did not say a word in answer to her. His disciples came and asked him, "Send her away, for she keeps calling out after us." 24 † He said in reply, "I was sent only to the lost sheep of the house of Israel." 25 * But the woman came and did him homage, saying, "Lord, help me." 26 He said in reply, "It is not right to take the food of the children † and throw it to the dogs." 27 She said, "Please, Lord, for even the dogs eat the scraps that fall from the table of their masters." 28 * Then Jesus said to her in reply, "O woman, great is your faith! † Let it be done for you as you wish." And her daughter was healed from that hour.

**The Healing of Many People.** 29 Moving on from there Jesus walked by the Sea of Galilee, went up on the mountain, and sat down there. 30 * Great crowds came to him, having with them the lame, the blind, the deformed, the mute, and many others. They placed them at his feet, and he cured them. 31 The crowds were amazed when they saw the mute speaking, the deformed made whole, the lame walking, and the blind able to see, and they glorified the God of Israel.

**The Feeding of the Four Thousand.** † 32 * Jesus summoned his disciples and said, "My heart is moved with pity for the crowd, for they have been with me now for three days and have nothing to eat. I do not want to send them away hungry, for fear they may collapse on

MT

---

**15:5** See note on Mk 7:11.
**15:8** The text of Is 29:13 is quoted approximately according to the Septuagint.
**15:13–14** Jesus leads his disciples away from the teaching authority of the Pharisees.
**15:15** Matthew specifies *Peter* as the questioner, unlike Mk 7:17. Given his tendency to present the disciples as more understanding than in his Marcan source, it is noteworthy that here he retains the Marcan rebuke, although in a slightly milder form. This may be due to his wish to correct the Jewish Christians within his church who still held to the food laws and thus separated themselves from Gentile Christians who did not observe them.
**15:19** The Marcan list of thirteen things that defile (Mk 7:21–22) is here reduced to seven that partially cover the content of the Decalogue.
**15:21–28** See note on Mt 8:5–13.
**15:24** See note on Mt 10:5–6.
**15:26** *The children*: the people of Israel. *Dogs*: see note on Mt 7:6.

**15:28** As in the case of the cure of the centurion's servant (Mt 8:10), Matthew ascribes Jesus' granting the request to the woman's *great faith*, a point not made equally explicit in the Marcan parallel (Mk 7:24–30).
**15:32–39** Most probably this story is a doublet of that of the feeding of the five thousand (Mt 14:13–21). It differs from it notably only in that Jesus takes the initiative, not the disciples (Mt 15:32), and in the numbers: the crowd has been with Jesus *three days* (Mt 15:32), *seven loaves* are multiplied (Mt 15:36), *seven baskets* of fragments remain after the feeding (Mt 15:37), and *four thousand* men are fed (Mt 15:38).

**15:4** Ex 20:12; 21:17; Lv 20:9; Dt 5:16; Prv 20:20.
**15:8** Is 29:13 LXX.
**15:9** Col 2:23.
**15:10** Mk 7:14.
**15:14** 23:16, 19, 24;
Lk 6:39; Jn 9:40.
**15:18** 12:34.
**15:21–28** Mk 7:24–30.
**15:25** 10:6.
**15:28** 8:10.
**15:30** Is 35:5–6.
**15:32–39** Mk 8:1–10.

the way." ³³ The disciples said to him, "Where could we ever get enough bread in this deserted place to satisfy such a crowd?" ³⁴ Jesus said to them, "How many loaves do you have?" "Seven," they replied, "and a few fish." ³⁵ He ordered the crowd to sit down on the ground. ³⁶ Then he took the seven loaves and the fish, gave thanks,† broke the loaves, and gave them to the disciples, who in turn gave them to the crowds. ³⁷* They all ate and were satisfied. They picked up the fragments left over—seven baskets full. ³⁸ Those who ate were four thousand men, not counting women and children. ³⁹ And when he had dismissed the crowds, he got into the boat and came to the district of Magadan.

## 16 The Demand for a Sign. ¹†* The Pharisees and Sadducees came and, to test him, asked him to show them a sign from heaven. ²† He said to them in reply, "[In the evening you say, 'Tomorrow will be fair, for the sky is red'; ³* and, in the morning, 'Today will be stormy, for the sky is red and threatening.' You know how to judge the appearance of the sky, but you cannot judge the signs of the times.] ⁴* An evil and unfaithful generation seeks a sign, but no sign will be given it except the sign of Jonah."† Then he left them and went away.

## The Leaven of the Pharisees and Sadducees.
⁵* In coming to the other side of the sea,† the disciples had forgotten to bring bread. ⁶* Jesus said to them, "Look out, and beware of the leaven† of the Pharisees and Sadducees." ⁷† They concluded among themselves, saying, "It is because we have brought no bread." ⁸ When Jesus became aware of this he said, "You of little faith, why do you conclude among yourselves that it is because you have no bread? ⁹* Do you not yet understand, and do you not remember the five loaves for the five thousand, and how many wicker baskets you took up? ¹⁰* Or the seven loaves for the four thousand, and how many baskets you took up? ¹¹ How do you not comprehend that I was not speaking to you about bread? Beware of the leaven of the Pharisees and Sadducees." ¹² Then they understood† that he was not telling them to beware of the leaven of bread, but of the teaching of the Pharisees and Sadducees.

## Peter's Confession About Jesus.† ¹³* When Jesus went into the region of Caesarea Philippi† he asked his disciples, "Who do people say that the Son of Man is?" ¹⁴* They replied, "Some say John the Baptist,† others Elijah, still others Jeremiah or one of the prophets." ¹⁵ He said to them, "But who do you say that I am?" ¹⁶†* Simon Peter said in reply, "You

---

**MT**

†

**15:36** *Gave thanks:* see Mt 14:19, "said the blessing." There is no difference in meaning. The thanksgiving was a blessing of God for his benefits.

**16:1** *A sign from heaven:* see note on Mt 12:38–42.

**16:2–3** The answer of Jesus in these verses is omitted in many important textual witnesses, and it is very uncertain that it is an original part of this gospel. It resembles Lk 12:54–56 and may have been inserted from there. It rebukes the Pharisees and Sadducees who are able to read indications of coming weather but not the indications of the coming kingdom in the signs that Jesus does offer, his mighty deeds and teaching.

**16:4** See notes on Mt 12:39, 40.

**16:5–12** Jesus' warning his disciples against *the teaching of the Pharisees and Sadducees* comes immediately before his promise to confer on Peter the authority to bind and to loose on earth (Mt 16:19), an authority that will be confirmed in heaven. Such authority most probably has to do, at least in part, with teaching. The rejection of the teaching authority of the Pharisees (see also Mt 12:12–14) prepares for a new one derived from Jesus.

**16:6** *Leaven:* see note on Mt 13:33. *Sadducees:* Matthew's Marcan source speaks rather of "the leaven of Herod" (Mk 8:15).

**16:7–11** The disciples, men *of little faith,* misunderstand Jesus' metaphorical use of *leaven,* forgetting that, as the feeding of the crowds shows, he is not at a loss to provide them with bread.

**16:12** After his rebuke, the disciples understand that by *leaven* he meant the corrupting influence of the *teaching of the Pharisees and Sadducees.* The evangelist probably understands this *teaching* as common to both groups. Since at the time of Jesus' ministry the two differed widely on points of *teaching,* e.g., the resurrection of the dead, and at the time of the evangelist the Sadducee party was no longer a force in Judaism, the supposed

common teaching fits neither period. The disciples' eventual understanding of Jesus' warning contrasts with their continuing obtuseness in the Marcan parallel (Mk 8:14–21).

**16:13–20** The Marcan confession of Jesus as Messiah, made by Peter as spokesman for the other disciples (Mk 8:27–29; cf. also Lk 9:18–20), is modified significantly here. The confession is of Jesus both as *Messiah* and as *Son of the living God* (Mt 16:16). Jesus' response, drawn principally from material peculiar to Matthew, attributes the confession to a divine revelation granted to Peter alone (Mt 16:17) and makes him the *rock* on which Jesus *will build his church* (Mt 16:18) and the disciple whose authority in the church *on earth* will be confirmed in *heaven,* i.e., by God (Mt 16:19).

**16:13** *Caesarea Philippi:* situated about twenty miles north of the Sea of Galilee in the territory ruled by Philip, a son of Herod the Great, tetrarch until his death in A.D. 34 (see note on Mt 14:1). He rebuilt the town of Paneas, naming it *Caesarea* in honor of the emperor, and *Philippi* ("of Philip") to distinguish it from the seaport in Samaria that was also called Caesarea. *Who do people say that the Son of Man is?:* although the question differs from the Marcan parallel (Mk 8:27: "Who...that I am?"), the meaning is the same, for Jesus here refers to himself as the *Son of Man* (cf. Mt 16:15).

**16:14** *John the Baptist:* see Mt 14:2. *Elijah:* cf. Mal 3:23–24; Sir 48:10; and see note on Mt 3:4. *Jeremiah:* an addition of Matthew to the Marcan source.

| | |
|---|---|
| **15:37** 16:10. | **16:9** 14:17–21; Jn 6:9. |
| **16:1–10** Mk 8:11–21. | **16:10** 15:34–38. |
| **16:3** Lk 12:54–56. | **16:13–16** Mk 8:27–29; Lk |
| **16:4** 12:39; Jon 2:1. | 9:18–20. |
| **16:5–12** Mk 8:14–21. | **16:14** 14:2. |
| **16:6** Lk 12:1. | **16:16** Jn 6:69. |

are the Messiah, the Son of the living God." [17] Jesus said to him in reply, "Blessed are you, Simon son of Jonah. For flesh and blood† has not revealed this to you, but my heavenly Father. [18]* And so I say to you, you are Peter, and upon this rock I will build my church,† and the gates of the netherworld shall not prevail against it. [19]* I will give you the keys to the kingdom of heaven.† Whatever you bind on earth shall be bound in heaven; and whatever you loose on earth shall be loosed in heaven." [20]†* Then he strictly ordered his disciples to tell no one that he was the Messiah.

### The First Prediction of the Passion.† [21]* From that time on, Jesus began to show his disciples

that he† must go to Jerusalem and suffer greatly from the elders, the chief priests, and the scribes, and be killed and on the third day be raised.* [22]† Then Peter took him aside and began to rebuke him, "God forbid, Lord! No such thing shall ever happen to you." [23]* He turned and said to Peter, "Get behind me, Satan! You are an obstacle to me. You are thinking not as God does, but as human beings do."

### The Conditions of Discipleship.† [24]* Then Jesus said to his disciples, "Whoever wishes to come after me must deny himself,† take up his cross, and follow me. [25]* For whoever wishes to save his life will lose it, but whoever loses his life for my sake will find

---

† **16:16** *The Son of the living God*: see Mt 2:15; 3:17. The addition of this exalted title to the Marcan confession eliminates whatever ambiguity was attached to the title Messiah. This, among other things, supports the view proposed by many scholars that Matthew has here combined his source's confession with a post-resurrectional confession of faith in Jesus as *Son of the living God* that belonged to the appearance of the risen Jesus to Peter; cf. 1 Cor 15:5; Lk 24:34.

**16:17** *Flesh and blood*: a Semitic expression for human beings, especially in their weakness. *Has not revealed this…but my heavenly Father*: that Peter's faith is spoken of as coming not through human means but through a revelation from God is similar to Paul's description of his recognition of who Jesus was; see Gal 1:15–16, "…when he [God]…was pleased to reveal his Son to me.…"

**16:18** *You are Peter, and upon this rock I will build my church*: the Aramaic word *kēpā'* meaning *rock* and transliterated into Greek as *Kēphas* is the name by which Peter is called in the Pauline letters (1 Cor 1:12; 3:22; 9:5; 15:4; Gal 1:18; 2:9, 11, 14) except in Gal 2:7–8 ("Peter"). It is translated as *Petros* ("Peter") in Jn 1:42. The presumed original Aramaic of Jesus' statement would have been, in English, "You are the Rock (*kēpā'*) and upon this rock (*kēpā'*) I will build my church." The Greek text probably means the same, for the difference in gender between the masculine noun *petros*, the disciple's new name, and the feminine noun *petra* (rock) may be due simply to the unsuitability of using a feminine noun as the proper name of a male. Although the two words were generally used with slightly different nuances, they were also used interchangeably with the same meaning, "rock." *Church*: this word (Greek *ekklēsia*) occurs in the gospels only here and in Mt 18:17 (twice). There are several possibilities for an Aramaic original. Jesus' *church* means the community that he will gather and that, like a building, will have Peter as its solid foundation. That function of Peter consists in his being witness to Jesus as *the Messiah, the Son of the living God. The gates of the netherworld shall not prevail against it*: the netherworld (Greek *Hades*, the abode of the dead) is conceived of as a walled city whose *gates* will not close in upon the church of Jesus, i.e., it will not be overcome by the power of death.

**16:19** *The keys to the kingdom of heaven*: the image of the keys is probably drawn from Is 22:15–25 where Eliakim, who succeeds Shebna as master of the palace, is given "the key of the House of David," which he authoritatively "opens" and "shuts" (Is 22:22). *Whatever you bind…loosed in heaven*: there are many instances in rabbinic literature of the binding-loosing imagery. Of the several meanings given there to the metaphor, two are of special importance here: the giving of authoritative teaching, and the lifting or imposing of the ban of excommunication. It is disputed whether the image of *the keys* and that of binding and loosing are different metaphors meaning the same thing. In any case, the promise of the keys is given to Peter alone. In Mt 18:18

all the disciples are given the power of binding and loosing, but the context of that verse suggests that there the power of excommunication alone is intended. That *the keys* are those of the *kingdom of heaven* and that Peter's exercise of authority in the church *on earth* will be confirmed *in heaven* show an intimate connection between, but not an identification of, the church and the *kingdom of heaven*.

**16:20** Cf. Mk 8:30. Matthew makes explicit that the prohibition has to do with speaking of Jesus as *the Messiah*; see note on Mk 8:27–30.

**16:21–23** This first prediction of the passion follows Mk 8:31–33 in the main and serves as a corrective to an understanding of Jesus' messiahship as solely one of glory and triumph. By his addition of *from that time on* (Mt 16:21) Matthew has emphasized that Jesus' revelation of his coming suffering and death marks a new phase of the gospel. Neither this nor the two later passion predictions (Mt 17:22–23; 20:17–19) can be taken as sayings that, as they stand, go back to Jesus himself. However, it is probable that he foresaw that his mission would entail suffering and perhaps death, but was confident that he would ultimately be vindicated by God (see Mt 26:29).

**16:21** *He*: the Marcan parallel (Mk 8:31) has "the Son of Man." Since Matthew has already designated Jesus by that title (Mt 15:13), its omission here is not significant. The Matthean prediction is equally about the sufferings of the Son of Man. *Must*: this necessity is part of the tradition of all the synoptics; cf. Mk 8:31; Lk 9:21. *The elders, the chief priests, and the scribes*: see note on Mk 8:31. *On the third day*: so also Lk 9:22, against the Marcan "after three days" (Mk 8:31). Matthew's formulation is, in the Greek, almost identical with the pre-Pauline fragment of the kerygma in 1 Cor 15:4 and also with Hos 6:2, which many take to be the Old Testament background to the confession that Jesus was raised *on the third day*. Josephus uses "after three days" and "on the third day" interchangeably (*Antiquities* 7:280–81; 8:214, 218) and there is probably no difference in meaning between the two phrases.

**16:22–23** Peter's refusal to accept Jesus' predicted suffering and death is seen as a satanic attempt to deflect Jesus from his God-appointed course, and the disciple is addressed in terms that recall Jesus' dismissal of the devil in the temptation account (Mt 4:10: "Get away, Satan!"). Peter's satanic purpose is emphasized by Matthew's addition to the Marcan source of the words *You are an obstacle to me*.

**16:24–28** A readiness to follow Jesus even to giving up one's life for him is the condition for true discipleship; this will be repaid by him at the final judgment.

**16:24** *Deny himself*: to deny someone is to disown him (see

**16:18** Jn 1:42.
**16:19** Is 22:22; Rev 3:7.
**16:20** Mk 8:30; Lk 9:21.
**16:21–28** Mk 8:31–9:1;
    Lk 9:22–27.

**16:21** 17:22–23; 20:17–19.
**16:23** 4:10.
**16:24** Lk 14:27.
**16:25** Lk 17:33; Jn 12:25.

it.† ²⁶What profit would there be for one to gain the whole world and forfeit his life? Or what can one give in exchange for his life? ²⁷†* For the Son of Man will come with his angels in his Father's glory, and then he will repay everyone according to his conduct. ²⁸† Amen, I say to you, there are some standing here who will not taste death until they see the Son of Man coming in his kingdom."

## 17 The Transfiguration of Jesus.† ¹* After six days Jesus took Peter, James, and John his brother, and led them up a high mountain by themselves.† ²†* And he was transfigured before them; his face shone like the sun and his clothes became white as light. ³† And behold, Moses and Elijah appeared to them, conversing with him. ⁴Then Peter said to Jesus in reply, "Lord, it is good that we are here. If you wish, I will make three tents† here, one for you, one for Moses, and one for Elijah." ⁵* While he was still speaking, behold, a bright cloud cast a shadow over them,† then from the cloud came a voice that said, "This is my beloved Son, with whom I am well pleased; listen to him." ⁶† When the disciples heard this, they fell prostrate and were very much afraid. ⁷But Jesus came and touched them, saying, "Rise, and do not be afraid." ⁸And when the disciples raised their eyes, they saw no one else but Jesus alone.

## The Coming of Elijah.† ⁹* As they were coming down from the mountain, Jesus charged them, "Do not tell the vision† to anyone until the Son of Man has been raised from the dead." ¹⁰†* Then the disciples asked him, "Why do the scribes say that Elijah must come first?" ¹¹* He said in reply,† "Elijah will indeed come and restore all things; ¹²* but I tell you that Elijah has already come, and they did not recognize him but did to him whatever they pleased. So also will the Son of Man suffer at their hands." ¹³† Then the disciples understood that he was speaking to them of John the Baptist.

## The Healing of a Boy with a Demon.†
¹⁴* When they came to the crowd a man approached, knelt down before him, ¹⁵and

---

† Mt 10:33; 26:34–35) and to deny oneself is to disown oneself as the center of one's existence.

**16:25** See notes on Mt 10:38, 39.

**16:27** The parousia and final judgment are described in Mt 25:31 in terms almost identical with these.

**16:28** *Coming in his kingdom:* since the *kingdom of the Son of Man* has been described as "the world" and Jesus' sovereignty precedes his final coming in glory (Mt 13:38, 41), the coming in this verse is not the parousia as in the preceding but the manifestation of Jesus' rule after his resurrection; see notes on Mt 13:38, 41.

**17:1–8** The account of the transfiguration confirms that Jesus is the *Son* of God (Mt 17:5) and points to fulfillment of the prediction that he will come *in his Father's glory* at the end of the age (Mt 16:27). It has been explained by some as a resurrection appearance retrojected into the time of Jesus' ministry, but that is not probable since the account lacks many of the usual elements of the resurrection-appearance narratives. It draws upon motifs from the Old Testament and noncanonical Jewish apocalyptic literature that express the presence of the heavenly and the divine, e.g., brilliant light, white garments, and the overshadowing cloud.

**17:1** These three disciples are also taken apart from the others by Jesus in Gethsemane (Mt 26:37). *A high mountain:* this has been identified with Tabor or Hermon, but probably no specific mountain was intended by the evangelist or by his Marcan source (Mk 9:2). Its meaning is theological rather than geographical, possibly recalling the revelation to Moses on Mount Sinai (Ex 24:12–18) and to Elijah at the same place (1 Kgs 19:8–18; Horeb = Sinai).

**17:2** *His face shone like the sun:* this is a Matthean addition; cf. Dn 10:6. *His clothes became white as light:* cf. Dn 7:9, where the clothing of God appears "snow bright." For the white garments of other heavenly beings, see Rev 4:4; 7:9; 19:14.

**17:3** See note on Mk 9:5.

**17:4** *Three tents:* the booths in which the Israelites lived during the feast of Tabernacles (cf. Jn 7:2) were meant to recall their ancestors' dwelling in booths during the journey from Egypt to the promised land (Lv 23:39–42). The same Greek word, *skēnē*, here translated *tents*, is used in the LXX for the booths of that feast, and some scholars have suggested that there is an allusion here to that liturgical custom.

**17:5** *Cloud cast a shadow over them:* see note on Mk 9:7. *This is my beloved Son...listen to him:* cf. Mt 3:17. The voice repeats the baptismal proclamation about Jesus, with the addition of the command *listen to him.* The latter is a reference to Dt 18:15 in which the Israelites are commanded to *listen to* the prophet like Moses whom God will raise up for them. The command to listen to Jesus is general, but in this context it probably applies particularly to the preceding predictions of his passion and resurrection (Mt 16:21) and of his coming (Mt 16:27, 28).

**17:6–7** A Matthean addition; cf. Dn 10:9–10, 18–19.

**17:9–13** In response to the disciples' question about the expected return of Elijah, Jesus interprets the mission of the Baptist as the fulfillment of that expectation. But that was not suspected by those who opposed and finally killed him, and Jesus predicts a similar fate for himself.

**17:9** *The vision:* Matthew alone uses this word to describe the transfiguration. *Until the Son of Man has been raised from the dead:* only in the light of Jesus' resurrection can the meaning of his life and mission be truly understood; until then no testimony to *the vision* will lead people to faith.

**17:10** See notes on Mt 3:4; 16:14.

**17:11–12** The preceding question and this answer may reflect later controversy with Jews who objected to the Christian claims for Jesus that Elijah had not yet come.

**17:13** See Mt 11:14.

**17:14–20** Matthew has greatly shortened the Marcan story (Mk 9:14–29). Leaving aside several details of the boy's illness, he concentrates on the need for faith, not so much on the part of

---

| | |
|---|---|
| **16:27** 25:31–33; Jb 34:11; Ps 62:13; Jer 17:10; 2 Thes 1:7–8. | **17:5** 3:17; Dt 18:15; 2 Pt 1:17. |
| **17:1–8** Mk 9:2–8; Lk 9:28–36. | **17:9–13** Mk 9:9–13. |
| **17:2** 28:3; Dn 7:9; 10:6; Rev 4:4; 7:9; 19:14. | **17:10** Mal 3:23–24. |
| | **17:11** Lk 1:17. |
| | **17:12–13** 11:14. |
| | **17:14–21** Mk 9:14–29; Lk 9:37–43. |

said, "Lord, have pity on my son, for he is a lunatic† and suffers severely; often he falls into fire, and often into water. ¹⁶ I brought him to your disciples, but they could not cure him." ¹⁷ * Jesus said in reply, "O faithless and perverse† generation, how long will I be with you? How long will I endure you? Bring him here to me." ¹⁸ Jesus rebuked him and the demon came out of him,† and from that hour the boy was cured. ¹⁹ Then the disciples approached Jesus in private and said, "Why could we not drive it out?" ²⁰ †* He said to them, "Because of your little faith. Amen, I say to you, if you have faith the size of a mustard seed, you will say to this mountain, 'Move from here to there,' and it will move. Nothing will be impossible for you." [²¹]†

**The Second Prediction of the Passion.**† ²² * As they were gathering in Galilee, Jesus said to them, "The Son of Man is to be handed over to men, ²³ and they will kill him, and he will be raised on the third day." And they were overwhelmed with grief.

**Payment of the Temple Tax.**† ²⁴ * When they came to Capernaum, the collectors of the temple tax† approached Peter and said, "Doesn't your teacher pay the temple tax?" ²⁵ "Yes," he said.† When he came into the house, before he had time to speak, Jesus asked him, "What is your opinion, Simon? From whom do the kings of the earth take tolls or census tax? From their subjects or from foreigners?" ²⁶ † When he said, "From foreigners," Jesus said to him, "Then the subjects are exempt. ²⁷ But that we may not offend them, † go to the sea, drop in a hook, and take the first fish that comes up. Open its mouth and you will find a coin worth twice the temple tax. Give that to them for me and for you."

# 18 †The Greatest in the Kingdom. ¹ * At that time the disciples† approached

---

† the boy's father (as does Mark, for Matthew omits Mk 9:22b–24) but on that of his own disciples whose inability to drive out the demon is ascribed to their *little faith* (Mt 17:20).

**17:15** *A lunatic*: this description of the boy is peculiar to Matthew. The word occurs in the New Testament only here and in Mt 4:24 and means one affected or struck by the moon. The symptoms of the boy's illness point to epilepsy, and attacks of this were thought to be caused by phases of the moon.

**17:17** *Faithless and perverse*: so Matthew and Luke (Lk 9:41) against Mark's *faithless* (Mk 9:19). The Greek word here translated *perverse* is the same as that in Dt 32:5 LXX, where Moses speaks to his people. There is a problem in knowing to whom the reproach is addressed. Since the Matthean Jesus normally chides his disciples for their *little faith* (as in Mt 17:20), it would appear that the charge of lack of faith could not be made against them and that the reproach is addressed to unbelievers among the Jews. However in Mt 17:20b (*if you have faith the size of a mustard seed*), which is certainly addressed to the disciples, they appear to have not even the smallest faith; if they had, they would have been able to cure the boy. In the light of Mt 17:20b the reproach of Mt 17:17 could have applied to the disciples. There seems to be an inconsistency between the charge of *little faith* in Mt 17:20a and that of not even a little in Mt 17:20b.

**17:18** *The demon came out of him*: not until this verse does Matthew indicate that the boy's illness is a case of demoniacal possession.

**17:20** The entire verse is an addition of Matthew who (according to the better attested text) omits the reason given for the disciples' inability in Mk 9:29. *Little faith*: see note on Mt 6:30. *Faith the size of a mustard seed…and it will move*: a combination of a Q saying (cf. Lk 17:6) with a Marcan saying (cf. Mk 11:23).

**17:21** Some manuscripts add, "But this kind does not come out except by prayer and fasting"; this is a variant of the better reading of Mk 9:29.

**17:22–23** The second passion prediction (cf. Mt 16:21–23) is the least detailed of the three and may be the earliest. In the Marcan parallel the disciples do not understand (Mk 9:32); here they understand and are *overwhelmed with grief* at the prospect of Jesus' death (Mt 17:23).

**17:24–27** Like Mt 14:28–31 and Mt 16:16b–19, this episode comes from Matthew's special material on Peter. Although the question of *the collectors* concerns Jesus' payment of the

*temple tax*, it is put to Peter. It is he who receives instruction from Jesus about freedom from the obligation of payment and yet why it should be made. The means of doing so is provided miraculously. The pericope deals with a problem of Matthew's church, whether its members should pay the temple tax, and the answer is given through a word of Jesus conveyed to Peter. Some scholars see here an example of the teaching authority of Peter exercised in the name of Jesus (see Mt 16:19). The specific problem was a Jewish Christian one and may have arisen when the Matthean church was composed largely of that group.

**17:24** *The temple tax*: before the destruction of the Jerusalem temple in A.D. 70 every male Jew above nineteen years of age was obliged to make an annual contribution to its upkeep (cf. Ex 30:11–16; Neh 10:33). After the destruction the Romans imposed upon Jews the obligation of paying that tax for the temple of Jupiter Capitolinus. There is disagreement about which period the story deals with.

**17:25** *From their subjects or from foreigners?*: the Greek word here translated *subjects* literally means "sons."

**17:26** *Then the subjects are exempt*: just as *subjects* are not bound by laws applying to *foreigners*, neither are Jesus and his disciples, who belong to the kingdom of heaven, bound by the duty of paying the temple tax imposed on those who are not of the kingdom. If the Greek is translated "sons," the freedom of Jesus, the Son of God, and of his disciples, children ("sons") of the kingdom (cf. Mt 13:38), is even more clear.

**17:27** *That we may not offend them*: though they are exempt (Mt 17:26), Jesus and his disciples are to avoid giving offense; therefore the tax is to be paid. *A coin worth twice the temple tax*: literally, "a stater," a Greek coin worth two double drachmas. Two double drachmas were equal to the Jewish shekel and the tax was a half-shekel. *For me and for you*: not only Jesus but Peter pays the tax, and this example serves as a standard for the conduct of all the disciples.

**18:1–35** This discourse of the fourth book of the gospel is often called the "church order" discourse, but it lacks most of the considerations usually connected with church order, such as

---

17:17 Dt 32:5 LXX.              17:24 Ex 30:11–16; Neh
17:20 21:21; Lk 17:6; 1 Cor          10:33.
        13:2.                  18:1–5 Mk 9:36–37; Lk
17:22–23 16:21; 20:18–19.              9:46–48.

Jesus and said, "Who is the greatest in the kingdom of heaven?" ² He called a child over, placed it in their midst, ³* and said, "Amen, I say to you, unless you turn and become like children,† you will not enter the kingdom of heaven. ⁴* Whoever humbles himself like this child is the greatest in the kingdom of heaven. ⁵† And whoever receives one child such as this in my name receives me.

**Temptations to Sin.** ⁶* "Whoever causes one of these little ones† who believe in me to sin, it would be better for him to have a great millstone hung around his neck and to be drowned in the depths of the sea. ⁷† Woe to the world because of things that cause sin! Such things must come, but woe to the one through whom they come! ⁸* If your hand or foot causes you to sin,† cut it off and throw it away. It is better for you to enter into life maimed or crippled than with two hands or

two feet to be thrown into eternal fire. ⁹ And if your eye causes you to sin, tear it out and throw it away. It is better for you to enter into life with one eye than with two eyes to be thrown into fiery Gehenna.

**The Parable of the Lost Sheep.** † ¹⁰* "See that you do not despise one of these little ones,† for I say to you that their angels in heaven always look upon the face of my heavenly Father. [¹¹]†* ¹² What is your opinion? If a man has a hundred sheep and one of them goes astray, will he not leave the ninety-nine in the hills and go in search of the stray? ¹³ And if he finds it, amen, I say to you, he rejoices more over it than over the ninety-nine that did not stray. ¹⁴ In just the same way, it is not the will of your heavenly Father that one of these little ones be lost.

**A Brother Who Sins.** † ¹⁵* "If your brother† sins [against you], go and tell him his fault

---

† . . . various offices in the church and the duties of each, and deals principally with the relations that must obtain among the members of the church. Beginning with the warning that greatness in the *kingdom of heaven* is measured not by power but by childlikeness (Mt 18:1–5), it deals with the care that the disciples must take not to cause the *little ones to sin* or to neglect them if they stray from the community (Mt 18:6–14), the correction of members who sin (Mt 18:15–18), the efficacy of the prayer of the disciples because of the presence of Jesus (Mt 18:19–20), and the forgiveness that must be repeatedly extended to sinful members who repent (Mt 18:21–35).

**18:1** The initiative is taken not by Jesus as in the Marcan parallel (Mk 9:33–34) but by the disciples. *Kingdom of heaven*: this may mean *the kingdom* in its fullness, i.e., after the parousia and the final judgment. But what follows about causes of sin, church discipline, and forgiveness, all dealing with the present age, suggests that the question has to do with rank also in the church, where the kingdom is manifested here and now, although only partially and by anticipation; see notes on Mt 3:2; 4:17.

**18:3** *Become like children*: the child is held up as a model for the disciples not because of any supposed innocence of children but because of their complete dependence on, and trust in, their parents. So must the disciples be, in respect to God.

**18:5** Cf. Mt 10:40.

**18:6** *One of these little ones*: the thought passes from the child of Mt 18:2–4 to the disciples, *little ones* because of their becoming *like children*. It is difficult to know whether this is a designation of all who are disciples or of those who are insignificant in contrast to others, e.g., the leaders of the community. Since apart from this chapter the designation *little ones* occurs in Matthew only in Mt 10:42 where it means disciples as such, that is its more likely meaning here. *Who believe in me*: since discipleship is impossible without at least some degree of faith, this further specification seems superfluous. However, it serves to indicate that the warning against causing a *little one* to sin is principally directed against whatever would lead such a one to a weakening or loss of faith. The Greek verb *skandalizein*, here translated *causes...to sin*, means literally "causes to stumble"; what the stumbling is depends on the context. It is used of falling away from faith in Mt 13:21. According to the better reading of Mk 9:42, *in me* is a Matthean addition to the Marcan source. *It would be better...depths of the sea*: cf. Mk 9:42.

**18:7** This is a Q saying; cf. Lk 17:1. The inevitability of *things that cause sin* (literally, "scandals") does not take away the re-

sponsibility of *the one through whom they come*.

**18:8–9** These verses are a doublet of Mt 5:29–30. In that context they have to do with causes of sexual sin. As in the Marcan source from which they have been drawn (Mk 9:42–48), they differ from the first warning about scandal, which deals with causing another person to sin, for they concern what *causes* oneself *to sin* and they do not seem to be related to another's loss of faith, as the first warning is. It is difficult to know how Matthew understood the logical connection between these verses and Mt 18:6–7.

**18:10–14** The first and last verses are peculiar to Matthew. The parable itself comes from Q; see Lk 15:3–7. In Luke it serves as justification for Jesus' table-companionship with sinners; here, it is an exhortation for the disciples to seek out fellow disciples who have gone *astray*. Not only must no one cause a fellow disciple to sin, but those who have strayed must be sought out and, if possible, brought back to the community. The joy of the shepherd on finding the sheep, though not absent in Mt 18:13 is more emphasized in Luke. By his addition of Mt 18:10, 14 Matthew has drawn out explicitly the application of the parable to the care of the *little ones*.

**18:10** *Their angels in heaven...my heavenly Father*: for the Jewish belief in angels as guardians of nations and individuals, see Dn 10:13, 20–21; Tb 5:4–7; 1QH 5:20–22; as intercessors who present the prayers of human beings to God, see Tb 13:12, 15. The high worth of the *little ones* is indicated by their being represented before God by these heavenly beings.

**18:11** Some manuscripts add, "For the Son of Man has come to save what was lost"; cf. Mt 9:13. This is practically identical with Lk 19:10 and is probably a copyist's addition from that source.

**18:15–20** Passing from the duty of Christian disciples toward those who have strayed from their number, the discourse now turns to how they are to deal with one who sins and yet remains within the community. First there is to be private correction (Mt 18:15); if this is unsuccessful, further correction before *two or three witnesses* (Mt 18:16); if this fails, the matter is to be brought before the assembled community (the church), and if the sinner refuses to attend to the correction of *the church*, he is to be

---

**18:3** 19:14; Mk 10:15; Lk 18:17.
**18:4** 23:12.
**18:6–7** Mk 9:42; Lk 17:1–2.
**18:8–9** 5:29–30; Mk 9:43–47.

**18:10–14** Ez 34:1–3, 16; Lk 15:3–7.
**18:11** Lk 19:10.
**18:15** Lv 19:17; Sir 19:13; Gal 6:1.

between you and him alone. If he listens to you, you have won over your brother. 16†* If he does not listen, take one or two others along with you, so that 'every fact may be established on the testimony of two or three witnesses.' 17* If he refuses to listen to them, tell the church.† If he refuses to listen even to the church, then treat him as you would a Gentile or a tax collector. 18†* Amen, I say to you, whatever you bind on earth shall be bound in heaven, and whatever you loose on earth shall be loosed in heaven. 19†* Again, [amen,] I say to you, if two of you agree on earth about anything for which they are to pray, it shall be granted to them by my heavenly Father. 20†* For where two or three are gathered together in my name, there am I in the midst of them."

## The Parable of the Unforgiving Servant.†

21* Then Peter approaching asked him, "Lord, if my brother sins against me, how often must I forgive him? As many as seven times?" 22† Jesus answered, "I say to you, not seven times but seventy-seven times. 23* That is why the kingdom of heaven may be likened to a king who decided to settle accounts with his servants. 24† When he began the accounting, a debtor was brought before him who owed him a huge amount. 25 Since he had no way of paying it back, his master ordered him to be sold, along with his wife, his children, and all his property, in payment of the debt. 26† At that, the servant fell down, did him homage, and said, 'Be patient with me, and I will pay you back in full.' 27 Moved with compassion the master of that servant let him go and forgave him the loan. 28 When that servant had left, he found one of his fellow servants who owed him a much smaller amount.† He seized him and started to choke him, demanding, 'Pay back what you owe.' 29 Falling to his knees, his fellow servant begged him, 'Be patient with me, and I will pay you back.' 30 But he refused. Instead, he had him put in prison until he paid back the debt. 31 Now when his fellow servants saw what had happened, they were deeply disturbed, and went to their master

---

† expelled (Mt 18:17). The church's judgment will be ratified *in heaven*, i.e., by God (Mt 18:18). This three-step process of correction corresponds, though not exactly, to the procedure of the Qumran community; see 1QS 5:25–6:1; 6:24–7:25; CD 9:2–8. The section ends with a saying about the favorable response of God to prayer, even to that of a very small number, for Jesus is in the midst of any gathering of his disciples, however small (Mt 18:19–20). Whether this prayer has anything to do with the preceding judgment is uncertain.

**18:15** *Your brother*: a fellow disciple; see Mt 23:8. The bracketed words, *against you*, are widely attested but they are not in the important codices Sinaiticus and Vaticanus or in some other textual witnesses. Their omission broadens the type of sin in question. *Won over*: literally, "gained."

**18:16** Cf. Dt 19:15.

**18:17** *The church*: the second of the only two instances of this word in the gospels; see note on Mt 16:18. Here it refers not to the entire *church* of Jesus, as in Mt 16:18, but to the local congregation. *Treat him...a Gentile or a tax collector*: just as the observant Jew avoided the company of Gentiles and tax collectors, so must the congregation of Christian disciples separate itself from the arrogantly sinful member who refuses to repent even when convicted of his sin by the whole *church*. Such a one is to be set outside the fellowship of the community. The harsh language about *Gentile* and *tax collector* probably reflects a stage of the Matthean *church* when it was principally composed of Jewish Christians. That time had long since passed, but the principle of exclusion for such a sinner remained. Paul makes a similar demand for excommunication in 1 Cor 5:1–13.

**18:18** Except for the plural of the verbs *bind* and *loose*, this verse is practically identical with Mt 16:19b and many scholars understand it as granting to all the disciples what was previously given to Peter alone. For a different view, based on the different contexts of the two verses, see note on Mt 16:19.

**18:19–20** Some take these verses as applying to prayer on the occasion of the church's gathering to deal with the sinner of Mt 18:17. Unless an *a fortiori* argument is supposed, this seems unlikely. God's answer to the prayer of *two or three* envisages a different situation from one that involves the entire congregation. In addition, the object of this prayer is expressed in most general terms as *anything for which they are to pray*.

**18:20** *For where two or three...midst of them*: the presence of Jesus guarantees the efficacy of the prayer. This saying is similar to one attributed to a rabbi executed in A.D. 135 at the time of the second Jewish revolt: "...When two sit and there are between them the words of the Torah, the divine presence (*Shekinah*) rests upon them" (*Pirqê 'Abôt* 3,3).

**18:21–35** The final section of the discourse deals with the forgiveness that the disciples are to give to their fellow disciples who sin against them. To the question of Peter how often forgiveness is to be granted (Mt 18:21), Jesus answers that it is to be given without limit (Mt 18:22) and illustrates this with the parable of the unmerciful servant (Mt 18:23–34), warning that his *heavenly Father* will give those who do not forgive the same treatment as that given to the unmerciful servant (Mt 18:35). Mt 18:21–22 correspond to Lk 17:4; the parable and the final warning are peculiar to Matthew. That the parable did not originally belong to this context is suggested by the fact that it really does not deal with repeated forgiveness, which is the point of Peter's question and Jesus' reply.

**18:22** *Seventy-seven times*: the Greek corresponds exactly to the LXX of Gn 4:24. There is probably an allusion, by contrast, to the limitless vengeance of Lamech in the Genesis text. In any case, what is demanded of the disciples is limitless forgiveness.

**18:24** *A huge amount*: literally, "ten thousand talents." The talent was a unit of coinage of high but varying value depending on its metal (gold, silver, copper) and its place of origin. It is mentioned in the New Testament only here and in Mt 25:14–30.

**18:26** *Pay you back in full*: an empty promise, given the size of the debt.

**18:28** *A much smaller amount*: literally, "a hundred denarii." A denarius was the normal daily wage of a laborer. The difference between the two debts is enormous and brings out the absurdity of the conduct of the Christian who has received the great forgiveness of God and yet refuses to forgive the relatively minor offenses done to him.

---

* 
**18:16** Dt 19:15; Jn 8:17;   **18:19** 7:7–8; Jn 15:7.
1 Tm 5:19.                     **18:20** 1 Cor 5:4.
**18:17** 1 Cor 5:1–13.       **18:21–22** 6:12; Lk 17:4.
**18:18** 16:19; Jn 20:23.    **18:23** 25:19.

MT

and reported the whole affair. 32 His master summoned him and said to him, 'You wicked servant! I forgave you your entire debt because you begged me to. 33* Should you not have had pity on your fellow servant, as I had pity on you?' 34 Then in anger his master handed him over to the torturers until he should pay back the whole debt.† 35†* So will my heavenly Father do to you, unless each of you forgives his brother from his heart.'

## VI. MINISTRY IN JUDEA AND JERUSALEM

**19** **Marriage and Divorce.** 1† When Jesus† finished these words,† he left Galilee and went to the district of Judea across the Jordan. 2 Great crowds followed him, and he cured them there. 3* Some Pharisees approached him, and tested him,† saying, "Is it lawful for a man to divorce his wife for any cause whatever?" 4†* He said in reply, "Have you not read that from the beginning the Creator 'made them male and female' 5* and said, 'For this reason a man shall leave his father and mother and be joined to his wife, and the two shall become one flesh'? 6 So they are no longer two, but one flesh. Therefore, what God has joined together, no human being must separate." 7†* They said to him, "Then why did Moses command that the man give the woman a bill of divorce and dismiss [her]?" 8 He said to them, "Because of the hardness of your hearts Moses allowed you to divorce your wives, but from the beginning it was not so. 9* I say to you,† whoever divorces his wife (unless the marriage is unlawful) and marries another commits adultery." 10 [His] disciples said to him, "If that is the case of a man with his wife, it is better not to marry." 11 He answered, "Not all can accept [this] word,† but only those to whom that is granted. 12 Some are incapable of marriage because they were born so; some, because they were made so by others; some, because they have renounced marriage† for

---

†

**18:34** Since the debt is so great as to be unpayable, the punishment will be endless.

**18:35** The Father's forgiveness, already given, will be withdrawn at the final judgment for those who have not imitated his forgiveness by their own.

**19:1–23:39** The narrative section of the fifth book of the gospel. The first part (Mt 19:1–20:34) has for its setting the journey of Jesus from Galilee to Jerusalem; the second (Mt 21:1–23:39) deals with Jesus' ministry in Jerusalem up to the final great discourse of the gospel (Mt 24–25). Matthew follows the Marcan sequence of events, though adding material both special to this gospel and drawn from Q. The second part ends with the denunciation of the scribes and Pharisees (Mt 23:1–36) followed by Jesus' lament over Jerusalem (Mt 23:37–39). This long and important speech raises a problem for the view that Matthew is structured around five other discourses of Jesus (see Introduction) and that this one has no such function in the gospel. However, it is to be noted that this speech lacks the customary concluding formula that follows the five discourses (see note on Mt 7:28), and that those discourses are all addressed either exclusively (Mt 10; 18; 24; 25) or primarily (Mt 5–7) to the disciples, whereas this is addressed primarily to the scribes and Pharisees (Mt 23:13–36). Consequently, it seems plausible to maintain that the evangelist did not intend to give it the structural importance of the five other discourses, and that, in spite of its being composed of sayings-material, it belongs to the narrative section of this book. In that regard, it is similar to the sayings-material of Mt 11:7–30. Some have proposed that Matthew wished to regard it as part of the final discourse of Mt 24–25, but the intervening material (Mt 24:1–4) and the change in matter and style of those chapters do not support that view.

**19:1** In giving Jesus' teaching on divorce (Mt 19:3–9), Matthew here follows his Marcan source (Mk 10:2–12) as he does Q in Mt 5:31–32 (cf. Lk 16:18). Mt 19:10–12 are peculiar to Matthew.

**19:1** *When Jesus finished these words*: see note on Mt 7:28–29. *The district of Judea across the Jordan*: an inexact designation of the territory. Judea did not extend *across the Jordan*; the territory east of the river was Perea. The route to Jerusalem by way of Perea avoided passage through Samaria.

**19:3** *Tested him*: the verb is used of attempts of Jesus' opponents to embarrass him by challenging him to do something they think impossible (Mt 16:1; Mk 8:11; Lk 11:16) or by having him

say something that they can use against him (Mt 22:18, 35; Mk 10:2; 12:15). *For any cause whatever*: this is peculiar to Matthew and has been interpreted by some as meaning that Jesus was being asked to take sides in the dispute between the schools of Hillel and Shammai on the reasons for divorce, the latter holding a stricter position than the former. It is unlikely, however, that to ask Jesus' opinion about the differing views of two Jewish schools, both highly respected, could be described as "testing" him, for the reason indicated above.

**19:4–6** Matthew recasts his Marcan source, omitting Jesus' question about Moses' command (Mk 10:3) and having him recall at once two Genesis texts that show the will and purpose of *the Creator* in making human beings *male and female* (Gn 1:27), namely, that a *man* may *be joined to his wife* in marriage in the intimacy of *one flesh* (Gn 2:24). *What God has* thus *joined* must not be separated by any human being. (The NAB translation of the Hebrew *bāśār* of Gn 2:24 as "body" rather than "flesh" obscures the reference of Matthew to that text.)

**19:7** See Dt 24:1–4.

**19:9** Moses' concession to human sinfulness (*the hardness of your hearts*, Mt 19:8) is repudiated by Jesus, and the original will of the Creator is reaffirmed against that concession. (*Unless the marriage is unlawful*): see note on Mt 5:31–32. There is some evidence suggesting that Jesus' absolute prohibition of divorce was paralleled in the Qumran community (see 11QTemple 57:17–19; CD 4:12b–5:14). Matthew removes Mark's setting of this verse as spoken to the disciples alone "in the house" (Mk 10:10) and also his extension of the divorce prohibition to the case of a woman's divorcing her husband (Mk 10:12), probably because in Palestine, unlike the places where Roman and Greek law prevailed, the woman was not allowed to initiate the divorce.

**19:11** [*This*] *word*: probably the disciples' "*it is better not to marry*" (Mt 19:10). Jesus agrees but says that celibacy is not for all but only for those *to whom that is granted* by God.

**19:12** *Incapable of marriage*: literally, "eunuchs." Three classes are mentioned, eunuchs from birth, eunuchs by castration, and those who have voluntarily *renounced marriage* (literally, "have made themselves eunuchs") *for the sake of the kingdom,*

---

18:33 Sir 28:4.
18:35 6:15; Jas 2:13.
19:3–9 Mk 10:2–12.
19:4 Gn 1:27.

19:5 Gn 2:24; 1 Cor 6:16;
　　Eph 5:31.
19:7 Dt 24:1–4.
19:9 5:32; Lk 16:18; 1 Cor
　　7:10–11.

the sake of the kingdom of heaven. Whoever can accept this ought to accept it."

### Blessing of the Children.† 13 * Then children were brought to him that he might lay his hands on them and pray. The disciples rebuked them, 14 * but Jesus said, "Let the children come to me, and do not prevent them; for the kingdom of heaven belongs to such as these." 15 After he placed his hands on them, he went away.

### The Rich Young Man.† 16 * Now someone approached him and said, "Teacher, what good must I do to gain eternal life?"† 17 He answered him, "Why do you ask me about the good? There is only One who is good.† If you wish to enter into life, keep the commandments." 18 †* He asked him, "Which ones?" And Jesus replied, " 'You shall not kill; you shall not commit adultery; you shall not steal; you shall not bear false witness; 19 honor your father and your mother'; and 'you shall love your neighbor as yourself.' " 20 † The young man said to him, "All of these I have observed.

What do I still lack?" 21 * Jesus said to him, "If you wish to be perfect,† go, sell what you have and give to [the] poor, and you will have treasure in heaven. Then come, follow me." 22 When the young man heard this statement, he went away sad, for he had many possessions. 23 † Then Jesus said to his disciples, "Amen, I say to you, it will be hard for one who is rich to enter the kingdom of heaven. 24 * Again I say to you, it is easier for a camel to pass through the eye of a needle than for one who is rich to enter the kingdom of God." 25 † When the disciples heard this, they were greatly astonished and said, "Who then can be saved?" 26 * Jesus looked at them and said, "For human beings this is impossible, but for God all things are possible." 27 * Then Peter said to him in reply, "We have given up everything and followed you. What will there be for us?" 28 †* Jesus said to them, "Amen, I say to you that you who have followed me, in the new age, when the Son of Man is seated on his throne of glory, will yourselves sit on twelve thrones, judging the twelve tribes of Israel. 29 And everyone who has given up houses

---

† i.e., to devote themselves entirely to its service. Some scholars take the last class to be those who have been divorced by their spouses and have refused to enter another marriage. But it is more likely that it is rather those who have chosen never to marry, since that suits better the optional nature of the decision: *whoever can…ought to accept it.*

**19:13–15** This account is understood by some as intended to justify the practice of infant baptism. That interpretation is based principally on the command not to *prevent* the children from coming, since that word sometimes has a baptismal connotation in the New Testament; see Acts 8:36.

**19:16–30** Cf. Mk 10:17–31. This story does not set up a "two-tier" morality, that of those who seek (only) *eternal life* (Mt 19:16) and that of those who *wish to be perfect* (Mt 19:21). It speaks rather of the obstacle that riches constitute for the following of Jesus and of the impossibility, humanly speaking, for one who has *many possessions* (Mt 19:22) *to enter the kingdom* (Mt 19:24). Actual renunciation of riches is not demanded of all; Matthew counts the rich Joseph of Arimathea as a disciple of Jesus (Mt 27:57). But only the poor in spirit (Mt 5:3) can *enter the kingdom* and, as here, such poverty may entail the sacrifice of one's *possessions.* The Twelve, who *have given up everything* (Mt 19:27) to follow Jesus, will have as their reward a share in Jesus' (the Son of Man's) *judging the twelve tribes of Israel* (Mt 19:28), and all who have similarly sacrificed family or property for his sake *will inherit eternal life* (Mt 19:29).

**19:16** *Gain eternal life:* this is equivalent to "entering into life" (Mt 19:17) and "being saved" (Mt 19:25); the *life* is that of the new age after the final judgment (see Mt 25:46). It probably is also equivalent here to "entering the kingdom of heaven" (Mt 19:23) or "the kingdom of God" (Mt 19:24), but see notes on Mt 3:2; 4:17; 18:1 for the wider reference of *the kingdom* in Matthew.

**19:17** By Matthew's reformulation of the Marcan question and reply (Mk 10:17–18) Jesus' repudiation of the term "good" for himself has been softened. Yet the Marcan assertion that "no one is good but God alone" stands, with only unimportant verbal modification.

**19:18–19** The first five commandments cited are from the

Decalogue (see Ex 20:12–16; Dt 5:16–20). Matthew omits Mark's "you shall not defraud" (Mk 10:19; see Dt 24:14) and adds Lv 19:18. This combination of commandments of the Decalogue with Lv 19:18 is partially the same as Paul's enumeration of the demands of Christian morality in Rom 13:9.

**19:20** *Young man:* in Matthew alone of the synoptics the questioner is said to be a *young man;* thus the Marcan "from my youth" (Mk 10:20) is omitted.

**19:21** *If you wish to be perfect: to be perfect* is demanded of all Christians; see Mt 5:48. In the case of this man, it involves selling his possessions and giving to the poor; only so can he *follow* Jesus.

**19:23–24** Riches are an obstacle to entering *the kingdom* that cannot be overcome by human power. The comparison with the impossibility of a camel's passing *through the eye of a needle* should not be mitigated by such suppositions as that *the eye of a needle* means a low or narrow gate. *The kingdom of God:* as in Mt 12:28; 21:31, 43 instead of Matthew's usual *kingdom of heaven.*

**19:25–26** See note on Mk 10:23–27.

**19:28** This saying, directed to the Twelve, is from Q; see Lk 22:29–30. *The new age:* the Greek word here translated "new age" occurs in the New Testament only here and in Ti 3:5. Literally, it means "rebirth" or "regeneration," and is used in Titus of spiritual rebirth through baptism. Here it means the "rebirth" effected by the coming of the kingdom. Since that coming has various stages (see notes on Mt 3:2; 4:17), the *new age* could be taken as referring to the time after the resurrection when the Twelve will govern the true Israel, i.e., the church of Jesus. (For "judge" in the sense of "govern," cf. Jgs 12:8, 9, 11; 15:20;

---

**19:13–15** Mk 10:13–16; Lk 18:15–17.
**19:14** 18:3; Acts 8:36.
**19:16–30** Mk 10:17–31; Lk 18:18–30.
**19:18–19** Ex 20:12–16; Dt 5:16–20 / Lv 19:18; Rom 13:9.
**19:21** 5:48; 6:20.
**19:24** 7:14.
**19:26** Gn 18:14; Jb 42:2; Lk 1:37.
**19:27** 4:20, 22.
**19:28** 25:31; Dn 7:9, 22; Lk 22:30; Rev 3:21; 20:4.

or brothers or sisters or father or mother or children or lands for the sake of my name will receive a hundred times more, and will inherit eternal life. [30]†* But many who are first will be last, and the last will be first.

# 20 The Workers in the Vineyard.†

[1] "The kingdom of heaven is like a landowner who went out at dawn to hire laborers for his vineyard. [2] After agreeing with them for the usual daily wage, he sent them into his vineyard. [3] Going out about nine o'clock, he saw others standing idle in the marketplace, [4]† and he said to them, 'You too go into my vineyard, and I will give you what is just.' [5] So they went off. [And] he went out again around noon, and around three o'clock, and did likewise. [6] Going out about five o'clock, he found others standing around, and said to them, 'Why do you stand here idle all day?' [7] They answered, 'Because no one has hired us.' He said to them, 'You too go into my vineyard.' [8]†* When it was evening the owner of the vineyard said to his foreman, 'Summon the laborers and give them their pay, beginning with the last and ending with the first.' [9] When those who had started about five o'clock came, each received the usual daily wage. [10] So when the first came, they thought that they would receive more, but each of them also got the usual wage. [11] And on receiving it they grumbled against the landowner, [12] saying, 'These last ones worked only one hour, and you have made them equal to us, who bore the day's burden and the heat.' [13] He said to one of them in reply, 'My friend, I am not cheating you.† Did you not agree with me for the usual daily wage? [14]† Take what is yours and go. What if I wish to give this last one the same as you? [15] [Or] am I not free to do as I wish with my own money? Are you envious because I am generous?' [16]† Thus, the last will be first, and the first will be last."

## The Third Prediction of the Passion.†

[17]* As Jesus was going up to Jerusalem, he took the twelve [disciples] aside by themselves, and said to them on the way, [18] "Behold, we are going up to Jerusalem, and the Son of Man will be handed over to the chief priests and the scribes, and they will condemn him to death, [19] and hand him over to the Gentiles to be mocked and scourged and crucified, and he will be raised on the third day."

## The Request of James and John.†

[20]* Then the mother† of the sons of Zebedee approached him with her sons and did him homage, wishing to ask him for something. [21] He said to her, "What do you wish?" She answered him, "Command that these two sons of mine sit, one at your right and the other at your left, in your kingdom." [22] Jesus said in reply, "You do not know what you are asking.† Can you drink the cup that I am going to drink?" They said to him, "We can." [23] He replied, "My cup you will

---

16:31; Ps 2:10). But since it is connected here with the time when the *Son of Man* will be *seated on his throne of glory*, language that Matthew uses in Mt 25:31 for the time of final judgment, it is more likely that what the Twelve are promised is that they will be joined with Jesus then in judging the people of Israel.

**19:30** Different interpretations have been given to this saying, which comes from Mk 10:31. In view of Matthew's associating it with the following parable (Mt 20:1–15) and substantially repeating it (in reverse order) at the end of that parable (Mt 20:16), it may be that his meaning is that all who respond to the call of Jesus, at whatever time (*first* or *last*), will be the same in respect to inheriting the benefits of the kingdom, which is the gift of God.

**20:1–16** This parable is peculiar to Matthew. It is difficult to know whether the evangelist composed it or received it as part of his traditional material and, if the latter is the case, what its original reference was. In its present context its close association with Mt 19:30 suggests that its teaching is the equality of all the disciples in the reward of inheriting eternal life.

**20:4** *What is just*: although the wage is not stipulated as in the case of those first hired, it will be fair.

**20:8** *Beginning with the last...the first*: this element of the parable has no other purpose than to show how *the first* knew what *the last* were given (Mt 20:12).

**20:13** *I am not cheating you*: literally, "I am not treating you unjustly."

**20:14–15** The owner's conduct involves no violation of justice (Mt 20:4, 13), and that all the workers receive the same wage

is due only to his generosity to the latest arrivals; the resentment of the first comes from envy.

**20:16** See note on Mt 19:30.

**20:17–19** Cf. Mk 10:32–34. This is the third and the most detailed of the passion predictions (Mt 16:21–23; 17:22–23). It speaks of Jesus' being *handed over to the Gentiles* (Mt 27:2), his being *mocked* (Mt 27:27–30), *scourged* (Mt 27:26), and *crucified* (Mt 27:31, 35). In all but the last of these points Matthew agrees with his Marcan source, but whereas Mark speaks of Jesus' being *killed* (Mk 10:34), Matthew has the specific *to be...crucified*.

**20:20–28** Cf. Mk 10:35–45. The request of the sons of Zebedee, made through their mother, for the highest places of honor in the *kingdom*, and the indignation of *the other ten* disciples at this request, show that neither *the two brothers* nor the others have understood that what makes for greatness in the kingdom is not lordly power but humble service. Jesus gives the example, and his ministry of service will reach its highest point when he gives his life for the deliverance of the human race from sin.

**20:20–21** The reason for Matthew's making the *mother* the petitioner (cf. Mk 10:35) is not clear. Possibly he intends an allusion to Bathsheba's seeking the kingdom for Solomon; see 1 Kgs 1:11–21. *Your kingdom*: see note on Mt 16:28.

**20:22** *You do not know what you are asking*: the Greek verbs

---

**19:30** 20:16.
**20:8** Lv 19:13; Dt 24:15.
**20:17–19** 16:21; 17:22–23;
Mk 10:32–34; Lk 18:31–33.
**20:20–28** Mk 10:35–45.

indeed drink, but to sit at my right and at my left [, this] is not mine to give but is for those for whom it has been prepared by my Father." 24* When the ten heard this, they became indignant at the two brothers. 25 But Jesus summoned them and said, "You know that the rulers of the Gentiles lord it over them, and the great ones make their authority over them felt. 26 But it shall not be so among you. Rather, whoever wishes to be great among you shall be your servant; 27* whoever wishes to be first among you shall be your slave. 28* Just so, the Son of Man did not come to be served but to serve and to give his life as a ransom† for many."

**The Healing of Two Blind Men.**† 29* As they left Jericho, a great crowd followed him. 30* Two blind men were sitting by the roadside, and when they heard that Jesus was passing by, they cried out, "[Lord,]† Son of David, have pity on us!" 31 The crowd warned them to be silent, but they called out all the more, "Lord, Son of David, have pity on us!" 32 Jesus stopped and called them and said, "What do you want me to do for you?" 33 They answered him, "Lord, let our eyes be opened." 34 Moved with pity,

Jesus touched their eyes. Immediately they received their sight, and followed him.

# 21 The Entry into Jerusalem.† 1* When they drew near Jerusalem and came to Bethphage† on the Mount of Olives, Jesus sent two disciples, 2 saying to them, "Go into the village opposite you, and immediately you will find an ass tethered, and a colt with her.† Untie them and bring them here to me. 3 And if anyone should say anything to you, reply, 'The master has need of them.' Then he will send them at once." 4† This happened so that what had been spoken through the prophet might be fulfilled:

5* 　　"Say to daughter Zion,
　　　'Behold, your king comes to you,
　　　　meek and riding on an ass,
　　　　　and on a colt, the foal of a beast of burden.'"

6 The disciples went and did as Jesus had ordered them. 7† They brought the ass and the colt and laid their cloaks over them, and he sat upon them. 8†* The very large crowd spread their cloaks on the road, while others

---

are plural and, with the rest of the verse, indicate that the answer is addressed not to the woman but to her sons. *Drink the cup:* see note on Mk 10:38–40. Matthew omits the Marcan "or be baptized with the baptism with which I am baptized" (Mk 10:38).
**20:28** *Ransom:* this noun, which occurs in the New Testament only here and in the Marcan parallel (Mk 10:45), does not necessarily express the idea of liberation by payment of some price. The cognate verb is used frequently in the LXX of God's liberating Israel from Egypt or from Babylonia after the Exile; see Ex 6:6; 15:13; Ps 77:16 (76 LXX); Is 43:1; 44:22. The liberation brought by Jesus' death will be *for many;* cf. Is 53:12. *Many* does not mean that some are excluded, but is a Semitism designating the collectivity who benefit from the service of the one, and is equivalent to "all." While there are few verbal contacts between this saying and the fourth Servant Song (Is 52:13–53:12), the ideas of that passage are reflected here.
**20:29–34** The cure of the blind men is probably symbolic of what will happen to the disciples, now blind to the meaning of Jesus' passion and to the necessity of their sharing his suffering. As the men are given sight, so, after the resurrection, will the disciples come to see that to which they are now blind. Matthew has abbreviated his Marcan source (Mk 10:46–52) and has made Mark's one man two. Such doubling is characteristic of this gospel; see Mt 8:28–34 (// Mk 5:1–20) and the note on Mt 9:27–31.
**20:30** *[Lord,]:* some important textual witnesses omit this, but that may be because copyists assimilated this verse to Mt 9:27. *Son of David:* see note on Mt 9:27.
**21:1–11** Jesus' coming to Jerusalem is in accordance with the divine will that he must go there (cf. Mt 16:21) to suffer, die, and be raised. He prepares for his entry into the city in such a way as to make it a fulfillment of the prophecy of Zec 9:9 (Mt 21:2) that emphasizes the humility of the *king* who *comes* (Mt 21:5). That prophecy, absent from the Marcan parallel account (Mk 11:1–11) although found also in the Johannine account of the entry (Jn 12:15), is the center of the Matthean story. During the procession from Bethphage to Jerusalem, Jesus is acclaimed as

the Davidic messianic king by the crowds who accompany him (Mt 21:9). On his arrival the *whole city was shaken,* and to the inquiry of the amazed populace about Jesus' identity the crowds with him reply that he is *the prophet, from Nazareth in Galilee* (Mt 21:10, 11).
**21:1** *Bethphage:* a village that can no longer be certainly identified. Mark mentions it before Bethany (Mk 11:1), which suggests that it lay to the east of the latter. *The Mount of Olives:* the hill east of Jerusalem that is spoken of in Zec 14:4 as the place where the Lord will come to rescue Jerusalem from the enemy nations.
**21:2** *An ass tethered, and a colt with her:* instead of the one animal of Mk 11:2, Matthew has two, as demanded by his understanding of Zec 9:9.
**21:4–5** *The prophet:* this fulfillment citation is actually composed of two distinct Old Testament texts, Is 62:11 (*Say to daughter Zion*) and Zec 9:9. The *ass* and the *colt* are the same animal in the prophecy, mentioned twice in different ways, the common Hebrew literary device of poetic parallelism. That Matthew takes them as two is one of the reasons why some scholars think that he was a Gentile rather than a Jewish Christian who would presumably not make that mistake (see Introduction).
**21:7** *Upon them:* upon the two animals; an awkward picture resulting from Matthew's misunderstanding of the prophecy.
**21:8** *Spread…on the road:* cf. 2 Kgs 9:13. There is a similarity between the cutting and strewing of the branches and the festivities of Tabernacles (Lv 23:39–40); see also 2 Mc 10:5–8 where the celebration of the rededication of the temple is compared to that of Tabernacles.

20:24–27 Lk 22:25–27.　　20:30 9:27.
20:27 Mk 9:35.　　21:1–11 Mk 11:1–11; Lk
20:28 26:28; Is 53:12; Rom　　19:28–38; Jn
5:6; 1 Tm 2:6.　　12:12–15.
20:29–34 Mk 10:46–52; Lk　　21:5 Is 62:11; Zec 9:9.
18:35–43.　　21:8 2 Kgs 9:13.

MT

cut branches from the trees and strewed them on the road. 9 * The crowds preceding him and those following kept crying out and saying:

"Hosanna† to the Son of David;
   blessed is he who comes in the name
      of the Lord;
   hosanna in the highest."

10 And when he entered Jerusalem the whole city was shaken† and asked, "Who is this?" 11 And the crowds replied, "This is Jesus the prophet,† from Nazareth in Galilee."

### The Cleansing of the Temple.† 12 * Jesus entered the temple area and drove out all those engaged in selling and buying there. He overturned the tables of the money changers and the seats of those who were selling doves.†* 13 * And he said to them, "It is written:

'My house shall be a house of
   prayer,'†
   but you are making it a den of
      thieves."

14 * The blind and the lame† approached him in the temple area, and he cured them.

15 When the chief priests and the scribes saw the wondrous things† he was doing, and the children crying out in the temple area, "Hosanna to the Son of David," they were indignant 16 †* and said to him, "Do you hear what they are saying?" Jesus said to them, "Yes; and have you never read the text, 'Out of the mouths of infants and nurslings you have brought forth praise'?" 17 And leaving them, he went out of the city to Bethany, and there he spent the night.

### The Cursing of the Fig Tree.† 18 * When he was going back to the city in the morning, he was hungry. 19 * Seeing a fig tree by the road, he went over to it, but found nothing on it except leaves. And he said to it, "May no fruit ever come from you again." And immediately the fig tree withered. 20 When the disciples saw this, they were amazed and said, "How was it that the fig tree withered immediately?" 21 †* Jesus said to them in reply, "Amen, I say to you, if you have faith and do not waver, not only will you do what has been done to the fig tree, but even if you say to this mountain, 'Be lifted up and thrown into the sea,' it will be done. 22 * Whatever you ask for in prayer with faith, you will receive."

---

**MT**

**21:9** *Hosanna*: the Hebrew means "(O LORD) grant salvation"; see Ps 118:25, but that invocation had become an acclamation of jubilation and welcome. *Blessed is he…in the name of the Lord*: see Ps 118:26 and the note on Jn 12:13. *In the highest*: probably only an intensification of the acclamation, although *Hosanna in the highest* could be taken as a prayer, "May God save (him)."

**21:10** *Was shaken*: in the gospels this verb is peculiar to Matthew where it is used also of the earthquake at the time of the crucifixion (Mt 27:51) and of the terror of the guards of Jesus' tomb at the appearance of the angel (Mt 28:4). For Matthew's use of the cognate noun, see note on Mt 8:24.

**21:11** *The prophet*: see Mt 16:14 ("one of the prophets") and 21:46.

**21:12–17** Matthew changes the order of (Mk 11:11, 12, 15) and places the cleansing of the temple on the same day as the entry into Jerusalem, immediately after it. The activities going on in *the temple area* were not secular but connected with the temple worship. Thus Jesus' attack on those so engaged and his charge that they were *making* God's *house of prayer a den of thieves* (Mt 21:12–13) constituted a claim to authority over the religious practices of Israel and were a challenge to the priestly authorities. Mt 21:14–17 are peculiar to Matthew. Jesus' healings and his countenancing the children's cries of praise rouse the indignation of the *chief priests and the scribes* (Mt 21:15). These two groups appear in the infancy narrative (Mt 2:4) and have been mentioned in the first and third passion predictions (Mt 16:21; 20:18). Now, as the passion approaches, they come on the scene again, exhibiting their hostility to Jesus.

**21:12** These activities were carried on in the court of the Gentiles, the outermost court of *the temple area*. Animals for sacrifice were sold; the *doves* were for those who could not afford a more expensive offering; see Lv 5:7. *Tables of the money changers*: only the coinage of Tyre could be used for the purchases; other

money had to be exchanged for that.

**21:13** *'My house…prayer'*: cf. Is 56:7. Matthew omits the final words of the quotation, "for all peoples" ("all nations"), possibly because for him the worship of the God of Israel by all nations belongs to the time after the resurrection; see Mt 28:19. *A den of thieves*: the phrase is taken from Jer 7:11.

**21:14** *The blind and the lame*: according to 2 Sm 5:8 LXX *the blind and the lame* were forbidden to enter "the house of the Lord," the temple. These are the last of Jesus' healings in Matthew.

**21:15** *The wondrous things*: the healings.

**21:16** *'Out of the mouths…praise'*: cf. Ps 8:3 LXX.

**21:18–22** In Mark the effect of Jesus' cursing the fig tree is not immediate; see Mk 11:14, 20. By making it so, Matthew has heightened the miracle. Jesus' act seems arbitrary and ill-tempered, but it is a prophetic action similar to those of Old Testament prophets that vividly symbolize some part of their preaching; see, e.g., Ez 12:1–20. It is a sign of the judgment that is to come upon the Israel that with all its apparent piety lacks the fruit of good deeds (Mt 3:10) and will soon bear the punishment of its fruitlessness (Mt 21:43). Some scholars propose that this story is the development in tradition of a parable of Jesus about the destiny of a fruitless tree, such as Lk 13:6–9. Jesus' answer to the question of the amazed disciples (Mt 21:20) makes the miracle an example of the power of prayer made with unwavering *faith* (Mt 21:21–22).

**21:21** See Mt 17:20.

---

| | |
|---|---|
| **21:9** Ps 118:25–26. | **21:16** Ps 8:2 LXX; Wis |
| **21:12–17** Mk 11:15–19; Lk | 10:21. |
| 19:45–48; Jn 2:14–22. | **21:18–22** Mk 11:12–14, 20–24. |
| **21:12** Lv 5:7. | **21:19** Jer 8:13; Lk 13:6–9. |
| **21:13** Is 56:7; Jer 7:11. | **21:21** 17:20; Lk 17:6. |
| **21:14** 2 Sm 5:8 LXX. | **21:22** 7:7; 1 Jn 3:22. |

**The Authority of Jesus Questioned.**† 23 * When he had come into the temple area, the chief priests and the elders of the people approached him as he was teaching and said, "By what authority are you doing these things?† And who gave you this authority?" * 24 Jesus said to them in reply, "I shall ask you one question,† and if you answer it for me, then I shall tell you by what authority I do these things. 25 Where was John's baptism from? Was it of heavenly or of human origin?" They discussed this among themselves and said, "If we say 'Of heavenly origin,' he will say to us, 'Then why did you not believe him?' 26 †* But if we say, 'Of human origin,' we fear the crowd, for they all regard John as a prophet." 27 So they said to Jesus in reply, "We do not know." He himself said to them, "Neither shall I tell you by what authority I do these things.†

**The Parable of the Two Sons.**† 28 "What is your opinion? A man had two sons. He came to the first and said, 'Son, go out and work in the vineyard today.' 29 He said in reply, 'I will not,' but afterwards he changed his mind and went.

30 The man came to the other son and gave the same order. He said in reply, 'Yes, sir,' but did not go. 31 † Which of the two did his father's will?" They answered, "The first." Jesus said to them, "Amen, I say to you, tax collectors and prostitutes are entering the kingdom of God before you. 32 †* When John came to you in the way of righteousness, you did not believe him; but tax collectors and prostitutes did. Yet even when you saw that, you did not later change your minds and believe him.

**The Parable of the Tenants.**† 33 * "Hear another parable. There was a landowner who planted a vineyard,† put a hedge around it, dug a wine press in it, and built a tower. Then he leased it to tenants and went on a journey. * 34 When vintage time drew near, he sent his servants† to the tenants to obtain his produce. 35 But the tenants seized the servants and one they beat, another they killed, and a third they stoned. 36 Again he sent other servants, more numerous than the first ones, but they treated them in the same way. 37 Finally, he sent his son to them, thinking, 'They will respect my son.' 38 † But

---

**21:23–27** Cf. Mk 11:27–33. This is the first of five controversies between Jesus and the religious authorities of Judaism in Mt 21:23–22:46, presented in the form of questions and answers.

**21:23** *These things*: probably his entry into the city, his cleansing of the temple, and his healings there.

**21:24** To reply by counterquestion was common in rabbinical debate.

**21:26** *We fear...as a prophet*: cf. Mt 14:5.

**21:27** Since through embarrassment on the one hand and fear on the other the religious authorities claim ignorance of the origin of John's baptism, they show themselves incapable of speaking with authority; hence Jesus refuses to discuss with them the grounds of his authority.

**21:28–32** The series of controversies is interrupted by three parables on the judgment of Israel (Mt 21:28–22:14) of which this, peculiar to Matthew, is the first. The second (Mt 21:33–46) comes from Mark (12:1–12), and the third (Mt 22:1–14) from Q; see Lk 14:15–24. This interruption of the controversies is similar to that in Mark, although Mark has only one parable between the first and second controversy. As regards Matthew's first parable, Mt 21:28–30 if taken by themselves could point simply to the difference between saying and doing, a theme of much importance in this gospel (cf. Mt 7:21; 12:50); that may have been the parable's original reference. However, it is given a more specific application by the addition of Mt 21:31–32. The two sons represent, respectively, the religious leaders and the religious outcasts who followed John's call to repentance. By the answer they give to Jesus' question (Mt 21:31) the leaders condemn themselves. There is much confusion in the textual tradition of the parable. Of the three different forms of the text given by important textual witnesses, one has the leaders answer that the son who agreed to go but did not was the one who did the father's will. Although some scholars accept that as the original reading, their arguments in favor of it seem unconvincing. The choice probably lies only between a reading that puts the son who agrees and then disobeys before the son who at first refuses and then obeys, and the reading followed in the present translation. The witnesses to the latter reading are

slightly better than those that support the other.

**21:31** *Entering...before you*: this probably means "they enter; you do not."

**21:32** Cf. Lk 7:29–30. Although the thought is similar to that of the Lucan text, the formulation is so different that it is improbable that the saying comes from Q. *Came to you...way of righteousness*: several meanings are possible: that John himself was righteous, that he taught righteousness to others, or that he had an important place in God's plan of salvation. For the last, see note on Mt 3:14–15.

**21:33–46** Cf. Mk 12:1–12. In this parable there is a close correspondence between most of the details of the story and the situation that it illustrates, the dealings of God with his people. Because of that heavy allegorizing, some scholars think that it does not in any way go back to Jesus, but represents the theology of the later church. That judgment applies to the Marcan parallel as well, although the allegorizing has gone farther in Matthew. There are others who believe that while many of the allegorical elements are due to church sources, they have been added to a basic parable spoken by Jesus. This view is now supported by the Gospel of Thomas 65, where a less allegorized and probably more primitive form of the parable is found.

**21:33** *Planted a vineyard...a tower*: cf. Is 5:1–2. The *vineyard* is defined in Is 5:7 as "the house of Israel."

**21:34–35** *His servants*: Matthew has two sendings of *servants* as against Mark's three sendings of a single servant (Mk 11:2–5a) followed by a statement about the sending of "many others" (Mk 11:2, 5b). That these servants stand for the prophets sent by God to Israel is clearly implied but not made explicit here, but see Mt 23:37. *His produce*: cf. Mk 12:2 "some of the produce." The *produce* is the good works demanded by God, and his claim to them is total.

**21:38** *Acquire his inheritance*: if a Jewish proselyte died

---

**21:23–27** Mk 11:27–33; Lk 20:1–8.
**21:23** Jn 2:18.
**21:26** 14:5.
**21:32** Lk 7:29–30.
**21:33–46** Mk 12:1–12; Lk 20:9–19.
**21:33** Is 5:1–2, 7.

MT

when the tenants saw the son, they said to one another, 'This is the heir. Come, let us kill him and acquire his inheritance.' ³⁹†* They seized him, threw him out of the vineyard, and killed him. ⁴⁰ What will the owner of the vineyard do to those tenants when he comes?" ⁴¹ They answered† him, "He will put those wretched men to a wretched death and lease his vineyard to other tenants who will give him the produce at the proper times." ⁴²†* Jesus said to them, "Did you never read in the scriptures:

'The stone that the builders rejected
    has become the cornerstone;
by the Lord has this been done,
    and it is wonderful in our eyes'?

⁴³† Therefore, I say to you, the kingdom of God will be taken away from you and given to a people that will produce its fruit. ⁴⁴ [† The one who falls on this stone will be dashed to pieces; and it will crush anyone on whom it falls.]" ⁴⁵ When the chief priests and the Pharisees† heard his parables, they knew that he was speaking about them. ⁴⁶ And although they were attempting to arrest him, they feared the crowds, for they regarded him as a prophet.

# 22 The Parable of the Wedding Feast.†
¹* Jesus again in reply spoke to them in parables, saying, ² "The kingdom of heaven may be likened to a king who gave a wedding feast† for his son. ³† He dispatched his servants to summon the invited guests to the feast, but they refused to come. ⁴ A second time he sent other servants, saying, 'Tell those invited: "Behold, I have prepared my banquet, my calves and fattened cattle are killed, and everything is ready; come to the feast."' ⁵ Some ignored the invitation and went away, one to his farm, another to his business. ⁶* The rest laid hold of his servants, mistreated them, and killed them. ⁷† The king was enraged and sent his troops, destroyed those murderers, and burned their city. ⁸ Then he said to his servants, 'The feast is ready, but those who were invited were not worthy to come. ⁹ Go out, therefore, into the main roads and invite to the feast whomever you find.' ¹⁰ The servants went out into the streets and gathered all they found, bad and good alike,† and the hall was filled with guests. ¹¹† But when the king came in to meet the guests he saw a man there not dressed in a wedding garment. ¹² He said to him, 'My friend, how is it that you came in here without a wedding garment?' But he was reduced to silence. ¹³†* Then the king said to his attendants, 'Bind his hands and feet, and cast him into the darkness outside, where there will be

---

†

without heir, the tenants of his land would have final claim on it.

**21:39** *Threw him out...and killed him:* the change in the Marcan order where the son is killed and his corpse then thrown out (Mk 12:8) was probably made because of the tradition that Jesus died outside the city of Jerusalem; see Jn 19:17; Heb 13:12.

**21:41** *They answered:* in Mk 12:9 the question is answered by Jesus himself; here the leaders answer and so condemn themselves; cf. Mt 21:31. Matthew adds that the new *tenants* to whom the vineyard will be transferred *will give the owner the produce at the proper times.*

**21:42** Cf. Ps 118:22–23. The psalm was used in the early church as a prophecy of Jesus' resurrection; see Acts 4:11; 1 Pt 2:7. If, as some think, the original parable ended at Mt 21:39 it was thought necessary to complete it by a reference to Jesus' vindication by God.

**21:43** Peculiar to Matthew. *Kingdom of God:* see note on Mt 19:23–24. Its presence here instead of Matthew's usual "kingdom of heaven" may indicate that the saying came from Matthew's own traditional material. *A people that will produce its fruit:* believing Israelites and Gentiles, the church of Jesus.

**21:44** The majority of textual witnesses omit this verse. It is probably an early addition to Matthew from Lk 20:18 with which it is practically identical.

**21:45** *The Pharisees:* Matthew inserts into the group of Jewish leaders (Mt 21:23) those who represented the Judaism of his own time.

**22:1–14** This parable is from Q; see Lk 14:15–24. It has been given many allegorical traits by Matthew, e.g., the burning of the *city* of the guests who refused the invitation (Mt 22:7), which corresponds to the destruction of Jerusalem by the Romans in A.D. 70. It has similarities with the preceding parable of the tenants:

the sending of two groups of *servants* (Mt 22:3, 4), the murder of the *servants* (Mt 22:6), the punishment of the *murderers* (Mt 22:7), and the entrance of a new group into a privileged situation of which the others had proved themselves unworthy (Mt 22:8–10). The parable ends with a section that is peculiar to Matthew (Mt 22:11–14), which some take as a distinct parable. Matthew presents the *kingdom* in its double aspect, already present and something that can be entered here and now (Mt 22:1–10), and something that will be possessed only by those present members who can stand the scrutiny of the final judgment (Mt 22:11–14). The parable is not only a statement of God's judgment on Israel but a warning to Matthew's church.

**22:2** *Wedding feast:* the Old Testament's portrayal of final salvation under the image of a banquet (Is 25:6) is taken up also in Mt 8:11; cf. Lk 13:15.

**22:3–4** *Servants...other servants:* probably Christian missionaries in both instances; cf. Mt 23:34.

**22:7** See note on Mt 22:1–14.

**22:10** *Bad and good alike:* cf. Mt 13:47.

**22:11** *A wedding garment:* the repentance, change of heart and mind, that is the condition for entrance into the kingdom (Mt 3:2; 4:17) must be continued in a life of good deeds (Mt 7:21–23).

**22:13** *Wailing and grinding of teeth:* the Christian who lacks the wedding garment of good deeds will suffer the same fate as those Jews who have rejected Jesus; see note on Mt 8:11–12.

---

*

**21:39** Heb 13:12.
**21:42** Ps 118:22–23; Is 28:16; Acts 4:11; 1 Pt 2:7.
**22:1–14** Lk 14:15–24.
**22:6** 21:35.
**22:13** 8:12; 25:30.

MT

wailing and grinding of teeth.' [14] Many are invited, but few are chosen."

**Paying Taxes to the Emperor.**† [15]* Then the Pharisees† went off and plotted how they might entrap him in speech. [16] They sent their disciples to him, with the Herodians,† saying, "Teacher, we know that you are a truthful man and that you teach the way of God in accordance with the truth. And you are not concerned with anyone's opinion, for you do not regard a person's status. [17]† Tell us, then, what is your opinion: Is it lawful to pay the census tax to Caesar or not?" [18] Knowing their malice, Jesus said, "Why are you testing me, you hypocrites? [19]† Show me the coin that pays the census tax." Then they handed him the Roman coin. [20] He said to them, "Whose image is this and whose inscription?" [21]* They replied, "Caesar's."† At that he said to them, "Then repay to Caesar what belongs to Caesar and to God what belongs to God." [22] When they heard this they were amazed, and leaving him they went away.

**The Question About the Resurrection.**†
[23]* On that day Sadducees approached him,

saying that there is no resurrection.† They put this question to him, [24]* saying, "Teacher, Moses said, 'If a man dies† without children, his brother shall marry his wife and raise up descendants for his brother.' [25] Now there were seven brothers among us. The first married and died and, having no descendants, left his wife to his brother. [26] The same happened with the second and the third, through all seven. [27] Finally the woman died. [28] Now at the resurrection, of the seven, whose wife will she be? For they all had been married to her." [29]† Jesus said to them in reply, "You are misled because you do not know the scriptures or the power of God. [30] At the resurrection they neither marry nor are given in marriage but are like the angels in heaven. [31] And concerning the resurrection of the dead, have you not read what was said to you† by God, [32]* 'I am the God of Abraham, the God of Isaac, and the God of Jacob'? He is not the God of the dead but of the living." [33] When the crowds heard this, they were astonished at his teaching.

**The Greatest Commandment.**† [34]* When the Pharisees heard that he had silenced the

---

† **22:15–22** The series of controversies between Jesus and the representatives of Judaism (see note on Mt 21:23–27) is resumed. As in the first (Mt 21:23–27), here and in the following disputes Matthew follows his Marcan source with few modifications.
**22:15** *The Pharisees*: while Matthew retains the Marcan union of Pharisees and Herodians in this account, he clearly emphasizes the Pharisees' part. They alone are mentioned here, and the Herodians are joined with them only in a prepositional phrase of Mt 22:16. *Entrap him in speech*: the question that they will pose is intended to force Jesus to take either a position contrary to that held by the majority of the people or one that will bring him into conflict with the Roman authorities.
**22:16** *Herodians*: see note on Mk 3:6. They would favor payment of the tax; the Pharisees did not.
**22:17** *Is it lawful*: the law to which they refer is the law of God.
**22:19** *They handed him the Roman coin*: their readiness in producing the money implies their use of it and their acceptance of the financial advantages of the Roman administration in Palestine.
**22:21** *Caesar's*: the emperor Tiberius (A.D. 14–37). *Repay to Caesar what belongs to Caesar*: those who willingly use the coin that is Caesar's should *repay* him in kind. The answer avoids taking sides in the question of the lawfulness of the tax. *To God what belongs to God*: Jesus raises the debate to a new level. Those who have hypocritically asked about tax in respect to its relation to the law of *God* should be concerned rather with repaying God with the good deeds that are his due; cf. Mt 21:41, 43.
**22:23–33** Here Jesus' opponents are the *Sadducees*, members of the powerful priestly party of his time; see note on Mt 3:7. Denying the resurrection of the dead, a teaching of relatively late origin in Judaism (cf. Dn 12:2), they appeal to a law of the Pentateuch (Dt 25:5–10) and present a case based on it that would make resurrection from the dead ridiculous (Mt 22:24–28). Jesus chides them for knowing neither *the scriptures* nor *the power of God* (Mt 22:29). His argument in respect to God's power contradicts the notion, held even by many proponents as well as by

opponents of the teaching, that the life of those raised from the dead would be essentially a continuation of the type of life they had had before death (Mt 22:30). His argument based on the scriptures (Mt 22:31–32) is of a sort that was accepted as valid among Jews of the time.
**22:23** *Saying that there is no resurrection*: in the Marcan parallel (Mk 22:12, 18) the Sadducees are correctly defined as those "who say there is no resurrection"; see also Lk 20:27. Matthew's rewording of Mark can mean that these particular Sadducees deny the resurrection, which would imply that he was not aware that the denial was characteristic of the party. For some scholars this is an indication of his being a Gentile Christian; see note on Mt 21:4–5.
**22:24** *'If a man dies…his brother'*: this is known as the "law of the levirate," from the Latin *levir*, "brother-in-law." Its purpose was to continue the family line of the deceased brother (Dt 25:6).
**22:29** The sexual relationships of this world will be transcended; the risen body will be the work of the creative *power of God*.
**22:31–32** Cf. Ex 3:6. In the Pentateuch, which the Sadducees accepted as normative for Jewish belief and practice, God speaks even now (*to you*) of himself as the God of the patriarchs who died centuries ago. He identifies himself in relation to them, and because of their relation to him, the living God, they too are alive. This might appear no argument for the resurrection, but simply for life after death as conceived in Wis 3:1–3. But the general thought of early first-century Judaism was not influenced by that conception; for it human immortality was connected with the existence of the body.
**22:34–40** The Marcan parallel (Mk 12:28–34) is an exchange between Jesus and a scribe who is impressed by the way in

---

*
22:15–22 Mk 12:13–17; Lk          22:24 Gn 38:8; Dt 25:5–6.
    20:20–26.                    22:32 Ex 3:6.
22:21 Rom 13:7.                    22:34–40 Mk 12:28–34; Lk
22:23–33 Mk 12:18–27; Lk              10:25–28.
    20:27–40.

M
T

Sadducees, they gathered together, ³⁵ and one of them [a scholar of the law]† tested him by asking, ³⁶ "Teacher,† which commandment in the law is the greatest?" ³⁷ * He said to him,† "You shall love the Lord, your God, with all your heart, with all your soul, and with all your mind. ³⁸ This is the greatest and the first commandment. ³⁹ * The second is like it:† You shall love your neighbor as yourself. ⁴⁰ † * The whole law and the prophets depend on these two commandments."

**The Question About David's Son.**† ⁴¹ * While the Pharisees were gathered together, Jesus questioned them,† ⁴² † saying, "What is your opinion about the Messiah? Whose son is he?" They replied, "David's." ⁴³ He said to them,

"How, then, does David, inspired by the Spirit, call him 'lord,' saying:

⁴⁴ *     'The Lord said to my lord,
           "Sit at my right hand
           until I place your enemies under your
                feet"'?

⁴⁵ † If David calls him 'lord,' how can he be his son?" ⁴⁶ * No one was able to answer him a word, nor from that day on did anyone dare to ask him any more questions.

# 23 †Denunciation of the Scribes and Pharisees. ¹ * Then Jesus spoke to the crowds and to his disciples, ² † saying, "The scribes and the Pharisees have taken their seat

---

†
which Jesus has conducted himself in the previous controversy (Mk 12:28), who compliments him for the answer he gives him (Mk 12:32), and who is said by Jesus to be "not far from the kingdom of God" (Mk 12:34). Matthew has sharpened that scene. The questioner, as the representative of other Pharisees, tests Jesus by his question (Mt 22:34–35), and both his reaction to Jesus' reply and Jesus' commendation of him are lacking.

**22:35** *[A scholar of the law]*: meaning "scribe." Although this reading is supported by the vast majority of textual witnesses, it is the only time that the Greek word so translated occurs in Matthew. It is relatively frequent in Luke, and there is reason to think that it may have been added here by a copyist since it occurs in the Lucan parallel (Lk 10:25–28). *Tested*: see note on Mt 19:3.

**22:36** For the devout Jew all the commandments were to be kept with equal care, but there is evidence of preoccupation in Jewish sources with the question put to Jesus.

**22:37–38** Cf. Dt 6:5. Matthew omits the first part of Mark's fuller quotation (Mk 12:29; Dt 6:4–5), probably because he considered its monotheistic emphasis needless for his church. The love of God must engage the total person (*heart, soul, mind*).

**22:39** Jesus goes beyond the extent of the question put to him and joins *to the greatest and the first commandment* a *second*, that of *love of neighbor*, Lv 19:18; see note on Mt 19:18–19. This combination of the two commandments may already have been made in Judaism.

**22:40** The double commandment is the source from which *the whole law and the prophets* are derived.

**22:41–46** Having answered the questions of his opponents in the preceding three controversies, Jesus now puts a question to them about the sonship of the Messiah. Their easy response (Mt 22:43a) is countered by his quoting a verse of Ps 110 that raises a problem for their response (43b–45). They are unable to solve it and *from that day on* their questioning of him is ended.

**22:41** *The Pharisees…questioned them*: Mark is not specific about who are questioned (Mk 12:35).

**22:42–44** *David's*: this view of the Pharisees was based on such Old Testament texts as Is 11:1–9; Jer 23:5; and Ez 34:23; see also the extrabiblical Psalms of Solomon 17:21. *How, then… saying*: Jesus cites Ps 110:1 accepting the Davidic authorship of the psalm, a common view of his time. The psalm was probably composed for the enthronement of a Davidic king of Judah. Matthew assumes that the Pharisees interpret it as referring to the Messiah, although there is no clear evidence that it was so interpreted in the Judaism of Jesus' time. It was widely used in the early church as referring to the exaltation of the risen Jesus. *My lord*: understood as the Messiah.

**22:45** Since Matthew presents Jesus both as Messiah (Mt 16:16) and as Son of David (Mt 1:1; see also note on Mt 9:27), the question is not meant to imply Jesus' denial of Davidic sonship. It probably means that although he is the Son of David, he

is someone greater, Son of Man and Son of God, and recognized as greater by David who calls him my *'lord.'*

**23:1–39** The final section of the narrative part of the fifth book of the gospel is a denunciation by Jesus of the scribes and the Pharisees (see note on Mt 3:7). It depends in part on Mark and Q (cf. Mk 12:38–39; Lk 11:37–52; 13:34–35), but in the main it is peculiar to Matthew. (For the reasons against considering this extensive body of sayings-material either as one of the structural discourses of this gospel or as part of the one that follows in Mt 24–25, see note on Mt 19:1–23:39.) While the tradition of a deep opposition between Jesus and the Pharisees is well founded, this speech reflects an opposition that goes beyond that of Jesus' ministry and must be seen as expressing the bitter conflict between Pharisaic Judaism and the church of Matthew at the time when the gospel was composed. The complaint often made that the speech ignores the positive qualities of Pharisaism and of its better representatives is true, but the complaint overlooks the circumstances that gave rise to the invective. Nor is the speech purely anti-Pharisaic. The evangelist discerns in his church many of the same faults that he finds in its opponents and warns his fellow Christians to look to their own conduct and attitudes.

**23:2–3** *Have taken their seat…Moses*: it is uncertain whether this is simply a metaphor for Mosaic teaching authority or refers to an actual *chair* on which the teacher sat. It has been proved that there was a seat so designated in synagogues of a later period than that of this gospel. *Do and observe…they tell you*: since the Matthean Jesus abrogates Mosaic law (Mt 5:31–42), warns his disciples against the teaching of the Pharisees (Mt 14:1–12), and, in this speech, denounces the Pharisees as blind guides in respect to their teaching on oaths (Mt 23:16–22), this commandment *to observe all things whatsoever they* (the scribes and Pharisees) *tell you* cannot be taken as the evangelist's understanding of the proper standard of conduct for his church. The saying may reflect a period when the Matthean community was largely Jewish Christian and was still seeking to avoid a complete break with the synagogue. Matthew has incorporated this traditional material into his speech in accordance with his view of the course of salvation history, in which he portrays the time of Jesus' ministry as marked by the fidelity to the law, although with significant pointers to the new situation that would exist after his death and resurrection (see note on Mt 5:17–20). The crowds and the disciples (Mt 23:1) are exhorted not to *follow* the *example* of the Jewish leaders, whose deeds do not conform to their teaching (Mt 23:3).

| | |
|---|---|
| **22:37** Dt 6:5. | **22:44** Ps 110:1; Acts 2:35; |
| **22:39** Lv 19:18; Jas 2:8. | Heb 1:13. |
| **22:40** Rom 13:8–10; Gal | **22:46** Lk 20:40. |
| 5:14. | **23:1–39** Mk 12:38–39; Lk |
| **22:41–46** Mk 12:35–37; Lk | 11:37–52; 13:34–35. |
| 20:41–44. | |

on the chair of Moses. ³Therefore, do and observe all things whatsoever they tell you, but do not follow their example. For they preach but they do not practice. ⁴* They tie up heavy burdens† [hard to carry] and lay them on people's shoulders, but they will not lift a finger to move them. ⁵†* All their works are performed to be seen. They widen their phylacteries and lengthen their tassels. ⁶†* They love places of honor at banquets, seats of honor in synagogues, ⁷greetings in marketplaces, and the salutation 'Rabbi.' ⁸† As for you, do not be called 'Rabbi.' You have but one teacher, and you are all brothers. ⁹Call no one on earth your father; you have but one Father in heaven. ¹⁰Do not be called 'Master'; you have but one master, the Messiah. ¹¹* The greatest among you must be your servant. ¹²* Whoever exalts himself will be humbled; but whoever humbles himself will be exalted.

¹³†* "Woe to you, scribes and Pharisees, you hypocrites. You lock the kingdom of heaven† before human beings. You do not enter yourselves, nor do you allow entrance to those trying to enter. [¹⁴]†

¹⁵† "Woe to you, scribes and Pharisees, you hypocrites. You traverse sea and land to make one convert, and when that happens you make him a child of Gehenna twice as much as yourselves.

¹⁶†* "Woe to you, blind guides, who say, 'If one swears by the temple, it means nothing, but if one swears by the gold of the temple, one is obligated.' ¹⁷Blind fools, which is greater, the gold, or the temple that made the gold sacred? ¹⁸And you say, 'If one swears by the altar, it means nothing, but if one swears by the gift on the altar, one is obligated.' ¹⁹You blind ones, which is greater, the gift, or the altar that makes the gift sacred? ²⁰* One who swears by the altar swears by it and all that is upon it; ²¹one who swears by the temple swears by it and by him who dwells in it; ²²one who swears by heaven swears by the throne of God and by him who is seated on it.

²³* "Woe to you, scribes and Pharisees, you hypocrites. You pay tithes† of mint and dill and cummin, and have neglected the weightier things of the law: judgment and mercy and fidelity. [But] these you should

---

† 23:4 *Tie up heavy burdens*: see note on Mt 11:28.
**23:5** To the charge of preaching but not practicing (Mt 23:3), Jesus adds that of acting in order to earn praise. The disciples have already been warned against this same fault (see note on Mt 6:1–18). *Phylacteries*: the Mosaic law required that during prayer small boxes containing parchments on which verses of scripture were written be worn on the left forearm and the forehead (see Ex 13:9, 16; Dt 6:8; 11:18). *Tassels*: see note on Mt 9:20. The widening of *phylacteries* and the lengthening of *tassels* were for the purpose of making these evidences of piety more noticeable.
**23:6–7** Cf. Mk 12:38–39. *'Rabbi'*: literally, "my great one," a title of respect for teachers and leaders.
**23:8–12** These verses, warning against the use of various titles, are addressed to the disciples alone. While only the title *'Rabbi'* has been said to be used in addressing the scribes and Pharisees (Mt 23:7), the implication is that *Father* and *'Master'* also were. The prohibition of these titles to the disciples suggests that their use was present in Matthew's church. The Matthean Jesus forbids not only the titles but the spirit of superiority and pride that is shown by their acceptance. *Whoever exalts…will be exalted*: cf. Lk 14:11.
**23:13–36** This series of seven "woes," directed against the *scribes and Pharisees* and addressed to them, is the heart of the speech. The phrase *woe to* occurs often in the prophetic and apocalyptic literature, expressing horror of a sin and punishment for those who commit it. See note on Mt 6:2. The hypocrisy of the *scribes and Pharisees* consists in the difference between their speech and action (Mt 23:3) and in demonstrations of piety that have no other purpose than to enhance their reputation as religious persons (Mt 23:5).
**23:13** *You lock the kingdom of heaven*: cf. Mt 16:19 where Jesus tells Peter that he will give him the keys to *the kingdom of heaven*. The purpose of the authority expressed by that metaphor is to give entrance into the kingdom (the kingdom is closed only to those who reject the authority); here the charge is made that the authority of the *scribes and Pharisees* is exercised in such a way as to be an obstacle to entrance. Cf. Lk 11:52 where the accusation against the "scholars of the law" (Matthew's *scribes*) is

that they "have taken away the key of knowledge."
**23:14** Some manuscripts add a verse here or after Mt 23:12, "Woe to you, scribes and Pharisees, you hypocrites. You devour the houses of widows and, as a pretext, recite lengthy prayers. Because of this, you will receive a very severe condemnation." Cf. Mk 12:40; Lk 20:47. This "woe" is almost identical with Mk 12:40 and seems to be an interpolation derived from that text.
**23:15** In the first century A.D. until the First Jewish Revolt against Rome (A.D. 66–70), many Pharisees conducted a vigorous missionary campaign among Gentiles. *Convert*: literally, "proselyte," a Gentile who accepted Judaism fully by submitting to circumcision and all other requirements of Mosaic law. *Child of Gehenna*: worthy of everlasting punishment; for *Gehenna*, see note on Mt 5:22. *Twice as much as yourselves*: possibly this refers simply to the zeal of the *convert*, surpassing that of the one who converted him.
**23:16–22** An attack on the casuistry that declared some oaths binding (*one is obligated*) and others not (*it means nothing*) and held the binding oath to be the one made by something of lesser value (*the gold; the gift on the altar*). Such teaching, which inverts the order of values, reveals the teachers to be *blind guides*; cf. Mt 15:14. Since the Matthean Jesus forbids all oaths to his disciples (Mt 5:33–37), this woe does not set up a standard for Christian moral conduct, but ridicules the Pharisees on their own terms.
**23:23** The Mosaic law ordered tithing of the produce of the land (Lv 27:30; Dt 14:22–23), and the scribal tradition is said here to have extended this law to even the smallest herbs. The practice is criticized not in itself but because it shows the Pharisees' preoccupation with matters of less importance while they neglect *the weightier things of the law*.

---

*
**23:4** Lk 11:46.
**23:5** 6:1–6; Ex 13:9, 16; Nm 15:38–39; Dt 6:8; 11:18.
**23:6–7** Mk 12:38–39; Lk 11:43; 20:46.
**23:11** 20:26.
**23:12** Lk 14:11; 18:14.
**23:13** Lk 11:52.
**23:16** 15:14.
**23:20–22** 5:34–35.
**23:23** Lv 27:30; Dt 14:22; Lk 11:42.

"Woe to you, scribes and Pharisees, you hypocrites. You are like whitewashed tombs, which appear beautiful on the outside, but inside are full of dead men's bones and every kind of filth" (Mt 23:27). Above, Hellenistic tombs in the Kidron Valley east of Jerusalem.

have done, without neglecting the others. <sup>24</sup>†* Blind guides, who strain out the gnat and swallow the camel!

<sup>25</sup>†* "Woe to you, scribes and Pharisees, you hypocrites. You cleanse the outside of cup and dish, but inside they are full of plunder and self-indulgence. <sup>26</sup>Blind Pharisee, cleanse first the inside of the cup, so that the outside also may be clean.

<sup>27</sup>† "Woe to you, scribes and Pharisees, you hypocrites. You are like whitewashed tombs, which appear beautiful on the outside, but inside are full of dead men's bones and every kind of filth. <sup>28</sup>* Even so, on the outside you appear righteous, but inside you are filled with hypocrisy and evildoing.

<sup>29</sup>† "Woe to you, scribes and Pharisees,† you hypocrites. You build the tombs of the prophets and adorn the memorials of the righteous, <sup>30</sup>* and you say, 'If we had lived in the days of our ancestors, we would not have joined them in shedding the prophets' blood.' <sup>31</sup>* Thus you bear witness against yourselves that you are the children of those who murdered the prophets; <sup>32</sup>now fill up what your ancestors measured out! <sup>33</sup>* You serpents, you brood of vipers, how can you flee from the judgment of Gehenna? <sup>34</sup>†* Therefore, behold, I send to

---

**23:24** Cf. Lv 11:41–45 that forbids the eating of any "swarming creature." The Pharisees' scrupulosity about minor matters and neglect of greater ones (Mt 23:23) is further brought out by this contrast between straining liquids that might contain a tiny "swarming creature" and yet swallowing *the camel*. The latter was one of the unclean animals forbidden by the law (Lv 11:4), but it is hardly possible that the scribes and Pharisees are being denounced as guilty of so gross a violation of the food laws. To *swallow the camel* is only a hyperbolic way of speaking of their neglect of what is important.

**23:25–26** The ritual washing of utensils for dining (cf. Mk 7:4) is turned into a metaphor illustrating a concern for appearances while inner purity is ignored. The *scribes and Pharisees* are compared to cups carefully washed on the outside but filthy within. *Self-indulgence*: the Greek word here translated means lack of self-control, whether in drinking or in sexual conduct.

**23:27–28** The sixth *woe*, like the preceding one, deals with concern for externals and neglect of what is *inside*. Since contact with dead bodies, even when one was unaware of it, caused ritual impurity (Nm 19:11–22), tombs were whitewashed so that

no one would contract such impurity inadvertently.

**23:29–36** The final *woe* is the most serious indictment of all. It portrays the *scribes and Pharisees* as standing in the same line as their *ancestors* who murdered *the prophets* and *the righteous*.

**23:29–32** In spite of honoring the slain dead by building their *tombs* and adorning their *memorials*, and claiming that they would not have joined in their ancestors' crimes if they *had lived in their days*, the *scribes and Pharisees* are true children of their ancestors and are defiantly ordered by Jesus to *fill up* what those *ancestors measured out*. This order reflects the Jewish notion that there was an allotted measure of suffering that had to be completed before God's final judgment would take place.

**23:34–36** There are important differences between the Matthean and the Lucan form of this Q material; cf. Lk 11:49–51.

---

**23:24** Lv 11:41–45.
**23:25–26** Mk 7:4; Lk 11:39.
**23:28** Lk 16:15; 18:9.
**23:30** Lk 11:47.
**23:31** Acts 7:52.
**23:33** 3:7; 12:34.
**23:34–36** 5:12; Gn 4:8; 2 Chr 24:20–22; Zec 1:1; Lk 11:49–51; Rev 18:24.

you prophets and wise men and scribes; some of them you will kill and crucify, some of them you will scourge in your synagogues and pursue from town to town, <sup>35</sup> so that there may come upon you all the righteous blood shed upon earth, from the righteous blood of Abel to the blood of Zechariah, the son of Barachiah, whom you murdered between the sanctuary and the altar. <sup>36</sup> Amen, I say to you, all these things will come upon this generation.

**The Lament over Jerusalem.**† <sup>37</sup>* "Jerusalem, Jerusalem, you who kill the prophets and stone those sent to you, how many times I yearned to gather your children together, as a hen gathers her young under her wings, but you were unwilling!* <sup>38</sup>* Behold, your house will be abandoned, desolate. <sup>39</sup>* I tell you, you will not see me again until you say, 'Blessed is he who comes in the name of the Lord.'"

**24** **The Destruction of the Temple Foretold.** <sup>1</sup>* Jesus left the temple area and was going away, when his disciples approached him to point out the temple buildings. <sup>2</sup>† He said to them in reply, "You see all these things, do you not? Amen, I say to you, there will not be left here a stone upon another stone that will not be thrown down."

**The Beginning of Calamities.** <sup>3</sup> As he was sitting on the Mount of Olives,† the disciples approached him privately and said, "Tell us, when will this happen, and what sign will there be of your coming, and of the end of the age?" <sup>4</sup>† Jesus said to them in reply, "See that no one deceives you. <sup>5</sup> For many will come in my name, saying, 'I am the Messiah,' and they will deceive many. <sup>6</sup>* You will hear of wars† and reports of wars; see that you are not alarmed, for these things must happen, but

---

In Luke the one who sends the emissaries is the "wisdom of God." If, as many scholars think, that is the original wording of Q, Matthew, by making Jesus the sender, has presented him as the personified divine wisdom. In Luke, wisdom's emissaries are the Old Testament "prophets" and the Christian "apostles." Matthew's *prophets and wise men and scribes* are probably Christian disciples alone; cf. Mt 10:41 and see note on Mt 13:52. *You will kill*: see Mt 24:9. *Scourge in your synagogues…town to town*: see Mt 10:17, 23 and the note on Mt 10:17. *All the righteous blood shed upon the earth*: the slaying of the disciples is in continuity with all the shedding of *righteous blood* beginning with that of *Abel*. The persecution of Jesus' disciples by *this generation* involves the persecutors in the guilt of their murderous ancestors. *The blood of Zechariah*: see note on Lk 11:51. By identifying him as *the son of Barachiah* Matthew understands him to be Zechariah the Old Testament minor prophet; see Zec 1:1.

**23:37–39** Cf. Lk 13:34–35. The denunciation of Pharisaic Judaism ends with this lament over *Jerusalem*, which has repeatedly rejected and murdered those whom God has *sent* to her. *How many times*: this may refer to various visits of Jesus to the city, an aspect of his ministry found in John but otherwise not in the synoptics. *As a hen…under her wings*: for imagery similar to this, see Ps 17:8; 91:4. *Your house…desolate*: an allusion to the destruction of the temple in A.D. 70. *You will not see me…in the name of the Lord*: Israel will not see Jesus again until he comes in glory for the final judgment. The acclamation has been interpreted in contrasting ways, as an indication that Israel will at last accept Jesus at that time, and as its troubled recognition of him as its dreaded judge who will pronounce its condemnation; in support of the latter view see Mt 24:30.

**24:1–25:46** The discourse of the fifth book, the last of the five around which the gospel is structured. It is called the "eschatological" discourse since it deals with the coming of the new age (the *eschaton*) in its fullness, with events that will precede it, and with how the disciples are to conduct themselves while awaiting an event that is as certain as its exact time is unknown to all but the Father (Mt 24:36). The discourse may be divided into two parts, Mt 24:1–44 and Mt 24:45–25:46. In the first, Matthew follows his Marcan source (Mk 13:1–37) closely. The second is drawn from Q and from the evangelist's own traditional material. Both parts show Matthew's editing of his sources by deletions, additions, and modifications. The vigilant waiting that is emphasized in the second part does not mean a cessation of ordinary activity and concentration only on what is to come, but a faithful accomplishment of duties at hand, with awareness

that the end, for which the disciples must always be ready, will entail the great judgment by which the everlasting destiny of all will be determined.

**24:2** As in Mark, Jesus predicts the destruction of the temple. By omitting the Marcan story of the widow's contribution (Mk 12:41–44) that immediately precedes the prediction in that gospel, Matthew has established a close connection between it and Mt 23:38, "…your house will be abandoned desolate."

**24:3** *The Mount of Olives*: see note on Mt 21:1. *The disciples*: cf. Mk 13:3–4 where only Peter, James, John, and Andrew put the question that is answered by the discourse. In both gospels, however, the question is put *privately*: the ensuing discourse is only for those who are *disciples* of Jesus. *When will this happen… end of the age?*: Matthew distinguishes carefully between the destruction of the temple (*this*) and the *coming* of Jesus that will bring *the end of the age*. In Mark the two events are more closely connected, a fact that may be explained by Mark's believing that the one would immediately succeed the other. *Coming*: this translates the Greek word *parousia*, which is used in the gospels only here and in Mt 24:27, 37, 39. It designated the official visit of a ruler to a city or the manifestation of a saving deity, and it was used by Christians to refer to the final coming of Jesus in glory, a term first found in the New Testament with that meaning in 1 Thes 2:19. *The end of the age*: see note on Mt 13:39.

**24:4–14** This section of the discourse deals with calamities in the world (Mt 24:6–7) and in the church (Mt 24:9–12). The former *must happen* before *the end* comes (Mt 24:6), but they are only the *beginning of the labor pains* (Mt 24:8). (It may be noted that the Greek word translated *the end* in Mt 24:6 and in Mt 24:13–14 is not the same as the phrase "the end of the age" in Mt 24:3, although the meaning is the same.) The latter are sufferings of the church, both from within and without, that will last until *the gospel is preached (this) and the coming of Jesus*…*to all nations. Then the end will come* and those who have endured the sufferings with fidelity *will be saved* (Mt 24:13–14).

**24:6–7** The disturbances mentioned here are a commonplace of apocalyptic language, as is the assurance that they *must happen* (see Dn 2:28 LXX), for that is the plan of God. *Kingdom against kingdom*: see Is 19:2.

---

**23:37–39** Lk 13:34–35;   **23:39** Ps 118:26.
  19:41–44.   **24:1–44** Mk 13:1–37; Lk
**23:37** 21:35.     21:5–36.
**23:38** Jer 12:7.   **24:6** Dn 2:28 LXX.

it will not yet be the end. 7* Nation will rise against nation, and kingdom against kingdom; there will be famines and earthquakes from place to place. 8† All these are the beginning of the labor pains. 9†* Then they will hand you over to persecution, and they will kill you. You will be hated by all nations because of my name. 10 And then many will be led into sin; they will betray and hate one another. 11 Many false prophets will arise and deceive many; 12 and because of the increase of evildoing, the love of many will grow cold. 13* But the one who perseveres to the end will be saved. 14* And this gospel of the kingdom will be preached throughout the world as a witness to all nations,† and then the end will come.

**The Great Tribulation.**† 15* "When you see the desolating abomination† spoken of through Daniel the prophet standing in the holy place (let the reader understand), 16 then those in Judea must flee† to the mountains, 17†* a

person on the housetop must not go down to get things out of his house, 18 a person in the field must not return to get his cloak. 19 Woe to pregnant women and nursing mothers in those days. 20† Pray that your flight not be in winter or on the sabbath, 21†* for at that time there will be great tribulation, such as has not been since the beginning of the world until now, nor ever will be. 22 And if those days had not been shortened, no one would be saved; but for the sake of the elect they will be shortened. 23* If anyone says to you then, 'Look, here is the Messiah!' or, 'There he is!' do not believe it. 24 False messiahs and false prophets will arise, and they will perform signs and wonders so great as to deceive, if that were possible, even the elect. 25 Behold, I have told it to you beforehand. 26 So if they say to you, 'He is in the desert,' do not go out there; if they say, 'He is in the inner rooms,' do not believe it.† 27* For just as lightning comes from the east and is seen as far as the west, so will the

---

† **24:8** *The labor pains*: the tribulations leading up to the end of the age are compared to the pains of a woman about to give birth. There is much attestation for rabbinic use of the phrase "the woes (or birth pains) of the Messiah" after the New Testament period, but in at least one instance it is attributed to a rabbi who lived in the late first century A.D. In this Jewish usage it meant the distress of the time preceding the coming of the Messiah; here, the *labor pains* precede the coming of the Son of Man in glory.

**24:9–12** Matthew has used Mk 13:9–12 in his missionary discourse (Mt 10:17–21) and omits it here. Besides the sufferings, including death, and the hatred of *all nations* that the disciples will have to endure, there will be worse affliction within the church itself. This is described in Mt 24:10–12, which are peculiar to Matthew. *Will be led into sin*: literally, "will be scandalized," probably meaning that they will become apostates; see Mt 13:21 where "fall away" translates the same Greek word as here. *Betray*: in the Greek this is the same word as the *hand over* of Mt 24:9. The handing over to persecution and hatred from outside will have their counterpart within the church. *False prophets*: these are Christians; see note on Mt 7:15–20. *Evildoing*: see Mt 7:23. Because of the apocalyptic nature of much of this discourse, the literal meaning of this description of the church should not be pressed too hard. However, there is reason to think that Matthew's addition of these verses reflects in some measure the condition of his community.

**24:14** Except for the last part (*and then the end will come*), this verse substantially repeats Mk 13:10. The Matthean addition raises a problem since what follows in Mt 24:15–23 refers to the horrors of the First Jewish Revolt including the destruction of the temple, and Matthew, writing after that time, knew that the parousia of Jesus was still in the future. A solution may be that the evangelist saw the events of those verses as foreshadowing the cosmic disturbances that he associates with the parousia (Mt 24:29) so that the period in which the former took place could be understood as belonging to *the end*.

**24:15–28** Cf. Mk 13:14–23; Lk 17:23–24, 37. A further stage in the tribulations that will precede the coming of the Son of Man, and an answer to the question of Mt 24:3a, "when will this (the destruction of the temple) happen?"

**24:15** *The desolating abomination*: in 167 B.C. the Syrian king Antiochus IV Epiphanes desecrated the temple by setting up in it a statue of Zeus Olympios (see 1 Mc 1:54). That event is referred to in Dn 12:11 LXX as the "desolating abomination"

(NAB "horrible abomination") and the same Greek term is used here; cf. also Dn 9:27; 11:31. Although the desecration had taken place before Daniel was written, it is presented there as a future event, and Matthew sees that "prophecy" fulfilled in the desecration of the temple by the Romans. *In the holy place*: the temple; more precise than Mark's *where he should not* (Mk 13:14). *Let the reader understand*: this parenthetical remark, taken from Mk 13:14 invites *the reader* to realize the meaning of Daniel's "prophecy."

**24:16** The tradition that the Christians of Jerusalem fled from that city to Pella, a city of Transjordan, at the time of the First Jewish Revolt is found in Eusebius (*Ecclesiastical History* 3.5.3), who attributes the flight to "a certain oracle given by revelation before the war." The tradition is not improbable but the Matthean command, derived from its Marcan source, is vague in respect to the place of flight (*to the mountains*), although some scholars see it as applicable to the flight to Pella.

**24:17–19** Haste is essential, and the journey will be particularly difficult for women who are burdened with unborn or infant children.

**24:20** *On the sabbath*: this addition to *in winter* (cf. Mk 13:18) has been understood as an indication that Matthew was addressed to a church still observing the Mosaic law of sabbath rest and the scribal limitations upon the length of journeys that might lawfully be made on that day. That interpretation conflicts with Matthew's view on sabbath observance (cf. Mt 12:1–14). The meaning of the addition may be that those undertaking on the sabbath a journey such as the one here ordered would be offending the sensibilities of law-observant Jews and would incur their hostility.

**24:21** For the unparalleled distress of that time, see Dn 12:1.

**24:26–28** Claims that the Messiah is to be found in some distant or secret place must be ignored. *The coming of the Son of Man* will be as clear as *lightning* is to all and as *the corpse* of an animal is to *vultures*; cf. Lk 17:24, 37. Here there is clear identification of *the Son of Man* and the Messiah; cf. Mt 24:23.

---

*

| 24:7 Is 19:2. | 12:11; Mk 13:14. |
| 24:9 10:17. | 24:17 Lk 17:31. |
| 24:13 10:22. | 24:21 Dn 12:1. |
| 24:14 28:19; Rom 10:18. | 24:23 Lk 17:23. |
| 24:15 Dn 9:27; 11:31; | 24:27–28 Lk 17:24, 37. |

MT

coming of the Son of Man be. 28 Wherever the corpse is, there the vultures will gather.

**The Coming of the Son of Man.** 29 †* "Immediately after the tribulation of those days,

> the sun will be darkened,
>> and the moon will not give its light,
> and the stars will fall from the sky,
>> and the powers of the heavens will be shaken.

30* And then the sign of the Son of Man† will appear in heaven, and all the tribes of the earth will mourn, and they will see the Son of Man coming upon the clouds of heaven with power and great glory. 31* And he will send out his angels† with a trumpet blast, and they will gather his elect from the four winds, from one end of the heavens to the other.

**The Lesson of the Fig Tree.**† 32 "Learn a lesson from the fig tree. When its branch becomes tender and sprouts leaves, you know that summer is near. 33 In the same way, when you see all these things, know that he is near, at the gates. 34 Amen, I say to you, this generation† will not pass away until all these things have taken place. 35* Heaven and earth will pass away, but my words will not pass away.

**The Unknown Day and Hour.**† 36* "But of that day and hour no one knows, neither the angels of heaven, nor the Son,† but the Father alone. 37 †* For as it was in the days of Noah, so it will be at the coming of the Son of Man. 38 In [those] days before the flood, they were eating and drinking, marrying and giving in marriage, up to the day that Noah entered the ark. 39 They did not know until the flood came and carried them all away. So will it be [also] at the coming of the Son of Man. 40 †* Two men will be out in the field; one will be taken, and one will be left. 41 Two women will be grinding at the mill; one will be taken, and one will be left. 42 †* Therefore, stay awake! For you do not know on which day your Lord will come. 43* Be sure of this: if the master of the house had known the hour of night when the thief was coming, he would have stayed awake and not let his house be broken into. 44 So too, you also must be prepared, for at an hour you do not expect, the Son of Man will come.

**The Faithful or the Unfaithful Servant.**† 45* "Who, then, is the faithful and prudent servant, whom the master has put in charge of his household to distribute to them their food at the proper time?† 46 Blessed is that servant whom his master on his arrival finds doing so. 47 Amen, I say to you, he will put

---

† **24:29** The answer to the question of Mt 24:3b, "What sign will there be of your coming?" *Immediately after…those days*: the shortening of time between the preceding *tribulation* and the parousia has been explained as Matthew's use of a supposed device of Old Testament prophecy whereby certainty that a predicted event will occur is expressed by depicting it as imminent. While it is questionable that that is an acceptable understanding of the Old Testament predictions, it may be applicable here, for Matthew knew that the parousia had not come *immediately after* the fall of Jerusalem, and it is unlikely that he is attributing a mistaken calculation of time to Jesus. *The sun…be shaken*: cf. Is 13:10, 13.

**24:30** *The sign of the Son of Man*: perhaps this means *the sign* that is the glorious appearance *of the Son of Man*; cf. Mt 12:39–40 where "the sign of Jonah" is Jonah's being in the "belly of the whale." *Tribes of the earth will mourn*: peculiar to Matthew; cf. Zec 12:12–14. *Coming upon the clouds…glory*: cf. Dn 7:13, although there the "one like a son of man" comes to God to receive kingship; here the *Son of Man* comes from heaven for judgment.

**24:31** *Send out his angels*: cf. Mt 13:41 where they are sent out to collect the wicked for punishment. *Trumpet blast*: cf. Is 27:13; 1 Thes 4:16.

**24:32–35** Cf. Mk 13:28–31.

**24:34** The difficulty raised by this verse cannot be satisfactorily removed by the supposition that *this generation* means the Jewish people throughout the course of their history, much less the entire human race. Perhaps for Matthew it means the *generation* to which he and his community belonged.

**24:36–44** The statement of Mt 24:34 is now counterbalanced by one that declares that the exact time of the parousia is known only to *the Father* (Mt 24:36), and the disciples are warned to be always ready for it. This section is drawn from Mark and Q (cf. Lk 17:26–27, 34–35; 12:39–40).

**24:36** Many textual witnesses omit *nor the Son*, which follows Mk 13:32. Since its omission can be explained by reluctance to attribute this ignorance to *the Son*, the reading that includes it is probably original.

**24:37–39** Cf. Lk 17:26–27. *In the days of Noah*: the Old Testament account of the flood lays no emphasis upon what is central for Matthew, i.e., the unexpected coming of the flood upon those who were unprepared for it.

**24:40–41** Cf. Lk 17:34–35. *Taken…left*: the former probably means *taken* into the kingdom; the latter, *left* for destruction. People in the same situation will be dealt with in opposite ways. In this context, the discrimination between them will be based on their readiness for the coming of the Son of Man.

**24:42–44** Cf. Lk 12:39–40. The theme of vigilance and readiness is continued with the bold comparison of the Son of Man to a thief who comes to break into a house.

**24:45–51** The second part of the discourse (see note on Mt 24:1–25:46) begins with this parable of *the faithful* or unfaithful *servant*; cf. Lk 12:41–46. It is addressed to the leaders of Matthew's church; *the servant has* been *put in charge* of his master's *household* (Mt 24:45) even though that household is composed of those who are his *fellow servants* (Mt 24:49).

**24:45** *To distribute…proper time*: readiness for the master's return means a vigilance that is accompanied by faithful performance of the duty assigned.

---

* **24:29** Is 13:10, 13; Ez 32:7; Am 8:9.
**24:30** Dn 7:13; Zec 12:12–14; Rev 1:7.
**24:31** Is 27:13; 1 Cor 15:52; 1 Thes 4:16.
**24:35** Is 40:8.
**24:36** Acts 1:7.
**24:37–39** Gn 6:5–7:23; Lk 17:26–27; 2 Pt 3:6.
**24:40–41** Lk 17:34–35.
**24:42–44** 25:13; Lk 12:39–40.
**24:43** 1 Thes 5:2.
**24:45–51** Lk 12:41–46.

MT

him in charge of all his property. [48]† But if that wicked servant says to himself, 'My master is long delayed,' [49] and begins to beat his fellow servants, and eat and drink with drunkards, [50] the servant's master will come on an unexpected day and at an unknown hour [51]* and will punish him severely† and assign him a place with the hypocrites, where there will be wailing and grinding of teeth.

# 25

**The Parable of the Ten Virgins.†** [1] "Then† the kingdom of heaven will be like ten virgins who took their lamps and went out to meet the bridegroom. [2]† Five of them were foolish and five were wise. [3] The foolish ones, when taking their lamps, brought no oil with them, [4] but the wise brought flasks of oil with their lamps. [5] Since the bridegroom was long delayed, they all became drowsy and fell asleep. [6] At midnight, there was a cry, 'Behold, the bridegroom! Come out to meet him!' [7] Then all those virgins got up and trimmed their lamps. [8] The foolish ones said to the wise, 'Give us some of your oil, for our lamps are going out.' [9] But the wise ones replied, 'No, for there may not be enough for us and you. Go instead to the merchants and buy some for yourselves.' [10] While they went off to buy it, the bridegroom came and those who were ready went into the wedding feast with him. Then the door was locked. [11]†* Afterwards the other virgins came and said, 'Lord, Lord, open the door for us!' [12] But he said in reply, 'Amen, I say to you, I do not know you.' [13]* Therefore, stay awake,† for you know neither the day nor the hour.

**The Parable of the Talents.**† [14]* "It will be as when a man who was going on a journey† called in his servants and entrusted his possessions to them. [15] To one he gave five talents;† to another, two; to a third, one—to each according to his ability. Then he went away. Immediately [16] the one who received five talents went and traded with them, and made another five. [17] Likewise, the one who received two made another two. [18]† But the man who received one went off and dug a hole in the ground and buried his master's money. [19] After a long time the master of those servants came back and settled accounts with them. [20] The one who had received five talents came forward bringing the additional five.† He said, 'Master, you gave me five talents. See, I have made five more.' [21]* His master said to him, 'Well done, my good and faithful servant. Since you were faithful in small matters, I will give you great responsibilities. Come, share your master's joy.' [22] [Then] the one who had received two talents also came forward and said, 'Master, you gave me two talents. See, I have made two more.' [23] His master said to him, 'Well done, my good and faithful servant. Since you were faithful in small matters, I will give you great responsibilities. Come, share your master's joy.' [24] Then the one who had received the one talent came forward and said, 'Master, I knew you were a demanding person, harvesting where you did not plant and gathering where you did not scatter; [25] so out of fear I went off and buried your talent in the ground. Here it is back.' [26] His master said to him in reply, 'You wicked, lazy servant!† So

---

† **24:48** *My master…delayed*: the note of delay is found also in the other parables of this section; cf. Mt 25:5, 19.

**24:51** *Punish him severely*: the Greek verb, found in the New Testament only here and in the Lucan parallel (Lk 12:46), means, literally, "cut in two." *With the hypocrites*: see note on Mt 6:2. Matthew classes the unfaithful Christian leader with the unbelieving leaders of Judaism. *Wailing and grinding of teeth*: see note on Mt 8:11–12.

**25:1–13** Peculiar to Matthew.

**25:1** *Then*: at the time of the parousia. *Kingdom…will be like*: see note on Mt 13:24–30.

**25:2–4** *Foolish…wise*: cf. the contrasted "wise man" and "fool" of Mt 7:24, 26, where the two are distinguished by good deeds and lack of them, and such deeds may be signified by the *oil* of this parable.

**25:11–12** *Lord, Lord*: cf. Mt 7:21. *I do not know you*: cf. Mt 7:23 where the Greek verb is different but synonymous.

**25:13** *Stay awake*: some scholars see this command as an addition to the original parable of Matthew's traditional material, since in Mt 25:5 all the virgins, wise and foolish, fall asleep. But the wise virgins are adequately equipped for their task, and stay awake may mean no more than to be prepared; cf. Mt 24:42, 44.

**25:14–30** Cf. Lk 19:12–27.

**25:14** *It will be as when…journey*: literally, "For just as a man who was going on a journey." Although the comparison is not completed, the sense is clear; the kingdom of heaven is like the situation here described. Faithful use of one's gifts will lead to participation in the fullness of the kingdom, lazy inactivity to exclusion from it.

**25:15** *Talents*: see note on Mt 18:24.

**25:18** *Buried his master's money*: see note on Mt 13:44.

**25:20–23** Although the first two servants have received and doubled large sums, their faithful trading is regarded by the master as fidelity *in small matters* only, compared with *the great responsibilities* now to be given to them. The latter are unspecified. *Share your master's joy*: probably the joy of the banquet of the kingdom; cf. Mt 8:11.

**25:26–28** *Wicked, lazy servant*: this man's inactivity is not negligible but seriously culpable. As punishment, he loses the gift he had received, that is now given to the first servant, whose possessions are already great.

---

* **24:51** 13:42; 25:30.     **25:13** 24:42; Mk 13:33.
**25:11–12** 7:21, 23; Lk     **25:14–30** Lk 19:12–27.
13:25–27.                      **25:21** Lk 16:10.

you knew that I harvest where I did not plant and gather where I did not scatter? [27] Should you not then have put my money in the bank so that I could have got it back with interest on my return? [28] Now then! Take the talent from him and give it to the one with ten. [29]†* For to everyone who has, more will be given and he will grow rich; but from the one who has not, even what he has will be taken away. [30]† And throw this useless servant into the darkness outside, where there will be wailing and grinding of teeth.'

**The Judgment of the Nations.**† [31]* "When the Son of Man comes in his glory, and all the angels with him, he will sit upon his glorious throne, [32]* and all the nations† will be assembled before him. And he will separate them one from another, as a shepherd separates the sheep from the goats. [33] He will place the sheep on his right and the goats on his left. [34] Then the king will say to those on his right, 'Come, you who are blessed by my Father. Inherit the kingdom prepared for you from the foundation of the world. [35]* For I was hungry and you gave me food, I was thirsty and you gave me drink, a stranger and you welcomed me, [36] naked and you clothed me, ill and you cared for me, in prison and you visited me.' [37] Then the righteous† will answer him and say, 'Lord, when did we see you hungry and feed you, or thirsty and give you drink? [38] When did we see you a stranger and welcome you, or naked and clothe you? [39] When did we see you ill or in prison, and visit you?' [40]* And the king will say to them in reply, 'Amen, I say to you, whatever you did for one of these least brothers of mine, you did for me.' [41]†* Then he will say to those on his left, 'Depart from me, you accursed, into the eternal fire prepared for the devil and his angels. [42]* For I was hungry and you gave me no food, I was thirsty and you gave me no drink, [43] a stranger and you gave me no welcome, naked and you gave me no clothing, ill and in prison, and you did not care for me.' [44]† Then they will answer and say, 'Lord, when did we see you hungry or thirsty or a stranger or naked or ill or in prison, and not minister to your needs?' [45] He will answer them, 'Amen, I say to you, what you did not do for one of these least ones, you did not do for me.' [46]* And these will go off to eternal punishment, but the righteous to eternal life."

## VII. THE PASSION AND RESURRECTION

# 26

**The Conspiracy Against Jesus.** [1]† When Jesus finished all these words,† he said to his disciples, [2]* "You know that in two days' time it will be Passover, and the Son of Man

---

† **25:29** See note on Mt 13:12 where there is a similar application of this maxim.

**25:30** See note on Mt 8:11–12.

**25:31–46** The conclusion of the discourse, which is peculiar to Matthew, portrays the final judgment that will accompany the parousia. Although often called a "parable," it is not really such, for the only parabolic elements are the depiction of *the Son of Man* as a *shepherd* and of *the righteous* and the wicked as *sheep* and *goats*, respectively (Mt 25:32–33). The criterion of judgment will be the deeds of mercy that have been done for the *least* of Jesus' *brothers* (Mt 25:40). A difficult and important question is the identification of these *least brothers*. Are they all people who have suffered hunger, thirst, etc. (Mt 25:35, 36) or a particular group of such sufferers? Scholars are divided in their response and arguments can be made for either side. But leaving aside the problem of what the traditional material that Matthew edited may have meant, it seems that a stronger case can be made for the view that in the evangelist's sense the sufferers are Christians, probably Christian missionaries whose sufferings were brought upon them by their preaching of the gospel. The criterion of judgment for *all the nations* is their treatment of those who have borne to the world the message of Jesus, and this means ultimately their acceptance or rejection of Jesus himself; cf. Mt 10:40, "Whoever receives you, receives me." See note on Mt 16:27.

**25:32** *All the nations*: before the end the gospel will have been preached throughout the world (Mt 24:14); thus the Gentiles will be judged on their response to it. But the phrase *all the nations* includes the Jews also, for at the judgment "the Son of Man...will repay everyone according to his conduct" (Mt 16:27).

**25:37–40** *The righteous* will be astonished that in caring for the needs of the sufferers they were ministering to the *Lord* himself. *One of these least brothers of mine*: cf. Mt 10:42.

**25:41** *Fire prepared...his angels*: cf. 1 Enoch 10:13 where it is said of the evil angels and Semyaza, their leader, "In those days they will lead them into the bottom of the fire—and in torment—in the prison (where) they will be locked up forever."

**25:44–45** The *accursed* (Mt 25:41) will be likewise astonished that their neglect of the sufferers was neglect of the *Lord* and will receive from him a similar answer.

**26:1–28:20** The five books with alternating narrative and discourse (Mt 3:1–25:46) that give this gospel its distinctive structure lead up to the climactic events that are the center of Christian belief and the origin of the Christian church, the passion and resurrection of Jesus. In his passion narrative (Mt 26 and 27) Matthew follows his Marcan source closely but with omissions (e.g., Mk 14:51–52) and additions (e.g., Mt 27:3–10, 19). Some of the additions indicate that he utilized traditions that he had received from elsewhere; others are due to his own theological insight (e.g., Mt 26:28, "...for the forgiveness of sins"; Mt 27:52). In his editing Matthew also altered Mark in some minor details. But there is no need to suppose that he knew any passion narrative other than Mark's.

**26:1–2** *When Jesus finished all these words*: see note on Mt 7:28–29. *"You know...crucified"*: Matthew turns Mark's statement of the time (Mk 14:1) into Jesus' final prediction of his passion. *Passover*: see note on Mk 14:1.

---

**25:29** 13:12; Mk 4:25; Lk 8:18; 19:26.
**25:31** 16:27; Dt 33:2 LXX.
**25:32** Ez 34:17.
**25:35–36** Is 58:7; Ez 18:7.
**25:40** 10:40, 42.
**25:41** 7:23; Lk 13:27.
**25:42–43** Jb 22:7; Jas 2:15–16.
**25:46** Dn 12:2.
**26:2–5** Mk 14:1–2; Lk 22:1–2.

M
T

will be handed over to be crucified." [3]† Then the chief priests and the elders of the people assembled in the palace of the high priest, who was called Caiaphas, [4]* and they consulted together to arrest Jesus by treachery and put him to death. [5] But they said, "Not during the festival,† that there may not be a riot among the people."

### The Anointing at Bethany.† [6]* Now when

Jesus was in Bethany in the house of Simon the leper, [7] a woman came up to him with an alabaster jar of costly perfumed oil, and poured it on his head while he was reclining at table. [8] When the disciples saw this, they were indignant and said, "Why this waste? [9] It could have been sold for much, and the money given to the poor." [10] Since Jesus knew this, he said to them, "Why do you make trouble for the woman? She has done a good thing for me. [11]* The poor you will always have with you; but you will not always have me. [12]† In pouring this perfumed oil upon my body, she did it to prepare me for burial. [13] Amen, I say to you, wherever this gospel is proclaimed in the whole world, what she has done will be spoken of, in memory of her."

### The Betrayal by Judas. [14]* Then one of the

Twelve, who was called Judas Iscariot,† went to the chief priests [15]†* and said, "What are you willing to give me if I hand him over to you?" They paid him thirty pieces of silver, [16] and from that time on he looked for an opportunity to hand him over.

### Preparations for the Passover. [17]* On the first

day of the Feast of Unleavened Bread,† the disciples approached Jesus and said, "Where do you want us to prepare for you to eat the Passover?"* [18]† He said, "Go into the city to a certain man and tell him, 'The teacher says, "My appointed time draws near; in your house I shall celebrate the Passover with my disciples."'" [19] The disciples then did as Jesus had ordered, and prepared the Passover.

### The Betrayer. [20] When it was evening, he re-

clined at table with the Twelve. [21] And while they were eating, he said, "Amen, I say to you, one of you will betray me."† [22] Deeply distressed at this, they began to say to him one after another, "Surely it is not I, Lord?" [23] He said in reply, "He who has dipped his hand into the dish with me is the one who will betray me. [24]†* The Son of Man indeed goes, as it is written of him, but woe to that man by whom the Son of Man is betrayed. It would be better for that man if he had never been born." [25]† Then Judas, his betrayer, said in reply, "Surely it is not I, Rabbi?" He answered, "You have said so."

### The Lord's Supper. [26]†* While they were eat-

ing, Jesus took bread, said the blessing, broke

---

**26:3** *Caiaphas* was high priest from A.D. 18 to 36.

**26:5** *Not during the festival*: the plan to delay Jesus' arrest and execution until after *the festival* was not carried out, for according to the synoptics he was arrested on the night of Nisan 14 and put to death the following day. No reason is given why the plan was changed.

**26:6–13** See notes on Mk 14:3–9 and Jn 12:1–8.

**26:12** *To prepare me for burial*: cf. Mk 14:8. In accordance with the interpretation of this act as Jesus' *burial* anointing, Matthew, more consistent than Mark, changes the purpose of the visit of the women to Jesus' tomb; they do not go to anoint him (Mk 16:1) but "to see the tomb" (Mt 28:1).

**26:14** *Iscariot*: see note on Lk 6:16.

**26:15** The motive of avarice is introduced by Judas's question about the price for betrayal, which is absent in the Marcan source (Mk 14:10–11). *Hand him over*: the same Greek verb is used to express the saving purpose of God by which Jesus is handed over to death (cf. Mt 17:22; 20:18; 26:2) and the human malice that hands him over. *Thirty pieces of silver*: the price of the betrayal is found only in Matthew. It is derived from Zec 11:12 where it is the wages paid to the rejected shepherd, a cheap price (Zec 11:13). That amount is also the compensation paid to one whose slave has been gored by an ox (Ex 21:32).

**26:17** *The first day of the Feast of Unleavened Bread*: see note on Mk 14:1. Matthew omits Mark's "when they sacrificed the Passover lamb."

**26:18** By omitting much of Mk 14:13–15, adding *My appointed time draws near*, and turning the question into a state-

ment, *in your house I shall celebrate the Passover*, Matthew has given this passage a solemnity and majesty greater than that of his source.

**26:21** Given Matthew's interest in the fulfillment of the Old Testament, it is curious that he omits the Marcan designation of Jesus' betrayer as "one who is eating with me" (Mk 14:18), since that is probably an allusion to Ps 41:10. However, the shocking fact that the betrayer is one who shares table fellowship with Jesus is emphasized in Mt 26:23.

**26:24** *It would be better…born*: the enormity of the deed is such that it would be better not to exist than to do it.

**26:25** Peculiar to Matthew. *You have said so*: cf. Mt 26:64; 27:11. This is a half-affirmative. Emphasis is laid on the pronoun and the answer implies that the statement would not have been made if the question had not been asked.

**26:26–29** See note on Mk 14:22–24. The Marcan-Matthean is one of the two major New Testament traditions of the words of Jesus when instituting the Eucharist. The other (and earlier) is the Pauline-Lucan (1 Cor 11:23–25; Lk 22:19–20). Each shows the influence of Christian liturgical usage, but the Marcan-Matthean is more developed in that regard than the Pauline-Lucan. The words

---

| | |
|---|---|
| **26:4** Jn 11:47–53. | **26:17–25** Mk 14:12–21; Lk |
| **26:6–13** Mk 14:3–9; Jn 12:1–8. | 22:7–23. |
| **26:11** Dt 15:11. | **26:17** Ex 12:14–20. |
| **26:14–16** Mk 14:10–11; Lk | **26:24** Is 53:8–10. |
| 22:3–6. | **26:26–30** Mk 14:22–26; Lk |
| **26:15** Zec 11:12. | 22:14–23; 1 Cor |
| | 11:23–25. |

it, and giving it to his disciples said, "Take and eat; this is my body."†* 27 Then he took a cup, gave thanks,† and gave it to them, saying, "Drink from it, all of you, 28* for this is my blood of the covenant, which will be shed on behalf of many for the forgiveness of sins. 29† I tell you, from now on I shall not drink this fruit of the vine until the day when I drink it with you new in the kingdom of my Father." 30† Then, after singing a hymn, they went out to the Mount of Olives.

**Peter's Denial Foretold.** 31* Then Jesus said to them, "This night all of you will have your faith in me shaken,† for it is written:*

'I will strike the shepherd,
   and the sheep of the flock will be
      dispersed';

32 but after I have been raised up, I shall go before you to Galilee." 33 Peter said to him in reply, "Though all may have their faith in you shaken, mine will never be." 34†* Jesus said to him, "Amen, I say to you, this very night before the cock crows, you will deny me three times."* 35 Peter said to him, "Even though I should have to die with you, I will not deny you." And all the disciples spoke likewise.

**The Agony in the Garden.** 36†* Then Jesus came with them to a place called Gethsemane,† and he said to his disciples, "Sit here while I go over there and pray."* 37* He took along Peter and the two sons of Zebedee,† and began to feel sorrow and distress. 38* Then he said to them, "My soul is sorrowful even to death.† Remain here and keep watch with me." 39* He advanced a little and fell prostrate in prayer, saying, "My Father,† if it is possible, let this cup pass from me; yet, not as I will, but as you will." 40 When he returned to his disciples he found them asleep. He said to Peter, "So you could not keep watch with me for one hour? 41 Watch and pray that you may not undergo the test.† The spirit is willing, but

---

† over the bread and cup succeed each other without the intervening meal mentioned in 1 Cor 11:25; Lk 22:20; and there is parallelism between the consecratory words (*this is my body…this is my blood*). Matthew follows Mark closely but with some changes.

**26:26** See note on Mt 14:19. *Said the blessing:* a prayer blessing God. *Take and eat:* literally, *Take, eat. Eat* is an addition to Mark's "take it" (literally, "take"; Mk 14:22). *This is my body:* the bread is identified with Jesus himself.

**26:27–28** *Gave thanks:* see note on Mt 15:36. *Gave it to them…all of you:* cf. Mk 14:23–24. In the Marcan sequence the disciples drink and then Jesus says the interpretative words. Matthew has changed this into a command to *drink* followed by those words. *My blood:* see Lv 17:11 for the concept that the *blood* is "the seat of life" and that when placed on the altar it "makes atonement." *Which will be shed:* the present participle, "being shed" or "going to be shed," is future in relation to the Last Supper. *On behalf of:* Greek *peri;* see note on Mk 14:24. *Many:* see note on Mt 20:28. *For the forgiveness of sins:* a Matthean addition. The same phrase occurs in Mk 1:4 in connection with John's baptism but Matthew avoids it there (Mt 3:11). He places it here probably because he wishes to emphasize that it is the sacrificial death of Jesus that brings *forgiveness of sins.*

**26:29** Although his death will interrupt the table fellowship he has had with the disciples, Jesus confidently predicts his vindication by God and a new table fellowship with them at the banquet of the kingdom.

**26:30** See note on Mk 14:26.

**26:31** *Will have…shaken:* literally, "will be scandalized in me"; see note on Mt 24:9–12. *I will strike…dispersed:* cf. Zec 13:7.

**26:34** *Before the cock crows:* see note on Mt 14:25. The third watch of the night was called "cockcrow." *Deny me:* see note on Mt 16:24.

**26:36–56** Cf. Mk 14:32–52. The account of Jesus in Gethsemane is divided between that of his agony (Mt 26:36–46) and that of his betrayal and arrest (Mt 26:47–56). Jesus' *sorrow and distress* (Mt 26:37) in face of death is unrelieved by the presence of his three disciples who, though urged to *watch with* him (Mt 26:38, 41), fall asleep (Mt 26:40, 43). He prays that *if…possible* his death may be avoided (Mt 26:39) but that his Father's will be done (Mt 26:39, 42, 44). Knowing then that his death must

take place, he announces to his companions that *the hour* for his being *handed over* has come (Mt 26:45). Judas arrives with an armed force provided by the Sanhedrin and greets Jesus with a kiss, the prearranged sign for his identification (Mt 26:47–49). After his arrest, he rebukes a disciple who has attacked the *high priest's servant* with a *sword* (Mt 26:51–54), and chides those who have come out to seize him with *swords and clubs* as if he were a *robber* (Mt 26:55–56). In both rebukes Jesus declares that the treatment he is now receiving is the fulfillment of the scriptures (Mt 26:55, 56). The subsequent flight of *all the disciples* is itself the fulfillment of his own prediction (cf. 31). In this episode, Matthew follows Mark with a few alterations.

**26:36** *Gethsemane:* the Hebrew name means "oil press" and designates an olive orchard on the western slope of the Mount of Olives; see note on Mt 21:1. The name appears only in Matthew and Mark. The place is called a "garden" in Jn 18:1.

**26:37** *Peter and the two sons of Zebedee:* cf. Mt 17:1.

**26:38** Cf. Ps 42:6, 12. In the Septuagint (Ps 41:5, 12) the same Greek word for *sorrowful* is used as here. *To death:* i.e., "enough to die"; cf. Jon 4:9.

**26:39** *My Father:* see note on Mk 14:36. Matthew omits the Aramaic *'abbā'* and adds the qualifier *my. This cup:* see note on Mk 10:38–40.

**26:41** *Undergo the test:* see note on Mt 6:13. In that verse "the final test" translates the same Greek word as is here translated *the test,* and these are the only instances of the use of that word in Matthew. It is possible that the passion of Jesus is seen here as an anticipation of the great tribulation that will precede the parousia (see notes on Mt 24:8; 24:21) to which Mt 6:13 refers, and that just as Jesus prays to be delivered from death (Mt 26:39), so he exhorts the disciples to pray that they will not have to *undergo* the great *test* that his passion would be for them. Some scholars, however, understand *not undergo* (literally, "not enter") *the test* as meaning not that the disciples may be spared

---

| | |
|---|---|
| **26:26–27** 1 Cor 10:16. | **26:36–46** Mk 14:32–42; Lk |
| **26:28** Ex 24:8; Is 53:12. | 22:39–46. |
| **26:31–35** Mk 14:7–31. | **26:36** Jn 18:1. |
| **26:31** Zec 13:7; Jn 16:32. | **26:37–39** Heb 5:7. |
| **26:34–35** Lk 22:33–34; Jn | **26:38** Ps 42:6, 12; Jon 4:9. |
| 13:37–38. | **26:39** Jn 4:34; 6:38; Phil |
| **26:34** 26:69–75. | 2:8. |

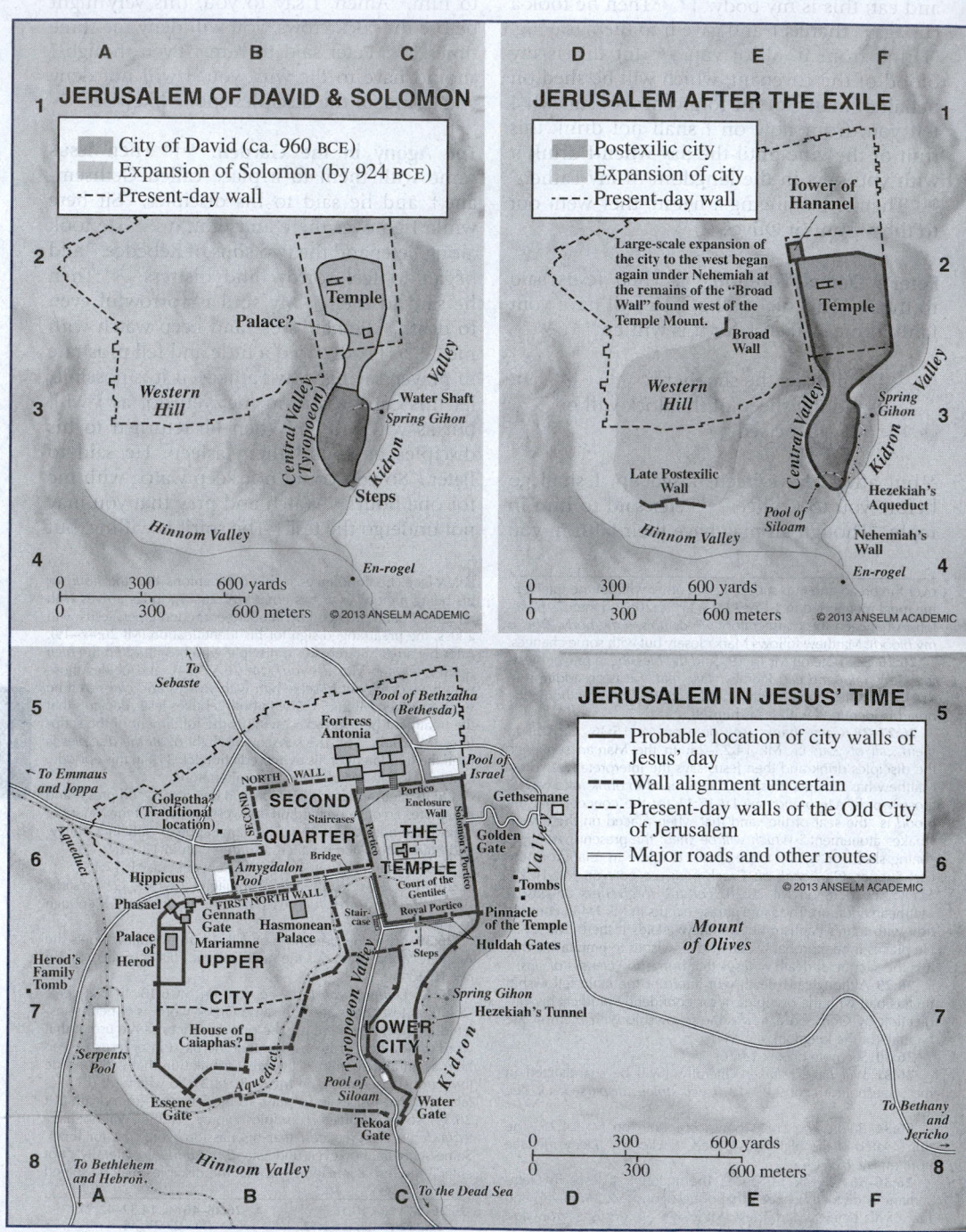

**JERUSALEM OF DAVID & SOLOMON**

- City of David (ca. 960 BCE)
- Expansion of Solomon (by 924 BCE)
- Present-day wall

Temple

Palace?

Western Hill

Central Valley (Tyropoeon)

Kidron

Water Shaft

Spring Gihon

Steps

Hinnom Valley

En-rogel

0   300   600 yards
0   300   600 meters   © 2013 ANSELM ACADEMIC

**JERUSALEM AFTER THE EXILE**

- Postexilic city
- Expansion of city
- Present-day wall

Tower of Hananel

Large-scale expansion of the city to the west began again under Nehemiah at the remains of the "Broad Wall" found west of the Temple Mount.

Broad Wall

Temple

Western Hill

Central Valley

Spring Gihon

Kidron

Late Postexilic Wall

Pool of Siloam

Hezekiah's Aqueduct

Nehemiah's Wall

Hinnom Valley

En-rogel

0   300   600 yards
0   300   600 meters   © 2013 ANSELM ACADEMIC

**JERUSALEM IN JESUS' TIME**

- Probable location of city walls of Jesus' day
- Wall alignment uncertain
- Present-day walls of the Old City of Jerusalem
- Major roads and other routes

© 2013 ANSELM ACADEMIC

To Sebaste

Pool of Bethzatha (Bethesda)

Fortress Antonia

Pool of Israel

To Emmaus and Joppa

Golgotha? (Traditional location)

NORTH WALL

SECOND

SECOND QUARTER

Portico

Enclosure Wall

Staircases

Gethsemane

Aqueduct

Hippicus

Amygdalon Pool

Bridge

Portico

THE TEMPLE

Solomon's Portico

Golden Gate

Phasael

FIRST NORTH WALL

Palace of Herod

Mariamne

Gennath Gate

Hasmonean Palace

Stair-case

'Court of the Gentiles

Royal Portico

Pinnacle of the Temple

Tombs

Herod's Family Tomb

UPPER

CITY

Steps

Huldah Gates

Mount of Olives

Serpents Pool

House of Caiaphas?

Tyropoeon Valley

LOWER CITY

Spring Gihon

Hezekiah's Tunnel

Kidron

Essene Gate

Aqueduct

Pool of Siloam

Tekoa Gate

Water Gate

To Bethany and Jericho

To Bethlehem and Hebron

Hinnom Valley

To the Dead Sea

0   300   600 yards
0   300   600 meters

the flesh is weak." [42] †* Withdrawing a second time, he prayed again, "My Father, if it is not possible that this cup pass without my drinking it, your will be done!" [43] Then he returned once more and found them asleep, for they could not keep their eyes open. [44] He left them and withdrew again and prayed a third time, saying the same thing again. [45]* Then he returned to his disciples and said to them, "Are you still sleeping and taking your rest? Behold, the hour is at hand when the Son of Man is to be handed over to sinners. [46] Get up, let us go. Look, my betrayer is at hand."

**The Betrayal and Arrest of Jesus.** [47]* While he was still speaking, Judas, one of the Twelve, arrived, accompanied by a large crowd, with swords and clubs, who had come from the chief priests and the elders of the people. [48] His betrayer had arranged a sign with them, saying, "The man I shall kiss is the one; arrest him." [49] Immediately he went over to Jesus and said, "Hail, Rabbi!" † and he kissed him. [50] Jesus answered him, "Friend, do what you have come for." Then stepping forward they laid hands on Jesus and arrested him. [51] And behold, one of those who accompanied Jesus put his hand to his sword, drew it, and struck the high priest's servant, cutting off his ear. [52] Then Jesus said to him, "Put your sword back into its sheath, for all who take the sword will perish by the sword. [53] Do you think that I cannot call upon my Father and he will not provide me at this moment with more than twelve legions of angels? [54] But then how would the scriptures be fulfilled which say that it must come to pass in this way?" [55] † At that hour Jesus said to the crowds, "Have you come out as against a robber, with swords and clubs to seize me? Day after day I sat teaching in the temple area, yet you did not arrest me. [56]* But all this has come to pass that the writings of the prophets may be fulfilled." Then all the disciples left him and fled.

**Jesus Before the Sanhedrin.** † [57]* Those who had arrested Jesus led him away to Caiaphas† the high priest, where the scribes and the elders were assembled. [58] Peter was following him at a distance as far as the high priest's courtyard, and going inside he sat down with the servants to see the outcome. [59] The chief priests and the entire Sanhedrin† kept trying to obtain false testimony against Jesus in order to put him to death, [60]* but they found none, though many false witnesses came forward. Finally two† came forward [61] who stated, "This man said, 'I can destroy the temple of God and within three days rebuild it.'" [62] The high priest rose and addressed him, "Have you no answer? What are these men testifying against you?" [63]* But Jesus was silent.† Then the high

MT

---

*the test* but that they may not yield to the temptation of falling away from Jesus because of his passion even though they will have to endure it.

**26:42** *Your will be done*: cf. Mt 6:10.

**26:49** *Rabbi*: see note on Mt 23:6–7. Jesus is so addressed twice in Matthew (Mt 26:25), both times by Judas. For the significance of the closely related address "teacher" in Matthew, see note on Mt 8:19.

**26:55** *Day after day…arrest me*: cf. Mk 14:49. This suggests that Jesus had taught for a relatively long period in Jerusalem, whereas Mt 21:1–11 puts his coming to the city for the first time only a few days before.

**26:57–68** Following Mk 14:53–65 Matthew presents the nighttime appearance of Jesus before the *Sanhedrin* as a real trial. After *many false witnesses* bring charges against him that do not suffice for the death sentence (Mt 26:60), *two came forward* who charge him with claiming to be able to *destroy the temple…and within three days rebuild it* (Mt 26:60–61). Jesus makes no answer even when challenged to do so by *the high priest*, who then orders him to declare *under oath…whether* he is the *Messiah, the Son of God* (Mt 26:62–63). Matthew changes Mark's clear affirmative response (Mk 14:62) to the same one as that given to Judas (Mt 26:25), but follows Mark almost verbatim in Jesus' predicting that his judges will see him (*the Son of Man*) seated *at the right hand* of God *and coming on the clouds of heaven* (Mt 26:64). *The high priest* then charges him with blasphemy (Mt 26:65), a charge with which the other members of *the Sanhedrin* agree by declaring that *he deserves to die* (Mt 26:66). They then attack him (Mt 26:67) and mockingly demand that he *prophesy* (Mt 26:68). This account contains elements that are contrary to

the judicial procedures prescribed in the Mishnah, the Jewish code of law that dates in written form from ca. A.D. 200, e.g., trial on a feast day, a night session of the court, pronouncement of a verdict of condemnation at the same session at which testimony was received. Consequently, some scholars regard the account entirely as a creation of the early Christians without historical value. However, it is disputable whether the norms found in the Mishnah were in force at the time of Jesus. More to the point is the question whether the Matthean-Marcan night trial derives from a combination of two separate incidents, a night-time preliminary investigation (cf. Jn 18:13, 19–24) and a formal trial on the following morning (cf. Lk 22:66–71).

**26:57** *Caiaphas*: see note on Mt 26:3.

**26:59** *Sanhedrin*: see note on Lk 22:66.

**26:60–61** *Two*: cf. Dt 19:15. *I can destroy…rebuild it*: there are significant differences from the Marcan parallel (Mk 14:58). Matthew omits "made with hands" and "not made with hands" and changes Mark's "will destroy" and "will build another" to *can destroy* and (can) *rebuild*. The charge is probably based on Jesus' prediction of the temple's destruction; see notes on Mt 23:37–39; 24:2; and Jn 2:19. A similar prediction by Jeremiah was considered as deserving death; cf. Jer 7:1–15; 26:1–8.

**26:63** *Silent*: possibly an allusion to Is 53:7. *I order you…living God*: peculiar to Matthew; cf. Mk 14:61.

---

| | |
|---|---|
| **26:42** 6:10; Heb 10:9. | **26:57–68** Mk 14:53–65; Lk |
| **26:45** Jn 12:23; 13:1; 17:1. | 22:54–55, 63–71; Jn |
| **26:47–56** Mk 14:43–50; Lk | 18:12–14, 19–24. |
| 22:47–53; Jn 18:3–11. | **26:60–61** Dt 19:15; Jn 2:19; |
| **26:56** 26:31. | Acts 6:14. |
| | **26:63** Is 53:7. |

priest said to him, "I order you to tell us under oath before the living God whether you are the Messiah, the Son of God." [64]* Jesus said to him in reply, "You have said so.† But I tell you:

> From now on you will see 'the Son of Man
> seated at the right hand of the Power'
> and 'coming on the clouds of heaven.'"

[65] Then the high priest tore his robes and said, "He has blasphemed!† What further need have we of witnesses? You have now heard the blasphemy; [66] what is your opinion?" They said in reply, "He deserves to die!" [67]†* Then they spat in his face and struck him, while some slapped him, [68] saying, "Prophesy for us, Messiah: who is it that struck you?"

**Peter's Denial of Jesus.** [69]* Now Peter was sitting outside in the courtyard. One of the maids came over to him and said, "You too were with Jesus the Galilean." [70]† But he denied it in front of everyone, saying, "I do not know what you are talking about!" [71] As he went out to the gate, another girl saw him and said to those who were there, "This man was with Jesus the Nazorean." [72] Again he denied it with an oath, "I do not know the man!" [73]† A little later the bystanders came over and said to Peter, "Surely you too are one of them; even your speech gives you away." [74] At that he began to curse and to swear, "I do not know the man." And immediately a cock crowed. [75]* Then Peter remembered the word that Jesus had spoken: "Before the cock crows you will deny me three times." He went out and began to weep bitterly.

# 27

**Jesus Before Pilate.** [1]† When it was morning,* all the chief priests and the elders of the people took counsel† against Jesus to put him to death. [2] They bound him, led him away, and handed him over to Pilate, the governor.

**The Death of Judas.** [3]* Then Judas, his betrayer, seeing that Jesus had been condemned, deeply regretted what he had done. He returned the thirty pieces of silver† to the chief priests and elders,* [4] saying, "I have sinned in betraying innocent blood." They said, "What is that to us? Look to it yourself." [5]† Flinging the money into the temple, he departed and went off and hanged himself. [6] The chief priests gathered up the money, but said, "It is not lawful to deposit this in the temple treasury, for it is the price of blood." [7] After consultation, they used it to buy the potter's field as a burial place for foreigners. [8] That is why that field even today is called the Field

---

† **26:64** *You have said so:* see note on Mt 26:25. *From now on…heaven:* the Son of Man who is to be crucified (cf. Mt 20:19) will be seen in glorious majesty (cf. Ps 110:1) and *coming on the clouds of heaven* (cf. Dn 7:13). *The Power:* see note on Mk 14:61–62.

**26:65** *Blasphemed:* the punishment for *blasphemy* was death by stoning (see Lv 24:10–16). According to the Mishnah, to be guilty of blasphemy one had to pronounce "the Name itself," i.e., Yahweh; cf. *Sanhedrin 7:4, 5.* Those who judge the gospel accounts of Jesus' trial by the later Mishnah standards point out that Jesus uses the surrogate "the Power," and hence no Jewish court would have regarded him as guilty of blasphemy; others hold that the Mishnah's narrow understanding of blasphemy was a later development.

**26:67–68** The physical abuse, apparently done to Jesus by the members of the Sanhedrin themselves, recalls the sufferings of the Isaian Servant of the Lord; cf. Is 50:6. The mocking challenge to *prophesy* is probably motivated by Jesus' prediction of his future glory (Mt 26:64).

**26:70** *Denied it in front of everyone:* see Mt 10:33. Peter's repentance (Mt 26:75) saves him from the fearful destiny of which Jesus speaks there.

**26:73** *Your speech…away:* Matthew explicates Mark's "you too are a Galilean" (Mk 14:70).

**27:1–31** Cf. Mk 15:1–20. Matthew's account of the Roman trial before *Pilate* is introduced by a consultation of the Sanhedrin after which Jesus is *handed over to…the governor* (Mt 27:1–2). Matthew follows his Marcan source closely but adds some material that is peculiar to him, the death of *Judas* (Mt 27:3–10), possibly the name *Jesus* as the name of *Barabbas* also

(Mt 27:16–17), the intervention of Pilate's *wife* (Mt 27:19), Pilate's washing *his hands* in token of his disclaiming responsibility for Jesus' death (Mt 27:24), and the assuming of that responsibility by *the whole people* (Mt 27:25).

**27:1** There is scholarly disagreement about the meaning of the Sanhedrin's taking *counsel* (*symboulion elabon*; cf. Mt 12:14; 22:15; 27:7; 28:12); see note on Mk 15:1. Some understand it as a discussion about the strategy for putting their death sentence against *Jesus* into effect since they lacked the right to do so themselves. Others see it as the occasion for their passing that sentence, holding that Matthew, unlike Mark (Mk 14:64), does not consider that it had been passed in the night session (Mt 26:66). Even in the latter interpretation, their handing *him over to Pilate* is best explained on the hypothesis that they did not have competence to put their sentence into effect, as is stated in Jn 18:31.

**27:3** *The thirty pieces of silver:* see Mt 26:15.

**27:5–8** For another tradition about the death of Judas, cf. Acts 1:18–19. The two traditions agree only in the purchase of a field with *the money* paid to Judas for his betrayal of Jesus and the name given to the field, *the Field of Blood.* In Acts Judas himself buys the field and its name comes from his own blood shed in his fatal accident on it. *The potter's field:* this designation of the field is based on the fulfillment citation in Mt 27:10.

---

**26:64** Ps 110:1; Dn 7:13.
**26:67** Wis 2:19; Is 50:6.
**26:69–75** Mk 14:66–72;
　　Lk 22:56–62; Jn
　　18:17–18, 25–27.

**26:75** 26:34.
**27:1–2** Mk 15:1; Lk 23:1; Jn
　　18:28.
**27:3–10** Acts 1:18–19.
**27:3** 26:15.

of Blood. [9] Then was fulfilled what had been said through Jeremiah the prophet,† "And they took the thirty pieces of silver, the value of a man with a price on his head, a price set by some of the Israelites, [10]* and they paid it out for the potter's field just as the Lord had commanded me."

### Jesus Questioned by Pilate.

[11]* Now Jesus stood before the governor, and he questioned him, "Are you the king of the Jews?"† Jesus said, "You say so." [12]* And when he was accused by the chief priests and elders,† he made no answer. [13] Then Pilate said to him, "Do you not hear how many things they are testifying against you?" [14] But he did not answer him one word, so that the governor was greatly amazed.

### The Sentence of Death.

[15]†* Now on the occasion of the feast the governor was accustomed to release to the crowd one prisoner whom they wished. [16]† And at that time they had a notorious prisoner called [Jesus] Barabbas. [17] So when they had assembled, Pilate said to them, "Which one do you want me to release to you, [Jesus] Barabbas, or Jesus called Messiah?" [18]† For he knew that it was out of envy that they had handed him over. [19]† While he was still seated on the bench, his wife sent him a message, "Have nothing to do with that righteous man. I suffered much in a dream today because of him." [20]* The chief priests and the elders persuaded the crowds to ask for Barabbas but to destroy Jesus. [21] The governor said to them in reply, "Which of the two do you want me to release to you?" They answered, "Barabbas!" [22]† Pilate said to them, "Then what shall I do with Jesus called Messiah?" They all said, "Let him be crucified!" [23] But he said, "Why? What evil has he done?" They only shouted the louder, "Let him be crucified!" [24]†* When Pilate saw that he was not succeeding at all, but that a riot was breaking out instead, he took water and washed his hands in the sight of the crowd, saying, "I am innocent of this man's blood. Look to it yourselves." [25] And the whole people said in reply, "His blood be upon us and upon our children." [26] Then he released Barabbas to them, but after he had Jesus scourged,† he handed him over to be crucified.

---

† **27:9–10** Cf. Mt 26:15. Matthew's attributing this text to Jeremiah is puzzling, for there is no such text in that book, and *the thirty pieces of silver* thrown by Judas "into the temple" (Mt 27:5) recall rather Zec 11:12–13. It is usually said that the attribution of the text to Jeremiah is due to Matthew's combining the Zechariah text with texts from Jeremiah that speak of a *potter* (Jer 18:2–3), the buying of a *field* (Jer 32:6–9), or the breaking of a potter's flask at Topheth in the valley of Ben-Hinnom with the prediction that it will become a burial place (Jer 19:1–13).

**27:11** *King of the Jews*: this title is used of Jesus only by pagans. The Matthean instances are, besides this verse, Mt 2:2; 27:29, 37. Matthew equates it with "Messiah"; cf. Mt 2:2, 4 and Mt 27:17, 22 where he has changed "the king of the Jews" of his Marcan source (Mk 15:9, 12) to "(Jesus) called Messiah." The normal political connotation of both titles would be of concern to the Roman *governor*. *You say so*: see note on Mt 26:25. An unqualified affirmative response is not made because Jesus' kingship is not what Pilate would understand it to be.

**27:12–14** Cf. Mt 26:62–63. As in the trial before the Sanhedrin, Jesus' silence may be meant to recall Is 53:7. *Greatly amazed*: possibly an allusion to Is 52:14–15.

**27:15–26** The choice that Pilate offers *the crowd* between *Barabbas* and *Jesus* is said to be in accordance with a custom of releasing at the Passover feast *one prisoner* chosen by *the crowd* (Mt 27:15). This custom is mentioned also in Mk 15:6 and Jn 18:39 but not in Luke; see note on Lk 23:17. Outside of the gospels there is no direct attestation of it, and scholars are divided in their judgment of the historical reliability of the claim that there was such a practice.

**27:16–17** *[Jesus] Barabbas*: it is possible that the double name is the original reading; *Jesus* was a common Jewish name; see note on Mt 1:21. This reading is found in only a few textual witnesses, although its absence in the majority can be explained as an omission of *Jesus* made for reverential reasons. That name is bracketed because of its uncertain textual attestation. The Aramaic name *Barabbas* means "son of the father"; the irony of the choice offered between him and Jesus, the true son of the Father, would be evident to those addressees of

Matthew who knew that.

**27:18** Cf. Mk 14:10. This is an example of the tendency, found in varying degree in all the gospels, to present Pilate in a relatively favorable light and emphasize the hostility of the Jewish authorities and eventually of the people.

**27:19** Jesus' innocence is declared by a Gentile woman. *In a dream*: in Matthew's infancy narrative, dreams are the means of divine communication; cf. Mt 1:20; 2:12, 13, 19, 22.

**27:22** *Let him be crucified*: incited by the chief priests and elders (Mt 27:20), the crowds demand that Jesus be executed by crucifixion, a peculiarly horrible form of Roman capital punishment. The Marcan parallel, "Crucify him" (Mk 15:3), addressed to Pilate, is changed by Matthew to the passive, probably to emphasize the responsibility of the crowds.

**27:24–25** Peculiar to Matthew. *Took water…blood*: cf. Dt 21:1–8, the handwashing prescribed in the case of a murder when the killer is unknown. The elders of the city nearest to where the corpse is found must wash their hands, declaring, "Our hands did not shed this blood." *Look to it yourselves*: cf. Mt 27:4. *The whole people*: Matthew sees in those who speak these words *the* entire *people* (Greek *laos*) of Israel. *His blood… and upon our children*: cf. Jer 26:15. The responsibility for Jesus' death is accepted by the nation that was God's special possession (Ex 19:5), his own people (Hos 2:25), and they thereby lose that high privilege; see Mt 21:43 and the note on that verse. The controversy between Matthew's church and Pharisaic Judaism about which was the true people of God is reflected here. As the Second Vatican Council has pointed out, guilt for Jesus' death is not attributable to all the Jews of his time or to any Jews of later times.

**27:26** *He had Jesus scourged*: the usual preliminary to crucifixion.

---

* **27:10** Zec 11:12–13.
**27:11–14** Mk 15:2–5; Lk 23:2–3; Jn 18:29–38.
**27:12** Is 53:7.
**27:15–26** Mk 15:6–15; Lk 23:17–25; Jn 18:39–19:16.
**27:20** Acts 3:14.
**27:24** Dt 21:1–8.

MT

**Mockery by the Soldiers.** 27 * Then the soldiers of the governor took Jesus inside the praetorium† and gathered the whole cohort around him. 28 They stripped off his clothes and threw a scarlet military cloak† about him. 29 * Weaving a crown out of thorns,† they placed it on his head, and a reed in his right hand. And kneeling before him, they mocked him, saying, "Hail, King of the Jews!" 30 * They spat upon him† and took the reed and kept striking him on the head. 31 And when they had mocked him, they stripped him of the cloak, dressed him in his own clothes, and led him off to crucify him.

**The Way of the Cross.**† 32 * As they were going out, they met a Cyrenian named Simon; this man they pressed into service to carry his cross.

**The Crucifixion.** 33 * And when they came to a place called Golgotha (which means Place of the Skull), 34 * they gave Jesus wine to drink mixed with gall.† But when he had tasted it, he refused to drink. 35 * After they had crucified him, they divided his garments† by casting lots; 36 then they sat down and kept watch over him there. 37 And they placed over his head the written charge† against him: This is Jesus, the King of the Jews. 38 Two revolutionaries† were crucified with him, one on his right and the other on his left. 39 †* Those passing by reviled him, shaking their heads 40 * and saying, "You who would destroy the temple and rebuild it in three days, save yourself, if you are the Son of God, [and] come down from the cross!" 41 Likewise the chief priests with the scribes and elders mocked him and said, 42 "He saved others; he cannot save himself. So he is the king of Israel!† Let him come down from the cross now, and we will believe in him. 43 †* He trusted in God; let him deliver him now if he wants him. For he said, 'I am the Son of God.'" 44 The revolutionaries who were crucified with him also kept abusing him in the same way.

**The Death of Jesus.** 45 †* From noon onward,* darkness came over the whole land until three in the afternoon. 46 * And about three o'clock Jesus cried out in a loud voice, "*Eli, Eli, lema sabachthani?*"† which means, "My God, my God, why have you forsaken me?" 47 † Some of the bystanders who heard it said, "This one is calling for Elijah." 48 * Immediately one

---

† **27:27** *The praetorium*: the residence of the Roman governor. His usual place of residence was at Caesarea Maritima on the Mediterranean coast, but he went to Jerusalem during the great feasts, when the influx of pilgrims posed the danger of a nationalistic riot. It is disputed whether the *praetorium* in Jerusalem was the old palace of Herod in the west of the city or the fortress of Antonia northwest of the temple area. *The whole cohort*: normally six hundred soldiers.

**27:28** *Scarlet military cloak*: so Matthew as against the royal purple of Mk 15:17 and Jn 19:2.

**27:29** *Crown out of thorns*: probably of long *thorns* that stood upright so that it resembled the "radiant" *crown*, a diadem with spikes worn by Hellenistic kings. The soldiers' purpose was mockery, not torture. *A reed*: peculiar to Matthew; a mock scepter.

**27:30** *Spat upon him*: cf. Mt 26:67 where there also is a possible allusion to Is 50:6.

**27:32** See note on Mk 15:21. *Cyrenian named Simon*: Cyrenaica was a Roman province on the north coast of Africa and Cyrene was its capital city. The city had a large population of Greek-speaking Jews. *Simon* may have been living in Palestine or have come there for the Passover as a pilgrim. *Pressed into service*: see note on Mt 5:41.

**27:34** *Wine...mixed with gall*: cf. Mk 15:23 where the drink is "wine drugged with myrrh," a narcotic. Matthew's text is probably an inexact allusion to Ps 69:22. That psalm belongs to the class called the individual lament, in which a persecuted just man prays for deliverance in the midst of great suffering and also expresses confidence that his prayer will be heard. That theme of the suffering Just One is frequently applied to the sufferings of Jesus in the passion narratives.

**27:35** The clothing of an executed criminal went to his executioner(s), but the description of that procedure in the case of Jesus, found in all the gospels, is plainly inspired by Ps 22:19. However, that psalm verse is quoted only in Jn 19:24.

**27:37** The offense of a person condemned to death by crucifixion was written on a tablet that was displayed on his cross. The *charge* against *Jesus* was that he had claimed to be the *King of the Jews* (cf. Mt 27:11), i.e., the Messiah (cf. Mt 27:17, 22).

**27:38** *Revolutionaries*: see note on Jn 18:40 where the same Greek word as that found here is used for Barabbas.

**27:39–40** *Reviled him...heads*: cf. Ps 22:8. *You who would destroy...three days*; cf. Mt 26:61. *If you are the Son of God*: the same words as those of the devil in the temptation of Jesus; cf. Mt 4:3, 6.

**27:42** *King of Israel*: in their mocking of Jesus the members of the Sanhedrin call themselves and their people not "the Jews" but *Israel*.

**27:43** Peculiar to Matthew. *He trusted in God...wants him*: cf. Ps 22:9. *He said...of God*: probably an allusion to Wis 2:12–20 where the theme of the suffering Just One appears.

**27:45** Cf. Am 8:9 where on the day of the Lord "the sun will set at midday."

**27:46** *Eli, Eli, lema sabachthani?*: Jesus cries out in the words of Ps 22:2a, a psalm of lament that is the Old Testament passage most frequently drawn upon in this narrative. In Mark the verse is cited entirely in Aramaic, which Matthew partially retains but changes the invocation of God to the Hebrew *Eli*, possibly because that is more easily related to the statement of the following verse about Jesus' calling for Elijah.

**27:47** *Elijah*: see note on Mt 3:4. This prophet, taken up into heaven (2 Kgs 2:11), was believed to come to the help of those

---

**27:27–31** Mk 15:16–20; Jn 19:2–3.
**27:29** 27:11.
**27:30** Is 50:6.
**27:32** Mk 15:21; Lk 23:26.
**27:33–44** Mk 15:22–32; Lk 23:32–38; Jn 19:17–19, 23–24.
**27:34** Ps 69:21.
**27:35** Ps 22:19.
**27:39** Ps 22:8.
**27:40** 4:3, 6; 26:61.
**27:43** Ps 22:9; Wis 2:12–20.
**27:45–46** Mk 15:33–41; Lk 23:44–49; Jn 19:28–30.
**27:45** Am 8:9.
**27:46** Ps 22:2.
**27:48** Ps 69:21.

of them ran to get a sponge; he soaked it in wine, and putting it on a reed, gave it to him to drink. [49] But the rest said, "Wait, let us see if Elijah comes to save him." [50] † But Jesus cried out again in a loud voice, and gave up his spirit. [51] * And behold, the veil of the sanctuary was torn in two from top to bottom. † The earth quaked, rocks were split, [52] * tombs were opened, and the bodies of many saints who had fallen asleep were raised. [53] And coming forth from their tombs after his resurrection, they entered the holy city and appeared to many. [54] † The centurion and the men with him who were keeping watch over Jesus feared greatly when they saw the earthquake and all that was happening, and they said, "Truly, this was the Son of God!" [55] There were many women there, looking on from a distance, † who had followed Jesus from Galilee, ministering to him. [56] * Among them were Mary Magdalene and Mary the mother of James and Joseph, and the mother of the sons of Zebedee.

**The Burial of Jesus.** † [57] * When it was evening, there came a rich man from Arimathea named Joseph, who was himself a disciple of Jesus. * [58] He went to Pilate and asked for the body of Jesus; then Pilate ordered it to be handed over. [59] Taking the body, Joseph wrapped it [in] clean linen [60] and laid it in his new tomb that he had hewn in the rock. Then he rolled a huge stone across the entrance to the tomb and departed. [61] But Mary Magdalene and the other Mary remained sitting there, facing the tomb.

**The Guard at the Tomb.** † [62] The next day, the one following the day of preparation, † the chief priests and the Pharisees gathered before Pilate [63] * and said, "Sir, we remember that this impostor while still alive said, 'After three days I will be raised up.' [64] Give orders, then, that the grave be secured until the third day, lest his disciples come and steal him and say to the people, 'He has been raised from the dead.' This last imposture would be worse than the first." † [65] Pilate said to them, "The guard is yours; † go secure it as best you can." [66] So they went and secured the tomb by fixing a seal to the stone and setting the guard.

---

† in distress, but the evidences of that belief are all later than the gospels.

**27:50** *Gave up his spirit*: cf. the Marcan parallel (Mk 15:37), "breathed his last." Matthew's alteration expresses both Jesus' control over his destiny and his obedient giving up of his life to God.

**27:51–53** *Veil of the sanctuary…bottom*: cf. Mk 15:38; Lk 23:45. Luke puts this event immediately before the death of Jesus. There were two veils in the Mosaic tabernacle on the model of which the temple was constructed, the outer one before the entrance of the Holy Place and the inner one before the Holy of Holies (see Ex 26:31–36). Only the high priest could pass through the latter and that only on the Day of Atonement (see Lv 16:1–18). Probably the torn veil of the gospels is the inner one. The meaning of the scene may be that now, because of Jesus' death, all people have access to the presence of God, or that the temple, its holiest part standing exposed, is now profaned and will soon be destroyed. *The earth quaked…appeared to many*: peculiar to Matthew. The earthquake, the splitting of the *rocks*, and especially the resurrection of the dead *saints* indicate the coming of the final age. In the Old Testament the coming of God is frequently portrayed with the imagery of an earthquake (see Ps 68:9; 77:19), and Jesus speaks of the earthquakes that will accompany the "labor pains" that signify the beginning of the dissolution of the old world (Mt 24:7–8). For the expectation of the resurrection of the dead at the coming of the new and final age, see Dn 12:1–3. Matthew knows that the end of the old age has not yet come (Mt 28:20), but the new age has broken in with the death (and resurrection; cf. the earthquake in Mt 28:2) of Jesus; see note on Mt 16:28. *After his resurrection*: this qualification seems to be due to Matthew's wish to assert the primacy of Jesus' *resurrection* even though he has placed the resurrection of the dead *saints* immediately after Jesus' death.

**27:54** Cf. Mk 15:39. The Christian confession of faith is made by Gentiles, not only *the centurion*, as in Mark, but the other soldiers *who were keeping watch over Jesus* (cf. Mt 27:36).

**27:55–56** *Looking on from a distance*: cf. Ps 38:12. *Mary Magdalene…Joseph*: these two women are mentioned again in Mt 27:61 and Mt 28:1 and are important as witnesses of the reality of the empty tomb. ∧ *James* and *Joseph* are referred to in Mt 13:55 as brothers of Jesus.

**27:57–61** Cf. Mk 15:42–47. Matthew drops Mark's designation of *Joseph* of *Arimathea* as "a distinguished member of the council" (the Sanhedrin), and makes him *a rich man* and a *disciple of Jesus*. The former may be an allusion to Is 53:9 (the Hebrew reading of that text is disputed and the one followed in the NAB OT has nothing about the rich, but they are mentioned in the LXX version). That the tomb was the *new tomb* of a *rich man* and that it was seen by the women are indications of an apologetic intent of Matthew; there could be no question about the identity of Jesus' burial place. *The other Mary*: the mother of James and Joseph (Mt 27:56).

**27:62–66** Peculiar to Matthew. The story prepares for Mt 28:11–15 and the Jewish charge that the tomb was empty because the disciples had stolen the body of Jesus (Mt 28:13, 15).

**27:62** *The next day…preparation*: the sabbath. According to the synoptic chronology, in that year *the day of preparation* (for the sabbath) was the Passover; cf. Mk 15:42. *The Pharisees*: the principal opponents of Jesus during his ministry and, in Matthew's time, of the Christian church, join with the *chief priests* to guarantee against a possible attempt of Jesus' *disciples* to steal his body.

**27:64** *This last imposture…the first*: the claim that Jesus *has been raised from the dead* is clearly the *last imposture*; the *first* may be either his claim that he would *be raised up* (Mt 27:63) or his claim that he was the one with whose ministry the kingdom of God had come (see Mt 12:28).

**27:65** *The guard is yours*: literally, "have a guard" or "you have a guard." Either the imperative or the indicative could mean that Pilate granted the petitioners some Roman soldiers as guards, which is the sense of the present translation. However, if

---

| | |
|---|---|
| **27:51** Ex 26:31–36; Ps 68:9; 77:19. | Lk 23:50–56; Jn 19:38–42. |
| **27:52** Dn 12:1–3. | **27:57** Is 53:9. |
| **27:56** 13:55. | **27:63** 12:40; 16:21; 17:23; 20:19. |
| **27:57–61** Mk 15:42–47; | |

M
T

# 28 † The Resurrection of Jesus.

¹* After the sabbath, as the first day of the week was dawning,† Mary Magdalene and the other Mary came to see the tomb. ²†* And behold, there was a great earthquake; for an angel of the Lord descended from heaven, approached, rolled back the stone, and sat upon it. ³* His appearance was like lightning and his clothing was white as snow. ⁴The guards were shaken with fear of him and became like dead men. ⁵Then the angel said to the women in reply, "Do not be afraid! I know that you are seeking Jesus the crucified. ⁶† He is not here, for he has been raised just as he said. Come and see the place where he lay. ⁷* Then go quickly and tell his disciples, 'He has been raised from the dead, and he is going before you to Galilee; there you will see him.' Behold, I have told you." ⁸Then they went away quickly from the tomb, fearful yet overjoyed, and ran to announce† this to his disciples. ⁹†* And behold, Jesus met them on their way and greeted them. They approached, embraced his feet, and did him homage. ¹⁰Then Jesus said to them, "Do not be afraid. Go tell my brothers to go to Galilee, and there they will see me."

## The Report of the Guard.†

¹¹While they were going, some of the guard went into the city and told the chief priests all that had happened. ¹²They assembled with the elders and took counsel; then they gave a large sum of money to the soldiers, ¹³telling them, "You are to say, 'His disciples came by night and stole him while we were asleep.' ¹⁴And if this gets to the ears of the governor, we will satisfy [him] and keep you out of trouble." ¹⁵The soldiers took the money and did as they were instructed. And this story has circulated among the Jews to the present [day].

## The Commissioning of the Disciples.†

¹⁶* The eleven† disciples went to Galilee, to the

---

† the verb is taken as an indicative it could also mean that Pilate told them to use their own Jewish guards.

**28:1–20** Except for Mt 28:1–8 based on Mk 16:1–8, the material of this final chapter is peculiar to Matthew. Even where he follows Mark, Matthew has altered his source so greatly that a very different impression is given from that of the Marcan account. The two points that are common to the resurrection testimony of all the gospels are that the tomb of Jesus had been found empty and that the risen Jesus had appeared to certain persons, or, in the original form of Mark, that such an appearance was promised as soon to take place (see Mk 16:7). On this central and all-important basis, Matthew has constructed an account that interprets the resurrection as the turning of the ages (Mt 28:2–4), shows the Jewish opposition to Jesus as continuing *to the present* in the claim that the resurrection is a deception perpetrated by the *disciples* who stole his body from the tomb (Mt 28:11–15), and marks a new stage in the mission of *the disciples* once limited to Israel (Mt 10:5–6); now they are to *make disciples of all nations*. In this work they will be strengthened by the presence of the exalted Son of Man, who will be with them *until* the kingdom comes in fullness at *the end of the age* (Mt 28:16–20).

**28:1** *After the sabbath...dawning*: since the sabbath ended at sunset, this could mean in the early evening, for *dawning* can refer to the appearance of the evening star; cf. Lk 23:54. However, it is probable that Matthew means the morning dawn of the day after the sabbath, as in the similar though slightly different text of Mark, "when the sun had risen" (Mk 16:2). *Mary Magdalene and the other Mary*: see notes on Mt 27:55–56; 57–61. *To see the tomb*: cf. Mk 16:1–2 where the purpose of the women's visit is to anoint Jesus' body.

**28:2–4** Peculiar to Matthew. *A great earthquake*: see note on Mt 27:51–53. *Descended from heaven*: this trait is peculiar to Matthew, although his interpretation of the "young man" of his Marcan source (Mk 16:5) as an *angel* is probably true to Mark's intention; cf. Lk 24:23 where the "two men" of Mt 24:4 are said to be "angels." *Rolled back the stone...upon it*: not to allow the risen Jesus to leave the tomb but to make evident that the tomb is empty (see Mt 24:6). Unlike the apocryphal Gospel of Peter (9:35—11:44), the New Testament does not describe the resurrection of Jesus, nor is there anyone who sees it. *His appearance was like lightning...snow*: see note on Mt 17:2.

**28:6–7** Cf. Mk 16:6–7. *Just as he said*: a Matthean addition referring to Jesus' predictions of his resurrection, e.g., Mt 16:21;

17:23; 20:19. *Tell his disciples*: like the angel of the Lord of the infancy narrative, the angel interprets a fact and gives a commandment about what is to be done; cf. Mt 1:20–21. Matthew omits Mark's "and Peter" (Mk 16:7); considering his interest in Peter, this omission is curious. Perhaps the reason is that the Marcan text may allude to a first appearance of Jesus to Peter alone (cf. 1 Cor 15:5; Lk 24:34) which Matthew has already incorporated into his account of Peter's confession at Caesarea Philippi; see note on Mt 16:16. *He is going...Galilee*: like Mk 16:7, a reference to Jesus' prediction at the Last Supper (Mt 26:32; Mk 14:28). Matthew changes Mark's "as he told you" to a declaration of the angel.

**28:8** Contrast Mk 16:8 where the women in their fear "said nothing to anyone."

**28:9–10** Although these verses are peculiar to Matthew, there are similarities between them and John's account of the appearance of Jesus to Mary Magdalene (Jn 20:17). In both there is a touching of Jesus' body, and a command of Jesus to bear a message to his disciples, designated as his *brothers*. Matthew may have drawn upon a tradition that appears in a different form in John. Jesus' words to the women are mainly a repetition of those of the angel (Mt 28:5a, 7b).

**28:11–15** This account indicates that the dispute between Christians and Jews about the empty tomb was not whether the tomb was empty but why.

**28:16–20** This climactic scene has been called a "proleptic parousia," for it gives a foretaste of the final glorious coming of the Son of Man (Mt 26:64). Then his triumph will be manifest to all; now it is revealed only to *the disciples*, who are commissioned to announce it to *all nations* and bring them to belief in Jesus and obedience to his commandments.

**28:16** *The eleven*: the number recalls the tragic defection of Judas Iscariot. *To the mountain...ordered them*: since the message to the *disciples* was simply that they were to go to Galilee (Mt 28:10), some think that *the mountain* comes from a tradition of the message known to Matthew and alluded to here. For the significance of *the mountain*, see note on Mt 17:1.

---

*
**28:1–10** Mk 16:1–8; Lk 24:1–12; Jn 20:1–10.
**28:2** 25:51.
**28:3** 17:2.
**28:7** 26:32.
**28:9–10** Jn 20:17.
**28:16–20** Mk 16:14–16; Lk 24:36–49; Jn 20:19–23.

MT

mountain to which Jesus had ordered them. 17† When they saw him, they worshiped, but they doubted. 18†* Then Jesus approached and said to them, "All power in heaven and on earth has been given to me. 19* Go, therefore,† and make disciples of all nations, baptizing them in the name of the Father, and of the Son, and of the holy Spirit, 20* teaching them to observe all that I have commanded you.† And behold, I am with you always, until the end of the age."

---

† **28:17** *But they doubted*: the Greek can also be translated, "but some doubted." The verb occurs elsewhere in the New Testament only in Mt 14:31 where it is associated with Peter's being of "little faith." For the meaning of that designation, see note on Mt 6:30.

**28:18** *All power...me*: the Greek word here translated *power* is the same as that found in the LXX translation of Dn 7:13–14 where one "like a son of man" is given *power* and an everlasting kingdom by God. The risen Jesus here claims universal power, i.e., *in heaven and on earth*.

**28:19** *Therefore*: since universal power belongs to the risen Jesus (Mt 28:18), he gives the eleven a mission that is universal. They are to *make disciples of all nations*. While *all nations* is understood by some scholars as referring only to all Gentiles, it is probable that it included the Jews as well. *Baptizing them*: baptism is the means of entrance into the community of the risen one, the Church. *In the name of the Father...holy Spirit*: this is

perhaps the clearest expression in the New Testament of trinitarian belief. It may have been the baptismal formula of Matthew's church, but primarily it designates the effect of baptism, the union of the one baptized with the Father, Son, and holy Spirit.

**28:20** *All that I have commanded you*: the moral teaching found in this gospel, preeminently that of the Sermon on the Mount (Mt 5–7). The commandments of Jesus are the standard of Christian conduct, not the Mosaic law as such, even though some of the Mosaic commandments have now been invested with the authority of Jesus. *Behold, I am with you always*: the promise of Jesus' real though invisible presence echoes the name Emmanuel given to him in the infancy narrative; see note on Mt 1:23. *End of the age*: see notes on Mt 13:39 and Mt 24:3.

---

**28:18** Dn 7:14 LXX.          **28:20** 1:23; 13:39; 24:3.
**28:19** Acts 1:8.

# The Gospel According to
# Mark

## INTRODUCTION

### James A. Kelhoffer

This introduction to the Gospel of Mark covers five points: the date of the book, its author, secrecy about Jesus' identity in Mark, the Twelve's lack of understanding about Jesus, and the importance of a readiness to suffer as Jesus' follower.

## The Date of Mark's Gospel

During the First Roman-Jewish War, the Romans captured the city of Jerusalem and burned the Jewish Temple. The traumatic fall of Jerusalem in the year 70 CE had profound implications for the development of the two religious traditions that would come to be known as "Judaism" and "Christianity." For Jews, the destruction of the Temple meant the cessation of sacrifices and other priestly functions prescribed in the Mosaic law, and therefore necessitated that a new understanding of the Abrahamic covenant emerge. For Jesus' followers, the fall of Jerusalem also resulted in a break with the Palestinian context of both the historical Jesus and the earliest communities of Jesus' followers in Palestine.

Most scholars date Mark, the earliest NT Gospel, to around 70 CE, holding that the predicted appearance of the "desolating abomination" (Mk 13:14) refers to the imminent or the recent destruction of the Temple in Jerusalem. Scholars debate whether this prediction best fits a context shortly before (ca. 67–70 CE) or after (ca. 70–75 CE) the destruction of the Temple. If an approximate date of 70 CE is accepted, between the time of Jesus' crucifixion and the writing of this Gospel, Mark and his community had approximately four decades to reflect on the meaning of Jesus' life, teachings, death, and Resurrection. Such a date also suggests that some of Jesus' followers faced a

recent or an ongoing context of hardship due to, or analogous to that of, the First Roman-Jewish War. The teaching requiring disciples to take up their cross and follow Jesus (8:34) may reflect an upheaval such as the one caused by this war.

## The Author of This Gospel

All four of the NT Gospels were written anonymously. At some point in the second century, the name "Mark" came to be associated with this Gospel. The earliest attribution to someone named "Mark" comes from a church leader named Papias from the town of Hierapolis (ca. 110/120 CE), four or five decades after Mark was written. Our source for Papias is the church historian Eusebius of Caesarea (d. ca. 339 CE), who wrote around 200 years after Papias. Papias describes "Mark" not as a disciple of Jesus, but as the "interpreter" of Peter.[1]

---

### Outline of Mark

**I.** **The Preparation for the Public Ministry of Jesus (1:1–13)**

**II.** **The Mystery of Jesus (1:14–8:26)**

**III.** **The Mystery Begins to Be Revealed (8:27–9:32)**

**IV.** **The Full Revelation of the Mystery (9:33–16:8)**
**The Longer Ending (16:9–20)**
**The Shorter Ending**
**The Freer Logion (in the note on 16:9–20)**

---

1. Eusebius, *Ecclesiastical History,* 3.39.15.

Notably, the author of Mark himself never suggests that he was a follower of the earthly Jesus, let alone an apostle. The identification of "Alexander and Rufus" as the sons of "Simon, a Cyrenian" (Mk 15:21) suggests that, subsequent to the crucifixion, at least one generation had passed before Mark was written.

Papias says that Mark did not write down Peter's recollections "in order" but "as needs dictated." That is to say, Papias recognizes Mark not merely as a collector of materials about Jesus but, rather, as an *author* who, after purportedly arranging Peter's "memoirs," wrote for the needs of a particular situation or community. Scholarship today holds that the author of Mark made use of a variety of earlier oral and written traditions about Jesus, shaping those traditions to emphasize certain points (e.g., secrecy, misunderstanding, and suffering, discussed below). Eusebius also reports that Papias preferred the apostles' "living and enduring voice" to traditions about Jesus taken "from books," since the origin and reliability of writings, including Gospels, can be uncertain.[2]

Understandably, scholars have questioned the reliability of an attribution of this Gospel to someone named "Mark" who, in fact, was Peter's "interpreter." Consider how plausible it would be for someone today to claim to accurately preserve a tradition from the time of the French revolutionary and dictator Napoleon Bonaparte (d. 1821) about the authorship of an early eighteenth-century novel. In any case, Papias's attribution of this work to Mark (whether historically accurate or not) attests to an identification that gained popularity in the second and later centuries, as well as in later copies of Mark bearing the title "According to Mark" or "the Gospel According to Mark."

## Secrecy about Jesus

At the beginning of Mark, Jesus proclaims, "This is the time of fulfillment. The kingdom of God is at hand. Repent, and believe in the gospel" (Mk 1:15). One might expect that "the gospel" and message about Jesus would be proclaimed openly thereafter. On the contrary, Jesus orders the demons he casts out not to identify him

as "the Holy One of God" (1:23–25; cf. 1:34; 3:11–12). Additionally, when Jesus heals a twelve-year-old girl, a miracle that only three disciples and the girl's parents witnessed, "he gave strict orders that no one should know" what had happened (5:41–43; cf. 5:37–40). Later in Mark, even when Peter (correctly, if vaguely) identifies Jesus as "the Messiah" (or God's "anointed one"), Jesus warns the disciples "not to tell anyone about him" (8:29–30). However prominent, the theme of secrecy in Mark is not consistently narrated. At one point, a man healed of leprosy actually ignores Jesus' command to "tell no one anything"; instead, the man "spread the report abroad" (1:40–45). In another instance, Jesus himself breaks the pattern of secrecy by commanding a former demoniac whom he has healed, "Go home to your family and announce to them all that the Lord in his pity has done for you" (5:18–20). One may consider this theme of secrecy in relation to another curious emphasis in this Gospel, namely the disciples' misunderstanding.

## The Disciples' Misunderstanding about Jesus

In addition to the need for secrecy about Jesus' miracles and about Jesus himself, Mark calls attention to the disciples' lack of understanding about Jesus' miracles and identity. Since Jesus appointed the Twelve as apostles to "be with him," to preach, and to drive out demons (Mk 3:14–15), it is noteworthy that in Mark the apostles themselves seem to comprehend so little about Jesus. They have a promising start as followers of Jesus: they accept Jesus' call to "follow" him (1:16–20; 2:13–14; cf. 10:28), and Jesus gives exclusively to them the secrets of God's kingdom (4:11–13). They even conduct a successful mission of preaching, exorcising demons, and healing (6:6b–13; cf. 6:30).

Nevertheless, Mark elsewhere offers an overwhelmingly negative depiction of the disciples. Three passages highlight their lack of faith and understanding (Mk 4:35–41; 6:47–52; 8:14–21). They fail to understand about the miraculous feeding of 5,000 men and

MK

their families (6:52a; cf. 6:34–44); instead, their "hearts were hardened" (6:52b). Their failure to understand what Jesus is about manifests itself in their squabbling for prominence and their resentment of the success of other miracle-workers (9:33–41; 10:35–41; 10:13–16). Jesus' arrest is preceded not only by Judas's betrayal (14:1–2, 10–11) but also by Peter, James, and John's failure to keep watch while Jesus prays in Gethsemane (14:32–42). When Jesus is arrested, the Twelve flee without offering any resistance or demonstration of loyalty to their teacher (14:43–52). Their collective betrayal of Jesus contrasts markedly with their earlier promise not to deny Jesus and, if necessary, to "die with" him (14:31). Subsequent to Peter's three denials of association with Jesus and his tearful remorse (14:66–72), none of the Twelve appears again in Mark's narrative. The Gospel's sudden ending at Mk 16:8, with a similarly unfavorable depiction of other fearful and silent followers of Jesus, precludes a narrated reconciliation between Jesus and the Twelve who had abandoned him.

## Following Jesus Requires a Readiness to Face Hardship

At an important turning point occurring roughly in the middle of this Gospel, Jesus reveals for the first time that it is necessary for him to suffer, die, and rise from the dead (Mk 8:31). Jesus also states that anyone who wishes to follow him must be prepared to "take up his [or her] cross" (8:34). Above we mentioned Jesus' command that Peter and the other disciples keep quiet about Jesus' identity as Messiah (8:29–30). Although Peter had answered correctly that Jesus was the Messiah, his answer did not include an acknowledgment that Jesus would be a *suffering* Messiah. Nor has it been clear until this point in Mark's narrative that following Jesus requires a readiness to face hardship. Jesus' newly disclosed requirements for understanding his mission and being his follower could account for the need for secrecy: for Mark, a message about Jesus as a miracle worker would be incomplete without a comprehension of his suffering.

To Mark's audience, taking up one's cross (Mk 8:34) would call to mind the Roman practice of crucifixion and how dangerous a wholehearted commitment to following Jesus could be. Jesus also teaches that saving one's life requires losing it, but assures his listeners that "whoever loses his [or her] life for my sake and that of the gospel will save it" (8:35). Thus Mark's message about Jesus stipulates that there is no easy and painless way to the kingdom of God—there is no "cheap grace." Those who embrace the benefits of Christ's sacrifice must themselves be prepared to emulate the self-sacrifice exemplified by Jesus' crucifixion.

How, then, shall we interpret the Markan disciples, who so often do not live up to, or even comprehend, Jesus' message and requirements for discipleship? Clearly, they are on the right track for having "given up everything and followed" Jesus (Mk 10:28), as well as in affirming a readiness to "die with" him (14:31). But their flight at Jesus' arrest (14:43–50) and Peter's denials of association with Jesus (14:66–72) would offer to Mark's community examples of how *not* to follow Jesus. Contrasting with the numerous failures of the Twelve in Mark are other characters who offer positive models. One of them is the anonymous woman who, despite the objections of "some" (possibly some of the Twelve), anointed Jesus' body for burial with a "perfumed oil" (14:3–9). There is also Simon of Cyrene, who carries Jesus' cross for him (15:21). Although Simon's service is not voluntary, the occurrences of the verb "take up/carry" and the noun "cross" in both 8:34 and 15:21 make clear Mark's allusion to Jesus' earlier invitation to discipleship by a readiness to take up one's cross in 8:34. Finally, it is perhaps ironic that a centurion, that is, a Gentile and a leader of the Roman military occupation, recognizes the crucified Jesus as "Son of God" (15:39). The centurion's identification of Jesus as a suffering Messiah is precisely what Peter, now conspicuously absent at the end of Mark, had earlier rejected (8:31–33). In this Gospel's overall message, the need for both a recognition of Jesus' suffering and a readiness to face hardship and danger as Jesus' follower offers both a promise to those who endure and a warning to others who, like the Markan disciples, may consider Jesus' experience of suffering to be incidental to their calling as Jesus' followers.

## Conclusion

We have touched upon Mark's date and author, as well as the author's handling of the themes of secrecy, misunderstanding, and suffering. As you read this Gospel, crafted by an anonymous author in a time of war and hardship, reflect on how these puzzle pieces could fit together in Mark's overall picture of Jesus. ■

# THE GOSPEL ACCORDING TO MARK

## New American Bible, Introduction

This shortest of all New Testament gospels is likely the first to have been written, yet it often tells of Jesus' ministry in more detail than either Matthew or Luke (for example, the miracle stories at Mk 5:1–20 or Mk 9:14–29). It recounts what Jesus did in a vivid style, where one incident follows directly upon another. In this almost breathless narrative, Mark stresses Jesus' message about the kingdom of God now breaking into human life as good news (Mk 1:14–15) and Jesus himself as the gospel of God (Mk 1:1; 8:35; 10:29). Jesus is the Son whom God has sent to rescue humanity by serving and by sacrificing his life (Mk 10:45).

The opening verse about good news in Mark (Mk 1:1) serves as a title for the entire book. The action begins with the appearance of John the Baptist, a messenger of God attested by scripture. But John points to a mightier one, Jesus, at whose baptism God speaks from heaven, declaring Jesus his Son. The Spirit descends upon Jesus, who eventually, it is promised, will baptize "with the holy Spirit." This presentation of who Jesus really is (Mk 1:1–13) is rounded out with a brief reference to the temptation of Jesus and how Satan's attack fails. Jesus as Son of God will be victorious, a point to be remembered as one reads of Jesus' death and the enigmatic ending to Mark's Gospel.

The key verses at Mk 1:14–15, which are programmatic, summarize what Jesus proclaims as gospel: fulfillment, the nearness of the kingdom, and therefore the need for repentance and for faith. After the call of the first four disciples, all fishermen (Mk 1:16–20), we see Jesus engaged in teaching (Mk 1:21, 22, 27), preaching (Mk 1:38, 39), and healing (Mk 1:29–31, 34, 40–45), and exorcising demons (Mk 1:22–27, 34–39). The content of Jesus' teaching is only rarely stated, and then chiefly in parables (Mk 4) about the kingdom. His cures, especially on the sabbath (Mk 3:1–5); his claim, like God, to forgive sins (Mk 2:3–12); his table fellowship with tax collectors and sinners (Mk 2:14–17); and the statement that his followers need not now fast but should rejoice while Jesus is present (Mk 2:18–22), all stir up opposition that will lead to Jesus' death (Mk 3:6).

In Mark, Jesus is portrayed as immensely popular with the people in Galilee during his ministry (Mk 2:2; 3:7; 4:1). He appoints twelve disciples to help preach and drive out demons, just as he does (Mk 3:13–19). He continues to work many miracles; the blocks Mk 4:35–6:44 and Mk 6:45–7:10 are cycles of stories about healings, miracles at the Sea of Galilee, and marvelous feedings of the crowds. Jesus' teaching in Mk 7 exalts the word of God over "the tradition of the elders" and sees defilement as a matter of the heart, not of unclean foods. Yet opposition mounts. Scribes charge that Jesus is possessed by Beelzebul (Mk 3:22). His relatives think him "out of his mind" (Mk 3:21). Jesus' kinship is with those who do the will of God, in a new eschatological family, not even with mother, brothers, or sisters by blood ties (Mk 3:31–35; cf. Mk 6:1–6). But all too often his own disciples do not understand Jesus (Mk 4:13, 40; 6:52; 8:17–21). The fate of John the Baptist (Mk 6:17–29) hints ominously at Jesus' own passion (Mk 9:13; cf. Mk 8:31).

A breakthrough seemingly comes with Peter's confession that Jesus is the Christ (Messiah; Mk 8:27–30). But Jesus himself emphasizes his passion (Mk 8:31; 9:31; 10:33–34), not glory in the kingdom (Mk 10:35–45). Momentarily he is glimpsed in his true identity when he is transfigured before three of the disciples (Mk 9:2–8), but by and large Jesus is depicted in Mark as moving obediently along the way to his cross in Jerusalem. Occasionally there are miracles (Mk 9:17–27; 10:46–52; 11:12–14, 20–21, the only such account in Jerusalem), sometimes teachings (Mk 10:2–11, 23–31), but the greatest concern is with discipleship (Mk 8:34–9:1; 9:33–50). For the disciples do not grasp the mystery being revealed (Mk 9:32; 10:32, 38). One of them will betray him, Judas (Mk 14:10–11, 43–45); one will deny him, Peter (Mk 14:27, 31, 54, 66–72); all eleven men will desert Jesus (Mk 14:27, 50).

The passion account, with its condemnation of Jesus by the Sanhedrin (Mk 14:53, 55–65; 15:1a) and sentencing by Pilate (Mk 15:1b–15), is prefaced with the entry into Jerusalem (Mk 11:1–11), ministry and controversies there (Mk 11:15–12:44), Jesus' Last Supper with the disciples (Mk 14:1–26), and his arrest at Gethsemane (Mk 14:32–52). A chapter of apocalyptic tone about the destruction of the temple (Mk 13:1–2, 14–23) and the coming of the Son of Man (Mk 13:24–27), a discourse filled with promises (Mk 13:11, 31) and admonitions to be watchful (Mk 13:2, 23, 37), is significant for Mark's Gospel, for it helps one see that God, in Jesus, will be victorious after the cross and at the end of history.

The Gospel of Mark ends in the most ancient manuscripts with an abrupt scene at Jesus' tomb, which the women find empty (Mk 16:1–8). His own prophecy of Mk 14:28 is reiterated, that Jesus goes before the disciples into Galilee; "there you will see him." These words may imply resurrection appearances there, or Jesus' parousia there, or the start of Christian mission, or a return to the roots depicted in Mk 1:9, 14–15 in Galilee. Other hands have attached additional endings after Mk 16:8; see note on Mk 16:9–20.

The framework of Mark's Gospel is partly geographical: Galilee (Mk 1:14–9:49), through the area "across the Jordan" (Mk 10:1) and through Jericho (Mk 10:46–52), to Jerusalem (Mk 11:1–16:8). Only rarely does Jesus go into Gentile territory (Mk 5:1–20; 7:24–37), but those who acknowledge him there and the centurion who confesses Jesus at the cross (Mk 15:39) presage the gospel's expansion into the world beyond Palestine.

Mark's Gospel is even more oriented to christology. Jesus is the Son of God (Mk 1:11; 9:7; 15:39; cf. Mk 1:1; 14:61). He is the Messiah, the anointed king of Davidic descent (Mk 12:35; 15:32), the Greek for which, Christos, has, by the time Mark wrote, become in effect a proper name (Mk 1:1; 9:41). Jesus is also seen as Son of Man, a term used in Mark not simply as a substitute for "I" or for humanity in general (cf. Mk 2:10, 27–28; 14:21) or with reference to a mighty figure who is to come (Mk 13:26; 14:62), but also in connection with Jesus' predestined, necessary path of suffering and vindication (Mk 8:31; 10:45).

The unfolding of Mark's story about Jesus is sometimes viewed by interpreters as centered around the term "mystery." The word is employed just once, at Mk 4:11, in the singular, and its content there is the kingdom, the open secret that God's reign is now breaking into human life with its reversal of human values. There is a related sense in which Jesus' real identity remained a secret during his lifetime, according to Mark, although demons and demoniacs knew it (Mk 1:24; 3:11; 5:7); Jesus warned against telling of his mighty deeds and revealing his identity (Mk 1:44; 3:12; 5:43; 7:36; 8:26, 30), an injunction sometimes broken (Mk 1:45; cf. Mk 5:19–20). Further, Jesus teaches by parables, according to Mark, in such a way that those "outside" the kingdom do not understand, but only those to whom the mystery has been granted by God.

Mark thus shares with Paul, as well as with other parts of the New Testament, an emphasis on election (Mk 13:20, 22) and upon the gospel as Christ and his cross (cf. 1 Cor 1:23). Yet in Mark the person of Jesus is also depicted with an unaffected naturalness. He reacts to events with authentic human emotion: pity (Mk 1:44), anger (Mk 3:5), triumph (Mk 4:40), sympathy (Mk 5:36; 6:34), surprise (Mk 6:9), admiration (Mk 7:29; 10:21), sadness (Mk 14:33–34), and indignation (Mk 14:48–49).

Although the book is anonymous, apart from the ancient heading "According to Mark" in manuscripts, it has traditionally been assigned to John Mark, in whose mother's house (at Jerusalem) Christians assembled (Acts 12:12). This Mark was a cousin of Barnabas (Col 4:10) and accompanied Barnabas and Paul on a missionary journey (Acts 12:25; 13:3; 15:36–39). He appears in Pauline letters (2 Tm 4:11; Phlm 24) and with Peter (1 Pt 5:13). Papias (ca. A.D. 135) described Mark as Peter's "interpreter," a view found in other patristic writers. Petrine influence should not, however, be exaggerated. The evangelist has put together various oral and possibly written sources—miracle stories, parables, sayings, stories of controversies, and the passion—so as to speak of the crucified Messiah for Mark's own day.

Traditionally, the gospel is said to have been

written shortly before A.D. 70 in Rome, at a time of impending persecution and when destruction loomed over Jerusalem. Its audience seems to have been Gentile, unfamiliar with Jewish customs (hence Mk 7:3–4, 11). The book aimed to equip such Christians to stand faithful in the face of persecution (Mk 13:9–13), while going on with the proclamation of the gospel begun in Galilee (Mk 13:10; 14:9). Modern research often proposes as the author an unknown Hellenistic Jewish Christian, possibly in Syria, and perhaps shortly after the year 70.

The principal divisions of the Gospel according to Mark are the following:

I. The Preparation for the Public Ministry of Jesus (1:1–13)
II. The Mystery of Jesus (1:14–8:26)
III. The Mystery Begins to Be Revealed (8:27–9:32)
IV. The Full Revelation of the Mystery (9:33–16:8)
The Longer Ending (16:9–20)
The Shorter Ending
The Freer Logion (in the note on 16:9–20) ∎

# Mark

## I. THE PREPARATION FOR THE PUBLIC MINISTRY OF JESUS†

**1** ¹The beginning of the gospel of Jesus Christ [the Son of God].†

**The Preaching of John the Baptist.** ²* As it is written in Isaiah the prophet:†*

> "Behold, I am sending my messenger
> ahead of you;
> he will prepare your way.
> ³* A voice of one crying out in the desert:
> 'Prepare the way of the Lord,
> make straight his paths.'"

⁴John [the] Baptist appeared in the desert proclaiming a baptism of repentance for the forgiveness of sins. ⁵People of the whole Judean countryside and all the inhabitants of Jerusalem were going out to him and were being baptized by him in the Jordan River as they acknowledged their sins. ⁶John was clothed in camel's hair, with a leather belt around his waist.† He fed on locusts and wild honey. ⁷And this is what he proclaimed: "One mightier than I is coming after me. I am not worthy to stoop and loosen the thongs of his sandals. ⁸†* I have baptized you with water; he will baptize you with the holy Spirit."

**The Baptism of Jesus.** ⁹* It happened in those days that Jesus came from Nazareth of Galilee and was baptized in the Jordan by John. ¹⁰On coming up out of the water he saw the heavens being torn open and the Spirit, like a dove, descending upon him.† ¹¹* And a voice came from the heavens, "You are my beloved Son; with you I am well pleased."

**The Temptation of Jesus.**† ¹²At once the Spirit drove him out into the desert,* ¹³and he remained in the desert for forty days, tempted by Satan. He was among wild beasts, and the angels ministered to him.

## II. THE MYSTERY OF JESUS

**The Beginning of the Galilean Ministry.** ¹⁴* After John had been arrested,† Jesus came to Galilee proclaiming the gospel of God: ¹⁵* "This is the time of fulfillment. The kingdom of God is at hand. Repent, and believe in the gospel."

---

**1:1–13** The prologue of the Gospel according to Mark begins with the title (Mk 1:1) followed by three events preparatory to Jesus' preaching: (1) the appearance in the Judean wilderness of John, baptizer, preacher of repentance, and precursor of Jesus (Mk 1:2–8); (2) the baptism of Jesus, at which a voice from heaven acknowledges Jesus to be God's Son, and the holy Spirit descends on him (Mk 1:9–11); (3) the temptation of Jesus by Satan (Mk 1:12–13).

**1:1** *The gospel of Jesus Christ [the Son of God]*: the "good news" of salvation in and through Jesus, crucified and risen, acknowledged by the Christian community as Messiah (Mk 8:29; 14:61–62) and Son of God (Mk 1:11; 9:7; 15:39), although some important manuscripts here omit *the Son of God*.

**1:2–3** Although Mark attributes the prophecy to Isaiah, the text is a combination of Mal 3:1; Is 40:3; Ex 23:20; cf. Mt 11:10; Lk 7:27. John's ministry is seen as God's prelude to the saving mission of his Son. *The way of the Lord*: this prophecy of Deutero-Isaiah concerning the end of the Babylonian exile is here applied to the coming of Jesus; John the Baptist is to prepare the way for him.

**1:6** *Clothed in camel's hair…waist*: the Baptist's garb recalls that of Elijah in 2 Kgs 1:8. Jesus speaks of the Baptist as Elijah who has already come (Mk 9:11–13; Mt 17:10–12; cf. Mal 3:23–24; Lk 1:17).

**1:8–9** Through the life-giving baptism with the holy Spirit (Mk 1:8), Jesus will create a new people of God. But first he identifies himself with the people of Israel in submitting to John's baptism of repentance and in bearing on their behalf the burden of God's decisive judgment (Mk 1:9; cf. Mk 1:4). As in the desert of Sinai, so here in the wilderness of Judea, Israel's sonship with God is to be renewed.

**1:10–11** *He saw the heavens…and the Spirit…upon him*: indicating divine intervention in fulfillment of promise. Here the descent of the Spirit on Jesus is meant, anointing him for his ministry; cf. Is 11:2; 42:1; 61:1; 63:9. *A voice…with you I am well pleased*: God's acknowledgment of Jesus as his unique Son, the object of his love. His approval of Jesus is the assurance that Jesus will fulfill his messianic mission of salvation.

**1:12–13** The same Spirit who descended on Jesus in his baptism now drives him into the desert for forty days. The result is radical confrontation and temptation by Satan who attempts to frustrate the work of God. The presence of wild beasts may indicate the horror and danger of the desert regarded as the abode of demons or may reflect the paradise motif of harmony among all creatures; cf. Is 11:6–9. The presence of ministering angels to sustain Jesus recalls the angel who guided the Israelites in the desert in the first Exodus (Ex 14:19; 23:20) and the angel who supplied nourishment to Elijah in the wilderness (1 Kgs 19:5–7). The combined forces of good and evil were present to Jesus in the desert. His sustained obedience brings forth the new Israel of God there where Israel's rebellion had brought death and alienation.

**1:14–15** *After John had been arrested*: in the plan of God, Jesus was not to proclaim the good news of salvation prior to the termination of the Baptist's active mission. *Galilee*: in the Marcan account, scene of the major part of Jesus' public ministry before his arrest and condemnation. *The gospel of God*: not only the good news from God but about God at work in Jesus Christ. *This is the time of fulfillment*: i.e., of God's promises. *The kingdom of God…Repent*: see note on Mt 3:2.

---

**1:2–8** Mt 3:1–11; Lk 3:2–16.
**1:2** Mal 3:1.
**1:3** Is 40:3; Jn 1:23.
**1:8** Jn 1:27; Acts 1:5; 11:16.
**1:9–11** Mt 3:13–17; Lk
3:21–23; Jn 1:32–33.
**1:11** Ps 2:7.
**1:12–13** Mt 4:1–11; Lk 4:1–13.
**1:14–15** Mt 4:12–17; Lk 4:14–15.
**1:15** Mt 3:2.

MK

**The Call of the First Disciples.†** [16]* As he passed by the Sea of Galilee, he saw Simon and his brother Andrew casting their nets into the sea; they were fishermen. [17] Jesus said to them, "Come after me, and I will make you fishers of men." [18] Then they abandoned their nets and followed him. [19] He walked along a little farther and saw James, the son of Zebedee, and his brother John. They too were in a boat mending their nets. [20] Then he called them. So they left their father Zebedee in the boat along with the hired men and followed him.

**The Cure of a Demoniac.** [21]†* Then they came to Capernaum, and on the sabbath he entered the synagogue and taught. [22]* The people were astonished at his teaching, for he taught them as one having authority and not as the scribes. [23]† In their synagogue was a man with an unclean spirit; [24]† he cried out, "What have you to do with us,† Jesus of Nazareth? Have you come to destroy us? I know who you are—the Holy One of God!" [25] Jesus rebuked him and said, "Quiet! Come out of him!" [26] The unclean spirit convulsed him and with a loud cry came out of him. [27] All were amazed and asked one another, "What is this? A new teaching with authority. He commands even the unclean spirits and they obey him." [28] His fame spread everywhere throughout the whole region of Galilee.

**The Cure of Simon's Mother-in-Law.** [29]* On leaving the synagogue he entered the house of Simon and Andrew with James and John. [30] Simon's mother-in-law lay sick with a fever. They immediately told him about her. [31] He approached, grasped her hand, and helped her up. Then the fever left her and she waited on them.

**Other Healings.** [32] When it was evening, after sunset, they brought to him all who were ill or possessed by demons. [33] The whole town was gathered at the door. [34] He cured many who were sick with various diseases, and he drove out many demons, not permitting them to speak because they knew him.

**Jesus Leaves Capernaum.** [35]* Rising very early before dawn, he left and went off to a deserted place, where he prayed. [36] Simon and those who were with him pursued him [37] and on finding him said, "Everyone is looking for you." [38] He told them, "Let us go on to the nearby villages that I may preach there also. For this purpose have I come." [39] So he went into their synagogues, preaching and driving out demons throughout the whole of Galilee.

**The Cleansing of a Leper.** [40]* A leper† came to him [and kneeling down] begged him and said, "If you wish, you can make me clean." [41] Moved with pity, he stretched out his hand, touched him, and said to him, "I do will it. Be made clean."* [42] The leprosy left him immediately, and he was made clean.* [43] Then, warning him sternly, he dismissed him at once. [44] Then he said to him, "See that you tell no one anything, but go, show yourself to the priest and offer for your cleansing what Moses prescribed; that will be proof for them."* [45] The man went away and began to publicize the whole matter. He spread the report abroad so that it was impossible for Jesus to enter a town openly. He remained outside in deserted places, and people kept coming to him from everywhere.

---

† 
**1:16–20** These verses narrate the call of the first Disciples. See notes on Mt 4:18–22 and Mt 4:20.

**1:21–45** The account of a single day's ministry of Jesus on a sabbath in and outside the synagogue of Capernaum (Mk 1:21–31) combines teaching and miracles of exorcism and healing. Mention is not made of the content of the teaching but of the effect of astonishment and alarm on the people. Jesus' teaching with authority, making an absolute claim on the hearer, was in the best tradition of the ancient prophets, not of the scribes. The narrative continues with events that evening (Mk 1:32–34; see notes on Mt 8:14–17) and the next day (Mk 1:35–39). The cleansing in Mk 1:40–45 stands as an isolated story.

**1:23** *An unclean spirit:* so called because of the spirit's resistance to the holiness of God. The spirit knows and fears the power of Jesus to destroy his influence; cf. Mk 1:32, 34; 3:11; 6:13.

**1:24–25** *The Holy One of God:* not a confession but an at-

tempt to ward off Jesus' power, reflecting the notion that use of the precise name of an opposing spirit would guarantee mastery over him. Jesus silenced the cry of the unclean spirit and drove him out of the man.

**1:24** *What have you to do with us?:* see note on Jn 2:4.

**1:40** *A leper:* for the various forms of skin disease, see Lv 13:1–50 and the note on Lv 13:2–4. There are only two instances in the Old Testament in which God is shown to have cured a leper (Nm 12:10–15; 2 Kgs 5:1–14). The law of Moses provided for the ritual purification of a leper. In curing the leper, Jesus assumes that the priests will reinstate the cured man into the religious community. See also note on Lk 5:14.

---

*
| | |
|---|---|
| **1:16–20** Mt 4:18–22; Lk 5:2–11. | **1:35–39** Lk 4:42–44. |
| **1:21–28** Lk 4:31–37. | **1:40–44** Mt 8:2–4; Lk 5:12–14. |
| **1:22** Mt 7:28–29. | **1:41** Lk 5:30. |
| **1:29–34** Mt 8:14–16; Lk 4:38–41. | **1:42** Lk 17:14. |
| | **1:44** Lv 14:2–32. |

# 2 The Healing of a Paralytic. [1]† When Jesus returned to Capernaum* after some days, it became known that he was at home.† [2] Many gathered together so that there was no longer room for them, not even around the door, and he preached the word to them. [3] They came bringing to him a paralytic carried by four men. [4] Unable to get near Jesus because of the crowd, they opened up the roof above him. After they had broken through, they let down the mat on which the paralytic was lying. [5]† When Jesus saw their faith, he said to the paralytic, "Child, your sins are forgiven." [6]† Now some of the scribes were sitting there asking themselves, [7] "Why does this man speak that way?† He is blaspheming. Who but God alone can forgive sins?"* [8] Jesus immediately knew in his mind what they were thinking to themselves, so he said, "Why are you thinking such things in your hearts? [9] Which is easier, to say to the paralytic, 'Your sins are forgiven,' or to say, 'Rise, pick up your mat and walk'? [10]† But that you may know that the Son of Man has authority to forgive sins on earth"— [11] he said to the paralytic, "I say to you, rise, pick up your mat, and go home." [12] He rose, picked up his mat at once, and went away in the sight of everyone. They were all astounded and glorified God, saying, "We have never seen anything like this."

## The Call of Levi. [13]†* Once again he went out along the sea. All the crowd came to him and he taught them. [14]* As he passed by,† he saw Levi, son of Alphaeus, sitting at the customs post. He said to him, "Follow me." And he got up and followed him. [15] While he was at table in his house,† many tax collectors and sinners sat with Jesus and his disciples; for there were many who followed him. [16]† Some scribes who were Pharisees saw that he was eating with sinners and tax collectors and said to his disciples, "Why does he eat with tax collectors and sinners?" [17] Jesus heard this and said to them [that], "Those who are well do not need a physician,† but the sick do. I did not come to call the righteous but sinners."

## The Question About Fasting.† [18] The disciples of John and of the Pharisees were accustomed to fast.* People came to him and objected, "Why do the disciples of John and the disciples of the Pharisees fast, but your disciples do not fast?" [19] Jesus answered them, "Can the wedding guests fast† while the bridegroom is with them? As long as they have the bridegroom with them they cannot fast. [20] But the days will come when the bridegroom is taken away from them, and then they will fast on that day. [21] No one sews a piece of unshrunken cloth on an old cloak. If he does, its fullness

---

† **2:1–3:6** This section relates a series of conflicts between Jesus and the scribes and Pharisees in which the growing opposition of the latter leads to their plot to put Jesus to death (Mk 3:6).

**2:1–2** *He was at home*: to the crowds that gathered in and outside the house Jesus *preached the word*, i.e., the gospel concerning the nearness of the kingdom and the necessity of repentance and faith (Mk 1:14).

**2:5** It was the faith of the paralytic and those who carried him that moved Jesus to heal the sick man. Accounts of other miracles of Jesus reveal more and more his emphasis on faith as the requisite for exercising his healing powers (Mk 5:34; 9:23–24; 10:52).

**2:6** *Scribes*: trained in oral interpretation of the written law; in Mark's gospel, adversaries of Jesus, with one exception (Mk 12:28, 34).

**2:7** *He is blaspheming*: an accusation made here and repeated during the trial of Jesus (Mk 14:60–64).

**2:10** *But that you may know that the Son of Man...on earth*: although Mk 2:8–9 are addressed to the scribes, the sudden interruption of thought and structure in Mk 2:10 seems not addressed to them nor to the paralytic. Moreover, the early public use of the designation "Son of Man" to unbelieving scribes is most unlikely. The most probable explanation is that Mark's insertion of Mk 2:10 is a commentary addressed to Christians for whom he recalls this miracle and who already accept in faith that Jesus is Messiah and Son of God.

**2:13** *He taught them*: see note on Mk 1:21–45.

**2:14** *As he passed by*: see note on Mk 1:16–20. *Levi, son of Alphaeus*: see note on Mt 9:9. *Customs post*: such tax collectors paid a fixed sum for the right to collect customs duties within their districts. Since whatever they could collect above this amount constituted their profit, the abuse of extortion was widespread among

them. Hence, Jewish customs officials were regarded as sinners (Mk 2:16), outcasts of society, and disgraced along with their families. *He got up and followed him*: i.e., became a disciple of Jesus.

**2:15** *In his house*: cf. Mk 2:1; Mt 9:10. Lk 5:29 clearly calls it Levi's house.

**2:16–17** This and the following conflict stories reflect a similar pattern: a statement of fact, a question of protest, and a reply by Jesus.

**2:17** *Do not need a physician*: this maxim of Jesus with its implied irony was uttered to silence his adversaries who objected that he ate with *tax collectors and sinners* (Mk 2:16). Because the scribes and Pharisees were self-righteous, they were not capable of responding to Jesus' call to repentance and faith in the gospel.

**2:18–22** This conflict over the question of fasting has the same pattern as Mk 2:16–17; see notes on Mt 9:15; 9:16–17.

**2:19** *Can the wedding guests fast?*: the bridal metaphor expresses a new relationship of love between God and his people in the person and mission of Jesus to his disciples. It is the inauguration of the new and joyful messianic time of fulfillment and the passing of the old. Any attempt at assimilating the Pharisaic practice of fasting, or of extending the preparatory discipline of John's disciples beyond the arrival of the bridegroom, would be as futile as sewing a *piece of unshrunken cloth on an old cloak* or pouring *new wine into old wineskins* with the resulting destruction of both cloth and wine (Mk 2:21–22). Fasting is rendered superfluous during the earthly ministry of Jesus; cf. Mk 2:20.

---

| | |
|---|---|
| **2:1–12** Mt 9:2–8; Lk 5:18–26. | **2:14–17** Mt 9:9–13; Lk 5:27–32. |
| **2:7** Is 43:25. | |
| **2:13** 4:1. | **2:18–22** Mt 9:14–17; Lk 5:33–39. |

M K

pulls away, the new from the old, and the tear gets worse. <sup>22</sup> Likewise, no one pours new wine into old wineskins. Otherwise, the wine will burst the skins, and both the wine and the skins are ruined. Rather, new wine is poured into fresh wineskins."

**The Disciples and the Sabbath.**† <sup>23</sup> As he was passing through a field of grain on the sabbath, his disciples began to make a path while picking the heads of grain.* <sup>24</sup> At this the Pharisees said to him, "Look, why are they doing what is unlawful on the sabbath?"* <sup>25</sup> He said to them, "Have you never read what David did† when he was in need and he and his companions were hungry? <sup>26</sup> How he went into the house of God when Abiathar was high priest and ate the bread of offering that only the priests could lawfully eat, and shared it with his companions?"* <sup>27</sup> Then he said to them, "The sabbath was made for man,† not man for the sabbath.* <sup>28</sup>† That is why the Son of Man is lord even of the sabbath."

**3** **A Man with a Withered Hand.** <sup>1</sup>† Again he entered the synagogue.* There was a man there who had a withered hand. <sup>2</sup> They watched him closely to see if he would cure him on the sabbath so that they might accuse him. <sup>3</sup> He said to the man with the withered hand, "Come up here before us." <sup>4</sup> Then he said to them, "Is it lawful to do good on the sabbath rather than to do evil, to save life rather than to destroy it?" But they remained silent. <sup>5</sup> Looking around at them with anger and grieved at their hardness of heart, he said to the man, "Stretch out your hand." He stretched it out and his hand was restored.* <sup>6</sup>† The Pharisees went out and immediately took counsel with the Herodians against him to put him to death.

**The Mercy of Jesus.** <sup>7</sup>† Jesus withdrew toward the sea with his disciples.* A large number of people [followed] from Galilee and from Judea. <sup>8</sup> Hearing what he was doing, a large number of people came to him also from Jerusalem, from Idumea, from beyond the Jordan, and from the neighborhood of Tyre and Sidon. <sup>9</sup> He told his disciples to have a boat ready for him because of the crowd, so that they would not crush him. <sup>10</sup> He had cured many and, as a result, those who had diseases were pressing upon him to touch him.* <sup>11</sup>† And whenever unclean spirits saw him they would fall down before him and shout, "You are the Son of God."* <sup>12</sup> He warned them sternly not to make him known.

**The Mission of the Twelve.** <sup>13</sup>* He went up the mountain† and summoned those whom he wanted and they came to him. <sup>14</sup>* He appointed twelve [whom he also named apostles] that they might be with him† and

---

† **2:23–28** This conflict regarding the sabbath follows the same pattern as in Mk 2:18–22.

**2:25–26** *Have you never read what David did?:* Jesus defends the action of his disciples on the basis of 1 Sm 21:2–7 in which an exception is made to the regulation of Lv 24:9 because of the extreme hunger of David and his men. According to 1 Samuel, the priest who gave the bread to David was Ahimelech, father of Abiathar.

**2:27** *The sabbath was made for man:* a reaffirmation of the divine intent of the sabbath to benefit Israel as contrasted with the restrictive Pharisaic tradition added to the law.

**2:28** *The Son of Man is lord even of the sabbath:* Mark's comment on the theological meaning of the incident is to benefit his Christian readers; see note on Mk 2:10.

**3:1–5** Here Jesus is again depicted in conflict with his adversaries over the question of sabbath-day observance. His opponents were already ill disposed toward him because they regarded Jesus as a violator of the sabbath. Jesus' question *Is it lawful to do good on the sabbath rather than to do evil?* places the matter in the broader theological context outside the casuistry of the scribes. The answer is obvious. Jesus heals the man with the withered hand in the sight of all and reduces his opponents to silence; cf. Jn 5:17–18.

**3:6** In reporting the plot of the Pharisees and Herodians to put Jesus to death after this series of conflicts in Galilee, Mark uses a pattern that recurs in his account of later controversies in Jerusalem (Mk 11:17–18; 12:13–17). The help of the Herodians, supporters of Herod Antipas, tetrarch of Galilee and Perea, is needed to take action against Jesus. Both series of conflicts point to their gravity and to the impending passion of Jesus.

**3:7–19** This overview of the Galilean ministry manifests the power of Jesus to draw people to himself through his teaching and deeds of power. The crowds of Jews from many regions surround Jesus (Mk 3:7–12). This phenomenon prepares the way for creating a new people of Israel. The choice and mission of the Twelve is the prelude (Mk 3:13–19).

**3:11–12** See note on Mk 1:24–25.

**3:13** *He went up the mountain:* here and elsewhere the mountain is associated with solemn moments and acts in the mission and self-revelation of Jesus (Mk 6:46; 9:2–8; 13:3). Jesus acts with authority as he *summoned those whom he wanted and they came to him.*

**3:14–15** *He appointed twelve [whom he also named apostles] that they might be with him:* literally "he made," i.e., instituted them as apostles to extend his messianic mission through them (Mk 6:7–13). See notes on Mt 10:1 and 10:2–4.

---

**2:23–28** Mt 12:1–8; Lk 6:1–5.
**2:24** 1 Dt 23:25.
**2:26** 1 Sm 21:2–7; Lv 24:5–9.
**2:27** 2 Mc 5:19.
**3:1–6** Mt 12:9–14; Lk 6:6–11.
**3:5** Lk 14:4.
**3:7–12** Mt 4:23–25; 12:15; Lk 6:17–19.
**3:10** 5:30.
**3:11** 1:34; Lk 4:41.
**3:13–19** Mt 10:1–4; Lk 6:12–16.
**3:14** 6:7.

he might send them forth to preach [15] and to have authority to drive out demons: [16]† [he appointed the twelve:] Simon, whom he named Peter; [17]James, son of Zebedee, and John the brother of James, whom he named Boanerges, that is, sons of thunder;* [18]Andrew, Philip, Bartholomew, Matthew, Thomas, James the son of Alphaeus; Thaddeus, Simon the Cananean, [19]and Judas Iscariot who betrayed him.

### Blasphemy of the Scribes.

[20]† He came home.† Again [the] crowd gathered, making it impossible for them even to eat.* [21]When his relatives heard of this they set out to seize him, for they said, "He is out of his mind."* [22]The scribes who had come from Jerusalem said, "He is possessed by Beelzebul,"† and "By the prince of demons he drives out demons."*

### Jesus and Beelzebul.

[23]Summoning them, he began to speak to them in parables, "How can Satan drive out Satan? [24]If a kingdom is divided against itself, that kingdom cannot stand. [25]And if a house is divided against itself, that house will not be able to stand. [26]And if Satan has risen up against himself and is divided, he cannot stand; that is the end of him. [27]But no one can enter a strong man's house to plunder his property unless he first ties up the strong man. Then he can plunder his house. [28]Amen, I say to you, all sins and all blasphemies that people utter will be forgiven them.* [29]But whoever blasphemes against the holy Spirit† will never have forgiveness, but is guilty of an everlasting sin." [30]For they had said, "He has an unclean spirit."

### Jesus and His Family.

[31]* His mother and his brothers arrived. Standing outside they sent word to him and called him. [32]A crowd seated around him told him, "Your mother and your brothers† [and your sisters] are outside asking for you." [33]But he said to them in reply, "Who are my mother and [my] brothers?" [34]And looking around at those seated in the circle he said, "Here are my mother and my brothers. [35][For] whoever does the will of God is my brother and sister and mother."

## 4 The Parable of the Sower.

[1]† On another occasion* he began to teach by the sea.† A very large crowd gathered around him so that he got into a boat on the sea and sat down. And the whole crowd was beside the sea on land.* [2]And he taught them at length in parables, and in the course of his instruction he said to them, [3]† "Hear this! A sower went out to sow. [4]And as he sowed, some seed fell on the path, and the birds came and ate it up. [5]Other seed fell on rocky ground where it had little soil. It sprang up at once because the soil was not deep. [6]And when the sun rose, it was scorched and it withered for lack of roots. [7]Some seed fell among thorns, and the thorns grew up and choked it and it produced no grain. [8]And some seed fell on rich soil and produced fruit. It came up and grew and yielded thirty, sixty,

---

**3:16** *Simon, whom he named Peter*: Mark indicates that Simon's name was changed on this occasion. Peter is first in all lists of the apostles (Mt 10:2; Lk 6:14; Acts 1:13; cf. 1 Cor 15:5–8).

**3:20–35** Within the narrative of the coming of Jesus' relatives (Mk 3:20–21) is inserted the account of the unbelieving scribes from Jerusalem who attributed Jesus' power over demons to Beelzebul (Mk 3:22–30); see note on Mk 5:21–43. There were those even among the relatives of Jesus who disbelieved and regarded Jesus as *out of his mind* (Mk 3:21). Against this background, Jesus is informed of the arrival of his mother and brothers [and sisters] (Mk 3:32). He responds by showing that not family ties but doing God's will (Mk 3:35) is decisive in the kingdom; cf. note on Mt 12:46–50.

**3:20** *He came home*: cf. Mk 2:1–2 and see note on Mk 2:15.

**3:22** *By Beelzebul*: see note on Mt 10:25. Two accusations are leveled against Jesus: (1) that *he is possessed* by an unclean spirit and (2) *by the prince of demons he drives out demons*. Jesus answers the second charge by a parable (Mk 3:24–27) and responds to the first charge in Mk 3:28–29.

**3:29** *Whoever blasphemes against the holy Spirit*: this sin is called *an everlasting sin* because it attributes to Satan, who is the power of evil, what is actually the work of the holy Spirit, namely, victory over the demons.

**3:32** *Your brothers*: see note on Mk 6:3.

**4:1–34** *In parables* (Mk 4:2): see note on Mt 13:3. The use of parables is typical of Jesus' enigmatic method of teaching the crowds (Mk 4:2–9, 12) as compared with the interpretation of the parables he gives to his disciples (Mk 4:10–25, 33–34) to each group according to its capacity to understand (Mk 4:9–11). The key feature of the parable at hand is the sowing of the seed (Mk 4:3), representing the breakthrough of the kingdom of God into the world. The various types of soil refer to the diversity of response accorded the word of God (Mk 4:4–7). The climax of the parable is the harvest of thirty, sixty, and a hundredfold, indicating the consummation of the kingdom (Mk 4:8). Thus both the present and the future action of God, from the initiation to the fulfillment of the kingdom, is presented through this and other parables (Mk 4:26–29, 30–32).

**4:1** *By the sea*: the shore of the Sea of Galilee or a boat near the shore (Mk 2:13; 3:7–8) is the place where Mark depicts Jesus teaching the crowds. By contrast the mountain is the scene of Jesus at prayer (Mk 6:46) or in the process of forming his disciples (Mk 3:13; 9:2).

**4:3–8** See note on Mt 13:3–8.

| | |
|---|---|
| **3:17** Mt 16:18; Jn 1:42. | **3:31–35** Mt 12:46–50; Lk |
| **3:20** 2:2. | 8:19–21. |
| **3:21** Jn 10:20. | **4:1–12** Mt 13:1–13; Lk |
| **3:22–30** Mt 12:24–32; Lk | 8:4–10. |
| 11:15–22; 12:10. | **4:1** 2:13; Lk 5:1. |
| **3:28** Lk 12:10. | |

MK

and a hundredfold." [9] He added, "Whoever has ears to hear ought to hear."

**The Purpose of the Parables.** [10] And when he was alone, those present along with the Twelve questioned him about the parables. [11] † He answered them, "The mystery of the kingdom of God has been granted to you. But to those outside everything comes in parables, [12] so that

> 'they may look and see but not perceive,
>     and hear and listen but not
>         understand,
>     in order that they may not be converted
>         and be forgiven.'" *

[13] † Jesus said to them, "Do you not understand this parable? * Then how will you understand any of the parables? [14] The sower sows the word. [15] These are the ones on the path where the word is sown. As soon as they hear, Satan comes at once and takes away the word sown in them. [16] And these are the ones sown on rocky ground who, when they hear the word, receive it at once with joy. [17] But they have no root; they last only for a time. Then when tribulation or persecution comes because of the word, they quickly fall away. [18] Those sown among thorns are another sort. They are the people who hear the word, [19] but worldly anxiety, the lure of riches, and the craving for other things intrude and choke the word, and it bears no fruit. [20] But those sown on rich soil are the ones who hear the word and accept it and bear fruit thirty and sixty and a hundredfold."

**Parable of the Lamp.** [21] * He said to them, "Is a lamp brought in to be placed under a bushel basket or under a bed, and not to be placed on a lampstand? * [22] For there is nothing hidden except to be made visible; nothing is secret except to come to light. * [23] Anyone who has ears to hear ought to hear." [24] He also told them, "Take care what you hear. The measure with which you measure will be measured out to you, and still more will be given to you. * [25] To the one who has, more will be given; from the one who has not, even what he has will be taken away." *

**Seed Grows of Itself.** [26] He said, "This is how it is with the kingdom of God; † it is as if a man were to scatter seed * on the land [27] and would sleep and rise night and day and the seed would sprout and grow, he knows not how. [28] Of its own accord the land yields fruit, first the blade, then the ear, then the full grain in the ear. [29] And when the grain is ripe, he wields the sickle at once, for the harvest has come."

**The Mustard Seed.** [30] * He said, "To what shall we compare the kingdom of God, or what parable can we use for it? [31] It is like a mustard seed that, when it is sown in the ground, is the smallest of all the seeds on the earth. [32] † But once it is sown, it springs up and becomes the largest of plants and puts forth large branches, so that the birds of the sky can dwell in its shade." [33] With many such parables * he spoke the word to them as they were able to understand it. [34] Without parables he did not speak to them, but to his own disciples he explained everything in private.

**The Calming of a Storm at Sea.** [35] † On that day, as evening drew on, he said to them, "Let us cross to the other side." * [36] Leaving the crowd, they took him with them in the boat just as he was. And other boats were with him. [37] A violent squall came up and waves were breaking over the boat, so that it was already

---

†
**4:11–12** These verses are to be viewed against their background in Mk 3:6, 22 concerning the unbelief and opposition Jesus encountered in his ministry. It is against this background that the distinction in Jesus' method becomes clear of presenting the kingdom to the disbelieving crowd in one manner and to the disciples in another. To the former it is presented in parables and the truth remains hidden; for the latter the parable is interpreted and the mystery is partially revealed because of their faith; see notes on Mt 13:11 and Mt 13:13.

**4:13–20** See note on Mt 13:18–23.

**4:26–29** Only Mark records the parable of the seed's growth. Sower and harvester are the same. The emphasis is on the power of the seed to grow of itself without human intervention (Mk 4:27). Mysteriously it produces *blade* and *ear* and *full grain* (Mk 4:28). Thus the kingdom of God initiated by Jesus in proclaiming the word develops quietly yet powerfully until

it is fully established by him at the final judgment (Mk 4:29); cf. Rev 14:15.

**4:32** The universality of the kingdom of God is indicated here; cf. Ez 17:23; 31:6; Dn 4:17–19.

**4:35–5:43** After the chapter on parables, Mark narrates four miracle stories: Mk 4:35–41; 5:1–20; and two joined together in Mk 5:21–43. See also notes on Mt 8:23–34 and 9:8–26.

---

*
| | |
|---|---|
| **4:12** Is 6:9; Jn 12:40; Acts 28:26; Rom 11:8. | **4:25** Mt 13:12; Lk 19:26. |
| **4:13–20** Mt 13:18–23; Lk 8:11–15. | **4:26–29** Jas 5:7. |
| **4:21–25** Lk 8:16–18. | **4:30–32** Mt 13:31–32; Lk 13:18–19. |
| **4:21** Mt 5:15; Lk 11:33. | **4:33–34** Mt 13:34. |
| **4:22** Mt 10:26; Lk 12:2. | **4:35–40** Mt 8:18, 23–37; Lk 8:22–25. |
| **4:24** Mt 7:2; Lk 6:38. | |

MK

filling up. [38] Jesus was in the stern, asleep on a cushion. They woke him and said to him, "Teacher, do you not care that we are perishing?" [39] He woke up, rebuked the wind, and said to the sea, "Quiet! Be still!"† The wind ceased and there was great calm. [40] Then he asked them, "Why are you terrified? Do you not yet have faith?" [41]†* They were filled with great awe and said to one another, "Who then is this whom even wind and sea obey?"

# 5 The Healing of the Gerasene Demoniac.

[1]†* They came to the other side of the sea, to the territory of the Gerasenes. [2] When he got out of the boat, at once a man† from the tombs who had an unclean spirit met him. [3] The man had been dwelling among the tombs, and no one could restrain him any longer, even with a chain. [4] In fact, he had frequently been bound with shackles and chains, but the chains had been pulled apart by him and the shackles smashed, and no one was strong enough to subdue him. [5] Night and day among the tombs and on the hillsides he was always crying out and bruising himself with stones. [6] Catching sight of Jesus from a distance, he ran up and prostrated himself before him, [7] crying out in a loud voice, "What have you to do with me,† Jesus, Son of the Most High God? I adjure you by God, do not torment me!" [8] (He had been saying to him, "Unclean spirit, come out of the man!") [9]† He asked him, "What is your name?" He replied, "Legion is my name. There are many of us."* [10] And he pleaded earnestly with him not to drive them away from that territory.

[11] Now a large herd of swine† was feeding there on the hillside. [12] And they pleaded with him, "Send us into the swine. Let us enter them." [13] And he let them, and the unclean spirits came out and entered the swine. The herd of about two thousand rushed down a steep bank into the sea, where they were drowned. [14] The swineherds ran away and reported the incident in the town and throughout the countryside. And people came out to see what had happened. [15] As they approached Jesus, they caught sight of the man who had been possessed by Legion, sitting there clothed and in his right mind. And they were seized with fear. [16] Those who witnessed the incident explained to them what had happened to the possessed man and to the swine. [17] Then they began to beg him to leave their district. [18] As he was getting into the boat, the man who had been possessed pleaded to remain with him. [19] But he would not permit him but told him instead, "Go home† to your family and announce to them all that the Lord in his pity has done for you." [20] Then the man went off and began to proclaim in the Decapolis what Jesus had done for him; and all were amazed.

## Jairus's Daughter and the Woman with a Hemorrhage.†

[21] When Jesus had crossed again [in the boat] to the other side, a large crowd gathered around him, and he stayed close to the sea.* [22] One of the synagogue officials, named Jairus, came forward.* Seeing him he fell at his feet [23] and pleaded earnestly with him, saying, "My daughter is at the point of death. Please, come lay your hands on her† that she may get well and live." [24] He went off with him, and a large crowd followed him and pressed upon him.

[25] There was a woman afflicted with hemorrhages for twelve years. [26] She had suffered greatly at the hands of many doctors and had

---

**4:39** *Quiet! Be still!*: as in the case of silencing a demon (Mk 1:25), Jesus rebukes the wind and subdues the turbulence of the sea by a mere word; see note on Mt 8:26.

**4:41** Jesus is here depicted as exercising power over wind and sea. In the Christian community this event was seen as a sign of Jesus' saving presence amid persecutions that threatened its existence.

**5:1** *The territory of the Gerasenes*: the reference is to pagan territory; cf. Is 65:1. Another reading is "Gadarenes"; see note on Mt 8:28.

**5:2–6** The man was an outcast from society, dominated by unclean spirits (Mk 5:8, 13), living among the tombs. The prostration before Jesus (Mk 5:6) indicates Jesus' power over evil spirits.

**5:7** *What have you to do with me?*: cf. Mk 1:24 and see note on Jn 2:4.

**5:9** *Legion is my name*: the demons were numerous and the condition of the possessed man was extremely serious; cf. Mt 12:45.

**5:11** *Herd of swine*: see note on Mt 8:30.

**5:19** *Go home*: Jesus did not accept the man's request *to remain with him* as a disciple (Mk 5:18), yet invited him to announce to his own people what the Lord had done for him, i.e., proclaim the gospel message to his pagan family; cf. Mk 1:14, 39; 3:14; 13:10.

**5:21–43** The story of the raising to life of Jairus's daughter is divided into two parts: Mk 5:21–24; 5:35–43. Between these two separated parts the account of the cure of the hemorrhage victim (Mk 5:25–34) is interposed. This technique of intercalating or sandwiching one story within another occurs several times in Mk 3:19b–21; 3:22–30; 3:31–35; 6:6b–13; 6:14–29; 6:30; 11:12–14; 11:15–19; 11:20–25; 14:53; 14:54; 14:55–65; 14:66–73.

**5:23** *Lay your hands on her*: this act for the purpose of healing is frequent in Mk 6:5; 7:32–35; 8:23–25; 16:18 and is also found in Mt 9:18; Lk 4:40; 13:13; Acts 9:17; 28:8.

---

| | |
|---|---|
| **4:41** 1:27. | Lk 8:2; 11:26. |
| **5:1–20** Mt 8:28–34; Lk | **5:21** 2:13. |
| 8:26–39. | **5:22–43** Mt 9:18–26; Lk |
| **5:9** Mt 12:45; | 8:41–56. |

spent all that she had. Yet she was not helped but only grew worse. ²⁷ She had heard about Jesus and came up behind him in the crowd and touched his cloak. ²⁸† She said, "If I but touch his clothes, I shall be cured." ²⁹ Immediately her flow of blood dried up. She felt in her body that she was healed of her affliction. ³⁰ Jesus, aware at once that power had gone out from him, turned around in the crowd and asked, "Who has touched my clothes?" ³¹ But his disciples said to him, "You see how the crowd is pressing upon you, and yet you ask, 'Who touched me?'" ³² And he looked around to see who had done it. ³³ The woman, realizing what had happened to her, approached in fear and trembling. She fell down before Jesus and told him the whole truth. ³⁴ He said to her, "Daughter, your faith has saved you. Go in peace and be cured of your affliction."*

³⁵† While he was still speaking, people from the synagogue official's house arrived and said, "Your daughter has died; why trouble the teacher any longer?" ³⁶ Disregarding the message that was reported, Jesus said to the synagogue official, "Do not be afraid; just have faith." ³⁷ He did not allow anyone to accompany him inside except Peter, James, and John, the brother of James. ³⁸ When they arrived at the house of the synagogue official, he caught sight of a commotion, people weeping and wailing loudly. ³⁹†* So he went in and said to them, "Why this commotion and weeping? The child is not dead but asleep." ⁴⁰ And they ridiculed him. Then he put them all out.

He took along the child's father and mother and those who were with him and entered the room where the child was. ⁴¹† He took the child by the hand and said to her, "*Talitha koum,*" which means, "Little girl, I say to you, arise!" ⁴² The girl, a child of twelve, arose immediately and walked around. [At that] they were utterly astounded. ⁴³ He gave strict orders that no one should know this and said that she should be given something to eat.

**6** **The Rejection at Nazareth.** ¹* He departed from there and came to his native place,† accompanied by his disciples. ²† When the sabbath came he began to teach in the synagogue, and many who heard him were astonished. They said, "Where did this man get all this? What kind of wisdom has been given him? What mighty deeds are wrought by his hands! ³* Is he not the carpenter,† the son of Mary, and the brother of James and Joses and Judas and Simon? And are not his sisters here with us?" And they took offense at him. ⁴†* Jesus said to them, "A prophet is not without honor except in his native place and among his own kin and in his own house." ⁵ So he was not able to perform any mighty deed there,† apart from curing a few sick people by laying his hands on them. ⁶ He was amazed at their lack of faith.

**The Mission of the Twelve.** He went around to the villages in the vicinity teaching. ⁷* He summoned the Twelve† and began to send

**5:28** Both in the case of Jairus and his daughter (Mk 5:23) and in the case of the hemorrhage victim, the inner conviction that physical contact (Mk 5:30) accompanied by faith in Jesus' saving power could effect a cure was rewarded.
**5:35** The faith of Jairus was put to a twofold test: (1) that his daughter might be cured and, now that she had died, (2) that she might be restored to life. His faith contrasts with the lack of faith of the crowd.
**5:39** *Not dead but asleep:* the New Testament often refers to death as sleep (Mt 27:52; Jn 11:11; 1 Cor 15:6; 1 Thes 4:13–15); see note on Mt 9:24.
**5:41** *Arise:* the Greek verb *egeirein* is the verb generally used to express resurrection from death (Mk 6:14, 16; Mt 11:5; Lk 7:14) and Jesus' own resurrection (Mk 16:6; Mt 28:6; Lk 24:6).
**6:1** *His native place:* the Greek word *patris* here refers to Nazareth (cf. Mk 1:9; Lk 4:16, 23–24) though it can also mean native land.
**6:2–6** See note on Mt 13:54–58.
**6:3** *Is he not the carpenter?:* no other gospel calls Jesus a carpenter. Some witnesses have "the carpenter's son," as in Mt 13:55. *Son of Mary:* contrary to Jewish custom, which calls a man the son of his father, this expression may reflect Mark's own faith that God is the Father of Jesus (Mk 1:1, 11; 8:38; 13:32; 14:36). The *brother of James…Simon:* in Semitic usage, the terms "brother," "sister" are applied not only to children of the same parents, but to nephews, nieces, cousins, half-brothers, and half-sisters; cf.

Gn 14:16; 29:15; Lv 10:4. While one cannot suppose that the meaning of a Greek word should be sought in the first place from Semitic usage, the Septuagint often translates the Hebrew *'āh* by the Greek word *adelphos,* "brother," as in the cited passages, a fact that may argue for a similar breadth of meaning in some New Testament passages. For instance, there is no doubt that in v 17, "brother" is used of Philip, who was actually the half-brother of Herod Antipas. On the other hand, Mark may have understood the terms literally; see also Mk 3:31–32; Mt 12:46; 13:55–56; Lk 8:19; Jn 7:3, 5. The question of meaning here would not have arisen but for the faith of the church in Mary's perpetual virginity.
**6:4** *A prophet is not without honor…in his own house:* a saying that finds parallels in other literatures, especially Jewish and Greek, but without reference to a prophet. Comparing himself to previous Hebrew prophets whom the people rejected, Jesus intimates his own eventual rejection by the nation especially in view of the dishonor his own relatives had shown him (Mk 3:21) and now his townspeople as well.
**6:5** *He was not able to perform any mighty deed there:* according to Mark, Jesus' power could not take effect because of a person's lack of faith.

* **5:34** Lk 7:30.
**5:39–40** Acts 9:40.
**6:1–6** Mt 13:54–58; Lk 4:16–30.
**6:3** 15:40; Mt 12:46; Jn 6:42.
**6:4** Jn 4:44.
**6:7–11** Mt 10:1, 9–14; Lk 9:15; 10:4–11.

them out two by two and gave them authority over unclean spirits. ⁸† He instructed them to take nothing for the journey but a walking stick—no food, no sack, no money in their belts. ⁹They were, however, to wear sandals but not a second tunic. ¹⁰† He said to them, "Wherever you enter a house, stay there until you leave from there. ¹¹Whatever place does not welcome you or listen to you, leave there and shake the dust off your feet in testimony against them." ¹²So they went off and preached repentance. ¹³† They drove out many demons, and they anointed with oil many who were sick* and cured them.

### Herod's Opinion of Jesus.† ¹⁴King Herod†

heard about it, for his fame had become widespread, and people were saying,* "John the Baptist has been raised from the dead; that is why mighty powers are at work in him."* ¹⁵Others were saying, "He is Elijah"; still others, "He is a prophet like any of the prophets."* ¹⁶But when Herod learned of it, he said, "It is John whom I beheaded. He has been raised up."

### The Death of John the Baptist.† ¹⁷Herod was

the one who had John arrested and bound in prison on account of Herodias, the wife of his brother Philip, whom he had married.* ¹⁸John had said to Herod, "It is not lawful for you to have your brother's wife."* ¹⁹Herodias† harbored a grudge against him and wanted to kill him but was unable to do so. ²⁰Herod

feared John, knowing him to be a righteous and holy man, and kept him in custody. When he heard him speak he was very much perplexed, yet he liked to listen to him. ²¹She had an opportunity one day when Herod, on his birthday, gave a banquet for his courtiers, his military officers, and the leading men of Galilee. ²²Herodias's own daughter came in and performed a dance that delighted Herod and his guests. The king said to the girl, "Ask of me whatever you wish and I will grant it to you." ²³He even swore [many things] to her, "I will grant you whatever you ask of me, even to half of my kingdom."* ²⁴She went out and said to her mother, "What shall I ask for?" She replied, "The head of John the Baptist." ²⁵The girl hurried back to the king's presence and made her request, "I want you to give me at once on a platter the head of John the Baptist." ²⁶The king was deeply distressed, but because of his oaths and the guests he did not wish to break his word to her. ²⁷* So he promptly dispatched an executioner with orders to bring back his head. He went off and beheaded him in the prison. ²⁸He brought in the head on a platter and gave it to the girl. The girl in turn gave it to her mother. ²⁹When his disciples heard about it, they came and took his body and laid it in a tomb.

### The Return of the Twelve. ³⁰The apostles†

gathered together with Jesus and reported all they had done and taught.* ³¹† He said to them, "Come away by yourselves to a deserted

---

**6:7–13** The preparation for the mission of the Twelve is seen in the call (1) of the first disciples to be fishers of men (Mk 1:16–20), (2) then of the Twelve set apart to be with Jesus and to receive authority to preach and expel demons (Mk 3:13–19). Now they are given the specific mission to exercise that authority in word and power as representatives of Jesus during the time of their formation.

**6:8–9** In Mark the use of a *walking stick* (Mk 6:8) and *sandals* (Mk 6:9) is permitted, but not in Mt 10:10 nor in Lk 10:4. Mark does not mention any prohibition to visit pagan territory and to enter Samaritan towns. These differences indicate a certain adaptation to conditions in and outside of Palestine and suggest in Mark's account a later activity in the church. For the rest, Jesus required of his apostles a total dependence on God for food and shelter; cf. Mk 6:35–44; 8:1–9.

**6:10–11** Remaining in the same house as a guest (Mk 6:10) rather than moving to another offering greater comfort avoided any impression of seeking advantage for oneself and prevented dishonor to one's host. Shaking the dust off one's feet served as testimony against those who rejected the call to repentance.

**6:13** *Anointed with oil...cured them:* a common medicinal remedy, but seen here as a vehicle of divine power for healing.

**6:14–16** The various opinions about Jesus anticipate the theme of his identity that reaches its climax in Mk 8:27–30.

**6:14** *King Herod:* see note on Mt 14:1.

**6:17–29** Similarities are to be noted between Mark's account

of the imprisonment and death of John the Baptist in this pericope, and that of the passion of Jesus (Mk 15:1–47). Herod and Pilate, each in turn, acknowledges the holiness of life of one over whom he unjustly exercises the power of condemnation and death (Mk 6:26–27; 15:9–10, 14–15). The hatred of Herodias toward John parallels that of the Jewish leaders toward Jesus. After the deaths of John and of Jesus, well-disposed persons request the bodies of the victims of Herod and of Pilate in turn to give them respectful burial (Mk 6:29; 15:45–46).

**6:19** *Herodias:* see note on Mt 14:3.

**6:30** *Apostles:* here, and in some manuscripts at Mk 3:14, Mark calls apostles (i.e., those sent forth) the Twelve whom Jesus sends as his emissaries, empowering them to preach, to expel demons, and to cure the sick (Mk 6:13). Only after Pentecost is the title used in the technical sense.

**6:31–34** The withdrawal of Jesus with his disciples to a desert place to rest attracts a great number of people to follow him. Toward this people of the new exodus Jesus is moved with pity; he satisfies their spiritual hunger by teaching them many things, thus gradually showing himself the faithful shepherd of a new Israel; cf. Nm 27:17; Ez 34:15.

*

| | |
|---|---|
| **6:13** Jas 5:14. | **6:18** Lv 18:16. |
| **6:14–29** Mt 14:1–12. | **6:23** Est 5:3. |
| **6:14–16** Lk 9:7–8. | **6:27–28** Lk 9:9. |
| **6:15** Mt 16:14. | **6:30** Lk 9:10. |
| **6:17** Lk 3:19–20. | |

place and rest a while." People were coming and going in great numbers, and they had no opportunity even to eat. * ³²So they went off in the boat by themselves to a deserted place. * ³³People saw them leaving and many came to know about it. They hastened there on foot from all the towns and arrived at the place before them.

**The Feeding of the Five Thousand.** ³⁴When he disembarked and saw the vast crowd, his heart was moved with pity for them, for they were like sheep without a shepherd; and he began to teach them many things. ³⁵† By now it was already late and his disciples approached him and said, "This is a deserted place and it is already very late. ³⁶Dismiss them so that they can go to the surrounding farms and villages and buy themselves something to eat." ³⁷He said to them in reply, "Give them some food yourselves." But they said to him, "Are we to buy two hundred days' wages worth of food and give it to them to eat?" ³⁸He asked them, "How many loaves do you have? Go and see." And when they had found out they said, "Five loaves and two fish." ³⁹So he gave orders to have them sit down in groups on the green grass. ⁴⁰† The people took their places in rows by hundreds and by fifties. ⁴¹Then, taking the five loaves and the two fish and looking up to heaven, he said the blessing, broke the loaves, and gave them to [his] disciples to set before the people; he also divided the two fish among them all. † ⁴²They all ate and were satisfied. ⁴³And they picked up twelve wicker baskets full of fragments and what was left of the fish. ⁴⁴Those who ate [of the loaves] were five thousand men.

**The Walking on the Water.**† ⁴⁵Then he made his disciples get into the boat * and precede him to the other side toward Bethsaida,† while he dismissed the crowd. ⁴⁶† And when he had taken leave of them, he went off to the mountain to pray. ⁴⁷When it was evening, the boat was far out on the sea and he was alone on shore. ⁴⁸Then he saw that they were tossed about while rowing, for the wind was against them. About the fourth watch of the night, he came toward them walking on the sea.† He meant to pass by them. ⁴⁹But when they saw him walking on the sea, they thought it was a ghost and cried out. ⁵⁰† They had all seen him and were terrified. But at once he spoke with them, "Take courage, it is I, do not be afraid!" ⁵¹He got into the boat with them and the wind died down. They were [completely] astounded. ⁵²They had not understood the incident of the loaves.† On the contrary, their hearts were hardened. *

**The Healings at Gennesaret.** ⁵³* After making the crossing, they came to land at Gennesaret and tied up there. ⁵⁴As they were leaving the boat, people immediately recognized him. ⁵⁵They scurried about the surrounding country and began to bring in the sick on mats to wherever they heard he was. ⁵⁶Whatever villages or towns or countryside he entered, they laid the sick in the marketplaces and begged him that they might touch only the tassel on his cloak; and as many as touched it were healed. *

**7** **The Tradition of the Elders.**† ¹Now when the Pharisees with some scribes who had come from Jerusalem gathered around him, *

---

† **6:35–44** See note on Mt 14:13–21. Compare this section with Mk 8:1–9. The various accounts of the multiplication of loaves and fishes, two each in Mark and in Matthew and one each in Luke and in John, indicate the wide interest of the early church in their eucharistic gatherings; see, e.g., Mk 6:41; 8:6; 14:22; and recall also the sign of bread in Ex 16; Dt 8:3–16; Ps 78:24–25; 105:40; Wis 16:20–21.

**6:40** *The people…in rows by hundreds and by fifties:* reminiscent of the groupings of Israelites encamped in the desert (Ex 18:21–25) and of the wilderness tradition of the prophets depicting the transformation of the wasteland into pastures where the true shepherd feeds his flock (Ez 34:25–26) and makes his people beneficiaries of messianic grace.

**6:41** On the language of this verse as eucharistic (cf. Mk 14:22), see notes on Mt 14:19, 20. Jesus observed the Jewish table ritual of blessing God before partaking of food.

**6:45–52** See note on Mt 14:22–33.

**6:45** *To the other side toward Bethsaida:* a village at the northeastern shore of the Sea of Galilee.

**6:46** *He went off to the mountain to pray:* see Mk 1:35–38. In Jn 6:15 Jesus withdrew to evade any involvement in the false messianic hopes of the multitude.

**6:48** *Walking on the sea:* see notes on Mt 14:22–33 and on Jn 6:19.

**6:50** *It is I, do not be afraid!:* literally, "I am." This may reflect the divine revelatory formula of Ex 3:14; Is 41:4, 10, 14; 43:1–3, 10, 13. Mark implies the hidden identity of Jesus as Son of God.

**6:52** *They had not understood…the loaves:* the revelatory character of this sign and that of the walking on the sea completely escaped the disciples. *Their hearts were hardened:* in Mk 3:5–6 hardness of heart was attributed to those who did not accept Jesus and plotted his death. Here the same disposition prevents the disciples from comprehending Jesus' self-revelation through signs; cf. Mk 8:17.

**7:1–23** See note on Mt 15:1–20. Against the Pharisees' narrow, legalistic, and external practices of piety in matters of purification (Mk 7:2–5), external worship (Mk 7:6–7), and observance

**6:31** 3:20; Mt 14:13; Lk 9:10.
**6:32–44** Mt 14:13–21; Lk 9:10–17; Jn 6:1–13.
**6:45–51** Mt 14:22–32;
Jn 6:15–21.
**6:52** 4:13.
**6:53–56** Mt 14:34–36.
**6:56** 5:27–28; Acts 5:15.
**7:1–23** Mt 15:1–20.

2 they observed that some of his disciples ate their meals with unclean, that is, unwashed, hands. 3 (For the Pharisees and, in fact, all Jews, do not eat without carefully washing their hands,† keeping the tradition of the elders. 4 And on coming from the marketplace they do not eat without purifying themselves. And there are many other things that they have traditionally observed, the purification of cups and jugs and kettles [and beds].) 5 So the Pharisees and scribes questioned him, "Why do your disciples not follow the tradition of the elders† but instead eat a meal with unclean hands?" 6 He responded, "Well did Isaiah prophesy about you hypocrites, as it is written:*

'This people honors me with their lips,
    but their hearts are far from me;
7   In vain do they worship me,
    teaching as doctrines human precepts.'

8 You disregard God's commandment but cling to human tradition." 9 He went on to say, "How well you have set aside the commandment of God in order to uphold your tradition! 10 For Moses said, 'Honor your father and your mother,' and 'Whoever curses father or mother shall die.'* 11 Yet you say, 'If a person says to father or mother, "Any support you might have had from me is qorban"'† (meaning, dedicated to God), 12 you allow him to do nothing more for his father or mother. 13 You nullify the word of God in favor of your tradition that you have handed on. And you do many such things." 14 * He summoned the crowd again and said to them, "Hear me, all of you, and understand. 15 Nothing that enters one from outside can defile that person; but the things that come out from within are what defile." [16]†

17 †* When he got home away from the crowd his disciples questioned him about the parable. 18 He said to them, "Are even you likewise without understanding? Do you not realize that everything that goes into a person from outside cannot defile, 19 †* since it enters not the heart but the stomach and passes out into the latrine?" (Thus he declared all foods clean.) 20 "But what comes out of a person, that is what defiles. 21 * From within people, from their hearts, come evil thoughts, unchastity, theft, murder, 22 adultery, greed, malice, deceit, licentiousness, envy, blasphemy, arrogance, folly. 23 All these evils come from within and they defile."

**The Syrophoenician Woman's Faith.** 24 * From that place he went off to the district of Tyre.† He entered a house and wanted no one to know about it, but he could not escape notice. 25 Soon a woman whose daughter had an unclean spirit heard about him. She came and fell at his feet. 26 The woman was a Greek, a Syrophoenician by birth, and she begged him to drive the demon out of her daughter. * 27 He said to her, "Let the children be fed first.† For it is not right to take the food of the children and throw it to the dogs." 28 She replied and said to him, "Lord, even the dogs under the table eat the children's scraps." 29 Then he said to her, "For saying this, you may go. The demon

---

of commandments, Jesus sets in opposition the true moral intent of the divine law (Mk 7:8–13). But he goes beyond contrasting the law and Pharisaic interpretation of it. The parable of Mk 7:14–15 in effect sets aside the law itself in respect to clean and unclean food. He thereby opens the way for unity between Jew and Gentile in the kingdom of God, intimated by Jesus' departure for pagan territory beyond Galilee. For similar contrast see Mk 2:1–3:6; 3:20–35; 6:1–6.

**7:3** *Carefully washing their hands*: refers to ritual purification.

**7:5** *Tradition of the elders*: the body of detailed, unwritten, human laws regarded by the scribes and Pharisees to have the same binding force as that of the Mosaic law; cf. Gal 1:14.

**7:11** *Qorban*: a formula for a gift to God, dedicating the offering to the temple, so that the giver might continue to use it for himself but not give it to others, even needy parents.

**7:16** Mk 7:16, "Anyone who has ears to hear ought to hear," is omitted because it is lacking in some of the best Greek manuscripts and was probably transferred here by scribes from Mk 4:9, 23.

**7:17** *Away from the crowd…the parable*: in this context of privacy the term *parable* refers to something hidden, about to be revealed to the disciples; cf. Mk 4:10-11, 34. Jesus sets the Mosaic food laws in the context of the kingdom of God where

they are abrogated, and he declares moral defilement the only cause of uncleanness.

**7:19** *(Thus he declared all foods clean)*: if this bold declaration goes back to Jesus, its force was not realized among Jewish Christians in the early church; cf. Acts 10:1–11:18.

**7:24–37** The withdrawal of Jesus to the district of Tyre may have been for a respite (Mk 7:24), but he soon moved onward to Sidon and, by way of the Sea of Galilee, to the Decapolis. These districts provided a Gentile setting for the extension of his ministry of healing because the people there acknowledged his power (Mk 7:29, 37). The actions attributed to Jesus (Mk 7:33–35) were also used by healers of the time.

**7:27–28** The figure of a household in which children at table are fed first and then their leftover food is given to the dogs under the table is used effectively to acknowledge the prior claim of the Jews to the ministry of Jesus; however, Jesus accedes to the Gentile woman's plea for the cure of her afflicted daughter because of her faith.

---

*
        7:6 Is 29:13.                         7:19 Acts 10:15.
       7:10 Ex 21:17; Lv 20:9; Dt            7:21 Jer 17:9.
            5:16; Eph 6:2.                    7:24–30 Mt 15:21–28.
    7:14–23 Mt 15:10–20.                      7:26 Mt 8:29.
       7:17 4:10, 13.

has gone out of your daughter." [30] When the woman went home, she found the child lying in bed and the demon gone.

**The Healing of a Deaf Man.** [31]* Again he left the district of Tyre and went by way of Sidon to the Sea of Galilee, into the district of the Decapolis. [32] And people brought to him a deaf man who had a speech impediment and begged him to lay his hand on him. [33] He took him off by himself away from the crowd. He put his finger into the man's ears and, spitting, touched his tongue; [34] then he looked up to heaven and groaned, and said to him, *"Ephphatha!"* (that is, "Be opened!") [35] And [immediately] the man's ears were opened, his speech impediment was removed, and he spoke plainly. [36]† He ordered them not to tell anyone. But the more he ordered them not to, the more they proclaimed it. [37] They were exceedingly astonished and they said, "He has done all things well. He makes the deaf hear and [the] mute speak."*

**8** **The Feeding of the Four Thousand.**† [1] In those days when there again was a great crowd without anything to eat,* he summoned the disciples and said, [2] "My heart is moved with pity for the crowd, because they have been with me now for three days and have nothing to eat. [3] If I send them away hungry to their homes, they will collapse on the way, and some of them have come a great distance." [4] His disciples answered him, "Where can anyone get enough bread to satisfy them here in this deserted place?" [5] Still he asked them, "How many loaves do you have?" "Seven," they replied. [6]† He ordered the crowd to sit down on the ground. Then, taking the seven loaves he gave thanks, broke them, and gave them to his disciples to

distribute, and they distributed them to the crowd. [7] They also had a few fish. He said the blessing over them and ordered them distributed also. [8] They ate and were satisfied. They picked up the fragments left over—seven baskets. [9] There were about four thousand people.

He dismissed them [10] and got into the boat with his disciples and came to the region of Dalmanutha.

**The Demand for a Sign.** [11]† The Pharisees came forward and began to argue with him,* seeking from him a sign from heaven to test him.* [12] He sighed from the depth of his spirit and said, "Why does this generation seek a sign? Amen, I say to you, no sign will be given to this generation." [13] Then he left them, got into the boat again, and went off to the other shore.

**The Leaven of the Pharisees.** [14]* They had forgotten to bring bread, and they had only one loaf with them in the boat. [15]† He enjoined them, "Watch out, guard against the leaven of the Pharisees and the leaven of Herod." [16] They concluded among themselves that it was because they had no bread. [17] When he became aware of this he said to them, "Why do you conclude that it is because you have no bread? Do you not yet understand or comprehend? Are your hearts hardened?* [18] Do you have eyes and not see, ears and not hear? And do you not remember,* [19] when I broke the five loaves for the five thousand, how many wicker baskets full of fragments you picked up?" They answered him, "Twelve." [20] "When I broke the seven loaves for the four thousand, how many full baskets of fragments did you pick up?" They answered [him], "Seven." [21] He said to them, "Do you still not understand?"

---

7:36 *The more they proclaimed it*: the same verb *proclaim* attributed here to the crowd in relation to the miracles of Jesus is elsewhere used in Mark for the preaching of the gospel on the part of Jesus, of his disciples, and of the Christian community (Mk 1:14; 13:10; 14:9). Implied in the action of the crowd is a recognition of the salvific mission of Jesus; see note on Mt 11:5–6.

8:1–10 The two accounts of the multiplication of loaves and fishes (Mk 8:1–10; 6:31–44) have eucharistic significance. Their similarity of structure and themes but dissimilarity of detail are considered by many to refer to a single event that, however, developed in two distinct traditions, one Jewish Christian and the other Gentile Christian, since Jesus in Mark's presentation (Mk 7:24–37) has extended his saving mission to the Gentiles.

8:6 See note on Mk 6:41.

8:11–12 The objection of the Pharisees that Jesus' miracles

are unsatisfactory for proving the arrival of God's kingdom is comparable to the request of the crowd for a sign in Jn 6:30–31. Jesus' response shows that a sign originating in human demand will not be provided; cf. Nm 14:11, 22.

8:15 *The leaven of the Pharisees...of Herod*: the corruptive action of leaven (1 Cor 5:6–8; Gal 5:9) was an apt symbol of the evil dispositions both of the Pharisees (Mk 8:11–13; 7:5–13) and of Herod (Mk 6:14–29) toward Jesus. The disciples of Jesus are warned against sharing such rebellious attitudes toward Jesus; cf. Mk 8:17, 21.

---

7:31–37 Mt 15:29–31.
7:37 Mt 15:31.
8:1–10 6:34–44; Mt 15:32–39.
8:11–13 Mt 12:38–39; 16:1–4.
8:11 Lk 11:16.
8:14–21 Mt 16:5–12; Lk 12:1.
8:17 4:13.
8:18 Jer 5:21; Ez 12:2.

MK

**The Blind Man of Bethsaida.**† ²²When they arrived at Bethsaida, they brought to him a blind man and begged him to touch him. ²³He took the blind man by the hand and led him outside the village. Putting spittle on his eyes he laid his hands on him and asked, "Do you see anything?"* ²⁴Looking up he replied, "I see people looking like trees and walking." ²⁵Then he laid hands on his eyes a second time and he saw clearly; his sight was restored and he could see everything distinctly. ²⁶Then he sent him home and said, "Do not even go into the village."

## III. THE MYSTERY BEGINS TO BE REVEALED

**Peter's Confession About Jesus.**† ²⁷Now Jesus and his disciples set out for the villages of Caesarea Philippi.* Along the way he asked his disciples, "Who do people say that I am?" ²⁸They said in reply, "John the Baptist, others Elijah, still others one of the prophets." ²⁹And he asked them, "But who do you say that I am?" Peter said to him in reply, "You are the Messiah." ³⁰Then he warned them not to tell anyone about him.

**The First Prediction of the Passion.** ³¹* He began to teach them that the Son of Man† must suffer greatly and be rejected by the elders, the chief priests, and the scribes, and be killed, and rise after three days. ³²He spoke this openly. Then Peter took him aside and began to rebuke him. ³³At this he turned around and, looking at his disciples, rebuked Peter and said, "Get behind me, Satan. You are thinking not as God does, but as human beings do."

**The Conditions of Discipleship.** ³⁴He summoned the crowd with his disciples and said† to them, "Whoever wishes to come after me must deny himself, take up his cross, and follow me.* ³⁵For whoever wishes to save his life will lose it, but whoever loses his life for my sake and that of the gospel† will save it.* ³⁶What profit is there for one to gain the whole world and forfeit his life? ³⁷What could one give in exchange for his life? ³⁸Whoever is ashamed of me and of my words in this faithless and sinful generation, the Son of Man will be ashamed of when he comes in his Father's glory with the holy angels."*

**9** ¹†* He also said to them, "Amen, I say to you, there are some standing here who will not taste death until they see that the kingdom of God has come in power."

**The Transfiguration of Jesus.**† ²After six days Jesus took Peter, James, and John and led them

---

**8:22–26** Jesus' actions and the gradual cure of the blind man probably have the same purpose as in the case of the deaf man (Mk 7:31–37). Some commentators regard the cure as an intended symbol of the gradual enlightenment of the disciples concerning Jesus' messiahship.

**8:27–30** This episode is the turning point in Mark's account of Jesus in his public ministry. Popular opinions concur in regarding him as a prophet. The disciples by contrast believe him to be the Messiah. Jesus acknowledges this identification but prohibits them from making his messianic office known to avoid confusing it with ambiguous contemporary ideas on the nature of that office. See further the notes on Mt 16:13–20.

**8:31** *Son of Man*: an enigmatic title. It is used in Dn 7:13–14 as a symbol of "the saints of the Most High," the faithful Israelites who receive the everlasting kingdom from the Ancient One (God). They are represented by a human figure that contrasts with the various beasts who represent the previous kingdoms of the earth. In the Jewish apocryphal books of 1 Enoch and 4 Ezra the "Son of Man" is not, as in Daniel, a group, but a unique figure of extraordinary spiritual endowments, who will be revealed as the one through whom the everlasting kingdom decreed by God will be established. It is possible though doubtful that this individualization of the Son of Man figure had been made in Jesus' time, and therefore his use of the title in that sense is questionable. Of itself, this expression means simply a human being, or, indefinitely, someone, and there are evidences of this use in pre-Christian times. Its use in the New Testament is probably due to Jesus' speaking of himself in that way, "a human being," and the later church's taking this in the sense of the Jewish apocrypha and applying it to him with that meaning. *Rejected by the elders, the chief priests, and the scribes*: the supreme council called

the Sanhedrin was made up of seventy-one members of these three groups and presided over by the high priest. It exercised authority over the Jews in religious matters. See note on Mt 8:20.

**8:34–35** This utterance of Jesus challenges all believers to authentic discipleship and total commitment to himself through self-renunciation and acceptance of the cross of suffering, even to the sacrifice of life itself. *Whoever wishes to save his life will lose it…will save it*: an expression of the ambivalence of life and its contrasting destiny. Life seen as mere self-centered earthly existence and lived in denial of Christ ends in destruction, but when lived in loyalty to Christ, despite earthly death, it arrives at fullness of life.

**8:35** *For my sake and that of the gospel*: Mark here, as at Mk 10:29 equates Jesus with the gospel.

**9:1** *There are some standing…come in power*: understood by some to refer to the establishment by God's power of his kingdom on earth in and through the church; more likely, as understood by others, to the imminent parousia.

**9:2–8** Mark and Mt 17:1 place the transfiguration of Jesus six days after the first prediction of his passion and death and his instruction to the disciples on the doctrine of the cross; Lk 9:28 has "about eight days." Thus the transfiguration counterbalances the prediction of the passion by affording certain of the disciples insight into the divine glory that Jesus possessed. His glory will overcome his death and that of his disciples; cf. 2 Cor 3:18; 2 Pt 1:16–19. The heavenly voice (Mk 9:7) prepares the disciples to

**8:23** 7:33; Jn 9:6.
**8:27–30** Mt 16:13–20; Lk 9:18–21.
**8:31–38** Mt 16:21–27; Lk 9:22–26.
**8:34** Mt 10:38–39; 16:24–27; Lk 14:26–27.
**8:35** Jn 12:25.
**8:38** Mt 10:33; Lk 12:8.
**9:1** Mt 16:28; Lk 9:27.

MK

up a high mountain apart by themselves. * And he was transfigured before them, 3 and his clothes became dazzling white, such as no fuller on earth could bleach them. 4 Then Elijah appeared to them along with Moses, and they were conversing with Jesus. 5 † Then Peter said to Jesus in reply, "Rabbi, it is good that we are here! Let us make three tents: one for you, one for Moses, and one for Elijah." 6 He hardly knew what to say, they were so terrified. 7 Then a cloud came, casting a shadow over them; † then from the cloud came a voice, "This is my beloved Son. Listen to him." 8 Suddenly, looking around, they no longer saw anyone but Jesus alone with them.

## The Coming of Elijah. † 9 As they were coming down from the mountain, he charged them not to relate what they had seen to anyone, except when the Son of Man had risen from the dead. * 10 So they kept the matter to themselves, questioning what rising from the dead meant. 11 * Then they asked him, "Why do the scribes say that Elijah must come first?" 12 He told them, "Elijah will indeed come first and restore all things, yet how is it written regarding the Son of Man that he must suffer greatly and be treated with contempt? 13 But I tell you that Elijah has come and they did to him whatever they pleased, as it is written of him." *

## The Healing of a Boy with a Demon. † 14 When they came to the disciples, * they saw a large crowd around them and scribes arguing with them. 15 Immediately on seeing him, the whole crowd was utterly amazed. They ran up to him and greeted him. 16 He asked them, "What are you arguing about with them?" 17 Someone

from the crowd answered him, "Teacher, I have brought to you my son possessed by a mute spirit. 18 Wherever it seizes him, it throws him down; he foams at the mouth, grinds his teeth, and becomes rigid. I asked your disciples to drive it out, but they were unable to do so." 19 He said to them in reply, "O faithless generation, how long will I be with you? How long will I endure you? Bring him to me." 20 They brought the boy to him. And when he saw him, the spirit immediately threw the boy into convulsions. As he fell to the ground, he began to roll around and foam at the mouth. 21 Then he questioned his father, "How long has this been happening to him?" He replied, "Since childhood. 22 It has often thrown him into fire and into water to kill him. But if you can do anything, have compassion on us and help us." 23 Jesus said to him, "'If you can!' Everything is possible to one who has faith." 24 Then the boy's father cried out, "I do believe, help my unbelief!" 25 Jesus, on seeing a crowd rapidly gathering, rebuked the unclean spirit and said to it, "Mute and deaf spirit, I command you: come out of him and never enter him again!" 26 Shouting and throwing the boy into convulsions, it came out. He became like a corpse, which caused many to say, "He is dead!" 27 But Jesus took him by the hand, raised him, and he stood up. 28 When he entered the house, his disciples asked him in private, "Why could we not drive it out?" 29 † He said to them, "This kind can only come out through prayer."

## The Second Prediction of the Passion. 30 * They left from there and began a journey through Galilee, but he did not wish anyone to know about it. * 31 He was teaching his disciples and

† understand that in the divine plan Jesus must die ignominiously before his messianic glory is made manifest; cf. Lk 24:25–27. See further the note on Mt 17:1–8.

9:5 Moses and Elijah represent, respectively, law and prophecy in the Old Testament and are linked to Mount Sinai; cf. Ex 19:16–20:17; 1 Kgs 19:2, 8–14. They now appear with Jesus as witnesses to the fulfillment of the law and the prophets taking place in the person of Jesus as he appears in glory.

9:7 A cloud came, casting a shadow over them: even the disciples enter into the mystery of his glorification. In the Old Testament the cloud covered the meeting tent, indicating the Lord's presence in the midst of his people (Ex 40:34–35) and came to rest upon the temple in Jerusalem at the time of its dedication (1 Kgs 8:10).

9:9–13 At the transfiguration of Jesus his disciples had seen Elijah. They were perplexed because, according to the rabbinical interpretation of Mal 3:23–24, Elijah was to come first. Jesus' response shows that Elijah has come, in the person of John the

Baptist, to prepare for the day of the Lord. Jesus must suffer greatly and be treated with contempt (Mk 9:12) like the Baptist (Mk 9:13); cf. Mk 6:17–29.

9:14–29 The disciples' failure to effect a cure seems to reflect unfavorably on Jesus (Mk 9:14–18, 22). In response Jesus exposes their lack of trust in God (Mk 9:19) and scores their lack of prayer (Mk 9:29), i.e., of conscious reliance on God's power when acting in Jesus' name. For Matthew, see note on Mt 17:14–20. Lk 9:37–43 centers attention on Jesus' sovereign power.

9:29 This kind can only come out through prayer: a variant reading adds "and through fasting."

| | |
|---|---|
| 9:2–13 Mt 17:1–13; Lk 9:28–36. | 9:14–29 Mt 17:14–21; Lk 9:37–43. |
| 9:9 8:31. | 9:30–32 8:31; Mt 17:22–23; Lk 9:43–45. |
| 9:11–12 Is 53:3; Mal 3:23. | 9:30 Jn 7:1. |
| 9:13 1 Kgs 19:2–10. | |

telling them, "The Son of Man is to be handed over to men and they will kill him, and three days after his death he will rise." [32] But they did not understand the saying, and they were afraid to question him.

## IV. THE FULL REVELATION OF THE MYSTERY

**The Greatest in the Kingdom.** † [33] They came to Capernaum and, once inside the house, he began to ask them, "What were you arguing about on the way?" * [34] But they remained silent. They had been discussing among themselves on the way who was the greatest. [35] Then he sat down, called the Twelve, and said to them, "If anyone wishes to be first, he shall be the last of all and the servant of all." * [36] Taking a child he placed it in their midst, and putting his arms around it he said to them, [37] "Whoever receives one child such as this in my name, receives me; and whoever receives me, receives not me but the One who sent me." *

**Another Exorcist.** † [38] John said to him, * "Teacher, we saw someone driving out demons in your name, and we tried to prevent him because he does not follow us." [39] Jesus replied, "Do not prevent him. There is no one who performs a mighty deed in my name who can at the same time speak ill of me. [40] For whoever is not against us is for us. * [41] Anyone who gives you a cup of water to drink because you belong to Christ, amen, I say to you, will surely not lose his reward. *

**Temptations to Sin.** [42] * "Whoever causes one of these little ones who believe [in me] to sin, it would be better for him if a great millstone were put around his neck and he were thrown into the sea. [43] If your hand causes you to sin, cut it off. It is better for you to enter into life maimed than with two hands to go into Gehenna, † into the unquenchable fire. [[44]] † [45] And if your foot causes you to sin, cut it off. It is better for you to enter into life crippled than with two feet to be thrown into Gehenna. [[46]] [47] And if your eye causes you to sin, pluck it out. Better for you to enter into the kingdom of God with one eye than with two eyes to be thrown into Gehenna, [48] where 'their worm does not die, and the fire is not quenched.' *

**The Simile of Salt.** [49] † "Everyone will be salted with fire. [50] Salt is good, but if salt becomes insipid, with what will you restore its flavor? Keep salt in yourselves and you will have peace with one another." *

# 10

**Marriage and Divorce.** [1] He set out from there and went into the district of Judea [and] across the Jordan. Again crowds gathered around him and, as was his custom, he again taught them. [2] † The Pharisees approached and asked, "Is it lawful for a husband to divorce his wife?" They were testing him. * [3] He said to them in reply, "What did Moses command you?" [4] They replied, "Moses permitted him to write a bill of divorce and dismiss her." * [5] But Jesus told them, "Because of the hardness of your hearts he wrote you this commandment. [6] But from the beginning of creation, 'God made them male and female. * [7] For this reason a man shall leave his father and mother [and be joined to his wife], * [8] and the two shall become one flesh.' So they are no longer two but one flesh.

---

† **9:33–37** Mark probably intends this incident and the sayings that follow as commentary on the disciples' lack of understanding (Mk 9:32). Their role in Jesus' work is one of service, especially to the poor and lowly. Children were the symbol Jesus used for the *anawim*, the poor in spirit, the lowly in the Christian community.

**9:38–41** Jesus warns against jealousy and intolerance toward others, such as exorcists who do *not follow us*. The saying in Mk 9:40 is a broad principle of the divine tolerance. Even the smallest courtesies shown to those who teach in Jesus' name do not go unrewarded.

**9:43, 45, 47** *Gehenna*: see note on Mt 5:22.

**9:44, 46** These verses, lacking in some important early manuscripts, are here omitted as scribal additions. They simply repeat Mk 9:48 itself a modified citation of Is 66:24.

**9:49** *Everyone will be salted with fire*: so the better manuscripts. Some add "every sacrifice will be salted with salt." The purifying and preservative use of salt in food (Lv 2:13) and the refinement effected through fire refer here to comparable effects in the spiritual life of the disciples of Jesus.

**10:2–9** In the dialogue between Jesus and the Pharisees on the subject of divorce, Jesus declares that the law of Moses permitted divorce (Dt 24:1) only *because of the hardness of your hearts* (Mk 10:4–5). In citing Gn 1:27 and 2:24 Jesus proclaims permanence to be the divine intent from the beginning concerning human marriage (Mk 10:6–8). He reaffirms this with the declaration that *what God has joined together, no human being must separate* (Mk 10:9). See further the notes on Mt 5:31–32; 19:3–9.

---

*

| | |
|---|---|
| **9:33–37** Mt 18:1–5; Lk 9:46–48. | **9:42–47** Mt 5:29–30; 18:6–9; Lk 17:1–2. |
| **9:35** Mt 20:27. | **9:48** Is 66:24. |
| **9:37** Mt 10:40; 18:5; Jn 13:20. | **9:50** Lv 2:13; Mt 5:13; Lk 14:34–35; Col 4:6. |
| **9:38–41** Nm 11:28; Lk 9:49–50; 1 Cor 12:3. | **10:2–12** Mt 19:3–9. |
| **9:40** Lk 12:30. | **10:4** Dt 24:1–4. |
| **9:41** Mt 10:42; 1 Cor 3:23. | **10:6** Gn 1:27. |
| | **10:7–8** Gn 2:24; 1 Cor 6:16; Eph 5:31. |

⁹Therefore what God has joined together, no human being must separate." ¹⁰In the house the disciples again questioned him about this. ¹¹* He said to them, "Whoever divorces his wife and marries another commits adultery against her; ¹²and if she divorces her husband and marries another, she commits adultery."

**Blessing of the Children.** ¹³* And people were bringing children to him that he might touch them, but the disciples rebuked them.* ¹⁴When Jesus saw this he became indignant and said to them, "Let the children come to me; do not prevent them, for the kingdom of God belongs to such as these. ¹⁵Amen, I say to you, whoever does not accept the kingdom of God like a child† will not enter it."* ¹⁶Then he embraced them and blessed them, placing his hands on them.

**The Rich Man.** ¹⁷* As he was setting out on a journey, a man ran up, knelt down before him, and asked him, "Good teacher, what must I do to inherit eternal life?" ¹⁸Jesus answered him, "Why do you call me good?† No one is good but God alone. ¹⁹You know the commandments: 'You shall not kill; you shall not commit adultery; you shall not steal; you shall not bear false witness; you shall not defraud; honor your father and your mother.'"* ²⁰He replied and said to him, "Teacher, all of these I have observed from my youth." ²¹Jesus, looking at him, loved him and said to him, "You are lacking in one thing. Go, sell what you have, and give to [the] poor and you will have treasure in heaven; then come, follow me." ²²At that statement his face fell, and he went away sad, for he had many possessions.

²³† Jesus looked around and said to his disciples, "How hard it is for those who have wealth to enter the kingdom of God!"* ²⁴The disciples were amazed at his words. So Jesus again said to them in reply, "Children, how hard it is to enter the kingdom of God! ²⁵It is easier for a camel to pass through [the] eye of [a] needle than for one who is rich to enter the kingdom of God." ²⁶They were exceedingly astonished and said among themselves, "Then who can be saved?" ²⁷Jesus looked at them and said, "For human beings it is impossible, but not for God. All things are possible for God." ²⁸Peter began to say to him, "We have given up everything and followed you." ²⁹Jesus said, "Amen, I say to you, there is no one who has given up house or brothers or sisters or mother or father or children or lands for my sake and for the sake of the gospel ³⁰who will not receive a hundred times more now in this present age: houses and brothers and sisters and mothers and children and lands, with persecutions, and eternal life in the age to come. ³¹But many that are first will be last, and [the] last will be first."*

**The Third Prediction of the Passion.** ³²* They were on the way, going up to Jerusalem, and Jesus went ahead of them. They were amazed, and those who followed were afraid. Taking the Twelve aside again, he began to tell them what was going to happen to him. ³³"Behold, we are going up to Jerusalem, and the Son of Man will be handed over to the chief priests and the scribes, and they will condemn him to death and hand him over to the Gentiles ³⁴who will mock him, spit upon him, scourge him, and put him to death, but after three days he will rise."

**Ambition of James and John.** ³⁵* Then James and John, the sons of Zebedee, came to him and said to him, "Teacher, we want you to do for us whatever we ask of you." ³⁶He replied, "What do you wish [me] to do for you?" ³⁷They answered him, "Grant that in your glory we may sit one at your right and the other at your left." ³⁸†* Jesus said to them,

---

† **10:15** *Whoever does not accept the kingdom of God like a child:* i.e., in total dependence upon and obedience to the gospel; cf. Mt 18:3–4.

**10:18** *Why do you call me good?:* Jesus repudiates the term "good" for himself and directs it to God, the source of all goodness who alone can grant the gift of eternal life; cf. Mt 19:16–17.

**10:23–27** In the Old Testament wealth and material goods are considered a sign of God's favor (Jb 1:10; Ps 128:1–2; Is 3:10). The words of Jesus in Mk 10:23–25 provoke astonishment among the disciples because of their apparent contradiction of the Old Testament concept (Mk 10:24, 26). Since wealth, power, and merit generate false security, Jesus rejects them utterly as a claim to enter the kingdom. Achievement of salvation is beyond human capability and depends solely on the goodness of God who offers it as a gift (Mk 10:27).

**10:38–40** *Can you drink the cup…I am baptized?:* the metaphor of drinking the cup is used in the Old Testament to refer to acceptance of the destiny assigned by God; see note on Psalm

---

*
10:11–12 Mt 5:32; Lk 16:18;
   1 Cor 7:10–11.
10:13–16 Mt 19:13–15; Lk
   18:15–17.
10:13 Lk 9:47.
10:15 Mt 18:3.
10:17–31 Mt 19:16–30; Lk
   18:18–30.

10:19 Ex 20:12–16; Dt
   5:16–21.
10:23 Prv 11:28.
10:31 Mt 19:30; Lk 13:30.
10:32–34 8:31; Mt 20:17–19; Lk
   18:31–33.
10:35–45 Mt 20:20–28.
10:38 Lk 12:50.

"You do not know what you are asking. Can you drink the cup that I drink or be baptized with the baptism with which I am baptized?" [39] They said to him, "We can." Jesus said to them, "The cup that I drink, you will drink, and with the baptism with which I am baptized, you will be baptized; [40] but to sit at my right or at my left is not mine to give but is for those for whom it has been prepared." [41] When the ten heard this, they became indignant at James and John. [42]† Jesus summoned them and said to them,* "You know that those who are recognized as rulers over the Gentiles lord it over them, and their great ones make their authority over them felt. [43] But it shall not be so among you. Rather, whoever wishes to be great among you will be your servant; [44] whoever wishes to be first among you will be the slave of all. [45] For the Son of Man did not come to be served but to serve and to give his life as a ransom for many."

**The Blind Bartimaeus.**† [46] They came to Jericho.* And as he was leaving Jericho with his disciples and a sizable crowd, Bartimaeus, a blind man, the son of Timaeus, sat by the roadside begging. [47] On hearing that it was Jesus of Nazareth, he began to cry out and say, "Jesus, son of David, have pity on me." [48] And many rebuked him, telling him to be silent. But he kept calling out all the more, "Son of David, have pity on me." [49] Jesus stopped and said, "Call him." So they called the blind man, saying to him, "Take courage; get up, he is calling you." [50] He threw aside his cloak, sprang up, and came to Jesus. [51] Jesus said to him in reply, "What do you want me to do for you?" The blind man replied to him, "Master, I want to see." [52] Jesus told him, "Go your way; your faith has saved you." Immediately he received his sight and followed him on the way.

## 11 The Entry into Jerusalem.† [1] When they drew near to Jerusalem,* to Bethphage and Bethany at the Mount of Olives, he sent two of his disciples [2] and said to them, "Go into the village opposite you, and immediately on entering it, you will find a colt tethered on which no one has ever sat. Untie it and bring it here. [3] If anyone should say to you, 'Why are you doing this?' reply, 'The Master has need of it and will send it back here at once.'" [4] So they went off and found a colt tethered at a gate outside on the street, and they untied it. [5] Some of the bystanders said to them, "What are you doing, untying the colt?" [6] They answered them just as Jesus had told them to, and they permitted them to do it. [7] So they brought the colt to Jesus and put their cloaks over it. And he sat on it. [8] Many people spread their cloaks on the road, and others spread leafy branches that they had cut from the fields. [9] Those preceding him as well as those following kept crying out:*

"Hosanna!
　Blessed is he who comes in the name
　　of the Lord!
[10]　Blessed is the kingdom of our father
　　David that is to come!
　Hosanna in the highest!"

[11] He entered Jerusalem and went into the temple area. He looked around at everything and, since it was already late, went out to Bethany with the Twelve.*

**Jesus Curses a Fig Tree.**† [12] The next day as they were leaving Bethany he was hungry.* [13] Seeing from a distance a fig tree in leaf, he went over to see if he could find anything on it. When he reached it he found nothing but leaves; it was not the time for figs. [14] And he said to it

---

†
11:6. In Jesus' case, this involves divine judgment on sin that Jesus the innocent one is to expiate on behalf of the guilty (Mk 14:24; Is 53:5). His baptism is to be his crucifixion and death for the salvation of the human race; cf. Lk 12:50. The request of James and John for a share in the glory (Mk 10:35–37) must of necessity involve a share in Jesus' sufferings, the endurance of tribulation and suffering for the gospel (Mk 10:39). The authority of assigning places of honor in the kingdom is reserved to God (Mk 10:40).

**10:42–45** Whatever authority is to be exercised by the disciples must, like that of Jesus, be rendered as service to others (Mk 10:45) rather than for personal aggrandizement (Mk 10:42–44). The service of Jesus is his passion and death for the sins of the human race (Mk 10:45); cf. Mk 14:24; Is 53:11–12; Mt 26:28; Lk 22:19–20.

**10:46–52** See notes on Mt 9:27–31 and 20:29–34.

**11:1–11** In Mark's account Jesus takes the initiative in order-ing the preparation for his entry into Jerusalem (Mk 11:1–6) even as he later orders the preparation of his last Passover supper (Mk 14:12–16). In Mk 10:9–10 the greeting receives stops short of proclaiming him Messiah. He is greeted rather as the prophet of the coming messianic kingdom. Contrast Mt 21:9.

**11:12–14** Jesus' search for fruit on the fig tree recalls the prophets' earlier use of this image to designate Israel; cf. Jer 8:13; 29:17; Jl 1:7; Hos 9:10, 16. Cursing the fig tree is a parable in action representing Jesus' judgment (Mk 11:20) on barren Israel and the fate of Jerusalem for failing to receive his teaching; cf. Is 34:4; Hos 2:14; Lk 13:6–9.

*
10:42–45 Lk 22:25–27.　　　　　11:9–10 2 Sm 7:16; Ps 118:26.
10:46–52 Mt 20:29–34; Lk　　　11:11 Mt 21:10, 17.
　　　18:35–43.　　　　　　　　11:12–14 Mt 21:18–20; Lk
11:1–10 Mt 21:1–9; Lk 19:29–　　　13:6–9.
　　　38; Jn 12:12–15.

MK

in reply, "May no one ever eat of your fruit again!" And his disciples heard it.

**Cleansing of the Temple.**† 15 They came to Jerusalem,* and on entering the temple area he began to drive out those selling and buying there. He overturned the tables of the money changers and the seats of those who were selling doves. 16 He did not permit anyone to carry anything through the temple area. 17 Then he taught them saying, "Is it not written:

'My house shall be called a house of
      prayer for all peoples'?
But you have made it a den of
      thieves.'"*

18 The chief priests and the scribes came to hear of it and were seeking a way to put him to death, yet they feared him because the whole crowd was astonished at his teaching. 19 When evening came, they went out of the city.*

**The Withered Fig Tree.** 20* Early in the morning, as they were walking along, they saw the fig tree withered to its roots. 21 Peter remembered and said to him, "Rabbi, look! The fig tree that you cursed has withered." 22 Jesus said to them in reply, "Have faith in God. 23 Amen, I say to you, whoever says to this mountain, 'Be lifted up and thrown into the sea,' and does not doubt in his heart but believes that what he says will happen, it shall be done for him.* 24 Therefore I tell you, all that you ask for in prayer, believe that you will receive it and it shall be yours.* 25 When you stand to pray, forgive anyone against whom you have a grievance, so that your heavenly Father may in turn forgive you your transgressions."* [26]†

**The Authority of Jesus Questioned.**† 27 They returned once more to Jerusalem.* As he was walking in the temple area, the chief priests, the scribes, and the elders approached him 28 and said to him, "By what authority are you doing these things? Or who gave you this authority to do them?" 29 Jesus said to them, "I shall ask you one question. Answer me, and I will tell you by what authority I do these things. 30 Was John's baptism of heavenly or of human origin? Answer me." 31 They discussed this among themselves and said, "If we say, 'Of heavenly origin,' he will say, '[Then] why did you not believe him?' 32 But shall we say, 'Of human origin'?"—they feared the crowd, for they all thought John really was a prophet. 33 So they said to Jesus in reply, "We do not know." Then Jesus said to them, "Neither shall I tell you by what authority I do these things."

# 12

**Parable of the Tenants.**† 1 He began to speak to them in parables.* "A man planted a vineyard, put a hedge around it, dug a wine press, and built a tower. Then he leased it to tenant farmers and left on a journey.* 2 At the proper time he sent a servant to the tenants to obtain from them some of the produce of the vineyard. 3 But they seized him, beat him, and sent him away empty-handed. 4 Again he sent them another servant. And that one they beat over the head and treated shamefully. 5 He sent yet another whom they killed. So, too, many others; some they beat, others they killed. 6 He had one other to send, a beloved son. He sent him to them last of all, thinking, 'They will respect my son.' 7 But those tenants said to one another, 'This is the heir. Come, let us kill him, and the inheritance will be ours.' 8 So they seized him and killed him, and threw him out of the vineyard. 9 What [then] will the owner of the vineyard do? He will come, put the tenants to death, and give the vineyard to others. 10 Have you not read this scripture passage:*

---

† **11:15–19** See note on Mt 21:12–17.
**11:26** This verse, which reads, "But if you do not forgive, neither will your heavenly Father forgive your transgressions," is omitted in the best manuscripts. It was probably added by copyists under the influence of Mt 6:15.
**11:27–33** The mounting hostility toward Jesus came from the chief priests, the scribes, and the elders (Mk 11:27); the Herodians and the Pharisees (Mk 12:13); and the Sadducees (Mk 12:18). By their rejection of God's messengers, John the Baptist and Jesus, they incurred the divine judgment implied in Mk 11:27–33 and confirmed in the parable of the vineyard tenants (Mk 12:1–12).
**12:1–12** The vineyard denotes Israel (Is 5:1–7). The tenant farmers are the religious leaders of Israel. God is the owner of

the vineyard. His servants are his messengers, the prophets. The beloved son is Jesus (Mk 1:11; 9:7; Mt 3:17; 17:5; Lk 3:22; 9:35). The punishment of the tenants refers to the religious leaders, and the transfer of the vineyard to others refers to the people of the new Israel.

---

* **11:15–18** Mt 21:12–13; Lk          **11:25** Mt 6:14; 18:35.
    19:45–46; Jn 2:14–16.             **11:27–33** Mt 21:23–27; Lk
  **11:17** Is 56:7; Jer 7:11.                20:1–8.
  **11:19** Lk 21:37.                 **12:1–12** Mt 21:33–46; Lk
**11:20–24** Mt 21:20–22.                     20:9–19.
  **11:23** Mt 17:20–21; Lk 17:6.     **12:1** Is 5:1–7; Jer 2:21.
  **11:24** Mt 7:7; Jn 11:22;         **12:10–11** Ps 118:22–23; Is
        14:13.                                28:16.

'The stone that the builders rejected
    has become the cornerstone;
11  by the Lord has this been done,
    and it is wonderful in our eyes'?"

12 They were seeking to arrest him, but they feared the crowd, for they realized that he had addressed the parable to them. So they left him and went away.

**Paying Taxes to the Emperor.** 13† They sent some Pharisees* and Herodians to him to ensnare him* in his speech.† 14 They came and said to him, "Teacher, we know that you are a truthful man and that you are not concerned with anyone's opinion. You do not regard a person's status but teach the way of God in accordance with the truth. Is it lawful to pay the census tax to Caesar or not? Should we pay or should we not pay?" 15 Knowing their hypocrisy he said to them, "Why are you testing me? Bring me a denarius to look at." 16 They brought one to him and he said to them, "Whose image and inscription is this?" They replied to him, "Caesar's." 17 So Jesus said to them, "Repay to Caesar what belongs to Caesar and to God what belongs to God." They were utterly amazed at him.*

**The Question About the Resurrection.** † 18 Some Sadducees, who say there is no resurrection, came to him and put this question to him, 19 saying, "Teacher, Moses wrote for us, 'If someone's brother dies, leaving a wife but no child, his brother must take the wife and raise up descendants for his brother.'* 20 Now there were seven brothers. The first married a woman and died, leaving no descendants. 21 So the second married her and died, leaving no descendants, and the third likewise. 22 And the seven left no descendants. Last of all the woman also died. 23 At the resurrection [when they arise] whose wife will she be? For all seven had been married to her." 24 Jesus said to them, "Are you not misled because you do not know the scriptures or the power of God? 25 When they rise from the dead, they neither marry nor are given in marriage, but they are like the angels in heaven. 26 As for the dead being raised, have you not read in the Book of Moses, in the passage about the bush, how God told him, 'I am the God of Abraham, [the] God of Isaac, and [the] God of Jacob'?* 27 He is not God of the dead but of the living. You are greatly misled."

**The Greatest Commandment.** † 28 One of the scribes,* when he came forward and heard them disputing and saw how well he had answered them, asked him, "Which is the first of all the commandments?" 29 Jesus replied, "The first is this: 'Hear, O Israel! The Lord our God is Lord alone! 30 You shall love the Lord your God with all your heart, with all your soul, with all your mind, and with all your strength.'* 31 The second is this: 'You shall love your neighbor as yourself.' There is no other commandment greater than these."* 32 The scribe said to him, "Well said, teacher. You are right in saying, 'He is One and there is no other than he.' 33 And 'to love him with all your heart, with all your understanding, with all your strength, and to love your neighbor as yourself' is worth more than all burnt offerings and sacrifices."* 34 And when Jesus saw that [he] answered with understanding, he said to him, "You are not far from the kingdom of God." And no one dared to ask him any more questions.*

**The Question About David's Son.** † 35 As Jesus was teaching in the temple area he said,* "How do the scribes claim that the Messiah is the son of David? 36 David himself, inspired by the holy Spirit, said:

'The Lord said to my lord,
    "Sit at my right hand
        until I place your enemies under your
            feet."'*

---

† **12:13–34** In the ensuing conflicts (cf. also Mk 2:1–3:6) Jesus vanquishes his adversaries by his responses to their questions and reduces them to silence (Mk 12:34).

**12:13–17** See note on Mt 22:15–22.

**12:18–27** See note on Mt 22:23–33.

**12:28–34** See note on Mt 22:34–40.

**12:35–37** Jesus questions the claim of the scribes about the Davidic descent of the Messiah, not to deny it (Mt 1:1; Acts 2:20, 34; Rom 1:3; 2 Tm 2:8) but to imply that he is more than this. His superiority derives from his transcendent origin, to which David himself attested when he spoke of the Messiah with the name "Lord" (Ps 110:1). See also note on Mt 22:41–46.

---

| | |
|---|---|
| **12:13–27** Mt 22:15–33; Lk | **12:30** Dt 6:4–5. |
| 20:20–39. | **12:31** Lv 19:18; Rom 13:9; |
| **12:13** 3:6. | Gal 5:14; Jas 2:8. |
| **12:17** Rom 13:7. | **12:33** Dt 6:4; Mi 40:7–9. |
| **12:19** Dt 25:5. | **12:34** Mt 22:46; Lk 20:40. |
| **12:26** Ex 3:6. | **12:35–37** Mt 22:41–45; Lk |
| **12:28–34** Mt 22:34–40; Lk | 20:41–44. |
| 10:25–28. | **12:36** Ps 110:1. |

37 David himself calls him 'lord'; so how is he his son?" [The] great crowd heard this with delight.

**Denunciation of the Scribes.**† 38 In the course of his teaching he said,* "Beware of the scribes, who like to go around in long robes and accept greetings in the marketplaces, 39 seats of honor in synagogues, and places of honor at banquets. 40 They devour the houses of widows and, as a pretext, recite lengthy prayers. They will receive a very severe condemnation."

**The Poor Widow's Contribution.**† 41 He sat down opposite the treasury and observed how the crowd put money into the treasury.* Many rich people put in large sums. 42 A poor widow also came and put in two small coins worth a few cents. 43 Calling his disciples to himself, he said to them, "Amen, I say to you, this poor widow put in more than all the other contributors to the treasury. 44 For they have all contributed from their surplus wealth, but she, from her poverty, has contributed all she had, her whole livelihood."

# 13 The Destruction of the Temple Foretold.† 1 As he was making his way out of the temple area one of his disciples said to him, "Look, teacher, what stones and what buildings!"* 2 Jesus said to him, "Do you see these great buildings? There will not be one stone left upon another that will not be thrown down."

**The Signs of the End.** 3† As he was sitting on the Mount of Olives opposite the temple area, Peter, James, John, and Andrew asked him privately,* 4 "Tell us, when will this happen, and what sign will there be when all these things are about to come to an end?" 5 Jesus began to say to them, "See that no one deceives you.* 6 Many will come in my name saying, 'I am he,' and they will deceive many. 7 When you hear of wars and reports of wars do not be alarmed; such things must happen, but it will not yet be the end. 8 Nation will rise against nation and kingdom against kingdom. There will be earthquakes from place to place and there will be famines. These are the beginnings of the labor pains.

**The Coming Persecution.** 9* "Watch out for yourselves. They will hand you over to the courts. You will be beaten in synagogues. You will be arraigned before governors and kings because of me, as a witness before them. 10 But the gospel must first be preached to all nations.† 11 When they lead you away and hand you over, do not worry beforehand about what you are to say.* But say whatever will be given to you at that hour. For it will not be you who are speaking but the holy Spirit. 12 Brother will hand over brother to death, and the father his child; children will rise up against parents and have them put to death. 13 You will be hated by all because of my name. But the one who perseveres to the end will be saved.

**The Great Tribulation.** 14* "When you see the desolating abomination standing† where he should not (let the reader understand), then those in Judea must flee to the mountains,* 15 [and] a person on a housetop must not go down or enter to get anything out of his house,* 16 and a person in a field must not return to get his cloak. 17 Woe to pregnant women and nursing mothers in those days. 18 Pray that this does not happen in winter.

**12:38–40** See notes on Mk 7:1–23 and Mt 23:1–39.
**12:41–44** See note on Lk 21:1–4.
**13:1–2** The reconstructed temple with its precincts, begun under Herod the Great ca. 20 B.C., was completed only some seven years before it was destroyed by fire in A.D. 70 at the hands of the Romans; cf. Jer 26:18; Mt 24:1–2. For the dating of the reconstruction of the temple, see further the note on Jn 2:20.
**13:3–37** Jesus' prediction of the destruction of the temple (Mk 13:2) provoked questions that the four named disciples put to him in private regarding the time and the sign when all *these things are about to come to an end* (Mk 13:3–4). The response to their questions was Jesus' eschatological discourse prior to his imminent death. It contained instruction and consolation exhorting the disciples and the church to faith and obedience through the trials that would confront them (Mk 13:5–13). The sign is the presence of *the desolating abomination* (Mk 13:14; see Dn 9:27), i.e., of the Roman power profaning the temple. Flight from Jerusalem is urged rather than defense of the city through misguided messianic hope (Mk 13:14–23). Intervention will occur only after destruction (Mk 13:24–27), which will happen before the end of the first Christian generation (Mk 13:28–31). No one but the Father knows the precise time, or that of the parousia (Mk 13:32); hence the necessity of constant vigilance (Mk 13:33–37). Luke sets the parousia at a later date, after "the time of the Gentiles" (Lk 21:24). See also notes on Mt 24:1–25:46.
**13:10** *The gospel...to all nations*: the period of the Christian mission.
**13:14** The participle *standing* is masculine, in contrast to the neuter at Mt 24:15.

**12:38–40** Mt 23:1–7; Lk 11:43; 20:45–47.
**12:41–44** Lk 21:1–4.
**13:1–2** Mt 24:1–2; Lk 21:5–6.
**13:3–8** Mt 24:3–8; Lk 21:7–11.
**13:5** Eph 5:6; 2 Thes 2:3.
**13:9–13** Mt 24:9–14; Lk 21:12–19.
**13:11–12** Mt 10:19–22; Lk 12:11–12.
**13:14–23** Mt 24:15–22; Lk 21:20–24.
**13:14** Dn 9:27; Mt 24:15.
**13:15** Lk 17:31.

© Anselm Academic / Brian Singer-Towns

When one of his disciples exclaims to him in awe over the Temple structures, Jesus responds, "Do you see these great buildings? There will not be one stone left upon another that will not be thrown down" (Mk 13:2). Above, debris pushed over the side of the Temple Mount in its destruction in 70 CE.

¹⁹ For those times will have tribulation such as has not been since the beginning of God's creation until now, nor ever will be.* ²⁰ If the Lord had not shortened those days, no one would be saved; but for the sake of the elect whom he chose, he did shorten the days. ²¹ If anyone says to you then, 'Look, here is the Messiah! Look, there he is!' do not believe it. ²² False messiahs and false prophets will arise and will perform signs and wonders in order to mislead, if that were possible, the elect. ²³ Be watchful! I have told it all to you beforehand.

**The Coming of the Son of Man.** ²⁴* "But in those days after that tribulation

> the sun will be darkened,
>     and the moon will not give its light,*
> ²⁵     and the stars will be falling from the sky,
>     and the powers in the heavens will be
>         shaken.

²⁶†* And then they will see 'the Son of Man coming in the clouds' with great power and glory, ²⁷ and then he will send out the angels and gather [his] elect from the four winds, from the end of the earth to the end of the sky.

**The Lesson of the Fig Tree.** ²⁸* "Learn a lesson from the fig tree. When its branch becomes tender and sprouts leaves, you know that summer is near. ²⁹ In the same way, when you see these things happening, know that he is near, at the gates. ³⁰ Amen, I say to you, this generation will not pass away until all these things have taken place. ³¹ Heaven and earth will pass away, but my words will not pass away.

**Need for Watchfulness.** ³² "But of that day or hour, no one knows, neither the angels in heaven, nor the Son, but only the Father. ³³* Be watchful! Be alert! You do not know when the time will come. ³⁴ It is like a man traveling abroad. He leaves home and places his servants in charge, each with his work, and orders the gatekeeper to be on the watch.* ³⁵ Watch, therefore; you do not know when the lord of the house is coming, whether in

MK

---

† **13:26** *Son of Man...with great power and glory:* Jesus cites this text from Dn 7:13 in his response to the high priest, *Are you the Messiah?* (Mk 14:61). In Ex 34:5; Lv 16:2; and Nm 11:25 the clouds indicate the presence of the divinity. Thus in his role of Son of Man, Jesus is a heavenly being who will come in power and glory.

*
**13:19** Dn 12:1.
**13:24–27** Mt 24:29–31; Lk 21:25–27.
**13:24** Is 13:10; Ez 32:7; Jl 2:10.
**13:26** 14:62; Dn 7:13–14.
**13:28–32** Mt 24:32–36; Lk 21:29–33.
**13:33–37** Mt 24:42; 25:13–15.
**13:34** Mt 25:14–30; Lk 19:12–27.

the evening, or at midnight, or at cockcrow, or in the morning. ³⁶May he not come suddenly and find you sleeping. ³⁷What I say to you, I say to all: 'Watch!'"

# 14 The Conspiracy Against Jesus. ¹† The Passover and the Feast of Unleavened Bread† were to take place in two days' time.* So the chief priests and the scribes were seeking a way to arrest him by treachery and put him to death. ²They said, "Not during the festival, for fear that there may be a riot among the people."

**The Anointing at Bethany.**† ³When he was in Bethany reclining at table in the house of Simon the leper,* a woman came with an alabaster jar of perfumed oil, costly genuine spikenard. She broke the alabaster jar and poured it on his head. ⁴There were some who were indignant. "Why has there been this waste of perfumed oil? ⁵It could have been sold for more than three hundred days' wages and the money given to the poor." They were infuriated with her. ⁶Jesus said, "Let her alone. Why do you make trouble for her? She has done a good thing for me. ⁷The poor you will always have with you, and whenever you wish you can do good to them, but you will not always have me. ⁸She has done what she could. She has anticipated anointing my body for burial. ⁹Amen, I say to you, wherever the gospel is proclaimed to the whole world, what she has done will be told in memory of her."

**The Betrayal by Judas.** ¹⁰* Then Judas Iscariot,

one of the Twelve, went off to the chief priests to hand him over to them. ¹¹When they heard him they were pleased and promised to pay him money. Then he looked for an opportunity to hand him over.

**Preparations for the Passover.** ¹²* On the first day of the Feast of Unleavened Bread, when they sacrificed the Passover lamb,† his disciples said to him, "Where do you want us to go and prepare for you to eat the Passover?" ¹³He sent two of his disciples and said to them, "Go into the city and a man will meet you, carrying a jar of water.† Follow him. ¹⁴Wherever he enters, say to the master of the house, 'The Teacher says, "Where is my guest room where I may eat the Passover with my disciples?"' ¹⁵Then he will show you a large upper room furnished and ready. Make the preparations for us there." ¹⁶The disciples then went off, entered the city, and found it just as he had told them; and they prepared the Passover.

**The Betrayer.** ¹⁷* When it was evening, he came with the Twelve. ¹⁸† And as they reclined at table and were eating, Jesus said, "Amen, I say to you, one of you will betray me, one who is eating with me." ¹⁹They began to be distressed and to say to him, one by one, "Surely it is not I?" ²⁰He said to them, "One of the Twelve, the one who dips with me into the dish. ²¹For the Son of Man indeed goes, as it is written of him,† but woe to that man by whom the Son of Man is betrayed. It would be better for that man if he had never been born."

---

† **14:1–16:8** In the movement of Mark's gospel the cross is depicted as Jesus' way to glory in accordance with the divine will. Thus the passion narrative is seen as the climax of Jesus' ministry.

**14:1** *The Passover and the Feast of Unleavened Bread*: the connection between the two festivals is reflected in Ex 12:3–20; 34:18; Lv 23:4–8; Nm 9:2–14; 28:16–17; Dt 16:1–8. The Passover commemorated the redemption from slavery and the departure of the Israelites from Egypt by night. It began at sundown after the Passover lamb was sacrificed in the temple in the afternoon of the fourteenth day of the month of Nisan. With the Passover supper on the same evening was associated the eating of unleavened bread. The latter was continued through Nisan 21, a reminder of the affliction of the Israelites and of the haste surrounding their departure. Praise and thanks to God for his goodness in the past were combined at this dual festival with the hope of future salvation. *The chief priests...to death*: the intent to put Jesus to death was plotted for a long time but delayed for fear of the crowd (Mk 3:6; 11:18; 12:12).

**14:3** At Bethany on the Mount of Olives, a few miles from Jerusalem, in *the house of Simon the leper*, Jesus defends a woman's loving action of anointing his head with perfumed oil in view of his impending death and burial as a criminal, in which case his body would not be anointed. See further the note on Jn

12:7. He assures the woman of the remembrance of her deed in the worldwide preaching of the good news.

**14:12** *The first day of the Feast of Unleavened Bread...the Passover lamb*: a less precise designation of the day for sacrificing the Passover lamb as evidenced by some rabbinical literature. For a more exact designation, see note on Mk 14:1. It was actually Nisan 14.

**14:13** *A man...carrying a jar of water*: perhaps a prearranged signal, for only women ordinarily carried water in jars. The Greek word used here, however, implies simply a person and not necessarily a male.

**14:18** *One of you will betray me, one who is eating with me*: contrasts the intimacy of table fellowship at the Passover meal with the treachery of the traitor; cf. 14:10.

**14:21** *The Son of Man indeed goes, as it is written of him*: a reference to Ps 41:10 cited by Jesus concerning Judas at the Last Supper; cf. Jn 13:18–19.

---

**14:1–2** Mt 26:2–5; Lk 22:1–2; Jn 11:45–53.
**14:3–9** Mt 26:6–13; Jn 12:1–8.
**14:10–11** Mt 26:14–16; Lk 22:3–6.
**14:12–16** Mt 26:17–19; Lk 22:7–13.
**14:17–21** Mt 26:20–24; Lk 22:21–23; Jn 13:21–26.

## The Lord's Supper. 22† While they were eating,* he took bread, said the blessing, broke it, and gave it to them, and said, "Take it; this is my body." 23 Then he took a cup, gave thanks, and gave it to them, and they all drank from it. 24 He said to them, "This is my blood of the covenant, which will be shed† for many. 25 Amen, I say to you, I shall not drink again the fruit of the vine until the day when I drink it new in the kingdom of God." 26 Then, after singing a hymn,† they went out to the Mount of Olives.*

## Peter's Denial Foretold.† 27 Then Jesus said to them, "All of you will have your faith shaken, for it is written:

'I will strike the shepherd,
    and the sheep will be dispersed.'*

28 But after I have been raised up, I shall go before you to Galilee." 29 Peter said to him, "Even though all should have their faith shaken, mine will not be." 30 Then Jesus said to him, "Amen, I say to you, this very night before the cock crows twice you will deny me three times." 31 But he vehemently replied, "Even though I should have to die with you, I will not deny you." And they all spoke similarly.

## The Agony in the Garden. 32† Then they came to a place named Gethsemane,* and he said to his disciples, "Sit here while I pray."* 33 He took with him Peter, James, and John, and began to be troubled and distressed. 34 Then

he said to them, "My soul is sorrowful even to death. Remain here and keep watch." 35 He advanced a little and fell to the ground and prayed that if it were possible the hour might pass by him; 36 he said, "Abba, Father,† all things are possible to you. Take this cup away from me, but not what I will but what you will." 37 When he returned he found them asleep. He said to Peter, "Simon, are you asleep? Could you not keep watch for one hour? 38† Watch and pray that you may not undergo the test.* The spirit is willing but the flesh is weak." 39 Withdrawing again, he prayed, saying the same thing. 40 Then he returned once more and found them asleep, for they could not keep their eyes open and did not know what to answer him. 41 He returned a third time and said to them, "Are you still sleeping and taking your rest? It is enough. The hour has come. Behold, the Son of Man is to be handed over to sinners. 42 Get up, let us go. See, my betrayer is at hand."

## The Betrayal and Arrest of Jesus. 43* Then, while he was still speaking, Judas, one of the Twelve, arrived, accompanied by a crowd with swords and clubs who had come from the chief priests, the scribes, and the elders. 44 His betrayer had arranged a signal with them, saying, "The man I shall kiss is the one; arrest him and lead him away securely." 45 He came and immediately went over to him and said, "Rabbi." And he kissed him. 46 At this they laid hands on him and arrested him. 47 One of the bystanders drew his sword, struck the

MK

---

† **14:22–24** The actions and words of Jesus express within the framework of the Passover meal and the transition to a new covenant the sacrifice of himself through the offering of his body and blood in anticipation of his passion and death. His *blood of the covenant* both alludes to the ancient rite of Ex 24:4–8 and indicates the new community that the sacrifice of Jesus will bring into being (Mt 26:26–28; Lk 22:19–20; 1 Cor 11:23–25).

**14:24** *Which will be shed*: see note on Mt 26:27–28. *For many*: the Greek preposition *hyper* is a different one from that at Mt 26:28 but the same as that found at Lk 22:19, 20 and 1 Cor 11:24. The sense of both words is vicarious, and it is difficult in Hellenistic Greek to distinguish between them. For *many* in the sense of "all," see note on Mt 20:28.

**14:26** *After singing a hymn*: Ps 114–118, thanksgiving songs concluding the Passover meal.

**14:27–31** Jesus predicted that the Twelve would waver in their faith, even abandon him, despite their protestations to the contrary. Yet he reassured them that after his resurrection he would regather them in Galilee (Mk 16:7; cf. Mt 26:32; 28:7, 10, 16; Jn 21), where he first summoned them to be his followers as he began to preach the good news (Mk 1:14–20).

**14:32–34** The disciples who had witnessed the raising to life of the daughter of Jairus (Mk 5:37) and the transfiguration of their

Master (Mk 9:2) were now invited to witness his degradation and agony and to watch and pray with him.

**14:36** *Abba, Father*: an Aramaic term, here also translated by Mark, Jesus' special way of addressing God with filial intimacy. The word *'abbā'* seems not to have been used in earlier or contemporaneous Jewish sources to address God without some qualifier. Cf. Rom 8:15; Gal 4:6 for other occurrences of the Aramaic word in the Greek New Testament. *Not what I will but what you will*: note the complete obedient surrender of the human will of Jesus to the divine will of the Father; cf. Jn 4:34; 8:29; Rom 5:19; Phil 2:8; Heb 5:8.

**14:38** *The spirit is willing but the flesh is weak*: the spirit is drawn to what is good yet found in conflict with the flesh, inclined to sin; cf. Ps 51:7, 12. Everyone is faced with this struggle, the full force of which Jesus accepted on our behalf and, through his bitter passion and death, achieved the victory.

---

**14:22–25** Mt 26:26–30; Lk 22:19–20; 1 Cor 11:23–25.
**14:26–31** Mt 26:30–35; Lk 22:34, 39; Jn 13:36–38.
**14:27** Zec 13:7; Jn 16:32.
**14:32–42** Mt 26:36–46; Lk 22:40–46.
**14:32** Jn 18:1.
**14:38** Rom 7:5.
**14:43–50** Mt 26:47–56; Lk 22:47–53; Jn 18:3–11.

high priest's servant, and cut off his ear. <sup>48</sup> Jesus said to them in reply, "Have you come out as against a robber, with swords and clubs, to seize me? <sup>49</sup> Day after day I was with you teaching in the temple area, yet you did not arrest me; but that the scriptures may be fulfilled." <sup>50</sup> And they all left him and fled. <sup>51</sup> Now a young man followed him wearing nothing but a linen cloth about his body. They seized him, <sup>52</sup> but he left the cloth behind and ran off naked.

**Jesus Before the Sanhedrin.** <sup>53</sup>†* They led Jesus away to the high priest, and all the chief priests and the elders and the scribes came together. <sup>54</sup> Peter followed him at a distance into the high priest's courtyard and was seated with the guards, warming himself at the fire. <sup>55</sup> The chief priests and the entire Sanhedrin kept trying to obtain testimony against Jesus in order to put him to death, but they found none. <sup>56</sup> Many gave false witness against him, but their testimony did not agree. <sup>57</sup>† Some took the stand and testified falsely against him, alleging, <sup>58</sup> "We heard him say, 'I will destroy this temple made with hands and within three days I will build another not made with hands.'"* <sup>59</sup> Even so their testimony did not agree. <sup>60</sup> The high priest rose before the assembly and questioned Jesus, saying, "Have you no answer? What are these men testifying against you?" <sup>61</sup>† But he was silent and answered nothing. Again the high priest asked him and said to him, "Are you the Messiah, the son of the Blessed One?" <sup>62</sup> Then Jesus answered, "I am;

and 'you will see the Son of Man
seated at the right hand of the Power

and coming with the clouds of
heaven.'"*

<sup>63</sup> At that the high priest tore his garments and said, "What further need have we of witnesses? <sup>64</sup> You have heard the blasphemy. What do you think?" They all condemned him as deserving to die. <sup>65</sup> Some began to spit on him. They blindfolded him and struck him and said to him, "Prophesy!" And the guards greeted him with blows.*

**Peter's Denial of Jesus.** <sup>66</sup>* While Peter was below in the courtyard, one of the high priest's maids came along. <sup>67</sup> Seeing Peter warming himself, she looked intently at him and said, "You too were with the Nazarene, Jesus." <sup>68</sup>† But he denied it saying, "I neither know nor understand what you are talking about." So he went out into the outer court. [Then the cock crowed.] <sup>69</sup> The maid saw him and began again to say to the bystanders, "This man is one of them." <sup>70</sup> Once again he denied it. A little later the bystanders said to Peter once more, "Surely you are one of them; for you too are a Galilean." <sup>71</sup> He began to curse and to swear, "I do not know this man about whom you are talking." <sup>72</sup> And immediately a cock crowed a second time. Then Peter remembered the word that Jesus had said to him, "Before the cock crows twice you will deny me three times." He broke down and wept.*

# 15

**Jesus Before Pilate.** <sup>1</sup>* As soon as morning came,* the chief priests with the elders and the scribes, that is, the whole Sanhedrin, held a council.† They bound Jesus, led him away, and handed him over to Pilate. <sup>2</sup> Pilate questioned him, "Are you the king of

---

† **14:53** *They led Jesus away…came together:* Mark presents a formal assembly of the whole Sanhedrin (chief priests, elders, and scribes) at night, leading to the condemnation of Jesus (Mk 14:64), in contrast to Lk 22:66, 71 where Jesus is condemned in a daytime meeting of the council; see also Jn 18:13, 19–24.

**14:57–58** See notes on Mt 26:60–61 and Jn 2:19.

**14:61–62** *The Blessed One:* a surrogate for the divine name, which Jews did not pronounce. *I am:* indicates Jesus' acknowledgment that he is the Messiah and Son of God; cf. Mk 1:1. Contrast Mt 26:64 and Lk 22:67–70, in which Jesus leaves his interrogators to answer their own question. *You will see the Son of Man…with the clouds of heaven:* an allusion to Dn 7:13 and Ps 110:1 portending the enthronement of Jesus as judge in the transcendent glory of God's kingdom. *The Power:* another surrogate for the name of God.

**14:68** *[Then the cock crowed]:* found in most manuscripts, perhaps in view of Mk 14:30, 72 but omitted in others.

**15:1** *Held a council:* the verb here, *poieō,* can mean either "convene a council" or "take counsel." This reading is preferred

to a variant "reached a decision" (cf. Mk 3:6), which Mk 14:64 describes as having happened at the night trial; see note on Mt 27:1–2. *Handed him over to Pilate:* lacking authority to execute their sentence of condemnation (Mk 14:64), the Sanhedrin had recourse to Pilate to have Jesus tried and put to death (Mk 15:15); cf. Jn 18:31.

**15:2** *The king of the Jews:* in the accounts of the evangelists a certain irony surrounds the use of this title as an accusation against Jesus (see note on Mk 15:26). While Pilate uses this term (Mk 15:2, 9, 12), he is aware of the evil motivation of the chief priests who handed Jesus over for trial and condemnation (Mk 15:10; Lk 23:14–16, 20; Mt 27:18, 24; Jn 18:38; 19:4, 6, 12).

---

**14:53–65** Mt 26:57–68; Lk 22:54–55, 63–65, 67–71; Jn 18:12–13.
**14:58** 15:29; 2 Cor 5:1.
**14:62** 13:26; Ps 110:1; Dn 7:13; Mt 24:30.
**14:65** Lk 22:63–65.

**14:66–72** Mt 26:69–75; Lk 22:56–62; Jn 18:16–18, 25–27.
**14:72** Jn 13:38.
**15:1–5** Mt 27:1–2, 11–14; Lk 23:1–3.
**15:1** Jn 18:28.

MK

the Jews?"† He said to him in reply, "You say so." ³The chief priests accused him of many things. ⁴Again Pilate questioned him, "Have you no answer? See how many things they accuse you of." ⁵Jesus gave him no further answer, so that Pilate was amazed.

**The Sentence of Death.**† ⁶Now on the occasion of the feast he used to release to them one prisoner whom they requested.* ⁷A man called Barabbas† was then in prison along with the rebels who had committed murder in a rebellion. ⁸The crowd came forward and began to ask him to do for them as he was accustomed. ⁹Pilate answered, "Do you want me to release to you the king of the Jews?" ¹⁰For he knew that it was out of envy that the chief priests had handed him over. ¹¹But the chief priests stirred up the crowd to have him release Barabbas for them instead. ¹²Pilate again said to them in reply, "Then what [do you want] me to do with [the man you call] the king of the Jews?" ¹³†They shouted again, "Crucify him." ¹⁴Pilate said to them, "Why? What evil has he done?" They only shouted the louder, "Crucify him." ¹⁵†So Pilate, wishing to satisfy the crowd, released Barabbas to them and, after he had Jesus scourged, handed him over to be crucified.

**Mockery by the Soldiers.** ¹⁶†*The soldiers led him away inside the palace, that is, the praetorium, and assembled the whole cohort. ¹⁷They clothed him in purple and, weaving a crown of thorns, placed it on him. ¹⁸They began to salute him with, "Hail, King of the Jews!" ¹⁹and kept striking his head with a reed and spitting upon him. They knelt before him in homage. ²⁰And when they had mocked him,

they stripped him of the purple cloak, dressed him in his own clothes, and led him out to crucify him.

**The Way of the Cross.** ²¹They pressed into service a passer-by, Simon, a Cyrenian,† who was coming in from the country, the father of Alexander and Rufus, to carry his cross.*

**The Crucifixion.** ²²*They brought him to the place of Golgotha (which is translated Place of the Skull). ²³They gave him wine drugged with myrrh, but he did not take it. ²⁴†*Then they crucified him and divided his garments by casting lots for them to see what each should take. ²⁵It was nine o'clock in the morning† when they crucified him. ²⁶†The inscription of the charge against him read, "The King of the Jews." ²⁷With him they crucified two revolutionaries, one on his right and one on his left.* [²⁸]† ²⁹†Those passing by reviled him, shaking their heads and saying,* "Aha! You who would destroy the temple and rebuild it in three days, ³⁰save yourself by coming down from the cross." ³¹Likewise the chief priests, with the scribes, mocked him among themselves and said, "He saved others; he cannot save himself. ³²Let the Messiah, the King of Israel, come down now from the cross that we may see and believe." Those who were crucified with him also kept abusing him.*

**The Death of Jesus.** ³³At noon darkness came over the whole land until three in the afternoon. ³⁴And at three o'clock Jesus cried out in a loud voice, *"Eloi, Eloi, lema sabachthani?"*† which is translated, "My God, my God, why have you forsaken me?"* ³⁵†Some of the bystanders who heard it said, "Look, he is

---

† **15:6–15** See note on Mt 27:15–26.
**15:7** *Barabbas:* see note on Mt 27:16–17.
**15:13** *Crucify him:* see note on Mt 27:22.
**15:15** See note on Mt 27:26.
**15:16** *Praetorium:* see note on Mt 27:27.
**15:21** *They pressed into service…Simon, a Cyrenian:* a condemned person was constrained to bear his own instrument of torture, at least the crossbeam. The precise naming of Simon and his sons is probably due to their being known among early Christian believers to whom Mark addressed his gospel. See also notes on Mt 27:32; Lk 23:26–32.
**15:24** See notes on Mt 27:35 and Jn 19:23–25a.
**15:25** *It was nine o'clock in the morning:* literally, "the third hour," thus between 9 a.m. and 12 noon. Cf. Mk 15:33, 34, 42 for Mark's chronological sequence, which may reflect liturgical or catechetical considerations rather than the precise historical sequence of events; contrast the different chronologies in the other gospels, especially Jn 19:14.
**15:26** *The inscription…the King of the Jews:* the political rea-

son for the death penalty falsely charged by the enemies of Jesus. See further the notes on Mt 27:37 and Jn 19:19.
**15:28** This verse, "And the scripture was fulfilled that says, 'And he was counted among the wicked,'" is omitted in the earliest and best manuscripts. It contains a citation from Is 53:12 and was probably introduced from Lk 22:37.
**15:29** See note on Mt 27:39–40.
**15:34** An Aramaic rendering of Ps 22:2. See also note on Mt 27:46.
**15:35** *Elijah:* a verbal link with *Eloi* (Mk 15:34). See note on Mk 9:9–13; cf. Mal 3:23–24. See also note on Mt 27:47.

---

* **15:6–15** Mt 27:15–26;      Lk 23:32–46; Jn
          Lk 23:17–25; Jn      19:17–30.
          18:39–40.          **15:24** Ps 22:18.
**15:16–20** Mt 27:27–31; Jn   **15:27** Lk 23:33.
          19:2–3.          **15:29** Jn 2:19.
    **15:21** Mt 27:32; Lk 23:26.  **15:32** Lk 23:39.
    **15:22–38** Mt 27:33–51;    **15:34** Ps 22:2.

calling Elijah." 36 One of them ran, soaked a sponge with wine, put it on a reed, and gave it to him to drink, saying, "Wait, let us see if Elijah comes to take him down." 37 Jesus gave a loud cry and breathed his last. 38† The veil of the sanctuary was torn in two from top to bottom. 39†* When the centurion who stood facing him saw how he breathed his last he said, "Truly this man was the Son of God!" 40† There were also women looking on from a distance.* Among them were Mary Magdalene, Mary the mother of the younger James and of Joses, and Salome. 41 These women had followed him when he was in Galilee and ministered to him. There were also many other women who had come up with him to Jerusalem.

**The Burial of Jesus.** 42* When it was already evening, since it was the day of preparation, the day before the sabbath, 43 Joseph of Arimathea,† a distinguished member of the council, who was himself awaiting the kingdom of God, came and courageously went to Pilate and asked for the body of Jesus. 44 Pilate was amazed that he was already dead. He summoned the centurion and asked him if Jesus had already died. 45 And when he learned of it from the centurion, he gave the body to Joseph. 46 Having bought a linen cloth, he took him down, wrapped him in the linen cloth and laid him in a tomb that had been hewn out of the rock. Then he rolled a stone against

the entrance to the tomb. 47 Mary Magdalene and Mary the mother of Joses watched where he was laid.

# 16 The Resurrection of Jesus.† 1 When the sabbath was over,* Mary Magdalene, Mary, the mother of James, and Salome bought spices so that they might go and anoint him.* 2 Very early when the sun had risen, on the first day of the week, they came to the tomb. 3 They were saying to one another, "Who will roll back the stone for us from the entrance to the tomb?" 4 When they looked up, they saw that the stone had been rolled back; it was very large. 5 On entering the tomb they saw a young man sitting on the right side, clothed in a white robe, and they were utterly amazed.* 6 He said to them, "Do not be amazed! You seek Jesus of Nazareth, the crucified. He has been raised; he is not here. Behold, the place where they laid him. 7 But go and tell his disciples and Peter, 'He is going before you to Galilee; there you will see him, as he told you.'* 8 Then they went out and fled from the tomb, seized with trembling and bewilderment. They said nothing to anyone, for they were afraid.

## THE LONGER ENDING†

**The Appearance to Mary Magdalene.** [9* When he had risen, early on the first day of the week,

---

**15:38** See note on Mt 27:51–53.

**15:39** The closing portion of Mark's gospel returns to the theme of its beginning in the Gentile centurion's climactic declaration of belief that Jesus *was the Son of God.* It indicates the fulfillment of the good news announced in the prologue (Mk 1:1) and may be regarded as the firstfruit of the passion and death of Jesus.

**15:40–41** See note on Mt 27:55–56.

**15:43** *Joseph of Arimathea*: see note on Mt 27:57–61.

**16:1–8** The purpose of this narrative is to show that the tomb is empty and that Jesus *has been raised* (Mk 16:6) and is *going before you to Galilee* (Mk 16:7) in fulfillment of Mk 14:28. The women find the tomb empty, and an angel stationed there announces to them what has happened. They are told to proclaim the news to Peter and the disciples in order to prepare them for a reunion with him. Mark's composition of the gospel ends at Mk 16:8 with the women telling no one, because they were afraid. This abrupt termination causes some to believe that the original ending of this gospel may have been lost. See the following note.

**16:9–20** This passage, termed the Longer Ending to the Marcan gospel by comparison with a much briefer conclusion found in some less important manuscripts, has traditionally been accepted as a canonical part of the gospel and was defined as such by the Council of Trent. Early citations of it by the Fathers indicate that it was composed by the second century, although vocabulary and style indicate that it was written by someone other than Mark. It is a general resume of the material concerning the appearances of the risen Jesus, reflecting, in particular,

traditions found in Lk 24 and Jn 20.

The Shorter Ending: Found after Mk 16:8 before the Longer Ending in four seventh-to-ninth-century Greek manuscripts as well as in one Old Latin version, where it appears alone without the Longer Ending.

The Freer Logion: Found after Mk 16:14 in a fourth-fifth century manuscript preserved in the Freer Gallery of Art, Washington, DC, this ending was known to Jerome in the fourth century. It reads: "And they excused themselves, saying, 'This age of lawlessness and unbelief is under Satan, who does not allow the truth and power of God to prevail over the unclean things dominated by the spirits [or, does not allow the unclean things dominated by the spirits to grasp the truth and power of God]. Therefore reveal your righteousness now.' They spoke to Christ. And Christ responded to them, 'The limit of the years of Satan's power is completed, but other terrible things draw near. And for those who sinned I was handed over to death, that they might return to the truth and no longer sin, in order that they might inherit the spiritual and incorruptible heavenly glory of righteousness. But….'"

---

**15:39–41** Mt 27:54–56; Lk 23:47–49.
**15:40** 6:3; Lk 8:2–3.
**15:42–47** Mt 27:57–61; Lk 23:50–56; Jn 19:38–42.
**16:1–8** Mt 28:1–8; Lk 24:1–10; Jn 20:1–10.
**16:1–2** Mt 28:1; Lk 23:56.
**16:5** Jn 20:12.
**16:7** 14:28.
**16:9–20** Mt 28:1–10; Jn 20:11–18.

© Anselm Academic / Brian Singer-Towns

"They were saying to one another, 'Who will roll back the stone for us from the entrance to the tomb?' When they looked up, they saw that the stone had been rolled back; it was very large" (Mk 16:3–4). Above, a tomb such as that in which Jesus was buried.

he appeared first to Mary Magdalene, out of whom he had driven seven demons. [10]* She went and told his companions who were mourning and weeping. [11] When they heard that he was alive and had been seen by her, they did not believe.

**The Appearance to Two Disciples.** [12]* After this he appeared in another form to two of them walking along on their way to the country. [13] They returned and told the others; but they did not believe them either.

**The Commissioning of the Eleven.** [14]* [But] later, as the eleven were at table, he appeared to them and rebuked them for their unbelief and hardness of heart because they had not believed those who saw him after he had been raised. [15]* He said to them, "Go into the whole world and proclaim the gospel to every creature. [16] Whoever believes and is baptized will be saved; whoever does not believe will be condemned. [17] These signs will accompany those who believe: in my name they will drive out demons, they will speak new

languages. [18] They will pick up serpents [with their hands], and if they drink any deadly thing, it will not harm them. They will lay hands on the sick, and they will recover."*

**The Ascension of Jesus.** [19] So then the Lord Jesus, after he spoke to them, was taken up into heaven and took his seat at the right hand of God.* [20] But they went forth and preached everywhere, while the Lord worked with them and confirmed the word through accompanying signs.]*

### THE SHORTER ENDING

[And they reported all the instructions briefly to Peter's companions. Afterwards Jesus himself, through them, sent forth from east to west the sacred and imperishable proclamation of eternal salvation. Amen.]

**16:10–11** Lk 24:10–11; Jn 20:18.
**16:12–14** Lk 24:13–35.
**16:14** Lk 24:36–49; 1 Cor 15:5.
**16:15–16** 13:10; Mt 28:18–20; Lk 24:47; Jn 20:21.
**16:18** Mt 10:1; Lk 10:19; Acts 28:3–6.
**16:19** Lk 24:50–53.
**16:20** 1 Tm 3:16.

MK

# The Gospel According to

# Luke

## INTRODUCTION

### Clare K. Rothschild

The Gospel of Luke is the longest of the four canonical Gospels. Its genre, a much-debated topic, is probably best described as hybrid, incorporating aspects of history, biography, philosophy, epic, and novels. While each of the four Gospels has unique features, the Gospel of Luke is widely appreciated for its stories about Zacchaeus, Mary and Martha, the Prodigal Son, the Good Samaritan, and the Road to Emmaus. It is also treasured for themes like the liberation of the poor and oppressed. It tends to be the favorite of feminists for its higher proportion of stories about women.

## Authorship

Scholars favor the hypothesis that Luke's Gospel is the first in a two-volume set of works, the second volume being the Acts of the Apostles. This connection is suggested by matching dedications in both Luke (Lk 1:3) and Acts (Acts 1:1) to "Theophilus"—either Luke's benefactor or every "lover of God" (based on the etymology of the name in Greek). Like the other canonical Gospels, the earliest extant manuscripts of the Third Gospel have no attributions, making it, technically speaking, anonymous. It is not attributed to "Luke" until Irenaeus, the priest of Lyons, in his book, *Against Heresies* written around the year 175 CE. This Gospel was clearly in use in the beginning of the second century, when we know that the teacher Marcion used it.

On the basis of the reference to a person named Luke in Phlm 24 (cf. 2 Tm 4:11), authorial attribution to Luke may be accurate and may correlate authorship with a companion of the Apostle Paul. Authorial attribution to Luke may also correlate authorship with Paul on the basis of the so-called "we-passages" in Acts (see Acts 16:10–17; 20:5–15; 21:1–18; 27:1–28:16

---

## Outline of Luke

I. The Prologue (1:1–4)

II. The Infancy Narrative (1:5–2:52)

III. The Preparation for the Public Ministry (3:1–4:13)

IV. The Ministry in Galilee (4:14–9:50)

V. The Journey to Jerusalem: Luke's Travel Narrative (9:51–19:27)

VI. The Teaching Ministry in Jerusalem (19:28–21:38)

VII. The Passion Narrative (22:1–23:56)

VIII. The Resurrection Narrative (24:1–53)

---

and the initial introduction to the Acts of the Apostles). In these passages, the author suddenly switches to speaking in the first person plural (we) as if he were with Paul at the scenes described. No evidence suggests that Luke was an eyewitness to Jesus' historical ministry.

The idea that Luke was a physician (see Col 4:14) is possible, although not provable on the basis of the Gospel's use of medical knowledge—contrary to the claims of a number of scholars in the past. As Henry Joel Cadbury demonstrated, equal amounts of legal and nautical language in this Gospel make it just as likely that Luke was a doctor, lawyer, or nautical engineer/skipper. What we can say about the author of Luke-Acts (the hyphenated expression for the two volume work was coined by Cadbury and is frequently used to refer to the two volumes together) is that he was a well-educated Hellenistic Jew or Gentile with knowledge of the Greek translation of the Jewish Scriptures and familiarity with other important literature of the day, including but not limited to history, drama, and poetry.

## Date/Provenance

The Gospel of Luke may have been written anytime between 56 and 140 CE. Over the past hundred years, scholarly judgment on the dating of Luke demonstrates a trend from the earlier to the later. Although a majority of scholars opt for a date of composition on or around the year 85 CE, some support a date of about 115 CE.[1] Technically speaking, if one accepts "Markan Priority," or the idea that the author of the Gospel of Luke relied on Mark as a source to write his Gospel, then the *terminus post quem*, or date after which the Gospel must have been written, is the Gospel of Mark. If Mark was composed during or near the end of the Jewish war with Rome in 70 CE, then Luke would have been written sometime after 70 as well. The *terminus ante quem* or date before which the Gospel *must* have been written is the second-century apologist Justin Martyr (103–165 CE), who cites this Gospel in his apologetic writing, the *Dialogue with Trypho* (103.8). The question of whether both Luke and Acts were composed at the same time is perhaps unsolvable. The important point is that many scholars believe that the prologue to the Gospel of Luke (Lk 1:1–4) introduces both books.

Finally, if time spent by Paul and details about Ephesus in Acts such as the "lecture hall of Tyrannus" (Acts 19:9) constitute an accurate metric, then it is likely that both the Gospel of Luke and Acts were written in or by someone from this city.

## Sources

The author of Luke probably relied on several sources for the composition of the Gospel. Consensus today holds that this author used a version of the Gospel of Mark not unlike our own. Most likely, the author also had other sources at his disposal. Today these sources are commonly categorized in two groups. The first is "Q" (for *Quelle*, German for "source"), a hypothetical source containing (mostly) sayings that demonstrate verbatim agreement with Matthew, but are absent from Mark. The other source consists of material unique to Luke, designated "Special L" or simply "L." This source may reflect any number of oral or written archival or non-archival reports. It is impossible, in hindsight, to say whether L represents just one or numerous additional sources. We can say, however, that many well-known parables, such as the Good Samaritan (Lk 10:25–37), the Rich Fool (12:13–21), the Lost Coin (15:8–10), the Lost Son (15:11–32), the Dishonest Steward (16:1–12), the Rich Man and Lazarus (16:19–31), the Widow and the Judge (18:1–8), and the Pharisee and the Tax Collector (18:9–14) represent L.

This source also contains all of the material in chapters 1 and 2 of this Gospel, including some of the most beautiful liturgical hymns, perhaps of the earliest layer of Christian tradition: the *Magnificat* (Lk 1:46–55), the *Benedictus* (1:67–79), the *Gloria in Excelsis* (2:14), and the *Nunc Dimittis* (2:29–32). Based on the noticeable emphasis on John the Baptist in Luke 1–3 (i.e., 1:5–25, 57–80; 3:10–14), some scholars speculate that the author of Luke possessed an early source about this important historical figure. Acts 19:1–7 suggests that the Baptist's followers, just like Jesus' followers, spread westward throughout the empire in the decades following John's death.

The author did not blindly copy his sources, but modified them to suit his style and purpose. For example, he improved aspects of the Greek style of the Gospel of Mark. It seems that Luke also made modifications to address a few debated theological beliefs in his sources. The most important such belief was the second coming or *parousia* of Christ. The Gospel of Mark and other early Christian texts like 1 Thessalonians (4:13–18) depict the onset of the second coming as soon. Luke, however, delays its arrival ("the kingdom of God is among you," Lk 17:21).

This so-called "delay of the *parousia*" is a very important concept of early Christianity. As far as we can tell, both John the Baptist and Jesus preached a gospel or "good news" message, featuring a warning that the end of the

---

1. Richard I. Pervo, *Dating Acts: Between the Evangelists and the Apologists* (Santa Rosa: Polebridge, 2006), esp. 15–17, 26, 343–46.

age was near (for John the Baptist, see Lk 3:7–18; for Jesus, see 21:31). Paul, too, preached such a message, emphasizing Jesus' return at the end. At points, Paul even seemed to believe that Jesus would return in Paul's own lifetime (1 Thes 4:13–18). When Paul died (perhaps 68 CE) and Jesus had not returned, many early Christians, it seems, felt forced to postpone gospel predictions, sometimes indefinitely. This postponement or delay helps scholars to date early Christian texts. The basic principle is that the more pressing the expectation of the end in a writing, the earlier the text; and likewise, the less pressing the expectation—that is, the farther the delay is pushed into the future even to the point of not speaking about it or viewing it as an existential phenomenon—the later the text. This principle is not foolproof, but often helpful.

Most likely the author combined sources in his Gospel because he felt that no single source sufficed, in either length or breadth, for his purpose (on Luke's purpose see below). Mark's unusually abrupt ending (Mk 16:8) and its overriding interest in Jesus' suffering and death (see the initial introduction to the Gospel According to Mark) were probably the chief reasons that Luke decided to rewrite it. Luke may also have felt that parts of Mark were redundant—for example, the so-called "Great Omission," a nickname for Luke's omission of Mk 6:45–8:26 or the "Lesser Omission," a nickname for Luke's omission of Mk 9:41–10:12. Ultimately, Luke adopts less than half of our present text of Mark.

In terms of his application of sources, Luke systematically alternates Q sayings with Markan material. Mark is adopted for Lk 3:1–6:1; Q is adopted for Lk 6:20–8:3; Mark, for Lk 8:4–9:50; Q, for Lk 9:51–18:14; and Mark, for Lk 18:15–24:11. In the heart of Luke's Gospel (Lk 9:51–19:48), the author draws upon Q to portray Jesus as an itinerant missionary. Today this section is known as the "Lukan Travel Narrative." Among other things, it has the important effect of setting a precedent for the itinerant gospel work of Jesus' disciples, especially Peter and Paul, in Acts. (More is said about the Lukan Travel Narrative below.)

# Key Themes and Purpose

In weaving Mark, Q, and L material together to create a single ornate tapestry, the author of Luke accents a number of significant subjects and themes under three general headings: early Christian practices, early Christian membership, and early Christian historiography.

Beginning with aspects of early Christian religious practice, Jerusalem—specifically the Temple (Lk 1:8–22; 24:53)—is the important starting and ending place of the Gospel (contrast Mark's focus on Galilee, Mk 16:7). In tandem with this focus on Jerusalem, the author places an unusual emphasis on food, dining, prayer, and worship. Luke narrates a total of nineteen meals, probably either as guidance on actual dining practices in his own Christian community or, more generally, as analogies for ethical behavior (see Jesus' parables about banquets, Lk 14:7–11, 12–14, 15–24; 15:25–32; 16:19–31 and other related teachings, 7:44–50; 22:27).

Jesus not only eats more in this Gospel (Lk 7:34), he also prays more. Prayer is an element of the narratives of Jesus' baptism (3:21), his selection of disciples (6:12), his inquiry of the disciples as to his identity (9:18), his transfiguration (9:28), and his prediction that Peter will deny him (22:32). In this Gospel, the disciples ask Jesus to teach them how to pray (11:1) and Jesus encourages them to pray often (18:1; 21:36; 22:40). This Gospel even features parables about praying (11:5–8; 18:1–8, 9–14).

In terms of the second major theme, membership, Luke's Gospel features women among the early band of Jesus' disciples and friends. Women unique to Luke include Elizabeth (the mother of John the Baptist, Lk 1:24–25, 41–45), Anna (2:36–38), the widow at Nain (7:11–17), the woman with the alabaster jar of ointment (7:36–50), the ministering women (8:1–3), the woman healed on the sabbath (13:10–17), and the widow in the parable with the judge (18:1–8). This Gospel also includes a special story about Mary and her sister Martha that is not found anywhere else in the New Testament (10:38–42).

For this special inclusion of more women, many readers are inclined to think of Luke as, if not exactly feminist, certainly ahead of his time. On one hand, this claim seems plausible; Luke does include more women in his book. The Apostle Paul may have influenced Luke in this regard. Paul incorporated women at all levels of his ministry. If Luke was Paul's co-worker, or even if he was simply influenced by a collection of Paul's letters, he may have felt he had permission to report stories about Jesus' work among female, in addition to male, followers.

On the other hand, we should probably not be too hasty to celebrate Luke as a premodern champion of women. True, he focuses on Mary over Joseph in the birth narrative (Lk 1:26–56; contrast Mt 1:18–25), but not in a liberating role as apostle, but in her traditional capacity as mother. True, also, Luke includes a unique story about Jesus' healing the son of a widow at Nain. However, the only role this woman has in the story (she does not speak) is as the object of Jesus' compassion. The group of women in Lk 8:1–3 might possess real influence in the movement, but we only hear that they financially support Jesus' ministry. No woman in Luke exercises a role of leadership as, for example, Phoebe seems to do, based on Paul's reference to her as a deacon or minister of the church at Cenchreae in Rom 16:1–2. Most are, rather, in need of Jesus' assistance. The story about Mary and Martha (Lk 10:38–42) seems to portray Mary as a genuine disciple kneeling at the feet of her Master (v. 39), yet the group of women (including Mary) giving an account of the empty tomb and resurrection are immediately dismissed as reporting "nonsense" (24:11).

We probably ought to conclude therefore that Luke includes women in his story of Jesus because he recognizes them as marginalized members of society and therefore in particular need of Jesus' message of salvation, just as he does the poor (Lk 1:53; 4:18; 6:20–21, 24–25; 12:16–21; 16:19–31) and other groups of oppressed people, including tax collectors (15:1–2; 18:9–14; 19:2–10) and Samaritans (9:51–56; 10:29–37; 17:11–19).

Finally, unlike Matthew and Mark, Luke advertises his purpose at the beginning of his work as competitive (Lk 1:1–4). He wants, he says, to improve upon other available Gospels (1:1). The author specifies that his account will demonstrate the "truth" of what at least one reader, Theophilus, already knows (1:4). Evidently, Theophilus has information, but lacks truth. This must mean that he has some but not all of the facts. It probably also means that the information he has does not impress him as truth, that is, as anything more than a string of details. One may wonder what Theophilus knew. If we speculate, for example, that he had read the Gospel of Mark, then we can safely assume that he knew certain sayings and miracles of Jesus, as well as the story of Jesus' crucifixion. How, we might ask, would this information lack truth? One possibility is that for Luke truth demands an explanation of how a Jewish movement became universal (came to include Gentiles or non-Jews).

Of course, Acts is Luke's chief means of answering this question, but the Gospel sets the stage for Acts' clarification through its Travel Narrative (Lk 9:51–19:27). The Travel Narrative provides the model of Jesus as an itinerant missionary that Peter and Paul subsequently imitate (see chart "The Gospel of Luke and Acts" in the introduction to the Acts of the Apostles). This imitation not only unites the two disparate parts of the story (Jesus in volume 1, Peter and Paul in volume 2) but lends them plausibility. Disciples should, after all, be expected to follow in their teacher's footsteps. Without the Travel Narrative (as in the case of the Gospel of Mark), Jesus does not appear to be an itinerant missionary of the type Peter, Paul, and other early Christians such as Apollos must certainly have been. So, Luke's Gospel plays an important role in his answer to the question of how Christianity came to be comprised primarily of Gentiles.

By integrating sources into a single, interesting, and plausible narrative that answers real questions held by the people of his day, the author we call Luke performs the classic work of an ancient historian. Historians advertise their works in prologues. Accuracy, beginning at the beginning, order, and truth are the conventional claims of ancient historians and the claims that Luke makes (Lk 1:1–4). Most ancient historians included their names in these opening lines; Luke, however, does not. His use of a conventional prologue form tells us that this author wishes readers to perceive his narrative as, at least in some sense, a true history of the Jesus movement. Of all four evangelists, this author is the most eager to position his work as history. Correspondingly, he is the only evangelist who explicitly designates the historical context of Jesus' ministry. He does so by orienting it to the time of John the Baptist: "In the fifteenth year of the reign of Tiberius Caesar, when Pontius Pilate was governor of Judea, and Herod was tetrarch of Galilee, and his brother Philip tetrarch of the region of Ituraea and Trachonitis, and Lysanias was tetrarch of Abilene, during the high priesthood of Annas and Caiaphas, the word of God came to John the son of Zechariah in the desert" (3:1–2; see also 1:5).

Prophecy and its fulfillment also help bolster the impression of this work as true history. Events—especially unusual, supernatural, or otherwise special—that take place after being predicted, impress readers as, if not inherently more likely, at least more truthful. Pagan historians accomplish this goal through the use of "fate" language. The births of John the Baptist (Lk 1:13) and Jesus (1:31–33), and Jesus' death and Resurrection (9:22, 43b–45; 18:31–33), are each foretold and fulfilled in the course of the Gospel narrative. Similarly, the Holy Spirit plays a special role in the unfolding of events in Luke. Not only does the Holy Spirit "fill" certain people, including John the Baptist

(1:15), Elizabeth (1:41), and John the Baptist's father, Zechariah (1:67), enabling them to take part in God's divine plan, but it conceives the baby Jesus (1:35) and anoints him at his baptism for ministry (3:22; 4:1, 14, 18). In Luke, Jesus also promises that God will give the Holy Spirit to those who ask (11:13).

Lastly, this author demonstrates clear interest in the trajectory and end of history, that is, the topic of salvation. Jesus is Savior (Lk 2:11; 19:10) and the day of salvation coincides with his birth (2:11; 4:21; 5:26; 19:5, 9; 23:43). For Luke, this theme is probably related to the etymology of Jesus' name (Yeshua, "Yahweh saves").

In conclusion, as a historian, Luke has a twofold aim. First, he wants his Gospel to explain Christianity as a missionary effort with at least three crucial claims about origins: (1) it originated with Jesus, but was continued first by Peter, then by Paul; (2) it originated in Jerusalem, but its center of gravity gradually shifted to Rome; and (3) it originated with Jews, incorporating Gentiles at an early stage and ultimately becoming a predominantly Gentile phenomenon. Second, the Gospel must legitimate Christianity as the rightful heir to Jewish salvation history and as a religion under the Roman government of its day. ∎

# THE GOSPEL ACCORDING TO LUKE

## New American Bible, Introduction

The Gospel according to Luke is the first part of a two-volume work that continues the biblical history of God's dealings with humanity found in the Old Testament, showing how God's promises to Israel have been fulfilled in Jesus and how the salvation promised to Israel and accomplished by Jesus has been extended to the Gentiles. The stated purpose of the two volumes is to provide Theophilus and others like him with certainty—assurance—about earlier instruction they have received (Lk 1:4). To accomplish his purpose, Luke shows that the preaching and teaching of the representatives of the early church are grounded in the preaching and teaching of Jesus, who during his historical ministry (Acts 1:21–22) prepared his specially chosen followers and commissioned them to be witnesses to his resurrection and to all else that he did (Acts 10:37–42). This continuity between the historical ministry of Jesus and the ministry of the apostles is Luke's way of guaranteeing the fidelity of the Church's teaching to the teaching of Jesus.

Luke's story of Jesus and the church is dominated by a historical perspective. This history is first of all salvation history. God's divine plan for human salvation was accomplished during the period of Jesus, who through the events of his life (Lk 22:22) fulfilled the Old Testament prophecies (Lk 4:21; 18:31; 22:37; 24:26–27, 44), and this salvation is now extended to all humanity in the period of the church (Acts 4:12). This salvation history, moreover, is a part of human history. Luke relates the story of Jesus and the church to events in contemporary Palestinian (Lk 1:5; 3:1–2; Acts 4:6) and Roman (Lk 2:1–2; 3:1; Acts 11:28; 18:2, 12) history for, as Paul says in Acts 26:26, "this was not done in a corner." Finally, Luke relates the story of Jesus and the church to contemporaneous church history. Luke is concerned with presenting Christianity as a legitimate form of worship in the Roman world, a religion that is capable of meeting the spiritual needs of a world empire like that of Rome. To this end, Luke depicts the Roman governor Pilate declaring Jesus innocent of any wrongdoing three times (Lk 23:4, 14, 22). At the same time Luke argues in Acts that Christianity is the logical development and proper fulfillment of Judaism and is therefore deserving of the same toleration and freedom traditionally accorded Judaism by Rome (Acts 13:16–41; 23:6–9; 24:10–21; 26:2–23).

The prominence given to the period of the church in the story has important consequences for Luke's interpretation of the teachings of Jesus. By presenting the time of the church as a distinct phase of salvation history, Luke accordingly shifts the early Christian emphasis away from the expectation of an imminent parousia to the day-to-day concerns of the Christian community in the world. He does this in the gospel by regularly emphasizing the words "each day" (Lk 9:23; cf. Mk 8:34; Lk 11:3; 16:19; 19:47) in the sayings of Jesus. Although Luke still believes the parousia to be a reality that will come unexpectedly (Lk 12:38, 45–46), he is more concerned with presenting the words and deeds of Jesus as guides for the conduct of Christian disciples in the interim period between the ascension and the parousia and with presenting Jesus himself as the model of Christian life and piety.

Throughout the gospel, Luke calls upon the Christian disciple to identify with the master Jesus, who is caring and tender toward the poor and lowly, the outcast, the sinner, and the afflicted, toward all those who recognize their dependence on God (Lk 4:18; 6:20–23; 7:36–50; 14:12–14; 15:1–32; 16:19–31; 18:9–14; 19:1–10; 21:1–4), but who is severe toward the proud and self-righteous, and particularly toward those who place their material wealth before the service of God and his people (Lk 6:24–26; 12:13–21; 16:13–15, 19–31; 18:9–14, 15–25; cf. Lk 1:50–53). No gospel writer is more concerned than Luke with the mercy and compassion of Jesus (Lk 7:41–43; 10:29–37; 13:6–9; 15:11–32). No gospel writer is more concerned with the role of the Spirit in the life of Jesus and the Christian disciple (Lk

1:35, 41; 2:25–27; 4:1, 14, 18; 10:21; 11:13; 24:49), with the importance of prayer (Lk 3:21; 5:16; 6:12; 9:28; 11:1–13; 18:1–8), or with Jesus' concern for women (Lk 7:11–17, 36–50; 8:2–3; 10:38–42). While Jesus calls all humanity to repent (Lk 5:32; 10:13; 11:32; 13:1–5; 15:7–10; 16:30; 17:3–4; 24:47), he is particularly demanding of those who would be his disciples. Of them he demands absolute and total detachment from family and material possessions (Lk 9:57–62; 12:32–34; 14:25–35). To all who respond in faith and repentance to the word Jesus preaches, he brings salvation (Lk 2:30–32; 3:6; 7:50; 8:48, 50; 17:19; 19:9) and peace (Lk 2:14; 7:50; 8:48; 19:38, 42) and life (Lk 10:25–28; 18:26–30).

Early Christian tradition, from the late second century on, identifies the author of this gospel and of the Acts of the Apostles as Luke, a Syrian from Antioch, who is mentioned in the New Testament in Col 4:14, Phlm 24 and 2 Tm 4:11. The prologue of the gospel makes it clear that Luke is not part of the first generation of Christian disciples but is himself dependent upon the traditions he received from those who were eyewitnesses and ministers of the word (Lk 1:2). His two-volume work marks him as someone who was highly literate both in the Old Testament traditions according to the Greek versions and in Hellenistic Greek writings.

Among the likely sources for the composition of this gospel (Lk 1:3) were the Gospel of Mark, a written collection of sayings of Jesus known also to the author of the Gospel of Matthew (Q; see Introduction to Matthew), and other special traditions that were used by Luke alone among the gospel writers. Some hold

that Luke used Mark only as a complementary source for rounding out the material he took from other traditions. Because of its dependence on the Gospel of Mark and because details in Luke's Gospel (Lk 13:35a; 19:43–44; 21:20; 23:28–31) imply that the author was acquainted with the destruction of the city of Jerusalem by the Romans in A.D. 70, the Gospel of Luke is dated by most scholars after that date; many propose A.D. 80–90 as the time of composition.

Luke's consistent substitution of Greek names for the Aramaic or Hebrew names occurring in his sources (e.g., Lk 23:33 // Mk 15:22; Lk 18:41 // Mk 10:51), his omission from the gospel of specifically Jewish Christian concerns found in his sources (e.g., Mk 7:1–23), his interest in Gentile Christians (Lk 2:30–32; 3:6, 38; 4:16–30; 13:28–30; 14:15–24; 17:11–19; 24:47–48), and his incomplete knowledge of Palestinian geography, customs, and practices are among the characteristics of this gospel that suggest that Luke was a non-Palestinian writing to a non-Palestinian audience that was largely made up of Gentile Christians.

The principal divisions of the Gospel according to Luke are the following:

I. The Prologue (1:1–4)
II. The Infancy Narrative (1:5–2:52)
III. The Preparation for the Public Ministry (3:1–4:13)
IV. The Ministry in Galilee (4:14–9:50)
V. The Journey to Jerusalem: Luke's Travel Narrative (9:51–19:27)
VI. The Teaching Ministry in Jerusalem (19:28–21:38)
VII. The Passion Narrative (22:1–23:56)
VIII. The Resurrection Narrative (24:1–53) ∎

# Luke

## I. THE PROLOGUE†

**1** ¹Since many have undertaken to compile a narrative of the events that have been fulfilled among us,* ²just as those who were eyewitnesses from the beginning and ministers of the word have handed them down to us,* ³I too have decided, after investigating everything accurately anew, to write it down in an orderly sequence for you, most excellent Theophilus, ⁴so that you may realize the certainty of the teachings you have received.

## II. THE INFANCY NARRATIVE†

**Announcement of the Birth of John.** ⁵In the days of Herod, King of Judea,† there was a priest named Zechariah of the priestly division of Abijah; his wife was from the daughters of Aaron, and her name was Elizabeth.* ⁶Both were righteous in the eyes of God, observing all the commandments and ordinances of the Lord blamelessly. ⁷But they had no child,† because Elizabeth was barren and both were advanced in years.* ⁸Once when he was serving as priest in his division's turn before God, ⁹according to the practice of the priestly service, he was chosen by lot to enter the sanctuary of the Lord to burn incense.* ¹⁰Then, when the whole assembly of the people was praying outside at the hour of the incense offering, ¹¹the angel of the Lord appeared to him, standing at the right of the altar of incense. ¹²Zechariah was troubled by what he saw, and fear came upon him. ¹³But the angel said to him, "Do not be afraid,† Zechariah, because your prayer has been heard. Your wife Elizabeth will bear you a son, and you shall name him John.* ¹⁴And you will have joy and gladness, and many will rejoice at his birth, ¹⁵for he will be great in the sight of [the] Lord. He will drink neither wine nor strong drink.† He will be filled with the holy Spirit even from his mother's womb,* ¹⁶and he will turn many of the children of Israel to the Lord their God. ¹⁷He

---

**1:1–4** The Gospel according to Luke is the only one of the synoptic gospels to begin with a literary prologue. Making use of a formal, literary construction and vocabulary, the author writes the prologue in imitation of Hellenistic Greek writers and, in so doing, relates his story about Jesus to contemporaneous Greek and Roman literature. Luke is not only interested in the words and deeds of Jesus, but also in the larger context of the birth, ministry, death, and resurrection of Jesus as the fulfillment of the promises of God in the Old Testament. As a second- or third-generation Christian, Luke acknowledges his debt to earlier *eyewitnesses* and *ministers of the word*, but claims that his contribution to this developing tradition is a complete and accurate account, told in an orderly manner, and intended to provide *Theophilus* ("friend of God," literally) and other readers with certainty about earlier teachings they have received.

**1:5–2:52** Like the Gospel according to Matthew, this gospel opens with an infancy narrative, a collection of stories about the birth and childhood of Jesus. The narrative uses early Christian traditions about the birth of Jesus, traditions about the birth and circumcision of John the Baptist, and canticles such as the Magnificat (Lk 1:46–55) and Benedictus (Lk 1:67–79), composed of phrases drawn from the Greek Old Testament. It is largely, however, the composition of Luke who writes in imitation of Old Testament birth stories, combining historical and legendary details, literary ornamentation and interpretation of scripture, to answer in advance the question, "Who is Jesus Christ?" The focus of the narrative, therefore, is primarily christological. In this section Luke announces many of the themes that will become prominent in the rest of the gospel: the centrality of Jerusalem and the temple, the journey motif, the universality of salvation, joy and peace, concern for the lowly, the importance of women, the presentation of Jesus as savior, Spirit-guided revelation and prophecy, and the fulfillment of Old Testament promises. The account presents parallel scenes (diptychs) of angelic announcements of the birth of John the Baptist and of Jesus, and of the birth, circumcision, and presentation of John and Jesus. In this parallelism, the ascendency of Jesus over John is stressed: John is prophet of the Most High (Lk 1:76); Jesus is Son of the Most

High (Lk 1:32). John is great in the sight of the Lord (Lk 1:15); Jesus will be Great (a LXX attribute, used absolutely, of God) (Lk 1:32). John will go before the Lord (Lk 1:16–17); Jesus will be Lord (Lk 1:43; 2:11).

**1:5** *In the days of Herod, King of Judea:* Luke relates the story of salvation history to events in contemporary world history. Here and in Lk 3:1–2 he connects his narrative with events in Palestinian history; in Lk 2:1–2 and Lk 3:1 he casts the Jesus story in the light of events of Roman history. Herod the Great, the son of the Idumean Antipater, was declared "King of Judea" by the Roman Senate in 40 B.C., but became the undisputed ruler of Palestine only in 37 B.C. He continued as king until his death in 4 B.C. *Priestly division of Abijah:* a reference to the eighth of the twenty-four divisions of priests who, for a week at a time, twice a year, served in the Jerusalem temple.

**1:7** *They had no child:* though childlessness was looked upon in contemporaneous Judaism as a curse or punishment for sin, it is intended here to present Elizabeth in a situation similar to that of some of the great mothers of important Old Testament figures: Sarah (Gn 15:3; 16:1); Rebekah (Gn 25:21); Rachel (Gn 29:31; 30:1); the mother of Samson and wife of Manoah (Jgs 13:2–3); Hannah (1 Sm 1:2).

**1:13** *Do not be afraid:* a stereotyped Old Testament phrase spoken to reassure the recipient of a heavenly vision (Gn 15:1; Jos 1:9; Dn 10:12, 19 and elsewhere in Lk 1:30; 2:10). *You shall name him John:* the name means "Yahweh has shown favor," an indication of John's role in salvation history.

**1:15** *He will drink neither wine nor strong drink:* like Samson (Jgs 13:4–5) and Samuel (1 Sm 1:11 LXX and 4QSamᵃ), John is to be consecrated by Nazirite vow and set apart for the Lord's service.

---

**1:1–4** Acts 1:1; 1 Cor 15:3.
**1:2** 24:48; Jn 15:27; Acts 1:21–22.
**1:5** 1 Chr 24:10.
**1:7** Gn 18:11; Jgs 13:2–5; 1 Sm 1:5–6.
**1:9** Ex 30:7.
**1:13** 1:57, 60, 63; Mt 1:20–21.
**1:15** 7:33; Nm 6:1–21; Jgs 13:4; 1 Sm 1:11 LXX.

will go before him in the spirit and power of Elijah† to turn the hearts of fathers toward children and the disobedient to the understanding of the righteous, to prepare a people fit for the Lord."* ¹⁸Then Zechariah said to the angel, "How shall I know this? For I am an old man, and my wife is advanced in years." ¹⁹And the angel said to him in reply, "I am Gabriel,† who stand before God. I was sent to speak to you and to announce to you this good news.* ²⁰But now you will be speechless and unable to talk† until the day these things take place, because you did not believe my words, which will be fulfilled at their proper time."*

²¹Meanwhile the people were waiting for Zechariah and were amazed that he stayed so long in the sanctuary. ²²But when he came out, he was unable to speak to them, and they realized that he had seen a vision in the sanctuary. He was gesturing to them but remained mute. ²³Then, when his days of ministry were completed, he went home. ²⁴After this time his wife Elizabeth conceived, and she went into seclusion for five months, saying, ²⁵"So has the Lord done for me at a time when he has seen fit to take away my disgrace before others."*

**Announcement of the Birth of Jesus.**† ²⁶In the sixth month, the angel Gabriel was sent from God to a town of Galilee called Nazareth, ²⁷to a virgin betrothed to a man named Joseph, of the house of David, and the virgin's name was Mary.* ²⁸And coming to her, he said, "Hail, favored one! The Lord is with you."* ²⁹But

she was greatly troubled at what was said and pondered what sort of greeting this might be. ³⁰Then the angel said to her, "Do not be afraid, Mary, for you have found favor with God. ³¹*Behold, you will conceive in your womb and bear a son, and you shall name him Jesus. ³²* He will be great and will be called Son of the Most High,† and the Lord God will give him the throne of David his father, ³³and he will rule over the house of Jacob forever, and of his kingdom there will be no end."* ³⁴But Mary said to the angel, "How can this be, since I have no relations with a man?"† ³⁵And the angel said to her in reply, "The holy Spirit will come upon you, and the power of the Most High will overshadow you. Therefore the child to be born will be called holy, the Son of God.* ³⁶And behold, Elizabeth, your relative, has also conceived† a son in her old age, and this is the sixth month for her who was called barren; ³⁷for nothing will be impossible for God."* ³⁸Mary said, "Behold, I am the handmaid of the Lord. May it be done to me according to your word." Then the angel departed from her.

**Mary Visits Elizabeth.** ³⁹During those days Mary set out and traveled to the hill country in haste to a town of Judah, ⁴⁰where she entered the house of Zechariah and greeted Elizabeth. ⁴¹When Elizabeth heard Mary's greeting, the infant leaped in her womb, and Elizabeth, filled with the holy Spirit,* ⁴²cried out in a loud voice and said, "Most blessed are you among women, and blessed is the fruit of

---

**1:17** *He will go before him in the spirit and power of Elijah*: John is to be the messenger sent before Yahweh, as described in Mal 3:1–2. He is cast, moreover, in the role of the Old Testament fiery reformer, the prophet Elijah, who according to Mal 3:23 (4:5) is sent before "the great and terrible day of the Lord comes."

**1:19** *I am Gabriel*: "the angel of the Lord" is identified as Gabriel, the angel who in Dn 9:20–25 announces the seventy weeks of years and the coming of an anointed one, a prince. By alluding to Old Testament themes in Lk 1:17, 19 such as the coming of the day of the Lord and the dawning of the messianic era, Luke is presenting his interpretation of the significance of the births of John and Jesus.

**1:20** *You will be speechless and unable to talk*: Zechariah's becoming mute is the sign given in response to his question in v 18. When Mary asks a similar question in Lk 1:34, unlike Zechariah who was punished for his doubt, she, in spite of her doubt, is praised and reassured (Lk 1:35–37).

**1:26–38** The announcement to Mary of the birth of Jesus is parallel to the announcement to Zechariah of the birth of John. In both the angel Gabriel appears to the parent who is troubled by the vision (Lk 1:11–12, 26–29) and then told by the angel not to fear (Lk 1:13, 30). After the announcement is made (Lk 1:14–17, 31–33) the parent objects (Lk 1:18, 34) and a sign is given to confirm the announcement (Lk 1:20, 36). The particular focus of the announcement of the birth of Jesus is on his identity as Son of David (Lk 1:32–33) and Son of God (Lk 1:32, 35).

**1:32** *Son of the Most High*: cf. Lk 1:76 where John is described as "prophet of the Most High." "Most High" is a title for God commonly used by Luke (Lk 1:35, 76; 6:35; 8:28; Acts 7:48; 16:17).

**1:34** Mary's questioning response is a denial of sexual relations and is used by Luke to lead to the angel's declaration about the Spirit's role in the conception of this child (Lk 1:35). According to Luke, the virginal conception of Jesus takes place through the holy Spirit, the power of God, and therefore Jesus has a unique relationship to Yahweh: he is Son of God.

**1:36–37** The sign given to Mary in confirmation of the angel's announcement to her is the pregnancy of her aged relative Elizabeth. If a woman past the childbearing age could become pregnant, why, the angel implies, should there be doubt about Mary's pregnancy, for *nothing will be impossible for God*.

**1:17** Sir 48:10; Mal 3:1; 3:23–24; Mt 11:14; 17:11–13.
**1:19** Dn 8:16; 9:21.
**1:20** 1:45.
**1:25** Gn 30:23.
**1:27** 2:5; Mt 1:16, 18.
**1:28** Jgs 6:12; Ru 2:4; Jdt 13:18.
**1:31** Gn 16:11; Jgs 13:3; Is 7:14; Mt 1:21–23.
**1:32–33** 2 Sm 7:12, 13, 16; Is 9:7.
**1:33** Dn 2:44; 7:14; Mi 4:7; Mt 28:18.
**1:35** Mt 1:20.
**1:37** Gn 18:14; Jer 32:27; Mt 19:26.
**1:41** 1:15; Gn 25:22 LXX.

your womb.* ⁴³And how does this happen to me, that the mother of my Lord† should come to me? ⁴⁴For at the moment the sound of your greeting reached my ears, the infant in my womb leaped for joy. ⁴⁵Blessed are you who believed† that what was spoken to you by the Lord would be fulfilled."*

**The Canticle of Mary.** ⁴⁶*And Mary said:†

"My soul proclaims the greatness of the
            Lord;*
⁴⁷      my spirit rejoices in God my savior.*
⁴⁸  For he has looked upon his handmaid's
            lowliness;
        behold, from now on will all ages call
            me blessed.*
⁴⁹  The Mighty One has done great things
            for me,
        and holy is his name.*
⁵⁰  His mercy is from age to age
        to those who fear him.*
⁵¹  He has shown might with his arm,
        dispersed the arrogant of mind and
            heart.*
⁵²  He has thrown down the rulers from
            their thrones
        but lifted up the lowly.*
⁵³  The hungry he has filled with good things;
        the rich he has sent away empty.*
⁵⁴  He has helped Israel his servant,
        remembering his mercy,*
⁵⁵      according to his promise to our fathers,

to Abraham and to his descendants
    forever."*

⁵⁶Mary remained with her about three months and then returned to her home.

**The Birth of John.**† ⁵⁷When the time arrived for Elizabeth to have her child she gave birth to a son. ⁵⁸Her neighbors and relatives heard that the Lord had shown his great mercy toward her, and they rejoiced with her.* ⁵⁹†When they came on the eighth day to circumcise* the child, they were going to call him Zechariah after his father, ⁶⁰but his mother said in reply, "No. He will be called John."* ⁶¹But they answered her, "There is no one among your relatives who has this name." ⁶²So they made signs, asking his father what he wished him to be called. ⁶³He asked for a tablet and wrote, "John is his name," and all were amazed. ⁶⁴Immediately his mouth was opened, his tongue freed, and he spoke blessing God.* ⁶⁵Then fear came upon all their neighbors, and all these matters were discussed throughout the hill country of Judea. ⁶⁶All who heard these things took them to heart, saying, "What, then, will this child be?" For surely the hand of the Lord was with him.

**The Canticle of Zechariah.** ⁶⁷Then Zechariah his father, filled with the holy Spirit, prophesied, saying:

---

† **1:43** Even before his birth, Jesus is identified in Luke as the Lord.

**1:45** *Blessed are you who believed*: Luke portrays Mary as a believer whose faith stands in contrast to the disbelief of Zechariah (Lk 1:20). Mary's role as believer in the infancy narrative should be seen in connection with the explicit mention of her presence among "those who believed" after the resurrection at the beginning of the Acts of the Apostles (Acts 1:14).

**1:46–55** Although Mary is praised for being the mother of the Lord and because of her belief, she reacts as the servant in a psalm of praise, the Magnificat. Because there is no specific connection of the canticle to the context of Mary's pregnancy and her visit to Elizabeth, the Magnificat (with the possible exception of v 48) may have been a Jewish Christian hymn that Luke found appropriate at this point in his story. Even if not composed by Luke, it fits in well with themes found elsewhere in Luke: joy and exultation in the Lord; the lowly being singled out for God's favor; the reversal of human fortunes; the fulfillment of Old Testament promises. The loose connection between the hymn and the context is further seen in the fact that a few Old Latin manuscripts identify the speaker of the hymn as Elizabeth, even though the overwhelming textual evidence makes Mary the speaker.

**1:57–66** The birth and circumcision of John above all emphasize John's incorporation into the people of Israel by the sign of the covenant (Gn 17:1–12). The narrative of John's circumcision also prepares the way for the subsequent description of the circumcision of Jesus in Lk 2:21. At the beginning of his

two-volume work Luke shows those who play crucial roles in the inauguration of Christianity to be wholly a part of the people of Israel. At the end of the Acts of the Apostles (Acts 21:20; 22:3; 23:6–9; 24:14–16; 26:2–8, 22–23) he will argue that Christianity is the direct descendant of Pharisaic Judaism.

**1:59** The practice of Palestinian Judaism at this time was to name the child at birth; moreover, though naming a male child after the father is not completely unknown, the usual practice was to name the child after the grandfather (see Lk 1:61). The naming of the child John and Zechariah's recovery from his loss of speech should be understood as fulfilling the angel's announcement to Zechariah in Lk 1:13, 20.

---

| | |
|---|---|
| **1:42** 11:27–28; Jgs 5:24; Jdt 13:18; Dt 28:4. | **1:52** 1 Sm 2:7; 2 Sm 22:28; Jb 5:11; 12:19; Ps 147:6; Sir 10:14; Jas 4:6; 1 Pt 5:5. |
| **1:45** 1:20. | |
| **1:46–55** 1 Sm 2:1–10. | **1:53** 1 Sm 2:5; Ps 107:9. |
| **1:46** Ps 35:9; Is 61:10; Heb 3:18. | **1:54** Ps 98:3; Is 41:8–9. |
| **1:47** Ti 3:4; Jude 25. | **1:55** Gn 13:15; 17:7; 18:18; 22:17–18; Mi 7:20. |
| **1:48** 11:27; 1 Sm 1:11; 2 Sm 16:12; 2 Kgs 14:26; Ps 113:7. | **1:58** 1:14. |
| **1:49** Dt 10:21; Ps 71:19; 111:9; 126:2–3. | **1:59** 2:21; Gn 17:10, 12; Lv 12:3. |
| **1:50** Ps 89:2; 103:13, 17. | **1:60** 1:13. |
| **1:51** Ps 89:10; 118:15; Jer 32:17 (39:17 LXX). | **1:64** 1:20. |

L
K

68†   "Blessed be the Lord, the God of Israel,
      for he has visited and brought
         redemption to his people.*

69†   He has raised up a horn for our
      salvation
      within the house of David his
         servant,*

70   even as he promised through the mouth
      of his holy prophets from of old:

71   salvation from our enemies and from
      the hand of all who hate us,*

72   to show mercy to our fathers*
      and to be mindful of his holy
        covenant*

73   and of the oath he swore to Abraham
      our father,*
      and to grant us that, 74 rescued from
      the hand of enemies,
    without fear we might worship him 75 in
      holiness and righteousness
      before him all our days.*

76   And you, child, will be called prophet of
      the Most High,
      for you will go before the Lord† to
        prepare his ways,*

77   to give his people knowledge of
      salvation
      through the forgiveness of their sins,

78   because of the tender mercy of our
      God*
      by which the daybreak from on high†
        will visit us*

79   to shine on those who sit in darkness
      and death's shadow,
      to guide our feet into the path of
        peace."

80 The child grew and became strong in spirit, and he was in the desert until the day of his manifestation to Israel.*

## 2 The Birth of Jesus.

¹† In those days a decree went out from Caesar Augustus† that the whole world should be enrolled. ² This was the first enrollment, when Quirinius was governor of Syria. ³ So all went to be enrolled, each to his own town. ⁴ And Joseph too went up from Galilee from the town of Nazareth to Judea, to the city of David that is called Bethlehem, because he was of the house and family of David,* ⁵ to be enrolled with Mary, his betrothed, who was with child.* ⁶ While they were there, the time came for her to have her child, ⁷ and she gave birth to her firstborn

---

**1:68–79** Like the canticle of Mary (Lk 1:46–55) the canticle of Zechariah is only loosely connected with its context. Apart from Lk 1:76–77, the hymn in speaking of *a horn for our salvation* (Lk 1:69) and *the daybreak from on high* (Lk 1:78) applies more closely to Jesus and his work than to John. Again like Mary's canticle, it is largely composed of phrases taken from the Greek Old Testament and may have been a Jewish Christian hymn of praise that Luke adapted to fit the present context by inserting Lk 1:76–77 to give Zechariah's reply to the question asked in Lk 1:66.

**1:69** *A horn for our salvation*: the horn is a common Old Testament figure for strength (Ps 18:3; 75:5–6; 89:18; 112:9; 148:14). This description is applied to God in Ps 18:3 and is here transferred to Jesus. The connection of the phrase with *the house of David* gives the title messianic overtones and may indicate an allusion to a phrase in Hannah's song of praise (1 Sm 2:10), "the horn of his anointed."

**1:76** *You will go before the Lord*: here *the Lord* is most likely a reference to Jesus (contrast Lk 1:15–17 where Yahweh is meant) and John is presented as the precursor of Jesus.

**1:78** *The daybreak from on high*: three times in the LXX (Jer 23:5; Zec 3:8; 6:12), the Greek word used here for *daybreak* translates the Hebrew word for "scion, branch," an Old Testament messianic title.

**2:1–2** Although universal registrations of Roman citizens are attested in 28 B.C., 8 B.C., and A.D. 14 and enrollments in individual provinces of those who are not Roman citizens are also attested, such a universal census of the Roman world under Caesar Augustus is unknown outside the New Testament. Moreover, there are notorious historical problems connected with Luke's dating the census *when Quirinius was governor of Syria*, and the various attempts to resolve the difficulties have proved unsuccessful. P. Sulpicius Quirinius became legate of the province of Syria in A.D. 6–7 when Judea was annexed to the province of Syria. At that time, a provincial census of Judea

was taken up. If Quirinius had been legate of Syria previously, it would have to have been before 10 B.C. because the various legates of Syria from 10 B.C. to 4 B.C. (the death of Herod) are known, and such a dating for an earlier census under Quirinius would create additional problems for dating the beginning of Jesus' ministry (Lk 3:1, 23): A previous legateship after 4 B.C. (and before A.D. 6) would not fit with the dating of Jesus' birth in the days of Herod (Lk 1:5; Mt 2:1). Luke may simply be combining Jesus' birth in Bethlehem with his vague recollection of a census under Quirinius (see also Acts 5:37) to underline the significance of this birth for the whole Roman world: through this child born in Bethlehem peace and salvation come to the empire.

**2:1** *Caesar Augustus*: the reign of the Roman emperor Caesar Augustus is usually dated from 27 B.C. to his death in A.D. 14. According to Greek inscriptions, Augustus was regarded in the Roman Empire as "savior" and "god," and he was credited with establishing a time of peace, the *pax Augusta*, throughout the Roman world during his long reign. It is not by chance that Luke relates the birth of Jesus to the time of Caesar Augustus: the real savior (Lk 2:11) and peace-bearer (Lk 2:14; see also Lk 19:38) is the child born in Bethlehem. The great emperor is simply God's agent (like the Persian king Cyrus in Is 44:28–45:1) who provides the occasion for God's purposes to be accomplished. *The whole world*: that is, the whole Roman world: Rome, Italy, and the Roman provinces.

---

**1:68** 7:16; Ps 41:13; 72:18;      **1:75** Ti 2:12.
    106:48; 111:9.               **1:76** Is 40:3; Mal 3:1; Mt
**1:69** Ps 18:3.                    3:3; 11:10.
**1:71** Ps 106:10.              **1:78–79** Is 60:1–2.
**1:72–73** Gn 17:7; Lv 26:42; Ps   **1:78** Mal 3:20.
    105:8–9; Mi 7:20.            **1:80** 2:40; Mt 3:1.
**1:72** Ps 106:45–46.          **2:4** Mi 5:2; Mt 2:6.
**1:73–74** Gn 22:16–17.        **2:5** 1:27; Mt 1:18.

Lk

son. † She wrapped him in swaddling clothes and laid him in a manger, because there was no room for them in the inn. *

⁸† Now there were shepherds in that region living in the fields and keeping the night watch over their flock. ⁹ The angel of the Lord appeared to them and the glory of the Lord shone around them, and they were struck with great fear. * ¹⁰ The angel said to them, "Do not be afraid; for behold, I proclaim to you good news of great joy that will be for all the people. ¹¹ †* For today in the city of David a savior has been born for you who is Messiah and Lord. ¹² And this will be a sign for you: you will find an infant wrapped in swaddling clothes and lying in a manger." ¹³ And suddenly there was a multitude of the heavenly host with the angel, praising God and saying:

¹⁴† "Glory to God in the highest *
        and on earth peace to those on whom
            his favor rests."

**The Visit of the Shepherds.** ¹⁵ When the angels went away from them to heaven, the shepherds said to one another, "Let us go, then, to Bethlehem to see this thing that has taken place, which the Lord has made known to us." ¹⁶ So they went in haste and found Mary and Joseph, and the infant lying in the manger. ¹⁷ When they saw this, they made known the message that had been told them about this child. ¹⁸ All who heard it were amazed by what had been told them by the shepherds. ¹⁹ And Mary kept all these things, reflecting on them in her heart. ²⁰ Then the shepherds returned, glorifying and praising God for all they had heard and seen, just as it had been told to them.

**The Circumcision and Naming of Jesus.** ²¹ When eight days were completed for his circumcision, † he was named Jesus, the name given him by the angel before he was conceived in the womb. *

**The Presentation in the Temple.** ²²† When the days were completed for their purification † according to the law of Moses, they took him up to Jerusalem to present him to the Lord, *

---

**2:7** *Firstborn son*: the description of Jesus as *firstborn* son does not necessarily mean that Mary had other sons. It is a legal description indicating that Jesus possessed the rights and privileges of the firstborn son (Gn 27; Ex 13:2; Nm 3:12–13; 18:15–16; Dt 21:15–17). See notes on Mt 1:25; Mk 6:3. *Wrapped him in swaddling clothes*: there may be an allusion here to the birth of another descendant of David, his son Solomon, who though a great king was wrapped in swaddling clothes like any other infant (Wis 7:4–6). *Laid him in a manger*: a feeding trough for animals. A possible allusion to Is 1:3 LXX.
**2:8–20** The basic message of Jesus' birth to the shepherds is in keeping with Luke's theme that the lowly are singled out as the recipients of God's favors and blessings (see also Lk 1:48, 52).
**2:11** The basic message of the infancy narrative is contained in the angel's announcement: this child is *savior, Messiah,* and *Lord*. Luke is the only synoptic gospel writer to use the title *savior* for Jesus (Lk 2:11; Acts 5:31; 13:23; see also Lk 1:69; 19:9; Acts 4:12). As savior, Jesus is looked upon by Luke as the one who rescues humanity from sin and delivers humanity from the condition of alienation from God. The title *christos*, "Christ," is the Greek equivalent of the Hebrew *māšîaḥ*, "Messiah," "anointed one." Among certain groups in first-century Palestinian Judaism, the title was applied to an expected royal leader from the line of David who would restore the kingdom to Israel (see Acts 1:6). The political overtones of the title are played down in Luke and instead the Messiah of the Lord (Lk 2:26) or the Lord's anointed is the one who now brings salvation to all humanity, Jew and Gentile (Lk 2:29–32). Lord is the most frequently used title for Jesus in Luke and Acts. In the New Testament it is also applied to Yahweh, as it is in the Old Testament. When used of Jesus it points to his transcendence and dominion over humanity.
**2:14** *On earth peace to those on whom his favor rests*: the peace that results from the Christ event is for those whom God has favored with his grace. This reading is found in the oldest representatives of the Western and Alexandrian text traditions and is the preferred one; the Byzantine text tradition, on the other hand, reads: "on earth peace, good will toward men." The peace of which Luke's gospel speaks (Lk 2:14; 7:50; 8:48; 10:5–6; 19:38,

42; 24:36) is more than the absence of war of the *pax Augusta*; it also includes the security and well-being characteristic of peace in the Old Testament.
**2:21** Just as John before him had been incorporated into the people of Israel through his circumcision, so too this child (see note on Lk 1:57–66).
**2:22–40** The presentation of Jesus in the temple depicts the parents of Jesus as devout Jews, faithful observers of the law of the Lord (Lk 2:23–24, 39), i.e., the law of Moses. In this respect, they are described in a fashion similar to the parents of John (Lk 1:6) and Simeon (Lk 2:25) and Anna (Lk 2:36–37).
**2:22** *Their purification*: syntactically, *their* must refer to Mary and Joseph, even though the Mosaic law never mentions the purification of the husband. Recognizing the problem, some Western scribes have altered the text to read "his purification," understanding the presentation of Jesus in the temple as a form of purification; the Vulgate version has a Latin form that could be either "his" or "her." According to the Mosaic law (Lv 12:2–8), the woman who gives birth to a boy is unable for forty days to touch anything sacred or to enter the temple area by reason of her legal impurity. At the end of this period she is required to offer a year-old lamb as a burnt offering and a turtledove or young pigeon as an expiation of sin. The woman who could not afford a lamb offered instead two turtledoves or two young pigeons, as Mary does here. *They took him up to Jerusalem to present him to the Lord*: as the firstborn son (Lk 2:7) Jesus was consecrated to the Lord as the law required (Ex 13:2, 12), but there was no requirement that this be done at the temple. The concept of a presentation at the temple is probably derived from 1 Sm 1:24–28, where Hannah offers the child Samuel for sanctuary services. The law further stipulated (Nm 3:47–48) that the firstborn son should be redeemed by the parents through their payment of five shekels to a member of a priestly family. About this legal requirement Luke is silent.

---

**2:7** Mt 1:25.
**2:9** 1:11, 26.
**2:11** Mt 1:21; 16:16; Jn 4:42; Acts 2:36; 5:31; Phil 2:11.
**2:14** 19:38.
**2:21** 1:31; Gn 17:12; Mt 1:21.
**2:22–24** Lv 12:2–8.

23 just as it is written in the law of the Lord, "Every male that opens the womb shall be consecrated to the Lord,"* 24 and to offer the sacrifice of "a pair of turtledoves or two young pigeons," in accordance with the dictate in the law of the Lord.

25 Now there was a man in Jerusalem whose name was Simeon. This man was righteous and devout, awaiting the consolation of Israel,† and the holy Spirit was upon him. 26 It had been revealed to him by the holy Spirit that he should not see death before he had seen the Messiah of the Lord. 27 He came in the Spirit into the temple; and when the parents brought in the child Jesus to perform the custom of the law in regard to him, 28 he took him into his arms and blessed God, saying:

29      "Now, Master, you may let your servant go
         in peace, according to your word,
30      for my eyes have seen your salvation,*
31      which you prepared in sight of all the peoples,
32      a light for revelation to the Gentiles,
         and glory for your people Israel."*

33 The child's father and mother were amazed at what was said about him; 34 and Simeon blessed them and said to Mary his mother, "Behold, this child is destined for the fall and rise of many in Israel, and to be a sign that will be contradicted* 35 (and you yourself a sword will pierce)† so that the thoughts of many hearts may be revealed." 36 There was also a prophetess, Anna, the daughter of Phanuel, of the tribe of Asher. She was advanced in years, having lived seven years with her husband after her marriage, 37 and then as a widow until she was eighty-four. She never left the temple, but worshiped night and day with fasting and prayer. 38 And coming forward at that very time, she gave thanks to God and spoke about the child to all who were awaiting the redemption of Jerusalem.*

**The Return to Nazareth.** 39 When they had fulfilled all the prescriptions of the law of the Lord, they returned to Galilee, to their own town of Nazareth.* 40 The child grew and became strong, filled with wisdom; and the favor of God was upon him.*

**The Boy Jesus in the Temple.**† 41 Each year his parents went to Jerusalem for the feast of Passover,* 42 and when he was twelve years old, they went up according to festival custom. 43 After they had completed its days, as they were returning, the boy Jesus remained behind in Jerusalem, but his parents did not know it. 44 Thinking that he was in the caravan, they journeyed for a day and looked for him among their relatives and acquaintances, 45 but not finding him, they returned to Jerusalem to look for him. 46 After three days they found him in the temple, sitting in the midst of the teachers, listening to them and asking them questions, 47 and all who heard him were astounded at his understanding and his answers. 48 When his parents saw him, they were astonished, and his mother said to him, "Son, why have you done this to us? Your father and I have been looking for you with great anxiety." 49 And he said to them, "Why were you looking for me? Did you not know that I must be in my Father's house?"† 50 But they did not understand what he said to them. 51 He went down with them and came to Nazareth, and was obedient to them; and his mother kept all these things in her heart.* 52 And Jesus advanced [in] wisdom and age and favor before God and man.*

---

† **2:25** *Awaiting the consolation of Israel:* Simeon here and later Anna who speak about the child to all who were awaiting the redemption of Jerusalem represent the hopes and expectations of faithful and devout Jews who at this time were looking forward to the restoration of God's rule in Israel. The birth of Jesus brings these hopes to fulfillment.

**2:35** *(And you yourself a sword will pierce):* Mary herself will not be untouched by the various reactions to the role of Jesus (Lk 2:34). Her blessedness as mother of the Lord will be challenged by her son who describes true blessedness as "hearing the word of God and observing it" (Lk 11:27–28 and Lk 8:20–21).

**2:41–52** This story's concern with an incident from Jesus' youth is unique in the canonical gospel tradition. It presents Jesus in the role of the faithful Jewish boy, raised in the traditions of Israel, and fulfilling all that the law requires. With this episode, the infancy narrative ends just as it began, in the setting of the Jerusalem temple.

**2:49** *I must be in my Father's house:* this phrase can also be translated, "I must be about my Father's work." In either translation, Jesus refers to God as his Father. His divine sonship, and his obedience to his heavenly Father's will, take precedence over his ties to his family.

---

**2:23** Ex 13:2, 12.
**2:30–31** 3:6; Is 40:5 LXX; 52:10.
**2:32** Is 42:6; 46:13; 49:6; Acts 13:47; 26:23.
**2:34** 12:51; Is 8:14; Jn 9:39; Rom 9:33; 1 Cor 1:23; 1 Pt 2:7–8.
**2:38** Is 52:9.
**2:39** Mt 2:23.
**2:40** 1:80; 2:52.
**2:41** Ex 12:24–27; 23:15; Dt 16:1–8.
**2:51** 2:19.
**2:52** 1:80; 2:40; 1 Sm 2:26.

LK

## III. THE PREPARATION FOR THE PUBLIC MINISTRY

**3** **The Preaching of John the Baptist.**† [1] In the fifteenth year of the reign of Tiberius Caesar,† when Pontius Pilate was governor of Judea,* and Herod was tetrarch of Galilee, and his brother Philip tetrarch of the region of Ituraea and Trachonitis, and Lysanias was tetrarch of Abilene, [2] during the high priesthood of Annas and Caiaphas,† the word of God came to John* the son of Zechariah in the desert. [3]† He went throughout [the] whole region of the Jordan, proclaiming a baptism of repentance for the forgiveness of sins,* [4]† as it is written in the book of the words of the prophet Isaiah:*

"A voice of one crying out in the desert:
    'Prepare the way of the Lord,*
        make straight his paths.
[5] Every valley shall be filled
        and every mountain and hill shall be
            made low.
    The winding roads shall be made
            straight,
        and the rough ways made smooth,
[6]     and all flesh shall see the salvation of
            God.'"*

[7] He said to the crowds who came out to be baptized by him, "You brood of vipers! Who warned you to flee from the coming wrath?* [8] Produce good fruits as evidence of your repentance; and do not begin to say to yourselves, 'We have Abraham as our father,' for I tell you, God can raise up children to Abraham from these stones.* [9] Even now the ax lies at the root of the trees. Therefore every tree that does not produce good fruit will be cut down and thrown into the fire."*

[10] And the crowds asked him, "What then should we do?" [11] He said to them in reply, "Whoever has two tunics should share with the person who has none. And whoever has food should do likewise." [12] Even tax collectors came to be baptized and they said to him, "Teacher, what should we do?"* [13] He answered them, "Stop collecting more than what is prescribed." [14] Soldiers also asked him, "And what is it that we should do?" He told them, "Do not practice extortion, do not falsely accuse anyone, and be satisfied with your wages."

[15]* Now the people were filled with expectation, and all were asking in their hearts whether John might be the Messiah. [16]† John answered them all, saying,* "I am baptizing

---

**3:1–20** Although Luke is indebted in this section to his sources, the Gospel of Mark and a collection of sayings of John the Baptist, he has clearly marked this introduction to the ministry of Jesus with his own individual style. Just as the gospel began with a long periodic sentence (Lk 1:1–4), so too this section (Lk 3:1–2). He casts the call of John the Baptist in the form of an Old Testament prophetic call (Lk 3:2) and extends the quotation from Isaiah found in Mk 1:3 (Is 40:3) by the addition of Is 40:4–5 in Lk 3:5–6. In doing so, he presents his theme of the universality of salvation, which he has announced earlier in the words of Simeon (Lk 2:30–32). Moreover, in describing the expectation of the people (Lk 3:15), Luke is characterizing the time of John's preaching in the same way as he had earlier described the situation of other devout Israelites in the infancy narrative (Lk 2:25–26, 37–38). In Lk 3:7–18 Luke presents the preaching of John the Baptist who urges the crowds to reform in view of *the coming wrath* (Lk 3:7, 9: eschatological preaching), and who offers the crowds certain standards for reforming social conduct (Lk 3:10–14: ethical preaching), and who announces to the crowds the coming of *one mightier than* he (Lk 3:15–18: messianic preaching).

**3:1** *Tiberius Caesar*: Tiberius succeeded Augustus as emperor in A.D. 14 and reigned until A.D. 37. The fifteenth year of his reign, depending on the method of calculating his first regnal year, would have fallen between A.D. 27 and 29. *Pontius Pilate*: prefect of Judea from A.D. 26 to 36. The Jewish historian Josephus describes him as a greedy and ruthless prefect who had little regard for the local Jewish population and their religious practices (see Lk 13:1). *Herod*: i.e., Herod Antipas, the son of Herod the Great. He ruled over Galilee and Perea from 4 B.C. to A.D. 39. His official title *tetrarch* means literally, "ruler of a quarter," but came to designate any subordinate prince. *Philip*: also a son of Herod the Great, tetrarch of the territory to the north and east of the Sea of Galilee from 4 B.C. to A.D. 34. Only two small areas of this territory are mentioned by Luke. *Lysanias*: nothing is

known about this Lysanias who is said here to have been tetrarch of Abilene, a territory northwest of Damascus.

**3:2** *During the high priesthood of Annas and Caiaphas*: after situating the call of John the Baptist in terms of the civil rulers of the period, Luke now mentions the religious leadership of Palestine (see note on Lk 1:5). Annas had been high priest A.D. 6–15. After being deposed by the Romans in A.D. 15 he was succeeded by various members of his family and eventually by his son-in-law, Caiaphas, who was high priest A.D. 18–36. Luke refers to Annas as high priest at this time (but see Jn 18:13, 19), possibly because of the continuing influence of Annas or because the title continued to be used for the ex-high priest. *The word of God came to John*: Luke is alone among the New Testament writers in associating the preaching of John with a call from God. Luke is thereby identifying John with the prophets whose ministries began with similar calls. In Lk 7:26 John will be described as "more than a prophet"; he is also the precursor of Jesus (Lk 7:27), a transitional figure inaugurating the period of the fulfillment of prophecy and promise.

**3:3** See note on Mt 3:2.

**3:4** The Essenes from Qumran used the same passage to explain why their community was in the desert studying and observing the law and the prophets (1QS 8:12–15).

**3:16** *He will baptize you with the holy Spirit and fire*: in contrast to John's baptism with water, Jesus is said to baptize with the holy Spirit and with fire. From the point of view of the early Christian community, the Spirit and fire must have been under-

---

**3:1–20** Mt 3:1–12; Mk 1:1–8;
        Jn 1:19–28.
**3:2** 1:80.
**3:3** Acts 13:24; 19:4.
**3:4–6** Is 40:3–5.
**3:4** Jn 1:23.
**3:6** 2:30–31.
**3:7** Mt 12:34.
**3:8** Jn 8:39.
**3:9** Mt 7:19; Jn 15:6.
**3:12** 7:29.
**3:15–16** Acts 13:25.
**3:16** 7:19–20; Jn 1:27; Acts
        1:5; 11:16.

you with water, but one mightier than I is coming. I am not worthy to loosen the thongs of his sandals. He will baptize you with the holy Spirit and fire. [17] His winnowing fan† is in his hand to clear his threshing floor and to gather the wheat into his barn, but the chaff he will burn with unquenchable fire."* [18] Exhorting them in many other ways, he preached good news to the people. [19]† Now Herod the tetrarch,* who had been censured by him because of Herodias, his brother's wife, and because of all the evil deeds Herod had committed, [20] added still another to these by [also] putting John in prison.

## The Baptism of Jesus.† [21]* After all the people had been baptized and Jesus also had been baptized and was praying,† heaven was opened [22]†* and the holy Spirit descended upon him in bodily form like a dove. And a voice came from heaven, "You are my beloved Son; with you I am well pleased."

## The Genealogy of Jesus.† [23]* When Jesus began his ministry he was about thirty years of age. He was the son, as was thought, of Joseph, the son of Heli,* [24] the son of Matthat, the son of Levi, the son of Melchi, the son of Jannai, the son of Joseph, [25] the son of Mattathias, the son of Amos, the son of Nahum, the son of Esli, the son of Naggai, [26] the son of Maath,

the son of Mattathias, the son of Semein, the son of Josech, the son of Joda, [27] the son of Joanan, the son of Rhesa, the son of Zerubbabel, the son of Shealtiel, the son of Neri,* [28] the son of Melchi, the son of Addi, the son of Cosam, the son of Elmadam, the son of Er, [29] the son of Joshua, the son of Eliezer, the son of Jorim, the son of Matthat, the son of Levi, [30] the son of Simeon, the son of Judah, the son of Joseph, the son of Jonam, the son of Eliakim, [31]* the son of Melea, the son of Menna, the son of Mattatha, the son of Nathan, the son of David,† [32] the son of Jesse,* the son of Obed, the son of Boaz, the son of Sala, the son of Nahshon, [33] the son of Amminadab, the son of Admin, the son of Arni, the son of Hezron, the son of Perez,* the son of Judah,* [34] the son of Jacob, the son of Isaac, the son of Abraham,* the son of Terah, the son of Nahor, [35] the son of Serug, the son of Reu, the son of Peleg, the son of Eber, the son of Shelah, [36] the son of Cainan, the son of Arphaxad, the son of Shem,* the son of Noah, the son of Lamech, [37] the son of Methuselah, the son of Enoch, the son of Jared, the son of Mahalaleel, the son of Cainan, [38] the son of Enos, the son of Seth, the son of Adam,* the son of God.

# 4 The Temptation of Jesus.† [1]* Filled with the holy Spirit,† Jesus returned from the Jordan and was led by the Spirit into the desert [2] for

---

† stood in the light of the fire symbolism of the pouring out of the Spirit at Pentecost (Acts 2:1–4); but as part of John's preaching, the Spirit and fire should be related to their purifying and refining characteristics (Ez 36:25–27; Mal 3:2–3). See note on Mt 3:11.

**3:17** *Winnowing fan:* see note on Mt 3:12.

**3:19–20** Luke separates the ministry of John the Baptist from that of Jesus by reporting the imprisonment of John before the baptism of Jesus (Lk 3:21–22). Luke uses this literary device to serve his understanding of the periods of salvation history. With John the Baptist, the time of promise, the period of Israel, comes to an end; with the baptism of Jesus and the descent of the Spirit upon him, the time of fulfillment, the period of Jesus, begins. In his second volume, the Acts of the Apostles, Luke will introduce the third epoch in salvation history, the period of the church.

**3:21–22** This episode in Luke focuses on the heavenly message identifying Jesus as Son and, through the allusion to Is 42:1, as Servant of Yahweh. The relationship of Jesus to the Father has already been announced in the infancy narrative (Lk 1:32, 35; 2:49); it occurs here at the beginning of Jesus' Galilean ministry and will reappear in Lk 9:35 before another major section of Luke's gospel, the travel narrative (Lk 9:51–19:27). Elsewhere in Luke's writings (Lk 4:18; Acts 10:38), this incident will be interpreted as a type of anointing of Jesus.

**3:21** *Was praying:* Luke regularly presents Jesus at prayer at important points in his ministry: here at his baptism; at the choice of the Twelve (Lk 6:12); before Peter's confession (Lk 9:18); at the transfiguration (Lk 9:28); when he teaches his disciples to pray (Lk 11:1); at the Last Supper (Lk 22:32); on the Mount of Olives (Lk 22:41); on the cross (Lk 23:46).

**3:22** *You are my beloved Son; with you I am well pleased:*

this is the best attested reading in the Greek manuscripts. The Western reading, "You are my Son, this day I have begotten you," is derived from Ps 2:7.

**3:23–38** Whereas Mt 1:2 begins the genealogy of Jesus with Abraham to emphasize Jesus' bonds with the people of Israel, Luke's universalism leads him to trace the descent of Jesus beyond Israel to Adam and beyond that to God (Lk 3:38) to stress again Jesus' divine sonship.

**3:31** *The son of Nathan, the son of David:* in keeping with Jesus' prophetic role in Luke and Acts (e.g., Lk 7:16, 39; 9:8; 13:33; 24:19; Acts 3:22–23; 7:37) Luke traces Jesus' Davidic ancestry through the prophet Nathan (see 2 Sm 7:2) rather than through King Solomon, as Mt 1:6–7.

**4:1–13** See note on Mt 4:1–11.

**4:1** *Filled with the holy Spirit:* as a result of the descent of the Spirit upon him at his baptism (Lk 3:21–22), Jesus is now equipped to overcome the devil. Just as the Spirit is prominent at this early stage of Jesus' ministry (Lk 4:1, 14, 18), so too it

| | |
|---|---|
| **3:17** Mt 3:12. | **3:31–32** 1 Sm 16:1, 18. |
| **3:19–20** Mt 14:3–4; Mk 6:17–18. | **3:31–33** Ru 4:17–22; 1 Chr 2:1–15. |
| **3:21–22** Mt 3:13–17; Mk 1:9–11. | **3:33** Gn 29:35; 38:29. |
| **3:22** 9:35; Ps 2:7; Is 42:1; Mt 12:18; 17:5; Mk 9:7; Jn 1:32; 2 Pt 1:17. | **3:34** Gn 21:3; 25:26; 1 Chr 1:34; 28:34. |
| | **3:34–36** Gn 11:10–26; 1 Chr 1:24–27. |
| **3:23–38** Mt 1:1–17. | **3:36–38** Gn 4:25–5:32; 1 Chr 1:1–4. |
| **3:23** 4:22; Jn 6:42. | **4:1–13** Mt 4:1–11; Mk 1:12–13. |
| **3:27** 1 Chr 3:17; Ez 2:3. | |
| **3:31** 2 Sm 5:14. | |

forty days,† to be tempted by the devil. He ate nothing during those days, and when they were over he was hungry.* ³ The devil said to him, "If you are the Son of God, command this stone to become bread." ⁴ Jesus answered him, "It is written, 'One does not live by bread alone.'"* ⁵ Then he took him up and showed him all the kingdoms of the world in a single instant. ⁶ The devil said to him, "I shall give to you all this power and their glory; for it has been handed over to me, and I may give it to whomever I wish.* ⁷ All this will be yours, if you worship me." ⁸ Jesus said to him in reply, "It is written:

'You shall worship the Lord, your God,
    and him alone shall you serve.'"*

⁹† Then he led him to Jerusalem, made him stand on the parapet of the temple, and said to him, "If you are the Son of God, throw yourself down from here, ¹⁰ for it is written:

'He will command his angels concerning you,
    to guard you,'*

¹¹ and:

'With their hands they will support you,
    lest you dash your foot against a stone.'"*

¹² Jesus said to him in reply, "It also says, 'You shall not put the Lord, your God, to the test.'"*

¹³† When the devil had finished every temptation,* he departed from him for a time.

## IV. THE MINISTRY IN GALILEE

### The Beginning of the Galilean Ministry.
¹⁴* Jesus returned to Galilee in the power of the Spirit, and news of him spread† throughout the whole region.* ¹⁵ He taught in their synagogues and was praised by all.

### The Rejection at Nazareth.†*
¹⁶ He came to Nazareth, where he had grown up, and went according to his custom† into the synagogue on the sabbath day. He stood up to read ¹⁷ and was handed a scroll of the prophet Isaiah. He unrolled the scroll and found the passage where it was written:

¹⁸     "The Spirit of the Lord is upon me,†
        because he has anointed me
            to bring glad tidings to the poor.*
        He has sent me to proclaim liberty to
            captives
        and recovery of sight to the blind,
            to let the oppressed go free,
¹⁹        and to proclaim a year acceptable to the
            Lord."

²⁰ Rolling up the scroll, he handed it back to the attendant and sat down, and the eyes of all in the synagogue looked intently at him. ²¹ He said to them, "Today this scripture passage is fulfilled in your hearing."† ²² And all spoke

---

† will be at the beginning of the period of the church in Acts (Acts 1:4; 2:4, 17).

**4:2** *For forty days*: the mention of forty days recalls the forty years of the wilderness wanderings of the Israelites during the Exodus (Dt 8:2).

**4:9** *To Jerusalem*: the Lucan order of the temptations concludes on the parapet of the temple in Jerusalem, the city of destiny in Luke-Acts. It is in Jerusalem that Jesus will ultimately face his destiny (Lk 9:51; 13:33).

**4:13** *For a time*: the devil's opportune time will occur before the passion and death of Jesus (Lk 22:3, 31–32, 53).

**4:14** *News of him spread*: a Lucan theme; see Lk 4:37; 5:15; 7:17.

**4:16–30** Luke has transposed to the beginning of Jesus' ministry an incident from his Marcan source, which situated it near the end of the Galilean ministry (Mk 6:1–6a). In doing so, Luke turns the initial admiration (Lk 4:22) and subsequent rejection of Jesus (Lk 4:28–29) into a foreshadowing of the whole future ministry of Jesus. Moreover, the rejection of Jesus in his own hometown hints at the greater rejection of him by Israel (Acts 13:46).

**4:16** *According to his custom*: Jesus' practice of regularly attending synagogue is carried on by the early Christians' practice of meeting in the temple (Acts 2:46; 3:1; 5:12).

**4:18** *The Spirit of the Lord is upon me, because he has anointed me*: see note on Lk 3:21–22. As this incident develops,

Jesus is portrayed as a prophet whose ministry is compared to that of the prophets Elijah and Elisha. Prophetic anointings are known in first-century Palestinian Judaism from the Qumran literature that speaks of prophets as God's anointed ones. *To bring glad tidings to the poor*: more than any other gospel writer Luke is concerned with Jesus' attitude toward the economically and socially poor (see Lk 6:20, 24; 12:16–21; 14:12–14; 16:19–26; 19:8). At times, in Luke's gospel are associated with the downtrodden, the oppressed and afflicted, the forgotten and the neglected (Lk 4:18; 6:20–22; 7:22; 14:12–14), and it is they who accept Jesus' message of salvation.

**4:21** *Today this scripture passage is fulfilled in your hearing*: this sermon inaugurates the time of fulfillment of Old Testament prophecy. Luke presents the ministry of Jesus as fulfilling Old Testament hopes and expectations (Lk 7:22); for Luke, even Jesus' suffering, death, and resurrection are done in fulfillment of the scriptures (Lk 24:25–27, 44–46; Acts 3:18).

---

*
| | |
|---|---|
| **4:2** Heb 4:15. | **4:13** 22:3; Jn 13:2, 27; Heb |
| **4:4** Dt 8:3. | 4:15. |
| **4:6** Jer 27:5; Mt 28:18. | **4:14–15** Mt 4:12–17; Mk |
| **4:8** Dt 6:13. | 1:14–15. |
| **4:10** Ps 91:11. | **4:14** 5:15; Mt 3:16. |
| **4:11** Ps 91:12. | **4:16–30** Mt 13:53–58; Mk |
| **4:12** Dt 6:16; 1 Cor 10:9. | 6:1–6. |
| | **4:18–19** Is 61:1–2; 58:6. |

highly of him and were amazed at the gracious words that came from his mouth. They also asked, "Isn't this the son of Joseph?"* 23 He said to them, "Surely you will quote me this proverb, 'Physician, cure yourself,' and say, 'Do here in your native place the things that we heard were done in Capernaum.'"† 24 And he said, "Amen, I say to you, no prophet is accepted in his own native place. 25† Indeed, I tell you, there were many widows in Israel in the days of Elijah when the sky was closed for three and a half years and a severe famine spread over the entire land.* 26† It was to none of these that Elijah was sent, but only to a widow in Zarephath* in the land of Sidon. 27 Again, there were many lepers in Israel during the time of Elisha the prophet; yet not one of them was cleansed, but only Naaman the Syrian."* 28 When the people in the synagogue heard this, they were all filled with fury. 29 They rose up, drove him out of the town, and led him to the brow of the hill on which their town had been built, to hurl him down headlong. 30 But he passed through the midst of them and went away.

**The Cure of a Demoniac.** 31† Jesus then went down to Capernaum,* a town of Galilee.* He taught them on the sabbath, 32 and they were astonished at his teaching because he spoke with authority.* 33 In the synagogue there was a man with the spirit of an unclean demon,* and he cried out in a loud voice, 34 "Ha! What have you to do with us, Jesus of Nazareth? Have you come to destroy us?† I know who

you are—the Holy One of God!"* 35 Jesus rebuked him and said, "Be quiet! Come out of him!" Then the demon threw the man down in front of them and came out of him without doing him any harm. 36 They were all amazed and said to one another, "What is there about his word? For with authority and power he commands the unclean spirits, and they come out." 37 And news of him spread everywhere in the surrounding region.

**The Cure of Simon's Mother-in-Law.** 38* After he left the synagogue, he entered the house of Simon.† Simon's mother-in-law was afflicted with a severe fever, and they interceded with him about her. 39 He stood over her, rebuked the fever, and it left her. She got up immediately and waited on them.

**Other Healings.** * 40 At sunset, all who had people sick with various diseases brought them to him. He laid his hands on each of them and cured them. 41† And demons also came out from many, shouting, "You are the Son of God."* But he rebuked them and did not allow them to speak because they knew that he was the Messiah.

**Jesus Leaves Capernaum.** * 42† At daybreak, Jesus left and went to a deserted place. The crowds went looking for him, and when they came to him, they tried to prevent him from leaving them. 43 But he said to them, "To the other towns also I must proclaim the good news of the kingdom of God, because for this

---

† **4:23** *The things that we heard were done in Capernaum*: Luke's source for this incident reveals an awareness of an earlier ministry of Jesus in Capernaum that Luke has not yet made use of because of his transposition of this Nazareth episode to the beginning of Jesus' Galilean ministry. It is possible that by use of the future tense *you will quote me…*, Jesus is being portrayed as a prophet.

**4:25–26** The references to Elijah and Elisha serve several purposes in this episode: they emphasize Luke's portrait of Jesus as a prophet like Elijah and Elisha; they help to explain why the initial admiration of the people turns to rejection; and they provide the scriptural justification for the future Christian mission to the Gentiles.

**4:26** *A widow in Zarephath in the land of Sidon*: like Naaman the Syrian in Lk 4:27, a non-Israelite becomes the object of the prophet's ministry.

**4:31–44** The next several incidents in Jesus' ministry take place in Capernaum and are based on Luke's source, Mk 1:21–39. To the previous portrait of Jesus as prophet (Lk 4:16–30) they now add a presentation of him as teacher (Lk 4:31–32), exorcist (Lk 4:32–37, 41), healer (Lk 4:38–40), and proclaimer of God's kingdom (Lk 4:43).

**4:34** *What have you to do with us?*: see note on Jn 2:4. *Have you come to destroy us?*: the question reflects the current belief

that before the day of the Lord control over humanity would be wrested from the evil spirits, evil destroyed, and God's authority over humanity reestablished. The synoptic gospel tradition presents Jesus carrying out this task.

**4:38** *The house of Simon*: because of Luke's arrangement of material, the reader has not yet been introduced to Simon (cf. Mk 1:16–18, 29–31. Situated as it is before the call of Simon (Lk 5:1–11), it helps the reader to understand Simon's eagerness to do what Jesus says (Lk 5:5) and to follow him (Lk 5:11).

**4:41** *They knew that he was the Messiah*: that is, the Christ (see note on Lk 2:11).

**4:42** *They tried to prevent him from leaving them*: the reaction of these strangers in Capernaum is presented in contrast to the reactions of those in his hometown who rejected him (Lk 4:28–30).

---

**4:22** 3:23; Jn 6:42.
**4:25** 1 Kgs 17:1–7; 18:1; Jas 5:17.
**4:26** 1 Kgs 17:9.
**4:27** 2 Kgs 5:1–14.
**4:31–37** Mk 1:21–28.
**4:31** Mt 4:13; Jn 2:12.
**4:32** Mt 7:28–29.
**4:33–34** 8:28; Mt 8:29; Mk 1:23–24; 5:7.
**4:34** 4:41; Jn 6:69.
**4:38–39** Mt 8:14–15; Mk 1:29–31.
**4:40–41** Mt 8:16; Mk 1:32–34.
**4:41** Mt 8:29; Mk 3:11–12.
**4:42–44** Mk 1:35–39.

purpose I have been sent."* ⁴⁴ And he was preaching in the synagogues of Judea.†

# 5 The Call of Simon the Fisherman.†*

¹* While the crowd was pressing in on Jesus and listening to the word of God, he was standing by the Lake of Gennesaret. ² He saw two boats there alongside the lake; the fishermen had disembarked and were washing their nets. ³ Getting into one of the boats, the one belonging to Simon, he asked him to put out a short distance from the shore. Then he sat down and taught the crowds from the boat. ⁴* After he had finished speaking, he said to Simon, "Put out into deep water and lower your nets for a catch." ⁵ Simon said in reply, "Master, we have worked hard all night and have caught nothing, but at your command I will lower the nets." ⁶ When they had done this, they caught a great number of fish and their nets were tearing. ⁷ They signaled to their partners in the other boat to come to help them. They came and filled both boats so that they were in danger of sinking. ⁸ When Simon Peter saw this, he fell at the knees of Jesus and said, "Depart from me, Lord, for I am a sinful man." ⁹ For astonishment at the catch of fish they had made seized him and all those with him, ¹⁰ and likewise James and John, the sons of Zebedee, who were partners of Simon. Jesus said to Simon, "Do not be afraid; from now on you will be catching men."* ¹¹ When they brought their boats to the shore, they left everything† and followed him.*

## The Cleansing of a Leper.*

¹² Now there was a man full of leprosy† in one of the towns where he was; and when he saw Jesus, he fell prostrate, pleaded with him, and said, "Lord, if you wish, you can make me clean." ¹³ Jesus stretched out his hand, touched him, and said, "I do will it. Be made clean." And the leprosy left him immediately. ¹⁴ Then he ordered him not to tell anyone, but "Go, show yourself to the priest and offer for your cleansing what Moses prescribed;† that will be proof for them."* ¹⁵ The report about him spread all the more, and great crowds assembled to listen to him and to be cured of their ailments, ¹⁶ but he would withdraw to deserted places to pray.*

## The Healing of a Paralytic.*

¹⁷† One day as Jesus was teaching, Pharisees† and teachers of the law were sitting there who had come from every village of Galilee and Judea and Jerusalem, and the power of the Lord was with him for healing. ¹⁸ And some men brought on a stretcher a man who was paralyzed; they were trying to bring him in and set [him] in his presence. ¹⁹ But not finding a way to bring him in because of the crowd, they went up on the roof and lowered him on the stretcher through the tiles† into the middle in front of Jesus. ²⁰ When he saw their faith, he said, "As for you,

---

† **4:44** *In the synagogues of Judea*: instead of *Judea*, which is the best reading of the manuscript tradition, the Byzantine text tradition and other manuscripts read "Galilee," a reading that harmonizes Luke with Mt 4:23 and Mk 1:39. Up to this point Luke has spoken only of a ministry of Jesus in Galilee. Luke may be using *Judea* to refer to the land of Israel, the territory of the Jews, and not to a specific portion of it.

**5:1–11** This incident has been transposed from his source, Mk 1:16–20, which places it immediately after Jesus makes his appearance in Galilee. By this transposition Luke uses this example of Simon's acceptance of Jesus to counter the earlier rejection of him by his hometown people, and since several incidents dealing with Jesus' power and authority have already been narrated, Luke creates a plausible context for the acceptance of Jesus by Simon and his partners. Many commentators have noted the similarity between the wondrous catch of fish reported here (Lk 4:4–9) and the post-resurrectional appearance of Jesus in Jn 21:1–11. There are traces in Luke's story that the post-resurrectional context is the original one: in Lk 4:8 Simon addresses Jesus as *Lord* (a post-resurrectional title for Jesus—see Lk 24:34; Acts 2:36—that has been read back into the historical ministry of Jesus) and recognizes himself as a sinner (an appropriate recognition for one who has denied Jesus—Lk 22:54–62). As used by Luke, the incident looks forward to Peter's leadership in Luke-Acts (Lk 6:14; 9:20; 22:31–32; 24:34; Acts 1:15; 2:14–40; 10:11–18; 15:7–12) and symbolizes the future success of Peter as fisherman (Acts 2:41).

**5:11** *They left everything*: in Mk 1:16–20 and Mt 4:18–22 the fishermen who follow Jesus leave their nets and their father; in Luke, they leave *everything* (see also Lk 5:28; 12:33; 14:33; 18:22), an indication of Luke's theme of complete detachment from material possessions.

**5:12** *Full of leprosy*: see note on Mk 1:40.

**5:14** *Show yourself to the priest...what Moses prescribed*: this is a reference to Lv 14:2–9 that gives detailed instructions for the purification of one who had been a victim of leprosy and thereby excluded from contact with others (see Lv 13:45–46, 49; Nm 5:2–3). *That will be proof for them*: see note on Mt 8:4.

**5:17–6:11** From his Marcan source, Luke now introduces a series of controversies with Pharisees: controversy over Jesus' power to forgive sins (Lk 5:17–26); controversy over his eating and drinking with tax collectors and sinners (Lk 5:27–32); controversy over not fasting (Lk 5:33–36); and finally two episodes narrating controversies over observance of the sabbath (Lk 5:1–11).

**5:17** *Pharisees*: see note on Mt 3:7.

**5:19** *Through the tiles*: Luke has adapted the story found in Mark to his non-Palestinian audience by changing "opened up the roof" (Mk 2:4, a reference to Palestinian straw and clay roofs) to *through the tiles*, a detail that reflects the Hellenistic Greco-Roman house with tiled roof.

**4:43** 8:1; Mk 1:14–15.
**5:1–11** Mt 4:18–22; Mk 1:16–20.
**5:1–3** Mt 13:1–2; Mk 2:13; 3:9–10; 4:1–2.
**5:4–9** Jn 21:1–11.
**5:10** Jer 16:16.
**5:11** Mt 19:27.
**5:12–16** Mt 8:2–4; Mk 1:40–45.
**5:14** 8:56; Lv 14:2–32; Mk 7:36.
**5:16** Mk 1:35.
**5:17–26** Mt 9:1–8; Mk 2:1–12.

your sins are forgiven."† ²¹Then the scribes†
and Pharisees began to ask themselves, "Who
is this who speaks blasphemies? Who but God
alone can forgive sins?"* ²²Jesus knew their
thoughts and said to them in reply, "What
are you thinking in your hearts?* ²³Which
is easier, to say, 'Your sins are forgiven,' or to
say, 'Rise and walk'? ²⁴†* But that you may
know that the Son of Man has authority on
earth to forgive sins"—he said to the man
who was paralyzed, "I say to you, rise, pick
up your stretcher, and go home." ²⁵He stood
up immediately before them, picked up what
he had been lying on, and went home, glorifying God. ²⁶Then astonishment seized them
all and they glorified God, and, struck with
awe, they said, "We have seen incredible things
today."

**The Call of Levi.*** ²⁷After this he went out and
saw a tax collector named Levi sitting at the
customs post. He said to him, "Follow me."
²⁸And leaving everything behind,† he got up
and followed him. ²⁹* Then Levi gave a great
banquet for him in his house, and a large
crowd of tax collectors and others were at table
with them. ³⁰The Pharisees and their scribes
complained to his disciples, saying, "Why do
you eat and drink with tax collectors and sinners?" ³¹Jesus said to them in reply, "Those
who are healthy do not need a physician, but
the sick do. ³²I have not come to call the righteous to repentance but sinners."

**The Question About Fasting.*** ³³And they said
to him, "The disciples of John fast often and
offer prayers, and the disciples of the Pharisees do the same; but yours eat and drink."
³⁴†Jesus answered them, "Can you make the
wedding guests† fast while the bridegroom

is with them? ³⁵But the days will come, and
when the bridegroom is taken away from
them, then they will fast in those days."
³⁶†And he also told them a parable. "No one
tears a piece from a new cloak to patch an old
one. Otherwise, he will tear the new and the
piece from it will not match the old cloak.
³⁷Likewise, no one pours new wine into old
wineskins. Otherwise, the new wine will burst
the skins, and it will be spilled, and the skins
will be ruined. ³⁸Rather, new wine must be
poured into fresh wineskins. ³⁹[And] no one
who has been drinking old wine desires new,
for he says, 'The old is good.'"†

**6** **Debates About the Sabbath.**† ¹* While he
was going through a field of grain on a
sabbath, his disciples were picking the heads
of grain, rubbing them in their hands, and
eating them.* ²Some Pharisees said, "Why are
you doing what is unlawful on the sabbath?"
³* Jesus said to them in reply, "Have you not
read what David did when he and those [who
were] with him were hungry? ⁴[How] he went
into the house of God, took the bread of offering,† which only the priests could lawfully eat,
ate of it, and shared it with his companions."*
⁵Then he said to them, "The Son of Man is
lord of the sabbath."

⁶* On another sabbath he went into the
synagogue and taught, and there was a man
there whose right hand was withered. ⁷The
scribes and the Pharisees watched him closely
to see if he would cure on the sabbath so that
they might discover a reason to accuse him.*
⁸But he realized their intentions and said to
the man with the withered hand, "Come up
and stand before us." And he rose and stood
there.* ⁹Then Jesus said to them, "I ask you, is
it lawful to do good on the sabbath rather than

---

**5:20** *As for you, your sins are forgiven*: literally, "O man, your
sins are forgiven you." The connection between the forgiveness
of sins and the cure of the paralytic reflects the belief of first-
century Palestine (based on the Old Testament: Ex 20:5; Dt 5:9)
that sickness and infirmity are the result of sin, one's own or that
of one's ancestors (see also Lk 13:2; Jn 5:14; 9:2).

**5:21** *The scribes*: see note on Mk 2:6.
**5:24** See notes on Mt 9:6 and Mk 2:10.
**5:28** *Leaving everything behind*: see note on Lk 5:11.
**5:34–35** See notes on Mt 9:15 and Mk 2:19.
**5:34** *Wedding guests*: literally, "sons of the bridal chamber."
**5:36–39** See notes on Mt 9:16–17 and Mk 2:19.
**5:39** *The old is good*: this saying is meant to be ironic and
offers an explanation for the rejection by some of the new wine
that Jesus offers: satisfaction with old forms will prevent one from
sampling the new.
**6:1–11** The two episodes recounted here deal with gath-

ering grain and healing, both of which were forbidden on the
sabbath. In his defense of his disciples' conduct and his own
charitable deed, Jesus argues that satisfying human needs such
as hunger and performing works of mercy take precedence even
over the sacred sabbath rest. See also notes on Mt 12:1–14 and
Mk 2:25–26.

**6:4** *The bread of offering*: see note on Mt 12:5–6.

---

*

| | |
|---|---|
| **5:21** 7:49; Is 43:25. | **6:1–5** Mt 12:1–8; Mk |
| **5:22** 6:8; 9:47. | 2:23–28. |
| **5:24–25** Jn 5:8–9, 27. | **6:1** Dt 23:26. |
| **5:27–32** Mt 9:9–13; Mk | **6:3–4** 1 Sm 21:1–6. |
| 2:13–17. | **6:4** Lv 24:5–9. |
| **5:29–30** 15:1–2. | **6:6–11** Mt 12:9–14; Mk |
| **5:33–39** Mt 9:14–17; Mk | 3:1–6. |
| 2:18–22. | **6:7** 14:1. |
| | **6:8** 5:22; 9:47. |

to do evil, to save life rather than to destroy it?" [10] Looking around at them all, he then said to him, "Stretch out your hand." He did so and his hand was restored. [11] But they became enraged and discussed together what they might do to Jesus.

### The Mission of the Twelve.† [12]* In those days he departed to the mountain to pray, and he spent the night in prayer† to God. [13] When day came, he called his disciples to himself, and from them he chose Twelve,† whom he also named apostles: [14]* Simon, whom he named Peter,† and his brother Andrew, James, John, Philip, Bartholomew, [15] Matthew, Thomas, James the son of Alphaeus, Simon who was called a Zealot,† [16] and Judas the son of James, and Judas Iscariot,† who became a traitor.

### Ministering to a Great Multitude.* [17]† And he came down with them and stood on a stretch of level ground. A great crowd of his disciples and a large number of the people from all Judea and Jerusalem and the coastal region of Tyre and Sidon [18] came to hear him and to be healed of their diseases; and even those who were tormented by unclean spirits were cured. [19] Everyone in the crowd sought to touch him because power came forth from him and healed them all.

### Sermon on the Plain.* [20]† And raising his eyes toward his disciples he said:

"Blessed are you who are poor,†
for the kingdom of God is yours.

[21]   Blessed are you who are now hungry,
for you will be satisfied.

Blessed are you who are now weeping,
for you will laugh.*

[22]   Blessed are you when people hate you,
and when they exclude and insult you,
and denounce your name as evil
on account of the Son of Man.*

[23] Rejoice and leap for joy on that day! Behold, your reward will be great in heaven. For their

---

† **6:12–16** See notes on Mt 10:1–11:1 and Mk 3:14–15.

**6:12** *Spent the night in prayer:* see note on Lk 3:21.

**6:13** *He chose Twelve:* the identification of this group as the *Twelve* is a part of early Christian tradition (see 1 Cor 15:5), and in Matthew and Luke, the *Twelve* are associated with the twelve tribes of Israel (Lk 22:29–30; Mt 19:28). After the fall of Judas from his position among the Twelve, the need is felt on the part of the early community to reconstitute this group before the Christian mission begins at Pentecost (Acts 1:15–26). From Luke's perspective, they are an important group who because of their association with Jesus from the time of his baptism to his ascension (Acts 1:21–22) provide the continuity between the historical Jesus and the church of Luke's day and who as the original eyewitnesses guarantee the fidelity of the church's beliefs and practices to the teachings of Jesus (Lk 1:1–4). *Whom he also named apostles:* only Luke among the gospel writers attributes to Jesus the bestowal of the name *apostles* upon the Twelve. See note on Mt 10:2–4. "Apostle" becomes a technical term in early Christianity for a missionary sent out to preach the word of God. Although Luke seems to want to restrict the title to the Twelve (only in Acts 4:4, 14 are Paul and Barnabas termed apostles), other places in the New Testament show an awareness that the term was more widely applied (1 Cor 15:5–7; Gal 1:19; 1 Cor 1:1; 9:1; Rom 16:7).

**6:14** *Simon, whom he named Peter:* see note on Mk 3:16.

**6:15** *Simon who was called a Zealot:* the Zealots were the instigators of the First Revolt of Palestinian Jews against Rome in A.D. 66–70. Because the existence of the Zealots as a distinct group during the lifetime of Jesus is the subject of debate, the meaning of the identification of Simon as a Zealot is unclear.

**6:16** *Judas Iscariot:* the name *Iscariot* may mean "man from Kerioth."

**6:17** *The coastal region of Tyre and Sidon:* not only Jews from Judea and Jerusalem, but even Gentiles from outside Palestine come to hear Jesus (Lk 2:31–32; 3:6; 4:24–27).

**6:20–49** Luke's "Sermon on the Plain" is the counterpart to Matthew's "Sermon on the Mount" (Mt 5:1–7:27). It is addressed to the disciples of Jesus, and, like the sermon in Matthew, it begins with beatitudes (Lk 6:20–22) and ends with the parable of the two houses (Lk 6:46–49). Almost all the words of Jesus reported by Luke are found in Matthew's version, but because Matthew includes sayings that were related to specifically Jewish Christian problems (e.g., Mt 5:17–20; 6:1–8, 16–18) that Luke did not find appropriate for his predominantly Gentile Christian audience, the "Sermon on the Mount" is considerably longer. Luke's sermon may be outlined as follows: an introduction consisting of blessings and woes (Lk 6:20–26); the love of one's enemies (Lk 6:27–36); the demands of loving one's neighbor (Lk 6:37–42); good deeds as proof of one's goodness (Lk 6:43–45); a parable illustrating the result of listening to and acting on the words of Jesus (Lk 6:46–49). At the core of the sermon is Jesus' teaching on the love of one's enemies (Lk 6:27–36) that has as its source of motivation God's graciousness and compassion for all humanity (Lk 6:35–36) and Jesus' teaching on the love of one's neighbor (Lk 6:37–42) that is characterized by forgiveness and generosity.

**6:20–26** The introductory portion of the sermon consists of blessings and woes that address the real economic and social conditions of humanity (the poor—the rich; the hungry—the satisfied; those grieving—those laughing; the outcast—the socially acceptable). By contrast, Matthew emphasizes the religious and spiritual values of disciples in the kingdom inaugurated by Jesus ("poor in spirit," Mt 5:3; "hunger and thirst for righteousness," Mt 5:6). In the sermon, *blessed* extols the fortunate condition of persons who are favored with the blessings of God; the woes, addressed as they are to the disciples of Jesus, threaten God's profound displeasure on those so blinded by their present fortunate situation that they do not recognize and appreciate the real values of God's kingdom. In all the blessings and woes, the present condition of the persons addressed will be reversed in the future.

---

**6:12–16** Mt 10:1–4; Mk 3:13–19.
**6:14–16** Acts 1:13.
**6:17–19** Mt 4:23–25; Mk 3:7–10.
**6:20–26** Mt 5:1–12.

**6:21** Ps 126:5–6; Is 61:3; Jer 31:25; Rev 7:16–17.
**6:22** Jn 15:19; 16:2; 1 Pt 4:14.

L K

ancestors treated the prophets in the same way.*

24　　But woe to you who are rich,
　　　　for you have received your
　　　　　consolation.*
25　　But woe to you who are filled now,
　　　　for you will be hungry.
　　　Woe to you who laugh now,
　　　　for you will grieve and weep.*
26　　Woe to you when all speak well of you,
　　　　for their ancestors treated the false
　　　　　prophets in this way.*

**Love of Enemies.**† 27* "But to you who hear I say, love your enemies, do good to those who hate you,* 28 bless those who curse you, pray for those who mistreat you.* 29 To the person who strikes you on one cheek, offer the other one as well, and from the person who takes your cloak, do not withhold even your tunic. 30 Give to everyone who asks of you, and from the one who takes what is yours do not demand it back. 31 Do to others as you would have them do to you.* 32 For if you love those who love you, what credit is that to you? Even sinners love those who love them. 33 And if you do good to those who do good to you, what credit is that to you? Even sinners do the same. 34 If you lend money to those from whom you expect repayment, what credit [is] that to you? Even sinners lend to sinners, and get back the same amount.* 35 But rather, love your enemies and do good to them, and lend expecting nothing back; then your reward will be great and you will be children of the Most High, for he himself is kind to the ungrateful and the wicked.* 36 Be merciful, just as [also] your Father is merciful.

**Judging Others.**† 37* "Stop judging and you will not be judged. Stop condemning and you will not be condemned. Forgive and you will be forgiven.* 38 Give and gifts will be given to you; a good measure, packed together, shaken down, and overflowing, will be poured into your lap. For the measure with which you measure will in return be measured out to you."* 39 And he told them a parable, "Can a blind person guide a blind person? Will not both fall into a pit?* 40 No disciple is superior to the teacher; but when fully trained, every disciple will be like his teacher.* 41 Why do you notice the splinter in your brother's eye, but do not perceive the wooden beam in your own? 42 How can you say to your brother, 'Brother, let me remove that splinter in your eye,' when you do not even notice the wooden beam in your own eye? You hypocrite! Remove the wooden beam from your eye first; then you will see clearly to remove the splinter in your brother's eye.

**A Tree Known by Its Fruit.*** 43† "A good tree does not bear rotten fruit, nor does a rotten tree bear good fruit. 44 For every tree is known by its own fruit. For people do not pick figs from thornbushes, nor do they gather grapes from brambles. 45 A good person out of the store of goodness in his heart produces good, but an evil person out of a store of evil produces evil; for from the fullness of the heart the mouth speaks.

**The Two Foundations.** 46* "Why do you call me, 'Lord, Lord,' but not do what I command? 47† I will show you what someone is like who comes to me, listens to my words, and acts on them.* 48 That one is like a person building a house, who dug deeply and laid the foundation on rock; when the flood came, the river burst against that house but could not shake it because it had been well built. 49 But the one who listens and does not act is like a person who built a house on the ground without a foundation. When the river burst against it, it collapsed at once and was completely destroyed."

---

† 6:27–36 See notes on Mt 5:43–48 and Mt 5:48.
6:37–42 See notes on Mt 7:1–12; 7:1; 7:5.
6:43–46 See notes on Mt 7:15–20 and 12:33.
6:47–49 See note on Mt 7:24–27.

* 6:23 11:47–48; 2 Chr 36:16; Mt 23:30–31.
6:24 Jas 5:1.
6:25 Is 65:13–14.
6:26 Jas 4:4.
6:27–36 Mt 5:38–48.

6:27 Prv 25:21; Rom 12:20–21.
6:28 Rom 12:14; 1 Pt 3:9.
6:31 Mt 7:12.
6:34 Dt 15:7–8.
6:35 Lv 25:35–36.
6:37–42 Mt 7:1–5.
6:37 Mt 6:14; Jas 2:13.
6:38 Mk 4:24.
6:39 Mt 15:14; 23:16–17, 24.
6:40 Mt 10:24–25; Jn 13:16; 15:20.
6:43–45 Mt 7:16–20; 12:33, 35.
6:46 Mt 7:21; Rom 2:13; Jas 1:22.
6:47–49 Mt 7:24–27.

# 7 The Healing of a Centurion's Slave.*

[1]† When he had finished all his words to the people, he entered Capernaum.† [2] A centurion† there had a slave who was ill and about to die, and he was valuable to him. [3] When he heard about Jesus, he sent elders of the Jews to him, asking him to come and save the life of his slave. [4] They approached Jesus and strongly urged him to come, saying, "He deserves to have you do this for him, [5] for he loves our nation and he built the synagogue for us." [6] And Jesus went with them, but when he was only a short distance from the house, the centurion sent friends to tell him, "Lord, do not trouble yourself, for I am not worthy to have you enter under my roof.† [7] Therefore, I did not consider myself worthy to come to you; but say the word and let my servant be healed. [8] For I too am a person subject to authority, with soldiers subject to me. And I say to one, 'Go,' and he goes; and to another, 'Come here,' and he comes; and to my slave, 'Do this,' and he does it." [9] When Jesus heard this he was amazed at him and, turning, said to the crowd following him, "I tell you, not even in Israel have I found such faith." [10] When the messengers returned to the house, they found the slave in good health.

## Raising of the Widow's Son.†

[11]* Soon afterward he journeyed to a city called Nain, and his disciples and a large crowd accompanied him. [12] As he drew near to the gate of the city, a man who had died was being carried out, the only son of his mother, and she was a widow. A large crowd from the city was with her.* [13] When the Lord saw her, he was moved with pity for her and said to her, "Do not weep." [14] He stepped forward and touched the coffin; at this the bearers halted, and he said, "Young man, I tell you, arise!" [15] The dead man sat up and began to speak, and Jesus gave him to his mother.* [16] Fear seized them all, and they glorified God, exclaiming, "A great prophet has arisen in our midst," and "God has visited his people."* [17] This report about him spread through the whole of Judea and in all the surrounding region.

## The Messengers from John the Baptist.†

[18]* The disciples of John told him about all these things. John summoned two of his disciples [19] and sent them to the Lord to ask, "Are you the one who is to come, or should we look for another?"* [20] When the men came to him, they said, "John the Baptist has sent us to you to ask, 'Are you the one who is to come, or should we look for another?'" [21] At that time he cured many of their diseases, sufferings, and evil spirits; he also granted sight to many who were blind. [22] And he said to them in reply, "Go and tell John what you have seen and heard: the blind regain their sight, the lame walk, lepers are cleansed, the deaf hear, the dead are raised, the poor have the good news proclaimed to them.* [23] And blessed is the one who takes no offense at me."†

## Jesus' Testimony to John.

[24]† When the messengers of John had left, Jesus began to speak

---

† **7:1–8:3** The episodes in this section present a series of reactions to the Galilean ministry of Jesus and reflect some of Luke's particular interests: the faith of a Gentile (Lk 7:1–10); the prophet Jesus' concern for a widowed mother (Lk 7:11–17); the ministry of Jesus directed to the afflicted and unfortunate of Is 61:1 (Lk 7:18–23); the relation between John and Jesus and their role in God's plan for salvation (Lk 7:24–35); a forgiven sinner's manifestation of love (Lk 7:36–50); the association of women with the ministry of Jesus (Lk 8:1–3).

**7:1–10** This story about the faith of the centurion, a Gentile who cherishes the Jewish nation (Lk 7:5), prepares for the story in Acts of the conversion by Peter of the Roman centurion Cornelius who is similarly described as one who is generous to the Jewish nation (Acts 10:2). See also Acts 10:34–35 in the speech of Peter: "God shows no partiality…whoever fears him and acts righteously is acceptable to him." See also notes on Mt 8:5–13 and Jn 4:43–54.

**7:2** *A centurion*: see note on Mt 8:5.

**7:6** *I am not worthy to have you enter under my roof*: to enter the house of a Gentile was considered unclean for a Jew; cf. Acts 10:28.

**7:11–17** In the previous incident Jesus' power was displayed for a Gentile whose servant was dying; in this episode it is displayed toward a widowed mother whose only son has already died. Jesus' power over death prepares for his reply to John's disciples in Lk 7:22: "the dead are raised." This resuscitation in alluding to the prophet Elijah's resurrection of the only son of a widow of Zarephath (1 Kgs 7:8–24) leads to the reaction of the crowd: "A great prophet has arisen in our midst" (Lk 7:16).

**7:18–23** In answer to John's question, *Are you the one who is to come?*—a probable reference to the return of the fiery prophet of reform, Elijah, "before the day of the Lord comes, the great and terrible day" (Mal 3:23)—Jesus responds that his role is rather to bring the blessings spoken of in Is 61:1 to the oppressed and neglected of society (Lk 7:22; cf. Lk 4:18).

**7:23** *Blessed is the one who takes no offense at me*: this beatitude is pronounced on the person who recognizes Jesus' true identity in spite of previous expectations of what "the one who is to come" would be like.

**7:24–30** In his testimony to John, Jesus reveals his understanding of the relationship between them: John is the precursor of Jesus (Lk 7:27); John is the messenger spoken of in Mal 3:1

---

*
| | |
|---|---|
| **7:1–10** Mt 8:5–13; Jn | 2 Kgs 4:36. |
| 4:43–54. | **7:16** 1:68; 19:44. |
| **7:11–17** 4:25–26; 1 Kgs | **7:18–23** Mt 11:2–6. |
| 17:8–24. | **7:19** Mal 3:1; Rev 1:4, 8; |
| **7:12** 8:42; 1 Kgs 17:17. | 4:8. |
| **7:15** 1 Kgs 17:23; | **7:22** 4:18; Is 35:5–6; 61:1. |

to the crowds about John.* "What did you go out to the desert to see—a reed swayed by the wind? 25 Then what did you go out to see? Someone dressed in fine garments? Those who dress luxuriously and live sumptuously are found in royal palaces. 26 Then what did you go out to see? A prophet? Yes, I tell you, and more than a prophet.* 27 This is the one about whom scripture says:

'Behold, I am sending my messenger
    ahead of you,
  he will prepare your way before you.'*

28 I tell you, among those born of women, no one is greater than John; yet the least in the kingdom of God is greater than he." 29 * (All the people who listened, including the tax collectors, and who were baptized with the baptism of John, acknowledged the righteousness of God; 30 but the Pharisees and scholars of the law, who were not baptized by him, rejected the plan of God for themselves.)

31 † "Then to what shall I compare the people of this generation? What are they like?* 32 They are like children who sit in the marketplace and call to one another,

'We played the flute for you, but you did
  not dance.
We sang a dirge, but you did not weep.'

33 For John the Baptist came neither eating food nor drinking wine, and you said, 'He is possessed by a demon.' 34 The Son of Man came eating and drinking and you said, 'Look, he is a glutton and a drunkard, a friend of tax collectors and sinners.'* 35 But wisdom is vindicated by all her children."

## The Pardon of the Sinful Woman.† 36 * A Pharisee invited him to dine with him, and he entered the Pharisee's house and reclined at table.† 37 Now there was a sinful woman in the city who learned that he was at table in the house of the Pharisee.* Bringing an alabaster flask of ointment,* 38 she stood behind him at his feet weeping and began to bathe his feet with her tears. Then she wiped them with her hair, kissed them, and anointed them with the ointment. 39 When the Pharisee who had invited him saw this he said to himself, "If this man were a prophet, he would know who and what sort of woman this is who is touching him, that she is a sinner." 40 Jesus said to him in reply, "Simon, I have something to say to you." "Tell me, teacher," he said. 41 "Two people were in debt to a certain creditor; one owed five hundred days' wages† and the other owed fifty. 42 Since they were unable to repay the debt, he forgave it for both. Which of them will love him more?" 43 Simon said in reply, "The one, I suppose, whose larger debt was forgiven." He said to him, "You have judged rightly." 44 Then he turned to the woman and said to Simon, "Do you see this woman? When I entered your house, you did not give me water for my feet, but she has bathed them with her tears and wiped them with her hair. 45 You did not give me a kiss, but she has not ceased kissing my feet since the time I entered. 46 You did not anoint my head with oil, but she anointed my feet with ointment. 47 So I tell you, her many sins have been forgiven; hence, she has shown great love.† But the one to whom little is forgiven, loves little." 48 He said to her, "Your sins are forgiven."* 49 The others at table said to themselves, "Who is this who even forgives sins?"* 50 But he said

---

† who in Mal 3:23 is identified as Elijah. Taken with the previous episode, it can be seen that Jesus identifies John as precisely the person John envisioned Jesus to be: the Elijah who prepares the way for the coming of the day of the Lord.

**7:31–35** See note on Mt 11:16–19.

**7:36–50** In this story of the pardoning of the sinful woman Luke presents two different reactions to the ministry of Jesus. A Pharisee, suspecting Jesus to be a prophet, invites Jesus to a festive banquet in his house, but the Pharisee's self-righteousness leads to little forgiveness by God and consequently little love shown toward Jesus. The sinful woman, on the other hand, manifests a faith in God (Lk 7:50) that has led her to seek forgiveness for her sins, and because so much has forgiven, she now overwhelms Jesus with her display of love; cf. the similar contrast in attitudes in Lk 18:9–14. The whole episode is a powerful lesson on the relation between forgiveness and love.

**7:36** Reclined at table: the normal posture of guests at a banquet. Other oriental banquet customs alluded to in this story

include the reception by the host with a kiss (Lk 7:45), washing the feet of the guests (Lk 7:44), and the anointing of the guests' heads (Lk 7:46).

**7:41** Days' wages: one denarius is the normal daily wage of a laborer.

**7:47** Her many sins have been forgiven; hence, she has shown great love: literally, "her many sins have been forgiven, seeing that she has loved much." That the woman's sins have been forgiven is attested by the great love she shows toward Jesus. Her love is the consequence of her forgiveness. This is also the meaning demanded by the parable in Lk 7:41–43.

| | |
|---|---|
| 7:24–30 Mt 11:7–15. | 7:36 11:37; 14:1. |
| 7:26 1:76. | 7:37 Mt 26:7; Mk 14:3. |
| 7:27 Mal 3:1 / Is 40:3. | 7:37–38 Jn 12:3. |
| 7:29–30 3:7, 12; Mt 21:32. | 7:48 5:20; Mt 9:20; Mk |
| 7:31–35 Mt 11:16–19. | 2:5. |
| 7:34 15:2. | 7:49 5:21. |

to the woman, "Your faith has saved you; go in peace."

## 8 Galilean Women Follow Jesus.† ¹ Afterward he journeyed from one town and village to another, preaching and proclaiming the good news of the kingdom of God.* Accompanying him were the Twelve ² * and some women who had been cured of evil spirits and infirmities, Mary, called Magdalene, from whom seven demons had gone out, ³ Joanna, the wife of Herod's steward Chuza, Susanna, and many others who provided for them out of their resources.

## The Parable of the Sower.* ⁴† When a large crowd gathered, with people from one town after another journeying to him, he spoke in a parable.† ⁵ "A sower went out to sow his seed. And as he sowed, some seed fell on the path and was trampled, and the birds of the sky ate it up. ⁶ Some seed fell on rocky ground, and when it grew, it withered for lack of moisture. ⁷ Some seed fell among thorns, and the thorns grew with it and choked it. ⁸ And some seed fell on good soil, and when it grew, it produced fruit a hundredfold." After saying this, he called out, "Whoever has ears to hear ought to hear."*

## The Purpose of the Parables.* ⁹ Then his disciples asked him what the meaning of this parable might be. ¹⁰ He answered, "Knowledge of the mysteries of the kingdom of God has been granted to you; but to the rest, they are made known through parables so that 'they may look but not see, and hear but not understand.'*

## The Parable of the Sower Explained.† ¹¹ * "This is the meaning of the parable. The seed is the word of God.* ¹² Those on the path are the ones who have heard, but the devil comes and takes away the word from their hearts that they may not believe and be saved. ¹³ Those on rocky ground are the ones who, when they hear, receive the word with joy, but they have no root; they believe only for a time and fall away in time of trial. ¹⁴ As for the seed that fell among thorns, they are the ones who have heard, but as they go along, they are choked by the anxieties and riches and pleasures of life, and they fail to produce mature fruit. ¹⁵ But as for the seed that fell on rich soil, they are the ones who, when they have heard the word, embrace it with a generous and good heart, and bear fruit through perseverance.

## The Parable of the Lamp.† ¹⁶ * "No one who lights a lamp conceals it with a vessel or sets it under a bed; rather, he places it on a lampstand so that those who enter may see the light.* ¹⁷ For there is nothing hidden that will not become visible, and nothing secret that will not be known and come to light. * ¹⁸ Take care, then, how you hear. To anyone who has, more will be given, and from the one who has not, even what he seems to have will be taken away."*

## Jesus and His Family.* ¹⁹ Then his mother and his brothers† came to him but were unable to join him because of the crowd. ²⁰ * He was told, "Your mother and your brothers are standing outside and they wish to see you." ²¹ He said to them in reply, "My mother and my brothers are those who hear the word of God and act on it."†

---

† 

**8:1–3** Luke presents Jesus as an itinerant preacher traveling in the company of the Twelve and of the Galilean women who are sustaining them out of their means. These Galilean women will later accompany Jesus on his journey to Jerusalem and become witnesses to his death (Lk 23:49) and resurrection (Lk 24:9–11, where Mary Magdalene and Joanna are specifically mentioned; cf. also Acts 1:14). The association of women with the ministry of Jesus is most unusual in the light of the attitude of first-century Palestinian Judaism toward women. The more common attitude is expressed in Jn 4:27, and early rabbinic documents caution against speaking with women in public.

**8:4–21** The focus in this section is on how one should hear the word of God and act on it. It includes the parable of the sower and its explanation (Lk 8:4–15), a collection of sayings on how one should act on the word that is heard (Lk 8:16–18), and the identification of the mother and brothers of Jesus as the ones who hear the word and act on it (Lk 8:19–21). See also notes on Mt 13:1–53 and Mk 4:1–34.

**8:4–8** See note on Mt 13:3–8.

**8:11–15** On the interpretation of the parable of the sower,

see note on Mt 13:18–23.

**8:16–18** These sayings continue the theme of responding to the word of God. Those who hear the word must become a light to others (Lk 8:16); even the mysteries of the kingdom that have been made known to the disciples (Lk 8:9–10) must come to light (Lk 8:17); a generous and persevering response to the word of God leads to a still more perfect response to the word.

**8:19** *His brothers:* see note on Mk 6:3.

**8:21** The family of Jesus is not constituted by physical

---

| | |
|---|---|
| **8:1** 4:43. | **8:11–15** Mt 13:18–23; Mk |
| **8:2–3** 23:49; 24:10; Mt | 4:13–20. |
| 27:55–56; Mk | **8:11** 1 Pt 1:23. |
| 15:40–41; Jn 19:5. | **8:16–18** Mk 4:21–25. |
| **8:4–8** Mt 13:1–9; Mk 4:1–9. | **8:16** 11:33; Mt 5:15. |
| **8:8** 14:35; Mt 11:15; | **8:17** 12:2; Mt 10:26. |
| 13:43; Mk 4:23. | **8:18** 19:26; Mt 13:12; |
| **8:9–10** Mt 13:10–13; Mk | 25:29. |
| 4:10–12. | **8:19–21** Mt 12:46–50; Mk |
| **8:10** Is 6:9. | 3:31–35. |
| | **8:20–21** 11:27–28. |

## The Calming of a Storm at Sea.* ²²† One day he got into a boat with his disciples and said to them, "Let us cross to the other side of the lake." So they set sail, ²³ and while they were sailing he fell asleep. A squall blew over the lake, and they were taking in water and were in danger. ²⁴ They came and woke him saying, "Master, master, we are perishing!" He awakened, rebuked the wind and the waves, and they subsided and there was a calm. ²⁵ Then he asked them, "Where is your faith?" But they were filled with awe and amazed and said to one another, "Who then is this, who commands even the winds and the sea, and they obey him?"

## The Healing of the Gerasene Demoniac.*
²⁶ Then they sailed to the territory of the Gerasenes,† which is opposite Galilee. ²⁷ When he came ashore a man from the town who was possessed by demons met him. For a long time he had not worn clothes; he did not live in a house, but lived among the tombs. ²⁸* When he saw Jesus, he cried out and fell down before him; in a loud voice he shouted, "What have you to do with me, Jesus, son of the Most High God? I beg you, do not torment me!" ²⁹ For he had ordered the unclean spirit to come out of the man. (It had taken hold of him many times, and he used to be bound with chains and shackles as a restraint, but he would break his bonds and be driven by the demon into deserted places.) ³⁰ Then Jesus asked him, "What is your name?"† He replied, "Legion," because many demons had entered him. ³¹ And they pleaded with him not to order them to depart to the abyss.†

³² A herd of many swine was feeding there on the hillside, and they pleaded with him to allow them to enter those swine; and he let them. ³³ The demons came out of the man and entered the swine, and the herd rushed down the steep bank into the lake and was drowned. ³⁴ When the swineherds saw what had happened, they ran away and reported the incident in the town and throughout the countryside. ³⁵ People came out to see what had happened and, when they approached Jesus, they discovered the man from whom the demons had come out sitting at his feet.† He was clothed and in his right mind, and they were seized with fear. ³⁶ Those who witnessed it told them how the possessed man had been saved. ³⁷ The entire population of the region of the Gerasenes asked Jesus to leave them because they were seized with great fear. So he got into a boat and returned. ³⁸ The man from whom the demons had come out begged to remain with him, but he sent him away, saying, ³⁹ "Return home and recount what God has done for you." The man went off and proclaimed throughout the whole town what Jesus had done for him.

## Jairus's Daughter and the Woman with a Hemorrhage.† ⁴⁰* When Jesus returned, the crowd welcomed him, for they were all waiting for him. ⁴¹ And a man named Jairus, an official of the synagogue, came forward. He fell at the feet of Jesus and begged him to come to his house, ⁴² because he had an only daughter,† about twelve years old, and she was dying. As he went, the crowds almost crushed him. ⁴³ And a woman afflicted

relationship with him but by obedience to the word of God. In this, Luke agrees with the Marcan parallel (Mk 3:31–35), although by omitting Mk 3:33 and especially Mk 3:20–21 Luke has softened the Marcan picture of Jesus' natural family. Probably he did this because Mary has already been presented in Lk 1:38 as the obedient handmaid of the Lord who fulfills the requirement for belonging to the eschatological family of Jesus; cf. also Lk 11:27–28.

**8:22–56** This section records four miracles of Jesus that manifest his power and authority: (1) the calming of a storm on the lake (Lk 8:22–25); (2) the exorcism of a demoniac (Lk 8:26–39); (3) the cure of a hemorrhaging woman (Lk 8:40–48); (4) the raising of Jairus's daughter to life (Lk 8:49–56). They parallel the same sequence of stories at Mk 4:35–5:43.

**8:26** *Gerasenes*: other manuscripts read Gadarenes or Gergesenes. See also note on Mt 8:28. *Opposite Galilee*: probably Gentile territory (note the presence in the area of pigs—unclean animals to Jews) and an indication that the person who receives salvation (Lk 8:36) is a Gentile.

**8:30** *What is your name?*: the question reflects the popular belief that knowledge of the spirit's name brought control over

the spirit. *Legion*: to Jesus' question the demon replies with a Latin word transliterated into Greek. The Roman legion at this period consisted of 5,000 to 6,000 foot soldiers; hence the name implies a very large number of demons.

**8:31** *Abyss*: the place of the dead (Rom 10:7) or the prison of Satan (Rev 20:3) or the subterranean "watery deep" that symbolizes the chaos before the order imposed by creation (Gn 1:2).

**8:35** *Sitting at his feet*: the former demoniac takes the position of a disciple before the master (Lk 10:39; Acts 22:3).

**8:40–56** Two interwoven miracle stories, one a healing and the other a resuscitation, present Jesus as master over sickness and death. In the Lucan account, faith in Jesus is responsible for the cure (Lk 8:48) and for the raising to life (Lk 8:50).

**8:42** *An only daughter*: cf. the son of the widow of Nain whom Luke describes as an "only" son (Lk 7:12; see also Lk 9:38).

| | |
|---|---|
| **8:22–25** Mt 8:18, 23–27; Mk 4:35–41. | **8:28–29** 4:33–35; Mt 8:29; Mk 1:23–24. |
| **8:26–39** Mt 8:28–34; Mk 5:1–20. | **8:40–56** Mt 9:18–26; Mk 5:21–43. |

with hemorrhages for twelve years,† who [had spent her whole livelihood on doctors and] was unable to be cured by anyone, ⁴⁴ came up behind him and touched the tassel on his cloak. Immediately her bleeding stopped. ⁴⁵ Jesus then asked, "Who touched me?" While all were denying it, Peter said, "Master, the crowds are pushing and pressing in upon you." ⁴⁶ But Jesus said, "Someone has touched me; for I know that power has gone out from me."* ⁴⁷ When the woman realized that she had not escaped notice, she came forward trembling. Falling down before him, she explained in the presence of all the people why she had touched him and how she had been healed immediately. ⁴⁸ He said to her, "Daughter, your faith has saved you; go in peace."*

⁴⁹ While he was still speaking, someone from the synagogue official's house arrived and said, "Your daughter is dead; do not trouble the teacher any longer." ⁵⁰ On hearing this, Jesus answered him, "Do not be afraid; just have faith and she will be saved." ⁵¹ When he arrived at the house he allowed no one to enter with him except Peter and John and James, and the child's father and mother. ⁵² †* All were weeping and mourning for her, when he said, "Do not weep any longer, for she is not dead, but sleeping." ⁵³ And they ridiculed him, because they knew that she was dead. ⁵⁴ But he took her by the hand and called to her, "Child, arise!" ⁵⁵ Her breath returned and she immediately arose. He then directed that she should be given something to eat. ⁵⁶ Her parents were astounded, and he instructed them to tell no one what had happened.

# 9 The Mission of the Twelve.† ¹* He summoned the Twelve and gave them power and authority over all demons and to cure diseases, ² and he sent them to proclaim the kingdom of God and to heal [the sick]. ³ He said to them, "Take nothing for the journey,† neither walking stick, nor sack, nor food, nor money, and let no one take a second tunic. ⁴ Whatever house you enter, stay there and leave from there.* ⁵ And as for those who do not welcome you, when you leave that town, shake the dust from your feet† in testimony against them."* ⁶ Then they set out and went from village to village proclaiming the good news and curing diseases everywhere.

## Herod's Opinion of Jesus.* ⁷† Herod the tetrarch† heard about all that was happening, and he was greatly perplexed because some were saying, "John has been raised from the dead";* ⁸ others were saying, "Elijah has appeared"; still others, "One of the ancient prophets has arisen." ⁹ †* But Herod said, "John I beheaded. Who then is this about whom I hear such things?" And he kept trying to see him.

## The Return of the Twelve and the Feeding of the Five Thousand.* ¹⁰ When the apostles returned, they explained to him what they had done. He took them and withdrew in private to a town called Bethsaida. ¹¹ The crowds, meanwhile, learned of this and followed him. He received them and spoke to them about the kingdom of God, and he healed those who needed to be cured. ¹² As the day was drawing to a close, the Twelve approached

---

† **8:43** *Afflicted with hemorrhages for twelve years:* according to the Mosaic law (Lv 15:25–30) this condition would render the woman unclean and unfit for contact with other people.

**8:52** *Sleeping:* her death is a temporary condition; cf. Jn 11:11–14.

**9:1–6** Armed with the power and authority that Jesus himself has been displaying in the previous episodes, the Twelve are now sent out to continue the work that Jesus has been performing throughout his Galilean ministry: (1) proclaiming the kingdom (Lk 4:43; 8:1); (2) exorcising demons (Lk 4:33–37, 41; 8:26–39) and (3) healing the sick (Lk 4:38–40; 5:12–16, 17–26; 6:6–10; 7:1–10, 17, 22; 8:40–56).

**9:3** *Take nothing for the journey:* the absolute detachment required of the disciple (Lk 14:33) leads to complete reliance on God (Lk 12:22–31).

**9:5** *Shake the dust from your feet:* see note on Mt 10:14.

**9:7–56** This section in which Luke gathers together incidents that focus on the identity of Jesus is introduced by a question that Herod is made to ask in this gospel: "Who then is this about whom I hear such things?"(Lk 9:9) In subsequent episodes, Luke reveals to the reader various answers to Herod's question: Jesus

is one in whom God's power is present and who provides for the needs of God's people (Lk 9:10–17); Peter declares Jesus to be "the Messiah of God" (Lk 9:18–21); Jesus says he is the suffering Son of Man (Lk 9:22, 43–45); Jesus is the Master to be followed, even to death (Lk 9:23–27); Jesus is God's son, his Chosen One (Lk 9:28–36).

**9:7** *Herod the tetrarch:* see note on Lk 3:1.

**9:9** *And he kept trying to see him:* this indication of Herod's interest in Jesus prepares for Lk 13:31–33 and for Lk 23:8–12 where Herod's curiosity about Jesus' power to perform miracles remains unsatisfied.

---

| | |
|---|---|
| **8:46** 6:19. | **9:7–9** Mt 14:1–12; Mk |
| **8:48** 7:50; 17:19; 18:42. | 6:14–29. |
| **8:52** 7:13. | **9:7–8** 9:19; Mt 16:14; Mk |
| **9:1–6** Mt 10:1, 5–15; Mk | 8:28. |
| 6:7–13. | **9:9** 23:8. |
| **9:4** 10:5–7. | **9:10–17** Mt 14:13–21; Mk |
| **9:5** 10:10–11; Acts 13:51. | 6:30–44; Jn 6:1–14. |

him and said, "Dismiss the crowd so that they can go to the surrounding villages and farms and find lodging and provisions; for we are in a deserted place here." 13* He said to them, "Give them some food yourselves." They replied, "Five loaves and two fish are all we have, unless we ourselves go and buy food for all these people." 14 Now the men there numbered about five thousand. Then he said to his disciples, "Have them sit down in groups of [about] fifty." 15 They did so and made them all sit down. 16 Then taking† the five loaves and the two fish, and looking up to heaven, he said the blessing over them, broke them, and gave them to the disciples to set before the crowd.* 17 They all ate and were satisfied. And when the leftover fragments were picked up, they filled twelve wicker baskets.

**Peter's Confession About Jesus.**† 18* Once when Jesus was praying in solitude,† and the disciples were with him, he asked them, "Who do the crowds say that I am?" 19 They said in reply, "John the Baptist; others, Elijah; still others, 'One of the ancient prophets has arisen.'"* 20 Then he said to them, "But who do you say that I am?" Peter said in reply, "The Messiah of God."† 21 He rebuked them and directed them not to tell this to anyone.

**The First Prediction of the Passion.** 22 He said, "The Son of Man must suffer greatly and be rejected by the elders, the chief priests, and the scribes, and be killed and on the third day be raised."*

**The Conditions of Discipleship.*** 23 Then he said to all, "If anyone wishes to come after me, he must deny himself and take up his cross daily† and follow me.* 24 For whoever wishes to save his life will lose it, but whoever loses his life for my sake will save it.* 25 What profit is there for one to gain the whole world yet lose or forfeit himself? 26 Whoever is ashamed of me and of my words, the Son of Man will be ashamed of when he comes in his glory and in the glory of the Father and of the holy angels.* 27 Truly I say to you, there are some standing here who will not taste death until they see the kingdom of God."

**The Transfiguration of Jesus.**† 28* About eight days after he said this, he took Peter, John, and James and went up the mountain to pray.† 29 While he was praying his face changed in appearance and his clothing became dazzling white. 30 And behold, two men were conversing with him, Moses and Elijah,† 31†* who appeared in glory and spoke of his exodus that he was going to accomplish in Jerusalem. 32 Peter and his companions had been overcome by sleep, but becoming fully awake, they saw his glory† and the two men standing with him.* 33 As they were about to part from him, Peter said to Jesus, "Master, it is good that we are here; let us make three tents,† one for you, one

---

† **9:16** *Then taking…:* the actions of Jesus recall the institution of the Eucharist in Lk 22:19; see also note on Mt 14:19.

**9:18–22** This incident is based on Mk 8:27–33, but Luke has eliminated Peter's refusal to accept Jesus as suffering Son of Man (Mk 8:32) and the rebuke of Peter by Jesus (Mk 8:33). Elsewhere in the gospel, Luke softens the harsh portrait of Peter and the other apostles found in his Marcan source (cf. Lk 22:39–46, which similarly lacks a rebuke of Peter that occurs in the source, Mk 14:37–38).

**9:18** *When Jesus was praying in solitude:* see note on Lk 3:21.

**9:20** *The Messiah of God:* on the meaning of this title in first-century Palestinian Judaism, see notes on Lk 2:11 and on Mt 16:13–20 and Mk 8:27–30.

**9:23** *Daily:* this is a Lucan addition to a saying of Jesus, removing the saying from a context that envisioned the imminent suffering and death of the disciple of Jesus (as does the saying in Mk 8:34–35) to one that focuses on the demands of daily Christian existence.

**9:28–36** Situated shortly after the first announcement of the passion, death, and resurrection, this scene of Jesus' transfiguration provides the heavenly confirmation to Jesus' declaration that his suffering will end in glory (Lk 9:32); see also notes on Mt 17:1–8 and Mk 9:2–8.

**9:28** *Up the mountain to pray:* the "mountain" is the regular place of prayer in Luke (see Lk 6:12; 22:39–41).

**9:30** *Moses and Elijah:* the two figures represent the Old Testament law and the prophets. At the end of this episode, the heavenly voice will identify Jesus as the one to be listened to now (Lk 9:35). See also note on Mk 9:5.

**9:31** *His exodus that he was going to accomplish in Jerusalem:* Luke identifies the subject of the conversation as the *exodus* of Jesus, a reference to the death, resurrection, and ascension of Jesus that will take place in Jerusalem, the city of destiny (see Lk 9:51). The mention of exodus, however, also calls to mind the Israelite Exodus from Egypt to the promised land.

**9:32** *They saw his glory:* the *glory* that is proper to God is here attributed to Jesus (see Lk 24:26).

**9:33** *Let us make three tents:* in a possible allusion to the feast of Tabernacles, Peter may be likening his joy on the occasion of the transfiguration to the joyful celebration of this harvest festival.

*

| | |
|---|---|
| **9:13–17** 2 Kgs 4:42–44. | **9:23–27** Mt 16:24–28; Mk |
| **9:16** 22:19; 24:30–31; Acts | 8:34–9:1. |
| 2:42; 20:11; 27:35. | **9:23** 14:27; Mt 10:38. |
| **9:18–21** Mt 16:13–20; Mk | **9:24** 17:33; Mt 10:39; Jn |
| 8:27–30. | 12:25. |
| **9:19** 9:7–8. | **9:26** 12:9; Mt 10:33; 2 Tm |
| **9:22** 24:7, 26; Mt 16:21; | 2:12. |
| 20:18–19; Mk 8:31; | **9:28–36** Mt 17:1–8; Mk 9:2–8. |
| 10:33–34. | **9:31** 9:22; 13:33. |
| | **9:32** Jn 1:14; 2 Pt 1:16. |

LK

© Daniel Blatt

In Lk 9:28–36, Jesus takes Peter, John, and James "up the mountain to pray." It is on the mountain, according to the Gospels, that Jesus is transfigured before the disciples' eyes. Above, Mount Tabor in Lower Galilee, believed by many Christians to be the site of Jesus' transfiguration.

for Moses, and one for Elijah." But he did not know what he was saying. [34]† While he was still speaking, a cloud came and cast a shadow over them, and they became frightened when they entered the cloud. [35]†* Then from the cloud came a voice that said, "This is my chosen Son; listen to him." [36] After the voice had spoken, Jesus was found alone. They fell silent and did not at that time† tell anyone what they had seen.

**The Healing of a Boy with a Demon.**† [37]* On the next day, when they came down from the mountain, a large crowd met him. [38] There was a man in the crowd who cried out, "Teacher, I beg you, look at my son; he is my only child. [39] For a spirit seizes him and he suddenly screams and it convulses him until he foams at the mouth; it releases him only with difficulty, wearing him out. [40] I begged your disciples to cast it out but they could not." [41] Jesus said in reply, "O faithless and perverse generation, how long will I be with you and endure you? Bring your son here." [42] As he was coming forward, the demon threw him to the ground in a convulsion; but Jesus rebuked the unclean spirit, healed the boy, and returned him to his father. [43] And all were astonished by the majesty of God.

**The Second Prediction of the Passion.*** While they were all amazed at his every deed, he said to his disciples, [44] "Pay attention to what I am telling you. The Son of Man is to be handed over to men." [45] But they did not understand this saying; its meaning was hidden from them so that they should not understand it, and they were afraid to ask him about this saying.

**The Greatest in the Kingdom.*** [46]† An argument arose among the disciples about which of them was the greatest.* [47] Jesus realized the

---

† **9:34** *Over them*: it is not clear whether *them* refers to Jesus, Moses, and Elijah, or to the disciples. For the cloud casting its shadow, see note on Mk 9:7.

**9:35** Like the heavenly voice that identified Jesus at his baptism prior to his undertaking the Galilean ministry (Lk 3:22), so too here before the journey to the city of destiny is begun (Lk 9:51) the heavenly voice again identifies Jesus as Son. *Listen to him*: the two representatives of Israel of old depart (Lk 9:33) and Jesus is left alone (Lk 9:36) as the teacher whose words must be heeded (see also Acts 3:22).

**9:36** *At that time*: i.e., before the resurrection.

**9:37–43a** See note on Mk 9:14–29.

**9:46–50** These two incidents focus on attitudes that are opposed to Christian discipleship: rivalry and intolerance of outsiders.

---

**9:35** 3:22; Dt 18:15; Ps 2:7; Is 42:1; Mt 3:17; 12:18; Mk 1:11; 2 Pt 1:17–18.
**9:37–43** Mt 17:14–18; Mk 9:14–27.
**9:43–45** 18:32–34; Mt 17:22–23; Mk 9:30–32.
**9:46–48** Mt 18:1–5; Mk 9:33–37.
**9:46** 22:24.

intention of their hearts and took a child and placed it by his side [48] and said to them, "Whoever receives this child in my name receives me, and whoever receives me receives the one who sent me. For the one who is least among all of you is the one who is the greatest."*

**Another Exorcist.*** [49] Then John said in reply, "Master, we saw someone casting out demons in your name and we tried to prevent him because he does not follow in our company." [50] Jesus said to him, "Do not prevent him, for whoever is not against you is for you."

## V. THE JOURNEY TO JERUSALEM: LUKE'S TRAVEL NARRATIVE†

**Departure for Jerusalem; Samaritan Inhospitality.** [51]† When the days for his being taken up† were fulfilled, he resolutely determined to journey to Jerusalem,* [52]† and he sent messengers ahead of him.* On the way they entered a Samaritan village to prepare for his reception there, [53] but they would not welcome him because the destination of his journey was Jerusalem. [54] When the disciples James and John saw this they asked, "Lord, do you want us to call down fire from heaven to consume them?"* [55] Jesus turned and rebuked them, [56] and they journeyed to another village.

**The Would-be Followers of Jesus.**† [57]* As they were proceeding on their journey someone said to him, "I will follow you wherever you go." [58] Jesus answered him, "Foxes have dens and birds of the sky have nests, but the Son of Man has nowhere to rest his head." [59] And to another he said, "Follow me." But he replied, "[Lord,] let me go first and bury my father." [60] But he answered him, "Let the dead bury their dead.† But you, go and proclaim the kingdom of God." [61]* And another said, "I will follow you, Lord, but first let me say farewell to my family at home." [62] [To him] Jesus said, "No one who sets a hand to the plow and looks to what was left behind is fit for the kingdom of God."

# 10

**The Mission of the Seventy-two.**† [1] After this the Lord appointed seventy[-two]† others whom he sent ahead of him in pairs to every town and place he intended to visit.* [2] He said to them, "The harvest is abundant but the laborers are few; so ask the master of the harvest to send out laborers for his harvest.* [3] Go on your way; behold, I am sending

---

**9:51–18:14** The Galilean ministry of Jesus finishes with the previous episode and a new section of Luke's gospel begins, the journey to Jerusalem. This journey is based on Mk 10:1–52 but Luke uses his Marcan source only in Lk 18:15–19:27. Before that point he has inserted into his gospel a distinctive collection of sayings of Jesus and stories about him that he has drawn from Q, a collection of sayings of Jesus used also by Matthew, and from his own special traditions. All of the material collected in this section is loosely organized within the framework of a journey of Jesus to Jerusalem, the city of destiny, where his exodus (suffering, death, resurrection, ascension) is to take place (Lk 9:31), where salvation is accomplished, and from where the proclamation of God's saving word is to go forth (Lk 24:47; Acts 1:8). Much of the material in the Lucan travel narrative is teaching for the disciples. During the course of this journey Jesus is preparing his chosen Galilean witnesses for the role they will play after his exodus (Lk 9:31); they are to be his witnesses to the people (Acts 10:39; 13:31) and thereby provide certainty to the readers of Luke's gospel that the teachings they have received are rooted in the teachings of Jesus (Lk 1:1–4).

**9:51–55** Just as the Galilean ministry began with a rejection of Jesus in his hometown, so too the travel narrative begins with the rejection of him by Samaritans. In this episode Jesus disassociates himself from the attitude expressed by his disciples that those who reject him are to be punished severely. The story alludes to 2 Kgs 1:10, 12 where the prophet Elijah takes the course of action Jesus rejects, and Jesus thereby rejects the identification of himself with Elijah.

**9:51** *Days for his being taken up*: like the reference to his exodus in Lk 9:31 this is probably a reference to all the events (suffering, death, resurrection, ascension) of his last days in Jerusalem. *He resolutely determined*: literally, "he set his face."

**9:52** *Samaritan*: Samaria was the territory between Judea and Galilee west of the Jordan river. For ethnic and religious reasons,

the Samaritans and the Jews were bitterly opposed to one another (see Jn 4:9).

**9:57–62** In these sayings Jesus speaks of the severity and the unconditional nature of Christian discipleship. Even family ties and filial obligations, such as burying one's parents, cannot distract one no matter how briefly from proclaiming the kingdom of God. The first two sayings are paralleled in Mt 8:19–22; see also notes there.

**9:60** *Let the dead bury their dead*: i.e., let the spiritually dead (those who do not follow) bury their physically dead. See also note on Mt 8:22.

**10:1–12** Only the Gospel of Luke contains two episodes in which Jesus sends out his followers on a mission: the first (Lk 9:1–6) is based on the mission in Mk 6:6b–13 and recounts the sending out of the Twelve; here in Lk 10:1–12 a similar report based on Q becomes the sending out of seventy-two in this gospel. The episode continues the theme of Jesus preparing witnesses to himself and his ministry. These witnesses include not only the Twelve but also the seventy-two who may represent the Christian mission in Luke's own day. Note that the instructions given to the Twelve and to the seventy-two are similar and that what is said to the seventy-two in Lk 10:4 is directed to the Twelve in Lk 22:35.

**10:1** *Seventy[-two]*: important representatives of the Alexandrian and Caesarean text types read "seventy," while other important Alexandrian texts and Western readings have "seventy-two."

---

* **9:48** 10:16; Mt 10:40; Jn 13:20.
**9:49–50** Mk 9:38–40.
**9:51** 9:53; 13:22, 33; 17:11; 18:31; 19:28; 24:51; Acts 1:2, 9–11, 22.

**9:52** Mal 3:1.
**9:54** 2 Kgs 1:10, 12.
**9:57–60** Mt 8:19–22.
**9:61–62** 1 Kgs 19:20.
**10:1** Mk 6:7.
**10:2** Mt 9:37–38; Jn 4:35.

you like lambs among wolves.* 4† Carry no money bag,* no sack, no sandals;* and greet no one along the way. 5 Into whatever house you enter, first say, 'Peace to this household.'† 6 If a peaceful person† lives there, your peace will rest on him; but if not, it will return to you. 7 Stay in the same house and eat and drink what is offered to you, for the laborer deserves his payment. Do not move about from one house to another.* 8 Whatever town you enter and they welcome you, eat what is set before you,* 9 cure the sick in it and say to them, 'The kingdom of God is at hand for you.'* 10 Whatever town you enter and they do not receive you, go out into the streets and say,* 11 'The dust of your town that clings to our feet, even that we shake off against you.' Yet know this: the kingdom of God is at hand.* 12 I tell you, it will be more tolerable for Sodom on that day than for that town.*

**Reproaches to Unrepentant Towns.**† 13* "Woe to you, Chorazin! Woe to you, Bethsaida!* For if the mighty deeds done in your midst had been done in Tyre and Sidon, they would long ago have repented, sitting in sackcloth and ashes. 14 But it will be more tolerable for Tyre and Sidon at the judgment than for you. 15†* And as for you, Capernaum, 'Will you be exalted to heaven? You will go down to the netherworld.' 16 Whoever listens to you listens to me. Whoever rejects you rejects me. And whoever rejects me rejects the one who sent me."*

**Return of the Seventy-two.** 17 The seventy[-two] returned rejoicing, and said, "Lord, even the demons are subject to us because of your name." 18 Jesus said, "I have observed Satan fall like lightning† from the sky.* 19 Behold, I have given you the power 'to tread upon serpents' and scorpions and upon the full force of the enemy and nothing will harm you.* 20 Nevertheless, do not rejoice because the spirits are subject to you, but rejoice because your names are written in heaven."*

**Praise of the Father.*** 21 At that very moment he rejoiced [in] the holy Spirit and said, "I give you praise, Father, Lord of heaven and earth, for although you have hidden these things from the wise and the learned you have revealed them to the childlike.† Yes, Father, such has been your gracious will.* 22 All things have been handed over to me by my Father. No one knows who the Son is except the Father, and who the Father is except the Son and anyone to whom the Son wishes to reveal him."*

**The Privileges of Discipleship.*** 23 Turning to the disciples in private he said, "Blessed are the eyes that see what you see. 24 For I say to you, many prophets and kings desired to see what you see, but did not see it, and to hear what you hear, but did not hear it."

**The Greatest Commandment.*** 25† There was a scholar of the law† who stood up to test him and said, "Teacher, what must I do to inherit

---

**10:4** *Carry no money bag…greet no one along the way*: because of the urgency of the mission and the singlemindedness required of missionaries, attachment to material possessions should be avoided and even customary greetings should not distract from the fulfillment of the task.

**10:5** *First say, 'Peace to this household'*: see notes on Lk 2:14 and Mt 10:13.

**10:6** *A peaceful person*: literally, "a son of peace."

**10:13–16** The call to repentance here is a part of the proclamation of the kingdom brings with it a severe judgment for those who hear it and reject it.

**10:15** *The netherworld*: the underworld, the place of the dead (Acts 2:27, 31) here contrasted with heaven; see also note on Mt 11:23.

**10:18** *I have observed Satan fall like lightning*: the effect of the mission of the seventy-two is characterized by the Lucan Jesus as a symbolic fall of Satan. As the kingdom of God is gradually being established, evil in all its forms is being defeated; the dominion of Satan over humanity is at an end.

**10:21** *Revealed them to the childlike*: a restatement of the theme announced in Lk 8:10: the mysteries of the kingdom are revealed to the disciples. See also note on Mt 11:25–27.

**10:25–37** In response to a question about inheriting eternal life, Jesus illustrates the superiority of love over legalism through the story of the good Samaritan.

The law of love proclaimed in the "Sermon on the Plain" (Lk 6:27–36) is exemplified by one whom the legal expert would have considered ritually impure (see Jn 4:9). Moreover, the identity of the "neighbor" requested by the legal expert (Lk 10:29) turns out to be a Samaritan, the enemy of the Jew (see note on Lk 9:52).

**10:25** *Scholar of the law*: an expert in the Mosaic law, and probably a member of the group elsewhere identified as the scribes (Lk 5:21).

---

**10:3** Mt 10:16.
**10:4–11** Mt 10:7–14.
**10:4** 9:3; 2 Kgs 4:29.
**10:7** 9:4; Mt 10:10; 1 Cor 9:6–14; 1 Tm 5:18.
**10:8** 1 Cor 10:27.
**10:9** Mt 3:2; 4:17; Mk 1:15.
**10:10–11** 9:5.
**10:11** Acts 13:51; 18:6.
**10:12** Mt 10:15; 11:24.
**10:13–15** Mt 11:20–24.
**10:13–14** Is 23; Ez 26–28; Jl 3:4–8; Am 1:1–10; Zec 9:2–4.
**10:15** Is 14:13–15.
**10:16** Mt 10:40; Jn 5:23; 13:20; 15:23.
**10:18** Is 14:12; Jn 12:31; Rev 12:7–12.
**10:19** Ps 91:13; Mk 16:18.
**10:20** Ex 32:32; Dn 12:1; Mt 7:22; Phil 4:3; Heb 12:23; Rev 3:5; 21:27.
**10:21–22** Mt 11:25–27.
**10:21** 1 Cor 1:26–28.
**10:22** Jn 3:35; 10:15.
**10:23–24** Mt 13:16–17.
**10:25–28** Mt 22:34–40; Mk 12:28–34.

eternal life?"* ²⁶Jesus said to him, "What is written in the law? How do you read it?" ²⁷He said in reply, "You shall love the Lord, your God, with all your heart, with all your being, with all your strength, and with all your mind, and your neighbor as yourself."* ²⁸He replied to him, "You have answered correctly; do this and you will live."*

**The Parable of the Good Samaritan.** ²⁹But because he wished to justify himself, he said to Jesus, "And who is my neighbor?" ³⁰Jesus replied, "A man fell victim to robbers as he went down from Jerusalem to Jericho. They stripped and beat him and went off leaving him half-dead. ³¹† A priest happened to be going down that road, but when he saw him, he passed by on the opposite side. ³²Likewise a Levite came to the place, and when he saw him, he passed by on the opposite side. ³³But a Samaritan traveler who came upon him was moved with compassion at the sight. ³⁴He approached the victim, poured oil and wine over his wounds and bandaged them. Then he lifted him up on his own animal, took him to an inn and cared for him. ³⁵The next day he took out two silver coins and gave them to the innkeeper with the instruction, 'Take care of him. If you spend more than what I have given you, I shall repay you on my way back.' ³⁶Which of these three, in your opinion, was neighbor to the robbers' victim?" ³⁷He answered, "The one who treated him with mercy." Jesus said to him, "Go and do likewise."

**Martha and Mary.**† ³⁸* As they continued their journey he entered a village where a woman whose name was Martha welcomed him. ³⁹† She had a sister named Mary [who] sat beside the Lord at his feet listening to him speak. ⁴⁰Martha, burdened with much serving, came to him and said, "Lord, do you not care that my sister has left me by myself to do the serving? Tell her to help me." ⁴¹The Lord said to her in reply, "Martha, Martha, you are anxious and worried about many things. ⁴²† There is need of only one thing. Mary has chosen the better part and it will not be taken from her."

**11** **The Lord's Prayer.*** ¹† He was praying in a certain place, and when he had finished, one of his disciples said to him, "Lord, teach us to pray just as John taught his disciples."† ²† He said to them, "When you pray, say:

> Father, hallowed be your name,
>     your kingdom come.
³   Give us each day our daily bread†
⁴   and forgive us our sins
>     for we ourselves forgive everyone in
>         debt to us,
>     and do not subject us to the final
>         test."

**Further Teachings on Prayer.*** ⁵And he said to them, "Suppose one of you has a friend to whom he goes at midnight and says, 'Friend, lend me three loaves of bread, ⁶for a friend of mine has arrived at my house from a journey and I have nothing to offer him,' ⁷and he says in reply from within, 'Do not bother me; the door has already been locked and my children and I are already in bed. I cannot get up to

---

**10:31–32** *Priest…Levite:* those religious representatives of Judaism who would have been expected to be models of "neighbor" to the victim pass him by.

**10:38–42** The story of Martha and Mary further illustrates the importance of hearing the words of the teacher and the concern with women in Luke.

**10:39** *Sat beside the Lord at his feet:* it is remarkable for first-century Palestinian Judaism that a woman would assume the posture of a disciple at the master's feet (see also Lk 8:35; Acts 22:3), and it reveals a characteristic attitude of Jesus toward women in this gospel (see Lk 8:2–3).

**10:42** *There is need of only one thing:* some ancient versions read, "there is need of few things"; another important, although probably inferior, reading found in some manuscripts is, "there is need of few things, or of one."

**11:1–13** Luke presents three episodes concerned with prayer. The first (Lk 11:1–4) recounts Jesus teaching his disciples the Christian communal prayer, the "Our Father"; the second (Lk 11:5–8), the importance of persistence in prayer; the third (Lk 11:9–13), the effectiveness of prayer.

**11:1–4** The Matthean form of the "Our Father" occurs in the "Sermon on the Mount" (Mt 6:9–15); the shorter Lucan version

is presented while Jesus is at prayer (see note on Lk 3:21) and his disciples ask him to teach them to pray just as John taught his disciples to pray. In answer to their question, Jesus presents them with an example of a Christian communal prayer that stresses the fatherhood of God and acknowledges him as the one to whom the Christian disciple owes daily sustenance (Lk 11:3), forgiveness (Lk 11:4), and deliverance from the final trial (Lk 11:4). See also notes on Mt 6:9–13.

**11:2** *Your kingdom come:* in place of this petition, some early church Fathers record: "May your holy Spirit come upon us and cleanse us," a petition that may reflect the use of the "Our Father" in a baptismal liturgy.

**11:3–4** *Daily bread:* see note on Mt 6:11. *The final test:* see note on Mt 6:13.

---

**10:25** 18:18; Mt 19:16; Mk 10:17.
**10:27** Lv 18:18; Dt 6:5; 10:12; Jos 22:5; Mt 19:19; 22:37–39; Rom 13:9; Gal 5:14;
Jas 2:8.
**10:28** Lv 18:5; Prv 19:16; Rom 10:5; Gal 3:12.
**10:38–39** Jn 11:1; 12:2–3.
**11:1–4** Mt 6:9–15.
**11:5–8** 18:1–5.

give you anything.' [8]I tell you, if he does not get up to give him the loaves because of their friendship, he will get up to give him whatever he needs because of his persistence.

### The Answer to Prayer.* [9]"And I tell you, ask and you will receive; seek and you will find; knock and the door will be opened to you.* [10]For everyone who asks, receives; and the one who seeks, finds; and to the one who knocks, the door will be opened. [11]What father among you would hand his son a snake when he asks for a fish? [12]Or hand him a scorpion when he asks for an egg? [13]If you then, who are wicked, know how to give good gifts to your children, how much more will the Father in heaven give the holy Spirit† to those who ask him?"

### Jesus and Beelzebul.* [14]He was driving out a demon [that was] mute, and when the demon had gone out, the mute person spoke and the crowds were amazed. [15]Some of them said, "By the power of Beelzebul, the prince of demons, he drives out demons."* [16]Others, to test him, asked him for a sign from heaven.* [17]But he knew their thoughts and said to them, "Every kingdom divided against itself will be laid waste and house will fall against house. [18]And if Satan is divided against himself, how will his kingdom stand? For you say that it is by Beelzebul that I drive out demons. [19]If I, then, drive out demons by Beelzebul, by whom do your own people† drive them out? Therefore they will be your judges. [20]But if it is by the finger of God that [I] drive out demons, then the kingdom of God has come upon you.* [21]When a strong man fully armed guards his palace, his possessions are safe. [22]But when one stronger† than he attacks and overcomes him, he takes away the armor on which he relied and distributes the spoils.

[23]Whoever is not with me is against me, and whoever does not gather with me scatters.*

### The Return of the Unclean Spirit.* [24]"When an unclean spirit goes out of someone, it roams through arid regions searching for rest but, finding none, it says, 'I shall return to my home from which I came.' [25]But upon returning, it finds it swept clean and put in order. [26]Then it goes and brings back seven other spirits more wicked than itself who move in and dwell there, and the last condition of that person is worse than the first."*

### True Blessedness.† [27]While he was speaking, a woman from the crowd called out and said to him, "Blessed is the womb that carried you and the breasts at which you nursed."* [28]He replied, "Rather, blessed are those who hear the word of God and observe it."

### The Demand for a Sign.† [29]While still more people gathered in the crowd, he said to them,* "This generation is an evil generation; it seeks a sign, but no sign will be given it, except the sign of Jonah.* [30]Just as Jonah became a sign to the Ninevites, so will the Son of Man be to this generation. [31]At the judgment the queen of the south will rise with the men of this generation and she will condemn them, because she came from the ends of the earth to hear the wisdom of Solomon, and there is something greater than Solomon here.* [32]At the judgment the men of Nineveh will arise with this generation and condemn it, because at the preaching of Jonah they repented, and there is something greater than Jonah here.*

### The Simile of Light. [33]"No one who lights a lamp hides it away or places it [under a bushel basket], but on a lampstand so that those who

---

† **11:13** *The holy Spirit*: this is a Lucan editorial alteration of a traditional saying of Jesus (see Mt 7:11). Luke presents the gift of the holy Spirit as the response of the Father to the prayer of the Christian disciple.

**11:19** *Your own people*: the Greek reads "your sons." Other Jewish exorcists (see Acts 19:13–20), who recognize that the power of God is active in the exorcism, would themselves convict the accusers of Jesus. See also note on Mt 12:27.

**11:22** *One stronger*: i.e., Jesus. Cf. Lk 3:16 where John the Baptist identifies Jesus as "mightier than I."

**11:27–28** The beatitude in Lk 11:28 should not be interpreted as a rebuke of the mother of Jesus; see note on Lk 8:21. Rather, it emphasizes (like Lk 2:35) that attentiveness to God's word is more important than biological relationship to Jesus.

**11:29–32** The "sign of Jonah" in Luke is the preaching of the

need for repentance by a prophet who comes from afar. Cf. Mt 12:38–42 (and see notes there) where the "sign of Jonah" is interpreted by Jesus as his death and resurrection.

---

| | |
|---|---|
| **11:9–13** Mt 7:7–11. | **11:24–26** Mt 12:43–45. |
| **11:9** Mt 21:22; Mk 11:24; Jn 14:13; 15:7; 1 Jn 5:14–15. | **11:26** Jn 5:14. |
| | **11:27** 1:28, 42, 48. |
| **11:14–23** Mt 12:22–30; Mk 3:20–27. | **11:29–32** Mt 12:38–42; Mk 8:12. |
| **11:15** Mt 9:34. | **11:29** Mt 16:1, 4; Jn 6:30; 1 Cor 1:22. |
| **11:16** Mt 12:38; 16:1; Mk 8:11; 1 Cor 1:22. | **11:31** 1 Kgs 10:1–10; 2 Chr 9:1–12. |
| **11:20** Ex 8:19. | **11:32** Jon 3:8, 10. |
| **11:23** 9:50; Mk 9:40. | |

enter might see the light.* ³⁴The lamp of the body is your eye.* When your eye is sound, then your whole body is filled with light, but when it is bad, then your body is in darkness. ³⁵Take care, then, that the light in you not become darkness. ³⁶If your whole body is full of light, and no part of it is in darkness, then it will be as full of light as a lamp illuminating you with its brightness."

**Denunciation of the Pharisees and Scholars of the Law.†** ³⁷*After he had spoken, a Pharisee invited him to dine at his home. He entered and reclined at table to eat.* ³⁸The Pharisee was amazed to see that he did not observe the prescribed washing before the meal.* ³⁹The Lord said to him, "Oh you Pharisees!* Although you cleanse the outside of the cup and the dish, inside you are filled with plunder and evil. ⁴⁰You fools! Did not the maker of the outside also make the inside? ⁴¹But as to what is within, give alms, and behold, everything will be clean for you. ⁴²Woe to you Pharisees! You pay tithes of mint and of rue and of every garden herb, but you pay no attention to judgment and to love for God. These you should have done, without overlooking the others.* ⁴³Woe to you Pharisees! You love the seat of honor in synagogues and greetings in marketplaces.* ⁴⁴Woe to you! You are like unseen graves† over which people unknowingly walk."*

⁴⁵Then one of the scholars of the law† said to him in reply, "Teacher, by saying this you are insulting us too."* ⁴⁶And he said, "Woe also to you scholars of the law! You impose on people burdens hard to carry, but you yourselves do not lift one finger to touch them. ⁴⁷*Woe to you! You build the memorials of the prophets

whom your ancestors killed. ⁴⁸Consequently, you bear witness and give consent to the deeds of your ancestors, for they killed them and you do the building. ⁴⁹*Therefore, the wisdom of God said, 'I will send to them prophets and apostles;† some of them they will kill and persecute' ⁵⁰in order that this generation might be charged with the blood of all the prophets shed since the foundation of the world, ⁵¹from the blood of Abel to the blood of Zechariah† who died between the altar and the temple building. Yes, I tell you, this generation will be charged with their blood!* ⁵²Woe to you, scholars of the law! You have taken away the key of knowledge. You yourselves did not enter and you stopped those trying to enter."* ⁵³When he left, the scribes and Pharisees began to act with hostility toward him and to interrogate him about many things,* ⁵⁴for they were plotting to catch him at something he might say.*

**12** **The Leaven of the Pharisees.†** ¹Meanwhile, so many people were crowding together that they were trampling one another underfoot.* He began to speak, first to his disciples, "Beware of the leaven—that is, the hypocrisy—of the Pharisees.

**Courage Under Persecution.†** ²*"There is nothing concealed that will not be revealed, nor secret that will not be known.* ³Therefore whatever you have said in the darkness will be heard in the light, and what you have whispered behind closed doors will be proclaimed on the housetops. ⁴I tell you, my friends, do not be afraid of those who kill the body but after that can do no more. ⁵I shall show you whom to fear. Be afraid of the one who after

**11:37–54** This denunciation of the Pharisees (Lk 11:39–44) and the scholars of the law (Lk 11:45–52) is set by Luke in the context of Jesus' dining at the home of a Pharisee. Controversies with or reprimands of Pharisees are regularly set by Luke within the context of Jesus' eating with Pharisees (see Lk 5:29–39; 7:36–50; 14:1–24). A different compilation of similar sayings is found in Mt 23 (see also notes there).

**11:44** *Unseen graves*: contact with the dead or with human bones or graves (see Nm 19:16) brought ritual impurity. Jesus presents the Pharisees as those who insidiously lead others astray through their seeming attention to the law.

**11:45** *Scholars of the law*: see note on Lk 10:25.

**11:49** *I will send to them prophets and apostles*: Jesus connects the mission of the church (apostles) with the mission of the Old Testament prophets who often suffered the rebuke of their contemporaries.

**11:51** *From the blood of Abel to the blood of Zechariah*: the murder of Abel is the first murder recounted in the Old Testament (Gn 4:8). The Zechariah mentioned here may be the Zechariah

whose murder is recounted in 2 Chr 24:20–22, the last murder presented in the Hebrew canon of the Old Testament.

**12:1** See notes on Mk 8:15 and Mt 16:5–12.

**12:2–9** Luke presents a collection of sayings of Jesus exhorting his followers to acknowledge him and his mission fearlessly and assuring them of God's protection even in times of persecution. They are paralleled in Mt 10:26–33.

**11:33** 8:16; Mt 5:15; Mk 4:21.
**11:34–36** Mt 6:22–23.
**11:37–54** 20:45–47; Mt 23:1–36; Mk 12:38–40.
**11:37** 7:36; 14:1.
**11:38** Mt 15:2; Mk 7:2–5.
**11:39–41** Mt 23:25–26.
**11:42** Lv 27:30; Mt 23:23.
**11:43** 20:46; Mt 23:6; Mk 12:38–39.
**11:44** Mt 23:27.
**11:45** Mt 23:4.
**11:47–48** Mt 23:29–32.
**11:49–51** Mt 23:34–36.
**11:51** Gn 4:8; 2 Chr 24:20–22.
**11:52** Mt 23:13.
**11:53** 6:11; Mt 22:15–22.
**11:54** 20:20.
**12:1** Mt 16:6; Mk 8:15.
**12:2–9** Mt 10:26–33.
**12:2** 8:17; Mk 4:22.

killing has the power to cast into Gehenna;† yes, I tell you, be afraid of that one. [6] Are not five sparrows sold for two small coins?† Yet not one of them has escaped the notice of God. [7] Even the hairs of your head have all been counted. Do not be afraid. You are worth more than many sparrows.* [8] I tell you, everyone who acknowledges me before others the Son of Man will acknowledge before the angels of God. [9] But whoever denies me before others will be denied before the angels of God.*

**Sayings About the Holy Spirit.**† [10] "Everyone who speaks a word against the Son of Man will be forgiven, but the one who blasphemes against the holy Spirit will not be forgiven.* [11] When they take you before synagogues and before rulers and authorities,* do not worry about how or what your defense will be or about what you are to say. [12] For the holy Spirit will teach you at that moment what you should say."

**Saying Against Greed.** [13]† Someone in the crowd said to him, "Teacher, tell my brother to share the inheritance with me." [14] He replied to him, "Friend, who appointed me as your judge and arbitrator?"* [15] Then he said to the crowd, "Take care to guard against all greed, for though one may be rich, one's life does not consist of possessions."*

**Parable of the Rich Fool.** [16] Then he told them a parable. "There was a rich man whose land produced a bountiful harvest. [17] He asked himself, 'What shall I do, for I do not have space to store my harvest?' [18] And he said, 'This is what I shall do: I shall tear down my barns and build larger ones. There I shall store all my grain and other goods [19]* and I shall say to myself, "Now as for you, you have so many good things stored up for many years, rest, eat, drink, be merry!"'* [20] But God said to him, 'You fool, this night your life will be demanded of you; and the things you have prepared, to whom will they belong?' [21] Thus will it be for the one who stores up treasure for himself but is not rich in what matters to God."†

**Dependence on God.** [22]* He said to [his] disciples, "Therefore I tell you, do not worry about your life and what you will eat, or about your body and what you will wear. [23] For life is more than food and the body more than clothing. [24] Notice the ravens: they do not sow or reap; they have neither storehouse nor barn, yet God feeds them. How much more important are you than birds!* [25] Can any of you by worrying add a moment to your lifespan? [26] If even the smallest things are beyond your control, why are you anxious about the rest? [27] Notice how the flowers grow. They do not toil or spin. But I tell you, not even Solomon in all his splendor was dressed like one of them.* [28] If God so clothes the grass in the field that grows today and is thrown into the oven tomorrow, will he not much more provide for you, O you of little faith? [29] As for you, do not seek what you are to eat and what you are to drink, and do not worry anymore. [30] All the nations of the world seek for these things, and your Father knows that you need them. [31] Instead, seek his kingdom, and these other things will be given you besides. [32] Do not be afraid any longer, little flock, for your Father is pleased to give you the kingdom.* [33] Sell your belongings and give alms. Provide money bags for yourselves that do not wear out, an inexhaustible treasure in heaven that no thief can reach nor moth destroy.* [34] For where your treasure is, there also will your heart be.

**Vigilant and Faithful Servants.**† [35]* "Gird your loins and light your lamps [36] and be like

---

† **12:5** *Gehenna*: see note on Mt 5:22.
**12:6** *Two small coins*: the Roman copper coin, the assarion (Latin *as*), was worth about one-sixteenth of a denarius (see note on Lk 7:41).
**12:10–12** The sayings about the holy Spirit are set in the context of fearlessness in the face of persecution (Lk 12:2–9; cf. Mt 12:31–32). The holy Spirit will be presented in Luke's second volume, the Acts of the Apostles, as the power responsible for the guidance of the Christian mission and the source of courage in the face of persecution.
**12:13–34** Luke has joined together sayings contrasting those whose focus and trust in life is on material possessions, symbolized here by the rich fool of the parable (Lk 12:16–21), with those who recognize their complete dependence on God (Lk 12:21), those whose radical detachment from material posses-

sions symbolizes their heavenly treasure (Lk 12:33–34).
**12:21** *Rich in what matters to God*: literally, "rich for God."
**12:35–48** This collection of sayings relates to Luke's understanding of the end time and the return of Jesus. Luke emphasizes

| | |
|---|---|
| **12:7** 12:24; 21:18; Acts 27:34. | **12:19–21** Mt 6:19–21; 1 Tm 6:17. |
| **12:9** 9:26; Mk 8:38; 2 Tm 2:12. | **12:19–20** Sir 11:19. |
| **12:10** Mt 12:31–32; Mk 3:28–29. | **12:22–32** Mt 6:25–34. |
| **12:11–12** 21:12–15; Mt 10:17–20; Mk 13:11. | **12:24** 12:7. |
| **12:14** Ex 2:14; Acts 7:27. | **12:27** 1 Kgs 10:4–7; 2 Chr 9:3–6. |
| **12:15** 1 Tm 6:9–10. | **12:32** 22:29; Rev 1:6. |
| | **12:33** 18:22; Mt 6:20–21; Mk 10:21. |
| | **12:35–46** Mt 24:45–51. |

LK

servants who await their master's return from a wedding, ready to open immediately when he comes and knocks.* ³⁷ Blessed are those servants whom the master finds vigilant on his arrival. Amen, I say to you, he will gird himself, have them recline at table, and proceed to wait on them. ³⁸ And should he come in the second or third watch and find them prepared in this way, blessed are those servants. ³⁹* Be sure of this: if the master of the house had known the hour when the thief was coming, he would not have let his house be broken into. ⁴⁰ You also must be prepared, for at an hour you do not expect, the Son of Man will come."

⁴¹ Then Peter said, "Lord, is this parable meant for us or for everyone?" ⁴² And the Lord replied, "Who, then, is the faithful and prudent steward whom the master will put in charge of his servants to distribute [the] food allowance at the proper time? ⁴³ Blessed is that servant whom his master on arrival finds doing so. ⁴⁴ Truly, I say to you, he will put him in charge of all his property. ⁴⁵ But if that servant says to himself, 'My master is delayed in coming,'† and begins to beat the menservants and the maidservants, to eat and drink and get drunk, ⁴⁶ then that servant's master will come on an unexpected day and at an unknown hour and will punish him severely and assign him a place with the unfaithful. ⁴⁷ That servant who knew his master's will but did not make preparations nor act in accord with his will shall be beaten severely;* ⁴⁸ and the servant who was ignorant of his master's will but acted in a way deserving of a severe beating shall be beaten only lightly. Much will be required of the person entrusted with much, and still more will be demanded of the person entrusted with more.

**Jesus: A Cause of Division.**† ⁴⁹ "I have come to set the earth on fire, and how I wish it were already blazing! ⁵⁰† There is a baptism with which I must be baptized, and how great is my anguish until it is accomplished!* ⁵¹ Do you think that I have come to establish peace on the earth?* No, I tell you, but rather division.* ⁵² From now on a household of five will be divided, three against two and two against three; ⁵³ a father will be divided against his son and a son against his father, a mother against her daughter and a daughter against her mother, a mother-in-law against her daughter-in-law and a daughter-in-law against her mother-in-law."*

**Signs of the Times.*** ⁵⁴ He also said to the crowds, "When you see [a] cloud rising in the west you say immediately that it is going to rain—and so it does; ⁵⁵ and when you notice that the wind is blowing from the south you say that it is going to be hot—and so it is. ⁵⁶ You hypocrites! You know how to interpret the appearance of the earth and the sky; why do you not know how to interpret the present time?

**Settlement with an Opponent.*** ⁵⁷ "Why do you not judge for yourselves what is right? ⁵⁸ If you are to go with your opponent before a magistrate, make an effort to settle the matter on the way; otherwise your opponent will turn you over to the judge, and the judge hand you over to the constable, and the constable throw you into prison. ⁵⁹ I say to you, you will not be released until you have paid the last penny."†

**13** **A Call to Repentance.**† ¹ At that time some people who were present there told him about the Galileans whose blood

---

† for his readers the importance of being faithful to the instructions of Jesus in the period before the parousia.

**12:45** *My master is delayed in coming:* this statement indicates that early Christian expectations for the imminent return of Jesus had undergone some modification. Luke cautions his readers against counting on such a delay and acting irresponsibly. Cf. the similar warning in Mt 24:48.

**12:49–53** Jesus' proclamation of the kingdom is a refining and purifying fire. His message that meets with acceptance or rejection will be a source of conflict and dissension even within families.

**12:50** *Baptism:* i.e., his death.

**12:59** *The last penny:* Greek, *lepton,* a very small amount. Mt 5:26 has for "the last penny" the Greek word *kodrantēs* (Latin *quadrans,* "farthing").

**13:1–5** The death of the Galileans at the hands of Pilate (Lk 13:1) and the accidental death of those on whom the tower fell (Lk 13:4) are presented by the Lucan Jesus as timely reminders of the need for all to repent, for the victims of these tragedies

should not be considered outstanding sinners who were singled out for punishment.

**13:1** The slaughter of the Galileans by Pilate is unknown outside Luke; but from what is known about Pilate from the Jewish historian Josephus, such a slaughter would be in keeping with the character of Pilate. Josephus reports that Pilate had disrupted a religious gathering of the Samaritans on Mount Gerizim with a slaughter of the participants (*Antiquities* 18:86–87), and that on another occasion Pilate had killed many Jews who had opposed him when he appropriated money from the temple treasury to build an aqueduct in Jerusalem (*Jewish War* 2:175–77; *Antiquities* 18:60–62).

| | |
|---|---|
| **12:36** Mt 25:1–13; Mk 13:35–37. | **12:51–53** Mt 10:34–35. |
| | **12:51** 2:14. |
| **12:39–40** Mt 24:43–44; 1 Thes 5:2. | **12:53** Mi 7:6. |
| | **12:54–56** Mt 16:2–3. |
| **12:47** Jas 4:17. | **12:57–59** Mt 5:25–26. |
| **12:50** Mk 10:38–39. | |

Pilate† had mingled with the blood of their sacrifices. [2] He said to them in reply, "Do you think that because these Galileans suffered in this way they were greater sinners than all other Galileans?* [3] By no means! But I tell you, if you do not repent,* you will all perish as they did! [4] Or those eighteen people who were killed when the tower at Siloam fell on them† —do you think they were more guilty than everyone else who lived in Jerusalem? [5] By no means! But I tell you, if you do not repent, you will all perish as they did!"

### The Parable of the Barren Fig Tree.† [6]* And he told them this parable: "There once was a person who had a fig tree planted in his orchard, and when he came in search of fruit on it but found none, [7] he said to the gardener, 'For three years now I have come in search of fruit on this fig tree but have found none. [So] cut it down. Why should it exhaust the soil?' [8] He said to him in reply, 'Sir, leave it for this year also, and I shall cultivate the ground around it and fertilize it; [9] it may bear fruit in the future. If not you can cut it down.'"

### Cure of a Crippled Woman on the Sabbath.†
[10] He was teaching in a synagogue on the sabbath. [11] And a woman was there who for eighteen years had been crippled by a spirit; she was bent over, completely incapable of standing erect. [12] When Jesus saw her, he called to her and said, "Woman, you are set free of your infirmity." [13] He laid his hands on her, and she at once stood up straight and glorified God.

[14]* But the leader of the synagogue, indignant that Jesus had cured on the sabbath, said to the crowd in reply, "There are six days when work should be done. Come on those days to be cured, not on the sabbath day." [15]† The Lord said to him in reply, "Hypocrites! Does not each one of you on the sabbath untie his ox or his ass from the manger and lead it out for watering?* [16]† This daughter of Abraham, whom Satan has bound for eighteen years now, ought she not to have been set free on the sabbath day from this bondage?"* [17] When he said this, all his adversaries were humiliated; and the whole crowd rejoiced at all the splendid deeds done by him.

### The Parable of the Mustard Seed.* [18]† Then he said, "What is the kingdom of God like? To what can I compare it? [19] It is like a mustard seed that a person took and planted in the garden. When it was fully grown, it became a large bush and 'the birds of the sky dwelt in its branches.'"*

### The Parable of the Yeast.* [20] Again he said, "To what shall I compare the kingdom of God? [21] It is like yeast that a woman took and mixed [in] with three measures of wheat flour until the whole batch of dough was leavened."

### The Narrow Door; Salvation and Rejection.†
[22] He passed through towns and villages, teaching as he went and making his way to Jerusalem. [23] Someone asked him, "Lord, will only a few people be saved?" He answered

---

**13:4** Like the incident mentioned in Lk 13:1 nothing of this accident in Jerusalem is known outside Luke and the New Testament.

**13:6–9** Following on the call to repentance in Lk 13:1–5, the parable of the barren fig tree presents a story about the continuing patience of God with those who have not yet given evidence of their repentance (see Lk 3:8). The parable may also be alluding to the delay of the end time, when punishment will be meted out, and the importance of preparing for the end of the age because the delay will not be permanent (Lk 13:8–9).

**13:10–17** The cure of the crippled woman on the sabbath and the controversy that results furnishes a parallel to an incident that will be reported by Luke in 14:1–6, the cure of the man with dropsy on the sabbath. A characteristic of Luke's style is the juxtaposition of an incident that reveals Jesus' concern for a man with an incident that reveals his concern for a woman; cf., e.g., Lk 7:11–17 and Lk 8:49–56.

**13:15–16** If the law as interpreted by Jewish tradition allowed the untying of bound animals on the sabbath, how much more should this woman who has been bound by Satan's power be freed on the sabbath from her affliction.

**13:16** *Whom Satan has bound*: affliction and infirmity are taken as evidence of Satan's hold on humanity. The healing ministry of Jesus reveals the gradual wresting from Satan of control

over humanity and the establishment of God's kingdom.

**13:18–21** Two parables are used to illustrate the future proportions of the kingdom of God that will result from its deceptively small beginning in the preaching and healing ministry of Jesus. They are paralleled in Mt 13:31–33 and Mk 4:30–32.

**13:22–30** These sayings of Jesus follow in Luke upon the parables of the kingdom (Lk 13:18–21) and stress that great effort is required for entrance into the kingdom (Lk 13:24) and that there is an urgency to accept the present opportunity to enter because the narrow door will not remain open indefinitely (Lk 13:25). Lying behind the sayings is the rejection of Jesus and his message by his Jewish contemporaries (Lk 13:26) whose places at table in the kingdom will be taken by Gentiles from the four corners of the world (Lk 13:29). Those called last (the Gentiles) will precede those to whom the invitation to enter was first extended (the Jews). See also Lk 14:15–24.

---

**13:2** Jn 9:2.
**13:3–5** Jn 8:24.
**13:6–9** Jer 8:13; Heb 3:17; Mt 21:19; Mk 11:13.
**13:14** 6:7; 14:3; Ex 20:8–11; Dt 5:12–15; Mt 12:10; Mk 3:2–4; Jn 5:16; 7:23; 9:14, 16.
**13:15** 14:5; Dt 22:4; Mt 12:11.
**13:16** 19:9.
**13:18–19** Mt 13:31–32; Mk 4:30–32.
**13:19** Ez 17:23–24; 31:6.
**13:20–21** Mt 13:33.

them, [24]* "Strive to enter through the narrow door, for many, I tell you, will attempt to enter but will not be strong enough.* [25] After the master of the house has arisen and locked the door, then will you stand outside knocking and saying, 'Lord, open the door for us.' He will say to you in reply, 'I do not know where you are from.'* [26] And you will say, 'We ate and drank in your company and you taught in our streets.' [27]* Then he will say to you, 'I do not know where [you] are from. Depart from me, all you evildoers!' [28]* And there will be wailing and grinding of teeth when you see Abraham, Isaac, and Jacob and all the prophets in the kingdom of God and you yourselves cast out. [29] And people will come from the east and the west and from the north and the south and will recline at table in the kingdom of God.* [30] For behold, some are last who will be first, and some are first who will be last."*

**Herod's Desire to Kill Jesus.** [31] At that time some Pharisees came to him and said, "Go away, leave this area because Herod wants to kill you." [32] He replied, "Go and tell that fox, 'Behold, I cast out demons and I perform healings today and tomorrow, and on the third day I accomplish my purpose.† [33]† Yet I must continue on my way today,* tomorrow, and the following day, for it is impossible that a prophet should die outside of Jerusalem.'

**The Lament over Jerusalem.*** [34] "Jerusalem, Jerusalem, you who kill the prophets and stone those sent to you, how many times I yearned to gather your children together as a hen gathers her brood under her wings, but you were unwilling! [35] Behold, your house will be abandoned. [But] I tell you, you will not see me until [the time comes when] you say, 'Blessed is he who comes in the name of the Lord.'"*

**14 Healing of the Man with Dropsy on the Sabbath.**† [1]* On a sabbath he went to dine at the home of one of the leading Pharisees, and the people there were observing him carefully.* [2] In front of him there was a man suffering from dropsy.† [3] Jesus spoke to the scholars of the law and Pharisees in reply, asking, "Is it lawful to cure on the sabbath or not?"* [4] But they kept silent; so he took the man and, after he had healed him, dismissed him. [5] Then he said to them, "Who among you, if your son or ox† falls into a cistern, would not immediately pull him out on the sabbath day?"* [6] But they were unable to answer his question.*

**Conduct of Invited Guests and Hosts.**† [7]* He told a parable to those who had been invited, noticing how they were choosing the places of honor at the table. [8]* "When you are invited by someone to a wedding banquet, do not recline at table in the place of honor. A more distinguished guest than you may have been invited by him, [9] and the host who invited both of you may approach you and say, 'Give your place to this man,' and then you would proceed with embarrassment to take the lowest place. [10] Rather, when you are invited, go and take the lowest place so that when the host comes to you he may say, 'My friend, move up to a higher position.' Then you will enjoy the esteem of your companions at the table. [11] For everyone who exalts himself will be humbled, but the one who humbles himself will be exalted."* [12] Then he said to the host who invited him, "When you hold a lunch or a dinner, do not invite your friends or your brothers or your relatives or your wealthy neighbors, in case they may invite you back and you have repayment.* [13] Rather, when you hold a banquet, invite the poor, the crippled,

---

† **13:32** Nothing, not even Herod's desire to kill Jesus, stands in the way of Jesus' role in fulfilling God's will and in establishing the kingdom through his exorcisms and healings.
**13:33** *It is impossible that a prophet should die outside of Jerusalem:* Jerusalem is the city of destiny and the goal of the journey of the prophet Jesus. Only when he reaches the holy city will his work be accomplished.
**14:1–6** See note on Lk 13:10–17.
**14:2** *Dropsy:* an abnormal swelling of the body because of the retention and accumulation of fluid.
**14:5** *Your son or ox:* this is the reading of many of the oldest and most important New Testament manuscripts. Because of the strange collocation of *son* and *ox*, some copyists have altered it to "your ass or ox," on the model of the saying in Lk 13:15.
**14:7–14** The banquet scene found only in Luke provides the

opportunity for these teachings of Jesus on humility and presents a setting to display Luke's interest in Jesus' attitude toward the rich and the poor (see notes on Lk 4:18; 6:20–26; 12:13–34).

---

**13:24–30** Mt 7:13–14, 21–23.
**13:24** Mk 10:25.
**13:25** Mt 25:10–12.
**13:27** Ps 6:9; Mt 7:23; 25:41.
**13:28–29** Mt 8:11–12.
**13:29** Ps 107:2–3.
**13:30** Mt 19:20; 20:16; Mk 10:31.
**13:33** 2:38; Jn 6:30; 8:20.
**13:34–35** 19:41–44; Mt 23:37–39.
**13:35** 19:38; 1 Kgs 9:7–8;

Ps 118:26; Jer 7:4–7, 13–15; 12:7; 22:5.
**14:1–6** 6:6–11; 13:10–17.
**14:1** 11:37.
**14:3** 6:9; Mk 3:4.
**14:5** 13:15; Dt 22:4; Mt 12:11.
**14:6** Mt 22:46.
**14:7** 11:43; Mt 23:6; Mk 12:38–39.
**14:8–10** Prv 25:6–7.
**14:11** 18:14.
**14:12** 6:32–35.

the lame, the blind; [14] blessed indeed will you be because of their inability to repay you. For you will be repaid at the resurrection of the righteous." *

### The Parable of the Great Feast.† [15] One of his fellow guests on hearing this said to him, "Blessed is the one who will dine in the kingdom of God." [16] * He replied to him, "A man gave a great dinner to which he invited many. [17] When the time for the dinner came, he dispatched his servant to say to those invited, 'Come, everything is now ready.' [18] But one by one, they all began to excuse themselves. The first said to him, 'I have purchased a field and must go to examine it; I ask you, consider me excused.' [19] And another said, 'I have purchased five yoke of oxen and am on my way to evaluate them; I ask you, consider me excused.' [20] And another said, 'I have just married a woman, and therefore I cannot come.' [21] The servant went and reported this to his master. Then the master of the house in a rage commanded his servant, 'Go out quickly into the streets and alleys of the town and bring in here the poor and the crippled, the blind and the lame.' [22] The servant reported, 'Sir, your orders have been carried out and still there is room.' [23] The master then ordered the servant, 'Go out to the highways and hedgerows and make people come in that my home may be filled. [24] For, I tell you, none of those men who were invited will taste my dinner.'"

### Sayings on Discipleship.† [25] Great crowds were traveling with him, and he turned and addressed them, [26] * "If any one comes to me without hating his father† and mother, wife and children, brothers and sisters, and even his own life, he cannot be my disciple. * [27] Whoever does not carry his own cross and come after me cannot be my disciple. * [28] Which of you wishing to construct a tower does not first sit down and calculate the cost to see if there is enough for its completion? [29] Otherwise, after laying the foundation and finding himself unable to finish the work the onlookers should laugh at him [30] and say, 'This one began to build but did not have the resources to finish.' [31] Or what king marching into battle would not first sit down and decide whether with ten thousand troops he can successfully oppose another king advancing upon him with twenty thousand troops? [32] But if not, while he is still far away, he will send a delegation to ask for peace terms. [33] In the same way, everyone of you who does not renounce all his possessions cannot be my disciple. *

### The Simile of Salt.† [34] "Salt is good, but if salt itself loses its taste, with what can its flavor be restored? * [35] It is fit neither for the soil nor for the manure pile; it is thrown out. Whoever has ears to hear ought to hear." *

## 15 The Parable of the Lost Sheep. * [1] † The tax collectors and sinners were all drawing near to listen to him, [2] but the Pharisees and scribes began to complain, saying, "This man welcomes sinners and eats with them." * [3] So to them he addressed this parable. [4] * "What man among you having a hundred sheep and losing one of them would not leave the ninety-nine in the desert and go after the lost one* until he finds it? * [5] And when he does find it, he sets it on his shoulders with great joy [6] and, upon his arrival home, he calls together his friends and neighbors and says to them, 'Rejoice with me

---

† **14:15–24** The parable of the great dinner is a further illustration of the rejection by Israel, God's chosen people, of Jesus' invitation to share in the banquet in the kingdom and the extension of the invitation to other Jews whose identification as the poor, crippled, blind, and lame (Lk 14:21) classifies them among those who recognize their need for salvation, and to Gentiles (Lk 14:23). A similar parable is found in Mt 22:1–10.

**14:25–33** This collection of sayings, most of which are peculiar to Luke, focuses on the total dedication necessary for the disciple of Jesus. No attachment to family (Lk 14:26) or possessions (Lk 14:33) can stand in the way of the total commitment demanded of the disciple. Also, acceptance of the call to be a disciple demands readiness to accept persecution and suffering (Lk 14:27) and a realistic assessment of the hardships and costs (Lk 14:28–32).

**14:26** *Hating his father…*: cf. the similar saying in Mt 10:37. The disciple's family must take second place to the absolute dedication involved in following Jesus (see also Lk 9:59–62).

**14:34–35** The simile of salt follows the sayings of Jesus that demanded of the disciple total dedication and detachment from family and possessions and illustrates the condition of one who does not display this total commitment. The halfhearted disciple is like salt that cannot serve its intended purpose. See the simile of salt in Mt 5:13 and the note there.

**15:1–32** To the parable of the lost sheep (Lk 15:1–7) that Luke shares with Matthew (Mt 18:12–14), Luke adds two parables (the lost coin, Lk 15:8–10; the prodigal son, Lk 15:11–32) from his own special tradition to illustrate Jesus' particular concern for the lost and God's love for the repentant sinner.

---

**14:14** Jn 5:29.
**14:16–24** Mt 22:2–10.
**14:26–27** Mt 10:37–38.
**14:26** 9:57–62; 18:29; Jn 12:25.
**14:27** 9:23; Mt 16:24; Mk 8:34.
**14:33** 5:11.
**14:34** Mt 5:13; Mk 9:50.
**14:35** 8:8; Mt 11:15; 13:9; Mk 4:9, 23.
**15:1–7** Mt 9:10–13.
**15:2** 5:30; 19:7.
**15:4–7** Mt 18:12–14.
**15:4–6** 19:10.
**15:4** Ez 34:11–12, 16.

LK

because I have found my lost sheep.' 7 I tell you, in just the same way there will be more joy in heaven over one sinner who repents than over ninety-nine righteous people who have no need of repentance.*

**The Parable of the Lost Coin.** 8 "Or what woman having ten coins† and losing one would not light a lamp and sweep the house, searching carefully until she finds it? 9 And when she does find it, she calls together her friends and neighbors and says to them, 'Rejoice with me because I have found the coin that I lost.' 10 In just the same way, I tell you, there will be rejoicing among the angels of God over one sinner who repents."

**The Parable of the Lost Son.** 11 Then he said, "A man had two sons, 12 and the younger son said to his father, 'Father, give me the share of your estate that should come to me.' So the father divided the property between them. 13 After a few days, the younger son collected all his belongings and set off to a distant country where he squandered his inheritance on a life of dissipation.* 14 When he had freely spent everything, a severe famine struck that country, and he found himself in dire need. 15 So he hired himself out to one of the local citizens who sent him to his farm to tend the swine. 16 And he longed to eat his fill of the pods on which the swine fed, but nobody gave him any. 17 Coming to his senses he thought, 'How many of my father's hired workers have more than enough food to eat, but here am I, dying from hunger. 18 I shall get up and go to my father and I shall say to him, "Father, I have sinned against heaven and against you. 19 I no longer deserve to be called your son; treat me as you would treat one of your hired workers."' 20 So he got up and went back to his father. While he was still a long way off, his father caught sight of him, and was filled with compassion. He ran to his son, embraced him and kissed him. 21 His son said to him, 'Father, I have sinned against heaven and against you; I

no longer deserve to be called your son.' 22 But his father ordered his servants, 'Quickly bring the finest robe and put it on him; put a ring on his finger and sandals on his feet. 23 Take the fattened calf and slaughter it. Then let us celebrate with a feast, 24 because this son of mine was dead, and has come to life again; he was lost, and has been found.' Then the celebration began. 25 Now the older son had been out in the field and, on his way back, as he neared the house, he heard the sound of music and dancing. 26 He called one of the servants and asked what this might mean. 27 The servant said to him, 'Your brother has returned and your father has slaughtered the fattened calf because he has him back safe and sound.' 28 He became angry, and when he refused to enter the house, his father came out and pleaded with him. 29 He said to his father in reply, 'Look, all these years I served you and not once did I disobey your orders; yet you never gave me even a young goat to feast on with my friends. 30 But when your son returns who swallowed up your property with prostitutes, for him you slaughter the fattened calf.' 31 He said to him, 'My son, you are here with me always; everything I have is yours. 32 But now we must celebrate and rejoice, because your brother was dead and has come to life again; he was lost and has been found.'"

**16** **The Parable of the Dishonest Steward.**† 1 Then he also said to his disciples, "A rich man had a steward who was reported to him for squandering his property. 2 He summoned him and said, 'What is this I hear about you? Prepare a full account of your stewardship, because you can no longer be my steward.' 3 The steward said to himself, 'What shall I do, now that my master is taking the position of steward away from me? I am not strong enough to dig and I am ashamed to beg. 4 I know what I shall do so that, when I am removed from the stewardship, they may welcome me into their homes.' 5 He called in his master's debtors one by one. To the first

---

† **15:8** *Ten coins:* literally, "ten drachmas." A drachma was a Greek silver coin.
**16:1–8a** The parable of the dishonest steward has to be understood in the light of the Palestinian custom of agents acting on behalf of their masters and the usurious practices common to such agents. The dishonesty of the steward consisted in the squandering of his master's property (Lk 16:1) and not in any subsequent graft. The master commends the dishonest steward who has forgone his own usurious commission on the business

transaction by having the debtors write new notes that reflected only the real amount owed the master (i.e., minus the steward's profit). The dishonest steward acts in this way in order to ingratiate himself with the debtors because he knows he is being dismissed from his position (Lk 16:3). The parable, then, teaches the prudent use of one's material goods in light of an imminent crisis.

**15:7** Ez 18:23.      **15:13** Prv 29:3.

he said, 'How much do you owe my master?' ⁶† He replied, 'One hundred measures of olive oil.' He said to him, 'Here is your promissory note. Sit down and quickly write one for fifty.' ⁷ Then to another he said, 'And you, how much do you owe?' He replied, 'One hundred kors† of wheat.' He said to him, 'Here is your promissory note; write one for eighty.' ⁸ And the master commended that dishonest steward for acting prudently.

**Application of the Parable.**† "For the children of this world are more prudent in dealing with their own generation than are the children of light.†* ⁹ I tell you, make friends for yourselves with dishonest wealth,† so that when it fails, you will be welcomed into eternal dwellings.* ¹⁰† The person who is trustworthy in very small matters is also trustworthy in great ones; and the person who is dishonest in very small matters is also dishonest in great ones.* ¹¹ If, therefore, you are not trustworthy with dishonest wealth, who will trust you with true wealth? ¹² If you are not trustworthy with what belongs to another, who will give you what is yours? ¹³ No servant can serve two masters.† He will either hate one and love the other, or be devoted to one and despise the other. You cannot serve God and mammon."*

**A Saying Against the Pharisees.** ¹⁴† The Pharisees, who loved money,† heard all these things

and sneered at him. ¹⁵ And he said to them, "You justify yourselves in the sight of others, but God knows your hearts; for what is of human esteem is an abomination in the sight of God.*

**Sayings About the Law.** ¹⁶ "The law and the prophets lasted until John;† but from then on the kingdom of God is proclaimed, and everyone who enters does so with violence.* ¹⁷ It is easier for heaven and earth to pass away than for the smallest part of a letter of the law to become invalid.*

**Sayings About Divorce.** ¹⁸ "Everyone who divorces his wife and marries another commits adultery, and the one who marries a woman divorced from her husband commits adultery.*

**The Parable of the Rich Man and Lazarus.**† ¹⁹ "There was a rich man† who dressed in purple garments and fine linen and dined sumptuously each day. ²⁰ And lying at his door was a poor man named Lazarus, covered with sores,* ²¹ who would gladly have eaten his fill of the scraps that fell from the rich man's table. Dogs even used to come and lick his sores. ²² When the poor man died, he was carried away by angels to the bosom of Abraham. The rich man also died and was buried, ²³ and from the netherworld,† where he was in torment, he raised

---

**16:6** *One hundred measures*: literally, "one hundred baths." A bath is a Hebrew unit of liquid measurement equivalent to eight or nine gallons.

**16:7** *One hundred kors*: a *kor* is a Hebrew unit of dry measure for grain or wheat equivalent to ten or twelve bushels.

**16:8b–13** Several originally independent sayings of Jesus are gathered here by Luke to form the concluding application of the parable of the dishonest steward.

**16:8b–9** The first conclusion recommends the prudent use of one's wealth (in the light of the coming of the end of the age) after the manner of the children of this world, represented in the parable by the dishonest steward.

**16:9** *Dishonest wealth*: literally, "mammon of iniquity." Mammon is the Greek transliteration of a Hebrew or Aramaic word that is usually explained as meaning "that in which one trusts." The characterization of this wealth as *dishonest* expresses a tendency of wealth to lead one to dishonesty. *Eternal dwellings*: or, "eternal tents," i.e., heaven.

**16:10–12** The second conclusion recommends constant fidelity to those in positions of responsibility.

**16:13** The third conclusion is a general statement about the incompatibility of serving God and being a slave to riches. To be dependent upon wealth is opposed to the teachings of Jesus who counseled complete dependence on the Father as one of the characteristics of the Christian disciple (Lk 12:22–39). *God and mammon*: see note on Lk 16:9. Mammon is used here as if it were itself a god.

**16:14–18** The two parables about the use of riches in chap.

16 are separated by several isolated sayings of Jesus on the hypocrisy of the Pharisees (Lk 16:14–15), on the law (Lk 16:16–17), and on divorce (Lk 16:18).

**16:14–15** The Pharisees are here presented as examples of those who are slaves to wealth (see Lk 16:13) and, consequently, they are unable to serve God.

**16:16** John the Baptist is presented in Luke's gospel as a transitional figure between the period of Israel, the time of promise, and the period of Jesus, the time of fulfillment. With John, the fulfillment of the Old Testament promises has begun.

**16:19–31** The parable of the rich man and Lazarus again illustrates Luke's concern with Jesus' attitude toward the rich and the poor. The reversal of the fates of the rich man and Lazarus (Lk 16:22–23) illustrates the teachings of Jesus in Luke's "Sermon on the Plain" (Lk 6:20–21, 24–25).

**16:19** The oldest Greek manuscript of Luke dating from ca. A.D. 175–225 records the name of the rich man as an abbreviated form of "Nineveh," but there is very little textual support in other manuscripts for this reading. "Dives" of popular tradition is the Latin Vulgate's translation for "rich man" (Lk 16:19–31).

**16:23** *The netherworld*: see note on Lk 10:15.

---

| | |
|---|---|
| **16:8** Eph 5:8; 1 Thes 5:5. | **16:17** Mt 5:18. |
| **16:9** 12:33. | **16:18** Mt 5:32; 19:9; Mk |
| **16:10** 19:17; Mt 25:20–23. | 10:11–12; 1 Cor |
| **16:13** Mt 6:24. | 7:10–11. |
| **16:15** 18:9–14. | **16:20** Mt 15:27; Mk 7:28. |
| **16:16** Mt 11:12–13. | |

his eyes and saw Abraham far off and Lazarus at his side. 24 And he cried out, 'Father Abraham, have pity on me. Send Lazarus to dip the tip of his finger in water and cool my tongue, for I am suffering torment in these flames.' 25 Abraham replied, 'My child, remember that you received what was good during your lifetime while Lazarus likewise received what was bad; but now he is comforted here, whereas you are tormented.* 26 Moreover, between us and you a great chasm is established to prevent anyone from crossing who might wish to go from our side to yours or from your side to ours.' 27 He said, 'Then I beg you, father, send him to my father's house, 28 for I have five brothers, so that he may warn them, lest they too come to this place of torment.' 29 But Abraham replied, 'They have Moses and the prophets. Let them listen to them.' 30† He said, 'Oh no, father Abraham, but if someone from the dead goes to them, they will repent.' 31 Then Abraham said, 'If they will not listen to Moses and the prophets, neither will they be persuaded if someone should rise from the dead.'"*

**17** **Temptations to Sin.** 1* He said to his disciples, "Things that cause sin will inevitably occur, but woe to the person through whom they occur. 2 It would be better for him if a millstone were put around his neck and he be thrown into the sea than for him to cause one of these little ones to sin. 3 Be on your guard!† If your brother sins, rebuke him; and if he repents, forgive him.* 4 And if he wrongs you seven times in one day and returns to you seven times saying, 'I am sorry,' you should forgive him."*

**Saying of Faith.** 5 And the apostles said to the Lord, "Increase our faith." 6 The Lord replied,

"If you have faith the size of a mustard seed, you would say to [this] mulberry tree, 'Be uprooted and planted in the sea,' and it would obey you.*

**Attitude of a Servant.**† 7 "Who among you would say to your servant who has just come in from plowing or tending sheep in the field, 'Come here immediately and take your place at table'? 8 Would he not rather say to him, 'Prepare something for me to eat. Put on your apron and wait on me while I eat and drink. You may eat and drink when I am finished'? 9 Is he grateful to that servant because he did what was commanded? 10 So should it be with you. When you have done all you have been commanded, say, 'We are unprofitable servants; we have done what we were obliged to do.'"

**The Cleansing of Ten Lepers.**† 11 As he continued his journey to Jerusalem,* he traveled through Samaria and Galilee.† 12 As he was entering a village, ten lepers met [him]. They stood at a distance from him 13 and raised their voice, saying, "Jesus, Master! Have pity on us!"* 14 And when he saw them, he said, "Go show yourselves to the priests."† As they were going they were cleansed.* 15 And one of them, realizing he had been healed, returned, glorifying God in a loud voice; 16 and he fell at the feet of Jesus and thanked him. He was a Samaritan. 17 Jesus said in reply, "Ten were cleansed, were they not? Where are the other nine? 18 Has none but this foreigner returned to give thanks to God?" 19 Then he said to him, "Stand up and go; your faith has saved you."*

**The Coming of the Kingdom of God.** 20† Asked by the Pharisees when the kingdom of God

---

16:30–31 A foreshadowing in Luke's gospel of the rejection of the call to repentance even after Jesus' resurrection.

17:3 *Be on your guard*: the translation takes Lk 17:3a as the conclusion to the saying on scandal in Lk 17:1–2. It is not impossible that it should be taken as the beginning of the saying on forgiveness in Lk 17:3b–4.

17:7–10 These sayings of Jesus, peculiar to Luke, which continue his response to the apostles' request to increase their faith (Lk 17:5–6), remind them that Christian disciples can make no claim on God's graciousness; in fulfilling the exacting demands of discipleship, they are only doing their duty.

17:11–19 This incident recounting the thankfulness of the cleansed Samaritan leper is narrated only in Luke's gospel and provides an instance of Jesus holding up a non-Jew (Lk 17:18) as an example to his Jewish contemporaries (cf. Lk 10:33 where a similar purpose is achieved in the story of the good Samaritan). Moreover, it is the faith in Jesus manifested by the foreigner that

has brought him salvation (Lk 17:19; cf. the similar relationship between faith and salvation in Lk 7:50; 8:48, 50).

17:11 *Through Samaria and Galilee*: or, "between Samaria and Galilee."

17:14 See note on Lk 5:14.

17:20–37 To the question of the Pharisees about the time of the coming of God's kingdom, Jesus replies that the kingdom is *among you* (Lk 17:20–21). The emphasis has thus been shifted from an imminent observable coming of the kingdom to some-

16:25 6:24–25.
16:31 Jn 5:46–47; 11:44–48.
17:1–2 Mt 18:6–7.
17:3 Mt 18:15.
17:4 Mt 6:14; 18:21–22, 35; Mk 11:25.
17:6 Mt 17:20; 21:21; Mk 11:23.
17:11 9:51–53; 13:22, 33; 18:31; 19:28; Jn 4:4.
17:13 18:38; Mt 9:27; 15:22.
17:14 5:14; Lv 14:2–32; Mt 8:4; Mk 1:44.
17:19 7:50; 18:42.

Admonishing his disciples regarding sin, Jesus used an analogy involving a grinding stone, a heavy, conical stone used to mill grain. "It would be better for him if a millstone were put around his neck and he be thrown into the sea than for him to cause one of these little ones to sin" (Lk 17:2).

would come, he said in reply, "The coming of the kingdom of God cannot be observed,* [21]† and no one will announce, 'Look, here it is,' or, 'There it is.'* For behold, the kingdom of God is among you."

**The Day of the Son of Man.** [22] Then he said to his disciples, "The days will come when you will long to see one of the days of the Son of Man, but you will not see it. [23] There will be those who will say to you, 'Look, there he is,' [or] 'Look, here he is.' Do not go off, do not run in pursuit.* [24] For just as lightning flashes and lights up the sky from one side to the other, so will the Son of Man be [in his day].* [25] But first he must suffer greatly and be rejected by this generation.* [26] As it was in the days of Noah,* so it will be in the days of the Son of Man; [27] they were eating and drinking, marrying and giving in marriage up to the day that Noah entered the ark, and the flood came and destroyed them all. [28]* Similarly, as it was in the days of Lot: they were eating, drinking,

buying, selling, planting, building; [29] on the day when Lot left Sodom, fire and brimstone rained from the sky to destroy them all. [30] So it will be on the day the Son of Man is revealed. [31]* On that day, a person who is on the housetop and whose belongings are in the house must not go down to get them, and likewise a person in the field must not return to what was left behind.* [32] Remember the wife of Lot. [33] Whoever seeks to preserve his life will lose it, but whoever loses it will save it.* [34] I tell you, on that night there will be two people in one bed; one will be taken, the other left. [35]* And there will be two women grinding meal together; one will be taken, the other left." [[36]]† [37] They said to him in reply, "Where, Lord?" He said to them, "Where the body is, there also the vultures will gather."*

# 18

**The Parable of the Persistent Widow.** [1]† Then he told them a parable about the necessity for them to pray always without becoming weary.* He said, [2] "There was

---

† thing that is already present in Jesus' preaching and healing ministry. Luke has also appended further traditional sayings of Jesus about the unpredictable suddenness of the day of the Son of Man, and assures his readers that in spite of the delay of that day (Lk 12:45), it will bring judgment unexpectedly on those who do not continue to be vigilant.

**17:21** *Among you:* the Greek preposition translated as *among* can also be translated as "within." In the light of other statements in Luke's gospel about the presence of the kingdom (see Lk 10:9, 11; 11:20) "among" is to be preferred.

**17:36** The inclusion of Lk 17:36, "There will be two men in the field; one will be taken, the other left behind," in some Western manuscripts appears to be a scribal assimilation to Mt 24:40.

**18:1–14** The particularly Lucan material in the travel narrative concludes with two parables on prayer. The first (Lk 18:1–8) teaches the disciples the need of persistent prayer so that they not fall victims to apostasy (Lk 18:8). The second (Lk 18:9–14)

condemns the self-righteous, critical attitude of the Pharisee and teaches that the fundamental attitude of the Christian disciple must be the recognition of sinfulness and complete dependence on God's graciousness. The second parable recalls the story of the pardoning of the sinful woman (Lk 7:36–50) where a similar

**17:20** Jn 3:3.
**17:21** 17:23; Mt 24:23; Mk 13:21.
**17:23** 17:21; Mt 24:23, 26; Mk 13:21.
**17:24** Mt 24:27.
**17:25** 9:22; 18:32–33; Mt 16:21; 17:22–23; 20:18–19; Mk 8:31; 9:31; 10:33–34.
**17:26–27** Gn 6–8; Mt 24:37–39.
**17:28–29** Gn 18:20–21; 19:1–29.
**17:31–32** Gn 19:17, 26.
**17:31** Mt 24:17–18; Mk 13:15–16.
**17:33** 9:24; Mt 10:39; 16:25; Mk 8:35; Jn 12:25.
**17:35** Mt 24:40–41.
**17:37** Jb 39:30; Mt 24:28.
**18:1** Rom 12:12; Col 4:2; 1 Thes 5:17.

a judge in a certain town who neither feared God nor respected any human being. ³And a widow in that town used to come to him and say, 'Render a just decision for me against my adversary.' ⁴For a long time the judge was unwilling, but eventually he thought, 'While it is true that I neither fear God nor respect any human being, ⁵†* because this widow keeps bothering me I shall deliver a just decision for her lest she finally come and strike me.'" ⁶The Lord said, "Pay attention to what the dishonest judge says. ⁷Will not God then secure the rights of his chosen ones who call out to him day and night? Will he be slow to answer them? ⁸I tell you, he will see to it that justice is done for them speedily. But when the Son of Man comes, will he find faith on earth?"

### The Parable of the Pharisee and the Tax Collector.

⁹He then addressed this parable to those who were convinced of their own righteousness and despised everyone else.* ¹⁰"Two people went up to the temple area to pray; one was a Pharisee and the other was a tax collector. ¹¹The Pharisee took up his position and spoke this prayer to himself, 'O God, I thank you that I am not like the rest of humanity—greedy, dishonest, adulterous—or even like this tax collector. ¹²I fast twice a week, and I pay tithes on my whole income.'* ¹³But the tax collector stood off at a distance and would not even raise his eyes to heaven but beat his breast and prayed, 'O God, be merciful to me a sinner.'* ¹⁴I tell you, the latter went home justified, not the former; for everyone who exalts himself will be humbled, and the one who humbles himself will be exalted."*

### Saying on Children and the Kingdom.

¹⁵† People were bringing even infants to him that he might touch them,† and when the disciples saw this, they rebuked them.* ¹⁶Jesus, however, called the children to himself and said, "Let the children come to me and do not prevent them; for the kingdom of God belongs to such as these. ¹⁷Amen, I say to you, whoever does not accept the kingdom of God like a child will not enter it."*

### The Rich Official.

¹⁸* An official asked him this question, "Good teacher, what must I do to inherit eternal life?"* ¹⁹Jesus answered him, "Why do you call me good? No one is good but God alone. ²⁰You know the commandments, 'You shall not commit adultery; you shall not kill; you shall not steal; you shall not bear false witness; honor your father and your mother.'"* ²¹And he replied, "All of these I have observed from my youth." ²²†* When Jesus heard this he said to him, "There is still one thing left for you: sell all that you have and distribute it to the poor, and you will have a treasure in heaven. Then come, follow me." ²³But when he heard this he became quite sad, for he was very rich.

### On Riches and Renunciation.

²⁴Jesus looked at him [now sad] and said, "How hard it is for those who have wealth to enter the kingdom of God! ²⁵For it is easier for a camel to pass through the eye of a needle than for a rich person to enter the kingdom of God." ²⁶Those who heard this said, "Then who can be saved?" ²⁷And he said, "What is impossible for human beings is possible for God."* ²⁸Then Peter said, "We have given up our possessions and followed you." ²⁹* He said to them, "Amen, I say to you, there is no one who has given up house or wife or brothers or parents or children for the sake of the kingdom of God ³⁰who will not receive [back] an overabundant return in this present age and eternal life in the age to come."

---

† contrast is presented between the critical attitude of the Pharisee Simon and the love shown by the pardoned sinner.

**18:5** *Strike me*: the Greek verb translated as strike means "to strike under the eye" and suggests the extreme situation to which the persistence of the widow might lead. It may, however, be used here in the much weaker sense of "to wear one out."

**18:15–19:27** Luke here includes much of the material about the journey to Jerusalem found in his Marcan source (Lk 10:1–52) and adds to it the story of Zacchaeus (Lk 19:1–10) from his own particular tradition and the parable of the gold coins (minas) (Lk 19:11–27) from Q, the source common to Luke and Matthew.

**18:15–17** The sayings on children furnish a contrast to the attitude of the Pharisee in the preceding episode (Lk 18:9–14) and that of the wealthy official in the following one (Lk 18:18–23) who think that they can lay claim to God's favor by their own

merit. The attitude of the disciple should be marked by the receptivity and trustful dependence characteristic of the child.

**18:22** Detachment from material possessions results in the total dependence on God demanded of one who would inherit eternal life. *Sell all that you have*: the original saying (cf. Mk 10:21) has characteristically been made more demanding by Luke's addition of "all."

---

**18:5** 11:8.
**18:9** 16:5; Mt 23:25–28.
**18:12** Mt 23:23.
**18:13** Ps 51:3.
**18:14** 14:11; Mt 23:12.
**18:15–17** Mt 19:13–15; Mk 10:13–16.
**18:17** Mt 18:3.
**18:18–30** Mt 19:16–30; Mk 10:17–31.
**18:18** 10:25.
**18:20** Ex 20:12–16; Dt 5:16–20.
**18:22** 12:33; Sir 29:11; Mt 6:20.
**18:27** Mk 14:36.
**18:29–30** 14:26.

L
K

**The Third Prediction of the Passion.*** [31†] Then he took the Twelve aside and said to them, "Behold, we are going up to Jerusalem and everything written by the prophets about the Son of Man will be fulfilled.† [32]* He will be handed over to the Gentiles and he will be mocked and insulted and spat upon; [33] and after they have scourged him they will kill him, but on the third day he will rise." [34] But they understood nothing of this; the word remained hidden from them and they failed to comprehend what he said.*

**The Healing of the Blind Beggar.*** [35] Now as he approached Jericho a blind man was sitting by the roadside begging, [36] and hearing a crowd going by, he inquired what was happening. [37] They told him, "Jesus of Nazareth is passing by." [38]* He shouted, "Jesus, Son of David,† have pity on me!" [39] The people walking in front rebuked him, telling him to be silent, but he kept calling out all the more, "Son of David, have pity on me!" [40] Then Jesus stopped and ordered that he be brought to him; and when he came near, Jesus asked him, [41] "What do you want me to do for you?" He replied, "Lord, please let me see."* [42] Jesus told him, "Have sight; your faith has saved you."* [43] He immediately received his sight and followed him, giving glory to God. When they saw this, all the people gave praise to God.

**19** **Zacchaeus the Tax Collector.**† [1] He came to Jericho and intended to pass through the town. [2] Now a man there named Zacchaeus, who was a chief tax collector and also a wealthy man, [3] was seeking to see who Jesus was; but he could not see him because of the crowd, for he was short in stature. [4] So he ran ahead and climbed a sycamore tree in order to see Jesus, who was about to pass that way. [5] When he reached the place, Jesus looked up and said to him, "Zacchaeus, come down quickly, for today I must stay at your house." [6] And he came down quickly and received him with joy. [7] When they all saw this, they began to grumble, saying, "He has gone to stay at the house of a sinner."* [8] But Zacchaeus stood there and said to the Lord, "Behold, half of my possessions, Lord, I shall give to the poor, and if I have extorted anything from anyone I shall repay it four times over."* [9]† And Jesus said to him, "Today salvation* has come to this house because this man too is a descendant of Abraham. [10]†* For the Son of Man has come to seek and to save what was lost."

**The Parable of the Ten Gold Coins.**† [11]* While they were listening to him speak, he proceeded

---

18:31–33 The details included in this third announcement of Jesus' suffering and death suggest that the literary formulation of the announcement has been directed by the knowledge of the historical passion and death of Jesus.

18:31 *Everything written by the prophets…will be fulfilled*: this is a Lucan addition to the words of Jesus found in the Marcan source (Mk 10:32–34). Luke understands the events of Jesus' last days in Jerusalem to be the fulfillment of Old Testament prophecy, but, as is usually the case in Luke-Acts, the author does not specify which Old Testament prophets he has in mind; cf. Lk 24:25, 27, 44; Acts 3:8; 13:27; 26:22–23.

18:38 *Son of David*: the blind beggar identifies Jesus with a title that is related to Jesus' role as Messiah (see note on Lk 2:11). Through this Son of David, salvation comes to the blind man. Note the connection between salvation and house of David mentioned earlier in Zechariah's canticle (Lk 1:69). See also note on Mt 9:27.

19:1–10 The story of the tax collector Zacchaeus is unique to this gospel. While a rich man (Lk 19:2), Zacchaeus provides a contrast to the rich man of Lk 18:18–23 who cannot detach himself from his material possessions to become a follower of Jesus. Zacchaeus, according to Luke, exemplifies the proper attitude toward wealth: he promises to give half of his possessions to the poor (Lk 19:8) and consequently is the recipient of salvation (Lk 19:9–10).

19:9 *A descendant of Abraham*: literally, "a son of Abraham." The tax collector Zacchaeus, whose repentance is attested by his determination to amend his former ways, shows himself to be a true descendant of Abraham, the true heir to the promises of God in the Old Testament. Underlying Luke's depiction of Zacchaeus as a descendant of Abraham, the father of the Jews (Lk 1:73;

16:22–31), is his recognition of the central place occupied by Israel in the plan of salvation.

19:10 This verse sums up for Luke his depiction of the role of Jesus as savior in this gospel.

19:11–27 In this parable Luke has combined two originally distinct parables: (1) a parable about the conduct of faithful and productive servants (Lk 19:13, 15b–26) and (2) a parable about a rejected king (Lk 19:12, 14–15a, 27). The story about the conduct of servants occurs in another form in Mt 25:14–20. The story about the rejected king may have originated with a contemporary historical event. After the death of Herod the Great, his son Archelaus traveled to Rome to receive the title of king. A delegation of Jews appeared in Rome before Caesar Augustus to oppose the request of Archelaus. Although not given the title of king, Archelaus was made ruler over Judea and Samaria. As the story is used by Luke, however, it furnishes a correction to the expectation of the imminent end of the age and of the establishment of the kingdom in Jerusalem (Lk 19:11). Jesus is not on his way to Jerusalem to receive the kingly power; for that, he must go away and only after returning from the distant country (a reference to the parousia) will reward and judgment take place.

---

18:31–34 24:25–27, 44;
          Mt 20:17–19; Mk
          10:32–34; Acts 3:18.
18:32–33 9:22, 44.
    18:34 Mk 9:32.
18:35–43 Mt 20:29–34; Mk
          10:46–52.
18:38–39 17:13; Mt 9:27;
          15:22.

    18:41 Mk 10:36.
    18:42 7:50; 17:19.
     19:7 5:30; 15:2.
     19:8 Ex 21:37; Nm 5:6–7;
          2 Sm 12:6.
     19:9 13:16; Mt 21:31.
    19:10 15:4–10; Ez 34:16.
19:11–27 Mt 25:14–30.

L
K

to tell a parable because he was near Jerusalem and they thought that the kingdom of God would appear there immediately. [12] So he said, "A nobleman went off to a distant country to obtain the kingship for himself and then to return.* [13] He called ten of his servants and gave them ten gold coins† and told them, 'Engage in trade with these until I return.' [14] His fellow citizens, however, despised him and sent a delegation after him to announce, 'We do not want this man to be our king.' [15] But when he returned after obtaining the kingship, he had the servants called, to whom he had given the money, to learn what they had gained by trading. [16] The first came forward and said, 'Sir, your gold coin has earned ten additional ones.' [17] He replied, 'Well done, good servant! You have been faithful in this very small matter; take charge of ten cities.'* [18] Then the second came and reported, 'Your gold coin, sir, has earned five more.' [19] And to this servant too he said, 'You, take charge of five cities.' [20] Then the other servant came and said, 'Sir, here is your gold coin; I kept it stored away in a handkerchief, [21] for I was afraid of you, because you are a demanding person; you take up what you did not lay down and you harvest what you did not plant.' [22] He said to him, 'With your own words I shall condemn you, you wicked servant. You knew I was a demanding person, taking up what I did not lay down and harvesting what I did not plant; [23] why did you not put my money in a bank? Then on my return I would have collected it with interest.' [24] And to those standing by he said, 'Take the gold coin from him and give it to the servant who has ten.' [25] But they said to him, 'Sir, he has ten gold coins.' [26] 'I tell you, to everyone who has, more will be given, but from the one who has not, even what he has will be taken away.* [27] Now as for those enemies of mine who did not want me as their king, bring them here and slay them before me.'"

## VI. THE TEACHING MINISTRY IN JERUSALEM†

**The Entry into Jerusalem.*** [28] After he had said this, he proceeded on his journey up to Jerusalem. [29] As he drew near to Bethphage and Bethany at the place called the Mount of Olives, he sent two of his disciples.* [30] He said, "Go into the village opposite you, and as you enter it you will find a colt tethered on which no one has ever sat. Untie it and bring it here.* [31] And if anyone should ask you, 'Why are you untying it?' you will answer, 'The Master has need of it.'" [32] So those who had been sent went off and found everything just as he had told them.* [33] And as they were untying the colt, its owners said to them, "Why are you untying this colt?" [34] They answered, "The Master has need of it." [35] * So they brought it to Jesus, threw their cloaks over the colt, and helped Jesus to mount. [36] As he rode along, the people were spreading their cloaks on the road; [37] and now as he was approaching the slope of the Mount of Olives, the whole multitude of his disciples began to praise God aloud with joy for all the mighty deeds they had seen. [38] They proclaimed:

"Blessed is the king who comes
　in the name of the Lord.†
Peace in heaven
　and glory in the highest."*

[39] Some of the Pharisees in the crowd said to him, "Teacher, rebuke your disciples."† [40] He said in reply, "I tell you, if they keep silent, the stones will cry out!"

---

**19:13** *Ten gold coins*: literally, "ten minas." A mina was a monetary unit that in ancient Greece was the equivalent of one hundred drachmas.
**19:28–21:38** With the royal entry of Jesus into Jerusalem, a new section of Luke's gospel begins, the ministry of Jesus in Jerusalem before his death and resurrection. Luke suggests that this was a lengthy ministry in Jerusalem (Lk 19:47; 20:1; 21:37–38; 22:53) and it is characterized by Jesus' daily teaching in the temple (Lk 21:37–38). For the story of the entry of Jesus into Jerusalem, see also Mt 21:1–11; Mk 11:1–10; Jn 12:12–19 and the notes there.
**19:38** *Blessed is the king who comes in the name of the Lord*: only in Luke is Jesus explicitly given the title *king* when he enters Jerusalem in triumph. Luke has inserted this title into the words of Ps 118:26 that heralded the arrival of the pilgrims coming to the holy city and to the temple. Jesus is thereby acclaimed as

*king* (see Lk 1:32) and as the one *who comes* (see Mal 3:1; Lk 7:19). *Peace in heaven…*: the acclamation of the disciples of Jesus in Luke echoes the announcement of the angels at the birth of Jesus (Lk 2:14). The peace Jesus brings is associated with the salvation to be accomplished here in Jerusalem.
**19:39** *Rebuke your disciples*: this command, found only in Luke, was given so that the Roman authorities would not interpret the acclamation of Jesus as king as an uprising against them; cf. Lk 23:2–3.

---

| | |
|---|---|
| **19:12** Mk 13:34. | **19:29** Zec 14:4. |
| **19:17** 16:10. | **19:30** Nm 19:2; Dt 21:3; |
| **19:26** 8:18; Mt 13:12; Mk | 　1 Sm 6:7; Zec 9:9. |
| 　4:25. | **19:32** 22:13. |
| **19:28–40** Mt 21:1–11; Mk | **19:35–36** 2 Kgs 9:13. |
| 　11:1–11; Jn 12:12–19. | **19:38** 2:14; Ps 118:26. |

**The Lament for Jerusalem.**† ⁴¹\* As he drew near, he saw the city and wept over it,\* ⁴²saying, "If this day you only knew what makes for peace—but now it is hidden from your eyes.\* ⁴³† For the days are coming upon you when your enemies will raise a palisade against you; they will encircle you and hem you in on all sides.\* ⁴⁴They will smash you to the ground and your children within you, and they will not leave one stone upon another within you because you did not recognize the time of your visitation."\*

**The Cleansing of the Temple.** ⁴⁵\* Then Jesus entered the temple area† and proceeded to drive out those who were selling things,\* ⁴⁶saying to them, "It is written, 'My house shall be a house of prayer, but you have made it a den of thieves.'"\* ⁴⁷And every day he was teaching in the temple area.\* The chief priests, the scribes, and the leaders of the people, meanwhile, were seeking to put him to death,\* ⁴⁸but they could find no way to accomplish their purpose because all the people were hanging on his words.

**20** † **The Authority of Jesus Questioned.**\* ¹ One day as he was teaching the people in the temple area and proclaiming the good news, the chief priests and scribes, together with the elders, approached him ²and said to him, "Tell us, by what authority are you doing these things? Or who is the one who gave you this authority?"\* ³He said to them in reply, "I shall ask you a question. Tell me, ⁴was John's baptism of heavenly or of human origin?"\* ⁵They discussed this among themselves, and said, "If we say, 'Of heavenly origin,' he will say, 'Why did you not believe him?'\* ⁶But if we say, 'Of human origin,' then all the people will stone us, for they are convinced that John was a prophet." ⁷So they answered that they did not know from where it came. ⁸Then Jesus said to them, "Neither shall I tell you by what authority I do these things."

**The Parable of the Tenant Farmers.**† ⁹\* Then he proceeded to tell the people this parable. "[A] man planted a vineyard, leased it to tenant farmers, and then went on a journey for a long time.\* ¹⁰At harvest time he sent a servant\* to the tenant farmers to receive some of the produce of the vineyard. But they beat the servant and sent him away empty-handed. ¹¹So he proceeded to send another servant, but him also they beat and insulted and sent away empty-handed. ¹²Then he proceeded to send a third, but this one too they wounded and threw out. ¹³The owner of the vineyard said, 'What shall I do? I shall send my beloved son; maybe they will respect him.'\* ¹⁴But when the tenant farmers saw him they said to one another, 'This is the heir. Let us kill him that the inheritance may become ours.' ¹⁵So they threw him out of the vineyard and killed him.† What will the owner of the vineyard do to them? ¹⁶He will come and put those tenant farmers to death and turn over the vineyard to others." When the people heard this, they exclaimed, "Let it not be so!" ¹⁷But he looked at them and asked, "What then does this scripture passage mean:

'The stone which the builders rejected
has become the cornerstone'?\*

---

† **19:41–44** The lament for Jerusalem is found only in Luke. By not accepting Jesus (the one who mediates peace), Jerusalem will not find peace but will become the victim of devastation.

**19:43–44** Luke may be describing the actual disaster that befell Jerusalem in A.D. 70 when it was destroyed by the Romans during the First Revolt.

**19:45–46** Immediately upon entering the holy city, Jesus in a display of his authority enters the temple (see Mal 3:1–3) and lays claim to it after cleansing it that it might become a proper place for his teaching ministry in Jerusalem (Lk 19:47; 20:1; 21:37; 22:53). See Mt 21:12–17; Mk 11:15–19; Jn 2:13–17 and the notes there.

**20:1–47** The Jerusalem religious leaders or their representatives, in an attempt to incriminate Jesus with the Romans and to discredit him with the people, pose a number of questions to him (about his authority, Lk 20:2; about payment of taxes, Lk 20:22; about the resurrection, Lk 20:28–33).

**20:9–19** This parable about an absentee landlord and a tenant farmers' revolt reflects the social and economic conditions of rural Palestine in the first century. The synoptic gospel writers use the parable to describe how the rejection of the landlord's son becomes the occasion for the vineyard to be taken away from

those to whom it was entrusted (the religious leadership of Judaism that rejects the teaching and preaching of Jesus; Lk 20:19).

**20:15** *They threw him out of the vineyard and killed him*: cf. Mk 12:8. Luke has altered his Marcan source and reports that the murder of the son takes place outside the vineyard to reflect the tradition of Jesus' death outside the walls of the city of Jerusalem (see Heb 13:12).

**19:41–44** 13:34–35.
**19:41** 2 Kgs 8:11–12; Jer 14:17; 15:5.
**19:42** 8:10; Is 6:9–10; Mt 13:14; Mk 4:12; Acts 28:26–27; Rom 11:8, 10.
**19:43** Is 29:3.
**19:44** 1:68; 21:6; Ps 137:9; Mt 24:2; Mk 13:2.
**19:45–46** Mt 21:12–13; Mk 11:15–17; Jn 2:13–17.
**19:45** 3:1 / Hos 9:15.
**19:46** Is 56:7; Jer 7:11.
**19:47–48** 20:19; 22:2; Mt 21:46;
Mk 11:18; 12:12; 14:1–2; Jn 5:18; 7:30.
**19:47** 21:37; 22:53; Jn 18:20.
**20:1–8** Mt 21:23–27; Mk 11:27–33.
**20:2** Acts 4:7.
**20:4** 3:3, 16.
**20:5** Mt 21:32.
**20:9–19** Mt 21:33–46; Mk 12:1–12.
**20:9** Is 5:1–7.
**20:10–12** 2 Chr 36:15–16.
**20:13** 3:22.
**20:17** Ps 118:22; Is 28:16.

[18] Everyone who falls on that stone will be dashed to pieces; and it will crush anyone on whom it falls." [19] The scribes and chief priests sought to lay their hands on him at that very hour, but they feared the people, for they knew that he had addressed this parable to them.*

**Paying Taxes to the Emperor.*** [20] † They watched him closely and sent agents pretending to be righteous who were to trap him in speech,* in order to hand him over to the authority and power of the governor. [21] They posed this question to him, "Teacher, we know that what you say and teach is correct, and you show no partiality, but teach the way of God in accordance with the truth.* [22] Is it lawful for us to pay tribute to Caesar or not?" † [23] Recognizing their craftiness he said to them, [24] "Show me a denarius; † whose image and name does it bear?" They replied, "Caesar's." [25] So he said to them, "Then repay to Caesar what belongs to Caesar and to God what belongs to God."* [26] They were unable to trap him by something he might say before the people, and so amazed were they at his reply that they fell silent.

**The Question About the Resurrection.*** [27] Some Sadducees, † those who deny that there is a resurrection, came forward and put this question to him,* [28] † saying, "Teacher, Moses wrote for us, 'If someone's brother dies leaving a wife but no child, his brother must take the wife and raise up descendants for his brother.'* [29] Now there were seven brothers; the first married a woman but died childless. [30] Then the second [31] and the third married her, and likewise all the seven died childless. [32] Finally the woman also died. [33] Now at the resurrection whose wife will that woman be? For all seven had been married to her." [34] Jesus said to them, "The children of this age marry and are given in marriage; [35] but those who are deemed worthy to attain to the coming age and to the resurrection of the dead neither marry nor are given in marriage. [36] They can no longer die, for they are like angels; and they are the children of God because they are the ones who will rise. † [37] That the dead will rise even Moses made known in the passage about the bush, when he called 'Lord' the God of Abraham, the God of Isaac, and the God of Jacob;* [38] and he is not God of the dead, but of the living, for to him all are alive."* [39] Some of the scribes said in reply, "Teacher, you have answered well." [40] And they no longer dared to ask him anything.*

**The Question About David's Son.** † [41] * Then he said to them, "How do they claim that the Messiah is the Son of David? [42] For David himself in the Book of Psalms says:*

'The Lord said to my lord,
"Sit at my right hand
[43]        till I make your enemies your
                footstool."'

[44] Now if David calls him 'lord,' how can he be his son?"

**Denunciation of the Scribes.*** [45] Then, within the hearing of all the people, he said to [his] disciples, [46] "Be on guard against the scribes, who like to go around in long robes and love greetings in marketplaces, seats of honor in synagogues, and places of honor at banquets.*

---

**20:20** The governor: i.e., Pontius Pilate, the Roman administrator responsible for the collection of taxes and maintenance of order in Palestine. See also note on Mt 22:15–22.

**20:22** Through their question the agents of the Jerusalem religious leadership hope to force Jesus to take sides on one of the sensitive political issues of first-century Palestine. The issue of nonpayment of taxes to Rome becomes one of the focal points of the First Jewish Revolt (A.D. 66–70) that resulted in the Roman destruction of Jerusalem and the temple. See also note on Mt 22:15–22.

**20:24** Denarius: a Roman silver coin (see note on Lk 7:41).

**20:27** Sadducees: see note on Mt 3:7.

**20:28–33** The Sadducees' question, based on the law of levirate marriage recorded in Dt 25:5–10, ridicules the idea of the resurrection. Jesus rejects their naive understanding of the resurrection (Lk 20:35–36) and then argues on behalf of the resurrection of the dead on the basis of the written law (Lk 20:37–38) that the Sadducees accept. See also notes on Mt 22:23–33.

**20:36** Because they are the ones who will rise: literally, "being sons of the resurrection."

**20:41–44** After successfully answering the three questions of his opponents, Jesus now asks them a question. Their inability to respond implies that they have forfeited their position and authority as the religious leaders of the people because they do not understand the scriptures. This series of controversies between the religious leadership of Jerusalem and Jesus reveals Jesus as the authoritative teacher whose words are to be listened to (see Lk 9:35). See also notes on Mt 22:41–46.

---

| | |
|---|---|
| **20:19** 19:47–48; 22:2; Mt 21:46; Mk 11:18; 12:12; 14:1–2; Jn 5:18; 7:30. | **20:27** Acts 23:8. |
| **20:20–26** Mt 22:15–22; Mk 12:13–17. | **20:28** Gn 38:8; Dt 25:5. |
| **20:20** 11:54. | **20:37** Ex 3:2, 6, 15–16. |
| **20:21** Jn 3:2. | **20:38** Rom 14:8–9. |
| **20:25** Rom 13:6–7. | **20:40** Mt 22:46; Mk 12:34. |
| **20:27–40** Mt 22:23–33; Mk 12:18–27. | **20:41–44** Mt 22:41–45; Mk 12:35–37. |
| | **20:42–43** Ps 110:1. |
| | **20:45–47** 11:37–54; Mt 23:1–36; Mk 12:38–40. |
| | **20:46** 14:7–11. |

[47] They devour the houses of widows and, as a pretext, recite lengthy prayers. They will receive a very severe condemnation."

# 21

### The Poor Widow's Contribution.†

[1]* When he looked up he saw some wealthy people putting their offerings into the treasury [2] and he noticed a poor widow putting in two small coins. [3] He said, "I tell you truly, this poor widow put in more than all the rest; [4] for those others have all made offerings from their surplus wealth, but she, from her poverty, has offered her whole livelihood."

### The Destruction of the Temple Foretold.*

[5]† While some people were speaking about how the temple was adorned with costly stones and votive offerings, he said, [6] "All that you see here—the days will come when there will not be left a stone upon another stone that will not be thrown down."*

### The Signs of the End.

[7]* Then they asked him, "Teacher, when will this happen? And what sign will there be when all these things are about to happen?" [8] He answered, "See that you not be deceived, for many will come in my name, saying, 'I am he,' and 'The time has come.'† Do not follow them!* [9] When you hear of wars and insurrections, do not be terrified; for such things must happen first, but it will not immediately be the end." [10] Then he said to them, "Nation will rise against nation, and kingdom against kingdom.* [11] There will be powerful earthquakes, famines, and plagues from place to place; and awesome sights and mighty signs will come from the sky.

### The Coming Persecution.

[12]* "Before all this happens,† however, they will seize and persecute you, they will hand you over to the synagogues and to prisons, and they will have you led before kings and governors because of my name.* [13] It will lead to your giving testimony. [14] Remember, you are not to prepare your defense beforehand, [15]* for I myself shall give you a wisdom in speaking† that all your adversaries will be powerless to resist or refute. [16]* You will even be handed over by parents, brothers, relatives, and friends, and they will put some of you to death.* [17] You will be hated by all because of my name, [18] but not a hair on your head will be destroyed.* [19] By your perseverance you will secure your lives.*

### The Great Tribulation.†

[20]* "When you see Jerusalem surrounded by armies, know that its desolation is at hand.* [21] Then those in Judea must flee to the mountains. Let those within the city escape from it, and let those in the countryside not enter the city,* [22] for these days are the time of punishment when all the scriptures are fulfilled. [23] Woe to pregnant women and nursing mothers in those days, for a terrible calamity will come upon the earth and a wrathful judgment upon this people.* [24] They will fall by the edge of the sword and be taken as captives to all the Gentiles; and

---

**21:1–4** The widow is another example of the poor ones in this gospel whose detachment from material possessions and dependence on God leads to their blessedness (Lk 6:20). Her simple offering provides a striking contrast to the pride and pretentiousness of the scribes denounced in the preceding section (Lk 20:45–47). The story is taken from Mk 12:41–44.

**21:5–36** Jesus' eschatological discourse in Luke is inspired by Mk 13 but Luke has made some significant alterations to the words of Jesus found there. Luke maintains, though in a modified form, the belief in the early expectation of the end of the age (see Lk 21:27, 28, 31, 32, 36), but, by focusing attention throughout the gospel on the importance of the day-to-day following of Jesus and by reinterpreting the meaning of some of the signs of the end from Mk 13 he has come to terms with what seemed to the early Christian community to be a delay of the parousia. Mark, for example, described the desecration of the Jerusalem temple by the Romans (Mk 13:14) as the apocalyptic symbol (see Dn 9:27; 12:11) accompanying the end of the age and the coming of the Son of Man. Luke (Lk 21:20–24), however, removes the apocalyptic setting and separates the historical destruction of Jerusalem from the signs of the coming of the Son of Man by a period that he refers to as "the times of the Gentiles" (Lk 21:24). See also notes on Mt 24:1–36 and Mk 13:1–37.

**21:8** The time has come: in Luke, the proclamation of the imminent end of the age has itself become a false teaching.

**21:12** Before all this happens…: to Luke and his community, some of the signs of the end just described (Lk 21:10–11) still lie in the future. Now in dealing with the persecution of the disciples (Lk 21:12–19) and the destruction of Jerusalem (Lk 21:20–24) Luke is pointing to eschatological signs that have already been fulfilled.

**21:15** A wisdom in speaking: literally, "a mouth and wisdom."

**21:20–24** The actual destruction of Jerusalem by Rome in A.D. 70 upon which Luke and his community look back provides the assurance that, just as Jesus' prediction of Jerusalem's destruction was fulfilled, so too will be his announcement of their final redemption (Lk 21:27–28).

---

**21:1–4** Mk 12:41–44.
**21:5–6** Mt 24:1–2; Mk 13:1–2.
**21:6** 19:44.
**21:7–19** Mt 24:3–14; Mk 13:3–13.
**21:8** 17:23; Mk 13:5, 6, 21; 1 Jn 2:18.
**21:10** 2 Chr 15:6; Is 19:2.
**21:12–15** 12:11–12; Mt 10:17–20; Mk 13:9–11.
**21:12** Jn 16:2; Acts 25:24.

**21:15** Acts 6:10.
**21:16–18** Mt 10:21–22.
**21:16** 12:52–53.
**21:18** 12:7; 1 Sm 14:45; Mt 10:30; Acts 27:34.
**21:19** 8:15.
**21:20–24** Mt 24:15–21; Mk 13:14–19.
**21:20–22** 19:41–44.
**21:21** 17:31.
**21:23** 1 Cor 7:26.

Jerusalem will be trampled underfoot by the Gentiles until the times of the Gentiles† are fulfilled.*

**The Coming of the Son of Man.** * 25 "There will be signs in the sun, the moon, and the stars, and on earth nations will be in dismay, perplexed by the roaring of the sea and the waves.* 26 People will die of fright in anticipation of what is coming upon the world, for the powers of the heavens† will be shaken.* 27 And then they will see the Son of Man coming in a cloud with power and great glory.* 28 But when these signs begin to happen, stand erect and raise your heads because your redemption is at hand."*

**The Lesson of the Fig Tree.** * 29 He taught them a lesson. "Consider the fig tree and all the other trees. 30 When their buds burst open, you see for yourselves and know that summer is now near; 31 in the same way, when you see these things happening, know that the kingdom of God is near. 32 Amen, I say to you, this generation will not pass away until all these things have taken place.* 33 Heaven and earth will pass away, but my words will not pass away.*

**Exhortation to Be Vigilant.** 34 "Beware that your hearts do not become drowsy from carousing and drunkenness and the anxieties of daily life, and that day catch you by surprise* 35 like a trap. For that day will assault everyone who lives on the face of the earth. 36 Be vigilant at all times and pray that you have the strength to escape the tribulations that are imminent and to stand before the Son of Man."*

**Ministry in Jerusalem.** 37 During the day, Jesus was teaching in the temple area, but at night he would leave and stay at the place called the Mount of Olives.* 38 And all the people would get up early each morning to listen to him in the temple area.

## VII. THE PASSION NARRATIVE†

**22** **The Conspiracy Against Jesus.** 1 * Now the feast of Unleavened Bread, called the Passover,† was drawing near, 2 * and the chief priests and the scribes were seeking a way to put him to death, for they were afraid of the people. 3 * Then Satan entered into Judas,† the one surnamed Iscariot, who was counted among the Twelve,* 4 and he went to the chief priests and temple guards to discuss a plan for handing him over to them. 5 They were pleased and agreed to pay him money. 6 He accepted their offer and sought a favorable opportunity to hand him over to them in the absence of a crowd.

**Preparations for the Passover.** * 7 When the day of the feast of Unleavened Bread arrived, the day for sacrificing the Passover lamb,* 8 he sent out Peter and John, instructing them, "Go and make preparations for us to eat the Passover." 9 They asked him, "Where do you want us to make the preparations?" 10 And he answered them, "When you go into the city, a man will meet you carrying a jar of water.† Follow him

† **21:24** *The times of the Gentiles*: a period of indeterminate length separating the destruction of Jerusalem from the cosmic signs accompanying the coming of the Son of Man.

**21:26** *The powers of the heavens*: the heavenly bodies mentioned in Lk 21:25 and thought of as cosmic armies.

**22:1–23:56a** The passion narrative. Luke is still dependent upon Mark for the composition of the passion narrative but has incorporated much of his own special tradition into the narrative. Among the distinctive sections in Luke are: (1) the tradition of the institution of the Eucharist (Lk 22:15–20); (2) Jesus' farewell discourse (Lk 22:21–38); (3) the mistreatment and interrogation of Jesus (Lk 22:63–71); (4) Jesus before Herod and his second appearance before Pilate (Lk 23:6–16); (5) words addressed to the women followers on the way to the crucifixion (Lk 23:27–32); (6) words to the penitent thief (Lk 23:39–41); (7) the death of Jesus (Lk 23:46, 47b–49). Luke stresses the innocence of Jesus (Lk 23:4, 14–15, 22) who is the victim of the powers of evil (Lk 22:3, 31, 53) and who goes to his death in fulfillment of his Father's will (Lk 22:42, 46). Throughout the narrative Luke emphasizes the mercy, compassion, and healing power of Jesus (Lk 22:51; 23:43) who does not go to death lonely and deserted, but is accom-

panied by others who follow him on the way of the cross (Lk 23:26–31, 49).

**22:1** *Feast of Unleavened Bread, called the Passover*: see note on Mk 14:1.

**22:3** *Satan entered into Judas*: see note on Lk 4:13.

**22:10** *A man will meet you carrying a jar of water*: see note on Mk 14:13.

| | |
|---|---|
| **21:24** Tb 14:5; Ps 79:1; Is 63:18; Jer 21:7; Rom 11:25; Rev 11:2. | **21:34** 12:45–46; Mt 24:48–50; 1 Thes 5:3, 6–7. |
| **21:25–28** Mt 24:29–31; Mk 13:24–27. | **21:36** Mk 13:33. |
| **21:25** Wis 5:22; Is 13:10; Ez 32:7; Jl 2:10; 3:3–4; 4:15; Rev 6:12–14. | **21:37** 19:47; 22:39. |
| | **22:1–2** Mk 14:1–2; Jn 11:47–53. |
| **21:26** Hg 2:6, 21. | **22:2** 19:47–48; 20:19; Mt 5:18; 7:30. |
| **21:27** Dn 7:13–14; Mt 26:64; Rev 1:7. | **22:3–6** Mt 26:14–16; Mk 14:10–11; Jn 13:2, 27. |
| **21:28** 2:38. | |
| **21:29–33** Mt 24:32–35; Mk 13:28–31. | **22:3** Acts 1:17. |
| | **22:7–13** Mt 26:17–19; Mk 14:12–16. |
| **21:32** 9:27; Mt 16:28. | |
| **21:33** 16:17. | **22:7** Ex 12:6, 14–20. |

into the house that he enters [11] and say to the master of the house, 'The teacher says to you, "Where is the guest room where I may eat the Passover with my disciples?"' [12] He will show you a large upper room that is furnished. Make the preparations there." [13] Then they went off and found everything exactly as he had told them, and there they prepared the Passover.*

**The Last Supper.**\* [14] When the hour came, he took his place at table with the apostles. [15] He said to them, "I have eagerly desired to eat this Passover† with you before I suffer, [16] for, I tell you, I shall not eat it [again] until there is fulfillment in the kingdom of God."* [17] Then he took a cup,† gave thanks, and said, "Take this and share it among yourselves; [18] for I tell you [that] from this time on I shall not drink of the fruit of the vine until the kingdom of God comes." [19]†* Then he took the bread, said the blessing, broke it, and gave it to them, saying, "This is my body, which will be given for you; do this in memory of me." [20] And likewise the cup after they had eaten, saying, "This cup is the new covenant in my blood, which will be shed for you.*

**The Betrayal Foretold.** [21] *"And yet behold, the hand of the one who is to betray me is with me on the table; [22] for the Son of Man indeed goes as it has been determined; but woe to that man by whom he is betrayed." [23] And they began to debate among themselves who among them would do such a deed.

**The Role of the Disciples.** [24]† Then an argument broke out among them* about which of them should be regarded as the greatest. [25]†* He said to them, "The kings of the Gentiles lord it over them and those in authority over them are addressed as 'Benefactors'; [26] but among you it shall not be so. Rather, let the greatest among you be as the youngest, and the leader as the servant.* [27] For who is greater: the one seated at table or the one who serves? Is it not the one seated at table? I am among you as the one who serves. [28] It is you who have stood by me in my trials; [29] and I confer a kingdom on you, just as my Father has conferred one on me,* [30] that you may eat and drink at my table in my kingdom; and you will sit on thrones judging the twelve tribes of Israel.*

**Peter's Denial Foretold.**\* [31]† "Simon, Simon, behold Satan has demanded to sift all of you† like wheat,* [32] but I have prayed that your own faith may not fail; and once you have turned back, you must strengthen your brothers." [33] He said to him, "Lord, I am prepared to go to prison and to die with you."* [34] But he replied, "I tell you, Peter, before the cock crows this day, you will deny three times that you know me."*

**Instructions for the Time of Crisis.** [35]* He said to them, "When I sent you forth without a money bag or a sack or sandals, were you in need of anything?" "No, nothing," they replied. [36]* He said to them,† "But now one who has a money bag should take it, and

---

† **22:15** *This Passover*: Luke clearly identifies this last supper of Jesus with the apostles as a Passover meal that commemorated the deliverance of the Israelites from slavery in Egypt. Jesus reinterprets the significance of the Passover by setting it in the context of the kingdom of God (Lk 22:16). The "deliverance" associated with the Passover finds its new meaning in the blood that will be shed (Lk 22:20).

**22:17** Because of a textual problem in Lk 22:19–20 some commentators interpret this cup as the eucharistic cup.

**22:19c–20** *Which will be given…do this in memory of me*: these words are omitted in some important Western text manuscripts and a few Syriac manuscripts. Other ancient text types, including the oldest papyrus manuscript of Luke dating from the late second or early third century, contain the longer reading presented here. The Lucan account of the words of institution of the Eucharist bears a close resemblance to the words of institution in the Pauline tradition (see 1 Cor 11:23–26). See also notes on Mt 26:26–29; 26:27–28; and Mk 14:22–24.

**22:24–38** The Gospel of Luke presents a brief farewell discourse of Jesus; compare the lengthy farewell discourses and prayer in Jn 13–17.

**22:25** *'Benefactors'*: this word occurs as a title of rulers in the Hellenistic world.

**22:31–32** Jesus' prayer for Simon's faith and the commission to strengthen his brothers anticipates the post-resurrectional prominence of Peter in the first half of Acts, where he appears as the spokesman for the Christian community and the one who begins the mission to the Gentiles (Acts 10–11).

**22:31** *All of you*: literally, "you." The translation reflects the meaning of the Greek text that uses a second person plural pronoun here.

**22:36** In contrast to the ministry of the Twelve and of the seventy-two during the period of Jesus (Lk 9:3; 10:4), in the future

| | |
|---|---|
| **22:13** 19:32. | **22:25–27** Mt 20:25–27; Mk |
| **22:14–20** Mt 26:20, 26–30; Mk | 10:42–44; Jn 13:3–16. |
| 14:17, 22–26; 1 Cor | **22:26** Mt 23:11; Mk 9:35. |
| 11:23–25. | **22:29** 12:32. |
| **22:16** 13:29. | **22:30** Mt 19:28. |
| **22:19** 24:30; Acts 27:35. | **22:31–34** Mt 26:33–35; |
| **22:20** Ex 24:8; Jer 31:31; | Mk 14:29–31; Jn |
| 32:40; Zec 9:11. | 13:37–38. |
| **22:21–23** Ps 41:10; Mt 26:21– | **22:31** Jb 1:6–12; Am 9:9. |
| 25; Mk 14:18–21; Jn | **22:33** 22:54. |
| 13:21–30. | **22:34** 22:54–62. |
| **22:24** 9:46; Mt 18:1; Mk | **22:35** 9:3; 10:4; Mt |
| 9:34. | 10:9–10; Mk 6:7–9. |
| | **22:36** 22:49. |

© Carolyn Osiek, RSCJ

"Then going out [Jesus] went, as was his custom, to the Mount of Olives, and the disciples followed him" (Lk 22:39). Above, stairs leading down from the upper city to the garden on the Mount of Olives, also known as the garden of Gethsemane, where Jesus was arrested.

likewise a sack, and one who does not have a sword should sell his cloak and buy one. 37 For I tell you that this scripture must be fulfilled in me, namely, 'He was counted among the wicked'; and indeed what is written about me is coming to fulfillment." * 38 Then they said, "Lord, look, there are two swords here." But he replied, "It is enough!" †

**The Agony in the Garden.** * 39 Then going out he went, as was his custom, to the Mount of Olives, and the disciples followed him. 40 When he arrived at the place he said to them, "Pray that you may not undergo the test." * 41 After withdrawing about a stone's throw from them and kneeling, he prayed, * 42 saying, "Father, if you are willing, take this cup away from me; still, not my will but yours be done." * †[43 And to strengthen him an angel from heaven appeared to him. 44 He was in such agony and he prayed so fervently that his sweat became like drops of blood falling on the ground.] 45 When he rose from prayer and returned to his disciples, he found them sleeping from grief. 46 He said to them, "Why are you sleeping? Get up and pray that you may not undergo the test." *

**The Betrayal and Arrest of Jesus.** * 47 While he was still speaking, a crowd approached and in front was one of the Twelve, a man named Judas. He went up to Jesus to kiss him. 48 Jesus said to him, "Judas, are you betraying the Son of Man with a kiss?" 49 His disciples realized what was about to happen, and they asked, "Lord, shall we strike with a sword?" * 50 And one of them struck the high priest's servant and cut off his right ear. * 51 † But Jesus said in reply, "Stop, no more of this!" Then he touched the servant's ear and healed him. 52 And Jesus said to the chief priests and temple guards and elders who had come for him,

---

† period of the church the missionaries must be prepared for the opposition they will face in a world hostile to their preaching.
**22:38** *It is enough!*: the farewell discourse ends abruptly with these words of Jesus spoken to the disciples when they take literally what was intended as figurative language about being prepared to face the world's hostility.
**22:43–44** These verses, though very ancient, were probably not part of the original text of Luke. They are absent from the oldest papyrus manuscripts of Luke and from manuscripts of wide geographical distribution.

**22:51** *And healed him*: only Luke recounts this healing of the injured servant.

---

* 
| | |
|---|---|
| **22:37** Is 53:12. | **22:42** Mt 6:10. |
| **22:39–46** Mt 26:30, 36–46; | **22:46** 22:40. |
|    Mk 14:26, 32–42; Jn | **22:47–53** Mt 26:47–56; Mk |
|    18:1–2. |    14:43–50; Jn 18:3–4. |
| **22:40** 22:46. | **22:49** 22:36. |
| **22:41** Heb 5:7–8. | **22:50** Jn 18:26. |

"Have you come out as against a robber, with swords and clubs?* ⁵³ Day after day I was with you in the temple area, and you did not seize me; but this is your hour, the time for the power of darkness."*

**Peter's Denial of Jesus.** ⁵⁴* After arresting him they led him away and took him into the house of the high priest; Peter was following at a distance.* ⁵⁵ They lit a fire in the middle of the courtyard and sat around it, and Peter sat down with them. ⁵⁶ When a maid saw him seated in the light, she looked intently at him and said, "This man too was with him." ⁵⁷ But he denied it saying, "Woman, I do not know him." ⁵⁸ A short while later someone else saw him and said, "You too are one of them"; but Peter answered, "My friend, I am not." ⁵⁹ About an hour later, still another insisted, "Assuredly, this man too was with him, for he also is a Galilean." ⁶⁰ But Peter said, "My friend, I do not know what you are talking about." Just as he was saying this, the cock crowed, ⁶¹ and the Lord turned and looked at Peter;† and Peter remembered the word of the Lord, how he had said to him, "Before the cock crows today, you will deny me three times."* ⁶² He went out and began to weep bitterly. ⁶³* The men who held Jesus in custody were ridiculing and beating him. ⁶⁴ They blindfolded him and questioned him, saying, "Prophesy! Who is it that struck you?" ⁶⁵ And they reviled him in saying many other things against him.

**Jesus Before the Sanhedrin.**† ⁶⁶* When day came the council of elders of the people met, both chief priests and scribes,* and they brought him before their Sanhedrin.† ⁶⁷ They said, "If you are the Messiah, tell us," but he replied to them, "If I tell you, you will not believe,* ⁶⁸ and if I question, you will not respond. ⁶⁹ But from this time on the Son of Man will be seated at the right hand of the power of God."* ⁷⁰ They all asked, "Are you then the Son of God?" He replied to them, "You say that I am." ⁷¹ Then they said, "What further need have we for testimony? We have heard it from his own mouth."

# 23

**Jesus Before Pilate.*** ¹† Then the whole assembly of them arose and brought him before Pilate. ² They brought charges against him, saying, "We found this man misleading our people; he opposes the payment of taxes to Caesar and maintains that he is the Messiah, a king."* ³ Pilate asked him, "Are you the king of the Jews?" He said to him in reply, "You say so."* ⁴ Pilate then addressed the chief priests and the crowds, "I find this man not guilty." ⁵ But they were adamant and said, "He is inciting the people with his teaching throughout all Judea, from Galilee where he began even to here."*

**Jesus Before Herod.** ⁶† On hearing this Pilate asked if the man was a Galilean; ⁷ and upon learning that he was under Herod's jurisdiction, he sent him to Herod who was in Jerusalem at that time.* ⁸ Herod was very glad to see Jesus; he had been wanting to see him for a long time, for he had heard about him and had been hoping to see him perform some sign.* ⁹ He questioned him at length, but he gave him no answer.* ¹⁰ The chief priests and

---

† **22:61** Only Luke recounts that *the Lord turned and looked at Peter*. This look of Jesus leads to Peter's weeping bitterly over his denial (Lk 22:62).

**22:66–71** Luke recounts one daytime trial of Jesus (Lk 22:66–71) and hints at some type of preliminary nighttime investigation (Lk 22:54–65). Mark (and Matthew who follows Mark) has transferred incidents of this day into the nighttime interrogation with the result that there appear to be two Sanhedrin trials of Jesus in Mark (and Matthew); see note on Mk 14:53.

**22:66** *Sanhedrin*: the word is a Hebraized form of a Greek word meaning a "council," and refers to the elders, chief priests, and scribes who met under the high priest's leadership to decide religious and legal questions that did not pertain to Rome's interests. Jewish sources are not clear on the competence of the Sanhedrin to sentence and to execute during this period.

**23:1–5, 13–25** Twice Jesus is brought before Pilate in Luke's account, and each time Pilate explicitly declares Jesus innocent of any wrongdoing (Lk 23:4, 14, 22). This stress on the innocence of Jesus before the Roman authorities is also characteristic of John's gospel (Jn 18:38; 19:4, 6). Luke presents the Jerusalem Jewish leaders as the ones who force the hand of the Roman authorities (Lk 23:1–2, 5, 10, 13, 18, 21, 23–25).

**23:6–12** The appearance of Jesus before Herod is found only in this gospel. Herod has been an important figure in Luke (Lk 9:7–9; 13:31–33) and has been presented as someone who has been curious about Jesus for a long time. His curiosity goes unrewarded. It is faith in Jesus, not curiosity, that is rewarded (Lk 7:50; 8:48, 50; 17:19).

---

| | |
|---|---|
| **22:52** 22:37. | **22:69** Ps 110:1; Dn |
| **22:53** 19:47; 21:37; Jn 7:30; | 7:13–14; Acts 7:56. |
| 8:20; Col 1:13. | **23:1–5** Mt 27:1–2, 11–14; Mk |
| **22:54–62** Mt 26:57–58, 69–75; | 15:1–5; Jn 18:28–38. |
| Mk 14:53–54, 66–72; | **23:2** 20:22–25; Acts 17:7; |
| Jn 18:12–18, 25–27. | 24:5. |
| **22:54** 22:33. | **23:3** 22:70; 1 Tm 6:13. |
| **22:61** 22:34. | **23:5** 23:14, 22, 41; Mt |
| **22:63–65** Mt 26:67–68; Mk | 27:24; Jn 19:4, 6; Acts |
| 14:65. | 13:28. |
| **22:66–71** Mt 26:59–66; Mk | **23:7** 3:1; 9:7. |
| 14:55–64. | **23:8** 9:9; Acts 4:27–28. |
| **22:66** Mt 27:1; Mk 15:1. | **23:9** Mk 15:5. |
| **22:67** Jn 3:12; 8:45; 10:24. | |

scribes, meanwhile, stood by accusing him harshly.* ¹¹ [Even] Herod and his soldiers treated him contemptuously and mocked him, and after clothing him in resplendent garb, he sent him back to Pilate.* ¹² Herod and Pilate became friends that very day, even though they had been enemies formerly. ¹³ Pilate then summoned the chief priests, the rulers, and the people ¹⁴ and said to them, "You brought this man to me and accused him of inciting the people to revolt. I have conducted my investigation in your presence and have not found this man guilty of the charges you have brought against him,* ¹⁵ nor did Herod, for he sent him back to us. So no capital crime has been committed by him. ¹⁶* Therefore I shall have him flogged and then release him." [¹⁷]†

**The Sentence of Death.*** ¹⁸ But all together they shouted out, "Away with this man! Release Barabbas to us." ¹⁹ (Now Barabbas had been imprisoned for a rebellion that had taken place in the city and for murder.) ²⁰ Again Pilate addressed them, still wishing to release Jesus, ²¹ but they continued their shouting, "Crucify him! Crucify him!" ²² Pilate addressed them a third time, "What evil has this man done? I found him guilty of no capital crime. Therefore I shall have him flogged and then release him." ²³ With loud shouts, however, they persisted in calling for his crucifixion, and their voices prevailed. ²⁴ The verdict of Pilate was that their demand should be granted. ²⁵ So he released the man who had been imprisoned for rebellion and murder, for whom they asked, and he handed Jesus over to them to deal with as they wished.

**The Way of the Cross.†** ²⁶* As they led him away they took hold of a certain Simon, a Cyrenian, who was coming in from the country; and after laying the cross on him, they made him carry it behind Jesus. ²⁷ A large crowd of people followed Jesus, including many women who mourned and lamented him. ²⁸* Jesus turned to them and said, "Daughters of Jerusalem, do not weep for me; weep instead for yourselves and for your children, ²⁹ for indeed, the days are coming when people will say, 'Blessed are the barren, the wombs that never bore and the breasts that never nursed.' ³⁰ At that time people will say to the mountains, 'Fall upon us!' and to the hills, 'Cover us!'* ³¹ for if these things are done when the wood is green what will happen when it is dry?" ³² Now two others, both criminals, were led away with him to be executed.

**The Crucifixion.*** ³³ When they came to the place called the Skull, they crucified him and the criminals there, one on his right, the other on his left.* ³⁴ [Then Jesus said, "Father, forgive them, they know not what they do."]† They divided his garments by casting lots.* ³⁵ The people stood by and watched; the rulers, meanwhile, sneered at him and said,* "He saved others, let him save himself if he is the chosen one, the Messiah of God."* ³⁶ Even the soldiers jeered at him. As they approached to offer him wine* ³⁷ they called out, "If you are King of the Jews, save yourself." ³⁸ Above him there was an inscription that read, "This is the King of the Jews."

³⁹† Now one of the criminals hanging there reviled Jesus, saying, "Are you not the Messiah? Save yourself and us." ⁴⁰ The other, however, rebuking him, said in reply, "Have you no fear of God, for you are subject to the same condemnation? ⁴¹ And indeed, we have been condemned justly, for the sentence we received corresponds to our crimes, but this man has done nothing criminal."* ⁴² Then he

---

**23:17** This verse, "He was obliged to release one prisoner for them at the festival," is not part of the original text of Luke. It is an explanatory gloss from Mk 15:6 (also Mt 27:15) and is not found in many early and important Greek manuscripts. On its historical background, see notes on Mt 27:15–26.
**23:26–32** An important Lucan theme throughout the gospel has been the need for the Christian disciple to follow in the footsteps of Jesus. Here this theme comes to the fore with the story of Simon of Cyrene who takes up the cross and follows Jesus (see Lk 9:23; 14:27) and with the large crowd who likewise follow Jesus on the way of the cross. See also note on Mk 15:21.
**23:34** [Then Jesus said, "Father, forgive them, they know not what they do."]: this portion of Lk 23:34 does not occur in the oldest papyrus manuscript of Luke and in other early Greek manuscripts and ancient versions of wide geographical distribution.
**23:39–43** This episode is recounted only in this gospel. The

penitent sinner receives salvation through the crucified Jesus. Jesus' words to the penitent thief reveal Luke's understanding that the destiny of the Christian is "to be with Jesus."

**23:10** Mt 27:12; Mk 15:3.
**23:11** Mt 27:28–30; Mk 15:17–19; Jn 19:2–3.
**23:14** 23:4, 22, 41.
**23:16** 23:22; Jn 19:12–14.
**23:18–25** Mt 27:20–26; Mk 15:6–7, 11–15; Jn 18:38b–40; 19:14–16; Acts 3:13–14.
**23:26–32** Mt 27:32, 38; Mk 15:21, 27; Jn 19:17.
**23:28–31** 19:41–44; 21:23–24.
**23:30** Hos 10:8; Rev 6:16.
**23:33–43** Mt 27:33–44; Mk 15:22–32; Jn 19:17–24.
**23:33** 22:37; Is 53:12.
**23:34** Nm 15:27–31; Ps 22:19; Mt 5:44; Acts 7:60.
**23:35–36** Ps 22:8–9.
**23:35** 4:23.
**23:36** Ps 69:22; Mt 27:48; Mk 15:36.
**23:41** 23:4, 14, 22.

said, "Jesus, remember me when you come into your kingdom."* ⁴³He replied to him, "Amen, I say to you, today you will be with me in Paradise."*

**The Death of Jesus.*** ⁴⁴† It was now about noon* and darkness came over the whole land until three in the afternoon ⁴⁵because of an eclipse of the sun. Then the veil of the temple was torn down the middle.* ⁴⁶Jesus cried out in a loud voice, "Father, into your hands I commend my spirit"; and when he had said this he breathed his last.* ⁴⁷The centurion who witnessed what had happened glorified God and said, "This man was innocent† beyond doubt." ⁴⁸When all the people who had gathered for this spectacle saw what had happened, they returned home beating their breasts;* ⁴⁹but all his acquaintances stood at a distance, including the women who had followed him from Galilee and saw these events.*

**The Burial of Jesus.*** ⁵⁰Now there was a virtuous and righteous man named Joseph who, though he was a member of the council, ⁵¹had not consented to their plan of action. He came from the Jewish town of Arimathea and was awaiting the kingdom of God.* ⁵²He went to Pilate and asked for the body of Jesus. ⁵³After he had taken the body down, he wrapped it in a linen cloth and laid him in a rock-hewn tomb in which no one had yet been buried.* ⁵⁴It was the day of preparation, and the sabbath was about to begin. ⁵⁵The women who had come from Galilee with him followed

behind, and when they had seen the tomb and the way in which his body was laid in it,* ⁵⁶they returned and prepared spices and perfumed oils. Then they rested on the sabbath according to the commandment.*

## VIII. THE RESURRECTION NARRATIVE†

**24** **The Resurrection of Jesus.** ¹* But at daybreak on the first day of the week they took the spices they had prepared and went to the tomb. ²They found the stone rolled away from the tomb; ³but when they entered, they did not find the body of the Lord Jesus. ⁴While they were puzzling over this, behold, two men in dazzling garments appeared to them.* ⁵They were terrified and bowed their faces to the ground. They said to them, "Why do you seek the living one among the dead?* ⁶He is not here, but he has been raised.† Remember what he said to you while he was still in Galilee, ⁷that the Son of Man must be handed over to sinners and be crucified, and rise on the third day."* ⁸And they remembered his words.* ⁹†* Then they returned from the tomb and announced all these things to the eleven and to all the others. ¹⁰The women were Mary Magdalene, Joanna, and Mary the mother of James; the others who accompanied them also told this to the apostles,* ¹¹but their story seemed like nonsense and they did not believe them. ¹²†* But Peter got up and ran to the tomb, bent down, and saw the burial cloths alone; then he went home amazed at what had happened.

---

† **23:44** *Noon…three in the afternoon:* literally, the sixth and ninth hours. See note on Mk 15:25.
 **23:47** *This man was innocent:* or, "This man was righteous."
 **24:1–53** The resurrection narrative in Luke consists of five sections: (1) the women at the empty tomb (Lk 23:56b–24:12); (2) the appearance to the two disciples on the way to Emmaus (Lk 24:13–35); (3) the appearance to the disciples in Jerusalem (Lk 24:36–43); (4) Jesus' final instructions (Lk 24:44–49); (5) the ascension (Lk 24:50–53). In Luke, all the resurrection appearances take place in and around Jerusalem; moreover, they are all recounted as having taken place on Easter Sunday. A consistent theme throughout the narrative is that the suffering, death, and resurrection of Jesus were accomplished in fulfillment of Old Testament promises and of Jewish hopes (Lk 24:19a, 21, 26–27, 44, 46). In his second volume, Acts, Luke will argue that Christianity is the fulfillment of the hopes of Pharisaic Judaism and its logical development (see Acts 24:10–21).
 **24:6** *He is not here, but he has been raised:* this part of the verse is omitted in important representatives of the Western text tradition, but its presence in other text types and the slight difference in wording from Mt 28:6 and Mk 16:6 argue for its retention.
 **24:9** The women in this gospel do not flee from the tomb

and tell no one, as in Mk 16:8 but return and tell the disciples about their experience. The initial reaction to the testimony of the women is disbelief (Lk 24:11).
 **24:12** This verse is missing from the Western textual tradition but is found in the best and oldest manuscripts of other text types.

---

*
| | |
|---|---|
| **23:42** 9:27; 23:2, 3, 38. | **23:55** 8:2; 23:49; 24:10. |
| **23:43** 2 Cor 12:3; Rev 2:7. | **23:56** Ex 12:16; 20:10; Dt |
| **23:44–49** Mt 27:45–56; | 5:14. |
| Mk 15:33–41; Jn | **24:1–8** Mt 28:1–8; Mk |
| 19:25–30. | 16:1–8; Jn 20:1–17. |
| **23:44–45** Am 8:9. | **24:4** 2 Mc 3:26; Acts 1:10. |
| **23:45** Ex 26:31–33; 36:35. | **24:5** Acts 2:9. |
| **23:46** Ps 31:6; Acts 7:59. | **24:7** 9:22, 44; 17:25; |
| **23:48** 18:13; Zec 12:10. | 18:32–33; Mt 16:21; |
| **23:49** 8:1–3; 23:55–56; | 17:22–23; Mk 9:31; |
| 24:10; Ps 38:12. | Acts 17:3. |
| **23:50–56** Mt 27:57–61; | **24:8** Jn 2:22. |
| Mk 15:42–47; Jn | **24:9–11** Mk 16:10–11; Jn |
| 19:38–42; Acts 13:29. | 20:18. |
| **23:51** 2:25, 38. | **24:10** 8:2–3; Mk 16:9. |
| **23:53** 19:30; Acts 13:29. | **24:12** Jn 20:3–7. |

## The Appearance on the Road to Emmaus.†

¹³ Now that very day two of them were going to a village seven miles† from Jerusalem called Emmaus,* ¹⁴ and they were conversing about all the things that had occurred. ¹⁵ And it happened that while they were conversing and debating, Jesus himself drew near and walked with them, ¹⁶†* but their eyes were prevented from recognizing him. ¹⁷ He asked them, "What are you discussing as you walk along?" They stopped, looking downcast. ¹⁸ One of them, named Cleopas, said to him in reply, "Are you the only visitor to Jerusalem who does not know of the things that have taken place there in these days?" ¹⁹ And he replied to them, "What sort of things?" They said to him, "The things that happened to Jesus the Nazarene, who was a prophet mighty in deed and word before God and all the people,* ²⁰ how our chief priests and rulers both handed him over to a sentence of death and crucified him. ²¹* But we were hoping that he would be the one to redeem Israel; and besides all this, it is now the third day since this took place. ²²* Some women from our group, however, have astounded us: they were at the tomb early in the morning ²³ and did not find his body; they came back and reported that they had indeed seen a vision of angels who announced that he was alive. ²⁴* Then some of those with us went to the tomb and found things just as the women had described, but him they did not see." ²⁵* And he said to them, "Oh, how foolish you are! How slow of heart to believe all that the prophets spoke! ²⁶ Was it not necessary that the Messiah should suffer† these things and enter into his glory?" ²⁷ Then beginning with Moses and all the prophets, he interpreted to them what referred to him in all the scriptures.* ²⁸ As they approached the village to which they were going, he gave the impression that he was going on farther. ²⁹ But they urged him, "Stay with us, for it is nearly evening and the day is almost over." So he went in to stay with them. ³⁰ And it happened that, while he was with them at table, he took bread, said the blessing, broke it, and gave it to them. ³¹ With that their eyes were opened and they recognized him, but he vanished from their sight. ³² Then they said to each other, "Were not our hearts burning [within us] while he spoke to us on the way and opened the scriptures to us?" ³³ So they set out at once and returned to Jerusalem where they found gathered together the eleven and those with them ³⁴ who were saying, "The Lord has truly been raised and has appeared to Simon!"* ³⁵ Then the two recounted what had taken place on the way and how he was made known to them in the breaking of the bread.

## The Appearance to the Disciples in Jerusalem.

³⁶† While they were still speaking about this,* he stood in their midst and said to them, "Peace be with you."* ³⁷ But they were startled and terrified and thought that they were seeing a ghost.* ³⁸ Then he said to them, "Why are you troubled? And why do questions arise in your hearts? ³⁹† Look at my hands and my feet, that it is I myself. Touch me and see, because a ghost does not have flesh and bones as you can see I have." ⁴⁰* And as he said this, he showed them his hands and his feet. ⁴¹ While they were still incredulous for joy and were amazed, he asked them, "Have you anything here to eat?" ⁴² They gave him a piece of baked fish;* ⁴³ he took it and ate it in front of them.

⁴⁴ He said to them, "These are my words

---

† **24:13–35** This episode focuses on the interpretation of scripture by the risen Jesus and the recognition of him in the breaking of the bread. The references to the quotations of scripture and explanation of it (Lk 24:25–27), the kerygmatic proclamation (Lk 24:34), and the liturgical gesture (Lk 24:30) suggest that the episode is primarily catechetical and liturgical rather than apologetic.

**24:13** *Seven miles*: literally, "sixty stades." A stade was 607 feet. Some manuscripts read "160 stades" or more than eighteen miles. The exact location of Emmaus is disputed.

**24:16** A consistent feature of the resurrection stories is that the risen Jesus was different and initially unrecognizable (Lk 24:37; Mk 16:12; Jn 20:14; 21:4).

**24:26** *That the Messiah should suffer…*: Luke is the only New Testament writer to speak explicitly of a suffering Messiah (Lk 24:26, 46; Acts 3:18; 17:3; 26:23). The idea of a suffering Messiah is not found in the Old Testament or in other Jewish literature prior to the New Testament period, although the idea is hinted at in Mk 8:31–33. See notes on Mt 26:63 and 26:67–68.

**24:36–43, 44–49** The Gospel of Luke, like each of the other gospels (Mt 28:16–20; Mk 16:14–15; Jn 20:19–23), focuses on an important appearance of Jesus to the Twelve in which they are commissioned for their future ministry. As in Lk 24:6, 12, so in Lk 24:36, 40 there are omissions in the Western text.

**24:39–42** The apologetic purpose of this story is evident in the concern with the physical details and the report that Jesus ate food.

| | |
|---|---|
| **24:13** Mk 16:12–13. | **24:27** 24:44; Dt 18:15; Ps |
| **24:16** Jn 20:14; 21:4. | 22:1–18; Is 53; 1 Pt |
| **24:19** Mt 2:23; 21:11; Acts | 1:10–11. |
| 2:22. | **24:34** 1 Cor 15:4–5. |
| **24:21** 1:54, 68; 2:38. | **24:36–53** Mk 16:14–19; Jn |
| **24:22–23** 24:1–11; Mt 28:1–8; | 20:19–20. |
| Mk 16:1–8. | **24:36** 1 Cor 15:5. |
| **24:24** Jn 20:3–10. | **24:37** Mt 14:26. |
| **24:25–26** 9:22; 18:31; 24:44; | **24:40–41** Jn 21:5, 9–10, 13. |
| Acts 3:24; 17:3. | **24:42** Acts 10:41. |

that I spoke to you while I was still with you, that everything written about me in the law of Moses and in the prophets and psalms must be fulfilled."* ⁴⁵Then he opened their minds to understand the scriptures.* ⁴⁶† And he said to them,* "Thus it is written that the Messiah would suffer and rise from the dead on the third day ⁴⁷and that repentance, for the forgiveness of sins, would be preached in his name to all the nations, beginning from Jerusalem.* ⁴⁸You are witnesses of these things.*

⁴⁹And [behold] I am sending the promise of my Father† upon you; but stay in the city until you are clothed with power from on high."*

**The Ascension.**† ⁵⁰* Then he led them [out] as far as Bethany, raised his hands, and blessed them. ⁵¹As he blessed them he parted from them and was taken up to heaven. ⁵²They did him homage and then returned to Jerusalem with great joy,* ⁵³and they were continually in the temple praising God.†

---

† 
**24:46** See note on Lk 24:26.
**24:49** *The promise of my Father*: i.e., the gift of the holy Spirit.
**24:50–53** Luke brings his story about the time of Jesus to a close with the report of the ascension. He will also begin the story of the time of the church with a recounting of the ascension. In the gospel, Luke recounts the ascension of Jesus on Easter Sunday night, thereby closely associating it with the resurrection. In Acts 1:3, 9–11; 13:31 he historicizes the ascension by speaking of a forty-day period between the resurrection and the ascension. The Western text omits some phrases in Lk 24:51,

52 perhaps to avoid any chronological conflict with Acts 1 about the time of the ascension.
**24:53** The Gospel of Luke ends as it began (Lk 1:9), in the Jerusalem temple.

---

| | |
|---|---|
| **24:44** 18:31; 24:27; Mt 16:21; Jn 5:39, 46. | **24:48** Acts 1:8. |
| **24:45** Jn 20:9. | **24:49** Jn 14:26; Acts 1:4; 2:3–4. |
| **24:46** 9:22; Is 53: Hos 6:2. | **24:50–51** Mk 16:19; Acts 1:9–11. |
| **24:47** Mt 3:2; 28 19–20; Mk 16:15–16; Acts 10:41. | **24:52** Acts 1:12. |

# The Gospel According to

# John

## INTRODUCTION

### Mary Coloe

When reading an ancient document, it helps to have some basic information about it: Who wrote it? When and where was it written? Who was the intended reader? Why was it written? Knowing the type of writing used also aids appreciation. Is the text poetry or an instruction manual? Is it a satirical essay or an editorial? The answer to such questions also provides key tools for scholars in interpreting the ancient biblical texts. The Vatican II document on biblical interpretation, *Dei Verbum*, explains:

> The interpreter must investigate what meaning the sacred writer intended to express and actually expressed in particular circumstances by using contemporary literary forms in accordance with the situation of his own time and culture. (*Dei Verbum* 11)

These guiding principles are particularly important when approaching the Gospel of John. This Gospel obviously differs from the three Synoptic Gospels. Though John contains fewer miracles than the Synoptics, those included in John are dramatic. In addition, these miracles are named "signs" in John, which emphasizes that these events are meant to lead to a deeper perception of Jesus' identity and mission. Jesus speaks long discourses to bring out the underlying meaning of these signs. Where the Synoptics describe a single journey from Galilee to Jerusalem, in John's Gospel Jesus travels back and forth between Galilee and Jerusalem several times. There are no narratives of his birth or scene of his baptism; instead, this Gospel introduces Jesus with a richly evocative Prologue (Jn 1:1–18) that clearly situates Jesus' origins in God from the beginning. The Fourth Gospel is remarkably Jewish in its details about Jesus' attendance at major Jewish festivals, and yet, the Jews are presented as distinctly "other" to Jesus and the disciples, suggesting the emergence of a new community centered on Jesus,

---

## Outline of John

I. **Prologue (1:1–18)**

II. **The Book of Signs (1:19–12:50)**

III. **The Book of Glory (13:1–20:31)**

IV. **Epilogue: The Resurrection Appearance in Galilee (21:1–25)**

---

not the synagogue. Understanding something of the historical and religious context for this Gospel will assist understanding the text.

## Date and Location

Scholars today date this Gospel as the last written, sometime in the late nineties CE. While this is the date of the final editing, there are indications, explored here, that this Gospel has gone through a long process of compiling the memories of Jesus, selecting and arranging them, and presenting them in a form to emphasize Jesus' identity and mission. The Gospel has its roots in the Galilean and Judean life of Jesus, but its final place of editing is likely to have been in the wider Greco-Roman world, such as Alexandria, Antioch, or Ephesus.

## Authorship

Twice in the Gospel we read of eyewitness testimony—"An eyewitness has testified, and his testimony is true" (Jn 19:35; cf. 21:24). These affirmations of truth are linked with an anonymous character in the text known only as "the disciple whom Jesus loved" (13:23; 19:25–27; 20:3–10). Opinions vary about the identity of this Beloved Disciple. In the second century, Irenaeus, the Bishop of Lyon (ca. 180–200), attributed the Gospel to John, the disciple of the Lord who leaned on his breast (13:23; *Against Heresies* 3.1.1). "John" was then identified with John, the son of Zebedee, who in the Synoptics is one of Jesus' earliest disciples (Mk 1:19) and his close companion (Mk 9:2; 14:33). Many scholars today question Irenaeus's interpretation. In the second century, questions were asked about which Gospels could be considered authentic; linking the Gospel to one of the original disciples may have been Irenaeus's strategy to bolster its authenticity. While some still identify John with the son of Zebedee, many scholars today consider him the unidentified eyewitness whose testimony and teaching are the basis for the Gospel's particular theological vision. Most commentaries will offer further details on this unresolved question.

The author's actual name, however, seems less important than the affirmations that the Gospel is based on the eyewitness testimony of a disciple who was with Jesus from the beginning, possibly the unnamed disciple of John the Baptist who first follows Jesus (Jn 1:35–39). This disciple, whom most scholars consider male, was possibly the leader and teacher of a group of believers, passing on and shaping memories about Jesus to meet the particular needs and circumstances of this community.

## Unity of the Text

Some strange breaks in the narrative, such as Jesus' command "Get up, let us go" (Jn 14:31), followed by three further chapters of discourse (chs. 15–17), suggest that this Gospel has gone through editorial stages before reaching its final form. In ch. 21, Peter asks about the destiny of the Beloved Disciple. Jesus replies, "What if I want him to remain until I come? What concern is it of yours?" To this the narrator adds that Jesus had not said that the Beloved Disciple would not die (21:23). The heightened importance of Peter, the apparent "ending" in 20:30–31, followed by a further ending in 21:24–25, along with a change in the vocabulary and writing style, have led scholars to consider that ch. 21 was an early addition to the original text by a final editor; the question

about the fate of the Beloved Disciple suggests the chapter was added following his death. This editorial work must have been early since we know of no manuscript tradition that lacks ch. 21. Such disjunctions in the text have led some to postulate that the Gospel had multiple authors, but the majority of scholars consider chs. 1–20 a literary unity based on writing style, vocabulary, and theological consistency.

## The Johannine Community

The fact that Jesus' first disciples are directed to him by John the Baptist (Jn 1:29, 35–36) and that John later affirms the superiority of Jesus (3:28–30), leads scholars to believe that this community includes former disciples of John the Baptist. Chapter 4, with its narrative about the Samaritan woman and Jesus being welcomed by the Samaritan village (4:40), suggests that there are also Samaritans in the community, along with many Jews and Gentiles. The destruction of Jerusalem and its Temple by Rome in 70 CE was a critical event for both Jews and Jesus' followers. Within Judaism, it brought an end to Temple worship, sacrifice, and the priesthood. Judaism from this time looked to the law and the teaching of the rabbis to maintain its religious identity. The followers of Jesus gradually established a religious identity focused on Jesus and moving apart from Judaism. Both groups, Jews and Christians, also needed to find somewhere to live within the Roman Empire with all its civic responsibilities and imperial cultic practices.[1]

John's Gospel highly values the practice of Judaism, its worship, Scriptures, and festivals, and yet there is marked conflict between Jesus, as well as his disciples, with the Jewish leadership, presented in the Gospel primarily as the Pharisees. The Gospel thus has continuity with the rich heritage of Israel, while at the same time the sharp polemic and negative treatment of characters called "the Jews" suggest that this community had its origins in Judaism but is now seeking to distance itself from the

JN

---

1. See Warren Carter, *John and Empire: Initial Explorations* (New York: T & T Clark, 2008) for a discussion of the social setting of the Johannine community.

Torah-centered synagogue, as it affirms faith in Jesus and "life in his name" (Jn 20:31)

An intriguing and much debated feature of this Gospel is the use of the term "the Jews." This is curious, given that, within the Gospel narrative, *all* the characters are Jews, with the exception of Pilate, possibly the royal official (Jn 4:46), and the Greeks (12:20). (The Samaritans are a special case and their situation will be discussed later.) Most frequently the term "the Jews" is used to refer to the Jewish authorities associated with Jerusalem (cf. 1:19; 2:13–22; 9:22; 11:45–53; 18:28–19:22) who are opponents of Jesus and his disciples (20:19). Many today consider that this term is part of the rhetorical strategy of the Gospel written for a community seeking its own religious identity over against emerging Rabbinic Judaism.

## Outline of the Gospel

John's Gospel can be divided into two major sections: chs. 1:19–12:50, the "Book of Signs," which concerns Jesus' miracles (called "signs," e.g., Jn 2:11; 4:54), and chs. 13:1–20:31, the "Book of Glory," which focuses on Jesus' return to the Father (called his "glorification," e.g., 13:31; 14:13; 17:1, 5, 24). These two major sections are introduced by a Prologue (1:1–18) and concluded with an Epilogue (21:1–25).[2]

Within the Book of Signs, smaller subdivisions are suggested by the text. Chapter 1 presents a sequence of "days" (designated by the repeated phrase, "the next day"; Jn 1:29, 35, 43) beginning with the ministry of John (1:19–34) and concluding with Jesus' promise to his disciples that they would see "greater things" (1:50–51). Chapter 2 begins in "Cana in Galilee" (2:1) and the changing of the water into wine is called "the beginning of his signs" (2:11). At the end of ch. 4 the narrative returns to "Cana in Galilee" (4:46) and the cure of the royal official's son is called "the second sign." These repetitions suggest that chs. 2, 3, and 4 are a literary unit, which Raymond Brown and others call "From Cana to Cana."

The next six chapters deal with issues linked to specific Jewish feasts: the sabbath (ch. 5), Passover (ch. 6), Tabernacles (7:1–10:21), and Dedication (10:22–42).

Chapters 11 and 12 focus on the person of Lazarus, his death and resurrection (Jn 11:1–44), and its consequences for Jesus (11:45–53; 12:10, 17–19). The death and raising of Lazarus provide a transition from the account of Jesus' public ministry to an account of his own death and Resurrection.

John begins the Book of Glory with Jesus' final meal (Jn 13:2), and proceeds to Jesus' instruction to his disciples about the meaning of his departure (chs. 13–16), his prayer to his Father for his disciples (ch. 17), his death (chs. 18–19), and his Resurrection (ch. 20). As noted above, many scholars today consider that the Gospel, at least in its earlier form, concluded with a brief statement of its purpose (20:30–31). Chapter 21 appears to be an early editor's addition to the original text, an Epilogue, which then has its own conclusion (21:24–25).

## Reading the Text

John's Gospel frequently leaves clues to guide the audience, not unlike an old style detective mystery where the crime occurs in the first chapter and the rest of the book involves a detective looking for clues. The reader is expected to notice the clues, so that in the final chapter, the reader and the detective have both worked out the perpetrator of the crime. Since this Gospel was written for an audience living somewhere in the eastern part of the Roman Empire toward the end of the first century, an audience familiar with the traditions and Scriptures of Israel, today's readers will need a contemporary guide to detect and understand these clues. Frequently the Gospel depends on the reader knowing an Old Testament text, either explicitly quoted (e.g., Jn 2:17; 6:31), or just alluded to (e.g., 1:51; cf. Gn 28:12). Often the reader is expected to know Jewish customs (e.g., foot washing) or the rituals and symbols associated with Jewish festivals. Without this knowledge, the modern reader can miss the point of a Johannine episode.

Take for example, the first miracle at Cana (Jn 2:1–12). At first glance, it appears to be a

---

2. This outline follows that of Raymond E. Brown, *The Gospel According to John*, 2 vols., Anchor Bible 29–29a (New York: Doubleday & Co., 1966, 1970).

simple miracle story—Jesus provides abundant wine at a wedding—but a closer reading reveals far more. The steward of the feast called the bridegroom to congratulate him on the provision of such abundant good wine toward the end of the feast (2:9–10). This indicates that, at a Jewish wedding ceremony, the bridegroom had the task of providing the wine. But, in this case, it was Jesus who provided the wine and so the evangelist is giving a clue, or a sign, that Jesus is the bridegroom at this feast. Within the Old Testament, the image of a bridegroom and bride was frequently used to speak of the loving relationship between God and Israel (Jer 2:2; Hos 2:19–24) and a feast was a symbol of the covenant (Ex 24:9–11; Is 25:6–9).

This miracle begins with the words "on the third day" (Jn 2:1) and concludes with the statement that this was the first sign when Jesus "revealed his glory" (2:11). These phrases, "the third day," "revealed his glory," echo the language found in the account of Israel's arrival at Mount Sinai and entrance into the solemn covenant with God. At Sinai the people were told to prepare for the third day (Ex 19:11 [twice], 15, 16), for on the third day God would descend upon the mountain in glory. The evangelist presumes that his audience is familiar with this important Old Testament text and so will understand the allusion, not unlike today when a line from a movie will immediately evoke the entire film. The first miracle at Cana, when read within this Exodus context, opens up a richer understanding of the narrative. Jesus is being presented as the covenanting God of Israel, the loving bridegroom providing abundant wine for the wedding feast. Since wine miracles were also associated with the Greek god Dionysus, presenting Jesus as the bridegroom and source of abundant wine would appeal to both Jewish and Greek traditions. This example demonstrates the depth of meaning in a Johannine passage, and the value of a good commentary to help the reader uncover that depth.

## "Cana to Cana"

One approach to interpreting this section is to focus on the way the characters in the text respond to Jesus. In chs. 2 and 3 the characters are Jews, while in ch. 4 the narrative moves outside Judaism to the Samaritans (Jn 4:1–42) and the Gentile official (4:46–54). Within the world of Judaism, the first significant character is the mother of Jesus. In spite of Jesus' retort, his mother directs the servants, "Do whatever he tells you" (2:5). She trusts Jesus' words and her trust leads to the bountiful supply of wine. She displays authentic faith in Jesus, at least in terms of this Gospel. With the mother of Jesus as a model, the reader then meets other characters and is implicitly invited to evaluate their faith response to Jesus: the Jews in the Temple (2:13–22), Nicodemus (2:23–3:10), and John the Baptist (3:25–30). The Jews are portrayed as completely rejecting Jesus' words (2:20); they display no faith in him. Nicodemus comes to Jesus (3:2), but fails to comprehend his words (3:4, 9) and so remains in a state of partial faith. He will appear again, however (7:50–52), and eventually he displays perfect faith in anointing the body of Jesus for burial (19:39–42). Following the first encounter with Nicodemus, John the Baptist testifies that Jesus is the "bridegroom" (3:29), and adds, "He must increase; I must decrease" (3:30). These words indicate that John has perfect faith.

Moving beyond the world of Judaism (Jn 4:1–42), note the gradual shift in the attitude of the Samaritan woman toward Jesus. At first she is dismissive of him (4:9) and shows no faith. But then she addresses him as "sir" and requests water from him (4:11, 15). At this stage, she is showing partial faith. Then she considers him a prophet (4:19), and finally, the Messiah/Christ (4:25). Showing full faith, she leaves Jesus to bring other villagers to him, and they also come to acknowledge Jesus as "the savior of the world" (4:42).

Chapter 4 concludes with Jesus back in Cana, where a "royal official," probably a Gentile, also shows complete faith when he trusts Jesus' word that his son will live (Jn 4:50). Like the mother of Jesus, this official is at first rebuffed by Jesus (4:48), but he too persists and his faith is rewarded. This Gentile official and the mother of Jesus serve as models of perfect Johannine faith. Between these two characters, the reader is introduced to others, both within and beyond Judaism, who display various faith responses to Jesus: full faith, partial faith, and no faith. The evangelist has crafted

JN

his narrative in this way to invite the reader—whether Jew, Samaritan, or Gentile—into a similar journey of faith.

## The Feasts of the Jews

Across chs. 5 to 10, the reader follows Jesus through the Jewish liturgical cycle as he participates in significant Jewish festivals (Jn 6:4; 7:2; 10:22). This cycle of Jewish festivals is introduced in Jn 5 with the weekly festival of the sabbath (5:9). The Jewish liturgical calendar begins with the spring festival of Passover and in Jn 6:4 we read, "The Jewish feast of Passover was near." A similar phrase is used in Jn 7:2 to introduce the fall (autumn) festival of Tabernacles. The religious context of this festival continues through chs. 7:1–10:21. The winter festival of Dedication is then announced at 10:22.

Why might the evangelist have shaped his narrative in this manner? The answer may lie in the historical situation of John's community. In the final decades of the first century, following the destruction of Jerusalem, Jewish leaders set about establishing a Jewish identity without the Temple. The Jewish members of the Johannine community had the painful choice of remaining within the Jewish synagogue or publicly joining the followers of Jesus, and, according to this Gospel, being expelled from the synagogue (Jn 9:22; 12:42; 16:2). Faced with this possibility, how could Jewish believers in Jesus retain and honor their heritage while professing faith in Jesus? Was this even possible? These chapters on the Jewish festivals express the pastoral sensitivity of the evangelist and his theological artistry as he presents Jesus as the one who brings the traditions and festivals of Judaism to their fulfillment.

On the sabbath, Jesus heals a man and commands him to sin no more (Jn 5:14). For these actions, Jesus is condemned by the Jewish leaders for working on the sabbath (5:16). Jesus defends his actions in the light of Jewish sabbath concessions, which recognize that God does not cease from work entirely on the sabbath either (5:17). The God who continues to work on the sabbath through giving life to the newborn and judgment to the deceased is now present in Jesus, who has been given authority to give life (5:26) and to judge (5:22).

In ch. 6 the Passover provides the context in this Gospel for the great feeding miracle (Jn 6:1–14), which is followed by a long discourse to bring out the meaning of this feast (6:25–59). The Exodus generation of Jews was fed in the wilderness by the manna, the bread from heaven (6:31). Behind the language of this discourse lies the gift of manna and the way the nourishment of the manna was identified in the first century with the nourishment of God's word and wisdom (Wis 16:20–26). The Gospel presents Jesus as the true bread that has come down from heaven (Jn 6:32, 38, 50).

In describing the festival of Tabernacles, the Mishnah (compiled around 200 CE) describes two of the rituals for the feast; one involved a water ceremony every morning (*m. Sukk.* 4.9) and then in the evening a celebration under large lights in the Temple courtyard (*m. Sukk.* 5.3). In this context, Jesus claims to be a source of living water (Jn 7:37–39) and the "light of the world" (8:12).

Then in the festival of Dedication, which commemorates the reconsecration of the Temple at the time of the Maccabees (164 BCE), Jesus identifies himself as the one sent and "consecrated" by his Father (Jn 10:36). Within the cycle of Jewish festivals, Jesus appropriates to himself the deeper meaning of the feasts and their great symbols: bread, light, water, the Temple. In this way, the evangelist reassures his community that in making a choice for Jesus they lose nothing of their Jewish heritage but in fact can now celebrate all that this heritage has promised in its fulfillment.

## Jesus' Farewell Discourse

Following the raising of Lazarus in ch. 11, Jesus' public ministry concludes with the Jewish leaders' ominous decision to put him to death (Jn 11:53). According to the Gospel, the leaders make this decision fearing the power of Rome (11:47–53), for they are entirely dependent on Roman good will to hold their elite positions. From ch. 13, Jesus gathers with "his own" (13:1). In chs. 5 and 6, the pattern of the narrative is a miracle followed by a discourse, which explores the theological meaning of the miracle. As Jesus approaches his "hour," which is both the crucifixion and Resurrection, the pattern reverses and the long discourse across chs. 13–17 provide the theological interpretation of the meaning of Jesus' death and Resurrection before the event.

The "hour" begins in ch. 13 with the act of Jesus washing the disciples' feet, then interpreting this action first as the only way disciples can have any part in him (Jn 13:9), then as a model or blueprint for their own behavior (13:15), and finally as an expression of love (13:34). In that society, foot washing was a common ritual of hospitality and welcome. Through this ritual, Jesus invites and welcomes disciples to participate in his coming "hour" and what it will mean for them.

Chapter 14 continues to unpack the particular Johannine understanding of Jesus' death. Earlier Jesus said, "Destroy this temple and in three days I will raise it up" (Jn 2:19). The narrator then explained that Jesus spoke of the temple of his body (2:21). In some way, Jesus' death will be the destroying of one temple (his body) and the raising of another. When Jesus speaks of "my Father's house" and its many dwellings in 14:2, we need to recall that he named the Temple, "my Father's house" (2:16).

In the Old Testament, the expression "my father's house" always refers to the people who make up the household and never to a building (e.g., Gn 24:38; 28:21; 46:31). In many modern translations the idiom "my father's house" is simply translated as "family" (e.g., Jos 2:13). The phrase conveys this double meaning in Jn 14:2—my Father's house(hold) and also Temple. The play on the phrase "my Father's house(hold)" continues as Jesus speaks of "many dwelling places," using a noun related to the verb menō (to dwell). The verb and the related noun are then repeated four times in ch. 14 to speak of the Father dwelling in Jesus (14:10), of the Spirit dwelling in believers (14:17), of the Father and Jesus dwelling in the believer (14:23), and of Jesus dwelling with the believer (14:25). In English translation it is easy to miss the "many dwelling places" Jesus speaks about in this chapter: the Father, the Spirit, and Jesus, dwelling in and with believers. As Jesus prepares to leave his disciples and return to the Father (13:1), he offers them the consolation (see 14:1, 18, 27) of the abiding presence of God, Father, Jesus, and Spirit, in and with the community.

In the Old Testament the great symbol of God's dwelling in Israel was the Temple, and so ch. 14 is introduced with the phrase Jesus used to speak of the Jerusalem Temple, namely, "my Father's house" (Jn 2:16; 14:2). We see in this chapter a reinterpretation of Israel's Temple traditions to speak of the future Christian community as the dwelling place of God. Somehow Jesus' departure to the Father, through his death, will bring about the indwelling of God in the community. Taking all this into consideration, Jn 14:2 is best understood as a statement about the Father's house(hold). At the end of ch. 14, Jesus says to the disciples, "Get up, let us go" (14:31). At the start of ch. 18, we find these words lead directly into Jesus' crossing the Kidron valley into the garden where he will be arrested. Scholars think that chs. 13 and 14 were the earliest form of Jesus' final discourse, and these chapters led directly into the passion. The evangelist then revised this earliest discourse by adding further words of explanation (chs. 15 to 17), and perhaps even these chapters underwent further editorial additions.

## The "Hour"

Three unique features of the Johannine passion narrative convey the particular Johannine theology of the cross: the creation symbolism, the meaning of the title on the cross (Jn 19:19), and the significance of the presence of Jesus' mother and the Beloved Disciple at the foot of the cross (19:25–27).

The Johannine passion uses a number of allusions to the Genesis creation account (Gn 2–3). Only John has Jesus arrested and buried in a garden (Jn 18:1; 19:41). John emphasizes that the cross is placed in the middle (Jn 19:18), just as the tree of life was situated in the middle of the garden in Genesis (Gn 2:9). At the foot of the cross stand a man and a woman, who is only named "woman" and "mother," the names given to Eve (Gn 2:23; 3:20). While the Synoptics portray the crucifixion drawing on Jewish atonement day symbolism (e.g., the tearing of the Temple veil, Mk 15:38), John draws on creation and Temple imagery to present his theology of the cross.

In this Gospel, the sign above Jesus' head is called a *titlon* (Jn 19:19), "title," although the NABRNT translates it as "inscription." It is different from the sign in the Synoptic Gospels where it is literally called an "inscription" (Mk 15:26; Lk 23:38), or a "charge" (Mt 27:37). Only John's Gospel has the words, *"Jesus the Nazorean, the King of the Jews."* The phrase, "Jesus the Nazorean" occurs three times in the passion, twice in the garden when Jesus is arrested (Jn 18:5, 7), and as the title on the cross (19:19). First-century Jews would understand the scriptural allusions behind the use of this title, "the Nazorean." First, it alludes to the words of Isaiah, "a shoot shall sprout from the stump of Jesse, and from his roots a bud (or "branch"; *netzer*) shall blossom" (Is 11:1). The word "branch" in Hebrew is formed from the same consonants (*nzr*) as the word "Nazorean." It is as if Jesus dies under the title "the Branch." Second, this is the symbolic title used by the prophet Zechariah to name the one who will build the new Temple in the final age. Zechariah states, "There is a man (literally "Behold the man") whose name is Branch . . . and he will build the temple of the LORD" (Zec 6:12). This verse from Zechariah is also hinted at in the words Pilate uses to announce Jesus to the crowd, "Behold the man" (Jn 19:5). Using these prophetic texts from Isaiah and Zechariah, readily familiar to first-century Jews, the Johannine title could be rephrased: Jesus the Branch, the Temple-builder.

In John's Gospel, Jesus speaks to his mother from the cross saying, "Woman, behold, your son" (Jn 19:26). He then says to the Beloved Disciple, "Behold, your mother" (19:27). These words establish a new relationship between the Beloved Disciple and the mother of Jesus. They are now mother and son. In changing their relationship, Jesus has also changed the relationship of the disciple to himself. If they

are now both "sons" of the one mother, then the Beloved Disciple is now a brother of Jesus. And if the disciple is now a brother of Jesus, it follows that the disciple is also drawn into Jesus' relationship as son of the Father. To use inclusive language, this scene portrays the divine filiation of all disciples, albeit a disciple's filiation is of a different nature than that of Jesus with the Father. In the death of Jesus, disciples become brothers and sisters of Jesus and children of God. Jesus confirms this in his first appearance to Mary Magdalene: "Go to my brothers [and sisters] and tell them, 'I am going to my Father and your Father'" (20:17).

Following this change of relationship, the reader is told, "the disciple took her into his home," literally, "to his own" (*eis ta idia*; Jn 19:27). This phrase was used in the Prologue: "He came to what was his own (*eis ta idia*), but his own people did not accept him; but to those who did accept him he gave power to become children of God, to those who believe in his name" (1:11–12). Here at the cross, these words of the Prologue are realized, as the Beloved Disciple, representative of all disciples, becomes brother to Jesus and child of God. The disciple is now drawn into the Father's house(hold). In this way, Jesus raises up a new Temple in "the hour"—the Temple of his Father's house(hold). On the cross, the Temple of his body is destroyed; from the cross, Jesus raises up a new Temple, the Father's house(hold) in the community of disciples.

## Conclusion

The Gospel of John is rich in its use of Jewish rituals, Scripture, and symbols. This can present problems for modern readers who are unaware of these allusions. If one is to appreciate the deep theological and spiritual gifts offered by this Gospel, one needs guidance to know its historical background and socio-religious context. ■

# THE GOSPEL ACCORDING TO JOHN

## New American Bible, Introduction

The Gospel according to John is quite different in character from the three synoptic gospels. It is highly literary and symbolic. It does not follow the same order or reproduce the same stories as the synoptic gospels. To a much greater degree, it is the product of a developed theological reflection and grows out of a different circle and tradition. It was probably written in the 90s of the first century.

The Gospel of John begins with a magnificent prologue, which states many of the major themes and motifs of the gospel, much as an overture does for a musical work. The prologue proclaims Jesus as the preexistent and incarnate Word of God who has revealed the Father to us. The rest of the first chapter forms the introduction to the gospel proper and consists of the Baptist's testimony about Jesus (there is no baptism of Jesus in this gospel—John simply points him out as the Lamb of God), followed by stories of the call of the first disciples, in which various titles predicated of Jesus in the early church are presented.

The gospel narrative contains a series of "signs"—the gospel's word for the wondrous deeds of Jesus. The author is primarily interested in the significance of these deeds, and so interprets them for the reader by various reflections, narratives, and discourses. The first sign is the transformation of water into wine at Cana (Jn 2:1–11); this represents the replacement of the Jewish ceremonial washings and symbolizes the entire creative and transforming work of Jesus. The second sign, the cure of the royal official's son (Jn 4:46–54) simply by the word of Jesus at a distance, signifies the power of Jesus' life-giving word. The same theme is further developed by other signs, probably for a total of seven. The third sign, the cure of the paralytic at the pool with five porticoes in chap. 5, continues the theme of water offering newness of life. In the preceding chapter, to the woman at the well in Samaria Jesus had offered living water springing up to eternal life, a symbol of the revelation that Jesus brings; here Jesus' life-giving word replaces the water of the pool that failed to bring life. Jn 6 contains two signs, the multiplication of loaves and the walking on the waters of the Sea of Galilee. These signs are connected much as the manna and the crossing of the Red Sea are in the Passover narrative and symbolize a new exodus. The multiplication of the loaves is interpreted for the reader by the discourse that follows, where the bread of life is used first as a figure for the revelation of God in Jesus and then for the Eucharist. After a series of dialogues reflecting Jesus' debates with the Jewish authorities at the Feast of Tabernacles in Jn 7; 8, the sixth sign is presented in Jn 9, the sign of the young man born blind. This is a narrative illustration of the theme of conflict in the preceding two chapters; it proclaims the triumph of light over darkness, as Jesus is presented as the Light of the world. This is interpreted by a narrative of controversy between the Pharisees and the young man who had been given his sight by Jesus, ending with a discussion of spiritual blindness and spelling out the symbolic meaning of the cure. And finally, the seventh sign, the raising of Lazarus in chap. 11, is the climax of signs. Lazarus is presented as a token of the real life that Jesus, the Resurrection and the Life, who will now ironically be put to death because of his gift of life to Lazarus, will give to all who believe in him once he has been raised from the dead.

After the account of the seven signs, the "hour" of Jesus arrives, and the author passes from sign to reality, as he moves into the discourses in the upper room that interpret the meaning of the passion, death, and resurrection narratives that follow. The whole gospel of John is a progressive revelation of the glory of God's only Son, who comes to reveal the Father and then returns in glory to the Father. The author's purpose is clearly expressed in what must have been the original ending of the gospel at the end of Jn 20: "Now Jesus did many other signs in the presence of [his] disciples that are not written in this book. But these are written that you may [come to] believe that Jesus is the Messiah, the Son of God, and that through this belief you may have life in his name."

Critical analysis makes it difficult to accept the idea that the gospel as it now stands was written by one person. Jn 21 seems to have been added after the gospel was completed; it exhibits a Greek style somewhat different from that of the rest of the work. The prologue (Jn 1:1–18) apparently contains an independent hymn, subsequently adapted to serve as a preface to the gospel. Within the gospel itself there are also some inconsistencies, e.g., there are two endings of Jesus' discourse in the upper room (Jn 14:31; 18:1). To solve these problems, scholars have proposed various rearrangements that would produce a smoother order. However, most have come to the conclusion that the inconsistencies were probably produced by subsequent editing in which homogeneous materials were added to a shorter original.

Other difficulties for any theory of eyewitness authorship of the gospel in its present form are presented by its highly developed theology and by certain elements of its literary style. For instance, some of the wondrous deeds of Jesus have been worked into highly effective dramatic scenes (Jn 9); there has been a careful attempt to have these followed by discourses that explain them (Jn 5; 6); and the sayings of Jesus have been woven into long discourses of a quasi-poetic form resembling the speeches of personified Wisdom in the Old Testament.

The gospel contains many details about Jesus not found in the synoptic gospels, e.g., that Jesus engaged in a baptizing ministry (Jn 3:22) before he changed to one of preaching and signs; that Jesus' public ministry lasted for several years (see note on Jn 2:13); that he traveled to Jerusalem for various festivals and met serious opposition long before his death (Jn 2:14–25; 5; 7–8); and that he was put to death on the day before Passover (Jn 18:28). These events are not always in chronological order because of the development and editing that took place. However, the accuracy of much of the detail of the fourth gospel constitutes a strong argument that the Johannine tradition rests upon the testimony of an eyewitness. Although tradition identified this person as John, the son of Zebedee, most modern scholars find that the evidence does not support this.

The fourth gospel is not simply history; the narrative has been organized and adapted to serve the evangelist's theological purposes as well. Among them are the opposition to the synagogue of the day and to John the Baptist's followers, who tried to exalt their master at Jesus' expense, the desire to show that Jesus was the Messiah, and the desire to convince Christians that their religious belief and practice must be rooted in Jesus. Such theological purposes have impelled the evangelist to emphasize motifs that were not so clear in the synoptic account of Jesus' ministry, e.g., the explicit emphasis on his divinity.

The polemic between synagogue and church produced bitter and harsh invective, especially regarding the hostility toward Jesus of the authorities—Pharisees and Sadducees—who are combined and referred to frequently as "the Jews" (see note on Jn 1:19). These opponents are even described in Jn 8:44 as springing from their father the devil, whose conduct they imitate in opposing God by rejecting Jesus, whom God has sent. On the other hand, the author of this gospel seems to take pains to show that women are not inferior to men in the Christian community: the woman at the well in Samaria (Jn 4) is presented as a prototype of a missionary (Jn 4:4–42), and the first witness of the resurrection is a woman (Jn 20:11–18).

The final editing of the gospel and arrangement in its present form probably dates from between A.D. 90 and 100. Traditionally, Ephesus has been favored as the place of composition, though many support a location in Syria, perhaps the city of Antioch, while some have suggested other places, including Alexandria.

The principal divisions of the Gospel according to John are the following:

I. Prologue (1:1–18)
II. The Book of Signs (1:19–12:50)
III. The Book of Glory (13:1–20:31)
IV. Epilogue: The Resurrection Appearance in Galilee (21:1–25) ∎

# John

## I. PROLOGUE†

**1** ¹ In the beginning† was the Word,
    and the Word was with God,
    and the Word was God.*
² He was in the beginning with God.
³† All things came to be through him,
    and without him nothing came
      to be.*
What came to be ⁴ through him was life,
    and this life was the light of the
      human race;*
⁵† the light shines in the darkness,*
    and the darkness has not overcome it.

⁶† A man named John was sent from God.*
⁷ He came for testimony,† to testify to the light,
so that all might believe through him.* ⁸ He
was not the light, but came to testify to the
light.* ⁹ The true light, which enlightens everyone, was coming into the world.*

¹⁰     He was in the world,
    and the world came to be through him,
    but the world did not know him.
¹¹     He came to what was his own,
    but his own people† did not accept
      him.

¹²* But to those who did accept him he gave
power to become children of God, to those
who believe in his name, ¹³†* who were born
not by natural generation nor by human
choice nor by a man's decision but by God.

¹⁴     And the Word became flesh†
    and made his dwelling among us,
    and we saw his glory,
    the glory as of the Father's only Son,
    full of grace and truth.*

¹⁵† John testified to him and cried out, saying,
"This was he of whom I said,* 'The one who is

---

† **1:1–18** The prologue states the main themes of the gospel: life, light, truth, the world, testimony, and the preexistence of Jesus Christ, the incarnate *Logos*, who reveals God the Father. In origin, it was probably an early Christian hymn. Its closest parallel is in other christological hymns, Col 1:15–20 and Phil 2:6–11. Its core (Jn 1:1–5, 10–11, 14) is poetic in structure, with short phrases linked by "staircase parallelism," in which the last word of one phrase becomes the first word of the next. Prose inserts (at least Jn 1:6–8, 15) deal with John the Baptist.

**1:1** *In the beginning*: also the first words of the Old Testament (Gn 1:1). *Was*: this verb is used three times with different meanings in this verse: existence, relationship, and predication. *The Word* (Greek *logos*): this term combines God's dynamic, creative word (Genesis), personified preexistent Wisdom as the instrument of God's creative activity (Proverbs), and the ultimate intelligibility of reality (Hellenistic philosophy). *With God*: the Greek preposition here connotes communication with another. *Was God*: lack of a definite article with "God" in Greek signifies predication rather than identification.

**1:3** *What came to be*: while the oldest manuscripts have no punctuation here, the corrector of Bodmer Papyrus P⁷⁵, some manuscripts, and the Ante-Nicene Fathers take this phrase with what follows, as staircase parallelism. Connection with Jn 1:3 reflects fourth-century anti-Arianism.

**1:5** The ethical dualism of light and darkness is paralleled in intertestamental literature and in the Dead Sea Scrolls. *Overcome*: "comprehend" is another possible translation, but cf. Jn 12:35; Wis 7:29–30.

**1:6** John was *sent* just as Jesus was "sent" (Jn 4:34) in divine mission. Other references to John the Baptist in this gospel emphasize the differences between them and John's subordinate role.

**1:7** *Testimony*: the testimony theme of John is introduced, which portrays Jesus as if on trial throughout his ministry. All testify to Jesus: John the Baptist, the Samaritan woman, scripture, his works, the crowds, the Spirit, and his disciples.

**1:11** *What was his own…his own people*: first a neuter, literally, "his own property/possession" (probably = Israel), then a masculine, "his own people" (the Israelites).

**1:13** Believers in Jesus become children of God not through any of the three natural causes mentioned but through God who is the immediate cause of the new spiritual life. *Were born*: the Greek verb can mean "begotten" (by a male) or "born" (from a female or of parents). The variant "he who was begotten," asserting Jesus' virginal conception, is weakly attested in Old Latin and Syriac versions.

**1:14** *Flesh*: the whole person, used probably against docetic tendencies (cf. 1 Jn 4:2; 2 Jn 7). *Made his dwelling*: literally, "pitched his tent/tabernacle." Cf. the tabernacle or tent of meeting that was the place of God's presence among his people (Ex 25:8–9). The incarnate Word is the new mode of God's presence among his people. The Greek verb has the same consonants as the Aramaic word for God's presence (Shekinah). *Glory*: God's visible manifestation of majesty in power, which once filled the tabernacle (Ex 40:34) and the temple (1 Kgs 8:10–11, 27), is now centered in Jesus. *Only Son*: Greek, *monogenēs*, but see note on Jn 1:18. *Grace and truth*: these words may represent two Old Testament terms describing Yahweh in covenant relationship with Israel (cf. Ex 34:6), thus God's "love" and "fidelity." The Word shares Yahweh's covenant qualities.

**1:15** This verse, interrupting Jn 1:14, 16 seems drawn from Jn 1:30.

---

**1:1** 10:30; Gn 1:1–5; Jb 28:12–27; Prv 8:22–25; Wis 9:1–2; 1 Jn 1:1–2; Col 1:1, 15; Rev 3:14; 19:13.
**1:3** Ps 33:9; Wis 9:1; Sir 42:15; 1 Cor 8:6; Col 1:16; Heb 1:2; Rev 3:14.
**1:4** 5:26; 8:12; 1 Jn 1:2.
**1:5** 3:19; 8:12; 9:5; 12:35, 46; Wis 7:29–30; 1 Thes 5:4; 1 Jn 2:8.
**1:6** Mt 3:1; Mk 1:4; Lk 3:2–3.
**1:7** 1:19–34; 5:33.
**1:8** 5:35.
**1:9** 3:19; 8:12; 9:39; 12:46.
**1:12** 3:11–12; 5:43–44; 12:46–50; Gal 3:26; 4:6–7; Eph 1:5; 1 Jn 3:2.
**1:13** 3:5–6.
**1:14** Ex 16:10; 24:17; 25:8–9; 33:22; 34:6; Sir 24:4, 8; Is 60:1; Ez 43:7; Jl 4:17; Heb 2:14; 1 Jn 1:2; 4:2; 2 Jn 7.
**1:15** 1:30; 3:27–30.

coming after me ranks ahead of me because he existed before me.'" [16] From his fullness we have all received, grace in place of grace,† [17] because while the law was given through Moses, grace and truth came through Jesus Christ.* [18] No one has ever seen God. The only Son, God,† who is at the Father's side, has revealed him.*

## II. THE BOOK OF SIGNS

**John the Baptist's Testimony to Himself.** [19]† And this is the testimony of John. When the Jews† from Jerusalem sent priests and Levites [to him] to ask him, "Who are you?" [20]† he admitted and did not deny it, but admitted,* "I am not the Messiah." [21] So they asked him, "What are you then? Are you Elijah?"† And he said, "I am not." "Are you the Prophet?" He answered, "No."* [22] So they said to him, "Who are you, so we can give an answer to those who sent us? What do you have to say for yourself?" [23] He said:

"I am 'the voice of one crying out in the desert,*

"Make straight the way of the Lord,'"†

as Isaiah the prophet said." [24] Some Pharisees† were also sent. [25] They asked him, "Why then do you baptize if you are not the Messiah or Elijah or the Prophet?"* [26] John answered them, "I baptize with water;† but there is one among you whom you do not recognize,* [27] the one who is coming after me, whose sandal strap I am not worthy to untie." [28] This happened in Bethany across the Jordan,† where John was baptizing.

**John the Baptist's Testimony to Jesus.** [29] The next day he saw Jesus coming toward him and said, "Behold, the Lamb of God,† who takes away the sin of the world.* [30]† He is the one of whom I said,* 'A man is coming after me who ranks ahead of me because he existed before me.' [31] I did not know him,† but the reason why I came baptizing with water was that he might be made known to Israel." [32] John testified further, saying, "I saw the Spirit come down like a dove† from the sky and remain upon him. [33] I did not know him,* but the one who sent me to baptize with water told me, 'On whomever you see the Spirit come down and remain, he is the one who will baptize

---

**1:16** *Grace in place of grace*: replacement of the Old Covenant with the New (cf. Jn 1:17). Other possible translations are "grace upon grace" (accumulation) and "grace for grace" (correspondence).

**1:18** *The only Son, God*: while the vast majority of later textual witnesses have another reading, "the Son, the only one" or "the only Son," the translation above follows the best and earliest manuscripts, *monogenēs theos*, but takes the first term to mean not just "Only One" but to include a filial relationship with the Father, as at Lk 9:38 ("only child") or Heb 11:17 ("only son") and as translated at Jn 1:14. The Logos is thus "only Son" and God but not Father/God.

**1:19–51** The testimony of John the Baptist about the Messiah and Jesus' self-revelation to the first disciples. This section constitutes the introduction to the gospel proper and is connected with the prose inserts in the prologue. It develops the major theme of testimony in four scenes: John's negative testimony about himself; his positive testimony about Jesus; the revelation of Jesus to Andrew and Peter; the revelation of Jesus to Philip and Nathanael.

**1:19** *The Jews*: throughout most of the gospel, the "Jews" does not refer to the Jewish people as such but to the hostile authorities, both Pharisees and Sadducees, particularly in Jerusalem, who refuse to believe in Jesus. The usage reflects the atmosphere, at the end of the first century, of polemics between church and synagogue, or possibly it refers to Jews as representative of a hostile world (Jn 1:10–11).

**1:20** *Messiah*: the anointed agent of Yahweh, usually considered to be of Davidic descent. See further the note on Jn 1:41.

**1:21** *Elijah*: the Baptist did not claim to be Elijah returned to earth (cf. Mal 3:19; Mt 11:14). *The Prophet*: probably the prophet like Moses (Dt 18:15; cf. Acts 3:22).

**1:23** This is a repunctuation and reinterpretation (as in the synoptic gospels and Septuagint) of the Hebrew text of Is 40:3 which reads, "A voice cries out: In the desert prepare the way of the LORD."

**1:24** *Some Pharisees*: other translations, such as "Now they

had been sent from the Pharisees," misunderstand the grammatical construction. This is a different group from that in Jn 1:19; the priests and Levites would have been Sadducees, not Pharisees.

**1:26** *I baptize with water*: the synoptics add "but he will baptize you with the holy Spirit" (Mk 1:8) or "…holy Spirit and fire" (Mt 3:11; Lk 3:16). John's emphasis is on purification and preparation for a better baptism.

**1:28** *Bethany across the Jordan*: site unknown. Another reading is "Bethabara."

**1:29** *The Lamb of God*: the background for this title may be the victorious apocalyptic lamb who would destroy evil in the world (Rev 5–7; 17:14); the paschal lamb, whose blood saved Israel (Ex 12); and/or the suffering servant led like a lamb to the slaughter as a sin-offering (Is 53:7, 10).

**1:30** *He existed before me*: possibly as Elijah (to come, Jn 1:27); for the evangelist and his audience, Jesus' preexistence would be implied (see note on Jn 1:1).

**1:31** *I did not know him*: this gospel shows no knowledge of the tradition (Lk 1) about the kinship of Jesus and John the Baptist. *The reason why I came baptizing with water*: in this gospel, John's baptism is not connected with forgiveness of sins; its purpose is revelatory, that Jesus may be made known to Israel.

**1:32** *Like a dove*: a symbol of the new creation (Gn 8:8) or the community of Israel (Hos 11:11). *Remain*: the first use of a favor-

---

| | |
|---|---|
| **1:17** 7:19; Ex 31:18; 34:28. | Mk 1:2; Lk 3:4. |
| **1:18** 5:37; 6:46; Ex 33:20; Jgs 13:21–22; 1 Tm 6:16; 1 Jn 4:12. | **1:25** Ez 36:25; Zec 13:1; Mt 16:14. |
| **1:20** 3:28; Lk 3:15; Acts 3:25. | **1:26** Mt 3:11; Mk 1:7–8; Lk 3:16; Acts 13:25. |
| **1:21** Dt 18:15, 18; 2 Kgs 2:11; Sir 48:10; Mal 3:1, 23; Mt 11:14; 17:11–13; Mk 9:13; Acts 3:22. | **1:29** 1:36; Ex 12; Is 53:7; Rev 5–7; 17:14. |
| | **1:30** 1:15; Mt 3:11; Mk 1:7; Lk 3:16. |
| **1:23** Is 40:3; Mt 3:3; | **1:33** Sg 5:2; Is 11:2; Hos 11:11; Mt 3:16; Mk 1:10; Lk 3:21–22. |

with the holy Spirit.'* ³⁴†* Now I have seen and testified that he is the Son of God."

### The First Disciples.* ³⁵ The next day John was there again with two of his disciples, ³⁶ and as he watched Jesus walk by, he said, "Behold, the Lamb of God."† ³⁷ The two disciples† heard what he said and followed Jesus. ³⁸ Jesus turned and saw them following him and said to them, "What are you looking for?" They said to him, "Rabbi" (which translated means Teacher), "where are you staying?" ³⁹ He said to them, "Come, and you will see." So they went and saw where he was staying, and they stayed with him that day. It was about four in the afternoon.† ⁴⁰ Andrew, the brother of Simon Peter, was one of the two who heard John and followed Jesus. ⁴¹ He first found his own brother Simon and told him, "We have found the Messiah"† (which is translated Anointed).* ⁴² Then he brought him to Jesus. Jesus looked at him and said, "You are Simon the son of John;† you will be called Cephas" (which is translated Peter).*

⁴³ The next day he† decided to go to Galilee, and he found Philip. And Jesus said to him, "Follow me." ⁴⁴ Now Philip was from Bethsaida, the town of Andrew and Peter. ⁴⁵ Philip found Nathanael and told him, "We have found the one about whom Moses wrote in the law, and also the prophets, Jesus son of Joseph, from Nazareth."* ⁴⁶ But Nathanael said to him, "Can anything good come from Nazareth?" Philip said to him, "Come and see." ⁴⁷ Jesus saw Nathanael coming toward him and said of him, "Here is a true Israelite.† There is no duplicity in him." ⁴⁸†* Nathanael said to him, "How do you know me?" Jesus answered and said to him, "Before Philip called you, I saw you under the fig tree." ⁴⁹ Nathanael answered him, "Rabbi, you are the Son of God;† you are the King of Israel."* ⁵⁰ Jesus answered and said to him, "Do you believe because I told you that I saw you under the fig tree?† You will see greater things than this." ⁵¹ And he said to him, "Amen, amen,† I say to you, you will see the sky opened and the angels of God ascending and descending on the Son of Man."*

## 2 The Wedding at Cana. ¹† On the third day there was a wedding† in Cana† in Galilee, and the mother of Jesus was there.* ² Jesus and his disciples were also invited to the wedding. ³ When the wine ran short, the mother of Jesus said to him, "They have no

---

1:49 *Son of God:* this title is used in the Old Testament, among other ways, as a title of adoption for the Davidic king (2 Sm 7:14; Ps 2:7; 89:27), and thus here, with *King of Israel*, in a messianic sense. For the evangelist, *Son of God* also points to Jesus' divinity (cf. Jn 20:28).

1:50 Possibly a statement: "You [singular] believe because I saw you under the fig tree."

1:51 The double "Amen" is characteristic of John. *You* is plural in Greek. The allusion is to Jacob's ladder (Gn 28:12).

2:1–6:71 Signs revealing Jesus as the Messiah to all Israel. "Sign" (*sēmeion*) is John's symbolic term for Jesus' wondrous deeds (see Introduction). The Old Testament background lies in the Exodus story (cf. Dt 11:3; 29:2). John is interested primarily in what the *sēmeia* signify: God's intervention in human history in a new way through Jesus.

2:1–11 The first sign. This story of replacement of Jewish ceremonial washings (Jn 2:6) presents the initial revelation about Jesus at the outset of his ministry. He manifests his glory; the disciples believe. There is no synoptic parallel.

2:1 *Cana:* unknown from the Old Testament. *The mother of Jesus:* she is never named in John.

---

ite verb in John, emphasizing the permanency of the relationship between Father and Son (as here) and between the Son and the Christian. Jesus is the permanent bearer of the Spirit.

1:34 *The Son of God:* this reading is supported by good Greek manuscripts, including the Chester Beatty and Bodmer Papyri and the Vatican Codex, but is suspect because it harmonizes this passage with the synoptic version: "This is my beloved Son" (Mt 3:17; Mk 1:11; Lk 3:22). The poorly attested alternate reading, "God's chosen One," is probably a reference to the Servant of Yahweh (Is 42:1).

1:36 John the Baptist's testimony makes his disciples' following of Jesus plausible.

1:37 *The two disciples:* Andrew (Jn 1:40) and, traditionally, John, son of Zebedee (see note on Jn 13:23).

1:39 *Four in the afternoon:* literally, the tenth hour, from sunrise, in the Roman calculation of time. Some suggest that the next day, beginning at sunset, was the sabbath; they would have stayed with Jesus to avoid travel on it.

1:41 *Messiah:* the Hebrew word *māšîaḥ*, "anointed one" (see note on Lk 2:11), appears in Greek as the transliterated *messias* only here and in Jn 4:25. Elsewhere the Greek translation *christos* is used.

1:42 *Simon, the son of John:* in Mt 16:17, Simon is called *Bariōna*, "son of Jonah," a different tradition for the name of Simon's father. *Cephas:* in Aramaic = the Rock; cf. Mt 16:18. Neither the Greek equivalent *Petros* nor, with one isolated exception, *Cephas* is attested as a personal name before Christian times.

1:43 *He:* grammatically, could be Peter, but logically is probably Jesus.

1:47 *A true Israelite. There is no duplicity in him:* Jacob was the first to bear the name "Israel" (Gn 32:29), but Jacob was a man of duplicity (Gn 27:35–36).

1:48 *Under the fig tree:* a symbol of messianic peace (cf. Mi 4:4; Zec 3:10).

---

1:33 Is 42:1; Mt 3:11; Mk 1:8; Lk 3:16.
1:34 Is 42:1; Mt 3:17; Mk 1:11; Lk 9:35.
1:35–51 Mt 4:18–22; Mk 1:16–20; Lk 5:1–11.
1:41 4:25.
1:42 Mt 16:18; Mk 3:16.
1:45 21:2.
1:48 Mi 4:4; Zec 3:10.
1:49 12:13; Ex 4:22; Dt 14:1; 2 Sm 7:14; Jb 1:6; 2:1; 38:7; Ps 2:7; 29:1; 89:27; Wis 2:18; Sir 4:10; Dn 3:92; Hos 11:1; Mt 14:33; 16:16; Mk 13:32.
1:51 Gn 28:10–17; Dn 7:13.
2:1 4:46; Jgs 14:12; Tb 11:8.

JN

© Carolyn Osiek, RSCJ

Above, the inside of the Stoa of Attalus, a restored center of public and commercial activity in the agora of Athens that is similar to the commercial area that surrounded the Jerusalem Temple, thought by many to be the site of Jesus' cleansing of the Temple (Jn 2:13–22).

wine." ⁴† [And] Jesus said to her, "Woman, how does your concern affect me? My hour has not yet come."* ⁵ His mother said to the servers, "Do whatever he tells you."* ⁶† Now there were six stone water jars there for Jewish ceremonial washings,* each holding twenty to thirty gallons. ⁷ Jesus told them, "Fill the jars with water." So they filled them to the brim. ⁸ Then he told them, "Draw some out now and take it to the headwaiter."† So they took it. ⁹ And when the headwaiter tasted the water that had become wine, without knowing where it came from (although the servers who had drawn the water knew), the headwaiter called the bridegroom ¹⁰ and said to him, "Everyone serves good wine first, and then when people have drunk freely, an inferior one; but you have kept the good wine until now." ¹¹ Jesus did this as the beginning of his signs† in Cana in Galilee and so revealed his glory, and his disciples began to believe in him.*

¹²† After this, he and his mother, [his] brothers, and his disciples went down to Capernaum and stayed there only a few days.†

**Cleansing of the Temple.** ¹³† Since the Passover† of the Jews was near,* Jesus went up to

---

† 
**2:4** This verse may seek to show that Jesus did not work miracles to help his family and friends, as in the apocryphal gospels. *Woman*: a normal, polite form of address, but unattested in reference to one's mother. Cf. also Jn 19:26. *How does your concern affect me?*: literally, "What is this to me and to you?"—a Hebrew expression of either hostility (Jgs 11:12; 2 Chr 35:21; 1 Kgs 17:18) or denial of common interest (Hos 14:9; 2 Kgs 3:13). Cf. Mk 1:24; 5:7 used by demons to Jesus. *My hour has not yet come*: the translation as a question ("Has not my hour now come?"), while preferable grammatically and supported by Greek Fathers, seems unlikely from a comparison with Jn 7:6, 30. The "hour" is that of Jesus' passion, death, resurrection, and ascension (Jn 13:1).
**2:6** *Twenty to thirty gallons*: literally, "two or three measures"; the Attic liquid measure contained 39.39 liters. The vast quantity recalls prophecies of abundance in the last days; cf. Am 9:13–14; Hos 14:7; Jer 31:12.
**2:8** *Headwaiter*: used of the official who managed a banquet, but there is no evidence of such a functionary in Palestine. Perhaps here a friend of the family acted as master of ceremonies; cf. Sir 32:1.

**2:11** *The beginning of his signs*: the first of seven (see Introduction).
**2:12–3:21** The next three episodes take place in Jerusalem. Only the first is paralleled in the synoptic gospels.
**2:12** This transitional verse may be a harmonization with the synoptic tradition in Lk 4:31 and Mt 4:13. There are many textual variants. John depicts no extended ministry in Capernaum as do the synoptics.
**2:13–22** This episode indicates the post-resurrectional replacement of the temple by the person of Jesus.
**2:13** *Passover*: this is the first Passover mentioned in John; a second is mentioned in Jn 6:4; a third in Jn 13:1. Taken literally, they point to a ministry of at least two years.

---

**2:4** 7:30; 8:20; 12:23; 13:1; Jgs 11:12; 1 Kgs 17:18; 2 Kgs 3:13; 2 Chr 35:21; Hos 14:9; Mk 1:24; 5:7; 7:30; 8:20; 12:23; 13:1.
**2:5** Gn 41:55.
**2:6** 3:25; Lv 11:33; Am 9:13–14; Mt 15:2; 23:25–26; Mk 7:2–4; Lk 11:38.
**2:11** 4:54.
**2:13–22** Mt 21:12–13; Mk 11:15–17; Lk 19:45–46.

JN

Jerusalem. [14]† He found in the temple area those who sold oxen, sheep, and doves,† as well as the money-changers seated there.* [15] He made a whip out of cords and drove them all out of the temple area, with the sheep and oxen, and spilled the coins of the money-changers and overturned their tables, [16] and to those who sold doves he said, "Take these out of here, and stop making my Father's house a marketplace."* [17]† His disciples recalled the words of scripture,* "Zeal for your house will consume me." [18] At this the Jews answered and said to him, "What sign can you show us for doing this?"* [19] Jesus answered and said to them,†* "Destroy this temple and in three days I will raise it up." [20] The Jews said, "This temple has been under construction for forty-six years,† and you will raise it up in three days?" [21] But he was speaking about the temple of his body. [22] Therefore, when he was raised from the dead, his disciples remembered that he had said this, and they came to believe the scripture and the word Jesus had spoken.*

[23] While he was in Jerusalem for the feast of Passover, many began to believe in his name when they saw the signs he was doing.* [24] But Jesus would not trust himself to them because he knew them all, [25] and did not need anyone to testify about human nature. He himself understood it well.*

## 3 Nicodemus.†

[1]* Now there was a Pharisee named Nicodemus, a ruler of the Jews.† [2] He came to Jesus at night and said to him, "Rabbi, we know that you are a teacher who has come from God, for no one can do these signs that you are doing unless God is with him."* [3] Jesus answered and said to him, "Amen, amen, I say to you, no one can see the kingdom of God without being born† from above." [4] Nicodemus said to him, "How can a person once grown old be born again? Surely he cannot reenter his mother's womb and be born again, can he?"* [5] Jesus answered, "Amen, amen, I say to you, no one can enter the kingdom of God without being born of water and Spirit.* [6] What is born of flesh is flesh and what is born of spirit is spirit.* [7] Do not be amazed that I told you, 'You must be born from above.' [8] The wind† blows where it wills, and you can hear the sound it makes, but you do not know where it comes from or where it goes; so it is with everyone who is born of the Spirit."* [9] Nicodemus answered and said to him, "How can this happen?" [10] Jesus answered and said to him, "You are the teacher of Israel and you do not understand this? [11] Amen, amen, I say to you, we speak of what we know and we testify to what we have seen, but you people do not accept our testimony.* [12] If I tell you about earthly things and you do not believe, how will you believe

---

† **2:14–22** The other gospels place the cleansing of the temple in the last days of Jesus' life (Matthew, on the day Jesus entered Jerusalem; Mark, on the next day). The order of events in the gospel narratives is often determined by theological motives rather than by chronological data.

**2:14** *Oxen, sheep, and doves*: intended for sacrifice. The doves were the offerings of the poor (Lv 5:7). *Money-changers*: for a temple tax paid by every male Jew more than nineteen years of age, with a half-shekel coin (Ex 30:11–16), in Syrian currency. See note on Mt 17:24.

**2:17** Ps 69:10, changed to future tense to apply to Jesus.

**2:19** This saying about the destruction of the temple occurs in various forms (Mt 24:2; 27:40; Mk 13:2; 15:29; Lk 21:6; cf. Acts 6:14). Mt 26:61 has: "I *can* destroy the temple of God…"; see note there. In Mk 14:58, there is a metaphorical contrast with a new temple: "I will destroy this temple *made with hands* and within three days I will build another *not made with hands*." Here it is symbolic of Jesus' resurrection and the resulting community (see Jn 2:21 and Rev 21:2). *In three days*: an Old Testament expression for a short, indefinite period of time; cf. Hos 6:2.

**2:20** *Forty-six years*: based on references in Josephus (*Jewish Wars* 1:401; *Antiquities* 15:380), possibly the spring of A.D. 28. Cf. note on Lk 3:1.

**3:1–21** Jesus instructs Nicodemus on the necessity of a new birth from above. This scene in Jerusalem at Passover exemplifies the faith engendered by signs (Jn 2:23). It continues the self-manifestation of Jesus in Jerusalem begun in Jn 2. This is the first of the Johannine discourses, shifting from dialogue to monologue

(Jn 3:11–15) to reflection of the evangelist (Jn 3:16–21). The shift from singular through Jn 3:10 to plural in Jn 3:11 may reflect the early church's controversy with the Jews.

**3:1** *A ruler of the Jews*: most likely a member of the Jewish council, the Sanhedrin; see note on Mk 8:31.

**3:3** *Born*: see note on Jn 1:13. *From above*: the Greek adverb *anōthen* means both "from above" and "again." Jesus means "from above" (see Jn 3:31) but Nicodemus misunderstands it as "again." This misunderstanding serves as a springboard for further instruction.

**3:8** *Wind*: the Greek word *pneuma* (as well as the Hebrew *rûah*) means both "wind" and "spirit." In the play on the double meaning, "wind" is primary.

| | |
|---|---|
| **2:14** Ex 30:11–16; Lv 5:7. | **3:1** 7:50–51; 19:39. |
| **2:16** Zec 14:21. | **3:2** 9:4, 16, 33; 10:21; |
| **2:17** Ps 69:9. | 11:10; 13:30; Mt |
| **2:18** 6:30. | 22:16; Mk 12:14; Lk |
| **2:19** Mt 24:2; 26:61; | 20:21. |
| 27:40; Mk 13:2; | **3:4** 1:13. |
| 14:58; 15:29; Lk 21:6; | **3:5** 1:32; 7:39; 19:30, |
| Acts 6:14. | 34–35; Is 32:15; 44:3; |
| **2:22** 5:39; 12:16; 14:26; | Ez 36:25–27; Jl 3:1–2. |
| 20:9; Mt 12:6; Lk | **3:6** 6:63; 1 Cor 15:44–50. |
| 24:6–8; Rev 21:22. | **3:8** Eccl 11:4–5; Acts |
| **2:23** 4:45. | 2:2–4. |
| **2:25** 1 Kgs 8:39; Ps 33:15; | **3:11** 3:32, 34; 8:14; Mt |
| 94:11; Sir 42:18; Jer | 11:27. |
| 17:10; 20:12. | |

JN

if I tell you about heavenly things? * ¹³ No one has gone up to heaven except the one who has come down from heaven, the Son of Man. * ¹⁴ And just as Moses lifted up† the serpent in the desert, so must the Son of Man be lifted up, * ¹⁵† so that everyone who believes in him may have eternal life."

¹⁶ For God so loved the world that he gave† his only Son, so that everyone who believes in him might not perish but might have eternal life. * ¹⁷ For God did not send his Son into the world to condemn† the world, but that the world might be saved through him. * ¹⁸ Whoever believes in him will not be condemned, but whoever does not believe has already been condemned, because he has not believed in the name of the only Son of God. * ¹⁹† And this is the verdict, * that the light came into the world, but people preferred darkness to light, because their works were evil. ²⁰ For everyone who does wicked things hates the light and does not come toward the light, so that his works might not be exposed. * ²¹ But whoever lives the truth comes to the light, so that his works may be clearly seen as done in God. *

**Final Witness of the Baptist.** ²²† After this, Jesus and his disciples went into the region of Judea, where he spent some time with them baptizing. * ²³ John was also baptizing in Aenon near Salim,† because there was an abundance of water there, and people came to be baptized, ²⁴†* for John had not yet been imprisoned. ²⁵ Now a dispute arose between the disciples of John and a Jew† about ceremonial washings. ²⁶ So they came to John and said to him, "Rabbi, the one who was with you across the Jordan, to whom you testified, here he is baptizing and everyone is coming to him." * ²⁷ John answered and said, "No one can receive anything except what has been given him from heaven. * ²⁸ You yourselves can testify that I said [that] I am not the Messiah, but that I was sent before him. * ²⁹ The one who has the bride is the bridegroom; the best man,† who stands and listens to him, rejoices greatly at the bridegroom's voice. So this joy of mine has been made complete. * ³⁰ He must increase; I must decrease." *

**The One from Heaven.**† ³¹ The one who comes from above is above all. The one who is of the earth is earthly and speaks of earthly things. But the one who comes from heaven [is above all]. * ³² He testifies to what he has seen and heard, but no one accepts his testimony. * ³³ Whoever does accept his testimony certifies that God is trustworthy. * ³⁴ For the one whom God sent speaks the words of God. He does not ration his gift† of the Spirit. ³⁵ The Father loves the Son and has given everything over to him. * ³⁶ Whoever believes in the Son has eternal life, but whoever disobeys the Son will not see life, but the wrath of God remains upon him. *

---

† **3:14** *Lifted up*: in Nm 21:9, Moses simply "mounted" a serpent upon a pole. John here substitutes a verb implying glorification. Jesus, exalted to glory at his cross and resurrection, represents healing for all.

**3:15** *Eternal life*: used here for the first time in John, this term stresses quality of life rather than duration.

**3:16** *Gave*: as a gift in the incarnation, and also "over to death" in the crucifixion; cf. Rom 8:32.

**3:17–19** *Condemn*: the Greek root means both judgment and condemnation. Jesus' purpose is to save, but his coming provokes judgment; some condemn themselves by turning from the light.

**3:19** Judgment is not only future but is partially realized here and now.

**3:22–26** Jesus' ministry in Judea is only loosely connected with Jn 2:13–3:21; cf. Jn 1:19–36. Perhaps John the Baptist's further testimony was transposed here to give meaning to "water" in Jn 3:5. Jesus is depicted as baptizing (Jn 3:22); contrast Jn 4:2.

**3:23** *Aenon near Salim*: site uncertain, either in the upper Jordan valley or in Samaria.

**3:24** A remark probably intended to avoid objections based on a chronology like that of the synoptics (Mt 4:12; Mk 1:14).

**3:25** *A Jew*: some think Jesus is meant. Many manuscripts read "Jews."

**3:29** *The best man*: literally, "the friend of the groom," the *shoshben* of Jewish tradition, who arranged the wedding.

Competition between him and the groom would be unthinkable.

**3:31–36** It is uncertain whether these are words by the Baptist, Jesus, or the evangelist. They are reflections on the two preceding scenes.

**3:34** *His gift*: of God or to Jesus, perhaps both. This verse echoes Jn 3:5, 8.

---

**3:12** 6:62–65; Wis 9:16–17; 1 Cor 15:40; 2 Cor 5:1; Phil 2:10; 3:19–20.
**3:13** 1:18; 6:62; Dn 7:13; Rom 10:6; Eph 4:9.
**3:14** 8:28; 12:32, 34; Nm 21:4–9; Wis 16:5–7.
**3:16** 1 Jn 4:9.
**3:17** 5:22, 30; 8:15–18; 12:47.
**3:18** 5:24; Mk 16:16.
**3:19** 1:5, 9–11; 8:12; 9:5.
**3:20** Jb 24:13–17.
**3:21** Gn 47:29 LXX; Jos 2:14 LXX; 2 Sm 2:6 LXX; 15:20 LXX; Tb 4:6 LXX; 13:6; Is 26:10 LXX;

Mt 5:14–16.
**3:22–23** 4:1–2.
**3:24** Mt 4:12; 14:3; Mk 1:14; 6:17; Lk 3:20.
**3:26** 1:26, 32–34, 36.
**3:27** 19:11; 1 Cor 4:7; 2 Cor 3:5; Heb 5:4.
**3:28** 1:20–23; Lk 3:15.
**3:29** 15:11; 17:13; Mt 9:15.
**3:30** 2 Sm 3:1.
**3:31** 8:23.
**3:32** 3:11.
**3:33–34** 8:26; 12:44–50; 1 Jn 5:10.
**3:35** 13:3; Mt 11:27; 28:18; Lk 10:22.
**3:36** 3:16; 1 Jn 5:13.

**4** [1]† Now when Jesus learned that the Pharisees had heard that Jesus was making and baptizing more disciples than John [2] (although Jesus himself was not baptizing, just his disciples),† [3] he left Judea and returned to Galilee.

**The Samaritan Woman.** [4] He had to† pass through Samaria. [5] So he came to a town of Samaria called Sychar,† near the plot of land that Jacob had given to his son Joseph.* [6] Jacob's well was there. Jesus, tired from his journey, sat down there at the well. It was about noon.

[7] A woman of Samaria came to draw water. Jesus said to her, "Give me a drink." [8] His disciples had gone into the town to buy food. [9]† The Samaritan woman said to him, "How can you, a Jew, ask me, a Samaritan woman, for a drink?"* (For Jews use nothing in common with Samaritans.) [10]† Jesus answered and said to her,* "If you knew the gift of God and who is saying to you, 'Give me a drink,' you would have asked him and he would have given you living water." [11] [The woman] said to him, "Sir,† you do not even have a bucket and the well is deep; where then can you get this living water? [12] Are you greater than our father Jacob, who gave us this well and drank from it himself with his children and his flocks?"* [13] Jesus answered and said to her, "Everyone who drinks this water will be thirsty again; [14] but whoever drinks the water I shall give will never thirst; the water I shall give will become in him a spring of water welling up to eternal life."* [15] The woman said to him, "Sir, give me this water, so that I may not be thirsty or have to keep coming here to draw water."

[16] Jesus said to her, "Go call your husband and come back." [17] The woman answered and said to him, "I do not have a husband." Jesus answered her, "You are right in saying, 'I do not have a husband.' [18] For you have had five husbands, and the one you have now is not your husband. What you have said is true."* [19] The woman said to him, "Sir, I can see that you are a prophet.* [20] Our ancestors worshiped on this mountain;† but you people say that the place to worship is in Jerusalem."* [21] Jesus said to her, "Believe me, woman, the hour is coming when you will worship the Father neither on this mountain nor in Jerusalem. [22] You people worship what you do not understand; we worship what we understand, because salvation is from the Jews.* [23] But the hour is coming, and is now here, when true worshipers will worship the Father in Spirit and truth;† and indeed the Father seeks such people to worship him. [24] God is Spirit, and those who worship him must worship in Spirit and truth."* [25]† The woman said to him, "I know that the Messiah is coming,* the one called the Anointed; when he comes, he will tell us everything." [26] Jesus said to her, "I am he,† the one who is speaking with you."*

[27] At that moment his disciples returned, and were amazed that he was talking with a woman,† but still no one said, "What are you looking for?" or "Why are you talking with

---

**4:1–42** Jesus in Samaria. The self-revelation of Jesus continues with his second discourse, on his mission to "half-Jews." It continues the theme of replacement, here with regard to cult (Jn 4:21). Water (Jn 4:7–15) serves as a symbol (as at Cana and in the Nicodemus episode).

**4:2** An editorial refinement of Jn 3:22, perhaps directed against followers of John the Baptist who claimed that Jesus imitated him.

**4:4** *He had to:* a theological necessity; geographically, Jews often bypassed Samaria by taking a route across the Jordan.

**4:5** *Sychar:* Jerome identifies this with Shechem, a reading found in Syriac manuscripts.

**4:9** Samaritan women were regarded by Jews as ritually impure, and therefore Jews were forbidden to drink from any vessel they had handled.

**4:10** *Living water:* the water of life, i.e., the revelation that Jesus brings; the woman thinks of "flowing water," so much more desirable than stagnant well water. On John's device of such misunderstanding, cf. note on Jn 3:3.

**4:11** *Sir:* the Greek *kyrios* means "master" or "lord," as a respectful mode of address for a human being or a deity; cf. Jn 4:19. It is also the word used in the Septuagint for the Hebrew *'adōnai*, substituted for the tetragrammaton YHWH.

**4:20** *This mountain:* Gerizim, on which a temple was erected in the fourth century B.C. by Samaritans to rival Mount Zion in Jerusalem; cf. Dt 27:4 (Mount Ebal = the Jews' term for Gerizim).

**4:23** *In Spirit and truth:* not a reference to an interior worship within one's own spirit. The Spirit is the spirit given by God that reveals truth and enables one to worship God appropriately (Jn 14:16–17). Cf. "born of water and Spirit" (Jn 3:5).

**4:25** The expectations of the Samaritans are expressed here in Jewish terminology. They did not expect a messianic king of the house of David but a prophet like Moses (Dt 18:15).

**4:26** *I am he:* it could also be translated "I am," an Old Testament self-designation of Yahweh (Is 43:3, etc.); cf. Jn 6:20; 8:24, 28, 58; 13:19; 18:5–6, 8. See note on Mk 6:50.

**4:27** *Talking with a woman:* a religious and social restriction that Jesus is pictured treating as unimportant.

---

| | |
|---|---|
| **4:5** Gn 33:18–19; 48:22; Jos 24:32. | **4:18** 2 Kgs 17:24–34. |
| **4:9** Sir 50:25–26; Mt 10:5. | **4:19** 9:17; Hos 1:3. |
| **4:10** Sir 24:20–21; Is 55:1; Jer 2:13. | **4:20** Dt 11:29; 27:4; Jos 8:33; Ps 122:1–5. |
| **4:12** 8:53; Mt 12:41. | **4:22** 2 Kgs 17:27; Ps 76:2–3. |
| **4:14** 6:35, 58; 7:37–39; Is 44:3; 49:10; Jl 4:18; Rev 7:16; 21:6. | **4:24** 2 Cor 3:17. |
| | **4:25** 1:41. |
| | **4:26** 9:37. |

her?" 28 The woman left her water jar and went into the town and said to the people, 29 "Come see a man who told me everything I have done. Could he possibly be the Messiah?" 30 They went out of the town and came to him. 31 Meanwhile, the disciples urged him, "Rabbi, eat." 32 But he said to them, "I have food to eat of which you do not know." 33 So the disciples said to one another, "Could someone have brought him something to eat?" 34 Jesus said to them, "My food is to do the will of the one who sent me and to finish his work.* 35 Do you not say, 'In four months† the harvest will be here'? I tell you, look up and see the fields ripe for the harvest.* 36 The reaper is already† receiving his payment and gathering crops for eternal life, so that the sower and reaper can rejoice together.* 37 For here the saying is verified that 'One sows and another reaps.'* 38 I sent you to reap what you have not worked for; others have done the work, and you are sharing the fruits of their work."

39 Many of the Samaritans of that town began to believe in him because of the word of the woman† who testified, "He told me everything I have done." 40 When the Samaritans came to him, they invited him to stay with them; and he stayed there two days. 41 Many more began to believe in him because of his word, 42 and they said to the woman, "We no longer believe because of your word; for we have heard for ourselves, and we know that this is truly the savior of the world."*

**Return to Galilee.** 43† After the two days, he left there for Galilee. 44†* For Jesus himself

testified that a prophet has no honor in his native place. 45 When he came into Galilee, the Galileans welcomed him, since they had seen all he had done in Jerusalem at the feast; for they themselves had gone to the feast.

**Second Sign at Cana.**† 46* Then he returned to Cana in Galilee, where he had made the water wine. Now there was a royal official whose son was ill in Capernaum. 47 When he heard that Jesus had arrived in Galilee from Judea, he went to him and asked him to come down and heal his son, who was near death. 48 Jesus said to him, "Unless you people see signs and wonders, you will not believe."* 49 The royal official said to him, "Sir, come down before my child dies." 50 Jesus said to him, "You may go; your son will live." The man believed what Jesus said to him and left.* 51 While he was on his way back, his slaves met him and told him that his boy would live. 52 He asked them when he began to recover. They told him, "The fever left him yesterday, about one in the afternoon." 53 The father realized that just at that time Jesus had said to him, "Your son will live," and he and his whole household came to believe. 54 [Now] this was the second sign Jesus did when he came to Galilee from Judea.*

**5** † **Cure on a Sabbath.** 1 After this, there was a feast† of the Jews, and Jesus went up to Jerusalem.* 2 Now there is in Jerusalem at the Sheep [Gate]† a pool called in Hebrew Bethesda, with five porticoes.* 3 In these lay a large number of ill, blind, lame, and

---

**4:35** 'In four months…': probably a proverb; cf. Mt 9:37–38.
**4:36** Already: this word may go with the preceding verse rather than with Jn 4:36.
**4:39** The woman is presented as a missionary, described in virtually the same words as the disciples are in Jesus' prayer (Jn 17:20).
**4:43–54** Jesus' arrival in Cana in Galilee; the second sign. This section introduces another theme, that of the life-giving word of Jesus. It is explicitly linked to the first sign (Jn 2:11). The royal official believes (Jn 4:50). The natural life given his son is a sign of eternal life.
**4:44** Probably a reminiscence of a tradition as in Mk 6:4. Cf. Gospel of Thomas 31: "No prophet is acceptable in his village, no physician heals those who know him."
**4:46–54** The story of the cure of the royal official's son may be a third version of the cure of the centurion's son (Mt 8:5–13) or servant (Lk 7:1–10). Cf. also Mt 15:21–28; Mk 7:24–30.
**5:1–47** The self-revelation of Jesus continues in Jerusalem at a feast. The third sign (Jn 2:11; 4:54) is performed, the cure of a paralytic by Jesus' life-giving word. The water of the pool fails to bring life; Jesus' word does.
**5:1** The reference in Jn 5:45–46 to Moses suggests that the feast was Pentecost. The connection of that feast with the giving

of the law to Moses on Sinai, attested in later Judaism, may already have been made in the first century. The feast could also be Passover (cf. Jn 6:4). John stresses that the day was a sabbath (Jn 5:9).
**5:2** There is no noun with Sheep. "Gate" is supplied on the grounds that there must have been a gate in the NE wall of the temple area where animals for sacrifice were brought in; cf. Neh 3:1, 32; 12:39. Hebrew: more precisely, Aramaic. Bethesda: preferred to variants "Be(th)zatha" and "Bethsaida"; bêt-'ešdatayin is given as the name of a double pool northeast of the temple area in the Qumran Copper Roll. Five porticoes: a pool excavated in Jerusalem actually has five porticoes.

---

| | |
|---|---|
| **4:34** 5:30, 36; 6:38; 9:4; 17:4. | Lk 4:24. |
| **4:35** Mt 9:37–38; Lk 10:2; Rev 14:15. | **4:46–54** 2:1–11; Mt 8:5–13; 15:21–28; Mk 7:24–30; Lk 7:1–10. |
| **4:36** Ps 126:5–6; Am 9:13–14. | **4:48** 2:18, 23; Wis 8:8; Mt 12:38; 1 Cor 1:22. |
| **4:37** Dt 20:6; 28:30; Jb 31:8; Mi 6:15. | **4:50** 1 Kgs 17:23. |
| **4:42** 1 Jn 4:14. | **4:54** 2:11. |
| **4:44** Mt 13:57; Mk 6:4; | **5:1** 6:4. |
| | **5:2** Neh 3:1, 32; 12:39. |

JN

crippled.† [4]† [5] One man was there who had been ill for thirty-eight years. [6] When Jesus saw him lying there and knew that he had been ill for a long time, he said to him, "Do you want to be well?" [7] The sick man answered him, "Sir, I have no one to put me into the pool when the water is stirred up; while I am on my way, someone else gets down there before me." [8] Jesus said to him, "Rise, take up your mat, and walk."* [9] Immediately the man became well, took up his mat, and walked.*

Now that day was a sabbath. [10] So the Jews said to the man who was cured, "It is the sabbath, and it is not lawful for you to carry your mat."* [11] He answered them, "The man who made me well told me, 'Take up your mat and walk.'" [12] They asked him, "Who is the man who told you, 'Take it up and walk'?" [13] The man who was healed did not know who it was, for Jesus had slipped away, since there was a crowd there.* [14]† After this Jesus found him in the temple area and said to him,* "Look, you are well; do not sin any more, so that nothing worse may happen to you." [15] The man went and told the Jews that Jesus was the one who had made him well. [16] Therefore, the Jews began to persecute Jesus because he did this on a sabbath.* [17]† But Jesus answered them,* "My Father is at work until now, so I am at work." [18] For this reason the Jews tried all the more to kill him, because he not only broke the sabbath but he also called God his own father, making himself equal to God.*

**The Work of the Son.** [19]† Jesus answered and said to them, "Amen, amen, I say to you, a son cannot do anything on his own, but only what he sees his father doing;* for what he does, his son will do also. [20] For the Father loves his Son and shows him everything that he himself does, and he will show him greater works than these, so that you may be amazed.* [21] For just as the Father raises the dead and gives life,† so also does the Son give life to whomever he wishes.* [22] Nor does the Father judge anyone, but he has given all judgment† to his Son,* [23] so that all may honor the Son just as they honor the Father. Whoever does not honor the Son does not honor the Father who sent him. [24] Amen, amen, I say to you, whoever hears my word and believes in the one who sent me has eternal life and will not come to condemnation, but has passed from death to life.* [25] Amen, amen, I say to you, the hour is coming and is now here when the dead will hear the voice of the Son of God, and those who hear will live.* [26] For just as the Father has life in himself, so also he gave to his Son the possession of life in himself.* [27] And he gave him power to exercise judgment, because he is the Son of Man.* [28]† Do not be amazed at this, because the hour is coming in which all who are in the tombs will hear his voice* [29] and will come out, those who have done good deeds to the resurrection of life, but those who have done wicked deeds to the resurrection of condemnation.*

---

**5:3** The Caesarean and Western recensions, followed by the Vulgate, add "waiting for the movement of the water." Apparently an intermittent spring in the pool bubbled up occasionally (see Jn 5:7). This turbulence was believed to cure.

**5:4** Toward the end of the second century in the West and among the fourth-century Greek Fathers, an additional verse was known: "For [from time to time] an angel of the Lord used to come down into the pool; and the water was stirred up, so the first one to get in [after the stirring of the water] was healed of whatever disease afflicted him." The angel was a popular explanation of the turbulence and the healing powers attributed to it. This verse is missing from all early Greek manuscripts and the earliest versions, including the original Vulgate. Its vocabulary is markedly non-Johannine.

**5:14** While the cure of the paralytic in Mk 2:1–12 is associated with the forgiveness of sins, Jesus never drew a one-to-one connection between sin and suffering (cf. Jn 9:3; Lk 12:1–5), as did Ez 18:20.

**5:17** Sabbath observance (Jn 5:10) was based on God's resting on the seventh day (cf. Gn 2:2–3; Ex 20:11). Philo and some rabbis insisted that God's providence remains active on the sabbath, keeping all things in existence, giving life in birth and taking it away in death. Other rabbis taught that God rested from creating, but not from judging (= ruling, governing). Jesus here claims the same authority to work as the Father, and, in the discourse that follows, the same divine prerogatives: power over life and death (Jn 5:21, 24–26) and judgment (Jn 5:22, 27).

**5:19** This proverb or parable is taken from apprenticeship in a trade: the activity of a son is modeled on that of his father. Jesus' dependence on the Father is justification for doing what the Father does.

**5:21** *Gives life*: in the Old Testament, a divine prerogative (Dt 32:39; 1 Sm 2:6; 2 Kgs 5:7; Tb 13:2; Is 26:19; Dn 12:2).

**5:22** *Judgment*: another divine prerogative, often expressed as acquittal or condemnation (Dt 32:36; Ps 43:1).

**5:28–29** While Jn 5:19–27 present realized eschatology, Jn 5:28–29 are future eschatology; cf. Dn 12:2.

---

| | |
|---|---|
| **5:8** Mt 9:6; Mk 2:11; Lk 5:24; Acts 3:6. | **5:20** 3:35. |
| **5:9** Mk 2:12; Lk 5:25; 9:14. | **5:21** 11:25; Dt 32:39; 1 Sm 2:6; 2 Kgs 5:7; Tb 13:2; Wis 16:13; Is 26:19; Dn 7:10, 13; 12:2; Rom 4:17; 2 Cor 1:9. |
| **5:10** Ex 20:8; Jer 17:21–27; Mk 3:2; Lk 13:10; 14:1. | |
| **5:13** Mt 8:18; 13:36; Mk 4:36; 7:17. | **5:22** Acts 10:42; 17:31. |
| **5:14** 8:11; 9:2; Ez 18:20. | **5:24** 3:18; 8:51; 1 Jn 3:14. |
| **5:16** 7:23; Mt 12:8. | **5:25** 5:28; 8:51; 11:25–26; Eph 2:1; 5:14; Rev 3:1. |
| **5:17** Ex 20:11. | **5:26** 1:4; 1 Jn 5:11. |
| **5:18** 7:1, 25; 8:37, 40; 10:33, 36; 14:28; Gn 3:5–6; Wis 2:16; Mt 26:4; 2 Thes 2:4. | **5:27** 5:22; Dn 7:13, 22; Mt 25:31; Lk 21:36. |
| **5:19** 3:34; 8:26; 12:49; 9:4; 10:30. | **5:28** 11:43. |
| | **5:29** Dn 12:2; Mt 16:27; 25:46; Acts 24:15; 2 Cor 5:10. |

JN

30 "I cannot do anything on my own; I judge as I hear, and my judgment is just, because I do not seek my own will but the will of the one who sent me.*

**Witnesses to Jesus.** 31*"If I testify on my own behalf, my testimony cannot be verified. 32 But there is another† who testifies on my behalf, and I know that the testimony he gives on my behalf is true. 33 You sent emissaries to John, and he testified to the truth.* 34 I do not accept testimony from a human being, but I say this so that you may be saved.* 35 He was a burning and shining lamp,† and for a while you were content to rejoice in his light.* 36 But I have testimony greater than John's. The works that the Father gave me to accomplish, these works that I perform testify on my behalf that the Father has sent me.* 37 Moreover, the Father who sent me has testified on my behalf. But you have never heard his voice nor seen his form,* 38 and you do not have his word remaining in you, because you do not believe in the one whom he has sent.* 39 You search† the scriptures, because you think you have eternal life through them; even they testify on my behalf.* 40 But you do not want to come to me to have life.

**Unbelief of Jesus' Hearers.** 41 "I do not accept human praise;† 42 moreover, I know that you do not have the love of God in you.* 43 I came in the name of my Father, but you do not accept me; yet if another comes in his own name, you will accept him.* 44 How can you believe, when you accept praise from one another and do not seek the praise that comes from the only God?* 45 Do not think that I will accuse you before the Father: the one who will accuse you is Moses, in whom you have placed your hope.* 46 For if you had believed Moses, you would have believed me, because he wrote about me.* 47 But if you do not believe his writings, how will you believe my words?"

**6 Multiplication of the Loaves.**† 1*After this, Jesus went across the Sea of Galilee [of Tiberias].† 2 A large crowd followed him, because they saw the signs he was performing on the sick. 3 Jesus went up on the mountain, and there he sat down with his disciples. 4 The Jewish feast of Passover was near.* 5† When Jesus raised his eyes and saw that a large crowd was coming to him, he said to Philip,* "Where can we buy enough food for them to eat?" 6† He said this to test him, because he himself knew what he was going to do. 7 Philip answered him, "Two hundred days' wages† worth of food would not be enough for each of them to have a little [bit]."* 8 One of his disciples, Andrew, the brother of Simon Peter, said to him, 9 "There is a boy here who has five barley loaves† and two fish; but what good are these for so many?"* 10 Jesus said, "Have the people recline." Now there was a great deal of grass† in that place. So the men reclined, about five thousand in number.* 11 Then Jesus took the loaves, gave thanks, and distributed

---

**5:32** *Another*: likely the Father, who in four different ways gives testimony to Jesus, as indicated in the verse groupings Jn 5:33–34, 36, 37–38, 39–40.

**5:35** *Lamp*: cf. Ps 132:17—"I will place a lamp for my anointed (= David)," and possibly the description of Elijah in Sir 48:1. But only *for a while*, indicating the temporary and subordinate nature of John's mission.

**5:39** *You search*: this may be an imperative: "Search the scriptures, because you think that you have eternal life through them."

**5:41** *Praise*: the same Greek word means "praise" or "honor" (from others) and "glory" (from God). There is a play on this in Jn 5:44.

**6:1–15** This story of the multiplication of the loaves is the fourth sign (cf. note on Jn 5:1–47). It is the only miracle story found in all four gospels (occurring twice in Mark and Matthew). See notes on Mt 14:13–21; 15:32–39. John differs on the roles of Philip and Andrew, the proximity of Passover (Jn 6:4), and the allusion to Elisha (see Jn 6:9). The story here symbolizes the food that is really available through Jesus. It connotes a new exodus and has eucharistic overtones.

**6:1** *[Of Tiberias]*: the awkward apposition represents a later name of the Sea of Galilee. It was probably originally a marginal gloss.

**6:5** Jesus takes the initiative (in the synoptics, the disciples

do), possibly pictured as (cf. Jn 6:14) the new Moses (cf. Nm 11:13).

**6:6** Probably the evangelist's comment; in this gospel Jesus is never portrayed as ignorant of anything.

**6:7** *Days' wages*: literally, "denarii"; a Roman denarius is a day's wage in Mt 20:2.

**6:9** *Barley loaves*: the food of the poor. There seems an allusion to the story of Elisha multiplying the barley bread in 2 Kgs 4:42–44.

**6:10** *Grass*: implies springtime, and therefore Passover. *Five thousand*: so Mk 6:39, 44 and parallels.

---

| | |
|---|---|
| **5:30** 6:38. | **5:42** 1 Jn 2:15. |
| **5:31–32** 8:13–14, 18. | **5:43** Mt 24:5, 24. |
| **5:33** 1:19–27; Mt | **5:44** 12:43. |
| 11:10–11. | **5:45** Dt 31:26. |
| **5:34** 1 Jn 5:9. | **5:46** 5:39; Dt 18:15; Lk |
| **5:35** 1:8; Ps 132:17; Sir | 16:31; 24:44. |
| 48:1. | **6:1–13** Mt 14:13–21; Mk |
| **5:36** 10:25. | 6:32–44; Lk 9:10–17. |
| **5:37** 8:18; Dt 4:12, 15; 1 Jn | **6:4** 2:13; 11:55. |
| 5:9. | **6:5** Nm 11:13. |
| **5:38** 1 Jn 2:14. | **6:7** Mt 20:2. |
| **5:39** 12:16; 19:28; 20:9; Lk | **6:9** 2 Kgs 4:42–44. |
| 24:27, 44; 1 Pt 1:10. | **6:10** Mt 14:21; Mk 6:44. |

JN

© Anselm Academic / Brian Singer-Towns

In Mt 14:13–21, Mk 6:34–44, and Jn 6:1–15, Jesus feeds the multitudes by multiplying five loaves and two fish. Above, the loaves and fish are depicted in a famous fifth-century mosaic by the Lake of Galilee.

them to those who were reclining, and also as much of the fish as they wanted.* ¹²When they had had their fill, he said to his disciples, "Gather the fragments left over, so that nothing will be wasted." ¹³So they collected them, and filled twelve wicker baskets† with fragments from the five barley loaves that had been more than they could eat. ¹⁴When the people saw the sign he had done, they said, "This is truly the Prophet,† the one who is to come into the world."* ¹⁵Since Jesus knew that they were going to come and carry him off to make him king, he withdrew again to the mountain alone.*

**Walking on the Water.**† ¹⁶*When it was evening, his disciples went down to the sea, ¹⁷embarked in a boat, and went across the sea to Capernaum. It had already grown dark, and Jesus had not yet come to them. ¹⁸The sea was stirred up because a strong wind was blowing. ¹⁹When they had rowed about three or four miles, they saw Jesus walking on the sea† and coming near the boat, and they began to be afraid.* ²⁰But he said to them, "It is I.† Do not be afraid." ²¹They wanted to take him into the boat, but the boat immediately arrived at the shore to which they were heading.

**The Bread of Life Discourse.** ²²† The next day, the crowd that remained across the sea saw that there had been only one boat there, and that Jesus had not gone along with his disciples in the boat, but only his disciples had left. ²³† Other boats came from Tiberias near the place where they had eaten the bread when the Lord gave thanks. ²⁴When the crowd saw that neither Jesus nor his disciples were there, they themselves got into boats and came to Capernaum looking for Jesus. ²⁵And when they found him across the sea they said to him, "Rabbi, when did you get here?" ²⁶Jesus answered them and said, "Amen, amen, I say to you, you are looking for me not because you saw signs but because you ate the loaves and were filled. ²⁷Do not work for food that perishes but for the food that endures for eternal life,† which the Son of Man will give you. For on him the Father, God, has set his seal."* ²⁸So they said to him, "What can we do to accomplish the works of God?" ²⁹Jesus answered and said to them, "This is the work of God, that you believe in the one he sent." ³⁰So they said to him, "What sign can you do, that we may see and believe in you? What can you do?* ³¹† Our ancestors ate manna in the desert, as it is written:*

> 'He gave them bread from heaven to eat.'"

† **6:13** *Baskets:* the word describes the typically Palestinian wicker basket, as in Mk 6:43 and parallels.

**6:14** *The Prophet:* probably the prophet like Moses (see note on Jn 1:21). *The one who is to come into the world:* probably Elijah; cf. Mal 3:1, 23.

**6:16–21** The fifth sign is a nature miracle, portraying Jesus sharing Yahweh's power. Cf. the parallel stories following the multiplication of the loaves in Mk 6:45–52 and Mt 14:22–33.

**6:19** *Walking on the sea:* although the Greek (cf. Jn 6:16) could mean "on the seashore" or "by the sea" (cf. Jn 21:1), the parallels, especially Mt 14:25, make clear that Jesus walked upon the water. John may allude to Jb 9:8: God "treads upon the crests of the sea."

**6:20** *It is I:* literally, "I am." See also notes on Jn 4:26 and Mk 6:50.

**6:22–71** Discourse on the bread of life; replacement of the manna. Jn 6:22–34 serve as an introduction, Jn 6:35–59 consti-

tute the discourse proper, Jn 6:60–71 portray the reaction of the disciples and Peter's confession.

**6:23** Possibly a later interpolation, to explain how the crowd got to Capernaum.

**6:27** *The food that endures for eternal life:* cf. Jn 4:14, on water "springing up to eternal life."

**6:31** *Bread from heaven:* cf. Ex 16:4, 15, 32–34 and the notes there; Ps 78:24. The manna, thought to have been hidden by Jeremiah (2 Mc 2:5–8), was expected to reappear miraculously at Passover, in the last days.

**6:11** 21:13.
**6:14** Dt 18:15, 18; Mal 3:1, 23; Acts 3:22.
**6:15** 18:36.
**6:16–21** Mt 14:22–27; Mk 6:45–52.
**6:19** Jb 9:8; Ps 29:3–4; 77:20; Is 43:16.
**6:27** 6:50, 51, 54, 58.
**6:30** Mt 16:1–4; Lk 11:29–30.
**6:31** Ex 16:4–5; Nm 11:7–9; Ps 78:24.

JN

³² So Jesus said to them, "Amen, amen, I say to you, it was not Moses who gave the bread from heaven; my Father gives you the true bread from heaven.* ³³ For the bread of God is that which comes down from heaven and gives life to the world."

³⁴* So they said to him, "Sir, give us this bread always." ³⁵† Jesus said to them, "I am the bread of life; whoever comes to me will never hunger, and whoever believes in me will never thirst.* ³⁶ But I told you that although you have seen [me], you do not believe.* ³⁷ Everything that the Father gives me will come to me, and I will not reject anyone who comes to me, ³⁸ because I came down from heaven not to do my own will but the will of the one who sent me.* ³⁹ And this is the will of the one who sent me, that I should not lose anything of what he gave me, but that I should raise it [on] the last day.* ⁴⁰ For this is the will of my Father, that everyone who sees the Son and believes in him may have eternal life, and I shall raise him [on] the last day."*

⁴¹ The Jews murmured about him because he said, "I am the bread that came down from heaven," ⁴² and they said, "Is this not Jesus, the son of Joseph? Do we not know his father and mother? Then how can he say, 'I have come down from heaven'?"* ⁴³ Jesus answered and said to them, "Stop murmuring† among yourselves.* ⁴⁴ No one can come to me unless the Father who sent me draw him, and I will raise him on the last day. ⁴⁵ It is written in the prophets:

'They shall all be taught by God.'

Everyone who listens to my Father and learns from him comes to me.* ⁴⁶ Not that anyone has seen the Father except the one who is from God; he has seen the Father.* ⁴⁷ Amen, amen, I say to you, whoever believes has eternal life. ⁴⁸ I am the bread of life. ⁴⁹ Your ancestors ate the manna in the desert, but they died;* ⁵⁰ this is the bread that comes down from heaven so that one may eat it and not die. ⁵¹ I am the living bread that came down from heaven; whoever eats this bread will live forever; and the bread that I will give is my flesh for the life of the world."*

⁵² The Jews quarreled among themselves, saying, "How can this man give us [his] flesh to eat?" ⁵³ Jesus said to them, "Amen, amen, I say to you, unless you eat the flesh of the Son of Man and drink his blood, you do not have life within you. ⁵⁴ Whoever eats† my flesh and drinks my blood has eternal life, and I will raise him on the last day. ⁵⁵ For my flesh is true food, and my blood is true drink. ⁵⁶ Whoever eats my flesh and drinks my blood remains in me and I in him. ⁵⁷ Just as the living Father sent me and I have life because of the Father, so also the one who feeds on me will have life because of me.* ⁵⁸ This is the bread that came down from heaven. Unlike your ancestors who ate and still died, whoever eats this bread will live forever." ⁵⁹ These things he said while teaching in the synagogue in Capernaum.

**The Words of Eternal Life.**† ⁶⁰ Then many of his disciples who were listening said, "This saying is hard; who can accept it?" ⁶¹ Since Jesus knew that his disciples were murmuring about this, he said to them, "Does this shock you? ⁶² What if you were to see the Son of Man ascending to where he was before?† ⁶³ It is the spirit that gives life, while the flesh† is of no avail. The words I have spoken to you are spirit and life. ⁶⁴ But there are some of you who do not believe." Jesus knew from the beginning the

---

†

**6:35–59** Up to Jn 6:50 "bread of life" is a figure for God's revelation in Jesus; in Jn 6:51–58, the eucharistic theme comes to the fore. There may thus be a break between Jn 6:50–51.

**6:43** *Murmuring:* the word may reflect the Greek of Ex 16:2, 7–8.

**6:54–58** *Eats:* the verb used in these verses is not the classical Greek verb used of human eating, but that of animal eating: "munch," "gnaw." This may be part of John's emphasis on the reality of the flesh and blood of Jesus (cf. Jn 6:55), but the same verb eventually became the ordinary verb in Greek meaning "eat."

**6:60–71** These verses refer more to themes of Jn 6:35–50 than to those of Jn 6:51–58 and seem to be addressed to members of the Johannine community who found it difficult to accept the high christology reflected in the bread of life discourse.

**6:62** This unfinished conditional sentence is obscure. Probably there is a reference to Jn 6:49–51. Jesus claims to be *the bread that comes down from heaven* (Jn 6:50); this claim provokes incredulity (Jn 6:60); and so Jesus is pictured as asking what his disciples will say when he goes up to heaven.

**6:63** *Spirit...flesh:* probably not a reference to the eucharistic body of Jesus but to the supernatural and the natural, as in Jn 3:6. *Spirit and life:* all Jesus said about the bread of life is the revelation of the Spirit.

---

| | |
|---|---|
| **6:32** Mt 6:11. | **6:42** Mt 13:54–57; Mk |
| **6:34** 4:15. | 6:1–4; Lk 4:22. |
| **6:35** Is 55:1–3; Am | **6:43** Ex 16:2, 7, 8; Lk 4:22. |
| 8:11–13. | **6:45** Is 54:13; Jer |
| **6:36** 20:29. | 31:33–34. |
| **6:38** 4:34; Mt 26:39; Heb | **6:46** 1:18; 7:29; Ex 33:20. |
| 10:9. | **6:49** 1 Cor 10:3, 5. |
| **6:39** 10:28–29; 17:12; | **6:51** Mt 26:26–27; Lk |
| 18:9. | 22:19. |
| **6:40** 1 Jn 2:25. | **6:57** 5:26. |

ones who would not believe and the one who would betray him.* [65] And he said, "For this reason I have told you that no one can come to me unless it is granted him by my Father."

[66] As a result of this, many [of] his disciples returned to their former way of life and no longer accompanied him. [67] Jesus then said to the Twelve, "Do you also want to leave?" [68] Simon Peter answered him, "Master, to whom shall we go? You have the words of eternal life. [69] We have come to believe and are convinced that you are the Holy One of God."* [70] Jesus answered them, "Did I not choose you twelve? Yet is not one of you a devil?" [71] He was referring to Judas, son of Simon the Iscariot; it was he who would betray him, one of the Twelve.*

# 7 The Feast of Tabernacles. [1]† After this, Jesus moved about within Galilee; but he did not wish to travel in Judea, because the Jews were trying to kill him.* [2] But the Jewish feast of Tabernacles was near.* [3] So his brothers† said to him, "Leave here and go to Judea, so that your disciples also may see the works you are doing. [4] No one works in secret if he wants to be known publicly. If you do these things, manifest yourself to the world."* [5] For his brothers did not believe in him. [6]† So Jesus said to them, "My time is not yet here, but the time is always right for you. [7] The world cannot hate you, but it hates me, because I testify to it that its works are evil.* [8] You go up to the feast. I am not going up† to this feast, because my time has not yet been fulfilled." [9] After he had said this, he stayed on in Galilee.

[10] But when his brothers had gone up to the feast, he himself also went up, not openly but [as it were] in secret. [11] The Jews were looking for him at the feast and saying, "Where is he?" [12] And there was considerable murmuring about him in the crowds. Some said, "He is a good man," [while] others said, "No; on the contrary, he misleads the crowd." [13] Still, no one spoke openly about him because they were afraid of the Jews.*

**The First Dialogue.**† [14] When the feast was already half over, Jesus went up into the temple area and began to teach. [15]†* The Jews were amazed and said, "How does he know scripture without having studied?" [16] Jesus answered them and said, "My teaching is not my own but is from the one who sent me. [17] Whoever chooses to do his will† shall know whether my teaching is from God or whether I speak on my own.* [18] Whoever speaks on his own seeks his own glory, but whoever seeks the glory of the one who sent him is truthful, and there is no wrong in him. [19] Did not Moses give you the law? Yet none of you keeps the law. Why are you trying to kill me?"* [20] The crowd answered, "You are possessed!† Who is trying to kill you?"* [21] Jesus answered and said to them, "I performed one work† and all of you are amazed* [22] because of it. Moses gave you circumcision—not that it came from Moses but rather from the patriarchs—and you circumcise a man on the sabbath.* [23] If a man can receive circumcision on a sabbath so that the law of Moses may not be broken, are you

---

† **7–8** These chapters contain events about the feast of Tabernacles (Sukkoth, Ingathering: Ex 23:16; Tents, Booths: Dt 16:13–16), with its symbols of booths (originally built to shelter harvesters), rain (water from Siloam poured on the temple altar), and lights (illumination of the four torches in the Court of the Women). They continue the theme of the replacement of feasts (Passover, Jn 2:13; 6:4; Hanukkah, Jn 10:22; Pentecost, Jn 5:1), here accomplished by Jesus as the Living Water. These chapters comprise seven miscellaneous controversies and dialogues. There is a literary inclusion with Jesus in hiding in Jn 7:4, 10; 8:59. There are frequent references to attempts on his life: Jn 7:1, 13, 19, 25, 30, 32, 44; 8:37, 40, 59.

**7:3** *Brothers:* these relatives (cf. Jn 2:12 and see note on Mk 6:3) are never portrayed as disciples until after the resurrection (Acts 1:14). Mt 13:55 and Mk 6:3 give the names of four of them. Jesus has already performed works/signs in Judea; cf. Jn 2:23; 3:2; 4:45; 5:8.

**7:6** *Time:* the Greek word means "opportune time," here a synonym for Jesus' "hour" (see note on Jn 2:4), his death and resurrection. In the wordplay, any time is suitable for Jesus' brothers, because they are not dependent on God's will.

**7:8** *I am not going up:* an early attested reading "not yet" seems a correction, since Jesus in the story does go up to the feast. "Go up," in a play on words, refers not only to going up

to Jerusalem but also to exaltation at the cross, resurrection, and ascension; cf. Jn 3:14; 6:62; 20:17.

**7:14–31** Jesus teaches in the temple; debate with the Jews.

**7:15** *Without having studied:* literally, "How does he know letters without having learned?" Children were taught to read and write by means of the scriptures. But here more than Jesus' literacy is being discussed; the people are wondering how he can teach like a rabbi. Rabbis were trained by other rabbis and traditionally quoted their teachers.

**7:17** *To do his will:* presumably a reference back to the "work" of Jn 6:29: belief in the one whom God has sent.

**7:20** *You are possessed:* literally, "You have a demon." The insane were thought to be possessed by a demoniacal spirit.

**7:21** *One work:* the cure of the paralytic (Jn 5:1–9) because of the reference to the sabbath (Jn 7:22; 5:9–10).

---

| | |
|---|---|
| **6:64** 13:11. | **7:7** 15:18. |
| **6:69** 11:27; Mt 16:16; Mk 1:24; Lk 4:34. | **7:13** 9:22; 19:38; 20:19. |
| **6:71** 12:4; 13:2, 27. | **7:15** Lk 2:47. |
| **7:1** 5:18; 8:37, 40. | **7:17** 6:29. |
| **7:2** Ex 23:16; Lv 23:34; Nm 29:12; Dt 16:13–16; Zec 14:16–19. | **7:19** Acts 7:53. |
| | **7:20** 8:48–49; 10:20. |
| | **7:21** 5:1–9. |
| **7:4** 14:22. | **7:22** Gn 17:10; Lv 12:3. |

angry with me because I made a whole person well on a sabbath?* ²⁴ Stop judging by appearances, but judge justly."*

²⁵ So some of the inhabitants of Jerusalem said, "Is he not the one they are trying to kill? ²⁶ And look, he is speaking openly and they say nothing to him. Could the authorities† have realized that he is the Messiah? ²⁷ But we know where he is from. When the Messiah comes, no one will know where he is from."* ²⁸ So Jesus cried out in the temple area as he was teaching and said, "You know me and also know where I am from. Yet I did not come on my own, but the one who sent me, whom you do not know, is true.* ²⁹ I know him, because I am from him, and he sent me."* ³⁰ So they tried to arrest him, but no one laid a hand upon him, because his hour had not yet come.* ³¹ But many of the crowd began to believe in him, and said, "When the Messiah comes, will he perform more signs than this man has done?"*

**Officers Sent to Arrest Jesus.**† ³² The Pharisees heard the crowd murmuring about him to this effect, and the chief priests and the Pharisees sent guards to arrest him. ³³ So Jesus said, "I will be with you only a little while longer, and then I will go to the one who sent me.* ³⁴ You will look for me but not find [me], and where I am you cannot come."* ³⁵ So the Jews said to one another, "Where is he going that we will not find him? Surely he is not going to the dispersion† among the Greeks to teach the Greeks, is he? ³⁶ What is the meaning of his saying, 'You will look for me and not find [me], and where I am you cannot come'?"

**Rivers of Living Water.**† ³⁷ On the last and greatest day of the feast, Jesus stood up and

exclaimed, "Let anyone who thirsts come to me and drink.* ³⁸ Whoever believes in me, as scripture says:

'Rivers of living water† will flow from within him.'"*

³⁹ He said this in reference to the Spirit that those who came to believe in him were to receive. There was, of course, no Spirit yet,† because Jesus had not yet been glorified.*

**Discussion About the Origins of the Messiah.**† ⁴⁰ Some in the crowd who heard these words said, "This is truly the Prophet."* ⁴¹ Others said, "This is the Messiah." But others said, "The Messiah will not come from Galilee, will he? ⁴² Does not scripture say that the Messiah will be of David's family and come from Bethlehem, the village where David lived?"* ⁴³ So a division occurred in the crowd because of him. ⁴⁴ Some of them even wanted to arrest him, but no one laid hands on him.

⁴⁵ So the guards went to the chief priests and Pharisees, who asked them, "Why did you not bring him?" ⁴⁶ The guards answered, "Never before has anyone spoken like this one." ⁴⁷ So the Pharisees answered them, "Have you also been deceived? ⁴⁸ Have any of the authorities or the Pharisees believed in him?* ⁴⁹ But this crowd, which does not know the law, is accursed." ⁵⁰ Nicodemus, one of their members who had come to him earlier, said to them,* ⁵¹ "Does our law condemn a person before it first hears him and finds out what he is doing?"* ⁵² They answered and said to him, "You are not from Galilee also, are you? Look and see that no prophet arises from Galilee."

---

**7:26** *The authorities*: the members of the Sanhedrin (same term as Jn 3:1).

**7:32–36** Jesus announces his approaching departure (cf. also Jn 8:21; 12:36; 13:33) and complete control over his destiny.

**7:35** *Dispersion*: or "diaspora": Jews living outside Palestine. *Greeks*: probably refers to the Gentiles in the Mediterranean area; cf. Jn 12:20.

**7:37, 39** Promise of living water through the Spirit.

**7:38** *Living water*: not an exact quotation from any Old Testament passage; in the gospel context the gift of the Spirit is meant; cf. Jn 3:5. *From within him*: either Jesus or the believer; if Jesus, it continues the Jesus-Moses motif (water from the rock, Ex 17:6; Nm 20:11) as well as Jesus as the new temple (cf. Ez 47:1). Grammatically, it goes better with the believer.

**7:39** *No Spirit yet*: Codex Vaticanus and early Latin, Syriac, and Coptic versions add "given." In this gospel, the sending of the Spirit cannot take place until Jesus' glorification through his death, resurrection, and ascension; cf. Jn 20:22.

**7:40–53** Discussion of the Davidic lineage of the Messiah.

| | |
|---|---|
| **7:23** 5:2–9, 16; Mt 12:11–12; Lk 14:5. | Prv 1:28; Is 55:6; Hos 5:6. |
| **7:24** 8:15; Lv 19:15; Is 11:3–4. | **7:37** Rev 21:6. |
| **7:27** Heb 7:3. | **7:38** 4:10, 14; 19:34; Is 12:3; Ez 47:1. |
| **7:28** 8:19. | **7:39** 16:7. |
| **7:29** 6:46; 8:55. | **7:40** Dt 18:15, 18. |
| **7:30** 7:44; 8:20; Lk 4:29–30. | **7:42** 2 Sm 7:12–14; Ps 89:3–4; 132:11; Mi 5:1; Mt 2:5–6. |
| **7:31** 2:11; 10:42; 11:45. | **7:48** 12:42. |
| **7:33** 13:33; 16:16. | **7:50** 3:1; 19:39. |
| **7:34** 8:21; 12:36; 13:33, 36; 16:5; Dt 4:29; | **7:51** Dt 1:16–17. |

**8** **A Woman Caught in Adultery.**† [⁷:⁵³Then each went to his own house, ¹while Jesus went to the Mount of Olives.†* ²But early in the morning he arrived again in the temple area, and all the people started coming to him, and he sat down and taught them. ³Then the scribes and the Pharisees brought a woman who had been caught in adultery and made her stand in the middle. ⁴They said to him, "Teacher, this woman was caught in the very act of committing adultery. ⁵Now in the law, Moses commanded us to stone such women.† So what do you say?"* ⁶They said this to test him, so that they could have some charge to bring against him. Jesus bent down and began to write on the ground with his finger.† ⁷†But when they continued asking him, he straightened up and said to them,* "Let the one among you who is without sin be the first to throw a stone at her." ⁸Again he bent down and wrote on the ground. ⁹And in response, they went away one by one, beginning with the elders. So he was left alone with the woman before him. ¹⁰Then Jesus straightened up and said to her, "Woman, where are they? Has no one condemned you?"* ¹¹She replied, "No one, sir." Then Jesus said, "Neither do I condemn you. Go, [and] from now on do not sin any more."]*

**The Light of the World.**† ¹²Jesus spoke to them again, saying, "I am the light of the world. Whoever follows me will not walk in darkness, but will have the light of life."* ¹³So the Pharisees said to him, "You testify on your own behalf, so your testimony cannot be verified." ¹⁴Jesus answered and said to them, "Even if I do testify on my own behalf, my testimony can be verified,† because I know where I came from and where I am going. But you do not know where I come from or where I am going.* ¹⁵You judge by appearances,† but I do not judge anyone.* ¹⁶And even if I should judge, my judgment is valid, because I am not alone, but it is I and the Father who sent me.* ¹⁷Even in your law† it is written that the testimony of two men can be verified.* ¹⁸I testify on my behalf and so does the Father who sent me."* ¹⁹So they said to him, "Where is your father?" Jesus answered, "You know neither me nor my Father. If you knew me, you would know my Father also."* ²⁰He spoke these words while teaching in the treasury in the temple area. But no one arrested him, because his hour had not yet come.*

**Jesus, the Father's Ambassador.**† ²¹He said to them again, "I am going away and you will look for me, but you will die in your sin.† Where I am going you cannot come."* ²²†So the Jews said, "He is not going to kill himself, is he, because he said, 'Where I am going you cannot come'?" ²³He said to them, "You belong to what is below, I belong to what is above. You belong to this world, but I do not belong to this world.* ²⁴That is why I told you

---

† **7:53–8:11** The story of the woman caught in adultery is a later insertion here, missing from all early Greek manuscripts. A Western text-type insertion, attested mainly in Old Latin translations, it is found in different places in different manuscripts: here, or after Jn 7:36 or at the end of this gospel, or after Lk 21:38, or at the end of that gospel. There are many non-Johannine features in the language, and there are also many doubtful readings within the passage. The style and motifs are similar to those of Luke, and it fits better with the general situation at the end of Lk 21, but it was probably inserted here because of the allusion to Jer 17:13 (cf. note on Jn 8:6) and the statement, "I do not judge anyone," in Jn 8:15. The Catholic Church accepts this passage as canonical scripture.

**8:1** *Mount of Olives*: not mentioned elsewhere in the gospel tradition outside of passion week.

**8:5** Lv 20:10 and Dt 22:22 mention only death, but Dt 22:23–24 prescribes stoning for a betrothed virgin.

**8:6** Cf. Jer 17:13 (RSV): "Those who turn away from thee shall be written in the earth, for they have forsaken the LORD, the fountain of living water"; cf. Jn 7:38.

**8:7** The first stones were to be thrown by the witnesses (Dt 17:7).

**8:12–20** Jesus the light of the world. Jesus replaces the four torches of the illumination of the temple as the light of joy.

**8:14** *My testimony can be verified*: this seems to contradict Jn 5:31, but the emphasis here is on Jesus' origin from the Father

and his divine destiny. *Where I am going*: indicates Jesus' passion and glorification.

**8:15** *By appearances*: literally, "according to the flesh." *I do not judge anyone*: superficial contradiction of Jn 5:22, 27, 30; here the emphasis is that the judgment is not by material standards.

**8:17** *Your law*: a reflection of later controversy between church and synagogue.

**8:21–30** He whose ambassador I am is with me. Jesus' origin is from God; he can reveal God.

**8:21** *You will die in your sin*: i.e., of disbelief; cf. Jn 8:24. *Where I am going you cannot come*: except through faith in Jesus' passion-resurrection.

**8:22** The Jews suspect that he is referring to his death. Johannine irony is apparent here; Jesus' death will not be self-inflicted but destined by God.

---

**8:1–2** Lk 21:37–38.
**8:5** Lv 20:10; Dt 22:22–29.
**8:7** Dt 17:7.
**8:10** Ez 33:11.
**8:11** 5:14.
**8:12** 1:4–5, 9; 12:46; Ex 13:22; Is 42:6; Zec 14:8.
**8:14** 5:31.

**8:15** 12:47; 1 Sm 16:7.
**8:16** 5:30.
**8:17** Dt 17:6; 19:15; Nm 35:30.
**8:18** 5:23, 37.
**8:19** 7:28; 14:7; 15:21.
**8:20** 7:30.
**8:21** 7:34; 13:33.
**8:23** 3:31; 17:14; 18:36.

that you will die in your sins. For if you do not believe that I AM,† you will die in your sins."* ²⁵† So they said to him, "Who are you?"* Jesus said to them, "What I told you from the beginning. ²⁶ I have much to say about you in condemnation. But the one who sent me is true, and what I heard from him I tell the world."* ²⁷ They did not realize that he was speaking to them of the Father. ²⁸ So Jesus said [to them], "When you lift up the Son of Man, then you will realize that I AM, and that I do nothing on my own, but I say only what the Father taught me.* ²⁹ The one who sent me is with me. He has not left me alone, because I always do what is pleasing to him." ³⁰ Because he spoke this way, many came to believe in him.

**Jesus and Abraham.**† ³¹ Jesus then said to those Jews who believed in him,† "If you remain in my word, you will truly be my disciples, ³² and you will know the truth, and the truth will set you free."* ³³ They answered him, "We are descendants of Abraham and have never been enslaved to anyone.† How can you say, 'You will become free'?"* ³⁴ Jesus answered them, "Amen, amen, I say to you, everyone who commits sin is a slave of sin.* ³⁵ A slave does not remain in a household forever, but a son† always remains.* ³⁶ So if a son frees you, then you will truly be free. ³⁷ I know that you are descendants of Abraham. But you are trying to kill me, because my word has no room among you. ³⁸† I tell you what I have seen in the Father's presence; then do what you have heard from the Father."

³⁹† They answered and said to him, "Our father is Abraham." Jesus said to them,* "If you were Abraham's children, you would be doing the works of Abraham. ⁴⁰ But now you are trying to kill me, a man who has told you the truth that I heard from God; Abraham did not do this. ⁴¹ You are doing the works of your father!" [So] they said to him, "We are not illegitimate. We have one Father, God."* ⁴² Jesus said to them, "If God were your Father, you would love me, for I came from God and am here; I did not come on my own, but he sent me.* ⁴³ Why do you not understand what I am saying? Because you cannot bear to hear my word. ⁴⁴ You belong to your father the devil and you willingly carry out your father's desires. He was a murderer from the beginning and does not stand in truth, because there is no truth in him. When he tells a lie, he speaks in character, because he is a liar and the father of lies.* ⁴⁵ But because I speak the truth, you do not believe me. ⁴⁶ Can any of you charge me with sin? If I am telling the truth, why do you not believe me?* ⁴⁷ Whoever belongs to God hears the words of God; for this reason you do not listen, because you do not belong to God."*

⁴⁸ The Jews answered and said to him, "Are we not right in saying that you are a Samaritan† and are possessed?" ⁴⁹ Jesus answered, "I am not possessed; I honor my Father, but you dishonor me. ⁵⁰ I do not seek my own glory; there is one who seeks it and he is the one who judges.* ⁵¹ Amen, amen, I say to you, whoever keeps my word will never see death."* ⁵² [So] the Jews said to him, "Now we are sure that you are possessed. Abraham died, as did the prophets, yet you say, 'Whoever keeps my word will never taste death.' ⁵³ Are you greater than our father Abraham,† who died? Or the prophets, who died? Who do you make

---

8:24, 28 *I AM:* an expression that late Jewish tradition understood as Yahweh's own self-designation (Is 43:10); see note on Jn 4:26. Jesus is here placed on a par with Yahweh.

8:25 *What I told you from the beginning:* this verse seems textually corrupt, with several other possible translations: "(I am) what I say to you"; "Why do I speak to you at all?" The earliest attested reading (Bodmer Papyrus P⁶⁶) has (in a second hand), "I told you at the beginning what I am also telling you (now)." The answer here (cf. Prv 8:22) seems to hinge on a misunderstanding of Jn 8:24 "that I AM" as "what I am."

8:31–59 Jesus' origin ("before Abraham") and destiny are developed; the truth will free them from sin (Jn 8:34) and death (Jn 8:51).

8:31 *Those Jews who believed in him:* a rough editorial suture, since in Jn 8:37 they are described as trying to kill Jesus.

8:33 *Have never been enslaved to anyone:* since, historically, the Jews were enslaved almost continuously, this verse is probably Johannine irony, about slavery to sin.

8:35 *A slave...a son:* an allusion to Ishmael and Isaac (Gn 16; 21), or to the release of a slave after six years (Ex 21:2; Dt 15:12).

8:38 *The Father:* i.e., God. It is also possible, however, to understand the second part of the verse as a sarcastic reference to descent of the Jews from the devil (Jn 8:44), "You do what you have heard from [your] father."

8:39 *The works of Abraham:* Abraham believed; cf. Rom 4:11–17; Jas 2:21–23.

8:48 *Samaritan:* therefore interested in magical powers; cf. Acts 7:14–24.

8:53 *Are you greater than our father Abraham?:* cf. Jn 4:12.

---

8:24 Ex 3:14; Dt 32:39; Is 43:10.
8:25 10:24.
8:26 12:44–50.
8:28 3:14; 12:32, 34.
8:32 Is 42:7; Gal 4:31.
8:33 Mt 3:9.
8:34 Rom 6:16–17.
8:35 Gn 21:10; Gal 4:30; Heb 3:5–6.
8:39 Gn 26:5; Rom 4:11–17; Jas 2:21–23.
8:41 Mal 2:10.
8:42 1 Jn 5:1.
8:44 Gn 3:4; Wis 1:13; 2:24; Acts 13:10; 1 Jn 3:8–15.
8:46 Heb 4:15; 1 Pt 2:22; 1 Jn 3:5.
8:47 10:26; 1 Jn 4:6.
8:50 7:18.
8:51 5:24–29; 6:40, 47; 11:25–26.

JN

yourself out to be?"* [54] Jesus answered, "If I glorify myself, my glory is worth nothing; but it is my Father who glorifies me, of whom you say, 'He is our God.' [55] You do not know him, but I know him. And if I should say that I do not know him, I would be like you a liar. But I do know him and I keep his word.* [56] Abraham your father rejoiced to see my day; he saw it† and was glad.* [57] So the Jews said to him, "You are not yet fifty years old and you have seen Abraham?"† [58]† Jesus said to them,* "Amen, amen, I say to you, before Abraham came to be, I AM." [59] So they picked up stones to throw at him; but Jesus hid and went out of the temple area.*

**9 The Man Born Blind.** [1]† As he passed by he saw a man blind from birth.* [2]† His disciples asked him,* "Rabbi, who sinned, this man or his parents, that he was born blind?" [3] Jesus answered, "Neither he nor his parents sinned; it is so that the works of God might be made visible through him.* [4] We have to do the works of the one who sent me while it is day. Night is coming when no one can work.* [5] While I am in the world, I am the light of the world."* [6] When he had said this, he spat on the ground and made clay with the saliva, and smeared the clay on his eyes,* [7] and said to him, "Go wash† in the Pool of Siloam" (which means Sent). So he went and washed, and came back able to see.*

[8] His neighbors and those who had seen him earlier as a beggar said, "Isn't this the one who used to sit and beg?" [9] Some said, "It is," but others said, "No, he just looks like him." He said, "I am." [10] So they said to him, "[So] how were your eyes opened?" [11] He replied, "The man called Jesus made clay and anointed my eyes and told me, 'Go to Siloam and wash.' So I went there and washed and was able to see." [12] And they said to him, "Where is he?" He said, "I don't know."

[13] They brought the one who was once blind to the Pharisees. [14] Now Jesus had made clay† and opened his eyes on a sabbath.* [15] So then the Pharisees also asked him how he was able to see. He said to them, "He put clay on my eyes, and I washed, and now I can see." [16] So some of the Pharisees said, "This man is not from God, because he does not keep the sabbath." [But] others said, "How can a sinful man do such signs?" And there was a division among them.* [17] So they said to the blind man again, "What do you have to say about him, since he opened your eyes?" He said, "He is a prophet."*

[18] Now the Jews did not believe that he had been blind and gained his sight until they summoned the parents of the one who had gained his sight. [19] They asked them, "Is this your son, who you say was born blind? How does he now see?" [20] His parents answered and said, "We know that this is our son and that he was born blind. [21] We do not know how he sees now, nor do we know who opened his eyes. Ask him, he is of age; he can speak for himself." [22]†* His parents said this because they were afraid of the Jews, for the Jews had already agreed that if anyone acknowledged him as the Messiah, he would be expelled from the synagogue. [23] For this reason his parents said, "He is of age; question him."*

[24] So a second time they called the man who

---

† 8:56 *He saw it*: this seems a reference to the birth of Isaac (Gn 17:7; 21:6), the beginning of the fulfillment of promises about Abraham's seed.

8:57 The evidence of the third-century Bodmer Papyrus P75 and the first hand of Codex Sinaiticus indicates that the text originally read: "How can Abraham have seen you?"

8:58 *Came to be, I AM*: the Greek word used for "came to be" is the one used of all creation in the prologue, while the word used for "am" is the one reserved for the Logos.

9:1–10:21 Sabbath healing of the man born blind. This sixth sign is introduced to illustrate the saying, "I am the light of the world" (Jn 8:12; 9:5). The narrative of conflict about Jesus contrasts Jesus (light) with the Jews (blindness, Jn 9:39–41). The theme of water is reintroduced in the reference to the pool of Siloam. Ironically, Jesus is being judged by the Jews, yet the Jews are judged by the Light of the world; cf. Jn 3:19–21.

9:2 See note on Jn 5:14, and Ex 20:5, that parents' sins were visited upon their children. Jesus denies such a cause and emphasizes the purpose: the infirmity was providential.

9:7 *Go wash*: perhaps a test of faith; cf. 2 Kgs 5:10–14. The

water tunnel Siloam (= Sent) is used as a symbol of Jesus, sent by his Father.

9:14 In using spittle, kneading clay, and healing, Jesus had broken the sabbath rules laid down by Jewish tradition.

9:22 This comment of the evangelist (in terms used again in Jn 12:42; 16:2) envisages a situation after Jesus' ministry. Rejection/excommunication from the synagogue of Jews who confessed Jesus as Messiah seems to have begun ca. A.D. 85, when the curse against the *mînîm* or heretics was introduced into the "Eighteen Benedictions."

8:53 4:12.
8:55 7:28–29.
8:56 Gn 17:17; Mt 13:17; Lk 17:22.
8:58 1:30; 17:5.
8:59 10:31, 39; 11:8; Lk 4:29–30.
9:1–2 Is 42:7.
9:2 Ex 20:5; Ez 18:20; Lk 13:2.
9:3 5:14; 11:4.

9:4 11:9–10; 12:35–36.
9:5 8:12.
9:6 5:11; Mk 7:33; 8:23.
9:7 2 Kgs 5:10–14.
9:14 5:9.
9:16 3:2; Mt 12:10–11; Lk 13:10–11; 14:1–4.
9:17 4:19.
9:22 7:13; 12:42; 16:2; 19:38.
9:23 12:42.

JN

had been blind and said to him, "Give God the praise!† We know that this man is a sinner."* ²⁵ He replied, "If he is a sinner, I do not know. One thing I do know is that I was blind and now I see." ²⁶ So they said to him, "What did he do to you? How did he open your eyes?" ²⁷ He answered them, "I told you already and you did not listen. Why do you want to hear it again? Do you want to become his disciples, too?" ²⁸ They ridiculed him and said, "You are that man's disciple; we are disciples of Moses! ²⁹ We know that God spoke to Moses, but we do not know where this one is from."* ³⁰ The man answered and said to them, "This is what is so amazing, that you do not know where he is from, yet he opened my eyes. ³¹ We know that God does not listen to sinners, but if one is devout and does his will, he listens to him.* ³²† It is unheard of that anyone ever opened the eyes of a person born blind. ³³ If this man were not from God, he would not be able to do anything."* ³⁴ They answered and said to him, "You were born totally in sin, and are you trying to teach us?" Then they threw him out.

³⁵ When Jesus heard that they had thrown him out, he found him and said, "Do you believe in the Son of Man?" ³⁶ He answered and said, "Who is he, sir, that I may believe in him?" ³⁷ Jesus said to him, "You have seen him and the one speaking with you is he."* ³⁸ He said, "I do believe, Lord," and he worshiped him. ³⁹† Then Jesus said, "I came into this world for judgment, so that those who do not see might see, and those who do see might become blind."*

⁴⁰ Some of the Pharisees who were with him heard this and said to him, "Surely we are not also blind, are we?"* ⁴¹ Jesus said to them, "If you were blind, you would have no sin; but now you are saying, 'We see,' so your sin remains.*

# 10

**The Good Shepherd.** ¹† "Amen, amen, I say to you,* whoever does not enter a sheepfold† through the gate but climbs over elsewhere is a thief and a robber. ² But whoever enters through the gate is the shepherd of the sheep. ³ The gatekeeper opens it for him, and the sheep hear his voice, as he calls his own sheep by name and leads them out. ⁴† When he has driven out all his own, he walks ahead of them, and the sheep follow him,* because they recognize his voice. ⁵ But they will not follow a stranger; they will run away from him, because they do not recognize the voice of strangers." ⁶ Although Jesus used this figure of speech,† they did not realize what he was trying to tell them.

⁷† So Jesus said again, "Amen, amen, I say to you, I am the gate for the sheep. ⁸† All who came [before me] are thieves and robbers, but the sheep did not listen to them. ⁹ I am the gate. Whoever enters through me will be saved, and will come in and go out and find pasture. ¹⁰ A thief comes only to steal and slaughter and destroy; I came so that they might have life and have it more abundantly. ¹¹ I am the good shepherd. A good shepherd lays down his life for the sheep.* ¹² A hired man, who is not a shepherd and whose sheep are not his own, sees a wolf coming and leaves the sheep and runs away, and the wolf catches and scatters them.* ¹³ This is because he works for pay and has no concern for the sheep. ¹⁴ I am the good shepherd, and I know mine and mine know me, ¹⁵ just as the Father knows me and I know the Father; and I will lay down my life for the sheep.* ¹⁶ I have other sheep† that

---

**9:24** *Give God the praise!*: an Old Testament formula of adjuration to tell the truth; cf. Jos 7:19; 1 Sm 6:5 LXX. Cf. Jn 5:41.

**9:32** *A person born blind*: the only Old Testament cure from blindness is found in Tobit (cf. Tb 7:7; 11:7–13; 14:1–2), but Tobit was not born blind.

**9:39–41** These verses spell out the symbolic meaning of the cure; the Pharisees are not the innocent blind, willing to accept the testimony of others.

**10:1–21** The good shepherd discourse continues the theme of attack on the Pharisees that ends Jn 9. The figure is allegorical: the hired hands are the Pharisees who excommunicated the cured blind man. It serves as a commentary on Jn 9. For the shepherd motif, used of Yahweh in the Old Testament, cf. Ex 34; Gn 48:15; 49:24; Mi 7:14; Ps 23:1–4; 80:1.

**10:1** *Sheepfold*: a low stone wall open to the sky.

**10:4** *Recognize his voice*: the Pharisees do not recognize Jesus, but the people of God, symbolized by the blind man, do.

**10:6** *Figure of speech*: John uses a different word for illustrative speech than the "parable" of the synoptics, but the idea is similar.

**10:7–10** In Jn 10:7–8, the figure is of a gate for the shepherd to come to the sheep; in Jn 10:9–10, the figure is of a gate for the sheep to *come in and go out.*

**10:8** *[Before me]*: these words are omitted in many good early manuscripts and versions.

**10:16** *Other sheep*: the Gentiles, possibly a reference to "God's dispersed children" of Jn 11:52 destined to be gathered into one, or "apostolic Christians" at odds with the community of the beloved disciple.

| | |
|---|---|
| **9:24** Jos 7:19; 1 Sm 6:5 LXX. | **9:41** 15:22. |
| **9:29** Ex 33:11. | **10:1–5** Gn 48:15; 49:24; Ps 23:1–4; 80:2; Jer 23:1–4; Ez 34:1–31; Mi 7:14. |
| **9:31** 10:21; Ps 34:16; 66:18; Prv 15:29; Is 1:15. | **10:4** Mi 2:12–13. |
| **9:33** 3:2. | **10:11** Ps 23:1–4; Is 40:11; 49:9–10; Heb 13:20; Rev 7:17. |
| **9:37** 4:26; Dn 7:13. | |
| **9:39** Mt 13:33–35. | **10:12** Zec 11:17. |
| **9:40** Mt 15:14; 23:26; Rom 2:19. | **10:15** 15:13; 1 Jn 3:16. |

do not belong to this fold. These also I must lead, and they will hear my voice, and there will be one flock, one shepherd.* ¹⁷This is why the Father loves me, because I lay down my life in order to take it up again.* ¹⁸No one takes it from me, but I lay it down on my own. I have power to lay it down, and power to take it up again.† This command I have received from my Father."*

¹⁹Again there was a division among the Jews because of these words.* ²⁰Many of them said, "He is possessed and out of his mind; why listen to him?"* ²¹Others said, "These are not the words of one possessed; surely a demon cannot open the eyes of the blind, can he?"*

**Feast of the Dedication.** ²²The feast of the Dedication† was then taking place in Jerusalem. It was winter.* ²³† And Jesus walked about in the temple area on the Portico of Solomon. ²⁴So the Jews gathered around him and said to him, "How long are you going to keep us in suspense?† If you are the Messiah, tell us plainly."* ²⁵Jesus answered them, "I told you† and you do not believe. The works I do in my Father's name testify to me.* ²⁶But you do not believe, because you are not among my sheep.* ²⁷My sheep hear my voice; I know them, and they follow me. ²⁸I give them eternal life, and they shall never perish. No one can take them out of my hand.* ²⁹My Father, who has given them to me, is greater than all,†

and no one can take them out of the Father's hand.* ³⁰† The Father and I are one."*

³¹The Jews again picked up rocks to stone him.* ³²Jesus answered them, "I have shown you many good works from my Father. For which of these are you trying to stone me?" ³³The Jews answered him, "We are not stoning you for a good work but for blasphemy. You, a man, are making yourself God."* ³⁴† Jesus answered them,* "Is it not written in your law, 'I said, "You are gods"'? ³⁵If it calls them gods to whom the word of God came, and scripture cannot be set aside, ³⁶can you say that the one whom the Father has consecrated† and sent into the world blasphemes because I said, 'I am the Son of God'?* ³⁷If I do not perform my Father's works, do not believe me; ³⁸but if I perform them, even if you do not believe me, believe the works, so that you may realize [and understand] that the Father is in me and I am in the Father."* ³⁹[Then] they tried again to arrest him; but he escaped from their power.

⁴⁰He went back across the Jordan to the place where John first baptized, and there he remained.* ⁴¹Many came to him and said, "John performed no sign,† but everything John said about this man was true." ⁴²And many there began to believe in him.*

**11** **The Raising of Lazarus.**† ¹Now a man was ill, Lazarus from Bethany,* the village of Mary and her sister Martha. ²Mary

---

† **10:18** *Power to take it up again:* contrast the role of the Father as the efficient cause of the resurrection in Acts 2:24; 4:10; etc.; Rom 1:4; 4:24. Yet even here is added: *This command I have received from my Father.*

**10:22** *Feast of the Dedication:* an eight-day festival of lights (Hebrew, Hanukkah) held in December, three months after the feast of Tabernacles (Jn 7:2), to celebrate the Maccabees' rededication of the altar and reconsecration of the temple in 164 B.C., after their desecration by Antiochus IV Epiphanes (Dn 8:13; 9:27; cf. 1 Mc 4:36–59; 2 Mc 1:18–2:19; 10:1–8).

**10:23** *Portico of Solomon:* on the east side of the temple area, offering protection against the cold winds from the desert.

**10:24** *Keep us in suspense:* literally, "How long will you take away our life?" Cf. Jn 11:48–50. *If you are the Messiah, tell us plainly:* cf. Lk 22:67. This is the climax of Jesus' encounters with the Jewish authorities. There has never yet been an open confession before them.

**10:25** *I told you:* probably at Jn 8:25 which was an evasive answer.

**10:29** The textual evidence for the first clause is very divided; it may also be translated: "As for the Father, what he has given me is greater than all," or "My Father is greater than all, in what he has given me."

**10:30** This is justification for Jn 10:29; it asserts unity of power and reveals that the words and deeds of Jesus are the words and deeds of God.

**10:34** This is a reference to the judges of Israel who, since they exercised the divine prerogative to judge (Dt 1:17), were

called "gods"; cf. Ex 21:6, besides Ps 82:6, from which the quotation comes.

**10:36** *Consecrated:* this may be a reference to the rededicated altar at the Hanukkah feast; see note on Jn 10:22.

**10:41** *Performed no sign:* this is to stress the inferior role of John the Baptist. The Transjordan topography recalls the great witness of John the Baptist to Jesus, as opposed to the hostility of the authorities in Jerusalem.

**11:1–44** The raising of Lazarus, the longest continuous narrative in John outside of the passion account, is the climax of the signs. It leads directly to the decision of the Sanhedrin to kill Jesus. The theme of life predominates. Lazarus is a token of the real life that Jesus dead and raised will give to all who believe in him. Johannine irony is found in the fact that Jesus' gift of life leads to his own death. The story is not found in the synoptics, but cf. Mk 5:21 and parallels; Lk 7:11–17. There are also paral-

**10:16** 11:52; Is 56:8; Jer 23:3; Ez 34:23; 37:24; Mi 2:12.
**10:17** Heb 10:10.
**10:18** 19:11.
**10:19** 7:43; 9:16.
**10:20** 7:20; 8:48.
**10:21** 3:2.
**10:22** 1 Mc 4:54, 59.
**10:24** Lk 22:67.
**10:25** 8:25 / 5:36; 10:38.
**10:26** 8:45, 47.
**10:28** Dt 32:39.
**10:29** Wis 3:1; Is 43:13.
**10:30** 1:1; 12:45; 14:9; 17:21.
**10:31** 8:59.
**10:33** 5:18; 19:7; Lv 24:16.
**10:34** Ps 82:6.
**10:36** 5:18.
**10:38** 14:10–11, 20.
**10:40** 1:28.
**10:42** 2:23; 7:31; 8:30.
**11:1–2** 12:1–8; Lk 10:38–42; 16:19–31.

was the one who had anointed the Lord with perfumed oil and dried his feet with her hair; it was her brother Lazarus who was ill. ³So the sisters sent word to him, saying, "Master, the one you love is ill." ⁴When Jesus heard this he said, "This illness is not to end in death,† but is for the glory of God, that the Son of God may be glorified through it."* ⁵Now Jesus loved Martha and her sister and Lazarus. ⁶So when he heard that he was ill, he remained for two days in the place where he was. ⁷Then after this he said to his disciples, "Let us go back to Judea." ⁸The disciples said to him, "Rabbi, the Jews were just trying to stone you, and you want to go back there?"* ⁹Jesus answered, "Are there not twelve hours in a day? If one walks during the day,* he does not stumble, because he sees the light of this world.* ¹⁰But if one walks at night, he stumbles, because the light is not in him."† ¹¹He said this, and then told them, "Our friend Lazarus is asleep, but I am going to awaken him." ¹²So the disciples said to him, "Master, if he is asleep, he will be saved." ¹³But Jesus was talking about his death, while they thought that he meant ordinary sleep.* ¹⁴So then Jesus said to them clearly, "Lazarus has died. ¹⁵And I am glad for you that I was not there, that you may believe. Let us go to him." ¹⁶So Thomas, called Didymus,† said to his fellow disciples, "Let us also go to die with him."*

¹⁷When Jesus arrived, he found that Lazarus had already been in the tomb for four days. ¹⁸Now Bethany was near Jerusalem, only about two miles† away. ¹⁹And many of the Jews had come to Martha and Mary to comfort them about their brother.* ²⁰When Martha heard that Jesus was coming, she went to meet him; but Mary sat at home. ²¹Martha said to Jesus, "Lord, if you had been here, my brother would not have died.* ²²[But] even now I know that whatever you ask of God, God will

give you." ²³Jesus said to her, "Your brother will rise." ²⁴Martha said to him, "I know he will rise, in the resurrection on the last day."* ²⁵Jesus told her, "I am the resurrection and the life; whoever believes in me, even if he dies, will live,* ²⁶and everyone who lives and believes in me will never die. Do you believe this?" ²⁷†* She said to him, "Yes, Lord. I have come to believe that you are the Messiah, the Son of God, the one who is coming into the world."

²⁸When she had said this, she went and called her sister Mary secretly, saying, "The teacher is here and is asking for you." ²⁹As soon as she heard this, she rose quickly and went to him. ³⁰For Jesus had not yet come into the village, but was still where Martha had met him. ³¹So when the Jews who were with her in the house comforting her saw Mary get up quickly and go out, they followed her, presuming that she was going to the tomb to weep there. ³²When Mary came to where Jesus was and saw him, she fell at his feet and said to him, "Lord, if you had been here, my brother would not have died." ³³When Jesus saw her weeping and the Jews who had come with her weeping, he became perturbed† and deeply troubled, ³⁴and said, "Where have you laid him?" They said to him, "Sir, come and see." ³⁵And Jesus wept.* ³⁶So the Jews said, "See how he loved him." ³⁷But some of them said, "Could not the one who opened the eyes of the blind man have done something so that this man would not have died?"

³⁸So Jesus, perturbed again, came to the tomb. It was a cave, and a stone lay across it. ³⁹Jesus said, "Take away the stone." Martha, the dead man's sister, said to him, "Lord, by now there will be a stench; he has been dead for four days." ⁴⁰Jesus said to her, "Did I not tell you that if you believe you will see the glory of God?" ⁴¹So they took away the stone.

---

lels between this story and Luke's parable of the rich man and poor Lazarus (Lk 16:19–31). In both a man named Lazarus dies; in Luke, there is a request that he return to convince his contemporaries of the need for faith and repentance, while in John, Lazarus does return and some believe but others do not.
**11:4** *Not to end in death*: this is misunderstood by the disciples as referring to physical death, but it is meant as spiritual death.
**11:10** *The light is not in him*: the ancients apparently did not grasp clearly the entry of light *through* the eye; they seem to have thought of it as being in the eye; cf. Lk 11:34; Mt 6:23.
**11:16** *Called Didymus*: Didymus is the Greek word for twin. Thomas is derived from the Aramaic word for twin; in an ancient Syriac version and in the Gospel of Thomas (80:11–12) his given name, Judas, is supplied.

**11:18** *About two miles*: literally, "about fifteen stades"; a stade was 607 feet.
**11:27** The titles here are a summary of titles given to Jesus earlier in the gospel.
**11:33** *Became perturbed*: a startling phrase in Greek, literally, "He snorted in spirit," perhaps in anger at the presence of evil (death).

---

**11:4** 9:3, 24.
**11:8** 8:59; 10:31.
**11:9–10** 12:35; 1 Jn 2:10.
**11:9** 8:12; 9:4.
**11:13** Mt 9:24.
**11:16** 14:5, 22.
**11:19** 12:9, 17–18.
**11:21** 11:32.

**11:24** 5:29; 6:39–40, 44, 54; 12:48; Is 2:2; Mi 4:1; Acts 23:8; 24:15.
**11:25** 5:24; 8:51; 14:6; Dn 12:2.
**11:27** 1:9; 6:69.
**11:35** Lk 19:41.

JN

And Jesus raised his eyes and said, "Father,† I thank you for hearing me. 42 I know that you always hear me; but because of the crowd here I have said this, that they may believe that you sent me."* 43 And when he had said this, he cried out in a loud voice,† "Lazarus, come out!" 44 The dead man came out, tied hand and foot with burial bands, and his face was wrapped in a cloth. So Jesus said to them, "Untie him and let him go."

**Session of the Sanhedrin.** 45 Now many of the Jews who had come to Mary and seen what he had done began to believe in him.* 46 But some of them went to the Pharisees and told them what Jesus had done. 47 So the chief priests and the Pharisees convened the Sanhedrin and said, "What are we going to do? This man is performing many signs.* 48 If we leave him alone, all will believe in him, and the Romans will come† and take away both our land and our nation." 49 * But one of them, Caiaphas, who was high priest that year,† said to them, "You know nothing, 50 nor do you consider that it is better for you that one man should die instead of the people, so that the whole nation may not perish." 51 He did not say this on his own, but since he was high priest for that year, he prophesied that Jesus was going to die for the nation, 52 and not only for the nation, but also to gather into one the dispersed children of God.† 53 So from that day on they planned to kill him.*

54 So Jesus no longer walked about in public among the Jews, but he left for the region near the desert, to a town called Ephraim,† and there he remained with his disciples.

**The Last Passover.** 55 Now the Passover of the Jews was near, and many went up from the country to Jerusalem before Passover to purify† themselves.* 56 They looked for Jesus and said to one another as they were in the temple area, "What do you think? That he will not come to the feast?" 57 For the chief priests and the Pharisees had given orders that if anyone knew where he was, he should inform them, so that they might arrest him.

**12** **The Anointing at Bethany.*** 1 † Six days before Passover Jesus came to Bethany, where Lazarus was, whom Jesus had raised from the dead.* 2 They gave a dinner for him there, and Martha served, while Lazarus was one of those reclining at table with him.* 3 Mary took a liter of costly perfumed oil made from genuine aromatic nard and anointed the feet of Jesus† and dried them with her hair; the house was filled with the fragrance of the oil.* 4 Then Judas the Iscariot, one [of] his disciples, and the one who would betray him, said, 5 "Why was this oil not sold for three hundred days' wages† and given to the poor?" 6 He said this not because he cared about the poor but because he was a thief and held the money bag and used to steal the contributions.* 7 So Jesus said, "Leave her alone. Let her keep this for the day of my burial.† 8 You always have the poor with you, but you do not always have me."*

9 [The] large crowd of the Jews found out that he was there and came, not only because of Jesus, but also to see Lazarus, whom he had raised from the dead.* 10 And the chief priests plotted to kill Lazarus too, 11 because many of

---

**11:41** *Father*: in Aramaic, *'abbā'*. See note on Mk 14:36.
**11:43** *Cried out in a loud voice*: a dramatization of Jn 5:28; "the hour is coming when all who are in the tombs will hear his voice."
**11:48** *The Romans will come*: Johannine irony; this is precisely what happened after Jesus' death.
**11:49** *That year*: emphasizes the conjunction of the office and the year. Actually, Caiaphas was high priest A.D. 18–36. The Jews attributed a gift of prophecy, sometimes unconscious, to the high priest.
**11:52** *Dispersed children of God*: perhaps the "other sheep" of Jn 10:16.
**11:54** Ephraim is usually located about twelve miles northeast of Jerusalem, where the mountains descend into the Jordan valley.
**11:55** *Purify*: prescriptions for purity were based on Ex 19:10–11, 15; Nm 9:6–14; 2 Chr 30:1–3, 15–18.
**12:1–8** This is probably the same scene of anointing found in Mk 14:3–9 (see note there) and Mt 26:6–13. The anointing by a penitent woman in Lk 7:36–38 is different. Details from these various episodes have become interchanged.

**12:3** *The feet of Jesus*: so Mk 14:3; but in Mt 26:6, Mary anoints Jesus' head as a sign of regal, messianic anointing.
**12:5** *Days' wages*: literally, "denarii." A denarius is a day's wage in Mt 20:2; see note on Jn 6:7.
**12:7** Jesus' response reflects the rabbinical discussion of what was the greatest act of mercy, almsgiving or burying the dead. Those who favored proper burial of the dead thought it an essential condition for sharing in the resurrection.

**11:42** 12:30.
**11:45** Lk 16:31.
**11:47** 12:19; Mt 26:3–5; Lk 22:2; Acts 4:16.
**11:49–50** 18:13–14.
**11:53** 5:18; 7:1; Mt 12:14.
**11:55** 2:13; 5:1; 6:4; 18:28; Ex 19:10–11, 15; Nm 9:6–14; 19:12; Dt 16:6;
2 Chr 30:1–3, 15–18.
**12:1–11** Mt 26:6–13; Mk 14:3–9.
**12:1–2** 11:1.
**12:2** Lk 10:38–42.
**12:3** 11:2.
**12:6** 13:29.
**12:8** Dt 15:11.
**12:9** 11:19.

the Jews were turning away and believing in Jesus because of him.*

**The Entry into Jerusalem.**† [12]*On the next day, when the great crowd that had come to the feast heard that Jesus was coming to Jerusalem, [13]they took palm branches† and went out to meet him, and cried out:

> "Hosanna!
> Blessed is he who comes in the name of the Lord,
> [even] the king of Israel."*

[14]Jesus found an ass and sat upon it, as is written:

> [15] "Fear no more, O daughter Zion;†
> see, your king comes, seated upon an ass's colt."*

[16]His disciples did not understand this at first, but when Jesus had been glorified they remembered that these things were written about him and that they had done this† for him.* [17]†So the crowd that was with him when he called Lazarus from the tomb and raised him from death continued to testify. [18]This was [also] why the crowd went to meet him, because they heard that he had done this sign. [19]So the Pharisees said to one another, "You see that you are gaining nothing. Look, the whole world† has gone after him."*

**The Coming of Jesus' Hour.**† [20]Now there were some Greeks† among those who had come up to worship at the feast.* [21]†They came to Philip, who was from Bethsaida in Galilee, and asked him, "Sir, we would like to see Jesus."* [22]Philip went and told Andrew; then Andrew and Philip went and told Jesus.* [23]†Jesus answered them,* "The hour has come for the Son of Man to be glorified. [24]†Amen, amen, I say to you, unless a grain of wheat falls to the ground and dies, it remains just a grain of wheat;* but if it dies, it produces much fruit. [25]Whoever loves his life† loses it, and whoever hates his life in this world will preserve it for eternal life.* [26]Whoever serves me must follow me, and where I am, there also will my servant be. The Father will honor whoever serves me.*

[27]"I am troubled† now. Yet what should I say? 'Father, save me from this hour'? But it was for this purpose that I came to this hour.* [28]Father, glorify your name." Then a voice came from heaven, "I have glorified it and will glorify it again."* [29]The crowd there heard it and said it was thunder; but others said, "An angel has spoken to him."* [30]Jesus answered and said, "This voice did not come

---

**12:12–19** In John, the entry into Jerusalem follows the anointing whereas in the synoptics it precedes. In John, the crowd, not the disciples, are responsible for the triumphal procession.

**12:13** Palm branches: used to welcome great conquerors; cf. 1 Mc 13:51; 2 Mc 10:7. They may be related to the *lûlāb*, the twig bundles used at the feast of Tabernacles. Hosanna: see Ps 118:25–26. The Hebrew word means: "(O Lord), grant salvation." He who comes in the name of the Lord: referred in Ps 118:26 to a pilgrim entering the temple gates, but here a title for Jesus (see notes on Mt 11:3 and Jn 6:14; 11:27). The king of Israel: perhaps from Zep 3:14–15, in connection with the next quotation from Zec 9:9.

**12:15** Daughter Zion: Jerusalem. Ass's colt: symbol of peace, as opposed to the war horse.

**12:16** They had done this: the antecedent of they is ambiguous.

**12:17–18** There seem to be two different crowds in these verses. There are some good witnesses to the text that have another reading for Jn 12:17: "Then the crowd that was with him began to testify that he had called Lazarus out of the tomb and raised him from the dead."

**12:19** The whole world: the sense is that everyone is following Jesus, but John has an ironic play on world; he alludes to the universality of salvation (Jn 3:17; 4:42).

**12:20–36** This announcement of glorification by death is an illustration of "the whole world" (Jn 12:19) going after him.

**12:20** Greeks: not used here in a nationalistic sense. These are probably Gentile proselytes to Judaism; cf. Jn 7:35.

**12:21–22** Philip…Andrew: the approach is made through disciples who have distinctly Greek names, suggesting that access to Jesus was mediated to the Greek world through his

disciples. Philip and Andrew were from Bethsaida (Jn 1:44); Galileans were mostly bilingual. See: here seems to mean "have an interview with."

**12:23** Jesus' response suggests that only after the crucifixion could the gospel encompass both Jew and Gentile.

**12:24** This verse implies that through his death Jesus will be accessible to all. It remains just a grain of wheat: this saying is found in the synoptic triple and double traditions (Mk 8:35; Mt 16:25; Lk 9:24; Mt 10:39; Lk 17:33). John adds the phrases (Jn 12:25) in this world and for eternal life.

**12:25** His life: the Greek word psychē refers to a person's natural life. It does not mean "soul," for Hebrew anthropology did not postulate body/soul dualism in the way that is familiar to us.

**12:27** I am troubled: perhaps an allusion to the Gethsemane agony scene of the synoptics.

---

**12:11** 11:45.
**12:12–19** Mt 21:1–16; Mk 11:1–10; Lk 19:28–40.
**12:13** 1:49; Lv 23:40; 1 Mc 13:51; 2 Mc 10:7; Rev 7:9.
**12:15** Is 40:9; Zec 9:9.
**12:16** 2:22.
**12:19** 11:47–48.
**12:20** Acts 10:2.
**12:21** 1:44.
**12:22** 1:40.
**12:23** 2:4.
**12:24** Is 53:10–12; 1 Cor 15:36.
**12:25** Mt 10:39; 16:25; Mk 8:35; Lk 9:24; 17:33.
**12:26** 14:3; 17:24; Mt 16:24; Mk 8:34; Lk 9:23.
**12:27** 6:38; 18:11; Mt 26:38–39; Mk 14:34–36; Lk 22:42; Heb 5:7–8.
**12:28** 2:11; 17:5; Dn 4:31, 34.
**12:29** Ex 9:28; 2 Sm 22:14; Jb 37:4; Ps 29:3; Lk 22:43; Acts 23:9.

for my sake but for yours.* ³¹ Now is the time of judgment on this world; now the ruler of this world† will be driven out.* ³² And when I am lifted up from the earth, I will draw everyone to myself."* ³³ He said this indicating the kind of death he would die. ³⁴ So the crowd answered him, "We have heard from the law that the Messiah remains forever.† Then how can you say that the Son of Man must be lifted up? Who is this Son of Man?"* ³⁵ Jesus said to them, "The light will be among you only a little while. Walk while you have the light, so that darkness may not overcome you. Whoever walks in the dark does not know where he is going.* ³⁶ While you have the light, believe in the light, so that you may become children of the light."*

**Unbelief and Belief Among the Jews.** After he had said this, Jesus left and hid from them. ³⁷†* Although he had performed so many signs in their presence they did not believe in him, ³⁸† in order that the word which Isaiah the prophet spoke might be fulfilled:

"Lord, who has believed our preaching,
  to whom has the might of the Lord
    been revealed?"*

³⁹ For this reason they could not believe, because again Isaiah said:

⁴⁰ "He blinded their eyes
  and hardened their heart,
  so that they might not see with their
    eyes

and understand with their heart and
  be converted,
  and I would heal them."*

⁴¹ Isaiah said this because he saw his glory† and spoke about him.* ⁴² Nevertheless, many, even among the authorities, believed in him, but because of the Pharisees they did not acknowledge it openly in order not to be expelled from the synagogue.* ⁴³ For they preferred human praise to the glory of God.*

**Recapitulation.** ⁴⁴ Jesus cried out and said, "Whoever believes in me believes not only in me but also in the one who sent me,* ⁴⁵ and whoever sees me sees the one who sent me.* ⁴⁶ I came into the world as light, so that everyone who believes in me might not remain in darkness.* ⁴⁷ And if anyone hears my words and does not observe them, I do not condemn him, for I did not come to condemn the world but to save the world.* ⁴⁸ Whoever rejects me and does not accept my words has something to judge him: the word that I spoke, it will condemn him on the last day,* ⁴⁹ because I did not speak on my own, but the Father who sent me commanded me what to say and speak.* ⁵⁰ And I know that his commandment is eternal life. So what I say, I say as the Father told me."

## III. THE BOOK OF GLORY†

# 13
**The Washing of the Disciples' Feet.†** ¹ Before the feast of Passover,† Jesus knew that his hour had come to pass from

---

**12:31** *Ruler of this world*: Satan.

**12:34** There is no passage in the Old Testament that states precisely that the *Messiah remains forever*. Perhaps the closest is Ps 89:37.

**12:37–50** These verses, on unbelief of the Jews, provide an epilogue to the Book of Signs.

**12:38–41** John gives a historical explanation of the disbelief of the Jewish people, not a psychological one. The Old Testament had to be fulfilled; the disbelief that met Isaiah's message was a foreshadowing of the disbelief that Jesus encountered. In Jn 12:42 and also in Jn 3:20 we see that there is no negation of freedom.

**12:41** *His glory*: Isaiah saw the glory of Yahweh enthroned in the heavenly temple, but in John the antecedent of *his* is Jesus.

**13:1–19:42** The Book of Glory. There is a major break here; the word "sign" is used again only in Jn 20:30. In this phase of Jesus' return to the Father, the discourses (Jn 13–17) precede the traditional narrative of the passion (Jn 18–20) to interpret them for the Christian reader. This is the only extended example of esoteric teaching of disciples in John.

**13:1–20** Washing of the disciples' feet. This episode occurs in

John at the place of the narration of the institution of the Eucharist in the synoptics. It may be a dramatization of Lk 22:27—"I am your servant." It is presented as a "model" ("pattern") of the crucifixion. It symbolizes cleansing from sin by sacrificial death.

**13:1** *Before the feast of Passover*: this would be Thursday evening, before the day of preparation; in the synoptics, the Last Supper is a Passover meal taking place, in John's chronology, on Friday evening. *To the end*: or, "completely."

| | |
|---|---|
| 12:30 11:42. | 12:40 Is 6:9–10; Mt |
| 12:31 16:11; Lk 10:18; Rev | 13:13–15; Mk 4:12. |
| 12:9. | 12:41 5:39; Is 6:1, 4. |
| 12:32 3:14; 8:28; Is 52:13. | 12:42 9:22. |
| 12:34 Ps 89:5; 110:4; Is | 12:43 5:44. |
| 9:7; Dn 7:13–14; Rev | 12:44 13:20; 14:1. |
| 20:1–6. | 12:45 14:7–9. |
| 12:35 9:4; 11:10; Jb 5:14. | 12:46 1:9; 8:12. |
| 12:36 Eph 5:8. | 12:47 3:17. |
| 12:37–43 Dt 29:2–4; Mk | 12:48 Lk 10:16; Heb 4:12. |
| 4:11–12; Rom 9–11. | 12:49 14:10, 31; Dt |
| 12:38 Is 53:1; Rom 10:16. | 18:18–19. |

this world to the Father. He loved his own in the world and he loved them to the end.* ²The devil had already induced† Judas, son of Simon the Iscariot, to hand him over. So, during supper,* ³fully aware that the Father had put everything into his power and that he had come from God and was returning to God,* ⁴he rose from supper and took off his outer garments. He took a towel and tied it around his waist. ⁵† Then he poured water into a basin and began to wash the disciples' feet* and dry them with the towel around his waist. ⁶He came to Simon Peter, who said to him, "Master, are you going to wash my feet?" ⁷Jesus answered and said to him, "What I am doing, you do not understand now, but you will understand later." ⁸Peter said to him, "You will never wash my feet." Jesus answered him, "Unless I wash you, you will have no inheritance with me."* ⁹Simon Peter said to him, "Master, then not only my feet, but my hands and head as well." ¹⁰Jesus said to him, "Whoever has bathed† has no need except to have his feet washed, for he is clean all over; so you are clean, but not all."* ¹¹For he knew who would betray him; for this reason, he said, "Not all of you are clean."*

¹²So when he had washed their feet [and] put his garments back on and reclined at table again, he said to them, "Do you realize what I have done for you? ¹³You call me 'teacher' and 'master,' and rightly so, for indeed I am.* ¹⁴If I, therefore, the master and teacher, have washed your feet, you ought to wash one another's feet. ¹⁵I have given you a model to follow, so that as I have done for you, you should also do.* ¹⁶Amen, amen, I say to you, no slave is greater than his master nor any messenger†

greater than the one who sent him.* ¹⁷If you understand this, blessed are you if you do it. ¹⁸I am not speaking of all of you. I know those whom I have chosen. But so that the scripture might be fulfilled, 'The one who ate my food has raised his heel against me.'* ¹⁹From now on I am telling you before it happens, so that when it happens you may believe that I AM. ²⁰Amen, amen, I say to you, whoever receives the one I send receives me, and whoever receives me receives the one who sent me."*

**Announcement of Judas's Betrayal.*** ²¹When he had said this, Jesus was deeply troubled and testified, "Amen, amen, I say to you, one of you will betray me." ²²The disciples looked at one another, at a loss as to whom he meant. ²³One of his disciples, the one whom Jesus loved,† was reclining at Jesus' side.* ²⁴So Simon Peter nodded to him to find out whom he meant. ²⁵He leaned back against Jesus' chest and said to him, "Master, who is it?"* ²⁶Jesus answered, "It is the one to whom I hand the morsel† after I have dipped it." So he dipped the morsel and [took it and] handed it to Judas, son of Simon the Iscariot. ²⁷After he took the morsel, Satan entered him. So Jesus said to him, "What you are going to do, do quickly."* ²⁸[Now] none of those reclining at table realized why he said this to him. ²⁹Some thought that since Judas kept the money bag, Jesus had told him, "Buy what we need for the feast," or to give something to the poor.* ³⁰So he took the morsel and left at once. And it was night.

**The New Commandment.** ³¹† When he had left, Jesus said,† "Now is the Son of Man

---

† **13:2** *Induced*: literally, "The devil put into the heart that Judas should hand him over."

**13:5** The act of washing another's feet was one that could not be required of the lowliest Jewish slave. It is an allusion to the humiliating death of the crucifixion.

**13:10** *Bathed*: many have suggested that this passage is a symbolic reference to baptism. The Greek root involved is used in baptismal contexts in 1 Cor 6:11; Eph 5:26; Ti 3:5; Heb 10:22.

**13:16** *Messenger*: the Greek has *apostolos*, the only occurrence of the term in John. It is not used in the technical sense here.

**13:23** *The one whom Jesus loved*: also mentioned in Jn 19:26; 20:2; 21:7. A disciple, called "another disciple" or "the other disciple," is mentioned in Jn 18:15 and Jn 20:2; in the latter reference he is identified with the disciple whom Jesus loved. There is also an unnamed disciple in Jn 1:35–40; see note on Jn 1:37.

**13:26** *Morsel*: probably the bitter herb dipped in salt water.

**13:31–17:26** Two farewell discourses and a prayer. These seem to be Johannine compositions, including sayings of Jesus at the Last Supper and on other occasions, modeled on similar

farewell discourses in Greek literature and the Old Testament (of Moses, Joshua, David).

**13:31–38** Introduction: departure and return. Terms of coming and going predominate. These verses form an introduction to the last discourse of Jesus, which extends through Jn 14–17. In it John has collected Jesus' words to his own (Jn 13:1). There are indications that several speeches have been fused together, e.g., in Jn 14:31 and Jn 17:1.

* **13:1** 2:4; 7:30; 8:20; Mt 26:17, 45; Mk 14:12, 41; Lk 22:7.
**13:2** 6:71; 17:12; Mt 26:20–21; Mk 14:17–18; Lk 22:3.
**13:3** 3:35.
**13:5** 1 Sm 25:41.
**13:8** 2 Sm 20:1.
**13:10** 15:3.
**13:11** 6:70.
**13:13** Mt 23:8, 10.
**13:15** Lk 22:27; 1 Pt 2:21.
**13:16** 15:20; Mt 10:24; Lk 6:40.
**13:18** Ps 41:10.
**13:20** Mt 10:40; Mk 9:37; Lk 9:48.
**13:21–30** Mt 26:21–25; Mk 14:18–21; Lk 22:21–23.
**13:23** 19:26; 20:2; 21:7, 20; Mt 10:37.
**13:25** 21:20.
**13:27** 13:2; Lk 22:3.
**13:29** 12:5–6.

glorified, and God is glorified in him. [32] [If God is glorified in him,] God will also glorify him in himself, and he will glorify him at once.* [33] My children, I will be with you only a little while longer. You will look for me, and as I told the Jews, 'Where I go you cannot come,' so now I say it to you.* [34] I give you a new commandment:† love one another. As I have loved you, so you also should love one another.* [35] This is how all will know that you are my disciples, if you have love for one another."

**Peter's Denial Predicted.** [36] Simon Peter said to him, "Master, where are you going?" Jesus answered [him], "Where I am going, you cannot follow me now, though you will follow later."* [37] Peter said to him, "Master, why can't I follow you now? I will lay down my life for you." [38] Jesus answered, "Will you lay down your life for me? Amen, amen, I say to you, the cock will not crow before you deny me three times."*

# 14

**Last Supper Discourses.** [1]† "Do not let your hearts be troubled. You have faith† in God; have faith also in me. [2] In my Father's house there are many dwelling places. If there were not, would I have told you that I am going to prepare a place for you? [3]† And if I go and prepare a place for you, I will come back again and take you to myself, so that where I am you also may be.* [4] Where [I] am going you know the way."† [5] Thomas said to him, "Master, we do not know where you are going; how can we know the way?" [6] Jesus said to him, "I am the way and the truth† and the life. No one comes to the Father except through me.* [7] If you know me, then you will also know my Father.† From now on you do know him and have seen him."* [8] Philip said to him, "Master, show us the Father,† and that will be enough for us."* [9] Jesus said to him, "Have I been with you for so long a time and you still do not know me, Philip? Whoever has seen me has seen the Father. How can you say, 'Show us the Father'?* [10] Do you not believe that I am in the Father and the Father is in me? The words that I speak to you I do not speak on my own. The Father who dwells in me is doing his works.* [11] Believe me that I am in the Father and the Father is in me, or else, believe because of the works themselves.* [12] Amen, amen, I say to you, whoever believes in me will do the works that I do, and will do greater ones than these, because I am going to the Father.* [13] And whatever you ask in my name, I will do, so that the Father may be glorified in the Son.* [14] If you ask anything of me in my name, I will do it.

**The Advocate.** [15] "If you love me, you will keep my commandments.* [16] And I will ask the Father, and he will give you another Advocate† to be with you always,* [17] the Spirit of truth,† which the world cannot accept, because it neither sees nor knows it. But you know it, because it remains with you, and will be in you.* [18] I will not leave you orphans; I will come to

13:34 *I give you a new commandment*: this puts Jesus on a par with Yahweh. The commandment itself is not new; cf. Lv 19:18 and the note there.

14:1–31 Jesus' departure and return. This section is a dialogue marked off by a literary inclusion in Jn 14:1, 27: "Do not let your hearts be troubled."

14:1 *You have faith*: could also be imperative: "Have faith."

14:3 *Come back again*: a rare Johannine reference to the parousia; cf. 1 Jn 2:28.

14:4 *The way*: here, of Jesus himself; also a designation of Christianity in Acts 9:2; 19:9, 23; 22:4; 24:14, 22.

14:6 *The truth*: in John, the divinely revealed reality of the Father manifested in the person and works of Jesus. The possession of truth confers knowledge and liberation from sin (Jn 8:32).

14:7 An alternative reading, "If you knew me, then you would have known my Father also," would be a rebuke, as in Jn 8:19.

14:8 *Show us the Father*: Philip is pictured asking for a theophany like Ex 24:9–10; 33:18.

14:16 *Another Advocate*: Jesus is the first advocate (*paraclete*); see 1 Jn 2:1, where Jesus is an advocate in the sense of intercessor in heaven. The Greek term derives from legal terminology for an advocate or defense attorney, and can mean spokesman, mediator, intercessor, comforter, consoler, although no one of these terms encompasses the meaning in John. The Paraclete in John is a teacher, a witness to Jesus, and a prosecutor of the world, who represents the continued presence on earth of the Jesus who has returned to the Father.

14:17 *The Spirit of truth*: this term is also used at Qumran, where it is a moral force put into a person by God, as opposed to the spirit of perversity. It is more personal in John; it will teach the realities of the new order (Jn 14:26), and testify to the truth (Jn 14:6). While it has been customary to use masculine personal pronouns in English for the Advocate, the Greek word for "spirit" is neuter, and the Greek text and manuscript variants fluctuate between masculine and neuter pronouns.

13:32 17:1–5.
13:33 7:33; 8:21.
13:34 15:12–13, 17; Lv 19:18; 1 Thes 4:9; 1 Jn 2:7–10; 3:23; 2 Jn 5.
13:36 Mk 14:27; Lk 22:23.
13:38 18:27; Mt 26:33–35; Mk 14:29–31; Lk 22:33–34.
14:3 12:26; 17:24; 1 Jn 2:28.
14:6 8:31–47.
14:7 8:19; 12:45.
14:8 Ex 24:9–10; 33:18.

14:9 1:18; 10:30; 12:45; 2 Cor 4:4; Col 1:15; Heb 1:3.
14:10 1:1; 10:37–38; 12:49.
14:11 10:38.
14:12 1:50; 5:20.
14:13 15:7, 16; 16:23–24; Mt 7:7–11.
14:15 15:10; Dt 6:4–9; Ps 119; Wis 6:18; 1 Jn 5:3; 2 Jn 6.
14:16 15:26; Lk 24:49; 1 Jn 2:1.
14:17 16:13; Mt 28:20; 2 Jn 1–2.

you.† [19] In a little while the world will no longer see me, but you will see me, because I live and you will live.* [20] On that day you will realize that I am in my Father and you are in me and I in you.* [21] Whoever has my commandments and observes them is the one who loves me. And whoever loves me will be loved by my Father, and I will love him and reveal myself to him."* [22] Judas, not the Iscariot,† said to him, "Master, [then] what happened that you will reveal yourself to us and not to the world?"* [23] Jesus answered and said to him, "Whoever loves me will keep my word, and my Father will love him, and we will come to him and make our dwelling with him.* [24] Whoever does not love me does not keep my words; yet the word you hear is not mine but that of the Father who sent me.

[25] "I have told you this while I am with you. [26] The Advocate, the holy Spirit that the Father will send in my name—he will teach you everything and remind you of all that [I] told you.* [27] Peace† I leave with you; my peace I give to you. Not as the world gives do I give it to you. Do not let your hearts be troubled or afraid.* [28] † You heard me tell you, 'I am going away and I will come back to you.'* If you loved me, you would rejoice that I am going to the Father; for the Father is greater than I. [29] And now I have told you this before it happens, so that when it happens you may believe.* [30] I will no longer speak much with you, for the ruler of the world† is coming. He has no power over me, [31] but the world must know that I love the Father and that I do just as the Father has commanded me. Get up, let us go.*

**15** **The Vine and the Branches.** [1] † "I am the true vine,† and my Father is the vine grower.* [2] He takes away every branch in me that does not bear fruit, and every one that does he prunes† so that it bears more fruit. [3] You are already pruned because of the word that I spoke to you.* [4] Remain in me, as I remain in you. Just as a branch cannot bear fruit on its own unless it remains on the vine, so neither can you unless you remain in me. [5] I am the vine, you are the branches. Whoever remains in me and I in him will bear much fruit, because without me you can do nothing. [6] †* Anyone who does not remain in me will be thrown out like a branch and wither; people will gather them and throw them into a fire and they will be burned. [7] If you remain in me and my words remain in you, ask for whatever you want and it will be done for you.* [8] By this is my Father glorified, that you bear much fruit and become my disciples.* [9] As the Father loves me, so I also love you. Remain in my love.* [10] If you keep my commandments, you will remain in my love, just as I have kept my Father's commandments and remain in his love.*

[11] "I have told you this so that my joy may be in you and your joy may be complete.* [12] This is my commandment: love one another as I love you.* [13] † No one has greater love than this,* to lay down one's life for one's friends. [14] You are my friends if you do what I command you. [15] I no longer call you slaves, because a slave does not know what his master is doing. I have called you friends,† because I have told you everything I have heard from

---

† **14:18** *I will come to you*: indwelling, not parousia.
**14:22** *Judas, not the Iscariot*: probably not the brother of Jesus in Mk 6:3 // Mt 13:55 or the apostle named Jude in Lk 6:16, but Thomas (see note on Jn 11:16), although other readings have "Judas the Cananean."
**14:27** *Peace*: the traditional Hebrew salutation šālôm; but Jesus' "Shalom" is a gift of salvation, connoting the bounty of messianic blessing.
**14:28** *The Father is greater than I*: because he *sent, gave,* etc., and Jesus is "a man who has told you the truth that I heard from God" (Jn 8:40).
**14:30** *The ruler of the world*: Satan; cf. Jn 12:31; 16:11.
**15:1–16:4** Discourse on the union of Jesus with his disciples. His words become a monologue and go beyond the immediate crisis of the departure of Jesus.
**15:1–17** Like Jn 10:1–5, this passage resembles a parable. Israel is spoken of as a vineyard at Is 5:1–7; Mt 21:33–46 and as a vine at Ps 80:9–17; Jer 2:21; Ez 15:2; 17:5–10; 19:10; Hos 10:1. The identification of the vine as the Son of Man in Ps 80:15 and Wisdom's description of herself as a vine in Sir 24:17 are further background for portrayal of Jesus by this figure. There may be secondary eucharistic symbolism here; cf. Mk 14:25, "the fruit of the vine."

**15:2** *Takes away...prunes*: in Greek there is a play on two related verbs.
**15:6** Branches were cut off and dried on the wall of the vineyard for later use as fuel.
**15:13** *For one's friends*: or: "those whom one loves." In Jn 15:9–13a, the words for love are related to the Greek *agapaō*. In Jn 15:13b–15, the words for love are related to the Greek *phileō*. For John, the two roots seem synonymous and mean "to love"; cf. also Jn 21:15–17. The word *philos* is used here.
**15:15** *Slaves...friends*: in the Old Testament, Moses (Dt 34:5),

---

* **14:19** 16:16.
**14:20** 10:38; 17:21; Is 2:17; 4:2–3.
**14:21** 16:27; 1 Jn 2:5; 3:24.
**14:22** 7:4; Acts 10:40–41.
**14:23** Rev 3:20.
**14:26** 15:26; 16:7, 13–14; Ps 51:13; Is 63:10.
**14:27** 16:33; Eph 2:14–18.
**14:28** 8:40.
**14:29** 13:19; 16:4.
**14:31** 6:38.

**15:1** Ps 80:9–17; Is 5:1–7; Jer 2:21; Ez 15:2; 17:5–10; 19:10.
**15:3** 13:10.
**15:6** Ez 15:6–7; 19:10–14.
**15:7** 14:13; Mt 7:7; Mk 11:24; 1 Jn 5:14.
**15:8** Mt 5:16.
**15:9** 17:23.
**15:10** 8:29; 14:15.
**15:11** 16:22; 17:13.
**15:12** 13:34.
**15:13** Rom 5:6–8; 1 Jn 3:16.

JN

my Father.* ¹⁶ It was not you who chose me, but I who chose you and appointed you to go and bear fruit that will remain, so that whatever you ask the Father in my name he may give you.* ¹⁷ This I command you: love one another.*

## The World's Hatred.†
¹⁸ "If the world hates you, realize that it hated me first.* ¹⁹ If you belonged to the world, the world would love its own; but because you do not belong to the world, and I have chosen you out of the world, the world hates you.* ²⁰ Remember the word I spoke to you,† 'No slave is greater than his master.' If they persecuted me, they will also persecute you. If they kept my word, they will also keep yours.* ²¹ And they will do all these things to you on account of my name,† because they do not know the one who sent me.* ²² If I had not come and spoken† to them, they would have no sin; but as it is they have no excuse for their sin.* ²³ Whoever hates me also hates my Father.* ²⁴ If I had not done works among them that no one else ever did, they would not have sin; but as it is, they have seen and hated both me and my Father.* ²⁵ But in order that the word written in their law† might be fulfilled, 'They hated me without cause.'*

²⁶ "When the Advocate comes whom I will send† you from the Father, the Spirit of truth that proceeds from the Father, he will testify to

me.* ²⁷ And you also testify, because you have been with me from the beginning.*

# 16
¹ "I have told you this so that you may not fall away. ² They will expel you from the synagogues; in fact, the hour† is coming when everyone who kills you will think he is offering worship to God.* ³ They will do this because they have not known either the Father or me.* ⁴ I have told you this so that when their hour comes you may remember that I told you.*

## Jesus' Departure; Coming of the Advocate.†
"I did not tell you this from the beginning, because I was with you. ⁵ But now I am going to the one who sent me, and not one of you asks me,† 'Where are you going?'* ⁶ But because I told you this, grief has filled your hearts. ⁷ But I tell you the truth, it is better for you that I go. For if I do not go, the Advocate will not come to you.* But if I go, I will send him to you. ⁸† And when he comes he will convict the world in regard to sin and righteousness and condemnation: ⁹ sin, because they do not believe in me;* ¹⁰ righteousness, because I am going to the Father and you will no longer see me; ¹¹ condemnation, because the ruler of this world has been condemned.*

¹² "I have much more to tell you, but you cannot bear it now. ¹³† But when he comes, the Spirit of truth, he will guide you to all

---

Joshua (Jos 24:29), and David (Ps 89:21) were called "servants" or "slaves of Yahweh"; only Abraham (Is 41:8; 2 Chr 20:7; cf. Jas 2:23) was called a "friend of God."

**15:18–16:4** The hostile reaction of the world. There are synoptic parallels, predicting persecution, especially at Mt 10:17–25; 24:9–10.

**15:20** *The word I spoke to you:* a reference to Jn 13:16.

**15:21** *On account of my name:* the idea of persecution for Jesus' name is frequent in the New Testament (Mt 10:22; 24:9; Acts 9:14). For John, association with Jesus' name implies union with Jesus.

**15:22, 24** Jesus' words (*spoken*) and deeds (*works*) are the great motives of credibility. *They have seen and hated:* probably means that they have seen his works and still have hated; but the Greek can be read: "have seen both me and my Father and still have hated both me and my Father." *Works…that no one else ever did:* so Yahweh in Dt 4:32–33.

**15:25** *In their law:* law is here used as a larger concept than the Pentateuch, for the reference is to Ps 35:19 or Ps 69:5. See notes on Jn 10:34; 12:34. *Their law* reflects the argument of the church with the synagogue.

**15:26** *Whom I will send:* in Jn 14:16, 26, the Paraclete is to be sent by the Father, at the request of Jesus. Here the Spirit comes from both Jesus and the Father in mission; there is no reference here to the eternal procession of the Spirit.

**16:2** *Hour:* of persecution, not Jesus' "hour" (see note on Jn 2:4).

**16:4b–33** A duplicate of Jn 14:1–31 on departure and return.

**16:5** *Not one of you asks me:* the difficulty of reconciling this

with Simon Peter's question in Jn 13:36 and Thomas' words in Jn 14:5 strengthens the supposition that the last discourse has been made up of several collections of Johannine material.

**16:8–11** These verses illustrate the forensic character of the Paraclete's role: in the forum of the disciples' conscience he prosecutes the world. He leads believers to see (a) that the basic sin was and is refusal to believe in Jesus; (b) that, although Jesus was found guilty and apparently died in disgrace, in reality righteousness has triumphed, for Jesus has returned to his Father; (c) finally, that it is the ruler of this world, Satan, who has been condemned through Jesus' death (Jn 12:32).

**16:13** *Declare to you the things that are coming:* not a reference to new predictions about the future, but interpretation of what has already occurred or been said.

---

| | |
|---|---|
| **15:15** Dt 34:5; Jos 24:29; 2 Chr 20:7; Ps 89:21; Is 41:8; Rom 8:15; Gal 4:7; Jas 2:23. | **15:24** 3:2; 9:32; Dt 4:32–33. |
| | **15:25** Ps 35:19; 69:4. |
| | **15:26** 14:16, 26; Mt 10:19–20. |
| **15:16** 14:13; Dt 7:6. | **15:27** Lk 1:2; Acts 1:8. |
| **15:17** 13:34; 1 Jn 3:23; 4:21. | **16:2** 9:22; 12:42; Mt 10:17; Lk 21:12; Acts 26:11. |
| **15:18** 7:7; 14:17; Mt 10:22; 24:9; Mk 13:13; Lk 6:22; 1 Jn 3:13. | **16:3** 15:21. |
| **15:19** 17:14–19; 14:29. | **16:4** 13:19; 14:29. |
| **15:20** 13:16; Mt 10:24. | **16:5** 7:33; 13:36; 14:5. |
| **15:21** 8:19; 16:3. | **16:7** 7:39; 14:16–17, 26; 15:26. |
| **15:22** 8:21, 24; 9:41. | **16:9** 8:21–24; 15:22. |
| **15:23** 5:23; Lk 10:16; 1 Jn 2:23. | **16:11** 12:31. |

truth.* He will not speak on his own, but he will speak what he hears, and will declare to you the things that are coming. [14] He will glorify me, because he will take from what is mine and declare it to you. [15] Everything that the Father has is mine; for this reason I told you that he will take from what is mine and declare it to you.

[16] "A little while and you will no longer see me, and again a little while later and you will see me."* [17] So some of his disciples said to one another, "What does this mean that he is saying to us, 'A little while and you will not see me, and again a little while and you will see me,' and 'Because I am going to the Father'?" [18] So they said, "What is this 'little while' [of which he speaks]? We do not know what he means." [19] Jesus knew that they wanted to ask him, so he said to them, "Are you discussing with one another what I said, 'A little while and you will not see me, and again a little while and you will see me'? [20] Amen, amen, I say to you, you will weep and mourn, while the world rejoices; you will grieve, but your grief will become joy.* [21] When a woman is in labor, she is in anguish because her hour has arrived; but when she has given birth to a child, she no longer remembers the pain because of her joy that a child has been born into the world.* [22] So you also are now in anguish. But I will see you again, and your hearts will rejoice, and no one will take your joy away from you.* [23] On that day you will not question me about anything. Amen, amen, I say to you, whatever you ask the Father in my name he will give you.* [24] Until now you have not asked anything in my name; ask and you will receive, so that your joy may be complete.

[25] †* "I have told you this in figures of speech. The hour is coming when I will no longer speak to you in figures but I will tell you clearly about the Father. [26] On that day you will ask in my name, and I do not tell you that I will ask the Father for you.* [27] For the Father himself loves you, because you have loved me and have come to believe that I came from God. [28] I came from the Father and have come into the world. Now I am leaving the world and going back to the Father."* [29] His disciples said, "Now you are talking plainly, and not in any figure of speech. [30] Now we realize that you know everything and that you do not need to have anyone question you. Because of this we believe that you came from God."† [31] Jesus answered them, "Do you believe now? [32] Behold, the hour is coming and has arrived when each of you will be scattered† to his own home and you will leave me alone. But I am not alone, because the Father is with me.* [33] I have told you this so that you might have peace in me. In the world you will have trouble, but take courage, I have conquered the world."*

## 17 The Prayer of Jesus.†

[1] When Jesus had said this, he raised his eyes to heaven† and said, "Father, the hour has come. Give glory to your son, so that your son may glorify you,* [2] † just as you gave him authority over all people,* so that he may give eternal life to all you gave him. [3] † Now this is eternal life,* that they should know you, the only true God, and the one whom you sent, Jesus Christ. [4] I glorified you on earth by accomplishing the work that you gave me to do. [5] Now glorify me,

---

† **16:25** See note on Jn 10:6. Here, possibly a reference to Jn 15:1–16 or Jn 16:21.

**16:30** The reference is seemingly to the fact that Jesus could anticipate their question in Jn 16:19. The disciples naively think they have the full understanding that is the climax of "the hour" of Jesus' death, resurrection, and ascension (Jn 16:25), but the only part of the hour that is at hand for them is their share in the passion (Jn 16:32).

**16:32** *You will be scattered*: cf. Mk 14:27 and Mt 26:31, where both cite Zec 13:7 about the sheep being dispersed.

**17:1–26** Climax of the last discourse(s). Since the sixteenth century, this chapter has been called the "high priestly prayer" of Jesus. He speaks as intercessor, with words addressed directly to the Father and not to the disciples, who supposedly only overhear. Yet the prayer is one of petition, for immediate (Jn 17:6–19) and future (Jn 17:20–21) disciples. Many phrases reminiscent of the Lord's Prayer occur. Although still in the world (Jn 17:13), Jesus looks on his earthly ministry as a thing of the past (Jn 17:4, 12). Whereas Jesus has up to this time stated that the disciples could follow him (Jn 13:33, 36), now he wishes them to be with

him in union with the Father (Jn 17:12–14).

**17:1** The action of looking up to heaven and the address Father are typical of Jesus at prayer; cf. Jn 11:41 and Lk 11:2.

**17:2** Another possible interpretation is to treat the first line of the verse as parenthetical and the second as an appositive to the clause that ends v 1: *so that your son may glorify you (just as… all people), so that he may give eternal life….*

**17:3** This verse was clearly added in the editing of the gospel as a reflection on the preceding verse; Jesus nowhere else refers to himself as Jesus Christ.

---

* 
| | |
|---|---|
| **16:13** 14:17, 26; 15:26; Ps 25:5; 143:10; 1 Jn 2:27; Rev 7:17. | **16:26** 14:13. |
| | **16:28** 1:1. |
| | **16:32** 8:29; Zec 13:7; Mt 26:31; Mk 14:27. |
| **16:16** 7:33; 14:19. | **16:33** 14:27. |
| **16:20** Ps 126:6. | **17:1** 13:31. |
| **16:21** Is 26:17–18; Jer 31:13; Mi 4:9. | **17:2** 3:35; Mt 28:18. |
| **16:22** 14:19; 15:11; 20:20. | **17:3** 1:17; Wis 14:7; 15:3; 1 Jn 5:20. |
| **16:23** 14:13. | |
| **16:25** Mt 13:34–35. | |

JN

Father, with you, with the glory that I had with you before the world began. *

6 "I revealed your name† to those whom you gave me out of the world. They belonged to you, and you gave them to me, and they have kept your word. 7 Now they know that everything you gave me is from you, 8 because the words you gave to me I have given to them, and they accepted them and truly understood that I came from you, and they have believed that you sent me. 9 I pray for them. I do not pray for the world but for the ones you have given me, because they are yours. * 10 and everything of mine is yours and everything of yours is mine, and I have been glorified in them. * 11 And now I will no longer be in the world, but they are in the world, while I am coming to you. Holy Father, keep them in your name that you have given me, so that they may be one just as we are. 12 When I was with them I protected them in your name that you gave me, and I guarded them, and none of them was lost except the son of destruction, in order that the scripture might be fulfilled. * 13 But now I am coming to you. I speak this in the world so that they may share my joy completely. * 14 I gave them your word, and the world hated them, because they do not belong to the world any more than I belong to the world. * 15 † I do not ask that you take them out of the world * but that you keep them from the evil one. 16 They do not belong to the world any more than I belong to the world. 17 Consecrate them in the truth. Your word is truth. * 18 As you sent me into the world, so I sent them into the world. * 19 And I consecrate myself for them, so that they also may be consecrated in truth.

20 "I pray not only for them, but also for those who will believe in me through their word, 21 so that they may all be one, as you, Father, are in me and I in you, that they also may be in us, that the world may believe that you sent me. * 22 And I have given them the glory you gave me, so that they may be one, as we are one, 23 I in them and you in me, that they may be brought to perfection as one, that the world may know that you sent me, and that you loved them even as you loved me. 24 Father, they are your gift to me. I wish that where I am† they also may be with me, that they may see my glory that you gave me, because you loved me before the foundation of the world. * 25 Righteous Father, the world also does not know you, but I know you, and they know that you sent me. * 26 I made known to them your name and I will make it known,† that the love with which you loved me may be in them and I in them."

# 18 Jesus Arrested.† 1 When he had said this, Jesus went out† with his disciples across the Kidron valley to where there was a garden, into which he and his disciples entered. * 2 Judas his betrayer also knew the place, because Jesus had often met there with his disciples. 3 So Judas got a band of soldiers† and guards from the chief priests and the Pharisees and went there with lanterns, torches, and weapons. * 4 Jesus, knowing everything that was going to happen to him, went out and said to them, "Whom are you looking for?" 5 They answered him, "Jesus the Nazorean."† He said to them, "I AM." Judas his betrayer was also with them. 6 When he said to them, "I AM," they turned away and fell to the ground. 7 So he again asked them, "Whom are you

---

**17:6** *I revealed your name*: perhaps the name *I AM*; cf. Jn 8:24, 28, 58; 13:19.

**17:15** Note the resemblance to the petition of the Lord's Prayer, "deliver us from the evil one." Both probably refer to the devil rather than to abstract evil.

**17:24** *Where I am*: Jesus prays for the believers ultimately to join him in heaven. Then they will not see his glory as in a mirror but clearly (2 Cor 3:18; 1 Jn 3:2).

**17:26** *I will make it known*: through the Advocate.

**18:1–14** John does not mention the agony in the garden and the kiss of Judas, nor does he identify the place as Gethsemane or the Mount of Olives.

**18:1** *Jesus went out*: see Jn 14:31, where it seems he is leaving the supper room. *Kidron valley*: literally, "the winter-flowing Kidron"; this wadi has water only during the winter rains.

**18:3** *Band of soldiers*: seems to refer to Roman troops, either the full cohort of 600 men (1/10 of a legion), or more likely the maniple of 200 under their tribune (Jn 18:12). In this case, John is hinting at Roman collusion in the action against Jesus before he

was brought to Pilate. The lanterns and torches may be symbolic of the hour of darkness.

**18:5** *Nazorean*: the form found in Mt 26:71 (see note on Mt 2:23) is here used, not *Nazarene* of Mark. *I AM*: or "I am he," but probably intended by the evangelist as an expression of divinity (cf. their appropriate response in Jn 18:6); see note on Jn 8:24. John sets the confusion of the arresting party against the background of Jesus' divine majesty.

| | |
|---|---|
| **17:5** 1:1, 2; 12:28; Phil 2:6, 9–11. | **17:17** 1 Pt 1:22 |
| **17:9** 17:20. | **17:18** 20:21–22. |
| **17:10** 16:15; 2 Thes 1:10, 12. | **17:21** 10:30; 14:10–11, 20. |
| **17:12** 13:18; 18:9; Ps 41:10; Mt 26:24; Acts 1:16. | **17:24** 14:3; 1 Thes 4:17. |
| | **17:25** 1:10. |
| **17:13** 15:11. | **18:1** 2 Sm 15:23; Mt 26:30, 36; Mk 14:26, 32; Lk 22:39. |
| **17:14** 15:19. | |
| **17:15** Mt 6:13; 2 Thes 3:3; 1 Jn 5:18. | **18:3** Mt 26:47–51; Mk 14:43–44; Lk 22:47. |

JN

looking for?" They said, "Jesus the Nazorean." [8]Jesus answered, "I told you that I AM. So if you are looking for me, let these men go." [9]†* This was to fulfill what he had said, "I have not lost any of those you gave me." [10]Then Simon Peter, who had a sword, drew it, struck the high priest's slave, and cut off his right ear. The slave's name was Malchus.† [11]Jesus said to Peter, "Put your sword into its scabbard. Shall I not drink the cup† that the Father gave me?"*

[12]* So the band of soldiers, the tribune, and the Jewish guards seized Jesus, bound him, [13]and brought him to Annas† first. He was the father-in-law of Caiaphas, who was high priest that year.* [14]It was Caiaphas who had counseled the Jews that it was better that one man should die rather than the people.*

### Peter's First Denial.*

[15]Simon Peter and another disciple† followed Jesus. Now the other disciple was known to the high priest, and he entered the courtyard of the high priest with Jesus. [16]But Peter stood at the gate outside. So the other disciple, the acquaintance of the high priest, went out and spoke to the gatekeeper and brought Peter in. [17]Then the maid who was the gatekeeper said to Peter, "You are not one of this man's disciples, are you?" He said, "I am not." [18]Now the slaves and the guards were standing around a charcoal fire that they had made, because it was cold, and were warming themselves. Peter was also standing there keeping warm.

### The Inquiry Before Annas.*

[19]The high priest questioned Jesus about his disciples and about his doctrine. [20]Jesus answered him, "I have spoken publicly to the world. I have always taught in a synagogue or in the temple area† where all the Jews gather, and in secret I have said nothing.* [21]Why ask me? Ask those who heard me what I said to them. They know what I said." [22]When he had said this, one of the temple guards standing there struck Jesus and said, "Is this the way you answer the high priest?"* [23]Jesus answered him, "If I have spoken wrongly, testify to the wrong; but if I have spoken rightly, why do you strike me?" [24]Then Annas sent him bound to Caiaphas† the high priest.*

### Peter Denies Jesus Again.*

[25]Now Simon Peter was standing there keeping warm. And they said to him, "You are not one of his disciples, are you?" He denied it and said, "I am not." [26]One of the slaves of the high priest, a relative of the one whose ear Peter had cut off, said, "Didn't I see you in the garden with him?" [27]Again Peter denied it. And immediately the cock crowed.†

### The Trial Before Pilate.

[28]* Then they brought Jesus from Caiaphas to the praetorium.† It was morning. And they themselves did not enter the praetorium, in order not to be defiled so that they could eat the Passover. [29]So Pilate came out to them and said, "What charge do you bring [against] this man?" [30]They answered and said to him, "If he were not a criminal, we would not have handed him over to you." [31]At this, Pilate said to them, "Take him yourselves, and judge him according to your law." The Jews answered him, "We do not have the right to execute anyone,"† [32]† in order that

---

† 18:9 The citation may refer to Jn 6:39; 10:28; or 17:12.

18:10 Only John gives the names of the two antagonists; both John and Luke mention the right ear.

18:11 The theme of the cup is found in the synoptic account of the agony (Mk 14:36 and parallels).

18:13 *Annas*: only John mentions an inquiry before Annas; cf. Jn 18:16, 19–24; see note on Lk 3:2. It is unlikely that this nighttime interrogation before Annas is the same as the trial before Caiaphas placed by Matthew and Mark at night and by Luke in the morning.

18:15–16 *Another disciple…the other disciple*: see note on Jn 13:23.

18:20 *I have always taught…in the temple area*: cf. Mk 14:49 for a similar statement.

18:24 *Caiaphas*: see Mt 26:3, 57; Lk 3:2; and the notes there. John may leave room here for the trial before Caiaphas described in the synoptic gospels.

18:27 Cockcrow was the third Roman division of the night, lasting from midnight to 3 a.m.

18:28 *Praetorium*: see note on Mt 27:27. *Morning*: literally, "the early hour," or fourth Roman division of the night, 3 to 6 a.m. *The Passover*: the synoptic gospels give the impression that the Thursday night supper was the Passover meal (Mk 14:12); for John that meal is still to be eaten Friday night.

18:31 *We do not have the right to execute anyone*: only John gives this reason for their bringing Jesus to Pilate. Jewish sources are not clear on the competence of the Sanhedrin at this period to sentence and to execute for political crimes.

18:32 The Jewish punishment for blasphemy was stoning (Lv 24:16). In coming to the Romans to ensure that Jesus would be crucified, the Jewish authorities fulfilled his prophecy that he would be exalted (Jn 3:14; 12:32–33). There is some historical evidence, however, for Jews crucifying Jews.

| | |
|---|---|
| **18:9** 6:39; 10:28; 17:12. | Mk 14:55–64; Lk |
| **18:11** Mt 20:22; 26:39; Mk | 22:66–71. |
| 10:38; Lk 22:42. | **18:20** 6:59; 7:14, 26; Is |
| **18:12–14** Mt 26:57–58; | 48:16; Mt 26:55; Mk |
| Mk 14:53–54; Lk | 4:23; Lk 19:47; 22:53. |
| 22:54–55. | **18:22** Acts 23:2. |
| **18:13** Lk 3:2. | **18:24** Mt 26:57. |
| **18:14** 11:49–50. | **18:25–27** Mt 26:71–75; |
| **18:15–18** Mt 26:58, 69–70; | Mk 14:69–72; Lk |
| Mk 14:54, 66–68; Lk | 22:58–62. |
| 22:54–57. | **18:28–38a** Mt 27:1–2, 11–25; Mk |
| **18:19–24** Mt 26:59–66; | 15:1–5; Lk 23:1–5. |

the word of Jesus might be fulfilled that he said indicating the kind of death* he would die. 33 So Pilate went back into the praetorium and summoned Jesus and said to him, "Are you the King of the Jews?" 34 Jesus answered, "Do you say this on your own or have others told you about me?" 35 Pilate answered, "I am not a Jew, am I? Your own nation and the chief priests handed you over to me. What have you done?"* 36 Jesus answered, "My kingdom does not belong to this world. If my kingdom did belong to this world, my attendants [would] be fighting to keep me from being handed over to the Jews. But as it is, my kingdom is not here."* 37 So Pilate said to him, "Then you are a king?" Jesus answered, "You say I am a king.† For this I was born and for this I came into the world, to testify to the truth. Everyone who belongs to the truth listens to my voice."* 38 Pilate said to him, "What is truth?"*

When he had said this, he again went out to the Jews and said to them, "I find no guilt in him. 39 But you have a custom that I release one prisoner to you at Passover.† Do you want me to release to you the King of the Jews?" 40 They cried out again, "Not this one but Barabbas!"† Now Barabbas was a revolutionary.

# 19

1†* Then Pilate took Jesus and had him scourged. 2 And the soldiers wove a crown out of thorns and placed it on his head, and clothed him in a purple cloak, 3 and they came to him and said, "Hail, King of the Jews!" And they struck him repeatedly. 4 Once more Pilate went out and said to them, "Look, I am bringing him out to you, so that you may know that I find no guilt in him."* 5 So Jesus came out, wearing the crown of thorns and the purple cloak. And he said to them, "Behold, the man!"* 6 When the chief priests and the guards saw him they cried out, "Crucify him, crucify him!" Pilate said to them, "Take him yourselves and crucify him. I find no guilt in him."* 7† The Jews answered,* "We have a law, and according to that law he ought to die, because he made himself the Son of God." 8 Now when Pilate heard this statement, he became even more afraid, 9 and went back into the praetorium and said to Jesus, "Where are you from?" Jesus did not answer him.* 10 So Pilate said to him, "Do you not speak to me? Do you not know that I have power to release you and I have power to crucify you?" 11 Jesus answered [him], "You would have no power over me if it had not been given to you from above. For this reason the one who handed me over to you has the greater sin."* 12 Consequently, Pilate tried to release him; but the Jews cried out, "If you release him, you are not a Friend of Caesar.† Everyone who makes himself a king opposes Caesar."*

13 When Pilate heard these words he brought Jesus out and seated him† on the judge's bench in the place called Stone Pavement, in Hebrew, Gabbatha. 14 It was preparation day for Passover, and it was about noon.† And he said to the Jews, "Behold, your king!" 15 They cried out, "Take him away, take him away! Crucify him!" Pilate said to them, "Shall I crucify your king?" The chief priests answered, "We have no king but Caesar." 16 Then he handed him over to them to be crucified.†

---

**18:37** *You say I am a king:* see Mt 26:64 for a similar response to the high priest. It is at best a reluctant affirmative.

**18:39** See note on Mt 27:15.

**18:40** *Barabbas:* see note on Mt 27:16–17. *Revolutionary:* a guerrilla warrior fighting for nationalistic aims, though the term can also denote a robber. See note on Mt 27:38.

**19:1** Luke places the mockery of Jesus at the midpoint in the trial when Jesus was sent to Herod. Mark and Matthew place the scourging and mockery at the end of the trial after the sentence of death. Scourging was an integral part of the crucifixion penalty.

**19:7** *Made himself the Son of God:* this question was not raised in John's account of the Jewish interrogations of Jesus as it was in the synoptic account. Nevertheless, see Jn 5:18; 8:53; 10:36.

**19:12** *Friend of Caesar:* a Roman honorific title bestowed upon high-ranking officials for merit.

**19:13** *Seated him:* others translate "(Pilate) sat down." In John's thought, Jesus is the real judge of the world, and John may here be portraying him seated on the judgment bench. *Stone Pavement:* in Greek *lithostrotos;* under the fortress Antonia, one of the conjectured locations of the praetorium, a massive stone pavement has been excavated. *Gabbatha* (Aramaic rather than Hebrew) probably means "ridge, elevation."

**19:14** *Noon:* Mk 15:25 has Jesus crucified "at the third hour," which means either 9 a.m. or the period from 9 to 12 noon, the time when, according to John, Jesus was sentenced to death, was the hour at which the priests began to slaughter Passover lambs in the temple; see Jn 1:29.

**19:16** *He handed him over to them to be crucified:* in context this would seem to mean "handed him over to the chief priests." Lk 23:25 has a similar ambiguity. There is a polemic tendency in the gospels to place the guilt of the crucifixion on the Jewish authorities and to exonerate the Romans from blame. But John later mentions the Roman soldiers (Jn 19:23), and it was to these soldiers that Pilate handed Jesus over.

---

**18:32** 3:14; 8:28; 12:32–33.
**18:35** 1:11.
**18:36** 1:10; 8:23.
**18:37** 8:7; 1 Tm 6:13.
**18:38b–40** Mt 27:15–26;
     Mk 15:6–15; Lk
     23:18–25; Acts 3:14.
**19:1–16** Mt 27:27–31; Mk
     15:16–20;

Lk 23:13–25.
**19:4** 18:38.
**19:5** Is 52:14.
**19:6** 18:31; 19:15.
**19:7** 10:33–36; Lv 24:16.
**19:9** 7:28.
**19:11** 3:27; 10:18; Rom
     13:1.
**19:12** Acts 17:7.

**The Crucifixion of Jesus.** So they took Jesus, [17]* and carrying the cross himself† he went out to what is called the Place of the Skull, in Hebrew, Golgotha. [18]There they crucified him, and with him two others, one on either side, with Jesus in the middle. [19]† Pilate also had an inscription written and put on the cross. It read, "Jesus the Nazorean, the King of the Jews." [20]Now many of the Jews read this inscription, because the place where Jesus was crucified was near the city; and it was written in Hebrew, Latin, and Greek. [21]So the chief priests of the Jews said to Pilate, "Do not write 'The King of the Jews,' but that he said, 'I am the King of the Jews.'"* [22]Pilate answered, "What I have written, I have written."

[23]† When the soldiers had crucified Jesus,* they took his clothes and divided them into four shares, a share for each soldier.* They also took his tunic, but the tunic was seamless, woven in one piece from the top down. [24]So they said to one another, "Let's not tear it, but cast lots for it to see whose it will be," in order that the passage of scripture might be fulfilled [that says]:

"They divided my garments among them,
and for my vesture they cast lots."

This is what the soldiers did. [25]†* Standing by the cross of Jesus were his mother and his mother's sister, Mary the wife of Clopas, and Mary of Magdala. [26]When Jesus saw his mother† and the disciple there whom he loved, he said to his mother, "Woman, behold, your son."* [27]Then he said to the disciple, "Behold, your mother." And from that hour the disciple took her into his home.

[28]* After this, aware that everything was now finished, in order that the scripture might be fulfilled,† Jesus said, "I thirst."* [29]There was a vessel filled with common wine.† So they put a sponge soaked in wine on a sprig of hyssop and put it up to his mouth. [30]† When Jesus had taken the wine, he said, "It is finished."* And bowing his head, he handed over the spirit.

**The Blood and Water.** [31]Now since it was preparation day, in order that the bodies might not remain on the cross on the sabbath, for the sabbath day of that week was a solemn one, the Jews asked Pilate that their legs be broken and they be taken down.* [32]So the soldiers came and broke the legs of the first and then of the other one who was crucified with Jesus. [33]But when they came to Jesus and saw that he was already dead, they did not break his legs, [34]†* but one soldier thrust his lance into

---

† **19:17** *Carrying the cross himself*: a different picture from that of the synoptics, especially Lk 23:26, where Simon of Cyrene is made to carry the cross, walking behind Jesus. In John's theology, Jesus remained in complete control and master of his destiny (cf. Jn 10:18). *Place of the Skull*: the Latin word for skull is *Calvaria*; hence "Calvary." *Golgotha* is actually an Aramaic rather than a Hebrew word.

**19:19** The inscription differs with slightly different words in each of the four gospels. John's form is fullest and gives the equivalent of the Latin *INRI = Iesus Nazarenus Rex Iudaeorum*. Only John mentions its polyglot character (Jn 19:20) and Pilate's role in keeping the title unchanged (Jn 19:21–22).

**19:23–25a** While all four gospels describe the soldiers casting lots to divide Jesus' garments (see note on Mt 27:35), only John quotes the underlying passage from Ps 22:19, and only John sees each line of the poetic parallelism literally carried out in two separate actions (Jn 19:23–24).

**19:25** It is not clear whether four women are meant, or three (i.e., *Mary the wife of Cl[e]opas* [cf. Lk 24:18] is in apposition with *his mother's sister*) or two (his mother and his mother's sister, i.e., Mary of Cl[e]opas and Mary of Magdala). Only John mentions the mother of Jesus here. The synoptics have a group of women looking on from a distance at the cross (Mk 15:40).

**19:26–27** This scene has been interpreted literally, of Jesus' concern for his mother; and symbolically, e.g., in the light of the Cana story in Jn 2 (the presence of the mother of Jesus, the address *woman*, and the mention of the *hour*) and of the upper room in Jn 13 (the presence of the beloved disciple; the *hour*). Now that the hour has come (Jn 19:28), Mary (a symbol of the church?) is given a role as the mother of Christians (personified by the beloved disciple); or, as a representative of those seeking salvation, she is supported by the disciple who interprets Jesus'

revelation; or Jewish and Gentile Christianity (or Israel and the Christian community) are reconciled.

**19:28** *The scripture...fulfilled*: either in the scene of Jn 19:25–27, or in the *I thirst* of Jn 19:28. If the latter, Ps 22:16; 69:22 deserve consideration.

**19:29** *Wine*: John does not mention the drugged wine, a narcotic that Jesus refused as the crucifixion began (Mk 15:23), but only this final gesture of kindness at the end (Mk 15:36). *Hyssop*, a small plant, is scarcely suitable for carrying a sponge (Mark mentions a reed) and may be a symbolic reference to the hyssop used to daub the blood of the paschal lamb on the doorpost of the Hebrews (Ex 12:22).

**19:30** *Handed over the spirit*: there is a double nuance of dying (giving up the last breath or spirit) and that of passing on the holy Spirit; see Jn 7:39, which connects the giving of the Spirit with Jesus' glorious return to the Father, and Jn 20:22, where the author portrays the conferral of the Spirit.

**19:34–35** John probably emphasizes these verses to show the reality of Jesus' death, against the docetic heretics. In the blood and water there may also be a symbolic reference to the Eucharist and baptism.

---

| | |
|---|---|
| **19:17–22** Mt 27:32–37; | Lk 8:2; 23:49. |
| Mk 15:21–26; Lk | **19:26** 13:23. |
| 23:26–35. | **19:28–30** Mt 27:45–56; |
| **19:21** 18:33; Lk 19:14. | Mk 15:33–41; Lk |
| **19:23–27** Mt 27:38–44; | 23:44–49. |
| Mk 15:27–32; Lk | **19:28** Ps 22:16; 69:22. |
| 23:36–43. | **19:30** 4:34; 10:18; 17:4; Lk |
| **19:23–24** Ps 22:19; Mt 27:35; | 23:46. |
| Mk 15:24; Lk 23:34. | **19:31** Ex 12:16; Dt 21:23. |
| **19:25** Mt 27:55; Mk | **19:34** Nm 20:11; 1 Jn 5:6. |
| 15:40–41; | |

his side, and immediately blood and water flowed out. [35] An eyewitness has testified, and his testimony is true; he knows† that he is speaking the truth, so that you also may [come to] believe.* [36] For this happened so that the scripture passage might be fulfilled:

"Not a bone of it will be broken."*

[37] And again another passage says:

"They will look upon him whom they have pierced."*

**The Burial of Jesus.**† [38]* After this, Joseph of Arimathea, secretly a disciple of Jesus for fear of the Jews, asked Pilate if he could remove the body of Jesus. And Pilate permitted it. So he came and took his body. [39] Nicodemus, the one who had first come to him at night, also came bringing a mixture of myrrh and aloes weighing about one hundred pounds.* [40] They took the body of Jesus and bound it with burial cloths along with the spices, according to the Jewish burial custom. [41] Now in the place where he had been crucified there was a garden, and in the garden a new tomb, in which no one had yet been buried. [42] So they laid Jesus there because of the Jewish preparation day; for the tomb was close by.

# 20 †**The Empty Tomb.**† [1] On the first day of the week,* Mary of Magdala came to the tomb early in the morning, while it was still dark,† and saw the stone removed from the tomb.* [2] So she ran† and went to Simon Peter and to the other disciple whom Jesus

loved, and told them, "They have taken the Lord from the tomb, and we don't know where they put him." [3]† So Peter and the other disciple went out and came to the tomb. [4] They both ran, but the other disciple ran faster than Peter and arrived at the tomb first; [5] he bent down and saw the burial cloths there, but did not go in. [6]* When Simon Peter arrived after him, he went into the tomb and saw the burial cloths† there, [7] and the cloth that had covered his head, not with the burial cloths but rolled up in a separate place.* [8] Then the other disciple also went in, the one who had arrived at the tomb first, and he saw and believed. [9]†* For they did not yet understand the scripture that he had to rise from the dead. [10] Then the disciples returned home.

**The Appearance to Mary of Magdala.**† [11] But Mary stayed outside the tomb weeping.* And as she wept, she bent over into the tomb [12] and saw two angels in white sitting there, one at the head and one at the feet where the body of Jesus had been. [13] And they said to her, "Woman, why are you weeping?" She said to them, "They have taken my Lord, and I don't know where they laid him." [14] When she had said this, she turned around and saw Jesus there, but did not know it was Jesus.* [15] Jesus said to her, "Woman, why are you weeping? Whom are you looking for?"* She thought it was the gardener and said to him, "Sir, if you carried him away, tell me where you laid him, and I will take him." [16] Jesus said to her, "Mary!" She turned and said to him in Hebrew, "Rabbouni,"† which means Teacher. [17] Jesus said to her, "Stop holding on to me,†

---

† **19:35** *He knows:* it is not certain from the Greek that this *he* is the *eyewitness* of the first part of the sentence. *May [come to] believe:* see note on Jn 20:31.

**19:38–42** In the first three gospels there is no anointing on Friday. In Matthew and Luke the women come to the tomb on Sunday morning precisely to anoint Jesus.

**20:1–31** The risen Jesus reveals his glory and confers the Spirit. This story fulfills the basic need for testimony to the resurrection. What we have here is not a record but a series of single stories.

**20:1–10** The story of the empty tomb is found in both the Matthean and the Lucan traditions; John's version seems to be a fusion of the two.

**20:1** *Still dark:* according to Mark the sun had risen, Matthew describes it as "dawning," and Luke refers to early dawn. Mary sees the stone removed, not the empty tomb.

**20:2** Mary runs away, not directed by an angel/young man as in the synoptic accounts. The plural "we" in the second part of her statement might reflect a tradition of more women going to the tomb.

**20:3–10** The basic narrative is told of Peter alone in Lk 24:12, a verse missing in important manuscripts and which may be borrowed from tradition similar to John. Cf. also Lk 24:24.

**20:6–8** Some special feature about the state of the burial cloths caused the beloved disciple to believe. Perhaps the details emphasized that the grave had not been robbed.

**20:9** Probably a general reference to the scriptures is intended, as in Lk 24:26 and 1 Cor 15:4. Some individual Old Testament passages suggested are Ps 16:10; Hos 6:2; Jon 2:1, 2, 10.

**20:11–18** This appearance to Mary is found only in John, but cf. Mt 28:8–10 and Mk 16:9–11.

**20:16** *Rabbouni:* Hebrew or Aramaic for "my master."

**20:17** *Stop holding on to me:* see Mt 28:9, where the women take hold of his feet. *I have not yet ascended:* for John and many

---

* **19:35** 7:37–39; 21:24.
**19:36** Ex 12:46; Nm 9:12; Ps 34:21.
**19:37** Nm 21:9; Zec 12:10; Rev 1:7.
**19:38–42** Mt 27:57–60; Mk 24:42–46; Lk 23:46–49.
**19:39** 3:1–2; 7:50; Ps 45:9.
**20:1–10** Mt 28:1–10; Mk 16:1–11; Lk 24:1–12.

**20:1** 19:25.
**20:6** Lk 24:12.
**20:7** 11:44; 19:40.
**20:9** Acts 2:26–27; 1 Cor 15:4.
**20:11–18** Mk 16:9–11.
**20:14** 21:4; Mk 16:12; Lk 24:16; 1 Cor 15:43–44.
**20:15–17** Mt 28:9–10.

for I have not yet ascended to the Father. But go to my brothers and tell them, 'I am going to my Father and your Father, to my God and your God.'"* ¹⁸Mary of Magdala went and announced to the disciples, "I have seen the Lord," and what he told her.

### Appearance to the Disciples.†

¹⁹On the evening of that first day of the week,* when the doors were locked, where the disciples† were, for fear of the Jews, Jesus came and stood in their midst and said to them, "Peace be with you." ²⁰When he had said this, he showed them his hands and his side.† The disciples rejoiced when they saw the Lord.* ²¹† [Jesus] said to them again,* "Peace be with you. As the Father has sent me, so I send you." ²²† And when he had said this, he breathed on them and said to them,* "Receive the holy Spirit. ²³** Whose sins you forgive are forgiven them, and whose sins you retain are retained."

### Thomas.

²⁴Thomas, called Didymus, one of the Twelve, was not with them when Jesus came. ²⁵So the other disciples said to him, "We have seen the Lord." But he said to them, "Unless I see the mark of the nails in his hands and put my finger into the nailmarks and put my hand into his side, I will not believe."* ²⁶Now a week later his disciples were again inside and Thomas was with them. Jesus came, although the doors were locked, and stood in their midst and said, "Peace be with you."* ²⁷Then he said to Thomas, "Put your finger here and see my hands, and bring your hand and put it into my side, and do not be unbelieving, but believe." ²⁸†* Thomas answered and said to him, "My Lord and my God!" ²⁹† Jesus said to him, "Have you come to believe because you have seen me?* Blessed are those who have not seen and have believed."

### Conclusion.†

³⁰Now Jesus did many other signs in the presence of [his] disciples that are not written in this book.* ³¹But these are written that you may [come to] believe that Jesus is the Messiah, the Son of God, and that through this belief you may have life in his name.*

## IV. EPILOGUE: THE RESURRECTION APPEARANCE IN GALILEE

**21** **The Appearance to the Seven Disciples.** ¹† After this, Jesus revealed

---

of the New Testament writers, the ascension in the theological sense of going to the Father to be glorified took place with the resurrection as one action. This scene in John dramatizes such an understanding, for by Easter night Jesus is glorified and can give the Spirit. Therefore his ascension takes place immediately after he has talked to Mary. In such a view, the ascension after forty days described in Acts 1:1–11 would be simply a termination of earthly appearances or, perhaps better, an introduction to the conferral of the Spirit upon the early church, modeled on Elisha's being able to have a (double) share in the spirit of Elijah if he saw him being taken up (same verb as ascending) into heaven (2 Kgs 2:9–12). *To my Father and your Father, my God and your God*: this echoes Ru 1:16: "Your people shall be my people, and your God my God." The Father of Jesus will now become the Father of the disciples because, once ascended, Jesus can give them the Spirit that comes from the Father and they can be reborn as God's children (Jn 3:5). That is why he calls them *my brothers*.

**20:19–29** The appearances to the disciples, without or with Thomas (cf. Jn 11:16; 14:5), have rough parallels in the other gospels only for Jn 20:19–23; cf. Lk 24:36–39; Mk 16:14–18.

**20:19** *The disciples*: by implication from Jn 20:24 this means ten of the Twelve, presumably in Jerusalem. *Peace be with you*: although this could be an ordinary greeting, John intends here to echo Jn 14:27. The theme of rejoicing in Jn 20:20 echoes Jn 16:22.

**20:20** *Hands and...side*: Lk 24:39–40 mentions "hands and feet," based on Ps 22:17.

**20:21** By means of this sending, the Eleven were made apostles, that is, "those sent" (cf. Jn 17:18), though John does not use the noun in reference to them (see note on Jn 13:16). A solemn mission or "sending" is also the subject of the post-resurrection appearances to the Eleven in Mt 28:19; Lk 24:47; Mk 16:15.

**20:22** This action recalls Gn 2:7, where God breathed on the first man and gave him life; just as Adam's life came from God, so now the disciples' new spiritual life comes from Jesus. Cf. also the revivification of the dry bones in Ez 37. This is the author's version of Pentecost. Cf. also the note on Jn 19:30.

**20:23** The Council of Trent defined that this power to forgive sins is exercised in the sacrament of penance. See Mt 16:19; 18:18.

**20:28** *My Lord and my God*: this forms a literary inclusion with the first verse of the gospel: "and the Word was God."

**20:29** This verse is a beatitude on future generations; faith, not sight, matters.

**20:30–31** These verses are clearly a conclusion to the gospel and express its purpose. While many manuscripts read *come to believe*, possibly implying a missionary purpose for John's gospel, a small number of quite early ones read "continue to believe," suggesting that the audience consists of Christians whose faith is to be deepened by the book; cf. Jn 19:35.

**21:1–23** There are many non-Johannine peculiarities in this chapter, some suggesting Lucan Greek style; yet this passage is closer to John than Jn 7:53–8:11. There are many Johannine features as well. Its closest parallels in the synoptic gospels are found in Lk 5:1–11 and Mt 14:28–31. Perhaps the tradition was ultimately derived from John but preserved by some disciple other than the writer of the rest of the gospel. The appearances narrated seem to be independent of those in Jn 20. Even if a later addition, the chapter was added before publication of the gospel, for it appears in all manuscripts.

---

20:17 Acts 1:9.
20:19–23 Mt 28:16–20;
　　　Mk 16:14–18; Lk
　　　24:36–44.
20:20 14:27.
20:21 17:18; Mt 28:19; Mk
　　　16:15; Lk 24:47–48.
20:22 Gn 2:7; Ez 37:9;
　　　1 Cor 15:45.
20:23 Mt 16:19; 18:18.
20:25 1 Jn 1:1.
20:26 21:14.
20:28 1:1.
20:29 4:48; Lk 1:45; 1 Pt
　　　1:8.
20:30 21:25.
20:31 3:14, 15; 1 Jn 5:13.

himself again to his disciples at the Sea of Tiberias. He revealed himself in this way.* ²Together were Simon Peter, Thomas called Didymus, Nathanael from Cana in Galilee, Zebedee's sons,† and two others of his disciples. ³† Simon Peter said to them, "I am going fishing." They said to him, "We also will come with you." So they went out and got into the boat, but that night they caught nothing.* ⁴When it was already dawn, Jesus was standing on the shore; but the disciples did not realize that it was Jesus.* ⁵Jesus said to them, "Children, have you caught anything to eat?" They answered him, "No."* ⁶So he said to them, "Cast the net over the right side of the boat and you will find something." So they cast it, and were not able to pull it in because of the number of fish. ⁷So the disciple whom Jesus loved said to Peter, "It is the Lord." When Simon Peter heard that it was the Lord, he tucked in his garment, for he was lightly clad, and jumped into the sea. ⁸The other disciples came in the boat, for they were not far from shore, only about a hundred yards, dragging the net with the fish. ⁹†* When they climbed out on shore, they saw a charcoal fire with fish on it and bread. ¹⁰Jesus said to them, "Bring some of the fish you just caught." ¹¹So Simon Peter went over and dragged the net ashore full of one hundred fifty-three† large fish. Even though there were so many, the net was not torn.* ¹²Jesus said to them, "Come, have breakfast." And none of the disciples dared to ask him,† "Who are you?" because they realized it was the Lord. ¹³Jesus came over and took the bread and gave it to them, and in like manner the fish.* ¹⁴† This was now the third time* Jesus was revealed to his disciples after being raised from the dead.

**Jesus and Peter.**† ¹⁵When they had finished breakfast, Jesus said to Simon Peter,† "Simon, son of John, do you love me more than these?"† He said to him, "Yes, Lord, you know that I love you." He said to him, "Feed my lambs." ¹⁶He then said to him a second time, "Simon, son of John, do you love me?" He said to him, "Yes, Lord, you know that I love you." He said to him, "Tend my sheep." ¹⁷He said to him the third time, "Simon, son of John, do you love me?" Peter was distressed that he had said to him a third time, "Do you love me?" and he said to him, "Lord, you know everything; you know that I love you." [Jesus] said to him, "Feed my sheep.* ¹⁸† Amen, amen, I say to you,* when you were younger, you used to dress yourself and go where you wanted; but when you grow old, you will stretch out your hands, and someone else will dress you and lead you where you do not want to go." ¹⁹He said this signifying by what kind of death he would glorify God. And when he had said this, he said to him, "Follow me."*

**The Beloved Disciple.** ²⁰Peter turned and saw the disciple following whom Jesus loved, the one who had also reclined upon his chest during the supper and had said, "Master, who is the one who will betray you?"* ²¹When Peter saw him, he said to Jesus, "Lord, what about

---

† **21:2** *Zebedee's sons:* the only reference to James and John in this gospel (but see note on Jn 1:37). Perhaps the phrase was originally a gloss to identify, among the five, the *two others of his disciples.* The anonymity of the latter phrase is more Johannine (Jn 1:35). The total of seven may suggest the community of the disciples in its fullness.

**21:3–6** This may be a variant of Luke's account of the catch of fish; see note on Lk 5:1–11.

**21:9, 12–13** It is strange that Jesus already has fish since none have yet been brought ashore. This meal may have had eucharistic significance for early Christians since Jn 21:13 recalls Jn 6:11 which uses the vocabulary of Jesus' action at the Last Supper; but see also note on Mt 14:19.

**21:11** The exact number 153 is probably meant to have a symbolic meaning in relation to the apostles' universal mission; Jerome claims that Greek zoologists catalogued 153 species of fish. Or 153 is the sum of the numbers from 1 to 17. Others invoke Ez 47:10.

**21:12** *None...dared to ask him:* is Jesus' appearance strange to them? Cf. Lk 24:16; Mk 16:12; Jn 20:14. The disciples do, however, recognize Jesus *before* the breaking of the bread (opposed to Lk 24:35).

**21:14** This verse connects Jn 20 and 21; cf. Jn 20:19, 26.

**21:15–23** This section constitutes Peter's rehabilitation and emphasizes his role in the church.

**21:15–17** In these three verses there is a remarkable variety of synonyms: two different Greek verbs for *love* (see note on Jn 15:13); two verbs for *feed/tend;* two nouns for *sheep;* two verbs for *know.* But apparently there is no difference of meaning. The threefold confession of Peter is meant to counteract his earlier threefold denial (Jn 18:17, 25, 27). The First Vatican Council cited these verses in defining that Jesus after his resurrection gave Peter the jurisdiction of supreme shepherd and ruler over the whole flock.

**21:15** *More than these:* probably "more than these disciples do" rather than "more than you love them" or "more than you love these things [fishing, etc.]."

**21:18** Originally probably a proverb about old age, now used as a figurative reference to the crucifixion of Peter.

---

**21:1** Mt 26:32; 28:7.
**21:3** Mt 4:18; Lk 5:4–10.
**21:4** 20:14; Mt 28:17; Lk 24:16.
**21:5** Lk 24:41.
**21:9** Lk 24:41–43.
**21:11** 2 Chr 2:16.
**21:13** Lk 24:42.
**21:14** 20:19, 26.
**21:17** 13:37–38; 18:15–18, 25–27; Mt 26:69–75; Mk 14:66–72; Lk 22:55–62.
**21:18** Acts 21:11, 14; 2 Pt 1:14.
**21:19** 13:36.
**21:20** 13:25.

J
N

him?" [22] Jesus said to him, "What if I want him to remain until I come?† What concern is it of yours? You follow me." * [23]† So the word spread among the brothers that that disciple would not die. But Jesus had not told him that he would not die, just "What if I want him to remain until I come? [What concern is it of yours?]"

**Conclusion.** [24] It is this disciple who testifies to these things and has written them,† and we know that his testimony is true. * [25] There are also many other things that Jesus did, but if these were to be described individually, I do not think the whole world would contain the books that would be written. *

---

† **21:22** *Until I come:* a reference to the parousia.

**21:23** This whole scene takes on more significance if the disciple is already dead. The death of the apostolic generation caused problems in the church because of a belief that Jesus was to have returned first. Loss of faith sometimes resulted; cf. 2 Pt 3:4.

**21:24** *Who...has written them:* this does not necessarily mean he wrote them with his own hand. The same expression is used in Jn 19:22 of Pilate, who certainly would not have written the inscription himself. *We know:* i.e., the Christian community; cf. Jn 1:14, 16.

---

* **21:22** Mt 16:28.  **21:25** 20:30.
 **21:24** 19:35.

# Sacred Time: Festivals, Feasts, and Fasts of Judaism Practiced by Jesus, the Apostles, and Their Contemporaries

Festivals include feasts to celebrate fertility, happiness, commitment, births, marriages, or victories. Times of fasting include penance and periods when feasting are forbidden.

| Event | Significance and Reference |
|---|---|
| **Sabbath** | The seventh day is a day of rest to honor God and family. No work is permitted (Ex 20:8–11; Lv 23:1–3; Dt 5:12–15). In the New Testament period, synagogue attendance on the sabbath is typical (Mk 1:21; 6:2; Lk 4:16; Acts 15:21; 18:4). Jesus often engages in disputes about how to honor the sabbath (Mt 12:1–12; Mk 2:23–28; 3:2–4; Lk 13:10–16; Jn 5:10–18). |
| | Christians celebrate Sunday instead of the sabbath to honor the Paschal mystery of Christ's life, death, and Resurrection (Mt 28:1–10; Mk 16:1–8; Lk 24:1–12; Jn 20:1–23; 1 Cor 16:2; Heb 4:9). |
| **New Year** | Rosh Hashanah marks the New Year with prayers and rest. It is a day of trumpets (Nm 29:1–6). |
| **Yom Kippur or Day of Atonement** | Ten days after the New Year, the Day of Atonement honors ancestors and is a day of repentance, symbolized by a scapegoat driven into the wilderness (Lv 16; 23:26–32; Nm 29:7–11). |
| **Sabbatical year** | Every seven years the land rests, slaves are freed, and all debts are suspended or erased (Ex 21:2; 23:10–11; Lv 25:1–7; Dt 15:1–6). |
| **Jubilee (fiftieth year)** | The seventh sabbatical year is honored with compassion to the poor, the freedom of slaves, erasure of debts, the return of property to its original owner, and resting the land (Lv 25:8–22; 2 Chr 36:21; Is 61:1–2). Jesus draws on this tradition in the synagogue at Nazareth (Lk 4:16–22). |
| **Feast of Passover or Unleavened Bread** | The memorial of the Exodus from Egypt is honored in a seder meal in which prayers and blessings are offered for Jews across the world (Ex 12:1–28; 34:18, 25; Lv 23:4–14; Nm 9:1–14; 28:16–25; Dt 16:1–8; Ez 45:18–24). It is also a time of pilgrimage to the Temple. |
| | Jesus gave new meaning to Passover when he offered himself as the bread of life in the Eucharist (Mt 26:17–19, 26–29; Jn 6:4–14, 22–59; 1 Cor 10:1; 11:23–26). |
| **Feast of Weeks (Shavuot or Pentecost)** | Shavuot ("weeks") concludes a period of seven weeks after the rite of Omer (the second day of Passover, on which the first sheaf of wheat is offered in thanks for the harvest). The Greek name for this feast, Pentecost ("fifty"), derives from the fact that the feast falls fifty days after Passover (Ex 23:16; 34:22; Lv 23:15–22; Nm 28:26–31; Dt 16:9–10). |
| | Pentecost, for Christians, marks the descent of the Holy Spirit and the beginning of the church (Acts 2:1–11; 20:16; 1 Cor 16:8). |
| **Feast of Tabernacles or Booths (Sukkoth)** | Autumn feast; gathering of the harvest on the fifteenth to the twenty-first days of the seventh month. The feast recalls Israel's experience of living in the wilderness during the Exodus (Lv 23:33–43; Nm 29:12–39; Dt 16:13–17; Ez 45:25; Zec 14:16–19). |
| | Jesus attended the feast of Tabernacles (feast of Booths) in the Temple (Jn 7:2–14, 37). |
| **Purim** | Holy day that marks the defeat of Haman of Persia by Esther and honors Mordecai's faith. The feast includes drama, fasting, feasting, and prayers for Israel (Est 9:20–32). |
| **Hanukkah** | The dedication of the second Temple and the defeat of Antiochus IV (167 BCE) in the Maccabean War is the mythic source of Hanukkah. The festival includes feasting and celebrations (1 Mc 4:1–59; 2 Mc 10:1–8; Jn 10:22). |

# Greco-Roman Rulers in the New Testament Period

The Greek and Roman rulers who occupied or conquered Palestine had a profound influence on the world of the New Testament. Some of their names are recorded in the Scriptures and others are remembered in histories of the age, but all play a significant role in understanding the Bible.

| Name and Date | Significance and Reference |
|---|---|
| Octavius (or Octavian) "Augustus" (27 BCE–14 CE) | Octavius Caesar,[1] known as Augustus ("majestic"), ruled Rome when Jesus of Nazareth was born. He was the first Caesar to be proclaimed a god. He and his wife, Livia Drusilla, played essential roles in Roman political and religious thought (Lk 2:1). |
| Quirinius (6 BCE–21 CE) | Roman governor of Syria who ruled Judea at the time of the birth of Christ. He was an advisor to Augustus and Tiberius (Lk 2:2). |
| Tiberius Claudius (14–37 CE) | Caesar Tiberius was the son of Tiberius Nero and Livia Drusilla and adopted by Octavius. John the Baptist and Jesus were killed during his rule (Lk 3:1). Romans called the Lake of Galilee Tiberias. The lake's major city, Tiberias, was built during his lifetime and named for him (Jn 6:23). |
| Pontius Pilate (26–36 CE) | Roman prefect of Judea with power to execute. John the Baptist and Jesus were killed during his rule (Lk 3:1; 13:1; 23:1-25; Jn 19:1-16). |
| Gaius "Caligula" (37–41 CE) | Caesar Gaius, known as Caligula ("little boots"), was the adopted grandson of Tiberius. He deified himself and ordered his divine statue erected in the Temple of Jerusalem. His blasphemous plan influenced apocalyptic writings. |
| Claudius (41–54 CE) | During this Caesar's reign there was famine and persecution of both Jews and Christians, including the martyrdom of Stephen and James (Acts 8:2; 11:28-29; 12:2; 18:2). |
| Nero (54–68 CE) | Claudius's son by Agrippina, Caesar Nero saw himself as a god. He blamed the burning of Rome on Christians and began the persecutions that killed Peter and Paul. The "number of the beast," 666 (Rev 13:18), is a numerological representation of Nero's name. The Epistles of Paul were written during his rule. |
| Felix (52–59 CE) | Roman governor of Judea. He worked with Festus and Bernice, daughter of Herod Agrippa I. He heard the case of Paul, when he was accused of desecrating the Temple, but failed to decide Paul's case. Paul was still in custody when Felix was replaced (Acts 24:1-27; 25:14). |
| Festus Porcius (60 CE) | Procurator of Judea, appointed by Nero to succeed Felix. Festus reviewed Paul's case; when Paul appealed to Caesar, Festus agreed to send Paul to Rome, that his case might be decided there (Acts 24:27–25:27; 26:24-32). Festus ruled for two years and died in office. |

1. Caesar was originally the name of a Roman family to which the first emperor, Julius Caesar, belonged. Subsequent emperors adopted the name as a way of indicating that they had inherited the imperial authority.

*(continued on next page)*

*(Greco-Roman Rulers in the New Testament Period – continued from previous page)*

| | |
|---|---|
| **Galba**<br>(68–69 CE) | Governor of Hispania, rose to become Caesar during the Roman civil wars when there were three Caesars in one year. |
| **Otho**<br>(69 CE) | Held the throne of Caesar for eight weeks, then committed suicide. Three days later, Vitellius was named emperor. |
| **Vitellius**<br>(69 CE) | Governor of Lower Germany who was proclaimed Caesar after Otho's suicide in the midst of Rome's civil wars. |
| **Titus Flavius Vespasianus**<br>(69–79 CE) | Counteracted the excesses of Nero, restored stability to Rome. Caesar at the time of the Jewish revolt. Vespasian began building the Colosseum. Titus deified him. |
| **Titus Flavius**<br>(79–81 CE) | The general who defeated the Jewish rebellion and demolished Jerusalem. He was Caesar during the eruption of Vesuvius, was poisoned by his brother Domitian, and then deified. |
| **Domitian**<br>(81–96 CE) | As Caesar, he accepted divine honors; he is reputed to have been the first emperor to demand that he be addressed as *Dominus et Deus* ("Lord and God") and to have encouraged the offering of sacrifices to his divinity. The Gospels of Matthew, Luke, and John, the Catholic Letters, and the book of Revelation may have been written during his reign. |
| **Nerva**<br>(96–98 CE) | A just Caesar who forbade indulgence and instituted social welfare programs throughout Rome. He named Trajan his adopted son and heir. He was deified at his death. |
| **Trajan**<br>(98–117 CE) | A native of Hispania, Caesar Trajan freed prisoners and returned property. The Gospel of John, the Catholic Epistles, and the book of Revelation may have been written during this time. Trajan and Pliny the Younger exchanged letters, which have survived, that deal with the correct procedure for arresting, questioning, and punishing persons accused of being Christians. |
| **Hadrian**<br>(117–138 CE) | This emperor was a man of art and science and respected as a statesman and soldier. He traveled extensively throughout the empire, leaving many monumental buildings that still stand. He was deified at his death. |

Festus Porcius

Otho | Vitellius

Galba

Titus Flavius

Nerva

| Nero | Vespasianus | Domitian | Trajan | Hadrian |

60 CE   70   80   90   100   110   120   130   140 CE

# Titles of Jesus of Nazareth

Those who wrote the Gospels honored Jesus with names, words, and titles that expressed faith in him.

| Title | Significance and Reference |
|---|---|
| **Jesus** | *Yeshua* (or Joshua) in Hebrew means "God saves" (Mt 1:21; Lk 1:31). |
| **Son of Mary** | This title identifies Jesus as born of woman and fully human (Mt 1:18; Mk 6:3; Lk 1:26–31). |
| **Rabbi or Rabbouni** | By addressing Jesus with this title, Jesus' disciples identified him as a Jewish wisdom teacher, healer, and scholar of the Torah. An equivalent title is "master" (*Didaskalos* in Greek) (Mk 9:5; 10:51; Jn 3:2; 20:16). |
| **Carpenter or craftsman** | Jesus was a craftsman like his father Joseph (Mt 13:55; Mk 6:3). |
| **Messiah (*Christos* in Greek)** | Christ (*Mashia* in Hebrew) means anointed one, a title used for kings, prophets, and war heroes. Jesus was called Messiah by his disciples and the Gospel writers (Mt 1:1, 18; 16:16; Mk 1:1; 8:29; Jn 4:25–26; Acts 2:38). Paul and other NT writers make it the title by which Jesus was most frequently known, with connotations well beyond those of the Jewish messiah. |
| **King of the Jews** | Jesus was born of David's royal line. Angels, shepherds, and the Magi adored the newborn king. Pilate mocked him with this title, having it nailed to the cross on which Christ was crucified (Mt 2:2; Mk 15:2; Lk 23:38; Jn 19:19). |
| **Son (Root) of David** | Jesus is a descendant of Israel's great King David, the fulfillment of the prophecy of Nathan, who said the Covenant would remain with the house of David (2 Sm 7:11–16; Mt 1:1; 12:23; Lk 18:38; Rev 5:5). |
| **Son of Abraham** | Jesus is the descendant of Israel's great patriarch and shares in the election of Israel and the eternal covenant (Mt 1:1; Lk 3:34). |
| **Son of Man** | This title is given to a heavenly yet human figure in Daniel's vision (Dn 7:13–14) and used in the Gospels to depict Jesus as vulnerable in his humanity and his passion (Mt 8:20; 17:9, 12, 22–23; Lk 9:22, 58; 18:8).<br><br>The Son of Man came as the "human one" from heaven with the authority to forgive sin (Mt 9:6; 12:32; Mk 2:10; Lk 5:24; 12:10; Jn 3:13). He will be condemned, die, be buried, offer his life to redeem many (Mt 20:18–19, 28; Mk 9:31), and rise from the dead (Mk 9:9). He will also be triumphant in his future return (Mt 13:41; 16:27; 19:28; Mk 14:62; Lk 12:8; Jn 1:51; 12:23; 13:31) to judge the living and the dead in the new age (Mt 19:28, 26:64; Lk 22:69; Jn 5:26–29). |
| **Son of God or Son of the Most High, Son of the Blessed One** | This title points to Jesus' unique connection to the Father: he is God's "only" Son (Mt 4:3; 14:33; 27:54; Mk 3:11; Lk 1:32; Jn 1:18). In the Hebrew Scriptures, the phrase was sometimes used with regard to Israel's king, who ruled on God's behalf as a sort of adopted son (Ps 2). In this sense, the phrase means much the same thing as Messiah/Christ (Mk 14:61; Jn 11:26; 20:31). |
| **Savior** | Jesus is savior of Israel and of the world, the one who releases humanity from bondage, from sin and death (Lk 2:11; Jn 4:42; Acts 5:31; 13:23). |
| **The Lord; I AM** | In Jesus' day, Jews typically substituted the word Lord (*kyrios* in Greek) for the unutterable divine name "Yahweh" (which is related to the Hebrew phrase "I am"; Ex 3:13–15). The New Testament writers assert that Jesus Christ is Lord, the Glory of God, the manifestation of God among us (Jn 1:1–18; 20:28–29; Acts 2:36; Phil 2:11).<br><br>Jesus is the "I am" of God; the bread of life; the light of the world; the door, the gate; the Good Shepherd; the resurrection and life; the way, the truth, and the life (Jn 6:35; 8:12, 58; 10:7, 11; 11:25; 14:6). |
| **Lamb of God** | Jesus is the worthy sacrifice who frees humanity from sin, who was slain (Jn 1:29, 36; Rev 5:6; 17:14). |
| **Word of God, Alpha and Omega** | Jesus is the Word (Logos) of God in the flesh. Jesus is the alpha and the omega, the beginning and end of all creation; the pre-existent one (Jn 1:1–3, 14; Rev 19:13; 21:6). |

# Wonders, Miracles, and Signs in the New Testament

The miraculous events in the Gospels and writings of the early Christians evidence the power of God working through Jesus and his followers. All the forces of nature submit in the name of Jesus.

| Wonders | Event and Reference |
|---|---|
| **Angelic annunciations, wondrous pregnancies** | Barren Elizabeth conceives John the Baptist (Lk 1:5–25). |
| | Mary is called by the angel Gabriel to be the mother of Christ and she conceives by the Holy Spirit (Lk 1:26–38). |
| | The Virgin Mary gives birth to Jesus (Lk 2:3–16). |
| **Signs of Jesus' destiny** | Elizabeth proclaims that Mary carries the Savior (Lk 1:39–45). |
| | John recognizes Jesus while in the womb (Lk 1:44). |
| | The child Jesus astonishes the teachers of the Law (Lk 2:42–49). |
| **Extraordinary interventions** | An angel warns Joseph of impending danger (Mt 2:1–9, 13–18). |
| | The apostles are released from jail (Acts 12:6–11; 16:26–36). |
| **Jesus heals** | Jesus heals the centurion's servant (Mt 8:5–13; Lk: 7:1–10); John tells a similar story of Jesus healing the son of a "royal official" (Jn 4:46–54). |
| | Peter's mother-in-law is cured of her fever (Mt 8:14–15; Mk 1:29–31; Lk 4:38–39). |
| | The crippled woman is raised up straight (Lk 13:10–13). |
| | A man who suffers from dropsy is healed (Lk 14:1–4). |
| | Lepers are cleansed (Mt 8:1–3; Mk 1:40–42; Lk 17:12–14). |
| | The ill and the lame are made whole. Limbs are restored (Mt 9:1–7; 12:9–13; Mk 2:1–12; 3:1–6; Lk 5:17–25; 6:6–11; 22:50–51; Jn 5:1–9). |
| | A woman's twelve-year hemorrhage is healed (Mt 9:20–22; Mk 5:25–29; Lk 8:43–44). |
| | The blind see, and the deaf hear, and the mute speak (Mt 9:27–35; 11:5; 15:29–31; 20:29–34; 21:14; Mk 7:31–37; 8:22–26; 10:46–52; Lk 18:35–43; Jn 9:1–41; Acts 9:3–18). |
| | General cures take place (Mt 14:34–36; Mk 6:53–56). |
| | The sick are healed, the possessed are freed, and demons are expelled (Mt 8:16, 28–33; 12:22; 15:21–28; 17:15–18; Mk 1:23–26; 5:1–20; 7:24–30; 9:20–28; Lk 4:33–35; 8:28–36; 9:37–42; 11:14). |
| **Jesus has power over nature** | Jesus rebukes the wind and calms the storms (Mt 8:23–26; Mk 4:35–39; Lk 8:22–24). |
| | Jesus walks on water (Mt 14:22–32; Mk 6:45–51; Jn 6:16–21). |
| | A coin appears in the mouth of a fish (Mt 17:24–27). |
| | Jesus causes a fig tree to wither (Mt 21:18–19; Mk 11:12–14, 20–21). |
| **Jesus' relationship with the Father is revealed** | God calls Jesus son (Mt 3:16–17; Mk 1:9–11; Lk 3:21–22). |
| | Jesus is transfigured before his apostles (Mt 17:1–2; Mk 9:2–3). |
| | Jesus is taken into glory (Mk 16:19; Lk 24:51 Acts 1:9–11). |
| **Jesus has power over death** | The daughter of Jairus is raised from death (Mt 9:18–25; Mk 5:22–24, 35–42; Lk 8:41–42, 49–55). |
| | The widow's son is raised on the way to the funeral (Lk 7:11–15). |
| | Lazarus is resurrected and called from the tomb (Jn 11:1–44). |
| | Jesus rises from the dead (Mk 16:5–6; Lk 24:2–7). |
| | The disciples encounter the resurrected Christ (Mt 28:1–10, 16–20; Lk 24:13–49; Jn 20:1–20, 24–29; 21:1–14). |
| **The Holy Spirit is sent** | The gift of the Holy Spirit descends upon the disciples (Jn 20:21–22; Acts 2:2–4, 17–41; 8:14–17). |
| **The disciples work wonders in the name of Jesus** | The disciples heal the sick, exorcise demons, and raise the dead (Acts 8:6–7; 9:40; 14:8–10; 16:18; 19:11–12; 20:9–12; 28:7–8). |

# The Men Who Followed Jesus

These men were among the first Christian witnesses who encountered Jesus of Nazareth, heard his teachings, witnessed his healings, and became his disciples. The evangelists would record their memories in the Gospels.

| Name | Significance | Reference |
|------|-------------|-----------|
| **John the Baptist** | Jesus' cousin, he prophesied the reign of God, condemned injustice, offered the baptism of repentance, called Jesus the Lamb of God, and was martyred by Herod Antipas. | Mt 3:1–17; 11:11; Mk 1:6, 14–15; 6:25 Lk 3:1–20; Jn 1:29–36 |
| **Simon Peter (Cephas)** | One of the first apostles and a Galilean fisherman, he was a man of faith, weakness, repentance, and hope. Jesus called him to lead the church and gave him the keys of the kingdom of heaven. | Mt 16:17–18; 26:69–75; Mk 8:29; Jn 1:40–42; 21:15–19; Gal 2:9 |
| **James, son of Zebedee** | A fisherman called with his brother John to be one of the Twelve. Jesus called them the sons of thunder. James was martyred by Agrippa I. | Mt 4:21–22; Mk 3:16–19; Lk 5:10–11; Acts 12:1–2 |
| **James, the Younger or the Less** | One of the Twelve, he was a member of Jesus' family—the son of Alphaeus (Cleopas) and Mary, the sister of Mary of Nazareth. James was the brother of Jose (Joseph) and Salome. | Mt 10:3; 27:55–56; Mk 3:18; 15:40; Lk 6:15; Acts 1:13 |
| **James, the Just** | Follower of Jesus honored with the title "brother of the Lord." Although not among the Twelve, he witnessed the resurrected Christ and was leader of the church of Jerusalem. Herod martyred him before the Roman destruction of 70 CE. | Mt 13:55; Mk 6:3; Acts 1:14; 15:13; 21:18; 1 Cor 15:7; Gal 1:19; 2:1–12 |
| **John, son of Zebedee** | The brother of James, he was a fisherman and one of the Twelve. Known as the beloved disciple, he was a primary leader in the early church. The Gospel of John is named for him. | Mt 4:21–22; Mk 3:17; Jn 19:26–27; Gal 2:9 |
| **Andrew** | A fisherman from Galilee and one of the Twelve, he was the brother of Simon Peter. | Mt 4:18–19; 10:2; Mk 1:16–17; Lk 6:14; Jn 1:40–44; 12:20–22 |
| **Philip** | One of the Twelve, he witnessed that Jesus was foretold by Moses and the prophets and brought Nathanael to the Lord. | Jn 1:43–46; 14:8–9 |
| **Bartholomew** | Also known as Nathanael, he was the friend of Philip who recognized Jesus as the Son of God and became one of the Twelve. | Mt 10:3; Mk 3:18; Lk 6:14; Jn 1:45–49 |
| **Matthew (Levi)** | Son of Alphaeus and brother of James, he was a Galilean tax collector and one of the Twelve. He was present for the descent of the Holy Spirit. | Mt 9:9–10; Mk 2:14; Lk 6:15; Acts 1:13 |
| **Thomas** | Also called Didymus (twin), he was one of the Twelve. He refused to believe in the risen Christ until he saw Jesus and touched his wounds. | Mt 10:3; Mk 3:18; Lk 6:15; Jn 11:16; 14:5; 20:24–29 |
| **Simon, the Zealot** | One of the Twelve, he may have been an insurgent from Cana who had belonged to an anti-Roman movement. | Lk 6:15; Acts 1:13 |
| **Judas Iscariot** | One of the Twelve, he was from Judea. He betrayed Jesus for thirty pieces of silver and then in grief hung himself. | Mt 26:14–16; 27:3–5; Lk 6:16; Acts 1:16–18 |
| **Jude (Judas) Thaddaeus** | One of the Twelve and a relative of Jesus and James, he was present at Pentecost. | Mt 13:55; Lk 6:16; Jn 14:22; Acts 1:13 |
| **Joseph of Arimathea** | A member of the Sanhedrin and disciple of Jesus, he secured Jesus' body from Pilate and provided Jesus with a tomb. | Mt 27:57–60; Jn 19:38–42 |
| **Nicodemus** | A Pharisee and a leader of the Judean people, he came to Jesus by night. He helped Joseph of Arimathea shroud and entomb Jesus. | Jn 3:1–4, 9; 19:39–42 |
| **Matthias** | A disciple who followed Jesus from his baptism to his Ascension. He was elected to replace Judas as one of the Twelve. | Acts 1:21–26 |

# The Women Who Followed Jesus

These women were among the first Christian witnesses of the mission of Jesus of Nazareth. Some of their names we know, and some remain a mystery. All of them, however, embraced the teachings of Jesus, witnessed his healings, and became his disciples.

| Name | Significance | Reference |
|---|---|---|
| Mary of Nazareth | Jesus' mother accepted her vocation at the invitation of the Archangel Gabriel, became the wife of Joseph, visited her cousin Elizabeth in her early pregnancy, prayed in solidarity with the poor (Lk 1:46–55; the prayer is known as the Magnificat), gave birth to Jesus in a stable, and consecrated Jesus to the Lord. After fleeing to Egypt to escape Herod, Mary and Joseph returned and settled in Nazareth. On one occasion, they lost Jesus for three days in the Temple. Mary prompted Jesus to perform his first miracle at a wedding in Cana and stood at the foot of the cross as he died. She was present at Pentecost. | Mt 1:16–25; 2:11, 13–23; Lk 1:39–56; 2:3–19, 21–24, 39, 42–51; Jn 2:1–12; 19:25–27; Acts 1:12–14; 2:1–4 |
| Mary of Magdala | After Jesus cast out seven demons from her, Mary became a patron of Jesus and the apostles. She stood at the cross with the holy women, laid Jesus in the tomb and kept watch, brought spices to anoint Jesus, and was a primal witness to Christ's Resurrection. She called Jesus Rabbouni, Master, and he commissioned her to tell the brothers he had risen. Her proclamation, "I have seen the Lord," became foundational for the Christian faith. | Mt 27:55–56; 28:1; Mk 15:40–47; 16:1–11; Lk 8:2–3; 24:1–11; Jn 19:25; 20:1–18 |
| Martha of Bethany | The sister of Mary and Lazarus of Bethany, Martha was a patron and disciple of Jesus who proclaimed that Jesus was "the Messiah, the Son of God" and witnessed Jesus raise Lazarus from the dead. | Lk 10:38–42; Jn 11:1–44; 12:2 |
| Mary of Bethany | The sister of Martha and Lazarus, not to be confused with Mary of Magdala, Mary sat at the Lord's feet as a disciple while Martha continued with the duties of hospitality. Mary anointed Jesus' feet with perfumed oil. The anointing in the Gospels of Matthew (26:6–13) and Mark (14:3–9) may be the same story as the one in John's Gospel. | Lk 10:38–42; Jn 11:1–44; 12:3–8 |
| Joanna, wife of Chuza | The wife of Chuza, Herod's steward, Joanna was a disciple of Jesus and served as patron for his community of followers. She was among the first to witness the Resurrection of Jesus. | Lk 8:1–3; 24:9–10 |
| Mary, wife of Cleopas | She was the sister of Mary of Nazareth, the wife of Alphaeus (Cleopas), and the mother of James the Less and Joses (Joseph). She stood at the foot of the cross and accompanied Mary of Magdala to the tomb to anoint Jesus' body, where they encountered angels who told them Jesus had risen. | Mt 27:55–61; 28:1–10; Mk 15:40–47; Jn 19:25 |
| Susanna | A patron and disciple of Jesus, she was listed among those healed from demons and other infirmities by Jesus. | Lk 8:1–3 |
| Samaritan woman | Unnamed woman who met Jesus at a well in Sychar, Samaria. Offering her "living water," Jesus revealed his mission as the Messiah to her. The Eastern Church remembers the Samaritan woman as Saint Photini. | Jn 4:1–28, 42 |
| Salome | One of the witnesses to the death of Jesus and the empty tomb. | Mk 15:40; 16:1 |
| The unnamed woman sinner | She burst in on a banquet to wash Jesus' feet with her tears and wipe them with her hair. Jesus assured her that her sins were forgiven because she loved much. | Lk 7:36–50 |
| Peter's mother-in-law | She was ill with a fever in Peter's house. Jesus cured her and she immediately rose and began to perform service for them. | Mt 8:14–15; Mk 1:29–31; Lk 4:38–39 |

# Beatitudes and Parables of Jesus

Jesus offered a vision of justice and compassion as sign of the reign of God, often conveying this vision in parables as well as in the Beatitudes.

## Beatitudes (Mt 5:1–12; Lk 6:20–26)

| Blessings | Woes |
|---|---|
| Blessed are the poor in spirit | Woe to the rich; Woe to those who are filled |
| Blessed are those who mourn | Woe to those who laugh now |
| Blessed are those who desire righteousness | |
| Blessed are the meek | |
| Blessed are the merciful | |
| Blessed are the clean of heart | |
| Blessed are the peacemakers | |
| Blessed are those who are persecuted for righteousness | |
| Blessed are those who are insulted, hated, and persecuted because of Christ | Woe to the praised |

| Parable Name | Matthew | Mark | Luke |
|---|---|---|---|
| The barren fig tree | | | 13:6–9 |
| The dishonest steward | | | 16:1–13 |
| Feasting and the bridegroom | 9:14–15 | 2:19–20 | 5:34–35 |
| The fig tree | 24:32–35 | 13:28–31 | 21:29–33 |
| The net | 13:47–50 | | |
| Good and faithful servants | 24:45–51 | | 12:42–46 |
| The household servants | | 13:34–37 | |
| The good Samaritan | | | 10:25–37 |
| The great feast | | | 14:16–24 |
| The lamp | 5:15 | 4:21 | 8:16–18 |
| The lost coin | | | 15:8–10 |
| The lost sheep | 18:12–14 | | 15:1–7 |
| The laborers in the vineyard | 20:1–16 | | |
| The head of a household | 13:51–52 | | |
| The mustard seed | 13:31–32 | 4:30–32 | 13:18–19 |

*(continued on next page)*

(Beatitudes and Parables of Jesus – continued from previous page)

| Parable Name | Matthew | Mark | Luke |
|---|---|---|---|
| New cloth | 9:16 | 2:21 | 5:36 |
| New wine | 9:17 | 2:22 | 5:37–39 |
| The persistent friend at midnight | | | 11:5–8 |
| The Pharisee and the tax collector | | | 18:9–14 |
| The prodigal son | | | 15:11–32 |
| The rejected stone | 21:42–46 | 12:10–11 | 20:17–19 |
| The rich fool | | | 12:13–31 |
| The rich man and Lazarus | | | 16:19–31 |
| The seed and the harvest | | 4:26–29 | |
| The sheep and the goats | 25:31–46 | | |
| The sower and soils | 13:3–23 | 4:1–20 | 8:4–15 |
| The talents | 25:14–30 | | 19:11–27 |
| The ten virgins | 25:1–13 | | |
| The thief at night | 24:43–44 | | 12:39–40 |
| The treasure and the pearl | 13:44–46 | | |
| The two debtors | | | 7:40–45 |
| Two sons | 21:28–32 | | |
| The unmerciful servant | 18:23–35 | | |
| Watchful slaves | | | 12:35–48 |
| The wheat and the weeds | 13:24–31, 36–43 | | |
| The wicked tenants | 21:33–41 | 12:1–9 | 20:9–16 |
| The widow and the judge | | | 18:1–8 |
| The wise and foolish builders | 7:24–27 | | 6:46–49 |
| The worthless salt | 5:13 | 9:50 | 14:34–35 |
| Yeast | 13:33 | | 13:20–21 |

# The Acts
## of the Apostles

## INTRODUCTION

### Clare K. Rothschild

Many people today understand the Acts of the Apostles as the first Christian history. Unlike any other early Christian text, Acts offers information (albeit selectively) about the nascent Christian movement in the days, weeks, months, and years after John the Baptist and Jesus were killed. The consensus of scholars is that Acts is a companion volume to the Gospel of Luke, intended, at least in some ways, as an extension of the Gospel's narrative. The debated literary genre of Acts shares important similarities and differences with Luke. Like Luke, it incorporates but is not limited to elements of history, biography, epic, and ancient novels. Unlike Luke, Acts focuses on the professional careers of the apostles, whereas Luke offers birth to death narratives of both John the Baptist and Jesus. Acts also shares certain themes in common with Luke's Gospel, including women, the poor and oppressed, the role of the Holy Spirit, and prophecy fulfillment (see below, "Key Themes and Purpose"). The primary goal of Acts is to demonstrate a smooth transfer of Christianity from Jesus to Peter and Paul, from Jews to Gentiles, and from Jerusalem to Rome.

## Authorship

As with the Gospel of Luke, Acts is, technically speaking, anonymous. Nevertheless, attribution of Acts to a writer named Luke may be accurate and may correlate authorship with a companion of the Apostle Paul (see Col 4:14; 2 Tm 4:11; Phlm 24). Such a correlation might have been made on the basis of literary connections between Luke and Acts (especially the mutual dedication to "Theophilus," either an otherwise unknown early Christian or every "lover of God," based on the etymology of this name in Greek, Lk 1:3; Acts 1:1). The

### Outline of Acts

I. **The Preparation for the Christian Mission (1:1–2:13)**

II. **The Mission in Jerusalem (2:14–8:3)**

III. **The Mission in Judea and Samaria (8:4–9:43)**

IV. **The Inauguration of the Gentile Mission (10:1–15:35)**

V. **The Mission of Paul to the Ends of the Earth (15:36–28:31)**

correlation might also have been made on the basis of Acts' so-called "we-passages," passages in which the author speaks in the first person plural (we), implying that he was present at the event he narrates (Acts 16:10; 20:5–15; 21:1–18; 27:1–28:16). Whatever the author's precise identity, it is safe to assume that he was a well-educated Hellenistic Jew or Gentile with knowledge of the Greek translation of the Jewish Scriptures, as well as other important works.

Around the year 1927, Henry Joel Cadbury, one of the most important commentators on Acts of the last century, coined the hyphenated expression "Luke-Acts" to express coherence between the two individual books Luke and Acts, especially with regard to authorship. There are some valid challenges to this claim, such as discrepancies between the ascension scenes in Lk 24:50–53 and Acts 1:6–11. Still, most scholars today find such discrepancies explainable, attributable in this case to the author's interest in the ascension as both the *end* of Jesus' career on earth (Luke) and the *beginning* of God's work on earth through the Spirit (Acts). Those scholars who dispute the hyphenated expression "Luke-Acts" usually have doubts about the degree of correlation between the two books, rather than their mutual authorship.

## Date/Provenance

As with the Gospel of Luke, scholars typically date Acts anywhere from 56 to 140 CE. Over the past hundred years, the dating of Acts demonstrates a clear trend from earlier to later. Although the majority opt for a date around 85 CE, today some scholars believe that both the Gospel of Luke and Acts were composed closer to the year 115 CE.[1] If one accepts "Markan Priority," or the idea that the author of the Gospel of Luke relied on Mark as a source to write his Gospel, then the Gospel of Luke's *terminus post quem*, or date after which the text *must* have been written, is the Gospel of Mark. If Mark was written during or near the end of the Jewish War with Rome, as most scholars believe, then Mark was written around the year 70 CE. The date of the Gospel of Luke would then postdate 70, allowing some time for Mark to circulate. If Acts was written at the same time as Luke, then Acts shares Luke's *terminus post quem* of 70 CE derived from Mark. Acts' *terminus ante quem*, or the date before which the text must have been written, is, as noted above, Irenaeus (around the year 180), who mentions it in his book *Against Heresies*.

If duration and details of the time spent by Paul in Ephesus in Acts 19 (such as the "hall of Tyrannus" in 19:9) constitute an accurate metric, it is possible that both the Gospel of Luke and Acts were composed in or by someone from Ephesus.

## Sources

Since the author relied on several sources for the composition of his first volume (see the initial introduction to the Gospel According to Luke), it seems highly unlikely that he would have composed the second volume without any sources. Yet the sources behind Acts remain a mystery. In fact, one scholar of the past became so disheartened attempting to discern the sources of Acts that he recommended the search be abandoned in favor of the study of Acts' style.[2] Stylistic examinations of Acts often focus on its many speeches (Acts 1:16–22; 2:14–36; 7:2–53; 11:5–17; 13:16–41; 15:7–11, 13–21; 17:22–31; 20:18–35; 22:1–21; 24:10–21; 26:2–23) because ancient historians were usually forced to invent the speeches delivered by the historical personages in their narratives.

If, as most scholars agree, the Lukan prologue (Lk 1:1–4) is intended to cover both Luke and Acts, then the author may have used oral or written accounts by "eyewitnesses . . . and ministers of the word" (Lk 1:2) to compose Acts. True, this claim stands in tension with the we-passages insofar as these passages portray the author *himself* as an eyewitness; but it is not impossible to imagine that the author views himself as one of his own eyewitness informants—albeit to Paul's, not Jesus' ministry. Alternatively, it is also possible that the we-passages constitute a diary belonging to someone other than the author, the first person plural pronoun being a vestige of the original piece. Currently scholars have no firm solutions to these puzzles.

In terms of the book's value for reconstructing the actual history of the early movement, scholars sometimes explore the author's possible use of an early collection of Paul's letters.[3] It is likely that the author wrote with knowledge of Paul's letters, although he frequently departs from the information that our versions of these letters provide. Just one example of general correspondences between Paul's letters and Acts: the Lukan Paul manages to visit every single one of the addresses of Paul's undisputed letters, including Thessalonica, Corinth, Galatia (specifically, Pisidian Antioch, Iconium, Lystra, Derbe), Philippi, and Rome, as well as the address of a disputed letter, Ephesus.

Similarities between Acts 15:1–41 and Gal 2:1–14 regarding the so-called "Jerusalem Council"/"Antioch Incident" offer perhaps the

---

1. Richard I. Pervo, *Dating Acts: Between the Evangelists and the Apologists* (Santa Rosa: Polebridge, 2006), esp. 15–17, 26, 343–46.

2. Martin Dibelius, *Studies in the Acts of the Apostles*, trans. Mary Ling (London: SCM, 1956), 1.

3. Pervo, *Dating Acts*, 51–147.

most important case in the question of specific correspondences between Paul's letters and Acts. Although the two accounts (Acts and Galatians) differ in specifics, both reports acknowledge that such events took place. Discrepancies between the two accounts suggest either that our versions of the letters are different from those in the author's possession or that the author freely emended the information in the letters to suit his particular goals. Such discrepancies may be seen in a comparison of Acts 15:30–41 and Gal 2:11–14 (the "Antioch Incident"). In Galatians, Paul describes the event as a bitter dispute with Peter over table fellowship with Gentiles. In Acts, however, the author describes the event as Paul's parting of the ways with Barnabas over a disagreement about whether to travel with "John called Mark."

Why would the author depart so dramatically from Paul's account? Scholars postulate that Luke might have changed both the participants and the nature of the dispute to avoid portraying Peter and Paul in opposition to one another. Despite such differences, a growing number of scholars believe that the author of Acts relied on an early collection of Paul's letters, finding it easier to imagine that Luke modified the letters to suit his interests than that he, as an early Christian with a clear interest in Paul's life, did not possess them. The author's willingness to adapt Mark and Q in composing Luke also suggests he did not copy sources blindly. If he modified Mark, he might also have modified Paul's letters to meet present historical, literary, and theological demands.

Interestingly, Acts has important correspondences with ancient novels in regard to the arrangement of various historical elements. Ancient novels are famous for scene types like trials, escapes, and shipwrecks—events that also take place in Acts. Like Acts, novels typically follow a protagonist through his career, rather than from birth to death. Finally, Acts resembles ancient novels in its adventurousness and in the interlacement and parallelism of some of its episodes. Such stories give the narrative a fast-paced excitement. The apostles are rarely in one place for long, often jailed, or chased out of town by authorities, whether Jewish or Roman.

## Key Themes and Purpose

As with its companion volume, most scholars today agree that the author of the Gospel of Luke wrote Acts to depict what took place among Jesus' followers after his death, showcasing smooth transitions of leadership: from Jesus to Peter and Paul; of demography: from Jews to Gentiles; and of geographical center: from Jerusalem to Rome. If the purpose of Luke, as stated in Lk 1:1–4, is, as many scholars think, intended to cover Acts, then the explicit purpose of Acts is to clarify, for Theophilus, the "truth" about "what he has been taught," most likely about both the words and deeds of Jesus (Gospel of Luke) *and* the origin and development of the movement in Jesus' name (Acts of the Apostles). (The movement's nickname in Acts is "the Way," Acts 9:2; 19:9; 22:4; 24:14, 22. It is also referred to as "Christian" in 11:26 and 26:28; elsewhere in the NT only at 1 Pt 4:16.) Such clarification comes, in Acts, in the form of miracles, legends, and other popular episodes about Peter, Paul, and other early Christian disciples, occurring after Jesus' death and in parallel with stories about Jesus in the Third Gospel (see "The Gospel of Luke and Acts" at the end of this introduction).

Concerning parallels between the Third Gospel and Acts, today many scholars endorse some version of the theory that the author relied on his first volume, Luke's Gospel, as the primary source or even template for the composition of Acts. Charts, such as the one below, suggest that the author depicted Peter (Acts 1–12) and Paul (chs. 13–28), collectively and individually, as imitating the life and ministry of the Lukan Jesus. By comparing boxes horizontally and vertically across the chart, it is not difficult to see that Peter and Paul perform many of the same deeds as the Lukan Jesus, often in the same order in which the Lukan Jesus performed them. Reliance on the Gospel of Luke as a model for the portrayals of Peter and Paul in Acts makes sense insofar as disciples typically imitate their teachers.

The depiction of Jews and Romans in Acts is also an important, if debated, theme. Some wonder whether Luke was more favorably disposed toward one or the other group. On the one hand, in the Gospel of Luke the author seems to exonerate the Romans for the death of Jesus. Luke's is the only Gospel in which Pilate agrees that Jesus did *not* conspire against the emperor (Lk 23:4). Also, Herod Antipas, tetrarch of Galilee, is "glad to see Jesus" when he is sent to him by Pilate and likewise finds Jesus not guilty of treason (Lk 23:6–11, 14–15). Similarly, in Acts, the author seems to want to demonstrate that Jews, not Romans, chase Paul from city to city across Asia Minor (modern Turkey) and into Greece, cutting short his ministry (in some cases, necessitating epistolary correspondence) in almost every town he visits (see Acts 13:50; 14:19; 17:5, 13). These observations have led to the assumption that Luke was pro-Roman. Yet not all evidence points in that direction. We see, for example, in Acts 22–23 that, although Luke narrates Paul's mistreatment by the Roman tribune Claudius Lysias in Acts 21:31–38, Claudius Lysias avoids mentioning his embarrassing role in his letter to the governor Felix in 23:26–30.[4] The discrepancy between these two reports, long acknowledged by scholars, may be Luke's indirect way of condemning, if not the Roman Empire or Roman law in general, certain local emissaries.

---

4. Trevor W. Thompson. "Writing in Character: Claudius Lysias to Felix as a Double-Pseudepigraphon (Acts 23:26–30)," in *The Interface of Orality and Writing: Speaking, Seeing, Writing in the Shaping of New Genres*, ed. A. Weissenrieder and R. B. Coote (Tübingen: Mohr Siebeck, 2010), 393–407, at 399–407.

Finally, as in the Gospel of Luke (see the initial introduction to the Gospel According to Luke), women, the poor and oppressed, the Holy Spirit, and prophecy fulfillment play important roles in Acts. Prominent women in Acts include Sapphira (Acts 5:1), Tabitha (9:36, 40), Lydia (16:14, 40), and Priscilla (18:2, 18, 26). The ideal community shares possessions (2:44–47; 4:32–35)—a model that both welcomes the poor and the oppressed and systematically alleviates these conditions. The community severely punishes those who hold back in any way on this ideal (4:36–5:11). In Acts, the Spirit occasionally halts the movement ("the Spirit of Jesus," 16:7), but usually guides or even propels it forward (see 8:29, 39; 11:12; 13:4; 20:22). Sometimes the Spirit utilizes dreams in this capacity (9:10–12; 10:3–6, 10–16; 11:5–10; 18:9–10). Prophecy fulfillment is a recurring motif seen in, for example: (1) the movement's predicted spread (1:8) from Jerusalem (2:14–36), to Judea and Samaria (8:1, 4–25), and to "the ends of the earth" (10:1–11:18 or 28:16); (2) Paul's call or conversion (9:1–31; 22:1–21; 26:2–23); and (3) Peter's conversion of Cornelius (10:1–48). Both the Spirit and prophecy fulfillment assist the author in conveying his aim to legitimate Gentile Christianity from Jerusalem to Rome and beyond. Canonization of this important book within the New Testament offers some measure of the author's success. ∎

# The Gospel of Luke and Acts

| Luke | Acts 1–12 | Acts 13–28 |
|---|---|---|
| Preface to Theophilus (Lk 1:1–4) | Preface to Theophilus (Acts 1:1–5) | |
| Jesus prays at his baptism (Lk 3:21) | Disciples pray as they await baptism by the Holy Spirit (Acts 1:14, 24) | |
| Spirit descends on Jesus, with physical form (Lk 3:21–22) | Spirit descends on disciples and Peter, with physical form (Acts 2:4; cf. 1:5 and 10:44) | Paul is sent by the Spirit (Acts 13:4) |
| Spirit sends Jesus out to wilderness (Lk 4:1–13) | | Paul is sent by the Spirit to Seleucia (Acts 13:4) |
| Jesus is tempted by the devil (Lk 4:2) | Peter confronts Simon Magus (Acts 8:9–24) | Paul is opposed by a "son of the devil" (Acts 13:10) |
| After John is arrested, Jesus' ministry begins (Lk 4:16–30) | | After Peter is arrested, Paul's ministry begins (Acts 12:4) |
| A sermon declares that a prophecy is fulfilled (Lk 4:16–30) | A sermon declares that a prophecy is fulfilled (Acts 2:14–40) | A sermon declares that prophecies are fulfilled (Acts 13:27, 32) |
| Jesus heals a man lame from birth (Lk 5:17–26) | Peter heals a man lame from birth (Acts 3:1–10) | Paul heals a man lame from birth (Acts 14:8) |
| Religious leaders attack Jesus (Lk 5:29–6:11) | Religious leaders attack Peter (and John) (Acts 4:1–4) | Religious leaders attack Paul (and Barnabas) (Acts 15:1–2) |
| A centurion invites Jesus to his house (Lk 7:1–10) | A centurion invites Peter to his house (Acts 10:1–23) | A jailor invites Paul to his house (Acts 16:34) |
| Jesus raises a widow's son from the dead (Lk 7:11–17) | Peter raises a widow from the dead (Acts 9:36–43) | Paul converts the unmarried woman Lydia (Acts 16:11–15) |
| Missionary journeys to the Gentiles prefigured (Lk 10:1–12) | Missionary journeys begin (Acts 13:1–19:20) | Missionary journeys clearly to the Gentiles begin (Acts 16:10ff.) |
| Jesus travels to Jerusalem (Lk 9:51–19:28) | Peter travels to Jerusalem (Acts 11:2) | Paul travels to Jerusalem (Acts 19:21–21:17) |
| Passion journey (Lk 9:31, 51; 12:50; 13:33; 18:31–33) under divine necessity (Lk 13:33) and characterized by disciples' lack of understanding (Lk 9:45; 18:34) | | Passion journey (Acts 20:3, 22–24, 37–38; 21:4, 10–11, 13) under divine necessity (Acts 20:22; 21:14) and characterized by Paul's friends' lack of understanding (Acts 21:4, 12–13) |
| Jesus received favorably in Jerusalem (Lk 19:37) | Peter received favorably in Jerusalem (Acts 11:18) | Paul received favorably in Jerusalem (Acts 21:17–20) |
| Jesus is devoted to the Temple (Lk 19:45–48) | | Paul is devoted to the Temple (Acts 21:26) |
| Sadducees oppose Jesus, but scribes support him (Lk 20:27–39; cf. 7:36–50) | Herod opposes James and Peter (Acts 12:1–3) | Sadducees oppose Paul, but Pharisees support him (Acts 23:6–9) |

*(continued on next page)*

(The Gospel of Luke and Acts – continued from previous page)

| Luke | Acts 1–12 | Acts 13–28 |
|---|---|---|
| Jesus breaks bread and gives thanks (Lk 22:19) | | Paul breaks bread and gives thanks (Acts 27:35) |
| Jesus is seized by an angry mob (Lk 22:54) | Peter is seized by an angry Herod (Acts 12:4–5) | Paul is seized by an angry mob (Acts 21:30) |
| Jesus is slapped by high priest's aides (Lk 22:63–64) | | Paul is slapped at high priest's command (Acts 23:2) |
| Jesus is tried four times and declared innocent three times (Lk 22:66–23:13) | | Paul is tried four times and declared innocent three times (Acts 23:1–26:32) |
| Pilate declares Jesus innocent three times (Lk 23:4, 14, 22) | | Three men, Lysias, Festus, and Agrippa, declare Paul innocent (Acts 23:29; 25:25; 26:31) |
| Jesus is rejected by the Jews (Lk 23:18) | | Paul is rejected by the Jews (Acts 21:36) |
| Pilate sends Jesus to Herod for questioning (Lk 23:6–12) | | Another Herod, Herod Agrippa, hears Paul with the permission of Festus (Acts 25:13–26:32) |
| Pilate says he will release Jesus (Lk 23:16, 22) | | Agrippa says: "This man could have been set free" (Acts 26:32) |
| Jews cry, "Away with this man!" (Lk 23:18) | | Jews cry, "Away with him!" (Acts 21:36) |
| Jesus is regarded favorably by a centurion (Lk 23:47) | | Paul is regarded favorably by a centurion (Acts 27:43) |
| Luke reports a final confirmation that the Scriptures have been fulfilled (Lk 24:45–47) | | Luke reports a final confirmation that the Scriptures have been fulfilled (Acts 28:23–28) |

# THE ACTS OF THE APOSTLES

## New American Bible, Introduction

The Acts of the Apostles, the second volume of Luke's two-volume work, continues Luke's presentation of biblical history, describing how the salvation promised to Israel in the Old Testament and accomplished by Jesus has now under the guidance of the holy Spirit been extended to the Gentiles. This was accomplished through the divinely chosen representatives (Acts 10:41) whom Jesus prepared during his historical ministry (Acts 1:21–22) and commissioned after his resurrection as witnesses to all that he taught (Acts 1:8; 10:37–43; Lk 24:48). Luke's preoccupation with the Christian community as the Spirit-guided bearer of the word of salvation rules out of his book detailed histories of the activity of most of the preachers. Only the main lines of the roles of Peter and Paul serve Luke's interest.

Peter was the leading member of the Twelve (Acts 1:13, 15), a miracle worker like Jesus in the gospel (Acts 3:1–10; 5:1–11, 15; 9:32–35, 36–42), the object of divine care (Acts 5:17–21; 12:6–11), and the spokesman for the Christian community (Acts 2:14–36; 3:12–26; 4:8–12; 5:29–32; 10:34–43; 15:7–11), who, according to Luke, was largely responsible for the growth of the community in the early days (Acts 2:4; 4:4). Paul eventually joined the community at Antioch (Acts 11:25–26), which subsequently commissioned him and Barnabas to undertake the spread of the gospel to Asia Minor. This missionary venture generally failed to win the Jews of the diaspora to the gospel but enjoyed success among the Gentiles (Acts 13:14–14:27).

Paul's refusal to impose the Mosaic law upon his Gentile converts provoked very strong objection among the Jewish Christians of Jerusalem (Acts 15:1), but both Peter and James supported his position (Acts 15:6–21). Paul's second and third missionary journeys (Acts 16:36–21:16) resulted in the same pattern of failure among the Jews generally but of some success among the Gentiles. Paul, like Peter, is presented as a miracle worker (Acts 14:8–18; 19:12; 20:7–12; 28:7–10) and the object of divine care (Acts 16:25–31).

In Acts, Luke has provided a broad survey of the church's development from the resurrection of Jesus to Paul's first Roman imprisonment, the point at which the book ends. In telling this story, Luke describes the emergence of Christianity from its origins in Judaism to its position as a religion of worldwide status and appeal. Originally a Jewish Christian community in Jerusalem, the church was placed in circumstances impelling it to include within its membership people of other cultures: the Samaritans (Acts 8:4–25), at first an occasional Gentile (Acts 8:26–30; 10:1–48), and finally the Gentiles on principle (Acts 11:20–21). Fear on the part of the Jewish people that Christianity, particularly as preached to the Gentiles, threatened their own cultural heritage caused them to be suspicious of Paul's gospel (Acts 13:42–45; 15:1–5; 28:17–24). The inability of Christian missionaries to allay this apprehension inevitably created a situation in which the gospel was preached more and more to the Gentiles. Toward the end of Paul's career, the Christian communities, with the exception of those in Palestine itself (Acts 9:31), were mainly of Gentile membership. In tracing the emergence of Christianity from Judaism, Luke is insistent upon the prominence of Israel in the divine plan of salvation (see note on Acts 1:26; see also Acts 2:5–6; 3:13–15; 10:36; 13:16–41; 24:14–15) and that the extension of salvation to the Gentiles has been a part of the divine plan from the beginning (see Acts 15:13–18; 26:22–23).

In the development of the church from a Jewish Christian origin in Jerusalem, with its roots in Jewish religious tradition, to a series of Christian communities among the Gentiles of the Roman empire, Luke perceives the action of God in history laying open the heart of all humanity to the divine message of salvation. His approach to the history of the church is motivated by his theological interests. His history of the apostolic church is the story of a Spirit-guided community and a Spirit-guided spread of the Word of God (Acts 1:8). The travels of Peter and Paul are in reality the travels of the Word of God as it spreads from Jerusalem, the city of destiny for Jesus, to Rome, the capital of the civilized world of Luke's day. Nonetheless, the historical data he utilizes are of value for the understanding of the church's early life and development and as general background to the Pauline epistles. In the interpretation of Acts, care must be exercised to determine Luke's theological aims and interests and to evaluate his historical data without either exaggerating their literal accuracy or underestimating their factual worth.

Finally, an apologetic concern is evident throughout Acts. By stressing the continuity between Judaism and Christianity (Acts 13:16–41; 23:6–9; 24:10–21; 26:2–23), Luke argues that Christianity is deserving of the same toleration accorded Judaism by Rome. Part of Paul's defense before Roman authorities is to show that Christianity is not a disturber of the peace of the Roman Empire (Acts 24:5, 12–13; 25:7–8). Moreover, when he stands before Roman authorities, he is declared innocent of any crime against the empire (Acts 18:13–15; 23:29; 25:25–27; 26:31–32). Luke tells his story with the hope that Christianity will be treated as fairly.

Concerning the date of Acts, see the Introduction to the Gospel according to Luke.

The principal divisions of the Acts of the Apostles are the following:

I. The Preparation for the Christian Mission (1:1–2:13)

II. The Mission in Jerusalem (2:14–8:3)

III. The Mission in Judea and Samaria (8:4–9:43)

IV. The Inauguration of the Gentile Mission (10:1–15:35)

V. The Mission of Paul to the Ends of the Earth (15:36–28:31) ∎

# Acts

## I. THE PREPARATION FOR THE CHRISTIAN MISSION

**1** †**The Promise of the Spirit.** ¹In the first book,* Theophilus, I dealt with all that Jesus did and taught ²until the day he was taken up, after giving instructions through the holy Spirit to the apostles whom he had chosen.* ³He presented himself alive to them by many proofs after he had suffered, appearing to them during forty days† and speaking about the kingdom of God.* ⁴While meeting with them, he enjoined them not to depart from Jerusalem, but to wait for "the promise of the Father† about which you have heard me speak;* ⁵for John baptized with water, but in a few days you will be baptized with the holy Spirit."*

**The Ascension of Jesus.** ⁶When they had gathered together they asked him, "Lord, are you at this time going† to restore the kingdom to Israel?" ⁷† He answered them,* "It is not for you to know the times or seasons that the Father has established by his own authority. ⁸† But you will receive power when the holy Spirit comes upon you,* and you will be my witnesses in Jerusalem, throughout Judea and Samaria, and to the ends of the earth." ⁹When he had said this, as they were looking on, he was lifted up, and a cloud took him from their sight.* ¹⁰While they were looking intently at the sky as he was going, suddenly two men dressed in white garments stood beside them.* ¹¹They said, "Men of Galilee, why are you standing there looking at the sky? This Jesus who has been taken up from you into heaven will return in the same way as you have seen him going into heaven."* ¹²* Then they returned to Jerusalem from the mount called Olivet, which is near Jerusalem, a sabbath day's journey away.

**The First Community in Jerusalem.** ¹³When they entered the city they went to the upper room where they were staying, Peter and John and James and Andrew, Philip and Thomas, Bartholomew and Matthew, James son of Alphaeus, Simon the Zealot, and Judas son of James. ¹⁴All these devoted themselves with one accord to prayer, together with some women, and Mary the mother of Jesus, and his brothers.*

**The Choice of Judas's Successor.** ¹⁵During those days Peter stood up in the midst of the brothers (there was a group of about one hundred and twenty persons in the one place). He said, ¹⁶"My brothers, the scripture had to be fulfilled which the holy Spirit spoke beforehand through the mouth of David, concerning

---

† **1:1–26** This introductory material (Acts 1:1–2) connects Acts with the Gospel of Luke, shows that the apostles were instructed by the risen Jesus (Acts 1:3–5), points out that the parousia or second coming in glory of Jesus will occur as certainly as his ascension occurred (Acts 1:6–11), and lists the members of the Twelve, stressing their role as a body of divinely mandated witnesses to his life, teaching, and resurrection (Acts 1:12–26).

**1:3** *Appearing to them during forty days*: Luke considered especially sacred the interval in which the appearances and instructions of the risen Jesus occurred and expressed it therefore in terms of the sacred number forty (cf. Dt 8:2). In his gospel, however, Luke connects the ascension of Jesus with the resurrection by describing the ascension on Easter Sunday evening (Lk 24:50–53). What should probably be understood as one event (resurrection, glorification, ascension, sending of the Spirit—the paschal mystery) has been historicized by Luke when he writes of a visible ascension of Jesus after forty days and the descent of the Spirit at Pentecost. For Luke, the ascension marks the end of the appearances of Jesus except for the extraordinary appearance to Paul. With regard to Luke's understanding of salvation history, the ascension also marks the end of the time of Jesus (Lk 24:50–53) and signals the beginning of the time of the church.

**1:4** *The promise of the Father*: the holy Spirit, as is clear from the next verse. This gift of the Spirit was first promised in Jesus' final instructions to his chosen witnesses in Luke's gospel (Lk 24:49) and formed part of the continuing instructions of the risen Jesus on the kingdom of God, of which Luke speaks in Acts 1:3.

**1:6** The question of the disciples implies that in believing Jesus to be the Christ (see note on Lk 2:11) they had expected him to be a political leader who would restore self-rule to Israel during his historical ministry. When this had not taken place, they ask if it is to take place at this time, the period of the church.

**1:7** This verse echoes the tradition that the precise time of the parousia is not revealed to human beings; cf. Mk 13:32; 1 Thes 5:1–3.

**1:8** Just as Jerusalem was the city of destiny in the Gospel of Luke (the place where salvation was accomplished), so here at the beginning of Acts, Jerusalem occupies a central position. It is the starting point for the mission of the Christian disciples to "the ends of the earth," the place where the apostles were situated and the doctrinal focal point in the early days of the community (Acts 15:2, 6). *The ends of the earth*: for Luke, this means Rome.

---

*
| | |
|---|---|
| **1:1** Lk 1:1–4. | **1:8** 2:1–13; 10:39; Is |
| **1:2** Mt 28:19–20; Lk | 43:10; Mt 28:19; Lk |
| 24:44–49; Jn 20:22; | 24:47–48. |
| 1 Tm 3:16. | **1:9** 2 Kgs 2:11; Mk 16:19; |
| **1:3** 10:41; 13:31. | Lk 24:51. |
| **1:4** Jn 14:16, 17, 26. | **1:10** Jn 20:17. |
| **1:5** 11:16; Mt 3:11; Mk | **1:11** Lk 24:51; Eph 4:8–10; |
| 1:8; Lk 3:16; Jn 1:26; | 1 Pt 3:22; Rev 1:7. |
| Eph 1:13. | **1:12–14** Lk 6:14–16. |
| **1:7** Mt 24:36; 1 Thes | **1:14** Lk 23:49. |
| 5:1–2. | |

Judas, who was the guide for those who arrested Jesus.* [17] He was numbered among us and was allotted a share in this ministry. [18]* He bought a parcel of land with the wages of his iniquity, and falling headlong, he burst open in the middle, and all his insides spilled out.† [19] This became known to everyone who lived in Jerusalem, so that the parcel of land was called in their language 'Akeldama,' that is, Field of Blood. [20] For it is written in the Book of Psalms:

'Let his encampment become desolate,
and may no one dwell in it.'

And:

'May another take his office.'*

[21] Therefore, it is necessary that one of the men who accompanied us the whole time the Lord Jesus came and went among us, [22] beginning from the baptism of John until the day on which he was taken up from us, become with us a witness to his resurrection."* [23] So they proposed two, Joseph called Barsabbas, who was also known as Justus, and Matthias. [24] Then they prayed, "You, Lord, who know the hearts of all, show which one of these two you have chosen [25] to take the place in this apostolic ministry from which Judas turned away to go to his own place." [26]†* Then they gave lots to them, and the lot fell upon Matthias, and he was counted with the eleven apostles.

**2** **The Coming of the Spirit.** [1]† When the time for Pentecost was fulfilled, they were all in one place together.* [2] And suddenly there came from the sky a noise like a strong driving wind,† and it filled the entire house in which they were.* [3] Then there appeared to them tongues as of fire,† which parted and came to rest on each one of them.* [4] And they were all filled with the holy Spirit and began to speak in different tongues,† as the Spirit enabled them to proclaim.*

[5] Now there were devout Jews from every nation under heaven staying in Jerusalem. [6] At this sound, they gathered in a large crowd, but they were confused because each one heard them speaking in his own language. [7] They were astounded, and in amazement they asked, "Are not all these people who are speaking Galileans?* [8] Then how does each of us hear them in his own native language? [9] We are Parthians, Medes, and Elamites, inhabitants of Mesopotamia, Judea and Cappadocia, Pontus and Asia, [10] Phrygia and Pamphylia, Egypt and the districts of Libya near Cyrene, as well as travelers from Rome, [11] both Jews and converts to Judaism, Cretans and Arabs, yet we hear them speaking in our own tongues of the mighty acts of God."* [12] They were all astounded and bewildered, and said to one another, "What does this mean?" [13] But others said, scoffing, "They have had too much new wine."*

## II. THE MISSION IN JERUSALEM

**Peter's Speech at Pentecost.** [14]† Then Peter stood up with the Eleven, raised his voice, and proclaimed to them, "You who are Jews, indeed all of you staying in Jerusalem. Let this be

---

1:18 Luke records a popular tradition about the death of Judas that differs from the one in Mt 27:5, according to which Judas hanged himself. Here, although the text is not certain, Judas is depicted as purchasing a piece of property with the betrayal money and being killed on it in a fall.

1:26 The need to replace Judas was probably dictated by the symbolism of the number twelve, recalling the twelve tribes of Israel. This symbolism also indicates that for Luke (see Lk 22:30) the Christian church is a reconstituted Israel.

2:1–41 Luke's pentecostal narrative consists of an introduction (Acts 2:1–13), a speech ascribed to Peter declaring the resurrection of Jesus and its messianic significance (Acts 2:14–36), and a favorable response from the audience (Acts 2:37–41). It is likely that the narrative telescopes events that took place over a period of time and on a less dramatic scale. The Twelve were not originally in a position to proclaim publicly the messianic office of Jesus without incurring immediate reprisal from those religious authorities in Jerusalem who had brought about Jesus' death precisely to stem the rising tide in his favor.

2:2 There came from the sky a noise like a strong driving wind: wind and spirit are associated in Jn 3:8. The sound of a great rush of wind would herald a new action of God in the history of salvation.

2:3 Tongues as of fire: see Ex 19:18 where fire symbolizes the presence of God to initiate the covenant on Sinai. Here the holy Spirit acts upon the apostles, preparing them to proclaim the new covenant with its unique gift of the Spirit (Acts 2:38).

2:4 To speak in different tongues: ecstatic prayer in praise of God, interpreted in Acts 2:6, 11 as speaking in foreign languages, symbolizing the worldwide mission of the church.

2:14–36 The first of six discourses in Acts (along with Acts 3:12–26; 4:8–12; 5:29–32; 10:34–43; 13:16–41) dealing with the resurrection of Jesus and its messianic import. Five of these are attributed to Peter, the final one to Paul. Modern scholars term these discourses in Acts the "kerygma," the Greek word for proclamation (cf. 1 Cor 15:11).

---

1:16 Ps 41:10; Lk 22:47.
1:18 Mt 27:3–10.
1:20 Ps 69:26; 109:8; Jn 17:12.
1:22 1:8–9; 10:39.
1:26 Prv 16:33.
2:1 Lv 23:15–21; Dt 16:9–11.
2:2–3 Jn 3:8.

2:3 Lk 3:16.
2:4 1:5; 4:31; 8:15, 17; 10:44; 11:15–16; 15:8; 19:6; Ps 104:30; Jn 20:33.
2:7 1:11.
2:11 10:46.
2:13 1 Cor 14:23.

known to you, and listen to my words. [15] These people are not drunk, as you suppose, for it is only nine o'clock in the morning. [16] No, this is what was spoken through the prophet Joel:

[17]　'It will come to pass in the last days,'
　　　　God says,
　　　'that I will pour out a portion of my
　　　　　spirit
　　　upon all flesh.
　　Your sons and your daughters shall
　　　　prophesy,
　　your young men shall see visions,
　　　your old men shall dream dreams.*
[18]　Indeed, upon my servants and my
　　　　handmaids
　　　I will pour out a portion of my spirit
　　　　in those days,
　　　and they shall prophesy.
[19]　And I will work wonders in the heavens
　　　　above
　　　and signs on the earth below:
　　　　blood, fire, and a cloud of smoke.
[20]　The sun shall be turned to darkness,
　　　and the moon to blood,
　　　　before the coming of the great and
　　　　　splendid day of the Lord,
[21]　and it shall be that everyone shall be
　　　　saved who calls on the name of
　　　　the Lord.'*

[22] You who are Israelites, hear these words. Jesus the Nazorean was a man commended to you by God with mighty deeds, wonders, and signs, which God worked through him in your midst, as you yourselves know.* [23] This man, delivered up by the set plan and foreknowledge of God, you killed, using lawless men to crucify him.* [24] But God raised him up, releasing him from the throes of death, because it was impossible for him to be held by it.* [25] For David says of him:

　　'I saw the Lord ever before me,*
　　　with him at my right hand I shall not
　　　　be disturbed.
[26]　Therefore my heart has been glad and
　　　　my tongue has exulted;
　　　my flesh, too, will dwell in hope,
[27]　because you will not abandon my soul
　　　　to the netherworld,
　　　nor will you suffer your holy one to
　　　　see corruption.*
[28]　You have made known to me the paths
　　　　of life;
　　　you will fill me with joy in your
　　　　presence.'

[29] My brothers, one can confidently say to you about the patriarch David that he died and was buried, and his tomb is in our midst to this day. [30] But since he was a prophet and knew that God had sworn an oath to him that he would set one of his descendants upon his throne,* [31] he foresaw and spoke of the resurrection of the Messiah, that neither was he abandoned to the netherworld nor did his flesh see corruption.* [32] God raised this Jesus; of this we are all witnesses. [33] Exalted at the right hand of God,† he received the promise of the holy Spirit from the Father and poured it forth, as you [both] see and hear.* [34] For David did not go up into heaven, but he himself said:

　　'The Lord said to my Lord,
　　　"Sit at my right hand*
[35]　　until I make your enemies your
　　　　footstool."'

[36] Therefore let the whole house of Israel know for certain that God has made him both Lord and Messiah, this Jesus whom you crucified."* [37] Now when they heard this, they were cut to the heart, and they asked Peter and the other apostles, "What are we to do, my

---

† **2:33** *At the right hand of God*: or "by the right hand of God."
　**2:38** *Repent and be baptized*: repentance is a positive concept, a change of mind and heart toward God reflected in the actual goodness of one's life. It is in accord with the apostolic teaching derived from Jesus (Acts 2:42) and ultimately recorded in the four gospels. Luke presents baptism in Acts as the expected response to the apostolic preaching about Jesus and associates it with the conferring of the Spirit (Acts 1:5; 10:44–48; 11:16).
　**2:42–47** The first of three summary passages (along with Acts 4:32–37; 5:12–16) that outline, somewhat idyllically, the chief characteristics of the Jerusalem community: adherence to the teachings of the Twelve and the centering of its religious life in the eucharistic liturgy (Acts 2:42); a system of distribution

of goods that led wealthier Christians to sell their possessions when the needs of the community's poor required it (Acts 2:44 and the note on Acts 4:32–37); and continued attendance at the temple, since in this initial stage there was little or no thought of any dividing line between Christianity and Judaism (Acts 2:46).

* **2:17** Is 2:2; 44:3; Jl 3:1–5.　**2:30** 2 Sm 7:12; Ps 132:11.
**2:21** Rom 10:13.　　　　　**2:31** 13:35; Ps 16:10.
**2:22** 10:38; Lk 24:19.　　**2:33** 1:4–5.
**2:23** 1 Thes 2:15.　　　　　**2:34–35** Ps 110:1.
**2:24** 13:34.　　　　　　　**2:36** 9:22; Rom 10:9; Phil
**2:25–28** Ps 16:8–11.　　　　2:11.
**2:27** 13:35.

brothers?"* ³⁸ Peter [said] to them, "Repent and be baptized,† every one of you, in the name of Jesus Christ for the forgiveness of your sins; and you will receive the gift of the holy Spirit.* ³⁹ For the promise is made to you and to your children and to all those far off, whomever the Lord our God will call."* ⁴⁰ He testified with many other arguments, and was exhorting them, "Save yourselves from this corrupt generation."* ⁴¹ Those who accepted his message were baptized, and about three thousand persons were added that day.*

**Communal Life.**† ⁴²* They devoted themselves to the teaching of the apostles and to the communal life, to the breaking of the bread and to the prayers.* ⁴³ Awe came upon everyone, and many wonders and signs were done through the apostles.* ⁴⁴ All who believed were together and had all things in common;* ⁴⁵ they would sell their property and possessions and divide them among all according to each one's need. ⁴⁶ Every day they devoted themselves to meeting together in the temple area and to breaking bread in their homes. They ate their meals with exultation and sincerity of heart, ⁴⁷ praising God and enjoying favor with all the people. And every day the Lord added to their number those who were being saved.

**3** **Cure of a Crippled Beggar.** ¹† Now Peter and John were going up to the temple area for the three o'clock hour of prayer.† ²* And a man crippled from birth was carried and placed at the gate of the temple called "the Beautiful Gate" every day to beg for alms from the people who entered the temple. ³ When he saw Peter and John about to go into the temple, he asked for alms. ⁴ But Peter looked intently at him, as did John, and said, "Look at us." ⁵ He paid attention to them, expecting to receive something from them. ⁶† Peter said, "I have neither silver nor gold, but what I do have I give you: in the name of Jesus Christ the Nazorean, [rise and] walk."* ⁷ Then Peter took him by the right hand and raised him up, and immediately his feet and ankles grew strong. ⁸ He leaped up, stood, and walked around, and went into the temple with them, walking and jumping and praising God.* ⁹ When all the people saw him walking and praising God, ¹⁰ they recognized him as the one who used to sit begging at the Beautiful Gate of the temple, and they were filled with amazement and astonishment at what had happened to him.

**Peter's Speech.** ¹¹ As he clung to Peter and John, all the people hurried in amazement toward them in the portico called "Solomon's Portico."* ¹² When Peter saw this, he addressed the people, "You Israelites, why are you amazed at this, and why do you look so intently at us as if we had made him walk by our own power or piety?* ¹³ The God of Abraham, [the God] of Isaac, and [the God] of Jacob, the God of our ancestors, has glorified† his servant Jesus whom you handed over and denied in Pilate's presence, when he had decided to release him.* ¹⁴ You denied the Holy and Righteous One† and asked that a murderer be released to

---

† **3:1–4:31** This section presents a series of related events: the dramatic cure of a lame beggar (Acts 3:1–10) produces a large audience for the kerygmatic discourse of Peter (Acts 3:11–26). The Sadducees, taking exception to the doctrine of resurrection, have Peter, John, and apparently the beggar as well, arrested (Acts 4:1–4) and brought to trial before the Sanhedrin. The issue concerns the authority by which Peter and John publicly teach religious doctrine in the temple (Acts 4:5–7). Peter replies with a brief summary of the kerygma, implying that his authority is prophetic (Acts 4:8–12). The court warns the apostles to abandon their practice of invoking prophetic authority in the name of Jesus (Acts 4:13–18). When Peter and John reply that the prophetic role cannot be abandoned to satisfy human objections, the court nevertheless releases them, afraid to do otherwise since the beggar, lame from birth and over forty years old, is a well-known figure in Jerusalem and the facts of his cure are common property (Acts 4:19–22). The narrative concludes with a prayer of the Christian community imploring divine aid against threats of persecution (Acts 4:23–31).
**3:1** *For the three o'clock hour of prayer*: literally, "at the ninth hour of prayer." With the day beginning at 6 a.m., the ninth hour would be 3 p.m.
**3:6–10** The miracle has a dramatic cast; it symbolizes the saving power of Christ and leads the beggar to enter the tem-

ple, where he hears Peter's proclamation of salvation through Jesus.
**3:13** *Has glorified*: through the resurrection and ascension of Jesus, God reversed the judgment against him on the occasion of his trial. *Servant*: the Greek word can also be rendered as "son" or even "child" here and also in Acts 3:26; 4:25 (applied to David); Acts 4:27; and Acts 4:30. Scholars are of the opinion, however, that the original concept reflected in the words identified Jesus with the suffering Servant of the Lord of Is 52:13–53:12.
**3:14** *The Holy and Righteous One*: so designating Jesus emphasizes his special relationship to the Father (see Lk 1:35; 4:34) and emphasizes his sinlessness and religious dignity that are placed in sharp contrast with the guilt of those who rejected him in favor of Barabbas.

---

*
| | |
|---|---|
| **2:37** Lk 3:10. | **2:43** 5:12–16. |
| **2:38** 3:19; 16:31; Lk 3:3. | **2:44** 4:32, 34–35. |
| **2:39** Is 57:19; Jl 3:5; Eph 2:17. | **3:2–8** 14:8–10. |
| | **3:6** 4:10. |
| **2:40** Dt 32:5; Ps 78:8; Lk 9:41; Phil 2:15. | **3:8** Is 35:6; Lk 7:22. |
| **2:41** 2:47; 4:4; 5:14; 6:7; 11:21, 24; 21:20. | **3:11** 5:12; Jn 10:23. |
| | **3:12** 14:15. |
| **2:42–47** 4:32–35. | **3:13** Ex 3:6, 15; Is 52:13; Lk 23:14–25. |
| **2:42** 1:14; 6:4. | |

**ACTS**

you.* ¹⁵† The author of life you put to death, but God raised him from the dead; of this we are witnesses.* ¹⁶ And by faith in his name, this man, whom you see and know, his name has made strong, and the faith that comes through it has given him this perfect health, in the presence of all of you. ¹⁷ Now I know, brothers, that you acted out of ignorance,† just as your leaders did;* ¹⁸ but God has thus brought to fulfillment what he had announced beforehand through the mouth of all the prophets,† that his Messiah would suffer.* ¹⁹ Repent, therefore, and be converted, that your sins may be wiped away,* ²⁰ and that the Lord may grant you times of refreshment and send you the Messiah already appointed for you, Jesus,† ²¹ whom heaven must receive until the times of universal restoration† of which God spoke through the mouth of his holy prophets from of old. ²² For Moses said:†

'A prophet like me will the Lord, your
        God, raise up for you
    from among your own kinsmen;
    to him you shall listen in all that he
        may say to you.*
²³     Everyone who does not listen to that
        prophet
    will be cut off from the people.'*

²⁴ Moreover, all the prophets who spoke, from Samuel and those afterwards, also announced these days. ²⁵ You are the children of the prophets and of the covenant that God made with your ancestors when he said to Abraham, 'In your offspring all the families of the earth shall be blessed.'* ²⁶ For you first, God raised up his servant and sent him to bless you by turning each of you from your evil ways."*

**4** ¹ While they were still speaking to the people, the priests, the captain of the temple guard, and the Sadducees† confronted them, ² disturbed that they were teaching the people and proclaiming in Jesus the resurrection of the dead.* ³ They laid hands on them and put them in custody until the next day, since it was already evening. ⁴ But many of those who heard the word came to believe and [the] number of men grew to [about] five thousand.

**Before the Sanhedrin.** ⁵ On the next day, their leaders, elders, and scribes were assembled in Jerusalem, ⁶ with Annas the high priest, Caiaphas, John, Alexander, and all who were of the high-priestly class. ⁷ They brought them into their presence and questioned them, "By what power or by what name have you done this?" ⁸ Then Peter, filled with the holy Spirit, answered them, "Leaders of the people and elders:* ⁹ If we are being examined today about a good deed done to a cripple, namely, by what means he was saved, ¹⁰ then all of you and all the people of Israel should know that it

---

**3:15** *The author of life*: other possible translations of the Greek title are "leader of life" or "pioneer of life." The title clearly points to Jesus as the source and originator of salvation.

**3:17** *Ignorance*: a Lucan motif, explaining away the actions not only of the people but also of their leaders in crucifying Jesus. On this basis the presbyters in Acts could continue to appeal to the Jews in Jerusalem to believe in Jesus, even while affirming their involvement in his death because they were unaware of his messianic dignity. See also Acts 13:27 and Lk 23:34.

**3:18** *Through the mouth of all the prophets*: Christian prophetic insight into the Old Testament saw the crucifixion and death of Jesus as the main import of messianic prophecy. The Jews themselves did not anticipate a suffering Messiah; they usually understood the Servant Song in Is 52:13–53:12 to signify their own suffering as a people. In his typical fashion (cf. Lk 18:31; 24:25, 27, 44), Luke does not specify the particular Old Testament prophecies that were fulfilled by Jesus. See also note on Lk 24:26.

**3:20** *The Lord...and send you the Messiah already appointed for you, Jesus*: an allusion to the parousia or second coming of Christ, judged to be imminent in the apostolic age. This reference to its nearness is the only explicit one in Acts. Some scholars believe that this verse preserves a very early christology, in which the title "Messiah" (Greek "Christ") is applied to him as of his parousia, his second coming (contrast Acts 2:36). This view of a future messiahship of Jesus is not found elsewhere in the New Testament.

**3:21** *The times of universal restoration*: like "the times of refreshment" (Acts 3:20), an apocalyptic designation of the messianic age, fitting in with the christology of Acts 3:20 that associates the messiahship of Jesus with his future coming.

**3:22** A loose citation of Dt 18:15, which teaches that the Israelites are to learn the will of Yahweh from no one but their prophets. At the time of Jesus, some Jews expected a unique prophet to come in fulfillment of this text. Early Christianity applied this tradition and text to Jesus and used them especially in defense of the divergence of Christian teaching from traditional Judaism.

**4:1** *The priests, the captain of the temple guard, and the Sadducees*: the priests performed the temple liturgy; the temple guard was composed of Levites, whose captain ranked next after the high priest. The Sadducees, a party within Judaism at this time, rejected those doctrines, including bodily resurrection, which they believed alien to the ancient Mosaic religion. The Sadducees were drawn from priestly families and from the lay aristocracy.

---

**3:14** Mt 27:20–21; Mk 15:11; Lk 23:18; Jn 18:40.
**3:15** 4:10; 5:31 / 1:8; 2:32.
**3:17** 13:27; Lk 23:34; 1 Cor 2:8; 1 Tm 1:13.
**3:18** Lk 18:31.
**3:19** 2:38.
**3:22** 7:37; Dt 18:15, 18.
**3:23** Lv 23:29; Dt 18:19.
**3:25** Gn 12:3; 18:18; 22:18; Sir 44:19–21; Gal 3:8–9.
**3:26** 13:46; Rom 1:16.
**4:2** 23:6–8; 24:21.
**4:8** Mt 10:20.

was in the name of Jesus Christ the Nazorean whom you crucified, whom God raised from the dead; in his name this man stands before you healed. [11]* He is 'the stone rejected by you,† the builders, which has become the cornerstone.' [12]†* There is no salvation through anyone else, nor is there any other name under heaven given to the human race by which we are to be saved."

[13] Observing the boldness of Peter and John and perceiving them to be uneducated, ordinary men, they were amazed, and they recognized them as the companions of Jesus. [14] Then when they saw the man who had been cured standing there with them, they could say nothing in reply. [15] So they ordered them to leave the Sanhedrin, and conferred with one another, saying, [16] "What are we to do with these men? Everyone living in Jerusalem knows that a remarkable sign was done through them, and we cannot deny it. [17] But so that it may not be spread any further among the people, let us give them a stern warning never again to speak to anyone in this name."*

[18] So they called them back and ordered them not to speak or teach at all in the name of Jesus. [19] Peter and John, however, said to them in reply, "Whether it is right in the sight of God for us to obey you rather than God, you be the judges.* [20] It is impossible for us not to speak about what we have seen and heard." [21] After threatening them further, they released them, finding no way to punish them, on account of the people who were all praising God for what had happened. [22] For the man on whom this sign of healing had been done was over forty years old.

**Prayer of the Community.** [23] After their release they went back to their own people and reported what the chief priests and elders had told them. [24] And when they heard it, they raised their voices to God with one accord and said, "Sovereign Lord, maker of heaven and earth and the sea and all that is in them, [25] you said by the holy Spirit through the mouth of our father David, your servant:

'Why did the Gentiles rage*
　　and the peoples entertain folly?
[26] The kings of the earth took their stand
　　and the princes gathered together
　　against the Lord and against his
　　anointed.'

[27] Indeed they gathered in this city against your holy servant Jesus whom you anointed, Herod† and Pontius Pilate, together with the Gentiles and the peoples of Israel,* [28] to do what your hand and [your] will had long ago planned to take place. [29] And now, Lord, take note of their threats, and enable your servants to speak your word with all boldness, [30] as you stretch forth [your] hand to heal, and signs and wonders are done through the name of your holy servant Jesus." [31]† As they prayed, the place where they were gathered shook, and they were all filled with the holy Spirit and continued to speak the word of God with boldness.*

**Life in the Christian Community.**† [32] The community of believers was of one heart and mind, and no one claimed that any of his possessions was his own, but they had everything in common. [33] With great power the apostles bore witness to the resurrection of the Lord Jesus, and great favor was accorded them all. [34]* There was no needy person among them, for those who owned property or houses would sell them, bring the proceeds of the sale, [35] and put them at the feet of the apostles,

---

**4:11** Early Christianity applied this citation from Ps 118:22 to Jesus; cf. Mk 12:10; 1 Pt 2:7.

**4:12** In the Roman world of Luke's day, salvation was often attributed to the emperor who was hailed as "savior" and "god." Luke, in the words of Peter, denies that deliverance comes through anyone other than Jesus.

**4:27** *Herod*: Herod Antipas, ruler of Galilee and Perea from 4 B.C. to A.D. 39, who executed John the Baptist and before whom Jesus was arraigned; cf. Lk 23:6–12.

**4:31** *The place…shook*: the earthquake is used as a sign of the divine presence in Ex 19:18; Is 6:4. Here the shaking of the building symbolizes God's favorable response to the prayer. Luke may have had as an additional reason for using the symbol in this sense the fact that it was familiar in the Hellenistic world. Ovid and Virgil also employ it.

**4:32–37** This is the second summary characterizing the Jeru-

salem community (see note on Acts 2:42–47). It emphasizes the system of the distribution of goods and introduces Barnabas, who appears later in Acts as the friend and companion of Paul, and who, as noted here (Acts 4:37), endeared himself to the community by a donation of money through the sale of property. This sharing of material possessions continues a practice that Luke describes during the historical ministry of Jesus (Lk 8:3) and is in accord with the sayings of Jesus in Luke's gospel (Lk 12:33; 16:9, 11, 13).

---

| | |
|---|---|
| **4:11** Ps 118:22; Is 28:16; | **4:19** 5:29–32. |
| Mt 21:42; Mk 12:10; | **4:25–26** Ps 2:1–2. |
| Lk 20:17; Rom 9:33; | **4:27** Lk 23:12–13. |
| 1 Pt 2:7. | **4:31** 2:4. |
| **4:12** Mt 1:21; 1 Cor 3:11. | **4:34–35** 2:44–45. |
| **4:17** 5:28. | |

and they were distributed to each according to need.

<sup>36</sup>* Thus Joseph, also named by the apostles Barnabas (which is translated "son of encouragement"), a Levite, a Cypriot by birth, <sup>37</sup> sold a piece of property that he owned, then brought the money and put it at the feet of the apostles.

# 5 Ananias and Sapphira.†

<sup>1</sup> A man named Ananias, however, with his wife Sapphira, sold a piece of property. <sup>2</sup> He retained for himself, with his wife's knowledge, some of the purchase price, took the remainder, and put it at the feet of the apostles. <sup>3</sup> But Peter said, "Ananias, why has Satan filled your heart so that you lied to the holy Spirit and retained part of the price of the land?* <sup>4</sup> While it remained unsold, did it not remain yours? And when it was sold, was it not still under your control? Why did you contrive this deed? You have lied not to human beings, but to God." <sup>5</sup> When Ananias heard these words, he fell down and breathed his last, and great fear came upon all who heard of it. <sup>6</sup> The young men came and wrapped him up, then carried him out and buried him.

<sup>7</sup> After an interval of about three hours, his wife came in, unaware of what had happened. <sup>8</sup> Peter said to her, "Tell me, did you sell the land for this amount?" She answered, "Yes, for that amount." <sup>9</sup> Then Peter said to her, "Why did you agree to test the Spirit of the Lord? Listen, the footsteps of those who have buried your husband are at the door, and they will carry you out." <sup>10</sup> At once, she fell down at his feet and breathed her last. When the young men entered they found her dead, so they carried her out and buried her beside her husband. <sup>11</sup> And great fear came upon the whole church and upon all who heard of these things.*

## Signs and Wonders of the Apostles.†

<sup>12</sup> Many signs and wonders were done among the people at the hands of the apostles. They were all together in Solomon's portico.* <sup>13</sup> None of the others dared to join them, but the people esteemed them. <sup>14</sup> Yet more than ever, believers in the Lord, great numbers of men and women, were added to them. <sup>15</sup> Thus they even carried the sick out into the streets and laid them on cots and mats so that when Peter came by, at least his shadow might fall on one or another of them.* <sup>16</sup> A large number of people from the towns in the vicinity of Jerusalem also gathered, bringing the sick and those disturbed by unclean spirits, and they were all cured.

## Trial Before the Sanhedrin.†

<sup>17</sup> Then the high priest rose up and all his companions, that is, the party of the Sadducees, and, filled with jealousy,* <sup>18</sup> laid hands upon the apostles and put them in the public jail. <sup>19</sup> But during the night, the angel of the Lord opened the doors of the prison, led them out, and said,* <sup>20</sup> "Go and take your place in the temple area, and tell the people everything about this life." <sup>21</sup> When they heard this, they went to the temple early in the morning and taught. When the high priest and his companions arrived, they convened the Sanhedrin, the full senate of the Israelites, and sent to the jail to have them brought in. <sup>22</sup> But the court officers who went did not find them in the prison, so they came back and reported, <sup>23</sup> "We found the jail securely locked and the guards stationed outside the doors, but when we opened them, we found no one inside." <sup>24</sup> When they heard this

---

† **5:1–11** The sin of Ananias and Sapphira did not consist in the withholding of part of the money but in their deception of the community. Their deaths are ascribed to a lie to the holy Spirit (Acts 5:3, 9), i.e., they accepted the honor accorded them by the community for their generosity, but in reality they were not deserving of it.

**5:12–16** This, the third summary portraying the Jerusalem community, underscores the Twelve as its bulwark, especially because of their charismatic power to heal the sick; cf. Acts 2:42–47; 4:32–37.

**5:17–42** A second action against the community is taken by the Sanhedrin in the arrest and trial of the Twelve; cf. Acts 4:1–3. The motive is the jealousy of the religious authorities over the popularity of the apostles (Acts 5:17) who are now charged with the defiance of the Sanhedrin's previous order to them to abandon their prophetic role (Acts 5:28; cf. Acts 4:18). In this crisis the apostles are favored by a miraculous release from prison

(Acts 5:18–24). (For similar incidents involving Peter and Paul, see Acts 12:6–11; 16:25–29.) The real significance of such an event, however, would be manifest only to people of faith, not to unbelievers; since the Sanhedrin already judged the Twelve to be inauthentic prophets, it could disregard reports of their miracles. When the Twelve immediately resumed public teaching, the Sanhedrin determined to invoke upon them the penalty of death (Acts 5:33) prescribed in Dt 13:6–10. Gamaliel's advice against this course finally prevailed, but it did not save the Twelve from the punishment of scourging (Acts 5:40) in a last endeavor to shake their conviction of their prophetic mission.

---

*
**4:36–37** 9:27; 11:22, 30;
    12:25; 13:15; 1 Cor
    9:6; Gal 2:1, 9, 13;
    Col 4:10.
**5:3** Lk 22:3; Jn 13:2.
**5:11** 2:43; 5:5; 19:17.

**5:12** 2:43; 6:8; 14:3;
    15:12.
**5:15** 19:11–12; Mk 6:56.
**5:17** 4:1–3, 6.
**5:19** 12:7–10; 16:25–26.

report, the captain of the temple guard and the chief priests were at a loss about them, as to what this would come to. 25 Then someone came in and reported to them, "The men whom you put in prison are in the temple area and are teaching the people." 26 Then the captain and the court officers went and brought them in, but without force, because they were afraid of being stoned by the people.*

27 When they had brought them in and made them stand before the Sanhedrin, the high priest questioned them, 28 "We gave you strict orders [did we not?] to stop teaching in that name. Yet you have filled Jerusalem with your teaching and want to bring this man's blood upon us."* 29 But Peter and the apostles said in reply, "We must obey God rather than men.* 30† The God of our ancestors raised Jesus,* though you had him killed by hanging him on a tree. 31 God exalted him at his right hand† as leader and savior to grant Israel repentance and forgiveness of sins.* 32 We are witnesses of these things, as is the holy Spirit that God has given to those who obey him."*

33 When they heard this, they became infuriated and wanted to put them to death. 34† But a Pharisee in the Sanhedrin named Gamaliel, a teacher of the law, respected by all the people, stood up, ordered the men to be put outside for a short time,* 35 and said to them, "Fellow Israelites, be careful what you are about to do to these men. 36† Some time ago, Theudas appeared, claiming to be someone important, and about four hundred men joined him, but he was killed, and all those who were loyal to him were disbanded and came to nothing. 37 After him came Judas the Galilean at the time of the census. He also drew people after him, but he too perished and all who were loyal to him were scattered. 38 So now I tell you, have nothing to do with these men, and let them go. For if this endeavor or this activity is of human origin, it will destroy itself. 39 But if it comes from God, you will not be able to destroy them; you may even find yourselves fighting against God." They were persuaded by him. 40 After recalling the apostles, they had them flogged, ordered them to stop speaking in the name of Jesus, and dismissed them.* 41 So they left the presence of the Sanhedrin, rejoicing that they had been found worthy to suffer dishonor for the sake of the name.* 42 And all day long, both at the temple and in their homes, they did not stop teaching and proclaiming the Messiah, Jesus.*

**6** **The Need for Assistants.** 1† At that time, as the number of disciples continued to grow, the Hellenists complained against the Hebrews because their widows were being neglected in the daily distribution.* 2† So the Twelve called together the community of the disciples and said, "It is not right for us to neglect the word of God to serve at table.† 3 Brothers, select from among you seven reputable men, filled with the Spirit and wisdom, whom we shall appoint to this task, 4 whereas we shall devote ourselves to prayer and to the ministry of the word." 5 The proposal was acceptable to the whole community, so they chose Stephen, a man filled with faith and the holy Spirit, also Philip, Prochorus, Nicanor, Timon, Parmenas, and Nicholas of Antioch, a convert to Judaism. 6* They presented these

---

† 

**5:30** *Hanging him on a tree*: that is, crucifying him (cf. also Gal 3:13).

**5:31** *At his right hand*: see note on Acts 2:33.

**5:34** *Gamaliel*: in Acts 22:3, Paul identifies himself as a disciple of this Rabbi Gamaliel I who flourished in Jerusalem between A.D. 25 and 50.

**5:36–37** Gamaliel offers examples of unsuccessful contemporary movements to argue that if God is not the origin of this movement preached by the apostles it will perish by itself. The movement initiated by Theudas actually occurred when C. Cuspius Fadus was governor, A.D. 44–46. Luke's placing of Judas the Galilean after Theudas and at the time of the census (see note on Lk 2:1–2) is an indication of the vagueness of his knowledge of these events.

**6:1–7** *The Hellenists…the Hebrews*: the Hellenists were not necessarily Jews from the diaspora, but were more probably Palestinian Jews who spoke only Greek. The Hebrews were Palestinian Jews who spoke Hebrew or Aramaic and who may also have spoken Greek. Both groups belong to the Jerusalem Jewish Christian community. The conflict between them leads to a restructuring of the community that will better serve the community's needs. The real purpose of the whole episode, however,

is to introduce Stephen as a prominent figure in the community whose long speech and martyrdom will be recounted in Acts 7.

**6:2–4** The essential function of the Twelve is the "service of the word," including development of the kerygma by formulation of the teachings of Jesus.

**6:2** *To serve at table*: some commentators think that it is not the serving of food that is described here but rather the keeping of the accounts that recorded the distribution of food to the needy members of the community. In any case, after Stephen and the others are chosen, they are never presented carrying out the task for which they were appointed (Acts 6:2–3). Rather, two of their number, Stephen and Philip, are presented as preachers of the Christian message. They, the Hellenist counterpart of the Twelve, are active in the ministry of the word.

**5:26** Lk 20:19.
**5:28** Mt 27:25.
**5:29** 4:19.
**5:30** 2:23–24.
**5:31** 2:38.
**5:32** Lk 24:48; Jn 15:26.
**5:34** 22:3.
**5:40** Mt 10:17;

Acts 4:17–18.
**5:41** Mt 5:10–11; 1 Pt 4:13.
**5:42** 2:46; 5:20–21, 25; 8:35; 17:3; 18:5, 28; 19:4–5.
**6:1** 2:45; 4:34–35.
**6:6** 1:24; 13:3; 14:23.

men to the apostles who prayed and laid hands on them. † [7] The word of God continued to spread, and the number of the disciples in Jerusalem increased greatly; even a large group of priests were becoming obedient to the faith. *

**Accusation Against Stephen.** [8] † Now Stephen, filled with grace and power, was working great wonders and signs among the people. [9] Certain members of the so-called Synagogue of Freedmen, Cyrenians, and Alexandrians, and people from Cilicia and Asia, came forward and debated with Stephen, [10] but they could not withstand the wisdom and the spirit with which he spoke. * [11] Then they instigated some men to say, "We have heard him speaking blasphemous words against Moses and God." * [12] They stirred up the people, the elders, and the scribes, accosted him, seized him, and brought him before the Sanhedrin. [13] They presented false witnesses † who testified, "This man never stops saying things against [this] holy place and the law. [14] For we have heard him claim that this Jesus the Nazorean will destroy this place and change the customs that Moses handed down to us." * [15] All those who sat in the Sanhedrin looked intently at him and saw that his face was like the face of an angel.

**7** **Stephen's Discourses.** [1] Then the high priest asked, "Is this so?" [2] * And he replied, † "My brothers and fathers, listen. The

God of glory appeared to our father Abraham while he was in Mesopotamia, † before he had settled in Haran, [3] and said to him, 'Go forth from your land and [from] your kinsfolk to the land that I will show you.' * [4] So he went forth from the land of the Chaldeans and settled in Haran. And from there, after his father died, he made him migrate to this land where you now dwell. * [5] Yet he gave him no inheritance in it, not even a foot's length, but he did promise to give it to him and his descendants as a possession, even though he was childless. * [6] And God spoke thus, * 'His descendants shall be aliens in a land not their own, where they shall be enslaved and oppressed for four hundred years; [7] but I will bring judgment on the nation they serve,' God said, 'and after that they will come out and worship me in this place.' * [8] Then he gave him the covenant of circumcision, and so he became the father of Isaac, and circumcised him on the eighth day, as Isaac did Jacob, and Jacob the twelve patriarchs. *

[9] "And the patriarchs, jealous of Joseph, sold him into slavery in Egypt; but God was with him * [10] and rescued him from all his afflictions. He granted him favor and wisdom before Pharaoh, the king of Egypt, who put him in charge of Egypt and [of] his entire household. * [11] Then a famine and great affliction struck all Egypt and Canaan, and our ancestors could find no food; * [12] but when Jacob heard that there was grain in Egypt, he sent our ancestors there a first time. * [13] The second time, Joseph

---

† 

**6:6** *They…laid hands on them:* the customary Jewish way of designating persons for a task and invoking upon them the divine blessing and power to perform it.

**6:8–8:1** The summary (Acts 6:7) on the progress of the Jerusalem community, illustrated by the conversion of the priests, is followed by a lengthy narrative regarding Stephen. Stephen's defense is not a response to the charges made against him but takes the form of a discourse that reviews the fortunes of God's word to Israel and leads to a prophetic declaration: a plea for the hearing of that word as announced by Christ and now possessed by the Christian community.

The charges that Stephen depreciated the importance of the temple and the Mosaic law and elevated Jesus to a stature above Moses (Acts 6:13–14) were in fact true. Before the Sanhedrin, no defense against them was possible. With Stephen, who thus perceived the fuller implications of the teachings of Jesus, the differences between Judaism and Christianity began to appear. Luke's account of Stephen's martyrdom and its aftermath shows how the major impetus behind the Christian movement passed from Jerusalem, where the temple and law prevailed, to Antioch in Syria, where these influences were less pressing.

**6:13** *False witnesses:* here, and in his account of Stephen's execution (Acts 7:54–60), Luke parallels the martyrdom of Stephen with the death of Jesus.

**7:2–53** Stephen's speech represents Luke's description of Christianity's break from its Jewish matrix. Two motifs become

prominent in the speech: (1) Israel's reaction to God's chosen leaders in the past reveals that the people have consistently rejected them; and (2) Israel has misunderstood God's choice of the Jerusalem temple as the place where he is to be worshiped.

**7:2** *God…appeared to our father Abraham…in Mesopotamia:* the first of a number of minor discrepancies between the data of the Old Testament and the data of Stephen's discourse. According to Gn 12:1, God first spoke to Abraham in Haran. The main discrepancies are these: in Acts 7:16 it is said that Jacob was buried in Shechem, whereas Gn 50:13 says he was buried at Hebron; in the same verse it is said that the tomb was purchased by Abraham, but in Gn 33:19 and Jos 24:32 the purchase is attributed to Jacob himself.

| | |
|---|---|
| **6:7** 9:31; 12:24; 16:5; 19:20; 28:30–31. | **7:5** Gn 12:7; 13:15; 15:2; 16:1; Dt 2:5. |
| **6:10** Lk 21:15. | **7:6–7** Gn 15:13–14. |
| **6:11** Mt 26:59–61; Mk 14:55–58; Acts 21:21. | **7:7** Ex 3:12. |
| | **7:8** Gn 17:10–14; 21:2–4. |
| **6:14** Mt 26:59–61; 27:40; Jn 2:19. | **7:9** Gn 37:11, 28; 39:2, 3, 21, 23. |
| **7:2** Gn 11:31; 12:1; Ps 29:3. | **7:10** Gn 41:37–43; Ps 105:21; Wis 10:13–14. |
| **7:3** Gn 12:1. | |
| **7:4** Gn 12:5; 15:7. | **7:11** Gn 41:54–57; 42:5. |
| | **7:12** Gn 42:1–2. |

made himself known to his brothers, and Joseph's family became known to Pharaoh.* <sup>14</sup>Then Joseph sent for his father Jacob, inviting him and his whole clan, seventy-five persons;* <sup>15</sup>and Jacob went down to Egypt. And he and our ancestors died* <sup>16</sup>and were brought back to Shechem and placed in the tomb that Abraham had purchased for a sum of money from the sons of Hamor at Shechem.*

<sup>17</sup> "When the time drew near for the fulfillment of the promise that God pledged to Abraham, the people had increased and become very numerous in Egypt,* <sup>18</sup>until another king who knew nothing of Joseph came to power [in Egypt].* <sup>19</sup>He dealt shrewdly with our people and oppressed [our] ancestors by forcing them to expose their infants, that they might not survive. <sup>20</sup>At this time Moses was born, and he was extremely beautiful. For three months he was nursed in his father's house;* <sup>21</sup>but when he was exposed, Pharaoh's daughter adopted him and brought him up as her own son.* <sup>22</sup>Moses was educated [in] all the wisdom of the Egyptians and was powerful in his words and deeds.

<sup>23</sup>* "When he was forty years old, he decided to visit his kinsfolk, the Israelites. <sup>24</sup>When he saw one of them treated unjustly, he defended and avenged the oppressed man by striking down the Egyptian. <sup>25</sup>He assumed [his] kinsfolk would understand that God was offering them deliverance through him, but they did not understand. <sup>26</sup>* The next day he appeared to them as they were fighting and tried to reconcile them peacefully, saying, 'Men, you are brothers. Why are you harming one another?' <sup>27</sup>Then the one who was harming his neighbor pushed him aside, saying, 'Who appointed you ruler and judge over us? <sup>28</sup>Are you thinking of killing me as you killed the Egyptian yesterday?' <sup>29</sup>Moses fled when he heard this and settled as an alien in the land of Midian, where he became the father of two sons.*

<sup>30</sup>* "Forty years later, an angel appeared to him in the desert near Mount Sinai in the flame of a burning bush. <sup>31</sup>When Moses saw it, he was amazed at the sight, and as he drew near to look at it, the voice of the Lord came,

<sup>32</sup>'I am the God of your fathers, the God of Abraham, of Isaac, and of Jacob.' Then Moses, trembling, did not dare to look at it. <sup>33</sup>But the Lord said to him, 'Remove the sandals from your feet, for the place where you stand is holy ground. <sup>34</sup>I have witnessed the affliction of my people in Egypt and have heard their groaning, and I have come down to rescue them. Come now, I will send you to Egypt.' <sup>35</sup>This Moses, whom they had rejected with the words, 'Who appointed you ruler and judge?' God sent as [both] ruler and deliverer, through the angel who appeared to him in the bush.* <sup>36</sup>This man led them out, performing wonders and signs in the land of Egypt, at the Red Sea, and in the desert for forty years.* <sup>37</sup>It was this Moses who said to the Israelites, 'God will raise up for you, from among your own kinsfolk, a prophet like me.'* <sup>38</sup>It was he who, in the assembly in the desert, was with the angel who spoke to him on Mount Sinai and with our ancestors, and he received living utterances to hand on to us.*

<sup>39</sup> "Our ancestors were unwilling to obey him; instead, they pushed him aside and in their hearts turned back to Egypt,* <sup>40</sup>saying to Aaron, 'Make us gods who will be our leaders. As for that Moses who led us out of the land of Egypt, we do not know what has happened to him.'* <sup>41</sup>So they made a calf in those days, offered sacrifice to the idol, and reveled in the works of their hands. <sup>42</sup>Then God turned and handed them over to worship the host of heaven, as it is written in the book of the prophets:*

'Did you bring me sacrifices and offerings
  for forty years in the desert, O house
    of Israel?*
<sup>43</sup>  No, you took up the tent of Moloch
    and the star of [your] god Rephan,
    the images that you made to
    worship.
  So I shall take you into exile beyond
    Babylon.'

<sup>44</sup>Our ancestors had the tent of testimony in the desert just as the One who spoke to

7:13 Gn 45:3–4, 16.   Jos 24:32.
7:14 Gn 45:9–11, 18–19;   7:17 Ex 1:7.
46:27; Ex 1:5 LXX; Dt   7:18 Ex 1:8.
10:22.   7:20 Ex 2:2; Heb 11:23.
7:15 Gn 46:5–6; 49:33.   7:21 Ex 2:3–10.
7:16 Gn 23:3–20; 33:19;   7:23–24 Ex 2:11–12.
49:29–30; 50:13;   7:26–28 Ex 2:13–14.
7:29 Ex 2:15, 21–22; 18:3–4.   7:38 Ex 19:3; 20:1–17; Dt 5:4–22; 6:4–25.
7:30–34 Ex 3:2–3.   7:39 Nm 14:3.
7:35 Ex 2:14.   7:40 Ex 32:1, 23.
7:36 Ex 7:3, 10; 14:21; Nm 14:33.   7:41 Ex 32:4–6.
7:37 Dt 18:15; Acts 3:22.   7:42–43 Am 5:25–27.
7:42 Jer 7:18; 8:2; 19:13.

Moses directed him to make it according to the pattern he had seen.* ⁴⁵ Our ancestors who inherited it brought it with Joshua when they dispossessed the nations that God drove out from before our ancestors, up to the time of David,* ⁴⁶ who found favor in the sight of God and asked that he might find a dwelling place for the house of Jacob.* ⁴⁷ But Solomon built a house for him.* ⁴⁸ Yet the Most High does not dwell in houses made by human hands. As the prophet says:*

49     'The heavens are my throne,
           the earth is my footstool.
       What kind of house can you build for
           me?
       says the Lord,
       or what is to be my resting place?*
50     Did not my hand make all these things?'

**Conclusion.** ⁵¹ "You stiff-necked people, uncircumcised in heart and ears, you always oppose the holy Spirit; you are just like your ancestors. ⁵² Which of the prophets did your ancestors not persecute? They put to death those who foretold the coming of the righteous one, whose betrayers and murderers you have now become.* ⁵³ You received the law as transmitted by angels, but you did not observe it."*

**Stephen's Martyrdom.** ⁵⁴ When they heard this, they were infuriated, and they ground their teeth at him. ⁵⁵* But he, filled with the holy Spirit, looked up intently to heaven and saw the glory of God and Jesus standing at the right hand of God,† ⁵⁶ and he said, "Behold, I see the heavens opened and the Son of Man standing at the right hand of God." ⁵⁷ But they cried out in a loud voice, covered their ears,† and rushed upon him together. ⁵⁸ They threw him out of the city, and began to stone him. The witnesses laid down their cloaks at the feet of a young man named Saul.* ⁵⁹ As they were stoning Stephen,* he called out, "Lord Jesus, receive my spirit."† ⁶⁰ Then he fell to his knees and cried out in a loud voice, "Lord, do not hold this sin against them"; and when he said this, he fell asleep.*

**8** ¹ Now Saul was consenting to his execution.*

**Persecution of the Church.** On that day, there broke out a severe persecution† of the church in Jerusalem, and all were scattered throughout the countryside of Judea and Samaria, except the apostles.† ² Devout men buried Stephen and made a loud lament over him. ³ Saul, meanwhile, was trying to destroy the church;† entering house after house and dragging out men and women, he handed them over for imprisonment.*

### III. THE MISSION IN JUDEA AND SAMARIA

**Philip in Samaria.** ⁴ Now those who had been scattered went about preaching the word.* ⁵ Thus Philip went down to [the] city of Samaria and proclaimed the Messiah to them.* ⁶ With one accord, the crowds paid attention to what was said by Philip when they heard it

---

**7:55** *He...saw...Jesus standing at the right hand of God*: Stephen affirms to the Sanhedrin that the prophecy Jesus made before them has been fulfilled (Mk 14:62).
**7:57** *Covered their ears*: Stephen's declaration, like that of Jesus, is a scandal to the court, which regards it as blasphemy.
**7:59** Compare Lk 23:34, 46.
**8:1–40** Some idea of the severity of the persecution that now breaks out against the Jerusalem community can be gathered from Acts 22:4 and Acts 26:9–11. Luke, however, concentrates on the fortunes of the word of God among people, indicating how the dispersal of the Jewish community resulted in the conversion of the Samaritans (Acts 8:4–17, 25). His narrative is further expanded to include the account of Philip's acceptance of an Ethiopian (Acts 8:26–39).
**8:1** *All were scattered...except the apostles*: this observation leads some modern scholars to conclude that the persecution was limited to the Hellenist Christians and that the Hebrew Christians were not molested, perhaps because their attitude toward the law and temple was still more in line with that of their fellow Jews (see the charge leveled against the Hellenist Stephen in Acts 6:13–14). Whatever the facts, it appears that the Twelve took no public stand regarding Stephen's position, choosing, instead, to await the development of events.

**8:3** *Saul...was trying to destroy the church*: like Stephen, Saul was able to perceive that the Christian movement contained the seeds of doctrinal divergence from Judaism. A pupil of Gamaliel, according to Acts 22:3, and totally dedicated to the law as the way of salvation (Gal 1:13–14), Saul accepted the task of crushing the Christian movement, at least insofar as it detracted from the importance of the temple and the law. His vehement opposition to Christianity reveals how difficult it was for a Jew of his time to accept a messianism that differed so greatly from the general expectation.

---

| | |
|---|---|
| **7:44** Ex 25:9, 40. | **7:55–56** Mt 26:64; Mk 14:62; |
| **7:45** Jos 3:14–17; 18:1; | Lk 22:69; Acts 2:34. |
| 2 Sm 7:5–7. | **7:58** 22:20. |
| **7:46** 2 Sm 7:1–2; 1 Kgs | **7:59** Ps 31:6; Lk 23:46. |
| 8:17; Ps 132:1–5. | **7:60** Mt 27:46, 50; Mk |
| **7:47** 1 Kgs 6:1; 1 Chr | 15:34; Lk 23:46. |
| 17:12. | **8:1** 22:20. |
| **7:48** 17:24. | **8:3** 9:1, 13; 22:4; |
| **7:49** Is 66:1–2. | 26:9–11; 1 Cor 5:9; |
| **7:52** 2 Chr 36:16; Mt | Gal 1:13. |
| 23:31, 34. | **8:4** 11:19. |
| **7:53** Gal 3:19; Heb 2:2. | **8:5** 6:5; 21:8–9. |

and saw the signs he was doing. ⁷For unclean spirits, crying out in a loud voice, came out of many possessed people, and many paralyzed and crippled people were cured.* ⁸There was great joy in that city.

**Simon the Magician.** ⁹A man named Simon used to practice magic† in the city and astounded the people of Samaria, claiming to be someone great. ¹⁰All of them, from the least to the greatest, paid attention to him, saying, "This man is the 'Power of God' that is called 'Great.'" ¹¹They paid attention to him because he had astounded them by his magic for a long time, ¹²but once they began to believe Philip as he preached the good news about the kingdom of God and the name of Jesus Christ, men and women alike were baptized.* ¹³Even Simon himself believed and, after being baptized, became devoted to Philip; and when he saw the signs and mighty deeds that were occurring, he was astounded.

¹⁴Now when the apostles in Jerusalem heard that Samaria had accepted the word of God, they sent them Peter and John, ¹⁵who went down and prayed for them, that they might receive the holy Spirit, ¹⁶for it had not yet fallen upon any of them; they had only been baptized in the name of the Lord Jesus.† ¹⁷Then they laid hands on them and they received the holy Spirit.*

¹⁸†When Simon saw that the Spirit was conferred by the laying on of the apostles' hands, he offered them money ¹⁹and said, "Give me this power too, so that anyone upon whom I lay my hands may receive the holy Spirit." ²⁰But Peter said to him, "May your money perish with you, because you thought that you could buy the gift of God with money. ²¹You have no share or lot in this matter, for your heart is not upright before God. ²²Repent of this wickedness of yours and pray to the Lord that, if possible, your intention may be forgiven. ²³For I see that you are filled with bitter gall and are in the bonds of iniquity." ²⁴Simon said in reply, "Pray for me to the Lord, that nothing of what you have said may come upon me." ²⁵So when they had testified and proclaimed the word of the Lord, they returned to Jerusalem and preached the good news to many Samaritan villages.

**Philip and the Ethiopian.**† ²⁶Then the angel of the Lord spoke to Philip, "Get up and head south on the road that goes down from Jerusalem to Gaza, the desert route." ²⁷So he got up and set out. Now there was an Ethiopian eunuch, a court official of the Candace,† that is, the queen of the Ethiopians, in charge of her entire treasury, who had come to Jerusalem to worship,* ²⁸and was returning home. Seated in his chariot, he was reading the prophet Isaiah. ²⁹The Spirit said to Philip, "Go and join up with that chariot." ³⁰†Philip ran up and heard him reading Isaiah the prophet and said, "Do you understand what you are reading?" ³¹He replied, "How can I, unless someone instructs me?" So he invited Philip to get in and sit with him.* ³²This was the scripture passage he was reading:*

> "Like a sheep he was led to the
>    slaughter,
>   and as a lamb before its shearer is
>    silent,
>     so he opened not his mouth.

---

**8:9–13, 18–24** Sorcerers were well known in the ancient world. Probably the incident involving Simon and his altercation with Peter is introduced to show that the miraculous charisms possessed by members of the Christian community (Acts 8:6–7) were not to be confused with the magic of sorcerers.

**8:16** Here and in Acts 10:44–48 and Acts 19:1–6, Luke distinguishes between baptism in the name of the Lord Jesus and the reception of the Spirit. In each case, the Spirit is conferred through members of the Twelve (Peter and John) or their representative (Paul). This may be Luke's way of describing the role of the church in the bestowal of the Spirit. Elsewhere in Acts, baptism and the Spirit are more closely related (Acts 1:5; 11:16).

**8:18–20** Simon attempts to buy the gift of God (Acts 8:20) with money. Peter's cursing of Simon's attempt so to use his money expresses a typically Lucan attitude toward material wealth (cf. Lk 6:24; 12:16–21; 16:13).

**8:26–40** In the account of the conversion of the Ethiopian eunuch, Luke adduces additional evidence to show that the spread of Christianity outside the confines of Judaism itself was in accord with the plan of God. He does not make clear whether

the Ethiopian was originally a convert to Judaism or, as is more probable, a "God-fearer" (Acts 10:1), i.e., one who accepted Jewish monotheism and ethic and attended the synagogue but did not consider himself bound by other regulations such as circumcision and observance of the dietary laws. The story of his conversion to Christianity is given a strong supernatural cast by the introduction of an angel (Acts 8:26), instruction from the holy Spirit (Acts 8:29), and the strange removal of Philip from the scene (8:39).

**8:27** *The Candace*: Candace is not a proper name here but the title of a Nubian queen.

**8:30–34** Philip is brought alongside the carriage at the very moment when the Ethiopian is pondering the meaning of Is 53:7–8, a passage that Christianity, from its earliest origins, has applied to Jesus; cf. note on Acts 3:13.

---

**8:7** Mk 16:17.                 **8:27** Is 56:3–5.
**8:12** 1:3; 19:8; 28:23, 31.      **8:31** Jn 16:13.
**8:17** 2:4; 4:31; 10:44–47;     **8:32–33** Is 53:7–8 LXX.
     15:8–9; 19:2, 6.

33
> In [his] humiliation justice was denied
>> him.
> Who will tell of his posterity?
>> For his life is taken from the earth."

34 Then the eunuch said to Philip in reply, "I beg you, about whom is the prophet saying this? About himself, or about someone else?" 35 Then Philip opened his mouth and, beginning with this scripture passage, he proclaimed Jesus to him. 36 * As they traveled along the road they came to some water, and the eunuch said, "Look, there is water. What is to prevent my being baptized?" [37] † 38 Then he ordered the chariot to stop, and Philip and the eunuch both went down into the water, and he baptized him. 39 When they came out of the water, the Spirit of the Lord snatched Philip away, and the eunuch saw him no more, but continued on his way rejoicing. * 40 Philip came to Azotus, and went about proclaiming the good news to all the towns until he reached Caesarea. *

## 9 Saul's Conversion.

1 † Now Saul, still breathing murderous threats against the disciples of the Lord, * went to the high priest * 2 and asked him for letters to the synagogues in Damascus, that, if he should find any men or women who belonged to the Way, † he might bring them back to Jerusalem in chains. 3 On his journey, as he was nearing Damascus, a light from the sky suddenly flashed around him. * 4 He fell to the ground and heard a voice saying to him, "Saul, Saul, why are you persecuting me?" * 5 He said, "Who are you, sir?" The reply came, "I am Jesus, whom you are persecuting. * 6 Now get up and go into the city and you will be told what you must do." * 7 The men who were traveling with him stood speechless, for they heard the voice but could see no one. * 8 Saul got up from the ground, but when he opened his eyes he could see nothing; † so they led him by the hand and brought him to Damascus. * 9 For three days he was unable to see, and he neither ate nor drank.

**Saul's Baptism.** 10 * There was a disciple in Damascus named Ananias, and the Lord said to him in a vision, "Ananias." He answered, "Here I am, Lord." 11 The Lord said to him, "Get up and go to the street called Straight and ask at the house of Judas for a man from Tarsus named Saul. He is there praying, * 12 and [in a vision] he has seen a man named Ananias come in and lay [his] hands on him, that he may regain his sight." 13 But Ananias replied, "Lord, I have heard from many sources about this man, what evil things he has done to your holy ones † in Jerusalem. * 14 And here he has authority from the chief priests to imprison all who call upon your name." * 15 But the Lord said to him, "Go, for this man is a chosen instrument of mine to carry my name before Gentiles, kings, and Israelites, * 16 and I will show him what he will have to suffer for my name." 17 So Ananias went and entered the house; laying his hands on him, he said, "Saul, my brother, the Lord has sent me, Jesus who appeared to you on the way by which you came, that you may regain your sight and be filled with the holy Spirit." 18 Immediately things like scales fell from his eyes and he

---

**8:37** The oldest and best manuscripts of Acts omit this verse, which is a Western text reading: "And Philip said, 'If you believe with all your heart, you may.' And he said in reply, 'I believe that Jesus Christ is the Son of God.'"

**9:1–19** This is the first of three accounts of Paul's conversion (with Acts 22:3–16 and Acts 26:2–18) with some differences of detail owing to Luke's use of different sources. Paul's experience was not visionary but was precipitated by the appearance of Jesus, as he insists in 1 Cor 15:8. The words of Jesus, "Saul, Saul, why are you persecuting me?" related by Luke with no variation in all three accounts, exerted a profound and lasting influence on the thought of Paul. Under the influence of this experience he gradually developed his understanding of justification by faith (see the letters to the Galatians and Romans) and of the identification of the Christian community with Jesus Christ (see 1 Cor 12:27). That Luke would narrate this conversion three times is testimony to the importance he attaches to it. This first account occurs when the word is first spread to the Gentiles. At this point, the conversion of the hero of the Gentile mission is recounted. The emphasis in the account is on Paul as a divinely chosen instrument (Acts 9:15).

**9:2** The Way: a name used by the early Christian community for itself (Acts 18:26; 19:9, 23; 22:4; 24:14, 22). The Essene community at Qumran used the same designation to describe its mode of life.

**9:8** He could see nothing: a temporary blindness (Acts 9:18) symbolizing the religious blindness of Saul as persecutor (cf. Acts 26:18).

**9:13** Your holy ones: literally, "your saints."

---

| | |
|---|---|
| **8:36** 10:47. | Mt 25:40. |
| **8:39** 1 Kgs 18:12. | **9:6** 22:10; 26:16. |
| **8:40** 21:8. | **9:7** 22:9; 26:13–14. |
| **9:1** 8:3; 9:13; 22:4; 1 Cor | **9:8** 22:11. |
| 15:9; Gal 1:13–14. | **9:10–19** 22:12–16. |
| **9:1–2** 9:14; 26:10. | **9:11** 21:39. |
| **9:3** 1 Cor 9:1; 15:8; Gal | **9:13** 8:3; 9:1. |
| 1:16. | **9:14** 9:1–2; 26:10; 1 Cor |
| **9:4** 22:6; 26:14. | 1:2; 2 Tm 2:22. |
| **9:5** 22:8; 26:15; | **9:15** 22:15; 26:1; 27:24. |

regained his sight. He got up and was baptized, [19] and when he had eaten, he recovered his strength.†

**Saul Preaches in Damascus.** He stayed some days with the disciples in Damascus, [20] and he began at once to proclaim Jesus in the synagogues, that he is the Son of God.† [21] All who heard him were astounded and said, "Is not this the man who in Jerusalem ravaged those who call upon this name, and came here expressly to take them back in chains to the chief priests?" [22] But Saul grew all the stronger and confounded [the] Jews who lived in Damascus, proving that this is the Messiah.

**Saul Visits Jerusalem.** [23] After a long time had passed, the Jews conspired to kill him, [24] * but their plot became known to Saul. Now they were keeping watch on the gates day and night so as to kill him, [25] but his disciples took him one night and let him down through an opening in the wall, lowering him in a basket.

[26] * When he arrived in Jerusalem† he tried to join the disciples, but they were all afraid of him, not believing that he was a disciple. [27] Then Barnabas took charge of him and brought him to the apostles, and he reported to them how on the way he had seen the Lord and that he had spoken to him, and how in Damascus he had spoken out boldly in the name of Jesus. [28] He moved about freely with them in Jerusalem, and spoke out boldly in the name of the Lord. [29] He also spoke and debated with the Hellenists,† but they tried to kill him. [30] And when the brothers learned of this, they took him down to Caesarea and sent him on his way to Tarsus. *

**The Church at Peace.** [31] † The church throughout all Judea, Galilee, and Samaria was at peace. It was being built up and walked in the fear of the Lord, and with the consolation of the holy Spirit it grew in numbers.

**Peter Heals Aeneas at Lydda.** [32] As Peter was passing through every region, he went down to the holy ones living in Lydda. [33] There he found a man named Aeneas, who had been confined to bed for eight years, for he was paralyzed. [34] Peter said to him, "Aeneas, Jesus Christ heals you. Get up and make your bed." He got up at once. [35] And all the inhabitants of Lydda and Sharon saw him, and they turned to the Lord.

**Peter Restores Tabitha to Life.** [36] Now in Joppa there was a disciple named Tabitha (which translated means Dorcas).† She was completely occupied with good deeds and almsgiving. [37] Now during those days she fell sick and died, so after washing her, they laid [her] out in a room upstairs. [38] Since Lydda was near Joppa, the disciples, hearing that Peter was there, sent two men to him with the request, "Please come to us without delay." [39] So Peter got up and went with them. When he arrived, they took him to the room upstairs where all the widows came to him weeping and showing him the tunics and cloaks that Dorcas had made while she was with them. [40] Peter sent them all out and knelt down and prayed. Then he turned to her body and said, "Tabitha, rise up." She opened her eyes, saw Peter, and sat up. * [41] He gave her his hand and raised her up, and when he had called the holy ones and the widows, he presented her alive. [42] This became known all over Joppa, and many came to believe in the Lord. [43] †* And he stayed a long time in Joppa with Simon, a tanner.

---

† **9:19–30** This is a brief resume of Paul's initial experience as an apostolic preacher. At first he found himself in the position of being regarded as an apostate by the Jews and suspect by the Christian community of Jerusalem. His acceptance by the latter was finally brought about through his friendship with Barnabas (Acts 9:27).
**9:20** *Son of God*: the title "Son of God" occurs in Acts only here, but cf. the citation of Ps 2:7 in Paul's speech at Antioch in Pisidia (Acts 13:33).
**9:26** This visit of Paul to Jerusalem is mentioned by Paul in Gal 1:18.
**9:29** *Hellenists*: see note on Acts 6:1–7.
**9:31–43** In the context of the period of peace enjoyed by the community through the cessation of Paul's activities against it, Luke introduces two traditions concerning the miraculous power exercised by Peter as he was making a tour of places where the Christian message had already been preached. The towns of Lydda, Sharon, and Joppa were populated by both Jews and Gentiles and their Christian communities may well have been mixed.
**9:36** *Tabitha* (*Dorcas*), respectively the Aramaic and Greek words for "gazelle," exemplifies the right attitude toward material possessions expressed by Jesus in the Lucan Gospel (Lk 6:30; 11:41; 12:33; 18:22; 19:8).
**9:43** The fact that Peter lodged with a tanner would have been significant to both the Gentile and Jewish Christians, for Judaism considered the tanning occupation unclean.

---

* **9:24–25** 2 Cor 11:32–33.      **9:40** Mk 5:40–41.
**9:26–27** Gal 1:18.      **9:43** 10:6.
**9:30** 11:25.

ACTS

## IV. THE INAUGURATION OF THE GENTILE MISSION

**10** **The Vision of Cornelius.*** ¹† Now in Caesarea there was a man named Cornelius, a centurion of the Cohort called the Italica,† ²devout and God-fearing along with his whole household, who used to give alms generously† to the Jewish people and pray to God constantly. ³One afternoon about three o'clock,† he saw plainly in a vision an angel of God come in to him and say to him, "Cornelius." ⁴He looked intently at him and, seized with fear, said, "What is it, sir?" He said to him, "Your prayers and almsgiving have ascended as a memorial offering before God. ⁵Now send some men to Joppa and summon one Simon who is called Peter. ⁶He is staying with another Simon, a tanner, who has a house by the sea."* ⁷When the angel who spoke to him had left, he called two of his servants and a devout soldier† from his staff, ⁸explained everything to them, and sent them to Joppa.

**The Vision of Peter.** ⁹† The next day, while they were on their way and nearing the city, Peter went up to the roof terrace to pray at about noontime.† ¹⁰He was hungry and wished to eat, and while they were making preparations he fell into a trance. ¹¹*He saw heaven opened and something resembling a large sheet coming down, lowered to the ground by its four corners. ¹²In it were all the earth's four-legged animals and reptiles and the birds of the sky. ¹³A voice said to him, "Get up, Peter. Slaughter

and eat." ¹⁴But Peter said, "Certainly not, sir. For never have I eaten anything profane and unclean."* ¹⁵The voice spoke to him again, a second time, "What God has made clean, you are not to call profane."* ¹⁶This happened three times, and then the object was taken up into the sky.

¹⁷† While Peter was in doubt about the meaning of the vision he had seen, the men sent by Cornelius asked for Simon's house and arrived at the entrance. ¹⁸They called out inquiring whether Simon, who is called Peter, was staying there. ¹⁹As Peter was pondering the vision, the Spirit said [to him], "There are three men here looking for you.* ²⁰So get up, go downstairs, and accompany them without hesitation, because I have sent them." ²¹Then Peter went down to the men and said, "I am the one you are looking for. What is the reason for your being here?" ²²They answered, "Cornelius, a centurion, an upright and God-fearing man, respected by the whole Jewish nation, was directed by a holy angel to summon you to his house and to hear what you have to say."* ²³So he invited them in and showed them hospitality.

The next day he got up and went with them, and some of the brothers from Joppa went with him. ²⁴† On the following day he entered Caesarea. Cornelius was expecting them and had called together his relatives and close friends. ²⁵*When Peter entered, Cornelius met him and, falling at his feet, paid him homage. ²⁶Peter, however, raised him up, saying, "Get up. I myself am also a human being." ²⁷While he conversed with him, he went in and found

---

† **10:1–48** The narrative centers on the conversion of Cornelius, a Gentile and a "God-fearer" (see note on Acts 8:26–40). Luke considers the event of great importance, as is evident from his long treatment of it. The incident is again related in Acts 11:1–18 where Peter is forced to justify his actions before the Jerusalem community and alluded to in Acts 15:7–11 where at the Jerusalem "Council" Peter supports Paul's missionary activity among the Gentiles. The narrative divides itself into a series of distinct episodes, concluding with Peter's presentation of the Christian kerygma (Acts 10:4–43) and a pentecostal experience undergone by Cornelius' household preceding their reception of baptism (Acts 10:44–48).

**10:1** *The Cohort called the Italica:* this battalion was an auxiliary unit of archers formed originally in Italy but transferred to Syria shortly before A.D. 69.

**10:2** *Used to give alms generously:* like Tabitha (Acts 9:36), Cornelius exemplifies the proper attitude toward wealth (see note on Acts 9:36).

**10:3** *About three o'clock:* literally, "about the ninth hour." See note on Acts 3:1.

**10:7** *A devout soldier:* by using this adjective, Luke probably intends to classify him as a "God-fearer" (see note on Acts 8:26–40).

**10:9–16** The vision is intended to prepare Peter to share the food of Cornelius' household without qualms of conscience (Acts 10:48). The necessity of such instructions to Peter reveals that at first not even the apostles fully grasped the implications of Jesus' teaching on the law. In Acts, the initial insight belongs to Stephen.

**10:9** *At about noontime:* literally, "about the sixth hour."

**10:17–23** The arrival of the Gentile emissaries with their account of the angelic apparition illuminates Peter's vision: he is to be prepared to admit Gentiles, who were considered unclean like the animals of his vision, into the Christian community.

**10:24–27** So impressed is Cornelius with the apparition that he invites close personal friends to join him in his meeting with Peter. But his understanding of the person he is about to meet is not devoid of superstition, suggested by his falling down before him. For a similar experience of Paul and Barnabas, see Acts 14:11–18.

---

10:1–8 10:30–33.
  10:6 9:43.
10:11–20 11:5–12.
  10:14 Lv 11:1–47; Ez 4:14.

10:15 Mk 7:15–19; Gal 2:12.
  10:19 13:2.
  10:22 Lk 7:4–5.
10:25–26 14:13–15; Rev 19:10.

many people gathered together [28]* and said to them, "You know that it is unlawful for a Jewish man to associate with, or visit, a Gentile, but God has shown me that I should not call any person profane or unclean.† [29] And that is why I came without objection when sent for. May I ask, then, why you summoned me?"

[30] Cornelius replied, "Four days ago† at this hour, three o'clock in the afternoon, I was at prayer in my house when suddenly a man in dazzling robes stood before me and said, [31] 'Cornelius, your prayer has been heard and your almsgiving remembered before God. [32] Send therefore to Joppa and summon Simon, who is called Peter. He is a guest in the house of Simon, a tanner, by the sea.' [33] So I sent for you immediately, and you were kind enough to come. Now therefore we are all here in the presence of God to listen to all that you have been commanded by the Lord."

**Peter's Speech.**† [34] Then Peter proceeded to speak and said,† "In truth, I see that God shows no partiality.* [35] Rather, in every nation whoever fears him and acts uprightly is acceptable to him. [36]† You know the word [that] he sent to the Israelites† as he proclaimed peace through Jesus Christ, who is Lord of all,* [37] what has happened all over Judea, beginning in Galilee after the baptism that John preached,* [38] how God anointed Jesus of Nazareth† with the holy Spirit and power. He went about doing good and healing all those oppressed by the devil,

for God was with him.* [39] We are witnesses† of all that he did both in the country of the Jews and [in] Jerusalem. They put him to death by hanging him on a tree. [40] This man God raised [on] the third day and granted that he be visible, [41] not to all the people, but to us, the witnesses chosen by God in advance, who ate and drank with him after he rose from the dead.* [42] He commissioned us* to preach to the people and testify that he is the one appointed by God as judge of the living and the dead.† [43] To him all the prophets bear witness, that everyone who believes in him will receive forgiveness of sins through his name."

**The Baptism of Cornelius.** [44]* While Peter was still speaking these things, the holy Spirit fell upon all who were listening to the word.† [45] The circumcised believers who had accompanied Peter were astounded that the gift of the holy Spirit should have been poured out on the Gentiles also, [46] for they could hear them speaking in tongues and glorifying God. Then Peter responded, [47] "Can anyone withhold the water for baptizing these people, who have received the holy Spirit even as we have?"* [48] He ordered them to be baptized in the name of Jesus Christ. [49] Then they invited him to stay for a few days.

**11** **The Baptism of the Gentiles Explained.**† [1] Now the apostles and the brothers who were in Judea heard that the Gentiles too

---

**10:28** Peter now fully understands the meaning of his vision; see note on Acts 10:17–23.

**10:30** *Four days ago*: literally, "from the fourth day up to this hour."

**10:34–43** Peter's speech to the household of Cornelius typifies early Christian preaching to Gentiles.

**10:34–35** The revelation of God's choice of Israel to be the people of God did not mean he withheld the divine favor from other people.

**10:36–43** These words are more directed to Luke's Christian readers than to the household of Cornelius, as indicated by the opening words, "You know." They trace the continuity between the preaching and teaching of Jesus of Nazareth and the proclamation of Jesus by the early community. The emphasis on this divinely ordained continuity (Acts 10:41) is meant to assure Luke's readers of the fidelity of Christian tradition to the words and deeds of Jesus.

**10:36** *To the Israelites*: Luke, in the words of Peter, speaks of the prominent position occupied by Israel in the history of salvation.

**10:38** *Jesus of Nazareth*: God's revelation of his plan for the destiny of humanity through Israel culminated in Jesus of Nazareth. Consequently, the ministry of Jesus is an integral part of God's revelation. This viewpoint explains why the early Christian communities were interested in conserving the historical substance of the ministry of Jesus, a tradition leading to the production of the four gospels.

**10:39** *We are witnesses*: the apostolic testimony was not restricted to the resurrection of Jesus but also included his historical ministry. This witness, however, was theological in character; the Twelve, divinely mandated as prophets, were empowered to interpret his sayings and deeds in the light of his redemptive death and resurrection. The meaning of these words and deeds was to be made clear to the developing Christian community as the bearer of the word of salvation (cf. Acts 1:21–26). *Hanging him on a tree*: see note on Acts 5:30.

**10:42** *As judge of the living and the dead*: the apostolic preaching to the Jews appealed to their messianic hope, while the preaching to Gentiles stressed the coming divine judgment; cf. 1 Thes 1:10.

**10:44** Just as the Jewish Christians received the gift of the Spirit, so too do the Gentiles.

**11:1–18** The Jewish Christians of Jerusalem were scandalized to learn of Peter's sojourn in the house of the Gentile Cornelius. Nonetheless, they had to accept the divine directions given to both Peter and Cornelius. They concluded that the setting aside

---

**10:28** Gal 2:11–16.
**10:34** Dt 10:17; 2 Chr 19:7; Jb 34:19; Wis 6:7; Rom 2:11; Gal 2:6; Eph 6:9; 1 Pt 1:17.
**10:36** Is 52:7; Na 2:1.
**10:37** Mt 4:12; Mk 1:14; Lk 4:14.
**10:38** Is 61:1; Lk 4:18.
**10:41** Lk 24:41–43.
**10:42** 1:8; 3:15; 17:31; Lk 24:48; Rom 14:9; 2 Tm 4:1.
**10:44** 11:15; 15:8.
**10:47** 8:36.

had accepted the word of God. ² So when Peter went up to Jerusalem the circumcised believers confronted him, ³ saying, "You entered† the house of uncircumcised people and ate with them." ⁴ Peter began and explained it to them step by step, saying, ⁵ * "I was at prayer in the city of Joppa when in a trance I had a vision, something resembling a large sheet coming down, lowered from the sky by its four corners, and it came to me. ⁶ Looking intently into it, I observed and saw the four-legged animals of the earth, the wild beasts, the reptiles, and the birds of the sky. ⁷ I also heard a voice say to me, 'Get up, Peter. Slaughter and eat.' ⁸ But I said, 'Certainly not, sir, because nothing profane or unclean has ever entered my mouth.' ⁹ But a second time a voice from heaven answered, 'What God has made clean, you are not to call profane.' ¹⁰ This happened three times, and then everything was drawn up again into the sky. ¹¹ Just then three men appeared at the house where we were, who had been sent to me from Caesarea. ¹² The Spirit told me to accompany them without discriminating. These six brothers† also went with me, and we entered the man's house. ¹³ He related to us how he had seen [the] angel standing in his house, saying, 'Send someone to Joppa and summon Simon, who is called Peter,* ¹⁴ who will speak words to you by which you and all your household will be saved.' ¹⁵ As I began to speak, the holy Spirit fell upon them as it had upon us at the beginning,* ¹⁶ and I remembered the word of the Lord, how he had said, 'John baptized with water but you will be baptized with the holy Spirit.'* ¹⁷ If then God gave them the same gift he gave to us when we came to believe in the Lord Jesus Christ, who was I to be able to hinder God?"* ¹⁸ When they heard this, they stopped objecting and glorified God, saying, "God has then granted life-giving repentance to the Gentiles too."

## The Church at Antioch.†

¹⁹ Now those who had been scattered by the persecution that arose because of Stephen went as far as Phoenicia, Cyprus, and Antioch, preaching the word to no one but Jews.* ²⁰ There were some Cypriots and Cyrenians among them, however, who came to Antioch and began to speak to the Greeks as well, proclaiming the Lord Jesus. ²¹ The hand of the Lord was with them and a great number who believed turned to the Lord. ²² The news about them reached the ears of the church in Jerusalem, and they sent Barnabas [to go] to Antioch. ²³ When he arrived and saw the grace of God, he rejoiced and encouraged them all to remain faithful to the Lord in firmness of heart, ²⁴ for he was a good man, filled with the holy Spirit and faith. And a large number of people was added to the Lord. ²⁵ Then he went to Tarsus to look for Saul, ²⁶ and when he had found him he brought him to Antioch. For a whole year they met with the church and taught a large number of people, and it was in Antioch that the disciples were first called Christians.†

## The Prediction of Agabus.†

²⁷ At that time some prophets came down from Jerusalem to Antioch, ²⁸ and one of them named Agabus stood up and predicted by the Spirit that there would be a severe famine all over the world, and it happened under Claudius.* ²⁹ So the disciples determined that, according to ability,* each should send relief to the brothers who lived in Judea. ³⁰† This they did, sending it to the presbyters in care of Barnabas and Saul.

---

† of the legal barriers between Jew and Gentile was an exceptional ordinance of God to indicate that the apostolic kerygma was also to be directed to the Gentiles. Only in Acts 15 at the "Council" in Jerusalem does the evangelization of the Gentiles become the official position of the church leadership in Jerusalem.

**11:3** *You entered...*: alternatively, this could be punctuated as a question.

**11:12** *These six brothers*: companions from the Christian community of Joppa (see Acts 10:23).

**11:19–26** The Jewish Christian antipathy to the mixed community was reflected by the early missionaries generally. The few among them who entertained a different view succeeded in introducing Gentiles into the community at Antioch (in Syria). When the disconcerted Jerusalem community sent Barnabas to investigate, he was so favorably impressed by what he observed that he persuaded his friend Saul to participate in the Antioch mission.

**11:26** *Christians*: "Christians" is first applied to the members of the community at Antioch because the Gentile members of the

community enable it to stand out clearly from Judaism.

**11:27–30** It is not clear whether the prophets from Jerusalem came to Antioch to request help in view of the coming famine or whether they received this insight during their visit there. The former supposition seems more likely. Suetonius and Tacitus speak of famines during the reign of Claudius (A.D. 41–54), while the Jewish historian Josephus mentions a famine in Judea in A.D. 46–48. Luke is interested, rather, in showing the charity of the Antiochene community toward the Jewish Christians of Jerusalem despite their differences on mixed communities.

**11:30** *Presbyters*: this is the same Greek word that elsewhere is translated "elders," primarily in reference to the Jewish community.

---

| | |
|---|---|
| **11:5–12** 10:11–20. | **11:17** 15:8–9. |
| **11:13** 10:3–5, 22, 30–32. | **11:19** 8:1–4. |
| **11:15** 10:44. | **11:28** 21:10. |
| **11:16** 1:5; 19:4; Lk 3:16. | **11:29–30** 12:25. |

# 12 Herod's Persecution of the Christians.[†]

[1] About that time King Herod laid hands upon some members of the church to harm them. [2] He had James, the brother of John,[†] killed by the sword, [3][†] and when he saw that this was pleasing to the Jews he proceeded to arrest Peter also. (It was [the] feast of Unleavened Bread.) [4] He had him taken into custody and put in prison under the guard of four squads of four soldiers each. He intended to bring him before the people after Passover. [5] Peter thus was being kept in prison, but prayer by the church was fervently being made to God on his behalf.*

[6] On the very night before Herod was to bring him to trial, Peter, secured by double chains, was sleeping between two soldiers, while outside the door guards kept watch on the prison. [7] Suddenly the angel of the Lord stood by him and a light shone in the cell. He tapped Peter on the side and awakened him, saying, "Get up quickly." The chains fell from his wrists. [8] The angel said to him, "Put on your belt and your sandals." He did so. Then he said to him, "Put on your cloak and follow me." [9] So he followed him out, not realizing that what was happening through the angel was real; he thought he was seeing a vision. [10] They passed the first guard, then the second, and came to the iron gate leading out to the city, which opened for them by itself. They emerged and made their way down an alley, and suddenly the angel left him. [11] Then Peter recovered his senses and said, "Now I know for certain that [the] Lord sent his angel and rescued me from the hand of Herod and from all that the Jewish people had been expecting." [12] When he realized this, he went to the house of Mary, the mother of John who is called Mark, where there were many people gathered in prayer.* [13] When he knocked on the gateway door, a maid named Rhoda came to answer it. [14] She was so overjoyed when she recognized Peter's voice that, instead of opening the gate, she ran in and announced that Peter was standing at the gate. [15] They told her, "You are out of your mind," but she insisted that it was so. But they kept saying, "It is his angel." [16] But Peter continued to knock, and when they opened it, they saw him and were astounded. [17] He motioned to them with his hand to be quiet and explained [to them] how the Lord had led him out of the prison, and said, "Report this to James[†] and the brothers." Then he left and went to another place. [18] At daybreak there was no small commotion among the soldiers over what had become of Peter.* [19] Herod, after instituting a search but not finding him, ordered the guards tried and executed. Then he left Judea to spend some time in Caesarea.

## Herod's Death.

[20][†] He had long been very angry with the people of Tyre and Sidon, who now came to him in a body. After winning over Blastus, the king's chamberlain, they sued for peace because their country was supplied with food from the king's territory. [21] On an appointed day, Herod, attired in royal robes, [and] seated on the rostrum, addressed them publicly. [22] The assembled crowd cried out, "This is the voice of a god, not of a man." [23] At once the angel of the Lord struck him down because he did not ascribe the honor to God, and he was eaten by worms and breathed his last. [24] But the word of God continued to spread and grow.*

## Mission of Barnabas and Saul.

[25] After Barnabas and Saul completed their relief mission, they returned to Jerusalem,[†] taking with them John, who is called Mark.*

---

† **12:1–19** Herod Agrippa ruled Judea A.D. 41–44. While Luke does not assign a motive for his execution of James and his intended execution of Peter, the broad background lies in Herod's support of Pharisaic Judaism. The Jewish Christians had lost the popularity they had had in Jerusalem (Acts 2:47), perhaps because of suspicions against them traceable to the teaching of Stephen.

**12:2** *James, the brother of John*: this James, the son of Zebedee, was beheaded by Herod Agrippa ca. A.D. 44.

**12:3–4** *Feast of Unleavened Bread...Passover*: see note on Lk 22:1.

**12:17** *To James*: this James is not the son of Zebedee mentioned in Acts 12:2, but is James, the "brother of the Lord" (Gal 1:19), who in Acts 15; 21 is presented as leader of the Jerusalem Christian community. *He left and went to another place*: the conjecture that Peter left for Rome at this time has nothing to recommend it. His chief responsibility was still the leadership of the Jewish Christian community in Palestine (see Gal 2:7). The concept of the great missionary effort of the church was yet to come (see Acts 13:1–3).

**12:20–23** Josephus gives a similar account of Herod's death that occurred in A.D. 44. Early Christian tradition considered the manner of it to be a divine punishment upon his evil life. See 2 Kgs 19:35 for the figure of the angel of the Lord in such a context.

**12:25** *They returned to Jerusalem*: many manuscripts read "from Jerusalem," since Acts 11:30 implies that Paul and Barnabas are already in Jerusalem. This present verse could refer to a return visit or subsequent relief mission.

---

*
**12:5** Jas 5:16.                                **12:24** 6:7.
**12:12** 12:25; 15:37.                      **12:25** 11:29–30.
**12:18** 5:22–24.

**PAUL'S JOURNEYS IN ACTS**

→ First missionary journey,
with Barnabas and Mark (ca. CE 46–48)

⤑ Second missionary journey,
with Silas (ca. CE 49–52)

© 2013 ANSELM ACADEMIC

# 13

¹ † Now there were in the church at Antioch prophets and teachers: Barnabas, Symeon who was called Niger, Lucius of Cyrene, Manaen who was a close friend of Herod the tetrarch, and Saul. ² While they were worshiping the Lord and fasting, the holy Spirit said, "Set apart for me Barnabas and Saul for the work to which I have called them." ³ Then, completing their fasting and prayer, they laid hands on them and sent them off.

**First Mission Begins in Cyprus.** ⁴ † So they, sent forth by the holy Spirit, went down to Seleucia and from there sailed to Cyprus. ⁵ When they arrived in Salamis, they proclaimed the word of God in the Jewish synagogues. They had John † also as their assistant. ⁶ When they had traveled through the whole island as far as Paphos, they met a magician named Bar-Jesus who was a Jewish false prophet. † ⁷ He was with the proconsul Sergius Paulus, a man of intelligence, who had summoned Barnabas and Saul and wanted to hear the word of God. ⁸ But Elymas the magician (for that is what his name means) opposed them in an attempt to turn the proconsul away from the faith. ⁹ But Saul, also known as Paul, † filled with the holy Spirit, looked intently at him ¹⁰ and said, "You son of the devil, you enemy of all that is right, full of every sort of deceit and fraud. Will you not stop twisting the straight paths of [the] Lord? ¹¹ Even now the hand of the Lord is upon you. You will be blind, and unable to see the sun for a time." Immediately a dark mist fell upon him, and he went about seeking people to lead him by the hand. ¹² When the proconsul saw what had happened, he came to believe, for he was astonished by the teaching about the Lord.

**Paul's Arrival at Antioch in Pisidia.** ¹³ From Paphos, Paul and his companions set sail and arrived at Perga in Pamphylia. But John left them and returned to Jerusalem. * ¹⁴ They continued on from Perga and reached Antioch in Pisidia. On the sabbath they entered [into] the synagogue and took their seats. ¹⁵ After the reading of the law and the prophets, the synagogue officials sent word to them, "My brothers, if one of you has a word of exhortation for the people, please speak."

**Paul's Address in the Synagogue.** ¹⁶ † So Paul got up, motioned with his hand, and said, "Fellow Israelites and you others who are God-fearing, † listen. ¹⁷ The God of this people Israel chose our ancestors and exalted the people during their sojourn in the land of Egypt. * With uplifted arm he led them out of it ¹⁸ and for about forty years he put up with † them in the desert. * ¹⁹ When he had destroyed seven nations in the land of Canaan, he gave them their land as an inheritance * ²⁰ at the end of about four hundred and fifty years. † After these things he provided judges up to Samuel [the] prophet. * ²¹ Then they asked for a king. God gave them Saul, son of Kish, a man from the tribe of Benjamin, for forty years. * ²² Then he removed him and raised up David as their king; of him he testified, 'I have found David,

---

**13:1–3** The impulse for the first missionary effort in Asia Minor is ascribed to the prophets of the Antiochene community, under the inspiration of the holy Spirit. Just as the Jerusalem community had earlier been the center of missionary activity, so too Antioch becomes the center from which the missionaries Barnabas and Saul are sent out.

**13:4–14:27** The key event in Luke's account of the first missionary journey is the experience of Paul and Barnabas at Pisidian Antioch (Acts 13:14–52). The Christian kerygma proclaimed by Paul in the synagogue was favorably received. Some Jews and "God-fearers" (see note on Acts 8:26–40) became interested and invited the missionaries to speak again on the following sabbath (Acts 13:42). By that time, however, the appearance of a large number of Gentiles from the city had so disconcerted the Jews that they became hostile toward the apostles (Acts 13:44–50). This hostility of theirs appears in all three accounts of Paul's missionary journeys in Acts, the Jews of Iconium (Acts 14:1–2) and Beroea (Acts 17:11) being notable exceptions.

**13:5** John: that is, John Mark (see Acts 12:12, 25).

**13:6** A magician named Bar-Jesus who was a Jewish false prophet: that is, he posed as a prophet. Again Luke takes the opportunity to dissociate Christianity from the magical acts of the time (Acts 13:7–11); see also Acts 8:18–24.

**13:9** Saul, also known as Paul: there is no reason to believe that his name was changed from Saul to Paul upon his conversion. The use of a double name, one Semitic (Saul), the other Greco-Roman (Paul), is well attested (cf. Acts 1:23, Joseph Justus; Acts 12:12, 25, John Mark).

**13:16–41** This is the first of several speeches of Paul to Jews proclaiming that the Christian church is the logical development of Pharisaic Judaism (see also Acts 24:10–21; 26:2–23).

**13:16** Who are God-fearing: see note on Acts 8:26–40.

**13:18** Put up with: some manuscripts read "sustained."

**13:20** At the end of about four hundred and fifty years: the manuscript tradition makes it uncertain whether the mention of four hundred and fifty years refers to the sojourn in Egypt before the Exodus, the wilderness period and the time of the conquest (see Ex 12:40–41), as the translation here suggests, or to the time between the conquest and the time of Samuel, the period of the judges, if the text is read, "After these things, for about four hundred and fifty years, he provided judges."

---

**13:13** 15:38.
**13:17** Ex 6:1, 6; 12:51.
**13:18** Ex 16:1, 35; Nm 14:34.
**13:19** Dt 7:1; Jos 14:1–2.
**13:20** Jgs 2:16; 1 Sm 3:20.
**13:21** 1 Sm 8:5, 19; 9:16; 10:1, 20–21, 24; 11:15.

son of Jesse, a man after my own heart; he will carry out my every wish.'* ²³ From this man's descendants God, according to his promise, has brought to Israel a savior, Jesus.* ²⁴ John heralded his coming by proclaiming a baptism of repentance to all the people of Israel;* ²⁵ and as John was completing his course, he would say, 'What do you suppose that I am? I am not he. Behold, one is coming after me; I am not worthy to unfasten the sandals of his feet.'*

²⁶ "My brothers, children of the family of Abraham, and those others among you who are God-fearing, to us this word of salvation has been sent. ²⁷ The inhabitants of Jerusalem and their leaders failed to recognize him, and by condemning him they fulfilled the oracles of the prophets that are read sabbath after sabbath. ²⁸ For even though they found no grounds for a death sentence, they asked Pilate to have him put to death,* ²⁹ and when they had accomplished all that was written about him, they took him down from the tree and placed him in a tomb.* ³⁰ But God raised him from the dead,* ³¹ and for many days he appeared to those who had come up with him from Galilee to Jerusalem.* These are [now] his witnesses before the people.† ³² We ourselves are proclaiming this good news to you that what God promised our ancestors ³³ he has brought to fulfillment for us, [their] children, by raising up Jesus, as it is written in the second psalm, 'You are my son; this day I have begotten you.'* ³⁴ And that he raised him from the dead never to return to corruption he declared in this way, 'I shall give you the benefits assured to David.'* ³⁵ That is why he also says in another psalm, 'You will not suffer your holy one to see corruption.'* ³⁶ Now David, after he had served the will of God in

his lifetime, fell asleep, was gathered to his ancestors, and did see corruption.* ³⁷ But the one whom God raised up did not see corruption. ³⁸ You must know, my brothers, that through him forgiveness of sins is being proclaimed to you, [and] in regard to everything from which you could not be justified† under the law of Moses, ³⁹ in him every believer is justified.* ⁴⁰ Be careful, then, that what was said in the prophets not come about:

⁴¹ 'Look on, you scoffers,
    be amazed and disappear.
For I am doing a work in your days,
    a work that you will never believe
      even if someone tells you.'"*

⁴² As they were leaving, they invited them to speak on these subjects the following sabbath. ⁴³ After the congregation had dispersed, many Jews and worshipers who were converts to Judaism followed Paul and Barnabas, who spoke to them and urged them to remain faithful to the grace of God.

**Address to the Gentiles.** ⁴⁴ On the following sabbath almost the whole city gathered to hear the word of the Lord. ⁴⁵ When the Jews saw the crowds, they were filled with jealousy and with violent abuse contradicted what Paul said. ⁴⁶* Both Paul and Barnabas spoke out boldly and said, "It was necessary that the word of God be spoken to you first, but since you reject it and condemn yourselves as unworthy of eternal life, we now turn to the Gentiles.† ⁴⁷ For so the Lord has commanded us, 'I have made you a light to the Gentiles, that you may be an instrument of salvation to the ends of the earth.'"* ⁴⁸ The Gentiles were delighted when they

---

† **13:31** The theme of the Galilean witnesses is a major one in the Gospel of Luke and in Acts and is used to signify the continuity between the teachings of Jesus and the teachings of the church and to guarantee the fidelity of the church's teachings to the words of Jesus.

**13:38–39** *Justified*: the verb is the same as that used in Paul's letters to speak of the experience of justification and, as in Paul, is here connected with the term "to have faith" ("every believer"). But this seems the only passage about Paul in Acts where justification is mentioned. In Lucan fashion it is paralleled with "forgiveness of sins" (a theme at Acts 2:38; 3:19; 5:31; 10:43) based on Jesus' resurrection (Acts 13:37) rather than his cross, and is put negatively (Acts 13:38). Therefore, some would translate, "in regard to everything from which you could not be acquitted... every believer is acquitted."

**13:46** The refusal to believe frustrates God's plan for his chosen people; however, no adverse judgment is made here

concerning their ultimate destiny. Again, Luke, in the words of Paul, speaks of the priority of Israel in the plan for salvation (see Acts 10:36).

* **13:22** 1 Sm 13:14; 16:12–13; Ps 89:20–21.
**13:23** Is 11:1.
**13:24** Mt 3:1–2; Mk 1:4–5; Lk 3:2–3.
**13:25** Mt 3:11; Mk 1:7; Lk 3:16; Jn 1:20, 27.
**13:28** Mt 27:20, 22–23; Mk 15:13–14; Lk 23:4, 14–15, 21–23; Jn 19:4–6, 15.
**13:29** Mt 27:59–60; Mk 15:46; Lk 23:53; Jn 19:38, 41–42.
**13:30** 2:24, 32; 3:15; 4:10; 17:31.
**13:31** 1:3, 8; 10:39, 41; Mt 28:8–10, 16–20; Mk 16:9, 12–20; Lk 24:13–53; Jn 20:11–29; 21:1–23.
**13:33** Ps 2:7.
**13:34** Is 55:3.
**13:35** Ps 16:10.
**13:36** 2:29; 1 Kgs 2:10.
**13:39** Rom 3:20.
**13:41** Heb 1:5.
**13:46** 3:26; Rom 1:16.
**13:47** Is 49:6.

heard this and glorified the word of the Lord. All who were destined for eternal life came to believe, 49 and the word of the Lord continued to spread through the whole region. 50 The Jews, however, incited the women of prominence who were worshipers and the leading men of the city, stirred up a persecution against Paul and Barnabas, and expelled them from their territory. 51,* So they shook the dust from their feet in protest against them and went to Iconium.† 52 The disciples were filled with joy and the holy Spirit.

# 14 Paul and Barnabas at Iconium. 1 In Iconium they entered the Jewish synagogue together and spoke in such a way that a great number of both Jews and Greeks came to believe, 2 although the disbelieving Jews stirred up and poisoned the minds of the Gentiles against the brothers. 3 So they stayed for a considerable period, speaking out boldly for the Lord, who confirmed the word about his grace by granting signs and wonders to occur through their hands.* 4 The people of the city were divided: some were with the Jews; others, with the apostles. 5 When there was an attempt by both the Gentiles and the Jews, together with their leaders, to attack and stone them,* 6 they realized it and fled to the Lycaonian cities of Lystra and Derbe and to the surrounding countryside, 7 where they continued to proclaim the good news.

**Paul and Barnabas at Lystra.** 8† At Lystra there was a crippled man, lame from birth, who had never walked. 9 He listened to Paul speaking, who looked intently at him, saw that he had the faith to be healed, 10 and called out in a loud voice, "Stand up straight on your feet." He jumped up and began to walk about. 11 When the crowds saw what Paul had done,

they cried out in Lycaonian, "The gods have come down to us in human form."* 12 They called Barnabas "Zeus"† and Paul "Hermes," because he was the chief speaker. 13 And the priest of Zeus, whose temple was at the entrance to the city, brought oxen and garlands to the gates, for he together with the people intended to offer sacrifice.

14 The apostles Barnabas and Paul tore their garments† when they heard this and rushed out into the crowd, shouting, 15† "Men, why are you doing this? We are of the same nature as you, human beings. We proclaim to you good news that you should turn from these idols to the living God, 'who made heaven and earth and sea and all that is in them.'* 16 In past generations he allowed all Gentiles to go their own ways;* 17 yet, in bestowing his goodness, he did not leave himself without witness, for he gave you rains from heaven and fruitful seasons, and filled you with nourishment and gladness for your hearts."* 18 Even with these words, they scarcely restrained the crowds from offering sacrifice to them.

19* However, some Jews from Antioch and Iconium arrived and won over the crowds. They stoned Paul and dragged him out of the city, supposing that he was dead. 20 But when the disciples gathered around him, he got up and entered the city. On the following day he left with Barnabas for Derbe.

**End of the First Mission.** 21 After they had proclaimed the good news to that city and made a considerable number of disciples, they returned to Lystra and to Iconium and to Antioch. 22 They strengthened the spirits of the disciples and exhorted them to persevere in the faith, saying, "It is necessary for us to undergo many hardships to enter the kingdom of God."* 23 They appointed presbyters†

---

† 

**13:51** See note on Lk 9:5.

**14:8–18** In an effort to convince his hearers that the divine power works through his word, Paul cures the cripple. However, the pagan tradition of the occasional appearance of gods among human beings leads the people astray in interpreting the miracle. The incident reveals the cultural difficulties with which the church had to cope. Note the similarity of the miracle worked here by Paul to the one performed by Peter in Acts 3:2–10.

**14:12** Zeus…Hermes: in Greek religion, Zeus was the chief of the Olympian gods, the "father of gods and men"; Hermes was a son of Zeus and was usually identified as the herald and messenger of the gods.

**14:14** Tore their garments: a gesture of protest.

**14:15–17** This is the first speech of Paul to Gentiles recorded by Luke in Acts (cf. Acts 17:22–31). Rather than showing how Christianity is the logical outgrowth of Judaism, as he does in

speeches before Jews, Luke says that God excuses past Gentile ignorance and then presents a natural theology arguing for the recognition of God's existence and presence through his activity in natural phenomena.

**14:23** They appointed presbyters: the communities are given their own religious leaders by the traveling missionaries. The structure in these churches is patterned on the model of the Jerusalem community (Acts 11:30; 15:2, 5, 22; 21:18).

---

**13:51** Mt 10:14; Mk 6:11; Lk 9:5; 10:11.
**14:3** Mk 16:17–20.
**14:5** 2 Tm 3:11.
**14:11** 28:6.
**14:15** 3:12; 10:26; Ex 20:11;

Ps 146:6.
**14:16** 17:30.
**14:17** Wis 13:1.
**14:19–20** 2 Cor 11:25; 2 Tm 3:11.
**14:22** 1 Thes 3:3.

for them in each church and, with prayer and fasting, commended them to the Lord in whom they had put their faith. ²⁴ Then they traveled through Pisidia and reached Pamphylia. ²⁵ After proclaiming the word at Perga they went down to Attalia. ²⁶ From there they sailed to Antioch, where they had been commended to the grace of God for the work they had now accomplished.* ²⁷ And when they arrived, they called the church together and reported what God had done with them and how he had opened the door of faith to the Gentiles. ²⁸ Then they spent no little time with the disciples.

**15 Council of Jerusalem.** ¹† Some who had come down from Judea were instructing the brothers,* "Unless you are circumcised according to the Mosaic practice,* you cannot be saved."† ² Because there arose no little dissension and debate by Paul and Barnabas with them, it was decided that Paul, Barnabas, and some of the others should go up to Jerusalem to the apostles and presbyters about this question. ³ They were sent on their journey by the church, and passed through Phoenicia and Samaria telling of the conversion of the Gentiles, and brought great joy to all the brothers. ⁴ When they arrived in Jerusalem, they were welcomed by the church, as well as by the apostles and the presbyters, and they reported what God had done with them. ⁵ But some from the party of the Pharisees who

had become believers stood up and said, "It is necessary to circumcise them and direct them to observe the Mosaic law."

⁶† The apostles and the presbyters met together to see about this matter. ⁷† After much debate had taken place, Peter got up and said to them, "My brothers, you are well aware that from early days God made his choice among you that through my mouth the Gentiles would hear the word of the gospel and believe.* ⁸ And God, who knows the heart, bore witness by granting them the holy Spirit just as he did us.* ⁹ He made no distinction between us and them, for by faith he purified their hearts.* ¹⁰ Why, then, are you now putting God to the test by placing on the shoulders of the disciples a yoke that neither our ancestors nor we have been able to bear?* ¹¹ On the contrary, we believe that we are saved through the grace of the Lord Jesus,* in the same way as they."† ¹² The whole assembly fell silent, and they listened while Paul and Barnabas described the signs and wonders God had worked among the Gentiles through them.

**James on Dietary Law.** ¹³† After they had fallen silent, James responded, "My brothers, listen to me. ¹⁴ Symeon† has described how God first concerned himself with acquiring from among the Gentiles a people for his name. ¹⁵ The words of the prophets agree with this, as is written:

---

† **15:1–35** The Jerusalem "Council" marks the official rejection of the rigid view that Gentile converts were obliged to observe the Mosaic law completely. From here to the end of Acts, Paul and the Gentile mission become the focus of Luke's writing.

**15:1–5** When some of the converted Pharisees of Jerusalem discover the results of the first missionary journey of Paul, they urge that the Gentiles be taught to follow the Mosaic law. Recognizing the authority of the Jerusalem church, Paul and Barnabas go there to settle the question of whether Gentiles can embrace a form of Christianity that does not include this obligation.

**15:6–12** The gathering is possibly the same as that recalled by Paul in Gal 2:1–10. Note that in Acts 15:2 it is only the apostles and presbyters, a small group, with whom Paul and Barnabas are to meet. Here Luke gives the meeting a public character because he wishes to emphasize its doctrinal significance (see Acts 15:22).

**15:7–11** Paul's refusal to impose the Mosaic law on the Gentile Christians is supported by Peter on the ground that within his own experience God bestowed the holy Spirit upon Cornelius and his household without preconditions concerning the adoption of the Mosaic law (see Acts 10:44–47).

**15:11** In support of Paul, Peter formulates the fundamental meaning of the gospel: that all are invited to be saved through faith in the power of Christ.

**15:13–35** Some scholars think that this apostolic decree suggested by James, the immediate leader of the Jerusalem community, derives from another historical occasion than the meeting in

question. This seems to be the case if the meeting is the same as the one related in Gal 2:1–10. According to that account, nothing was imposed upon Gentile Christians in respect to Mosaic law; whereas the decree instructs Gentile Christians of mixed communities to abstain from meats sacrificed to idols and from blood-meats, and to avoid marriage within forbidden degrees of consanguinity and affinity (Lv 18), all of which practices were especially abhorrent to Jews. Luke seems to have telescoped two originally independent incidents here: the first a Jerusalem "Council" that dealt with the question of circumcision, and the second a Jerusalem decree dealing mainly with Gentile observance of dietary laws (see Acts 21:25 where Paul seems to be learning of the decree for the first time).

**15:14** *Symeon:* elsewhere in Acts he is called either Peter or Simon. The presence of the name Symeon here suggests that, in the source Luke is using for this part of the Jerusalem "Council" incident, the name may have originally referred to someone other than Peter (see Acts 13:1 where the Antiochene Symeon Niger is mentioned). As the text now stands, however, it is undoubtedly a reference to Simon Peter (Acts 15:7).

---

**14:26** 13:1–3.
**15:1–4** Gal 2:1–9.
**15:1** Lv 12:3; Gal 5:2.
**15:7** 10:27–43.
**15:8** 10:44–48.

**15:9** 10:34–35.
**15:10** Mt 23:4; Gal 5:1.
**15:11** Gal 2:16; 3:11; Eph 2:5–8.

16 'After this I shall return*
  and rebuild the fallen hut of David;
from its ruins I shall rebuild it
  and raise it up again,
17 so that the rest of humanity may seek
  out the Lord,
even all the Gentiles on whom my
  name is invoked.
Thus says the Lord who accomplishes
  these things,
18 known from of old.'

19 * It is my judgment, therefore, that we ought to stop troubling the Gentiles who turn to God, 20 but tell them by letter to avoid pollution from idols, unlawful marriage, the meat of strangled animals, and blood.* 21 For Moses, for generations now, has had those who proclaim him in every town, as he has been read in the synagogues every sabbath."

**Letter of the Apostles.** 22 Then the apostles and presbyters, in agreement with the whole church, decided to choose representatives and to send them to Antioch with Paul and Barnabas. The ones chosen were Judas, who was called Barsabbas, and Silas, leaders among the brothers. 23 This is the letter delivered by them: "The apostles and the presbyters, your brothers, to the brothers in Antioch, Syria, and Cilicia of Gentile origin: greetings. 24 Since we have heard that some of our number [who went out] without any mandate from us have upset you with their teachings and disturbed your peace of mind, 25 we have with one accord decided to choose representatives and to send them to you along with our beloved Barnabas and Paul, 26 who have dedicated their lives to the name of our Lord Jesus Christ. 27 So we are sending Judas and Silas who will also convey this same message by word of mouth: 28 * 'It is the decision of the holy Spirit and of us not to place on you any burden beyond these necessities, 29 namely, to abstain from meat sacrificed to idols, from blood, from meats of strangled animals, and from unlawful marriage. If you keep free of these, you will be doing what is right. Farewell.'"*

**Delegates at Antioch.** 30 And so they were sent on their journey. Upon their arrival in Antioch they called the assembly together and delivered the letter. 31 When the people read it, they were delighted with the exhortation. 32 Judas and Silas, who were themselves prophets, exhorted and strengthened the brothers with many words. 33 After they had spent some time there, they were sent off with greetings of peace from the brothers to those who had commissioned them. [34]† 35 But Paul and Barnabas remained in Antioch, teaching and proclaiming with many others the word of the Lord.

## V. THE MISSION OF PAUL TO THE ENDS OF THE EARTH

**Paul and Barnabas Separate.** 36 † After some time, Paul said to Barnabas, "Come, let us make a return visit to see how the brothers are getting on in all the cities where we proclaimed the word of the Lord." 37 Barnabas wanted to take with them also John, who was called Mark, 38 but Paul insisted that they should not take with them someone who had deserted them at Pamphylia and who had not continued with them in their work.* 39 So sharp was their disagreement that they separated. Barnabas took Mark and sailed to Cyprus. 40 But Paul chose Silas and departed after being commended by the brothers to the grace of the Lord. 41 He traveled through Syria and Cilicia bringing strength to the churches.

**16** **Paul in Lycaonia: Timothy.** 1 He reached [also] Derbe and Lystra where there was a disciple named Timothy, the son of a Jewish woman who was a believer, but his father was a Greek.* 2 The brothers in Lystra

† **15:34** Some manuscripts add, in various wordings, "But Silas decided to remain there."
**15:36–18:22** This continuous narrative recounts Paul's second missionary journey. On the internal evidence of the Lucan account, it lasted about three years. Paul first visited the communities he had established on his first journey (Acts 16:1–5), then pushed on into Macedonia, where he established communities at Philippi, Thessalonica, and Beroea (Acts 16:7–17:5). To escape the hostility of the Jews of Thessalonica, he left for Greece and while resident in Athens attempted, without success, to establish an effective Christian community there. From Athens he proceeded to Corinth and, after a stay of a year and a half, returned to Antioch by way of Ephesus and Jerusalem (Acts 17:16–18:22). Luke does not concern himself with the structure or statistics of the communities but aims to show the general progress of the gospel in the Gentile world as well as its continued failure to take root in the Jewish community.

* **15:16–17** Am 9:11–12.
**15:19–20** 15:28–29; 21:25.
**15:20** Gn 9:4; Lv 3:17; 17:10–14.
**15:28–29** 15:19–20.
**15:29** Gn 9:4; Lv 3:17; 17:10–14.
**15:38** 13:13.
**16:1** 1 Tm 1:2; 2 Tm 1:5.

**ACTS**

and Iconium spoke highly of him,* 3 and Paul wanted him to come along with him. On account of the Jews of that region, Paul had him circumcised,† for they all knew that his father was a Greek. 4 As they traveled from city to city, they handed on to the people for observance the decisions reached by the apostles and presbyters in Jerusalem. 5 Day after day the churches grew stronger in faith and increased in number.

**Through Asia Minor.** 6 They traveled through the Phrygian and Galatian territory because they had been prevented by the holy Spirit from preaching the message in the province of Asia. 7 When they came to Mysia, they tried to go on into Bithynia, but the Spirit of Jesus† did not allow them, 8 so they crossed through Mysia and came down to Troas. 9 During [the] night Paul had a vision. A Macedonian stood before him and implored him with these words, "Come over to Macedonia and help us." 10 When he had seen the vision, we† sought passage to Macedonia at once, concluding that God had called us to proclaim the good news to them.

**Into Europe.** 11† We set sail from Troas, making a straight run for Samothrace, and on the next day to Neapolis, 12 and from there to Philippi, a leading city in that district of Macedonia and a Roman colony. We spent some time in that city. 13 On the sabbath we went outside the city gate along the river where we thought there would be a place of prayer. We sat and spoke with the women who had gathered there. 14 One of them, a woman named Lydia, a dealer in purple cloth, from the city of Thyatira, a worshiper of God,† listened, and

the Lord opened her heart to pay attention to what Paul was saying. 15 After she and her household had been baptized, she offered us an invitation, "If you consider me a believer in the Lord, come and stay at my home," and she prevailed on us.

**Imprisonment at Philippi.** 16 As we were going to the place of prayer, we met a slave girl with an oracular spirit,† who used to bring a large profit to her owners through her fortune-telling. 17 She began to follow Paul and us, shouting, "These people are slaves of the Most High God, who proclaim to you a way of salvation." 18 She did this for many days. Paul became annoyed, turned, and said to the spirit, "I command you in the name of Jesus Christ to come out of her." Then it came out at that moment.

19 When her owners saw that their hope of profit was gone, they seized Paul and Silas and dragged them to the public square before the local authorities. 20 They brought them before the magistrates† and said, "These people are Jews and are disturbing our city 21 and are advocating customs that are not lawful for us Romans to adopt or practice." 22* The crowd joined in the attack on them, and the magistrates had them stripped and ordered them to be beaten with rods. 23 After inflicting many blows on them, they threw them into prison and instructed the jailer to guard them securely. 24 When he received these instructions, he put them in the innermost cell and secured their feet to a stake.

**Deliverance from Prison.** 25 About midnight, while Paul and Silas were praying and singing hymns to God as the prisoners listened, 26 there was suddenly such a severe earthquake

---

† **16:3** *Paul had him circumcised:* he did this in order that Timothy might be able to associate with the Jews and so perform a ministry among them. Paul did not object to the Jewish Christians' adherence to the law. But he insisted that the law could not be imposed on the Gentiles. Paul himself lived in accordance with the law, or as exempt from the law, according to particular circumstances (see 1 Cor 9:19–23).

**16:7** *The Spirit of Jesus:* this is an unusual formulation in Luke's writings. The parallelism with Acts 16:6 indicates its meaning, the holy Spirit.

**16:10–17** This is the first of the so-called "we-sections" in Acts, where Luke writes as one of Paul's companions. The other passages are Acts 20:5–15; 21:1–18; 27:1–28:16. Scholars debate whether Luke may not have used the first person plural simply as a literary device to lend color to the narrative. The realism of the narrative, however, lends weight to the argument that the "we" includes Luke or another companion of Paul whose data Luke used as a source.

**16:11–40** The church at Philippi became a flourishing community to which Paul addressed one of his letters (see Introduction to the Letter to the Philippians).

**16:14** *A worshiper of God:* a "God-fearer." See note on Acts 8:26–40.

**16:16** *With an oracular spirit:* literally, "with a Python spirit." The Python was the serpent or dragon that guarded the Delphic oracle. It later came to designate a "spirit that pronounced oracles" and also a ventriloquist who, it was thought, had such a spirit in the belly.

**16:20** *Magistrates:* in Greek, *stratēgoi,* the popular designation of the *duoviri,* the highest officials of the Roman colony of Philippi.

---

**16:2** Phil 2:20.        **16:22–23** 2 Cor 11:25; Phil 1:30; 1 Thes 2:2.

that the foundations of the jail shook; all the doors flew open, and the chains of all were pulled loose. 27 When the jailer woke up and saw the prison doors wide open, he drew [his] sword and was about to kill himself, thinking that the prisoners had escaped. 28 But Paul shouted out in a loud voice, "Do no harm to yourself; we are all here." 29 He asked for a light and rushed in and, trembling with fear, he fell down before Paul and Silas. 30 Then he brought them out and said, "Sirs, what must I do to be saved?" 31 And they said, "Believe in the Lord Jesus and you and your household will be saved." 32 So they spoke the word of the Lord to him and to everyone in his house. 33 He took them in at that hour of the night and bathed their wounds; then he and all his family were baptized at once. 34 He brought them up into his house and provided a meal and with his household rejoiced at having come to faith in God.

35 But when it was day, the magistrates sent the lictors† with the order, "Release those men." 36 The jailer reported the[se] words to Paul, "The magistrates have sent orders that you be released. Now, then, come out and go in peace." 37 But Paul said to them, "They have beaten us publicly, even though we are Roman citizens and have not been tried, and have thrown us into prison.* And now, are they going to release us secretly? By no means. Let them come themselves and lead us out."† 38 The lictors reported these words to the magistrates, and they became alarmed when they heard that they were Roman citizens.* 39 So they came and placated them, and led them out and asked that they leave the city. 40 When they had come out of the prison, they went to Lydia's house where they saw and encouraged the brothers, and then they left.

# 17

**Paul in Thessalonica.** 1 When they took the road through Amphipolis and Apollonia, they reached Thessalonica, where there was a synagogue of the Jews.* 2 Following his usual custom, Paul joined them, and for three sabbaths he entered into discussions with them from the scriptures, 3 expounding and demonstrating that the Messiah had to suffer and rise from the dead, and that "This is the Messiah, Jesus, whom I proclaim to you."* 4 Some of them were convinced and joined Paul and Silas; so, too, a great number of Greeks who were worshipers, and not a few of the prominent women. 5 But the Jews became jealous and recruited some worthless men loitering in the public square, formed a mob, and set the city in turmoil. They marched on the house of Jason,* intending to bring them before the people's assembly. 6† When they could not find them, they dragged Jason and some of the brothers before the city magistrates, shouting, "These people who have been creating a disturbance all over the world have now come here, 7 and Jason has welcomed them.* They all act in opposition to the decrees of Caesar and claim instead that there is another king, Jesus."† 8 They stirred up the crowd and the city magistrates who, upon hearing these charges, 9 took a surety payment from Jason and the others before releasing them.

**Paul in Beroea.** 10 The brothers immediately sent Paul and Silas to Beroea during the night. Upon arrival they went to the synagogue of the Jews. 11 These Jews were more fair-minded than those in Thessalonica, for they received the word with all willingness and examined the scriptures daily to determine whether these things were so.* 12 Many of them became believers, as did not a few of the influential Greek women and men. 13 But when the Jews of Thessalonica learned that the word of God had now been proclaimed by Paul in Beroea also, they came there too to cause a commotion and stir up the crowds. 14 So the brothers at once sent Paul on his way to the seacoast, while Silas and Timothy remained behind.* 15 After Paul's escorts had taken him to Athens, they came away with instructions for Silas and Timothy to join him as soon as possible.

**16:35** *The lictors:* the equivalent of police officers, among whose duties were the apprehension and punishment of criminals.

**16:37** Paul's Roman citizenship granted him special privileges in regard to criminal process. Roman law forbade under severe penalty the beating of Roman citizens (see also Acts 22:25).

**17:6–7** The accusations against Paul and his companions echo the charges brought against Jesus in Lk 23:2.

**17:7** *There is another king, Jesus:* a distortion into a political sense of the apostolic proclamation of Jesus and the kingdom of God (see Acts 8:12).

**16:37** 22:25.
**16:38** 22:29.
**17:1** 1 Thes 2:1–2.
**17:3** 3:18; Lk 24:25–26, 46.
**17:5** Rom 16:21.
**17:7** Lk 23:2; Jn 19:12–15.
**17:11** Jn 5:39.
**17:14** 1 Thes 3:1–2.

ACTS

**Paul in Athens.†** [16] While Paul was waiting for them in Athens, he grew exasperated at the sight of the city full of idols. [17] So he debated in the synagogue with the Jews and with the worshipers, and daily in the public square with whoever happened to be there. [18] Even some of the Epicurean and Stoic philosophers† engaged him in discussion. Some asked, "What is this scavenger trying to say?" Others said, "He sounds like a promoter of foreign deities," because he was preaching about 'Jesus' and 'Resurrection.' [19] They took him and led him to the Areopagus† and said, "May we learn what this new teaching is that you speak of?* [20] For you bring some strange notions to our ears; we should like to know what these things mean." [21] Now all the Athenians as well as the foreigners residing there used their time for nothing else but telling or hearing something new.

**Paul's Speech at the Areopagus.** [22] Then Paul stood up at the Areopagus and said:†

"You Athenians, I see that in every respect you are very religious. [23] For as I walked around looking carefully at your shrines, I even discovered an altar inscribed, 'To an Unknown God.'† What therefore you unknowingly worship, I proclaim to you. [24] The God who made the world and all that is in it, the Lord of heaven and earth, does not dwell in sanctuaries made by human hands,* [25] nor is he served by human hands because he needs anything. Rather it is he who gives to everyone life and breath and everything. [26] He made from one† the whole human race to dwell on the entire surface of the earth, and he fixed the ordered seasons and the boundaries of their regions, [27] so that people might seek God, even perhaps grope for him and find him, though indeed he is not far from any one of us.* [28] For 'In him we live and move and have our being,'† as even some of your poets have said, 'For we too are his offspring.' [29] Since therefore we are the offspring of God, we ought not to think that the divinity is like an image fashioned from gold, silver, or stone by human art and imagination.* [30] God has overlooked the times of ignorance, but now he demands that all people everywhere repent [31] because he has established a day on which he will 'judge the world with justice' through a man he has appointed, and he has provided confirmation for all by raising him from the dead."*

[32] When they heard about resurrection of the dead, some began to scoff, but others said, "We should like to hear you on this some other time." [33] And so Paul left them. [34] But some did join him, and became believers. Among them were Dionysius, a member of the Court of the Areopagus, a woman named Damaris, and others with them.

---

† **17:16–21** Paul's presence in Athens sets the stage for the great discourse before a Gentile audience in Acts 17:22–31. Although Athens was a politically insignificant city at this period, it still lived on the glories of its past and represented the center of Greek culture. The setting describes the conflict between Christian preaching and Hellenistic philosophy.

**17:18** *Epicurean and Stoic philosophers*: for the followers of Epicurus (342–271 B.C.), the goal of life was happiness attained through sober reasoning and the searching out of motives for all choice and avoidance. The Stoics were followers of Zeno, a younger contemporary of Alexander the Great. Zeno and his followers believed in a type of pantheism that held that the spark of divinity was present in all reality and that, in order to be free, each person must live "according to nature." *This scavenger*: literally, "seed-picker," as of a bird that picks up grain. The word is later used of scrap collectors and of people who take other people's ideas and propagate them as if they were their own. *Promoter of foreign deities*: according to Xenophon, Socrates was accused of promoting new deities. The accusation against Paul echoes the charge against Socrates. *'Jesus' and 'Resurrection'*: the Athenians are presented as misunderstanding Paul from the outset; they think he is preaching about Jesus and a goddess named *Anastasis*, i.e., Resurrection.

**17:19** *To the Areopagus*: the "Areopagus" refers either to the Hill of Ares west of the Acropolis or to the Council of Athens, which at one time met on the hill but which at this time assembled in the Royal Colonnade (*Stoa Basileios*).

**17:22–31** In Paul's appearance at the Areopagus he preaches his climactic speech to Gentiles in the cultural center of the an-

cient world. The speech is more theological than christological. Paul's discourse appeals to the Greek world's belief in divinity as responsible for the origin and existence of the universe. It contests the common belief in a multiplicity of gods supposedly exerting their powers through their images. It acknowledges that the attempt to find God is a constant human endeavor. It declares, further, that God is the judge of the human race, that the time of the judgment has been determined, and that it will be executed through a man whom God raised from the dead. The speech reflects sympathy with pagan religiosity, handles the subject of idol worship gently, and appeals for a new examination of divinity, not from the standpoint of creation but from the standpoint of judgment.

**17:23** *'To an Unknown God'*: ancient authors such as Pausanias, Philostratus, and Tertullian speak of Athenian altars with no specific dedication as altars of "unknown gods" or "nameless altars."

**17:26** *From one*: many manuscripts read "from one blood." *Fixed...seasons*: or "fixed limits to the epochs."

**17:28** *'In him we live and move and have our being'*: some scholars understand this saying to be based on an earlier saying of Epimenides of Knossos (6th century B.C.). *'For we too are his offspring'*: here Paul is quoting Aratus of Soli, a third-century B.C. poet from Cilicia.

**17:19** 1 Cor 1:22.
**17:24** 7:48–50; Gn 1:1; 1 Kgs 8:27; Is 42:5.
**17:27** Jer 23:23; Wis 13:6; Rom 1:19.
**17:29** 19:26; Is 40:18–20; 44:10–17; Rom 1:22–23.
**17:31** 10:42.

# 18 Paul in Corinth.

¹After this he left Athens and went to Corinth. ²There he met a Jew named Aquila,* a native of Pontus, who had recently come from Italy with his wife Priscilla† because Claudius had ordered all the Jews to leave Rome. He went to visit them ³and, because he practiced the same trade, stayed with them and worked, for they were tentmakers by trade. ⁴Every sabbath, he entered into discussions in the synagogue, attempting to convince both Jews and Greeks.

⁵When Silas and Timothy came down from Macedonia, Paul began to occupy himself totally with preaching the word, testifying to the Jews that the Messiah was Jesus. ⁶When they opposed him and reviled him, he shook out his garments† and said to them, "Your blood be on your heads! I am clear of responsibility. From now on I will go to the Gentiles."* ⁷So he left there and went to a house belonging to a man named Titus Justus, a worshiper of God;† his house was next to a synagogue.* ⁸Crispus,† the synagogue official,* came to believe in the Lord along with his entire household, and many of the Corinthians who heard believed and were baptized. ⁹*One night in a vision the Lord said to Paul, "Do not be afraid. Go on speaking, and do not be silent, ¹⁰for I am with you. No one will attack and harm you, for I have many people in this city." ¹¹He settled there for a year and a half and taught the word of God among them.

**Accusations Before Gallio.** ¹²But when Gallio was proconsul of Achaia,† the Jews rose up together against Paul and brought him to the tribunal, ¹³saying, "This man is inducing people to worship God contrary to the law."†

¹⁴When Paul was about to reply, Gallio spoke to the Jews, "If it were a matter of some crime or malicious fraud, I should with reason hear the complaint of you Jews; ¹⁵but since it is a question of arguments over doctrine and titles and your own law, see to it yourselves. I do not wish to be a judge of such matters." ¹⁶And he drove them away from the tribunal. ¹⁷They all seized Sosthenes, the synagogue official, and beat him in full view of the tribunal. But none of this was of concern to Gallio.

**Return to Syrian Antioch.** ¹⁸Paul remained for quite some time, and after saying farewell to the brothers he sailed for Syria, together with Priscilla and Aquila. At Cenchreae he had his hair cut* because he had taken a vow.† ¹⁹When they reached Ephesus, he left them there, while he entered the synagogue and held discussions with the Jews. ²⁰Although they asked him to stay for a longer time, he did not consent, ²¹but as he said farewell he promised, "I shall come back to you again, God willing." Then he set sail from Ephesus. ²²Upon landing at Caesarea, he went up and greeted the church† and then went down to Antioch. ²³†After staying there some time, he left and traveled in orderly sequence through the Galatian country and Phrygia, bringing strength to all the disciples.

**Apollos.** ²⁴A Jew named Apollos,* a native of Alexandria, an eloquent speaker, arrived in Ephesus. He was an authority on the scriptures.† ²⁵He had been instructed in the Way of the Lord and, with ardent spirit, spoke and taught accurately about Jesus, although he knew only the baptism of John. ²⁶He began

---

† **18:2** *Aquila…Priscilla*: both may already have been Christians at the time of their arrival in Corinth (see Acts 18:26). According to 1 Cor 16:19, their home became a meeting place for Christians. *Claudius*: the Emperor Claudius expelled the Jews from Rome ca. A.D. 49. The Roman historian Suetonius gives as reason for the expulsion disturbances among the Jews "at the instigation of Chrestos," probably meaning disputes about the messiahship of Jesus.

**18:6** *Shook out his garments*: a gesture indicating Paul's repudiation of his mission to the Jews there; cf. Acts 28:17–31.

**18:7** *A worshiper of God*: see note on Acts 8:26–40.

**18:8** *Crispus*: in 1 Cor 1:14 Paul mentions that Crispus was one of the few he himself baptized at Corinth.

**18:12** *When Gallio was proconsul of Achaia*: Gallio's proconsulship in Achaia is dated to A.D. 51–52 from an inscription discovered at Delphi. This has become an important date in establishing a chronology of the life and missionary work of Paul.

**18:13** *Contrary to the law*: Gallio (Acts 18:15) understands this to be a problem of Jewish, not Roman, law.

**18:18** *He had his hair cut because he had taken a vow*: a

reference to a Nazirite vow (see Nm 6:1–21, especially Nm 6:18) taken by Paul (see also Acts 21:23–27).

**18:22** *He went up and greeted the church*: "going up" suggests a visit to the church in Jerusalem.

**18:23–21:16** Luke's account of Paul's third missionary journey devotes itself mainly to his work at Ephesus (Acts 19:1–20:1). There is a certain restiveness on Paul's part and a growing conviction that the Spirit bids him return to Jerusalem and prepare to go to Rome (Acts 19:21).

**18:24–25** Apollos appears as a preacher who knows the teaching of Jesus in the context of John's baptism of repentance. Aquila and Priscilla instruct him more fully. He is referred to in 1 Cor 1:12; 3:5–6, 22.

---

| | |
|---|---|
| **18:2** Rom 16:3. | **18:8** 1 Cor 1:14. |
| **18:6** 13:51; Mt 10:14; | **18:9–10** Jer 1:8. |
| 27:24–25; Mk 6:11; | **18:18** 21:24; Nm 6:18. |
| Lk 9:5; 10:10–11. | **18:24** 1 Cor 1:12. |
| **18:7** 13:46–47; 28:28. | |

to speak boldly in the synagogue; but when Priscilla and Aquila heard him, they took him aside and explained to him the Way [of God]† more accurately. ²⁷And when he wanted to cross to Achaia, the brothers encouraged him and wrote to the disciples there to welcome him. After his arrival he gave great assistance to those who had come to believe through grace. ²⁸He vigorously refuted the Jews in public, establishing from the scriptures that the Messiah is Jesus.

**19** **Paul in Ephesus.** ¹† While Apollos was in Corinth, Paul traveled through the interior of the country and came [down] to Ephesus where he found some disciples. ²He said to them, "Did you receive the holy Spirit when you became believers?" They answered him, "We have never even heard that there is a holy Spirit." ³He said, "How were you baptized?" They replied, "With the baptism of John." ⁴Paul then said, "John baptized with a baptism of repentance, telling the people to believe in the one who was to come after him, that is, in Jesus."* ⁵When they heard this, they were baptized in the name of the Lord Jesus. ⁶And when Paul laid [his] hands on them, the holy Spirit came upon them, and they spoke in tongues and prophesied.* ⁷Altogether there were about twelve men.

⁸He entered the synagogue, and for three months debated boldly with persuasive arguments about the kingdom of God. ⁹But when some in their obstinacy and disbelief disparaged the Way before the assembly, he withdrew and took his disciples with him and began to hold daily discussions in the lecture hall of Tyrannus. ¹⁰This continued for two years with the result that all the inhabitants of the province of Asia heard the word of the Lord, Jews and Greeks alike. ¹¹So extraordinary were the mighty deeds God accomplished at the hands of Paul ¹²that when face cloths or aprons that touched his skin were applied to the sick, their diseases left them and the evil spirits came out of them.*

**The Jewish Exorcists.** ¹³Then some itinerant Jewish exorcists tried to invoke the name of the Lord Jesus over those with evil spirits, saying, "I adjure you by the Jesus whom Paul preaches." ¹⁴When the seven sons of Sceva, a Jewish high priest, tried to do this, ¹⁵the evil spirit said to them in reply, "Jesus I recognize, Paul I know, but who are you?" ¹⁶The person with the evil spirit then sprang at them and subdued them all. He so overpowered them that they fled naked and wounded from that house. ¹⁷When this became known to all the Jews and Greeks who lived in Ephesus, fear fell upon them all, and the name of the Lord Jesus was held in great esteem. ¹⁸Many of those who had become believers came forward and openly acknowledged their former practices. ¹⁹Moreover, a large number of those who had practiced magic collected their books and burned them in public. They calculated their value and found it to be fifty thousand silver pieces. ²⁰Thus did the word of the Lord continue to spread with influence and power.

**Paul's Plans.** ²¹When this was concluded, Paul made up his mind to travel through Macedonia and Achaia, and then to go on to Jerusalem, saying, "After I have been there, I must visit Rome also."* ²²Then he sent to Macedonia two of his assistants, Timothy and Erastus, while he himself stayed for a while in the province of Asia.

**The Riot of the Silversmiths.** ²³About that time a serious disturbance broke out concerning the Way. ²⁴There was a silversmith named Demetrius who made miniature silver shrines of Artemis† and provided no little work for the craftsmen. ²⁵He called a meeting of these and other workers in related crafts and said, "Men, you know well that our prosperity derives from this work. ²⁶As you can now see and hear, not only in Ephesus but throughout most of the province of Asia this Paul has persuaded and misled a great number of people

---

† **18:26** *The Way [of God]:* for the Way, see note on Acts 9:2. Other manuscripts here read "the Way of the Lord," "the word of the Lord," or simply "the Way."

**19:1–6** Upon his arrival in Ephesus, Paul discovers other people at the same religious stage as Apollos, though they seem to have considered themselves followers of Christ, not of the Baptist. On the relation between baptism and the reception of the Spirit, see note on Acts 8:16.

**19:24** *Miniature silver shrines of Artemis:* the temple of Artemis at Ephesus was one of the seven wonders of the ancient

world. Artemis, originally the Olympian virgin hunter, moon goddess, and goddess of wild nature, was worshiped at Ephesus as an Asian mother goddess and goddess of fertility. She was one of the most widely worshiped female deities in the Hellenistic world (see Acts 18:27).

---

**19:4** 1:5; 11:16; 13:24–25; Mt 3:11; Mk 1:8; Lk 3:16.
**19:6** 8:15–17; 10:44, 46.
**19:12** 5:15–16; Lk 8:44–47.
**19:21** 23:11; Rom 1:13; 15:22–32.

by saying that gods made by hands are not gods at all.* ²⁷ The danger grows, not only that our business will be discredited, but also that the temple of the great goddess Artemis will be of no account, and that she whom the whole province of Asia and all the world worship will be stripped of her magnificence."

²⁸ When they heard this, they were filled with fury and began to shout, "Great is Artemis of the Ephesians!" ²⁹ The city was filled with confusion, and the people rushed with one accord into the theater, seizing Gaius and Aristarchus, the Macedonians, Paul's traveling companions.* ³⁰ Paul wanted to go before the crowd, but the disciples would not let him, ³¹ and even some of the Asiarchs† who were friends of his sent word to him advising him not to venture into the theater. ³² Meanwhile, some were shouting one thing, others something else; the assembly was in chaos, and most of the people had no idea why they had come together. ³³ Some of the crowd prompted Alexander, as the Jews pushed him forward, and Alexander signaled with his hand that he wished to explain something to the gathering. ³⁴ But when they recognized that he was a Jew, they all shouted in unison, for about two hours, "Great is Artemis of the Ephesians!" ³⁵ Finally the town clerk restrained the crowd and said, "You Ephesians, what person is there who does not know that the city of the Ephesians is the guardian of the temple† of the great Artemis and of her image that fell from the sky? ³⁶ Since these things are undeniable, you must calm yourselves and not do anything rash. ³⁷ The men you brought here are not temple robbers, nor have they insulted our goddess. ³⁸ If Demetrius and his fellow craftsmen have a complaint against anyone, courts are in session, and there are proconsuls. Let them bring charges against one another. ³⁹ If you have anything further to investigate, let the matter be settled in the lawful assembly, ⁴⁰ for, as it is, we are in danger of being charged with rioting because of today's conduct. There is no cause for it. We shall [not]† be able to give a reason for this demonstration." With these words he dismissed the assembly.

# 20 Journey to Macedonia and Greece.
¹ When the disturbance was over, Paul had the disciples summoned and, after encouraging them, he bade them farewell and set out on his journey to Macedonia.* ² As he traveled throughout those regions, he provided many words of encouragement for them. Then he arrived in Greece, ³ where he stayed for three months. But when a plot was made against him by the Jews as he was about to set sail for Syria, he decided to return by way of Macedonia.

**Return to Troas.** ⁴* Sopater, the son of Pyrrhus, from Beroea, accompanied him, as did Aristarchus and Secundus from Thessalonica, Gaius from Derbe, Timothy, and Tychicus and Trophimus from Asia ⁵ who went on ahead and waited for us† at Troas.* ⁶ We sailed from Philippi after the feast of Unleavened Bread,† and rejoined them five days later in Troas, where we spent a week.

**Eutychus Restored to Life.** ⁷ On the first day of the week† when we gathered to break bread, Paul spoke to them because he was going to leave on the next day, and he kept on speaking until midnight. ⁸ There were many lamps in the upstairs room where we were gathered, ⁹ and a young man named Eutychus who was sitting on the window sill was sinking into a deep sleep as Paul talked on and on. Once overcome by sleep, he fell down from the third story and when he was picked up, he was dead. ¹⁰* Paul went down,† threw

---

**19:31** *Asiarchs*: the precise status and role of the Asiarchs is disputed. They appear to have been people of wealth and influence who promoted the Roman imperial cult and who may also have been political representatives in a league of cities in the Roman province of Asia.

**19:35** *Guardian of the temple*: this title was accorded by Rome to cities that provided a temple for the imperial cult. Inscriptional evidence indicates that Ephesus was acknowledged as the temple keeper of Artemis and of the imperial cult. *That fell from the sky*: many scholars think that this refers to a meteorite that was worshiped as an image of the goddess.

**19:40** Some manuscripts omit the negative in *[not]* be able, making the meaning, "There is no cause for which we shall be able to give a reason for this demonstration."

**20:5** The second "we-section" of Acts begins here. See note on Acts 16:10–17.

**20:6** *Feast of Unleavened Bread*: see note on Lk 22:1.

**20:7** *The first day of the week*: the day after the sabbath and the first day of the Jewish week, apparently chosen originally by the Jerusalem community for the celebration of the liturgy of the Eucharist in order to relate it to the resurrection of Christ.

**20:10** The action of Paul in throwing himself upon the dead boy recalls that of Elijah in 1 Kgs 17:21 where the son of the widow of Zarephath is revived and that of Elisha in 2 Kgs 4:34 where the Shunammite woman's son is restored to life.

---

**19:26** 17:29.
**19:29** Col 4:10.
**20:1** 1 Cor 16:1.
**20:4** Rom 16:21.
**20:5** 21:29; 2 Tm 4:20.
**20:10** 1 Kgs 17:17–24; 2 Kgs 4:30–37; Mt 9:24; Mk 5:39; Lk 8:52.

himself upon him, and said as he embraced him, "Don't be alarmed; there is life in him." [11] Then he returned upstairs, broke the bread, and ate; after a long conversation that lasted until daybreak, he departed. [12] And they took the boy away alive and were immeasurably comforted.

**Journey to Miletus.** [13] We went ahead to the ship and set sail for Assos where we were to take Paul on board, as he had arranged, since he was going overland. [14] When he met us in Assos, we took him aboard and went on to Mitylene. [15] We sailed away from there on the next day and reached a point off Chios, and a day later we reached Samos, and on the following day we arrived at Miletus. [16]† Paul had decided to sail past Ephesus in order not to lose time in the province of Asia, for he was hurrying to be in Jerusalem, if at all possible, for the day of Pentecost.

**Paul's Farewell Speech at Miletus.** [17] From Miletus he had the presbyters of the church at Ephesus summoned. [18] When they came to him, he addressed them, "You know how I lived among you the whole time from the day I first came to the province of Asia. [19] I served the Lord with all humility and with the tears and trials that came to me because of the plots of the Jews, [20] and I did not at all shrink from telling you what was for your benefit, or from teaching you in public or in your homes. [21] I earnestly bore witness for both Jews and Greeks to repentance before God and to faith in our Lord Jesus. [22] But now, compelled by the Spirit, I am going to Jerusalem. What will happen to me there I do not know, [23] except that in one city after another the holy Spirit has been warning me that imprisonment and hardships await me.* [24] Yet I consider life of no importance to me, if only I may finish my course and the ministry that I received from the Lord Jesus, to bear witness to the gospel of God's grace.*

[25] "But now I know that none of you to whom I preached the kingdom during my travels will ever see my face again. [26] And so I solemnly declare to you this day that I am not responsible for the blood of any of you, [27] for I did not shrink from proclaiming to you the entire plan of God. [28]* Keep watch over yourselves and over the whole flock of which the holy Spirit has appointed you overseers,† in which you tend the church of God that he acquired with his own blood. [29] I know that after my departure savage wolves will come among you, and they will not spare the flock.* [30] And from your own group, men will come forward perverting the truth to draw the disciples away after them.* [31] So be vigilant and remember that for three years, night and day, I unceasingly admonished each of you with tears.* [32] And now I commend you to God and to that gracious word of his that can build you up and give you the inheritance among all who are consecrated. [33] I have never wanted anyone's silver or gold or clothing. [34] You know well that these very hands have served my needs and my companions.* [35] In every way I have shown you that by hard work of that sort we must help the weak, and keep in mind the words of the Lord Jesus who himself said, 'It is more blessed to give than to receive.'"*

[36] When he had finished speaking he knelt down and prayed with them all. [37] They were all weeping loudly as they threw their arms around Paul and kissed him, [38] for they were deeply distressed that he had said that they would never see his face again. Then they escorted him to the ship.

# 21

**Arrival at Tyre.** [1]† When we had taken leave of them we set sail, made a straight run for Cos, and on the next day for Rhodes, and from there to Patara. [2] Finding a

---

† **20:16–35** Apparently aware of difficulties at Ephesus and neighboring areas, Paul calls the presbyters together at Miletus, about thirty miles from Ephesus. He reminds them of his dedication to the gospel (Acts 20:18–21), speaks of what he is about to suffer for the gospel (Acts 20:22–27), and admonishes them to guard the community against false prophets, sure to arise upon his departure (Acts 20:28–31). He concludes by citing a saying of Jesus (Acts 20:35) not recorded in the gospel tradition. Luke presents this farewell to the Ephesian presbyters as Paul's last will and testament.
**20:28** *Overseers:* see note on Phil 1:1. *The church of God:* because the clause "that he acquired with his own blood" fol-

lowing "the church of God" suggests that "his own blood" refers to God's blood, some early copyists changed "the church of God" to "the church of the Lord." Some prefer the translation "acquired with the blood of his own," i.e., Christ.
**21:1–18** The third "we-section" of Acts (see note on Acts 16:10–17).

**20:23** 9:16.
**20:24** 2 Tm 4:7.
**20:28** Jn 21:15–17; 1 Pt 5:2.
**20:29** Jn 10:12.
**20:30** Mt 7:15; 2 Pt 2:1–3;

1 Jn 2:18–19.
**20:31** 1 Thes 2:11.
**20:34** 1 Cor 4:12; 1 Thes 2:9; 2 Thes 3:8.
**20:35** Sir 4:31.

ship crossing to Phoenicia, we went on board and put out to sea. ³We caught sight of Cyprus but passed by it on our left and sailed on toward Syria and put in at Tyre where the ship was to unload cargo. ⁴There we sought out the disciples and stayed for a week. They kept telling Paul through the Spirit not to embark for Jerusalem. ⁵At the end of our stay we left and resumed our journey. All of them, women and children included, escorted us out of the city, and after kneeling on the beach to pray, ⁶we bade farewell to one another. Then we boarded the ship, and they returned home.

**Arrival at Ptolemais and Caesarea.** ⁷We continued the voyage and came from Tyre to Ptolemais, where we greeted the brothers and stayed a day with them. ⁸On the next day we resumed the trip and came to Caesarea, where we went to the house of Philip the evangelist, who was one of the Seven,† and stayed with him.* ⁹He had four virgin daughters gifted with prophecy. ¹⁰We had been there several days when a prophet named Agabus† came down from Judea. ¹¹* He came up to us, took Paul's belt, bound his own feet and hands with it, and said, "Thus says the holy Spirit: This is the way the Jews will bind the owner of this belt in Jerusalem, and they will hand him over to the Gentiles."† ¹²When we heard this, we and the local residents begged him not to go up to Jerusalem. ¹³Then Paul replied, "What are you doing, weeping and breaking my heart? I am prepared not only to be bound but even to die in Jerusalem for the name of the Lord Jesus." ¹⁴* Since he would not be dissuaded we let the matter rest, saying,* "The Lord's will be done."†

**Paul and James in Jerusalem.** ¹⁵After these days we made preparations for our journey, then went up to Jerusalem. ¹⁶Some of the disciples from Caesarea came along to lead us to the house of Mnason, a Cypriot, a disciple of long standing, with whom we were to stay. ¹⁷† When we reached Jerusalem the brothers welcomed us warmly. ¹⁸The next day, Paul accompanied us on a visit to James, and all the presbyters were present. ¹⁹He greeted them, then proceeded to tell them in detail what God had accomplished among the Gentiles through his ministry. ²⁰They praised God when they heard it but said to him, "Brother, you see how many thousands of believers there are from among the Jews, and they are all zealous observers of the law. ²¹They have been informed that you are teaching all the Jews who live among the Gentiles to abandon Moses and that you are telling them not to circumcise their children or to observe their customary practices. ²²What is to be done? They will surely hear that you have arrived. ²³† So do what we tell you. We have four men who have taken a vow.* ²⁴Take these men and purify yourself with them, and pay their expenses† that they may have their heads shaved. In this way everyone will know that there is nothing to the reports they have been given about you but that you yourself live in observance of the law. ²⁵* As for the Gentiles who have come to believe, we sent them our decision that they abstain from meat sacrificed to idols, from blood, from the meat of strangled animals, and from unlawful marriage."† ²⁶So Paul took the men, and on the next day after purifying himself together with them entered the temple to give notice of the day when the purification would be completed and the offering made for each of them.*

**Paul's Arrest.** ²⁷When the seven days were nearly completed, the Jews from the province

---

† **21:8** *One of the Seven*: see note on Acts 6:2–4.

**21:10** *Agabus*: mentioned in Acts 11:28 as the prophet who predicted the famine that occurred when Claudius was emperor.

**21:11** The symbolic act of Agabus recalls those of Old Testament prophets. Compare Is 20:2; Ez 4:1; Jer 13:1.

**21:14** The Christian disciples' attitude reflects that of Jesus (see Lk 22:42).

**21:17–26** The leaders of the Jewish Christians of Jerusalem inform Paul that the Jews there believe he has encouraged the Jews of the diaspora to abandon the Mosaic law. According to Acts, Paul had no objection to the retention of the law by the Jewish Christians of Jerusalem and left the Jews of the diaspora who accepted Christianity free to follow the same practice.

**21:23–26** The leaders of the community suggest that Paul, on behalf of four members of the Jerusalem community, make the customary payment for the sacrifices offered at the termination of the Nazirite vow (see Nm 6:1–24) in order to impress favorably

the Jewish Christians in Jerusalem with his high regard for the Mosaic law. Since Paul himself had once made this vow (Acts 18:18), his respect for the law would be on public record.

**21:24** *Pay their expenses*: according to Nm 6:14–15 the Nazirite had to present a yearling lamb for a holocaust, a yearling ewe lamb for a sin offering, and a ram for a peace offering, along with food and drink offerings, upon completion of the period of the vow.

**21:25** Paul is informed about the apostolic decree, seemingly for the first time (see note on Acts 15:13–35). The allusion to the decree was probably introduced here by Luke to remind his readers that the Gentile Christians themselves were asked to respect certain Jewish practices deriving from the law.

---

**21:8** 6:5; 8:5–6.
**21:11** 11:28; 20:23.
**21:14** 19:15–16.
**21:14** Mt 6:10; 26:39;

Mk 14:36; Lk 22:42.
**21:23–27** 18:18; Nm 6:1–21.
**21:25** 15:19–20, 28–29.
**21:26** 1 Cor 9:20.

Paul is arrested while in the Temple in Jerusalem, accused by the Jews of "teaching everyone everywhere against the people and the law and this place," as well as bringing "Greeks" (non-Jews) into a prohibited area of the Temple (Acts 21:27–30). Above, a model of the Temple area as it would have appeared at that time.

of Asia noticed him in the temple, stirred up the whole crowd, and laid hands on him, [28] * shouting, "Fellow Israelites, help us. This is the man who is teaching everyone everywhere against the people and the law and this place, and what is more, he has even brought Greeks into the temple and defiled this sacred place." † [29] For they had previously seen Trophimus the Ephesian in the city with him and supposed that Paul had brought him into the temple. [30] The whole city was in turmoil with people rushing together. They seized Paul and dragged him out of the temple, and immediately the gates were closed. [31] While they were trying to kill him, a report reached the cohort commander † that all Jerusalem was rioting. [32] He immediately took soldiers and centurions and charged down on them. When they saw the commander and the soldiers they stopped beating Paul. [33] The cohort commander came forward, arrested him, and ordered him to be secured with two chains; he tried to find out who he might be and what he had done. [34] Some in the mob shouted one thing, others something else; so, since he was unable to ascertain the truth because of the uproar, he ordered Paul to be brought into the compound. [35] When he reached the steps, he was carried by the soldiers because of the violence of the mob, [36] †* for a crowd of people followed and shouted, "Away with him!"

[37] Just as Paul was about to be taken into the compound, he said to the cohort commander, "May I say something to you?" He replied, "Do you speak Greek? [38] So then you are not the Egyptian † who started a revolt some time ago and led the four thousand assassins into the desert?" * [39] Paul answered, "I am a Jew,

---

† **21:28** The charges against Paul by the diaspora Jews are identical to the charges brought against Stephen by diaspora Jews in Acts 6:13. *Brought Greeks into the temple:* non-Jews were forbidden, under penalty of death, to go beyond the Court of the Gentiles. Inscriptions in Greek and Latin on a stone balustrade marked off the prohibited area.

**21:31** *Cohort commander:* literally, "the leader of a thousand in a cohort." At this period the Roman cohort commander usually led six hundred soldiers, a tenth of a legion; but the number in a cohort varied.

**21:36** *"Away with him!":* at the trial of Jesus before Pilate in Lk 23:18, the people similarly shout, "Away with this man."

**21:38** *The Egyptian:* according to the Jewish historian Josephus, an Egyptian gathered a large crowd on the Mount of Olives to witness the destruction of the walls of Jerusalem that would fall at the Egyptian "prophet's" word. The commotion was put down by the Roman authorities and the Egyptian escaped, but only after thousands had been killed. *Four thousand assassins:* literally, *sicarii.* According to Josephus, these were political nationalists who removed their opponents by assassination with a short dagger, called in Latin a *sica.*

**21:28** Rom 15:31.                                Jn 19:15.
**21:36** 22:22; Lk 23:18;                   **21:38** 5:36–37.

of Tarsus in Cilicia, a citizen of no mean city; I request you to permit me to speak to the people." [40] When he had given his permission, Paul stood on the steps and motioned with his hand to the people; and when all was quiet he addressed them in Hebrew. †

# 22 Paul's Defense Before the Jerusalem Jews. † [1] "My brothers and fathers, listen to what I am about to say to you in my defense." [2] When they heard him addressing them in Hebrew they became all the more quiet. And he continued, [3] "I am a Jew, born in Tarsus in Cilicia, but brought up in this city. At the feet of Gamaliel I was educated strictly in our ancestral law and was zealous for God, just as all of you are today. * [4] I persecuted this Way to death, binding both men and women and delivering them to prison. * [5] Even the high priest and the whole council of elders can testify on my behalf. For from them I even received letters to the brothers and set out for Damascus to bring back to Jerusalem in chains for punishment those there as well.

[6] "On that journey as I drew near to Damascus, about noon a great light from the sky suddenly shone around me. * [7] I fell to the ground and heard a voice saying to me, 'Saul, Saul, why are you persecuting me?' * [8] I replied, 'Who are you, sir?' And he said to me, 'I am Jesus the Nazorean whom you are persecuting.' * [9] My companions saw the light but did not hear the voice of the one who spoke to me. * [10] I asked, 'What shall I do, sir?' The Lord answered me, 'Get up and go into Damascus, and there you will be told about everything appointed for you to do.' * [11] Since I could see nothing because of the brightness of that light, I was led by hand by my companions and entered Damascus. *

[12] * "A certain Ananias, a devout observer of the law, and highly spoken of by all the Jews who lived there, [13] came to me and stood there and said, 'Saul, my brother, regain your sight.' And at that very moment I regained my sight and saw him. [14] Then he said, 'The God of our ancestors designated you to know his will, to see the Righteous One, and to hear the sound of his voice; [15] for you will be his witness † before all to what you have seen and heard. [16] Now, why delay? Get up and have yourself baptized and your sins washed away, calling upon his name.'

[17] "After I had returned to Jerusalem and while I was praying in the temple, I fell into a trance [18] and saw the Lord saying to me, 'Hurry, leave Jerusalem at once, because they will not accept your testimony about me.' [19] But I replied, 'Lord, they themselves know that from synagogue to synagogue I used to imprison and beat those who believed in you. * [20] And when the blood of your witness Stephen was being shed, I myself stood by giving my approval and keeping guard over the cloaks of his murderers.' * [21] Then he said to me, * 'Go, I shall send you far away to the Gentiles.'" †

**Paul Imprisoned.** [22] * They listened to him until he said this, but then they raised their voices and shouted, "Take such a one as this away from the earth. It is not right that he should live." † [23] And as they were yelling and throwing off their cloaks and flinging dust into the air, [24] the cohort commander ordered him to be brought into the compound and gave instruction that he be interrogated under the lash to determine the reason why they were making such an outcry against him. [25] * But when they had stretched him out for the whips, Paul said to the centurion on duty, "Is it lawful for you to scourge a man who is a Roman citizen and has not been tried?" † [26] When

---

21:40 *In Hebrew:* meaning, perhaps, in Aramaic, which at this time was the Semitic tongue in common use.

22:1–21 Paul's first defense speech is presented to the Jerusalem crowds. Luke here presents Paul as a devout Jew (Acts 22:3) and zealous persecutor of the Christian community (Acts 22:4–5), and then recounts the conversion of Paul for the second time in Acts (see note on Acts 9:1–19).

22:15 *His witness:* like the Galilean followers during the historical ministry of Jesus, Paul too, through his experience of the risen Christ, is to be a witness to the resurrection (compare Acts 1:8; 10:39–41; Lk 24:48).

22:21 Paul endeavors to explain that his position on the law has not been identical with that of his audience because it has been his prophetic mission to preach to the Gentiles to whom the law was not addressed and who had no faith in it as a way of salvation.

22:22 Paul's suggestion that his prophetic mission to the Gentiles did not involve his imposing the law on the Gentiles provokes the same opposition as occurred in Pisidian Antioch (Acts 13:45).

22:25 *Is it lawful for you to scourge a man who is a Roman citizen and has not been tried?:* see note on Acts 16:37.

---

| | |
|---|---|
| 22:3 5:34; 26:4–5; 2 Cor 11:22; Gal 1:13–14; Phil 3:5–6. | 22:10 9:6; 26:16. |
| | 22:11 9:8. |
| | 22:12–16 9:10–19. |
| 22:4 8:3; 9:1–2; 22:19; 26:9–11; Phil 3:6. | 22:19 8:3; 9:1–2; 22:4–5; 26:9–11. |
| 22:6 9:3; 26:13; 1 Cor 15:8. | 22:20 7:58; 8:1. |
| 22:7 9:4; 26:14. | 22:21 9:15; Gal 2:7–9. |
| 22:8 9:5; 26:15; Mt 25:40. | 22:22 21:36; Lk 23:18; Jn 19:15. |
| 22:9 9:7; 26:13–14. | 22:25 16:37. |

the centurion heard this, he went to the cohort commander and reported it, saying, "What are you going to do? This man is a Roman citizen." [27] Then the commander came and said to him, "Tell me, are you a Roman citizen?" "Yes," he answered. [28] The commander replied, "I acquired this citizenship for a large sum of money." Paul said, "But I was born one." [29] At once those who were going to interrogate him backed away from him, and the commander became alarmed when he realized that he was a Roman citizen and that he had had him bound.

**Paul Before the Sanhedrin.** [30] The next day, wishing to determine the truth about why he was being accused by the Jews, he freed him and ordered the chief priests and the whole Sanhedrin to convene. Then he brought Paul down and made him stand before them.

**23** [1] Paul looked intently at the Sanhedrin and said, "My brothers, I have conducted myself with a perfectly clear conscience before God to this day."* [2] The high priest Ananias† ordered his attendants to strike his mouth. [3] Then Paul said to him, "God will strike you,† you whitewashed wall. Do you indeed sit in judgment upon me according to the law and yet in violation of the law order me to be struck?"* [4] The attendants said, "Would you revile God's high priest?" [5] Paul answered, "Brothers, I did not realize he was the high priest. For it is written,* 'You shall not curse a ruler of your people.'"†

[6] Paul was aware that some were Sadducees and some Pharisees, so he called out before the Sanhedrin, "My brothers, I am a Pharisee, the son of Pharisees; [I] am on trial for hope in the resurrection of the dead."* [7] When he said this, a dispute broke out between the Pharisees and Sadducees, and the group became divided. [8] For the Sadducees say that there is no resurrection or angels or spirits, while the Pharisees acknowledge all three.*

[9] A great uproar occurred, and some scribes belonging to the Pharisee party stood up and sharply argued, "We find nothing wrong with this man. Suppose a spirit or an angel has spoken to him?" [10] The dispute was so serious that the commander, afraid that Paul would be torn to pieces by them, ordered his troops to go down and rescue him from their midst and take him into the compound. [11]†* The following night the Lord stood by him and said, "Take courage. For just as you have borne witness to my cause in Jerusalem, so you must also bear witness in Rome."

**Transfer to Caesarea.** [12] When day came, the Jews made a plot and bound themselves by oath not to eat or drink until they had killed Paul. [13] There were more than forty who formed this conspiracy. [14] They went to the chief priests and elders and said, "We have bound ourselves by a solemn oath to taste nothing until we have killed Paul. [15] You, together with the Sanhedrin, must now make an official request to the commander to have him bring him down to you, as though you meant to investigate his case more thoroughly. We on our part are prepared to kill him before he arrives." [16] The son of Paul's sister, however, heard about the ambush; so he went and entered the compound and reported it to Paul. [17] Paul then called one of the centurions† and requested, "Take this young man to the commander; he has something to report to him." [18] So he took him and brought him to the commander and explained, "The prisoner Paul called me and asked that I bring this young man to you; he has something to say to you." [19] The commander took him by the hand, drew him aside, and asked him privately, "What is it you have to report to me?" [20] He replied, "The Jews have conspired to ask you to bring Paul down to the Sanhedrin tomorrow, as though they meant to inquire about him more thoroughly, [21] but do not believe them. More than forty of them are lying in wait for him; they

---

† **23:2** *The high priest Ananias*: Ananias, son of Nedebaeus, was high priest from A.D. 47 to 59.
**23:3** *God will strike you*: Josephus reports that Ananias was later assassinated in A.D. 66 at the beginning of the First Revolt.
**23:5** Luke portrays Paul as a model of one who is obedient to the Mosaic law. Paul, because of his reverence for the law (Ex 22:27), withdraws his accusation of hypocrisy, "whitewashed wall" (cf. Mt 23:27), when he is told Ananias is the high priest.
**23:11** The occurrence of the vision of Christ consoling Paul and assuring him that he will be his witness in Rome prepares the reader for the final section of Acts: the journey of Paul and the word he preaches to Rome under the protection of the Romans.
**23:17** *Centurions*: a centurion was a military officer in charge of one hundred soldiers.

*
| | |
|---|---|
| **23:1** 24:16. | **23:6** 24:15, 21; 26:5; Phil |
| **23:2** Ez 13:10–15; Mt | 3:5. |
| 23:27. | **23:8** Mt 22:23; Lk 20:27. |
| **23:5** Ex 22:27. | **23:11** 19:21. |

have bound themselves by oath not to eat or drink until they have killed him. They are now ready and only wait for your consent." ²²As the commander dismissed the young man he directed him, "Tell no one that you gave me this information."

²³Then he summoned two of the centurions and said, "Get two hundred soldiers ready to go to Caesarea by nine o'clock tonight,† along with seventy horsemen and two hundred auxiliaries. ²⁴Provide mounts for Paul to ride and give him safe conduct to Felix the governor." ²⁵Then he wrote a letter with this content: ²⁶† "Claudius Lysias to his excellency the governor Felix, greetings.† ²⁷This man, seized by the Jews and about to be murdered by them, I rescued after intervening with my troops when I learned that he was a Roman citizen.* ²⁸I wanted to learn the reason for their accusations against him so I brought him down to their Sanhedrin. ²⁹I discovered that he was accused in matters of controversial questions of their law and not of any charge deserving death or imprisonment.* ³⁰Since it was brought to my attention that there will be a plot against the man, I am sending him to you at once, and have also notified his accusers to state [their case] against him before you."

³¹So the soldiers, according to their orders, took Paul and escorted him by night to Antipatris. ³²The next day they returned to the compound, leaving the horsemen to complete the journey with him. ³³When they arrived in Caesarea they delivered the letter to the governor and presented Paul to him. ³⁴When he had read it and asked to what province he belonged, and learned that he was from Cilicia, ³⁵he said, "I shall hear your case when your accusers arrive." Then he ordered that he be held in custody in Herod's praetorium.

# 24

**Trial Before Felix.** ¹Five days later the high priest Ananias came down with some elders and an advocate, a certain Tertullus, and they presented formal charges against Paul to the governor. ²When he was called, Tertullus began to accuse him, saying, "Since we have attained much peace through you, and reforms have been accomplished in this nation through your provident care, ³we acknowledge this in every way and everywhere, most excellent Felix, with all gratitude. ⁴But in order not to detain you further, I ask you to give us a brief hearing with your customary graciousness. ⁵* We found this man to be a pest; he creates dissension among Jews all over the world and is a ringleader of the sect of the Nazoreans.† ⁶He even tried to desecrate our temple, but we arrested him.* [⁷]† ⁸If you examine him you will be able to learn from him for yourself about everything of which we are accusing him." ⁹The Jews also joined in the attack and asserted that these things were so.

¹⁰† Then the governor motioned to him to speak and Paul replied, "I know that you have been a judge over this nation for many years and so I am pleased to make my defense before you. ¹¹As you can verify, not more than twelve days have passed since I went up to Jerusalem to worship. ¹²Neither in the temple, nor in the synagogues, nor anywhere in the city did they find me arguing with anyone or instigating a riot among the people. ¹³Nor can they prove to you the accusations they are now making against me. ¹⁴But this I do admit to you, that according to the Way, which they call a sect, I worship the God of our ancestors and I believe everything that is in accordance with the law and written in the prophets.* ¹⁵I have the same hope in God as they themselves have that there will be a resurrection of the righteous and the unrighteous.* ¹⁶Because of this, I always strive to keep my conscience clear before God and man.* ¹⁷After many years, I came to bring alms for my nation and offerings.* ¹⁸While I was so engaged, they found me, after my purification,

---

† **23:23** *By nine o'clock tonight*: literally, "by the third hour of the night." The night hours began at 6 p.m. *Two hundred auxiliaries*: the meaning of the Greek is not certain. It seems to refer to spearmen from the local police force and not from the cohort of soldiers, which would have numbered only 500–1000 men.
**23:26–30** The letter emphasizes the fact that Paul is a Roman citizen and asserts the lack of evidence that he is guilty of a crime against the empire. The tone of the letter implies that the commander became initially involved in Paul's case because of his Roman citizenship, but this is not an exact description of what really happened (see Acts 21:31–33; 22:25–29).
**23:26** M. Antonius Felix was procurator of Judea from A.D. 52 to 60. His procuratorship was marked by cruelty toward and

oppression of his Jewish subjects.
**24:5** *Nazoreans*: that is, followers of Jesus of Nazareth.
**24:7** The Western text has added here a verse (really Acts 24:6b–8a) that is not found in the best Greek manuscripts. It reads, "and would have judged him according to our own law, but the cohort commander Lysias came and violently took him out of our hands and ordered his accusers to come before you."
**24:10–21** Whereas the advocate Tertullus referred to Paul's

---

**23:27** 21:30–34; 22:27.
**23:29** 18:14–15; 25:18–19.
**24:5** 24:14; Lk 23:2.
**24:6** 21:28.
**24:14** 24:5.
**24:15** Dn 12:2; Jn 5:28–29.
**24:16** 23:1.
**24:17** Rom 15:25–26; Gal 2:10.

in the temple without a crowd or disturbance. * [19] But some Jews from the province of Asia, who should be here before you to make whatever accusation they might have against me— [20] or let these men themselves state what crime they discovered when I stood before the Sanhedrin, [21] unless it was my one outcry as I stood among them, that 'I am on trial before you today for the resurrection of the dead.'" *

[22] Then Felix, who was accurately informed about the Way, postponed the trial, saying, "When Lysias the commander comes down, I shall decide your case." [23] He gave orders to the centurion that he should be kept in custody but have some liberty, and that he should not prevent any of his friends from caring for his needs.

**Captivity in Caesarea.** [24] † Several days later Felix came with his wife Drusilla, who was Jewish. He had Paul summoned and listened to him speak about faith in Christ Jesus. [25] But as he spoke about righteousness and self-restraint and the coming judgment, Felix became frightened and said, "You may go for now; when I find an opportunity I shall summon you again." [26] At the same time he hoped that a bribe would be offered him by Paul, and so he sent for him very often and conversed with him.

[27] Two years passed and Felix was succeeded by Porcius Festus. Wishing to ingratiate himself with the Jews, Felix left Paul in prison. †

# 25

**Appeal to Caesar.** [1] Three days after his arrival in the province, Festus went up from Caesarea to Jerusalem [2] where the chief priests and Jewish leaders presented him their formal charges against Paul. † They asked him [3] as a favor to have him sent to Jerusalem, for they were plotting to kill him along the way. [4] Festus replied that Paul was being held in custody in Caesarea and that he himself would be returning there shortly. [5] He said, "Let your authorities come down with me, and if this man has done something improper, let them accuse him."

[6] After spending no more than eight or ten days with them, he went down to Caesarea, and on the following day took his seat on the tribunal and ordered that Paul be brought in. [7] When he appeared, the Jews who had come down from Jerusalem surrounded him and brought many serious charges against him, which they were unable to prove. [8] In defending himself Paul said, "I have committed no crime either against the Jewish law or against the temple or against Caesar." [9] † Then Festus, wishing to ingratiate himself with the Jews, said to Paul in reply, "Are you willing to go up to Jerusalem and there stand trial before me on these charges?" [10] Paul answered, "I am standing before the tribunal of Caesar; this is where I should be tried. I have committed no crime against the Jews, as you very well know. [11] If I have committed a crime or done anything deserving death, I do not seek to escape the death penalty; but if there is no substance to the charges they are bringing against me, then no one has the right to hand me over to them. I appeal to Caesar." [12] Then Festus, after conferring with his council, replied, "You have appealed to Caesar. To Caesar you will go."

**Paul Before King Agrippa.** [13] When a few days had passed, King Agrippa and Bernice † arrived in Caesarea on a visit to Festus. [14] Since they spent several days there, Festus referred Paul's case to the king, saying, "There is a man here left in custody by Felix. * [15] When I was in Jerusalem the chief priests and the elders of the Jews brought charges against him and demanded his condemnation. [16] I answered them that it was not Roman practice to hand over an

---

† activities on his missionary journeys, the apostle narrowed the charges down to the riot connected with the incident in the temple (see Acts 21:27–30; 24:17–20). In his defense, Paul stresses the continuity between Christianity and Judaism.

**24:24–25** The way of Christian discipleship greatly disquiets Felix, who has entered into an adulterous marriage with Drusilla, daughter of Herod Agrippa I. This marriage provides the background for the topics Paul speaks about and about which Felix does not want to hear.

**24:27** Very little is known of Porcius Festus who was a procurator of Judea from A.D. 60 to 62.

**25:2** Even after two years this animosity toward Paul in Jerusalem had not subsided (see Acts 24:27).

**25:9–12** Paul refuses to acknowledge that the Sanhedrin in Jerusalem has any jurisdiction over him now (Acts 25:11). Paul uses his right as a Roman citizen to appeal his case to the jurisdiction of the Emperor (Nero, ca. A.D. 60) (Acts 25:12). This move broke the deadlock between Roman protective custody of Paul and the plan of his enemies to kill him (25:3).

**25:13** *King Agrippa and Bernice*: brother and sister, children of Herod Agrippa I whose activities against the Jerusalem community are mentioned in Acts 12:1–19. Agrippa II was a petty ruler over small areas in northern Palestine and some villages in Perea. His influence on the Jewish population of Palestine was insignificant.

**24:18–19** 21:26–30.                    **25:14** 24:27.
**24:21** 23:6; 24:15.

accused person before he has faced his accusers and had the opportunity to defend himself against their charge. 17 So when [they] came together here, I made no delay; the next day I took my seat on the tribunal and ordered the man to be brought in. 18 * His accusers stood around him, but did not charge him with any of the crimes I suspected. 19 Instead they had some issues with him about their own religion and about a certain Jesus who had died but who Paul claimed was alive. 20 Since I was at a loss how to investigate this controversy, I asked if he were willing to go to Jerusalem and there stand trial on these charges. 21 And when Paul appealed that he be held in custody for the Emperor's decision, I ordered him held until I could send him to Caesar." 22 Agrippa said to Festus, "I too should like to hear this man." He replied, "Tomorrow you will hear him."

23 The next day Agrippa and Bernice came with great ceremony and entered the audience hall in the company of cohort commanders and the prominent men of the city and, by command of Festus, Paul was brought in. 24 And Festus said, "King Agrippa and all you here present with us, look at this man about whom the whole Jewish populace petitioned me here and in Jerusalem, clamoring that he should live no longer. 25 I found, however, that he had done nothing deserving death, and so when he appealed to the Emperor, I decided to send him. 26 But I have nothing definite to write about him to our sovereign; therefore I have brought him before all of you, and particularly before you, King Agrippa, so that I may have something to write as a result of this investigation. 27 For it seems senseless to me to send up a prisoner without indicating the charges against him."

# 26 King Agrippa Hears Paul. 1 Then Agrippa said to Paul, "You may now speak on your own behalf." So Paul stretched out his hand and began his defense. 2 † "I

count myself fortunate, King Agrippa, that I am to defend myself before you today against all the charges made against me by the Jews, 3 especially since you are an expert in all the Jewish customs and controversies. And therefore I beg you to listen patiently. 4 My manner of living from my youth, a life spent from the beginning among my people † and in Jerusalem, all [the] Jews know. 5 * They have known about me from the start, if they are willing to testify, that I have lived my life as a Pharisee, the strictest party of our religion. 6 * But now I am standing trial because of my hope in the promise made by God to our ancestors. 7 Our twelve tribes hope to attain to that promise as they fervently worship God day and night; and on account of this hope I am accused by Jews, O king. 8 Why is it thought unbelievable among you that God raises the dead? 9 * I myself once thought that I had to do many things against the name of Jesus the Nazorean, 10 and I did so in Jerusalem. I imprisoned many of the holy ones with the authorization I received from the chief priests, and when they were to be put to death I cast my vote against them. * 11 Many times, in synagogue after synagogue, I punished them in an attempt to force them to blaspheme; I was so enraged against them that I pursued them even to foreign cities.

12 "On one such occasion I was traveling to Damascus with the authorization and commission of the chief priests. 13 * At midday, along the way, O king, I saw a light from the sky, brighter than the sun, shining around me and my traveling companions. * 14 We all fell to the ground and I heard a voice saying to me in Hebrew, 'Saul, Saul, why are you persecuting me? * It is hard for you to kick against the goad.' † 15 And I said, 'Who are you, sir?' And the Lord replied, 'I am Jesus whom you are persecuting. * 16 Get up now, and stand on your feet. * I have appeared to you for this purpose, to appoint you as a servant and witness of what you have seen [of me] and what you will be shown. † 17 I

---

† **26:2–23** Paul's final defense speech in Acts is now made before a king (see Acts 9:15). In the speech Paul presents himself as a zealous Pharisee and Christianity as the logical development of Pharisaic Judaism. The story of his conversion is recounted for the third time in Acts in this speech (see note on Acts 9:1–19).

**26:4** *Among my people:* that is, among the Jews.

**26:14** *In Hebrew:* see note on Acts 21:40. *It is hard for you to kick against the goad:* this proverb is commonly found in Greek literature and in this context signifies the senselessness and ineffectiveness of any opposition to the divine influence in his life.

**26:16** The words of Jesus directed to Paul here reflect the dialogues between Christ and Ananias (Acts 9:15) and between Ananias and Paul (Acts 22:14–15) in the two previous accounts of Paul's conversion.

| | |
|---|---|
| 25:18–19 18:14–15; 23:29. | 26:10 9:14. |
| 26:5 Phil 3:5–6; Gal | 26:13–14 9:7. |
| 1:13–14; 2 Cor 11:22. | 26:13 9:3; 22:6. |
| 26:6–8 23:6; 24:15, 21; | 26:14 9:4; 22:7. |
| 28:20. | 26:15 9:5; 22:8; Mt 25:40. |
| 26:9–11 8:3; 9:1–2; 22:19; Phil | 26:16 9:6; 22:10; Ez 2:1. |
| 3:6. | |

shall deliver you from this people and from the Gentiles to whom I send you,* [18]to open their eyes† that they may turn from darkness to light and from the power of Satan to God, so that they may obtain forgiveness of sins and an inheritance among those who have been consecrated by faith in me.'*

[19]"And so, King Agrippa, I was not disobedient to the heavenly vision. [20]On the contrary, first to those in Damascus and in Jerusalem and throughout the whole country of Judea, and then to the Gentiles, I preached the need to repent and turn to God, and to do works giving evidence of repentance. [21]* That is why the Jews seized me [when I was] in the temple and tried to kill me. [22]* But I have enjoyed God's help to this very day, and so I stand here testifying to small and great alike, saying nothing different from what the prophets and Moses foretold,† [23]that the Messiah must suffer† and that, as the first to rise from the dead, he would proclaim light both to our people and to the Gentiles."*

**Reactions to Paul's Speech.** [24]While Paul was so speaking in his defense, Festus said in a loud voice, "You are mad, Paul; much learning is driving you mad." [25]But Paul replied, "I am not mad, most excellent Festus; I am speaking words of truth and reason. [26]The king knows about these matters and to him I speak boldly, for I cannot believe that [any] of this has escaped his notice; this was not done in a corner.† [27]King Agrippa, do you believe the prophets?† I know you believe." [28]Then Agrippa said to Paul, "You will soon persuade me to play the Christian." [29]Paul replied, "I

would pray to God that sooner or later not only you but all who listen to me today might become as I am except for these chains."

[30]Then the king rose, and with him the governor and Bernice and the others who sat with them. [31]† And after they had withdrawn they said to one another, "This man is doing nothing [at all] that deserves death or imprisonment." [32]And Agrippa said to Festus, "This man could have been set free if he had not appealed to Caesar."*

# 27 Departure for Rome. [1]† When it was decided that we should sail to Italy, they handed Paul and some other prisoners over to a centurion named Julius of the Cohort Augusta.† [2]We went on board a ship from Adramyttium bound for ports in the province of Asia and set sail. Aristarchus, a Macedonian from Thessalonica, was with us.* [3]On the following day we put in at Sidon where Julius was kind enough to allow Paul to visit his friends who took care of him. [4]From there we put out to sea and sailed around the sheltered side of Cyprus because of the headwinds, [5]and crossing the open sea off the coast of Cilicia and Pamphylia we came to Myra in Lycia.

**Storm and Shipwreck.** [6]There the centurion found an Alexandrian ship that was sailing to Italy and put us on board. [7]For many days we made little headway, arriving at Cnidus only with difficulty, and because the wind would not permit us to continue our course we sailed for the sheltered side of Crete off Salmone. [8]We sailed past it with difficulty and reached

---

26:18 *To open their eyes*: though no mention is made of Paul's blindness in this account (cf. Acts 9:8–9, 12, 18; 22:11–13), the task he is commissioned to perform is the removal of other people's spiritual blindness.

26:22 *Saying nothing different from what the prophets and Moses foretold*: see note on Lk 18:31.

26:23 *That the Messiah must suffer*: see note on Lk 24:26.

26:26 *Not done in a corner*: for Luke, this Greek proverb expresses his belief that he is presenting a story about Jesus and the church that is already well known. As such, the entire history of Christianity is public knowledge and incontestable. Luke presents his story in this way to provide "certainty" to his readers about the instructions they have received (Lk 1:4).

26:27–28 If the Christian missionaries proclaim nothing different from what the Old Testament prophets had proclaimed (Acts 26:22–23), then the logical outcome for the believing Jew, according to Luke, is to become a Christian.

26:31–32 In recording the episode of Paul's appearance before Agrippa, Luke wishes to show that, when Paul's case was judged impartially, no grounds for legal action against him were

found (see Acts 23:29; 25:25).

27:1–28:16 Here Luke has written a stirring account of adventure on the high seas, incidental to his main purpose of showing how well Paul got along with his captors and how his prophetic influence saved the lives of all on board. The recital also establishes the existence of Christian communities in Puteoli and Rome. This account of the voyage and shipwreck also constitutes the final "we-section" in Acts (see note on Acts 16:10–17).

27:1 *Cohort Augusta*: the presence of a Cohort Augusta in Syria during the first century A.D. is attested in inscriptions. Whatever the historical background to this information given by Luke may be, the name Augusta serves to increase the prominence and prestige of the prisoner Paul whose custodians bear so important a Roman name.

---

| | |
|---|---|
| 26:17 Jer 1:7. | 44–47. |
| 26:18 Is 42:7, 16; 61:1 LXX; | 26:23 Is 42:6; 49:6; Lk 2:32; |
| Col 1:13. | 1 Cor 15:20–23. |
| 26:21 21:31. | 26:32 25:11–12. |
| 26:22–23 3:18; Lk 24:26–27, | 27:2 19:29; 20:4. |

ACTS

PAUL'S JOURNEYS IN ACTS

→ Third missionary journey (ca. CE 53–57)
⇢ Journey to prison in Rome (ca. CE 59–62)

© 2013 ANSELM ACADEMIC

ITALY

Rome
Forum
of Appius
Three Inns

Puteoli

Malta

Sicily

Syracuse

Rhegium

Adriatic Sea

The Great Sea
(Mediterranean Sea)

Fair Havens

Crete

GREECE

MACEDONIA

Thessalonica
Amphipolis
Berea
Apollonia
Philippi
Neapolis

Corinth

Athens

Troas
Assos
Mitylene

Ephesus
Colossae
Miletus
Cos
Cnidus
Rhodes

Patara

Myra
Attalia
Perga

Lystra
Derbe
Iconium
Antioch

GALATIA

Tarsus

Cyprus
Paphos
Salamis

Antioch
Seleucia

SYRIA

Sidon
Tyre
Ptolemais

Caesarea
Antipatris

Jerusalem

ATLANTIC
OCEAN

0      500 miles
0   500 kilometers

North
Sea

Rome

Mediterranean
Sea

Jerusalem

Black
Sea

Roman Empire
First Century CE

0      200      400 miles
0      200      400 kilometers

a place called Fair Havens, near which was the city of Lasea.

⁹ Much time had now passed and sailing had become hazardous because the time of the fast† had already gone by, so Paul warned them,* ¹⁰ "Men, I can see that this voyage will result in severe damage and heavy loss not only to the cargo and the ship, but also to our lives." ¹¹ The centurion, however, paid more attention to the pilot and to the owner of the ship than to what Paul said. ¹² Since the harbor was unfavorably situated for spending the winter, the majority planned to put out to sea from there in the hope of reaching Phoenix, a port in Crete facing west-northwest, there to spend the winter.

¹³ A south wind blew gently, and thinking they had attained their objective, they weighed anchor and sailed along close to the coast of Crete. ¹⁴ Before long an offshore wind of hurricane force called a "Northeaster" struck. ¹⁵ Since the ship was caught up in it and could not head into the wind we gave way and let ourselves be driven. ¹⁶ We passed along the sheltered side of an island named Cauda and managed only with difficulty to get the dinghy under control. ¹⁷ They hoisted it aboard, then used cables to undergird the ship. Because of their fear that they would run aground on the shoal of Syrtis, they lowered the drift anchor and were carried along in this way. ¹⁸ We were being pounded by the storm so violently that the next day they jettisoned some cargo, ¹⁹ and on the third day with their own hands they threw even the ship's tackle overboard. ²⁰ Neither the sun nor the stars were visible for many days, and no small storm raged. Finally, all hope of our surviving was taken away.

²¹ When many would no longer eat, Paul stood among them and said, "Men, you should have taken my advice and not have set sail from Crete and you would have avoided this disastrous loss. ²² I urge you now to keep up your courage; not one of you will be lost, only the ship. ²³ For last night an angel of the God to whom [I] belong and whom I serve stood by me ²⁴ and said, 'Do not be afraid, Paul. You are destined to stand before Caesar; and behold, for your sake, God has granted safety

to all who are sailing with you.'* ²⁵ Therefore, keep up your courage, men; I trust in God that it will turn out as I have been told. ²⁶ We are destined to run aground on some island."

²⁷ On the fourteenth night, as we were still being driven about on the Adriatic Sea, toward midnight the sailors began to suspect that they were nearing land. ²⁸ They took soundings and found twenty fathoms; a little farther on, they again took soundings and found fifteen fathoms. ²⁹ Fearing that we would run aground on a rocky coast, they dropped four anchors from the stern and prayed for day to come. ³⁰ The sailors then tried to abandon ship; they lowered the dinghy to the sea on the pretext of going to lay out anchors from the bow. ³¹ But Paul said to the centurion and the soldiers, "Unless these men stay with the ship, you cannot be saved." ³² So the soldiers cut the ropes of the dinghy and set it adrift.

³³ Until the day began to dawn, Paul kept urging all to take some food. He said, "Today is the fourteenth day that you have been waiting, going hungry and eating nothing. ³⁴ I urge you, therefore, to take some food; it will help you survive. Not a hair of the head of anyone of you will be lost." ³⁵ When he said this, he took bread,† gave thanks to God in front of them all, broke it, and began to eat.* ³⁶ They were all encouraged, and took some food themselves. ³⁷ In all, there were two hundred seventy-six of us on the ship. ³⁸ After they had eaten enough, they lightened the ship by throwing the wheat into the sea.

³⁹ When day came they did not recognize the land, but made out a bay with a beach. They planned to run the ship ashore on it, if they could. ⁴⁰ So they cast off the anchors and abandoned them to the sea, and at the same time they unfastened the lines of the rudders, and hoisting the foresail into the wind, they made for the beach. ⁴¹ But they struck a sandbar and ran the ship aground. The bow was wedged in and could not be moved, but the stern began to break up under the pounding [of the waves]. ⁴² The soldiers planned to kill the prisoners so that none might swim away and escape, ⁴³ but the centurion wanted to save Paul and so kept them from carrying out

---

† **27:9** *The time of the fast*: the fast kept on the occasion of the Day of Atonement (Lv 16:29–31), which occurred in late September or early October.

**27:35** *He took bread…*: the words recall the traditional language of the celebration of the Eucharist (see Lk 22:19).

* **27:9** Lv 16:29–31.
**27:24** 23:11.
**27:35** Mt 15:36;

Mk 6:41; 8:6;
Lk 22:19; 1 Cor 11:23–24.

their plan. He ordered those who could swim to jump overboard first and get to the shore, [44] and then the rest, some on planks, others on debris from the ship. In this way, all reached shore safely.

# 28 Winter in Malta.

[1] Once we had reached safety we learned that the island was called Malta. [2] The natives showed us extraordinary hospitality; they lit a fire and welcomed all of us because it had begun to rain and was cold. [3] Paul had gathered a bundle of brushwood and was putting it on the fire when a viper, escaping from the heat, fastened on his hand. [4] When the natives saw the snake hanging from his hand, they said to one another, "This man must certainly be a murderer; though he escaped the sea, Justice† has not let him remain alive." [5] But he shook the snake off into the fire and suffered no harm. [6] They were expecting him to swell up or suddenly to fall down dead but, after waiting a long time and seeing nothing unusual happen to him, they changed their minds and began to say that he was a god.* [7] In the vicinity of that place were lands belonging to a man named Publius, the chief of the island. He welcomed us and received us cordially as his guests for three days. [8] It so happened that the father of Publius was sick with a fever and dysentery. Paul visited him and, after praying, laid his hands on him and healed him. [9] After this had taken place, the rest of the sick on the island came to Paul and were cured. [10] They paid us great honor and when we eventually set sail they brought us the provisions we needed.

**Arrival in Rome.** [11] Three months later we set sail on a ship that had wintered at the island. It was an Alexandrian ship with the Dioscuri† as its figurehead. [12] We put in at Syracuse and stayed there three days, [13] and from there we sailed round the coast and arrived at Rhegium.

After a day, a south wind came up and in two days we reached Puteoli. [14] There we found some brothers and were urged to stay with them for seven days. And thus we came to Rome. [15] The brothers from there heard about us and came as far as the Forum of Appius and Three Taverns to meet us. On seeing them, Paul gave thanks to God and took courage. [16] When he entered Rome,† Paul was allowed to live by himself, with the soldier who was guarding him.

**Testimony to Jews in Rome.** [17]† Three days later he called together the leaders of the Jews. When they had gathered he said to them, "My brothers, although I had done nothing against our people or our ancestral customs, I was handed over to the Romans as a prisoner from Jerusalem.* [18] After trying my case the Romans wanted to release me, because they found nothing against me deserving the death penalty.* [19] But when the Jews objected, I was obliged to appeal to Caesar, even though I had no accusation to make against my own nation.* [20] This is the reason, then, I have requested to see you and to speak with you, for it is on account of the hope of Israel† that I wear these chains."* [21] They answered him, "We have received no letters from Judea about you, nor has any of the brothers arrived with a damaging report or rumor about you. [22] But we should like to hear you present your views, for we know that this sect is denounced everywhere."*

[23] So they arranged a day with him and came to his lodgings in great numbers. From early morning until evening, he expounded his position to them, bearing witness to the kingdom of God and trying to convince them about Jesus from the law of Moses and the prophets. [24] Some were convinced by what he had said, while others did not believe. [25]† Without reaching any agreement among

---

† **28:4** *Justice*: in Greek mythology, the pursuing goddess of vengeance and justice.

**28:11** *Dioscuri*: that is, the Twin Brothers, Castor and Pollux, the sons of Zeus and the patrons of the sailors.

**28:16** With Paul's arrival in Rome, the programmatic spread of the word of the Lord to "the ends of the earth" (Acts 1:8) is accomplished. In Rome, Paul is placed under house arrest, and under this mild form of custody he is allowed to proclaim the word in the capital of the civilized world of his day.

**28:17–22** Paul's first act in Rome is to learn from the leaders of the Jewish community whether the Jews of Jerusalem plan to pursue their case against him before the Roman jurisdiction. He is informed that no such plan is afoot, but that the Jews of Rome

have heard the Christian teaching denounced. Paul's offer to explain it to them is readily accepted.

**28:20** *The hope of Israel*: in the words of Paul (Acts 23:6), Luke has identified this hope as hope in the resurrection of the dead.

**28:25–28** Paul's final words in Acts reflect a major concern of Luke's writings: how the salvation promised in the Old Testament, accomplished by Jesus, and offered first to Israel (Acts

---

*
| **28:6** 14:11. | **28:19** 25:11. |
| **28:17** 24:12–13; 25:8. | **28:20** 23:6; 24:15, 21; |
| **28:18** 23:29; 25:25; | 26:6–8. |
| 26:31–32. | **28:22** 24:5, 14. |

ACTS

themselves they began to leave; then Paul made one final statement. "Well did the holy Spirit speak to your ancestors through the prophet Isaiah, saying:

26 'Go to this people and say:*
    You shall indeed hear but not
        understand.
    You shall indeed look but never see.
27 Gross is the heart of this people;
        they will not hear with their ears;
        they have closed their eyes,
        so they may not see with their eyes

and hear with their ears
and understand with their heart and be
    converted,
and I heal them.'

28* Let it be known to you that this salvation of God has been sent to the Gentiles; they will listen." [29]†

30† He remained for two full years in his lodgings. He received all who came to him, 31 and with complete assurance and without hindrance he proclaimed the kingdom of God and taught about the Lord Jesus Christ.

13:26), has now been offered to and accepted by the Gentiles. Quoting Is 6:9–10, Paul presents the scriptural support for his indictment of his fellow Jews who refuse to accept the message he proclaims. Their rejection leads to its proclamation among the Gentiles.

**28:29** The Western text has added here a verse that is not found in the best Greek manuscripts: "And when he had said this, the Jews left, seriously arguing among themselves."

**28:30–31** Although the ending of Acts may seem to be abrupt, Luke has now completed his story with the establish-

ment of Paul and the proclamation of Christianity in Rome. Paul's confident and unhindered proclamation of the gospel in Rome forms the climax to the story whose outline was provided in Acts 1:8—"You will be my witnesses in Jerusalem…and to the ends of the earth."

**28:26** Is 6:9–10; Mt 13:14–15; Mk 4:12; Lk 8:10; Jn 12:40; Rom 11:8.   **28:28** 13:46; 18:6; Ps 67:2; Is 40:5 LXX; Lk 3:6.

# Introduction to Pauline Literature

## Laurie Brink, OP

Twenty-one of the twenty-seven books of the New Testament are called "letters" and comprise nearly a third of the New Testament texts. Traditionally, fourteen of these letters are collectively identified as Pauline Literature. The remaining seven are classified as Catholic Epistles. Pauline Literature is identified by the community or the individual addressed; the Catholic Epistles are identified by their authors. The traditional list of Pauline Literature includes the "Letter" to the Hebrews. Hebrews is neither a true letter, nor written by Paul. It was unlikely originally addressed to "Hebrews." [Ed. note: This NAB translation includes Hebrews in the Pauline corpus, as explained in the NAB introduction to the New Testament Letters.]

The canonical order of the Pauline letters is not based on chronology but according to the length of each letter. Longer letters come before shorter ones. Letters addressed to churches (Romans, 1 and 2 Corinthians, Galatians, Ephesians, Philippians, Colossians, 1 and 2 Thessalonians) are placed ahead of those written to individuals (1 and 2 Timothy, Titus, Philemon). Hebrews does not state in its text that it was written by Paul; it follows after those that claim Paul as the author.

The actual authorship of all but seven of the thirteen letters that identify Paul as author is disputed. The undisputed letters include: Romans, 1 and 2 Corinthians, Galatians, Philippians, 1 Thessalonians, and Philemon.

## Authorship

### The Apostle Paul

Less than two decades after the Resurrection of Jesus, an unlikely apostle proclaimed the folly of the cross as the very wisdom of God (1 Cor 1:21). In the first-century Mediterranean world, where religion defined one's ethnicity and one's patriotism, this foolhardy preacher was himself a living paradox. A self-proclaimed Hebrew, a Pharisee, a zealous Jew and admitted persecutor of the church (Phil 3:5–6), Paul came to recognize his religious pedigree, all that he valued, as "loss because of Christ" (Phil 3:7).

Not since the Books of the Prophets had the individual's voice sounded in Scripture. The Gospels and Acts of the Apostles that precede the Letters from Paul in the canon report the teachings and deeds of Jesus and his apostles. But beginning with the Letter to the Romans, the reader hears the actual voice of the writers, not mediated through narrative, but directed to the church of that day. The result is a personal, somewhat provocative and always cross-centered view of the developing faith in Christ.

Paul did not intend to be an apostle to the Gentiles (Rom 11:13; Gal 2:8). By his own admission, he was a persecutor of the church (1 Cor 15:9; Gal 1:13; Phil 3:6), zealous for his Jewish faith (Gal 1:14). Like the prophet Jeremiah before him, he had been called while in his mother's womb (Gal 1:15), but through a revelation from God he recognized his mission to proclaim the gospel to the Gentiles (Gal 1:12, 16). Three years following his initial revelation, Paul went to Jerusalem to meet with Cephas (Aramaic term for Rock = Peter) and remained with him for fifteen days. At that time, he also met James, "the brother of the Lord" (Gal 1:18–19). Fourteen years later, Paul returned to Jerusalem and met with James, Cephas, and John, who approved of Paul's mission to the Gentiles (Gal 2:9), requiring only that they remember the poor (Gal 2:10). Sometime later in Antioch, Paul chastised Cephas for refusing to eat with the Gentiles after the arrival of those from the circumcision party (Gal 2:11–12).

His remarkable revelation cost him dearly. He was imprisoned, suffered beatings by lashes and rods, was stoned, thrice shipwrecked, and was adrift at sea for a night and a day (2 Cor 11:24–25). He enumerated the multiple dangers he endured, including hunger, thirst, cold, and exposure (2 Cor 11:26–27).

The Acts of the Apostles characterizes Paul from the lens of the late first-century author known as Luke. Paul's conversion is dramatically told in three separate accounts (Acts 9:1–19; 22:3–21; 26:9–20). He identifies himself as a citizen of Tarsus (Acts 21:39; 22:3) and a Roman citizen (Acts 22:25). He received a strict religious education at the feet of Gamaliel (Acts 22:3). His family includes a sister and a nephew who warns him about a planned ambush (Acts 23:16). Though Paul often dismisses his oral abilities (1 Cor 2:1–4) or is criticized for them (2 Cor 10:10), Luke presents him as a persuasive speaker (Acts 17:34). Paul possesses the ability to heal (Acts 14:8–10; 19:11–12) and to cast out demons (Acts 16:18). The Acts of the Apostles concludes with Paul in Rome under house arrest. The apocryphal *Acts of Paul* narrates Paul's martyrdom in Rome at the behest of the emperor Nero.

The early church father John Chrysostom (ca. 349–407) readily admitted that, of all the saints, he loved Paul the most.[1] Few are lukewarm when it comes to an evaluation of this apostle-come-lately. On issues of gender and sexuality, his proponents call him a "proto-feminist," citing Gal 3:28, while detractors argue that he is a misogynist who thought it better if women were quiet in church (1 Cor 14:33b–36). His apparent pro-Gentile stance gains him the title "marginal Jew," while his apocalyptic perspectives place him in good stead with other apocalyptic Jews of his day. Romans 13 is cited as demonstrating Paul's conservative political views. But others see his creation of communities and encouragement to refrain from participating in public religion (the eating of meat sacrificed to idols) as examples of his anti-imperial attitude. He is seen as anti-slavery when he supports the runaway slave, Onesimus, in the Letter to Philemon. This stance is hard to support, however, when reading 1 Cor 7:21–24, where Paul seems to urge slaves not to be concerned to gain their freedom because they are already free in the Lord.

An overview of Paul's first-century Mediterranean world will provide a context in which

to read the archive of letters left to us from this irascible preacher.

## The Religious Marketplace

Paul uses a variety of terms to talk about the Christian community. The earliest nomenclature appears to be *ekklēsia* found in 1 Thes 1:1, utilized by Mt 16:18; 18:17 and perpetuated by Luke in Acts 5:11; 8:1, 3; 9:31; 11:22, 26; 14:23, 27; 15:3, 4, 22, 41; 16:5; 18:22; 20:17, 28. The word *ekklēsia* is the Greek term for assembly, or gathering, which is translated as "church," though in Paul's time the present understanding of church was not formed. By the turn of the century, this *ekklēsia* has a formal structure, as seems to be indicated by Acts 14:23 where the churches appoint elders at Antioch of Pisidia and in Acts 15:4, where the *ekklēsia*, apostles, and elders gather to meet Paul in Jerusalem. Other terms used by Paul include "those called" (*klētoi*, Rom 1:7; 1 Cor 1:2), which may be paired with "the saints" (*hagioi*, e.g., Rom 1:7; 1 Cor 1:2; 16:1); "the elect" (*eklogē*, Rom 11:7), "the believers" (*pisteuontes*, e.g., 1 Thes 1:7; 2:10), and "brothers/sisters" (*adelphoi*, e.g., 1 Cor 1:10; 1 Thes 1:4).

This *ekklēsia* was just one of many religions competing for attention in the religious marketplace of the first century. One need only read the Acts of the Apostles to hear about the religious competition: Zeus and Hermes in Lystra (Acts 14:11–13), the nameless gods in Athens (Acts 17:22–23), and the great goddess Artemis in Ephesus (Acts 19:23–41). In addition to the temples that encircled the forum of any Greco-Roman city in the East—the locale of much of Paul's mission work—the hospital was dedicated to the healing god Asclepius, the meat sold in the market most often had originally been sacrificed in a pagan temple, and the daily visit to one's patron often meant participating in their household cults.

Romans allowed for the practice of various religions as long as the state gods were not ignored. In fact, Rome often adapted and adopted the divinities they found in other parts of the empire. The Egyptian Isis became "Romanized" and redressed as a more modest matron. Another religious ritual with strong

1. Margaret M. Mitchell, *The Heavenly Trumpet: John Chrysostom and the Art of Pauline Interpretation* (Louisville, KY: Westminster John Knox, 2002), 1.

ties to the state was the worship of the emperor as a god. The imperial cult, though only in its infancy during Paul's lifetime, would become a serious challenge to Christian faith. Even in Paul's day, the emperor claimed the title "lord" and "savior," so Paul's use of these titles for Jesus Christ (e.g., Rom 1:4; 4:24; 16:2; Phil 2:11; 3:20) stand in direct opposition to Caesar.

## Snapshots of the Society

The Corinthian correspondence provides a unique glimpse into some of the social concerns of the Pauline *ekklēsia*. Though a bit like listening to half a conversation, the letters show Paul's response to questions about immorality (1 Cor 5), lawsuits (1 Cor 6), marriage (1 Cor 7), and women's roles (1 Cor 11:2–16).

Paul believed that Christ would return imminently and that the community of believers was living in the last days. This sense of eager expectation is part of his eschatology and informed his social teachings. Salvation would be completed (1 Cor 5:5; 1 Thes 5:1-11) with Christ's return, but those who were in Christ had already begun their new life. They were a new creation (2 Cor 5:17). As such, they had a different set of moral expectations.

The term that is often translated as "immorality" is *porneia* in the Greek, used for an array of illicit sexual activities. Paul responds to a report he has received that a man is living with his father's wife (1 Cor 5:1). Paul declares such behavior as appalling—even the Gentiles would not engage in such acts. The context suggests that the man may have married his stepmother either after his father's death or after the couple's divorce. Marriage between a stepson and stepmother was illegal by both Jewish and Roman standards.[2] The members of the *ekklēsia* were not to associate with a fellow member who was an immoral person, or any fellow member who was greedy or an idolater, reveler, drunkard, or robber (1 Cor 5:11).

Catalogues of virtues and vices were common in Greco-Roman (Plutarch, *De Stoicorum repugnantiis*, 1034c; Epictetus, *Diatribai*,

2.16.11–17; Cicero, *Tusculanae disputations*, 4.3.5) and Hellenistic Jewish writings (Wisdom of Solomon; Philo, *Who Is the Heir?* 168–73). Such lists were used to demonstrate clear boundaries of good moral behavior. In the undisputed Pauline letters, catalogues are found in Rom 1:29–31; 13:13; 1 Cor 6:9–10; 2 Cor 12:20–21; and Gal 5:19–21. The ethical behavior expected of members extended to their legal affairs as well. Paul chastises the Corinthian community for using the civic legal system to work out their disagreements (1 Cor 6:6–8).

In the first-century world, Paul's statement that it is well for a man not to touch a woman (1 Cor 7:1) would have seemed anti-social. Augustan legislation provided incentives for women to have children. Judaism saw marriage and the procreation of children as a holy command (Philo, *On the Special Laws*, 3.1–82). But Paul's sense of imminent eschatology (1 Cor 7:31) meant that the believers were living in a "here and not yet reality." The reign of God was in process but not yet complete. In this context, Paul offers his "concession" to the Corinthians' questions about marriage, that is, that marriage is not forbidden but is not his personal preference.

Paul claims that wives as well as husbands have the right to sexual gratification (1 Cor 7:3–4). But gender equality does not seem to extend in the case of public worship. Women who prophesy are to cover their heads (1 Cor 11:5). Women should keep silent in the churches, and if they have questions, ask their husbands at home (1 Cor 14:34–35). However, some scholars argue that 1 Cor 14:34–35 is an interpolation inserted later to create conformity with 1 Tim 2:11–12.

The role of women in the first-century Mediterranean world was far from homogenous. In general, Roman women exercised more authority than did their Greek counterparts. Roman women could own property, inherit, and, in some cases, be independent of a male guardian. The extent to which Roman gender customs spread to the Greek east is unknown. Paul does name women as active participants in the church. Of the twenty-seven names listed in Rom 16, ten belong to women who are variously titled as "diakonos" or minister

_____
2. Conzelmann, Hans, *1 Corinthians* (Philadelphia: Fortress Press, 1975), 96.

(Phoebe, Rom 16:1), fellow worker (Prisca, along with her husband Aquila, v. 3), hard workers (Mary v. 6, Tryphaena, Tryphosa, and Persis, v. 12), relative and fellow prisoner and "prominent among the apostles" (Junia, v. 7), Rufus's mother (v. 13), and saints (Julia and Nereus's sister, v. 15).

# The Pauline Epistolary Archive

## Letter-Writing and the Ancient Postal Service

The books of the New Testament are remarkable for their content, which is made all the more amazing given the vagaries of history. One wonders how many other letters from the apostles might have been penned but were never preserved, sent but were never received. A brief excursus into letter writing and delivery in the first century serves to accent the extraordinary existence of the Pauline corpus.

The letters that appear in the New Testament for the most part were written by reed pens on papyrus rolls. The scribe would select a length of papyrus depending on the anticipated contents. The message would be written on the inside of the scroll with delivery instructions on the outside. Since secretaries or professional letter-writers penned most letters, likely Paul's epistles were not written by his hand. In fact, one such secretary added his own personal note in Rom 16:22, "I, Tertius, the writer of this letter, greet you in the Lord." On occasion, Paul does add his own postscript (1 Cor 16:21; Phlm 19) and in Gal 6:11, Paul notes his penmanship: "See with what large letters I am writing to you in my own hand!" Personal interjections in the author's own hand may have served to authenticate the letter.

While Paul appears to be the mastermind behind the content of the letters, he is not alone. In 1 Thes 1:1 and 2 Thes 1:1, he includes Silvanus and Timothy as co-senders. First Corinthians is written by Paul and Sosthenes. Timothy is the co-sender of 2 Corinthians, Philippians, Philemon, and Colossians. The Letter to the Galatians is being sent by Paul and all the brothers (fellow Christians) with him (Gal 1:2).

The postal system of the Roman Empire was restricted to governmental agents, so private correspondence had to be sent by couriers or trusted travelers. The cache of papyri discovered in the trash heaps of Egypt testifies to the happenstance of much personal correspondence. Letters were sent home when one happened upon a traveler going that direction. Paul's letters give only occasional indications of who his courier may have been. Chloe's people bring a report to Paul (1 Cor 1:11), which may have been in letter-form or given orally. Perhaps these same people carried Paul's earlier letter to the Corinthians (1 Cor 5:9). The tearful letter that Paul mentions in 2 Cor 2:4 was likely carried to the church of Corinth by Titus, whose return Paul anxiously awaited (2 Cor 7:6–13). Delicate details concerning the business or controversy under discussion were often left to the trusted emissary.

"For this reason I am sending you Timothy, who is my beloved and faithful son in the Lord; he will remind you of my ways in Christ [Jesus], just as I teach them everywhere in every church." (1 Cor 4:17)

Paul follows standard epistolary form when dictating his letters. Most ancient epistles included a prescript and greeting, followed by a health wish or thanksgiving section, the body of the letter, greetings, and a closing formula. Paul adds his own personal touch to the standard *chairein* (greetings). He incorporates the Jewish formula of shalom, so that the greeting becomes grace (*charis*) and peace (shalom, *eirēnē* in Greek). All of Paul's genuine epistles include the various parts of a standard letter, save the Letter to the Galatians. Paul is furious; he has nothing to be thankful about in his chastising letter to the churches of Galatia. Romans 16 closes with an extensive greetings section in which Paul sends his regards to twenty-four individuals and two family groups.

## The Undisputed Letters Written by Paul

Scholarly consensus attributes seven letters to Paul (and his co-senders) Romans, 1 and 2 Corinthians, Galatians, Philippians, 1 Thessalonians, and Philemon. By reconstructing

Paul's itinerary from his genuine letters and the Acts of the Apostles, an approximate date and origin of these letters can be mapped.[3]

First Thessalonians is believed to have been written early in Paul's apostolic career when he resided in Corinth (approximately 50–51 CE). The Corinthian correspondence followed in 54–56 CE. Acts of the Apostles records Paul's two-year stay in Ephesus (Acts 19:10), following his preaching in Corinth (Acts 18:1–17). Given his lengthy stay, Paul may have penned several letters here, including 1 and 2 Corinthians, and Galatians (55–56 CE). Paul wrote the Letter to the Romans from Corinth (56–57 CE). Determining the date and place of origin for Philippians and Philemon depends on the location of Paul's imprisonment at the time of writing. If Paul is writing from Ephesus, the letters could have been composed between 53 and 55 CE. If Paul is in the custody of Felix and then Festus in Caesarea, he may be writing shortly before he is taken to Rome. If Paul writes from Rome, then Philippians and Philemon become the last letters preserved from the Apostle Paul. According to Eusebius, the fourth-century church historian, Paul was martyred under Nero, who reigned from 54 to 68 CE.

## Letters Written in the Name of Paul

The Pauline corpus found within the New Testament includes letters that were attributed to Paul but actually were written long after his death. The deuteropauline letters of Thessalonians, Colossians, and Ephesians appear to have been written between 70 and 100 CE, though some scholars argue that one or all of these are genuinely Pauline. First and Second Timothy and Titus, also known as the Pastoral Epistles because of their concern about matters of church management, demonstrate by their vocabulary and content a late first-century to early second-century date. While 1 Timothy and Titus appear to be by the same hand and address similar concerns, 2 Timothy is markedly different and may have another author. For Paul and the earliest Christian communities,

the church gathers in the households of members (Rom 16:5; 1 Cor 16:19). The church anticipating the end time ("citizenship . . . in heaven" in Phil 3:20) had no need for structures or even developed ministries beyond "apostles"—those sent to preach the coming reign of God. Hence, little source material is found in Paul's own letters concerning the internal functioning of the churches. Intra-church differentiation of ministries includes apostles (2 Cor 8:23; Phil 2:25), prophets (Rom 12:6; 1 Cor 12:28; 14:1–5; 1 Thes 5:20), teachers (Rom 12:7; Gal 6:6), overseers and ministers, both male and female (Phil 1:1; Rom 16:1), and leaders (Rom 12:8; 1 Cor 12:28; 1 Thes 5:12). Those members who had the means to host the Lord's Supper rose in responsibility and authority in the early communities. Some of these house church patrons were women (1 Cor 16:19).

As time went on, the delay of the *parousia* and the growing number of believers led to the development of institutional elements. For the next generation of Pauline communities, the church that met in the household of a Christian patron readily developed into the "household of God" (Eph 2:19). Like other households of the time, order and proper management were vital for the welfare of the members of that household. Codes of behavior were common in the Greco-Roman world and provided directives for ethical behavior as well as good order among social classes. These "household codes" were adapted to fit the growing Christian communities and are found in Eph 5:21–6:9; Col 3:18–4:1; 1 Tm 2:8–15; 5:1-2; 6:1–2; Ti 2:1–10; 3:1 (cf. 1 Pt 2:11–3:12).

By the time of the Pastoral Epistles (1 and 2 Timothy and Titus), the "household of God" had developed a hierarchical ministry of bishops (1 Tm 3:1–7; Ti 1:7–9), presbyters (1 Tm 5:17–22; Ti 1:5), deacons (1 Tm 3:8–13), and widows (1 Tm 5:3–16), with set standards for their selection and their behavior.

## "In Regard to the Matters about Which You Wrote" (1 Cor 7:1)

A quick survey of the life of the Apostle Paul

---

3. Klauck, Hans-Josef, *Ancient Letters and the New Testament* (Waco, TX: Baylor University Press, 2006), 299–408.

and his religious and social context provides the backdrop on which to read the Pauline corpus found in the New Testament. None of the letters in the canon are simply "notes," meant to send greetings to acquaintances at a distance, though they do that. Each letter, whether genuinely authored by Paul or written in the tradition of Paul, is addressed to a specific community with specific concerns and questions. The Thessalonians are worried that their beloved dead will be left behind when Jesus returns (1 Thes 4:13–18). The Corinthian correspondence concludes myriad questions about right behavior within a polytheistic urban environment. The Letter to the Galatians shows Paul's temper as he chastises the churches for their fickle faith. "O stupid Galatians! Who has bewitched you, before whose eyes Jesus Christ was publicly portrayed as crucified?" (Gal 3:1). The Philippians seem to have been favored by Paul. He is effusive in his praise of them (Phil 1:3–11), while admonishing two of their leaders to resolve their differences (Phil 4:2–3). The shortest of the genuine letters is addressed not to a church but to an individual. Paul attempts to mediate between Onesimus the runaway slave and his owner, Philemon, both of whom

are believers. And finally, Paul's Letter to the Romans is addressed to a community he did not establish. It summarizes and expands his theological thinking to date, particularly with respect to the question of Israel and God's righteousness to Jews and Gentiles. Many scholars sense that one major issue in Romans is to try to mediate between Gentile Christian communities and Christian Jews who were returning after Nero lifted Claudius's edict that expelled at least one community of Jews from Rome.

But specific issues and local concerns notwithstanding, the Pauline letters do share common ground. They are attempts to shore up the faith of new believers, correct the misunderstandings created by false apostles, and encourage a virtuous life. They are christocentric, or more correctly, cross-centric (1 Cor 1:18; Gal 6:14; Phil 2:8), focused on the saving act of Christ Jesus.

For I handed on to you as of first importance what I also received: that Christ died for our sins in accordance with the scriptures; that he was buried; that he was raised on the third day in accordance with the scriptures. (1 Cor 15:3–4) ∎

# NEW TESTAMENT LETTERS
## New American Bible, Introduction

In the New Testament canon, between the Acts of the Apostles and Revelation, there are twenty-one documents that take the form of letters or epistles. Most of these are actual letters, but some are more like treatises in the guise of letters. In a few cases even some of the more obvious elements of the letter form are absent; see the Introductions to Hebrews and to 1 John.

The virtually standard form found in these documents, though with some variation, is dependent upon the conventions of letter writing common in the ancient world, but these were modified to suit the purposes of Christian writers. The New Testament letters usually begin with a greeting including an identification of the sender or senders and of the recipients. Next comes a prayer, usually in the form of a thanksgiving. The body of the letter provides an exposition of Christian teaching, usually provoked by concrete circumstances, and generally also draws conclusions regarding ethical behavior. There often follows a discussion of practical matters, such as the writer's travel plans, and the letter concludes with further advice and a formula of farewell.

Fourteen of the twenty-one letters have been traditionally attributed to Paul. One of these, the Letter to the Hebrews, does not itself claim to be the work of Paul; when it was accepted into the canon after much discussion, it was attached at the very end of the Pauline corpus. The other thirteen identify Paul as their author, but most scholars believe that some of them were actually written by his disciples; see the Introductions to Ephesians, Colossians, 2 Thessalonians, and 1 Timothy.

Four of the letters in the Pauline corpus (Ephesians, Philippians, Colossians, and Philemon) are called the "Captivity Epistles" because in each of them the author speaks of being in prison at the time of writing. Three others (1–2 Timothy and Titus) are known as the "Pastoral Epistles" because, addressed to individuals rather than communities, they give advice to disciples about caring for the flock. The letters of the Pauline corpus are arranged in roughly descending order of length from Romans to Philemon, with Hebrews added at the end.

The other seven letters of the New Testament that follow the Pauline corpus are collectively referred to as the "Catholic Epistles." This term, which means "universal," refers to the fact that most of them are directed not to a single Christian community, as are most of the Pauline letters, but to a wider audience; see the Introduction to the catholic letters. Three of them (1–2–3 John) are closely related to the fourth gospel and thus belong to the Johannine corpus. The catholic letters, like those of the Pauline corpus, are also arranged in roughly descending order of length, but the three Johannine letters are kept together and Jude is placed at the end.

The genuine letters of Paul are earlier in date than any of our written gospels. The dates of the other New Testament letters are more difficult to determine, but for the most part they belong to the second and third Christian generations rather than to the first. ∎

# The Letter to the

# Romans

## INTRODUCTION

### Laurie Brink, OP

Paul's Letter to the Romans has been the cornerstone for much theological inquiry throughout history. The church father Augustine of Hippo used Rom 5 as support for his concept of original sin. Martin Luther's understanding of justification by faith was rooted in his reading of Rom 3–4. Studying Rom 9–11 led John Calvin to espouse the concept of double predestination. From Karl Barth to N. T. Wright, theologians and biblical scholars alike have attempted to understand the righteousness of God as expressed in Rom 1–2. The theological and ethical impact notwithstanding, Paul's Letter to the Romans must first be understood within its original context.

Only seven of the fourteen epistles attributed to the Apostle Paul in the New Testament are generally held to be authentic (see the introduction to Pauline Literature). Romans stands as a litmus test by which others are judged.[1] In the current New Testament canon, Romans follows Acts of the Apostles. Earlier Greek manuscripts placed Romans and the other Pauline Epistles after the Catholic Letters, perhaps owing to the fact that the Catholic Letters were attributed to the pillars of the church (Peter, James, and John). By Paul's own admission, he was "the least of the apostles" (1 Cor 15:9).

Since Paul believed that Christ Jesus would return imminently, he was eager to bring both Jew and Gentile to faith in Christ. Paul wrote to the communities he had founded to encourage them in their new faith as they anticipated the day that they would "all stand before the judgment seat of God" (Rom 14:10). But why did Paul write to the church in Rome, a community he did not found and had never

---

---

visited? Who were these "beloved of God" (1:7), and what did he hope to gain by penning his longest and what may have been one of his last epistles?

## Authorship

Paul appears to be the sole author of the Letter to the Romans, since no co-senders are named. Paul introduces himself in the prescript as "Paul, a slave of Christ Jesus, called to be an apostle and set apart for the gospel of God" (Rom 1:1). He is an apostle to the Gentiles (11:13). He further describes his Jewish identity: "I too am an Israelite, a descendant of Abraham, of the tribe of Benjamin" (11:1).

Romans is a letter composed late in Paul's preaching career, probably in Corinth between 56 and 57 CE. By the time Paul wrote he had completed his missionary work in the eastern Mediterranean (Rom 15:19) and was anticipating a trip to Jerusalem (Rom 15:25) where he

---

1. Charles D. Myers, "Romans, Epistle to the," in *Anchor Bible Dictionary*, ed. David Noel Freedman (New York: Doubleday, 1992), 816.

would deliver the financial contributions he had been collecting throughout his apostolate (1 Cor 16:1–4; 2 Cor 8–9; Gal 2:10). After his Jerusalem visit, he intended to stop in Rome on his way to Spain (Rom 15:28). According to Acts of the Apostles, Paul's visit to Jerusalem did not go as planned. He was arrested for allegedly bringing Greeks into the sacred area of the Temple (Acts 21:28) and was taken to the imperial headquarters in Caesarea, where he was imprisoned for two years (Acts 24:27). He did eventually sail to Rome, where he was held for another two years under Roman custody (Acts 28:30).

## Recipients

The second part of the prescript identifies the recipients of the letter: "to all the beloved of God in Rome, called to be holy" (Rom 1:7). With the exception of Philippians, Romans is the only letter from Paul not addressed explicitly to a "church" (see 1 Cor 1:2; 2 Cor 1:1; Gal 1:2; 1 Thes 1:1; Phlm 2).

Who were these "beloved of God in Rome" and did they include both Jewish Christians and Gentile Christians? The identity of the addressees has caused considerable scholarly debate. Paul speaks of Jews and Gentiles (Rom 1:16; 2:9–10; 3:9, 29; 9:24; 10:12), and Paul's discussion on the election of Israel (Rom 9–11) suggests that Jewish Christians were among the audience. In Rom 11:13, Paul seems to single out the Gentiles when he writes, "Now I am speaking to you Gentiles." More recently, some scholars have argued against the long-held idea of a mixed community, proposing that the implied readers were Gentiles, perhaps even former God-fearers, well-versed in the Jewish Scriptures and tradition.[2]

## Context

The difficulty in determining the make-up of Paul's addressees is related to the question of the origin of the church in Rome. How the Christian message originally reached Rome and by whom is unknown. Likely the first believers were Jewish. Paul's co-workers Prisca and Aquila arrived in Corinth after having been expelled from Rome because of the edict of Claudius (Acts 18:2). The Roman historian Suetonius recorded that in 49 CE the emperor Claudius banished the Jews from Rome for disturbances instigated by a certain person named Chrestus (*Divus Claudius* 25.4). Suetonius may have mistaken the Greek word *Christos* for the Latin *Chrestus,* a common slave name. Paul sends greetings to Aquila and Prisca in this letter (Rom 16:3), suggesting that they have returned to Rome.

While the Jewish Christians were in exile, the leadership of the churches shifted to the remaining Gentile members. After the death of Claudius, Jewish Christians may have returned (Prisca and Aquila may be prime examples), but the church they had left was decidedly different from the one to which they returned. Under Gentile leadership, the community had likely moved beyond its Jewish roots. Romans 14:1 and 15:1, 7 may indicate that tension existed between the returning Jewish Christians and the Gentile Christians.

## Reasons for Writing

The contents of Romans suggest that Paul had more than one reason for writing to this community.[3] In keeping with his designation as "apostle," Paul was set on expanding his missionary territory west (Rom 15:20). He anticipated preaching in Rome (1:15) with the hope of reaping a harvest among the Gentiles there (1:13). He had completed his work in the eastern Mediterranean and longed to travel to Spain (15:24, 28) where he would no doubt continue to preach to the Gentiles (15:18–24, 28). Paul may have anticipated that the Roman community would serve as a financial base for his western exploits.

Other aspects of the letter demonstrate Paul's apologetic purpose. He states that he is not ashamed of the gospel (Rom 1:16) and that some have slandered him (3:8). Indeed, his integrity must have been under attack for

2. A. Andrew Das, *Solving the Romans Debate* (Minneapolis: Fortress Press, 2007), 53–114.

3. J. D. G. Dunn, "Romans, Letter to the," in *Dictionary of Paul and His Letters*, ed. Gerald F. Hawthorne et al. (Downers Grove, IL: Intervarsity Press, 1993), 839–41.

he states, "I speak the truth in Christ, I do not lie; my conscience joins with the holy Spirit in bearing me witness" (9:1). Paul frequently uses diatribes, a mode of argumentation in which an imaginary opponent presents hypothetical objections and false conclusions (2:1–5, 17–29; 3:1–9; 3:27–4:25; 6:1–16; 9:19–21; 11:17–24; 14:4–10). This indicates that Paul felt a need to justify his understanding of the gospel and his role in its proclamation.

Finally, Paul may be writing to heal divisions within the Roman Christian community. Romans 14:1–15:6 addresses the disparity between the "strong" and "weak" concerning issues of food. Paul urges that the community live in harmony with one another, "May the God of endurance and encouragement grant you to think in harmony with one another, in keeping with Christ Jesus" (Rom 15:5). Similar language is found in 1 Corinthians where Paul is addressing the schisms among the believers (1 Cor 1:10). The social setting proposed by scholars includes several diverse Christian groups with no central organization. Paul's letter indicates at least five separate house churches (Rom 16:5, 10–11, 14–15). Among the various house communities, some may have held more closely to Jewish traditions than others. Paul exhorts his Roman readers to "welcome one another, then, as Christ welcomed you, for the glory of God" (15:7).

## Content

Questions arise whether the Letter to the Romans is a single letter penned by Paul or a combination of earlier letters edited together by a later hand. By the second century, Paul's Letter to the Romans seems to have circulated in three versions: a 14-chapter letter, a 15-chapter letter, and a 16-chapter letter. The doxology in Rom 16:25–27 served as an appropriate ending to the various versions. Since these verses are absent in one group of manuscripts and found in a variety of locations in another group, the doxology may not have been originally part of Paul's letter. Some scholars have argued that the whole of Rom 16 is a separate letter written to the church of Ephesus. By Paul's own admission, he had never visited Rome, so how would he have known

the twenty-six people to whom he sends greetings (16:3–15)? The original ending of the letter has implications for understanding the text. If the letter concludes with ch. 15, then Paul may not have had knowledge about the church in Rome. However, if ch. 16 is original to his letter, Paul may have gained knowledge about the Roman community from those he names. This outline assumes the integrity of the canonical letter.

Following the standard epistolary format, Paul's Letter to the Romans includes a prescript (1:1–7), thanksgiving (1:8–15), body of the letter (1:16–15:33), greetings (16:1–24), and closing (16:25–27). In Rom 1:1–7, Paul identifies himself and includes a lengthy definition of the gospel of God. He addresses his letter to the "beloved of God in Rome, called to be holy." Some manuscripts do not include "in Rome," in an effort to universalize the message by removing reference to a more specific audience. First Corinthians includes the address to those "called to be holy," but only in Romans does Paul call his readers "beloved of God." Within the thanksgiving (Rom 1:8–15), Paul acknowledges his longing to visit the Roman communities.

The body of the letter opens with the theme Paul will develop throughout. Paul is not ashamed of the gospel, for "it is the power of God for the salvation of everyone who believes: for Jew first, and then Greek. For in it is revealed the righteousness of God from faith to faith" (Rom 1:16–17). The key terms "salvation," "righteousness of God," and "faith" introduced here will be developed more fully throughout the letter. But first, Paul demonstrates the universal need for salvation by delineating the dire moral state of both Gentiles (1:18–32) and Jews (2:1–3:9).

Neither observance of the Law (Torah) nor human effort can make one just before God (Rom 3:20), Paul declares. The righteousness of God is found only in the saving act of Christ Jesus who served as an expiation for sins (3:25). The terms "just," "justify," and "righteousness" share the same Greek root: *dikaios*. God's justice/righteousness cannot be obtained by individual effort. Nonetheless, the Israelites were commanded to strive to be just, as God was just. The Law provided the parameters by which the faithful Israelite was to pursue righteousness. The Law makes one conscious of sin (3:20), but is insufficient to justify all of humanity since it excludes the Gentiles (3:29–30). Paul's discussion of the Law is rhetorical, designed to counter claims that adherence and study of the Torah alone granted one salvation. As he states, "Are we then annulling the law by this faith? Of course not! On the contrary, we are supporting the law" (3:31).

To further explain that justification is separate from the observance of the Law, Paul uses Abraham as a model of faithfulness in Rom 4:1–25. "Abraham believed God, and it was credited to him as righteousness" (4:3). Abraham stands as the father of both the uncircumcised who believe and the circumcised who believe, since his faith preceded his own circumcision. Reaching further back into biblical history, Paul demonstrates how the sin of Adam is overcome by the gift of Christ (5:15).

In ch. 6, Paul explains that through baptism the believer participates in the paschal mystery. Baptism into Christ Jesus is a baptism into his death, so as to be raised with him in resurrection (Rom 6:5). Therefore, the old self should be crucified with Christ so that one might no longer be enslaved to sin, but alive for God (6:11). The grace of God does not free the believer to now sin anew, however (6:1, 15). Once a slave to sin, the believer is now a servant of obedience (6:16).

Life in Christ frees one from the Law in order to live in the Spirit (Rom 7:1–6). The Law served to point out what was sinful, Paul writes, though the Law itself was not sinful (7:7–13). The follower of the Law is incapable of choosing the good (7:14–24). Knowing what is right and doing what is right are impossible without recourse to the Spirit (8:2). The ethical "impossibility" presented in 7:14–25 is then compared to the ethical "possibility" found in 8:1–13.[4] Borrowing from the Greek philosophical tradition, Paul describes the sinful condition of humanity as "flesh," while the "spirit" represents the new life in Christ. Those led by the spirit of God are children of God,

who received not a spirit of slavery but one of adoption (8:14–15). The Spirit itself testifies that the believers are heirs of God and joint heirs with Christ through suffering with him (8:16–17). Creation, too, awaits the full revelation of God (8:19–22). No power on earth or in heaven will be able to separate the faithful from the love of God in Christ Jesus (8:39).

But what of Israel? And how do the Gentiles fit within God's plan? In Rom 9–11, Paul addresses the perplexing questions of God's fidelity to the Jews and Israel's salvation. "For I could wish that I myself were accursed and separated from Christ for the sake of my brothers, my kin according to the flesh" (Rom 9:3). But not all of Israel is Israel (9:6). Paul redefines Israel as a theological entity, not simply a historical and ethnic one. Through Israel's history, God made choices (Isaac over Ishmael, 9:7–9; Jacob over Esau, 9:10–13). God shows mercy upon those whom God wills (9:18), but God will not abandon Israel (11:1). The Gentiles have benefited from the Jews' unbelief, but once the Gentiles have come to faith, Israel will be saved (11:25–26).

In the final section of the letter (Rom 12:1–15:13) Paul exhorts believers to be transformed so that they may know God's will. Paul engages the metaphor of the body and its many parts to encourage humility among the members (Rom 12:3–8). The body metaphor is also found in 1 Corinthians, where it serves as a symbol of unity (1 Cor 12:12–26). Romans 13 continues to describe how the believer is to live within the world. Verses 1–7 direct the community to be good citizens within the imperial realm and to respect civil authority— good advice for a minority community within the heart of the imperial world of Rome. Romans 14:1–15:13 concerns reconciliation and unity. Paul identifies weak members (Rom 14:1–2; 15:1) among the strong (Rom 15:1) and encourages a spirit of welcome and consideration.

Chapter 15 closes with Paul's travel plans (Rom 15:24–28). He hopes to find hospitality and financial support when he visits Rome and asks for the community's prayers for his successful trip to Jerusalem (15:30–33).

The letter closes with a recommendation for Phoebe, a minister (*diakonos*) at Cenchreae,

---

4. Brendan Byrne, *Romans* (Collegeville, MN: Liturgical Press, 1996), 224–47.

one of the ports of the city of Corinth (Rom 16:1–2). Likely Phoebe carried Paul's letter, which also served to introduce her to the community. Paul sends greetings to numerous members of the Roman churches, twenty-six of whom he names (16:3–15). Since Paul has not visited Rome, it is surprising that he knows so many individuals now residing there. In fact, he appears to have ministered with them, since he calls them co-workers, apostles, fellow prisoners, and "firstfruits." The list of Jewish and Gentile names, along with Paul's descriptions, provide valuable social information about the early church in Rome. In 16:21–23, he sends greetings from Timothy and Paul's relatives. The final doxology in 16:25–27 summarizes various Pauline themes found through the letter. ■

# THE LETTER TO THE ROMANS

## New American Bible, Introduction

Of all the letters of Paul, that to the Christians at Rome has long held pride of place. It is the longest and most systematic unfolding of the apostle's thought, expounding the gospel of God's righteousness that saves all who believe (Rom 1:16–17); it reflects a universal outlook, with special implications for Israel's relation to the church (Rom 9–11). Yet, like all Paul's letters, Romans too arose out of a specific situation, when the apostle wrote from Greece, likely Corinth, between A.D. 56 and 58 (cf. Acts 20:2–3).

Paul at that time was about to leave for Jerusalem with a collection of funds for the impoverished Jewish Christian believers there, taken up from his predominantly Gentile congregations (Rom 15:25–27). He planned then to travel on to Rome and to enlist support there for a mission to Spain (Rom 15:24, 28). Such a journey had long been on his mind (Rom 1:9–13; 15:23). Now, with much missionary preaching successfully accomplished in the East (Rom 15:19), he sought new opportunities in the West (Rom 15:20–21), in order to complete the divine plan of evangelization in the Roman world. Yet he recognized that the visit to Jerusalem would be hazardous (Rom 15:30–32), and we know from Acts that Paul was arrested there and came to Rome only in chains, as a prisoner (Acts 21–28, especially Acts 21:30–33 and Acts 28:14, 30–31).

The existence of a Christian community in Rome antedates Paul's letter there. When it arose, likely within the sizable Jewish population at Rome, and how, we do not know. The Roman historian Suetonius mentions an edict of the Emperor Claudius about A.D. 49 ordering the expulsion of Jews from Rome in connection with a certain "Chrestus," probably involving a dispute in the Jewish community over Jesus as the Messiah ("Christus"). According to Acts 18:2, Aquila and Priscilla (or Prisca, as in Rom 16:3) were among those driven out; from them, in Corinth, Paul may have learned about conditions in the church at Rome.

Opinions vary as to whether Jewish or Gentile Christians predominated in the house churches (cf. Rom 16:5) in the capital city of the empire at the time Paul wrote. Perhaps already by then Gentile Christians were in the majority. Paul speaks in Romans of both Jews and Gentiles (Rom 3:9, 29; see note on Rom 1:14). The letter also refers to those "weak in faith" (Rom 14:1) and those "who are strong" (Rom 15:1); this terminology may reflect not so much differences between believers of Jewish and of Gentile background, respectively, as an ascetic tendency in some converts (Rom 14:2) combined with Jewish laws about clean and unclean foods (Rom 14:14, 20). The issues were similar to problems that Paul had faced in Corinth (1 Cor 8). If Rom 16 is part of the letter to Rome (see note on Rom 16:1–23), then Paul had considerable information about conditions in Rome through all these people there whom he knew, and our letter does not just reflect a generalized picture of an earlier situation in Corinth.

In any case, Paul writes to introduce himself and his message to the Christians at Rome, seeking to enlist their support for the proposed mission to Spain. He therefore employs formulations likely familiar to the Christians at Rome; see note on the confessional material at Rom 1:3–4 and compare Rom 3:25–26; 4:25. He cites the Old Testament frequently (Rom 1:17; 3:10–18; 4; 9:7, 12–13, 15, 17, 25–29, 33; 10:5–13, 15–21; 15:9–12). The gospel Paul presents is meant to be a familiar one to those in Rome, even though they heard it first from other preachers.

As the outline below shows, this gospel of Paul (see Rom 16:25) finds its center in salvation and justification through faith in Christ (Rom 1:16–17). While God's wrath is revealed against all sin and wickedness of Gentile and Jew alike (Rom 1:18–3:20), God's power to save by divine righteous or justifying action in Christ is also revealed (Rom 1:16–17; 3:21–5:21). The consequences and implications for those who believe are set forth (Rom 6:1–8:39), as are results for those in Israel (Rom

9–11) who, to Paul's great sorrow (Rom 9:1–5), disbelieve. The apostle's hope is that, just as rejection of the gospel by some in Israel has led to a ministry of salvation for non-Jews, so one day, in God's mercy, "all Israel" will be saved (Rom 11:11–15, 25–29, 30–32). The fuller ethical response of believers is also drawn out, both with reference to life in Christ's body (Rom 12) and with regard to the world (Rom 13:1–7), on the basis of the eschatological situation (Rom 13:11–14) and conditions in the community (Rom 14:1–15:13).

Others have viewed Romans more in the light of Paul's earlier, quite polemical Letter to the Galatians and so see the theme as the relationship between Judaism and Christianity, a topic judged to be much in the minds of the Roman Christians. Each of these religious faiths claimed to be the way of salvation based upon a covenant between God and a people chosen and made the beneficiary of divine gifts. But Christianity regarded itself as the prophetic development and fulfillment of the faith of the Old Testament, declaring that the preparatory Mosaic covenant must now give way to the new and more perfect covenant in Jesus Christ. Paul himself had been the implacable advocate of freedom of Gentiles from the laws of the Mosaic covenant and, especially in Galatia, had refused to allow attempts to impose them on Gentile converts to the gospel. He had witnessed the personal hostilities that developed between the adherents of the two faiths and had written his strongly worded Letter to the Galatians against those Jewish Christians who were seeking to persuade Gentile Christians to adopt the religious practices of Judaism. For him, the purity of the religious understanding of Jesus as the source of salvation would be seriously impaired if Gentile Christians were obligated to amalgamate the two religious faiths.

Still others find the theme of Israel and the church as expressed in Rom 9–11 to be the heart of Romans. Then the implication of Paul's exposition of justification by faith rather than by means of law is that the divine plan of salvation works itself out on a broad theological plane to include the whole of humanity, despite the differences in the content of the given religious system to which a human culture is heir. Romans presents a plan of salvation stretching from Adam through Abraham and Moses to Christ (Rom 4; 5) and on to the future revelation at Christ's parousia (Rom 8:18–25). Its outlook is universal.

Paul's Letter to the Romans is a powerful exposition of the doctrine of the supremacy of Christ and of faith in Christ as the source of salvation. It is an implicit plea to the Christians at Rome, and to all Christians, to hold fast to that faith. They are to resist any pressure put on them to accept a doctrine of salvation through works of the law (see note on Rom 10:4). At the same time they are not to exaggerate Christian freedom as an abdication of responsibility for others (Rom 12:1–2) or as a repudiation of God's law and will (see notes on Rom 3:9–26; 3:31; 7:7–12, 13–25).

The principal divisions of the Letter to the Romans are the following:

I. Address (1:1–15)

II. Humanity Lost Without the Gospel (1:16–3:20)

III. Justification Through Faith in Christ (3:21–5:21)

IV. Justification and the Christian Life (6:1–8:39)

V. Jews and Gentiles in God's Plan (9:1–11:36)

VI. The Duties of Christians (12:1–15:13)

VII. Conclusion (15:14–16:27) ∎

# ROMANS

## I. ADDRESS

**Greeting.** † ¹ Paul, a slave of Christ Jesus, † called to be an apostle and set apart for the gospel of God, * ² which he promised previously through his prophets in the holy scriptures, * ³ † the gospel about his Son, descended from David according to the flesh, * ⁴ but established as Son of God in power according to the spirit of holiness through resurrection from the dead, Jesus Christ our Lord. * ⁵ † Through him we have received the grace of apostleship, to bring about the obedience of faith, for the sake of his name, among all the Gentiles, * ⁶ among whom are you also, who are called to belong to Jesus Christ; * ⁷ to all the beloved of God in Rome, called to be holy. †

Grace to you and peace from God our Father and the Lord Jesus Christ. *

**Thanksgiving.** ⁸ First, I give thanks † to my God through Jesus Christ for all of you, because your faith is heralded throughout the world. * ⁹ God is my witness, whom I serve with my spirit in proclaiming the gospel of his Son, that I remember you constantly, * ¹⁰ † always asking in my prayers that somehow by God's will I may at last find my way clear to come to you. * ¹¹ For I long to see you, that I may share with you some spiritual gift so that you may be strengthened, * ¹² that is, that you and I may be mutually encouraged by one another's faith, yours and mine. ¹³ I do not want you to be unaware, brothers, † that I often planned to come to you, though I was prevented until now, that I might harvest some fruit among you, too, as among the rest of the Gentiles. * ¹⁴ To Greeks † and non-Greeks alike, to the wise and the ignorant, I am under obligation; ¹⁵ that is why I

---

**1:1–7** In Paul's letters the greeting or *praescriptio* follows a standard form, though with variations. It is based upon the common Greco-Roman epistolary practice, but with the addition of Semitic and specifically Christian elements. The three basic components are: name of sender; name of addressee; greeting. In identifying himself, Paul often adds phrases to describe his apostolic mission; this element is more developed in Romans than in any other letter. Elsewhere he associates co-workers with himself in the greeting: Sosthenes (1 Corinthians), Timothy (2 Corinthians; Philippians; Philemon) Silvanus (1 Thessalonians–2 Thessalonians). The standard secular greeting was the infinitive *chairein*, "greetings." Paul uses instead the similar-sounding *charis*, "grace," together with the Semitic greeting *šālôm* (Greek *eirēnē*), "peace." These gifts, foreshadowed in God's dealings with Israel (see Nm 6:24–26), have been poured out abundantly in Christ, and Paul wishes them to his readers. In Romans the Pauline *praescriptio* is expanded and expressed in a formal tone; it emphasizes Paul's office as apostle to the Gentiles. Rom 1:3–4 stress the gospel or *kerygma*, Rom 1:2 the fulfillment of God's promise, and Rom 1:1, 5 Paul's office. On his call, see Gal 1:15–16; 1 Cor 9:1; 15:8–10; Acts 9:1–22; 22:3–16; 26:4–18.

**1:1** *Slave of Christ Jesus*: Paul applies the term slave to himself in order to express his undivided allegiance to the Lord of the church, the Master of all, including slaves and masters. "No one can serve (i.e., be a slave to) two masters," said Jesus (Mt 6:24). It is this aspect of the slave-master relationship rather than its degrading implications that Paul emphasizes when he discusses Christian commitment.

**1:3–4** Paul here cites an early confession that proclaims Jesus' sonship as messianic descendant of David (cf. Mt 22:42; 2 Tm 2:8; Rev 22:16) and as Son of God by the resurrection. As "life-giving spirit" (1 Cor 15:45), Jesus Christ is able to communicate the Spirit to those who believe in him.

**1:5** Paul recalls his apostolic office, implying that the Romans know something of his history. *The obedience of faith*: as Paul will show at length in chaps. 6–8 and 12–15, faith in God's justifying action in Jesus Christ relates one to God's gift of the new life that is made possible through the death and resurrection of Jesus Christ and the activity of the holy Spirit (see especially Rom 8:1–11).

**1:7** *Called to be holy*: Paul often refers to Christians as "the holy ones" or "the saints." The Israelite community was called

a "holy assembly" because they had been separated for the worship and service of the Lord (see Lv 11:44; 23:1–44). The Christian community regarded its members as sanctified by baptism (Rom 6:22; 15:16; 1 Cor 6:11; Eph 5:26–27). Christians are called to holiness (1 Cor 1:2; 1 Thes 4:7), that is, they are called to make their lives conform to the gift they have already received.

**1:8** In Greco-Roman letters, the greeting was customarily followed by a prayer. The Pauline letters usually include this element (except Galatians and 1 Timothy, 2 Timothy) expressed in Christian thanksgiving formulas and usually stating the principal theme of the letter. In 2 Corinthians the thanksgiving becomes a blessing, and in Ephesians it is preceded by a lengthy blessing. Sometimes the thanksgiving is blended into the body of the letter, especially in 1 Thessalonians. In Romans it is stated briefly.

**1:10–12** Paul lays the groundwork for his more detailed statement in Rom 15:22–24 about his projected visit to Rome.

**1:13** *Brothers* is idiomatic for all Paul's "kin in Christ," all those who believe in the gospel; it includes women as well as men (cf. Rom 4:3).

**1:14** *Greeks and non-Greeks*: literally, "Greeks and barbarians." As a result of Alexander's conquests, Greek became the standard international language of the Mediterranean world. *Greeks* in Paul's statement therefore means people who know Greek or who have been influenced by Greek culture. *Non-Greeks* were people whose cultures remained substantially unaffected by Greek influences. Greeks called such people "barbarians" (cf. Acts 28:2), meaning people whose speech was foreign. Roman citizens would scarcely classify themselves as such, and Nero, who was reigning when Paul wrote this letter,

---

**1:1** Gal 1:10; Phil 1:1; Jas 1:1 / Acts 9:15; 13:2; 1 Cor 1:1; Gal 1:15; Ti 1:1.

**1:2** 16:25–26; Ti 1:2.

**1:3** 9:5; 2 Sm 7:12; Mt 1:1; Mk 12:35; Jn 7:42; Acts 13:22–23; 2 Tm 2:8; Rev 22:16.

**1:4** 10:9; Acts 13:33; Phil 3:10.

**1:5** 15:15; Gal 2:7, 9 / 15:18; Acts 9:15; 26:16–18;

Gal 1:16; 2:7, 9.

**1:6** 1 Cor 1:9.

**1:7** Nm 6:25–26; 1 Cor 1:2–3; 2 Cor 1:1–2.

**1:8** 16:19; 1 Thes 1:8.

**1:9** 2 Cor 1:23; Eph 1:16; Phil 1:8; 1 Thes 1:2; 2:5, 10; 2 Tm 1:3.

**1:10** 15:23, 32; Acts 18:21; 1 Cor 4:19; 1 Thes 2:17.

**1:11** 1 Thes 2:17; 3:10.

**1:13** 15:22; Jn 15:16; Acts 19:21.

am eager to preach the gospel also to you in Rome.*

## II. HUMANITY LOST WITHOUT THE GOSPEL

**God's Power for Salvation.**† ¹⁶For I am not ashamed of the gospel. It is the power of God for the salvation of everyone who believes: for Jew first, and then Greek.* ¹⁷For in it is revealed the righteousness of God from faith to faith;† as it is written, "The one who is righteous by faith will live."*

**Punishment of Idolaters.** ¹⁸† The wrath† of God† is indeed being revealed from heaven against every impiety and wickedness* of those who suppress the truth by their wickedness. ¹⁹For what can be known about God is evident to them, because God made it evident to them.* ²⁰Ever since the creation of the world, his invisible attributes of eternal power and divinity have been able to be understood and perceived in what he has made.* As a result, they have no excuse; ²¹for although they knew God they did not accord him glory as God or give him thanks. Instead, they became

vain in their reasoning, and their senseless minds were darkened.* ²²While claiming to be wise,* they became fools ²³and exchanged the glory of the immortal God for the likeness of an image of mortal man or of birds or of four-legged animals or of snakes.*

²⁴Therefore, God handed them over to impurity through the lusts of their hearts† for the mutual degradation of their bodies.* ²⁵They exchanged the truth of God for a lie and revered and worshiped the creature rather than the creator, who is blessed forever. Amen.* ²⁶Therefore, God handed them over to degrading passions. Their females exchanged natural relations for unnatural, ²⁷and the males likewise gave up natural relations with females and burned with lust for one another. Males did shameful things with males and thus received in their own persons the due penalty for their perversity.* ²⁸And since they did not see fit to acknowledge God, God handed them over to their undiscerning mind to do what is improper. ²⁹*They are filled with every form of wickedness, evil, greed, and malice; full of envy, murder, rivalry, treachery, and spite. They are gossips ³⁰and scandalmongers and they hate

---

†
prided himself on his admiration for Greek culture. *Under obligation:* Paul will expand on the theme of obligation in Rom 13:8; 15:1, 27.
**1:16–17** The principal theme of the letter is salvation through faith. *I am not ashamed of the gospel:* Paul is not ashamed to proclaim the gospel, despite the criticism that Jews and Gentiles leveled against the proclamation of the crucified savior; cf. 1 Cor 1:23–24. Paul affirms, however, that it is precisely through the crucifixion and resurrection of Jesus that God's saving will and power become manifest. *Jew first* (cf. Rom 2:9–10) means that Jews especially, in view of the example of Abraham (Rom 4), ought to be the leaders in the response of faith.
**1:17** *In it is revealed the righteousness of God from faith to faith:* the gospel centers in Jesus Christ, in whom God's saving presence and righteousness in history have been made known. Faith is affirmation of the basic purpose and meaning of the Old Testament as proclamation of divine promise (Rom 1:2; 4:13) and exposure of the inability of humanity to effect its salvation even through covenant law. Faith is the gift of the holy Spirit and denotes acceptance of salvation as God's righteousness, that is, God's gift of a renewed relationship in forgiveness and power for a new life. Faith is response to God's total claim on people and their destiny. *The one who is righteous by faith will live:* see note on Heb 2:4.
**1:18–3:20** Paul aims to show that all humanity is in a desperate plight and requires God's special intervention if it is to be saved.
**1:18–32** In this passage Paul uses themes and rhetoric common in Jewish-Hellenistic mission proclamation (cf. Wis 13:1–14:31) to indict especially the non-Jewish world. The close association of idolatry and immorality is basic, but the generalization needs in all fairness to be balanced against the fact that non-Jewish Christian society on many levels displayed moral attitudes and performance whose quality would challenge much of contemporary Christian culture. Romans themselves expressed abhorrence over devotion accorded to animals in Egypt. Paul's

main point is that the wrath of God does not await the end of the world but goes into action at each present moment in humanity's history when misdirected piety serves as a facade for self-interest.
**1:18** *The wrath of God:* God's reaction to human sinfulness, an Old Testament phrase that expresses the irreconcilable opposition between God and evil (see Is 9:11, 16, 18, 20; 10:4; 30:27). It is not contrary to God's universal love for his creatures, but condemns Israel's turning aside from the covenant obligations. Hosea depicts Yahweh as suffering intensely at the thought of having to punish Israel (Hos 11:8–9). God's wrath was to be poured forth especially on the "Day of Yahweh" and thus took on an eschatological connotation (see Zep 1:15).
**1:24** In order to expose the depth of humanity's rebellion against the Creator, *God handed them over to impurity through the lusts of their hearts.* Instead of curbing people's evil interests, God abandoned them to self-indulgence, thereby removing the facade of apparent conformity to the divine will. Subsequently Paul will show that the Mosaic law produces the same effect; cf. Rom 5:20; 7:13–24. The divine judgment expressed here is related to the theme of hardness of heart described in Rom 9:17–18.

---

**1:15** Acts 28:30–31.
**1:16** Ps 119:46; 1 Cor 1:18, 24 / Rom 2:9; Acts 3:26; 13:46.
**1:17** 3:21–22; Heb 2:4; Gal 3:11; Heb 10:38.
**1:18** 2:5, 8–9; Is 66:15; Eph 5:6; Col 3:6.
**1:19–32** Wis 13–19; Acts 14:15–17; 17:23–29.
**1:20** Jb 12:7–9; Ps 8:4; 19:2; Sir 17:7–9; Is 40:26; Acts 14:17; 17:25–28.
**1:21** Eph 4:17–18.
**1:22** Wis 13:1–9; Is 5:21;

Jer 10:14; Acts 17:29–30; 1 Cor 1:19–21.
**1:23** Dt 4:15–19; Ps 106:20; Wis 11:15; 12:24; 13:10–19; Jer 2:11.
**1:24** Wis 12:25; 14:22–31; Acts 7:41–42; Eph 4:19.
**1:25** 9:5; Jer 13:25–27.
**1:27** Lv 18:22; 20:13; Wis 14:26; 1 Cor 6:9; 1 Tm 1:10.
**1:29–31** 13:13; Mt 15:19; Mk 7:21–22; Gal 5:19–21; 2 Tm 3:2–4.

God. They are insolent, haughty, boastful, ingenious in their wickedness, and rebellious toward their parents. [31] They are senseless, faithless, heartless, ruthless. [32] Although they know the just decree of God that all who practice such things deserve death, they not only do them but give approval to those who practice them.*

**God's Just Judgment.** [1]† Therefore, you are without excuse,* every one of you who passes judgment.† For by the standard by which you judge another you condemn yourself, since you, the judge, do the very same things. [2] We know that the judgment of God on those who do such things is true. [3] Do you suppose, then, you who judge those who engage in such things and yet do them yourself, that you will escape the judgment of God?* [4] Or do you hold his priceless kindness, forbearance, and patience in low esteem, unaware that the kindness of God would lead you to repentance?* [5] By your stubbornness and impenitent heart,* you are storing up wrath for yourself for the day of wrath and revelation of the just judgment of God, [6]* who will repay everyone according to his works:† [7] eternal life to those who seek glory, honor, and immortality through perseverance in good works, [8] but wrath and fury to those who selfishly disobey the truth and obey wickedness.* [9] Yes, affliction and distress will come upon every human being who does evil, Jew first and then Greek. [10]* But there will be glory, honor, and peace for everyone who does good, Jew first and then Greek. [11]†* There is no partiality with God.

**Judgment by the Interior Law.**† [12] All who sin outside the law will also perish without reference to it, and all who sin under the law will be judged in accordance with it.* [13] For it is not those who hear the law who are just in the sight of God; rather, those who observe the law will be justified.* [14] For when the Gentiles who do not have the law by nature observe the prescriptions of the law, they are a law for themselves even though they do not have the law.* [15] They show that the demands of the law are written in their hearts,† while their conscience also bears witness and their conflicting thoughts accuse or even defend them [16] on the day when, according to my gospel, God will judge people's hidden works through Christ Jesus.*

**Judgment by the Mosaic Law.**† [17] Now if you call yourself a Jew and rely on the law and boast of God* [18] and know his will and are able to discern what is important since you are instructed from the law,* [19] and if you are confident that you are a guide for the blind and a light for those in darkness,* [20] that you are a trainer of the foolish and teacher of the simple,* because in the law you have the formulation of knowledge and truth— [21] then you who teach another, are you failing to teach yourself? You who preach against stealing, do you steal?* [22] You who forbid adultery, do you commit adultery? You who detest idols, do

---

† **2:1–3:20** After his general indictment of the Gentile, Paul shows that in spite of special revelation Jews enjoy no advantage in moral status before God (Rom 3:1–8). With the entire human race now declared guilty before God (Rom 3:9–20), Paul will then be able to display the solution for the total problem: salvation through God's redemptive work that is revealed in Christ Jesus for all who believe (Rom 3:21–31).

**2:1–11** As a first step in his demonstration that Jews enjoy no real moral supremacy over Gentiles, Paul explains that the final judgment will be a review of performance, not of privilege. From this perspective Gentiles stand on an equal footing with Jews, and Jews cannot condemn the sins of Gentiles without condemning themselves.

**2:6** *Will repay everyone according to his works*: Paul reproduces the Septuagint text of Ps 62:12 and Prv 24:12.

**2:11** *No partiality with God*: this sentence is not at variance with the statements in Rom 2:9–10. Since Jews are the first to go under indictment, it is only fair that they be given first consideration in the distribution of blessings. Basic, of course, is the understanding that God accepts no bribes (Dt 10:17).

**2:12–16** Jews cannot reasonably demand from Gentiles the standard of conduct inculcated in the Old Testament since God did not address its revelation to them. Rather, God made it possible for Gentiles to know instinctively the difference between right and wrong. But, as Paul explained in Rom 1:18–32,

humanity misread the evidence of God's existence, power, and divinity, and "while claiming to be wise, they became fools" (Rom 1:22).

**2:15** Paul expands on the thought of Jer 31:33; Wis 17:11.

**2:17–29** Mere possession of laws is no evidence of virtue. By eliminating circumcision as an elitist moral sign, Paul clears away the last obstacle to his presentation of justification through faith without claims based on the receipt of circumcision and its attendant legal obligations.

---

**1:32** Acts 8:1; 2 Thes 2:12.
**2:1** Mt 7:1–2.
**2:3** Wis 16:15–16.
**2:4** 3:25–26; 9:22; Wis 11:23; 15:1; 2 Pt 3:9, 15.
**2:5** Ex 33:3; Acts 7:51; Rev 6:17; 11:18.
**2:6** Ps 62:12; Prv 24:12; Sir 16:14; Mt 16:27; Jn 5:29; 2 Cor 5:10.
**2:8** 2 Thes 1:8.
**2:10** 1:16; 3:9.
**2:11** Dt 10:17; 2 Chr 19:7; Sir 35:12–13; Acts 10:34; Gal 2:6;

Eph 6:9; Col 3:25; 1 Pt 1:17.
**2:12** 3:19.
**2:13** Mt 7:21; Lk 6:46–49; 8:21; Jas 1:22–25; 1 Jn 3:7.
**2:14** Acts 10:35.
**2:16** Acts 10:42; 17:31.
**2:17** Is 48:1–2; Mi 3:11; Phil 3:4–6.
**2:18** Phil 1:10.
**2:19** Mt 15:14; Lk 6:39.
**2:20** 2 Tm 3:15.
**2:21** Ps 50:16–21; Mt 23:3–4.

ROM

you rob temples? <sup>23</sup> You who boast of the law, do you dishonor God by breaking the law? <sup>24</sup> * For, as it is written, "Because of you the name of God is reviled among the Gentiles." † <sup>25</sup> * Circumcision, to be sure, has value if you observe the law; but if you break the law, your circumcision has become uncircumcision. * <sup>26</sup> Again, if an uncircumcised man keeps the precepts of the law, will he not be considered circumcised? * <sup>27</sup> Indeed, those who are physically uncircumcised but carry out the law will pass judgment on you, with your written law and circumcision, who break the law. <sup>28</sup> One is not a Jew outwardly. True circumcision is not outward, in the flesh. * <sup>29</sup> Rather, one is a Jew inwardly, and circumcision is of the heart, in the spirit, not the letter; his praise is not from human beings but from God. *

**3** **Answers to Objections.** <sup>1</sup> † What advantage is there then in being a Jew? Or what is the value of circumcision? <sup>2</sup> Much, in every respect. [For] in the first place, they were entrusted with the utterances of God. * <sup>3</sup> What if some were unfaithful? Will their infidelity nullify the fidelity of God? * <sup>4</sup> Of course not! God must be true, though every human being is a liar, † as it is written:

"That you may be justified in your
     words,
and conquer when you are judged." *

<sup>5</sup> But if our wickedness provides proof of God's righteousness, what can we say? Is God unjust, humanly speaking, to inflict his wrath? * <sup>6</sup> Of course not! For how else is God to judge the world? <sup>7</sup> But if God's truth redounds to his glory through my falsehood, why am I still being condemned as a sinner? <sup>8</sup> And why not say—as we are accused and as some claim we say—that we should do evil that good may come of it? Their penalty is what they deserve. *

**Universal Bondage to Sin.** † <sup>9</sup> Well, then, are we better off? Not entirely, for we have already brought the charge against Jews and Greeks alike that they are all under the domination of sin, * <sup>10</sup> as it is written: *

"There is no one just, not one,
<sup>11</sup>   there is no one who understands,
    there is no one who seeks God.
<sup>12</sup>   All have gone astray; all alike are
      worthless;
   there is not one who does good,
    [there is not] even one.
<sup>13</sup>   Their throats are open graves;
   they deceive with their tongues;
  the venom of asps is on their lips; *
<sup>14</sup>    their mouths are full of bitter cursing. *
<sup>15</sup>   Their feet are quick to shed blood; *
<sup>16</sup>   ruin and misery are in their ways,
<sup>17</sup>   and the way of peace they know not.
<sup>18</sup>   There is no fear of God before their
      eyes." *

<sup>19</sup> Now we know that what the law † says is addressed to those under the law, so that every mouth may be silenced and the whole world stand accountable to God, * <sup>20</sup> since no human being will be justified in his sight † by observing the law; for through the law comes consciousness of sin. *

---

† **2:24** According to Is 52:5 the suffering of Israel prompts her enemies to revile God. Paul uses the passage in support of his point that the present immorality of Israelites is the cause of such defamation.

**3:1–4** In keeping with the popular style of diatribe, Paul responds to the objection that his teaching on the sinfulness of all humanity detracts from the religious prerogatives of Israel. He stresses that Jews have remained the vehicle of God's revelation despite their sins, though this depends on the fidelity of God.

**3:4** *Though every human being is a liar:* these words reproduce the Greek text of Ps 116:11. The rest of the verse is from Ps 51:6.

**3:9–20** *Well, then, are we better off?:* this phrase can also be translated "Are we at a disadvantage?" but the latter version does not substantially change the overall meaning of the passage. Having explained that Israel's privileged status is guaranteed by God's fidelity, Paul now demonstrates the infidelity of the Jews by a catena of citations from scripture, possibly derived from an existing collection of *testimonia.* These texts show that all human beings share the common burden of sin. They are linked together by mention of organs of the body: throat, tongue, lips, mouth, feet, eyes.

**3:19** *The law:* Paul here uses the term in its broadest sense to mean all of the scriptures; none of the preceding texts is from the Torah or Pentateuch.

**3:20** *No human being will be justified in his sight:* these words are freely cited from Ps 143:2. In place of the psalmist's "no living person," Paul substitutes "no human being" (literally "no flesh," a Hebraism), and he adds "by observing the law."

**2:24** Is 52:5; Ez 36:20; 2 Pt 2:2.
**2:25–29** Jer 4:4; 9:24–25.
**2:25** 1 Cor 7:19; Gal 5:3.
**2:26** Gal 5:6.
**2:28** Jn 7:24; 8:15, 39.
**2:29** Dt 30:6; Jer 4:4; 9:25; Col 2:11 / 1 Cor 4:5; 2 Cor 10:18.
**3:2** 9:4; Dt 4:7–8; Ps 103:7; 147:19–20.
**3:3** 9:6; 11:1, 29; Ps 89:30–37; 2 Tm 2:13.
**3:4** Ps 116:11 / Ps 51:6.
**3:5** 9:14; Jb 34:12–17.
**3:8** 6:1.
**3:9** 1:18–2:25; 3:23; Sir 8:5.
**3:10–11** Ps 14:1–3; 53:2–4; Eccl 7:20.
**3:13** Ps 5:10; 140:4.
**3:14** Ps 10:7.
**3:15–17** Prv 1:16; Is 59:7–8.
**3:18** Ps 36:2.
**3:19** 7:7.
**3:20** Ps 143:2; Gal 2:16 / 7:7.

## III. JUSTIFICATION THROUGH FAITH IN CHRIST

**Justification Apart from the Law.**† ²¹But now† the righteousness of God has been manifested apart from the law, though testified to by the law and the prophets, * ²²the righteousness of God through faith in Jesus Christ for all who believe. For there is no distinction; * ²³all have sinned and are deprived of the glory of God. * ²⁴They are justified freely by his grace through the redemption in Christ Jesus, * ²⁵whom God set forth as an expiation,† through faith, by his blood, to prove his righteousness because of the forgiveness of sins previously committed, * ²⁶through the forbearance of God—to prove his righteousness in the present time, that he might be righteous and justify the one who has faith in Jesus.

²⁷*What occasion is there then for boasting?† It is ruled out. On what principle, that of works? No, rather on the principle of faith.† ²⁸For we consider that a person is justified by faith apart from works of the law. * ²⁹Does God belong to Jews alone? Does he not belong to Gentiles, too? Yes, also to Gentiles, * ³⁰for God is one and will justify the circumcised on the basis of faith and the uncircumcised through faith. * ³¹Are we then annulling the law by this faith? Of course not! * On the contrary, we are supporting the law.†

**4** †**Abraham Justified by Faith.** ¹What then can we say that Abraham found, our ancestor according to the flesh? * ²†Indeed, if Abraham was justified on the basis of his works, he has reason to boast; but this was not so in the sight of God. ³*For what does the scripture say? "Abraham believed God, and it was credited to him as righteousness."† ⁴A worker's wage is credited not as a gift, but as something due. * ⁵But when one does not work, yet believes in the one who justifies the ungodly, his faith is credited as righteousness. ⁶So also David declares the blessedness of the person to whom God credits righteousness apart from works:

⁷    "Blessed are they whose iniquities are forgiven *
     and whose sins are covered.

---

† **3:21–31** These verses provide a clear statement of Paul's "gospel," i.e., the principle of justification by faith in Christ. God has found a means of rescuing humanity from its desperate plight: Paul's general term for this divine initiative is the righteousness of God (Rom 3:21). Divine mercy declares the guilty innocent and makes them so. God does this not as a result of the law but apart from it (Rom 3:21), and not because of any merit in human beings but through forgiveness of their sins (Rom 3:24), in virtue of the redemption wrought in Christ Jesus for all who believe (Rom 3:22, 24–25). God has manifested his righteousness in the coming of Jesus Christ, whose saving activity inaugurates a new era in human history.

**3:21** *But now*: Paul adopts a common phrase used by Greek authors to describe movement from disaster to prosperity. The expressions indicate that Rom 3:21–26 are the consolatory answer to Rom 3:9–20.

**3:25** *Expiation*: this rendering is preferable to "propitiation," which suggests hostility on the part of God toward sinners. As Paul will be at pains to point out (Rom 5:8–10), it is humanity that is hostile to God.

**3:27–31** People cannot boast of their own holiness, since it is God's free gift (Rom 3:27), both to the Jew who practices circumcision out of faith and to the Gentile who accepts faith without the Old Testament religious culture symbolized by circumcision (Rom 3:29–30).

**3:27** *Principle of faith*: literally, "law of faith." Paul is fond of wordplay involving the term "law"; cf. Rom 7:21, 23; 8:2. Since "law" in Greek may also connote "custom" or "principle," his readers and hearers would have sensed no contradiction in the use of the term after the negative statement concerning law in Rom 3:20.

**3:31** *We are supporting the law*: giving priority to God's intentions. God is the ultimate source of law, and the essence of law is fairness. On the basis of the Mosaic covenant, God's justice is in question if those who sinned against the law are permitted to go free (see Rom 3:23–26). In order to rescue all humanity rather than condemn it, God thinks of an alternative: the law or

"principle" of faith (Rom 3:27). What can be more fair than to admit everyone into the divine presence on the basis of forgiveness grasped by faith? Indeed, this principle of faith antedates the Mosaic law, as Paul will demonstrate in Rom 4, and does not therefore mark a change in divine policy.

**4:1–25** This is an expanded treatment of the significance of Abraham's faith, which Paul discusses in Gal 3:6–18; see notes there.

**4:2–5** Rom 4:2 corresponds to Rom 4:4, and Rom 4:3–5. The Greek term here rendered *credited* means "made an entry." The context determines whether it is credit or debit. Rom 4:8 speaks of "recording sin" as a debit. Paul's repeated use of accountants' terminology in this and other passages can be traced both to the Old Testament texts he quotes and to his business activity as a tentmaker. The commercial term in Gn 15:6, "credited it to him," reminds Paul in Rom 4:7–8 of Ps 32:2, in which the same term is used and applied to forgiveness of sins. Thus Paul is able to argue that Abraham's faith involved receipt of forgiveness of sins and that all believers benefit as he did through faith.

**4:3** Jas 2:24 appears to conflict with Paul's statement. However, James combats the error of extremists who used the doctrine of justification through faith as a screen for moral self-determination. Paul discusses the subject of holiness in greater detail than does James and beginning with Rom 6 shows how justification through faith introduces one to the gift of a new life in Christ through the power of the holy Spirit.

---

**3:21** Is 51:6–8; Acts 10:43.
**3:22** 1:17; Gal 2:16; Phil 3:9.
**3:23** 3:9; 5:12.
**3:24** Eph 2:8; Ti 3:7 / Rom 5:1–2; Eph 1:7.
**3:25** Lv 16:12–15; Acts 17:31; 1 Jn 4:10.
**3:27** 8:2; 1 Cor 1:29–31.
**3:28** 5:1; Gal 2:16.
**3:29** 10:12.
**3:30** Dt 6:4; Gal 3:20; Jas 2:19 / Rom 4:11–12.
**3:31** 8:4; Mt 5:17.
**4:1** Gal 3:6–9.
**4:3** Gn 15:6; Gal 3:6; Jas 2:14, 20–24.
**4:4** 11:6.
**4:7–8** Ps 32:1–2.

ROM

8　　Blessed is the man whose sin the Lord does not record."

9 Does this blessedness† apply only to the circumcised, or to the uncircumcised as well? Now we assert that "faith was credited to Abraham as righteousness."* 10 Under what circumstances was it credited? Was he circumcised or not? He was not circumcised, but uncircumcised. 11 And he received the sign of circumcision as a seal on the righteousness received through faith while he was uncircumcised. Thus he was to be the father of all the uncircumcised who believe, so that to them [also] righteousness might be credited,* 12 as well as the father of the circumcised who not only are circumcised but also follow the path of faith that our father Abraham walked while still uncircumcised.

**Inheritance Through Faith.** 13 It was not through the law that the promise was made to Abraham and his descendants that he would inherit the world, but through the righteousness that comes from faith.* 14 For if those who adhere to the law are the heirs, faith is null and the promise is void.* 15 For the law produces wrath;* but where there is no law, neither is there violation.† 16 For this reason, it depends on faith, so that it may be a gift, and the promise may be guaranteed to all his descendants, not to those who only adhere to the law but to those who follow the faith of Abraham, who is the father of all of us,* 17 as it is written, "I have made you father of many nations." He is our father in the sight of God, in whom he believed, who gives life to the dead and calls into being what does not exist.* 18 He believed, hoping against hope,* that he would become "the father of many nations," according to what was said, "Thus shall your descendants be." 19* He did not weaken in faith when he considered his own body as [already] dead (for he was almost a hundred years old) and the dead womb of Sarah. 20 He did not doubt God's promise in unbelief;† rather, he was empowered by faith and gave glory to God 21 and was fully convinced that what he had promised he was also able to do.* 22 That is why "it was credited to him as righteousness."* 23 But it was not for him alone that it was written that "it was credited to him"; 24 it was also for us, to whom it will be credited, who believe in the one who raised Jesus our Lord from the dead,* 25 who was handed over for our transgressions and was raised for our justification.*

5 **Faith, Hope, and Love.**† 1 Therefore, since we have been justified by faith, we have peace† with God through our Lord Jesus Christ,* 2 through whom we have gained access [by faith] to this grace in which we stand, and we boast in hope of the glory of God.* 3 Not only that, but we even boast of our afflictions, knowing that affliction produces endurance, 4 and endurance, proven character, and proven character, hope,* 5 and hope does not disappoint, because the love of God has been poured out into our hearts through the holy Spirit that has been given to us.* 6 For Christ, while we were still helpless, yet died at the

---

† 4:9 *Blessedness*: evidence of divine favor.

4:15 Law has the negative function of bringing the deepseated rebellion against God to the surface in specific sins; see note on Rom 1:18–32.

4:20 *He did not doubt God's promise in unbelief*: any doubts Abraham might have had were resolved in commitment to God's promise. Heb 11:8–12 emphasizes the faith of Abraham and Sarah.

5:1–11 Popular piety frequently construed reverses and troubles as punishment for sin; cf. Jn 9:2. Paul therefore assures believers that God's justifying action in Jesus Christ is a declaration of peace. The crucifixion of Jesus Christ displays God's initiative in certifying humanity for unimpeded access into the divine presence. Reconciliation is God's gift of pardon to the entire human race. Through faith one benefits personally from this pardon or, in Paul's term, is justified. The ultimate aim of God is to liberate believers from the pre-Christian self as described in Rom 1–3. Since this liberation will first find completion in the believer's resurrection, salvation is described as future in Rom 5:10. Because this fullness of salvation belongs to the future it is called the Christian hope. Paul's Greek term for hope does not, however, suggest a note of uncertainty, to the effect: "I wonder whether God really means it." Rather, God's promise in the gospel fills believers with expectation and anticipation for the climactic gift of unalloyed commitment in the holy Spirit to the performance of the will of God. The persecutions that attend Christian commitment are to teach believers patience and to strengthen this hope, which will not disappoint them because the holy Spirit dwells in their hearts and imbues them with God's love (Rom 5:5).

5:1 *We have peace*: a number of manuscripts, versions, and church Fathers read "Let us have peace"; cf. Rom 14:19.

---

| | |
|---|---|
| 4:9 4:3. | 4:21 Gn 18:14; Lk 1:37. |
| 4:11 Gn 17:10–11; Gal 3:6–8. | 4:22 Gn 15:6. |
| | 4:24 10:9; 1 Pt 1:21. |
| 4:13 Gn 12:7; 18:18; 22:17–18; Sir 44:21; Gal 3:16–18, 29. | 4:25 Is 53:4–5, 12; 1 Cor 15:17; 1 Pt 1:3 / Rom 8:11. |
| 4:14 Gn 3:18. | 5:1 3:24–28; Gal 2:16. |
| 4:15 3:20; 5:13; 7:8; Gal 3:19. | 5:2 Eph 2:18; 3:12. |
| 4:16 Sir 44:19; Gal 3:7–9. | 5:4 2 Cor 12:9–10; Jas 1:2–4; 1 Pt 1:5–7; 4:12–14. |
| 4:17 Gn 17:5; Heb 11:19 / Is 48:13. | 5:5 8:14–16; Ps 22:5–6; 25:20. |
| 4:18 Gn 15:5. | |
| 4:19–20 Gn 17:17; Heb 11:11. | |

appointed time for the ungodly. [7] Indeed, only with difficulty does one die for a just person, though perhaps for a good person one might even find courage to die.† [8] But God proves his love for us in that while we were still sinners Christ died for us.* [9] How much more then, since we are now justified by his blood, will we be saved through him from the wrath.* [10] Indeed, if, while we were enemies, we were reconciled to God through the death of his Son, how much more, once reconciled, will we be saved by his life.* [11] Not only that, but we also boast of God through our Lord Jesus Christ, through whom we have now received reconciliation.

**Humanity's Sin Through Adam.** [12]† Therefore, just as through one person sin entered the world,* and through sin, death, and thus death came to all, inasmuch as all sinned†— [13] for up to the time of the law, sin was in the world, though sin is not accounted when there is no law.* [14] But death reigned from Adam to Moses, even over those who did not sin after the pattern of the trespass of Adam, who is the type of the one who was to come.*

**Grace and Life Through Christ.** [15] But the gift is not like the transgression. For if by that one person's transgression the many died, how much more did the grace of God and the gracious gift of the one person Jesus Christ overflow for the many. [16] And the gift is not like the result of the one person's sinning. For after

one sin there was the judgment that brought condemnation; but the gift, after many transgressions, brought acquittal. [17] For if, by the transgression of one person, death came to reign through that one, how much more will those who receive the abundance of grace and of the gift of justification come to reign in life through the one person Jesus Christ. [18] In conclusion, just as through one transgression condemnation came upon all, so through one righteous act acquittal and life came to all.* [19] For just as through the disobedience of one person the many were made sinners, so through the obedience of one the many will be made righteous.* [20] The law entered in† so that transgression might increase but, where sin increased, grace overflowed all the more,* [21] so that, as sin reigned in death, grace also might reign through justification for eternal life through Jesus Christ our Lord.*

## IV. JUSTIFICATION AND THE CHRISTIAN LIFE

**6** **Freedom from Sin; Life in God.** [1]† What then shall we say? Shall we persist in sin that grace may abound? Of course not!* [2] How can we who died to sin yet live in it?* [3] Or are you unaware that we who were baptized into Christ Jesus were baptized into his death?* [4] We were indeed buried with him through baptism into death, so that, just as Christ was raised from the dead by the glory of the Father, we too might live in newness of life.*

---

† **5:7** In the world of Paul's time the *good person* is especially one who is magnanimous to others.

**5:12–21** Paul reflects on the sin of Adam (Gn 3:1–13) in the light of the redemptive mystery of Christ. Sin, as used in the singular by Paul, refers to the dreadful power that has gripped humanity, which is now in revolt against the Creator and engaged in the exaltation of its own desires and interests. But no one has a right to say, "Adam made me do it," for all are culpable (Rom 5:12): Gentiles under the demands of the law written in their hearts (Rom 2:14–15), and Jews under the Mosaic covenant. Through the Old Testament law, the sinfulness of humanity that was operative from the beginning (Rom 5:13) found further stimulation, with the result that sins were generated in even greater abundance. According to Rom 5:15–21, God's act in Christ is in total contrast to the disastrous effects of the virus of sin that invaded humanity through Adam's crime.

**5:12** *Inasmuch as all sinned*: others translate "because all sinned," and understand Rom 5:13 as a parenthetical remark. Unlike Wis 2:24, Paul does not ascribe the entry of death to the devil.

**5:20** *The law entered in*: sin had made its entrance (Rom 5:12); now the law comes in alongside sin. See notes on Rom 1:18–32; 5:12–21. *Where sin increased, grace overflowed all the more*: Paul declares that grace outmatches the productivity of sin.

**6:1–11** To defend the gospel against the charge that it pro-

motes moral laxity (cf. Rom 3:5–8), Paul expresses himself in the typical style of spirited diatribe. God's display of generosity or grace is not evoked by sin but, as stated in Rom 5:8 is the expression of God's love, and this love pledges eternal life to all believers (Rom 5:21). Paul views the present conduct of the believers from the perspective of God's completed salvation when the body is resurrected and directed totally by the holy Spirit. Through baptism believers share the death of Christ and thereby escape from the grip of sin. Through the resurrection of Christ the power to live anew becomes reality for them, but the fullness of participation in Christ's resurrection still lies in the future. But life that is lived in dedication to God now is part and parcel of that future. Hence anyone who sincerely claims to be interested in that future will scarcely be able to say, "Let us sin so that grace may prosper" (cf. Rom 6:1).

---

**5:8** Jn 3:16; 1 Jn 4:10, 19.
**5:9** 1:18; 1 Thes 1:10.
**5:10** 8:7–8; 2 Cor 5:18; Col 1:21–22.
**5:12** Gn 2:17; 3:1–19; Wis 2:24 / Rom 3:19, 23.
**5:13** 4:15.
**5:14** 1 Cor 15:21.
**5:18** 1 Cor 15:21–22.
**5:19** Is 53:11; Phil 2:8–9.
**5:20** 4:15; 7:7–8; Gal 3:19.
**5:21** 6:23.
**6:1** 3:5–8.
**6:2** 1 Pt 4:1.
**6:3** Gal 3:27.
**6:4** Col 2:12; 1 Pt 3:21–22.

⁵ For if we have grown into union with him through a death like his, we shall also be united with him in the resurrection.* ⁶ We know that our old self was crucified with him, so that our sinful body might be done away with, that we might no longer be in slavery to sin.* ⁷ For a dead person has been absolved from sin. ⁸ If, then, we have died with Christ, we believe that we shall also live with him.* ⁹ We know that Christ, raised from the dead, dies no more; death no longer has power over him.* ¹⁰ As to his death, he died to sin once and for all; as to his life, he lives for God.* ¹¹ Consequently, you too must think of yourselves as [being] dead to sin and living for God in Christ Jesus.*

¹²† Therefore, sin must not reign over your mortal bodies so that you obey their desires.* ¹³ And do not present the parts of your bodies to sin as weapons for wickedness, but present yourselves to God as raised from the dead to life and the parts of your bodies to God as weapons for righteousness.* ¹⁴ For sin is not to have any power over you, since you are not under the law but under grace.*

¹⁵ What then? Shall we sin because we are not under the law but under grace? Of course not!* ¹⁶ Do you not know that if you present yourselves to someone as obedient slaves,* you are slaves of the one you obey, either of sin, which leads to death, or of obedience, which leads to righteousness?* ¹⁷ But thanks be to God that, although you were once slaves of sin, you have become obedient from the heart to the pattern of teaching to which you were entrusted.† ¹⁸ Freed from sin, you have become slaves of righteousness. ¹⁹ I am speaking in human terms because of the weakness of your nature. For just as you presented the parts of your bodies as slaves to impurity and to lawlessness for lawlessness, so now present them as slaves to righteousness for sanctification. ²⁰* For when you were slaves of sin, you were free from righteousness.† ²¹ But what profit did you get then from the things of which you are now ashamed? For the end of those things is death.* ²² But now that you have been freed from sin and have become slaves of God, the benefit that you have leads to sanctification,† and its end is eternal life.* ²³ For the wages of sin is death, but the gift of God is eternal life in Christ Jesus our Lord.*

## 7 Freedom from the Law.†

¹ Are you unaware, brothers (for I am speaking to people who know the law), that the law has jurisdiction over one as long as one lives? ² Thus a married woman is bound by law to her living husband; but if her husband dies, she is released from the law in respect to her husband.* ³ Consequently, while her husband is alive she will be called an adulteress if she consorts with another man. But if her husband dies she is free from that law, and she is not an adulteress if she consorts with another man.

⁴ In the same way, my brothers, you also were put to death to the law through the body of Christ, so that you might belong to another, to the one who was raised from the dead in order that we might bear fruit for God. ⁵ For when we were in the flesh, our sinful passions, awakened by the law, worked in our members to bear fruit for death.* ⁶ But now we are released from the law, dead to what held us captive, so that we may serve in the newness of the spirit and not under the obsolete letter.*

---

**6:12–19** Christians have been released from the grip of sin, but sin endeavors to reclaim its victims. The antidote is constant remembrance that divine grace has claimed them and identifies them as people who are alive only for God's interests.

**6:17** In contrast to humanity, which was handed over to self-indulgence (Rom 1:24–32), believers are *entrusted* ("handed over") to God's *pattern of teaching*, that is, the new life God aims to develop in Christians through the productivity of the holy Spirit. Throughout this passage Paul uses the slave-master model in order to emphasize the fact that one cannot give allegiance to both God and sin.

**6:20** *You were free from righteousness*: expressed ironically, for such freedom is really tyranny. The commercial metaphors in Rom 6:21–23 add up only one way: sin is a bad bargain.

**6:22** *Sanctification*: or holiness.

**7:1–6** Paul reflects on the fact that Christians have a different understanding of the law because of their faith in Christ. Law binds the living, not the dead, as exemplified in marriage, which binds in life but is dissolved through death. Similarly, Christians who through baptism have died with Christ to sin

(cf. Rom 6:2–4) are freed from the law that occasioned transgressions, which in turn were productive of death. Now that Christians are joined to Christ, the power of Christ's resurrection makes it possible for them to bear the fruit of newness of life for God.

---

**6:5** Phil 3:10–11; 2 Tm 2:11.
**6:6** Gal 5:24; 6:14; Eph 4:22–23.
**6:8** 1 Thes 4:17.
**6:9** Acts 13:34; 1 Cor 15:26; 2 Tm 1:10; Rev 1:18.
**6:10** Heb 9:26–28; 1 Pt 3:18.
**6:11** 2 Cor 5:15; 1 Pt 2:24.
**6:12** Gn 4:7.
**6:13** 12:1; Eph 2:5; 5:14 / Col 3:5.
**6:14** Gal 5:18; 1 Jn 3:6.
**6:15** 5:17, 21.
**6:16–18** Jn 8:32–36.
**6:16** Jn 8:31–34; 2 Pt 2:19.
**6:20** Jn 8:34.
**6:21** 8:6, 13; Prv 12:28; Ez 16:61, 63.
**6:22** 1 Pt 1:9.
**6:23** Gn 2:17; Gal 6:7–9; Jas 1:15.
**7:1** 1 Cor 7:39.
**7:5** 6:21; 8:6, 13.
**7:6** 8:2; 2 Cor 3:6.

## Acquaintance with Sin Through the Law.

[7]† What then can we say? That the law is sin? Of course not!† Yet I did not know sin except through the law, and I did not know what it is to covet except that the law said, "You shall not covet."* [8] But sin, finding an opportunity in the commandment, produced in me every kind of covetousness. Apart from the law sin is dead.* [9] I once lived outside the law, but when the commandment came, sin became alive; [10] then I died, and the commandment that was for life turned out to be death for me.* [11] For sin, seizing an opportunity in the commandment, deceived me and through it put me to death.* [12] So then the law is holy, and the commandment is holy and righteous and good.*

## Sin and Death.†

[13] Did the good, then, become death for me? Of course not! Sin, in order that it might be shown to be sin, worked death in me through the good, so that sin might become sinful beyond measure through the commandment.* [14] We know that the law is spiritual; but I am carnal, sold into slavery to sin.* [15] What I do, I do not understand. For I do not do what I want, but I do what I hate. [16] Now if I do what I do not want, I concur that the law is good. [17] So now it is no longer I who do it, but sin that dwells in me. [18] For I know that good does not dwell in me, that is, in my flesh. The willing is ready at hand, but doing the good is not.* [19] For I do not do the good I want, but I do the evil I do not want. [20] Now if

[I] do what I do not want, it is no longer I who do it, but sin that dwells in me. [21] So, then, I discover the principle that when I want to do right, evil is at hand. [22] For I take delight in the law of God, in my inner self, [23]* but I see in my members another principle at war with the law of my mind, taking me captive to the law of sin that dwells in my members.† [24] Miserable one that I am! Who will deliver me from this mortal body? [25] Thanks be to God through Jesus Christ our Lord. Therefore, I myself, with my mind, serve the law of God but, with my flesh, the law of sin.*

## 8 The Flesh and the Spirit.†

[1] Hence, now there is no condemnation for those who are in Christ Jesus. [2] For the law of the spirit of life in Christ Jesus has freed you from the law of sin and death.* [3] For what the law, weakened by the flesh, was powerless to do, this God has done: by sending his own Son in the likeness of sinful flesh and for the sake of sin, he condemned sin in the flesh,* [4] so that the righteous decree of the law might be fulfilled in us, who live not according to the flesh but according to the spirit.* [5] For those who live according to the flesh are concerned with the things of the flesh, but those who live according to the spirit with the things of the spirit. [6] The concern of the flesh is death, but the concern of the spirit is life and peace.* [7] For the concern of the flesh is hostility toward God; it does not submit to the law of God, nor can it;*

---

† **7:7–25** In this passage Paul uses the first person singular in the style of diatribe for the sake of argument. He aims to depict the disastrous consequences when a Christian reintroduces the law as a means to attain the objective of holiness pronounced in Rom 6:22.

**7:7–12** The apostle defends himself against the charge of identifying the law with sin. Sin does not exist in law but in human beings, whose sinful inclinations are not overcome by the proclamation of law.

**7:13–25** Far from improving the sinner, law encourages sin to expose itself in transgressions or violations of specific commandments (see Rom 1:24; 5:20). Thus persons who do not experience the justifying grace of God, and Christians who revert to dependence on law as the criterion for their relationship with God, will recognize a rift between their reasoned desire for the goodness of the law and their actual performance that is contrary to the law. Unable to free themselves from the slavery of sin and the power of death, they can only be rescued from defeat in the conflict by the power of God's grace working through Jesus Christ.

**7:23** As in Rom 3:27, Paul plays on the term *law*, which in Greek can connote custom, system, or *principle*.

**8:1–13** After his warning in Rom 7 against the wrong route to fulfillment of the objective of holiness expressed in Rom 6:22, Paul points his addressees to the correct way. Through the redemptive work of Christ, Christians have been liberated from the terrible forces of sin and death. Holiness was impossible so long as the *flesh* (or our "old self"), that is, self-interested hostility

toward God (Rom 8:7), frustrated the divine objectives expressed in the law. What is worse, sin used the law to break forth into all manner of lawlessness (Rom 8:8). All this is now changed. At the cross God broke the power of sin and pronounced sentence on it (Rom 8:3). Christians still retain the flesh, but it is alien to their new being, which is life in the spirit, namely the new self, governed by the holy Spirit. Under the direction of the holy Spirit Christians are able to fulfill the divine will that formerly found expression in the law (Rom 8:4). The same Spirit who enlivens Christians for holiness will also resurrect their bodies at the last day (Rom 8:11). Christian life is therefore the experience of a constant challenge to put to death the evil deeds of the body through life of the spirit (Rom 8:13).

---

| | |
|---|---|
| **7:7** 3:20; Ex 20:17; Dt 5:21. | **7:25** 1 Cor 15:57. |
| **7:8** 5:13, 20; 1 Cor 15:56 / Rom 4:15. | **8:2** 7:23–24; 2 Cor 3:17. |
| **7:10** Lv 18:5. | **8:3** Acts 13:38; 15:10 / Jn 3:16–17; 2 Cor 5:21; |
| **7:11** Gn 3:13; Heb 3:13. | Gal 3:13; 4:4; Phil |
| **7:12** 1 Tm 1:8. | 2:7; Col 1:22; Heb |
| **7:13** 4:15; 5:20. | 2:17; 4:15; 1 Jn 4:9. |
| **7:14** 8:7–8; Ps 51:7. | **8:4** Gal 5:16–25. |
| **7:18** Gn 6:5; 8:21; Phil 2:13. | **8:6** 6:21; 7:5; 8:13; Gal 6:8. |
| **7:23** Gal 5:17; 1 Pt 2:11. | **8:7** 5:10; Jas 4:4. |

8 and those who are in the flesh cannot please God.* 9 But you are not in the flesh; on the contrary, you are in the spirit, if only the Spirit of God dwells in you. Whoever does not have the Spirit of Christ does not belong to him.* 10 But if Christ is in you, although the body is dead because of sin, the spirit is alive because of righteousness.* 11 If the Spirit of the one who raised Jesus from the dead dwells in you, the one who raised Christ from the dead will give life to your mortal bodies also, through his Spirit that dwells in you. 12 Consequently, brothers, we are not debtors to the flesh, to live according to the flesh. 13 For if you live according to the flesh, you will die, but if by the spirit you put to death the deeds of the body, you will live.*

**Children of God Through Adoption.†** 14 For those who are led by the Spirit of God are children of God.* 15 For you did not receive a spirit of slavery to fall back into fear, but you received a spirit of adoption, through which we cry, "Abba,† Father!"* 16 The Spirit itself bears witness with our spirit that we are children of God,* 17 and if children, then heirs, heirs of God and joint heirs with Christ, if only we suffer with him so that we may also be glorified with him.*

**Destiny of Glory.†** 18 I consider that the sufferings of this present time are as nothing compared with the glory to be revealed for us.* 19 For creation awaits with eager expectation the revelation of the children of God; 20 for creation was made subject to futility, not of its own accord but because of the one who subjected it,* in hope 21 that creation itself would be set free from slavery to corruption and share in the glorious freedom of the children of God.* 22 We know that all creation is groaning in labor pains even until now;* 23 and not only that, but we ourselves, who have the firstfruits of the Spirit, we also groan within ourselves as we wait for adoption, the redemption of our bodies.* 24 For in hope we were saved. Now hope that sees for itself is not hope. For who hopes for what one sees?* 25 But if we hope for what we do not see, we wait with endurance.

26 In the same way, the Spirit too comes to the aid of our weakness; for we do not know how to pray as we ought, but the Spirit itself intercedes with inexpressible groanings. 27 And the one who searches hearts knows what is the intention of the Spirit, because it intercedes for the holy ones according to God's will.*

**God's Indomitable Love in Christ.** 28 † We know that all things work for good for those who love God,† who are called according to his purpose.* 29 † For those he foreknew he also predestined to be conformed to the image of his Son, so that he might be the firstborn among many brothers.* 30 And those he predestined he also called; and those he called he also justified; and those he justified he also glorified.* 31 † What then shall we say to this? If God

---

† **8:14–17** Christians, by reason of the Spirit's presence within them, enjoy not only new life but also a new relationship to God, that of adopted children and heirs through Christ, whose sufferings and glory they share.

**8:15** *Abba:* see note on Mk 14:36.

**8:18–27** The glory that believers are destined to share with Christ far exceeds the sufferings of the present life. Paul considers the destiny of the created world to be linked with the future that belongs to the believers. As it shares in the penalty of corruption brought about by sin, so also will it share in the benefits of redemption and future glory that comprise the ultimate liberation of God's people (Rom 8:19–22). After patient endurance in steadfast expectation, the full harvest of the Spirit's presence will be realized. On earth believers enjoy the firstfruits, i.e., the Spirit, as a guarantee of the total liberation of their bodies from the influence of the rebellious old self (Rom 8:23).

**8:28–30** These verses outline the Christian vocation as it was designed by God: *to be conformed to the image of his Son,* who is to *be the firstborn among many brothers* (Rom 8:29). God's redemptive action on behalf of the believers has been in process before the beginning of the world. Those whom God chooses are *those he foreknew* (Rom 8:29) or elected. Those who are *called* (Rom 8:30) are *predestined* or predetermined. These expressions do not mean that God is arbitrary. Rather, Paul uses them to emphasize the thought and care that God has taken for the Christian's salvation.

**8:28** *We know that all things work for good for those who love God:* a few ancient authorities have God as the subject of the verb, and some translators render: "We know that God makes everything work for good for those who love God...."

**8:29** *Image:* while man and woman were originally created in God's image (Gn 1:26–27), it is through baptism into Christ, the image of God (2 Cor 4:4; Col 1:15), that we are renewed according to the image of the Creator (Col 3:10).

**8:31–39** The all-conquering power of God's love has overcome every obstacle to Christians' salvation and every threat to separate them from God. That power manifested itself fully when God's own Son was delivered up to death for their salvation. Through him Christians can overcome all their afflictions and trials.

---

**8:8** 1 Jn 2:16.
**8:9** 1 Cor 3:16.
**8:10** Gal 2:20; 1 Pt 4:6.
**8:13** Gal 5:24; 6:8; Eph 4:22–24.
**8:14** Gal 5:18.
**8:15** Mk 14:36; Gal 4:5–6; 2 Tm 1:7.
**8:16** Jn 1:12; Gal 3:26–29.
**8:17** Gal 4:7; 1 Pt 4:13; 5:1.
**8:18** 2 Cor 4:17.
**8:20** Gn 3:17–19.
**8:21** 2 Pt 3:12–13; Rev 21:1.
**8:22** 2 Cor 5:2–5.
**8:23** 2 Cor 1:22; Gal 5:5.
**8:24** 2 Cor 5:7; Heb 11:1.
**8:27** Ps 139:1; 1 Cor 4:5.
**8:28–29** Eph 1:4–14; 3:11.
**8:29** Eph 1:5; 1 Pt 1:2.
**8:30** Is 45:25; 2 Thes 2:13–14.

is for us, who can be against us?* ³²He who did not spare his own Son but handed him over for us all, how will he not also give us everything else along with him?* ³³Who will bring a charge against God's chosen ones? It is God who acquits us.* ³⁴Who will condemn? It is Christ [Jesus] who died, rather, was raised, who also is at the right hand of God, who indeed intercedes for us.* ³⁵What will separate us from the love of Christ? Will anguish, or distress, or persecution, or famine, or nakedness, or peril, or the sword? ³⁶As it is written:*

> "For your sake we are being slain all the
>       day;
>    we are looked upon as sheep to be
>       slaughtered."

³⁷No, in all these things we conquer overwhelmingly through him who loved us.* ³⁸For I am convinced that neither death, nor life, nor angels, nor principalities, nor present things,† nor future things, nor powers,* ³⁹nor height, nor depth,† nor any other creature will be able to separate us from the love of God in Christ Jesus our Lord.

## V. JEWS AND GENTILES IN GOD'S PLAN†

**9** **Paul's Love for Israel.**† ¹I speak the truth in Christ, I do not lie; my conscience joins with the holy Spirit in bearing me witness*

²that I have great sorrow and constant anguish in my heart. ³For I could wish that I myself were accursed and separated from Christ for the sake of my brothers, my kin according to the flesh.* ⁴They are Israelites; theirs the adoption, the glory, the covenants, the giving of the law, the worship, and the promises;* ⁵theirs the patriarchs, and from them, according to the flesh, is the Messiah. God who is over all† be blessed forever. Amen.*

**God's Free Choice.** ⁶But it is not that the word of God has failed. For not all who are of Israel are Israel,* ⁷nor are they all children of Abraham because they are his descendants; but "It is through Isaac that descendants shall bear your name."* ⁸This means that it is not the children of the flesh who are the children of God, but the children of the promise are counted as descendants.* ⁹For this is the wording of the promise, "About this time I shall return and Sarah will have a son."* ¹⁰And not only that,* but also when Rebecca had conceived children by one husband, our father Isaac†—¹¹before they had yet been born or had done anything, good or bad, in order that God's elective plan might continue, ¹²not by works but by his call—she was told, "The older shall serve the younger."* ¹³As it is written:*

> "I loved Jacob
>    but hated Esau."†

---

**8:38** *Present things* and *future things* may refer to astrological data. Paul appears to be saying that the gospel liberates believers from dependence on astrologers.

**8:39** *Height, depth* may refer to positions in the zodiac, positions of heavenly bodies relative to the horizon. In astrological documents the term for "height" means "exaltation" or the position of greatest influence exerted by a planet. Since hostile spirits were associated with the planets and stars, Paul includes *powers* (Rom 8:38) in his list of malevolent forces.

**9:1–11:36** Israel's unbelief and its rejection of Jesus as savior astonished and puzzled Christians. It constituted a serious problem for them in view of God's specific preparation of Israel for the advent of the Messiah. Paul addresses himself here to the essential question of how the divine plan could be frustrated by Israel's unbelief. At the same time, he discourages both complacency and anxiety on the part of Gentiles. To those who might boast of their superior advantage over Jews, he warns that their enjoyment of the blessings assigned to Israel can be terminated. To those who might anxiously ask, "How can we be sure that Israel's fate will not be ours?" he replies that only unbelief can deprive one of salvation.

**9:1–5** The apostle speaks in strong terms of the depth of his grief over the unbelief of his own people. He would willingly undergo a curse himself for the sake of their coming to the knowledge of Christ (Rom 9:3; cf. Lv 27:28–29). His love for them derives from God's continuing choice of them and from the spiritual benefits that God bestows on them and through them on all of humanity (Rom 9:4–5).

**9:5** Some editors punctuate this verse differently and prefer

the translation, "Of whom is Christ according to the flesh, who is God over all." However, Paul's point is that God *who is over all* aimed to use Israel, which had been entrusted with every privilege, in outreach to the entire world through the Messiah.

**9:10** *Children by one husband, our father Isaac:* Abraham had two children, Ishmael and Isaac, by two wives, Hagar and Sarah, respectively. In that instance Isaac, although born later than Ishmael, became the bearer of the messianic promise. In the case of twins born to Rebecca, God's elective procedure is seen even more dramatically, and again the younger, contrary to Semitic custom, is given the preference.

**9:13** The literal rendering, *"Jacob I loved, but Esau I hated,"* suggests an attitude of divine hostility that is not implied in Paul's statement. In Semitic usage "hate" means to love less; cf. Lk 14:26 with Mt 10:37. Israel's unbelief reflects the mystery of the divine election that is always operative within it. Mere

---

**8:31** Ps 118:6; Heb 13:6.
**8:32** Jn 3:16.
**8:33–34** Is 50:8.
**8:34** Ps 110:1; Heb 7:25;
1 Jn 2:1.
**8:36** Ps 44:23; 1 Cor 4:9;
15:30; 2 Cor 4:11;
2 Tm 3:12.
**8:37** 1 Jn 5:4.
**8:38–39** 1 Cor 3:22; Eph 1:21;
1 Pt 3:22.
**9:1** 2 Cor 11:31; 1 Tm
2:7.
**9:3** Ex 32:32.

**9:4–5** 3:2; Ex 4:22; Dt 7:6;
14:1–2.
**9:5** Mt 1:1–16; Lk
3:23–38 / Rom 1:25;
Ps 41:14.
**9:6** Nm 23:19 / Mt 3:9.
**9:7** Gn 21:12; Gal 3:29.
**9:8** Gal 4:23, 28.
**9:9** Gn 18:10, 14.
**9:10** Gn 25:21.
**9:12** 11:5–6 / Gn
25:23–24.
**9:13** Mal 1:3.

14† What then are we to say? Is there injustice on the part of God? Of course not!* 15For he says to Moses:

"I will show mercy to whom I will,
   I will take pity on whom I will."*

16So it depends not upon a person's will or exertion, but upon God, who shows mercy.* 17For the scripture says to Pharaoh, "This is why I have raised you up, to show my power through you that my name may be proclaimed throughout the earth."* 18Consequently, he has mercy upon whom he wills,* and he hardens whom he wills.†

19† You will say to me then, "Why [then] does he still find fault? For who can oppose his will?"* 20But who indeed are you, a human being, to talk back to God?* Will what is made say to its maker, "Why have you created me so?" 21Or does not the potter have a right over the clay, to make out of the same lump one vessel for a noble purpose and another for an ignoble one? 22What if God, wishing to show his wrath and make known his power, has endured with much patience the vessels of wrath made for destruction?* 23This was to make known the riches of his glory to the vessels of mercy, which he has prepared previously for glory, 24namely, us whom he has called, not only from the Jews but also from the Gentiles.

**Witness of the Prophets.** 25As indeed he says in Hosea:

"Those who were not my people I will
      call 'my people,'
   and her who was not beloved† I will
      call 'beloved.'*
26 And in the very place where it was
      said to them, 'You are not my
      people,'
   there they shall be called children of
      the living God."*

27* And Isaiah cries out concerning Israel, "Though the number of the Israelites were like the sand of the sea, only a remnant will be saved; 28for decisively and quickly will the Lord execute sentence upon the earth." 29And as Isaiah predicted:

"Unless the Lord of hosts had left us
      descendants,
   we would have become like
      Sodom
   and have been made like
      Gomorrah."*

**Righteousness Based on Faith.**† 30What then shall we say? That Gentiles, who did not pursue righteousness, have achieved it, that is, righteousness that comes from faith;* 31but that Israel, who pursued the law of righteousness, did not attain to that law?* 32Why not? Because they did it not by faith, but as if it could be done by works.* They stumbled over the stone that causes stumbling,† 33as it is written:

---

† natural descent from Abraham does not ensure the full possession of the divine gifts; it is God's sovereign prerogative to bestow this fullness upon, or to withhold it from, whomsoever he wishes; cf. Mt 3:9; Jn 8:39. The choice of Jacob over Esau is a case in point.

**9:14–18** The principle of divine election does not invite Christians to theoretical inquiry concerning the nonelected, nor does this principle mean that God is unfair in his dealings with humanity. The instruction concerning divine election is a part of the gospel and reveals that the gift of faith is the enactment of God's mercy (Rom 9:16). God raised up Moses to display that mercy, and Pharaoh to display divine severity in punishing those who obstinately oppose their Creator.

**9:18** The basic biblical principle is: those who will not see or hear *shall* not see or hear. On the other hand, the same God who thus makes stubborn or hardens the heart can reconstruct it through the work of the holy Spirit.

**9:19–29** The apostle responds to the objection that if God rules over faith through the principle of divine election, God cannot then accuse unbelievers of sin (Rom 9:19). For Paul, this objection is in the last analysis a manifestation of human insolence, and his "answer" is less an explanation of God's ways than the rejection of an argument that places humanity on a level with God. At the same time, Paul shows that God is far less arbitrary than appearances suggest, for God endures *with much patience* (Rom 9:22) a person like the Pharaoh of the Exodus.

**9:25** *Beloved*: in Semitic discourse means "preferred" or "favorite" (cf. Rom 9:13). See Hos 2:1.

**9:30–33** In the conversion of the Gentiles and, by contrast, of relatively few Jews, the Old Testament prophecies are seen to be fulfilled; cf. Rom 9:25–29. Israel feared that the doctrine of justification through faith would jeopardize the validity of the Mosaic law, and so they never reached their goal of righteousness that they had sought to attain through meticulous observance of the law (Rom 9:31). Since Gentiles, including especially Greeks and Romans, had a great regard for righteousness, Paul's statement concerning Gentiles in Rom 9:30 is to be understood from a Jewish perspective: quite evidently they had not been interested in "God's" righteousness, for it had not been revealed to them; but now in response to the proclamation of the gospel they respond in faith.

**9:32** Paul discusses Israel as a whole from the perspective

---

| | |
|---|---|
| **9:14** Dt 32:4. | **9:22** 2:4; Wis 12:20–21; Jer |
| **9:15** Ex 33:19. | 50:25. |
| **9:16** Eph 2:8; Ti 3:5. | **9:25** Hos 2:25. |
| **9:17** Ex 9:16. | **9:26** Hos 2:1. |
| **9:18** 11:30–32; Ex 4:21; | **9:27–28** Is 10:22–23; Hos 2:1 / |
| 7:3. | Rom 11:5 / Is 28:22. |
| **9:19** 3:7; Wis 12:12. | **9:29** Is 1:9; Mt 10:15. |
| **9:20–21** Wis 15:7; Is 29:16; | **9:30** 10:4, 20. |
| 45:9; Jer 18:6. | **9:31** 10:3. |
| | **9:32** Is 8:14. |

"Behold, I am laying a stone in Zion
    that will make people stumble
  and a rock that will make them fall,
and whoever believes in him shall not
    be put to shame."*

**10** ¹† Brothers, my heart's desire and prayer to God on their behalf is for salvation.* ²I testify with regard to them that they have zeal for God, but it is not discerning.* ³For, in their unawareness of the righteousness that comes from God and their attempt to establish their own [righteousness], they did not submit to the righteousness of God.* ⁴For Christ is the end† of the law for the justification of everyone who has faith.*

⁵† Moses writes about the righteousness that comes from [the] law, "The one who does these things will live by them."* ⁶But the righteousness that comes from faith says,* "Do not say in your heart, 'Who will go up into heaven?' (that is, to bring Christ down) ⁷† or 'Who will go down into the abyss?' (that is, to bring Christ up from the dead)."* ⁸But what does it say?

"The word is near you,
    in your mouth and in your heart"*

(that is, the word of faith that we preach), ⁹for, if you confess† with your mouth that Jesus is Lord and believe in your heart that God raised him from the dead, you will be saved.* ¹⁰For one believes with the heart and

so is justified, and one confesses with the mouth and so is saved. ¹¹For the scripture says, "No one who believes in him will be put to shame."* ¹²For there is no distinction between Jew and Greek; the same Lord is Lord of all, enriching all who call upon him.* ¹³For "everyone who calls on the name of the Lord will be saved."*

¹⁴† But how can they call on him in whom they have not believed? And how can they believe in him of whom they have not heard? And how can they hear without someone to preach?* ¹⁵And how can people preach unless they are sent? As it is written,* "How beautiful are the feet of those who bring [the] good news!"† ¹⁶But not everyone has heeded the good news; for Isaiah says, "Lord, who has believed what was heard from us?"* ¹⁷Thus faith comes from what is heard, and what is heard comes through the word of Christ.* ¹⁸But I ask, did they not hear? Certainly they did; for

"Their voice has gone forth to all the
    earth,
  and their words to the ends of the
    world."*

¹⁹But I ask, did not Israel understand?* First Moses says:

"I will make you jealous of those who
    are not a nation;
  with a senseless nation I will make
    you angry."

---

† of contemporary Jewish rejection of Jesus as Messiah. The Old Testament and much of Jewish noncanonical literature in fact reflect a fervent faith in divine mercy.

**10:1–13** Despite Israel's lack of faith in God's act in Christ, Paul does not abandon hope for her salvation (Rom 10:1). However, Israel must recognize that the Messiah's arrival in the person of Jesus Christ means the termination of the Mosaic law as the criterion for understanding oneself in a valid relationship to God. Faith in God's saving action in Jesus Christ takes precedence over any such legal claim (Rom 10:6).

**10:4** The Mosaic legislation has been superseded by God's action in Jesus Christ. Others understand end here in the sense that Christ is the goal of the law, i.e., the true meaning of the Mosaic law, which cannot be correctly understood apart from him. Still others believe that both meanings are intended.

**10:5–6** The subject of the verb *says* (Rom 10:6) is *righteousness* personified. Both of the statements in Rom 10:5, 6 derive from Moses, but Paul wishes to contrast the language of law and the language of faith.

**10:7** Here Paul blends Dt 30:13 and Ps 107:26.

**10:9–11** To confess Jesus as Lord was frequently quite hazardous in the first century (cf. Mt 10:18; 1 Thes 2:2; 1 Pt 2:18–21; 3:14). For a Jew it could mean disruption of normal familial and other social relationships, including great economic sacrifice. In

the face of penalties imposed by the secular world, Christians are assured that *no one who believes in Jesus will be put to shame* (Rom 10:11).

**10:14–21** The gospel has been sufficiently proclaimed to Israel, and Israel has adequately understood God's plan for the messianic age, which would see the gospel brought to the uttermost parts of the earth. As often in the past, Israel has not accepted the prophetic message; cf. Acts 7:51–53.

**10:15** *How beautiful are the feet of those who bring [the] good news*: in Semitic fashion, the parts of the body that bring the messenger with welcome news are praised; cf. Lk 11:27.

**9:33** Is 28:16; 1 Pt 2:6–8.
**10:1** 9:1, 3.
**10:2** Acts 22:3.
**10:3** 9:31–32; Phil 3:9.
**10:4** Acts 13:38–39; 2 Cor 3:14; Heb 8:13.
**10:5** Lv 18:5; Gal 3:12.
**10:6** Dt 9:4; 30:12.
**10:7** Dt 30:13; 1 Pt 3:19.
**10:8** Dt 30:14.
**10:9** 1 Cor 12:3.
**10:11** 9:33; Is 28:16.
**10:12** 1:16; 3:22, 29; Acts 10:34; 15:9, 11; Gal 3:28; Eph 2:14.
**10:13** Jl 3:5; Acts 2:21.
**10:14** Acts 8:31.
**10:15** Is 52:7; Na 2:1; Eph 6:15.
**10:16** Is 53:1; Jn 12:38.
**10:17** Jn 17:20.
**10:18** Ps 19:5; Mt 24:14.
**10:19** 11:11, 14; Dt 32:21.

20 * Then Isaiah speaks boldly and says:

"I was found [by] those who were not
    seeking me;
I revealed myself to those who were
    not asking for me."

21 But regarding Israel he says, "All day long I stretched out my hands to a disobedient and contentious people."

# 11 The Remnant of Israel.†

1 I ask, then, has God rejected his people? Of course not! * For I too am an Israelite, a descendant of Abraham, of the tribe of Benjamin. * 2 God has not rejected his people whom he foreknew. Do you not know what the scripture says about Elijah, how he pleads with God against Israel? 3 "Lord, they have killed your prophets, they have torn down your altars, and I alone am left, and they are seeking my life." * 4 But what is God's response to him? "I have left for myself seven thousand men who have not knelt to Baal." * 5 So also at the present time there is a remnant, chosen by grace. * 6 But if by grace, it is no longer because of works; otherwise grace would no longer be grace. * 7 What then? What Israel was seeking it did not attain, but the elect attained it; the rest were hardened, * 8 as it is written:

"God gave them a spirit of deep sleep,
    eyes that should not see
    and ears that should not hear,
down to this very day." *

9 And David says: *

"Let their table become a snare and a
    trap,

a stumbling block and a retribution
    for them;
10     let their eyes grow dim so that they may
        not see,
    and keep their backs bent forever."

**The Gentiles' Salvation.** 11 † Hence I ask, did they stumble so as to fall? Of course not! But through their transgression salvation has come to the Gentiles, so as to make them jealous. * 12 Now if their transgression is enrichment for the world, and if their diminished number is enrichment for the Gentiles, how much more their full number.

13 Now I am speaking to you Gentiles. Inasmuch then as I am the apostle to the Gentiles, I glory in my ministry * 14 in order to make my race jealous and thus save some of them. 15 For if their rejection is the reconciliation of the world, what will their acceptance be but life from the dead? 16 † If the firstfruits are holy, so is the whole batch of dough; and if the root is holy, so are the branches. *

17 But if some of the branches were broken off, and you, a wild olive shoot, were grafted in their place and have come to share in the rich root of the olive tree, * 18 do not boast against the branches. If you do boast, consider that you do not support the root; the root supports you. * 19 Indeed you will say, "Branches were broken off so that I might be grafted in." 20 That is so. They were broken off because of unbelief, but you are there because of faith. So do not become haughty, but stand in awe. * 21 For if God did not spare the natural branches, [perhaps] he will not spare you either. * 22 See, then, the kindness and severity of God: severity toward those who fell, but God's kindness to you, provided you remain in his kindness; otherwise you too will be cut off. *

---

† **11:1–10** Although Israel has been unfaithful to the prophetic message of the gospel (Rom 10:14–21), God remains faithful to Israel. Proof of the divine fidelity lies in the existence of Jewish Christians like Paul himself. The unbelieving Jews, says Paul, have been blinded by the Christian teaching concerning the Messiah.

**11:11–15** The unbelief of the Jews has paved the way for the preaching of the gospel to the Gentiles and for their easier acceptance of it outside the context of Jewish culture. Through his mission to the Gentiles Paul also hopes to fill his fellow Jews with jealousy. Hence he hastens to fill the entire Mediterranean world with the gospel. Once all the Gentile nations have heard the gospel, Israel as a whole is expected to embrace it. This will be tantamount to resurrection of the dead, that is, the reappearance of Jesus Christ with all the believers at the end of time.

**11:16–24** Israel remains holy in the eyes of God and stands as a witness to the faith described in the Old Testament because of the firstfruits (or the first piece baked) (Rom 11:16), that is,

the converted remnant, and the root that is holy, that is, the patriarchs (Rom 11:16). The Jews' failure to believe in Christ is a warning to Gentile Christians to be on guard against any semblance of anti-Jewish arrogance, that is, failure to recognize their total dependence on divine grace.

---

* **10:20–21** 9:30; Is 65:1–2.
**11:1–2** 1 Sm 12:22; Ps 94:14.
**11:1** 2 Cor 11:22; Phil 3:5.
**11:3** 1 Kgs 19:10, 14.
**11:4** 1 Kgs 19:18.
**11:5** 9:27.
**11:6** 4:4; Gal 3:18.
**11:7** 9:31.
**11:8** Dt 29:3; Is 29:10; Mt 13:13–15; Acts 28:26–27.
**11:9–10** Ps 69:23–24; 35:8.

**11:11** Acts 13:46; 18:6; 28:28 / Rom 10:19; Dt 32:21.
**11:13** 1:5.
**11:16** Nm 15:17–21; Ez 44:30; Neh 10:36–38.
**11:17** Eph 2:11–19.
**11:18** 1 Cor 1:31.
**11:20** 12:16.
**11:21** 1 Cor 10:12.
**11:22** Jn 15:2, 4; Heb 3:14.

23 And they also, if they do not remain in unbelief, will be grafted in, for God is able to graft them in again.* 24 For if you were cut from what is by nature a wild olive tree, and grafted, contrary to nature, into a cultivated one, how much more will they who belong to it by nature be grafted back into their own olive tree.

**God's Irrevocable Call.**† 25 I do not want you to be unaware of this mystery, brothers, so that you will not become wise [in] your own estimation: a hardening has come upon Israel in part, until the full number of the Gentiles comes in,* 26 and thus all Israel will be saved,* as it is written:*

> "The deliverer will come out of Zion,
>     he will turn away godlessness from
>     Jacob;
27     and this is my covenant with them
>     when I take away their sins."*

28 In respect to the gospel, they are enemies on your account; but in respect to election, they are beloved because of the patriarchs.* 29 For the gifts and the call of God are irrevocable.*

**Triumph of God's Mercy.** 30 † Just as you once disobeyed God but have now received mercy because of their disobedience, 31 so they have now disobeyed in order that, by virtue of the mercy shown to you, they too may [now] receive mercy. 32 For God delivered all to disobedience, that he might have mercy upon all.*

33 † Oh, the depth of the riches and wisdom and knowledge of God! How inscrutable are his judgments and how unsearchable his ways!*

34     "For who has known the mind of the
>         Lord†
>     or who has been his counselor?"*
35 †   "Or who has given him anything*
>         that he may be repaid?"

36 For from him and through him and for him are all things. To him be glory forever. Amen.*

## VI. THE DUTIES OF CHRISTIANS†

**12** **Sacrifice of Body and Mind.** 1 † I urge you therefore, brothers, by the mercies of God, to offer your bodies as a living sacrifice, holy and pleasing to God, your spiritual worship.* 2 Do not conform yourselves to this age but be transformed by the renewal of your mind, that you may discern what is the will of God, what is good and pleasing and perfect.*

**Many Parts in One Body.** 3 * For by the grace given to me I tell everyone among you not to think of himself more highly than one ought to think, but to think soberly, each according

---

**11:25–29** In God's design, Israel's unbelief is being used to grant the light of faith to the Gentiles. Meanwhile, Israel remains dear to God (cf. Rom 9:13), still the object of special providence, the mystery of which will one day be revealed.
**11:30–32** Israel, together with the Gentiles who have been handed over to all manner of vices (Rom 1), *has been delivered…to disobedience*. The conclusion of Rom 11:32 repeats the thought of Rom 5:20, "Where sin increased, grace overflowed all the more."
**11:33–36** This final reflection celebrates the wisdom of God's plan of salvation. As Paul has indicated throughout these chapters, both Jew and Gentile, despite the religious recalcitrance of each, have received the gift of faith. The methods used by God in making this outreach to the world stagger human comprehension but are at the same time a dazzling invitation to abiding faith.
**11:34** The citation is from the Greek text of Is 40:13. Paul does not explicitly mention Isaiah in this verse, nor Job in Rom 11:35.
**11:35** Paul quotes from an old Greek version of Jb 41:3a, which differs from the Hebrew text (Jb 41:11a).
**12:1–13:14** Since Christ marks the termination of the Mosaic law as the primary source of guidance for God's people (Rom 10:4), the apostle explains how Christians can function, in the light of the gift of justification through faith, in their relation to one another and the state.
**12:1–8** The Mosaic code included elaborate directions on sacrifices and other cultic observances. The gospel, however, invites believers to present their *bodies as a living sacrifice* (Rom

12:1). Instead of being limited by specific legal maxims, Christians are liberated for the exercise of good judgment as they are confronted with the many and varied decisions required in the course of daily life. To assist them, God distributes a variety of gifts to the fellowship of believers, including those of prophecy, teaching, and exhortation (Rom 12:6–8). Prophets assist the community to understand the will of God as it applies to the present situation (Rom 12:6). Teachers help people to understand themselves and their responsibilities in relation to others (Rom 12:7). One who *exhorts* offers encouragement to the community to exercise their faith in the performance of all that is pleasing to God (Rom 12:8). Indeed, this very section, beginning with Rom 12:1, is a specimen of Paul's own style of exhortation.

---

**11:23** 2 Cor 3:16.
**11:25** Prv 3:7 / Rom 12:16;
    Mk 13:10; Lk 21:24;
    Jn 10:16.
**11:26–27** Ps 14:7; Is 59:20–21.
**11:26** Mt 23:39.
**11:27** Is 27:9; Jer 31:33–34.
**11:28** 15:8; 1 Thes 2:15–16.
**11:29** 9:6; Nm 23:19; Is 54:10.
**11:32** Gal 3:22; 1 Tm 2:4.
**11:33** Jb 11:7–8; Ps 139:6, 17–18; Wis 17:1; Is 55:8–9.

**11:34** Jb 15:8; Wis 9:13;
    Is 40:13; Jer 23:18;
    1 Cor 2:11–16.
**11:35** Jb 41:3; Is 40:14.
**11:36** 1 Cor 8:6; Col 1:16–17.
**12:1** 2 Cor 1:3 / Rom 6:13;
    1 Pt 2:5.
**12:2** Eph 4:17, 22–23; 1 Pt 1:14 / Eph 5:10, 17;
    Phil 1:10.
**12:3** 15:15 / Phil 2:3 / 1 Cor 12:11; Eph 4:7.

to the measure of faith that God has apportioned. [4]* For as in one body we have many parts, and all the parts do not have the same function, [5]so we, though many, are one body in Christ† and individually parts of one another. [6]* Since we have gifts that differ according to the grace given to us, let us exercise them:† if prophecy, in proportion to the faith; [7]if ministry, in ministering; if one is a teacher, in teaching; [8]if one exhorts, in exhortation; if one contributes, in generosity; if one is over others,† with diligence; if one does acts of mercy, with cheerfulness.

**Mutual Love.** [9]Let love be sincere; hate what is evil, hold on to what is good;* [10]love one another with mutual affection; anticipate one another in showing honor.* [11]Do not grow slack in zeal, be fervent in spirit, serve the Lord.* [12]Rejoice in hope, endure in affliction, persevere in prayer.* [13]Contribute to the needs of the holy ones,* exercise hospitality. [14]† Bless those who persecute [you],* bless and do not curse them.* [15]Rejoice with those who rejoice, weep with those who weep.* [16]Have the same regard for one another; do not be haughty but associate with the lowly; do not be wise in your own estimation.* [17]Do not repay anyone evil for evil; be concerned for what is noble in the sight of all.* [18]If possible, on your part, live at peace with all.* [19]Beloved, do not look for revenge but leave room for the wrath; for it is written, "Vengeance is mine, I will repay, says the Lord."* [20]Rather, "if your enemy is hungry, feed him; if he is thirsty, give him something to drink; for by so doing you will heap burning coals upon his head."* [21]Do not be conquered by evil but conquer evil with good.

**13** **Obedience to Authority.**† [1]Let every person be subordinate to the higher authorities, for there is no authority except from God, and those that exist have been established by God.* [2]Therefore, whoever resists authority opposes what God has appointed, and those who oppose it will bring judgment upon themselves. [3]For rulers are not a cause of fear to good conduct, but to evil.* Do you wish to have no fear of authority? Then do what is good and you will receive approval from it, [4]for it is a servant of God for your good. But if you do evil, be afraid, for it does not bear the sword without purpose; it is the servant of God to inflict wrath on the evildoer.* [5]Therefore, it is necessary to be subject not only because of the wrath but also because of conscience.* [6]This is why you also pay taxes, for the authorities are ministers of God, devoting themselves to this very thing. [7]Pay to all their dues, taxes to whom taxes are due, toll to whom toll is due, respect to whom respect is due, honor to whom honor is due.*

---

† **12:5** *One body in Christ*: on the church as the body of Christ, see 1 Cor 12:12–27.

**12:6** Everyone has some gift that can be used for the benefit of the community. When the instruction on justification through faith is correctly grasped, the possessor of a gift will understand that it is not an instrument of self-aggrandizement. Possession of a gift is not an index to quality of faith. Rather, the gift is a challenge to faithful use.

**12:8** *Over others*: usually taken to mean "rule over" but possibly "serve as a patron." Wealthier members in Greco-Roman communities were frequently asked to assist in public service projects. In view of the references to contributing *in generosity* and to *acts of mercy*, Paul may have in mind people like Phoebe (Rom 16:1–2), who is called a *benefactor* (or "patron") because of the services she rendered to many Christians, including Paul.

**12:14–21** Since God has justified the believers, it is not necessary for them to take justice into their own hands by taking vengeance. God will ultimately deal justly with all, including those who inflict injury on the believers. This question of personal rights as a matter of justice prepares the way for more detailed consideration of the state as adjudicator.

**13:1–7** Paul must come to grips with the problem raised by a message that declares people free from the law. How are they to relate to Roman authority? The problem was exacerbated by the fact that imperial protocol was interwoven with devotion to various deities. Paul builds on the traditional instruction exhibited in Wis 6:1–3, according to which kings and magistrates rule by consent of God. From this perspective, then, believers who render obedience to the governing authorities are obeying the one who is highest in command. At the same time, it is recognized that Caesar has the responsibility to make just ordinances and to commend uprightness; cf. Wis 6:4–21. That Caesar is not entitled to obedience when such obedience would nullify God's prior claim to the believers' moral decision becomes clear in the light of the following verses.

| | |
|---|---|
| **12:4–5** 1 Cor 12:12, 27; Eph 4:25. | **12:16** 15:5; Phil 2:2–3 / Rom 11:20; Prv 3:7; Is 5:21. |
| **12:6–8** 1 Cor 12:4–11, 28–31; Eph 4:7–12; 1 Pt 4:10–11 / 2 Cor 9:7. | **12:17** Prv 3:4; 1 Thes 5:15; 1 Pt 3:9. |
| | **12:18** Heb 12:14. |
| **12:9** 2 Cor 6:6; 1 Tm 1:5; 1 Pt 1:22 / Am 5:15. | **12:19** Lv 19:18; Dt 32:35, 41; Mt 5:39; 1 Cor 6:6–7; Heb 10:30. |
| **12:10** Jn 13:34; 1 Thes 4:9; 1 Pt 2:17; 2 Pt 1:7 / Phil 2:3. | **12:20** Prv 25:21–22; Mt 5:44. |
| **12:11** Acts 18:25. | **13:1** Prv 8:15–16; Wis 6:3; Jn 19:11; 1 Pt 2:13–17; Ti 3:1. |
| **12:12** 5:2–3; Col 4:2; 1 Thes 5:17. | |
| **12:13** Heb 13:2; 1 Pt 4:9. | **13:3** 1 Pt 2:13–14; 3:13. |
| **12:14–21** Mt 5:38–48; 1 Cor 4:12; 1 Pt 3:9. | **13:4** 12:19. |
| **12:14** Lk 6:27–28. | **13:5** 1 Pt 2:19. |
| **12:15** Ps 35:13; Sir 7:34; 1 Cor 12:26. | **13:7** Mt 22:21; Mk 12:17; Lk 20:25. |

**Love Fulfills the Law.**† 8 Owe nothing to anyone, except to love one another; for the one who loves another has fulfilled the law.* 9 The commandments, "You shall not commit adultery; you shall not kill; you shall not steal; you shall not covet," and whatever other commandment there may be, are summed up in this saying, [namely] "You shall love your neighbor as yourself."* 10 Love does no evil to the neighbor; hence, love is the fulfillment of the law.*

**Awareness of the End of Time.**† 11 And do this because you know the time; it is the hour now for you to awake from sleep. For our salvation is nearer now than when we first believed;* 12 the night is advanced, the day is at hand. Let us then throw off the works of darkness [and] put on the armor of light;* 13 let us conduct ourselves properly as in the day,† not in orgies and drunkenness, not in promiscuity and licentiousness, not in rivalry and jealousy.* 14 But put on the Lord Jesus Christ, and make no provision for the desires of the flesh.*

**14** **To Live and Die for Christ.** 1† Welcome anyone who is weak in faith,* but not for disputes over opinions.* 2 One person believes that one may eat anything, while the weak person eats only vegetables.* 3 The one who eats must not despise the one who abstains, and the one who abstains must not pass judgment on the one who eats; for God has welcomed him.* 4 Who are you to pass judgment on someone else's servant? Before his own master he stands or falls. And he will be upheld, for the Lord is able to make him stand.* 5 [For] one person considers one day more important than another, while another person considers all days alike.* Let everyone be fully persuaded in his own mind.† 6 Whoever observes the day, observes it for the Lord. Also whoever eats, eats for the Lord, since he gives thanks to God; while whoever abstains, abstains for the Lord and gives thanks to God. 7 None of us lives for oneself, and no one dies for oneself. 8 For if we live, we live for the Lord,† and if we die, we die for the Lord; so then, whether we live or die, we are the Lord's.* 9 For this is why Christ died and came to life, that he might be Lord of both the dead and the living.* 10 Why then do you judge your brother? Or you, why do you look down on your brother? For we shall all stand before the judgment seat of God;* 11 for it is written:

"As I live, says the Lord, every knee shall
        bend before me,
    and every tongue shall give praise to
        God."*

12 So [then] each of us shall give an account of himself [to God].*

---

† **13:8–10** When love directs the Christian's moral decisions, the interest of law in basic concerns, such as familial relationships, sanctity of life, and security of property, is safeguarded (Rom 13:9). Indeed, says Paul, the same applies to any *other commandment* (Rom 13:9), whether one in the Mosaic code or one drawn up by local magistrates under imperial authority. Love anticipates the purpose of public legislation, namely, to secure the best interests of the citizenry. Since Caesar's obligation is to punish the wrongdoer (Rom 13:4), the Christian who acts in love is free from all legitimate indictment.

**13:11–14** These verses provide the motivation for the love that is encouraged in Rom 13:8–10.

**13:13** *Let us conduct ourselves properly as in the day*: the behavior described in Rom 1:29–30 is now to be reversed. Secular moralists were fond of making references to people who could not wait for nightfall to do their carousing. Paul says that Christians claim to be people of the new day that will dawn with the return of Christ. Instead of planning for nighttime behavior they should be concentrating on conduct that is consonant with avowed interest in the Lord's return.

**14:1–15:6** Since Christ spells termination of the law, which included observance of specific days and festivals as well as dietary instruction, the jettisoning of long-practiced customs was traumatic for many Christians brought up under the Mosaic code. Although Paul acknowledges that in principle no food is a source of moral contamination (Rom 14:14), he recommends that the consciences of Christians who are scrupulous in this regard be respected by other Christians (Rom 14:21). On the other hand, those who have scruples are not to sit in judgment on those who know that the gospel has liberated them from such ordinances (Rom 14:10). See 1 Cor 8; 10.

**14:5** Since the problem to be overcome was humanity's perverted mind or judgment (Rom 1:28), Paul indicates that the *mind* of the Christian is now able to function with appropriate discrimination (cf. Rom 12:2).

**14:8** *The Lord*: Jesus, our Master. The same Greek word, *kyrios*, was applied to both rulers and holders of slaves. Throughout the Letter to the Romans Paul emphasizes God's total claim on the believer; see note on Rom 1:1.

**13:8** Jn 13:34; Gal 5:14.
**13:9** Ex 20:13–17 / Lv 19:18; Dt 5:17–21; Mt 5:43–44; 19:18–19; 22:39; Mk 12:31; Lk 10:27; Gal 5:14; Jas 2:8.
**13:10** Mt 22:40; 1 Cor 13:4–7.
**13:11** Eph 5:8–16; 1 Thes 5:5–7.
**13:12** Jn 8:12; 1 Thes 5:4–8; 1 Jn 2:8 / 2 Cor 6:7; 10:4; Eph 5:11; 6:13–17.
**13:13** Lk 21:34; Eph 5:18.
**13:14** Gal 3:27; 5:16;

Eph 4:24; 6:11.
**14:1–23** 1 Cor 8:1–13.
**14:1** 15:1, 7; 1 Cor 9:22.
**14:2** Gn 1:29; 9:3; 1 Cor 8:1–13; 10:14–33.
**14:3** Col 2:16.
**14:4** 2:1; Mt 7:11; Jas 4:11–12.
**14:5** Gal 4:10.
**14:8** Lk 20:38; 2 Cor 5:15; Gal 2:20; 1 Thes 5:10.
**14:9** Acts 10:42.
**14:10** Acts 17:31; 2 Cor 5:10.
**14:11** Is 49:18 / Is 45:23; Phil 2:10–11.
**14:12** Gal 6:5.

ROM

ROM

## Consideration for the Weak Conscience.

13 Then let us no longer judge one another, but rather resolve never to put a stumbling block or hindrance in the way of a brother. * 14 I know and am convinced in the Lord Jesus that nothing is unclean in itself; still, it is unclean for someone who thinks it unclean. * 15 If your brother is being hurt by what you eat, your conduct is no longer in accord with love. Do not because of your food destroy him for whom Christ died. * 16 So do not let your good be reviled. * 17 For the kingdom of God is not a matter of food and drink, but of righteousness, peace, and joy in the holy Spirit; * 18 whoever serves Christ in this way is pleasing to God and approved by others. 19 Let us † then pursue what leads to peace and to building up one another. * 20 For the sake of food, do not destroy the work of God. * Everything is indeed clean, but it is wrong for anyone to become a stumbling block by eating; 21 it is good not to eat meat or drink wine or do anything that causes your brother to stumble. 22 Keep the faith [that] you have to yourself in the presence of God; blessed is the one who does not condemn himself for what he approves. 23 * But whoever has doubts is condemned if he eats, because this is not from faith; for whatever is not from faith is sin. †

15 **Patience and Self-Denial.** 1 We who are strong ought to put up with the failings of the weak and not to please ourselves; * 2 let each of us please our neighbor for the good, for building up. * 3 For Christ did not please himself; but, as it is written, * "The insults of those who insult you fall upon me." † 4 For whatever was written previously was written for our instruction, that by endurance and by the encouragement of the scriptures we might have hope. * 5 May the God of endurance and encouragement grant you to think in harmony † with one another, in keeping with Christ Jesus, * 6 that with one accord you may with one voice glorify the God and Father of our Lord Jesus Christ.

## God's Fidelity and Mercy. †

7 Welcome one another, then, as Christ welcomed you, for the glory of God. * 8 For I say that Christ became a minister of the circumcised to show God's truthfulness, to confirm the promises to the patriarchs, * 9 but so that the Gentiles might glorify God for his mercy. As it is written:

> "Therefore, I will praise you among the Gentiles
>   and sing praises to your name." *

10 And again it says: *

> "Rejoice, O Gentiles, with his people." †

11 And again:

> "Praise the Lord, all you Gentiles,
>   and let all the peoples praise him." *

12 And again Isaiah says:

> "The root of Jesse shall come,
>   raised up to rule the Gentiles;
> in him shall the Gentiles hope." *

13 May the God of hope fill you with all joy and peace in believing, so that you may abound in hope by the power of the holy Spirit. *

---

**14:19** Some manuscripts, versions, and church Fathers read, "We then pursue…"; cf. Rom 5:1.

**14:23** *Whatever is not from faith is sin*: Paul does not mean that all the actions of unbelievers are sinful. He addresses himself to the question of intracommunity living. *Sin* in the singular is the dreadful power described in Rom 5:12–14.

**15:3** Liberation from the law of Moses does not make the scriptures of the old covenant irrelevant. Much consolation and motivation for Christian living can be derived from the Old Testament, as in the citation from Ps 69:10. Because this psalm is quoted several times in the New Testament, it has been called indirectly messianic.

**15:5** *Think in harmony*: a Greco-Roman ideal. Not rigid uniformity of thought and expression but thoughtful consideration of other people's views finds expression here.

**15:7–13** True oneness of mind is found in pondering the ultimate mission of the church: to bring it about that God's name be glorified throughout the world and that Jesus Christ be univer-sally recognized as God's gift to all humanity. Paul here prepares his addressees for the climactic appeal he is about to make.

**15:10** Paul's citation of Dt 32:43 follows the Greek version.

| | |
|---|---|
| **14:13** 1 Cor 8:9, 13. | **15:4** 4:23–24; 1 Mc 12:9; |
| **14:14** Mk 7:5, 20; Acts | 1 Cor 10:11; 2 Tm |
| 10:15; 1 Cor | 3:16. |
| 10:25–27; 1 Tm 4:4. | **15:5** 12:16; Phil 2:2; 4:2. |
| **14:15** 1 Cor 8:11–13. | **15:7** 14:1. |
| **14:16** 2:24; Ti 2:5. | **15:8** Mt 15:24 / Mi 7:20; |
| **14:17** 1 Cor 8:8. | Acts 3:25. |
| **14:19** 12:18 / 15:2. | **15:9** 11:30 / 2 Sm 22:50; |
| **14:20–21** 1 Cor 8:11–13; | Ps 18:50. |
| 10:28–29; Ti 1:15. | **15:10** Dt 32:43. |
| **14:23** Ti 1:15; Jas 4:17. | **15:11** Ps 117:1. |
| **15:1** 14:1–2. | **15:12** Is 11:10; Rev 5:5; |
| **15:2** 14:1, 19; 1 Cor 9:19; | 22:16. |
| 10:24, 33. | **15:13** 5:1–2. |
| **15:3** Ps 69:10. | |

## VII. CONCLUSION

**Apostle to the Gentiles.** [14] † I myself am convinced about you, my brothers, that you yourselves are full of goodness, † filled with all knowledge, and able to admonish one another. [15] But I have written to you rather boldly in some respects to remind you, because of the grace given me by God * [16] to be a minister of Christ Jesus to the Gentiles in performing the priestly service of the gospel of God, so that the offering up of the Gentiles may be acceptable, sanctified by the holy Spirit. * [17] In Christ Jesus, then, I have reason to boast in what pertains to God. [18] For I will not dare to speak of anything except what Christ has accomplished through me to lead the Gentiles to obedience by word and deed, * [19] by the power of signs and wonders, by the power of the Spirit [of God], so that from Jerusalem all the way around to Illyricum † I have finished preaching the gospel of Christ. [20] Thus I aspire † to proclaim the gospel not where Christ has already been named, so that I do not build on another's foundation, * [21] but as it is written: *

"Those who have never been told of him
shall see,
and those who have never heard of
him shall understand." †

**Paul's Plans; Need for Prayers.** [22] That is why I have so often been prevented from coming to you. [23] But now, since I no longer have any opportunity in these regions and since I have desired to come to you for many years, * [24] I hope to see you in passing as I go to Spain and to be sent on my way there by you, after I have enjoyed being with you for a time. * [25] † Now, however, I am going to Jerusalem to minister to the holy ones. * [26] For Macedonia and Achaia † have decided to make some contribution for the poor among the holy ones in Jerusalem; * [27] they decided to do it, and in fact they are indebted to them, for if the Gentiles have come to share in their spiritual blessings, they ought also to serve them in material blessings. * [28] So when I have completed this and safely handed over this contribution to them, I shall set out by way of you to Spain; [29] and I know that in coming to you I shall come in the fullness of Christ's blessing.

[30] I urge you, [brothers,] by our Lord Jesus Christ and by the love of the Spirit, to join me in the struggle by your prayers to God on my behalf, * [31] that I may be delivered from the disobedient in Judea, and that my ministry for Jerusalem may be acceptable to the holy ones, [32] so that I may come to you with joy by the will of God and be refreshed together with you. [33] The God of peace be with all of you. Amen. *

**16** **Phoebe Commended.** [1] † I commend to you Phoebe our sister, who is [also] a minister † of the church at Cenchreae, * [2] that

---

† **15:14–33** Paul sees himself as apostle and benefactor in the priestly service of the gospel and so sketches plans for a mission in Spain, supported by those in Rome.

**15:14** *Full of goodness*: the opposite of what humanity was filled with according to Rom 1:29–30.

**15:19** *Illyricum*: Roman province northwest of Greece on the eastern shore of the Adriatic.

**15:20** *I aspire*: Paul uses terminology customarily applied to philanthropists. Unlike some philanthropists of his time, Paul does not engage in cheap competition for public acclaim. This explanation of his missionary policy is to assure the Christians in Rome that he is also not planning to remain in that city and build on other people's foundations (cf. 2 Cor 10:12–18). However, he does solicit their help in sending him on his way to Spain, which was considered the limit of the western world. Thus Paul's addressees realize that evangelization may be understood in the broader sense of mission or, as in Rom 1:15, of instruction within the Christian community that derives from the gospel.

**15:21** The citation from Is 52:15 concerns the Servant of the Lord. According to Isaiah, the Servant is first of all Israel, which was to bring the knowledge of Yahweh to the nations. In Rom 9–11 Paul showed how Israel failed in this mission. Therefore, he himself undertakes almost singlehandedly Israel's responsibility as the Servant and moves as quickly as possible with the gospel through the Roman empire.

**15:25–27** Paul may have viewed the contribution he was gathering from Gentile Christians for the poor in Jerusalem (cf. 2 Cor 8–9) as a fulfillment of the vision of Is 60:5–6. In confidence that the messianic fulfillment was taking place, Paul stresses in Rom 14–16 the importance of harmonious relationships between Jews and Gentiles.

**15:26** *Achaia*: the Roman province of southern Greece.

**16:1–23** Some authorities regard these verses as a later addition to the letter, but in general the evidence favors the view that they were included in the original. Paul endeavors through the long list of greetings (Rom 16:3–16, 21–23) to establish strong personal contact with congregations that he has not personally encountered before. The combination of Jewish and Gentile names dramatically attests the unity in the gospel that transcends previous barriers of nationality, religious ceremony, or racial status.

**16:1** *Minister*: in Greek, *diakonos*; see note on Phil 1:1.

---

**15:15** 1:5; 12:3.
**15:16** 11:13; Phil 2:17.
**15:18** Acts 15:12; 2 Cor 12:12.
**15:20** 2 Cor 10:13–18.
**15:21** Is 52:15.
**15:23** 1:10–13; Acts 19:21–22.
**15:24** 1 Cor 16:6.
**15:25** Acts 19:21; 20:22.

**15:26** 1 Cor 16:1; 2 Cor 8:1–4; 9:2, 12.
**15:27** 9:4 / 1 Cor 9:11.
**15:30** 2 Cor 1:11; Phil 1:27; Col 4:3; 2 Thes 3:1.
**15:33** 16:20; 2 Cor 13:11; Phil 4:9; 1 Thes 5:23; 2 Thes 3:16; Heb 13:20.
**16:1** Acts 18:18.

you may receive her in the Lord in a manner worthy of the holy ones, and help her in whatever she may need from you, for she has been a benefactor to many and to me as well.

**Paul's Greetings.** ³Greet Prisca and Aquila,† my co-workers in Christ Jesus,* ⁴who risked their necks for my life, to whom not only I am grateful but also all the churches of the Gentiles; ⁵greet also the church at their house.† Greet my beloved Epaenetus, who was the firstfruits in Asia for Christ.* ⁶Greet Mary, who has worked hard for you. ⁷Greet Andronicus and Junia,† my relatives and my fellow prisoners; they are prominent among the apostles and they were in Christ before me. ⁸Greet Ampliatus, my beloved in the Lord. ⁹Greet Urbanus, our co-worker in Christ, and my beloved Stachys. ¹⁰Greet Apelles, who is approved in Christ. Greet those who belong to the family of Aristobulus. ¹¹Greet my relative Herodion. Greet those in the Lord who belong to the family of Narcissus. ¹²Greet those workers in the Lord, Tryphaena and Tryphosa. Greet the beloved Persis, who has worked hard in the Lord. ¹³Greet Rufus,† chosen in the Lord, and his mother and mine.* ¹⁴Greet Asyncritus, Phlegon, Hermes, Patrobas, Hermas, and the brothers who are with them. ¹⁵Greet Philologus, Julia, Nereus and his sister, and Olympas, and all the holy ones who are with them. ¹⁶Greet one another with a holy kiss. All the churches of Christ greet you.*

**Against Factions.** ¹⁷†I urge you, brothers, to watch out for those who create dissensions and obstacles, in opposition to the teaching that you learned; avoid them.* ¹⁸For such people do not serve our Lord Christ but their own appetites, and by fair and flattering speech they deceive the hearts of the innocent.* ¹⁹For while your obedience is known to all, so that I rejoice over you, I want you to be wise as to what is good, and simple as to what is evil;* ²⁰then the God of peace will quickly crush Satan† under your feet. The grace of our Lord Jesus be with you.*

**Greetings from Corinth.** ²¹Timothy, my co-worker, greets you; so do Lucius and Jason and Sosipater, my relatives.* ²²I, Tertius, the writer of this letter, greet you in the Lord. ²³*Gaius, who is host to me and to the whole church, greets you. Erastus,† the city treasurer, and our brother Quartus greet you. [²⁴]†

**Doxology.**† [²⁵Now to him who can strengthen you, according to my gospel and the proclamation of Jesus Christ,* according to the revelation of the mystery kept secret for long ages† ²⁶but now manifested through the prophetic writings and, according to the command of the eternal God, made known to all nations to bring about the obedience of faith,* ²⁷to the only wise God, through Jesus Christ be glory forever and ever. Amen.]*

---

† **16:3** *Prisca and Aquila*: presumably the couple mentioned at Acts 18:2; 1 Cor 16:19; 2 Tm 4:19.

**16:5** *The church at their house*: i.e., that meets there. Such local assemblies (cf. 1 Cor 16:19; Col 4:15; Phlm 2) might consist of only one or two dozen Christians each. It is understandable, therefore, that such smaller groups might experience difficulty in relating to one another on certain issues. *Firstfruits*: cf. Rom 8:23; 11:16; 1 Cor 16:15.

**16:7** The name Junia is a woman's name. One ancient Greek manuscript and a number of ancient versions read the name "Julia." Most editors have interpreted it as a man's name, Junias.

**16:13** This Rufus cannot be identified to any degree of certainty with the Rufus of Mk 15:21.

**16:17–18** Paul displays genuine concern for the congregations in Rome by warning them against self-seeking teachers. It would be a great loss, he intimates, if their obedience, which is known to all (cf. Rom 1:8), would be diluted.

**16:20** This verse contains the only mention of Satan in Romans.

**16:23** This Erastus is not necessarily to be identified with the Erastus of Acts 19:22 or of 2 Tm 4:20.

**16:24** Some manuscripts add, similarly to Rom 16:20, "The grace of our Lord Jesus Christ be with you all. Amen."

**16:25–27** This doxology is assigned variously to the end of Rom 14; 15; 16 in the manuscript tradition. Some manuscripts omit it entirely. Whether written by Paul or not, it forms an admirable conclusion to the letter at this point.

**16:25** Paul's gospel reveals *the mystery kept secret for long ages*: justification and salvation through faith, with all the implications for Jews and Gentiles that Paul has developed in the letter.

* **16:3** Acts 18:2, 18–26; 1 Cor 16:19; 2 Tm 4:19.
**16:5** 1 Cor 16:19; Col 4:15; Phlm 2 / 1 Cor 16:15.
**16:13** Mk 15:21.
**16:16** 1 Cor 16:20; 2 Cor 13:12; 1 Thes 5:26; 1 Pt 5:14.
**16:17** Mt 7:15; Ti 3:10.
**16:18** Phil 3:18–19; Col 2:4; 2 Pt 2:3.
**16:19** 1:8; Mt 10:16; 1 Cor 14:20.
**16:20** 15:33; Gn 3:15; Lk 10:19 / 1 Cor 16:23; 1 Thes 5:28;
2 Thes 3:18.
**16:21** Acts 16:1–2; 19:22; 20:4; 1 Cor 4:17; 16:10; Phil 2:19–22; Heb 13:23.
**16:23** Acts 19:29; 1 Cor 1:14 / 2 Tm 4:20.
**16:25** 1 Cor 2:7; Eph 1:9; 3:3–9; Col 1:26.
**16:26** 2 Tm 1:10 / Rom 1:5; Eph 3:4–5, 9; 1 Pt 1:20.
**16:27** 11:36; Gal 1:5; Eph 3:20–21; Phil 4:20; 1 Tm 1:17; 2 Tm 4:18; Heb 13:21; 1 Pt 4:11; 2 Pt 3:18; Jude 25; Rev 1:6.

The First Letter to the

# Corinthians

## INTRODUCTION

### Laurie Brink, OP

The canonical letter called 1 Corinthians is part of a larger Corinthian correspondence that includes not only letters but communiqués from envoys and personal visits. Within 1 Corinthians itself, Paul mentions an earlier letter in which he instructed the Corinthians not to associate with immoral people (1 Cor 5:9). The correspondence was not one-sided. In 1 Cor 7:1 Paul refers directly to a letter he had received from the community. Oral reports came from Chloe's people (1:11), and Paul mentions Stephanas, Fortunatus, and Achaicus, who have recently arrived in Ephesus (16:17). Paul sends his own envoys, as seems to be the case with Timothy in 1 Cor 16:10. The canonical 1 Corinthians should be read with an understanding that it is part of a larger archive of communication between the churches in Corinth and the apostle who founded them.

Within the New Testament, 1 Corinthians and 2 Corinthians provide insights into an important period in the history of the church. In fact, we find the earliest tradition of the institution of the Eucharist in 1 Cor 11:23–26. Paul's definition of the gospel he preaches is given in 1 Cor 15:1–7 and abbreviated elsewhere (1:17). Chapter 14 presents a view into the liturgical celebration of the mid-first-century church. First Corinthians itself is a treasure-trove of information about the social concerns of believers attempting to live the Christian life within a thoroughly Greco-Roman world. These are not anonymous believers, for we have the names of sixteen Corinthians with whom Paul worked and prayed.[1] The problems that beset the original community were not wholly resolved in Paul's day. By the end of the first century, the community of Corinth

## Outline of 1 Corinthians

I. **Address (1:1–9)**

II. **Disorders in the Corinthian Community (1:10–6:20)**

  A. **Divisions in the Church (1:10–4:21)**

  B. **Moral Disorders (5:1–6:20)**

III. **Answers to the Corinthians' Questions (7:1–11:1)**

  A. **Marriage and Virginity (7:1–40)**

  B. **Offerings to Idols (8:1–11:1)**

IV. **Problems in Liturgical Assemblies (11:2–14:40)**

  A. **Women's Headdresses (11:3–16)**

  B. **The Lord's Supper (11:17–34)**

  C. **Spiritual Gifts (12:1–14:40)**

V. **The Resurrection (15:1–58)**

  A. **The Resurrection of Christ (15:1–11)**

  B. **The Resurrection of the Dead (15:12–34)**

  C. **The Manner of the Resurrection (15:35–58)**

VI. **Conclusion (16:1–24)**

continued to fight about its ministers, necessitating a letter from Clement of Rome. In it, Clement asks the community if they have forgotten Paul's letter to them.[2] So it would seem that the Corinthians had returned to their fractious ways.

---

1. Gerd Theissen, *The Social Setting of Pauline Christianity: Essays on Corinth* (Philadelphia: Fortress Press: 1982), 94–95.

2. 1 Clem. 47:1–3.

# Authorship

Paul wrote 1 Corinthians from Ephesus where he was awaiting Pentecost (1 Cor 16:8), the Jewish spring harvest festival fifty days after Passover. Sosthenes, a former synagogue leader in Corinth, was the co-sender of the letter (1:1). At the letter's conclusion, Paul added a postscript, acknowledging that he was writing the greeting in his own hand (16:21), which suggests that the rest of the letter was written by dictation to a secretary.

According to Acts of the Apostles, Paul arrived in Corinth after leaving Athens (Acts 18:1) and remained in the city for a year and a half (Acts 18:11). In Corinth Paul met the Jewish couple Aquila and Priscilla (Acts 18:2; in 1 Cor 16:19 and Rom 16:3 she is called Prisca). He resided and worked with them, since they shared the same trade (Acts 18:3). Every sabbath, Paul took his message to the synagogue, where he attempted to persuade both Jews and Greeks to the gospel (Acts 18:4). Many were baptized (Acts 18:8, 10), but opposition from the Jews forced him to appear before the Roman proconsul Gallio (18:12–17). When Gallio refused the case, the complainants seized Sosthenes, the synagogue official, and beat him (Acts 18:17). After founding the community in Corinth, Paul, Priscilla, and Aquila travel to Ephesus. Since Sosthenes is listed as co-author with Paul, he may have relocated to Ephesus as well. First Corinthians was written probably between 54 and 56 CE.

# Recipients

Paul writes "to the church of God that is in Corinth, to you who have been sanctified in Christ Jesus, called to be holy" (1 Cor 1:2). Paul establishes that his recipients are part of the larger community of believers: "all those everywhere who call upon the name of our Lord Jesus Christ" (1:2). Throughout the letter, Paul emphasizes being sanctified, called, and holy. He reminds the church community that they have been sanctified (6:11), a sanctification rooted in Christ (1:30). They have been called by God to fellowship (1:9), both "Jews and Greeks alike" (1:24). They are God's holy temple (3:17), the holy ones who will judge the world (6:2).

Earlier social scientific investigations proposed that the majority of the Corinthians whose names are known belonged to the upper classes.[3] More recent investigations have tempered that proposal. The limited economic information known about the Corinthian believers suggests that the vast majority lived at a subsistence level, with a few who did possess surplus resources.[4] Paul notes that few of the Corinthians were well-born (1 Cor 1:26–28), which seems to imply that some may have been. The membership of the Corinthian Christian community includes both Gentiles and Jews (12:13). Some of the Gentile believers had been accustomed to eating food offered to idols (8:7, 10). Acts 18:8 identifies Crispus (whom Paul says in 1 Cor 1:14 that he baptized) as the leader of the local synagogue.

# Context

Because of its strategic location, straddling the isthmus that separates the Peloponnese from the rest of Greece, the city of Corinth had an extensive battle history. Refusing to obey Rome's command to disband the Achaian league, Corinth was destroyed in 146 BCE. Until its reestablishment by Julius Caesar nearly a hundred years later, the city stood virtually empty. In 27 BCE, Corinth became the capital of the senatorial province of Achaia and the seat of the ruling proconsul, who in Paul's day was Gallio (June 51–May 52). A few miles east of Corinth was the port city of Isthmia, which biannually held athletic competitions similar to the Olympic games. By the first century CE, the city had eclipsed Athens in economic and political importance. A few decades before Paul, the first-century geographer Strabo wrote of Corinth:

> Corinth is called "wealthy" because of its commerce, since it is situated on the Isthmus and is master of two harbors, of which the one leads straight to Asia, and the other

---

3. Theissen, *Social Setting*, 95.

4. Steven J. Friesen, "Prospects for a Demography of the Pauline Mission: Corinth among the Churches," in *Urban Religion in Roman Corinth: Interdisciplinary Approaches*, by Daniel N. Schowalter and Steven J. Friesen, (Cambridge, MA: Harvard University Press, 2005), 367.

to Italy; and it makes easy the exchange of merchandise from both countries that are so far distant from each other. . . .The city of the Corinthians, then, was always great and wealthy, and it was well equipped with men skilled both in the affairs of state and in the craftsman's arts.[5]

Though little of Greek Corinth existed after the Roman destruction, its unsavory reputation continued. In classical times, the city was noted for its sanctuary of Aphrodite perched on its acrocorinth or escarpment, rising 1,750 feet above the city. In Paul's day, the temple of Aphrodite was still in use but considerably smaller. Writing around 160 CE Pausanias remarks that several temples dotted the acrocorinth, including those to Aphrodite, Isis, Sarapis, Demeter, and Kore.[6] Today only the remnants of the temple of Apollo hint at its once glorious pagan history.

## Reason for Writing

Though 1 Corinthians addresses a variety of issues, Paul's chief concern is the divisions that have arisen in the young community. Chloe's people have brought a report to Paul that the community has dissolved into factions (1 Cor 1:11). As a response, 1 Corinthians sets forth Paul's argument for unity.

> I urge you, brothers, in the name of our Lord Jesus Christ, that all of you agree in what you say, and that there be no divisions among you, but that you be united in the same mind and in the same purpose. (1 Cor 1:10)

Paul addresses disturbances in the Corinthian community: divisions and rival groups (1 Cor 1:10–17; 3:1–4:5; 11:18), immorality (5:1–13), litigious action (6:1–8), disregard for the "weaker" Christian (8:11), liturgical abuses (11:17–22), and diverse understandings of resurrection (ch. 15). When Paul's authority is questioned (ch. 9), he urges unity and concord (1:10) and encourages that love guide the community (16:14). To these crises and conflicts, Paul offers his advice, addressing each one separately. A man of his times, Paul employs rhetoric in order to persuade his community toward good. A staple in his rhetorical arsenal, metaphors like that of the body and its various parts are meant to strengthen the Corinthians' sense of common purpose (12:12–26). Paul's ultimate answer to the schisms among his community is rooted not in the parts, but in the whole. He uses an ancient rhetorical topic of unity. The metaphor of the body is a political device used to combat factionalism.

Like the great philosophers before him—Socrates, Plato, Aristotle—Paul recognized that the answer to *stasis*, or factionalism, is love. In, 1 Cor 8:1, he admonishes that love builds up. Paul means for love to be a binding force in the community, an antidote to schism (13:1–13). He concludes his letter with an exhortation: "Be on your guard, stand firm in the faith, be courageous, be strong. Your every act should be done with love" (16:13–14).

## Contents

As seen in other letters from Paul, 1 Corinthians follows the standard epistolary format found in Greco-Roman correspondence. There is a prescript (1 Cor 1:1–3), a thanksgiving section (1:4–9), followed by the body of the letter (1:10–15:58). Paul concludes his letter with a discussion of his plans and final exhortations and greetings (16:1–24). The variety of topics addressed and the changes in tone have led some scholars to question the unity of canonical 1 Corinthians. However, a systematic analysis of its contents through the lens of ancient rhetoric demonstrates a cohesive deliberative argument designed to foster unity among the divided Corinthian communities.[7]

Paul, who identifies himself as one "called to be an apostle of Christ Jesus by the will of God," and Sosthenes, the brother, greet the church of God in Corinth (1 Cor 1:1–2). Paul uses the singular term "church" to establish from the outset that the believers are to be of one body. He is aware that some locations

---

5. *Geogr.* 8.6.20; 8.6.23.

6. *Description of Greece*, 2.5.1.

7. Margaret M. Mitchell, *Paul and the Rhetoric of Reconciliation: An Exegetical Investigation of the Language and Composition of 1 Corinthians* (Tubingen: Mohr/Paul Siebeck; Louisville, KY: Westminster John Knox, 1991).

1
C
O
R

have multiple churches (Gal 1:2). The theme presented in 1 Cor 1:10 confirms Paul's concern for unity.

> I urge you, brothers, in the name of our Lord Jesus Christ, that all of you agree in what you say, and that there be no divisions among you, but that you be united in the same mind and in the same purpose.

Chloe's people have reported that the Corinthian believers are claiming different founders (1 Cor 1:11). Paul's immediate answer is to remind them that they belong to Christ, in whom they were baptized. The gospel which he preaches is the message of the cross, "foolishness to those who are perishing, but to us who are being saved it is the power of God" (1:18). The Corinthians have become haughty in their Christian calling, so Paul reminds them that they were neither wise nor powerful, nor of noble birth (1:26). But it is exactly these unlikely ones whom God choses—the foolish, the weak, the lowly and despised—so as to shame the wise, the strong, and the powerful (1:27–28). If anyone feels a need to boast, he or she should boast in the Lord (1:31). Boasting about oneself is to be avoided since it leads to divisions within the community.[8]

Paul critiques the type of wisdom so prized in Greco-Roman philosophical circles. But his is a wisdom not of this age or of the past (1 Cor 2:6). Rather, it is God's wisdom, which is mysterious, hidden, and unknown by the rulers of this age (2:8–9). Believers have access to this wisdom of God through the spirit of God (2:10–12). But they are not yet mature as "spiritual people." Paul calls them infants since they continue to behave like children with jealous rivalries among themselves (3:1–4).

To correct their misunderstandings about their leaders, Paul engages a series of metaphors. Paul planted, Apollos watered, but God gave the growth (1 Cor 3:6). Paul lays the foundation like a master builder but another builds upon it (3:10). The Corinthians are the very temple of God in which the Spirit dwells (3:16–17). Boasting about to whom they belong is needless, since everything belongs to them and they belong to Christ (3:21–23). The

phrase "I belong to" had cultic significance in the ancient world. It identified one's affiliation to a particular god. For example, inscriptions on votive offerings found in Corinth read "I belong to Aphrodite."[9] The Corinthians have mistakenly taken up pagan practices when they argue among themselves about to whom they owe allegiance. Paul and Apollos are merely servants of Christ and stewards of the mysteries (4:1); the Corinthians should follow their example. Contrary to the Corinthians' boasting, Paul and Apollos are fools on Christ's account (4:10), willingly going without food, drink, or homes. When they are ridiculed, persecuted, and slandered, they do not retaliate or defend themselves (4:11–13). Paul offers his own life as an appropriate model (4:16).

In 1 Cor 1:18–4:21, Paul has treated the Corinthians as one group whom he sees as beloved children. In the following chapters, he turns to the issues that divide the community. Chapters 5 and 6 address the immorality among the community members. Paul responds to a report he has received about a man who is living with his father's wife (5:1). Such behavior is appalling—even the Gentiles would not engage in such acts, Paul writes. The members of the *ekklēsia* (Greek for "an assembly," which is translated as "church") were not to associate with a fellow member who was an immoral person, or any fellow member who was greedy or an idolater, reveler, drunkard, or robber (5:10). Believers are taking each other to court rather than settling their differences (6:1–6). Paul advises that it is better to put up with injustice rather than inflict it on others (6:7–8). Paul returns to the metaphor of the body as a temple when he chastises those who engage in immorality.

> Do you not know that your body is a temple of the holy Spirit within you, whom you have from God, and that you are not your own? [20] For you have been purchased at a price. Therefore, glorify God in your body. (1 Cor 6:19–20)

In an earlier letter, the Corinthians had sent a series of questions to Paul, which he attempts

---

8. Mitchell, *Rhetoric of Reconciliation*, 91–95.

9. Robert M. Grant, *Paul in the Roman World: Conflict in Corinth* (Louisville, KY: Westminster John Knox, 2001), 25.

to answer in ch. 7. The first question Paul addresses appears to result from an overzealous ascetical group among the believers. This group advocates "It is a good thing for a man not to touch a woman" (1 Cor 7:1). Paul's sense of imminent eschatology (7:31) meant that the believers were living in a here-and-not-yet reality. In this context, Paul offers his "concession" to the Corinthians' questions about marriage. How is the believer to avoid immorality during this in-between time? Each man should have his own wife and each woman her own husband (7:2). But for those who are unmarried they should remain as they are. However, if they lack self-control, "it is better to marry than to be on fire" (7:9). Paul urges the members to remain in the state in which God called them (7:20). The circumcised should not try to "undo" his circumcision nor the uncircumcised seek to be circumcised (7:18–19). Nor should slaves be concerned about their status. Admitting that he has no commandment from the Lord, Paul offers his own opinion concerning the state of affairs for virgins, widows, and other unmarried people (7:25–39).

The next question to which Paul responds is a dietary one. The concern about eating meat must be placed within the first-century context. Meat was not a regular part of most people's diets. On celebratory occasions, a non-believer might sacrifice an animal to the gods. Such a celebration was accompanied by a feast to which friends and family were invited. Being invited to such a banquet was an honor. Knowing one would be served meat was a rare delight. Should a believer attend one of these meals and eat the meat sacrificed to idols? Paul reminds the Corinthians that idols do not exist (1 Cor 8:5); however, eating such meat may cause a weaker brother or sister to stumble (8:7–10). The problem is made clearer in ch. 10, where eating idol meat means participating in an idolatrous ritual (10:19–22).

Paul changes the subject in ch. 9, launching into a defense of his rights as an apostle (1 Cor 9:1–18) and expounding on his sense of freedom (9:19–27). Some Corinthians may not view Paul's apostleship to be on par with that of other apostles (9:5). Paul counters with examples that show that one's efforts merit

payment (9:7). He cites the Law of Moses that an ox should not be muzzled while it is working (9:9), and then concludes, "If we have sown spiritual seed for you, is it a great thing that we reap a material harvest from you?" (9:11). Despite his right to compensation, Paul does not take it, but offers the gospel free of charge (9:15, 18). He is under obligation to preach the gospel (9:16–17). For the sake of his own salvation, he must drive himself as an athlete would: "No, I drive my body and train it, for fear that, after having preached to others, I myself should be disqualified" (9:27). The Corinthians would have been familiar with athletic imagery since Olympic-style games were held biannually at nearby Isthmia.

Paul criticizes the boastful Corinthians (1 Cor 10:12) and reminds them to seek the good of their neighbor (10:24), again setting himself as the example (10:33–11:1). He next turns to liturgical concerns, specifically appropriate head coverings (11:3–16) and abuses at the Lord's Supper (11:17–22). The earliest institution of the Eucharist is found in 11:23–26.

In chs. 12–14, Paul counters the Corinthian community's overzealous valuing of certain charismatic activities. He explains that spiritual gifts are for the good of the whole (1 Cor 12:1–11; 14:14–25). The metaphor of the body and its parts was another attempt to show the community the value of all its members (12:12–26). Paul saves his best example of unity for last. Chapter 13 is Paul's litany on love—the antidote to schism and the chief theological virtue (13:4–13). Paul then returns to the questions of liturgy (14:26–40).

The final Corinthian concern that Paul addresses has to do with questions about the resurrection of the dead. In an early kerygmatic statement or teaching about the faith, Paul explains that the gospel which he preached, which the community received, and in which they now stand had been handed on to him. It is namely that:

> Christ died for our sins in accordance with the scriptures; that he was buried; that he was raised on the third day in accordance with the scriptures; that he appeared to Cephas, then to the Twelve. (1 Cor 15:3–5)

The Resurrection of Christ is the foundation

of all belief (1 Cor 15:14, 17). Christ is the firstfruits. Those believers who have died will likewise be raised (15:20). Nonetheless the Corinthians wonder how the dead are raised and what kind of body they then possess (15:35).

As Paul concludes his lengthy letter, he reminds the fractious Corinthian church that they are part of the larger *ekklēsia*. So he tells of the collection he intends for the saints in Jerusalem (1 Cor 16:1–4), outlines his travel plans (16:5–9), and sends final exhortations and greetings (16:10–24). He continues to keep them conscious of other churches by mention of those in Asia and the church that meets in the house of Aquila and Prisca (16:19), adding, "All the brothers greet you. Greet one another with a holy kiss" (16:20). According to the second-century apologist Justin Martyr, a kiss was part of the liturgical celebration of the Lord's Supper (*First Apology* 65). Paul often concludes his letters with this liturgical reminder of their faith (Rom 16:16; 2 Cor 13:12; 1 Thes 5:26). Finally, those who would not follow Paul's direction are to be excluded. Should someone not "love the Lord," Paul concludes, that person is to be accursed (1 Cor 16:22). ■

# THE FIRST LETTER TO THE CORINTHIANS

## New American Bible, Introduction

Paul's first letter to the church of Corinth provides us with a fuller insight into the life of an early Christian community of the first generation than any other book of the New Testament. Through it we can glimpse both the strengths and the weaknesses of this small group in a great city of the ancient world, men and women who had accepted the good news of Christ and were now trying to realize in their lives the implications of their baptism. Paul, who had founded the community and continued to look after it as a father, responds both to questions addressed to him and to situations of which he had been informed. In doing so, he reveals much about himself, his teaching, and the way in which he conducted his work of apostleship. Some things are puzzling because we have the correspondence only in one direction. For the person studying this letter, it seems to raise as many questions as it answers, but without it our knowledge of church life in the middle of the first century would be much poorer.

Paul established a Christian community in Corinth about the year 51, on his second missionary journey. The city, a commercial crossroads, was a melting pot full of devotees of various pagan cults and marked by a measure of moral depravity not unusual in a great seaport. The Acts of the Apostles suggests that moderate success attended Paul's efforts among the Jews in Corinth at first, but that they soon turned against him (Acts 18:1–8). More fruitful was his year and a half spent among the Gentiles (Acts 18:11), which won to the faith many of the city's poor and underprivileged (1 Cor 1:26). After his departure the eloquent Apollos, an Alexandrian Jewish Christian, rendered great service to the community, expounding "from the scriptures that the Messiah is Jesus" (Acts 18:24–28).

While Paul was in Ephesus on his third journey (1 Cor 16:8; Acts 19:1–20), he received disquieting news about Corinth. The community there was displaying open factionalism, as certain members were identifying themselves exclusively with individual Christian leaders and interpreting Christian teaching as a superior wisdom for the initiated few (1 Cor 1:10–4:21). The community lacked the decisiveness to take appropriate action against one of its members who was living publicly in an incestuous union (1 Cor 5:1–13). Other members engaged in legal conflicts in pagan courts of law (1 Cor 6:1–11); still others may have participated in religious prostitution (1 Cor 6:12–20) or temple sacrifices (1 Cor 10:14–22).

The community's ills were reflected in its liturgy. In the celebration of the Eucharist certain members discriminated against others, drank too freely at the agape, or fellowship meal, and denied Christian social courtesies to the poor among the membership (1 Cor 11:17–22). Charisms such as ecstatic prayer, attributed freely to the impulse of the holy Spirit, were more highly prized than works of charity (1 Cor 13:1–2, 8), and were used at times in a disorderly way (1 Cor 14:1–40). Women appeared at the assembly without the customary head-covering (1 Cor 11:3–16), and perhaps were quarreling over their right to address the assembly (1 Cor 14:34–35).

Still other problems with which Paul had to deal concerned matters of conscience discussed among the faithful members of the community: the eating of meat that had been sacrificed to idols (1 Cor 8:1–13), the use of sex in marriage (1 Cor 7:1–7), and the attitude to be taken by the unmarried toward marriage in view of the possible proximity of Christ's second coming (1 Cor 7:25–40). There was also a doctrinal matter that called for Paul's attention, for some members of the community, despite their belief in the resurrection of Christ, were denying the possibility of general bodily resurrection.

To treat this wide spectrum of questions, Paul wrote this letter from Ephesus about the year A.D. 56. The majority of the Corinthian Christians may well have been quite faithful. Paul writes on their behalf to guard against the threats posed to the community by the views and conduct of various minorities. He writes with confidence in the authority of his apostolic mission, and he presumes that the Corinthians, despite their deficiencies, will recognize and accept it. On the other hand, he does not hesitate to exercise his authority as his judgment dictates in each situation, even going so far as to promise a direct confrontation with recalcitrants, should the abuses he scores remain uncorrected (1 Cor 4:18–21).

The letter illustrates well the mind and character of Paul. Although he is impelled to insist on his office as founder of the community, he recognizes that he is only one servant of God among many and generously acknowledges the labors of Apollos (1 Cor 3:5–8). He provides us in this letter with many valuable examples of his method of theological reflection and exposition. He always treats the questions at issue on the level of the purity of Christian teaching and conduct. Certain passages of the letter are of the greatest importance for the understanding of early Christian teaching on the Eucharist (1 Cor 10:14–22; 11:17–34) and on the resurrection of the body (1 Cor 15:1–58).

Paul's authorship of 1 Corinthians, apart from a few verses that some regard as later interpolations, has never been seriously questioned. Some scholars have proposed, however, that the letter as we have it contains portions of more than one original Pauline

letter. We know that Paul wrote at least two other letters to Corinth (see 1 Cor 5:9; 2 Cor 2:3–4) in addition to the two that we now have; this theory holds that the additional letters are actually contained within the two canonical ones. Most commentators, however, find 1 Corinthians quite understandable as a single coherent work.

The principal divisions of the First Letter to the Corinthians are the following:

I. Address (1:1–9)
II. Disorders in the Corinthian Community (1:10–6:20)
  A. Divisions in the Church (1:10–4:21)
  B. Moral Disorders (5:1–6:20)
III. Answers to the Corinthians' Questions (7:1–11:1)
  A. Marriage and Virginity (7:1–40)
  B. Offerings to Idols (8:1–11:1)
IV. Problems in Liturgical Assemblies (11:2–14:40)
  A. Women's Headdresses (11:3–16)
  B. The Lord's Supper (11:17–34)
  C. Spiritual Gifts (12:1–14:40)
V. The Resurrection (15:1–58)
  A. The Resurrection of Christ (15:1–11)
  B. The Resurrection of the Dead (15:12–34)
  C. The Manner of the Resurrection (15:35–58)
VI. Conclusion (16:1–24) ∎

# FIRST CORINTHIANS

## I. ADDRESS†

**1 Greeting.** [1] Paul, called to be an apostle of Christ Jesus by the will of God,† and Sosthenes our brother,* [2] to the church of God that is in Corinth, to you who have been sanctified in Christ Jesus, called to be holy, with all those everywhere who call upon the name of our Lord Jesus Christ, their Lord and ours.* [3] Grace to you and peace from God our Father and the Lord Jesus Christ.

**Thanksgiving.** [4] I give thanks to my God always on your account for the grace of God bestowed on you in Christ Jesus, [5] that in him you were enriched in every way, with all discourse and all knowledge, [6] as the testimony† to Christ was confirmed among you, [7] so that you are not lacking in any spiritual gift as you wait for the revelation of our Lord Jesus Christ.* [8] He will keep you firm to the end, irreproachable on the day of our Lord Jesus [Christ].* [9] God is faithful, and by him you were called to fellowship with his Son, Jesus Christ our Lord.*

## II. DISORDERS IN THE CORINTHIAN COMMUNITY

### A. Divisions in the Church†

**Groups and Slogans.** [10] I urge you, brothers, in the name of our Lord Jesus Christ, that all of you agree in what you say, and that there be no divisions among you, but that you be united in the same mind and in the same purpose.* [11] For it has been reported to me about you, my brothers, by Chloe's people, that there are rivalries among you. [12] I mean that each of you is saying, "I belong to† Paul," or "I belong to Apollos," or "I belong to Cephas," or "I belong to Christ."* [13]† Is Christ divided? Was Paul crucified for you? Or were you baptized in the name of Paul? [14] I give thanks [to God] that I baptized none of you except Crispus and Gaius,* [15] so that no one can say you were baptized in my name. [16] (I baptized the household of Stephanas also; beyond that I do not know whether I baptized anyone else.)* [17]† For Christ did not send me to baptize but to preach the gospel, and not with the wisdom of human eloquence,† so that the cross of Christ might not be emptied of its meaning.*

**Paradox of the Cross.** [18] The message of the cross is foolishness to those who are perishing,

---

† 1:1–9 Paul follows the conventional form for the opening of a Hellenistic letter (cf. Rom 1:1–7), but expands the opening with details carefully chosen to remind the readers of their situation and to suggest some of the issues the letter will discuss.

**1:1** *Called…by the will of God*: Paul's mission and the church's existence are grounded in God's initiative. God's call, grace, and fidelity are central ideas in this introduction, emphasized by repetition and wordplays in the Greek.

**1:6** *The testimony*: this defines the purpose of Paul's mission (see also 1 Cor 15:15 and the note on 1 Cor 2:1). The forms of his testimony include oral preaching and instruction, his letters, and the life he leads as an apostle.

**1:10–4:21** The first problem Paul addresses is that of divisions within the community. Although we are unable to reconstruct the situation in Corinth completely, Paul clearly traces the divisions back to a false self-image on the part of the Corinthians, coupled with a false understanding of the apostles who preached to them (cf. 1 Cor 4:6, 9; 9:1–5) and of the Christian message itself. In these chapters he attempts to deal with those underlying factors and to bring the Corinthians back to a more correct perspective.

**1:12** *I belong to*: the activities of Paul and Apollos in Corinth are described in Acts 18. *Cephas* (i.e., "the Rock," a name by which Paul designates Peter also in 1 Cor 3:22; 9:5; 15:5 and in Gal 1:18; 2:9, 11, 14) may well have passed through Corinth; he could have baptized some members of the community either there or elsewhere. The reference to *Christ* may be intended ironically here.

**1:13–17** The reference to baptism and the contrast with preaching the gospel in v 17a suggest that some Corinthians were paying special allegiance to the individuals who initiated them into the community.

**1:17b–18** The basic theme of 1 Cor 1–4 is announced. Adher-

ence to individual leaders has something to do with differences in rhetorical ability and also with certain presuppositions regarding wisdom, eloquence, and effectiveness (power), which Paul judges to be in conflict with the gospel and the cross.

**1:17b** *Not with the wisdom of human eloquence*: both of the nouns employed here involve several levels of meaning, on which Paul deliberately plays as his thought unfolds. *Wisdom* (*sophia*) may be philosophical and speculative, but in biblical usage the term primarily denotes practical knowledge such as is demonstrated in the choice and effective application of means to achieve an end. The same term can designate the arts of building (cf. 1 Cor 3:10) or of persuasive speaking (cf. 1 Cor 2:4) or effectiveness in achieving salvation. *Eloquence* (*logos*): this translation emphasizes one possible meaning of the term *logos* (cf. the references to rhetorical style and persuasiveness in 1 Cor 2:1, 4). But the term itself may denote an internal reasoning process, plan, or intention, as well as an external word, speech, or message. So by his expression *ouk en sophia logou* in the context of gospel preaching, Paul may intend to exclude both human ways of reasoning or thinking about things and human rhetorical technique. *Human*: this adjective does not stand in the Greek text but is supplied from the context. Paul will begin immediately to distinguish between *sophia* and *logos* from their divine counterparts and play them off against each other.

---

**1:1** Rom 1:1.
**1:2** Acts 18:1–11.
**1:7** Ti 2:13.
**1:8** Phil 1:6.
**1:9** 1 Jn 1:3.
**1:10** Phil 2:2.
**1:12** 3:4, 22; 16:12; Acts 18:24–28.
**1:14** Acts 18:8 / Rom 16:23.
**1:16** 16:15–17.
**1:17** 2:1, 4.

but to us who are being saved it is the power of God.* ¹⁹For it is written:

> "I will destroy the wisdom of the wise,
>   and the learning of the learned I will
>     set aside."*

²⁰Where is the wise one? Where is the scribe? Where is the debater of this age? Has not God made the wisdom of the world foolish?* ²¹† For since in the wisdom of God the world did not come to know God through wisdom, it was the will of God through the foolishness of the proclamation to save those who have faith. ²²For Jews demand signs and Greeks look for wisdom,* ²³but we proclaim Christ crucified, a stumbling block to Jews and foolishness to Gentiles,* ²⁴but to those who are called, Jews and Greeks alike, Christ the power of God and the wisdom of God. ²⁵For the foolishness of God is wiser than human wisdom, and the weakness of God is stronger than human strength.

**The Corinthians and Paul.**† ²⁶Consider your own calling, brothers. Not many of you were wise by human standards, not many were powerful, not many were of noble birth. ²⁷Rather, God chose the foolish of the world to shame the wise, and God chose the weak of the world

to shame the strong,* ²⁸and God chose the lowly and despised of the world, those who count for nothing, to reduce to nothing those who are something, ²⁹so that no human being might boast† before God.* ³⁰It is due to him that you are in Christ Jesus, who became for us wisdom from God, as well as righteousness, sanctification, and redemption,* ³¹so that, as it is written, "Whoever boasts, should boast in the Lord."*

**2** ¹When I came to you, brothers, proclaiming the mystery of God,† I did not come with sublimity of words or of wisdom.* ²For I resolved to know nothing while I was with you except Jesus Christ, and him crucified.* ³I came to you in weakness† and fear and much trembling, ⁴and my message and my proclamation were not with persuasive [words of] wisdom,† but with a demonstration of spirit and power,* ⁵so that your faith might rest not on human wisdom but on the power of God.*

**The True Wisdom.**† ⁶Yet we do speak a wisdom to those who are mature, but not a wisdom of this age, nor of the rulers of this age who are passing away. ⁷Rather, we speak God's wisdom,† mysterious, hidden, which God predetermined before the ages for our glory, ⁸and which none of the rulers of this age† knew;

---

**1:21–25** True wisdom and power are to be found paradoxically where one would least expect them, in the place of their apparent negation. To human eyes the crucified Christ symbolizes impotence and absurdity.

**1:26–2:5** The pattern of God's wisdom and power is exemplified in their own experience, if they interpret it rightly (1 Cor 1:26–31), and can also be read in their experience of Paul as he first appeared among them preaching the gospel (1 Cor 2:1–5).

**1:29–31** "Boasting (about oneself)" is a Pauline expression for the radical sin, the claim to autonomy on the part of a creature, the illusion that we live and are saved by our own resources. "Boasting in the Lord" (1 Cor 1:31), on the other hand, is the acknowledgment that we live only from God and for God.

**2:1** The mystery of God: God's secret, known only to himself, is his plan for the salvation of his people; it is clear from 1 Cor 1:18–25; 2:2, 8–10 that this secret involves Jesus and the cross. In place of mystery, other good manuscripts read "testimony" (cf. 1 Cor 1:6).

**2:3** The weakness of the crucified Jesus is reflected in Paul's own bearing (cf. 2 Cor 10–13). Fear and much trembling: reverential fear based on a sense of God's transcendence permeates Paul's existence and preaching. Compare his advice to the Philippians to work out their salvation with "fear and trembling" (Phil 2:12), because God is at work in them just as his exalting power was paradoxically at work in the emptying, humiliation, and obedience of Jesus to death on the cross (Phil 2:6–11).

**2:4** Among many manuscript readings here the best is either "not with the persuasion of wisdom" or "not with persuasive words of wisdom," which differ only by a nuance. Whichever reading is accepted, the inefficacy of human wisdom for salvation is contrasted with the power of the cross.

**2:6–3:4** Paul now asserts paradoxically what he has previously been denying. To the Greeks who "are looking for wisdom" (1 Cor 1:22), he does indeed bring a wisdom, but of a higher order and an entirely different quality, the only wisdom really worthy of the name. The Corinthians would be able to grasp Paul's preaching as wisdom and enter into a wisdom-conversation with him if they were more open to the Spirit and receptive to the new insight and language that the Spirit teaches.

**2:7–10a** God's wisdom: his plan for our salvation. This was his own eternal secret that no one else could fathom, but in this new age of salvation he has graciously revealed it to us. For the pattern of God's secret, hidden to others and now revealed to the Church, cf. also Rom 11:25–36; 16:25–27; Eph 1:3–10; 3:3–11; Col 1:25–28.

**2:8** The rulers of this age: this suggests not only the political leaders of the Jews and Romans under whom Jesus was crucified (cf. Acts 4:25–28) but also the cosmic powers behind them (cf. Eph 1:20–23; 3:10). They would not have crucified the Lord of glory: they became the unwitting executors of God's plan, which will paradoxically bring about their own conquest and submission (1 Cor 15:24–28).

---

**1:18** 2:14 / Rom 1:16.
**1:19** Is 29:14.
**1:20** Is 19:12.
**1:22** Mt 12:38; 16:1 / Acts 17:18–21.
**1:23** 2:2; Gal 3:1 / Gal 5:11.
**1:27** Jas 2:5.
**1:29** Eph 2:9.
**1:30** Rom 4:17 / 6:11; Rom 3:24–26; 2 Cor 5:21 / Eph 1:7; Col 1:14; 1 Thes 5:23.
**1:31** Jer 9:23; 2 Cor 10:17.
**2:1** 1:17.
**2:2** 1:23; Gal 6:14.
**2:4** 4:20; Rom 15:19; 1 Thes 1:5.
**2:5** 2 Cor 4:7.

for, if they had known it, they would not have crucified the Lord of glory. 9 But as it is written:

> "What eye has not seen, and ear has not heard,
>     and what has not entered the human heart,
>     what God has prepared for those who love him,"*

10* this God has revealed to us through the Spirit.

For the Spirit scrutinizes everything, even the depths of God. 11 Among human beings, who knows what pertains to a person except the spirit of the person that is within? Similarly, no one knows what pertains to God except the Spirit of God. 12 We have not received the spirit of the world but the Spirit that is from God, so that we may understand the things freely given us by God. 13 And we speak about them not with words taught by human wisdom, but with words taught by the Spirit, describing spiritual realities in spiritual terms.†

14 Now the natural person† does not accept what pertains to the Spirit of God, for to him it is foolishness, and he cannot understand it, because it is judged spiritually. 15 The spiritual person, however, can judge everything but is not subject to judgment† by anyone.

16 For "who has known the mind of the Lord, so as to counsel him?" But we have the mind of Christ.*

**3** 1† Brothers, I could not talk to you as spiritual people, but as fleshly people,† as infants in Christ. 2 I fed you milk, not solid food, because you were unable to take it. Indeed, you are still not able, even now,* 3 for you are still of the flesh. While there is jealousy and rivalry among you,† are you not of the flesh and behaving in an ordinary human way?* 4 Whenever someone says, "I belong to Paul," and another, "I belong to Apollos," are you not merely human?*

**The Role of God's Ministers.**† 5 What is Apollos, after all, and what is Paul? Ministers† through whom you became believers, just as the Lord assigned each one. 6 I planted, Apollos watered, but God caused the growth.* 7 Therefore, neither the one who plants nor the one who waters is anything, but only God, who causes the growth. 8 The one who plants and the one who waters are equal, and each will receive wages in proportion to his labor. 9 For we are God's co-workers; you are God's field, God's building.*

10† According to the grace of God given to me, like a wise master builder I laid a foundation, and another is building upon it. But each

---

† **2:13** *In spiritual terms:* the Spirit teaches spiritual people a new mode of perception (1 Cor 2:12) and an appropriate language by which they can share their self-understanding, their knowledge about what God has done in them. The final phrase in 1 Cor 2:13 can also be translated "describing spiritual realities to spiritual people," in which case it prepares for 1 Cor 2:14–16.

**2:14** *The natural person:* see note on 1 Cor 3:1.

**2:15** *The spiritual person...is not subject to judgment:* since spiritual persons have been given knowledge of what pertains to God (1 Cor 2:11–12), they share in God's own capacity to judge. One to whom the mind of the Lord (and of Christ) is revealed (1 Cor 2:16) can be said to share in some sense in God's exemption from counseling and criticism.

**3:1–4** The Corinthians desire a sort of wisdom dialogue or colloquy with Paul; they are looking for solid, adult food, and he appears to disappoint their expectations. Paul counters: if such a dialogue has not yet taken place, the reason is that they are still at an immature stage of development (cf. 1 Cor 2:6).

**3:1** *Spiritual people...fleshly people:* Paul employs two clusters of concepts and terms to distinguish what later theology will call the "natural" and the "supernatural." (1) The natural person (1 Cor 2:14) is one whose existence, perceptions, and behavior are determined by purely natural principles, the *psychē* (1 Cor 2:14) and the *sarx* (flesh, a biblical term that connotes creatureliness, 1 Cor 3:1, 3). Such persons are only infants (1 Cor 3:1); they remain on a purely human level (*anthrōpoi*, 1 Cor 3:4). (2) On the other hand, they are called to be animated by a higher principle, the *pneuma*, God's spirit. They are to become spiritual (*pneumatikoi*, 1 Cor 3:1) and mature (1 Cor 2:6) in their perceptions and behavior (cf. Gal 5:16–26). The culmination of

existence in the Spirit is described in 1 Cor 15:44–49.

**3:3–4** Jealousy, rivalry, and divisions in the community are symptoms of their arrested development; they reveal the immaturity both of their self-understanding (1 Cor 3:4) and of the judgments about their apostles (1 Cor 3:21).

**3:5–4:5** The Corinthians tend to evaluate their leaders by the criteria of human wisdom and to exaggerate their importance. Paul views the role of the apostles in the light of his theology of spiritual gifts (cf. 1 Cor 12–14, where the charism of the apostle heads the lists). The essential aspects of all spiritual gifts (1 Cor 12:4–6 presents them as gifts of grace, as services, and as modes of activity) are exemplified by the apostolate, which is a gift of grace (1 Cor 3:10) through which God works (1 Cor 3:9) and a form of service (1 Cor 3:5) for the common good (elsewhere expressed by the verb "build up," suggested here by the image of the building, 1 Cor 3:9). The apostles serve the church, but their accountability is to God and to Christ (1 Cor 4:1–5).

**3:5** *Ministers:* for other expressions of Paul's understanding of himself as minister or steward to the church, cf. 1 Cor 4:1; 9:17, 19–27; 2 Cor 3:6–9; 4:1; 5:18; 6:3–4; and 2 Cor 11:23 (the climax of Paul's defense).

**3:10–11** There are diverse functions in the service of the community, but each individual's task is serious, and each will stand accountable for the quality of his contribution.

---

* **2:9** Is 64:3.
**2:10** Mt 11:25; 13:11; 16:17.
**2:16** Wis 9:13; Is 40:13; Rom 11:34.

**3:2** Heb 5:12–14.
**3:3** Jas 3:13–16.
**3:4** 1:12.
**3:6** Acts 18:1–11, 24–28.
**3:9** Eph 2:20–22; 1 Pt 2:5.

one must be careful how he builds upon it, [11] for no one can lay a foundation other than the one that is there, namely, Jesus Christ. [12] If anyone builds on this foundation with gold, silver, precious stones, wood, hay, or straw, [13] the work of each will come to light, for the Day† will disclose it. It will be revealed with fire, and the fire [itself] will test the quality of each one's work.* [14] If the work stands that someone built upon the foundation, that person will receive a wage. [15] But if someone's work is burned up, that one will suffer loss; the person will be saved,† but only as through fire. [16] Do you not know that you are the temple of God, and that the Spirit of God dwells in you?* [17] If anyone destroys God's temple, God will destroy that person; for the temple of God, which you are, is holy.†

[18] Let no one deceive himself. If anyone among you considers himself wise in this age, let him become a fool so as to become wise.* [19] For the wisdom of this world is foolishness in the eyes of God, for it is written:*

"He catches the wise in their own ruses,"

[20] and again:

"The Lord knows the thoughts of the wise, that they are vain."*

[21]† So let no one boast about human beings, for everything belongs to you,* [22] Paul or Apollos or Cephas, or the world or life or death, or the present or the future: all belong to you, [23] and you to Christ, and Christ to God.

**4** [1] Thus should one regard us: as servants of Christ and stewards of the mysteries of God.* [2] Now it is of course required of stewards that they be found trustworthy. [3] It does not concern me in the least that I be judged by you or any human tribunal; I do not even pass judgment on myself; [4] I am not conscious of anything against me, but I do not thereby stand acquitted; the one who judges me is the Lord.* [5] Therefore, do not make any judgment before the appointed time, until the Lord comes, for he will bring to light what is hidden in darkness and will manifest the motives of our hearts, and then everyone will receive praise from God.

**Paul's Life as Pattern.**† [6] I have applied these things to myself and Apollos for your benefit, brothers, so that you may learn from us not to go beyond what is written,† so that none of you will be inflated with pride in favor of one person over against another. [7] Who confers distinction upon you? What do you possess that you have not received? But if you have received it, why are you boasting as if you did not receive it? [8] You are already satisfied; you have already grown rich; you have become kings† without us! Indeed, I wish that you had become kings, so that we also might become kings with you.

---

**3:13** *The Day:* the great day of Yahweh, the day of judgment, which can be a time of either gloom or joy. *Fire* both destroys and purifies.

**3:15** *Will be saved:* although Paul can envision very harsh divine punishment (cf. 1 Cor 3:17), he appears optimistic about the success of divine corrective means both here and elsewhere (cf. 1 Cor 5:5; 11:32 [discipline]). The text of 1 Cor 3:15 has sometimes been used to support the notion of purgatory, though it does not envisage this.

**3:17** *Holy:* i.e., "belonging to God." The cultic sanctity of the community is a fundamental theological reality to which Paul frequently alludes (cf. 1 Cor 1:2, 30; 6:11; 7:14).

**3:21–23** These verses pick up the line of thought of 1 Cor 1:10–13. If the Corinthians were genuinely wise (1 Cor 3:18–20), their perceptions would be reversed, and they would see everything in the world and all those with whom they exist in the church in their true relations with one another. Paul assigns all the persons involved in the theological universe a position on a scale: God, Christ, church members, church leaders. Read from top to bottom, the scale expresses ownership; read from bottom to top, the obligation to serve. This picture should be complemented by similar statements such as those in 1 Cor 8:6 and 1 Cor 15:20–28.

**4:6–21** This is an emotionally charged peroration to the discussion about divisions. It contains several exhortations and statements of Paul's purpose in writing (cf. 1 Cor 4:6, 14–17, 21) that counterbalance the initial exhortation at 1 Cor 1:10.

**4:6** *That you may learn from us not to go beyond what is written:* the words "to go" are not in the Greek, but have here been added as the minimum necessary to elicit sense from this difficult passage. It probably means that the Corinthians should avoid the false wisdom of vain speculation, contenting themselves with Paul's proclamation of the cross, which is the fulfillment of God's promises in the Old Testament (what is written). *Inflated with pride:* literally, "puffed up," i.e., arrogant, filled with a sense of self-importance. The term is particularly Pauline, found in the New Testament only in 1 Cor 4:6, 18–19; 5:2; 8:1; 13:4; Col 2:18 (cf. the related noun at 2 Cor 12:20). It sometimes occurs in conjunction with the theme of "boasting," as in 1 Cor 4:6–7 here.

**4:8** *Satisfied…rich…kings:* these three statements could also be punctuated as questions continuing the series begun in v 7. In any case these expressions reflect a tendency at Corinth toward an overrealized eschatology, a form of self-deception that draws Paul's irony. The underlying attitude has implications for the Corinthians' thinking about other issues, notably morality and the resurrection, that Paul will address later in the letter.

**3:13** Mt 3:11–12; 2 Thes 1:7–10.
**3:16** 6:19; 2 Cor 6:16; Eph 2:20–22.
**3:18** 8:2; Is 5:21; Gal 6:3.
**3:19** 1:20 / Jb 5:13.
**3:20** Ps 94:11.
**3:21** 4:6 / Rom 8:32.
**4:1** Ti 1:7; 1 Pt 4:10.
**4:4** 2 Cor 1:12 / Rom 2:16; 2 Cor 5:10.

⁹† For as I see it, God has exhibited us apostles as the last of all, like people sentenced to death, since we have become a spectacle to the world, to angels and human beings alike.* ¹⁰We are fools on Christ's account, but you are wise in Christ; we are weak, but you are strong; you are held in honor, but we in disrepute.* ¹¹To this very hour we go hungry and thirsty, we are poorly clad and roughly treated, we wander about homeless* ¹²and we toil, working with our own hands. When ridiculed, we bless; when persecuted, we endure;* ¹³when slandered, we respond gently. We have become like the world's rubbish, the scum of all, to this very moment.

¹⁴I am writing you this not to shame you, but to admonish you as my beloved children.† ¹⁵Even if you should have countless guides to Christ, yet you do not have many fathers, for I became your father in Christ Jesus through the gospel.* ¹⁶Therefore, I urge you, be imitators of me.* ¹⁷For this reason I am sending you Timothy, who is my beloved and faithful son in the Lord; he will remind you of my ways in Christ [Jesus], just as I teach them everywhere in every church.*

¹⁸† Some have become inflated with pride,

as if I were not coming to you. ¹⁹But I will come to you soon, if the Lord is willing, and I shall ascertain not the talk of these inflated people but their power. ²⁰For the kingdom of God is not a matter of talk but of power.* ²¹Which do you prefer? Shall I come to you with a rod, or with love and a gentle spirit?*

## B. Moral Disorders†

# 5 A Case of Incest.†

¹It is widely reported that there is immorality among you, and immorality of a kind not found even among pagans—a man living with his father's wife.* ²And you are inflated with pride.† Should you not rather have been sorrowful? The one who did this deed should be expelled from your midst. ³I, for my part, although absent in body but present in spirit, have already, as if present, pronounced judgment on the one who has committed this deed,* ⁴in the name of [our] Lord Jesus: when you have gathered together and I am with you in spirit with the power of the Lord Jesus, ⁵you are to deliver this man to Satan† for the destruction of his flesh, so that his spirit may be saved on the day of the Lord.*

---

**4:9–13** A rhetorically effective catalogue of the circumstances of apostolic existence, in the course of which Paul ironically contrasts his own sufferings with the Corinthians' illusion that they have passed beyond the folly of the passion and have already reached the condition of glory. His language echoes that of the beatitudes and woes, which assert a future reversal of present conditions. Their present sufferings ("to this very hour," 11) place the apostles in the class of those to whom the beatitudes promise future relief (Mt 5:3–11; Lk 6:20–23); whereas the Corinthians' image of themselves as "already" filled, rich, ruling (1 Cor 4:8), as wise, strong, and honored (1 Cor 4:10) places them paradoxically in the position of those whom the woes threaten with future undoing (Lk 6:24–26). They have lost sight of the fact that the reversal is predicted for the future.

**4:14–17** *My beloved children*: the close of the argument is dominated by the tender metaphor of the father who not only gives his children life but also educates them. Once he has begotten them through his preaching, Paul continues to present the gospel to them existentially, by his life as well as by his word, and they are to learn, as children do, by imitating their parents (1 Cor 4:16). The reference to the *rod* in 1 Cor 4:21 belongs to the same image-complex. So does the image of the *ways* in 1 Cor 4:17: the ways that Paul teaches everywhere, "his ways in Christ Jesus," mean a behavior pattern quite different from the human ways along which the Corinthians are walking (1 Cor 3:3).

**4:18–21** 1 Cor 4:20 picks up the contrast between a certain kind of talk (*logos*) and true power (*dynamis*) from 1 Cor 1:17–18 and 1 Cor 2:4–5. The kingdom, which many of them imagine to be fully present in their lives (1 Cor 4:8), will be rather unexpectedly disclosed in the strength of Paul's encounter with them, if they make a powerful intervention on his part necessary. Compare the similar ending to an argument in 2 Cor 13:1–4, 10.

**5:1–6:20** Paul now takes up a number of other matters that require regulation. These have come to his attention by hearsay

(1 Cor 5:1), probably in reports brought by "Chloe's people" (1 Cor 1:11).

**5:1–13** Paul first deals with the incestuous union of a man with his stepmother (1 Cor 5:1–8) and then attempts to clarify general admonitions he has given about associating with fellow Christians guilty of immorality (1 Cor 5:9–13). Each of these three brief paragraphs expresses the same idea: the need of separation between the holy and the unholy.

**5:2** *Inflated with pride*: this remark and the reference to *boasting* in 1 Cor 5:6 suggest that they are proud of themselves despite the infection in their midst, tolerating and possibly even approving the situation. The attitude expressed in 1 Cor 6:2, 13 may be influencing their thinking in this case.

**5:5** *Deliver this man to Satan*: once the sinner is expelled from the church, the sphere of Jesus' lordship and victory over sin, he will be in the region outside over which Satan is still master. *For the destruction of his flesh*: the purpose of the penalty is medicinal: through affliction, sin's grip over him may be destroyed and the path to repentance and reunion laid open. With Paul's instructions for an excommunication ceremony here, contrast his recommendations for the reconciliation of a sinner in 2 Cor 2:5–11.

---

| | |
|---|---|
| **4:9** 15:31; Rom 8:36; 2 Cor 4:8–12; 11:23 / Heb 10:33. | **4:15** Gal 4:19; Phlm 10. |
| **4:10** 1:18; 3:18; 2 Cor 11:19 / 1 Cor 2:3; 2 Cor 13:9. | **4:16** 11:1; Phil 3:17; 4:9; 1 Thes 1:6; 2 Thes 3:7, 9. |
| **4:11** Rom 8:35; 2 Cor 11:23–27. | **4:17** 16:10; Acts 19:22. |
| **4:12** Acts 9:6–14; 18:3; 20:34; 1 Thes 2:9 / 1 Pt 3:9. | **4:20** 2:4; 1 Thes 1:5. |
| | **4:21** 2 Cor 1:23; 10:2. |
| | **5:1** Lv 18:7–8; 20:11; Dt 27:20. |
| | **5:3** Col 2:5. |
| | **5:5** 1 Tm 1:20. |

6 * Your boasting is not appropriate. Do you not know that a little yeast† leavens all the dough? 7† Clear out the old yeast, so that you may become a fresh batch of dough, inasmuch as you are unleavened. For our paschal lamb, Christ, has been sacrificed.* 8 Therefore, let us celebrate the feast, not with the old yeast, the yeast of malice and wickedness, but with the unleavened bread of sincerity and truth.*

9† I wrote you in my letter not to associate with immoral people, 10 not at all referring to the immoral of this world or the greedy and robbers or idolaters; for you would then have to leave the world.* 11 But I now write to you not to associate with anyone named a brother, if he is immoral, greedy, an idolater, a slanderer, a drunkard, or a robber, not even to eat with such a person.* 12 For why should I be judging outsiders? Is it not your business to judge those within? 13 God will judge those outside. "Purge the evil person from your midst."*

# 6 Lawsuits Before Unbelievers.† 1 How can any one of you with a case against another dare to bring it to the unjust for judgment instead of to the holy ones? 2† Do you not know that the holy ones will judge the world? If the world is to be judged by you, are you unqualified for the lowest law courts?* 3 Do you not know that we will judge angels? Then why not everyday matters? 4 If, therefore, you have courts for everyday matters, do you seat as judges people of no standing in the church? 5 I say this to shame you. Can it be that there is not one among you wise enough to be able to settle a case between brothers? 6 But rather brother goes to court against brother, and that before unbelievers?

7 Now indeed [then] it is, in any case, a failure on your part that you have lawsuits against one another. Why not rather put up with injustice? Why not rather let yourselves be cheated?* 8 Instead, you inflict injustice and cheat, and this to brothers. 9† Do you not know that the unjust will not inherit the kingdom of God? Do not be deceived; neither fornicators nor idolaters nor adulterers nor boy prostitutes† nor sodomites* 10 nor thieves nor the greedy nor drunkards nor slanderers nor robbers will inherit the kingdom of God. 11 That is what some of you used to be; but now you have had yourselves washed, you were sanctified, you were justified in the name of the Lord Jesus Christ and in the Spirit of our God.*

## Sexual Immorality.† 12 "Everything is lawful for me,"† but not everything is beneficial.

---

†

**5:6** A little yeast: yeast, which induces fermentation, is a natural symbol for a source of corruption that becomes all-pervasive. The expression is proverbial.

**5:7–8** In the Jewish calendar, Passover was followed immediately by the festival of Unleavened Bread. In preparation for this feast all traces of old bread were removed from the house, and during the festival only unleavened bread was eaten. The sequence of these two feasts provides Paul with an image of Christian existence: Christ's death (the true Passover celebration) is followed by the life of the Christian community, marked by newness, purity, and integrity (a perpetual feast of unleavened bread). Paul may have been writing around Passover time (cf. 1 Cor 16:5); this is a little Easter homily, the earliest in Christian literature.

**5:9–13** Paul here corrects a misunderstanding of his earlier directives against associating with immoral fellow Christians. He concedes the impossibility of avoiding contact with sinners in society at large but urges the Corinthians to maintain the inner purity of their own community.

**6:1–11** Christians at Corinth are suing one another before pagan judges in Roman courts. A barrage of rhetorical questions (1 Cor 6:1–9) betrays Paul's indignation over this practice, which he sees as an infringement upon the holiness of the Christian community.

**6:2–3** The principle to which Paul appeals is an eschatological prerogative promised to Christians: they are to share with Christ the judgment of the world (cf. Dn 7:22, 27). Hence they ought to be able to settle minor disputes within the community.

**6:9–10** A catalogue of typical vices that exclude from the kingdom of God and that should be excluded from God's church. Such lists (cf. 1 Cor 5:10) reflect the common moral sensibility of the New Testament period.

**6:9** The Greek word translated as boy prostitutes may refer to catamites, i.e., boys or young men who were kept for purposes of prostitution, a practice not uncommon in the Greco-Roman world. In Greek mythology this was the function of Ganymede, the "cupbearer of the gods," whose Latin name was Catamitus. The term translated sodomites refers to adult males who indulged in homosexual practices with such boys. See similar condemnations of such practices in Rom 1:26–27; 1 Tm 1:10.

**6:12–20** Paul now turns to the opinion of some Corinthians that sexuality is a morally indifferent area (1 Cor 6:12–13). This leads him to explain the mutual relation between the Lord Jesus and our bodies (1 Cor 6:13b) in a densely packed paragraph that contains elements of a profound theology of sexuality (1 Cor 6:15–20).

**6:12–13** Everything is lawful for me: the Corinthians may have derived this slogan from Paul's preaching about Christian freedom, but they mean something different by it: they consider sexual satisfaction a matter as indifferent as food, and they attribute no lasting significance to bodily functions (1 Cor 6:13a). Paul begins to deal with the slogan by two qualifications, which suggest principles for judging sexual activity. Not everything is beneficial: cf. 1 Cor 10:23, and the whole argument of 1 Cor 8–10 on the finality of freedom and moral activity. Not let myself be dominated: certain apparently free actions may involve in fact a secret servitude in conflict with the lordship of Jesus.

---

*

| | |
|---|---|
| **5:6** Gal 5:9. | **6:2** Wis 3:8; Mt 19:28; |
| **5:7** Ex 12:1–13; Dt | Rev 20:4. |
| 16:1–2; 1 Pt 1:19. | **6:7** Mt 5:38–42; Rom |
| **5:8** Ex 12:15–20; 13:7; Dt | 12:17–21; 1 Thes |
| 16:3. | 5:15. |
| **5:10** 10:27; Jn 17:15. | **6:9** 15:50; Gal 5:19–21; |
| **5:11** Mt 18:17; 2 Thes 3:6, | Eph 5:5. |
| 14; 2 Jn 10. | **6:11** Ti 3:3–7. |
| **5:13** Dt 13:6; 17:7; 22:24. | |

"Everything is lawful for me," but I will not let myself be dominated by anything.* ¹³"Food for the stomach and the stomach for food," but God will do away with both the one and the other. The body, however, is not for immorality, but for the Lord, and the Lord is for the body; ¹⁴God raised the Lord and will also raise us by his power.*

¹⁵Do you not know that your bodies are members of Christ? Shall I then take Christ's members and make them the members of a prostitute?† Of course not!* ¹⁶[Or] do you not know that anyone who joins himself to a prostitute becomes one body with her? For "the two," it says, "will become one flesh."* ¹⁷But whoever is joined to the Lord becomes one spirit with him.* ¹⁸Avoid immorality. Every other sin a person commits is outside the body, but the immoral person sins against his own body.† ¹⁹Do you not know that your body is a temple† of the holy Spirit within you, whom you have from God, and that you are not your own?* ²⁰For you have been purchased at a price. Therefore glorify God in your body.*

# III. ANSWERS TO THE CORINTHIANS' QUESTIONS

## A. Marriage and Virginity†

**7** **Advice to the Married.**† ¹Now in regard to the matters about which you wrote: "It is a good thing for a man not to touch a woman,"† ²but because of cases of immorality every man should have his own wife, and every woman her own husband. ³The husband should fulfill his duty toward his wife, and likewise the wife toward her husband. ⁴A wife does not have authority over her own body, but rather her husband, and similarly a husband does not have authority over his own body, but rather his wife. ⁵Do not deprive each other, except perhaps by mutual consent for a time, to be free for prayer, but then return to one another, so that Satan may not tempt you through your lack of self-control. ⁶This I say by way of concession,† however, not as a command. ⁷Indeed, I wish everyone to be as I am, but each has a particular gift from God,† one of one kind and one of another.*

⁸†* Now to the unmarried and to widows

---

**6:15b–16** *A prostitute*: the reference may be specifically to religious prostitution, an accepted part of pagan culture at Corinth and elsewhere; but the prostitute also serves as a symbol for any sexual relationship that conflicts with Christ's claim over us individually. *The two...will become one flesh*: the text of Gn 2:24 is applied positively to human marriage in Matthew and Mark, and in Eph 5:29–32: love of husband and wife reflect the love of Christ for his church. The application of the text to union with a prostitute is jarring, for such a union is a parody, an antitype of marriage, which does conflict with Christ's claim over us. This explains the horror expressed in 1 Cor 6:15b.

**6:18** *Against his own body*: expresses the intimacy and depth of sexual disorder, which violates the very orientation of our bodies.

**6:19–20** Paul's vision becomes trinitarian. *A temple*: sacred by reason of God's gift, his indwelling Spirit. *Not your own*: but "for the Lord," who acquires ownership by the act of redemption. *Glorify God in your body*: the argument concludes with a positive imperative to supplement the negative "avoid immorality" of 1 Cor 6:18. Far from being a terrain that is morally indifferent, the area of sexuality is one in which our relationship with God (and his Christ and his Spirit) is very intimately expressed: he is either highly glorified or deeply offended.

**7:1–40** Paul now begins to answer questions addressed to him by the Corinthians (1 Cor 7:1–11:1). The first of these concerns marriage. This chapter contains advice both to the married (1–16) and to the unmarried (1 Cor 7:25–38) or widowed (1 Cor 7:39–40); these two parts are separated by 1 Cor 7:17–24, which enunciate a principle applicable to both.

**7:1–16** It seems that some Christians in Corinth were advocating asceticism in sexual matters. The pattern *it is a good thing...*, but occurs twice (1 Cor 7:1–2, 8–9; cf. 1 Cor 7:26), suggesting that in this matter as in others the Corinthians have seized upon a genuine value but are exaggerating or distorting it in some way. Once again Paul calls them to a more correct per-

spective and a better sense of their own limitations. The phrase it is a *good thing* (1 Cor 7:1) may have been the slogan of the ascetic party at Corinth.

**7:1–7** References to Paul's own behavior (1 Cor 7:7–8) suggest that his celibate way of life and his preaching to the unmarried (cf. 1 Cor 7:25–35) have given some the impression that asceticism within marriage, i.e., suspension of normal sexual relations, would be a laudable ideal. Paul points to their experience of widespread immorality to caution them against overestimating their own strength (1 Cor 7:2); as individuals they may not have the particular gift that makes such asceticism feasible (1 Cor 7:7) and hence are to abide by the principle to be explained in 1 Cor 7:17–24.

**7:6** *By way of concession*: this refers most likely to the concession mentioned in 1 Cor 7:5a: temporary interruption of relations for a legitimate purpose.

**7:7** *A particular gift from God*: use of the term *charisma* suggests that marriage and celibacy may be viewed in the light of Paul's theology of spiritual gifts (1 Cor 12:12–14).

**7:8** Paul was obviously unmarried when he wrote this verse. Some interpreters believe that he had previously been married and widowed; there is no clear evidence either for or against this view, which was expressed already at the end of the second century by Clement of Alexandria.

---

**6:12** 10:23.
**6:14** Rom 8:11; 2 Cor 4:14.
**6:15** 12:27; Rom 6:12–13; 12:5; Eph 5:30.
**6:16** Gn 2:24; Mt 19:5; Mk 10:8; Eph 5:31.
**6:17** Rom 8:9–10; 2 Cor 3:17.
**6:19** 3:16–17; Rom 5:5.
**6:20** 3:23; 7:23; Acts 20:28 / Rom 12:1; Phil 1:20.
**7:7** Mt 19:11–12.
**7:8** 1 Tm 5:11–16 / 9:5.

I say: it is a good thing for them to remain as they are, as I do, 9 but if they cannot exercise self-control they should marry, for it is better to marry than to be on fire. 10* To the married, however, I give this instruction (not I, but the Lord):† A wife should not separate from her husband 11 —and if she does separate she must either remain single or become reconciled to her husband—and a husband should not divorce his wife.

12 To the rest† I say (not the Lord): if any brother has a wife who is an unbeliever, and she is willing to go on living with him, he should not divorce her; 13 and if any woman has a husband who is an unbeliever, and he is willing to go on living with her, she should not divorce her husband. 14 For the unbelieving husband is made holy through his wife, and the unbelieving wife is made holy through the brother. Otherwise your children would be unclean, whereas in fact they are holy.*

15 If the unbeliever separates,† however, let him separate. The brother or sister is not bound in such cases; God has called you to peace. 16 For how do you know, wife, whether you will save your husband; or how do you know, husband, whether you will save your wife?

**The Life That the Lord Has Assigned.**† 17 Only, everyone should live as the Lord has assigned, just as God called each one. I give this order in all the churches. 18 Was someone called after he had been circumcised? He should not try to undo his circumcision. Was an uncircumcised person called? He should not be circumcised.* 19 Circumcision means nothing, and uncircumcision means nothing; what matters is keeping God's commandments.* 20 Everyone should remain in the state in which he was called.

21 Were you a slave when you were called? Do not be concerned but, even if you can gain your freedom, make the most of it. 22 For the slave called in the Lord is a freed person in the Lord, just as the free person who has been called is a slave of Christ.* 23 You have been purchased at a price. Do not become slaves to human beings.* 24 Brothers, everyone should continue before God in the state in which he was called.

**Advice to Virgins and Widows.** 25 Now in regard to virgins I have no commandment from the Lord,† but I give my opinion as one who by the Lord's mercy is trustworthy. 26 So this is what I think best because of the present distress: that it is a good thing for a person to remain as he is.* 27 Are you bound to a wife? Do not seek a separation. Are you free of a wife? Then do not look for a wife. 28 If you marry, however, you do not sin, nor does an unmarried woman sin if she marries; but such people will experience affliction in their earthly life, and I would like to spare you that.

29† I tell you, brothers, the time is running out. From now on, let those having wives act as not having them,* 30 those weeping as not weeping, those rejoicing as not rejoicing, those buying as not owning, 31 those using the world as not using it fully. For the world in its present form is passing away.

32 I should like you to be free of anxieties. An unmarried man is anxious about the things of the Lord, how he may please the Lord. 33 But a married man is anxious about the things of the world, how he may please his wife,* 34 and he is divided. An unmarried woman or a virgin is anxious about the things of the Lord, so that she may be holy in both body and spirit. A married woman, on the other hand,

---

† **7:10–11** (Not I, but the Lord): Paul reminds the married of Jesus' principle of nonseparation (Mk 10:9). This is one of his rare specific references to the teaching of Jesus.
**7:12–14** To the rest: marriages in which only one partner is a baptized Christian. Jesus' prohibition against divorce is not addressed to them, but Paul extends the principle of nonseparation to such unions, provided they are marked by peacefulness and shared sanctification.
**7:15–16** If the unbeliever separates: the basis of the "Pauline privilege" in Catholic marriage legislation.
**7:17–24** On the ground that distinct human conditions are less significant than the whole new existence opened up by God's call, Paul urges them to be less concerned with changing their states of life than with answering God's call where it finds them. The principle applies both to the married state (1 Cor 7:1–16) and to the unmarried (1 Cor 7:25–38).
**7:25–28** Paul is careful to explain that the principle of 1 Cor

7:17 does not bind under sin but that present earthly conditions make it advantageous for the unmarried to remain as they are (1 Cor 7:28). These remarks must be complemented by the statement about "particular gifts" from 1 Cor 7:7.
**7:29–31** The world…is passing away: Paul advises Christians to go about the ordinary activities of life in a manner different from those who are totally immersed in them and unaware of their transitoriness.

---

| | |
|---|---|
| **7:10–11** Mt 5:32; 19:9. | **7:22** Eph 6:5–9; Col 3:11; |
| **7:14** Rom 11:16. | Phlm 16. |
| **7:18** 1 Mc 1:15 / Acts | **7:23** 6:20. |
| 15:1–2. | **7:26** 7:8. |
| **7:19** Rom 2:25, 29; Gal | **7:29** Rom 13:11. |
| 5:6; 6:15. | **7:33** Lk 14:20. |

is anxious about the things of the world, how she may please her husband.* ³⁵ I am telling you this for your own benefit, not to impose a restraint upon you, but for the sake of propriety and adherence to the Lord without distraction.*

³⁶† If anyone thinks he is behaving improperly toward his virgin, and if a critical moment has come† and so it has to be, let him do as he wishes. He is committing no sin; let them get married. ³⁷ The one who stands firm in his resolve, however, who is not under compulsion but has power over his own will, and has made up his mind to keep his virgin, will be doing well. ³⁸ So then, the one who marries his virgin does well; the one who does not marry her will do better.

³⁹† A wife is bound to her husband as long as he lives. But if her husband dies, she is free to be married to whomever she wishes, provided that it be in the Lord.* ⁴⁰ She is more blessed, though, in my opinion, if she remains as she is, and I think that I too have the Spirit of God.*

### B. Offerings to Idols†

**8** **Knowledge Insufficient.** ¹ Now in regard to meat sacrificed to idols:† we realize that "all of us have knowledge"; knowledge inflates

with pride, but love builds up.* ² If anyone supposes he knows something, he does not yet know as he ought to know. ³ But if one loves God, one is known by him.*

⁴ So about the eating of meat sacrificed to idols: we know that "there is no idol in the world," and that "there is no God but one."* ⁵ Indeed, even though there are so-called gods in heaven and on earth (there are, to be sure, many "gods" and many "lords"), ⁶† yet for us there is

> one God, the Father,
>> from whom all things are and for
>> whom we exist,
> and one Lord, Jesus Christ,
>> through whom all things are and
>> through whom we exist.*

**Practical Rules.** ⁷ But not all have this knowledge. There are some who have been so used to idolatry up until now that, when they eat meat sacrificed to idols, their conscience, which is weak, is defiled.*

⁸† Now food will not bring us closer to God. We are no worse off if we do not eat, nor are we better off if we do.* ⁹ But make sure that this liberty of yours in no way becomes a stumbling block to the weak.* ¹⁰ If someone sees you, with your knowledge, reclining at

---

† **7:36–38** The passage is difficult to interpret, because it is unclear whether Paul is thinking of a father and his unmarried daughter (or slave), or of a couple engaged in a betrothal or spiritual marriage. The general principles already enunciated apply: there is no question of sin, even if they should marry, but staying as they are is "better" (for the reasons mentioned in 1 Cor 7:28–35). Once again the *charisma* of 1 Cor 7:7 which applies also to the unmarried (1 Cor 7:8–9), is to be presupposed.

**7:36** *A critical moment has come*: either because the woman will soon be beyond marriageable age, or because their passions are becoming uncontrollable (cf. 1 Cor 7:9).

**7:39–40** Application of the principles to the case of widows. If they do choose to remarry, they ought to prefer Christian husbands.

**8:1–11:1** The Corinthians' second question concerns meat that has been sacrificed to idols; in this area they were exhibiting a disordered sense of liberation that Paul here tries to rectify. These chapters contain a sustained and unified argument that illustrates Paul's method of theological reflection on a moral dilemma. Although the problem with which he is dealing is dated, the guidelines for moral decisions that he offers are of lasting validity. Essentially Paul urges them to take a communitarian rather than an individualistic view of their Christian freedom. Many decisions that they consider pertinent only to their private relationship with God have, in fact, social consequences. Nor can moral decisions be determined by merely theoretical considerations; they must be based on concrete circumstances, specifically on the value and needs of other individuals and on mutual responsibility within the community. Paul here introduces the theme of "building up" (*oikodomē*), i.e., of contributing by individual action to the welfare and growth of the community. This theme will be further developed in 1 Cor 14; see note on 1 Cor 14:3b–5. Several years later Paul would again deal with the problem of

meat sacrificed to idols in Rom 14:1–15:6.

**8:1a** *Meat sacrificed to idols*: much of the food consumed in the city could have passed through pagan religious ceremonies before finding its way into markets and homes. *"All of us have knowledge"*: a slogan, similar to 1 Cor 6:12, which reveals the self-image of the Corinthians. 1 Cor 8:4 will specify the content of this knowledge.

**8:6** This verse rephrases the monotheistic confession of 1 Cor 8:4 in such a way as to contrast it with polytheism (1 Cor 8:5) and to express our relationship with the one God in concrete, i.e., in personal and Christian terms. *And for whom we exist*: since the Greek contains no verb here and the action intended must be inferred from the preposition *eis*, another translation is equally possible: "toward whom we return." *Through whom all things*: the earliest reference in the New Testament to Jesus' role in creation.

**8:8–9** Although the food in itself is morally neutral, extrinsic circumstances may make the eating of it harmful. *A stumbling block*: the image is that of tripping or causing someone to fall (cf. 1 Cor 8:13; 9:12; 10:12, 32; 2 Cor 6:3; Rom 14:13, 20–1). This is a basic moral imperative for Paul, a counterpart to the positive imperative to "build one another up"; compare the expression "giving offense" as opposed to "pleasing" in 1 Cor 10:32–33.

---

**7:34** 1 Tm 5:5.
**7:35** Lk 10:39–42.
**7:39** Rom 7:2.
**7:40** 7:25.
**8:1** Rom 15:14 / 1 Cor 13:1–13; Rom 14:15, 19.
**8:3** Rom 8:29; Gal 4:9;
**8:4** 10:19; Dt 6:4.

**8:6** Mal 2:10 / Rom 11:36; Eph 4:5–6 / 1 Cor 1:2–3 / Jn 1:3; Col 1:16.
**8:7** 10:28; Rom 14:23 / Rom 14:1; 15:1.
**8:8** Rom 14:17.
**8:9** Rom 14:13, 20–21.

table in the temple of an idol, may not his conscience too, weak as it is, be "built up" to eat the meat sacrificed to idols? [11] Thus through your knowledge, the weak person is brought to destruction, the brother for whom Christ died.* [12] When you sin in this way against your brothers and wound their consciences, weak as they are, you are sinning against Christ. [13] †* Therefore, if food causes my brother to sin, I will never eat meat again, so that I may not cause my brother to sin.

## 9 †Paul's Rights as an Apostle. [1] Am I not free? Am I not an apostle? Have I not seen Jesus our Lord? Are you not my work in the Lord?* [2] Although I may not be an apostle for others, certainly I am for you, for you are the seal of my apostleship in the Lord.

[3] My defense against those who would pass judgment on me† is this. [4] † Do we not have the right to eat and drink? [5] Do we not have the right to take along a Christian wife, as do the rest of the apostles, and the brothers of the Lord, and Cephas? [6] Or is it only myself and Barnabas who do not have the right not to work?* [7] Who ever serves as a soldier at his own expense? Who plants a vineyard without eating its produce? Or who shepherds a flock without using some of the milk from the flock?* [8] Am I saying this on human authority, or does not the law also speak of these things? [9] It is written in the law of Moses, "You shall not muzzle an ox while it is treading out the grain."* Is God concerned about oxen, [10] or is he not really speaking for our sake? It was written for our sake, because the plowman should plow in hope, and the thresher in hope of receiving a share.* [11] If we have sown spiritual seed for you, is it a great thing that we reap a material harvest from you?* [12] If others share this rightful claim on you, do not we still more?*

### Reason for Not Using His Rights. Yet we have not used this right.† On the contrary, we endure everything so as not to place an obstacle to the gospel of Christ. [13] † Do you not know that those who perform the temple services eat [what] belongs to the temple, and those who minister at the altar share in the sacrificial offerings?* [14] In the same way, the Lord ordered that those who preach the gospel should live by the gospel.*

[15] † I have not used any of these rights, however, nor do I write this that it be done so in my case. I would rather die. Certainly no one is going to nullify my boast.* [16] If I preach the gospel, this is no reason for me to boast,

---

† **8:13** His own course is clear: he will avoid any action that might harm another Christian. This statement prepares for the paradigmatic development in 1 Cor 9.

**9:1–27** This chapter is an emotionally charged expansion of Paul's appeal to his own example in 1 Cor 8:13; its purpose is to reinforce the exhortation of 1 Cor 8:9. The two opening questions introduce the themes of Paul's freedom and his apostleship (1 Cor 9:1), themes that the chapter will develop in reverse order, 1 Cor 9:1–18 treating the question of his apostleship and the rights that flow from it, and 1 Cor 9:19–27 exploring dialectically the nature of Paul's freedom. The language is highly rhetorical, abounding in questions, wordplays, paradoxes, images, and appeals to authority and experience. The argument is unified by repetitions; its articulations are highlighted by inclusions and transitional verses.

**9:3** *My defense against those who would pass judgment on me:* the reference to a defense (*apologia*) is surprising, and suggests that Paul is incorporating some material here that he has previously used in another context. The defense will touch on two points: the fact of Paul's rights as an apostle (1 Cor 9:4–12a and 1 Cor 9:13–14) and his nonuse of those rights (1 Cor 9:12b and 1 Cor 9:15–18).

**9:4–12a** Apparently some believe that Paul is not equal to the other apostles and therefore does not enjoy equal privileges. His defense on this point (here and in 1 Cor 9:13–14) reinforces the assertion of his apostolic character in 1 Cor 9:2. It consists of a series of analogies from natural equity (1 Cor 9:7) and religious custom (1 Cor 9:13) designed to establish his equal right to support from the churches (1 Cor 9:4–6, 11–12a); these analogies are confirmed by the authority of the law (1 Cor 9:8–10) and of Jesus himself (1 Cor 9:14).

**9:12b** It appears, too, that suspicion or misunderstanding has been created by Paul's practice of not living from his preaching. The first reason he asserts in defense of this practice is an entirely apostolic one; it anticipates the developments to follow in 1 Cor 9:19–22. He will give a second reason in 1 Cor 9:15–18.

**9:13–14** The position of these verses produces an interlocking of the two points of Paul's defense. These arguments by analogy (1 Cor 9:13) and from authority (1 Cor 9:14) belong with those of 1 Cor 9:7–10 and ground the first point. But Paul defers them until he has had a chance to mention "the gospel of Christ" (1 Cor 9:12b), after which it is more appropriate to mention Jesus' injunction to his preachers and to argue by analogy from the sacred temple service to his own liturgical service, the preaching of the gospel (cf. Rom 1:9; 15:16).

**9:15–18** Paul now assigns a more personal motive to his nonuse of his right to support. His preaching is not a service spontaneously undertaken on his part but a stewardship imposed by a sort of divine compulsion. Yet to merit any reward he must bring some spontaneous quality to his service, and this he does by freely renouncing his right to support. The material here is quite similar to that contained in Paul's "defense" at 2 Cor 11:5–12; 12:11–18.

---

| | |
|---|---|
| **8:11** Rom 14:15, 20. | **9:9** Dt 25:4; 1 Tm 5:18. |
| **8:13** Mt 18:6; Rom 14:20–21. | **9:10** 2 Tm 2:6. |
| **9:1** 1 Cor 9:19 / 2 Cor 12:12 / 1 Cor 15:8–9 / Acts 9:17; 26:16. | **9:11** Rom 15:27. |
| | **9:12** 2 Cor 11:7–12; 12:13–18; 2 Thes 3:6–12. |
| **9:6** Acts 4:36–37; 13:1–2; Gal 2:1, 9, 13; Col 4:10. | **9:13** Nm 18:8, 31; Dt 18:1–5. |
| **9:7** 2 Tm 2:3–4. | **9:14** Mt 10:10; Lk 10:7–8. |
| | **9:15** 2 Cor 11:9–10. |

for an obligation has been imposed on me, and woe to me if I do not preach it!* <sup>17</sup> If I do so willingly, I have a recompense, but if unwillingly, then I have been entrusted with a stewardship.* <sup>18</sup> What then is my recompense? That, when I preach, I offer the gospel free of charge so as not to make full use of my right in the gospel.*

**All Things to All.** <sup>19</sup>† Although I am free in regard to all, I have made myself a slave to all so as to win over as many as possible.* <sup>20</sup> To the Jews I became like a Jew to win over Jews; to those under the law I became like one under the law—though I myself am not under the law—to win over those under the law. <sup>21</sup> To those outside the law I became like one outside the law—though I am not outside God's law but within the law of Christ—to win over those outside the law. <sup>22</sup> To the weak I became weak, to win over the weak. I have become all things to all, to save at least some.* <sup>23</sup> All this I do for the sake of the gospel, so that I too may have a share in it.

<sup>24</sup>† Do you not know that the runners in the stadium all run in the race, but only one wins the prize? Run so as to win.* <sup>25</sup> Every athlete exercises discipline in every way. They do it to win a perishable crown, but we an imperishable one.* <sup>26</sup> Thus I do not run aimlessly; I do not fight as if I were shadowboxing. <sup>27</sup> No, I drive my body and train it, for fear that, after

having preached to others, I myself should be disqualified.†

**10** **Warning Against Overconfidence.** <sup>1</sup>† I do not want you to be unaware, brothers, that our ancestors were all under the cloud and all passed through the sea,* <sup>2</sup> and all of them were baptized into Moses in the cloud and in the sea.* <sup>3</sup> All ate the same spiritual food, <sup>4</sup> and all drank the same spiritual drink, for they drank from a spiritual rock that followed them,† and the rock was the Christ.* <sup>5</sup> Yet God was not pleased with most of them, for they were struck down in the desert.*

<sup>6</sup>† These things happened as examples for us, so that we might not desire evil things, as they did.* <sup>7</sup> And do not become idolaters, as some of them did, as it is written, "The people sat down to eat and drink, and rose up to revel."* <sup>8</sup> Let us not indulge in immorality as some of them did, and twenty-three thousand fell within a single day.* <sup>9</sup> Let us not test Christ† as some of them did, and suffered death by serpents.* <sup>10</sup> Do not grumble as some of them did, and suffered death by the destroyer.* <sup>11</sup> These things happened to them as an example, and they have been written down as a warning to us, upon whom the end of the ages has come.† <sup>12</sup> Therefore, whoever thinks he is standing secure should take care not to fall.† <sup>13</sup> No trial has come to you but what is human. God is faithful and will not let you be

---

† **9:19–23** In a rhetorically balanced series of statements Paul expands and generalizes the picture of his behavior and explores the paradox of apostolic freedom. It is not essentially freedom from restraint but freedom for service—a possibility of constructive activity.

**9:24–27** A series of miniparables from sports, appealing to readers familiar with Greek gymnasia and the nearby Isthmian games.

**9:27** *For fear that…I myself should be disqualified*: a final paradoxical turn to the argument: what appears at first a free, spontaneous renunciation of rights (1 Cor 9:12–18) seems subsequently to be required for fulfillment of Paul's stewardship (to preach effectively he must reach his hearers wherever they are, 1 Cor 9:19–22), and finally is seen to be necessary for his own salvation (1 Cor 9:23–27). Mention of the possibility of disqualification provides a transition to 1 Cor 10.

**10:1–5** Paul embarks unexpectedly upon a panoramic survey of the events of the Exodus period. The privileges of Israel in the wilderness are described in terms that apply strictly only to the realities of the new covenant ("baptism," "spiritual food and drink"); interpreted in this way they point forward to the Christian experience (1 Cor 10:1–4). But those privileges did not guarantee God's permanent pleasure (1 Cor 10:5).

**10:4** *A spiritual rock that followed them*: the Torah speaks only about a rock from which water issued, but rabbinic legend amplified this into a spring that followed the Israelites throughout their migration. Paul uses this legend as a literary type: he makes the rock itself accompany the Israelites, and he gives it a spiritual sense. *The rock was the Christ*: in the Old Testament, Yahweh is

the Rock of his people (cf. Dt 32, Moses' song to Yahweh the Rock). Paul now applies this image to the Christ, the source of the living water, the true Rock that accompanied Israel, guiding their experiences in the desert.

**10:6–13** This section explicitates the typological value of these Old Testament events: the desert experiences of the Israelites are examples, meant as warnings, to deter us from similar sins (idolatry, immorality, etc.) and from a similar fate.

**10:9** *Christ*: to avoid Paul's concept of Christ present in the wilderness events, some manuscripts read "the Lord."

**10:11** *Upon whom the end of the ages has come*: it is our period in time toward which past ages have been moving and in which they arrive at their goal.

**10:12–13** *Take care not to fall*: the point of the whole comparison with Israel is to caution against overconfidence, a sense of complete security (1 Cor 10:12). This warning is immediately balanced by a reassurance, based, however, on God (1 Cor 10:13).

---

* **9:16** Acts 26:14–18.
**9:17** 4:1; Gal 2:7.
**9:18** 2 Cor 11:7–12.
**9:19** Mt 20:26–27.
**9:22** 10:33; Rom 15:1; 2 Cor 11:29.
**9:24** Heb 12:1.
**9:25** 2 Tm 2:5 / 2 Tm 4:7–8; Jas 1:12; 1 Pt 5:4.
**10:1** Ex 13:21–22; 14:19–20 /

Ex 14:21–22, 26–30.
**10:2** Rom 6:3; Gal 3:27 / Ex 16:4–35.
**10:4** Ex 17:1–7; Nm 20:7–11; Dt 8:15.
**10:5** Nm 14:28–38; Jude 5.
**10:6** Nm 11:4, 34.
**10:7** Ex 32:6.
**10:8** Nm 25:1–9.
**10:9** Nm 21:5–9.
**10:10** Nm 14:2–37; 16:1–35.

tried beyond your strength; but with the trial he will also provide a way out, so that you may be able to bear it. *

**Warning Against Idolatry.**† ¹⁴Therefore, my beloved, avoid idolatry. * ¹⁵I am speaking as to sensible people; judge for yourselves what I am saying. ¹⁶The cup of blessing that we bless, is it not a participation in the blood of Christ? The bread that we break, is it not a participation in the body of Christ? * ¹⁷Because the loaf of bread is one, we, though many, are one body, for we all partake of the one loaf. *

¹⁸Look at Israel according to the flesh; are not those who eat the sacrifices participants in the altar? * ¹⁹So what am I saying? That meat sacrificed to idols is anything? Or that an idol is anything? ²⁰No, I mean that what they sacrifice, [they sacrifice] to demons,† not to God, and I do not want you to become participants with demons. * ²¹You cannot drink the cup of the Lord and also the cup of demons. You cannot partake of the table of the Lord and of the table of demons. * ²²Or are we provoking the Lord to jealous anger? Are we stronger than he? *

**Seek the Good of Others.**† ²³"Everything is lawful," but not everything is beneficial. † "Everything is lawful," but not everything builds up. * ²⁴No one should seek his own advantage, but that of his neighbor. * ²⁵†Eat anything

sold in the market, without raising questions on grounds of conscience, ²⁶for "the earth and its fullness are the Lord's." * ²⁷If an unbeliever invites you and you want to go, eat whatever is placed before you, without raising questions on grounds of conscience. ²⁸But if someone says to you, "This was offered in sacrifice," do not eat it on account of the one who called attention to it and on account of conscience; ²⁹I mean not your own conscience, but the other's. For why should my freedom be determined by someone else's conscience? ³⁰If I partake thankfully, why am I reviled for that over which I give thanks? *

³¹So whether you eat or drink, or whatever you do, do everything for the glory of God. ³²†Avoid giving offense, whether to Jews or Greeks or the church of God, ³³just as I try to please everyone in every way, not seeking my own benefit but that of the many, that they may be saved. *

# 11

¹Be imitators of me, as I am of Christ. *

## IV. PROBLEMS IN LITURGICAL ASSEMBLIES†

²I praise you because you remember me in everything and hold fast to the traditions, just as I handed them on to you. *

---

† **10:14–22** The warning against idolatry from 1 Cor 10:7 is now repeated (1 Cor 10:14) and explained in terms of the effect of sacrifices: all sacrifices, Christian (1 Cor 10:16–17), Jewish (1 Cor 10:18), or pagan (1 Cor 10:20), establish communion. But communion with Christ is exclusive, incompatible with any other such communion (1 Cor 10:21). Compare the line of reasoning at 1 Cor 6:15.

**10:20** *To demons*: although Jews denied divinity to pagan gods, they often believed that there was some nondivine reality behind the idols, such as the dead, or angels, or demons. The explanation Paul offers in 1 Cor 10:20 is drawn from Dt 32:17: the power behind the idols, with which the pagans commune, consists of demonic powers hostile to God.

**10:23–11:1** By way of peroration Paul returns to the opening situation (1 Cor 8) and draws conclusions based on the intervening considerations (1 Cor 9–10).

**10:23–24** He repeats in the context of this new problem the slogans of liberty from 1 Cor 6:12, with similar qualifications. Liberty is not merely an individual perfection, nor an end in itself, but is to be used for the common good. The language of 1 Cor 10:24 recalls the descriptions of Jesus' self-emptying in Phil 2.

**10:25–30** A summary of specific situations in which the eating of meat sacrificed to idols could present problems of conscience. Three cases are considered. In the first (the marketplace, 1 Cor 10:25–26) and the second (at table, 1 Cor 10:27), there is no need to be concerned with whether food has passed through a pagan sacrifice or not, for the principle of 1 Cor 8:4–6 still stands, and the whole creation belongs to the one God. But in the third case (1 Cor 10:28), the situation changes if someone present explicitly raises the question of the sacrificial origin of the food;

eating in such circumstances may be subject to various interpretations, some of which could be harmful to individuals. Paul is at pains to insist that the enlightened Christian conscience need not change its judgment about the neutrality, even the goodness, of the food in itself (1 Cor 10:29–30); yet the total situation is altered to the extent that others are potentially endangered, and this calls for a different response, for the sake of others.

**10:32–11:1** In summary, the general rule of mutually responsible use of their Christian freedom is enjoined first negatively (1 Cor 10:32), then positively, as exemplified in Paul (1 Cor 10:33), and finally grounded in Christ, the pattern for Paul's behavior and theirs (1 Cor 11:1; cf. Rom 15:1–3).

**11:2–14:40** This section of the letter is devoted to regulation of conduct at the liturgy. The problems Paul handles have to do with the dress of women in the assembly (1 Cor 11:3–16), improprieties in the celebration of community meals (1 Cor 11:17–34), and the use of charisms or spiritual gifts (1 Cor 12:1–14:40). The statement in 1 Cor 11:2 introduces all of these discussions, but applies more appropriately to the second (cf. the mention of praise in 1 Cor 11:17 and of tradition in 1 Cor 11:23).

---

**10:13** Mt 6:13; Jas 1:13–14 / 1 Cor 1:9.
**10:14** 1 Jn 5:21.
**10:16** Mt 26:26–29; Acts 2:42.
**10:17** Rom 12:5; Eph 4:4.
**10:18** Lv 7:6.
**10:20** Dt 32:17.
**10:21** 2 Cor 6:14–18.
**10:22** Dt 32:21 / Eccl 6:10.
**10:23** 6:12.
**10:24** Rom 15:2; Phil 2:4, 21.
**10:26** Ps 24:1; 50:12.
**10:30** Rom 14:6; 1 Tm 4:3–4.
**10:33** 9:22; Rom 15:2.
**11:1** 4:16; Phil 3:17.
**11:2** 15:3; 2 Thes 2:15.

## A. Women's Headdresses†

**Man and Woman.** ³But I want you to know that Christ is the head of every man, and a husband the head of his wife,† and God the head of Christ.* ⁴†Any man who prays or prophesies with his head covered brings shame upon his head. ⁵But any woman who prays or prophesies with her head unveiled brings shame upon her head, for it is one and the same thing as if she had had her head shaved. ⁶For if a woman does not have her head veiled, she may as well have her hair cut off. But if it is shameful for a woman to have her hair cut off or her head shaved, then she should wear a veil.

⁷†A man, on the other hand, should not cover his head, because he is the image and glory of God, but woman is the glory of man.* ⁸For man did not come from woman, but woman from man;* ⁹nor was man created for woman, but woman for man;* ¹⁰for this reason a woman should have a sign of authority† on her head, because of the angels. ¹¹†Woman is not independent of man or man of woman in the Lord.* ¹²For just as woman came from man, so man is born of woman; but all things are from God.*

¹³†Judge for yourselves: is it proper for a woman to pray to God with her head unveiled? ¹⁴Does not nature itself teach you that if a man wears his hair long it is a disgrace to him, ¹⁵whereas if a woman has long hair it is her glory, because long hair has been given [her] for a covering? ¹⁶But if anyone is inclined to be argumentative, we do not have such a custom, nor do the churches of God.

## B. The Lord's Supper†

**An Abuse at Corinth.** ¹⁷In giving this instruction, I do not praise the fact that your meetings are doing more harm than good. ¹⁸First of all, I hear that when you meet as a church there are divisions among you, and to a degree I believe it;* ¹⁹there have to be factions among you in order that [also] those who are approved among you may become known.† ²⁰When you meet in one place, then, it is not to eat the Lord's supper, ²¹for in eating, each one goes ahead with his own supper, and one goes hungry while another gets drunk.

---

**11:3–16** Women have been participating in worship at Corinth without the head-covering normal in Greek society of the period. Paul's stated goal is to bring them back into conformity with contemporary practice and propriety. In his desire to convince, he reaches for arguments from a variety of sources, though he has space to develop them only sketchily and is perhaps aware that they differ greatly in persuasiveness.

**11:3** *A husband the head of his wife*: the specific problem suggests to Paul the model of the head as a device for clarifying relations within a hierarchical structure. The model is similar to that developed later in greater detail and nuance in Eph 5:21–33. It is a hybrid model, for it grafts onto a strictly theological scale of existence (cf. 1 Cor 3:21–23) the hierarchy of sociosexual relations prevalent in the ancient world: men, dominant, reflect the active function of Christ in relation to his church; women, submissive, reflect the passive role of the church with respect to its savior. This gives us the functional scale: God, Christ, man, woman.

**11:4–6** From man's direct relation to Christ, Paul infers that his head should not be covered. But woman, related not directly to Christ on the scale but to her husband, requires a covering as a sign of that relationship. *Shameful...to have her hair cut off*: certain less honored classes in society, such as lesbians and prostitutes, are thought to have worn their hair close-cropped.

**11:7–9** The hierarchy of v 3 is now expressed in other metaphors: the image (*eikōn*) and the reflected glory (*doxa*). Paul is alluding basically to the text of Gn 1:27, in which mankind as a whole, the male-female couple, is created in God's image and given the command to multiply and together dominate the lower creation. But Gn 1:24 is interpreted here in the light of the second creation narrative in Gn 2, in which each of the sexes is created separately (first the man and then the woman from man and for him, to be his helpmate, Gn 2:20–23), and under the influence of the story of the fall, as a result of which the husband rules over the woman (Gn 3:16). This interpretation splits the single image of God into two, at different degrees of closeness.

**11:10** *A sign of authority*: "authority" (*exousia*) may possibly be due to mistranslation of an Aramaic word for "veil"; in any case, the connection with 1 Cor 11:9 indicates that the covering is a sign of woman's subordination. *Because of the angels*: a surprising additional reason, which the context does not clarify. Presumably the reference is to cosmic powers who might inflict harm on women or whose function is to watch over women or the cult.

**11:11–12** These parenthetical remarks relativize the argument from Gn 2–3. *In the Lord*: in the Christian economy the relation between the sexes is characterized by a mutual dependence, which is not further specified. And even in the natural order conditions have changed: the mode of origin described in Gn 2 has been reversed (1 Cor 11:12a). But the ultimately significant fact is the origin that all things have in common (1 Cor 11:12b).

**11:13–16** The argument for conformity to common church practice is summed up and pressed home. 1 Cor 11:14–15 contain a final appeal to the sense of propriety that contemporary Greek society would consider "natural" (cf. 1 Cor 11:5–6).

**11:17–34** Paul turns to another abuse connected with the liturgy, and a more serious one, for it involves neglect of basic Christian tradition concerning the meaning of the Lord's Supper. Paul recalls that tradition for them and reminds them of its implications.

**11:19** *That...those who are approved among you may become known*: Paul situates their divisions within the context of the eschatological separation of the authentic from the inauthentic and the final revelation of the difference. The notion of authenticity-testing recurs in the injunction to self-examination in view of present and future judgment (1 Cor 11:28–32).

---

**11:3** Eph 5:23.
**11:7** Gn 1:26–27; 5:1.
**11:8** Gn 2:21–23.
**11:9** Gn 2:18.
**11:11** Gal 3:27–28.
**11:12** 8:6; Rom 11:36.
**11:18** 1:10–12; Gal 5:20.

<sup>22</sup> Do you not have houses in which you can eat and drink? Or do you show contempt for the church of God and make those who have nothing feel ashamed? What can I say to you? Shall I praise you? In this matter I do not praise you.*

**Tradition of the Institution.** <sup>23</sup>† For I received from the Lord what I also handed on to you,* that the Lord Jesus, on the night he was handed over, took bread, <sup>24</sup> and, after he had given thanks, broke it and said, "This is my body that is for you. Do this in remembrance of me." <sup>25</sup> In the same way also the cup, after supper, saying, "This cup is the new covenant in my blood. Do this, as often as you drink it, in remembrance of me."* <sup>26</sup> For as often as you eat this bread and drink the cup, you proclaim the death of the Lord until he comes.

<sup>27</sup> Therefore whoever eats the bread or drinks the cup of the Lord unworthily will have to answer for the body and blood of the Lord.† <sup>28</sup> A person should examine himself,† and so eat the bread and drink the cup. <sup>29</sup> For anyone who eats and drinks without discerning the body, eats and drinks judgment† on himself. <sup>30</sup> That is why many among you are ill and infirm, and a considerable number are dying. <sup>31</sup> If we discerned ourselves, we would not be under judgment; <sup>32</sup> but since we are judged by [the] Lord, we are being disciplined so that we may not be condemned along with the world.*

<sup>33</sup> Therefore, my brothers, when you come together to eat, wait for one another. <sup>34</sup> If anyone is hungry, he should eat at home, so that your meetings may not result in judgment. The other matters I shall set in order when I come.

## C. Spiritual Gifts†

**12 Unity and Variety.** <sup>1</sup> Now in regard to spiritual gifts, brothers, I do not want you to be unaware. <sup>2</sup>† You know how, when you were pagans, you were constantly attracted and led away to mute idols.* <sup>3</sup> Therefore, I tell you that nobody speaking by the spirit of God says, "Jesus be accursed." And no one can say, "Jesus is Lord," except by the holy Spirit.*

<sup>4</sup>† There are different kinds of spiritual gifts but the same Spirit;* <sup>5</sup> there are different forms of service but the same Lord; <sup>6</sup> there are different workings but the same God who produces all of them in everyone. <sup>7</sup> To each individual the manifestation of the Spirit is given for some benefit. <sup>8</sup> To one is given through the Spirit the expression of wisdom; to another the expression of knowledge according to the same Spirit;* <sup>9</sup> to another faith by the same

---

† **11:23–25** This is the earliest written account of the institution of the Lord's Supper in the New Testament. The narrative emphasizes Jesus' action of self-giving (expressed in the words over the bread and the cup) and his double command to repeat his own action.

**11:27** It follows that the only proper way to celebrate the Eucharist is one that corresponds to Jesus' intention, which fits with the meaning of his command to reproduce his action in the proper spirit. If the Corinthians eat and drink unworthily, i.e., without having grasped and internalized the meaning of his death for them, *they will have to answer for the body and blood*, i.e., will be guilty of a sin against the Lord himself (cf. 1 Cor 8:12).

**11:28** *Examine himself*: the Greek word is similar to that for "approved" in 1 Cor 11:19, which means "having been tested and found true." The self-testing required for proper eating involves *discerning the body* (1 Cor 11:29), which, from the context, must mean understanding the sense of Jesus' death (1 Cor 11:26), perceiving the imperative to unity that follows from the fact that Jesus gives himself to all and requires us to repeat his sacrifice in the same spirit (1 Cor 11:18–25).

**11:29–32** *Judgment*: there is a series of wordplays in these verses that would be awkward to translate literally into English; it includes all the references to judgment (*krima*, 1 Cor 11:29, 34; *krinō*, 1 Cor 11:31, 32) discernment (*diakrinō*, 1 Cor 11:29, 31), and condemnation (*katakrinō*, 1 Cor 11:32). The judgment is concretely described as the illness, infirmity, and death that have visited the community. These are signs that the power of Jesus' death is not yet completely recognized and experienced. Yet even the judgment incurred is an expression of God's concern; it is a medicinal measure meant to rescue us from condemnation with God's enemies.

**12:1–14:40** Ecstatic and charismatic activity were common in early Christian experience, as they were in other ancient religions. But the Corinthians seem to have developed a disproportionate esteem for certain phenomena, especially tongues, to the detriment of order in the liturgy. Paul's response to this development provides us with the fullest exposition we have of his theology of the charisms.

**12:2–3** There is an experience of the Spirit and an understanding of ecstatic phenomena that are specifically Christian and that differ, despite apparent similarities, from those of the pagans. It is necessary to discern which spirit is leading one; ecstatic phenomena must be judged by their effect (1 Cor 12:2). 1 Cor 12:3 illustrates this by an example: power to confess Jesus as Lord can come only from the Spirit, and it is inconceivable that the Spirit would move anyone to curse the Lord.

**12:4–6** There are some features common to all charisms, despite their diversity: all are *gifts* (*charismata*), grace from outside ourselves; all are forms of *service* (*diakoniai*), an expression of their purpose and effect; and all are *workings* (*energēmata*), in which God is at work. Paul associates each of these aspects with what later theology will call one of the persons of the Trinity, an early example of "appropriation."

---

**11:22** Jas 2:1–7.
**11:23** 11:2; 15:3 / 10:16–17; Mt 26:26–29; Mk 14:22–25; Lk 22:14–20.
**11:25** Ex 24:8; 2 Cor 3:6; Heb 8:6–13.
**11:32** Dt 8:5; Heb 12:5–11.
**12:2** Eph 2:11–18.
**12:3** Rom 10:9; 1 Jn 4:2–3.
**12:4** Rom 12:6; Eph 4:7, 11.
**12:8** 2:6–13.

Spirit; to another gifts of healing by the one Spirit; [10] to another mighty deeds; to another prophecy; to another discernment of spirits; to another varieties of tongues; to another interpretation of tongues.* [11] But one and the same Spirit produces all of these, distributing them individually to each person as he wishes.*

**One Body, Many Parts.**† [12] As a body is one though it has many parts, and all the parts of the body, though many, are one body, so also Christ.* [13] For in one Spirit we were all baptized into one body, whether Jews or Greeks, slaves or free persons, and we were all given to drink of one Spirit.*

[14] Now the body is not a single part, but many. [15] If a foot should say, "Because I am not a hand I do not belong to the body," it does not for this reason belong any less to the body. [16] Or if an ear should say, "Because I am not an eye I do not belong to the body," it does not for this reason belong any less to the body. [17] If the whole body were an eye, where would the hearing be? If the whole body were hearing, where would the sense of smell be? [18] But as it is, God placed the parts, each one of them, in the body as he intended. [19] If they were all one part, where would the body be? [20] But as it is, there are many parts, yet one body. [21] The eye cannot say to the hand, "I do not need you," nor again the head to the feet, "I do not need you." [22] Indeed, the parts of the body that seem to be weaker are all the more necessary, [23] and those parts of the body that we consider less honorable we surround with greater honor, and our less presentable parts

are treated with greater propriety, [24] whereas our more presentable parts do not need this. But God has so constructed the body as to give greater honor to a part that is without it, [25] so that there may be no division in the body, but that the parts may have the same concern for one another. [26] If [one] part suffers, all the parts suffer with it; if one part is honored, all the parts share its joy.

**Application to Christ.**† [27] Now you are Christ's body, and individually parts of it.* [28] Some people God has designated in the church to be, first, apostles;† second, prophets; third, teachers; then, mighty deeds; then, gifts of healing, assistance, administration, and varieties of tongues.* [29] Are all apostles? Are all prophets? Are all teachers? Do all work mighty deeds? [30] Do all have gifts of healing? Do all speak in tongues? Do all interpret? [31] Strive eagerly for the greatest spiritual gifts.

**The Way of Love.** But I shall show you a still more excellent way.

**13** †[1] If I speak in human and angelic tongues† but do not have love, I am a resounding gong or a clashing cymbal.* [2] And if I have the gift of prophecy and comprehend all mysteries and all knowledge; if I have all faith so as to move mountains but do not have love, I am nothing.* [3] If I give away everything I own, and if I hand my body over so that I may boast but do not have love, I gain nothing.*

[4] † Love is patient, love is kind. It is not jealous, [love] is not pompous, it is not inflated,*

---

† **12:12–26** The image of a *body* is introduced to explain Christ's relationship with believers (1 Cor 12:12). 1 Cor 12:13 applies this model to the church: by baptism all, despite diversity of ethnic or social origins, are integrated into one organism. 1 Cor 12:14–26 then develop the need for diversity of function among the parts of a body without threat to its unity.

**12:27–30** Paul now applies the image again to the church as a whole and its members (1 Cor 12:27). The lists in 1 Cor 12:28–30 spell out the parallelism by specifying the diversity of functions found in the church (cf. Rom 12:6–8; Eph 4:11).

**12:28** *First, apostles*: apostleship was not mentioned in 1 Cor 12:8–10, nor is it at issue in these chapters, but Paul gives it pride of place in his listing. It is not just one gift among others but a prior and fuller gift that includes the others. They are all demonstrated in Paul's apostolate, but he may have developed his theology of charisms by reflecting first of all on his own grace of apostleship (cf. 1 Cor 3:5–4:14; 9:1–27; 2 Cor 2:14–6:13; 10:1–13:30, esp. 1 Cor 11:23 and 12:12).

**13:1–13** This chapter involves a shift of perspective and a new point. All or part of the material may once have been an independent piece in the style of Hellenistic eulogies of virtues, but it is now integrated, by editing, into the context of 1 Cor 12–14 (cf. the reference to tongues and prophecy) and into the letter

as a whole (cf. the references to knowledge and to behavior). The function of 1 Cor 13 within the discussion of spiritual gifts is to relativize all the charisms by contrasting them with the more basic, pervasive, and enduring value that gives them their purpose and their effectiveness. The rhetoric of this chapter is striking.

**13:1–3** An inventory of gifts, arranged in careful gradation: neither tongues (on the lowest rung), nor prophecy, knowledge, or faith, nor even self-sacrifice has value unless informed by love.

**13:4–7** This paragraph is developed by personification and enumeration, defining love by what it does or does not do. The Greek contains fifteen verbs; it is natural to translate many of them by adjectives in English.

---

* | | |
|---|---|
| **12:10** 14:5, 26, 39; Acts 2:4. | **12:28** Eph 2:20; 3:5; 4:11. |
| **12:11** 7:7; Eph 4:7. | **13:1** 8:1; 16:14; Rom |
| **12:12** 10:17; Rom 12:4–5; | 12:9–10; 13:8–10. |
| Eph 2:16; Col 3:15. | **13:2** 4:1; 14:2 / 1:5; 8:1–3; |
| **12:13** Gal 3:28; Eph | 12:8 / Mt 17:20; |
| 2:13–18; Col 3:11 / Jn | 21:21; Col 2:3. |
| 7:37–39. | **13:3** Mt 6:2. |
| **12:27** Rom 12:5–8; Eph | **13:4** Eph 4:2 / 1 Cor 4:6, |
| 1:23; 4:12; 5:30; Col | 18; 5:2; 8:1. |
| 1:18, 24. | |

1 COR

[5] it is not rude, it does not seek its own interests, it is not quick-tempered, it does not brood over injury,* [6] it does not rejoice over wrongdoing but rejoices with the truth. [7] It bears all things, believes all things, hopes all things, endures all things.*

[8] † Love never fails. If there are prophecies, they will be brought to nothing; if tongues, they will cease; if knowledge, it will be brought to nothing. [9] For we know partially and we prophesy partially, [10] but when the perfect comes, the partial will pass away. [11] When I was a child, I used to talk as a child, think as a child, reason as a child; when I became a man, I put aside childish things. [12] At present we see indistinctly, as in a mirror, but then face to face. At present I know partially; then I shall know fully, as I am fully known.* [13] † So faith, hope, love remain, these three;* but the greatest of these is love.

# 14

**Prophecy Greater than Tongues.** [1] † Pursue love, but strive eagerly for the spiritual gifts, above all that you may prophesy.* [2] † For one who speaks in a tongue does not speak to human beings but to God, for no one listens; he utters mysteries in spirit. [3] On the other hand, one who prophesies does speak to human beings, for their building up, † encouragement, and solace.* [4] Whoever speaks in a tongue builds himself up, but whoever

prophesies builds up the church. [5] Now I should like all of you to speak in tongues, but even more to prophesy. One who prophesies is greater than one who speaks in tongues, unless he interprets, so that the church may be built up.

[6] † Now, brothers, if I should come to you speaking in tongues, what good will I do you if I do not speak to you by way of revelation, or knowledge, or prophecy, or instruction? [7] Likewise, if inanimate things that produce sound, such as flute or harp, do not give out the tones distinctly, how will what is being played on flute or harp be recognized? [8] And if the bugle gives an indistinct sound, who will get ready for battle? [9] Similarly, if you, because of speaking in tongues, do not utter intelligible speech, how will anyone know what is being said? For you will be talking to the air. [10] It happens that there are many different languages in the world, and none is meaningless; [11] but if I do not know the meaning of a language, I shall be a foreigner to one who speaks it, and one who speaks it a foreigner to me. [12] So with yourselves: since you strive eagerly for spirits, seek to have an abundance of them for building up the church.

**Need for Interpretation.** † [13] Therefore, one who speaks in a tongue should pray to be able to interpret. [14] [For] if I pray in a tongue, my spirit † is at prayer but my mind is

---

**13:8–13** The final paragraph announces its topic, *Love never fails* (1 Cor 13:8), then develops the permanence of love in contrast to the charisms (1 Cor 13:9–12), and finally asserts love's superiority even over the other "theological virtues" (1 Cor 13:13).

**13:13** In speaking of love, Paul is led by spontaneous association to mention faith and hope as well. They are already a well-known triad (cf. 1 Thes 1:3), three interrelated (cf. 1 Cor 13:7) features of Christian life, more fundamental than any particular charism. *The greatest…is love*: love is operative even within the other members of the triad (1 Cor 13:7), so that it has a certain primacy among them. Or, if the perspective is temporal, love will remain (cf. "never fails," 1 Cor 13:8) even when faith has yielded to sight and hope to possession.

**14:1–5** 1 Cor 14:1b returns to the thought of 1 Cor 12:31a and reveals Paul's primary concern. The series of contrasts in 1 Cor 14:2–5 discloses the problem at Corinth: a disproportionate interest in tongues, with a corresponding failure to appreciate the worth of prophecy. Paul attempts to clarify the relative values of those gifts by indicating the kind of communication achieved in each and the kind of effect each produces.

**14:2–3a** They involve two kinds of communication: tongues, private speech toward God in inarticulate terms that need interpretation to be intelligible to others (see 1 Cor 14:27–28); prophecy, communication with others in the community.

**14:3b–5** They produce two kinds of effect. One who speaks in tongues *builds himself up*; it is a matter of individual experience and personal perfection, which inevitably recalls Paul's previous remarks about being inflated, seeking one's own good, pleasing oneself. But a prophet *builds up the church*: the theme of "building up" or "edifying" others, the main theme of the let-

ter, comes to clearest expression in this chapter (1 Cor 14:3, 4, 5, 12, 17). It has been anticipated at 1 Cor 8:1 and 1 Cor 10:23, and by the related concept of "the beneficial" in 1 Cor 6:12; 10:23; 12:7; etc.

**14:6–12** Sound, in order to be useful, must be intelligible. This principle is illustrated by a series of analogies from music (1 Cor 14:7–8) and from ordinary human speech (1 Cor 14:10–11); it is applied to the case at hand in 1 Cor 14:9, 12.

**14:13–19** The charism of interpretation lifts tongues to the level of intelligibility, enabling them to produce the same effect as prophecy (cf. 1 Cor 14:5, 26–28).

**14:14–15** *My spirit*: Paul emphasizes the exclusively ecstatic, nonrational quality of tongues. The tongues at Pentecost are also described as an ecstatic experience (Acts 2:4, 12–13), though Luke superimposes further interpretations of his own. *My mind*: the ecstatic element, dominant in earliest Old Testament prophecy as depicted in 1 Sm 10:5–13; 19:20–24, seems entirely absent from Paul's notion of prophecy and completely relegated to tongues. He emphasizes the role of reason when he specifies instruction as a function of prophecy (1 Cor 14:6, 19, 31). But he does not exclude intuition and emotion; cf. references to encouragement and consolation (1 Cor 14:3, 31) and the scene describing the ideal exercise of prophecy (1 Cor 14:24–25).

---

* 
**13:5** 10:24, 33; Phil 2:4, 21; 1 Thes 5:15.
**13:7** Prv 10:12; 1 Pt 4:8.
**13:12** 2 Cor 5:7; Heb 11:1 / 2 Tm 2:19; 1 Jn 3:2.
**13:13** Col 1:4; 1 Thes 1:3; 5:8.
**14:1** 14:5, 12, 39.
**14:3** 14:4–5, 12, 17, 26; 3:9; 8:1, 10; 10:23.

unproductive. [15] So what is to be done? I will pray with the spirit, but I will also pray with the mind. I will sing praise with the spirit, but I will also sing praise with the mind. * [16] Otherwise, if you pronounce a blessing [with] the spirit, how shall one who holds the place of the uninstructed say the "Amen" to your thanksgiving, since he does not know what you are saying? [17] For you may be giving thanks very well, but the other is not built up. [18] I give thanks to God that I speak in tongues more than any of you, [19] but in the church I would rather speak five words with my mind, so as to instruct others also, than ten thousand words in a tongue.

### Functions of These Gifts.

[20] † Brothers, stop being childish in your thinking. In respect to evil be like infants, but in your thinking be mature. * [21] It is written in the law:

"By people speaking strange tongues
    and by the lips of foreigners
I will speak to this people,
    and even so they will not listen
        to me, *

says the Lord." [22] Thus, tongues are a sign not for those who believe but for unbelievers, whereas prophecy is not for unbelievers but for those who believe.

[23] † So if the whole church meets in one place and everyone speaks in tongues, and then un-instructed people or unbelievers should come in, will they not say that you are out of your minds? * [24] But if everyone is prophesying, and an unbeliever or uninstructed person should come in, he will be convinced by everyone and judged by everyone, [25] and the secrets of his heart will be disclosed, and so he will fall down and worship God, declaring, "God is really in your midst." *

### Rules of Order.

[26] † So what is to be done, brothers? When you assemble, one has a psalm, another an instruction, a revelation, a tongue, or an interpretation. Everything should be done for building up. * [27] If anyone speaks in a tongue, let it be two or at most three, and each in turn, and one should inter-pret. [28] But if there is no interpreter, the person should keep silent in the church and speak to himself and to God.

[29] Two or three prophets should speak, and the others discern. [30] But if a revelation is given to another person sitting there, the first one should be silent. [31] For you can all prophesy one by one, so that all may learn and all be encouraged. [32] Indeed, the spirits of prophets are under the prophets' control, [33] since he is not the God of disorder but of peace.

As in all the churches of the holy ones, † [34] women should keep silent in the churches, for they are not allowed to speak, but should be subordinate, as even the law says. * [35] But if they want to learn anything, they should ask their husbands at home. For it is improper for a woman to speak in the church. [36] Did

---

† **14:20–22** The Corinthians pride themselves on tongues as a sign of God's favor, a means of direct communication with him (2:28). To challenge them to a more mature appraisal, Paul draws from scripture a less flattering explanation of what speaking in tongues may signify. Isaiah threatened the people that if they failed to listen to their prophets, the Lord would speak to them (in punishment) through the lips of Assyrian conquerors (Is 28:11–12). Paul compresses Isaiah's text and makes God address his people directly. Equating tongues with foreign languages (cf. 1 Cor 14:10–11), Paul concludes from Isaiah that *tongues are a sign not for those who believe*, i.e., not a mark of God's pleasure for those who listen to him but a mark of his displeasure with those in the community who are faithless, who have not heeded the message that he has sent through the prophets.

**14:23–25** Paul projects the possible missionary effect of two hypothetical liturgical experiences, one consisting wholly of tongues, the other entirely of prophecy. *Uninstructed (idiōtai):* the term may simply mean people who do not speak or understand tongues, as in 1 Cor 14:16, where it seems to designate Christians. But coupled with the term "unbelievers" it may be another way of designating those who have not been initiated into the community of faith; some believe it denotes a special class of non-Christians who are close to the community, such as catechumens. *Unbelievers (apistoi):* he has shifted from the inner-community perspective of 1 Cor 14:22; the term here designates non-Christians (cf. 1 Cor 6:6; 7:15; 10:27).

**14:26–33a** Paul concludes with specific directives regarding exercise of the gifts in their assemblies. Verse 26 enunciates the basic criterion in the use of any gift: it must contribute to "building up."

**14:33b–36** Verse 33b may belong with what precedes, so that the new paragraph would begin only with 1 Cor 14:34. 1 Cor 14:34–35 change the subject. These two verses have the theme of submission in common with 1 Cor 14:11 despite differences in vocabulary, and a concern with what is or is not becoming; but it is difficult to harmonize the injunction to silence here with 1 Cor 11 which appears to take it for granted that women do pray and prophesy aloud in the assembly (cf. 1 Cor 11:5, 13). Hence the verses are often considered an interpolation, reflecting the discipline of later churches; such an interpolation would have to have antedated our manuscripts, all of which contain them, though some transpose them to the very end of the chapter.

**14:15** Eph 5:19; Col 3:16.
**14:20** Mt 10:16; Rom 16:19; Eph 4:14.
**14:21** Is 28:11–12; Dt 28:49.
**14:23** Acts 2:6, 13.
**14:25** 4:5 / Is 45:14; Zec 8:23.
**14:26** Eph 4:12.
**14:34** 1 Tm 2:11–15; 1 Pt 3:1.

the word of God go forth from you? Or has it come to you alone?

[37] If anyone thinks that he is a prophet or a spiritual person, he should recognize that what I am writing to you is a commandment of the Lord. [38] If anyone does not acknowledge this, he is not acknowledged. [39] So, [my] brothers, strive eagerly to prophesy, and do not forbid speaking in tongues, [40] but everything must be done properly and in order.

## V. THE RESURRECTION

### A. The Resurrection of Christ

**15** †The Gospel Teaching.† [1] Now I am reminding you, brothers, of the gospel I preached to you, which you indeed received and in which you also stand. [2] Through it you are also being saved, if you hold fast to the word I preached to you, unless you believed in vain. [3]† For I handed on to you as of first importance what I also received: that Christ died for our sins in accordance with the scriptures;* [4] that he was buried; that he was raised on the third day in accordance with the scriptures;* [5] that he appeared to Cephas, then to the Twelve.* [6] After that, he appeared to more than five hundred brothers at once, most of whom are still living, though some have fallen asleep. [7] After that he appeared to James, then to all the apostles. [8] Last of all, as to one born abnormally, he appeared to me.*  [9] For I am the least† of the apostles, not fit to be called an apostle, because I persecuted the church of God.*  [10] But by the grace of God I am what I am, and his grace to me has not been ineffective. Indeed, I have toiled harder than all of them; not I, however, but the grace of God [that is] with me. [11] Therefore, whether it be I or they, so we preach and so you believed.

### B. The Resurrection of the Dead

**Results of Denial.**† [12] But if Christ is preached as raised from the dead, how can some among you say there is no resurrection of the dead? [13] If there is no resurrection of the dead, then neither has Christ been raised.* [14] And if Christ has not been raised, then empty [too] is our preaching; empty, too, your faith. [15] Then we are also false witnesses to God, because we testified against God that he raised Christ, whom he did not raise if in fact the dead are not raised.* [16] For if the dead are not raised, neither has Christ been raised, [17] and if Christ has not been raised,† your faith is vain; you are still in your sins. [18] Then those who have fallen asleep in Christ have perished. [19] If for this life only we have hoped in Christ, we are the most pitiable people of all.

---

† 15:1–58 Some consider this chapter an earlier Pauline composition inserted into the present letter. The problem that Paul treats is clear to a degree: some of the Corinthians are denying the resurrection of the dead (1 Cor 15:12), apparently because of their inability to imagine how any kind of bodily existence could be possible after death (1 Cor 15:35). It is plausibly supposed that their attitude stems from Greek anthropology, which looks with contempt upon matter and would be content with the survival of the soul, and perhaps also from an overrealized eschatology of gnostic coloration, such as that reflected in 2 Tm 2:18, which considers the resurrection a purely spiritual experience already achieved in baptism and in the forgiveness of sins. Paul, on the other hand, will affirm both the essential corporeity of the resurrection and its futurity. His response moves through three steps: a recall of the basic kerygma about Jesus' resurrection (1 Cor 15:1–11), an assertion of the logical inconsistencies involved in denial of the resurrection (1 Cor 15:12–34), and an attempt to perceive theologically what the properties of the resurrected body must be (1 Cor 15:35–58).

15:1–11 Paul recalls the tradition (1 Cor 15:3–7), which he can presuppose as common ground and which provides a starting point for his argument. This is the fundamental content of all Christian preaching and belief (1 Cor 15:1–2, 11).

15:3–7 The language by which Paul expresses the essence of the "gospel" (1 Cor 15:1) is not his own but is drawn from older credal formulas. This credo highlights Jesus' death for our sins (confirmed by his burial) and Jesus' resurrection (confirmed by his appearances) and presents both of them as fulfillment of prophecy. In accordance with the scriptures: conformity of Jesus' passion with the scriptures is asserted in Mt 16:1; Lk 24:25–27,

32, 44–46. Application of some Old Testament texts (Ps 2:7; 16:8–11) to his resurrection is illustrated by Acts 2:27–31; 13:29–39; and Is 52:13–53:12 and Hos 6:2 may also have been envisaged.

15:9–11 A persecutor may have appeared disqualified (ouk... hikanos) from apostleship, but in fact God's grace has qualified him. Cf. the remarks in 2 Corinthians about his qualifications (2 Cor 2:16; 3:5) and his greater labors (2 Cor 11:23). These verses are parenthetical, but a nerve has been touched (the references to his abnormal birth and his activity as a persecutor may echo taunts from Paul's opponents), and he is instinctively moved to self-defense.

15:12–19 Denial of the resurrection (1 Cor 15:12) involves logical inconsistencies. The basic one, stated twice (1 Cor 15:13, 16), is that if there is no such thing as (bodily) resurrection, then it has not taken place even in Christ's case.

15:17–18 The consequences for the Corinthians are grave: both forgiveness of sins and salvation are an illusion, despite their strong convictions about both. Unless Christ is risen, their faith does not save.

---

*
15:3 11:23 / 1 Pt 2:24; 3:18 / Is 53:4–12.
15:4 Acts 2:23–24 / Ps 16:8–11; Hos 6:1–2; Jon 2:1.
15:5 Mk 16:14; Mt 28:16–17; Lk 24:36; Jn 20:19.
15:8 9:1; Acts 9:3–6; Gal 1:16.
15:9 Acts 8:3; 9:1–2; Gal 1:23; Eph 3:8; 1 Tm 1:15.
15:13 1 Thes 4:14.
15:15 Acts 5:32.

**Christfruits the Firstfruits.**† [20]* But now Christ has been raised from the dead, the firstfruits† of those who have fallen asleep. [21]† For since death came through a human being, the resurrection of the dead came also through a human being. [22] For just as in Adam all die, so too in Christ shall all be brought to life,* [23] but each one in proper order: Christ the firstfruits; then, at his coming, those who belong to Christ;* [24] then comes the end,† when he hands over the kingdom to his God and Father, when he has destroyed every sovereignty and every authority and power.* [25] For he must reign until he has put all his enemies under his feet.* [26]† The last enemy* to be destroyed is death, [27]† for "he subjected everything under his feet."* But when it says that everything has been subjected, it is clear that it excludes the one who subjected everything to him. [28] When everything is subjected to him, then the Son himself will [also] be subjected to the one who subjected everything to him, so that God may be all in all.*

**Practical Arguments.**† [29] Otherwise, what will people accomplish by having themselves baptized for the dead?† If the dead are not raised at all, then why are they having themselves baptized for them?

[30]† Moreover, why are we endangering ourselves all the time?* [31] Every day I face death; I swear it by the pride in you [brothers] that I have in Christ Jesus our Lord.* [32] If at Ephesus I fought with beasts, so to speak, what benefit was it to me? If the dead are not raised:

"Let us eat and drink,
    for tomorrow we die."*

[33] Do not be led astray:

"Bad company corrupts good morals."

[34] Become sober as you ought and stop sinning. For some have no knowledge of God; I say this to your shame.*

### C. The Manner of the Resurrection†

[35]† But someone may say, "How are the dead raised? With what kind of body will they come back?"

---

† **15:20–28** After a triumphant assertion of the reality of Christ's resurrection (1 Cor 15:20a), Paul explains its positive implications and consequences. As a soteriological event of both human (1 Cor 15:20–23) and cosmic (1 Cor 15:24–28) dimensions, Jesus' resurrection logically and necessarily involves ours as well.

**15:20** The firstfruits: the portion of the harvest offered in thanksgiving to God implies the consecration of the entire harvest to come. Christ's resurrection is not an end in itself; its finality lies in the whole harvest, ourselves.

**15:21–22** Our human existence, both natural and supernatural, is corporate, involves solidarity. In Adam...in Christ: the Hebrew word ādām in Genesis is both a common noun for mankind and a proper noun for the first man. Paul here presents Adam as at least a literary type of Christ; the parallelism and contrast between them will be developed further in 1 Cor 15:45–49 and in Rom 5:12–21.

**15:24–28** Paul's perspective expands to cosmic dimensions, as he describes the climax of history, the end. His viewpoint is still christological, as in 1 Cor 15:20–23. 1 Cor 15:24, 28 describe Christ's final relations to his enemies and his Father in language that is both royal and military; 1 Cor 15:25–28 insert a proof from scripture (Ps 110:1; 8:6) into this description. But the viewpoint is also theological, for God is the ultimate agent and end, and likewise soteriological, for we are the beneficiaries of all the action.

**15:26** The last enemy...is death: a parenthesis that specifies the final fulfillment of the two Old Testament texts just referred to, Ps 110:1 and Ps 8:7. Death is not just one cosmic power among many, but the ultimate effect of sin in the universe (cf. 1 Cor 15:56; Rom 5:12). Christ defeats death where it prevails, in our bodies. The destruction of the last enemy is concretely the "coming to life" (1 Cor 15:22) of "those who belong to Christ" (1 Cor 15:23).

**15:27b–28** The one who subjected everything to him: the Father is the ultimate agent in the drama, and the final end of the process, to whom the Son and everything else is ordered (1 Cor 15:24, 28). That God may be all in all: his reign is a dynamic exercise of creative power, an outpouring of life and energy through the universe, with no further resistance. This is the supremely positive meaning of "subjection": that God may fully be God.

**15:29–34** Paul concludes his treatment of logical inconsistencies with a listing of miscellaneous Christian practices that would be meaningless if the resurrection were not a fact.

**15:29** Baptized for the dead: this practice is not further explained here, nor is it necessarily mentioned with approval, but Paul cites it as something in their experience that attests in one more way to belief in the resurrection.

**15:30–34** A life of sacrifice, such as Paul describes in 1 Cor 4:9–13 and 2 Corinthians, would be pointless without the prospect of resurrection; a life of pleasure, such as that expressed in the Epicurean slogan of 1 Cor 15:32, would be far more consistent. I fought with beasts: since Paul does not elsewhere mention a combat with beasts at Ephesus, he may be speaking figuratively about struggles with adversaries.

**15:35–58** Paul imagines two objections that the Corinthians could raise: one concerning the manner of the resurrection (how?), the other pertaining to the qualities of the risen body (what kind?). These questions probably lie behind their denial of the resurrection (1 Cor 15:12), and seem to reflect the presumption that no kind of body other than the one we now possess would be possible. Paul deals with these objections in inverse order, in 1 Cor 15:36–49 and 1 Cor 15:50–58. His argument is fundamentally theological and its appeal is to the understanding.

**15:35–49** Paul approaches the question of the nature of the risen body (what kind of body?) by means of two analogies: the seed (1 Cor 15:36–44) and the first man, Adam (1 Cor 15:45–49).

---

* **15:20** Rom 8:11; Col 1:18; 1 Thes 4:14.
**15:22** Gn 3:17–19; Rom 5:12–19.
**15:23** 1 Thes 4:15–17.
**15:24** Eph 1:22.
**15:25** Ps 110:1.
**15:26** Rom 6:9; 2 Tm 1:10; Rev 20:14; 21:4.
**15:27** Ps 8:7; Eph 1:22; Phil 3:21.
**15:28** Eph 4:6; Col 3:11.
**15:30** 2 Cor 4:8–12; 11:23–27.
**15:31** Ps 44:23; Rom 8:36.
**15:32** 4:9; 2 Cor 4:10–11 / Wis 2:5–7; Is 22:13.
**15:34** Mt 22:29; Mk 12:24.

**The Resurrection Body.** 36† You fool! What you sow is not brought to life unless it dies.* 37 And what you sow is not the body that is to be but a bare kernel of wheat, perhaps, or of some other kind; 38* but God gives it a body as he chooses, and to each of the seeds its own body. 39† Not all flesh is the same, but there is one kind for human beings, another kind of flesh for animals, another kind of flesh for birds, and another for fish. 40 There are both heavenly bodies and earthly bodies, but the brightness of the heavenly is one kind and that of the earthly another. 41 The brightness of the sun is one kind, the brightness of the moon another, and the brightness of the stars another. For star differs from star in brightness.

42† So also is the resurrection of the dead. It is sown corruptible; it is raised incorruptible. 43 It is sown dishonorable; it is raised glorious. It is sown weak; it is raised powerful.* 44 It is sown a natural body; it is raised a spiritual body. If there is a natural body, there is also a spiritual one.

45 So, too, it is written, "The first man, Adam,† became a living being," the last Adam a life-giving spirit.* 46 But the spiritual was not first; rather the natural and then the spiritual. 47 The first man was from the earth, earthly; the second man, from heaven. 48 As was the earthly one, so also are the earthly, and as is the heavenly one, so also are the heavenly. 49 Just as we have borne the image of the earthly one, we shall also bear the image† of the heavenly one.*

**The Resurrection Event.** 50† This I declare, brothers: flesh and blood cannot inherit the kingdom of God, nor does corruption† inherit incorruption.* 51† Behold, I tell you a mystery. We shall not all fall asleep, but we will all be changed,* 52 in an instant, in the blink of an eye, at the last trumpet. For the trumpet will sound, the dead will be raised incorruptible, and we shall be changed.* 53 For that which is corruptible must clothe itself with incorruptibility, and that which is mortal must clothe itself with immortality.* 54† And when this which is corruptible clothes itself with incorruptibility and this which is mortal clothes itself with immortality, then the word that is written shall come about:*

"Death is swallowed up in victory.
55    Where, O death, is your victory?
      Where, O death, is your sting?"*

56 The sting of death is sin,† and the power of sin is the law.* 57 But thanks be to God who

---

15:36–38 The analogy of the seed: there is a change of attributes from seed to plant; the old life-form must be lost for the new to emerge. By speaking about the seed as a *body* that dies and comes to life, Paul keeps the point of the analogy before the reader's mind.

15:39–41 The expression "its own body" (1 Cor 15:38) leads to a development on the marvelous diversity evident in bodily life.

15:42–44 The principles of qualitative difference before and after death (1 Cor 15:36–38) and of diversity on different levels of creation (1 Cor 15:39–41) are now applied to the human body. Before: a body animated by a lower, natural life-principle (*psyche*) and endowed with the properties of natural existence (corruptibility, lack of glory, weakness). After: a body animated by a higher life-principle (*pneuma*; cf. 1 Cor 15:45) and endowed with other qualities (incorruptibility, glory, power, spirituality), which are properties of God himself.

15:45 The analogy of *the first man, Adam*, is introduced by a citation from Gn 2:7. Paul alters the text slightly, adding the adjective *first*, and translating the Hebrew *'ādām* twice, so as to give it its value both as a common noun (*man*) and as a proper name (*Adam*). 1 Cor 15:45b then specifies similarities and differences between the two Adams. *The last Adam*, Christ (cf. 1 Cor 15:21–22) has become a…*spirit* (*pneuma*), a life-principle transcendent with respect to the natural soul (*psyche*) of the first Adam (on the terminology here, cf. note on 1 Cor 3:1). Further, he is not just alive, but life-giving, a source of life for others.

15:49 *We shall also bear the image*: although it has less manuscript support, this reading better fits the context's emphasis on futurity and the transforming action of God; on future transformation as conformity to the image of the Son, cf. Rom 8:29; Phil 3:21. The majority reading, "let us bear the image," suggests that the image of the heavenly man is already present and exhorts us to conform to it.

15:50–57 These verses, an answer to the first question of 1 Cor 15:35, explain theologically how the change of properties from one image to another will take place: God has the power to transform, and he will exercise it.

15:50–53 *Flesh and blood…corruption*: living persons and the corpses of the dead, respectively. In both cases, the gulf between creatures and God is too wide to be bridged unless God himself transforms us.

15:51–52 *A mystery*: the last moment in God's plan is disclosed; cf. notes on 1 Cor 2:1, 7–10a. The final trumpet and the awakening of the dead are stock details of the apocalyptic scenario. *We shall not all fall asleep*: Paul expected that some of his contemporaries might still be alive at Christ's return; after the death of Paul and his whole generation, copyists altered this statement in various ways. *We will all be changed*: the statement extends to all Christians, for Paul is not directly speaking about anyone else. Whether they have died before the end or happen still to be alive, all must be transformed.

15:54–55 *Death is swallowed up in victory*: scripture itself predicts death's overthrow. *O death*: in his prophetic vision Paul may be making Hosea's words his own, or imagining this cry of triumph on the lips of the risen church.

15:56 *The sting of death is sin*: an explanation of Hosea's metaphor. Death, scorpion-like, is equipped with a sting, sin, by

---

15:36 Jn 12:24.
15:38 Gn 1:11.
15:43 Phil 3:20–21; Col 3:4.
15:45 Gn 2:7 / Jn 5:21–29;
          2 Cor 3:6, 17.
15:49 Gn 5:3 / Rom 8:29;
          Phil 3:21.
15:50 Jn 3:3–6.
15:51 1 Thes 4:14–17.
15:52 Jl 2:1; Zec 9:14; Mt
          24:31; Rev 11:15–18.
15:53 2 Cor 5:2–4.
15:54 Is 25:8; 2 Cor 5:4;
          2 Tm 1:10; Heb
          2:14–15.
15:55 Hos 13:14.
15:56 Rom 4:15; 7:7, 13.

gives us the victory through our Lord Jesus Christ.*

58 Therefore, my beloved brothers, be firm, steadfast, always fully devoted to the work of the Lord, knowing that in the Lord your labor is not in vain.

## VI. CONCLUSION

# 16

**The Collection.**† ¹ Now in regard to the collection† for the holy ones, you also should do as I ordered the churches of Galatia.* ² On the first day of the week each of you should set aside and save whatever he can afford, so that collections will not be going on when I come. ³ And when I arrive, I shall send those whom you have approved with letters of recommendation to take your gracious gift to Jerusalem. ⁴ If it seems fitting that I should go also,† they will go with me.

**Paul's Travel Plans.**† ⁵ I shall come to you after I pass through Macedonia (for I am going to pass through Macedonia),* ⁶ and perhaps I shall stay or even spend the winter with you, so that you may send me on my way wherever I may go. ⁷ For I do not wish to see you now just in passing, but I hope to spend some time with you, if the Lord permits.* ⁸ † I shall stay in Ephesus* until Pentecost, ⁹ because a door has opened for me wide and productive for work, but there are many opponents.*

¹⁰ If Timothy comes, see that he is without fear in your company, for he is doing the work

of the Lord just as I am.* ¹¹ Therefore, no one should disdain him. Rather, send him on his way in peace that he may come to me, for I am expecting him with the brothers. ¹² Now in regard to our brother Apollos, I urged him strongly to go to you with the brothers, but it was not at all his will that he go now. He will go when he has an opportunity.*

**Exhortation and Greetings.** ¹³ Be on your guard, stand firm in the faith, be courageous, be strong. ¹⁴ Your every act should be done with love.

¹⁵ I urge you, brothers—you know that the household of Stephanas* is the firstfruits of Achaia and that they have devoted themselves to the service of the holy ones— ¹⁶ be subordinate to such people and to everyone who works and toils with them. ¹⁷ I rejoice in the arrival of Stephanas, Fortunatus, and Achaicus, because they made up for your absence, ¹⁸ for they refreshed my spirit as well as yours. So give recognition to such people.*

¹⁹ † The churches of Asia send you greetings. Aquila and Prisca together with the church at their house send you many greetings in the Lord.* ²⁰ All the brothers greet you. Greet one another with a holy kiss.*

²¹ I, Paul, write you this greeting in my own hand.* ²² If anyone does not love the Lord, let him be accursed.† *Marana tha.** ²³ The grace of the Lord Jesus be with you.* ²⁴ My love to all of you in Christ Jesus.

1 COR

---

† which it injects its poison. Christ defeats sin, the cause of death (Gn 3:19; Rom 5:12).

**16:1–4** This paragraph contains our earliest evidence for a project that became a major undertaking of Paul's ministry. The collection for the church at Jerusalem was a symbol in his mind for the unity of Jewish and Gentile Christianity. Cf. Gal 2:10; Rom 15:25–29; 2 Cor 8–9 and the notes to this last passage.

**16:1** *In regard to the collection*: it has already begun in Galatia and Macedonia (cf. 2 Cor 8), and presumably he has already instructed the Corinthians about its purpose.

**16:4** *That I should go also*: presumably Paul delivered the collection on his final visit to Jerusalem; cf. Rom 15:25–32; Acts 24:14.

**16:5–12** The travel plans outlined here may not have materialized precisely as Paul intended; cf. 2 Cor 1:8–2:13; 7:4–16.

**16:8** *In Ephesus until Pentecost*: this tells us the place from which he wrote the letter and suggests he may have composed it about Easter time (cf. 1 Cor 5:7–8).

**16:19–24** These paragraphs conform to the normal epistolary conclusion, but their language is overlaid with liturgical coloration as well. The *greetings* of the Asian churches are probably to be read, along with the letter, in the liturgy at Corinth, and the union of the church is to be expressed by a holy kiss (1 Cor 16:19–20). Paul adds to this his own greeting (1 Cor 16:21) and blessings (1 Cor 16:23–24).

**16:22** *Accursed*: literally, "anathema." This expression (cf. 1 Cor 12:3) is a formula for exclusion from the community; it may imply here a call to self-examination before celebration of the Eucharist, in preparation for the Lord's coming and judgment (cf. 1 Cor 11:17–34). *Marana tha*: an Aramaic expression, probably used in the early Christian liturgy. As understood here ("O Lord, come!"), it is a prayer for the early return of Christ. If the Aramaic words are divided differently (*Maran atha*, "Our Lord has come"), it becomes a credal declaration. The former interpretation is supported by what appears to be a Greek equivalent of this acclamation in Rev 22:20 "Amen. Come, Lord Jesus!"

---

**15:57** Jn 16:33; 1 Jn 5:4.
**16:1** Acts 24:17; Rom 15:25–32; 2 Cor 8–9; Gal 2:10.
**16:5** Acts 19:21; Rom 15:26; 2 Cor 1:15–16.
**16:7** Acts 18:21.
**16:8** 15:32; Acts 18:19; 19:1–10.
**16:9** Acts 14:27; 2 Cor 2:12.
**16:10** 4:17; Acts 16:1; 19:22; Phil 2:19–23.
**16:12** 1:12; 3:4–6, 22; Acts 18:24–28.
**16:15** 1:16.
**16:18** 1 Thes 5:12–13.
**16:19** Acts 18:2, 18, 26; Rom 16:3–5.
**16:20** Rom 16:16; 2 Cor 13:12; 1 Thes 5:26; 1 Pt 5:14.
**16:21** Gal 6:11; Col 4:18; 2 Thes 3:17.
**16:22** 12:3; Rom 9:3; Gal 1:8–9; Rev 22:20.
**16:23** Rom 16:20.

# The Second Letter to the

# Corinthians

## INTRODUCTION

### Laurie Brink, OP

Correspondence between Paul and the Corinthian community exceeded the two canonical letters, 1 and 2 Corinthians, evincing an involved and tumultuous relationship between the apostle and the church he founded at Corinth. Prior to the first canonical letter, Paul wrote at least one letter no longer extant but mentioned in 1 Cor 5:9. In 1 Cor 7:1, Paul responded to a letter sent to him from the Corinthians concerning various questions of decorum. News of the community was brought to him by Chloe's people (1 Cor 1:11) and by Stephanas, Fortunatus, and Achaicus (1 Cor 16:17). Following the writing of canonical 1 Corinthians, Paul sent the so-called "Letter of Tears" (mentioned in 2 Cor 2:4) and 2 Corinthians, which may be composed of five separate letter fragments. He sent envoys, Timothy (1 Cor 4:17; 16:10) and Titus (2 Cor 12:18). He visited the city at least twice and planned a third visit (2 Cor. 12:14; 13:1–2). The Corinthian correspondence thus represents an "epistolary archive" from the early church.

The first canonical letter addresses disturbances in the Corinthian community: divisions and rival groups (1 Cor 1:10–17; 3:1–4:5; 11:18), immorality (5:1–13), litigious action (6:1–8), disregard for the "weaker" Christian (8:11), liturgical abuses (11:17–22), and resurrection (ch. 15). When Paul's authority is questioned (ch. 9), he urges unity and concord (1:10) and encourages the Corinthians to let love guide the community (16:14).

Various parts of the second canonical letter evidence differences in topic, tone, and rhetorical strategy. Scholars have suggested a variety of explanations to account for the inconsistencies. The traditional view purported that the letter was a whole, major disruptions in thought and argument being blamed on Paul's having had a "sleepless night," or having been

## Outline of 2 Corinthians

interrupted in mid-sentence. In this line of thought, 2 Corinthians is a whole composition written after Titus returned from Corinth, and contains no earlier fragments. However, many scholars partition 2 Corinthians into two letters, the first found in chs. 1–9 and the second in chs. 10–13.[1] Others propose the five-letter hypothesis.[2] According to this theory, after canonical 1 Corinthians, 2 Cor 2:14–7:4 (minus 6:14–7:1) was written, then there was a disastrous visit followed by the letter found in 2 Cor 10–13, perhaps the so-called "Letter of Tears." A letter of reconciliation is found in 2 Cor 1:1–2:3, 7:5–16, and 13:11–13. Chapter 8 and

---

1. C. K. Barrett, *A Commentary on the Second Epistle to the Corinthians* (London: Black, 1973); Victor Paul Furnish, *II Corinthians: A New Translation with Introduction and Commentary* (Garden City, NY: Doubleday, 1984).

2. Gunther Bornkamm, "The History of the Origin of the So-Called Second Letter to the Corinthians," *New Testament Studies* 8 (1962): 258–64; H. D. Betz, *2 Corinthians 8 and 9: A Commentary on Two Administrative Letters of the Apostle Paul* (Philadelphia: Fortress, 1985).

ch. 9 are two separate fund-raising letters. A later redactor gathered the various fragments, compiling what would become 2 Corinthians. The date and occasion for 2 Corinthians depends on the theory to which one subscribes.

Its complicated history notwithstanding, the present form of 2 Corinthians has been received and revered by the believing community since the second century. As such this article will examine the canonical text as a unitary letter.

## Authorship

Paul and Timothy are the co-senders of 2 Corinthians. Paul is terse in his self-designation. He is simply "an apostle of Christ Jesus by the will of God" (2 Cor 1:1). Paul emphasizes his status as "apostle" when he plans on defending his authority or asserting his legitimacy, as seen in Rom 1:1, 1 Cor 1:1, and Gal 1:1.[3] In 1 Thessalonians, Paul states only his name. In Philippians, he is Paul, a servant of Christ Jesus. In Philemon, he is Paul, the prisoner.

Timothy is simply "the brother," which could refer to his Christian membership or his role with Paul in the missionary effort. Timothy is variously called "brother" (2 Cor 1:1; 1 Thes 3:2; Phlm 1), "co-worker" (Rom 16:21; 1 Thes 3:2), and Paul's "beloved and faithful son in the Lord" (1 Cor 4:17). In addition to 2 Corinthians, he is listed as a co-sender in Philippians, 1 Thessalonians, and Philemon. Timothy was known to the community, having preached among them along with Silvanus and Paul (2 Cor 1:19). According to 1 Cor 4:17, Timothy was sent to Corinth to remind the church of Paul's teachings. Paul tells the Corinthians to take care of Timothy when he arrives and not to let anyone despise him (1 Cor 16:10–11). Acts of the Apostles describes Timothy as a native of Lystra, born of a Jewish mother and a Greek father (Acts 16:1). He had not been circumcised, so Paul had this done (Acts 16:3). The Second Letter to Timothy names his mother as "Eunice" and his grandmother as "Lois," and identifies them as Christians (2 Tm 1:5). Later tradition placed Timothy as the first bishop of Ephesus (*Hist. Eccl.* 3.4).[4]

## Recipients

Paul's Second Letter to the Corinthians is addressed "to the church of God at Corinth along with all the holy ones throughout Achaia" (2 Cor 1:1). Paul claims to have brought the gospel to the Corinthians (2 Cor 10:14) and sees himself as their spiritual father (1 Cor 4:15). Paul frequently refers to Christians as the holy ones (1 Cor 1:2; 6:1, 2; 14:33; 16:15; 2 Cor 1:1; 13:12). In this instance he is including all the holy ones within the Roman senatorial province of Achaia, a region that included all of central Greece and the Peloponnese. In 1 Corinthians, Paul addresses the local church along with "all those everywhere who call upon the name of our Lord Jesus Christ" (1 Cor 1:2). Acts of the Apostles mentions a few converts in nearby Athens (Acts 17:34) and Rom 16:1 indicates that a church existed at Cenchreae, one of the seaports of Corinth, where Phoebe served as deacon. When Paul says "everywhere" in 1 Cor 1:2, he likely intends that such neighboring church communities be included in his letter.

## Context

See the initial introduction to 1 Corinthians.

## Reason for Writing

All is not well with the church in Corinth. Opponents have challenged Paul's authority, necessitating a difficult visit that did not go well (2 Cor 2:1). He responded by writing the "Letter of Tears" (2:4), which Titus carried to the community. Upon his return, Titus brought news of the community's response to the tearful letter (7:6–8). The Corinthians regretted their earlier actions and longed for Paul to visit. Paul sent Titus again with two co-workers (8:16–24). In these back and forth exchanges, Paul attempted to defend his apostleship and authority, his right to raise funds for the saints

---

3. Margaret E. Thrall, *The Second Epistle to the Corinthians* (Edinburgh: T & T Clark, 1994), 79.

4. Eusebius, *Church History*, 3.4.

in Jerusalem, and the very gospel which he preached.

The opponents who unsettled the evangelical efforts of Paul among the Corinthians have been variously identified as gnostics, legalists, so called "divine-men" who possess spiritual gifts, and religious enthusiasts. Paul calls them "superapostles" (2 Cor 11:5) and "false apostles" (11:13). These rival teachers have presented themselves to the Corinthians as legitimate apostles and have challenged Paul's apostleship. They are Jewish, perhaps even from Palestine, since Paul refers to them as "Hebrews" (11:22). Unlike the opponents in Galatia, these Jewish Christians are not encouraging circumcision and do not seem concerned that the Gentile converts keep the Law. Rather, their focus is on Paul's credibility. They are effective rhetoricians who criticize Paul's lack of speaking skills (11:6). They may also claim outstanding charismatic experiences, which Paul counters with comments on his own visions and revelations (12:1–4). The rival teachers preach "another" Jesus (11:4) and are peddlers of God's word (2:17). According to his opponents, Paul's refusal to accept financial support undermines his credibility (11:7–11; 12:13–15). Paul's ultimate answer to these "superapostles" is his list of sufferings (11:23–29) and his constant thorn in the flesh (12:7), which allow him to participate in Christ's sufferings. He concludes, "Therefore, I am content with weaknesses, insults, hardships, persecutions, and constraints, for the sake of Christ; for when I am weak, then I am strong" (12:10).

## Contents

Paul and Timothy address the Christians of Corinth and those in the neighboring churches as well. Paul opens his letter with a blessing to God, the "Father of our Lord Jesus Christ, the Father of compassion and God of all encouragement" (2 Cor 1:3). Ten times in just five verses (1:3–7) Paul will use the word for encouragement, drawing attention to the sufferings and afflictions that both Paul and the Corinthians have experienced. While in Asia (the Roman province in western Asia Minor), Paul, and presumably Timothy, came close to

death (1:8). God delivered them from the situation (1:10), but Paul asks that the Corinthians continue to pray for them (1:11).

The Corinthians must have doubted Paul's sincerity when he had to postpone a promised visit, for he defends himself, saying, "So when I intended this, did I act lightly? Or do I make my plans according to human considerations, so that with me it is 'yes, yes' and 'no, no'?" (2 Cor 1:17). Paul explains that he has postponed his promised visit because he wanted to spare the Corinthians (1:23). The last trip didn't go well, and in response Paul had written a tearful letter: "For out of much affliction and anguish of heart I wrote to you with many tears, not that you might be pained but that you might know the abundant love I have for you" (2:4). Part of that letter included Paul's directive that the community chastise a member who has done wrong, but he now tells them that the offender has been punished enough. They are to forgive him and comfort him (2:6–8). The "Letter of Tears" was also meant to test their obedience to Paul (2:9).

Titus might have been the bearer of the "Letter of Tears" since Paul acknowledges that he was anxious to have him return (2 Cor 2:12–13). Paul uses the image of an imperial triumph to describe the paradox of Christ. God leads Paul in triumph, a military image of success for the victorious when the general and his troops return to the welcoming city. But the processional imagery could reflect both a military triumph where Paul is captive and a religious procession where he is manifesting the deity.[5] Paul's imagery of sacrifice shames his opponents, whom he calls peddlers of God's word, people who sell the gospel as a commodity (2:17).

Paul then turns to the topic of letters of recommendation, which in the Greco-Roman world served to verify one's character and authority. Paul asks if such letters are even necessary, since the Corinthians themselves are his letter of recommendation (2 Cor 3:1–3). Paul's confidence comes through Christ toward God (3:4), who has made Paul a minister of a

---

5. Paul Duff, "Metaphor, Motif, and Meaning: The Rhetorical Strategy Behind the Image 'Led in Triumph' in 2 Corinthians 2:14." *CBQ* (1991): 79–92.

new covenant in the Spirit. Throughout 2 Corinthians, Paul references the Old Testament and covenantal language, demonstrating that the Corinthians would have been familiar with such images and that perhaps his opponents used them as well. Paul compares the radiance of Moses' face when he beheld God with the splendor of the Spirit (3:7–11). Moses had to wear a veil to hide the fact that his brightness faded, but the radiance of the Spirit is permanent (3:12–18). If the gospel appears veiled, it is only to those who are perishing (4:3).

In defending himself, Paul critiques his opponents when he says, "We have renounced shameful, hidden things; not acting deceitfully or falsifying the word of God, but by the open declaration of the truth we commend ourselves to everyone's conscience in the sight of God" (2 Cor 4:2). Paul uses the metaphor of earthen vessels to describe the power of God at work in him (4:7). Suffering is a constant companion and Paul makes a remarkable claim: that he is "always carrying about in the body the dying of Jesus, so that the life of Jesus may also be manifested in our body" (4:10). One's physical nature may be wasting away, but God is preparing a more permanent dwelling (5:1). Until then, Paul and his companions endure, walking by faith, being of good courage, awaiting the judgment of Christ (5:6–10).

The theme of recommendation continues, though, more appropriately, Paul calls it a non-recommendation (2 Cor 5:12). Paul's opponents pride themselves in a person's status, so he reminds the community that it is the heart that should be weighed. Paul is controlled by his love of Christ (5:14), who died and was raised for them (5:15). No longer seeing things from a human perspective, the apostle now expounds on being the new creation (5:17), which results from God's reconciling the world to himself through Christ (5:18). Paul and his companions are invited to participate in that message of reconciliation, becoming ambassadors for Christ (5:19–20).

Paul now returns to the theme of suffering for the sake of the gospel. The recommendation that he provides is his life of endurance in afflictions, his sincerity in speech, and his witness to the power of God with weapons of righteousness (2 Cor 6:3–10).

Having reestablished his apostolic credentials, he concludes this section of the letter with a command not to marry unbelievers but to be cleansed from every defilement (6:14–7:1). Since this section stands in direct opposition with 1 Cor 7:12–15, scholars propose that it is a later interpolation. Further evidence that 2 Cor 6:14–7:1 was not originally part of the letter is found in the fact that 7:2–4 picks up where 6:13 left off. Paul had advised the Corinthians to widen their hearts (6:13); now he encourages them to open their hearts to him (7:2). He is confident and proud of the Corinthians, with whom he is overjoyed (7:4).

Paul's so called "Letter of Tears" did the trick. Titus returns to Paul with news that the Corinthians have reaffirmed their confidence in Paul (2 Cor 7:7). They were grieved into a godly repentance (7:10). The initial reason for the letter, Paul states, was not because of the one who had done wrong or his victim; rather Paul sought to reignite the community's zeal before God (7:12). The theme of comfort, introduced in the thanksgiving section (1:3–7), returns here. God comforts the downcast (7:6). Paul is comforted by the return of Titus, who was comforted by the Corinthians (7:7). The Corinthians' response has comforted Paul (7:13). Paul's confidence in the Corinthian church has been confirmed and renewed (7:16).

Chapters 8 and 9 are both stewardship letters, requesting that the community provide financial support for the saints, presumably those in Jerusalem. In ch. 8, Paul sets before the Corinthians the example of the generosity of the churches of Macedonia, hoping to encourage their own liberal response (2 Cor 8:1–5). Titus is going to the Corinthians to direct the appeal (2 Cor 8:16). In ch. 9, the Corinthians are now an inspiration to the Macedonians (2 Cor 9:2). Paul is sending other brothers as an advance team to organize the collection (2 Cor 9:3), so that if some Macedonians accompany Paul to Corinth, Paul won't be embarrassed upon their arrival. Paul cites Scripture to encourage the Corinthians' generosity, for "God loves a cheerful giver!" (2 Cor 9:7; Prv 22:8 LXX). The Corinthians will glorify God by their obedience to the gospel and their generous contribution (2 Cor 9:13), declares Paul.

The last chapters in canonical 2 Corinthians

2 COR

evidence a drastic change in tone. Here Paul is engaging in a well-argued defense of his apostleship against opponents who belittle his skills and reject his authority. Paul begins his apology by rallying the troops. Using military imagery, Paul exhorts the Corinthians as a general would his troops before a battle (2 Cor 10:1–6). Paul's opponents grant that his letters are strong, he says, but call him a lightweight when it comes to personal presence (10:10). Paul won't stoop to their level by comparing himself to them (10:12), however. He asserts that he has followed the legitimate boundaries of his apostolic mandate (10:13). He was the first to bring the gospel to the Corinthians (10:14). He is not boasting of work done by others, which suggests that his opponents were doing so (10:16). Commendation comes from the Lord, declares Paul, not self-congratulating interlopers (10:18).

To defend himself, Paul must list his own accomplishments (2 Cor 11:6-7, 18, 21–33), but to boast in oneself was considered inappropriate.[6] Plutarch did single out occasions when one may boast.[7] In order to defend one's reputation, the wronged one could legitimately talk of his or her accomplishments. The Greek words for boasting are found more than twenty times in canonical 2 Corinthians (1:12, 14; 5:12; 7:4, 14; 8:24; 9:2, 3; 10:8, 13, 15, 16, 17; 11:10, 12, 16, 17, 18, 30; 12:1, 5, 6, 9). But one's boasting should be useful and not offensive. The authority of which Paul boasts has been given to him for the up-building of the community and not its destruction. In 2 Cor 11:1–15, Paul enumerates the boasts of the so-called "superapostles" (11:5). He then defends his own right to boast but does so in the guise

of the fool (11:16–21). Ironically, the stuff of Paul's boasts is not superlative accomplishments but a litany of his sufferings (11:22–33). Though there is nothing to be gained by boasting, Paul nonetheless discusses the visions and revelations of the Lord (12:1–5). But the only divine communiqué that Paul recounts is the Lord's invitation to embrace his weakness (12:9). Paul plays the fool because the Corinthians have failed to support him (12:11). He has demonstrated the signs of a true apostle with the exception of not taking their money (12:12–13). And this latter point seems to be crucial to his opponents (12:13).

For a third time, Paul promises to come to the Corinthians, but not in search of payment (2 Cor 12:14). They accuse him of being crafty (12:16) and seem to distrust Titus and the brother sent to them (12:17–18). Paul fears that a return visit might be a disappointment for both sides (12:20–21). Paul ends with a warning. Upon his next visit, he will deal mightily with those who have sinned (13:1–2). He has been defending himself throughout chs. 10–13. Now he puts the Corinthians on trial. They are to examine and test themselves, remembering that Jesus Christ is within them (13:5). Paul writes to correct the Corinthians by letter, so that upon his visit he won't have to be so severe (13:10). The authority he has from the Lord is, after all, for their betterment and not for their ruin. In closing, he gives a summary of his directives: "Rejoice. Mend your ways, encourage one another, agree with one another, live in peace, and the God of love and peace will be with you" (13:11). The unusual triadic final blessing in 13:13, "The grace of the Lord Jesus Christ and the love of God and the fellowship of the holy Spirit be with all of you," replaces his usual dual greeting from God the Father and the Lord Jesus Christ. ∎

---

6. Margaret M. Mitchell, "A Patristic Perspective on Pauline Periautologia," *NTS* (2001): 354–71.

7. *Mor.* 540c, 545a.

# THE SECOND LETTER TO THE CORINTHIANS

## New American Bible, Introduction

The Second Letter to the Corinthians is the most personal of all of Paul's extant writings, and it reveals much about his character. In it he deals with one or more crises that have arisen in the Corinthian church. The confrontation with these problems caused him to reflect deeply on his relationship with the community and to speak about it frankly. One moment he is venting his feelings of frustration and uncertainty, the next he is pouring out his relief and affection. The importance of the issues at stake between them calls forth from him an enormous effort of personal persuasion, as well as doctrinal considerations that are of great value for us. Paul's ability to produce profound theological foundations for what may at first sight appear to be rather commonplace circumstances is perhaps nowhere better exemplified than in Second Corinthians. The emotional tone of the letter, its lack of order, and our ignorance of some of its background do not make it easy to follow, but it amply repays the effort required of the reader.

Second Corinthians is rich and varied in content. The interpretation of Exodus in chapter 3, for instance, offers a striking example of early apologetic use of the Old Testament. Paul's discussion of the collection in chaps. 8–9 contains a theology of sharing of possessions, of community of goods among Christian churches, which is both balanced and sensitive. Furthermore, the closing chapters provide an illustration of early Christian invective and polemic, because the conflict with intruders forces Paul to assert his authority. But in those same chapters Paul articulates the vision and sense of values that animate his own apostolate, revealing his faith that Jesus' passion and resurrection are the pattern for all Christian life and expressing a spirituality of ministry unsurpassed in the New Testament.

The letter is remarkable for its rhetoric. Paul falls naturally into the style and argumentation of contemporary philosophic preachers, employing with ease the stock devices of the "diatribe." By a barrage of questions, by challenges both serious and ironic, by paradox heaped upon paradox, even by insults hurled at his opponents, he strives to awaken in his hearers a true sense of values and an appropriate response. All his argument centers on the destiny of Jesus, in which a paradoxical reversal of values is revealed. But Paul appeals to his own personal experience as well. In passages of great rhetorical power (2 Cor 4:7–15; 6:3–10; 11:21–29; 12:5–10; 13:3–4) he enumerates the circumstances of his ministry and the tribulations he has had to endure for Jesus and the gospel, in the hope of illustrating the pattern of Jesus' existence in his own and of drawing the Corinthians into a reappraisal of the values they cherish. Similar passages in the same style in his other letters (cf. especially Rom 8:31–39; 1 Cor 1:26–31; 4:6–21; 9:1–27; 13:1–13; Phil 4:10–19) confirm Paul's familiarity with contemporary rhetoric and demonstrate how effectively it served to express his vision of Christian life and ministry.

Second Corinthians was occasioned by events and problems that developed after Paul's first letter reached Corinth. We have no information about these circumstances except what is contained in the letter itself, which of course supposes that they are known to the readers. Consequently the reconstruction of the letter's background is an uncertain enterprise about which there is not complete agreement.

The letter deals principally with these three topics: (1) a crisis between Paul and the Corinthians, occasioned at least partially by changes in his travel plans (2 Cor 1:12–2:13), and the successful resolution of that crisis (2 Cor 7:5–16); (2) further directives and encouragement in regard to the collection for the church in Jerusalem (2 Cor 8:1–9:15); (3) the definition and defense of Paul's ministry as an apostle. Paul's reflections on this matter are occasioned by visitors from other churches who passed through Corinth, missionaries who differed from Paul in a variety of ways, both in theory and in practice. Those differences led to comparisons. Either the visitors themselves or some of the local church members appear to have sown confusion among the Corinthians with regard to Paul's authority or his style, or both. Paul deals at length with aspects of this situation in 2 Cor 2:14–7:4 and again in 2 Cor 10:1–13:10, though the manner of treatment and the thrust of the argument differ in each of these sections.

Scholars have noticed a lack of continuity in this document. For example, the long section of 2 Cor 2:14–7:4 seems abruptly spliced into the narrative of a crisis and its resolution. Identical or similar topics, moreover, seem to be treated several times during the letter (compare 2 Cor 2:14–7:4 with 2 Cor 10:1–13:10, and 2 Cor 8:1–24 with 2 Cor 9:1–15). Many judge, therefore, that this letter as it stands incorporates several briefer letters sent to Corinth over a certain span of time. If this is so, then Paul himself or, more likely, some other editor clearly took care to gather those letters together and impose some literary unity upon the collection, thus producing the document that has come down to us as the Second Letter

to the Corinthians. Others continue to regard it as a single letter, attributing its inconsistencies to changes of perspective in Paul that may have been occasioned by the arrival of fresh news from Corinth during its composition. The letter, or at least some sections of it, appears to have been composed in Macedonia (2 Cor 2:12–13; 7:5–6; 8:1–4; 9:2–4). It is generally dated about the autumn of A.D. 57; if it is a compilation, of course, the various parts may have been separated by intervals of at least some months.

The principal divisions of the Second Letter to the Corinthians are the following:

I. Address (1:1–11)
II. The Crisis Between Paul and the Corinthians (1:12–7:16)
  A. Past Relationships (1:12–2:13)
  B. Paul's Ministry (2:14–7:4)
  C. Resolution of the Crisis (7:5–16)
III. The Collection for Jerusalem (8:1–9:15)
IV. Paul's Defense of His Ministry (10:1–13:10)
V. Conclusion (13:11–13) ∎

# SECOND CORINTHIANS

## I. ADDRESS

**1** **Greeting.** [1]† Paul, an apostle of Christ Jesus by the will of God, and Timothy our brother, to the church of God that is in Corinth, with all the holy ones throughout Achaia:* [2] grace to you and peace from God our Father and the Lord Jesus Christ.

**Thanksgiving.** [3]* Blessed be the God and Father of our Lord Jesus Christ, the Father of compassion and God of all encouragement,† [4] who encourages us in our every affliction, so that we may be able to encourage those who are in any affliction with the encouragement with which we ourselves are encouraged by God.* [5] For as Christ's sufferings overflow to us, so through Christ† does our encouragement also overflow. [6] If we are afflicted, it is for your encouragement and salvation; if we are encouraged, it is for your encouragement, which enables you to endure the same sufferings that we suffer. [7] Our hope for you is firm, for we know that as you share in the sufferings, you also share in the encouragement.†

[8] We do not want you to be unaware, brothers, of the affliction that came to us in the province of Asia;† we were utterly weighed down beyond our strength, so that we despaired even of life.* [9] Indeed, we had accepted within ourselves the sentence of death,† that we might trust not in ourselves but in God who raises the dead.* [10] He rescued us from such great danger of death, and he will continue to rescue us; in him we have put our hope [that] he will also rescue us again,* [11] as you help us with prayer, so that thanks may be given by many on our behalf for the gift granted us through the prayers of many.*

## II. THE CRISIS BETWEEN PAUL AND THE CORINTHIANS

### A. Past Relationships†

**Paul's Sincerity and Constancy.** [12]† For our boast is this, the testimony of our conscience that we have conducted ourselves in the world, and especially toward you, with the simplicity and sincerity of God, [and] not by human wisdom but by the grace of God. [13] For we write you nothing but what you can read and understand, and I hope that you will understand completely, [14] as you have come to understand us partially, that we are your boast as you also are ours, on the day of [our] Lord Jesus.*

[15] With this confidence I formerly intended to come† to you so that you might receive a double favor, [16] namely, to go by way of you

---

† **1:1–11** The opening follows the usual Pauline form, except that the thanksgiving takes the form of a doxology or glorification of God (2 Cor 1:3). This introduces a meditation on the experience of suffering and encouragement shared by Paul and the Corinthians (2 Cor 1:4–7), drawn, at least in part, from Paul's reflections on a recent affliction (2 Cor 1:8–10). The section ends with a modified and delayed allusion to thanksgiving (2 Cor 1:11).

**1:3** *God of all encouragement*: Paul expands a standard Jewish blessing so as to state the theme of the paragraph. The theme of "encouragement" or "consolation" (*paraklēsis*) occurs ten times in this opening, against a background formed by multiple references to "affliction" and "suffering."

**1:5** *Through Christ*: the Father of compassion is the Father of our Lord Jesus (2 Cor 1:3); Paul's sufferings and encouragement (or "consolation") are experienced in union with Christ. Cf. Lk 2:25: the "consolation of Israel" is Jesus himself.

**1:7** *You also share in the encouragement*: the eschatological reversal of affliction and encouragement that Christians expect (cf. Mt 5:4; Lk 6:24) permits some present experience of reversal in the Corinthians' case, as in Paul's.

**1:8** *Asia*: a Roman province in western Asia Minor, the capital of which was Ephesus.

**1:9–10** *The sentence of death*: it is unclear whether Paul is alluding to a physical illness or to an external threat to life. The result of the situation was to produce an attitude of faith in God alone. *God who raises the dead*: rescue is the constant pattern of God's activity; his final act of encouragement is the resurrection.

**1:12–2:13** The autobiographical remarks about the crisis in Asia Minor lead into consideration of a crisis that has arisen between Paul and the Corinthians. Paul will return to this question, after a long digression, in 2 Cor 7:5–16. Both of these sections deal with travel plans Paul had made, changes in the plans, alternative measures adopted, a breach that opened between him and the community, and finally a reconciliation between them.

**1:12–14** Since Paul's own conduct will be under discussion here, he prefaces the section with a statement about his habitual behavior and attitude toward the community. He protests his openness, single-mindedness, and conformity to God's grace; he hopes that his relationship with them will be marked by mutual understanding and pride, which will constantly increase until it reaches its climax at the judgment. Two references to boasting frame this paragraph (2 Cor 1:12, 14), the first appearances of a theme that will be important in the letter, especially in 2 Cor 10–13; the term is used in a positive sense here (cf. note on 1 Cor 1:29–31).

**1:15** *I formerly intended to come*: this plan reads like a revision of the one mentioned in 1 Cor 16:5. Not until 2 Cor 1:23–2:1 will Paul tell us something his original readers already knew, that he has canceled one or the other of these projected visits.

*
**1:1** Eph 1:1; Col 1:1 / 2 Cor 1:19; Acts 16 / Rom 1:7; 1 Cor 1:2.
**1:3** 1 Cor 15:24; Eph 1:3; 1 Pt 1:3 / Rom 15:5.
**1:4** 7:6–7, 13; 1 Thes 3:6–8; 2 Thes 2:16.
**1:8** Acts 20:18–19; 1 Cor 15:32.
**1:9** 4:7–11; Rom 4:17.
**1:10** 2 Tm 4:18.
**1:11** 4:15; 9:12.
**1:14** Phil 2:16; 1 Thes 2:19–20.

to Macedonia, and then to come to you again on my return from Macedonia, and have you send me on my way to Judea.* ¹⁷So when I intended this, did I act lightly?† Or do I make my plans according to human considerations, so that with me it is "yes, yes" and "no, no"?* ¹⁸As God is faithful,† our word to you is not "yes" and "no." ¹⁹For the Son of God, Jesus Christ, who was proclaimed to you by us, Silvanus and Timothy and me, was not "yes" and "no," but "yes" has been in him.* ²⁰For however many are the promises of God, their Yes is in him; therefore, the Amen from us also goes through him to God for glory.* ²¹† But the one who gives us security with you in Christ and who anointed us is God;* ²²he has also put his seal upon us and given the Spirit in our hearts as a first installment.*

**Paul's Change of Plan.** ²³* But I call upon God as witness, on my life, that it is to spare you that I have not yet gone to Corinth.† ²⁴Not that we lord it over your faith; rather, we work together for your joy, for you stand firm in the faith.

**2** ¹For I decided not to come to you again in painful circumstances. ²For if I inflict pain upon you, then who is there to cheer me except the one pained by me? ³And I wrote as I did† so that when I came I might not be pained by those in whom I should have rejoiced, confident about all of you that my joy is that of all of you. ⁴For out of much affliction and anguish of heart I wrote to you with many tears, not that you might be pained but that you might know the abundant love I have for you.

**The Offender.**† ⁵If anyone has caused pain, he has caused it not to me, but in some measure (not to exaggerate) to all of you. ⁶This punishment by the majority is enough for such a person, ⁷so that on the contrary you should forgive and encourage him instead, or else the person may be overwhelmed by excessive pain.* ⁸Therefore, I urge you to reaffirm your love for him. ⁹For this is why I wrote, to know your proven character, whether you were obedient in everything.* ¹⁰Whomever you forgive anything, so do I. For indeed what I have forgiven, if I have forgiven anything, has been for you in the presence of Christ, ¹¹so that we might not be taken advantage of by Satan, for we are not unaware of his purposes.*

**† 1:17** *Did I act lightly?*: the subsequent change of plans casts suspicion on the original intention, creating the impression that Paul is vacillating and inconsistent or that *human considerations* keep dictating shifts in his goals and projects (cf. the counter-claim of 2 Cor 1:12). *"Yes, yes" and "no, no"*: stating something and denying it in the same or the next breath; being of two minds at once, or from one moment to the next.
**1:18–22** *As God is faithful*: unable to deny the change in plans, Paul nonetheless asserts the firmness of the original plan and claims a profound constancy in his life and work. He grounds his defense in God himself, who is firm and reliable; this quality can also be predicated in various ways of those who are associated with him. Christ, Paul, and the Corinthians all participate in analogous ways in the constancy of God. A number of the terms here, which appear related only conceptually in Greek or English, would be variations of the same root, *'mn*, in a Semitic language, and thus naturally associated in a Semitic mind, such as Paul's. These include the words *yes* (2 Cor 1:17–20), *faithful* (2 Cor 1:18), *Amen* (2 Cor 1:20), *gives us security* (2 Cor 1:21), *faith, stand firm* (2 Cor 1:24).
**1:21–22** The commercial terms *gives us security, seal, first installment* are here used analogously to refer to the process of initiation into the Christian life, perhaps specifically to baptism. The passage is clearly trinitarian. The Spirit is the *first installment* or "down payment" of the full messianic benefits that God guarantees to Christians. Cf. Eph 1:13–14.
**1:23–24** *I have not yet gone to Corinth*: some suppose that Paul received word of some affair in Corinth, which he decided to regulate by letter even before the first of his projected visits (cf. 2 Cor 1:16). Others conjecture that he did pay the first visit, was offended there (cf. 2 Cor 2:5), returned to Ephesus, and sent a letter (2 Cor 2:3–9) in place of the second visit. The expressions *to spare you* (2 Cor 1:23) and *work together for your joy* (2 Cor 1:24) introduce the major themes of the next two paragraphs,

which are remarkable for insistent repetition of key words and ideas. These form two clusters of terms in the English translation: (1) cheer, rejoice, encourage, joy; (2) pain, affliction, anguish. These clusters reappear when Paul resumes treatment of this subject in 2 Cor 7:5–16.
**2:3–4** *I wrote as I did*: we learn for the first time about the sending of a letter in place of the proposed visit. Paul mentions the letter in passing, but emphasizes his motivation in sending it: to avoid being saddened by them (cf. 1 Cor 2:1), and to help them realize the depth of his love. Another motive will be added in 2 Cor 7:12: to bring to light their own concern for him. *With many tears*: it has been suggested that we may have all or part of this "tearful letter" somewhere in the Corinthian correspondence, either in 1 Cor 5 (the case of the incestuous man), or in 1 Corinthians as a whole, or in 2 Cor 2:10–13. None of these hypotheses is entirely convincing. See note on 2 Cor 13:1.
**2:5–11** The nature of the *pain* (2 Cor 2:5) is unclear, though some believe an individual at Corinth rejected Paul's authority, thereby scandalizing many in the community. In any case, action has been taken, and Paul judges the measures adequate to right the situation (2 Cor 2:6). The follow-up directives he now gives are entirely positive: forgive, encourage, love. *Overwhelmed* (2 Cor 2:7): a vivid metaphor (literally "swallowed") that Paul employs positively at 2 Cor 5:4 and in 1 Cor 15:54 (2 Cor 2:7). It is often used to describe satanic activity (cf. 1 Pt 5:8); note the reference to Satan here in 2 Cor 2:11.

* **1:16** 1 Cor 15:5–9; Acts 19:21.
**1:17** Mt 5:37; Jas 5:12.
**1:19** Acts 16:1–3; 1 Thes 1:1; 2 Thes 1:1.
**1:20** 1 Cor 14:16; Rev 3:14.
**1:21** 1 Jn 2:20, 27.
**1:22** Eph 1:13–14; 4:30 / 2 Cor 5:5; Rom 5:5; 8:16, 23.
**1:23** 13:2.
**2:7** Col 3:13.
**2:9** 7:15.
**2:11** Eph 4:27.

**Paul's Anxiety.**† ¹²When I went to Troas for the gospel of Christ, although a door was opened for me in the Lord,* ¹³† I had no relief in my spirit because I did not find my brother Titus.* So I took leave of them and went on to Macedonia.

## B. Paul's Ministry†

**Ministers of a New Covenant.** ¹⁴† But thanks be to God,† who always leads us in triumph in Christ† and manifests through us the odor of the knowledge of him† in every place. ¹⁵For we are the aroma of Christ for God among those who are being saved and among those who are perishing,* ¹⁶to the latter an odor of death that leads to death, to the former an odor of life that leads to life. Who is qualified† for this? ¹⁷For we are not like the many who trade on the word of God; but as out of sincerity, indeed as from God and in the presence of God, we speak in Christ.*

**3** ¹†* Are we beginning to commend ourselves again? Or do we need, as some do, letters of recommendation to you or from you? ²You are our letter,† written on our hearts, known and read by all, ³†* shown to be a letter of Christ administered by us, written not in ink but by the Spirit of the living God, not on tablets of stone but on tablets that are hearts of flesh.

⁴† Such confidence we have through Christ toward God. ⁵Not that of ourselves we are

---

† **2:12–13** *I had no relief*: Paul does not explain the reason for his anxiety until he resumes the thread of his narrative at 2 Cor 7:5: he was waiting to hear how the Corinthians would respond to his letter. Since 2 Cor 7:5–16 describes their response in entirely positive terms, we never learn in detail why he found it necessary to defend and justify his change of plans, as in 2 Cor 1:15–24. Was this portion of the letter written before the arrival of Titus with his good news (2 Cor 7:6–7)?

**2:13** *Macedonia*: a Roman province in northern Greece.

**2:14–7:4** This section constitutes a digression within the narrative of the crisis and its resolution (2 Cor 1:12–2:13 and 2 Cor 7:5–16). The main component (2 Cor 2:14–6:10) treats the nature of Paul's ministry and his qualifications for it; this material bears some similarity to the defense of his ministry in chaps. 10–13, but it may well come from a period close to the crisis. This is followed by a supplementary block of material quite different in character and tone (2 Cor 6:14–7:1). These materials may have been brought together into their present position during final editing of the letter; appeals to the Corinthians link them to one another (2 Cor 6:11–13) and lead back to the interrupted narrative (2 Cor 7:2–4).

**2:14–6:10** The question of Paul's adequacy (2 Cor 2:16; cf. 2 Cor 3:5) and his credentials (2 Cor 3:1–2) has been raised. Paul responds by an extended treatment of the nature of his ministry. It is a ministry of glory (2 Cor 3:7–4:6), of life (2 Cor 4:7–5:10), of reconciliation (2 Cor 5:11–6:10).

**2:14–16a** The initial statement plunges us abruptly into another train of thought. Paul describes his personal existence and his function as a preacher in two powerful images (2 Cor 2:14) that constitute a prelude to the development to follow.

**2:14a** *Leads us in triumph in Christ*: this metaphor of a festive parade in honor of a conquering military hero can suggest either a positive sharing in Christ's triumph or an experience of defeat, being led in captivity and submission (cf. 2 Cor 4:8–11; 1 Cor 4:9). Paul is probably aware of the ambiguity, as he is in the case of the next metaphor.

**2:14b–16a** *The odor of the knowledge of him*: incense was commonly used in triumphal processions. The metaphor suggests the gradual diffusion of the knowledge of God through the apostolic preaching. *The aroma of Christ*: the image shifts from the fragrance Paul diffuses to the aroma that he is. Paul is probably thinking of the "sweet odor" of the sacrifices in the Old Testament (e.g., Gn 8:21; Ex 29:18) and perhaps of the metaphor of wisdom as a sweet odor (Sir 24:15). *Death...life*: the aroma of Christ that comes to them through Paul is perceived differently by various classes of people. To some his preaching and his life (cf. 1 Cor 1:17–2:6) are perceived as death, and the effect is death for them; others perceive him, despite appearances, as *life*, and the effect is life for them. This fragrance thus produces a separation and a judgment (cf. the function of the "light" in John's gospel).

**2:16b–17** *Qualified*: Paul may be echoing either the self-satisfied claims of other preachers or their charges about Paul's deficiencies. No one is really qualified, but the apostle contrasts himself with those who dilute or falsify the preaching for personal advantage and insists on his totally good conscience: his ministry is from God, and he has exercised it with fidelity and integrity (cf. 2 Cor 3:5–6).

**3:1** Paul seems to allude to certain preachers who pride themselves on their written credentials. Presumably they reproach him for not possessing similar credentials and compel him to spell out his own qualifications (2 Cor 4:2; 5:12; 6:4). The Corinthians themselves should have performed this function for Paul (2 Cor 5:12; cf. 2 Cor 12:11). Since he is forced to find something that can recommend him, he points to them: their very existence constitutes his *letter* of recommendation (2 Cor 3:1–2). Others who engage in self-commendation will also be mentioned in 2 Cor 10:12–18.

**3:2–3** Mention of "letters of recommendation" generates a series of metaphors in which Paul plays on the word "letter": (1) the community is Paul's letter of recommendation (2 Cor 3:2a); (2) they are a letter engraved on his affections for all to see and read (2 Cor 3:2b); (3) they are a letter from Christ that Paul merely delivers (2 Cor 3:3a); (4) they are a letter written by the Spirit on the tablets of human hearts (2 Cor 3:3b). One image dissolves into another.

**3:3b** This verse contrasts Paul's letter with those *written...in ink* (like the credentials of other preachers) and those *written... on tablets of stone* (like the law of Moses). These contrasts suggest that the other preachers may have claimed special relationship with Moses. If they were Judaizers zealous for the Mosaic law, that would explain the detailed contrast between the old and the new covenants (2 Cor 3:6; 4:7–6:10). If they were charismatics who claimed Moses as their model, that would explain the extended treatment of Moses himself and his glory (2 Cor 3:7–4:6). *Hearts of flesh*: cf. Ezekiel's contrast between the heart of flesh that the Spirit gives and the heart of stone that it replaces (Ez 36:26); the context is covenant renewal and purification that makes observance of the law possible.

**3:4–6** These verses resume 2 Cor 2:1–3:3. Paul's confidence (2 Cor 3:4) is grounded in his sense of God-given mission (2 Cor 2:17), the specifics of which are described in 2 Cor 3:1–3. 2 Cor 3:5–6 return to the question of his qualifications (2 Cor 2:16), attributing them entirely to God. 2 Cor 3:6 further spells out the situation described in 2 Cor 3:3b and "names" it: Paul is living within a *new covenant*, characterized by the Spirit, which *gives* life. The usage of a *new covenant* is derived from Jer 31:31–33 a passage that also speaks of writing on the heart; cf. 2 Cor 3:2.

---

*

**2:12** Acts 16:8.  
**2:13** 7:6; 1 Tm 1:3.  
**2:15** 4:3; 1 Cor 1:18.  
**2:17** 4:2; 1 Cor 5:8.  

**3:1** Acts 18:27; Rom 16:1;  
    1 Cor 16:3.  
**3:3** Ex 24:12; 31:18;  
    32:15–19 / Jer 31:33;  
    Ez 11:19; 36:26–27.

2 COR

qualified to take credit for anything as coming from us; rather, our qualification comes from God,* 6 who has indeed qualified us as ministers of a new covenant, not of letter but of spirit;* for the letter brings death, but the Spirit gives life.†

### Contrast with the Old Covenant.
7† Now if the ministry of death,† carved in letters on stone, was so glorious that the Israelites could not look intently at the face of Moses because of its glory that was going to fade,* 8 how much more† will the ministry of the Spirit be glorious? 9 For if the ministry of condemnation was glorious, the ministry of righteousness will abound much more in glory. 10 Indeed, what was endowed with glory has come to have no glory in this respect because of the glory that surpasses it. 11 For if what was going to fade was glorious, how much more will what endures be glorious.

12 Therefore, since we have such hope,† we act very boldly 13 and not like Moses,† who put a veil over his face so that the Israelites could not look intently at the cessation of what was fading. 14 Rather, their thoughts were rendered dull, for to this present day† the same veil remains unlifted when they read the old covenant, because through Christ it is taken away. 15 To this day, in fact, whenever Moses is read, a veil lies over their hearts,* 16 but whenever a person turns to the Lord the veil is removed.* 17 Now the Lord is the Spirit,† and where the Spirit of the Lord is, there is freedom. 18† All of us, gazing with unveiled face on the glory of the Lord, are being transformed into the same image from glory to glory, as from the Lord who is the Spirit.*

### 4 Integrity in the Ministry.
1† Therefore, since we have this ministry through the mercy shown us, we are not discouraged. 2 Rather, we have renounced shameful, hidden things; not acting deceitfully or falsifying the

---

†

**3:6** This verse serves as a topic sentence for 2 Cor 3:7–6:10. For the contrast between *letter* and *spirit*, cf. Rom 2:29; 7:5–6.

**3:7–4:6** Paul now develops the contrast enunciated in 2 Cor 3:6b in terms of the relative glory of the two covenants, insisting on the greater glory of the new. His polemic seems directed against individuals who appeal to the glorious Moses and fail to perceive any comparable glory either in Paul's life as an apostle or in the gospel he preaches. He asserts in response that Christians have a glory of their own that far surpasses that of Moses.

**3:7** The *ministry of death*: from his very first words, Paul describes the Mosaic covenant and ministry from the viewpoint of their limitations. They lead to *death* rather than life (2 Cor 3:6–7; cf. 2 Cor 4:7–5:10), to *condemnation* rather than reconciliation (2 Cor 3:9; cf. 2 Cor 5:11–6:10). *Was so glorious*: the basic text to which Paul alludes is Ex 34:29–35 to which his opponents have undoubtedly laid claim. *Going to fade*: Paul concedes the glory of Moses' covenant and ministry, but grants them only temporary significance.

**3:8–11** *How much more*: the argument "from the less to the greater" is repeated three times (2 Cor 3:8, 9, 11). 2 Cor 3:10 expresses another point of view: the difference in glory is so great that only the new covenant and ministry can properly be called "glorious" at all.

**3:12** *Such hope*: the glory is not yet an object of experience, but that does not lessen Paul's confidence. *Boldly*: the term *parrēsia* expresses outspoken declaration of Christian conviction (cf. 2 Cor 4:1–2). Paul has nothing to hide and no reason for timidity.

**3:13–14a** *Not like Moses*: in Exodus Moses veiled his face to protect the Israelites from God's reflected glory. Without impugning Moses' sincerity, Paul attributes another effect to the veil. Since it lies between God's glory and the Israelites, it explains how they could fail to notice the glory disappearing. *Their thoughts were rendered dull*: the problem lay with their understanding. This will be expressed in 2 Cor 3:14b–16 by a shift in the place of the veil: it is no longer over Moses' face but over their perception.

**3:14b–16** The parallelism in these verses makes it necessary to interpret corresponding parts in relation to one another. *To this present day*: this signals the shift of Paul's attention to his contemporaries; his argument is typological, as in 1 Cor 10. The Israelites of Moses' time typify the Jews of Paul's time, and

perhaps also Christians of Jewish origin or mentality who may not recognize the temporary character of Moses' glory. *When they read the old covenant*: the lasting dullness prevents proper appraisal of Moses' person and covenant. When his writings are read in the synagogue, a veil still impedes their understanding. *Through Christ*: i.e., in the new covenant. *Whenever a person turns to the Lord*: Moses in Exodus appeared before God without the veil and gazed on his face unprotected. Paul applies that passage to converts to Christianity: when they turn to the Lord fully and authentically, the impediment to their understanding is removed.

**3:17** *The Lord is the Spirit*: the "Lord" to whom the Christian turns (2 Cor 3:16) is the Spirit of whom Paul has been speaking, the life-giving Spirit of the living God (2 Cor 3:6, 8), the inaugurator of the new covenant and ministry, who is also the Spirit of Christ. *The Spirit of the Lord*: the Lord here is the living God (2 Cor 3:3), but there may also be an allusion to Christ as Lord (2 Cor 3:14, 16). *Freedom*: i.e., from the ministry of death (2 Cor 3:7) and the covenant that condemned (2 Cor 3:9).

**3:18** Another application of the veil image. *All of us...with unveiled face*: Christians (Israelites from whom the veil has been removed) are like Moses, standing in God's presence, beholding and reflecting his glory. *Gazing*: the verb may also be translated "contemplating as in a mirror"; 2 Cor 4:6 would suggest that the mirror is Christ himself. *Are being transformed*: elsewhere Paul speaks of transformation, conformity to Jesus, God's image, as a reality of the end time, and even 2 Cor 3:12 speaks of the glory as an object of hope. But the life-giving Spirit, the distinctive gift of the new covenant, is already present in the community (cf. 2 Cor 1:22, the "first installment"), and the process of transformation has already begun. *Into the same image*: into the image of God, which is Christ (2 Cor 4:4).

**4:1–2** A ministry of this sort generates confidence and forthrightness; cf. 2 Cor 1:12–14; 2:17.

---

*

**3:5** Jn 3:27.
**3:6** Eph 3:7 / Jer 31:31–34.
**3:7** Ex 34:29–35.
**3:15** Rom 11:7–10.
**3:16** Ex 34:34.

**3:18** Rom 8:29–30; 12:2; Gal 4:19; Phil 3:10, 20–21 / 2 Cor 4:4–6; 1 Cor 15:49; Col 1:15; 3:9–11; 1 Jn 3:2.

word of God, but by the open declaration of the truth we commend ourselves to everyone's conscience in the sight of God.* ³And even though our gospel is veiled,† it is veiled for those who are perishing,* ⁴in whose case the god of this age has blinded the minds of the unbelievers, so that they may not see the light of the gospel of the glory of Christ, who is the image of God.* ⁵For we do not preach ourselves† but Jesus Christ as Lord, and ourselves as your slaves for the sake of Jesus. ⁶† For God who said, "Let light shine out of darkness," has shone in our hearts to bring to light the knowledge of the glory of God on the face of [Jesus] Christ.*

**The Paradox of the Ministry.** ⁷† But we hold this treasure† in earthen vessels, that the surpassing power may be of God and not from us. ⁸† We are afflicted in every way, but not constrained; perplexed, but not driven to despair;* ⁹persecuted, but not abandoned; struck down, but not destroyed; ¹⁰†* always carrying about in the body the dying of Jesus,

so that the life of Jesus may also be manifested in our body. ¹¹For we who live are constantly being given up to death for the sake of Jesus, so that the life of Jesus may be manifested in our mortal flesh.*

¹²† So death is at work in us, but life in you. ¹³† Since, then, we have the same spirit of faith, according to what is written, "I believed, therefore I spoke," we too believe and therefore speak,* ¹⁴knowing that the one who raised the Lord Jesus will raise us also with Jesus and place us with you in his presence.* ¹⁵Everything indeed is for you, so that the grace bestowed in abundance on more and more people may cause the thanksgiving to overflow for the glory of God.*

¹⁶† Therefore, we are not discouraged;† rather, although our outer self is wasting away, our inner self is being renewed day by day.* ¹⁷For this momentary light affliction is producing for us an eternal weight of glory beyond all comparison,* ¹⁸as we look not to what is seen but to what is unseen; for what is seen is transitory, but what is unseen is eternal.*

---

**4:3–4** *Though our gospel is veiled*: the final application of the image. Paul has been reproached either for obscurity in his preaching or for his manner of presenting the gospel. But he confidently asserts that there is no veil over his gospel. If some fail to perceive its light, that is because of unbelief. The veil lies over their eyes (2 Cor 3:14), a blindness induced by Satan, and a sign that they are headed for destruction (cf. 2 Cor 2:15).

**4:5** *We do not preach ourselves*: the light seen in his gospel is the glory of Christ (2 Cor 4:4). Far from preaching himself, the preacher should be a transparent medium through whom Jesus is perceived (cf. 2 Cor 4:10–11). *Your slaves*: Paul draws attention away from individuals as such and toward their role in relation to God, Christ, and the community; cf. 1 Cor 3:5; 2 Cor 4:1.

**4:6** Autobiographical allusion to the episode at Damascus clarifies the origin and nature of Paul's service; cf. Acts 9:1–19; 22:3–16; 26:2–18. *"Let light shine out of darkness"*: Paul seems to be thinking of Gn 1:3 and presenting his apostolic ministry as a new creation. There may also be an allusion to Is 9:1 suggesting his prophetic calling as servant of the Lord and light to the nations; cf. Is 42:6, 16; 49:6; 60:1–2, and the use of light imagery in Acts 26:13–23. *To bring to light the knowledge*: Paul's role in the process of revelation, expressed at the beginning under the image of the odor and aroma (2 Cor 2:14–15), is restated now, at the end of this first moment of the development, in the imagery of light and glory (2 Cor 4:3–6).

**4:7–5:10** Paul now confronts the difficulty that his present existence does not appear glorious at all; it is marked instead by suffering and death. He deals with this by developing the topic already announced in 2 Cor 3:3, 6, asserting his faith in the presence and ultimate triumph of life, in his own and every Christian existence, despite the experience of death.

**4:7** *This treasure*: the glory that he preaches and into which they are being transformed. *In earthen vessels*: the instruments God uses are human and fragile; some imagine small terracotta lamps in which light is carried.

**4:8–9** A catalogue of his apostolic trials and afflictions. Yet in these the negative never completely prevails; there is always some experience of rescue, of salvation.

**4:10–11** Both the negative and the positive sides of the experience are grounded christologically. The logic is similar to that of 2 Cor 1:3–11. His sufferings are connected with Christ's, and his deliverance is a sign that he is to share in Jesus' resurrection.

**4:12–15** His experience does not terminate in himself, but in others (2 Cor 4:12, 15; cf. 2 Cor 1:4–5). Ultimately, everything is ordered even beyond the community, toward God (2 Cor 4:15; cf. 2 Cor 1:11).

**4:13–14** Like the psalmist, Paul clearly proclaims his faith, affirming life within himself despite death (2 Cor 4:10–11) and the life-giving effect of his experience upon the church (2 Cor 4:12, 14–15). *And place us with you in his presence*: Paul imagines God presenting him and them to Jesus at the parousia and the judgment; cf. 2 Cor 11:2; Rom 14:10.

**4:16–18** In a series of contrasts Paul explains the extent of his faith in life. Life is not only already present and revealing itself (2 Cor 4:8–11, 16) but will outlast his experience of affliction and dying: it is eternal (2 Cor 4:17–18).

**4:16** *Not discouraged*: i.e., despite the experience of death. Paul is still speaking of himself personally, but he assumes his faith and attitude will be shared by all Christians. *Our outer self*: the individual subject of ordinary perception and observation, in contrast to the interior and hidden self, which undergoes renewal. *Is being renewed day by day*: this suggests a process that has already begun; cf. 2 Cor 3:18. The renewal already taking place even in Paul's dying is a share in the life of Jesus, but this is recognized only by faith (2 Cor 4:13, 18; 2 Cor 5:7).

| | |
|---|---|
| **4:2** 2:17; 1 Thes 2:4–7. | 1 Cor 15:31. |
| **4:3** 2:15–16; 2 Thes 2:10. | **4:13** Ps 116:10. |
| **4:4** Jn 12:31–36 / 1 Tm 1:11. | **4:14** Rom 4:24–25; 8:11; 1 Cor 6:14; 1 Thes 4:14. |
| **4:6** Gn 1:3; Is 9:1; Acts 26:13–23; Gal 1:15–16 / Jn 8:12; Heb 1:3. | **4:15** 1:11. |
| | **4:16** 4:1. |
| **4:8** 6:4–10; 1 Cor 4:9–13. | **4:17** Mt 5:11–12; Rom 8:18. |
| **4:10** Col 1:24. | **4:18** Rom 8:24–25; Heb 11:1. |
| **4:11** Rom 8:36; | |

# 5 Our Future Destiny.

**5** **Our Future Destiny.** [1]* For we know that if our earthly dwelling,† a tent, should be destroyed, we have a building from God, a dwelling not made with hands, eternal in heaven. [2]† For in this tent we groan, longing to be further clothed with our heavenly habitation* [3] if indeed, when we have taken it off,† we shall not be found naked. [4] For while we are in this tent we groan and are weighed down, because we do not wish to be unclothed† but to be further clothed, so that what is mortal may be swallowed up by life.* [5] Now the one who has prepared us for this very thing is God,* who has given us the Spirit as a first installment.†

[6]† So we are always courageous, although we know that while we are at home in the body we are away from the Lord, [7] for we walk by faith, not by sight. [8] Yet we are courageous, and we would rather leave the body and go home to the Lord.* [9] Therefore, we aspire to please him, whether we are at home or away. [10] For we must all appear† before the judgment seat of Christ, so that each one may receive recompense, according to what he did in the body, whether good or evil.*

## The Ministry of Reconciliation.

[11]† Therefore, since we know the fear of the Lord, we try to persuade others; but we are clearly apparent to God, and I hope we are also apparent to your consciousness.* [12] We are not commending ourselves to you again but giving you an opportunity to boast of us, so that you may have something to say to those who boast of external appearance rather than of the heart.* [13] For if we are out of our minds,† it is for God; if we are rational, it is for you. [14]† For the love of Christ impels us, once we have come to the conviction that one died for all; therefore, all have died.* [15] He indeed died for all, so that those who live might no longer live for themselves but for him who for their sake died and was raised.*

[16] Consequently,† from now on we regard no one according to the flesh; even if we once knew Christ according to the flesh, yet now we

---

**5:1** *Our earthly dwelling*: the same contrast is restated in the imagery of a dwelling. The language recalls Jesus' saying about the destruction of the temple and the construction of another building *not made with hands* (Mk 14:58), a prediction later applied to Jesus' own body (Jn 2:20).

**5:2–5** 2 Cor 5:2–3 and 4 are largely parallel in structure. *We groan, longing*: see note on 2 Cor 5:5. *Clothed with our heavenly habitation*: Paul mixes his metaphors, adding the image of the garment to that of the building. *Further clothed*: the verb means strictly "to put one garment on over another." Paul may desire to put the resurrection body on over his mortal body, without dying; 2 Cor 5:2, 4 permit this meaning but do not impose it. Or perhaps he imagines the resurrection body as a garment put on over the Christ-garment first received in baptism (Gal 3:27) and preserved by moral behavior (Rom 13:12–14; Col 3:12; cf. Mt 22:11–13). Some support for this interpretation may be found in the context; cf. the references to baptism (2 Cor 5:5), to judgment according to works (2 Cor 5:10), and to present renewal (2 Cor 4:16), an idea elsewhere combined with the image of "putting on" a new nature (Eph 4:22–24; Col 3:1–5, 9–10).

**5:3** *When we have taken it off*: the majority of witnesses read "when we have put it on," i.e., when we have been clothed (in the resurrection body), then we shall not be without a body (naked). This seems mere tautology, though some understand it to mean: whether we are "found" (by God at the judgment) clothed or naked depends upon whether we have preserved or lost our original investiture in Christ (cf. the previous note). In this case to "put it on" does not refer to the resurrection body, but to keeping intact the Christ-garment of baptism. The translation follows the western reading (Codex Bezae, Tertullian), the sense of which is clear: to "take it off" is to shed our mortal body in death, after which we shall be clothed in the resurrection body and hence not "naked" (cf. 1 Cor 15:51–53).

**5:4** *We do not wish to be unclothed*: a clear allusion to physical death (2 Cor 4:16; 5:1). Unlike the Greeks, who found dissolution of the body desirable (cf. Socrates), Paul has a Jewish horror of it. He seems to be thinking of the "intermediate period," an interval between death and resurrection. *Swallowed up by life*: cf. 1 Cor 15:54.

**5:5** God has created us for resurrected bodily life and already prepares us for it by the gift of the Spirit in baptism. *The Spirit as a*

*first installment*: the striking parallel to 2 Cor 5:1–5 in Rom 8:17–30 describes Christians who have received the "firstfruits" (cf. "first installment" here) of the Spirit as "groaning" (cf. 2 Cor 5:2, 4 here) for the resurrection, the complete redemption of their bodies. In place of clothing and building, Rom 8 uses other images for the resurrection: adoption and conformity to the image of the Son.

**5:6–9** Tension between present and future is expressed by another spatial image, the metaphor of the country and its citizens. At present we are like citizens in exile or far away from home. The Lord is the distant homeland, believed in but unseen (2 Cor 5:7).

**5:10** *We must all appear*: the verb is ambiguous: we are scheduled to "appear" for judgment, at which we will be "revealed" as we are (cf. 2 Cor 11; 2:14; 4:10–11).

**5:11–15** This paragraph is transitional. Paul sums up much that has gone before. Still playing on the term "appearance," he reasserts his transparency before God and the Corinthians, in contrast to the self-commendation, boasting, and preoccupation with externals that characterize some others (cf. 2 Cor 1:12–14; 2:14; 3:1; 3:7–4:6). 2 Cor 5:14 recalls 2 Cor 3:7–4:6, and sums up 2 Cor 4:7–5:10.

**5:13** *Out of our minds*: this verse confirms that a concern for ecstasy and charismatic experience may lie behind the discussion about "glory" in 2 Cor 3:7–4:6. Paul also enjoys such experiences but, unlike others, does not make a public display of them or consider them ends in themselves. *Rational*: the Greek virtue *sōphrosynē*, to which Paul alludes, implies reasonableness, moderation, good judgment, self-control.

**5:14–15** These verses echo 2 Cor 4:14 and resume the treatment of "life despite death" from 2 Cor 4:7–5:10.

**5:16–17** *Consequently*: the death of Christ described in 2 Cor 5:14–15 produces a whole new order (2 Cor 5:17) and a new mode of perception (2 Cor 5:16). *According to the flesh*: the natu-

| | |
|---|---|
| **5:1** Is 38:12 / Col 3:1–4 / Mk 14:58; Col 2:11; Heb 9:11, 24. | **5:10** Mt 16:27; 25:31–46; Rom 2:16; 14:10–11. |
| **5:2** Rom 8:23 / 1 Cor 15:51–54. | **5:11** 1:12–14. |
| **5:4** Is 25:8; 1 Cor 15:54. | **5:12** 3:1 / 2 Cor 1:14; Phil 1:26. |
| **5:5** 1:22. | **5:14** Rom 6:1–6. |
| **5:8** Phil 1:21–23. | **5:15** Rom 4:25; 6:4–11; 14:9; Col 3:3–4. |

know him so no longer. <sup>17</sup>* So whoever is in Christ is a new creation: the old things have passed away; behold, new things have come. <sup>18</sup>† And all this is from God, who has reconciled us to himself through Christ and given us the ministry of reconciliation, <sup>19</sup> namely, God was reconciling the world to himself in Christ, not counting their trespasses against them and entrusting to us the message of reconciliation.* <sup>20</sup> So we are ambassadors for Christ, as if God were appealing through us. We implore you on behalf of Christ, be reconciled to God.* <sup>21</sup>† For our sake he made him to be sin who did not know sin,* so that we might become the righteousness of God in him.

## 6 The Experience of the Ministry. <sup>1</sup>† Working together,* then, we appeal to you not to receive the grace of God in vain.† <sup>2</sup> For he says:

> "In an acceptable time† I heard you,
>     and on the day of salvation I helped you."*

Behold, now is a very acceptable time; behold, now is the day of salvation. <sup>3</sup>* We cause no one to stumble† in anything, in order that no fault may be found with our ministry; <sup>4</sup>† on the contrary, in everything we commend ourselves as ministers of God, through much endurance,† in afflictions, hardships, constraints,* <sup>5</sup> beatings, imprisonments, riots, labors, vigils, fasts;* <sup>6</sup>† by purity, knowledge, patience, kindness, in a holy spirit, in unfeigned love,* <sup>7</sup> in truthful speech, in the power of God; with weapons of righteousness at the right and at the left;* <sup>8</sup> through glory and dishonor, insult and praise. We are treated as deceivers and yet are truthful;† <sup>9</sup> as unrecognized and yet acknowledged; as dying and behold we live; as chastised and yet not put to death;* <sup>10</sup> as sorrowful yet always rejoicing; as poor yet enriching many; as having nothing and yet possessing all things.*

<sup>11</sup>† We have spoken frankly to you, Corinthians; our heart is open wide. <sup>12</sup> You are not constrained by us; you are constrained by your

---

† ral mode of perception, characterized as "fleshly," is replaced by a mode of perception proper to the Spirit. Elsewhere Paul contrasts what Christ looks like according to the old criteria (weakness, powerlessness, folly, death) and according to the new (wisdom, power, life); cf. 2 Cor 5:15, 21; 1 Cor 1:17–3:3. Similarly, he describes the paradoxical nature of Christian existence, e.g., in 2 Cor 4:10–11, 14. *A new creation:* rabbis used this expression to describe the effect of the entrance of a proselyte or convert into Judaism or of the remission of sins on the Day of Atonement. The new order created *in Christ* is the new covenant (2 Cor 3:6).

**5:18–21** Paul attempts to explain the meaning of God's action by a variety of different categories; his attention keeps moving rapidly back and forth from God's act to his own ministry as well. *Who has reconciled us to himself:* i.e., he has brought all into oneness. *Not counting their trespasses:* the reconciliation is described as an act of justification (cf. "righteousness," 2 Cor 5:21); this contrasts with the covenant that condemned (2 Cor 3:8). *The ministry of reconciliation:* Paul's role in the wider picture is described: entrusted with the message of reconciliation (2 Cor 5:19), he is Christ's ambassador, through whom God appeals (2 Cor 5:20a). In v 20b Paul acts in the capacity just described.

**5:21** This is a statement of God's purpose, expressed paradoxically in terms of sharing and exchange of attributes. As Christ became our righteousness (1 Cor 1:30), we become God's righteousness (cf. 2 Cor 5:14–15).

**6:1–10** This paragraph is a single long sentence in the Greek, interrupted by the parenthesis of 2 Cor 5:2. The one main verb is "we appeal." In this paragraph Paul both exercises his ministry of reconciliation (cf. 2 Cor 5:20) and describes how his ministry is exercised: the "message of reconciliation" (2 Cor 5:19) is lived existentially in his apostolic experience.

**6:1** *Not to receive…in vain:* i.e., conform to the gift of justification and new creation. The context indicates how this can be done concretely: become God's righteousness (2 Cor 5:21), not live for oneself (2 Cor 5:15) be reconciled with Paul (2 Cor 6:11–13; 7:2–3).

**6:2** *In an acceptable time:* Paul cites the Septuagint text of Is 49:8; the Hebrew reads "in a time of favor"; it is parallel to "on the day of salvation." *Now:* God is bestowing favor and salvation at this very moment, as Paul is addressing his letter to them.

**6:3** *Cause no one to stumble:* the language echoes that of 1 Cor 8–10 as does the expression "no longer live for themselves" in 2 Cor 5:15. *That no fault may be found:* i.e., at the eschatological judgment (cf. 1 Cor 4:2–5).

**6:4a** This is the central assertion, the topic statement for the catalogue that follows. *We commend ourselves:* Paul's self-commendation is ironical (with an eye on the charges mentioned in 2 Cor 3:1–3) and paradoxical (pointing mostly to experiences that would not normally be considered points of pride but are perceived as such by faith). Cf. also the self-commendation in 2 Cor 11:23–29. *As ministers of God:* the same Greek word, *diakonos,* means "minister" and "servant"; cf. 2 Cor 11:23, the central assertion in a similar context, and 1 Cor 3:5.

**6:4b–5** *Through much endurance:* this phrase functions as a subtitle; it is followed by an enumeration of nine specific types of trials endured.

**6:6–7a** A list of virtuous qualities in two groups of four, the second fuller than the first.

**6:8b–10** A series of seven rhetorically effective antitheses, contrasting negative external impressions with positive inner reality. Paul perceives his existence as a reflection of Jesus' own and affirms an inner reversal that escapes outward observation. The final two members illustrate two distinct kinds of paradox or apparent contradiction that are characteristic of apostolic experience.

**6:11–13** Paul's tone becomes quieter, but his appeal for acceptance and affection is emotionally charged. References to the heart and their mutual relations bring the development begun in 2 Cor 2:14–3:3 to an effective conclusion.

---

*

| | |
|---|---|
| **5:17** Gal 6:15; Eph 2:15 / Is 43:18–21; Rev 21:5. | **6:3** 1 Cor 9:12; 10:32 / 2 Cor 8:20–21. |
| **5:19** Rom 5:10–11; Col 1:20. | **6:4** 4:8–11; 11:23–27; 1 Cor 4:9–13. |
| **5:20** Eph 6:20; Phlm 9. | **6:5** Acts 16:23. |
| **5:21** Is 53:6–9; Gal 3:13 / Rom 3:24–26; 1 Cor 1:30; 1 Pt 2:24; 1 Jn 3:5–8. | **6:6** Gal 5:22–23. |
| | **6:7** 10:4; Rom 13:12; Eph 6:11–17. |
| **6:1** 1 Cor 3:9; 1 Thes 3:2. | **6:9** 4:10–11; Rom 8:36. |
| **6:2** Is 49:8. | **6:10** Rom 8:32; 1 Cor 3:21. |

2 COR

own affections. * [13] As recompense in kind (I speak as to my children), be open yourselves. *

**Call to Holiness.** [14] † Do not be yoked with those who are different, with unbelievers. † For what partnership do righteousness and lawlessness have? Or what fellowship does light have with darkness? [15] What accord has Christ with Beliar? Or what has a believer in common with an unbeliever? [16] * What agreement has the temple of God with idols? For we are the temple of the living God; as God said:

> "I will live with them and move among them, †
> and I will be their God
> and they shall be my people.

[17]  Therefore, come forth from them
> and be separate," says the Lord,
> "and touch nothing unclean;
> then I will receive you *

[18]  and I will be a father to you,
> and you shall be sons and daughters to me,
> says the Lord Almighty." *

**7** [1] Since we have these promises, beloved, let us cleanse ourselves from every defilement

of flesh and spirit, making holiness perfect in the fear of God.

[2] † Make room for us; we have not wronged anyone, or ruined anyone, or taken advantage of anyone. [3] I do not say this in condemnation, for I have already said that you are in our hearts, that we may die together and live together. * [4] I have great confidence in you, I have great pride in you; I am filled with encouragement, I am overflowing with joy all the more because of all our affliction.

## C. Resolution of the Crisis †

**Paul's Joy in Macedonia.** [5] † For even when we came into Macedonia, † our flesh had no rest, but we were afflicted in every way—external conflicts, internal fears. * [6] But God, who encourages the downcast, encouraged us by the arrival of Titus, * [7] and not only by his arrival but also by the encouragement with which he was encouraged in regard to you, as he told us of your yearning, your lament, your zeal for me, so that I rejoiced even more. [8] † For even if I saddened you by my letter, I do not regret it; and if I did regret it ([for] I see that that letter saddened you, if only for a while), * [9] I rejoice now, not because you were saddened, but because you were saddened into repentance;

---

† **6:14–7:1** Language and thought shift noticeably here. Suddenly we are in a different atmosphere, dealing with a quite different problem. Both the vocabulary and the thought, with their contrast between good and evil, are more characteristic of Qumran documents or the Book of Revelation than they are of Paul. Hence, critics suspect that this section was inserted by another hand.

**6:14–16a** The opening injunction to separate from unbelievers is reinforced by five rhetorical questions to make the point that Christianity is not compatible with paganism. Their opposition is emphasized also by the accumulation of five distinct designations for each group. These verses are a powerful statement of God's holiness and the exclusiveness of his claims.

**6:16c–18** This is a chain of scriptural citations carefully woven together. God's covenant relation to his people and his presence among them (2 Cor 6:16) is seen as conditioned on cultic separation from the profane and cultically impure (2 Cor 6:17); that relation is translated into the personal language of the parent-child relationship, an extension to the community of the language of 2 Sm 7:14 (2 Cor 6:18). Some remarkable parallels to this chain are found in the final chapters of Revelation. God's presence among his people (Rev 21:22) is expressed there, too, by applying 2 Sm 7:14 to the community (Rev 21:7). There is a call to separation (Rev 18:4) and exclusion of the unclean from the community and its liturgy (Rev 21:27). The title "Lord Almighty" (*Pantokratōr*) occurs in the New Testament only here in 2 Cor 6:18 and nine times in Revelation.

**7:2–4** These verses continue the thought of 2 Cor 6:11–13, before the interruption of 2 Cor 6:14–7:1. 2 Cor 7:4 serves as a transition to the next section: the four themes it introduces (confidence; pride or "boasting"; encouragement; joy in affliction) are developed in 2 Cor 7:5–16. All have appeared previously in the letter.

**7:5–16** This section functions as a peroration or formal summing up of the whole first part of the letter, 2 Cor 1–7. It deals with the restoration of right relations between Paul and the Corinthians, and it is marked by fullness and intensity of emotion.

**7:5–7** Paul picks up the thread of the narrative interrupted at 2 Cor 2:13 (2 Cor 7:5) and describes the resolution of the tense situation there depicted (2 Cor 7:6–7). Finally Titus arrives and his coming puts an end to Paul's restlessness (2 Cor 2:13; 2 Cor 7:5), casts out his fears, and reverses his mood. The theme of encouragement and affliction is reintroduced (cf. 2 Cor 1:3–11; here, too, encouragement is traced back to God and is described as contagious (2 Cor 7:6). The language of joy and sorrow also reappears in 2 Cor 7:7 (cf. 2 Cor 1:23–2:1 and the note on 2 Cor 1:23–24).

**7:5** *Macedonia:* see note on 2 Cor 2:13.

**7:8–12** Paul looks back on the episode from the viewpoint of its ending. The goal of their common activity, promotion of their joy (2 Cor 1:24), has been achieved, despite and because of the sorrow they felt. That sorrow was God-given. Its salutary effects are enumerated fully and impressively in 2 Cor 7:10–11; not the least important of these is that it has revealed to them the attachment they have to Paul.

---

| | |
|---|---|
| **6:12** 7:3. | **6:18** 2 Sm 7:14; Ps 2:7; Is |
| **6:13** Gal 4:19. | 43:6; Jer 31:9; Rev |
| **6:16** 1 Cor 10:20–21 / | 21:7 / Rev 4:8; 11:17; |
| 1 Cor 3:16–17; 6:19 | 15:3; 21:22. |
| / Ex 25:8; 29:45; | **7:3** 6:11–13. |
| Lv 26:12; Jer 31:1; | **7:5** 2:13. |
| 32:38; Ez 37:27. | **7:6** 7:13–14; 1 Thes |
| **6:17** Is 52:11; Ez 20:34, | 3:6–8. |
| 41; Rev 18:4; 21:27. | **7:8** 2:2–4; Heb 12:11. |

for you were saddened in a godly way, so that you did not suffer loss in anything because of us. [10] For godly sorrow produces a salutary repentance without regret, but worldly sorrow produces death. [11] For behold what earnestness this godly sorrow has produced for you, as well as readiness for a defense, and indignation, and fear, and yearning, and zeal, and punishment. In every way you have shown yourselves to be innocent in the matter. [12] So then even though I wrote to you, it was not on account of the one who did the wrong, or on account of the one who suffered the wrong, but in order that your concern for us might be made plain to you in the sight of God. * [13] For this reason we are encouraged.

And besides our encouragement, † we rejoice even more because of the joy of Titus, since his spirit has been refreshed by all of you. [14] For if I have boasted to him about you, I was not put to shame. No, just as everything we said to you was true, so our boasting before Titus proved to be the truth. [15] And his heart goes out to you all the more, as he remembers the obedience of all of you, when you received him with fear and trembling. * [16] I rejoice, because I have confidence in you in every respect.

## III. THE COLLECTION FOR JERUSALEM†

**8** **Generosity in Giving.** [1] † We want you to know, brothers, † of the grace of God † that has been given to the churches of Macedonia, * [2] † for in a severe test of affliction, the abundance of their joy and their profound poverty overflowed in a wealth of generosity on their part. [3] † For according to their means, I can testify, and beyond their means, spontaneously, [4] they begged us insistently for the favor of taking part in the service to the holy ones, * [5] and this, not as we expected, but they gave themselves first to the Lord and to us † through the will of God, [6] so that we urged Titus † that, as he had already begun, he should also complete for you this gracious act also. * [7] † Now as you excel in every respect, in faith, discourse, knowledge, all earnestness, and in the love we

---

† **7:13–16** Paul summarizes the effect of the experience on Titus: encouragement, joy, love, relief. Finally, he describes its effects on himself: encouragement, joy, confidence, pride or "boasting" (i.e., the satisfaction resulting from a boast that proves well-founded; cf. 2 Cor 7:4; 1:12, 14).

**8:1–9:15** Paul turns to a new topic, the collection for the church in Jerusalem. There is an early precedent for this project in the agreement mentioned in Gal 2:6–10. According to Acts, the church at Antioch had sent Saul and Barnabas to Jerusalem with relief (Acts 11:27–30). Subsequently Paul organized a project of relief for Jerusalem among his own churches. Our earliest evidence for it comes in 1 Cor 16:1–4—after it had already begun (see notes there); by the time Paul wrote Rom 15:25–28 the collection was completed and ready for delivery. 2 Cor 8–9 contain what appear to be two letters on the subject. In them Paul gives us his fullest exposition of the meaning he sees in the enterprise, presenting it as an act of Christian charity and as an expression of the unity of the church, both present and eschatological. These chapters are especially rich in the recurrence of key words, on which Paul plays; it is usually impossible to do justice to these wordplays in the translation.

**8:1–24** This is a letter of recommendation for Titus and two unnamed companions, written from Macedonia probably at least a year later than 1 Cor 16. The recommendation proper is prefaced by remarks about the ideals of sharing and equality within the Christian community (2 Cor 8:1–15). Phil 4:10–20 shows that Paul has reflected on his personal experience of need and relief in his relations with the community at Philippi; he now develops his reflections on the larger scale of relations between his Gentile churches and the mother church in Jerusalem.

**8:1–5** The example of the Macedonians, a model of what ought to be happening at Corinth, provides Paul with the occasion for expounding his theology of "giving."

**8:1** *The grace of God:* the fundamental theme is expressed by the Greek noun *charis,* which will be variously translated throughout these chapters as "grace" (2 Cor 8:1; 9:8, 14), "favor" (2 Cor 8:4), "gracious act" (2 Cor 8:6, 7, 9) or "gracious work" (2 Cor 8:19), to be compared to "gracious gift" (1 Cor 16:3). The related term, *eucharistia,* "thanksgiving," also occurs at 2 Cor

9:11, 12. The wordplay is not superficial; various mutations of the same root signal inner connection between aspects of a single reality, and Paul consciously exploits the similarities in vocabulary to highlight that connection.

**8:2** Three more terms are now introduced. *Test (dokimē):* the same root is translated as "to test" (2 Cor 8:8) and "evidence" (2 Cor 9:13); it means to be tried and found genuine. *Abundance:* variations on the same root lie behind "overflow" (2 Cor 8:2; 9:12), "excel" (2 Cor 8:7), "surplus" (2 Cor 8:14), "superfluous" (2 Cor 9:1) "make abundant" and "have an abundance" (2 Cor 9:8). These expressions of fullness contrast with references to need (2 Cor 8:14; 9:12). *Generosity:* the word *haplotēs* has nuances of both simplicity and sincerity; here and in 2 Cor 9:11, 13 it designates the singleness of purpose that manifests itself in generous giving.

**8:3–4** Paul emphasizes the spontaneity of the Macedonians and the nature of their action. *They begged us insistently:* the same root is translated as "urge," "appeal," "encourage" (2 Cor 8:6, 17; 9:5). *Taking part:* the same word is translated "contribution" in 2 Cor 9:13 and a related term as "partner" in 2 Cor 8:23. *Service (diakonia):* this word occurs also in 2 Cor 9:1, 13 as "service"; in 2 Cor 9:12 it is translated "administration," and in 2 Cor 8:19, 20 the corresponding verb is rendered "administer."

**8:5** *They gave themselves…to the Lord and to us:* on its deepest level their attitude is one of self-giving.

**8:6** *Titus:* 1 Cor 16 seemed to leave the organization up to the Corinthians, but apparently Paul has sent Titus to initiate the collection as well; 2 Cor 8:16–17 will describe Titus' attitude as one of shared concern and cooperation.

**8:7** The charitable service Paul is promoting is seen briefly and in passing within the perspective of Paul's theology of the charisms. *Earnestness (spoudē):* this or related terms occur also in 2 Cor 8:22 ("earnest") and 2 Cor 8:8, 16, 17 ("concern").

---

\* 
**7:12** 2:3, 9; 7:8.     **8:4** Acts 24:17; Rom
**7:15** 2:9.               15:31.
   **8:1** 11:9; Rom 15:26.   **8:6** 2:13; 7:6–7, 13–14;
                                8:16, 23; 12:18.

2 COR

2 COR

have for you,* may you excel in this gracious act also.

⁸ I say this not by way of command, but to test the genuineness of your love by your concern for others. ⁹†* For you know the gracious act of our Lord Jesus Christ, that for your sake he became poor although he was rich, so that by his poverty you might become rich. ¹⁰ And I am giving counsel in this matter, for it is appropriate for you who began not only to act but to act willingly last year:* ¹¹ complete it now, so that your eager† willingness may be matched by your completion of it out of what you have. ¹²† For if the eagerness is there, it is acceptable according to what one has, not according to what one does not have; ¹³ not that others should have relief while you are burdened, but that as a matter of equality ¹⁴ your surplus at the present time should supply their needs, so that their surplus may also supply your needs, that there may be equality. ¹⁵ As it is written:

> "Whoever had much did not have more,
>     and whoever had little did not have
>         less."*

### Titus and His Collaborators.†

¹⁶ But thanks be to God who put the same concern for you into the heart of Titus, ¹⁷ for he not only welcomed our appeal but, since he is very concerned, he has gone to you of his own accord. ¹⁸ With him we have sent the brother† who is praised in all the churches for his preaching of the gospel.* ¹⁹ And not only that, but he has also been appointed our traveling companion by the churches in this gracious work administered by us for the glory of the Lord [himself] and for the expression of our eagerness.* ²⁰ This we desire to avoid, that anyone blame us† about this lavish gift administered by us, ²¹ for we are concerned for what is honorable not only in the sight of the Lord but also in the sight of others.* ²² And with them we have sent our brother whom we often tested in many ways and found earnest, but who is now much more earnest because of his great confidence in you. ²³ As for Titus, he is my partner and co-worker for you; as for our brothers, they are apostles of the churches, the glory of Christ. ²⁴ So give proof before the churches of your love and of our boasting about you to them.†

## 9 God's Indescribable Gift.†

¹ Now about the service to the holy ones, it is superfluous for me to write to you, ² for I know your eagerness, about which I boast of you to the Macedonians, that Achaia† has been ready since last year; and your zeal has stirred up most of them.* ³ Nonetheless, I sent the brothers† so that our boast about you might not prove empty in this case, so that you might be ready, as I said, ⁴ for fear that if any Macedonians come with me and find you not ready we

---

† **8:9** The dialectic of Jesus' experience, expressed earlier in terms of life and death (2 Cor 5:15), sin and righteousness (2 Cor 5:21), is now rephrased in terms of poverty and wealth. Many scholars think this is a reference to Jesus' preexistence with God (his "wealth") and to his incarnation and death (his "poverty"), and they point to the similarity between this verse and Phil 2:6–8. Others interpret the wealth and poverty as succeeding phases of Jesus' earthly existence, e.g., his sense of intimacy with God and then the desolation and the feeling of abandonment by God in his death (cf. Mk 15:34).

**8:11** *Eager*: the word *prothymia* also occurs in 2 Cor 8:12, 19; 9:2.

**8:12–15** Paul introduces the principle of *equality* into the discussion. The goal is not impoverishment but sharing of resources; balance is achieved at least over the course of time. In 2 Cor 8:15 Paul grounds his argument unexpectedly in the experience of Israel gathering manna in the desert: equality was achieved, independently of personal exertion, by God, who gave with an even hand according to need. Paul touches briefly here on the theme of "living from God."

**8:16–24** In recommending Titus and his companions, Paul stresses their personal and apostolic qualities, their good dispositions toward the Corinthians, and their authority as messengers of the churches and representatives of Christ.

**8:18** *The brother*: we do not know the identity of this co-worker of Paul, nor of the third companion mentioned below in 2 Cor 8:22.

**8:20–22** *That anyone blame us*: 2 Cor 12:16–18 suggests that misunderstandings may indeed have arisen concerning Paul's management of the collection through the messengers mentioned here, but those same verses seem to imply that the Corinthians by and large would recognize the honesty of Paul's conduct in this area as in others (cf. 2 Cor 6:3).

**8:24** As Paul began by holding up the Macedonians as examples to be imitated, he closes by exhorting the Corinthians to show their love (by accepting the envoys and by cooperating as the Macedonians do), thus justifying the pride Paul demonstrates because of them before other churches.

**9:1–15** Quite possibly this was originally an independent letter, though it deals with the same subject and continues many of the same themes. In that case, it may have been written a few weeks later than 2 Cor 8, while the delegation there mentioned was still on its way.

**9:2** *Achaia*: see note on Rom 15:26.

**9:3** *I sent the brothers*: the Greek aorist tense here could be epistolary, referring to the present; in that case Paul would be sending them now, and 2 Cor 9 would merely conclude the letter of recommendation begun in 2 Cor 8. But the aorist may also refer to a sending that is past as Paul writes; then 2 Cor 9, with its apparently fresh beginning, is a follow-up message entrusted to another carrier.

---

*
| | |
|---|---|
| **8:7** 1 Cor 1:5. | **8:18** 12:18. |
| **8:9** 6:10; Phil 2:6–8. | **8:19** 1 Cor 16:3–4. |
| **8:10** 9:2; 1 Cor 16:1–4. | **8:21** Rom 12:17. |
| **8:15** Ex 16:18. | **9:2** 8:10; Rom 15:26. |

might be put to shame (to say nothing of you) in this conviction. ⁵ So I thought it necessary to encourage the brothers to go on ahead to you and arrange in advance for your promised gift, so that in this way it might be ready as a bountiful gift and not as an exaction.

⁶ Consider this: whoever sows sparingly will also reap sparingly, and whoever sows bountifully will also reap bountifully.* ⁷ Each must do as already determined, without sadness or compulsion, for God loves a cheerful giver.* ⁸† Moreover, God is able to make every grace abundant for you, so that in all things, always having all you need, you may have an abundance for every good work. ⁹ As it is written:

"He scatters abroad, he gives to the
        poor;
    his righteousness endures forever."*

¹⁰ The one who supplies seed to the sower and bread for food will supply and multiply your seed and increase the harvest of your righteousness.*

¹¹† You are being enriched in every way for all generosity, which through us produces thanksgiving to God, ¹² for the administration of this public service is not only supplying the needs of the holy ones but is also overflowing in many acts of thanksgiving to God. ¹³ Through the evidence of this service, you are glorifying God for your obedient confession of the gospel of Christ and the generosity of your contribution to them and to all others,* ¹⁴ while in prayer on your behalf they long for you, because of the surpassing grace of God upon you. ¹⁵ Thanks be to God for his indescribable gift!*

## IV. PAUL'S DEFENSE OF HIS MINISTRY†

**10** **Accusation of Weakness.**† ¹ Now I myself, Paul, urge you through the gentleness and clemency of Christ,† I who am humble when face to face with you, but brave toward you when absent, ²†* I beg you that, when present, I may not have to be brave with that confidence with which I intend to act boldly against some who consider us as acting according to the flesh. ³ For, although we are in the flesh, we do not battle according to the flesh,† ⁴ for the weapons of our battle are not of flesh but are enormously powerful, capable of destroying fortresses. We destroy

---

† **9:8–10** The behavior to which he exhorts them is grounded in God's own pattern of behavior. God is capable of overwhelming generosity, as scripture itself attests (2 Cor 9:9), so that they need not fear being short. He will provide in abundance, both supplying their natural needs and increasing their righteousness. Paul challenges them to godlike generosity and reminds them of the fundamental motive for encouragement: God himself cannot be outdone.

**9:11–15** Paul's vision broadens to take in all the interested parties in one dynamic picture. His language becomes liturgically colored and conveys a sense of fullness. With a final play on the words *charis* and *eucharistia* (see note on 2 Cor 8:1), he describes a circle that closes on itself: the movement of grace overflowing from God to them and handed on from them through Paul to others is completed by the prayer of praise and thanksgiving raised on their behalf to God.

**10:1–13:10** These final chapters have their own unity of structure and theme and could well have formed the body of a separate letter. They constitute an *apologia* on Paul's part, i.e., a legal defense of his behavior and his ministry; the writing is emotionally charged and highly rhetorical. In the central section (2 Cor 11:16–12:10), the *apologia* takes the form of a boast. This section is prepared for by a prologue (2 Cor 11:1–15) and followed by an epilogue (2 Cor 12:11–18), which are similar in content and structure. These sections, in turn, are framed by an introduction (2 Cor 10:1–18) and a conclusion (2 Cor 12:19–13:10), both of which assert Paul's apostolic authority and confidence and define the purpose of the letter. The structure that results from this disposition of the material is chiastic, i.e., the first element corresponds to the last, the second to the second last, etc., following the pattern a b c b´ a´.

**10:1–18** Paul asserts his apostolic authority and expresses the confidence this generates in him. He writes in response to certain opinions that have arisen in the community and certain charges raised against him and in preparation for a forthcoming visit in which he intends to set things in order. This section gives us an initial glimpse of the situation in Corinth that Paul must address; much of its thematic material will be taken up again in the finale (2 Cor 12:19–13:10).

**10:1–2** A strong opening plunges us straight into the conflict. Contrasts dominate here: presence versus absence, gentleness-clemency-humility versus boldness-confidence-bravery. *Through the gentleness and clemency of Christ*: the figure of the gentle Christ, presented in a significant position before any specifics of the situation are suggested, forms a striking contrast to the picture of the bold and militant Paul (2 Cor 10:2–6); this tension is finally resolved in 2 Cor 13:3–4. *Absent…present*: this same contrast, with a restatement of the purpose of the letter, recurs in 2 Cor 13:10, which forms an inclusion with 2 Cor 10:1–2.

**10:2b–4a** *Flesh*: the Greek word *sarx* can express both the physical life of the body without any pejorative overtones (as in "we are in the flesh," 3) and our natural life insofar as it is marked by limitation and weakness (as in the other expressions) in contrast to the higher life and power conferred by the Spirit; cf. note on 1 Cor 3:1. The wordplay is intended to express the paradoxical situation of a life already taken over by the Spirit but not yet seen as such except by faith. Lack of empirical evidence of the Spirit permits misunderstanding and misjudgment, but Paul resolutely denies that his behavior and effectiveness are as limited as some suppose.

**10:3b–6** Paul is involved in combat. The strong military language and imagery are both an assertion of his confidence in the divine power at his disposal and a declaration of war against those who underestimate his resources. The threat is echoed in 2 Cor 13:2–3.

---

*
**9:6** Prv 11:24–25.      **9:13** 8:4; Rom 15:31.
**9:7** Prv 22:8 LXX.      **9:15** Rom 5:15–16.
**9:9** Ps 112:9.          **10:2** 13:2, 10; 1 Cor 4:21.
**9:10** Is 55:10.

arguments* ⁵and every pretension raising itself against the knowledge of God, and take every thought captive in obedience to Christ, ⁶and we are ready to punish every disobedience, once your obedience is complete.*

⁷* Look at what confronts you. Whoever is confident of belonging to Christ should consider that as he belongs to Christ, so do we.† ⁸* And even if I should boast a little too much of our authority, which the Lord gave for building you up and not for tearing you down, I shall not be put to shame. ⁹† May I not seem as one frightening you through letters. ¹⁰For someone will say, "His letters are severe and forceful, but his bodily presence is weak, and his speech contemptible."* ¹¹Such a person must understand that what we are in word through letters when absent, that we also are in action when present.*

¹²† Not that we dare to class or compare ourselves with some of those who recommend themselves. But when they measure themselves by one another and compare themselves with one another, they are without understanding.* ¹³But we will not boast beyond measure but will keep to the limits† God has apportioned

us, namely, to reach even to you. ¹⁴For we are not overreaching ourselves, as though we did not reach you; we indeed first came to you with the gospel of Christ. ¹⁵We are not boasting beyond measure, in other people's labors; yet our hope is that, as your faith increases, our influence among you may be greatly enlarged, within our proper limits, ¹⁶so that we may preach the gospel even beyond you, not boasting of work already done in another's sphere.* ¹⁷* "Whoever boasts, should boast in the Lord."† ¹⁸For it is not the one who recommends himself who is approved,† but the one whom the Lord recommends.*

# 11 Preaching Without Charge.† ¹If only you would put up with a little foolishness from me!† Please put up with me.* ²† For I am jealous of you with the jealousy of God, since I betrothed you to one husband to present you as a chaste virgin to Christ.* ³But I am afraid that, as the serpent deceived Eve† by his cunning, your thoughts may be corrupted from a sincere [and pure] commitment to Christ.* ⁴For if someone comes and preaches another Jesus† than the one we preached,* or

---

**10:7–8** *Belonging to Christ…so do we*: these phrases already announce the pattern of Paul's boast in 2 Cor 11:21b–29, especially 2 Cor 11:22–23. *For building you up and not for tearing you down*: Paul draws on the language by which Jeremiah described the purpose of the prophetic power the Lord gave to him (Jer 1:9–10; 12:16–17; 24:6). Though Paul's power may have destructive effects on others (2 Cor 10:2–6), its intended effect on the community is entirely constructive (cf. 2 Cor 13:10). *I shall not be put to shame*: his assertions will not be refuted; they will be revealed as true at the judgment.

**10:9–10** Paul cites the complaints of some who find him lacking in personal forcefulness and holds out the threat of a personal *parousia* (both "return" and "presence") that will be forceful, indeed will be a demonstration of Christ's own power (cf. 2 Cor 13:2–4).

**10:12–18** Paul now qualifies his claim to boldness, indicating its limits. He distinguishes his own behavior from that of others, revealing those "others" as they appear to him: as self-recommending, immoderately boastful, encroaching on territory not assigned to them, and claiming credit not due to them.

**10:13** *Will keep to the limits*: the notion of proper limits is expressed here by two terms with overlapping meanings, *metron* and *kanōn*, which are played off against several expressions denoting overreaching or expansion beyond a legitimate sphere.

**10:17** *Boast in the Lord*: there is a legitimate boasting, in contrast to the immoderate boasting to which 2 Cor 10:13, 15 allude. God's work through Paul in the community is the object of his boast (2 Cor 10:13–16; 2 Cor 1:12–14) and constitutes his recommendation (2 Cor 3:1–3). Cf. notes on 2 Cor 1:12–14 and 1 Cor 1:29–31.

**10:18** *Approved*: to be approved is to come successfully through the process of testing for authenticity (cf. 2 Cor 13:3–7 and the note on 2 Cor 8:2). *Whom the Lord recommends*: self-commendation is a premature and unwarranted anticipation of the final judgment, which the Lord alone will pass (cf. 1 Cor 4:3–5). Paul alludes to this judgment throughout 2 Cor 10–13, frequently in final or transitional positions; cf. 2 Cor 11:15; 12:19a; 13:3–7.

**11:1–15** Although these verses continue to reveal information about Paul's opponents and the differences he perceives between them and himself, 2 Cor 11:1 signals a turn in Paul's thought. This section constitutes a prologue to the boasting that he will undertake in 2 Cor 11:16–12:10, and it bears remarkable similarities to the section that follows the central boast, 2 Cor 12:11–18.

**11:1** *Put up with a little foolishness from me*: this verse indicates more clearly than the general statement of intent in 2 Cor 10:13 the nature of the project Paul is about to undertake. He alludes ironically to the Corinthians' toleration for others. *Foolishness*: Paul qualifies his project as folly from beginning to end; see note on 2 Cor 11:16–12:10.

**11:2** Paul gives us a sudden glimpse of the theological values that are at stake. *The jealousy of God*: the perspective is that of the covenant, described in imagery of love and marriage, as in the prophets; cf. 1 Cor 10:22. *I betrothed you*: Paul, like a father (cf. 2 Cor 12:14), betroths the community to Christ as his bride (cf. Eph 5:21–33) and will present her to him at his second coming. Cf. Mt 25:1–13 and the nuptial imagery in Rev 21.

**11:3** *As the serpent deceived Eve*: before Christ can return for the community Paul fears a repetition of the primal drama of seduction. Corruption of minds is satanic activity (see 2 Cor 2:11; 4:4). Satanic imagery recurs in 2 Cor 11:13–15, 20; 12:7b, 16–17; see notes on these passages.

**11:4** *Preaches another Jesus*: the danger is specified, and Paul's opponents are identified with the cunning serpent. The battle for minds has to do with the understanding of Jesus, the Spirit, the gospel; the Corinthians have flirted with another un-

---

| | |
|---|---|
| **10:4** 6:7; 13:2–3; 1 Cor 1:25; Eph 6:10–14. | **10:16** Rom 15:20–21. |
| **10:6** 2:9. | **10:17** Jer 9:22–23; 1 Cor 1:31. |
| **10:7** 1 Cor 1:12. | **10:18** 13:3–9. |
| **10:8** 13:10. | **11:1** 11:21; 12:11. |
| **10:10** 1 Cor 2:3. | **11:2** Hos 2:21–22; Eph 5:26–27. |
| **10:11** 13:1–2. | **11:3** Gn 3:1–6. |
| **10:12** 3:1–2; 4:2; 5:12; 6:4; 10:18; 12:11. | **11:4** Gal 1:6–9. |

if you receive a different spirit from the one you received or a different gospel from the one you accepted, you put up with it well enough. [5] †* For I think that I am not in any way inferior to these "superapostles." [6] Even if I am untrained in speaking, I am not so in knowledge; * in every way we have made this plain to you in all things. †

[7] † Did I make a mistake when I humbled myself so that you might be exalted, because I preached the gospel of God to you without charge? * [8] I plundered other churches by accepting from them in order to minister to you. [9] And when I was with you and in need, I did not burden anyone, for the brothers who came from Macedonia supplied my needs. So I refrained and will refrain from burdening you in any way. * [10] By the truth of Christ in me, this boast of mine shall not be silenced in the regions of Achaia. * [11] † And why? Because I do not love you? God knows I do! *

[12] And what I do I will continue to do, in order to end this pretext of those who seek a pretext for being regarded as we are in the mission of which they boast. [13] † For such people are false apostles, deceitful workers, who masquerade as apostles of Christ. [14] And no wonder, for even Satan masquerades as an angel of light. [15] So it is not strange that his ministers also masquerade as ministers of righteousness. Their end will correspond to their deeds.

### Paul's Boast: His Labors.

[16] † I repeat, no one should consider me foolish; † but if you do, accept me as a fool, so that I too may boast a little. † [17] What I am saying I am not saying according to the Lord but as in foolishness, in this boastful state. [18] Since many boast according to the flesh, I too will boast. [19] For you gladly put up with fools, since you are wise yourselves. [20] † For you put up with it if someone enslaves you, or devours you, or gets the better of you, or puts on airs, or slaps you in the face. [21] To my shame I say that we were too weak! †

But what anyone dares to boast of (I am

---

derstanding than the one that Paul handed on to them as traditional and normative.

**11:5** These "superapostles": this term, employed again in 2 Cor 12:11b, designates the opponents of whom Paul has spoken in 2 Cor 10 and again in 2 Cor 11:4. They appear to be intruders at Corinth. Their preaching is marked at least by a different emphasis and style, and they do not hesitate to accept support from the community. Perhaps these itinerants appeal to the authority of church leaders in Jerusalem and even carry letters of recommendation from them. But it is not those distant leaders whom Paul is attacking here. The intruders are "superapostles" not in the sense of the "pillars" at Jerusalem (Gal 2), but in their own estimation. They consider themselves superior to Paul as apostles and ministers of Christ, and they are obviously enjoying some success among the Corinthians. Paul rejects their claim to be apostles in any superlative sense (hyperlian), judging them bluntly as "false apostles," ministers of Satan masquerading as apostles of Christ (2 Cor 11:13–15). On the contrary, he himself will claim to be a superminister of Christ (hyper egō, 2 Cor 11:23).

**11:6** Apparently found deficient in both rhetorical ability (cf. 2 Cor 10:10) and knowledge (cf. 2 Cor 10:5), Paul concedes the former charge but not the latter. In every way: in all their contacts with him revelation has been taking place. Paul, through whom God reveals the knowledge of himself (2 Cor 2:14), and in whom the death and life of Jesus are revealed (2 Cor 4:10–11; cf. 2 Cor 6:4), also demonstrates his own role as the bearer of true knowledge. Cf. 1 Cor 1:18–2:16.

**11:7–10** Abruptly Paul passes to another reason for complaints: his practice of preaching without remuneration (cf. 1 Cor 9:3–18). He deftly defends his practice by situating it from the start within the pattern of Christ's own self-humiliation (cf. 2 Cor 10:1) and reduces objections to absurdity by rhetorical questions (cf. 2 Cor 12:13).

**11:11–12** Paul rejects lack of affection as his motive (possibly imputed to him by his opponents) and states his real motive, a desire to emphasize the disparity between himself and the others (cf. 2 Cor 11:19–21). The topic of his gratuitous service will be taken up once more in 2 Cor 12:13–18. 1 Cor 9:15–18 gives a different but complementary explanation of his motivation.

**11:13–15** Paul picks up again the imagery of 2 Cor 11:3 and

applies it to the opponents: they are false apostles of Christ, really serving another master. Deceitful...masquerade: deception and simulation, like cunning (2 Cor 11:3), are marks of the satanic. Angel of light: recalls the contrast between light and darkness, Christ and Beliar at 2 Cor 6:14–15. Ministers of righteousness: recalls the earlier contrast between the ministry of condemnation and that of righteousness (2 Cor 3:9). Their end: the section closes with another allusion to the judgment, when all participants in the final conflict will be revealed or unmasked and dealt with as they deserve.

**11:16–12:10** Paul now accepts the challenge of his opponents and indulges in boasting similar to theirs, but with differences that he has already signaled in 2 Cor 10:12–18 and that become clearer as he proceeds. He defines the nature of his project and unmistakably labels it as folly at the beginning and the end (2 Cor 11:16–23; 12:11). Yet his boast does not spring from ignorance (2 Cor 11:21; 12:6) nor is it concerned merely with human distinctions (2 Cor 11:18). Paul boasts "in moderation" (2 Cor 10:13, 15) and "in the Lord" (2 Cor 10:17).

**11:16–29** The first part of Paul's boast focuses on labors and afflictions, in which authentic service of Christ consists.

**11:16–21** These verses recapitulate remarks already made about the foolishness of boasting and the excessive toleration of the Corinthians. They form a prelude to the boast proper.

**11:20** Paul describes the activities of the "others" in terms that fill out the picture drawn in vv 3–4, 13–15. Much of the vocabulary suggests fleshly or even satanic activity. Enslaves: cf. Gal 2:4. Devours: cf. 1 Pt 5:8. Gets the better: the verb lambanō means "to take," but is used in a variety of senses; here it may imply financial advantage, as in the English colloquialism "to take someone." It is similarly used at 2 Cor 12:16 and is there connected with cunning and deceit. Puts on airs: the same verb is rendered "raise oneself" (2 Cor 10:5) and "be too elated" (2 Cor 12:7).

**11:21** Paul ironically concedes the charge of personal weakness from 2 Cor 10:1–18 but will refute the other charge there

---

| | |
|---|---|
| **11:5** 12:11. | **11:9** Phil 4:15, 18. |
| **11:6** 1 Cor 1:5, 17; 2:1–5. | **11:10** 1 Cor 9:15. |
| **11:7** 12:13–18; Acts 18:3; 1 Cor 9:6–18. | **11:11** 12:15. |

speaking in foolishness) I also dare. [22]† Are they Hebrews? So am I. Are they Israelites? So am I. Are they descendants of Abraham? So am I.* [23]† Are they ministers of Christ? (I am talking like an insane person.)* I am still more,† with far greater labors, far more imprisonments, far worse beatings, and numerous brushes with death. [24] Five times at the hands of the Jews I received forty lashes minus one.* [25] Three times I was beaten with rods, once I was stoned, three times I was shipwrecked, I passed a night and a day on the deep;* [26] on frequent journeys, in dangers from rivers, dangers from robbers, dangers from my own race, dangers from Gentiles, dangers in the city, dangers in the wilderness, dangers at sea, dangers among false brothers; [27] in toil and hardship, through many sleepless nights, through hunger and thirst, through frequent fastings, through cold and exposure.* [28] And apart from these things, there is the daily pressure upon me of my anxiety for all the churches. [29] Who is weak, and I am not weak? Who is led to sin, and I am not indignant?*

**Paul's Boast: His Weakness.**† [30] If I must boast, I will boast of the things that show my weakness. [31]† The God and Father of the Lord Jesus knows, he who is blessed forever, that I do not lie. [32] At Damascus, the governor under King Aretas guarded the city of Damascus, in order to seize me, [33] but I was lowered in a basket through a window in the wall and escaped his hands.*

# 12

[1]† I must boast; not that it is profitable, but I will go on to visions and revelations of the Lord. [2] I know someone in Christ who, fourteen years ago (whether in the body or out of the body I do not know, God knows), was caught up to the third heaven. [3] And I know that this person (whether in the body or out of the body I do not know, God knows) [4] was caught up into Paradise and heard ineffable things, which no one may utter.* [5] About this person† I will boast, but about myself I will not boast, except about my weaknesses. [6] Although if I should wish to boast, I would not be foolish, for I would be telling the truth. But I refrain, so that no one may think more of me than what he sees in me or hears from me [7] because of the abundance of the revelations. Therefore, that I might not become too elated,† a thorn in the flesh was given to me,

---

† mentioned, that lack of boldness, accepting the challenge to demonstrate it by his boast.

**11:22** The opponents apparently pride themselves on their "Jewishness." Paul, too, can claim to be a Jew by race, religion, and promise. *Descendants of Abraham:* elsewhere Paul distinguishes authentic from inauthentic heirs of Abraham and the promise (Rom 4:13–18; 9:7–13; 11:1; Gal 3:9, 27–29; cf. Jn 8:33–47). Here he grants his opponents this title in order to concentrate on the principal claim that follows.

**11:23a** *Ministers of Christ…I am still more:* the central point of the boast (cf. note on 2 Cor 11:5). *Like an insane person:* the climax of his folly.

**11:23b–29** Service of the humiliated and crucified Christ is demonstrated by trials endured for him. This rhetorically impressive catalogue enumerates many of the labors and perils Paul encountered on his missionary journeys.

**11:30–12:10** The second part of Paul's boast, marked by a change of style and a shift in focus. After recalling the project in which he is engaged, he states a new topic: his weaknesses as matter for boasting. Everything in this section, even the discussion of privileges and distinctions, will be integrated into this perspective.

**11:31–32** The episode at Damascus is symbolic. It aptly illustrates Paul's weakness but ends in deliverance (cf. 2 Cor 4:7–11).

**12:1–4** *In the body or out of the body:* he seemed no longer confined to bodily conditions, but he does not claim to understand the mechanics of the experience. *Caught up:* i.e., in ecstasy. *The third heaven…Paradise:* ancient cosmologies depicted a multitiered universe. Jewish intertestamental literature contains much speculation about the number of heavens. Seven is the number usually mentioned, but the Testament of Levi (2:7–10; 3:1–4) speaks of three; God himself dwelt in the third of these. Without giving us any clear picture of the cosmos, Paul indicates a mental journey to a nonearthly space, set apart by God, in which secrets were revealed to him. *Ineffable things:*

i.e., privileged knowledge, which it was not possible or permitted to divulge.

**12:5–7** *This person:* the indirect way of referring to himself has the effect of emphasizing the distance between that experience and his everyday life, just as the indirect *someone in Christ* (2 Cor 12:2) and all the passive verbs emphasize his passivity and receptivity in the experience. The revelations were not a personal achievement, nor were they meant to draw attention to any quality of his own.

**12:7** *That I might not become too elated:* God assures that there is a negative component to his experience, so that he cannot lose proper perspective; cf. 2 Cor 1:9; 4:7–11. *A thorn in the flesh:* variously interpreted as a sickness or physical disability, a temptation, or a handicap connected with his apostolic activity. But since Hebrew "thorn in the flesh," like English "thorn in my side," refers to persons (cf. Nm 33:55; Ez 28:24), Paul may be referring to some especially persistent and obnoxious opponent. The language of 2 Cor 12:7–8 permits this interpretation. If this is correct, the frequent appearance of singular pronouns in depicting the opposition may not be merely a stylistic variation; the singular may be provoked and accompanied by the image of one individual in whom criticism of Paul's preaching, way of life, and apostolic consciousness is concentrated, and who embodies all the qualities Paul attributes to the group. *An angel of Satan:* a personal messenger from Satan; cf. the satanic language already applied to the opponents in 2 Cor 11:3, 13–15, 20.

---

*    **11:22** Acts 22:3 / Rom 11:1; Phil 3:5–6.      **11:25** Acts 14:19; 27:43–44.
**11:23** 6:5; Acts 16:22–24; 1 Cor 15:31–32.    **11:27** 1 Cor 4:11.
**11:29** 1 Cor 9:22.
**11:33** Acts 9:23–25.
**11:24** Dt 25:2–3.    **12:4** Lk 23:43; Rev 2:7.

an angel of Satan, to beat me, to keep me from being too elated.* ⁸Three times† I begged the Lord about this, that it might leave me,* ⁹† but he said to me, "My grace is sufficient for you, for power is made perfect in weakness." I will rather boast most gladly of my weaknesses,† in order that the power of Christ may dwell with me.* ¹⁰Therefore, I am content with weaknesses, insults, hardships, persecutions, and constraints, for the sake of Christ;* for when I am weak, then I am strong.†

**Selfless Concern for the Church.**† ¹¹I have been foolish. You compelled me, for I ought to have been commended by you. For I am in no way inferior to these "superapostles,"* even though I am nothing. ¹²† The signs of an apostle were performed among you with all endurance, signs and wonders, and mighty deeds.* ¹³† In what way were you less privileged than the rest of the churches, except that on my part I did not burden you? Forgive me this wrong!*

¹⁴ Now I am ready to come to you this third time. And I will not be a burden, for I want not what is yours, but you. Children ought not to save for their parents, but parents for their children. ¹⁵I will most gladly spend and be utterly spent for your sakes. If I love you more, am I to be loved less? ¹⁶But granted that I myself did not burden you, yet I was crafty and got the better of you by deceit.* ¹⁷Did I take advantage of you through any of those I sent to you? ¹⁸I urged Titus to go and sent the brother with him. Did Titus take advantage of you? Did we not walk in the same spirit? And in the same steps?*

**Final Warnings and Appeals.**† ¹⁹Have you been thinking all along that we are defending† ourselves before you? In the sight of God we are speaking in Christ, and all for building you up, beloved. ²⁰For I fear that† when I come I may find you not such as I wish, and that you may find me not as you wish; that there may be rivalry, jealousy, fury, selfishness, slander, gossip, conceit, and disorder.* ²¹I fear that when I come again† my God may humiliate me before you, and I may have to mourn over

---

**12:8** *Three times*: his prayer was insistent, like that of Jesus in Gethsemane, a sign of how intolerable he felt the thorn to be.

**12:9** *But he said to me*: Paul's petition is denied; release and healing are withheld for a higher purpose. The Greek perfect tense indicates that Jesus' earlier response still holds at the time of writing. *My grace is sufficient for you*: this is not a statement about the sufficiency of grace in general. Jesus speaks directly to Paul's situation. *Is made perfect*: i.e., is given most fully and manifests itself fully.

**12:9b–10a** Paul draws the conclusion from the autobiographical anecdote and integrates it into the subject of this part of the boast. *Weaknesses*: the apostolic hardships he must endure, including active personal hostility, as specified in a final catalogue (2 Cor 12:10a). *That the power of Christ may dwell with me*: Paul pinpoints the ground for the paradoxical strategy he has adopted in his self-defense.

**12:10** *When I am weak, then I am strong*: Paul recognizes a twofold pattern in the resolution of the weakness-power (and death-life) dialectic, each of which looks to Jesus as the model and is experienced in him. The first is personal, involving a reversal in oneself (Jesus, 2 Cor 13:4a; Paul, 2 Cor 1:9–10; 4:10–11; 6:9). The second is apostolic, involving an effect on others (Jesus, 2 Cor 5:14–15; Paul, 2 Cor 1:6; 4:12; 13:9). The specific kind of "effectiveness in ministry" that Paul promises to demonstrate on his arrival (2 Cor 13:4b; cf. 2 Cor 10:1–11) involves elements of both; this, too, will be modeled on Jesus' experience and a participation in that experience (2 Cor 9; 13:3b).

**12:11–18** This brief section forms an epilogue or concluding observation to Paul's boast, corresponding to the prologue in 2 Cor 11:1–15. A four-step sequence of ideas is common to these two sections: Paul qualifies his boast as folly (2 Cor 11:1; 12:11a), asserts his noninferiority to the "superapostles" (2 Cor 11:5; 12:11b), exemplifies this by allusion to charismatic endowments (2 Cor 11:6; 12:12), and finally denies that he has been a financial burden to the community (2 Cor 11:7–12; 12:13–18).

**12:12** Despite weakness and affliction (suggested by the mention *of endurance*), his ministry has been accompanied by demonstrations of power (cf. 1 Cor 2:3–4). *Signs of an apostle*: visible proof of belonging to Christ and of mediating Christ's

power, which the opponents require as touchstones of apostleship (2 Cor 12:11; cf. 2 Cor 13:3).

**12:13–18** Paul insists on his intention to continue refusing support from the community (cf. 2 Cor 11:8–12). In defending his practice and his motivation, he once more protests his love (cf. 2 Cor 11:11) and rejects the suggestion of secret self-enrichment. He has recourse here again to language applied to his opponents earlier: "cunning" (2 Cor 11:3), "deceit" (2 Cor 11:13), "got the better of you" (see note on 2 Cor 11:20), "take advantage" (2 Cor 2:11).

**12:19–13:10** This concludes the development begun in 2 Cor 10. In the chiastic arrangement of the material (see note on 2 Cor 10:1–13:10), this final part corresponds to the opening; there are important similarities of content between the two sections as well.

**12:19** This verse looks back at the previous chapters and calls them by their proper name, a defense, an *apologia* (cf. 1 Cor 9:3). Yet Paul insists on an important distinction: he has indeed been speaking for their benefit, but the ultimate judgment to which he submits is God's (cf. 1 Cor 4:3–5). This verse also leads into the final section, announcing two of its themes: judgment and building up.

**12:20** *I fear that...*: earlier Paul expressed fear that the Corinthians were being victimized, exploited, seduced from right thinking by his opponents (2 Cor 11:3–4, 19–21). Here he alludes unexpectedly to moral disorders among the Corinthians themselves. The catalogue suggests the effects of factions that have grown up around rival apostles.

**12:21** *Again*: one can also translate, "I fear that when I come my God may again humiliate me." Paul's allusion to the humiliation and mourning that may await him recall the mood he described in 2 Cor 2:1–4, but there is no reference here to any individual such as there is in 2 Cor 2:5–11. The crisis of 2 Cor 2

---

| | |
|---|---|
| **12:7** Nm 33:55; Jos 23:13; Ez 28:24. | **12:12** Rom 15:19; 1 Thes 1:5. |
| **12:8** Mt 26:39–44. | **12:13** 11:9–12. |
| **12:9** 4:7. | **12:16** 11:3, 13. |
| **12:10** 6:4–5; Rom 5:3 / Phil 4:13. | **12:18** 2:13; 8:16, 23. |
| **12:11** 11:5. | **12:20** 1 Cor 1:11; 3:3. |

many of those who sinned earlier and have not repented of the impurity, immorality, and licentiousness they practiced.

# 13

¹This third time I am coming† to you. "On the testimony of two or three witnesses a fact shall be established."* ²I warned those who sinned earlier† and all the others, and I warn them now while absent, as I did when present on my second visit, that if I come again I will not be lenient, ³† since you are looking for proof of Christ speaking in me. He is not weak toward you but powerful in you. ⁴For indeed he was crucified out of weakness, but he lives by the power of God. So also we are weak in him, but toward you we shall live with him by the power of God.

⁵† Examine yourselves to see whether you are living in faith. Test yourselves. Do you not realize that Jesus Christ is in you?—unless, of course, you fail the test. ⁶I hope you will discover that we have not failed. ⁷But we pray to God that you may not do evil, not that we may appear to have passed the test but that you may do what is right, even though we may seem to have failed. ⁸For we cannot do anything against the truth, but only for the truth. ⁹For we rejoice when we are weak but you are strong. What we pray for is your improvement.

¹⁰†* I am writing this while I am away, so that when I come I may not have to be severe in virtue of the authority that the Lord has given me to build up and not to tear down.

## V. CONCLUSION†

¹¹Finally, brothers, rejoice. Mend your ways, encourage one another, agree with one another, live in peace, and the God of love and peace will be with you. ¹²Greet one another with a holy kiss. All the holy ones greet you.*

¹³The grace of the Lord Jesus Christ and the love of God and the fellowship of the holy Spirit be with all of you.*

---

† has happily been resolved by integration of the offender and repentance (2 Cor 7:4–16), whereas 2 Cor 12:21 is preoccupied with still unrepentant sinners. The sexual sins recall 1 Cor 5–7.

**13:1** *This third time I am coming*: designation of the forthcoming visit as the "third" (cf. 2 Cor 12:14) may indicate that, in addition to his founding sojourn in Corinth, Paul had already made the first of two visits mentioned as planned in 2 Cor 1:15, and the next visit will be the long-postponed second of these. If so, the materials in 2 Cor 1:12–2:13 plus 2 Cor 7:4–16 and 2 Cor 10–13 may date from the same period of time, presumably of some duration, between Paul's second and third visit, though it is not clear that they are addressing the same crisis. The chronology is too unsure and the relations between sections of 2 Corinthians too unclear to yield any certainty. The hypothesis that 2 Cor 10–13 are themselves the "tearful letter" mentioned at 2 Cor 2:3–4 creates more problems than it solves.

**13:2** *I warned those who sinned earlier*: mention of unrepentant sinners (2 Cor 12:21 and here) and of an oral admonition given them on an earlier visit complicates the picture at the very end of Paul's development. It provides, in fact, a second explanation for the show of power that has been threatened from the beginning (2 Cor 10:1–6), but a different reason for it, quite unsuspected until now. It is not clear whether Paul is merely alluding to a dimension of the situation that he has not previously had occasion to mention, or whether some other community crisis, not directly connected with that behind 2 Cor 10–13, has influenced the final editing. *I will not be lenient*: contrast Paul's hesitation and reluctance to inflict pain in 2 Cor 1:23 and 2 Cor 2:1–4. The next visit will bring the showdown.

**13:3–4** Paul now gives another motive for severity when he comes, the charge of weakness leveled against him as an apostle. The motive echoes more closely the opening section (2 Cor 10:1–18) and the intervening development (especially 2 Cor 11:30–12:10). *Proof of Christ speaking in me*: the threat of 2 Cor 10:1–2 is reworded to recall Paul's conformity with the pattern of Christ, his insertion into the interplay of death and life, weakness and power (cf. note on 2 Cor 12:10b).

**13:5–9** Paul turns the challenge mentioned in 2 Cor 13:3 on them: they are to put themselves to the test to demonstrate whether Christ is in them. These verses involve a complicated series of plays on the theme of *dokimē* (testing, proof, passing and failing a test). Behind this stands the familiar distinction between present human judgment and final divine judgment. This is the final appearance of the theme (cf. 2 Cor 10:18; 11:15; 12:19).

**13:10** *Authority…to build up and not to tear down*: Paul restates the purpose of his letter in language that echoes 2 Cor 10:2, 8, emphasizing the positive purpose of his authority in their regard. This verse forms an inclusion with the topic sentence of the section (2 Cor 12:19), as well as with the opening of this entire portion of the letter (2 Cor 10:1–2).

**13:11–13** These verses may have originally concluded 2 Cor 10–13, but they have nothing specifically to do with the material of that section. It is also possible to consider them a conclusion to the whole of 2 Corinthians in its present edited form. The exhortations are general, including a final appeal for peace in the community. The letter ends calmly, after its many storms, with the prospect of ecclesial unity and divine blessing. The final verse is one of the clearest trinitarian passages in the New Testament.

---

*

| | |
|---|---|
| **13:1** Dt 19:15; Mt 18:16; Jn 8:17; Heb 10:28. | 1 Thes 5:26; 1 Pt 5:14. |
| **13:10** 10:8. | **13:13** Rom 16:20; 1 Cor 16:23. |
| **13:12** Rom 16:16; 1 Cor 16:20 / Phil 4:22; | |

# The Letter to the
# Galatians

## INTRODUCTION

### Tatha Wiley

Reading the Apostle Paul's letters puts to rest the idea that the development of the earliest communities was problem-free. The very function of his letters is to respond to problems, questions, and conflicts in the Christ assemblies he had established. The conflict we see in his Letter to the Galatians was new to them but not to him. This was not the first time that Paul exchanged heated words with persons who disagreed with him (Gal 2:4–5, 11–14) over what the Gentiles have to do to be part of Israel.

Evangelists whom Paul considers rivals have come into these assemblies and are proceeding to challenge directly what Paul had told his Gentile converts about belonging to Israel. Since salvation and belonging to the covenant are identical, in effect what the other evangelists are saying is that Paul is wrong about the salvation of the Gentiles.

Paul's anxiety is so acute that he places a curse on those he says are preaching "a different gospel" (Gal 1:6) and "wish to pervert the gospel of Christ" (1:7). He repeats the curse for emphasis (1:8–9).

Paul's Letter to the Galatians is dated in the early fifties, and is the only one of his letters written to assemblies spread out over a region, rather than concentrated in a single city. This undisputed letter is Paul through and through—devoted to Christ, passionate, supremely confident, highly defensive about his apostleship and message. He was sometimes abrasive even to the assembly members themselves: "O stupid Galatians!" (Gal 3:1); "Are you so stupid?" (3:3). In between these exclamations is the fundamental question he wanted them to answer. "I want to learn only this from you: did you receive the Spirit from works of the law, or from faith in what you heard?" (3:2).

## Outline of Galatians

I.  **Address (1:1–5)**

II. **Loyalty to the Gospel (1:6–10)**

III. **Paul's Defense of His Gospel and His Authority (1:11–2:21)**

IV. **Faith and Liberty (3:1–4:31)**

V.  **Exhortation to Christian Living (5:1–6:10)**

VI. **Conclusion (6:11–18)**

All they have to do is attend to their experience in order to reject Paul's rivals and stay loyal to Paul. Paul's assemblies are charismatic—Spirit-filled. By "the Spirit" is meant the divine Spirit. Sometimes he talks of the Spirit as God's Spirit, sometimes as the Spirit of Christ (Rom 8:9–14; 1 Cor 6:11; Gal 4:6). As we know from other letters, roles of ministry are gifts of the Spirit, leadership is a gift of the Spirit, prophecy is a gift of the Spirit, and so on (cf. 1 Cor 12). But Paul is not talking here about roles or functions generated by the Spirit within the community. He is talking about a foundational experience of divine mystery that they all have been given on the basis of their faith in Christ.

Paul's challengers' message of "circumcision" stands for much more than the physical act itself. It first evokes Gn 17:10 and God's demand that Abraham circumcise males as the sign of the covenant, the bond between God and the people of Israel. Second, it evokes the distinctive Jewish way of life, living as a Jewish woman according to the commands of the Torah for women, and living as a Jewish man according to the commands for men. If Gentiles want to belong to the covenant people of God, they can do so; but as the dominant rabbinic view of the time argued, they have to become Jewish to do so.

"What do the Gentiles have to do?" was a lively question among Jews long before Paul entered into the conversation. But when he did, his perspective came not from a school or group but from his own mystical experience. In this letter, before he even extends his normal greeting, he establishes his authority on the basis of God's revelation to him of the risen Christ (Gal 1:1). He reminds his audience that what he has preached to them has not come through human beings—James, the brother of Jesus in Jerusalem, for instance—but directly from this revelation (1:11–12).

Paul experienced this revelation as a prophetic call to proclaim Christ to Gentiles (Gal 1:15–16). The prophet Jeremiah described his call this way:

The word of the LORD came to me:
Before I formed you in the womb I knew
   you,
before you were born I dedicated you,
   a prophet to the nations I appointed you.
                                         (Jer 1:5)

Paul uses similar language:

But when [God], who from my mother's womb had set me apart and called me through his grace, was pleased to reveal his Son to me, so that I might proclaim him to the Gentiles . . . . (Gal 1:15–16)

They are both set aside from the womb for a task to "the nations," or "to the Gentiles," as Paul says. The fact that they conceive their call in these terms says something about their similar conception of God. One way of thinking about God was from the perspective of Israel. God was exclusively the God of Israel. Another view was from the perspective of creation. God is the creator of all nations. Jeremiah and Paul share this second view. Their prophetic call takes them beyond Israel, while each remains firmly rooted in it.[1]

What did Paul proclaim? He preached that

God now accepted Gentiles and they were now part of the covenant. This message, what he calls "the truth of the gospel" (Gal 2:5, 14), was the source of disagreement with his fellow Jesus evangelists. The rival evangelists shared Paul's conviction that Jesus is God's Messiah, Paul's hope in resurrection, and Paul's expectation that Jesus would return and bring divine judgment. But they did not agree about what was required of Gentiles or, more accurately, what Paul did not require. In Paul's view, God had already validated their inclusion in Israel's covenant on the basis of their faith in Christ (3:2). They had experienced the gift of God's self. They did not have this experience by becoming Jewish (i.e., by performing "works of the law"). Paul does not dismiss the law for Jews—as some Christian theologians would later mistakenly claim—but he does reject its normativity for justification. To be justified is to be right before God. For Paul, one need not become Jewish in order to share in God's covenant with Israel.

Contemporary Paul scholars such as Krister Stendahl and E. P. Sanders recovered the Jewishness of Paul and contributed to an understanding of the Jewishness of the Jesus movement. For example, what was formerly termed Paul's "conversion" is now more aptly termed his "call." He did not convert from one religion to another. Christianity does not separate from Judaism until the second century CE, and even that is quite early if we are talking about outsiders recognizing the difference between the two groups. Rabbinic Judaism develops out of Pharisaic Judaism, and Christianity develops out of what we might call "Messianic Judaism." Second Temple Judaism, the Judaism of Paul's day, is rich in the diversity of interpretations of its past and its symbols, and Paul's vehement disagreement with his rival evangelists in Galatia remains an intra-Jewish conflict.

Stendahl, Sanders, and others realized that theological terms like *justification* have a social meaning as well. One does not become right with God through some abstract formula but because one belongs to the covenant people of Israel. Paul and his opponents held two contrasting conditions for belonging. Do Gentiles belong by doing the works of the law (as Paul's opponents insisted)? Or do Gentiles

---

1. Helmut Koester, *Paul and His World: Interpreting the New Testament in Context* (Minneapolis: Fortress Press, 2007), 4.

belong through their faith in Christ (as Paul proclaimed)? The issue was not only theological but social. How does a Gentile woman or man become and remain a member of the covenant community?

Paul's co-evangelists in the Jesus movement—perhaps especially those connected with James in Jerusalem, but we need not limit Paul's opponents to Jerusalem—were apparently scandalized by his inclusion of Gentiles without demanding full conversion to Judaism and subsequent observance of the law. Who were these Gentiles? If Paul's practice was consistent, he started preaching in the Jewish synagogue (cf. Acts 13:5). Some Gentiles attracted to Judaism were called "God fearers." This was a Jewish name for people attracted to Judaism but whose joining stopped short of full conversion. Apparently many of them were attracted to the messianic proclamation of Jesus. They became the Christ-believers in Paul's assemblies.

Paul uses the Hebrew Scriptures with ease in this letter. He expects his audience to know the figures and stories to which he refers. He is surely speaking to Gentiles who already were familiar with the Hebrew Scriptures. God fearers would be likely candidates.

But ultimately Gentiles, even God fearers, were considered outsiders to Israel. Without becoming Jewish themselves, they could be included only so far. Deep within Paul's thinking there was an analogy between Jesus and Gentiles in that both were outside the law. A sinner is one who is outside the law, and the Torah asserts that a person who dies by crucifixion is a sinner and accursed by God (Gal 3:13; cf. Dt 21:23). Gentiles are outsiders to the circle of those who are identified as Jewish not simply by their birth but by their not observing the commands of the Torah. God's raising the crucified Jesus from the dead validated Jesus, who was outside the law, and signaled the beginning of eschatological time in which all nations will be called into the covenant. Paul was called to offer God's salvation to Gentiles. Those who accepted underwent baptism. Paul is convinced that he is right about faith as the only condition for belonging because he has witnessed God at work in these Gentile converts.

For Israel, Torah observance created a circle around Israel: the observant were insiders and the non-observant were outsiders. Surely real life was a little messier than this, but the image served to distinguish one from the other. Paul reconceived the circle for the eschatological Israel, also including as insiders women and men who became members through the egalitarian initiation rite of baptism. The fragment of their baptismal ritual preserved in Gal 3:28 contrasted two worlds. The old world of sin—the world of religious, class, and gender privilege—is "no more." The new world is characterized by the relationships of equality and mutuality—not hierarchy and domination—shared by those who believe in Christ. Ultimately, Paul may have felt the very character of Christian community, this "new creation" (6:15), was jeopardized by the opponents' preaching.

With baptism, women and men believers become "Abraham's descendant, heirs according to the promise" (Gal 3:29). If one is "in Christ Jesus" (3:26), that is, a member of the assembly, one is part of the people of God. To justify his stance scripturally, Paul bypasses the stories of Moses and the Law as well as of Abraham and the sign of the covenant to concentrate on Abraham's trusting God: "Realize then that it is those who have faith who are children of Abraham" (3:7). He is determined they will see his point: "The blessing of Abraham [will] be extended to the Gentiles through Christ Jesus, so that we might receive the promise of the Spirit through faith" (3:14).

Paul's anxiety about losing these assemblies looms like a dark cloud over this whole letter. At least some were convinced by other evangelists that salvation required circumcision. Paul speaks directly to them: "Tell me, you who want to be under the law . . ." (Gal 4:21). He tells them what is expected of them: "Once again I declare to every man who has himself circumcised that he is bound to observe the entire law" (5:3). Yet, he counters, real righteousness—justification—is not dependent on following the law but, as they have seen, on the Spirit which they have already received (5:5). He offers a compliment laced with lament: "You were running well; who hindered you from following [the] truth?" (5:7).

GAL

By "truth" Paul evoked what he called earlier "the truth of the gospel" (Gal 2:5, 14). The agreement that Paul thought he had made in Jerusalem was that he would go to the "uncircumcised," Gentile women and men, and their inclusion was to be free of the law (2:7–9). They were not to be asked to adopt Torah-observance. This is the "truth of the gospel." Paul's mission would not be to all, however. Peter would go to the "circumcised" (2:7). The Jerusalem leaders saw no contradiction or conflict between Jewish women and men living the way of the Torah and proclamation of Jesus as Messiah.

Neither did Paul's opponents, the evangelists who were insisting on the link between circumcision and membership in Israel's covenant. Paul's reference to them is always hostile and bitter, but we should take this in the context of anger and affront. His description of them was not meant to be historically accurate but polemical, intended to devalue them in the eyes of his Galatian converts. For our part, we should interpret them neutrally. They were concerned about the inclusion and salvation of the Gentiles. To the question of membership in the covenant, they believed—genuinely, we presume—that Gentile women and men can share in Israel's covenant only if they adopt the way of life mandated by the Torah.

In Paul's view, a view that he saw early on would be opposed (Gal 2:4, 12), God accepts persons in their social, cultural, and ethnic uniqueness. The Christ-believers in Galatia *know* this to be true. It has already been confirmed for them. To meet the power of scriptural authority that his opponents have in the command to circumcise, Paul needs only that the Galatian believers answer his one question from their *experience*: "I want to learn only this from you: did you receive the Spirit from works of the law, or from faith in what you heard?" (3:2). ∎

# THE LETTER TO THE GALATIANS

## New American Bible, Introduction

The Galatians to whom the letter is addressed were Paul's converts, most likely among the descendants of Celts who had invaded western and central Asia Minor in the third century B.C. and had settled in the territory around Ancyra (modern Ankara, Turkey). Paul had passed through this area on his second missionary journey (Acts 16:6) and again on his third (Acts 18:23). It is less likely that the recipients of this letter were Paul's churches in the southern regions of Pisidia, Lycaonia, and Pamphylia where he had preached earlier in the Hellenized cities of Perge, Iconium, Pisidian Antioch, Lystra, and Derbe (Acts 13:13–14:27); this area was part of the Roman province of Galatia, and some scholars think that South Galatia was the destination of this letter.

If it is addressed to the Galatians in the north, the letter was probably written around A.D. 54 or 55, most likely from Ephesus after Paul's arrival there for a stay of several years on his third missionary journey (Acts 19; 20:31). On the South Galatian theory, the date would be earlier, perhaps A.D. 48–50. Involved is the question of how one relates the events of Gal 2:1–10 to the "Council of Jerusalem" described in Acts 15 (see notes on each passage).

In any case, the new Christians whom Paul is addressing were converts from paganism (Gal 4:8–9) who were now being enticed by other missionaries to add the observances of the Jewish law, including the rite of circumcision, to the cross of Christ as a means of salvation. For, since Paul's visit, some other interpretation of Christianity had been brought to these neophytes, probably by converts from Judaism (the name "Judaizers" is sometimes applied to them); it has specifically been suggested that they were Jewish Christians who had come from the austere Essene sect.

These interlopers insisted on the necessity of following certain precepts of the Mosaic law along with faith in Christ. They were undermining Paul's authority also, asserting that he had not been trained by Jesus himself, that his gospel did not agree with that of the original

and true apostles in Jerusalem, that he had kept from his converts in Galatia the necessity of accepting circumcision and other key obligations of the Jewish law, in order more easily to win them to Christ, and that his gospel was thus not the full and authentic one held by "those of repute" in Jerusalem (Gal 2:2). Some scholars also see in Galatians 5; 6 another set of opponents against whom Paul writes, people who in their emphasis on the Spirit set aside all norms for conduct and became libertines in practice.

When Paul learned of the situation, he wrote this defense of his apostolic authority and of the correct understanding of the faith. He set forth the unique importance of Christ and his redemptive sacrifice on the cross, the freedom that Christians enjoy from the old burdens of the law, the total sufficiency of Christ and of faith in Christ as the way to God and to eternal life, and the beauty of the new life of the Spirit. Galatians is thus a summary of basic Pauline theology. Its themes were more fully and less polemically developed in the Letter to the Romans.

Autobiographically, the letter gives us Paul's own accounts of how he came to faith (Gal 1:15–24), the agreement in "the truth of the gospel" (Gal 2:5, 14) that he shared with the Jewish Christian leaders in Jerusalem, James, Cephas, and John (Gal 2:1–10), and the rebuke he had to deliver to Cephas in Antioch for inconsistency, contrary to the gospel, on the issue of table fellowship in the racially mixed church of Jewish and Gentile Christians in Antioch (Gal 2:11–14; cf. Gal 2:15–21). At the conclusion of the letter (Gal 6:11–18), Paul wrote in his own hand (cf. 2 Thes 3:17–18) a vivid summary of the message to the Galatians.

In his vigorous emphasis on the absolute preeminence of Christ and his cross as God's way to salvation and holiness, Paul stresses Christian freedom and the ineffectiveness of the Mosaic law for gaining divine favor and blessings (Gal 3:19–29). The pious Jew saw in the law a way established by God to win divine approval by a life of meticulous observance of ritual, social, and moral regulations. But Paul's profound insight into the higher designs of God in Christ led him to understand and welcome the priority of promise and faith (shown in the experience of Abraham, Gal 3:6–18) and the supernatural gifts of the Spirit (Gal 3:2–5; 5:16–6:10). His enthusiasm for this new vision of the life of grace in Christ and of the uniquely salvific role of Christ's redemptive death on the cross shines through this whole letter.

The principal divisions of the Letter to the Galatians are the following:

I. Address (1:1–5)
II. Loyalty to the Gospel (1:6–10)
III. Paul's Defense of His Gospel and His Authority (1:11–2:21)
IV. Faith and Liberty (3:1–4:31)
V. Exhortation to Christian Living (5:1–6:10)
VI. Conclusion (6:11–18) ■

# GALATIANS

## I. ADDRESS

1 **Greeting.**† ¹* Paul, an apostle† not from human beings nor through a human being but through Jesus Christ and God the Father who raised him from the dead,* ²† and all the brothers who are with me, to the churches of Galatia: ³ grace to you and peace from God our Father and the Lord Jesus Christ, ⁴† who gave himself for our sins that he might rescue us from the present evil age in accord with the will of our God and Father,* ⁵ to whom be glory forever and ever. Amen.*

## II. LOYALTY TO THE GOSPEL†

⁶* I am amazed that you are so quickly forsaking the one who called you† by [the] grace [of Christ] for a different gospel ⁷(not that there is another). But there are some who are disturbing you and wish to pervert the gospel of Christ. ⁸* But even if we or an angel from heaven should preach [to you] a gospel other than the one that we preached to you, let that one be accursed!† ⁹ As we have said before, and now I say again, if anyone preaches to you a gospel other than the one that you received, let that one be accursed!

¹⁰* Am I now currying favor with human beings or God? Or am I seeking to please people? If I were still trying to please people, I would not be a slave of Christ.†

## III. PAUL'S DEFENSE OF HIS GOSPEL AND HIS AUTHORITY†

**His Call by Christ.** ¹¹* Now I want you to know, brothers, that the gospel preached by me is not of human origin. ¹² For I did not receive it from a human being, nor was I taught it, but it came through a revelation of Jesus Christ.†

¹³† For you heard of my former way of life in Judaism, how I persecuted the church of God beyond measure and tried to destroy it,* ¹⁴ and progressed in Judaism beyond many of my contemporaries among my race, since I was even more a zealot for my ancestral traditions.* ¹⁵ But when [God], who from my mother's womb had set me apart and called me through his grace, was pleased* ¹⁶ to reveal

---

† **1:1–5** See note on Rom 1:1–7, concerning the greeting.
**1:1** *Apostle*: because of attacks on his authority in Galatia, Paul defends his apostleship. He is not an apostle commissioned by a congregation (Phil 2:25; 2 Cor 8:23) or even by prophets (1 Tm 1:18; 4:14) but *through Jesus Christ and God the Father*.
**1:2** *All the brothers*: fellow believers in Christ, male and female; cf. Gal 3:27–28. Paul usually mentions the co-sender(s) at the start of a letter, but the use of *all* is unique, adding weight to the letter. *Galatia*: central Turkey more likely than the Roman province of Galatia; see Introduction.
**1:4** The greeting in Gal 1:3 is expanded by a christological formula that stresses deliverance through the Lord Jesus from a world dominated by Satan; cf. 2 Cor 4:4; Eph 2:2; 6:12.
**1:6–10** In place of the usual thanksgiving (see note on Rom 1:8), Paul, with little to be thankful for in the Galatian situation, expresses amazement at the way his converts are deserting the gospel of Christ for a perverted message. He reasserts the one gospel he has preached (Gal 1:7–9) and begins to defend himself (Gal 1:10).
**1:6** *The one who called you*: God or Christ, though in actuality Paul was the divine instrument to call the Galatians.
**1:8** *Accursed*: in Greek, *anathema*; cf. Rom 9:3; 1 Cor 12:3; 16:22.
**1:10** This charge by Paul's opponents, that he sought to conciliate people with flattery and to curry favor with God, might refer to his mission practices (cf. 1 Cor 9:19–23) but the word *still* suggests it refers to his pre-Christian days (cf. Gal 1:14; Phil 3:6). The self-description *slave of Christ* is one Paul often uses in a greeting (Rom 1:1).
**1:11–2:21** Paul's presentation on behalf of his message and of his apostleship reflects rhetorical forms of his day: he first narrates the facts about certain past events (Gal 1:12–2:14) and then states his contention regarding justification by faith as the gospel message (Gal 2:15–21). Further arguments follow from both

experience and scripture in Galatians 3; 4, before he draws out the ethical consequences (Gal 5:1–6:10). The specific facts that he takes up here to show that his gospel is not a human invention (Gal 1:11) but *came through a revelation of Jesus Christ* (Gal 1:12) deal with his own calling as a Christian missionary (Gal 1:13–17), his initial relations with the apostles in Jerusalem (Gal 1:18–24), a later journey to Jerusalem (Gal 2:1–10), and an incident in Antioch involving Cephas and persons from James (Gal 2:11–14). The content of Paul's revealed gospel is then set forth in the heart of the letter (Gal 2:15–21).
**1:12** Although Paul received his gospel *through a revelation* from Christ, this did not exclude his use of early Christian confessional formulations. See note on Gal 1:4.
**1:13–17** Along with Phil 3:4–11, which also moves from autobiography to its climax in a discussion on justification by faith (cf. Gal 2:15–21), this passage is Paul's chief account of the change from his *former way of life* (Gal 1:13) to service as a Christian missionary (Gal 1:16); cf. Acts 9:1–22; 22:4–16; 26:9–18. Paul himself does not use the term "conversion" but stresses revelation (Gal 1:12, 16). In Gal 1:15 his language echoes the Old Testament prophetic call of Jeremiah. Unlike the account in Acts (cf. Acts 22:4–16), the calling of Paul here includes the mission to proclaim Christ *to the Gentiles* (Gal 1:16).

---

*
| | |
|---|---|
| **1:1–3** Rom 1:1–7; 1 Cor 1:1–3. | **1:8–9** 1 Cor 16:22 / Gal 5:3, 21; 2 Cor 13:2. |
| **1:1** 1:11–12. | **1:10** 2 Cor 5:11 / 1 Thes 2:4. |
| **1:4** 2:20; Eph 5:2; 1 Tm 2:6 / 1 Jn 5:19 / Rom 12:2; Eph 5:16; Heb 10:10. | **1:11–12** 1 Cor 15:1 / Gal 1:1; Eph 3:3. |
| **1:5** Rom 16:27; 2 Tm 4:18. | **1:13** Acts 8:1–3; 9:1–2; 1 Cor 15:9. |
| **1:6–7** 5:8, 10; Acts 15:1, 24; 2 Cor 11:4. | **1:14** Acts 26:4–5. |
| | **1:15** Is 49:1; Jer 1:4. |

his Son to me,* so that I might proclaim him to the Gentiles, I did not immediately consult flesh and blood,† 17 nor did I go up to Jerusalem to those who were apostles before me; rather, I went into Arabia† and then returned to Damascus.

18 † Then after three years† I went up to Jerusalem to confer with Cephas and remained with him for fifteen days.* 19 But I did not see any other of the apostles,* only James the brother of the Lord.† 20 (As to what I am writing to you, behold, before God, I am not lying.)* 21 Then I went into the regions of Syria and Cilicia.* 22 And I was unknown personally to the churches of Judea that are in Christ; 23 they only kept hearing that "the one who once was persecuting us is now preaching the faith he once tried to destroy."* 24 So they glorified God because of me.

**2** **The Council of Jerusalem.**† 1 Then after fourteen years I again went up to Jerusalem with Barnabas,† taking Titus along also.*

2 I went up in accord with a revelation,† and I presented to them the gospel that I preach to the Gentiles—but privately to those of repute—so that I might not be running, or have run, in vain.* 3 Moreover, not even† Titus, who was with me, although he was a Greek, was compelled to be circumcised,* 4 but because of the false brothers† secretly brought in, who slipped in to spy on our freedom that we have in Christ Jesus,* that they might enslave us— 5 to them we did not submit even for a moment, so that the truth of the gospel† might remain intact for you.* 6 But from those who were reputed to be important (what they once were makes no difference to me; God shows no partiality)—those of repute made me add nothing.* 7 † On the contrary, when they saw that I had been entrusted with the gospel to the uncircumcised, just as Peter to the circumcised,* 8 for the one who worked in Peter for an apostolate to the circumcised worked also in me for the Gentiles, 9 and when they recognized the grace bestowed upon me, James and

---

**1:16** *Flesh and blood*: human authorities (cf. Mt 16:17; 1 Cor 15:50). Paul's apostleship comes from God (Gal 1:1).

**1:17** *Arabia*: probably the region of the Nabataean Arabs, east and south of Damascus.

**1:18–24** Paul's first journey to Jerusalem as a Christian, according to Galatians (cf. Acts 9:23–31 and the note on Acts 12:25). He is quite explicit about contacts there, testifying under oath (Gal 1:20). On returning to *Syria* (perhaps specifically Damascus, cf. Gal 1:17) *and Cilicia* (including his home town Tarsus, cf. Acts 9:30; 22:3), Paul most likely engaged in missionary work. He underscores the fact that Christians in Judea knew of him only by reputation.

**1:18** *After three years*: two years and more, since Paul's call. To *confer* with Cephas may mean simply "pay a visit" or more specifically "get information from" him about Jesus, over a two-week period. *Cephas*: Aramaic name of Simon (Peter); cf. Mt 16:16–18 and the notes there.

**1:19** *James the brother of the Lord*: not one of the Twelve, but a brother of Jesus (see note on Mk 6:3). He played an important role in the Jerusalem church (see note on Gal 2:9), the leadership of which he took over from Peter (Acts 12:17). Paul may have regarded James as an apostle.

**2:1–10** Paul's second journey to Jerusalem, according to Galatians, involved a private meeting with *those of repute* (Gal 2:2). At issue was a Gentile, Titus, and the question of circumcision, which *false brothers* (Gal 2:4) evidently demanded for him. Paul insists that the gospel he preaches (Gal 2:2; cf. Gal 1:9, 11) remained intact with no addition by those of repute (Gal 2:6); that *Titus* was not *compelled* to accept circumcision (Gal 2:3); and that he and the reputed *pillars* in Jerusalem agreed on how each would advance the missionary task (Gal 1:7–10). Usually, Gal 1:1–10 is equated with the "Council of Jerusalem," as it is called, described in Acts 15. See notes on Acts 15:6–12, 13–35, the latter concerning the "decree" that Paul does not mention.

**2:1** *After fourteen years*: thirteen or more years, probably reckoned from the return to Syria and Cilicia (Gal 1:21), though possibly from Paul's calling as a Christian (Gal 1:15). *Barnabas*: cf. Gal 2:9, 13; 1 Cor 9:6. A Jewish Christian missionary, with whom Paul worked (Acts 4:36–37; 11:22, 25, 30; 12:25; 13:1–3; 15:2). *Titus*: a missionary companion of Paul (2 Cor 2:13; 7:6,

13–15; 8:6, 16, 23; 12:18), non-Jewish (Gal 2:3), never mentioned in Acts.

**2:2** *A revelation*: cf. Gal 1:1, 12. Paul emphasizes it was God's will, not Jerusalem authority, that led to the journey. Acts 15:2 states that the church in Antioch appointed Paul and Barnabas for the task. *Those of repute*: leaders of the Jerusalem church; the term, while positive, may be slightly ironic (cf. Gal 1:6, 9). *Run, in vain*: while Paul presents a positive picture in what follows, his missionary work in Galatia would have been to no purpose if his opponents were correct that circumcision is needed for complete faith in Christ.

**2:3** *Not even* a Gentile Christian like Titus was compelled to receive the rite of circumcision. The Greek text could be interpreted that he voluntarily accepted circumcision, but this is unlikely in the overall argument.

**2:4** *False brothers*: Jewish Christians who took the position that Gentile Christians must first become Jews through circumcision and observance of the Mosaic law in order to become Christians; cf. Acts 15:1.

**2:5** *The truth of the gospel*: the true gospel, in contrast to the false one of the opponents (Gal 1:6–9); the gospel of grace, used as a norm (Gal 2:14).

**2:7–9** Some think that actual "minutes" of the meeting are here quoted. Paul's apostleship to the Gentiles (Gal 1:16) is recognized alongside that of Peter to the Jews. Moreover, the right to proclaim the gospel without requiring circumcision and the Jewish law is sealed by a handshake. That Paul and colleagues *should go to the Gentiles* did not exclude his preaching to Jews as well (Rom 1:13–16) or Cephas to Gentile areas.

---

**1:16** 1:11–12; Rom 1:5; 1 Cor 15:10; Acts 9:3–9 / Gal 2:2, 7 / Mt 16:17.
**1:18** Acts 9:26–30 / Jn 1:42.
**1:19** 2:9; Mt 13:55; Acts 12:17.
**1:20** Rom 9:1; 2 Cor 11:31.
**1:21** Acts 9:30.
**1:23** 1:13.
**2:1** Acts 15:2.

**2:2** 1:11–12, 16 / 1:16 / Phil 2:16.
**2:3** 2 Cor 2:13; 7:6–7; 8:16–17; 12:18; Ti 1:4 / Gal 2:14; 6:12.
**2:4** 5:1; Acts 15:1, 24.
**2:5** 2:14; 4:16.
**2:6** Dt 10:17; Rom 2:11.
**2:7** 1:15–16; Acts 9:15; 15:12; 22:21; Rom 1:5.

Cephas and John,† who were reputed to be pillars, gave me and Barnabas their right hands in partnership, that we should go to the Gentiles and they to the circumcised.* 10 Only, we were to be mindful of the poor,† which is the very thing I was eager to do.*

### Peter's Inconsistency at Antioch.†

11* And when Cephas came to Antioch, I opposed him to his face because he clearly was wrong.† 12 For, until some people came from James,† he used to eat with the Gentiles; but when they came, he began to draw back and separated himself, because he was afraid of the circumcised.* 13 And the rest of the Jews† [also] acted hypocritically along with him, with the result that even Barnabas was carried away by their hypocrisy.* 14 But when I saw that they were not on the right road in line with the truth of the gospel, I said to Cephas in front of all,* "If you, though a Jew, are living like a Gentile and not like a Jew, how can you compel the Gentiles to live like Jews?"†

### Faith and Works.†

15 We, who are Jews by nature and not sinners from among the Gentiles,

16* [yet] who know that a person is not justified by works of the law but through faith in Jesus Christ, even we have believed in Christ Jesus that we may be justified by faith in Christ and not by works of the law, because by works of the law no one will be justified.† 17 But if, in seeking to be justified in Christ, we ourselves are found to be sinners, is Christ then a minister of sin?† Of course not! 18 But if I am building up again those things that I tore down, then I show myself to be a transgressor.† 19 For through the law I died to the law,† that I might live for God. I have been crucified with Christ;* 20 yet I live, no longer I, but Christ lives in me; insofar as I now live in the flesh, I live by faith in the Son of God who has loved me and given himself up for me.* 21 I do not nullify the grace of God; for if justification comes through the law, then Christ died for nothing.*

## IV. FAITH AND LIBERTY

### Justification by Faith.†

3 1 O stupid† Galatians! Who has bewitched you, before whose eyes Jesus Christ was publicly portrayed

---

† **2:9** *James and Cephas and John*: see notes on Gal 1:18, 19; on Peter and John as leaders in the Jerusalem church, cf. Acts 3:1 and 8:14. The order here, with James first, may reflect his prominence in Jerusalem after Peter (Cephas) departed (Acts 12:17).

**2:10** *The poor*: Jerusalem Christians or a group within the church there (cf. Rom 15:26). The collection for them was extremely important in Paul's thought and labor (cf. Rom 15:25–28; 1 Cor 16:1–4; 2 Cor 8–9).

**2:11–14** The decision reached in Jerusalem (Gal 2:3–7) recognized the freedom of Gentile Christians from the Jewish law. But the problem of table fellowship between Jewish Christians, who possibly still kept kosher food regulations, and Gentile believers was not yet settled. When Cephas first came to the racially mixed community of Jewish and Gentile Christians in Antioch (Gal 2:12), he ate with non-Jews. Pressure from persons arriving later from Jerusalem caused him and Barnabas to draw back. Paul therefore publicly rebuked Peter's inconsistency toward the gospel (Gal 2:14). Some think that what Paul said on that occasion extends through Gal 2:16, 21.

**2:11** *Clearly was wrong*: literally, "stood condemned," by himself and also by Paul. His action in breaking table fellowship was especially grievous if the eating involved the meal at the Lord's supper (cf. 1 Cor 11:17–25).

**2:12** *Some people came from James*: strict Jewish Christians (cf. Acts 15:1, 5; 21:20–21), either sent by James (Gal 1:19; 2:9) or claiming to be from the leader of the Jerusalem church. *The circumcised*: presumably Jewish Christians, not Jews.

**2:13** *The Jews*: Jewish Christians, like Barnabas. *Hypocrisy*: literally, "pretense," "play-acting"; moral insincerity.

**2:14** *Compel the Gentiles to live like Jews*: that is, conform to Jewish practices, such as circumcision (Gal 2:3–5) or regulations about food (Gal 2:12).

**2:15–21** Following on the series of incidents cited above, Paul's argument, whether spoken to Cephas at Antioch or only now articulated, is pertinent to the Galatian situation, where believers were having themselves circumcised (Gal 6:12–13) and obeying other aspects of Jewish law (Gal 4:9–10; 5:1–4). He

insists that salvation is by faith in Christ, not by works of the law. His teaching on the gospel concerns justification by faith (Gal 2:16) in relation to sin (Gal 2:17), law (Gal 2:19), life in Christ (Gal 2:19–20), and grace (Gal 2:21).

**2:16** *No one will be justified*: Ps 143:2 is reflected.

**2:17** *A minister of sin*: literally, "a servant of sin" (cf. Rom 15:8), an agent of sin, one who promotes it. This is possibly a claim by opponents that justification on the basis of faith in Christ makes Christ an abettor of sin when Christians *are found to be sinners*. Paul denies the conclusion (cf. Rom 6:1–4).

**2:18** To return to observance of the law as the means to salvation would entangle one not only in inevitable transgressions of it but also in the admission that it was wrong to have abandoned the law in the first place.

**2:19** *Through the law I died to the law*: this is variously explained: the law revealed sin (Rom 7:7–9) and led to death and then to belief in Christ; or, the law itself brought the insight that law cannot justify (Gal 2:16; Ps 143:2); or, the "law of Christ" (Gal 6:2) led to abandoning the Mosaic law; or, the law put Christ to death (cf. Gal 3:13) and so provided a way to our salvation, through baptism into Christ, through which we die (*crucified with Christ*; see Rom 6:6). Cf. also Gal 3:19–25 on the role of the law in reference to salvation.

**3:1–14** Paul's contention that justification comes not through the law or the works of the law but by faith in Christ and in his death (Gal 2:16, 21) is supported by appeals to Christian experience (Gal 3:1–5) and to scripture (Gal 3:6–14). The gift of

---

**2:9** Rom 15:15 / Gal 1:18–19; Jn 1:42; Acts 12:17 / Gal 2:1.
**2:10** Acts 11:29–30; Rom 15:25–28; 1 Cor 16:1–4; 2 Cor 8:9.
**2:11** 1:18 / Acts 11:19–30; 15:1–2.
**2:12** Acts 10:15, 28; 11:3.
**2:13** 2:1, 9.

**2:14** 2:5 / 1:18; 2:9 / 2:3.
**2:16** 3:2, 11; Ps 143:1–2; Rom 3:20, 28; 4:5; 11:6; Eph 2:8–9; Phil 3:9.
**2:19** 6:14; Rom 6:6, 8, 10; 7:6.
**2:20** 1:4; Rom 8:10–11; Col 3:3–4.
**2:21** 5:2.

as crucified?* ²I want to learn only this from you:* did you receive the Spirit from works of the law, or from faith in what you heard?† ³Are you so stupid?* After beginning with the Spirit, are you now ending with the flesh?† ⁴Did you experience so many things† in vain?—if indeed it was in vain. ⁵Does, then, the one who supplies the Spirit to you and works mighty deeds among you do so from works of the law or from faith in what you heard?* ⁶Thus Abraham "believed God,* and it was credited to him as righteousness."†

⁷† Realize then that it is those who have faith who are children of Abraham.* ⁸Scripture, which saw in advance that God would justify the Gentiles by faith, foretold the good news to Abraham, saying, "Through you shall all the nations be blessed."* ⁹Consequently, those who have faith are blessed along with Abraham who had faith.* ¹⁰† For all who depend on works of the law are under a curse; for it is written, "Cursed be everyone who does not persevere in doing all the things written in the book of the law."* ¹¹And that no one is justified before God by the law is clear, for "the one who is righteous by faith will live."*

¹²But the law does not depend on faith; rather, "the one who does these things will live by them."* ¹³Christ ransomed us from the curse of the law by becoming a curse for us, for it is written, "Cursed be everyone who hangs on a tree,"* ¹⁴that the blessing of Abraham might be extended to the Gentiles through Christ Jesus, so that we might receive the promise of the Spirit through faith.*

## The Law Did Not Nullify the Promise.
¹⁵† Brothers, in human terms I say that no one can annul or amend even a human will once ratified.* ¹⁶Now the promises were made to Abraham and to his descendant.† It does not say, "And to descendants," as referring to many, but as referring to one, "And to your descendant," who is Christ.* ¹⁷This is what I mean: the law, which came four hundred and thirty years afterward,† does not annul a covenant previously ratified by God, so as to cancel the promise.* ¹⁸For if the inheritance comes from the law,* it is no longer from a promise; but God bestowed it on Abraham through a promise.†

¹⁹† Why, then, the law? It was added for

† God's Spirit to the Galatians came from the gospel received in faith, not from doing what the law enjoins. The story of Abraham shows that faith in God brings *righteousness* (Gal 3:6; Gn 15:6). The promise to Abraham (Gal 3:8; Gn 12:3) extends to the Gentiles (Gal 3:14).

**3:1** *Stupid*: not just senseless, for they were in danger of deserting their salvation.

**3:2** *Faith in what you heard*: Paul's message received with faith. The Greek can also mean "the proclamation of the faith" or "a hearing that comes from faith."

**3:3** On the contrast of *Spirit* and *flesh*, cf. Rom 8:1–11. Having received the Spirit, they need not be circumcised now.

**3:4** *Experience so many things*: probably the *mighty deeds* of Gal 1:5 but possibly the experience of sufferings.

**3:6** *Abraham...righteousness*: see Gn 15:6; Rom 4:3. The Galatians like Abraham heard with faith and experienced justification. This first argument forms the basis for the further scriptural evidence that follows.

**3:7–9** *Faith* is what matters, for *Abraham* and the *children of Abraham*, in contrast to the claims of the opponents that circumcision and observance of the law are needed to bring the promised blessing of Gn 12:3; cf. Gn 18:18; Sir 44:21; Acts 3:25.

**3:10–14** Those *who depend* not on promise and faith but *on works of the law are under a curse* because they *do not persevere in doing all the things written in the book of the law* (Gal 3:10; Dt 27:26) in order to gain life (Gal 3:12; Lv 18:5; cf. Rom 10:5). But scripture teaches that *no one is justified before God by the law* (Gal 3:11; Heb 2:4, adapted from the Greek version of Habakkuk; cf. Rom 1:17; Heb 10:38). Salvation, then, depends on faith in Christ who died on the cross (Gal 3:13), taking upon himself a curse found in Dt 21:23 (about executed criminals hanged in public view), to free us from *the curse of the law* (Gal 3:13). That the Gentile Galatians have received the promised Spirit (Gal 3:14) by faith and in no other way returns the argument to the experience cited in Gal 3:1–5.

**3:15–18** A third argument to support Paul's position that salvation is not through the law but by promise (Gal 3:1–14) comes

from legal practice and scriptural history. A legal agreement or *human will*, duly *ratified*, is unalterable (Gal 3:15). God's *covenant* with *Abraham* and its repeated promises (Gn 12:2–3, 7; 13:15; 17:7–8; 22:16–18; 24:7) is not superseded by *the law*, which came much later, in the time of Moses. *The inheritance* (of the Spirit and the blessings) is by promise, not by law (Gal 3:18). Paul's argument hinges on the fact that the same Greek word, *diathēkē*, can be rendered as *will* or testament (Gal 3:15) and as *covenant* (Gal 3:17).

**3:16** *Descendant*: literally, "and to his seed." The Hebrew, as in Gn 12:7; 15:18; 22:17–18, is a collective singular, traditionally rendered as a plural, *descendants*, but taken by Paul in its literal number to refer to *Christ* as descendant of Abraham.

**3:17** *Four hundred and thirty years afterward*: follows Ex 12:40 in the Greek (Septuagint) version, in contrast to Gn 15:13 and Acts 7:6, for chronology.

**3:18** This refutes the opponents' contention that the promises of God are fulfilled only as a reward for human observance of the law.

**3:19–22** A digression: if the Mosaic law, then, does not save or *bring life*, why was it given? Elsewhere, Paul says the law served to show what sin is (Rom 3:20; 7:7–8). Here the further implication is that the law in effect served to produce transgressions. Moreover, it was received at second hand *by angels*, through a *mediator*, not directly from God (Gal 3:19). The law

| | |
|---|---|
| **3:1** 5:7; 1 Cor 1:23. | **3:11** 2:16; Heb 2:4; Rom |
| **3:2** 2:16 / 3:14; Rom | 1:17. |
| 10:17. | **3:12** Lv 18:5; Rom 10:5. |
| **3:3** 5:16–18. | **3:13** Dt 21:23; Rom 8:3; |
| **3:5** 2:16. | 2 Cor 5:21. |
| **3:6** Gn 15:6; Rom 4:3; Jas | **3:14** 3:2–3, 5; Is 44:3; Jl |
| 2:23. | 3:1–2; Acts 2:33. |
| **3:7** 3:29; Rom 4:11–12 / | **3:15** Rom 3:5 / Heb |
| Sir 44:19–21. | 9:16–17. |
| **3:8** Gn 12:3; 18:17–19; | **3:16** Gn 12:7; 13:15; 17:8; |
| Acts 3:25. | 22:17; 24:7; Mt 1:1. |
| **3:9** Rom 4:16. | **3:17** Ex 12:40. |
| **3:10** Dt 27:26; Jas 2:10. | **3:18** Rom 4:16; 11:6. |

GAL

transgressions, until the descendant† came to whom the promise had been made; it was promulgated by angels at the hand of a mediator.* 20 Now there is no mediator when only one party is involved, and God is one.* 21 Is the law then opposed to the promises [of God]? Of course not! For if a law had been given that could bring life, then righteousness would in reality come from the law.* 22 But scripture confined all things under the power of sin, that through faith in Jesus Christ the promise might be given to those who believe.*

**What Faith Has Brought Us.**† 23 Before faith came, we were held in custody under law, confined for the faith that was to be revealed.* 24 Consequently, the law was our disciplinarian† for Christ, that we might be justified by faith.* 25 But now that faith has come, we are no longer under a disciplinarian.* 26 For through faith you are all children of God† in Christ Jesus.* 27† For all of you who were baptized into Christ* have clothed yourselves with Christ.† 28 There is neither Jew nor Greek, there is neither slave nor free person, there is not male and female; for you are all one in Christ Jesus.* 29 And if you belong to Christ,

then you are Abraham's descendant, heirs according to the promise.*

**4 God's Free Children in Christ.**† 1 I mean that as long as the heir is not of age,† he is no different from a slave, although he is the owner of everything, 2 but he is under the supervision of guardians and administrators until the date set by his father. 3* In the same way we also, when we were not of age, were enslaved to the elemental powers of the world.† 4 But when the fullness of time had come, God sent his Son, born of a woman, born under the law,* 5 to ransom those under the law, so that we might receive adoption.* 6 As proof that you are children,† God sent the spirit of his Son into our hearts, crying out, "Abba, Father!"* 7 So you are no longer a slave but a child, and if a child then also an heir, through God.*

**Do Not Throw This Freedom Away.**† 8* At a time when you did not know God, you became slaves to things that by nature are not gods;† 9 but now that you have come to know God, or rather to be known by God, how can you turn back again to the weak and destitute elemental powers? Do you want to be slaves to them all over again?* 10 You are observing days,* months, seasons,

---

† does not, however, oppose God's purposes, for it carries out its function (Gal 3:22), so that *righteousness* comes by *faith* and *promise*, not by human works of the law.

**3:19** *The descendant*: Christ (Gal 3:16). *By angels*: Dt 33:2–4 stressed their presence as enhancing the importance of the law; Paul uses their role to diminish its significance (cf. Acts 7:38, 53). *A mediator*: Moses. But in a covenant of promise, where all depends on the one God, no mediator is needed (Gal 3:20).

**3:23–29** Paul adds a further argument in support of righteousness or justification by faith and through God's promise rather than by works of the law (Gal 2:16; 3:22): as *children of God, baptized into Christ*, the Galatians are all *Abraham's descendant* and *heirs* of *the promise* to Abraham (Gal 3:8, 14, 16–18, 29). The teaching in Gal 3:23–25, that since *faith* (Christianity) *has come, we are no longer under* the law, could be taken with the previous paragraph on the role of the Mosaic law, but it also fits here as a contrast between the situation *before faith* (Gal 3:23) and the results after faith has come (Gal 3:25–29).

**3:24–25** *Disciplinarian*: the Greek *paidagōgos* referred to a slave who escorted a child to school but did not teach or tutor; hence, a guardian or monitor. Applying this to the law fits the role of the law described in Gal 3:19–25.

**3:26** *Children of God*: literally "sons," in contrast to the young child under the disciplinarian in Gal 3:24–25. The term includes males and females (Gal 3:28).

**3:27–28** Likely a formula used at baptism that expresses racial, social-economic, and sexual equality in Christ (cf. Col 3:11).

**3:27** *Clothed yourselves with Christ*: literally, "have put on Christ"; cf. Rom 13:14; Eph 4:24; Col 3:10. Baptismal imagery, traceable to the Old Testament (Jb 29:14; Is 59:17) but also found in pagan mystery cults.

**4:1–7** What Paul has argued in Gal 3:26–29 is now elaborated in terms of the Christian as *the heir* (Gal 4:1, 7; cf. Gal

3:18, 29) freed from control by others. Again, as in Gal 3:2–5, the proof that Christians are children of God is the gift of the Spirit of Christ relating them intimately to God.

**4:1, 3** *Not of age*: an infant or minor.

**4:3** *The elemental powers of the world*: while the term can refer to "elements" like earth, air, fire, and water or to elementary forms of religion, the sense here is more likely that of celestial beings that were thought in pagan circles to control the world; cf. Gal 4:8; Col 2:8, 20.

**4:6** *Children*: see note on Gal 3:26; here in contrast to the infant or young person *not of age* (Gal 3:1, 3). *Abba*: cf. Mk 14:36 and the note; Rom 8:15.

**4:8–11** On the basis of the arguments advanced from Gal 3:1 through Gal 4:7, Paul now launches his appeal to the Galatians with the question, *how can you turn back* to the slavery of the law (Gal 4:9)? The question is posed with reference to bondage to the *elemental powers* (see note on Gal 4:3) because the Galatians had originally been converted to Christianity from paganism, not Judaism (Gal 4:8). The use of the direct question is like Gal 3:3–5.

**4:8** *Things that by nature are not gods*: or "gods that by nature do not exist."

---

| | |
|---|---|
| **3:19** Rom 4:15; 5:20; 7:7, 13 / Acts 7:38, 53. | 12:13; Col 3:11. |
| **3:20** Dt 6:4. | **3:29** 3:7, 14, 16, 18; Rom 4:16–17; 9:7 / Gal 4:1, |
| **3:21** Rom 7:7, 10; 8:2–4. | 7; Rom 4:13–14; 8:17; |
| **3:22** Rom 3:9–20, 23; 11:32. | Heb 6:12; Jas 2:5. |
| **3:23** 4:3–5; 5:18. | **4:3** 3:23 / 4:9; Col 2:20. |
| **3:24** 2:16. | **4:4** Mk 1:15. |
| **3:25** Rom 10:4. | **4:5** 3:13, 26. |
| **3:26** 4:5–7; Jn 1:12; Rom 8:14–17. | **4:6** 3:26; Rom 8:15. |
| | **4:7** 3:29; Rom 8:16–17. |
| **3:27** Rom 6:3; 13:14; Eph 4:24. | **4:8** 1 Cor 12:2. |
| | **4:9** 4:3; Col 2:20. |
| **3:28** Rom 10:12; 1 Cor | **4:10** Col 2:16–20. |

and years.† ¹¹ I am afraid on your account that perhaps I have labored for you in vain.†

**Appeal to Former Loyalty.**† ¹² I implore you, brothers, be as I am, because I have also become as you are.† You did me no wrong;* ¹³ you know that it was because of a physical illness† that I originally preached the gospel to you, ¹⁴ and you did not show disdain or contempt because of the trial caused you by my physical condition, but rather you received me as an angel of God, as Christ Jesus. ¹⁵ Where now is that blessedness of yours?† Indeed, I can testify to you that, if it had been possible, you would have torn out your eyes and given them to me. ¹⁶ So now have I become your enemy by telling you the truth? ¹⁷ They show interest in you, but not in a good way; they want to isolate you,† so that you may show interest in them.* ¹⁸ Now it is good to be shown interest for good reason at all times, and not only when I am with you. ¹⁹ My children, for whom I am again in labor until Christ be formed in you!* ²⁰ I would like to be with you now and to change my tone, for I am perplexed because of you.

**An Allegory on Christian Freedom.**† ²¹ Tell me, you who want to be under the law, do you not listen to the law? ²² For it is written that Abraham had two sons, one by the slave woman and the other by the freeborn woman.* ²³ The son of the slave woman was born naturally,

the son of the freeborn through a promise.* ²⁴ Now this is an allegory. These women represent two covenants. One was from Mount Sinai, bearing children for slavery; this is Hagar.* ²⁵ Hagar represents Sinai,† a mountain in Arabia; it corresponds to the present Jerusalem, for she is in slavery along with her children. ²⁶ But the Jerusalem above is freeborn, and she is our mother.* ²⁷ For it is written:

> "Rejoice, you barren one who bore no
> children;*
> break forth and shout, you who were
> not in labor;
> for more numerous are the children of
> the deserted one
> than of her who has a husband."†

²⁸ Now you, brothers, like Isaac, are children of the promise.* ²⁹ But just as then the child of the flesh persecuted the child of the spirit, it is the same now. ³⁰ But what does the scripture say?

> "Drive out the slave woman and her son!
> For the son of the slave woman shall
> not share the inheritance with the
> son"*

of the freeborn. ³¹ Therefore, brothers, we are children not of the slave woman but of the freeborn woman.*

---

**4:10** This is likely a reference to ritual observances from the Old Testament, promoted by opponents: sabbaths or Yom Kippur, new moon, Passover or Pentecost, sabbatical years.

**4:11** Cf. Gal 2:2. If the Galatians become *slaves…all over again* to the law (Gal 4:9), Paul will have worked in vain among them.

**4:12–20** A strongly personal section. Paul appeals to past ties between the Galatians and himself. He speaks sharply of the opponents (Gal 4:17–18) and pastorally to the Galatians (Gal 4:19–20).

**4:12** *Because I have also become as you are*: a terse phrase in Greek, meaning "Be as I, Paul, am," i.e., living by faith, independent of the law, for, in spite of my background in Judaism (Gal 1:13), I have become as you Galatians are now, a brother in Christ.

**4:13** *Physical illness*: because its nature is not described, some assume an eye disease (Gal 4:15); others, epilepsy; some relate it to 2 Cor 12:7–9. *Originally*: this may also be translated "formerly" or "on the first (of two) visit(s)"; cf. Acts 16:6; 18:23.

**4:15** *That blessedness of yours*: possibly a reference to the Galatians' initial happy reception of Paul (Gal 4:14) and of his gospel (Gal 1:6; 3:1–4) and their felicitation at such blessedness, but the phrase could also refer ironically to earlier praise by Paul of the Galatians, no longer possible when they turn from the gospel to the claims of the opponents (Gal 4:17–18; 1:7). If the word is a more literal reference to a beatitude, Gal 3:26–28 may be in view.

**4:17** *Isolate you*: that is, from the blessings of the gospel and/ or from Paul.

**4:21–31** Paul supports his appeal for the gospel (Gal 4:9; 1:6–9; 2:16; 3:2) by a further argument from scripture (cf. Gal 3:6–18). It involves the relationship of *Abraham* (Gal 3:6–16) to his wife, Sarah, the *freeborn woman*, and to Hagar, *the slave woman*, and the contrast between the sons born to each, *Isaac*, child of promise, and Ishmael, son of Hagar (Gn 16; 21). Only through Isaac is the promise of God preserved. This *allegory* (Gal 4:24), with its equation of the Sinai covenant and Mosaic law with slavery and of the promise of God with freedom, Paul uses only in light of previous arguments. His quotation of Gn 21:10 at Gal 4:30 suggests on a scriptural basis that the Galatians should expel those who are troubling them (Gal 1:7).

**4:25** *Hagar represents Sinai…*: some manuscripts have what seems a geographical note, "For Sinai is a mountain in Arabia."

**4:27** Is 54:1 in the Septuagint translation is applied to Sarah as the *barren one* (in Gn 15) who ultimately becomes the mother not only of Isaac but now of numerous children, i.e., of all those who believe, the *children of the promise* (Gal 4:28).

---

**4:12** 1 Cor 11:1.
**4:17** 1:7; 6:12; Acts 20:30.
**4:19** 1 Cor 4:14–15; 2 Cor 6:13; 1 Thes 2:7–8.
**4:22** Gn 16:15; 21:2–3.
**4:23** Gn 17:16; Rom 4:19–20; 9:7–9.
**4:24** 3:17 / Ex 19:20 / Gn 16:1.
**4:26** Heb 12:22; Rev 21:2.
**4:27** Is 54:1.
**4:28** Rom 9:8.
**4:30** Gn 21:10.
**4:31** 3:29; Jn 8:35.

## V. EXHORTATION TO CHRISTIAN LIVING

**5** **The Importance of Faith.**† ¹For freedom† Christ set us free; so stand firm and do not submit again to the yoke of slavery. *

²It is I, Paul, who am telling you that if you have yourselves circumcised, Christ will be of no benefit to you.* ³Once again I declare to every man who has himself circumcised* that he is bound to observe the entire law.† ⁴You are separated from Christ, you who are trying to be justified by law; you have fallen from grace. ⁵* For through the Spirit, by faith, we await the hope of righteousness. ⁶* For in Christ Jesus, neither circumcision nor uncircumcision counts for anything, but only faith working through love.†

**Be Not Misled.**† ⁷You were running well;† who hindered you from following [the] truth? ⁸* That enticement does not come from the one who called you.† ⁹A little yeast leavens the whole batch of dough.* ¹⁰I am confident of you in the Lord that you will not take a different view, and that the one who is troubling you will bear the condemnation, whoever he may be.* ¹¹As for me, brothers, if I am still preaching circumcision,† why am I still being persecuted? In that case, the stumbling block of the cross has been abolished.* ¹²Would

that those who are upsetting you might also castrate themselves!†

**Freedom for Service.**† ¹³For you were called for freedom, brothers.* But do not use this freedom as an opportunity for the flesh; rather, serve† one another through love. ¹⁴For the whole law* is fulfilled in one statement, namely, "You shall love your neighbor as yourself."† ¹⁵But if you go on biting and devouring one another, beware that you are not consumed by one another.

¹⁶* I say, then: live by the Spirit and you will certainly not gratify the desire of the flesh.† ¹⁷For the flesh has desires against the Spirit, and the Spirit against the flesh; these are opposed to each other, so that you may not do what you want.* ¹⁸But if you are guided by the Spirit, you are not under the law.* ¹⁹† Now the works of the flesh are obvious: immorality, impurity, licentiousness,* ²⁰idolatry, sorcery, hatreds, rivalry, jealousy, outbursts of fury, acts of selfishness, dissensions, factions,* ²¹occasions of envy,† drinking bouts, orgies, and the like. I warn you, as I warned you before, that those who do such things will not inherit the kingdom of God. ²²In contrast, the fruit of the Spirit is love, joy, peace, patience, kindness, generosity, faithfulness,* ²³gentleness, self-control. Against such there is no law.* ²⁴Now

---

† **5:1–6** Paul begins the exhortations, continuing through Gal 6:10, with an appeal to the Galatians to side with freedom instead of slavery (Gal 5:1). He reiterates his message of justification or righteousness by faith instead of law and circumcision (Gal 5:2–5); cf. Gal 2:16; 3:3. Faith, not circumcision, is what counts (Gal 5:6).

**5:1** *Freedom*: Paul stresses as the conclusion from the allegory in Gal 4:21–31 this result of Christ's work for us. It is a principle previously mentioned (Gal 2:4), the responsible use of which Gal 5:13 will emphasize.

**5:3** Cf. Gal 3:10–12. Just as those who seek to live by the law must carry out all its contents, so those who have faith and live by promise must stand firm in their freedom (Gal 5:1, 13).

**5:6** Cf. Rom 2:25–26; 1 Cor 7:19; Gal 6:15. The Greek for *faith working through love* or "faith expressing itself through love" can also be rendered as "faith energized by (God's) love."

**5:7–12** Paul addresses the Galatians directly: with questions (Gal 5:7, 11), a proverb (Gal 5:9), a statement (Gal 5:8), and biting sarcasm (Gal 5:12), seeking to persuade the Galatians to break with those trying to add law and circumcision to Christ as a basis for salvation.

**5:7** *Running well*: as in an athletic contest; cf. Gal 2:2; 1 Cor 9:24–26; Phil 2:16; 3:14.

**5:8** *The one who called you*: see note on Gal 1:6.

**5:11** *Preaching circumcision*: this could refer to Paul's preChristian period (possibly as a missionary for Judaism); more probably it arose as a charge from opponents, based perhaps on the story in Acts 16:1–3 that Paul had circumcised Timothy "on account of the Jews." Unlike the Gentile Titus in Gal 2:3, Timothy was the son of a Jewish mother. *The stumbling block of the cross*: cf. 1 Cor 1:23.

**5:12** A sarcastic half-wish that their knife would go beyond

mere circumcision; cf. Phil 3:2 and the note there.

**5:13–26** In light of another reminder of the freedom of the gospel (Gal 5:13; cf. Gal 5:1), Paul elaborates on what believers are called to do and be: they fulfill the law by love of neighbor (Gal 5:14–15), walking in the Spirit (Gal 5:16–26), as is illustrated by concrete *fruit of the Spirit* in their lives.

**5:13** *Serve...through love*: cf. Gal 5:6.

**5:14** Lv 19:18, emphasized by Jesus (Mt 22:39; Lk 10:27); cf. Rom 13:8–10.

**5:16–25** *Spirit...flesh*: cf. Gal 3:3 and the note on Rom 8:1–13.

**5:19–23** Such lists of vices and virtues (cf. Rom 1:29–31; 1 Cor 6:9–10) were common in the ancient world. Paul contrasts *works of the flesh* (Gal 5:19) with *fruit* (not "works") of the Spirit (Gal 5:22). Not law, but the Spirit, leads to such traits.

**5:21** *Occasions of envy*: after the Greek word *phthonoi*, "envies," some manuscripts add a similar sounding one, *phonoi*, "murders."

---

| | |
|---|---|
| **5:1** 2:4; 4:5, 9; Jn 8:32, 36. | 1 Cor 8:9; 1 Pt 2:16. |
| **5:2** 2:21; Acts 15:1–29. | **5:14** Lv 19:18; Mt 22:39; Rom 13:8–10. |
| **5:3** 3:10; Rom 2:25; Jas 2:10. | **5:16** 5:24–25; Rom 8:5. |
| **5:5** Rom 8:23, 25. | **5:17** Rom 7:15, 23; 8:6. |
| **5:6** 3:28; 6:15; 1 Cor 7:19. | **5:18** Rom 6:14; 8:14. |
| **5:8** 1:6. | **5:19–21** Rom 1:29–31; 1 Cor 6:9–10; Col 3:5–6, 8. |
| **5:9** 1 Cor 5:6. | **5:20** Rev 22:15. |
| **5:10** 1:7. | **5:22** Eph 5:9 / 1 Cor 13:4–7; 2 Cor 6:6; |
| **5:11** 6:12, 14; 1 Cor 1:23. | 1 Tm 4:12; 2 Pt 1:6. |
| **5:13** 5:1 / Rom 6:18; | **5:23** 1 Tm 1:9. |

those who belong to Christ [Jesus] have crucified their flesh with its passions and desires.* ²⁵ If we live in the Spirit, let us also follow the Spirit.* ²⁶ Let us not be conceited, provoking one another, envious of one another.*

**6** **Life in the Community of Christ.**† ¹ Brothers, even if a person is caught in some transgression, you who are spiritual should correct that one in a gentle spirit, looking to yourself, so that you also may not be tempted.* ² Bear one another's burdens,* and so you will fulfill the law of Christ.† ³* For if anyone thinks he is something when he is nothing, he is deluding himself. ⁴† Each one must examine his own work, and then he will have reason to boast with regard to himself alone, and not with regard to someone else; ⁵ for each will bear his own load.*

⁶* One who is being instructed in the word should share all good things with his instructor.† ⁷ Make no mistake: God is not mocked, for a person will reap only what he sows, ⁸ because the one who sows for his flesh will reap corruption from the flesh, but the one who sows for the spirit will reap eternal life from the spirit.* ⁹ Let us not grow tired of doing good, for in due time we shall reap our harvest, if we do not give up.* ¹⁰ So then, while we have the opportunity, let us do good to all,* but especially to those who belong to the family of the faith.†

## VI. CONCLUSION

**Final Appeal.**† ¹¹ See with what large letters† I am writing to you in my own hand!* ¹²† It is those who want to make a good appearance in the flesh who are trying to compel you to have yourselves circumcised, only that they may not be persecuted for the cross of Christ.* ¹³ Not even those having themselves circumcised† observe the law themselves; they only want you to be circumcised so that they may boast of your flesh. ¹⁴ But may I never boast except in the cross of our Lord Jesus Christ, through which† the world has been crucified to me, and I to the world.* ¹⁵ For neither does circumcision mean anything, nor does uncircumcision,* but only a new creation.† ¹⁶ Peace and mercy be to all who follow this rule† and to the Israel of God.*

¹⁷ From now on, let no one make troubles for me; for I bear the marks of Jesus† on my body.*

¹⁸ The grace of our Lord Jesus Christ be with your spirit, brothers. Amen.*

---

†

**6:1–10** The ethical exhortations begun at Gal 5:1 continue with a variety of admonitions to the community (*brothers*: see note on Gal 1:2). Nearly every sentence contains a separate item of practical advice; the faith and freedom of the gospel underlie each maxim. Tensions and temptation within communal life have previously been addressed in Gal 5:15, 26, and Gal 6:1 continues with a case in which a *person is caught in some transgression* such as those in Gal 5:19–21; cf. Gal 2:17.

**6:2** *The law of Christ*: cf. Rom 8:2; 1 Cor 9:21; Gal 5:14. The principle of love for others is meant. To *bear one another's burdens* is to "serve one another through love" (Gal 5:13).

**6:4–5** Self-examination is the cure for self-deception. Compare what you are with what you were before, and give the glory to God; cf. Rom 6:19–22. *Load*: used elsewhere of a soldier's pack. Correcting one's own conduct avoids burdening others with it.

**6:6** Implies oral instruction in the faith by catechists; these are to be remunerated for their service; cf. Rom 15:27.

**6:10** *The family of the faith*: the Christian household or church. Doing good has a universal object (*to all*), but the local community makes specific the reality of those to be served.

**6:11–18** A postscript in Paul's own hand, as was his practice (see 1 Cor 16:21; 2 Thes 3:17). Paul summarizes his appeal against his opponents (Gal 6:12–13), then returns to his message of glorying in the cross, not in circumcision, as the means of salvation (Gal 6:14–15; cf. Gal 5:11). A benediction follows at Gal 6:16. In the polemical spirit that the attack on his apostleship called forth (Gal 1:11–2:21), Paul reasserts his missionary credentials (Gal 6:17) before giving a final benediction (Gal 6:18).

**6:11** *Large letters*: in contrast to the finer hand of the scribe who wrote the letter up to this point. The larger Greek letters make Paul's message even more emphatic. Some find a hint of poor eyesight on Paul's part. See note on Gal 4:13.

**6:12–15** The Jewish Christian opponents wished *not* to *be persecuted*, possibly by Jews. But since Judaism seems to have had a privileged status as a religion in the Roman empire, circumcised Christians might, if taken as Jews, thereby avoid persecution from the Romans. In any case, Paul instead stresses conformity with *the cross of our Lord Jesus Christ*; cf. Gal 2:19–21; 5:11.

**6:13** *Those having themselves circumcised*: other manuscripts read, "those who have had themselves circumcised."

**6:14** *Through which*: or "through whom."

**6:15** *New creation*: or "new creature"; cf. 2 Cor 5:17.

**6:16** *This rule*: the principle in Gal 6:14–15. *The Israel of God*: while the church may be meant (the phrase can be translated "to all who follow this rule, even the Israel of God"; cf. Gal 6:10; 1 Cor 10:18), the reference may also be to God's ancient people, Israel; cf. Ps 125:5; 128:6.

**6:17** *The marks of Jesus*: slaves were often branded by marks (*stigmata*) burned into their flesh to show to whom they belonged; so also were devotees of pagan gods. Paul implies that instead of outdated circumcision, his body bears the scars of his apostolic labors (2 Cor 11:22–31), such as floggings (Acts 16:22; 2 Cor 11:25) and stonings (Acts 14:19), that mark him as belonging to the Christ who suffered (cf. Rom 6:3; 2 Cor 4:10; Col 1:24) and will protect his own.

---

**5:24** 2:19; Rom 6:6; 8:13.
**5:25** 5:16.
**5:26** Phil 2:3.
**6:1** Mt 18:15; Jas 5:19 / 1 Cor 10:12–13.
**6:2** Col 3:13 / 1 Cor 9:21.
**6:3–4** 1 Cor 3:18; 8:2; 2 Cor 12:11.
**6:5** Rom 14:12.
**6:6** 1 Cor 9:14.
**6:8** Prv 11:18; Rom 8:6, 13.

**6:9** 2 Thes 3:13; Heb 12:1–3.
**6:10** 1 Thes 5:15.
**6:11** 1 Cor 16:21.
**6:12** 5:2, 11.
**6:14** 2:20; 1 Cor 2:2.
**6:15** 5:6; 1 Cor 7:19 / 2 Cor 5:17.
**6:16** Ps 125:5; 128:6.
**6:17** 2 Cor 4:10.
**6:18** Phil 4:23; 2 Tm 4:22; Phlm 25.

GAL

## INTRODUCTION

### Raymond F. Collins

The Letter to the Ephesians is addressed not to a specific local community, but rather generally, to all God's holy ones in Ephesus (Eph 1:1). Ephesus, a port city, was the capital of the Roman province of Asia. Mentioned some twenty times in the New Testament, Ephesus served as the Apostle Paul's base of operations for more than two years (Acts 19:8–10), but Paul was not the founder of the church in Ephesus. According to Acts, there were already disciples in Ephesus when Paul first arrived there (Acts 19:1). Hence, Paul was not the apostle to the Ephesians in the same way that he was the apostle to the Corinthians (1 Cor 9:2), being the founder of that faith community.

## Ephesians and Colossians

In many ways it is best to read Ephesians as a new, revised, and expanded edition of the Letter to the Colossians. The two letters are remarkably similar. The structure of Ephesians is similar to that of Colossians. About one third of the vocabulary of Colossians recurs in Ephesians, where it comprises about a quarter of the text. The elaborate writing style and the length of the sentences make Ephesians more akin to Colossians than to the undisputed Pauline letters. Striking examples are Eph 1:3–14 and 3:1–7. Both of these passages constitute but a single sentence in Greek.

The two letters are also remarkably similar in imagery and theology. Sometimes the text of Colossians appears to have been repeated almost verbatim in Ephesians. A case in point would be the similar recommendations of Tychicus, named as the letter-carrier in both texts (Eph 6:21–22; Col 4:7–8).

Apart from Paul, the identified author, Tychicus is the only person named in the text. The letter lacks the customary epistolary greetings

## Outline of Ephesians

I.   **Address (1:1–14)**

II.  **Unity of the Church in Christ (1:15–2:22)**

III. **World Mission of the Church (3:1–4:24)**

IV.  **Daily Conduct, an Expression of Unity (4:25–6:20)**

V.   **Conclusion (6:21–24)**

that appear in the conclusions of all of Paul's undisputed letters except Galatians. The letter does not even once address its recipients as "brothers and sisters" (*adelphoi*), the familiar form of address found in all of the undisputed letters except for the Letter to Philemon, which uses the same noun in the singular as a form of address (Phlm 7, 20). For an increasing number of scholars, the absence of any echo of a personal relationship between Paul and those to whom the letter is addressed raises serious doubts about Paul's authorship of the letter.

The absence of personal names, the impersonal style, and the letter's general failure to engage with any particular situation at Ephesus make it unlikely that the letter was written to a community with which Paul had considerable interaction for more than two years. Moreover, Eph 1:15 suggests that the author's knowledge of the faith and love of the Ephesians is based on hearsay while Eph 3:2 suggests that their knowledge of Paul and his ministry is something that they have only heard about.

The central and seemingly exclusive role assigned to Paul in the communication of God's revelation in Eph 3:2–3 in some ways parallels a similar focus on Paul in Ti 1:1–3. Some authors would see this kind of focus on Paul as a sign that the texts were written one or two generations after Paul had died, probably by one of his disciples sometime during the final decades of the first century CE. That Ephesians is apparently so dependent on Colossians enhances the likelihood of this scenario.

Ephesians also is much longer than Colossians and includes additional material, expansions that are not found in Colossians. A good example is the similar "household codes" found in both texts (Eph 5:21–6:9; Col 3:18–4:1). Not only do the two passages have a similar literary form; they also appear in similar positions within the rhetorical flow of the respective letters and have a similar function. When compared with the household code of Colossians, the text of Ephesians has been significantly expanded, particularly in regard to the wife-husband relationship (Col 3:18–20). The motif is developed in such a way as to describe the relationship between Christ and the church by means of marital imagery (Eph 5:21–32). The other two elements of the household code, pertaining to the child-parent and slave-master relationships, have also been expanded, albeit not as extensively.

## A Treatise on the Church

In some ways Ephesians can be considered a theological tract within an epistolary framework, i.e., a kind of theological essay inserted into a letter template. The framework consists of just six verses, the opening greeting (Eph 1:1–2) and the closing conventions (6:21–24). The main theme of theological exposition is cosmic reconciliation achieved by means of the church whose head is Christ. In traditional Roman Catholic terminology, the church can be described as the sacrament of cosmic reconciliation insofar as it is both a sign and means of that reconciliation.

The church is first mentioned in the letter in Eph 1:22–23, which speaks of the church as the body of Christ. The language is Pauline (Rom 12:4–5; 1 Cor 12:12–13, 27) but the image of the church as the body of Christ in Ephesians is different from that of Paul's major letters in three respects. First, the church (ekklēsia) is the church universal rather than a local assembly. Second, the body is distinguished from its head. Christ is the head; the

church, the torso. Third, the church as body of Christ is presented within a cosmic perspective whereas in the letters actually written by Paul some thirty years prior to Ephesians the body imagery serves as an analogy for the unity of the local community.

The body image recurs, without mention of Christ as head of the church, at the beginning of the part of the letter that encourages its readers to live a Christian lifestyle (Eph 4:1–6). The recipients of the letter are urged to live in a manner worthy of their calling. They are exhorted to preserve the unity of the spirit through the bond of peace. There follow seven reasons for the unity of the church. The seven—a number that symbolizes fullness and perfection—are presented in two triads and a climactic finale, "one God and Father of all, who is over all and through all and in all." Aspects of the unity of the church are one body, one Spirit, and one hope, the first triad; and one Lord, one faith, one baptism, the second triad. Given the emphasis on the unity of the church, it is not surprising that the epistle often stresses the importance of love and the avoidance of socially disruptive vices (4:31). Were it not for the nine times that "love" (agapē) is mentioned in 1 Cor 13, the word would occur more often in Ephesians than in any other letter in the Pauline corpus.

In 1 Corinthians, Paul exploits body imagery to speak about the unity and diversity of function within the church. The author of Ephesians also does so. He writes that "grace was given to each of us according to the measure of Christ's gift" (Eph 4:7) and says that the risen Christ "gave some as apostles, others as prophets, others as evangelists, others as pastors and teachers . . . for building up the body of Christ" (4:11–12). The description of the diversity of gifts within the community comes to a hortatory conclusion when the recipients of the letter are urged to "grow in every way into him who is the head, Christ, from whom the whole body, joined and held together by every supporting ligament, with the proper functioning of each part, brings about the body's growth and builds itself up in love" (4:15–16). In this context, Christ's headship of the body means that the church derives its vitality from Christ.

The list of gifts given to the members of the

body of Christ recalls similar lists in Rom 12:6–8 and 1 Cor 12:8–10, 28–30, but there are significant differences. First, the gifts are called "grace" (*charis*) rather than "gift" (*charisma*), as they are in 1 Corinthians and in Romans. Second, the gifts are said to come from the risen Christ rather than from the Spirit. Third, the gifts that are cited are exclusively gifts of leadership, gifts of proclaiming and teaching the gospel.

Ephesians' exploitation of the wife-husband relationship in Eph 5:21–32 is the letter's third exposition of the theme of the church, the body of Christ. Again, the church is identified as the body (5:30) and Christ as its head (5:23). In this passage, the headship of Christ is developed in such a way as to underscore the authority of Christ over the church. Christ loves the church, but the church is subordinate to Christ, as a wife in the culture of the day was expected to be subordinate to her husband. The marital imagery of the text reflects the Old Testament imagery of Yahweh as the spouse of Israel. The way in which Christ prepares the church, his bride, for the marital union (5:25–27) is replete with baptismal imagery.

While the body of Christ is the major image used of the church in Ephesians the letter also includes another image that recalls the analogy used by Paul in 1 Corinthians. In Eph 2:19–22, the church is described as a building, which is a temple because God in the Spirit dwells in it (cf. 1 Cor 3:10–17). In the letter that clearly came from Paul's hand the foundation of the church is Jesus Christ (1 Cor 3:11). Now apostles and (Christian) prophets are the foundation of the church, with Christ as the capstone (Eph 2:20).

## Jews and Gentiles

Ephesians uses the construction imagery to teach that Gentile believers are no longer outsiders, strangers, and sojourners, but are now fellow citizens with the holy ones and members of the household of God (Eph 2:19). The reconciliation of Jews and Gentiles, accomplished through Christ's death and Resurrection, is a major theme of this letter (3:4–6). Prior to Christ's death and Resurrection, Gentiles were without hope and without God (2:12). That is no longer the case. This reconciliation of Gentiles and Jews is not only an important element of the unity of the church, it is also a major dimension of cosmic reconciliation.

The author uses two striking images to make his point. He describes Christ, our peace, as breaking down the wall of enmity that had separated Jews from Gentiles (Eph 2:14). Enmity and alienation are destroyed. Then the author describes Christ as creating one new person (*heis kainos anthrōpos*, 2:15; cf. 4:24) in place of the two. This reconciliation is peace, the peace which Christ preached, the peace which he established, and the peace which he is. Through him Jews and Gentiles have access to God in the one Spirit (2:14–18).

## The Cosmic Perspective

The author's cosmic vision of an exalted Christ is noteworthy. It imparts a dimension to Christology that is unparalleled in the rest of the New Testament. Particularly striking is the description of the Resurrection of Jesus in Eph 1:20–23 (cf. 2:6–7; 4:8–10). Having raised Jesus from the dead, God has seated Jesus at the right hand of God (see Ps 110:1) in the heavens, above every principality, authority, power, and dominion. All things are under his feet. His name will endure forever.

The author introduces his rich theological exposition with a prayer of praise (Eph 1:3–14) that serves as a kind of foreword to what is to come. The prayer of praise blesses the God of Israel, who is identified as the Father of our Lord Jesus Christ. The all-encompassing cosmic and temporal dimensions of God's plan of salvation are introduced for the reader to ponder. The prayer introduces the promised holy Spirit as the first installment, a down payment (*arrabōn*), on our inheritance (1:14). The heart of the prayer is found in 1:8–10, "In all wisdom and insight, he has made known to us the mystery (*mystērion*, cf. 3:3, 4, 9; 5:32; 6:19) of his will in accord with his favor that he set forth in him as a plan for the fullness of times, to sum up all things in Christ, in heaven and on earth." These words succinctly state the theme of the entire letter. The rest is explanation. ∎

EPH

# THE LETTER TO THE EPHESIANS

## New American Bible, Introduction

Ephesians is the great Pauline letter about the church. It deals, however, not so much with a congregation in the city of Ephesus in Asia Minor as with the worldwide church, the head of which is Christ (Eph 4:15), the purpose of which is to be the instrument for making God's plan of salvation known throughout the universe (Eph 3:9–10). Yet this ecclesiology is anchored in God's saving love, shown in Jesus Christ (Eph 2:4–10), and the whole of redemption is rooted in the plan and accomplishment of the triune God (Eph 1:3–14). The language is often that of doxology (Eph 1:3–14) and prayer (cf. Eph 1:15–23; 3:14–19), indeed of liturgy and hymns (Eph 3:20–21; 5:14).

The majestic chapters of Ephesians emphasize the unity in the church of Christ that has come about for both Jews and Gentiles within God's household (Eph 1:15–2:22, especially Eph 2:11–22) and indeed the "seven unities" of church, Spirit, hope; one Lord, faith, and baptism; and the one God (Eph 4:4–6). Yet the concern is not with the church for its own sake but rather as the means for mission in the world (Eph 3:1–4:24). The gifts Christ gives its members are to lead to growth and renewal (Eph 4:7–24). Ethical admonition is not lacking either; all aspects of human life and relationships are illumined by the light of Christ (Eph 4:25–6:20).

The letter is seemingly addressed by Paul to Christians in Ephesus (Eph 1:1), a place where the apostle labored for well over two years (Acts 19:10). Yet there is a curiously impersonal tone to the writing for a community with which Paul was so intimately acquainted (cf. Eph 3:2 and Eph 4:21). There are no personal greetings (cf. Eph 6:23). More significantly, important early manuscripts omit the words "in

Ephesus" (see note on Eph 1:1). Many therefore regard the letter as an encyclical or "circular letter" sent to a number of churches in Asia Minor, the addressees to be designated in each place by its bearer, Tychicus (Eph 6:21–22). Others think that Ephesians is the letter referred to in Col 4:16 as "to the Laodiceans."

Paul, who is designated as the sole author at Eph 1:1, is described in almost unparalleled terms with regard to the significant role he has in God's plan for bringing the Gentiles to faith in Christ (Eph 3:1–12). Yet at the time of writing he is clearly in prison (Eph 3:1; 4:1; 6:20), suffering afflictions (Eph 3:13). Traditionally this "Captivity Epistle" has, along with Colossians, Philippians, and Philemon, been dated to an imprisonment in Rome, likely in A.D. 61–63. Others appeal to an earlier imprisonment, perhaps in Caesarea (Acts 23:27–27:2). Since the early nineteenth century, however, much of critical scholarship has considered the letter's style and use of words (especially when compared with Colossians), its concept of the church, and other points of doctrine put forward by the writer as grounds for serious doubt about authorship by Paul. The letter may then be the work of a secretary writing at the apostle's direction or of a later disciple who sought to develop Paul's ideas for a new situation around A.D. 80–100.

The principal divisions of the Letter to the Ephesians are the following:

I. Address (1:1–14)
II. Unity of the Church in Christ (1:15–2:22)
III. World Mission of the Church (3:1–4:24)
IV. Daily Conduct, an Expression of Unity (4:25–6:20)
V. Conclusion (6:21–24) ∎

# EPHESIANS

## I. ADDRESS

**Greeting.**† ¹Paul, an apostle of Christ Jesus by the will of God, to the holy ones who are [in Ephesus]† faithful in Christ Jesus: * ²grace to you and peace from God our Father and the Lord Jesus Christ. *

**The Father's Plan of Salvation.** ³† Blessed be the God and Father of our Lord Jesus Christ, * who has blessed us in Christ with every spiritual blessing in the heavens,† ⁴as he chose us in him, before the foundation of the world, to be holy and without blemish before him. * In love ⁵he destined us for adoption to himself through Jesus Christ, in accord with the favor of his will, * ⁶for the praise of the glory of his grace that he granted us in the beloved. *

**Fulfillment Through Christ.** ⁷In him we have redemption by his blood, the forgiveness of transgressions, in accord with the riches of his grace* ⁸that he lavished upon us. In all wisdom and insight, * ⁹he has made known to us the mystery† of his will in accord with his favor that he set forth in him* ¹⁰as a plan for the fullness of times, to sum up all things in Christ, in heaven and on earth. *

**Inheritance Through the Spirit.** ¹¹In him we were also chosen, destined in accord with the purpose of the One who accomplishes all things according to the intention of his will, * ¹²so that we might exist for the praise of his glory, we who first hoped† in Christ. ¹³In him you also, who have heard the word of truth, the gospel of your salvation, and have believed in him, were sealed† with the promised holy Spirit, * ¹⁴which is the first installment† of our inheritance toward redemption as God's possession, to the praise of his glory. *

## II. UNITY OF THE CHURCH IN CHRIST

**The Church as Christ's Body.**† ¹⁵Therefore, I, too, hearing of your faith in the Lord Jesus and of your love† for all the holy ones, * ¹⁶do

---

**1:1–2** For the epistolary form used at the beginning of letters, see note on Rom 1:1–7. Twenty-two of the thirty Greek words in Eph 1:1–2 also occur in Col 1:1–2.

**1:1** *[In Ephesus]*: the phrase is lacking in important early witnesses such as P⁴⁶ (3rd cent.), and Sinaiticus and Vaticanus (4th cent.), appearing in the latter two as a fifth-century addition. Basil and Origen mention its absence from manuscripts. See Introduction. Without the phrase, the Greek can be rendered, as in Col 1:2, "to the holy ones and faithful brothers in Christ."

**1:3–14** While a Pauline letter usually continues after the greeting with a prayer of thanksgiving, as in Eph 1:15–23 below, Ephesians first inserts a blessing of God for the blessings Christians have experienced, as in 2 Cor 1:3–4 and 1 Pt 1:3–12. The blessing here, akin to a Jewish *berakah*, is rich in images almost certainly drawn from hymns and liturgy. Many ideas here are also found in Col 1:3–23. Certain phrases are frequently repeated, such as *in Christ* (Eph 1:3, 10, 12) or *in him* (Eph 1:4, 7, 9, 11, 13) or *in the beloved* (Eph 1:6) and *(for) the praise of (his) glory* (Eph 1:6, 12, 14). Some terms like *chose* (Eph 1:4) and *destined* (Eph 1:5) reflect Old Testament theology (cf. Dt 7:7; 9:4–6; 23:5) or Pauline themes (*redemption*, Eph 1:7, 14; *grace*, Eph 1:6, 7) or specific emphases in Colossians (*forgiveness*, Col 1:14). A triadic structure is discernible in Eph 1:3–14: *God the Father* (Eph 1:3–6, 8, 11), *Christ* (Eph 1:3, 5, 7–10, 12), and the *Spirit* (Eph 1:13–14). The spiritual blessings Christians have received through Christ (Eph 1:3) are gratefully enumerated: the call to holiness (Eph 1:4; cf. Col 1:22); the gift of divine *adoption* establishing a unique spiritual relationship with God the Father through Christ (Eph 1:5; cf. Gal 4:5); liberation from sin through Christ's sacrificial death (Eph 1:7); revelation of God's plan of salvation in Christ (Eph 1:9; cf. Eph 3:3–4; Rom 16:25); the gift of election and faith in Christ bestowed upon Jewish Christians (see note on Eph 1:12, *we who first hoped in Christ*); and finally, the same gift granted to Gentiles (Eph 1:13, *you also*). In the Christ-centered faith and existence of the Christian communities the apostle sees the predetermined *plan* of God to bring all creation under the final rule of Christ (Eph 1:4–5, 9–10) being *made known* (Eph 1:9)

and carried through, to God's *glory* (Eph 1:6, 12, 14).

**1:3** *In the heavens*: literally, "in the heavenlies" or "in the heavenly places," a term in Ephesians for the divine realm.

**1:9** *Mystery*: as in Rom 16:25; Col 1:26–27 and elsewhere, a secret of God now revealed in the *plan* to save and *sum up all things in Christ* (Eph 1:10); cf. Eph 3:3–6.

**1:12** *We who first hoped*: probably Jewish Christians (contrast Eph 1:13, *you*, the Gentiles); possibly the people of Israel, "we who already enjoyed the hope of Christ," or perhaps present hope in contrast to future redemption (cf. Eph 1:14).

**1:13** *Sealed*: by God, in baptism; cf. Eph 4:30; 2 Cor 1:22.

**1:14** *First installment*: down payment by God on full salvation, as at 2 Cor 1:22.

**1:15–23** See note on Rom 1:8 for the thanksgiving form in a letter. Much of the content parallels thoughts in Col 1:3–20. The prayer moves from God and Christ (Eph 1:17, 20–21) to the Ephesians (Eph 1:17–19) and the church (Eph 1:22–23). Paul asks that the blessing imparted by God the Father (Eph 1:3) to the Ephesians will be strengthened in them through the message of the gospel (Eph 1:13, 17–19). Those blessings are seen in the context of God's *might* in establishing the sovereignty of Christ over all other creatures (Eph 1:19–21) and in appointing him *head* of the church (Eph 1:22–23). For the allusion to angelic spirits in Eph 1:21, see Rom 8:38 and Col 1:16. Here, as in 1 Cor 15:24–25 and Col 2:15, every such *principality* and *power* is made subject to Christ.

**1:15** *Your faith…your love*: some manuscripts omit the latter phrase, but cf. Col 1:4.

---

| | |
|---|---|
| **1:1** Rom 1:7; 1 Cor 1:1–2; Col 1:1. | Col 1:14, 20. |
| | **1:8** Col 1:9. |
| **1:2** Col 1:2. | **1:9** 3:3, 9; Rom 16:25. |
| **1:3** 2:6; 2 Cor 1:3. | **1:10** Gal 4:4; Col 1:16, 20. |
| **1:4** Is 5:27; Jn 15:16; 17:24; Rom 8:29; 2 Thes 2:13. | **1:11** Is 46:10; Rom 8:28; Col 1:12; Rev 4:11. |
| | **1:13** 4:30; Acts 2:33; Col 1:5–6. |
| **1:5** Jn 1:12; 1 Jn 3:1. | |
| **1:6** Mt 3:17; Col 1:13. | **1:14** 2 Cor 1:22; 5:5. |
| **1:7** 2:7–13; Rom 3:24; | **1:15** Col 1:3–4; Phlm 4–5. |

EPH

not cease giving thanks for you, remembering you in my prayers, * [17] that the God of our Lord Jesus Christ, the Father of glory, may give you a spirit of wisdom and revelation resulting in knowledge of him. * [18] May the eyes of [your] hearts be enlightened, that you may know what is the hope that belongs to his call, what are the riches of glory in his inheritance among the holy ones, * [19] and what is the surpassing greatness of his power for us who believe, in accord with the exercise of his great might, * [20] which he worked in Christ, raising him from the dead and seating him at his right hand in the heavens, * [21] far above every principality, authority, power, and dominion, and every name that is named not only in this age but also in the one to come. * [22] And he put all things beneath his feet and gave him as head over all things to the church, * [23] which is his body, † the fullness of the one who fills all things in every way. *

## 2 †Generosity of God's Plan.† [1] * You were dead in your transgressions and sins† [2] in which you once lived following the age of

this world, † following the ruler of the power of the air, the spirit that is now at work in the disobedient. * [3] All of us once lived among them in the desires of our flesh, following the wishes of the flesh and the impulses, and we were by nature children of wrath, like the rest. * [4] But God, who is rich in mercy, because of the great love he had for us, [5] * even when we were dead in our transgressions, brought us to life with Christ † (by grace you have been saved), [6] raised us up with him, and seated us with him in the heavens in Christ Jesus, * [7] that in the ages to come he might show the immeasurable riches of his grace in his kindness to us in Christ Jesus. * [8] For by grace you have been saved through faith, and this is not from you; it is the gift of God; * [9] it is not from works, so no one may boast. * [10] For we are his handiwork, created in Christ Jesus for the good works that God has prepared in advance, that we should live in them. *

## One in Christ.† [11] Therefore, remember that at one time you, Gentiles in the flesh, called the uncircumcision by those called

**1:23** *His body*: the church (Eph 1:22); cf. note on Col 1:18. Only in Ephesians and Colossians is Christ the *head* of the *body*, in contrast to the view in 1 Cor 12 and Rom 12:4–8 where Christ is equated with the entire body or community. *Fullness*: see note on Col 1:19. Some take *the one who fills* as God, others as Christ (cf. Eph 4:10). If in Christ "dwells the fullness of the deity bodily" (Col 2:9), then, as God "fills" Christ, Christ in turn fills the church and the believer (Eph 3:19; 5:18). But the difficult phrases here may also allow the church to be viewed as the "complement" of Christ who is "being filled" as God's plan for the universe is carried out through the church (cf. Eph 3:9–10).

**2:1–22** The gospel of *salvation* (Eph 1:13) that God *worked in Christ* (Eph 1:20) is reiterated in terms of what God's *great love* (Eph 2:4), expressed in Christ, means for us. The passage sometimes addresses *you*, Gentiles (Eph 2:1–2, 8, 11–13, 19, 22), but other times speaks of *all of us* who believe (Eph 2:3–7, 10, 14, 18). In urging people to *remember* their grim past when they were *dead* in sins (Eph 2:1–3, 11–12) and what they are *now in Christ* (Eph 2:4–10, 13), the author sees both Jew and Gentile reconciled with God, now *one new person*, a new humanity, *one body*, *the household of God*, *a temple* and *dwelling place* of God's Spirit (Eph 2:15–16, 19–22). The presentation falls into two parts, the second stressing more the meaning for the church.

**2:1–10** The recipients of Paul's letter have experienced, in their redemption from *transgressions and sins*, the effect of Christ's supremacy over the power of the devil (Eph 2:1–2; cf. Eph 6:11–12), who rules not from the netherworld but from the *air* between God in heaven and human beings on earth. Both Jew and Gentile have experienced, through Christ, God's free gift of salvation that already marks them for a future heavenly destiny (Eph 2:3–7). The language *dead, raised us up*, and *seated us...in the heavens* closely parallels Jesus' own passion and Easter experience. The terms in Eph 2:8–9 describe salvation in the way Paul elsewhere speaks of justification: *by grace, through faith, the gift of God, not from works*; cf. Gal 2:16–21; Rom 3:24–28. Christians are a newly created people in Christ, fashioned by God for a life of goodness (Eph 2:10).

**2:1–7** These verses comprise one long sentence in Greek, the

main verb coming in Eph 2:5, God *brought us to life*, the object you/us *dead in...transgressions* being repeated in Eph 2:1, 5; cf. Col 2:13.

**2:2** *Age of this world*: or "aeon," a term found in gnostic thought, possibly synonymous with the *rulers of this world*, but also reflecting the Jewish idea of "two ages," this present evil age and "the age to come"; cf. 1 Cor 3:19; 5:10; 7:31; Gal 1:4; Ti 2:12. *The disobedient*: literally, "the sons of disobedience," a Semitism as at Is 30:9.

**2:5** Our relation through baptism *with Christ*, the risen Lord, is depicted in terms of realized eschatology, as already exaltation, though Eph 2:7 brings in the future aspect too.

**2:11–22** The Gentiles lacked Israel's messianic expectation, lacked the various *covenants* God made with *Israel*, lacked *hope* of salvation and knowledge of the true *God* (Eph 2:11–12); but through Christ all these religious barriers between Jew and Gentile have been transcended (Eph 2:13–14) by the abolition of the Mosaic covenant-law (Eph 2:15) for the sake of uniting Jew and Gentile into a single religious community (Eph 2:15–16), imbued with the same holy *Spirit* and worshiping the same *Father* (Eph 2:18). The Gentiles are now included in God's *household* (Eph 2:19) as it arises upon the *foundation* of *apostles* assisted by those endowed with the prophetic gift (Eph 3:5), the preachers of Christ (Eph 2:20; cf. 1 Cor 12:28). With Christ as the *capstone* (Eph 2:20; cf. Is 28:16; Mt 21:42), they are being built into the holy *temple* of God's people where the divine presence dwells (Eph 2:21–22).

**1:16** Col 1:3, 9.
     Col 1:19.
**1:17** 3:14, 16; Col 1:9–10; 1 Jn 5:20.
**2:1** Col 1:21; 2:13.
**2:2** 6:12; Jn 12:31; Col 1:13.
**1:18** 4:4; Col 1:12, 27.
**2:3** Col 3:6–7.
**1:19** 2 Cor 13:4; Col 1:11; 2:12.
**2:5** Rom 5:8; 6:13; Col 2:13.
**1:20** Ps 110:1; Heb 1:3.
**2:6** Rom 8:10–11; Phil 3:20; Col 2:12.
**1:21** Phil 2:9; Col 1:16; 1 Pt 3:22.
**2:7** 1:7.
**1:22** 4:15; Ps 8:7; Mt 28:18; Col 1:18.
**2:8** Rom 3:24; Gal 2:16.
**1:23** 4:10, 12; Rom 12:5; 1 Cor 12:27;
**2:9** 1 Cor 1:29.
**2:10** 4:24; Ti 2:14.

the circumcision, which is done in the flesh by human hands, [12] were at that time without Christ, alienated from the community of Israel† and strangers to the covenants of promise, without hope and without God in the world. * [13] But now in Christ Jesus you who once were far off have become near by the blood of Christ. *

[14] † For he is our peace, he who made both one and broke down the dividing wall of enmity, through his flesh, * [15] abolishing the law with its commandments and legal claims, that he might create in himself one new person† in place of the two, thus establishing peace, * [16] and might reconcile both with God, in one body, through the cross, putting that enmity to death by it. * [17] He came and preached peace to you who were far off and peace to those who were near, * [18] for through him we both have access in one Spirit to the Father. *

[19] So then you are no longer strangers and sojourners, but you are fellow citizens with the holy ones and members of the household of God, * [20] built upon the foundation of the apostles and prophets, * with Christ Jesus himself as the capstone.† [21] Through him the whole structure is held together and grows into a temple sacred in the Lord; * [22] in him you also are being built together into a dwelling place of God in the Spirit. *

## III. WORLD MISSION OF THE CHURCH

**3 Commission to Preach God's Plan.** † [1] Because of this, * I, Paul, a prisoner of Christ† [Jesus] for you Gentiles— [2] if, as I suppose, you have heard of the stewardship† of God's grace that was given to me for your benefit, * [3] [namely, that] the mystery† was made known to me by revelation, as I have written briefly earlier. * [4] When you read this you can understand my insight into the mystery of Christ, [5] which was not made known to human beings in other generations as it has now been revealed to his holy apostles and prophets by the Spirit, * [6] that the Gentiles are coheirs, members of the same body, and copartners in the promise in Christ Jesus through the gospel. *

[7] Of this I became a minister by the gift of God's grace that was granted me in accord with the exercise of his power. * [8] To me, the very least of all the holy ones, this grace was given, to preach to the Gentiles the inscrutable riches of Christ, * [9] and to bring to light [for all]† what is the plan of the mystery hidden from ages past in God who created all things, * [10] so that the manifold wisdom of God might now be made known through the church to the principalities and authorities† in the heavens. * [11] This was according to the eternal purpose that he accomplished in Christ Jesus our

---

2:12 *The community of Israel:* or "commonwealth"; cf. Eph 4:18. *The covenants:* cf. Rom 9:4: with Abraham, with Moses, with David.

2:14–16 The elaborate imagery here combines pictures of Christ as *our peace* (Is 9:5), his crucifixion, the ending of the Mosaic law (cf. Col 2:14), reconciliation (2 Cor 5:18–21), and the destruction of *the dividing wall* such as kept people from God in the temple or a barrier in the heavens.

2:15 *One new person:* a corporate body, the Christian community, made up of Jews and Gentiles, replacing ancient divisions; cf. Rom 1:16.

2:20 *Capstone:* the Greek can also mean cornerstone or keystone.

3:1–13 Paul reflects on his mission to the Gentiles. He alludes to his call and appointment to the apostolic office (Eph 3:2–3) and how his *insight* through revelation, as well as that of the other apostles and charismatic prophets in the church (Eph 3:4–5), has deepened understanding of God's plan of salvation in Christ. Paul is the special herald (Eph 3:7) of a new *promise* to the *Gentiles* (Eph 3:6): that the divine plan includes them in the spiritual benefits promised to Israel. Not only is this unique apostolic role his; Paul also has been given the task of explaining to all the divine *plan* (Eph 3:8–9), once *hidden.* Through *the church,* God's plan to save through Christ is becoming manifest to angelic beings (Eph 3:10; cf. Eph 1:21), in accord with God's *purpose* (Eph 3:11). The fulfillment of the plan in Christ gives the whole church more *confidence* through *faith* in God (Eph 3:12). The readers of this letter are also thereby encouraged to greater confidence despite Paul's imprisonment (Eph 3:13).

3:1 *A prisoner of Christ:* see Introduction. Paul abruptly departs from his train of thought at the end of Eph 3:1, leaving an incomplete sentence.

3:2 *Stewardship:* the Greek is the same term employed at Eph 1:10 for the *plan* that God administers (Col 1:25) and in which Paul plays a key role.

3:3–4 *The mystery:* God's resolve to deliver Gentiles along with Israel through Christ; cf. notes on Eph 1:10; 3:9.

3:9 *[For all]:* while some think this phrase was added so as to yield the sense "to enlighten all about the plan...," it is more likely that some manuscripts and Fathers omitted it accidentally or to avoid the idea that *all* conflicted with Paul's assignment to preach to *the Gentiles* (Eph 3:8) specifically.

3:10 *Principalities and authorities:* see note on Eph 1:15–23 regarding Eph 3:21.

---

| | |
|---|---|
| 2:12 Rom 9:4; Col 1:21, 27. | 3:1 Phil 1:7, 13; Col 1:24–29; 4:18; Phlm 9; 2 Tm 2:9. |
| 2:13 2:17; Is 57:19; Col 1:20. | 3:2 Col 1:25. |
| 2:14 Gal 3:28. | 3:3 1:9–10; Col 1:26. |
| 2:15 2 Cor 5:17; Col 2:14. | 3:5 Col 1:26. |
| 2:16 Col 1:20, 22. | 3:6 2:13, 18–19. |
| 2:17 Is 57:19; Zec 9:10. | 3:7 Rom 15:15; Col 1:25, 29. |
| 2:18 3:12. | |
| 2:19 Heb 12:22–23. | 3:8 1 Cor 15:8–10; Gal 1:16; 2:7–9. |
| 2:20 Is 28:16; Rev 21:14. | |
| 2:21 1 Cor 3:16; Col 2:19. | 3:9 Rom 16:25; Col 1:26–27. |
| 2:22 1 Pt 2:5. | |
| | 3:10 1 Pt 1:12. |

EPH

Lord, 12 in whom we have boldness of speech and confidence of access through faith in him.* 13 So I ask you not to lose heart over my afflictions for you; this is your glory.*

**Prayer for the Readers.**† 14 For this reason I kneel before the Father, 15 from whom every family† in heaven and on earth is named, 16 that he may grant you in accord with the riches of his glory to be strengthened with power through his Spirit in the inner self,* 17 and that Christ may dwell in your hearts through faith; that you, rooted and grounded in love,* 18 may have strength to comprehend with all the holy ones what is the breadth and length and height and depth,* 19 and to know the love of Christ that surpasses knowledge, so that you may be filled with all the fullness of God.*

20 Now to him who is able to accomplish far more than all we ask or imagine, by the power at work within us,* 21 to him be glory in the church and in Christ Jesus to all generations, forever and ever. Amen.

**4** **Unity in the Body.** 1 † I, then, a prisoner for the Lord, urge you to live in a manner worthy of the call you have received,* 2 with all humility and gentleness, with patience, bearing with one another through love,* 3 striving to preserve the unity of the spirit through the

bond of peace:* 4 † one body and one Spirit, as you were also called to the one hope of your call;* 5 one Lord, one faith, one baptism;* 6 one God and Father of all, who is over all and through all and in all.*

**Diversity of Gifts.** 7 But grace was given to each of us according to the measure of Christ's gift.* 8 Therefore, it says:

"He ascended† on high and took
    prisoners captive;
he gave gifts to men."*

9 What does "he ascended" mean except that he also descended into the lower [regions] of the earth? 10 The one who descended is also the one who ascended far above all the heavens, that he might fill all things.

11 † And he gave some as apostles, others as prophets, others as evangelists, others as pastors and teachers,* 12 to equip the holy ones for the work of ministry,† for building up the body of Christ, 13 until we all attain to the unity of faith and knowledge of the Son of God, to mature manhood,† to the extent of the full stature of Christ,* 14 so that we may no longer be infants, tossed by waves and swept along by every wind of teaching arising from human trickery, from their cunning in the interests of deceitful scheming.* 15 Rather, living

---

**3:14–21** The apostle prays that those he is addressing may, like the rest of the church, deepen their understanding of God's plan of salvation in Christ. It is a plan that affects the whole universe (Eph 3:15) with *the breadth and length and height and depth* of God's love in Christ (Eph 3:18) or possibly the universe in all its dimensions. The apostle prays that they may perceive the redemptive love of Christ for them and be completely immersed in the fullness of God (Eph 3:19). The prayer concludes with a doxology to God (Eph 3:20–21).
**3:14–15** *Every family*: in the Greek there is wordplay on the word for *the Father* (*patria, patēr*). The phrase could also mean "God's whole family" (cf. Eph 2:21).
**4:1–16** A general plea for unity in the church. Christians have been fashioned through the *Spirit* into a single harmonious religious community (*one body*, Eph 4:4, 12; cf. Eph 4:16), belonging to a single *Lord* (in contrast to the many gods of the pagan world), and by one way of salvation through *faith*, brought out especially by the significance of *baptism* (Eph 4:1–6; cf. Rom 6:1–11). But Christian unity is more than adherence to a common belief. It is manifested in the exalted Christ's gifts to individuals to serve so as to make the community more Christlike (Eph 4:11–16). This teaching on Christ as the source of the gifts is introduced by a citation of Ps 68:18, which depicts Yahweh triumphantly leading Israel to salvation in Jerusalem. It is here understood of Christ, ascending *above all the heavens*, the *head* of the church; through his redemptive death, resurrection, and ascension he has become the source of the church's spiritual gifts. The "descent" of Christ (Eph 4:9–10) refers more probably to the incarnation (cf. Phil 2:6–8) than to Christ's presence after his death in the world of the dead (cf. 1 Pt 3:19).

**4:4–6** The "seven unities" (church, *Spirit*, hope; *Lord*, *faith* in Christ [Eph 1:13], *baptism*; *one God*) reflect the triune structure of later creeds in reverse.
**4:8–10** While the emphasis is on an ascension and gift-giving by Christ, there is also a reference in taking *prisoners captive* to the aeons and powers mentioned at Eph 1:21; 2:2; 3:10; 6:12.
**4:11** Concerning this list of ministers, cf. 1 Cor 12:28 and Rom 12:6–8. *Evangelists*: missionary preachers (cf. Acts 21:8; 2 Tm 4:5), not those who wrote gospels. *Pastors and teachers*: a single group in the Greek, shepherding congregations.
**4:12** The ministerial leaders in Eph 4:11 are to equip the whole people of God for their *work of ministry*.
**4:13** *Mature manhood*: literally, "a perfect man" (cf. Col 1:28), possibly the "one new person" of Eph 2:15, though there *anthrōpos* suggests humanity, while here *anēr* is the term for male. This personage becomes visible in the church's growing to its fullness in the unity of those who believe in Christ.

---

| | |
|---|---|
| **3:12** Rom 5:1–2; Heb 4:16. | **4:3** Col 3:14–15. |
| **3:13** Col 1:22, 24; 2 Tm 2:10. | **4:4** Rom 12:5; 1 Cor 10:17; 12:12–13. |
| **3:16** 6:10; Rom 7:22; 2 Cor 4:16; Col 1:11. | **4:5** 1 Cor 8:6. |
| **3:17** Jn 14:23; Col 1:23; 2:7. | **4:6** 1 Cor 12:6. |
| | **4:7** Rom 12:3, 6; 1 Cor 12:28. |
| **3:18** Col 2:2. | **4:8** Ps 68:19; Col 2:15. |
| **3:19** Col 2:3, 9. | **4:11** 1 Cor 12:28. |
| **3:20** Rom 16:25–27; Col 1:29. | **4:13** Col 1:28. |
| **4:1** 3:1; Col 1:10. | **4:14** 1 Cor 14:20; Col 2:4, 8; Heb 13:9; Jas 1:6. |
| **4:2** Col 3:12–13. | |

the truth in love, we should grow in every way into him who is the head,* Christ,† ¹⁶from whom the whole body, joined and held together by every supporting ligament, with the proper functioning of each part, brings about the body's growth and builds itself up in love.*

**Renewal in Christ.†** ¹⁷So I declare and testify in the Lord that you must no longer live as the Gentiles do, in the futility of their minds;* ¹⁸darkened in understanding, alienated from the life of God because of their ignorance, because of their hardness of heart,* ¹⁹they have become callous and have handed themselves over to licentiousness for the practice of every kind of impurity to excess.* ²⁰That is not how you learned Christ, ²¹assuming that you have heard of him and were taught in him, as truth is in Jesus, ²²that you should put away the old self of your former way of life, corrupted through deceitful desires,* ²³and be renewed in the spirit of your minds,* ²⁴and put on† the new self, created in God's way in righteousness and holiness of truth.*

## IV. DAILY CONDUCT, AN EXPRESSION OF UNITY†

**Rules for the New Life.** ²⁵Therefore, putting away falsehood, speak the truth, each one to his neighbor, for we are members one of another.* ²⁶Be angry but do not sin;* do not let the sun set on your anger,† ²⁷and do not leave room for the devil.* ²⁸The thief must no longer steal, but rather labor, doing honest work† with his [own] hands, so that he may have something to share with one in need.*

²⁹No foul language should come out of your mouths, but only such as is good for needed edification, that it may impart grace to those who hear.* ³⁰And do not grieve the holy Spirit of God, with which you were sealed for the day of redemption.† ³¹All bitterness, fury, anger, shouting, and reviling must be removed from you, along with all malice.* ³²[And] be kind to one another, compassionate, forgiving one another as God has forgiven you in Christ.*

**5** ¹So be imitators of God,† as beloved children,* ²and live in love, as Christ loved us and handed himself over for us as a sacrificial offering to God for a fragrant aroma.* ³Immorality or any impurity or greed must not even be mentioned among you, as is fitting among holy ones,* ⁴no obscenity or silly or suggestive talk, which is out of place, but instead, thanksgiving.* ⁵Be sure of this, that no immoral or impure or greedy person, that is, an idolater, has any inheritance in the kingdom of Christ and of God.*

**Duty to Live in the Light.** ⁶*Let no one deceive you with empty arguments, for because of these things the wrath of God is coming upon the disobedient.† ⁷So do not be associated with them. ⁸For you were once darkness, but now you are light in the Lord. Live as children of light,* ⁹for light produces every kind of goodness and righteousness and truth.* ¹⁰Try to learn what is pleasing to the Lord.* ¹¹Take no part in the fruitless works of darkness; rather expose them,* ¹²for it is shameful even to mention the things done by them in secret;

---

**4:15–16** *The head, Christ*: cf. Col 1:18 and contrast 1 Cor 12:12–27 and Rom 12:4–5 where Christ is identified with the whole body, including the head. The imagery may derive from ancient views in medicine, the *head* coordinating and caring for the body, each *ligament* (perhaps the ministers of Eph 4:11) supporting the whole. But as at Eph 2:19–22, where the temple is depicted as a growing organism, there may also be the idea here of growing toward the capstone, Christ.

**4:17–24** Paul begins to indicate how the new life in Christ contrasts with the Gentiles' old way of existence. Literally, *the old self* (Eph 4:22) and *the new self* (Eph 4:24) are "the old man" and "the new man" (*anthrōpos*, person), as at Eph 2:15; cf. note on Eph 4:13.

**4:24** *Put on*: in baptism. See note on Gal 3:27.

**4:25–6:20** For similar exhortations to a morally good life in response to God's gift of faith, see notes on Rom 12:1–13:14 and Gal 5:13–26.

**4:26** If angry, seek reconciliation that day, not giving the devil (Eph 6:11) opportunity to lead into sin.

**4:28** *Honest work*: literally, "the good." *His [own] hands*: some manuscripts have the full phrase as in 1 Cor 4:12.

**4:30** See note on Eph 1:13.

**5:1** *Imitators of God*: in forgiving (Eph 4:32) and in loving (as exhibited in how *Christ loved us*).

**5:6** See note on Eph 2:2.

---

**4:15** 1 Cor 11:3; Col 1:18; 2:19.
**4:16** Col 2:19.
**4:17** Rom 1:21.
**4:18** Col 1:21; 1 Pt 1:14.
**4:19** Col 3:5.
**4:22** Rom 8:13; Gal 6:8; Col 3:9.
**4:23** Rom 12:2.
**4:24** Gn 1:26–27; Col 3:10.
**4:25** Zec 8:16.
**4:26** Ps 4:5 LXX; Mt 5:22.
**4:27** 2 Cor 2:11.
**4:28** 1 Thes 4:11.
**4:29** 5:4; Col 3:16; 4:6.
**4:31** Col 3:8.
**4:32** Mt 6:14; Col 3:12–13.
**5:1** Mt 5:45, 48.
**5:2** Ex 29:18; Ps 40:7; Gal 2:20; 1 Jn 3:16.
**5:3** Gal 5:19; Col 3:5.
**5:4** 4:29; Col 3:8.
**5:5** 1 Cor 6:9–10; Gal 5:21; Col 3:5.
**5:6** Rom 1:18; Col 2:4, 8.
**5:8** 2:11–13; Jn 12:36; Col 1:12–13.
**5:9** Gal 5:22.
**5:10** Rom 12:2.
**5:11** Rom 13:12.

¹³but everything exposed by the light becomes visible,* ¹⁴for everything that becomes visible is light. Therefore, it says:*

"Awake, O sleeper,
    and arise from the dead,
    and Christ will give you light."†

¹⁵† Watch carefully then how you live, not as foolish persons but as wise,* ¹⁶making the most of the opportunity, because the days are evil. ¹⁷Therefore, do not continue in ignorance, but try to understand what is the will of the Lord. ¹⁸And do not get drunk on wine, in which lies debauchery, but be filled with the Spirit,* ¹⁹addressing one another [in] psalms and hymns and spiritual songs, singing and playing to the Lord in your hearts,* ²⁰giving thanks always and for everything in the name of our Lord Jesus Christ to God the Father.*

**Wives and Husbands.** ²¹† Be subordinate to one another* out of reverence for Christ.† ²²Wives should be subordinate to their husbands as to the Lord.* ²³For the husband is head of his wife just as Christ is head of the church, he himself the savior of the body.* ²⁴As the church is subordinate to Christ, so wives should be subordinate to their husbands in everything. ²⁵Husbands, love your wives, even as Christ loved the church and handed himself over for her* ²⁶to sanctify her, cleansing her by the bath of water with the word,* ²⁷that he might present to himself the church in splendor, without spot or wrinkle or any such thing, that she might be holy and without blemish.* ²⁸So [also] husbands should love their wives as their own bodies. He who

loves his wife loves himself. ²⁹For no one hates his own flesh but rather nourishes and cherishes it, even as Christ does the church, ³⁰because we are members of his body.*

³¹    "For this reason a man shall leave [his]
        father and [his] mother
        and be joined to his wife,
        and the two shall become one flesh."*

³²This is a great mystery, but I speak in reference to Christ and the church.* ³³In any case, each one of you should love his wife as himself, and the wife should respect her husband.

**6** **Children and Parents.** ¹Children, obey your parents [in the Lord], for this is right.* ²"Honor your father and mother."* This is the first commandment with a promise, ³"that it may go well with you and that you may have a long life on earth." ⁴Fathers, do not provoke your children to anger, but bring them up with the training and instruction of the Lord.*

**Slaves and Masters.** ⁵Slaves, be obedient to your human masters with fear and trembling, in sincerity of heart, as to Christ,* ⁶not only when being watched, as currying favor, but as slaves of Christ, doing the will of God from the heart,* ⁷willingly serving the Lord and not human beings, ⁸knowing that each will be requited from the Lord for whatever good he does, whether he is slave or free. ⁹Masters, act in the same way toward them, and stop bullying, knowing that both they and you have a Master in heaven and that with him there is no partiality.*

---

† **5:14** An early Christian hymn, possibly from a baptismal liturgy. For the content compare Eph 2:5–6; 3:9 and Is 60:1.
**5:15–16, 19–20** The wording is similar to Col 4:5 and Eph 3:16–17.
**5:21–6:9** Cf. notes on Col 3:18–4:1 and 1 Pt 2:18–3:7 for a similar listing of household duties where the inferior is admonished first (*wives*, Eph 5:22; *children*, Eph 6:1; *slaves*, Eph 6:5), then the superior (*husbands*, Eph 5:25; *fathers*, Eph 6:4; *masters*, Eph 6:9). Paul varies this pattern by an emphasis on mutuality (see Eph 5:20); use of Old Testament material about *father and mother* in Eph 6:2; the judgment to come for slave-owners (*you have a Master in heaven*, Eph 6:9); and above all the initial principle of subordination *to one another* under *Christ*, thus effectively undermining exclusive claims to domination by one party. Into the section on *wives* and *husbands* an elaborate teaching on *Christ* and *the church* has been woven (Eph 5:22–33).
**5:21–33** The apostle exhorts married Christians to a strong mutual love. Holding with Gn 2:24 that marriage is a divine institution (Eph 5:31), Paul sees Christian marriage as taking on a new meaning symbolic of the intimate relationship of love between

Christ and the church. The wife should serve her husband in the same spirit as that of the church's service to Christ (Eph 5:22, 24), and the husband should care for his wife with the devotion of Christ to the church (Eph 5:25–30). Paul gives to the Genesis passage its highest meaning in the light of the union of Christ and the church, of which Christlike loyalty and devotion in Christian marriage are a clear reflection (Eph 5:31–33).

**5:13** Jn 3:20–21.
**5:14** Is 26:19; 60:1.
**5:15–16** Col 4:5.
**5:18** Prv 23:31 LXX; Lk 21:34.
**5:19** Ps 33:2–3; Col 3:16.
**5:20** Col 3:17.
**5:21** 1 Pt 5:5.
**5:22** Col 3:18–4:1; 1 Pt 3:1–7.
**5:23** 1 Cor 11:3; Col 1:18.
**5:25** Col 3:19; 1 Tm 2:6.
**5:26** Rom 6:4; Ti 3:5–7.
**5:27** 2 Cor 11:2; Col 1:22.
**5:30** Rom 12:5; 1 Cor 6:15.
**5:31** Gn 2:24; Mt 19:5; Mk 10:7–8.
**5:32** Rev 19:7.
**6:1** Prv 6:20; Sir 3:1–6; Col 3:20.
**6:2–3** Ex 20:12; Dt 5:16.
**6:4** Col 3:21–22.
**6:5** Col 3:22–25; 1 Tm 6:1–2; Ti 2:9–10.
**6:6** 1 Pt 2:18.
**6:9** Col 4:1.

**Battle Against Evil.** [10]† Finally, draw your strength from the Lord and from his mighty power. [11] Put on the armor of God so that you may be able to stand firm against the tactics of the devil.* [12] For our struggle is not with flesh and blood but with the principalities, with the powers, with the world rulers of this present darkness, with the evil spirits in the heavens.* [13] Therefore, put on the armor of God, that you may be able to resist on the evil day and, having done everything, to hold your ground.* [14] So stand fast with your loins girded in truth, clothed with righteousness as a breastplate,* [15] and your feet shod in readiness for the gospel of peace.* [16] In all circumstances, hold faith as a shield, to quench all [the] flaming arrows of the evil one.* [17] And take the helmet of salvation and the sword of the Spirit, which is the word of God.*

**Constant Prayer.** [18] With all prayer and supplication, pray at every opportunity in the Spirit.

To that end, be watchful with all perseverance and supplication for all the holy ones* [19] and also for me, that speech may be given me to open my mouth, to make known with boldness the mystery of the gospel* [20] for which I am an ambassador in chains, so that I may have the courage to speak as I must.*

## V. CONCLUSION

**A Final Message.**† [21] So that you also may have news of me and of what I am doing, Tychicus, my beloved brother and trustworthy minister in the Lord, will tell you everything.* [22] I am sending him to you for this very purpose, so that you may know about us and that he may encourage your hearts.*

[23] Peace be to the brothers, and love with faith, from God the Father and the Lord Jesus Christ. [24] Grace be with all who love our Lord Jesus Christ in immortality.*

---

† **6:10–20** A general exhortation to courage and prayer. Drawing upon the imagery and ideas of Is 11:5; 59:16–17; and Wis 5:17–23, Paul describes the Christian in terms of the dress and equipment of Roman soldiers. He observes, however, that the Christian's readiness for combat is not directed against human beings but against the spiritual powers of evil (Eph 6:10–17; cf. Eph 1:21; 2:2; 3:10). Unique importance is placed upon prayer (Eph 6:18–20).

**6:21–24** *Tychicus*: the bearer of the letter; see note on Col 4:7. Eph 6:21–22 parallel Col 4:7–8, often word for word. If Ephesians is addressed to several Christian communities (see

Introduction), it is understandable that no greetings to individual members of these communities should have been included in it.

---

*

| | |
|---|---|
| **6:11** Rom 13:12; 2 Cor 6:7; 10:4; Jas 4:7. | **6:18** Mt 26:41; Col 4:2–3. |
| **6:12** 1:21; 2:2; Col 1:13. | **6:19** Acts 4:29; Col 4:3; 2 Thes 3:1. |
| **6:13** Rom 13:12. | **6:20** 2 Cor 5:20; Col 4:4. |
| **6:14** Wis 5:17–20; Is 11:5; Lk 12:35; 1 Thes 5:8. | **6:21** Acts 20:4; Col 4:7; 2 Tm 4:12. |
| **6:15** Is 52:7. | **6:22** Col 4:8. |
| **6:16** 1 Pt 5:9. | **6:24** 1 Pt 1:8. |
| **6:17** Is 59:17; 1 Thes 5:8. | |

E
P
H

# The Letter to the
# Philippians

## INTRODUCTION

### Tatha Wiley

The Letter of Paul to the Philippians is commonly dated after his Letter to the Galatians, which is thought to have been written in the early fifties of the first century CE. Because Philippians so clearly shares features of the so-called undisputed letters—expectation of the day of the Lord (Phil 1:6), hope for resurrection (3:11), experience of the Spirit (3:3)—the letter has generated little doubt that its author is Paul. It is a warm, friendly letter to an assembly of believers with whom Paul is on comfortable terms and who have done much for him. He is not afraid to show his desire to be with them, "how I long for all of you" (1:8), nor his uncertainty about continuing his own life (1:22).

There is a lingering question among biblical scholars whether the text we have was originally a single letter or a composite of several fragments of letters. If the former, it reflects one place and time in Paul's relationship to the assembly. But if it is a composite, the original letters would reflect different times, situations, and possibly places. Are there clues for the latter?

Helmut Koester argues there are such clues; for example, two sentences that are conclusions in form and should end the letter (Phil 3:1; 4:9) are then followed by new topics. In another example Koester cites, Epaphroditus is noted in 4:18 as the bearer of a gift of money from the Philippians, but already in 2:25 Paul had introduced him in the text, expressing the need to send Epaphroditus back to Philippi because he had been very sick. [1]

The third example is a section that fits oddly with the rest. In a sudden angry outburst, Paul exclaims, "Beware of the dogs! Beware of the evil workers! Beware of the mutilation!" (Phil 3:2). This harsh language does not fit with

---

## Outline of Philippians

---

the rest of the letter. If this is one letter, is this part original to it? Is it a fragment from another letter? For Paul to call people "dogs" is shocking. So, too, for a Jew like Paul to refer to circumcision, the sign of the covenant given to Abraham (Gn 17:10)—by God, no less, as a mutilation is shocking as well. If it is Paul, such polemical language reflects the threat that these other evangelists posed to him. He redefines Israel as the Spirit-filled Gentile assembly of Christ-believers (Phil 3:3).

The literary question, however, remains unresolved. The disjointed nature of the letter could point simply to different reactions to topics as Paul wrote or it could be that several fragments of letters have been pieced together and presented as one letter. [2]

---

1. Helmut Koester, *Paul and His World: Interpreting the New Testament in Context* (Minneapolis: Fortress Press, 2007), 73–74.

2. For a view that stresses the rhetorical arguments for unity, see Carolyn Osiek, *Philippians and Philemon,* Abingdon New Testament Commentaries (Nashville: Abingdon Press, 2000).

PHIL

That Paul was imprisoned when he wrote to the Philippian assembly is evident from the several references he makes (Phil 1:7, 12–17). But where he was in prison remains unknown. It was once thought that the "praetorium" (1:13), the imperial guard he mentions, must be housed in Rome with the emperor; so Paul was in Rome. But now scholars know that the praetorium could be any place that represented imperial power, not just with the emperor and not just in Rome. Paul could have been imprisoned in any number of places.

Paul integrates what is thought to be a liturgical hymn at Phil 2:6–11. He may have written it, but the scholarly consensus is that the hymn predates his letter and that he uses it rather than writes it. Much can be made of the hymn. It shows, for instance, that the early Jesus-followers were not restricted to the concept of resurrection in conceiving of God's vindication of Jesus after his death. This hymn represents a distinct tradition. Jesus is exalted rather than resurrected (2:9). Exaltation and resurrection are different, but Paul goes easily back and forth between them as forms of validation.

The hymn offers Paul a contrast and a parallel. The contrast is between the values of Christ and the values of the ancient world. In the hierarchically-structured world of the first century, honor was all-important. Honor implied power. The hymn suggests that Christ's status would carry honor, but he did not choose it. He took on the form of the lowest of the low in the social order. A slave was so marginalized as to be a nonperson (Phil 2:7).[3] While a slave, functioning as his master's administrator, for example, could share his master's status, he was still an owned being, still subject to all the vulnerabilities of one enslaved—sexual use, being bought and sold, beaten, tortured, killed. Orlando Patterson defines slavery as total powerlessness: "Slavery is one of the most extreme forms of the relation of domination, approaching the limits of total power from the viewpoint of the master and of total powerlessness from the viewpoint of the slave."[4]

From whatever community this hymn came, one can presume that there were slaves among the members, as slavery was ubiquitous in the Greco-Roman world. The hymn is self-affirming: *Jesus identified with us*. To start with this would make for a distinctive theology of incarnation indeed. An ancient person, convinced of the intrinsic relation between honor and power, would be deeply perplexed by God's exaltation of one without honor—one who dies as a criminal—and power. Yet in the end, the power that Jesus receives is what an emperor could only hope for:

> Because of this, God greatly exalted him and bestowed on him the name that is above every name, that at the name of Jesus every knee should bend, of those in heaven and on earth and under the earth, and every tongue confess that Jesus Christ is Lord, to the glory of God the Father. (Phil 2:9–11)

Paul draws a parallel between himself and the Philippian believers. They both suffer for Christ and share in the same struggle (Phil 1:29–30). Paul imitates Christ, and the assembly imitates Paul (3:17). He assures them that their obedience guarantees God's presence: "Keep on doing what you have learned and received and heard and seen in me. Then the God of peace will be with you" (4:9). They are to conduct themselves according to the model they have in him (3:17). They complete his joy, he says, "by being of the same mind, with the same love, united in heart, thinking one thing" (2:2). "Sameness" is positive in this context: they are to have "the same mind within themselves that Christ Jesus had, the mind that will lead them to think of the interests of others rather than of themselves and their own interests."[5]

But "sameness" implies complete agreement. What if a person did not share complete agreement with Paul? What if she or he understood the gospel differently?[6] Such questions are not allowed. Paul had eliminated debate early on: "Do everything without grumbling or questioning" (Phil 2:14). Otherwise, he implies, there is divisiveness (1:27). He divides

---

3. The term is Orlando Patterson's. See his *Slavery and Social Death* (Cambridge: Harvard University Press, 1982), 1.

4. Ibid.

5. A. Katherine Grieb, "Philippians and the Politics of God," *Interpretation* 61 no. 3 (July 2007): 256–69, at 267.

6. Joseph A. Marchal, "Imperial Intersections and Initial Inquiries: Toward a Feminist, Postcolonial Analysis of Philippians," *Journal of Feminist Studies in Religion* 22 no. 2 (2006): 5–32.

people into two groups. Some, he says, "proclaim the word fearlessly" (1:14). But others, unnamed opponents, he describes in very negative terms. They preach Christ from envy and rivalry (1:15), proclaim Christ out of selfish ambition (1:17), and are "enemies of the cross of Christ" (3:18).

What "enemies of the cross of Christ" could mean is truly perplexing. An explanation may be found in the reference to those who preach Christ from envy (Phil 1:15), explored from the perspective of the meaning of envy in the ancient world. Envy occurs in people who share the same kind of work. Calling oneself a victim of envy draws attention to the good that one possesses and that others want. "We [moderns] emphasize that aspect of envy which desires to possess what someone else has, while the envious person in antiquity wished even more that the possessor be stripped of the valued object. This evil wish turned the envious person into an enemy."[7] Alluding to envy allowed Paul indirectly to refer to his success in preaching the gospel in prison.

Paul does not say exactly how he is being opposed by these figures he describes in such derogatory terms. One can presume that they, too, are Christ believers since they are preaching Christ. They could be Jewish believers, given Paul's later redefinition of the covenant of Israel as the charismatic assembly, "We are the circumcision, we who worship through the Spirit of God . . ." (Phil 3:3). But Paul's allusions to "your opponents" (1:28), to the Philippians' suffering (1:29), and to their struggle (1:30) suggests that they are experiencing opposition from outside as well.

Contemporary interest in Paul's relation to the Roman Empire has produced much of value in this regard. Israel had a long history of suffering conquest and foreign rule and a long tradition of resistance against those who ruled over them. Seeing the eschatological expectations and hopes from the Israelite tradition as a "strategy of resistance," the Christ-hymn in Phil 2:6–11 seems to stand in that tradition and

to exemplify resistance literature at its finest.[8] Paul appropriates and then reverses imperial terms and imagery, positioning the one put to death by the empire as "Lord" (2:11). The emperor is Lord. Paul writes that "at the name of Jesus every knee should bend," but in the imperial order it is to the emperor that all have the obligation to kneel. Now it is Jesus, rather than the emperor, whose name is "above every name."

Extending honor to Jesus even further, Paul uses the hymn's merism, a figure of speech that evokes everything or totality: every knee should bend "of those in heaven and on earth and under the earth" (Phil 2:10). That God would raise from the dead one crucified by the empire subverts imperial claims of power. In a triumphant note, Paul writes that Christ will "bring all things into subjection to himself" (3:21)—"all things" meaning imperial powers, too.

In addition, by establishing a number of Christ assemblies, Paul in effect established a resistance network. He gave them ethical instruction cast in eschatological terms: "Discern what is of value, so that you may be pure and blameless for the day of Christ" (Phil 1:10). He also forbade the worship of idols, a prohibition not only of local deities but also of the imperial cult. Beginning with Octavian Augustus, the first emperor to follow the Roman dictator Julius Caesar, emperors were divinized at their deaths.

In fact, Paul appropriated the whole imperial vocabulary. He put Jesus in a competition that relegated the emperor to the realm of the finite while giving Jesus the cosmos. Resistance language runs throughout the undisputed letters. Even Paul's conviction that Christ "will change our lowly body to conform with his glorified body" is cast in imperial language; this change will be made "by the power that enables him [i.e., Christ] also to bring all things into subjection to himself" (Phil 3:21). Paul's own reference to doing things "for your benefit" (1:24) and "for your progress" (1:25) echoes

---

7. David E. Fredrickson, "Envious Enemies of the Cross of Christ (Philippians 3:18)," *Word & World* 28 no. 1 (Winter 2008), 22–8, at 24.

8. Abraham Smith, "Unmasking the Powers: Toward a Postcolonial Analysis of 1 Thessalonians," in *Paul and the Roman Imperial Order*, ed. Richard A. Horsley (Harrisburg, PA: Trinity Press International, 2004), 47–66, at 53.

the empire's descriptions of the benefits to those it defeats and the progress it brings them. Imperial authorities would be quite at home with Paul's directive against questioning (2:14).

But the employment of imperial terms was not without cost. Paul constructed his resistance strategy almost as a parody of imperial power by picking up imperial terms for one who, in the words of the hymn, "emptied himself, taking the form of a slave" (Phil 2:7). But

it was not the image of a powerless slave that was of lasting influence for the tradition to come. It is of the powerful Lord of the cosmos who makes everything subject to himself. It is the image of the triumphal Christ that is most deeply influential in the subsequent tradition. The powerless Jesus, however, does not entirely disappear. Those who know powerlessness first-hand—like the slaves in the Philippian congregation—will also celebrate him. ■

P
H
I
L

# THE LETTER TO THE PHILIPPIANS

## New American Bible, Introduction

Philippi, in northeastern Greece, was a city of some importance in the Roman province of Macedonia. Lying on the great road from the Adriatic coast to Byzantium, the Via Egnatia, and in the midst of rich agricultural plains near the gold deposits of Mt. Pangaeus, it was in Paul's day a Roman town (Acts 16:21), with a Greek-Macedonian population and a small group of Jews (see Acts 16:13). Originally founded in the sixth century B.C. as Krenides by the Thracians, the town was taken over after 360 B.C. by Philip II of Macedon, the father of Alexander the Great, and was renamed for himself, "Philip's City." The area became Roman in the second century B.C. On the plains near Philippi in October 42 B.C., Antony and Octavian decisively defeated the forces of Brutus and Cassius, the slayers of Julius Caesar. Octavian (Augustus) later made Philippi a Roman colony and settled many veterans of the Roman armies there.

Paul, according to Acts (Acts 16:9–40), established at Philippi the first Christian community in Europe. He came to Philippi, via its harbor town of Neapolis (modern Kavalla), on his second missionary journey, probably in A.D. 49 or 50, accompanied by Silas and Timothy (Acts 15:40; 16:3; cf. Phil 1:1) and Luke, if he is to be included in the "we" references of Acts 16:10–17. The Acts account tells of the conversion of a business woman, Lydia; the exorcism of a slave girl; and, after an earthquake, while Paul and Silas were imprisoned in Philippi, the faith and baptism of a jailer and his family. None of these persons, however, is directly mentioned in Philippians (cf. the notes on Phil 4:2 and Phil 4:3). Acts 16 concludes its account by describing how Paul (and Silas), asked by the magistrates to leave Philippi, went on to Thessalonica (Acts 17:1–10), where several times his loyal Philippians continued to support him with financial aid (Phil 4:16). Later, Paul may have passed through Philippi on his way from Ephesus to Greece (Acts 20:1–2), and he definitely stopped there on his fateful trip to Jerusalem (Acts 20:6).

Paul's letter to the Christians at Philippi was written while he was in a prison somewhere (Phil 1:7, 13, 14, 17), indeed in danger of death (Phil 1:20–23). Although under guard for preaching Christ, Paul rejoices at the continuing progress of the gospel (Phil 1:12–26) and expresses gratitude for the Philippians' renewed concern and help in an expression of thanks most clearly found at Phil 4:10–20. Much of the letter is devoted to instruction about unity and humility within the Christian community at Philippi (Phil 1:27–2:18) and exhortations to growth, joy, and peace in their life together (Phil 4:1–9). The letter seems to be drawing to a close at the end of what we number as Phil 2, as Paul reports the plans of his helper Timothy and of Epaphroditus (whom the Philippians had sent to aid Paul) to come to Philippi (Phil 2:19–3:1), and even Paul's own expectation that he will go free and come to Philippi (Phil 1:25–26; 2:24). Yet quite abruptly at Phil 3:2, Paul erupts into warnings against false teachers who threaten to impose on the Philippians the burdens of the Mosaic law, including circumcision. The section that follows, Phil 3:2–21, is a vigorous attack on these Judaizers (cf. Gal 2:11–3:29) or Jewish Christian teachers (cf. 2 Cor 11:12–23), giving us insights into Paul's own life story (Phil 3:4–6) and into the doctrine of justification, the Christian life, and ultimate hope (Phil 3:7–21).

The location of Paul's imprisonment when he wrote to the Philippians, and thus the date of the letter, are uncertain. The traditional view has been that it stems from Paul's confinement in Rome, between A.D. 59 and 63 (cf. Acts 28:14–31). One modern view suggests the period when he was imprisoned at Caesarea, on the coast of Palestine, A.D. 57 or 58 (Acts 23:23–26:32); another suggests Corinth (cf. 2 Cor 11:9). Much recent scholarship favors Ephesus, around A.D. 55, a situation referred to in 2 Cor 1:8 concerning "the affliction that came to us" in Asia Minor (cf. also 1 Cor 15:32). The reference at Phil 1:13 to the "praetorium" (cf. also Phil 4:22) can be understood to mean the imperial guard or government house at Ephesus (or Caesarea), or the praetorian camp in Rome. Involved in a decision are the several journeys back and forth between Philippi and wherever Paul is imprisoned, mentioned in the letter (Phil 2:25–28; 4:14); this factor causes many to prefer Ephesus because of its proximity to Philippi. The Ephesian hypothesis dates the composition of Philippians to the mid-50s when most of Paul's major letters were written.

There is also a likelihood, according to some scholars, that the letter as we have it is a composite from parts of three letters by Paul to the Philippians. Seemingly Phil 4:10–20 is a brief note of appreciation for help sent through Epaphroditus. The long section from Phil 1:3 to Phil 3:1 is then another letter, with news of Paul's imprisonment and reports on Timothy and Epaphroditus (who has fallen ill while with Paul), along with exhortations to the Philippians about Christian conduct; and Phil 3:2–21 a third communication warning about threats to Philippian Christianity. The other verses in Phil 4 and Phil 1:1–2, are variously assigned by critics to these three underlying letters, which an editor presumably put together to produce a picture of Paul writing earnestly from prison (Phil 1–2), facing opponents of the faith (Phil 3), and with serene joy advising and thanking his Philippians (Phil 4). If all four chapters were originally a unity, then one must assume that a break occurred between the writing of Phil 3:1 and Phil 3:2, possibly involving the receipt of bad news from Philippi, and that Paul had some reasons for delaying his words of thanks for the aid brought by Epaphroditus till the end of his letter.

This beautiful letter is rich in insights into Paul's theology and his apostolic love and concern for the gospel and his converts. In Philippians, Paul reveals his human sensitivity and tenderness, his enthusiasm for Christ as the key to life and death (Phil 1:21), and his deep feeling for those in Christ who dwell in Philippi. With them he shares his hopes and convictions, his anxieties and fears, revealing the total confidence in Christ that constitutes faith (Phil 3:8–10). The letter incorporates a hymn about the salvation that God has brought about through Christ (Phil 2:6–11), applied by Paul to the relations of Christians with one another (Phil 2:1–5). Philippians has been termed "the letter of joy" (Phil 4:4, 10). It is the rejoicing of faith, based on true understanding of Christ's unique role in the salvation of all who profess his lordship (Phil 2:11; 3:8–12, 14, 20–21).

The principal divisions of the Letter to the Philippians are the following:

I. Address (1:1–11)
II. Progress of the Gospel (1:12–26)
III. Instructions for the Community (1:27–2:18)
IV. Travel Plans of Paul and His Assistants (2:19–3:1)
V. Polemic: Righteousness and the Goal in Christ (3:2–21)
VI. Instructions for the Community (4:1–9)
VII. Gratitude for the Philippians' Generosity (4:10–20)
VIII. Farewell (4:21–23)

# PHILIPPIANS

## I. ADDRESS

**1** **Greeting.**† ¹Paul and Timothy, slaves† of Christ Jesus, to all the holy ones in Christ Jesus who are in Philippi, with the overseers and ministers: * ² * grace to you and peace from God our Father and the Lord Jesus Christ. †

**Thanksgiving.**† ³I give thanks to my God at every remembrance of you, * ⁴praying always with joy in my every prayer for all of you, ⁵because of your partnership for the gospel from the first day until now. ⁶ * I am confident of this, that the one who began a good work in you will continue to complete it until the day of Christ Jesus. † ⁷It is right that I should think this way about all of you, because I hold you in my heart, you who are all partners with me in grace, both in my imprisonment and in the defense and confirmation of the gospel. ⁸For God is my witness, how I long for all of you

with the affection of Christ Jesus. * ⁹And this is my prayer: that your love may increase ever more and more in knowledge and every kind of perception, * ¹⁰to discern what is of value, so that you may be pure and blameless for the day of Christ, * ¹¹filled with the fruit of righteousness that comes through Jesus Christ for the glory and praise of God. *

## II. PROGRESS OF THE GOSPEL†

¹² * I want you to know, brothers, that my situation has turned out rather to advance the gospel, ¹³so that my imprisonment has become well known in Christ throughout the whole praetorium† and to all the rest, * ¹⁴† and so that the majority of the brothers, having taken encouragement in the Lord from my imprisonment, dare more than ever to proclaim the word fearlessly.

¹⁵Of course, some preach Christ from envy and rivalry, others from good will. ¹⁶The latter act out of love, aware that I am here for the defense of the gospel; ¹⁷the former proclaim Christ out of selfish ambition, not from pure motives, thinking that they will cause me trouble in my imprisonment. ¹⁸What difference

---

† **1:1–2** See note on Rom 1:1–7, concerning the greeting.

**1:1** *Slaves*: Paul usually refers to himself at the start of a letter as an apostle. Here he substitutes a term suggesting the unconditional obligation of himself and Timothy to the service of Christ, probably because, in view of the good relationship with the Philippians, he wishes to stress his status as a co-servant rather than emphasize his apostolic authority. Reference to Timothy is a courtesy: Paul alone writes the letter, as the singular verb throughout shows (Phil 1:3–26), and the reference (Phil 2:19–24) to Timothy in the third person. *Overseers*: the Greek term *episkopos* literally means "one who oversees" or "one who supervises," but since the second century it has come to designate the "bishop," the official who heads a local church. In New Testament times this office had not yet developed into the form that it later assumed, though it seems to be well on the way to such development in the Pastorals; see 1 Tm 3:2 and Ti 1:7, where it is translated bishop. At Philippi, however (and at Ephesus, according to Acts 20:28), there was more than one *episkopos*, and the precise function of these officials is uncertain. In order to distinguish this office from the later stages into which it developed, the term is here translated as *overseers*. *Ministers*: the Greek term *diakonoi* is used frequently in the New Testament to designate "servants," "attendants," or "ministers." Paul refers to himself and to other apostles as "ministers of God" (2 Cor 6:4) or "ministers of Christ" (2 Cor 11:23). In the Pastorals (1 Tm 3:8, 12) the *diakonos* has become an established official in the local church; hence the term is there translated as *deacon*. The *diakonoi* at Philippi seem to represent an earlier stage of development of the office; we are uncertain about their precise functions. Hence the term is here translated as *ministers*. See Rom 16:1, where Phoebe is described as a *diakonos* (minister) of the church of Cenchreae.

**1:2** The gifts come *from* Christ the Lord, not simply through him from the Father; compare the christology in Phil 2:6–11.

**1:3–11** As in Rom 1:8–15 and all the Pauline letters except Galatians, a thanksgiving follows, including a direct prayer for

the Philippians (Phil 1:9–11); see note on Rom 1:8. On their *partnership for the gospel* (Phil 1:5), cf. Phil 1:29–30; 4:10–20. Their devotion to the faith and to Paul made them his pride and joy (Phil 4:1). The characteristics thus manifested are evidence of the community's continuing preparation for the Lord's parousia (Phil 1:6, 10). Paul's especially warm relationship with the Philippians is suggested here (Phil 1:7–8) as elsewhere in the letter. The eschatology serves to underscore a concern for ethical growth (Eph 1:9–11), which appears throughout the letter.

**1:6** *The day of Christ Jesus*: the parousia or triumphant return of Christ, when those loyal to him will be with him and share in his eternal glory; cf. Phil 1:10; 2:16; 3:20–21; 1 Thes 4:17; 5:10; 2 Thes 1:10; 1 Cor 1:8.

**1:12–26** The body of the letter begins with an account of Paul's present *situation*, i.e., his *imprisonment* (Phil 1:12–13; see Introduction), and then goes on with advice for the Philippians (Phil 1:27–2:18). The *advance* of *the gospel* (Phil 1:12) and the *progress* of the Philippians *in the faith* (Phil 1:25) frame what is said.

**1:13** *Praetorium*: either the praetorian guard in the city where Paul was imprisoned or the governor's official residence in a Roman province (cf. Mk 15:16; Acts 23:35). See Introduction on possible sites.

**1:14–18** Although Paul is imprisoned, Christians there nonetheless go on preaching Christ. But they do so with varied motives, *some* with personal hostility toward Paul, others out of personal ambition.

---

\* 
| | |
|---|---|
| **1:1** Rom 1:1; 2 Cor 1:1; 1 Thes 1:1; Phlm 1 / 1 Tm 3:1–13. | **1:8** Rom 1:9; 2 Cor 1:23; 1 Thes 2:5. |
| **1:2** Rom 1:7; Gal 1:3; Phlm 3. | **1:9** Eph 3:14–19; Col 1:9–10; Phlm 6. |
| **1:3** Rom 1:8; 1 Cor 1:4; 1 Thes 1:2. | **1:10** Rom 2:18; 12:2 / 1:6. **1:11** Jn 15:8. |
| **1:6** 2:13 / 1:10; 2:16; 1 Cor 1:8. | **1:12–13** Eph 3:1; 6:20; 2 Tm 2:9; Phlm 9. **1:13** 4:22. |

does it make, as long as in every way, whether in pretense or in truth, Christ is being proclaimed?* And in that I rejoice.†

Indeed I shall continue to rejoice, [19]† for I know that this will result in deliverance for me† through your prayers and support from the Spirit of Jesus Christ.* [20] My eager expectation and hope is that I shall not be put to shame in any way, but that with all boldness, now as always, Christ will be magnified in my body, whether by life or by death.* [21] For to me life is Christ, and death is gain.* [22] If I go on living in the flesh, that means fruitful labor for me. And I do not know which I shall choose.* [23] I am caught between the two. I long to depart this life and be with Christ, [for] that is far better.* [24] Yet that I remain [in] the flesh is more necessary for your benefit. [25] And this I know with confidence, that I shall remain and continue in the service of all of you for your progress and joy in the faith, [26] so that your boasting in Christ Jesus may abound on account of me when I come to you again.

### III. INSTRUCTIONS FOR THE COMMUNITY

**Steadfastness in Faith.**† [27] Only, conduct yourselves in a way worthy of the gospel of Christ, so that, whether I come and see you or am absent, I may hear news of you, that you are standing firm in one spirit, with one mind struggling together for the faith of the gospel,* [28] not intimidated in any way by your opponents. This is proof to them of destruction, but of your salvation. And this is God's doing. [29] For to you has been granted, for the sake of Christ, not only to believe in him but also to suffer for him.* [30] Yours is the same struggle* as you saw in me and now hear about me.†

## 2 Plea for Unity and Humility.† [1] If there is any encouragement in Christ, any solace in love, any participation in the Spirit, any compassion and mercy, [2] complete my joy by being of the same mind, with the same love, united in heart, thinking one thing.* [3] Do nothing out of selfishness or out of vainglory; rather, humbly regard others as more important than yourselves,* [4] each looking out not for his own interests, but [also] everyone for those of others.*

[5] Have among yourselves the same attitude that is also yours in Christ Jesus,†

[6]      Who,† though he was in the form of
              God,*
         did not regard equality with God
              something to be grasped.†

---

† 1:18 *Rejoice*: a major theme in the letter; see Introduction.

**1:19–25** Paul earnestly debates his prospects of martyrdom or continued missionary labor. While he may *long to depart this life* and thus *be with Christ* (Phil 1:23), his overall and final expectation is that he will be delivered from this imprisonment and *continue in the service* of the Philippians and of others (Phil 1:19, 25; Phil 2:24). In either case, Christ is central (Phil 1:20–21); if to live means Christ for Paul, death means to be united with Christ in a deeper sense.

**1:19** *Result in deliverance for me*: an echo of Jb 13:16, hoping that God will turn suffering to ultimate good and deliverance from evil.

**1:27–30** Ethical admonition begins at this early point in the letter, emphasizing steadfastness and congregational unity in the face of possible suffering. The *opponents* (Phil 1:28) are those in Philippi, probably pagans, who oppose the gospel cause. *This is proof…* (Phil 1:28) may refer to the whole outlook and conduct of the Philippians, turning out for their salvation but to the judgment of the opponents (cf. 2 Cor 2:15–16), or possibly the sentence refers to the opinion of the opponents, who hold that the obstinacy of the Christians points to the destruction of such people as defy Roman authority (though in reality, Paul holds, such faithfulness leads to salvation).

**1:30** A reference to Paul's earlier imprisonment in Philippi (Acts 16:19–24; 1 Thes 2:2) and to his present confinement.

**2:1–11** The admonition to likemindedness and unity (Phil 2:2–5) is based on the believers' threefold experience with Christ, God's love, and the Spirit. The appeal to humility (Phil 2:3) and to obedience (Phil 2:12) is rooted in christology, specifically in a statement about Christ Jesus (Phil 2:6–11) and his humbling of self and obedience to the point of death (Phil 2:8).

**2:5** *Have…the same attitude that is also yours in Christ Jesus*:

or, "that also Christ Jesus had." While it is often held that Christ here functions as a model for moral imitation, it is not the historical Jesus but the entire Christ event that Phil 2:6–11 depict. Therefore, the appeal is to have in relations among yourselves that same relationship you have in Christ Jesus, i.e., serving one another as you serve Christ (Phil 2:4).

**2:6–11** Perhaps an early Christian hymn quoted here by Paul. The short rhythmic lines fall into two parts, Phil 2:6–8 where the subject of every verb is Christ, and Phil 2:9–11 where the subject is God. The general pattern is thus of Christ's humiliation and then exaltation. More precise analyses propose a division into six three-line stanzas (Phil 2:6; 7abc, 7d–8, 9, 10, 11) or into three stanzas (Phil 2:6–7ab, 7cd–8, 9–11). Phrases such as *even death on a cross* (Phil 2:8c) are considered by some to be additions (by Paul) to the hymn, as are Phil 2:10c, 11c.

**2:6** Either a reference to Christ's preexistence and those aspects of divinity that he was willing to give up in order to serve in human form, or to what the man Jesus refused to grasp at to attain divinity. Many see an allusion to the Genesis story: unlike Adam, Jesus, *though…in the form of God* (Gn 1:26–27), did not reach out for *equality with God*, in contrast with the first Adam in Gn 3:5–6.

---

* **1:18** 4:10.
**1:19** Jb 13:16 / 2 Cor 1:11.
**1:20** 1 Cor 6:20; 1 Pt 4:16.
**1:21** Gal 2:20.
**1:22** Rom 1:13.
**1:23** 2 Cor 5:8.
**1:27** Eph 4:1; Col 1:10;
       1 Thes 2:12 / 4:3.

**1:29** Mt 5:10; 10:38; Mk
       8:34; Acts 5:41.
**1:30** 1:13; Acts 16:22–24.
**2:2** Rom 15:5; 1 Cor 1:10.
**2:3** Rom 12:3, 10; Gal
       5:26.
**2:4** 1 Cor 10:24, 33; 13:5.
**2:6** Jn 1:1–2; 17:5; Col
       2:9; Heb 1:3.

7 Rather, he emptied himself,
   taking the form of a slave,
   coming in human likeness;†
   and found human in appearance,*
8 he humbled himself,*
   becoming obedient to death,
   even death on a cross.†
9 Because of this, God greatly exalted him
   and bestowed on him the name†
   that is above every name,*
10 that at the name of Jesus
   every knee should bend,†
   of those in heaven and on earth and
     under the earth,*
11 and every tongue confess that
   Jesus Christ is Lord,†
   to the glory of God the Father.*

**Obedience and Service in the World.**† 12* So then, my beloved, obedient as you have always been, not only when I am present but all the more now when I am absent, work out your salvation with fear and trembling.† 13 For God is the one who, for his good purpose, works in you both to desire and to work.* 14 Do everything without grumbling or questioning,* 15 that you may be blameless and innocent, children of God without blemish in the midst of a crooked and perverse generation,† among whom you shine like lights in the world,* 16 as

you hold on to the word of life, so that my boast for the day of Christ may be that I did not run in vain or labor in vain.* 17 But, even if I am poured out as a libation† upon the sacrificial service of your faith, I rejoice and share my joy with all of you.* 18 In the same way you also should rejoice and share your joy with me.*

## IV. TRAVEL PLANS OF PAUL AND HIS ASSISTANTS†

**Timothy and Paul.** 19 I hope, in the Lord Jesus, to send Timothy† to you soon, so that I too may be heartened by hearing news of you.* 20 For I have no one comparable to him for genuine interest in whatever concerns you. 21 For they all seek their own interests, not those of Jesus Christ.* 22 But you know his worth, how as a child with a father he served along with me in the cause of the gospel. 23 He it is, then, whom I hope to send as soon as I see how things go with me, 24 but I am confident in the Lord that I myself will also come soon.†

**Epaphroditus.** 25 With regard to Epaphroditus,† my brother and co-worker and fellow soldier, your messenger and minister in my need, I consider it necessary to send him to

---

**2:7** *Taking the form of a slave, coming in human likeness:* or "…taking the form of a slave. Coming in human likeness, and found human in appearance." While it is common to take Phil 2:6–7 as dealing with Christ's preexistence and Phil 2:8 with his incarnate life, so that lines Phil 2:7b–7c are parallel, it is also possible to interpret so as to exclude any reference to preexistence (see note on Phil 2:6) and to take Phil 2:6–8 as presenting two parallel stanzas about Jesus' human state (Phil 2:6–7b; 7cd–8); in the latter alternative, *coming in human likeness* begins the second stanza and parallels 6a to some extent.
**2:8** There may be reflected here language about the servant of the Lord, Is 52:13–53:12 especially Is 53:12.
**2:9** *The name:* "Lord" (Phil 2:11), revealing the true nature of the one who is named.
**2:10–11** *Every knee should bend…every tongue confess:* into this language of Is 45:23 there has been inserted a reference to the three levels in the universe, according to ancient thought, *heaven, earth, under the earth.*
**2:11** *Jesus Christ is Lord:* a common early Christian acclamation; cf. 1 Cor 12:3; Rom 10:9. But doxology to God the Father is not overlooked here (Phil 2:11c) in the final version of the hymn.
**2:12–18** Paul goes on to draw out further ethical implications for daily life (Phil 2:14–18) from the salvation God works in Christ.
**2:12** *Fear and trembling:* a common Old Testament expression indicating awe and seriousness in the service of God (cf. Ex 15:16; Jdt 2:28; Ps 2:11; Is 19:16).
**2:15–16** *Generation…as you hold on to…:* or "…generation. Among them shine like lights in the world because you hold the word of life…."

**2:17** *Libation:* in ancient religious ritual, the pouring out on the ground of a liquid offering as a sacrifice. Paul means that he may be facing death.
**2:19–3:1** The plans of Paul and his assistants for future travel are regularly a part of a Pauline letter near its conclusion; cf. Rom 15:22–29; 1 Cor 16:5–12.
**2:19** *Timothy:* already known to the Philippians (Acts 16:1–15; cf. 1 Cor 4:17; 16:10).
**2:24** *I myself will also come soon:* cf. Phil 1:19–25 for the significance of this statement.
**2:25** *Epaphroditus:* sent by the Philippians as their *messenger* (literally, "apostle") to aid Paul in his imprisonment, he had fallen seriously ill; Paul commends him as he sends him back to Philippi.

---

**2:7** Is 53:3, 11; Jn 1:14; Rom 8:3; 2 Cor 8:9; Gal 4:4; Heb 2:14, 17.
**2:8** Mt 26:39; Jn 10:17; Heb 5:8; 12:2.
**2:9** Acts 2:33; Mt 23:12; Eph 1:20–21; Heb 1:3–4.
**2:10** Is 45:23; Jn 5:23; Rom 14:11; Rev 5:13.
**2:11** Acts 2:36; Rom 10:9; 1 Cor 12:3.
**2:12** Ps 2:11; 1 Cor 2:3; 2 Cor 7:15.
**2:13** 1:6; 1 Cor 12:6; 15:10; 2 Cor 3:5.
**2:14** 1 Cor 10:10; 1 Pt 4:9.
**2:15** 1 Thes 3:13 / Dt 32:5; Mt 10:16; Acts 2:40 / Dn 12:3; Mt 5:14, 16; Eph 5:8.
**2:16** 1 Thes 2:19 / Is 49:4; 65:23; Gal 2:2.
**2:17** Rom 15:16; 2 Tm 4:6.
**2:18** 3:1; 4:4.
**2:19** Acts 16:1–3; 17:14–15; 1 Cor 4:17; 16:10.
**2:21** 1 Cor 13:5; 2 Tm 4:10.

you.* ²⁶ For he has been longing for all of you and was distressed because you heard that he was ill. ²⁷ He was indeed ill, close to death; but God had mercy on him, not just on him but also on me, so that I might not have sorrow upon sorrow. ²⁸ I send him therefore with the greater eagerness, so that, on seeing him, you may rejoice again, and I may have less anxiety. ²⁹ Welcome him then in the Lord with all joy and hold such people in esteem,* ³⁰ because for the sake of the work of Christ he came close to death, risking his life to make up for those services to me that you could not perform.

# 3 Concluding Admonitions. ¹ Finally, my brothers, rejoice† in the Lord. Writing the same things to you is no burden for me but is a safeguard for you.*

## V. POLEMIC: RIGHTEOUSNESS AND THE GOAL IN CHRIST†

**Against Legalistic Teachers.** ²† Beware of the dogs! Beware of the evil-workers!* Beware of the mutilation!† ³ For we are the circumcision,† we who worship through the Spirit of God, who boast in Christ Jesus and do not put our confidence in flesh,* ⁴ although I myself have grounds for confidence even in the flesh.*

**Paul's Autobiography.** If anyone else thinks he can be confident in flesh, all the more can I. ⁵ Circumcised on the eighth day,† of the race of Israel, of the tribe of Benjamin, a Hebrew of Hebrew parentage, in observance of the law a Pharisee,* ⁶ in zeal I persecuted the church, in righteousness based on the law I was blameless.*

**Righteousness from God.** ⁷ [But] whatever gains I had, these I have come to consider a loss† because of Christ.* ⁸ More than that, I even consider everything as a loss because of the supreme good of knowing Christ Jesus my Lord. For his sake I have accepted the loss of all things and I consider them so much rubbish, that I may gain Christ ⁹ and be found in him, not having any righteousness of my own based on the law but that which comes through faith in Christ,* the righteousness from God, depending on faith ¹⁰ to know him and the power of his resurrection and [the] sharing of his sufferings by being conformed to his death,* ¹¹ if somehow I may attain the resurrection from the dead.*

**Forward in Christ.**† ¹²* It is not that I have already taken hold of it or have already attained perfect maturity,† but I continue my pursuit in hope that I may possess it, since I have

PHIL

---

3:1 *Finally…rejoice*: the adverb often signals the close of a letter; cf. Phil 4:8; 2 Cor 13:11. While the verb could also be translated "good-bye" or "farewell," although it is never so used in Greek epistolography, the theme of joy has been frequent in the letter (Phil 1:18; 2:2, 18); note also Phil 4:4 and the addition of "always" as evidence for the meaning "rejoice." To write *the same things* may refer to what Paul has previously taught in Philippi or to what he has just written or to what follows.

3:2–21 An abrupt change in content and tone, either because Paul at this point responds to disturbing news he has just heard about a threat to the faith of the Philippians in the form of false teachers, or because part of another Pauline letter was inserted here; see Introduction. The chapter describes these teachers in strong terms as *dogs*. The persons meant are evidently different from the rival preachers of Phil 1:14–18 and the opponents of Phil 1:28. Since Phil 3:2–4 emphasize Jewish terms like *circumcision* (Phil 3:2–3, 5), some relate them to the "Judaizers" of the Letter to the Galatians. Other phrases make them appear more like the false teachers of 2 Cor 11:12–15, the *evil-workers*. The latter part of the chapter depicts the *many* who are *enemies* of Christ's cross in terms that may sound more Gentile or even "gnostic" than Jewish (Phil 3:18–19). Accordingly, some see two groups of false teachers in Phil 3, others one group characterized by a claim of having attained "perfect maturity" (Phil 3:12–15).

3:2–11 Paul sets forth the Christian claim, especially using personal, autobiographical terms that are appropriate to the situation. He presents his own experience in coming to know Christ Jesus in terms of *righteousness* or justification (cf. Rom 1:16–17; 3:21–5:11; Gal 2:5–11), contrasting the *righteousness from God* through faith and that of one's own *based on the law* as two exclusive ways of pleasing God.

3:2 *Beware of the mutilation*: literally, "incision," an ironic wordplay on "circumcision"; cf. Gal 5:12. There may be an association with the self-inflicted mutilations of the prophets of Baal (1 Kgs 18:28) and of devotees of Cybele who slashed themselves in religious frenzy.

3:3 *We are the circumcision*: the true people of God, seed and offspring of Abraham (Gal 3:7, 29; 6:15). *Spirit of God*: some manuscripts read "worship God by the Spirit."

3:5 *Circumcised on the eighth day*: as the law required (Gn 17:12; Lv 12:3).

3:7 *Loss*: his knowledge of Christ led Paul to reassess the ways of truly pleasing and serving God. His reevaluation indicates the profound and lasting effect of his experience of the meaning of Christ on the way to Damascus some twenty years before (Gal 1:15–16; Acts 9:1–22).

3:12–16 To be *taken possession of by Christ* does not mean that one has already arrived at perfect spiritual maturity. Paul and the Philippians instead press on, trusting in God.

3:12 *Attained perfect maturity*: possibly an echo of the concept in the mystery religions of being an initiate, admitted to divine secrets.

---

| | |
|---|---|
| 2:25 4:10–11, 15–16, 18. | Acts 22:3; 23:6; 26:5. |
| 2:29 1 Cor 16:18. | 3:6 Acts 8:3; 22:4; |
| 3:1 2:18; 4:4. | 26:9–11. |
| 3:2 Ps 22:17, 21; Rev | 3:7 Mt 13:44, 46; Lk 14:33. |
| 22:15 / 2 Cor 11:13 / | 3:9 Rom 3:21–22. |
| Gal 5:6, 12. | 3:10 Rom 6:3–5; 8:17; Gal |
| 3:3 Rom 2:28–29; Col | 6:17. |
| 2:11. | 3:11 Jn 11:23–26; Acts 4:2; |
| 3:4 2 Cor 11:18, 21–23. | Rev 20:5–6. |
| 3:5 Lk 1:59; 2:21 / | 3:12 1 Tm 6:12, 19. |

indeed been taken possession of by Christ [Jesus]. ¹³ Brothers, I for my part do not consider myself to have taken possession. Just one thing: forgetting what lies behind but straining forward to what lies ahead, ¹⁴ I continue my pursuit toward the goal, the prize of God's upward calling, in Christ Jesus.* ¹⁵ Let us, then, who are "perfectly mature" adopt this attitude. And if you have a different attitude, this too God will reveal to you. ¹⁶ Only, with regard to what we have attained, continue on the same course.†

**Wrong Conduct and Our Goal.**† ¹⁷ Join with others in being imitators of me,† brothers, and observe those who thus conduct themselves according to the model you have in us.* ¹⁸ For many, as I have often told you and now tell you even in tears, conduct themselves as enemies of the cross of Christ.* ¹⁹ Their end is destruction. Their God is their stomach; their glory is in their "shame." Their minds are occupied with earthly things.* ²⁰ But our citizenship† is in heaven, and from it we also await a savior, the Lord Jesus Christ.* ²¹ He will change our lowly body to conform with his glorified body by the power that enables him also to bring all things into subjection to himself.*

## VI. INSTRUCTIONS FOR THE COMMUNITY†

**4** **Live in Concord.** ¹ Therefore, my brothers, whom I love and long for, my joy and crown, in this way stand firm in the Lord, beloved.*

² I urge Euodia and I urge Syntyche† to come to a mutual understanding in the Lord. ³ Yes, and I ask you also, my true yokemate,† to help them, for they have struggled at my side in promoting the gospel, along with Clement and my other co-workers, whose names are in the book of life.*

**Joy and Peace.** ⁴ Rejoice† in the Lord always. I shall say it again: rejoice!* ⁵ Your kindness† should be known to all. The Lord is near.* ⁶ Have no anxiety at all, but in everything, by prayer and petition, with thanksgiving, make your requests known to God.* ⁷ Then the peace of God that surpasses all understanding will guard your hearts and minds in Christ Jesus.*

⁸* Finally, brothers, whatever is true, whatever is honorable, whatever is just, whatever is pure, whatever is lovely, whatever is gracious, if there is any excellence and if there is anything worthy of praise, think about these things.† ⁹ Keep on doing what you have learned and received and heard and seen in me.* Then the God of peace will be with you.†

## VII. GRATITUDE FOR THE PHILIPPIANS' GENEROSITY†

¹⁰ I rejoice greatly in the Lord that now at last you revived your concern for me. You were, of course, concerned about me but lacked an opportunity.* ¹¹ Not that I say this because of

---

**3:16** Some manuscripts add, probably to explain Paul's cryptic phrase, "thinking alike."

**3:17–21** Paul and those who live a life centered in Christ, envisaging both his suffering and resurrection, provide a model that is the opposite of opponents who reject Christ's cross (cf. 1 Cor 1:23).

**3:17** *Being imitators of me*: not arrogance, but humble simplicity, since all his converts know that Paul is wholly dedicated to imitating Christ (1 Cor 11:1; cf. also Phil 4:9; 1 Thes 1:6; 2 Thes 3:7, 9; 1 Cor 4:6).

**3:20** *Citizenship*: Christians constitute a colony of heaven, as Philippi was a *colonia* of Rome (Acts 16:12). The hope Paul expresses involves the final coming of Christ, not a status already attained, such as the opponents claim.

**4:1–9** This series of ethical admonitions rests especially on the view of Christ and his coming (cf. Phil 4:5) in Phil 3:20–21. Paul's instructions touch on unity within the congregation, joy, prayer, and the Christian outlook on life.

**4:2** *Euodia...Syntyche*: two otherwise unknown women in the Philippian congregation; on the advice to them, cf. Phil 2:2–4.

**4:3** *Yokemate*: or "comrade," although the Greek *syzygos* could also be a proper name. *Clement*: otherwise unknown, although later writers sought to identify him with Clement, bishop of Rome (Eusebius, *Ecclesiastical History* 3.15.1).

**4:4** *Rejoice*: see note on Phil 3:1.

**4:5** *Kindness*: considerateness, forbearance, fairness. *The Lord is near*: most likely a reference to Christ's parousia (Phil 1:6, 10; 3:20–21; 1 Cor 16:22), although some sense an echo of Ps 119:151 and the perpetual presence of the Lord.

**4:8** The language employs terms from Roman Stoic thought.

**4:9** Cf. note on Phil 3:17.

**4:10–20** Paul, more directly than anywhere else in the letter (cf. Phil 1:3–5), here thanks the Philippians for their gift of money sent through Epaphroditus (Phil 2:25). Paul's own policy was to

---

| | |
|---|---|
| **3:14** 1 Cor 9:24–25; 2 Tm 4:7. | Lk 10:20; Rev 3:5; 13:8; 17:8; 20:12, 15; 21:27. |
| **3:17** 1 Cor 4:16; 11:1; 1 Thes 1:7; 1 Pt 5:3. | **4:4** 2:18; 3:1. |
| **3:18** 1 Cor 1:17, 23; Gal 6:12. | **4:5** Ti 3:2 / Ps 145:18; Heb 10:37; Jas 5:8–9. |
| **3:19** Rom 8:5–6; 16:18. | **4:6** Mt 6:25–34; 1 Pt 5:7 / Col 4:2. |
| **3:20** Eph 2:6, 19; Col 3:1–3; Heb 12:22. | **4:7** Jn 14:27; Col 3:15. |
| **3:21** Rom 8:23, 29; 1 Cor 15:42–57; 2 Cor 3:18; 5:1–5 / 1 Cor 15:27–28. | **4:8** Rom 12:17. |
| **4:1** 1 Thes 2:19–20. | **4:9** 1 Thes 4:1 / Rom 15:33; 16:20; 1 Cor 14:33; 1 Thes 5:23. |
| **4:3** Ex 32:32–33; Ps 69:29; Dn 12:1; | **4:10** 1:18; 2:25; 1 Cor 9:11; 2 Cor 11:9. |

need, for I have learned, in whatever situation I find myself, to be self-sufficient.* ¹²I know indeed how to live in humble circumstances; I know also how to live with abundance. In every circumstance and in all things I have learned the secret of being well fed and of going hungry, of living in abundance and of being in need. ¹³I have the strength for everything through him who empowers me.* ¹⁴Still, it was kind of you to share in my distress.

¹⁵You Philippians indeed know that at the beginning of the gospel,† when I left Macedonia, not a single church shared with me in an account of giving and receiving, except you alone. ¹⁶For even when I was at Thessalonica you sent me something for my needs, not only once but more than once. ¹⁷It is not that I am eager for the gift; rather, I am eager

for the profit that accrues to your account. ¹⁸I have received full payment and I abound. I am very well supplied because of what I received from you through Epaphroditus, "a fragrant aroma," an acceptable sacrifice,† pleasing to God.* ¹⁹My God will fully supply whatever you need, in accord with his glorious riches in Christ Jesus.* ²⁰To our God and Father, glory forever and ever. Amen.*

## VIII. FAREWELL†

²¹Give my greetings to every holy one in Christ Jesus. The brothers who are with me send you their greetings; ²²* all the holy ones send you their greetings, especially those of Caesar's household.† ²³The grace of the Lord Jesus Christ be with your spirit.

---

be self-sufficient as a missionary, supporting himself by his own labor (1 Thes 2:5–9; 1 Cor 9:15–18; cf. Acts 18:2–3). In spite of this reliance on self and on God to provide (Phil 4:11–13) Paul accepted gifts from the Philippians *not only once but more than once* (Phil 4:16) when he was in Thessalonica (Acts 17:1–9), as he does now, in prison (*my distress*, Phil 4:14). While commercial terms appear in the passage, like *an account of giving and receiving* (Phil 4:15) and *received full payment* (Phil 4:18), Paul is most concerned about the spiritual growth of the Philippians (Phil 4:10, 17, 19); he emphasizes that God will care for their needs, through Christ.

**4:15** *The beginning of the gospel*: it was at Philippi that Paul first preached Christ in Europe, going on from there to Thessalonica and Beroea (Acts 16:9–17:14).

**4:18** *Aroma...sacrifice*: Old Testament cultic language (cf.

Gn 8:21; Ex 29:18, 25, 41; Lv 1:9, 13; Ez 20:41) applied to the Philippians' gift; cf. Eph 5:2; 2 Cor 2:14–16.

**4:21–23** On the usual greetings at the conclusion of a letter, see note on 1 Cor 16:19–24. Inclusion of greetings from *all the holy ones* in the place from which Paul writes would involve even the Christians of Phil 1:14–18 who had their differences with Paul.

**4:22** *Those of Caesar's household*: minor officials or even slaves and freedmen, found in Ephesus or Rome, among other places.

---

| | |
|---|---|
| **4:11–12** 1 Cor 4:11; 2 Cor 6:10; 11:27 / 2 Cor 12:9–10. | **4:18** Gn 8:21; Ex 29:18; Eph 5:2; Heb 13:16. |
| **4:13** Col 1:29; 2 Tm 4:17. | **4:19** 1 Thes 3:11, 13. |
| | **4:20** Rom 16:27; Eph 5:20. |
| | **4:22** 1:13. |

# The Letter to the
# Colossians

## INTRODUCTION
### Raymond F. Collins

Within the corpus of New Testament epistles, the Letter to the Colossians has close ties with both Paul's Letter to Philemon and the deuteropauline Letter to the Ephesians. These texts, along with Paul's Letter to the Philippians, are often called the "Letters from Prison" since each of them describes its stated author as a prisoner (Col 4:3, 10, 18; cf. Eph 3:1; 4:1; 6:20; Phil 1:7, 13, 14, 17; Phlm 9, 10, 13).

Paul was not the founder of the community of believers at Colossae, a city in the Lycus Valley, located in the Western part of what is now Asian Turkey. The apostle most likely had not even visited the area (Col 2:1). He learned about the community's faith from Epaphras (1:4, 8, 9), a fellow slave of Jesus Christ, who initially evangelized the Colossians (1:7; 4:12).

## The Situation at Colossae

The opening thanksgiving of the letter is occasioned by what the author has heard about the faith, love, and hope of the community (Col 1:3–8). This gives rise to a prayer that the community be filled with knowledge of God's will and live a life in keeping with their relationship with the Lord (1:9–14). There were, nonetheless, some concerns even if these did not rise to the level of a major crisis. Colossians 2:8 mentions an "empty, seductive philosophy according to human tradition, according to the elemental powers of the world and not according to Christ." Colossians 2:20 asks, "Why do you submit to regulations as if you were still living in the world?"

The two verses suggest that the source of the trouble was a popular philosophy, associated with the "worship of angels" (Col 2:18) espoused by people who were bound to follow prescribed ascetical practices with regard to food and the observance of calendar-related

---

## Outline of Colossians

I. **Address (1:1–14)**

II. **The Preeminence of Christ (1:15–2:3)**

III. **Warnings Against False Teachers (2:4–23)**

IV. **The Ideal Christian Life in the World (3:1–4:6)**

V. **Conclusion (4:7–18)**

---

festivals (2:16). The adherents of this captivating philosophy took issue with the predominantly Gentile group of believers at Colossae because they seem to have rejected some elements of traditional wisdom and did not espouse the self-abasing practices followed by these critics. In addition these critics appear to have accused believers of not observing customary festivals.

## A Rich Christology

Rather than confronting these concerns head-on, the letter articulates a vision of Christ that ought to dominate the thinking and the practice of Colossian believers. This vision is beautifully expressed in a christological hymn (Col 1:15–20) whose focus is cosmological. The hymn has some similarity with the prologue of the Fourth Gospel (Jn 1:1–18) and the christological hymn of Phil 2:6–11.

Presenting Christ as the firstborn of all creation, the hymn says that in Christ are created all things in heaven and on earth. The hymn's primary intent is not polemical but its assertion that the thrones, dominions, principalities, and powers are created through and for him suggests that Christ is superior to any other entity, save the invisible God. In a second movement of thought, the hymn presents Christ as the firstborn from the dead—an implicit reference to the Resurrection—and the head of a cosmic body that is identified with the church. Using the term "fullness" (plērōma), popular in Gnosticism—from the Greek gnōsis, "knowledge," a kind of philosophy that exalted inspired knowledge—the hymn also proclaims that Christ is the reconciler of all things. The term suggests that Christ is everything that God is. Since Christ is the image (eikōn) of the invisible God, he is the one in whom humans encounter God.

The idea that the fullness of the deity dwells in Christ is reprised in Col 2:9, the first verse in another subunit of the letter (2:9–15) that has a rich and varied Christology. The section begins with the affirmation that the fullness of the deity abides in Christ bodily (sōmatikōs), a notion that appears to prepare for the later development of the doctrine of the Incarnation. Believers share in the fullness that dwells in Christ. With Christ believers have been buried in baptism; with him they are raised through faith in the power of God (cf. 3:1). Christ brings believers to life (cf. 3:3–4) and has forgiven their transgressions. Although focused on believers' participation in Christ, this section of Colossians retains the cosmological aspect of the christological hymn. It affirms that Christ is the head of every principality and power (2:10) and that he has made a public spectacle of them (2:15).

The profound Christology of Col 1:15–20 and 2:9–15 should not lead the reader of the letter to overlook other important christological ideas expressed by its author. The letter speaks about the kingdom of God's beloved Son (1:13–14). It presents Christ as the mystery of God (2:2; cf. 1:26–27; 4:3). It says that Christ is all in all; in him there is no Greek and Jew, circumcision and uncircumcision, barbarian, Scythian, slave and free (3:11).

## The Life of Believers

The idea that Christ is victorious over astral forces allows the author to draw an important inference, namely, that believers should not respond to the ascetical taunts of the troublemakers by adopting similar ascetical practices (Col 2:16–23). Having died with Christ, believers have been freed from this kind of obligation (2:14, 20; cf. 3:9), which, after all, deals only with things that are perishing. In baptism believers have been buried with Christ (2:12). With Christ, they have been raised and put on a new self which is being renewed in the image of the creator (3:1, 10; cf. 1:15).

That Christ renders null the power of any heavenly force and has freed believers from undue ascetical practices does not mean that that they are free from moral responsibility. The third chapter of the letter is an exhortation to do everything in the name of the Lord Jesus, giving thanks to God the Father through him (Col 3:17). Believers must put to death whatever is earthly (3:5). They are to put on a new person that is being renewed (3:9–10). Two catalogues of vices illustrate the kinds of things that believers must avoid (3:5, 8–9). The household code of Col 3:18–4:1 suggests that within the context of the usual social structures of the times believers are to act so as to please the Lord. Above all, believers are to put on love, the bond of perfection (3:14).

The reality of Christ dominates the letter's vision. This same reality should define the life of believers.

## Development of Paul's Thought

The deep Christology and extensive moral exhortation of the letter represent a development of the thought of the Apostle Paul. A glance at the way that the author uses the word "church" may serve as an illustration. The word "church" (ekklēsia) does not appear in the opening greeting of the letter. Like the Letter to the Ephesians (Eph 1:1; cf. Phil 1:1; Rom 1:7), the letter is not addressed to a church, but to the holy ones who are described as faithful brothers [and sisters] (Col 1:2).

In the final greetings of Colossians the word "church" clearly refers to a local assembly, as it does in Paul's uncontested letters. The author of Colossians sends greetings to the church that gathers in Nympha's house (Col 4:15;

COL

cf. Rom 16:5; 1 Cor 16:19; Phlm 2) and asks that the missive be read in the church of the Laodiceans (Col 4:16). On the other hand, in Col 1:18 and 24 the church is identified as the body (*sōma*), of which Christ is the head. In both of these earlier instances, the "church" is the universal church, localized neither in any particular city nor in anyone's home. In this respect, the ecclesiology of Colossians is similar to that of Ephesians, whose teaching about the church is far more developed than is the ecclesiology of Colossians.

## The Occasion of the Letter

In the course of recent decades there has been much discussion of the problematic situation in Colossae that prompted the writing of the letter. Was the "empty, seductive philosophy according to human tradition" (Col 2:8) that might have seemed attractive to Colossian believers some form of Judaism, with its dietary regulations and sabbath observance (cf. 2:16)? Ancient authors sometimes referred to the various forms of Judaism as "philosophies." Some synagogues in Gentile areas attracted God-fearing people who thought that Jewish practices were a way to achieve spiritual perfection. Was the philosophy of Col 2:8 a kind of Gnosticism or gnosticizing syncretism that tended to denigrate the body and things material (cf. 2:23)? And what did the author mean by the "worship of angels" (2:18)? Is this a reference to humans worshiping angels or is it a reference to visions of heavenly angels worshiping God?

The letter offers a theological and philosophical critique of false asceticism (Col 2:14, 22–23) but it does not attempt to argue directly with the philosophy itself. This makes it difficult to determine with any precision the exact nature of the problematic situation. It certainly does not appear to have been a Christian heresy; rather it seems to be a criticism of Christian beliefs and practices coming from people who objected that believers had abandoned traditional beliefs and the way of life that ensued from these beliefs.

## Relationship with Ephesians and Philemon

With Ephesians, the Letter to the Colossians shares a similar vocabulary, style, content, and outline. Philemon shares none of these similarities with Colossians; rather, the mention of various named individuals is the link between Philemon and Colossians. "Timothy our brother" is the named fellow-greeter, if not co-author of both texts (Col 1:1; Phlm 1:1). The brief Letter to Philemon, written on behalf of Onesimus, is addressed not only to Philemon but also to several others, one of whom is Archippus, Paul's "fellow soldier" (Phlm 2). At the conclusion of his Letter to Philemon, Paul sends greetings on behalf of a fellow prisoner, Epaphras, and four missionaries who had worked with him, Mark, Aristarchus, Demas, and Luke (cf. Phlm 23). Toward the end of the Letter to the Colossians, just before the appended hand-written salutation, the Colossians are asked to urge Archippus, presumably the very same Archippus mentioned in the greeting of Philemon, to fulfill the ministry that he had received in the Lord (Col. 4:17). In Colossians Onesimus is described as a beloved brother (Col. 4:9; cf. Phlm 16) and "one of you." Along with Tychicus (cf. Eph 6:21–22), he is sent to Colossae to tell the Colossians about Paul (Col. 4:7–9).

The names of Paul's fellow workers mentioned in Phlm 23 reappear in the closing section of Colossians. Aristarchus is described as Paul's fellow prisoner who sends greetings to the Colossians, as does Mark, now identified as the cousin of Barnabas (Col. 4:10; cf. Acts 15:37–39). Luke, identified as the beloved physician, likewise sends greetings, as does Demas, who is not further qualified. The descriptive epithets attributed to Aristarchus, Mark, and Luke suggest that these persons were unknown to the Colossian community.

Greetings are also sent by Epaphras, whom the author commends to the Colossians because of his work among the Colossians, the Laodiceans, and the inhabitants of Hierapolis (Col. 4:12–13). The three cities are within a few miles of one another in the Lycus Valley. The commendation suggests that Epaphras, previously identified as the one who preached the gospel to the Colossians (1:7), probably evangelized the other two cities as well.

## Did Paul Write the Letter to the Colossians?

Many commentators believe that Colossians was not actually written by Paul. Among their reasons for thinking this is that much of the vocabulary and certainly the style of the letter are different from those of the letters definitely written by the apostle. Moreover, particularly in the understanding of Christ and the church and the use of a spatial rather than a temporal frame of reference, the letter expresses some ideas that are significantly different from those expressed in Paul's uncontested letters.

If the Letter to the Colossians was not written by Paul, mention of the apostle's imprisonment may be a literary device employed by the author to account for Paul's absence due to the fact that the apostle had already died. Some who believe that the letter was not actually written by the apostle—that it was, in fact, a pseudepigraphic composition—think that the encouragement of an exchange of the letter addressed to the Colossians with that addressed to the Laodiceans (Col 4:16) was the pseudonymous author's way of dealing with the fact that Colossae was not an inhabited locale at the time the text was written. The exchange of letters motif was a literary device employed to say that the text was really intended for the Laodiceans. In any case, history has not preserved the referenced Letter to the Laodiceans.

Why was Colossae possibly uninhabited at the time? A major earthquake that occurred in the Lycus Valley left the city in ruins. The earthquake is generally dated to 60–61 CE, but it may have occurred a few years later.

If Paul himself wrote the letter, he would most likely have mentioned the earthquake, had it already occurred. Hence, if Paul wrote the letter, he would have done so before the earthquake. Should the letter have been written by Paul, its failure to make any mention of the earthquake suggests that the imprisonment to which reference is made in Colossians was not Paul's house arrest in Rome (Acts 28:16–31) but an earlier imprisonment (cf. 2 Cor 6:5; 11:23), perhaps in Ephesus (cf. 1 Cor 15:32; 2 Cor 1:8–10), a relatively short five-day journey from Colossae.

Scholars continue to dispute the authorship and dating of this letter, but there is little doubt that the Letter to the Colossians stands within the Pauline tradition and that it was written in the later part of the first century CE. ◼

# THE LETTER TO THE COLOSSIANS

## New American Bible, Introduction

This letter is addressed to a congregation at Colossae in the Lycus Valley in Asia Minor, east of Ephesus. At the time of writing, Paul had not visited there, the letter says (Col 1:4; 2:1). The community had apparently been established by Epaphras of Colossae (Col 1:7; 4:12; Phlm 23). Problems, however, had arisen, brought on by teachers who emphasized Christ's relation to the universe (cosmos). Their teachings stressed angels (Col 2:18; "principalities and powers," Col 2:15), which were connected with astral powers and cultic practices (see note on Col 2:16) and rules about food and drink and ascetical disciplines (Col 2:16, 18). These teachings, Paul insists, detract from the person and work of Christ for salvation as set forth magnificently in a hymnic passage at Col 1:15–20 and reiterated throughout the letter. Such teachings are but "shadows"; Christ is "reality" (Col 2:17).

For help in dealing with these problems that the new teachers posed at Colossae, Epaphras sought out Paul, who was then imprisoned (Col 4:10, 18) at a place that the letter does not mention. Paul, without entering into debate over the existence of angelic spirits or their function, simply affirms that Christ possesses the sum total of redemptive power (Col 1:19) and that the spiritual renewal of the human person occurs through contact in baptism with the person of Christ, who died and rose again (Col 2:9–14). It is unnecessary for the Christian to be concerned about placating spirits (Col 2:15) or avoiding imagined defilement through ascetical practices in regard to food and drink (Col 2:20–23). True Christian asceticism consists in the conquering of personal sins (Col 3:5–10) and the practice of love of neighbor in accordance with the standard set by Christ (Col 3:12–16).

Paul commends the community as a whole (Col 1:3–8); this seems to indicate that, though the Colossians have been under pressure to adopt the false doctrines, they have not yet succumbed. The apostle expresses his prayerful concern for them (Col 1:9–14). His preaching has cost him persecution, suffering, and imprisonment, but he regards these as reflective of the sufferings of Christ, a required discipline for the sake of the gospel (see note on 1:24; cf. 1:29; 2:1). His instructions to the Christian family and to slaves and masters require a new spirit of reflection and action. Love, obedience, and service are to be rendered "in the Lord" (Col 3:18–4:1).

Colossians follows the outline of a typical Pauline letter. It is distinguished by the poetic lines in Col 1:15–20 concerning who Christ is and what Christ means in creation and redemption. This hymn may be compared with similar passages in Phil 2:6–11; 1 Tm 3:16; and Jn 1:1–18. It was apparently familiar liturgical material to the author, the audience, and the false teachers. In Col 1:21–2:7, however, Paul interprets the relation between the body of Christ, which he insists is the church (Col 1:18), and the world or cosmos to be one not simply of Christ's preexistence and rule but one of missionary advance into the world by the spreading of the word (Col 1:25, 28). In this labor of the missionary body of Christ, Paul as a minister plays a prime part in bringing Christ and the gospel as hope to the Gentiles (Col 1:23, 25, 27). To "every creature under heaven" the word is to be proclaimed, so that everyone receives Christ, is established in faith, and walks in Christ (Col 1:28; 2:6, 7).

Paul wrote the Letter to the Colossians while in prison, but his several imprisonments leave the specific place and date of composition uncertain. On this point the same problem exists as with Ephesians and Philippians (see the Introductions to these letters). Traditionally the house arrest at Rome, in which Paul enjoyed a certain restricted freedom in preaching (see Acts 28:16–28), or a second Roman imprisonment has been claimed as the setting. Others suggest a still earlier imprisonment at Caesarea (see Acts 23:12–27:1) or in Ephesus (see Acts 19). Still others regard the letter as the work of some pupil or follower of Paul, writing in his name. In any case, the contents are often closely paralleled by thoughts in Ephesians.

The principal divisions of the Letter to the Colossians are the following:

I. Address (1:1–14)

II. The Preeminence of Christ (1:15–2:3)

III. Warnings Against False Teachers (2:4–23)

IV. The Ideal Christian Life in the World (3:1–4:6)

V. Conclusion (4:7–18) ∎

# COLOSSIANS

## I. ADDRESS

**1** **Greeting.**† ¹Paul, an apostle of Christ Jesus by the will of God, and Timothy our brother,* ²to the holy ones and faithful brothers in Christ in Colossae: grace to you and peace from God our Father.

**Thanksgiving.**† ³We always give thanks to God, the Father of our Lord Jesus Christ, when we pray for you,* ⁴for we have heard of your faith in Christ Jesus and the love that you have for all the holy ones ⁵because of the hope reserved for you in heaven. Of this you have already heard through the word of truth, the gospel,* ⁶that has come to you. Just as in the whole world it is bearing fruit and growing, so also among you, from the day you heard it and came to know the grace of God in truth, ⁷* as you learned it from Epaphras† our beloved fellow slave, who is a trustworthy minister of Christ on your behalf ⁸and who also told us of your love in the Spirit.

**Prayer for Continued Progress.**† ⁹Therefore, from the day we heard this, we do not cease praying for you and asking that you may be filled with the knowledge of his will through all spiritual wisdom and understanding* ¹⁰to live in a manner worthy of the Lord, so as to be fully pleasing, in every good work bearing fruit and growing in the knowledge of God, ¹¹strengthened with every power, in accord with his glorious might, for all endurance and patience, with joy ¹²† giving thanks to the Father, who has made you fit to share in the inheritance of the holy ones in light.* ¹³He delivered us from the power of darkness and transferred us to the kingdom of his beloved Son, ¹⁴in whom we have redemption, the forgiveness of sins.*

## II. THE PREEMINENCE OF CHRIST

### His Person and Work

¹⁵† He is the image† of the invisible God,
the firstborn of all creation.*

¹⁶ For in him† were created all things in heaven and on earth,
the visible and the invisible,
whether thrones or dominions or principalities or powers;
all things were created through him and for him.*

¹⁷ He is before all things,
and in him all things hold together.

---

† **1:1–2** For the epistolary form used by Paul at the beginning of his letters, see note on Rom 1:1–7. On *holy ones* or "God's people," see note on Rom 1:7. Awareness of their calling helps this group to be *faithful brothers* and sisters *in Christ*, i.e., dedicated to the tasks implied in their calling.

**1:3–8** On thanksgiving at the start of a letter, see note on Rom 1:8. The apostle, recalling his own prayers for them and the good report about them he has received (Col 1:3–4), congratulates the Colossians upon their acceptance of Christ and their faithful efforts to live the gospel (Col 3:6–8). To encourage them he mentions the success of the gospel elsewhere (Col 1:6) and assures them that his knowledge of their community is accurate, since he has been in personal contact with Epaphras (Col 1:7–8), who likely had evangelized Colossae and other cities in the Lycus Valley of Asia Minor (cf. Col 4:12, 13; Phlm 23). On *faith, love,* and *hope* (Col 1:4, 5, 8), see note on 1 Cor 13:13; cf. 1 Thes 1:3; 5:8.

**1:7** *Epaphras:* now with Paul but a Colossian, founder of the church there.

**1:9–14** Moved by Epaphras' account, the apostle has prayed and continues to pray fervently for the Colossians that, in their response to the gospel, they *may be filled with the knowledge of God's will* (Col 1:9; cf. Col 3:10). Paul expects a mutual interaction between their life according to the gospel and this knowledge (Col 1:10), yielding results (*fruit,* Col 1:10; cf. Col 1:6) *in every good work:* growth, strength, *endurance, patience, with joy* (Col 1:11), and the further giving of thanks (Col 1:12).

**1:12–14** A summary about *redemption by the Father* precedes the statement in Col 1:15–20 about the *beloved Son* who is God's love in person (Col 1:13). Christians share *the inheritance…in light* with *the holy ones,* here probably the angels (Col 1:12). The imagery reflects the Exodus (*delivered…transferred*) and Jesus' theme of the *kingdom. Redemption* is explained as *forgiveness of sins* (cf. Acts 2:38; Rom 3:24–25; Eph 1:7).

**1:15–20** As the poetic arrangement indicates, these lines are probably an early Christian hymn, known to the Colossians and taken up into the letter from liturgical use (cf. Phil 2:6–11; 1 Tm 3:16). They present Christ as the mediator of creation (Col 1:15–18a) and of redemption (Col 1:18b–20). There is a parallelism between *firstborn of all creation* (Col 1:15) and *firstborn from the dead* (Col 1:18). While many of the phrases were at home in Greek philosophical use and even in gnosticism, the basic ideas also reflect Old Testament themes about Wisdom found in Prv 8:22–31; Wis 7:22–8:1; and Sir 1:4. See also notes on what is possibly a hymn in Jn 1:1–18.

**1:15** *Image:* cf. Gn 1:27. Whereas the man and the woman were originally created in the image and likeness of God (see also Gn 1:26), Christ as image (2 Cor 4:4) of *the invisible God* (Jn 1:18) now shares this new nature in baptism with those redeemed (cf. Col 3:10–11).

**1:16–17** Christ (though not mentioned by name) is preeminent and supreme as God's agent in the creation of *all things* (cf. Jn 1:3), as prior to *all things* (Col 1:17; cf. Heb 1:3).

---

**1:1** Eph 1:1.
**1:3** Eph 1:15–16; Phlm 4–5.
**1:5** Eph 1:13, 18; 1 Pt 1:4.
**1:7** Phlm 23.
**1:9** Eph 1:15–17; 5:17; Phil 1:9.
**1:12** 3:17; Jn 8:12; Acts 26:18; 1 Tm 6:16; 1 Pt 2:9.
**1:14** Eph 1:7.
**1:15** Ps 89:28; Jn 1:3, 18; 2 Cor 4:4.
**1:16** 1 Cor 8:6; Eph 1:10, 21.

18    He is the head of the body, the church.†

He is the beginning, the firstborn
     from the dead,

that in all things he himself might be
     preeminent.*

19    For in him all the fullness† was pleased
     to dwell,

20    and through him to reconcile all things
     for him,

making peace by the blood of his
     cross†

[through him], whether those on
     earth or those in heaven.*

21† And you who once were alienated and hostile in mind because of evil deeds* 22 he has now reconciled in his fleshly body through his death, to present you holy, without blemish, and irreproachable before him, 23 provided that you persevere in the faith, firmly grounded, stable, and not shifting from the hope of the gospel that you heard, which has been preached to every creature under heaven, of which I, Paul, am a minister.

**Christ in Us.**† 24 Now I rejoice in my sufferings for your sake, and in my flesh I am filling up what is lacking† in the afflictions of Christ on behalf of his body, which is the church, 25 of which I am a minister in accordance with

God's stewardship given to me to bring to completion for you the word of God, 26 the mystery hidden from ages and from generations past. But now it has been manifested to his holy ones,* 27 to whom God chose to make known the riches of the glory of this mystery among the Gentiles; it is Christ in you, the hope for glory.* 28 It is he whom we proclaim, admonishing everyone and teaching everyone with all wisdom, that we may present everyone perfect in Christ.* 29 For this I labor and struggle, in accord with the exercise of his power working within me.*

**2** 1 For I want you to know how great a struggle I am having for you and for those in Laodicea† and all who have not seen me face to face, 2 that their hearts may be encouraged as they are brought together in love, to have all the richness of fully assured understanding, for the knowledge of the mystery of God, Christ,* 3 in whom are hidden all the treasures of wisdom and knowledge.*

## III. WARNINGS AGAINST FALSE TEACHERS†

**A General Admonition.** 4 I say this so that no one may deceive you by specious arguments.* 5 For even if I am absent in the flesh, yet I am

---

**1:18** *Church:* such a reference seemingly belongs under "redemption" in the following lines, not under the "creation" section of the hymn. Stoic thought sometimes referred to the world as "the body of Zeus." Pauline usage is to speak of the church as the body of Christ (1 Cor 12:12–27; Rom 12:4–5). Some think that the author of Colossians has inserted the reference to the church here so as to define "head of the body" in Paul's customary way. See Col 1:24. *Preeminent:* when Christ was raised by God as *firstborn from the dead* (cf. Acts 26:23; Rev 1:5), he was placed over the community, the church, that he had brought into being, but he is also indicated as crown of the whole new creation, over *all* things. His further role is to *reconcile all things* (Col 1:20) for God or possibly "to himself."

**1:19** *Fullness:* in gnostic usage this term referred to a spiritual world of beings above, between God and the world; many later interpreters take it to refer to *the fullness of the deity* (Col 2:9); the reference could also be to the fullness of grace (cf. Jn 1:16).

**1:20** *The blood of his cross:* the most specific reference in the hymn to redemption through Christ's death, a central theme in Paul; cf. Col 2:14–15; 1 Cor 1:17, 18, 23. *[Through him]:* the phrase, lacking in some manuscripts, seems superfluous but parallels the reference to reconciliation through Christ earlier in the verse.

**1:21–23** Paul, in applying this hymn to the Colossians, reminds them that they have experienced the reconciling effect of Christ's death. He sees the effects of the cross in the redemption of human beings, not of cosmic powers such as those referred to in Col 1:16, 20 (*all things*). Paul also urges adherence to Christ in faith and begins to point to his own role as minister (Col 1:23), sufferer (Col 1:24), and proclaimer (Col 1:27–28) of this gospel.

**1:24–2:3** As the community at Colossae was not personally known to Paul (see Introduction), he here invests his teaching

with greater authority by presenting a brief sketch of his apostolic ministry and sufferings as they reflect those of Christ on behalf of the church (Col 1:24). The preaching of God's word (Col 1:25) carries out the divine plan (*the mystery*, Col 1:26) to make Christ known to the Gentiles (Col 1:27). It teaches the God-given wisdom about Christ (Col 1:28), whose power works mightily in the apostle (Col 1:29). Even in those communities that do not know him personally (Col 2:1), he can increase the perception of God in Christ, unite the faithful more firmly in love, and so bring encouragement to them (Col 2:2). He hopes that his apostolic authority will make the Colossians perceive more readily the defects in the teaching of others who have sought to delude them, the next concern in the letter.

**1:24** *What is lacking:* although variously interpreted, this phrase does not imply that Christ's atoning death on the cross was defective. It may refer to the apocalyptic concept of a quota of "messianic woes" to be endured before the end comes; cf. Mk 13:8, 19–20, 24 and the note on Mt 23:29–32. Others suggest that Paul's mystical unity with Christ allowed him to call his own *sufferings the afflictions of Christ.*

**2:1** *Laodicea:* chief city in Phrygia, northwest of Colossae; cf. Col 4:13, 16; Rev 3:14–22.

**2:4–23** In face of the threat posed by false teachers (Col 2:4), the Colossians are admonished to adhere to the gospel as it was

---

**1:18** 1 Cor 11:3; 12:12, 27; 15:20; Eph 1:22–23; Rev 1:5.
**1:20** 2 Cor 5:18–19; Eph 1:10.
**1:21** Eph 2:14–16.
**1:26** Rom 16:25–26; 1 Cor 2:7; Eph 3:3, 9.

**1:27** 3:4; Rom 8:10.
**1:28** Eph 4:13.
**1:29** 2:1; 4:12; Phil 4:13.
**2:2** 1:26–27; Eph 3:18–19.
**2:3** Prv 2:4–5; Is 45:3; Rom 11:33; 1 Cor 1:30.
**2:4** Eph 4:14.

with you in spirit, rejoicing as I observe your good order and the firmness of your faith in Christ.* ⁶ So, as you received Christ Jesus the Lord, walk in him, ⁷ rooted in him and built upon him and established in the faith as you were taught, abounding in thanksgiving.* ⁸ See to it that no one captivate you with an empty, seductive philosophy according to human tradition, according to the elemental powers of the world† and not according to Christ.*

**Sovereign Role of Christ.** ⁹* For in him dwells the whole fullness of the deity† bodily, ¹⁰ and you share in this fullness in him, who is the head of every principality and power. ¹¹* In him† you were also circumcised with a circumcision not administered by hand, by stripping off the carnal body, with the circumcision of Christ. ¹² You were buried with him in baptism, in which you were also raised with him through faith in the power of God, who raised him from the dead.* ¹³* And even when you were dead [in] transgressions and the uncircumcision of your flesh, he brought you to life along with him, having forgiven us all our transgressions; ¹⁴† obliterating the bond against us, with its legal claims, which was opposed to us, he also removed it from our midst, nailing it to the cross;* ¹⁵ despoiling the principalities and the powers, he made a public spectacle of them,* leading them away in triumph by it.†

**Practices Contrary to Faith.** ¹⁶* Let no one, then, pass judgment on you in matters of food and drink or with regard to a festival or new moon or sabbath.† ¹⁷ These are shadows of things to come; the reality belongs to Christ.* ¹⁸ Let no one disqualify you, delighting in self-abasement and worship of angels, taking his stand on visions,† inflated without reason by his fleshly mind,* ¹⁹ and not holding closely to the head, from whom the whole body, supported and held together by its ligaments and bonds, achieves the growth that comes from God.*

²⁰ If you died with Christ to the elemental powers of the world, why do you submit to regulations as if you were still living in the world? ²¹ "Do not handle! Do not taste! Do not touch!" ²² These are all things destined to perish with use; they accord with human precepts and teachings.* ²³ While they have a semblance of wisdom in rigor of devotion and self-abasement [and] severity to the body, they are of no value against gratification of the flesh.

## IV. THE IDEAL CHRISTIAN LIFE IN THE WORLD

**3 Mystical Death and Resurrection.**† ¹ If then you were raised with Christ, seek what is above, where Christ is seated at the

---

first preached to them (Col 2:6), steeping themselves in it with grateful hearts (Col 2:7). They must reject religious teachings originating in any source except the gospel (Col 2:8) because in Christ alone will they have access to God, the *deity* (Col 2:9). So fully has Christ enlightened them that they need no other source of religious knowledge or virtue (Col 2:10). They do not require *circumcision* (Col 2:11), for *in baptism* their whole being has been affected by Christ (Col 2:12) through forgiveness of sin and resurrection to a new life (Col 2:13; cf. Col 3:1 and Rom 6:1–11).

On the cross Christ canceled the record of the debt that stood against us with all its claims (Col 2:14), i.e., he eliminated the law (cf. Eph 2:15) that human beings could not observe—and that could not save them. He forgave sins against the law (Col 2:14) and exposed as false and misleading (Col 2:15) all other powers (cf. Col 1:16) that purport to offer salvation. Therefore, the Colossians are not to accept judgments from such teachers on *food and drink* or to keep certain religious festivals or engage in certain cultic practices (Col 2:16), for the Colossians would thereby risk severing themselves from Christ (Col 2:19). If, when they accepted the gospel, they believed in Christ as their savior, they must be convinced that their salvation cannot be achieved by appeasing ruling spirits through dietary practices or through a wisdom gained simply by means of harsh asceticism (Col 2:20–23).

**2:8** *Elemental powers of the world*: see note on Gal 4:3.

**2:9** *Fullness of the deity*: the divine nature, not just attributes; see note on Col 1:19.

**2:11** A description of baptism (Col 2:12) in symbolic terms of the Old Testament rite for entry into the community. The false teachers may have demanded physical circumcision of the Colossians.

**2:14** The elaborate metaphor here about how God canceled the legal claims against us through Christ's cross depicts not Christ being nailed to the cross by men but *the bond…with its legal claims* being nailed to the cross by God.

**2:15** The picture derives from the *public spectacle* and *triumph* of a Roman emperor's victory parade, where captives marched in subjection. *The principalities and the powers* are here conquered, not reconciled (cf. Col 1:16, 20). An alternate rendering for *by it* (the cross) is "by him" (Christ).

**2:16** *Festival or new moon or sabbath*: yearly, monthly, and weekly observances determined by religious powers associated with a calendar set by the heavenly bodies, sun, moon, and stars (cf. Col 2:8).

**2:18** Ascetic practices encouraged by the false teachers included subjection of self humbly to their rules, worship of angels, and cultivation of visions, though exact details are unclear.

**3:1–4** By retaining the message of the gospel that the risen, living Christ is the source of their salvation, the Colossians will be free from false religious evaluations of the things of the world (Col 3:1–2). They have died to these; but one day *when Christ…appears*, they will live with Christ in the presence of God (Col 3:3–4).

---

*
| 2:5 1 Cor 5:3; Phil 1:27. | 2:15 1:16, 20; 2 Cor 2:14; |
| 2:7 Eph 2:20–22; 3:17. | Eph 1:21. |
| 2:9 1:19; Eph 3:19. | 2:16 Rom 14:3–4; 1 Tm |
| 2:11 1:22; Jer 4:4; Rom | 4:3. |
| 2:25–29; Phil 3:3. | 2:17 Heb 8:5; 10:1. |
| 2:12 Rom 6:3–4. | 2:18 2:23; Mt 24:4. |
| 2:13 Eph 2:1, 5. | 2:19 Eph 2:21–22; 4:16. |
| 2:14 Eph 2:14–15. | 2:22 Is 29:13. |

right hand of God.* ² Think of what is above, not of what is on earth. ³ For you have died, and your life is hidden with Christ in God.* ⁴ When Christ your life appears, then you too will appear with him in glory.

### Renunciation of Vice.†

⁵ Put to death, then, the parts of you that are earthly:* immorality, impurity, passion, evil desire, and the greed that is idolatry.† ⁶ Because of these the wrath of God† is coming [upon the disobedient].* ⁷ By these you too once conducted yourselves, when you lived in that way. ⁸ But now you must put them all away:† anger, fury, malice, slander, and obscene language out of your mouths.* ⁹ Stop lying to one another, since you have taken off the old self with its practices* ¹⁰† and have put on the new self, which is being renewed, for knowledge, in the image of its creator.* ¹¹ Here there is not Greek and Jew, circumcision and uncircumcision, barbarian, Scythian,† slave, free; but Christ is all and in all.*

¹² Put on then, as God's chosen ones, holy and beloved, heartfelt compassion, kindness, humility, gentleness, and patience,* ¹³ bearing with one another and forgiving one another, if one has a grievance against another; as the Lord has forgiven you, so must you also do.* ¹⁴ And over all these put on love, that is, the bond of perfection.* ¹⁵ And let the peace of Christ control your hearts, the peace into which you were also called in one body. And be thankful.* ¹⁶ Let the word of Christ dwell in you richly, as in all wisdom you teach and admonish one another, singing psalms, hymns, and spiritual songs with gratitude in your hearts to God.* ¹⁷ And whatever you do, in word or in deed, do everything in the name of the Lord Jesus, giving thanks to God the Father through him.*

### The Christian Family.

¹⁸† Wives, be subordinate to your husbands, as is proper in the Lord.* ¹⁹ Husbands, love your wives, and avoid any bitterness toward them. ²⁰ Children, obey your parents in everything, for this is pleasing to the Lord.* ²¹ Fathers, do not provoke your children, so they may not become discouraged.*

### Slaves and Masters.

²² Slaves,† obey your human masters in everything, not only when being watched, as currying favor, but in simplicity of heart, fearing the Lord.* ²³ Whatever you do, do from the heart, as for the Lord and not for others, ²⁴ knowing that you will receive from the Lord the due payment of the inheritance; be slaves of the Lord Christ. ²⁵ For the wrongdoer will receive recompense for the wrong he committed, and there is no partiality.*

**4** ¹ Masters, treat your slaves justly and fairly, realizing that you too have a Master in heaven.

### Prayer and Apostolic Spirit.

² Persevere in prayer, being watchful in it with thanksgiving;* ³ at the same time, pray for us, too, that God may open a door to us for the word, to speak of the mystery of Christ, for which I am

---

† **3:5–17** In lieu of false asceticism and superstitious festivals, the apostle reminds the Colossians of the moral life that is to characterize their response to God through Christ. He urges their participation in the liturgical hymns and prayers that center upon God's plan of salvation in Christ (Col 3:16).

**3:5, 8** The two lists of five vices each are similar to enumerations at Rom 1:29–31 and Gal 5:19–21.

**3:6** *The wrath of God:* see note on Rom 1:18. Many manuscripts add, as at Eph 5:6, "upon the disobedient."

**3:8–10** *Put…away; have taken off; have put on:* the terms may reflect baptismal practice, taking off garments and putting on new ones after being united with Christ, here translated into ethical terms.

**3:10** *Image:* see note on Col 1:15.

**3:11** *Scythian:* a barbarous people from north of the Black Sea.

**3:18–4:6** After general recommendations that connect family life and the social condition of slavery with the service of Christ (Col 3:18–4:1), Paul requests prayers for himself, especially in view of his imprisonment (Col 3:2–3), and recommends friendly relations and meaningful discussions of Christian teaching with *outsiders,* i.e., non-Christians (Col 3:5–6). See note on Eph 5:21–6:9.

**3:22–25** *Slaves:* within this table of duties in family and societal relations, involving wives and husbands, children and parents (Col 3:18–21), such as also appears in Eph 5:22–6:9, slaves here receive special attention because of the case of Onesimus the slave returning to his master (Col 4:9; Phlm 10–12).

---

*

| | |
|---|---|
| **3:1** 2:12; Ps 110:1; Phil 3:20; Eph 2:6. | Eph 4:32. |
| **3:3** Rom 6:2–5. | **3:14** Rom 13:8–10. |
| **3:5** Mt 15:19; Rom 1:29–30; Gal 5:19–21; Eph 5:3, 5. | **3:15** Rom 12:5; 1 Cor 12:12; Eph 2:16; 4:3–4; Phil 4:7. |
| **3:6** Rom 1:18. | **3:16** Eph 5:19–20. |
| **3:8** Eph 4:22, 25, 31. | **3:17** 1 Cor 10:31. |
| **3:9** Rom 6:4, 6; Eph 4:22–25; Heb 12:1; 1 Pt 2:1; 4:2. | **3:18** Eph 5:22; Ti 2:5; 1 Pt 3:1. |
| **3:10** Gn 1:26–27. | **3:20** Eph 6:1. |
| **3:11** 1 Cor 12:13; Gal 3:27–28. | **3:21** Eph 6:4. |
| **3:12** Eph 4:1–2, 32; 1 Thes 5:15. | **3:22** Eph 6:5; 1 Tm 6:1; Ti 2:9–10; 1 Pt 2:18. |
| **3:13** Mt 6:14; 18:21–35; | **3:25** Rom 2:11. |
| | **4:2** Lk 18:1; Rom 12:12; Eph 6:18–20; 1 Thes 5:17. |

in prison,* ⁴ that I may make it clear, as I must speak. ⁵ Conduct yourselves wisely toward outsiders, making the most of the opportunity.* ⁶ Let your speech always be gracious, seasoned with salt, so that you know how you should respond to each one.

## V. CONCLUSION†

**Tychicus and Onesimus.** ⁷ Tychicus,† my beloved brother, trustworthy minister, and fellow slave in the Lord, will tell you all the news of me.* ⁸ I am sending him to you for this very purpose, so that you may know about us and that he may encourage your hearts, ⁹ together with Onesimus, a trustworthy and beloved brother, who is one of you. They will tell you about everything here.*

**From Paul's Co-Workers.** ¹⁰ Aristarchus,† my fellow prisoner, sends you greetings, as does Mark the cousin of Barnabas (concerning whom you have received instructions; if he comes to you, receive him),* ¹¹ and Jesus,† who is called Justus, who are of the circumcision; these alone are my co-workers for the kingdom of God, and they have been a comfort to me. ¹² Epaphras† sends you greetings; he is one of you, a slave of Christ [Jesus], always striving for you in his prayers so that you may be perfect and fully assured in all the will of God.* ¹³ For I can testify that he works very hard for you and for those in Laodicea† and those in Hierapolis. ¹⁴ Luke† the beloved physician sends greetings, as does Demas.*

**A Message for the Laodiceans.** ¹⁵ Give greetings to the brothers in Laodicea and to Nympha and to the church in her house.† ¹⁶ And when this letter is read before you, have it read also in the church of the Laodiceans, and you yourselves read the one from Laodicea.† ¹⁷ And tell Archippus, "See that you fulfill the ministry† that you received in the Lord."*

¹⁸ The greeting is in my own hand,† Paul's. Remember my chains. Grace be with you.*

---

† **4:7–18** Paul concludes with greetings and information concerning various Christians known to the Colossians.

**4:7** *Tychicus*: Acts 20:4 mentions his role in the collection for Jerusalem; Eph 6:21 repeats what is said here; see also 2 Tm 4:12; Ti 3:12.

**4:10** *Aristarchus*: a Thessalonian who was with Paul at Ephesus and Caesarea and on the voyage to Rome (Acts 19:29; 20:4; 27:2). *Mark*: also referred to at Phlm 24 and 2 Tm 4:11 and, as "John Mark," in Acts (Acts 12:12, 25; 13:13; 15:37–40). See also 1 Pt 5:13 and the note there. Traditionally the author of the second gospel.

**4:11** *Jesus*: a then common Jewish name, the Greek form of Joshua.

**4:12** *Epaphras*: see notes on Col 1:3–8 and Col 1:7.

**4:13** *Laodicea*: see note on Col 2:1. *Hierapolis*: a city northeast of Laodicea and northwest of Colossae.

**4:14** *Luke*: only here described as a medical doctor; cf. Phlm 24 and 2 Tm 4:11. Traditionally the author of the third gospel. *Demas*: cf. Phlm 24; he later deserted Paul (2 Tm 4:10).

**4:15** *Nympha and…her house*: some manuscripts read a masculine for the house-church leader, "Nymphas and…his house."

**4:16** *The one from Laodicea*: either a letter by Paul that has been lost or the Letter to the Ephesians (cf. note on Eph 1:1 *in Ephesus*).

**4:17** *Fulfill the ministry*: usually taken to mean that *Archippus*, the son of Philemon and Apphia (Phlm 1–2), is "pastor" at Colossae. An alternate interpretation is that Archippus, not Philemon, is the owner of the slave Onesimus and that Paul is asking Archippus to complete the service he has received in the Lord by sending Onesimus back to minister to Paul in his captivity (cf. Phlm 20).

**4:18** *My own hand*: a postscript in Paul's own hand was his custom; cf. Gal 6:11–18 and 2 Thes 3:17–18.

---

| | |
|---|---|
| **4:3** Rom 15:30; 1 Cor 16:9; Eph 6:19; 2 Thes 3:1. | 2 Tm 4:11; Phlm 24; 1 Pt 5:13. |
| **4:5** Eph 5:15–16. | **4:12** 1:7; Rom 15:30. |
| **4:7** Acts 20:4; Eph 6:21–22; Phil 1:12. | **4:14** Phlm 24; 2 Tm 4:10–11. |
| **4:9** Phlm 10–11. | **4:17** Phlm 2. |
| **4:10** Acts 19:29; 20:4; 27:2 / Acts 12:12, 25; 13:13; 15:37, 40; | **4:18** 1 Cor 16:21; Gal 6:11; Eph 3:1; 2 Thes 3:17. |

# Thessalonians

## INTRODUCTION

### Tatha Wiley

The first surviving Christian writings were composed twenty years after Jesus' death—in the fifties and sixties of the first century CE—but they were not the stories of Jesus' life. They were letters written by the Apostle Paul to assemblies of Jesus' followers that he had established around the Mediterranean region. They were sent to residents of an important city, Thessalonica, the provincial capital of Macedonia. Thessalonica had been under Roman rule for two centuries but culturally remained a Greek city. Rome allowed it to be a "free city" and to have its own local government. It was a port city and also located on a major Roman highway, the Via Egnatia.[1]

When we use the words *Christianity* and *Christian* for Paul's time, we wrongly collapse a historical development that actually took generations to occur. While the term *Christian* was first used at Antioch at the time of Paul and *church* translates the word *ekklēsia* found in the Pauline letters, today they evoke images of members of a distinct religion separated from Judaism (and a building in which they meet). The terms *Jesus movement* and *assembly* are neutral descriptions of the historical reality that do not evoke these images. Similarly, historians of first-century Judaism no longer refer to *late Judaism*—as if Judaism were about to end, replaced by Christianity—but by the time period *Second Temple Judaism*, in between the first Temple's destruction by the Babylonians (sixth century BCE) and the destruction of the rebuilt second Temple by the Romans (late first century CE).

The historical reality we need to remember is the Jewish context of a messianic movement after the death of Jesus. The Jesus movement was one of the Judaisms—along with Pharisaic

---

1. Beverly Gaventa, *First and Second Thessalonians* (Louisville: Westminister John Knox, 1998), 3.

## Outline of 1 Thessalonians

I. **Address (1:1–10)**

II. **Previous Relations with the Thessalonians (2:1–3:13)**

III. **Specific Exhortations (4:1–5:25)**

IV. **Final Greeting (5:26–28)**

Judaism—that survived the Jewish-Roman War in 70 CE. The Judaisms competed for the attention and allegiance of the people, each vying to be the major interpreter of Israel's history and symbols after the war. Pharasaic Judaism developed into Rabbinic Judaism. Only gradually did the Jesus movement become a predominantly non-Jewish religion, Christianity, distinct from Judaism. While Paul considered himself firmly in the context of Israel, his denial that Gentiles had to observe the Torah was bound to have consequences in a community that defined itself by living the way of the law.

In 1 Thessalonians, Paul's earliest letter, Jesus is the Lord Jesus Christ, a cosmic figure. A number of terms used to describe him carried political overtones and were appropriated from the imperial regime. The exception is *Messiah* (*Christ* in Greek), the Jewish figure of God's anointed one and Israel's liberator from foreign occupation.

Paul describes Jesus, crucified by imperial authorities, as Lord of the universe. He will "come down from heaven" (1 Thes 4:16) to punish the evil and vindicate the good. He will save believers "from the coming wrath" (1:10). The *Pax Romana*—the peace proclaimed by the emperor—was conceived as salvation for all. But Paul writes that "sudden disaster" will come upon those who say "peace and security" (5:3). His subtle reference to the *Pax Romana* unmasks the false peace imposed on Rome's colonized. The word *gospel* (1:5; 2:2, 4, 8, 9; 3:2) was also appropriated from the imperial realm, meaning an important announcement made by the emperor. So, too, *parousia* (2:19; 3:13; 4:15; 5:23)—the "coming of the Lord." This was a political term used for a community's readiness for an emperor's arrival and the sending out of a delegation to greet him. To say to the Thessalonians that God calls them "into his kingdom" (2:12) was likewise a challenge. For one kingdom to begin, another must end.

Like letters today, letters in the ancient world served many functions, conveying greetings or news or information and expressing friendship among senders and recipients. Paul's letters responded to difficulties in the assemblies he had established. Paul followed the general form of a private letter, expanding the thanksgiving section and adding moral and eschatological instruction. Eschatological hopes and expectations shaped the horizon of some forms of Judaism of Paul's time.

*Eschaton* means "end-time." Eschatological hopes are natural in times of crisis—the hope for freedom and liberation, for independence from foreign occupation, for justice, for a savior. The eschatological time is not the end of history but the beginning of a new stage when the reign of evil that distorts all of creation is ended at last. Common eschatological images are of a future wrath and judgment, the second coming or "day of the Lord," a new covenant, and all nations worshiping the true God of Israel.

One does not have to read far to discover that Paul expected something dramatic to happen in the future. God's intervention will change the structures of the world, replacing injustice with justice and inequality with equality. Jesus, who is with God in heaven, will return, delivering the Thessalonian believers—who have learned from Paul how they should conduct themselves to please God (1 Thes 4:1)—from the "coming wrath" (1:10), God's anger at human evil (2:16). Destruction or salvation (5:9) are the only options.

Who were these believers that Paul had convinced of Jesus' significance? That the assembly members were non-Jews is clear by Paul's comment that they have "turned to God from idols, to serve the living and true God" (1 Thes 1:9). Paul does not take credit for their belief. God has chosen them, and the gospel came to them "not . . . in word alone, but also in power and in the holy Spirit and [with] much conviction" (1:5). He does not portray his role as apostle as superior to theirs. Rather, in their proclamation of the word, they share equally in the process of salvation. In Macedonia and Achaia and everywhere their faith has become known because "the word of the Lord has sounded forth" from them (1:8).

In this letter, Paul makes a promise to believers and imposes an obligation upon them. His promise is that salvation from God's wrath is a realistic hope (1 Thes 1:10; 2:19; 3:13) *if* they conduct themselves as worthy of God (2:12), *if* they conduct themselves to please God (4:1), *if* they refrain from immorality (4:3), *if* they avoid impurity (4:7), *if* they love one another (4:9), *if* they conduct themselves properly toward outsiders (4:12), *if* they encourage one another and build one another up (5:11), *if* they always seek what is good for each other and for all (5:15), *if* they avoid evil (5:22). In other words, *if they create an assembly of justice and equality*, they will be saved. Then they will be with Jesus forever (4:17).

Paul envisions a new, just society in which total equality is the basis for ethical conduct:

> What matters—and all that matters—is how one relates to one's brothers and sisters in the community of the new age that endeavors to make God's justice a reality already now in this world. Here only one principle determines what its members have to do: to follow the commandment of love regardless of all distinctions of ethnic, social, and gender identity. Mutual respect is required of all.[2]

Obligation is the other side of promise. Paul's ethical instruction is an intrinsic part of the gospel (1 Thes 4:4–8). God calls the Thessalonian

---

2. Helmut Koester, *Paul and His World: Interpreting the New Testament in Context* (Minneapolis: Fortress Press, 2007), 13.

believers to holiness (4:7). The concept of holiness was familiar to Jews from the Torah. It was a moral imperative: Be holy as God is holy (Lv 19:2). Honor was a more familiar cultural ideal for Gentiles. But to be worthy of God requires not only right behavior, Paul emphasizes, but a transformation of their values and orientation that results in being *blameless* before God (1 Thes 3:13). If they desire salvation, they are to be "perfectly holy" and "preserved blameless" for the return of Jesus (5:23). For now, divine judgment is still in the future. No one knows when it will become present. But Paul does not seem concerned. They are not in darkness, he says, they are children of light and of the day (5:4–5). They are destined for salvation (5:8). They are ready for eschatological battle. The weapons are defensive, the breastplate and helmet (5:8). They are connected with the virtues of faith, hope, and love (1:3). Paul is not worried about the surprise arrival of the day of the Lord because in the community's faith, hope, and love it is already being realized. Salvation is already a present reality.

Paul does not expect his converts to produce this transformation by themselves. God will accomplish it (1 Thes 5:24). The power of the Holy Spirit is moral conversion generated by God (1:5). This is the process of sanctification.

In addition to the gift of God's Spirit, Paul gives another answer, though somewhat indirect, as to how they are to achieve this moral change. They are to become imitators of himself and the Lord (1 Thes 1:6). What do they imitate in Paul? He gives only hints: by suffering ill treatment and still having courage to preach (2:2); by not deluding, deceiving, or working from impure motives (2:3); by pleasing God, not human beings (2:4); by not using flattery to win people or the gospel for one's own greed (2:5); by not seeking praise for oneself but by being gentle (2:6–7); by working hard and not being a burden to anyone (2:9);

by being devout, just, and blameless toward others (2:10); by encouraging others to live in ways worthy of God (2:12).

Paul responds to a number of problems in the Thessalonian assembly. His comment, "Be at peace among yourselves" (1 Thes 5:13), suggests the presence of noticeable conflict in the assembly. His call "to respect those who are laboring among you and who are over you in the Lord and who admonish you" (1 Thes 5:12) implies difficulty with leadership in the group. This certainly occurred in other Pauline assemblies (cf. 1 Cor 1:12). A further problem might have been his worry over the place of prophecy, an important ministry in the early Jesus movement: "Do not despise prophetic utterances" (1 Thes 5:20).

But the major question of the assembly members that Timothy brought back to Paul regarded the members who had died (1 Thes 4:13–18). Two services provided by voluntary associations in the ancient world were sharing a common meal and helping with burial costs. After death, people remained members as ancestors. The question posed to Timothy when he visited them (3:2) and that Paul addresses was one of belonging, rather than the theological question of resurrection. Were the members who had died still to be included in salvation when Christ comes again?

Paul answers with an enthusiastic yes. Not only will they be included, he assures them, but Jesus will first gather up those who have died. Then, in an expression charged with joy, Paul draws everyone into the image: "We who are alive, who are left, will be caught up together with them in the clouds to meet the Lord in the air. Thus we shall always be with the Lord" (1 Thes 4:17). This is an example of development in Paul's own thinking. Chances are he had not yet thought about the death of assembly members. But when confronted with the question, he seeks first to calm anxieties and then to formulate an answer consistent with other eschatological images and language. ■

# THE FIRST LETTER TO THE THESSALONIANS

## New American Bible, Introduction

When Paul parted from Barnabas (Acts 15:36–41) at the beginning of what is called his second missionary journey, he chose Silvanus (Silas) as his traveling companion. Soon afterwards he took Timothy along with him (Acts 16:1–3). Paul was now clearly at the head of his own missionary band. About A.D. 50, he arrived in Greece for the first time. In making converts in Philippi and, soon afterwards, in Thessalonica, he was beset by persecution from Jews and Gentiles alike. Moving on to Beroea, he was again harassed by enemies from Thessalonica and hurriedly left for Athens (Acts 16:11–17:15). Silvanus and Timothy remained behind for a while. Paul soon sent Timothy back to Thessalonica to strengthen that community in its trials (1 Thes 3:1–5). Timothy and Silvanus finally returned to Paul when he reached Corinth (Acts 18:1–18), probably in the early summer of A.D. 51. Timothy's return with a report on conditions at Thessalonica served as the occasion for Paul's first letter (1 Thes 3:6–8).

The letter begins with a brief address (1 Thes 1:1) and concludes with a greeting (1 Thes 5:26–28). The body of the letter consists of two major parts. The first (1 Thes 1:2–3:13) is a set of three sections of thanksgiving connected by two *apologiae* (defenses) dealing, respectively, with the missionaries' previous conduct and their current concerns. Paul's thankful optimism regarding the Thessalonians' spiritual welfare is tempered by his insistence on their recognition of the selfless love shown by the missionaries. In an age of itinerant peddlers of new religions, Paul found it necessary to emphasize not only the content of his gospel but also his manner of presenting it, for both attested to God's grace as freely bestowed and powerfully effected.

The second part of the letter (1 Thes 4:1–5:25) is specifically hortatory or parenetic. The superabundant love for which Paul has just prayed (1 Thes 3:12–13) is to be shown practically by living out the norms of conduct that he has communicated to them. Specific "imperatives" of Christian life, principles for acting morally, stem from the "indicative" of one's relationship to God through Christ by the sending of the holy Spirit. Thus, moral conduct is the practical, personal expression of one's Christian faith, love, and hope.

The principal divisions of the First Letter to the Thessalonians are the following:

 I. Address (1:1–10)
 II. Previous Relations with the Thessalonians (2:1–3:13)
 III. Specific Exhortations (4:1–5:25)
 IV. Final Greeting (5:26–28) ■

# FIRST THESSALONIANS

## I. ADDRESS

**1** **Greeting.** ¹†* Paul, Silvanus, and Timothy to the church of the Thessalonians in God the Father and the Lord Jesus Christ: grace to you and peace.

**Thanksgiving for Their Faith.** ²We give thanks to God always for all of you, remembering you in our prayers, unceasingly* ³calling to mind your work of faith and labor of love and endurance in hope† of our Lord Jesus Christ, before our God and Father, ⁴knowing, brothers loved by God, how you were chosen.* ⁵For our gospel did not come to you in word alone, but also in power and in the holy Spirit and [with] much conviction. You know what sort of people we were [among] you for your sake.* ⁶And you became imitators† of us and of the Lord, receiving the word in great affliction, with joy from the holy Spirit, ⁷so that you became a model for all the believers in Macedonia and in Achaia.* ⁸For from you the word of the Lord has sounded forth not only in Macedonia and [in] Achaia, but in every place your faith in God has gone forth, so that we have no need to say anything.* ⁹For they themselves openly declare about us what sort of reception we had among you, and how you turned to God from idols to serve the living and true God* ¹⁰and to await his Son from heaven, whom he raised from [the] dead, Jesus, who delivers us from the coming wrath.*

## II. PREVIOUS RELATIONS WITH THE THESSALONIANS

**2** **Paul's Ministry Among Them.** ¹For you yourselves know, brothers, that our reception among you was not without effect. ²Rather, after we had suffered and been insolently treated, as you know, in Philippi, we drew courage through our God to speak to you the gospel of God with much struggle.* ³Our exhortation was not from delusion or impure motives, nor did it work through deception. ⁴But as we were judged worthy† by God to be entrusted with the gospel, that is how we speak, not as trying to please human beings, but rather God, who judges our hearts.* ⁵Nor, indeed, did we ever appear with flattering speech, as you know, or with a pretext for greed—God is witness— ⁶nor did we seek praise from human beings, either from you or from others,* ⁷although we were able to impose our weight as apostles of Christ. Rather, we were gentle† among you, as a nursing mother cares for her children. ⁸With such affection for you, we were determined to share with you not only the gospel of God, but our very selves as well, so dearly beloved had you become to us. ⁹You recall, brothers, our toil and drudgery. Working night and day in order not to burden any of you, we proclaimed to you the gospel of God.* ¹⁰You are witnesses, and so is God, how devoutly and justly and blamelessly we behaved toward you believers. ¹¹As you know, we treated each one of you as a father treats his children,* ¹²exhorting and encouraging you and insisting that you conduct yourselves as worthy of the God who calls you into his kingdom and glory.*

---

† **1:1** On the address, see note on Rom 1:1–7.
**1:3** *Faith…love…hope*: this, along with 1 Thes 5:8, is the earliest mention in Christian literature of the three "theological virtues" (see 1 Cor 13:13). The order here stresses eschatological hope, in line with the letter's emphasis on the Lord's second, triumphal coming, or parousia (1 Thes 1:10; 2:12, 19; 3:13; 4:13–5:11; 5:23).
**1:6** *Imitators*: the Pauline theme of "imitation" (see 1 Thes 2:14; 1 Cor 4:16; 11:1; 2 Thes 3:9) is rooted in Paul's view of solidarity in Christ through sharing in Jesus' cross and in the Spirit of the risen Lord.
**2:4** *Judged worthy*: Paul regards "worthiness" not as grounded in one's own talent or moral self-righteousness but in God's discernment of genuinely selfless attitudes and actions (see 2 Cor 10:17–18).

**2:7** *Gentle*: many excellent manuscripts read "infants" (*nēpioi*), but "gentle" (*ēpioi*) better suits the context here.

---

* **1:1** Acts 15:40; 16:1–3, 19; 17:14–15; 2 Thes 1:1–2.
**1:2** 2 Thes 1:3.
**1:4** 2 Thes 2:13.
**1:5** Acts 13:52; 17:1–9.
**1:7** 2 Thes 1:4; 1 Cor 4:16; 11:1 / 2:14; Phil 3:17.
**1:8** Rom 1:8.
**1:9** Acts 14:15; Gal 4:8 / 4:5.
**1:10** Rom 2:1–16; 5:9; 13:4 / 5:9.
**2:2** Acts 16:19–17:10.
**2:4** Gal 1:10.
**2:6** Jn 5:41, 44; 1 Cor 10:31; 2 Cor 4:17.
**2:9** Acts 20:34; 1 Cor 4:12; 9:3–18; 2 Thes 3:7–9.
**2:11** Acts 20:31.
**2:12** 1 Pt 5:10 / 4:7; 2 Thes 2:14.

**Further Thanksgiving.** [13] And for this reason we too give thanks to God unceasingly, that, in receiving the word of God from hearing us, you received not a human word but, as it truly is, the word of God, which is now at work in you who believe. [14]† For you, brothers, have become imitators of the churches of God that are in Judea in Christ Jesus. For you suffer the same things from your compatriots as they did from the Jews, [15]† who killed both the Lord Jesus and the prophets and persecuted us; they do not please God, and are opposed to everyone,* [16] trying to prevent us from speaking to the Gentiles that they may be saved, thus constantly filling up the measure of their sins. But the wrath of God has finally begun to come upon them.*

**Paul's Recent Travel Plans.** [17] Brothers, when we were bereft of you for a short time, in person, not in heart, we were all the more eager in our great desire to see you in person.* [18] We decided to go to you—I, Paul, not only once but more than once—yet Satan thwarted us.* [19] For what is our hope or joy or crown to boast of in the presence of our Lord Jesus at his coming if not you yourselves?* [20] For you are our glory and joy.

**3** [1] That is why, when we could bear it no longer, we decided to remain alone in Athens* [2] and sent Timothy, our brother and co-worker for God in the gospel of Christ, to strengthen and encourage you in your faith,* [3] so that no one be disturbed in these afflictions. For you yourselves know that we are destined† for this. [4] For even when we were among you, we used to warn you in advance that we would undergo affliction, just as has

happened, as you know.* [5] For this reason, when I too could bear it no longer, I sent to learn about your faith, for fear that somehow the tempter had put you to the test and our toil might come to nothing.

[6] But just now Timothy has returned to us from you, bringing us the good news of your faith and love, and that you always think kindly of us and long to see us as we long to see you. [7] Because of this, we have been reassured about you, brothers, in our every distress and affliction, through your faith. [8] For we now live, if you stand firm in the Lord.

**Concluding Thanksgiving and Prayer.** [9]† What thanksgiving, then, can we render to God for you, for all the joy we feel on your account before our God? [10] Night and day we pray beyond measure to see you in person and to remedy the deficiencies of your faith. [11] Now may God himself, our Father, and our Lord Jesus direct our way to you, [12] and may the Lord make you increase and abound in love for one another and for all, just as we have for you,* [13] so as to strengthen your hearts, to be blameless in holiness before our God and Father at the coming of our Lord Jesus with all his holy ones. [Amen.]*

### III. SPECIFIC EXHORTATIONS

**4** **General Exhortations.** [1] Finally, brothers, we earnestly ask and exhort you in the Lord Jesus that, as you received from us how you should conduct yourselves to please God—and as you are conducting yourselves—you do so even more. [2] For you know what instructions† we gave you through the Lord Jesus.

---

**2:14** Luke's picture of the persecutions at Philippi (by Gentiles) and in Thessalonica and Beroea (by Jews) seems to be considerably schematized (Acts 16:11–40; 17:1–15). Paul pictures the Thessalonian community as composed of converts from paganism (1 Thes 1:9) and speaks here of persecution by their (pagan) compatriots rather than by Jews.

**2:15–16** Paul is speaking of historical opposition on the part of Palestinian Jews in particular and does so only some twenty years after Jesus' crucifixion. Even so, he quickly proceeds to depict the persecutors typologically, in apocalyptic terms. His remarks give no grounds for anti-Semitism to those willing to understand him, especially in view of Paul's pride in his own ethnic and religious background (Rom 9:1–5; 10:1; 11:1–3; Phil 3:4–6). Sinful conduct (1 Thes 2:16) is itself an anticipation of the ultimate wrath or judgment of God (Rom 1:18–2:5), whether or not it is perceived as such.

**3:3** *We are destined*: the Greek phraseology and the context suggest Paul's concern to alert his readers to difficulties he knew they would necessarily face and to enable them to see their present experience in the light of what he warned them would happen

in the future. This line of thought is followed in 2 Thes 2:1–15.

**3:9–10** The tension between Paul's optimism concerning the Thessalonians' faith and his worries about their perseverance remains unresolved. Perhaps this is accounted for not only by the continuing harassment but also by the shortness of his own stay in Thessalonica (even if that were over twice as long as the conventional three weeks that Luke assigns to it, Acts 17:2).

**4:2** *Instructions*: these include specific guidelines on the basis of the Lord's authority, not necessarily sayings Jesus actually uttered. More profoundly, as 1 Thes 4:8 implies, the instructions are practical principles that Paul worked out in accordance with his understanding of the role of the Spirit.

---

*

**2:15** Acts 2:23; 7:52.
**2:16** Gn 15:16; 2 Mc 6:14 / Rom 1:18; 2:5–6.
**2:17** 3:10; Rom 1:10–11.
**2:18** Rom 15:22.
**2:19** 2 Cor 1:14; Phil 2:16; 4:1.

**3:1** Acts 17:14.
**3:2** Acts 16:1–2; 1 Cor 3:5–9.
**3:4** Acts 14:22; 2 Thes 2:5–7; 2 Tm 3:12.
**3:12** 4:9–10; 2 Thes 1:3.
**3:13** 5:23; 1 Cor 1:8.

**Holiness in Sexual Conduct.**† ³This is the will of God, your holiness: that you refrain from immorality, ⁴that each of you know how to acquire a wife for himself in holiness and honor, ⁵not in lustful passion as do the Gentiles who do not know God;* ⁶not to take advantage of or exploit a brother in this matter, for the Lord is an avenger in all these things, as we told you before and solemnly affirmed. ⁷For God did not call us to impurity but to holiness. ⁸Therefore, whoever disregards this, disregards not a human being but God, who [also] gives his holy Spirit to you.*

**Mutual Charity.** ⁹On the subject of mutual charity you have no need for anyone to write you, for you yourselves have been taught by God to love one another.* ¹⁰Indeed, you do this for all the brothers throughout Macedonia. Nevertheless we urge you, brothers, to progress even more,* ¹¹and to aspire to live a tranquil life, to mind your own affairs, and to work with your [own] hands, as we instructed you, ¹²that you may conduct yourselves properly toward outsiders and not depend on anyone.

**Hope for the Christian Dead.** ¹³We do not want you to be unaware, brothers, about those who have fallen asleep, so that you may not grieve like the rest, who have no hope. ¹⁴For if we believe that Jesus died and rose, so too will God, through Jesus, bring with him those who have fallen asleep.* ¹⁵Indeed, we tell you this, on the word of the Lord, that we who are alive, who are left until the coming of the

Lord,† will surely not precede those who have fallen asleep.* ¹⁶For the Lord himself, with a word of command, with the voice of an archangel and with the trumpet of God, will come down from heaven, and the dead in Christ will rise first.* ¹⁷Then we who are alive, who are left, will be caught up together† with them in the clouds to meet the Lord in the air. Thus we shall always be with the Lord. ¹⁸Therefore, console one another with these words.

**5** **Vigilance.** ¹Concerning times and seasons, brothers, you have no need for anything to be written to you.* ²For you yourselves know very well that the day of the Lord will come like a thief at night.* ³When people are saying, "Peace and security," then sudden disaster comes upon them, like labor pains upon a pregnant woman, and they will not escape.

⁴But you, brothers, are not in darkness, for that day to overtake you like a thief.* ⁵For all of you are children of the light† and children of the day. We are not of the night or of darkness. ⁶Therefore, let us not sleep as the rest do, but let us stay alert and sober.* ⁷Those who sleep go to sleep at night, and those who are drunk get drunk at night. ⁸But since we are of the day, let us be sober, putting on the breastplate of faith and love and the helmet that is hope for salvation.* ⁹For God did not destine us for wrath, but to gain salvation through our Lord Jesus Christ, ¹⁰who died for us, so that whether we are awake or asleep we may live together with him.† ¹¹Therefore, encourage

---

† **4:3–8** Many think that this passage deals with a variety of moral regulations (fornication, adultery, sharp business practices). It can be more specifically interpreted as bringing general norms to bear on a specific problem, namely, marriage within degrees of consanguinity (as between uncle and niece) forbidden in Jewish law but allowed according to a Greek heiress law, which would insure retention of an inheritance within the family and perhaps thereby occasion divorce. In that case, "immorality" (1 Thes 4:3) should be rendered as "unlawful marriage" and "this matter" (1 Thes 4:6) as "a lawsuit." The phrase in 1 Thes 4:4, "acquire a wife for himself," has often been interpreted to mean "control one's body."

**4:15** *Coming of the Lord*: Paul here assumes that the second coming, or parousia, will occur within his own lifetime but insists that the time or season is unknown (1 Thes 5:1–2). Nevertheless, the most important aspect of the parousia for him was the fulfillment of union with Christ. His pastoral exhortation focuses first on hope for the departed faithful, then (1 Thes 5:1–3) on the need of preparedness for those who have to achieve their goal.

**4:17** *Will be caught up together*: literally, snatched up, carried off; cf. 2 Cor 12:2; Rev 12:5. From the Latin verb here used, *rapiemur*, has come the idea of "the rapture," when believers will be transported away from the woes of the world; this construc-

tion combines this verse with Mt 24:40–41 (see note there) // Lk 17:34–35 and passages from Revelation in a scheme of millennial dispensationalism.

**5:5** *Children of the light*: that is, belonging to the daylight of God's personal revelation and expected to achieve it (an analogous development of imagery that appears in Jn 12:36).

**5:10** Characteristically, Paul plays on words suggesting ultimate and anticipated death and life. Union with the crucified and risen Lord at his parousia is anticipated in some measure in contrasted states of our temporal life. The essential element he urges is our indestructible personal union in Christ's own life (see Rom 5:1–10).

---

* **4:5** Ps 79:6; Jer 10:25; 2 Thes 1:8; 1 Pt 3:7.
**4:8** Lk 10:16.
**4:9** Jn 6:45; 13:34; 1 Jn 2:20–21, 27; 4:7.
**4:10** 2 Thes 3:6–12.
**4:14** 1 Cor 15:3–4, 12, 20.
**4:15** 1 Cor 15:51; Rev 14:13; 20:4–6.

**4:16** Mt 24:31; 1 Cor 15:23, 52.
**5:1** Mt 24:36–45.
**5:2** 2 Pt 3:10.
**5:4** Eph 5:8–9.
**5:6** Mt 24:42; Rom 13:12–13; 1 Pt 5:8.
**5:8** Is 59:17; Rom 13:11–14; Eph 6:11, 14–17.

one another and build one another up, as indeed you do. *

**Church Order.** [12] We ask you, brothers, to respect those who are laboring among you and who are over you in the Lord and who admonish you, [13] and to show esteem for them with special love on account of their work. Be at peace among yourselves.

[14] We urge you, brothers, admonish the idle, cheer the fainthearted, support the weak, be patient with all. [15] See that no one returns evil for evil; rather, always seek what is good [both] for each other and for all. * [16] Rejoice always. [17] Pray without ceasing. [18] In all circumstances give thanks, for this is the will of God for you in Christ Jesus. * [19] † Do not quench the Spirit.

---

† **5:19–21** Paul's buoyant encouragement of charismatic freedom sometimes occasioned excesses that he or others had to remedy (see 1 Cor 14; 2 Thes 2:1–15; 2 Pt 3:1–16).

**5:23** Another possible translation is, "May the God of peace himself make you perfectly holy and sanctify your spirit fully, and may both soul and body be preserved blameless for the coming of our Lord Jesus Christ." In either case, Paul is not offering an anthropological or philosophical analysis of human nature. Rather, he looks to the wholeness of what may be called the supernatural and natural aspects of a person's service of God.

[20] Do not despise prophetic utterances. [21] Test everything; retain what is good. [22] Refrain from every kind of evil.

**Concluding Prayer.** [23] † May the God of peace himself make you perfectly holy and may you entirely, spirit, soul, and body, be preserved blameless for the coming of our Lord Jesus Christ. * [24] The one who calls you is faithful, and he will also accomplish it. [25] Brothers, pray for us [too].

## IV. FINAL GREETING

[26] Greet all the brothers with a holy kiss. † [27] I adjure you by the Lord that this letter be read to all the brothers. [28] The grace of our Lord Jesus Christ be with you.

---

† **5:26** *Kiss:* the holy embrace (see Rom 16:16; 1 Cor 16:20; 2 Cor 13:12; 1 Pt 5:14) was a greeting of respect and affection, perhaps given during a liturgy at which Paul's letter would have been read.

---

**5:11** Rom 15:2; 1 Cor 8:1;
14:12, 26; Eph 4:29.
**5:15** Prv 20:22; Mt

**5:38–42;** Rom 12:17.
**5:18** Eph 5:20.
**5:23** 2 Thes 3:16.

# The Second Letter to the
# Thessalonians

## INTRODUCTION

### Tatha Wiley

While Paul is convinced that Christ's coming is imminent, the assembly in Thessalonica may be looking to Christ's return a bit more fervently than even Paul. These believers see in their own persecution (1:4–10) a sign that the end time is here and that God is now ending the reign of evil that has distorted creation. Their apocalyptic expectation is intense.

In his First Letter to the Thessalonians, Paul portrayed the assembly's experience of tribulation as a sign of the presence of the gospel. In its affliction the community shared with Paul the presence of salvation.[1] As Paul emphasized in the first letter, the day of the Lord will spell deliverance for his followers (1 Thes 5:1–9). It was also a politically charged message, as in his First Letter to the Corinthians: Christ will destroy "every sovereignty and every authority and power" (1 Cor 15:24). Paul "reads events in light of an eschatological vision of God bringing a new era of justice for those who have faced alienation and oppression."[2] But in 2 Thessalonians, he seems to recede from that conviction.

Given noticeable differences between 1 and 2 Thessalonians, scholars have raised the question whether Paul is the actual writer of the second letter. Is this letter an example of *pseudepigrapha*, writings in which an anonymous writer uses someone else's name to give authority to his work? Unlike 1 Thessalonians, which is considered an undisputed letter, without question written by Paul, many scholars consider this second letter of disputable authorship.

---

1. Helmut Koester, *Paul and His World: Interpreting the New Testament in Context* (Minneapolis: Fortress Press, 2007), 24.

2. Abraham Smith, "Unmasking the Powers: Toward a Postcolonial Analysis of 1 Thessalonians," in *Paul and the Roman Imperial Order*, ed. Richard A. Horsley (Harrisburg, PA: Trinity Press International, 2004), 47–66, at 55.

## Outline of 2 Thessalonians

I. **Address (1:1–12)**

II. **Warning Against Deception Concerning the Parousia (2:1–17)**

III. **Concluding Exhortations (3:1–16)**

IV. **Final Greetings (3:17–18)**

Authorship becomes a question for biblical scholars when something—wording, style, tone, perspective—does not fit the Paul of the undisputed letters. The letters themselves become the basis for comparison. While each letter is written to a different assembly with its own distinctive problems, they share characteristic themes of Paul's, for example, the centrality of the Gentiles, phrases such as the "truth of the gospel," such basic contrasts as "works of the law" and "faith in Christ," the import of this contrast for justification, and ethical instruction—often about sexual immorality—that emphasizes the moral transformation entailed in being worthy before God. Sometimes reversals are the clue. For example, Paul expects the day of the Lord in his lifetime; he does not speculate about the date, but he believes it to be imminent. For Paul suddenly to place the day of the Lord far into the future would be odd. Or possibly Paul is not the author here.

Indeed, observing such differences raises the question of authorship. But settling the question is not a prelude to dismissal. Rather it opens the way to the discovery of yet another author and community in the first century of the Christian tradition.

Both letters name Paul, Silvanus, and Timothy as their authors. With some repetition, the church is described in the same way and the same greeting is extended here (2 Thes 1:1). The thanksgiving in each letter shares the same words but uses them differently. The first letter thanks God for the Thessalonians' "work of faith and labor of love and endurance in hope" in Christ (1 Thes 1:3). The second letter gives thanks because "your faith flourishes ever more, and the love of every one of you for one another grows ever greater" (2 Thes 1:3). The author then boasts of their "endurance and faith" during persecution (2 Thes 1:4). The differences are so slight here that a compelling case could be not be made that Paul did not write the second letter.

A clearer contrast can be seen in the relationship of the author to the community. In the undisputed letter, Paul longs for the community. He is the lover seeking his beloved: "With such affection for you, we were determined to share with you not only the gospel of God, but our very selves as well, so dearly beloved had you become to us" (1 Thes 2:8). He wants to be with them: "When we were bereft of you for a short time, in person, not in heart, we were all the more eager in our great desire to see you in person" (2:17). Timothy has told him that "you always think kindly of us and long to see us as we long to see you" (3:6). Words fall short of what he wants to express: "What thanksgiving, then, can we render to God for you, for all the joy we feel on your account before our God?" (3:9). Such joy, however, does not diminish his corrective tendency: "Night and day we pray beyond measure to see you in person and to remedy the deficiencies of your faith" (3:10). He praises them several times for the love they have for one another (3:6; 4:9): "May the Lord make you increase and abound in love for one another and for all, just as we have for you" (3:12).

The second letter never mentions the author's desire to see the community, nor does it express any expectation that he will be with them. In the first letter, the status of the believers is assured: they are loved and chosen by God (1 Thes 1:4). But for the second, their worthiness is ambiguous, something yet to be settled: "We always pray for you, that our God may make you worthy of his calling" (2 Thes 1:11).

In both letters, believers are encouraged to become imitators of Paul (2 Thes 1:6; 2 Thes 3:7). But for the second author, imitation requires obedience: "If anyone does not obey our word as expressed in this letter, take note of this person not to associate with him, that he may be put to shame" (3:14). This threat is followed by an even stronger one about nonbelievers: "Those who do not obey the gospel of our Lord Jesus . . . will pay the penalty of eternal ruin" (1:8–9). Instruction in this letter is less about encouragement and more about imperatives: "For you know how one must imitate us. For we did not act in a disorderly way among you, nor did we eat food received free from anyone" (3:7–8). He instructed them, "If anyone was unwilling to work, neither should that one eat" (3:10).

A further difference regards proclamation of the gospel. In the first letter, the community was commended for its work apart from Paul: "For from you the word of the Lord has sounded forth" (1 Thes 1:8). The apostle and assembly were partners in preaching the word. In the second letter, however, only Paul and his co-workers spread the word. The assembly prays for them, "so that the word of the Lord may speed forward and be glorified" (2 Thes 3:1).

Do these differences constitute sufficient evidence that Paul did not write the second letter? Could it be the same person, enthusiastic at one time and somber at another? Or do these letters reflect the concerns and convictions of different persons who have different relationships with their communities? Consider a further question, the writer's purpose in writing.

If the second letter is a pseudepigraph, it originates in a community after Paul's death, and its concerns would not be those of the earlier community. Still, an anonymous writer could not make the later situation transparent or his audience would know the letter to be false. The first assembly's primary concern regarded their members who had died. Will the dead rise on the last day? The problem described in the second letter is a letter falsely attributed to Paul (2 Thes 2:1–2). In the false letter, Paul is announcing—incorrectly, we are told—that the day of the Lord is here. If indeed

2 Thessalonians is not written by Paul, one has to be amazed that the author has employed a pseudepigraph to combat a problem caused by a pseudepigraph! What is the author doing? One hypothesis is that the author uses Paul as a literary device to respond to persons whose apocalyptic intensity has exceeded his personal tolerance.

But a deeper problem for this community may be this writer's fixation with divine violence. Divine retribution is portrayed as the appropriate response to the persecution of believers: "It is surely just on God's part to repay with afflictions those who are afflicting you" (2 Thes 1:6). The Lord Jesus will inflict punishment on those "who do not acknowledge God" (1:8). The second letter is striking for its harshness. The Lord Jesus will "kill [the lawless one] with the breath of his mouth," rendering him "powerless by the manifestation of his coming" (2:8).[3] This desire for revenge and legitimation of divine vengeance seems to go beyond Paul's own use of hostile, polemical language elsewhere to describe his opponents.

Then, after saying how "the power of Satan" is involved in "every wicked deceit" of those who will not be saved because "they have not accepted the love of truth" (2 Thes 2:9–10), the writer of 2 Thessalonians makes this odd statement about God:

Therefore, God is sending them a deceiving

power so that they may believe the lie, that all who have not believed the truth but have approved wrongdoing may be condemned. (2 Thes 2:11–12)

A God who is duplicitous? Who plays a game with human beings so that when they believe the deception served to them they are condemned? The emphasis on a God of retribution thus continues, a harsh theology exceeding anything the undisputed Pauline letters would suggest.

Why would someone appropriate Paul's identity in the first place? A first reason is authority. The community that this writer speaks to must value Paul. A letter carrying his name strengthens the letter's reception. But the writer's use of Paul is not without ambiguity. Paul's communities were charismatic, Spirit-filled groups. They were egalitarian. Women received gifts of the Spirit, as did men. By contrast, the second author does not prize the natural messiness that comes with a charismatic community. Instead, he values continuity and stability. He tells the assembly to "hold fast to the traditions that you were taught" (2 Thes 2:15). How is the writer using Paul? Is it simple imitation? Or is he using Paul to reverse himself on matters of eschatological expectation and the shape of the community? Is he involved in subtly but effectively changing the dynamics of the community and using Paul's own authority to do so? By stressing the assembly's obedience, the writer shapes a more passive than active community (3:14). ■

---

3. Just who is meant by "the lawless one" is an open question.

# THE SECOND LETTER TO THE THESSALONIANS

## New American Bible, Introduction

This letter is addressed to the same church as the letter that precedes it in the canon and contains many expressions parallel to those in the First Letter to the Thessalonians, indeed verbatim with them. Yet other aspects of the contents of the Second Letter to the Thessalonians suggest a more impersonal tone and changed circumstances in the situation at Thessalonica.

The letter begins with an address (2 Thes 1:1–2) that expands only slightly on that of 1 Thes 1:1. It ends with a greeting insisting on its Pauline authority in the face of false claims made in Paul's name (see note on 2 Thes 2:2). The body of the letter falls into three short parts, of which the second is notoriously difficult (2 Thes 2).

The opening thanksgiving and prayer (2 Thes 1:3–12) speak of the Thessalonians' increasing faith and love in the face of outside persecution. God's eventual judgment against persecutors and his salvation for the faithful are already evidenced by the very fact of persecution. The second part (2 Thes 2:1–17), the heart of the letter, deals with a problem threatening the faith of the community. A message involving a prophetic oracle and apparently a forged letter, possibly presented at a liturgical gathering (cf. 2 Thes 2:2 and 1 Cor 14:26–33), to the effect that the day of the Lord and all that it means have already come, has upset the life of the Thessalonian church.

The writer counters their preoccupation with the date of the parousia (or coming again of the Lord Jesus from heaven, 2 Thes 2:1) by recalling Paul's teaching concerning what must happen first and by going on to describe what will happen at the Lord's coming (2 Thes 2:8); he indicates the twofold process by which the "activity of Satan" and God's actions (2 Thes 2:9–11) are working out, namely, a growing division between believers and those who succumb to false prophecy and "the lie." He concludes by insisting on Pauline traditions and by praying for divine strength (2 Thes 2:13–17). The closing part of the letter (2 Thes 3:1–16) deals in particular with the apostle's directives and model style of life and with correction of disorderly elements within the community.

Traditional opinion holds that this letter was written shortly after 1 Thessalonians. Occasionally it has been argued that 2 Thessalonians was written first or that the two letters are addressed to different segments within the church at Thessalonica (2 Thessalonians being directed to the Jewish Christians there) or even that 2 Thessalonians was originally written to some other nearby place where Paul carried out mission work, such as Philippi or Beroea. Increasingly in recent times, however, the opinion has been advanced that 2 Thessalonians is a pseudepigraph, that is, a letter written authoritatively in Paul's name, to maintain apostolic traditions in a later period, perhaps during the last two decades of the first century.

In any case, the presumed audience of Second Thessalonians and certain features of its style and content require that it be read and studied in a Pauline context, particularly that provided by 1 Thessalonians. At the same time, and especially if the letter is regarded as not by Paul himself, its apocalyptic presentation of preconditions for the parousia (2 Thes 2:1–12) may profit from and require recourse to a wider biblical basis for interpretation, namely Old Testament books such as Daniel and Isaiah and especially, in the New Testament, the synoptic apocalyptic discourse (Mk 13; Mt 24–25; Lk 21:5–36) and the Book of Revelation.

The principal divisions of the Second Letter to the Thessalonians are the following:

I. Address (1:1–12)
II. Warning Against Deception Concerning the Parousia (2:1–17)
III. Concluding Exhortations (3:1–16)
IV. Final Greetings (3:17–18) ∎

# SECOND THESSALONIANS

## I. ADDRESS

**1** **Greeting.**† ¹Paul, Silvanus, and Timothy to the church of the Thessalonians in God our Father and the Lord Jesus Christ:* ²grace to you and peace from God [our] Father and the Lord Jesus Christ.

**Thanksgiving.** ³† We ought to thank God always for you, brothers, as is fitting, because your faith flourishes ever more, and the love of every one of you for one another grows ever greater.* ⁴Accordingly, we ourselves boast of you in the churches of God regarding your endurance and faith in all your persecutions and the afflictions you endure.

⁵This is evidence of the just judgment of God, so that you may be considered worthy of the kingdom of God for which you are suffering.* ⁶For it is surely just on God's part to repay with afflictions those who are afflicting you, ⁷and to grant rest along with us to you who are undergoing afflictions, at the revelation of the Lord Jesus from heaven with his mighty angels, ⁸in blazing fire, inflicting punishment on those who do not acknowledge God and on those who do not obey the gospel of our Lord Jesus.* ⁹These will pay the penalty of eternal ruin, separated from the presence of the Lord and from the glory of his power,* ¹⁰when he comes to be glorified among his holy ones† and to be marveled at on that day among all who have believed, for our testimony to you was believed.*

**Prayer.** ¹¹To this end, we always pray for you, that our God may make you worthy of his calling and powerfully bring to fulfillment every good purpose and every effort of faith,* ¹²† that the name of our Lord Jesus may be glorified in you, and you in him,* in accord with the grace of our God and Lord Jesus Christ.

## II. WARNING AGAINST DECEPTION CONCERNING THE PAROUSIA

**2** **Christ and the Lawless One.**† ¹We ask you, brothers, with regard to the coming of our Lord Jesus Christ and our assembling with him,* ²not to be shaken out of your minds suddenly, or to be alarmed either by a "spirit,"† or by an oral statement, or by a

---

1:1–2 On the address, see note on Rom 1:1–7 and cf. 1 Thes 1:1.

1:3–12 On the thanksgiving, see note on Rom 1:8 and cf. 1 Thes 1:2–10. Paul's gratitude to God for the faith and love of the Thessalonians (2 Thes 1:3) and his Christian pride in their faithful endurance (2 Thes 1:4–5) contrast with the condemnation announced for those who afflict them, a judgment to be carried out at the parousia (2 Thes 1:6–10), which is described in vivid language drawn from Old Testament apocalyptic. A prayer for the fulfillment of God's purpose in the Thessalonians (2 Thes 1:11–12) completes the section, as is customary in a Pauline letter (cf. 1 Thes 1:2–3).

1:10 *Among his holy ones*: in the Old Testament, this term can refer to an angelic throng (cf. also Jude 14), but here, in parallel with *among all who have believed*, it can refer to the triumphant people of God.

1:12 *The grace of our God and Lord Jesus Christ*: the Greek can also be translated, "the grace of our God and of the Lord Jesus Christ."

2:1–17 The Thessalonians have been *shaken* by a message purporting to come from Paul himself that *the day of the Lord* is already present. He warns against this deception in eschatology by citing a scenario of events that must first occur (2 Thes 2:3–12) before the end will come. The overall point Paul makes is the need to reject such lies as Satan sends; he also reaffirms the Thessalonians in their calling (2 Thes 2:13–14). They are to uphold what Paul himself has taught (2 Thes 2:15). There is a concluding prayer for their strengthening (2 Thes 2:16–17). As in 2 Thes 1:8–10, the Old Testament provides a good deal of coloring; cf. especially Is 14:13–14; 66:15, 18–21; Ez 28:2–9; Dn 11:36–37. The contents of 2 Thes 2:3b–8 may come from a previously existing apocalypse. The details have been variously interpreted. An alternative to the possibilities noted below understands that an oracular utterance, supposedly coming from a prophetic spirit (2 Thes 2:2–3a), has so disrupted the community's thinking that its effects may be compared to those of the mania connected with the worship of the Greek god Dionysus. On this view, the writer seems to allude in 2 Thes 2:6–8 to Dionysiac "seizure," although, of course, ironically, somewhat as Paul alludes to witchcraft ("an evil eye") in Gal 3:1 in speaking of the threat to faith posed by those disturbing the Galatians (Gal 1:6–7; 5:10b). On this view of 2 Thes 2, the Greek participles *katechon* (rendered above as *what is restraining*) and *katechōn* (*the one who restrains*) are to be translated "the seizing power" in 2 Thes 2:6 and "the seizer" in 2 Thes 2:7. They then allude to a pseudocharismatic force or spirit of Dionysiac character that has suddenly taken hold of the Thessalonian community (see 2 Thes 2:2). The addressees *know* (2 Thes 2:6) this force or spirit because of the problem it is causing. This pseudocharismatic force or spirit is a kind of anticipation and advance proof of the ultimate, climactic figure (*the lawless one* or the rebel, 2 Thes 2:3), of which the community has been warned (see note on 1 Thes 3:3). It is, however, only the beginning of the end that the latter's manifestation entails; the end is not yet. For in the course of *the mystery of lawlessness* (2 Thes 2:7), false prophetism, after it ceases in the Thessalonian community, will be manifested in the world at large (2 Thes 2:8–12), where it will also be eliminated in turn by the Lord Jesus.

2:2 *"Spirit"*: a Spirit-inspired utterance or ecstatic revelation. *An oral statement*: literally, a "word" or pronouncement, not

---

1:1 1 Thes 1:1.
1:3 1 Cor 1:4; 1 Thes 1:2; 3:12.
1:5 Phil 1:28; 1 Thes 2:12.
1:8 Ps 79:5–6; Is 66:15; Jer 10:25.
1:9 Is 2:10, 19, 21.
1:10 Ps 89:8; Dn 7:18–22, 27; 1 Thes 3:13.
1:11 1 Thes 1:2–3.
1:12 Is 66:5.
2:1 1 Thes 4:13–17.

2
T
H
E
S

letter allegedly from us to the effect that the day of the Lord is at hand.* ³Let no one deceive you in any way. For unless the apostasy comes first and the lawless one is revealed,† the one doomed to perdition, ⁴* who opposes and exalts himself above every so-called god and object of worship, so as to seat himself in the temple of God,† claiming that he is a god— ⁵do you not recall that while I was still with you I told you these things? ⁶And now you know what is restraining,† that he may be revealed in his time. ⁷† For the mystery of lawlessness is already at work. But the one who restrains is to do so only for the present, until he is removed from the scene.* ⁸And then the lawless one will be revealed, whom the Lord [Jesus] will kill with the breath of his mouth and render powerless by the manifestation of his coming,* ⁹the one whose coming springs from the power of Satan in every mighty deed and in signs and wonders that lie,* ¹⁰and in every wicked deceit for those who are perishing because they have not accepted the love of truth so that they may be saved. ¹¹Therefore, God is sending them a deceiving power so that they may believe the lie, ¹²that all who

have not believed the truth but have approved wrongdoing may be condemned.

¹³But we ought to give thanks to God for you always, brothers loved by the Lord, because God chose you as the firstfruits† for salvation through sanctification by the Spirit and belief in truth.* ¹⁴To this end he has [also] called you through our gospel to possess the glory of our Lord Jesus Christ.* ¹⁵Therefore, brothers, stand firm and hold fast to the traditions that you were taught, either by an oral statement or by a letter of ours.†

¹⁶May our Lord Jesus Christ himself and God our Father, who has loved us and given us everlasting encouragement and good hope through his grace, ¹⁷encourage your hearts and strengthen them in every good deed and word.

### III. CONCLUDING EXHORTATIONS

3 †**Request for Prayers.** ¹Finally, brothers, pray for us, so that the word of the Lord may speed forward and be glorified, as it did among you,* ²and that we may be delivered from perverse and wicked people, for not all have faith. ³But the Lord is faithful; he will

---

necessarily of ecstatic origin. *A letter allegedly sent by us*: possibly a forged letter, so that Paul calls attention in 2 Thes 3:17 to his practice of concluding a genuine letter with a summary note or greeting in his own hand, as at Gal 6:11–18 and elsewhere.

**2:3b–5** This incomplete sentence (anacoluthon, 2 Thes 2:4) recalls what the Thessalonians had already been taught, an apocalyptic scenario depicting, in terms borrowed especially from Dn 11:36–37 and related verses, human self-assertiveness against God in *the temple of God* itself. *The lawless one* represents the climax of such activity in this account.

**2:4** *Seat himself in the temple of God*: a reflection of the language in Dn 7:23–25; 8:9–12; 9:27; 11:36–37; 12:11 about the attempt of Antiochus IV Epiphanes to set up a statue of Zeus in the Jerusalem temple and possibly of the Roman emperor Caligula to do a similar thing (Mk 13:14). Here the imagery suggests an attempt to install someone in the place of God, *claiming that he is a god* (cf. Ez 28:2). Usually, it is the Jerusalem temple that is assumed to be meant; on the alternative view sketched above (see note on 2 Thes 2:1–17), *the temple* refers to the Christian community.

**2:6–7** *What is restraining…the one who restrains*: neuter and masculine, respectively, of a force and person holding back the lawless one. The Thessalonians know what is meant (2 Thes 2:6), but the terms, seemingly found only in this passage and in writings dependent on it, have been variously interpreted. Traditionally, 2 Thes 2:6 has been applied to the Roman empire and 2 Thes 2:7 to the Roman emperor (in Paul's day, Nero) as bulwarks holding back chaos (cf. Rom 13:1–7). A second interpretation suggests that cosmic or angelic powers are binding Satan (2 Thes 2:9) and so restraining him; some relate this to an anti-Christ figure (1 Jn 2:18) or to Michael the archangel (Rev 12:7–9; 20:1–3). A more recent view suggests that it is the preaching of the Christian gospel that restrains the end, for in God's plan the end cannot come until the gospel is preached to all nations (Mk 13:10); in that case, Paul as missionary preacher par excellence is "the one who restrains," whose removal (death) will bring the end (2 Thes 2:7). On the alternative view (see note

on 2 Thes 2:1–17), the phrases should be referred to that which and to him who seizes (a prophet) in ecstasy so as to have him speak pseudo-oracles.

**2:7–12** *The lawless one* and *the one who restrains* are involved in an activity or process, *the mystery of lawlessness*, behind which *Satan* stands (2 Thes 2:9). The action of the *Lord [Jesus]* in overcoming the lawless one is described in Old Testament language (*with the breath of his mouth*; cf. Is 11:4; Jb 4:9; Rev 19:15). His *coming* is literally the Lord's "parousia." The biblical concept of the "holy war," eschatologically conceived, may underlie the imagery.

**2:13** *As the firstfruits*: there is also strong manuscript evidence for the reading, "God chose you from the beginning," thus providing a focus on God's activity from beginning to end; *firstfruits* is a Pauline term, however; cf. Rom 8:23; 11:16; 16:5 among other references.

**2:15** Reference to *an oral statement* and *a letter* (2 Thes 2:2) and the content here, including a formula of conclusion (cf. 1 Cor 16:13; Gal 5:1), suggest that 2 Thes 2:1–15 or even 2 Thes 2:1–17 are to be taken as a literary unit, notwithstanding the incidental thanksgiving formula in 2 Thes 2:13.

**3:1–18** The final chapter urges the Thessalonians to pray for Paul and his colleagues (2 Thes 3:1–2) and reiterates confidence in the Thessalonians (2 Thes 3:3–5), while admonishing them about a specific problem in their community that has grown out of the intense eschatological speculation, namely, not to work but to become instead disorderly busybodies (2 Thes 3:6–15). A benediction (2 Thes 3:16) and postscript in Paul's own hand round out the letter. On 2 Thes 3:17–18, cf. note on 2 Thes 2:2.

---

**2:2** Mt 24:6; 1 Cor 14:26, 32–33; 1 Thes 5:1–2.
**2:4** Dn 11:36–37; Ez 28:2.
**2:7** Mt 13:36–43; Acts 20:29; Gal 5:10; 2 Pt 2:1; Rev 22:11.
**2:8** Is 11:4; Rev 19:15.
**2:9** Mt 24:24; Rev 13:13.
**2:13** 1 Thes 2:13; 5:9.
**2:14** Rom 5:1–10; 8:29–30; 1 Thes 4:7; 5:9.
**3:1** Eph 6:19; Col 4:3.

strengthen you and guard you from the evil one.* ⁴We are confident of you in the Lord that what we instruct you, you [both] are doing and will continue to do.* ⁵May the Lord direct your hearts to the love of God and to the endurance of Christ.

**Neglect of Work.** ⁶We instruct you, brothers, in the name of [our] Lord Jesus Christ, to shun any brother who conducts himself in a disorderly way and not according to the tradition they received from us.† ⁷For you know how one must imitate us. For we did not act in a disorderly way among you, ⁸nor did we eat food received free from anyone. On the contrary, in toil and drudgery, night and day we worked, so as not to burden any of you.* ⁹Not that we do not have the right. Rather, we wanted to present ourselves as a model for you, so that you might imitate us.* ¹⁰In fact, when we were with you, we instructed you that if anyone was unwilling to work, neither should that one eat.* ¹¹We hear that some are conducting themselves among you in a disorderly way, by not keeping busy but minding the business of others.* ¹²Such people we instruct and urge in the Lord Jesus Christ to work quietly and to eat their own food. ¹³But you, brothers, do not be remiss in doing good. ¹⁴If anyone does not obey our word as expressed in this letter, take note of this person not to associate with him, that he may be put to shame. ¹⁵Do not regard him as an enemy but admonish him as a brother.* ¹⁶May the Lord of peace himself give you peace at all times and in every way. The Lord be with all of you.*

## IV. FINAL GREETINGS

¹⁷This greeting is in my own hand, Paul's. This is the sign in every letter; this is how I write.* ¹⁸The grace of our Lord Jesus Christ be with all of you.

---

**3:6** Some members of the community, probably because they regarded the parousia as imminent or the new age of the Lord to be already here (2 Thes 2:2), had apparently ceased to work for a living. The disciplinary problem they posed could be rooted in distorted thinking about Paul's own teaching (cf. 1 Thes 2:16; 3:3–4; 5:4–5) or, more likely, in a forged letter (2 Thes 2:2) and the type of teaching dealt with in 2 Thes 2:1–15. The apostle's own moral teaching, reflected in his selfless labors for others, was rooted in a deep doctrinal concern for the gospel message (cf. 1 Thes 2:3–10).

---

| | |
|---|---|
| **3:3** 1 Thes 5:24 / 1 Cor 16:13 / Mt 6:13. | **3:10** 1 Thes 4:11. |
| **3:4** 2 Cor 7:16; 1 Thes 4:1–2. | **3:11** Thes 5:14. |
| **3:8** 1 Thes 2:9. | **3:15** 2 Cor 2:7; Gal 6:1. |
| **3:9** Mt 10:10; Phil 3:17. | **3:16** Jn 14:27; Rom 15:33. |
| | **3:17** 1 Cor 16:21; Gal 6:11. |

# The First Letter to
# Timothy

## INTRODUCTION

### Raymond F. Collins

The First Letter to Timothy appears in the New Testament as the first of four "personal" letters ostensibly written by the Apostle Paul to various individuals. These are the three Pastoral Epistles and the Letter to Philemon. First Timothy's appearance as the first of these letters has more to do with the fact that it is longer than the other letters than with the sequence in which the letters were written. Second Timothy comes after 1 Timothy because it is addressed to the same person. Many scholars hold that the first of the Pastoral Letters to have been written was the shortest of them, the Letter to Titus, rather than 1 Timothy.

## A Pseudepigraphic Text

In recent decades, a consensus has developed among biblical scholars that 1 Timothy was not written by the Apostle Paul himself. Most New Testament scholars consider that the text was written by a second-generation disciple of Paul, that is, a disciple of a disciple of Paul. This means that 1 Timothy is a pseudepigraphic text, one not written by the person to whom it is ascribed. The letter was most probably written close to the turn of the first century CE.

Scholars who hold that 1 Timothy is pseudepigraphic note that at the time the text was written pseudepigraphy was not always held in disregard. It was considered wrong to attribute a text to someone else for a base motive, but writing a text in another's name to pay honor to that person or to show how his thought was relevant to a new set of circumstances was considered noble. The author of 1 Timothy intended to carry on the Pauline tradition and demonstrate how the apostle's legacy was important for a Pauline church that was still in existence a couple of generations after the apostle's death.

## Outline of 1 Timothy

I.  **Address (1:1–2)**

II. **Sound Teaching (1:3–20)**

III. **Problems of Discipline (2:1–4:16)**

IV. **Duties Toward Others (5:1–6:2a)**

V.  **False Teaching and True Wealth (6:2b–19)**

VI. **Final Recommendation and Warning (6:20–21)**

One reason for the view that 1 Timothy was not written by Paul is the difference of vocabulary between 1 Timothy and the letters that are generally considered to be authentic: Romans, 1 and 2 Corinthians, Galatians, Philippians, 1 Thessalonians, and Philemon. Equally important is the difference of theology between those letters and this text. The way that Paul writes about Christ in those letters is different from the way that 1 Timothy speaks about Christ. In many of those texts the eschatological appearance of Jesus as Lord, the *parousia*, seems to be imminent, but that is not the case with 1 Timothy.

The final greeting of 1 Timothy, 1 Tm 6:21, written in the plural, betrays the fact that the text is really intended for a community rather than an individual. That church is obviously much more organized and structured than were the churches to which Paul had written in the undisputed seven letters. The fact that Hymenaeus and Alexander, who appear to have been excommunicated by Paul (1:20), do not otherwise appear in the New Testament literature by or about Paul creates a historical dilemma that must be addressed.

# The Epistolary Greeting (1 Tm 1:1-2)

The consensus view that 1 Timothy is not an authentic letter of Paul to Timothy, his missionary companion, occasional emissary, and co-sender of several of his letters (2 Corinthians, Philippians, 1 Thessalonians, and Philemon), requires that the traditional designation of this text as the First Letter of Paul to Timothy be carefully evaluated.

That the letter is attributed to Paul is an indication of the authority that Paul continued to hold in Ephesus, the pre-eminent church of Asia Minor (1 Tm 1:3). Ephesus was the capital of the Roman province of Asia at the end of the first century CE. Paul spent more than two years there (Acts 19:8–10). From this city he wrote several letters, especially his two extant letters to the Corinthians. Paul is the apostolic authority under whose aegis the teaching and instruction of 1 Timothy are conveyed. The author of the text adopted the persona of Paul as he formulated teaching and set out instructions for the church in Paul's absence (1 Tm 3:15; 4:13). That church had to cope with new theological issues and with social circumstances that were different from those that existed a few decades earlier. In 1 Tm 1:12–17, the author offers a cameo reflection on the persecutor of the church who became an apostle (2:7) to the readers of his text.

Timothy had probably died before this letter was written. That the letter is said to have been written to him indicates the respect in which Timothy, Paul's chief lieutenant, was held even after his death. Timothy was, by that time, a revered figure from the past who carried on Paul's work. By invoking the name of Timothy, the author provides us with early evidence of the developing tradition of the church. The author's "Timothy" stands for those leaders of the church who continue Paul's work.

The first and last verses of the text show that its ostensible literary form is that of a letter. This demonstrates the importance of the "apostolic letter," first used by Paul, as a means of teaching and instruction during the first century CE. The "letter," however, is not a real letter, a written communication from one person to another. It is a document of church order, written to provide guidelines for the church as it develops structures and organizes itself toward the end of the first century CE. The author's choice of the Pauline apostolic letter form enhances the work's authority.

# Theology and Ethics

That the text has most likely not been written by Paul in no way detracts from its canonicity or authority. It is an apostolic writing composed under the inspiration of the Holy Spirit (*Dei Verbum*, 24). As such it is important to read and study the text as instructions that have been promulgated under the authority of Paul.

Several passages in the text imply that it was written to counteract erroneous teaching (1 Tm 1:18–19; 4:7; 6:3, 20–21), but apart from error with regard to sex and diet (4:1–4) it is almost impossible to determine the precise nature of that false teaching. The author of 1 Timothy uses characteristic expressions to qualify the importance of the teaching that he is conveying. He calls his teaching "sound" (1:10; 6:3) and "trustworthy" (1:15; 3:1; 4:9). "Sound" indicates that his teaching is correct and that it results in good behavior. "Trustworthy" points to the reliability and traditional nature of the teaching.

The way that the letter speaks about Christ is also striking. The author uses the traditional titles "Christ" and "Lord," but he also uses distinctive language to speak about Jesus' manifestation or appearance, which he terms his *epiphaneia*. This language would have made an impression upon first-century readers since the term was often used in reference to the solemn appearance of an emperor with pomp and splendor. First Timothy 3:16 speaks about the manifestation of Jesus in the flesh while 1 Tm 6:14 talks about the appearance of Jesus as Christ and Lord at the proper time, that is, the end time. Believers live between these two "epiphanies" of Jesus.

Not to be overlooked in the author's distinctive picture of Jesus are a short hymn and a hymnic confession of faith that are unique within the New Testament. The author does not specifically speak about the Resurrection of Jesus from the dead, as Paul did so often.

Absent the language of Resurrection, the short hymn in 1 Tm 3:16 sets out six different but complementary facets of the significance of the Resurrection. The hymnic confession of 2:5 echoes the Jewish *Shema*, the confession that God is one, but adds a three-fold confession about Jesus, namely, that he is the only mediator between God and humankind, that he is human, and that he offered himself as a ransom for all.

Commentators on 1 Timothy often note that its ethical teaching has a "bourgeois" character, a preoccupation with the rules of conventional morality. The letter employs lists of common virtues (1 Tm 2:15; 3:2–5, 8–12; 6:11) and vices (1:9–10; 3:3), sometimes in reference to the leaders of the church (3:2–5, 8–12). Similar lists, sometimes called "catalogues," were used in the philosophic discourse of the times to encourage good behavior or to condemn bad behavior. Philosophers also made use of lists to describe how a functional household should be organized. The author of 1 Timothy writes in similar fashion in 1 Tm 5:1–2; 6:1–2.

The letter seems to suggest that "devotion" (*eusebeia*; 1 Tm 2:2; 3:16; 4:7, 8; 6:3, 5, 6, 11) is the most important virtue, as it is in many Hellenistic writings. First Timothy also often mentions the importance of good works (2:10; 3:1; 5:10 [twice], 25; 6:18) and includes an important exhortation on wealth that echoes the treatment of that literary theme in popular moral teaching. This common-place approach to morality and ethics must be seen within the context of the church's need to be respected by those outside the community (cf. 3:7; 6:1). The use of common ethical themes shows that believers share the high moral standards taught by Stoics and other Hellenistic moralists.

## Ecclesiology

Undoubtedly the most distinctive teaching of 1 Timothy is its ecclesiology, its teaching about the church. The ethical instruction imparted throughout the letter is provided in order that the recipients might "know how to behave in the household of God, which is the church of the living God, the pillar and foundation of truth" (1 Tm 3:15). This succinct ecclesiological formulation identifies the church as a household, compares it to the assembly of Israel at the time of the Exodus, says that it belongs to God who is characterized as "living," the biblical God's primal trait, and functionally speaks of the church as being the foundation of truth. This latter note sets the church in opposition to those who have made shipwreck of the faith (1:19).

The identification of the church as a household reflects the fact that the church was organized on the model of the Greco-Roman household. The snippets of household codes found in 1 Tm 5:1–12 and 6:1–2 show the importance of household structures for the church at this time. That the church respected these structures enhanced its acceptability in society as a whole.

Emerging structures of church leadership appear in 1 Tm 3:1–13, which uses catalogues of virtues and vices to identify the qualities expected of "bishops" (*episkopoi*) and "deacons" (*diakonoi*). These offices should not be equated with bishops and deacons of later centuries. It is better to think of the *episkopoi* of that era as overseers or supervisors, and of the *diakonoi* as assistants or servants. The "women" (*gynaikai*) referred to in the passage (3:11) are arguably female assistants. The attention to the virtuous life of church leaders and the way in which they fulfilled their own household responsibilities demonstrates how keen the church was to assure that its leaders be well respected in society.

First Timothy 3:11 is not the only passage in the letter to speak about women. First Timothy 5:3–16 talks about widows and distinguishes three categories of widows: (1) those who are truly widows, without any means of support apart from the assistance of the church; (2) widows who should be able to rely on family members; and (3) young widows who are urged to remarry, have children, and take care of their homes. The exhortation that young widows remarry concurs with the rejection of that false asceticism that denigrates marriage (4:3), the rejection of which may also have motivated the reference to motherhood in 1 Tm 2:15.

This last reference comes at the end of a series of liturgical instructions (1 Tm 2:1–15). The first subunit within these instructions (vv.

1–7) identifies different modes of the believer's prayer and states that prayer be offered for everyone, especially kings and those who hold political authority. The second subunit (vv. 8–15) speaks about the respective demeanor of men and women at prayer. It concludes with a midrashic exposition on the Genesis 2 story of Adam and Eve; the precise meaning of this exposition continues to be the subject of much exegetical debate today. ■

# THE FIRST LETTER TO TIMOTHY

## New American Bible, Introduction

The three letters, First and Second Timothy and Titus, form a distinct group within the Pauline corpus. In the collection of letters by the Apostle to the Gentiles, they differ from the others in form and contents. All three suggest they were written late in Paul's career. The opponents are not "Judaizers" as in Galatians but false teachers stressing "knowledge" (*gnōsis*; see note on 1 Tm 6:20–21). Attention is given especially to correct doctrine and church organization. Jesus' second coming recedes into the background compared to references in Paul's earlier letters (though not Colossians and Ephesians). The three letters are addressed not to congregations but to those who shepherd congregations (Latin, *pastores*). These letters were first named "Pastoral Epistles" in the eighteenth century because they all are concerned with the work of a pastor in caring for the community or communities under his charge.

The first of the Pastorals, 1 Timothy, is presented as having been written from Macedonia. Timothy, whom Paul converted, was of mixed Jewish and Gentile parentage (Acts 16:1–3). He was the apostle's companion on both the second and the third missionary journeys (Acts 16:3; 19:22) and was often sent by him on special missions (Acts 19:22; 1 Cor 4:17; 1 Thes 3:2). In 1 Timothy (1 Tm 1:3), he is described as the administrator of the entire Ephesian community.

The letter instructs Timothy on his duty to restrain false and useless teaching (1 Tm 1:3–11; 4:1–5; 6:3–16) and proposes principles pertaining to his relationship with the older members of the community (1 Tm 5:1–2) and with the presbyters (1 Tm 5:17–22). It gives rules for aid to widows (1 Tm 5:3–8) and their selection for charitable ministrations (1 Tm 5:9–16) and also deals with liturgical celebrations (1 Tm 2:1–15), selections for the offices of bishop and deacon (1 Tm 3:1–13), relation of slaves with their masters (1 Tm 6:1–2), and obligations of the wealthier members of the community (1 Tm 6:17–19). This letter also reminds Timothy of the prophetic character of

his office (1 Tm 1:12–20) and encourages him in his exercise of it (1 Tm 4:6–16). The central passage of the letter (1 Tm 3:14–16) expresses the principal motive that should guide the conduct of Timothy—preservation of the purity of the church's doctrine against false teaching. On this same note the letter concludes (1 Tm 6:20–21).

From the late second century to the nineteenth, Pauline authorship of the three Pastoral Epistles went unchallenged. Since then, the attribution of these letters to Paul has been questioned. Most scholars are convinced that Paul could not have been responsible for the vocabulary and style, the concept of church organization, or the theological expressions found in these letters. A second group believes, on the basis of statistical evidence, that the vocabulary and style are Pauline, even if at first sight the contrary seems to be the case. They state that the concept of church organization in the letters is not as advanced as the questioners of Pauline authorship hold since the notion of hierarchical order in a religious community existed in Israel before the time of Christ, as evidenced in the Dead Sea Scrolls. Finally, this group sees affinities between the theological thought of the Pastorals and that of the unquestionably genuine letters of Paul. Other scholars, while conceding a degree of validity to the positions mentioned above, suggest that the apostle made use of a secretary who was responsible for the composition of the letters. A fourth group of scholars believes that these letters are the work of a compiler, that they are based on traditions about Paul in his later years, and that they include, in varying amounts, actual fragments of genuine Pauline correspondence.

If Paul is considered the more immediate author, the Pastorals are to be dated between the end of his first Roman imprisonment (Acts 28:16) and his execution under Nero (A.D. 63–67); if they are regarded as only more remotely Pauline, their date may be as late as the early second century. In spite of these problems of authorship and dating, the Pastorals are illustrative of early Christian life and remain an important element of canonical scripture.

The principal divisions of the First Letter to Timothy are the following:

I. Address (1:1–2)
II. Sound Teaching (1:3–20)
III. Problems of Discipline (2:1–4:16)
IV. Duties Toward Others (5:1–6:2a)
V. False Teaching and True Wealth (6:2b–19)
VI. Final Recommendation and Warning (6:20–21) ■

# FIRST TIMOTHY

**1**
**T**
**M**

## I. ADDRESS

**1** **Greeting.**† ¹Paul, an apostle of Christ Jesus by command of God our savior and of Christ Jesus our hope,* ²to Timothy, my true child in faith: grace, mercy, and peace from God the Father and Christ Jesus our Lord.*

## II. SOUND TEACHING

**Warning Against False Doctrine.** ³† I repeat the request I made of you when I was on my way to Macedonia,* that you stay in Ephesus to instruct certain people not to teach false doctrines ⁴† or to concern themselves with myths and endless genealogies, which promote speculations rather than the plan of God that is to be received by faith.* ⁵The aim of this instruction is love from a pure heart, a good conscience, and a sincere faith.* ⁶Some people have deviated from these and turned to meaningless talk,* ⁷wanting to be teachers of the law, but without understanding either what they are saying or what they assert with such assurance.

⁸† We know that the law is good, provided that one uses it as law,* ⁹with the understanding that law is meant not for a righteous person but for the lawless and unruly, the godless and sinful, the unholy and profane, those who kill their fathers or mothers, murderers, ¹⁰the unchaste, sodomites,† kidnappers, liars, perjurers, and whatever else is opposed to sound teaching,* ¹¹according to the glorious gospel of the blessed God, with which I have been entrusted.*

**Gratitude for God's Mercy.**† ¹²I am grateful to him who has strengthened me, Christ Jesus our Lord, because he considered me trustworthy in appointing me to the ministry.* ¹³I was once a blasphemer and a persecutor and an arrogant man, but I have been mercifully treated because I acted out of ignorance in my unbelief.* ¹⁴Indeed, the grace of our Lord has been abundant, along with the faith and love that are in Christ Jesus.* ¹⁵This saying is trustworthy† and deserves full acceptance: Christ Jesus came into the world to save sinners. Of these I am the foremost.* ¹⁶But for that reason I was mercifully treated, so that in me, as the foremost, Christ Jesus might display all his patience as an example for those who would come to believe in him for everlasting life. ¹⁷To the king of ages,† incorruptible, invisible, the only God, honor and glory forever and ever. Amen.*

**Responsibility of Timothy.**† ¹⁸I entrust this charge to you, Timothy, my child, in

---

† **1:1–2** For the Pauline use of the conventional epistolary form, see note on Rom 1:1–7.

**1:3–7** Here Timothy's initial task *in Ephesus* (cf. Acts 20:17–35) is outlined: to suppress the idle religious speculations, probably about Old Testament figures (1 Tm 1:3–4, but see note on 1 Tm 6:20–21), which do not contribute to the development of love within the community (1 Tm 1:5) but rather encourage similar useless conjectures (1 Tm 1:6–7).

**1:4** The *plan of God that is to be received by faith*: the Greek may also possibly mean "God's trustworthy plan" or "the training in faith that God requires."

**1:8–11** Those responsible for the speculations that are to be suppressed by Timothy do not present the Old Testament from the Christian viewpoint. The Christian values the Old Testament not as a system of law but as the first stage in God's revelation of his saving plan, which is brought to fulfillment in the good news of salvation through faith in Jesus Christ.

**1:10** *Sodomites*: see 1 Cor 6:9 and the note there.

**1:12–17** Present gratitude for the Christian apostleship leads Paul to recall an earlier time when he had been a fierce persecutor of the Christian communities (cf. Acts 26:9–11) until his conversion by intervention of divine mercy through the appearance of Jesus. And this and his subsequent apostolic experience testify to the saving purpose of Jesus' incarnation. The fact of his former ignorance of the truth has not kept the apostle from regarding himself as having been the worst of sinners (1 Tm 1:15). Yet he was chosen to be an apostle, that God might manifest his firm will to save sinful humanity through Jesus Christ (1 Tm 1:16). The recounting of so great a mystery leads to a spontaneous outpouring of adoration (1 Tm 1:17).

**1:15** *This saying is trustworthy*: this phrase regularly introduces in the Pastorals a basic truth of early Christian faith; cf. 1 Tm 3:1; 4:9; 2 Tm 2:11; Ti 3:8.

**1:17** *King of ages*: through Semitic influence, the Greek expression could mean "everlasting king"; it could also mean "king of the universe."

**1:18–20** Timothy is to be mindful of his calling, which is here compared to the way Barnabas and Saul were designated by Christ as prophets for missionary service; cf. Acts 13:1–3. Such is probably the sense of the allusion to the prophetic words (1 Tm 1:18). His task is not to yield, whether in doctrine or in conduct, to erroneous opinions, taking warning from what has already happened at Ephesus in the case of Hymenaeus and Alexander (1 Tm 1:19–20).

---

* **1:1** 2:3; Lk 1:47; Ti 1:3; 2:10 / Col 1:27.
**1:2** 2 Tm 1:2; Ti 1:4.
**1:3** Acts 20:1.
**1:4** 4:7; Ti 1:14; 3:9; 2 Pt 1:16.
**1:5** Rom 13:10.
**1:6** 6:4, 20; Ti 1:10.
**1:8** Rom 7:12, 16.
**1:10** 4:6; 6:3; 2 Tm 4:3; Ti 1:9; 2:1.
**1:11** Ti 1:3.
**1:12** Phil 4:13 / Acts 9:15; Gal 1:15–16.
**1:13** Acts 8:3; 9:1–2; 1 Cor 15:9; Gal 1:13.
**1:14** Rom 5:20; 2 Tm 1:13.
**1:15** Lk 15:2; 19:10.
**1:17** Rom 16:27.

accordance with the prophetic words once spoken about you.† Through them may you fight a good fight* [19]by having faith and a good conscience. Some, by rejecting conscience, have made a shipwreck of their faith,* [20]among them Hymenaeus† and Alexander, whom I have handed over to Satan to be taught not to blaspheme.*

### III. PROBLEMS OF DISCIPLINE

2 **Prayer and Conduct.** [1]† First of all, then, I ask that supplications, prayers, petitions, and thanksgivings be offered for everyone,* [2]for kings and for all in authority, that we may lead a quiet and tranquil life in all devotion and dignity. [3]This is good and pleasing to God our savior,* [4]who wills everyone to be saved and to come to knowledge of the truth.*

[5]     For there is one God.
        There is also one mediator between God
              and the human race,
        Christ Jesus, himself human,*
[6]     who gave himself as ransom for all.

This was the testimony† at the proper time.* [7]For this I was appointed preacher and apostle (I am speaking the truth, I am not lying), teacher of the Gentiles in faith and truth.*

[8]† It is my wish, then, that in every place the men should pray, lifting up holy hands, without anger or argument. [9]Similarly, [too,] women should adorn themselves with proper conduct, with modesty and self-control, not with braided hairstyles and gold ornaments, or pearls, or expensive clothes,* [10]but rather, as befits women who profess reverence for God, with good deeds.* [11]A woman must receive instruction silently and under complete control.* [12]I do not permit a woman to teach or to have authority over a man.† She must be quiet. [13]For Adam was formed first, then Eve.* [14]Further, Adam was not deceived, but the woman was deceived and transgressed.* [15]But she will be saved through motherhood, provided women persevere in faith and love and holiness, with self-control.*

3 **Qualifications of Various Ministers.** [1]† This saying is trustworthy:† whoever

---

† **1:18** *The prophetic words once spoken about you*: the Greek may also be translated, "the prophecies that led (me) to you." It probably refers to testimonies given by charismatic figures in the Christian communities. *Fight a good fight*: this translation preserves the play on words in Greek. The Greek terms imply a lengthy engagement in battle and might well be translated "wage a good campaign."

**1:20** *Hymenaeus*: mentioned in 2 Tm 2:17 as saying that the resurrection has already taken place (in baptism). *Alexander*: probably the Alexander mentioned in 2 Tm 4:14 as the coppersmith who "did me a great deal of harm." *Whom I have handed over to Satan*: the same terms are used in the condemnation of the incestuous man in 1 Cor 5:5.

**2:1–7** This marked insistence that the liturgical prayer of the community concern itself with the needs of all, whether Christian or not, and especially of those in authority, may imply that a disposition existed at Ephesus to refuse prayer for pagans. In actuality, such prayer aids the community to achieve peaceful relationships with non-Christians (1 Tm 2:2) and contributes to salvation, since it derives its value from the presence within the community of Christ, who is the one and only savior of all (1 Tm 2:3–6). The vital apostolic mission to the Gentiles (1 Tm 2:7) reflects Christ's purpose of universal salvation. 1 Tm 2:5 contains what may well have been a very primitive creed. Some interpreters have called it a Christian version of the Jewish *shema*: "Hear, O Israel, the LORD is our God, the LORD alone..." (Dt 6:4–5). The assertion in 1 Tm 2:7, "I am speaking the truth, I am not lying," reminds one of similar affirmations in Rom 9:1; 2 Cor 11:31; and Gal 1:20.

**2:6** *The testimony*: to make sense of this overly concise phrase, many manuscripts supply "to which" (or "to whom"); two others add "was given." The translation has supplied "this was."

**2:8–15** The prayer of the community should be unmarred by internal dissension (1 Tm 2:8); cf. Mt 5:21–26; 6:14; Mk 11:25. At the liturgical assembly the dress of women should be appropriate to the occasion (1 Tm 2:9); their chief adornment is to be reputation for good works (1 Tm 2:10). Women are not to take

part in the charismatic activity of the assembly (1 Tm 2:11–12; cf. 1 Cor 14:34) or exercise authority; their conduct there should reflect the role of man's helpmate (1 Tm 2:13; cf. Gn 2:18) and not the later relationship of Eve to Adam (1 Tm 2:14; cf. Gn 3:6–7). As long as women perform their role as wives and mothers in faith and love, their salvation is assured (1 Tm 2:15).

**2:12** *A man*: this could also mean "her husband."

**3:1–7** The passage begins by commending those who aspire to the office of bishop (*episkopos*; see note on Phil 1:1) within the community, but this first sentence (1 Tm 3:1) may also imply a warning about the great responsibilities involved. The writer proceeds to list the qualifications required: personal stability and graciousness; talent for teaching (1 Tm 3:2); moderation in habits and temperament (1 Tm 3:3); managerial ability (1 Tm 3:4); and experience in Christian living (1 Tm 3:5–6). Moreover, the candidate's previous life should provide no grounds for the charge that he did not previously practice what he now preaches. No list of qualifications for presbyters appears in 1 Timothy. The presbyter-bishops here and in Titus (see note on Ti 1:5–9) lack certain functions reserved here for Paul and Timothy.

**3:1** *This saying is trustworthy*: the saying introduced is so unlike others after this phrase that some later Western manuscripts read, "This saying is popular." It is understood by some interpreters as concluding the preceding section (1 Tm 2:8–15). *Bishop*: literally, "overseer"; see note on Phil 1:1.

---

* **1:18** 4:14 / 6:12; 2 Tm 4:7; Jude 3.
**1:19** 3:9.
**1:20** 2 Tm 2:17; 4:14 / 1 Cor 5:5.
**2:1** Eph 6:18; Phil 4:6.
**2:3** 1:1; 4:10.
**2:4** 2 Tm 3:7; 2 Pt 3:9.
**2:5** 1 Cor 8:6; Heb 8:6; 9:15; 12:24 / Rom 5:15.
**2:6** Mk 10:45;

Gal 1:4; 2:20; Eph 5:25; Ti 2:14.
**2:7** Acts 9:15; 1 Cor 9:1; Gal 2:7–8.
**2:9** 1 Pt 3:3–5.
**2:10** 5:10; 1 Pt 3:1.
**2:11–12** 1 Cor 14:34–35.
**2:13** Gn 1:27; 2:7, 22; 1 Cor 11:8–9.
**2:14** Gn 3:6, 13; 2 Cor 11:3.
**2:15** 5:14.

aspires to the office of bishop desires a noble task.* ²Therefore, a bishop must be irreproachable, married only once, temperate, self-controlled, decent, hospitable, able to teach, ³not a drunkard, not aggressive, but gentle, not contentious, not a lover of money.* ⁴He must manage his own household well, keeping his children under control with perfect dignity; ⁵for if a man does not know how to manage his own household, how can he take care of the church of God? ⁶He should not be a recent convert, so that he may not become conceited and thus incur the devil's punishment.† ⁷He must also have a good reputation among outsiders, so that he may not fall into disgrace, the devil's trap.*

⁸† Similarly, deacons must be dignified, not deceitful, not addicted to drink, not greedy for sordid gain, ⁹holding fast to the mystery of the faith with a clear conscience. ¹⁰Moreover, they should be tested first; then, if there is nothing against them, let them serve as deacons. ¹¹Women,† similarly, should be dignified, not slanderers, but temperate and faithful in everything.* ¹²Deacons may be married only once and must manage their children and their households well. ¹³Thus those who serve well as deacons gain good standing and much confidence in their faith in Christ Jesus.

### The Mystery of Our Religion.† ¹⁴I am writing you about these matters, although I hope to

visit you soon. ¹⁵But if I should be delayed, you should know how to behave in the household of God, which is the church of the living God, the pillar and foundation of truth.* ¹⁶Undeniably great is the mystery of devotion,

> Who† was manifested in the flesh,
> vindicated in the spirit,
> seen by angels,
> proclaimed to the Gentiles,
> believed in throughout the world,
> taken up in glory.*

**4 False Asceticism.**† ¹Now the Spirit explicitly says that in the last times some will turn away from the faith by paying attention to deceitful spirits and demonic instructions* ²through the hypocrisy of liars with branded consciences. ³They forbid marriage and require abstinence from foods that God created to be received with thanksgiving by those who believe and know the truth.* ⁴For everything created by God is good, and nothing is to be rejected when received with thanksgiving,* ⁵for it is made holy by the invocation of God in prayer.†

### Counsel to Timothy. ⁶† If you will give these instructions to the brothers, you will be a good minister of Christ Jesus, nourished on the words of the faith and of the sound teaching

---

† **3:6** *The devil's punishment*: this phrase could mean the punishment once incurred by the devil (objective genitive) or a punishment brought about by the devil (subjective genitive).

**3:8–13** Deacons, besides possessing the virtue of moderation (1 Tm 3:8), are to be outstanding for their faith (1 Tm 3:9) and well respected within the community (1 Tm 3:10). Women in the same role, although some interpreters take them to mean wives of deacons, must be dignified, temperate, dedicated, and not given to malicious talebearing (1 Tm 3:11). Deacons must have shown stability in marriage and have a good record with their families (1 Tm 3:12), for such experience prepares them well for the exercise of their ministry on behalf of the community (1 Tm 3:13). See further the note on Phil 1:1.

**3:11** *Women*: this seems to refer to women deacons but may possibly mean wives of deacons. The former is preferred because the word is used absolutely; if deacons' wives were meant, a possessive "their" would be expected. Moreover, they are also introduced by the word "similarly," as in 1 Tm 3:8; this parallel suggests that they too exercised ecclesiastical functions.

**3:14–16** In case there is some delay in the visit to Timothy at Ephesus planned for the near future, the present letter is being sent on ahead to arm and enlighten him in his task of preserving sound Christian conduct in the Ephesian church. The care he must exercise over this community is required by the profound nature of Christianity. It centers in Christ, appearing in human flesh, vindicated by the holy Spirit; the mystery of his person was revealed to the angels, announced to the Gentiles, and accepted by them in faith. He himself was taken up (through his resurrection and ascension) to the divine glory (1 Tm 3:16). This passage

apparently includes part of a liturgical hymn used among the Christian communities in and around Ephesus. It consists of three couplets in typical Hebrew balance: flesh-spirit (contrast), seen-proclaimed (complementary), world-glory (contrast).

**3:16** *Who*: the reference is to Christ, who is himself "the mystery of our devotion." Some predominantly Western manuscripts read "which," harmonizing the gender of the pronoun with that of the Greek word for mystery; many later (eighth/ninth century on), predominantly Byzantine manuscripts read "God," possibly for theological reasons.

**4:1–5** Doctrinal deviations from the true Christian message within the church have been prophesied, though the origin of the prophecy is not specified (1 Tm 4:1–2); cf. Acts 20:29–30. The letter warns against a false asceticism that prohibits marriage and regards certain foods as forbidden, though they are part of God's good creation (1 Tm 4:3).

**4:5** *The invocation of God in prayer*: literally, "the word of God and petition." The use of "word of God" without an article in Greek suggests that it refers to the name of God being invoked in blessing rather than to the "word of God" proclaimed to the community.

**4:6–10** Timothy is urged to be faithful, both in his teaching and in his own life, as he looks only to God for salvation.

---

| | |
|---|---|
| **3:1–7** Ti 1:6–9. | **3:16** Jn 1:14; Rom 1:3–4. |
| **3:3** Heb 13:5. | **4:1** 2 Tm 3:1; 4:3; 2 Pt |
| **3:7** 2 Cor 8:21; 2 Tm | 3:3; Jude 18. |
| 2:26. | **4:3** Gn 9:3; Rom 14:6; |
| **3:11** Ti 2:3. | 1 Cor 10:30–31. |
| **3:15** Eph 2:19–22. | **4:4** Gn 1:31; Acts 10:15. |

you have followed. [7] Avoid profane and silly myths. Train yourself for devotion,* [8] for, while physical training is of limited value, devotion is valuable in every respect, since it holds a promise of life both for the present and for the future.* [9] This saying is trustworthy and deserves full acceptance.* [10] For this we toil and struggle,† because we have set our hope on the living God, who is the savior of all, especially of those who believe.*

[11] † Command and teach these things. [12] Let no one have contempt for your youth,† but set an example for those who believe, in speech, conduct, love, faith, and purity.* [13] Until I arrive, attend to the reading,† exhortation, and teaching. [14] Do not neglect the gift you have, which was conferred on you through the prophetic word† with the imposition of hands of the presbyterate.* [15] Be diligent in these matters, be absorbed in them, so that your progress may be evident to everyone. [16] Attend to yourself and to your teaching; persevere in both tasks, for by doing so you will save both yourself and those who listen to you.

## IV. DUTIES TOWARD OTHERS

**5** [1] † Do not rebuke an older man, but appeal to him as a father. Treat younger men as brothers,* [2] older women as mothers, and younger women as sisters with complete purity.

**Rules for Widows.** [3] Honor widows who are truly widows. [4] But if a widow has children or grandchildren, let these first learn to perform their religious duty to their own family and to make recompense to their parents, for this is pleasing to God. [5] The real widow, who is all alone, has set her hope on God and continues in supplications and prayers night and day.* [6] But the one who is self-indulgent is dead while she lives. [7] Command this, so that they may be irreproachable. [8] And whoever does not provide for relatives and especially family members has denied the faith and is worse than an unbeliever.

[9] Let a widow be enrolled if she is not less than sixty years old, married only once, [10] with a reputation for good works, namely, that she has raised children, practiced hospitality, washed the feet of the holy ones, helped those in distress, involved herself in every good work.* [11] But exclude younger widows, for when their sensuality estranges them from Christ, they want to marry [12] and will incur condemnation for breaking their first pledge. [13] And furthermore, they learn to be idlers, going about from house to house, and not only idlers but gossips and busybodies as well, talking about things that ought not to be mentioned.* [14] So I would like younger widows to marry, have children, and manage a home, so as to give the adversary no pretext for maligning us.* [15] For some have already turned away to follow Satan. [16] If any woman believer† has widowed relatives, she must assist them; the church is not to be burdened, so that it will be able to help those who are truly widows.

---

**4:10** *Struggle*: other manuscripts and patristic witnesses read "suffer reproach."

**4:11–16** Timothy is urged to preach and teach with confidence, relying on the gifts and the mission that God has bestowed on him.

**4:12** *Youth*: some commentators find this reference a sign of pseudepigraphy. Timothy had joined Paul as a missionary already in A.D. 49, some fifteen years before the earliest supposed date of composition.

**4:13** *Reading*: the Greek word refers to private or public reading. Here, it probably designates the public reading of scripture in the Christian assembly.

**4:14** *Prophetic word*: this may mean the utterance of a Christian prophet designating the candidate or a prayer of blessing accompanying the rite. *Imposition of hands*: this gesture was used in the Old Testament to signify the transmission of authority from Moses to Joshua (Nm 27:18–23; Dt 34:9). The early Christian community used it as a symbol of installation into an office: the Seven (Acts 6:6) and Paul and Barnabas (Acts 13:3). *Of the presbyterate*: this would mean that each member of the college of presbyters imposed hands and appears to contradict 2 Tm 1:6, in which Paul says that he imposed hands on Timothy. This latter text, however, does not exclude participation by others in the rite. Some prefer to translate "for the presbyterate," and thus understand it to designate the office into which Timothy was installed rather than the agents who installed him.

**5:1–16** After a few words of general advice based on common sense (1 Tm 5:1–2), the letter takes up, in its several aspects, the subject of widows. The first responsibility for their care belongs to the family circle, not to the Christian community as such (1 Tm 5:3–4, 16). The widow left without the aid of relatives may benefit the community by her prayer, and the community should consider her material sustenance its responsibility (1 Tm 5:5–8). Widows who wish to work directly for the Christian community should not be accepted unless they are well beyond the probability of marriage, i.e., sixty years of age, married only once, and with a reputation for good works (1 Tm 5:9–10). Younger widows are apt to be troublesome and should be encouraged to remarry (1 Tm 5:11–15).

**5:16** *Woman believer*: some early Latin manuscripts and Fathers have a masculine here, while most later manuscripts and patristic quotations conflate the two readings, perhaps to avoid unfair restriction to women.

---

| | |
|---|---|
| **4:7** 1:4; 2 Tm 2:16; Ti 1:14. | **4:14** 5:22; Acts 6:6; 8:17; 2 Tm 1:6. |
| **4:8** 6:6. | **5:1** Lv 19:32; Ti 2:2. |
| **4:9** 1:15; 2 Tm 2:11; Ti 3:8. | **5:5** Jer 49:11; Lk 2:37; 18:7. |
| **4:10** 2:4; Ti 2:11. | **5:10** Jn 13:14; Heb 13:2. |
| **4:12** 1 Cor 16:11; Ti 2:15 / Phil 3:17. | **5:13** 2 Thes 3:11. |
| | **5:14** 1 Cor 7:9. |

**Rules for Presbyters.**† ¹⁷Presbyters who preside well deserve double honor, especially those who toil in preaching and teaching.* ¹⁸For the scripture says, "You shall not muzzle an ox when it is threshing," and, "A worker deserves his pay."* ¹⁹Do not accept an accusation against a presbyter unless it is supported by two or three witnesses.* ²⁰Reprimand publicly those who do sin, so that the rest also will be afraid.* ²¹I charge you before God and Christ Jesus and the elect angels to keep these rules without prejudice, doing nothing out of favoritism. ²²Do not lay hands too readily on anyone, and do not share in another's sins. Keep yourself pure.* ²³Stop drinking only water, but have a little wine for the sake of your stomach and your frequent illnesses.

²⁴Some people's sins are public, preceding them to judgment; but other people are followed by their sins. ²⁵Similarly, good works are also public; and even those that are not cannot remain hidden.

**6** **Rules for Slaves.** ¹†Those who are under the yoke of slavery must regard their masters as worthy of full respect, so that the name of God and our teaching† may not suffer abuse.* ²Those whose masters are believers must not take advantage of them because they are brothers but must give better service because those who will profit from their work are believers and are beloved.*

## V. FALSE TEACHING AND TRUE WEALTH

Teach and urge these things.† ³Whoever teaches something different and does not agree with the sound words of our Lord Jesus Christ and the religious teaching* ⁴is conceited, understanding nothing, and has a morbid disposition for arguments and verbal disputes. From these come envy, rivalry, insults, evil suspicions, ⁵and mutual friction among people with corrupted minds, who are deprived of the truth, supposing religion to be a means of gain.* ⁶†Indeed, religion with contentment is a great gain.* ⁷For we brought nothing into the world, just as we shall not be able to take anything out of it.* ⁸If we have food and clothing, we shall be content with that.* ⁹Those who want to be rich are falling into temptation and into a trap and into many foolish and harmful desires, which plunge them into ruin and destruction.* ¹⁰For the love of money is the root of all evils, and some people in their desire for it have strayed from the faith and have pierced themselves with many pains.

**Exhortations to Timothy.**† ¹¹But you, man of God,† avoid all this. Instead, pursue righteousness, devotion, faith, love, patience, and gentleness.* ¹²Compete well for the faith. Lay hold of eternal life, to which you were called when you made the noble confession in the

---

**5:17–25** The function of presbyters is not exactly the same as that of the *episkopos*, "bishop" (1 Tm 3:1); in fact, the relation of the two at the time of this letter is obscure (but cf. note on Ti 1:5–9). The Pastorals seem to reflect a transitional stage that developed in many regions of the church into the monarchical episcopate of the second and third centuries. The presbyters possess the responsibility of preaching and teaching, for which functions they are supported by the community (1 Tm 5:17–18). The realization that their position subjects them to adverse criticism is implied in the direction to Timothy (1 Tm 5:19–20) to make sure of the truth of any accusation against them before public reproof is given. He must be as objective as possible in weighing charges against presbyters (1 Tm 5:21), learning from his experience to take care in selecting them (1 Tm 5:22). Some scholars take 1 Tm 5:22 as a reference not to ordination of presbyters but to reconciliation of public sinners. The letter now sounds an informal note of personal concern in its advice to Timothy not to be so ascetic that he even avoids wine (1 Tm 5:23). Judgment concerning the fitness of candidates to serve as presbyters is easy with persons of open conduct, more difficult and prolonged with those of greater reserve (1 Tm 5:24–25).
**6:1–2** Compare the tables for household duties, such as that of Col 3:18–4:1. Domestic relationships derive new meaning from the Christian faith.
**6:1** *Our teaching*: this refers to the teaching of the Christian community.
**6:2b–10** Timothy is exhorted to maintain steadfastly the position outlined in this letter, not allowing himself to be pressured

into any other course. He must realize that false teachers can be discerned by their pride, envy, quarrelsomeness, and greed for material gain. 1 Tm 6:6 is rather obscure and is interpreted, and therefore translated, variously. The suggestion seems to be that the important gain that religion brings is spiritual, but that there is material gain, too, up to the point of what is needed for physical sustenance (cf. 1 Tm 6:17–19).
**6:6** *Contentment*: the word *autarkeia* is a technical Greek philosophical term for the virtue of independence from material goods (Aristotle, Cynics, Stoics).
**6:11–16** Timothy's position demands total dedication to God and faultless witness to Christ (1 Tm 6:11–14) operating from an awareness, through faith, of the coming revelation in Jesus of the invisible God (1 Tm 6:15–16).
**6:11** *Man of God*: a title applied to Moses and the prophets (Dt 33:1; 1 Sm 2:27; 1 Kgs 12:22; 13:1; etc.).

**5:17** 1 Cor 16:18; Phil 2:29.
**5:18** Dt 25:4; 1 Cor 9:8 / Mt 10:10; Lk 10:7.
**5:19** Dt 17:6; 19:15; Mt 18:16; 2 Cor 13:1.
**5:20** Gal 2:14; Eph 5:11; 2 Tm 4:2; Ti 1:9, 13.
**5:22** 4:14; 2 Tm 1:6.
**6:1** Eph 6:5; Ti 2:9–10.
**6:2** Phlm 16.
**6:3** Gal 1:6–9; 2 Tm 1:13; Ti 1:1.
**6:5** 2 Tm 3:8; 4:4; Ti 1:14.
**6:6** 4:8; Phil 4:11–12; Heb 13:5.
**6:7** Jb 1:21; Eccl 5:14.
**6:8** Prv 30:8.
**6:9** Prv 23:4; 28:22.
**6:11** 2 Tm 2:22.

presence of many witnesses. * [13] I charge [you] before God, who gives life to all things, and before Christ Jesus, who gave testimony under Pontius Pilate for the noble confession, * [14] to keep the commandment without stain or reproach until the appearance of our Lord Jesus Christ [15] that the blessed and only ruler will make manifest at the proper time, the King of kings and Lord of lords, * [16] who alone has immortality, who dwells in unapproachable light, and whom no human being has seen or can see. To him be honor and eternal power. Amen. *

**Right Use of Wealth.**† [17] Tell the rich in the present age not to be proud and not to rely on so uncertain a thing as wealth but rather on God, who richly provides us with all things for our enjoyment. * [18] Tell them to do good, to be rich in good works, to be generous, ready to share, [19] thus accumulating as treasure a good foundation for the future, so as to win the life that is true life. *

## VI. FINAL RECOMMENDATION AND WARNING†

[20] O Timothy, guard what has been entrusted to you. Avoid profane babbling and the absurdities of so-called knowledge. * [21] By professing it, some people have deviated from the faith.
Grace be with all of you. *

---

† **6:17–19** Timothy is directed to instruct the rich, advising them to make good use of their wealth by aiding the poor.
**6:20–21** A final solemn warning against the heretical teachers, with what seems to be a specific reference to gnosticism, the great rival and enemy of the church for two centuries and more (the Greek word for "knowledge" is *gnōsis*). If gnosticism is being referred to here, it is probable that the warnings against "speculations" and "myths and genealogies" (cf. especially 1 Tm 1:4; Ti 3:9) involve allusions to that same kind of heresy. Characteristic of the various gnostic systems of speculation was an elaborate mythology of innumerable superhuman interme-diaries, on a descending scale ("genealogies"), between God and the world. Thus would be explained the emphasis upon Christ's being the one mediator (as in 1 Tm 2:5). Although fully developed gnosticism belonged to the second and later centuries, there are signs that incipient forms of it belonged to Paul's own period.

---

* **6:12** 1 Cor 9:26; 2 Tm 4:7.  **6:17** Ps 62:11; Lk 12:20.
**6:13** Jn 18:36–37; 19:11.  **6:19** Mt 6:20.
**6:15** 2 Mc 13:4; Rev 17:14.  **6:20** 2 Tm 1:14 / 1 Tm 4:7.
**6:16** Ex 33:20; Ps 104:2.  **6:21** 1:6; 2 Tm 2:18.

# The Second Letter to
# Timothy

## INTRODUCTION

### Raymond F. Collins

Many affinities link 2 Timothy with 1 Timothy, the most obvious of which are their respective epistolary salutations. Both texts identify their purported sender, Paul, as an apostle of Christ Jesus by the will of God. Both texts identify their recipient, Timothy, as Paul's "child." Both texts have the same three-part opening epistolary greeting, a wish prayer for mercy, grace, and peace, which is not found in any of the undisputed letters of Paul. Although 2 Timothy incorporates "The Lord be with your Spirit" into the epistolary farewell (2 Tm 4:23a), both texts conclude with "Grace be with all of you." The final "you" (*hymin*) is in the plural but the "your" (*tou*) of the first part of the farewell greeting is in the singular, in keeping with the personal tone of the opening salutation.

## A Pastoral Epistle

Some of the characteristic expressions of 1 Timothy are to be found in the body of the letter that tradition has identified as the Second Letter to Timothy. Among these is the affirmative formula, "This saying is trustworthy" (2 Tm 2:11; see 1 Tm 1:15; 3:1; 4:9; cf. Ti 3:8). The "epiphany" language of 1 Timothy also recurs in 2 Timothy. Second Timothy 1:10 mentions "the appearance (*epiphaneia*) of our savior Christ Jesus" in the past while 2 Tm 4:1 and 8 speak about an "appearance" in the future when Christ Jesus the Lord will appear as a just judge. As in 1 Timothy, therefore, Christian existence is placed between these two epiphanies. The teaching that both letters proposed is identified by the code word "truth" (2 Tm 2:15, 18, 25; 3:7, 8; 4:4; cf. 1 Tm 2:4, 7 [twice]; 3:15; 4:3; 6:5) and as "sound" (2 Tm 1:13; 4:3; cf. 1 Tm 1:10; 6:3). Both 1 and 2 Timothy describe Paul as a preacher, apostle, and teacher (1 Tm 2:7; 2 Tm 1:11), seemingly

## Outline of 2 Timothy

I.  **Address (1:1–5)**

II. **Exhortations to Timothy (1:6–2:13)**

III. **Instructions Concerning False Teaching (2:14–4:8)**

IV. **Personal Requests and Final Greetings (4:9–22)**

adding the epithets of preacher and teacher to the traditional designation of Paul as an apostle to clarify the meaning of "apostle" for a later generation. These and other similarities between 1 and 2 Timothy suggest that they belong to the same corpus of literature, the Pastoral Epistles, even if not necessarily written by the same author.

## A Personal Letter

A number of scholars who maintain that 1 Timothy was not written by Paul hold that 2 Timothy was written in whole or in part by Paul. The reason for this is that 2 Timothy is such a personal letter with so many personal reminiscences that it could not have been written by anyone other than the apostle himself. The idea that 2 Timothy was partially written by Paul goes back to 1921 when the British scholar P. N. Harrison suggested that four fragments of Paul's own letters are preserved in the canonical 2 Timothy. The theory of incorporated notes by Paul or of parts of letters by him has taken many forms during the past century. Among them can be cited the 2009 commentary by Michel Gourgues, who proposed that 2 Tm 1:1–2:12; 4:6–22 was written by Paul.

For Gourgues the use of Paul's own writing by the anonymous author/editor of 2 Timothy was the point of contact between the apostle and the corpus of the Pastoral Epistles that allowed the entire corpus to become part of the canonical New Testament.

The number of persons who are mentioned by name in the text contributes to the personal quality of the letter. It is addressed to Timothy, identified as "my dear child," Paul's chief co-worker (2 Tm 1:2). Hellenistic letters often included such things as "so-and-so says hello," a third-person greeting, or "give my regards to," a second-person greeting, just before the final salutation. The author of 2 Timothy asks that greetings be extended to Prisca and Aquila (4:19). This couple is well known. They hosted house churches in Rome and in Ephesus and on at least one occasion they risked their necks for Paul (Rom 16:3–5; 1 Cor 16:19). Luke, who uses the diminutive, Priscilla, to identify the wife, says that Paul met them in Corinth and that he worked as a tentmaker with them (Acts 18:1–3). They left Corinth with Paul, and accompanied him as far as Ephesus. After Paul's departure from Ephesus they continued to minister there (Acts 18:18–26). Second Timothy also sends greetings to Onesiphorus (2 Tm 4:19), who is previously described as having encouraged Paul and not being ashamed of his imprisonment (1:16–18). He is said to have searched for Paul in Rome and had helped Paul in Ephesus. "Paul" offered prayers on his behalf but, apart from 2 Timothy, Onesiphorus is not mentioned in the New Testament.

Third-person greetings are sent by Eubulus, Pudens, Linus, and Claudia (2 Tm 4:21), none of whom appears elsewhere in the New Testament. Between the second- and third-person final greetings there is a mention of Erastus, who remained in Corinth (2 Tm 4:20) where he was city treasurer (Rom 16:24), and of a sick Trophimus, left behind in Miletus, who had accompanied Paul from Greece to Troas (Acts 20:4–5).

Several other individuals are also named in 2 Timothy. Lois and Eunice are respectively identified as the grandmother and mother of Timothy in 2 Tm 1:5. Phygelus and Hermogenes are said to have deserted Paul (2 Tm 1:15). Hymenaeus and Philetus are said to have deviated from the truth (2 Tm 2:17). Demas (Phlm 24) deserted Paul while Crescens and Titus went to Galatia and Dalmatia respectively (2 Tm 4:10). "Paul" sent Tychicus to Ephesus (2 Tm 4:11). He left his cloak with Carpus in Troas (2 Tm 4:13). Only Luke (Phlm 24; cf. Col 4:14) remained with "Paul," who asks that Mark come to him (2 Tm 4:11). This Mark is most likely to be identified with the John Mark of Acts (Acts 12:12, 25; 15:37, 39) and the Mark of Phlm 24 (cf. Col 4:10). There is also a coppersmith named Alexander who may be the Alexander of 1 Tm 1:20.

Jannes and Jambres, who opposed Moses (2 Tm 3:8), belong to another era. The pair of names appear in rabbinic and early Christian literature as those of the magicians who competed with Moses and Aaron in producing wonders before the Exodus (Ex 7:11 passim). Not otherwise mentioned in the New Testament, they provide a precedent for opposition to an appointed leader of God's people.

This impressive list of names, many of whom are associated with places where Paul had ministered, adds much to the personal quality of the letter. That so many of these individuals are otherwise unknown adds to the puzzle of the letter's authenticity. If the letter has not been written by Paul, as the majority of contemporary scholars hold, the names add to its verisimilitude. The mixture of known with otherwise unknown individuals provides credibility for the existence of these unknown individuals.

## An Epistolary Testament

The letter repeatedly suggests that Paul is in prison (2 Tm 1:8, 16; 2:9; cf. 1:12). Should the letter be pseudonymous, this detail accounts for the absence of Paul and the need for a letter to substitute for his personal presence.

The opening and closing epistolary conventions of the text (2 Tm 1:1–2; 4:19–22), along with the initial thanksgiving, which differs from Paul's typical expressions of thanksgiving (1:3), provide the letter with an epistolary format that is even more pronounced than that of 1 Timothy. The bodies of the two "letters" are, however, radically different from one another. The body of 1 Timothy is largely concerned with the church and its organization; the body of 2 Timothy is for the most part a kind of reflection on Paul's life and ministry (see 2 Tm 3:10–11). Second Timothy 4:6–8 portrays Paul as a person who is about to die. He has accomplished his ministry and is awaiting the appearance of the Lord, his judge. The absence of so many named individuals leaves Paul to face this prospect all alone.

As a text attributed to someone about to depart this life, the body of the letter has a literary form similar to that of the farewell discourses of Old Testament, intertestamental, and New Testament literature. Typically this kind of literature was anonymously composed and was attributed to the departing person as a testimony to that person's importance. One feature of such literature is the passing on of the person's work, the continuance of the legacy. In this case, the heir apparent is Timothy, strikingly described in 2 Tm 1:2 as Paul's "dear child" (cf. 2:1). There is some suggestion that Timothy is relatively young, at least in comparison with Paul (1:5; 2:22; 3:15). As the departing Jesus prayed in the Farewell Discourse of the Fourth Gospel for those who would succeed him in ministry (Jn 17:9, 15–17, 20–21), so Paul prays for Timothy (2 Tm 1:3).

## Theological Motifs

Timothy is a link in a chain of tradition that begins with Paul's ancestors (2 Tm 1:3), is passed along by Paul and by Timothy's ancestors (1:5) to Timothy, who is to entrust it to others (2:2). Two significant images are used to describe the succession in ministry. First, Timothy is urged "to stir into flame the gift of God that you have through the imposition of my hands" (1:6). The gesture (cf. 1 Tm 4:14), symbolizing the communication of power, is similar to one used in ordination rituals that were about to be developed in rabbinic and Christian circles. Second, Timothy is exhorted to "guard this rich trust" (2 Tm 1:14; cf. 1:12). The language of this passage will give rise to the later theological notion of the deposit of faith.

Succession in ministry takes place in the troubled final times (2 Tm 3:1–5, 13; 4:3–4). Timothy is exhorted to avoid the vices that are prevalent in those times. Much of the body of

the letter consists of a series of exhortations addressed to Timothy (1:6–8, 13–14; 2:2–8, 14–17; 3:5, 14; 4:1–5). Paul is presented as the person from whom Timothy should learn and whose example he should follow. Negative examples portray the kind of conduct that Timothy is to avoid.

An exhortation found in 2 Tm 3:14–17 has proved to be particularly important for the later tradition of the church. Timothy is exhorted to remain faithful to what he has learned and to believe and hold on to the sacred scriptures that he received from infancy. The scriptures provide salvific wisdom, are inspired, and are useful for teaching, refutation, correction, and training in righteousness. When 2 Timothy was written, the "sacred scriptures" were basically what is known today as the Old Testament. The passage provides the biblical foundation for the doctrine of the inspiration of sacred Scripture (*Catechism of the Catholic Church*, 105–7).

Second Timothy shares with 1 Timothy elements of an "epiphany" Christology but differs from it with regard to another christological element, that of savior. All three Pastoral Epistles use the epithet "Savior." In the uncontested letters, Paul uses the title just once, when writing about the expectation of the return of the Lord Jesus Christ (Phil 3:20). Second Timothy 1:10 reprises this Pauline usage by applying the title to Christ, whereas 1 Timothy uses the title only in reference to God (1 Tm 1:1; 2:3; 4:10).

Through the example of Paul and Timothy, beleaguered disciples are encouraged to remain steadfast in their adherence to the gospel. Often this encouragement is merely implicit. It becomes explicit in a short hymn introduced by the formulaic "this saying is trustworthy" (2 Tm 2:11–13). The first part of the hymn (2:11b–12a) echoes what Paul wrote in Rom 6:8. In this life we die and live with Christ. If we persevere we shall reign with him. The second part of the hymn is a strong exhortation for believers to remain faithful. A kind of holy law, expressing the kind of justice found in the law of talion—a law in which the stipulated punishment corresponds exactly to the crime, as in "an eye for an eye"—says that if we deny Christ, he will deny us, notwithstanding his essential fidelity. ■

# THE SECOND LETTER TO TIMOTHY

## New American Bible, Introduction

The authorship and date of this letter, as one of the Pastoral Epistles, are discussed in the Introduction to the First Letter to Timothy.

The tone here is more personal than in First Timothy, for this letter addresses Timothy in vivid terms (2 Tm 1:6–14; 2:1–13) and depicts Paul's courage and hope in the face of discouragements late in the course of his apostolic ministry (2 Tm 1:15–18; 3:10–17; 4:9–18). Indeed, the letter takes on the character of a final exhortation and testament from Paul to the younger Timothy (2 Tm 4:1–8). Paul is portrayed as a prisoner (2 Tm 1:8, 16; 2:9) in Rome (2 Tm 1:17), and there is a hint that Timothy may be in Ephesus (2 Tm 2:17). The letter reveals that, with rare exceptions, Christians have not rallied to Paul's support (2 Tm 1:15–18) and takes a pessimistic view of the outcome of his case (2 Tm 4:6). It describes Paul as fully aware of what impends, looking to God, not to human beings, for his deliverance (2 Tm 4:3–8, 18). It recalls his mission days with Timothy (2 Tm 1:3–5; cf. Acts 16:1–4). It points to his preaching of the gospel as the reason for his imprisonment and offers Timothy, as a motive for steadfastness, his own example of firmness in faith despite adverse circumstances (2 Tm 1:6–14). The letter suggests that Timothy should prepare others to replace himself as Paul has prepared Timothy to replace him (2 Tm 2:1–2). Paul urges him not to desist out of fear from preserving and spreading the Christian message (2 Tm 2:3–7). It presents the resurrection of Jesus and his messianic role as the heart of the gospel for which Paul has been ready to lay down his life (2 Tm 2:8–9) and thus not only to express his own conviction fully but to support the conviction of others (2 Tm 2:10–13).

This letter, like the preceding one, urges Timothy to protect the community from the inevitable impact of false teaching (2 Tm 2:14–3:9), without fear of the personal attacks that may result (2 Tm 3:10–13). It recommends that he rely on the power of the scriptures, on proclamation of the word, and on sound doctrine (2 Tm 3:14–4:2), without being troubled by those who do not accept him (2 Tm 4:3–5). The letter poignantly observes in passing that Paul has need of his reading materials and his cloak (2 Tm 4:13) and, what will be best of all, a visit from Timothy.

On the theory of authorship by Paul himself, Second Timothy appears to be the last of the three Pastoral Epistles. The many scholars who argue that the Pastorals are products of the Pauline school often incline toward Second Timothy as the earliest of the three and the one most likely to have actual fragments of material from Paul himself.

The principal divisions of the Second Letter to Timothy are the following:

I. Address (1:1–5)
II. Exhortations to Timothy (1:6–2:13)
III. Instructions Concerning False Teaching (2:14–4:8)
IV. Personal Requests and Final Greetings (4:9–22) ∎

# SECOND TIMOTHY

## I. ADDRESS

**1** **Greeting.**† ¹Paul, an apostle of Christ Jesus by the will of God* for the promise of life in Christ Jesus,† ²to Timothy, my dear child: grace, mercy, and peace from God the Father and Christ Jesus our Lord.

**Thanksgiving.** ³* I am grateful to God, whom I worship with a clear conscience as my ancestors did,† as I remember you constantly in my prayers, night and day. ⁴† I yearn to see you again, recalling your tears, so that I may be filled with joy, ⁵as I recall your sincere faith that first lived in your grandmother Lois and in your mother Eunice and that I am confident lives also in you.*

## II. EXHORTATIONS TO TIMOTHY

**The Gifts Timothy Has Received.** ⁶For this reason, I remind you to stir into flame the gift of God† that you have through the imposition of my hands.* ⁷For God did not give us a spirit of cowardice but rather of power and love and self-control.* ⁸So do not be ashamed of your testimony to our Lord,† nor of me, a prisoner for his sake; but bear your share of hardship for the gospel with the strength that comes from God.*

⁹† He saved us and called us to a holy life, not according to our works but according to his own design and the grace bestowed on us in Christ Jesus before time began,* ¹⁰but now made manifest through the appearance of our savior Christ Jesus, who destroyed death and brought life and immortality to light through the gospel,* ¹¹† for which I was appointed preacher and apostle* and teacher. ¹²† On this account I am suffering these things; but I am not ashamed,* for I know him in whom I have believed and am confident that he is able to guard what has been entrusted to me until that day. ¹³Take as your norm the sound words that you heard from me, in the faith and love that are in Christ Jesus.* ¹⁴Guard this rich trust with the help of the holy Spirit that dwells within us.*

**Paul's Suffering.** ¹⁵†* You know that everyone in Asia deserted me, including Phygelus and Hermogenes. ¹⁶† May the Lord grant mercy to the family of Onesiphorus* because he often gave me new heart and was not ashamed of my chains. ¹⁷But when he came to Rome, he promptly searched for me and found me. ¹⁸May the Lord grant him to find mercy from the Lord† on that day. And you know very well the services he rendered in Ephesus.*

---

**1:1–2** For the formula of address and greeting, see note on Rom 1:1–7.

**1:1** *The promise of life in Christ Jesus*: that God grants through union with Christ in faith and love; cf. Col 3:4; 1 Tm 4:8.

**1:3** *As my ancestors did*: this emphasizes the continuity of Judaism and Christianity; for a similar view, see Rom 9:3–5; Phil 3:4–6.

**1:4–5** Purportedly written from prison in Rome (2 Tm 1:8, 17; 4:6–8) shortly before the writer's death, the letter recalls the earlier sorrowful parting from Timothy, commending him for his faith and expressing the longing to see him again.

**1:6** *The gift of God*: the grace resulting from the conferral of an ecclesiastical office. *The imposition of my hands*: see note on 1 Tm 4:14.

**1:8** *Do not be ashamed of your testimony to our Lord*: i.e., of preaching and suffering for the sake of the gospel.

**1:9–10** Redemption from sin and the call to holiness of life are not won by personal deeds but are freely and graciously bestowed according to God's eternal plan; cf. Eph 1:4.

**1:11** *Teacher*: the overwhelming majority of manuscripts and Fathers read "teacher of the nations," undoubtedly a harmonization with 1 Tm 2:7.

**1:12** *He is able to guard...until that day*: the intervening words can also be translated "what I have entrusted to him" (i.e., the fruit of his ministry) as well as "what has been entrusted to me" (i.e., the faith). The same difficult term occurs in 2 Tm 1:14, where it is modified by the adjective "rich" and used without a possessive.

**1:15** Keen disappointment is expressed, here and later (2 Tm 4:16), that the Christians of the province of Asia, especially Phygelus and Hermogenes, should have abandoned the writer and done nothing to defend his case in court.

**1:16–18** *The family of Onesiphorus because he...of my chains*: Onesiphorus seems to have died before this letter was written. His family is mentioned twice (here and in 2 Tm 4:19), though it was Onesiphorus himself who was helpful to Paul in prison and rendered much service to the community of Ephesus. Because the apostle complains of abandonment by all in Asia during his second imprisonment and trial, the assistance of Onesiphorus seems to have been given to Paul during his first Roman imprisonment (A.D. 61–63).

**1:18** *Lord...Lord*: the first "Lord" here seems to refer to Christ, the second "Lord" to the Father.

---

*

| | |
|---|---|
| **1:1** 1 Tm 4:8. | 2 Pt 1:11 / 1 Cor |
| **1:3** 1 Tm 3:9 / Phil 3:5. | 15:54–55; Heb 2:14 / |
| **1:5** 1 Tm 1:5 / Acts 16:1. | 1 Cor 15:53–54. |
| **1:6** 1 Tm 4:14; 5:22 / Acts | **1:11** 1 Tm 2:7. |
| 6:6; 8:17. | **1:12** 1 Pt 4:16 / 1 Tm |
| **1:7** Rom 5:5; 8:15; 1 Cor | 1:10–11. |
| 2:4. | **1:13** 1 Tm 1:14. |
| **1:8** 2:3, 15; Rom 1:16. | **1:14** 1 Tm 6:20 / Rom |
| **1:9** Eph 2:8–9; Ti 3:5 / | 8:11. |
| Eph 1:4; Ti 1:2. | **1:15** 4:16. |
| **1:10** Rom 16:26; 1 Pt 1:20 | **1:16** 4:19. |
| / 1 Tm 6:14 / Phil | **1:18** Jude 21. |
| 3:20; Ti 1:4; 2:13; | |

**2 Timothy's Conduct.** †So you, my child, be strong in the grace that is in Christ Jesus. [2] And what you heard from me through many witnesses entrust to faithful people who will have the ability to teach others as well. [3] Bear your share of hardship along with me like a good soldier of Christ Jesus.* [4] To satisfy the one who recruited him, a soldier does not become entangled in the business affairs of life.* [5] Similarly, an athlete cannot receive the winner's crown except by competing according to the rules.* [6] The hardworking farmer ought to have the first share of the crop.* [7] Reflect on what I am saying, for the Lord will give you understanding in everything.*

[8] †Remember Jesus Christ, raised from the dead, a descendant of David: such is my gospel,* [9] for which I am suffering, even to the point of chains, like a criminal. But the word of God is not chained.* [10] Therefore, I bear with everything for the sake of those who are chosen, so that they too may obtain the salvation that is in Christ Jesus, together with eternal glory.* [11] This saying is trustworthy:

If we have died with him
    we shall also live with him;*
[12] if we persevere
    we shall also reign with him.
But if we deny him
    he will deny us.*
[13] If we are unfaithful
    he remains faithful,
    for he cannot deny himself.*

## III. INSTRUCTIONS CONCERNING FALSE TEACHING

**Warning Against Useless Disputes.** [14] †Remind people of these things and charge them before God† to stop disputing about words. This serves no useful purpose since it harms those who listen.* [15] Be eager to present yourself as acceptable to God, a workman who causes no disgrace, imparting the word of truth without deviation.* [16] Avoid profane, idle talk, for such people will become more and more godless,* [17] and their teaching will spread like gangrene. Among them are Hymenaeus and Philetus,* [18] who have deviated from the truth by saying that [the] resurrection has already taken place and are upsetting the faith of some.* [19] Nevertheless, God's solid foundation stands, bearing this inscription, "The Lord knows those who are his"; and, "Let everyone who calls upon the name of the Lord avoid evil."*

[20] In a large household there are vessels not only of gold and silver but also of wood and clay, some for lofty and others for humble use. [21] If anyone cleanses himself of these things, he will be a vessel for lofty use, dedicated, beneficial to the master of the house, ready for every good work.* [22] So turn from youthful desires and pursue righteousness, faith, love, and peace, along with those who call on the Lord† with purity of heart.* [23] Avoid foolish and ignorant debates, for you know that they breed quarrels.* [24] A slave of the Lord should not quarrel, but should be gentle with everyone,

---

**2:1–7** This passage manifests a characteristic deep concern for safeguarding the faith and faithfully transmitting it through trustworthy people (2 Tm 2:1–2; cf. 2 Tm 1:14; 1 Tm 6:20; Ti 1:9). Comparisons to the soldier's detachment, the athlete's sportsmanship, and the farmer's arduous work as the price of recompense (2 Tm 2:4–6) emphasize the need of singleness of purpose in preaching the word, even at the cost of hardship, for the sake of Christ (2 Tm 2:3).

**2:8–13** The section begins with a sloganlike summary of Paul's gospel about Christ (2 Tm 2:8) and concludes with what may be part of an early Christian hymn (2 Tm 2:11b–12a; most exegetes include the rest of 2 Tm 2:12 and all of 2 Tm 2:13 as part of the quotation). The poetic lines suggest that through baptism Christians die spiritually with Christ and hope to live with him and reign with him forever, but the Christian life includes endurance, witness, and even suffering, as the final judgment will show and as Paul's own case makes clear; while he is imprisoned for preaching the gospel (2 Tm 2:9), his sufferings are helpful to the elect for obtaining the salvation and glory available in Christ (2 Tm 2:10), who will be true to those who are faithful and will disown those who deny him (2 Tm 2:12–13).

**2:14–19** For those who dispute about mere words (cf. 2 Tm 2:23–24) and indulge in irreligious talk to the detriment of their listeners (2 Tm 2:16–19), see notes on 1 Tm 1:3–7; 6:20–21. Hymenaeus and Philetus (2 Tm 2:17), while accepting the Chris-

tian's mystical death and resurrection in Christ through baptism, claimed that baptized Christians are already risen with Christ in this life and thus that there is no future bodily resurrection or eternal glory to come. The first quotation in 2 Tm 2:19 is from Nm 16:5; the other quotation is from some unidentified Jewish or Christian writing.

**2:14** *Before God*: many ancient manuscripts read "before the Lord."

**2:22** *Those who call on the Lord*: those who believe in Christ and worship him as Lord, i.e., Christians (Acts 9:14–16, 20–21; Rom 10:12–13; cf. 2 Tm 2:19, literally, "Everyone who names the name of the Lord").

---

* 
**2:3** 1:8; 4:5; Phlm 2.
**2:4** 1 Cor 9:6.
**2:5** 1 Cor 9:25.
**2:6** 1 Cor 9:7–10.
**2:7** Prv 2:6.
**2:8** Rom 1:3; 1 Cor 15:4, 20 / Rom 2:16; Gal 1:11; 2:2.
**2:9** Phil 1:12–14.
**2:10** Col 1:24; 1 Tm 1:15.
**2:11** Rom 6:8.
**2:12** Mt 10:22, 33; Lk 12:9.
**2:13** Nm 23:19; Rom 3:3–4; 1 Cor 10:13; Ti 1:2.

**2:14** 1 Tm 6:4.
**2:15** 1:8; 2 Cor 6:7; Eph 1:13; Col 1:5.
**2:16** 1 Tm 4:7.
**2:17** 1 Tm 1:20.
**2:18** 2 Thes 2:2.
**2:19** Is 28:16; 1 Cor 3:10–15 / Nm 16:5; Jn 10:14.
**2:21** 3:17.
**2:22** Gal 5:22; 1 Tm 6:11 / Rom 10:13; 1 Cor 1:2.
**2:23** 1 Tm 1:4; 4:7; 6:4; Ti 3:9.

able to teach, tolerant,* ²⁵correcting opponents with kindness. It may be that God will grant them repentance that leads to knowledge of the truth,* ²⁶† and that they may return to their senses out of the devil's snare,* where they are entrapped by him, for his will.

# 3 The Dangers of the Last Days.† ¹But understand this: there will be terrifying times in the last days.* ²People will be self-centered and lovers of money, proud, haughty, abusive, disobedient to their parents, ungrateful, irreligious,* ³callous, implacable, slanderous, licentious, brutal, hating what is good, ⁴traitors, reckless, conceited, lovers of pleasure rather than lovers of God, ⁵as they make a pretense of religion but deny its power. Reject them.* ⁶For some of these slip into homes and make captives of women weighed down by sins, led by various desires,* ⁷always trying to learn but never able to reach a knowledge of the truth.* ⁸Just as Jannes and Jambres opposed Moses, so they also oppose the truth—people of depraved mind, unqualified in the faith.* ⁹But they will not make further progress, for their foolishness will be plain to all, as it was with those two.

**Paul's Example and Teaching.**† ¹⁰You have followed my teaching, way of life, purpose, faith, patience, love, endurance, ¹¹persecutions, and sufferings, such as happened to me in Antioch, Iconium, and Lystra, persecutions that I endured. Yet from all these things the Lord delivered me.* ¹²In fact, all who want to live religiously in Christ Jesus will be persecuted.* ¹³But wicked people and charlatans will go from bad to worse, deceivers and deceived. ¹⁴But you, remain faithful to what you have learned and believed, because you know from whom you learned it,* ¹⁵and that from infancy you have known [the] sacred scriptures, which are capable of giving you wisdom for salvation through faith in Christ Jesus.* ¹⁶† All scripture* is inspired by God and is useful for teaching, for refutation, for correction, and for training in righteousness,† ¹⁷so that one who belongs to God may be competent, equipped for every good work.*

# 4 Solemn Charge.† ¹I charge you in the presence of God and of Christ Jesus, who will judge the living and the dead, and by his appearing and his kingly power:* ²proclaim the word; be persistent whether it is convenient or inconvenient; convince, reprimand, encourage through all patience and teaching.* ³For the time will come when people will not tolerate sound doctrine but, following their own desires and insatiable curiosity,† will accumulate teachers* ⁴and will stop listening to the truth and will be diverted to myths.* ⁵But you, be self-possessed in all circumstances; put up with hardship; perform the work of an evangelist; fulfill your ministry.

**Reward for Fidelity.** ⁶†* For I am already being poured out like a libation, and the time of my

---

**2:26** Some interpreters would render this passage, "Thus they may come to their senses and, forced to do his (i.e., God's) will, may escape the devil's trap." This interpretation of the Greek is possible, but the one accepted in the text seems more likely.

**3:1–9** The moral depravity and false teaching that will be rampant in the last days are already at work (2 Tm 3:1–5). The frivolous and superficial, too, devoid of the true spirit of religion, will be easy victims of those who pervert them by falsifying the truth (2 Tm 3:6–8), just as Jannes and Jambres, Pharaoh's magicians of Egypt (Ex 7:11–12, 22), discredited the truth in Moses' time. Exodus does not name the magicians, but the two names are widely found in much later Jewish, Christian, and even pagan writings. Their origins are legendary.

**3:10–17** Paul's example for Timothy includes persecution, a frequent emphasis in the Pastorals. Timothy is to be steadfast to what he has been taught and to scripture. The scriptures are the source of wisdom, i.e., of belief in and loving fulfillment of God's word revealed in Christ, through whom salvation is given.

**3:16–17** *Useful for teaching...every good work*: because as God's word the scriptures share his divine authority. It is exercised through those who are ministers of the word.

**3:16** *All scripture is inspired by God*: this could possibly also be translated, "All scripture inspired by God is useful for…." In this classic reference to inspiration, God is its principal author, with the writer as the human collaborator. Thus the scriptures are the word of God in human language. See also 2 Pt 1:20–21.

**4:1–5** The gravity of the obligation incumbent on Timothy to preach the word can be gauged from the solemn adjuration: in the presence of God, and of Christ coming as universal judge, and by his appearance and *his kingly power* (2 Tm 4:1). Patience, courage, constancy, and endurance are required despite the opposition, hostility, indifference, and defection of many to whom the truth has been preached (2 Tm 4:2–5).

**4:3** *Insatiable curiosity*: literally, "with itching ears."

**4:6** The apostle recognizes his death through martyrdom to be imminent. He regards it as an act of worship in which his blood will be poured out in sacrifice; cf. Ex 29:38–40; Phil 2:17.

---

**2:24** 1 Tm 3:2–3.
**2:25** 3:7; 1 Tm 2:4.
**2:26** 1 Tm 3:7.
　**3:1** 1 Tm 4:1; 2 Pt 3:3; Jude 18.
**3:2–4** Rom 1:29–31.
**3:5** Rom 2:20–22; Ti 1:16.
**3:6** Ti 1:11.
**3:7** 2:25.
**3:8** Ex 7:11, 22; 1 Tm 6:5.
**3:11** Acts 13:50; 14:5, 19 / Ps 34:20.
**3:12** Jn 15:20; Acts 14:22.

**3:14** 2:2.
**3:15** Jn 5:39.
**3:16** Rom 15:4; 2 Pt 1:19–21.
**3:17** 2:21.
**4:1** 1 Tm 5:21; 6:14 / Acts 10:42; Rom 14:9–10; 1 Pt 4:5.
**4:2** Acts 20:20, 31; 1 Tm 5:20.
**4:3** 1 Tm 4:1.
**4:4** 1 Tm 1:4; 4:7; Ti 1:14.
**4:6** Phil 2:17.

departure is at hand. [7] † I have competed well; I have finished the race; * I have kept the faith. [8] † From now on the crown of righteousness awaits me, which the Lord, the just judge, will award to me on that day, * and not only to me, but to all who have longed for his appearance.

## IV. PERSONAL REQUESTS AND FINAL GREETINGS

**Paul's Loneliness.** [9] † Try to join me soon, [10] for Demas, enamored of the present world, deserted me and went to Thessalonica, Crescens to Galatia, † and Titus to Dalmatia. * [11] Luke is the only one with me. Get Mark and bring him with you, for he is helpful to me in the ministry. * [12] I have sent Tychicus to Ephesus. * [13] When you come, bring the cloak I left with Carpus in Troas, the papyrus rolls, and especially the parchments. *

[14] Alexander † the coppersmith did me a great deal of harm; the Lord will repay him according to his deeds. * [15] You too be on guard against him, for he has strongly resisted our preaching.

[16] At my first defense no one appeared on my behalf, but everyone deserted me. May it not be held against them! * [17] But the Lord stood by me and gave me strength, so that through me the proclamation might be completed and all the Gentiles might hear it. And I was rescued from the lion's mouth. * [18] The Lord will rescue me from every evil threat and will bring me safe to his heavenly kingdom. To him be glory forever and ever. Amen. *

**Final Greeting.** [19] Greet Prisca and Aquila † and the family of Onesiphorus. * [20] Erastus † remained in Corinth, while I left Trophimus sick at Miletus. * [21] Try to get here before winter. Eubulus, Pudens, Linus, † Claudia, and all the brothers send greetings.

[22] The Lord be with your spirit. Grace be with all of you. *

**4:7** At the close of his life Paul could testify to the accomplishment of what Christ himself foretold concerning him at the time of his conversion, "I will show him what he will have to suffer for my name" (Acts 9:16).

**4:8** When the world is judged at the parousia, all who have eagerly looked for the Lord's appearing and have sought to live according to his teachings will be rewarded. The crown is a reference to the laurel wreath placed on the heads of victorious athletes and conquerors in war; cf. 2 Tm 2:5; 1 Cor 9:25.

**4:9–13** Demas either abandoned the work of the ministry for worldly affairs or, perhaps, gave up the faith itself (2 Tm 4:10). Luke (2 Tm 4:11) may have accompanied Paul on parts of his second and third missionary journeys (Acts 16:10–12; 20:5–7). Notice the presence of the first personal pronoun "we" in these Acts passages, suggesting to some that Luke (or at least some traveling companion of Paul's) was the author of Acts. Mark, once rejected by Paul (Acts 13:13; 15:39), is now to render him a great service (2 Tm 4:11); cf. Col 4:10; Phlm 24. For Tychicus, see Eph 6:21; cf. also Acts 20:4; Col 4:7.

**4:10** *Galatia*: some manuscripts read "Gaul" or "Gallia."

**4:14–18** *Alexander*: an opponent of Paul's preaching (2 Tm 4:14–15), perhaps the one who is mentioned in 1 Tm 1:20. Despite Paul's abandonment by his friends in the province of Asia (cf. 2 Tm 1:15–16), the divine assistance brought this first trial to a successful issue, even to the point of making the gospel message known to those who participated in or witnessed the trial (2 Tm 4:16–17).

**4:19** *Prisca and Aquila*: they assisted Paul in his ministry in Corinth (Acts 18:2–3) and Ephesus (Acts 18:19, 26; 1 Cor 16:19). They risked death to save his life, and all the Gentile communities are indebted to them (Rom 16:3–5).

**4:20** *Erastus*: he was the treasurer of the city of Corinth (Rom 16:24); cf. also Acts 19:22. *Trophimus*: from the province of Asia, he accompanied Paul from Greece to Troas (Acts 20:4–5).

**4:21** *Linus*: Western tradition sometimes identified this Linus with the supposed successor of Peter as bishop of Rome, and Claudia as the mother of Linus (*Apostolic Constitutions*, fourth century).

**4:7** 1 Tm 1:18; 6:12; Jude 3 / Acts 20:24; 1 Cor 9:24; Heb 12:1.
**4:8** 2:5; Wis 5:16; 1 Cor 9:25; Phil 3:14; Jas 1:12; 1 Pt 5:4; Rev 2:10.
**4:10** Col 4:14; Phlm 24 / 2 Cor 2:13; 7:6–7; 8:23; Gal 2:3; Ti 1:4.
**4:11** Col 4:14; Phlm 24 / Col 4:10; Phlm 24.
**4:12** Acts 20:4; Eph 6:21; Col 4:7.
**4:13** Acts 16:8; 20:6.
**4:14** 1 Tm 1:20 / 2 Sm 3:39;
Ps 28:4; 62:12; Prv 24:12; Rom 2:6.
**4:16** 1:15.
**4:17** Acts 23:11; 27:23; Phil 4:13 / 1 Mc 2:60; Ps 22:22; Dn 6:23.
**4:18** 2 Cor 1:10 / Rom 16:27.
**4:19** Acts 18:2; Rom 16:3; 1 Cor 16:19 / 2 Tm 1:16.
**4:20** Acts 19:22; Rom 16:24 / Acts 20:4; 21:29.
**4:22** Gal 6:18; Phil 4:23; Col 4:18; 1 Tm 6:21; Ti 3:15.

# The Letter to

# Titus

## INTRODUCTION

### Raymond F. Collins

The Letter to Titus belongs to the same corpus of New Testament literature as do the two Letters to Timothy. All three texts are addressed to Paul's closest co-workers, asking them to carry on the work that Paul had begun. For this reason all three letters have been called the "Pastoral Epistles," letters written to pastors of local churches. The Letter to Titus provides directives to Titus, who is charged with organizing the church on Crete (Ti 1:5).

## Similarities with the Other Pastoral Epistles

The letter shares many similarities with 1 and 2 Timothy. Among these is an epiphany Christology (Ti 2:13; cf. 1 Tm 6:14; 2 Tm 1:10; 4:1, 8). Peculiar to Titus is the use of a noun, "appearance" (epiphaneia), to refer to the future manifestation of Jesus as Lord and the use of the related verb, "appear" (epiphainō), to refer to Jesus' manifestation in the past (Ti 2:11).

Titus shares with the other Pastoral Epistles the use of the title "Savior." Once again, however, Titus uses the title in a slightly different way from the other letters. Titus uses the title of both God (Ti 1:3; 2:10; 3:4) and Jesus (1:4; 2:13; 3:6) whereas 1 Timothy uses the title only of God (1 Tm 1:1; 2:3; 4:10) and 2 Timothy uses it only of Jesus (2 Tm 1:10). The use of the Savior title in the Pastoral Epistles is to be understood within the socio-political context within which these texts were written, that is, an era in which the title typically referred to the divinized Roman emperor. In the Pastoral Epistles, the title reminded believers that God and his Christ were Savior; the Roman emperor was not.

Many of the ideas associated with the idea of Savior come together in the epiphaneia passage found in Ti 2:11–14. This is one of

## Outline of Titus

I. Address (1:1–4)

II. Pastoral Charge (1:5–16)

III. Teaching the Christian Life (2:1–3:15)

the rare passages in the New Testament that explicitly speak of Jesus as God. Some authors have held that the expression "the glory of the great God and our savior Jesus Christ" (2:13) speaks about God and Jesus, but the wording in Greek and the fact that "god and savior" was an epithet used of gods and divinized human beings in the Hellenistic world suggest that the phrase pertains to Jesus, who is called "great God and Savior."

With the other two Pastorals, Titus employs the striking formula, "This saying is trustworthy" (Ti 3:8a). Even more than the other Pastorals, Titus borrows a metaphor from the domain of health to speak about the "sound doctrine," the healthy teaching, to which believers should adhere and which they should pass along (1:9, 13; 2:1, 2). Like the other Pastorals, Titus uses "truth" (alētheia, 1:1, 14) as a code word to speak about the orthodox content of the community's belief. Titus uses the word "faith" (pistis) in similar fashion (1:1; 4, 13; 2:2, 10; 3:15). First and Second Timothy employ the terminology in virtually the same way. (cf. 1 Tm 1:2, 4, 5, 14, 19 [twice]; 2:7, 15; 3:9, 13; 4:1, 6, 12; 5:8, 12; 6:10, 11, 12, 21; 2 Tm 1:5, 13; 2:18, 22; 3:8, 10, 15; 4:7). The way that the Pastoral Epistles speak about faith is different from the way that Paul does. In Paul's undisputed letters, "faith" and "belief" are used to describe the believer's personal relationship with God and Jesus. In the

Pastoral Epistles, "faith" describes the content of a person's belief, the orthodox faith of the community.

That Titus belongs to the same corpus of letters as 1 and 2 Timothy is also evident in its use of catalogues of virtues (Ti 1:8; 3:2) and vices (1:7; 3:3) and a household code (2:1–10). Like the other Pastorals, Titus clearly has the form of a letter. The final salutation of the letter (3:15b) is in the plural, just like the final salutations of 1 and 2 Timothy (1 Tm 6:21b; 2 Tm 4:22b). Its second- and third-person greetings (Ti 3:15a) are generalized; they do not contain the names of specific individuals, as do the greetings of 2 Tm 4:19–21.

Personal names nonetheless appear in Titus in the brief travelogue with directives that is found in Ti 3:12–14. "Paul" writes that he intends to send Artemas or Tychicus to join Titus (3:12), apparently to take Titus's place while he visits Paul. Artemas does not appear elsewhere in the New Testament but Tychicus is mentioned in four other New Testament texts that most contemporary scholarship holds to have been written after Paul (Acts 20:4; Eph 6:21; Col 4:7; 2 Tm 4:12). "Titus" is instructed to send Apollos and a lawyer named Zeno to Paul (Ti 3:13). The latter is unknown in the New Testament, whereas Apollos is a well-known figure (Acts 18:24–19:1; 1 Cor 1:12; 3:4–6, 22; 4:6; 16:12). As is the case with the bevy of names at the end of 2 Timothy, this short mixture of names, known and unknown, seems to add an aura of verisimilitude to a text that most of today's biblical scholars believe to be pseudepigraphic.

## The Opening Salutation (Ti 1:1–4)

Within the corpus of New Testament letters, the opening salutation of Titus is distinctive. The letter is addressed to Titus, "my true child in our common faith" (Ti 1:4). The designation of Titus as Paul's child is related to the belief that they share (cf. 1 Tm 1:2). The letter's epistolary greeting (Ti 1:4) resembles the greetings of the undisputed Pauline letters more than do the greetings of 1 and 2 Timothy (1 Tm 1:2b;

2 Tm 1:2b), but it introduces "Savior" language into the text from its outset.

Most striking, however, is how "Paul" is described in Ti 1:1–3. For the author of the text, Paul appears to be the only apostle. The author of a Hellenistic letter often added a word or two ("father," "king," etc.) to his name—always the first word in a letter—to identify the relationship between himself and the one to whom he was writing. The author's "title" in this work is a concise but comprehensive description of Paul's apostolate. Seemingly out of place in a letter ostensibly addressed to one of Paul's closest aides, it identifies Paul in relationship to God and Jesus but then it places Paul virtually at the center of time, situated between before time began and the eternal life for which we hope. The concisely expressed theology, ecclesiology, and understanding of Paul's apostolate of these verses deserve careful unpacking.

## Its Teaching

Between the epistolary salutation and its letter closing, Titus is more similar to 1 Timothy than it is to 2 Timothy. That the purported recipient of both Titus and 1 Timothy is described as Paul's true child in faith—Paul's legitimate heir—may provide a hint of the similarity of contents (Ti 1:4; cf. 1 Tm 1:2). The body of the "letter," like the body of 1 Timothy, is a document that deals with church order (Ti 1:5).

The letter sets down the qualifications of the one who is to serve as supervisor or overseer of a community (Ti 1:1–6). He is initially called "presbyter," elder, but is also identified as "bishop" and "God's steward." The bishop and the presbyter are one and the same person. Titus does not mention "deacons." The seemingly less-developed leadership structure of the church that is reflected in Titus is sometimes cited as a reason in favor of the view that Titus was the first of the Pastorals to have been written.

The bishop's responsibility is to teach sound doctrine and refute opponents, whose maliciousness is described at length (Ti 1:10–16) but in general terms. The description includes a paradoxical quotation, apparently from the sixth-century BCE Epimenides. The quotation, apparently intended to show that doctrinal error leads to moral misconduct, is a rare instance of a pagan author being quoted in the New Testament.

The household code in Ti 2:1–10 spells out some responsibilities of older men and women, younger men and women, and slaves. It is noteworthy that a mention of faith is added to the secular responsibilities of all five groups. Also noteworthy and to be related to the secular ethic of Titus is an exhortation to obey secular authority, an exhortation that is coupled with a broad social outlook (3:1; cf. 1 Tm 4:1–4). With the other two Pastorals, Titus uses the language of "good works" to speak about the ethical implications of adherence to sound doctrine (1:16 [twice], 2:7, 14; 3:1, 5, 8, 14; cf. 1 Tm 2:10, 3:1; 5:10 [twice], 25; 6:18; 2 Tm 1:9; 2:21; 3:17; 4:5).

The baptismal hymn in Ti 3:4–7, identified as a trustworthy saying (3:8a), may be the most important expression of sound doctrine in Titus. Its rich soteriology, or teaching about salvation, deserves to be carefully unpacked. The hymn speaks of the appearance of Jesus as due to the kindness and gracious mercy of God, of salvation coming from God's mercy rather than from righteous deeds, of baptism and the outpouring of the Holy Spirit as the means by which one is saved, of being justified by grace, and of the hope of eternal life to which all are heirs. All of these are important elements in the writings of the Apostle Paul, especially in his letters to the Romans and to the Galatians, but nowhere do they receive a more beautiful hymnic expression than they do in Ti 3:4–7. ■

# THE LETTER TO TITUS

## New American Bible, Introduction

The third of the Pastoral Epistles in the New Testament is addressed to a different co-worker of Paul than are First and Second Timothy. The situation is different, too, for Titus is addressed as the person in charge of developing the church on the large Mediterranean island of Crete (Ti 1:5), a place Paul had never, according to the New Testament, visited. The tone is closer to that of First Timothy as three topics of church life and structure are discussed: presbyter-bishops (see note on Ti 1:5–9), groups with which one must work in the church (Ti 2:1–10), and admonitions for conduct based on the grace and love of God that appeared in Jesus Christ (Ti 2:11–3:10). The warmer personal tone of Second Timothy is replaced by emphasis on church office and on living in the society of the day, in which deceivers and heretics abound (Ti 1:10–16; 3:9–10).

The Pauline assistant who is addressed, Titus, was a Gentile Christian, but we are nowhere informed of his place of birth or residence. He went from Antioch with Paul and Barnabas to Jerusalem (Gal 2:1; cf. Acts 15:2). According to 2 Corinthians (2 Cor 2:13; 7:6, 13–14), he was with Paul on his third missionary journey; his name, however, does not appear in Acts. Besides being the bearer of Paul's severe letter to the Corinthians (2 Cor 7:6–8), he had the responsibility of taking up the collection in Corinth for the Christian community of Jerusalem (2 Cor 8:6, 16–19, 23). In the present letter (Ti 1:5), he is mentioned as the administrator of the Christian community in Crete, charged with the task of organizing it through the appointment of presbyters and bishops (Ti 1:5–9; here the two terms refer to the same personages).

The letter instructs Titus about the character of the assistants he is to choose in view of the pastoral difficulties peculiar to Crete (Ti 1:5–16). It suggests the special individual and social virtues that the various age groups and classes in the Christian community should be encouraged to acquire (Ti 2:1–10). The motivation for transformation of their lives comes from christology, especially the redemptive sacrifice of Christ and his future coming, as applied through baptism and justification (Ti 2:11–14; 3:4–8). The community is to serve as a leaven for Christianizing the social world about it (Ti 3:1–3). Good works are to be the evidence of their faith in God (Ti 3:8); those who engage in religious controversy are, after suitable warning, to be ignored (Ti 3:9–11).

The authorship and date of the Letter to Titus are discussed in the Introduction to 1 Timothy. Those who assume authorship by Paul himself usually place Titus after 1 Timothy and before 2 Timothy. Others see it as closely related to 1 Timothy, in a growing emphasis on church structure and opposition to heresy, later than the letters of Paul himself and 2 Timothy. It has also been suggested that, if the three Pastorals once circulated as a literary unit, Titus was meant to be read ahead of 1 and 2 Timothy.

The principal divisions of the Letter to Titus are the following:

I. Address (1:1–4)

II. Pastoral Charge (1:5–16)

III. Teaching the Christian Life (2:1–3:15)

# TITUS

## I. ADDRESS

**1** **Greeting.**† ¹Paul, a slave of God and apostle of Jesus Christ for the sake of the faith of God's chosen ones and the recognition of religious truth,* ²in the hope of eternal life that God, who does not lie, promised before time began,* ³who indeed at the proper time revealed his word in the proclamation with which I was entrusted by the command of God our savior,* ⁴to Titus, my true child in our common faith: grace and peace from God the Father and Christ Jesus our savior.*

## II. PASTORAL CHARGE

**Titus in Crete.** ⁵† For this reason I left you in Crete so that you might set right what remains to be done and appoint presbyters in every town, as I directed you, ⁶* on condition that a man be blameless, married only once, with believing children who are not accused of licentiousness or rebellious. ⁷For a bishop as God's steward must be blameless, not arrogant, not irritable, not a drunkard, not aggressive, not greedy for sordid gain, ⁸but hospitable, a lover of goodness, temperate, just, holy, and self-controlled, ⁹holding fast to the true message as taught so that he will be able both to exhort with sound doctrine and to refute opponents.* ¹⁰† For there are also many rebels, idle talkers and deceivers, especially the Jewish Christians.† ¹¹It is imperative to silence them, as they are upsetting whole families by teaching for sordid gain what they should not. ¹²One of them, a prophet of their own, once said, "Cretans have always been liars, vicious beasts, and lazy gluttons."† ¹³That testimony is true. Therefore, admonish them sharply, so that they may be sound in the faith,* ¹⁴instead of paying attention to Jewish myths and regulations of people who have repudiated the truth.* ¹⁵To the clean all things are clean, but to those who are defiled and unbelieving nothing is clean; in fact, both their minds and their consciences are tainted.* ¹⁶They claim to know God, but by their deeds they deny him. They are vile and disobedient and unqualified for any good deed.

## III. TEACHING THE CHRISTIAN LIFE

**2** **Christian Behavior.**† ¹As for yourself, you must say what is consistent with sound doctrine, namely,* ²that older men should be temperate, dignified, self-controlled, sound in faith, love, and endurance. ³Similarly, older women should be reverent in their behavior, not slanderers, not addicted to drink, teaching what is good, ⁴so that they may train younger women to love their husbands and children, ⁵to be self-controlled, chaste, good homemakers, under the control of their husbands, so that the word of God may not be discredited.*

⁶Urge the younger men, similarly, to control themselves, ⁷showing yourself as a model of good deeds in every respect, with integrity in your teaching, dignity, ⁸and sound speech that cannot be criticized, so that the opponent will be put to shame without anything bad to say about us.

---

**1:1–4** On the epistolary form, see note on Rom 1:1–7. The apostolate is the divinely appointed mission to lead others to the true faith and through it to eternal salvation (Ti 1:1–3).

**1:5–9** This instruction on the selection and appointment of presbyters, substantially identical with that in 1 Tm 3:1–7 on a bishop (see note there), was aimed at strengthening the authority of Titus by apostolic mandate; cf. Ti 2:15. In Ti 1:5, 7 and Acts 20:17, 28, the terms *episkopos* and *presbyteros* ("bishop" and "presbyter") refer to the same persons. Deacons are not mentioned in Titus. See also note on Phil 1:1.

**1:10–16** This adverse criticism of the defects within the community is directed especially against certain Jewish Christians, who busy themselves with useless speculations over persons mentioned in the Old Testament, insist on the observance of Jewish ritual purity regulations, and thus upset whole families by teaching things they have no right to teach; cf. Ti 3:9; 1 Tm 1:3–10.

**1:10** *Jewish Christians*: literally, "those of the circumcision."

**1:12** *Cretans…gluttons*: quoted from Epimenides, a Cretan poet of the sixth century B.C.

**2:1–10** One of Titus' main tasks in Crete is to become acquainted with the character of the Cretans and thereby learn to cope with its deficiencies (see Ti 1:12). The counsel is not only for Titus himself but for various classes of people with whom he must deal: older men and women (Ti 2:2–4), younger women and men (Ti 2:4–7), and slaves (Ti 2:9–10); cf. Eph 6:1–9; Col 3:18–4:1.

---

**1:1** 1 Tm 2:4; 4:3; 2 Tm 2:25; 3:7; Heb 10:26.
**1:2** 3:7; 2 Tm 1:1; 1 Jn 2:25.
**1:3** 2:10; 3:4; Ps 24:5; 1 Tm 1:1; 2:3; 4:10; Jude 25.
**1:4** 2:13; 3:6; Phil 3:20; 2 Tm 1:10; 2 Pt 1:11; 2:20; 3:2, 18.
**1:6–7** 1 Tm 3:2–7; 2 Tm 2:24–26.
**1:9** 1:13; 2:1–2, 8; 1 Tm 1:10; 6:3;

**2 Tm** 1:13; 4:3.
**1:13** 1:9.
**1:14** 3:9; 1 Tm 1:4; 4:7; 2 Tm 4:4; 2 Pt 1:16.
**1:15** Mk 7:18–23; Acts 10:15; Rom 14:14–23.
**2:1** 1:9, 13; 2:8; 1 Tm 1:10; 6:3; 2 Tm 1:13; 4:3.
**2:5** 1 Cor 11:3; 14:34; Eph 5:22–24; Col 3:18; 1 Tm 2:11–15; 1 Pt 3:1–6.

[9] Slaves are to be under the control of their masters in all respects, giving them satisfaction, not talking back to them* [10] or stealing from them, but exhibiting complete good faith, so as to adorn the doctrine of God our savior in every way.*

**Transformation of Life.** [11]† For the grace of God has appeared, saving all* [12] and training us to reject godless ways and worldly desires and to live temperately, justly, and devoutly in this age, [13] as we await the blessed hope, the appearance† of the glory of the great God and of our savior Jesus Christ,* [14] who gave himself for us to deliver us from all lawlessness and to cleanse for himself a people as his own, eager to do what is good.*

[15] Say these things. Exhort and correct with all authority. Let no one look down on you.*

**3** [1]† Remind them to be under the control of magistrates and authorities,† to be obedient, to be open to every good enterprise.* [2] They are to slander no one, to be peaceable, considerate, exercising all graciousness toward everyone. [3] For we ourselves were once foolish, disobedient, deluded, slaves to various desires and pleasures, living in malice and envy, hateful ourselves and hating one another.*

[4]      But when the kindness and generous love
        of God our savior appeared,*
[5]      not because of any righteous deeds we had done

     but because of his mercy,
he saved us through the bath of rebirth
     and renewal by the holy Spirit,*
[6]      whom he richly poured out on us
     through Jesus Christ our savior,*
[7]      so that we might be justified by his grace
     and become heirs in hope of eternal life.*

[8] This saying is trustworthy.

**Advice to Titus.** † I want you to insist on these points, that those who have believed in God be careful to devote themselves to good works; these are excellent and beneficial to others.* [9] † Avoid foolish arguments, genealogies, rivalries, and quarrels about the law,* for they are useless and futile. [10] After a first and second warning, break off contact with a heretic,* [11] realizing that such a person is perverted and sinful and stands self-condemned.

**Directives, Greetings, and Blessing.** † [12] When I send Artemas to you, or Tychicus, try to join me at Nicopolis, where I have decided to spend the winter.* [13] Send Zenas the lawyer and Apollos on their journey soon, and see to it that they have everything they need.* [14] But let our people, too, learn to devote themselves to good works to supply urgent needs, so that they may not be unproductive.*

[15] All who are with me send you greetings. Greet those who love us in the faith. Grace be with all of you.*

---

**2:11–15** Underlying the admonitions for moral improvement in Ti 2:1–10 as the moving force is the constant appeal to God's revelation of salvation in Christ, with its demand for transformation of life.

**2:13** *The blessed hope, the appearance*: literally, "the blessed hope and appearance," but the use of a single article in Greek strongly suggests an epexegetical, i.e., explanatory sense. *Of the great God and of our savior Jesus Christ*: another possible translation is "of our great God and savior Jesus Christ."

**3:1–8** The list of Christian duties continues from Ti 2:9–10, undergirded again as in Ti 2:11–13 by appeal to what God in Christ has done (Ti 2:4–7; cf. Ti 2:11–14). The spiritual renewal of the Cretans, signified in God's merciful gift of baptism (Ti 3:4–7), should be reflected in their improved attitude toward civil authority and in their Christian relationship with all (Ti 3:1–3).

**3:1** *Magistrates and authorities*: some interpreters understand these terms as referring to the principalities and powers of the heavenly hierarchy. *To be open to every good enterprise*: this implies being good citizens. It could also be translated "ready to do every sort of good work" (as Christians); cf. Ti 3:14.

**3:8–11** In matters of good conduct and religious doctrine, Titus is to stand firm.

**3:9** See note on 1 Tm 6:20–21.

**3:12–15** *Artemas* or *Tychicus* (2 Tm 4:12) is to replace Titus,

who will join Paul in his winter sojourn at Nicopolis in Epirus, on the western coast of Greece.

| | |
|---|---|
| **2:9** 1 Cor 7:21–22; Eph 6:5–8; Col 3:22–25; 1 Tm 6:1–2; 1 Pt 2:18. | Jude 25. |
| **2:10** 1:3; 3:4; Ps 24:5; 1 Tm 1:1; 2:3; 4:10; Jude 25. | **3:5** Dt 9:5; Eph 2:4–5, 8–9; 2 Tm 1:9. |
| **2:11** 1 Tm 2:4; 4:10. | **3:6** 1:4; 2:13; Phil 3:20; 2 Tm 1:10; 2 Pt 1:1, 11; 2:20; 3:2, 18. |
| **2:13** 1 Cor 1:7; Phil 3:20; 1 Thes 1:10 / 2 Tm 1:10 / Ti 1:4; 3:6; 2 Pt 1:11; 2:20; 3:2, 18. | **3:7** 1:2; 2 Tm 1:1; 1 Jn 2:25. |
| **2:14** Gal 1:4; 2:20; Eph 5:2, 25; 1 Tm 2:6; 1 Pt 1:18–19 / Ps 130:8. | **3:8** 1 Tm 1:15; 3:1; 4:9; 2 Tm 2:11. |
| **2:15** 1 Tm 4:12. | **3:9** 1 Tm 1:4; 4:7; 2 Tm 2:23. |
| **3:1** Rom 13:1–7; 1 Tm 2:1–2; 1 Pt 2:13–14. | **3:10** Mt 18:15–18; Rom 16:17; 1 Cor 5:11; 2 Thes 3:6, 14–15. |
| **3:3** 1 Cor 6:9–11; Eph 2:1–3; 5:8; Col 3:5–7; 1 Pt 4:3. | **3:12** Acts 20:4; Eph 6:21; Col 4:7; 2 Tm 4:12. |
| **3:4** 1:3; 2:10; Ps 24:5; 1 Tm 1:1; 2:3; 4:10; | **3:13** Acts 18:24–26; 1 Cor 1:12; 3:4–6, 22; 4:6; 16:12. |
| | **3:14** 2:14; 3:8; Heb 10:24; 1 Pt 3:13. |
| | **3:15** Heb 13:25. |

# The Letter to
# Philemon

## INTRODUCTION

### Tatha Wiley

The Apostle Paul was perfectly capable of giving people orders. He often did so. Yet in his Letter to Philemon, he suggests, he hints, but he refuses to tell Philemon what to do. Without question, he wanted something from Philemon, and discovering what it was has become a key interpretive challenge. So it is valuable to examine clues found in the letter against the backdrop of what we know about Paul's assumptions and values.

Paul was about one thing: creating communities, new communities. The ekklēsia—meaning assembly or church—is a "new creation" (Gal 6:15), Paul writes in Galatians, governed by a new power and new values. Paul's subtlety in writing to Philemon is deliberate. It forces Philemon to acknowledge the difference between the world in which he lives and the community that Christ-followers are called to create.

The authorship of Philemon is undisputed. A mere 25 verses, it is meticulously crafted, alternating praise with challenge, gradually increasing in pressure until Paul's challenge to Philemon becomes unavoidable. The pressure begins with the greeting itself. Paul writes to Philemon about a personal matter, yet he addresses the letter "to the church at your house" (Phlm 2). Paul makes this matter not just an individual affair but a test of communal self-definition.

Paul had met Philemon's slave Onesimus in prison—the location is unknown but the overlap of names with Colossians suggests western Asia Minor. Paul had converted Onesimus to Christ. The dominant interpretation in the tradition is, as Paul says himself, that he is "sending" Onesimus back to Philemon (Phlm 12). Was he returning Onesimus to resume his life as Philemon's slave? Or is the letter a subtle but powerful appeal for manumission? Since much of the subsequent tradition accepted the legitimacy of slavery, it was difficult for Paul's interpreters to imagine that he was asking for Onesimus's freedom.

As a prisoner himself, of course, Paul's "returning" Onesimus is only metaphorical. But by virtue of someone or some means, Onesimus is being returned to Philemon. If Onesimus was a runaway slave, Paul would have known that Onesimus's future was perilous, for "cruelty of a master toward his slave can never be ruled out in the Greco-Roman world, where severity bordering on sadism was a commonplace of the servile relationship. Mildness and forbearance in this respect would have made Philemon not only an exception but an oddity in his own world, conditioned as it was by violence against all purported inferiors."[1]

Not everyone thinks Onesimus was a slave or that the relation between Philemon and Onesimus was of master and slave. An alternate interpretation is that they are estranged brothers and Paul's mission in the letter was to reconcile them not only as brothers but as "beloved brothers" (Phlm 16).[2] The only indication that Onesimus is a slave rests on the description of him: "no longer as a slave but more than a slave, a brother" (v. 16). The slavery terminology is not uncommon for Paul. He takes the social and familial alienation of the slave as an analogy for the alienation of humanity from God through sin.[3] Just as the slave is socially dead, to use Orlando Patterson's phrase (see the initial introduction to

---

1. Allen Dwight Callahan, "Paul's Epistle to Philemon: Toward an Alternative *Argumentum*," *Harvard Theological Review* 86, no. 4 (1993), 357–76, at 358. Callahan's thesis below that they are brothers is on pp. 362, 369–72. On alienation and the analogy between slavery and sinful humanity, see 370.

2. Ibid., 362, 369–72.

3. Ibid., 370.

Philippians), humankind is spiritually dead in sin.

However cogent this thesis, the dominant view is that Onesimus was a slave, Philemon was his master, and Paul met Onesimus in prison. We do not have to settle the question why Onesimus was there. Paul puts such effort into paving the way for Onesimus to be received back with kindness that, if indeed he is a runaway slave, this would have been a concerted effort to avoid having violence done to him.

To maintain the institution of slavery required extreme violence. No one wanted to be a slave, and slave owners used various techniques of dehumanization to keep their slaves in line. They were bought and sold, beaten and tortured. But now, like Philemon himself, Onesimus is a Christ-follower. Whatever Paul wants for Onesimus, he wants for a member of the *ekklēsia*. He even offers to make good Onesimus's debt: "If he . . . owes you anything, charge it to me" (Phlm 18).

Paul circles around what he wants but leaves it to Philemon to draw the conclusion. Paul hopes Philemon's faith will become "effective" (Phlm 6). He wants "the good" that Philemon does to be "voluntary" (v. 14). Paul could "order" him to do "what is proper" (v. 8), he says, but he would rather appeal to Philemon on the basis of love (v. 9). Paul refers to himself as Onesimus's "father" (v. 10). Paul's use of familial language is not uncommon. But it does make for competing fathers, since legally Philemon was *paterfamilias* of his household. If Onesimus was his slave, Philemon owned him just as he owned the land, animals, and equipment of his household. Paul subverts the structure of the household grounded in hierarchy and difference.

Onesimus is coming back, Paul writes, as "more than a slave, a brother, beloved especially to me, but even more so to you" (Phlm 16). The relation of slave owner and slave cannot accommodate equality. There is no equality in the patriarchal household. Applying even more pressure, Paul identifies further with Onesimus, calling him "my own heart" (v. 12)

and asking Philemon to "welcome him as you would me" (v. 17). Philemon would welcome Paul as a free man.

"May I not tell you," Paul writes, "that you owe me your very self?" (Phlm 19). Paul may "not tell" Philemon about owing his very salvation to him, but he says it in front of Apphia and Archippus and the whole assembly who meets in Philemon's house as well as Epaphras, Mark, Aristarchus, Demas, and Luke, who are with Paul (vv. 2, 23–24). As if an afterthought, Paul tells Philemon he will be there: "Prepare a guest room for me" (v. 22). If Philemon's faith is truly effective (v. 6), Paul will verify it himself.

Faith is effective in building up the new community. The communal self-definition proclaims that "in the Christian community all distinctions of religion, race, class, nationality, and gender are insignificant. All the baptized are equal, they are one in Christ."[4] Paul envisions the new community as a social and political entity in its own right. It is a "new just society."[5] It is not the patriarchal household. "There must be total equality for all."[6] Paul writes in Galatians that there is no such thing as slave and freeman (Gal 3:28), no longer the sinful possession of one by another.

What did Paul want from Philemon? Given his vision of the *ekklēsia*, it is reasonable to speculate that Paul wanted Philemon to realize for himself that he had joined an assembly whose purpose was to "make God's justice a reality already now in this world."[7] For Philemon's faith to be effective, he must turn from the injustice endemic in the old creation to the justice created in the new creation of acceptance and inclusion. ◼

P
H
L
M

---

4. Elisabeth Schüssler Fiorenza, "The Praxis of Coequal Discipleship," in *Paul and Empire: Religion and Power in Imperial Society*, ed. Richard A. Horsley (Harrisburg, PA: Trinity Press International, 1997), 228.

5. Helmut Koester, *Paul and His World: Interpreting the New Testament in Context* (Minneapolis: Fortress Press, 2007), 14, 13.

6. Ibid., 13.

7. Ibid.

# THE LETTER TO PHILEMON

## New American Bible, Introduction

This short letter addressed to three specific individuals was written by Paul during an imprisonment, perhaps in Rome between A.D. 61 and 63 (see the Introduction to Colossians for other possible sites). It concerns Onesimus, a slave from Colossae (Col 4:9), who had run away from his master, perhaps guilty of theft in the process (Phlm 18). Onesimus was converted to Christ by Paul (Phlm 10). Paul sends him back to his master (Phlm 12) with this letter asking that he be welcomed willingly by his old master (Phlm 8–10, 14, 17) not just as a slave but as a brother in Christ (Phlm 16). Paul uses very strong arguments (especially Phlm 19) in his touching appeal on behalf of Onesimus. It is unlikely that Paul is subtly hinting that he would like to retain Onesimus as his own slave, lent to Paul by his master. Rather, he suggests he would like to have Onesimus work

with him for the gospel (Phlm 13, 20–21). There is, however, little evidence connecting this Onesimus with a bishop of Ephesus of the same name mentioned by Ignatius of Antioch (ca. A.D. 110).

Paul's letter deals with an accepted institution of antiquity, human slavery. But Paul breathes into this letter the spirit of Christ and of equality within the Christian community. He does not attack slavery directly, for this is something the Christian communities of the first century were in no position to do, and the expectation that Christ would soon come again militated against social reforms. Yet Paul, by presenting Onesimus as "brother, beloved . . . to me, but even more so to you" (Phlm 16), voiced an idea revolutionary in that day and destined to break down worldly barriers of division "in the Lord." ∎

# PHILEMON

**Address and Greeting.** [1]† Paul, a prisoner for Christ Jesus, and Timothy our brother, to Philemon, our beloved and our co-worker,* [2] to Apphia our sister,† to Archippus our fellow soldier, and to the church at your house.* [3] Grace to you and peace† from God our Father and the Lord Jesus Christ.*

**Thanksgiving.** [4]†* I give thanks to my God always, remembering you in my prayers, [5] as I hear of the love and the faith you have in the Lord Jesus and for all the holy ones,† [6] so that your partnership in the faith may become effective in recognizing every good there is in us† that leads to Christ.*

**Plea for Onesimus.** [7] For I have experienced much joy and encouragement† from your love, because the hearts of the holy ones have been refreshed by you, brother.* [8] Therefore, although I have the full right† in Christ to order you to do what is proper, [9] I rather urge you out of love, being as I am, Paul, an old man,† and now also a prisoner for Christ Jesus.* [10] I urge you on behalf of my child Onesimus, whose father I have become in my imprisonment,* [11] who was once useless to you but is now useful† to [both] you and me. [12] I am sending him, that is, my own heart, back to you. [13] I should have liked to retain him for myself, so that he might serve† me on your behalf in my imprisonment for the gospel,* [14] but I did not want to do anything without your consent, so that the good you do might not be forced but voluntary.* [15] Perhaps this is why he was away from† you for a while, that you might have him back forever, [16] no longer as a slave but more than a slave, a brother, beloved especially to me, but even more so to you, as a man† and in the Lord.* [17] So if you regard me as a partner, welcome him as you would me. [18]† And if he has done you any injustice or owes you anything, charge it to me. [19] I, Paul, write this in my own hand: I will pay. May I not tell you that you owe me your very self.* [20] Yes, brother, may I profit from you in the Lord. Refresh my heart in Christ.

[21] With trust in your compliance I write to you, knowing that you will do even more than I say. [22] At the same time prepare a guest room for me, for I hope to be granted to you through your prayers.*

---

† **1** *Prisoner*: as often elsewhere (cf. Romans, 1 Corinthians, Galatians especially), the second word in Greek enunciates the theme and sets the tone of the letter. Here it is the prisoner appealing rather than the apostle commanding.

**2** *Apphia our sister*: sister is here used (like brother) to indicate a fellow Christian. *The church at your house*: *your* here is singular. It more likely refers to Philemon than to the last one named, Archippus; Philemon is then the owner of the slave Onesimus (Phlm 10). An alternate view is that the actual master of the slave is Archippus and that the one to whom the letter is addressed, Philemon, is the most prominent Christian there; see note on Col 4:17.

**3** *Grace…and peace*: for this greeting, which may be a combination of Greek and Aramaic epistolary formulae, see note on Rom 1:1–7.

**4** *In my prayers*: literally, "at the time of my prayers."

**5** *Holy ones*: a common term for members of the Christian community (so also Phlm 7).

**6** *In us*: some good ancient manuscripts have *in you* (plural). *That leads to Christ*: *leads to* translates the Greek preposition *eis*, indicating direction or purpose.

**7** *Encouragement*: the Greek word *paraklēsis* is cognate with the verb translated "urge" in Phlm 9–10, and serves as an introduction to Paul's plea. *Hearts*: literally, "bowels," expressing in Semitic fashion the seat of the emotions, one's "inmost self." The same Greek word is used in Phlm 12 and again in Phlm 20, where it forms a literary inclusion marking off the body of the letter.

**8** *Full right*: often translated "boldness," the Greek word *parrēsia* connotes the full franchise of speech, as the right of a citizen to speak before the body politic, claimed by the Athenians as their privilege (Euripides).

**9** *Old man*: some editors conjecture that Paul here used a similar Greek word meaning "ambassador" (cf. Eph 6:20). This conjecture heightens the contrast with "prisoner" but is totally without manuscript support.

**11** *Useless…useful*: here Paul plays on the name Onesimus, which means "useful" or "beneficial." The verb translated "profit" in Phlm 20 is cognate.

**13** *Serve*: the Greek *diakoneō* could connote a ministry.

**15** *Was away from*: literally, "was separated from," but the same verb means simply "left" in Acts 18:1. It is a euphemism for his running away.

**16** *As a man*: literally, "in the flesh." With this and the following phrase, Paul describes the natural and spiritual orders.

**18–19** *Charge it to me…I will pay*: technical legal and commercial terms in account keeping and acknowledgment of indebtedness.

---

*

**1** 9; Eph 3:1; 4:1; Phil 1:7, 13.
**2** Col 4:17.
**3** Rom 1:7; Gal 1:3; Phil 1:2.
**4–5** Rom 1:8–9; Eph 1:15–16.
**6** Phil 1:9; Col 1:9.
**7** 2 Cor 7:4.

**9** 1; Eph 3:1; 4:1; Phil 1:7, 13.
**10** 1 Cor 4:14–15; Gal 4:19; Col 4:9.
**13** Phil 2:30.
**14** 2 Cor 9:7; 1 Pt 5:2.
**16** 1 Tm 6:2.
**19** Gal 6:11; 2 Thes 3:17.
**22** Heb 13:19.

**Final Greetings.** [23] Epaphras, † my fellow prisoner in Christ Jesus, greets you, * [24] as well as Mark, Aristarchus, Demas, and Luke, my co-workers. [25] The grace of the Lord Jesus Christ be with your spirit. *

---

**23–24** *Epaphras:* a Colossian who founded the church there (Col 1:7) and perhaps also in Laodicea and Hierapolis (Col 2:1; 4:12–13). *Aristarchus:* a native of Thessalonica and fellow worker of Paul (Acts 19:29; 20:4; 27:2). For Mark, Demas, and Luke, see 2 Tm 4:9–13 and the note there.

**23** Col 1:7; 4:12–13.
**25** Acts 12:12, 15; 13:13; 15:37–39; 19:29;
20:4; 27:2; Col 4:10, 14; 2 Tm 4:10–13.

# The Letter to the
# Hebrews

## INTRODUCTION

### Mary Katherine Birge, SSJ

Whoever the author of the Letter to the Hebrews was, he was deeply conversant with the text and symbols of the Old Testament.[1] Whoever his audience was, they too must have been as widely conversant with the Old Testament as the author (or at least he thought they were) since he wove Old Testament quotations, characters, images, themes, symbols, and allusions throughout his homily-called-letter. Without such knowledge and understanding, the audience (it would have been read aloud to the community) would be at a loss to understand its argument or to recognize the beauty of its language. Indeed, both author and audience needed to possess a thorough Hellenistic education to compose and, in turn, understand and appreciate the elegant prose and rhetorical flourishes found in Hebrews.

More important than the homily's graceful style and language, however, is the effect they would have had on the minds and spirits of its audience. The audience seems to have reached a crossroads after experiencing extended hostility from non-Christian neighbors, because of which members of the Christian community may have lost possessions, experienced abuse, physical or verbal, and even been imprisoned (Heb 10:32–34; 13:3, 13). The author was aware of the wearying effect of such treatment on their psyche and the possible weakening of their commitment to communal life, and so he urged them to "hold fast" to their faith and practice (4:14; cf. 2:1, 3; 3:6; 10:23, 25, 35).[2] He seeks to renew his audience's spirit and strengthen their resolve to follow Christ through his thoughtful and creative use of the

---

1. Quoting from the Old Testament, the author of Hebrews largely uses its Greek translation, the Septuagint, abbreviated LXX.

2. Craig R. Koester, *Hebrews,* Anchor Bible (New York: Doubleday, 2001), 67–71.

## Outline of Hebrews

I.   Introduction (1:1–4)

II.  The Son Higher Than the Angels (1:5–2:18)

III. Jesus, Faithful and Compassionate High Priest (3:1–5:10)

IV.  Jesus' Eternal Priesthood and Eternal Sacrifice (5:11–10:39)

V.   Examples, Discipline, Disobedience (11:1–12:29)

VI.  Final Exhortation, Blessing, Greetings (13:1–25)

---

Old Testament to explain how God has now become accessible to them through Christ.

In the first two verses, the author begins what will become his practice throughout the homily as he argues for continued fidelity to Christ. He starts with God having first spoken incompletely to their "ancestors through the prophets" and then moves to the present and to the son and heir through whom God has now spoken, the one "through whom [God] created the universe" (Heb 1:1–2). The author follows a pattern of argument, moving "from the lesser to the greater" point (a rhetorical pattern called *a minore ad maiorem* in classical rhetoric), drawing attention to where the elements he is comparing converge and diverge. The point of convergence here is God's desire to communicate in speech with the Jews and their descendants through divinely empowered agents (God's prophets and son). The divergence emerges in the "fullness" or "completeness" of that communication. Unspoken but understood in v. 2 is that the son's speech has revealed completely whatever had been obscured in the prophets' initial speech.

Then, the author issues a torrent of Old Testament quotations (Heb 1:3–12) that explore the son's identity in relationship to God and the angels. These quotations culminate in the son's enthronement in v. 13, forming an *inclusio* (a literary "sandwich" where two similar ideas or phrases enclose different subject matter and help interpret the meaning of the enclosed material) with v. 3 where he has taken a seat at the right hand of God. The rhetorical question in v. 14 makes clear that angels, with whom the author has been comparing the son throughout vv. 3–13, do not serve at the throne of God as they do in the Old Testament, but are in service to "those who are to inherit salvation" (v. 14). The author declares that the son is superior to the angels (cf. v. 4) and suggests that his inheritance as son "makes [the audience's salvation] possible."[3] The author frequently employs this title "son" for Jesus (1:2, 5, 8; 3:6; 5:5, 8; 7:28), as well as its almost synonymous counterpart, "son of God" (4:14; 6:6; 7:3; 10:29). The title he gives Jesus that becomes the work's controlling image, however, is "priest"/"high priest" (2:17; 3:1; 4:14; 5:5, 10; 6:20; 7:26; 8:1; 9:11; 10:21). The Letter to the Hebrews is alone among all the New Testament writings to use this designation for Jesus, and that alone would make the letter interesting. What the author does with it, however, makes it especially important for understanding the background for Christian theology's claims about Jesus' priesthood and self-sacrifice.

In the Old Testament priests and high priests were charged with casting the sacred divining lots, the Urim and the Thummim (Lv 16:8; Dt 33:8), and with instructing the people in the Law (Dt 33:10). In addition to regulating ritual purity laws (Lv 13–15) and the sanctuary and later Temple (Nm 3:38), they also offered sacrifices (Lv 16:6; Dt 33:10). By applying the title "high priest" to Jesus, the author asserts unambiguously that Jesus' priesthood surpasses that of all other priests.[4] Yet when he mentions Jesus' priesthood for the first time, he connects it with his solidarity with the human condition ("he had to become like his brothers [and sisters] in every way," Heb 2:17). Jesus' own experience of physical suffering (v. 18) enables him to be "a merciful and faithful high priest" (v. 17) who will always be able to intercede for those who seek God (7:25).

One of the specific duties of the high priest had been to enter the innermost part of the sanctuary on the Day of Atonement and make a sacrifice to atone for his and the people's sins (Lv 16). Unlike Israel's high priests, who had been set apart from the people in order to perform their ministry, Jesus has been made "at one" with the people so that he may make the people "at one" with God by removing their sins.[5] Later, in Heb 4:15, the author articulates this explicitly when he writes of Jesus, "We do not have a high priest who is unable to sympathize with our weaknesses, but one who has similarly been tested in every way, yet without sin," and then invites the people to draw near to Jesus with confidence for the help they seek in finding "at one-ment" with God (cf. 4:16).

The next section (Heb 3:1–6) begins with the author naming Jesus as "apostle and high priest" (v. 1) as he compares and contrasts Jesus with Moses (vv. 1–6). An "apostle" in the New Testament is someone who is charged and sent by Jesus (e.g., Mt 10:2; Mk 3:14; Lk 6:13; Acts 1:2; 14:14)—and so by God—to announce the gospel, while the high priest is someone who is sent from humanity to communicate with God (cf. Heb 5:1). By placing these two titles for Jesus together—apostle and high priest—the writer establishes the basis for his later development of Jesus as the mediator between God and humanity in a "new covenant" (8:6; 9:15; 12:24).[6] Scripture never calls Moses a high priest, but Exodus does note his priestly descent (Ex 2:1), and in Nm 12:7–8 God declares that they meet and speak "face to face" (as the high priest will on the Day of Atonement; see above). Moses has also been chosen by God to initiate Israel into the Sinai covenant (Ex 24:3–8). The author recognizes that he must establish Jesus as the absolute high priest and

3. Alan C. Mitchell, *Hebrews,* Sacra Pagina 13 (Collegeville, MN: Liturgical Press, 2007), 51.

4. Luke Timothy Johnson, *Hebrews,* New Testament Library (Louisville: Westminster John Knox, 2006), 103.

5. Koester, *Hebrews,* 241.

6. Johnson, *Hebrews,* 106–7.

mediator of this "new covenant," which Jeremiah had spoken of (Jer 31:31) and God has established in Jesus (Heb 8:8, 13; 9:15; 12:24). Moses is the obvious person with whom the author can compare Jesus in order to show how Jesus surpasses even the tradition's ultimate figure, much as he had to establish in ch. 1 that Jesus is exalted far above the angels.[7]

Beginning in Heb 5:1 and extending to 10:39, the author of Hebrews engages in a sustained reflection on Jesus' ongoing ministry to the people as a new kind of high priest whose effectiveness as mediator for the people with God far exceeds any other mediator's achievement. Since Jesus shares in their humanity, has "been tested in every way, yet [is] without sin" (4:15), and at the same time is the Son of God who has been called by God to be high priest (5:4), he opens the way for the people to "approach the throne of grace to receive mercy" (4:16) as "the source of eternal salvation for all who obey him" (5:9). In 5:1–4 the author presents the characteristics that all high priests had to possess. Then he lists Jesus' personal qualities in 5:5–10 that meet those general characteristics, but in reverse order. Priests and high priests have to be from the tribe of Levi, but Jesus is from the tribe of Judah through his descent from David (7:14). The author has to develop a different basis for Jesus' priesthood; to do so, he turns to Melchizedek, a mysterious and little known figure from Gn 14:18 and Ps 110:4.

The standard in Heb 5:1 for the high priest—to be chosen from "among [the people] and made their representative before God"—is met and surpassed in v. 10 by Jesus who has been "declared by God high priest according to the order of Melchizedek." The writer has taken the reference to Melchizedek from Ps 110:4. He first mentions this passage in Heb 5:6, quoting it directly. He adapts it in 5:10, changing the title from "priest" to "high priest." After raising the theme of Jesus as high priest and developing it in an intriguing direction, he drops the subject of Melchizedek and begins to exhort his audience about the sluggish or tepid quality of their spiritual life (Heb 5:11–6:19). He takes up the theme of Jesus as

high priest in 6:20–7:1 again and does not rest from it until 10:39.

Only after establishing for his audience the absolute authenticity of Jesus' status as priest (Heb 7:1–28) can the homilist begin the argument (8:1–10:39) that is both central to his homily and crucial to its purpose. There is a new covenant, which the prophet Jeremiah foretold (8:8–12; see Jer 31:31–34) and for which Jesus is mediator as the heavenly high priest (Heb 8:1b–2, 6). The high priest exercised his ministry in a sanctuary and tabernacle that was a model, however imperfect, of the true, perfect one in heaven (8:5; 9:1–10). Jesus, now in the perfect, heavenly sanctuary, has made the perfect sacrifice with his own blood, thereby removing perfectly the barrier of sin that separates humanity from God (9:11–10:7) that the long line of the first covenant's high priests had been unable to accomplish. No further sacrifice ever need be offered (10:18) because Jesus Christ has been that offering "once for all" (10:10). As the homilist draws to a close the central portion of his teaching, he begins again to urge his audience to hold on to their faith in Jesus, to support one another in the practice of Christian virtue, and to return to their communal assemblies that some had apparently abandoned (10:19–39). In his exhortation he reveals the catalyst behind his writing a homily that instructs and tries to comfort; he is afraid for this community.

This fear and worry for their future life with God lead him in the next section to compose a stirring encomium to faith that encompasses the whole of Jewish salvation history (Heb 11:1–40). He links his audience to the historic exemplars of faith through their shared experiences of alienation, suffering, and tribulation. The homilist points out to the audience that although these heroes of faith "did not receive what had been promised" (vv. 13, 39)—as the audience themselves had not yet either—because of their faith they would join the audience in "what had been promised," entry into the presence of God enabled by Jesus Christ. For anyone who might have thought the homilist's persistent emphasis on the failure of the first covenant, its priests and sacrifices, excluded these ancestors in faith from "the assembly of the firstborn enrolled

7. Harold W. Attridge, *Hebrews*, Hermeneia (Philadelphia: Fortress, 1989), 104.

HEB

in heaven . . . and the spirits of the just made perfect" (12:23) had not reckoned on the potency of God's justice. As the homilist moves to his final series of exhortation and instruction to persuade them to stay the course in their new faith and the consequences of not doing so (12:1–13:25), he recalls once more for his audience their heroes in faith and urges them to imitate their strength and fortitude (12:1).

# THE LETTER TO THE HEBREWS

## New American Bible, Introduction

As early as the second century, this treatise, which is of great rhetorical power and force in its admonition to faithful pilgrimage under Christ's leadership, bore the title "To the Hebrews." It was assumed to be directed to Jewish Christians. Usually Hebrews was attached in Greek manuscripts to the collection of letters by Paul. Although no author is mentioned (for there is no address), a reference to Timothy (Heb 13:23) suggested connections to the circle of Paul and his assistants. Yet the exact audience, the author, and even whether Hebrews is a letter have long been disputed.

The author saw the addressees in danger of apostasy from their Christian faith. This danger was due not to any persecution from outsiders but to a weariness with the demands of Christian life and a growing indifference to their calling (Heb 2:1; 4:14; 6:1–12; 10:23–32). The author's main theme, the priesthood and sacrifice of Jesus (Heb 3–10), is not developed for its own sake but as a means of restoring their lost fervor and strengthening them in their faith. Another important theme of the letter is that of the pilgrimage of the people of God to the heavenly Jerusalem (Heb 11:10; 12:1–3, 18–29; 13:14). This theme is intimately connected with that of Jesus' ministry in the heavenly sanctuary (Heb 9:11–10:22).

The author calls this work a "message of encouragement" (Heb 13:22), a designation that is given to a synagogue sermon in Acts 13:15. Hebrews is probably therefore a written homily, to which the author gave an epistolary ending (Heb 13:22–25).

The author begins with a reminder of the preexistence, incarnation, and exaltation of Jesus (Heb 1:3) that proclaimed him the climax of God's word to humanity (Heb 1:1–3). He dwells upon the dignity of the person of Christ, superior to the angels (Heb 1:4–2:2). Christ is God's final word of salvation communicated (in association with accredited witnesses to his teaching: cf. Heb 2:3–4) not merely by word but through his suffering in the humanity common to him and to all others (Heb 2:5–16). This enactment of salvation went beyond the pattern known to Moses, faithful prophet of God's word though he was, for Jesus as high priest expiated sin and was faithful to God with the faithfulness of God's own Son (Heb 2:17–3:6).

Just as the infidelity of the people thwarted Moses' efforts to save them, so the infidelity of any Christian may thwart God's plan in Christ (Heb 3:6–4:13). Christians are to reflect that it is their humanity that Jesus took upon himself, with all its defects save sinfulness, and that he bore the burden of it until death out of obedience to God. God declared this work of his Son to be the cause of salvation for all (Heb 4:14–5:10). Although Christians recognize this fundamental teaching, they may grow weary of it and of its implications, and therefore require other reflections to stimulate their faith (Heb 5:11–6:20).

Therefore, the author presents to the readers for their reflection the everlasting priesthood of Christ (Heb 7:1–28), a priesthood that fulfills the promise of the Old Testament (Heb 8:1–13). It also provides the meaning God ultimately intended in the sacrifices of the Old Testament (Heb 9:1–28): these pointed to the unique sacrifice of Christ, which alone obtains forgiveness of sins (Heb 10:1–18). The trial of faith experienced by the readers should resolve itself through their consideration of Christ's ministry in the heavenly sanctuary and his perpetual intercession there on their behalf (Heb 7:25; 8:1–13). They should also be strengthened by the assurance of his foreordained parousia, and by the fruits of faith that they have already enjoyed (Heb 10:19–39).

It is in the nature of faith to recognize the reality of what is not yet seen and is the object of hope, and the saints of the Old Testament give striking example of that faith (Heb 11:1–40). The perseverance to which the author exhorts the readers is shown forth in the early life of Jesus. Despite the afflictions of his ministry and the supreme trial of his suffering and death, he remained confident of the triumph that God would bring him (Heb 12:1–3). The difficulties of human life have meaning when they are accepted as God's discipline (Heb 12:4–13), and if Christians persevere in fidelity to the word in which they have believed, they are assured of possessing forever the unshakable kingdom of God (Heb 12:14–29).

The letter concludes with specific moral commandments (Heb 13:1–17), in the course of which the author recalls again his central theme of the sacrifice of Jesus and the courage needed to associate oneself with it in faith (Heb 13:9–16).

As early as the end of the second century, the church of Alexandria in Egypt accepted Hebrews as a letter of Paul, and that became the view commonly held in the East. Pauline authorship was contested in the West into the fourth century, but then accepted. In the sixteenth century, doubts about that position were again raised, and the modern consensus is that the letter was not written by Paul. There is, however, no widespread agreement on any of the other suggested authors, e.g., Barnabas, Apollos, or Prisc(ill)a and Aquila. The document itself has no statement about its author.

Among the reasons why Pauline authorship has been abandoned are the great difference of vocabulary and style between Hebrews and Paul's letters, the alternation of doctrinal teaching with moral exhortation, the different manner of citing the Old Testament, and the resemblance between the thought of Hebrews and that of Alexandrian Judaism. The Greek of the letter is in many ways the best in the New Testament.

Since the letter of Clement of Rome to the Corinthians, written about A.D. 96, most probably cites Hebrews, the upper limit for the date of composition is reasonably certain. While the letter's references in the present tense to the Old Testament sacrificial worship do not necessarily show that temple worship was still going on, many older commentators and a growing number of recent ones favor the view that it was and that the author wrote before the destruction of the temple of Jerusalem in A.D. 70. In that case, the argument of the letter is more easily explained as directed toward Jewish Christians rather than those of Gentile origin, and the persecutions they have suffered in the past (cf. Heb 10:32–34) may have been connected with the disturbances that preceded the expulsion of the Jews from Rome in A.D. 49 under the emperor Claudius. These were probably caused by disputes between Jews who accepted Jesus as the Messiah and those who did not.

The principal divisions of the Letter to the Hebrews are the following:

# HEBREWS

## I. INTRODUCTION†

**1** ¹ In times past, God spoke in partial and various ways to our ancestors through the prophets; ² in these last days, he spoke to us through a son, whom he made heir of all things and through whom he created the universe, *

³ who is the refulgence of his glory,
     the very imprint of his being,
and who sustains all things by his
     mighty word.
When he had accomplished purification
     from sins,
he took his seat at the right hand of the
     Majesty on high, *

⁴ as far superior to the angels
     as the name he has inherited is more
         excellent than theirs. *

## II. THE SON HIGHER THAN THE ANGELS

**Messianic Enthronement.**† ⁵ For to which of the angels did God ever say:

"You are my son; this day I have
     begotten you"? *

Or again:

"I will be a father to him, and he shall
     be a son to me"?

⁶ And again, when he leads† the first-born into the world, he says:

"Let all the angels of God worship
     him." *

⁷ Of the angels he says:

"He makes his angels winds
     and his ministers a fiery flame"; *

⁸ but of the Son:

"Your throne, O God, † stands forever
     and ever;
and a righteous scepter is the scepter
     of your kingdom. *

⁹ You loved justice and hated wickedness;
     therefore God, your God, anointed
         you
with the oil of gladness above your
     companions";

---

† **1:1–4** The letter opens with an introduction consisting of a reflection on the climax of God's revelation to the human race in his Son. The divine communication was initiated and maintained during Old Testament times in fragmentary and varied ways through *the prophets* (Heb 1:1), including Abraham, Moses, and all through whom God spoke. But now *in these last days* (Heb 1:2) the final age, God's revelation of his saving purpose is achieved *through a son*, i.e., one who is Son, whose role is redeemer and mediator of creation. He was made *heir of all things* through his death and exaltation to glory, yet he existed before he appeared as man; through him God *created the universe*. Heb 1:3–4, which may be based upon a liturgical hymn, assimilate the Son to the personified Wisdom of the Old Testament as *refulgence* of God's *glory* and *imprint of his being* (Heb 1:3; cf. Wis 7:26). These same terms are used of the Logos in Philo. The author now turns from the cosmological role of the preexistent Son to the redemptive work of Jesus: he brought about purification from sins and has been exalted to the right hand of God (see Ps 110:1). The once-humiliated and crucified Jesus has been declared God's Son, and this name shows his superiority to the angels. The reason for the author's insistence on that superiority is, among other things, that in some Jewish traditions angels were mediators of the old covenant (see Acts 7:53; Gal 3:19). Finally, Jesus' superiority to the angels emphasizes the superiority of the new covenant to the old because of the heavenly priesthood of Jesus.

**1:5–14** Jesus' superiority to the angels is now demonstrated by a series of seven Old Testament texts. Some scholars see in the stages of Jesus' exaltation an order corresponding to that of enthronement ceremonies in the ancient Near East, especially in Egypt, namely, elevation to divine status (Heb 1:5–6); presenta-

tion to the angels and proclamation of everlasting lordship (Heb 1:7–12); enthronement and conferral of royal power (Heb 1:13). The citations from the Psalms in Heb 1:5, 13 were traditionally used of Jesus' messianic sonship (cf. Acts 13:33) through his resurrection and exaltation (cf. Acts 2:33–35); those in Heb 1:8, 10–12 are concerned with his divine kingship and his creative function. The central quotation in Heb 1:7 serves to contrast the angels with the Son. The author quotes it according to the Septuagint translation, which is quite different in meaning from that of the Hebrew ("You make the winds your messengers, and flaming fire your ministers"). The angels are only *sent to serve… those who are to inherit salvation* (Heb 1:14).

**1:6** *And again, when he leads*: the Greek could also be translated "And when he again leads" in reference to the parousia.

**1:8–12** *O God*: the application of the name "God" to the Son derives from the preexistence mentioned in Heb 1:2–3; the psalmist had already used it of the Hebrew king in the court style of the original. See note on Ps 45:7. It is also important for the author's christology that in Heb 1:10–12 an Old Testament passage addressed to God is redirected to Jesus.

---

<sup>10</sup> and:

> "At the beginning, O Lord, you
>     established the earth,*
> and the heavens are the works of your
>     hands.
> <sup>11</sup>   They will perish, but you remain;
>     and they will all grow old like a
>         garment.
> <sup>12</sup>   You will roll them up like a cloak,
>     and like a garment they will be
>         changed.
> But you are the same, and your years
>     will have no end."

<sup>13</sup> But to which of the angels has he ever said:

> "Sit at my right hand
>     until I make your enemies your
>         footstool"?*

<sup>14</sup> Are they not all ministering spirits sent to serve, for the sake of those who are to inherit salvation?*

## 2 Exhortation to Faithfulness.† <sup>1</sup> Therefore, we must attend all the more to what we have heard, so that we may not be carried away. <sup>2</sup> For if the word announced through angels proved firm, and every transgression and disobedience received its just recompense,*

<sup>3</sup> how shall we escape if we ignore so great a salvation? Announced originally through the Lord, it was confirmed for us by those who had heard.* <sup>4</sup> God added his testimony by signs, wonders, various acts of power, and distribution of the gifts of the holy Spirit according to his will.*

**Exaltation Through Abasement.**† <sup>5</sup> For it was not to angels that he subjected the world to come, of which we are speaking. <sup>6</sup> Instead, someone has testified somewhere:

> "What is man that you are mindful of
>     him,
> or the son of man that you care for
>     him?*
> <sup>7</sup>   You made him for a little while lower
>         than the angels;
>     you crowned him with glory and
>         honor,
> <sup>8</sup>       subjecting all things under his feet."

In "subjecting" all things [to him], he left nothing not "subject to him." Yet at present we do not see "all things subject to him,"* <sup>9</sup> but we do see Jesus "crowned with glory and honor" because he suffered death, he who "for a little while" was made "lower than the angels," that by the grace of God he might taste death for everyone.*

---

† **2:1–4** The author now makes a transition into exhortation, using an a fortiori argument (as at Heb 7:21–22; 9:13–14; 10:28–29; 12:25). The *word announced through angels* (Heb 2:2), the Mosaic law, is contrasted with the more powerful word that Christians have received (Heb 2:3–4). Christ's supremacy strengthens Christians against being *carried away* from their faith.

**2:5–18** The humanity and the suffering of Jesus do not constitute a valid reason for relinquishing the Christian faith. Ps 8:6–7 is also applied to Jesus in 1 Cor 15:27; Eph 1:22; and probably 1 Pt 3:22. This christological interpretation, therefore, probably reflects a common early Christian tradition, which may have originated in the expression *the son of man* (Heb 2:6). The psalm contrasts God's greatness with man's relative insignificance but also stresses the superiority of man to the rest of creation, of which he is lord. Hebrews applies this christologically: Jesus lived a truly human existence, *lower than the angels*, in the days of his earthly life, particularly in his suffering and death; now, *crowned with glory and honor*, he is raised above all creation. The author considers all things as already *subject to him* because of his exaltation (Heb 2:8–9), though *we do not see* this yet. The reference to Jesus as *leader* (Heb 2:10) sounds the first note of an important leitmotif in Hebrews: the journey of the people of God to the sabbath rest (Heb 4:9), the heavenly sanctuary, following Jesus, their "forerunner" (Heb 6:20). It was fitting that God should make him *perfect through suffering*, consecrated by obedient suffering. Because he is perfected as high priest, Jesus is then able to consecrate his people (Heb 2:11); access to God is made possible by each of these two consecrations. If Jesus is able to help human beings, it is because he has become one of us; we are his "brothers." The author then

cites three Old Testament texts as proofs of this unity between ourselves and the Son. Ps 22:23 is interpreted so as to make Jesus the singer of this lament, which ends with joyful praise of the Lord in the assembly of "brothers." The other two texts are from Is 8:17, 18. The first of these seems intended to display in Jesus an example of the trust in God that his followers should emulate. The second curiously calls these followers "children"; probably this is to be understood to mean children of Adam, but the point is our solidarity with Jesus. By sharing human nature, including the ban of death, Jesus broke the power of the devil over death (Heb 2:14); the author shares the view of Hellenistic Judaism that death was not intended by God and that it had been introduced into the world by the devil. The *fear of death* (Heb 2:15) is a religious fear based on the false conception that death marks the end of a person's relations with God (cf. Ps 115:17–18; Is 38:18). Jesus deliberately allied himself with the *descendants of Abraham* (Heb 2:16) in order to be a *merciful and faithful high priest*. This is the first appearance of the central theme of Hebrews, Jesus the great high priest expiating the *sins of the people* (Heb 2:17), as one who experienced the same tests as they (Heb 2:18).

---

**1:10–12** Ps 102:26–28.  
   **1:13** Ps 110:1.  
   **1:14** Ps 91:11; Dn 7:10.  
    **2:2** Acts 7:38, 53; Gal  
      3:19.  
   **2:3** 10:29; 12:25.  
   **2:4** Mk 16:20;  

     Acts 14:3; 19:11.  
   **2:6** Ps 8:5–7.  
   **2:8** Mt 28:18; 1 Cor  
     15:25–28; Eph  
     1:20–23; Phil 3:21;  
     1 Pt 3:22.  
   **2:9** Phil 2:6–11.

[10] For it was fitting that he, for whom and through whom all things exist, in bringing many children to glory, should make the leader to their salvation perfect through suffering.* [11] He who consecrates and those who are being consecrated all have one origin. Therefore, he is not ashamed to call them "brothers," [12] saying:

"I will proclaim your name to my
    brothers,
  in the midst of the assembly I will
    praise you";*

[13] and again:

"I will put my trust in him";

and again:

"Behold, I and the children God has
    given me."*

[14] Now since the children share in blood and flesh, he likewise shared in them, that through death he might destroy the one who has the power of death, that is, the devil,* [15] and free those who through fear of death had been subject to slavery all their life. [16] Surely he did not help angels but rather the descendants of Abraham; [17] therefore, he had to become like his brothers in every way, that he might be a merciful and faithful high priest before God to expiate the sins of the people.* [18] Because he himself was tested through what he suffered, he is able to help those who are being tested.

## III. JESUS, FAITHFUL AND COMPASSIONATE HIGH PRIEST

**3 Jesus, Superior to Moses.**† [1] Therefore, holy "brothers," sharing in a heavenly calling, reflect on Jesus, the apostle and high priest of our confession, [2] who was faithful to the one who appointed him, just as Moses was "faithful in [all] his house."* [3] But he is worthy of more "glory" than Moses, as the founder of a house has more "honor" than the house itself.* [4] Every house is founded by someone, but the founder of all is God. [5] Moses was "faithful in all his house" as a "servant" to testify to what would be spoken, [6]†* but Christ was faithful as a son placed over his house. We are his house, if [only] we hold fast to our confidence and pride in our hope.

**Israel's Infidelity a Warning.** [7]† Therefore, as the holy Spirit says:

---

† **3:1–6** The author now takes up the two qualities of Jesus mentioned in Heb 2:17, but in inverse order: faithfulness (Heb 3:1–4:13) and mercy (Heb 4:14–5:10). Christians are called *holy "brothers"* because of their common relation to him (Heb 2:11), *the apostle*, a designation for Jesus used only here in the New Testament (cf. Jn 13:16; 17:3), meaning one sent as God's final word to us (Heb 1:2). He is compared with Moses probably because he is seen as mediator of the new covenant (Heb 9:15) just as Moses was of the old (Heb 9:19–22, including his sacrifice). But when the author of Hebrews speaks of Jesus' sacrifice, he does not consider Moses as the Old Testament antitype, but rather the high priest on the Day of Atonement (Heb 9:6–15). Moses' faithfulness *"in [all] his house"* refers back to Nm 12:7, on which this section is a midrashic commentary. In Heb 3:3–6, the author does not indicate that he thinks of either Moses or Christ as the founder of the household. *His house* (Heb 3:2, 5, 6) means God's house, not that of Moses or Christ; in the case of Christ, compare Heb 3:6 with Heb 10:21. The *house* of Heb 3:6 is the Christian community; the author suggests its continuity with Israel by speaking not of two houses but of only one. Heb 3:6 brings out the reason why Jesus is superior to Moses: the latter was the faithful *servant* laboring *in* the house founded by God, but Jesus is God's *son*, placed *over* the house.

**3:6** The majority of manuscripts add "firm to the end," but these words are not found in the three earliest and best witnesses and are probably an interpolation derived from Heb 3:14.

**3:7–4:13** The author appeals for steadfastness of faith in Jesus, basing his warning on the experience of Israel during the Exodus. In the Old Testament the Exodus had been invoked as a symbol of the return of Israel from the Babylonian exile (Is 42:9; 43:16–21; 51:9–11). In the New Testament the redemption was similarly understood as a new exodus, both in the experience of Jesus himself (Lk 9:31) and in that of his followers (1 Cor 10:1–4). The author cites Ps 95:7–11, a salutary example of hardness of heart, as a warning against the danger of growing weary and giving up the journey. To call God *living* (Heb 3:12) means that he reveals himself in his works (cf. Jos 3:10; Jer 10:11). The *rest* (Heb 3:11) into which Israel was to enter was only a foreshadowing of that rest to which Christians are called. They are to remember the example of Israel's revolt in the desert that cost a whole generation the loss of the promised land (Heb 3:15–19; cf. Nm 14:20–29). In Heb 4:1–11, the symbol of *rest* is seen in deeper dimension: because the promise to the ancient Hebrews foreshadowed that given to Christians, it is *good news*; and because the promised land was the place of rest that God provided for his people, it was a share in his own rest, which he enjoyed after he had finished his creative work (Heb 3:3–4; cf. Gn 2:2). The author attempts to read this meaning of God's rest into Ps 95:7–11 (Heb 3:6–9). The Greek form of the name of Joshua, who led Israel into the promised land, is Jesus (Heb 3:8). The author plays upon the name but stresses the superiority of Jesus, who leads his followers into heavenly rest. Heb 3:12, 13 are meant as a continuation of the warning, for the word of God brings judgment as well as salvation. Some would capitalize *the word of God* and see it as a personal title of Jesus, comparable to that of Jn 1:1–18.

---

* 
**2:10** 12:2; Is 53:4 / Rom 11:36; 1 Cor 8:6.
**2:12** Ps 22:23.
**2:13** Is 8:17, 18.
**2:14** Is 25:8; Hos 13:14; Jn 12:31; Rom 6:9; 1 Cor 15:54–55; 2 Tm 1:10;

Rev 12:10.
**2:17** 4:15; 5:1–3.
**3:2** Nm 12:7.
**3:3** 2 Cor 3:7–8.
**3:6** 10:21; Eph 2:19; 1 Tm 3:15; 1 Pt 4:17.

HEB

> "Oh, that today you would hear his
>     voice, *
> 8  'Harden not your hearts as at the
>         rebellion
>     in the day of testing in the desert,
> 9  where your ancestors tested and tried
>         me
>     and saw my works * 10 for forty years.
> Because of this I was provoked with
>         that generation
>     and I said, "They have always been
>         of erring heart,
>     and they do not know my ways."
> 11  As I swore in my wrath,
>     "They shall not enter into my
>         rest."'"

12 Take care, brothers, that none of you may have an evil and unfaithful heart, so as to forsake the living God. 13 Encourage yourselves daily while it is still "today," so that none of you may grow hardened by the deceit of sin. 14 We have become partners of Christ if only we hold the beginning of the reality firm until the end, * 15 for it is said:

> "Oh, that today you would hear his
>     voice:
>     'Harden not your hearts as at the
>         rebellion.'" *

16 * Who were those who rebelled when they heard? Was it not all those who came out of Egypt under Moses? 17 With whom was he "provoked for forty years"? Was it not those who had sinned, whose corpses fell in the desert? * 18 And to whom did he "swear that they should not enter into his rest," if not to those who were disobedient? * 19 And we see that they could not enter for lack of faith.

## 4 The Sabbath Rest.

1 Therefore, let us be on our guard while the promise of entering into his rest remains, that none of you seem to have failed. 2 For in fact we have received the good news just as they did. But the word that they heard did not profit them, for they were not united in faith with those who listened. 3 For we who believed enter into [that] rest, just as he has said: *

> "As I swore in my wrath,
>     'They shall not enter into my rest,'"

and yet his works were accomplished at the foundation of the world. 4 For he has spoken somewhere about the seventh day in this manner, "And God rested on the seventh day from all his works"; * 5 and again, in the previously mentioned place, "They shall not enter into my rest." * 6 Therefore, since it remains that some will enter into it, and those who formerly received the good news did not enter because of disobedience, 7 he once more set a day, "today," when long afterwards he spoke through David, as already quoted: *

> "Oh, that today you would hear his
>     voice:
>     'Harden not your hearts.'"

8 Now if Joshua had given them rest, he would not have spoken afterwards of another day. * 9 Therefore, a sabbath rest still remains for the people of God. 10 And whoever enters into God's rest, rests from his own works as God did from his. 11 Therefore, let us strive to enter into that rest, so that no one may fall after the same example of disobedience.

12 Indeed, the word of God is living and effective, sharper than any two-edged sword, penetrating even between soul and spirit, joints and marrow, and able to discern reflections and thoughts of the heart. * 13 No creature is concealed from him, but everything is naked and exposed to the eyes of him to whom we must render an account. *

## Jesus, Compassionate High Priest.

14 † Therefore, since we have a great high priest who has

---

**4:14–16** These verses, which return to the theme first sounded in Heb 2:16–3:1, serve as an introduction to the section that follows. The author here alone calls Jesus *a great high priest* (Heb 4:14), a designation used by Philo for the Logos; perhaps he does so in order to emphasize Jesus' superiority over the Jewish high priest. He has *been tested in every way, yet without sin* (Heb 4:15); this indicates an acquaintance with the tradition of Jesus' temptations, not only at the beginning (as in Mk 1:13) but throughout his public life (cf. Lk 22:28). Although the reign of the exalted Jesus is a theme that occurs elsewhere in Hebrews, and

3:7–11 Ps 95:7–11.
3:9 Ex 17:7; Nm 20:2–5.
3:14 Rom 8:17.
3:15 Ps 95:7–8.
3:16–19 Nm 14:1–38; Dt 1:19–40.
3:17 Nm 14:29.
3:18 Nm 14:22–23; Dt 1:35.
4:3 3:11; Ps 95:11.
4:4 Gn 2:2.
4:5 Ps 95:11.
4:7 3:7–8, 15; Ps 95:7–8.
4:8 Dt 31:7; Jos 22:4.
4:12 Wis 18:15–16; Is 49:2; Eph 6:17; Rev 1:16; 2:12.
4:13 Jb 34:21–22; Ps 90:8; 139:2–4.

passed through the heavens, Jesus, the Son of God, let us hold fast to our confession. * [15] For we do not have a high priest who is unable to sympathize with our weaknesses, but one who has similarly been tested in every way, yet without sin. * [16] So let us confidently approach the throne of grace to receive mercy and to find grace for timely help. *

**5** [1] † Every high priest is taken from among men and made their representative before God, to offer gifts and sacrifices for sins. † [2] He is able to deal patiently† with the ignorant and erring, for he himself is beset by weakness [3] and so, for this reason, must make sin offerings for himself as well as for the people. * [4] No one takes this honor upon himself but only when called by God, just as Aaron was. * [5] In the same way, it was not Christ who glorified himself in becoming high priest, but rather the one who said to him:

"You are my son;
    this day I have begotten you"; *

[6] just as he says in another place: †

    "You are a priest forever
    according to the order of
    Melchizedek." *

[7] In the days when he was in the flesh, he offered prayers and supplications with loud cries and tears to the one who was able to save him from death, † and he was heard because of his reverence. * [8] Son though he was,† he learned obedience from what he suffered; * [9] and when he was made perfect, he became the source of eternal salvation for all who obey him, * [10] declared by God high priest according to the order of Melchizedek. *

## IV. JESUS' ETERNAL PRIESTHOOD AND ETERNAL SACRIFICE

**Exhortation to Spiritual Renewal.** [11] † About this we have much to say, and it is difficult to explain, for you have become sluggish in hearing. [12] Although you should be teachers by this time, you need to have someone teach you again the basic elements of the utterances of God. You need milk, [and] not solid food. * [13] Everyone who lives on milk lacks experience

---

†
Jesus' throne is mentioned in Heb 1:8, *the throne of grace* (Heb 4:16) refers to the throne of God. The similarity of Heb 4:16 to Heb 10:19–22 indicates that the author is thinking of our confident access to God, made possible by the priestly work of Jesus.

**5:1–10** The true humanity of Jesus (see note on Heb 2:5–18) makes him a more rather than a less effective high priest to the Christian community. In Old Testament tradition, the high priest was identified with the people, guilty of personal sin just as they were (Heb 5:1–3). Even so, the office was of divine appointment (Heb 5:4), as was also the case with the sinless Christ (Heb 5:5). For Heb 5:6, see note on Ps 110:4. Although Jesus was Son of God, he was destined as a human being to learn obedience by accepting the suffering he had to endure (Heb 5:8). Because of his perfection through this experience of human suffering, he is the cause of salvation for all (Heb 5:9), a *high priest according to the order of Melchizedek* (Heb 5:10; cf. Heb 5:6 and Heb 7:3).

**5:1** *To offer gifts and sacrifices for sins*: the author is thinking principally of the Day of Atonement rite, as is clear from Heb 9:7. This ritual was celebrated to atone for "all the sins of the Israelites" (Lv 16:34).

**5:2** *Deal patiently*: the Greek word *metriopathein* occurs only here in the Bible; this term was used by the Stoics to designate the golden mean between excess and defect of passion. Here it means rather the ability to sympathize.

**5:6–8** The author of Hebrews is the only New Testament writer to cite Ps 110:4, here and in Heb 7:17, 21, to show that Jesus has been called by God to his role as priest. Heb 5:7–8 deal with his ability to sympathize with sinners, because of his own experience of the trials and weakness of human nature, especially fear of death. In his present exalted state, weakness is foreign to him, but he understands what we suffer because of his previous earthly experience.

**5:7** *He offered prayers…to the one who was able to save him from death*: at Gethsemane (cf. Mk 14:35), though some see a broader reference (see note on Jn 12:27).

**5:8** *Son though he was*: two different though not incompat-

ible views of Jesus' sonship coexist in Hebrews, one associating it with his exaltation, the other with his preexistence. The former view is the older one (cf. Rom 1:4).

**5:11–6:20** The central section of Hebrews (5:11–10:39) opens with a reprimand and an appeal. Those to whom the author directs his teaching about Jesus' priesthood, which is *difficult to explain*, have become *sluggish in hearing* and forgetful of even *the basic elements* (Heb 5:12). But rather than treating of basic teachings, the author apparently believes that the challenge of more advanced ones may shake them out of their inertia (*therefore*, Heb 6:1). The six examples of *basic teaching* in Heb 6:1–3 are probably derived from a traditional catechetical list. No effort is made to address apostates, for their very hostility to the Christian message cuts them off completely from Christ (Heb 6:4–8). This harsh statement seems to rule out repentance after apostasy, but perhaps the author deliberately uses hyperbole in order to stress the seriousness of abandoning Christ. With Heb 6:9 a milder tone is introduced, and the criticism of the community (Heb 6:1–3, 9) is now balanced by an expression of confidence that its members are living truly Christian lives, and that God will justly reward their efforts (Heb 6:10). The author is concerned especially about their persevering (Heb 6:11–12), citing in this regard the achievement of Abraham, who relied on God's promise and on God's oath (Heb 6:13–18; cf. Gn 22:16), and proposes to them as a firm anchor of Christian hope the high priesthood of Christ, who is now living with God (Heb 6:19–20).

---

**4:14** 9:11, 24.
**4:15** 2:17–18; 5:2.
**4:16** 8:1; 10:19, 22, 35; 12:2; Eph 3:12.
**5:3** Lv 9:7; 16:15–17, 30, 34.
**5:4** Ex 28:1.
**5:5** Ps 2:7.
**5:6** Ps 110:4.
**5:7** Mt 26:38–44; Mk 14:34–40; Lk 22:41–46; Jn 12:27.
**5:8** Rom 5:19; Phil 2:8.
**5:9** 7:24–25, 28.
**5:10** 6:20; Ps 110:4.
**5:12** 1 Cor 3:1–3.

HEB

of the word of righteousness, for he is a child. [14] But solid food is for the mature, for those whose faculties are trained by practice to discern good and evil.

**6** [1] Therefore, let us leave behind the basic teaching about Christ and advance to maturity, without laying the foundation all over again: repentance from dead works and faith in God,* [2] instruction about baptisms† and laying on of hands, resurrection of the dead and eternal judgment.* [3] And we shall do this, if only God permits. [4] For it is impossible in the case of those who have once been enlightened and tasted the heavenly gift† and shared in the holy Spirit* [5] and tasted the good word of God and the powers of the age to come,† [6] and then have fallen away, to bring them to repentance again, since they are recrucifying the Son of God for themselves† and holding him up to contempt.* [7] Ground that has absorbed the rain falling upon it repeatedly and brings forth crops useful to those for whom it is cultivated receives a blessing from God.* [8] But if it produces thorns and thistles, it is rejected; it will soon be cursed and finally burned.*

[9] But we are sure in your regard, beloved, of better things related to salvation, even though we speak in this way. [10] For God is not unjust so as to overlook your work and the love you have demonstrated for his name by having served and continuing to serve the holy ones.

[11] We earnestly desire each of you to demonstrate the same eagerness for the fulfillment of hope until the end,* [12] so that you may not become sluggish, but imitators of those who, through faith and patience,* are inheriting the promises.†

**God's Promise Immutable.** [13]†* When God made the promise to Abraham, since he had no one greater by whom to swear, "he swore by himself," [14] and said, "I will indeed bless you and multiply" you.* [15] And so, after patient waiting,* he obtained the promise.† [16] Human beings swear by someone greater than themselves; for them an oath serves as a guarantee and puts an end to all argument. [17] So when God wanted to give the heirs of his promise an even clearer demonstration of the immutability of his purpose, he intervened with an oath,* [18] so that by two immutable things,† in which it was impossible for God to lie, we who have taken refuge might be strongly encouraged to hold fast to the hope that lies before us.* [19] This we have as an anchor of the soul,* sure and firm, which reaches into the interior behind the veil,† [20] where Jesus has entered on our behalf as forerunner, becoming high priest forever according to the order of Melchizedek.*

**7** **Melchizedek, a Type of Christ.** [1]† This "Melchizedek, king of Salem and priest of God Most High,"† "met Abraham as he

---

† **6:2** *Instruction about baptisms*: not simply about Christian baptism but about the difference between it and similar Jewish rites, such as proselyte baptism, John's baptism, and the washings of the Qumran sectaries. *Laying on of hands*: in Acts 8:17; 19:6 this rite effects the infusion of the holy Spirit; in Acts 6:6; 13:3; 1 Tm 4:14; 5:22; 2 Tm 1:6 it is a means of conferring some ministry or mission in the early Christian community.

**6:4** *Enlightened and tasted the heavenly gift*: this may refer to baptism and the Eucharist, respectively, but more probably means the neophytes' enlightenment by faith and their experience of salvation.

**6:5** *Tasted the good word of God and the powers of the age to come*: the proclamation of the *word of God* was accompanied by signs of the Spirit's power (1 Thes 1:5; 1 Cor 2:4).

**6:6** *They are recrucifying the Son of God for themselves*: a colorful description of the malice of apostasy, which is portrayed as again crucifying and deriding the Son of God.

**6:12** *Imitators of those…inheriting the promises*: the author urges the addressees to imitate the faith of the holy people of the Old Testament, who now possess the promised goods of which they lived in hope. This theme will be treated fully in Heb 6:11.

**6:13** *He swore by himself*: God's promise to Abraham, which he confirmed by an oath ("I swear by myself," Gn 22:16) was the basis for the hope of all Abraham's descendants.

**6:15** *He obtained the promise*: this probably refers not to Abraham's temporary possession of the land but to the eschatological blessings that Abraham and the other patriarchs have now come to possess.

**6:18** *Two immutable things*: the promise and the oath, both made by God.

**6:19** *Anchor…into the interior behind the veil*: a mixed metaphor. The Holy of Holies, beyond the veil that separates it from the Holy Place (Ex 26:31–33), is seen as the earthly counterpart of the heavenly abode of God. This theme will be developed in Heb 9.

**7:1–3** Recalling the meeting between Melchizedek and Abraham described in Gn 14:17–20, the author enhances the significance of this priest by providing the popular etymological meaning of his name and that of the city over which he ruled (Heb 7:2). Since Genesis gives no information on the parentage or the death of Melchizedek, he is seen here as a type of Christ, representing a priesthood that is unique and eternal (Heb 7:3).

**7:1** The author here assumes that Melchizedek was a priest of the God of Israel (cf. Gn 14:22 and the note there).

* 
**6:1** 9:14.
**6:2** 9:10; Mk 7:4 / Acts 6:6; 8:17; 13:3; 19:6; 1 Tm 4:14; 5:22; 2 Tm 1:6.
**6:4** 10:26, 32; Ps 34:6; 2 Cor 4:6.
**6:6** 2 Pt 2:21.
**6:7** Gn 1:11–12; Dt 11:11.
**6:8** Gn 3:17–18; Mt 7:16; 13:7; Mk 4:7; Lk 8:7.
**6:11** 3:14.

**6:12** 5:11; Gal 3:14; Eph 1:13–14.
**6:13** Gn 22:16.
**6:14** Gn 22:17.
**6:15** 6:12; Rom 4:20.
**6:17** 6:12.
**6:18** Nm 23:19; 1 Sm 15:29; Jn 8:17; 2 Tm 2:13.
**6:19** 10:20; Ex 26:31–33; Lv 16:2.
**6:20** 5:10; Ps 110:4.

returned from his defeat of the kings" and "blessed him."* ²† And Abraham apportioned to him "a tenth of everything." His name first means righteous king, and he was also "king of Salem," that is, king of peace. ³ Without father, mother, or ancestry, without beginning of days or end of life,† thus made to resemble the Son of God, he remains a priest forever.*

⁴† See how great he is to whom the patriarch "Abraham [indeed] gave a tenth" of his spoils.* ⁵ The descendants of Levi who receive the office of priesthood have a commandment according to the law to exact tithes from the people, that is, from their brothers, although they also have come from the loins of Abraham.* ⁶ But he who was not of their ancestry received tithes from Abraham and blessed him who had received the promises. ⁷ Unquestionably, a lesser person is blessed by a greater.† ⁸ In the one case, mortal men receive tithes; in the other, a man of whom it is testified that he lives on. ⁹ One might even say that Levi† himself, who receives tithes, was tithed through Abraham, ¹⁰ for he was still in his father's loins when Melchizedek met him.

¹¹† If, then, perfection came through the levitical priesthood, on the basis of which the people received the law, what need would there still have been for another priest to arise according to the order of Melchizedek, and not reckoned according to the order of Aaron?* ¹² When there is a change of priesthood, there is necessarily a change of law as well. ¹³ Now he of whom these things are said† belonged to a different tribe, of which no member ever officiated at the altar. ¹⁴ It is clear that our Lord arose from Judah,† and in regard to that tribe Moses said nothing about priests.* ¹⁵† It is even more obvious if another priest is raised up after the likeness of Melchizedek, ¹⁶ who has become so, not by a law expressed in a commandment concerning physical descent but by the power of a life that cannot be destroyed.† ¹⁷ For it is testified:

> "You are a priest forever
> according to the order of
> Melchizedek."*

¹⁸ On the one hand, a former commandment is annulled because of its weakness and uselessness,* ¹⁹ for the law brought nothing to perfection; on the other hand, a better hope† is introduced, through which we draw near to

---

**7:2** In Gn 14, the Hebrew text does not state explicitly who gave tithes to whom. The author of Hebrews supplies Abraham as the subject, according to a contemporary interpretation of the passage. This supports the argument of the midrash and makes it possible to see in Melchizedek a type of Jesus. The messianic blessings of righteousness and peace are foreshadowed in the names "Melchizedek" and "Salem."

**7:3** *Without father, mother, or ancestry, without beginning of days or end of life:* this is perhaps a quotation from a hymn about Melchizedek. The rabbis maintained that anything not mentioned in the Torah does not exist. Consequently, since the Old Testament nowhere mentions Melchizedek's ancestry, birth, or death, the conclusion can be drawn that he *remains…forever.*

**7:4–10** The tithe that Abraham gave to Melchizedek (Heb 7:4), a practice later followed by the levitical priesthood (Heb 7:5), was a gift (Heb 7:6) acknowledging a certain superiority in Melchizedek, the foreign priest (Heb 7:7). This is further indicated by the fact that the institution of the levitical priesthood was sustained by hereditary succession in the tribe of Levi, whereas the absence of any mention of Melchizedek's death in Genesis implies that his personal priesthood is permanent (Heb 7:8). The levitical priesthood itself, through Abraham, its ancestor, paid tithes to Melchizedek, thus acknowledging the superiority of his priesthood over its own (Heb 7:9–10).

**7:7** *A lesser person is blessed by a greater:* though this sounds like a principle, there are some examples in the Old Testament that do not support it (cf. 2 Sm 14:22; Jb 31:20). The author may intend it as a statement of a liturgical rule.

**7:9** *Levi:* for the author this name designates not only the son of Jacob mentioned in Genesis but the priestly tribe that was thought to be descended from him.

**7:11–14** The levitical priesthood was not typified by the priesthood of Melchizedek, for Ps 110:4 speaks of a priesthood of a new order, the order of Melchizedek, to arise in messianic times (Heb 7:11). Since the levitical priesthood served the Mosaic law, a new priesthood (Heb 7:12) would not come into being without a change in the law itself. Thus Jesus was not associated with the Old Testament priesthood, for he was a descendant of the tribe of Judah, which had never exercised the priesthood (Heb 7:13–14).

**7:13** *He of whom these things are said:* Jesus, the priest "according to the order of Melchizedek." According to the author's interpretation, Ps 110 spoke prophetically of Jesus.

**7:14** *Judah:* the author accepts the early Christian tradition that Jesus was descended from the family of David (cf. Mt 1:1–2, 16, 20; Lk 1:27; 2:4; Rom 1:3). The Qumran community expected two Messiahs, one descended from Aaron and one from David; Hebrews shows no awareness of this view or at least does not accept it. Our author's view is not attested in contemporaneous Judaism.

**7:15–19** Jesus does not exercise a priesthood through family lineage but through his immortal existence (Heb 7:15–16), fulfilling Ps 110:4 (Heb 7:17; cf. Heb 7:3). Thus he abolishes forever both the levitical priesthood and the law it serves, because neither could effectively sanctify people (Heb 7:18) by leading them into direct communication with God (Heb 7:19).

**7:16** *A life that cannot be destroyed:* the life to which Jesus has attained by virtue of his resurrection; it is his exaltation rather than his divine nature that makes him priest. The Old Testament speaks of the Aaronic priesthood as eternal (see Ex 40:15); our author does not explicitly consider this possible objection to his argument but implicitly refutes it in Heb 7:23–24.

**7:19** *A better hope:* this hope depends upon the sacrifice of the Son of God; through it we "approach the throne of grace" (Heb 4:16); cf. Heb 6:19, 20.

---

**7:1** Gn 14:17–20.
**7:3** 4:14; 6:6; 10:29.
**7:4** Gn 14:20.
**7:5** Nm 18:21 / Gn 35:11.
**7:11** 5:6; Ps 110:4.

**7:14** Gn 49:10; Is 11:1; Mt 1:1–2, 16, 20; 2:6; Lk 1:27; 2:4; Rom 1:3; Rev 5:5.
**7:17** 5:6; Ps 110:4.
**7:18** 10:1.

God. [20]† And to the degree that this happened not without the taking of an oath†—for others became priests without an oath, [21] but he with an oath, through the one who said to him:

> "The Lord has sworn, and he will not repent:*
> 'You are a priest forever'"—

[22]* to that same degree has Jesus [also] become the guarantee of an [even] better covenant.† [23] Those priests were many because they were prevented by death from remaining in office, [24] but he, because he remains forever, has a priesthood that does not pass away.* [25]† Therefore, he is always able to save those who approach God through him, since he lives forever to make intercession for them.*

[26]* It was fitting that we should have such a high priest:† holy, innocent, undefiled, separated from sinners, higher than the heavens.† [27] He has no need, as did the high priests, to offer sacrifice day after day,†* first for his own sins and then for those of the people; he did that once for all when he offered himself. [28] For the law appoints men subject to weakness to be high priests, but the word of the oath, which was taken after the law, appoints a son, who has been made perfect forever.*

# 8 Heavenly Priesthood of Jesus.† [1] The main point of what has been said is this: we have such a high priest, who has taken his seat at the right hand of the throne of the Majesty in heaven,* [2] a minister of the sanctuary† and of the true tabernacle that the Lord, not man, set up.* [3] Now every high priest is appointed to offer gifts and sacrifices; thus the necessity for this one also to have something to offer.* [4] If then he were on earth, he would not be a priest, since there are those who offer gifts according to the law.* [5] They worship in a copy and shadow of the heavenly sanctuary, as Moses was warned when he was about to erect the tabernacle. For he says, "See that you make everything according to the pattern shown you on the mountain."* [6] Now he has obtained so much more excellent a ministry as he is mediator of a better covenant, enacted on better promises.*

## Old and New Covenants.† [7] For if that first covenant had been faultless, no place would

---

**7:20–25** As was the case with the promise to Abraham (Heb 6:13), though not with the levitical priesthood, the eternal priesthood of the order of Melchizedek was confirmed by God's oath (Heb 7:20–21); cf. Ps 110:4. Thus Jesus becomes the guarantee of a permanent covenant (Heb 7:22) that does not require a succession of priests as did the levitical priesthood (Heb 7:23) because his high priesthood is eternal and unchangeable (Heb 7:24). Consequently, Jesus is able to save all who draw near to God through him since he is their ever-living intercessor (Heb 7:25).

**7:20** *An oath:* God's oath in Ps 110:4.

**7:22** *An [even] better covenant:* better than the Mosaic covenant because it will be eternal, like the priesthood of Jesus upon which it is based. Heb 7:12 argued that a change of priesthood involves a change of law; since "law" and "covenant" are used correlatively, a new covenant is likewise instituted.

**7:25** *To make intercession:* the intercession of the exalted Jesus, not the sequel to his completed sacrifice but its eternal presence in heaven; cf. Rom 8:34.

**7:26** This verse with its list of attributes is reminiscent of Heb 7:3 and is perhaps a hymnic counterpart to it, contrasting the exalted Jesus with Melchizedek.

**7:26–28** Jesus is precisely the high priest whom the human race requires, holy and sinless, installed far above humanity (Heb 7:26); one having no need to offer sacrifice daily for sins but making a single offering of himself (Heb 7:27) once for all. The law could only appoint high priests with human limitations, but the fulfillment of God's oath regarding the priesthood of Melchizedek (Ps 110:4) makes the Son of God the perfect priest forever (Heb 7:28).

**7:27** Such daily sacrifice is nowhere mentioned in the Mosaic law; only on the Day of Atonement is it prescribed that the high priest must *offer sacrifice...for his own sins and then for those of the people* (Lv 16:11–19). *Once for all:* this translates the Greek words *ephapax/hapax* that occur eleven times in Hebrews.

**8:1–6** The Christian community has in Jesus the kind of high priest described in Heb 7:26–28. In virtue of his ascension Jesus has taken his place at God's right hand in accordance with Ps

110:1 (Heb 8:1), where he presides over the heavenly sanctuary established by God himself (Heb 8:2). Like every high priest, he has his offering to make (Heb 8:3; cf. Heb 9:12, 14), but it differs from that of the levitical priesthood in which he had no share (Heb 8:4) and which was in any case but a shadowy reflection of the true offering in the heavenly sanctuary (Heb 8:5). But Jesus' ministry in the heavenly sanctuary is that of mediator of a superior covenant that accomplishes what it signifies (Heb 8:6).

**8:2** *The sanctuary:* the Greek term could also mean "holy things" but bears the meaning "sanctuary" elsewhere in Hebrews (Heb 9:8, 12, 24, 25; 10:19; 13:11). *The true tabernacle:* the heavenly tabernacle *that the Lord...set up* is contrasted with the earthly tabernacle that Moses set up in the desert. *True* means "real" in contradistinction to a mere "copy and shadow" (Heb 8:5); compare the Johannine usage (e.g., Jn 1:9; 6:32; 15:1). The idea that the earthly sanctuary is a reflection of a heavenly model may be based upon Ex 25:9, but probably also derives from the Platonic concept of a real world of which our observable world is merely a shadow.

**8:7–13** Since the first covenant was deficient in accomplishing what it signified, it had to be replaced (Heb 8:7), as Jeremiah (Jer 31:31–34) had prophesied (Heb 8:8–12). Even in the time of Jeremiah, the first covenant was antiquated (Heb 8:13). In Heb 7:22–24, the superiority of the new covenant was seen in the permanence of its priesthood; here the superiority is based on better promises, made explicit in the citation of Jer 31:31–34

---

**7:21** Ps 110:4.
**7:22** 8:6–10; 9:15–20; 10:29; 12:24; 13:20.
**7:24** 5:6; 13:8.
**7:25** Rom 8:34; 1 Jn 2:1; Rev 1:18.
**7:26** 4:14, 15.
**7:27** 5:3; 9:12, 25–28; 10:11–14; Ex 29:38–39; Lv 16:6, 11, 15–17;

Nm 28:3–4; Is 53:10; Rom 6:10.
**7:28** 5:1, 2, 9.
**8:1** 1:3; 4:14; 7:26–28.
**8:2** 9:11; Ex 33:7; Nm 24:6 LXX.
**8:3** 5:1.
**8:4** 7:13.
**8:5** 9:23; Ex 25:40; Acts 7:44; Col 2:17.
**8:6** 7:22; 9:15.

have been sought for a second one. ⁸But he finds fault with them and says:†

> "Behold, the days are coming, says the
>     Lord,*
> when I will conclude a new covenant
>     with the house of Israel and the
>     house of Judah.
> ⁹ It will not be like the covenant I made
>     with their fathers
> the day I took them by the hand to
>     lead them forth from the land of
>     Egypt;
> for they did not stand by my covenant
>     and I ignored them, says the Lord.
> ¹⁰ But this is the covenant I will establish
>     with the house of Israel
> after those days, says the Lord:
> I will put my laws in their minds
>     and I will write them upon their
>     hearts.
> I will be their God,
>     and they shall be my people.*
> ¹¹ And they shall not teach, each one his
>     fellow citizen
> and kinsman, saying, 'Know the Lord,'
> for all shall know me,
>     from least to greatest.
> ¹² For I will forgive their evildoing
>     and remember their sins no more."

¹³†* When he speaks of a "new" covenant, he declares the first one obsolete. And what has become obsolete and has grown old is close to disappearing.

## 9 The Worship of the First Covenant.† ¹Now [even] the first covenant had regulations for worship and an earthly sanctuary. ²For a tabernacle was constructed, the outer one,† in which were the lampstand, the table, and the bread of offering; this is called the Holy Place.* ³† Behind the second veil was the tabernacle called the Holy of Holies,* ⁴in which were the gold altar of incense† and the ark of the covenant entirely covered with gold. In it were the gold jar containing the manna, the staff of Aaron that had sprouted, and the tablets of the covenant.* ⁵† Above it were the cherubim of glory overshadowing the place of expiation. Now is not the time to speak of these in detail.*

⁶With these arrangements for worship, the priests, in performing their service,† go into the outer tabernacle repeatedly,* ⁷but the high priest alone goes into the inner one once a year, not without blood† that he offers for himself and for the sins of the people.* ⁸In this way the holy Spirit shows that the way into the sanctuary had not yet been revealed while the outer tabernacle still had its place. ⁹This is a symbol of the present time,† in

---

(LXX: 38), namely, in the immediacy of the people's knowledge of God (Heb 8:11) and in the forgiveness of sin (Heb 8:12).

**8:8–12** In citing Jeremiah the author follows the Septuagint; some apparent departures from it may be the result of a different Septuagintal text rather than changes deliberately introduced.

**8:13** *Close to disappearing*: from the prophet's perspective, not that of the author of Hebrews.

**9:1–10** The regulations for worship under the old covenant permitted all the priests to enter the Holy Place (Heb 2:6), but only the high priest to enter the Holy of Holies and then only once a year (Heb 9:3–5, 7). The description of the sanctuary and its furnishings is taken essentially from Ex 25–26. This exclusion of the people from the Holy of Holies signified that they were not allowed to stand in God's presence (Heb 9:8) because their offerings and sacrifices, which were merely symbols of their need of spiritual renewal (Heb 9:10), could not obtain forgiveness of sins (Heb 9:9).

**9:2** *The outer one*: the author speaks of *the outer tabernacle* (Heb 9:6) and *the inner one* (Heb 9:7) rather than of one Mosaic tabernacle divided into two parts or sections.

**9:3** *The second veil*: what is meant is the veil that divided the Holy Place from the Holy of Holies. It is here called *the second*, because there was another veil at the entrance to the Holy Place, or "outer tabernacle" (Ex 26:36).

**9:4** *The gold altar of incense*: Ex 30:6 locates this altar in the Holy Place, the first tabernacle, rather than in the Holy of Holies. Neither is there any Old Testament support for the assertion that the jar of manna and the staff of Aaron were in the ark of the covenant. For the tablets of the covenant, see Ex 25:16.

**9:5** *The place of expiation*: the gold "mercy seat" (Greek *hilastērion*, as in Rom 3:25), where the blood of the sacrificial animals was sprinkled on the Day of Atonement (Lv 16:14–15). This rite achieved "expiation" or atonement for the sins of the preceding year.

**9:6** *In performing their service*: the priestly services that had to be performed regularly in the Holy Place or *outer tabernacle* included burning incense on the incense altar twice each day (Ex 30:7), replacing the loaves on the table of the bread of offering once each week (Lv 24:8), and constantly caring for the lamps on the lampstand (Ex 27:21).

**9:7** *Not without blood*: blood was essential to Old Testament sacrifice because it was believed that life was located in the blood. Hence blood was especially sacred, and its outpouring functioned as a meaningful symbol of cleansing from sin and reconciliation with God. Unlike Hebrews, the Old Testament never says that the blood is "offered." The author is perhaps retrojecting into his description of Mosaic ritual a concept that belongs to the New Testament antitype, as Paul does when he speaks of the Israelites' passage through the sea as a "baptism" (1 Cor 10:2).

**9:9** *The present time*: this expression is equivalent to the "present age," used in contradistinction to the "age to come."

---

**8:8** Jer 31:31–34.
**8:10** 10:16–17.
**8:13** Rom 10:4.
**9:2** Ex 25:23–30.
**9:3** Ex 26:31–34.
**9:4** Ex 16:32–34; 25:10, 16, 21; 30:1–10;
Lv 16:12–13; Nm 17:2–7, 16–26.
**9:5** Ex 25:16–22; 26:34; Lv 16:14–15.
**9:6** Ex 27:21; 30:7; Lv 24:8.
**9:7** Ex 30:10; Lv 16:1–14.

which gifts and sacrifices are offered that cannot perfect the worshiper in conscience [10] but only in matters of food and drink and various ritual washings: regulations concerning the flesh, imposed until the time of the new order.*

**Sacrifice of Jesus.** [11]† But when Christ came as high priest of the good things that have come to be,† passing through the greater and more perfect tabernacle not made by hands, that is, not belonging to this creation,* [12] he entered once for all into the sanctuary, not with the blood of goats and calves but with his own blood, thus obtaining eternal redemption.* [13] For if the blood of goats and bulls and the sprinkling of a heifer's ashes† can sanctify those who are defiled so that their flesh is cleansed,* [14] how much more will the blood of Christ, who through the eternal spirit† offered himself unblemished to God, cleanse our consciences from dead works to worship the living God.*

[15]† For this reason he is mediator of a new covenant: since a death has taken place for deliverance from transgressions under the first covenant, those who are called may receive the promised eternal inheritance.* [16]† Now where there is a will, the death of the testator must be established. [17] For a will takes effect only at death; it has no force while the testator is alive. [18] Thus not even the first covenant was inaugurated without blood. [19]† When every commandment had been proclaimed by Moses to all the people according to the law, he took the blood of calves [and goats], together with water and crimson wool and hyssop, and sprinkled both the book itself and all the people,* [20] saying, "This is 'the blood of the covenant which God has enjoined upon you.'"* [21] In the same way, he sprinkled also the tabernacle† and all the vessels of worship with blood.* [22]† According to the law almost everything is purified by blood,* and without the shedding of blood there is no forgiveness.

[23]† Therefore, it was necessary for the copies of the heavenly things to be purified by these

---

† **9:11–14** Christ, the high priest of the spiritual blessings foreshadowed in the Old Testament sanctuary, has actually entered the true sanctuary of heaven that is not of human making (Heb 9:11). His place there is permanent, and his offering is his own blood that won eternal redemption (Heb 9:12). If the sacrifice of animals could bestow legal purification (Heb 9:13), how much more effective is the blood of the sinless, divine Christ who spontaneously offered himself to purge the human race of sin and render it fit for the service of God (Heb 9:14).

**9:11** *The good things that have come to be*: the majority of later manuscripts here read "the good things to come"; cf. Heb 10:1.

**9:13** *A heifer's ashes*: ashes from a red heifer that had been burned were mixed with water and used for the cleansing of those who had become ritually defiled by touching a corpse; see Nm 19:9, 14–21.

**9:14** *Through the eternal spirit*: this expression does not refer either to the holy Spirit or to the divine nature of Jesus but to the life of the risen Christ, "a life that cannot be destroyed" (Heb 7:16).

**9:15–22** Jesus' role as *mediator of the new covenant* is based upon his sacrificial *death* (cf. Heb 8:6). His death has effected *deliverance from transgressions*, i.e., deliverance from sins committed under the old covenant, which the Mosaic sacrifices were incapable of effacing. Until this happened, the *eternal inheritance* promised by God could not be obtained (Heb 9:15). This effect of his work follows the human pattern by which a last will and testament becomes effective only with the death of the testator (Heb 9:16–17). The Mosaic covenant was also associated with death, for Moses made use of blood to seal the pact between God and the people (Heb 9:18–21). In Old Testament tradition, guilt could normally not be remitted without the use of blood (Heb 9:22; cf. Lv 17:11).

**9:16–17** *A will…death of the testator*: the same Greek word *diathēkē*, meaning "covenant" in Heb 9:15, 18, is used here with the meaning *will*. The new covenant, unlike the old, is at the same time a will that requires the *death of the testator*. Jesus as eternal Son is the one who established the new covenant together with his Father, author of both covenants; at the same time he is the testator whose death puts his *will* into effect.

**9:19–20** A number of details here are different from the description of this covenant rite in Ex 24:5–8. Exodus mentions only calves ("young bulls," NAB), not goats (but this addition in Hebrews is of doubtful authenticity), says nothing of the use of *water and crimson wool and hyssop* (these features probably came from a different rite; cf. Lv 14:3–7; Nm 19:6–18), and describes Moses as splashing blood on the altar, whereas Hebrews says he sprinkled it on the book (but both book and altar are meant to symbolize the agreement of God). The words of Moses are also slightly different from those in Exodus and are closer to the words of Jesus at the Last Supper in Mk 14:24 // Mt 26:28.

**9:21** According to Exodus, the tabernacle did not yet exist at the time of the covenant rite. Moreover, nothing is said of sprinkling it with blood at its subsequent dedication (Ex 40:9–11).

**9:22** *Without the shedding of blood there is no forgiveness*: in fact, ancient Israel did envisage other means of obtaining forgiveness; the Old Testament mentions contrition of heart (Ps 51:17), fasting (Jl 2:12), and almsgiving (Sir 3:29). The author is limiting his horizon to the sacrificial cult, which did always involve the shedding of blood for its expiatory and unitive value.

**9:23–28** Since the blood of animals became a cleansing symbol among Old Testament prefigurements, it was necessary that the realities foreshadowed be brought into being by a shedding of blood that was infinitely more effective by reason of its worth (Heb 9:23). Christ did not simply prefigure the heavenly realities (Heb 9:24) by performing an annual sacrifice with a blood not his own (Heb 9:25); he offered the single sacrifice of himself as the final annulment of sin (Heb 9:26). Just as death is the unrepeatable act that ends a person's life, so Christ's offering of himself for all is the unrepeatable sacrifice that has once for all achieved redemption (Heb 9:27–28).

---

**9:10** 13:9; Lv 11; 14:8; Nm 19:11–21; Col 2:16.
**9:11** 4:14; 10:1, 20.
**9:12** 7:27; Mt 26:28.
**9:13** 10:4; Lv 16:6–16; Nm 19:9, 14–21.
**9:14** 10:10; Rom 5:9; 1 Tm 3:9; Ti 2:14;

1 Pt 1:18–19; 1 Jn 1:7; Rev 1:5.
**9:15** 1 Tm 2:5.
**9:19** 9:12–13.
**9:20** Ex 24:3–8; Mt 26:28; Mk 14:24.
**9:21** Ex 40:9; Lv 8:15, 19.
**9:22** Lv 17:11.

rites, but the heavenly things themselves by better sacrifices than these.* ²⁴ For Christ did not enter into a sanctuary made by hands, a copy of the true one, but heaven itself, that he might now appear before God on our behalf.* ²⁵ Not that he might offer himself repeatedly, as the high priest enters each year into the sanctuary with blood that is not his own; ²⁶ if that were so, he would have had to suffer repeatedly from the foundation of the world. But now once for all he has appeared at the end of the ages† to take away sin by his sacrifice.* ²⁷ Just as it is appointed that human beings die once, and after this the judgment,* ²⁸ so also Christ, offered once to take away the sins of many,† will appear a second time, not to take away sin but to bring salvation to those who eagerly await him.*

**10** **One Sacrifice Instead of Many.** ¹† Since the law has only a shadow of the good things to come,† and not the very image of them, it can never make perfect those who come to worship by the same sacrifices that they offer continually each year.* ² Otherwise, would not the sacrifices have ceased to be offered, since the worshipers, once cleansed, would no longer have had any consciousness

of sins? ³ But in those sacrifices there is only a yearly remembrance of sins,* ⁴ for it is impossible that the blood of bulls and goats take away sins.* ⁵ For this reason, when he came into the world, he said:†

"Sacrifice and offering you did not
　　desire,*
　but a body you prepared for me;
⁶　holocausts and sin offerings you took no
　　delight in.
⁷　Then I said, 'As is written of me in the
　　scroll,
　Behold, I come to do your will,
　　O God.'"

⁸ First he says, "Sacrifices and offerings, holocausts and sin offerings,† you neither desired nor delighted in." These are offered according to the law.* ⁹ Then he says, "Behold, I come to do your will." He takes away the first to establish the second.* ¹⁰ By this "will," we have been consecrated through the offering of the body of Jesus Christ once for all.*

¹¹† Every priest stands daily at his ministry, offering frequently those same sacrifices that can never take away sins.* ¹² But this one offered one sacrifice for sins, and took his seat

H
E
B

---

**9:26** *At the end of the ages*: the use of expressions such as this shows that the author of Hebrews, despite his interest in the Platonic concept of an eternal world above superior to temporal reality here below, nevertheless still clings to the Jewish Christian eschatology with its sequence of "the present age" and "the age to come."

**9:28** *To take away the sins of many*: the reference is to Is 53:12. Since the Greek verb *anapherō* can mean both "to take away" and "to bear," the author no doubt intended to play upon both senses: Jesus took away sin by bearing it himself. See the similar wordplay in Jn 1:29. *Many* is used in the Semitic meaning of "all" in the inclusive sense, as in Mk 14:24. *To those who eagerly await him*: Jesus will appear *a second time* at the parousia, as the high priest reappeared on the Day of Atonement, emerging from the Holy of Holies, which he had entered *to take away sin*. This dramatic scene is described in Sir 50:5–11.

**10:1–10** Christian faith now realizes that the Old Testament sacrifices did not effect the spiritual benefits to come but only prefigured them (Heb 10:1). For if the sacrifices had actually effected the forgiveness of sin, there would have been no reason for their constant repetition (Heb 10:2). They were rather a continual reminder of the people's sins (Heb 10:3). It is not reasonable to suppose that human sins could be removed by the blood of animal sacrifices (Heb 10:4). Christ, therefore, is here shown to understand his mission in terms of Ps 40:6–8, cited according to the Septuagint (Heb 10:5–7). Jesus acknowledged that the Old Testament sacrifices did not remit the sins of the people and so, perceiving the will of God, offered his own body for this purpose (Heb 10:8–10).

**10:1** *A shadow of the good things to come*: the term *shadow* was used in Heb 8:5 to signify the earthly counterpart of the Platonic heavenly reality. But here it means a prefiguration of what is to come in Christ, as it is used in the Pauline literature; cf. Col 2:17.

**10:5–7** A passage from Ps 40:7–9 is placed in the mouth of the Son at his incarnation. As usual, the author follows the Septuagint text. There is a notable difference in Heb 10:5 (Ps 40:6), where the Masoretic text reads "ears you have dug for me" ("ears open to obedience you gave me," NAB), but most Septuagint manuscripts have "a body you prepared for me," a reading obviously more suited to the interpretation of Hebrews.

**10:8** *Sacrifices and offerings, holocausts and sin offerings*: these four terms taken from the preceding passage of Ps 40 (with the first two changed to plural forms) are probably intended as equivalents to the four principal types of Old Testament sacrifices: peace offerings (Lv 3, here called *sacrifices*); cereal offerings (Lv 2, here called *offerings*); holocausts (Lv 1); and *sin offerings* (Lv 4–5). This last category includes the guilt offerings of Lv 5:14–19.

**10:11–18** Whereas the levitical priesthood offered daily sacrifices that were ineffectual in remitting sin (Heb 10:11), Jesus offered a single sacrifice that won him a permanent place at God's right hand. There he has only to await the final outcome of his work (Heb 10:12–13; cf. Ps 110:1). Thus he has brought into being in his own person the new covenant prophesied by Jeremiah (Jer 31:33–34) that has rendered meaningless all other offerings for sin (Heb 10:14–18).

---

**9:23** Jb 15:15.
**9:24** 7:25; Rom 8:34; 1 Jn 2:1–2.
**9:26** 7:27; Jn 1:29; Gal 4:4.
**9:27** Gn 3:19.
**9:28** 10:10; Is 53:12.
**10:1** 8:5; Col 2:17.
**10:3** Lv 16:21; Nm 5:15 LXX.

**10:4** Is 1:11; Mi 6:6–8.
**10:5–7** Ps 40:7–9.
**10:8** 10:5–6; Ps 40:7.
**10:9** 7; Ps 40:8; Mt 26:39; Mk 14:36; Lk 22:42; Jn 6:38.
**10:10** 9:12, 14.
**10:11** 7:27; Dt 10:8; 18:7.

forever at the right hand of God;* ¹³† now he waits until his enemies are made his footstool. ¹⁴ For by one offering he has made perfect forever those who are being consecrated.* ¹⁵† The holy Spirit also testifies to us, for after saying:

¹⁶     "This is the covenant I will establish
            with them after those days, says
            the Lord:
         'I will put my laws in their hearts,
         and I will write them upon their
            minds,'"*

¹⁷ he also says:†

    "Their sins and their evildoing
         I will remember no more."*

¹⁸ Where there is forgiveness of these, there is no longer offering for sin.

**Recalling the Past.**† ¹⁹ Therefore, brothers, since through the blood of Jesus we have confidence of entrance into the sanctuary* ²⁰† by the new and living way he opened for us

through the veil,* that is, his flesh, ²¹†* and since we have "a great priest over the house of God," ²² let us approach with a sincere heart and in absolute trust, with our hearts sprinkled clean from an evil conscience† and our bodies washed in pure water.* ²³ Let us hold unwaveringly to our confession that gives us hope, for he who made the promise is trustworthy.* ²⁴ We must consider how to rouse one another to love and good works. ²⁵ We should not stay away from our assembly,† as is the custom of some, but encourage one another, and this all the more as you see the day drawing near.*

²⁶†* If we sin deliberately after receiving knowledge of the truth, there no longer remains sacrifice for sins ²⁷ but a fearful prospect of judgment and a flaming fire that is going to consume the adversaries.* ²⁸ Anyone who rejects the law of Moses† is put to death without pity on the testimony of two or three witnesses.* ²⁹ Do you not think that a much worse punishment is due the one who has contempt for the Son of God, considers unclean the covenant-blood by which he was

---

†
**10:13** *Until his enemies are made his footstool*: Ps 110:1 is again used; the reference here is to the period of time between the enthronement of Jesus and his second coming. The identity of the *enemies* is not specified; cf. 1 Cor 15:25–27.

**10:15–17** The testimony of the scriptures is now invoked to support what has just preceded. The passage cited is a portion of the new covenant prophecy of Jer 31:31–34, which the author previously used in Heb 8:8–12.

**10:17** *He also says*: these words are not in the Greek text, which has only *kai*, "also," but the expression *"after saying"* in Heb 10:15 seems to require such a phrase to divide the Jeremiah text into two sayings. Others understand "the Lord says" of Heb 10:16 (here rendered *says the Lord*) as outside the quotation and consider Heb 10:16b as part of the second saying. Two ancient versions and a number of minuscules introduce the words "then he said" or a similar expression at the beginning of Heb 10:17.

**10:19–39** Practical consequences from these reflections on the priesthood and the sacrifice of Christ should make it clear that Christians may now have direct and confident access to God through the person of Jesus (Heb 10:19–20), who rules God's house as high priest (Heb 10:21). They should approach God with sincerity and faith, in the knowledge that through baptism their sins have been remitted (Heb 10:22), reminding themselves of the hope they expressed in Christ at that event (Heb 10:23). They are to encourage one another to Christian love and activity (Heb 10:24), not refusing, no matter what the reason, to participate in the community's assembly, especially in view of the parousia (Heb 10:25; cf. 1 Thes 4:13–18). If refusal to participate in the assembly indicates rejection of Christ, no sacrifice exists to obtain forgiveness for so great a sin (Heb 10:26); only the dreadful judgment of God remains (Heb 10:27). For if violation of the Mosaic law could be punished by death, how much worse will be the punishment of those who have turned their backs on Christ by despising his sacrifice and disregarding the gifts of the holy Spirit (Heb 10:28–29). Judgment belongs to the Lord, and he enacts it by his living presence (Heb 10:30–31). There was a time when the spirit of their community caused them to welcome and share their sufferings (Heb 10:32–34). To revitalize that spirit

is to share in the courage of the Old Testament prophets (cf. Is 26:20; Heb 2:3–4), the kind of courage that must distinguish the faith of the Christian (Heb 10:35–39).

**10:20** *Through the veil, that is, his flesh*: the term *flesh* is used pejoratively. As the temple veil kept people from entering the Holy of Holies (it was rent at Christ's death, Mk 15:38), so the flesh of Jesus constituted an obstacle to approaching God.

**10:21** *The house of God*: this refers back to Heb 3:6, "we are his house."

**10:22** *With our hearts sprinkled clean from an evil conscience*: as in Heb 9:13 (see note there), the sprinkling motif refers to the Mosaic rite of cleansing from ritual impurity. This could produce only an external purification, whereas sprinkling with the blood of Christ (Heb 9:14) cleanses the *conscience*. *Washed in pure water*: baptism is elsewhere referred to as a washing; cf. 1 Cor 6:11; Eph 5:26.

**10:25** *Our assembly*: the liturgical *assembly* of the Christian community, probably for the celebration of the Eucharist. *The day*: this designation for the parousia also occurs in the Pauline letters, e.g., Rom 2:16; 1 Cor 3:13; 1 Thes 5:2.

**10:26** *If we sin deliberately*: verse 29 indicates that the author is here thinking of apostasy; cf. Heb 3:12; 6:4–8.

**10:28** *Rejects the law of Moses*: evidently not any sin against the law, but idolatry. Dt 17:2–7 prescribed capital punishment for idolaters who were convicted on the testimony of two or three witnesses.

---

*
| | |
|---|---|
| **10:12–13** Ps 110:1. | **10:22** 9:13–14; Ez 36:25; |
| **10:14** 9:28. | 1 Cor 6:11; Ti 3:5; |
| **10:16** 8:10; Jer 31:33. | 1 Pt 3:21. |
| **10:17** 8:12; Jer 31:34. | **10:23** 3:1, 6; 4:14; 1 Cor |
| **10:19** 3:6; 4:16; 6:19–20; | 10:13. |
| Eph 1:7; 3:12. | **10:25** Rom 13:12; 1 Cor |
| **10:20** Jn 14:6 / Heb | 3:13. |
| 6:19–20; 9:8, 11–12; | **10:26** 3:12; 6:4–8. |
| Mt 27:51; Mk 15:38; | **10:27** 10:31; 9:27; Is 26:11 |
| Lk 23:45. | LXX; Zep 1:18. |
| **10:21** 3:6. | **10:28** Dt 17:6. |

consecrated, and insults the spirit of grace? * ³⁰ We know the one who said:

"Vengeance is mine; I will repay,"

and again:

"The Lord will judge his people." *

³¹ It is a fearful thing to fall into the hands of the living God. *

³² Remember the days past when, after you had been enlightened, † you endured a great contest of suffering. * ³³ At times you were publicly exposed to abuse and affliction; at other times you associated yourselves with those so treated. * ³⁴ You even joined in the sufferings of those in prison and joyfully accepted the confiscation of your property, knowing that you had a better and lasting possession. * ³⁵ Therefore, do not throw away your confidence; it will have great recompense. * ³⁶ You need endurance to do the will of God and receive what he has promised. *

³⁷ "For, after just a brief moment, †
　　he who is to come shall come;
　　he shall not delay. *

³⁸ But my just one shall live by faith,
　　and if he draws back I take no
　　　　pleasure in him." *

³⁹ We are not among those who draw back and perish, but among those who have faith and will possess life.

## V. EXAMPLES, DISCIPLINE, DISOBEDIENCE

# 11
† **Faith of the Ancients.** ¹ Faith is the realization of what is hoped for and evidence † of things not seen. * ² Because of it the ancients were well attested. ³ * By faith we understand that the universe was ordered by the word of God, † so that what is visible came into being through the invisible. ⁴ † By faith Abel offered to God a sacrifice greater than Cain's. Through this he was attested to be righteous, God bearing witness to his gifts, and through this, though dead, he still speaks. * ⁵ By faith Enoch was taken up so that he should not see death, and "he was found no more because God had taken him." Before he was taken up, he was attested to have pleased God. * ⁶ † But without faith it is impossible to please him, * for anyone who approaches God

---

**10:32** *After you had been enlightened*: "enlightenment" is an ancient metaphor for baptism (cf. Eph 5:14; Jn 9:11), but see Heb 6:4 and the note there.

**10:37–38** In support of his argument, the author uses Hb 2:3–4 in a wording almost identical with the text of the Codex Alexandrinus of the Septuagint but with the first and second lines of Heb 10:4 inverted. He introduces it with a few words from Is 26:20: *after just a brief moment*. Note the Pauline usage of Hb 2:4 in Rom 1:17; Gal 3:11.

**11:1–40** This chapter draws upon the people and events of the Old Testament to paint an inspiring portrait of religious faith, firm and unyielding in the face of any obstacles that confront it. These pages rank among the most eloquent and lofty to be found in the Bible. They expand the theme announced in Heb 6:12, to which the author now returns (Heb 10:39). The material of this chapter is developed chronologically. Heb 11:3–7 draw upon the first nine chapters of Genesis (Gn 1–9); Heb 11:8–22, upon the period of the patriarchs; Heb 11:23–31, upon the time of Moses; Heb 11:32–38, upon the history of the judges, the prophets, and the Maccabean martyrs. The author gives the most extensive description of faith provided in the New Testament, though his interest does not lie in a technical, theological definition. In view of the needs of his audience he describes what authentic faith does, not what it is in itself. Through faith God guarantees the blessings to be hoped for from him, providing evidence in the gift of faith that what he promises will eventually come to pass (Heb 11:1). Because they accepted in faith God's guarantee of the future, the biblical personages discussed in Heb 11:3–38 were themselves commended by God (Heb 11:2). Christians have even greater reason to remain firm in faith since they, unlike the Old Testament men and women of faith, have perceived the beginning of God's fulfillment of his messianic promises (Heb 11:39–40).

**11:1** *Faith is the realization…evidence*: the author is not attempting a precise definition. There is dispute about the mean-

ing of the Greek words *hypostasis* and *elenchos*, here translated *realization* and *evidence*, respectively. *Hypostasis* usually means "substance," "being" (as translated in Heb 1:3), or "reality" (as translated in Heb 3:14); here it connotes something more subjective, and so *realization* has been chosen rather than "assurance" (RSV). *Elenchos*, usually "proof," is used here in an objective sense and so translated *evidence* rather than the transferred sense of "(inner) conviction" (RSV).

**11:3** *By faith…God*: this verse does not speak of the faith of the Old Testament men and women but is in the first person plural. Hence it seems out of place in the sequence of thought.

**11:4** The "Praise of the Ancestors" in Sir 44:1–50:21 gives a similar list of heroes. The Cain and Abel narrative in Gn 4:1–16 does not mention Abel's faith. It says, however, that God "looked with favor on Abel and his offering" (Gn 4:4); in view of Heb 11:6 the author probably understood God's favor to have been activated by Abel's faith. *Though dead, he still speaks*: possibly because his blood "cries out to me from the soil" (Gn 4:10), but more probably a way of saying that the repeated story of Abel provides ongoing witness to faith.

**11:6** One must believe not only that God *exists* but that he is concerned about human conduct; the Old Testament defines folly as the denial of this truth; cf. Ps 52:2.

---

**10:29** 6:6.
**10:30** Dt 32:35, 36; Rom 12:19.
**10:31** 10:27; Mt 10:28; Lk 12:4–5.
**10:32** 6:4.
**10:33** 1 Cor 4:9.
**10:34** 13:3; Mt 6:19–20; Lk 12:33–34.
**10:35** 4:16.
**10:36** Lk 21:19.

**10:37** Is 26:20; Heb 2:3.
**10:38** Heb 2:4; Rom 1:17; Gal 3:11.
**11:1** 1:3; 3:14; Rom 8:24; 2 Cor 4:18.
**11:3** Gn 1:3; Ps 33:6; Wis 9:1; Jn 1:3.
**11:4** 12:24; Gn 4:4, 10.
**11:5** Gn 5:24; Sir 44:16.
**11:6** Wis 4:10.

must believe that he exists and that he rewards those who seek him. [7] By faith Noah, warned about what was not yet seen, with reverence built an ark for the salvation of his household. Through this he condemned the world and inherited the righteousness that comes through faith.*

[8] By faith Abraham obeyed when he was called to go out to a place that he was to receive as an inheritance; he went out, not knowing where he was to go.* [9] By faith he sojourned in the promised land as in a foreign country, dwelling in tents with Isaac and Jacob, heirs of the same promise;* [10] for he was looking forward to the city with foundations, whose architect and maker is God.* [11] By faith he received power to generate, even though he was past the normal age—and Sarah herself was sterile—for he thought that the one who had made the promise was trustworthy.* [12] So it was that there came forth from one man, himself as good as dead, descendants as numerous as the stars in the sky and as countless as the sands on the seashore.*

[13] All these died in faith. They did not receive what had been promised but saw it and greeted it from afar and acknowledged themselves to be strangers and aliens on earth,* [14] for those who speak thus show that they are seeking a homeland. [15] If they had been thinking of the land from which they had come, they would have had opportunity to return. [16] But now they desire a better homeland, a heavenly one. Therefore, God is not ashamed to be called their God, for he has prepared a city for them.*

[17] By faith Abraham, when put to the test, offered up Isaac, and he who had received the promises was ready to offer his only son,* [18] of whom it was said, "Through Isaac descendants shall bear your name."* [19]† He reasoned that God was able to raise even from the dead,* and he received Isaac back as a symbol. [20] By faith regarding things still to come Isaac† blessed Jacob and Esau.* [21] By faith Jacob, when dying, blessed each of the sons of Joseph and "bowed in worship, leaning on the top of his staff."* [22] By faith Joseph, near the end of his life, spoke of the Exodus of the Israelites and gave instructions about his bones.*

[23]* By faith Moses was hidden by his parents for three months after his birth, because they saw that he was a beautiful child, and they were not afraid of the king's edict. [24]† By faith Moses, when he had grown up, refused to be known as the son of Pharaoh's daughter;* [25] he chose to be ill-treated along with the people of God rather than enjoy the fleeting pleasure of sin. [26] He considered the reproach of the Anointed greater wealth than the treasures of Egypt, for he was looking to the recompense. [27] By faith he left Egypt, not fearing the king's fury, for he persevered as if seeing the one who is invisible.* [28] By faith he kept the Passover and sprinkled the blood, that the Destroyer of the firstborn might not touch them.* [29] By faith they crossed the Red Sea as if it were dry land, but when the Egyptians attempted it they were drowned.* [30] By faith the walls of Jericho fell after being encircled for seven days.* [31] By faith Rahab the harlot did not perish with the disobedient, for she had received the spies in peace.*

[32] What more shall I say? I have not time to tell of Gideon, Barak, Samson, Jephthah, of David and Samuel and the prophets,* [33] who by faith conquered kingdoms, did what was righteous, obtained the promises; they closed the mouths of lions,* [34] put out raging fires, escaped the devouring sword; out of weakness they were made powerful, became strong in battle, and turned back foreign invaders.*

---

**11:19** *As a symbol*: Isaac's "return from death" is seen as a *symbol* of Christ's resurrection. Others understand the words *en parabolē* to mean "in figure," i.e., the word *dead* is used figuratively of Isaac, since he did not really die. But in the one other place that *parabolē* occurs in Hebrews, it means symbol (Heb 9:9).

**11:20–22** Each of these three patriarchs, Isaac, Jacob, and Joseph, had faith in the future fulfillment of God's promise and renewed this faith when near death.

**11:24–27** The reason given for Moses' departure from Egypt differs from the account in Ex 2:11–15. The author also gives a christological interpretation of his decision to share the trials of his people.

---

**11:7** Gn 6:8–22; Sir 44:17–18; Mt 24:37–39; Lk 17:26–27; 1 Pt 3:20;

2 Pt 2:5.

**11:8** Gn 12:1–4; 15:7–21; Sir 44:19–22;

Acts 7:2–8; Rom 4:16–22.

**11:9** Gn 12:8; 13:12; 23:4; 26:3; 35:27.

**11:10** 12:22; 13:14; Rev 21:10–22.

**11:11** Gn 17:19; 21:2; Rom 4:19–21 / 1 Cor 10:13.

**11:12** Gn 15:5; 22:17; 32:13; Ex 32:13; Dt 10:22; Dn 3:36 LXX.

**11:13** Gn 23:4; Ps 39:13.

**11:16** 13:14; Ex 3:6.

**11:17** Gn 22:1–10; Sir 44:20; 1 Mc 2:52; Jas 2:21.

**11:18** Gn 21:12 LXX; Rom 9:7.

**11:19** Rom 4:16–22.

**11:20** Gn 27:27–40.

**11:21** Gn 27:38–40; 47:31 LXX; 48:15–16.

**11:22** Gn 50:24–25.

**11:23** Ex 2:2; Acts 7:20.

**11:24–25** Ex 2:10–15; Acts 7:23–29.

**11:27** Ex 2:15; Acts 7:29.

**11:28** Ex 12:21–23; Wis 18:25; 1 Cor 10:10.

**11:29** Ex 14:22–28.

**11:30** Jos 6:12–21.

**11:31** Jos 2:1–21; 6:22–25; Jas 2:25.

**11:32** Jgs 4:6–22; 6:11–8:32; 11:1–12:7.

**11:33** Dn 6:23.

**11:34** Dn 3:22–25, 49–50.

35 Women received back their dead through resurrection. Some were tortured and would not accept deliverance, in order to obtain a better resurrection.* 36 Others endured mockery, scourging, even chains and imprisonment.* 37 They were stoned, sawed in two, put to death at sword's point; they went about in skins of sheep or goats, needy, afflicted, tormented.* 38 The world was not worthy of them. They wandered about in deserts and on mountains, in caves and in crevices in the earth.*

39 Yet all these, though approved because of their faith, did not receive what had been promised. 40 God had foreseen something better for us, so that without us they should not be made perfect.†

**12** **God Our Father.**† 1 Therefore, since we are surrounded by so great a cloud of witnesses, let us rid ourselves of every burden and sin that clings to us† and persevere in running the race that lies before us 2 while keeping our eyes fixed on Jesus, the leader and perfecter of faith. For the sake of the joy that lay before him he endured the cross, despising its shame, and has taken his seat at the right of the throne of God.* 3 Consider how he endured such opposition from sinners, in order that you may not grow weary and lose heart. 4 In your struggle against sin you have not yet resisted to the point of shedding blood. 5 You have also forgotten the exhortation addressed to you as sons:

"My son, do not disdain the discipline
of the Lord*
or lose heart when reproved by him;

6     for whom the Lord loves, he disciplines;
he scourges every son he
acknowledges."

7 Endure your trials as "discipline"; God treats you as sons. For what "son" is there whom his father does not discipline?* 8 If you are without discipline, in which all have shared, you are not sons but bastards. 9 Besides this, we have had our earthly fathers to discipline us, and we respected them. Should we not [then] submit all the more to the Father of spirits and live?* 10 They disciplined us for a short time as seemed right to them, but he does so for our benefit, in order that we may share his holiness. 11 At the time, all discipline seems a cause not for joy but for pain, yet later it brings the peaceful fruit of righteousness to those who are trained by it.*

12 So strengthen your drooping hands and your weak knees.* 13 Make straight paths for your feet, that what is lame may not be dislocated but healed.*

**Penalties of Disobedience.** 14* Strive for peace with everyone, and for that holiness without which no one will see the Lord. 15† See to it that no one be deprived of the grace of God, that no bitter root spring up and cause trouble, through which many may become defiled,* 16 that no one be an immoral or profane person like Esau, who sold his birthright for a single meal.* 17 For you know that later, when he wanted to inherit his father's blessing, he was rejected because he found no opportunity to change his mind, even though he sought the blessing with tears.*

18† You have not approached that which

---

† **11:40** *So that without us they should not be made perfect*: the heroes of the Old Testament obtained their recompense only after the saving work of Christ had been accomplished. Thus they already enjoy what Christians who are still struggling do not yet possess in its fullness.
**12:1–13** Christian life is to be inspired not only by the Old Testament men and women of faith (Heb 12:1) but above all by Jesus. As the architect of Christian faith, he had himself to endure the cross before receiving the glory of his triumph (Heb 12:2). Reflection on his sufferings should give his followers courage to continue the struggle, if necessary even to the shedding of blood (Heb 12:3–4). Christians should regard their own sufferings as the affectionate correction of the Lord, who loves them as a father loves his children.
**12:1** *That clings to us*: the meaning is uncertain, since the Greek word *euperistatos*, translated *cling*, occurs only here. The papyrus P46 and one minuscule read *euperispastos*, "easily distracting," which also makes good sense.
**12:15–17** Esau serves as an example in two ways: his *profane* attitude illustrates the danger of apostasy, and his inability to se-

cure a blessing afterward illustrates the impossibility of repenting after falling away (see Heb 6:4–6).
**12:18–29** As a final appeal for adherence to Christian teaching, the two covenants, of Moses and of Christ, are compared. The Mosaic covenant, the author argues, is shown to have originated in fear of God and threats of divine punishment (Heb 12:18–21). The covenant in Christ gives us direct access to God (Heb 12:22), makes us members of the Christian community, God's children, a sanctified people (Heb 12:23), who have Jesus

* **11:35** 1 Kgs 17:17–24; 2 Kgs 4:18–37; 2 Mc 6:18–7:42.
**11:36** 2 Chr 36:16; Jer 20:2; 37:15.
**11:37** 2 Chr 24:21.
**11:38** 1 Mc 2:28–30.
**12:2** 2:10; Ps 110:1; Phil 2:6–8.
**12:5–6** Prv 3:11–12 / Dt 8:5; 1 Cor 11:32.
**12:7** Prv 13:24; Sir 30:1.
**12:9** Nm 16:22; 27:16 LXX.
**12:11** 2 Cor 4:17; Phil 1:11; Jas 3:18.
**12:12** Is 35:3; Sir 25:23; Jb 4:3–4.
**12:13** Prv 4:26 LXX.
**12:14** Rom 12:18; 14:19.
**12:15** Dt 29:18 (17 LXX).
**12:16** Gn 25:33.
**12:17** Gn 27:34–38.

could be touched†* and a blazing fire and gloomy darkness and storm ¹⁹and a trumpet blast and a voice speaking words such that those who heard begged that no message be further addressed to them,* ²⁰for they could not bear to hear the command: "If even an animal touches the mountain, it shall be stoned."* ²¹Indeed, so fearful was the spectacle that Moses said, "I am terrified and trembling."* ²²No, you have approached Mount Zion and the city of the living God, the heavenly Jerusalem, and countless angels in festal gathering,* ²³and the assembly of the firstborn enrolled in heaven,† and God the judge of all, and the spirits of the just made perfect,* ²⁴and Jesus, the mediator of a new covenant, and the sprinkled blood that speaks more eloquently† than that of Abel.*

²⁵See that you do not reject the one who speaks. For if they did not escape when they refused the one who warned them on earth, how much more in our case if we turn away from the one who warns from heaven.* ²⁶His voice shook the earth at that time, but now he has promised, "I will once more shake not only earth but heaven."* ²⁷That phrase, "once more," points to [the] removal of shaken, created things, so that what is unshaken may remain.* ²⁸Therefore, we who are receiving the unshakable kingdom should have gratitude, with which we should offer worship pleasing to God in reverence and awe.* ²⁹For our God is a consuming fire.*

## VI. FINAL EXHORTATION, BLESSING, GREETINGS

**13** ¹† Let mutual love continue. ²Do not neglect hospitality, for through it some have unknowingly entertained angels.* ³Be mindful of prisoners as if sharing their imprisonment, and of the ill-treated as of yourselves, for you also are in the body.* ⁴Let marriage be honored among all and the marriage bed be kept undefiled, for God will judge the immoral and adulterers.* ⁵Let your life be free from love of money but be content with what you have, for he has said, "I will never forsake you or abandon you."* ⁶Thus we may say with confidence:

> "The Lord is my helper,
> [and] I will not be afraid.
> What can anyone do to me?"*

⁷Remember your leaders who spoke the word of God to you. Consider the outcome of their way of life and imitate their faith. ⁸Jesus Christ is the same yesterday, today, and forever.*

⁹Do not be carried away by all kinds of strange teaching.† It is good to have our hearts strengthened by grace and not by foods, which do not benefit those who live by them.* ¹⁰We have an altar† from which those who serve the tabernacle have no right to eat. ¹¹The bodies of the animals whose blood the high priest brings into the sanctuary as a sin offering are

---

† as mediator to speak for us (Heb 12:24). Not to heed the voice of the risen Christ is a graver sin than the rejection of the word of Moses (Heb 12:25–26). Though Christians fall away, God's kingdom in Christ will remain and his justice will punish those guilty of deserting it (Heb 12:28–29).

**12:18** This remarkably beautiful passage contrasts two great assemblies of people: that of the Israelites gathered at Mount Sinai for the sealing of the old covenant and the promulgation of the Mosaic law, and that of the followers of Jesus gathered at *Mount Zion, the heavenly Jerusalem*, the assembly of the *new covenant*. This latter scene, marked by the presence of *countless angels* and of *Jesus* with his redeeming *blood*, is reminiscent of the celestial liturgies of the Book of Revelation.

**12:23** *The assembly of the firstborn enrolled in heaven*: this expression may refer to the angels of Heb 12:22, or to the heroes of the Old Testament (see Heb 11), or to the entire assembly of the new covenant.

**12:24** *Speaks more eloquently*: the blood of Abel, the first human blood to be shed, is contrasted with that of Jesus. Abel's blood cried out from the earth for vengeance, but the blood of Jesus has opened the way for everyone, providing cleansing and access to God (Heb 10:19).

**13:1–16** After recommendations on social and moral matters (Heb 13:1–6), the letter turns to doctrinal issues. The fact that the original leaders are dead should not cause the recipients of this letter to lose their faith (Heb 13:7), for Christ still lives and he remains always the same (Heb 13:8). They must not rely for their

personal sanctification on regulations concerning foods (Heb 13:9), nor should they entertain the notion that Judaism and Christianity can be intermingled (Heb 13:10; cf. notes on Gal 2:11–14; 2:15–21). As Jesus died separated from his own people, so must the Christian community remain apart from the religious doctrines of Judaism (Heb 13:11–14). Christ must be the heart and center of the community (Heb 13:15–16).

**13:9** *Strange teaching*: this doctrine about *foods* probably refers to the Jewish food laws; in view of Heb 13:10, however, the author may be thinking of the Mosaic sacrificial banquets.

**13:10** *We have an altar*: this does not refer to the Eucharist, which is never clearly mentioned in Hebrews, but to the sacrifice of Christ.

---

| | |
|---|---|
| **12:18** Ex 19:12–14; Dt 4:11; 5:22–23. | **12:27** Is 66:22; Mt 24:35; Mk 13:31; Lk 21:33. |
| **12:19** Ex 19:16, 19; 20:18–19. | **12:28** Dn 7:14, 18 / Rom 1:9. |
| **12:20** Ex 19:12–13. | **12:29** Dt 4:24; Is 33:14. |
| **12:21** Dt 9:19. | **13:2** Gn 18:3; 19:2–3; Jgs 6:11–22; Tb 5:4. |
| **12:22** Gal 4:26; Rev 21:2. | **13:3** Mt 25:36. |
| **12:23** Lk 10:20; Rev 5:11. | **13:4** 1 Cor 5:13; Eph 5:5. |
| **12:24** 7:22; 8:6; 9:15 / 11:4; Gn 4:10. | **13:5** Dt 31:6, 8; Jos 1:5. |
| **12:25** Ex 20:19. | **13:6** Ps 27:1–3; 118:6. |
| **12:26** Ex 19:18; Jgs 5:4–5; Ps 68:9; Hg 2:6. | **13:8** 1:12; 7:24; Rev 1:17. |
| | **13:9** Rom 14:17; 1 Cor 8:8; Eph 4:14; Col 2:16. |

burned outside the camp.* [12] Therefore, Jesus also suffered outside the gate, to consecrate the people by his own blood.* [13] Let us then go to him outside the camp, bearing the reproach that he bore. [14] For here we have no lasting city, but we seek the one that is to come.* [15] Through him [then] let us continually offer God a sacrifice of praise, that is, the fruit of lips that confess his name.* [16] Do not neglect to do good and to share what you have; God is pleased by sacrifices of that kind.*

[17] † Obey your leaders and defer to them, for they keep watch over you and will have to give an account, that they may fulfill their task with joy and not with sorrow, for that would be of no advantage to you.

[18] Pray for us, for we are confident that we have a clear conscience, wishing to act rightly in every respect. [19] I especially ask for your prayers that I may be restored to you very soon.

[20] † May the God of peace, who brought up from the dead the great shepherd of the sheep by the blood of the eternal covenant, Jesus our Lord,* [21] furnish you with all that is good, that you may do his will. May he carry out in you what is pleasing to him through Jesus Christ, to whom be glory forever [and ever]. Amen.

[22] Brothers, I ask you to bear with this message of encouragement, for I have written to you rather briefly. [23] I must let you know that our brother Timothy has been set free. If he comes soon, I shall see you together with him.* [24] Greetings to all your leaders and to all the holy ones. Those from Italy send you greetings. [25] Grace be with all of you.*

---

† **13:17–25** Recommending obedience to the leaders of the community, the author asks for prayers (Heb 13:17–19). The letter concludes with a blessing (Heb 13:20–21), a final request for the acceptance of its message (Heb 13:22), information regarding Timothy (Heb 13:23), and general greetings (Heb 13:24–25).

**13:20–21** These verses constitute one of the most beautiful blessings in the New Testament. The resurrection of Jesus is presupposed throughout Hebrews, since it is included in the author's frequently expressed idea of his exaltation, but this is the only place where it is explicitly mentioned.

---

**13:11** Ex 29:14; Lv 16:27.
**13:12** Mt 21:39; Mk 12:8; Lk 20:15; Jn 19:17.
**13:14** 11:10, 14.
**13:15** Hos 14:3.
**13:16** Phil 4:18.
**13:20** Is 63:11; Zec 9:11; Jn 10:11; Acts 2:24; Rom 15:33.
**13:23** Acts 16:1.
**13:25** Ti 3:15.

HEB

# Introduction to the Catholic Letters and the Letter to the Hebrews

## Mary Katherine Birge, SSJ

The collection of New Testament writings entitled the "Catholic Letters" (1 and 2 Peter, James, Jude, 1, 2, and 3 John, and the Letter to the Hebrews) represents an expression of early Christianity distinct from that encountered in the Pauline letters.[1] These works are difficult to categorize: they are not all letters (e.g., Hebrews and 1 John), and even when they do follow the form of a letter, sometimes their contents suggest a purpose broader than that associated with a simple letter (e.g., James). With the exception of Hebrews and 1 John, each letter has a sender's name or title attached to it, yet each one's authorial provenance is unsure.[2] Due to such complicating factors, and the relative anonymity of each letter's recipient, scholars have had difficulty reaching a consensus regarding the audience or date of composition for any of the letters.

For much of the twentieth century, scholars primarily used the historical-critical method when studying the Bible; because of that focus on historical issues, these letters were often overlooked. In the late twentieth and early twenty-first centuries, methods of biblical scholarship expanded widely beyond a historical lens; as a result, scholars began to look at the Catholic Letters with new eyes and discovered a treasure trove of material produced by early Christianity.

The collection's title "catholic" has variously been construed in Christian history as: (1) pointing to the letters' "general" or "universal" Christian audience since, with the exception of 1 Peter, they do not name the location of their recipients;[3] (2) indicating the letters are universally or widely read by the Christian community; or (3) denoting nascent church structures and traditions absent from (presumed) earlier and more loosely organized Pauline churches. The last reason is not based on evidence from the texts themselves, and so is insupportable. The first reason, while initially appealing, becomes less persuasive after careful reading of the texts reveals that the letters were indeed written for specific audiences, even though their identity remains unknown. The remaining argument for titling the collection "catholic" is accurate in that all Christians accept these letters as part of the New Testament canon, even though they may not read them as frequently as other books and letters of the New Testament.

All these letters, except for 1 Peter and 1 John, were accepted only gradually by the early church into the New Testament canon. Much of the reluctance sprang from a suspicion that their authors were not the actual apostolic witnesses their prescripts indicated. Eastern Christianity seemed to accept these letters into the canon more readily than Western Christianity, as indicated by Origen (d. 253), who cited them as Scripture. By the late fourth and early fifth centuries, with support for them

---

1. The Letter to the Hebrews was not among those letters that fourth-century church historian Eusebius labeled "catholic" (*Ecclesiastical History* 2.23.25), but it is included here because, like them, it is not written by Paul nor is its intended audience known. This Study Bible, however, follows the NAB arrangement of including Hebrews in the Pauline corpus; thus the Anselm and NAB introductions to Hebrews and the Letter to the Hebrews appear just prior to these Catholic Letters.

2. The Letter to the Hebrews is anonymous, but some Christian tradition associated it with Paul, perhaps on the strength of the reference to Timothy (a co-worker of Paul) in 13:23. Scholars now concur that Paul did not write Hebrews.

3. While 1 Peter does name its target audience, this "audience" consists of small, local Christian communities in five different regions widely scattered across ancient Asia Minor (cf. 1:1). Thus one could argue that 1 Peter was written for a general audience.

as Scripture from both Augustine and Jerome, most hurdles to their acceptance in Western and Eastern churches had been surmounted.

# The Letter to the Hebrews

The Letter to the Hebrews is not a letter, its author is unknown, and scholars continue to argue whether early Jewish Christians were its intended audience. The "letter" does not begin with the standard greeting with which all Greco-Roman letters begin (see 1:1–2), although it does conclude with a few standard remarks found in many early Christian letters: words of encouragement, mention of someone's name who is known to the audience, a greeting from some who are absent from the community, and a very brief final prayer or blessing (13:22–25). Its title "To the Hebrews" was most likely added after its composition and probably reflects early efforts to identify its audience from the contents. The work alternates throughout between an explanation about Christ and an exhortation that supports the explanation, so that the letter's genre resembles a sermon or homily whose purpose is a "message of encouragement" (13:22). The writer takes a significant number of quotations from the Old Testament and uses them in two ways: he constructs his argument based on the quotations themselves, and then uses them to advance the argument forcefully.

The writer of Hebrews begins immediately in the prologue (Heb 1:1–4) to lay out his argument and how he will pursue it. He starts with how God has communicated in the past to humanity through the prophets only "in partial . . . ways," and then moves to proclaim how God has now communicated through his Son and heir, who possesses the characteristics of Wisdom (Prv 8:22–31; Wis 7:22, 25–27; 9:2, 9). In Heb 1:1–4 (all one sentence in Greek) the writer establishes continuity between God's speech in the past and God's speech in the present through his Son. But he also establishes discontinuity between God's utterance through the many Old Testament prophets long ago and God's final, definitive utterance through the one agent of his Son.

In the Platonic philosophical worldview of the writer and audience of Hebrews, many agents speaking multiple ways would imply some sort of deficiency in their activity (cf. Heb 10:1), whereas the absolute revelation of God's word through a single actor would imply the opposite. In addition, the adequacy with which an agent bears and interprets the whole divine word to humanity depends as much upon the bearer's ability to share fully in humanity's experience and understand it as upon his capacity to participate in and comprehend God's spirit. The author of Hebrews argues that the prophets possessed only the experience of being human, and so their communication of God's speech had naturally been incomplete and imperfect. The Son, however, embodies both capacities, and so the writer can repeatedly claim that the Son is the only agent who can fully and completely mediate the new covenant between humanity and God (cf. 9:15). The Son is the one who will purify sins as high priest because he has been raised up to sit at God's right hand (cf. 8:1–6).

As already noted, dating the work and identifying the location of its audience prove difficult. Clement of Rome quotes from Hebrews in his first letter (ca. 96 CE), which provides the latest possible date for composition. There is, however, no equivalent evidence to establish its earliest possible date, except that it has to have been written some years after Jesus' death, which most scholars agree occurred sometime around 30 CE. On the basis of internal evidence, some have proposed that Hebrews was written in response to the suffering of Jewish Christians expelled from Rome by Emperor Claudius in 49 CE (cf. Heb 10:32–34). Others suggest that it was directed to Jewish Christians in Rome who were experiencing persecution, fear, and loss following the destruction of the Jerusalem Temple in 70 CE, and possibly were contemplating abandoning Christianity altogether (cf. 2:1; 4:14; 6:4–8; 10:23, 26–31; 11:1–40). Still others think that it was directed to a mixed community of Jewish and Gentile Christians at Alexandria.[4]

---

4. Paul Ellingworth, *The Epistle to the Hebrews*, New International Greek Testament Commentary (Grand Rapids, MI: Eerdmans, 1993), 28.

# The Letter of James

The Letter of James begins, "James, a slave of God and of the Lord Jesus Christ, to the twelve tribes in the dispersion, greetings" (Jas 1:1). There are three people named James in the New Testament to whom this letter can be attributed, but only one makes sense as its author, either in actuality or pseudonymously. The Synoptic Gospels count two persons with the name of James among the Twelve who make up Jesus' inner circle (Mt 10:2–3; Mk 3:17–18; Lk 6:14–15), but James, son of Zebedee, was beheaded by Herod Agrippa I in 44 CE (too early for such a letter to have been written by him; Acts 12:2), and James, son of Alphaeus, is never mentioned after the Synoptic Gospels, making him an unlikely candidate for the authorship of this work. That leaves James, a relative of Jesus (Mt 13:55; Mk 6:3), often called "brother of the Lord" (e.g., Gal 1:19), who became leader of the Jerusalem community (Acts 15:13–21; 21:17–26; Gal 2:9, 12) after Peter escaped from Herod Agrippa I's prison (Acts 12:17–19) and whose death by stoning (ca. 62 CE under the direction of the high priest Ananus the Younger) is recounted by Josephus (*Jewish Antiquities* 20.200). Anyone in contemporary Western society who is called "brother of" someone else is presumed to share the same parentage with that person. In the ancient Mediterranean world, however, as often is true in societies of contemporary Africa, members of an extended kinship network are called "brother" or "sister" to indicate they belong to the same extended family group. Mostly likely James bore the title "brother" in this extended sense.[5]

Whoever the writer of this letter is, he is a Christian Jew writing to other Christian Jews who live outside the traditional boundaries of ancient Israel, as indicated by the salutation: "to the twelve tribes in the dispersion, greetings" (Jas 1:1b). The letter begins with the requisite Hellenistic epistolary opening, yet does not conform to the usual elements associated with an actual letter, nor does it end with the standard closing expected of a letter. The body of the letter is comprised of several different literary styles that reflect its author's Jewish identity, as well as his familiarity with a number of Hellenistic rhetorical forms. The author recalls much of Old Testament Wisdom literature's moral exhortation and teaching when he employs pithy maxims and proverbs (e.g., 1:12; 2:26; 3:3–5, 12) to instruct his audience in right conduct. He also draws on elements from the rhetorical genre of diatribe, which is not an attack, but rather a didactic conversation usually consisting of a thesis followed by a series of rhetorical questions, examples, paradoxes, objections, and answering of objections. The reader encounters the densest collection of these diatribal characteristics in 2:1–7, 14–17; 4:1–5, 13–16. Yet the author's use of these two literary styles seems to be in service to another rhetorical form whose function reveals the purpose of the letter, i.e., moral exhortation to pursue a specific occupation or vocation because it is superior to another. The whole Letter of James urges its readers to adopt behaviors and attitudes counter to prevailing societal norms that privilege wealth and status (e.g., 1:9–11; 2:2–4; 3:13–18). The author writes to convince his readers to engage in conduct and cultivate attitudes requisite among disciples of Jesus ("the noble name that was invoked over you," 2:7). Since he writes to persuade his readers to pursue a specific profession or vocation, his writing constitutes a form of moral exhortation.

# The First Letter of Peter

Irenaeus (ca. 180 CE) is the first Christian author to cite 1 Peter by name, but *1 Clement* (ca. 96) demonstrates through common use of words and themes that its author, Clement of Rome, probably possessed knowledge of 1 Peter. The author of 2 Peter also knows of the existence of 1 Peter (cf. 2 Pt 3:1). Polycarp in *To the Philippians* (before 140) directly cites 1 Peter at least fourteen times, and Clement of Alexandria (d. 215) quotes from it frequently. It is no surprise, then, that Eusebius accepts it without question as one of the genuine apostolic writings from earliest Christianity (*Ecclesiastical History* 3.3.1). The Syriac Church,

---

5. James Hartin, *James*, Sacra Pagina 14 (Collegeville, MN: Liturgical Press, 2003), 16–17.

however, did not accept it as a canonical book until the fifth century.

The majority of contemporary scholars do not believe that Simon Peter wrote 1 Peter. John H. Elliot summarizes the reasons against Petrine authorship: (1) Its language usage—classical Greek word choice, style, and use of rhetoric—reveals one of the most linguistically sophisticated pieces of writing in the New Testament and so makes it most improbable that a first-century Galilean fisherman would have been its author. (2) The author quotes the Old Testament according to the LXX, as opposed to the Aramaic translations of the Old Testament (Targums) that would have been more familiar to an uneducated Galilean worker like Simon Peter (cf. Acts 4:13). (3) The letter does not refer directly to any specific teaching of Jesus, nor does it mention any experience from Jesus' life and ministry that Peter, one of Jesus' closest associates, would have shared with him. (4) The writer's use of the title "fellow presbyter," sometimes translated "co-elder" (1 Pt 5:1), is unique to this letter; had this been the historical Peter, such an expression would have been more widely used. Also, the assertion to be a "witness to the sufferings of Christ" (5:1) does not claim eyewitness status, but rather designates its bearer as one who gives witness to Christ's sufferings by being a disciple. (5) If Peter had written this letter from Rome, it would have been written when Paul was in Rome as well, yet it is most strange that Peter would have written a letter to various Christian communities that he had not visited, but which were personally well-known to Paul, without including some mention of Paul.[6]

It is likely that 1 Peter is a pseudonymous letter written after Peter's death during the 64–65 persecution of Christians in Rome by Nero. The name "Babylon" (cf. 1 Pt 5:13) is a code word for Rome used by Christians and Jews after the Romans destroyed Jerusalem and the Temple during the Jewish War (66–70 CE), as the Babylonians had done many years before. It is possible, then, that there was a "Petrine circle" in Rome that survived the persecutions and sent the letter out under Peter's name some

time after 70 CE to small, rural, mostly Gentile Christian communities scattered throughout Asia Minor (cf. 1:1). Christians are a small minority community which, because of their monotheistic beliefs and practice, stand out as alien, bizarre, and even dangerous to the larger, polytheistic society, which views failure to worship the local and imperial gods as a threat to public welfare and safety. These Christian communities have begun experiencing confusion, fear, and doubt about following Christ because of painful scorn and oppression directed against them by mainstream society. First Peter addresses the questions raised by their pain and suffering.

# The Second Letter of Peter

The acceptance of 2 Peter into the New Testament canon came late and with great hesitation from early Christian commentators. Christian writers practically disregard it (allusions to it by Clement, Cyprian, and Irenaeus are uncertain) until Origen (d. 253) notes it and its debated authorship. Eastern Christianity accepted it more easily than the West, and it was not until Athanasius included it as part of the canon in his *Thirty-Ninth Festal Letter* (367) that Western Christianity began to accept it. Jerome acknowledged that the radically differing literary and theological styles of 1 and 2 Peter had led earlier Christian authors to dispute the possibility that Simon Peter was the author of 2 Peter and, on those grounds, to reject it as unfit for the New Testament canon. Nevertheless, Jerome asserted that both works originated with Simon Peter; he attributed their literary and theological differences to the different secretaries Peter employed while writing them. As with the letter from Jude, the Syriac Church did not accept 2 Peter in the canon until the sixth century. While contemporary scholars continue to debate whether Simon Peter was the author of 1 Peter, almost all agree that he was not the author of 2 Peter. But if Peter did not write 2 Peter, who did?

Most commentators accept that the writer of 2 Peter was a Christian Hellenized Jew. They say Christian because of his frequent

6. John H. Elliott, *1 Peter,* Anchor Bible 37B (New York: Doubleday, 2000), 120–21.

use of phrases like "our Lord and savior Jesus Christ" and his promotion of Christianity; a Jew because of his frequent reference to figures and events from the Hebrew Scriptures, and because of the format of farewell discourse he chooses for the letter; and, finally, Hellenized because of his knowledge and use of elaborate Greek syntax and rhetoric, Greek philosophical ideas, and the breadth of his Greek vocabulary (he employs the highest number of Greek words not found elsewhere in the New Testament). He writes to a Gentile Christian community that has been visited by Gentile Christian teachers who are teaching a type of Christianity that is very attractive to other Gentile Christians, especially those newly converted ("those who have barely escaped from people who live in error," 2 Pt 2:18). The visiting teachers have derided their hope in Jesus' return and a final judgment (3:3–4) and promoted behaviors and attitudes reflective of Gentile values rather than Christian ethics (2:17–19). The author of 2 Peter writes to this newly Christian Gentile community in the guise of giving them his "last will and testament" to correct the false teaching to which they have been exposed and which they have found attractive and, in some sense, to "re-catechize" these new Christians with language, ideas, and imagery familiar to them from their Hellenistic Gentile world.

Significant passages in 2 Peter, in which the author berates the falseness of the visiting teachers (2 Pt 2:1–18; 3:1–3), agree with substantial sections in Jude (Jude 4–13, 16–18 respectively) in which that author rails against intruders in his own community. The most likely explanation for this agreement is that one author had the work of the other author in front of him when he was writing. A key difference between the two works suggests which author borrowed from the other. Jude alludes to the apocryphal book of *1 Enoch* in Jude 6 (cf. *1 Enoch* 6–19) and quotes it directly in Jude 14–15 (cf. *1 Enoch* 1:9). Second Peter omits all reference to *1 Enoch* and refocuses the purpose of Jude 6–8. This suggests that the author of 2 Peter has adapted the text of Jude; given the ethnicity of 2 Peter's readers, they probably would not have recognized material from *1 Enoch*. The majority of scholars conclude that 2 Peter uses Jude.[7]

# The Johannine Letters

Christian writing does not indicate awareness of the Johannine Letters until the middle of the second century, although the letters are generally dated to ca. 100 CE. Polycarp's *To the Philippians* (no later than 140) provides one of the earliest parallels (7.1–2) to the ideas and themes of the Johannine Letters (2 Jn 7; 1 Jn 4:2–3). With Irenaeus of Lyons in his *Against Heresies*, Christian writers begin directly citing 1 and 2 John. There is no mention of 3 John until Eusebius (*Ecclesiastical History* 6.25.10) reports that Origen (d. 253) was acquainted with 2 and 3 John, but did not believe they were authentic. By the late fourth century, however, the three Johannine Letters are accepted as having been written by the Apostle John, as seen in Athanasius's *Thirty-Ninth Festal Letter* (367), the Synod of Hippo (393), and the Council of Carthage (397). Important biblical codices of the fourth and fifth centuries included these three letters, demonstrating their broad recognition within Greek- and Latin-speaking Christianity.

The Letters of John, the Gospel of John, and the book of Revelation in some way are related, but how is difficult to establish. Scholars believe that a community of Johannine Christianity produced these books and letters, most likely in the late first century. Yet they have not resolved who wrote them, if the same person wrote all of them, or in what order they were written. Asia Minor appears to be where the community resided, but agreement on a more precise location has proven elusive. Lack of agreement on who wrote the letters, in what sequence they were written, and the community's precise location has produced many theories, some of which the reader can examine in the introduction before each letter in this Study Bible.

The community, which two of the letters directly address, seems to have undergone

---

7. Richard J. Bauckham, *Jude, 2 Peter* (Word Biblical Commentary 50; Nashville, TN: Thomas Nelson, 1996), 142.

a painful division from which two Christian groups, hostile to one another, emerged. The third letter is addressed to an individual member of the community who has been caught on the front lines of that clash and has acted in a way that supports the letter writer and those sympathetic to him. The conflict which led to this division was about two essential beliefs and practices of Christianity: (1) who Jesus was and is, and what he did and continues to do (Christology), and (2) how one ought to behave in light of one's belief in Jesus as the Messiah and Son of God who has come in human flesh (ethics). The letters draw on major motifs, also found in the Gospel of John, that heighten the contrast between the two groups: light versus darkness, truth versus lie, life versus death. Those who have remained faithful, that is those for whom the letters have been written, the author(s) associates with light, truth, and life. Those who have deserted the true community, the author(s) consigns to darkness, lies, and death. These three letters afford contemporary readers of the New Testament a rare look into a very early Christian community as it struggled to sort through what it means for members to understand who Jesus is in ways that contradict one another. They also show that how Christians, both early and contemporary, understand Jesus' identity will radically shape the way they live.

## The Letter of Jude

Tertullian of North Africa, Clement of Alexandria (late second century), and Origen of Alexandria (early third century) accepted the Letter of Jude as a canonical book of the New Testament, and the Muratorian Canon (Italy, ca. 170 CE) included it as well. Only later in the third and fourth centuries were questions raised by Jerome, Didymus, and Eusebius about Jude's canonicity. Their doubts seem to have been triggered by the letter's heavy reliance on two non-canonical works (1 Enoch in Jude 6, 14–15 and the Assumption of Moses in Jude 9). Yet Athanasius included it as part of the canon in his Thirty-Ninth Festal Letter (367), and with his endorsement both Eastern and Western Christianity came to accept it as part of their biblical canon. Syriac Christianity

took longer to accept Jude, but did so in the sixth century.

Several scholars have argued that Jude is written for a general audience because it is not addressed to any group more specific than those "called, beloved in God the Father and kept safe for Jesus Christ" (Jude 1b). When the purpose for the letter is closely considered and the various characterizations of the false teachers noted, however, it becomes clear that the author wrote to a specific community that was being visited by a group of Christians professing and practicing a Christianity at odds with what the author had preached to the community. Where that community lived and what its ethnic and socio-economic composition were, scholars cannot precisely say. These same scholars often draw on v. 17 ("remember the words spoken beforehand by the apostles of our Lord Jesus Christ") as evidence to establish a late, post-apostolic date for the letter. Yet this statement can also be understood as simply pointing to the instruction received in the past at the community's founding and does not require a late first-century date to be true. The author modestly calls himself "a slave of Jesus Christ and brother of James" (v. 1). A good case can be made for the author as another "brother" (cf. Mt 13:55; Mk 6:3) from the same extended family network as James and Jesus (see the explanation of the term "brother" in the NAB introduction to James), and an equally good case can be made for the letter as pseudonymous. The "when," "to whom," and "by whom" questions about the Letter of Jude cannot be readily or satisfactorily answered. Yet these uncertainties do not detract from the letter's power to witness to the hopes, concerns, and values of early Christianity.

The Letter of Jude is a real letter (unlike Hebrews or 1 John). It has the standard Hellenistic epistolary opening (Jude 1–2) in which the author identifies himself and the intended recipient, expresses a wish or hope for the recipient's good health, and briefly signals the purpose of the letter (vv. 3–4). He has adapted the standard letter format, as other Christian letter writers have done (cf. Paul's letters). Thus his self-identification includes a statement of his own relationship to Christ ("slave"); his recipients' identification recalls their fundamental nature in relationship to the Father and Jesus ("called, beloved in God the Father and kept safe for Jesus Christ"); the author's wish or hope for the letter's recipients becomes a wish-prayer for them ("may mercy, peace, and love be yours in abundance"), while the statement announcing the reason for the letter remains unchanged. The author develops the body or content of the letter into a short homily that begs his audience to spurn the theological advances of these "godless persons" (v. 4) in two ways. First he condemns these theological intruders and

their outrageous behavior by likening them to a host of figures from the Old Testament and Apocrypha whose various rebellions against God brought terrible judgment and punishment upon them (vv. 5–16). Then he strives to rally them by recalling words of early Christian preaching (v. 18) and encouraging them in steadfast fidelity to God and the practice of mercy, even on those whom he has condemned (vv. 20–22). He crowns the missive with a sweeping doxology, which exults in the power of God to save them through Jesus Christ (vv. 24–25). ■

# THE CATHOLIC LETTERS

## New American Bible, Revised Edition

In addition to the thirteen letters attributed to Paul and the Letter to the Hebrews, the New Testament contains seven other letters. Three of these are attributed to John, two to Peter, and one each to James and Jude, all personages of the apostolic age. The term "catholic letter" first appears, with reference only to 1 John, in the writings of Apollonius of Ephesus, a second-century apologist, known only from a citation in Eusebius's *Ecclesiastical History*. Eusebius himself (A.D. 260–340) used the term to refer to all seven letters.

The reason for the term "catholic," which means "universal," was the perception that these letters, unlike those of Paul, which were directed to a particular local church, were apparently addressed more generally to the universal church. This designation is not entirely accurate, however. On the one hand, Hebrews has no specifically identified addressees, and originally this was probably true of Ephesians as well. On the other hand, 3 John is addressed to a named individual, 2 John to a specific, though unnamed, community, and 1 Peter to a number of churches that are specified as being located in Asia Minor.

While all seven of these writings begin with an epistolary formula, several of them do not appear to be real letters in the modern sense of the term. In the ancient world it was not unusual to cast an exhortation in the form of a letter for literary effect, a phenomenon comparable to the "open letter" that is sometimes used today.

With the exception of 1 Peter and 1 John, the ancient church showed reluctance to include the catholic letters in the New Testament canon. The reason for this was widespread doubt whether they had actually been written by the apostolic figures to whom they are attributed. The early Christians saw the New Testament as the depository of apostolic faith; therefore, they wished to include only the testimony of apostles. Today we distinguish more clearly between the authorship of a work and its canonicity: even though written by other, later witnesses than those whose names they bear, these writings nevertheless testify to the apostolic faith and constitute canonical scripture. By the late fourth or early fifth centuries, most objections had been overcome in both the Greek and Latin churches (though not in the Syriac), and all seven of the catholic letters have since been acknowledged as canonical. ■

# The Letter of

# James

## INTRODUCTION

### Mary Katherine Birge, SSJ

In the *New American Bible* introduction to James that immediately precedes the letter, the author writes, "Ethical norms [in James] are derived not primarily from christology, as in Paul, but from a concept of salvation that involves conversion, baptism, forgiveness of sin, and expectation of judgment (Jas 1:17; 4:12)." What that author describes as "a concept of salvation" is a compressed definition of Christian discipleship lived out through an eschatological hope. For James the hope that a life lived in imitation of Jesus' obedience to his Father will culminate in eternal life at the final judgment (cf. 1:11–12, 21; 2:12–13; 5:7–9, 20) depends ultimately on a faith expressed in deeds (2:14–17). As the prophets of the Old Testament did before him, James criticizes faith void of moral action and urges his audience to "be doers of the word and not hearers only" (1:22). He does not advocate replacing "faith" with "works," as many of his interpreters, beginning with Martin Luther, have argued. Rather, he says that faith is incomplete, empty, and imperfect without deeds of love that directly welcome and care for the poorest of one's community as well as the wealthiest (2:1–5, 14–17). These deeds of love reveal the depth of a faith that strives to imitate the faith of Jesus. Moral action is not simply a sign of faith, but it is faith itself in action.[1]

This faith in action reveals whether James's audience has chosen friendship with God or friendship with "the world" (the NABRE uses the word "lover" rather than "friendship" or "friend" in Jas 4:4). The "world" that James names and disparages in 1:27; 2:5; 3:6; and 4:4 comprises whatever opposes God and what God values (5:1–6). In Matthew's Gospel Jesus offers the same kind of choice: "You

## Outline of James

I.   **Address (1:1)**

II.  **The Value of Trials and Temptation (1:2–18)**

III. **Exhortations and Warnings (1:19–5:12)**

IV.  **The Power of Prayer (5:13–20)**

cannot serve God and mammon" (Mt 6:24). To befriend God and be befriended by God does not require Christians to live apart from other members of society nor to maintain ritual purity by avoiding some item. James presumes they will participate in society around them, own property, and render judgments. Or how else would they have the wherewithal to share their possessions with the poor, pay just wages to workers, and care for orphans and widows—actions that he reminds them, in both affirmative and negative ways, are living faith (Jas 1:27; 5:1–6)?

These three activities, especially regarding the care of the orphan and widow, reflect the covenantal demands found in the Torah and the Prophets (e.g., Ex 23:10–11; Lv 19:9–10; Dt 14:28–29; 26:12–15; Hos 12:7–9; Am 2:6–8; Mi 3:1–3). Indeed, James underscores his audience's breach of covenantal behavior by addressing them as "adulterers" (Jas 4:4), an epithet used by prophets for Israel, who have been unfaithful to God (e.g., Jer 3:20; Ez 16:23–26; Hos 9:1).[2] The authority of the Torah and Prophets perdures for James and his Christian community, so that anyone who acts in ways opposite to Torah and prophetic

---

1. Patrick Hartin, *James,* SP 14 (Collegeville, MN: Liturgical Press, 2003), 31, 117.

2. Ibid., 198.

injunctions (Jas 4:2–3) reveals an empty faith and the simultaneous embrace of friendship of "the world" and rejection of God (4:4).[3]

Unlike in today's world, where friendship often designates spontaneous relationships of goodwill, kindness, or shared purpose, in the Hellenistic world of the New Testament friendship denotes a kind of a deliberate bond between persons who have become so intimate as to share between them one soul or one self.[4] For James friendship with God means that the fundamental orientation of a person's heart is in union with God; what she values is at one with what God values; how she perceives reality follows God's perception of reality.[5] Because of this intimate union, a person's every "work" or deed announces her rejection of the "world's" basic presumption, i.e., that her worth resides in the value of her possessions and her associates' social status. In contrast, the basic presumption of someone who is at one with God is that "all good giving and every perfect gift is from above, coming down from the Father of lights, with whom there is not alteration or shadow caused by change" (Jas 1:17). God's generosity is without measure and the world's is not. For James no one can be "of two minds" (1:8); that is, no one can want friendship with God and friendship with the world at the same time. The shared intimacy required of true friends will manifest itself in

their "works" or actions, and these actions will always reveal their shared hopes and desires. Actions that "dishonor [. . .] the poor person" (2:6) and demonstrate "bitter jealousy and selfish ambition" (3:14) arise from the "wisdom" of this world and mark their actor as an "enemy" of God. James counters this image of enmity with God by offering his audience the figure of Abraham as a model for friendship with God.

In 2:21–23 James presents Abraham as a friend of God, not in the sense of being God's friend, but rather as someone who has acted as a friend toward God or whose actions proclaim that he has befriended God (see 2 Chr 20:7; Is 41:8). When God asks him to sacrifice his cherished and beloved son, Isaac, on Mount Moriah (Gn 22:1–18), he responds from a faith that is "perfect and complete, lacking in nothing" (Jas 1:4). Abraham's orientation toward God, which allows him to view the world through the eyes of God, leads him to obey. Had he been in union with the values of the world, Abraham would have scorned such a call as meaningless because it would not have advanced what he wanted. His faith in God was tested (1:3) and "completed by the works" (2:22).[6] Abraham is counted a "friend of God" because he "is not double-minded" and "thinks and acts according to the measure of God."[7] James challenges his audience throughout his letter to live according to the standard of friendship with God. ∎

3. Luke Timothy Johnson, *Brother of Jesus, Friend of God: Studies in the Letter of James* (Grand Rapids, MI: Eerdmans, 2004), 212–13

4. Ibid., 214.

5. Hartin, *James*, 198, 213

6. Johnson, *Brother*, 215.

7. Luke Timothy Johnson, *The Letter of James* (Anchor Bible 37A; New York: Doubleday, 1995), 248.

JAS

# THE LETTER OF JAMES
## New American Bible, Introduction

The person to whom this letter is ascribed can scarcely be one of the two members of the Twelve who bore the name James (see Mt 10:2–3; Mk 3:17–18; Lk 6:14–15), for he is not identified as an apostle but only as "slave of God and of the Lord Jesus Christ" (Jas 1:1). This designation most probably refers to the third New Testament personage named James, a relative of Jesus who is usually called "brother of the Lord" (see Mt 13:55; Mk 6:3). He was the leader of the Jewish Christian community in Jerusalem whom Paul acknowledged as one of the "pillars" (Gal 2:9). In Acts he appears as the authorized spokesman for the Jewish Christian position in the early Church (Acts 12:17; 15:13–21). According to the Jewish historian Josephus (*Antiquities* 20:201–203), he was stoned to death by the Jews under the high priest Ananus II in A.D. 62.

The letter is addressed to "the twelve tribes in the dispersion." In Old Testament terminology the term "twelve tribes" designates the people of Israel; the "dispersion" or "diaspora" refers to the non-Palestinian Jews who had settled throughout the Greco-Roman world (see Jn 7:35). Since in Christian thought the church is the new Israel, the address probably designates the Jewish Christian churches located in Palestine, Syria, and elsewhere. Or perhaps the letter is meant more generally for all Christian communities, and the "dispersion" has the symbolic meaning of exile from our true home, as it has in the address of 1 Peter (1 Pt 1:1). The letter is so markedly Jewish in character that some scholars have regarded it as a Jewish document subsequently "baptized" by a few Christian insertions, but such an origin is scarcely tenable in view of the numerous contacts discernible between the Letter of James and other New Testament literature.

From the viewpoint of its literary form, James is a letter only in the most conventional sense; it has none of the characteristic features of a real letter except the address. It belongs rather to the genre of parenesis or exhortation and is concerned almost exclusively with ethical conduct. It therefore falls within the tradition of Jewish wisdom literature, such as can be found in the Old Testament (Proverbs, Sirach) and in the extracanonical Jewish literature (Testaments of the Twelve Patriarchs, the Books of Enoch, the Manual of Discipline found at Qumran). More specifically, it consists of sequences of didactic proverbs, comparable to Tb 4:5–19, to many passages in Sirach, and to sequences of sayings in the synoptic gospels. Numerous passages in James treat of subjects that also appear in the synoptic sayings of Jesus, especially in Matthew's Sermon on the Mount, but the correspondences are too general to establish any literary dependence. James represents a type of early Christianity that emphasized sound teaching and responsible moral behavior. Ethical norms are derived not primarily from christology, as in Paul, but from a concept of salvation that involves conversion, baptism, forgiveness of sin, and expectation of judgment (Jas 1:17; 4:12).

Paradoxically, this very Jewish work is written in an excellent Greek style, which ranks among the best in the New Testament and appears to be the work of a trained Hellenistic writer. Those who continue to regard James of Jerusalem as its author are therefore obliged to suppose that a secretary must have put the letter into its present literary form. This assumption is not implausible in the light of ancient practice. Some regard the letter as one of the earliest writings in the New Testament and feel that its content accurately reflects what we would expect of the leader of Jewish Christianity. Moreover, they argue that the type of Jewish Christianity reflected in the letter cannot be situated historically after the fall of Jerusalem in A.D. 70.

Others, however, believe it more likely that James is a pseudonymous work of a later period. In addition to its Greek style, they observe further that (a) the prestige that the writer is assumed to enjoy points to the later legendary reputation of James; (b) the discussion of the importance of good works seems to presuppose a debate subsequent to that in

Paul's own day; (c) the author does not rely upon prescriptions of the Mosaic law, as we would expect from the historical James; (d) the letter contains no allusions to James's own history and to his relationship with Jesus or to the early Christian community of Jerusalem. For these reasons, many recent interpreters assign James to the period A.D. 90–100.

The principal divisions of the Letter of James are the following:

I. Address (1:1)
II. The Value of Trials and Temptation (1:2–18)
III. Exhortations and Warnings (1:19–5:12)
IV. The Power of Prayer (5:13–20) ■

# JAMES

## I. ADDRESS

1 [1]† James, a slave of God and of the Lord Jesus Christ, to the twelve tribes in the dispersion, greetings. *

## II. THE VALUE OF TRIALS AND TEMPTATION

**Perseverance in Trial.** [2]* Consider it all joy, my brothers, when you encounter various trials,† [3]for you know that the testing† of your faith produces perseverance. [4]And let perseverance be perfect, so that you may be perfect and complete, lacking in nothing. [5]But if any of you lacks wisdom,† he should ask God who gives to all generously and ungrudgingly, and he will be given it. * [6]But he should ask in faith, not doubting, for the one who doubts is like a wave of the sea that is driven and tossed about by the wind. * [7]For that person must not suppose that he will receive anything from the Lord, [8]since he is a man of two minds, unstable in all his ways.

[9]The brother in lowly circumstances† should take pride in his high standing, * [10]and the rich one in his lowliness, for he will pass away "like the flower of the field." * [11]For the sun comes up with its scorching heat and dries up the grass, its flower droops, and the beauty of its appearance vanishes. So will the rich person fade away in the midst of his pursuits.

**Temptation.** [12]* Blessed is the man who perseveres in temptation,† for when he has been proved he will receive the crown of life that he promised to those who love him. [13]† No one experiencing temptation should say, "I am being tempted by God"; for God is not subject to temptation to evil, and he himself tempts no one. * [14]Rather, each person is tempted when he is lured and enticed by his own desire. [15]Then desire conceives and brings forth sin, and when sin reaches maturity it gives birth to death.

[16]† Do not be deceived, my beloved brothers: [17]all good giving and every perfect gift† is from above, coming down from the Father of lights, with whom there is no alteration or shadow caused by change. [18]* He willed to give us birth by the word of truth that we may be a kind of firstfruits of his creatures.†

## III. EXHORTATIONS AND WARNINGS

**Doers of the Word.** [19]Know this, my dear brothers: everyone should be quick to hear,†

---

†

**1:1** *James, a slave of God and of the Lord Jesus Christ*: a declaration of the writer's authority for instructing the Christian communities; cf. Rom 1:1. Regarding the identity of the author, see Introduction. *Dispersion*: see Introduction.

**1:2** *Consider it all joy…various trials*: a frequent teaching of the New Testament derived from the words and sufferings of Jesus (Mt 5:10–12; Jn 10:11; Acts 5:41).

**1:3–8** The sequence of testing, perseverance, and being perfect and complete indicates the manner of attaining spiritual maturity and full preparedness for the coming of Christ (Jas 5:7–12; cf. 1 Pt 1:6–7; Rom 5:3–5). These steps require wisdom (Jas 1:5).

**1:5** *Wisdom*: a gift that God readily grants to all who ask in faith and that sustains the Christian in times of trial. It is a kind of knowledge or understanding not accessible to the unbeliever or those who doubt, which gives the recipient an understanding of the real importance of events. In this way a Christian can deal with adversity with great calm and hope (cf. 1 Cor 2:6–12).

**1:9–11** Throughout his letter (see Jas 2:5; 4:10, 13–16; 5:1–6), the author reaffirms the teaching of Jesus that worldly prosperity is not necessarily a sign of God's favor but can even be a hindrance to proper humility before God (cf. Lk 6:20–25; 12:16–21; 16:19–31).

**1:12** *Temptation*: the Greek word used here is the same one used for "trials" in Jas 1:2. *The crown of life*: in ancient Palestine, crowns or wreaths of flowers were worn at festive occasions as signs of joy and honor. In the Hellenistic world, wreaths were given as a reward to great statesmen, soldiers, athletes. *Life*: here means eternal life. *He promised*: some manuscripts read "God" or "the Lord," while the best witnesses do not specify the subject of "promised."

**1:13–15** It is contrary to what we know of God for God to be the author of human temptation (Jas 1:13). In the commission of a sinful act, one is first beguiled by passion (Jas 1:14), then consent is given, which in turn causes the sinful act. When sin permeates the entire person, it incurs the ultimate penalty of death (Jas 1:15).

**1:16–18** The author here stresses that God is the source of all good and of good alone, and the evil of temptation does not come from him.

**1:17** *All good giving and every perfect gift* may be a proverb written in hexameter. *Father of lights*: God is here called the Father of the heavenly luminaries, i.e., the stars, sun, and moon that he created (Gn 1:14–18). Unlike orbs moving from nadir to zenith, he never changes or diminishes in brightness.

**1:18** Acceptance of the gospel message, *the word of truth*, constitutes new birth (Jn 3:5–6) and makes the recipient the *firstfruits* (i.e., the cultic offering of the earliest grains, symbolizing the beginning of an abundant harvest) of a new creation; cf. 1 Cor 15:20; Rom 8:23.

**1:19–25** To *be quick to hear* the gospel is to accept it readily and to act in conformity with it, removing from one's soul whatever is opposed to it, so that it may take root and effect salvation (Jas 1:19–21). To listen to the gospel message but not practice it

---

**1:1** Jn 7:35; 1 Pt 1:1.
**1:2** Rom 5:3–5; 1 Pt 1:6; 4:13–16.
**1:5** Prv 2:2–6; Wis 9:4, 9–12.
**1:6** Mt 7:7; Mk 11:24.
**1:9** 2:5.

**1:10** Is 40:6–7.
**1:12** 1 Cor 9:25; 2 Tm 4:8; 1 Pt 5:4; Rev 2:10.
**1:13** Sir 15:11–20; 1 Cor 10:13.
**1:18** Jn 1:12–13; 1 Pt 1:23.

slow to speak, slow to wrath,* [20] for the wrath of a man does not accomplish the righteousness of God.* [21] Therefore, put away all filth and evil excess and humbly welcome the word that has been planted in you and is able to save your souls.*

[22] Be doers of the word and not hearers only, deluding yourselves.* [23] For if anyone is a hearer of the word and not a doer, he is like a man who looks at his own face in a mirror. [24] He sees himself, then goes off and promptly forgets what he looked like. [25] But the one who peers into the perfect law† of freedom and perseveres, and is not a hearer who forgets but a doer who acts, such a one shall be blessed in what he does.*

[26] † If anyone thinks he is religious and does not bridle his tongue† but deceives his heart, his religion is vain.* [27] Religion that is pure and undefiled before God and the Father is this: to care for orphans and widows† in their affliction and to keep oneself unstained by the world.*

## 2 Sin of Partiality.† [1] My brothers, show no partiality as you adhere to the faith in our glorious Lord Jesus Christ. [2] For if a man with gold rings on his fingers and in fine clothes comes into your assembly, and a poor person in shabby clothes also comes in, [3] and you pay attention to the one wearing the fine clothes and say, "Sit here, please," while you say to the poor one, "Stand there," or "Sit at my feet," [4] have you not made distinctions among yourselves and become judges with evil designs?†

[5] Listen, my beloved brothers. Did not God choose those who are poor† in the world to be rich in faith and heirs of the kingdom that he promised to those who love him?* [6] But you dishonored the poor person. Are not the rich oppressing you? And do they themselves not haul you off to court? [7] Is it not they who blaspheme the noble name that was invoked over you?* [8] However, if you fulfill the royal† law according to the scripture, "You shall love your neighbor as yourself," you are doing well.* [9] But if you show partiality, you commit sin, and are convicted by the law as transgressors.* [10] For whoever keeps the whole law, but falls short in one particular, has become guilty in respect to all of it.* [11] For he who said, "You shall not commit adultery," also said, "You shall not kill."* Even if you do not commit adultery but kill, you have become a transgressor of the law. [12] * So speak and so act as people who will be judged by the law of freedom.† [13] For the judgment is merciless to one who has not shown mercy; mercy triumphs over judgment.*

### Faith and Works.† [14] What good is it, my brothers, if someone says he has faith but does

---

† is failure to improve oneself (Jas 1:22–24). Only conformity of life to the perfect law of true freedom brings happiness (Jas 1:25).

**1:25** *Peers into the perfect law*: the image of a person doing this is paralleled to that of hearing God's word. The *perfect law* applies the Old Testament description of the Mosaic law to the gospel of Jesus Christ that brings freedom.

**1:26–27** A practical application of Jas 1:22 is now made.

**1:26** For control of the tongue, see note on Jas 3:1–12.

**1:27** In the Old Testament, orphans and widows are classical examples of the defenseless and oppressed.

**2:1–13** In the Christian community there must be no discrimination or favoritism based on status or wealth (Jas 2:2–4; cf. Mt 5:3; 11:5; 23:6; 1 Cor 1:27–29). Divine favor rather consists in God's election and promises (Jas 2:5). The rich who oppress the poor blaspheme the name of Christ (Jas 2:6–7). By violating one law of love of neighbor, they offend against the whole law (Jas 2:8–11). On the other hand, conscious awareness of the final judgment helps the faithful to fulfill the whole law (Jas 2:12).

**2:4** When Christians show favoritism to the rich they are guilty of the worst kind of prejudice and discrimination. The author says that such Christians set themselves up as judges who judge not by divine law but by the basest, self-serving motives.

**2:5** The poor, "God's poor" of the Old Testament, were seen by Jesus as particularly open to God for belief in and reliance on him alone (Lk 6:20). God's law cannot tolerate their oppression in any way (Jas 2:9).

**2:8** *Royal*: literally, "kingly"; because the Mosaic law came from God, the universal king. There may be an allusion to Jesus' uses of this commandment in his preaching of the kingdom of God (Mt 22:39; Mk 12:31; Lk 10:27).

**2:12–13** The law upon which the last judgment will be based is the law of freedom. As Jesus taught, mercy (which participates in God's own loving mercy) includes forgiveness of those who wrong us (see Mt 6:12, 14–15).

**2:14–26** The theme of these verses is the relationship of faith and works (deeds). It has been argued that the teaching here contradicts that of Paul (see especially Rom 4:5–6). The problem can only be understood if the different viewpoints of the two authors are seen. Paul argues against those who claim to participate in God's salvation because of their good deeds as well as because they have committed themselves to trust in God through Jesus Christ (Paul's concept of faith). Paul certainly understands, however, the implications of true faith for a life of love and generosity (see Gal 5:6, 13–15). The author of James is well aware that proper conduct can only come about with an authentic commitment to God in faith (Jas 2:18, 26). Many think he was seeking to correct a misunderstanding of Paul's view.

---

**1:19** Prv 14:17; Sir 5:11.
**1:20** Eph 4:26.
**1:21** Col 3:8.
**1:22** Mt 7:26; Rom 2:13.
**1:25** 2:12; Ps 19:8; Rom 8:2.
**1:26** 3:2; Ps 34:14.
**1:27** Ex 22:21.
**2:5** 1 Cor 1:26–28; Rev 2:9.
**2:7** 1 Pt 4:4.
**2:8** Lv 19:18; Mt 22:39; Rom 13:9.
**2:9** Dt 1:17.
**2:10** Gal 3:10.
**2:11** Ex 20:13–14; Dt 5:17–18.
**2:12** 1:25; Rom 8:2.
**2:13** Mt 5:7; 6:14–15; 18:32–33.

not have works? Can that faith save him?* ¹⁵If a brother or sister has nothing to wear and has no food for the day, ¹⁶and one of you says to them, "Go in peace, keep warm, and eat well," but you do not give them the necessities of the body, what good is it?* ¹⁷So also faith of itself, if it does not have works, is dead.

¹⁸Indeed someone may say, "You have faith and I have works." Demonstrate your faith to me without works, and I will demonstrate my faith to you from my works. ¹⁹You believe that God is one. You do well. Even the demons believe that and tremble. ²⁰Do you want proof, you ignoramus, that faith without works is useless? ²¹Was not Abraham our father justified by works when he offered his son Isaac upon the altar?* ²²You see that faith was active along with his works, and faith was completed by the works. ²³Thus the scripture was fulfilled that says, "Abraham believed God, and it was credited to him as righteousness," and he was called "the friend of God."* ²⁴See how a person is justified by works and not by faith alone. ²⁵And in the same way, was not Rahab the harlot also justified by works when she welcomed the messengers and sent them out by a different route?* ²⁶For just as a body without a spirit is dead, so also faith without works is dead.

**3** **Power of the Tongue.**† ¹Not many of you should become teachers, my brothers, for you realize that we will be judged more strictly, ²for we all fall short in many respects. If anyone does not fall short in speech, he is a perfect man, able to bridle his whole body also.* ³If we put bits into the mouths of horses to make them obey us, we also guide their whole bodies. ⁴It is the same with ships: even though they are so large and driven by fierce winds, they are steered by a very small rudder wherever the pilot's inclination wishes.

⁵In the same way the tongue is a small member and yet has great pretensions.

Consider how small a fire can set a huge forest ablaze. ⁶The tongue is also a fire. It exists among our members as a world of malice, defiling the whole body and setting the entire course of our lives on fire, itself set on fire by Gehenna. ⁷For every kind of beast and bird, of reptile and sea creature, can be tamed and has been tamed by the human species, ⁸but no human being can tame the tongue. It is a restless evil, full of deadly poison.* ⁹With it we bless the Lord and Father, and with it we curse human beings who are made in the likeness of God. ¹⁰From the same mouth come blessing and cursing. This need not be so, my brothers. ¹¹Does a spring gush forth from the same opening both pure and brackish water? ¹²Can a fig tree, my brothers, produce olives, or a grapevine figs? Neither can salt water yield fresh.*

**True Wisdom.**† ¹³Who among you is wise and understanding? Let him show his works by a good life in the humility that comes from wisdom.* ¹⁴But if you have bitter jealousy and selfish ambition in your hearts, do not boast and be false to the truth. ¹⁵Wisdom of this kind does not come down from above but is earthly, unspiritual, demonic. ¹⁶For where jealousy and selfish ambition exist, there is disorder and every foul practice. ¹⁷But the wisdom from above is first of all pure, then peaceable, gentle, compliant, full of mercy and good fruits, without inconstancy or insincerity.* ¹⁸And the fruit of righteousness is sown in peace for those who cultivate peace.*

**4** **Causes of Division.**† ¹Where do the wars and where do the conflicts among you come from? Is it not from your passions† that make war within your members?* ²You covet

---

† **3:1–12** The use and abuse of the important role of teaching in the church (Jas 3:1) are here related to the good and bad use of the tongue (Jas 3:9–12), the instrument through which teaching was chiefly conveyed (see Sir 5:11–6:1; 28:12–26).

**3:13–18** This discussion of true wisdom is related to the previous reflection on the role of the teacher as one who is in control of his speech. The qualities of the wise man endowed from above are detailed (Jas 3:17–18; cf. Gal 5:22–23), in contrast to the qualities of earthbound wisdom (Jas 3:14–16; cf. 2 Cor 12:20).

**4:1–12** The concern here is with the origin of conflicts in the Christian community. These are occasioned by love of *the world,* which *means enmity with God* (Jas 4:4). Further, the conflicts are bound up with failure to pray properly (cf. Mt 7:7–11; Jn 14:13; 15:7; 16:23), that is, not asking God at all or using God's kind-

ness only for one's pleasure (Jas 4:2–3). In contrast, the proper dispositions are submission to God, repentance, humility, and resistance to evil (Jas 4:7–10).

**4:1–3** *Passions:* the Greek word here (literally, "pleasures") does not indicate that pleasure is evil. Rather, as the text points out (Jas 4:2–3), it is the manner in which one deals with needs and desires that determines good or bad. The motivation for any

---

**2:14** Mt 25:31–46; Gal 5:6.
**2:16** 1 Jn 3:17.
**2:21** Gn 22:9–12; Heb 11:17.
**2:23** Gn 15:6; Rom 4:3; Gal 3:6 / 2 Chr 20:7; Is 41:8.
**2:25** Jos 2:1–21.
**3:2** 1:26; Prv 13:3; Sir 28:12–26.
**3:8** Ps 140:4.
**3:12** Mt 7:16–17.
**3:13** Eph 4:1–2.
**3:17** 1:17; Wis 7:22–23.
**3:18** Mt 5:9.
**4:1** Rom 7:23; 1 Pt 2:11.

JAS

but do not possess. You kill and envy but you cannot obtain; you fight and wage war. You do not possess because you do not ask. ³ You ask but do not receive, because you ask wrongly, to spend it on your passions. ⁴ Adulterers!† Do you not know that to be a lover of the world means enmity with God? Therefore, whoever wants to be a lover of the world makes himself an enemy of God.* ⁵ Or do you suppose that the scripture speaks without meaning when it says, "The spirit that he has made to dwell in us tends toward jealousy"?† ⁶ But he bestows a greater grace; therefore, it says:*

"God resists the proud,
  but gives grace to the humble."†

⁷ So submit yourselves to God. Resist the devil, and he will flee from you.* ⁸ Draw near to God, and he will draw near to you. Cleanse your hands, you sinners, and purify your hearts, you of two minds.* ⁹ Begin to lament, to mourn, to weep. Let your laughter be turned into mourning and your joy into dejection. ¹⁰ Humble yourselves before the Lord and he will exalt you.*

¹¹ Do not speak evil of one another, brothers. Whoever speaks evil of a brother or judges his brother speaks evil of the law and judges the law.† If you judge the law, you are not a doer of the law but a judge. ¹² There is one lawgiver and judge who is able to save or to destroy. Who then are you to judge your neighbor?*

**Warning Against Presumption.**† ¹³ Come now, you who say, "Today or tomorrow we shall go into such and such a town, spend a year there doing business, and make a profit"— ¹⁴ you have no idea what your life will be like tomorrow.† You are a puff of smoke that appears briefly and then disappears.* ¹⁵ Instead you should say, "If the Lord wills it,† we shall live to do this or that." ¹⁶ But now you are boasting in your arrogance. All such boasting is evil. ¹⁷* So for one who knows the right thing to do and does not do it, it is a sin.†

**5** **Warning to the Rich.**† ¹ Come now, you rich, weep and wail over your impending miseries.* ² Your wealth has rotted away, your clothes have become moth-eaten,* ³ your gold and silver have corroded, and that corrosion will be a testimony against you; it will devour your flesh like a fire. You have stored up treasure for the last days.* ⁴ Behold, the wages you withheld from the workers who harvested your fields are crying aloud, and the cries of the harvesters have reached the ears of the Lord of hosts.* ⁵ You have lived on earth in luxury and pleasure; you have fattened your hearts for the day of slaughter.* ⁶ You have condemned; you have murdered the righteous one;* he offers you no resistance.†

J A S

---

† action can be wrong, especially if one does not pray properly but seeks only selfish enjoyment (Jas 4:3).
**4:4** *Adulterers*: a common biblical image for the covenant between God and his people is the marriage bond. In this image, breaking the covenant with God is likened to the unfaithfulness of adultery.
**4:5** The meaning of this saying is difficult because the author of James cites, probably from memory, a passage that is not in any extant manuscript of the Bible. Other translations of the text with a completely different meaning are possible: "The Spirit that he (God) made to dwell in us yearns (for us) jealously," or, "He (God) yearns jealously for the spirit that he has made to dwell in us." If this last translation is correct, the author perhaps had in mind an apocryphal religious text that echoes the idea that God is zealous for his creatures; cf. Ex 20:5; Dt 4:24; Zec 8:2.
**4:6** The point of this whole argument is that God wants the happiness of all, but that selfishness and pride can make that impossible. We must work with him in humility (Jas 4:10).
**4:11** Slander of a fellow Christian does not break just one commandment but makes mockery of the authority of law in general and therefore of God.
**4:13–17** The uncertainty of life (Jas 4:14), its complete dependence on God, and the necessity of submitting to God's will (Jas 4:15) all help one know and do what is right (Jas 4:17). To disregard this is to live in pride and arrogance (Jas 4:16); failure to do what is right is a sin (Jas 4:17).
**4:14** Some important Greek manuscripts here have, "You who have no idea what tomorrow will bring. Why, what is your life?"

**4:15** *If the Lord wills it*: often in piety referred to as the "conditio Jacobaea," the condition James says we should employ to qualify all our plans.
**4:17** *It is a sin*: those who live arrogantly, forgetting the contingency of life and our dependence on God (Jas 4:13–16), are guilty of sin.
**5:1–6** Continuing with the theme of the transitory character of life on earth, the author points out the impending ruin of the godless. He denounces the unjust rich, whose victims cry to heaven for judgment on their exploiters (Jas 5:4–6). The decay and corrosion of the costly garments and metals, which symbolize wealth, prove them worthless and portend the destruction of their possessors (Jas 5:2–3).
**5:6** The author does not have in mind any specific crime in his readers' communities but rather echoes the Old Testament theme of the harsh oppression of the righteous poor (see Prv 1:11; Wis 2:10, 12, 20)

---

**4:4** Mt 6:24; Lk 16:13; Rom 8:7; 1 Jn 2:15–16.
**4:6** Jb 22:29; Prv 3:34; Mt 23:12; 1 Pt 5:5.
**4:7** 1 Pt 5:8–9.
**4:8** Zec 1:3; Mal 3:7.
**4:10** Jb 5:11; Mt 23:12; Lk 14:11; 18:14; 1 Pt 5:6.
**4:12** Mt 7:1;

Rom 2:1; 14:4.
**4:14** Prv 27:1 / Ps 39:6–7.
**4:17** Lk 12:47.
**5:1** Lk 6:24.
**5:2** Mt 6:19.
**5:3** Ps 21:10; Prv 11:4; Jdt 16:17.
**5:4** Lv 19:13; Dt 24:14–15; Mal 3:5.
**5:5** Jer 12:3; Lk 16:19–25.
**5:6** Wis 2:10–20.

**Patience and Oaths.** [7]† Be patient, therefore, brothers, until the coming of the Lord. See how the farmer waits for the precious fruit of the earth, being patient with it until it receives the early and the late rains.† [8]You too must be patient. Make your hearts firm, because the coming of the Lord is at hand.* [9]Do not complain, brothers, about one another, that you may not be judged. Behold, the Judge is standing before the gates. [10]Take as an example of hardship and patience, brothers, the prophets who spoke in the name of the Lord. [11]Indeed we call blessed those who have persevered. You have heard of the perseverance of Job, and you have seen the purpose of the Lord, because "the Lord is compassionate and merciful."*

[12]* But above all, my brothers, do not swear, either by heaven or by earth or with any other oath, but let your "Yes" mean "Yes" and your "No" mean "No," that you may not incur condemnation.†

## IV. THE POWER OF PRAYER

**Anointing of the Sick.** [13]Is anyone among you suffering? He should pray. Is anyone in good spirits? He should sing praise. [14]Is anyone among you sick?† He should summon the presbyters of the church, and they should pray over him and anoint [him] with oil in the name of the Lord,* [15]and the prayer of faith will save the sick person, and the Lord will raise him up. If he has committed any sins, he will be forgiven.†

**Confession and Intercession.** [16]Therefore, confess your sins to one another and pray for one another, that you may be healed. The fervent prayer of a righteous person is very powerful. [17]Elijah was a human being like us; yet he prayed earnestly that it might not rain, and for three years and six months it did not rain upon the land.* [18]Then he prayed again, and the sky gave rain and the earth produced its fruit.*

**Conversion of Sinners.** [19]* My brothers, if anyone among you should stray from the truth and someone bring him back, [20]* he should know that whoever brings back a sinner from the error of his way will save his soul from death and will cover a multitude of sins.†

---

† **5:7–11** Those oppressed by the unjust rich are reminded of the need for patience, both in bearing the sufferings of human life (Jas 5:9) and in their expectation of the coming of the Lord. It is then that they will receive their reward (Jas 5:7–8, 10–11; cf. Heb 10:25; 1 Jn 2:18).

**5:7** *The early and the late rains*: an expression related to the agricultural season in ancient Palestine (see Dt 11:14; Jer 5:24; Jl 2:23).

**5:12** This is the threat of condemnation for the abuse of swearing oaths (cf. Mt 5:33–37). *By heaven or by earth*: these words were substitutes for the original form of an oath, to circumvent its binding force and to avoid pronouncing the holy name of God (see Ex 22:10).

**5:14** In case of sickness a Christian should ask for the presbyters of the church, i.e., those who have authority in the church (cf. Acts 15:2, 22–23; 1 Tm 5:17; Ti 1:5). They are to pray over the person and anoint with oil; oil was used for medicinal pur-

poses in the ancient world (see Is 1:6; Lk 10:34). In Mk 6:13, the Twelve anoint the sick with oil on their missionary journey. *In the name of the Lord*: by the power of Jesus Christ.

**5:15** The results of the prayer and anointing are physical health and forgiveness of sins. The Roman Catholic Church (Council of Trent, Session 14) declared that this anointing of the sick is a sacrament "instituted by Christ and promulgated by blessed James the apostle."

**5:20** When a Christian is instrumental in the conversion of a sinner, the result is forgiveness of sins and a reinstatement of the sinner to the life of grace.

---

* 
**5:8** Lk 21:19; Heb 10:36 / Heb 10:25; 1 Pt 4:7.
**5:11** Ex 34:6; Ps 103:8.
**5:12** Mt 5:34–37.
**5:14** Mk 6:13.

**5:17** 1 Kgs 17:1; Lk 4:25.
**5:18** 1 Kgs 18:45.
**5:19** Mt 18:15; Gal 6:1.
**5:20** Prv 10:12; 1 Pt 4:8.

J A S

# The First Letter of

# Peter

## INTRODUCTION

### Mary Katherine Birge, SSJ

The author of 1 Peter has written a letter of encouragement to Christian communities that stretch across the Anatolian peninsula (today's western Turkey). He names them "the chosen sojourners of the dispersion" (1 Pt 1:1), signaling a significant development in Christian theology and a likely reason for the letter. The word "chosen" recalls the Old Testament description of Israel as the chosen people of God (e.g., Dt 7:6; 14:2; Neh 1:9; Ps 33:12; 105:6, 43; Is 41:8, 9; 43:20). The word "sojourners" describes persons who live in a land not their own, without prospects of becoming permanent residents of it, and the word "dispersion" refers to the Jewish diaspora, the state of Jewish people now living outside the historical boundaries of Israel, often under some form of persecution.

The author of 1 Peter makes clear in his letter that his audience is comprised of Gentile converts (1 Pt 1:14, 18; 4:2–4), yet he applies to them here and in other places (e.g., 3:6, 10–12; 5:2) Old Testament allusions and metaphors for Israel. He even applies to them God's own declaration to Israel to be holy because God is holy (1:15–16; cf. Lv 11:44; 19:2). By drawing on such language and imagery, he knows, or at least presumes, that his addressees have an extensive knowledge either of the Old Testament itself or of those themes and events in it that directly touch on the Christian story. In other places in the New Testament Christians are identified as "heirs" of Israel and its promises (Gal 3:29; Eph 3:6; Heb 6:17), but in 1 Peter members of the Christian church *are* Israel, the chosen people of God. In 1 Pt 1:10–12 the author has written the reason for this: their election was the aim of God from the beginning, just as the author of Ephesians notes (Eph 1:4–5), but with a significant difference: 1 Peter folds

---

## Outline of 1 Peter

I.   **Address (1:1–2)**

II.  **The Gift and Call of God in Baptism (1:3–2:10)**

III. **The Christian in a Hostile World (2:11–4:11)**

IV.  **Advice to the Persecuted (4:12–5:11)**

V.   **Conclusion (5:12–14)**

---

Christianity and Israel into one reality without the language of attack or judgment.[1]

As converts to Christianity (1 Pt 1:14, 18; 4:2–4) who have abandoned former practices, both religious and civic, these believers have come to the attention of their one-time co-religionists who "are surprised that [they] do not plunge into the same swamp of profligacy," and consequently "vilify" them (4:4). These new Christians now reside as "aliens and sojourners" in societies they once navigated with a sure sense of belonging (2:11). Their everyday relationships with neighbors, co-workers, and even spouses have been changed by their new identity as Christians, and they are now outsiders and strangers to them and subject to abusive speech fraught with hostility and conflict (2:12, 21–23; 3:9, 16; 4:14).

The suffering such treatment evokes in them may likely be accompanied by loss of social status for those among them who have it and may also negatively affect their economic

1. Paul Achtemeier, *1 Peter*, Hermeneia (Minneapolis, MN: Fortress, 1996), 69–72; Donald P. Senior, *1 Peter*, Sacra Pagina 15 (Collegeville, MN: Liturgical Press, 2003), 28.

1
P
T

situation.[2] The believers are bewildered from this suffering at the hands of those they once knew, whom 1 Peter calls "Gentiles" (1 Pt 2:12; 4:3). Between the new patterns of living that they have had to learn as Christians and their rejection and vilification by many they once knew, their sense of identity has been shaken. The author of 1 Peter has shaped his letter to encourage these communities to hold fast to their faith in Jesus in the face of persecution and the suffering that follows it (1:6–7, 13; 2:19; 3:16), but he also provides them with a way to understand their suffering that neither seeks out a martyrdom echoing Jesus' own death nor anxiously awaits the triumphant arrival of God as final judge. [3]

He exhorts them to consider how Jesus had conducted himself while enduring suffering for which "he committed no sin" (1 Pt 2:22) and to "arm [themselves] also with the same attitude" (4:1) as Christ's: "When he was insulted, he returned no insult; when he suffered, he did not threaten" (2:23). By approaching their suffering in this way, they will participate in Jesus' own sufferings (4:13), and this suffering for the sake of faith will be transformed (4:13–14). Yet 1 Peter provides them with an additional way to comprehend their suffering without retaliating against their tormentors; their Gentile persecutors will observe their exemplary conduct and "be put to shame" (3:16). He regards those who vilify them as possessing some sort of fairness or rationality when he asks his audience, "Now who is going to harm you if you are enthusiastic for what is good?" (3:13). He even

recognizes the potential that Gentile husbands of Christian wives present for conversion when he writes that husbands "may be won over without a word by their wives' conduct" (3:1).[4]

The circumstances under which Christian citizens, slaves, and wives lived, the last two in particular, were precarious in the best of times. The author urges cooperation with the civil government for all (1 Pt 2:13–17); he instructs slaves to submit to good and evil masters alike and to bear with patience unjust suffering (2:18–20), and he charges wives to give their unbelieving husbands no cause for concern or opportunity for conflict by their conduct or attitude (3:1–6). The principle underlying each of these injunctions derives neither from a theology that conflates obedience to God with obedience to the state, nor from one that accepts and approves slavery, nor even from one that envisions women as inherently inferior to their husbands or needing to revere them.

Each of these constituents, Christian citizens, slaves, and wives, by virtue of their conversion were liable to be viewed as insubordinate and ran the risk of attracting scorn, possible death, and sure censure. The author of 1 Peter is trying to find a way for them to maintain their Christian faith and practice that rejects major premises of the culture: one's support for a city's or locale's primary gods or the adoption of a master's or husband's gods. He provides them with a defense: practice conduct that is most acceptable to their society in every area of their life but one—their faith. The cost to the new Christians is hostility, suffering, and grief, but they can maintain their faith and might yet bring about the conversion of others.[5] ∎

2. Lewis R. Donelson, *I & II Peter and Jude,* New Testament Library (Louisville: Westminster John Knox, 2010), 13; Senior, *1 Peter*, 13.

3. Earl J. Richard, *Reading 1 Peter, Jude, and 2 Peter* (Macon, GA: Smyth & Helwys, 2000), 20.

4. Donelson, *I & II Peter and Jude*, 90.

5. Achtemeier, *1 Peter*, 222.

# THE FIRST LETTER OF PETER

## New American Bible, Introduction

This letter begins with an address by Peter to Christian communities located in five provinces of Asia Minor (1 Pt 1:1), including areas evangelized by Paul (Acts 16:6–7; 18:23). Christians there are encouraged to remain faithful to their standards of belief and conduct in spite of threats of persecution. Numerous allusions in the letter suggest that the churches addressed were largely of Gentile composition (1 Pt 1:14, 18; 2:9–10; 4:3–4), though considerable use is made of the Old Testament (1 Pt 1:24; 2:6–7, 9–10, 22; 3:10–12).

The contents following the address both inspire and admonish these "chosen sojourners" (1 Pt 1:1) who, in seeking to live as God's people, feel an alienation from their previous religious roots and the society around them. Appeal is made to Christ's resurrection and the future hope it provides (1 Pt 1:3–5) and to the experience of baptism as new birth (1 Pt 1:3, 23–25; 3:21). The suffering and death of Christ serve as both source of salvation and example (1 Pt 1:19; 2:21–25; 3:18). What Christians are in Christ, as a people who have received mercy and are to proclaim and live according to God's call (1 Pt 2:9–10), is repeatedly spelled out for all sorts of situations in society (1 Pt 2:11–17), work (even as slaves, 1 Pt 2:18–20), the home (1 Pt 3:1–7), and general conduct (1 Pt 3:8–12; 4:1–11). But over all hangs the possibility of suffering as a Christian (1 Pt 3:13–17). In 1 Pt 4:12–19 persecution is described as already occurring, so that some have supposed the letter was addressed both to places where such a "trial by fire" was already present and to places where it might break out.

The letter constantly mingles moral exhortation (*paraklēsis*) with its catechetical summaries of mercies in Christ. Encouragement to fidelity in spite of suffering is based upon a vision of the meaning of Christian existence. The emphasis on baptism and allusions to various features of the baptismal liturgy suggest that the author has incorporated into his exposition numerous homiletic, credal, hymnic, and sacramental elements of the baptismal rite that had become traditional at an early date.

From Irenaeus in the late second century until modern times, Christian tradition regarded Peter the apostle as author of this document. Since he was martyred at Rome during the persecution of Nero between A.D. 64 and 67, it was supposed that the letter was written from Rome shortly before his death. This is supported by its reference to "Babylon" (1 Pt 5:13), a code name for Rome in the early church.

Some modern scholars, however, on the basis of a number of features that they consider incompatible with Petrine authenticity, regard the letter as the work of a later Christian writer. Such features include the cultivated Greek in which it is written, difficult to attribute to a Galilean fisherman, together with its use of the Greek Septuagint translation when citing the Old Testament; the similarity in both thought and expression to the Pauline literature; and the allusions to widespread persecution of Christians, which did not occur until at least the reign of Domitian (A.D. 81–96). In this view the letter would date from the end of the first century or even the beginning of the second, when there is evidence for persecution of Christians in Asia Minor (the letter of Pliny the Younger to Trajan, A.D. 111–12).

Other scholars believe, however, that these objections can be met by appeal to use of a secretary, Silvanus, mentioned in 1 Pt 5:12. Such secretaries often gave literary expression to the author's thoughts in their own style and language. The persecutions may refer to local harassment rather than to systematic repression by the state. Hence there is nothing in the document incompatible with Petrine authorship in the 60s.

Still other scholars take a middle position. The many literary contacts with the Pauline literature, James, and 1 John suggest a common fund of traditional formulations rather than direct dependence upon Paul. Such liturgical and catechetical traditions must have been very ancient and in some cases of Palestinian origin.

Yet it is unlikely that Peter addressed a letter to the Gentile churches of Asia Minor while Paul was still alive. This suggests a period after the death of the two apostles, perhaps A.D. 70–90. The author would be a disciple of Peter in Rome, representing a Petrine group that served as a bridge between the Palestinian origins of Christianity and its flowering in the Gentile world. The problem addressed would not be official persecution but the difficulty of living the Christian life in a hostile, secular environment that espoused different values and subjected the Christian minority to ridicule and oppression.

The principal divisions of the First Letter of Peter are the following:

I. Address (1:1–2)

II. The Gift and Call of God in Baptism (1:3–2:10)

III. The Christian in a Hostile World (2:11–4:11)

IV. Advice to the Persecuted (4:12–5:11)

V. Conclusion (5:12–14) ■

# FIRST PETER

## I. ADDRESS

**Greeting.**† 1 Peter, an apostle of Jesus Christ, to the chosen sojourners of the dispersion† in Pontus, Galatia, Cappadocia, Asia, and Bithynia, * 2 in the foreknowledge of God the Father, through sanctification by the Spirit, for obedience and sprinkling with the blood of Jesus Christ: may grace and peace be yours in abundance. *

## II. THE GIFT AND CALL OF GOD IN BAPTISM

**Blessing.** 3 † Blessed be the God and Father of our Lord Jesus Christ, who in his great mercy gave us a new birth to a living hope through the resurrection of Jesus Christ from the dead, * 4 to an inheritance that is imperishable, undefiled, and unfading, kept in heaven for you * 5 who by the power of God are safeguarded through faith, to a salvation that is ready to be revealed in the final time. 6 † In this you rejoice, although now for a little while you may have to suffer through various trials, * 7 so that the genuineness of your faith, more precious than gold that is perishable even though tested by fire, may prove to be for praise, glory, and honor at the revelation of Jesus Christ. * 8 Although you have not seen him you love him; even though you do not see him now yet believe in him, you rejoice with an indescribable and glorious joy, * 9 as you attain the goal of [your] faith, the salvation of your souls.

10 † Concerning this salvation, prophets who prophesied about the grace that was to be yours searched and investigated it, 11 investigating the time and circumstances that the Spirit of Christ within them indicated when it testified in advance to the sufferings destined for Christ and the glories to follow them. * 12 It was revealed to them that they were serving not themselves but you with regard to the things that have now been announced to you by those who preached the good news to you [through] the holy Spirit sent from heaven, things into which angels longed to look.

**Obedience.** 13 † Therefore, gird up the loins of your mind,† live soberly, and set your hopes completely on the grace to be brought to you at the revelation of Jesus Christ. 14 Like obedient children, do not act in compliance with the desires of your former ignorance† 15 but, as he who called you is holy, be holy yourselves in every aspect of your conduct, * 16 for it is written, "Be holy because I [am] holy." *

**Reverence.** 17 Now if you invoke as Father him who judges impartially according to each one's works, conduct yourselves with reverence during the time of your sojourning, * 18 realizing that you were ransomed from your futile conduct, handed on by your ancestors, not with perishable things like silver or gold *

---

† **1:1–2** The introductory formula names *Peter* as the writer (but see Introduction). In his comments to the presbyters (1 Pt 5:1), the author calls himself a "fellow presbyter." He addresses himself to the Gentile converts of Asia Minor. Their privileged status as a *chosen* and sanctified people makes them worthy of God's *grace* and *peace*. In contrast is their actual existence as aliens and *sojourners*, scattered among pagans, far from their true country.
**1:1** *Dispersion*: literally, diaspora; see Jas 1:1 and Introduction to that letter. *Pontus…Bithynia*: five provinces in Asia Minor, listed in clockwise order from the north, perhaps in the sequence in which a messenger might deliver the letter.
**1:3–5** A prayer of praise and thanksgiving to God who bestows the gift of new life and hope in baptism (*new birth*, 1 Pt 1:3) *through the resurrection of Jesus Christ from the dead*. The new birth is a sign of an *imperishable inheritance* (1 Pt 1:4), of *salvation* that is still in the future (*to be revealed in the final time*, 1 Pt 1:5).
**1:6–9** As the glory of Christ's resurrection was preceded by his sufferings and death, the new life of faith that it bestows is to be subjected to many *trials* (1 Pt 1:6) while achieving its goal: the glory of the fullness of *salvation* (1 Pt 1:9) at the coming of Christ (1 Pt 1:7).
**1:10–12** The *Spirit of Christ* (1 Pt 1:11) is here shown to have been present in the prophets, moving them to search, investigate, and prophesy about the *grace* of *salvation* that was to come (1 Pt 1:10), and in the apostles impelling them to preach the fulfillment of salvation in the message of Christ's sufferings and glory (1 Pt 1:12).
**1:13–25** These verses are concerned with the call of God's people to holiness and to mutual love by reason of their redemption through the blood of Christ (1 Pt 1:18–21).
**1:13** *Gird up the loins of your mind*: a figure reminiscent of the rite of Passover when the Israelites were in flight from their oppressors (Ex 12:11), and also suggesting the vigilance of the Christian people in expectation of the parousia of Christ (Lk 12:35).
**1:14–16** The *ignorance* here referred to (1 Pt 1:14) was their former lack of knowledge of God, leading inevitably to godless conduct. Holiness (1 Pt 1:15–16), on the contrary, is the result of their call to the knowledge and love of God.

---

*

| | |
|---|---|
| **1:1** Jas 1:1. | **1:11** Is 52:13–53:12; Dn 9:24. |
| **1:2** Rom 8:29. | |
| **1:3** Ti 3:5. | **1:15** Mt 5:48; 1 Jn 3:3. |
| **1:4** Mt 6:19–20. | **1:16** Lv 11:44; 19:2. |
| **1:6** Jas 1:2–3. | **1:17** 2:11. |
| **1:7** 1 Cor 3:13. | **1:18** Is 52:3; 1 Cor 6:20. |
| **1:8** 2 Cor 5:6–7. | |

1 PT

¹⁹but with the precious blood of Christ* as of a spotless unblemished lamb.† ²⁰He was known before the foundation of the world but revealed in the final time for you, ²¹who through him believe in God who raised him from the dead and gave him glory, so that your faith and hope are in God.

**Mutual Love.**† ²²Since you have purified yourselves by obedience to the truth for sincere mutual love, love one another intensely from a [pure] heart.* ²³You have been born anew,* not from perishable but from imperishable seed, through the living and abiding word of God,† ²⁴for:

> "All flesh is like grass,
>> and all its glory like the flower of the
>> field;
> the grass withers,
>> and the flower wilts;*
²⁵> but the word of the Lord remains
>> forever."

This is the word that has been proclaimed to you.

**2** **God's House and People.** ¹† Rid yourselves of all malice and all deceit, insincerity, envy, and all slander;* ²like newborn infants, long for pure spiritual milk so that through it you may grow into salvation, ³* for you have tasted that the Lord is good.† ⁴Come to him, a living stone,† rejected by human beings but chosen and precious in the sight of God,* ⁵and, like living stones, let yourselves be built† into a spiritual house to be a holy priesthood to offer spiritual sacrifices acceptable to God through Jesus Christ.* ⁶For it says in scripture:

> "Behold, I am laying a stone in Zion,
>> a cornerstone, chosen and precious,
> and whoever believes in it shall not be
>> put to shame."*

⁷Therefore, its value is for you who have faith, but for those without faith:

> "The stone which the builders rejected
>> has become the cornerstone,"*

⁸and

> "A stone that will make people stumble,
>> and a rock that will make them fall."

They stumble by disobeying the word, as is their destiny.*

⁹† But you are "a chosen race, a royal priesthood, a holy nation, a people of his own, so that you may announce the praises" of him who called you out of darkness into his wonderful light.*

¹⁰> Once you were "no people"
>> but now you are God's people;
> you "had not received mercy"
>> but now you have received mercy.*

---

**1:19** Christians have received the redemption prophesied by Isaiah (Is 52:3), through the blood (Jewish symbol of life) of the spotless lamb (Is 53:7, 10; Jn 1:29; Rom 3:24–25; cf. 1 Cor 6:20).

**1:22–25** The new birth of Christians (1 Pt 1:23) derives from Christ, the *imperishable seed* or sowing that produces a new and lasting existence in those who accept the gospel (1 Pt 1:24–25), with the consequent duty of loving *one another* (1 Pt 1:22).

**1:23** *The living and abiding word of God*: or, "the word of the living and abiding God."

**2:1–3** Growth toward salvation is seen here as two steps: first, stripping away all that is contrary to the new life in Christ; second, the nourishment (*pure spiritual milk*) that the newly baptized have received.

**2:3** *Tasted that the Lord is good*: cf. Ps 34:9.

**2:4–8** Christ is the cornerstone (cf. Is 28:16) that is the foundation of the spiritual edifice of the Christian community (1 Pt 2:5). To unbelievers, Christ is an obstacle and a stumbling block on which they are destined to fall (1 Pt 2:8); cf. Rom 11:11.

**2:5** *Let yourselves be built*: the form of the Greek word could also be indicative passive, "you are being built" (cf. 1 Pt 2:9).

**2:9–10** The prerogatives of ancient Israel mentioned here are now more fully and fittingly applied to the Christian people: "a chosen race" (cf. Is 43:20–21) indicates their divine election (Eph 1:4–6); "a royal priesthood" (cf. Ex 19:6) to serve and worship God in Christ, thus continuing the priestly functions of his life, passion, and resurrection; "a holy nation" (Ex 19:6) reserved for God, a people he claims for his own (cf. Mal 3:17) in virtue of their baptism into his death and resurrection. This transcends all natural and national divisions and unites the people into one community to glorify the one who led them from the darkness of paganism to the light of faith in Christ. From being "no people" deprived of all mercy, they have become the very people of God, the chosen recipients of his mercy (cf. Hos 1:9; 2:25).

---

**1:19** Ex 12:5; Jn 1:29; Heb 9:14.
**1:22** Rom 12:10.
**1:23** 1 Jn 3:9.
**1:24** Is 40:6–8.
**2:1–2** Jas 1:21.
**2:3** Ps 34:9.
**2:4** Ps 118:22; Mt 21:42; Acts 4:11.
**2:5** Eph 2:21–22.
**2:6** Is 28:16.
**2:7** Ps 118:22; Mt 21:42; Lk 20:17; Acts 4:11.
**2:8** Is 8:14; Rom 9:33.
**2:9** Ex 19:6; Is 61:6; Rev 1:6; 20:6.
**2:10** Hos 1:9; 2:25 / Hos 1:6.

## III. THE CHRISTIAN IN A HOSTILE WORLD

**Christian Examples.** [11]† Beloved, I urge you as aliens and sojourners† to keep away from worldly desires that wage war against the soul.* [12] Maintain good conduct among the Gentiles, so that if they speak of you as evildoers, they may observe your good works and glorify God on the day of visitation.

**Christian Citizens.**† [13] Be subject to every human institution for the Lord's sake, whether it be to the king as supreme* [14] or to governors as sent by him for the punishment of evildoers and the approval of those who do good. [15] For it is the will of God that by doing good you may silence the ignorance of foolish people. [16] Be free, yet without using freedom as a pretext for evil, but as slaves of God.* [17] Give honor to all, love the community, fear God, honor the king.*

**Christian Slaves.** [18]† Slaves, be subject to your masters with all reverence, not only to those who are good and equitable but also to those who are perverse.* [19] For whenever anyone bears the pain of unjust suffering because of consciousness of God, that is a grace. [20] But what credit is there if you are patient when beaten for doing wrong? But if you are patient when you suffer for doing what is good, this is a grace before God. [21] For to this you have been called, because Christ also suffered† for you, leaving you an example that you should follow in his footsteps.*

22        "He committed no sin,*
              and no deceit was found in his
                   mouth."†

[23] When he was insulted, he returned no insult; when he suffered, he did not threaten; instead, he handed himself over to the one who judges justly.* [24] He himself bore our sins in his body upon the cross, so that, free from sin, we might live for righteousness. By his wounds you have been healed.* [25] For you had gone astray like sheep,* but you have now returned to the shepherd and guardian of your souls.†

**3** **Christian Spouses.** [1]† Likewise, you wives should be subordinate to your husbands so that, even if some disobey the word, they may be won over without a word by their wives' conduct [2] when they observe your reverent and chaste behavior.* [3] Your adornment should not be an external one: braiding the hair, wearing gold jewelry, or dressing in fine clothes,* [4] but rather the hidden character of the heart, expressed in the imperishable beauty of a gentle and calm disposition, which is precious in the sight of God. [5] For this is also

† **2:11–3:12** After explaining the doctrinal basis for the Christian community, the author makes practical applications in terms of the virtues that should prevail in all the social relationships of the members of the community: good example to Gentile neighbors (1 Pt 2:11–12); respect for human authority (1 Pt 2:13–17); obedience, patience, and endurance of hardship in domestic relations (1 Pt 2:18–25); Christian behavior of husbands and wives (1 Pt 3:1–7); mutual charity (1 Pt 3:8–12).

**2:11** *Aliens and sojourners*: no longer signifying absence from one's native land (Gn 23:4), this image denotes rather their estrangement from the world during their earthly pilgrimage (see also 1 Pt 1:1, 17).

**2:13–17** True Christian freedom is the result of being servants of God (1 Pt 2:16; see note on 1 Pt 2:18–23). It includes reverence for God, esteem for every individual, and committed love for fellow Christians (1 Pt 2:17). Although persecution may threaten, subjection to human government is urged (1 Pt 2:13, 17) and concern for the impact of Christians' conduct on those who are not Christians (1 Pt 2:12, 15).

**2:18–21** Most of the labor in the commercial cities of first-century Asia Minor was performed by a working class of slaves. The sense of freedom contained in the gospel undoubtedly caused great tension among Christian slaves: witness the special advice given concerning them here and in 1 Cor 7:21–24; Eph 6:5–8; Col 3:22–25; Phlm. The point made here does not have so much to do with the institution of slavery, which the author does not challenge, but with the nonviolent reaction (1 Pt 2:20) of slaves to unjust treatment. Their patient suffering is compared to that of Jesus (1 Pt 2:21), which won righteousness for all humanity.

**2:21** *Suffered*: some ancient manuscripts and versions read "died" (cf. 1 Pt 3:18).

**2:22–25** After the quotation of Is 53:9b, the passage describes Jesus' passion with phrases concerning the Suffering Servant from Is 53:4–12, perhaps as employed in an early Christian confession of faith; cf. 1 Pt 1:18–21 and 1 Pt 3:18–22.

**2:25** *The shepherd and guardian of your souls*: the familiar shepherd and flock figures express the care, vigilance, and love of God for his people in the Old Testament (Ps 23; Is 40:11; Jer 23:4–5; Ez 34:11–16) and of Jesus for all humanity in the New Testament (Mt 18:10–14; Lk 15:4–7; Jn 10:1–16; Heb 13:20).

**3:1–6** The typical marital virtues of women of the ancient world, obedience, reverence, and chastity (1 Pt 3:1–2), are outlined here by the author, who gives them an entirely new motivation: Christian wives are to be virtuous so that they may be instrumental in the conversion of their husbands. In imitation of *holy women* in the past (1 Pt 3:5) they are to cultivate the interior life (1 Pt 3:4) instead of excessive concern with their appearance (1 Pt 3:3).

*
| | |
|---|---|
| **2:11** Gal 5:24. | **2:23** Mt 5:39. |
| **2:13** Is 53:1–7. | **2:24** Is 53:4, 12 / Is 53:5. |
| **2:16** Gal 5:13. | **2:25** Is 53:6. |
| **2:17** Prv 24:21; Mt 22:21. | **3:2** 1 Cor 7:12–16; Eph |
| **2:18** Eph 6:5. | 5:22–24; Col 3:18; |
| **2:21** Mt 16:24. | 1 Tm 2:9–15. |
| **2:22** Is 53:9. | **3:3** 1 Tm 2:9–10. |

how the holy women who hoped in God once used to adorn themselves and were subordinate to their husbands; ⁶thus Sarah obeyed Abraham, calling him "lord." You are her children when you do what is good and fear no intimidation.

⁷* Likewise, you husbands should live with your wives in understanding, showing honor to the weaker female sex, since we are joint heirs of the gift of life, so that your prayers may not be hindered.†

**Christian Conduct.**† ⁸Finally, all of you, be of one mind, sympathetic, loving toward one another, compassionate, humble. ⁹Do not return evil for evil, or insult for insult; but, on the contrary, a blessing, because to this you were called, that you might inherit a blessing.* ¹⁰For:

"Whoever would love life*
　　and see good days
must keep the tongue from evil
　　and the lips from speaking deceit,
¹¹　must turn from evil and do good,
　　seek peace and follow after it.
¹²　For the eyes of the Lord are on the righteous
　　and his ears turned to their prayer,
but the face of the Lord is against evildoers."

**Christian Suffering.**† ¹³Now who is going to harm you if you are enthusiastic for what is good? ¹⁴But even if you should suffer because

of righteousness, blessed are you. Do not be afraid or terrified with fear of them, ¹⁵but sanctify Christ as Lord in your hearts. Always be ready to give an explanation to anyone who asks you for a reason for your hope,* ¹⁶but do it with gentleness and reverence, keeping your conscience clear, so that, when you are maligned, those who defame your good conduct in Christ may themselves be put to shame. ¹⁷For it is better to suffer for doing good, if that be the will of God, than for doing evil.

¹⁸For Christ also suffered† for sins once, the righteous for the sake of the unrighteous, that he might lead you to God. Put to death in the flesh, he was brought to life in the spirit.* ¹⁹In it he also went to preach to the spirits in prison,† ²⁰who had once been disobedient while God patiently waited in the days of Noah during the building of the ark, in which a few persons, eight in all, were saved through water.* ²¹This prefigured baptism, which saves you now. It is not a removal of dirt from the body but an appeal to God† for a clear conscience, through the resurrection of Jesus Christ,* ²²who has gone into heaven and is at the right hand of God, with angels, authorities, and powers subject to him.*

4 **Christian Restraint.**† ¹Therefore, since Christ suffered in the flesh, arm yourselves also with the same attitude (for whoever suffers in the flesh has broken with sin), ²so as not to spend what remains of one's life in the flesh on human desires, but on the will of God. ³For the time that has passed is sufficient

---

**3:7** Husbands who do not respect their wives will have as little success in prayer as those who, according to Paul, have no love: their prayers will be "a resounding gong or a clashing cymbal" (1 Cor 13:1). Consideration for others is shown as a prerequisite for effective prayer also in Mt 5:23–24; 1 Cor 11:20–22; Jas 4:3. After all, whatever the social position of women in the world and in the family, they are equal recipients of the gift of God's salvation. Paul is very clear on this point, too (see 1 Cor 11:11–12; Gal 3:28).

**3:8–12** For the proper ordering of Christian life in its various aspects as described in 1 Pt 2:11–3:9, there is promised the blessing expressed in Ps 34:13–17. In the Old Testament this refers to longevity and prosperity; here, it also refers to eternal life.

**3:13–22** This exposition, centering on 1 Pt 3:17, runs as follows: by his suffering and death Christ the righteous one saved the unrighteous (1 Pt 3:18); by his resurrection he received new life in the spirit, which he communicates to believers through the baptismal bath that cleanses their consciences from sin. As Noah's family was saved *through water,* so Christians are saved through the waters of baptism (1 Pt 3:19–22). Hence they need not share the fear of sinners; they should rather rejoice in suffering because of their hope in Christ. Thus their innocence disappoints their accusers (1 Pt 3:13–16; cf. Mt 10:28; Rom 8:35–39).

**3:18** *Suffered*: very many ancient manuscripts and versions read "died." *Put to death in the flesh*: affirms that Jesus truly died as a human being. *Brought to life in the spirit*: that is, in the new and transformed existence freed from the limitations and weaknesses of natural human life (cf. 1 Cor 15:45).

**3:19** *The spirits in prison*: it is not clear just who these spirits are. They may be the spirits of the sinners who died in the flood, or angelic powers, hostile to God, who have been overcome by Christ (cf. 1 Pt 3:22; Gn 6:4; Enoch 6–36, especially 21:6; 2 Enoch 7:1–5).

**3:21** *Appeal to God*: this could also be translated "pledge," that is, a promise on the part of Christians to live with a good conscience before God, or a pledge from God of forgiveness and therefore a good conscience for us.

**4:1–6** Willingness to suffer with Christ equips the Christian with the power to conquer sin (1 Pt 4:1). Christ is here portrayed as the judge to whom those guilty of pagan vices must render an account (1 Pt 4:5; cf. Jn 5:22–27; Acts 10:42; 2 Tm 4:1).

---

**3:7** Eph 5:25–33; Col 3:19.
**3:9** Mt 5:44; Lk 6:28; Rom 12:14.
**3:10–12** Ps 34:13–17.
**3:15** Is 8:12.
**3:18** 1 Cor 15:45.
**3:20** Gn 7:7, 17; 2 Pt 2:5.
**3:21** Eph 5:26; Heb 10:22.
**3:22** Eph 1:20–21.

for doing what the Gentiles like to do: living in debauchery, evil desires, drunkenness, orgies, carousing, and wanton idolatry.* ⁴They are surprised that you do not plunge into the same swamp of profligacy, and they vilify you; ⁵but they will give an account to him who stands ready to judge the living and the dead.* ⁶For this is why the gospel was preached even to the dead† that, though condemned in the flesh in human estimation, they might live in the spirit in the estimation of God.

### Christian Charity.† ⁷The end of all things is at hand. Therefore, be serious and sober for prayers. ⁸* Above all, let your love for one another be intense, because love covers a multitude of sins.† ⁹Be hospitable to one another without complaining.* ¹⁰As each one has received a gift, use it to serve one another as good stewards of God's varied grace.* ¹¹Whoever preaches, let it be with the words of God; whoever serves, let it be with the strength that God supplies, so that in all things God may be glorified through Jesus Christ,* to whom belong glory and dominion forever and ever. Amen.†

## IV. ADVICE TO THE PERSECUTED

### Trial of Persecution.† ¹²Beloved, do not be surprised that a trial by fire is occurring among you, as if something strange were happening to you.* ¹³But rejoice to the extent that you share in the sufferings of Christ, so that when his glory is revealed you may also rejoice exultantly.* ¹⁴If you are insulted for the name of Christ, blessed are you, for the Spirit of glory and of God rests upon you.* ¹⁵But let no one among you be made to suffer as a murderer, a thief, an evildoer, or as an intriguer. ¹⁶But whoever is made to suffer as a Christian should not be ashamed but glorify God because of the name. ¹⁷For it is time for the judgment to begin with the household of God; if it begins with us, how will it end for those who fail to obey the gospel of God?*

¹⁸　　"And if the righteous one is barely saved,
　　　where will the godless and the sinner
　　　appear?"*

¹⁹As a result, those who suffer in accord with God's will hand their souls over to a faithful creator as they do good.

## 5 Advice to Presbyters.† ¹So I exhort the presbyters† among you, as a fellow presbyter and witness to the sufferings of Christ and one who has a share in the glory to be revealed. ²Tend the flock of God in your midst, [overseeing] not by constraint but willingly, as God would have it, not for shameful profit but eagerly.* ³Do not lord it over those assigned to you, but be examples to the flock. ⁴* And when the chief Shepherd is revealed, you will receive the unfading crown of glory.†

### Advice to the Community.† ⁵Likewise, you younger members,† be subject to the presbyters. And all of you, clothe yourselves with

---

4:6 *The dead*: these may be the sinners of the flood generation who are possibly referred to in 1 Pt 3:19. But many scholars think that there is no connection between these two verses, and that *the dead* here are Christians who have died since hearing the preaching of the gospel.

4:7–11 The inner life of the eschatological community is outlined as *the end* (the parousia of Christ) and the judgment draws near in terms of seriousness, sobriety, prayer, and love expressed through hospitality and the use of one's gifts for the glory of God and of Christ.

4:8 *Love covers a multitude of sins*: a maxim based on Prv 10:12; see also Ps 32:1; Jas 5:20.

4:11 Some scholars feel that this doxology concludes the part of the homily addressed specifically to the newly baptized, begun in 1 Pt 1:3; others that it concludes a baptismal liturgy. Such doxologies do occur within a New Testament letter, e.g., Rom 9:5. Some propose that 1 Pt 4:11 was an alternate ending, with 1 Pt 4:12–5:14 being read in places where persecution was more pressing. But such doxologies usually do not occur at the end of letters (the only examples are 2 Pt 3:18, Jude 25, and Rom 16:27, the last probably a liturgical insertion).

4:12–19 The suffering to which the author has already frequently referred is presented in more severe terms. This has led some scholars to see these verses as referring to an actual persecution. Others see the heightening of the language as only a rhetorical device used at the end of the letter to emphasize the suffering motif.

5:1–4 In imitation of Christ, the chief shepherd, those entrusted with a pastoral office are to tend the flock by their care and example.

5:1 *Presbyters*: the officially appointed leaders and teachers of the Christian community (cf. 1 Tm 5:17–18; Ti 1:5–8; Jas 5:14).

5:4 See note on 1 Pt 2:25.

5:5–11 The community is to be subject to the presbyters and to show humility toward one another and trust in God's love and care (1 Pt 5:5–7). With sobriety, alertness, and steadfast faith they must resist the evil one: their sufferings are shared with Christians everywhere (1 Pt 5:8–9). They will be strengthened and called to eternal glory (1 Pt 5:10–11).

5:5 *Younger members*: this may be a designation for officeholders of lesser rank.

---

4:3 Eph 2:2–3; 4:17–19;
　　Col 3:7; Ti 3:3.
4:5 Acts 10:42; 2 Tm 4:1.
4:8 Prv 10:12; Jas 5:20.
4:9 Heb 13:2.
4:10 Rom 12:6–8; 1 Cor
　　12:4–11.
4:11 1 Cor 10:31.
4:12 1:6–7; 3:14, 17.

4:13 Rom 5:3–5; 8:17;
　　2 Tm 2:12.
4:14 Acts 5:41 / Is 11:2.
4:17 Lk 23:31; 2 Thes 1:8.
4:18 Prv 11:31 LXX.
5:2 Acts 20:28; Ti 1:7.
5:4 Wis 5:15–16; 1 Cor
　　9:25; 2 Tm 4:8; Jas
　　1:12.

humility in your dealings with one another, for:

"God opposes the proud
    but bestows favor on the humble."*

6 So humble yourselves under the mighty hand of God, that he may exalt you in due time.* 7 Cast all your worries upon him because he cares for you.*

8 Be sober and vigilant. Your opponent the devil is prowling around like a roaring lion looking for [someone] to devour.* 9 Resist him, steadfast in faith, knowing that your fellow believers throughout the world undergo the same sufferings. 10 The God of all grace who called you to his eternal glory through Christ [Jesus] will himself restore, confirm, strengthen, and establish you after you have suffered a little.* 11 To him be dominion forever. Amen.

## V. CONCLUSION

12 I write you this briefly through Silvanus,† whom I consider a faithful brother, exhorting you and testifying that this is the true grace of God. Remain firm in it. 13 The chosen one† at Babylon sends you greeting, as does Mark, my son. 14 Greet one another with a loving kiss. Peace to all of you who are in Christ.*

---

† **5:12** *Silvanus*: the companion of Paul (see 2 Cor 1:19; 1 Thes 1:1; 2 Thes 1:1). Jews and Jewish Christians, like Paul, often had a Hebrew name (Saoul, Silas) and a Greek or Latin name (Paul, Silvanus). On Silvanus's possible role as amanuensis, see Introduction.

**5:13** *The chosen one*: feminine, referring to the Christian community (*ekklēsia*) at *Babylon*, the code name for Rome in Rev 14:8; 17:5; 18:2. *Mark, my son*: traditionally a prominent disciple of Peter and co-worker at the church in Rome, perhaps the John Mark referred to in Acts 12:12, 25; 13:5, 13; and in Acts 15:37–39, a companion of Barnabas. Perhaps this is the same Mark mentioned as Barnabas's cousin in Col 4:10, a co-worker with Paul in Phlm 24 (see also 2 Tm 4:11).

---

*

| | |
|---|---|
| **5:5** Prv 3:34. | **5:8** 1 Thes 5:6. |
| **5:6** Jb 22:29; Jas 4:10. | **5:10** Rom 8:18; 2 Cor 4:17. |
| **5:7** Ps 55:23; Mt 6:25–33; | **5:14** Rom 16:16; 1 Cor |
| Lk 12:22–31; Phil 4:6. | 16:20; 2 Cor 13:12. |

# The Second Letter of

# Peter

## INTRODUCTION

### Mary Katherine Birge, SSJ

In 2 Peter the reader encounters the work of a Jewish Christian writer who has been well educated in both Jewish thought and Hellenistic literature. This background provides him with a unique advantage as he tries to "translate" the idiom of Jewish Christianity into an idiom more familiar to his audience of Gentile Christians whose native milieu, until their conversion, has always been Hellenism. These men and women, likely recent converts to Christianity, seem to have become captivated by the ideas and practices that a group of visiting Christians (2 Pt 2:1, 20–21) have been teaching them and that, the author believes, assault basic premises of Christianity. This is part of the writer's motivation for adopting language, figures of speech, and philosophical concepts of the first-century Hellenistic world.[1] He employs them as tools in his struggle to persuade his audience to turn away from these "false prophets" and "false teachers" (2:1) and to turn back to true "knowledge of God and of Jesus our Lord" (1:2).

Well before 2 Peter wrote in the latter quarter of the first century CE, Hellenistic Jews had adopted and adapted Hellenistic religious and philosophical vocabulary "to express [their] own religious tradition in terms appropriate to its Hellenistic environment,"[2] multiple examples of which can be seen in Jewish literature of the period (cf. the Wisdom of Solomon, various works of Philo, 4 Maccabees). The author of 2 Peter is not the first to have refashioned the religious and philosophical language of Hellenism and to embrace its values and practices (as seen above) in order to co-opt and subvert its power to attract, even to entice

## Outline of 2 Peter

I. Address (1:1–2)

II. Exhortation to Christian Virtue (1:3–21)

III. Condemnation of the False Teachers (2:1–22)

IV. The Delay of the Second Coming (3:1–16)

V. Final Exhortation and Doxology (3:17–18)

those living outside of its system. Nor is he the only early Christian writer to employ such a linguistic and rhetorical strategy in writing to Gentile Christians (cf. *1–2 Clement* and *The Shepherd of Hermas*, especially the "Visions"). He is, however, the only writer in the New Testament to engage his audience deliberately in this way as an attempt to dissolve a Christian community's attraction to renegade teachers and restore the community's understanding of God (2 Pt 1:3) to its original state

The first few verses of 2 Pt 1 alone offer significant examples of his practice of "borrowing" from Hellenism's religious and literary terminology. The author of 2 Peter reminds his audience in 1:3 that God's "divine power" has provided everything that they need in order to live a life of godliness. The phrase "divine power" is a religious term familiar from Greek literature and adopted by Hellenistic Jewish authors, yet it appears nowhere else in Christian literature until significantly later writers such as Justin and Clement of Alexandria.[3] In some Greek and Hellenistic Jewish writings, e.g., Plato's *Laws* (3.691E), Philo's *Worse* (23 §83) and the *Letter of Aristeas* (155–57), the

1. Daniel J. Harrington, *Jude and 2 Peter*, Sacra Pagina 15 (Collegeville, MN: Liturgical Press, 2003), 232–34.

2. Richard J. Bauckham, *Jude, 2 Peter*, Word Biblical Commentary 50 (Nashville: Thomas Nelson, 1983), 180.

3. Ibid., 177.

2
PT

authors employ this phrase when discussing "the nature of the divine in relationship to human nature,"[4] which is exactly what the author of 2 Peter is doing in this verse and in the next.

He takes another word, "devotion" (2 Pt 1:3), which both Greeks and Hellenistic Jews employ throughout their literature, and continues his effort to use the language of his audience's culture.[5] The Greeks use this word in speaking about reverence or piety toward the gods, as do Hellenistic Jews, but the latter, along with early Christians, also employ it to expound on the necessity of living an ethical life and rendering obedience to God's desires, both of which themes the author of 2 Peter will bring up throughout the rest of his letter.[6] For Jews and Christians, these practices are integral components of showing devotion to God, something that the false teachers seem to have rejected according to 2 Peter's attacks against them in 2:1–22 and 3:3–7. In this same verse (1:3), he includes one more word that bears dual Greek and Hellenistic Jewish meanings. When the author asserts that God has "called us by his own glory and power," he employs a phrase, "glory and power," that is found frequently in Greek literature (e.g., Plutarch, Pausanias, Dionysius of Halicarnassus) and usually indicates military deeds of great renown. In Hellenistic Jewish literature the phrase always refers to God's great acts of power. Here the author of 2 Peter has picked up language that would have been used in the Greek world to honor a patron with a formal decree acknowledging his beneficence and largess to clients, and he applies it to God, implying to his audience that God is their patron

and benefactor.[7] He continues to draw on both these Greek and Hellenistic Jewish traditions when he reminds his audience that they "may come to share in the divine nature" (1:4).

There was within Greek literature a robust strain of thought that claimed the spiritual part of a human being actually belonged to the divine sphere and that it was possible to recover this essential part of its nature and take part in divine immortality after having disposed of one's inferior flesh. Hellenistic Judaism had already worked with this Greek concept by the time 2 Peter was written, having employed such religious vocabulary to communicate an expressly Jewish understanding that the destiny of human life is found in the imperishability of the soul (e.g., Wis 2:23). The author of 2 Peter would have been familiar with this strain of Greek thought and well aware that his audience knew it, too.[8] In 2 Pt 1:4b he takes language to which his audience's recently Gentile ears are accustomed and may find soothing amid the strangeness of new Christian vocabulary and notions about the world, and he joins it to the deeply Jewish Christian notion that corruption exists in this world because of sin (1:4c). This kind of corruption exists not because of the inherently physical nature of humanity, a concept Greek thought advanced and Judaism and Christianity rejected.[9] His choice of Hellenistic-sounding language, especially in ch. 1, helps him to establish a rapport with his audience, so that by the time he reaches an all-out polemic against the false teachers in chs. 2 and 3, the author of 2 Peter has prepared the audience to accept as right and just his devastating critique of the false teachers and to assent to his own instruction about Christian living. ■

4. Gene L. Green, *Jude & 2 Peter,* Baker Exegetical Commentary on the New Testament (Grand Rapids, MI: Baker Academic, 2008), 181.

5. Harrington, *Jude and 2 Peter,* 247.

6. Bauckham, *Jude, 2 Peter,* 178.

7. Green, *Jude & 2 Peter,* 184.

8. Bauckham, *Jude, 2 Peter,* 180.

9. Ibid., 184.

# THE SECOND LETTER OF PETER

## New American Bible, Introduction

This letter can be appreciated both for its positive teachings and for its earnest warnings. It seeks to strengthen readers in faith (2 Pt 1:1), hope for the future (2 Pt 3:1–10), knowledge (2 Pt 1:2, 6, 8), love (2 Pt 1:7), and other virtues (2 Pt 1:5–6). This aim is carried out especially by warning against false teachers, the condemnation of whom occupies the long central section of the letter (2 Pt 2:1–22). A particular crisis is the claim by "scoffers" that there will be no second coming of Jesus, a doctrine that the author vigorously affirms (2 Pt 3:1–10). The concept of God's "promises" is particularly precious in the theology of 2 Peter (2 Pt 1:4; 3:4, 9, 13). Closing comments at 2 Pt 3:17–18 well sum up the twin concerns: that you not "be led into" error and "fall" but instead "grow in grace" and "knowledge" of Jesus Christ.

Second Peter is clearly structured in its presentation of these points. It reminds its readers of the divine authenticity of Christ's teaching (2 Pt 1:3–4), continues with reflections on Christian conduct (2 Pt 1:5–15), then returns to the exalted dignity of Jesus by incorporating into the text the apostolic witness to his transfiguration (2 Pt 1:16–18). It takes up the question of the interpretation of scripture by pointing out that it is possible to misunderstand the sacred writings (2 Pt 1:19–21) and that divine punishment will overtake false teachers (2 Pt 2:1–22). It proclaims that the parousia is the teaching of the Lord and of the apostles and is therefore an eventual certainty (2 Pt 3:1–13). At the same time, it warns that the meaning of Paul's writings on this question should not be distorted (2 Pt 3:14–18).

In both content and style this letter is very different from 1 Peter, which immediately precedes it in the canon. The opening verse attributes it to "Symeon Peter, a slave and apostle of Jesus Christ." Moreover, the author in 2 Pt 3:1 calls his work a "second letter," referring probably to 1 Peter as his first, and in 2 Pt 1:18 counts himself among those present at the transfiguration of Jesus.

Nevertheless, acceptance of 2 Peter into the New Testament canon met with great resistance in the early church. The oldest certain reference to it comes from Origen in the early third century. While he himself accepted both Petrine letters as canonical, he testifies that others rejected 2 Peter. As late as the fifth century some local churches still excluded it from the canon, but eventually it was universally adopted. The principal reason for the long delay was the persistent doubt that the letter stemmed from the apostle Peter.

Among modern scholars there is wide agreement that 2 Peter is a pseudonymous work, i.e., one written by a later author who attributed it to Peter according to a literary convention popular at the time. It gives the impression of being more remote in time from the apostolic period than 1 Peter; indeed, many think it is the latest work in the New Testament and assign it to the first or even the second quarter of the second century.

The principal reasons for this view are the following. The author refers to the apostles and "our ancestors" as belonging to a previous generation, now dead (2 Pt 3:2–4). A collection of Paul's letters exists and appears to be well known, but disputes have arisen about the interpretation of them (2 Pt 3:14–16). The passage about false teachers (2 Pt 2:1–18) contains a number of literary contacts with Jude 4–16, and it is generally agreed that 2 Peter depends upon Jude, not vice versa. Finally, the principal problem exercising the author is the false teaching of "scoffers" who have concluded from the delay of the parousia that the Lord is not going to return. This could scarcely have been an issue during the lifetime of Simon Peter.

The Christians to whom the letter is addressed are not identified, though it may be the intent of 2 Pt 3:1 to identify them with the churches of Asia Minor to which 1 Peter was sent. Except for the epistolary greeting in 2 Pt 1:1–2, 2 Peter does not have the features of a genuine letter at all, but is rather a general exhortation cast in the form of a letter. The author must have been a Jewish Christian of the dispersion for, while his Jewish heritage is evident in various features of his thought and style, he writes in the rather stilted literary Greek of the Hellenistic period. He appeals to tradition against the twin threat of doctrinal error and moral laxity, which appear to reflect an early stage of what later developed into full-blown gnosticism. Thus he forms a link between the apostolic period and the church of subsequent ages.

The principal divisions of the Second Letter of Peter are the following:

I. Address (1:1–2)

II. Exhortation to Christian Virtue (1:3–21)

III. Condemnation of the False Teachers (2:1–22)

IV. The Delay of the Second Coming (3:1–16)

V. Final Exhortation and Doxology (3:17–18) ∎

# SECOND PETER

## I. ADDRESS

**1** **Greeting.** [1]† Symeon Peter, a slave and apostle of Jesus Christ, to those who have received a faith of equal value to ours through the righteousness of our God and savior Jesus Christ: [2] may grace and peace be yours in abundance through knowledge† of God and of Jesus our Lord.

## II. EXHORTATION TO CHRISTIAN VIRTUE

**The Power of God's Promise.**† [3] His divine power has bestowed on us everything that makes for life and devotion, through the knowledge of him* who called us by his own glory and power.† [4] Through these, he has bestowed on us the precious and very great promises, so that through them you may come to share in the divine nature, after escaping from the corruption that is in the world because of evil desire.* [5]† For this very reason, make every effort to supplement your faith with virtue, virtue with knowledge,* [6] knowledge with self-control, self-control with endurance, endurance with devotion, [7] devotion with mutual affection, mutual affection with love. [8] If these are yours and increase in abundance, they will keep you from being idle or unfruitful in the knowledge of our Lord Jesus Christ. [9]* Anyone who lacks them is blind and shortsighted, forgetful of the cleansing of his past sins. [10]† Therefore, brothers, be all the more eager to make your call and election firm, for, in doing so, you will never stumble. [11] For, in this way, entry into the eternal kingdom of our Lord and savior Jesus Christ will be richly provided for you.

**Apostolic Witness.** [12]† Therefore, I will always remind you of these things, even though you already know them and are established in the truth you have. [13] I think it right, as long as I am in this "tent,"† to stir you up by a reminder, [14] since I know that I will soon have to put it aside, as indeed our Lord Jesus Christ has shown me.* [15] I shall also make every effort to enable you always to remember these things after my departure.

[16] We did not follow cleverly devised myths when we made known to you the power and coming† of our Lord Jesus Christ, but we had been eyewitnesses of his majesty.* [17] For he received honor and glory from God the Father† when that unique declaration came to him from the majestic glory, "This is my Son, my beloved, with whom I am well pleased."*

---

**1:1** *Symeon Peter*: on the authorship of 2 Peter, see Introduction; on the spelling here of the Hebrew name *Šim'ôn*, cf. Acts 15:14. The greeting is especially similar to those in 1 Peter and Jude. The words translated *our God and savior Jesus Christ* could also be rendered "our God and the savior Jesus Christ"; cf. 2 Pt 1:11; 2:20; 3:2, 18.

**1:2** *Knowledge*: a key term in the letter (2 Pt 1:3, 8; 2:20; 3:18), perhaps used as a Christian emphasis against gnostic claims.

**1:3–4** Christian life in its fullness is a gift of divine power effecting a knowledge of Christ and the bestowal of divine promises (2 Pt 3:4, 9). *To share in the divine nature*, escaping from a corrupt world, is a thought found elsewhere in the Bible but expressed only here in such Hellenistic terms (2 Pt 1:3); cf. 2 Pt 1:2; 2:20; but see also Jn 15:4; 17:22–23; Rom 8:14–17; Heb 3:14; 1 Jn 1:3; 3:2.

**1:3** *By his own glory and power*: the most ancient papyrus and the best codex read "through glory and power."

**1:5–9** Note the climactic gradation of qualities (2 Pt 1:5–7), beginning with faith and leading to the fullness of Christian life, which is love; cf. Rom 5:3–4; Gal 5:6, 22 for a similar series of "virtues," though the program and sense here are different than in Paul. The fruit of these is knowledge of Christ (2 Pt 1:8) referred to in 2 Pt 1:3; their absence is spiritual blindness (2 Pt 1:9).

**1:10–11** Perseverance in the Christian vocation is the best preventative against losing it and the safest provision for attaining its goal, the kingdom. *Kingdom of...Christ*, instead of "God," is unusual; cf. Col 1:13 and Mt 13:41, as well as the *righteousness of...Christ* (2 Pt 1:1).

**1:12–19** The purpose in writing is to call to mind the apostle's witness to the truth, even as he faces the end of his life (2 Pt 1:12–15), his eyewitness testimony to Christ (1 Pt 1:16–18), and the true prophetic message (2 Pt 1:19) through the Spirit in scripture (2 Pt 1:20–21), in contrast to what false teachers are setting forth (2 Pt 2).

**1:13** *Tent*: a biblical image for transitory human life (Is 38:12), here combined with a verb that suggests not folding or packing up a tent but its being discarded in death (cf. 2 Cor 5:1–4).

**1:16** *Coming*: in Greek *parousia*, used at 2 Pt 3:4, 12 of the second coming of Christ. The word was used in the extrabiblical writings for the visitation of someone in authority; in Greek cult and Hellenistic Judaism it was used for the manifestation of the divine presence. That the apostles *made known* has been interpreted to refer to Jesus' transfiguration (2 Pt 1:17) or to his entire first coming or to his future coming in power (2 Pt 3).

**1:17** The author assures the readers of the reliability of the apostolic message (including Jesus' power, glory, and coming; cf. note on 2 Pt 1:16) by appeal to the transfiguration of Jesus in glory (cf. Mt 17:1–8 and parallels) and by appeal to the prophetic message (2 Pt 1:19; perhaps Nm 24:17). Here, as elsewhere, the New Testament insists on continued reminders as necessary to preserve the historical facts about Jesus and the truths of the faith; cf. 2 Pt 3:1–2; 1 Cor 11:2; 15:1–3. *My Son, my beloved*: or, "my beloved Son."

---

**1:3** 2 Cor 4:6; 1 Pt 2:9.     **1:14** Is 38:12; Jn 21:18–19.
**1:4** 2 Cor 7:1; 1 Jn 2:15.     **1:16** Lk 9:28–36; Jn 1:14.
**1:5–7** Gal 5:22–23.           **1:17** Ps 2:7; Mt 17:4–6.
**1:9** 1 Jn 2:9, 11.

[18] We† ourselves heard this voice come from heaven while we were with him on the holy mountain. [19]* Moreover, we possess the prophetic message that is altogether reliable. You will do well to be attentive to it, as to a lamp shining in a dark place, until day dawns and the morning star rises in your hearts. [20]† Know this first of all, that there is no prophecy of scripture that is a matter of personal interpretation, [21] for no prophecy ever came through human will; but rather human beings moved by the holy Spirit spoke under the influence of God.

## III. CONDEMNATION OF THE FALSE TEACHERS

**2** **False Teachers.**† [1] There were also false prophets among the people, just as there will be false teachers among you, who will introduce destructive heresies and even deny the Master who ransomed them, bringing swift destruction on themselves. * [2] Many will follow their licentious ways, and because of them the way of truth will be reviled.* [3] In their greed they will exploit you with fabrications, but from of old their condemnation has not been idle and their destruction does not sleep.*

**Lessons from the Past.** [4]† For if God did not spare the angels when they sinned, but condemned them to the chains of Tartarus† and handed them over to be kept for judgment;* [5]† and if he did not spare the ancient world, even though he preserved Noah, a herald of righteousness, together with seven others, when he brought a flood upon the godless world;* [6] and if he condemned the cities of Sodom and Gomorrah [to destruction], reducing them to ashes, making them an example for the godless [people] of what is coming;* [7] and if he rescued Lot, a righteous man oppressed by the licentious conduct of unprincipled people [8] (for day after day that righteous man living among them was tormented in his righteous soul at the lawless deeds that he saw and heard), [9] then the Lord knows how to rescue the devout from trial and to keep the unrighteous under punishment for the day of judgment, * [10] and especially those who follow the flesh with its depraved desire and show contempt for lordship.*

**False Teachers Denounced.**† Bold and arrogant, they are not afraid to revile glorious beings,† [11]† whereas angels,* despite their superior strength and power, do not bring a reviling judgment against them from the Lord. [12] But these people, like irrational animals born by nature for capture and destruction, revile things that they do not understand, and in their destruction they will also be destroyed,* [13] suffering wrong† as payment for

---

†

**1:18** *We:* at Jesus' transfiguration, referring to Peter, James, and John (Mt 17:1).

**1:20–21** Often cited, along with 2 Tm 3:16, on the "inspiration" of scripture or against private interpretation, these verses in context are directed against the false teachers of 2 Pt 2 and clever tales (2 Pt 1:16). The prophetic word in scripture comes admittedly through *human beings* (2 Pt 1:21), but *moved by the holy Spirit,* not from their own interpretation, and is a matter of what the author and Spirit intended, not the *personal interpretation* of false teachers. Instead of *under the influence of God,* some manuscripts read "holy ones of God."

**2:1–3** The pattern of *false prophets* among the Old Testament people of God will recur through *false teachers* in the church. Such destructive opinions of heretical sects bring loss of faith in Christ, contempt for the way of salvation (cf. 2 Pt 2:21), and immorality.

**2:4–6** The false teachers will be punished just as surely and as severely as were the fallen *angels* (2 Pt 2:4; cf. Jude 6; Gn 6:1–4), the sinners of Noah's day (2 Pt 2:5; Gn 7:21–23), and the inhabitants of the cities of the Plain (2 Pt 2:6; Jude 7; Gn 19:25). Whereas there are three examples in Jude 5–7 (Exodus and wilderness; rebellious angels; Sodom and Gomorrah), 2 Peter omitted the first of these, has inserted a new illustration about Noah (2 Pt 2:5) between Jude's second and third examples, and listed the resulting three examples in their Old Testament order (Gn 6; 7; 19).

**2:4** *Chains of Tartarus:* cf. Jude 6; other manuscripts in 2 Peter read "pits of Tartarus." *Tartarus:* a term borrowed from Greek mythology to indicate the infernal regions.

**2:5–10a** Although God did not spare the sinful, he kept and saved the righteous, such as *Noah* (2 Pt 2:5) and *Lot* (2 Pt 2:7), and *he knows how to rescue the devout* (2 Pt 2:9), who are contrasted with the false teachers of the author's day. On Noah, cf. Gn 5:32–9:29, especially 7:1. On Lot, cf. Gn 13 and 19.

**2:10b–22** Some take 2 Pt 2:10b, 11 with the preceding paragraph. Others begin the new paragraph with 2 Pt 2:10a, supplying from 2 Pt 2:9 *The Lord knows how…to keep…under punishment,* with reference to God and probably specifically Christ (2 Pt 2:1). The conduct of the false teachers is described and condemned in language similar to that of Jude 8–16. This arrogance knows no bounds; animal-like, they are due to be caught and destroyed. They seduce even those who have knowledge of Christ (2 Pt 2:20).

**2:10b** *Glorious beings:* literally, "glories"; cf. Jude 8. While some think that illustrious personages are meant or even political officials behind whom (fallen) angels stand, it is more likely that the reference is to glorious angelic beings (cf. Jude 9).

**2:11** *From the Lord:* some manuscripts read "before the Lord"; cf. Jude 9.

**2:13** *Suffering wrong:* some manuscripts read "receiving a reward." *In their deceits:* some manuscripts read "in their love feasts" (Jude 12).

---

*

| | |
|---|---|
| **1:19** Lk 1:78–79; Rev 2:28. | Heb 11:7. |
| **2:1** Mt 24:11, 24; 1 Tm 4:1; Jude 4. | **2:6** Gn 19:24–25; Jude 7. |
| **2:2** Is 52:5. | **2:9** 1 Cor 10:13; Rev 3:10. |
| **2:3** Rom 16:18. | **2:10** Jude 8. |
| **2:4** Jude 6. | **2:11** Jude 9. |
| **2:5** Gn 8:15–19; | **2:12** Ps 49:13–15; Jude 10. |

wrongdoing. Thinking daytime revelry a delight, they are stains and defilements as they revel in their deceits while carousing with you.* 14 Their eyes are full of adultery and insatiable for sin. They seduce unstable people, and their hearts are trained in greed. Accursed children! 15 Abandoning the straight road, they have gone astray, following the road of Balaam, the son of Bosor,† who loved payment for wrongdoing,* 16 but he received a rebuke for his own crime: a mute beast spoke with a human voice and restrained the prophet's madness.*

17 These people are waterless springs and mists driven by a gale; for them the gloom of darkness has been reserved.* 18 For, talking empty bombast, they seduce with licentious desires of the flesh those who have barely escaped† from people who live in error.* 19 They promise them freedom, though they themselves are slaves of corruption, for a person is a slave of whatever overcomes him.* 20 For if they, having escaped the defilements of the world through the knowledge of [our] Lord and savior Jesus Christ, again become entangled and overcome by them, their last condition is worse than their first.* 21 For it would have been better for them not to have known the way of righteousness than after knowing it to turn back from the holy commandment handed down† to them.* 22† What

is expressed in the true proverb has happened to them,* "The dog returns to its own vomit," and "A bathed sow returns to wallowing in the mire."

## IV. THE DELAY OF THE SECOND COMING

**3 Denial of the Parousia.** 1† This is now, beloved, the second letter I am writing to you; through them by way of reminder I am trying to stir up your sincere disposition, 2 to recall the words previously spoken by the holy prophets and the commandment of the Lord and savior through your apostles.* 3 Know this first of all, that in the last days scoffers† will come [to] scoff, living according to their own desires* 4 and saying, "Where is the promise of his coming?† From the time when our ancestors fell asleep, everything has remained as it was from the beginning of creation."* 5 They deliberately ignore the fact that the heavens existed of old and earth was formed out of water† and through water† by the word of God;* 6 through these the world that then existed was destroyed,* deluged with water.† 7 The present heavens and earth have been reserved by the same word for fire, kept for the day of judgment and of destruction of the godless.*

8† But do not ignore this one fact, beloved, that with the Lord one day is like a thousand years† and a thousand years like one day.*

---

2:15 *Balaam, the son of Bosor*: in Nm 22:5, Balaam is said to be the son of Beor, and it is this name that turns up in a few ancient Greek manuscripts by way of "correction" of the text. Balaam is not portrayed in such a bad light in Nm 22. His evil reputation and his *madness* (2 Pt 2:16), and possibly his surname Bosor, may have come from a Jewish tradition about him in the first/second century, of which we no longer have any knowledge.

2:18 *Barely escaped*: some manuscripts read "really escaped."

2:21 *Commandment handed down*: cf. 2 Pt 3:2 and Jude 3.

2:22 The second proverb is of unknown origin, while the first appears in Prv 26:11.

3:1–4 The false teachers not only flout Christian morality (cf. Jude 8–19); they also deny the second coming of Christ and the judgment (2 Pt 3:4; cf. 2 Pt 3:7). They seek to justify their licentiousness by arguing that the promised return of Christ has not been realized and the world is the same, no better than it was before (2 Pt 3:3–4). The author wishes to strengthen the faithful against such errors by reminding them in this *second letter* of the instruction in 1 Peter and of the teaching of the *prophets* and of Christ, conveyed through the *apostles* (2 Pt 3:1–2; cf. Jude 17); cf. 1 Pt 1:10–12, 16–21, especially 16–21; Eph 2:20.

3:3 *Scoffers*: cf. Jude 18, where, however, only the passions of the scoffers are mentioned, not a denial on their part of Jesus' parousia.

3:4–7 The false teachers tried to justify their immorality by pointing out that the promised *coming* (*parousia*) of the Lord has not yet occurred, even though early Christians expected it in

their day. They thus insinuate that God is not guiding the world's history anymore, since nothing has changed and the first generation of Christians, *our ancestors* (2 Pt 3:4), has all died by this time. The author replies that, just as God destroyed the earth by water in the flood (2 Pt 3:5–6, cf. 2 Pt 2:5), so he will destroy it along with the false teachers on judgment day (2 Pt 3:7). *The word of God*, which called the world into being (Gn 1; Ps 33:6) and *destroyed* it by the waters of a flood, will destroy it again by fire on *the day of judgment* (2 Pt 3:5–7).

3:5 *Formed out of water and through water*: Gn 1:2, 6–8 is reflected as well as Greek views that water was the basic element from which all is derived.

3:6 *Destroyed, deluged with water*: cf. 2 Pt 2:5; Gn 7:11–8:2.

3:8–10 The scoffers' objection (2 Pt 3:4) is refuted also by showing that *delay* of the Lord's second coming is not a failure to fulfill his word but rather a sign of his patience: God is giving time for repentance before the final judgment (cf. Wis 11:23–26; Ez 18:23; 33:11).

3:8 Cf. Ps 90:4.

---

2:13 Jude 12.
2:15 Nm 31:16; Jude 11.
2:16 Nm 22:28–33.
2:17 Jude 12–13.
2:18 Jude 16.
2:19 Jn 8:34; Rom 6:16–17.
2:20 Mt 12:45.
2:21 Ez 3:20.
2:22 Prv 26:11.
3:2 Jude 17.
3:3 1 Tm 4:1; 2 Tm 3:1; Jude 18.
3:4 Is 5:19.
3:5 Gn 1:2, 6, 8; Ps 24:2.
3:6 Gn 7:21.
3:7 Is 51:6; Mt 3:12.
3:8 Ps 90:4.

2
PT

⁹ The Lord does not delay his promise, as some regard "delay," but he is patient with you, not wishing that any should perish but that all should come to repentance.* ¹⁰ But the day of the Lord will come like a thief,† and then the heavens will pass away with a mighty roar and the elements will be dissolved by fire, and the earth and everything done on it will be found out.*

**Exhortation to Preparedness.**† ¹¹ Since everything is to be dissolved in this way, what sort of persons ought [you] to be, conducting yourselves in holiness and devotion,* ¹²† waiting for and hastening the coming of the day of God,* because of which the heavens will be dissolved in flames and the elements melted by fire. ¹³ But according to his promise we await new heavens and a new earth† in which righteousness dwells.*

¹⁴ Therefore, beloved, since you await these things, be eager to be found without spot or blemish before him, at peace. ¹⁵ And consider the patience of our Lord as salvation, as our beloved brother Paul, according to the wisdom given to him, also wrote to you,* ¹⁶ speaking of these things† as he does in all his letters. In them there are some things hard to understand that the ignorant and unstable distort to their own destruction, just as they do the other scriptures.

## V. FINAL EXHORTATION AND DOXOLOGY†

¹⁷ Therefore, beloved, since you are forewarned, be on your guard not to be led into the error of the unprincipled and to fall from your own stability.* ¹⁸ But grow in grace and in the knowledge of our Lord and savior Jesus Christ. To him be glory now and to the day of eternity. [Amen.]*

---

† **3:10** *Like a thief*: Mt 24:43; 1 Thes 5:2; Rev 3:3. *Will be found out*: cf. 1 Cor 3:13–15. Some few versions read, as the sense may demand, "will not be found out"; many manuscripts read "will be burned up"; there are further variants in other manuscripts, versions, and Fathers. Total destruction is assumed (2 Pt 3:11).

**3:11–16** The second coming of Christ and the judgment of the world are the doctrinal bases for the moral exhortation to readiness through vigilance and a virtuous life; cf. Mt 24:42, 50–51; Lk 12:40; 1 Thes 5:1–11; Jude 20–21.

**3:12** *Flames…fire*: although this is the only New Testament passage about a final conflagration, the idea was common in apocalyptic and Greco-Roman thought. *Hastening*: eschatology is here used to motivate ethics (2 Pt 3:11), as elsewhere in the New Testament. Jewish sources and Acts 3:19–20 assume that proper ethical conduct can help bring the promised day of the Lord; cf. 2 Pt 3:9. Some render the phrase, however, "desiring it earnestly."

**3:13** *New heavens and a new earth*: cf. Is 65:17; 66:22. The divine promises will be fulfilled after the day of judgment will have passed. The universe will be transformed by the reign of God's *righteousness* or justice; cf. Is 65:17–18; Acts 3:21; Rom 8:18–25; Rev 21:1.

**3:16** *These things*: the teachings of this letter find parallels in Paul, e.g., God's will to save (Rom 2:4; 9:22–23; 1 Cor 1:7–8), the coming of Christ (1 Thes 4:16–17; 1 Cor 15:23–52), and preparedness for the judgment (Col 1:22–23; Eph 1:4–14; 4:30; 5:5–14). *Other scriptures*: used to guide the faith and life of the Christian community. The letters of Paul are thus here placed on the same level as books of the Old Testament. Possibly other New Testament writings could also be included.

**3:17–18** To avoid the dangers *of error* and loss of *stability*, Christians are *forewarned* to be *on guard* and to *grow in grace and knowledge* (2 Pt 1:2) of Christ. The doxology (2 Pt 3:18) recalls 1 Pt 4:11. Some manuscripts add *Amen*.

---

*
| | |
|---|---|
| **3:9** Ez 18:23; 1 Tm 2:4. | **3:13** Is 65:17; 66:22; Rom |
| **3:10** Is 66:15–16; Mt | 8:21; Rev 21:1, 27. |
| 24:29. | **3:15** Rom 8:19; Jude 24. |
| **3:11** Acts 3:19–21. | **3:17** Mk 13:5; Heb 2:1. |
| **3:12** Is 34:4; Heb 10:27. | **3:18** Rom 16:27. |

# The First Letter of
# John

## INTRODUCTION

### Mary Katherine Birge, SSJ

First John is not a letter in the sense that 2 and 3 John are letters. First John does not follow the literary conventions of a Greco-Roman letter; it has neither the opening greeting nor the closing salutation traditionally found in such letters. Rather, it appears to be a treatise or homily written to the same community to which John's Gospel had been written. This Johannine community seems to have undergone a recent schism in which a significant portion of its members has seceded, leaving its remaining members traumatized in the wake of their departure. The author writes with a twofold purpose: to oppose former members' false teachings about Jesus and to reassure the remaining members that they are following the true path to salvation. The false teachings of the former members, now opponents, seem to have centered around two central points for Christians: (1) the identity of Jesus and (2) the conduct of someone who believes that Jesus is the Messiah, son of God the Father, who became human.

As John writes, he alternates between a tone that is, on the one hand, polemical and, on the other, pastoral.[1] He attacks those who have deserted the community, associating them with darkness (1 Jn 2:8, 11 [x3]), calling them "antichrists" (2:18, 22), "liars" (2:4, 22; 4:20) and "children of the devil" (3:10), and claiming they do not belong to God (4:5, 6). Yet he comforts those who have remained, addressing them as "children" (2:1, 12, 14, 18, 28; 3:7, 18; 4:4) and "beloved" (2:7; 3:2, 21; 4:1, 7, 11), urging them to remain in union with God (1:6; 2:5–6, 24; 4:15–16) so that they will be in union with one another (1:7; 3:24), and reminding them that they have been cleansed of sin by Jesus (1:7; 2:2, 12; 4:10).

## Outline of 1 John

I.   Prologue (1:1–4)

II.  God as Light (1:5–3:10)

III. Love for One Another (3:11–5:12)

IV.  Epilogue (5:13–21)

The structure of 1 John follows the structure of the Gospel of John and seems to act almost as a commentary on the Gospel.[2] It has a prologue (1 Jn 1:1–4) that recalls the prologue of the Gospel (Jn 1:18) and an epilogue (1 Jn 5:13–21) that echoes and expands upon the first conclusion to the Gospel (Jn 20:30–31). Most scholars divide the central portion of the letter into two parts, recognizing that each section (1 Jn 1:5; 3:11) begins with the phrase, "this is the message." These two parts appear to follow the division of the Gospel. Within each of these sections, however, the author does not appear to have organized his treatise or homily in an ordered, rhetorical argument in the way Paul constructs his arguments. Rather the various units that make up these sections could easily be switched around without compromising the message of the letter. Within most of these units the author alternates between affirming his audience's choice to persevere in the truth and condemning his opponents' decision to become, as he sees it, liars, sinners, and consorters with the devil. As a result, readers may find some portions of the letter repetitious. But they must remember that John is trying to persuade members of his deeply shaken community that their decision to remain is the

---

1. John Painter, *1, 2, and 3 John*, Sacra Pagina 18 (Collegeville, MN: Liturgical Press, 2002), 116.

2. Raymond E. Brown, *The Epistles of John*, AB 30 (New York: Doubleday, 1982), 90–91.

right one. His repetitions demonstrate how critically important it is for him to bring stability to the faith of his community.[3]

In the prologue (1 Jn 1:1-4), John establishes the grounds for the argument he will make later in the letter against the opponents of his community. Here he begins with his credentials; by employing the first person plural 16 times (v. 1 [x5], v. 2 [x4], v. 3 [x4], v. 4 [x3]) he announces that he belongs to that band who had seen, heard, and known the first eyewitnesses to Jesus, the disciples. As a result, he has the knowledge and authority to preach the message (v. 5) that eternal life (v. 2) only comes through "fellowship" (v. 3, better translated "union") with those who remain in continuity with the apostolic tradition, who in turn are in union with "the Father and with his Son, Jesus Christ" (v. 3). Union with God and Christ, and so salvation for John's audience, depends on their union with the direct heirs of the eyewitnesses to Jesus. And John is that direct heir, not those who have deserted the community.[4] In the next two portions of the letter (1:5–3:10; 3:11–5:12) he plunges into the theological fray about who Jesus is and what he has accomplished (Christology), and why his opponents are in serious error.

For John the effect of Jesus' death and Resurrection "is expiation for [his community's] sins, and not for [his community's] sins only but for those of the whole world" (1 Jn 2:2). John makes clear that only by acknowledging Jesus as true Messiah and true Son of the Father (2:22b–23) can anyone achieve "eternal life" (3:15). But simply proclaiming Jesus so does not make them "children of God" (3:1). It requires much more than simple lip service. For John, "whoever claims to abide in [Jesus] ought to live [just] as he lived" (2:6). The marks of a true follower of Jesus are seen in one's actions, for "[i]f someone who has worldly means sees a brother in need and refuses him compassion, how can the love of God remain in him?" (3:17). Such an understanding that faith in Jesus and how one lives (ethics) can never be separated leads John to exhort his followers, "Children, let us love not in word or speech but in deed and truth" (3:18).

The phrasing of John's attacks against the dissenters, as well as the content of his comforting words to his community's shaky remaining members, likely provide the salient points to these opponents' problematic claims. The opponents have claimed to be without sin, and so in union with God (1 Jn 1:6, 8, 10), but seem to have rejected the notion that their claim (to be sinless and in union with God) rests on their active, concrete demonstration of love for their brother and sister (2:6, 9; 3:7, 11, 17, 23; 4:20–21). In addition, these opponents appear to have denied that Jesus was the incarnation of God (and so neither divine nor the Messiah) and that Jesus' death (4:9–10) made a difference in human salvation. Without these two principles, Jesus' death becomes simply an act of human love devoid of God's love and participation.[5] ∎

3. Painter, 1, 2, and 3 John, 86.

4. Ibid., 130.

5. Ibid., 91–92.

# THE FIRST LETTER OF JOHN

## New American Bible, Introduction

Early Christian tradition identified this work as a letter of John the apostle. Because of its resemblance to the fourth gospel in style, vocabulary, and ideas, it is generally agreed that both works are the product of the same school of Johannine Christianity. The terminology and the presence or absence of certain theological ideas in 1 John suggest that it was written after the gospel; it may have been composed as a short treatise on ideas that were developed more fully in the fourth gospel. To others, the evidence suggests that 1 John was written after the fourth gospel as part of a debate on the proper interpretation of that gospel. Whatever its relation to the gospel, 1 John may be dated toward the end of the first century. Unlike 2 and 3 John, it lacks in form the salutation and epistolary conclusion of a letter. These features, its prologue, and its emphasis on doctrinal teaching make it more akin to a theological treatise than to most other New Testament letters.

The purpose of the letter is to combat certain false ideas, especially about Jesus, and to deepen the spiritual and social awareness of the Christian community (1 Jn 3:17). Some former members (1 Jn 2:19) of the community refused to acknowledge Jesus as the Christ (1 Jn 2:22) and denied that he was a true man (1 Jn 4:2). The specific heresy described in this letter cannot be identified exactly, but it is a form of docetism or gnosticism; the former doctrine denied the humanity of Christ to insure that his divinity was untainted, and the latter viewed the appearance of Christ as a mere stepping-stone to higher knowledge of God. These theological errors are rejected by an appeal to the reality and continuity of the apostolic witness to Jesus. The author affirms that authentic Christian love, ethics, and faith take place only within the historical revelation and sacrifice of Jesus Christ. The fullness of Christian life as fellowship with the Father must be based on true belief and result in charitable living; knowledge of God and love for one another are inseparable, and error in one area inevitably affects the other. Although the author recognizes that Christian doctrine presents intangible mysteries of faith about Christ, he insists that the concrete Christian life brings to light the deeper realities of the gospel.

The structure and language of the letter are straightforward yet repetitious. The author sets forth the striking contrasts between light and darkness, Christians and the world, and truth and error to illustrate the threats and responsibilities of Christian life. The result is not one of theological argument but one of intense religious conviction expressed in simple truths. The letter is of particular value for its declaration of the humanity and divinity of Christ as an apostolic teaching and for its development of the intrinsic connection between Christian moral conduct and Christian doctrine.

The principal divisions of the First Letter of John are the following:

   I. Prologue (1:1–4)
  II. God as Light (1:5–3:10)
 III. Love for One Another (3:11–5:12)
 IV. Epilogue (5:13–21) ◼

# FIRST JOHN

## I. PROLOGUE

# 1

## The Word of Life†

1 What was from the beginning,
    what we have heard,
    what we have seen with our eyes,
    what we looked upon
    and touched with our hands
    concerns the Word of life—*

2 for the life was made visible;
    we have seen it and testify to it
    and proclaim to you the eternal life
    that was with the Father and was
        made visible to us—*

3 what we have seen and heard
    we proclaim now to you,
    so that you too may have fellowship
        with us;
    for our fellowship is with the Father
    and with his Son, Jesus Christ.*

4 We are writing this so that our joy may
    be complete.*

## II. GOD AS LIGHT

**God Is Light.** ⁵ Now this is the message that we have heard from him and proclaim to you: God is light,† and in him there is no darkness at all. ⁶ If we say, "We have fellowship with him," while we continue to walk in darkness, we lie and do not act in truth.* ⁷ But if we walk in the light as he is in the light, then we have fellowship with one another, and the blood of his Son Jesus cleanses us from all sin.* ⁸ If we say, "We are without sin," we deceive ourselves,† and the truth is not in us.* ⁹ If we acknowledge our sins, he is faithful and just and will forgive our sins and cleanse us from every wrongdoing.* ¹⁰ If we say, "We have not sinned," we make him a liar, and his word is not in us.*

# 2

**Christ and His Commandments.** ¹ My children,† I am writing this to you so that you may not commit sin. But if anyone does sin, we have an Advocate with the Father, Jesus Christ the righteous one.* ² He is expiation for our sins, and not for our sins only but for those of the whole world.* ³ The way we may be sure† that we know him is to keep his commandments.* ⁴ Whoever says, "I know him," but does not keep his commandments is a liar, and the truth is not in him.* ⁵ But whoever keeps his word, the love of God is truly perfected in him. This is the way we may know that we are in union with him:* ⁶ whoever claims to abide in him ought to live [just] as he lived.

**The New Commandment.†** ⁷ Beloved, I am writing no new commandment to you but an old commandment that you had from the

---

**1:1–4** There is a striking parallel to the prologue of the gospel of John (Jn 1:1–18), but the emphasis here is not on the preexistent Word but rather on the apostles' witness to the incarnation of life by their experience of the historical Jesus. He is *the Word of life* (1 Jn 1:1; cf. Jn 1:4), *the eternal life that was with the Father and was made visible* (1 Jn 1:2; cf. Jn 1:14), and was *heard, seen, looked upon,* and *touched* by the apostles. The purpose of their teaching is to share that *life,* called *fellowship…with the Father and with his Son, Jesus Christ,* with those who receive their witness (1 Jn 1:3; Jn 1:14, 16).

**1:5–7** *Light* is to be understood here as truth and goodness; *darkness* here is error and depravity (cf. Jn 3:19–21; 17:17; Eph 5:8). To *walk* in light or darkness is to live according to truth or error, not merely intellectual but moral as well. Fellowship with God and with one another consists in a life according to the truth as found in God and in Christ.

**1:8–10** Denial of the condition of sin is self-deception and even contradictory of divine revelation; there is also the continual possibility of sin's recurrence. Forgiveness and deliverance from sin through Christ are assured through acknowledgment of them and repentance.

**2:1** *Children*: like the term "beloved," this is an expression of pastoral love (cf. Jn 13:33; 21:5; 1 Cor 4:14). *Advocate*: for the use of the term, see Jn 14:16. Forgiveness of sin is assured through Christ's intercession and expiation or "offering"; the death of Christ effected the removal of sin.

**2:3–6** *The way we may be sure*: to those who claim, "I have known Christ and therefore I know him," our author insists on not mere intellectual knowledge but obedience to God's commandments in a life conformed to the example of Christ; this confirms our knowledge of him and is *the love of God…perfected*. Disparity between moral life and the commandments proves improper belief.

**2:7–11** The author expresses the continuity and freshness of mutual charity in Christian experience. Through Christ the commandment of love has become the *light* defeating the *darkness* of evil in a new age. All hatred as darkness is incompatible with the light and Christian life. Note also the characteristic Johannine polemic in which a positive assertion is emphasized by the negative statement of its opposite.

---

**1:1** 2:13; Jn 1:1, 14; 20:20, 25, 27.
**1:2** Jn 15:27; 17:5.
**1:3** Jn 17:21; Acts 4:20.
**1:4** Jn 15:11; 2 Jn 12.
**1:6** Jn 12:35.
**1:7** Mt 26:28; Rom 3:24–25; Heb 9:14; 1 Pt 1:19; Rev 1:5.
**1:8** 2 Chr 6:36; Prv 20:9.
**1:9** Prv 28:13; Jas 5:16.
**1:10** 5:10.
**2:1** Jn 14:16; Heb 7:25.
**2:2** 4:10.
**2:3** Jn 14:15; 15:10.
**2:4** 4:20.
**2:5** Jn 14:23.

beginning. The old commandment is the word that you have heard.* [8] And yet I do write a new commandment to you, which holds true in him and among you,† for the darkness is passing away, and the true light is already shining.* [9] Whoever says he is in the light, yet hates his brother, is still in the darkness.* [10] Whoever loves his brother remains in the light, and there is nothing in him to cause a fall.* [11] Whoever hates his brother is in darkness; he walks in darkness and does not know where he is going because the darkness has blinded his eyes.

### Members of the Community.† [12] I am writing to you, children, because your sins have been forgiven* for his name's sake.†

[13] I am writing to you, fathers, because you know him who is from the beginning.

I am writing to you, young men, because you have conquered the evil one.*

[14] I write to you, children, because you know the Father.

I write to you, fathers, because you know him who is from the beginning.

I write to you, young men, because you are strong and the word of God remains in you, and you have conquered the evil one.

[15] Do not love the world or the things of the world.† If anyone loves the world, the love of the Father is not in him.* [16] For all that is in the world, sensual lust,† enticement for the eyes, and a pretentious life, is not from the Father but is from the world. [17] Yet the world and its enticement are passing away. But whoever does the will of God remains forever.*

### Antichrists. [18] Children, it is the last hour;† and just as you heard that the antichrist was coming, so now many antichrists have appeared. Thus we know this is the last hour.* [19] They went out from us, but they were not really of our number;† if they had been, they would have remained with us. Their desertion shows that none of them was of our number. [20] But you have the anointing that comes from the holy one,† and you all have knowledge.* [21] I write to you not because you do not know the truth but because you do, and because every lie is alien to the truth.* [22]† Who is the liar? Whoever denies that Jesus is the Christ. Whoever denies the Father and the Son, this is the antichrist.* [23] No one who denies the Son has the Father, but whoever confesses the Son has the Father as well.*

### Life from God's Anointing. [24]* Let what you heard from the beginning remain in you. If what you heard from the beginning remains in you, then you will remain in the Son and in the Father.† [25] And this is the promise that he made us: eternal life.* [26] I write you these things about those who would deceive you. [27] As for you, the anointing that you received from him remains in you, so that you do not need anyone to teach you. But his anointing teaches you about everything and is true and not false; just as it taught you, remain in him.

### Children of God. [28]† And now, children, remain in him, so that when he appears we may have confidence and not be put to shame by

---

† **2:8** *Which holds true in him and among you:* literally, "a thing that holds true in him and in you."

**2:12–17** The Christian community that has experienced the grace of God through forgiveness of sin and knowledge of Christ is armed against the evil one.

**2:12** *For his name's sake:* because of Christ our sins are forgiven.

**2:15** *The world:* all that is hostile toward God and alienated from him. Love of the *world* and love of God are thus mutually exclusive; cf. Jas 4:4.

**2:16** *Sensual lust:* literally, "the lust of the flesh," inordinate desire for physical gratification. *Enticement for the eyes:* literally, "the lust of the eyes," avarice or covetousness; the eyes are regarded as the windows of the soul. *Pretentious life:* literally, "pride of life," arrogance or ostentation in one's earthly style of life that reflects a willful independence from God and others.

**2:18** *It is the last hour:* literally, "a last hour," the period between the death and resurrection of Christ and his second coming. *The antichrist:* opponent or adversary of Christ; the term appears only in 1 John–2 John, but "pseudochrists" (translated "false messiahs") in Mt 24:24 and Mk 13:22, and Paul's "lawless one" in 2 Thes 2:3, are similar figures. *Many antichrists:* Matthew, Mark, and Revelation seem to indicate a collectivity of persons, here related to the false teachers.

**2:19** *Not really of our number:* the apostate teachers only proved their lack of faith by leaving the community.

**2:20** *The anointing that comes from the holy one:* this anointing is in the Old Testament sense of receiving the Spirit of God. The *holy one* probably refers to Christ. True knowledge is the gift of the Spirit (cf. Is 11:2), and the function of the Spirit is to lead Christians to the truth (Jn 14:17, 26; 16:13).

**2:22–23** Certain gnostics denied that the earthly Jesus was the Christ; to deny knowledge of the Son is to deny the Father, since only through the Son has God been fully revealed (Jn 1:18; 14:8–9).

**2:24** Continuity with the apostolic witness as proclaimed in the prologue is the safeguard of right belief.

**2:28–29** Our confidence at his judgment is based on the daily assurance of salvation. Our actions reflect our true relation to him.

---

*
| | |
|---|---|
| **2:7** 3:11; Dt 6:5; Mt 22:37–40. | **2:17** Is 40:8; Mt 7:21; 1 Cor 7:31; 1 Pt 4:2. |
| **2:8** Jn 13:34 / Jn 1:5; Rom 13:12. | **2:18** 1 Tm 4:1. |
| **2:9** Jn 8:12. | **2:20** Jn 14:26. |
| **2:10** Eccl 2:14; Jn 11:10. | **2:21** 3:19; 2 Pt 1:12. |
| **2:12** 1 Cor 6:11. | **2:22** 2 Thes 2:4. |
| **2:13** 1:1; Jn 1:1. | **2:23** Jn 14:7–9. |
| **2:15** Rom 8:7–8; Jas 4:4; 2 Pt 1:4. | **2:24** Jn 14:23. |
| | **2:25** Jn 5:24; 10:28; 17:2. |

1 J N

him at his coming. ²⁹ If you consider that he is righteous, you also know that everyone who acts in righteousness is begotten by him.

3 ¹† See what love the Father has bestowed on us that we may be called the children of God. Yet so we are. The reason the world does not know us is that it did not know him.* ² Beloved, we are God's children now; what we shall be has not yet been revealed. We do know that when it is revealed† we shall be like him, for we shall see him as he is.* ³ Everyone who has this hope based on him makes himself pure, as he is pure.*

**Avoiding Sin.** ⁴ Everyone who commits sin commits lawlessness, for sin is lawlessness.† ⁵ You know that he was revealed to take away sins, and in him there is no sin.* ⁶ No one who remains in him sins; no one who sins has seen him or known him. ⁷ Children, let no one deceive you. The person who acts in righteousness is righteous, just as he is righteous. ⁸ Whoever sins belongs to the devil, because the devil has sinned from the beginning. Indeed, the Son of God was revealed to destroy the works of the devil.* ⁹ No one who is begotten by God commits sin, because God's seed remains in him; he cannot sin because he is begotten by God.† ¹⁰ In this way, the children of God and the children of the devil are made plain; no one who fails to act in righteousness belongs to God, nor anyone who does not love his brother.

## III. LOVE FOR ONE ANOTHER

¹¹† For this is the message you have heard from the beginning: we should love one another,* ¹² unlike Cain who belonged to the evil one and slaughtered his brother. Why did he slaughter him? Because his own works were evil, and those of his brother righteous.* ¹³ Do not be amazed, [then,] brothers, if the world hates you.* ¹⁴ We know that we have passed from death to life because we love our brothers. Whoever does not love remains in death.* ¹⁵ Everyone who hates his brother is a murderer, and you know that no murderer has eternal life remaining in him.* ¹⁶ The way we came to know love was that he laid down his life for us; so we ought to lay down our lives for our brothers.* ¹⁷ If someone who has worldly means sees a brother in need and refuses him compassion, how can the love of God remain in him?* ¹⁸ Children, let us love not in word or speech but in deed and truth.*

**Confidence Before God.**† ¹⁹ [Now] this is how we shall know that we† belong to the truth and reassure our hearts before him ²⁰ in whatever our hearts condemn, for God is greater than our hearts and knows everything. ²¹ Beloved, if [our] hearts do not condemn us, we have confidence in God ²² and receive from him whatever we ask, because we keep his commandments and do what pleases him.* ²³ And his commandment is this: we should believe in the name of his Son, Jesus Christ,

---

† **3:1–3** The greatest sign of God's love is the gift of his Son (Jn 3:16) that has made Christians true children of God. This relationship is a present reality and also part of the life to come; true knowledge of God will ultimately be gained, and Christians prepare themselves now by virtuous lives in imitation of the Son.

**3:2** *When it is revealed*: or "when he is revealed" (the subject of the verb could be Christ).

**3:4** *Lawlessness*: a reference to the activity of the antichrist, so it is expressed as hostility toward God and a rejection of Christ. The author goes on to contrast the states of sin and righteousness. Christians do not escape sin but realize that when they sin they cease to have fellowship with God. Virtue and sin distinguish the children of God from the children of the devil.

**3:9** A habitual sinner is a child of the devil, while a child of God, who by definition is in fellowship with God, cannot sin. *Seed*: Christ or the Spirit who shares the nature of God with the Christian.

**3:11–18** Love, even to the point of self-sacrifice, is the point of the commandment. The story of Cain and Abel (1 Jn 3:12–15; Gn 4:1–16) presents the rivalry of two brothers, in a contrast of evil and righteousness, where envy led to murder. For Christians, proof of deliverance is love toward others, after the example of Christ. This includes concrete acts of charity, out of our material abundance.

**3:19–24** Living a life of faith in Jesus and of Christian love assures us of abiding in God no matter what our feelings may at times tell us. Our obedience gives us confidence in prayer and trust in God's judgment. This obedience includes our belief in Christ and love for one another.

**3:19b–20** This difficult passage may also be translated "we shall be at peace before him in whatever our hearts condemn, for..." or "and before God we shall convince our hearts, if our hearts condemn us, that God is greater than our hearts."

---

**3:1** Jn 1:12; Eph 1:5 / Jn 15:21; 17:25.
**3:2** Phil 3:21.
**3:3** 2:6.
**3:5** Is 53:9; Jn 1:29; 8:46; 1 Pt 2:22.
**3:8** Jn 8:44; 12:31–32.
**3:11** 2:7; Jn 13:34; 15:12, 17.
**3:12** Gn 4:8; Jude 11.
**3:13** Mt 24:9; Jn 15:18; 17:14.
**3:14** Lv 19:17; Jn 5:24.
**3:15** Jn 8:44.
**3:16** Mt 20:28; Jn 10:11; 15:13.
**3:17** Dt 15:7, 11; Jas 2:15–16.
**3:18** Jas 1:22.
**3:22** 5:15; Mt 7:7–11; 21:22; Jn 14:13–14.

and love one another just as he commanded us.* [24] Those who keep his commandments remain in him, and he in them, and the way we know that he remains in us is from the Spirit that he gave us.*

**Testing the Spirits.**† [1] Beloved, do not trust every spirit but test the spirits to see whether they belong to God, because many false prophets have gone out into the world.* [2] This is how you can know the Spirit of God: every spirit that acknowledges Jesus Christ come in the flesh belongs to God,* [3] and every spirit that does not acknowledge Jesus† does not belong to God. This is the spirit of the antichrist that, as you heard, is to come, but in fact is already in the world.* [4] You belong to God, children, and you have conquered them, for the one who is in you is greater than the one who is in the world. [5] They belong to the world; accordingly, their teaching belongs to the world, and the world listens to them.* [6] We belong to God, and anyone who knows God listens to us, while anyone who does not belong to God refuses to hear us. This is how we know the spirit of truth and the spirit of deceit.*

**God's Love and Christian Life.** [7]† Beloved, let us love one another, because love is of God; everyone who loves is begotten by God and knows God. [8] Whoever is without love does not know God, for God is love. [9] In this way the love of God was revealed to us: God sent his only Son into the world so that we might have life through him.* [10] In this is love: not that we have loved God, but that he loved us and sent his Son as expiation for our sins.* [11] Beloved, if God so loved us, we also must love one another. [12] No one has ever seen God. Yet, if we love one another, God remains in us, and his love is brought to perfection in us.*

[13]† This is how we know that we remain in him and he in us, that he has given us of his Spirit. [14] Moreover, we have seen and testify that the Father sent his Son as savior of the world. [15] Whoever acknowledges that Jesus is the Son of God, God remains in him and he in God. [16] We have come to know and to believe in the love God has for us.

God is love, and whoever remains in love remains in God and God in him. [17] In this is love brought to perfection among us, that we have confidence on the day of judgment because as he is, so are we in this world.* [18] There is no fear in love, but perfect love drives out fear because fear has to do with punishment, and so one who fears is not yet perfect in love. [19] We love because he first loved us. [20] If anyone says, "I love God," but hates his brother, he is a liar; for whoever does not love a brother whom he has seen cannot love God† whom he has not seen.* [21] This is the commandment we have from him: whoever loves God must also love his brother.*

**Faith Is Victory over the World.** [1]† Everyone who believes that Jesus is the Christ is begotten by God, and everyone who loves the father loves [also] the one begotten by him.* [2] In this way we know that we love the children of God when we love God and obey

---

† **4:1–6** Deception is possible in spiritual phenomena and may be tested by its relation to Christian doctrine (cf. 1 Cor 12:3): those who fail to acknowledge Jesus Christ in the flesh are false prophets and belong to the antichrist. Even though these false prophets are well received in the world, the Christian who belongs to God has a greater power in the truth.

**4:3** *Does not acknowledge Jesus*: some ancient manuscripts add "Christ" and/or "to have come in the flesh" (cf. 1 Jn 4:2), and others read "every spirit that annuls (or severs) Jesus."

**4:7–12** Love as we share in it testifies to the nature of God and to his presence in our lives. One who loves shows that one is a child of God and knows God, for God's very being is love; one without love is without God. The revelation of the nature of God's love is found in the free gift of his Son to us, so that we may share life with God and be delivered from our sins. The love we have for one another must be of the same sort: authentic, merciful; this unique Christian love is our proof that we know God and can "see" the invisible God.

**4:13–21** The testimony of the Spirit and that of faith join the testimony of love to confirm our knowledge of God. Our love is grounded in the confession of Jesus as the Son of God and the example of God's love for us. Christian life is founded on the knowledge of God as love and on his continuing presence that

relieves us from fear of judgment (1 Jn 4:16–18). What Christ is gives us confidence, even as we live and love in this world. Yet Christian love is not abstract but lived in the concrete manner of love for one another.

**4:20** *Cannot love God*: some ancient manuscripts read "how can he love…?"

**5:1–5** Children of God are identified not only by their love for others (1 Jn 4:7–9) and for God (1 Jn 5:1–2) but by their belief in the divine sonship of Jesus Christ. Faith, the acceptance of Jesus in his true character and the obedience in love to God's commands (1 Jn 5:3), is the source of the Christian's power in the world and conquers the world of evil (1 Jn 5:4–5), even as Christ overcame the world (Jn 16:33).

---

* **3:23** Jn 13:34; 15:17.
**3:24** 4:13; Jn 14:21–23.
**4:1** 2:18; Mt 24:24.
**4:2** 1 Cor 12:3; 1 Thes 5:21.
**4:3** 3:22.
**4:5** Jn 15:19.
**4:6** Jn 8:47; 10:16.
**4:9** Jn 3:16.
**4:10** Rom 5:8.
**4:12** Jn 1:18; 1 Tm 6:16.
**4:17** 2:28.
**4:20** 2:4.
**4:21** Jn 13:34; 14:15, 21; 15:17.
**5:1** Jn 8:42; 1 Pt 1:23.

1 JN

his commandments. ³For the love of God is this, that we keep his commandments. And his commandments are not burdensome, * ⁴for whoever is begotten by God conquers the world. And the victory that conquers the world is our faith. * ⁵Who [indeed] is the victor over the world but the one who believes that Jesus is the Son of God? *

⁶This is the one who came through water and blood,† Jesus Christ, not by water alone, but by water and blood. The Spirit is the one that testifies, and the Spirit is truth. * ⁷So there are three that testify, ⁸the Spirit, the water, and the blood, and the three are of one accord. * ⁹If we accept human testimony, the testimony of God is surely greater. Now the testimony of God is this, that he has testified on behalf of his Son. * ¹⁰Whoever believes in the Son of God has this testimony within himself. Whoever does not believe God has made him a liar by not believing the testimony God has given about his Son. * ¹¹And this is the testimony: God gave us eternal life, and this life is in his Son. * ¹²Whoever possesses the Son has life; whoever does not possess the Son of God does not have life.

## IV. EPILOGUE†

**Prayer for Sinners.** ¹³I write these things to you so that you may know that you have eternal life, you who believe in the name of the Son of God. * ¹⁴And we have this confidence in him, that if we ask anything according to his will, he hears us. * ¹⁵And if we know that he hears us in regard to whatever we ask, we know that what we have asked him for is ours. ¹⁶If anyone sees his brother sinning, if the sin is not deadly, he should pray to God and he will give him life. This is only for those whose sin is not deadly. There is such a thing as deadly sin, about which I do not say that you should pray. * ¹⁷All wrongdoing is sin, but there is sin that is not deadly.

¹⁸We know that no one begotten by God sins; but the one begotten by God he protects, and the evil one cannot touch him. ¹⁹We know that we belong to God, and the whole world is under the power of the evil one. ²⁰We also know that the Son of God has come and has given us discernment to know the one who is true. And we are in the one who is true, in his Son Jesus Christ. He is the true God and eternal life. * ²¹Children, be on your guard against idols.

---

† **5:6–12** *Water and blood* (1 Jn 5:6) refers to Christ's baptism (Mt 3:16–17) and to the shedding of his blood on the cross (Jn 19:34). *The Spirit* was present at the baptism (Mt 3:16; Mk 1:10; Lk 3:22; Jn 1:32, 34). *The testimony* to Christ as the Son of God is confirmed by divine witness (1 Jn 5:7–9), greater by far than the two legally required human witnesses (Dt 17:6). To deny this is to deny God's truth; cf. Jn 8:17–18. The gist of the divine witness or *testimony* is that *eternal life* (1 Jn 5:11–12) is given in Christ and nowhere else. To *possess the Son* is not acceptance of a doctrine but of a person who lives now and provides life.

**5:13–21** As children of God we have confidence in prayer because of our intimate relationship with him (1 Jn 5:14–15). In love, we pray (1 Jn 5:16–17) for those who are in *sin*, but not in *deadly sin* (literally, "sin unto death"), probably referring to apostasy or activities brought on under the antichrist; cf. Mk 3:29; Heb 6:4–6; 10:26–31. Even in the latter case, however,

prayer, while not enjoined, is not forbidden. The letter concludes with a summary of the themes of the letter (1 Jn 5:18–20). There is a sharp antithesis between the children of God and those belonging to the world and to the evil one. The Son reveals the God of truth; Christians dwell in the true God, *in his Son*, and have eternal life. The final verse (1 Jn 5:21) voices a perennial warning about *idols*, any type of rival to God.

---

* **5:3** Jn 14:15.
**5:4** Jn 16:33.
**5:5** 1 Cor 15:57.
**5:6** Jn 15:26; 19:34.
**5:8** Jn 5:32, 36; 15:26.
**5:9** Jn 5:32, 37.
**5:10** Jn 3:33.

**5:11** 1:2; Jn 1:4; 5:21, 26; 17:3.
**5:13** Jn 1:12; 20:31.
**5:14** 3:21–22; Mt 7:7; Jn 14:13–14.
**5:16** Mt 12:31.
**5:20** Jer 24:7; Jn 17:3; Eph 1:17.

# John

## INTRODUCTION

### Mary Katherine Birge, SSJ

Unlike 1 John, 2 John provides the reader with an example of a typical Hellenistic letter in its length and identification of the sender and recipients in the first verse. It demonstrates its Christian origin when the writer includes a wish-prayer for the recipients and himself by invoking the "grace, mercy, and peace" of God the Father and Jesus Christ (2 Jn 3), a practice first encountered in Paul's letters. As is often the case in Pauline letters, 2 John's author hints at what compels him to write this letter in the final words of the wish-prayer: "truth and love." Three times (vv. 4, 6 [twice]) he employs phrases that evoke injunction, common in the Old Testament, to walk in the statutes of the Lord (e.g., Ex 16:4; Lv 18:4; 26:3; Dt 5:33). In the Old Testament such phrases signal a preoccupation with right conduct according to the Torah. In 2 John as well it signals a preoccupation with right conduct, but it is right conduct according to the Johannine Jesus' commandment (Jn 13:34; 15:12, 17) and 1 John's reiteration of it (1 Jn 3:11, 23; 4:7, 11, 12); that is, to "love one another" (2 Jn 5). Just as in 1 John the author proclaims that membership in the community requires the practice of right conduct modeled on how Jesus lived (1 Jn 2:6), so here in 2 John the author reminds his listeners that their practice of the love commandment is the evidence that they are "walking in the truth" (2 Jn 4). He turns, also, to an issue that 1 John deals with (1 Jn 4:2): those who disturb and disquiet members of the community with their rejection of Jesus Christ's incarnation, his coming in the flesh (2 Jn 7).

Such "deceivers" (2 Jn 7) must be rejected by the members of the community if they encounter them, lest they too become contaminated by such false teaching and thinking. In fact, the author of 2 John forbids his listeners to offer them the hospitality of their homes (v. 10), which at first glance seems aberrant given the emphasis early Christianity always placed on the need to care for the stranger and traveler. But those whom 2 John identifies as "deceivers" were not strangers or the poor, widowed, or orphaned. Rather it seems they endangered the spiritual life of the community because they brought a reverse kind of evangelization with them when they visited, preaching a deficient and dangerous form of Christianity. Second John's admonition in vv. 7–11, then, is not that different from the directions Matthew has Jesus give the Twelve about letting their peace descend only upon a worthy house and shaking from their feet the dust of a town that has rejected their message (Mt 10:13–14). Here it is simply the reverse; members of 2 John's community, like the Twelve of Matthew, are the true followers of Jesus. They must protect their "peace," their true relationship with Jesus and the Father, by a preemptive "shaking off" of the spiritual corruption such purveyors of fraud would bring to them. In short, 2 John's author seeks to protect his vulnerable community from becoming "prey" to false teachings. ◾

# THE SECOND LETTER OF JOHN

## New American Bible, Introduction

Written in response to similar problems, the Second and Third Letters of John are of the same length, perhaps determined by the practical consideration of the writing space on one piece of papyrus. In each letter the writer calls himself "the Presbyter," and their common authorship is further evidenced by internal similarities in style and wording, especially in the introductions and conclusions. The literary considerations that link 2 John and 3 John also link them with the First Letter and the Gospel of John. The concern with "truth," christology, mutual love, the new commandment, antichrist, and the integrity of witness to the earthly Jesus mark these works as products of the Johannine school. The identity of the Presbyter is problematic. The use of the title implies more than age, and refers to his position of leadership in the early church. The absence of a proper name indicates that he was well known and acknowledged in authority by the communities to which he writes. Although traditionally attributed to John the apostle, these letters were probably written by a disciple or scribe of an apostle. The traditional place and

date of composition, Ephesus at the end of the first century, are plausible for both letters.

The Second Letter is addressed to "the chosen Lady" and "to her children." This literary image of a particular Christian community reflects the specific destination and purpose of the letter. Unlike 1 John, this brief letter is not a theological treatise but a reply to problems within the church. The Johannine themes of love and truth are used to support practical advice on Christian living. The Presbyter encourages community members to show their Christianity by adhering to the great commandment of mutual love and to the historical truth about Jesus. The false teaching present among them is a spiritualizing christology that may tempt some members to discount teachings about the incarnation and death of Jesus the Christ; cf. 1 Jn 4:2. For their protection the Presbyter forbids hospitality toward unknown or "progressive" Christians to prevent their infiltration of the community. The Second Letter preserves the Johannine concerns of doctrinal purity and active love in the form of pastoral advice to a threatened community. ■

# SECOND JOHN

[1]†* The Presbyter to the chosen Lady and to her children whom I love in truth—and not only I but also all who know the truth— [2] because of the truth that dwells in us and will be with us forever. [3] Grace, mercy, and peace† will be with us from God the Father and from Jesus Christ the Father's Son in truth and love.

[4] I rejoiced greatly to find some of your children† walking in the truth just as we were commanded by the Father.* [5] But now, Lady, I ask you, not as though I were writing a new commandment but the one we have had from the beginning: let us love one another.* [6] For this is love, that we walk according to his commandments;† this is the commandment, as you heard from the beginning, in which you should walk.*

[7]* Many deceivers have gone out into the world, those who do not acknowledge Jesus Christ as coming in the flesh; such is the deceitful one and the antichrist.† [8] Look to yourselves that you† do not lose what we worked for but may receive a full recompense. [9]* Anyone who is so "progressive"† as not to remain in the teaching of the Christ does not have God; whoever remains in the teaching has the Father and the Son. [10]† If anyone comes to you and does not bring this doctrine, do not receive him in your house or even greet him;* [11] for whoever greets him shares in his evil works.

[12]† Although I have much to write to you, I do not intend to use paper and ink. Instead, I hope to visit you and to speak face to face so that our joy may be complete.* [13] The children of your chosen sister† send you greetings.

---

† **1** *The chosen Lady*: literally, "elected"; this could also be translated "Kyria (a woman's name) chosen (by God)" or "the lady Electa" or "Electa Kyria." The adjective "chosen" is applied to all Christians at the beginning of other New Testament letters (1 Pt 1:1; Ti 1:1). The description is of a specific community with "children" who are its members. *The truth*: the affirmation of Jesus in the flesh and in contrast to false teaching (2 Jn 7).

**3** *Grace, mercy, and peace*: like 1 Timothy; 2 Timothy this letter adds *mercy* to the terms used frequently in a salutation to describe Christian blessing; it appears only here in the Johannine writings. The author also puts the blessing in relation to *truth* and *love*, the watchwords of the Johannine teaching. *The Father's Son*: the title that affirms the close relationship of Christ to God; similar variations of this title occur elsewhere (Jn 1:14; 3:35), but the precise wording is not found elsewhere in the New Testament.

**4** *Some of your children*: this refers to those whom the Presbyter has recently encountered, but it may also indicate the presence of false doctrine in the community: the Presbyter encourages those who have remained faithful. *Walking in the truth*: an expression used in the Johannine writings to describe a way of living in which the Christian faith is visibly expressed; cf. 1 Jn 1:6–7; 2:6, 11; 3 Jn 3.

**6** *His commandments*: cf. 1 Jn 3:23; 2:7–8; 4:21; obedience to the commandment of faith and love includes all others.

**7** *The antichrist*: see 1 Jn 2:18–19, 22; 4:3.

**8** *You* (plural): it is not certain whether this means the Chris-

tians addressed or includes the Presbyter, since some of the ancient Greek manuscripts and Greek Fathers have "we."

**9** *Anyone who is so "progressive"*: literally, "Anyone who goes ahead." Some gnostic groups held the doctrine of the Christ come in the flesh to be a first step in belief, which the more advanced and spiritual believer surpassed and abandoned in his knowledge of the spiritual Christ. The author affirms that fellowship with God may be gained only by holding to the complete doctrine of Jesus Christ (1 Jn 2:22–23; 4:2; 5:5–6).

**10–11** At this time false teachers were considered so dangerous and divisive as to be shunned completely. From this description they seem to be wandering preachers. We see here a natural suspicion of early Christians concerning such itinerants and can envisage the problems faced by missionaries such as those mentioned in 3 Jn 10.

**12** *Our joy*: a number of other Greek manuscripts read "your joy."

**13** *Chosen sister*: the community of which the Presbyter is now a part greets you (singular), the community of the Lady addressed.

---

**1** Jn 8:32; 3 Jn 1.
**4** 3 Jn 3.
**5** Jn 13:34; 15:12; 1 Jn 4:7.
**6** Jn 13:34; 14:15; 1 Jn 5:3.
**7** 1 Jn 2:22; 4:2.
**9** Jn 8:31; 1 Jn 2:23; 4:15.
**10** Rom 16:17; 2 Thes 3:6.
**12** Jn 15:11; 1 Jn 1:4; 3 Jn 13.

# The Third Letter of

# John

## INTRODUCTION

### Mary Katherine Birge, SSJ

Like 2 John, 3 John follows the format and length of a conventional Greco-Roman letter. He names four persons including himself: the Presbyter (3 Jn 1; writer of this letter as well as that of 2 John), Gaius (3 Jn 1; recipient of this letter), Diotrephes (v. 9; possibly a leader of one of the Johannine house churches), and Demetrius (the probable bearer of this letter, whom the Presbyter recommends in v. 12 as trustworthy). The situation the reader encounters in 3 John seems to be the reverse of 2 John, where the Presbyter urges the letter's recipients to reject "anyone [who] comes to you and does not bring this doctrine [that Jesus had become human flesh]" and not to "receive him in your house or even greet him" (2 Jn 10). In 3 John the Presbyter is on the receiving end of the very practice he recommends to the audience of 2 John.

Diotrephes, who has not acknowledged a letter the Presbyter had previously sent to him (3 Jn 9), apparently was the leader of a house-church or at least the master of the household in which one of the small Johannine churches meets. Certain itinerant Christian missionaries who were known to the Presbyter had sought hospitality (a safe place to sleep, food, and perhaps some financial aid) from members of Diotrephes's house church, and he had decided that that they must be refused (v. 10). It seems that both Diotrephes and the Presbyter were known to Gaius. But Gaius did not agree with Diotrephes's negative evaluation of the Presbyter or of the "brothers" who had been

sent out by the Presbyter "for the sake of the Name" (v. 7). Gaius has received these brothers with hospitality without knowing them personally, for which the author of 3 John praises him (vv. 5–6).

It is possible that Demetrius, whom the Presbyter recommends to Gaius (3 Jn 12), had been among those "brothers" whom Diotrephes had refused. Such recommendations of a letter carrier unknown to the recipient of the letter were standard in Christian letter writing (e.g., Rom 16:1–2). Diotrephes, besides having denied hospitality to these Christian missionaries himself, also required members of his community to reject them under pain of being expelled from their local church (3 Jn 10). If Diotrephes was not the actual leader of this community, but rather the master of the household where the local Christian community has been accustomed to gather, he could simply have refused entrance to his house to those members of the community who did not comply with his demands. In any event, Diotrephes had some power if not authority to determine to whom members of his community might or might not offer hospitality.[1]

This briefest of all the New Testament letters reveals little about the exact nature of the Presbyter's and Diotrephes's dispute with one another or the theological or historical circumstances surrounding it. It does, however,

---

1. John Painter, *1, 2, and 3 John,* Sacra Pagina 18 (Collegeville, MN: Liturgical Press, 2002), 368–69.

provide the modern reader with a small window into the late first-century world of house churches, the abuse of their hospitality by traveling Christians that generated the need for recommendation letters,[2] the decentralized nature of their leadership and authority, and the difficulty such decentralization could produce for itinerant teachers or emissaries from

other Christian communities when they were trying to visit house churches to which they were unknown or which had been warned against receiving them because they were perceived as teaching falsely (cf. 2 Jn 10; Jude 4, 10–11, 18–19; 2 Pt 1:16; 2:1–3; 3:3–4).[3] ∎

---

2. Ibid., 362.

3. Gerard S. Sloyan, *Walking in the Truth: Perseverers and Deserters—The First, Second, And Third Letters of John* (New Testament In Context; Valley Forge, PA: Trinity Press International, 1995), 70.

# THE THIRD LETTER OF JOHN

## New American Bible, Introduction

The Third Letter of John preserves a brief glimpse into the problems of missionary activity and local autonomy in the early church. In contrast to the other two letters of John, this work was addressed to a specific individual, Gaius. This letter is less theological in content and purpose. The author's goal was to secure hospitality and material support for his missionaries, and the Presbyter is writing to another member of the church who has welcomed missionaries in the past. The Presbyter commends Gaius for his hospitality and encourages his future help. He indicates he may come to challenge the policy of Diotrephes that is based on evil gossip.

The problems of the Presbyter in this short letter provide us with valuable evidence of the flexible and personal nature of authority in the early church. The Presbyter writes to Gaius, whom perhaps he had converted or instructed, on the basis of their personal links. The brothers have also confirmed him as a loyal Christian in action and belief. Gaius accepted the missionaries from the Presbyter and presumably will accept Demetrius on the Presbyter's recommendation. In contrast, Diotrephes refuses to receive either letters or friends of the Presbyter. Although he is portrayed as ambitious and hostile, he perhaps exemplifies the cautious and sectarian nature of early Christianity; for its own protection the local community mistrusted missionaries as false teachers. Most interestingly, Diotrephes seems comfortable in ignoring the requests of the Presbyter. The Presbyter seems to acknowledge that only a personal confrontation with Diotrephes will remedy the situation (3 Jn 10). The division, however, may also rest on doctrinal disagreement in which Gaius and the other "friends" accept the teaching of the Presbyter, and Diotrephes does not; the missionaries are not received for suspicion of theological error. Diotrephes has thus been viewed by some as an overly ambitious local upstart trying to thwart the advance of orthodox Christianity, by others as an orthodox church official suspicious of the teachings of the Presbyter and those in the Johannine school who think as he does, or by still others as a local leader anxious to keep the debates in the Johannine community out of his own congregation.

This brief letter and the situation that it mirrors show us how little we know about some details of early development in the church: schools of opinion existed around which questions of faith and life were discussed, and personal ties as well as doctrine and authority played a role in what happened amid divisions and unity. ■

# THIRD JOHN

¹† The Presbyter to the beloved Gaius whom I love in truth.*

² Beloved, I hope you are prospering in every respect and are in good health, just as your soul is prospering. ³ I rejoiced greatly when some of the brothers† came and testified to how truly you walk in the truth.* ⁴ Nothing gives me greater joy than to hear that my children are walking in the truth.*

⁵ Beloved, you are faithful in all you do† for the brothers, especially for strangers;* ⁶ they have testified to your love before the church.* Please help them in a way worthy of God to continue their journey.† ⁷ For they have set out for the sake of the Name† and are accepting nothing from the pagans. ⁸ Therefore, we ought to support such persons, so that we may be co-workers in the truth.

⁹ I wrote to the church, but Diotrephes, who loves to dominate,† does not acknowledge us. ¹⁰ Therefore, if I come,† I will draw attention to what he is doing, spreading evil nonsense about us. And not content with that, he will not receive the brothers, hindering those who wish to do so and expelling them from the church.

¹¹ Beloved, do not imitate evil† but imitate good. Whoever does what is good is of God; whoever does what is evil has never seen God.* ¹² Demetrius† receives a good report from all, even from the truth itself. We give our testimonial as well, and you know our testimony is true.*

¹³ I have much to write to you, but I do not wish to write with pen and ink.* ¹⁴ Instead, I hope to see you soon, when we can talk face to face. ¹⁵ Peace be with you. The friends greet you; greet the friends† there each by name.*

---

† **1** *Beloved Gaius*: a frequent form of address for fellow Christians in New Testament epistolary literature.

**3** *The brothers*: in this letter, the term may refer to Christians who have been missionaries and received hospitality from Gaius (3 Jn 5–6). *Walk in the truth*: the common Johannine term to describe Christian living; this description presents Gaius as following the teachings of the Presbyter in contrast to Diotrephes.

**5** *You are faithful in all you do*: Gaius's aid to the missionaries is a manifestation of his true Christian faith.

**6** *Help them…to continue their journey*: the Presbyter asks Gaius not only to continue to welcome the missionaries to his community but also to equip them for further travels.

**7** *The Name*: of Jesus Christ (cf. Acts 5:41; 1 Jn 2:12; 3:23; 5:13). *Accepting nothing*: not expecting support from the pagans to whom they preach the gospel, so that they will not be considered as beggars; they required support from other Christians; cf. Paul's complaints to the Corinthians (1 Cor 9:3–12).

**9** *Who loves to dominate*: the Presbyter does not deny Diotrephes' place as leader but indicates that his ambition may have caused him to disregard his letter and his influence.

**10** *If I come*: the Presbyter may visit the community to challenge the actions of Diotrephes toward himself and the missionaries. *Will not receive the brothers*: Diotrephes may have been critical of the teachings of the Presbyter and sought to maintain doctrinal purity; cf. 1 Jn 2:19 and 2 Jn 10–11.

**11** *Do not imitate evil*: Gaius should not be influenced by the behavior of Diotrephes.

**12** *Demetrius*: because of the fear of false teachers, Demetrius, perhaps the bearer of the letter, is provided with a recommendation from the Presbyter; cf. 2 Cor 3:1; Rom 16:1. *Even from the truth itself*: this refers probably to the manner of Demetrius's life that testifies to his true belief; cf. Gaius above (3 Jn 3).

**15** *Friends*: although a Johannine term for Christians (Jn 15:15), the word here may refer to those in the community loyal to the Presbyter and to Gaius.

---

*

**1** 2 Jn 1.
**3** 5; Gal 6:10; 2 Jn 4.
**4** 1 Thes 2:11–12; 1 Tm 1:2; 2 Tm 1:2; 1 Jn 2:1; 2 Jn 4.
**5** Rom 12:13; Gal 6:10; Heb 13:2.

**6** Acts 15:3; Col 1:10; 1 Thes 2:12.
**11** 1 Jn 2:29; 3:6, 10.
**12** Jn 19:35; 21:24; 1 Tm 3:7.
**13** 2 Jn 12.
**15** Jn 20:19, 21, 26; Eph 6:23; 1 Pt 5:14.

# The Letter of

# Jude

## INTRODUCTION

### Mary Katherine Birge, SSJ

The Letter of Jude, in all of the New Testament surpassed in brevity only by the Letters of 2 and 3 John and Philemon, provides today's readers with a window into some texts that early Jewish Christians knew and accepted as authoritative. In addition to making references to the Torah and Prophets, Jude refers to two apocryphal works: the *Assumption of Moses* (most likely the tail end of a larger work called the *Testament of Moses*) and *1 Enoch* which he even quotes in Jude 14–15 (*1 Enoch* 1.9). His use of these non-canonical works along-side canonical ones (i.e., Genesis, Exodus, Zechariah, etc.) suggests he is writing at an early period of Christianity before distinctions had begun to be made between what was and was not canonical. It also signals that his likely audience is made up of Jewish Christians since he presumes its members were very familiar with an extensive list of Old Testament books, among them Numbers, Psalms, Proverbs, Isaiah, Ezekiel, Amos, and Hosea, as well as Jewish Apocrypha.[1]

Before he refers to the story of the archangel Michael arguing with the devil over the body of Moses in Jude 9 (found in the *Assumption of Moses*), Jude recalls three moments in biblical history when humans or angels have rebelled against God and attempted to wreak havoc among those who remain faithful to God (vv. 5–7). He compares the "intruders" (v. 4), against whom he is warning his audience, to these unfaithful creatures who bring about their own judgment and destruction through their rejection of God. Jude recalls the Israelites' doubt and disobedience while in the desert and their subsequent punishment (v. 5 = Ex 32:25–29; cf. Nm 14:20–35; Ps 95:8–11).

In v. 6 he reviews the rebellion of the angels in Gn 6:1–4 and includes material from *1 Enoch* in which fallen angels are chained "in gloom" awaiting the final judgment. As he concludes this triad of biblical and apocryphal examples, Jude cites the punishment of the cities of "Sodom, Gomorrah and the surrounding towns" by "eternal fire" in v. 7 for their attempted gang rape of two angels visiting Lot (Gn 19:1–29).[2] He sums up his comparison of these three groups with the intruders who threaten the salvation and faith of his audience (Jude 4) when he writes: "Similarly, these dreamers nevertheless also defile the flesh, scorn lordship, and revile glorious beings" (v. 8). The sins of the intruders (v. 8) parallel those Jude depicts in vv. 5–7, but not in a one-to-one correlation. They all, Israelites in the desert, rebellious angels, and inhabitants of Sodom and Gomorrah, have "scorned" the Lord's authority; the rebellious angels and city-dwellers of Sodom and Gomorrah have engaged in or attempted to "defile the flesh," but only the men from the two cities have "revile[d]" angels, "glorious beings."[3]

In v. 4 Jude has already denounced these "intruders" for engaging in "licentiousness" and for rejecting the authority of their "only Master and Lord, Jesus Christ." Most likely Jude has represented the intruders' rejection of local religious leaders' authority as their rejection of Jesus as "Master and Lord," from whom the local leaders would derive their authority. The "licentiousness" of which Jude accuses the intruders may have to do with sexual immorality or license (with which it is generally associated), but it may allude as well to the third

---

1. Lewis R. Donelson, *I & II Peter and Jude*, New Testament Library (Louisville: Westminster John Knox, 2010), 165.

2. Daniel J. Harrington, *Jude and 2 Peter*, Sacra Pagina 15 (Collegeville, MN: Liturgical Press, 2003), 179.

3. Richard J. Bauckham, *Jude, 2 Peter*, Word Biblical Commentary 50 (Nashville: Thomas Nelson, 1996), 55.

indictment, "revil[ing] glorious beings" (v. 8). References to angelic and human coupling in vv. 6 and 7 and the following dispute between the archangel Michael and the devil in v. 9 suggest that at issue is "the order of nature and the place of angels and of humans within it."[4] It may be, because of an exaggerated sense of already having been saved or a conception of no longer being held to the Law of Moses, that these intruders have come to understand themselves as greater than the "glorious beings," who share in the presence of God, with the consequence that they hold angelic creatures in lower regard than humans and have disparaged or slandered them. From Jude's withering description of the intruders and his comparison of them with unsavory figures from the Old Testament and Apocrypha, the reader may infer that the letter writer views their behavior with members of his audience as a perversion of Christian conduct and dangerous to his audience's salvation (v. 4; cf. v. 12). Moreover, they likely have shared with members of Jude's audience their malformed notions about an already realized salvation, and he must dissuade his audience from adopting the false teachers' distorted claims about Jesus (cf. vv. 16–17).[5]

Jude recalls the story (Jude 9) about the archangel Michael's argument with the devil over who might claim Moses' body, a story which he presumes his audience knows well (*Assumption of Moses*). This argument includes the devil slandering or proclaiming a judgment against Moses.[6] Jude focuses on the behavior and words of the archangel in the dispute: he "did not venture to pronounce a reviling judgment upon him [i.e., Satan] but said, 'May the Lord rebuke you!'" The archangel does not respond in kind to the devil by judging him as he had judged Moses, but rather quotes from the prophet Zechariah, "May the LORD . . . rebuke you!" (Zec 3:2). In this verse Jude seems to look back to his admonitions against the intrusive false teachers in their reviling of angels by holding up the archangel as an exemplar who refuses to judge even a fallen angel like the devil despite his blaspheming of Moses. With the archangel's appeal to God to exercise judgment, he also reminds his audience that judgment belongs to God alone. Jude may even be looking forward to Jude 22–23, where he urges his audience to practice mercy toward these offending intruders without condemnation.[7] ◾

---

4. Harrington, *Jude and 2 Peter*, 206.

5. Bauckham, *Jude, 2 Peter*, 57–59; Harrington, *Jude and 2 Peter*, 206–7.

6. Harrington, *Jude and 2 Peter*, 208–9; Jerome H. Neyrey, *2 Peter, Jude*, Anchor Bible 37C (New York: Doubleday, 1993), 65–66.

7. Donelson, *I & II Peter and Jude*, 184.

# THE LETTER OF JUDE

## New American Bible, Introduction

This letter is by its address attributed to "Jude, a slave of Jesus Christ and brother of James" (Jude 1). Since he is not identified as an apostle, this designation can hardly be meant to refer to the Jude or Judas who is listed as one of the Twelve (Lk 6:16; Acts 1:13; cf. Jn 14:22). The person intended is almost certainly the other Jude, named in the gospels among the relatives of Jesus (Mt 13:55; Mk 6:3), and the James who is listed there as his brother is the one to whom the Letter of James is attributed (see the Introduction to James). Nothing else is known of this Jude, and the apparent need to identify him by reference to his better-known brother indicates that he was a rather obscure personage in the early church.

The letter is addressed in the most general terms to "those who are called, beloved in God the Father and kept safe for Jesus Christ" (Jude 1), hence apparently to all Christians. But since its purpose is to warn the addressees against false teachers, the author must have had in mind one or more specific Christian communities located in the unidentified region where the errors in question constituted a danger. While the letter contains some Semitic features, there is nothing to identify the addressees specifically as Jewish Christians; indeed, the errors envisaged seem to reflect an early form of gnosticism, opposed to law, that points rather to the cultural context of the Gentile world. Like James and 2 Peter, the Letter of Jude manifests none of the typical features of the letter form except the address.

There is so much similarity between Jude and 2 Peter, especially Jude 4–16 and 2 Pt 2:1–18, that there must be a literary relationship between them. Since there is no evidence for the view that both authors borrowed from the same source, it is usually supposed that one of them borrowed from the other. Most scholars believe that Jude is the earlier of the two, principally because he quotes two apocryphal Jewish works, the Assumption of Moses (Jude 9) and the Book of Enoch (Jude 14–15) as part of his structured argument, whereas 2 Peter omits both references. Since there was controversy in the early church about the propriety of citing noncanonical literature that included legendary material, it is more probable that a later writer would omit such references than that he would add them.

Many interpreters today consider Jude a pseudonymous work dating from the end of the first century or even later. In support of this view they adduce the following arguments: (a) the apostles are referred to as belonging to an age that has receded into the past (Jude 17–18); (b) faith is understood as a body of doctrine handed down by a process of tradition (Jude 3); (c) the author's competent Greek style shows that he must have had a Hellenistic cultural formation; (d) the gnostic character of the errors envisaged fits better into the early second century than into a period several decades earlier. While impressive, these arguments are not entirely compelling and do not completely rule out the possibility of composition around the year A.D. 80, when the historical Jude may still have been alive.

This little letter is an urgent note by an author who intended to write more fully about salvation to an unknown group of readers, but who was forced by dangers from false teachers worming their way into the community (Jude 3–4) to dash off a warning against them (Jude 5–16) and to deliver some pressing Christian admonitions (Jude 17–23). The letter is justly famous for its majestic closing doxology (Jude 24–25). ■

# JUDE

**Address and Greeting.** ¹† Jude, a slave of Jesus Christ and brother of James, to those who are called, beloved in God the Father and kept safe for Jesus Christ:* ² may mercy, peace, and love be yours in abundance.*

**Occasion for Writing.** ³ Beloved, although I was making every effort to write to you about our common salvation,† I now feel a need to write to encourage you to contend for the faith that was once for all handed down to the holy ones.* ⁴ For there have been some intruders, who long ago were designated for this condemnation, godless persons, who pervert the grace of our God into licentiousness and who deny our only Master and Lord, Jesus Christ.*

**The False Teachers.** ⁵* I wish to remind you, although you know all things, that [the] Lord who once saved a people from the land of Egypt later destroyed those who did not believe.† ⁶* The angels too, who did not keep to their own domain but deserted their proper dwelling, he has kept in eternal chains, in gloom, for the judgment of the great day.† ⁷ Likewise, Sodom, Gomorrah, and the surrounding towns, which, in the same manner as they, indulged in sexual promiscuity and practiced unnatural vice,† serve as an example by undergoing a punishment of eternal fire.*

⁸ Similarly, these dreamers† nevertheless also defile the flesh, scorn lordship, and revile glorious beings. ⁹ Yet the archangel Michael, when he argued with the devil in a dispute over the body of Moses, did not venture to pronounce a reviling judgment† upon him but said, "May the Lord rebuke you!"* ¹⁰ But these people revile what they do not understand and are destroyed by what they know by nature like irrational animals.* ¹¹ Woe to them!* They followed the way of Cain, abandoned themselves to Balaam's error for the sake of gain, and perished in the rebellion of Korah.† ¹² These are blemishes on your love feasts,† as they carouse fearlessly and look after themselves. They are waterless clouds blown about by winds, fruitless trees in late autumn, twice dead and uprooted.* ¹³ They are like wild waves of the sea, foaming up their shameless deeds, wandering stars for whom the gloom of darkness has been reserved forever.

---

† **1** *Jude…brother of James:* for the identity of the author of this letter, see Introduction. *To those who are called:* the vocation to the Christian faith is God's free gift to those whom he loves and whom he safely protects in Christ until the Lord's second coming.

**3–4** *Our common salvation:* the teachings of the Christian faith derived from the apostolic preaching and to be kept by the Christian community.

**5** For this first example of divine punishment on those who had been saved but did not then keep faith, see Nm 14:28–29 and the note there. Some manuscripts have the word "once" (*hapax* as at Jude 3) after "you know"; some commentators have suggested that it means "knowing one thing" or "you know all things once for all." Instead of "[the] Lord" manuscripts vary, having "Jesus," "God," or no subject stated.

**6** This second example draws on Gn 6:1–4 as elaborated in the apocryphal Book of Enoch (cf. Jude 14): heavenly beings came to earth and had sexual intercourse with women. God punished them by casting them out of heaven into darkness and bondage.

**7** *Practiced unnatural vice:* literally, "went after alien flesh." This example derives from Gn 19:1–25, especially 4–11, when the townsmen of Sodom violated both hospitality and morality by demanding that Lot's two visitors (really messengers of Yahweh) be handed over to them so that they could abuse them sexually. *Unnatural vice:* this refers to the desire for intimacies by human beings with angels (the reverse of the example in Jude 6). Sodom (whence "sodomy") and Gomorrah became proverbial as object lessons for God's punishment on sin (Is 1:9; Jer 50:40; Am 4:11; Mt 10:15; 2 Pt 2:6).

**8** *Dreamers:* the writer returns to the false teachers of Jude 4, applying charges from the three examples in Jude 5, 6, 7. This may apply to claims they make for revelations they have received by night (to the author, hallucinations). *Defile the flesh:* this may mean bodily pollutions from the erotic dreams of sexual license

(Jude 7). *Lordship…glorious beings:* these may reflect the Lord (Jude 5; Jesus, Jude 4) whom they spurn and the angels (Jude 6; cf. note on 2 Pt 2:10, here, as there, literally, "glories").

**9** *The archangel Michael…judgment:* a reference to an incident in the apocryphal Assumption of Moses. Dt 34:6 had said of Moses, literally in Greek, "they buried him" or "he (God?) buried him" (taken to mean "he was buried"). The later account tells how Michael, who was sent to bury him, was challenged by the devil's interest in the body. Our author draws out the point that if an archangel refrained from reviling even the devil, how wrong it is for mere human beings to revile glorious beings (angels).

**11** *Cain…Balaam…Korah:* examples of rebellious men and of the punishment their conduct incurred; cf. Gn 4:8–16; Nm 16:1–35; 31:16. See note on 2 Pt 2:15.

**12** *Blemishes on your love feasts:* or "hidden rocks" or "submerged reefs" (cf. Jude 13). The opponents engaged in scandalous conduct in connection with community gatherings called *love feasts* (agape meals), which were associated with eucharistic celebrations at certain stages of early Christian practice; cf. 1 Cor 11:18–34 and the note on 2 Pt 2:13.

---

*

| | |
|---|---|
| **1** Mt 13:55; Mk 6:3; Acts 12:17; Rom 1:7. | **7** Dt 29:22–24; Mt 25:41; 2 Thes 1:8–9; 2 Pt 2:6; 3:7. |
| **2** Gal 6:16; 1 Tm 1:2; 2 Pt 1:2. | **9** Dn 10:21; 12:1. |
| **3** 17, 20; 1 Tm 6:12. | **10** 2 Pt 2:12. |
| **4** Gal 2:4; 2 Tm 3:6; 2 Pt 2:1. | **11** Gn 4:8–16; 1 Jn 3:12 / Nm 31:15–16; 2 Pt 2:15; Rev 2:14 / Nm 16:19–35. |
| **5** Nm 14:35; 1 Cor 10:5; Heb 3:16, 17. | **12** 2 Pt 2:13, 17. |
| **6** 2 Pt 2:4, 9. | |

**14**† Enoch, of the seventh generation from Adam, prophesied also about them when he said,* "Behold, the Lord has come with his countless holy ones **15** to execute judgment on all and to convict everyone for all the godless deeds that they committed and for all the harsh words godless sinners have uttered against him." **16** These people are complainers, disgruntled ones who live by their desires; their mouths utter bombast as they fawn over people to gain advantage.*

**Exhortations.** **17** But you, beloved, remember the words spoken beforehand by the apostles of our Lord Jesus Christ,* **18** for they told you,* "In [the] last time there will be scoffers who will live according to their own godless desires."† **19** These are the ones who cause divisions; they live on the natural plane, devoid of the Spirit.* **20** But you, beloved, build yourselves up in your most holy faith; pray in the holy Spirit.* **21** Keep yourselves in the love of God and wait for the mercy of our Lord Jesus Christ that leads to eternal life.* **22** On those who waver, have mercy;† **23** save others by snatching them out of the fire; on others have mercy with fear,† abhorring even the outer garment stained by the flesh.

**Doxology.**† **24** To the one who is able to keep you from stumbling and to present you unblemished and exultant, in the presence of his glory,* **25** to the only God, our savior, through Jesus Christ our Lord be glory, majesty, power, and authority from ages past, now, and for ages to come. Amen.*

---

† **14–15** Cited from the apocryphal Book of Enoch 1:9.

**18** This is the substance of much early Christian preaching rather than a direct quotation of any of the various New Testament passages on this theme (see Mk 13:22; Acts 20:30; 1 Tm 4:1–3; 2 Pt 3:3).

**22** *Have mercy*: some manuscripts read "convince," "confute," or "reprove." Others have "even though you waver" or "doubt" instead of *who waver*.

**23** *With fear*: some manuscripts connect the phrase "with fear" with the imperative "save" or with the participle "snatching." Other manuscripts omit the phrase "on others have mercy," so that only two groups are envisioned. Rescue of those led astray and caution in the endeavor are both enjoined. *Outer garment stained by the flesh*: the imagery may come from Zec 3:3–5, just as that of *snatching…out of the fire* comes from Zec

3:2; the very garments of the godless are to be abhorred because of their contagion.

**24–25** With this liturgical statement about the power of God to keep the faithful from stumbling, and praise to him through Jesus Christ, the letter reaches its conclusion by returning to the themes with which it began (Jude 1–2).

---

* **14–15** Mt 16:27; Heb 12:22–23.
  **16** 18; 1 Cor 10:10; 2 Pt 2:10, 18.
  **17** Heb 2:3; 2 Pt 3:2.
  **18** 1 Tm 4:1; 2 Tm 3:1–5; 2 Pt 3:3.
  **19** 1 Cor 2:14; Jas 3:15.
  **20** 2; Eph 6:18; Col 2:7.
  **21** Ti 2:13.
  **24** 2 Cor 4:14; 1 Pt 4:13.
  **25** Rom 11:36; 1 Tm 1:17.

# The Book of
# Revelation

## INTRODUCTION

### Jean-Pierre Ruiz

With its vivid imagery—from a seven-headed dragon and armored locusts to trumpeting angels and white-robed multitudes, from cataclysmic earthquakes to a river of life-giving water—Revelation leaves some readers thrilled, others terrified, still others perplexed. Some pore over its symbolism seeking clues to the future, while others draw strength for their daily living in its promises of ultimate victory for those who remain faithful. Still others find in its pages stirring testimony to the struggles faced by early Christians living under Roman subjugation. One way or another, it is all but impossible to be indifferent to the rich and complex book with which the canon of the New Testament concludes.

The brilliant but irascible fourth-century scholar Saint Jerome remarked that Revelation contains as many mysteries as it has words. The sixteenth-century reformer Martin Luther claimed that it was "neither apostolic nor prophetic," and that Christ "was neither taught nor known in it." The nineteenth-century German philosopher Friedrich Nietzsche claimed that the book of Revelation was "the most rabid outburst of vindictiveness in all recorded history."[1] Yet in 2006 Pope Benedict XVI explained that, for Christians, the book of Revelation's emphasis on Christ's "victory over death brings the message and guarantee of victory that they too will undoubtedly obtain," and "the whole of the vividly imaginative language that John uses aims to offer this consolation."[2] For Latin American Christians, the praise song "Alabaré" echoes Revelation's

## Outline of Revelation

heavenly choruses and invites worshipers to unite their voices with those who sing around God's throne (Rev 5:11–12). Reading Revelation through African American culture, Brian Blount testifies to the power of Revelation's hymns for energizing resistance against overwhelming injustice: "In oppressive camps where the powers concentrated against you appear limitless in their scope and evil intent where, defenseless, you stand with neither ally nor hope, where, although you cannot realistically fight back, you refuse to give up and give in, you still can resist. You can sing."[3]

The book of Revelation (also known as the Revelation to John and the Apocalypse) lends its name to a literary genre ("apocalyptic") that is amply represented in Jewish and Christian writings. Comparing features commonly found in these writings, biblical scholars define

1. As cited in Richard B. Hays, *The Moral Vision of the New Testament: A Contemporary Introduction to New Testament Ethics* (New York: Harper Collins, 1996), 169.

2. Pope Benedict XVI, General Audience (August 23, 2006): http://www.vatican.va/holy_father/benedict_xvi/audiences/2006/documents/hf_ben-xvi_aud_20060823_en.html.

3. Brian K. Blount, *Can I Get a Witness? Reading Revelation through African American Culture* (Louisville: Westminster John Knox Press, 2005), 117.

apocalypse as "a genre of revelatory literature with a narrative framework, in which a revelation is mediated by an otherworldly being to a human recipient, disclosing a transcendent reality which is both temporal, insofar as it envisages eschatological salvation, and spatial insofar as it involves another, supernatural world."[4] Daniel 7–12 and the book of Revelation are the only apocalypses in the canon of the Bible. Extracanonical apocalypses include portions of *1 Enoch, 4 Ezra, 2 Baruch, 3 Baruch,* the *Apocalypse of Abraham,* and the *Apocalypse of Peter.*

## Authorship

Most apocalypses are pseudonymous; the claim to authority stems from the attribution of the work to some storied figure from the past (such as Adam, Enoch, or Abraham). The book of Revelation is different. The seer-author identifies himself by name—John—four times: 1:1, 4, 9; 22:8. The author's name first occurs in the prologue, where he is identified as a participant in the transmission of the book's prophetic message: "The revelation of Jesus Christ which God gave to him, to show his servants what must happen soon. He made it known by sending his angel to his servant John, who gives witness to the word of God and to the testimony of Jesus Christ by reporting what he saw" (Rev 1:1–2). Then, in what resembles the sort of epistolary prologue found in the Pauline letters, the author greets his addressees: "John, to the seven churches in Asia: grace to you and peace from him who is and who was and who is to come, and from the seven spirits before his throne" (1:4).

Internal evidence does not help us to identify the author much more specifically, except to suggest that he was a leading figure well-known to Revelation's original audiences, Christians living in cities of the Roman province of Asia, part of present-day Turkey. In Rev 1:9 John provides information about his relationship with his addressees and about the geographical location of Revelation's inaugural vision: "I, John, your brother, who share with you the distress, the kingdom, and the endurance we have in Jesus, found myself on the island called Patmos because I proclaimed God's word and gave testimony to Jesus." By identifying himself as "your brother," John emphasizes his equality with his addressees, an equality confirmed by their shared experience. He shares their precarious condition, the experience of distress, and the attitude of endurance or perseverance (cf. 4 *Macc.* 1:11). That expression is found seven times in Revelation, most frequently in the messages specifically directed to each of seven local Christian communities (Rev 2:2, 3, 19; 3:10).

The inaugural vision takes place while John is on Patmos, a small island located fifty miles from Ephesus that was sparsely populated during the first century CE. Since antiquity, interpreters of Revelation have suggested that John was exiled to Patmos as punishment because he "proclaimed God's word and gave testimony to Jesus" (Rev 1:9; see Eusebius, *Ecclesiastical History* 3.18.1). Despite indications that deportation and permanent banishment from one's homeland were penalties imposed on transgressors by the Roman imperial authorities, sometimes as an alternative to the death penalty, John does not explicitly tell us that he has suffered this fate. It might also be possible that John visited Patmos in order to proclaim God's word and give testimony to Jesus in keeping with his role as a prophet. Or perhaps he fled to Patmos to escape his opponents on the mainland.[5]

The rest of the book is silent about the author-visionary's specific geographical location. We are not told whether he remained on Patmos or whether he returned to the Asian mainland. On several occasions, he is transported "in the spirit," an expression that recalls the ecstatic experiences of the prophet Ezekiel (see Ez 2:2; 8:3; 37:1). At the beginning of Rev 4, for example, John sees a vision of an open door to heaven. He hears the voice of the risen Jesus (identified as "the trumpetlike voice that had spoken to me before," that is, in 1:10). The voice commands, "Come up here and I will

---

4. John J. Collins, *The Apocalyptic Imagination: An Introduction to Jewish Apocalyptic Literature,* 2nd ed. (Grand Rapids, MI: Eerdmans, 1998), 5.

5. See David Aune. *Revelation 1–5,* WBC 52a (Dallas: Word Books, 1997), 76–82.

show you what must happen afterwards" (4:1). Caught up in the spirit, John receives a vision of the heavenly court. In 17:3 an angel carries him "in spirit to a deserted place where I saw a woman seated on a scarlet beast." In 21:10 an angel "took me in spirit to a great, high mountain and showed me the holy city Jerusalem coming down out of heaven from God."

After the three mentions of the author's name in the first chapter of Revelation, John is mentioned once more in the epilogue to underscore the authority of the book's message. After the beatitude in Rev 22:7, "Blessed is the one who keeps the prophetic message of this book," the narrator explains, "It is I, John, who heard and saw these things" (22:8). In a way that subverts the strategy of pseudonymous attribution that was used in other Jewish and Christian apocalypses, the authority of Revelation is bound up with the person of John and his original addressees' personal acquaintance with him.

Beginning around the middle of the second century CE with Justin Martyr (*Dialogue with Trypho* 81.4), early Christian interpreters identified the John of Revelation with the Apostle John, the son of Zebedee and the brother of James, to whom they also attributed the Fourth Gospel and the Johannine Epistles. Tertullian reports that Marcion, however, did not attribute Revelation to the Apostle John (*Against Marcion* 4.5). Eusebius reports Dionysius of Alexandria's observation (third century) that there were many others named John beside John the apostle and son of Zebedee, and while there were similarities between the Gospel of John and the First Letter of John, there are no such connections between these documents and Revelation (*Ecclesiastical History* 7.25.22).

Indirect evidence within Revelation points away from identifying its author as the Apostle John. In Revelation, the apostles are heroic figures whose names are inscribed on the foundation stones of the new Jerusalem (Rev 21:14), while John indirectly numbers himself among the prophets. In 22:9, when John prostrates himself before the angel in an act of misdirected worship, the angel admonishes him, "Don't! I am a fellow servant of yours and of your brothers the prophets and of those who keep the message of this book. Worship God."

John's role as a prophet is reconfirmed in Rev 10:8–11; in a scene that echoes Ez 3:1–3, he consumes a scroll and is told that he "must prophesy again." By consuming the scroll, the person of the prophet and the contents of the prophecy become coextensive.

## Recipients

John hears "a voice as loud as a trumpet" that commands, "Write on a scroll what you see and send it to the seven churches: to Ephesus, Smyrna, Pergamum, Thyatira, Sardis, Philadelphia, and Laodicea" (Rev 1:10–11). These seven cities all belonged to the Roman province of Asia, located in the western portion of what is Turkey today. Why these seven communities are identified as the recipients of John's Revelation is not known; the suggestion that they were all connected by a road that functioned as a sort of postal route is purely speculative.[6] Ephesus, Smyrna, and Pergamum were important cities located on or near the Aegean coast, while the other four are farther inland. Several of these cities were important centers of the imperial cult, with temples and priesthoods in honor of the emperor and of the city of Rome personified as the goddess Roma.[7] Each congregation is addressed specifically: Ephesus (2:1–7); Smyrna (2:8–11); Pergamum (2:12–17); Thyatira (2:18–29); Sardis (3:1–6); Philadelphia (3:7–13); and Laodicea (3:14–22). There is no evidence that any of these messages circulated independently. On the contrary, each message includes an admonition that suggests that all seven were to be read together: "Whoever has ears ought to hear what the Spirit says to the churches" (2:7, 11, 17, 29; 3:6, 13, 22).

## Date and Context

Two views predominate regarding the date of the composition of Revelation. Some suggest

---

6. William Ramsay, *The Letters to the Seven Churches of Asia and their Place in the Plan of the Apocalypse* (London: Hodder & Stoughton, 1904; repr. Grand Rapids, MI: Baker, 1979), 185–96.

7. Steven J. Friesen, *Imperial Cults and the Apocalypse of John: Reading Revelation in the Ruins* (New York: Oxford University Press, 2001).

the book was written during the reign of the Roman emperor Nero (54–68 CE), perhaps in response to his persecution of Christians, whom he executed as scapegoats for the great fire of Rome in 64 CE (Tacitus, *Annales*, 15.38, 44). Many suggest that 666, the "number of the beast" (Rev 13:18), is a numerological reference to Caesar Nero and that three references (13:3, 12, 14) to a beast whose mortal wound had been healed alludes to Nero's suicide in 68 CE and to the legend that he would return to life. Others, following Irenaeus (*Against Heresies* 5.30.3), maintain that Revelation was written during the latter part of the reign of the emperor Domitian (81–96 CE). Those who argue for a date of composition before the destruction of the Jerusalem Temple in 70 CE find support for this view in the mention of the "temple of God" in the "great city" where the "Lord was crucified" (11:1, 8). The "great city" is supposed to be destroyed by an earthquake (11:13), whereas the city and its Temple were actually destroyed by Rome's armies in 70 CE. Some find further support for a pre-70 CE date in the call for faithful endurance in the face of imminent death by the sword (13:10) and in the call for vengeance by those "who had been slaughtered because of the witness they bore to the word of God" (6:9). Revelation 20:4 likewise mentions "the souls of those who had been beheaded for their witness to Jesus and for the word of God."

Internal evidence in favor of a later (post-70 CE) date of composition includes six occurrences of "Babylon," a symbolic reference to Rome (Rev 14:8; 16:19; 17:5; 18:2, 10, 21). Babylon had destroyed Jerusalem and the first Temple in 587 BCE (2 Kgs 25); Rome earned that symbolic name for destroying the second Temple in 70 CE. First Peter 5:13 also uses this symbolic name, as do several post-70 CE Jewish apocalypses (for example, *4 Ezra* 3:1–2; *2 Baruch* 10:1–3). Revelation 13:4 refers to emperor worship, a practice widely attested in the cities of the province of Asia to which Revelation was addressed, with a temple at Ephesus dedicated to the emperor Domitian in 89/90 CE.[8] Many proponents of a Domitianic dating for

Revelation have relied on the assumption that this emperor was especially aggressive in his persecution of Christians. Revelation's message to Pergamum mentions one such victim of anti-Christian violence: "Antipas, my faithful witness, who was martyred [literally, "was killed"] among you" (2:13). More recent reconsideration of the evidence, however, leads to the conclusion that while there may have been sporadic and local outbreaks of violence against Christians, there does not seem to have been widespread and systematic persecution of Christians during this period.

Whether or not there was a policy or a practice of aggressive Roman persecution of Christians at the time Revelation was written, there can be no doubt that the power of Rome loomed large among the concerns of John and his fellow Christians. Even at a distance, the empire exerted its influence over every dimension of life in its far-flung provinces. For John and for other imperial subjects who belonged to religious minorities, the memory of what the new Babylon had done to Jerusalem in 70 CE was lesson enough of how precarious matters were.

## Contents

The complexity of the book of Revelation—with its successive series of seven seals, seven trumpets, seven bowls, and so forth—is such that there exist almost as many proposed outlines as there are readers seeking to understand the book's structure. Even so, this much is clear. The book begins with a prologue (Rev 1:1–3), an epistolary salutation (1:4–8), and the seer's report of his inaugural vision of the risen Christ (1:9–20). Messages from the risen Christ to each of the seven churches follow in 2:1–3:22, diagnosing the specific challenges each community faced. In 4:1–5:14 John reports his vision of the heavenly throne room in a scene that consciously emulates the pageantry of Roman imperial court protocols. In the course of this vision, he sees a seven-sealed scroll in the hand of the one seated on the throne, a scroll which no one but the "lion of the tribe of Judah, the root of David" (5:5) is worthy to open. This lion is actually "a Lamb that seemed to have been slain" (5:6),

---

8. See Friesen, *Imperial Cults and the Apocalypse of John*, 43–55, 147–151.

Revelation's most important symbolic representation of the crucified and risen Jesus. Revelation 6:1 to 16:21 then presents the unsealing of each of the seven seals of the scroll first mentioned in 5:1, the sounding of seven trumpets, and the outpouring of each of seven bowls of God's fury. Revelation 17:1–22:5 offers a tale of two cities—the demise of Rome (metaphorically identified as Babylon, the Great Prostitute), and the advent of the new creation, with the descent from heaven of the new Jerusalem. Revelation closes with an epilogue (22:6–21) that echoes themes that were introduced in the book's first chapter, focusing especially on the authority that the book claims over its addressees.

While some puzzle over the relationship between the messages to the seven churches in Rev 2:1–3:22 and the vision reports that follow them in chs. 4–22, what resonates throughout is the call to endurance. What that means in more practical terms becomes clear when we note that John's message was but one of several competing for attention in the province of Asia. John identifies the propagator of one such competing message in Thyatira as "Jezebel, who calls herself a prophetess" (2:20). By labeling his opponent as "Jezebel," he alludes to the wife of the idolatrous King Ahab, nemesis of the prophet Elijah (see 1 Kgs 19, 21). John says of his opponent in Thyatira that she "teaches and misleads my servants to play the harlot and to eat food sacrificed to idols" (Rev 2:20). Here John borrows from the prophetic literature of the Old Testament the use of the language of sexual misconduct as a metaphor for religious infidelity, that is, the worship of other gods. As for eating food sacrificed to idols, such food "could have been encountered by the average person in a variety of contexts. One would find it in the temple of a deity or in the context of a public festival; one might find it in the home of a nonmonotheistic neighbor; or one might find it at . . . the ancient meat market."[9] Paul addressed the same problem in Corinth, advising Christians there, "If an unbeliever invites you and you want to go, eat whatever is placed before you, without raising questions on grounds of conscience. But if someone says to you, 'This was offered in sacrifice,' do not eat it on account of the one who called attention to it and on account of conscience; I mean not your own conscience, but the other's" (1 Cor 10:27–29).

John was of a different mind, regarding even the smallest accommodation as a perilous concession, urging the churches to avoid any possible entanglement with Rome, its politics and its polytheism. With its inaugural vision "on the Lord's day" (Rev 1:10), a blessing pronounced on the reader and on those who listen to its prophetic message, and with its frequent scenes of heavenly worship, Revelation challenged its first-century Asian audiences to recognize that despite all appearances to the contrary, worship of Rome and of its emperor constituted idolatry. To that end, the vision reports in chs. 4–22 encouraged John's addressees to maintain their exclusive allegiance to Christ by showing them that the challenges they faced fit into the bigger picture, God's unfolding cosmic struggle against all those who opposed the divine plan. John reassured them that victory has already been achieved in the crucifixion and Resurrection of Jesus, the "Lamb that seemed to have been slain" (5:6). ■

---

9. Paul B. Duff, *Who Rides the Beast? Prophetic Rivalry and the Rhetoric of Crisis in the Churches of the Apocalypse* (New York: Oxford University Press, 2001), 52.

# THE BOOK OF REVELATION

## New American Bible, Introduction

The Apocalypse, or Revelation to John, the last book of the Bible, is one of the most difficult to understand because it abounds in unfamiliar and extravagant symbolism, which at best appears unusual to the modern reader. Symbolic language, however, is one of the chief characteristics of apocalyptic literature, of which this book is an outstanding example. Such literature enjoyed wide popularity in both Jewish and Christian circles from ca. 200 B.C. to A.D. 200.

This book contains an account of visions in symbolic and allegorical language borrowed extensively from the Old Testament, especially Ezekiel, Zechariah, and Daniel. Whether or not these visions were real experiences of the author or simply literary conventions employed by him is an open question.

This much, however, is certain: symbolic descriptions are not to be taken as literal descriptions, nor is the symbolism meant to be pictured realistically. One would find it difficult and repulsive to visualize a lamb with seven horns and seven eyes; yet Jesus Christ is described in precisely such words (Rev 5:6). The author used these images to suggest Christ's universal (seven) power (horns) and knowledge (eyes). A significant feature of apocalyptic writing is the use of symbolic colors, metals, garments (Rev 1:13–16; 3:18; 4:4; 6:1–8; 17:4; 19:8), and numbers (*four* signifies the world, *six* imperfection, *seven* totality or perfection, *twelve* Israel's tribes or the apostles, *one thousand* immensity). Finally the vindictive language in the book (Rev 6:9–10; 18:1–19:4) is also to be understood symbolically and not literally. The cries for vengeance on the lips of Christian martyrs that sound so harsh are in fact literary devices the author employed to evoke in the reader and hearer a feeling of horror for apostasy and rebellion that will be severely punished by God.

The lurid descriptions of the punishment of Jezebel (Rev 2:22) and of the destruction of the great harlot, Babylon (Rev 16:9–19:2), are likewise literary devices. The metaphor of Babylon as harlot would be wrongly construed if interpreted literally. On the other hand, the stylized figure of the woman clothed with the sun (Rev 12:1–6), depicting the New Israel, may seem to be a negative stereotype. It is necessary to look beyond the literal meaning to see that these images mean to convey a sense of God's wrath at sin in the former case and trust in God's providential care over the church in the latter.

The Book of Revelation cannot be adequately understood except against the historical background that occasioned its writing. Like Daniel and other apocalypses, it was composed as resistance literature to meet a crisis. The book itself suggests that the crisis was ruthless persecution of the early church by the Roman authorities; the harlot Babylon symbolizes pagan Rome, the city on seven hills (Rev 17:9). The book is, then, an exhortation and admonition to Christians of the first century to stand firm in the faith and to avoid compromise with paganism, despite the threat of adversity and martyrdom; they are to await patiently the fulfillment of God's mighty promises. The triumph of God in the world of men and women remains a mystery, to be accepted in faith and longed for in hope. It is a triumph that unfolded in the history of Jesus of Nazareth and continues to unfold in the history of the individual Christian who follows the way of the cross, even, if necessary, to a martyr's death.

Though the perspective is eschatological—ultimate salvation and victory are said to take place at the end of the present age when Christ will come in glory at the parousia—the book presents the decisive struggle of Christ and his followers against Satan and his cohorts as already over. Christ's overwhelming defeat of the kingdom of Satan ushered in the everlasting reign of God (Rev 11:15; 12:10). Even the forces of evil unwittingly carry out the divine plan (Rev 17:17), for God is the sovereign Lord of history.

The Book of Revelation had its origin in a

time of crisis, but it remains valid and meaningful for Christians of all time. In the face of apparently insuperable evil, either from within or from without, all Christians are called to trust in Jesus' promise, "Behold, I am with you always, until the end of the age" (Mt 28:20). Those who remain steadfast in their faith and confidence in the risen Lord need have no fear. Suffering, persecution, even death by martyrdom, though remaining impenetrable mysteries of evil, do not comprise an absurd dead end. No matter what adversity or sacrifice Christians may endure, they will in the end triumph over Satan and his forces because of their fidelity to Christ the victor. This is the enduring message of the book; it is a message of hope and consolation and challenge for all who dare to believe.

The author of the book calls himself John (Rev 1:1, 4, 9; 22:8), who because of his Christian faith has been exiled to the rocky island of Patmos, a Roman penal colony. Although he never claims to be John the apostle, whose name is attached to the fourth gospel, he was so identified by several of the early church Fathers, including Justin, Irenaeus, Clement of Alexandria, Tertullian, Cyprian, and Hippolytus. This identification, however, was denied by other Fathers, including Denis of Alexandria, Eusebius of Caesarea, Cyril of Jerusalem, Gregory Nazianzen, and John Chrysostom. Indeed, vocabulary, grammar, and style make it doubtful that the book could have been put into its present form by the same person(s) responsible for the fourth gospel. Nevertheless, there are definite linguistic and theological affinities between the two books. The tone of the letters to the seven churches (Rev 1:4–3:22) is indicative of the great authority the author enjoyed over the Christian communities in Asia. It is possible, therefore, that he was a disciple of John the apostle, who is traditionally associated with that part of the world. The date of the book in its present form is probably near the end of the reign of Domitian (A.D. 81–96), a fierce persecutor of the Christians.

The principal divisions of the Book of Revelation are the following:

I. Prologue (1:1–3)

II. Letters to the Churches of Asia (1:4–3:22)

III. God and the Lamb in Heaven (4:1–5:14)

IV. The Seven Seals, Trumpets, and Plagues, with Interludes (6:1–16:21)

V. The Punishment of Babylon and the Destruction of Pagan Nations (17:1–20:15)

VI. The New Creation (21:1–22:5)

VII. Epilogue (22:6–21) ■

R
E
V

# REVELATION

## I. PROLOGUE†

**1** ¹The revelation of Jesus Christ, which God gave to him, to show his servants what must happen soon. He made it known by sending his angel to his servant John, * ²who gives witness to the word of God and to the testimony of Jesus Christ by reporting what he saw. ³Blessed is the one† who reads aloud and blessed are those who listen to this prophetic message and heed what is written in it, for the appointed time is near. *

## II. LETTERS TO THE CHURCHES OF ASIA

**Greeting.**† ⁴John, to the seven churches in Asia:† grace to you and peace from him who is and who was and who is to come, and from the seven spirits before his throne, * ⁵and from Jesus Christ, the faithful witness, the firstborn of the dead and ruler of the kings of the earth. To him who loves us and has freed us† from our sins by his blood, * ⁶who has made us into a kingdom, priests for his God and Father, to him be glory and power forever [and ever]. Amen. *

⁷ Behold, he is coming amid the clouds,
　and every eye will see him,
　　even those who pierced him.
All the peoples of the earth will lament him.
Yes. Amen. *

⁸"I am the Alpha and the Omega,"† says the Lord God, "the one who is and who was and who is to come, the almighty." *

**The First Vision.**† ⁹I, John, your brother, who share with you the distress, the kingdom, and the endurance we have in Jesus, found myself on the island called Patmos† because I proclaimed God's word and gave testimony to Jesus. ¹⁰I was caught up in spirit on the Lord's day† and heard behind me a voice as loud as a trumpet, ¹¹which said, "Write on a scroll† what you see and send it to the seven churches: to Ephesus, Smyrna, Pergamum, Thyatira, Sardis, Philadelphia, and Laodicea." ¹²† Then I turned to see whose voice it was that spoke to me, and when I turned, I saw seven gold lampstands ¹³and in the midst of the lampstands one like a son of man,† wearing an ankle-length robe, with a gold sash around his chest. * ¹⁴The hair of his head was as white as white wool or as snow,† and his eyes were like a fiery flame. ¹⁵His feet were like polished

---

† **1:1–3** This prologue describes the source, contents, and audience of the book and forms an inclusion with the epilogue (Rev 22:6–21), with its similar themes and expressions.

**1:3** *Blessed is the one*: this is the first of seven beatitudes in this book; the others are in Rev 14:13; 16:15; 19:9; 20:6; 22:7, 14. *This prophetic message*: literally, "the words of the prophecy"; so Rev 22:7, 10, 18, 19 by inclusion. *The appointed time*: when Jesus will return in glory; cf. Rev 1:7; 3:11; 22:7, 10, 12, 20.

**1:4–8** Although Revelation begins and ends (Rev 22:21) with Christian epistolary formulae, there is nothing between Rev 4; 22 resembling a letter. The author here employs the standard word order for greetings in Greek letter writing: "N. to N., greetings…"; see note on Rom 1:1.

**1:4** *Seven churches in Asia*: Asia refers to the Roman province of that name in western Asia Minor (modern Turkey); these representative churches are mentioned by name in Rev 1:11, and each is the recipient of a message (Rev 2:1–3:22). *Seven* is the biblical number suggesting fullness and completeness; thus the seer is writing for the whole church.

**1:5** *Freed us*: the majority of Greek manuscripts and several early versions read "washed us"; but "freed us" is supported by the best manuscripts and fits well with Old Testament imagery, e.g., Is 40:2.

**1:8** *The Alpha and the Omega*: the first and last letters of the Greek alphabet. In Rev 22:13 the same words occur together with the expressions "the First and the Last, the Beginning and the End"; cf. Rev 1:17; 2:8; 21:6; Is 41:4; 44:6.

**1:9–20** In this first vision, the seer is commanded to write what he sees to the seven churches (Rev 1:9–11). He sees Christ in glory, whom he depicts in stock apocalyptic imagery (Rev 1:12–16), and hears him describe himself in terms meant to encourage Christians by emphasizing his victory over death (Rev 1:17–20).

**1:9** *Island called Patmos*: one of the Sporades islands in the Aegean Sea, some fifty miles south of Ephesus, used by the Romans as a penal colony. *Because I proclaimed God's word*: literally, "on account of God's word."

**1:10** *The Lord's day*: Sunday. *As loud as a trumpet*: the imagery is derived from the theophany at Sinai (Ex 19:16, 19; cf. Heb 12:19 and the trumpet in other eschatological settings in Is 27:13; Jl 2:1; Mt 24:31; 1 Cor 15:52; 1 Thes 4:16).

**1:11** *Scroll*: a papyrus roll.

**1:12–16** A symbolic description of Christ in glory. The metaphorical language is not to be understood literally; cf. Introduction.

**1:13** *Son of man*: see note on Mk 8:31. *Ankle-length robe*: Christ is priest; cf. Ex 28:4; 29:5; Wis 18:24; Zec 3:4. *Gold sash*: Christ is king; cf. Ex 28:4; 1 Mc 10:89; 11:58; Dn 10:5.

**1:14** *Hair…as white as white wool or as snow*: Christ is eternal, clothed with the dignity that belonged to the "Ancient of Days"; cf. Rev 1:18; Dn 7:9. *His eyes were like a fiery flame*: Christ is portrayed as all-knowing; cf. Rev 2:23; Ps 7:10; Jer 17:10; and similar expressions in Rev 2:18; 19:12; cf. Dn 10:6.

---

**1:1** 22:6–8, 20; Dn 2:28 / Rev 19:10.
**1:3** 22:7 / Lk 11:28.
**1:4** 8; 4:8; 11:17; 16:5; Ex 3:14.
**1:5** 3:14; 1 Cor 15:20; Col 1:18 / Heb 9:14;
1 Pt 1:19; 1 Jn 1:7.
**1:6** Ex 19:6; 1 Pt 2:9.
**1:7** Dn 7:13 / Zec 12:10; Mt 24:30; Jn 19:37.
**1:8** 17; 21:6; 22:13; Is 41:4; 44:6; 48:12.
**1:13** Dn 7:13; 10:5.

©W Wittman, Ltd

The author of the book of Revelation calls himself John and claims to have been exiled to the island of Patmos (above), a Roman penal colony, for his Christian faith. The author's precise circumstances are debated but not his motive, to encourage seven fledgling churches during a time of heavy persecution.

brass refined in a furnace,† and his voice was like the sound of rushing water. ¹⁶ In his right hand he held seven stars.† A sharp two-edged sword came out of his mouth, and his face shone like the sun at its brightest.*

¹⁷ When I caught sight of him, I fell down at his feet as though dead.† He touched me with his right hand and said, "Do not be afraid. I am the first and the last, * ¹⁸ the one who lives. Once I was dead, but now I am alive forever and ever. I hold the keys to death and the netherworld.† ¹⁹ Write down, therefore, what

you have seen, and what is happening, and what will happen afterwards.† ²⁰ This is the secret meaning† of the seven stars you saw in my right hand, and of the seven gold lampstands: the seven stars are the angels of the seven churches, and the seven lampstands are the seven churches.

**2** **To Ephesus.** ¹† "To the angel of the church† in Ephesus,† write this:

"'The one who holds the seven stars in his right hand and walks in the midst of the

---

† **1:15** *His feet…furnace*: Christ is depicted as unchangeable; cf. Ez 1:27; Dn 10:6. The Greek word translated "refined" is unconnected grammatically with any other word in the sentence. *His voice…water*: Christ speaks with divine authority; cf. Ez 1:24.

**1:16** *Seven stars*: in the pagan world, Mithras and the Caesars were represented with seven stars in their right hand, symbolizing their universal dominion. *A sharp two-edged sword*: this refers to the word of God (cf. Eph 6:17; Heb 4:12) that will destroy unrepentant sinners; cf. Rev 2:16; 19:15; Wis 18:15; Is 11:4; 49:2. *His face…brightest*: this symbolizes the divine majesty of Christ; cf. Rev 10:1; 21:23; Jgs 5:31; Is 60:19; Mt 17:2.

**1:17** It was an Old Testament belief that for sinful human beings to see God was to die; cf. Ex 19:21; 33:20; Jgs 6:22–23; Is 6:5.

**1:18** *Netherworld*: Greek Hades, Hebrew Sheol, the abode of the dead; cf. Rev 20:13–14; Nm 16:33.

**1:19** *What you have seen, and what is happening, and what will happen afterwards*: the three parts of the Book of Revelation, the vision (Rev 1:10–20), the situation in the seven churches (Rev 2–3), and the events of Rev 6–22.

**1:20** *Secret meaning*: literally, "mystery." *Angels*: these are the presiding spirits of the seven churches. Angels were thought to be in charge of the physical world (cf. Rev 7:1; 14:18; 16:5) and of nations (Dn 10:13; 12:1), communities (the seven churches),

and individuals (Mt 18:10; Acts 12:15). Some have seen in the "angel" of each of the seven churches its pastor or a personification of the spirit of the congregation.

**2:1–3:22** Each of the seven letters follows the same pattern: address; description of the exalted Christ; blame and/or praise for the church addressed; threat and/or admonition; final exhortation and promise to all Christians.

**2:1–7** The letter to Ephesus praises the members of the church there for their works and virtues, including discerning false teachers (Rev 2:2–3), but admonishes them to repent and return to their former devotion (Rev 2:4–5). It concludes with a reference to the Nicolaitans (see note on Rev 2:6) and a promise that the victor will have access to eternal life (Rev 2:7).

**2:1** *Ephesus*: this great ancient city had a population of ca. 250,000; it was the capital of the Roman province of Asia and the commercial, cultural, and religious center of Asia. The other six churches were located in the same province, situated roughly in a circle; they were selected for geographical reasons rather than for the size of their Christian communities. *Walks in the midst of the seven gold lampstands*: this signifies that Christ is always present in the church; see note on Rev 1:4.

---

Smyrna, modern Izmir, located about thirty miles north of Ephesus, was an important commercial center renowned for its loyalty to Rome. Christians there were a much persecuted minority. Pictured above are some ruins from the agora, which served as the commercial, judicial, and political center of the city.

seven gold lampstands says this: ² "I know your works, your labor, and your endurance, and that you cannot tolerate the wicked; you have tested those who call themselves apostles but are not, and discovered that they are impostors.† ³ Moreover, you have endurance and have suffered for my name, and you have not grown weary. ⁴ Yet I hold this against you: you have lost the love you had at first. ⁵ Realize how far you have fallen. Repent, and do the works you did at first. Otherwise, I will come to you and remove your lampstand from its place, unless you repent. ⁶ But you have this in your favor: you hate the works of the Nicolaitans,† which I also hate.

⁷ " ' "Whoever has ears ought to hear what the Spirit says to the churches. To the victor† I will give the right to eat from the tree of life that is in the garden of God." ' *

**To Smyrna.**† ⁸ "To the angel of the church in Smyrna,† write this:

" 'The first and the last, who once died but came to life, says this: ⁹ "I know your tribulation and poverty, but you are rich.† I know the slander of those who claim to be Jews and are not, but rather are members of the assembly of Satan.* ¹⁰ Do not be afraid of anything that you are going to suffer. Indeed, the devil will throw some of you into prison, that you may

**2:2** *Who call themselves…impostors*: this refers to unauthorized and perverse missionaries; cf. Acts 20:29–30.

**2:6** *Nicolaitans*: these are perhaps the impostors of Rev 2:2; see note on Rev 2:14–15. There is little evidence for connecting this group with Nicolaus, the proselyte from Antioch, mentioned in Acts 6:5.

**2:7** *Victor*: referring to any Christian individual who holds fast to the faith and does God's will in the face of persecution. *The tree of life that is in the garden of God*: this is a reference to the tree in the primeval paradise (Gn 2:9); cf. Rev 22:2, 14, 19. The decree excluding humanity from the tree of life has been revoked by Christ.

**2:8–11** The letter to Smyrna encourages the Christians in this important commercial center by telling them that although they are impoverished, they are nevertheless rich, and calls those Jews who are slandering them members of the assembly of Satan (Rev

2:9). There is no admonition; rather, the Christians are told that they will suffer much, even death, but the time of tribulation will be short compared to their eternal reward (Rev 2:10), and they will thus escape final damnation (Rev 2:11).

**2:8** *Smyrna*: modern Izmir, ca. thirty miles north of Ephesus, and the chief city of Lydia, with a temple to the goddess Roma. It was renowned for its loyalty to Rome, and it also had a large Jewish community very hostile toward Christians.

**2:9–10** The church in Smyrna was materially poor but spiritually rich. Accusations made by Jewish brethren there occasioned the persecution of Christians; cf. Acts 14:2, 19; 17:5, 13.

**2:7** 11, 17, 29; 3:6, 13, 22; 13:9; Mt 11:15.     **2:9** Jas 2:5.

be tested, and you will face an ordeal for ten days. Remain faithful until death, and I will give you the crown of life.

[11] """Whoever has ears ought to hear what the Spirit says to the churches.* The victor shall not be harmed by the second death."'†

**To Pergamum.**† [12] "To the angel of the church in Pergamum,† write this:

"'The one with the sharp two-edged sword says this: [13] "I know that you live where Satan's throne† is, and yet you hold fast to my name and have not denied your faith in me, not even in the days of Antipas, my faithful witness, who was martyred among you, where Satan lives. [14]† Yet I have a few things against you. You have some people there who hold to the teaching of Balaam, who instructed Balak to put a stumbling block before the Israelites: to eat food sacrificed to idols and to play the harlot.* [15] Likewise, you also have some people who hold to the teaching of [the] Nicolaitans. [16] Therefore, repent. Otherwise, I will come to you quickly and wage war against them with the sword of my mouth.

[17] """Whoever has ears ought to hear what the Spirit says to the churches. To the victor I shall give some of the hidden manna;† I shall also give a white amulet upon which is inscribed a new name, which no one knows except the one who receives it."'*

**To Thyatira.**† [18] "To the angel of the church in Thyatira,† write this:

"'The Son of God, whose eyes are like a fiery flame and whose feet are like polished brass, says this: [19] "I know your works, your love, faith, service, and endurance, and that your last works are greater than the first. [20] Yet I hold this against you, that you tolerate the woman Jezebel, who calls herself a prophetess, who teaches and misleads my servants to play the harlot and to eat food sacrificed to idols.† [21] I have given her time to repent, but she refuses to repent of her harlotry. [22] So I will cast her on a sickbed and plunge those who commit adultery with her into intense suffering unless they repent of her works. [23] I will also put her children† to death. Thus shall all the churches come to know that I am the searcher of hearts and minds and that I will give each of you what your works deserve.* [24] But I say to the rest of you in Thyatira, who do not uphold this teaching and know nothing of the so-called deep secrets of Satan:† on you I will place no further burden, [25] except that you must hold fast to what you have until I come.

[26]     """To the victor,† who keeps to my
             ways† until the end,
         I will give authority over the nations.*
[27]     He will rule them with an iron rod.
         Like clay vessels will they be smashed,

---

† **2:11** *The second death:* this refers to the eternal death, when sinners will receive their final punishment; cf. Rev 20:6, 14–15; 21:8.

**2:12–17** The letter to Pergamum praises the members of the church for persevering in their faith in Christ even in the midst of a pagan setting and in face of persecution and martyrdom (Rev 2:13). But it admonishes them about members who advocate an unprincipled morality (Rev 2:14; cf. 2 Pt 2:15; Jude 11) and others who follow the teaching of the Nicolaitans (Rev 2:15; see note there). It urges them to repent (Rev 2:16) and promises them the hidden manna and Christ's amulet (Rev 2:17).

**2:12** *Pergamum:* modern Bergama, ca. forty-five miles northeast of Smyrna, a center for various kinds of pagan worship. It also had an outstanding library (the word *parchment* is derived from its name).

**2:13** *Satan's throne:* the reference is to emperor worship and other pagan practices that flourished in Pergamum, perhaps specifically to the white marble altar erected and dedicated to Zeus by Eumenes II (197–160 B.C.).

**2:14–15** Like Balaam, the biblical prototype of the religious compromiser (cf. Nm 25:1–3; 31:16; 2 Pt 2:15; Jude 11), the Nicolaitans in Pergamum and Ephesus (Rev 2:6) accommodated their Christian faith to paganism. They abused the principle of liberty enunciated by Paul (1 Cor 9:19–23).

**2:17** *The hidden manna:* this is the food of life; cf. Ps 78:24–25. *White amulet:* literally, "white stone," on which was written a magical name, whose power could be tapped by one who knew the secret name. It is used here as a symbol of victory and joy; cf. Rev 3:4–5. *New name:* this is a reference to the Christian's rebirth in Christ; cf. Rev 3:12; 19:12; Is 62:2; 65:15.

**2:18–29** The letter to Thyatira praises the progress in virtue of this small Christian community (Rev 2:19) but admonishes them for tolerating a false prophet who leads them astray (Rev 2:20). Her fate is sealed, but there is hope of repentance for her followers (Rev 2:21–22). Otherwise, they too shall die (Rev 2:23). They are warned against Satanic power or knowledge (Rev 2:24–25). Those who remain faithful will share in the messianic reign, having authority over nations (Rev 2:26–27), and will in fact possess Christ himself (Rev 2:28).

**2:18** *Thyatira:* modern Akhisar, ca. forty miles southeast of Pergamum, a frontier town famous for its workers' guilds (cf. Acts 16:14), membership in which may have involved festal meals in pagan temples.

**2:20** The scheming and treacherous Jezebel of old (cf. 1 Kgs 19:1–2; 21:1–14; 2 Kgs 9:22, 30–34) introduced pagan customs into the religion of Israel; this new Jezebel was doing the same to Christianity.

**2:23** *Children:* spiritual descendants.

**2:24** *The so-called deep secrets of Satan:* literally, "the deep things of Satan," a scathing reference to the perverse teaching of the Nicolaitans (Rev 2:15).

**2:26–28** The Christian who perseveres in faith will share in Christ's messianic authority (cf. Ps 2:8–9) and resurrection victory over death, symbolized by the morning star; cf. Rev 22:16.

**2:26** *Who keeps to my ways:* literally, "who keeps my works."

---

| | |
|---|---|
| **2:11** 20:6, 14; 21:8. | **2:17** Is 62:2; 65:15. |
| **2:14** Nm 22–24; 25:1–3; 31:16; 2 Pt 2:15; Jude 11. | **2:23** 1 Sm 16:7; Jer 11:20; 17:10. |
| | **2:26** 12:5; Ps 2:8–9. |

<sup>28</sup> just as I received authority from my Father. And to him I will give the morning star.

<sup>29</sup> """Whoever has ears ought to hear what the Spirit says to the churches."'

**3** **To Sardis.**† <sup>1</sup> "To the angel of the church in Sardis,† write this:

"'The one who has the seven spirits of God and the seven stars says this: "I know your works, that you have the reputation of being alive, but you are dead. <sup>2</sup> Be watchful and strengthen what is left, which is going to die, for I have not found your works complete in the sight of my God. <sup>3</sup> Remember then how you accepted and heard; keep it, and repent. If you are not watchful, I will come like a thief, and you will never know at what hour I will come upon you.* <sup>4</sup> However, you have a few people in Sardis who have not soiled their garments; they will walk with me dressed in white, because they are worthy.*

<sup>5</sup> """The victor will thus be dressed in white,† and I will never erase his name from the book of life but will acknowledge his name in the presence of my Father and of his angels.*

<sup>6</sup> """Whoever has ears ought to hear what the Spirit says to the churches."'

**To Philadelphia.**† <sup>7</sup> "To the angel of the church in Philadelphia,† write this:

"'The holy one, the true,
     who holds the key of David,

who opens and no one shall close,
     who closes and no one shall open,*

says this:

<sup>8</sup> """I know your works (behold, I have left an open door† before you, which no one can close). You have limited strength, and yet you have kept my word and have not denied my name. <sup>9</sup> Behold, I will make those of the assembly of Satan who claim to be Jews and are not, but are lying, behold I will make them come and fall prostrate at your feet, and they will realize that I love you.* <sup>10</sup> Because you have kept my message of endurance,† I will keep you safe in the time of trial that is going to come to the whole world to test the inhabitants of the earth. <sup>11</sup> I am coming quickly. Hold fast to what you have, so that no one may take your crown.*

<sup>12</sup> """The victor I will make into a pillar† in the temple of my God, and he will never leave it again. On him I will inscribe the name of my God and the name of the city of my God, the new Jerusalem, which comes down out of heaven from my God, as well as my new name.*

<sup>13</sup> """Whoever has ears ought to hear what the Spirit says to the churches."'

**To Laodicea.**† <sup>14</sup> "To the angel of the church in Laodicea,† write this:

"'The Amen, the faithful and true witness, the source of God's creation, says this:* <sup>15</sup> "I

---

<sup>†</sup>

**3:1–6** The letter to Sardis does not praise the community but admonishes its members to watchfulness, mutual support, and repentance (Rev 3:2–3). The few who have remained pure and faithful will share Christ's victory and will be inscribed in the book of life (Rev 3:4–5).

**3:1** *Sardis*: this city, located ca. thirty miles southeast of Thyatira, was once the capital of Lydia, known for its wealth at the time of Croesus (6th century B.C.). Its citadel, reputed to be unassailable, was captured by surprise, first by Cyrus and later by Antiochus. The church is therefore warned to be on guard.

**3:5** *In white*: white is a sign of victory and joy as well as resurrection; see note on Rev 2:17. *The book of life*: the roll in which the names of the redeemed are kept; cf. Rev 13:8; 17:8; 20:12, 15; 21:27; Phil 4:3; Dn 12:1. They will be acknowledged by Christ in heaven; cf. Mt 10:32.

**3:7–13** The letter to Philadelphia praises the Christians there for remaining faithful even with their limited strength (Rev 3:8). Members of the assembly of Satan are again singled out (Rev 3:9; see Rev 2:9). There is no admonition; rather, the letter promises that they will be kept safe at the great trial (Rev 3:10–11) and that the victors will become pillars of the heavenly temple, upon which three names will be inscribed: God, Jerusalem, and Christ (Rev 3:12).

**3:7** *Philadelphia*: modern Alasehir, ca. thirty miles southeast of Sardis, founded by Attalus II Philadelphus of Pergamum to be an "open door" (Rev 3:8) for Greek culture; it was destroyed by an earthquake in A.D. 17. Rebuilt by money from the Emperor Tiberius, the city was renamed Neo-Caesarea; this may explain the allusions to "name" in Rev 3:12. *Key of David*: to the heav-

enly city of David (cf. Is 22:22), "the new Jerusalem" (Rev 3:12), over which Christ has supreme authority.

**3:8** *An open door*: opportunities for sharing and proclaiming the faith; cf. Acts 14:27; 1 Cor 16:9; 2 Cor 2:12.

**3:10** *My message of endurance*: this does not refer to a saying of Jesus about patience but to the example of Christ's patient endurance. *The inhabitants of the earth*: literally, "those who live on the earth." This expression, which also occurs in Rev 6:10; 8:13; 11:10; 13:8, 12, 14; 17:2, 8, always refers to the pagan world.

**3:12** *Pillar*: this may be an allusion to the rebuilding of the city; see note on v 7. *New Jerusalem*: it is described in Rev 21:10–22:5.

**3:14–22** The letter to Laodicea reprimands the community for being lukewarm (Rev 3:15–16), but no particular faults are singled out. Their material prosperity is contrasted with their spiritual poverty, the violet tunics that were the source of their wealth with the white robe of baptism, and their famous eye ointment with true spiritual perception (Rev 3:17–18). But Christ's chastisement is inspired by love and a desire to be allowed to share the messianic banquet with his followers in the heavenly kingdom (Rev 3:19–21).

**3:14** *Laodicea*: ca. forty miles southeast of Philadelphia and

---

*

| | |
|---|---|
| **3:3** Mt 24:42–44; Mk 13:33; 1 Thes 5:2; 2 Pt 3:10. | **3:7** Is 22:22; Mt 16:19. |
| | **3:9** 2:9 / Is 45:14; 60:14. |
| **3:4** 7:13–14. | **3:11** 2:25; 22:7, 20. |
| **3:5** Ps 69:29; Dn 12:1 / Mt 10:32. | **3:12** 21:2–3; Ez 48:35 / Rev 19:13. |
| | **3:14** 1:5. |

know your works; I know that you are neither cold nor hot.† I wish you were either cold or hot. ¹⁶† So, because you are lukewarm, neither hot nor cold, I will spit you out of my mouth. ¹⁷†* For you say, 'I am rich and affluent and have no need of anything,' and yet do not realize that you are wretched, pitiable, poor, blind, and naked. ¹⁸ I advise you to buy from me gold refined by fire† so that you may be rich, and white garments to put on so that your shameful nakedness may not be exposed, and buy ointment to smear on your eyes so that you may see. ¹⁹ Those whom I love, I reprove and chastise. Be earnest, therefore, and repent. *

²⁰ "'"Behold, I stand at the door and knock. If anyone hears my voice and opens the door, [then] I will enter his house and dine with him, and he with me.† ²¹ I will give the victor the right to sit with me on my throne, as I myself first won the victory and sit with my Father on his throne. *

²² "'"Whoever has ears ought to hear what the Spirit says to the churches."'"

## III. GOD AND THE LAMB IN HEAVEN

**4 Vision of Heavenly Worship.**† ¹ After this I had a vision of an open door† to heaven, and I heard the trumpetlike voice that had spoken to me before, saying, "Come up here and I will show you what must happen afterwards."

² † At once I was caught up in spirit. * A throne was there in heaven, and on the throne sat ³ one whose appearance sparkled like jasper and carnelian. Around the throne was a halo as brilliant as an emerald. ⁴ Surrounding the throne I saw twenty-four other thrones on which twenty-four elders† sat, dressed in white garments and with gold crowns on their heads. * ⁵ From the throne came flashes of lightning, rumblings, and peals of thunder.† Seven flaming torches burned in front of the throne, which are the seven spirits of God. ⁶ * In front of the throne was something that resembled a sea of glass like crystal.†

In the center and around the throne, there were four living creatures covered with eyes in front and in back. ⁷ The first creature resembled a lion, the second was like a calf, the third had a face like that of a human being, and the fourth looked like an eagle† in flight. ⁸ The four living creatures, each of them with six wings,† were covered with eyes inside and out. Day and night they do not stop exclaiming:

"Holy, holy, holy is the Lord God
　　almighty,
　　who was, and who is, and who is to
　　　come." *

⁹ Whenever the living creatures give glory and honor and thanks to the one who sits on

---

ca. eighty miles east of Ephesus, a wealthy industrial and commercial center, with a renowned medical school. It exported fine woolen garments and was famous for its eye salves. It was so wealthy that it was proudly rebuilt without outside aid after the devastating earthquake of A.D. 60/61. *The Amen*: this is a divine title (cf. Hebrew text of Is 65:16) applied to Christ; cf. 2 Cor 1:20. *Source of God's creation*: literally, "the beginning of God's creation," a concept found also in Jn 1:3; Col 1:16–17; Heb 1:2; cf. Prv 8:22–31; Wis 9:1–2.

**3:15–16** Halfhearted commitment to the faith is nauseating to Christ; cf. Rom 12:11.

**3:16** *Spit*: literally, "vomit." The image is that of a beverage that should be either hot or cold. Perhaps there is an allusion to the hot springs of Hierapolis across the Lycus river from Laodicea, which would have been lukewarm by the time they reached Laodicea.

**3:17** Economic prosperity occasioned spiritual bankruptcy.

**3:18** *Gold…fire*: God's grace. *White garments*: symbol of an upright life; the city was noted for its violet/purple cloth. *Ointment…eyes*: to remove spiritual blindness; one of the city's exports was eye ointment (see note on Rev 3:14).

**3:20** Christ invites all to the messianic banquet in heaven; cf. Is 25:6; Lk 14:15; 22:30.

**4:1–11** The seer now describes a vision of the heavenly court in worship of God enthroned. He reverently avoids naming or describing God but pictures twenty-four elders in priestly and regal attire (Rev 4:4) and God's throne and its surroundings made of precious gems and other symbols that traditionally express the majesty of God (Rev 4:5–6). Universal creation is represented by the four living creatures (Rev 4:6–7). Along with

the twenty-four elders, they praise God unceasingly in humble adoration (Rev 4:8–11).

**4:1** The ancients viewed heaven as a solid vault, entered by way of actual doors.

**4:2–8** Much of the imagery here is taken from Ez 1 and 10.

**4:4** *Twenty-four elders*: these represent the twelve tribes of Israel and the twelve apostles; cf. Rev 21:12–14.

**4:5** *Flashes of lightning, rumblings, and peals of thunder*: as in other descriptions of God's appearance or activity; cf. Rev 8:5; 11:19; 16:18; Ex 19:16; Ez 1:4, 13. *The seven spirits of God*: the seven "angels of the presence" as in Rev 8:2 and Tb 12:15.

**4:6** *A sea of glass like crystal*: an image adapted from Ez 1:22–26. *Four living creatures*: these are symbols taken from Ez 1:5–21; they are identified as cherubim in Ez 10:20. *Covered with eyes*: these suggest God's knowledge and concern.

**4:7** *Lion…calf…human being…eagle*: these symbolize, respectively, what is noblest, strongest, wisest, and swiftest in creation. *Calf*: traditionally translated "ox," the Greek word refers to a heifer or young bull. Since the second century, these four creatures have been used as symbols of the evangelists Mark, Luke, Matthew, and John, respectively.

**4:8** *Six wings*: like the seraphim of Is 6:2.

---

**3:17** Prv 13:7; Lk 12:21.
**3:19** Prv 3:11–12; 1 Cor 11:32; Heb 12:5–11.
**3:21** Lk 22:28–30; Mt 19:28.
**4:2–3** Is 6:1 / Ez 1:26–28.
**4:4** Is 24:23.
**4:6** Ex 24:10.
**4:8** Is 6:2–3 / Rev 1:4, 8; 11:17; 16:5.

the throne, who lives forever and ever, ¹⁰ the twenty-four elders fall down before the one who sits on the throne and worship him, who lives forever and ever. They throw down their crowns before the throne, exclaiming:

¹¹    "Worthy are you, Lord our God,
       to receive glory and honor and power,
    for you created all things;
       because of your will they came to be
          and were created."*

**5** **The Scroll and the Lamb.**† ¹ I saw a scroll† in the right hand of the one who sat on the throne. It had writing on both sides and was sealed with seven seals.* ² Then I saw a mighty angel who proclaimed in a loud voice, "Who is worthy to open the scroll and break its seals?" ³ But no one in heaven or on earth or under the earth was able to open the scroll or to examine it. ⁴ I shed many tears because no one was found worthy to open the scroll or to examine it. ⁵ One of the elders said to me, "Do not weep. The lion of the tribe of Judah, the root of David,† has triumphed, enabling him to open the scroll with its seven seals."*

⁶ Then I saw standing in the midst of the throne and the four living creatures and the elders a Lamb† that seemed to have been slain. He had seven horns and seven eyes; these are the [seven] spirits of God sent out into the whole world.* ⁷ He came and received the scroll from the right hand of the one who sat on the throne. ⁸ When he took it, the four living creatures and the twenty-four elders fell down before the Lamb. Each of the elders held a harp and gold bowls filled with incense, which are the prayers of the holy ones. ⁹ They sang a new hymn:

    "Worthy are you to receive the scroll
       and to break open its seals,
    for you were slain and with your
       blood you purchased for God
    those from every tribe and tongue,
       people and nation.
¹⁰     You made them a kingdom and priests
          for our God,
    and they will reign on earth."*

¹¹ I looked again and heard the voices of many angels who surrounded the throne and the living creatures and the elders. They were countless† in number,* ¹² and they cried out in a loud voice:

    "Worthy is the Lamb that was slain
       to receive power and riches, wisdom
          and strength,
    honor and glory and blessing."

¹³ Then I heard every creature in heaven and on earth and under the earth and in the sea, everything in the universe, cry out:

    "To the one who sits on the throne and
       to the Lamb
    be blessing and honor, glory and
       might,
    forever and ever."

¹⁴ The four living creatures answered, "Amen," and the elders fell down and worshiped.

---

† **5:1–14** The seer now describes a papyrus roll in God's right hand (Rev 5:1) with seven seals indicating the importance of the message. A mighty angel asks who is worthy to open the scroll, i.e., who can accomplish God's salvific plan (Rev 5:2). There is despair at first when no one in creation can do it (Rev 5:3–4). But the seer is comforted by an elder who tells him that Christ, called the lion of the tribe of Judah, has won the right to open it (Rev 5:5). Christ then appears as a Lamb, coming to receive the scroll from God (Rev 5:6–7), for which he is acclaimed as at a coronation (Rev 5:8–10). This is followed by a doxology of the angels (Rev 5:11–12) and then finally by the heavenly church united with all of creation (Rev 5:13–14).

**5:1** A scroll: a papyrus roll possibly containing a list of afflictions for sinners (cf. Ez 2:9–10) or God's plan for the world. Sealed with seven seals: it is totally hidden from all but God. Only the Lamb (Rev 5:7–9) has the right to carry out the divine plan.

**5:5** The lion of the tribe of Judah, the root of David: these are the messianic titles applied to Christ to symbolize his victory; cf. Rev 22:16; Gn 49:9; Is 11:1, 10; Mt 1:1.

**5:6** Christ is the Paschal Lamb without blemish, whose blood saved the new Israel from sin and death; cf. Ex 12; Is 53:7; Jn 1:29, 36; Acts 8:32; 1 Pt 1:18–19. This is the main title for Christ in Revelation, used twenty-eight times. Seven horns and seven eyes: Christ has the fullness (see note on Rev 1:4) of power (horns) and knowledge (eyes); cf. Zec 4:7. [Seven] spirits: as in Rev 1:4; 3:1; 4:5.

**5:11** Countless: literally, "100,000,000 plus 1,000,000," used by the author to express infinity.

---

**4:11** Rom 4:17; 16:27.          **5:6** Jn 1:29.
**5:1** Is 29:11.                  **5:10** 1:6; Ex 19:6; Is 61:6.
**5:5** Is 11:1, 10; Rom          **5:11** Dn 7:10; Jude 14–15.
     15:12.

## IV. THE SEVEN SEALS, TRUMPETS, AND PLAGUES, WITH INTERLUDES†

**6** †**The First Six Seals.** [1]† Then I watched while the Lamb broke open the first of the seven seals, and I heard one of the four living creatures cry out in a voice like thunder, "Come forward." [2] I looked, and there was a white horse, and its rider had a bow.† He was given a crown, and he rode forth victorious to further his victories.*

[3] When he broke open the second seal, I heard the second living creature cry out, "Come forward." [4]†* Another horse came out, a red one. Its rider was given power to take peace away from the earth, so that people would slaughter one another. And he was given a huge sword.

[5] When he broke open the third seal, I heard the third living creature cry out, "Come forward." I looked, and there was a black horse,† and its rider held a scale in his hand. [6] I heard what seemed to be a voice in the midst of the four living creatures. It said, "A ration of wheat costs a day's pay,† and three rations of barley cost a day's pay. But do not damage the olive oil or the wine."*

[7] When he broke open the fourth seal, I heard the voice of the fourth living creature cry out, "Come forward." [8] I looked, and there was a pale green† horse. Its rider was named Death, and Hades accompanied him. They were given authority over a quarter of the earth, to kill with sword, famine, and plague, and by means of the beasts of the earth.*

[9] When he broke open the fifth seal, I saw underneath the altar† the souls of those who had been slaughtered because of the witness they bore to the word of God. [10] They cried out in a loud voice, "How long will it be, holy and true master,† before you sit in judgment and avenge our blood on the inhabitants of the earth?" [11] Each of them was given a white robe, and they were told to be patient a little while longer until the number was filled of their fellow servants and brothers who were going to be killed as they had been.

[12]† Then I watched while he broke open the sixth seal, and there was a great earthquake; the sun turned as black as dark sackcloth† and the whole moon became like blood.* [13] The stars in the sky fell to the earth like unripe figs† shaken loose from the tree in a strong wind. [14] Then the sky was divided† like a torn scroll curling up, and every mountain and island was moved from its place.* [15] The

---

† **6:1–16:21** A series of seven disasters now begins as each seal is broken (Rev 6:1–8:1), followed by a similar series as seven trumpets sound (Rev 8:2–11:19) and as seven angels pour bowls on the earth causing plagues (Rev 15:1–16:21). These gloomy sequences are interrupted by longer or shorter scenes suggesting the triumph of God and his witnesses (e.g., Rev 7; 10; 11; 12; 13; 14).

**6:1–17** This chapter provides a symbolic description of the contents of the sealed scroll. The breaking of the first four seals reveals four riders. The first rider (of a white horse) is a conquering power (Rev 6:1–2), the second (red horse) a symbol of bloody war (Rev 6:3–4), the third (black horse) a symbol of famine (Rev 6:5–6), the fourth (pale green horse) a symbol of Death himself, accompanied by Hades (the netherworld) as his page (Rev 6:7–8). Rev 6:8b summarizes the role of all four riders. The breaking of the fifth seal reveals Christian martyrs in an attitude of sacrifice as blood poured out at the foot of an altar begging God for vindication, which will come only when their quota is filled; but they are given a white robe symbolic of victory (Rev 6:9–11). The breaking of the sixth seal reveals typical apocalyptic signs in the sky and the sheer terror of all people at the imminent divine judgment (Rev 6:12–17).

**6:1–8** The imagery is adapted from Zec 1:8–10; 6:1–8.

**6:2** *White horse…bow*: this may perhaps allude specifically to the Parthians on the eastern border of the Roman empire. Expert in the use of the bow, they constantly harassed the Romans and won a major victory in A.D. 62; see note on Rev 9:13–21. But the Old Testament imagery typifies the history of oppression of God's people at all times.

**6:4** *Huge sword*: this is a symbol of war and violence; cf. Ez 21:14–17.

**6:5** *Black horse*: this is a symbol of famine, the usual accompaniment of war in antiquity; cf. Lv 26:26; Ez 4:12–13. The

scale is a symbol of shortage of food with a corresponding rise in price.

**6:6** *A day's pay*: literally, "a denarius," a Roman silver coin that constitutes a day's wage in Mt 20:2. Because of the famine, food was rationed and sold at an exorbitant price. A liter of flour was considered a day's ration in the Greek historians Herodotus and Diogenes Laertius. *Barley*: food of the poor (Jn 6:9, 13; cf. 2 Kgs 7:1, 16, 18); it was also used to feed animals; cf. 1 Kgs 5:8. *Do not damage*: the olive and the vine are to be used more sparingly in time of famine.

**6:8** *Pale green*: symbol of death and decay; cf. Ez 14:21.

**6:9** *The altar*: this altar corresponds to the altar of holocausts in the temple in Jerusalem; see also Rev 11:1. *Because of the witness…word of God*: literally, "because of the word of God and the witness they had borne."

**6:10** *Holy and true master*: Old Testament usage as well as the context indicates that this is addressed to God rather than to Christ.

**6:12–14** Symbolic rather than literal description of the cosmic upheavals attending the day of the Lord when the martyrs' prayer for vindication (Rev 6:10) would be answered; cf. Am 8:8–9; Is 34:4; 50:3; Jl 2:10; 3:3–4; Mt 24:4–36; Mk 13:5–37; Lk 21:8–36.

**6:12** *Dark sackcloth*: for mourning, sackcloth was made from the skin of a black goat.

**6:13** *Unripe figs*: literally, "summer (or winter) fruit."

**6:14** *Was divided*: literally, "was split," like a broken papyrus roll torn in two, each half then curling up to form a roll on either side.

---

* **6:2** Zec 1:8–10; 6:1–3.　　　**6:8** Ez 14:21.
**6:4** Ez 21:14–16.　　　**6:12** Jl 3:4; Mt 24:29.
**6:6** Lv 26:26; Ez 4:16–17.　　　**6:14** Is 34:4 / Rev 16:20.

kings of the earth, the nobles,† the military officers, the rich, the powerful, and every slave and free person hid themselves in caves and among mountain crags. ¹⁶They cried out to the mountains and the rocks, "Fall on us and hide us from the face of the one who sits on the throne and from the wrath of the Lamb,* ¹⁷because the great day of their† wrath has come and who can withstand it?"

**7** †**The 144,000 Sealed.** ¹After this I saw four angels standing at the four corners of the earth,† holding back the four winds of the earth so that no wind could blow on land or sea or against any tree.* ²Then I saw another angel come up from the East,† holding the seal of the living God. He cried out in a loud voice to the four angels who were given power to damage the land and the sea, ³"Do not damage the land or the sea or the trees until we put the seal on the foreheads of the servants of our God."* ⁴I heard the number of those who had been marked with the seal, one hundred and forty-four thousand marked† from every tribe of the Israelites:* ⁵twelve thousand were marked from the tribe of Judah,† twelve thousand from the tribe of Reuben, twelve thousand from the tribe of Gad, ⁶twelve thousand from the tribe of Asher, twelve thousand from the tribe of Naphtali, twelve thousand from the tribe of Manasseh, ⁷twelve thousand from the tribe of Simeon, twelve thousand from the tribe of Levi, twelve thousand from the tribe of Issachar, ⁸twelve thousand from the tribe of Zebulun, twelve thousand from the tribe of Joseph, and twelve thousand were marked from the tribe of Benjamin.

**Triumph of the Elect.** ⁹After this I had a vision of a great multitude, which no one could count, from every nation, race, people, and tongue. They stood before the throne and before the Lamb, wearing white robes and holding palm branches† in their hands. ¹⁰They cried out in a loud voice:

> "Salvation comes from† our God, who
>      is seated on the throne,
>      and from the Lamb."

¹¹All the angels stood around the throne and around the elders and the four living creatures. They prostrated themselves before the throne, worshiped God, ¹²and exclaimed:

> "Amen. Blessing and glory, wisdom and
>      thanksgiving,
> honor, power, and might
>      be to our God forever and ever. Amen."

¹³Then one of the elders spoke up and said to me, "Who are these wearing white robes, and where did they come from?" ¹⁴I said to him, "My lord, you are the one who knows." He said to me, "These are the ones who have survived the time of great distress;† they have washed their robes and made them white in the blood of the Lamb.*

¹⁵    "For this reason they stand before God's
>           throne
>      and worship him day and night in his
>           temple.
> The one who sits on the throne will
>      shelter them.

---

**6:15** *Nobles*: literally, "courtiers," "grandees." *Military officers*: literally, "commanders of 1,000 men," used in Josephus and other Greek authors as the equivalent of the Roman *tribunus militum*. The listing of various ranks of society represents the universality of terror at the impending doom.
**6:17** *Their*: this reading is attested in the best manuscripts, but the vast majority read "his" in reference to the wrath of the Lamb in the preceding verse.
**7:1–17** An interlude of two visions precedes the breaking of the seventh seal, just as two more will separate the sixth and seventh trumpets (Rev 10). In the first vision (Rev 7:1–8), the elect receive the seal of the living God as protection against the coming cataclysm; cf. Rev 14:1; Ez 9:4–6; 2 Cor 1:22; Eph 1:13; 4:30. The second vision (Rev 7:9–17) portrays the faithful Christians before God's throne to encourage those on earth to persevere to the end, even to death.
**7:1** *The four corners of the earth*: the earth is seen as a table or rectangular surface.
**7:2** *East*: literally, "rising of the sun." The east was considered the source of light and the place of paradise (Gn 2:8). *Seal*: whatever was marked by the impression of one's signet ring belonged to that person and was under his protection.

**7:4–9** *One hundred and forty-four thousand*: the square of twelve (the number of Israel's tribes) multiplied by a thousand, symbolic of the new Israel (cf. Rev 14:1–5; Gal 6:16; Jas 1:1) that embraces people *from every nation, race, people, and tongue* (Rev 7:9).
**7:5–8** Judah is placed first because of Christ; cf. "the Lion of the tribe of Judah" (Rev 5:5). Dan is omitted because of a later tradition that the antichrist would arise from it.
**7:9** *White robes…palm branches*: symbols of joy and victory; see note on Rev 3:5.
**7:10** *Salvation comes from*: literally, "(let) salvation (be ascribed) to." A similar hymn of praise is found at the fall of the dragon (Rev 12:10) and of Babylon (Rev 19:1).
**7:14** *Time of great distress*: fierce persecution by the Romans; cf. Introduction.

**6:16** Is 2:19; Hos 10:8; Lk 23:30.
**7:1** Jer 49:36; Zec 6:5.
**7:3** Ex 12:7–14; Ez 9:4;
2 Cor 1:22; Eph 1:13; 4:30.
**7:4** Rev 14:1.
**7:14** Mt 24:21.

16 They will not hunger or thirst anymore,
     nor will the sun or any heat strike
        them.*
17 For the Lamb who is in the center of the
     throne will shepherd them
     and lead them to springs of life-giving
        water,†
     and God will wipe away every tear
        from their eyes."*

# 8 †The Seven Trumpets.

¹When he broke open the seventh seal, there was silence in heaven† for about half an hour.* ²And I saw that the seven angels who stood before God were given seven trumpets.*

## The Gold Censer.

³Another angel came and stood at the altar,† holding a gold censer. He was given a great quantity of incense to offer, along with the prayers of all the holy ones, on the gold altar that was before the throne.* ⁴The smoke of the incense along with the prayers of the holy ones went up before God from the hand of the angel. ⁵Then the angel took the censer, filled it with burning coals from the altar, and hurled it down to the earth. There were peals of thunder, rumblings, flashes of lightning, and an earthquake.*

## The First Four Trumpets.

⁶The seven angels who were holding the seven trumpets prepared to blow them.*

⁷When the first one blew his trumpet, there came hail and fire mixed with blood, which was hurled down to the earth. A third of the land was burned up, along with a third of the trees and all green grass.†

⁸† When the second angel blew his trumpet, something like a large burning mountain was hurled into the sea. A third of the sea turned to blood,* ⁹a third of the creatures living in the sea† died, and a third of the ships were wrecked.

¹⁰When the third angel blew his trumpet, a large star burning like a torch fell from the sky. It fell on a third of the rivers and on the springs of water.* ¹¹The star was called "Wormwood,"† and a third of all the water turned to wormwood. Many people died from this water, because it was made bitter.*

¹²When the fourth angel blew his trumpet, a third of the sun, a third of the moon, and a third of the stars were struck, so that a third of them became dark. The day lost its light for a third of the time, as did the night.*

¹³Then I looked again and heard an eagle flying high overhead cry out in a loud voice, "Woe! Woe! Woe† to the inhabitants of the earth from the rest of the trumpet blasts that the three angels are about to blow!"

# 9 The Fifth Trumpet.

† ¹Then the fifth angel blew his trumpet, and I saw a star† that had fallen from the sky to the earth. It was given the key for the passage to the abyss. ²It opened the passage to the abyss,* and smoke

---

7:17 *Life-giving water*: literally, "the water of life," God's grace, which flows from Christ; cf. Rev 21:6; 22:1, 17; Jn 4:10, 14.

8:1–13 The breaking of the seventh seal produces at first silence and then seven symbolic disasters, each announced by a trumpet blast, of which the first four form a unit as did the first four seals. A minor liturgy (Rev 8:3–5) is enclosed by a vision of seven angels (Rev 8:2, 6). Then follow the first four trumpet blasts, each heralding catastrophes modeled on the plagues of Egypt affecting the traditional prophetic third (cf. Ez 5:12) of the earth, sea, fresh water, and stars (Rev 8:7–12). Finally, there is a vision of an eagle warning of the last three trumpet blasts (Rev 8:13).

8:1 *Silence in heaven*: as in Zep 1:7, a prelude to the eschatological woes that are to follow; cf. Introduction.

8:3 *Altar*: there seems to be only one altar in the heavenly temple, corresponding to the altar of holocausts in Rev 6:9, and here to the altar of incense in Jerusalem; cf. also Rev 9:13; 11:1; 14:18; 16:7.

8:7 This woe resembles the seventh plague of Egypt (Ex 9:23–24); cf. Jl 3:3.

8:8–11 The background of these two woes is the first plague of Egypt (Ex 7:20–21).

8:9 *Creatures living in the sea*: literally, "creatures in the sea that had souls."

8:11 *Wormwood*: an extremely bitter and malignant plant symbolizing the punishment God inflicts on the ungodly;

cf. Jer 9:12–14; 23:15.

8:13 *Woe! Woe! Woe*: each of the three woes pronounced by the angel represents a separate disaster; cf. Rev 9:12; 11:14. The final woe, released by the seventh trumpet blast, includes the plagues of Rev 16.

9:1–12 The fifth trumpet heralds a woe containing elements from the eighth and ninth plagues of Egypt (Ex 10:12–15, 21–23) but specifically reminiscent of the invasion of locusts in Jl 1:4–2:10.

9:1 *A star*: late Judaism represented fallen powers as stars (Is 14:12–15; Lk 10:18; Jude 13), but a comparison with Rev 1:20 and Rev 20:1 suggests that here it means an angel. *The passage to the abyss*: referring to Sheol, the netherworld, where Satan and the fallen angels are kept for a thousand years, to be cast afterwards into the pool of fire; cf. Rev 20:7–10. The abyss was conceived of as a vast subterranean cavern full of fire. Its only link with the earth was a kind of passage or mine shaft, which was kept locked.

---

* —

7:16 Is 49:10.
7:17 21:4; Is 25:8.
8:1 Heb 2:20; Zep 1:7;
   Zec 2:17.
8:2 4:5; Tb 12:15.
8:3 Ps 141:2; Tb 12:12.
8:5 Ez 10:2; Ps 11:6 /

Rev 4:5; 11:19; 16:18.
8:6 16:1–21.
8:8 Ex 7:20.
8:10 Is 14:12.
8:11 Jer 9:14.
8:12 Ex 10:21–23.
9:2 20:1.

came up out of the passage like smoke from a huge furnace. The sun and the air were darkened by the smoke from the passage.* [3] Locusts came out of the smoke onto the land, and they were given the same power as scorpions† of the earth.* [4] They were told not to harm the grass of the earth or any plant or any tree, but only those people who did not have the seal of God on their foreheads. [5] They were not allowed to kill them but only to torment them for five months;† the torment they inflicted was like that of a scorpion when it stings a person. [6] During that time these people will seek death but will not find it, and they will long to die but death will escape them.*

[7]† The appearance of the locusts was like that of horses ready for battle. On their heads they wore what looked like crowns of gold; their faces were like human faces,* [8] and they had hair like women's hair. Their teeth were like lions' teeth,* [9] and they had chests like iron breastplates. The sound of their wings was like the sound of many horse-drawn chariots racing into battle. [10] They had tails like scorpions, with stingers; with their tails they had power to harm people for five months. [11] They had as their king the angel of the abyss, whose name in Hebrew is Abaddon† and in Greek Apollyon.

[12] The first woe has passed, but there are two more to come.

**The Sixth Trumpet.**† [13] Then the sixth angel blew his trumpet, and I heard a voice coming from the [four]† horns of the gold altar before God,* [14] telling the sixth angel who held the trumpet, "Release the four angels† who are bound at the banks of the great river Euphrates." [15] So the four angels were released, who were prepared for this hour, day, month, and year to kill a third of the human race. [16] The number of cavalry troops was two hundred million; I heard their number. [17] Now in my vision this is how I saw the horses and their riders. They wore red, blue, and yellow breastplates,† and the horses' heads were like heads of lions, and out of their mouths came fire, smoke, and sulfur.* [18] By these three plagues of fire, smoke, and sulfur that came out of their mouths a third of the human race was killed. [19] For the power of the horses is in their mouths and in their tails; for their tails are like snakes, with heads that inflict harm.

[20] The rest of the human race, who were not killed by these plagues, did not repent of the works of their hands,† to give up the worship of demons and idols made from gold, silver, bronze, stone, and wood, which cannot see or hear or walk.* [21] Nor did they repent of their murders, their magic potions, their unchastity, or their robberies.

# 10 The Angel with the Small Scroll.

[1]† Then I saw another mighty angel come down from heaven wrapped in a cloud, with a halo around his head; his face was like the sun and his feet were like pillars of fire. [2] In his hand he held a small scroll that had been opened. He placed his right foot on the sea and his left foot on the land,† [3] and then he cried out in a loud voice as a lion roars. When he cried out, the seven thunders† raised their voices, too.* [4] When the seven thunders had spoken, I was about to write it down; but

---

† **9:3** *Scorpions:* their poisonous sting was proverbial; Ez 2:6; Lk 11:12.

**9:5** *For five months:* more or less corresponding to the lifespan of locusts.

**9:7–10** Eight characteristics are listed to show the eschatological and diabolical nature of these locusts.

**9:11** *Abaddon:* Hebrew (more precisely, Aramaic) for destruction or ruin. *Apollyon:* Greek for the "Destroyer."

**9:13–21** The sixth trumpet heralds a woe representing another diabolical attack symbolized by an invasion by the Parthians living east of the Euphrates; see note on Rev 6:2. At the appointed time (Rev 9:15), the frightful horses act as God's agents of judgment. The imaginative details are not to be taken literally; see Introduction and the note on Rev 6:12–14.

**9:13** *[Four]:* many Greek manuscripts and versions omit the word. The horns were situated at the four corners of the altar (Ex 27:2; 30:2–3); see note on Rev 8:3.

**9:14–15** *The four angels:* they are symbolic of the destructive activity that will be extended throughout the universe.

**9:17** *Blue:* literally, "hyacinth-colored." *Yellow:* literally, "sulfurous."

**9:20** *The works of their hands:* i.e., the gods their hands had made.

**10:1–11:14** An interlude in two scenes (Rev 10:1–11 and Rev 11:1–14) precedes the sounding of the seventh trumpet; cf. Rev 7:1–17. The first vision describes an angel astride sea and land like a colossus, with a small scroll open, the contents of which indicate that the end is imminent (Rev 10). The second vision is of the measuring of the temple and of two witnesses, whose martyrdom means that the kingdom of God is about to be inaugurated.

**10:2** *He placed…on the land:* this symbolizes the universality of the angel's message, as does the figure of the small scroll open to be read.

**10:3** *The seven thunders:* God's voice announcing judgment and doom; cf. Ps 29:3–9, where thunder, as the voice of Yahweh, is praised seven times.

---

**9:2** Gn 19:28.
**9:3** Ex 10:12–15; Wis 16:9.
**9:6** Jb 3:21.
**9:7** Jl 2:4.
**9:8** Jl 1:6.
**9:13** Ex 30:1–3.
**9:17** Jb 41:10–13.
**9:20** Ps 135:15–17; Is 17:8; Dn 5:4.
**10:3** Ps 29:3–9; Jer 25:30; Am 3:8.

I heard a voice from heaven say, "Seal up what the seven thunders have spoken, but do not write it down." ⁵Then the angel I saw standing on the sea and on the land raised his right hand to heaven ⁶and swore by the one who lives forever and ever, who created heaven and earth and sea† and all that is in them, "There shall be no more delay.* ⁷At the time when you hear the seventh angel blow his trumpet, the mysterious plan of God† shall be fulfilled, as he promised to his servants the prophets."*

⁸Then the voice that I had heard from heaven spoke to me again and said, "Go, take the scroll that lies open in the hand of the angel who is standing on the sea and on the land." ⁹So I went up to the angel and told him to give me the small scroll. He said to me, "Take and swallow it. It will turn your stomach sour, but in your mouth it will taste as sweet† as honey." ¹⁰I took the small scroll from the angel's hand and swallowed it. In my mouth it was like sweet honey, but when I had eaten it, my stomach turned sour.* ¹¹Then someone said to me, "You must prophesy again about many peoples, nations, tongues, and kings."†

# 11 The Two Witnesses.

¹†* Then I was given a measuring rod like a staff and I was told, "Come and measure the temple of God and the altar, and count those who are worshiping in it. ²But exclude the outer court† of the temple; do not measure it, for it has been handed over to the Gentiles, who will trample the holy city for forty-two months. ³I will commission my two witnesses† to prophesy for those twelve hundred and sixty days, wearing sackcloth." ⁴* These are the two olive trees and the two lampstands† that stand before the Lord of the earth. ⁵† If anyone wants to harm them, fire comes out of their mouths and devours their enemies. In this way, anyone wanting to harm them is sure to be slain. ⁶They have the power to close up the sky so that no rain can fall during the time of their prophesying. They also have power to turn water into blood and to afflict the earth with any plague as often as they wish.*

⁷When they have finished their testimony, the beast that comes up from the abyss† will wage war against them and conquer them and kill them.* ⁸Their corpses will lie in the main street of the great city,† which has the symbolic names "Sodom" and "Egypt," where indeed their Lord was crucified. ⁹† Those from every people, tribe, tongue, and nation will gaze on their corpses for three and a half days, and they will not allow their corpses to be buried. ¹⁰The inhabitants of the earth will gloat over them and be glad and exchange gifts because these two prophets tormented the inhabitants of the earth. ¹¹But after the three and a half days, a breath of life from God entered them. When they stood on their feet, great fear fell on those who saw them.* ¹²Then they

---

**10:6** *Heaven and earth and sea*: the three parts of the universe. *No more delay*: cf. Dn 12:7; Heb 2:3.

**10:7** *The mysterious plan of God*: literally, "the mystery of God," the end of the present age when the forces of evil will be put down (Rev 17:1–19:4, 11–21; 20:7–10; cf. 2 Thes 2:6–12; Rom 16:25–26), and the establishment of the reign of God when all creation will be made new (Rev 21:1–22:5).

**10:9–10** The small scroll was sweet because it predicted the final victory of God's people; it was sour because it also announced their sufferings. Cf. Ez 3:1–3.

**10:11** This further prophecy is contained in chaps. 12–22.

**11:1** The temple and altar symbolize the new Israel; see note on Rev 7:4–9. The worshipers represent Christians. The measuring of the temple (cf. Ez 40:3–42:20; 47:1–12; Zec 2:5–6) suggests that God will preserve the faithful remnant (cf. Is 4:2–3) who remain true to Christ (Rev 14:1–5).

**11:2** *The outer court*: the Court of the Gentiles. *Trample... forty-two months*: the duration of the vicious persecution of the Jews by Antiochus IV Epiphanes (Dn 7:25; 12:7); this persecution of three and a half years (half of seven, counted as 1260 days in Rev 11:3; 12:6) became the prototype of periods of trial for God's people; cf. Lk 4:25; Jas 5:17. The reference here is to the persecution by the Romans; cf. Introduction.

**11:3** The two witnesses, wearing sackcloth symbolizing lamentation and repentance, cannot readily be identified. Do they represent Moses and Elijah, or the Law and the Prophets, or Peter and Paul? Most probably they refer to the universal church, especially the Christian martyrs, fulfilling the office of witness (two because of Dt 19:15; cf. Mk 6:7; Jn 8:17).

**11:4** *The two olive trees and the two lampstands*: the martyrs who stand in the presence of the Lord; the imagery is taken from Zec 4:8–14, where the olive trees refer to Zerubbabel and Joshua.

**11:5–6** These details are derived from stories of Moses, who turned *water into blood* (Ex 7:17–20), and of Elijah, who called down fire from heaven (1 Kgs 18:36–40; 2 Kgs 1:10) and closed up the sky for three years (1 Kgs 17:1; cf. 18:1).

**11:7** *The beast...from the abyss*: the Roman emperor Nero, who symbolizes the forces of evil, or the antichrist (Rev 13:1, 8; 17:8); cf. Dn 7:2–8, 11–12, 19–22 and Introduction.

**11:8** *The great city*: this expression is used constantly in Revelation for Babylon, i.e., Rome; cf. Rev 14:8; 16:19; 17:18; 18:2, 10, 21. *"Sodom" and "Egypt"*: symbols of immorality (cf. Is 1:10) and oppression of God's people (cf. Ex 1:11–14). *Where indeed their Lord was crucified*: not the geographical but the symbolic Jerusalem that rejects God and his witnesses, i.e., Rome, called Babylon in Rev 16–18; see note on Rev 17:9 and Introduction.

**11:9–12** Over the martyrdom (Rev 11:7) of the two witnesses, now called prophets, the ungodly rejoice *for three and a half days*, a symbolic period of time; see note on Rev 11:2. Afterwards they go in triumph to heaven, as did Elijah (2 Kgs 2:11).

---

*

| | |
|---|---|
| **10:6** Dt 32:40; Dn 12:7 / | **Zec** 2:5–9. |
| Ez 12:28. | **11:4** Zec 4:3, 14. |
| **10:7** Am 3:7. | **11:6** Ex 7:17. |
| **10:10** Ez 3:1–3. | **11:7** Dn 7:21. |
| **11:1** Ez 40:3–5 / | **11:11** Ez 37:5, 10. |

heard a loud voice from heaven say to them, "Come up here." So they went up to heaven in a cloud as their enemies looked on.* ¹³At that moment there was a great earthquake, and a tenth of the city fell in ruins. Seven thousand people† were killed during the earthquake; the rest were terrified and gave glory to the God of heaven.

¹⁴The second woe has passed, but the third is coming soon.

**The Seventh Trumpet.** † ¹⁵Then the seventh angel blew his trumpet. There were loud voices in heaven, saying, "The kingdom of the world now belongs to our Lord and to his Anointed, and he will reign forever and ever." ¹⁶The twenty-four elders who sat on their thrones before God prostrated themselves and worshiped God ¹⁷and said:

> "We give thanks to you, Lord God almighty,
>     who are and who were.
> For you have assumed your great power
>     and have established your reign.
¹⁸     The nations raged,
>     but your wrath has come,
>     and the time for the dead to be judged,
> and to recompense your servants, the prophets,
>     and the holy ones and those who fear your name,
>     the small and the great alike,

and to destroy those who destroy the earth."*

¹⁹Then God's temple in heaven was opened, and the ark of his covenant could be seen in the temple. There were flashes of lightning, rumblings, and peals of thunder, an earthquake, and a violent hailstorm.

**12** **The Woman and the Dragon.** ¹† A great sign appeared in the sky, a woman† clothed with the sun, with the moon under her feet, and on her head a crown of twelve stars.* ²She was with child and wailed aloud in pain as she labored to give birth.† ³Then another sign appeared in the sky; it was a huge red dragon,† with seven heads and ten horns, and on its heads were seven diadems.* ⁴Its tail swept away a third of the stars in the sky and hurled them down to the earth. Then the dragon stood before the woman about to give birth, to devour her child when she gave birth.* ⁵She gave birth to a son, a male child, destined to rule all the nations with an iron rod.† Her child was caught up to God and his throne.* ⁶The woman herself fled into the desert where she had a place prepared by God, that there she might be taken care of for twelve hundred and sixty days.†

⁷† Then war broke out in heaven; Michael† and his angels battled against the dragon. The dragon and its angels fought back, ⁸but they did not prevail and there was no longer any place for them in heaven. ⁹The huge dragon,

---

**11:13** *Seven thousand people*: a symbolic sum to represent all social classes (seven) and large numbers (thousands); cf. Introduction.

**11:15–19** The seventh trumpet proclaims the coming of God's reign after the victory over diabolical powers; see note on Rev 10:7.

**12:1–14:20** This central section of Revelation portrays the power of evil, represented by a dragon, in opposition to God and his people. First, the dragon pursues the woman about to give birth, but her son is saved and "caught up to God and his throne" (Rev 12:5). Then Michael and his angels cast the dragon and his angels out of heaven (Rev 12:7–9). After this, the dragon tries to attack the boy indirectly by attacking members of his church (Rev 12:13–17). A beast, symbolizing the Roman empire, then becomes the dragon's agent, mortally wounded but restored to life and worshiped by all the world (Rev 13:1–10). A second beast arises from the land, symbolizing the antichrist, which leads people astray by its prodigies to idolize the first beast (Rev 13:11–18). This is followed by a vision of the Lamb and his faithful ones, and the proclamation of imminent judgment upon the world in terms of the wine of God's wrath (Rev 14:1–20).

**12:1–6** The woman adorned with the sun, the moon, and the stars (images taken from Gn 37:9–10) symbolizes God's people in the Old and the New Testament. The Israel of old gave birth to the Messiah (Rev 12:5) and then became the new Israel, the church, which suffers persecution by the dragon (Rev 12:6, 13–

17); cf. Is 50:1; 66:7; Jer 50:12. This corresponds to a widespread myth throughout the ancient world that a goddess pregnant with a savior was pursued by a horrible monster; by miraculous intervention, she bore a son who then killed the monster.

**12:2** Because of Eve's sin, the woman gives birth in distress and pain (Gn 3:16; cf. Is 66:7–14).

**12:3** *Huge red dragon*: the Devil or Satan (cf. Rev 12:9; 20:2), symbol of the forces of evil, a mythical monster known also as Leviathan (Ps 74:13–14) or Rahab (Jb 26:12–13; Ps 89:11). *Seven diadems*: these are symbolic of the fullness of the dragon's sovereignty over the kingdoms of this world; cf. Christ with many diadems (Rev 19:12).

**12:5** *Rule…iron rod*: fulfilled in Rev 19:15; cf. Ps 2:9. *Was caught up to God*: reference to Christ's ascension.

**12:6** God protects the persecuted church in the desert, the traditional Old Testament place of refuge for the afflicted, according to the typology of the Exodus; see note on Rev 11:2.

**12:7–12** Michael, mentioned only here in Revelation, wins a victory over the dragon. A hymn of praise follows.

**12:7** *Michael*: the archangel, guardian and champion of Israel; cf. Dn 10:13, 21; 12:1; Jude 9. In Hebrew, the name Michael means "Who can compare with God?"; cf. Rev 13:4.

---

**11:12** 2 Kgs 2:11.          **12:3** Dn 7:7.
**11:18** Ps 2:1, 5 / Am 3:7.   **12:4** Dn 8:10.
**12:1** Gn 37:9.              **12:5** Is 66:7 / Ps 2:9.

the ancient serpent,† who is called the Devil and Satan, who deceived the whole world, was thrown down to earth, and its angels were thrown down with it.*

¹⁰ Then I heard a loud voice in heaven say:

"Now have salvation and power come,
    and the kingdom of our God
    and the authority of his Anointed.
For the accuser† of our brothers is cast
        out,
    who accuses them before our God day
        and night.
¹¹ They conquered him by the blood of the
        Lamb
    and by the word of their testimony;
    love for life did not deter them from
        death.
¹² Therefore, rejoice, you heavens,
    and you who dwell in them.
But woe to you, earth and sea,
    for the Devil has come down to you
        in great fury,
    for he knows he has but a short time."

¹³ When the dragon saw that it had been thrown down to the earth, it pursued the woman who had given birth to the male child.* ¹⁴ But the woman was given the two wings of the great eagle,† so that she could fly to her place in the desert, where, far from the serpent, she was taken care of for a year, two years, and a half-year.* ¹⁵ The serpent,† however, spewed a torrent of water out of his mouth after the woman to sweep her away with the current. ¹⁶ But the earth helped the woman and opened its mouth and swallowed the flood that the dragon spewed out of its mouth. ¹⁷ Then the dragon became angry with the woman and went off to wage war against the rest of her offspring, those who keep God's commandments and bear witness to Jesus.†* ¹⁸ It took its position† on the sand of the sea.

# 13 The First Beast.†

¹ Then I saw a beast come out of the sea with ten horns and seven heads; on its horns were ten diadems, and on its heads blasphemous name[s].* ² The beast I saw was like a leopard, but it had feet like a bear's, and its mouth was like the mouth of a lion.†* To it the dragon gave its own power and throne, along with great authority. ³ I saw that one of its heads seemed to have been mortally wounded, but this mortal wound was healed.† Fascinated, the whole world followed after the beast. ⁴ They worshiped the dragon because it gave its authority to the beast; they also worshiped the beast† and said, "Who can compare with the beast or who can fight against it?"

⁵† The beast was given a mouth uttering proud boasts and blasphemies,* and it was given authority to act for forty-two months.† ⁶ It opened its mouth to utter blasphemies against God, blaspheming his name and his dwelling and those who dwell in heaven. ⁷ It was also allowed to wage war against the holy ones and conquer them, and it was granted authority over every tribe, people, tongue, and nation.* ⁸ All the inhabitants of the earth will worship it, all whose names were not written from the foundation of the world in the book

---

**12:9** *The ancient serpent*: who seduced Eve (Gn 3:1–6), mother of the human race; cf. Rev 20:2; Eph 6:11–12. *Was thrown down*: allusion to the expulsion of Satan from heaven; cf. Lk 10:18.

**12:10** *The accuser*: the meaning of the Hebrew word "Satan," found in Rev 12:9; Jb 1–2; Zec 3:1; 1 Chr 21:1; he continues to accuse Christ's disciples.

**12:14** *Great eagle*: symbol of the power and swiftness of divine help; cf. Ex 19:4; Dt 32:11; Is 40:31.

**12:15** The serpent is depicted as the sea monster; cf. Rev 13:1; Is 27:1; Ez 32:2; Ps 74:13–14.

**12:17** Although the church is protected by God's special providence (Rev 12:16), the individual Christian is to expect persecution and suffering.

**12:18** *It took its position*: many later manuscripts and versions read "I took my position," thus connecting the sentence to the following paragraph.

**13:1–10** This wild beast, combining features of the four beasts in Dn 7:2–28, symbolizes the Roman empire; the seven heads represent the emperors; see notes on Rev 17:10 and Rev 17:12–14. The blasphemous names are the divine titles assumed by the emperors.

**13:2** Satan (Rev 12:9), the prince of this world (Jn 12:31),

commissioned the beast to persecute the church (Rev 13:5–7).

**13:3** This may be a reference to the popular legend that Nero would come back to life and rule again after his death (which occurred in A.D. 68 from a self-inflicted stab wound in the throat); cf. Rev 13:14; Rev 17:8. Domitian (A.D. 81–96) embodied all the cruelty and impiety of Nero. Cf. Introduction.

**13:4** *Worshiped the beast*: allusion to emperor worship, which Domitian insisted upon and ruthlessly enforced. *Who can compare with the beast*: perhaps a deliberate parody of the name Michael; see note on Rev 12:7.

**13:5–6** Domitian, like Antiochus IV Epiphanes (Dn 7:8, 11, 25), demanded that he be called by divine titles such as "our lord and god" and "Jupiter." See note on Rev 11:2.

**13:5** *Forty-two months*: this is the same duration as the profanation of the holy city (Rev 11:2), the prophetic mission of the two witnesses (Rev 11:3), and the retreat of the woman into the desert (Rev 12:6, 14).

---

**12:9** Gn 3:1–4; Lk 10:18.
**12:13** Gn 3:15.
**12:14** Ex 19:4; Dn 7:25; 12:7.
**12:17** Gn 3:15.

**13:1** 2 Thes 2:3–12.
**13:2** Dn 7:3–6.
**13:5** Dn 7:8, 11, 25; 8:14; 9:27; 11:36; 12:7.
**13:7** Dn 7:21.

of life, which belongs to the Lamb who was slain.*

9 Whoever has ears ought to hear these words.*

10 Anyone destined for captivity goes into captivity.
   Anyone destined to be slain by the sword shall be slain by the sword.*

Such is the faithful endurance of the holy ones.

**The Second Beast.**† ¹¹Then I saw another beast come up out of the earth; it had two horns like a lamb's but spoke like a dragon. ¹²It wielded all the authority of the first beast in its sight and made the earth and its inhabitants worship the first beast, whose mortal wound had been healed. ¹³It performed great signs, even making fire come down from heaven to earth in the sight of everyone.* ¹⁴It deceived the inhabitants of the earth with the signs it was allowed to perform in the sight of the first beast, telling them to make an image for the beast who had been wounded by the sword and revived. ¹⁵It was then permitted to breathe life into the beast's image, so that the beast's image could speak and [could] have anyone who did not worship it put to death.* ¹⁶It forced all the people, small and great, rich and poor, free and slave, to be given a stamped image on their right hands or their foreheads,* ¹⁷so that no one could buy or sell except one who had the stamped image of the beast's name or the number that stood for its name.

¹⁸† * Wisdom is needed here; one who understands can calculate the number of the beast, for it is a number that stands for a person. His number is six hundred and sixty-six.

# 14 **The Lamb's Companions.**† ¹Then I looked and there was the Lamb standing on Mount Zion,† and with him a hundred and forty-four thousand who had his name and his Father's name written on their foreheads.* ²I heard a sound from heaven like the sound of rushing water or a loud peal of thunder. The sound I heard was like that of harpists playing their harps. ³They were singing [what seemed to be] a new hymn before the throne, before the four living creatures and the elders. No one could learn this hymn except the hundred and forty-four thousand who had been ransomed from the earth.* ⁴These are they who were not defiled with women; they are virgins† and these are the ones who follow the Lamb wherever he goes. They have been ransomed as the firstfruits of the human race for God and the Lamb.* ⁵On their lips no deceit† has been found; they are unblemished.*

**The Three Angels.**† ⁶Then I saw another angel flying high overhead, with everlasting good news† to announce to those who dwell on earth, to every nation, tribe, tongue, and people. ⁷He said in a loud voice, "Fear God and

---

† **13:11–18** The second beast is described in terms of the false prophets (cf. Rev 16:13; 19:20; 20:10) who accompany the false messiahs (the first beast); cf. Mt 24:24; Mk 13:22; 2 Thes 2:9; cf. also Dt 13:2–4. Christians had either to worship the emperor and his image or to suffer martyrdom.

**13:18** Each of the letters of the alphabet in Hebrew as well as in Greek has a numerical value. Many possible combinations of letters will add up to 666, and many candidates have been nominated for this infamous number. The most likely is the emperor Caesar Nero (see note on Rev 13:3), the Greek form of whose name in Hebrew letters gives the required sum. (The Latin form of this name equals 616, which is the reading of a few manuscripts.) Nero personifies the emperors who viciously persecuted the church. It has also been observed that "6" represents imperfection, falling short of the perfect number "7," and is represented here in a triple or superlative form.

**14:1–5** Now follows a tender and consoling vision of the Lamb and his companions.

**14:1** *Mount Zion*: in Jerusalem, the traditional place where the true remnant, the Israel of faith, is to be gathered in the messianic reign; cf. 2 Kgs 19:30–31; Jl 3:5; Ob 17; Mi 4:6–8; Zep 3:12–20. *A hundred and forty-four thousand*: see note on Rev 7:4–9. *His Father's name…foreheads*: in contrast to the pagans who were marked with the name or number of the beast (Rev 13:16–17).

**14:4** *Virgins*: metaphorically, because they never indulged in any idolatrous practices, which are considered in the Old Testament to be adultery and fornication (Rev 2:14–15, 20–22; 17:1–6; cf. Ez 16:1–58; 23:1–49). The parallel passages (Rev 7:3; 22:4) indicate that the 144,000 whose foreheads are sealed represent all Christian people.

**14:5** *No deceit*: because they did not deny Christ or do homage to the beast. Lying is characteristic of the opponents of Christ (Jn 8:44), but the Suffering Servant spoke no falsehood (Is 53:9; 1 Pt 2:22). *Unblemished*: a cultic term taken from the vocabulary of sacrificial ritual.

**14:6–13** Three angels proclaim imminent judgment on the pagan world, calling all peoples to worship God the creator. Babylon (Rome) will fall, and its supporters will be tormented forever.

**14:6** *Everlasting good news*: that God's eternal reign is about to begin; see note on Rev 10:7.

---

* **13:8** 3:5; 17:8; 20:12.
**13:9** Mt 13:9.
**13:10** Jer 15:2.
**13:13** Dt 13:2–4; Mt 24:24; 2 Thes 2:9–10.
**13:15** Dn 3:5–7, 15.
**13:16** 14:9; 16:2; 19:20; 20:4.
**13:18** 17:9.
**14:1** Jl 3:5; Ob 17; Acts 2:21.
**14:3** Ps 33:3; 96:1; 98:1; Is 42:10.
**14:4** Jer 2:2; Jas 1:18.
**14:5** Zep 3:13.

give him glory, for his time has come to sit in judgment. Worship him who made heaven and earth and sea and springs of water."*

⁸ A second angel followed, saying:

"Fallen, fallen is Babylon the great,*
    that made all the nations drink
    the wine of her licentious passion."†

⁹ A third angel followed them and said in a loud voice, "Anyone who worships the beast or its image, or accepts its mark on forehead or hand, ¹⁰ will also drink the wine of God's fury,† poured full strength into the cup of his wrath, and will be tormented in burning sulfur before the holy angels and before the Lamb. ¹¹ The smoke of the fire that torments them will rise forever and ever, and there will be no relief day or night for those who worship the beast or its image or accept the mark of its name."* ¹² Here is what sustains the holy ones who keep God's commandments* and their faith in Jesus.†

¹³ * I heard a voice from heaven say, "Write this: Blessed are the dead who die in the Lord from now on." "Yes," said the Spirit, "let them find rest from their labors, for their works accompany them."†

**The Harvest of the Earth.**† ¹⁴ Then I looked and there was a white cloud, and sitting on the cloud one who looked like a son of man, with a gold crown on his head and a sharp sickle in his hand.* ¹⁵ Another angel came out of the temple, crying out in a loud voice to the one sitting on the cloud, "Use your sickle and reap the harvest, for the time to reap has come, because the earth's harvest is fully ripe."* ¹⁶ So the one who was sitting on the cloud swung his sickle over the earth, and the earth was harvested.

¹⁷ Then another angel came out of the temple in heaven who also had a sharp sickle. ¹⁸ Then another angel [came] from the altar,† [who] was in charge of the fire, and cried out in a loud voice to the one who had the sharp sickle, "Use your sharp sickle and cut the clusters from the earth's vines, for its grapes are ripe." ¹⁹ So the angel swung his sickle over the earth and cut the earth's vintage. He threw it into the great wine press of God's fury.* ²⁰ The wine press was trodden outside the city and blood poured out of the wine press to the height of a horse's bridle for two hundred miles.†

# 15

**The Seven Last Plagues.** ¹† Then I saw in heaven another sign,† great and awe-inspiring: seven angels with the seven last plagues, for through them God's fury is accomplished.

² Then I saw something like a sea of glass mingled with fire.† On the sea of glass were standing those who had won the victory over the beast and its image and the number that signified its name. They were holding God's harps,* ³ and they sang the song of Moses,† the servant of God, and the song of the Lamb:

"Great and wonderful are your works,
    Lord God almighty.
Just and true are your ways,
    O king of the nations.*

---

14:8 This verse anticipates the lengthy dirge over Babylon (Rome) in Rev 18:1–19:4. The oracle of Is 21:9 to Babylon is applied here.

14:10–11 *The wine of God's fury:* image taken from Is 51:17; Jer 25:15–16; 49:12; 51:7; Ez 23:31–34. Eternal punishment in the fiery pool of burning sulfur (or "fire and brimstone"; cf. Gn 19:24) is also reserved for the Devil, the beast, and the false prophet (Rev 19:20; 20:10; 21:8).

14:12 In addition to *faith in Jesus*, the seer insists upon the necessity and value of works, as in Rev 2:23; 20:12–13; 22:12; cf. Mt 16:27; Rom 2:6.

14:13 See note on Rev 1:3. According to Jewish thought, people's actions followed them as witnesses before the court of God.

14:14–20 The reaping of the harvest symbolizes the gathering of the elect in the final judgment, while the reaping and treading of the grapes symbolizes the doom of the ungodly (cf. Jl 4:12–13; Is 63:1–6) that will come in Rev 19:11–21.

14:18 *Altar:* there was only one altar in the heavenly temple; see notes on Rev 6:9; 8:3; 11:1.

14:20 *Two hundred miles:* literally sixteen hundred stades. The *stadion,* a Greek unit of measurement, was about 607 feet in length, approximately the length of a furlong.

15:1–16:21 The seven bowls, the third and last group of seven after the seven seals and the seven trumpets, foreshadow the final cataclysm. Again, the series is introduced by a heavenly prelude, in which the victors over the beast sing the canticle of Moses (Rev 15:2–4).

15:1–4 A vision of the victorious martyrs precedes the vision of woe in Rev 15:5–16:21; cf. Rev 7:9–12.

15:2 *Mingled with fire:* fire symbolizes the sanctity involved in facing God, reflected in the trials that have prepared the victorious Christians or in God's wrath.

15:3 *The song of Moses:* the song that Moses and the Israelites sang after their escape from the oppression of Egypt (Ex 15:1–18). The martyrs have escaped from the oppression of the Devil. *Nations:* many other Greek manuscripts and versions read "ages."

---

| | |
|---|---|
| 14:7 2:10; Mt 10:28. | 2 Thes 1:7; Heb 4:10. |
| 14:8 18:2–3; Is 21:9; Jer 51:8 / Is 51:17; Jer 25:15–17. | 14:14 1:7; Dn 7:13. |
| | 14:15 Jl 4:13; Mt 13:36–43. |
| 14:11 19:3. | 14:19 19:15; Is 63:1–6. |
| 14:12 12:17. | 15:2 7:9, 14; 13:15–18. |
| 14:13 Mt 11:28–29; | 15:3 Ps 92:6; 98:1 / Dt 32:4; Ps 145:17. |

⁴ Who will not fear you, Lord,
    or glorify your name?
For you alone are holy.
All the nations will come
and worship before you,
    for your righteous acts have been
        revealed."*

⁵† After this I had another vision. The temple that is the heavenly tent of testimony† opened, ⁶ and the seven angels with the seven plagues came out of the temple. They were dressed in clean white linen, with a gold sash around their chests.* ⁷ One of the four living creatures gave the seven angels seven gold bowls filled with the fury of God, who lives forever and ever. ⁸ Then the temple became so filled with the smoke from God's glory and might that no one could enter it until the seven plagues of the seven angels had been accomplished.*

**16** **The Seven Bowls.**† ¹ I heard a loud voice speaking from the temple to the seven angels, "Go and pour out the seven bowls of God's fury upon the earth."

² The first angel went and poured out his bowl on the earth. Festering and ugly sores broke out on those who had the mark of the beast or worshiped its image.†

³† The second angel poured out his bowl on the sea. The sea turned to blood like that from a corpse; every creature living in the sea died.

⁴ The third angel poured out his bowl on the rivers and springs of water. These also turned to blood.* ⁵ Then I heard the angel in charge of the waters say:

"You are just, O Holy One,
    who are and who were,
    in passing this sentence.*

⁶ For they have shed the blood of the holy
    ones and the prophets,
and you [have] given them blood to
        drink;
    it is what they deserve."*

⁷ Then I heard the altar cry out,

"Yes, Lord God almighty,
    your judgments are true and just."*

⁸ The fourth angel poured out his bowl on the sun. It was given the power to burn people with fire. ⁹ People were burned by the scorching heat and blasphemed the name of God who had power over these plagues, but they did not repent or give him glory.*

¹⁰* The fifth angel poured out his bowl on the throne of the beast.† Its kingdom was plunged into darkness, and people bit their tongues in pain ¹¹ and blasphemed the God of heaven because of their pains and sores. But they did not repent of their works.*

¹² The sixth angel emptied his bowl on the great river Euphrates. Its water was dried up to prepare the way for the kings of the East.† ¹³ I saw three unclean spirits like frogs† come from the mouth of the dragon, from the mouth of the beast, and from the mouth of the false prophet.* ¹⁴ These were demonic spirits who performed signs. They went out to the kings of the whole world to assemble them for the battle on the great day of God the almighty.* ¹⁵ ("Behold, I am coming like a thief."† Blessed is the one who watches and keeps his clothes ready, so that he may not go naked and people see him exposed.)* ¹⁶ They then assembled the kings in the place that is named Armageddon† in Hebrew.

¹⁷ The seventh angel poured out his bowl

---

† **15:5–8** Seven angels receive the bowls of God's wrath.
**15:5** *Tent of testimony*: the name of the meeting tent in the Greek text of Ex 40. Cf. 2 Mc 2:4–7.
**16:1–21** These seven bowls, like the seven seals (Rev 6:1–17; 8:1) and the seven trumpets (Rev 8:2–9:21; 11:15–19), bring on a succession of disasters modeled in part on the plagues of Egypt (Ex 7–12). See note on Rev 6:12–14.
**16:2** Like the sixth Egyptian plague (Ex 9:8–11).
**16:3–4** Like the first Egyptian plague (Ex 7:20–21). The same woe followed the blowing of the second trumpet (Rev 8:8–9).
**16:10** *The throne of the beast*: symbol of the forces of evil. *Darkness*: like the ninth Egyptian plague (Ex 10:21–23); cf. Rev 9:2.
**16:12** *The kings of the East*: Parthians; see notes on Rev 6:2 and Rev 17:12–13. *East*: literally, "rising of the sun," as in Rev 7:2.
**16:13** *Frogs*: possibly an allusion to the second Egyptian

plague (Ex 7:26–8:11). *The false prophet*: identified with the two-horned second beast (Rev 13:11–18 and the note there).
**16:15** *Like a thief*: as in Rev 3:3 (cf. Mt 24:42–44; 1 Thes 5:2). *Blessed*: see note on Rev 1:3.
**16:16** *Armageddon*: in Hebrew, this means "Mountain of Megiddo." Since Megiddo was the scene of many decisive battles in antiquity (Jgs 5:19–20; 2 Kgs 9:27; 2 Chr 35:20–24), the town became the symbol of the final disastrous rout of the forces of evil.

* **15:4** Ps 86:9–10; Jer 10:7.          **16:9** Am 4:6.
**15:6** 19:8.                            **16:10** Ex 10:21–23.
**15:8** 1 Kgs 8:10; Is 6:4.              **16:11** Ex 9:8–11 / Jer 5:3.
**16:4** Ex 7:14–24.                       **16:13** Ex 8:2–3.
**16:5** 1:4.                             **16:14** 1 Cor 1:8.
**16:6** Ez 35:6; Mt 23:34–35.            **16:15** Mt 24:42–44 / 3:17.
**16:7** Dn 3:27; Tb 3:2.

into the air. A loud voice came out of the temple from the throne, saying, "It is done."* [18] Then there were lightning flashes, rumblings, and peals of thunder, and a great earthquake. It was such a violent earthquake that there has never been one like it since the human race began on earth.* [19] The great city† was split into three parts, and the gentile cities fell. But God remembered great Babylon, giving it the cup filled with the wine of his fury and wrath. [20]† Every island fled, and mountains disappeared. [21] Large hailstones like huge weights came down from the sky on people, and they blasphemed God for the plague of hail because this plague was so severe.*

## V. THE PUNISHMENT OF BABYLON AND THE DESTRUCTION OF PAGAN NATIONS

**17** **Babylon the Great.** [1]† Then one of the seven angels who were holding the seven bowls came and said to me, "Come here. I will show you the judgment on the great harlot† who lives near the many waters.* [2]† The kings of the earth have had intercourse with her,* and the inhabitants of the earth became drunk on the wine of her harlotry." [3] Then he carried me away in spirit to a deserted place where I saw a woman seated on a scarlet beast† that was covered with blasphemous names, with seven heads and ten horns.* [4] The woman was wearing purple and scarlet and adorned with gold, precious stones, and pearls.* She held in her hand a gold cup that was filled with the abominable and sordid deeds of her harlotry. [5] On her forehead was written a name, which is a mystery, "Babylon the great, the mother of harlots and of the abominations of the earth." [6]† I saw that the woman was drunk on the blood of the holy ones and on the blood of the witnesses to Jesus.

### Meaning of the Beast and Harlot.† When I saw her I was greatly amazed. [7] The angel said to me, "Why are you amazed? I will explain to you the mystery of the woman and of the beast that carries her, the beast with the seven heads and the ten horns. [8]†* The beast that you saw existed once but now exists no longer. It will come up from the abyss and is headed for destruction. The inhabitants of the earth whose names have not been written in the book of life from the foundation of the world shall be amazed when they see the beast, because it existed once but exists no longer, and yet it will come again. [9] Here is a clue† for one who has wisdom. The seven heads represent seven hills upon which the woman sits. They also represent seven kings:* [10] five have already fallen, one still lives, and the last has not yet come,† and when he comes he must remain only a short while. [11] The beast† that existed once but exists no longer is an eighth king, but really belongs to the seven and is headed for destruction. [12] The ten horns that you saw represent ten kings who have not yet been crowned;† they will receive royal authority along with the beast for one hour.* [13] They are of one mind and will give their power and authority to the beast. [14] They will fight with the Lamb, but the Lamb will conquer them, for he is Lord of lords and king of kings, and those with him are called, chosen, and faithful."*

[15] Then he said to me, "The waters that you saw where the harlot lives represent large

---

† **16:19** *The great city*: Rome and the empire.
**16:20–21** See note on Rev 6:12–14. *Hailstones*: as in the seventh Egyptian plague (Ex 9:23–24); cf. Rev 8:7. *Like huge weights*: literally, "weighing a talent," about one hundred pounds.
**17:1–19:10** The punishment of Babylon is now described as a past event and, metaphorically, under the image of the great harlot who leads people astray into idolatry.
**17:1–6** Babylon, the symbolic name (Rev 17:5) of Rome, is graphically described as "the great harlot."
**17:2** *Intercourse…harlotry*: see note on Rev 14:4. The pagan kings subject to Rome adopted the cult of the emperor.
**17:3** *Scarlet beast*: see note on Rev 13:1–10. *Blasphemous names*: divine titles assumed by the Roman emperors; see note on Rev 13:5–6.
**17:4** Reference to the great wealth and idolatrous cults of Rome.
**17:6b–18** An interpretation of the vision is here given.
**17:8** Allusion to the belief that the dead Nero would return to power (Rev 17:11); see note on Rev 13:3.

**17:9** *Here is a clue*: literally, "Here a mind that has wisdom." *Seven hills*: of Rome.
**17:10** There is little agreement as to the identity of the Roman emperors alluded to here. The number seven (Rev 17:9) suggests that all the emperors are meant; see note on Rev 1:4.
**17:11** *The beast*: Nero; see note on Rev 17:8.
**17:12–13** *Ten kings who have not yet been crowned*: perhaps Parthian satraps who are to accompany the revived Nero (the beast) in his march on Rome to regain power; see note on Rev 13:3. In Rev 19:11–21, the Lamb and his companions will conquer them.

---

**16:17** Is 66:6.
**16:18** Mk 13:19.
**16:21** Ex 9:22–26.
**17:1** Jer 50:38; 51:13.
**17:2** Jer 51:7.
**17:3** 13:1.
**17:4** 18:16.
**17:8** 13:3–4 / 3:5; 13:8; 20:12.
**17:9** 13:18.
**17:12** Dn 7:24.
**17:14** 19:11–21; 2 Mc 13:4; 1 Tm 6:15 / Rom 1:6; 1 Pt 2:9; Jude 1.

R
E
V

numbers of peoples, nations, and tongues. [16] The ten horns† that you saw and the beast will hate the harlot; they will leave her desolate and naked; they will eat her flesh and consume her with fire.* [17] For God has put it into their minds to carry out his purpose and to make them come to an agreement to give their kingdom to the beast until the words of God are accomplished. [18] The woman whom you saw represents the great city that has sovereignty over the kings of the earth."

# 18 The Fall of Babylon.†

[1] After this I saw another angel coming down from heaven, having great authority, and the earth became illumined by his splendor.* [2]† He cried out in a mighty voice:

> "Fallen, fallen is Babylon the great.*
> She has become a haunt for demons.
> She is a cage for every unclean spirit,
> a cage for every unclean bird,
> [a cage for every unclean] and
> disgusting [beast].
> [3] For all the nations have drunk†
> the wine of her licentious passion.
> The kings of the earth had intercourse
> with her,
> and the merchants of the earth grew
> rich from her drive for luxury."*

[4] Then I heard another voice from heaven say:

> "Depart from her,† my people,
> so as not to take part in her sins
> and receive a share in her plagues,*
> [5] for her sins are piled up to the sky,
> and God remembers her crimes.*
> [6] Pay her back as she has paid others.
> Pay her back double for her deeds.
> Into her cup pour double what she
> poured.*

> [7] To the measure of her boasting and
> wantonness
> repay her in torment and grief;
> for she said to herself,
> 'I sit enthroned as queen;
> I am no widow,
> and I will never know grief.'*
> [8] Therefore, her plagues will come in one
> day,
> pestilence, grief, and famine;
> she will be consumed by fire.
> For mighty is the Lord God who judges
> her."

[9] The kings of the earth who had intercourse with her in their wantonness will weep and mourn over her when they see the smoke of her pyre. [10] They will keep their distance for fear of the torment inflicted on her, and they will say:

> "Alas, alas, great city,
> Babylon, mighty city.
> In one hour your judgment has
> come."

[11] The merchants of the earth will weep and mourn for her, because there will be no more markets† for their cargo: [12] their cargo of gold, silver, precious stones, and pearls; fine linen, purple silk, and scarlet cloth; fragrant wood of every kind, all articles of ivory and all articles of the most expensive wood, bronze, iron, and marble; [13] cinnamon, spice,† incense, myrrh, and frankincense; wine, olive oil, fine flour, and wheat; cattle and sheep, horses and chariots, and slaves, that is, human beings.

> [14] "The fruit you craved
> has left you.
> All your luxury and splendor are gone,
> never again will one find them."*

† **17:16–18** *The ten horns*: the ten pagan kings (Rev 17:12) who unwittingly fulfill God's will against harlot Rome, the great city; cf. Ez 16:37.

**18:1–19:4** A stirring dirge over the fall of Babylon-Rome. The perspective is prophetic, as if the fall of Rome had already taken place. The imagery here, as elsewhere in this book, is not to be taken literally. The vindictiveness of some of the language, borrowed from the scathing Old Testament prophecies against Babylon, Tyre, and Nineveh (Is 23; 24; 27; Jer 50–51; Ez 26–27), is meant to portray symbolically the inexorable demands of God's holiness and justice; cf. Introduction. The section concludes with a joyous canticle on the future glory of heaven.

**18:2** Many Greek manuscripts and versions omit *a cage for every unclean…beast*.

**18:3–24** Rome is condemned for her immorality, symbol of idolatry (see note on Rev 14:4), and for persecuting the church; cf. Rev 19:2.

**18:4** *Depart from her*: not evacuation of the city but separation from sinners, as always in apocalyptic literature.

**18:11** Ironically, the merchants weep not so much for Babylon-Rome, but for their lost markets; cf. Ez 27:36.

**18:13** *Spice*: an unidentified spice plant called in Greek *amōmon*.

* **17:16** Ez 16:37–41;      **18:4** Is 48:20; Jer 50:8.
     23:25–29.                   **18:5** Jer 51:9.
**18:1** Ez 43:2.            **18:6** Jer 50:15 / Jer 16:18.
**18:2** 14:8; Is 21:9; Jer     **18:7** Is 47:8–9.
     50:2–3; 51:8.            **18:14** Hos 10:5 / Am 6:7.
**18:3** 17:2; Jer 51:7.

15 The merchants who deal in these goods, who grew rich from her, will keep their distance for fear of the torment inflicted on her. Weeping and mourning, 16 they cry out:

"Alas, alas, great city,
        wearing fine linen, purple and
            scarlet,
        adorned [in] gold, precious stones,
            and pearls. *
17      In one hour this great wealth has been
            ruined."

Every captain of a ship, every traveler at sea, sailors, and seafaring merchants stood at a distance 18 and cried out when they saw the smoke of her pyre, "What city could compare with the great city?" 19 * They threw dust on their heads and cried out, weeping and mourning:

"Alas, alas, great city,
        in which all who had ships at sea
        grew rich from her wealth.
    In one hour she has been ruined.
20    Rejoice over her, heaven,
        you holy ones, apostles, and
            prophets.
    For God has judged your case against
        her." *

21 A mighty angel picked up a stone like a huge millstone and threw it into the sea and said:

"With such force will Babylon the great
        city be thrown down,
    and will never be found again. *
22    No melodies of harpists and musicians,
        flutists and trumpeters,
    will ever be heard in you again.
    No craftsmen in any trade
        will ever be found in you again.
    No sound of the millstone
        will ever be heard in you again. *
23    No light from a lamp
        will ever be seen in you again.
    No voices of bride and groom

will ever be heard in you again.
Because your merchants were the great
        ones of the world,
    all nations were led astray by your
        magic potion. *
24    In her was found the blood of prophets
        and holy ones
    and all who have been slain on the
        earth." *

# 19

1 After this I heard what sounded like the loud voice of a great multitude in heaven, saying:

"Alleluia! †
    Salvation, glory, and might belong to
        our God,
2        for true and just are his judgments.
    He has condemned the great harlot
        who corrupted the earth with her
            harlotry.
    He has avenged on her the blood of his
        servants." *

3 They said a second time:

"Alleluia! Smoke will rise from her
        forever and ever." *

4 The twenty-four elders and the four living creatures fell down and worshiped God who sat on the throne, saying, "Amen. Alleluia."

**The Victory Song.** † 5 A voice coming from the throne said:

"Praise our God, all you his servants,
    [and] you who revere him, small and
        great." *

6 Then I heard something like the sound of a great multitude or the sound of rushing water or mighty peals of thunder, as they said:

"Alleluia!
    The Lord has established his reign,
    [our] God, the almighty.

† **19:1, 3, 4, 6** *Alleluia:* found only here in the New Testament, this frequent exclamation of praise in the Hebrew psalms was important in Jewish liturgy.
**19:5–10** A victory song follows, sung by the entire church, celebrating the marriage of the Lamb, the union of the Messiah with the community of the elect.

**18:16** 17:4.
**18:19** Ez 27:27–32.
**18:20** 19:1–2; Dt 32:43.
**18:21** Jer 51:63–64; Ez 26:21.
**18:22** Is 24:8; Ez 26:13.
**18:23** Jer 7:34; 16:9; 25:10.
**18:24** 16:6.
**19:2** Dn 3:27 / Jer 51:48–49.
**19:3** 14:11; Is 34:10.
**19:5** 11:18; Ps 115:13.

7　Let us rejoice and be glad
　　　and give him glory.
　　For the wedding day of the Lamb† has
　　　come,
　　　his bride has made herself ready.*
8　She was allowed to wear
　　　a bright, clean linen garment."*

(The linen represents the righteous deeds of the holy ones.)†

⁹Then the angel said to me, "Write this: Blessed† are those who have been called to the wedding feast of the Lamb." And he said to me, "These words are true; they come from God."* ¹⁰I fell at his feet to worship him. But he said to me, "Don't! I am a fellow servant of yours and of your brothers who bear witness to Jesus. Worship God.* Witness to Jesus is the spirit of prophecy."†

**The King of Kings.** ¹¹† Then I saw the heavens opened, and there was a white horse; its rider was [called] "Faithful and True." He judges and wages war in righteousness.* ¹²His eyes were [like] a fiery flame, and on his head were many diadems. He had a name† inscribed that no one knows except himself.* ¹³He wore a cloak that had been dipped in† blood, and his name was called the Word of God.* ¹⁴The armies of heaven followed him, mounted on white horses and wearing clean white linen.* ¹⁵Out of his mouth came a sharp sword to strike the nations. He will rule them with an iron rod, and he himself will tread out in the wine press† the wine of the fury and wrath of God the almighty.* ¹⁶He has a name written on his cloak and on his thigh, "King of kings and Lord of lords."*

¹⁷† Then I saw an angel standing on the sun. He cried out [in] a loud voice to all the birds flying high overhead, "Come here. Gather for God's great feast, ¹⁸to eat the flesh of kings, the flesh of military officers, and the flesh of warriors, the flesh of horses and of their riders, and the flesh of all, free and slave, small and great."* ¹⁹Then I saw the beast and the kings of the earth and their armies gathered to fight against the one riding the horse and against his army. ²⁰The beast was caught and with it the false prophet† who had performed in its sight the signs by which he led astray those who had accepted the mark of the beast and those who had worshiped its image. The two were thrown alive into the fiery pool burning with sulfur.* ²¹The rest were killed by the sword that came out of the mouth of the one riding the horse, and all the birds gorged themselves on their flesh.

# 20 The Thousand-year Reign. ¹† Then I saw an angel come down from heaven, holding in his hand the key to the abyss† and a heavy chain.* ²He seized the dragon, the ancient serpent, which is the Devil or Satan,† and tied it up for a thousand years* ³and threw it into the abyss, which he locked over it and sealed, so that it could no longer lead the nations astray until the thousand years are

---

† **19:7** *The wedding day of the Lamb*: symbol of God's reign about to begin (Rev 21:1–22:5); see note on Rev 10:7. *His bride*: the church; cf. 2 Cor 11:2; Eph 5:22–27. Marriage is one of the biblical metaphors used to describe the covenant relationship between God and his people; cf. Hos 2:16–22; Is 54:5–6; 62:5; Ez 16:6–14. Hence, idolatry and apostasy are viewed as adultery and harlotry (Hos 2:4–15; Ez 16:15–63); see note on Rev 14:4.
**19:8** See note on Rev 14:12.
**19:9** *Blessed*: see note on Rev 1:3.
**19:10** *The spirit of prophecy*: as the prophets were inspired to proclaim God's word, so the Christian is called to give witness to the Word of God (Rev 19:13) made flesh; cf. Rev 1:2; 6:9; 12:17.
**19:11–16** Symbolic description of the exalted Christ (cf. Rev 1:13–16) who together with the armies of heaven overcomes the beast and its followers; cf. Rev 17:14.
**19:12** *A name*: in Semitic thought, the name conveyed the reality of the person; cf. Mt 11:27; Lk 10:22.
**19:13** *Had been dipped in*: other Greek manuscripts and versions read "had been sprinkled with"; cf. Rev 19:15. *The Word of God*: Christ is the revelation of the Father; cf. Jn 1:1, 14; 1 Jn 2:14.
**19:15** The treading of the wine press is a prophetic symbol used to describe the destruction of God's enemies; cf. Is 63:1–6; Jl 4:13.
**19:17–21** The certainty of Christ's victory is proclaimed by an angel, followed by a reference to the mustering of enemy forces and a fearsome description of their annihilation. The gruesome imagery is borrowed from Ez 39:4, 17–20.
**19:20** *Beast...false prophet*: see notes on Rev 13. *The fiery pool...sulfur*: symbol of God's punishment (Rev 14:10; 20:10, 14–15), different from the abyss; see note on Rev 9:1.
**20:1–6** Like the other numerical values in this book, the thousand years are not to be taken literally; they symbolize the long period of time between the chaining up of Satan (a symbol for Christ's resurrection-victory over death and the forces of evil) and the end of the world. During this time God's people share in the glorious reign of God that is present to them by virtue of their baptismal victory over death and sin; cf. Rom 6:1–8; Jn 5:24–25; 16:33; 1 Jn 3:14; Eph 2:1.
**20:1** *Abyss*: see note on Rev 9:1.
**20:2** *Dragon...serpent...Satan*: see notes on Rev 12:3, 9, 10, 15.

---

| | |
|---|---|
| **19:7** Mt 22:9; Eph 5:27. | **19:13** Is 63:1 / Jn 1:1. |
| **19:8** 15:6; Is 61:10; Mt 22:11–12. | **19:14** 15:6; 19:8. |
| | **19:15** 14:20; Is 63:3. |
| **19:9** Mt 8:11; Lk 14:15. | **19:16** 17:14; 2 Mc 13:4. |
| **19:10** 22:8–9. | **19:18** Ez 39:17–20. |
| **19:11** Is 11:4. | **19:20** 14:10. |
| **19:12** 1:14–16; 2:18 / Lk 10:22. | **20:1** 9:1. |
| | **20:2** Gn 3:1. |

completed. After this, it is to be released for a short time.

⁴ Then I saw thrones; those who sat on them were entrusted with judgment. I also saw the souls of those who had been beheaded for their witness to Jesus and for the word of God, and who had not worshiped the beast or its image nor had accepted its mark† on their foreheads or hands. They came to life and they reigned with Christ for a thousand years.* ⁵ The rest of the dead did not come to life until the thousand years were over. This is the first resurrection. ⁶ Blessed† and holy is the one who shares in the first resurrection. The second death has no power over these; they will be priests of God and of Christ, and they will reign with him for [the] thousand years.

⁷† When the thousand years are completed, Satan will be released from his prison. ⁸ He will go out to deceive the nations at the four corners of the earth, Gog and Magog,† to gather them for battle; their number is like the sand of the sea.* ⁹ They invaded the breadth of the earth† and surrounded the camp of the holy ones and the beloved city. But fire came down from heaven and consumed them.* ¹⁰ The Devil who had led them astray was thrown into the pool of fire and sulfur, where the beast and the false prophet were. There they will be tormented day and night forever and ever.

**The Large White Throne.**† ¹¹ Next I saw a large white throne and the one who was sitting on it. The earth and the sky fled from his presence and there was no place for them.* ¹² I saw the dead, the great and the lowly, standing before the throne, and scrolls were opened. Then another scroll was opened, the book of life.† The dead were judged according to their deeds, by what was written in the scrolls.* ¹³ The sea gave up its dead; then Death and Hades† gave up their dead. All the dead were judged according to their deeds. ¹⁴* Then Death and Hades were thrown into the pool of fire. (This pool of fire is the second death.†) ¹⁵ Anyone whose name was not found written in the book of life was thrown into the pool of fire.

## VI. THE NEW CREATION†

# 21 The New Heaven and the New Earth.
¹* Then I saw a new heaven and a new earth. The former heaven and the former earth had passed away, and the sea was no more.† ² I also saw the holy city, a new Jerusalem,† coming down out of heaven from God, prepared as a bride adorned for her husband.* ³ I heard a loud voice from the throne saying, "Behold, God's dwelling is with the human race.* He will dwell with them and they will be his people† and God himself will always be with them [as their God].† ⁴ He will wipe every tear from their eyes, and there shall be no more death or mourning, wailing or pain, [for] the old order has passed away."*

⁵ The one who sat on the throne† said, "Behold, I make all things new." Then he said, "Write these words down, for they are trustworthy and true."* ⁶ He said to me, "They are accomplished.† I [am] the Alpha and the Omega, the beginning and the end. To the thirsty I will give a gift from the spring of life-giving water.* ⁷ The victor† will inherit these

---

20:4 *Beast...mark*: see Rev 13 and its notes.
20:6 *Blessed*: see note on Rev 1:3. *Second death*: see note on Rev 2:11. *Priests*: as in Rev 1:6; 5:10; cf. 1 Pt 2:9.
20:7–10 A description of the symbolic battle to take place when Satan is released at the end of time, when the thousand years are over; see note on Rev 20:1–6.
20:8 *Gog and Magog*: symbols of all pagan nations; the names are taken from Ez 38:1–39:20.
20:9 *The breadth of the earth*: Palestine. *The beloved city*: Jerusalem; see note on Rev 14:1.
20:11–15 A description of the final judgment. After the intermediate reign of Christ, all the dead are raised and judged, thus inaugurating the new age.
20:12 *The book of life*: see note on Rev 3:5. *Judged...scrolls*: see note on Rev 14:12.
20:13 *Hades*: the netherworld; see note on Rev 1:18.
20:14 *Second death*: see note on Rev 2:11.
21:1–22:5 A description of God's eternal kingdom in heaven under the symbols of a new heaven and a new earth; cf. Is 65:17–25; 66:22; Mt 19:28.
21:1 *Sea...no more*: because as home of the dragon it was doomed to disappear; cf. Jb 7:12.

21:2 *New Jerusalem...bride*: symbol of the church (Gal 4:26); see note on Rev 19:7.
21:3–4 Language taken from Ez 37:27; Is 25:8; 35:10; cf. Rev 7:17.
21:3 *People*: other ancient manuscripts read a plural, "peoples."
21:5 *The one...on the throne*: God himself; cf. Rev 4:1–11.
21:6 *They are accomplished*: God's reign has already begun; see note on Rev 20:1–6. *Alpha...Omega*: see note on Rev 1:8. *Life-giving water*: see note on Rev 7:17.
21:7 *The victor*: over the forces of evil; see the conclusions of the seven letters (Rev 2:7, 11, 17, 26; 3:5, 12, 21). *He will be my son*: the victorious Christian enjoys divine affiliation by adoption (Gal 4:4–7; Rom 8:14–17); see note on Rev 2:26–28.

---

| | |
|---|---|
| 20:4 Mt 19:28. | 8:19–23; 2 Pt 3:13. |
| 20:8 Ez 38:2, 9, 16. | 21:2 19:7–9. |
| 20:9 Ez 38:22. | 21:3 Ez 37:27. |
| 20:11 2 Pt 3:7, 10, 12. | 21:4 7:17; Is 25:8; 35:10. |
| 20:12 Rom 2:6. | 21:5 Is 43:19; 2 Cor 5:17. |
| 20:14 1 Cor 15:26, 54–55. | 21:6 22:17; Ps 36:8–9; Is |
| 21:1 Is 65:17; 66:22; Rom | 55:1. |

gifts, and I shall be his God, and he will be my son. * 8 But as for cowards, † the unfaithful, the depraved, murderers, the unchaste, sorcerers, idol-worshipers, and deceivers of every sort, their lot is in the burning pool of fire and sulfur, which is the second death." *

**The New Jerusalem.** † 9 One of the seven angels who held the seven bowls filled with the seven last plagues came and said to me, "Come here. I will show you the bride, the wife of the Lamb." † 10 He took me in spirit to a great, high mountain and showed me the holy city Jerusalem coming down out of heaven from God. * 11 It gleamed with the splendor of God. Its radiance was like that of a precious stone, like jasper, clear as crystal. * 12 It had a massive, high wall, with twelve gates where twelve angels were stationed and on which names were inscribed, [the names] of the twelve tribes of the Israelites. 13 There were three gates facing east, three north, three south, and three west. * 14 The wall of the city had twelve courses of stones as its foundation, on which were inscribed the twelve names of the twelve apostles † of the Lamb. *

15 † The one who spoke to me held a gold measuring rod to measure the city, its gates, and its wall. 16 The city was square, its length the same as [also] its width. He measured the city with the rod and found it fifteen hundred miles † in length and width and height. 17 He also measured its wall: one hundred and forty-four cubits † according to the standard unit of measurement the angel used. 18 † The wall was constructed of jasper, while the city was pure

gold, clear as glass. 19 The foundations of the city wall were decorated with every precious stone; the first course of stones was jasper, the second sapphire, the third chalcedony, the fourth emerald, * 20 the fifth sardonyx, the sixth carnelian, the seventh chrysolite, the eighth beryl, the ninth topaz, the tenth chrysoprase, the eleventh hyacinth, and the twelfth amethyst. 21 The twelve gates were twelve pearls, each of the gates made from a single pearl; and the street of the city was of pure gold, transparent as glass.

22 † * I saw no temple in the city, for its temple is the Lord God almighty and the Lamb. 23 † The city had no need of sun or moon to shine on it, * for the glory of God gave it light, and its lamp was the Lamb. 24 The nations will walk by its light, † and to it the kings of the earth will bring their treasure. * 25 During the day its gates will never be shut, and there will be no night there. 26 The treasure and wealth of the nations will be brought there, 27 but nothing unclean will enter it, nor any[one] who does abominable things or tells lies. Only those will enter whose names are written in the Lamb's book of life. *

22 1 Then the angel showed me the river of life-giving water, † sparkling like crystal, flowing from the throne of God and of the Lamb * 2 down the middle of its street. On either side of the river grew the tree of life † that produces fruit twelve times a year, once each month; the leaves of the trees serve as medicine for the nations. 3 Nothing accursed will be found there anymore. The throne of

---

**21:8** *Cowards:* their conviction is so weak that they deny Christ in time of trial and become traitors. *Second death:* see note on Rev 2:11.

**21:9–22:5** Symbolic descriptions of the new Jerusalem, the church. Most of the images are borrowed from Ez 40–48.

**21:9** *the bride, the wife of the Lamb:* the church (Rev 21:2), the new Jerusalem (Rev 21:10); cf. 2 Cor 11:2.

**21:14** *Courses of stones…apostles:* literally, "twelve foundations"; cf. Eph 2:19–20.

**21:15–17** The city is shaped like a gigantic cube, a symbol of perfection (cf. 1 Kgs 6:19–20). The measurements of the city and its wall are multiples of the symbolic number twelve; see note on Rev 7:4–9.

**21:16** *Fifteen hundred miles:* literally, twelve thousand stades, about 12,000 furlongs (see note on Rev 14:20); the number is symbolic: twelve (the apostles as leaders of the new Israel) multiplied by 1,000 (the immensity of Christians); cf. Introduction. *In length and width and height:* literally, "its length and width and height are the same."

**21:17** *One hundred and forty-four cubits:* the cubit was about eighteen inches in length. *Standard unit of measurement the angel used:* literally, "by a human measure, i.e., an angel's."

**21:18–21** The gold and precious gems symbolize the beauty and excellence of the church; cf. Ex 28:15–21; Tb 13:16–17; Is 54:11–12.

**21:22** Christ is present throughout the church; hence, no temple is needed as an earthly dwelling for God; cf. Mt 18:20; 28:20; Jn 4:21.

**21:23** *Lamp…Lamb:* cf. Jn 8:12.

**21:24–27** All men and women of good will are welcome in the church; cf. Is 60:1, 3, 5, 11. *The…book of life:* see note on Rev 3:5.

**22:1, 17** *Life-giving water:* see note on Rev 7:17.

**22:2** *The tree of life:* cf. Rev 22:14; see note on Rev 2:7. *Fruit…medicine:* cf. Ez 47:12.

**21:7** 2 Sm 7:14.
**21:8** 22:15; Rom 1:29–32.
**21:10** Ez 40:2.
**21:11** Heb 11:10.
**21:13** Ez 48:31–35.
**21:14** Eph 2:20.
**21:19** Is 54:11–12.
**21:22** Jn 2:19–20.
**21:23** Is 60:1–2, 19–20.
**21:24** Is 60:11.
**21:27** Is 35:8; 52:1; Zec 13:2 / Rev 3:5; 20:12.
**22:1** Ez 47:1–12.

God and of the Lamb will be in it, and his servants will worship him. [4] They will look upon his face, † and his name will be on their foreheads. [5] Night will be no more, nor will they need light from lamp or sun, for the Lord God shall give them light, and they shall reign forever and ever. *

## VII. EPILOGUE†

[6] And he said to me, "These words are trustworthy and true, and the Lord, the God of prophetic spirits, sent his angel to show his servants what must happen soon." * † "Behold, I am coming soon." † Blessed is the one who keeps the prophetic message of this book. *

[8] It is I, John, who heard and saw these things, and when I heard and saw them I fell down to worship at the feet of the angel who showed them to me. [9] But he said to me, "Don't! I am a fellow servant of yours and of your brothers the prophets and of those who keep the message of this book. Worship God." *

[10] Then he said to me, "Do not seal up the prophetic words of this book, for the appointed time† is near. [11] Let the wicked still act wickedly, and the filthy still be filthy. The righteous must still do right, and the holy still be holy."

[12] "Behold, I am coming soon. I bring with me the recompense I will give to each according to his deeds. * [13] I am the Alpha and the Omega, * the first and the last, the beginning and the end." †

[14] Blessed are they who wash their robes so as to have the right to the tree of life and enter the city† through its gates. * [15] Outside are the dogs, the sorcerers, the unchaste, the murderers, the idol-worshipers, and all who love and practice deceit. *

[16] "I, Jesus, sent my angel to give you this testimony for the churches. I am the root and offspring of David, † the bright morning star." *

[17] The Spirit and the bride† say, "Come." Let the hearer say, "Come." Let the one who thirsts come forward, and the one who wants it receive the gift of life-giving water. *

[18] I warn everyone who hears the prophetic words in this book: if anyone adds to them, God will add to him the plagues described in this book, [19] and if anyone takes away from the words in this prophetic book, God will take away his share in the tree of life and in the holy city described in this book. *

[20] † * The one who gives this testimony says, "Yes, I am coming soon." Amen! Come, Lord Jesus!

[21] The grace of the Lord Jesus be with all.

---

† 22:4 *Look upon his face*: cf. Mt 5:8; 1 Cor 13:12; 1 Jn 3:2.
22:6–21 The book ends with an epilogue consisting of a series of warnings and exhortations and forming an inclusion with the prologue by resuming its themes and expressions; see note on Rev 1:1–3.
22:7, 12, 20 *I am coming soon*: Christ is the speaker; see note on Rev 1:3.
22:7, 14 *Blessed*: see note on Rev 1:3.
22:10 *The appointed time*: see note on Rev 1:3.
22:13 Christ applies to himself words used by God in Rev 1:8.
22:14 *The city*: heavenly Jerusalem; see note on Rev 21:2.
22:16 *The root...of David*: see note on Rev 5:5. *Morning star*: see note on Rev 2:26–28.

22:17 *Bride*: the church; see note on Rev 21:2.
22:20 *Come, Lord Jesus*: a liturgical refrain, similar to the Aramaic expression *Marana tha*—"Our Lord, come!"—in 1 Cor 16:22; cf. note there. It was a prayer for the coming of Christ in glory at the parousia: see note on Rev 1:3.

| | |
|---|---|
| 22:5 Is 60:20. | 22:14 7:14–15; 22:2. |
| 22:6 1:1. | 22:15 21:8; Rom 1:29–32. |
| 22:7 12, 20 / 1:3. | 22:16 1:1, 11–12; 22:6 / |
| 22:9 19:10. | 2:28. |
| 22:12 7, 20 / Ps 62:12; 2 Tm | 22:17 21:6; Is 55:1. |
| 4:14. | 22:19 Dt 4:2. |
| 22:13 1:8; 21:6; Is 41:4; | 22:20 7, 12 / Acts 3:20–21; |
| 44:6. | 1 Cor 15:23; 16:22. |

# Index

# Index

Special features are indicated using lower case letters after the page number: i (illustrations), m (maps), cap (captions), c (charts) and time line (time lines)

anointing rituals, 251
anthropology, 30–31
Antioch (Syria), 70, 1566, 1724
Antioch Incident, 1771–72
Antiochus III, king of Seleucid
    Kingdom, 770, 806
Antiochus IV Epiphanes, king
    of Seleucid Kingdom
  anti-Jewish policies of, 63,
    401, 772, 807, 1404
  imperial worship of, 400
  Maccabean Revolt and, 770
  military campaigns of, 806
anti-Semitism, 49–53, 81, 1560
antithetical parallelism, 836
aphorisms, 62–63
Aphrodite, 1857
Apis, 389
Apocalypse. *See* Revelation,
    book of
*Apocalypse of Abraham*, 41, 2080
*Apocalypse of Adam*, 1403
*Apocalypse of John*, 45
*Apocalypse of Moses*, 40
*Apocalypse of Noah*, 41
*Apocalypse of Peter*, 45, 2080
*Apocalypses of Paul*, 45
apocalyptic literature
  canonical texts as (*see*
    Daniel, book of;
    Revelation, book of)
  characteristics of, 2084
  definition, 2080
  history and overview, 1404
  noncanonical, 40, 41, 45,
    1330, 1403, 2080
  popularity of, 2084
  purpose, 2084
apocrypha. *See also*
    pseudepigrapha
  associated with Ezra, 678,
    678c
  as biblical book sources,
    2028, 2029
  as deuterocanonical books,
    39, 47, 55–56, 396, 399,
    400, 401
  of early Christians, 43–45,
    1822, 2028, 2029, 2074
  intertestamental texts, 39, 47
  overview, 396
  reception of, 45–46
  word origins and usage, 44
*Apocryphon of James*, 44
*Apocryphon of John*, 44

apodictic laws, 122
Apollonius of Ephesus, 2031
Apollos, 1858, 1861
apostles. *See also* false apostles
  canonical history and
    authority of, 102–3
  church foundation, 1923
  definition, 2002
  of Jesus, biographical
    significance and biblical
    references, 1766c
  Jesus as, 2002
  job description of Paul, 1859
  miracle-working capacity of,
    62
  Paul's authority and job
    description, 1859,
    1886–87, 1888
Apostles' Creed, 102
*Apostolic Constitutions*, 78
apostolic gospel tradition, 1552
apostolicity, as canon criteria,
    24, 103
Aquila, 1829, 1833, 1856, 1983
Aquinas, Thomas, 101
Aramaic, 25, 54, 62, 677, 1401
*Aramaic Levi Document*, 41
archaeology, 30–32
archangels, 399, 2074, 2075
Archippus, 1946, 1997
architecture, 28, 563i
Arch of Titus, C9i
Aristarchus, 1946, 1997
Arius of Alexandria, 72
ark of the covenant, 199
Arphaxad, king of the Medes,
    400
art, 73–74
Artaxerxes I, king of Persia, 398,
    677, 692, 695
Artaxerxes II, king of Persia,
    677
Artemis, 1822
artisans, as social class, 36
Asa, king of Judah, 392
*Ascension of Isaiah*, 44–45, 1403
asceticism, false, 1944, 1945,
    1946, 1948
Asclepius, 1822
Asher, 391
Asher, tribe of, C11m
Asherah, 389
Ashtart/Astarte/Ashtaroth/
    Ashtoreth, 389

assimilation, 405, 433, 463,
    1473
assonance, 991
*Assumption of Moses*, 22, 2029,
    2074, 2075, 2076
Assyrian Empire
  conflicts with, 536, 1165,
    1168, 1429, 1490, 1492
  defeat of Israel, North
    Kingdom, 537, 1165
  fall of, 1247
  geographic location, C13m
  geography of, 27
  as God's punishment for
    infidelity, 1426
  Israelite exile route, C13m
  palace sculptural art of,
    1347i
  prophesy in, 1155
  prophets during rule of, 394
  tribute payments to, 1427
Astruc, Jean, 84, 120
Athaliah, queen of Judah, 393,
    537
Athanasius, 72, 881, 2028,
    2029
atonement, 250–51, 1761, 2002
Augustine of Hippo
  canon formation and
    influence of, 39, 46, 400
  Gospel authorship theories,
    1550–51
  Jewish biblical
    interpretation, 48, 57
  original sin and Scripture
    support, 1828
Azariah (Uzziah), king of
    Judah, 393, 1164–65,
    1168, 1451

# B

Baal
  agriculture and worship of,
    29, 433
  biblical references and
    significance, 389
  description of, 1518
  God descriptions as, 1497
  royal worship of, 393, 537
  worship of, as infidelity,
    1427, 1428
Baasha, king of Israel, Northern
    Kingdom, 392

Babylon (code name for Rome), 2027, 2043, 2082, 2083, 2084

Babylonian Empire
conquest and destruction of Jerusalem, 538, 639, 1165, 1251, 1318, 1342, C4timeline
conquest of Judah, 536, 537–38, 641, 1248, 1251, 1318
deities of, 389c
dialogues with God on evil of, 1496–97
geographic location, 598m, C10m, C13m
geography of, 27
literary texts as sources from, 838, 1037
occupation of Jerusalem, 1318, 1342
revolt against, 536

Babylonian Exile
chronology, C4–C5timeline
historical account, 538, 1165, 1248, 1318, 1342
prophets of, 1156–57, 1165
routes, C13m

Babylonian Talmud, 1342

*Babylonian Theodicy, The*, 838

Bagoas, 735

Balaam, 292–93, C8cap

Balak, king of Moab, 292

baptism, 1831, 1909, 1945, 2043

Barnabas, 1772, 1776

Bartholomew, 1766

*2 Baruch*, 42, 1330, 2080, 2082

*3 Baruch*, 1330, 2080

*4 Baruch*, 1330

Baruch (scribe of Jeremiah), 41–42, 1249, 1330, 2080, 2082

Baruch, book of
canonical history, 39, 396, 1157, 1162, 1330
composition, 1330, 1332
Letter of Jeremiah, 1331, 1332
narrative introduction, 1330
narrative summary, 1330
original manuscript translations, 116, 118
outline and divisions, 1330, 1332

as prophetic literature, 1157
themes and theology, 1330–32

baskets of wickedness, 1517

Bathsheba, 471

*Bavli*, 57–58

Beatitudes, 1768c

Behemoth, 844

"Bel" (book of Daniel), 1402, 1404

Beloved Disciple, 1716–17, 1722

Ben Bag-Bag, 54

Benedict XVI, 2079

Benjamin, 391

Benjamin, tribe of, 435, C11m

Ben Sira (Ecclesiasticus, Sirach, Wisdom of Ben Sira)
canonical history, 23, 55, 398, 1094
character of, 840
collectivist references, 33
composition, 833, 840, 1091, 1094
Ezra omissions, 679
foreword of, 1091–92
historical context, 1091
history of, 1094
literary context, 836
literary forms, 837, 1091
as New Testament source, 1091
original manuscript translations, 116, 118
purpose, 1091, 1092–93
school settings for wisdom in, 838
sources for, 1091
themes, 1091–93
title origins, 1094
universalistic outlooks in, 834

*Bereshit*, 132

Beruriah, 54

Bethesda Pools, C9i

Bethulia, 732–33, 735

betrayal, 1628, 1630

Bible, overview. *See also related topics*
archaeology and historicity of, 30–32
authorship, 99–101
books of, alphabetical order, C16c

formation of, 19–26, 47–48
geography of, 27–29
reading, 128
social context of, 33–38
translations, 25–26, 39
word origins, 19

*Bible de Jérusalem*, 26

*Biblical Antiquities*, 40

biblical criticism, 84–91, 92c

biblical inspiration, 95–96, 99–101

biblical interpretation
anti-Semitism and rethinking, 51–53
archaeology supporting, 32
biblical criticism for, 84–91, 92c
canonical order affecting, 55–56
critical issues in, 93–97
historical and cultural context analyses, 30, 50, 53, 86, 105, 107–9
Jewish, 54–60
methods and criteria of Catholic Church, 101–2, 1716
punctuation affecting, 55
text analysis and, 105–7
transformative, 109–10
translation affecting, 55

Bilhah, 390

biographies, 1549–50, 1557–58

*Birth of Mary*, 44

*Birth of the Virgin Mary*, 44

birthright narratives, 133, 1466, 1468

births, miraculous, 395

bishops, 1972, 1991–92

blessing
Israel as, 293, 463, 1518
kingdoms as, among nations, 1518
as literary form, 121
as obedience reward, 297, 346
theology of, 123
as treaty sanction, 342

Blessing of Moses, 342, 345

blood, 251

Blount, Brian, 2079

boasting, 1858, 1888

Boaz, 462, 463, 464

body imagery

church symbolism, 1922–23, 1945

unity symbolism, 1831, 1834, 1857, 1858, 1859

Book of Doom, 1478, 1479

Book of Glory, 1718

*Book of Hekhalot*, 41

Book of Signs, 1718

book of the law, 20, 341, 346, 537

Book of the Twelve, 1155, 1162, 1453–54, 1471

*Book of Thomas the Contender, The*, 44

Booths (Sukkoth, Tabernacles), Feast of, 1720, 1761

branch metaphors, 1722

bread, 1720, 1723

brother (title), 1996, 1998, 2026, 2029, 2080

bull imagery, 199

# C

Cadbury, Henry Joel, 1660, 1770

Caesar Gaius, emperor of Roman Empire, 1762

calf imagery, 199

Caligula, emperor of Roman Empire, 1762

call narratives, 121, 1908

Calvin, John, 1828

Cana, wedding at, 1718–20, 1723

Canaan (promised land)
agriculture and religion, 433
biblical narratives and historical evidence, 30, 292, 406
deities of, 389c (*see also* Baal)
excavation sites in, 30, 32
geographic location, C10m
as promised land, 344–45
war preparation and conquest of, 290, 291, 292, 406, 407

canon. *See also* Apocrypha
biblical interpretation affected by, 55–56, 106–7, 108
Catholic Bible inclusions, 19, 25, 39, 47, 55–56, 396
criteria for, 24, 102–3
definition, 19

formation, 19–25, 102–3
Hebrew Bible inclusions, 19, 22–23, 47, 396, 400, 462, 465
of lectionary, 77–83
Protestant Bible inclusions, 19, 39, 47, 396–97

canonical meanings of interpretation, 106–7

Captivity Epistles, 1827. *See also* Colossians; Ephesians; Philemon; Philippians

casuistic laws, 122

catalogues (morality lists), 1972, 1991

*Catechism of the Catholic Church*, 98

Catholic Bible
biblical criticism and interpretations, 85–86, 87, 1716
canon comparisons, 19, 25, 47
deuterocanonical books of, 39, 47, 55–56, 396, 399, 400, 401
translations, 25–26, 115, 117

Catholic Bible Association, 115, 117

Catholic Church, 98–99, 99. *See also* Christian church, early

catholicity, as canon criteria, 24, 103

Catholic Letters
introduction overview, 2024–31
James, 1543, 2026, 2032–35
1 John, 24, 2028, 2059–61
2 John, 2028, 2031, 2067–68
3 John, 2028, 2031, 2068–69, 2070–72
Jude, 1543, 2028, 2029–30, 2053, 2074–76
1 Peter, 24, 1543, 2026–27, 2031, 2034, 2041–44
2 Peter, 294, 1543, 2027–28, 2051–54

caves, 500i

CCD (Confraternity of Christian Doctrine), 115, 117

censuses, 290–91, 294, 471

Cephas. *See* Peter

Chaldeans, 1496

chariots, prophetic visions of, 1517

charisms, 1859, 1861, 1886, 1907

cherubim, 199, 1347i

childbirth, 129

children
as cultural expectation, 1823
of the devil, 2059
early Christians as, 1858, 1909, 1957, 2059, 2060
of God, 1546, 1722, 1831

Christian church, early. *See also* christology; ecclesiology
apocryphal works accepted by, 43–45, 2028, 2029, 2074, 2075
conflicts of doctrine, 2029
disciple requirements, 1665–66
forgiveness of sin agency, 1563
gifts of, 1923
Gospels as history of, 1663, 1664
household codes, 1922, 1945, 1972, 1992
Judaism separation from, 47, 51
legitimization of, 1664, 1665, 1772, 1773, 1776–77
marriage doctrine, 1823, 1859, 1861, 1887
membership division (*see* factionalism)
membership inclusion, 1564, 1662–63, 1721, 1722, 1776–77, 1997
mission of, 1563–64
morality doctrine, 1823, 1858–59, 1861, 1933, 1945, 1948, 1956–57, 1958, 1964, 2033, 2034
movement terminology for, 47, 1772
as New Temple, 1722
Paul's authority in, 1859, 1886–87, 1888, 1889–90, 1911
perception in society, 2027, 2041–42, 2043
religious competition of, 1822–23, 1948

religious practices, 1662
  spiritual ancestors of,
    390–91c
  stewardship, 1887
  Stoicist philosophy and, 71
  terminology used, 1822
Christians, early
  apocrypha, of, 43–46, 2028,
    2029, 2074, 2075
  art of, 74
  Bible formation debates, 48
  biblical interpretation
    comparisons, 54–60
  daily life under Roman rule,
    1560–61
  images of Jesus, 69
  lectionary history, 78
  oppression of, 2027,
    2041–42, 2043
  persecution of, 2082, 2084,
    2085
  relationship with Jews, 48,
    51–53
  term usage, 47, 1772, 1955
christology. See also Messiah/
    Christ
  cosmological developments,
    1923, 1944–45
  epiphany, 171, 1984, 1990
  exaltation, 1933, 1934–35,
    2003, 2005, 2053
1 Chronicles (Chronicler's
    History), 64, 398, 402,
    607–9
2 Chronicles (Chronicler's
    History), 398, 402, 607,
    608, 639–41
Chronistic school, 679
church (ekklēsia), term usage,
    1822, 1858, 1945–46,
    1955
Church of England (Anglicans),
    56
church order discourse, 1564
Cicognani, A. G., 115, 116
circumcision
  early Christian church and,
    1859, 1907–8, 1910, 1911,
    1932
  forced, 772
  Jewish covenant practice of,
    49, 130, 404
  laws on, 57
  patriarchal models of, 1831
  Philo on symbolism of, 59

  as war preparation, 403
Claudius, emperor of Roman
    Empire, 1762, 1829,
    1833, 2006
Claudius Lysias, 1773
cleanliness, 249–50, 252
1 Clement (Clement of Rome),
    2026
Clement of Alexandria, 74,
    2026, 2029, 2051
Clement of Rome, 1855, 2006,
    2026
Codex Sinaiticus, 715–16
collectivism, 33–34
Colossae (Turkey), 1944, 1947,
    1948
Colossians, Letter to
  authorship, 1824, 1825,
    1946, 1947–48
  composition location and
    context, 1944, 1947, 1948
  contents summary, 1944–45
  intended audience, 1944,
    1947, 1948
  outline and divisions, 1944,
    1949
  Pauline literature
    comparisons, 1921, 1922,
    1946–47
  purpose, 1946, 1948
common good, 122
communal meanings of
    interpretation, 107
community
  biblical interpretation based
    on, 107, 110
  Christian emphasis on, 99
  early Christian church as,
    1564–65, 1721, 1776–77,
    1997
  identity and solidarity of,
    882
  Israelites as, 343, 405
complaints, 291, 1496–97
concealment, 756
Confraternity Bible, 25
Confraternity of Christian
    Doctrine (CCD), 115, 117
consecration rituals, 251
Constantine, emperor of Rome,
    24
Constitution on the Liturgy, The
    (Sacrosanctum Concilium),
    77, 79–80

contextual approach of
    interpretation
  Catholic teaching on, 101
  importance of, 50, 53, 86,
    105
  methodology of, 89, 95–97,
    107–9
conversion
  attraction to Judaism
    without, 1909, 1946
  call vs., 1908
  divine retribution for, C7cap
  early Christian, 2042
  to Judaism, 462, 465
  transformative interpretation
    and, 109
Corinth (Greece), 1856–57,
    1861, 1886, 1921
1 Corinthians
  authorship, 1821, 1824,
    1856, 1862
  composition, 1856, 1861,
    1890
  contents summary, 1826,
    1855, 1857–60, 1861,
    1884, 1889
  historical context, 1856–57
  intended audience/
    recipients, 1856
  literary context, 1855
  Old Testament references in,
    134, 294
  outline and divisions, 1855,
    1862
  purpose, 1830, 1857–58,
    1861
  Resurrection accounts and
    distinctiveness of Jesus, 67
2 Corinthians
  authorship, 1821, 1824,
    1885
  contents summary, 1826,
    1886–88
  historical context, 1856–57
  intended audience/
    recipients, 1885
  literary context, 1884–85
  outline and divisions, 1884,
    1890
  purpose, 1885–86
3 Corinthians, 43
cosmology, 1923, 1944–45
Council for the
    Implementation of the
    Constitution of the Sacred

of Israel, Northern Kingdom, 346, 401, 537

of Jerusalem, 1345, 1478, 1479, 1492, 1504, 1505

of nations/enemies, 1490–92, 1504, 1505

as punishment for disobedience, 345, 346, C7cap

of Temple, 538, 639, 1559

*Deus absconditus*, 713

deuterocanonical books, 39, 47, 55–56, 396, 399, 400, 401

Deutero-Isaiah (2 Isaiah), 1157, 1164, 1169, 1555

Deuteronomic Code, 341, 342

Deuteronomic School, 342, 344

Deuteronomist (D), 20, 85, 121, 126, 197

Deuteronomistic History of Israel

biblical books as introductions to, 341

books comprising, 246

composition and development, 20, 341, 397, 404, 540

contents summary, 397–98, 402, 404, 539, 540

major themes, 404, 473

as source, 540, 1249

Deuteronomy, book of

animal laws, C8cap

book order theories, 126

composition and development, 121, 341–42, 346

contents summary, 120, 341, 346

as Deuteronomistic History introduction, 341

false prophets, definition of, 1471

harvesting process and generosity laws, 464

levirate marriage laws, 463

literary forms and language of, 342–43, 346

location of centralized worship, 536

marriage laws, 694

monarchy laws, 472

outline and divisions, 341, 346

poems of, 342, 345

themes and theologies, 122, 124, 198, 341, 343–46

title origins, 346

Deutero-Zechariah, 1518

devil, 1561, 1630, 2075. *See also* Satan

devotion, 2052

*Dialogue of Pessimism*, 838

*Dialogue with Trypho* (Justin Martyr), 48, 1661, 2081

Diaspora audiences

encouragement messages, 2026, 2034, 2041–43

fidelity and faithfulness messages, 399, 712–13, 754, 1472

*Diatessaron* (Tatian), 24

didactic literature, 711, 713, 733, 833–40. *See also* Wisdom literature, overview

Didymus, 2029

*Dies Irae*, 42

Dinah, 41, 390

Dionysius of Alexandria, 2081

Dionysus, 1719

Diotrephes, 2070, 2072

disciples

and church organization, 1563–65

hardship readiness requirements, 1628–29

inclusivity dialogues, 1564, 1722

of Jesus, 1766–67c

miracle-working capacity of, 62

negative portrayals of, 1627–29, 1630

positive models of, 1628, 1719

divine power, term usage, 2051–52

*Divino afflante Spiritu* (Pius XII), 85, 101, 115, 116, 117

divorce, 1533

docetism, 2061

Documentary Hypothesis, 121

"Dogmatic Constitution on Divine Revelation" *(Dei Verbum),* 85–86, 87, 100, 711, 1552–53, 1716

dominion, 123

Domitian, emperor of Roman Empire, 1763, 2082

donkeys, 292–93, 1473, C8i

*Dormitio Mariae (Mary's Last Sleep)*, 45

*Douay-Rheims Bible*, 25, 93

doublets, 121

"Dragon, The," 1402, 1404

dream motif, 123

Dumuzi, 389

dwelling analogies, 1721, 1722

# E

Eastern Orthodox Bible, 47, 2027

Ecclesiastes (Qoheleth)

characteristics of, 840, 1036–37

composition, 833–34, 990, 1036, 1037, 1038

historical context and sources, 1037–38

literary forms and context, 833, 836, 837, 1037

outline and divisions, 1036, 1040

sources of, 838

themes, 835, 1038–38

title origins, 1040

*Ecclesiastical History* (Eusebius of Caesarea), 43, 2026, 2028, 2031, 2081

Ecclesiasticus. *See* Ben Sira

ecclesiology

apostolic foundation, 99, 1564, 1776, 1923

body of Christ analogies, 1922–23, 1945

church, term usage and description, 1858, 1922, 1945–46, 1955, 1972

leadership roles, 1972, 1984, 1985, 1991, 1993

liturgical development, 1855, 1859

liturgical practices, 1860

meeting locations, 1825, 1830

unity and community development, 1831, 1834, 1857, 1858, 1859, 1922–23, 1924, 1933, 1936

worship rules, 1822, 1823

ecumenical councils. *See also* Vatican II
  canon development, 25, 39, 45, 102, 396, 735, 2028
  overview and history, 72–73
Edom, 1452, 1466–66, 1468, 1533
efficaciousness, 123
Egypt, 838, 1037, 1165
Ehud, 433
Eichhorn, Johann Gottfried, 120
*ekklēsia*, 1822, 1858, 1945–46, 1955
El, 389
Elah, king of Israel, Northern Kingdom, 392
election
  covenant and, 343–44
  divine sonship of Israel and fidelity to, 64, 1533
  early Christians and Israel inclusion, 2041
  fidelity failures of, 472
  Jesus and, 1631
  theology of love and, 124, 1167, 1533
Eliezer, 392c
Elijah, 62, 392, 537, 540, 1156, 1534, C6cap
Elisha, 62, 393, 537, 540, 1156
elites, as social class, 36–37
Elliot, John H., 2027
*Elohim*, 130, 834, 1036
Elohist (E)
  biblical criticism and identification of, 85
  Exodus authorship, 196–97
  Genesis authorship, 130–31, 132
  Numbers authorship, 290
  Pentateuch authorship, 20, 120, 121, 126
Emmaus, road to, 103
emperor worship, 400, 1822–23, 1934–35, 2082
encouragement, messages of, 2005, 2025, 2041, 2042, 2043
enemies. *See also* war
  assimilation of, 463
  condemnation of, 1504
  of the cross of Christ as early Christian opponents, 1934

genocide of pagans, 407
Israel as blessing and light to, 463
Jews as, 49–52
judgment of, 1444
justice and evil of, 1496
oracles against the nations, 463, 1452, 1455, 1490, 1504
En-gedi cave, 500i
English Bibles, 25–26, 93, 678, 678c
Enoch, 40–41
*1 Enoch*
  canonical history, 22
  Catholic letters citing, 2028, 2029, 2074, 2076
  literary forms, 2080
  as pseudepigraphical text, description, 40
*2 Enoch*, 41
*3 Enoch*, 41
envy, 1934
Epaphras, 1944, 1946–47, 1948
Epaphroditus, 1932, 1936
Ephesians, Letter to, 1825, 1921–24, 1946
Ephesus (Asia Minor), 1856, 1921, 1971, 2081
Ephraim, tribe of, C11m
*Epic of Gilgamesh*, 1037
epiphany christology, 1971, 1984, 1990
*Epistle of Peter to James*, 44
*Epistle of Peter to Philip*, 44
*Epistle of the Apostles*, 45
*Epistle of Titus*, 44
*Epistle to the Laodiceans*, 43
equality, 123, 1909, 1956, 1997, 1998
Erastus, 1983
Esau, 123, 133, 390, 1466, 1468
eschatology
  definition, 1956
  perception of, 1511, 1519, 1934, 1956
  prophetic messages of judgment, 1453, 1467, 1503–4, 1532, 1534
  second coming (*see* parousia)
*1 Esdras*, 676, 678
*2 Esdras (4 Esdras)*, 678, 679

*3 Esdras*, 678
Esther, book of
  canonical history, 39, 55, 396, 400, 753, 756–57
  composition, 753, 756
  Greek translations and verse additions, 400, 753, 756, 757
  intended audience, 754
  literary forms, 711, 754, 756
  narrative summary, 400, 711, 753, 756
  original manuscript translations, 116, 118
  outlines and divisions, 753, 757
  portrayal of main character, 755
  purpose, 711
  setting, 400, 753
  themes, 753–56
ethnocentrism, 147
etiologies, 121
*euangelion/evangelium*, 23, 76, 1553–54
Eucharist, 103–4, 1855
Eunice, 1983
Eusebius of Caesarea
  canon formation and influence of, 24–25, 43, 46, 2029
  Catholic Letters citations, 2026, 2028, 2031
  Gospel authorship attributions, 1626, 1627
  martyrdom of Paul dating, 1825
  Revelation authorship theories, 2081
evangelists, 1552
Eve, Adam and, 40, 57, 128, C2time line
evil
  dialogue with God on, 1496–97
  divine retribution confusion, 835, 1038
  parousia and judgment of, 1934, 1955–56, 1966
  theodicy and justice of, 713, 843–44, 845, 1496–98, 1533–34
Ewald, Heinrich, 121

fires, 395

First *biblical books. See specific names of biblical books, e.g., Chronicles, Corinthians, Enoch, etc.*

First Jewish-Roman War, 1557, 1559, 1626, 1717, 1955, 2082

fish, 74, 1473

Flood, 27, 131, 132, C7cap

folktales, 399

food and oil, multiplication of, 395

foods, biblical, C7i

foot washing, 1721

foreigners (sojourners), 122, 250, 1923, 2041, 2043

foreign policy, 1427, 1429, 1466

foreshadowing, 107, 539

forgiveness, 123, 1563, 1565

form criticism, 90, 92

Former Prophets, 396, 404, 432, 535

four (number), 2084

Fourth *biblical books. See specific names of biblical books, e.g., Chronicles, Corinthians, Enoch, etc.*

Fragmentary Hypothesis, 120

free prophets, 1156

"From Cana to Cana," 1718–20

fuller meanings of interpretation, 106–7

fullness, 1945

fundamentalism, 88, 95–97, 101

# G

Gad, 391, 392

Gad, tribe of, C11m

Gaius, 2070, 2072

Galatians, Letter to
  authorship, 1821, 1824
  composition, 1907, 1911
  contents summary, 1826, 1907–10, 1911–12
  intended audience/ recipients, 1907, 1909, 1911
  literary style and structure, 1824
  outline and divisions, 1907, 1912

purpose, 1907

Resurrection accounts, 67

Son of Man references, 66

as source, 1772

Galba, 1763

Gallio, 1856

Gaza Strip, C15m

Gedaliah, 538, 1248, 1318

Geddes, Alexander, 120

gematria, 59

gender, 35, 93–95, 123, 400. *See also* women

genealogies
  collectivism and, 33
  human relationship illustrations, 464, 465
  kinship themes, 37–38, 129, 130, 1063
  as legitimacy, 398
  as Pentateuch literary form and theme, 121, 129, 130

Genesis, book of
  composition, 120, 130–31, 132
  geographic locations of nations, C10m
  Jonah references as faith statements, 1472
  in later biblical books, 133–34
  literary forms, 121, 129
  narrative summary, 119–20, 125
  outline and divisions, 119, 128, 132, 134
  significance of, 128–29
  themes and theologies, 122, 123, 129–30, 132, 133
  title origins, 132

*Genesis Apocryphon*, 22, 41

genocide, 292, 404, 406, 407, 756

Gentile Christians
  as intended audience, 2027, 2028, 2051
  Jewish law and, 1776, 1822, 1826, 1834
  reconciliation between Jewish Christians and, 1923
  universal salvation including, 1776, 1830–31, 1833, 1907–10, 1911

Gentiles

Christian community inclusion, 1776

early Christian term usage, 2042

intermarriage bans, 399, 678, 693–94, 1533

Judaism attraction without conversion, 1909, 1946

New Testament inclusion of, 1161

Old Testament perception of, 399–400, 405, 772

as Pauline literature audience, 1829

Paul's mission and reception, 1776, 1861

segregation *vs.* assimilation, 405, 463

geography. *See also* land
  collectivist identities and, 33–34
  livelihoods and, 29
  natural barriers and boundary markers, 27, C6cap
  of Palestine and the Levant, 27–29
  themes of, 405
  weather patterns and, 27, 29

German Bibles, 25

Gethsemane, garden of, 1710i

Gibeon, 403

Gideon, 433

gifts, 433, 1923, C7cap

"glory and power," 2052

Gnosticism, 23–24, 44, 70–71, 1945, 2054, 2061

goats, C8i

God. *See also* fidelity; Holy Spirit; obedience; retribution, divine; Word of God

Bible formation and view of, 48

biblical authorship, 99–101

collectivist references to, 33

covenant and relationship with, 129, 343, 344, 401, 1426, 1428, 1452

descriptions of, Pentateuch, 124, 131, 197, 198, 291–92, 343, 733

descriptions of, Prophets, 1160, 1249, 1427–28

Hananiah, 394, 1160, 1251

Hanukkah, 773, 809, 1761

*Harper's Song,* 1037

Harrison, P. N., 1982

Hasmonean Dynasty, 771, 808, C5time line

healings, 395, 1765

*hebel,* 1037, 1038, 1040

*Hebraica veritas,* 25

*Hebrew Apocalypse of Enoch,* 41

Hebrew Bible. *See also* Old Testament; Torah
  ancestral territory of, 34
  biblical book order and centralized worship, 398
  canon and book order, 47, 396
  canonical exclusion, 56, 399, 400, 401
  canonical inclusions, 462, 465
  description of Masoretic Text, 55
  Masoretic Text of, 21, 55, 1248, 1319
  Samuel divisions, 470
  Son of God references, 64
  Son of Man references, 63

Hebrews, Letter to the
  authorship, 1827, 2001, 2005, 2006
  canonical history and order, 24, 1821, 1825
  composition and dating, 2006, 2025
  contents summary, 2001–4, 2005, 2025
  intended audience, 2001, 2006, 2025, 2031
  literary forms, 2001, 2005, 2025
  in literature tradition, 1821
  Old Testament references, 2001, 2002, 2005, 2025
  outline and divisions, 2001, 2006
  Platonic references, 70
  purpose, 2001, 2005, 2025

Heliodorus, 807

Hellenistic empires and Hellenization
  cultural threat, perception of, 808

early Christian writing style traditions adapted from, 2051–52

Holy Land occupation of, 27

Judah as province during, 770

noncanonical texts popular with Christians in, 44

reinterpretation of tradition in culture of, 1062, 1063–64

social cultural patterns of, 33–38

tombs of, 1610i

Heracleon, 24

Heraclitus, 71, 76

*herem,* 292, 404, 406, 407

hermeneutics, 89, 105

Hermes, 1822

Hermogenes, 1983

Herod Agrippa I, 2026

Herod Antipas (King Herod), 1562, 1773, C5time line

Herod the Great, C5time line, C9cap

heroes, 711, 1093

Hezekiah, king of Judah
  Assyrian conflicts, 537, 1165, 1168
  biography, 394
  kingdom unification attempts, 639, 641
  prophets during reign of, 1481

historical books
  arrangement and canon, 396–97
  books of, 397–401
  composition and development, 20, 397, 401
  contents summary, 402
  historical value, 401, 402
  history of biblical formation and, 20–21
  literary forms, 397
  purpose, 401
  term origins and usage, 397
  themes, 397

historical-critical method of interpretation, 88, 92c, 101, 106

history, human, C3c

history books, as literary form, 119, 132–33, 609

*Hodayoth,* 42

holiness, 122, 124, 249–52, 1957, 2041

Holiness Code, 122, 249, 252

Holocaust, 51

Holofernes, 399–400, 733, 735

Holy Land (Levant and Palestine), 27–29, C15m

Holy Spirit (Spirit of God)
  biblical inspiration of, 99–101
  charismatic assemblies as filled with, 1861, 1907
  Christian community guidance in, 1664, 1665, 1773, 1957
  and creation, 123
  disciples and gifts of, 1765
  righteousness and, 1831

holy war, 292

homilies, 2001, 2005, 2059

homogenity, 405, 433, 463, 1473

honor, 34–35, 1933, 1957

hope
  early Christian messages of endurance through, 2005, 2025, 2041, 2042, 2043
  eschatological, 1511
  to exiles, 1063, 1066–1167, 1249, 1250, 1319, 1331, 1332
  faith as, 2005–6
  reconstruction of Temple, 1511
  restoration and salvation, 1167, 1444, 1453, 1471, 1479–80, 1504, 1505

horns, visions of, 1516

horses, visions of, 1516

Hosea (prophet), 393, 1159, 1429

Hosea, book of
  Genesis references in, 134
  historical context, 1427
  narrative summary, 1426–28
  outline and divisions, 1426, 1429
  prophet biography, 393, 1429
  prophet experience, 1159
  Song of Songs interpretation, 1054
  Son of God references, 64

symbolic acts, 1426
themes, 537, 1426, 1427, 1429
translation issues, 1429
wilderness tradition, 291, 1426
Hoshea, king of Israel, Northern Kingdom, 393, 1427
hospitality, 2067, 2068, 2070–71, 2072
Host of Heaven, 389
household codes, 1922, 1945, 1972, 1992, 2070–71
households of God, 1825, 1830
Huldah, 341
human relationships, 835
humans in creation, 123
hymns
  divine origin of Jesus Christ in, 66–68
  exaltation of Jesus, 1933, 1944–45, 1948, 1972, 1984, 1992
  as Psalms literary form, 885
hypocrisy, 1455, 1479, 1560, 1563

## I

I AM (title), 1764
"I belong to," 1858
*ichthys*, 74
identity
  of Christian church, 1945–46
  of Israelites, 33–34, 405, 473, 676, 677–78, 693
  of Jesus, 73–75, 1559, 1627, 1630, 1631, 2059, 2060, 2067, 2068
  liturgy and communal, 882
idolatry
  covenant laws against, 124, 199, 343, 344
  emperor worship as, 2083
  foreign alliances and international trade as, 1427
  foreign god worship as, 433
  God's honor and, 35
  as infidelity, 537, 1426–27
  prophetic messages on, 1159, 1166, 1331, 1332, 1345, 1505

punishments for, 345, 438, 1426–27
sacrificial meat eating practices as, 1859, 1861, 2083
weather and agricultural production promoting, 29
Ilgen, Karl David, 120
image of God, 123
immigrants, 122, 250
immortality, 1063
Inanna, 389
incarnation, 44–45, 1945, 2060, 2061, 2067, 2068
inclusive language, 93–95
inclusivity
  Christian church membership, 1564, 1662–63, 1721, 1722, 1776–77, 1997
  of discipleship, 1564, 1722
  of salvation, 72, 1909
incorruptibility, 1063
individualism, 33, 99
inerrancy, 100–101
*Infancy Gospel of Thomas*, 75
infidelity
  foreign policies as, 1427, 1429
  idolatry as, 537, 1426–27, 1428
  leadership failures as, 432, 434, 435, 537–39
  personifications of, 1426, 1429, 2083
*Instruction of Amen-em-ope, The*, 838, 993
*Instruction of Prince Hardjedef, The*, 838
*Instruction on the Historical Truth of the Gospels* (Pontifical Biblical Commission), 1552
intermarriage
  biblical examples, 130, 465, 693
  collectivist societies view on, 34
  Deuteronomy laws on, 694
  oracles challenging, 1533
  preserving identity and bans on, 399, 678, 693–94
  problems due to, 694
  Torah laws on, 693

interpretation. *See* biblical interpretation
"Interpretation of the Bible in the Church, The" (Pontifical Biblical Commission), 88
intertestamental books, 39, 47
interventions, miraculous, 395
intimacy, origins of, 129
Irenaeus of Lyon
  apocrypha rejections, 44
  biblical book citations and composition dating, 1771, 2026, 2028
  gnostic teachings by, 70
  Gospel authorship attributions, 1660, 1717
  Revelation composition dating theories, 2082
  rule of faith doctrine, 24
  "Scripture," term origins, 24
  Testament distinctions, 20
Isaac, 130, 390, C2 time line
Isaac, sacrifice of, 128, 2033
1 Isaiah (Proto-Isaiah), 1164, 1169
2 Isaiah (Deutero-Isaiah), 1157, 1164, 1169, 1555
3 Isaiah (Trito-Isaiah), 1157, 1164, 1169
Isaiah (prophet)
  biographical information, 21, 393, 1156, 1168
  in noncanonical texts, 22, 41–42, 44–45, 1403
  stories of kings featuring, 540
Isaiah, book of
  biblical interpretation affected by punctuation, 55
  call narrative comparisons, 1343, 1344
  composition, 21, 1166, 1168, 1169
  good news references in, 1553, 1555
  historical context, 1164–66, 1168–69
  historical periods and subdivisions, 1164
  intended audience, 1167
  Jesus Christ prophecies, 1722

future of, 346, 607–8, 639, 640, 676

geographic location, 559m, C11m, C12m

independence of, 536

Israel, Northern Kingdom relationship with, 536, 639–40, 641, 676

kings of, 392–93c, 639, C2–C3time line, C5time line

prophets of, 394c, 1156, C2–C4time line

Judaism

bibles of (see Hebrew Bible)

biblical interpretation comparisons, 54–60

Christianity separation from, 47, 51, 1908

conversion process, 462

festivals and feasts of, 1761c

Gentile attraction to, 1909, 1946

Gentile Christians and laws of, 1776, 1826, 1834

identity and definition, 806, 808

Jesus as fulfillment of Jewish tradition, 1720

Jesus movement as sect of, 1955

law of (see Torah)

marriage views, 1823

New Testament view of, 49

Roman destruction of Jerusalem impact on, 1717

sects of, first-century, 1908, 1955

spiritual ancestors of, 390–91c

term usage, 808

Judaizers, 1911, 1936

Judas Iscariot, 43, 1766

Judas Maccabees, 711, 773

Jude, Letter of, 1543, 2028, 2029–30, 2053, 2074–76

Jude (Judas) Thaddaeus, 1766

Judges, book of

Canaanites in, 292

canon comparisons and views of, 19

chronology, 435, C3time line

composition, 397

in Deuteronomistic History collection, 341

historical context, 432–33

literary structure, 432–33, 435

narrative summary, 402, 435

outline and divisions, 432, 435

themes, 433–34, 435

title origins, 432, 435

judgment day, 1444, 1453, 1467, 1503–5, 1534, 1564

*Judith*, 41

Judith, book of

canonical history, 39, 55, 396, 400, 732, 735

composition, 400, 732

Gentiles in, view of, 399–400

history of, 735

honor acquisition, 34

interbiblical references, 733, 735

Judith portraits in, 733–34

literary forms, 400, 711, 732–33

narrative summary, 711, 732

original manuscript translations, 116, 118

purpose, 711

sources for, 711

themes, 130, 733, 734

justice

laws regarding, 250

prophetic messages on social, 1452–53, 1455

themes of vengeance and, 1490–91

theodicy and questioning God's, 713, 843–44, 845, 1496–98, 1533–34

in wisdom literature, 1062

justification (righteousness), 834–35, 1563, 1830–31, 1833–34, 1908–9

Justin Martyr

apocrypha rejections, 44

divine power, term usage, 2051

early liturgical practices, 1860

Gospel dating and citation of, 1661

*gospel/euangelion*, word usage, 1554

Gospel writings, 43

Greek philosophy and Christian thought compatibility, 71

Jewish biblical interpretation, 48, 55

lectionary history, 78

Revelation authorship theories, 2081

# K

Kabbalah, 59

Kadesh, 319cap

Kenyon, Kathleen, 31

*kerygma*, 1552. See also good news

Keturah, 390

Kidron Valley tombs, 1610i

kingdom of God, 62, 1404, 1630, 1631

*King James Version*, 25, 93

King of the Jews, 1764

kings, 392–94c, 400, 680, C2–C5time line. See also names of specific kings

1 Kings

composition, 397

in Deuteronomistic History collection, 341

Greek translations and book division, 535

literary forms and techniques, 539

narrative summary, 402, 535–36

outline and divisions, 535, 540

themes and theology, 199, 434, 537, 539–40

2 Kings

composition, 397

in Deuteronomistic History collection, 341

Greek translations and book division, 535

law code discoveries, 341

literary forms, 539

narrative summary, 402, 536–38

outline and divisions, 535, 540

prophets in, 1471

themes and theology, 199, 434, 536, 537–38, 539–40

kinship, 37–38, 129, 130, 1063

*kippur*, 251

kissing, as early liturgical
practice, 1860
*Knesseth Yisra'el*, 993
knowledge of God, 1063
Koester, Helmut, 1932
Korah, 291

# L

"L" (Lukan/authorship source),
1551, 1661
Laban, 133, 390
Lachish (Judah), 1478, 1479
Lady (Woman) Wisdom, 82,
834, 840, 991–93, 994,
1063–64, 1092
Lake of Galilee/Gennesaret/
Kinneret, C6i
Lamb of God (title), 1764
lamentations, 885, 1249, 1331,
1443, 1472–73
Lamentations, book of, 1157,
1162, 1318–20
lampstands, visions of, 1517
land
    enemies contesting claims
        of, 433
    geography themes, 403, 405
    inheritance laws, 38, 463
    loss of, as punishment for
        disobedience, 433, 535
    natural barriers and
        boundary markers, C6cap
    promised (see Canaan)
    theology of, 344–45
    tribal allotments and
        territories, 403–4, C11m
language
    aphorisms and translations,
        62–63
    biblical interpretation
        comparisons, 56
    and dating, 677, 833
    inclusive, 93–95
    of suzerainty treaty forms,
        342–43
Laodiceans and Laodicea, 1946,
    1947, 2081
Latin Bible translations, 25
Latter Prophets, 396
law codes
    celebrations, 198
    Covenant Code, 122
    Decalogue (Ten
        Commandments), 122,
        198, 344

Deuteronomic Code, 341,
    342
Holiness Code, 122, 249,
    252
Priestly Code, 122
Ritual Decalogue, 122
laws. *See also* Torah
    cleanliness and holiness,
        249–52
    covenant and giving of,
        198–99
    development theories, 252
    festivals, 251
    land inheritance, 38, 463
    as literary form, 121
    in Numbers, 291
    Pentateuch themes of, 122
    priests, 251
    sacrifices, 250–51
    Sermon on the Mount on,
        1563
    slavery, 38
    types of, 122
lawsuits, 842
Lazarus, 1718, 1723
leadership
    centralized, 471
    charismatic models of, 433
    Christianity developments
        and transition of, 1772
    criticism of, 291, 400, 434,
        1479, 1559
    early Christian church
        succession, 1984, 1985
    early Christian expectations
        of, 1972, 1984, 1991
    gifts of, 1923
    God and, 433
    idolatry and, 537
    justice and, 1481
    models of, 405, 432, 435,
        1167
    shepherding analogies, 74,
        1518, C8cap
Leah, 390
lectio divina, 110–11
lectionary, 50, 77–83, 104
legal affairs, 1823
Leo XIII, 85
*Letter of Aristeas*, 21, 2051
Letter of Jeremiah, 42, 1331,
    1332
Letter of Tears, 1884, 1885,
    1886, 1887, 1993

Letters from Prison, 1944. *See
    also* Colossians; Ephesians;
    Philemon; Philippians
*Letter to Marcellinus*
    (Athanasius), 881
letter-writing conventions,
    1824
Levant (Holy Land), 27–29,
    C15m
Levi, 41, 391
Levi (Matthew), 1766
Leviathan, 844, 1473
levirate marriage, 463
Levites, 251, 291, 391
Leviticus, book of, 120, 198,
    249–53
*lex talionis*, 122
liberation, 124, 197–98
*Liber Psalmorum*, 116
life, as theme, 1038–39, 1040
*Life of Adam and Eve*, 40
*Life of Andrew* (Gregory of
    Tours), 46
light of the world, 1720, 1723
literalist interpretations, 88,
    105–6
literal sense of interpretation,
    88, 101, 105–6
literary criticism, 91
literary forms, as contextual
    interpretation component,
    108
liturgy
    biblical interpretation and,
        56, 103–4
    canon criteria and, 24, 103
    development of, 1855
    early Christian church
        development of, 1972–73
    role of Psalms in, 882, 886
Liturgy of the Word, 104
livelihoods, 29
loaves and fish, multiplication
    of, 1627–28, 1720, 1735i
locations, biblical, C6i
locusts, 1443, 1444
*Logos*, 71
*logos spermatikos*, 71–72
Lois, 1983
Lord (title), 1764
Lot, 129, 390, 463
*loudaioi*, 771–72
love
    commandments of, 250,
        1559, 1948, 2067, 2068

election and God's, 124,
1167, 1426, 1428
as factionalism remedy,
1857, 1922
faith as, 2032
marriage metaphors of
God's, 1054, 1426, 1429,
1719
universalistic outlook of
God's, 464, 465
loyalty, 462, 465, 1480
Lukan Travel Narrative, 1662,
1663
Luke, Gospel of
Acts comparisons, 1770,
1774–75
authorship theories and title
origins, 1553, 1660–61,
1666
biblical book combination
theories, 1660, 1661
canonical history, 43
composition, 1550–53,
1661, 1662, 1666
literary form, 1660
outline and divisions, 1660,
1666
prologue and historical
claims, 1663–64
prophetic literature
references, 1161
purpose, 1663, 1664, 1665,
1772
sources for, 1566, 1661–62,
1666
themes, 1660, 1661–62,
1664, 1665
Luke-Acts, 1660, 1661, 1770–71
Luther, Martin
apocrypha, 39, 42
Bible translations, 25
canonicity controversies,
396–97, 399, 400, 401
Chronicles title by, 607
faith with works
interpretations, 2032
justification by faith, 1828
on Revelation, 2079
Lutherans, 56
Lysimachus, 807

# M

"M" (Matthean/authorship
source), 1551, 1566

Maccabean revolt, 770–73,
806–7, 1761
1 Maccabees
canonical history, 39, 55,
396, 773
composition, 773
historical context, 770
Judean categories in, 772,
773
2 Maccabees comparisons,
773, 806, 807, 808
narrative summary, 401, 402,
771
original manuscript
translations, 116, 118
outline and divisions, 770,
773
purpose, 401, 771
setting, 401
themes, 770, 771, 773
title origins, 773
2 Maccabees
canonical history, 39, 55,
396, 773
composition, 401, 809
historical context, 770, 806
1 Maccabees comparisons,
773, 806, 807, 808
narrative summary, 401, 402,
807
original manuscript
translations, 116, 118
outline and divisions, 806,
809
purpose, 401, 809
themes, 770, 806–9
3 Maccabees, 39, 42, 401
4 Maccabees, 39, 42, 401
maiorem, 2001
Major Prophets, 1155, 1162
Malachi, book of, 1157,
1532–35
Man and His God, 838
Manasseh, king of Judah,
41–42, 394, 537, 539, 639
Manesseh, tribe of, C11m
man measuring Jerusalem
(vision), 1516
manna, 1720, 1723
Marcion, 23, 48, 1660, 2081
Marduk, 389
Mark, Gospel of
authorship and title origins,
1553, 1626–27, 1631,
1632

canonical history, 43
composition, 1550–53,
1566, 1626, 1631–32
gospel/euangelion, word usage,
1554, 1555
literary form and influences,
1550
literary structure, 1631
narrative summary, 1630
outline and divisions, 1626,
1632
Son of Man references, 64
as source, 1557, 1566,
1661–62, 1666, 1772
themes, 1627–29, 1630,
1631
translation, 1543
Markean Priority, 1661, 1771
marriage. See also intermarriage
Christ and Church analogies,
1429, 1922, 1923
Christian conversion within,
2042
covenant relationship
analogies, 1054, 1426,
1429, 1719
cultural practices of, 130
didactic themes of perfect,
714
early Christian restrictions
on, 1823, 1859, 1861,
1887
honor codes and, 35
levirate, 463
and sexuality, 1054
slavery laws and, 38
of widows in early Christian
church, 1972
Martha of Bethany, 1767
martyrdom, 42, 809, 2042,
2084, 2085
Martyrdom and Ascension of
Isaiah, 22
Martyrdom of Isaiah, 42
Martyrdom of Matthew, 45
Mary Magdalene, 43, 1767
Mary of Nazareth, Mother of
God
as disciple model, 1719
as disciple of Jesus, 1767
inclusivity dialogue at
crucifixion, 1722
noncanonical texts about,
43, 44, 45, 1554
in Qu'ran, 75

wilderness experience and complaints of, 291
Mount of Olives, 1710i
Mount Sinai (Mount Horeb), 120, 198, 224i, 342, 1719, C6i
Mount Tabor, 1687i
Mount Zion, 771
Muratorian Canon (Fragment), 24, 45, 2029
Murphy, Roland, 837
"my father's house," 1721
mystery, 844, 1631, 1923
myths, as literary form, 121, 129, 132–33

## N

Nabonidus, king of Babylon, 1467
Naboth's vineyard, 537
Nadab, king of Israel, Northern Kingdom, 392
Nag Hammadi Codices, 44, 45, 70–71
Nahum, book of, 116, 394, 463, 1156–57, 1490–92
name symbolism, 121, 714, 1426, 1474, 1557
Naomi, 462
Naphtali, 391
Naphtali, tribe of, C11m
Nathan, 471, 1156
nationhood, 129–30, 132, 133, 199–200, 201, 404, 405
nations
geographic location of, C10m
oracles against, 463, 1452, 1455, 1490–92, 1504
punishment of, 1444
nature, power over, 395, 1765
Nazorean, the (title), 1722
Nebuchadnezzar, king of Babylon
conquest of Judah, 537–38, 711, 1248, 1251, 1342, 1345
dream representations of, 1402
exile of Jews, 538, 1165
as historical context of Judith, 537–38, 732
Jerusalem invasion and destruction, 394, 1165, 1251, 1318

worship of king, 400
Negeb (Negev), C6i
Nehemiah, book of, 398, 399, 402, 676, 679, 692–95
Nero, emperor of Roman Empire, 1762, 1822, 1825, 2082
Nerva, emperor of Roman Empire, 1763
*New American Bible* (NAB)
Acts of the Apostles, 1776–77
Amos, 1455
Baruch, 1332
biblical novellas, 711
1 Chronicles, 609
2 Chronicles, 641
Colossians, 1948–49
1 Corinthians, 1861–62
2 Corinthians, 1889–90
Daniel, 1404
Deuteronomy, 346
Ecclesiastes, 1040
Esther, 756–57
Exodus, 201
Ezekiel, 1345
Ezra, 679
Galatians, 1911–12
Genesis, 132–34
Gospels, 1555
Habakkuk, 1498
Haggai, 1512
historical books, 402
Hosea, 1429
Isaiah, 1168–69
James, 2034–35
Jeremiah, 1251
Job, 845
Joel, 1445
1 John, 2061
2 John, 2068
3 John, 2072
Jonah, 1474
Joshua, 407
Jude, 2076
Judges, 435
Judith, 735
Kings, 539–40
Lamentations, 1320
Letter to the Hebrews, 2005–6
Leviticus, 253
Luke, 1665–66
1 Maccabees, 773
2 Maccabees, 809

Malachi, 1535
Mark, 1630–32
Matthew, 1562–66
Micah, 1481
Nahum, 1492
Nehemiah, 695
New Testament Letters, 1827
New Testament preface, 1543–44
Numbers, 294
Obadiah, 1468
Old Testament preface, 115–16
Pentateuch, 125–27
1 Peter, 2043–44
2 Peter, 2053–54
Philemon, 1998
Philippians, 1936–37
Prophetic Books, 1162–63
Proverbs, 995–96
Psalms, 885–86
Revelation, 2084–85
Romans, 1833–34
Ruth, 465
Samuel, 473
1 Thessalonians, 1958
2 Thessalonians, 1966
1 Timothy, 1974–75
2 Timothy, 1985
Titus, 1993
Tobit, 715–16
translation history, 26
Wisdom, 1065
Wisdom Books, 840–41
Zechariah, 1519
Zephaniah, 1505
*New American Bible Revised Edition* (NABRE)
Catholic Letters introduction, 2031
deuterocanonical books in, 39, 47
New Testament preface, 1545–48
Old Testament preface, 117–18
translation history, 26
translation method for, 93
*New International Version*, 26
New Testament, overview
archaeology and historical accuracy of, 30
canon formation, 19, 23–25, 102
composition, 47

marriage instructions and, 1823, 1859, 1861, 1887

perception and expectation of, 1934, 1955–56, 1966

postponement of, 1661–62, 1665

prediction timing as dating evidence, 1661–62, 2053

Revelation theme of, 2084

term origin and usage, 1956

Passion, 50–52, 1565, 1628, 1631, 1721–22. *See also* death of Jesus Christ

Passover (Unleavened Bread), Feast of

animal sacrifices, C8cap

celebrations in Joshua, 403

Gospel references and Jewish tradition, 1720

legal codes for, 198, 251

significance and biblical references, 1761

Pastoral Epistles, 1825, 1827, 1970–75, 1982–85, 1990–93

Patmos (Greece), 2080, 2087i

patriarchs, 120, 129, 131, 390–91c

patriarchy, 37, 130

patronage, 37

Patterson, Orlando, 1933, 1996

Pauline Letters, overview.

*See also* Colossians; 1 Corinthians; 2 Corinthians; Ephesians; Galatians; Letter to the Hebrews; Philemon, Letter to; Philippians; Romans, Letter to the; 1 Thessalonians; 2 Thessalonians; 1 Timothy; 2 Timothy; Titus

authorship, 1821–22, 1824–25, 1827

canonical history, 24, 43, 47

canonical order, 1821, 1827

categories of, 1827

collectivist attitudes toward out-groups, 34

composition and dating, 1555, 1825, 1955

content summaries, 1826

description, 1827

epistolary writing style of, 1824

*gospel/euangelion*, first Christian literature usage, 1554, 1555

Habakkuk verse references, 1497

Holy Spirit as biblical inspiration, 99

Jesus as Son of God, 65–66

letter-delivery methods, 1824

letter-writing conventions and style, 1824, 1827, 1956

purpose, 1956

religious marketplace and, 1822–23

Sinai metaphors of, C6cap

social context of, 1823–24

Son of Man references, 66

as source, 1771–72

typological comparisons of Jesus, 69

vocabulary development and usage, 1955–56

Paul (Saul) of Tarsus

ancestry of, 391

apostleship descriptions, 1859, 1886–87, 1888

arrest of, 1829, 1833

biographical information, 1776, 1821–22, 1856, 1936

call narrative, 1908, 1911

goal of, 1996

on immorality, 1823

imprisonment, 1933, 1936–37, 1944, 1947, 1948, 1985

Luke as associate of, 1660, 1663, 1946

Mark as associate of, 1631, 1946

ministerial inclusion of women, 1663

as miracle-worker, 62, 1776

missionary journeys of, 1796m, 1817m, 1958, 1971

noncanonical texts associated with, 43–44, 45, 1822

reception to mission of, 1776

on second coming, 1823

second coming predictions and death of, 1662

self-identification, 1885

treatment by Jews, 1773

Paul VI, 26, 79

*Pax Romana*, 1955–56

peasants, as social class, 36

Pekah, king of Israel, Northern Kingdom, 393, 1165

Pekahiah, king of Israel, Northern Kingdom, 393

Pentateuch

composition, 20, 120–21, 126, 127

contents summary, 125

history of biblical formation and, 20, 119

literary forms of, 119, 121–22, 125

reading strategies, 126–27

themes within, 122–23

theologies of, 123–24

title and books of, 119–20, 125–26

Pentecost (Feast of Weeks/ Shavuot), 165, 251, 462, 1444, 1445, 1761

Pergamum (Asia Minor), 2081

Persia (Persian Empire)

biblical books with setting in, 400, 753, 754

geographic location, C10m

Jewish autonomy and restoration, 398–99, 676–77, 692, 695, 1432

kings of, list, 680

*pesher*, 59–60

1 Peter, 24, 1543, 2026–27, 2031, 2034, 2041–44

2 Peter, 294, 1543, 2027–28, 2051–54

Peter (Simon Peter, Cephas)

Antioch Incident, 1772

Aramaic name for, 1821

betrayal of, 1628

biographical information, 1776

as church leader, 99, 1564

death of, 2026, 2027, 2043

as disciple of Jesus, 99, 1766

Jesus' identity, 1559, 1630

leadership commissions and shepherding metaphors, C8cap

letter authorship theories, 2043–44, 2053

historical books of, 397
Protestant Reformation, 396
Protestants, 58, 396
*Protoevangelium of James*, 24, 44, 58
Proto-Isaiah, 1164, 1169
Proto-Zechariah, 1516–18
Proverbs, book of
  character of, 840
  composition and editing, 833–34, 990–91, 995
  contents summary, 990, 991–94, 995
  Genesis references in, 134
  intended audience, 996
  literary context, 836
  literary forms, 837, 991
  literary structure, 991
  modern role of, 995–96
  original manuscript translations, 116
  outline and divisions, 990, 996
  purpose, 991, 995
  as source, 1091
  sources for, 838, 993
  universalistic outlooks in, 834
proverbs, definition, 991
*Providentissimus Deus* (Leo XIII), 85
*Psalm 151*, 39, 42
Psalms, book of, 64, 116, 129, 840, 881–86
*Psalms of Solomon*, 42
pseudepigrapha
  definition, 39
  New Testament canon and theories of, 1947, 1963–65, 1966, 1970, 2053, 2076
  Old Testament, 39–43
*Pseudo Philo*, 41
Pseudo-Solomon, 1062
Ptolemy Empire, 770
Ptolemy II Philadelphus, king of Egypt, 21
Puah, 123
punctuation, and biblical interpretation, 55
purification, 249–50, 252, 292
Purim, 711, 753, 756, 1761

# Q

Q (authorship source), 1551, 1557, 1566, 1661, 1662, 1772
*qal vahomer*, 59
*Qinah*, 1320
Qoheleth. *See* Ecclesiastes
Quirinius, 1762
Qumran
  Chronicles copies at, 640
  discoveries assisting in biblical interpretation, 55
  interpretation strategies associated with finding at, 59–60
  Jeremiah copies at, 1248
  noncanonical texts associated with texts found at, 42
  Old Testament canonization evidence, 22
  original biblical manuscripts from, 115–16, 118
  Tobit copies at, 399, 715
Qu'ran, 75–76

# R

Rabbinic Judaism, 1908, 1955
Rabbi/Rabbouni (title), 1764
Rachel, 133, 390
racism, 756
Rad, Gerhard von, 20
rape, 471–72, 1491
Raphael, 399
reader interpretation methods, 109–11
reason, 71–72, 108
Rebekah, 41, 123, 130, 390, C2time line
rebellion against God, 120, 291–92, 293
reciprocity, 37
recommendations, letters of, 1886, 1887
reconciliation, 123, 1923
redaction criticism, 90, 92
*regula fidei* doctrine, 24
Rehoboam, king of Judah, 392, 535–36
rejection of Jesus Christ, 1564, 1630, 1719
religious continuity, 676

remembering, theologies of, 124
Rendtorff, Rolf, 121
repentance, 251, 1249, 1443, 1444, 1516, 1533
resistance literature, 1934–35, 2084
restitution, 251
Restoration Period
  historical context, 1165–66
  hope, themes of, 1167, 1444, 1453, 1471, 1479–80, 1504, 1505
  Jerusalem conditions during, 1510
  political and administrative restoration, 692–93, 695
  prophetic activity during, 1157, 1166
  prophetic messages, 1343, 1345, 1467
  religious restoration, 398–99, 676–77
  Temple reconstruction, 399, 676–77, 679, 1157, 1166, 1343, 1344, 1345, 1510–12, 1519
Resurrection
  christology developments based on, 1923, 1945
  distinctiveness of Jesus, 67
  Gospel accounts, 1565, 1631
  Jonah's fish symbolism and, 1473
  tombs and, 1659cap
  and universal resurrection, 1859–60, 1861, 1923
  as validation, 1933
resurrection
  of the dead, early church beliefs of, 1859–60, 1861, 1957
  through faith, 1945
retainers, as social class, 36
retribution, divine. *See also* destruction; suffering
  abandonment as punishment, 1532–34
  blessings for obedience, 297, 346
  complexity and confusion of, 835–36, 843, 1038
  day of the Lord as, 1444, 1453, 1467, 1503–5, 1534

preparation themes, 290, 291, 292, 403

Roman conquests, 1557, 1559, 1626, 1717, 1955, 2082

violence themes, 405–6, 434

warrior roles of God, 292, 405–6, 1160, 1490–91, 1492, 1518

war spoils and laws, 292, 404, 406, 407, C9i

*wasf*, 1051

water, power over, 395, 1765, C6cap

Way, the, 47, 1772

weather, 27, 29

weddings, 1718–20, 1723

Weeks, Feast of. *See* Pentecost

Wellhausen, Julius, 20, 85, 121, 130

we-passages, 1660, 1770, 1771

Wheeler-Kenyon excavation method, 31

widows, 38, 122, 462–65, 1972, 2032

wilderness experience, 291–92, 319cap

wine, 1719, C7i

Wisdom, book of, 39, 833–34, 835, 836, 990, 1062–65

wisdom in crisis, 835–36

Wisdom literature, overview, 833–41, 2034

Wisdom of Ben Sira. *See* Ben Sira

Wisdom of God, 1331, 1332, 1858

Wisdom of Solomon, 39, 833–34, 835, 836, 990, 1062–65

woe oracles, 1249, 1451, 1453, 1479, 1497, 1504, 1510

"woman of worth," 994

woman sinner, the unnamed, 1767

Woman (Lady) Wisdom, 82, 834, 840, 991–93, 994, 1063–64, 1092

women

as disciples of Jesus, 1767c

disparagement of, 1092–93

early church marriage roles and metaphors, 1923

early church membership, 1662–63, 1724, 1773, 1823–23

early church roles, 82–83, 1663, 1823–24, 1972

early church worship and conduct of, 82–83, 1822

Gospels favored by, 1660

honor cultures and roles of, 35

Israelite society and roles of, 130

Jesus Christ and, 73

lectionary omissions, 81–83

male leadership commentary and victory of, 400

pseudepigraphical texts focusing on, 40

Roman society and roles of, 1823–24

savior characters, 400, 733–34, 755

and Scripture study, 54

suffering of Christian wives, advice for, 2042

widows, 38, 122, 464, 1972, 2032

Word of God

community of, 99

early Christian community development and, 1777

hymns indicating divine Jesus and, 67

Jesus identification with, 71

as prophetic message, 1159, 1249, 1342–43

as title of Jesus, 1764

worship as living context of, 103–4

wordplay, 836

*Words of Ahiqar, The,* 838

works (actions), 2032–33, 2060

World Catholic Biblical Federation, 26

worship

centralization of, 343–44, 346, 398, 536, 538, 540, 607–9, 641

church view of, 103–4

early church and women's conduct in, 82–83, 1822, 1823

laws of proper, 199, 200

as prophetic message, 1452

theology of, 124

Writings, 396

Wycliffe, John, 25

# X

Xerxes, king of Persia, 711, 754, 756

# Y

Yahweh, 84, 130. *See also* God

Yahwism, 537

Yahwist (J)

biblical criticism and identification of, 85

Exodus authorship, 196–97

Genesis authorship, 130–31, 132

Numbers authorship, 290

Pentateuch authorship, 20, 120, 121, 123, 124, 126

Yehud (Judah), 677–78

*Yerushalmi*, 57

*Yeshua* (Joshua), 69, 1664, 1764

Yom Kippur (Day of Atonement), 251, 1761, 2002

# Z

Zebulun, 391

Zebulun, tribe of, C11m

1 Zechariah (Proto-Zechariah), 1516–18

2 Zechariah (Deutero-Zechariah), 1518

3 Zechariah (Trito-Zechariah), 1516

Zechariah, book of

composition, 1519

contents summary, 1516–19

historical context, 1157, 1516

Jesus Christ prophesies, 1722, C8cap

Jude references to, 2075

original manuscript translations, 116

prophet biography, 1516

Second Temple rebuilding, 677, 1510

themes, 1519

# Additional Study Aids

# Time Line of Biblical History

The history of the Israelite tribes begins in the Late Bronze Age with the settlement of the central highlands in the southern Levant. The Merneptah stele indicates that there was a socioethnic group called "Yasir'il" (Israel) in that region around 1230–1205 BCE. Thus, an "historical timeline" for Israel can begin with the 13th century BCE. The first truly datable event in the history of Israel is the fall of Jerusalem in the 6th century. *Any dates assigned to figures or events prior to that time are approximate.*

| PREHISTORY | 2000 BCE | 1900 BCE | 1800 BCE | 1700 BCE |
|---|---|---|---|---|

Jacob's descendants settle in Egypt. (1750)

Abraham and Sarah arrive in Canaan. (1850)

### FOUNDATION FIGURES

Adam and Eve
Cain and Abel
Noah

### SPIRITUAL ANCESTORS OF THE MONOTHEISTIC FAITHS

Abraham and Sarah
Isaac and Rebekah
Jacob, Leah, and Rachel
Joseph and Asenath

## Prophets of Israel and Judah (*All Dates are BCE*)

| Ahijah (10th cen.) | Shemaiah Jehu (10th cen.) | Eliezer (9th cen.) | Elijah (9th cen.) | Micaiah, son of Imlah (9th cen.) | Zedekiah (9th cen.) | Elisha (9th cen.) | Amos (8th cen.) | Jonah (8th cen.) |
|---|---|---|---|---|---|---|---|---|

## Kings of Judah (*All Dates are BCE*)

| Rehoboam (931–913) | Abijam (Abijah) (913–911) | Asa (911–870) | Jehoshaphat (870–848) | Jehoram (Joram) (848–841) | Ahaziah (841) |
|---|---|---|---|---|---|

## Kings of Israel (*All Dates are BCE*)

| Jeroboam (931–910) | Nadab (910–909) | Baasha (909–886) | Elah (886–885) | Zimri (885) | Omri (885–874) | Ahab (875–854) |
|---|---|---|---|---|---|---|

## A Few Key Dates in Human History

- ca. 3800 BCE—City-states and river-valley civilizations begin with Bronze Age.
- ca. 3000 BCE—First pharaohs rule Egypt. Hieroglyphic writing is invented.
- ca. 2500 BCE—Great pyramids are built.
- ca. 1792 BCE—Hammurabi develops code of law in Babylon.
- ca. 1550 BCE—Canaanites invent alphabet.

- ca. 563 BCE—Buddha is born in India.
- ca. 551 BCE—Confucius is born in China.
- 500 to 300 BCE—Height of golden age of Greece.
- 43 BCE—Roman Empire is established.
- 476 CE—Roman Empire falls.
- 622 CE—Muhammad founds Islam in Arabia.

| 1600 BCE | 1500 BCE | 1400 BCE | 1300 BCE | 1200 BCE | 1100 BCE |
|---|---|---|---|---|---|

Judges lead Israelite tribes in Canaan. (1200)

Moses leads Exodus from Egypt. (1290)

Joshua invades Canaan. (1250)

**TIME IN EGYPT AND THE EXODUS**

Important Biblical Figures
Moses
Aaron
Miriam

**TIME OF THE JUDGES**

Important Biblical Figures
Deborah
Gideon
Samson
Samuel

| Hosea (8th cen.) | Isaiah of Jerusalem (8th cen.) | Micah (8th cen.) | Nahum (7th cen.) | Zephaniah (6th cen.) | Jeremiah (7th–6th cen.) | Uriah (7th cen.) | Hananiah (6th cen.) | Ezekiel (6th cen.) |
|---|---|---|---|---|---|---|---|---|

| Athaliah (841–835) | Joash (Jehoash) (835–796) | Amaziah (796–767) | Azariah (Uzziah) (767–740) | Jotham (740–732) | Ahaz (732–716) |
|---|---|---|---|---|---|

| Ahaziah (853–852) | Jehoram (Joram) (852–841) | Jehu (841–814) | Jehoahaz (814–798) | Jehoash (Joash) (798–782) | Jeroboam II (782–753) |
|---|---|---|---|---|---|

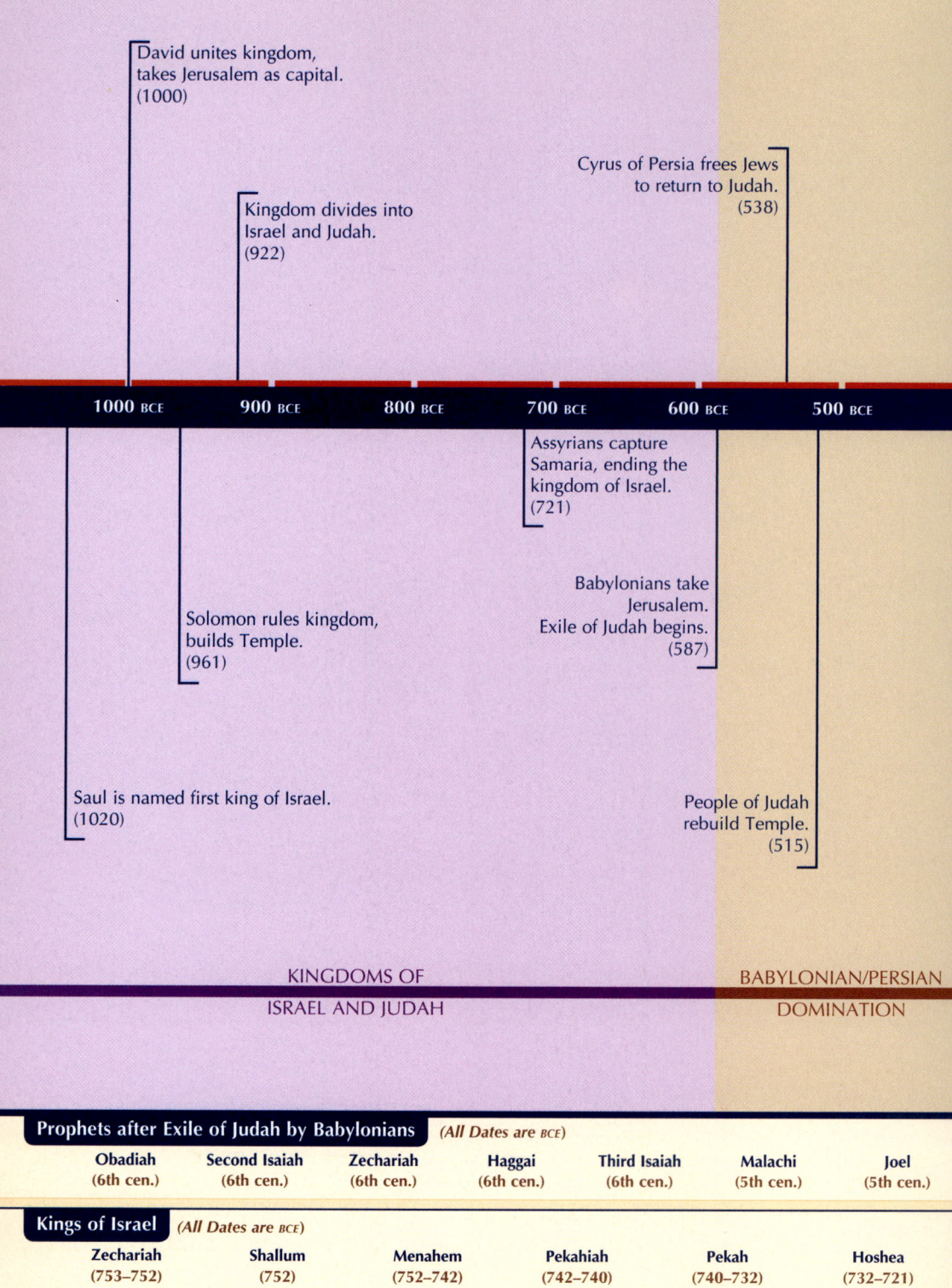

David unites kingdom, takes Jerusalem as capital. (1000)

Kingdom divides into Israel and Judah. (922)

Cyrus of Persia frees Jews to return to Judah. (538)

| 1000 BCE | 900 BCE | 800 BCE | 700 BCE | 600 BCE | 500 BCE |

Assyrians capture Samaria, ending the kingdom of Israel. (721)

Babylonians take Jerusalem. Exile of Judah begins. (587)

Solomon rules kingdom, builds Temple. (961)

Saul is named first king of Israel. (1020)

People of Judah rebuild Temple. (515)

KINGDOMS OF
ISRAEL AND JUDAH

BABYLONIAN/PERSIAN
DOMINATION

| Prophets after Exile of Judah by Babylonians | *(All Dates are BCE)* | | | | | |
|---|---|---|---|---|---|---|
| Obadiah (6th cen.) | Second Isaiah (6th cen.) | Zechariah (6th cen.) | Haggai (6th cen.) | Third Isaiah (6th cen.) | Malachi (5th cen.) | Joel (5th cen.) |

| Kings of Israel | *(All Dates are BCE)* | | | | |
|---|---|---|---|---|---|
| Zechariah (753–752) | Shallum (752) | Menahem (752–742) | Pekahiah (742–740) | Pekah (740–732) | Hoshea (732–721) |

Pontius Pilate is
Prefect of Judea.
(26–36)

The Jewish
revolt ends in
destruction of
Jerusalem and
Temple by
Romans.
(70)

Herod the Great dies, Herod Antipas
rules Galilee and Perea (the "Herod"
of Jesus' ministry). (4)

Greeks conquer
Holy Land.
(333)

Herod rules as
King of the Jews.
(37–4)

Saul the Pharisee
becomes Paul the
Apostle of Jesus. (31)

Temple is
rededicated.
(165)

Herod is named
tetrarch of Galilee.
(40)

| 400 BCE | 300 BCE | 200 BCE | 100 BCE | 0 | 100 CE |

Romans
conquer
Holy Land.
(63)

Jesus is
crucified.
(30)

Revolt against Greeks
by Maccabees begins.
(166)

Jesus is
born.
(5 BCE)

Ezra brings Torah
to Jerusalem.
(398) *

Simon establishes
Hasmonean
dynasty. (142)

Gospels and
other New
Testament
books are
written.
(80s and 90s)

Paul writes 1 Thessalonians,
Galatians, Philippians,
Philemon, 1-2 Corinthians,
Romans. (51–58)

Nehemiah becomes
governor of Judah,
starts renewal.
(445) *

James is martyred. (61)

Domitian
persecutes
Christians.
(95)

* There is no consensus about the
precise dating of the missions of Ezra and
Nehemiah, or whether Ezra preceded
Nehemiah or vice versa.

Peter and Paul are
martyred in Rome under
Nero. (64–68)

GREEK

HASMONEAN

ROMAN

DOMINATION

DYNASTY
(Free From Foreign
Domination)

DOMINATION

| Kings of Judah: Post-Destruction of Israel | | | | (All Dates are BCE) | | | |
|---|---|---|---|---|---|---|---|
| Hezekiah (716–687) | Manasseh (687–642) | Amon (642–640) | Josiah (640–608) | Jehoahaz (608) | Jehoiakim (609–597) | Jehoiachin (Jeconiah) (597) | Zedekiah (Mattaniah) (597–586) |

# Biblical Places

© leospek / Shutterstock.com

© Daniel Blatt

**Negeb:** Negeb (or Negev) means "south." Rolling, open plains and dramatic canyons, the Negeb is the area between Judah and the Red Sea (Jos 15:1) where Abraham and his family journeyed (Gn 20:1). Winter rains would cause its dry riverbeds to overflow (Ps 126:4). Prophetic oracles often recalled its inhabitants (Jer 13:19; Ob 19–20; Zec 7:7). Beer-sheba was its principal city (2 Sm 3:10).

**Sinai:** In Exodus, the revelation of God takes place on Sinai (Mount Horeb), possibly located in a range in the Sinai peninsula. Here Moses encounters the burning bush (Ex 3) and later receives the ten commandments (Ex 20:1–17) and other revelation. Here Elijah flees Jezebel and encounters God in the "light silent sound" (1 Kgs 19:8–12). In a complex metaphor, Paul sees Sinai as representing bondage to the law (Gal 4:24–26).

© Daniel Blatt

© Zev Radovan

**River Jordan:** Long a natural boundary (e.g., Is 8:23; Ez 47:18) and still so today, the River Jordan is fed by springs on Mount Hermon, flows through upper Galilee, enters the Lake of Galilee from the north, flows out from the lake's southern end, travels down the Jordan Valley and into the Dead Sea. Crossing the Jordan signals entry into the promised land (Dt 2:29), a line Moses may not cross (Dt 3:25–28). The Jordan is the place of John the Baptist's activity and where Jesus is baptized (Mt 3:13, Mk 1:5, 9; Lk 3:21).

**Lake of Galilee:** The Lake or Sea of Galilee, also called Sea of Chinnereth (Jos 12:3), Lake of Gennesaret (Lk 5:1), Sea of Tiberias (Jn 6:1; 21:1), or, today, Lake Kinneret, is located in northern Israel. The OT mentions it as a boundary marker (Nm 34:11; Jos 12:3; 13:27), but it is best known for Jesus' ministry on its shores. Here he calls his first disciples (Mt 4:18–22; Mk 1:16–20; Lk 5:1–11), preaches from a boat (Mk 4:1), calms a storm (Mt 8:23–27), walks on water (Mt 14:22–34), and encounters his disciples after the Resurrection (Jn 21:1).

# Biblical Plants

© Anselm Academic / Brian Singer-Towns

© Daniel Blatt

**Grapes:** Grapes were cultivated mainly to produce wine, which gladdens the heart (Ps 104:15). The nation Israel was sometimes portrayed as a vineyard or a choice vine (Ps 80:9–17; Is 5:1–7). Jesus drew on this imagery to compare himself to the best vine that gives life through its branches (Jn 15:1–8).

**Figs:** The vision of peace and security is to sit under one's own vine and fig tree (1 Mc 14:12; Mi 4:4). The fig is one of the few deciduous trees native to the Holy Land, so that its putting forth new leaves is a sign of approaching summer (Mt 24:32; Mk 13:28). The barren fig tree, which Jesus cursed, symbolizes lack of faith (Mt 21:19–22; Mk 11:12–14, 20–24).

© Carolyn Osiek, RSCJ

© Photobac / Shutterstock.com

**Olives:** Because the olive tree grows slowly, requiring several years before it produces fruit, it symbolizes stability and promise. Its fruit gives food, fuel, lubricant, and is used for medicinal purposes. It is the plant that first grows after the great flood (Gn 8:11), a metaphor for strength and greatness (Sir 50:10) and for happy family life (Ps 128:3). To bring about conversion, God punishes the unfaithful by blighting vines, figs, and olives (Am 4:9).

**Pomegranates:** The pomegranate with its many seeds is symbolic of fertility and a long and fruitful life. Spiced wine and pomegranate juice are luxurious drinks (Sg 8:2). Grain, wine, olive oil, figs, and pomegranates are offered as gifts to the Levites in the Temple (Tb 1:7), and are among the staples of fruitfulness in the land (Dt 8:8).

# Biblical Animals

© Daniel Blatt

© Zev Radovan

**Donkeys:** The patient donkey, or ass, was the main beast of burden in biblical times, carrying both baggage and people across dry and rocky terrain. Balaam had a talking donkey who could see an angel on the path that her rider could not (Nm 22:21–35). The prophecy of Zechariah (9:9) paved the way for the evangelists' description of Jesus' triumphant entry into Jerusalem astride a donkey (Mk 11:1–11).

**Sheep:** Pliable and obedient, sheep were a favorite herd animal for meat and milk. The nation of Israel is often referred to as sheep and their leaders as shepherds (Nm 27:17; 2 Sm 24:17; Ps 44:12; Mt 10:6). Jesus characterizes himself as the good shepherd who takes care of the sheep (Jn 10:11–16) and continues the metaphor of shepherding for leadership in his commissioning of Peter (Jn 21:15–17).

© Zev Radovan

© Zev Radovan

**Goats:** Goats, along with sheep, were raised for milk and meat; unlike sheep, goats are inquisitive, resilient, and stubborn. The Passover lamb could be either a young sheep or goat (Ex 12:5). A goat was sacrificed in the annual sacrifice for sin (Lv 16:20–22). In Matthew's parable of the last judgment, goats play the role of those who refuse to receive the needy, and thereby refuse to receive Jesus (Mt 25:32–33).

**Oxen:** Oxen were important: they did the heavy work of plowing and pulling wagons (1 Sm 11:5; 1 Kgs 19:19–21), and were used for major sacrifice as well (2 Sm 24:22). One might even rescue oxen on the sabbath (Lk 14:5). Plowers must not muzzle oxen, so that they could snack as they worked (Dt 25:4), a precept later used to justify material support of pastoral workers (1 Cor 9:9; 1 Tm 5:18).

# Biblical Sites and Artifacts

© Carolyn Osiek, RSCJ

© Daniel Blatt

**Tomb of the Patriarchs:** When Sarah dies at Kiriath-arba near Hebron, according to Genesis, Abraham needs to acquire a burial plot that will be on his own land. He purchases a cave in the field of Machpelah (Gn 23), negotiating the purchase with the resident Hittites. In the first century BCE, Herod the Great builds a monumental shrine over the traditional site, constructing its walls to replicate the renovated Temple Mount. They still stand today.

**Horned Altar:** Exact instructions were given for building the horned altar in wood (Ex 27:2; 38:2), but the shape was also copied in stone. The horns of the altar in the Tabernacle and later the Temple seem to have been a place of refuge for someone whose life was threatened (1 Kgs 1:50–51). The horns symbolized the altar and the Temple itself for pilgrims (Ps 118:27) and their destruction meant the destruction of the people (Am 3:14).

© W Wittman, Ltd

© Carolyn Osiek, RSCJ

**Menorah:** Exodus elaborately instructs fashioning the seven-branched lampstand from pure gold, with oil lamps (Ex 25:31–37; 37:17–24) to burn constantly with pure olive oil. It was thrice replaced, the third time after the armies of Antiochus carried it off from the Second Temple, ca. 165 BCE (1 Mc 1:21; 4:49). The final version became Roman spoil in 70 CE when the Romans destroyed the Temple and carted the lampstand off to Rome, a scene depicted here on the Arch of Titus in the Roman Forum. Recent study reveals that this menorah was originally covered with gold paint.

**Bethesda Pools:** In the Hellenistic period, two huge rectangular pools, shown here in a model of Jerusalem, were installed north of the Temple Mount to provide water for the Temple, in a region already full of springs thought to have healing properties. By the time of Jesus, the pools no longer served the Temple, but were still filled with water and surrounded by smaller pools, fed by springs. The paralytic is healed at a pool near the Sheep Gate named Bethesda, perhaps meaning "house of mercy" (Jn 5:2–9).

# MAP 1

LUD
(LYDIA)

JAVAN
(GREEKS)

GOMER

TOGARMAH

HITTITES

ASHKENAZ
(SCYTHIANS)

MADAI
(MEDES)

Caspian
Sea

ELAM
(PERSIA)

Persian
Gulf

ARPHAXAD

Ur.

ASSHUR
(ASSYRIA)

River Tigris

River Euphrates

Babylon.

Mari.

PADDAN-ARAM
Haran.

ARAM
(SYRIA)

Damascus.

AMORITES

Penuel.
CANAAN
Shechem.
Hebron.
Beer-sheba.

PHILISTINES

Gaza.

KITTIM
(CYPRUS)

The Great Sea
(Mediterranean Sea)

Red Sea

JOKTAN
(ARABIA)

Zoan.
On.

MIZRAIM
(EGYPT)

River Nile

PUT

Map 1:
THE TABLE OF NATIONS

JAVAN Descendants of Japheth (Gn 10:2–5)
PUT Descendants of Ham (Gn 10:6–20)
LUD Descendants of Shem (Gn 10:21–31)
(Egypt) Later biblical name

0      100      200 miles
0    100   200 kilometers

C10

MAP 2

Map 2:
THE TRIBAL TERRITORIES
© 2013 ANSELM ACADEMIC

0    20    40 miles
0    20    40 kilometers

Mt. Hermon

DAN

Tyre

ASHER

Hazor

NAPHTALI

Geshur

Lake of
Galilee

The Great Sea
(Mediterranean Sea)

ZEBULUN

Megiddo

ISSACHAR

Hepher

MANESSEH

GAD

Jordan River

Jabbok River

Aphek

EPHRAIM

Bethel

DAN

Gezer

BENJAMIN

Jericho

Jerusalem

Pisgah Peak

JUDAH

REUBEN

Lachish

Hebron

Judean Desert

Salt
Sea
(Dead
Sea)

Arnon River

SIMEON

The Negev

Mt. Halak

The Jordan Valley

Mt. Seir

# MAP 3

Map 3:
## THE KINGDOM YEARS

Probable extent of Israelite control during the kingdom of Solomon, ca. 950 BCE

The kingdoms of Israel and Judah, ca. 860 BCE

- - - - Boundary between Israel and Judah

? Exact location questionable

© 2013 ANSELM ACADEMIC

Riblah

ZOBAH

Byblos

Mt. Lebanon

Sidon

PHOENICIA

Damascus

Tyre

Mt. Hermon

Kedesh

Dan

ARAM
(Syria)

Acco

Hazor

Sea of Chinnereth

Ashtaroth

The Great Sea
(Mediterranean Sea)

Mt. Carmel

Golan?

River Yarmuk

Dor

Jokneam

Jezreel

Ramoth-gilead

Megiddo

Taanach

Mt. Gilboa

Dothan

Jabesh-gilead

Samaria

Tirzah

Zaphon

River Jordan

Shechem

Succoth

Aphek

Shiloh

ISRAEL

AMMON

Joppa

Bethel

Northern Kingdom

Gezer

Mizpah

Heshbon

PHILISTIA

Azekah

Jerusalem

Ashkelon

Bethlehem

Medeba

Adullam

Tekoa

Dibon

Gaza

Eglon?

Hebron

Aroer

Debir

Dead
Sea
(Salt
Sea)

River Arnon

Ziklag?

Arad

MOAB

Beer-sheba

Kir-hareseth

Zoar

Brook Zered

JUDAH
Southern Kingdom

Brook of Egypt

Kadesh-barnea

Bozrah

EDOM

Teman

0                    75 miles

0                    75 kilometers

Ezion-geber   Elath

Map 4:
**THE ASSYRIAN EMPIRE (ca. 700 BCE)**

→ Exiles from Israel into Assyrian captivity (721 BCE)

© 2013 ANSELM ACADEMIC

Map 5:
**THE BABYLONIAN EMPIRE (ca. 600 BCE)**

→ Exiles from Judah into Babylonian captivity (605, 597, 587 BCE)
→ Return of exiles under Shesbazzar and Zerubbabel (538 BCE)
→ Return of exiles under Ezra and Nehemiah (445 BCE)

© 2013 ANSELM ACADEMIC

# MAP 6

Map 6:
## THE MINISTRY OF JESUS AND ACTS OF THE APOSTLES

| | |
|---|---|
| *(1,742)* | Elevation, in feet |
| ? | Exact location questionable |

© 2013 ANSELM ACADEMIC

Sidon

Damascus

Zarephath

*Mt. Lebanon (11,000)* +

*Mt. Hermon (9,200)* +

ITUREA

Tyre  PHOENICIA

Panias (Caesarea Philippi)

TRACHONITIS

*The Great Sea (Mediterranean Sea)*

GALILEE

Ptolemais

Chorazin    Bethsaida
Capernaum
Magdala      Gergesa

Cana       *Lake of Galilee*
Nazareth   Tiberias    *River Yarmuk*

*Mt. Carmel (1,742)* +

*River Kishon*

Nain    +*Mt. Tabor (1,843)*   Gadara?

Esdraelon

*R. Jezreel*

Caesarea    Scythopolis

*Mt. Gilboa* + *(1,696)*

DECAPOLIS

SAMARIA

Samaria
Sychar                    Gerasa

*Mt. Gerizim* + *(2,890)*   *River Jordan*   *River Jabbok*

Joppa   Antipatris

PEREA

Arimathea   Ephraim      Gadara?

Philadelphia

Emmaus?

Jericho
Jerusalem         Bethabara

Azotus    Bethany
Ashkelon  Bethlehem
          Herodium

JUDEA      Machaerus

Gaza      Hebron

*Dead Sea (Salt Sea) (-1,300)*   *River Arnon*

IDUMEA    Masada

0 ____ 30 miles
0 ____ 30 kilometers

Beer-sheba

C14

MAP 7

CYPRUS

Map 7:
# THE HOLY LAND IN MODERN TIMES

Area occupied by Israel since June 1967
Gaza Strip. Palestinian territory; Israel completed withdrawal in 2005

© 2013 ANSELM ACADEMIC

0        75 miles
0        75 kilometers

LEBANON

Tripoli

SYRIA

Beirut

LEBANON MOUNTAINS
BEKAA VALLEY
ANTI-LEBANON MOUNTAINS

Sidon
Damascus

Tyre
Dan  Banyas (Caesarea Philippi)
Qiryat Shemona
Quneitra
Nahariya
GOLAN HEIGHTS
Akko  Safad
1973 Line
Haifa
1967 Cease-Fire Line
Tiberias
Lake of Galilee
Nazareth
Dera
Afula
Beth Shean

The Great Sea
(Mediterranean Sea)

Hadera  Tulkarm
Netanya
River Jordan
Nablus
Herzliya
WEST
Tel Aviv  Petah  BANK
Yafo  Tiqwa
Rishon le Zion  Lod  Ramallah
Ramla
Amman
Ashdod  Jericho
Ashqelon  Jerusalem
Bethlehem  Madaba
Hebron  Dhiban
Gaza  Kiriath
GAZA  Gat
STRIP  En Gedi
Beer-sheba  Dead Sea
(Salt Sea)
Al-Arish  Karak

ISRAEL

JORDAN

EGYPT

Negev  Arabah

Sinai

SAUDI ARABIA

Elat  Aqaba

# Biblical Books in Alphabetical Order

| Book | Abbreviation | Page | Book | Abbreviation | Page |
|---|---|---|---|---|---|
| Acts | Acts | 1770 | 1 Kings | 1 Kgs | 535 |
| Amos | Am | 1451 | 2 Kings | 2 Kgs | 575 |
| Baruch | Bar | 1330 | Lamentations | Lam | 1318 |
| Ben Sira | Sir | 1091 | Leviticus | Lv | 249 |
| 1 Chronicles | 1 Chr | 607 | Luke | Lk | 1660 |
| 2 Chronicles | 2 Chr | 639 | 1 Maccabees | 1 Mc | 770 |
| Colossians | Col | 1944 | 2 Maccabees | 2 Mc | 806 |
| 1 Corinthians | 1 Cor | 1855 | Malachi | Mal | 1532 |
| 2 Corinthians | 2 Cor | 1884 | Mark | Mk | 1626 |
| Daniel | Dn | 1401 | Matthew | Mt | 1557 |
| Deuteronomy | Dt | 341 | Micah | Mi | 1478 |
| Ecclesiastes | Eccl | 1036 | Nahum | Na | 1490 |
| Ephesians | Eph | 1921 | Nehemiah | Neh | 692 |
| Esther | Est | 753 | Numbers | Nm | 290 |
| Exodus | Ex | 196 | Obadiah | Ob | 1466 |
| Ezekiel | Ez | 1342 | 1 Peter | 1 Pt | 2041 |
| Ezra | Ezr | 676 | 2 Peter | 2 Pt | 2051 |
| Galatians | Gal | 1907 | Philemon | Phlm | 1996 |
| Genesis | Gn | 128 | Philippians | Phil | 1932 |
| Habakkuk | Hb | 1496 | Proverbs | Prv | 990 |
| Haggai | Hg | 1510 | Psalms | Ps(s) | 881 |
| Hebrews | Heb | 2001 | Revelation | Rev | 2079 |
| Hosea | Hos | 1426 | Romans | Rom | 1828 |
| Isaiah | Is | 1164 | Ruth | Ru | 462 |
| James | Jas | 2032 | 1 Samuel | 1 Sm | 470 |
| Jeremiah | Jer | 1247 | 2 Samuel | 2 Sm | 508 |
| Job | Jb | 842 | Song of Songs | Sg | 1051 |
| Joel | Jl | 1443 | 1 Thessalonians | 1 Thes | 1955 |
| 1 John | 1 Jn | 2059 | 2 Thessalonians | 2 Thes | 1963 |
| 2 John | 2 Jn | 2067 | 1 Timothy | 1 Tm | 1970 |
| 3 John | 3 Jn | 2070 | 2 Timothy | 2 Tm | 1982 |
| John | Jn | 1716 | Titus | Ti | 1990 |
| Jonah | Jon | 1471 | Tobit | Tb | 712 |
| Joshua | Jos | 403 | Wisdom | Wis | 1062 |
| Jude | Jude | 2074 | Zechariah | Zec | 1516 |
| Judges | Jgs | 432 | Zephaniah | Zep | 1503 |
| Judith | Jdt | 732 | | | |